The Hispanic Databook

2013

Third Edition

The Hispanic Databook

Detailed Profiles of States and 782 Places with Hispanic Population, including 23 Ethnic Backgrounds from Argentinean to Venezuelan, with Rankings and Comparisons of States, Counties and Places

A UNIVERSAL REFERENCE BOOK

PUBLISHER: Leslie Mackenzie
EDITORIAL DIRECTOR: Laura Mars
SENIOR EDITOR: David Garoogian
MARKETING DIRECTOR: Jessica Moody

Grey House Publishing, Inc.
4919 Route 22
Amenia, NY 12501
518.789.8700
FAX 845.373.6390
www.greyhouse.com
e-mail: books @greyhouse.com

First edition published 1994
Printed in Canada

ISBN 978-1-61925-004-8

Table of Contents

Introduction . . . vii
Hispanic Political Leadership Facts . . . ix
Why Latinos Need to Register and Vote. . . . xi
User's Guide. . . . xiii

SECTION ONE:
National Profile

2010 Census Profile . . . 3
Top Congressional Districts by Latino Share of Population . . . 5
National Profile . . . 7
Hispanic/Latino Population for the United States and States: 1980 to 2010 . . . 11
National Maps Showing Percent of State Population for All 23 Hispanic/Latino Groups. . . . 15

SECTION TWO:
State & Place Profiles

For a place (city, town, etc.) to be included in this section, it must meet one of two criteria. Either its overall population is at least 125,000, OR its overall population is at least 25,000 and its Hispanic/ Latino population is at least 20% of the overall population. For those states where less than five places meet either of these criteria, we have included places with total population of 10,000 or more with the highest percentage of Hispanic/Latino population, so that each state is represented by at least five places. This section starts with the state profile, followed by place profiles that meet the criteria above. Places are listed alphabetically within each state. Each profile contains data for 26 topics, if available.

Alabama . . . 41
Alaska . . . 48
Arizona . . . 54
Arkansas. . . . 82
California . . . 89
Colorado. . . . 323
Connecticut . . . 341
Delaware . . . 360
District of Columbia. . . . 366
Florida . . . 369
Georgia. . . . 488
Hawaii . . . 501
Idaho . . . 507
Illinois . . . 513
Indiana . . . 540
Iowa . . . 549
Kansas . . . 556
Kentucky . . . 565
Louisiana . . . 572
Maine . . . 581
Maryland . . . 586
Massachusetts . . . 599
Michigan . . . 615
Minnesota. . . . 624
Mississippi . . . 632
Missouri . . . 638
Montana . . . 646
Nebraska . . . 651
Nevada . . . 659
New Hampshire . . . 677
New Jersey . . . 683

New Mexico . . . 729
New York . . . 741
North Carolina . . . 805
North Dakota . . . 821
Ohio . . . 826
Oklahoma . . . 837
Oregon . . . 845
Pennsylvania . . . 854
Rhode Island . . . 869
South Carolina . . . 878
South Dakota . . . 886
Tennessee . . . 891
Texas . . . 900
Utah . . . 984
Vermont . . . 993
Virginia . . . 998
Washington . . . 1020
West Virginia . . . 1034
Wisconsin . . . 1039
Wyoming . . . 1047

SECTION THREE:
Rankings & Comparisons

This section contains top 10 rankings for all states and counties, plus places (cities, towns, etc.) that are profiled in this edition. Rankings and comparisons are arranged by topic for each of the 23 Hispanic/Latino groups.

Population . . . 1055
Population Growth: 2000-2010 . . . 1101
Males per 100 Females . . . 1125
Average Household Size . . . 1149
Median Age . . . 1173
High School Graduates . . . 1197
Four-Year College Graduates . . . 1221
Population Age 3-17 Enrolled in Public School . . . 1245
Population Age 3-17 Enrolled in Private School . . . 1269
Foreign-Born Population . . . 1293
Foreign-Born Naturalized Citizens . . . 1317
Language Spoken at Home: English Only . . . 1341
Language Spoken at Home: Spanish . . . 1365
Unemployment Rate . . . 1389
Class of Worker: Private Wage and Salary . . . 1413
Class of Worker: Government . . . 1437
Means of Transportation to Work: Car, Truck or Van . . . 1461
Means of Transportation to Work: Public Transportation . . . 1485
Homeownship Rate . . . 1509
Median Home Value . . . 1533
Median Gross Rent . . . 1557
Median Household Income . . . 1581
Per Capita Income . . . 1605
Households with $100,000+ Income . . . 1629
Households with Food Stamps/SNAP Benefits During Past 12 Months . . . 1653
Poverty Rate . . . 1677

Alphabetical Place Name Index . . . 1703

Introduction

This is the third edition of *The Hispanic Databook.* The second edition coincided with the Hispanic/Latino population becoming America's largest minority at 38.8 million. Today, the number of Hispanics/Latinos has surpassed 50 million, and is the fastest growing group in America.

This premier reference book includes detailed data on national, state, county, and place (city, town, etc.) levels. It contains profiles on 782 places with the highest concentrations of Hispanic/Latino population, comprising 23 ethnic backgrounds from Argentinean to Venezuelan, and includes 26 topics, including Homeownership, Income, Language Spoken, Jobs, Rent, and Poverty. In addition to providing significant facts and figures, *The Hispanic Databook* also compares and ranks all states, counties and places by all topics—allowing users to get to exactly the data they need in minutes.

New Features

Data in this edition is arranged alphabetically by state, then place, making it easy to research by place or region. There are 26 topics covered—11 more than the last edition—for a detailed look at where and how Hispanics live, work, and learn in America. Also new to this edition are four-color U.S. maps—one for each ethnic background, showing at-a-glance where in America each group is concentrated.

In addition to being easy to use, with more topics and color maps, this edition includes informative articles from NALEO—National Association of Latino Elected Officials—that discuss Hispanic Political Leadership, the Latino vote, and 2010 Census data.

More Data on Companion Web Site

In an effort to keep this print edition to a manageable size, our inclusion criteria for places is overall population of 125,000 OR Hispanic/Latino population of at least 25,000 where Hispanics/Latinos comprise at least 20% of the total population. For those states where less than five places meet either of these criteria, we have included places with total population of 10,000 or more with the highest percentage of Hispanic population, so that each state is represented by at least five places. This includes 782 places plus all 50 states and the District of Columbia.

To address places with Hispanic/Latino population that did not meet our population cutoff, we have developed a website that includes, not only 11,242 more places than the print edition, but also 10 more topics. Access to this incredible amount of valuable data is available at no additional cost, with the purchase of this print edition. Visit the following website for more information: http://gold.greyhouse.com/page/info_hispanic

Section One: National Profile

Starting with a census summary of the Hispanic/Latino population, this section provides national numbers for the 23 Hispanic/Latino backgrounds that comprise this demographic as they relate to each of the 26 topics. In addition, this section includes 23 maps to easily see where each ethnicity lives. This section also includes the top congressional districts by Latino share of the population, and a historic look at the Hispanic/Latino population for the entire United States as well as the 50 states from 1980 to 2010.

Section Two: State & Place Profiles

Arranged by state, this section profiles all places (cities, towns, etc.) where the overall population is at least 125,000, OR the overall population is at least 25,000 and its Hispanic/Latino population is at least 20% of the overall population. For those states where less than five places meet either of these criteria, we have included places with total population of 10,000 or more with the highest percentage of Hispanic population, so that each state is represented by at least five places.

Each place is then arranged by topic (High School Graduates, Homeownership Rate, Language Spoken at Home, etc.), and each topic provides the number/percentage of each ethnicity (Cuban, Mexican, Chilean, etc.) in that place. Using the profiles, researchers will learn that the median household income of Chileans in Miami, FL is $60,915 and that 35.2% of Bolivians in Providence, RI are four-year college graduates.

Section Three: Rankings & Comparisons

This section contains 1,988 charts that rank the top 10 states, counties and places for all 26 topics and 23 Hispanic groups. All topics are ranked by number and many also by percentage, in both ascending and descending order. For comparative purposes, the U.S. figures are included in each table. Using the rankings, researchers will learn that Charlotte, NC showed the greatest growth in the Argentinean population between 2000 and 2010 (317.9%) and Yonkers, NY has the highest median home value for Hondurans ($875,000).

An alphabetical list of all 782 places in *The Hispanic Databook,* with its county and state, appears after this section.

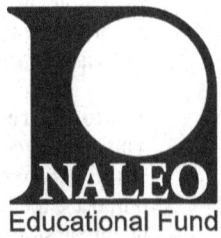

Hispanic Political Leadership Facts

NALEO Educational Fund

5,850 Latinos currently serve in elected offices nationwide, in all levels of government.
9 Hispanics serve in statewide offices, including the office of governor.

U.S. Senate:
Robert Menendez (D), New Jersey
Marco Rubio (R), Florida

U.S. House of Representatives:
24 Latinos serve in the 112th Congress
17 are Democrats
7 are Republican
7 are Latina

State Senates:
68 Latino state senators serve in state legislatures across the country

State Lower Houses:
183 Latinos state representatives serve in state legislatures across the country

Currently, we can report that 5,850 Latinos are serving in elected office. The top four states with the largest number of Latino elected officials were Texas, California, New Mexico, and Arizona. However, there was rapid growth in regions outside the Southwest, including Illinois, New Jersey, and other states which have emerging Latino populations.

In the last 15 years, there has been a 53% increase in the total number of Latinos serving in elected office from 3,743 in 1996 to 5,850 in 2011.

In 1996, Latino elected officials served in 34 states; by 2010, that number had increased to 43. Between 1996 and 2010, the number of Latina elected officials grew faster than the number of male Latino officials û the number of Latinas increased by 105%, compared to 37% for male Latinos. As a result, the Latina share of all Latino elected officials grew from 24% in 1996 to 32% in 2010.

Why Latinos Need to Register and Vote

by Arturo Vargas

Latinos are the fastest-growing and second largest population group in the United States. According to projections from the National Association of Latino Elected and Appointed Officials (NALEO) Educational Fund, more than 12.2 million Latino voters are expected to cast ballots on Election Day, an increase of 26 percent from 2008.

Despite the ability of the Latino voter to shape America's political landscape, more than 10 million Latinos are expected not to vote this November. Imagine the electoral potential if all 23.5 million Latino citizens of voting-age were not only registered, but voted.

Voting does not just send a candidate to Washington D.C., the state legislature or city hall; it speaks to the issues most pressing in a voter's life such as the economy, education, and healthcare.

We can bring change to our communities, but we need to vote. In order to secure funding for schools, to create new jobs and safer streets we must cast our ballot in every election including the next one on November 6.

Ensuring today's voter is informed, empowered, and inspired to own this year's election means continuing to eliminate the barriers that prevent participation. Now more than ever, the need to register to vote is high.

Registering to vote has never been easier. NALEO Educational Fund, in collaboration with other national Latino organizations and Spanish-language media, coordinates the historic non-partisan Latino ya es hora ("It's Time") civic participation campaign, which helps voters navigate the registration process.

Individuals interested in registering to vote can call ya es hora's national bilingual hotline, 1-888-VE-Y-VOTA, which is operational year-round to help voters with electoral information. While the Post Office and libraries provide voter registration forms, citizens can also register to vote easily online at www.YaEsHora.info. It takes less than 5 minutes to complete, and once complete, must be printed, stamped, and mailed. In addition, the California Department of Motor Vehicles (DMV) will offer Californians the ability to register to vote online without needing to print the form by visiting www.dmv.ca.gov.

Registering to vote is the first step towards bettering communities and country. The second is making an informed vote on November 6 that speaks on what matters most to you. The next is continued engagement. Only through active participation, year after year, will we continue strengthening our democracy and our country.

	Projected Latino Voters	Increase From 2008	Projected Share of Latino Vote
NATIONAL	12,237,000	25.60%	8.70%
Arizona	359,000	23.20%	12.00%
California	3,911,000	32.10%	26.30%
Colorado	224,000	15.00%	8.70%
Florida	1,650,000	34.50%	18.30%
Illinois	433,000	37.80%	7.60%
New Jersey	392,000	16.20%	10.40%
New Mexico	329,000	14.00%	35.00%
New York	845,000	13.70%	10.80%
Texas	1,987,000	17.10%	21.30%

User's Guide

Areas Covered in Print Edition

United States

All 50 States plus the District of Columbia

782 Places with overall population of at least 125,000, OR overall population of at least 25,000 where the Hispanic/Latino population is at least 20% of the overall population. For those states where less than five places meet either of these criteria, we have included places with total population of 10,000 or more with the highest percentage of Hispanic/Latino population, so that each state is represented by at least five places.

These places fall into several categories:

- Incorporated Municipalities: Depending on the state, municipalities are incorporated as either cities, towns, villages, or boroughs. A few municipalities have a form of government combined with another entity (e.g. county) and are listed as consolidated or metropolitan governments.
- Independent Cities: Baltimore MD, St. Louis MO, and eight independent cities in Virginia.
- Census Designated Places (CDP). The U.S. Bureau of the Census defines a CDP as "a statistical entity, defined for each decennial census according to Census Bureau guidelines, comprising a densely settled concentration of population that is not within an incorporated place, but is locally identified by a name. CDPs are delineated cooperatively by state and local officials and the Census Bureau, following Census Bureau guidelines."
- Minor Civil Divisions (MCD). Called towns, townships, districts, gores, locations, and plantations for the states where the Census Bureau has determined that they serve as general-purpose governments. Those states are Connecticut, Maine, Massachusetts, Michigan, Minnesota, New Hampshire, New Jersey, New York, Pennsylvania, Rhode Island, Vermont, and Wisconsin. In some states incorporated municipalities are part of minor civil divisions and in some states they are independent of them.

Areas Covered in Online Version

United States

All 50 States plus the District of Columbia

2,746 Counties and Parishes

12,024 Places

To offer more information on the Hispanic/Latino population than in this print book, we have developed a unique web site with more data for more places. Online, you'll find 14,821 states/counties/places and 36 topics vs. 833 states/counties/places and 26 topics covered in this print edition. The online topics are noted in the Topics section of this User's Guide, beginning on page xv. Access to this wealth of information is free with purchase of the print book. For details, go to http://gold.greyhouse.com/page/info_hispanic

Note: *Counties and places with no Hispanic/Latino residents have been excluded from both the print and online products. For a more in-depth discussion of geographic areas, please refer to the Census Bureau's Geographic Areas Reference Manual at http://www.census.gov/geo/www/garm.html.*

Source of Data

Data for this publication was derived from two sources: *U.S. Census Bureau, Profile of General Population and Housing Characteristics 2010: Summary File 2* and *U.S. Census Bureau, American Community Survey, 2006–2010, 5-Year Estimates.* The American Community Survey (ACS) is a relatively new survey conducted by the U.S. Census Bureau. It uses a series of monthly samples to produce annually updated data for the same small areas (census tracts and block groups) formerly surveyed via the decennial census long-form sample. American Community Survey 5-year estimates are period estimates, which means they represent the characteristics of the population and housing over a specific data collection period. The ACS data used in this book covers 2006 to 2010.

Population Groups Covered

This publication focuses on the following 23 population groups:

- Hispanic or Latino (of any race)
    - Central American, excluding Mexican
        - Costa Rican
        - Guatemalan
        - Honduran
        - Nicaraguan
        - Panamanian
        - Salvadoran
    - Cuban
    - Dominican (Dominican Republic)
    - Mexican
    - Puerto Rican
    - South American
        - Argentinean
        - Bolivian
        - Chilean
        - Colombian
        - Ecuadorian
        - Paraguayan
        - Peruvian
        - Uruguayan
        - Venezuelan
    - Spaniard

Please note that the above list only includes Spanish-speaking population groups. Groups such as Brazilian, Belizean and Guyanese are not included because Spanish is not their official language.

Data for a population group is subject to a threshold of 100 or more people. This means that data will not be shown for population groups with less than 100 people in a specified geographic area.

To maintain confidentiality, the Census Bureau applies statistical procedures that introduce some uncertainty into data for small geographic areas with small population groups. Therefore, tables may contain both sampling and nonsampling error.

Tables based on *households* and *occupied housing units* are classified by the race or ethnic group of the householder. In any population table where there is no note, the universe classification is always based on the race or ethnicity of the person. In all housing tables, the universe classification is based on the race or ethnicity of the householder.

Topics

POPULATION

Total Population: 100% count of total population.

Hispanic Population: The data on the Hispanic or Latino population were derived from answers to a question that was asked of all people. The terms "Hispanic," "Latino," and "Spanish" are used interchangeably. Some respondents identify with all three terms, while others may identify with only one of these three specific terms. People who identify with the terms "Hispanic," "Latino," or "Spanish" are those who classify themselves in one of the specific Hispanic, Latino, or Spanish categories listed on the questionnaire ("Mexican," "Puerto Rican," or "Cuban") as well as those who indicate that they are "another Hispanic, Latino, or Spanish origin." People who do not identify with one of the specific origins listed on the questionnaire but indicate that they are "another Hispanic, Latino, or Spanish origin" are those whose origins are from Spain, the Spanish-speaking countries of Central or South America, or the Dominican Republic. Up to two write-in responses to the "another Hispanic, Latino, or Spanish origin" category are coded.

Origin can be viewed as the heritage, nationality group, lineage, or country of birth of the person or the person's parents or ancestors before their arrival in the United States. People who identify their origin as Hispanic, Latino, or Spanish may be any race.

Some tabulations are shown by the origin of the householder. In all cases where the origin of households, families, or occupied housing units is classified as Hispanic, Latino, or Spanish, the origin of the householder is used.

If an individual did not provide a Hispanic origin response, his or her origin was allocated using specific rules of precedence of household relationship. For example, if origin was missing for a natural-born child in the household, then either the origin of the householder, another natural-born child, or spouse of the householder was allocated.

If Hispanic origin was not reported for anyone in the household and origin could not be obtained from a response to the race question, then their origin was assigned based on their prior census record (either from Census 2000 or the American Community Survey), if available. If not, then the Hispanic origin of a householder in a previously processed household with the same race was allocated. As in Census 2000, surnames (Spanish and non-Spanish) were used to assist in allocating an origin or race.

Population groups whose primary language is not Spanish are not classified as Hispanic by the Bureau of the Census and are not included in this publication (eg. Brazilian). *Source: U.S. Census Bureau, Profile of General Population and Housing Characteristics 2010: Summary File 2*

POPULATION GROWTH

Population Growth: Shows the change in population from 2000 to 2010. *Source: U.S. Census Bureau, Profile of General Population and Housing Characteristics 2010: Summary File 2; U.S. Census Bureau, Profile of General Demographic Characteristics 2000: Summary File 2*

SEX

Males per 100 Females: The sex ratio represents the balance between the male and female populations. Ratios above 100 indicate a larger male population, and ratios below 100 indicate a larger female population. This measure is derived by dividing the total number of males by the total number of females and then multiplying by 100. It is rounded to the nearest tenth.

Individuals were asked to mark either "male" or "female" to indicate their sex. For most cases in which sex was not reported, the appropriate entry was determined from the person's given (i.e., first) name and household relationship. Otherwise, sex was allocated according to the relationship to the householder and the age of the person. *Source: U.S. Census Bureau, Profile of General Population and Housing Characteristics 2010: Summary File 2*

HOUSEHOLD SIZE

Average Household Size: Average household size is a measure obtained by dividing the number of people in households by the number of households. In cases where people in households are crossclassified by race or Hispanic origin, people in the household are classified by the race or Hispanic origin of the householder rather than the race or Hispanic origin of each individual. Average household size is rounded to the nearest hundredth. *Source: U.S. Census Bureau, Profile of General Population and Housing Characteristics 2010: Summary File 2*

AGE

Median Age: Divides the age distribution into two equal parts: one-half of the cases falling below the median age and one-half above the median. Median age is computed on the basis of a single year-of-age distribution using a linear interpolation method.

The data on age were derived from answers to a two-part question (i.e., age and date of birth). The age classification for a person in census tabulations is the age of the person in completed years as of April 1, 2010, the census reference date. Both age and date of birth responses are used in combination to determine the most accurate age for the person as of the census reference date. Inconsistently reported and missing values are assigned or allocated based on the values of other variables for that person, from other people in the household or from people in other households. *Source: U.S. Census Bureau, Profile of General Population and Housing Characteristics 2010: Summary File 2*

EDUCATIONAL ATTAINMENT

High School Graduates: Number and percentage of the population age 25 and over who have a high school diploma or higher. This category includes people whose highest degree was a high school diploma or its equivalent, people who attended college but did not receive a degree, and people who received a college, university, or professional degree. People who reported completing the 12th grade but not receiving a diploma are not included.

4-Years College Graduates: Number and percentage of the population age 25 and over who have a 4-year college, university, or professional degree.

Data on educational attainment were derived from answers to Question 11, which was asked of all respondents. Respondents are classified according to the highest degree or the highest level of school completed. The question included instructions for persons currently enrolled in school to report the level of the previous grade attended or the highest degree received.

The educational attainment question included a response category that allowed people to report completing the 12th grade without receiving a high school diploma. Respondents who received a regular high school diploma and did not attend college were instructed to report "Regular high school diploma." Respondents who received the equivalent of a high school diploma (for example, passed the test of General Educational Development (G.E.D.)), and did not attend college, were instructed to report "GED or alternative credential." "Some college" is in two categories: "Some college credit, but less than 1 year of college credit" and "1 or more years of college credit, no degree." The category "Associate's degree" included people whose highest degree is an associate's degree, which generally requires 2 years of college level work and is either in an occupational program that prepares them for a specific occupation, or an academic program primarily in the arts and sciences. The course work may or may not be transferable to a bachelor's degree. Master's degrees include the traditional MA and MS degrees and field-specific degrees, such as MSW, MEd, MBA, MLS, and MEng. Instructions included in the respondent instruction guide for mailout/mailback respondents only provided the following examples of professional school degrees: Medicine, dentistry, chiropractic, optometry, osteopathic medicine, pharmacy, podiatry, veterinary medicine, law, and theology. The order in which degrees were listed suggested that doctorate degrees were "higher" than professional school degrees, which were "higher" than master's degrees. If more than one box was filled, the response was edited to the highest level or degree reported. *Source: U.S. Census Bureau, American Community Survey, 2006–2010, 5-Year Estimates*

SCHOOL ENROLLMENT

Population Age 3–17 Enrolled in Public School and **Population Age 3–17 Enrolled in Private School:** Includes people who attended school in the reference period and indicated they were enrolled by marking one of the questionnaire categories for "public school, public college," or "private school, private college, home school." The instruction guide defines a public school as "any school or college controlled and supported primarily by a local, county, state, or federal government." Private schools are defined as schools supported and controlled primarily by religious organizations or other private groups. Home schools are defined as "parental-guided education outside of public or private school for grades 1-12." Respondents who marked both the "public" and "private" boxes are edited to the first entry, "public."

Data on school enrollment and grade or level attending were derived from answers to Question 10. People were classified as enrolled in school if they were attending a public or private school or college at any time during the 3 months prior to the time of interview. The question included instructions to "include only nursery or preschool, kindergarten, elementary school, home school, and schooling which leads to a high school diploma, or a college degree." Respondents who did not answer the enrollment question were assigned the enrollment status and type of school of a person with the same age, sex, race, and Hispanic or Latino origin whose residence was in the same or nearby area. *Source: U.S. Census Bureau, American Community Survey, 2006–2010, 5-Year Estimates*

FOREIGN-BORN

Foreign Born: Number and percentage of foreign-born population. The foreign-born population includes anyone who was not a U.S. citizen or a U.S. national at birth. This includes respondents who indicated they were a U.S. citizen by naturalization or not a U.S. citizen.

Foreign-Born Naturalized Citizens: Number and percentage of foreign-born population who were not U.S. citizens at birth but became U.S. citizens by naturalization.

The data on citizenship status were derived from answers to Question 8. This question was asked about Persons 1 through 5 in the ACS. Respondents were asked to select one of five categories: (1) born in the United States, (2) born in Puerto Rico, Guam, the U.S. Virgin Islands, or Northern Marianas, (3) born abroad of U.S. citizen parent or parents, (4) U.S. citizen by naturalization, or (5) not a U.S citizen. Respondents indicating they are a U.S. citizen by naturalization are also asked to print their year of naturalization. People born in American Samoa, although not explicitly listed, are included in the second response category.

When no information on citizenship status was reported for a person, information for other household members, if available, was used to assign a citizenship status to the respondent. All cases of nonresponse that were not assigned a citizenship status based on information from other household members were allocated the citizenship status of another person with similar characteristics who provided complete information. In cases of conflicting responses, place of birth information is used to edit citizenship status. For example, if a respondent states he or she was born in Puerto Rico but was not a U.S. citizen, the edits use the response to the place of birth question to change the respondent's status to "U.S. citizen at birth."

The American Community Survey questionnaires do not ask about immigration status. The population surveyed includes all people who indicated that the United States was their usual place of residence on the survey date. The foreign-born population includes naturalized U.S. citizens, lawful permanent residents (i.e. immigrants), temporary migrants (e.g., foreign students), humanitarian migrants (e.g., refugees), and unauthorized migrants (i.e. people illegally present in the United States). *Source: U.S. Census Bureau, American Community Survey, 2006–2010, 5-Year Estimates*

LANGUAGE SPOKEN AT HOME

English Only: Number and percentage of population 5 years and over who report speaking English-only at home.

Spanish: Number and percentage of population 5 years and over who report speaking Spanish at home.

Data on language spoken at home were derived from answers to questions 14a and 14b. These questions were asked only of persons 5 years of age and older. Instructions mailed with the American Community Survey questionnaire instructed respondents to mark "Yes" on Question 14a if they sometimes or always spoke a language other than English at home, and "No" if a language was spoken only at school—or if speaking was limited to a few expressions or slang. For Question 14b, respondents printed the name of the non-English language they spoke at home. If the person spoke more than one non-English language, they reported the language spoken most often. If the language spoken most frequently could not be determined, the respondent reported the language learned first. This category excluded respondents who spoke a language other than English exclusively outside of the home. *Source: U.S. Census Bureau, American Community Survey, 2006–2010, 5-Year Estimates*

UNEMPLOYMENT

Unemployment Rate: Represents the number of unemployed people as a percentage of the civilian labor force. For example, if the civilian labor force equals 100 people and 7 people are unemployed, then the unemployment rate would be 7 percent. Tabulations relate to people 16 years old and over.

The data on employment status were derived from Questions 29 and 35 to 37 in the 2010 American Community Survey. The series of questions on employment status was designed to identify, in this sequence: (1) people who worked at any time during the reference week; (2) people on temporary layoff who were available for work; (3) people who did not work during the reference week but who had jobs or businesses from which they were temporarily absent (excluding layoff); (4) people who did not work during the reference week, but who were looking for work during the last four weeks and were available for work during the reference week; and (5) people not in the labor force. *Source: U.S. Census Bureau, American Community Survey, 2006–2010, 5-Year Estimates*

CLASS OF WORKER

Private Wage and Salary: Includes people who worked for wages, salary, commission, tips, pay-in-kind, or piece rates for a private, for-profit employer or a private not-for-profit, tax-exempt or charitable organization. Self-employed people whose business was incorporated are included with private wage and salary workers because they are paid employees of their own companies.

Government: Includes people who were employees of any local, state, or Federal governmental unit, regardless of the activity of the particular agency. For ACS tabulations, the data are presented separately for the three levels of government. Employees of Indian tribal governments, foreign governments, the United Nations, or other formal international organizations controlled by governments were classified as "Federal government workers." The government categories include all government workers, though government workers may work in different industries. For example, people who work in a public elementary school or city owned bus line are coded as local government class of workers.

Self-employed in Own Not Incorporated Business Workers: Includes people who worked for profit or fees in their own unincorporated business, profession, or trade, or who operated a farm. *Data available online only.*

Class of worker categorizes people according to the type of ownership of the employing organization. Class of worker data were derived from answers to question 41. Question 41 provides respondents with 8 class of worker categories from which they are to select one. These categories are:

- An employee of a private, for-profit company or business, or of an individual, for wages, salary, or commissions.
- An employee of a private, not-for-profit, tax-exempt, or charitable organization.
- A local government employee (city, county, etc.).
- A state government employee.
- A Federal government employee.
- Self-employed in own not incorporated business, professional practice, or farm.

- Self-employed in own incorporated business, professional practice, or farm.
- Working without pay in a family business or farm.

These questions were asked of all people 16 years old and over who had worked in the past 5 years. For employed people, the data refer to the person's job during the previous week. For those who worked two or more jobs, the data refer to the job where the person worked the greatest number of hours. For unemployed people and people who are not currently employed but report having a job within the last five years, the data refer to their last job. *Source: U.S. Census Bureau, American Community Survey, 2006–2010, 5-Year Estimates*

MEANS OF TRANSPORTATION TO WORK

Car, Truck, or Van: Includes workers using a car (including company cars but excluding taxicabs), a truck of one-ton capacity or less, or a van.

Public Transportation: Includes workers who used a bus or trolley bus, streetcar or trolley car, subway or elevated, railroad, or ferryboat, even if each mode is not shown separately in the tabulation. Numbers exclude taxicabs.

Walked: Includes workers who walked to work. *Data available online only.*

Worked from Home: Includes workers who worked from home. *Data available online only.*

The data on means of transportation to work were derived from answers to Question 31, which was asked of people who indicated in Question 29 that they worked at some time during the reference week. Means of transportation to work refers to the principal mode of travel or type of conveyance that the worker usually used to get from home to work during the reference week.

People who used different means of transportation on different days of the week were asked to specify the one they used most often, that is, the greatest number of days. People who used more than one means of transportation to get to work each day were asked to report the one used for the longest distance during the work trip.

The means of transportation data for some areas may show workers using modes of public transportation that are not available in those areas (for example, subway or elevated riders in a metropolitan area where there is no subway or elevated service). This result is largely due to people who worked during the reference week at a location that was different from their usual place of work (such as people away from home on business in an area where subway service was available), and people who used more than one means of transportation each day but whose principal means was unavailable where they lived (for example, residents of nonmetropolitan areas who drove to the fringe of a metropolitan area, and took the commuter railroad most of the distance to work). *Source: U.S. Census Bureau, American Community Survey, 2006–2010, 5-Year Estimates*

MEAN TRAVEL TIME TO WORK

Mean Travel Time to Work: The average travel time, in minutes, that workers usually took to get from home to work (one way) during the reference week. This measure is obtained by dividing the total number of minutes taken to get from home to work (the aggregate travel time) by the number of workers 16 years old and over who did not work at home. The travel time includes time spent waiting for public transportation, picking up passengers and carpools, and time spent in other activities related to getting to work. Mean travel times of workers having specific characteristics also are computed. For example, the mean travel time of workers traveling 45 or more minutes to work is computed by dividing the aggregate travel time of workers whose travel times were 45 or more minutes by the number of workers whose travel times were 45 or more minutes. The aggregate travel time to work used to calculate mean travel time to work is rounded. Mean travel time is rounded to the nearest tenth of a minute. *Data available online only.*

The data on travel time to work were derived from answers to Question 34. This question was asked of people who indicated in Question 29 that they worked at some time during the reference week, and who reported in Question 31 that they worked outside their home. Travel time to work refers to the total number of minutes that it usually took the worker to get from home to work during the reference week. The elapsed time includes time spent waiting for public transportation, picking up passengers in carpools, and time spent in other activities related to getting to work. *Source: U.S. Census Bureau, American Community Survey, 2006–2010, 5-Year Estimates*

HOUSING

Homeownership Rate: Percentage of housing units that are owner-occupied.

Tenure was asked at all occupied housing units. All occupied housing units are classified as either owner-occupied or renter-occupied. A housing unit is owner occupied if the owner or co-owner lives in the unit even if it is mortgaged or not fully paid for. The owner or co-owner must live in the unit and usually is Person 1 on the questionnaire. The unit is "Owned by you or someone in this household with a mortgage or loan" if it is being purchased with a mortgage or some other debt arrangement, such as a deed of trust, trust deed, contract to purchase, land contract, or purchase agreement. The unit is also considered owned with a mortgage if it is built on leased land and there is a mortgage on the unit. *Source: U.S. Census Bureau, Profile of General Population and Housing Characteristics 2010: Summary File 2*

Median Home Value: Median home value in dollars.

The data on value (also referred to as "price asked" for vacant units) were obtained from Housing Question 16 in the 2010 American Community Survey. The question was asked at housing units that were owned, being bought, vacant for sale, or sold not occupied at the time of the survey. Value is the respondent's estimate of how much the property (house and lot, mobile home and lot, or condominium unit) would sell for if it were for sale. If the house or mobile home was owned or being bought, but the land on which it sits was not, the respondent was asked to estimate the combined value of the house or mobile home and the land. For vacant units, value was the price asked for the property. Value was tabulated separately for all owner-occupied and vacant-for-sale housing units, as well as owner-occupied and vacant-for-sale mobile homes. The median divides the value distribution into two equal parts: one-half of the cases falling below the median value of the property (house and lot, mobile home and lot, or condominium unit) and one-half above the median. Median value is computed on the basis of a standard distribution. Median value calculations are rounded to the nearest hundred dollars. A hyphen indicates that the median estimate falls in the lowest interval of an open-ended distribution.

The value of a home provides information on neighborhood quality, housing affordability, and wealth. These data provide socioeconomic information not captured by household income and comparative information on the state of local housing markets. The data also serve to aid in the development of housing programs designed to meet the housing needs of persons at different economic levels. *Source: U.S. Census Bureau, Profile of General Population and Housing Characteristics 2010: Summary File 2*

Median Gross Rent: Median gross monthly rent in dollars.

The data on gross rent were obtained from answers to Housing Questions 11a-d and 15a in the 2010 American Community Survey. Gross rent is the contract rent plus the estimated average monthly cost of utilities (electricity, gas, and water and sewer) and fuels (oil, coal, kerosene, wood, etc.) if these are paid by the renter (or paid for the renter by someone else). Gross rent is intended to eliminate differentials that result from varying practices with respect to the inclusion of utilities and fuels as part of the rental payment. The estimated costs of water and sewer, and fuels are reported on a 12-month basis but are converted to monthly figures for the tabulations. Renter units occupied without payment of rent are shown separately as "No rent paid" in the tabulations. Median gross rent divides the gross rent distribution into two equal parts: one-half of the cases falling below the median gross rent and one-half above the median. Median gross rent is computed on the basis of a standard distribution. Median gross rent is rounded to the nearest whole dollar. A hyphen indicates that the median estimate falls in the lowest interval of an open-ended distribution.

Gross rent provides information on the monthly housing cost expenses for renters. When the data is used in conjunction with income data, the information offers an excellent measure of housing affordability and excessive shelter costs. The data also serve to aid in the development of housing programs to meet the needs of people at different economic levels, and to provide assistance to agencies in determining policies on fair rent. *Source: U.S. Census Bureau, Profile of General Population and Housing Characteristics 2010: Summary File 2*

INCOME AND POVERTY

The data on income were derived from answers to Questions 47 and 48, which were asked of the population 15 years old and over. "Total income" is the sum of the amounts reported separately for wage or salary income; net self-employment income; interest, dividends, or net rental or royalty income or income from estates and trusts; Social Security or Railroad Retirement income; Supplemental Security Income (SSI); public assistance or welfare payments; retirement, survivor, or disability pensions; and all other income.

Receipts from the following sources are not included as income: capital gains, money received from the sale of property (unless the recipient was engaged in the business of selling such property); the value of income "in kind" from food stamps, public housing subsidies, medical care, employer contributions for individuals, etc.; withdrawal of bank deposits; money borrowed; tax refunds; exchange of money between relatives living in the same household; gifts and lump-sum inheritances, insurance payments, and other types of lump-sum receipts.

Adjusting Income for Inflation—Income components were reported for the 12 months preceding the interview month. Monthly Consumer Price Indices (CPI) factors were used to inflation-adjust these components to a reference calendar year (January through December). For example, a household interviewed in March 2010 reports their income for March 2009 through February 2010. Their income is adjusted to the 2010 reference calendar year by multiplying their reported income by 2010 average annual CPI (January-December 2010) and then dividing by the average CPI for March 2009–February 2010. In order to inflate income amounts from previous years, the dollar values on individual records are inflated to the latest year's dollar values by multiplying by a factor equal to the average annual CPI-U-RS factor for the current year, divided by the average annual CPI-U-RS factor for the earlier/earliest year.

Median Income: The median divides the income distribution into two equal parts: one-half of the cases falling below the median income and one-half above the median. For households and families, the median income is based on the distribution of the total number of households and families including those with no income. The median income for individuals is based on individuals 15 years old and over with income. Median income for households, families, and individuals is computed on the basis of a standard distribution. Median income is rounded to the nearest whole dollar. Median income figures are calculated using linear interpolation. *Source: U.S. Census Bureau, Profile of General Population and Housing Characteristics 2010: Summary File 2*

Mean Income: Mean income is the amount obtained by dividing the aggregate income of a particular statistical universe by the number of units in that universe. For example, mean household income is obtained by dividing total household income by the total number of households. *Data available online only. Source: U.S. Census Bureau, Profile of General Population and Housing Characteristics 2010: Summary File 2*

Per Capita Income: Per capita income is the mean income computed for every man, woman, and child in a particular group including those living in group quarters. It is derived by dividing the aggregate income of a particular group by the total population in that group. Per capita income is rounded to the nearest whole dollar. *Source: U.S. Census Bureau, Profile of General Population and Housing Characteristics 2010: Summary File 2*

Households with $100,000+ Income: The number and percentage of households with income of $100,000 or more. *Source: U.S. Census Bureau, Profile of General Population and Housing Characteristics 2010: Summary File 2*

Households with Food Stamps/SNAP Benefits During Past 12 Months: Number and percentage of households where one or more current members received food stamps or a food stamp benefit card during the past 12 months.

The data on Food Stamp benefits were obtained from Housing Question 12 in the 2010 American Community Survey. The Food Stamp Act of 1977 defines this federally-funded program as one intended to "permit low-income households to obtain a more nutritious diet" (from Title XIII of Public Law 95-113, The Food Stamp Act of 1977, declaration of policy). Food purchasing power is increased by providing eligible households with coupons or cards that can be used to purchase food. The Food and Nutrition Service (FNS) of the U.S. Department of Agriculture (USDA) administers the Food Stamp Program through state and local welfare offices. The Food Stamp Program is the major national income support program to which all low-income and low-resource households, regardless of household characteristics, are eligible. On October 1, 2008, the Federal Food Stamp program was renamed SNAP (Supplemental Nutrition Assistance Program). *Source: U.S. Census Bureau, Profile of General Population and Housing Characteristics 2010: Summary File 2*

Households with Cash Public Assistance Income: Number and percentage of households in which one or more current members received public assistance during the past 12 months. Data are for households, not individuals. If any person living at the sample address at the time of the interview received public assistance in the past 12 months, then the household is included in the estimate of public assistance participation. *Data available online only. Source: U.S. Census Bureau, Profile of General Population and Housing Characteristics 2010: Summary File 2*

Mean Cash Public Assistance Income: Dollar value of cash public assistance income received. *Data available online only.*

Public assistance income provides cash payments to poor families and includes General Assistance and Temporary Assistance to Needy Families (TANF), which replaced Aid to Families with Dependent Children (AFDC) in 1997. Public assistance income does not include Supplemental Security Income (SSI), noncash benefits such as Food Stamps/SNAP, or separate payments received for hospital or other medical care. To qualify for public assistance benefits, the income and assets of an individual or family must fall below specified thresholds. However, unlike AFDC benefits, TANF benefits are time-limited, require most adult recipients to work, and give states increased flexibility in program design. *Source: U.S. Census Bureau, Profile of General Population and Housing Characteristics 2010: Summary File 2*

Poverty Rate—All People: Number and percentage of population with income in past 12 months below poverty level. Based on individuals for whom poverty status is determined. Poverty status was determined for all people except institutionalized people, people in military group quarters, people in college dormitories, and unrelated individuals under 15 years old. These groups were excluded from the numerator and denominator when calculating poverty rates. *Source: U.S. Census Bureau, Profile of General Population and Housing Characteristics 2010: Summary File 2*

Poverty Rate—Under 18 Years Old: Number and percentage of population under 18 years old living in a household with income in past 12 months below poverty level. *Data available online only. Source: U.S. Census Bureau, Profile of General Population and Housing Characteristics 2010: Summary File 2*

Poverty Rate—18 to 64 Years Old: Number and percentage of population 18 to 64 years old living in a household with income in past 12 months below poverty level. *Data available online only. Source: U.S. Census Bureau, Profile of General Population and Housing Characteristics 2010: Summary File 2*

Poverty Rate—65 Years Old and Over: Number and percentage of population 65 years old and over living in a household with income in past 12 months below poverty level. *Data available online only. Source: U.S. Census Bureau, Profile of General Population and Housing Characteristics 2010: Summary File 2*

Poverty statistics in ACS products adhere to the standards specified by the Office of Management and Budget in Statistical Policy Directive 14. The Census Bureau uses a set of dollar value thresholds that vary by family size and composition to determine who is in poverty. Further, poverty thresholds for people living alone or with nonrelatives (unrelated individuals) vary by age (under 65 years or 65 years and older). The poverty thresholds for two-person families also vary by the age of the householder. If a family's total income is less than the dollar value of the appropriate threshold, then that family and every individual in it are considered to be in poverty. Similarly, if an unrelated individual's total income is less than the appropriate threshold, then that individual is considered to be in poverty.

In determining the poverty status of families and unrelated individuals, the Census Bureau uses thresholds (income cutoffs) arranged in a two-dimensional matrix. The matrix consists of family size (from one person to nine or more people) cross-classified by presence and number of family members under 18 years old (from no children present to eight or more children present). Unrelated individuals and two-person families are further differentiated by age of reference person (RP) (under 65 years old and 65 years old and over).

To determine a person's poverty status, one compares the person's total family income in the last 12 months with the poverty threshold appropriate for that person's family size and composition (see example below). If the total income of that person's family is less than the threshold appropriate for that family, then the person is considered "below the poverty level," together with every member of his or her family. If a person is not living with anyone related by birth, marriage, or adoption, then the person's own income is compared with his or her poverty threshold. The total number of people below the poverty level is the sum of people in families and the number of unrelated individuals with incomes in the last 12 months below the poverty threshold.

Since ACS is a continuous survey, people respond throughout the year. Because the income questions specify a period covering the last 12 months, the appropriate poverty thresholds are determined by multiplying the base-year poverty thresholds (1982) by the average of the monthly inflation factors for the 12 months preceding the data collection. See the table in Appendix A titled "Poverty Thresholds in 1982, by Size of Family and Number of Related Children Under 18 Years (Dollars)," for appropriate base thresholds.

For example, consider a family of three with one child under 18 years of age, interviewed in July 2010 and reporting a total family income of $14,000 for the last 12 months (July 2009 to June 2010). The base year (1982) threshold for such a family is $7,765, while the average of the 12 inflation factors is 2.24574 Multiplying $7,765 by 2.24574 determines the appropriate poverty threshold for this family type, which is $17,438 Comparing the family's income of $14,000 with the poverty threshold shows that the family and all people in the family are considered to have been in poverty. The only difference for determining poverty status for unrelated individuals is that the person's individual total income is compared with the threshold rather than the family's income.

Since poverty is defined at the family level and not the household level, the poverty status of the household is determined by the poverty status of the householder. Households are classified as poor when the total income of the householder's family in the last 12 months is below the appropriate poverty threshold. (For nonfamily householders, their own income is compared with the appropriate threshold.) The income of people living in the household who are unrelated to the householder is not considered when determining the poverty status of a household, nor does their presence affect the family size in determining the appropriate threshold. The poverty thresholds vary depending upon three criteria: size of family, number of children, and, for one- and two- person families, age of the householder.

SECTION ONE:
National Profile

2010 CENSUS PROFILES
UNITED STATES

TOTAL POPULATION: 308,745,538
LATINO POPULATION: 50,477,594

LATINO SHARE OF POPULATION: 16.3%

POPULATION GROWTH BETWEEN 2000 AND 2010

Between 2000 and 2010, the nation's population grew from 281.4 million to 308.7 million, an increase of 10%. During the same period, the Latino population grew from 35.3 million to 50.5 million, an increase of 43%.

The increase in the U.S. Latino population contributed significantly to the nation's overall growth during the last decade. Between 2000 and 2010, the Latino population increase accounted for over half (56%) of the nation's total population growth.

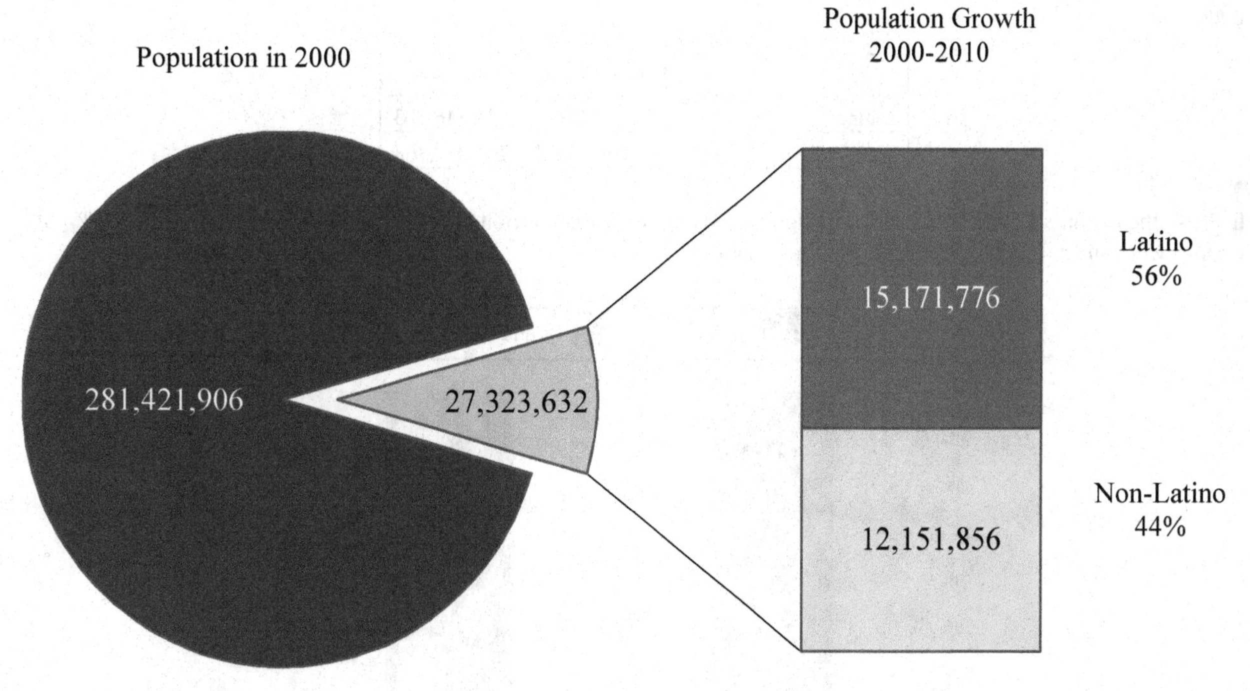

ETHNIC COMPOSITION OF POPULATION

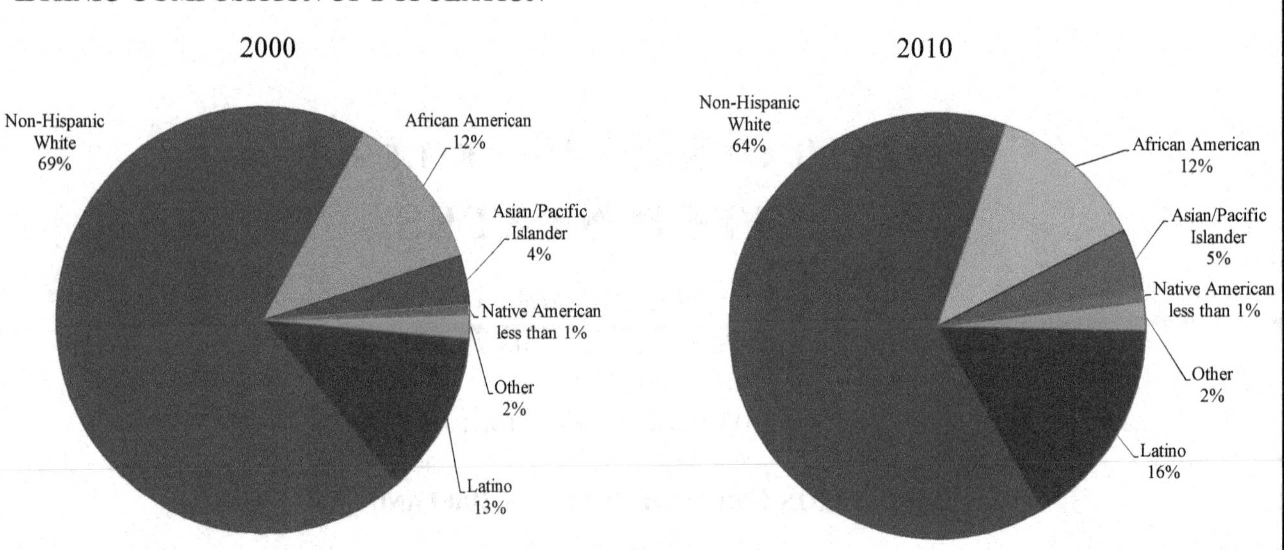

Between 2000 and 2010, the Latino share of the population grew from 13% to 16%, and one out of six of the nation's residents is Latino. In 2000, 69% of U.S. residents were Non-Hispanic White; in 2010, Non-Hispanic Whites were 64% of the nation's population.

AGE OF POPULATION: 2010

In 2010, 17.1 million Latinos were under 18, and 33.3 million were 18 and older. Latinos comprise 23% of all U.S. residents under 18.

	Under 18	18 and older
Latino	17,130,891	33,346,703
Non-Latino	57,050,576	201,217,368

In 2010, the nation's Latino population was significantly younger than its non-Latino population. Over one-third (34%) of Latinos were under 18, compared to 22% of non-Latinos.

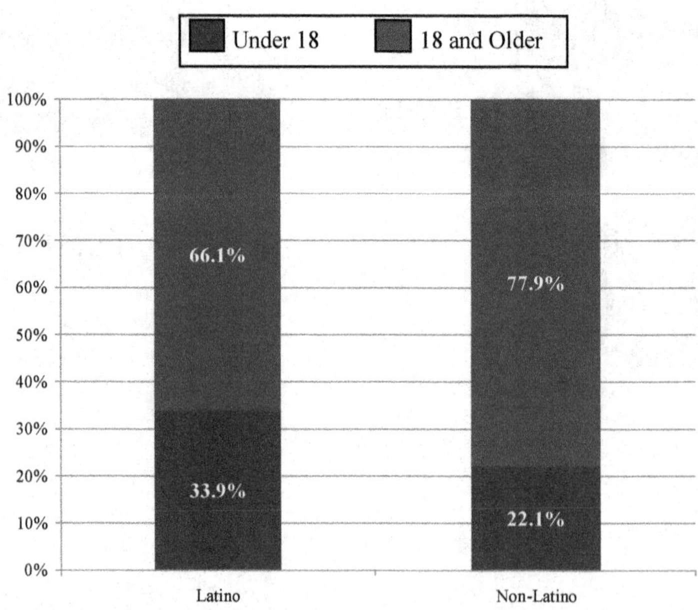

Congressional Districts: 2010

Census 2010 data reveal that Latinos comprise at least 40% of the population in 44 of the nation's Congressional districts.

Top Congressional Districts by Latino Share of Population

State	District	Total Population	Latino Population	Latino Share of Population	U.S. Representative
TX	15	787,124	649,297	82.5%	Rubén Hinojosa (D)
TX	16	757,427	617,465	81.5%	Silvestre Reyes (D)
TX	28	851,824	672,129	78.9%	Henry Cuellar (D)
CA	34	654,303	515,167	78.7%	Lucille Roybal-Allard (D)
TX	29	677,032	514,861	76.0%	Gene Green (D)
FL	21	693,501	524,005	75.6%	Mario Diaz-Balart (R)
CA	38	641,410	483,490	75.4%	Grace F. Napolitano (D)
IL	4	601,156	442,018	73.5%	Luis V. Gutierrez (D)
TX	27	741,993	543,306	73.2%	Blake Farenthold (R)
FL	25	807,176	577,998	71.6%	David Rivera (R)
TX	20	711,705	509,208	71.5%	Charlie Gonzalez (D)
CA	20	744,350	523,705	70.4%	Jim Costa (D)
CA	43	735,581	510,693	69.4%	Joe Baca (D)
CA	31	611,336	417,183	68.2%	Xavier Becerra (D)
CA	47	631,422	426,869	67.6%	Loretta Sanchez (D)
FL	18	712,790	476,672	66.9%	Ileana Ros-Lehtinen (R)
NY	16	693,819	461,580	66.5%	José E. Serrano (D)
CA	39	643,115	427,353	66.5%	Linda T. Sánchez (D)
TX	23	847,651	562,913	66.4%	Francisco "Quico" Canseco (R)
CA	32	642,236	412,275	64.2%	Judy Chu (D)
AZ	4	698,314	446,159	63.9%	Ed Pastor (D)
CA	51	757,891	473,224	62.4%	Bob Filner (D)
CA	28	660,194	379,697	57.5%	Howard L. Berman (D)
AZ	7	855,769	479,014	56.0%	Raúl M. Grijalva (D)
CA	35	662,413	360,796	54.5%	Maxine Waters (D)
CA	18	723,607	381,039	52.7%	Dennis Cardoza (D)
NM	2	663,956	343,856	51.8%	Steve Pearce (R)
CA	21	784,176	401,194	51.2%	Devin Nunes (R)
NJ	13	684,965	346,294	50.6%	Albio Sires (D)

table continued on next page

CONGRESSIONAL DISTRICTS: 2010, *continued*

State	District	Total Population	Latino Population	Latino Share of Population	U.S. Representative
CA	17	664,240	334,955	50.4%	Sam Farr (D)
CA	23	695,404	344,083	49.5%	Lois Capps (D)
CA	37	648,847	320,630	49.4%	Laura Richardson (D)
NM	1	701,939	339,430	48.4%	Martin Heinrich (D)
NY	15	639,873	295,284	46.1%	Charles B. Rangel (D)
CA	45	914,209	413,441	45.2%	Mary Bono Mack (R)
NY	12	672,358	299,572	44.6%	Nydia M. Velázquez (D)
NY	7	667,632	296,455	44.4%	Joseph Crowley (D)
TX	18	720,991	313,533	43.5%	Sheila Jackson Lee (D)
CA	44	844,756	367,158	43.5%	Ken Calvert (R)
TX	32	640,419	271,442	42.4%	Pete Sessions (R)
TX	9	733,796	310,931	42.4%	Al Green (D)
CA	27	684,496	289,529	42.3%	Brad Sherman (D)
CA	16	676,880	270,191	39.9%	Zoe Lofgren (D)
TX	30	706,469	280,508	39.7%	Eddie Bernice Johnson (D)

For more information about this 2010 Census Profile or other NALEO Educational Fund policy and research activities, please contact Rosalind Gold, Senior Director of Policy, Research and Advocacy, rgold@naleo.org. Copies of Census 2010 Profiles for individual states are available at www.naleo.org. Reprinted with permission from NALEO Educational Fund.

United States

Population

Group	Number	%TP[1]	%HP[2]
Total Population	308,745,538	100.0	-
Hispanic or Latino (of any race)	50,477,594	16.3	100.0
Central American, ex. Mexican	3,998,280	1.3	7.9
Costa Rican	126,418	<0.1	0.3
Guatemalan	1,044,209	0.3	2.1
Honduran	633,401	0.2	1.3
Nicaraguan	348,202	0.1	0.7
Panamanian	165,456	0.1	0.3
Salvadoran	1,648,968	0.5	3.3
Cuban	1,785,547	0.6	3.5
Dominican Republic	1,414,703	0.5	2.8
Mexican	31,798,258	10.3	63.0
Puerto Rican	4,623,716	1.5	9.2
South American	2,769,434	0.9	5.5
Argentinean	224,952	0.1	0.4
Bolivian	99,210	<0.1	0.2
Chilean	126,810	<0.1	0.3
Colombian	908,734	0.3	1.8
Ecuadorian	564,631	0.2	1.1
Paraguayan	20,023	<0.1	<0.1
Peruvian	531,358	0.2	1.1
Uruguayan	56,884	<0.1	0.1
Venezuelan	215,023	0.1	0.4
Spaniard	635,253	0.2	1.3

Population Growth: 2000–2010

Group	%
Total Population	9.7
Hispanic or Latino (of any race)	43.0
Central American, ex. Mexican	137.0
Costa Rican	84.3
Guatemalan	180.3
Honduran	191.1
Nicaraguan	96.0
Panamanian	80.4
Salvadoran	151.7
Cuban	43.8
Dominican Republic	84.9
Mexican	54.1
Puerto Rican	35.7
South American	104.6
Argentinean	123.0
Bolivian	135.8
Chilean	84.2
Colombian	93.1
Ecuadorian	116.7
Paraguayan	128.3
Peruvian	127.1
Uruguayan	202.5
Venezuelan	135.0
Spaniard	534.4

Males per 100 Females

Group	Number
Total Population	96.7
Hispanic or Latino (of any race)	103.1
Central American, ex. Mexican	108.9
Costa Rican	93.4
Guatemalan	133.7
Honduran	110.9
Nicaraguan	89.4
Panamanian	71.5
Salvadoran	104.7
Cuban	98.8
Dominican Republic	85.3
Mexican	106.2
Puerto Rican	94.1
South American	90.1
Argentinean	99.3
Bolivian	92.6
Chilean	93.0
Colombian	80.5
Ecuadorian	104.8
Paraguayan	85.0
Peruvian	89.0
Uruguayan	101.4
Venezuelan	84.9
Spaniard	91.9

Average Household Size

Group	People
Total Population	2.58
Hispanic or Latino (of any race)	3.52
Central American, ex. Mexican	3.91
Costa Rican	3.02
Guatemalan	4.16
Honduran	3.82
Nicaraguan	3.51
Panamanian	2.69
Salvadoran	4.14
Cuban	2.79
Dominican Republic	3.40
Mexican	3.78
Puerto Rican	2.87
South American	3.10
Argentinean	2.72
Bolivian	3.36
Chilean	2.79
Colombian	2.95
Ecuadorian	3.64
Paraguayan	3.06
Peruvian	3.23
Uruguayan	2.91
Venezuelan	2.86
Spaniard	2.63

Median Age

Group	Years
Total Population	37.2
Hispanic or Latino (of any race)	27.3
Central American, ex. Mexican	30.2
Costa Rican	32.8
Guatemalan	28.5
Honduran	29.6
Nicaraguan	33.8
Panamanian	35.2
Salvadoran	30.6
Cuban	40.1
Dominican Republic	30.0
Mexican	25.5
Puerto Rican	28.0
South American	35.0
Argentinean	36.6
Bolivian	33.9
Chilean	36.6
Colombian	35.6
Ecuadorian	32.9
Paraguayan	30.2
Peruvian	36.4
Uruguayan	36.1
Venezuelan	33.4
Spaniard	35.2

High School Graduates

(Universe: Population 25 Years and Over)

Group	Number	%
Total Population	169,828,176	85.0
Hispanic or Latino (of any race)	15,729,225	61.5
Central American, ex. Mexican	1,229,291	53.1
Costa Rican	62,430	79.4
Guatemalan	261,380	45.5
Honduran	183,875	51.4
Nicaraguan	163,713	73.6
Panamanian	90,726	90.9
Salvadoran	441,975	46.8
Cuban	893,728	76.0
Dominican Republic	487,188	64.6
Mexican	8,617,825	55.5
Puerto Rican	1,792,697	73.4
South American	1,500,164	83.8
Argentinean	131,501	87.7
Bolivian	56,563	88.7
Chilean	73,302	89.2
Colombian	492,011	85.1
Ecuadorian	257,111	70.5
Paraguayan	9,345	81.3
Peruvian	304,661	89.1
Uruguayan	28,000	74.9
Venezuelan	122,521	93.4
Spaniard	311,644	87.7

Four-Year College Graduates

(Universe: Population 25 Years and Over)

Group	Number	%
Total Population	55,726,999	27.9
Hispanic or Latino (of any race)	3,329,326	13.0
Central American, ex. Mexican	259,600	11.2
Costa Rican	19,902	25.3
Guatemalan	49,972	8.7
Honduran	36,825	10.3
Nicaraguan	43,076	19.4
Panamanian	30,742	30.8
Salvadoran	73,221	7.8
Cuban	294,051	25.0
Dominican Republic	114,831	15.2
Mexican	1,421,023	9.1
Puerto Rican	387,923	15.9
South American	547,657	30.6
Argentinean	58,342	38.9
Bolivian	21,696	34.0
Chilean	29,501	35.9
Colombian	180,693	31.3
Ecuadorian	66,496	18.2
Paraguayan	3,321	28.9
Peruvian	104,165	30.5
Uruguayan	7,721	20.6
Venezuelan	65,185	49.7
Spaniard	107,497	30.3

Population Age 3–17 Enrolled in Public School

(Universe: Population Age 3–17 Enrolled in School)

Group	Number	%
Total Population	48,352,782	86.4
Hispanic or Latino (of any race)	10,886,462	93.0
Central American, ex. Mexican	700,787	92.6
Costa Rican	20,289	83.4
Guatemalan	172,787	90.5
Honduran	104,642	94.2
Nicaraguan	52,697	89.2
Panamanian	26,230	87.1
Salvadoran	312,416	95.3
Cuban	219,287	81.2
Dominican Republic	285,040	91.7
Mexican	7,641,087	94.9
Puerto Rican	993,926	90.0
South American	434,809	85.0
Argentinean	28,593	79.6
Bolivian	16,501	83.6
Chilean	18,439	82.0
Colombian	144,999	85.4
Ecuadorian	94,696	88.6
Paraguayan	3,400	77.4
Peruvian	80,130	85.0
Uruguayan	8,612	87.9
Venezuelan	32,485	82.0
Spaniard	86,626	83.5

Population Age 3–17 Enrolled in Private School

(Universe: Population Age 3–17 Enrolled in School)

Group	Number	%
Total Population	7,635,968	13.6
Hispanic or Latino (of any race)	814,030	7.0
Central American, ex. Mexican	55,721	7.4
Costa Rican	4,037	16.6
Guatemalan	18,054	9.5
Honduran	6,435	5.8
Nicaraguan	6,358	10.8
Panamanian	3,884	12.9
Salvadoran	15,573	4.7

Notes: (1) Percent of total population; (2) Percent of Hispanic population; Profiles include counties with populations greater than or equal to 250,000, cities with populations greater than or equal to 125,000 or counties/places with total Hispanic populations greater than or equal to 50,000; Please refer to the User's Guide for a full explanation of data

Group	Number	%
Cuban	50,835	18.8
Dominican Republic	25,638	8.3
Mexican	413,757	5.1
Puerto Rican	110,897	10.0
South American	76,510	15.0
Argentinean	7,330	20.4
Bolivian	3,235	16.4
Chilean	4,048	18.0
Colombian	24,831	14.6
Ecuadorian	12,191	11.4
Paraguayan	992	22.6
Peruvian	14,152	15.0
Uruguayan	1,188	12.1
Venezuelan	7,143	18.0
Spaniard	17,167	16.5

Foreign-Born Population

Group	Number	%
Total Population	38,675,012	12.7
Hispanic or Latino (of any race)	18,203,058	38.1
Central American, ex. Mexican	2,581,953	65.6
Costa Rican	74,872	59.5
Guatemalan	704,059	69.3
Honduran	425,875	69.7
Nicaraguan	220,730	64.5
Panamanian	76,484	48.1
Salvadoran	1,040,817	64.5
Cuban	999,690	59.2
Dominican Republic	777,554	58.0
Mexican	11,484,169	37.4
Puerto Rican	50,753	1.1
South American	1,872,507	67.7
Argentinean	146,004	67.5
Bolivian	68,572	66.7
Chilean	78,755	63.2
Colombian	597,006	66.8
Ecuadorian	384,474	66.4
Paraguayan	13,369	68.5
Peruvian	365,695	70.0
Uruguayan	41,778	73.9
Venezuelan	150,031	71.9
Spaniard	80,388	14.6

Foreign-Born Naturalized U.S. Citizens

Group	Number	%
Total Population	16,653,874	43.1
Hispanic or Latino (of any race)	5,226,941	28.7
Central American, ex. Mexican	735,326	28.5
Costa Rican	29,747	39.7
Guatemalan	161,189	22.9
Honduran	87,415	20.5
Nicaraguan	101,087	45.8
Panamanian	47,616	62.3
Salvadoran	292,250	28.1
Cuban	574,825	57.5
Dominican Republic	364,573	46.9
Mexican	2,548,167	22.2
Puerto Rican	25,495	50.2
South American	776,192	41.5
Argentinean	60,178	41.2
Bolivian	27,677	40.4
Chilean	36,557	46.4
Colombian	276,096	46.2
Ecuadorian	147,890	38.5
Paraguayan	6,063	45.4
Peruvian	152,366	41.7
Uruguayan	11,688	28.0
Venezuelan	42,508	28.3
Spaniard	40,848	50.8

Language Spoken at Home: English Only
(Universe: Population 5 Years and Over)

Group	Number	%
Total Population	226,738,479	79.9
Hispanic or Latino (of any race)	10,070,161	23.6
Central American, ex. Mexican	364,729	10.2
Costa Rican	26,114	22.6
Guatemalan	79,842	8.8
Honduran	46,543	8.5
Nicaraguan	38,709	12.1
Panamanian	53,775	36.4
Salvadoran	111,815	7.6
Cuban	274,415	17.2
Dominican Republic	100,224	8.1
Mexican	6,364,824	23.4
Puerto Rican	1,363,661	33.8
South American	330,673	12.9
Argentinean	32,840	16.3
Bolivian	12,798	13.6
Chilean	25,158	21.6
Colombian	103,982	12.5
Ecuadorian	50,198	9.5
Paraguayan	4,548	25.0
Peruvian	60,210	12.4
Uruguayan	5,142	9.9
Venezuelan	26,260	13.6
Spaniard	329,412	64.3

Language Spoken at Home: Spanish
(Universe: Population 5 Years and Over)

Group	Number	%
Total Population	35,470,765	12.5
Hispanic or Latino (of any race)	32,517,599	76.1
Central American, ex. Mexican	3,189,144	89.4
Costa Rican	89,133	77.0
Guatemalan	825,152	90.5
Honduran	502,536	91.3
Nicaraguan	280,317	87.6
Panamanian	93,044	62.9
Salvadoran	1,348,423	92.2
Cuban	1,309,854	82.3
Dominican Republic	1,126,270	91.5
Mexican	20,807,289	76.4
Puerto Rican	2,652,253	65.8
South American	2,216,454	86.4
Argentinean	164,105	81.7
Bolivian	80,512	85.4
Chilean	89,784	77.0
Colombian	727,528	87.2
Ecuadorian	477,869	90.1
Paraguayan	13,135	72.3
Peruvian	423,220	87.1
Uruguayan	45,802	88.4
Venezuelan	164,193	85.0
Spaniard	170,755	33.3

Unemployment Rate
(Universe: Population 16 Years and Over)

Group	%
Total Population	7.9
Hispanic or Latino (of any race)	9.6
Central American, ex. Mexican	9.1
Costa Rican	9.1
Guatemalan	8.7
Honduran	10.5
Nicaraguan	9.1
Panamanian	8.8
Salvadoran	8.8
Cuban	8.5
Dominican Republic	11.7
Mexican	9.5
Puerto Rican	12.5
South American	7.7
Argentinean	6.4
Bolivian	6.9
Chilean	6.6
Colombian	8.1
Ecuadorian	8.0
Paraguayan	8.1
Peruvian	7.6
Uruguayan	8.1
Venezuelan	7.9
Spaniard	9.2

Class of Worker: Private Wage and Salary
(Universe: Civilian Employed Population 16 Years and Over)

Group	Number	%
Total Population	111,303,933	78.5
Hispanic or Latino (of any race)	16,885,499	83.2
Central American, ex. Mexican	1,735,651	85.8
Costa Rican	50,429	81.1
Guatemalan	459,613	87.0
Honduran	268,965	86.2
Nicaraguan	148,230	83.2
Panamanian	57,807	74.6
Salvadoran	724,552	86.9
Cuban	629,005	80.7
Dominican Republic	488,117	84.4
Mexican	10,604,462	83.9
Puerto Rican	1,356,636	79.9
South American	1,195,277	82.5
Argentinean	92,107	79.3
Bolivian	45,728	82.1
Chilean	50,903	78.9
Colombian	381,844	82.6
Ecuadorian	255,883	85.2
Paraguayan	7,915	77.0
Peruvian	232,048	82.5
Uruguayan	23,505	80.0
Venezuelan	87,720	82.9
Spaniard	189,956	74.8

Class of Worker: Government
(Universe: Civilian Employed Population 16 Years and Over)

Group	Number	%
Total Population	21,024,265	14.8
Hispanic or Latino (of any race)	2,135,316	10.5
Central American, ex. Mexican	120,877	6.0
Costa Rican	6,463	10.4
Guatemalan	21,854	4.1
Honduran	13,908	4.5
Nicaraguan	14,861	8.3
Panamanian	16,015	20.7
Salvadoran	44,561	5.3
Cuban	94,604	12.1
Dominican Republic	55,159	9.5
Mexican	1,262,016	10.0
Puerto Rican	283,831	16.7
South American	131,556	9.1
Argentinean	12,024	10.3
Bolivian	4,998	9.0
Chilean	7,943	12.3
Colombian	44,077	9.5
Ecuadorian	22,643	7.5
Paraguayan	767	7.5
Peruvian	24,716	8.8
Uruguayan	2,129	7.2
Venezuelan	9,240	8.7
Spaniard	46,709	18.4

Means of Transportation to Work: Car, Truck or Van
(Universe: Workers 16 Years and Over)

Group	Number	%
Total Population	120,259,023	86.4
Hispanic or Latino (of any race)	16,597,731	83.4
Central American, ex. Mexican	1,549,435	78.0
Costa Rican	49,391	81.2
Guatemalan	384,713	74.1
Honduran	230,424	75.3
Nicaraguan	142,809	81.5
Panamanian	58,971	76.4
Salvadoran	658,199	80.6
Cuban	671,804	87.7
Dominican Republic	323,251	57.5
Mexican	10,758,657	86.9
Puerto Rican	1,279,483	76.3
South American	1,063,488	75.2
Argentinean	88,574	78.2
Bolivian	44,555	82.2
Chilean	50,425	79.8
Colombian	354,212	78.4
Ecuadorian	180,050	61.3
Paraguayan	6,983	69.7
Peruvian	213,120	77.7
Uruguayan	21,478	75.3
Venezuelan	86,535	83.5
Spaniard	211,423	84.6

Means of Transportation to Work: Public Transportation (ex. Taxicab)
(Universe: Workers 16 Years and Over)

Group	Number	%
Total Population	6,872,730	4.9
Hispanic or Latino (of any race)	1,589,344	8.0
Central American, ex. Mexican	248,277	12.5

Notes: (1) Percent of total population; (2) Percent of Hispanic population; Profiles include counties with populations greater than or equal to 250,000, cities with populations greater than or equal to 125,000 or counties/places with total Hispanic populations greater than or equal to 50,000; Please refer to the User's Guide for a full explanation of data

Costa Rican	5,006	8.2
Guatemalan	73,231	14.1
Honduran	42,849	14.0
Nicaraguan	18,044	10.3
Panamanian	11,417	14.8
Salvadoran	93,589	11.5
Cuban	32,279	4.2
Dominican Republic	165,574	29.4
Mexican	625,271	5.1
Puerto Rican	243,076	14.5
South American	211,741	15.0
Argentinean	10,827	9.6
Bolivian	5,465	10.1
Chilean	6,026	9.5
Colombian	56,401	12.5
Ecuadorian	82,656	28.1
Paraguayan	1,841	18.4
Peruvian	35,642	13.0
Uruguayan	3,213	11.3
Venezuelan	7,299	7.0
Spaniard	13,801	5.5

Homeownership Rate
(Universe: Occupied Housing Units)

Group	%
Total Population	65.1
Hispanic or Latino (of any race)	47.3
Central American, ex. Mexican	39.7
Costa Rican	46.8
Guatemalan	31.9
Honduran	31.9
Nicaraguan	46.4
Panamanian	48.8
Salvadoran	43.9
Cuban	57.1
Dominican Republic	26.8
Mexican	49.8
Puerto Rican	37.9
South American	48.8
Argentinean	55.0
Bolivian	56.4
Chilean	52.7
Colombian	50.3
Ecuadorian	40.8
Paraguayan	42.7
Peruvian	47.8
Uruguayan	44.1
Venezuelan	52.4
Spaniard	63.7

Median Home Value

Group	Dollars
Total Population	188,400
Hispanic or Latino (of any race)	185,900
Central American, ex. Mexican	244,100
Costa Rican	267,200
Guatemalan	246,100
Honduran	194,200
Nicaraguan	247,100
Panamanian	236,300
Salvadoran	254,000
Cuban	268,500
Dominican Republic	282,200
Mexican	155,200
Puerto Rican	219,100
South American	290,800
Argentinean	323,800
Bolivian	357,200
Chilean	294,700
Colombian	260,900
Ecuadorian	336,100
Paraguayan	285,300
Peruvian	296,500
Uruguayan	271,300
Venezuelan	258,400
Spaniard	241,000

Median Gross Rent

Group	Dollars
Total Population	841
Hispanic or Latino (of any race)	877
Central American, ex. Mexican	944
Costa Rican	1,038
Guatemalan	941
Honduran	886
Nicaraguan	1,022
Panamanian	958
Salvadoran	947
Cuban	920
Dominican Republic	944
Mexican	842
Puerto Rican	864
South American	1,101
Argentinean	1,118
Bolivian	1,240
Chilean	1,120
Colombian	1,092
Ecuadorian	1,102
Paraguayan	1,169
Peruvian	1,081
Uruguayan	1,033
Venezuelan	1,132
Spaniard	959

Median Household Income
(2010 Inflation-Adjusted Dollars)

Group	Dollars
Total Population	51,914
Hispanic or Latino (of any race)	41,534
Central American, ex. Mexican	43,332
Costa Rican	50,197
Guatemalan	41,272
Honduran	37,901
Nicaraguan	49,335
Panamanian	49,834
Salvadoran	44,322
Cuban	43,857
Dominican Republic	34,925
Mexican	40,588
Puerto Rican	38,426
South American	51,747
Argentinean	56,918
Bolivian	61,501
Chilean	58,579
Colombian	50,731
Ecuadorian	49,755
Paraguayan	50,930
Peruvian	50,179
Uruguayan	46,991
Venezuelan	52,435
Spaniard	54,275

Per Capita Income
(2010 Inflation-Adjusted Dollars)

Group	Dollars
Total Population	27,334
Hispanic or Latino (of any race)	15,638
Central American, ex. Mexican	15,838
Costa Rican	20,657
Guatemalan	14,281
Honduran	14,264
Nicaraguan	19,311
Panamanian	23,572
Salvadoran	15,416
Cuban	24,144
Dominican Republic	14,986
Mexican	13,925
Puerto Rican	17,556
South American	22,420
Argentinean	31,616
Bolivian	23,689
Chilean	26,551
Colombian	21,619
Ecuadorian	18,651
Paraguayan	23,507
Peruvian	21,529
Uruguayan	22,297
Venezuelan	24,842
Spaniard	27,912

Households with $100,000+ Income

Group	Number	%
Total Population	23,850,374	20.9
Hispanic or Latino (of any race)	1,605,309	12.5
Central American, ex. Mexican	126,726	12.0
Costa Rican	6,840	17.7
Guatemalan	26,906	10.5
Honduran	14,741	9.2
Nicaraguan	16,352	16.7
Panamanian	10,050	18.4
Salvadoran	48,507	11.4
Cuban	110,896	18.4
Dominican Republic	37,904	9.5
Mexican	838,495	10.9
Puerto Rican	184,689	13.1
South American	165,425	19.1
Argentinean	21,197	26.5
Bolivian	7,624	25.1
Chilean	9,788	23.5
Colombian	48,775	17.4
Ecuadorian	26,975	16.2
Paraguayan	1,028	18.5
Peruvian	28,095	17.7
Uruguayan	2,905	15.0
Venezuelan	14,836	21.6
Spaniard	48,174	22.1

Households with Food Stamps/SNAP Benefits During Past 12 Months

Group	Number	%
Total Population	10,583,720	9.3
Hispanic or Latino (of any race)	2,019,816	15.7
Central American, ex. Mexican	111,818	10.6
Costa Rican	3,042	7.9
Guatemalan	27,422	10.7
Honduran	23,632	14.7
Nicaraguan	11,786	12.0
Panamanian	5,602	10.3
Salvadoran	38,438	9.0
Cuban	108,226	17.9
Dominican Republic	121,131	30.4
Mexican	1,155,415	15.1
Puerto Rican	344,445	24.4
South American	70,886	8.2
Argentinean	4,313	5.4
Bolivian	1,103	3.6
Chilean	2,164	5.2
Colombian	24,038	8.6
Ecuadorian	20,562	12.3
Paraguayan	307	5.5
Peruvian	11,947	7.5
Uruguayan	1,378	7.1
Venezuelan	4,390	6.4
Spaniard	18,301	8.4

Poverty Rate
(Income in Past 12 Months Below Poverty Level)

Group	%
Total Population	13.8
Hispanic or Latino (of any race)	22.4
Central American, ex. Mexican	19.8
Costa Rican	14.4
Guatemalan	23.4
Honduran	25.4
Nicaraguan	14.0
Panamanian	14.0
Salvadoran	17.8
Cuban	15.2
Dominican Republic	25.7
Mexican	24.0
Puerto Rican	25.1
South American	12.3
Argentinean	10.7
Bolivian	8.7
Chilean	9.0
Colombian	11.9
Ecuadorian	15.3
Paraguayan	12.3
Peruvian	12.1
Uruguayan	13.5
Venezuelan	12.6
Spaniard	12.2

NATIONAL PROFILE

Notes: (1) Percent of total population; (2) Percent of Hispanic population; Profiles include counties with populations greater than or equal to 250,000, cities with populations greater than or equal to 125,000 or counties/places with total Hispanic populations greater than or equal to 50,000; Please refer to the User's Guide for a full explanation of data

Hispanic Population for the United States and States: 1980 to 2010

Sorted Alphabetically by State

Area	Hispanic Origin (of any race)							
	Number				Percent of Total Population			
	1980	1990	2000	2010	1980	1990	2000	2010
United States	14,608,673	22,354,059	35,305,818	50,477,594	6.4	9.0	12.5	16.3
Alabama	33,299	24,629	75,830	185,602	0.9	0.6	1.7	3.9
Alaska	9,507	17,803	25,852	39,249	2.4	3.2	4.1	5.5
Arizona	440,701	688,338	1,295,617	1,895,149	16.2	18.8	25.3	29.6
Arkansas	17,904	19,876	86,866	186,050	0.8	0.8	3.2	6.4
California	4,544,331	7,687,938	10,966,556	14,013,719	19.2	25.8	32.4	37.6
Colorado	339,717	424,302	735,601	1,038,687	11.8	12.9	17.1	20.7
Connecticut	124,499	213,116	320,323	479,087	4.0	6.5	9.4	13.4
Delaware	9,661	15,820	37,277	73,221	1.6	2.4	4.8	8.2
District of Columbia	17,679	32,710	44,953	54,749	2.8	5.4	7.9	9.1
Florida	858,158	1,574,143	2,682,715	4,223,806	8.8	12.2	16.8	22.5
Georgia	61,260	108,922	435,227	853,689	1.1	1.7	5.3	8.8
Hawaii	71,263	81,390	87,699	120,842	7.4	7.3	7.2	8.9
Idaho	36,615	52,927	101,690	175,901	3.9	5.3	7.9	11.2
Illinois	635,602	904,446	1,530,262	2,027,578	5.6	7.9	12.3	15.8
Indiana	87,047	98,788	214,536	389,707	1.6	1.8	3.5	6.0
Iowa	25,536	32,647	82,473	151,544	0.9	1.2	2.8	5.0
Kansas	63,339	93,670	188,252	300,042	2.7	3.8	7.0	10.5
Kentucky	27,406	21,984	59,939	132,836	0.7	0.6	1.5	3.1
Louisiana	99,134	93,044	107,738	192,560	2.4	2.2	2.4	4.2
Maine	5,005	6,829	9,360	16,935	0.4	0.6	0.7	1.3
Maryland	64,746	125,102	227,916	470,632	1.5	2.6	4.3	8.2
Massachusetts	141,043	287,549	428,729	627,654	2.5	4.8	6.8	9.6
Michigan	162,440	201,596	323,877	436,358	1.8	2.2	3.3	4.4
Minnesota	32,123	53,884	143,382	250,258	0.8	1.2	2.9	4.7
Mississippi	24,731	15,931	39,569	81,481	1.0	0.6	1.4	2.7
Missouri	51,653	61,702	118,592	212,470	1.1	1.2	2.1	3.5
Montana	9,974	12,174	18,081	28,565	1.3	1.5	2.0	2.9
Nebraska	28,025	36,969	94,425	167,405	1.8	2.3	5.5	9.2
Nevada	53,879	124,419	393,970	716,501	6.7	10.4	19.7	26.5
New Hampshire	5,587	11,333	20,489	36,704	0.6	1.0	1.7	2.8
New Jersey	491,883	739,861	1,117,191	1,555,144	6.7	9.6	13.3	17.7
New Mexico	477,222	579,224	765,386	953,403	36.6	38.2	42.1	46.3
New York	1,659,300	2,214,026	2,867,583	3,416,922	9.5	12.3	15.1	17.6
North Carolina	56,667	76,726	378,963	800,120	1.0	1.2	4.7	8.4
North Dakota	3,902	4,665	7,786	13,467	0.6	0.7	1.2	2.0
Ohio	119,883	139,696	217,123	354,674	1.1	1.3	1.9	3.1
Oklahoma	57,419	86,160	179,304	332,007	1.9	2.7	5.2	8.9
Oregon	65,847	112,707	275,314	450,062	2.5	4.0	8.0	11.7
Pennsylvania	153,961	232,262	394,088	719,660	1.3	2.0	3.2	5.7
Rhode Island	19,707	45,752	90,820	130,655	2.1	4.6	8.7	12.4
South Carolina	33,426	30,551	95,076	235,682	1.1	0.9	2.4	5.1
South Dakota	4,023	5,252	10,903	22,119	0.6	0.8	1.4	2.7
Tennessee	34,077	32,741	123,838	290,059	0.7	0.7	2.2	4.6
Texas	2,985,824	4,339,905	6,669,666	9,460,921	21.0	25.5	32.0	37.6
Utah	60,302	84,597	201,559	358,340	4.1	4.9	9.0	13.0
Vermont	3,304	3,661	5,504	9,208	0.6	0.7	0.9	1.5
Virginia	79,868	160,288	329,540	631,825	1.5	2.6	4.7	7.9
Washington	120,016	214,570	441,509	755,790	2.9	4.4	7.5	11.2
West Virginia	12,707	8,489	12,279	22,268	0.7	0.5	0.7	1.2
Wisconsin	62,972	93,194	192,921	336,056	1.3	1.9	3.6	5.9
Wyoming	24,499	25,751	31,669	50,231	5.2	5.7	6.4	8.9

Source: U.S. Census Bureau, Decennial Census of Population, 1980 to 2010

Hispanic Population for the United States and States: 1980 to 2010

Sorted by 2010 Population

Area	Hispanic Origin (of any race)							
	Population				Percent of Total Population			
	1980	1990	2000	2010	1980	1990	2000	2010
United States	14,608,673	22,354,059	35,305,818	50,477,594	6.4	9.0	12.5	16.3
California	4,544,331	7,687,938	10,966,556	14,013,719	19.2	25.8	32.4	37.6
Texas	2,985,824	4,339,905	6,669,666	9,460,921	21.0	25.5	32.0	37.6
Florida	858,158	1,574,143	2,682,715	4,223,806	8.8	12.2	16.8	22.5
New York	1,659,300	2,214,026	2,867,583	3,416,922	9.5	12.3	15.1	17.6
Illinois	635,602	904,446	1,530,262	2,027,578	5.6	7.9	12.3	15.8
Arizona	440,701	688,338	1,295,617	1,895,149	16.2	18.8	25.3	29.6
New Jersey	491,883	739,861	1,117,191	1,555,144	6.7	9.6	13.3	17.7
Colorado	339,717	424,302	735,601	1,038,687	11.8	12.9	17.1	20.7
New Mexico	477,222	579,224	765,386	953,403	36.6	38.2	42.1	46.3
Georgia	61,260	108,922	435,227	853,689	1.1	1.7	5.3	8.8
North Carolina	56,667	76,726	378,963	800,120	1.0	1.2	4.7	8.4
Washington	120,016	214,570	441,509	755,790	2.9	4.4	7.5	11.2
Pennsylvania	153,961	232,262	394,088	719,660	1.3	2.0	3.2	5.7
Nevada	53,879	124,419	393,970	716,501	6.7	10.4	19.7	26.5
Virginia	79,868	160,288	329,540	631,825	1.5	2.6	4.7	7.9
Massachusetts	141,043	287,549	428,729	627,654	2.5	4.8	6.8	9.6
Connecticut	124,499	213,116	320,323	479,087	4.0	6.5	9.4	13.4
Maryland	64,746	125,102	227,916	470,632	1.5	2.6	4.3	8.2
Oregon	65,847	112,707	275,314	450,062	2.5	4.0	8.0	11.7
Michigan	162,440	201,596	323,877	436,358	1.8	2.2	3.3	4.4
Indiana	87,047	98,788	214,536	389,707	1.6	1.8	3.5	6.0
Utah	60,302	84,597	201,559	358,340	4.1	4.9	9.0	13.0
Ohio	119,883	139,696	217,123	354,674	1.1	1.3	1.9	3.1
Wisconsin	62,972	93,194	192,921	336,056	1.3	1.9	3.6	5.9
Oklahoma	57,419	86,160	179,304	332,007	1.9	2.7	5.2	8.9
Kansas	63,339	93,670	188,252	300,042	2.7	3.8	7.0	10.5
Tennessee	34,077	32,741	123,838	290,059	0.7	0.7	2.2	4.6
Minnesota	32,123	53,884	143,382	250,258	0.8	1.2	2.9	4.7
South Carolina	33,426	30,551	95,076	235,682	1.1	0.9	2.4	5.1
Missouri	51,653	61,702	118,592	212,470	1.1	1.2	2.1	3.5
Louisiana	99,134	93,044	107,738	192,560	2.4	2.2	2.4	4.2
Arkansas	17,904	19,876	86,866	186,050	0.8	0.8	3.2	6.4
Alabama	33,299	24,629	75,830	185,602	0.9	0.6	1.7	3.9
Idaho	36,615	52,927	101,690	175,901	3.9	5.3	7.9	11.2
Nebraska	28,025	36,969	94,425	167,405	1.8	2.3	5.5	9.2
Iowa	25,536	32,647	82,473	151,544	0.9	1.2	2.8	5.0
Kentucky	27,406	21,984	59,939	132,836	0.7	0.6	1.5	3.1
Rhode Island	19,707	45,752	90,820	130,655	2.1	4.6	8.7	12.4
Hawaii	71,263	81,390	87,699	120,842	7.4	7.3	7.2	8.9
Mississippi	24,731	15,931	39,569	81,481	1.0	0.6	1.4	2.7
Delaware	9,661	15,820	37,277	73,221	1.6	2.4	4.8	8.2
District of Columbia	17,679	32,710	44,953	54,749	2.8	5.4	7.9	9.1
Wyoming	24,499	25,751	31,669	50,231	5.2	5.7	6.4	8.9
Alaska	9,507	17,803	25,852	39,249	2.4	3.2	4.1	5.5
New Hampshire	5,587	11,333	20,489	36,704	0.6	1.0	1.7	2.8
Montana	9,974	12,174	18,081	28,565	1.3	1.5	2.0	2.9
West Virginia	12,707	8,489	12,279	22,268	0.7	0.5	0.7	1.2
South Dakota	4,023	5,252	10,903	22,119	0.6	0.8	1.4	2.7
Maine	5,005	6,829	9,360	16,935	0.4	0.6	0.7	1.3
North Dakota	3,902	4,665	7,786	13,467	0.6	0.7	1.2	2.0
Vermont	3,304	3,661	5,504	9,208	0.6	0.7	0.9	1.5

Source: U.S. Census Bureau, Decennial Census of Population, 1980 to 2010

Hispanic Population for the United States and States: 1980 to 2010

Sorted by Percent of Total Population in 2010

Area	Hispanic Origin (of any race)							
	Population				Percent of Total Population			
	1980	1990	2000	2010	1980	1990	2000	2010
New Mexico	477,222	579,224	765,386	953,403	36.6	38.2	42.1	46.3
California	4,544,331	7,687,938	10,966,556	14,013,719	19.2	25.8	32.4	37.6
Texas	2,985,824	4,339,905	6,669,666	9,460,921	21.0	25.5	32.0	37.6
Arizona	440,701	688,338	1,295,617	1,895,149	16.2	18.8	25.3	29.6
Nevada	53,879	124,419	393,970	716,501	6.7	10.4	19.7	26.5
Florida	858,158	1,574,143	2,682,715	4,223,806	8.8	12.2	16.8	22.5
Colorado	339,717	424,302	735,601	1,038,687	11.8	12.9	17.1	20.7
New Jersey	491,883	739,861	1,117,191	1,555,144	6.7	9.6	13.3	17.7
New York	1,659,300	2,214,026	2,867,583	3,416,922	9.5	12.3	15.1	17.6
United States	14,608,673	22,354,059	35,305,818	50,477,594	6.4	9.0	12.5	16.3
Illinois	635,602	904,446	1,530,262	2,027,578	5.6	7.9	12.3	15.8
Connecticut	124,499	213,116	320,323	479,087	4.0	6.5	9.4	13.4
Utah	60,302	84,597	201,559	358,340	4.1	4.9	9.0	13.0
Rhode Island	19,707	45,752	90,820	130,655	2.1	4.6	8.7	12.4
Oregon	65,847	112,707	275,314	450,062	2.5	4.0	8.0	11.7
Washington	120,016	214,570	441,509	755,790	2.9	4.4	7.5	11.2
Idaho	36,615	52,927	101,690	175,901	3.9	5.3	7.9	11.2
Kansas	63,339	93,670	188,252	300,042	2.7	3.8	7.0	10.5
Massachusetts	141,043	287,549	428,729	627,654	2.5	4.8	6.8	9.6
Nebraska	28,025	36,969	94,425	167,405	1.8	2.3	5.5	9.2
District of Columbia	17,679	32,710	44,953	54,749	2.8	5.4	7.9	9.1
Oklahoma	57,419	86,160	179,304	332,007	1.9	2.7	5.2	8.9
Hawaii	71,263	81,390	87,699	120,842	7.4	7.3	7.2	8.9
Wyoming	24,499	25,751	31,669	50,231	5.2	5.7	6.4	8.9
Georgia	61,260	108,922	435,227	853,689	1.1	1.7	5.3	8.8
North Carolina	56,667	76,726	378,963	800,120	1.0	1.2	4.7	8.4
Maryland	64,746	125,102	227,916	470,632	1.5	2.6	4.3	8.2
Delaware	9,661	15,820	37,277	73,221	1.6	2.4	4.8	8.2
Virginia	79,868	160,288	329,540	631,825	1.5	2.6	4.7	7.9
Arkansas	17,904	19,876	86,866	186,050	0.8	0.8	3.2	6.4
Indiana	87,047	98,788	214,536	389,707	1.6	1.8	3.5	6.0
Wisconsin	62,972	93,194	192,921	336,056	1.3	1.9	3.6	5.9
Pennsylvania	153,961	232,262	394,088	719,660	1.3	2.0	3.2	5.7
Alaska	9,507	17,803	25,852	39,249	2.4	3.2	4.1	5.5
South Carolina	33,426	30,551	95,076	235,682	1.1	0.9	2.4	5.1
Iowa	25,536	32,647	82,473	151,544	0.9	1.2	2.8	5.0
Minnesota	32,123	53,884	143,382	250,258	0.8	1.2	2.9	4.7
Tennessee	34,077	32,741	123,838	290,059	0.7	0.7	2.2	4.6
Michigan	162,440	201,596	323,877	436,358	1.8	2.2	3.3	4.4
Louisiana	99,134	93,044	107,738	192,560	2.4	2.2	2.4	4.2
Alabama	33,299	24,629	75,830	185,602	0.9	0.6	1.7	3.9
Missouri	51,653	61,702	118,592	212,470	1.1	1.2	2.1	3.5
Ohio	119,883	139,696	217,123	354,674	1.1	1.3	1.9	3.1
Kentucky	27,406	21,984	59,939	132,836	0.7	0.6	1.5	3.1
Montana	9,974	12,174	18,081	28,565	1.3	1.5	2.0	2.9
New Hampshire	5,587	11,333	20,489	36,704	0.6	1.0	1.7	2.8
Mississippi	24,731	15,931	39,569	81,481	1.0	0.6	1.4	2.7
South Dakota	4,023	5,252	10,903	22,119	0.6	0.8	1.4	2.7
North Dakota	3,902	4,665	7,786	13,467	0.6	0.7	1.2	2.0
Vermont	3,304	3,661	5,504	9,208	0.6	0.7	0.9	1.5
Maine	5,005	6,829	9,360	16,935	0.4	0.6	0.7	1.3
West Virginia	12,707	8,489	12,279	22,268	0.7	0.5	0.7	1.2

Source: U.S. Census Bureau, Decennial Census of Population, 1980 to 2010

Hispanic or Latino

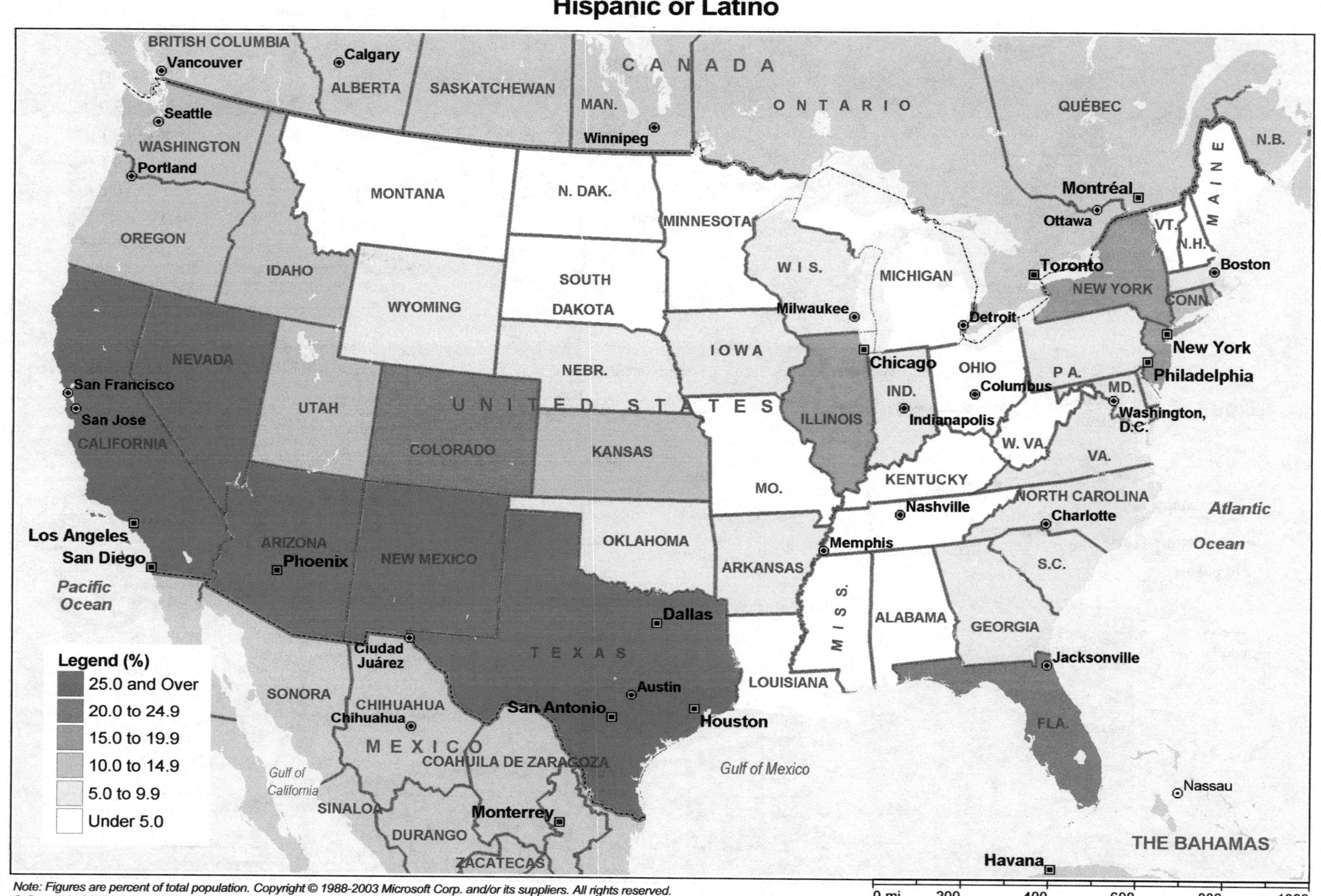

Note: Figures are percent of total population. Copyright © 1988-2003 Microsoft Corp. and/or its suppliers. All rights reserved.
© Copyright 2002 by Geographic Data Technology, Inc. All rights reserved. © 2002 Navigation Technologies. All rights reserved.

NATIONAL PROFILE

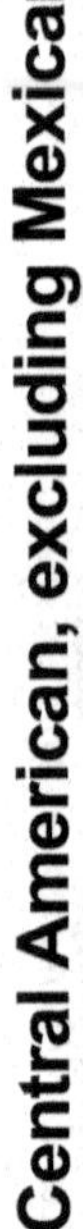

Central American, excluding Mexican

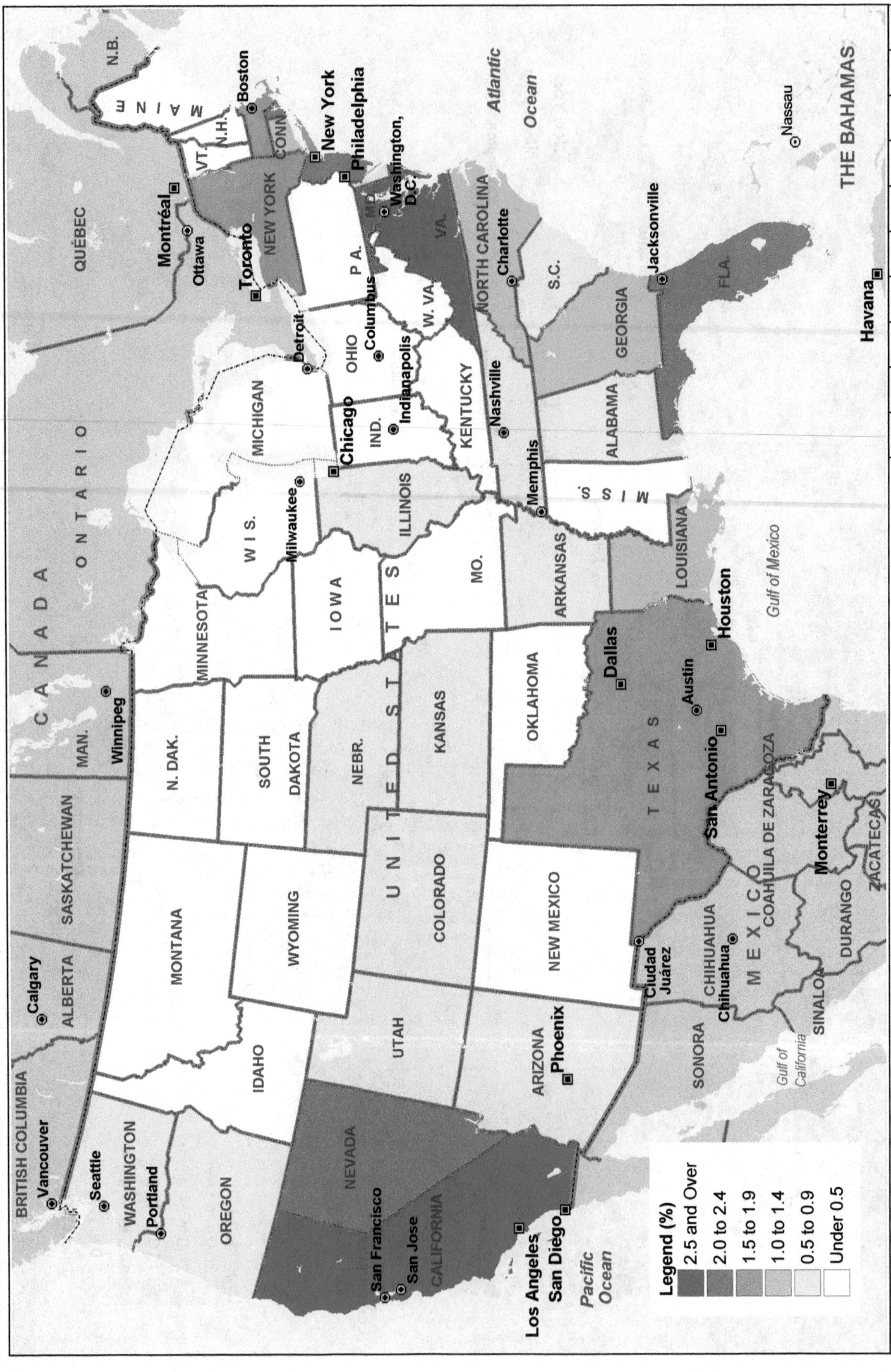

Legend (%)
- 2.5 and Over
- 2.0 to 2.4
- 1.5 to 1.9
- 1.0 to 1.4
- 0.5 to 0.9
- Under 0.5

Note: Figures are percent of total population.

Central American: Costa Rican

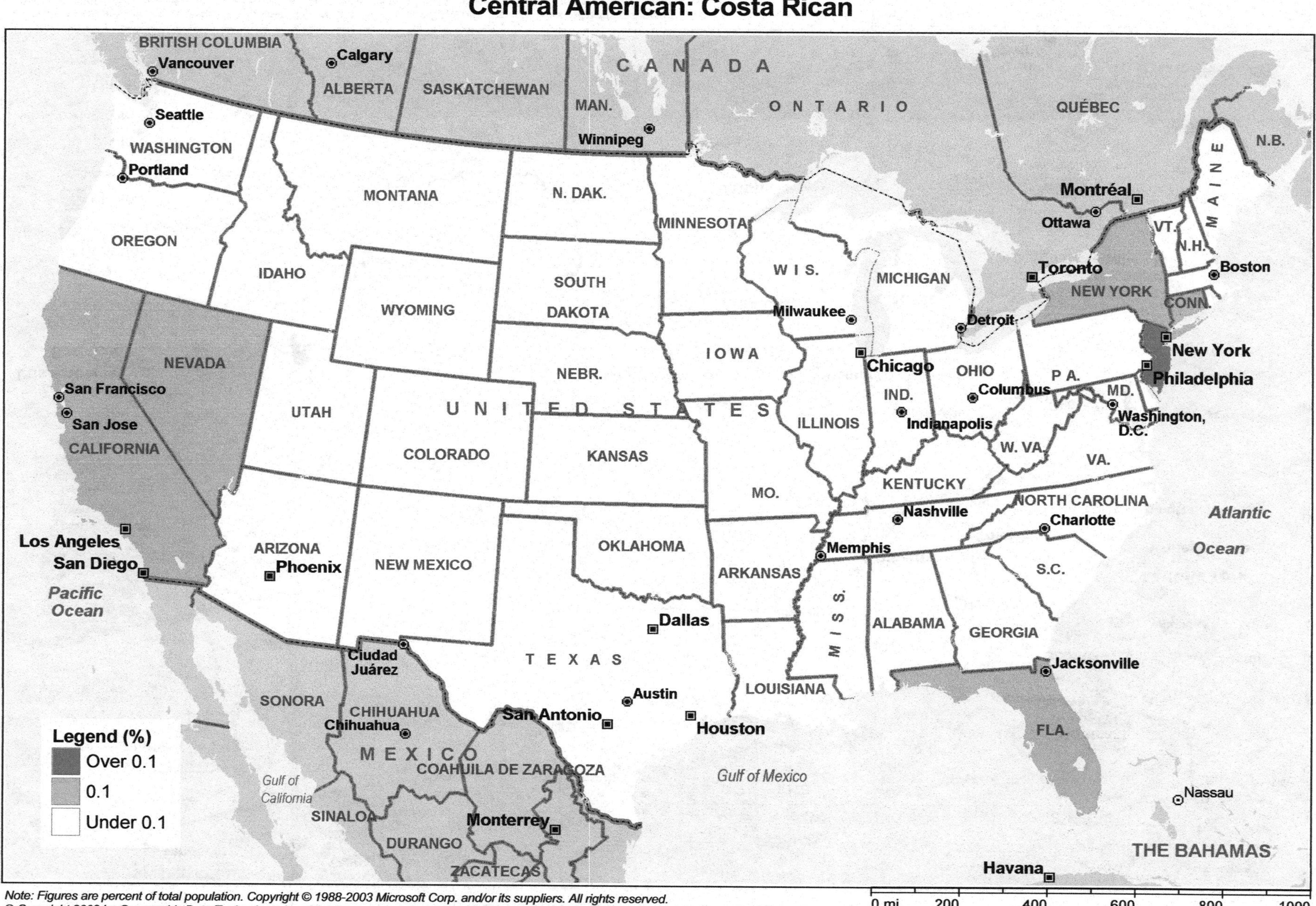

Note: Figures are percent of total population.

Central American: Guatemalan

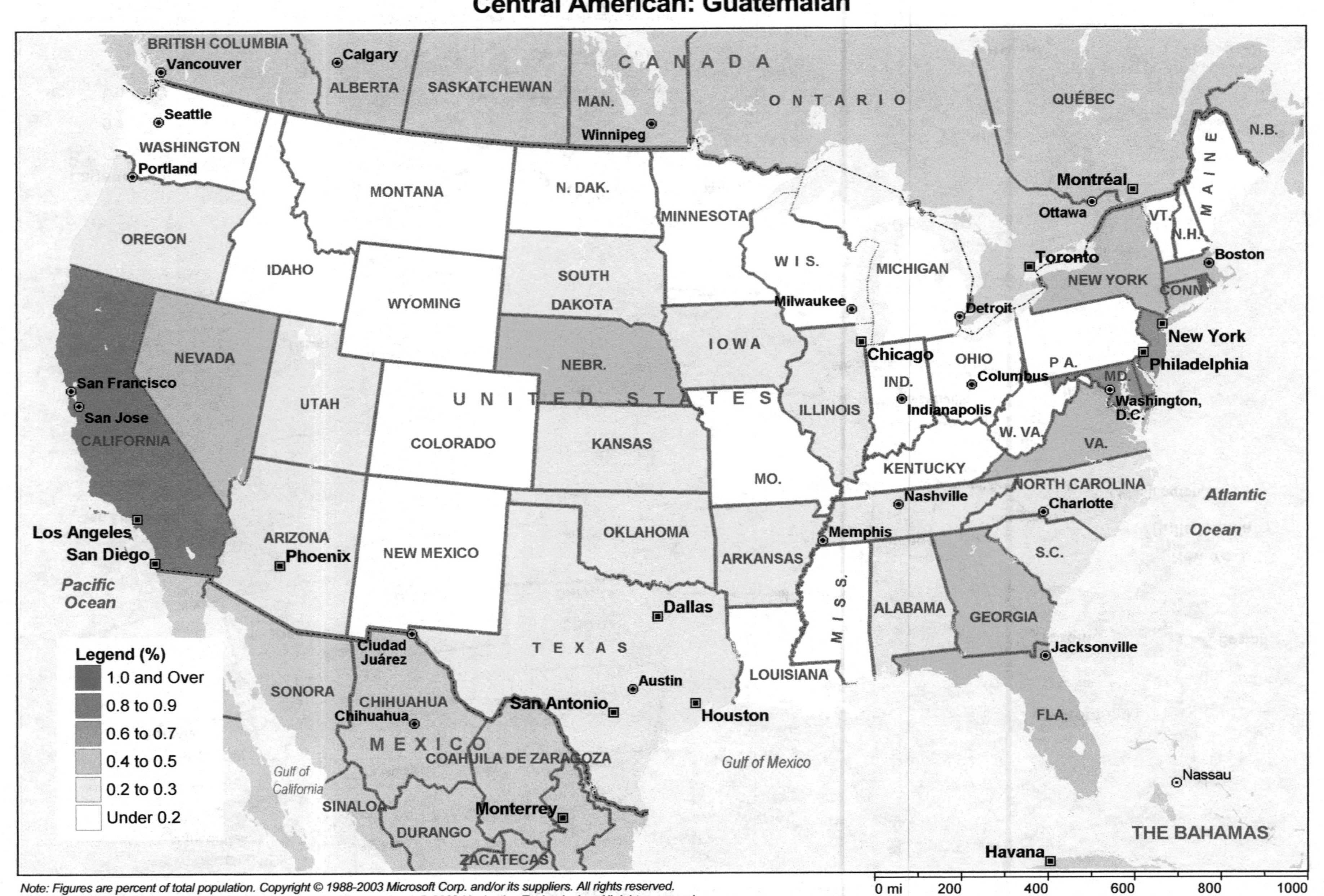

Note: Figures are percent of total population. Copyright © 1988-2003 Microsoft Corp. and/or its suppliers. All rights reserved.

Central American: Honduran

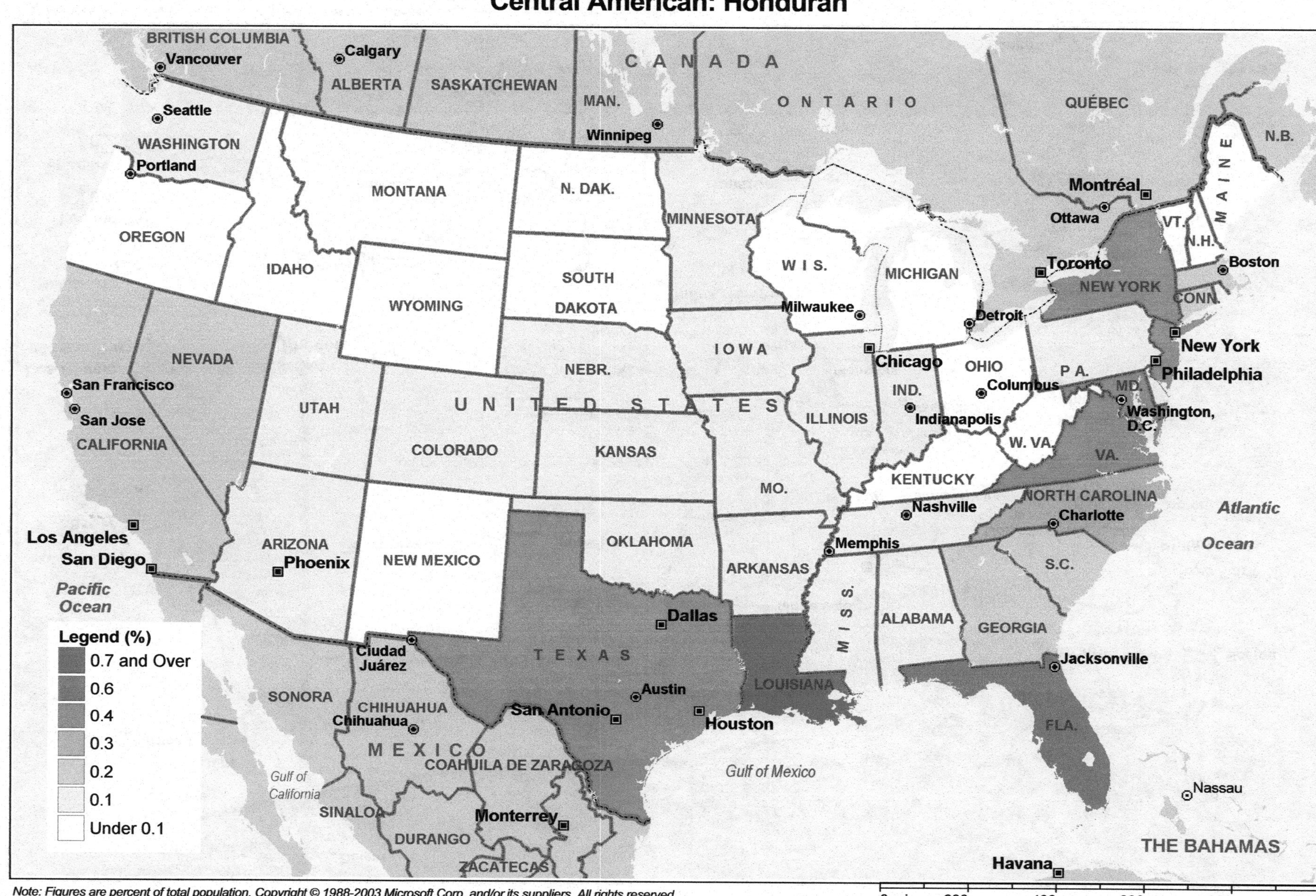

Note: Figures are percent of total population.

Central American: Nicaraguan

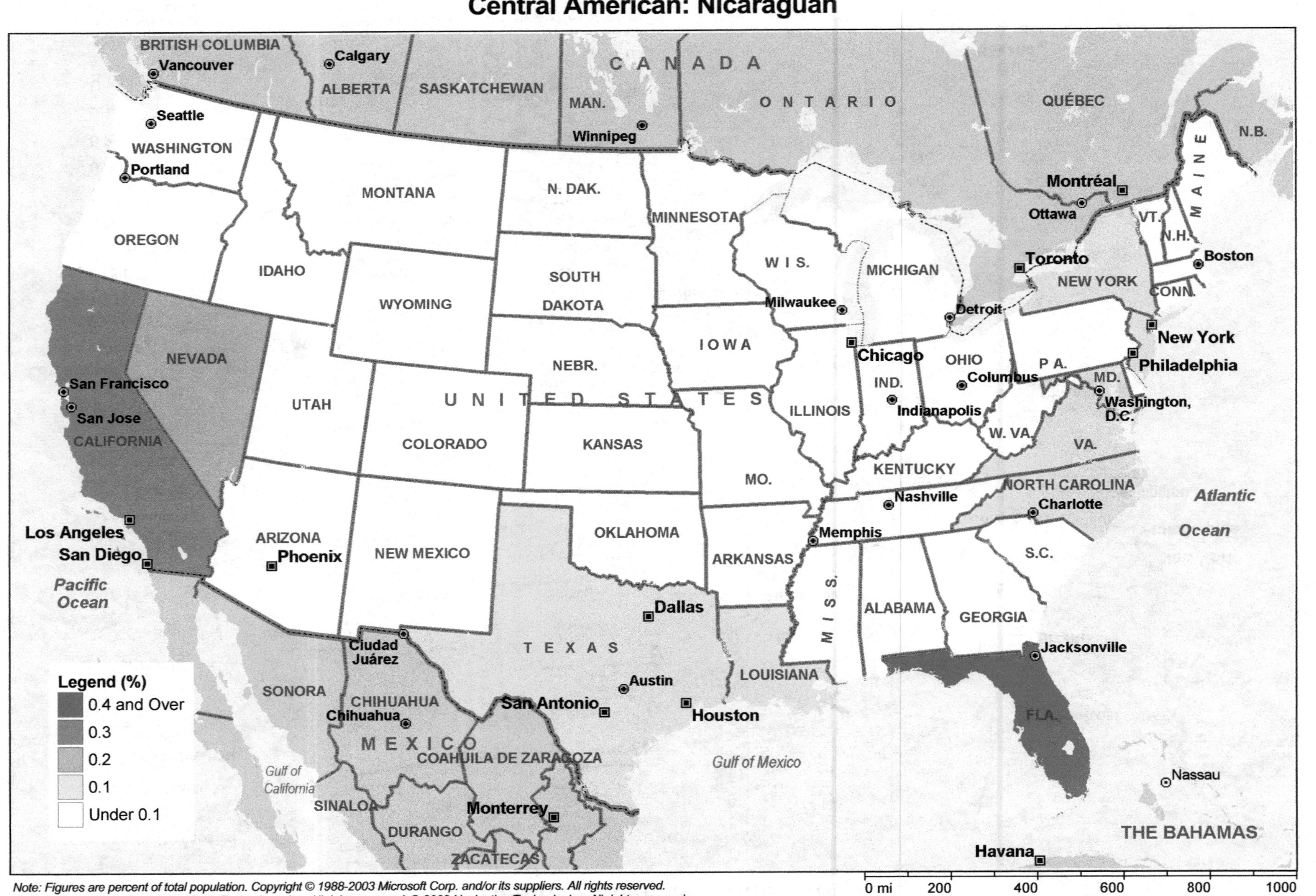

Note: Figures are percent of total population.

Central American: Panamanian

Note: Figures are percent of total population.

Central American: Salvadoran

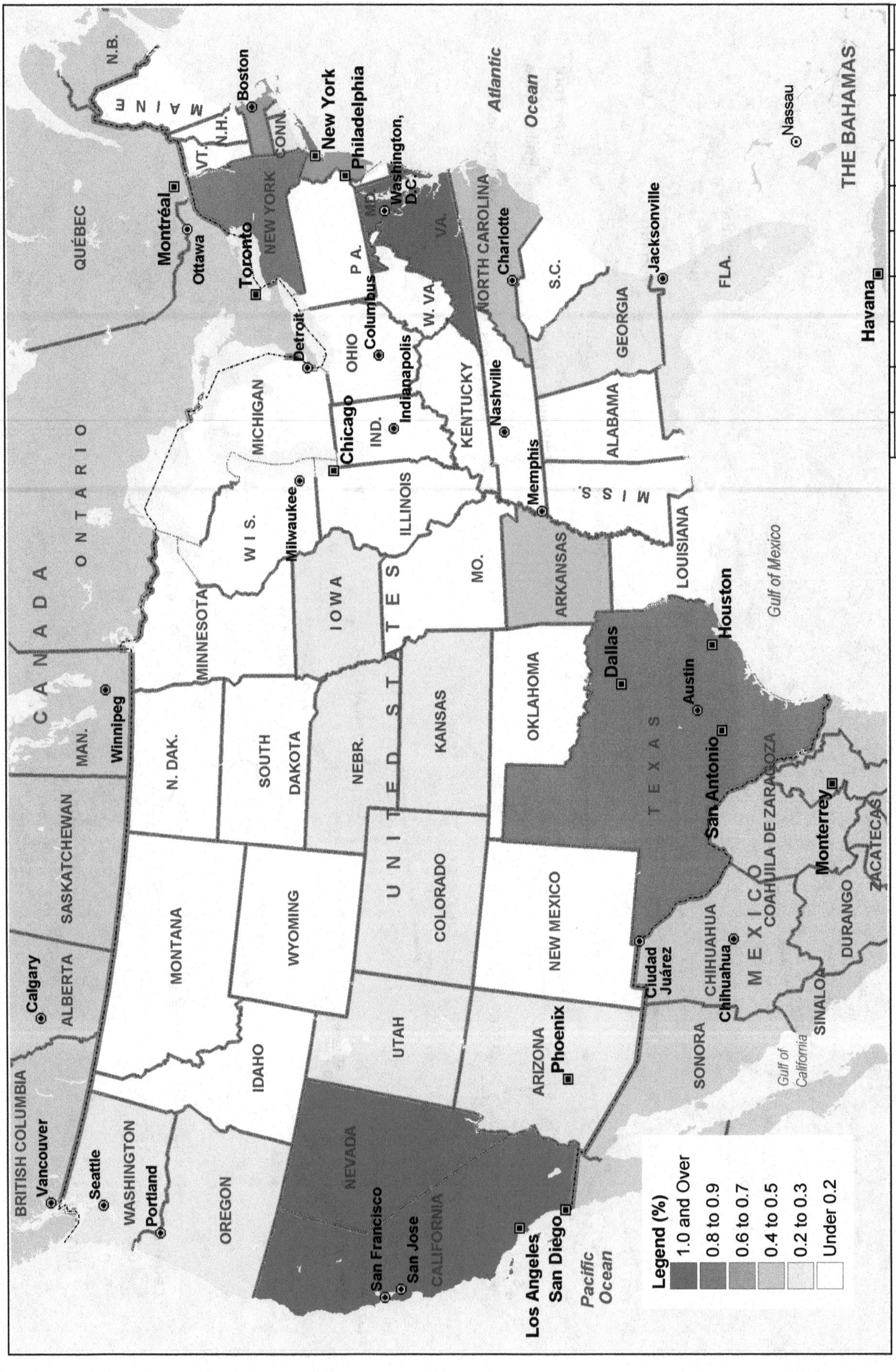

Legend (%)

- 1.0 and Over
- 0.8 to 0.9
- 0.6 to 0.7
- 0.4 to 0.5
- 0.2 to 0.3
- Under 0.2

0 mi 200 400 600 800 1000

Note: Figures are percent of total population.

Cuban

Note: Figures are percent of total population.

NATIONAL PROFILE

Dominican Republic

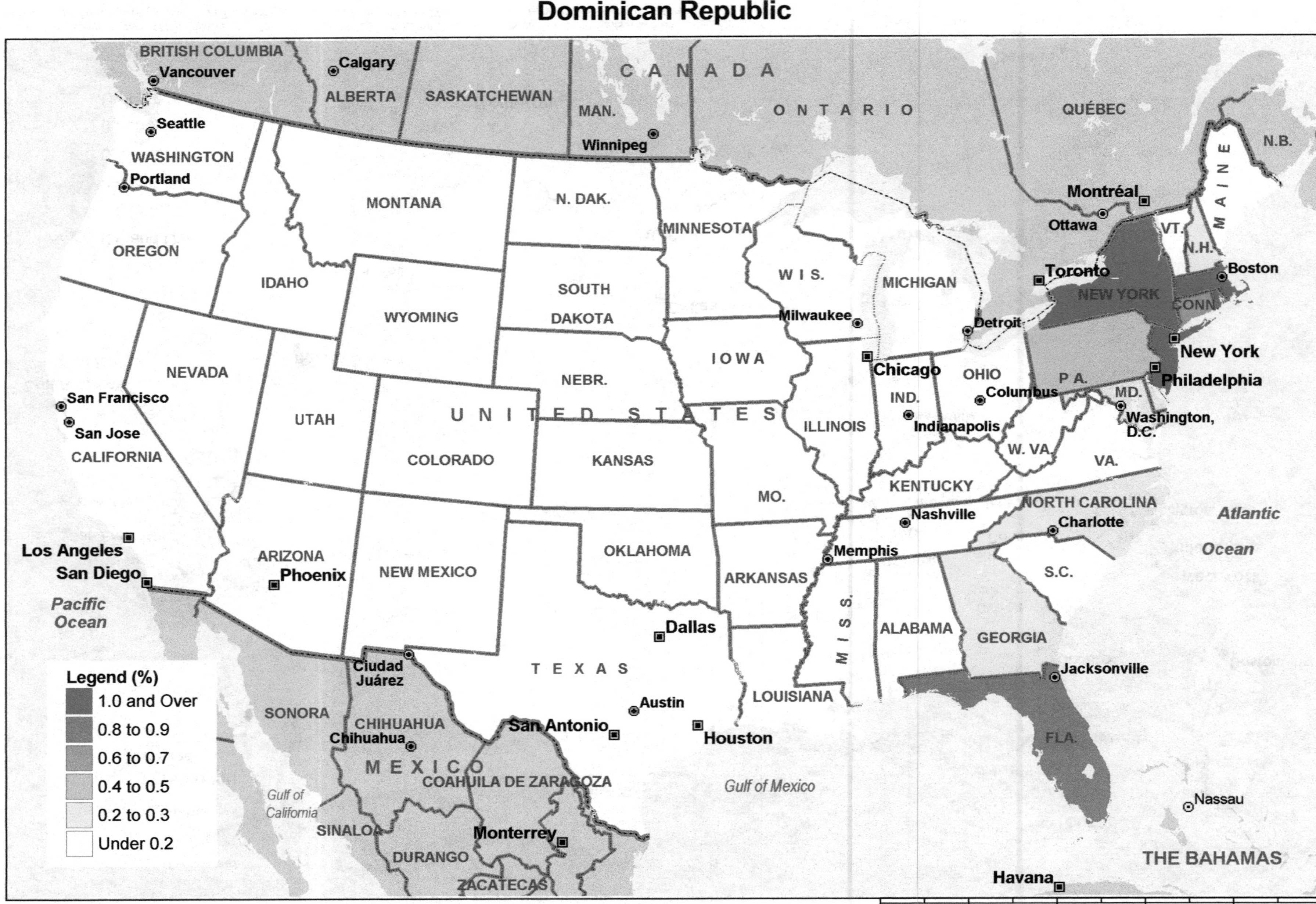

Note: Figures are percent of total population. Copyright © 1988-2003 Microsoft Corp. and/or its suppliers. All rights reserved.

Mexican

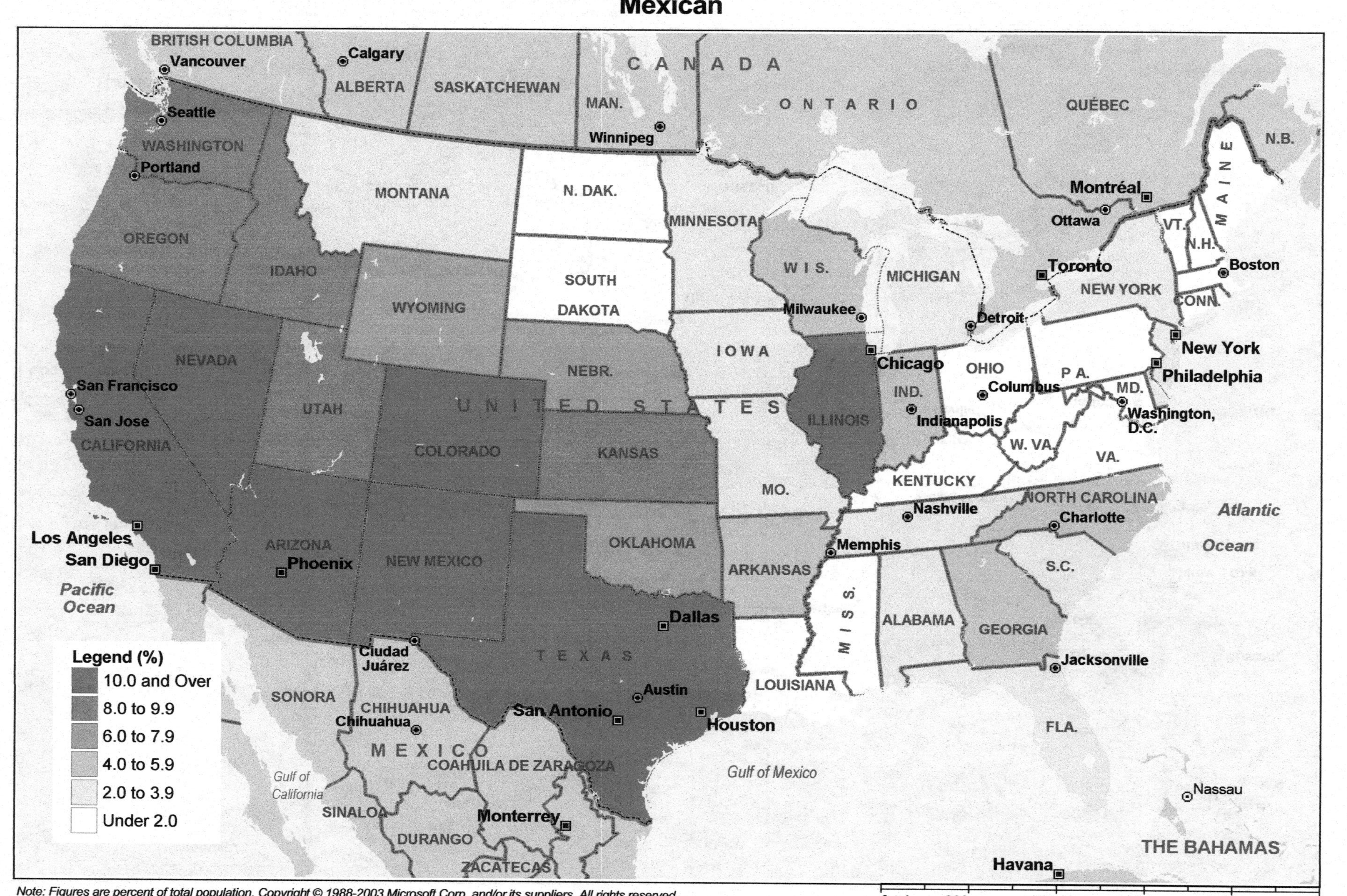

Note: Figures are percent of total population. Copyright © 1988-2003 Microsoft Corp. and/or its suppliers. All rights reserved.

Puerto Rican

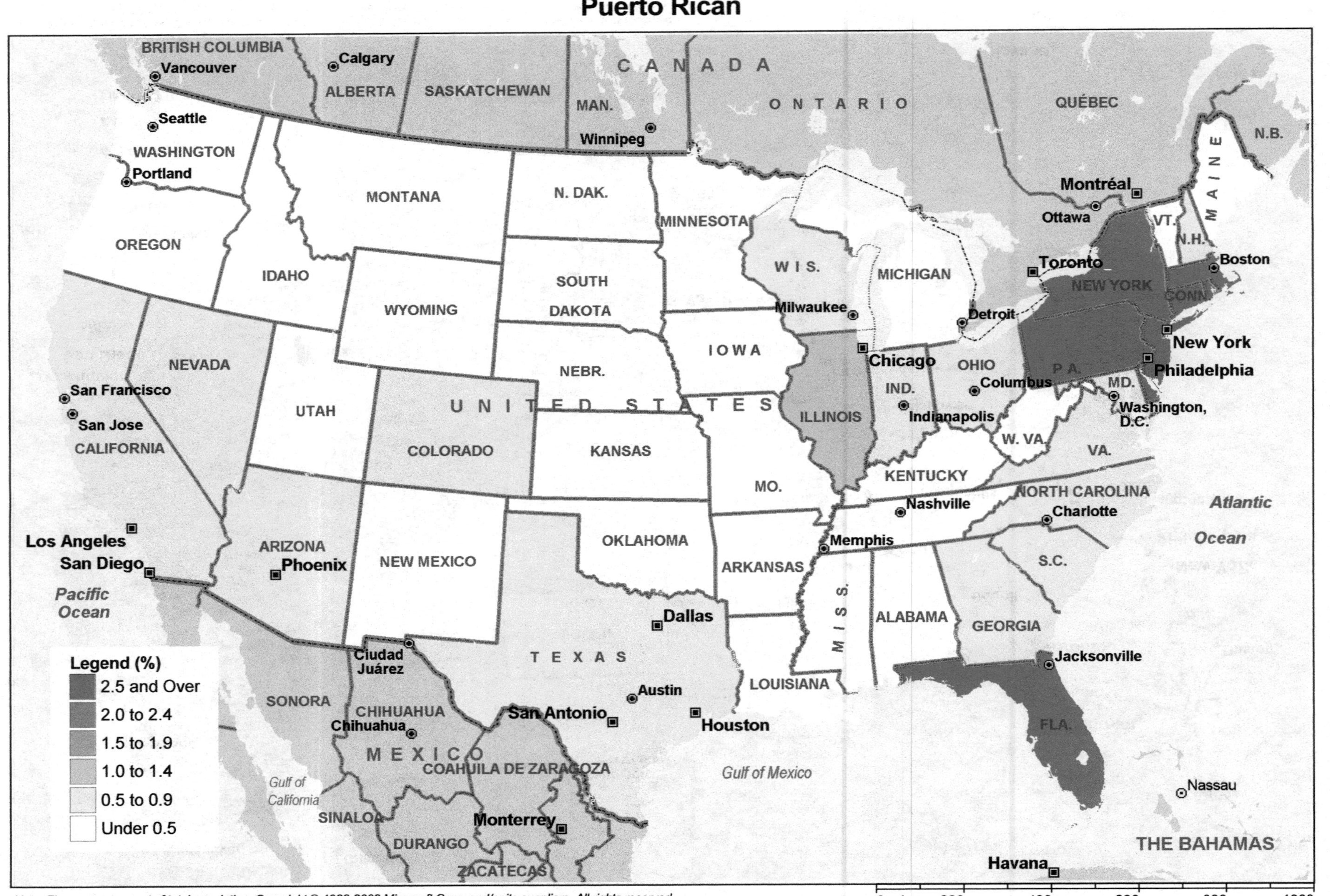

Note: Figures are percent of total population.

South American

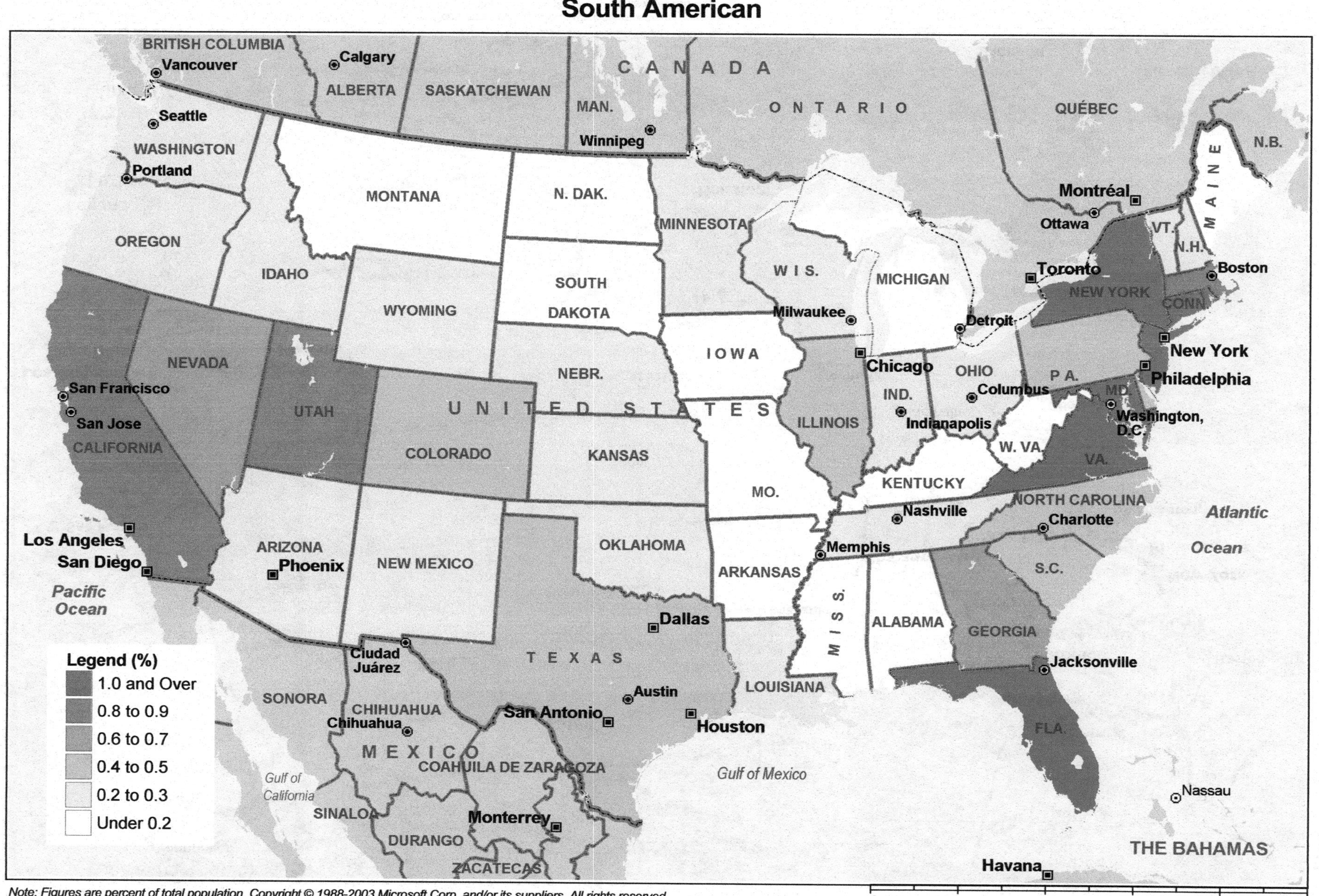

Note: Figures are percent of total population. Copyright © 1988-2003 Microsoft Corp. and/or its suppliers. All rights reserved. © Copyright 2002 by Geographic Data Technology, Inc. All rights reserved. © 2002 Navigation Technologies. All rights reserved.

South American: Argentinean

Note: Figures are percent of total population.

South American: Bolivian

Note: Figures are percent of total population.

South American: Chilean

Note: Figures are percent of total population. Copyright © 1988-2003 Microsoft Corp. and/or its suppliers. All rights reserved.

South American: Colombian

Note: Figures are percent of total population.

South American: Ecuadorian

Note: Figures are percent of total population.

South American: Paraguayan

Note: Figures are percent of total population.

South American: Peruvian

Note: Figures are percent of total population.

South American: Uruguayan

Note: Figures are percent of total population.

South American: Venezuelan

Note: Figures are percent of total population.

Spaniard

Note: Figures are percent of total population. Copyright © 1988-2003 Microsoft Corp. and/or its suppliers. All rights reserved.

SECTION TWO:
State & Place Profiles

Alabama

EDITOR'S NOTE: For a place to be included in this edition, it must meet one of two criteria. Either its overall population is at least 125,000, OR its overall population is at least 25,000 and its Hispanic/Latino population is at least 20% of the overall population. In Alabama, less than five places meet either of these criteria. In an effort to include at least five places for each state, we have included places with at least 10,000 total population with the highest percentage of Hispanic/Latino population. These places are identified with an asterisk (*). For the state of Alabama, the following locations are included:

- Albertville*
- Birmingham
- Huntsville
- Mobile
- Montgomery

Section Two: State & Place Profiles starts with the state profile, followed by place profiles that meet the criteria above. Places are listed alphabetically within each state. All states, all counties and places that meet the above criteria are ranked and compared in *Section Three: Rankings & Comparisons*, on page 1055.

For a more detailed look at the Hispanic/Latino population in Alabama, a companion web site is available at no additional charge with purchase of this print edition. Visit http://gold.greyhouse.com/page/info_hispanic for more information.

The web site includes data for all counties and places in Alabama with Hispanic/Latino population, plus ten additional topics: Self Employed Worker; Walked to Work; Worked from Home; Mean Travel Time to Work; Mean Household Income; Households with Cash Public Assistance; Mean Cash Pubic Assistance; Poverty Rates for 18 and Under, 18 to 64, and 65 and Over.

Population

Group	Number	%TP[1]	%HP[2]
Total Population	4,779,736	100.0	–
Hispanic or Latino (of any race)	185,602	3.9	100.0
Central American, ex. Mexican	22,800	0.5	12.3
Costa Rican	504	<0.1	0.3
Guatemalan	14,282	0.3	7.7
Honduran	3,280	0.1	1.8
Nicaraguan	739	<0.1	0.4
Panamanian	1,450	<0.1	0.8
Salvadoran	2,419	0.1	1.3
Cuban	4,064	0.1	2.2
Dominican Republic	852	<0.1	0.5
Mexican	122,911	2.6	66.2
Puerto Rican	12,225	0.3	6.6
South American	5,938	0.1	3.2
Argentinean	496	<0.1	0.3
Bolivian	292	<0.1	0.2
Chilean	451	<0.1	0.2
Colombian	2,052	<0.1	1.1
Ecuadorian	466	<0.1	0.3
Paraguayan	121	<0.1	0.1
Peruvian	1,116	<0.1	0.6
Uruguayan	129	<0.1	0.1
Venezuelan	757	<0.1	0.4
Spaniard	2,079	<0.1	1.1

Population Growth: 2000–2010

Group	%
Total Population	7.5
Hispanic or Latino (of any race)	144.8
Central American, ex. Mexican	380.8
Costa Rican	131.2
Guatemalan	482.2
Honduran	513.1
Nicaraguan	310.6
Panamanian	94.9
Salvadoran	421.3
Cuban	72.6
Dominican Republic	189.8
Mexican	176.1
Puerto Rican	93.4
South American	184.9
Argentinean	213.9
Chilean	194.8
Colombian	164.8
Ecuadorian	193.1
Peruvian	269.5
Venezuelan	166.5
Spaniard	766.3

Males per 100 Females

Group	Number
Total Population	94.3
Hispanic or Latino (of any race)	126.8
Central American, ex. Mexican	141.8
Costa Rican	80.0
Guatemalan	167.6
Honduran	137.7
Nicaraguan	85.7
Panamanian	64.2
Salvadoran	121.3
Cuban	104.2
Dominican Republic	86.4
Mexican	133.0
Puerto Rican	101.0
South American	86.8
Argentinean	79.7
Bolivian	105.6
Chilean	105.0
Colombian	78.1
Ecuadorian	98.3
Paraguayan	98.4
Peruvian	87.9
Uruguayan	92.5
Venezuelan	85.1
Spaniard	92.7

Average Household Size

Group	People
Total Population	2.48
Hispanic or Latino (of any race)	3.60
Central American, ex. Mexican	4.13
Costa Rican	2.82
Guatemalan	4.69
Honduran	3.64
Nicaraguan	3.08
Panamanian	2.66
Salvadoran	3.80
Cuban	2.65
Dominican Republic	2.90
Mexican	3.83
Puerto Rican	2.74
South American	2.77
Argentinean	2.72
Bolivian	2.94
Chilean	2.74
Colombian	2.72
Ecuadorian	2.91
Paraguayan	2.40
Peruvian	2.90
Uruguayan	2.52
Venezuelan	2.80
Spaniard	2.46

Median Age

Group	Years
Total Population	37.9
Hispanic or Latino (of any race)	24.7
Central American, ex. Mexican	25.8
Costa Rican	32.0
Guatemalan	24.6
Honduran	27.8
Nicaraguan	31.1
Panamanian	31.4
Salvadoran	28.0
Cuban	29.9
Dominican Republic	26.9
Mexican	23.7
Puerto Rican	26.2
South American	31.9
Argentinean	32.4
Bolivian	28.4
Chilean	32.9
Colombian	32.3
Ecuadorian	28.2
Paraguayan	20.3
Peruvian	34.8
Uruguayan	36.8
Venezuelan	32.3
Spaniard	35.1

High School Graduates

(Universe: Population 25 Years and Over)

Group	Number	%
Total Population	2,529,295	81.4
Hispanic or Latino (of any race)	44,368	55.5
Central American, ex. Mexican	4,096	41.1
Guatemalan	1,378	24.2
Honduran	745	47.6
Panamanian	801	90.3
Salvadoran	595	55.6
Cuban	1,848	77.7
Dominican Republic	345	90.1
Mexican	25,812	48.7
Puerto Rican	4,998	87.4
South American	3,436	90.8
Colombian	1,292	93.3
Peruvian	740	93.8
Spaniard	1,206	83.5

Four-Year College Graduates

(Universe: Population 25 Years and Over)

Group	Number	%
Total Population	675,076	21.7
Hispanic or Latino (of any race)	9,841	12.3
Central American, ex. Mexican	854	8.6
Guatemalan	191	3.3
Honduran	162	10.3
Panamanian	143	16.1
Salvadoran	60	5.6
Cuban	693	29.1
Dominican Republic	120	31.3
Mexican	3,844	7.3
Puerto Rican	1,800	31.5
South American	1,569	41.5
Colombian	798	57.6
Peruvian	287	36.4
Spaniard	382	26.5

Population Age 3–17 Enrolled in Public School

(Universe: Population Age 3–17 Enrolled in School)

Group	Number	%
Total Population	730,629	85.8
Hispanic or Latino (of any race)	31,635	90.8
Central American, ex. Mexican	3,012	84.3
Guatemalan	1,934	89.4
Honduran	333	94.9
Panamanian	224	77.2
Salvadoran	306	61.8
Cuban	556	84.6
Dominican Republic	175	88.4
Mexican	22,780	94.3
Puerto Rican	2,135	84.2
South American	1,425	77.7
Colombian	459	64.0
Peruvian	232	92.4
Spaniard	261	96.0

Population Age 3–17 Enrolled in Private School

(Universe: Population Age 3–17 Enrolled in School)

Group	Number	%
Total Population	121,031	14.2
Hispanic or Latino (of any race)	3,194	9.2
Central American, ex. Mexican	561	15.7
Guatemalan	230	10.6
Honduran	18	5.1

Notes: (1) Percent of total population; (2) Percent of Hispanic/Latino population; Profiles include places with an overall population of at least 125,000, OR an overall population of at least 25,000 where the Hispanic/Latino population is at least 20% of the overall population. In states where less than five places meet either of these criteria, we have included places with at least 10,000 total population with the highest percentage of Hispanic/Latino population. These places are identified with an asterisk (*); Please refer to the User's Guide for a full explanation of data.

Group	Number	%
Panamanian	66	22.8
Salvadoran	189	38.2
Cuban	101	15.4
Dominican Republic	23	11.6
Mexican	1,383	5.7
Puerto Rican	402	15.8
South American	410	22.3
Colombian	258	36.0
Peruvian	19	7.6
Spaniard	11	4.0

Foreign-Born Population

Group	Number	%
Total Population	157,935	3.4
Hispanic or Latino (of any race)	81,235	50.0
Central American, ex. Mexican	12,340	63.2
Guatemalan	7,973	67.0
Honduran	1,861	69.7
Panamanian	708	44.8
Salvadoran	1,013	49.7
Cuban	1,698	42.3
Dominican Republic	346	47.5
Mexican	61,055	54.7
Puerto Rican	130	1.2
South American	4,016	55.7
Colombian	1,427	52.5
Peruvian	856	63.9
Spaniard	389	19.0

Foreign-Born Naturalized U.S. Citizens

Group	Number	%
Total Population	45,532	28.8
Hispanic or Latino (of any race)	10,077	12.4
Central American, ex. Mexican	2,119	17.2
Guatemalan	862	10.8
Honduran	345	18.5
Panamanian	294	41.5
Salvadoran	325	32.1
Cuban	639	37.6
Dominican Republic	126	36.4
Mexican	5,171	8.5
Puerto Rican	41	31.5
South American	1,310	32.6
Colombian	577	40.4
Peruvian	258	30.1
Spaniard	153	39.3

Language Spoken at Home: English Only
(Universe: Population 5 Years and Over)

Group	Number	%
Total Population	4,194,045	95.1
Hispanic or Latino (of any race)	34,431	24.7
Central American, ex. Mexican	2,934	17.4
Guatemalan	1,039	10.3
Honduran	461	18.9
Panamanian	666	48.9
Salvadoran	378	22.0
Cuban	1,549	43.1
Dominican Republic	155	23.9
Mexican	19,022	20.1
Puerto Rican	4,513	46.2
South American	1,777	27.1
Colombian	693	29.0
Peruvian	180	14.6
Spaniard	1,394	70.5

Language Spoken at Home: Spanish
(Universe: Population 5 Years and Over)

Group	Number	%
Total Population	137,617	3.1
Hispanic or Latino (of any race)	104,149	74.6
Central American, ex. Mexican	13,465	79.7
Guatemalan	8,572	85.0
Honduran	1,977	81.1
Panamanian	695	51.1
Salvadoran	1,323	76.8
Cuban	2,018	56.1
Dominican Republic	494	76.1
Mexican	75,597	79.8
Puerto Rican	5,207	53.3
South American	4,755	72.5
Colombian	1,675	70.2
Peruvian	1,053	85.4
Spaniard	511	25.8

Unemployment Rate
(Universe: Population 16 Years and Over)

Group	%
Total Population	8.7
Hispanic or Latino (of any race)	8.7
Central American, ex. Mexican	10.5
Guatemalan	13.7
Honduran	3.0
Panamanian	3.3
Salvadoran	11.1
Cuban	10.0
Dominican Republic	5.0
Mexican	8.1
Puerto Rican	13.0
South American	9.1
Colombian	8.1
Peruvian	2.0
Spaniard	5.1

Class of Worker: Private Wage and Salary
(Universe: Civilian Employed Population 16 Years and Over)

Group	Number	%
Total Population	1,577,910	77.5
Hispanic or Latino (of any race)	63,736	89.1
Central American, ex. Mexican	8,630	90.7
Guatemalan	5,262	95.0
Honduran	1,221	86.7
Panamanian	644	80.5
Salvadoran	991	93.4
Cuban	1,491	81.6
Dominican Republic	314	91.3
Mexican	45,655	92.0
Puerto Rican	2,887	69.4
South American	2,228	77.3
Colombian	738	76.4
Peruvian	458	70.8
Spaniard	544	63.0

Class of Worker: Government
(Universe: Civilian Employed Population 16 Years and Over)

Group	Number	%
Total Population	332,613	16.3
Hispanic or Latino (of any race)	4,114	5.8
Central American, ex. Mexican	410	4.3
Guatemalan	95	1.7
Honduran	30	2.1
Panamanian	140	17.5
Salvadoran	47	4.4
Cuban	292	16.0
Dominican Republic	30	8.7
Mexican	1,478	3.0
Puerto Rican	1,007	24.2
South American	497	17.2
Colombian	158	16.4
Peruvian	176	27.2
Spaniard	177	20.5

Means of Transportation to Work: Car, Truck or Van
(Universe: Workers 16 Years and Over)

Group	Number	%
Total Population	1,894,534	94.7
Hispanic or Latino (of any race)	67,210	94.7
Central American, ex. Mexican	8,884	95.1
Guatemalan	5,235	97.0
Honduran	1,348	95.8
Panamanian	587	85.4
Salvadoran	1,058	95.1
Cuban	1,640	87.6
Dominican Republic	345	94.5
Mexican	46,564	95.3
Puerto Rican	4,134	94.2
South American	2,693	92.6
Colombian	914	90.5
Peruvian	606	97.7
Spaniard	862	90.0

Means of Transportation to Work: Public Transportation (ex. Taxicab)
(Universe: Workers 16 Years and Over)

Group	Number	%
Total Population	9,062	0.5
Hispanic or Latino (of any race)	198	0.3
Central American, ex. Mexican	55	0.6
Guatemalan	35	0.6
Honduran	5	0.4
Panamanian	0	0.0
Salvadoran	0	0.0
Cuban	2	0.1
Dominican Republic	5	1.4
Mexican	50	0.1
Puerto Rican	13	0.3
South American	33	1.1
Colombian	19	1.9
Peruvian	14	2.3
Spaniard	6	0.6

Homeownership Rate
(Universe: Occupied Housing Units)

Group	%
Total Population	69.7
Hispanic or Latino (of any race)	42.2
Central American, ex. Mexican	33.3
Costa Rican	52.4
Guatemalan	25.2
Honduran	33.1
Nicaraguan	52.9
Panamanian	53.7
Salvadoran	46.9
Cuban	58.5
Dominican Republic	45.1
Mexican	39.2
Puerto Rican	53.1
South American	53.9
Argentinean	56.1
Bolivian	59.3
Chilean	46.3
Colombian	59.3
Ecuadorian	54.3
Paraguayan	35.0
Peruvian	48.2
Uruguayan	56.3
Venezuelan	50.6
Spaniard	66.5

Median Home Value

Group	Dollars
Total Population	117,600
Hispanic or Latino (of any race)	95,000
Central American, ex. Mexican	98,800
Guatemalan	68,800
Honduran	123,800
Panamanian	129,500
Salvadoran	136,600
Cuban	127,900
Dominican Republic	127,500
Mexican	70,400
Puerto Rican	131,500
South American	181,900
Colombian	158,700
Peruvian	207,900
Spaniard	151,500

Median Gross Rent

Group	Dollars
Total Population	644
Hispanic or Latino (of any race)	636
Central American, ex. Mexican	648
Guatemalan	603
Honduran	884
Panamanian	622
Salvadoran	774
Cuban	599
Dominican Republic	695
Mexican	622
Puerto Rican	642
South American	866
Colombian	746
Peruvian	969
Spaniard	943

Median Household Income
(2010 Inflation-Adjusted Dollars)

Group	Dollars
Total Population	42,081
Hispanic or Latino (of any race)	35,234
Central American, ex. Mexican	32,722
Guatemalan	30,711
Honduran	33,866
Panamanian	29,938

Notes: (1) Percent of total population; (2) Percent of Hispanic/Latino population; Profiles include places with an overall population of at least 125,000, OR an overall population of at least 25,000 where the Hispanic/Latino population is at least 20% of the overall population. In states where less than five places meet either of these criteria, we have included places with at least 10,000 total population with the highest percentage of Hispanic/Latino population. These places are identified with an asterisk (*); Please refer to the User's Guide for a full explanation of data.

Salvadoran	32,917
Cuban	48,458
Dominican Republic	47,167
Mexican	33,170
Puerto Rican	47,765
South American	55,938
Colombian	51,117
Peruvian	75,686
Spaniard	38,974

Per Capita Income
(2010 Inflation-Adjusted Dollars)

Group	Dollars
Total Population	22,984
Hispanic or Latino (of any race)	12,872
Central American, ex. Mexican	11,288
Guatemalan	9,813
Honduran	11,722
Panamanian	14,058
Salvadoran	12,982
Cuban	18,704
Dominican Republic	21,784
Mexican	11,113
Puerto Rican	19,873
South American	22,823
Colombian	26,829
Peruvian	20,567
Spaniard	31,752

Households with $100,000+ Income

Group	Number	%
Total Population	264,625	14.5
Hispanic or Latino (of any race)	3,263	8.0
Central American, ex. Mexican	334	7.0
Guatemalan	179	6.8
Honduran	29	3.8
Panamanian	30	6.1
Salvadoran	22	3.9
Cuban	213	16.7
Dominican Republic	46	16.2
Mexican	1,591	6.0
Puerto Rican	439	12.9
South American	346	17.5
Colombian	133	16.4
Peruvian	67	22.9
Spaniard	129	15.9

Households with Food Stamps/SNAP Benefits During Past 12 Months

Group	Number	%
Total Population	206,852	11.4
Hispanic or Latino (of any race)	5,194	12.8
Central American, ex. Mexican	659	13.9
Guatemalan	456	17.3
Honduran	68	9.0
Panamanian	96	19.6
Salvadoran	32	5.6
Cuban	182	14.3
Dominican Republic	0	0.0
Mexican	3,587	13.5
Puerto Rican	416	12.2
South American	65	3.3
Colombian	3	0.4
Peruvian	9	3.1
Spaniard	109	13.5

Poverty Rate
(Income in Past 12 Months Below Poverty Level)

Group	%
Total Population	17.1
Hispanic or Latino (of any race)	30.5
Central American, ex. Mexican	38.2
Guatemalan	47.0
Honduran	26.4
Panamanian	20.6
Salvadoran	33.4
Cuban	20.1
Dominican Republic	18.5
Mexican	32.6
Puerto Rican	17.2
South American	14.9
Colombian	15.9
Peruvian	14.8
Spaniard	15.2

Albertville*

Population

Group	Number	%TP[1]	%HP[2]
Total Population	21,160	100.0	–
Hispanic or Latino (of any race)	5,899	27.9	100.0
Central American, ex. Mexican	1,856	8.8	31.5
Guatemalan	1,740	8.2	29.5
Mexican	3,457	16.3	58.6

Population Growth: 2000–2010

Group	%
Total Population	22.7
Hispanic or Latino (of any race)	112.7
Central American, ex. Mexican	474.6
Guatemalan	468.6
Mexican	55.6

Males per 100 Females

Group	Number
Total Population	97.2
Hispanic or Latino (of any race)	127.8
Central American, ex. Mexican	144.2
Guatemalan	144.7
Mexican	121.3

Average Household Size

Group	People
Total Population	2.79
Hispanic or Latino (of any race)	4.69
Central American, ex. Mexican	5.23
Guatemalan	5.31
Mexican	4.51

Median Age

Group	Years
Total Population	32.3
Hispanic or Latino (of any race)	23.1
Central American, ex. Mexican	24.2
Guatemalan	24.0
Mexican	21.7

High School Graduates
(Universe: Population 25 Years and Over)

Group	Number	%
Total Population	8,956	69.9
Hispanic or Latino (of any race)	319	16.2
Central American, ex. Mexican	59	7.8
Guatemalan	46	6.2
Mexican	214	18.9

Four-Year College Graduates
(Universe: Population 25 Years and Over)

Group	Number	%
Total Population	1,708	13.3
Hispanic or Latino (of any race)	21	1.1
Central American, ex. Mexican	0	0.0
Guatemalan	0	0.0
Mexican	0	0.0

Population Age 3–17 Enrolled in Public School
(Universe: Population Age 3–17 Enrolled in School)

Group	Number	%
Total Population	3,297	93.5
Hispanic or Latino (of any race)	1,089	100.0
Central American, ex. Mexican	487	100.0
Guatemalan	461	100.0
Mexican	602	100.0

Population Age 3–17 Enrolled in Private School
(Universe: Population Age 3–17 Enrolled in School)

Group	Number	%
Total Population	229	6.5
Hispanic or Latino (of any race)	0	0.0
Central American, ex. Mexican	0	0.0
Guatemalan	0	0.0
Mexican	0	0.0

Foreign-Born Population

Group	Number	%
Total Population	3,338	16.3
Hispanic or Latino (of any race)	2,910	61.0
Central American, ex. Mexican	1,071	59.1
Guatemalan	1,058	59.6
Mexican	1,768	61.8

Foreign-Born Naturalized U.S. Citizens

Group	Number	%
Total Population	240	7.2
Hispanic or Latino (of any race)	130	4.5
Central American, ex. Mexican	11	1.0
Guatemalan	11	1.0
Mexican	119	6.7

Language Spoken at Home: English Only
(Universe: Population 5 Years and Over)

Group	Number	%
Total Population	14,300	77.2
Hispanic or Latino (of any race)	296	7.5
Central American, ex. Mexican	45	2.8
Guatemalan	45	2.9
Mexican	238	10.5

Language Spoken at Home: Spanish
(Universe: Population 5 Years and Over)

Group	Number	%
Total Population	3,790	20.5
Hispanic or Latino (of any race)	3,526	89.1
Central American, ex. Mexican	1,429	89.5
Guatemalan	1,390	89.2
Mexican	2,026	89.5

Unemployment Rate
(Universe: Population 16 Years and Over)

Group	%
Total Population	5.5
Hispanic or Latino (of any race)	5.3
Central American, ex. Mexican	9.2
Guatemalan	9.3
Mexican	1.1

Class of Worker: Private Wage and Salary
(Universe: Civilian Employed Population 16 Years and Over)

Group	Number	%
Total Population	7,613	82.8
Hispanic or Latino (of any race)	2,068	94.1
Central American, ex. Mexican	892	100.0
Guatemalan	879	100.0
Mexican	1,140	91.6

Class of Worker: Government
(Universe: Civilian Employed Population 16 Years and Over)

Group	Number	%
Total Population	935	10.2
Hispanic or Latino (of any race)	25	1.1
Central American, ex. Mexican	0	0.0
Guatemalan	0	0.0
Mexican	0	0.0

Means of Transportation to Work: Car, Truck or Van
(Universe: Workers 16 Years and Over)

Group	Number	%
Total Population	8,473	96.3
Hispanic or Latino (of any race)	1,963	96.8
Central American, ex. Mexican	800	99.1
Guatemalan	787	99.1
Mexican	1,117	96.4

Means of Transportation to Work: Public Transportation (ex. Taxicab)
(Universe: Workers 16 Years and Over)

Group	Number	%
Total Population	0	0.0
Hispanic or Latino (of any race)	0	0.0
Central American, ex. Mexican	0	0.0
Guatemalan	0	0.0
Mexican	0	0.0

Homeownership Rate
(Universe: Occupied Housing Units)

Group	%
Total Population	60.9
Hispanic or Latino (of any race)	30.1
Central American, ex. Mexican	18.5
Guatemalan	15.9
Mexican	35.2

Median Home Value

Group	Dollars
Total Population	99,800

Notes: (1) Percent of total population; (2) Percent of Hispanic/Latino population; Profiles include places with an overall population of at least 125,000, OR an overall population of at least 25,000 where the Hispanic/Latino population is at least 20% of the overall population. In states where less than five places meet either of these criteria, we have included places with at least 10,000 total population with the highest percentage of Hispanic/Latino population. These places are identified with an asterisk (*); Please refer to the User's Guide for a full explanation of data.

Hispanic or Latino (of any race)	63,500
Central American, ex. Mexican	67,900
Guatemalan	68,800
Mexican	46,300

Median Gross Rent

Group	Dollars
Total Population	605
Hispanic or Latino (of any race)	672
Central American, ex. Mexican	737
Guatemalan	737
Mexican	650

Median Household Income
(2010 Inflation-Adjusted Dollars)

Group	Dollars
Total Population	35,843
Hispanic or Latino (of any race)	28,668
Central American, ex. Mexican	29,596
Guatemalan	32,857
Mexican	27,098

Per Capita Income
(2010 Inflation-Adjusted Dollars)

Group	Dollars
Total Population	16,839
Hispanic or Latino (of any race)	7,215
Central American, ex. Mexican	6,552
Guatemalan	6,509
Mexican	7,005

Households with $100,000+ Income

Group	Number	%
Total Population	616	8.6
Hispanic or Latino (of any race)	18	2.0
Central American, ex. Mexican	10	3.0
Guatemalan	10	3.1
Mexican	8	1.5

Households with Food Stamps/SNAP Benefits During Past 12 Months

Group	Number	%
Total Population	885	12.4
Hispanic or Latino (of any race)	136	15.4
Central American, ex. Mexican	86	26.0
Guatemalan	73	23.0
Mexican	50	9.5

Poverty Rate
(Income in Past 12 Months Below Poverty Level)

Group	%
Total Population	23.6
Hispanic or Latino (of any race)	50.3
Central American, ex. Mexican	71.4
Guatemalan	70.7
Mexican	37.5

Birmingham

Population

Group	Number	%TP[1]	%HP[2]
Total Population	212,237	100.0	–
Hispanic or Latino (of any race)	7,704	3.6	100.0
Central American, ex. Mexican	841	0.4	10.9
Guatemalan	331	0.2	4.3
Honduran	273	0.1	3.5
Salvadoran	106	<0.1	1.4
Cuban	101	<0.1	1.3
Mexican	5,237	2.5	68.0
Puerto Rican	338	0.2	4.4
South American	253	0.1	3.3

Population Growth: 2000–2010

Group	%
Total Population	-12.6
Hispanic or Latino (of any race)	104.7
Central American, ex. Mexican	578.2
Mexican	111.9
Puerto Rican	35.2

Males per 100 Females

Group	Number
Total Population	88.0
Hispanic or Latino (of any race)	150.2

Central American, ex. Mexican	164.5
Guatemalan	267.8
Honduran	152.8
Salvadoran	140.9
Cuban	110.4
Mexican	164.5
Puerto Rican	95.4
South American	93.1

Average Household Size

Group	People
Total Population	2.27
Hispanic or Latino (of any race)	3.28
Central American, ex. Mexican	3.49
Guatemalan	4.18
Honduran	3.72
Salvadoran	3.24
Cuban	1.98
Mexican	3.60
Puerto Rican	2.28
South American	2.20

Median Age

Group	Years
Total Population	35.4
Hispanic or Latino (of any race)	26.0
Central American, ex. Mexican	27.3
Guatemalan	25.7
Honduran	27.2
Salvadoran	31.2
Cuban	33.3
Mexican	25.4
Puerto Rican	26.9
South American	30.2

High School Graduates
(Universe: Population 25 Years and Over)

Group	Number	%
Total Population	118,538	82.4
Hispanic or Latino (of any race)	1,910	55.2
Mexican	1,356	50.1

Four-Year College Graduates
(Universe: Population 25 Years and Over)

Group	Number	%
Total Population	30,659	21.3
Hispanic or Latino (of any race)	558	16.1
Mexican	184	6.8

Population Age 3–17 Enrolled in Public School
(Universe: Population Age 3–17 Enrolled in School)

Group	Number	%
Total Population	30,233	86.1
Hispanic or Latino (of any race)	770	93.2
Mexican	683	95.4

Population Age 3–17 Enrolled in Private School
(Universe: Population Age 3–17 Enrolled in School)

Group	Number	%
Total Population	4,884	13.9
Hispanic or Latino (of any race)	56	6.8
Mexican	33	4.6

Foreign-Born Population

Group	Number	%
Total Population	7,813	3.6
Hispanic or Latino (of any race)	4,284	62.6
Mexican	3,798	67.6

Foreign-Born Naturalized U.S. Citizens

Group	Number	%
Total Population	1,549	19.8
Hispanic or Latino (of any race)	405	9.5
Mexican	276	7.3

Language Spoken at Home: English Only
(Universe: Population 5 Years and Over)

Group	Number	%
Total Population	191,848	94.9
Hispanic or Latino (of any race)	1,071	18.2
Mexican	706	14.8

Language Spoken at Home: Spanish
(Universe: Population 5 Years and Over)

Group	Number	%
Total Population	6,670	3.3
Hispanic or Latino (of any race)	4,810	81.8
Mexican	4,063	85.2

Unemployment Rate
(Universe: Population 16 Years and Over)

Group	%
Total Population	12.9
Hispanic or Latino (of any race)	7.0
Mexican	6.7

Class of Worker: Private Wage and Salary
(Universe: Civilian Employed Population 16 Years and Over)

Group	Number	%
Total Population	71,905	77.5
Hispanic or Latino (of any race)	3,036	85.3
Mexican	2,633	90.8

Class of Worker: Government
(Universe: Civilian Employed Population 16 Years and Over)

Group	Number	%
Total Population	15,646	16.9
Hispanic or Latino (of any race)	164	4.6
Mexican	64	2.2

Means of Transportation to Work: Car, Truck or Van
(Universe: Workers 16 Years and Over)

Group	Number	%
Total Population	84,085	92.9
Hispanic or Latino (of any race)	3,211	92.9
Mexican	2,677	94.4

Means of Transportation to Work: Public Transportation (ex. Taxicab)
(Universe: Workers 16 Years and Over)

Group	Number	%
Total Population	2,278	2.5
Hispanic or Latino (of any race)	68	2.0
Mexican	22	0.8

Homeownership Rate
(Universe: Occupied Housing Units)

Group	%
Total Population	49.3
Hispanic or Latino (of any race)	17.3
Central American, ex. Mexican	16.7
Guatemalan	10.0
Honduran	6.7
Salvadoran	38.2
Cuban	48.9
Mexican	12.9
Puerto Rican	26.9
South American	32.8

Median Home Value

Group	Dollars
Total Population	85,800
Hispanic or Latino (of any race)	84,600
Mexican	65,900

Median Gross Rent

Group	Dollars
Total Population	683
Hispanic or Latino (of any race)	690
Mexican	681

Median Household Income
(2010 Inflation-Adjusted Dollars)

Group	Dollars
Total Population	31,827
Hispanic or Latino (of any race)	36,079
Mexican	35,410

Per Capita Income
(2010 Inflation-Adjusted Dollars)

Group	Dollars
Total Population	19,775
Hispanic or Latino (of any race)	14,767
Mexican	11,891

Households with $100,000+ Income

Group	Number	%
Total Population	7,091	7.8
Hispanic or Latino (of any race)	182	9.1
Mexican	80	5.3

Notes: (1) Percent of total population; (2) Percent of Hispanic/Latino population; Profiles include places with an overall population of at least 125,000, OR an overall population of at least 25,000 where the Hispanic/Latino population is at least 20% of the overall population. In states where less than five places meet either of these criteria, we have included places with at least 10,000 total population with the highest percentage of Hispanic/Latino population. These places are identified with an asterisk (*); Please refer to the User's Guide for a full explanation of data.

Households with Food Stamps/SNAP Benefits During Past 12 Months		
Group	Number	%
Total Population	15,704	17.4
Hispanic or Latino (of any race)	173	8.6
Mexican	145	9.7

Poverty Rate (Income in Past 12 Months Below Poverty Level)	
Group	%
Total Population	26.4
Hispanic or Latino (of any race)	27.1
Mexican	27.8

Huntsville

Population			
Group	Number	%TP[1]	%HP[2]
Total Population	180,105	100.0	–
Hispanic or Latino (of any race)	10,512	5.8	100.0
Central American, ex. Mexican	886	0.5	8.4
Guatemalan	445	0.2	4.2
Honduran	141	0.1	1.3
Panamanian	159	0.1	1.5
Cuban	257	0.1	2.4
Dominican Republic	104	0.1	1.0
Mexican	7,151	4.0	68.0
Puerto Rican	1,036	0.6	9.9
South American	350	0.2	3.3
Colombian	111	0.1	1.1
Spaniard	149	0.1	1.4

Population Growth: 2000–2010	
Group	%
Total Population	13.8
Hispanic or Latino (of any race)	226.0
Central American, ex. Mexican	467.9
Cuban	87.6
Mexican	336.0
Puerto Rican	95.1
South American	175.6

Males per 100 Females	
Group	Number
Total Population	94.6
Hispanic or Latino (of any race)	132.2
Central American, ex. Mexican	133.2
Guatemalan	192.8
Honduran	176.5
Panamanian	47.2
Cuban	84.9
Dominican Republic	136.4
Mexican	142.7
Puerto Rican	108.0
South American	94.4
Colombian	105.6
Spaniard	88.6

Average Household Size	
Group	People
Total Population	2.25
Hispanic or Latino (of any race)	3.18
Central American, ex. Mexican	3.21
Guatemalan	3.78
Honduran	3.10
Panamanian	2.56
Cuban	2.28
Dominican Republic	3.12
Mexican	3.53
Puerto Rican	2.39
South American	2.26
Colombian	2.02
Spaniard	2.21

Median Age	
Group	Years
Total Population	36.5
Hispanic or Latino (of any race)	25.0
Central American, ex. Mexican	25.8
Guatemalan	24.9
Honduran	26.0
Panamanian	28.2
Cuban	27.2
Dominican Republic	25.5
Mexican	24.4
Puerto Rican	25.9
South American	32.7
Colombian	31.6
Spaniard	40.7

High School Graduates (Universe: Population 25 Years and Over)		
Group	Number	%
Total Population	101,176	86.7
Hispanic or Latino (of any race)	2,387	50.4
Mexican	1,210	37.2
Puerto Rican	431	92.9

Four-Year College Graduates (Universe: Population 25 Years and Over)		
Group	Number	%
Total Population	44,200	37.9
Hispanic or Latino (of any race)	640	13.5
Mexican	251	7.7
Puerto Rican	132	28.4

Population Age 3–17 Enrolled in Public School (Universe: Population Age 3–17 Enrolled in School)		
Group	Number	%
Total Population	23,452	81.4
Hispanic or Latino (of any race)	1,155	81.1
Mexican	891	91.8
Puerto Rican	136	60.7

Population Age 3–17 Enrolled in Private School (Universe: Population Age 3–17 Enrolled in School)		
Group	Number	%
Total Population	5,355	18.6
Hispanic or Latino (of any race)	270	18.9
Mexican	80	8.2
Puerto Rican	88	39.3

Foreign-Born Population		
Group	Number	%
Total Population	11,896	6.8
Hispanic or Latino (of any race)	4,380	49.6
Mexican	3,591	57.5
Puerto Rican	0	0.0

Foreign-Born Naturalized U.S. Citizens		
Group	Number	%
Total Population	4,847	40.7
Hispanic or Latino (of any race)	542	12.4
Mexican	232	6.5
Puerto Rican	0	0.0

Language Spoken at Home: English Only (Universe: Population 5 Years and Over)		
Group	Number	%
Total Population	151,783	92.2
Hispanic or Latino (of any race)	2,120	27.9
Mexican	1,114	20.8
Puerto Rican	381	51.1

Language Spoken at Home: Spanish (Universe: Population 5 Years and Over)		
Group	Number	%
Total Population	6,724	4.1
Hispanic or Latino (of any race)	5,420	71.3
Mexican	4,205	78.6
Puerto Rican	364	48.9

Unemployment Rate (Universe: Population 16 Years and Over)	
Group	%
Total Population	9.5
Hispanic or Latino (of any race)	7.5
Mexican	8.5
Puerto Rican	4.1

Class of Worker: Private Wage and Salary (Universe: Civilian Employed Population 16 Years and Over)		
Group	Number	%
Total Population	65,008	77.7
Hispanic or Latino (of any race)	3,976	88.2
Mexican	2,913	92.2
Puerto Rican	294	78.8

Class of Worker: Government (Universe: Civilian Employed Population 16 Years and Over)		
Group	Number	%
Total Population	14,043	16.8
Hispanic or Latino (of any race)	372	8.3
Mexican	147	4.7
Puerto Rican	73	19.6

Means of Transportation to Work: Car, Truck or Van (Universe: Workers 16 Years and Over)		
Group	Number	%
Total Population	77,489	93.7
Hispanic or Latino (of any race)	4,204	95.4
Mexican	3,007	95.5
Puerto Rican	313	100.0

Means of Transportation to Work: Public Transportation (ex. Taxicab) (Universe: Workers 16 Years and Over)		
Group	Number	%
Total Population	554	0.7
Hispanic or Latino (of any race)	0	0.0
Mexican	0	0.0
Puerto Rican	0	0.0

Homeownership Rate (Universe: Occupied Housing Units)	
Group	%
Total Population	58.0
Hispanic or Latino (of any race)	31.7
Central American, ex. Mexican	28.4
Guatemalan	9.4
Honduran	23.1
Panamanian	54.4
Cuban	52.9
Dominican Republic	57.6
Mexican	24.7
Puerto Rican	45.5
South American	49.2
Colombian	49.0
Spaniard	67.1

Median Home Value	
Group	Dollars
Total Population	146,800
Hispanic or Latino (of any race)	116,800
Mexican	105,100
Puerto Rican	112,000

Median Gross Rent	
Group	Dollars
Total Population	655
Hispanic or Latino (of any race)	593
Mexican	593
Puerto Rican	460

Median Household Income (2010 Inflation-Adjusted Dollars)	
Group	Dollars
Total Population	47,153
Hispanic or Latino (of any race)	38,068
Mexican	33,957
Puerto Rican	43,571

Per Capita Income (2010 Inflation-Adjusted Dollars)	
Group	Dollars
Total Population	29,255
Hispanic or Latino (of any race)	15,345
Mexican	12,097
Puerto Rican	17,993

Households with $100,000+ Income		
Group	Number	%
Total Population	15,206	20.8
Hispanic or Latino (of any race)	231	9.7
Mexican	101	6.5
Puerto Rican	24	8.8

Households with Food Stamps/SNAP Benefits During Past 12 Months		
Group	Number	%
Total Population	5,996	8.2
Hispanic or Latino (of any race)	98	4.1

STATE & PLACE PROFILES

Notes: (1) Percent of total population; (2) Percent of Hispanic/Latino population; Profiles include places with an overall population of at least 125,000, OR an overall population of at least 25,000 where the Hispanic/Latino population is at least 20% of the overall population. In states where less than five places meet either of these criteria, we have included places with at least 10,000 total population with the highest percentage of Hispanic/Latino population. These places are identified with an asterisk (*); Please refer to the User's Guide for a full explanation of data.

Mexican	89	5.8
Puerto Rican	9	3.3

Poverty Rate
(Income in Past 12 Months Below Poverty Level)

Group	%
Total Population	15.4
Hispanic or Latino (of any race)	29.8
Mexican	37.1
Puerto Rican	20.0

Mobile

Population

Group	Number	%TP[1]	%HP[2]
Total Population	195,111	100.0	–
Hispanic or Latino (of any race)	4,600	2.4	100.0
Central American, ex. Mexican	570	0.3	12.4
Guatemalan	159	0.1	3.5
Honduran	162	0.1	3.5
Salvadoran	101	0.1	2.2
Cuban	380	0.2	8.3
Mexican	1,677	0.9	36.5
Puerto Rican	562	0.3	12.2
South American	555	0.3	12.1
Colombian	111	0.1	2.4
Peruvian	148	0.1	3.2
Spaniard	152	0.1	3.3

Population Growth: 2000–2010

Group	%
Total Population	-1.9
Hispanic or Latino (of any race)	62.7
Central American, ex. Mexican	175.4
Cuban	45.0
Mexican	77.6
Puerto Rican	83.1
South American	113.5

Males per 100 Females

Group	Number
Total Population	88.8
Hispanic or Latino (of any race)	112.4
Central American, ex. Mexican	117.6
Guatemalan	224.5
Honduran	110.4
Salvadoran	98.0
Cuban	112.3
Mexican	129.1
Puerto Rican	93.8
South American	94.1
Colombian	79.0
Peruvian	102.7
Spaniard	108.2

Average Household Size

Group	People
Total Population	2.40
Hispanic or Latino (of any race)	2.73
Central American, ex. Mexican	3.09
Guatemalan	4.09
Honduran	2.80
Salvadoran	3.36
Cuban	2.45
Mexican	2.91
Puerto Rican	2.51
South American	2.78
Colombian	2.51
Peruvian	2.85
Spaniard	2.26

Median Age

Group	Years
Total Population	35.7
Hispanic or Latino (of any race)	28.4
Central American, ex. Mexican	27.5
Guatemalan	22.8
Honduran	30.5
Salvadoran	27.6
Cuban	33.3
Mexican	26.1
Puerto Rican	28.0
South American	35.0
Colombian	34.3
Peruvian	39.0
Spaniard	42.3

High School Graduates
(Universe: Population 25 Years and Over)

Group	Number	%
Total Population	106,522	85.5
Hispanic or Latino (of any race)	1,502	77.8
Mexican	485	67.5

Four-Year College Graduates
(Universe: Population 25 Years and Over)

Group	Number	%
Total Population	32,221	25.9
Hispanic or Latino (of any race)	456	23.6
Mexican	118	16.4

Population Age 3–17 Enrolled in Public School
(Universe: Population Age 3–17 Enrolled in School)

Group	Number	%
Total Population	28,555	76.9
Hispanic or Latino (of any race)	372	54.6
Mexican	91	51.1

Population Age 3–17 Enrolled in Private School
(Universe: Population Age 3–17 Enrolled in School)

Group	Number	%
Total Population	8,554	23.1
Hispanic or Latino (of any race)	309	45.4
Mexican	87	48.9

Foreign-Born Population

Group	Number	%
Total Population	7,227	3.7
Hispanic or Latino (of any race)	1,862	48.7
Mexican	838	54.5

Foreign-Born Naturalized U.S. Citizens

Group	Number	%
Total Population	2,274	31.5
Hispanic or Latino (of any race)	298	16.0
Mexican	86	10.3

Language Spoken at Home: English Only
(Universe: Population 5 Years and Over)

Group	Number	%
Total Population	172,409	94.6
Hispanic or Latino (of any race)	1,073	31.4
Mexican	320	24.5

Language Spoken at Home: Spanish
(Universe: Population 5 Years and Over)

Group	Number	%
Total Population	3,845	2.1
Hispanic or Latino (of any race)	2,327	68.2
Mexican	985	75.5

Unemployment Rate
(Universe: Population 16 Years and Over)

Group	%
Total Population	11.2
Hispanic or Latino (of any race)	5.3
Mexican	6.7

Class of Worker: Private Wage and Salary
(Universe: Civilian Employed Population 16 Years and Over)

Group	Number	%
Total Population	66,294	80.6
Hispanic or Latino (of any race)	1,751	87.5
Mexican	804	88.9

Class of Worker: Government
(Universe: Civilian Employed Population 16 Years and Over)

Group	Number	%
Total Population	12,880	15.7
Hispanic or Latino (of any race)	141	7.0
Mexican	42	4.6

Means of Transportation to Work: Car, Truck or Van
(Universe: Workers 16 Years and Over)

Group	Number	%
Total Population	76,186	94.6
Hispanic or Latino (of any race)	1,823	92.8
Mexican	836	94.5

Means of Transportation to Work: Public Transportation (ex. Taxicab)
(Universe: Workers 16 Years and Over)

Group	Number	%
Total Population	586	0.7
Hispanic or Latino (of any race)	0	0.0
Mexican	0	0.0

Homeownership Rate
(Universe: Occupied Housing Units)

Group	%
Total Population	56.4
Hispanic or Latino (of any race)	36.8
Central American, ex. Mexican	32.9
Guatemalan	22.9
Honduran	16.3
Salvadoran	42.4
Cuban	42.9
Mexican	30.1
Puerto Rican	30.9
South American	39.6
Colombian	46.3
Peruvian	37.0
Spaniard	72.8

Median Home Value

Group	Dollars
Total Population	120,600
Hispanic or Latino (of any race)	147,400
Mexican	106,700

Median Gross Rent

Group	Dollars
Total Population	701
Hispanic or Latino (of any race)	724
Mexican	671

Median Household Income
(2010 Inflation-Adjusted Dollars)

Group	Dollars
Total Population	37,056
Hispanic or Latino (of any race)	35,516
Mexican	32,984

Per Capita Income
(2010 Inflation-Adjusted Dollars)

Group	Dollars
Total Population	22,401
Hispanic or Latino (of any race)	20,109
Mexican	13,716

Households with $100,000+ Income

Group	Number	%
Total Population	9,410	12.4
Hispanic or Latino (of any race)	113	9.6
Mexican	12	2.2

Households with Food Stamps/SNAP Benefits During Past 12 Months

Group	Number	%
Total Population	12,697	16.8
Hispanic or Latino (of any race)	120	10.2
Mexican	62	11.5

Poverty Rate
(Income in Past 12 Months Below Poverty Level)

Group	%
Total Population	21.5
Hispanic or Latino (of any race)	18.0
Mexican	24.9

Montgomery

Population

Group	Number	%TP[1]	%HP[2]
Total Population	205,764	100.0	–
Hispanic or Latino (of any race)	7,998	3.9	100.0
Central American, ex. Mexican	821	0.4	10.3
Guatemalan	343	0.2	4.3
Honduran	233	0.1	2.9
Salvadoran	136	0.1	1.7
Cuban	160	0.1	2.0
Mexican	5,298	2.6	66.2
Puerto Rican	555	0.3	6.9

Notes: (1) Percent of total population; (2) Percent of Hispanic/Latino population; Profiles include places with an overall population of at least 125,000, OR an overall population of at least 25,000 where the Hispanic/Latino population is at least 20% of the overall population. In states where less than five places meet either of these criteria, we have included places with at least 10,000 total population with the highest percentage of Hispanic/Latino population. These places are identified with an asterisk (*); Please refer to the User's Guide for a full explanation of data.

South American	225	0.1	2.8
Spaniard	100	<0.1	1.3

Population Growth: 2000–2010

Group	%
Total Population	2.1
Hispanic or Latino (of any race)	222.0
Central American, ex. Mexican	403.7
Cuban	11.9
Mexican	442.8
Puerto Rican	57.7
South American	53.1

Males per 100 Females

Group	Number
Total Population	88.6
Hispanic or Latino (of any race)	131.2
Central American, ex. Mexican	135.2
Guatemalan	203.5
Honduran	140.2
Salvadoran	78.9
Cuban	110.5
Mexican	139.5
Puerto Rican	109.4
South American	78.6
Spaniard	108.3

Average Household Size

Group	People
Total Population	2.44
Hispanic or Latino (of any race)	3.65
Central American, ex. Mexican	4.02
Guatemalan	4.43
Honduran	4.00
Salvadoran	4.11
Cuban	2.70
Mexican	4.00
Puerto Rican	2.54
South American	2.81
Spaniard	2.39

Median Age

Group	Years
Total Population	34.0
Hispanic or Latino (of any race)	24.5
Central American, ex. Mexican	27.6
Guatemalan	25.3
Honduran	29.7
Salvadoran	27.5
Cuban	26.7
Mexican	23.7
Puerto Rican	23.8
South American	29.7
Spaniard	30.5

High School Graduates
(Universe: Population 25 Years and Over)

Group	Number	%
Total Population	109,795	85.1
Hispanic or Latino (of any race)	2,106	62.1
Central American, ex. Mexican	359	81.2
Mexican	1,115	50.2
Puerto Rican	329	80.8

Four-Year College Graduates
(Universe: Population 25 Years and Over)

Group	Number	%
Total Population	39,448	30.6
Hispanic or Latino (of any race)	545	16.1
Central American, ex. Mexican	43	9.7
Mexican	247	11.1
Puerto Rican	127	31.2

Population Age 3–17 Enrolled in Public School
(Universe: Population Age 3–17 Enrolled in School)

Group	Number	%
Total Population	30,855	80.6
Hispanic or Latino (of any race)	1,005	77.8
Central American, ex. Mexican	108	90.0
Mexican	554	75.6
Puerto Rican	124	62.6

Population Age 3–17 Enrolled in Private School
(Universe: Population Age 3–17 Enrolled in School)

Group	Number	%
Total Population	7,411	19.4
Hispanic or Latino (of any race)	286	22.2
Central American, ex. Mexican	12	10.0
Mexican	179	24.4
Puerto Rican	74	37.4

Foreign-Born Population

Group	Number	%
Total Population	8,499	4.2
Hispanic or Latino (of any race)	3,245	47.1
Central American, ex. Mexican	562	58.7
Mexican	2,515	56.7
Puerto Rican	8	1.0

Foreign-Born Naturalized U.S. Citizens

Group	Number	%
Total Population	2,694	31.7
Hispanic or Latino (of any race)	511	15.7
Central American, ex. Mexican	104	18.5
Mexican	391	15.5
Puerto Rican	8	100.0

Language Spoken at Home: English Only
(Universe: Population 5 Years and Over)

Group	Number	%
Total Population	179,380	94.3
Hispanic or Latino (of any race)	1,374	23.6
Central American, ex. Mexican	111	15.0
Mexican	580	15.6
Puerto Rican	413	58.7

Language Spoken at Home: Spanish
(Universe: Population 5 Years and Over)

Group	Number	%
Total Population	5,769	3.0
Hispanic or Latino (of any race)	4,260	73.1
Central American, ex. Mexican	447	60.5
Mexican	3,130	84.1
Puerto Rican	291	41.3

Unemployment Rate
(Universe: Population 16 Years and Over)

Group	%
Total Population	8.3
Hispanic or Latino (of any race)	3.8
Central American, ex. Mexican	0.0
Mexican	3.3
Puerto Rican	15.8

Class of Worker: Private Wage and Salary
(Universe: Civilian Employed Population 16 Years and Over)

Group	Number	%
Total Population	65,825	71.9
Hispanic or Latino (of any race)	2,946	90.3
Central American, ex. Mexican	422	92.7
Mexican	2,011	92.0
Puerto Rican	208	72.2

Class of Worker: Government
(Universe: Civilian Employed Population 16 Years and Over)

Group	Number	%
Total Population	21,490	23.5
Hispanic or Latino (of any race)	200	6.1
Central American, ex. Mexican	33	7.3
Mexican	112	5.1
Puerto Rican	55	19.1

Means of Transportation to Work: Car, Truck or Van
(Universe: Workers 16 Years and Over)

Group	Number	%
Total Population	86,136	95.1
Hispanic or Latino (of any race)	3,108	94.8
Central American, ex. Mexican	452	97.6
Mexican	2,059	94.8
Puerto Rican	254	100.0

Means of Transportation to Work: Public Transportation (ex. Taxicab)
(Universe: Workers 16 Years and Over)

Group	Number	%
Total Population	725	0.8
Hispanic or Latino (of any race)	0	0.0
Central American, ex. Mexican	0	0.0
Mexican	0	0.0
Puerto Rican	0	0.0

Homeownership Rate
(Universe: Occupied Housing Units)

Group	%
Total Population	58.9
Hispanic or Latino (of any race)	33.9
Central American, ex. Mexican	39.1
Guatemalan	25.0
Honduran	44.1
Salvadoran	58.3
Cuban	40.0
Mexican	27.8
Puerto Rican	43.9
South American	58.8
Spaniard	51.5

Median Home Value

Group	Dollars
Total Population	118,100
Hispanic or Latino (of any race)	118,800
Central American, ex. Mexican	123,200
Mexican	109,500
Puerto Rican	255,300

Median Gross Rent

Group	Dollars
Total Population	761
Hispanic or Latino (of any race)	724
Central American, ex. Mexican	735
Mexican	672
Puerto Rican	874

Median Household Income
(2010 Inflation-Adjusted Dollars)

Group	Dollars
Total Population	42,992
Hispanic or Latino (of any race)	37,870
Central American, ex. Mexican	36,111
Mexican	26,719
Puerto Rican	55,481

Per Capita Income
(2010 Inflation-Adjusted Dollars)

Group	Dollars
Total Population	24,409
Hispanic or Latino (of any race)	13,622
Central American, ex. Mexican	9,859
Mexican	11,650
Puerto Rican	19,257

Households with $100,000+ Income

Group	Number	%
Total Population	12,237	15.2
Hispanic or Latino (of any race)	193	11.5
Central American, ex. Mexican	14	8.2
Mexican	80	8.1
Puerto Rican	33	13.6

Households with Food Stamps/SNAP Benefits During Past 12 Months

Group	Number	%
Total Population	11,881	14.8
Hispanic or Latino (of any race)	265	15.8
Central American, ex. Mexican	34	20.0
Mexican	207	20.8
Puerto Rican	24	9.9

Poverty Rate
(Income in Past 12 Months Below Poverty Level)

Group	%
Total Population	19.7
Hispanic or Latino (of any race)	34.7
Central American, ex. Mexican	41.0
Mexican	40.6
Puerto Rican	11.9

Notes: (1) Percent of total population; (2) Percent of Hispanic/Latino population; Profiles include places with an overall population of at least 125,000, OR an overall population of at least 25,000 where the Hispanic/Latino population is at least 20% of the overall population. In states where less than five places meet either of these criteria, we have included places with at least 10,000 total population with the highest percentage of Hispanic/Latino population. These places are identified with an asterisk (*); Please refer to the User's Guide for a full explanation of data.

Alaska

EDITOR'S NOTE: For a place to be included in this edition, it must meet one of two criteria. Either its overall population is at least 125,000, OR its overall population is at least 25,000 and its Hispanic/Latino population is at least 20% of the overall population. In Alaska, less than five places meet either of these criteria. In an effort to include at least five places for each state, we have included places with at least 10,000 total population with the highest percentage of Hispanic/Latino population. These places are identified with an asterisk (*). For the state of Alaska, the following locations are included:

Anchorage
Badger*
College*
Fairbanks*
Juneau*

Section Two: State & Place Profiles starts with the state profile, followed by place profiles that meet the criteria above. Places are listed alphabetically within each state. All states, all counties and places that meet the above criteria are ranked and compared in *Section Three: Rankings & Comparisons*, on page 1055.

For a more detailed look at the Hispanic/Latino population in Alaska, a companion web site is available at no additional charge with purchase of this print edition. Visit http://gold.greyhouse.com/page/info_hispanic for more information.

The web site includes data for all counties and places in Alaska with Hispanic/Latino population, plus ten additional topics: Self Employed Worker; Walked to Work; Worked from Home; Mean Travel Time to Work; Mean Household Income; Households with Cash Public Assistance; Mean Cash Pubic Assistance; Poverty Rates for 18 and Under, 18 to 64, and 65 and Over.

Population

Group	Number	%TP[1]	%HP[2]
Total Population	710,231	100.0	–
Hispanic or Latino (of any race)	39,249	5.5	100.0
Central American, ex. Mexican	2,509	0.4	6.4
Costa Rican	140	<0.1	0.4
Guatemalan	508	0.1	1.3
Honduran	272	<0.1	0.7
Nicaraguan	176	<0.1	0.4
Panamanian	446	0.1	1.1
Salvadoran	938	0.1	2.4
Cuban	927	0.1	2.4
Dominican Republic	1,909	0.3	4.9
Mexican	21,642	3.0	55.1
Puerto Rican	4,502	0.6	11.5
South American	2,345	0.3	6.0
Argentinean	149	<0.1	0.4
Chilean	223	<0.1	0.6
Colombian	867	0.1	2.2
Ecuadorian	189	<0.1	0.5
Peruvian	611	0.1	1.6
Venezuelan	140	<0.1	0.4
Spaniard	1,513	0.2	3.9

Population Growth: 2000–2010

Group	%
Total Population	13.3
Hispanic or Latino (of any race)	51.8
Central American, ex. Mexican	108.9
Guatemalan	180.7
Honduran	90.2
Panamanian	89.8
Salvadoran	109.8
Cuban	67.6
Dominican Republic	117.7
Mexican	62.3
Puerto Rican	70.0
South American	104.8
Chilean	79.8
Colombian	97.0
Peruvian	119.8
Spaniard	769.5

Males per 100 Females

Group	Number
Total Population	108.5
Hispanic or Latino (of any race)	105.3
Central American, ex. Mexican	99.4
Costa Rican	94.4
Guatemalan	109.9
Honduran	76.6
Nicaraguan	100.0
Panamanian	67.7
Salvadoran	121.7
Cuban	112.1
Dominican Republic	101.4
Mexican	109.2
Puerto Rican	110.6
South American	82.3
Argentinean	104.1
Chilean	102.7
Colombian	74.8
Ecuadorian	78.3
Peruvian	81.8
Venezuelan	62.8
Spaniard	89.8

Average Household Size

Group	People
Total Population	2.65
Hispanic or Latino (of any race)	2.98
Central American, ex. Mexican	3.23
Costa Rican	2.67
Guatemalan	3.46
Honduran	3.29
Nicaraguan	3.15
Panamanian	2.50
Salvadoran	3.61
Cuban	2.79
Dominican Republic	3.49
Mexican	3.02
Puerto Rican	2.95
South American	2.78
Argentinean	2.44
Chilean	2.61
Colombian	2.78
Ecuadorian	2.68
Peruvian	3.00
Venezuelan	2.85
Spaniard	2.79

Median Age

Group	Years
Total Population	33.8
Hispanic or Latino (of any race)	24.4
Central American, ex. Mexican	25.9
Costa Rican	26.5
Guatemalan	25.0
Honduran	26.3
Nicaraguan	25.6
Panamanian	26.5
Salvadoran	25.8
Cuban	26.1
Dominican Republic	23.9
Mexican	23.6
Puerto Rican	22.7
South American	30.1
Argentinean	35.6
Chilean	29.7
Colombian	30.8
Ecuadorian	26.9
Peruvian	28.4
Venezuelan	31.0
Spaniard	29.6

High School Graduates

(Universe: Population 25 Years and Over)

Group	Number	%
Total Population	390,034	90.7
Hispanic or Latino (of any race)	14,451	76.7
Central American, ex. Mexican	862	64.3
Salvadoran	334	53.4
Dominican Republic	610	73.2
Mexican	7,871	73.2
Puerto Rican	1,598	80.5
South American	1,194	84.0
Colombian	475	73.8
Spaniard	855	96.6

Four-Year College Graduates

(Universe: Population 25 Years and Over)

Group	Number	%
Total Population	116,112	27.0
Hispanic or Latino (of any race)	3,433	18.2
Central American, ex. Mexican	275	20.5
Salvadoran	101	16.2
Dominican Republic	52	6.2
Mexican	1,580	14.7
Puerto Rican	322	16.2
South American	662	46.6
Colombian	254	39.4
Spaniard	241	27.2

Population Age 3–17 Enrolled in Public School

(Universe: Population Age 3–17 Enrolled in School)

Group	Number	%
Total Population	121,462	90.0
Hispanic or Latino (of any race)	8,441	90.2
Central American, ex. Mexican	331	68.4
Salvadoran	151	83.0
Dominican Republic	395	98.5
Mexican	4,595	89.2
Puerto Rican	1,332	99.2
South American	568	93.6
Colombian	116	86.6
Spaniard	444	97.6

Population Age 3–17 Enrolled in Private School

(Universe: Population Age 3–17 Enrolled in School)

Group	Number	%
Total Population	13,425	10.0
Hispanic or Latino (of any race)	917	9.8
Central American, ex. Mexican	153	31.6
Salvadoran	31	17.0
Dominican Republic	6	1.5
Mexican	554	10.8
Puerto Rican	11	0.8
South American	39	6.4
Colombian	18	13.4
Spaniard	11	2.4

Foreign-Born Population

Group	Number	%
Total Population	49,762	7.2
Hispanic or Latino (of any race)	8,643	22.5
Central American, ex. Mexican	1,069	43.3
Salvadoran	465	43.8
Dominican Republic	947	54.0
Mexican	4,438	20.1
Puerto Rican	41	0.9
South American	1,612	60.0
Colombian	660	66.5
Spaniard	54	3.0

Foreign-Born Naturalized U.S. Citizens

Group	Number	%
Total Population	24,772	49.8
Hispanic or Latino (of any race)	3,649	42.2
Central American, ex. Mexican	510	47.7
Salvadoran	149	32.0
Dominican Republic	660	69.7
Mexican	1,428	32.2
Puerto Rican	31	75.6
South American	760	47.1
Colombian	389	58.9

Notes: (1) Percent of total population; (2) Percent of Hispanic/Latino population; Profiles include places with an overall population of at least 125,000, OR an overall population of at least 25,000 where the Hispanic/Latino population is at least 20% of the overall population. In states where less than five places meet either of these criteria, we have included places with at least 10,000 total population with the highest percentage of Hispanic/Latino population. These places are identified with an asterisk (*); Please refer to the User's Guide for a full explanation of data.

Spaniard	9	16.7

Language Spoken at Home: English Only
(Universe: Population 5 Years and Over)

Group	Number	%
Total Population	534,077	83.5
Hispanic or Latino (of any race)	17,168	51.1
Central American, ex. Mexican	633	30.0
Salvadoran	136	15.3
Dominican Republic	158	9.4
Mexican	10,521	55.4
Puerto Rican	2,353	59.5
South American	361	15.0
Colombian	173	19.3
Spaniard	1,205	77.7

Language Spoken at Home: Spanish
(Universe: Population 5 Years and Over)

Group	Number	%
Total Population	22,447	3.5
Hispanic or Latino (of any race)	15,583	46.4
Central American, ex. Mexican	1,471	69.8
Salvadoran	752	84.4
Dominican Republic	1,466	87.4
Mexican	8,129	42.8
Puerto Rican	1,529	38.7
South American	1,842	76.5
Colombian	715	79.9
Spaniard	333	21.5

Unemployment Rate
(Universe: Population 16 Years and Over)

Group	%
Total Population	8.6
Hispanic or Latino (of any race)	9.0
Central American, ex. Mexican	1.5
Salvadoran	0.0
Dominican Republic	23.3
Mexican	7.3
Puerto Rican	15.8
South American	9.8
Colombian	2.7
Spaniard	14.1

Class of Worker: Private Wage and Salary
(Universe: Civilian Employed Population 16 Years and Over)

Group	Number	%
Total Population	222,955	67.1
Hispanic or Latino (of any race)	12,743	76.2
Central American, ex. Mexican	950	69.9
Salvadoran	535	81.3
Dominican Republic	684	83.8
Mexican	7,623	80.1
Puerto Rican	1,048	70.1
South American	903	66.9
Colombian	424	70.4
Spaniard	498	64.9

Class of Worker: Government
(Universe: Civilian Employed Population 16 Years and Over)

Group	Number	%
Total Population	84,606	25.5
Hispanic or Latino (of any race)	3,096	18.5
Central American, ex. Mexican	273	20.1
Salvadoran	61	9.3
Dominican Republic	92	11.3
Mexican	1,500	15.8
Puerto Rican	333	22.3
South American	364	27.0
Colombian	118	19.6
Spaniard	180	23.5

Means of Transportation to Work: Car, Truck or Van
(Universe: Workers 16 Years and Over)

Group	Number	%
Total Population	268,281	80.3
Hispanic or Latino (of any race)	13,500	77.3
Central American, ex. Mexican	1,018	70.7
Salvadoran	424	61.1
Dominican Republic	714	93.5
Mexican	7,166	73.1
Puerto Rican	1,486	82.8
South American	1,201	89.9
Colombian	576	95.2
Spaniard	636	82.2

Means of Transportation to Work: Public Transportation (ex. Taxicab)
(Universe: Workers 16 Years and Over)

Group	Number	%
Total Population	4,446	1.3
Hispanic or Latino (of any race)	228	1.3
Central American, ex. Mexican	12	0.8
Salvadoran	12	1.7
Dominican Republic	16	2.1
Mexican	96	1.0
Puerto Rican	36	2.0
South American	26	1.9
Colombian	0	0.0
Spaniard	10	1.3

Homeownership Rate
(Universe: Occupied Housing Units)

Group	%
Total Population	63.1
Hispanic or Latino (of any race)	47.2
Central American, ex. Mexican	48.9
Costa Rican	52.4
Guatemalan	45.5
Honduran	50.0
Nicaraguan	52.7
Panamanian	50.4
Salvadoran	47.8
Cuban	42.7
Dominican Republic	35.5
Mexican	47.9
Puerto Rican	34.9
South American	59.0
Argentinean	55.6
Chilean	63.6
Colombian	56.5
Ecuadorian	46.8
Peruvian	64.3
Venezuelan	67.5
Spaniard	61.8

Median Home Value

Group	Dollars
Total Population	229,100
Hispanic or Latino (of any race)	232,600
Central American, ex. Mexican	137,700
Salvadoran	137,500
Dominican Republic	234,000
Mexican	225,400
Puerto Rican	211,200
South American	324,200
Colombian	296,700
Spaniard	243,900

Median Gross Rent

Group	Dollars
Total Population	972
Hispanic or Latino (of any race)	995
Central American, ex. Mexican	1,204
Salvadoran	1,315
Dominican Republic	967
Mexican	993
Puerto Rican	1,150
South American	896
Colombian	1,259
Spaniard	936

Median Household Income
(2010 Inflation-Adjusted Dollars)

Group	Dollars
Total Population	66,521
Hispanic or Latino (of any race)	57,006
Central American, ex. Mexican	46,007
Salvadoran	47,326
Dominican Republic	50,231
Mexican	58,342
Puerto Rican	50,431
South American	66,414
Colombian	82,803
Spaniard	80,966

Per Capita Income
(2010 Inflation-Adjusted Dollars)

Group	Dollars
Total Population	30,726
Hispanic or Latino (of any race)	20,010
Central American, ex. Mexican	21,586
Salvadoran	22,515
Dominican Republic	15,664
Mexican	18,130
Puerto Rican	19,939
South American	27,243
Colombian	26,068
Spaniard	24,443

Households with $100,000+ Income

Group	Number	%
Total Population	71,518	28.8
Hispanic or Latino (of any race)	1,920	19.1
Central American, ex. Mexican	66	12.0
Salvadoran	31	15.8
Dominican Republic	28	6.7
Mexican	948	17.4
Puerto Rican	190	14.5
South American	180	20.5
Colombian	108	25.7
Spaniard	192	34.5

Households with Food Stamps/SNAP Benefits During Past 12 Months

Group	Number	%
Total Population	21,968	8.8
Hispanic or Latino (of any race)	1,200	11.9
Central American, ex. Mexican	120	21.8
Salvadoran	0	0.0
Dominican Republic	87	20.7
Mexican	683	12.5
Puerto Rican	154	11.8
South American	14	1.6
Colombian	3	0.7
Spaniard	95	17.1

Poverty Rate
(Income in Past 12 Months Below Poverty Level)

Group	%
Total Population	9.5
Hispanic or Latino (of any race)	11.6
Central American, ex. Mexican	3.6
Salvadoran	2.3
Dominican Republic	8.6
Mexican	14.2
Puerto Rican	12.6
South American	4.7
Colombian	4.1
Spaniard	6.3

Anchorage

Population

Group	Number	%TP[1]	%HP[2]
Total Population	291,826	100.0	–
Hispanic or Latino (of any race)	22,061	7.6	100.0
Central American, ex. Mexican	1,475	0.5	6.7
Guatemalan	354	0.1	1.6
Honduran	199	0.1	0.9
Nicaraguan	106	<0.1	0.5
Panamanian	254	0.1	1.2
Salvadoran	474	0.2	2.1
Cuban	521	0.2	2.4
Dominican Republic	1,626	0.6	7.4
Mexican	11,526	3.9	52.2
Puerto Rican	2,703	0.9	12.3
South American	1,500	0.5	6.8
Chilean	140	<0.1	0.6
Colombian	557	0.2	2.5
Ecuadorian	110	<0.1	0.5
Peruvian	447	0.2	2.0
Spaniard	799	0.3	3.6

Population Growth: 2000–2010

Group	%
Total Population	12.1
Hispanic or Latino (of any race)	49.1
Central American, ex. Mexican	138.7

Notes: (1) Percent of total population; (2) Percent of Hispanic/Latino population; Profiles include places with an overall population of at least 125,000, OR an overall population of at least 25,000 where the Hispanic/Latino population is at least 20% of the overall population. In states where less than five places meet either of these criteria, we have included places with at least 10,000 total population with the highest percentage of Hispanic/Latino population. These places are identified with an asterisk (*); Please refer to the User's Guide for a full explanation of data.

Group	Number
Guatemalan	190.2
Panamanian	111.7
Salvadoran	164.8
Cuban	51.9
Dominican Republic	105.3
Mexican	59.1
Puerto Rican	63.6
South American	97.1
Colombian	94.1
Peruvian	106.9

Males per 100 Females

Group	Number
Total Population	103.2
Hispanic or Latino (of any race)	99.1
Central American, ex. Mexican	94.8
Guatemalan	108.2
Honduran	65.8
Nicaraguan	100.0
Panamanian	76.4
Salvadoran	113.5
Cuban	101.2
Dominican Republic	99.0
Mexican	101.5
Puerto Rican	108.1
South American	82.9
Chilean	97.2
Colombian	75.7
Ecuadorian	77.4
Peruvian	87.8
Spaniard	84.1

Average Household Size

Group	People
Total Population	2.64
Hispanic or Latino (of any race)	3.02
Central American, ex. Mexican	3.21
Guatemalan	3.44
Honduran	3.43
Nicaraguan	3.14
Panamanian	2.41
Salvadoran	3.54
Cuban	2.77
Dominican Republic	3.51
Mexican	3.07
Puerto Rican	2.93
South American	2.77
Chilean	2.51
Colombian	2.77
Ecuadorian	2.75
Peruvian	2.99
Spaniard	2.79

Median Age

Group	Years
Total Population	32.9
Hispanic or Latino (of any race)	24.1
Central American, ex. Mexican	26.2
Guatemalan	26.0
Honduran	25.5
Nicaraguan	25.0
Panamanian	31.5
Salvadoran	25.1
Cuban	25.7
Dominican Republic	23.9
Mexican	23.2
Puerto Rican	21.9
South American	31.3
Chilean	32.0
Colombian	31.9
Ecuadorian	29.2
Peruvian	29.9
Spaniard	27.5

High School Graduates
(Universe: Population 25 Years and Over)

Group	Number	%
Total Population	162,873	91.9
Hispanic or Latino (of any race)	7,635	76.1
Central American, ex. Mexican	573	73.5
Dominican Republic	473	68.9
Mexican	3,808	73.3
Puerto Rican	927	75.9
South American	703	78.7
Spaniard	436	100.0

Four-Year College Graduates
(Universe: Population 25 Years and Over)

Group	Number	%
Total Population	58,411	33.0
Hispanic or Latino (of any race)	1,986	19.8
Central American, ex. Mexican	102	13.1
Dominican Republic	10	1.5
Mexican	1,040	20.0
Puerto Rican	215	17.6
South American	370	41.4
Spaniard	93	21.3

Population Age 3–17 Enrolled in Public School
(Universe: Population Age 3–17 Enrolled in School)

Group	Number	%
Total Population	48,760	90.3
Hispanic or Latino (of any race)	5,016	92.1
Central American, ex. Mexican	272	70.3
Dominican Republic	370	100.0
Mexican	2,456	90.6
Puerto Rican	875	99.4
South American	309	94.5
Spaniard	263	98.1

Population Age 3–17 Enrolled in Private School
(Universe: Population Age 3–17 Enrolled in School)

Group	Number	%
Total Population	5,210	9.7
Hispanic or Latino (of any race)	433	7.9
Central American, ex. Mexican	115	29.7
Dominican Republic	0	0.0
Mexican	254	9.4
Puerto Rican	5	0.6
South American	18	5.5
Spaniard	5	1.9

Foreign-Born Population

Group	Number	%
Total Population	26,273	9.2
Hispanic or Latino (of any race)	4,791	22.8
Central American, ex. Mexican	649	42.2
Dominican Republic	847	55.3
Mexican	2,091	19.3
Puerto Rican	8	0.3
South American	944	56.8
Spaniard	35	3.8

Foreign-Born Naturalized U.S. Citizens

Group	Number	%
Total Population	14,173	53.9
Hispanic or Latino (of any race)	2,296	47.9
Central American, ex. Mexican	364	56.1
Dominican Republic	654	77.2
Mexican	717	34.3
Puerto Rican	8	100.0
South American	394	41.7
Spaniard	4	11.4

Language Spoken at Home: English Only
(Universe: Population 5 Years and Over)

Group	Number	%
Total Population	220,304	83.7
Hispanic or Latino (of any race)	8,771	47.9
Central American, ex. Mexican	428	32.3
Dominican Republic	81	5.5
Mexican	5,003	54.4
Puerto Rican	1,454	58.6
South American	156	10.8
Spaniard	643	75.0

Language Spoken at Home: Spanish
(Universe: Population 5 Years and Over)

Group	Number	%
Total Population	11,769	4.5
Hispanic or Latino (of any race)	8,896	48.6
Central American, ex. Mexican	899	67.7
Dominican Republic	1,332	91.2
Mexican	3,965	43.1
Puerto Rican	980	39.5
South American	1,094	75.6
Spaniard	210	24.5

Unemployment Rate
(Universe: Population 16 Years and Over)

Group	%
Total Population	7.4
Hispanic or Latino (of any race)	10.8
Central American, ex. Mexican	2.6
Dominican Republic	25.4
Mexican	8.0
Puerto Rican	18.3
South American	9.8
Spaniard	19.3

Class of Worker: Private Wage and Salary
(Universe: Civilian Employed Population 16 Years and Over)

Group	Number	%
Total Population	102,494	71.6
Hispanic or Latino (of any race)	6,555	76.3
Central American, ex. Mexican	440	56.3
Dominican Republic	562	83.6
Mexican	3,432	79.3
Puerto Rican	675	78.8
South American	616	76.2
Spaniard	227	59.0

Class of Worker: Government
(Universe: Civilian Employed Population 16 Years and Over)

Group	Number	%
Total Population	31,046	21.7
Hispanic or Latino (of any race)	1,543	18.0
Central American, ex. Mexican	205	26.2
Dominican Republic	70	10.4
Mexican	783	18.1
Puerto Rican	128	14.9
South American	150	18.6
Spaniard	75	19.5

Means of Transportation to Work: Car, Truck or Van
(Universe: Workers 16 Years and Over)

Group	Number	%
Total Population	130,139	89.1
Hispanic or Latino (of any race)	7,907	88.4
Central American, ex. Mexican	720	87.0
Dominican Republic	602	93.6
Mexican	3,927	88.4
Puerto Rican	863	84.5
South American	717	90.5
Spaniard	327	83.6

Means of Transportation to Work: Public Transportation (ex. Taxicab)
(Universe: Workers 16 Years and Over)

Group	Number	%
Total Population	2,121	1.5
Hispanic or Latino (of any race)	170	1.9
Central American, ex. Mexican	0	0.0
Dominican Republic	16	2.5
Mexican	86	1.9
Puerto Rican	19	1.9
South American	26	3.3
Spaniard	0	0.0

Homeownership Rate
(Universe: Occupied Housing Units)

Group	%
Total Population	59.9
Hispanic or Latino (of any race)	46.5
Central American, ex. Mexican	50.1
Guatemalan	44.0
Honduran	50.0
Nicaraguan	55.6
Panamanian	55.3
Salvadoran	49.2
Cuban	40.7
Dominican Republic	35.0
Mexican	47.7
Puerto Rican	34.8
South American	62.0
Chilean	65.9
Colombian	61.0
Ecuadorian	46.4
Peruvian	64.6
Spaniard	56.8

Notes: (1) Percent of total population; (2) Percent of Hispanic/Latino population; Profiles include places with an overall population of at least 125,000, OR an overall population of at least 25,000 where the Hispanic/Latino population is at least 20% of the overall population. In states where less than five places meet either of these criteria, we have included places with at least 10,000 total population with the highest percentage of Hispanic/Latino population. These places are identified with an asterisk (*); Please refer to the User's Guide for a full explanation of data.

Median Home Value	
Group	Dollars
Total Population	269,500
Hispanic or Latino (of any race)	235,000
Central American, ex. Mexican	135,200
Dominican Republic	238,900
Mexican	225,200
Puerto Rican	192,000
South American	338,600
Spaniard	237,200

Median Gross Rent	
Group	Dollars
Total Population	1,009
Hispanic or Latino (of any race)	994
Central American, ex. Mexican	1,344
Dominican Republic	943
Mexican	990
Puerto Rican	1,083
South American	931
Spaniard	950

Median Household Income (2010 Inflation-Adjusted Dollars)	
Group	Dollars
Total Population	73,004
Hispanic or Latino (of any race)	57,181
Central American, ex. Mexican	55,339
Dominican Republic	51,713
Mexican	60,408
Puerto Rican	46,250
South American	66,197
Spaniard	70,000

Per Capita Income (2010 Inflation-Adjusted Dollars)	
Group	Dollars
Total Population	34,678
Hispanic or Latino (of any race)	20,668
Central American, ex. Mexican	22,307
Dominican Republic	15,756
Mexican	18,551
Puerto Rican	18,657
South American	31,490
Spaniard	27,398

Households with $100,000+ Income		
Group	Number	%
Total Population	34,103	32.7
Hispanic or Latino (of any race)	989	17.3
Central American, ex. Mexican	66	17.0
Dominican Republic	26	7.0
Mexican	484	17.1
Puerto Rican	91	11.2
South American	116	21.0
Spaniard	86	28.1

Households with Food Stamps/SNAP Benefits During Past 12 Months		
Group	Number	%
Total Population	7,449	7.1
Hispanic or Latino (of any race)	755	13.2
Central American, ex. Mexican	120	30.8
Dominican Republic	87	23.3
Mexican	341	12.1
Puerto Rican	130	16.0
South American	14	2.5
Spaniard	37	12.1

Poverty Rate (Income in Past 12 Months Below Poverty Level)	
Group	%
Total Population	7.9
Hispanic or Latino (of any race)	11.5
Central American, ex. Mexican	5.6
Dominican Republic	8.8
Mexican	12.7
Puerto Rican	17.9
South American	3.0
Spaniard	6.4

Badger*

Population			
Group	Number	%TP[1]	%HP[2]
Total Population	19,482	100.0	–
Hispanic or Latino (of any race)	880	4.5	100.0
Mexican	547	2.8	62.2
Puerto Rican	127	0.7	14.4

Population Growth: 2000–2010	
Group	%
Total Population	n/a

Males per 100 Females	
Group	Number
Total Population	109.9
Hispanic or Latino (of any race)	103.7
Mexican	101.8
Puerto Rican	104.8

Average Household Size	
Group	People
Total Population	2.84
Hispanic or Latino (of any race)	3.10
Mexican	3.15
Puerto Rican	2.93

Median Age	
Group	Years
Total Population	31.4
Hispanic or Latino (of any race)	22.9
Mexican	21.3
Puerto Rican	25.4

High School Graduates (Universe: Population 25 Years and Over)		
Group	Number	%
Total Population	10,134	93.7

Four-Year College Graduates (Universe: Population 25 Years and Over)		
Group	Number	%
Total Population	1,917	17.7

Population Age 3–17 Enrolled in Public School (Universe: Population Age 3–17 Enrolled in School)		
Group	Number	%
Total Population	2,953	83.8

Population Age 3–17 Enrolled in Private School (Universe: Population Age 3–17 Enrolled in School)		
Group	Number	%
Total Population	569	16.2

Foreign-Born Population		
Group	Number	%
Total Population	528	2.9

Foreign-Born Naturalized U.S. Citizens		
Group	Number	%
Total Population	276	52.3

Language Spoken at Home: English Only (Universe: Population 5 Years and Over)		
Group	Number	%
Total Population	15,634	94.5

Language Spoken at Home: Spanish (Universe: Population 5 Years and Over)		
Group	Number	%
Total Population	195	1.2

Unemployment Rate (Universe: Population 16 Years and Over)	
Group	%
Total Population	7.0

Class of Worker: Private Wage and Salary (Universe: Civilian Employed Population 16 Years and Over)		
Group	Number	%
Total Population	5,542	65.1

Class of Worker: Government (Universe: Civilian Employed Population 16 Years and Over)		
Group	Number	%
Total Population	2,452	28.8

Means of Transportation to Work: Car, Truck or Van (Universe: Workers 16 Years and Over)		
Group	Number	%
Total Population	8,184	91.0

Means of Transportation to Work: Public Transportation (ex. Taxicab) (Universe: Workers 16 Years and Over)		
Group	Number	%
Total Population	95	1.1

Homeownership Rate (Universe: Occupied Housing Units)	
Group	%
Total Population	76.0
Hispanic or Latino (of any race)	61.7
Mexican	61.0
Puerto Rican	55.2

Median Home Value	
Group	Dollars
Total Population	197,200

Median Gross Rent	
Group	Dollars
Total Population	1,240

Median Household Income (2010 Inflation-Adjusted Dollars)	
Group	Dollars
Total Population	82,283

Per Capita Income (2010 Inflation-Adjusted Dollars)	
Group	Dollars
Total Population	29,659

Households with $100,000+ Income		
Group	Number	%
Total Population	1,985	32.7

Households with Food Stamps/SNAP Benefits During Past 12 Months		
Group	Number	%
Total Population	155	2.6

Poverty Rate (Income in Past 12 Months Below Poverty Level)	
Group	%
Total Population	5.0

College*

Population			
Group	Number	%TP[1]	%HP[2]
Total Population	12,964	100.0	–
Hispanic or Latino (of any race)	687	5.3	100.0
Mexican	388	3.0	56.5

Population Growth: 2000–2010	
Group	%
Total Population	13.7
Hispanic or Latino (of any race)	73.5
Mexican	76.4

Males per 100 Females	
Group	Number
Total Population	109.8
Hispanic or Latino (of any race)	115.4
Mexican	124.3

Average Household Size	
Group	People
Total Population	2.44
Hispanic or Latino (of any race)	2.81
Mexican	2.76

Notes: (1) Percent of total population; (2) Percent of Hispanic/Latino population; Profiles include places with an overall population of at least 125,000, OR an overall population of at least 25,000 where the Hispanic/Latino population is at least 20% of the overall population. In states where less than five places meet either of these criteria, we have included places with at least 10,000 total population with the highest percentage of Hispanic/Latino population. These places are identified with an asterisk (*); Please refer to the User's Guide for a full explanation of data.

Median Age

Group	Years
Total Population	30.1
Hispanic or Latino (of any race)	23.4
Mexican	22.2

High School Graduates
(Universe: Population 25 Years and Over)

Group	Number	%
Total Population	7,693	94.5
Hispanic or Latino (of any race)	323	74.4

Four-Year College Graduates
(Universe: Population 25 Years and Over)

Group	Number	%
Total Population	3,165	38.9
Hispanic or Latino (of any race)	125	28.8

Population Age 3–17 Enrolled in Public School
(Universe: Population Age 3–17 Enrolled in School)

Group	Number	%
Total Population	1,768	92.6
Hispanic or Latino (of any race)	97	88.2

Population Age 3–17 Enrolled in Private School
(Universe: Population Age 3–17 Enrolled in School)

Group	Number	%
Total Population	142	7.4
Hispanic or Latino (of any race)	13	11.8

Foreign-Born Population

Group	Number	%
Total Population	1,331	10.0
Hispanic or Latino (of any race)	212	25.5

Foreign-Born Naturalized U.S. Citizens

Group	Number	%
Total Population	661	49.7
Hispanic or Latino (of any race)	152	71.7

Language Spoken at Home: English Only
(Universe: Population 5 Years and Over)

Group	Number	%
Total Population	10,394	84.4
Hispanic or Latino (of any race)	368	48.7

Language Spoken at Home: Spanish
(Universe: Population 5 Years and Over)

Group	Number	%
Total Population	506	4.1
Hispanic or Latino (of any race)	361	47.8

Unemployment Rate
(Universe: Population 16 Years and Over)

Group	%
Total Population	8.1
Hispanic or Latino (of any race)	3.1

Class of Worker: Private Wage and Salary
(Universe: Civilian Employed Population 16 Years and Over)

Group	Number	%
Total Population	3,970	60.2
Hispanic or Latino (of any race)	389	81.7

Class of Worker: Government
(Universe: Civilian Employed Population 16 Years and Over)

Group	Number	%
Total Population	2,251	34.2
Hispanic or Latino (of any race)	73	15.3

Means of Transportation to Work: Car, Truck or Van
(Universe: Workers 16 Years and Over)

Group	Number	%
Total Population	5,433	82.6
Hispanic or Latino (of any race)	427	92.8

Means of Transportation to Work: Public Transportation (ex. Taxicab)
(Universe: Workers 16 Years and Over)

Group	Number	%
Total Population	74	1.1
Hispanic or Latino (of any race)	0	0.0

Homeownership Rate
(Universe: Occupied Housing Units)

Group	%
Total Population	58.4
Hispanic or Latino (of any race)	48.9
Mexican	44.1

Median Home Value

Group	Dollars
Total Population	218,500
Hispanic or Latino (of any race)	230,400

Median Gross Rent

Group	Dollars
Total Population	967
Hispanic or Latino (of any race)	956

Median Household Income
(2010 Inflation-Adjusted Dollars)

Group	Dollars
Total Population	72,061
Hispanic or Latino (of any race)	74,120

Per Capita Income
(2010 Inflation-Adjusted Dollars)

Group	Dollars
Total Population	34,290
Hispanic or Latino (of any race)	18,591

Households with $100,000+ Income

Group	Number	%
Total Population	1,537	32.5
Hispanic or Latino (of any race)	83	30.9

Households with Food Stamps/SNAP Benefits During Past 12 Months

Group	Number	%
Total Population	312	6.6
Hispanic or Latino (of any race)	0	0.0

Poverty Rate
(Income in Past 12 Months Below Poverty Level)

Group	%
Total Population	9.6
Hispanic or Latino (of any race)	4.8

Fairbanks*

Population

Group	Number	%TP[1]	%HP[2]
Total Population	31,535	100.0	–
Hispanic or Latino (of any race)	2,837	9.0	100.0
Central American, ex. Mexican	176	0.6	6.2
Mexican	1,520	4.8	53.6
Puerto Rican	524	1.7	18.5
South American	159	0.5	5.6

Population Growth: 2000–2010

Group	%
Total Population	4.3
Hispanic or Latino (of any race)	53.0
Central American, ex. Mexican	69.2
Mexican	72.7
Puerto Rican	50.6

Males per 100 Females

Group	Number
Total Population	113.9
Hispanic or Latino (of any race)	105.9
Central American, ex. Mexican	74.3
Mexican	111.4
Puerto Rican	115.6
South American	78.7

Average Household Size

Group	People
Total Population	2.52
Hispanic or Latino (of any race)	2.99
Central American, ex. Mexican	2.79
Mexican	3.03
Puerto Rican	3.15
South American	2.90

Median Age

Group	Years
Total Population	27.9
Hispanic or Latino (of any race)	22.6
Central American, ex. Mexican	22.6
Mexican	21.6
Puerto Rican	22.9
South American	32.8

High School Graduates
(Universe: Population 25 Years and Over)

Group	Number	%
Total Population	15,698	89.3
Hispanic or Latino (of any race)	839	81.5
Mexican	493	82.3

Four-Year College Graduates
(Universe: Population 25 Years and Over)

Group	Number	%
Total Population	3,254	18.5
Hispanic or Latino (of any race)	97	9.4
Mexican	57	9.5

Population Age 3–17 Enrolled in Public School
(Universe: Population Age 3–17 Enrolled in School)

Group	Number	%
Total Population	4,338	85.4
Hispanic or Latino (of any race)	303	88.1
Mexican	264	93.0

Population Age 3–17 Enrolled in Private School
(Universe: Population Age 3–17 Enrolled in School)

Group	Number	%
Total Population	742	14.6
Hispanic or Latino (of any race)	41	11.9
Mexican	20	7.0

Foreign-Born Population

Group	Number	%
Total Population	1,846	5.9
Hispanic or Latino (of any race)	415	18.4
Mexican	177	12.8

Foreign-Born Naturalized U.S. Citizens

Group	Number	%
Total Population	968	52.4
Hispanic or Latino (of any race)	153	36.9
Mexican	52	29.4

Language Spoken at Home: English Only
(Universe: Population 5 Years and Over)

Group	Number	%
Total Population	24,686	86.4
Hispanic or Latino (of any race)	751	39.2
Mexican	549	47.5

Language Spoken at Home: Spanish
(Universe: Population 5 Years and Over)

Group	Number	%
Total Population	1,837	6.4
Hispanic or Latino (of any race)	1,110	57.9
Mexican	569	49.2

Unemployment Rate
(Universe: Population 16 Years and Over)

Group	%
Total Population	7.6
Hispanic or Latino (of any race)	5.9
Mexican	4.3

Class of Worker: Private Wage and Salary
(Universe: Civilian Employed Population 16 Years and Over)

Group	Number	%
Total Population	9,768	73.1
Hispanic or Latino (of any race)	637	80.1
Mexican	302	79.5

Class of Worker: Government
(Universe: Civilian Employed Population 16 Years and Over)

Group	Number	%
Total Population	2,951	22.1
Hispanic or Latino (of any race)	127	16.0
Mexican	69	18.2

Notes: (1) Percent of total population; (2) Percent of Hispanic/Latino population; Profiles include places with an overall population of at least 125,000, OR an overall population of at least 25,000 where the Hispanic/Latino population is at least 20% of the overall population. In states where less than five places meet either of these criteria, we have included places with at least 10,000 total population with the highest percentage of Hispanic/Latino population. These places are identified with an asterisk (*); Please refer to the User's Guide for a full explanation of data.

Means of Transportation to Work: Car, Truck or Van
(Universe: Workers 16 Years and Over)

Group	Number	%
Total Population	12,963	81.7
Hispanic or Latino (of any race)	992	85.2
Mexican	480	82.3

Means of Transportation to Work: Public Transportation (ex. Taxicab)
(Universe: Workers 16 Years and Over)

Group	Number	%
Total Population	311	2.0
Hispanic or Latino (of any race)	0	0.0
Mexican	0	0.0

Homeownership Rate
(Universe: Occupied Housing Units)

Group	%
Total Population	35.8
Hispanic or Latino (of any race)	20.4
Central American, ex. Mexican	21.1
Mexican	21.6
Puerto Rican	11.6
South American	34.7

Median Home Value

Group	Dollars
Total Population	192,500
Hispanic or Latino (of any race)	223,800
Mexican	228,600

Median Gross Rent

Group	Dollars
Total Population	1,000
Hispanic or Latino (of any race)	1,196
Mexican	1,167

Median Household Income
(2010 Inflation-Adjusted Dollars)

Group	Dollars
Total Population	51,320
Hispanic or Latino (of any race)	47,535
Mexican	30,625

Per Capita Income
(2010 Inflation-Adjusted Dollars)

Group	Dollars
Total Population	26,373
Hispanic or Latino (of any race)	18,800
Mexican	16,534

Households with $100,000+ Income

Group	Number	%
Total Population	2,206	18.2
Hispanic or Latino (of any race)	33	5.2
Mexican	0	0.0

Households with Food Stamps/SNAP Benefits During Past 12 Months

Group	Number	%
Total Population	928	7.6
Hispanic or Latino (of any race)	31	4.9
Mexican	31	8.6

Poverty Rate
(Income in Past 12 Months Below Poverty Level)

Group	%
Total Population	11.0
Hispanic or Latino (of any race)	12.3
Mexican	15.2

Juneau*

Population

Group	Number	%TP[1]	%HP[2]
Total Population	31,275	100.0	–
Hispanic or Latino (of any race)	1,588	5.1	100.0
Mexican	1,009	3.2	63.5
Puerto Rican	143	0.5	9.0

Population Growth: 2000–2010

Group	%
Total Population	1.8
Hispanic or Latino (of any race)	52.7
Mexican	61.2

Males per 100 Females

Group	Number
Total Population	104.1
Hispanic or Latino (of any race)	107.0
Mexican	108.9
Puerto Rican	113.4

Average Household Size

Group	People
Total Population	2.49
Hispanic or Latino (of any race)	2.82
Mexican	2.91
Puerto Rican	2.75

Median Age

Group	Years
Total Population	38.1
Hispanic or Latino (of any race)	26.3
Mexican	24.5
Puerto Rican	26.3

High School Graduates
(Universe: Population 25 Years and Over)

Group	Number	%
Total Population	19,635	95.3
Hispanic or Latino (of any race)	780	90.9
Mexican	461	85.5

Four-Year College Graduates
(Universe: Population 25 Years and Over)

Group	Number	%
Total Population	7,157	34.7
Hispanic or Latino (of any race)	161	18.8
Mexican	86	16.0

Population Age 3–17 Enrolled in Public School
(Universe: Population Age 3–17 Enrolled in School)

Group	Number	%
Total Population	4,996	89.6
Hispanic or Latino (of any race)	394	96.6
Mexican	210	93.8

Population Age 3–17 Enrolled in Private School
(Universe: Population Age 3–17 Enrolled in School)

Group	Number	%
Total Population	577	10.4
Hispanic or Latino (of any race)	14	3.4
Mexican	14	6.3

Foreign-Born Population

Group	Number	%
Total Population	2,142	6.9
Hispanic or Latino (of any race)	379	23.0
Mexican	257	25.5

Foreign-Born Naturalized U.S. Citizens

Group	Number	%
Total Population	1,217	56.8
Hispanic or Latino (of any race)	126	33.2
Mexican	47	18.3

Language Spoken at Home: English Only
(Universe: Population 5 Years and Over)

Group	Number	%
Total Population	25,896	89.1
Hispanic or Latino (of any race)	786	53.6
Mexican	449	51.3

Language Spoken at Home: Spanish
(Universe: Population 5 Years and Over)

Group	Number	%
Total Population	921	3.2
Hispanic or Latino (of any race)	675	46.0
Mexican	427	48.7

Unemployment Rate
(Universe: Population 16 Years and Over)

Group	%
Total Population	5.8
Hispanic or Latino (of any race)	8.6
Mexican	7.8

Class of Worker: Private Wage and Salary
(Universe: Civilian Employed Population 16 Years and Over)

Group	Number	%
Total Population	9,081	52.7
Hispanic or Latino (of any race)	365	48.7
Mexican	240	51.8

Class of Worker: Government
(Universe: Civilian Employed Population 16 Years and Over)

Group	Number	%
Total Population	6,878	39.9
Hispanic or Latino (of any race)	309	41.2
Mexican	147	31.7

Means of Transportation to Work: Car, Truck or Van
(Universe: Workers 16 Years and Over)

Group	Number	%
Total Population	13,096	77.2
Hispanic or Latino (of any race)	494	63.6
Mexican	238	51.9

Means of Transportation to Work: Public Transportation (ex. Taxicab)
(Universe: Workers 16 Years and Over)

Group	Number	%
Total Population	928	5.5
Hispanic or Latino (of any race)	26	3.3
Mexican	0	0.0

Homeownership Rate
(Universe: Occupied Housing Units)

Group	%
Total Population	62.3
Hispanic or Latino (of any race)	46.7
Mexican	46.9
Puerto Rican	39.6

Median Home Value

Group	Dollars
Total Population	291,600
Hispanic or Latino (of any race)	343,800
Mexican	372,500

Median Gross Rent

Group	Dollars
Total Population	1,084
Hispanic or Latino (of any race)	1,067
Mexican	990

Median Household Income
(2010 Inflation-Adjusted Dollars)

Group	Dollars
Total Population	75,517
Hispanic or Latino (of any race)	68,750
Mexican	76,157

Per Capita Income
(2010 Inflation-Adjusted Dollars)

Group	Dollars
Total Population	34,923
Hispanic or Latino (of any race)	22,031
Mexican	24,206

Households with $100,000+ Income

Group	Number	%
Total Population	3,880	32.3
Hispanic or Latino (of any race)	168	29.9
Mexican	122	32.9

Households with Food Stamps/SNAP Benefits During Past 12 Months

Group	Number	%
Total Population	691	5.8
Hispanic or Latino (of any race)	71	12.6
Mexican	28	7.5

Poverty Rate
(Income in Past 12 Months Below Poverty Level)

Group	%
Total Population	6.5
Hispanic or Latino (of any race)	19.8
Mexican	28.8

Notes: (1) Percent of total population; (2) Percent of Hispanic/Latino population; Profiles include places with an overall population of at least 125,000, OR an overall population of at least 25,000 where the Hispanic/Latino population is at least 20% of the overall population. In states where less than five places meet either of these criteria, we have included places with at least 10,000 total population with the highest percentage of Hispanic/Latino population. These places are identified with an asterisk (*); Please refer to the User's Guide for a full explanation of data.

Arizona

EDITOR'S NOTE: For a place to be included in this edition, it must meet one of two criteria. Either its overall population is at least 125,000, OR its overall population is at least 25,000 and its Hispanic/Latino population is at least 20% of the overall population. For the state of Arizona, the following locations are included:

Avondale
Buckeye
Bullhead City
Casa Grande
Casas Adobes
Chandler
Drexel Heights
El Mirage
Florence
Fortuna Foothills
Gilbert
Glendale
Goodyear
Marana
Maricopa
Mesa
Peoria
Phoenix
Sahuarita
San Luis
San Tan Valley
Scottsdale
Tempe
Tucson
Yuma

Section Two: State & Place Profiles starts with the state profile, followed by place profiles that meet the criteria above. Places are listed alphabetically within each state. All states, all counties and places that meet the above criteria are ranked and compared in *Section Three: Rankings & Comparisons*, on page 1055.

For a more detailed look at the Hispanic/Latino population in Arizona, a companion web site is available at no additional charge with purchase of this print edition. Visit http://gold.greyhouse.com/page/info_hispanic for more information.

The web site includes data for all counties and places in Arizona with Hispanic/Latino population, plus ten additional topics: Self Employed Worker; Walked to Work; Worked from Home; Mean Travel Time to Work; Mean Household Income; Households with Cash Public Assistance; Mean Cash Pubic Assistance; Poverty Rates for 18 and Under, 18 to 64, and 65 and Over.

Population

Group	Number	%TP[1]	%HP[2]
Total Population	6,392,017	100.0	–
Hispanic or Latino (of any race)	1,895,149	29.6	100.0
Central American, ex. Mexican	36,642	0.6	1.9
Costa Rican	1,573	<0.1	0.1
Guatemalan	13,426	0.2	0.7
Honduran	3,968	0.1	0.2
Nicaraguan	2,813	<0.1	0.1
Panamanian	2,251	<0.1	0.1
Salvadoran	12,225	0.2	0.6
Cuban	10,692	0.2	0.6
Dominican Republic	3,103	<0.1	0.2
Mexican	1,657,668	25.9	87.5
Puerto Rican	34,787	0.5	1.8
South American	21,895	0.3	1.2
Argentinean	2,775	<0.1	0.1
Bolivian	750	<0.1	<0.1
Chilean	1,955	<0.1	0.1
Colombian	6,706	0.1	0.4
Ecuadorian	2,516	<0.1	0.1
Paraguayan	175	<0.1	<0.1
Peruvian	4,658	0.1	0.2
Uruguayan	422	<0.1	<0.1
Venezuelan	1,707	<0.1	0.1
Spaniard	21,561	0.3	1.1

Population Growth: 2000–2010

Group	%
Total Population	24.6
Hispanic or Latino (of any race)	46.3
Central American, ex. Mexican	180.2
Costa Rican	124.1
Guatemalan	208.2
Honduran	190.7
Nicaraguan	232.1
Panamanian	94.4
Salvadoran	230.0
Cuban	102.8
Dominican Republic	247.9
Mexican	55.6
Puerto Rican	97.8
South American	169.9
Argentinean	189.4
Bolivian	190.7
Chilean	147.2
Colombian	175.2
Ecuadorian	231.1
Peruvian	210.9
Uruguayan	189.0
Venezuelan	145.6
Spaniard	869.5

Males per 100 Females

Group	Number
Total Population	98.7
Hispanic or Latino (of any race)	100.9
Central American, ex. Mexican	102.6
Costa Rican	80.0
Guatemalan	120.5
Honduran	93.9
Nicaraguan	89.3
Panamanian	68.5
Salvadoran	100.5
Cuban	108.8
Dominican Republic	110.2
Mexican	101.4
Puerto Rican	104.0
South American	84.3
Argentinean	96.3
Bolivian	91.8
Chilean	78.2
Colombian	75.8
Ecuadorian	86.4
Paraguayan	84.2
Peruvian	86.3
Uruguayan	86.7
Venezuelan	94.9
Spaniard	90.2

Average Household Size

Group	People
Total Population	2.63
Hispanic or Latino (of any race)	3.51
Central American, ex. Mexican	3.65
Costa Rican	2.86
Guatemalan	4.05
Honduran	3.51
Nicaraguan	3.34
Panamanian	2.54
Salvadoran	3.69
Cuban	2.73
Dominican Republic	2.98
Mexican	3.59
Puerto Rican	2.74
South American	2.77
Argentinean	2.56
Bolivian	2.88
Chilean	2.71
Colombian	2.70
Ecuadorian	2.99
Paraguayan	2.44
Peruvian	2.94
Uruguayan	2.78
Venezuelan	2.78
Spaniard	2.66

Median Age

Group	Years
Total Population	35.9
Hispanic or Latino (of any race)	25.4
Central American, ex. Mexican	30.6
Costa Rican	31.6
Guatemalan	28.9
Honduran	30.2
Nicaraguan	32.2
Panamanian	34.4
Salvadoran	32.0
Cuban	34.1
Dominican Republic	26.4
Mexican	25.0
Puerto Rican	27.7
South American	34.6
Argentinean	39.4
Bolivian	33.0
Chilean	35.6
Colombian	34.0
Ecuadorian	32.4
Paraguayan	26.1
Peruvian	34.1
Uruguayan	39.9
Venezuelan	32.3
Spaniard	33.9

High School Graduates

(Universe: Population 25 Years and Over)

Group	Number	%
Total Population	3,413,275	85.0
Hispanic or Latino (of any race)	565,554	62.2
Central American, ex. Mexican	11,521	55.5
Costa Rican	863	92.6
Guatemalan	3,281	43.3
Honduran	1,159	54.1
Nicaraguan	957	75.5
Panamanian	1,398	90.6
Salvadoran	3,465	52.0
Cuban	4,940	82.6
Dominican Republic	1,144	91.7
Mexican	484,752	60.2
Puerto Rican	14,291	86.7
South American	12,000	89.3
Argentinean	1,685	90.2
Chilean	1,013	92.7
Colombian	3,936	89.9
Ecuadorian	1,377	93.0
Peruvian	2,452	91.1
Venezuelan	748	82.4
Spaniard	10,019	86.5

Four-Year College Graduates

(Universe: Population 25 Years and Over)

Group	Number	%
Total Population	1,057,375	26.3
Hispanic or Latino (of any race)	93,714	10.3
Central American, ex. Mexican	2,536	12.2
Costa Rican	287	30.8
Guatemalan	523	6.9
Honduran	296	13.8
Nicaraguan	238	18.8
Panamanian	349	22.6
Salvadoran	758	11.4
Cuban	1,848	30.9
Dominican Republic	240	19.2
Mexican	71,755	8.9
Puerto Rican	4,048	24.5
South American	5,644	42.0
Argentinean	762	40.8
Chilean	434	39.7
Colombian	1,856	42.4
Ecuadorian	580	39.2
Peruvian	1,174	43.6

Notes: (1) Percent of total population; (2) Percent of Hispanic/Latino population; Profiles include places with an overall population of at least 125,000, OR an overall population of at least 25,000 where the Hispanic/Latino population is at least 20% of the overall population. In states where less than five places meet either of these criteria, we have included places with at least 10,000 total population with the highest percentage of Hispanic/Latino population. These places are identified with an asterisk (*); Please refer to the User's Guide for a full explanation of data.

Group	Number	%
Venezuelan	363	40.0
Spaniard	2,608	22.5

Population Age 3–17 Enrolled in Public School
(Universe: Population Age 3–17 Enrolled in School)

Group	Number	%
Total Population	1,056,579	90.8
Hispanic or Latino (of any race)	450,245	95.4
Central American, ex. Mexican	6,732	95.1
Costa Rican	327	87.2
Guatemalan	2,641	92.4
Honduran	694	97.3
Nicaraguan	446	100.0
Panamanian	512	100.0
Salvadoran	1,975	96.8
Cuban	1,362	90.4
Dominican Republic	648	87.8
Mexican	413,039	95.8
Puerto Rican	7,172	93.7
South American	3,659	83.0
Argentinean	275	62.2
Chilean	150	58.8
Colombian	1,236	92.9
Ecuadorian	578	85.0
Peruvian	974	96.2
Venezuelan	202	79.2
Spaniard	2,652	86.4

Population Age 3–17 Enrolled in Private School
(Universe: Population Age 3–17 Enrolled in School)

Group	Number	%
Total Population	107,146	9.2
Hispanic or Latino (of any race)	21,910	4.6
Central American, ex. Mexican	350	4.9
Costa Rican	48	12.8
Guatemalan	217	7.6
Honduran	19	2.7
Nicaraguan	0	0.0
Panamanian	0	0.0
Salvadoran	66	3.2
Cuban	145	9.6
Dominican Republic	90	12.2
Mexican	18,276	4.2
Puerto Rican	482	6.3
South American	752	17.0
Argentinean	167	37.8
Chilean	105	41.2
Colombian	95	7.1
Ecuadorian	102	15.0
Peruvian	38	3.8
Venezuelan	53	20.8
Spaniard	419	13.6

Foreign-Born Population

Group	Number	%
Total Population	884,625	14.2
Hispanic or Latino (of any race)	594,658	32.8
Central American, ex. Mexican	21,933	60.9
Costa Rican	704	42.3
Guatemalan	8,844	65.5
Honduran	2,443	60.3
Nicaraguan	1,170	57.2
Panamanian	1,080	44.0
Salvadoran	7,207	63.1
Cuban	4,383	49.0
Dominican Republic	992	38.3
Mexican	546,405	33.5
Puerto Rican	535	1.8
South American	12,850	57.9
Argentinean	1,659	62.7
Chilean	868	46.9
Colombian	4,237	60.2
Ecuadorian	1,473	50.2
Peruvian	2,802	62.0
Venezuelan	918	62.7
Spaniard	1,429	7.9

Foreign-Born Naturalized U.S. Citizens

Group	Number	%
Total Population	289,578	32.7
Hispanic or Latino (of any race)	139,783	23.5
Central American, ex. Mexican	6,432	29.3
Costa Rican	396	56.3
Guatemalan	2,065	23.3
Honduran	558	22.8
Nicaraguan	656	56.1
Panamanian	560	51.9
Salvadoran	2,040	28.3
Cuban	1,500	34.2
Dominican Republic	630	63.5
Mexican	120,171	22.0
Puerto Rican	276	51.6
South American	7,013	54.6
Argentinean	1,147	69.1
Chilean	420	48.4
Colombian	2,403	56.7
Ecuadorian	915	62.1
Peruvian	1,157	41.3
Venezuelan	337	36.7
Spaniard	814	57.0

Language Spoken at Home: English Only
(Universe: Population 5 Years and Over)

Group	Number	%
Total Population	4,215,749	72.9
Hispanic or Latino (of any race)	478,652	29.8
Central American, ex. Mexican	5,907	17.9
Costa Rican	706	44.9
Guatemalan	1,401	11.5
Honduran	696	19.1
Nicaraguan	556	28.4
Panamanian	900	39.6
Salvadoran	1,490	14.2
Cuban	2,891	34.5
Dominican Republic	680	29.6
Mexican	403,596	28.0
Puerto Rican	15,193	55.6
South American	5,098	25.3
Argentinean	712	28.1
Chilean	538	30.4
Colombian	1,381	21.5
Ecuadorian	486	18.8
Peruvian	986	24.8
Venezuelan	323	24.7
Spaniard	11,081	66.8

Language Spoken at Home: Spanish
(Universe: Population 5 Years and Over)

Group	Number	%
Total Population	1,199,689	20.7
Hispanic or Latino (of any race)	1,125,650	70.0
Central American, ex. Mexican	26,851	81.5
Costa Rican	868	55.1
Guatemalan	10,636	87.6
Honduran	2,940	80.9
Nicaraguan	1,345	68.7
Panamanian	1,342	59.1
Salvadoran	9,039	85.8
Cuban	5,438	64.9
Dominican Republic	1,619	70.4
Mexican	1,036,366	71.9
Puerto Rican	11,998	43.9
South American	14,847	73.6
Argentinean	1,797	71.0
Chilean	1,224	69.2
Colombian	5,009	78.0
Ecuadorian	2,006	77.6
Peruvian	2,968	74.6
Venezuelan	938	71.7
Spaniard	5,093	30.7

Unemployment Rate
(Universe: Population 16 Years and Over)

Group	%
Total Population	7.7
Hispanic or Latino (of any race)	9.3
Central American, ex. Mexican	7.5
Costa Rican	5.1
Guatemalan	4.7
Honduran	10.2
Nicaraguan	11.4
Panamanian	12.7
Salvadoran	7.9
Cuban	9.6
Dominican Republic	7.2
Mexican	9.5
Puerto Rican	6.6
South American	5.4
Argentinean	5.8
Chilean	2.6
Colombian	5.8
Ecuadorian	3.0
Peruvian	7.4
Venezuelan	5.9
Spaniard	9.3

Class of Worker: Private Wage and Salary
(Universe: Civilian Employed Population 16 Years and Over)

Group	Number	%
Total Population	2,154,992	78.4
Hispanic or Latino (of any race)	581,032	81.2
Central American, ex. Mexican	15,685	85.1
Costa Rican	751	81.5
Guatemalan	5,548	85.5
Honduran	1,595	85.2
Nicaraguan	978	85.3
Panamanian	878	74.9
Salvadoran	5,571	88.1
Cuban	3,316	78.6
Dominican Republic	769	82.2
Mexican	515,641	81.4
Puerto Rican	10,139	76.6
South American	8,322	76.6
Argentinean	992	72.6
Chilean	850	82.4
Colombian	2,456	75.2
Ecuadorian	939	71.7
Peruvian	1,897	81.1
Venezuelan	584	75.4
Spaniard	6,768	79.6

Class of Worker: Government
(Universe: Civilian Employed Population 16 Years and Over)

Group	Number	%
Total Population	416,233	15.1
Hispanic or Latino (of any race)	91,951	12.9
Central American, ex. Mexican	1,698	9.2
Costa Rican	112	12.2
Guatemalan	423	6.5
Honduran	224	12.0
Nicaraguan	135	11.8
Panamanian	229	19.5
Salvadoran	444	7.0
Cuban	746	17.7
Dominican Republic	111	11.9
Mexican	79,898	12.6
Puerto Rican	2,454	18.5
South American	1,695	15.6
Argentinean	212	15.5
Chilean	181	17.6
Colombian	589	18.0
Ecuadorian	226	17.3
Peruvian	329	14.1
Venezuelan	72	9.3
Spaniard	1,293	15.2

Means of Transportation to Work: Car, Truck or Van
(Universe: Workers 16 Years and Over)

Group	Number	%
Total Population	2,381,095	88.2
Hispanic or Latino (of any race)	628,658	89.5
Central American, ex. Mexican	15,692	86.7
Costa Rican	806	88.3
Guatemalan	5,404	84.6
Honduran	1,505	83.6
Nicaraguan	862	78.2
Panamanian	1,075	91.3
Salvadoran	5,676	91.3
Cuban	3,696	87.7
Dominican Republic	882	93.8
Mexican	557,098	89.6
Puerto Rican	11,716	88.4
South American	9,482	88.5
Argentinean	1,112	81.3
Chilean	927	88.1
Colombian	2,901	89.2
Ecuadorian	1,104	90.4
Peruvian	2,070	89.1
Venezuelan	738	96.9
Spaniard	7,516	89.2

Notes: (1) Percent of total population; (2) Percent of Hispanic/Latino population; Profiles include places with an overall population of at least 125,000, OR an overall population of at least 25,000 where the Hispanic/Latino population is at least 20% of the overall population. In states where less than five places meet either of these criteria, we have included places with at least 10,000 total population with the highest percentage of Hispanic/Latino population. These places are identified with an asterisk (*); Please refer to the User's Guide for a full explanation of data.

Means of Transportation to Work: Public Transportation (ex. Taxicab)
(Universe: Workers 16 Years and Over)

Group	Number	%
Total Population	54,275	2.0
Hispanic or Latino (of any race)	20,610	2.9
Central American, ex. Mexican	1,083	6.0
Costa Rican	16	1.8
Guatemalan	435	6.8
Honduran	168	9.3
Nicaraguan	141	12.8
Panamanian	41	3.5
Salvadoran	196	3.2
Cuban	106	2.5
Dominican Republic	16	1.7
Mexican	18,231	2.9
Puerto Rican	429	3.2
South American	154	1.4
Argentinean	18	1.3
Chilean	47	4.5
Colombian	0	0.0
Ecuadorian	11	0.9
Peruvian	78	3.4
Venezuelan	0	0.0
Spaniard	146	1.7

Homeownership Rate
(Universe: Occupied Housing Units)

Group	%
Total Population	66.0
Hispanic or Latino (of any race)	54.4
Central American, ex. Mexican	53.6
Costa Rican	56.1
Guatemalan	48.2
Honduran	46.2
Nicaraguan	58.4
Panamanian	59.9
Salvadoran	58.8
Cuban	51.2
Dominican Republic	44.4
Mexican	54.7
Puerto Rican	50.1
South American	62.0
Argentinean	63.7
Bolivian	63.3
Chilean	60.8
Colombian	61.6
Ecuadorian	66.1
Paraguayan	54.2
Peruvian	61.4
Uruguayan	67.7
Venezuelan	57.1
Spaniard	63.5

Median Home Value

Group	Dollars
Total Population	215,000
Hispanic or Latino (of any race)	165,800
Central American, ex. Mexican	190,400
Costa Rican	282,700
Guatemalan	178,400
Honduran	189,900
Nicaraguan	211,600
Panamanian	220,900
Salvadoran	177,700
Cuban	225,500
Dominican Republic	250,900
Mexican	161,400
Puerto Rican	225,600
South American	237,200
Argentinean	270,800
Chilean	187,000
Colombian	212,400
Ecuadorian	251,600
Peruvian	232,700
Venezuelan	288,800
Spaniard	201,600

Median Gross Rent

Group	Dollars
Total Population	856
Hispanic or Latino (of any race)	777
Central American, ex. Mexican	783
Costa Rican	829
Guatemalan	777
Honduran	694
Nicaraguan	796
Panamanian	979
Salvadoran	786
Cuban	746
Dominican Republic	764
Mexican	770
Puerto Rican	937
South American	936
Argentinean	828
Chilean	1,069
Colombian	982
Ecuadorian	1,098
Peruvian	876
Venezuelan	904
Spaniard	906

Median Household Income
(2010 Inflation-Adjusted Dollars)

Group	Dollars
Total Population	50,448
Hispanic or Latino (of any race)	39,076
Central American, ex. Mexican	41,766
Costa Rican	38,008
Guatemalan	40,981
Honduran	39,016
Nicaraguan	50,595
Panamanian	52,791
Salvadoran	39,689
Cuban	45,804
Dominican Republic	42,472
Mexican	38,239
Puerto Rican	47,867
South American	60,479
Argentinean	66,067
Chilean	66,538
Colombian	64,521
Ecuadorian	51,953
Peruvian	48,145
Venezuelan	51,211
Spaniard	50,536

Per Capita Income
(2010 Inflation-Adjusted Dollars)

Group	Dollars
Total Population	25,680
Hispanic or Latino (of any race)	14,104
Central American, ex. Mexican	16,178
Costa Rican	20,439
Guatemalan	13,738
Honduran	16,844
Nicaraguan	21,851
Panamanian	18,805
Salvadoran	16,356
Cuban	23,934
Dominican Republic	15,739
Mexican	13,470
Puerto Rican	21,422
South American	23,210
Argentinean	34,897
Chilean	23,441
Colombian	21,544
Ecuadorian	20,878
Peruvian	20,966
Venezuelan	18,831
Spaniard	25,030

Households with $100,000+ Income

Group	Number	%
Total Population	440,994	19.0
Hispanic or Latino (of any race)	47,552	9.8
Central American, ex. Mexican	1,426	13.0
Costa Rican	128	20.0
Guatemalan	378	11.3
Honduran	230	20.2
Nicaraguan	102	12.5
Panamanian	110	14.1
Salvadoran	378	9.7
Cuban	657	20.0
Dominican Republic	105	15.4
Mexican	38,229	9.0
Puerto Rican	1,731	17.8
South American	1,483	21.7
Argentinean	325	30.9
Chilean	82	13.4
Colombian	588	27.4
Ecuadorian	164	21.3
Peruvian	133	9.9
Venezuelan	83	18.3
Spaniard	1,229	16.9

Households with Food Stamps/SNAP Benefits During Past 12 Months

Group	Number	%
Total Population	212,791	9.1
Hispanic or Latino (of any race)	84,788	17.5
Central American, ex. Mexican	1,293	11.8
Costa Rican	0	0.0
Guatemalan	408	12.2
Honduran	281	24.7
Nicaraguan	40	4.9
Panamanian	96	12.3
Salvadoran	400	10.3
Cuban	533	16.2
Dominican Republic	175	25.6
Mexican	76,625	18.0
Puerto Rican	1,522	15.6
South American	415	6.1
Argentinean	36	3.4
Chilean	70	11.4
Colombian	197	9.2
Ecuadorian	12	1.6
Peruvian	78	5.8
Venezuelan	14	3.1
Spaniard	866	11.9

Poverty Rate
(Income in Past 12 Months Below Poverty Level)

Group	%
Total Population	15.3
Hispanic or Latino (of any race)	24.4
Central American, ex. Mexican	15.9
Costa Rican	0.7
Guatemalan	17.0
Honduran	23.3
Nicaraguan	11.8
Panamanian	13.0
Salvadoran	16.4
Cuban	18.1
Dominican Republic	20.2
Mexican	25.5
Puerto Rican	14.7
South American	10.7
Argentinean	8.4
Chilean	9.0
Colombian	13.9
Ecuadorian	11.3
Peruvian	6.7
Venezuelan	16.7
Spaniard	10.4

Avondale

Population

Group	Number	%TP[1]	%HP[2]
Total Population	76,238	100.0	–
Hispanic or Latino (of any race)	38,340	50.3	100.0
Central American, ex. Mexican	854	1.1	2.2
Guatemalan	249	0.3	0.6
Salvadoran	371	0.5	1.0
Mexican	34,041	44.7	88.8
Puerto Rican	614	0.8	1.6
South American	330	0.4	0.9
Colombian	128	0.2	0.3
Spaniard	310	0.4	0.8

Population Growth: 2000–2010

Group	%
Total Population	112.5
Hispanic or Latino (of any race)	131.1
Central American, ex. Mexican	705.7
Mexican	143.4
Puerto Rican	250.9

Males per 100 Females

Group	Number
Total Population	98.6
Hispanic or Latino (of any race)	98.5
Central American, ex. Mexican	90.2

Notes: (1) Percent of total population; (2) Percent of Hispanic/Latino population; Profiles include places with an overall population of at least 125,000, OR an overall population of at least 25,000 where the Hispanic/Latino population is at least 20% of the overall population. In states where less than five places meet either of these criteria, we have included places with at least 10,000 total population with the highest percentage of Hispanic/Latino population. These places are identified with an asterisk (*); Please refer to the User's Guide for a full explanation of data.

Guatemalan	93.0
Salvadoran	87.4
Mexican	99.4
Puerto Rican	96.2
South American	100.0
Colombian	93.9
Spaniard	85.6

Average Household Size

Group	People
Total Population	3.25
Hispanic or Latino (of any race)	3.86
Central American, ex. Mexican	3.88
Guatemalan	4.04
Salvadoran	4.01
Mexican	3.90
Puerto Rican	3.22
South American	3.31
Colombian	3.35
Spaniard	3.14

Median Age

Group	Years
Total Population	28.6
Hispanic or Latino (of any race)	24.4
Central American, ex. Mexican	29.7
Guatemalan	31.8
Salvadoran	29.7
Mexican	24.1
Puerto Rican	26.6
South American	32.1
Colombian	28.8
Spaniard	31.5

High School Graduates
(Universe: Population 25 Years and Over)

Group	Number	%
Total Population	30,853	78.0
Hispanic or Latino (of any race)	10,302	61.1
Central American, ex. Mexican	423	61.3
Mexican	8,805	59.4

Four-Year College Graduates
(Universe: Population 25 Years and Over)

Group	Number	%
Total Population	7,952	20.1
Hispanic or Latino (of any race)	1,691	10.0
Central American, ex. Mexican	50	7.2
Mexican	1,440	9.7

Population Age 3–17 Enrolled in Public School
(Universe: Population Age 3–17 Enrolled in School)

Group	Number	%
Total Population	15,640	93.7
Hispanic or Latino (of any race)	8,907	95.2
Central American, ex. Mexican	230	100.0
Mexican	7,579	95.4

Population Age 3–17 Enrolled in Private School
(Universe: Population Age 3–17 Enrolled in School)

Group	Number	%
Total Population	1,043	6.3
Hispanic or Latino (of any race)	452	4.8
Central American, ex. Mexican	0	0.0
Mexican	366	4.6

Foreign-Born Population

Group	Number	%
Total Population	11,452	16.3
Hispanic or Latino (of any race)	8,896	25.8
Central American, ex. Mexican	642	60.1
Mexican	7,872	26.1

Foreign-Born Naturalized U.S. Citizens

Group	Number	%
Total Population	4,255	37.2
Hispanic or Latino (of any race)	2,999	33.7
Central American, ex. Mexican	153	23.8
Mexican	2,607	33.1

Language Spoken at Home: English Only
(Universe: Population 5 Years and Over)

Group	Number	%
Total Population	40,332	63.9
Hispanic or Latino (of any race)	10,255	34.1
Central American, ex. Mexican	231	23.4
Mexican	8,576	32.6

Language Spoken at Home: Spanish
(Universe: Population 5 Years and Over)

Group	Number	%
Total Population	20,554	32.6
Hispanic or Latino (of any race)	19,804	65.8
Central American, ex. Mexican	756	76.6
Mexican	17,731	67.3

Unemployment Rate
(Universe: Population 16 Years and Over)

Group	%
Total Population	8.5
Hispanic or Latino (of any race)	10.8
Central American, ex. Mexican	5.2
Mexican	11.5

Class of Worker: Private Wage and Salary
(Universe: Civilian Employed Population 16 Years and Over)

Group	Number	%
Total Population	26,270	81.1
Hispanic or Latino (of any race)	11,214	85.2
Central American, ex. Mexican	378	90.2
Mexican	9,962	85.4

Class of Worker: Government
(Universe: Civilian Employed Population 16 Years and Over)

Group	Number	%
Total Population	5,053	15.6
Hispanic or Latino (of any race)	1,408	10.7
Central American, ex. Mexican	11	2.6
Mexican	1,218	10.4

Means of Transportation to Work: Car, Truck or Van
(Universe: Workers 16 Years and Over)

Group	Number	%
Total Population	29,511	92.7
Hispanic or Latino (of any race)	11,986	92.3
Central American, ex. Mexican	389	92.8
Mexican	10,661	92.8

Means of Transportation to Work: Public Transportation (ex. Taxicab)
(Universe: Workers 16 Years and Over)

Group	Number	%
Total Population	319	1.0
Hispanic or Latino (of any race)	103	0.8
Central American, ex. Mexican	0	0.0
Mexican	90	0.8

Homeownership Rate
(Universe: Occupied Housing Units)

Group	%
Total Population	61.5
Hispanic or Latino (of any race)	59.5
Central American, ex. Mexican	58.2
Guatemalan	52.6
Salvadoran	62.5
Mexican	60.1
Puerto Rican	53.8
South American	65.0
Colombian	67.7
Spaniard	66.1

Median Home Value

Group	Dollars
Total Population	206,500
Hispanic or Latino (of any race)	167,800
Central American, ex. Mexican	208,200
Mexican	165,700

Median Gross Rent

Group	Dollars
Total Population	1,123
Hispanic or Latino (of any race)	1,088
Central American, ex. Mexican	1,046
Mexican	1,078

Median Household Income
(2010 Inflation-Adjusted Dollars)

Group	Dollars
Total Population	60,907
Hispanic or Latino (of any race)	47,363
Central American, ex. Mexican	48,454
Mexican	44,843

Per Capita Income
(2010 Inflation-Adjusted Dollars)

Group	Dollars
Total Population	21,331
Hispanic or Latino (of any race)	14,323
Central American, ex. Mexican	13,033
Mexican	14,395

Households with $100,000+ Income

Group	Number	%
Total Population	4,660	21.8
Hispanic or Latino (of any race)	1,061	12.3
Central American, ex. Mexican	15	5.3
Mexican	915	12.1

Households with Food Stamps/SNAP Benefits During Past 12 Months

Group	Number	%
Total Population	2,586	12.1
Hispanic or Latino (of any race)	1,550	18.0
Central American, ex. Mexican	27	9.5
Mexican	1,337	17.7

Poverty Rate
(Income in Past 12 Months Below Poverty Level)

Group	%
Total Population	14.6
Hispanic or Latino (of any race)	20.2
Central American, ex. Mexican	3.6
Mexican	21.8

Buckeye

Population

Group	Number	%TP[1]	%HP[2]
Total Population	50,876	100.0	–
Hispanic or Latino (of any race)	19,489	38.3	100.0
Central American, ex. Mexican	569	1.1	2.9
Guatemalan	132	0.3	0.7
Salvadoran	279	0.5	1.4
Mexican	17,133	33.7	87.9
Puerto Rican	452	0.9	2.3
South American	181	0.4	0.9
Spaniard	157	0.3	0.8

Population Growth: 2000–2010

Group	%
Total Population	678.3
Hispanic or Latino (of any race)	713.4
Mexican	785.4

Males per 100 Females

Group	Number
Total Population	120.1
Hispanic or Latino (of any race)	122.5
Central American, ex. Mexican	93.5
Guatemalan	97.0
Salvadoran	92.4
Mexican	125.4
Puerto Rican	100.9
South American	92.6
Spaniard	93.8

Average Household Size

Group	People
Total Population	3.17
Hispanic or Latino (of any race)	3.94
Central American, ex. Mexican	3.96
Guatemalan	3.98
Salvadoran	3.94
Mexican	4.00
Puerto Rican	3.49
South American	3.09
Spaniard	2.88

Median Age

Group	Years
Total Population	30.7
Hispanic or Latino (of any race)	25.5
Central American, ex. Mexican	33.3
Guatemalan	33.8
Salvadoran	33.6

Notes: (1) Percent of total population; (2) Percent of Hispanic/Latino population; Profiles include places with an overall population of at least 125,000, OR an overall population of at least 25,000 where the Hispanic/Latino population is at least 20% of the overall population. In states where less than five places meet either of these criteria, we have included places with at least 10,000 total population with the highest percentage of Hispanic/Latino population. These places are identified with an asterisk (*); Please refer to the User's Guide for a full explanation of data.

Mexican	25.3
Puerto Rican	23.5
South American	34.6
Spaniard	32.6

High School Graduates
(Universe: Population 25 Years and Over)

Group	Number	%
Total Population	20,983	84.5
Hispanic or Latino (of any race)	4,784	65.2
Mexican	4,037	64.1

Four-Year College Graduates
(Universe: Population 25 Years and Over)

Group	Number	%
Total Population	4,922	19.8
Hispanic or Latino (of any race)	555	7.6
Mexican	415	6.6

Population Age 3–17 Enrolled in Public School
(Universe: Population Age 3–17 Enrolled in School)

Group	Number	%
Total Population	8,797	93.3
Hispanic or Latino (of any race)	4,124	97.1
Mexican	3,809	97.1

Population Age 3–17 Enrolled in Private School
(Universe: Population Age 3–17 Enrolled in School)

Group	Number	%
Total Population	636	6.7
Hispanic or Latino (of any race)	125	2.9
Mexican	113	2.9

Foreign-Born Population

Group	Number	%
Total Population	4,924	11.2
Hispanic or Latino (of any race)	3,576	22.2
Mexican	3,079	21.3

Foreign-Born Naturalized U.S. Citizens

Group	Number	%
Total Population	2,244	45.6
Hispanic or Latino (of any race)	1,570	43.9
Mexican	1,272	41.3

Language Spoken at Home: English Only
(Universe: Population 5 Years and Over)

Group	Number	%
Total Population	28,059	72.9
Hispanic or Latino (of any race)	4,704	34.9
Mexican	4,046	33.7

Language Spoken at Home: Spanish
(Universe: Population 5 Years and Over)

Group	Number	%
Total Population	9,340	24.3
Hispanic or Latino (of any race)	8,772	65.1
Mexican	7,973	66.3

Unemployment Rate
(Universe: Population 16 Years and Over)

Group	%
Total Population	7.8
Hispanic or Latino (of any race)	9.0
Mexican	8.1

Class of Worker: Private Wage and Salary
(Universe: Civilian Employed Population 16 Years and Over)

Group	Number	%
Total Population	13,279	74.9
Hispanic or Latino (of any race)	4,630	84.4
Mexican	4,060	84.2

Class of Worker: Government
(Universe: Civilian Employed Population 16 Years and Over)

Group	Number	%
Total Population	3,400	19.2
Hispanic or Latino (of any race)	531	9.7
Mexican	460	9.5

Means of Transportation to Work: Car, Truck or Van
(Universe: Workers 16 Years and Over)

Group	Number	%
Total Population	16,362	92.9
Hispanic or Latino (of any race)	5,194	95.0
Mexican	4,555	94.8

Means of Transportation to Work: Public Transportation (ex. Taxicab)
(Universe: Workers 16 Years and Over)

Group	Number	%
Total Population	29	0.2
Hispanic or Latino (of any race)	13	0.2
Mexican	13	0.3

Homeownership Rate
(Universe: Occupied Housing Units)

Group	%
Total Population	75.6
Hispanic or Latino (of any race)	71.5
Central American, ex. Mexican	82.0
Guatemalan	83.3
Salvadoran	83.0
Mexican	71.0
Puerto Rican	74.8
South American	80.4
Spaniard	75.0

Median Home Value

Group	Dollars
Total Population	194,500
Hispanic or Latino (of any race)	173,900
Mexican	166,700

Median Gross Rent

Group	Dollars
Total Population	1,128
Hispanic or Latino (of any race)	1,006
Mexican	1,069

Median Household Income
(2010 Inflation-Adjusted Dollars)

Group	Dollars
Total Population	62,046
Hispanic or Latino (of any race)	58,365
Mexican	58,087

Per Capita Income
(2010 Inflation-Adjusted Dollars)

Group	Dollars
Total Population	22,305
Hispanic or Latino (of any race)	14,190
Mexican	13,320

Households with $100,000+ Income

Group	Number	%
Total Population	2,615	19.8
Hispanic or Latino (of any race)	428	11.5
Mexican	354	11.0

Households with Food Stamps/SNAP Benefits During Past 12 Months

Group	Number	%
Total Population	1,126	8.5
Hispanic or Latino (of any race)	431	11.6
Mexican	386	12.0

Poverty Rate
(Income in Past 12 Months Below Poverty Level)

Group	%
Total Population	12.4
Hispanic or Latino (of any race)	14.1
Mexican	14.2

Bullhead City

Population

Group	Number	%TP[1]	%HP[2]
Total Population	39,540	100.0	–
Hispanic or Latino (of any race)	9,386	23.7	100.0
Central American, ex. Mexican	192	0.5	2.0
Mexican	8,203	20.7	87.4
Puerto Rican	161	0.4	1.7
Spaniard	138	0.3	1.5

Population Growth: 2000–2010

Group	%
Total Population	17.1
Hispanic or Latino (of any race)	37.9
Mexican	47.6

Males per 100 Females

Group	Number
Total Population	97.7
Hispanic or Latino (of any race)	99.6
Central American, ex. Mexican	102.1
Mexican	99.7
Puerto Rican	111.8
Spaniard	66.3

Average Household Size

Group	People
Total Population	2.35
Hispanic or Latino (of any race)	3.24
Central American, ex. Mexican	3.24
Mexican	3.32
Puerto Rican	2.28
Spaniard	2.29

Median Age

Group	Years
Total Population	48.2
Hispanic or Latino (of any race)	27.6
Central American, ex. Mexican	37.5
Mexican	26.4
Puerto Rican	38.5
Spaniard	46.3

High School Graduates
(Universe: Population 25 Years and Over)

Group	Number	%
Total Population	23,213	79.9
Hispanic or Latino (of any race)	2,087	52.9
Mexican	1,725	50.1

Four-Year College Graduates
(Universe: Population 25 Years and Over)

Group	Number	%
Total Population	3,542	12.2
Hispanic or Latino (of any race)	190	4.8
Mexican	148	4.3

Population Age 3–17 Enrolled in Public School
(Universe: Population Age 3–17 Enrolled in School)

Group	Number	%
Total Population	5,505	96.2
Hispanic or Latino (of any race)	2,023	99.1
Mexican	1,915	99.1

Population Age 3–17 Enrolled in Private School
(Universe: Population Age 3–17 Enrolled in School)

Group	Number	%
Total Population	216	3.8
Hispanic or Latino (of any race)	18	0.9
Mexican	18	0.9

Foreign-Born Population

Group	Number	%
Total Population	4,204	10.5
Hispanic or Latino (of any race)	2,711	32.9
Mexican	2,464	32.5

Foreign-Born Naturalized U.S. Citizens

Group	Number	%
Total Population	1,769	42.1
Hispanic or Latino (of any race)	947	34.9
Mexican	790	32.1

Language Spoken at Home: English Only
(Universe: Population 5 Years and Over)

Group	Number	%
Total Population	31,477	83.3
Hispanic or Latino (of any race)	2,323	32.2
Mexican	2,030	31.1

Language Spoken at Home: Spanish
(Universe: Population 5 Years and Over)

Group	Number	%
Total Population	5,181	13.7
Hispanic or Latino (of any race)	4,841	67.2
Mexican	4,504	68.9

Notes: (1) Percent of total population; (2) Percent of Hispanic/Latino population; Profiles include places with an overall population of at least 125,000, OR an overall population of at least 25,000 where the Hispanic/Latino population is at least 20% of the overall population. In states where less than five places meet either of these criteria, we have included places with at least 10,000 total population with the highest percentage of Hispanic/Latino population. These places are identified with an asterisk (*); Please refer to the User's Guide for a full explanation of data.

Unemployment Rate
(Universe: Population 16 Years and Over)

Group		%
Total Population		13.6
Hispanic or Latino (of any race)		12.1
Mexican		12.7

Class of Worker: Private Wage and Salary
(Universe: Civilian Employed Population 16 Years and Over)

Group	Number	%
Total Population	12,487	82.1
Hispanic or Latino (of any race)	2,657	85.1
Mexican	2,454	86.6

Class of Worker: Government
(Universe: Civilian Employed Population 16 Years and Over)

Group	Number	%
Total Population	1,577	10.4
Hispanic or Latino (of any race)	298	9.5
Mexican	214	7.5

Means of Transportation to Work: Car, Truck or Van
(Universe: Workers 16 Years and Over)

Group	Number	%
Total Population	13,678	93.7
Hispanic or Latino (of any race)	2,946	96.0
Mexican	2,672	95.6

Means of Transportation to Work: Public Transportation (ex. Taxicab)
(Universe: Workers 16 Years and Over)

Group	Number	%
Total Population	147	1.0
Hispanic or Latino (of any race)	45	1.5
Mexican	45	1.6

Homeownership Rate
(Universe: Occupied Housing Units)

Group	%
Total Population	60.8
Hispanic or Latino (of any race)	51.8
Central American, ex. Mexican	55.6
Mexican	52.2
Puerto Rican	43.1
Spaniard	59.3

Median Home Value

Group	Dollars
Total Population	139,200
Hispanic or Latino (of any race)	113,400
Mexican	103,700

Median Gross Rent

Group	Dollars
Total Population	794
Hispanic or Latino (of any race)	722
Mexican	718

Median Household Income
(2010 Inflation-Adjusted Dollars)

Group	Dollars
Total Population	36,549
Hispanic or Latino (of any race)	30,713
Mexican	30,761

Per Capita Income
(2010 Inflation-Adjusted Dollars)

Group	Dollars
Total Population	20,768
Hispanic or Latino (of any race)	11,226
Mexican	10,833

Households with $100,000+ Income

Group	Number	%
Total Population	1,436	8.4
Hispanic or Latino (of any race)	141	5.8
Mexican	141	6.7

Households with Food Stamps/SNAP Benefits During Past 12 Months

Group	Number	%
Total Population	2,672	15.7
Hispanic or Latino (of any race)	671	27.8
Mexican	619	29.4

Poverty Rate
(Income in Past 12 Months Below Poverty Level)

Group	%
Total Population	20.7
Hispanic or Latino (of any race)	41.3
Mexican	42.9

Casa Grande

Population

Group	Number	%TP[1]	%HP[2]
Total Population	48,571	100.0	–
Hispanic or Latino (of any race)	18,932	39.0	100.0
Central American, ex. Mexican	225	0.5	1.2
Salvadoran	117	0.2	0.6
Mexican	16,939	34.9	89.5
Puerto Rican	280	0.6	1.5
South American	156	0.3	0.8
Spaniard	172	0.4	0.9

Population Growth: 2000–2010

Group	%
Total Population	92.6
Hispanic or Latino (of any race)	91.8
Mexican	106.2

Males per 100 Females

Group	Number
Total Population	94.0
Hispanic or Latino (of any race)	96.7
Central American, ex. Mexican	80.0
Salvadoran	88.7
Mexican	97.4
Puerto Rican	127.6
South American	64.2
Spaniard	91.1

Average Household Size

Group	People
Total Population	2.74
Hispanic or Latino (of any race)	3.56
Central American, ex. Mexican	3.82
Salvadoran	4.24
Mexican	3.58
Puerto Rican	2.99
South American	3.50
Spaniard	3.09

Median Age

Group	Years
Total Population	36.0
Hispanic or Latino (of any race)	23.7
Central American, ex. Mexican	32.5
Salvadoran	30.3
Mexican	23.4
Puerto Rican	27.5
South American	31.5
Spaniard	29.5

High School Graduates
(Universe: Population 25 Years and Over)

Group	Number	%
Total Population	22,137	83.4
Hispanic or Latino (of any race)	4,935	67.3
Mexican	4,325	65.6

Four-Year College Graduates
(Universe: Population 25 Years and Over)

Group	Number	%
Total Population	5,217	19.7
Hispanic or Latino (of any race)	599	8.2
Mexican	413	6.3

Population Age 3–17 Enrolled in Public School
(Universe: Population Age 3–17 Enrolled in School)

Group	Number	%
Total Population	8,517	95.2
Hispanic or Latino (of any race)	5,307	97.9
Mexican	5,046	98.1

Population Age 3–17 Enrolled in Private School
(Universe: Population Age 3–17 Enrolled in School)

Group	Number	%
Total Population	433	4.8
Hispanic or Latino (of any race)	113	2.1
Mexican	100	1.9

Foreign-Born Population

Group	Number	%
Total Population	4,878	11.3
Hispanic or Latino (of any race)	3,349	20.3
Mexican	3,092	20.3

Foreign-Born Naturalized U.S. Citizens

Group	Number	%
Total Population	1,403	28.8
Hispanic or Latino (of any race)	748	22.3
Mexican	635	20.5

Language Spoken at Home: English Only
(Universe: Population 5 Years and Over)

Group	Number	%
Total Population	28,995	73.5
Hispanic or Latino (of any race)	6,288	42.8
Mexican	5,630	41.6

Language Spoken at Home: Spanish
(Universe: Population 5 Years and Over)

Group	Number	%
Total Population	9,115	23.1
Hispanic or Latino (of any race)	8,391	57.1
Mexican	7,907	58.4

Unemployment Rate
(Universe: Population 16 Years and Over)

Group	%
Total Population	9.2
Hispanic or Latino (of any race)	11.4
Mexican	11.5

Class of Worker: Private Wage and Salary
(Universe: Civilian Employed Population 16 Years and Over)

Group	Number	%
Total Population	13,547	74.8
Hispanic or Latino (of any race)	5,336	78.8
Mexican	4,911	78.9

Class of Worker: Government
(Universe: Civilian Employed Population 16 Years and Over)

Group	Number	%
Total Population	3,812	21.1
Hispanic or Latino (of any race)	1,316	19.4
Mexican	1,199	19.3

Means of Transportation to Work: Car, Truck or Van
(Universe: Workers 16 Years and Over)

Group	Number	%
Total Population	15,575	90.8
Hispanic or Latino (of any race)	5,850	93.2
Mexican	5,393	93.6

Means of Transportation to Work: Public Transportation (ex. Taxicab)
(Universe: Workers 16 Years and Over)

Group	Number	%
Total Population	13	0.1
Hispanic or Latino (of any race)	0	0.0
Mexican	0	0.0

Homeownership Rate
(Universe: Occupied Housing Units)

Group	%
Total Population	67.5
Hispanic or Latino (of any race)	56.7
Central American, ex. Mexican	57.3
Salvadoran	56.1
Mexican	56.8
Puerto Rican	60.4
South American	68.4
Spaniard	66.2

Median Home Value

Group	Dollars
Total Population	153,400
Hispanic or Latino (of any race)	157,500
Mexican	155,300

STATE & PLACE PROFILES

Notes: (1) Percent of total population; (2) Percent of Hispanic/Latino population; Profiles include places with an overall population of at least 125,000, OR an overall population of at least 25,000 where the Hispanic/Latino population is at least 20% of the overall population. In states where less than five places meet either of these criteria, we have included places with at least 10,000 total population with the highest percentage of Hispanic/Latino population. These places are identified with an asterisk (*); Please refer to the User's Guide for a full explanation of data.

Median Gross Rent

Group	Dollars
Total Population	801
Hispanic or Latino (of any race)	813
Mexican	818

Median Household Income
(2010 Inflation-Adjusted Dollars)

Group	Dollars
Total Population	45,009
Hispanic or Latino (of any race)	39,470
Mexican	38,755

Per Capita Income
(2010 Inflation-Adjusted Dollars)

Group	Dollars
Total Population	21,071
Hispanic or Latino (of any race)	13,175
Mexican	12,304

Households with $100,000+ Income

Group	Number	%
Total Population	2,067	12.5
Hispanic or Latino (of any race)	341	7.8
Mexican	273	6.8

Households with Food Stamps/SNAP Benefits During Past 12 Months

Group	Number	%
Total Population	2,124	12.9
Hispanic or Latino (of any race)	769	17.5
Mexican	735	18.4

Poverty Rate
(Income in Past 12 Months Below Poverty Level)

Group	%
Total Population	17.5
Hispanic or Latino (of any race)	22.6
Mexican	23.7

Casas Adobes

Population

Group	Number	%TP[1]	%HP[2]
Total Population	66,795	100.0	–
Hispanic or Latino (of any race)	13,956	20.9	100.0
Central American, ex. Mexican	197	0.3	1.4
Cuban	104	0.2	0.7
Mexican	11,965	17.9	85.7
Puerto Rican	312	0.5	2.2
South American	286	0.4	2.0
Spaniard	237	0.4	1.7

Population Growth: 2000–2010

Group	%
Total Population	23.7
Hispanic or Latino (of any race)	87.7
Mexican	113.7
Puerto Rican	36.2
South American	132.5

Males per 100 Females

Group	Number
Total Population	90.7
Hispanic or Latino (of any race)	91.9
Central American, ex. Mexican	95.0
Cuban	92.6
Mexican	92.8
Puerto Rican	106.6
South American	84.5
Spaniard	83.7

Average Household Size

Group	People
Total Population	2.34
Hispanic or Latino (of any race)	2.90
Central American, ex. Mexican	2.94
Cuban	2.28
Mexican	2.96
Puerto Rican	2.56
South American	2.31
Spaniard	2.50

Median Age

Group	Years
Total Population	41.6
Hispanic or Latino (of any race)	28.0
Central American, ex. Mexican	27.3
Cuban	28.5
Mexican	27.7
Puerto Rican	26.2
South American	36.4
Spaniard	38.2

High School Graduates
(Universe: Population 25 Years and Over)

Group	Number	%
Total Population	44,381	94.8
Hispanic or Latino (of any race)	6,625	92.5
Mexican	5,548	93.2

Four-Year College Graduates
(Universe: Population 25 Years and Over)

Group	Number	%
Total Population	16,630	35.5
Hispanic or Latino (of any race)	1,435	20.0
Mexican	1,207	20.3

Population Age 3–17 Enrolled in Public School
(Universe: Population Age 3–17 Enrolled in School)

Group	Number	%
Total Population	9,409	85.0
Hispanic or Latino (of any race)	3,276	85.6
Mexican	2,908	84.7

Population Age 3–17 Enrolled in Private School
(Universe: Population Age 3–17 Enrolled in School)

Group	Number	%
Total Population	1,662	15.0
Hispanic or Latino (of any race)	551	14.4
Mexican	524	15.3

Foreign-Born Population

Group	Number	%
Total Population	4,885	7.2
Hispanic or Latino (of any race)	1,832	13.1
Mexican	1,414	11.6

Foreign-Born Naturalized U.S. Citizens

Group	Number	%
Total Population	2,701	55.3
Hispanic or Latino (of any race)	970	52.9
Mexican	796	56.3

Language Spoken at Home: English Only
(Universe: Population 5 Years and Over)

Group	Number	%
Total Population	53,813	85.0
Hispanic or Latino (of any race)	7,010	55.6
Mexican	5,986	55.0

Language Spoken at Home: Spanish
(Universe: Population 5 Years and Over)

Group	Number	%
Total Population	6,865	10.8
Hispanic or Latino (of any race)	5,597	44.4
Mexican	4,907	45.0

Unemployment Rate
(Universe: Population 16 Years and Over)

Group	%
Total Population	6.4
Hispanic or Latino (of any race)	7.0
Mexican	7.0

Class of Worker: Private Wage and Salary
(Universe: Civilian Employed Population 16 Years and Over)

Group	Number	%
Total Population	25,341	76.2
Hispanic or Latino (of any race)	4,889	75.5
Mexican	4,158	76.9

Class of Worker: Government
(Universe: Civilian Employed Population 16 Years and Over)

Group	Number	%
Total Population	5,911	17.8
Hispanic or Latino (of any race)	1,251	19.3
Mexican	1,011	18.7

Means of Transportation to Work: Car, Truck or Van
(Universe: Workers 16 Years and Over)

Group	Number	%
Total Population	29,735	90.8
Hispanic or Latino (of any race)	5,888	92.4
Mexican	4,950	93.1

Means of Transportation to Work: Public Transportation (ex. Taxicab)
(Universe: Workers 16 Years and Over)

Group	Number	%
Total Population	529	1.6
Hispanic or Latino (of any race)	73	1.1
Mexican	73	1.4

Homeownership Rate
(Universe: Occupied Housing Units)

Group	%
Total Population	66.4
Hispanic or Latino (of any race)	58.5
Central American, ex. Mexican	43.8
Cuban	53.1
Mexican	59.5
Puerto Rican	39.3
South American	63.5
Spaniard	70.9

Median Home Value

Group	Dollars
Total Population	224,600
Hispanic or Latino (of any race)	221,400
Mexican	217,800

Median Gross Rent

Group	Dollars
Total Population	918
Hispanic or Latino (of any race)	922
Mexican	936

Median Household Income
(2010 Inflation-Adjusted Dollars)

Group	Dollars
Total Population	57,156
Hispanic or Latino (of any race)	54,732
Mexican	54,881

Per Capita Income
(2010 Inflation-Adjusted Dollars)

Group	Dollars
Total Population	29,578
Hispanic or Latino (of any race)	18,924
Mexican	18,444

Households with $100,000+ Income

Group	Number	%
Total Population	6,080	22.1
Hispanic or Latino (of any race)	676	18.7
Mexican	581	18.9

Households with Food Stamps/SNAP Benefits During Past 12 Months

Group	Number	%
Total Population	1,419	5.2
Hispanic or Latino (of any race)	381	10.5
Mexican	340	11.1

Poverty Rate
(Income in Past 12 Months Below Poverty Level)

Group	%
Total Population	9.0
Hispanic or Latino (of any race)	10.8
Mexican	11.2

Chandler

Population

Group	Number	%TP[1]	%HP[2]
Total Population	236,123	100.0	–
Hispanic or Latino (of any race)	51,808	21.9	100.0
Central American, ex. Mexican	1,418	0.6	2.7
Costa Rican	129	0.1	0.2
Guatemalan	479	0.2	0.9
Honduran	153	0.1	0.3

Notes: (1) Percent of total population; (2) Percent of Hispanic/Latino population; Profiles include places with an overall population of at least 125,000, OR an overall population of at least 25,000 where the Hispanic/Latino population is at least 20% of the overall population. In states where less than five places meet either of these criteria, we have included places with at least 10,000 total population with the highest percentage of Hispanic/Latino population. These places are identified with an asterisk (*); Please refer to the User's Guide for a full explanation of data.

Nicaraguan	132	0.1	0.3
Salvadoran	428	0.2	0.8
Cuban	371	0.2	0.7
Dominican Republic	221	0.1	0.4
Mexican	42,911	18.2	82.8
Puerto Rican	1,543	0.7	3.0
South American	1,265	0.5	2.4
Argentinean	130	0.1	0.3
Chilean	110	<0.1	0.2
Colombian	434	0.2	0.8
Ecuadorian	112	<0.1	0.2
Peruvian	281	0.1	0.5
Venezuelan	103	<0.1	0.2
Spaniard	1,115	0.5	2.2

Population Growth: 2000–2010

Group	%
Total Population	33.7
Hispanic or Latino (of any race)	39.8
Central American, ex. Mexican	191.2
Guatemalan	247.1
Salvadoran	219.4
Cuban	112.0
Mexican	46.3
Puerto Rican	119.8
South American	211.6
Colombian	226.3

Males per 100 Females

Group	Number
Total Population	96.5
Hispanic or Latino (of any race)	99.3
Central American, ex. Mexican	96.9
Costa Rican	76.7
Guatemalan	117.7
Honduran	68.1
Nicaraguan	91.3
Salvadoran	99.1
Cuban	87.4
Dominican Republic	92.2
Mexican	100.6
Puerto Rican	93.4
South American	87.1
Argentinean	103.1
Chilean	83.3
Colombian	76.4
Ecuadorian	64.7
Peruvian	93.8
Venezuelan	123.9
Spaniard	92.2

Average Household Size

Group	People
Total Population	2.71
Hispanic or Latino (of any race)	3.42
Central American, ex. Mexican	3.46
Costa Rican	3.00
Guatemalan	4.01
Honduran	3.04
Nicaraguan	3.09
Salvadoran	3.49
Cuban	2.80
Dominican Republic	2.78
Mexican	3.53
Puerto Rican	2.79
South American	2.89
Argentinean	2.65
Chilean	2.59
Colombian	2.66
Ecuadorian	3.30
Peruvian	3.25
Venezuelan	3.36
Spaniard	2.75

Median Age

Group	Years
Total Population	34.1
Hispanic or Latino (of any race)	25.6
Central American, ex. Mexican	31.5
Costa Rican	29.5
Guatemalan	28.0
Honduran	30.2
Nicaraguan	35.0
Salvadoran	33.5
Cuban	32.9
Dominican Republic	26.9
Mexican	24.9
Puerto Rican	27.5
South American	34.0
Argentinean	36.7
Chilean	35.5
Colombian	35.4
Ecuadorian	32.3
Peruvian	33.5
Venezuelan	31.3
Spaniard	29.9

High School Graduates
(Universe: Population 25 Years and Over)

Group	Number	%
Total Population	133,523	92.2
Hispanic or Latino (of any race)	17,683	72.3
Central American, ex. Mexican	457	64.0
Mexican	13,875	69.5
Puerto Rican	884	84.4
South American	669	100.0

Four-Year College Graduates
(Universe: Population 25 Years and Over)

Group	Number	%
Total Population	57,090	39.4
Hispanic or Latino (of any race)	5,192	21.2
Central American, ex. Mexican	229	32.1
Mexican	3,646	18.3
Puerto Rican	404	38.6
South American	323	48.3

Population Age 3–17 Enrolled in Public School
(Universe: Population Age 3–17 Enrolled in School)

Group	Number	%
Total Population	41,620	88.7
Hispanic or Latino (of any race)	12,512	94.3
Central American, ex. Mexican	311	96.3
Mexican	10,344	94.3
Puerto Rican	578	89.5
South American	294	98.0

Population Age 3–17 Enrolled in Private School
(Universe: Population Age 3–17 Enrolled in School)

Group	Number	%
Total Population	5,296	11.3
Hispanic or Latino (of any race)	750	5.7
Central American, ex. Mexican	12	3.7
Mexican	629	5.7
Puerto Rican	68	10.5
South American	6	2.0

Foreign-Born Population

Group	Number	%
Total Population	31,512	13.7
Hispanic or Latino (of any race)	12,512	24.8
Central American, ex. Mexican	709	53.9
Mexican	10,570	25.2
Puerto Rican	0	0.0
South American	677	56.9

Foreign-Born Naturalized U.S. Citizens

Group	Number	%
Total Population	14,160	44.9
Hispanic or Latino (of any race)	3,229	25.8
Central American, ex. Mexican	225	31.7
Mexican	2,360	22.3
Puerto Rican	0	0.0
South American	283	41.8

Language Spoken at Home: English Only
(Universe: Population 5 Years and Over)

Group	Number	%
Total Population	164,057	78.1
Hispanic or Latino (of any race)	18,593	42.7
Central American, ex. Mexican	174	14.5
Mexican	14,800	41.1
Puerto Rican	965	52.4
South American	306	28.5

Language Spoken at Home: Spanish
(Universe: Population 5 Years and Over)

Group	Number	%
Total Population	27,092	12.9
Hispanic or Latino (of any race)	24,835	57.0
Central American, ex. Mexican	1,030	85.5
Mexican	21,150	58.7
Puerto Rican	876	47.6
South American	762	70.9

Unemployment Rate
(Universe: Population 16 Years and Over)

Group	%
Total Population	6.4
Hispanic or Latino (of any race)	7.8
Central American, ex. Mexican	1.6
Mexican	8.6
Puerto Rican	3.3
South American	7.4

Class of Worker: Private Wage and Salary
(Universe: Civilian Employed Population 16 Years and Over)

Group	Number	%
Total Population	99,455	82.4
Hispanic or Latino (of any race)	18,840	84.2
Central American, ex. Mexican	677	93.8
Mexican	15,257	83.9
Puerto Rican	589	69.1
South American	517	81.2

Class of Worker: Government
(Universe: Civilian Employed Population 16 Years and Over)

Group	Number	%
Total Population	15,341	12.7
Hispanic or Latino (of any race)	2,649	11.8
Central American, ex. Mexican	4	0.6
Mexican	2,276	12.5
Puerto Rican	179	21.0
South American	41	6.4

Means of Transportation to Work: Car, Truck or Van
(Universe: Workers 16 Years and Over)

Group	Number	%
Total Population	105,913	90.0
Hispanic or Latino (of any race)	19,781	91.2
Central American, ex. Mexican	667	93.5
Mexican	15,991	90.8
Puerto Rican	759	89.0
South American	588	100.0

Means of Transportation to Work: Public Transportation (ex. Taxicab)
(Universe: Workers 16 Years and Over)

Group	Number	%
Total Population	1,633	1.4
Hispanic or Latino (of any race)	300	1.4
Central American, ex. Mexican	36	5.0
Mexican	255	1.4
Puerto Rican	9	1.1
South American	0	0.0

Homeownership Rate
(Universe: Occupied Housing Units)

Group	%
Total Population	66.3
Hispanic or Latino (of any race)	53.1
Central American, ex. Mexican	54.1
Costa Rican	65.7
Guatemalan	48.8
Honduran	32.6
Nicaraguan	57.4
Salvadoran	55.0
Cuban	63.4
Dominican Republic	50.0
Mexican	52.5
Puerto Rican	50.2
South American	66.6
Argentinean	63.0
Chilean	64.1
Colombian	73.4
Ecuadorian	66.7
Peruvian	63.5
Venezuelan	63.6
Spaniard	64.0

Median Home Value

Group	Dollars
Total Population	278,300
Hispanic or Latino (of any race)	244,200
Central American, ex. Mexican	313,300

Notes: (1) Percent of total population; (2) Percent of Hispanic/Latino population; Profiles include places with an overall population of at least 125,000, OR an overall population of at least 25,000 where the Hispanic/Latino population is at least 20% of the overall population. In states where less than five places meet either of these criteria, we have included places with at least 10,000 total population with the highest percentage of Hispanic/Latino population. These places are identified with an asterisk (*); Please refer to the User's Guide for a full explanation of data.

Group	
Mexican	232,300
Puerto Rican	351,000
South American	234,400

Median Gross Rent

Group	Dollars
Total Population	1,034
Hispanic or Latino (of any race)	936
Central American, ex. Mexican	1,058
Mexican	921
Puerto Rican	909
South American	1,027

Median Household Income
(2010 Inflation-Adjusted Dollars)

Group	Dollars
Total Population	70,775
Hispanic or Latino (of any race)	54,831
Central American, ex. Mexican	51,500
Mexican	54,743
Puerto Rican	48,456
South American	56,250

Per Capita Income
(2010 Inflation-Adjusted Dollars)

Group	Dollars
Total Population	32,559
Hispanic or Latino (of any race)	19,607
Central American, ex. Mexican	16,463
Mexican	18,634
Puerto Rican	21,916
South American	23,538

Households with $100,000+ Income

Group	Number	%
Total Population	26,623	31.3
Hispanic or Latino (of any race)	2,637	20.4
Central American, ex. Mexican	118	27.7
Mexican	1,936	18.8
Puerto Rican	110	19.3
South American	124	34.6

Households with Food Stamps/SNAP Benefits During Past 12 Months

Group	Number	%
Total Population	4,036	4.8
Hispanic or Latino (of any race)	1,309	10.1
Central American, ex. Mexican	56	13.1
Mexican	1,138	11.1
Puerto Rican	71	12.5
South American	8	2.2

Poverty Rate
(Income in Past 12 Months Below Poverty Level)

Group	%
Total Population	7.3
Hispanic or Latino (of any race)	14.1
Central American, ex. Mexican	25.7
Mexican	14.5
Puerto Rican	13.9
South American	2.8

Drexel Heights

Population

Group	Number	%TP[1]	%HP[2]
Total Population	27,749	100.0	–
Hispanic or Latino (of any race)	19,586	70.6	100.0
Central American, ex. Mexican	108	0.4	0.6
Mexican	17,992	64.8	91.9
Puerto Rican	142	0.5	0.7
Spaniard	118	0.4	0.6

Population Growth: 2000–2010

Group	%
Total Population	16.4
Hispanic or Latino (of any race)	36.7
Mexican	46.2

Males per 100 Females

Group	Number
Total Population	96.1
Hispanic or Latino (of any race)	94.6
Central American, ex. Mexican	92.9

Group	
Mexican	95.0
Puerto Rican	94.5
Spaniard	76.1

Average Household Size

Group	People
Total Population	3.14
Hispanic or Latino (of any race)	3.56
Central American, ex. Mexican	3.60
Mexican	3.56
Puerto Rican	3.70
Spaniard	3.15

Median Age

Group	Years
Total Population	33.0
Hispanic or Latino (of any race)	28.1
Central American, ex. Mexican	40.3
Mexican	28.2
Puerto Rican	27.5
Spaniard	33.0

High School Graduates
(Universe: Population 25 Years and Over)

Group	Number	%
Total Population	12,635	76.2
Hispanic or Latino (of any race)	6,861	68.5
Mexican	6,426	67.6

Four-Year College Graduates
(Universe: Population 25 Years and Over)

Group	Number	%
Total Population	1,756	10.6
Hispanic or Latino (of any race)	810	8.1
Mexican	694	7.3

Population Age 3–17 Enrolled in Public School
(Universe: Population Age 3–17 Enrolled in School)

Group	Number	%
Total Population	6,355	95.0
Hispanic or Latino (of any race)	5,144	96.1
Mexican	4,962	96.0

Population Age 3–17 Enrolled in Private School
(Universe: Population Age 3–17 Enrolled in School)

Group	Number	%
Total Population	335	5.0
Hispanic or Latino (of any race)	207	3.9
Mexican	207	4.0

Foreign-Born Population

Group	Number	%
Total Population	4,624	16.0
Hispanic or Latino (of any race)	4,330	22.0
Mexican	4,275	22.8

Foreign-Born Naturalized U.S. Citizens

Group	Number	%
Total Population	1,882	40.7
Hispanic or Latino (of any race)	1,738	40.1
Mexican	1,695	39.6

Language Spoken at Home: English Only
(Universe: Population 5 Years and Over)

Group	Number	%
Total Population	13,011	49.6
Hispanic or Latino (of any race)	4,986	28.4
Mexican	4,573	27.3

Language Spoken at Home: Spanish
(Universe: Population 5 Years and Over)

Group	Number	%
Total Population	12,900	49.2
Hispanic or Latino (of any race)	12,547	71.4
Mexican	12,128	72.5

Unemployment Rate
(Universe: Population 16 Years and Over)

Group	%
Total Population	12.5
Hispanic or Latino (of any race)	12.7
Mexican	13.0

Class of Worker: Private Wage and Salary
(Universe: Civilian Employed Population 16 Years and Over)

Group	Number	%
Total Population	8,549	70.8
Hispanic or Latino (of any race)	5,691	70.4
Mexican	5,370	70.2

Class of Worker: Government
(Universe: Civilian Employed Population 16 Years and Over)

Group	Number	%
Total Population	2,373	19.6
Hispanic or Latino (of any race)	1,525	18.9
Mexican	1,421	18.6

Means of Transportation to Work: Car, Truck or Van
(Universe: Workers 16 Years and Over)

Group	Number	%
Total Population	10,835	91.3
Hispanic or Latino (of any race)	7,276	91.0
Mexican	6,885	91.1

Means of Transportation to Work: Public Transportation (ex. Taxicab)
(Universe: Workers 16 Years and Over)

Group	Number	%
Total Population	203	1.7
Hispanic or Latino (of any race)	138	1.7
Mexican	130	1.7

Homeownership Rate
(Universe: Occupied Housing Units)

Group	%
Total Population	78.7
Hispanic or Latino (of any race)	77.0
Central American, ex. Mexican	77.5
Mexican	77.2
Puerto Rican	75.0
Spaniard	90.0

Median Home Value

Group	Dollars
Total Population	148,400
Hispanic or Latino (of any race)	146,800
Mexican	146,300

Median Gross Rent

Group	Dollars
Total Population	858
Hispanic or Latino (of any race)	899
Mexican	943

Median Household Income
(2010 Inflation-Adjusted Dollars)

Group	Dollars
Total Population	48,587
Hispanic or Latino (of any race)	49,010
Mexican	49,155

Per Capita Income
(2010 Inflation-Adjusted Dollars)

Group	Dollars
Total Population	17,090
Hispanic or Latino (of any race)	14,607
Mexican	14,374

Households with $100,000+ Income

Group	Number	%
Total Population	1,043	12.1
Hispanic or Latino (of any race)	613	12.2
Mexican	588	12.4

Households with Food Stamps/SNAP Benefits During Past 12 Months

Group	Number	%
Total Population	1,275	14.8
Hispanic or Latino (of any race)	768	15.3
Mexican	736	15.5

Poverty Rate
(Income in Past 12 Months Below Poverty Level)

Group	%
Total Population	18.1
Hispanic or Latino (of any race)	16.4
Mexican	16.6

Notes: (1) Percent of total population; (2) Percent of Hispanic/Latino population; Profiles include places with an overall population of at least 125,000, OR an overall population of at least 25,000 where the Hispanic/Latino population is at least 20% of the overall population. In states where less than five places meet either of these criteria, we have included places with at least 10,000 total population with the highest percentage of Hispanic/Latino population. These places are identified with an asterisk (*); Please refer to the User's Guide for a full explanation of data.

El Mirage

Population

Group	Number	%TP[1]	%HP[2]
Total Population	31,797	100.0	–
Hispanic or Latino (of any race)	15,120	47.6	100.0
Central American, ex. Mexican	305	1.0	2.0
Guatemalan	115	0.4	0.8
Salvadoran	113	0.4	0.7
Mexican	13,305	41.8	88.0
Puerto Rican	364	1.1	2.4
Spaniard	112	0.4	0.7

Population Growth: 2000–2010

Group	%
Total Population	317.9
Hispanic or Latino (of any race)	197.4
Mexican	199.1

Males per 100 Females

Group	Number
Total Population	98.3
Hispanic or Latino (of any race)	99.0
Central American, ex. Mexican	111.8
Guatemalan	150.0
Salvadoran	101.8
Mexican	99.0
Puerto Rican	104.5
Spaniard	119.6

Average Household Size

Group	People
Total Population	3.38
Hispanic or Latino (of any race)	4.13
Central American, ex. Mexican	4.12
Guatemalan	5.21
Salvadoran	3.82
Mexican	4.20
Puerto Rican	3.40
Spaniard	3.22

Median Age

Group	Years
Total Population	28.1
Hispanic or Latino (of any race)	23.3
Central American, ex. Mexican	31.3
Guatemalan	32.3
Salvadoran	28.9
Mexican	23.2
Puerto Rican	21.0
Spaniard	30.0

High School Graduates
(Universe: Population 25 Years and Over)

Group	Number	%
Total Population	11,062	75.3
Hispanic or Latino (of any race)	3,082	50.5
Mexican	2,613	48.0

Four-Year College Graduates
(Universe: Population 25 Years and Over)

Group	Number	%
Total Population	1,686	11.5
Hispanic or Latino (of any race)	282	4.6
Mexican	197	3.6

Population Age 3–17 Enrolled in Public School
(Universe: Population Age 3–17 Enrolled in School)

Group	Number	%
Total Population	6,162	95.1
Hispanic or Latino (of any race)	3,596	98.4
Mexican	3,371	98.3

Population Age 3–17 Enrolled in Private School
(Universe: Population Age 3–17 Enrolled in School)

Group	Number	%
Total Population	320	4.9
Hispanic or Latino (of any race)	58	1.6
Mexican	58	1.7

Foreign-Born Population

Group	Number	%
Total Population	5,214	18.7
Hispanic or Latino (of any race)	4,113	31.1
Mexican	3,784	31.8

Foreign-Born Naturalized U.S. Citizens

Group	Number	%
Total Population	1,295	24.8
Hispanic or Latino (of any race)	957	23.3
Mexican	862	22.8

Language Spoken at Home: English Only
(Universe: Population 5 Years and Over)

Group	Number	%
Total Population	16,690	69.0
Hispanic or Latino (of any race)	4,873	42.8
Mexican	4,344	42.1

Language Spoken at Home: Spanish
(Universe: Population 5 Years and Over)

Group	Number	%
Total Population	6,575	27.2
Hispanic or Latino (of any race)	6,491	57.0
Mexican	5,976	57.9

Unemployment Rate
(Universe: Population 16 Years and Over)

Group	%
Total Population	6.7
Hispanic or Latino (of any race)	7.6
Mexican	8.0

Class of Worker: Private Wage and Salary
(Universe: Civilian Employed Population 16 Years and Over)

Group	Number	%
Total Population	9,409	81.9
Hispanic or Latino (of any race)	3,822	82.1
Mexican	3,413	81.5

Class of Worker: Government
(Universe: Civilian Employed Population 16 Years and Over)

Group	Number	%
Total Population	1,419	12.4
Hispanic or Latino (of any race)	473	10.2
Mexican	424	10.1

Means of Transportation to Work: Car, Truck or Van
(Universe: Workers 16 Years and Over)

Group	Number	%
Total Population	10,751	94.3
Hispanic or Latino (of any race)	4,279	93.3
Mexican	3,812	92.5

Means of Transportation to Work: Public Transportation (ex. Taxicab)
(Universe: Workers 16 Years and Over)

Group	Number	%
Total Population	79	0.7
Hispanic or Latino (of any race)	65	1.4
Mexican	65	1.6

Homeownership Rate
(Universe: Occupied Housing Units)

Group	%
Total Population	71.3
Hispanic or Latino (of any race)	66.6
Central American, ex. Mexican	80.7
Guatemalan	75.0
Salvadoran	84.8
Mexican	66.1
Puerto Rican	67.0
Spaniard	75.6

Median Home Value

Group	Dollars
Total Population	171,400
Hispanic or Latino (of any race)	159,100
Mexican	152,000

Median Gross Rent

Group	Dollars
Total Population	1,114
Hispanic or Latino (of any race)	1,055
Mexican	1,045

Median Household Income
(2010 Inflation-Adjusted Dollars)

Group	Dollars
Total Population	48,726
Hispanic or Latino (of any race)	38,714
Mexican	37,865

Per Capita Income
(2010 Inflation-Adjusted Dollars)

Group	Dollars
Total Population	15,973
Hispanic or Latino (of any race)	10,866
Mexican	10,311

Households with $100,000+ Income

Group	Number	%
Total Population	831	10.4
Hispanic or Latino (of any race)	212	7.1
Mexican	143	5.4

Households with Food Stamps/SNAP Benefits During Past 12 Months

Group	Number	%
Total Population	967	12.1
Hispanic or Latino (of any race)	596	20.1
Mexican	567	21.5

Poverty Rate
(Income in Past 12 Months Below Poverty Level)

Group	%
Total Population	20.2
Hispanic or Latino (of any race)	29.0
Mexican	31.5

Florence

Population

Group	Number	%TP[1]	%HP[2]
Total Population	25,536	100.0	–
Hispanic or Latino (of any race)	7,978	31.2	100.0
Central American, ex. Mexican	122	0.5	1.5
Mexican	6,998	27.4	87.7
Puerto Rican	190	0.7	2.4

Population Growth: 2000–2010

Group	%
Total Population	49.7
Hispanic or Latino (of any race)	32.1
Central American, ex. Mexican	-48.3
Mexican	57.3

Males per 100 Females

Group	Number
Total Population	457.2
Hispanic or Latino (of any race)	603.5
Central American, ex. Mexican	771.4
Mexican	609.0
Puerto Rican	804.8

Average Household Size

Group	People
Total Population	2.35
Hispanic or Latino (of any race)	2.83
Central American, ex. Mexican	3.00
Mexican	2.82
Puerto Rican	2.73

Median Age

Group	Years
Total Population	36.2
Hispanic or Latino (of any race)	32.4
Central American, ex. Mexican	35.0
Mexican	32.2
Puerto Rican	33.1

High School Graduates
(Universe: Population 25 Years and Over)

Group	Number	%
Total Population	12,817	67.0
Hispanic or Latino (of any race)	3,639	48.4
Mexican	3,244	48.0

Four-Year College Graduates
(Universe: Population 25 Years and Over)

Group	Number	%
Total Population	945	4.9
Hispanic or Latino (of any race)	104	1.4
Mexican	80	1.2

Notes: (1) Percent of total population; (2) Percent of Hispanic/Latino population; Profiles include places with an overall population of at least 125,000, OR an overall population of at least 25,000 where the Hispanic/Latino population is at least 20% of the overall population. In states where less than five places meet either of these criteria, we have included places with at least 10,000 total population with the highest percentage of Hispanic/Latino population. These places are identified with an asterisk (*); Please refer to the User's Guide for a full explanation of data.

Population Age 3–17 Enrolled in Public School
(Universe: Population Age 3–17 Enrolled in School)

Group	Number	%
Total Population	754	93.5
Hispanic or Latino (of any race)	425	95.5
Mexican	419	95.4

Population Age 3–17 Enrolled in Private School
(Universe: Population Age 3–17 Enrolled in School)

Group	Number	%
Total Population	52	6.5
Hispanic or Latino (of any race)	20	4.5
Mexican	20	4.6

Foreign-Born Population

Group	Number	%
Total Population	5,003	21.2
Hispanic or Latino (of any race)	4,523	44.1
Mexican	4,074	43.8

Foreign-Born Naturalized U.S. Citizens

Group	Number	%
Total Population	576	11.5
Hispanic or Latino (of any race)	380	8.4
Mexican	354	8.7

Language Spoken at Home: English Only
(Universe: Population 5 Years and Over)

Group	Number	%
Total Population	13,915	59.8
Hispanic or Latino (of any race)	2,472	24.6
Mexican	2,274	25.0

Language Spoken at Home: Spanish
(Universe: Population 5 Years and Over)

Group	Number	%
Total Population	8,258	35.5
Hispanic or Latino (of any race)	7,548	75.0
Mexican	6,825	74.9

Unemployment Rate
(Universe: Population 16 Years and Over)

Group	%
Total Population	8.1
Hispanic or Latino (of any race)	6.8
Mexican	7.2

Class of Worker: Private Wage and Salary
(Universe: Civilian Employed Population 16 Years and Over)

Group	Number	%
Total Population	876	54.7
Hispanic or Latino (of any race)	253	45.0
Mexican	229	43.5

Class of Worker: Government
(Universe: Civilian Employed Population 16 Years and Over)

Group	Number	%
Total Population	686	42.8
Hispanic or Latino (of any race)	302	53.7
Mexican	290	55.1

Means of Transportation to Work: Car, Truck or Van
(Universe: Workers 16 Years and Over)

Group	Number	%
Total Population	1,350	85.1
Hispanic or Latino (of any race)	464	83.5
Mexican	434	82.5

Means of Transportation to Work: Public Transportation (ex. Taxicab)
(Universe: Workers 16 Years and Over)

Group	Number	%
Total Population	0	0.0
Hispanic or Latino (of any race)	0	0.0
Mexican	0	0.0

Homeownership Rate
(Universe: Occupied Housing Units)

Group	%
Total Population	75.9
Hispanic or Latino (of any race)	60.3
Central American, ex. Mexican	83.3
Mexican	59.5
Puerto Rican	63.6

Median Home Value

Group	Dollars
Total Population	118,200
Hispanic or Latino (of any race)	131,400
Mexican	137,800

Median Gross Rent

Group	Dollars
Total Population	648
Hispanic or Latino (of any race)	642
Mexican	650

Median Household Income
(2010 Inflation-Adjusted Dollars)

Group	Dollars
Total Population	41,642
Hispanic or Latino (of any race)	47,575
Mexican	47,766

Per Capita Income
(2010 Inflation-Adjusted Dollars)

Group	Dollars
Total Population	8,577
Hispanic or Latino (of any race)	6,840
Mexican	6,716

Households with $100,000+ Income

Group	Number	%
Total Population	179	7.4
Hispanic or Latino (of any race)	42	7.9
Mexican	33	7.0

Households with Food Stamps/SNAP Benefits During Past 12 Months

Group	Number	%
Total Population	105	4.3
Hispanic or Latino (of any race)	31	5.8
Mexican	31	6.6

Poverty Rate
(Income in Past 12 Months Below Poverty Level)

Group	%
Total Population	12.6
Hispanic or Latino (of any race)	22.6
Mexican	24.0

Fortuna Foothills

Population

Group	Number	%TP[1]	%HP[2]
Total Population	26,265	100.0	–
Hispanic or Latino (of any race)	5,270	20.1	100.0
Mexican	4,694	17.9	89.1
Puerto Rican	111	0.4	2.1

Population Growth: 2000–2010

Group	%
Total Population	28.3
Hispanic or Latino (of any race)	102.0
Mexican	113.2

Males per 100 Females

Group	Number
Total Population	95.8
Hispanic or Latino (of any race)	93.0
Mexican	92.9
Puerto Rican	117.6

Average Household Size

Group	People
Total Population	2.19
Hispanic or Latino (of any race)	3.39
Mexican	3.46
Puerto Rican	2.97

Median Age

Group	Years
Total Population	59.4
Hispanic or Latino (of any race)	27.4
Mexican	26.9
Puerto Rican	27.8

High School Graduates
(Universe: Population 25 Years and Over)

Group	Number	%
Total Population	18,371	84.5
Hispanic or Latino (of any race)	1,997	70.1
Mexican	1,775	71.2

Four-Year College Graduates
(Universe: Population 25 Years and Over)

Group	Number	%
Total Population	3,493	16.1
Hispanic or Latino (of any race)	312	11.0
Mexican	302	12.1

Population Age 3–17 Enrolled in Public School
(Universe: Population Age 3–17 Enrolled in School)

Group	Number	%
Total Population	2,736	90.4
Hispanic or Latino (of any race)	1,688	94.8
Mexican	1,484	95.1

Population Age 3–17 Enrolled in Private School
(Universe: Population Age 3–17 Enrolled in School)

Group	Number	%
Total Population	289	9.6
Hispanic or Latino (of any race)	92	5.2
Mexican	76	4.9

Foreign-Born Population

Group	Number	%
Total Population	3,568	13.0
Hispanic or Latino (of any race)	1,640	28.5
Mexican	1,474	29.1

Foreign-Born Naturalized U.S. Citizens

Group	Number	%
Total Population	1,148	32.2
Hispanic or Latino (of any race)	712	43.4
Mexican	642	43.6

Language Spoken at Home: English Only
(Universe: Population 5 Years and Over)

Group	Number	%
Total Population	21,741	84.6
Hispanic or Latino (of any race)	1,591	32.6
Mexican	1,340	30.7

Language Spoken at Home: Spanish
(Universe: Population 5 Years and Over)

Group	Number	%
Total Population	3,528	13.7
Hispanic or Latino (of any race)	3,284	67.2
Mexican	3,030	69.3

Unemployment Rate
(Universe: Population 16 Years and Over)

Group	%
Total Population	5.4
Hispanic or Latino (of any race)	5.0
Mexican	5.6

Class of Worker: Private Wage and Salary
(Universe: Civilian Employed Population 16 Years and Over)

Group	Number	%
Total Population	5,913	72.6
Hispanic or Latino (of any race)	1,636	73.5
Mexican	1,414	71.9

Class of Worker: Government
(Universe: Civilian Employed Population 16 Years and Over)

Group	Number	%
Total Population	1,745	21.4
Hispanic or Latino (of any race)	437	19.6
Mexican	437	22.2

Means of Transportation to Work: Car, Truck or Van
(Universe: Workers 16 Years and Over)

Group	Number	%
Total Population	7,493	91.7
Hispanic or Latino (of any race)	2,011	91.7
Mexican	1,782	92.6

Notes: (1) Percent of total population; (2) Percent of Hispanic/Latino population; Profiles include places with an overall population of at least 125,000, OR an overall population of at least 25,000 where the Hispanic/Latino population is at least 20% of the overall population. In states where less than five places meet either of these criteria, we have included places with at least 10,000 total population with the highest percentage of Hispanic/Latino population. These places are identified with an asterisk (*); Please refer to the User's Guide for a full explanation of data.

Means of Transportation to Work: Public Transportation (ex. Taxicab)
(Universe: Workers 16 Years and Over)

Group	Number	%
Total Population	43	0.5
Hispanic or Latino (of any race)	0	0.0
Mexican	0	0.0

Homeownership Rate
(Universe: Occupied Housing Units)

Group	%
Total Population	83.6
Hispanic or Latino (of any race)	73.7
Mexican	74.8
Puerto Rican	60.0

Median Home Value

Group	Dollars
Total Population	139,200
Hispanic or Latino (of any race)	212,200
Mexican	206,700

Median Gross Rent

Group	Dollars
Total Population	993
Hispanic or Latino (of any race)	1,007
Mexican	873

Median Household Income
(2010 Inflation-Adjusted Dollars)

Group	Dollars
Total Population	47,879
Hispanic or Latino (of any race)	49,932
Mexican	48,459

Per Capita Income
(2010 Inflation-Adjusted Dollars)

Group	Dollars
Total Population	24,851
Hispanic or Latino (of any race)	16,133
Mexican	15,608

Households with $100,000+ Income

Group	Number	%
Total Population	1,315	10.5
Hispanic or Latino (of any race)	243	15.6
Mexican	174	13.1

Households with Food Stamps/SNAP Benefits During Past 12 Months

Group	Number	%
Total Population	617	4.9
Hispanic or Latino (of any race)	296	19.0
Mexican	296	22.3

Poverty Rate
(Income in Past 12 Months Below Poverty Level)

Group	%
Total Population	11.7
Hispanic or Latino (of any race)	24.2
Mexican	26.1

Gilbert

Population

Group	Number	%TP[1]	%HP[2]
Total Population	208,453	100.0	–
Hispanic or Latino (of any race)	31,074	14.9	100.0
Central American, ex. Mexican	1,006	0.5	3.2
Guatemalan	266	0.1	0.9
Honduran	130	0.1	0.4
Nicaraguan	124	0.1	0.4
Salvadoran	307	0.1	1.0
Cuban	353	0.2	1.1
Dominican Republic	190	0.1	0.6
Mexican	23,846	11.4	76.7
Puerto Rican	1,357	0.7	4.4
South American	1,276	0.6	4.1
Argentinean	180	0.1	0.6
Colombian	396	0.2	1.3
Ecuadorian	113	0.1	0.4
Peruvian	305	0.1	1.0
Venezuelan	115	0.1	0.4
Spaniard	925	0.4	3.0

Population Growth: 2000–2010

Group	%
Total Population	90.0
Hispanic or Latino (of any race)	138.6
Central American, ex. Mexican	408.1
Cuban	212.4
Mexican	161.3
Puerto Rican	146.3
South American	377.9

Males per 100 Females

Group	Number
Total Population	97.0
Hispanic or Latino (of any race)	92.7
Central American, ex. Mexican	82.2
Guatemalan	95.6
Honduran	113.1
Nicaraguan	65.3
Salvadoran	83.8
Cuban	99.4
Dominican Republic	118.4
Mexican	93.9
Puerto Rican	92.2
South American	79.0
Argentinean	109.3
Colombian	64.3
Ecuadorian	82.3
Peruvian	84.8
Venezuelan	82.5
Spaniard	88.4

Average Household Size

Group	People
Total Population	3.00
Hispanic or Latino (of any race)	3.36
Central American, ex. Mexican	3.53
Guatemalan	3.78
Honduran	3.30
Nicaraguan	3.62
Salvadoran	3.57
Cuban	2.99
Dominican Republic	3.44
Mexican	3.41
Puerto Rican	3.15
South American	3.11
Argentinean	3.31
Colombian	3.01
Ecuadorian	2.67
Peruvian	3.38
Venezuelan	3.13
Spaniard	3.05

Median Age

Group	Years
Total Population	31.9
Hispanic or Latino (of any race)	25.0
Central American, ex. Mexican	30.3
Guatemalan	27.0
Honduran	31.2
Nicaraguan	33.0
Salvadoran	30.2
Cuban	30.4
Dominican Republic	29.6
Mexican	24.2
Puerto Rican	24.8
South American	34.5
Argentinean	35.5
Colombian	34.8
Ecuadorian	31.4
Peruvian	35.3
Venezuelan	31.5
Spaniard	29.0

High School Graduates
(Universe: Population 25 Years and Over)

Group	Number	%
Total Population	110,292	95.4
Hispanic or Latino (of any race)	11,323	85.1
Mexican	8,254	82.9
Puerto Rican	534	94.5
South American	762	88.9

Four-Year College Graduates
(Universe: Population 25 Years and Over)

Group	Number	%
Total Population	44,850	38.8
Hispanic or Latino (of any race)	3,299	24.8
Mexican	2,176	21.9
Puerto Rican	252	44.6
South American	291	34.0

Population Age 3–17 Enrolled in Public School
(Universe: Population Age 3–17 Enrolled in School)

Group	Number	%
Total Population	42,756	88.3
Hispanic or Latino (of any race)	6,341	91.9
Mexican	4,921	93.7
Puerto Rican	237	95.2
South American	285	84.3

Population Age 3–17 Enrolled in Private School
(Universe: Population Age 3–17 Enrolled in School)

Group	Number	%
Total Population	5,642	11.7
Hispanic or Latino (of any race)	559	8.1
Mexican	329	6.3
Puerto Rican	12	4.8
South American	53	15.7

Foreign-Born Population

Group	Number	%
Total Population	17,164	8.8
Hispanic or Latino (of any race)	4,853	18.8
Mexican	3,438	17.4
Puerto Rican	40	4.4
South American	717	46.9

Foreign-Born Naturalized U.S. Citizens

Group	Number	%
Total Population	8,960	52.2
Hispanic or Latino (of any race)	2,444	50.4
Mexican	1,418	41.2
Puerto Rican	40	100.0
South American	511	71.3

Language Spoken at Home: English Only
(Universe: Population 5 Years and Over)

Group	Number	%
Total Population	150,393	84.9
Hispanic or Latino (of any race)	11,158	49.2
Mexican	8,618	49.2
Puerto Rican	522	58.9
South American	375	28.9

Language Spoken at Home: Spanish
(Universe: Population 5 Years and Over)

Group	Number	%
Total Population	13,773	7.8
Hispanic or Latino (of any race)	11,475	50.6
Mexican	8,902	50.8
Puerto Rican	365	41.1
South American	924	71.1

Unemployment Rate
(Universe: Population 16 Years and Over)

Group	%
Total Population	5.8
Hispanic or Latino (of any race)	5.6
Mexican	5.7
Puerto Rican	0.0
South American	4.6

Class of Worker: Private Wage and Salary
(Universe: Civilian Employed Population 16 Years and Over)

Group	Number	%
Total Population	81,067	82.2
Hispanic or Latino (of any race)	9,890	79.7
Mexican	7,820	80.5
Puerto Rican	396	71.4
South American	488	69.8

Class of Worker: Government
(Universe: Civilian Employed Population 16 Years and Over)

Group	Number	%
Total Population	12,380	12.5
Hispanic or Latino (of any race)	1,872	15.1
Mexican	1,380	14.2

Notes: (1) Percent of total population; (2) Percent of Hispanic/Latino population; Profiles include places with an overall population of at least 125,000, OR an overall population of at least 25,000 where the Hispanic/Latino population is at least 20% of the overall population. In states where less than five places meet either of these criteria, we have included places with at least 10,000 total population with the highest percentage of Hispanic/Latino population. These places are identified with an asterisk (*); Please refer to the User's Guide for a full explanation of data.

Group	Number	%
Puerto Rican	159	28.6
South American	143	20.5

Means of Transportation to Work: Car, Truck or Van
(Universe: Workers 16 Years and Over)

Group	Number	%
Total Population	87,669	91.6
Hispanic or Latino (of any race)	11,346	93.7
Mexican	8,934	94.2
Puerto Rican	555	100.0
South American	640	91.6

Means of Transportation to Work: Public Transportation (ex. Taxicab)
(Universe: Workers 16 Years and Over)

Group	Number	%
Total Population	605	0.6
Hispanic or Latino (of any race)	85	0.7
Mexican	52	0.5
Puerto Rican	0	0.0
South American	18	2.6

Homeownership Rate
(Universe: Occupied Housing Units)

Group	%
Total Population	75.3
Hispanic or Latino (of any race)	66.7
Central American, ex. Mexican	64.8
Guatemalan	71.6
Honduran	63.6
Nicaraguan	64.9
Salvadoran	59.3
Cuban	73.7
Dominican Republic	56.5
Mexican	66.8
Puerto Rican	63.5
South American	75.0
Argentinean	76.3
Colombian	79.8
Ecuadorian	66.7
Peruvian	73.8
Venezuelan	74.4
Spaniard	68.5

Median Home Value

Group	Dollars
Total Population	298,400
Hispanic or Latino (of any race)	283,800
Mexican	275,500
Puerto Rican	282,500
South American	323,500

Median Gross Rent

Group	Dollars
Total Population	1,231
Hispanic or Latino (of any race)	1,126
Mexican	1,124
Puerto Rican	1,281
South American	1,269

Median Household Income
(2010 Inflation-Adjusted Dollars)

Group	Dollars
Total Population	79,989
Hispanic or Latino (of any race)	67,997
Mexican	65,133
Puerto Rican	79,900
South American	67,857

Per Capita Income
(2010 Inflation-Adjusted Dollars)

Group	Dollars
Total Population	31,476
Hispanic or Latino (of any race)	22,503
Mexican	22,429
Puerto Rican	31,553
South American	21,340

Households with $100,000+ Income

Group	Number	%
Total Population	23,581	36.7
Hispanic or Latino (of any race)	1,720	24.3
Mexican	1,290	23.9
Puerto Rican	87	28.1
South American	83	17.1

Households with Food Stamps/SNAP Benefits During Past 12 Months

Group	Number	%
Total Population	2,261	3.5
Hispanic or Latino (of any race)	567	8.0
Mexican	446	8.3
Puerto Rican	0	0.0
South American	18	3.7

Poverty Rate
(Income in Past 12 Months Below Poverty Level)

Group	%
Total Population	5.5
Hispanic or Latino (of any race)	7.9
Mexican	8.8
Puerto Rican	0.0
South American	0.0

Glendale

Population

Group	Number	%TP[1]	%HP[2]
Total Population	226,721	100.0	–
Hispanic or Latino (of any race)	80,501	35.5	100.0
Central American, ex. Mexican	1,843	0.8	2.3
Guatemalan	662	0.3	0.8
Honduran	232	0.1	0.3
Nicaraguan	125	0.1	0.2
Salvadoran	663	0.3	0.8
Cuban	765	0.3	1.0
Mexican	69,929	30.8	86.9
Puerto Rican	1,346	0.6	1.7
South American	778	0.3	1.0
Argentinean	113	<0.1	0.1
Colombian	243	0.1	0.3
Ecuadorian	111	<0.1	0.1
Peruvian	165	0.1	0.2
Spaniard	798	0.4	1.0

Population Growth: 2000–2010

Group	%
Total Population	3.6
Hispanic or Latino (of any race)	48.1
Central American, ex. Mexican	191.2
Guatemalan	221.4
Salvadoran	274.6
Cuban	278.7
Mexican	63.1
Puerto Rican	27.6
South American	80.1
Colombian	68.8
Spaniard	425.0

Males per 100 Females

Group	Number
Total Population	96.6
Hispanic or Latino (of any race)	98.5
Central American, ex. Mexican	97.3
Guatemalan	106.9
Honduran	82.7
Nicaraguan	104.9
Salvadoran	99.7
Cuban	110.7
Mexican	98.9
Puerto Rican	105.2
South American	88.4
Argentinean	126.0
Colombian	86.9
Ecuadorian	68.2
Peruvian	71.9
Spaniard	86.0

Average Household Size

Group	People
Total Population	2.82
Hispanic or Latino (of any race)	3.69
Central American, ex. Mexican	3.80
Guatemalan	4.08
Honduran	3.68
Nicaraguan	3.57
Salvadoran	3.87
Cuban	3.11
Mexican	3.77
Puerto Rican	2.72
South American	2.84
Argentinean	2.74
Colombian	2.62
Ecuadorian	3.08
Peruvian	3.22
Spaniard	2.96

Median Age

Group	Years
Total Population	32.5
Hispanic or Latino (of any race)	23.8
Central American, ex. Mexican	30.7
Guatemalan	31.0
Honduran	29.0
Nicaraguan	32.3
Salvadoran	31.1
Cuban	35.7
Mexican	23.3
Puerto Rican	25.9
South American	34.4
Argentinean	39.3
Colombian	35.5
Ecuadorian	29.8
Peruvian	35.5
Spaniard	31.4

High School Graduates
(Universe: Population 25 Years and Over)

Group	Number	%
Total Population	114,001	82.7
Hispanic or Latino (of any race)	23,377	61.0
Central American, ex. Mexican	638	64.8
Mexican	19,895	59.1
Puerto Rican	560	81.4
South American	577	82.9
Spaniard	493	84.1

Four-Year College Graduates
(Universe: Population 25 Years and Over)

Group	Number	%
Total Population	28,953	21.0
Hispanic or Latino (of any race)	3,462	9.0
Central American, ex. Mexican	98	10.0
Mexican	2,732	8.1
Puerto Rican	190	27.6
South American	186	26.7
Spaniard	44	7.5

Population Age 3–17 Enrolled in Public School
(Universe: Population Age 3–17 Enrolled in School)

Group	Number	%
Total Population	42,987	92.3
Hispanic or Latino (of any race)	19,398	95.4
Central American, ex. Mexican	208	100.0
Mexican	17,728	95.7
Puerto Rican	216	83.4
South American	231	100.0
Spaniard	68	100.0

Population Age 3–17 Enrolled in Private School
(Universe: Population Age 3–17 Enrolled in School)

Group	Number	%
Total Population	3,606	7.7
Hispanic or Latino (of any race)	931	4.6
Central American, ex. Mexican	0	0.0
Mexican	793	4.3
Puerto Rican	43	16.6
South American	0	0.0
Spaniard	0	0.0

Foreign-Born Population

Group	Number	%
Total Population	37,709	16.4
Hispanic or Latino (of any race)	25,633	32.3
Central American, ex. Mexican	975	63.9
Mexican	23,355	33.0
Puerto Rican	99	7.0
South American	659	54.1
Spaniard	99	9.1

Foreign-Born Naturalized U.S. Citizens

Group	Number	%
Total Population	11,776	31.2
Hispanic or Latino (of any race)	5,073	19.8

Notes: (1) Percent of total population; (2) Percent of Hispanic/Latino population; Profiles include places with an overall population of at least 125,000, OR an overall population of at least 25,000 where the Hispanic/Latino population is at least 20% of the overall population. In states where less than five places meet either of these criteria, we have included places with at least 10,000 total population with the highest percentage of Hispanic/Latino population. These places are identified with an asterisk (*); Please refer to the User's Guide for a full explanation of data.

Group	Number	%
Central American, ex. Mexican	307	31.5
Mexican	4,181	17.9
Puerto Rican	12	12.1
South American	369	56.0
Spaniard	60	60.6

Language Spoken at Home: English Only
(Universe: Population 5 Years and Over)

Group	Number	%
Total Population	146,786	69.7
Hispanic or Latino (of any race)	21,043	30.4
Central American, ex. Mexican	132	9.4
Mexican	17,558	28.4
Puerto Rican	569	48.1
South American	172	17.6
Spaniard	759	78.7

Language Spoken at Home: Spanish
(Universe: Population 5 Years and Over)

Group	Number	%
Total Population	49,743	23.6
Hispanic or Latino (of any race)	48,118	69.4
Central American, ex. Mexican	1,259	89.6
Mexican	44,119	71.5
Puerto Rican	588	49.7
South American	792	80.9
Spaniard	169	17.5

Unemployment Rate
(Universe: Population 16 Years and Over)

Group	%
Total Population	9.4
Hispanic or Latino (of any race)	12.1
Central American, ex. Mexican	5.1
Mexican	11.8
Puerto Rican	6.9
South American	0.0
Spaniard	40.1

Class of Worker: Private Wage and Salary
(Universe: Civilian Employed Population 16 Years and Over)

Group	Number	%
Total Population	84,701	80.8
Hispanic or Latino (of any race)	25,891	83.3
Central American, ex. Mexican	833	87.7
Mexican	23,027	83.7
Puerto Rican	504	81.7
South American	353	82.1
Spaniard	296	74.9

Class of Worker: Government
(Universe: Civilian Employed Population 16 Years and Over)

Group	Number	%
Total Population	14,194	13.5
Hispanic or Latino (of any race)	3,467	11.2
Central American, ex. Mexican	91	9.6
Mexican	2,901	10.5
Puerto Rican	113	18.3
South American	20	4.7
Spaniard	63	15.9

Means of Transportation to Work: Car, Truck or Van
(Universe: Workers 16 Years and Over)

Group	Number	%
Total Population	92,853	89.9
Hispanic or Latino (of any race)	28,321	92.4
Central American, ex. Mexican	750	82.9
Mexican	25,151	92.6
Puerto Rican	572	95.3
South American	412	95.8
Spaniard	383	97.0

Means of Transportation to Work: Public Transportation (ex. Taxicab)
(Universe: Workers 16 Years and Over)

Group	Number	%
Total Population	2,660	2.6
Hispanic or Latino (of any race)	693	2.3
Central American, ex. Mexican	44	4.9
Mexican	614	2.3
Puerto Rican	10	1.7
South American	0	0.0
Spaniard	0	0.0

Homeownership Rate
(Universe: Occupied Housing Units)

Group	%
Total Population	58.6
Hispanic or Latino (of any race)	48.0
Central American, ex. Mexican	52.1
Guatemalan	55.2
Honduran	46.2
Nicaraguan	52.3
Salvadoran	53.4
Cuban	51.5
Mexican	48.4
Puerto Rican	38.7
South American	50.9
Argentinean	50.0
Colombian	47.8
Ecuadorian	51.4
Peruvian	55.9
Spaniard	62.9

Median Home Value

Group	Dollars
Total Population	207,400
Hispanic or Latino (of any race)	168,400
Central American, ex. Mexican	196,300
Mexican	168,200
Puerto Rican	263,900
South American	130,800
Spaniard	120,000

Median Gross Rent

Group	Dollars
Total Population	832
Hispanic or Latino (of any race)	777
Central American, ex. Mexican	826
Mexican	768
Puerto Rican	949
South American	1,617
Spaniard	757

Median Household Income
(2010 Inflation-Adjusted Dollars)

Group	Dollars
Total Population	51,103
Hispanic or Latino (of any race)	39,822
Central American, ex. Mexican	60,226
Mexican	38,646
Puerto Rican	56,176
South American	33,065
Spaniard	73,542

Per Capita Income
(2010 Inflation-Adjusted Dollars)

Group	Dollars
Total Population	23,373
Hispanic or Latino (of any race)	14,186
Central American, ex. Mexican	22,563
Mexican	13,617
Puerto Rican	30,467
South American	13,326
Spaniard	18,041

Households with $100,000+ Income

Group	Number	%
Total Population	14,875	18.5
Hispanic or Latino (of any race)	2,245	10.7
Central American, ex. Mexican	43	8.6
Mexican	1,789	9.8
Puerto Rican	120	26.4
South American	25	7.9
Spaniard	128	37.8

Households with Food Stamps/SNAP Benefits During Past 12 Months

Group	Number	%
Total Population	10,627	13.2
Hispanic or Latino (of any race)	4,560	21.8
Central American, ex. Mexican	116	23.2
Mexican	4,046	22.1
Puerto Rican	114	25.1
South American	76	23.9
Spaniard	17	5.0

Poverty Rate
(Income in Past 12 Months Below Poverty Level)

Group	%
Total Population	16.6
Hispanic or Latino (of any race)	26.4
Central American, ex. Mexican	4.8
Mexican	27.7
Puerto Rican	4.4
South American	43.4
Spaniard	5.8

Goodyear

Population

Group	Number	%TP[1]	%HP[2]
Total Population	65,275	100.0	–
Hispanic or Latino (of any race)	18,136	27.8	100.0
Central American, ex. Mexican	484	0.7	2.7
Guatemalan	143	0.2	0.8
Salvadoran	191	0.3	1.1
Cuban	102	0.2	0.6
Mexican	15,412	23.6	85.0
Puerto Rican	491	0.8	2.7
South American	273	0.4	1.5
Spaniard	231	0.4	1.3

Population Growth: 2000–2010

Group	%
Total Population	245.2
Hispanic or Latino (of any race)	361.1
Mexican	388.5

Males per 100 Females

Group	Number
Total Population	88.4
Hispanic or Latino (of any race)	85.1
Central American, ex. Mexican	100.0
Guatemalan	93.2
Salvadoran	109.9
Cuban	117.0
Mexican	82.8
Puerto Rican	118.2
South American	90.9
Spaniard	87.8

Average Household Size

Group	People
Total Population	2.86
Hispanic or Latino (of any race)	3.68
Central American, ex. Mexican	3.75
Guatemalan	3.92
Salvadoran	3.97
Cuban	2.70
Mexican	3.76
Puerto Rican	3.15
South American	3.15
Spaniard	2.76

Median Age

Group	Years
Total Population	34.9
Hispanic or Latino (of any race)	25.7
Central American, ex. Mexican	30.3
Guatemalan	30.5
Salvadoran	30.1
Cuban	35.0
Mexican	25.2
Puerto Rican	29.8
South American	34.1
Spaniard	36.8

High School Graduates
(Universe: Population 25 Years and Over)

Group	Number	%
Total Population	32,853	90.0
Hispanic or Latino (of any race)	6,384	75.6
Mexican	5,438	73.7

Four-Year College Graduates
(Universe: Population 25 Years and Over)

Group	Number	%
Total Population	10,484	28.7
Hispanic or Latino (of any race)	1,370	16.2
Mexican	1,106	15.0

STATE & PLACE PROFILES

Notes: (1) Percent of total population; (2) Percent of Hispanic/Latino population; Profiles include places with an overall population of at least 125,000, OR an overall population of at least 25,000 where the Hispanic/Latino population is at least 20% of the overall population. In states where less than five places meet either of these criteria, we have included places with at least 10,000 total population with the highest percentage of Hispanic/Latino population. These places are identified with an asterisk (*); Please refer to the User's Guide for a full explanation of data.

Population Age 3–17 Enrolled in Public School
(Universe: Population Age 3–17 Enrolled in School)

Group	Number	%
Total Population	11,335	93.6
Hispanic or Latino (of any race)	4,663	95.3
Mexican	4,179	95.4

Population Age 3–17 Enrolled in Private School
(Universe: Population Age 3–17 Enrolled in School)

Group	Number	%
Total Population	778	6.4
Hispanic or Latino (of any race)	230	4.7
Mexican	202	4.6

Foreign-Born Population

Group	Number	%
Total Population	6,740	11.6
Hispanic or Latino (of any race)	3,644	21.9
Mexican	2,948	20.0

Foreign-Born Naturalized U.S. Citizens

Group	Number	%
Total Population	3,412	50.6
Hispanic or Latino (of any race)	1,536	42.2
Mexican	1,297	44.0

Language Spoken at Home: English Only
(Universe: Population 5 Years and Over)

Group	Number	%
Total Population	40,911	77.1
Hispanic or Latino (of any race)	5,800	39.0
Mexican	5,070	38.6

Language Spoken at Home: Spanish
(Universe: Population 5 Years and Over)

Group	Number	%
Total Population	9,749	18.4
Hispanic or Latino (of any race)	9,033	60.8
Mexican	8,022	61.1

Unemployment Rate
(Universe: Population 16 Years and Over)

Group	%
Total Population	6.8
Hispanic or Latino (of any race)	9.0
Mexican	8.0

Class of Worker: Private Wage and Salary
(Universe: Civilian Employed Population 16 Years and Over)

Group	Number	%
Total Population	19,693	76.0
Hispanic or Latino (of any race)	4,607	74.1
Mexican	4,051	73.7

Class of Worker: Government
(Universe: Civilian Employed Population 16 Years and Over)

Group	Number	%
Total Population	4,525	17.5
Hispanic or Latino (of any race)	965	15.5
Mexican	914	16.6

Means of Transportation to Work: Car, Truck or Van
(Universe: Workers 16 Years and Over)

Group	Number	%
Total Population	23,476	91.1
Hispanic or Latino (of any race)	5,735	92.8
Mexican	5,063	92.8

Means of Transportation to Work: Public Transportation (ex. Taxicab)
(Universe: Workers 16 Years and Over)

Group	Number	%
Total Population	107	0.4
Hispanic or Latino (of any race)	0	0.0
Mexican	0	0.0

Homeownership Rate
(Universe: Occupied Housing Units)

Group	%
Total Population	76.2
Hispanic or Latino (of any race)	69.7
Central American, ex. Mexican	71.7
Guatemalan	65.8
Salvadoran	77.8
Cuban	63.6
Mexican	69.8
Puerto Rican	66.2
South American	81.3
Spaniard	80.6

Median Home Value

Group	Dollars
Total Population	271,500
Hispanic or Latino (of any race)	218,900
Mexican	214,500

Median Gross Rent

Group	Dollars
Total Population	1,193
Hispanic or Latino (of any race)	1,161
Mexican	1,151

Median Household Income
(2010 Inflation-Adjusted Dollars)

Group	Dollars
Total Population	76,221
Hispanic or Latino (of any race)	65,166
Mexican	65,365

Per Capita Income
(2010 Inflation-Adjusted Dollars)

Group	Dollars
Total Population	28,141
Hispanic or Latino (of any race)	18,082
Mexican	17,774

Households with $100,000+ Income

Group	Number	%
Total Population	5,900	32.4
Hispanic or Latino (of any race)	879	23.9
Mexican	832	25.4

Households with Food Stamps/SNAP Benefits During Past 12 Months

Group	Number	%
Total Population	934	5.1
Hispanic or Latino (of any race)	485	13.2
Mexican	476	14.5

Poverty Rate
(Income in Past 12 Months Below Poverty Level)

Group	%
Total Population	7.5
Hispanic or Latino (of any race)	8.9
Mexican	9.9

Marana

Population

Group	Number	%TP[1]	%HP[2]
Total Population	34,961	100.0	–
Hispanic or Latino (of any race)	7,730	22.1	100.0
Central American, ex. Mexican	166	0.5	2.1
Mexican	6,478	18.5	83.8
Puerto Rican	251	0.7	3.2
South American	154	0.4	2.0
Spaniard	108	0.3	1.4

Population Growth: 2000–2010

Group	%
Total Population	157.9
Hispanic or Latino (of any race)	190.3
Mexican	208.6

Males per 100 Females

Group	Number
Total Population	99.6
Hispanic or Latino (of any race)	98.6
Central American, ex. Mexican	71.1
Mexican	100.8
Puerto Rican	99.2
South American	97.4
Spaniard	92.9

Average Household Size

Group	People
Total Population	2.63
Hispanic or Latino (of any race)	3.23
Central American, ex. Mexican	3.45
Mexican	3.29
Puerto Rican	2.86
South American	2.71
Spaniard	2.43

Median Age

Group	Years
Total Population	37.7
Hispanic or Latino (of any race)	26.9
Central American, ex. Mexican	34.8
Mexican	26.6
Puerto Rican	29.8
South American	36.7
Spaniard	35.0

High School Graduates
(Universe: Population 25 Years and Over)

Group	Number	%
Total Population	20,197	93.1
Hispanic or Latino (of any race)	3,445	86.4
Mexican	2,795	85.3

Four-Year College Graduates
(Universe: Population 25 Years and Over)

Group	Number	%
Total Population	7,931	36.6
Hispanic or Latino (of any race)	952	23.9
Mexican	762	23.3

Population Age 3–17 Enrolled in Public School
(Universe: Population Age 3–17 Enrolled in School)

Group	Number	%
Total Population	4,836	84.4
Hispanic or Latino (of any race)	2,214	88.3
Mexican	1,999	89.2

Population Age 3–17 Enrolled in Private School
(Universe: Population Age 3–17 Enrolled in School)

Group	Number	%
Total Population	893	15.6
Hispanic or Latino (of any race)	294	11.7
Mexican	243	10.8

Foreign-Born Population

Group	Number	%
Total Population	2,865	9.1
Hispanic or Latino (of any race)	1,367	17.9
Mexican	1,162	17.7

Foreign-Born Naturalized U.S. Citizens

Group	Number	%
Total Population	1,647	57.5
Hispanic or Latino (of any race)	692	50.6
Mexican	572	49.2

Language Spoken at Home: English Only
(Universe: Population 5 Years and Over)

Group	Number	%
Total Population	23,644	81.5
Hispanic or Latino (of any race)	3,360	49.0
Mexican	2,902	49.2

Language Spoken at Home: Spanish
(Universe: Population 5 Years and Over)

Group	Number	%
Total Population	3,901	13.4
Hispanic or Latino (of any race)	3,479	50.7
Mexican	3,002	50.8

Unemployment Rate
(Universe: Population 16 Years and Over)

Group	%
Total Population	7.0
Hispanic or Latino (of any race)	8.3
Mexican	8.6

Class of Worker: Private Wage and Salary
(Universe: Civilian Employed Population 16 Years and Over)

Group	Number	%
Total Population	10,646	76.2
Hispanic or Latino (of any race)	2,414	77.4
Mexican	1,986	76.8

Notes: (1) Percent of total population; (2) Percent of Hispanic/Latino population; Profiles include places with an overall population of at least 125,000, OR an overall population of at least 25,000 where the Hispanic/Latino population is at least 20% of the overall population. In states where less than five places meet either of these criteria, we have included places with at least 10,000 total population with the highest percentage of Hispanic/Latino population. These places are identified with an asterisk (*); Please refer to the User's Guide for a full explanation of data.

Class of Worker: Government
(Universe: Civilian Employed Population 16 Years and Over)

Group	Number	%
Total Population	2,493	17.8
Hispanic or Latino (of any race)	510	16.4
Mexican	406	15.7

Means of Transportation to Work: Car, Truck or Van
(Universe: Workers 16 Years and Over)

Group	Number	%
Total Population	12,456	90.5
Hispanic or Latino (of any race)	2,768	89.4
Mexican	2,236	87.2

Means of Transportation to Work: Public Transportation (ex. Taxicab)
(Universe: Workers 16 Years and Over)

Group	Number	%
Total Population	57	0.4
Hispanic or Latino (of any race)	0	0.0
Mexican	0	0.0

Homeownership Rate
(Universe: Occupied Housing Units)

Group	%
Total Population	80.8
Hispanic or Latino (of any race)	71.9
Central American, ex. Mexican	71.1
Mexican	72.1
Puerto Rican	76.4
South American	81.3
Spaniard	83.3

Median Home Value

Group	Dollars
Total Population	259,600
Hispanic or Latino (of any race)	279,800
Mexican	284,200

Median Gross Rent

Group	Dollars
Total Population	1,143
Hispanic or Latino (of any race)	1,076
Mexican	1,034

Median Household Income
(2010 Inflation-Adjusted Dollars)

Group	Dollars
Total Population	67,542
Hispanic or Latino (of any race)	66,498
Mexican	65,347

Per Capita Income
(2010 Inflation-Adjusted Dollars)

Group	Dollars
Total Population	30,802
Hispanic or Latino (of any race)	19,885
Mexican	18,443

Households with $100,000+ Income

Group	Number	%
Total Population	3,199	27.8
Hispanic or Latino (of any race)	540	29.3
Mexican	383	25.2

Households with Food Stamps/SNAP Benefits During Past 12 Months

Group	Number	%
Total Population	620	5.4
Hispanic or Latino (of any race)	129	7.0
Mexican	119	7.8

Poverty Rate
(Income in Past 12 Months Below Poverty Level)

Group	%
Total Population	4.4
Hispanic or Latino (of any race)	4.7
Mexican	5.4

Maricopa

Population

Group	Number	%TP[1]	%HP[2]
Total Population	43,482	100.0	–
Hispanic or Latino (of any race)	10,617	24.4	100.0
Central American, ex. Mexican	371	0.9	3.5
Salvadoran	159	0.4	1.5
Cuban	139	0.3	1.3
Mexican	8,539	19.6	80.4
Puerto Rican	502	1.2	4.7
South American	271	0.6	2.6
Spaniard	188	0.4	1.8

Population Growth: 2000–2010

Group	%
Total Population	4,081.0
Hispanic or Latino (of any race)	1,350.4
Mexican	1,207.7

Males per 100 Females

Group	Number
Total Population	98.5
Hispanic or Latino (of any race)	95.5
Central American, ex. Mexican	86.4
Salvadoran	89.3
Cuban	87.8
Mexican	95.1
Puerto Rican	111.8
South American	96.4
Spaniard	72.5

Average Household Size

Group	People
Total Population	3.03
Hispanic or Latino (of any race)	3.69
Central American, ex. Mexican	3.95
Salvadoran	4.23
Cuban	3.43
Mexican	3.75
Puerto Rican	3.44
South American	3.49
Spaniard	2.65

Median Age

Group	Years
Total Population	31.2
Hispanic or Latino (of any race)	24.3
Central American, ex. Mexican	29.5
Salvadoran	30.6
Cuban	25.9
Mexican	23.5
Puerto Rican	24.7
South American	32.3
Spaniard	29.0

High School Graduates
(Universe: Population 25 Years and Over)

Group	Number	%
Total Population	20,562	93.4
Hispanic or Latino (of any race)	3,386	79.5
Mexican	2,594	79.3

Four-Year College Graduates
(Universe: Population 25 Years and Over)

Group	Number	%
Total Population	5,943	27.0
Hispanic or Latino (of any race)	699	16.4
Mexican	436	13.3

Population Age 3–17 Enrolled in Public School
(Universe: Population Age 3–17 Enrolled in School)

Group	Number	%
Total Population	5,938	86.8
Hispanic or Latino (of any race)	1,888	94.6
Mexican	1,571	93.6

Population Age 3–17 Enrolled in Private School
(Universe: Population Age 3–17 Enrolled in School)

Group	Number	%
Total Population	905	13.2
Hispanic or Latino (of any race)	108	5.4
Mexican	108	6.4

Foreign-Born Population

Group	Number	%
Total Population	3,852	11.1
Hispanic or Latino (of any race)	1,873	21.8
Mexican	1,387	19.5

Foreign-Born Naturalized U.S. Citizens

Group	Number	%
Total Population	2,413	62.6
Hispanic or Latino (of any race)	1,193	63.7
Mexican	829	59.8

Language Spoken at Home: English Only
(Universe: Population 5 Years and Over)

Group	Number	%
Total Population	24,297	79.7
Hispanic or Latino (of any race)	2,996	41.5
Mexican	2,537	43.5

Language Spoken at Home: Spanish
(Universe: Population 5 Years and Over)

Group	Number	%
Total Population	4,635	15.2
Hispanic or Latino (of any race)	4,218	58.5
Mexican	3,294	56.5

Unemployment Rate
(Universe: Population 16 Years and Over)

Group	%
Total Population	4.8
Hispanic or Latino (of any race)	3.7
Mexican	4.1

Class of Worker: Private Wage and Salary
(Universe: Civilian Employed Population 16 Years and Over)

Group	Number	%
Total Population	13,996	80.3
Hispanic or Latino (of any race)	2,810	77.7
Mexican	2,260	77.7

Class of Worker: Government
(Universe: Civilian Employed Population 16 Years and Over)

Group	Number	%
Total Population	2,874	16.5
Hispanic or Latino (of any race)	776	21.5
Mexican	619	21.3

Means of Transportation to Work: Car, Truck or Van
(Universe: Workers 16 Years and Over)

Group	Number	%
Total Population	16,205	93.4
Hispanic or Latino (of any race)	3,475	96.3
Mexican	2,817	97.1

Means of Transportation to Work: Public Transportation (ex. Taxicab)
(Universe: Workers 16 Years and Over)

Group	Number	%
Total Population	47	0.3
Hispanic or Latino (of any race)	15	0.4
Mexican	15	0.5

Homeownership Rate
(Universe: Occupied Housing Units)

Group	%
Total Population	79.7
Hispanic or Latino (of any race)	75.6
Central American, ex. Mexican	76.5
Salvadoran	80.9
Cuban	70.3
Mexican	75.2
Puerto Rican	76.3
South American	79.5
Spaniard	87.9

Median Home Value

Group	Dollars
Total Population	188,300
Hispanic or Latino (of any race)	166,500
Mexican	165,600

Median Gross Rent

Group	Dollars
Total Population	1,222
Hispanic or Latino (of any race)	1,164

Notes: (1) Percent of total population; (2) Percent of Hispanic/Latino population; Profiles include places with an overall population of at least 125,000, OR an overall population of at least 25,000 where the Hispanic/Latino population is at least 20% of the overall population. In states where less than five places meet either of these criteria, we have included places with at least 10,000 total population with the highest percentage of Hispanic/Latino population. These places are identified with an asterisk (*); Please refer to the User's Guide for a full explanation of data.

Mexican	869

Median Household Income
(2010 Inflation-Adjusted Dollars)

Group	Dollars
Total Population	65,790
Hispanic or Latino (of any race)	53,862
Mexican	52,661

Per Capita Income
(2010 Inflation-Adjusted Dollars)

Group	Dollars
Total Population	26,609
Hispanic or Latino (of any race)	16,964
Mexican	16,041

Households with $100,000+ Income

Group	Number	%
Total Population	2,714	21.2
Hispanic or Latino (of any race)	361	14.5
Mexican	227	11.5

Households with Food Stamps/SNAP Benefits During Past 12 Months

Group	Number	%
Total Population	369	2.9
Hispanic or Latino (of any race)	129	5.2
Mexican	116	5.9

Poverty Rate
(Income in Past 12 Months Below Poverty Level)

Group	%
Total Population	5.6
Hispanic or Latino (of any race)	10.6
Mexican	12.9

Mesa

Population

Group	Number	%TP[1]	%HP[2]
Total Population	439,041	100.0	–
Hispanic or Latino (of any race)	115,753	26.4	100.0
Central American, ex. Mexican	3,147	0.7	2.7
Costa Rican	180	<0.1	0.2
Guatemalan	1,446	0.3	1.2
Honduran	300	0.1	0.3
Nicaraguan	198	<0.1	0.2
Panamanian	108	<0.1	0.1
Salvadoran	885	0.2	0.8
Cuban	455	0.1	0.4
Dominican Republic	257	0.1	0.2
Mexican	99,666	22.7	86.1
Puerto Rican	2,441	0.6	2.1
South American	1,747	0.4	1.5
Argentinean	242	0.1	0.2
Chilean	141	<0.1	0.1
Colombian	422	0.1	0.4
Ecuadorian	196	<0.1	0.2
Peruvian	467	0.1	0.4
Venezuelan	179	<0.1	0.2
Spaniard	1,447	0.3	1.3

Population Growth: 2000–2010

Group	%
Total Population	10.8
Hispanic or Latino (of any race)	47.9
Central American, ex. Mexican	177.0
Guatemalan	219.9
Salvadoran	212.7
Cuban	14.3
Mexican	56.9
Puerto Rican	61.3
South American	115.4
Colombian	97.2
Peruvian	138.3
Spaniard	839.6

Males per 100 Females

Group	Number
Total Population	96.8
Hispanic or Latino (of any race)	102.7
Central American, ex. Mexican	99.8
Costa Rican	76.5
Guatemalan	109.9
Honduran	98.7
Nicaraguan	92.2
Panamanian	80.0
Salvadoran	94.5
Cuban	111.6
Dominican Republic	104.0
Mexican	104.1
Puerto Rican	96.2
South American	78.4
Argentinean	87.6
Chilean	46.9
Colombian	68.1
Ecuadorian	108.5
Peruvian	78.2
Venezuelan	96.7
Spaniard	88.7

Average Household Size

Group	People
Total Population	2.63
Hispanic or Latino (of any race)	3.61
Central American, ex. Mexican	3.81
Costa Rican	2.98
Guatemalan	4.33
Honduran	3.44
Nicaraguan	3.21
Panamanian	2.52
Salvadoran	3.75
Cuban	2.58
Dominican Republic	2.67
Mexican	3.71
Puerto Rican	2.57
South American	2.94
Argentinean	2.84
Chilean	2.56
Colombian	3.09
Ecuadorian	3.12
Peruvian	2.87
Venezuelan	3.18
Spaniard	2.72

Median Age

Group	Years
Total Population	34.6
Hispanic or Latino (of any race)	24.2
Central American, ex. Mexican	28.6
Costa Rican	30.0
Guatemalan	26.6
Honduran	30.0
Nicaraguan	30.4
Panamanian	38.0
Salvadoran	30.0
Cuban	32.9
Dominican Republic	26.4
Mexican	23.7
Puerto Rican	27.9
South American	34.4
Argentinean	35.7
Chilean	35.4
Colombian	36.2
Ecuadorian	29.8
Peruvian	34.1
Venezuelan	29.8
Spaniard	32.6

High School Graduates
(Universe: Population 25 Years and Over)

Group	Number	%
Total Population	242,299	86.1
Hispanic or Latino (of any race)	31,534	58.1
Central American, ex. Mexican	845	44.3
Guatemalan	183	26.7
Salvadoran	350	42.8
Mexican	26,482	55.9
Puerto Rican	909	80.1
South American	1,055	91.5
Spaniard	707	88.8

Four-Year College Graduates
(Universe: Population 25 Years and Over)

Group	Number	%
Total Population	66,077	23.5
Hispanic or Latino (of any race)	4,816	8.9
Central American, ex. Mexican	168	8.8
Guatemalan	33	4.8
Salvadoran	76	9.3
Mexican	3,595	7.6
Puerto Rican	226	19.9
South American	418	36.3
Spaniard	100	12.6

Population Age 3–17 Enrolled in Public School
(Universe: Population Age 3–17 Enrolled in School)

Group	Number	%
Total Population	75,019	93.0
Hispanic or Latino (of any race)	27,115	97.1
Central American, ex. Mexican	806	100.0
Guatemalan	319	100.0
Salvadoran	281	100.0
Mexican	24,787	97.4
Puerto Rican	347	83.6
South American	255	95.9
Spaniard	132	79.5

Population Age 3–17 Enrolled in Private School
(Universe: Population Age 3–17 Enrolled in School)

Group	Number	%
Total Population	5,633	7.0
Hispanic or Latino (of any race)	811	2.9
Central American, ex. Mexican	0	0.0
Guatemalan	0	0.0
Salvadoran	0	0.0
Mexican	649	2.6
Puerto Rican	68	16.4
South American	11	4.1
Spaniard	34	20.5

Foreign-Born Population

Group	Number	%
Total Population	61,500	14.0
Hispanic or Latino (of any race)	43,813	39.5
Central American, ex. Mexican	2,444	64.0
Guatemalan	906	60.2
Salvadoran	1,112	66.3
Mexican	39,950	40.6
Puerto Rican	10	0.5
South American	998	57.3
Spaniard	93	7.2

Foreign-Born Naturalized U.S. Citizens

Group	Number	%
Total Population	15,057	24.5
Hispanic or Latino (of any race)	6,301	14.4
Central American, ex. Mexican	405	16.6
Guatemalan	199	22.0
Salvadoran	126	11.3
Mexican	5,198	13.0
Puerto Rican	10	100.0
South American	495	49.6
Spaniard	81	87.1

Language Spoken at Home: English Only
(Universe: Population 5 Years and Over)

Group	Number	%
Total Population	316,551	77.9
Hispanic or Latino (of any race)	27,639	28.4
Central American, ex. Mexican	521	14.8
Guatemalan	141	10.7
Salvadoran	245	15.5
Mexican	23,065	26.8
Puerto Rican	774	46.4
South American	446	26.6
Spaniard	672	61.2

Language Spoken at Home: Spanish
(Universe: Population 5 Years and Over)

Group	Number	%
Total Population	74,934	18.4
Hispanic or Latino (of any race)	69,546	71.5
Central American, ex. Mexican	2,989	85.2
Guatemalan	1,180	89.3
Salvadoran	1,334	84.5
Mexican	62,939	73.2
Puerto Rican	895	53.6
South American	1,225	73.0
Spaniard	426	38.8

Notes: (1) Percent of total population; (2) Percent of Hispanic/Latino population; Profiles include places with an overall population of at least 125,000, OR an overall population of at least 25,000 where the Hispanic/Latino population is at least 20% of the overall population. In states where less than five places meet either of these criteria, we have included places with at least 10,000 total population with the highest percentage of Hispanic/Latino population. These places are identified with an asterisk (*); Please refer to the User's Guide for a full explanation of data.

Unemployment Rate
(Universe: Population 16 Years and Over)

Group	%
Total Population	6.9
Hispanic or Latino (of any race)	8.4
Central American, ex. Mexican	6.1
Guatemalan	9.3
Salvadoran	3.0
Mexican	8.5
Puerto Rican	4.9
South American	4.6
Spaniard	9.9

Class of Worker: Private Wage and Salary
(Universe: Civilian Employed Population 16 Years and Over)

Group	Number	%
Total Population	169,818	83.6
Hispanic or Latino (of any race)	42,904	87.6
Central American, ex. Mexican	2,101	92.8
Guatemalan	730	91.0
Salvadoran	1,104	94.8
Mexican	37,259	87.6
Puerto Rican	830	91.2
South American	999	83.5
Spaniard	523	80.1

Class of Worker: Government
(Universe: Civilian Employed Population 16 Years and Over)

Group	Number	%
Total Population	22,562	11.1
Hispanic or Latino (of any race)	3,875	7.9
Central American, ex. Mexican	73	3.2
Guatemalan	19	2.4
Salvadoran	32	2.7
Mexican	3,320	7.8
Puerto Rican	80	8.8
South American	144	12.0
Spaniard	130	19.9

Means of Transportation to Work: Car, Truck or Van
(Universe: Workers 16 Years and Over)

Group	Number	%
Total Population	177,988	89.9
Hispanic or Latino (of any race)	42,724	89.1
Central American, ex. Mexican	1,956	87.3
Guatemalan	690	86.0
Salvadoran	1,025	88.1
Mexican	37,234	89.4
Puerto Rican	777	91.4
South American	1,056	90.3
Spaniard	547	86.7

Means of Transportation to Work: Public Transportation (ex. Taxicab)
(Universe: Workers 16 Years and Over)

Group	Number	%
Total Population	4,027	2.0
Hispanic or Latino (of any race)	1,688	3.5
Central American, ex. Mexican	160	7.1
Guatemalan	32	4.0
Salvadoran	128	11.0
Mexican	1,432	3.4
Puerto Rican	8	0.9
South American	49	4.2
Spaniard	0	0.0

Homeownership Rate
(Universe: Occupied Housing Units)

Group	%
Total Population	63.2
Hispanic or Latino (of any race)	44.7
Central American, ex. Mexican	47.0
Costa Rican	48.1
Guatemalan	45.6
Honduran	36.4
Nicaraguan	55.8
Panamanian	52.3
Salvadoran	49.8
Cuban	58.9
Dominican Republic	40.7
Mexican	44.3
Puerto Rican	42.7
South American	59.9
Argentinean	55.7
Chilean	60.4
Colombian	60.9
Ecuadorian	64.4
Peruvian	57.7
Venezuelan	55.4
Spaniard	58.3

Median Home Value

Group	Dollars
Total Population	200,300
Hispanic or Latino (of any race)	199,200
Central American, ex. Mexican	180,400
Guatemalan	155,300
Salvadoran	211,700
Mexican	199,300
Puerto Rican	237,100
South American	148,400
Spaniard	211,000

Median Gross Rent

Group	Dollars
Total Population	856
Hispanic or Latino (of any race)	812
Central American, ex. Mexican	788
Guatemalan	824
Salvadoran	781
Mexican	808
Puerto Rican	935
South American	757
Spaniard	911

Median Household Income
(2010 Inflation-Adjusted Dollars)

Group	Dollars
Total Population	50,079
Hispanic or Latino (of any race)	42,113
Central American, ex. Mexican	38,095
Guatemalan	62,337
Salvadoran	27,031
Mexican	41,815
Puerto Rican	51,506
South American	48,750
Spaniard	64,375

Per Capita Income
(2010 Inflation-Adjusted Dollars)

Group	Dollars
Total Population	24,647
Hispanic or Latino (of any race)	14,650
Central American, ex. Mexican	15,877
Guatemalan	15,387
Salvadoran	16,563
Mexican	14,066
Puerto Rican	17,732
South American	26,498
Spaniard	22,930

Households with $100,000+ Income

Group	Number	%
Total Population	28,533	17.2
Hispanic or Latino (of any race)	2,918	9.9
Central American, ex. Mexican	136	12.1
Guatemalan	59	16.9
Salvadoran	38	6.8
Mexican	2,259	8.9
Puerto Rican	151	19.3
South American	57	9.6
Spaniard	118	21.0

Households with Food Stamps/SNAP Benefits During Past 12 Months

Group	Number	%
Total Population	10,481	6.3
Hispanic or Latino (of any race)	2,895	9.8
Central American, ex. Mexican	54	4.8
Guatemalan	23	6.6
Salvadoran	31	5.6
Mexican	2,601	10.3
Puerto Rican	27	3.5
South American	0	0.0
Spaniard	83	14.7

Poverty Rate
(Income in Past 12 Months Below Poverty Level)

Group	%
Total Population	11.9
Hispanic or Latino (of any race)	20.3
Central American, ex. Mexican	13.9
Guatemalan	12.0
Salvadoran	16.0
Mexican	21.1
Puerto Rican	18.7
South American	5.9
Spaniard	15.4

Peoria

Population

Group	Number	%TP[1]	%HP[2]
Total Population	154,065	100.0	–
Hispanic or Latino (of any race)	28,629	18.6	100.0
Central American, ex. Mexican	638	0.4	2.2
Guatemalan	150	0.1	0.5
Salvadoran	228	0.1	0.8
Cuban	172	0.1	0.6
Mexican	23,791	15.4	83.1
Puerto Rican	963	0.6	3.4
South American	597	0.4	2.1
Colombian	205	0.1	0.7
Spaniard	505	0.3	1.8

Population Growth: 2000–2010

Group	%
Total Population	42.2
Hispanic or Latino (of any race)	71.4
Central American, ex. Mexican	279.8
Mexican	90.0
Puerto Rican	121.9
South American	231.7

Males per 100 Females

Group	Number
Total Population	92.2
Hispanic or Latino (of any race)	96.0
Central American, ex. Mexican	85.5
Guatemalan	97.4
Salvadoran	88.4
Cuban	95.5
Mexican	97.8
Puerto Rican	92.2
South American	74.1
Colombian	64.0
Spaniard	70.0

Average Household Size

Group	People
Total Population	2.66
Hispanic or Latino (of any race)	3.42
Central American, ex. Mexican	3.38
Guatemalan	3.76
Salvadoran	3.51
Cuban	2.60
Mexican	3.52
Puerto Rican	2.89
South American	3.04
Colombian	2.87
Spaniard	2.76

Median Age

Group	Years
Total Population	38.1
Hispanic or Latino (of any race)	25.6
Central American, ex. Mexican	33.3
Guatemalan	30.0
Salvadoran	36.0
Cuban	33.8
Mexican	24.9
Puerto Rican	28.0
South American	33.8
Colombian	31.8
Spaniard	35.7

Notes: (1) Percent of total population; (2) Percent of Hispanic/Latino population; Profiles include places with an overall population of at least 125,000, OR an overall population of at least 25,000 where the Hispanic/Latino population is at least 20% of the overall population. In states where less than five places meet either of these criteria, we have included places with at least 10,000 total population with the highest percentage of Hispanic/Latino population. These places are identified with an asterisk (*); Please refer to the User's Guide for a full explanation of data.

High School Graduates
(Universe: Population 25 Years and Over)

Group	Number	%
Total Population	87,719	89.9
Hispanic or Latino (of any race)	10,607	74.0
Mexican	8,932	73.1

Four-Year College Graduates
(Universe: Population 25 Years and Over)

Group	Number	%
Total Population	25,658	26.3
Hispanic or Latino (of any race)	1,692	11.8
Mexican	1,167	9.6

Population Age 3–17 Enrolled in Public School
(Universe: Population Age 3–17 Enrolled in School)

Group	Number	%
Total Population	27,067	92.1
Hispanic or Latino (of any race)	8,361	94.6
Mexican	7,341	95.0

Population Age 3–17 Enrolled in Private School
(Universe: Population Age 3–17 Enrolled in School)

Group	Number	%
Total Population	2,327	7.9
Hispanic or Latino (of any race)	477	5.4
Mexican	386	5.0

Foreign-Born Population

Group	Number	%
Total Population	14,104	9.5
Hispanic or Latino (of any race)	6,253	21.0
Mexican	5,134	19.8

Foreign-Born Naturalized U.S. Citizens

Group	Number	%
Total Population	7,650	54.2
Hispanic or Latino (of any race)	2,523	40.3
Mexican	1,738	33.9

Language Spoken at Home: English Only
(Universe: Population 5 Years and Over)

Group	Number	%
Total Population	117,865	85.3
Hispanic or Latino (of any race)	14,134	53.9
Mexican	12,318	54.3

Language Spoken at Home: Spanish
(Universe: Population 5 Years and Over)

Group	Number	%
Total Population	13,164	9.5
Hispanic or Latino (of any race)	12,086	46.1
Mexican	10,334	45.6

Unemployment Rate
(Universe: Population 16 Years and Over)

Group	%
Total Population	6.3
Hispanic or Latino (of any race)	9.9
Mexican	10.1

Class of Worker: Private Wage and Salary
(Universe: Civilian Employed Population 16 Years and Over)

Group	Number	%
Total Population	56,347	80.0
Hispanic or Latino (of any race)	10,189	83.4
Mexican	8,804	83.4

Class of Worker: Government
(Universe: Civilian Employed Population 16 Years and Over)

Group	Number	%
Total Population	9,933	14.1
Hispanic or Latino (of any race)	1,446	11.8
Mexican	1,239	11.7

Means of Transportation to Work: Car, Truck or Van
(Universe: Workers 16 Years and Over)

Group	Number	%
Total Population	63,338	91.6
Hispanic or Latino (of any race)	11,362	94.5
Mexican	9,881	95.3

Means of Transportation to Work: Public Transportation (ex. Taxicab)
(Universe: Workers 16 Years and Over)

Group	Number	%
Total Population	458	0.7
Hispanic or Latino (of any race)	61	0.5
Mexican	61	0.6

Homeownership Rate
(Universe: Occupied Housing Units)

Group	%
Total Population	73.7
Hispanic or Latino (of any race)	64.2
Central American, ex. Mexican	65.5
Guatemalan	66.7
Salvadoran	72.4
Cuban	66.1
Mexican	64.5
Puerto Rican	67.7
South American	68.9
Colombian	69.8
Spaniard	74.6

Median Home Value

Group	Dollars
Total Population	238,900
Hispanic or Latino (of any race)	215,600
Mexican	211,700

Median Gross Rent

Group	Dollars
Total Population	1,143
Hispanic or Latino (of any race)	1,131
Mexican	1,135

Median Household Income
(2010 Inflation-Adjusted Dollars)

Group	Dollars
Total Population	63,535
Hispanic or Latino (of any race)	55,724
Mexican	57,962

Per Capita Income
(2010 Inflation-Adjusted Dollars)

Group	Dollars
Total Population	29,279
Hispanic or Latino (of any race)	17,519
Mexican	16,899

Households with $100,000+ Income

Group	Number	%
Total Population	13,798	25.4
Hispanic or Latino (of any race)	1,504	20.0
Mexican	1,270	20.2

Households with Food Stamps/SNAP Benefits During Past 12 Months

Group	Number	%
Total Population	2,871	5.3
Hispanic or Latino (of any race)	838	11.1
Mexican	762	12.1

Poverty Rate
(Income in Past 12 Months Below Poverty Level)

Group	%
Total Population	7.3
Hispanic or Latino (of any race)	11.2
Mexican	11.9

Phoenix

Population

Group	Number	%TP[1]	%HP[2]
Total Population	1,445,632	100.0	–
Hispanic or Latino (of any race)	589,877	40.8	100.0
Central American, ex. Mexican	14,788	1.0	2.5
Costa Rican	348	<0.1	0.1
Guatemalan	6,722	0.5	1.1
Honduran	1,535	0.1	0.3
Nicaraguan	888	0.1	0.2
Panamanian	444	<0.1	0.1
Salvadoran	4,697	0.3	0.8
Cuban	3,975	0.3	0.7
Dominican Republic	865	0.1	0.1
Mexican	519,635	35.9	88.1
Puerto Rican	8,103	0.6	1.4
South American	5,116	0.4	0.9
Argentinean	608	<0.1	0.1
Bolivian	180	<0.1	<0.1
Chilean	320	<0.1	0.1
Colombian	1,687	0.1	0.3
Ecuadorian	628	<0.1	0.1
Peruvian	1,048	0.1	0.2
Uruguayan	106	<0.1	<0.1
Venezuelan	434	<0.1	0.1
Spaniard	4,863	0.3	0.8

Population Growth: 2000–2010

Group	%
Total Population	9.4
Hispanic or Latino (of any race)	31.1
Central American, ex. Mexican	143.0
Costa Rican	64.2
Guatemalan	180.4
Honduran	146.0
Nicaraguan	191.1
Panamanian	118.7
Salvadoran	153.1
Cuban	103.6
Dominican Republic	177.2
Mexican	38.5
Puerto Rican	59.2
South American	132.7
Argentinean	142.2
Chilean	154.0
Colombian	133.7
Ecuadorian	130.9
Peruvian	155.0
Venezuelan	180.0
Spaniard	688.2

Males per 100 Females

Group	Number
Total Population	100.6
Hispanic or Latino (of any race)	102.8
Central American, ex. Mexican	112.8
Costa Rican	74.0
Guatemalan	133.7
Honduran	99.9
Nicaraguan	94.3
Panamanian	79.0
Salvadoran	101.2
Cuban	114.6
Dominican Republic	106.0
Mexican	103.0
Puerto Rican	99.9
South American	85.6
Argentinean	106.1
Bolivian	87.5
Chilean	71.1
Colombian	75.9
Ecuadorian	85.3
Peruvian	86.1
Uruguayan	107.8
Venezuelan	95.5
Spaniard	94.1

Average Household Size

Group	People
Total Population	2.77
Hispanic or Latino (of any race)	3.81
Central American, ex. Mexican	3.85
Costa Rican	2.76
Guatemalan	4.21
Honduran	3.83
Nicaraguan	3.53
Panamanian	2.50
Salvadoran	3.73
Cuban	2.82
Dominican Republic	2.88
Mexican	3.91
Puerto Rican	2.67
South American	2.72
Argentinean	2.37
Bolivian	2.86
Chilean	2.59
Colombian	2.63
Ecuadorian	2.97
Peruvian	3.00

Notes: (1) Percent of total population; (2) Percent of Hispanic/Latino population; Profiles include places with an overall population of at least 125,000, OR an overall population of at least 25,000 where the Hispanic/Latino population is at least 20% of the overall population. In states where less than five places meet either of these criteria, we have included places with at least 10,000 total population with the highest percentage of Hispanic/Latino population. These places are identified with an asterisk (*); Please refer to the User's Guide for a full explanation of data.

Group	
Uruguayan	2.73
Venezuelan	2.55
Spaniard	2.76

Median Age

Group	Years
Total Population	32.2
Hispanic or Latino (of any race)	24.1
Central American, ex. Mexican	30.7
Costa Rican	32.5
Guatemalan	29.0
Honduran	30.8
Nicaraguan	32.3
Panamanian	33.4
Salvadoran	33.5
Cuban	35.4
Dominican Republic	26.8
Mexican	23.6
Puerto Rican	28.5
South American	35.0
Argentinean	39.4
Bolivian	32.9
Chilean	36.1
Colombian	34.4
Ecuadorian	34.9
Peruvian	34.6
Uruguayan	38.7
Venezuelan	33.8
Spaniard	32.3

High School Graduates
(Universe: Population 25 Years and Over)

Group	Number	%
Total Population	706,360	79.8
Hispanic or Latino (of any race)	151,459	54.3
Central American, ex. Mexican	3,760	47.2
Guatemalan	1,258	34.9
Honduran	434	50.5
Salvadoran	1,284	53.6
Cuban	1,943	79.7
Mexican	132,117	52.6
Puerto Rican	3,272	86.9
South American	2,357	88.6
Colombian	805	82.6
Peruvian	505	98.1
Spaniard	1,852	86.3

Four-Year College Graduates
(Universe: Population 25 Years and Over)

Group	Number	%
Total Population	225,330	25.5
Hispanic or Latino (of any race)	21,757	7.8
Central American, ex. Mexican	692	8.7
Guatemalan	182	5.0
Honduran	163	19.0
Salvadoran	145	6.0
Cuban	506	20.8
Mexican	17,197	6.8
Puerto Rican	694	18.4
South American	1,101	41.4
Colombian	352	36.1
Peruvian	254	49.3
Spaniard	550	25.6

Population Age 3–17 Enrolled in Public School
(Universe: Population Age 3–17 Enrolled in School)

Group	Number	%
Total Population	267,314	91.4
Hispanic or Latino (of any race)	148,255	96.5
Central American, ex. Mexican	2,637	92.7
Guatemalan	1,176	90.7
Honduran	414	100.0
Salvadoran	774	95.2
Cuban	407	92.3
Mexican	138,159	96.9
Puerto Rican	1,703	94.0
South American	790	86.1
Colombian	443	95.1
Peruvian	146	100.0
Spaniard	543	82.6

Population Age 3–17 Enrolled in Private School
(Universe: Population Age 3–17 Enrolled in School)

Group	Number	%
Total Population	25,293	8.6

Group	Number	%
Hispanic or Latino (of any race)	5,412	3.5
Central American, ex. Mexican	208	7.3
Guatemalan	121	9.3
Honduran	0	0.0
Salvadoran	39	4.8
Cuban	34	7.7
Mexican	4,469	3.1
Puerto Rican	108	6.0
South American	128	13.9
Colombian	23	4.9
Peruvian	0	0.0
Spaniard	114	17.4

Foreign-Born Population

Group	Number	%
Total Population	315,354	21.7
Hispanic or Latino (of any race)	238,167	41.1
Central American, ex. Mexican	8,752	62.3
Guatemalan	4,061	66.7
Honduran	1,116	56.5
Salvadoran	2,702	62.4
Cuban	2,394	71.5
Mexican	221,549	41.8
Puerto Rican	188	2.7
South American	2,484	57.5
Colombian	911	54.3
Peruvian	497	54.6
Spaniard	244	7.2

Foreign-Born Naturalized U.S. Citizens

Group	Number	%
Total Population	76,252	24.2
Hispanic or Latino (of any race)	39,922	16.8
Central American, ex. Mexican	1,701	19.4
Guatemalan	573	14.1
Honduran	191	17.1
Salvadoran	605	22.4
Cuban	507	21.2
Mexican	35,120	15.9
Puerto Rican	143	76.1
South American	1,216	49.0
Colombian	478	52.5
Peruvian	238	47.9
Spaniard	148	60.7

Language Spoken at Home: English Only
(Universe: Population 5 Years and Over)

Group	Number	%
Total Population	837,361	63.1
Hispanic or Latino (of any race)	111,030	21.9
Central American, ex. Mexican	1,525	11.9
Guatemalan	271	4.9
Honduran	351	21.0
Salvadoran	446	11.2
Cuban	624	19.4
Mexican	95,214	20.5
Puerto Rican	3,396	54.3
South American	970	24.6
Colombian	340	21.5
Peruvian	124	18.0
Spaniard	2,020	66.4

Language Spoken at Home: Spanish
(Universe: Population 5 Years and Over)

Group	Number	%
Total Population	411,840	31.0
Hispanic or Latino (of any race)	395,689	77.9
Central American, ex. Mexican	11,198	87.6
Guatemalan	5,257	94.8
Honduran	1,317	79.0
Salvadoran	3,540	88.8
Cuban	2,575	80.1
Mexican	367,728	79.3
Puerto Rican	2,811	44.9
South American	2,935	74.5
Colombian	1,225	77.3
Peruvian	563	82.0
Spaniard	944	31.1

Unemployment Rate
(Universe: Population 16 Years and Over)

Group	%
Total Population	7.4
Hispanic or Latino (of any race)	8.5
Central American, ex. Mexican	8.0

Group	%
Guatemalan	3.1
Honduran	17.1
Salvadoran	10.1
Cuban	7.8
Mexican	8.5
Puerto Rican	7.0
South American	3.0
Colombian	2.5
Peruvian	0.0
Spaniard	3.4

Class of Worker: Private Wage and Salary
(Universe: Civilian Employed Population 16 Years and Over)

Group	Number	%
Total Population	560,126	82.9
Hispanic or Latino (of any race)	190,920	85.2
Central American, ex. Mexican	6,114	84.3
Guatemalan	2,671	85.2
Honduran	617	79.7
Salvadoran	2,114	87.6
Cuban	1,639	89.3
Mexican	172,512	85.6
Puerto Rican	2,378	80.6
South American	1,626	74.0
Colombian	516	74.4
Peruvian	407	83.4
Spaniard	1,294	76.3

Class of Worker: Government
(Universe: Civilian Employed Population 16 Years and Over)

Group	Number	%
Total Population	73,898	10.9
Hispanic or Latino (of any race)	18,605	8.3
Central American, ex. Mexican	702	9.7
Guatemalan	172	5.5
Honduran	130	16.8
Salvadoran	199	8.2
Cuban	124	6.8
Mexican	15,834	7.9
Puerto Rican	392	13.3
South American	267	12.2
Colombian	102	14.7
Peruvian	70	14.3
Spaniard	328	19.4

Means of Transportation to Work: Car, Truck or Van
(Universe: Workers 16 Years and Over)

Group	Number	%
Total Population	582,095	87.8
Hispanic or Latino (of any race)	195,495	88.8
Central American, ex. Mexican	6,022	85.1
Guatemalan	2,498	82.4
Honduran	613	79.2
Salvadoran	2,161	90.6
Cuban	1,631	89.6
Mexican	176,260	88.9
Puerto Rican	2,476	85.3
South American	1,938	88.3
Colombian	683	98.4
Peruvian	417	85.5
Spaniard	1,469	88.0

Means of Transportation to Work: Public Transportation (ex. Taxicab)
(Universe: Workers 16 Years and Over)

Group	Number	%
Total Population	23,122	3.5
Hispanic or Latino (of any race)	10,043	4.6
Central American, ex. Mexican	539	7.6
Guatemalan	241	8.0
Honduran	120	15.5
Salvadoran	59	2.5
Cuban	91	5.0
Mexican	8,956	4.5
Puerto Rican	130	4.5
South American	19	0.9
Colombian	0	0.0
Peruvian	0	0.0
Spaniard	84	5.0

Homeownership Rate
(Universe: Occupied Housing Units)

Group	%
Total Population	57.6

Notes: (1) Percent of total population; (2) Percent of Hispanic/Latino population; Profiles include places with an overall population of at least 125,000, OR an overall population of at least 25,000 where the Hispanic/Latino population is at least 20% of the overall population. In states where less than five places meet either of these criteria, we have included places with at least 10,000 total population with the highest percentage of Hispanic/Latino population. These places are identified with an asterisk (*); Please refer to the User's Guide for a full explanation of data.

Hispanic or Latino (of any race)	47.4
Central American, ex. Mexican	48.0
Costa Rican	48.7
Guatemalan	40.7
Honduran	42.1
Nicaraguan	54.9
Panamanian	58.3
Salvadoran	56.5
Cuban	40.7
Dominican Republic	38.1
Mexican	47.7
Puerto Rican	41.5
South American	58.3
Argentinean	60.4
Bolivian	61.4
Chilean	56.7
Colombian	56.3
Ecuadorian	64.5
Peruvian	56.9
Uruguayan	60.0
Venezuelan	56.5
Spaniard	58.2

Median Home Value

Group	Dollars
Total Population	221,800
Hispanic or Latino (of any race)	166,700
Central American, ex. Mexican	177,900
Guatemalan	174,200
Honduran	225,900
Salvadoran	168,400
Cuban	230,800
Mexican	163,500
Puerto Rican	195,800
South American	197,000
Colombian	144,800
Peruvian	217,400
Spaniard	185,600

Median Gross Rent

Group	Dollars
Total Population	847
Hispanic or Latino (of any race)	782
Central American, ex. Mexican	782
Guatemalan	763
Honduran	783
Salvadoran	767
Cuban	684
Mexican	776
Puerto Rican	907
South American	930
Colombian	743
Peruvian	902
Spaniard	949

Median Household Income
(2010 Inflation-Adjusted Dollars)

Group	Dollars
Total Population	48,823
Hispanic or Latino (of any race)	36,297
Central American, ex. Mexican	36,695
Guatemalan	35,671
Honduran	31,250
Salvadoran	36,648
Cuban	47,131
Mexican	35,726
Puerto Rican	42,337
South American	48,393
Colombian	36,793
Peruvian	62,734
Spaniard	44,519

Per Capita Income
(2010 Inflation-Adjusted Dollars)

Group	Dollars
Total Population	24,460
Hispanic or Latino (of any race)	12,551
Central American, ex. Mexican	14,266
Guatemalan	13,654
Honduran	11,808
Salvadoran	13,929
Cuban	21,702
Mexican	12,070
Puerto Rican	19,035
South American	22,520
Colombian	16,784
Peruvian	18,882
Spaniard	25,748

Households with $100,000+ Income

Group	Number	%
Total Population	98,199	19.0
Hispanic or Latino (of any race)	11,830	8.1
Central American, ex. Mexican	459	10.9
Guatemalan	143	8.2
Honduran	99	21.1
Salvadoran	128	9.6
Cuban	180	14.0
Mexican	9,852	7.5
Puerto Rican	307	13.8
South American	187	14.4
Colombian	48	10.2
Peruvian	0	0.0
Spaniard	166	12.7

Households with Food Stamps/SNAP Benefits During Past 12 Months

Group	Number	%
Total Population	54,789	10.6
Hispanic or Latino (of any race)	26,237	17.9
Central American, ex. Mexican	624	14.9
Guatemalan	245	14.0
Honduran	169	36.0
Salvadoran	144	10.8
Cuban	255	19.8
Mexican	23,609	18.1
Puerto Rican	453	20.4
South American	110	8.4
Colombian	53	11.3
Peruvian	16	7.6
Spaniard	219	16.8

Poverty Rate
(Income in Past 12 Months Below Poverty Level)

Group	%
Total Population	19.1
Hispanic or Latino (of any race)	29.6
Central American, ex. Mexican	20.4
Guatemalan	19.3
Honduran	33.5
Salvadoran	17.9
Cuban	18.6
Mexican	30.6
Puerto Rican	13.9
South American	18.3
Colombian	26.7
Peruvian	11.6
Spaniard	11.2

Sahuarita

Population

Group	Number	%TP[1]	%HP[2]
Total Population	25,259	100.0	–
Hispanic or Latino (of any race)	8,077	32.0	100.0
Central American, ex. Mexican	141	0.6	1.7
Mexican	6,979	27.6	86.4
Puerto Rican	265	1.0	3.3
South American	141	0.6	1.7
Spaniard	101	0.4	1.3

Population Growth: 2000–2010

Group	%
Total Population	679.1
Hispanic or Latino (of any race)	930.2
Mexican	933.9

Males per 100 Females

Group	Number
Total Population	95.3
Hispanic or Latino (of any race)	89.6
Central American, ex. Mexican	101.4
Mexican	89.5
Puerto Rican	119.0
South American	53.3
Spaniard	77.2

Average Household Size

Group	People
Total Population	2.79
Hispanic or Latino (of any race)	3.41
Central American, ex. Mexican	3.71
Mexican	3.46
Puerto Rican	3.05
South American	2.65
Spaniard	2.79

Median Age

Group	Years
Total Population	34.4
Hispanic or Latino (of any race)	26.4
Central American, ex. Mexican	32.3
Mexican	25.9
Puerto Rican	29.1
South American	34.8
Spaniard	31.5

High School Graduates
(Universe: Population 25 Years and Over)

Group	Number	%
Total Population	14,077	96.4
Hispanic or Latino (of any race)	2,509	90.9
Mexican	2,295	91.8

Four-Year College Graduates
(Universe: Population 25 Years and Over)

Group	Number	%
Total Population	5,263	36.0
Hispanic or Latino (of any race)	707	25.6
Mexican	648	25.9

Population Age 3–17 Enrolled in Public School
(Universe: Population Age 3–17 Enrolled in School)

Group	Number	%
Total Population	3,874	88.1
Hispanic or Latino (of any race)	1,212	85.9
Mexican	1,055	85.1

Population Age 3–17 Enrolled in Private School
(Universe: Population Age 3–17 Enrolled in School)

Group	Number	%
Total Population	525	11.9
Hispanic or Latino (of any race)	199	14.1
Mexican	184	14.9

Foreign-Born Population

Group	Number	%
Total Population	1,519	7.0
Hispanic or Latino (of any race)	728	13.9
Mexican	598	12.9

Foreign-Born Naturalized U.S. Citizens

Group	Number	%
Total Population	762	50.2
Hispanic or Latino (of any race)	338	46.4
Mexican	248	41.5

Language Spoken at Home: English Only
(Universe: Population 5 Years and Over)

Group	Number	%
Total Population	16,059	81.4
Hispanic or Latino (of any race)	1,572	35.3
Mexican	1,375	34.4

Language Spoken at Home: Spanish
(Universe: Population 5 Years and Over)

Group	Number	%
Total Population	3,148	16.0
Hispanic or Latino (of any race)	2,872	64.5
Mexican	2,608	65.3

Unemployment Rate
(Universe: Population 16 Years and Over)

Group	%
Total Population	6.0
Hispanic or Latino (of any race)	7.6
Mexican	7.0

Class of Worker: Private Wage and Salary
(Universe: Civilian Employed Population 16 Years and Over)

Group	Number	%
Total Population	6,302	70.4
Hispanic or Latino (of any race)	1,451	64.5

Notes: (1) Percent of total population; (2) Percent of Hispanic/Latino population; Profiles include places with an overall population of at least 125,000, OR an overall population of at least 25,000 where the Hispanic/Latino population is at least 20% of the overall population. In states where less than five places meet either of these criteria, we have included places with at least 10,000 total population with the highest percentage of Hispanic/Latino population. These places are identified with an asterisk (*); Please refer to the User's Guide for a full explanation of data.

Mexican	1,395	67.5

Class of Worker: Government
(Universe: Civilian Employed Population 16 Years and Over)

Group	Number	%
Total Population	2,125	23.7
Hispanic or Latino (of any race)	646	28.7
Mexican	564	27.3

Means of Transportation to Work: Car, Truck or Van
(Universe: Workers 16 Years and Over)

Group	Number	%
Total Population	8,352	93.7
Hispanic or Latino (of any race)	2,140	97.6
Mexican	1,969	97.9

Means of Transportation to Work: Public Transportation (ex. Taxicab)
(Universe: Workers 16 Years and Over)

Group	Number	%
Total Population	0	0.0
Hispanic or Latino (of any race)	0	0.0
Mexican	0	0.0

Homeownership Rate
(Universe: Occupied Housing Units)

Group	%
Total Population	84.4
Hispanic or Latino (of any race)	80.0
Central American, ex. Mexican	85.4
Mexican	79.9
Puerto Rican	87.2
South American	87.5
Spaniard	72.7

Median Home Value

Group	Dollars
Total Population	249,700
Hispanic or Latino (of any race)	254,100
Mexican	253,000

Median Gross Rent

Group	Dollars
Total Population	1,228
Hispanic or Latino (of any race)	1,091
Mexican	1,127

Median Household Income
(2010 Inflation-Adjusted Dollars)

Group	Dollars
Total Population	73,827
Hispanic or Latino (of any race)	73,208
Mexican	74,667

Per Capita Income
(2010 Inflation-Adjusted Dollars)

Group	Dollars
Total Population	28,962
Hispanic or Latino (of any race)	20,827
Mexican	21,875

Households with $100,000+ Income

Group	Number	%
Total Population	2,254	28.7
Hispanic or Latino (of any race)	467	33.1
Mexican	452	35.4

Households with Food Stamps/SNAP Benefits During Past 12 Months

Group	Number	%
Total Population	118	1.5
Hispanic or Latino (of any race)	89	6.3
Mexican	74	5.8

Poverty Rate
(Income in Past 12 Months Below Poverty Level)

Group	%
Total Population	5.3
Hispanic or Latino (of any race)	6.8
Mexican	4.3

San Luis

Population

Group	Number	%TP[1]	%HP[2]
Total Population	25,505	100.0	–
Hispanic or Latino (of any race)	25,171	98.7	100.0
Mexican	24,543	96.2	97.5

Population Growth: 2000–2010

Group	%
Total Population	66.5
Hispanic or Latino (of any race)	84.3
Mexican	93.0

Males per 100 Females

Group	Number
Total Population	98.1
Hispanic or Latino (of any race)	97.4
Mexican	97.0

Average Household Size

Group	People
Total Population	4.20
Hispanic or Latino (of any race)	4.21
Mexican	4.21

Median Age

Group	Years
Total Population	25.5
Hispanic or Latino (of any race)	25.4
Mexican	25.5

High School Graduates
(Universe: Population 25 Years and Over)

Group	Number	%
Total Population	5,663	45.3
Hispanic or Latino (of any race)	4,689	41.4
Mexican	4,620	41.1

Four-Year College Graduates
(Universe: Population 25 Years and Over)

Group	Number	%
Total Population	775	6.2
Hispanic or Latino (of any race)	708	6.3
Mexican	708	6.3

Population Age 3–17 Enrolled in Public School
(Universe: Population Age 3–17 Enrolled in School)

Group	Number	%
Total Population	6,445	99.3
Hispanic or Latino (of any race)	6,445	99.3
Mexican	6,425	99.3

Population Age 3–17 Enrolled in Private School
(Universe: Population Age 3–17 Enrolled in School)

Group	Number	%
Total Population	47	0.7
Hispanic or Latino (of any race)	47	0.7
Mexican	47	0.7

Foreign-Born Population

Group	Number	%
Total Population	10,879	45.7
Hispanic or Latino (of any race)	10,859	48.8
Mexican	10,848	49.0

Foreign-Born Naturalized U.S. Citizens

Group	Number	%
Total Population	2,822	25.9
Hispanic or Latino (of any race)	2,802	25.8
Mexican	2,791	25.7

Language Spoken at Home: English Only
(Universe: Population 5 Years and Over)

Group	Number	%
Total Population	2,636	12.1
Hispanic or Latino (of any race)	1,107	5.5
Mexican	1,044	5.2

Language Spoken at Home: Spanish
(Universe: Population 5 Years and Over)

Group	Number	%
Total Population	19,035	87.7
Hispanic or Latino (of any race)	19,017	94.5
Mexican	18,980	94.8

Unemployment Rate
(Universe: Population 16 Years and Over)

Group	%
Total Population	19.5
Hispanic or Latino (of any race)	19.7
Mexican	19.7

Class of Worker: Private Wage and Salary
(Universe: Civilian Employed Population 16 Years and Over)

Group	Number	%
Total Population	4,844	78.0
Hispanic or Latino (of any race)	4,768	77.7
Mexican	4,745	77.6

Class of Worker: Government
(Universe: Civilian Employed Population 16 Years and Over)

Group	Number	%
Total Population	1,284	20.7
Hispanic or Latino (of any race)	1,284	20.9
Mexican	1,284	21.0

Means of Transportation to Work: Car, Truck or Van
(Universe: Workers 16 Years and Over)

Group	Number	%
Total Population	4,772	79.1
Hispanic or Latino (of any race)	4,752	79.8
Mexican	4,729	79.7

Means of Transportation to Work: Public Transportation (ex. Taxicab)
(Universe: Workers 16 Years and Over)

Group	Number	%
Total Population	924	15.3
Hispanic or Latino (of any race)	868	14.6
Mexican	868	14.6

Homeownership Rate
(Universe: Occupied Housing Units)

Group	%
Total Population	71.8
Hispanic or Latino (of any race)	72.0
Mexican	72.3

Median Home Value

Group	Dollars
Total Population	120,900
Hispanic or Latino (of any race)	120,900
Mexican	120,600

Median Gross Rent

Group	Dollars
Total Population	488
Hispanic or Latino (of any race)	488
Mexican	488

Median Household Income
(2010 Inflation-Adjusted Dollars)

Group	Dollars
Total Population	25,622
Hispanic or Latino (of any race)	25,622
Mexican	25,500

Per Capita Income
(2010 Inflation-Adjusted Dollars)

Group	Dollars
Total Population	7,868
Hispanic or Latino (of any race)	8,200
Mexican	8,203

Households with $100,000+ Income

Group	Number	%
Total Population	92	1.5
Hispanic or Latino (of any race)	92	1.5
Mexican	92	1.5

Households with Food Stamps/SNAP Benefits During Past 12 Months

Group	Number	%
Total Population	2,034	33.5
Hispanic or Latino (of any race)	2,034	33.5
Mexican	2,034	33.6

Notes: (1) Percent of total population; (2) Percent of Hispanic/Latino population; Profiles include places with an overall population of at least 125,000, OR an overall population of at least 25,000 where the Hispanic/Latino population is at least 20% of the overall population. In states where less than five places meet either of these criteria, we have included places with at least 10,000 total population with the highest percentage of Hispanic/Latino population. These places are identified with an asterisk (*); Please refer to the User's Guide for a full explanation of data.

Poverty Rate
(Income in Past 12 Months Below Poverty Level)

Group	%
Total Population	35.2
Hispanic or Latino (of any race)	35.4
Mexican	35.4

San Tan Valley

Population

Group	Number	%TP[1]	%HP[2]
Total Population	81,321	100.0	–
Hispanic or Latino (of any race)	18,995	23.4	100.0
Central American, ex. Mexican	519	0.6	2.7
Guatemalan	118	0.1	0.6
Salvadoran	196	0.2	1.0
Cuban	118	0.1	0.6
Dominican Republic	129	0.2	0.7
Mexican	15,678	19.3	82.5
Puerto Rican	697	0.9	3.7
South American	444	0.5	2.3
Colombian	114	0.1	0.6
Peruvian	131	0.2	0.7
Spaniard	309	0.4	1.6

Population Growth: 2000–2010

Group	%
Total Population	n/a

Males per 100 Females

Group	Number
Total Population	97.9
Hispanic or Latino (of any race)	99.0
Central American, ex. Mexican	92.9
Guatemalan	114.5
Salvadoran	88.5
Cuban	114.5
Dominican Republic	92.5
Mexican	100.4
Puerto Rican	98.0
South American	83.5
Colombian	70.1
Peruvian	70.1
Spaniard	98.1

Average Household Size

Group	People
Total Population	3.29
Hispanic or Latino (of any race)	3.89
Central American, ex. Mexican	3.85
Guatemalan	4.74
Salvadoran	3.87
Cuban	3.23
Dominican Republic	3.85
Mexican	4.00
Puerto Rican	3.36
South American	3.60
Colombian	3.53
Peruvian	3.70
Spaniard	3.07

Median Age

Group	Years
Total Population	28.6
Hispanic or Latino (of any race)	22.2
Central American, ex. Mexican	31.3
Guatemalan	24.7
Salvadoran	33.8
Cuban	23.3
Dominican Republic	29.3
Mexican	21.2
Puerto Rican	27.0
South American	29.5
Colombian	31.2
Peruvian	28.6
Spaniard	27.9

High School Graduates
(Universe: Population 25 Years and Over)

Group	Number	%
Total Population	32,858	92.1
Hispanic or Latino (of any race)	5,204	79.2
Mexican	4,115	76.5

Four-Year College Graduates
(Universe: Population 25 Years and Over)

Group	Number	%
Total Population	7,579	21.2
Hispanic or Latino (of any race)	913	13.9
Mexican	826	15.3

Population Age 3–17 Enrolled in Public School
(Universe: Population Age 3–17 Enrolled in School)

Group	Number	%
Total Population	14,344	90.2
Hispanic or Latino (of any race)	4,306	94.3
Mexican	3,622	94.1

Population Age 3–17 Enrolled in Private School
(Universe: Population Age 3–17 Enrolled in School)

Group	Number	%
Total Population	1,557	9.8
Hispanic or Latino (of any race)	261	5.7
Mexican	226	5.9

Foreign-Born Population

Group	Number	%
Total Population	4,863	7.6
Hispanic or Latino (of any race)	2,803	19.0
Mexican	2,211	18.0

Foreign-Born Naturalized U.S. Citizens

Group	Number	%
Total Population	1,920	39.5
Hispanic or Latino (of any race)	1,002	35.7
Mexican	718	32.5

Language Spoken at Home: English Only
(Universe: Population 5 Years and Over)

Group	Number	%
Total Population	45,857	81.9
Hispanic or Latino (of any race)	5,956	47.5
Mexican	4,905	47.3

Language Spoken at Home: Spanish
(Universe: Population 5 Years and Over)

Group	Number	%
Total Population	7,449	13.3
Hispanic or Latino (of any race)	6,493	51.8
Mexican	5,403	52.1

Unemployment Rate
(Universe: Population 16 Years and Over)

Group	%
Total Population	6.5
Hispanic or Latino (of any race)	6.9
Mexican	6.4

Class of Worker: Private Wage and Salary
(Universe: Civilian Employed Population 16 Years and Over)

Group	Number	%
Total Population	23,042	78.9
Hispanic or Latino (of any race)	4,206	75.0
Mexican	3,511	74.6

Class of Worker: Government
(Universe: Civilian Employed Population 16 Years and Over)

Group	Number	%
Total Population	4,755	16.3
Hispanic or Latino (of any race)	1,177	21.0
Mexican	1,021	21.7

Means of Transportation to Work: Car, Truck or Van
(Universe: Workers 16 Years and Over)

Group	Number	%
Total Population	26,345	92.9
Hispanic or Latino (of any race)	5,220	94.2
Mexican	4,436	94.5

Means of Transportation to Work: Public Transportation (ex. Taxicab)
(Universe: Workers 16 Years and Over)

Group	Number	%
Total Population	47	0.2
Hispanic or Latino (of any race)	19	0.3
Mexican	19	0.4

Homeownership Rate
(Universe: Occupied Housing Units)

Group	%
Total Population	77.3
Hispanic or Latino (of any race)	76.3
Central American, ex. Mexican	79.3
Guatemalan	81.5
Salvadoran	81.5
Cuban	74.3
Dominican Republic	88.5
Mexican	75.9
Puerto Rican	76.2
South American	83.3
Colombian	82.4
Peruvian	81.8
Spaniard	78.8

Median Home Value

Group	Dollars
Total Population	196,900
Hispanic or Latino (of any race)	187,200
Mexican	180,500

Median Gross Rent

Group	Dollars
Total Population	1,172
Hispanic or Latino (of any race)	965
Mexican	956

Median Household Income
(2010 Inflation-Adjusted Dollars)

Group	Dollars
Total Population	62,297
Hispanic or Latino (of any race)	61,517
Mexican	63,029

Per Capita Income
(2010 Inflation-Adjusted Dollars)

Group	Dollars
Total Population	22,462
Hispanic or Latino (of any race)	15,587
Mexican	15,459

Households with $100,000+ Income

Group	Number	%
Total Population	3,251	15.2
Hispanic or Latino (of any race)	587	16.0
Mexican	476	16.3

Households with Food Stamps/SNAP Benefits During Past 12 Months

Group	Number	%
Total Population	1,354	6.3
Hispanic or Latino (of any race)	187	5.1
Mexican	135	4.6

Poverty Rate
(Income in Past 12 Months Below Poverty Level)

Group	%
Total Population	7.4
Hispanic or Latino (of any race)	9.4
Mexican	10.4

Scottsdale

Population

Group	Number	%TP[1]	%HP[2]
Total Population	217,385	100.0	–
Hispanic or Latino (of any race)	19,225	8.8	100.0
Central American, ex. Mexican	461	0.2	2.4
Guatemalan	138	0.1	0.7
Cuban	317	0.1	1.6
Mexican	14,398	6.6	74.9
Puerto Rican	827	0.4	4.3
South American	1,093	0.5	5.7
Argentinean	172	0.1	0.9
Colombian	392	0.2	2.0
Peruvian	191	0.1	1.0
Spaniard	679	0.3	3.5

Population Growth: 2000–2010

Group	%
Total Population	7.2
Hispanic or Latino (of any race)	36.2

Notes: (1) Percent of total population; (2) Percent of Hispanic/Latino population; Profiles include places with an overall population of at least 125,000, OR an overall population of at least 25,000 where the Hispanic/Latino population is at least 20% of the overall population. In states where less than five places meet either of these criteria, we have included places with at least 10,000 total population with the highest percentage of Hispanic/Latino population. These places are identified with an asterisk (*); Please refer to the User's Guide for a full explanation of data.

Central American, ex. Mexican	163.4
Cuban	42.8
Mexican	42.4
Puerto Rican	41.9
South American	118.6
Colombian	132.0

Males per 100 Females

Group	Number
Total Population	93.3
Hispanic or Latino (of any race)	94.2
Central American, ex. Mexican	87.4
Guatemalan	112.3
Cuban	95.7
Mexican	98.2
Puerto Rican	81.8
South American	81.3
Argentinean	132.4
Colombian	73.5
Peruvian	81.9
Spaniard	81.1

Average Household Size

Group	People
Total Population	2.14
Hispanic or Latino (of any race)	2.86
Central American, ex. Mexican	2.61
Guatemalan	2.89
Cuban	2.26
Mexican	3.06
Puerto Rican	2.33
South American	2.53
Argentinean	2.39
Colombian	2.44
Peruvian	2.87
Spaniard	2.20

Median Age

Group	Years
Total Population	45.4
Hispanic or Latino (of any race)	28.4
Central American, ex. Mexican	31.6
Guatemalan	25.4
Cuban	37.9
Mexican	26.8
Puerto Rican	32.4
South American	38.2
Argentinean	49.3
Colombian	37.7
Peruvian	32.8
Spaniard	39.8

High School Graduates
(Universe: Population 25 Years and Over)

Group	Number	%
Total Population	155,608	95.6
Hispanic or Latino (of any race)	7,909	77.4
Mexican	5,353	71.3
South American	802	100.0

Four-Year College Graduates
(Universe: Population 25 Years and Over)

Group	Number	%
Total Population	84,423	51.9
Hispanic or Latino (of any race)	3,386	33.1
Mexican	2,116	28.2
South American	528	65.8

Population Age 3–17 Enrolled in Public School
(Universe: Population Age 3–17 Enrolled in School)

Group	Number	%
Total Population	25,257	80.2
Hispanic or Latino (of any race)	3,894	87.3
Mexican	3,341	87.5
South American	69	61.1

Population Age 3–17 Enrolled in Private School
(Universe: Population Age 3–17 Enrolled in School)

Group	Number	%
Total Population	6,230	19.8
Hispanic or Latino (of any race)	565	12.7
Mexican	478	12.5
South American	44	38.9

Foreign-Born Population

Group	Number	%
Total Population	23,399	10.7
Hispanic or Latino (of any race)	6,465	34.0
Mexican	5,161	34.3
South American	710	63.2

Foreign-Born Naturalized U.S. Citizens

Group	Number	%
Total Population	10,972	46.9
Hispanic or Latino (of any race)	1,514	23.4
Mexican	844	16.4
South American	388	54.6

Language Spoken at Home: English Only
(Universe: Population 5 Years and Over)

Group	Number	%
Total Population	180,496	86.4
Hispanic or Latino (of any race)	6,567	38.2
Mexican	4,532	33.8
South American	393	35.0

Language Spoken at Home: Spanish
(Universe: Population 5 Years and Over)

Group	Number	%
Total Population	13,912	6.7
Hispanic or Latino (of any race)	10,542	61.2
Mexican	8,850	66.0
South American	705	62.8

Unemployment Rate
(Universe: Population 16 Years and Over)

Group	%
Total Population	4.8
Hispanic or Latino (of any race)	5.4
Mexican	5.9
South American	0.0

Class of Worker: Private Wage and Salary
(Universe: Civilian Employed Population 16 Years and Over)

Group	Number	%
Total Population	93,123	83.3
Hispanic or Latino (of any race)	8,596	90.1
Mexican	6,604	91.5
South American	668	85.2

Class of Worker: Government
(Universe: Civilian Employed Population 16 Years and Over)

Group	Number	%
Total Population	9,648	8.6
Hispanic or Latino (of any race)	510	5.3
Mexican	341	4.7
South American	74	9.4

Means of Transportation to Work: Car, Truck or Van
(Universe: Workers 16 Years and Over)

Group	Number	%
Total Population	93,051	85.2
Hispanic or Latino (of any race)	7,435	80.2
Mexican	5,559	78.8
South American	657	85.5

Means of Transportation to Work: Public Transportation (ex. Taxicab)
(Universe: Workers 16 Years and Over)

Group	Number	%
Total Population	1,455	1.3
Hispanic or Latino (of any race)	492	5.3
Mexican	437	6.2
South American	0	0.0

Homeownership Rate
(Universe: Occupied Housing Units)

Group	%
Total Population	68.1
Hispanic or Latino (of any race)	44.0
Central American, ex. Mexican	46.5
Guatemalan	41.7
Cuban	60.9
Mexican	40.9
Puerto Rican	48.4
South American	56.3
Argentinean	72.2
Colombian	52.3
Peruvian	61.3
Spaniard	57.8

Median Home Value

Group	Dollars
Total Population	457,700
Hispanic or Latino (of any race)	327,400
Mexican	280,500
South American	390,400

Median Gross Rent

Group	Dollars
Total Population	1,100
Hispanic or Latino (of any race)	911
Mexican	912
South American	858

Median Household Income
(2010 Inflation-Adjusted Dollars)

Group	Dollars
Total Population	71,564
Hispanic or Latino (of any race)	53,256
Mexican	52,408
South American	66,280

Per Capita Income
(2010 Inflation-Adjusted Dollars)

Group	Dollars
Total Population	51,090
Hispanic or Latino (of any race)	24,662
Mexican	21,166
South American	43,748

Households with $100,000+ Income

Group	Number	%
Total Population	35,793	35.6
Hispanic or Latino (of any race)	1,340	22.7
Mexican	899	20.4
South American	102	29.7

Households with Food Stamps/SNAP Benefits During Past 12 Months

Group	Number	%
Total Population	2,029	2.0
Hispanic or Latino (of any race)	313	5.3
Mexican	273	6.2
South American	0	0.0

Poverty Rate
(Income in Past 12 Months Below Poverty Level)

Group	%
Total Population	6.9
Hispanic or Latino (of any race)	14.1
Mexican	16.1
South American	5.9

Tempe

Population

Group	Number	%TP[1]	%HP[2]
Total Population	161,719	100.0	–
Hispanic or Latino (of any race)	34,092	21.1	100.0
Central American, ex. Mexican	679	0.4	2.0
Guatemalan	181	0.1	0.5
Salvadoran	193	0.1	0.6
Cuban	324	0.2	1.0
Mexican	28,204	17.4	82.7
Puerto Rican	1,040	0.6	3.1
South American	914	0.6	2.7
Argentinean	134	0.1	0.4
Colombian	285	0.2	0.8
Peruvian	188	0.1	0.6
Spaniard	687	0.4	2.0

Population Growth: 2000–2010

Group	%
Total Population	2.0
Hispanic or Latino (of any race)	19.7
Central American, ex. Mexican	107.0
Cuban	80.0
Mexican	27.2
Puerto Rican	58.5
South American	68.6
Colombian	68.6

Notes: (1) Percent of total population; (2) Percent of Hispanic/Latino population; Profiles include places with an overall population of at least 125,000, OR an overall population of at least 25,000 where the Hispanic/Latino population is at least 20% of the overall population. In states where less than five places meet either of these criteria, we have included places with at least 10,000 total population with the highest percentage of Hispanic/Latino population. These places are identified with an asterisk (*); Please refer to the User's Guide for a full explanation of data.

Males per 100 Females	
Group	Number
Total Population	108.6
Hispanic or Latino (of any race)	106.4
Central American, ex. Mexican	101.5
Guatemalan	108.0
Salvadoran	107.5
Cuban	121.9
Mexican	106.2
Puerto Rican	118.0
South American	103.1
Argentinean	86.1
Colombian	82.7
Peruvian	135.0
Spaniard	96.8

Average Household Size	
Group	People
Total Population	2.30
Hispanic or Latino (of any race)	2.94
Central American, ex. Mexican	2.63
Guatemalan	3.41
Salvadoran	2.89
Cuban	2.43
Mexican	3.04
Puerto Rican	2.34
South American	2.30
Argentinean	2.37
Colombian	2.25
Peruvian	2.23
Spaniard	2.35

Median Age	
Group	Years
Total Population	28.1
Hispanic or Latino (of any race)	24.4
Central American, ex. Mexican	26.1
Guatemalan	25.8
Salvadoran	27.3
Cuban	23.0
Mexican	24.4
Puerto Rican	23.2
South American	28.5
Argentinean	30.4
Colombian	28.8
Peruvian	29.0
Spaniard	27.0

High School Graduates (Universe: Population 25 Years and Over)		
Group	Number	%
Total Population	83,346	89.8
Hispanic or Latino (of any race)	10,021	64.2
Mexican	7,861	59.6

Four-Year College Graduates (Universe: Population 25 Years and Over)		
Group	Number	%
Total Population	38,388	41.3
Hispanic or Latino (of any race)	2,934	18.8
Mexican	1,915	14.5

Population Age 3–17 Enrolled in Public School (Universe: Population Age 3–17 Enrolled in School)		
Group	Number	%
Total Population	19,793	89.7
Hispanic or Latino (of any race)	6,934	95.7
Mexican	6,216	96.2

Population Age 3–17 Enrolled in Private School (Universe: Population Age 3–17 Enrolled in School)		
Group	Number	%
Total Population	2,281	10.3
Hispanic or Latino (of any race)	310	4.3
Mexican	247	3.8

Foreign-Born Population		
Group	Number	%
Total Population	25,064	15.3
Hispanic or Latino (of any race)	10,378	31.4
Mexican	9,461	33.2

Foreign-Born Naturalized U.S. Citizens		
Group	Number	%
Total Population	6,169	24.6
Hispanic or Latino (of any race)	1,609	15.5
Mexican	1,268	13.4

Language Spoken at Home: English Only (Universe: Population 5 Years and Over)		
Group	Number	%
Total Population	119,194	76.7
Hispanic or Latino (of any race)	11,697	38.9
Mexican	9,218	35.8

Language Spoken at Home: Spanish (Universe: Population 5 Years and Over)		
Group	Number	%
Total Population	19,942	12.8
Hispanic or Latino (of any race)	18,190	60.5
Mexican	16,417	63.8

Unemployment Rate (Universe: Population 16 Years and Over)	
Group	%
Total Population	7.9
Hispanic or Latino (of any race)	8.4
Mexican	8.4

Class of Worker: Private Wage and Salary (Universe: Civilian Employed Population 16 Years and Over)		
Group	Number	%
Total Population	71,296	79.7
Hispanic or Latino (of any race)	13,578	84.9
Mexican	11,665	86.2

Class of Worker: Government (Universe: Civilian Employed Population 16 Years and Over)		
Group	Number	%
Total Population	14,059	15.7
Hispanic or Latino (of any race)	1,894	11.8
Mexican	1,522	11.2

Means of Transportation to Work: Car, Truck or Van (Universe: Workers 16 Years and Over)		
Group	Number	%
Total Population	70,652	80.7
Hispanic or Latino (of any race)	12,807	81.5
Mexican	10,902	82.1

Means of Transportation to Work: Public Transportation (ex. Taxicab) (Universe: Workers 16 Years and Over)		
Group	Number	%
Total Population	4,601	5.3
Hispanic or Latino (of any race)	1,269	8.1
Mexican	977	7.4

Homeownership Rate (Universe: Occupied Housing Units)	
Group	%
Total Population	44.5
Hispanic or Latino (of any race)	34.6
Central American, ex. Mexican	30.8
Guatemalan	28.6
Salvadoran	33.8
Cuban	38.1
Mexican	35.5
Puerto Rican	19.5
South American	35.9
Argentinean	42.3
Colombian	36.8
Peruvian	33.3
Spaniard	44.6

Median Home Value	
Group	Dollars
Total Population	248,500
Hispanic or Latino (of any race)	215,200
Mexican	201,100

Median Gross Rent	
Group	Dollars
Total Population	886
Hispanic or Latino (of any race)	825
Mexican	815

Median Household Income (2010 Inflation-Adjusted Dollars)	
Group	Dollars
Total Population	47,443
Hispanic or Latino (of any race)	40,017
Mexican	38,908

Per Capita Income (2010 Inflation-Adjusted Dollars)	
Group	Dollars
Total Population	26,234
Hispanic or Latino (of any race)	16,213
Mexican	14,840

Households with $100,000+ Income		
Group	Number	%
Total Population	12,073	18.8
Hispanic or Latino (of any race)	1,257	12.9
Mexican	746	9.5

Households with Food Stamps/SNAP Benefits During Past 12 Months		
Group	Number	%
Total Population	4,713	7.3
Hispanic or Latino (of any race)	1,286	13.2
Mexican	1,146	14.6

Poverty Rate (Income in Past 12 Months Below Poverty Level)	
Group	%
Total Population	20.6
Hispanic or Latino (of any race)	25.7
Mexican	26.9

Tucson

Population			
Group	Number	%TP[1]	%HP[2]
Total Population	520,116	100.0	–
Hispanic or Latino (of any race)	216,308	41.6	100.0
Central American, ex. Mexican	2,527	0.5	1.2
Costa Rican	125	<0.1	0.1
Guatemalan	672	0.1	0.3
Honduran	336	0.1	0.2
Nicaraguan	277	0.1	0.1
Panamanian	319	0.1	0.1
Salvadoran	778	0.1	0.4
Cuban	992	0.2	0.5
Dominican Republic	223	<0.1	0.1
Mexican	193,994	37.3	89.7
Puerto Rican	3,359	0.6	1.6
South American	1,973	0.4	0.9
Argentinean	265	0.1	0.1
Bolivian	103	<0.1	<0.1
Chilean	293	0.1	0.1
Colombian	570	0.1	0.3
Ecuadorian	147	<0.1	0.1
Peruvian	382	0.1	0.2
Venezuelan	153	<0.1	0.1
Spaniard	1,987	0.4	0.9

Population Growth: 2000–2010	
Group	%
Total Population	6.9
Hispanic or Latino (of any race)	24.4
Central American, ex. Mexican	98.7
Guatemalan	140.9
Honduran	143.5
Nicaraguan	102.2
Panamanian	24.6
Salvadoran	150.2
Cuban	55.0
Mexican	33.6
Puerto Rican	60.2
South American	97.5
Argentinean	132.5
Chilean	79.8
Colombian	131.7
Peruvian	82.8
Spaniard	745.5

Males per 100 Females	
Group	Number
Total Population	97.9

Notes: (1) Percent of total population; (2) Percent of Hispanic/Latino population; Profiles include places with an overall population of at least 125,000, OR an overall population of at least 25,000 where the Hispanic/Latino population is at least 20% of the overall population. In states where less than five places meet either of these criteria, we have included places with at least 10,000 total population with the highest percentage of Hispanic/Latino population. These places are identified with an asterisk (*); Please refer to the User's Guide for a full explanation of data.

Hispanic or Latino (of any race)	96.1
Central American, ex. Mexican	97.7
Costa Rican	89.4
Guatemalan	114.7
Honduran	106.1
Nicaraguan	108.3
Panamanian	66.1
Salvadoran	94.0
Cuban	113.3
Dominican Republic	134.7
Mexican	96.2
Puerto Rican	111.4
South American	89.7
Argentinean	94.9
Bolivian	80.7
Chilean	90.3
Colombian	78.7
Ecuadorian	113.0
Peruvian	95.9
Venezuelan	101.3
Spaniard	84.8

Average Household Size

Group	People
Total Population	2.43
Hispanic or Latino (of any race)	3.06
Central American, ex. Mexican	3.11
Costa Rican	2.46
Guatemalan	3.47
Honduran	2.89
Nicaraguan	3.25
Panamanian	2.29
Salvadoran	3.34
Cuban	2.43
Dominican Republic	2.65
Mexican	3.11
Puerto Rican	2.44
South American	2.36
Argentinean	2.18
Bolivian	2.91
Chilean	2.30
Colombian	2.38
Ecuadorian	2.87
Peruvian	2.25
Venezuelan	2.69
Spaniard	2.35

Median Age

Group	Years
Total Population	33.0
Hispanic or Latino (of any race)	26.9
Central American, ex. Mexican	30.4
Costa Rican	29.5
Guatemalan	31.5
Honduran	27.9
Nicaraguan	29.1
Panamanian	34.1
Salvadoran	30.6
Cuban	28.4
Dominican Republic	24.5
Mexican	26.8
Puerto Rican	26.8
South American	32.3
Argentinean	35.6
Bolivian	29.5
Chilean	33.5
Colombian	29.5
Ecuadorian	28.8
Peruvian	35.5
Venezuelan	27.9
Spaniard	31.5

High School Graduates
(Universe: Population 25 Years and Over)

Group	Number	%
Total Population	271,154	83.7
Hispanic or Latino (of any race)	75,847	68.2
Central American, ex. Mexican	1,068	59.5
Mexican	67,843	67.3
Puerto Rican	1,354	87.4
South American	1,255	88.4
Spaniard	626	82.3

Four-Year College Graduates
(Universe: Population 25 Years and Over)

Group	Number	%
Total Population	81,415	25.1
Hispanic or Latino (of any race)	12,397	11.1
Central American, ex. Mexican	281	15.7
Mexican	10,103	10.0
Puerto Rican	427	27.5
South American	574	40.4
Spaniard	199	26.1

Population Age 3–17 Enrolled in Public School
(Universe: Population Age 3–17 Enrolled in School)

Group	Number	%
Total Population	78,582	90.9
Hispanic or Latino (of any race)	46,371	94.0
Central American, ex. Mexican	540	91.7
Mexican	43,495	94.2
Puerto Rican	667	95.7
South American	204	84.3
Spaniard	54	50.9

Population Age 3–17 Enrolled in Private School
(Universe: Population Age 3–17 Enrolled in School)

Group	Number	%
Total Population	7,835	9.1
Hispanic or Latino (of any race)	2,984	6.0
Central American, ex. Mexican	49	8.3
Mexican	2,673	5.8
Puerto Rican	30	4.3
South American	38	15.7
Spaniard	52	49.1

Foreign-Born Population

Group	Number	%
Total Population	82,843	16.0
Hispanic or Latino (of any race)	59,837	28.6
Central American, ex. Mexican	1,644	55.6
Mexican	55,437	29.0
Puerto Rican	84	2.6
South American	1,463	65.7
Spaniard	160	14.3

Foreign-Born Naturalized U.S. Citizens

Group	Number	%
Total Population	28,208	34.0
Hispanic or Latino (of any race)	16,530	27.6
Central American, ex. Mexican	737	44.8
Mexican	14,486	26.1
Puerto Rican	34	40.5
South American	713	48.7
Spaniard	58	36.3

Language Spoken at Home: English Only
(Universe: Population 5 Years and Over)

Group	Number	%
Total Population	319,445	66.2
Hispanic or Latino (of any race)	56,361	29.9
Central American, ex. Mexican	737	26.3
Mexican	48,993	28.4
Puerto Rican	1,496	53.9
South American	461	22.5
Spaniard	615	58.6

Language Spoken at Home: Spanish
(Universe: Population 5 Years and Over)

Group	Number	%
Total Population	138,886	28.8
Hispanic or Latino (of any race)	132,036	69.9
Central American, ex. Mexican	2,032	72.5
Mexican	123,177	71.4
Puerto Rican	1,266	45.6
South American	1,554	76.0
Spaniard	398	37.9

Unemployment Rate
(Universe: Population 16 Years and Over)

Group	%
Total Population	8.6
Hispanic or Latino (of any race)	10.9
Central American, ex. Mexican	12.8
Mexican	11.0
Puerto Rican	8.4
South American	13.9
Spaniard	9.2

Class of Worker: Private Wage and Salary
(Universe: Civilian Employed Population 16 Years and Over)

Group	Number	%
Total Population	173,729	74.3
Hispanic or Latino (of any race)	64,905	75.9
Central American, ex. Mexican	1,135	78.3
Mexican	58,814	75.8
Puerto Rican	1,041	76.3
South American	873	75.6
Spaniard	299	79.7

Class of Worker: Government
(Universe: Civilian Employed Population 16 Years and Over)

Group	Number	%
Total Population	44,029	18.8
Hispanic or Latino (of any race)	14,112	16.5
Central American, ex. Mexican	206	14.2
Mexican	12,777	16.5
Puerto Rican	208	15.2
South American	209	18.1
Spaniard	44	11.7

Means of Transportation to Work: Car, Truck or Van
(Universe: Workers 16 Years and Over)

Group	Number	%
Total Population	196,425	84.3
Hispanic or Latino (of any race)	72,181	85.9
Central American, ex. Mexican	1,331	90.1
Mexican	65,559	86.0
Puerto Rican	1,055	75.8
South American	982	83.8
Spaniard	343	89.8

Means of Transportation to Work: Public Transportation (ex. Taxicab)
(Universe: Workers 16 Years and Over)

Group	Number	%
Total Population	8,362	3.6
Hispanic or Latino (of any race)	3,228	3.8
Central American, ex. Mexican	52	3.5
Mexican	2,966	3.9
Puerto Rican	103	7.4
South American	0	0.0
Spaniard	13	3.4

Homeownership Rate
(Universe: Occupied Housing Units)

Group	%
Total Population	51.9
Hispanic or Latino (of any race)	48.5
Central American, ex. Mexican	52.6
Costa Rican	50.0
Guatemalan	54.5
Honduran	42.9
Nicaraguan	57.1
Panamanian	54.5
Salvadoran	53.6
Cuban	35.9
Dominican Republic	34.1
Mexican	49.3
Puerto Rican	38.5
South American	48.7
Argentinean	42.5
Bolivian	53.1
Chilean	51.6
Colombian	49.5
Ecuadorian	52.7
Peruvian	52.8
Venezuelan	41.0
Spaniard	50.2

Median Home Value

Group	Dollars
Total Population	171,200
Hispanic or Latino (of any race)	146,300
Central American, ex. Mexican	154,700
Mexican	145,100
Puerto Rican	171,700
South American	217,200
Spaniard	125,000

Median Gross Rent

Group	Dollars
Total Population	690

Notes: (1) Percent of total population; (2) Percent of Hispanic/Latino population; Profiles include places with an overall population of at least 125,000, OR an overall population of at least 25,000 where the Hispanic/Latino population is at least 20% of the overall population. In states where less than five places meet either of these criteria, we have included places with at least 10,000 total population with the highest percentage of Hispanic/Latino population. These places are identified with an asterisk (*); Please refer to the User's Guide for a full explanation of data.

Hispanic or Latino (of any race)	664
Central American, ex. Mexican	663
Mexican	662
Puerto Rican	706
South American	779
Spaniard	730

Median Household Income
(2010 Inflation-Adjusted Dollars)

Group	Dollars
Total Population	37,025
Hispanic or Latino (of any race)	32,087
Central American, ex. Mexican	31,900
Mexican	32,203
Puerto Rican	28,368
South American	55,673
Spaniard	28,594

Per Capita Income
(2010 Inflation-Adjusted Dollars)

Group	Dollars
Total Population	20,243
Hispanic or Latino (of any race)	13,448
Central American, ex. Mexican	15,960
Mexican	13,137
Puerto Rican	15,569
South American	20,335
Spaniard	25,436

Households with $100,000+ Income

Group	Number	%
Total Population	20,568	9.9
Hispanic or Latino (of any race)	3,852	5.9
Central American, ex. Mexican	84	7.1
Mexican	3,302	5.6
Puerto Rican	86	7.7
South American	160	17.8
Spaniard	55	10.5

Households with Food Stamps/SNAP Benefits During Past 12 Months

Group	Number	%
Total Population	27,720	13.4
Hispanic or Latino (of any race)	13,940	21.3
Central American, ex. Mexican	187	15.8
Mexican	12,621	21.5
Puerto Rican	367	32.7
South American	40	4.4
Spaniard	62	11.8

Poverty Rate
(Income in Past 12 Months Below Poverty Level)

Group	%
Total Population	21.3
Hispanic or Latino (of any race)	26.8
Central American, ex. Mexican	22.0
Mexican	27.1
Puerto Rican	32.9
South American	15.1
Spaniard	20.2

Yuma

Population

Group	Number	%TP[1]	%HP[2]
Total Population	93,064	100.0	–
Hispanic or Latino (of any race)	51,033	54.8	100.0
Central American, ex. Mexican	447	0.5	0.9
Salvadoran	246	0.3	0.5
Cuban	105	0.1	0.2
Mexican	47,190	50.7	92.5
Puerto Rican	669	0.7	1.3
South American	233	0.3	0.5
Spaniard	273	0.3	0.5

Population Growth: 2000–2010

Group	%
Total Population	20.1
Hispanic or Latino (of any race)	44.2
Central American, ex. Mexican	134.0
Mexican	54.7
Puerto Rican	58.5
South American	113.8

Males per 100 Females

Group	Number
Total Population	103.4
Hispanic or Latino (of any race)	98.5
Central American, ex. Mexican	119.1
Salvadoran	129.9
Cuban	191.7
Mexican	98.2
Puerto Rican	128.3
South American	82.0
Spaniard	87.0

Average Household Size

Group	People
Total Population	2.86
Hispanic or Latino (of any race)	3.51
Central American, ex. Mexican	3.75
Salvadoran	3.91
Cuban	2.37
Mexican	3.55
Puerto Rican	2.90
South American	2.82
Spaniard	2.66

Median Age

Group	Years
Total Population	31.3
Hispanic or Latino (of any race)	25.2
Central American, ex. Mexican	28.9
Salvadoran	28.0
Cuban	27.9
Mexican	25.2
Puerto Rican	25.4
South American	28.5
Spaniard	26.7

High School Graduates
(Universe: Population 25 Years and Over)

Group	Number	%
Total Population	41,007	77.1
Hispanic or Latino (of any race)	15,106	62.5
Mexican	14,076	61.9

Four-Year College Graduates
(Universe: Population 25 Years and Over)

Group	Number	%
Total Population	8,438	15.9
Hispanic or Latino (of any race)	1,848	7.6
Mexican	1,673	7.4

Population Age 3–17 Enrolled in Public School
(Universe: Population Age 3–17 Enrolled in School)

Group	Number	%
Total Population	17,338	92.2
Hispanic or Latino (of any race)	12,474	94.8
Mexican	11,829	94.7

Population Age 3–17 Enrolled in Private School
(Universe: Population Age 3–17 Enrolled in School)

Group	Number	%
Total Population	1,458	7.8
Hispanic or Latino (of any race)	683	5.2
Mexican	660	5.3

Foreign-Born Population

Group	Number	%
Total Population	18,964	20.8
Hispanic or Latino (of any race)	15,709	31.5
Mexican	15,228	32.5

Foreign-Born Naturalized U.S. Citizens

Group	Number	%
Total Population	6,455	34.0
Hispanic or Latino (of any race)	5,475	34.9
Mexican	5,252	34.5

Language Spoken at Home: English Only
(Universe: Population 5 Years and Over)

Group	Number	%
Total Population	46,625	55.7
Hispanic or Latino (of any race)	10,979	24.6
Mexican	9,763	23.3

Language Spoken at Home: Spanish
(Universe: Population 5 Years and Over)

Group	Number	%
Total Population	34,784	41.6
Hispanic or Latino (of any race)	33,537	75.2
Mexican	32,037	76.5

Unemployment Rate
(Universe: Population 16 Years and Over)

Group	%
Total Population	9.1
Hispanic or Latino (of any race)	10.8
Mexican	11.0

Class of Worker: Private Wage and Salary
(Universe: Civilian Employed Population 16 Years and Over)

Group	Number	%
Total Population	25,642	70.6
Hispanic or Latino (of any race)	15,681	76.0
Mexican	14,903	76.6

Class of Worker: Government
(Universe: Civilian Employed Population 16 Years and Over)

Group	Number	%
Total Population	8,569	23.6
Hispanic or Latino (of any race)	3,945	19.1
Mexican	3,580	18.4

Means of Transportation to Work: Car, Truck or Van
(Universe: Workers 16 Years and Over)

Group	Number	%
Total Population	34,598	90.4
Hispanic or Latino (of any race)	19,305	92.2
Mexican	18,103	92.6

Means of Transportation to Work: Public Transportation (ex. Taxicab)
(Universe: Workers 16 Years and Over)

Group	Number	%
Total Population	249	0.7
Hispanic or Latino (of any race)	83	0.4
Mexican	67	0.3

Homeownership Rate
(Universe: Occupied Housing Units)

Group	%
Total Population	62.0
Hispanic or Latino (of any race)	57.8
Central American, ex. Mexican	44.4
Salvadoran	41.5
Cuban	42.9
Mexican	59.0
Puerto Rican	50.5
South American	57.0
Spaniard	51.1

Median Home Value

Group	Dollars
Total Population	159,600
Hispanic or Latino (of any race)	166,300
Mexican	164,700

Median Gross Rent

Group	Dollars
Total Population	773
Hispanic or Latino (of any race)	726
Mexican	705

Median Household Income
(2010 Inflation-Adjusted Dollars)

Group	Dollars
Total Population	43,343
Hispanic or Latino (of any race)	40,262
Mexican	39,409

Per Capita Income
(2010 Inflation-Adjusted Dollars)

Group	Dollars
Total Population	20,472
Hispanic or Latino (of any race)	15,271
Mexican	14,949

Households with $100,000+ Income

Group	Number	%
Total Population	4,221	12.4

Notes: (1) Percent of total population; (2) Percent of Hispanic/Latino population; Profiles include places with an overall population of at least 125,000, OR an overall population of at least 25,000 where the Hispanic/Latino population is at least 20% of the overall population. In states where less than five places meet either of these criteria, we have included places with at least 10,000 total population with the highest percentage of Hispanic/Latino population. These places are identified with an asterisk (*); Please refer to the User's Guide for a full explanation of data.

Hispanic or Latino (of any race)	1,495	9.5
Mexican	1,288	8.8

Households with Food Stamps/SNAP Benefits During Past 12 Months

Group	Number	%
Total Population	5,351	15.7
Hispanic or Latino (of any race)	3,612	23.0
Mexican	3,345	23.0

Poverty Rate
(Income in Past 12 Months Below Poverty Level)

Group	%
Total Population	18.5
Hispanic or Latino (of any race)	24.2
Mexican	24.6

Notes: (1) Percent of total population; (2) Percent of Hispanic/Latino population; Profiles include places with an overall population of at least 125,000, OR an overall population of at least 25,000 where the Hispanic/Latino population is at least 20% of the overall population. In states where less than five places meet either of these criteria, we have included places with at least 10,000 total population with the highest percentage of Hispanic/Latino population. These places are identified with an asterisk (*); Please refer to the User's Guide for a full explanation of data.

Arkansas

EDITOR'S NOTE: For a place to be included in this edition, it must meet one of two criteria. Either its overall population is at least 125,000, OR its overall population is at least 25,000 and its Hispanic/Latino population is at least 20% of the overall population. In Arkansas, less than five places meet either of these criteria. In an effort to include at least five places for each state, we have included places with at least 10,000 total population with the highest percentage of Hispanic/Latino population. These places are identified with an asterisk (*). For the state of Arkansas, the following locations are included:

- Hope*
- Little Rock
- Rogers
- Siloam Springs*
- Springdale

Section Two: State & Place Profiles starts with the state profile, followed by place profiles that meet the criteria above. Places are listed alphabetically within each state. All states, all counties and places that meet the above criteria are ranked and compared in *Section Three: Rankings & Comparisons*, on page 1055.

For a more detailed look at the Hispanic/Latino population in Arkansas, a companion web site is available at no additional charge with purchase of this print edition. Visit http://gold.greyhouse.com/page/info_hispanic for more information.

The web site includes data for all counties and places in Arkansas with Hispanic/Latino population, plus ten additional topics: Self Employed Worker; Walked to Work; Worked from Home; Mean Travel Time to Work; Mean Household Income; Households with Cash Public Assistance; Mean Cash Pubic Assistance; Poverty Rates for 18 and Under, 18 to 64, and 65 and Over.

Population

Group	Number	%TP[1]	%HP[2]
Total Population	2,915,918	100.0	–
Hispanic or Latino (of any race)	186,050	6.4	100.0
Central American, ex. Mexican	23,216	0.8	12.5
Costa Rican	333	<0.1	0.2
Guatemalan	4,533	0.2	2.4
Honduran	2,076	0.1	1.1
Nicaraguan	704	<0.1	0.4
Panamanian	485	<0.1	0.3
Salvadoran	14,980	0.5	8.1
Cuban	1,493	0.1	0.8
Dominican Republic	384	<0.1	0.2
Mexican	138,194	4.7	74.3
Puerto Rican	4,789	0.2	2.6
South American	3,028	0.1	1.6
Argentinean	338	<0.1	0.2
Bolivian	260	<0.1	0.1
Chilean	219	<0.1	0.1
Colombian	888	<0.1	0.5
Ecuadorian	302	<0.1	0.2
Peruvian	650	<0.1	0.3
Venezuelan	300	<0.1	0.2
Spaniard	1,902	0.1	1.0

Population Growth: 2000–2010

Group	%
Total Population	9.1
Hispanic or Latino (of any race)	114.2
Central American, ex. Mexican	303.5
Costa Rican	150.4
Guatemalan	334.2
Honduran	323.7
Nicaraguan	304.6
Panamanian	98.8
Salvadoran	331.6
Cuban	57.2
Mexican	125.8
Puerto Rican	93.7
South American	183.3
Colombian	165.9
Peruvian	240.3
Venezuelan	177.8
Spaniard	1,025.4

Males per 100 Females

Group	Number
Total Population	96.5
Hispanic or Latino (of any race)	114.4
Central American, ex. Mexican	115.1
Costa Rican	95.9
Guatemalan	142.0
Honduran	124.7
Nicaraguan	108.9
Panamanian	63.9
Salvadoran	109.7
Cuban	127.6
Dominican Republic	93.9
Mexican	116.3
Puerto Rican	101.1
South American	89.5
Argentinean	100.0
Bolivian	78.1
Chilean	92.1
Colombian	87.7
Ecuadorian	91.1
Peruvian	86.8
Venezuelan	94.8
Spaniard	91.2

Average Household Size

Group	People
Total Population	2.47
Hispanic or Latino (of any race)	3.72
Central American, ex. Mexican	3.85
Costa Rican	2.97
Guatemalan	3.93
Honduran	3.76
Nicaraguan	3.56
Panamanian	2.84
Salvadoran	3.92
Cuban	2.62
Dominican Republic	2.85
Mexican	3.86
Puerto Rican	2.83
South American	2.65
Argentinean	2.65
Bolivian	2.73
Chilean	2.52
Colombian	2.56
Ecuadorian	2.85
Peruvian	2.74
Venezuelan	2.52
Spaniard	2.77

Median Age

Group	Years
Total Population	37.4
Hispanic or Latino (of any race)	23.5
Central American, ex. Mexican	28.0
Costa Rican	25.9
Guatemalan	26.9
Honduran	27.3
Nicaraguan	29.3
Panamanian	32.1
Salvadoran	28.5
Cuban	30.6
Dominican Republic	27.0
Mexican	22.3
Puerto Rican	24.5
South American	31.0
Argentinean	33.9
Bolivian	23.1
Chilean	31.8
Colombian	31.6
Ecuadorian	31.5
Peruvian	33.7
Venezuelan	28.8
Spaniard	32.0

High School Graduates
(Universe: Population 25 Years and Over)

Group	Number	%
Total Population	1,544,903	81.9
Hispanic or Latino (of any race)	38,287	49.0
Central American, ex. Mexican	3,466	33.9
Guatemalan	796	37.3
Honduran	590	67.2
Salvadoran	1,686	25.6
Cuban	318	63.5
Mexican	26,467	46.0
Puerto Rican	2,348	88.0
South American	2,032	93.6
Colombian	639	95.7
Spaniard	995	84.8

Four-Year College Graduates
(Universe: Population 25 Years and Over)

Group	Number	%
Total Population	360,760	19.1
Hispanic or Latino (of any race)	6,966	8.9
Central American, ex. Mexican	626	6.1
Guatemalan	158	7.4
Honduran	82	9.3
Salvadoran	185	2.8
Cuban	142	28.3
Mexican	3,494	6.1
Puerto Rican	766	28.7
South American	1,144	52.7
Colombian	427	63.9
Spaniard	262	22.3

Population Age 3–17 Enrolled in Public School
(Universe: Population Age 3–17 Enrolled in School)

Group	Number	%
Total Population	476,186	90.4
Hispanic or Latino (of any race)	42,866	95.0
Central American, ex. Mexican	4,366	93.8
Guatemalan	744	83.9
Honduran	453	88.5
Salvadoran	2,935	98.7
Cuban	119	100.0
Mexican	34,505	96.0
Puerto Rican	1,068	91.3
South American	549	73.2
Colombian	156	67.2
Spaniard	254	81.9

Population Age 3–17 Enrolled in Private School
(Universe: Population Age 3–17 Enrolled in School)

Group	Number	%
Total Population	50,607	9.6
Hispanic or Latino (of any race)	2,274	5.0
Central American, ex. Mexican	291	6.2
Guatemalan	143	16.1
Honduran	59	11.5
Salvadoran	40	1.3
Cuban	0	0.0
Mexican	1,447	4.0
Puerto Rican	102	8.7
South American	201	26.8
Colombian	76	32.8
Spaniard	56	18.1

Foreign-Born Population

Group	Number	%
Total Population	122,446	4.3
Hispanic or Latino (of any race)	78,318	46.5
Central American, ex. Mexican	13,227	65.0
Guatemalan	3,125	74.5
Honduran	1,208	64.6
Salvadoran	8,211	63.2
Cuban	288	38.2
Mexican	60,320	46.9
Puerto Rican	157	3.3
South American	2,183	58.0
Colombian	784	67.4

Notes: (1) Percent of total population; (2) Percent of Hispanic/Latino population; Profiles include places with an overall population of at least 125,000, OR an overall population of at least 25,000 where the Hispanic/Latino population is at least 20% of the overall population. In states where less than five places meet either of these criteria, we have included places with at least 10,000 total population with the highest percentage of Hispanic/Latino population. These places are identified with an asterisk (*); Please refer to the User's Guide for a full explanation of data.

Group	Number	%
Spaniard	194	8.4

Foreign-Born Naturalized U.S. Citizens

Group	Number	%
Total Population	34,745	28.4
Hispanic or Latino (of any race)	13,648	17.4
Central American, ex. Mexican	2,446	18.5
Guatemalan	684	21.9
Honduran	130	10.8
Salvadoran	1,389	16.9
Cuban	237	82.3
Mexican	9,379	15.5
Puerto Rican	50	31.8
South American	739	33.9
Colombian	239	30.5
Spaniard	69	35.6

Language Spoken at Home: English Only
(Universe: Population 5 Years and Over)

Group	Number	%
Total Population	2,498,432	93.3
Hispanic or Latino (of any race)	33,788	23.4
Central American, ex. Mexican	1,731	9.9
Guatemalan	437	12.1
Honduran	429	27.4
Salvadoran	680	6.0
Cuban	355	52.2
Mexican	24,021	21.9
Puerto Rican	2,162	51.3
South American	961	28.9
Colombian	201	18.7
Spaniard	1,351	71.1

Language Spoken at Home: Spanish
(Universe: Population 5 Years and Over)

Group	Number	%
Total Population	131,717	4.9
Hispanic or Latino (of any race)	110,216	76.4
Central American, ex. Mexican	15,783	90.0
Guatemalan	3,153	87.5
Honduran	1,137	72.6
Salvadoran	10,624	94.0
Cuban	325	47.8
Mexican	85,735	78.0
Puerto Rican	2,049	48.7
South American	2,352	70.8
Colombian	863	80.4
Spaniard	490	25.8

Unemployment Rate
(Universe: Population 16 Years and Over)

Group	%
Total Population	7.8
Hispanic or Latino (of any race)	7.5
Central American, ex. Mexican	4.8
Guatemalan	3.2
Honduran	2.5
Salvadoran	4.3
Cuban	10.0
Mexican	7.9
Puerto Rican	6.8
South American	3.1
Colombian	1.7
Spaniard	16.0

Class of Worker: Private Wage and Salary
(Universe: Civilian Employed Population 16 Years and Over)

Group	Number	%
Total Population	960,643	76.6
Hispanic or Latino (of any race)	60,997	88.1
Central American, ex. Mexican	8,880	89.8
Guatemalan	1,894	83.3
Honduran	762	85.1
Salvadoran	5,771	92.7
Cuban	190	73.1
Mexican	45,872	89.1
Puerto Rican	1,590	83.0
South American	1,298	75.4
Colombian	377	73.6
Spaniard	760	80.3

Class of Worker: Government
(Universe: Civilian Employed Population 16 Years and Over)

Group	Number	%
Total Population	202,409	16.1
Hispanic or Latino (of any race)	3,806	5.5
Central American, ex. Mexican	281	2.8
Guatemalan	29	1.3
Honduran	49	5.5
Salvadoran	171	2.7
Cuban	46	17.7
Mexican	2,333	4.5
Puerto Rican	302	15.8
South American	313	18.2
Colombian	114	22.3
Spaniard	172	18.2

Means of Transportation to Work: Car, Truck or Van
(Universe: Workers 16 Years and Over)

Group	Number	%
Total Population	1,144,320	93.0
Hispanic or Latino (of any race)	62,561	92.2
Central American, ex. Mexican	9,154	93.7
Guatemalan	1,952	88.8
Honduran	894	99.9
Salvadoran	5,870	95.0
Cuban	253	97.3
Mexican	46,411	92.2
Puerto Rican	1,730	88.9
South American	1,431	84.6
Colombian	479	93.6
Spaniard	874	91.8

Means of Transportation to Work: Public Transportation (ex. Taxicab)
(Universe: Workers 16 Years and Over)

Group	Number	%
Total Population	5,321	0.4
Hispanic or Latino (of any race)	308	0.5
Central American, ex. Mexican	21	0.2
Guatemalan	0	0.0
Honduran	0	0.0
Salvadoran	21	0.3
Cuban	0	0.0
Mexican	231	0.5
Puerto Rican	5	0.3
South American	28	1.7
Colombian	0	0.0
Spaniard	7	0.7

Homeownership Rate
(Universe: Occupied Housing Units)

Group	%
Total Population	67.0
Hispanic or Latino (of any race)	48.1
Central American, ex. Mexican	53.5
Costa Rican	51.5
Guatemalan	40.5
Honduran	42.2
Nicaraguan	52.5
Panamanian	52.5
Salvadoran	58.7
Cuban	53.2
Dominican Republic	40.0
Mexican	46.9
Puerto Rican	46.0
South American	52.9
Argentinean	57.6
Bolivian	31.5
Chilean	54.4
Colombian	52.5
Ecuadorian	65.7
Peruvian	50.5
Venezuelan	50.5
Spaniard	62.7

Median Home Value

Group	Dollars
Total Population	102,300
Hispanic or Latino (of any race)	100,100
Central American, ex. Mexican	113,900
Guatemalan	85,900
Honduran	102,100
Salvadoran	116,200
Cuban	153,400
Mexican	91,100
Puerto Rican	149,000
South American	165,900
Colombian	176,200
Spaniard	170,100

Median Gross Rent

Group	Dollars
Total Population	617
Hispanic or Latino (of any race)	588
Central American, ex. Mexican	598
Guatemalan	617
Honduran	577
Salvadoran	580
Cuban	581
Mexican	587
Puerto Rican	617
South American	569
Colombian	491
Spaniard	544

Median Household Income
(2010 Inflation-Adjusted Dollars)

Group	Dollars
Total Population	39,267
Hispanic or Latino (of any race)	32,712
Central American, ex. Mexican	34,589
Guatemalan	35,345
Honduran	40,652
Salvadoran	31,881
Cuban	30,078
Mexican	31,878
Puerto Rican	47,500
South American	38,380
Colombian	40,238
Spaniard	35,603

Per Capita Income
(2010 Inflation-Adjusted Dollars)

Group	Dollars
Total Population	21,274
Hispanic or Latino (of any race)	11,290
Central American, ex. Mexican	11,042
Guatemalan	12,118
Honduran	10,253
Salvadoran	10,273
Cuban	25,130
Mexican	10,056
Puerto Rican	23,941
South American	24,337
Colombian	22,947
Spaniard	20,307

Households with $100,000+ Income

Group	Number	%
Total Population	131,232	11.7
Hispanic or Latino (of any race)	2,286	5.4
Central American, ex. Mexican	152	2.8
Guatemalan	80	7.6
Honduran	20	4.1
Salvadoran	21	0.6
Cuban	19	5.6
Mexican	1,278	4.2
Puerto Rican	332	21.4
South American	249	18.7
Colombian	46	14.5
Spaniard	150	16.4

Households with Food Stamps/SNAP Benefits During Past 12 Months

Group	Number	%
Total Population	140,510	12.6
Hispanic or Latino (of any race)	5,851	13.8
Central American, ex. Mexican	610	11.4
Guatemalan	114	10.8
Honduran	47	9.6
Salvadoran	351	10.2
Cuban	76	22.6
Mexican	4,348	14.3
Puerto Rican	220	14.2
South American	80	6.0
Colombian	29	9.1
Spaniard	233	25.5

Poverty Rate
(Income in Past 12 Months Below Poverty Level)

Group	%
Total Population	18.0
Hispanic or Latino (of any race)	30.6

Notes: (1) Percent of total population; (2) Percent of Hispanic/Latino population; Profiles include places with an overall population of at least 125,000, OR an overall population of at least 25,000 where the Hispanic/Latino population is at least 20% of the overall population. In states where less than five places meet either of these criteria, we have included places with at least 10,000 total population with the highest percentage of Hispanic/Latino population. These places are identified with an asterisk (*); Please refer to the User's Guide for a full explanation of data.

Central American, ex. Mexican	31.1
Guatemalan	29.2
Honduran	29.2
Salvadoran	31.4
Cuban	39.7
Mexican	31.8
Puerto Rican	14.8
South American	13.3
Colombian	20.5
Spaniard	37.5

Hope*

Population

Group	Number	%TP[1]	%HP[2]
Total Population	10,095	100.0	–
Hispanic or Latino (of any race)	2,096	20.8	100.0
Mexican	1,919	19.0	91.6

Population Growth: 2000–2010

Group	%
Total Population	-4.9
Hispanic or Latino (of any race)	46.5
Mexican	49.7

Males per 100 Females

Group	Number
Total Population	86.3
Hispanic or Latino (of any race)	111.3
Mexican	108.8

Average Household Size

Group	People
Total Population	2.61
Hispanic or Latino (of any race)	4.18
Mexican	4.25

Median Age

Group	Years
Total Population	32.5
Hispanic or Latino (of any race)	22.1
Mexican	21.6

High School Graduates
(Universe: Population 25 Years and Over)

Group	Number	%
Total Population	4,262	72.2
Hispanic or Latino (of any race)	402	48.2
Mexican	362	45.8

Four-Year College Graduates
(Universe: Population 25 Years and Over)

Group	Number	%
Total Population	679	11.5
Hispanic or Latino (of any race)	40	4.8
Mexican	16	2.0

Population Age 3–17 Enrolled in Public School
(Universe: Population Age 3–17 Enrolled in School)

Group	Number	%
Total Population	2,098	95.7
Hispanic or Latino (of any race)	587	100.0
Mexican	587	100.0

Population Age 3–17 Enrolled in Private School
(Universe: Population Age 3–17 Enrolled in School)

Group	Number	%
Total Population	95	4.3
Hispanic or Latino (of any race)	0	0.0
Mexican	0	0.0

Foreign-Born Population

Group	Number	%
Total Population	1,104	10.8
Hispanic or Latino (of any race)	1,044	50.8
Mexican	1,044	52.4

Foreign-Born Naturalized U.S. Citizens

Group	Number	%
Total Population	127	11.5
Hispanic or Latino (of any race)	71	6.8
Mexican	71	6.8

Language Spoken at Home: English Only
(Universe: Population 5 Years and Over)

Group	Number	%
Total Population	7,470	82.0
Hispanic or Latino (of any race)	118	7.0
Mexican	106	6.4

Language Spoken at Home: Spanish
(Universe: Population 5 Years and Over)

Group	Number	%
Total Population	1,534	16.8
Hispanic or Latino (of any race)	1,524	90.3
Mexican	1,492	90.8

Unemployment Rate
(Universe: Population 16 Years and Over)

Group	%
Total Population	9.5
Hispanic or Latino (of any race)	16.5
Mexican	17.2

Class of Worker: Private Wage and Salary
(Universe: Civilian Employed Population 16 Years and Over)

Group	Number	%
Total Population	2,704	73.0
Hispanic or Latino (of any race)	551	82.1
Mexican	527	82.5

Class of Worker: Government
(Universe: Civilian Employed Population 16 Years and Over)

Group	Number	%
Total Population	790	21.3
Hispanic or Latino (of any race)	26	3.9
Mexican	18	2.8

Means of Transportation to Work: Car, Truck or Van
(Universe: Workers 16 Years and Over)

Group	Number	%
Total Population	3,335	92.8
Hispanic or Latino (of any race)	536	88.6
Mexican	504	88.0

Means of Transportation to Work: Public Transportation (ex. Taxicab)
(Universe: Workers 16 Years and Over)

Group	Number	%
Total Population	32	0.9
Hispanic or Latino (of any race)	0	0.0
Mexican	0	0.0

Homeownership Rate
(Universe: Occupied Housing Units)

Group	%
Total Population	52.0
Hispanic or Latino (of any race)	49.5
Mexican	49.5

Median Home Value

Group	Dollars
Total Population	54,300
Hispanic or Latino (of any race)	43,700
Mexican	43,500

Median Gross Rent

Group	Dollars
Total Population	564
Hispanic or Latino (of any race)	579
Mexican	581

Median Household Income
(2010 Inflation-Adjusted Dollars)

Group	Dollars
Total Population	29,774
Hispanic or Latino (of any race)	35,785
Mexican	35,959

Per Capita Income
(2010 Inflation-Adjusted Dollars)

Group	Dollars
Total Population	12,902
Hispanic or Latino (of any race)	8,620
Mexican	8,315

Households with $100,000+ Income

Group	Number	%
Total Population	158	4.6
Hispanic or Latino (of any race)	0	0.0
Mexican	0	0.0

Households with Food Stamps/SNAP Benefits During Past 12 Months

Group	Number	%
Total Population	934	27.0
Hispanic or Latino (of any race)	82	16.0
Mexican	78	15.5

Poverty Rate
(Income in Past 12 Months Below Poverty Level)

Group	%
Total Population	35.1
Hispanic or Latino (of any race)	29.9
Mexican	30.3

Little Rock

Population

Group	Number	%TP[1]	%HP[2]
Total Population	193,524	100.0	–
Hispanic or Latino (of any race)	13,076	6.8	100.0
Central American, ex. Mexican	1,529	0.8	11.7
Guatemalan	694	0.4	5.3
Honduran	257	0.1	2.0
Nicaraguan	147	0.1	1.1
Salvadoran	357	0.2	2.7
Cuban	151	0.1	1.2
Mexican	9,714	5.0	74.3
Puerto Rican	342	0.2	2.6
South American	343	0.2	2.6
Spaniard	134	0.1	1.0

Population Growth: 2000–2010

Group	%
Total Population	5.7
Hispanic or Latino (of any race)	167.5
Central American, ex. Mexican	561.9
Mexican	188.0
Puerto Rican	51.3
South American	168.0

Males per 100 Females

Group	Number
Total Population	91.1
Hispanic or Latino (of any race)	132.6
Central American, ex. Mexican	150.7
Guatemalan	182.1
Honduran	159.6
Nicaraguan	116.2
Salvadoran	121.7
Cuban	143.5
Mexican	136.2
Puerto Rican	83.9
South American	86.4
Spaniard	78.7

Average Household Size

Group	People
Total Population	2.30
Hispanic or Latino (of any race)	3.55
Central American, ex. Mexican	3.67
Guatemalan	3.78
Honduran	3.66
Nicaraguan	3.37
Salvadoran	3.87
Cuban	2.34
Mexican	3.74
Puerto Rican	2.36
South American	2.49
Spaniard	2.20

Median Age

Group	Years
Total Population	35.1
Hispanic or Latino (of any race)	25.5
Central American, ex. Mexican	27.4
Guatemalan	26.3
Honduran	28.9
Nicaraguan	28.8

Notes: (1) Percent of total population; (2) Percent of Hispanic/Latino population; Profiles include places with an overall population of at least 125,000, OR an overall population of at least 25,000 where the Hispanic/Latino population is at least 20% of the overall population. In states where less than five places meet either of these criteria, we have included places with at least 10,000 total population with the highest percentage of Hispanic/Latino population. These places are identified with an asterisk (*); Please refer to the User's Guide for a full explanation of data.

Group		%
Salvadoran		27.5
Cuban		38.1
Mexican		24.8
Puerto Rican		26.6
South American		31.8
Spaniard		30.5

High School Graduates
(Universe: Population 25 Years and Over)

Group	Number	%
Total Population	110,473	88.7
Hispanic or Latino (of any race)	3,325	54.6
Central American, ex. Mexican	217	29.2
Mexican	2,371	51.7

Four-Year College Graduates
(Universe: Population 25 Years and Over)

Group	Number	%
Total Population	47,415	38.1
Hispanic or Latino (of any race)	832	13.7
Central American, ex. Mexican	21	2.8
Mexican	378	8.2

Population Age 3–17 Enrolled in Public School
(Universe: Population Age 3–17 Enrolled in School)

Group	Number	%
Total Population	27,379	76.8
Hispanic or Latino (of any race)	1,976	78.1
Central American, ex. Mexican	277	70.7
Mexican	1,533	88.5

Population Age 3–17 Enrolled in Private School
(Universe: Population Age 3–17 Enrolled in School)

Group	Number	%
Total Population	8,274	23.2
Hispanic or Latino (of any race)	554	21.9
Central American, ex. Mexican	115	29.3
Mexican	200	11.5

Foreign-Born Population

Group	Number	%
Total Population	14,205	7.4
Hispanic or Latino (of any race)	7,550	62.0
Central American, ex. Mexican	1,114	66.7
Mexican	6,005	68.0

Foreign-Born Naturalized U.S. Citizens

Group	Number	%
Total Population	3,704	26.1
Hispanic or Latino (of any race)	973	12.9
Central American, ex. Mexican	186	16.7
Mexican	708	11.8

Language Spoken at Home: English Only
(Universe: Population 5 Years and Over)

Group	Number	%
Total Population	158,539	89.7
Hispanic or Latino (of any race)	1,059	10.0
Central American, ex. Mexican	22	1.5
Mexican	430	5.5

Language Spoken at Home: Spanish
(Universe: Population 5 Years and Over)

Group	Number	%
Total Population	11,618	6.6
Hispanic or Latino (of any race)	9,552	90.0
Central American, ex. Mexican	1,399	98.5
Mexican	7,459	94.5

Unemployment Rate
(Universe: Population 16 Years and Over)

Group	%
Total Population	7.4
Hispanic or Latino (of any race)	6.6
Central American, ex. Mexican	10.1
Mexican	6.7

Class of Worker: Private Wage and Salary
(Universe: Civilian Employed Population 16 Years and Over)

Group	Number	%
Total Population	71,015	74.7
Hispanic or Latino (of any race)	5,603	88.7
Central American, ex. Mexican	711	80.5
Mexican	4,316	91.6

Class of Worker: Government
(Universe: Civilian Employed Population 16 Years and Over)

Group	Number	%
Total Population	19,594	20.6
Hispanic or Latino (of any race)	270	4.3
Central American, ex. Mexican	23	2.6
Mexican	143	3.0

Means of Transportation to Work: Car, Truck or Van
(Universe: Workers 16 Years and Over)

Group	Number	%
Total Population	87,204	93.5
Hispanic or Latino (of any race)	5,723	93.3
Central American, ex. Mexican	771	89.2
Mexican	4,309	94.6

Means of Transportation to Work: Public Transportation (ex. Taxicab)
(Universe: Workers 16 Years and Over)

Group	Number	%
Total Population	1,068	1.1
Hispanic or Latino (of any race)	36	0.6
Central American, ex. Mexican	0	0.0
Mexican	36	0.8

Homeownership Rate
(Universe: Occupied Housing Units)

Group	%
Total Population	56.2
Hispanic or Latino (of any race)	39.4
Central American, ex. Mexican	39.9
Guatemalan	39.3
Honduran	33.8
Nicaraguan	53.5
Salvadoran	40.6
Cuban	54.2
Mexican	37.4
Puerto Rican	40.0
South American	54.0
Spaniard	67.3

Median Home Value

Group	Dollars
Total Population	145,300
Hispanic or Latino (of any race)	85,900
Central American, ex. Mexican	14,300
Mexican	79,200

Median Gross Rent

Group	Dollars
Total Population	743
Hispanic or Latino (of any race)	664
Central American, ex. Mexican	708
Mexican	659

Median Household Income
(2010 Inflation-Adjusted Dollars)

Group	Dollars
Total Population	44,068
Hispanic or Latino (of any race)	29,619
Central American, ex. Mexican	31,932
Mexican	27,944

Per Capita Income
(2010 Inflation-Adjusted Dollars)

Group	Dollars
Total Population	29,229
Hispanic or Latino (of any race)	14,455
Central American, ex. Mexican	10,872
Mexican	12,248

Households with $100,000+ Income

Group	Number	%
Total Population	14,058	17.7
Hispanic or Latino (of any race)	193	5.6
Central American, ex. Mexican	20	4.3
Mexican	118	4.7

Households with Food Stamps/SNAP Benefits During Past 12 Months

Group	Number	%
Total Population	8,748	11.0
Hispanic or Latino (of any race)	441	12.8
Central American, ex. Mexican	136	28.9
Mexican	289	11.6

Poverty Rate
(Income in Past 12 Months Below Poverty Level)

Group	%
Total Population	17.4
Hispanic or Latino (of any race)	34.3
Central American, ex. Mexican	39.5
Mexican	35.7

Rogers

Population

Group	Number	%TP[1]	%HP[2]
Total Population	55,964	100.0	–
Hispanic or Latino (of any race)	17,619	31.5	100.0
Central American, ex. Mexican	3,612	6.5	20.5
Guatemalan	373	0.7	2.1
Honduran	121	0.2	0.7
Salvadoran	2,951	5.3	16.7
Mexican	12,414	22.2	70.5
Puerto Rican	180	0.3	1.0
South American	238	0.4	1.4
Spaniard	105	0.2	0.6

Population Growth: 2000–2010

Group	%
Total Population	44.1
Hispanic or Latino (of any race)	135.2
Central American, ex. Mexican	314.2
Salvadoran	346.4
Mexican	126.2

Males per 100 Females

Group	Number
Total Population	96.2
Hispanic or Latino (of any race)	103.1
Central American, ex. Mexican	104.0
Guatemalan	113.1
Honduran	89.1
Salvadoran	105.4
Mexican	103.6
Puerto Rican	73.1
South American	87.4
Spaniard	98.1

Average Household Size

Group	People
Total Population	2.82
Hispanic or Latino (of any race)	4.14
Central American, ex. Mexican	3.92
Guatemalan	4.06
Honduran	4.16
Salvadoran	3.93
Mexican	4.34
Puerto Rican	3.40
South American	2.93
Spaniard	3.19

Median Age

Group	Years
Total Population	31.7
Hispanic or Latino (of any race)	23.2
Central American, ex. Mexican	29.5
Guatemalan	29.3
Honduran	26.3
Salvadoran	29.5
Mexican	21.6
Puerto Rican	23.6
South American	34.3
Spaniard	21.8

High School Graduates
(Universe: Population 25 Years and Over)

Group	Number	%
Total Population	24,007	75.8
Hispanic or Latino (of any race)	2,808	36.4
Central American, ex. Mexican	534	34.3
Salvadoran	367	31.7
Mexican	1,876	33.8

Notes: (1) Percent of total population; (2) Percent of Hispanic/Latino population; Profiles include places with an overall population of at least 125,000, OR an overall population of at least 25,000 where the Hispanic/Latino population is at least 20% of the overall population. In states where less than five places meet either of these criteria, we have included places with at least 10,000 total population with the highest percentage of Hispanic/Latino population. These places are identified with an asterisk (*); Please refer to the User's Guide for a full explanation of data.

Four-Year College Graduates
(Universe: Population 25 Years and Over)

Group	Number	%
Total Population	8,209	25.9
Hispanic or Latino (of any race)	465	6.0
Central American, ex. Mexican	123	7.9
Salvadoran	67	5.8
Mexican	166	3.0

Population Age 3–17 Enrolled in Public School
(Universe: Population Age 3–17 Enrolled in School)

Group	Number	%
Total Population	10,053	87.6
Hispanic or Latino (of any race)	3,883	95.9
Central American, ex. Mexican	612	94.7
Salvadoran	477	100.0
Mexican	3,019	97.4

Population Age 3–17 Enrolled in Private School
(Universe: Population Age 3–17 Enrolled in School)

Group	Number	%
Total Population	1,429	12.4
Hispanic or Latino (of any race)	167	4.1
Central American, ex. Mexican	34	5.3
Salvadoran	0	0.0
Mexican	82	2.6

Foreign-Born Population

Group	Number	%
Total Population	10,338	19.4
Hispanic or Latino (of any race)	9,110	55.8
Central American, ex. Mexican	1,945	66.8
Salvadoran	1,435	66.2
Mexican	6,736	55.4

Foreign-Born Naturalized U.S. Citizens

Group	Number	%
Total Population	2,424	23.4
Hispanic or Latino (of any race)	1,908	20.9
Central American, ex. Mexican	308	15.8
Salvadoran	225	15.7
Mexican	1,456	21.6

Language Spoken at Home: English Only
(Universe: Population 5 Years and Over)

Group	Number	%
Total Population	34,100	70.9
Hispanic or Latino (of any race)	1,551	11.2
Central American, ex. Mexican	45	1.8
Salvadoran	45	2.3
Mexican	1,212	11.8

Language Spoken at Home: Spanish
(Universe: Population 5 Years and Over)

Group	Number	%
Total Population	12,891	26.8
Hispanic or Latino (of any race)	12,322	88.8
Central American, ex. Mexican	2,516	98.2
Salvadoran	1,902	97.7
Mexican	9,101	88.2

Unemployment Rate
(Universe: Population 16 Years and Over)

Group	%
Total Population	5.8
Hispanic or Latino (of any race)	5.2
Central American, ex. Mexican	1.6
Salvadoran	1.3
Mexican	6.6

Class of Worker: Private Wage and Salary
(Universe: Civilian Employed Population 16 Years and Over)

Group	Number	%
Total Population	22,288	88.2
Hispanic or Latino (of any race)	6,751	92.6
Central American, ex. Mexican	1,465	95.2
Salvadoran	1,210	96.6
Mexican	4,833	92.5

Class of Worker: Government
(Universe: Civilian Employed Population 16 Years and Over)

Group	Number	%
Total Population	1,753	6.9
Hispanic or Latino (of any race)	194	2.7
Central American, ex. Mexican	31	2.0
Salvadoran	19	1.5
Mexican	129	2.5

Means of Transportation to Work: Car, Truck or Van
(Universe: Workers 16 Years and Over)

Group	Number	%
Total Population	22,482	90.3
Hispanic or Latino (of any race)	6,452	89.7
Central American, ex. Mexican	1,419	92.9
Salvadoran	1,180	95.1
Mexican	4,517	88.3

Means of Transportation to Work: Public Transportation (ex. Taxicab)
(Universe: Workers 16 Years and Over)

Group	Number	%
Total Population	36	0.1
Hispanic or Latino (of any race)	0	0.0
Central American, ex. Mexican	0	0.0
Salvadoran	0	0.0
Mexican	0	0.0

Homeownership Rate
(Universe: Occupied Housing Units)

Group	%
Total Population	59.2
Hispanic or Latino (of any race)	55.0
Central American, ex. Mexican	55.7
Guatemalan	49.1
Honduran	43.8
Salvadoran	57.7
Mexican	55.6
Puerto Rican	44.2
South American	56.1
Spaniard	54.8

Median Home Value

Group	Dollars
Total Population	156,000
Hispanic or Latino (of any race)	131,400
Central American, ex. Mexican	127,500
Salvadoran	122,700
Mexican	125,900

Median Gross Rent

Group	Dollars
Total Population	748
Hispanic or Latino (of any race)	612
Central American, ex. Mexican	602
Salvadoran	651
Mexican	615

Median Household Income
(2010 Inflation-Adjusted Dollars)

Group	Dollars
Total Population	46,897
Hispanic or Latino (of any race)	36,074
Central American, ex. Mexican	49,228
Salvadoran	51,779
Mexican	34,261

Per Capita Income
(2010 Inflation-Adjusted Dollars)

Group	Dollars
Total Population	24,687
Hispanic or Latino (of any race)	11,216
Central American, ex. Mexican	12,213
Salvadoran	12,439
Mexican	10,432

Households with $100,000+ Income

Group	Number	%
Total Population	3,570	18.5
Hispanic or Latino (of any race)	152	3.7
Central American, ex. Mexican	8	1.1
Salvadoran	8	1.5
Mexican	126	4.3

Households with Food Stamps/SNAP Benefits During Past 12 Months

Group	Number	%
Total Population	1,683	8.7
Hispanic or Latino (of any race)	446	10.9
Central American, ex. Mexican	90	11.8
Salvadoran	75	14.0
Mexican	310	10.7

Poverty Rate
(Income in Past 12 Months Below Poverty Level)

Group	%
Total Population	14.4
Hispanic or Latino (of any race)	24.7
Central American, ex. Mexican	24.6
Salvadoran	16.2
Mexican	24.9

Siloam Springs*

Population

Group	Number	%TP[1]	%HP[2]
Total Population	15,039	100.0	–
Hispanic or Latino (of any race)	3,128	20.8	100.0
Central American, ex. Mexican	1,094	7.3	35.0
Guatemalan	198	1.3	6.3
Salvadoran	796	5.3	25.4
Mexican	1,686	11.2	53.9

Population Growth: 2000–2010

Group	%
Total Population	38.7
Hispanic or Latino (of any race)	106.1
Central American, ex. Mexican	317.6
Salvadoran	306.1
Mexican	78.4

Males per 100 Females

Group	Number
Total Population	96.1
Hispanic or Latino (of any race)	115.6
Central American, ex. Mexican	125.6
Guatemalan	175.0
Salvadoran	116.9
Mexican	114.5

Average Household Size

Group	People
Total Population	2.73
Hispanic or Latino (of any race)	3.93
Central American, ex. Mexican	4.08
Guatemalan	3.87
Salvadoran	4.12
Mexican	3.87

Median Age

Group	Years
Total Population	28.7
Hispanic or Latino (of any race)	23.1
Central American, ex. Mexican	27.2
Guatemalan	26.2
Salvadoran	28.7
Mexican	21.5

High School Graduates
(Universe: Population 25 Years and Over)

Group	Number	%
Total Population	6,271	80.6
Hispanic or Latino (of any race)	443	36.2
Mexican	315	32.9

Four-Year College Graduates
(Universe: Population 25 Years and Over)

Group	Number	%
Total Population	1,851	23.8
Hispanic or Latino (of any race)	78	6.4
Mexican	34	3.6

Population Age 3–17 Enrolled in Public School
(Universe: Population Age 3–17 Enrolled in School)

Group	Number	%
Total Population	2,492	94.0
Hispanic or Latino (of any race)	591	94.3
Mexican	478	93.0

Population Age 3–17 Enrolled in Private School
(Universe: Population Age 3–17 Enrolled in School)

Group	Number	%
Total Population	158	6.0
Hispanic or Latino (of any race)	36	5.7
Mexican	36	7.0

Notes: (1) Percent of total population; (2) Percent of Hispanic/Latino population; Profiles include places with an overall population of at least 125,000, OR an overall population of at least 25,000 where the Hispanic/Latino population is at least 20% of the overall population. In states where less than five places meet either of these criteria, we have included places with at least 10,000 total population with the highest percentage of Hispanic/Latino population. These places are identified with an asterisk (*); Please refer to the User's Guide for a full explanation of data.

Foreign-Born Population		
Group	Number	%
Total Population	1,561	10.9
Hispanic or Latino (of any race)	1,386	50.0
Mexican	980	46.4

Foreign-Born Naturalized U.S. Citizens		
Group	Number	%
Total Population	348	22.3
Hispanic or Latino (of any race)	273	19.7
Mexican	163	16.6

Language Spoken at Home: English Only (Universe: Population 5 Years and Over)		
Group	Number	%
Total Population	10,790	81.9
Hispanic or Latino (of any race)	547	21.7
Mexican	460	24.2

Language Spoken at Home: Spanish (Universe: Population 5 Years and Over)		
Group	Number	%
Total Population	2,209	16.8
Hispanic or Latino (of any race)	1,974	78.3
Mexican	1,443	75.8

Unemployment Rate (Universe: Population 16 Years and Over)	
Group	%
Total Population	8.5
Hispanic or Latino (of any race)	12.8
Mexican	13.2

Class of Worker: Private Wage and Salary (Universe: Civilian Employed Population 16 Years and Over)		
Group	Number	%
Total Population	5,194	81.2
Hispanic or Latino (of any race)	1,044	88.6
Mexican	775	88.1

Class of Worker: Government (Universe: Civilian Employed Population 16 Years and Over)		
Group	Number	%
Total Population	871	13.6
Hispanic or Latino (of any race)	91	7.7
Mexican	62	7.0

Means of Transportation to Work: Car, Truck or Van (Universe: Workers 16 Years and Over)		
Group	Number	%
Total Population	5,562	88.7
Hispanic or Latino (of any race)	1,085	94.8
Mexican	801	94.7

Means of Transportation to Work: Public Transportation (ex. Taxicab) (Universe: Workers 16 Years and Over)		
Group	Number	%
Total Population	9	0.1
Hispanic or Latino (of any race)	0	0.0
Mexican	0	0.0

Homeownership Rate (Universe: Occupied Housing Units)	
Group	%
Total Population	53.0
Hispanic or Latino (of any race)	45.5
Central American, ex. Mexican	52.8
Guatemalan	23.3
Salvadoran	61.7
Mexican	40.7

Median Home Value	
Group	Dollars
Total Population	117,300
Hispanic or Latino (of any race)	108,700
Mexican	103,700

Median Gross Rent	
Group	Dollars
Total Population	584
Hispanic or Latino (of any race)	555
Mexican	548

Median Household Income (2010 Inflation-Adjusted Dollars)	
Group	Dollars
Total Population	38,750
Hispanic or Latino (of any race)	31,393
Mexican	32,480

Per Capita Income (2010 Inflation-Adjusted Dollars)	
Group	Dollars
Total Population	17,057
Hispanic or Latino (of any race)	10,579
Mexican	10,436

Households with $100,000+ Income		
Group	Number	%
Total Population	553	11.4
Hispanic or Latino (of any race)	38	5.1
Mexican	9	1.7

Households with Food Stamps/SNAP Benefits During Past 12 Months		
Group	Number	%
Total Population	408	8.4
Hispanic or Latino (of any race)	43	5.8
Mexican	11	2.0

Poverty Rate (Income in Past 12 Months Below Poverty Level)	
Group	%
Total Population	19.5
Hispanic or Latino (of any race)	18.6
Mexican	13.3

Springdale

Population			
Group	Number	%TP[1]	%HP[2]
Total Population	69,797	100.0	–
Hispanic or Latino (of any race)	24,692	35.4	100.0
Central American, ex. Mexican	4,092	5.9	16.6
Guatemalan	455	0.7	1.8
Honduran	188	0.3	0.8
Salvadoran	3,316	4.8	13.4
Mexican	18,404	26.4	74.5
Puerto Rican	305	0.4	1.2
South American	182	0.3	0.7

Population Growth: 2000–2010	
Group	%
Total Population	52.4
Hispanic or Latino (of any race)	174.2
Central American, ex. Mexican	367.1
Salvadoran	390.5
Mexican	167.6

Males per 100 Females	
Group	Number
Total Population	98.8
Hispanic or Latino (of any race)	109.3
Central American, ex. Mexican	110.1
Guatemalan	127.5
Honduran	93.8
Salvadoran	110.1
Mexican	110.2
Puerto Rican	99.3
South American	80.2

Average Household Size	
Group	People
Total Population	3.02
Hispanic or Latino (of any race)	4.22
Central American, ex. Mexican	3.97
Guatemalan	4.19
Honduran	3.91
Salvadoran	3.96
Mexican	4.37
Puerto Rican	3.20
South American	2.89

Median Age	
Group	Years
Total Population	29.6
Hispanic or Latino (of any race)	22.1
Central American, ex. Mexican	27.7
Guatemalan	27.0
Honduran	29.1
Salvadoran	27.8
Mexican	20.6
Puerto Rican	23.4
South American	31.3

High School Graduates (Universe: Population 25 Years and Over)		
Group	Number	%
Total Population	26,442	69.9
Hispanic or Latino (of any race)	4,033	38.3
Central American, ex. Mexican	437	22.0
Salvadoran	265	15.8
Mexican	3,004	38.8

Four-Year College Graduates (Universe: Population 25 Years and Over)		
Group	Number	%
Total Population	6,676	17.6
Hispanic or Latino (of any race)	393	3.7
Central American, ex. Mexican	47	2.4
Salvadoran	35	2.1
Mexican	223	2.9

Population Age 3–17 Enrolled in Public School (Universe: Population Age 3–17 Enrolled in School)		
Group	Number	%
Total Population	14,053	93.6
Hispanic or Latino (of any race)	6,297	97.4
Central American, ex. Mexican	713	100.0
Salvadoran	638	100.0
Mexican	5,306	96.9

Population Age 3–17 Enrolled in Private School (Universe: Population Age 3–17 Enrolled in School)		
Group	Number	%
Total Population	957	6.4
Hispanic or Latino (of any race)	168	2.6
Central American, ex. Mexican	0	0.0
Salvadoran	0	0.0
Mexican	168	3.1

Foreign-Born Population		
Group	Number	%
Total Population	15,978	24.0
Hispanic or Latino (of any race)	12,660	54.1
Central American, ex. Mexican	2,547	71.0
Salvadoran	2,164	70.8
Mexican	9,543	52.3

Foreign-Born Naturalized U.S. Citizens		
Group	Number	%
Total Population	2,653	16.6
Hispanic or Latino (of any race)	1,959	15.5
Central American, ex. Mexican	239	9.4
Salvadoran	200	9.2
Mexican	1,509	15.8

Language Spoken at Home: English Only (Universe: Population 5 Years and Over)		
Group	Number	%
Total Population	37,322	63.0
Hispanic or Latino (of any race)	2,050	10.4
Central American, ex. Mexican	96	3.1
Salvadoran	96	3.6
Mexican	1,623	10.6

Language Spoken at Home: Spanish (Universe: Population 5 Years and Over)		
Group	Number	%
Total Population	18,646	31.5
Hispanic or Latino (of any race)	17,622	89.6
Central American, ex. Mexican	3,015	96.9
Salvadoran	2,563	96.4
Mexican	13,682	89.4

Unemployment Rate (Universe: Population 16 Years and Over)	
Group	%
Total Population	8.3
Hispanic or Latino (of any race)	9.9
Central American, ex. Mexican	3.9
Salvadoran	4.1
Mexican	11.0

STATE & PLACE PROFILES

Notes: (1) Percent of total population; (2) Percent of Hispanic/Latino population; Profiles include places with an overall population of at least 125,000, OR an overall population of at least 25,000 where the Hispanic/Latino population is at least 20% of the overall population. In states where less than five places meet either of these criteria, we have included places with at least 10,000 total population with the highest percentage of Hispanic/Latino population. These places are identified with an asterisk (*); Please refer to the User's Guide for a full explanation of data.

Class of Worker: Private Wage and Salary
(Universe: Civilian Employed Population 16 Years and Over)

Group	Number	%
Total Population	25,872	85.7
Hispanic or Latino (of any race)	8,705	90.5
Central American, ex. Mexican	1,672	92.0
Salvadoran	1,463	96.8
Mexican	6,421	89.8

Class of Worker: Government
(Universe: Civilian Employed Population 16 Years and Over)

Group	Number	%
Total Population	2,749	9.1
Hispanic or Latino (of any race)	275	2.9
Central American, ex. Mexican	48	2.6
Salvadoran	48	3.2
Mexican	205	2.9

Means of Transportation to Work: Car, Truck or Van
(Universe: Workers 16 Years and Over)

Group	Number	%
Total Population	28,183	95.5
Hispanic or Latino (of any race)	9,008	95.6
Central American, ex. Mexican	1,776	99.1
Salvadoran	1,495	98.9
Mexican	6,722	95.7

Means of Transportation to Work: Public Transportation (ex. Taxicab)
(Universe: Workers 16 Years and Over)

Group	Number	%
Total Population	124	0.4
Hispanic or Latino (of any race)	86	0.9
Central American, ex. Mexican	0	0.0
Salvadoran	0	0.0
Mexican	86	1.2

Homeownership Rate
(Universe: Occupied Housing Units)

Group	%
Total Population	54.4
Hispanic or Latino (of any race)	41.7
Central American, ex. Mexican	48.1
Guatemalan	35.9
Honduran	33.9
Salvadoran	50.5
Mexican	40.7
Puerto Rican	20.2
South American	62.3

Median Home Value

Group	Dollars
Total Population	147,000
Hispanic or Latino (of any race)	131,200
Central American, ex. Mexican	134,600
Salvadoran	131,400
Mexican	130,200

Median Gross Rent

Group	Dollars
Total Population	677
Hispanic or Latino (of any race)	680
Central American, ex. Mexican	575
Salvadoran	554
Mexican	693

Median Household Income
(2010 Inflation-Adjusted Dollars)

Group	Dollars
Total Population	42,879
Hispanic or Latino (of any race)	34,883
Central American, ex. Mexican	36,154
Salvadoran	35,104
Mexican	33,890

Per Capita Income
(2010 Inflation-Adjusted Dollars)

Group	Dollars
Total Population	18,582
Hispanic or Latino (of any race)	10,009
Central American, ex. Mexican	10,897
Salvadoran	10,724
Mexican	9,586

Households with $100,000+ Income

Group	Number	%
Total Population	2,479	11.2
Hispanic or Latino (of any race)	166	2.9
Central American, ex. Mexican	0	0.0
Salvadoran	0	0.0
Mexican	124	2.9

Households with Food Stamps/SNAP Benefits During Past 12 Months

Group	Number	%
Total Population	2,093	9.4
Hispanic or Latino (of any race)	600	10.6
Central American, ex. Mexican	33	3.3
Salvadoran	0	0.0
Mexican	524	12.4

Poverty Rate
(Income in Past 12 Months Below Poverty Level)

Group	%
Total Population	19.5
Hispanic or Latino (of any race)	27.4
Central American, ex. Mexican	22.0
Salvadoran	24.3
Mexican	28.8

Notes: (1) Percent of total population; (2) Percent of Hispanic/Latino population; Profiles include places with an overall population of at least 125,000, OR an overall population of at least 25,000 where the Hispanic/Latino population is at least 20% of the overall population. In states where less than five places meet either of these criteria, we have included places with at least 10,000 total population with the highest percentage of Hispanic/Latino population. These places are identified with an asterisk (*); Please refer to the User's Guide for a full explanation of data.

California

EDITOR'S NOTE: For a place to be included in this edition, it must meet one of two criteria. Either its overall population is at least 125,000, OR its overall population is at least 25,000 and its Hispanic/Latino population is at least 20% of the overall population. For the state of California, the following locations are included:

Adelanto
Alhambra
Altadena
Anaheim
Antioch
Apple Valley
Atwater
Azusa
Bakersfield
Baldwin Park
Banning
Beaumont
Bell
Bell Gardens
Bellflower
Brea
Brentwood
Buena Park
Burbank
Calexico
Camarillo
Carson
Cathedral City
Ceres
Chino
Chino Hills
Chula Vista
Clovis
Coachella
Colton
Compton
Concord
Corona
Costa Mesa
Covina
Culver City
Daly City
Delano
Desert Hot Springs
Diamond Bar
Downey
East Los Angeles
East Palo Alto
Eastvale
El Cajon
El Centro
El Monte
El Paso de Robles (Paso Robles)
Elk Grove
Escondido
Fairfield
Fallbrook
Florence-Graham
Florin
Fontana
Foothill Farms
Fremont
Fresno
Fullerton
Garden Grove
Gardena
Gilroy
Glendale
Glendora
Goleta
Hacienda Heights
Hanford
Hawthorne
Hayward
Hemet
Hesperia
Highland
Hollister
Huntington Beach
Huntington Park
Imperial Beach
Indio
Inglewood
Irvine
La Habra
La Mesa
La Mirada
La Presa
La Puente
La Quinta
La Verne
Laguna Hills
Lake Elsinore
Lake Forest
Lakewood
Lancaster
Lawndale
Lemon Grove
Livermore
Lodi
Lompoc
Long Beach
Los Angeles
Los Banos
Lynwood
Madera
Manteca
Maywood
Menifee
Merced
Modesto
Monrovia
Montclair
Montebello
Monterey Park
Moorpark
Moreno Valley
Morgan Hill
Mountain View
Murrieta
Napa
National City
Newark
Norco
North Highlands
Norwalk
Novato
Oakland
Oakley
Oceanside
Ontario
Orange
Orcutt
Oxnard
Palm Desert
Palm Springs
Palmdale
Paramount
Pasadena
Perris
Petaluma
Pico Rivera
Pittsburg
Placentia
Pomona
Porterville
Rancho Cucamonga
Redlands
Redwood City
Rialto
Richmond
Riverside
Rohnert Park
Rosemead
Rowland Heights
Rubidoux
Sacramento
Salinas
San Bernardino
San Bruno
San Buenaventura (Ventura)
San Diego
San Dimas
San Francisco
San Gabriel
San Jacinto
San Jose
San Juan Capistrano
San Leandro
San Marcos
San Mateo
San Pablo
San Rafael
Santa Ana
Santa Barbara
Santa Clarita
Santa Maria
Santa Paula
Santa Rosa
Seaside
Simi Valley
Soledad
South Gate
South San Francisco
South Whittier
Spring Valley
Stanton
Stockton
Suisun City
Sunnyvale
Temecula
Thousand Oaks
Torrance
Tracy
Tulare
Turlock
Tustin
Twentynine Palms
Union City
Upland
Vacaville
Vallejo
Victorville
Visalia
Vista
Wasco
Watsonville
West Covina
West Sacramento
West Whittier-Los Nietos
Westminster
Westmont
Whittier
Wildomar
Willowbrook
Windsor
Woodland
Yuba City
Yucaipa

Notes: (1) Percent of total population; (2) Percent of Hispanic/Latino population; Profiles include places with an overall population of at least 125,000, OR an overall population of at least 25,000 where the Hispanic/Latino population is at least 20% of the overall population. In states where less than five places meet either of these criteria, we have included places with at least 10,000 total population with the highest percentage of Hispanic/Latino population. These places are identified with an asterisk (*); Please refer to the User's Guide for a full explanation of data.

Section Two: State & Place Profiles starts with the state profile, followed by place profiles that meet the criteria above. Places are listed alphabetically within each state. All states, all counties and places that meet the above criteria are ranked and compared in *Section Three: Rankings & Comparisons*, on page 1055.

For a more detailed look at the Hispanic/Latino population in California, a companion web site is available at no additional charge with purchase of this print edition. Visit http://gold.greyhouse.com/page/info_hispanic for more information.

The web site includes data for all counties and places in California with Hispanic/Latino population, plus ten additional topics: Self Employed Worker; Walked to Work; Worked from Home; Mean Travel Time to Work; Mean Household Income; Households with Cash Public Assistance; Mean Cash Pubic Assistance; Poverty Rates for 18 and Under, 18 to 64, and 65 and Over.

Population

Group	Number	%TP[1]	%HP[2]
Total Population	37,253,956	100.0	–
Hispanic or Latino (of any race)	14,013,719	37.6	100.0
Central American, ex. Mexican	1,132,520	3.0	8.1
Costa Rican	22,469	0.1	0.2
Guatemalan	332,737	0.9	2.4
Honduran	72,795	0.2	0.5
Nicaraguan	100,790	0.3	0.7
Panamanian	17,768	<0.1	0.1
Salvadoran	573,956	1.5	4.1
Cuban	88,607	0.2	0.6
Dominican Republic	11,455	<0.1	0.1
Mexican	11,423,146	30.7	81.5
Puerto Rican	189,945	0.5	1.4
South American	293,880	0.8	2.1
Argentinean	44,410	0.1	0.3
Bolivian	13,351	<0.1	0.1
Chilean	24,006	0.1	0.2
Colombian	64,416	0.2	0.5
Ecuadorian	35,750	0.1	0.3
Paraguayan	1,228	<0.1	<0.1
Peruvian	91,511	0.2	0.7
Uruguayan	4,110	<0.1	<0.1
Venezuelan	11,100	<0.1	0.1
Spaniard	142,194	0.4	1.0

Population Growth: 2000–2010

Group	%
Total Population	10.0
Hispanic or Latino (of any race)	27.8
Central American, ex. Mexican	96.5
Costa Rican	69.8
Guatemalan	131.9
Honduran	139.7
Nicaraguan	96.3
Panamanian	66.2
Salvadoran	110.2
Cuban	22.6
Dominican Republic	127.0
Mexican	35.1
Puerto Rican	35.1
South American	81.6
Argentinean	91.3
Bolivian	101.7
Chilean	77.4
Colombian	93.6
Ecuadorian	97.4
Paraguayan	109.6
Peruvian	107.0
Uruguayan	150.8
Venezuelan	101.4
Spaniard	533.1

Males per 100 Females

Group	Number
Total Population	98.8
Hispanic or Latino (of any race)	102.1
Central American, ex. Mexican	97.8
Costa Rican	85.0
Guatemalan	112.3
Honduran	92.3
Nicaraguan	86.2
Panamanian	76.7
Salvadoran	94.2
Cuban	99.5
Dominican Republic	97.7
Mexican	103.0
Puerto Rican	99.1
South American	88.6
Argentinean	99.2
Bolivian	85.9
Chilean	90.0
Colombian	80.7
Ecuadorian	88.3
Paraguayan	74.2
Peruvian	89.2
Uruguayan	101.4
Venezuelan	87.9
Spaniard	90.0

Average Household Size

Group	People
Total Population	2.90
Hispanic or Latino (of any race)	3.93
Central American, ex. Mexican	3.97
Costa Rican	3.01
Guatemalan	4.20
Honduran	4.01
Nicaraguan	3.55
Panamanian	2.67
Salvadoran	4.01
Cuban	2.65
Dominican Republic	2.75
Mexican	4.06
Puerto Rican	2.83
South American	2.98
Argentinean	2.66
Bolivian	3.17
Chilean	2.77
Colombian	2.89
Ecuadorian	3.18
Paraguayan	2.82
Peruvian	3.25
Uruguayan	2.70
Venezuelan	2.70
Spaniard	2.71

Median Age

Group	Years
Total Population	35.2
Hispanic or Latino (of any race)	27.1
Central American, ex. Mexican	32.7
Costa Rican	36.2
Guatemalan	31.4
Honduran	31.3
Nicaraguan	35.1
Panamanian	37.0
Salvadoran	33.2
Cuban	37.3
Dominican Republic	28.9
Mexican	26.2
Puerto Rican	28.9
South American	37.4
Argentinean	39.1
Bolivian	37.6
Chilean	38.1
Colombian	35.7
Ecuadorian	38.2
Paraguayan	33.3
Peruvian	37.7
Uruguayan	39.8
Venezuelan	33.9
Spaniard	36.8

High School Graduates
(Universe: Population 25 Years and Over)

Group	Number	%
Total Population	18,958,197	80.7
Hispanic or Latino (of any race)	4,060,139	57.0
Central American, ex. Mexican	383,210	54.0
Costa Rican	12,067	85.2
Guatemalan	94,581	46.8
Honduran	20,622	48.3
Nicaraguan	46,811	74.6
Panamanian	10,269	89.6
Salvadoran	187,315	52.3
Cuban	45,039	80.9
Dominican Republic	4,937	87.6
Mexican	3,146,911	54.5
Puerto Rican	83,784	82.1
South American	170,801	87.6
Argentinean	26,641	87.4
Bolivian	8,377	92.8
Chilean	14,285	89.8
Colombian	35,056	87.4
Ecuadorian	20,416	82.1
Paraguayan	558	94.4
Peruvian	50,156	87.6
Uruguayan	1,711	74.7
Venezuelan	7,118	95.0
Spaniard	65,718	88.0

Four-Year College Graduates
(Universe: Population 25 Years and Over)

Group	Number	%
Total Population	7,063,690	30.1
Hispanic or Latino (of any race)	730,285	10.2
Central American, ex. Mexican	76,505	10.8
Costa Rican	4,180	29.5
Guatemalan	18,216	9.0
Honduran	3,804	8.9
Nicaraguan	11,875	18.9
Panamanian	3,739	32.6
Salvadoran	32,428	9.1
Cuban	16,535	29.7
Dominican Republic	1,638	29.1
Mexican	488,479	8.5
Puerto Rican	22,404	21.9
South American	66,592	34.1
Argentinean	11,467	37.6
Bolivian	3,277	36.3
Chilean	5,323	33.5
Colombian	15,073	37.6
Ecuadorian	7,042	28.3
Paraguayan	301	50.9
Peruvian	16,885	29.5
Uruguayan	637	27.8
Venezuelan	3,934	52.5
Spaniard	21,279	28.5

Population Age 3–17 Enrolled in Public School
(Universe: Population Age 3–17 Enrolled in School)

Group	Number	%
Total Population	6,273,823	88.2
Hispanic or Latino (of any race)	3,257,353	94.2
Central American, ex. Mexican	210,194	93.4
Costa Rican	3,417	80.0
Guatemalan	60,983	94.9
Honduran	13,954	95.2
Nicaraguan	14,956	87.5
Panamanian	2,525	83.8
Salvadoran	109,836	94.2
Cuban	10,858	78.0
Dominican Republic	1,550	92.3
Mexican	2,846,741	94.9
Puerto Rican	32,394	87.2
South American	42,840	82.5
Argentinean	5,239	76.9
Bolivian	1,981	81.2
Chilean	3,404	81.0
Colombian	9,202	82.7
Ecuadorian	5,514	83.7
Paraguayan	151	95.0
Peruvian	13,526	83.5
Uruguayan	393	80.0
Venezuelan	1,657	87.5
Spaniard	15,355	82.7

Population Age 3–17 Enrolled in Private School
(Universe: Population Age 3–17 Enrolled in School)

Group	Number	%
Total Population	842,757	11.8
Hispanic or Latino (of any race)	200,929	5.8
Central American, ex. Mexican	14,916	6.6
Costa Rican	856	20.0
Guatemalan	3,289	5.1
Honduran	704	4.8
Nicaraguan	2,146	12.5
Panamanian	487	16.2
Salvadoran	6,816	5.8
Cuban	3,062	22.0

Notes: (1) Percent of total population; (2) Percent of Hispanic/Latino population; Profiles include places with an overall population of at least 125,000, OR an overall population of at least 25,000 where the Hispanic/Latino population is at least 20% of the overall population. In states where less than five places meet either of these criteria, we have included places with at least 10,000 total population with the highest percentage of Hispanic/Latino population. These places are identified with an asterisk (*); Please refer to the User's Guide for a full explanation of data.

Group	Number	%
Dominican Republic	130	7.7
Mexican	153,722	5.1
Puerto Rican	4,770	12.8
South American	9,105	17.5
Argentinean	1,577	23.1
Bolivian	459	18.8
Chilean	801	19.0
Colombian	1,921	17.3
Ecuadorian	1,070	16.3
Paraguayan	8	5.0
Peruvian	2,665	16.5
Uruguayan	98	20.0
Venezuelan	237	12.5
Spaniard	3,219	17.3

Foreign-Born Population

Group	Number	%
Total Population	9,962,472	27.2
Hispanic or Latino (of any race)	5,324,223	39.6
Central American, ex. Mexican	730,456	63.1
Costa Rican	10,754	48.3
Guatemalan	223,690	66.7
Honduran	48,622	67.3
Nicaraguan	56,218	58.1
Panamanian	8,236	47.9
Salvadoran	366,066	62.5
Cuban	37,420	45.2
Dominican Republic	3,911	42.0
Mexican	4,282,066	38.1
Puerto Rican	4,401	2.5
South American	177,838	61.3
Argentinean	26,865	62.1
Bolivian	8,322	60.6
Chilean	12,916	55.1
Colombian	34,995	58.2
Ecuadorian	20,712	56.8
Paraguayan	575	67.5
Peruvian	57,694	66.0
Uruguayan	2,143	67.4
Venezuelan	7,482	67.9
Spaniard	13,031	11.8

Foreign-Born Naturalized U.S. Citizens

Group	Number	%
Total Population	4,472,020	44.9
Hispanic or Latino (of any race)	1,594,493	29.9
Central American, ex. Mexican	259,341	35.5
Costa Rican	6,207	57.7
Guatemalan	60,691	27.1
Honduran	12,171	25.0
Nicaraguan	30,262	53.8
Panamanian	5,482	66.6
Salvadoran	137,025	37.4
Cuban	27,376	73.2
Dominican Republic	2,463	63.0
Mexican	1,165,060	27.2
Puerto Rican	2,266	51.5
South American	92,923	52.3
Argentinean	14,447	53.8
Bolivian	5,040	60.6
Chilean	6,860	53.1
Colombian	18,599	53.1
Ecuadorian	12,516	60.4
Paraguayan	372	64.7
Peruvian	26,944	46.7
Uruguayan	974	45.5
Venezuelan	3,111	41.6
Spaniard	7,564	58.0

Language Spoken at Home: English Only
(Universe: Population 5 Years and Over)

Group	Number	%
Total Population	19,429,309	57.0
Hispanic or Latino (of any race)	2,790,012	23.0
Central American, ex. Mexican	92,079	8.6
Costa Rican	5,737	27.9
Guatemalan	18,550	6.0
Honduran	4,584	6.9
Nicaraguan	14,189	15.6
Panamanian	6,274	39.0
Salvadoran	39,579	7.3
Cuban	26,026	33.5
Dominican Republic	3,013	34.9
Mexican	2,272,329	22.6
Puerto Rican	86,652	54.5

Group	Number	%
South American	51,942	19.1
Argentinean	7,979	19.7
Bolivian	2,316	18.1
Chilean	4,999	22.5
Colombian	10,802	19.3
Ecuadorian	6,526	19.0
Paraguayan	298	36.4
Peruvian	13,297	16.2
Uruguayan	824	26.7
Venezuelan	2,065	19.8
Spaniard	74,570	72.1

Language Spoken at Home: Spanish
(Universe: Population 5 Years and Over)

Group	Number	%
Total Population	9,706,949	28.5
Hispanic or Latino (of any race)	9,296,159	76.7
Central American, ex. Mexican	977,048	91.2
Costa Rican	14,732	71.6
Guatemalan	290,126	93.7
Honduran	61,440	92.8
Nicaraguan	76,400	84.0
Panamanian	9,593	59.6
Salvadoran	501,736	92.6
Cuban	50,832	65.5
Dominican Republic	5,467	63.3
Mexican	7,774,326	77.2
Puerto Rican	70,874	44.6
South American	217,643	79.9
Argentinean	31,738	78.4
Bolivian	10,281	80.5
Chilean	16,892	76.2
Colombian	44,728	79.8
Ecuadorian	27,617	80.3
Paraguayan	497	60.7
Peruvian	68,483	83.3
Uruguayan	2,228	72.3
Venezuelan	8,129	77.8
Spaniard	26,342	25.5

Unemployment Rate
(Universe: Population 16 Years and Over)

Group	%
Total Population	9.0
Hispanic or Latino (of any race)	10.6
Central American, ex. Mexican	9.6
Costa Rican	8.1
Guatemalan	9.7
Honduran	10.9
Nicaraguan	8.8
Panamanian	9.5
Salvadoran	9.5
Cuban	7.6
Dominican Republic	12.3
Mexican	10.9
Puerto Rican	11.6
South American	7.3
Argentinean	5.9
Bolivian	6.7
Chilean	7.8
Colombian	8.9
Ecuadorian	6.1
Paraguayan	6.3
Peruvian	7.6
Uruguayan	9.8
Venezuelan	6.8
Spaniard	11.1

Class of Worker: Private Wage and Salary
(Universe: Civilian Employed Population 16 Years and Over)

Group	Number	%
Total Population	12,729,790	76.5
Hispanic or Latino (of any race)	4,575,525	81.6
Central American, ex. Mexican	478,921	81.7
Costa Rican	8,003	75.0
Guatemalan	140,058	81.3
Honduran	29,091	82.6
Nicaraguan	39,062	80.1
Panamanian	6,157	74.9
Salvadoran	244,392	82.4
Cuban	28,815	76.0
Dominican Republic	3,076	73.6
Mexican	3,738,169	82.2
Puerto Rican	57,170	75.2
South American	114,081	75.8

Group	Number	%
Argentinean	17,066	73.1
Bolivian	5,882	78.4
Chilean	8,790	73.8
Colombian	22,924	76.6
Ecuadorian	13,967	76.8
Paraguayan	350	81.2
Peruvian	35,206	76.9
Uruguayan	1,160	69.5
Venezuelan	4,503	75.3
Spaniard	35,546	71.1

Class of Worker: Government
(Universe: Civilian Employed Population 16 Years and Over)

Group	Number	%
Total Population	2,425,341	14.6
Hispanic or Latino (of any race)	612,035	10.9
Central American, ex. Mexican	44,417	7.6
Costa Rican	1,643	15.4
Guatemalan	9,925	5.8
Honduran	1,903	5.4
Nicaraguan	6,062	12.4
Panamanian	1,634	19.9
Salvadoran	21,912	7.4
Cuban	6,410	16.9
Dominican Republic	764	18.3
Mexican	494,871	10.9
Puerto Rican	13,637	17.9
South American	19,382	12.9
Argentinean	2,902	12.4
Bolivian	808	10.8
Chilean	1,692	14.2
Colombian	3,994	13.4
Ecuadorian	2,921	16.1
Paraguayan	33	7.7
Peruvian	5,042	11.0
Uruguayan	223	13.4
Venezuelan	810	13.5
Spaniard	9,844	19.7

Means of Transportation to Work: Car, Truck or Van
(Universe: Workers 16 Years and Over)

Group	Number	%
Total Population	13,810,537	84.9
Hispanic or Latino (of any race)	4,640,511	85.0
Central American, ex. Mexican	445,021	77.6
Costa Rican	9,007	86.0
Guatemalan	120,308	71.4
Honduran	25,687	74.4
Nicaraguan	38,619	80.9
Panamanian	6,649	80.5
Salvadoran	232,885	80.4
Cuban	31,650	85.2
Dominican Republic	3,514	79.5
Mexican	3,803,879	85.9
Puerto Rican	64,118	84.5
South American	122,542	83.3
Argentinean	19,011	83.1
Bolivian	6,334	86.0
Chilean	9,092	79.2
Colombian	24,536	83.4
Ecuadorian	15,076	84.4
Paraguayan	388	90.0
Peruvian	37,084	83.5
Uruguayan	1,422	86.4
Venezuelan	4,710	79.6
Spaniard	41,707	86.1

Means of Transportation to Work: Public Transportation (ex. Taxicab)
(Universe: Workers 16 Years and Over)

Group	Number	%
Total Population	834,363	5.1
Hispanic or Latino (of any race)	364,353	6.7
Central American, ex. Mexican	80,674	14.1
Costa Rican	533	5.1
Guatemalan	31,511	18.7
Honduran	5,427	15.7
Nicaraguan	5,369	11.3
Panamanian	717	8.7
Salvadoran	35,329	12.2
Cuban	1,798	4.8
Dominican Republic	460	10.4
Mexican	257,943	5.8
Puerto Rican	4,192	5.5

Notes: (1) Percent of total population; (2) Percent of Hispanic/Latino population; Profiles include places with an overall population of at least 125,000, OR an overall population of at least 25,000 where the Hispanic/Latino population is at least 20% of the overall population. In states where less than five places meet either of these criteria, we have included places with at least 10,000 total population with the highest percentage of Hispanic/Latino population. These places are identified with an asterisk (*); Please refer to the User's Guide for a full explanation of data.

South American	9,505	6.5
Argentinean	971	4.2
Bolivian	580	7.9
Chilean	799	7.0
Colombian	1,824	6.2
Ecuadorian	1,169	6.5
Paraguayan	19	4.4
Peruvian	3,511	7.9
Uruguayan	61	3.7
Venezuelan	389	6.6
Spaniard	1,683	3.5

Homeownership Rate
(Universe: Occupied Housing Units)

Group	%
Total Population	55.9
Hispanic or Latino (of any race)	44.5
Central American, ex. Mexican	36.0
Costa Rican	50.7
Guatemalan	30.6
Honduran	28.1
Nicaraguan	43.2
Panamanian	46.9
Salvadoran	37.6
Cuban	49.8
Dominican Republic	36.6
Mexican	45.4
Puerto Rican	42.4
South American	49.0
Argentinean	54.0
Bolivian	56.4
Chilean	51.0
Colombian	47.2
Ecuadorian	53.8
Paraguayan	47.1
Peruvian	45.1
Uruguayan	49.6
Venezuelan	41.6
Spaniard	58.5

Median Home Value

Group	Dollars
Total Population	458,500
Hispanic or Latino (of any race)	366,300
Central American, ex. Mexican	392,600
Costa Rican	468,200
Guatemalan	377,000
Honduran	394,200
Nicaraguan	445,700
Panamanian	405,700
Salvadoran	383,600
Cuban	512,100
Dominican Republic	435,700
Mexican	352,800
Puerto Rican	437,300
South American	487,900
Argentinean	505,300
Bolivian	482,900
Chilean	535,100
Colombian	479,900
Ecuadorian	477,900
Paraguayan	419,000
Peruvian	468,900
Uruguayan	425,000
Venezuelan	457,500
Spaniard	452,500

Median Gross Rent

Group	Dollars
Total Population	1,147
Hispanic or Latino (of any race)	1,031
Central American, ex. Mexican	1,002
Costa Rican	1,197
Guatemalan	991
Honduran	991
Nicaraguan	1,123
Panamanian	1,146
Salvadoran	987
Cuban	1,076
Dominican Republic	1,176
Mexican	1,021
Puerto Rican	1,151
South American	1,223
Argentinean	1,306
Bolivian	1,310
Chilean	1,241
Colombian	1,232
Ecuadorian	1,154
Paraguayan	1,222
Peruvian	1,173
Uruguayan	1,085
Venezuelan	1,407
Spaniard	1,241

Median Household Income
(2010 Inflation-Adjusted Dollars)

Group	Dollars
Total Population	60,883
Hispanic or Latino (of any race)	47,180
Central American, ex. Mexican	45,430
Costa Rican	58,989
Guatemalan	41,894
Honduran	41,053
Nicaraguan	59,588
Panamanian	57,455
Salvadoran	45,098
Cuban	56,167
Dominican Republic	48,971
Mexican	46,493
Puerto Rican	56,154
South American	58,729
Argentinean	61,831
Bolivian	62,917
Chilean	62,895
Colombian	58,621
Ecuadorian	57,484
Paraguayan	29,091
Peruvian	53,557
Uruguayan	50,307
Venezuelan	60,246
Spaniard	58,906

Per Capita Income
(2010 Inflation-Adjusted Dollars)

Group	Dollars
Total Population	29,188
Hispanic or Latino (of any race)	15,670
Central American, ex. Mexican	16,414
Costa Rican	24,759
Guatemalan	14,592
Honduran	14,664
Nicaraguan	21,724
Panamanian	27,151
Salvadoran	16,023
Cuban	31,864
Dominican Republic	26,198
Mexican	14,765
Puerto Rican	23,768
South American	26,844
Argentinean	33,997
Bolivian	26,318
Chilean	28,387
Colombian	26,558
Ecuadorian	24,641
Paraguayan	51,943
Peruvian	22,894
Uruguayan	28,701
Venezuelan	28,297
Spaniard	30,825

Households with $100,000+ Income

Group	Number	%
Total Population	3,458,070	27.9
Hispanic or Latino (of any race)	510,555	15.5
Central American, ex. Mexican	43,083	13.6
Costa Rican	1,794	25.2
Guatemalan	9,676	10.9
Honduran	2,237	12.2
Nicaraguan	6,580	23.5
Panamanian	1,451	22.8
Salvadoran	19,829	12.5
Cuban	8,020	26.4
Dominican Republic	568	18.9
Mexican	385,639	14.6
Puerto Rican	13,638	24.0
South American	24,491	25.4
Argentinean	4,446	27.1
Bolivian	1,250	27.4
Chilean	2,270	28.6
Colombian	5,109	25.7
Ecuadorian	3,100	25.7
Paraguayan	26	8.3
Peruvian	5,648	21.4
Uruguayan	250	19.5
Venezuelan	1,036	27.5
Spaniard	11,920	26.0

Households with Food Stamps/SNAP Benefits During Past 12 Months

Group	Number	%
Total Population	673,449	5.4
Hispanic or Latino (of any race)	333,839	10.1
Central American, ex. Mexican	24,968	7.9
Costa Rican	229	3.2
Guatemalan	7,487	8.5
Honduran	2,383	13.0
Nicaraguan	1,558	5.6
Panamanian	272	4.3
Salvadoran	12,476	7.9
Cuban	1,117	3.7
Dominican Republic	231	7.7
Mexican	289,756	10.9
Puerto Rican	4,620	8.1
South American	3,025	3.1
Argentinean	361	2.2
Bolivian	89	2.0
Chilean	311	3.9
Colombian	535	2.7
Ecuadorian	590	4.9
Paraguayan	9	2.9
Peruvian	896	3.4
Uruguayan	37	2.9
Venezuelan	89	2.4
Spaniard	2,535	5.5

Poverty Rate
(Income in Past 12 Months Below Poverty Level)

Group	%
Total Population	13.7
Hispanic or Latino (of any race)	19.9
Central American, ex. Mexican	18.3
Costa Rican	7.9
Guatemalan	22.1
Honduran	25.8
Nicaraguan	12.0
Panamanian	8.6
Salvadoran	17.1
Cuban	9.6
Dominican Republic	16.2
Mexican	20.8
Puerto Rican	15.3
South American	10.4
Argentinean	8.5
Bolivian	6.4
Chilean	7.3
Colombian	11.4
Ecuadorian	11.5
Paraguayan	10.3
Peruvian	12.3
Uruguayan	8.6
Venezuelan	8.3
Spaniard	12.1

Adelanto

Population

Group	Number	%TP[1]	%HP[2]
Total Population	31,765	100.0	–
Hispanic or Latino (of any race)	18,513	58.3	100.0
Central American, ex. Mexican	1,244	3.9	6.7
Guatemalan	298	0.9	1.6
Honduran	104	0.3	0.6
Salvadoran	707	2.2	3.8
Mexican	15,471	48.7	83.6
Puerto Rican	240	0.8	1.3
South American	120	0.4	0.6
Spaniard	133	0.4	0.7

Population Growth: 2000–2010

Group	%
Total Population	75.2
Hispanic or Latino (of any race)	123.1
Central American, ex. Mexican	411.9

Notes: (1) Percent of total population; (2) Percent of Hispanic/Latino population; Profiles include places with an overall population of at least 125,000, OR an overall population of at least 25,000 where the Hispanic/Latino population is at least 20% of the overall population. In states where less than five places meet either of these criteria, we have included places with at least 10,000 total population with the highest percentage of Hispanic/Latino population. These places are identified with an asterisk (*); Please refer to the User's Guide for a full explanation of data.

Salvadoran	525.7
Mexican	141.2
Puerto Rican	60.0

Males per 100 Females

Group	Number
Total Population	105.6
Hispanic or Latino (of any race)	110.6
Central American, ex. Mexican	105.3
Guatemalan	108.4
Honduran	96.2
Salvadoran	106.7
Mexican	109.7
Puerto Rican	122.2
South American	84.6
Spaniard	118.0

Average Household Size

Group	People
Total Population	3.84
Hispanic or Latino (of any race)	4.37
Central American, ex. Mexican	4.13
Guatemalan	4.26
Honduran	3.87
Salvadoran	4.28
Mexican	4.43
Puerto Rican	3.68
South American	3.97
Spaniard	3.89

Median Age

Group	Years
Total Population	25.3
Hispanic or Latino (of any race)	23.2
Central American, ex. Mexican	31.5
Guatemalan	30.7
Honduran	39.7
Salvadoran	31.0
Mexican	22.7
Puerto Rican	23.3
South American	35.8
Spaniard	32.1

High School Graduates
(Universe: Population 25 Years and Over)

Group	Number	%
Total Population	9,534	65.2
Hispanic or Latino (of any race)	3,619	50.8
Central American, ex. Mexican	261	48.1
Mexican	2,972	48.1

Four-Year College Graduates
(Universe: Population 25 Years and Over)

Group	Number	%
Total Population	1,198	8.2
Hispanic or Latino (of any race)	434	6.1
Central American, ex. Mexican	63	11.6
Mexican	278	4.5

Population Age 3–17 Enrolled in Public School
(Universe: Population Age 3–17 Enrolled in School)

Group	Number	%
Total Population	8,501	95.4
Hispanic or Latino (of any race)	4,350	97.2
Central American, ex. Mexican	173	100.0
Mexican	3,873	97.4

Population Age 3–17 Enrolled in Private School
(Universe: Population Age 3–17 Enrolled in School)

Group	Number	%
Total Population	412	4.6
Hispanic or Latino (of any race)	124	2.8
Central American, ex. Mexican	0	0.0
Mexican	102	2.6

Foreign-Born Population

Group	Number	%
Total Population	6,251	21.0
Hispanic or Latino (of any race)	4,979	32.5
Central American, ex. Mexican	509	51.6
Mexican	4,306	31.9

Foreign-Born Naturalized U.S. Citizens

Group	Number	%
Total Population	2,047	32.7
Hispanic or Latino (of any race)	1,200	24.1
Central American, ex. Mexican	166	32.6
Mexican	935	21.7

Language Spoken at Home: English Only
(Universe: Population 5 Years and Over)

Group	Number	%
Total Population	14,500	54.1
Hispanic or Latino (of any race)	3,098	22.6
Central American, ex. Mexican	41	5.0
Mexican	2,624	21.7

Language Spoken at Home: Spanish
(Universe: Population 5 Years and Over)

Group	Number	%
Total Population	11,151	41.6
Hispanic or Latino (of any race)	10,582	77.1
Central American, ex. Mexican	773	93.9
Mexican	9,419	77.9

Unemployment Rate
(Universe: Population 16 Years and Over)

Group	%
Total Population	19.7
Hispanic or Latino (of any race)	18.1
Central American, ex. Mexican	8.9
Mexican	19.1

Class of Worker: Private Wage and Salary
(Universe: Civilian Employed Population 16 Years and Over)

Group	Number	%
Total Population	6,464	78.8
Hispanic or Latino (of any race)	3,645	84.5
Central American, ex. Mexican	279	82.3
Mexican	3,201	85.3

Class of Worker: Government
(Universe: Civilian Employed Population 16 Years and Over)

Group	Number	%
Total Population	1,287	15.7
Hispanic or Latino (of any race)	455	10.5
Central American, ex. Mexican	14	4.1
Mexican	404	10.8

Means of Transportation to Work: Car, Truck or Van
(Universe: Workers 16 Years and Over)

Group	Number	%
Total Population	7,056	90.0
Hispanic or Latino (of any race)	3,821	91.5
Central American, ex. Mexican	264	83.3
Mexican	3,390	92.6

Means of Transportation to Work: Public Transportation (ex. Taxicab)
(Universe: Workers 16 Years and Over)

Group	Number	%
Total Population	150	1.9
Hispanic or Latino (of any race)	84	2.0
Central American, ex. Mexican	53	16.7
Mexican	16	0.4

Homeownership Rate
(Universe: Occupied Housing Units)

Group	%
Total Population	57.8
Hispanic or Latino (of any race)	63.0
Central American, ex. Mexican	67.3
Guatemalan	70.9
Honduran	74.2
Salvadoran	63.0
Mexican	62.7
Puerto Rican	64.0
South American	72.7
Spaniard	55.6

Median Home Value

Group	Dollars
Total Population	170,500
Hispanic or Latino (of any race)	192,600
Central American, ex. Mexican	185,900
Mexican	187,900

Median Gross Rent

Group	Dollars
Total Population	988
Hispanic or Latino (of any race)	794
Central American, ex. Mexican	831
Mexican	794

Median Household Income
(2010 Inflation-Adjusted Dollars)

Group	Dollars
Total Population	43,305
Hispanic or Latino (of any race)	43,154
Central American, ex. Mexican	38,750
Mexican	43,925

Per Capita Income
(2010 Inflation-Adjusted Dollars)

Group	Dollars
Total Population	12,337
Hispanic or Latino (of any race)	10,538
Central American, ex. Mexican	12,073
Mexican	10,416

Households with $100,000+ Income

Group	Number	%
Total Population	534	7.6
Hispanic or Latino (of any race)	167	5.6
Central American, ex. Mexican	13	6.8
Mexican	120	4.6

Households with Food Stamps/SNAP Benefits During Past 12 Months

Group	Number	%
Total Population	1,600	22.7
Hispanic or Latino (of any race)	599	19.9
Central American, ex. Mexican	32	16.8
Mexican	528	20.1

Poverty Rate
(Income in Past 12 Months Below Poverty Level)

Group	%
Total Population	25.6
Hispanic or Latino (of any race)	23.6
Central American, ex. Mexican	36.8
Mexican	22.5

Alhambra

Population

Group	Number	%TP[1]	%HP[2]
Total Population	83,089	100.0	–
Hispanic or Latino (of any race)	28,582	34.4	100.0
Central American, ex. Mexican	2,842	3.4	9.9
Costa Rican	110	0.1	0.4
Guatemalan	713	0.9	2.5
Honduran	128	0.2	0.4
Nicaraguan	509	0.6	1.8
Salvadoran	1,286	1.5	4.5
Cuban	417	0.5	1.5
Mexican	22,159	26.7	77.5
Puerto Rican	346	0.4	1.2
South American	961	1.2	3.4
Argentinean	112	0.1	0.4
Colombian	225	0.3	0.8
Ecuadorian	249	0.3	0.9
Peruvian	248	0.3	0.9
Spaniard	295	0.4	1.0

Population Growth: 2000–2010

Group	%
Total Population	-3.2
Hispanic or Latino (of any race)	-6.1
Central American, ex. Mexican	53.7
Guatemalan	80.5
Nicaraguan	59.6
Salvadoran	77.9
Cuban	-2.3
Mexican	-3.1
Puerto Rican	4.8
South American	50.6
Colombian	44.2
Ecuadorian	107.5
Peruvian	54.0

Males per 100 Females

Group	Number
Total Population	89.9
Hispanic or Latino (of any race)	90.1

Notes: (1) Percent of total population; (2) Percent of Hispanic/Latino population; Profiles include places with an overall population of at least 125,000, OR an overall population of at least 25,000 where the Hispanic/Latino population is at least 20% of the overall population. In states where less than five places meet either of these criteria, we have included places with at least 10,000 total population with the highest percentage of Hispanic/Latino population. These places are identified with an asterisk (*); Please refer to the User's Guide for a full explanation of data.

Group	
Central American, ex. Mexican	85.6
Costa Rican	59.4
Guatemalan	87.6
Honduran	82.9
Nicaraguan	87.1
Salvadoran	86.1
Cuban	96.7
Mexican	91.2
Puerto Rican	92.2
South American	82.0
Argentinean	107.4
Colombian	75.8
Ecuadorian	72.9
Peruvian	74.6
Spaniard	75.6

Average Household Size

Group	People
Total Population	2.82
Hispanic or Latino (of any race)	3.01
Central American, ex. Mexican	3.32
Costa Rican	2.59
Guatemalan	3.60
Honduran	3.30
Nicaraguan	3.17
Salvadoran	3.37
Cuban	2.74
Mexican	3.01
Puerto Rican	2.52
South American	2.88
Argentinean	2.71
Colombian	2.64
Ecuadorian	2.85
Peruvian	3.25
Spaniard	2.67

Median Age

Group	Years
Total Population	39.3
Hispanic or Latino (of any race)	34.0
Central American, ex. Mexican	37.4
Costa Rican	52.0
Guatemalan	38.7
Honduran	36.2
Nicaraguan	39.2
Salvadoran	35.4
Cuban	42.8
Mexican	33.2
Puerto Rican	37.2
South American	39.7
Argentinean	40.8
Colombian	39.5
Ecuadorian	40.7
Peruvian	37.5
Spaniard	39.6

High School Graduates
(Universe: Population 25 Years and Over)

Group	Number	%
Total Population	47,562	78.8
Hispanic or Latino (of any race)	14,551	79.3
Central American, ex. Mexican	1,711	72.6
Guatemalan	315	62.4
Salvadoran	853	71.1
Mexican	10,963	79.2
South American	799	89.5

Four-Year College Graduates
(Universe: Population 25 Years and Over)

Group	Number	%
Total Population	19,033	31.6
Hispanic or Latino (of any race)	3,524	19.2
Central American, ex. Mexican	527	22.3
Guatemalan	74	14.7
Salvadoran	298	24.8
Mexican	2,556	18.5
South American	319	35.7

Population Age 3–17 Enrolled in Public School
(Universe: Population Age 3–17 Enrolled in School)

Group	Number	%
Total Population	10,347	85.3
Hispanic or Latino (of any race)	4,562	82.1
Central American, ex. Mexican	408	64.9
Guatemalan	117	100.0
Salvadoran	255	68.4
Mexican	3,652	85.1
South American	135	67.8

Population Age 3–17 Enrolled in Private School
(Universe: Population Age 3–17 Enrolled in School)

Group	Number	%
Total Population	1,785	14.7
Hispanic or Latino (of any race)	993	17.9
Central American, ex. Mexican	221	35.1
Guatemalan	0	0.0
Salvadoran	118	31.6
Mexican	641	14.9
South American	64	32.2

Foreign-Born Population

Group	Number	%
Total Population	43,960	52.7
Hispanic or Latino (of any race)	9,330	32.8
Central American, ex. Mexican	2,189	64.2
Guatemalan	518	70.8
Salvadoran	1,035	58.9
Mexican	6,079	27.8
South American	738	62.0

Foreign-Born Naturalized U.S. Citizens

Group	Number	%
Total Population	27,365	62.2
Hispanic or Latino (of any race)	4,915	52.7
Central American, ex. Mexican	1,262	57.7
Guatemalan	267	51.5
Salvadoran	678	65.5
Mexican	2,883	47.4
South American	490	66.4

Language Spoken at Home: English Only
(Universe: Population 5 Years and Over)

Group	Number	%
Total Population	20,306	25.8
Hispanic or Latino (of any race)	7,284	27.8
Central American, ex. Mexican	318	10.1
Guatemalan	21	3.0
Salvadoran	161	10.3
Mexican	5,708	28.3
South American	191	16.6

Language Spoken at Home: Spanish
(Universe: Population 5 Years and Over)

Group	Number	%
Total Population	19,559	24.8
Hispanic or Latino (of any race)	18,886	72.0
Central American, ex. Mexican	2,787	88.9
Guatemalan	645	92.5
Salvadoran	1,403	89.7
Mexican	14,413	71.5
South American	961	83.4

Unemployment Rate
(Universe: Population 16 Years and Over)

Group	%
Total Population	7.6
Hispanic or Latino (of any race)	8.6
Central American, ex. Mexican	6.7
Guatemalan	13.5
Salvadoran	4.9
Mexican	9.7
South American	0.0

Class of Worker: Private Wage and Salary
(Universe: Civilian Employed Population 16 Years and Over)

Group	Number	%
Total Population	31,088	76.7
Hispanic or Latino (of any race)	10,317	72.8
Central American, ex. Mexican	1,429	77.4
Guatemalan	241	65.8
Salvadoran	727	80.9
Mexican	7,808	72.2
South American	535	73.6

Class of Worker: Government
(Universe: Civilian Employed Population 16 Years and Over)

Group	Number	%
Total Population	6,385	15.7
Hispanic or Latino (of any race)	2,771	19.6
Central American, ex. Mexican	209	11.3
Guatemalan	57	15.6
Salvadoran	78	8.7
Mexican	2,224	20.6
South American	181	24.9

Means of Transportation to Work: Car, Truck or Van
(Universe: Workers 16 Years and Over)

Group	Number	%
Total Population	34,157	87.1
Hispanic or Latino (of any race)	11,500	83.4
Central American, ex. Mexican	1,520	84.3
Guatemalan	299	88.5
Salvadoran	790	89.4
Mexican	8,623	82.1
South American	677	94.8

Means of Transportation to Work: Public Transportation (ex. Taxicab)
(Universe: Workers 16 Years and Over)

Group	Number	%
Total Population	2,267	5.8
Hispanic or Latino (of any race)	1,222	8.9
Central American, ex. Mexican	134	7.4
Guatemalan	19	5.6
Salvadoran	72	8.1
Mexican	1,003	9.6
South American	27	3.8

Homeownership Rate
(Universe: Occupied Housing Units)

Group	%
Total Population	40.8
Hispanic or Latino (of any race)	35.2
Central American, ex. Mexican	28.2
Costa Rican	58.5
Guatemalan	27.8
Honduran	24.3
Nicaraguan	27.2
Salvadoran	27.0
Cuban	42.7
Mexican	36.2
Puerto Rican	34.7
South American	40.3
Argentinean	43.6
Colombian	48.1
Ecuadorian	44.7
Peruvian	25.8
Spaniard	45.7

Median Home Value

Group	Dollars
Total Population	514,800
Hispanic or Latino (of any race)	515,000
Central American, ex. Mexican	524,100
Guatemalan	594,600
Salvadoran	492,200
Mexican	512,000
South American	514,300

Median Gross Rent

Group	Dollars
Total Population	1,126
Hispanic or Latino (of any race)	1,126
Central American, ex. Mexican	1,108
Guatemalan	1,341
Salvadoran	1,085
Mexican	1,142
South American	1,083

Median Household Income
(2010 Inflation-Adjusted Dollars)

Group	Dollars
Total Population	51,527
Hispanic or Latino (of any race)	52,372
Central American, ex. Mexican	58,375
Guatemalan	80,429
Salvadoran	42,104
Mexican	52,813
South American	64,112

Per Capita Income
(2010 Inflation-Adjusted Dollars)

Group	Dollars
Total Population	24,327
Hispanic or Latino (of any race)	22,938

Notes: (1) Percent of total population; (2) Percent of Hispanic/Latino population; Profiles include places with an overall population of at least 125,000, OR an overall population of at least 25,000 where the Hispanic/Latino population is at least 20% of the overall population. In states where less than five places meet either of these criteria, we have included places with at least 10,000 total population with the highest percentage of Hispanic/Latino population. These places are identified with an asterisk (*); Please refer to the User's Guide for a full explanation of data.

Central American, ex. Mexican	21,429	
Guatemalan	21,961	
Salvadoran	19,419	
Mexican	22,832	
South American	29,743	

Households with $100,000+ Income

Group	Number	%
Total Population	5,602	19.4
Hispanic or Latino (of any race)	1,680	18.1
Central American, ex. Mexican	173	15.4
Guatemalan	42	20.2
Salvadoran	54	8.8
Mexican	1,333	19.0
South American	147	32.1

Households with Food Stamps/SNAP Benefits During Past 12 Months

Group	Number	%
Total Population	957	3.3
Hispanic or Latino (of any race)	406	4.4
Central American, ex. Mexican	39	3.5
Guatemalan	0	0.0
Salvadoran	39	6.4
Mexican	331	4.7
South American	0	0.0

Poverty Rate
(Income in Past 12 Months Below Poverty Level)

Group	%
Total Population	12.7
Hispanic or Latino (of any race)	9.2
Central American, ex. Mexican	13.7
Guatemalan	8.5
Salvadoran	19.7
Mexican	9.4
South American	0.9

Altadena

Population

Group	Number	%TP[1]	%HP[2]
Total Population	42,777	100.0	–
Hispanic or Latino (of any race)	11,502	26.9	100.0
Central American, ex. Mexican	1,496	3.5	13.0
Guatemalan	275	0.6	2.4
Honduran	185	0.4	1.6
Nicaraguan	102	0.2	0.9
Salvadoran	783	1.8	6.8
Cuban	170	0.4	1.5
Mexican	8,477	19.8	73.7
Puerto Rican	196	0.5	1.7
South American	459	1.1	4.0
Argentinean	114	0.3	1.0
Colombian	139	0.3	1.2
Spaniard	101	0.2	0.9

Population Growth: 2000–2010

Group	%
Total Population	0.4
Hispanic or Latino (of any race)	32.4
Central American, ex. Mexican	119.0
Guatemalan	152.3
Salvadoran	162.8
Cuban	31.8
Mexican	36.9
Puerto Rican	60.7
South American	92.1

Males per 100 Females

Group	Number
Total Population	93.1
Hispanic or Latino (of any race)	98.1
Central American, ex. Mexican	89.6
Guatemalan	89.7
Honduran	94.7
Nicaraguan	70.0
Salvadoran	95.3
Cuban	93.2
Mexican	101.1
Puerto Rican	83.2
South American	100.4
Argentinean	132.7
Colombian	78.2
Spaniard	80.4

Average Household Size

Group	People
Total Population	2.78
Hispanic or Latino (of any race)	3.98
Central American, ex. Mexican	4.21
Guatemalan	4.45
Honduran	4.49
Nicaraguan	3.59
Salvadoran	4.53
Cuban	3.00
Mexican	4.11
Puerto Rican	2.48
South American	3.15
Argentinean	2.50
Colombian	3.41
Spaniard	2.38

Median Age

Group	Years
Total Population	41.8
Hispanic or Latino (of any race)	30.0
Central American, ex. Mexican	34.4
Guatemalan	34.8
Honduran	33.4
Nicaraguan	39.0
Salvadoran	32.1
Cuban	37.5
Mexican	28.8
Puerto Rican	36.7
South American	40.3
Argentinean	40.0
Colombian	42.8
Spaniard	43.5

High School Graduates
(Universe: Population 25 Years and Over)

Group	Number	%
Total Population	26,776	86.0
Hispanic or Latino (of any race)	4,399	63.7
Central American, ex. Mexican	576	60.5
Mexican	3,235	61.2

Four-Year College Graduates
(Universe: Population 25 Years and Over)

Group	Number	%
Total Population	12,968	41.7
Hispanic or Latino (of any race)	1,235	17.9
Central American, ex. Mexican	183	19.2
Mexican	749	14.2

Population Age 3–17 Enrolled in Public School
(Universe: Population Age 3–17 Enrolled in School)

Group	Number	%
Total Population	5,219	60.5
Hispanic or Latino (of any race)	2,346	73.4
Central American, ex. Mexican	333	80.0
Mexican	1,906	75.2

Population Age 3–17 Enrolled in Private School
(Universe: Population Age 3–17 Enrolled in School)

Group	Number	%
Total Population	3,401	39.5
Hispanic or Latino (of any race)	849	26.6
Central American, ex. Mexican	83	20.0
Mexican	629	24.8

Foreign-Born Population

Group	Number	%
Total Population	8,830	19.4
Hispanic or Latino (of any race)	3,862	30.6
Central American, ex. Mexican	932	54.2
Mexican	2,653	27.2

Foreign-Born Naturalized U.S. Citizens

Group	Number	%
Total Population	5,356	60.7
Hispanic or Latino (of any race)	1,741	45.1
Central American, ex. Mexican	323	34.7
Mexican	1,169	44.1

Language Spoken at Home: English Only
(Universe: Population 5 Years and Over)

Group	Number	%
Total Population	29,255	69.0
Hispanic or Latino (of any race)	3,277	28.6
Central American, ex. Mexican	145	9.3
Mexican	2,829	32.0

Language Spoken at Home: Spanish
(Universe: Population 5 Years and Over)

Group	Number	%
Total Population	8,749	20.6
Hispanic or Latino (of any race)	8,120	70.9
Central American, ex. Mexican	1,379	88.9
Mexican	5,987	67.7

Unemployment Rate
(Universe: Population 16 Years and Over)

Group	%
Total Population	7.3
Hispanic or Latino (of any race)	7.2
Central American, ex. Mexican	3.7
Mexican	8.3

Class of Worker: Private Wage and Salary
(Universe: Civilian Employed Population 16 Years and Over)

Group	Number	%
Total Population	15,392	70.1
Hispanic or Latino (of any race)	4,253	74.7
Central American, ex. Mexican	631	77.6
Mexican	3,277	75.4

Class of Worker: Government
(Universe: Civilian Employed Population 16 Years and Over)

Group	Number	%
Total Population	3,785	17.2
Hispanic or Latino (of any race)	705	12.4
Central American, ex. Mexican	104	12.8
Mexican	452	10.4

Means of Transportation to Work: Car, Truck or Van
(Universe: Workers 16 Years and Over)

Group	Number	%
Total Population	18,574	86.8
Hispanic or Latino (of any race)	4,857	88.3
Central American, ex. Mexican	687	87.6
Mexican	3,706	88.0

Means of Transportation to Work: Public Transportation (ex. Taxicab)
(Universe: Workers 16 Years and Over)

Group	Number	%
Total Population	966	4.5
Hispanic or Latino (of any race)	276	5.0
Central American, ex. Mexican	29	3.7
Mexican	211	5.0

Homeownership Rate
(Universe: Occupied Housing Units)

Group	%
Total Population	71.6
Hispanic or Latino (of any race)	60.1
Central American, ex. Mexican	58.2
Guatemalan	64.6
Honduran	29.8
Nicaraguan	70.4
Salvadoran	58.8
Cuban	76.9
Mexican	59.1
Puerto Rican	56.3
South American	75.0
Argentinean	72.7
Colombian	90.9
Spaniard	66.7

Median Home Value

Group	Dollars
Total Population	639,600
Hispanic or Latino (of any race)	541,300
Central American, ex. Mexican	610,800
Mexican	521,900

Median Gross Rent

Group	Dollars
Total Population	1,222
Hispanic or Latino (of any race)	1,326
Central American, ex. Mexican	1,454
Mexican	1,239

Notes: (1) Percent of total population; (2) Percent of Hispanic/Latino population; Profiles include places with an overall population of at least 125,000, OR an overall population of at least 25,000 where the Hispanic/Latino population is at least 20% of the overall population. In states where less than five places meet either of these criteria, we have included places with at least 10,000 total population with the highest percentage of Hispanic/Latino population. These places are identified with an asterisk (*); Please refer to the User's Guide for a full explanation of data.

Median Household Income
(2010 Inflation-Adjusted Dollars)

Group	Dollars
Total Population	82,839
Hispanic or Latino (of any race)	67,542
Central American, ex. Mexican	70,714
Mexican	57,622

Per Capita Income
(2010 Inflation-Adjusted Dollars)

Group	Dollars
Total Population	38,541
Hispanic or Latino (of any race)	22,645
Central American, ex. Mexican	18,316
Mexican	19,605

Households with $100,000+ Income

Group	Number	%
Total Population	6,108	39.3
Hispanic or Latino (of any race)	846	29.8
Central American, ex. Mexican	93	20.9
Mexican	592	27.8

Households with Food Stamps/SNAP Benefits During Past 12 Months

Group	Number	%
Total Population	526	3.4
Hispanic or Latino (of any race)	238	8.4
Central American, ex. Mexican	0	0.0
Mexican	226	10.6

Poverty Rate
(Income in Past 12 Months Below Poverty Level)

Group	%
Total Population	9.2
Hispanic or Latino (of any race)	19.9
Central American, ex. Mexican	30.1
Mexican	19.9

Anaheim

Population

Group	Number	%TP[1]	%HP[2]
Total Population	336,265	100.0	–
Hispanic or Latino (of any race)	177,467	52.8	100.0
Central American, ex. Mexican	9,074	2.7	5.1
Costa Rican	296	0.1	0.2
Guatemalan	3,474	1.0	2.0
Honduran	636	0.2	0.4
Nicaraguan	543	0.2	0.3
Panamanian	100	<0.1	0.1
Salvadoran	3,957	1.2	2.2
Cuban	945	0.3	0.5
Dominican Republic	114	<0.1	0.1
Mexican	154,554	46.0	87.1
Puerto Rican	1,439	0.4	0.8
South American	3,763	1.1	2.1
Argentinean	519	0.2	0.3
Bolivian	211	0.1	0.1
Chilean	181	0.1	0.1
Colombian	884	0.3	0.5
Ecuadorian	417	0.1	0.2
Peruvian	1,365	0.4	0.8
Spaniard	1,001	0.3	0.6

Population Growth: 2000–2010

Group	%
Total Population	2.5
Hispanic or Latino (of any race)	15.7
Central American, ex. Mexican	80.9
Costa Rican	44.4
Guatemalan	112.1
Honduran	108.5
Nicaraguan	73.5
Salvadoran	98.6
Cuban	5.4
Mexican	22.6
Puerto Rican	10.2
South American	56.4
Argentinean	87.4
Bolivian	91.8
Chilean	54.7
Colombian	80.0
Ecuadorian	87.8
Peruvian	55.8
Spaniard	447.0

Males per 100 Females

Group	Number
Total Population	99.0
Hispanic or Latino (of any race)	102.0
Central American, ex. Mexican	96.2
Costa Rican	91.0
Guatemalan	107.4
Honduran	85.4
Nicaraguan	83.4
Panamanian	66.7
Salvadoran	91.9
Cuban	85.7
Dominican Republic	90.0
Mexican	103.2
Puerto Rican	90.1
South American	84.5
Argentinean	102.7
Bolivian	85.1
Chilean	77.5
Colombian	88.5
Ecuadorian	78.2
Peruvian	79.8
Spaniard	81.7

Average Household Size

Group	People
Total Population	3.38
Hispanic or Latino (of any race)	4.47
Central American, ex. Mexican	4.30
Costa Rican	3.12
Guatemalan	4.66
Honduran	4.60
Nicaraguan	3.67
Panamanian	2.74
Salvadoran	4.25
Cuban	2.72
Dominican Republic	2.76
Mexican	4.61
Puerto Rican	2.90
South American	3.36
Argentinean	3.01
Bolivian	3.83
Chilean	2.62
Colombian	3.23
Ecuadorian	3.60
Peruvian	3.59
Spaniard	3.03

Median Age

Group	Years
Total Population	32.4
Hispanic or Latino (of any race)	26.2
Central American, ex. Mexican	32.2
Costa Rican	38.4
Guatemalan	31.3
Honduran	28.9
Nicaraguan	34.5
Panamanian	40.5
Salvadoran	32.8
Cuban	41.1
Dominican Republic	32.1
Mexican	25.5
Puerto Rican	29.7
South American	37.8
Argentinean	39.6
Bolivian	38.2
Chilean	36.8
Colombian	36.3
Ecuadorian	39.4
Peruvian	38.5
Spaniard	34.7

High School Graduates
(Universe: Population 25 Years and Over)

Group	Number	%
Total Population	150,557	73.7
Hispanic or Latino (of any race)	45,714	51.8
Central American, ex. Mexican	2,708	47.4
Guatemalan	672	31.7
Salvadoran	1,219	54.5
Cuban	596	88.4
Mexican	38,317	50.1
Puerto Rican	621	73.5
South American	1,962	86.4
Colombian	347	76.6
Peruvian	934	87.2

Four-Year College Graduates
(Universe: Population 25 Years and Over)

Group	Number	%
Total Population	47,167	23.1
Hispanic or Latino (of any race)	7,457	8.5
Central American, ex. Mexican	499	8.7
Guatemalan	152	7.2
Salvadoran	217	9.7
Cuban	154	22.8
Mexican	5,735	7.5
Puerto Rican	157	18.6
South American	605	26.6
Colombian	136	30.0
Peruvian	288	26.9

Population Age 3–17 Enrolled in Public School
(Universe: Population Age 3–17 Enrolled in School)

Group	Number	%
Total Population	62,980	90.2
Hispanic or Latino (of any race)	43,725	95.0
Central American, ex. Mexican	2,210	96.1
Guatemalan	785	98.9
Salvadoran	750	100.0
Cuban	138	71.1
Mexican	39,265	95.5
Puerto Rican	364	97.3
South American	840	90.6
Colombian	93	55.7
Peruvian	316	100.0

Population Age 3–17 Enrolled in Private School
(Universe: Population Age 3–17 Enrolled in School)

Group	Number	%
Total Population	6,812	9.8
Hispanic or Latino (of any race)	2,279	5.0
Central American, ex. Mexican	89	3.9
Guatemalan	9	1.1
Salvadoran	0	0.0
Cuban	56	28.9
Mexican	1,857	4.5
Puerto Rican	10	2.7
South American	87	9.4
Colombian	74	44.3
Peruvian	0	0.0

Foreign-Born Population

Group	Number	%
Total Population	127,652	38.3
Hispanic or Latino (of any race)	80,397	46.6
Central American, ex. Mexican	5,751	58.7
Guatemalan	2,225	62.0
Salvadoran	2,253	60.6
Cuban	402	44.3
Mexican	70,622	46.3
Puerto Rican	129	9.1
South American	2,473	64.1
Colombian	503	69.1
Peruvian	1,178	69.5

Foreign-Born Naturalized U.S. Citizens

Group	Number	%
Total Population	50,223	39.3
Hispanic or Latino (of any race)	18,886	23.5
Central American, ex. Mexican	1,713	29.8
Guatemalan	539	24.2
Salvadoran	591	26.2
Cuban	306	76.1
Mexican	15,331	21.7
Puerto Rican	40	31.0
South American	1,083	43.8
Colombian	156	31.0
Peruvian	639	54.2

Language Spoken at Home: English Only
(Universe: Population 5 Years and Over)

Group	Number	%
Total Population	122,661	40.0
Hispanic or Latino (of any race)	23,814	15.4
Central American, ex. Mexican	706	7.8

Notes: (1) Percent of total population; (2) Percent of Hispanic/Latino population; Profiles include places with an overall population of at least 125,000, OR an overall population of at least 25,000 where the Hispanic/Latino population is at least 20% of the overall population. In states where less than five places meet either of these criteria, we have included places with at least 10,000 total population with the highest percentage of Hispanic/Latino population. These places are identified with an asterisk (*); Please refer to the User's Guide for a full explanation of data.

Guatemalan	106	3.2
Salvadoran	315	9.2
Cuban	418	48.7
Mexican	20,045	14.7
Puerto Rican	606	44.5
South American	519	14.5
Colombian	80	12.3
Peruvian	66	4.1

Language Spoken at Home: Spanish
(Universe: Population 5 Years and Over)

Group	Number	%
Total Population	133,288	43.5
Hispanic or Latino (of any race)	130,605	84.4
Central American, ex. Mexican	8,275	91.6
Guatemalan	3,150	96.2
Salvadoran	3,077	89.8
Cuban	440	51.3
Mexican	116,063	85.2
Puerto Rican	755	55.5
South American	3,060	85.5
Colombian	573	87.7
Peruvian	1,554	95.9

Unemployment Rate
(Universe: Population 16 Years and Over)

Group	%
Total Population	9.6
Hispanic or Latino (of any race)	11.3
Central American, ex. Mexican	8.3
Guatemalan	2.8
Salvadoran	8.1
Cuban	5.9
Mexican	11.5
Puerto Rican	12.1
South American	13.1
Colombian	8.9
Peruvian	17.3

Class of Worker: Private Wage and Salary
(Universe: Civilian Employed Population 16 Years and Over)

Group	Number	%
Total Population	131,607	84.5
Hispanic or Latino (of any race)	67,331	88.4
Central American, ex. Mexican	4,439	86.3
Guatemalan	1,669	89.5
Salvadoran	1,781	86.2
Cuban	397	80.0
Mexican	59,171	88.8
Puerto Rican	550	84.5
South American	1,386	84.9
Colombian	301	89.1
Peruvian	621	87.1

Class of Worker: Government
(Universe: Civilian Employed Population 16 Years and Over)

Group	Number	%
Total Population	14,748	9.5
Hispanic or Latino (of any race)	5,121	6.7
Central American, ex. Mexican	329	6.4
Guatemalan	66	3.5
Salvadoran	144	7.0
Cuban	82	16.5
Mexican	4,375	6.6
Puerto Rican	74	11.4
South American	151	9.3
Colombian	0	0.0
Peruvian	71	10.0

Means of Transportation to Work: Car, Truck or Van
(Universe: Workers 16 Years and Over)

Group	Number	%
Total Population	135,013	88.6
Hispanic or Latino (of any race)	64,271	86.2
Central American, ex. Mexican	4,282	85.9
Guatemalan	1,449	79.9
Salvadoran	1,813	88.8
Cuban	433	94.1
Mexican	56,107	86.0
Puerto Rican	544	83.6
South American	1,511	93.7
Colombian	310	91.7
Peruvian	635	90.8

Means of Transportation to Work: Public Transportation (ex. Taxicab)
(Universe: Workers 16 Years and Over)

Group	Number	%
Total Population	7,315	4.8
Hispanic or Latino (of any race)	5,452	7.3
Central American, ex. Mexican	448	9.0
Guatemalan	260	14.3
Salvadoran	117	5.7
Cuban	13	2.8
Mexican	4,783	7.3
Puerto Rican	84	12.9
South American	64	4.0
Colombian	0	0.0
Peruvian	64	9.2

Homeownership Rate
(Universe: Occupied Housing Units)

Group	%
Total Population	48.5
Hispanic or Latino (of any race)	34.0
Central American, ex. Mexican	32.1
Costa Rican	40.5
Guatemalan	30.8
Honduran	24.8
Nicaraguan	42.9
Panamanian	38.5
Salvadoran	31.4
Cuban	47.6
Dominican Republic	32.4
Mexican	33.6
Puerto Rican	40.0
South American	41.6
Argentinean	42.6
Bolivian	50.0
Chilean	44.2
Colombian	34.1
Ecuadorian	55.4
Peruvian	38.1
Spaniard	48.6

Median Home Value

Group	Dollars
Total Population	503,000
Hispanic or Latino (of any race)	461,800
Central American, ex. Mexican	434,400
Guatemalan	368,900
Salvadoran	436,500
Cuban	625,000
Mexican	455,700
Puerto Rican	559,700
South American	500,000
Colombian	391,700
Peruvian	503,400

Median Gross Rent

Group	Dollars
Total Population	1,262
Hispanic or Latino (of any race)	1,253
Central American, ex. Mexican	1,261
Guatemalan	1,272
Salvadoran	1,202
Cuban	986
Mexican	1,256
Puerto Rican	1,097
South American	1,234
Colombian	1,318
Peruvian	1,210

Median Household Income
(2010 Inflation-Adjusted Dollars)

Group	Dollars
Total Population	57,807
Hispanic or Latino (of any race)	49,495
Central American, ex. Mexican	48,014
Guatemalan	43,500
Salvadoran	48,646
Cuban	61,250
Mexican	49,335
Puerto Rican	37,457
South American	55,685
Colombian	60,417
Peruvian	35,859

Per Capita Income
(2010 Inflation-Adjusted Dollars)

Group	Dollars
Total Population	22,911
Hispanic or Latino (of any race)	14,397
Central American, ex. Mexican	15,362
Guatemalan	13,823
Salvadoran	15,640
Cuban	32,728
Mexican	14,082
Puerto Rican	18,677
South American	17,197
Colombian	19,340
Peruvian	14,790

Households with $100,000+ Income

Group	Number	%
Total Population	23,864	24.0
Hispanic or Latino (of any race)	5,914	15.1
Central American, ex. Mexican	286	12.5
Guatemalan	129	15.2
Salvadoran	53	6.4
Cuban	109	29.1
Mexican	5,133	15.2
Puerto Rican	40	7.8
South American	218	18.9
Colombian	49	20.9
Peruvian	64	16.0

Households with Food Stamps/SNAP Benefits During Past 12 Months

Group	Number	%
Total Population	5,890	5.9
Hispanic or Latino (of any race)	3,910	10.0
Central American, ex. Mexican	152	6.7
Guatemalan	49	5.8
Salvadoran	68	8.2
Cuban	29	7.7
Mexican	3,567	10.6
Puerto Rican	55	10.7
South American	67	5.8
Colombian	0	0.0
Peruvian	9	2.3

Poverty Rate
(Income in Past 12 Months Below Poverty Level)

Group	%
Total Population	13.7
Hispanic or Latino (of any race)	19.1
Central American, ex. Mexican	18.3
Guatemalan	20.7
Salvadoran	18.9
Cuban	18.2
Mexican	19.7
Puerto Rican	13.6
South American	9.6
Colombian	3.1
Peruvian	15.2

Antioch

Population

Group	Number	%TP[1]	%HP[2]
Total Population	102,372	100.0	–
Hispanic or Latino (of any race)	32,436	31.7	100.0
Central American, ex. Mexican	4,289	4.2	13.2
Guatemalan	452	0.4	1.4
Honduran	150	0.1	0.5
Nicaraguan	1,269	1.2	3.9
Salvadoran	2,212	2.2	6.8
Cuban	185	0.2	0.6
Mexican	23,110	22.6	71.2
Puerto Rican	1,204	1.2	3.7
South American	1,083	1.1	3.3
Peruvian	748	0.7	2.3
Spaniard	635	0.6	2.0

Population Growth: 2000–2010

Group	%
Total Population	13.1
Hispanic or Latino (of any race)	62.0
Central American, ex. Mexican	242.8
Guatemalan	253.1

Notes: (1) Percent of total population; (2) Percent of Hispanic/Latino population; Profiles include places with an overall population of at least 125,000, OR an overall population of at least 25,000 where the Hispanic/Latino population is at least 20% of the overall population. In states where less than five places meet either of these criteria, we have included places with at least 10,000 total population with the highest percentage of Hispanic/Latino population. These places are identified with an asterisk (*); Please refer to the User's Guide for a full explanation of data.

Nicaraguan	279.9
Salvadoran	312.7
Cuban	54.2
Mexican	69.7
Puerto Rican	52.0
South American	200.8
Peruvian	322.6

Males per 100 Females

Group	Number
Total Population	94.8
Hispanic or Latino (of any race)	98.7
Central American, ex. Mexican	87.3
Guatemalan	89.9
Honduran	89.9
Nicaraguan	85.3
Salvadoran	89.2
Cuban	98.9
Mexican	101.9
Puerto Rican	96.1
South American	101.7
Peruvian	103.8
Spaniard	76.9

Average Household Size

Group	People
Total Population	3.15
Hispanic or Latino (of any race)	3.83
Central American, ex. Mexican	3.92
Guatemalan	3.82
Honduran	4.15
Nicaraguan	3.99
Salvadoran	3.93
Cuban	2.72
Mexican	3.96
Puerto Rican	3.25
South American	3.77
Peruvian	4.21
Spaniard	2.98

Median Age

Group	Years
Total Population	33.8
Hispanic or Latino (of any race)	26.5
Central American, ex. Mexican	32.2
Guatemalan	32.5
Honduran	29.8
Nicaraguan	32.1
Salvadoran	32.1
Cuban	32.2
Mexican	25.2
Puerto Rican	25.6
South American	35.5
Peruvian	34.4
Spaniard	37.6

High School Graduates
(Universe: Population 25 Years and Over)

Group	Number	%
Total Population	50,132	84.2
Hispanic or Latino (of any race)	11,255	68.5
Central American, ex. Mexican	2,087	80.1
Nicaraguan	824	77.9
Salvadoran	921	78.6
Mexican	7,488	64.3
Puerto Rican	553	84.2

Four-Year College Graduates
(Universe: Population 25 Years and Over)

Group	Number	%
Total Population	11,976	20.1
Hispanic or Latino (of any race)	1,225	7.5
Central American, ex. Mexican	194	7.4
Nicaraguan	95	9.0
Salvadoran	45	3.8
Mexican	780	6.7
Puerto Rican	131	19.9

Population Age 3–17 Enrolled in Public School
(Universe: Population Age 3–17 Enrolled in School)

Group	Number	%
Total Population	20,101	91.7
Hispanic or Latino (of any race)	7,680	95.9
Central American, ex. Mexican	948	97.0
Nicaraguan	450	97.4
Salvadoran	473	96.5
Mexican	5,808	95.6
Puerto Rican	361	94.0

Population Age 3–17 Enrolled in Private School
(Universe: Population Age 3–17 Enrolled in School)

Group	Number	%
Total Population	1,809	8.3
Hispanic or Latino (of any race)	332	4.1
Central American, ex. Mexican	29	3.0
Nicaraguan	12	2.6
Salvadoran	17	3.5
Mexican	265	4.4
Puerto Rican	23	6.0

Foreign-Born Population

Group	Number	%
Total Population	22,008	22.1
Hispanic or Latino (of any race)	12,005	38.1
Central American, ex. Mexican	2,270	47.7
Nicaraguan	1,028	55.6
Salvadoran	929	39.5
Mexican	8,902	39.1
Puerto Rican	55	4.2

Foreign-Born Naturalized U.S. Citizens

Group	Number	%
Total Population	11,435	52.0
Hispanic or Latino (of any race)	4,274	35.6
Central American, ex. Mexican	1,461	64.4
Nicaraguan	702	68.3
Salvadoran	570	61.4
Mexican	2,434	27.3
Puerto Rican	11	20.0

Language Spoken at Home: English Only
(Universe: Population 5 Years and Over)

Group	Number	%
Total Population	61,419	66.8
Hispanic or Latino (of any race)	8,935	31.4
Central American, ex. Mexican	1,003	22.6
Nicaraguan	260	14.8
Salvadoran	551	25.9
Mexican	5,941	29.1
Puerto Rican	698	57.6

Language Spoken at Home: Spanish
(Universe: Population 5 Years and Over)

Group	Number	%
Total Population	20,413	22.2
Hispanic or Latino (of any race)	19,494	68.4
Central American, ex. Mexican	3,443	77.4
Nicaraguan	1,498	85.2
Salvadoran	1,578	74.1
Mexican	14,389	70.6
Puerto Rican	503	41.5

Unemployment Rate
(Universe: Population 16 Years and Over)

Group	%
Total Population	10.3
Hispanic or Latino (of any race)	12.7
Central American, ex. Mexican	17.8
Nicaraguan	15.5
Salvadoran	20.7
Mexican	12.2
Puerto Rican	7.2

Class of Worker: Private Wage and Salary
(Universe: Civilian Employed Population 16 Years and Over)

Group	Number	%
Total Population	34,401	78.4
Hispanic or Latino (of any race)	10,948	83.6
Central American, ex. Mexican	1,655	78.0
Nicaraguan	649	74.6
Salvadoran	722	74.6
Mexican	7,908	85.1
Puerto Rican	532	93.3

Class of Worker: Government
(Universe: Civilian Employed Population 16 Years and Over)

Group	Number	%
Total Population	6,729	15.3
Hispanic or Latino (of any race)	1,428	10.9
Central American, ex. Mexican	354	16.7
Nicaraguan	201	23.1
Salvadoran	153	15.8
Mexican	854	9.2
Puerto Rican	24	4.2

Means of Transportation to Work: Car, Truck or Van
(Universe: Workers 16 Years and Over)

Group	Number	%
Total Population	37,592	88.2
Hispanic or Latino (of any race)	11,229	88.8
Central American, ex. Mexican	1,808	89.6
Nicaraguan	669	83.2
Salvadoran	855	91.9
Mexican	8,038	89.5
Puerto Rican	464	83.2

Means of Transportation to Work: Public Transportation (ex. Taxicab)
(Universe: Workers 16 Years and Over)

Group	Number	%
Total Population	2,340	5.5
Hispanic or Latino (of any race)	695	5.5
Central American, ex. Mexican	109	5.4
Nicaraguan	99	12.3
Salvadoran	10	1.1
Mexican	487	5.4
Puerto Rican	42	7.5

Homeownership Rate
(Universe: Occupied Housing Units)

Group	%
Total Population	64.3
Hispanic or Latino (of any race)	56.4
Central American, ex. Mexican	63.8
Guatemalan	66.9
Honduran	51.2
Nicaraguan	65.7
Salvadoran	63.2
Cuban	61.2
Mexican	54.1
Puerto Rican	51.0
South American	66.8
Peruvian	62.2
Spaniard	76.1

Median Home Value

Group	Dollars
Total Population	388,300
Hispanic or Latino (of any race)	396,300
Central American, ex. Mexican	381,300
Nicaraguan	327,100
Salvadoran	407,500
Mexican	388,900
Puerto Rican	450,500

Median Gross Rent

Group	Dollars
Total Population	1,213
Hispanic or Latino (of any race)	1,202
Central American, ex. Mexican	1,592
Nicaraguan	1,174
Salvadoran	1,674
Mexican	1,189
Puerto Rican	1,106

Median Household Income
(2010 Inflation-Adjusted Dollars)

Group	Dollars
Total Population	66,351
Hispanic or Latino (of any race)	59,227
Central American, ex. Mexican	71,633
Nicaraguan	105,313
Salvadoran	68,615
Mexican	54,560
Puerto Rican	73,150

Per Capita Income
(2010 Inflation-Adjusted Dollars)

Group	Dollars
Total Population	25,458
Hispanic or Latino (of any race)	18,056
Central American, ex. Mexican	22,488
Nicaraguan	28,130
Salvadoran	18,111
Mexican	16,368

Notes: (1) Percent of total population; (2) Percent of Hispanic/Latino population; Profiles include places with an overall population of at least 125,000, OR an overall population of at least 25,000 where the Hispanic/Latino population is at least 20% of the overall population. In states where less than five places meet either of these criteria, we have included places with at least 10,000 total population with the highest percentage of Hispanic/Latino population. These places are identified with an asterisk (*); Please refer to the User's Guide for a full explanation of data.

Puerto Rican	24,423	

Households with $100,000+ Income

Group	Number	%
Total Population	8,752	28.1
Hispanic or Latino (of any race)	1,654	22.1
Central American, ex. Mexican	354	27.0
Nicaraguan	243	50.4
Salvadoran	91	15.8
Mexican	1,061	20.6
Puerto Rican	109	34.4

Households with Food Stamps/SNAP Benefits During Past 12 Months

Group	Number	%
Total Population	2,252	7.2
Hispanic or Latino (of any race)	574	7.7
Central American, ex. Mexican	85	6.5
Nicaraguan	5	1.0
Salvadoran	80	13.9
Mexican	417	8.1
Puerto Rican	45	14.2

Poverty Rate
(Income in Past 12 Months Below Poverty Level)

Group	%
Total Population	13.4
Hispanic or Latino (of any race)	14.9
Central American, ex. Mexican	10.0
Nicaraguan	1.6
Salvadoran	17.0
Mexican	17.7
Puerto Rican	5.3

Apple Valley

Population

Group	Number	%TP[1]	%HP[2]
Total Population	69,135	100.0	–
Hispanic or Latino (of any race)	20,156	29.2	100.0
Central American, ex. Mexican	986	1.4	4.9
Guatemalan	329	0.5	1.6
Salvadoran	421	0.6	2.1
Cuban	214	0.3	1.1
Mexican	16,217	23.5	80.5
Puerto Rican	518	0.7	2.6
South American	288	0.4	1.4
Spaniard	360	0.5	1.8

Population Growth: 2000–2010

Group	%
Total Population	27.5
Hispanic or Latino (of any race)	100.2
Central American, ex. Mexican	362.9
Mexican	116.6
Puerto Rican	76.8

Males per 100 Females

Group	Number
Total Population	96.0
Hispanic or Latino (of any race)	98.7
Central American, ex. Mexican	86.7
Guatemalan	105.6
Salvadoran	77.6
Cuban	96.3
Mexican	100.5
Puerto Rican	89.7
South American	97.3
Spaniard	82.7

Average Household Size

Group	People
Total Population	2.91
Hispanic or Latino (of any race)	3.75
Central American, ex. Mexican	4.05
Guatemalan	4.21
Salvadoran	3.98
Cuban	3.60
Mexican	3.82
Puerto Rican	3.21
South American	3.54
Spaniard	2.81

Median Age

Group	Years
Total Population	37.0
Hispanic or Latino (of any race)	24.0
Central American, ex. Mexican	31.1
Guatemalan	30.6
Salvadoran	30.1
Cuban	28.5
Mexican	23.3
Puerto Rican	26.9
South American	32.0
Spaniard	29.2

High School Graduates
(Universe: Population 25 Years and Over)

Group	Number	%
Total Population	34,735	84.0
Hispanic or Latino (of any race)	6,057	66.0
Central American, ex. Mexican	335	47.5
Mexican	5,096	65.8

Four-Year College Graduates
(Universe: Population 25 Years and Over)

Group	Number	%
Total Population	6,714	16.2
Hispanic or Latino (of any race)	596	6.5
Central American, ex. Mexican	25	3.5
Mexican	487	6.3

Population Age 3–17 Enrolled in Public School
(Universe: Population Age 3–17 Enrolled in School)

Group	Number	%
Total Population	13,381	93.2
Hispanic or Latino (of any race)	5,646	96.5
Central American, ex. Mexican	492	90.6
Mexican	4,807	97.3

Population Age 3–17 Enrolled in Private School
(Universe: Population Age 3–17 Enrolled in School)

Group	Number	%
Total Population	969	6.8
Hispanic or Latino (of any race)	207	3.5
Central American, ex. Mexican	51	9.4
Mexican	134	2.7

Foreign-Born Population

Group	Number	%
Total Population	6,140	9.1
Hispanic or Latino (of any race)	4,010	20.9
Central American, ex. Mexican	572	39.9
Mexican	3,248	19.9

Foreign-Born Naturalized U.S. Citizens

Group	Number	%
Total Population	2,888	47.0
Hispanic or Latino (of any race)	1,467	36.6
Central American, ex. Mexican	209	36.5
Mexican	1,144	35.2

Language Spoken at Home: English Only
(Universe: Population 5 Years and Over)

Group	Number	%
Total Population	50,722	81.9
Hispanic or Latino (of any race)	8,204	48.4
Central American, ex. Mexican	302	22.5
Mexican	7,096	49.4

Language Spoken at Home: Spanish
(Universe: Population 5 Years and Over)

Group	Number	%
Total Population	9,216	14.9
Hispanic or Latino (of any race)	8,753	51.6
Central American, ex. Mexican	1,041	77.5
Mexican	7,261	50.6

Unemployment Rate
(Universe: Population 16 Years and Over)

Group	%
Total Population	12.9
Hispanic or Latino (of any race)	17.0
Central American, ex. Mexican	15.3
Mexican	17.5

Class of Worker: Private Wage and Salary
(Universe: Civilian Employed Population 16 Years and Over)

Group	Number	%
Total Population	17,878	71.1
Hispanic or Latino (of any race)	4,003	69.5
Central American, ex. Mexican	260	68.2
Mexican	3,409	69.2

Class of Worker: Government
(Universe: Civilian Employed Population 16 Years and Over)

Group	Number	%
Total Population	5,298	21.1
Hispanic or Latino (of any race)	1,171	20.3
Central American, ex. Mexican	61	16.0
Mexican	1,037	21.1

Means of Transportation to Work: Car, Truck or Van
(Universe: Workers 16 Years and Over)

Group	Number	%
Total Population	21,721	91.0
Hispanic or Latino (of any race)	5,080	90.5
Central American, ex. Mexican	339	91.6
Mexican	4,335	90.1

Means of Transportation to Work: Public Transportation (ex. Taxicab)
(Universe: Workers 16 Years and Over)

Group	Number	%
Total Population	347	1.5
Hispanic or Latino (of any race)	77	1.4
Central American, ex. Mexican	22	5.9
Mexican	45	0.9

Homeownership Rate
(Universe: Occupied Housing Units)

Group	%
Total Population	69.1
Hispanic or Latino (of any race)	60.3
Central American, ex. Mexican	63.5
Guatemalan	63.2
Salvadoran	63.8
Cuban	53.3
Mexican	61.1
Puerto Rican	55.8
South American	64.6
Spaniard	62.0

Median Home Value

Group	Dollars
Total Population	262,100
Hispanic or Latino (of any race)	271,500
Central American, ex. Mexican	270,800
Mexican	274,100

Median Gross Rent

Group	Dollars
Total Population	976
Hispanic or Latino (of any race)	939
Central American, ex. Mexican	2,000+
Mexican	942

Median Household Income
(2010 Inflation-Adjusted Dollars)

Group	Dollars
Total Population	50,066
Hispanic or Latino (of any race)	39,892
Central American, ex. Mexican	35,286
Mexican	40,330

Per Capita Income
(2010 Inflation-Adjusted Dollars)

Group	Dollars
Total Population	22,410
Hispanic or Latino (of any race)	13,303
Central American, ex. Mexican	10,855
Mexican	13,644

Households with $100,000+ Income

Group	Number	%
Total Population	4,692	20.9
Hispanic or Latino (of any race)	603	13.3
Central American, ex. Mexican	32	10.4
Mexican	547	14.2

STATE & PLACE PROFILES

Notes: (1) Percent of total population; (2) Percent of Hispanic/Latino population; Profiles include places with an overall population of at least 125,000, OR an overall population of at least 25,000 where the Hispanic/Latino population is at least 20% of the overall population. In states where less than five places meet either of these criteria, we have included places with at least 10,000 total population with the highest percentage of Hispanic/Latino population. These places are identified with an asterisk (*); Please refer to the User's Guide for a full explanation of data.

Households with Food Stamps/SNAP Benefits During Past 12 Months

Group	Number	%
Total Population	2,063	9.2
Hispanic or Latino (of any race)	761	16.8
Central American, ex. Mexican	29	9.4
Mexican	686	17.8

Poverty Rate
(Income in Past 12 Months Below Poverty Level)

Group	%
Total Population	17.9
Hispanic or Latino (of any race)	27.5
Central American, ex. Mexican	4.1
Mexican	30.0

Atwater

Population

Group	Number	%TP[1]	%HP[2]
Total Population	28,168	100.0	–
Hispanic or Latino (of any race)	14,808	52.6	100.0
Central American, ex. Mexican	159	0.6	1.1
Mexican	13,829	49.1	93.4
Puerto Rican	132	0.5	0.9
Spaniard	124	0.4	0.8

Population Growth: 2000–2010

Group	%
Total Population	21.9
Hispanic or Latino (of any race)	54.3
Mexican	66.0

Males per 100 Females

Group	Number
Total Population	95.7
Hispanic or Latino (of any race)	102.4
Central American, ex. Mexican	89.3
Mexican	102.8
Puerto Rican	106.3
Spaniard	77.1

Average Household Size

Group	People
Total Population	3.18
Hispanic or Latino (of any race)	3.94
Central American, ex. Mexican	3.84
Mexican	3.98
Puerto Rican	2.52
Spaniard	3.05

Median Age

Group	Years
Total Population	30.0
Hispanic or Latino (of any race)	23.4
Central American, ex. Mexican	32.6
Mexican	23.1
Puerto Rican	26.0
Spaniard	37.0

High School Graduates
(Universe: Population 25 Years and Over)

Group	Number	%
Total Population	11,634	73.5
Hispanic or Latino (of any race)	3,280	54.0
Mexican	3,034	52.5

Four-Year College Graduates
(Universe: Population 25 Years and Over)

Group	Number	%
Total Population	1,936	12.2
Hispanic or Latino (of any race)	380	6.3
Mexican	359	6.2

Population Age 3–17 Enrolled in Public School
(Universe: Population Age 3–17 Enrolled in School)

Group	Number	%
Total Population	5,998	95.1
Hispanic or Latino (of any race)	3,988	97.7
Mexican	3,881	98.7

Population Age 3–17 Enrolled in Private School
(Universe: Population Age 3–17 Enrolled in School)

Group	Number	%
Total Population	312	4.9
Hispanic or Latino (of any race)	93	2.3
Mexican	53	1.3

Foreign-Born Population

Group	Number	%
Total Population	6,077	22.0
Hispanic or Latino (of any race)	4,587	35.1
Mexican	4,444	35.4

Foreign-Born Naturalized U.S. Citizens

Group	Number	%
Total Population	2,396	39.4
Hispanic or Latino (of any race)	1,491	32.5
Mexican	1,389	31.3

Language Spoken at Home: English Only
(Universe: Population 5 Years and Over)

Group	Number	%
Total Population	13,885	55.9
Hispanic or Latino (of any race)	2,674	23.5
Mexican	2,450	22.6

Language Spoken at Home: Spanish
(Universe: Population 5 Years and Over)

Group	Number	%
Total Population	9,068	36.5
Hispanic or Latino (of any race)	8,706	76.5
Mexican	8,411	77.4

Unemployment Rate
(Universe: Population 16 Years and Over)

Group	%
Total Population	14.7
Hispanic or Latino (of any race)	16.0
Mexican	16.2

Class of Worker: Private Wage and Salary
(Universe: Civilian Employed Population 16 Years and Over)

Group	Number	%
Total Population	7,494	74.1
Hispanic or Latino (of any race)	3,685	83.1
Mexican	3,573	84.0

Class of Worker: Government
(Universe: Civilian Employed Population 16 Years and Over)

Group	Number	%
Total Population	1,697	16.8
Hispanic or Latino (of any race)	333	7.5
Mexican	313	7.4

Means of Transportation to Work: Car, Truck or Van
(Universe: Workers 16 Years and Over)

Group	Number	%
Total Population	8,804	90.5
Hispanic or Latino (of any race)	3,909	92.1
Mexican	3,766	92.8

Means of Transportation to Work: Public Transportation (ex. Taxicab)
(Universe: Workers 16 Years and Over)

Group	Number	%
Total Population	38	0.4
Hispanic or Latino (of any race)	24	0.6
Mexican	24	0.6

Homeownership Rate
(Universe: Occupied Housing Units)

Group	%
Total Population	55.5
Hispanic or Latino (of any race)	46.9
Central American, ex. Mexican	52.9
Mexican	46.8
Puerto Rican	64.5
Spaniard	50.0

Median Home Value

Group	Dollars
Total Population	214,600
Hispanic or Latino (of any race)	205,400
Mexican	201,100

Median Gross Rent

Group	Dollars
Total Population	869
Hispanic or Latino (of any race)	856
Mexican	844

Median Household Income
(2010 Inflation-Adjusted Dollars)

Group	Dollars
Total Population	42,226
Hispanic or Latino (of any race)	37,556
Mexican	37,624

Per Capita Income
(2010 Inflation-Adjusted Dollars)

Group	Dollars
Total Population	17,768
Hispanic or Latino (of any race)	11,794
Mexican	11,657

Households with $100,000+ Income

Group	Number	%
Total Population	1,114	13.5
Hispanic or Latino (of any race)	248	8.1
Mexican	248	8.6

Households with Food Stamps/SNAP Benefits During Past 12 Months

Group	Number	%
Total Population	1,030	12.5
Hispanic or Latino (of any race)	486	15.9
Mexican	462	16.0

Poverty Rate
(Income in Past 12 Months Below Poverty Level)

Group	%
Total Population	23.4
Hispanic or Latino (of any race)	29.3
Mexican	29.4

Azusa

Population

Group	Number	%TP[1]	%HP[2]
Total Population	46,361	100.0	–
Hispanic or Latino (of any race)	31,328	67.6	100.0
Central American, ex. Mexican	1,630	3.5	5.2
Guatemalan	513	1.1	1.6
Honduran	112	0.2	0.4
Nicaraguan	207	0.4	0.7
Salvadoran	707	1.5	2.3
Cuban	157	0.3	0.5
Mexican	27,377	59.1	87.4
Puerto Rican	230	0.5	0.7
South American	581	1.3	1.9
Argentinean	131	0.3	0.4
Peruvian	179	0.4	0.6
Spaniard	146	0.3	0.5

Population Growth: 2000–2010

Group	%
Total Population	3.7
Hispanic or Latino (of any race)	9.8
Central American, ex. Mexican	93.6
Guatemalan	123.0
Salvadoran	95.8
Cuban	21.7
Mexican	14.9
Puerto Rican	10.6
South American	110.5

Males per 100 Females

Group	Number
Total Population	96.0
Hispanic or Latino (of any race)	99.2
Central American, ex. Mexican	95.0
Guatemalan	122.1
Honduran	93.1
Nicaraguan	81.6
Salvadoran	85.1
Cuban	91.5
Mexican	100.4
Puerto Rican	103.5
South American	83.3

Notes: (1) Percent of total population; (2) Percent of Hispanic/Latino population; Profiles include places with an overall population of at least 125,000, OR an overall population of at least 25,000 where the Hispanic/Latino population is at least 20% of the overall population. In states where less than five places meet either of these criteria, we have included places with at least 10,000 total population with the highest percentage of Hispanic/Latino population. These places are identified with an asterisk (*); Please refer to the User's Guide for a full explanation of data.

Group	
Argentinean	92.6
Peruvian	86.5
Spaniard	65.9

Average Household Size

Group	People
Total Population	3.43
Hispanic or Latino (of any race)	4.03
Central American, ex. Mexican	4.11
Guatemalan	4.32
Honduran	4.18
Nicaraguan	4.03
Salvadoran	4.06
Cuban	3.17
Mexican	4.08
Puerto Rican	2.89
South American	3.43
Argentinean	3.35
Peruvian	3.68
Spaniard	3.09

Median Age

Group	Years
Total Population	29.3
Hispanic or Latino (of any race)	27.3
Central American, ex. Mexican	32.7
Guatemalan	32.4
Honduran	29.5
Nicaraguan	32.5
Salvadoran	33.4
Cuban	34.5
Mexican	26.8
Puerto Rican	32.7
South American	34.3
Argentinean	33.2
Peruvian	35.6
Spaniard	26.5

High School Graduates
(Universe: Population 25 Years and Over)

Group	Number	%
Total Population	18,775	74.7
Hispanic or Latino (of any race)	10,512	65.0
Central American, ex. Mexican	580	61.2
Mexican	9,080	64.3

Four-Year College Graduates
(Universe: Population 25 Years and Over)

Group	Number	%
Total Population	4,666	18.6
Hispanic or Latino (of any race)	1,694	10.5
Central American, ex. Mexican	90	9.5
Mexican	1,394	9.9

Population Age 3–17 Enrolled in Public School
(Universe: Population Age 3–17 Enrolled in School)

Group	Number	%
Total Population	7,807	89.6
Hispanic or Latino (of any race)	6,918	90.5
Central American, ex. Mexican	263	90.4
Mexican	6,318	90.6

Population Age 3–17 Enrolled in Private School
(Universe: Population Age 3–17 Enrolled in School)

Group	Number	%
Total Population	909	10.4
Hispanic or Latino (of any race)	723	9.5
Central American, ex. Mexican	28	9.6
Mexican	654	9.4

Foreign-Born Population

Group	Number	%
Total Population	14,889	32.4
Hispanic or Latino (of any race)	11,562	37.6
Central American, ex. Mexican	840	55.5
Mexican	10,212	37.4

Foreign-Born Naturalized U.S. Citizens

Group	Number	%
Total Population	5,745	38.6
Hispanic or Latino (of any race)	3,726	32.2
Central American, ex. Mexican	316	37.6
Mexican	3,085	30.2

Language Spoken at Home: English Only
(Universe: Population 5 Years and Over)

Group	Number	%
Total Population	17,751	41.9
Hispanic or Latino (of any race)	6,839	24.6
Central American, ex. Mexican	130	8.6
Mexican	5,953	24.2

Language Spoken at Home: Spanish
(Universe: Population 5 Years and Over)

Group	Number	%
Total Population	21,235	50.2
Hispanic or Latino (of any race)	20,966	75.3
Central American, ex. Mexican	1,364	90.8
Mexican	18,591	75.7

Unemployment Rate
(Universe: Population 16 Years and Over)

Group	%
Total Population	8.5
Hispanic or Latino (of any race)	9.5
Central American, ex. Mexican	10.6
Mexican	8.8

Class of Worker: Private Wage and Salary
(Universe: Civilian Employed Population 16 Years and Over)

Group	Number	%
Total Population	18,390	82.4
Hispanic or Latino (of any race)	11,818	84.2
Central American, ex. Mexican	840	91.3
Mexican	10,294	84.3

Class of Worker: Government
(Universe: Civilian Employed Population 16 Years and Over)

Group	Number	%
Total Population	2,646	11.9
Hispanic or Latino (of any race)	1,445	10.3
Central American, ex. Mexican	19	2.1
Mexican	1,283	10.5

Means of Transportation to Work: Car, Truck or Van
(Universe: Workers 16 Years and Over)

Group	Number	%
Total Population	18,834	86.8
Hispanic or Latino (of any race)	11,911	87.5
Central American, ex. Mexican	786	86.2
Mexican	10,392	87.8

Means of Transportation to Work: Public Transportation (ex. Taxicab)
(Universe: Workers 16 Years and Over)

Group	Number	%
Total Population	905	4.2
Hispanic or Latino (of any race)	671	4.9
Central American, ex. Mexican	65	7.1
Mexican	594	5.0

Homeownership Rate
(Universe: Occupied Housing Units)

Group	%
Total Population	53.5
Hispanic or Latino (of any race)	47.8
Central American, ex. Mexican	50.0
Guatemalan	45.1
Honduran	45.5
Nicaraguan	44.3
Salvadoran	53.2
Cuban	66.0
Mexican	47.6
Puerto Rican	46.7
South American	54.8
Argentinean	45.9
Peruvian	58.9
Spaniard	57.4

Median Home Value

Group	Dollars
Total Population	385,200
Hispanic or Latino (of any race)	376,300
Central American, ex. Mexican	366,900
Mexican	374,500

Median Gross Rent

Group	Dollars
Total Population	1,172
Hispanic or Latino (of any race)	1,159
Central American, ex. Mexican	1,152
Mexican	1,160

Median Household Income
(2010 Inflation-Adjusted Dollars)

Group	Dollars
Total Population	51,894
Hispanic or Latino (of any race)	48,941
Central American, ex. Mexican	73,693
Mexican	46,641

Per Capita Income
(2010 Inflation-Adjusted Dollars)

Group	Dollars
Total Population	18,576
Hispanic or Latino (of any race)	16,022
Central American, ex. Mexican	20,575
Mexican	15,522

Households with $100,000+ Income

Group	Number	%
Total Population	2,202	17.4
Hispanic or Latino (of any race)	1,125	14.9
Central American, ex. Mexican	91	16.7
Mexican	905	14.1

Households with Food Stamps/SNAP Benefits During Past 12 Months

Group	Number	%
Total Population	587	4.6
Hispanic or Latino (of any race)	440	5.8
Central American, ex. Mexican	13	2.4
Mexican	427	6.7

Poverty Rate
(Income in Past 12 Months Below Poverty Level)

Group	%
Total Population	17.4
Hispanic or Latino (of any race)	18.8
Central American, ex. Mexican	10.1
Mexican	19.4

Bakersfield

Population

Group	Number	%TP[1]	%HP[2]
Total Population	347,483	100.0	–
Hispanic or Latino (of any race)	158,205	45.5	100.0
Central American, ex. Mexican	7,497	2.2	4.7
Costa Rican	139	<0.1	0.1
Guatemalan	1,804	0.5	1.1
Honduran	545	0.2	0.3
Nicaraguan	239	0.1	0.2
Salvadoran	4,654	1.3	2.9
Cuban	405	0.1	0.3
Mexican	137,102	39.5	86.7
Puerto Rican	1,860	0.5	1.2
South American	1,747	0.5	1.1
Argentinean	212	0.1	0.1
Colombian	425	0.1	0.3
Ecuadorian	136	<0.1	0.1
Peruvian	534	0.2	0.3
Venezuelan	259	0.1	0.2
Spaniard	1,237	0.4	0.8

Population Growth: 2000–2010

Group	%
Total Population	40.6
Hispanic or Latino (of any race)	97.3
Central American, ex. Mexican	281.7
Guatemalan	369.8
Honduran	332.5
Salvadoran	280.5
Cuban	114.3
Mexican	111.9
Puerto Rican	102.0
South American	270.9
Colombian	226.9
Peruvian	229.6
Spaniard	610.9

Notes: (1) Percent of total population; (2) Percent of Hispanic/Latino population; Profiles include places with an overall population of at least 125,000, OR an overall population of at least 25,000 where the Hispanic/Latino population is at least 20% of the overall population. In states where less than five places meet either of these criteria, we have included places with at least 10,000 total population with the highest percentage of Hispanic/Latino population. These places are identified with an asterisk (*); Please refer to the User's Guide for a full explanation of data.

Males per 100 Females

Group	Number
Total Population	96.0
Hispanic or Latino (of any race)	99.4
Central American, ex. Mexican	104.5
Costa Rican	78.2
Guatemalan	108.6
Honduran	113.7
Nicaraguan	92.7
Salvadoran	103.7
Cuban	108.8
Mexican	99.3
Puerto Rican	99.8
South American	104.8
Argentinean	100.0
Colombian	91.4
Ecuadorian	156.6
Peruvian	124.4
Venezuelan	83.7
Spaniard	89.1

Average Household Size

Group	People
Total Population	3.10
Hispanic or Latino (of any race)	3.85
Central American, ex. Mexican	4.10
Costa Rican	3.18
Guatemalan	4.21
Honduran	4.13
Nicaraguan	3.52
Salvadoran	4.13
Cuban	3.22
Mexican	3.88
Puerto Rican	3.45
South American	3.28
Argentinean	2.77
Colombian	3.27
Ecuadorian	3.59
Peruvian	3.54
Venezuelan	3.00
Spaniard	2.94

Median Age

Group	Years
Total Population	30.0
Hispanic or Latino (of any race)	23.9
Central American, ex. Mexican	30.7
Costa Rican	35.2
Guatemalan	32.2
Honduran	29.3
Nicaraguan	30.4
Salvadoran	30.1
Cuban	26.8
Mexican	23.5
Puerto Rican	24.9
South American	33.3
Argentinean	34.4
Colombian	33.3
Ecuadorian	30.3
Peruvian	33.1
Venezuelan	35.1
Spaniard	32.0

High School Graduates
(Universe: Population 25 Years and Over)

Group	Number	%
Total Population	148,256	78.1
Hispanic or Latino (of any race)	41,823	60.1
Central American, ex. Mexican	2,502	55.0
Guatemalan	798	67.9
Salvadoran	1,298	46.3
Mexican	35,659	59.2
Puerto Rican	647	81.5
South American	988	85.8
Spaniard	574	89.1

Four-Year College Graduates
(Universe: Population 25 Years and Over)

Group	Number	%
Total Population	37,723	19.9
Hispanic or Latino (of any race)	5,647	8.1
Central American, ex. Mexican	292	6.4
Guatemalan	82	7.0
Salvadoran	118	4.2
Mexican	4,328	7.2
Puerto Rican	208	26.2
South American	364	31.6
Spaniard	108	16.8

Population Age 3–17 Enrolled in Public School
(Universe: Population Age 3–17 Enrolled in School)

Group	Number	%
Total Population	72,068	91.4
Hispanic or Latino (of any race)	39,885	95.4
Central American, ex. Mexican	1,521	96.3
Guatemalan	490	97.6
Salvadoran	853	100.0
Mexican	36,230	95.7
Puerto Rican	338	69.5
South American	236	92.2
Spaniard	233	100.0

Population Age 3–17 Enrolled in Private School
(Universe: Population Age 3–17 Enrolled in School)

Group	Number	%
Total Population	6,796	8.6
Hispanic or Latino (of any race)	1,936	4.6
Central American, ex. Mexican	58	3.7
Guatemalan	12	2.4
Salvadoran	0	0.0
Mexican	1,625	4.3
Puerto Rican	148	30.5
South American	20	7.8
Spaniard	0	0.0

Foreign-Born Population

Group	Number	%
Total Population	60,457	18.2
Hispanic or Latino (of any race)	43,019	29.6
Central American, ex. Mexican	5,052	64.9
Guatemalan	1,115	58.8
Salvadoran	3,322	67.3
Mexican	35,995	28.0
Puerto Rican	26	1.5
South American	1,039	65.2
Spaniard	121	11.4

Foreign-Born Naturalized U.S. Citizens

Group	Number	%
Total Population	23,285	38.5
Hispanic or Latino (of any race)	13,612	31.6
Central American, ex. Mexican	1,768	35.0
Guatemalan	358	32.1
Salvadoran	1,136	34.2
Mexican	10,886	30.2
Puerto Rican	0	0.0
South American	502	48.3
Spaniard	72	59.5

Language Spoken at Home: English Only
(Universe: Population 5 Years and Over)

Group	Number	%
Total Population	191,835	63.6
Hispanic or Latino (of any race)	40,408	31.5
Central American, ex. Mexican	523	7.3
Guatemalan	246	13.6
Salvadoran	156	3.4
Mexican	36,282	32.1
Puerto Rican	832	55.0
South American	109	7.8
Spaniard	724	70.5

Language Spoken at Home: Spanish
(Universe: Population 5 Years and Over)

Group	Number	%
Total Population	91,547	30.3
Hispanic or Latino (of any race)	87,598	68.3
Central American, ex. Mexican	6,651	92.3
Guatemalan	1,530	84.6
Salvadoran	4,373	96.6
Mexican	76,620	67.8
Puerto Rican	671	44.3
South American	1,220	86.9
Spaniard	293	28.5

Unemployment Rate
(Universe: Population 16 Years and Over)

Group	%
Total Population	10.2
Hispanic or Latino (of any race)	12.7
Central American, ex. Mexican	10.6
Guatemalan	15.8
Salvadoran	10.0
Mexican	13.0
Puerto Rican	19.5
South American	1.1
Spaniard	9.3

Class of Worker: Private Wage and Salary
(Universe: Civilian Employed Population 16 Years and Over)

Group	Number	%
Total Population	102,593	73.4
Hispanic or Latino (of any race)	44,156	78.5
Central American, ex. Mexican	3,228	86.5
Guatemalan	634	72.8
Salvadoran	2,202	91.4
Mexican	38,362	78.2
Puerto Rican	473	76.0
South American	494	69.4
Spaniard	351	69.5

Class of Worker: Government
(Universe: Civilian Employed Population 16 Years and Over)

Group	Number	%
Total Population	26,624	19.1
Hispanic or Latino (of any race)	8,220	14.6
Central American, ex. Mexican	247	6.6
Guatemalan	182	20.9
Salvadoran	45	1.9
Mexican	7,341	15.0
Puerto Rican	139	22.3
South American	117	16.4
Spaniard	125	24.8

Means of Transportation to Work: Car, Truck or Van
(Universe: Workers 16 Years and Over)

Group	Number	%
Total Population	126,156	93.3
Hispanic or Latino (of any race)	51,374	93.7
Central American, ex. Mexican	3,310	91.8
Guatemalan	848	97.4
Salvadoran	2,161	94.7
Mexican	44,880	93.9
Puerto Rican	554	88.9
South American	694	98.9
Spaniard	494	97.8

Means of Transportation to Work: Public Transportation (ex. Taxicab)
(Universe: Workers 16 Years and Over)

Group	Number	%
Total Population	1,539	1.1
Hispanic or Latino (of any race)	695	1.3
Central American, ex. Mexican	87	2.4
Guatemalan	14	1.6
Salvadoran	10	0.4
Mexican	571	1.2
Puerto Rican	12	1.9
South American	8	1.1
Spaniard	0	0.0

Homeownership Rate
(Universe: Occupied Housing Units)

Group	%
Total Population	59.7
Hispanic or Latino (of any race)	52.9
Central American, ex. Mexican	57.8
Costa Rican	68.4
Guatemalan	57.8
Honduran	45.7
Nicaraguan	54.5
Salvadoran	59.1
Cuban	48.8
Mexican	53.0
Puerto Rican	44.7
South American	58.2
Argentinean	51.9
Colombian	56.4
Ecuadorian	66.7
Peruvian	59.0
Venezuelan	59.3
Spaniard	60.3

Notes: (1) Percent of total population; (2) Percent of Hispanic/Latino population; Profiles include places with an overall population of at least 125,000, OR an overall population of at least 25,000 where the Hispanic/Latino population is at least 20% of the overall population. In states where less than five places meet either of these criteria, we have included places with at least 10,000 total population with the highest percentage of Hispanic/Latino population. These places are identified with an asterisk (*); Please refer to the User's Guide for a full explanation of data.

Median Home Value

Group	Dollars
Total Population	245,100
Hispanic or Latino (of any race)	218,000
Central American, ex. Mexican	205,500
Guatemalan	244,400
Salvadoran	162,800
Mexican	217,900
Puerto Rican	232,600
South American	236,600
Spaniard	197,200

Median Gross Rent

Group	Dollars
Total Population	906
Hispanic or Latino (of any race)	854
Central American, ex. Mexican	851
Guatemalan	540
Salvadoran	833
Mexican	853
Puerto Rican	1,317
South American	790
Spaniard	1,289

Median Household Income
(2010 Inflation-Adjusted Dollars)

Group	Dollars
Total Population	53,997
Hispanic or Latino (of any race)	44,717
Central American, ex. Mexican	44,208
Guatemalan	39,119
Salvadoran	39,563
Mexican	44,312
Puerto Rican	51,976
South American	54,563
Spaniard	48,333

Per Capita Income
(2010 Inflation-Adjusted Dollars)

Group	Dollars
Total Population	23,022
Hispanic or Latino (of any race)	14,623
Central American, ex. Mexican	15,265
Guatemalan	14,710
Salvadoran	12,891
Mexican	14,244
Puerto Rican	17,920
South American	26,367
Spaniard	23,665

Households with $100,000+ Income

Group	Number	%
Total Population	22,381	21.2
Hispanic or Latino (of any race)	4,157	11.4
Central American, ex. Mexican	99	4.4
Guatemalan	35	5.9
Salvadoran	22	1.6
Mexican	3,534	11.2
Puerto Rican	104	23.3
South American	203	36.4
Spaniard	32	9.9

Households with Food Stamps/SNAP Benefits During Past 12 Months

Group	Number	%
Total Population	9,688	9.2
Hispanic or Latino (of any race)	5,152	14.2
Central American, ex. Mexican	258	11.4
Guatemalan	88	14.9
Salvadoran	165	11.9
Mexican	4,594	14.5
Puerto Rican	81	18.1
South American	0	0.0
Spaniard	12	3.7

Poverty Rate
(Income in Past 12 Months Below Poverty Level)

Group	%
Total Population	17.3
Hispanic or Latino (of any race)	23.5
Central American, ex. Mexican	27.1
Guatemalan	19.8
Salvadoran	29.6
Mexican	23.7
Puerto Rican	10.4
South American	19.0
Spaniard	8.3

Baldwin Park

Population

Group	Number	%TP[1]	%HP[2]
Total Population	75,390	100.0	–
Hispanic or Latino (of any race)	60,403	80.1	100.0
Central American, ex. Mexican	4,065	5.4	6.7
Guatemalan	924	1.2	1.5
Honduran	262	0.3	0.4
Nicaraguan	440	0.6	0.7
Salvadoran	2,272	3.0	3.8
Cuban	173	0.2	0.3
Mexican	52,803	70.0	87.4
Puerto Rican	267	0.4	0.4
South American	526	0.7	0.9
Colombian	147	0.2	0.2
Ecuadorian	113	0.1	0.2
Peruvian	144	0.2	0.2
Spaniard	213	0.3	0.4

Population Growth: 2000–2010

Group	%
Total Population	-0.6
Hispanic or Latino (of any race)	1.2
Central American, ex. Mexican	77.0
Guatemalan	98.3
Nicaraguan	70.5
Salvadoran	95.9
Cuban	-18.0
Mexican	7.7
Puerto Rican	-4.0
South American	26.7
Ecuadorian	-6.6

Males per 100 Females

Group	Number
Total Population	98.5
Hispanic or Latino (of any race)	99.3
Central American, ex. Mexican	89.6
Guatemalan	93.3
Honduran	83.2
Nicaraguan	75.3
Salvadoran	92.9
Cuban	92.2
Mexican	100.1
Puerto Rican	85.4
South American	94.1
Colombian	86.1
Ecuadorian	73.8
Peruvian	114.9
Spaniard	97.2

Average Household Size

Group	People
Total Population	4.36
Hispanic or Latino (of any race)	4.71
Central American, ex. Mexican	4.60
Guatemalan	4.73
Honduran	4.21
Nicaraguan	3.91
Salvadoran	4.78
Cuban	3.48
Mexican	4.77
Puerto Rican	2.85
South American	3.92
Colombian	3.93
Ecuadorian	3.51
Peruvian	4.22
Spaniard	3.84

Median Age

Group	Years
Total Population	30.5
Hispanic or Latino (of any race)	28.0
Central American, ex. Mexican	36.3
Guatemalan	37.1
Honduran	35.1
Nicaraguan	39.4
Salvadoran	35.6
Cuban	43.8
Mexican	27.4
Puerto Rican	33.1
South American	41.8
Colombian	42.5
Ecuadorian	44.9
Peruvian	38.5
Spaniard	31.8

High School Graduates
(Universe: Population 25 Years and Over)

Group	Number	%
Total Population	24,967	56.7
Hispanic or Latino (of any race)	16,711	49.7
Central American, ex. Mexican	1,506	47.3
Guatemalan	501	53.7
Salvadoran	542	41.4
Mexican	14,363	49.5

Four-Year College Graduates
(Universe: Population 25 Years and Over)

Group	Number	%
Total Population	5,113	11.6
Hispanic or Latino (of any race)	2,070	6.2
Central American, ex. Mexican	301	9.5
Guatemalan	61	6.5
Salvadoran	127	9.7
Mexican	1,576	5.4

Population Age 3–17 Enrolled in Public School
(Universe: Population Age 3–17 Enrolled in School)

Group	Number	%
Total Population	16,773	95.6
Hispanic or Latino (of any race)	15,027	96.6
Central American, ex. Mexican	625	96.0
Guatemalan	219	92.8
Salvadoran	292	97.0
Mexican	13,904	96.8

Population Age 3–17 Enrolled in Private School
(Universe: Population Age 3–17 Enrolled in School)

Group	Number	%
Total Population	775	4.4
Hispanic or Latino (of any race)	522	3.4
Central American, ex. Mexican	26	4.0
Guatemalan	17	7.2
Salvadoran	9	3.0
Mexican	459	3.2

Foreign-Born Population

Group	Number	%
Total Population	34,569	45.9
Hispanic or Latino (of any race)	27,013	44.3
Central American, ex. Mexican	3,285	70.8
Guatemalan	1,022	76.6
Salvadoran	1,326	63.8
Mexican	22,748	42.2

Foreign-Born Naturalized U.S. Citizens

Group	Number	%
Total Population	14,914	43.1
Hispanic or Latino (of any race)	9,791	36.2
Central American, ex. Mexican	1,519	46.2
Guatemalan	471	46.1
Salvadoran	581	43.8
Mexican	7,923	34.8

Language Spoken at Home: English Only
(Universe: Population 5 Years and Over)

Group	Number	%
Total Population	12,783	18.3
Hispanic or Latino (of any race)	7,664	13.7
Central American, ex. Mexican	70	1.6
Guatemalan	15	1.2
Salvadoran	34	1.8
Mexican	6,897	14.0

Language Spoken at Home: Spanish
(Universe: Population 5 Years and Over)

Group	Number	%
Total Population	48,412	69.5
Hispanic or Latino (of any race)	47,976	85.8
Central American, ex. Mexican	4,200	98.1
Guatemalan	1,275	97.9
Salvadoran	1,833	98.2
Mexican	42,436	86.0

Notes: (1) Percent of total population; (2) Percent of Hispanic/Latino population; Profiles include places with an overall population of at least 125,000, OR an overall population of at least 25,000 where the Hispanic/Latino population is at least 20% of the overall population. In states where less than five places meet either of these criteria, we have included places with at least 10,000 total population with the highest percentage of Hispanic/Latino population. These places are identified with an asterisk (*); Please refer to the User's Guide for a full explanation of data.

Unemployment Rate
(Universe: Population 16 Years and Over)

Group	%
Total Population	10.2
Hispanic or Latino (of any race)	11.0
Central American, ex. Mexican	8.5
Guatemalan	14.7
Salvadoran	8.5
Mexican	11.5

Class of Worker: Private Wage and Salary
(Universe: Civilian Employed Population 16 Years and Over)

Group	Number	%
Total Population	25,304	81.6
Hispanic or Latino (of any race)	20,219	83.1
Central American, ex. Mexican	2,027	82.6
Guatemalan	619	84.1
Salvadoran	869	78.7
Mexican	17,272	83.1

Class of Worker: Government
(Universe: Civilian Employed Population 16 Years and Over)

Group	Number	%
Total Population	3,719	12.0
Hispanic or Latino (of any race)	2,614	10.7
Central American, ex. Mexican	267	10.9
Guatemalan	70	9.5
Salvadoran	197	17.8
Mexican	2,267	10.9

Means of Transportation to Work: Car, Truck or Van
(Universe: Workers 16 Years and Over)

Group	Number	%
Total Population	26,587	87.7
Hispanic or Latino (of any race)	20,871	87.3
Central American, ex. Mexican	1,943	81.2
Guatemalan	505	72.0
Salvadoran	948	87.9
Mexican	18,081	88.4

Means of Transportation to Work: Public Transportation (ex. Taxicab)
(Universe: Workers 16 Years and Over)

Group	Number	%
Total Population	1,462	4.8
Hispanic or Latino (of any race)	1,071	4.5
Central American, ex. Mexican	98	4.1
Guatemalan	38	5.4
Salvadoran	8	0.7
Mexican	973	4.8

Homeownership Rate
(Universe: Occupied Housing Units)

Group	%
Total Population	60.2
Hispanic or Latino (of any race)	56.4
Central American, ex. Mexican	57.6
Guatemalan	60.4
Honduran	45.2
Nicaraguan	54.3
Salvadoran	59.4
Cuban	59.4
Mexican	56.7
Puerto Rican	44.9
South American	55.7
Colombian	53.3
Ecuadorian	61.5
Peruvian	56.1
Spaniard	49.1

Median Home Value

Group	Dollars
Total Population	358,800
Hispanic or Latino (of any race)	362,300
Central American, ex. Mexican	312,100
Guatemalan	244,000
Salvadoran	348,700
Mexican	365,800

Median Gross Rent

Group	Dollars
Total Population	1,156
Hispanic or Latino (of any race)	1,155
Central American, ex. Mexican	1,107
Guatemalan	971
Salvadoran	1,155
Mexican	1,167

Median Household Income
(2010 Inflation-Adjusted Dollars)

Group	Dollars
Total Population	50,346
Hispanic or Latino (of any race)	48,276
Central American, ex. Mexican	54,250
Guatemalan	60,268
Salvadoran	52,281
Mexican	48,367

Per Capita Income
(2010 Inflation-Adjusted Dollars)

Group	Dollars
Total Population	15,228
Hispanic or Latino (of any race)	13,559
Central American, ex. Mexican	16,641
Guatemalan	18,547
Salvadoran	17,320
Mexican	13,241

Households with $100,000+ Income

Group	Number	%
Total Population	2,737	15.6
Hispanic or Latino (of any race)	1,878	14.1
Central American, ex. Mexican	175	13.5
Guatemalan	38	10.7
Salvadoran	118	19.6
Mexican	1,628	14.2

Households with Food Stamps/SNAP Benefits During Past 12 Months

Group	Number	%
Total Population	1,611	9.2
Hispanic or Latino (of any race)	1,358	10.2
Central American, ex. Mexican	85	6.5
Guatemalan	34	9.6
Salvadoran	0	0.0
Mexican	1,273	11.1

Poverty Rate
(Income in Past 12 Months Below Poverty Level)

Group	%
Total Population	15.9
Hispanic or Latino (of any race)	17.5
Central American, ex. Mexican	13.0
Guatemalan	8.5
Salvadoran	16.2
Mexican	18.3

Banning

Population

Group	Number	%TP[1]	%HP[2]
Total Population	29,603	100.0	–
Hispanic or Latino (of any race)	12,181	41.1	100.0
Central American, ex. Mexican	310	1.0	2.5
Salvadoran	137	0.5	1.1
Mexican	10,855	36.7	89.1
Puerto Rican	110	0.4	0.9

Population Growth: 2000–2010

Group	%
Total Population	25.6
Hispanic or Latino (of any race)	71.1
Central American, ex. Mexican	171.9
Mexican	79.1

Males per 100 Females

Group	Number
Total Population	93.4
Hispanic or Latino (of any race)	101.6
Central American, ex. Mexican	83.4
Salvadoran	107.6
Mexican	103.6
Puerto Rican	86.4

Average Household Size

Group	People
Total Population	2.61
Hispanic or Latino (of any race)	3.68
Central American, ex. Mexican	3.66
Salvadoran	3.64
Mexican	3.73
Puerto Rican	2.75

Median Age

Group	Years
Total Population	42.3
Hispanic or Latino (of any race)	26.5
Central American, ex. Mexican	36.2
Salvadoran	32.9
Mexican	26.0
Puerto Rican	32.8

High School Graduates
(Universe: Population 25 Years and Over)

Group	Number	%
Total Population	16,674	81.1
Hispanic or Latino (of any race)	3,558	62.3
Mexican	2,656	56.5

Four-Year College Graduates
(Universe: Population 25 Years and Over)

Group	Number	%
Total Population	3,611	17.6
Hispanic or Latino (of any race)	470	8.2
Mexican	262	5.6

Population Age 3–17 Enrolled in Public School
(Universe: Population Age 3–17 Enrolled in School)

Group	Number	%
Total Population	4,361	90.8
Hispanic or Latino (of any race)	2,709	98.3
Mexican	2,196	98.4

Population Age 3–17 Enrolled in Private School
(Universe: Population Age 3–17 Enrolled in School)

Group	Number	%
Total Population	442	9.2
Hispanic or Latino (of any race)	48	1.7
Mexican	35	1.6

Foreign-Born Population

Group	Number	%
Total Population	5,684	19.6
Hispanic or Latino (of any race)	3,609	35.0
Mexican	2,777	32.2

Foreign-Born Naturalized U.S. Citizens

Group	Number	%
Total Population	2,309	40.6
Hispanic or Latino (of any race)	1,046	29.0
Mexican	596	21.5

Language Spoken at Home: English Only
(Universe: Population 5 Years and Over)

Group	Number	%
Total Population	18,479	67.7
Hispanic or Latino (of any race)	2,861	30.3
Mexican	2,331	29.9

Language Spoken at Home: Spanish
(Universe: Population 5 Years and Over)

Group	Number	%
Total Population	6,772	24.8
Hispanic or Latino (of any race)	6,574	69.6
Mexican	5,467	70.1

Unemployment Rate
(Universe: Population 16 Years and Over)

Group	%
Total Population	9.5
Hispanic or Latino (of any race)	9.0
Mexican	10.0

Class of Worker: Private Wage and Salary
(Universe: Civilian Employed Population 16 Years and Over)

Group	Number	%
Total Population	6,719	72.3
Hispanic or Latino (of any race)	2,729	77.7
Mexican	2,205	76.3

Class of Worker: Government
(Universe: Civilian Employed Population 16 Years and Over)

Group	Number	%
Total Population	1,612	17.3

Notes: (1) Percent of total population; (2) Percent of Hispanic/Latino population; Profiles include places with an overall population of at least 125,000, OR an overall population of at least 25,000 where the Hispanic/Latino population is at least 20% of the overall population. In states where less than five places meet either of these criteria, we have included places with at least 10,000 total population with the highest percentage of Hispanic/Latino population. These places are identified with an asterisk (*); Please refer to the User's Guide for a full explanation of data.

Group	Number	%
Hispanic or Latino (of any race)	505	14.4
Mexican	429	14.8

Means of Transportation to Work: Car, Truck or Van
(Universe: Workers 16 Years and Over)

Group	Number	%
Total Population	8,050	88.4
Hispanic or Latino (of any race)	3,182	91.7
Mexican	2,598	90.9

Means of Transportation to Work: Public Transportation (ex. Taxicab)
(Universe: Workers 16 Years and Over)

Group	Number	%
Total Population	86	0.9
Hispanic or Latino (of any race)	57	1.6
Mexican	57	2.0

Homeownership Rate
(Universe: Occupied Housing Units)

Group	%
Total Population	68.4
Hispanic or Latino (of any race)	54.7
Central American, ex. Mexican	58.0
Salvadoran	45.2
Mexican	55.1
Puerto Rican	66.7

Median Home Value

Group	Dollars
Total Population	233,200
Hispanic or Latino (of any race)	212,700
Mexican	203,900

Median Gross Rent

Group	Dollars
Total Population	920
Hispanic or Latino (of any race)	796
Mexican	797

Median Household Income
(2010 Inflation-Adjusted Dollars)

Group	Dollars
Total Population	38,979
Hispanic or Latino (of any race)	36,295
Mexican	33,087

Per Capita Income
(2010 Inflation-Adjusted Dollars)

Group	Dollars
Total Population	21,020
Hispanic or Latino (of any race)	14,457
Mexican	13,801

Households with $100,000+ Income

Group	Number	%
Total Population	1,137	9.6
Hispanic or Latino (of any race)	296	10.3
Mexican	223	9.4

Households with Food Stamps/SNAP Benefits During Past 12 Months

Group	Number	%
Total Population	499	4.2
Hispanic or Latino (of any race)	248	8.7
Mexican	223	9.4

Poverty Rate
(Income in Past 12 Months Below Poverty Level)

Group	%
Total Population	14.6
Hispanic or Latino (of any race)	16.1
Mexican	18.1

Beaumont

Population

Group	Number	%TP[1]	%HP[2]
Total Population	36,877	100.0	–
Hispanic or Latino (of any race)	14,864	40.3	100.0
Central American, ex. Mexican	622	1.7	4.2
Guatemalan	176	0.5	1.2
Salvadoran	317	0.9	2.1
Cuban	124	0.3	0.8
Mexican	12,727	34.5	85.6
Puerto Rican	189	0.5	1.3
South American	225	0.6	1.5
Spaniard	148	0.4	1.0

Population Growth: 2000–2010

Group	%
Total Population	223.9
Hispanic or Latino (of any race)	260.6
Mexican	263.2

Males per 100 Females

Group	Number
Total Population	95.2
Hispanic or Latino (of any race)	95.1
Central American, ex. Mexican	79.8
Guatemalan	85.3
Salvadoran	84.3
Cuban	113.8
Mexican	96.4
Puerto Rican	94.8
South American	84.4
Spaniard	89.7

Average Household Size

Group	People
Total Population	3.08
Hispanic or Latino (of any race)	3.78
Central American, ex. Mexican	3.96
Guatemalan	4.04
Salvadoran	4.15
Cuban	2.80
Mexican	3.85
Puerto Rican	2.80
South American	3.21
Spaniard	3.31

Median Age

Group	Years
Total Population	32.5
Hispanic or Latino (of any race)	25.7
Central American, ex. Mexican	33.7
Guatemalan	35.2
Salvadoran	32.9
Cuban	29.0
Mexican	25.0
Puerto Rican	30.8
South American	35.6
Spaniard	30.5

High School Graduates
(Universe: Population 25 Years and Over)

Group	Number	%
Total Population	17,600	84.6
Hispanic or Latino (of any race)	4,388	64.8
Mexican	3,461	61.9

Four-Year College Graduates
(Universe: Population 25 Years and Over)

Group	Number	%
Total Population	5,020	24.1
Hispanic or Latino (of any race)	818	12.1
Mexican	599	10.7

Population Age 3–17 Enrolled in Public School
(Universe: Population Age 3–17 Enrolled in School)

Group	Number	%
Total Population	6,647	93.1
Hispanic or Latino (of any race)	3,642	96.5
Mexican	3,131	96.4

Population Age 3–17 Enrolled in Private School
(Universe: Population Age 3–17 Enrolled in School)

Group	Number	%
Total Population	494	6.9
Hispanic or Latino (of any race)	132	3.5
Mexican	117	3.6

Foreign-Born Population

Group	Number	%
Total Population	6,140	18.7
Hispanic or Latino (of any race)	3,769	29.2
Mexican	3,049	27.8

Foreign-Born Naturalized U.S. Citizens

Group	Number	%
Total Population	2,661	43.3
Hispanic or Latino (of any race)	1,400	37.1
Mexican	1,046	34.3

Language Spoken at Home: English Only
(Universe: Population 5 Years and Over)

Group	Number	%
Total Population	19,655	66.8
Hispanic or Latino (of any race)	3,775	33.8
Mexican	3,158	33.9

Language Spoken at Home: Spanish
(Universe: Population 5 Years and Over)

Group	Number	%
Total Population	7,646	26.0
Hispanic or Latino (of any race)	7,380	66.2
Mexican	6,170	66.1

Unemployment Rate
(Universe: Population 16 Years and Over)

Group	%
Total Population	6.8
Hispanic or Latino (of any race)	7.5
Mexican	8.8

Class of Worker: Private Wage and Salary
(Universe: Civilian Employed Population 16 Years and Over)

Group	Number	%
Total Population	9,068	67.9
Hispanic or Latino (of any race)	3,628	78.8
Mexican	2,983	80.1

Class of Worker: Government
(Universe: Civilian Employed Population 16 Years and Over)

Group	Number	%
Total Population	3,141	23.5
Hispanic or Latino (of any race)	627	13.6
Mexican	514	13.8

Means of Transportation to Work: Car, Truck or Van
(Universe: Workers 16 Years and Over)

Group	Number	%
Total Population	12,087	92.9
Hispanic or Latino (of any race)	4,160	93.5
Mexican	3,357	93.2

Means of Transportation to Work: Public Transportation (ex. Taxicab)
(Universe: Workers 16 Years and Over)

Group	Number	%
Total Population	17	0.1
Hispanic or Latino (of any race)	17	0.4
Mexican	17	0.5

Homeownership Rate
(Universe: Occupied Housing Units)

Group	%
Total Population	75.0
Hispanic or Latino (of any race)	67.2
Central American, ex. Mexican	61.2
Guatemalan	64.7
Salvadoran	62.8
Cuban	77.3
Mexican	67.1
Puerto Rican	63.6
South American	76.7
Spaniard	71.4

Median Home Value

Group	Dollars
Total Population	278,000
Hispanic or Latino (of any race)	250,700
Mexican	229,000

Median Gross Rent

Group	Dollars
Total Population	909
Hispanic or Latino (of any race)	885
Mexican	919

Notes: (1) Percent of total population; (2) Percent of Hispanic/Latino population; Profiles include places with an overall population of at least 125,000, OR an overall population of at least 25,000 where the Hispanic/Latino population is at least 20% of the overall population. In states where less than five places meet either of these criteria, we have included places with at least 10,000 total population with the highest percentage of Hispanic/Latino population. These places are identified with an asterisk (*); Please refer to the User's Guide for a full explanation of data.

Median Household Income
(2010 Inflation-Adjusted Dollars)

Group	Dollars
Total Population	66,121
Hispanic or Latino (of any race)	47,857
Mexican	48,527

Per Capita Income
(2010 Inflation-Adjusted Dollars)

Group	Dollars
Total Population	24,755
Hispanic or Latino (of any race)	16,369
Mexican	15,568

Households with $100,000+ Income

Group	Number	%
Total Population	2,574	23.3
Hispanic or Latino (of any race)	528	15.9
Mexican	451	16.3

Households with Food Stamps/SNAP Benefits During Past 12 Months

Group	Number	%
Total Population	488	4.4
Hispanic or Latino (of any race)	288	8.7
Mexican	224	8.1

Poverty Rate
(Income in Past 12 Months Below Poverty Level)

Group	%
Total Population	11.0
Hispanic or Latino (of any race)	16.0
Mexican	14.9

Bell

Population

Group	Number	%TP[1]	%HP[2]
Total Population	35,477	100.0	–
Hispanic or Latino (of any race)	33,028	93.1	100.0
Central American, ex. Mexican	3,894	11.0	11.8
Guatemalan	1,041	2.9	3.2
Honduran	268	0.8	0.8
Nicaraguan	381	1.1	1.2
Salvadoran	2,082	5.9	6.3
Cuban	774	2.2	2.3
Mexican	26,606	75.0	80.6
Puerto Rican	139	0.4	0.4
South American	293	0.8	0.9
Peruvian	118	0.3	0.4

Population Growth: 2000–2010

Group	%
Total Population	-3.2
Hispanic or Latino (of any race)	-0.9
Central American, ex. Mexican	42.0
Guatemalan	58.9
Honduran	74.0
Nicaraguan	54.3
Salvadoran	48.0
Cuban	-17.6
Mexican	8.3
Puerto Rican	-22.8
South American	29.1

Males per 100 Females

Group	Number
Total Population	101.7
Hispanic or Latino (of any race)	100.6
Central American, ex. Mexican	95.2
Guatemalan	107.0
Honduran	76.3
Nicaraguan	80.6
Salvadoran	94.0
Cuban	100.0
Mexican	101.8
Puerto Rican	95.8
South American	123.7
Peruvian	140.8

Average Household Size

Group	People
Total Population	3.93
Hispanic or Latino (of any race)	4.01
Central American, ex. Mexican	3.87
Guatemalan	3.77
Honduran	4.30
Nicaraguan	3.82
Salvadoran	3.99
Cuban	2.41
Mexican	4.16
Puerto Rican	3.44
South American	3.27
Peruvian	3.41

Median Age

Group	Years
Total Population	28.9
Hispanic or Latino (of any race)	28.5
Central American, ex. Mexican	35.6
Guatemalan	36.1
Honduran	31.8
Nicaraguan	38.1
Salvadoran	35.5
Cuban	56.9
Mexican	27.2
Puerto Rican	36.5
South American	41.9
Peruvian	41.8

High School Graduates
(Universe: Population 25 Years and Over)

Group	Number	%
Total Population	8,427	42.3
Hispanic or Latino (of any race)	6,988	39.1
Central American, ex. Mexican	1,251	45.2
Guatemalan	200	47.7
Salvadoran	861	45.8
Cuban	341	47.5
Mexican	5,095	36.8

Four-Year College Graduates
(Universe: Population 25 Years and Over)

Group	Number	%
Total Population	754	3.8
Hispanic or Latino (of any race)	550	3.1
Central American, ex. Mexican	83	3.0
Guatemalan	0	0.0
Salvadoran	37	2.0
Cuban	13	1.8
Mexican	398	2.9

Population Age 3–17 Enrolled in Public School
(Universe: Population Age 3–17 Enrolled in School)

Group	Number	%
Total Population	8,817	99.1
Hispanic or Latino (of any race)	8,286	99.1
Central American, ex. Mexican	572	97.1
Guatemalan	170	100.0
Salvadoran	358	95.5
Cuban	38	100.0
Mexican	7,442	99.2

Population Age 3–17 Enrolled in Private School
(Universe: Population Age 3–17 Enrolled in School)

Group	Number	%
Total Population	79	0.9
Hispanic or Latino (of any race)	79	0.9
Central American, ex. Mexican	17	2.9
Guatemalan	0	0.0
Salvadoran	17	4.5
Cuban	0	0.0
Mexican	62	0.8

Foreign-Born Population

Group	Number	%
Total Population	16,721	46.9
Hispanic or Latino (of any race)	16,007	48.9
Central American, ex. Mexican	2,725	67.5
Guatemalan	502	59.3
Salvadoran	1,777	67.0
Cuban	746	85.5
Mexican	12,203	45.4

Foreign-Born Naturalized U.S. Citizens

Group	Number	%
Total Population	3,952	23.6
Hispanic or Latino (of any race)	3,614	22.6
Central American, ex. Mexican	656	24.1
Guatemalan	159	31.7
Salvadoran	288	16.2
Cuban	390	52.3
Mexican	2,422	19.8

Language Spoken at Home: English Only
(Universe: Population 5 Years and Over)

Group	Number	%
Total Population	3,509	10.9
Hispanic or Latino (of any race)	1,895	6.4
Central American, ex. Mexican	130	3.4
Guatemalan	12	1.6
Salvadoran	118	4.7
Cuban	30	3.4
Mexican	1,586	6.6

Language Spoken at Home: Spanish
(Universe: Population 5 Years and Over)

Group	Number	%
Total Population	27,800	86.4
Hispanic or Latino (of any race)	27,555	93.6
Central American, ex. Mexican	3,664	96.6
Guatemalan	729	98.4
Salvadoran	2,397	95.3
Cuban	843	96.6
Mexican	22,396	93.4

Unemployment Rate
(Universe: Population 16 Years and Over)

Group	%
Total Population	10.5
Hispanic or Latino (of any race)	10.0
Central American, ex. Mexican	8.3
Guatemalan	5.7
Salvadoran	8.5
Cuban	7.2
Mexican	10.4

Class of Worker: Private Wage and Salary
(Universe: Civilian Employed Population 16 Years and Over)

Group	Number	%
Total Population	11,937	86.9
Hispanic or Latino (of any race)	11,300	87.2
Central American, ex. Mexican	1,887	85.6
Guatemalan	285	82.1
Salvadoran	1,367	86.8
Cuban	259	79.9
Mexican	8,925	87.8

Class of Worker: Government
(Universe: Civilian Employed Population 16 Years and Over)

Group	Number	%
Total Population	1,217	8.9
Hispanic or Latino (of any race)	1,121	8.7
Central American, ex. Mexican	123	5.6
Guatemalan	17	4.9
Salvadoran	82	5.2
Cuban	65	20.1
Mexican	901	8.9

Means of Transportation to Work: Car, Truck or Van
(Universe: Workers 16 Years and Over)

Group	Number	%
Total Population	11,294	83.7
Hispanic or Latino (of any race)	10,579	83.2
Central American, ex. Mexican	1,730	80.5
Guatemalan	255	77.3
Salvadoran	1,307	85.1
Cuban	230	71.0
Mexican	8,409	84.2

Means of Transportation to Work: Public Transportation (ex. Taxicab)
(Universe: Workers 16 Years and Over)

Group	Number	%
Total Population	1,141	8.5
Hispanic or Latino (of any race)	1,106	8.7
Central American, ex. Mexican	254	11.8
Guatemalan	32	9.7
Salvadoran	140	9.1
Cuban	12	3.7
Mexican	810	8.1

Notes: (1) Percent of total population; (2) Percent of Hispanic/Latino population; Profiles include places with an overall population of at least 125,000, OR an overall population of at least 25,000 where the Hispanic/Latino population is at least 20% of the overall population. In states where less than five places meet either of these criteria, we have included places with at least 10,000 total population with the highest percentage of Hispanic/Latino population. These places are identified with an asterisk (*); Please refer to the User's Guide for a full explanation of data.

Homeownership Rate
(Universe: Occupied Housing Units)

Group	%
Total Population	29.0
Hispanic or Latino (of any race)	27.6
Central American, ex. Mexican	24.3
Guatemalan	22.1
Honduran	19.4
Nicaraguan	18.8
Salvadoran	27.8
Cuban	21.6
Mexican	28.8
Puerto Rican	33.3
South American	27.6
Peruvian	19.5

Median Home Value

Group	Dollars
Total Population	340,300
Hispanic or Latino (of any race)	345,800
Central American, ex. Mexican	368,500
Guatemalan	446,900
Salvadoran	353,000
Cuban	454,500
Mexican	335,400

Median Gross Rent

Group	Dollars
Total Population	950
Hispanic or Latino (of any race)	951
Central American, ex. Mexican	1,000
Guatemalan	934
Salvadoran	1,058
Cuban	874
Mexican	952

Median Household Income
(2010 Inflation-Adjusted Dollars)

Group	Dollars
Total Population	38,473
Hispanic or Latino (of any race)	38,121
Central American, ex. Mexican	41,332
Guatemalan	29,583
Salvadoran	45,269
Cuban	18,903
Mexican	38,056

Per Capita Income
(2010 Inflation-Adjusted Dollars)

Group	Dollars
Total Population	12,671
Hispanic or Latino (of any race)	12,442
Central American, ex. Mexican	17,772
Guatemalan	12,131
Salvadoran	18,018
Cuban	17,795
Mexican	11,483

Households with $100,000+ Income

Group	Number	%
Total Population	511	5.7
Hispanic or Latino (of any race)	480	5.8
Central American, ex. Mexican	109	9.3
Guatemalan	26	9.0
Salvadoran	67	9.3
Cuban	10	2.4
Mexican	361	5.6

Households with Food Stamps/SNAP Benefits During Past 12 Months

Group	Number	%
Total Population	833	9.3
Hispanic or Latino (of any race)	788	9.6
Central American, ex. Mexican	92	7.8
Guatemalan	59	20.4
Salvadoran	21	2.9
Cuban	22	5.4
Mexican	665	10.4

Poverty Rate
(Income in Past 12 Months Below Poverty Level)

Group	%
Total Population	22.6
Hispanic or Latino (of any race)	22.2
Central American, ex. Mexican	17.7
Guatemalan	28.8
Salvadoran	15.6
Cuban	10.8
Mexican	22.9

Bell Gardens

Population

Group	Number	%TP[1]	%HP[2]
Total Population	42,072	100.0	–
Hispanic or Latino (of any race)	40,271	95.7	100.0
Central American, ex. Mexican	3,670	8.7	9.1
Guatemalan	934	2.2	2.3
Honduran	257	0.6	0.6
Nicaraguan	414	1.0	1.0
Salvadoran	1,967	4.7	4.9
Cuban	149	0.4	0.4
Mexican	34,509	82.0	85.7
Puerto Rican	131	0.3	0.3
South American	258	0.6	0.6
Peruvian	107	0.3	0.3

Population Growth: 2000–2010

Group	%
Total Population	-4.5
Hispanic or Latino (of any race)	-2.1
Central American, ex. Mexican	51.1
Guatemalan	70.7
Honduran	87.6
Nicaraguan	27.4
Salvadoran	75.0
Cuban	1.4
Mexican	5.0
Puerto Rican	19.1
South American	47.4

Males per 100 Females

Group	Number
Total Population	99.7
Hispanic or Latino (of any race)	99.5
Central American, ex. Mexican	98.8
Guatemalan	111.3
Honduran	100.8
Nicaraguan	96.2
Salvadoran	92.5
Cuban	88.6
Mexican	99.9
Puerto Rican	79.5
South American	98.5
Peruvian	114.0

Average Household Size

Group	People
Total Population	4.31
Hispanic or Latino (of any race)	4.41
Central American, ex. Mexican	4.15
Guatemalan	4.28
Honduran	4.33
Nicaraguan	4.39
Salvadoran	4.04
Cuban	2.73
Mexican	4.48
Puerto Rican	3.53
South American	3.11
Peruvian	3.41

Median Age

Group	Years
Total Population	27.3
Hispanic or Latino (of any race)	26.7
Central American, ex. Mexican	34.8
Guatemalan	35.0
Honduran	32.8
Nicaraguan	34.6
Salvadoran	35.3
Cuban	43.8
Mexican	25.9
Puerto Rican	30.1
South American	42.0
Peruvian	38.4

High School Graduates
(Universe: Population 25 Years and Over)

Group	Number	%
Total Population	9,524	42.1
Hispanic or Latino (of any race)	8,614	40.3
Central American, ex. Mexican	1,153	46.4
Guatemalan	417	46.4
Salvadoran	604	46.7
Mexican	7,115	39.0

Four-Year College Graduates
(Universe: Population 25 Years and Over)

Group	Number	%
Total Population	1,025	4.5
Hispanic or Latino (of any race)	843	3.9
Central American, ex. Mexican	111	4.5
Guatemalan	65	7.2
Salvadoran	39	3.0
Mexican	689	3.8

Population Age 3–17 Enrolled in Public School
(Universe: Population Age 3–17 Enrolled in School)

Group	Number	%
Total Population	11,187	96.9
Hispanic or Latino (of any race)	11,010	96.9
Central American, ex. Mexican	759	100.0
Guatemalan	338	100.0
Salvadoran	253	100.0
Mexican	9,987	96.7

Population Age 3–17 Enrolled in Private School
(Universe: Population Age 3–17 Enrolled in School)

Group	Number	%
Total Population	363	3.1
Hispanic or Latino (of any race)	349	3.1
Central American, ex. Mexican	0	0.0
Guatemalan	0	0.0
Salvadoran	0	0.0
Mexican	342	3.3

Foreign-Born Population

Group	Number	%
Total Population	19,914	47.0
Hispanic or Latino (of any race)	19,531	47.9
Central American, ex. Mexican	2,584	66.1
Guatemalan	810	56.9
Salvadoran	1,391	74.9
Mexican	16,524	46.2

Foreign-Born Naturalized U.S. Citizens

Group	Number	%
Total Population	4,881	24.5
Hispanic or Latino (of any race)	4,543	23.3
Central American, ex. Mexican	803	31.1
Guatemalan	145	17.9
Salvadoran	561	40.3
Mexican	3,573	21.6

Language Spoken at Home: English Only
(Universe: Population 5 Years and Over)

Group	Number	%
Total Population	2,551	6.6
Hispanic or Latino (of any race)	1,560	4.2
Central American, ex. Mexican	126	3.4
Guatemalan	43	3.1
Salvadoran	64	3.6
Mexican	1,343	4.2

Language Spoken at Home: Spanish
(Universe: Population 5 Years and Over)

Group	Number	%
Total Population	35,444	92.2
Hispanic or Latino (of any race)	35,271	95.7
Central American, ex. Mexican	3,601	96.6
Guatemalan	1,329	96.9
Salvadoran	1,703	96.4
Mexican	30,898	95.8

Unemployment Rate
(Universe: Population 16 Years and Over)

Group	%
Total Population	8.1
Hispanic or Latino (of any race)	8.0
Central American, ex. Mexican	11.1
Guatemalan	7.7

STATE & PLACE PROFILES

Notes: (1) Percent of total population; (2) Percent of Hispanic/Latino population; Profiles include places with an overall population of at least 125,000, OR an overall population of at least 25,000 where the Hispanic/Latino population is at least 20% of the overall population. In states where less than five places meet either of these criteria, we have included places with at least 10,000 total population with the highest percentage of Hispanic/Latino population. These places are identified with an asterisk (*); Please refer to the User's Guide for a full explanation of data.

Salvadoran		11.1
Mexican		7.3

Class of Worker: Private Wage and Salary
(Universe: Civilian Employed Population 16 Years and Over)

Group	Number	%
Total Population	15,200	90.4
Hispanic or Latino (of any race)	14,791	90.9
Central American, ex. Mexican	1,612	91.0
Guatemalan	528	92.1
Salvadoran	892	91.6
Mexican	12,968	91.2

Class of Worker: Government
(Universe: Civilian Employed Population 16 Years and Over)

Group	Number	%
Total Population	895	5.3
Hispanic or Latino (of any race)	815	5.0
Central American, ex. Mexican	45	2.5
Guatemalan	14	2.4
Salvadoran	16	1.6
Mexican	744	5.2

Means of Transportation to Work: Car, Truck or Van
(Universe: Workers 16 Years and Over)

Group	Number	%
Total Population	13,766	83.5
Hispanic or Latino (of any race)	13,353	83.6
Central American, ex. Mexican	1,570	88.7
Guatemalan	486	84.8
Salvadoran	896	92.0
Mexican	11,544	82.9

Means of Transportation to Work: Public Transportation (ex. Taxicab)
(Universe: Workers 16 Years and Over)

Group	Number	%
Total Population	1,457	8.8
Hispanic or Latino (of any race)	1,424	8.9
Central American, ex. Mexican	108	6.1
Guatemalan	35	6.1
Salvadoran	43	4.4
Mexican	1,304	9.4

Homeownership Rate
(Universe: Occupied Housing Units)

Group	%
Total Population	24.0
Hispanic or Latino (of any race)	23.1
Central American, ex. Mexican	19.8
Guatemalan	20.8
Honduran	9.8
Nicaraguan	13.2
Salvadoran	22.1
Cuban	21.0
Mexican	23.8
Puerto Rican	22.5
South American	18.5
Peruvian	16.2

Median Home Value

Group	Dollars
Total Population	394,600
Hispanic or Latino (of any race)	388,900
Central American, ex. Mexican	387,700
Guatemalan	293,000
Salvadoran	370,500
Mexican	370,400

Median Gross Rent

Group	Dollars
Total Population	997
Hispanic or Latino (of any race)	999
Central American, ex. Mexican	1,036
Guatemalan	1,138
Salvadoran	919
Mexican	991

Median Household Income
(2010 Inflation-Adjusted Dollars)

Group	Dollars
Total Population	39,167
Hispanic or Latino (of any race)	39,495
Central American, ex. Mexican	37,250
Guatemalan	41,131
Salvadoran	34,196
Mexican	40,084

Per Capita Income
(2010 Inflation-Adjusted Dollars)

Group	Dollars
Total Population	12,146
Hispanic or Latino (of any race)	11,919
Central American, ex. Mexican	14,671
Guatemalan	14,999
Salvadoran	15,717
Mexican	11,611

Households with $100,000+ Income

Group	Number	%
Total Population	647	6.4
Hispanic or Latino (of any race)	583	6.1
Central American, ex. Mexican	61	5.3
Guatemalan	22	5.3
Salvadoran	34	5.5
Mexican	522	6.4

Households with Food Stamps/SNAP Benefits During Past 12 Months

Group	Number	%
Total Population	1,026	10.2
Hispanic or Latino (of any race)	984	10.3
Central American, ex. Mexican	22	1.9
Guatemalan	0	0.0
Salvadoran	22	3.6
Mexican	932	11.5

Poverty Rate
(Income in Past 12 Months Below Poverty Level)

Group	%
Total Population	22.7
Hispanic or Latino (of any race)	22.5
Central American, ex. Mexican	23.7
Guatemalan	27.2
Salvadoran	13.5
Mexican	22.2

Bellflower

Population

Group	Number	%TP[1]	%HP[2]
Total Population	76,616	100.0	–
Hispanic or Latino (of any race)	40,085	52.3	100.0
Central American, ex. Mexican	3,104	4.1	7.7
Guatemalan	898	1.2	2.2
Honduran	184	0.2	0.5
Nicaraguan	297	0.4	0.7
Salvadoran	1,563	2.0	3.9
Cuban	295	0.4	0.7
Mexican	32,587	42.5	81.3
Puerto Rican	445	0.6	1.1
South American	867	1.1	2.2
Argentinean	116	0.2	0.3
Colombian	203	0.3	0.5
Ecuadorian	174	0.2	0.4
Peruvian	250	0.3	0.6
Spaniard	196	0.3	0.5

Population Growth: 2000–2010

Group	%
Total Population	5.1
Hispanic or Latino (of any race)	27.2
Central American, ex. Mexican	100.4
Guatemalan	142.7
Nicaraguan	52.3
Salvadoran	131.9
Cuban	32.3
Mexican	33.4
Puerto Rican	-8.2
South American	66.1
Colombian	59.8
Peruvian	51.5

Males per 100 Females

Group	Number
Total Population	94.4
Hispanic or Latino (of any race)	97.8
Central American, ex. Mexican	92.3
Guatemalan	102.3
Honduran	60.0
Nicaraguan	82.2
Salvadoran	94.9
Cuban	84.4
Mexican	98.5
Puerto Rican	88.6
South American	96.2
Argentinean	110.9
Colombian	97.1
Ecuadorian	109.6
Peruvian	85.2
Spaniard	100.0

Average Household Size

Group	People
Total Population	3.21
Hispanic or Latino (of any race)	3.89
Central American, ex. Mexican	3.97
Guatemalan	4.14
Honduran	3.63
Nicaraguan	4.15
Salvadoran	4.00
Cuban	2.89
Mexican	3.97
Puerto Rican	3.13
South American	3.30
Argentinean	2.74
Colombian	2.94
Ecuadorian	3.58
Peruvian	3.62
Spaniard	2.94

Median Age

Group	Years
Total Population	31.9
Hispanic or Latino (of any race)	26.9
Central American, ex. Mexican	33.2
Guatemalan	33.7
Honduran	33.7
Nicaraguan	32.5
Salvadoran	33.2
Cuban	31.8
Mexican	26.1
Puerto Rican	30.1
South American	39.8
Argentinean	39.3
Colombian	41.4
Ecuadorian	42.7
Peruvian	38.0
Spaniard	42.5

High School Graduates
(Universe: Population 25 Years and Over)

Group	Number	%
Total Population	34,830	77.1
Hispanic or Latino (of any race)	12,185	61.7
Central American, ex. Mexican	1,201	64.3
Salvadoran	503	55.8
Mexican	9,503	60.1

Four-Year College Graduates
(Universe: Population 25 Years and Over)

Group	Number	%
Total Population	8,016	17.7
Hispanic or Latino (of any race)	1,616	8.2
Central American, ex. Mexican	214	11.5
Salvadoran	106	11.8
Mexican	1,151	7.3

Population Age 3–17 Enrolled in Public School
(Universe: Population Age 3–17 Enrolled in School)

Group	Number	%
Total Population	15,477	91.5
Hispanic or Latino (of any race)	9,962	94.7
Central American, ex. Mexican	959	100.0
Salvadoran	660	100.0
Mexican	8,204	94.4

Population Age 3–17 Enrolled in Private School
(Universe: Population Age 3–17 Enrolled in School)

Group	Number	%
Total Population	1,443	8.5
Hispanic or Latino (of any race)	553	5.3
Central American, ex. Mexican	0	0.0
Salvadoran	0	0.0

Notes: (1) Percent of total population; (2) Percent of Hispanic/Latino population; Profiles include places with an overall population of at least 125,000, OR an overall population of at least 25,000 where the Hispanic/Latino population is at least 20% of the overall population. In states where less than five places meet either of these criteria, we have included places with at least 10,000 total population with the highest percentage of Hispanic/Latino population. These places are identified with an asterisk (*); Please refer to the User's Guide for a full explanation of data.

Mexican	483	5.6

Foreign-Born Population

Group	Number	%
Total Population	22,810	30.0
Hispanic or Latino (of any race)	14,101	36.5
Central American, ex. Mexican	1,899	53.1
Salvadoran	895	47.7
Mexican	11,200	35.7

Foreign-Born Naturalized U.S. Citizens

Group	Number	%
Total Population	9,780	42.9
Hispanic or Latino (of any race)	5,261	37.3
Central American, ex. Mexican	916	48.2
Salvadoran	456	50.9
Mexican	3,722	33.2

Language Spoken at Home: English Only
(Universe: Population 5 Years and Over)

Group	Number	%
Total Population	31,986	45.9
Hispanic or Latino (of any race)	7,171	20.8
Central American, ex. Mexican	463	14.0
Salvadoran	320	18.1
Mexican	5,526	20.0

Language Spoken at Home: Spanish
(Universe: Population 5 Years and Over)

Group	Number	%
Total Population	28,328	40.7
Hispanic or Latino (of any race)	27,223	79.2
Central American, ex. Mexican	2,835	86.0
Salvadoran	1,447	81.9
Mexican	22,144	80.0

Unemployment Rate
(Universe: Population 16 Years and Over)

Group	%
Total Population	7.3
Hispanic or Latino (of any race)	8.0
Central American, ex. Mexican	6.6
Salvadoran	7.3
Mexican	7.5

Class of Worker: Private Wage and Salary
(Universe: Civilian Employed Population 16 Years and Over)

Group	Number	%
Total Population	27,014	79.6
Hispanic or Latino (of any race)	13,067	81.6
Central American, ex. Mexican	1,393	84.1
Salvadoran	747	87.1
Mexican	10,512	81.8

Class of Worker: Government
(Universe: Civilian Employed Population 16 Years and Over)

Group	Number	%
Total Population	5,308	15.6
Hispanic or Latino (of any race)	1,983	12.4
Central American, ex. Mexican	171	10.3
Salvadoran	94	11.0
Mexican	1,599	12.4

Means of Transportation to Work: Car, Truck or Van
(Universe: Workers 16 Years and Over)

Group	Number	%
Total Population	30,226	90.8
Hispanic or Latino (of any race)	14,185	90.7
Central American, ex. Mexican	1,390	87.1
Salvadoran	734	91.0
Mexican	11,535	91.8

Means of Transportation to Work: Public Transportation (ex. Taxicab)
(Universe: Workers 16 Years and Over)

Group	Number	%
Total Population	1,245	3.7
Hispanic or Latino (of any race)	526	3.4
Central American, ex. Mexican	147	9.2
Salvadoran	27	3.3
Mexican	282	2.2

Homeownership Rate
(Universe: Occupied Housing Units)

Group	%
Total Population	40.0
Hispanic or Latino (of any race)	36.7
Central American, ex. Mexican	34.9
Guatemalan	42.3
Honduran	22.6
Nicaraguan	32.5
Salvadoran	33.1
Cuban	41.1
Mexican	37.7
Puerto Rican	30.0
South American	41.7
Argentinean	43.5
Colombian	32.4
Ecuadorian	48.3
Peruvian	35.1
Spaniard	49.4

Median Home Value

Group	Dollars
Total Population	423,400
Hispanic or Latino (of any race)	419,600
Central American, ex. Mexican	428,200
Salvadoran	405,800
Mexican	422,700

Median Gross Rent

Group	Dollars
Total Population	1,094
Hispanic or Latino (of any race)	1,090
Central American, ex. Mexican	1,227
Salvadoran	1,269
Mexican	1,064

Median Household Income
(2010 Inflation-Adjusted Dollars)

Group	Dollars
Total Population	50,565
Hispanic or Latino (of any race)	52,285
Central American, ex. Mexican	49,464
Salvadoran	49,576
Mexican	51,771

Per Capita Income
(2010 Inflation-Adjusted Dollars)

Group	Dollars
Total Population	20,345
Hispanic or Latino (of any race)	15,877
Central American, ex. Mexican	15,753
Salvadoran	16,210
Mexican	15,648

Households with $100,000+ Income

Group	Number	%
Total Population	4,189	17.4
Hispanic or Latino (of any race)	1,399	14.6
Central American, ex. Mexican	170	18.7
Salvadoran	71	14.3
Mexican	1,123	14.8

Households with Food Stamps/SNAP Benefits During Past 12 Months

Group	Number	%
Total Population	1,663	6.9
Hispanic or Latino (of any race)	951	9.9
Central American, ex. Mexican	97	10.7
Salvadoran	65	13.1
Mexican	767	10.1

Poverty Rate
(Income in Past 12 Months Below Poverty Level)

Group	%
Total Population	13.1
Hispanic or Latino (of any race)	15.7
Central American, ex. Mexican	22.5
Salvadoran	22.5
Mexican	15.4

Brea

Population

Group	Number	%TP[1]	%HP[2]
Total Population	39,282	100.0	–
Hispanic or Latino (of any race)	9,817	25.0	100.0
Central American, ex. Mexican	370	0.9	3.8
Guatemalan	105	0.3	1.1
Salvadoran	146	0.4	1.5
Cuban	139	0.4	1.4
Mexican	8,000	20.4	81.5
Puerto Rican	190	0.5	1.9
South American	444	1.1	4.5
Peruvian	150	0.4	1.5
Spaniard	195	0.5	2.0

Population Growth: 2000–2010

Group	%
Total Population	10.9
Hispanic or Latino (of any race)	36.3
Central American, ex. Mexican	122.9
Mexican	39.1
Puerto Rican	37.7
South American	74.1

Males per 100 Females

Group	Number
Total Population	95.2
Hispanic or Latino (of any race)	97.2
Central American, ex. Mexican	84.1
Guatemalan	56.7
Salvadoran	105.6
Cuban	95.8
Mexican	100.0
Puerto Rican	88.1
South American	82.7
Peruvian	82.9
Spaniard	78.9

Average Household Size

Group	People
Total Population	2.75
Hispanic or Latino (of any race)	3.26
Central American, ex. Mexican	3.39
Guatemalan	3.45
Salvadoran	3.65
Cuban	2.63
Mexican	3.33
Puerto Rican	2.94
South American	3.02
Peruvian	3.56
Spaniard	2.88

Median Age

Group	Years
Total Population	38.7
Hispanic or Latino (of any race)	30.1
Central American, ex. Mexican	30.6
Guatemalan	32.8
Salvadoran	28.0
Cuban	29.5
Mexican	29.2
Puerto Rican	34.0
South American	38.5
Peruvian	39.7
Spaniard	38.8

High School Graduates
(Universe: Population 25 Years and Over)

Group	Number	%
Total Population	24,163	92.5
Hispanic or Latino (of any race)	3,815	77.2
Mexican	3,084	74.9

Four-Year College Graduates
(Universe: Population 25 Years and Over)

Group	Number	%
Total Population	10,675	40.9
Hispanic or Latino (of any race)	773	15.6
Mexican	622	15.1

STATE & PLACE PROFILES

Notes: (1) Percent of total population; (2) Percent of Hispanic/Latino population; Profiles include places with an overall population of at least 125,000, OR an overall population of at least 25,000 where the Hispanic/Latino population is at least 20% of the overall population. In states where less than five places meet either of these criteria, we have included places with at least 10,000 total population with the highest percentage of Hispanic/Latino population. These places are identified with an asterisk (*); Please refer to the User's Guide for a full explanation of data.

Population Age 3–17 Enrolled in Public School
(Universe: Population Age 3–17 Enrolled in School)

Group	Number	%
Total Population	5,834	83.4
Hispanic or Latino (of any race)	1,893	88.2
Mexican	1,681	89.1

Population Age 3–17 Enrolled in Private School
(Universe: Population Age 3–17 Enrolled in School)

Group	Number	%
Total Population	1,160	16.6
Hispanic or Latino (of any race)	254	11.8
Mexican	205	10.9

Foreign-Born Population

Group	Number	%
Total Population	8,336	21.7
Hispanic or Latino (of any race)	2,441	28.3
Mexican	2,059	28.1

Foreign-Born Naturalized U.S. Citizens

Group	Number	%
Total Population	4,569	54.8
Hispanic or Latino (of any race)	1,196	49.0
Mexican	942	45.8

Language Spoken at Home: English Only
(Universe: Population 5 Years and Over)

Group	Number	%
Total Population	25,661	70.3
Hispanic or Latino (of any race)	3,509	44.0
Mexican	3,002	44.1

Language Spoken at Home: Spanish
(Universe: Population 5 Years and Over)

Group	Number	%
Total Population	4,869	13.3
Hispanic or Latino (of any race)	4,473	56.0
Mexican	3,810	55.9

Unemployment Rate
(Universe: Population 16 Years and Over)

Group	%
Total Population	6.9
Hispanic or Latino (of any race)	11.8
Mexican	11.3

Class of Worker: Private Wage and Salary
(Universe: Civilian Employed Population 16 Years and Over)

Group	Number	%
Total Population	15,435	78.1
Hispanic or Latino (of any race)	3,174	80.8
Mexican	2,753	80.9

Class of Worker: Government
(Universe: Civilian Employed Population 16 Years and Over)

Group	Number	%
Total Population	3,139	15.9
Hispanic or Latino (of any race)	585	14.9
Mexican	490	14.4

Means of Transportation to Work: Car, Truck or Van
(Universe: Workers 16 Years and Over)

Group	Number	%
Total Population	17,897	92.2
Hispanic or Latino (of any race)	3,510	91.9
Mexican	3,013	91.2

Means of Transportation to Work: Public Transportation (ex. Taxicab)
(Universe: Workers 16 Years and Over)

Group	Number	%
Total Population	236	1.2
Hispanic or Latino (of any race)	65	1.7
Mexican	58	1.8

Homeownership Rate
(Universe: Occupied Housing Units)

Group	%
Total Population	65.0
Hispanic or Latino (of any race)	51.7
Central American, ex. Mexican	49.0
Guatemalan	35.5
Salvadoran	52.5
Cuban	53.5
Mexican	51.1
Puerto Rican	57.7
South American	51.7
Peruvian	55.8
Spaniard	68.7

Median Home Value

Group	Dollars
Total Population	598,600
Hispanic or Latino (of any race)	594,800
Mexican	586,800

Median Gross Rent

Group	Dollars
Total Population	1,351
Hispanic or Latino (of any race)	1,288
Mexican	1,268

Median Household Income
(2010 Inflation-Adjusted Dollars)

Group	Dollars
Total Population	79,647
Hispanic or Latino (of any race)	61,250
Mexican	62,224

Per Capita Income
(2010 Inflation-Adjusted Dollars)

Group	Dollars
Total Population	36,115
Hispanic or Latino (of any race)	22,415
Mexican	22,543

Households with $100,000+ Income

Group	Number	%
Total Population	5,380	37.4
Hispanic or Latino (of any race)	666	27.3
Mexican	551	27.5

Households with Food Stamps/SNAP Benefits During Past 12 Months

Group	Number	%
Total Population	174	1.2
Hispanic or Latino (of any race)	114	4.7
Mexican	86	4.3

Poverty Rate
(Income in Past 12 Months Below Poverty Level)

Group	%
Total Population	5.7
Hispanic or Latino (of any race)	6.8
Mexican	6.8

Brentwood

Population

Group	Number	%TP[1]	%HP[2]
Total Population	51,481	100.0	–
Hispanic or Latino (of any race)	13,779	26.8	100.0
Central American, ex. Mexican	934	1.8	6.8
Guatemalan	183	0.4	1.3
Nicaraguan	233	0.5	1.7
Salvadoran	438	0.9	3.2
Mexican	10,521	20.4	76.4
Puerto Rican	618	1.2	4.5
South American	348	0.7	2.5
Peruvian	112	0.2	0.8
Spaniard	384	0.7	2.8

Population Growth: 2000–2010

Group	%
Total Population	120.9
Hispanic or Latino (of any race)	109.9
Central American, ex. Mexican	691.5
Mexican	99.8
Puerto Rican	202.9

Males per 100 Females

Group	Number
Total Population	94.2
Hispanic or Latino (of any race)	97.6
Central American, ex. Mexican	96.2
Guatemalan	98.9
Nicaraguan	99.1
Salvadoran	94.7
Mexican	99.5
Puerto Rican	87.8
South American	94.4
Peruvian	86.7
Spaniard	83.7

Average Household Size

Group	People
Total Population	3.11
Hispanic or Latino (of any race)	3.76
Central American, ex. Mexican	3.93
Guatemalan	4.27
Nicaraguan	4.03
Salvadoran	3.75
Mexican	3.90
Puerto Rican	3.39
South American	3.37
Peruvian	3.67
Spaniard	2.83

Median Age

Group	Years
Total Population	35.6
Hispanic or Latino (of any race)	26.5
Central American, ex. Mexican	30.5
Guatemalan	31.6
Nicaraguan	30.5
Salvadoran	29.9
Mexican	25.6
Puerto Rican	25.1
South American	35.4
Peruvian	30.5
Spaniard	39.3

High School Graduates
(Universe: Population 25 Years and Over)

Group	Number	%
Total Population	25,050	89.3
Hispanic or Latino (of any race)	4,529	71.1
Mexican	3,234	67.6

Four-Year College Graduates
(Universe: Population 25 Years and Over)

Group	Number	%
Total Population	7,907	28.2
Hispanic or Latino (of any race)	875	13.7
Mexican	578	12.1

Population Age 3–17 Enrolled in Public School
(Universe: Population Age 3–17 Enrolled in School)

Group	Number	%
Total Population	11,153	91.0
Hispanic or Latino (of any race)	3,479	92.6
Mexican	3,015	92.1

Population Age 3–17 Enrolled in Private School
(Universe: Population Age 3–17 Enrolled in School)

Group	Number	%
Total Population	1,098	9.0
Hispanic or Latino (of any race)	276	7.4
Mexican	259	7.9

Foreign-Born Population

Group	Number	%
Total Population	7,053	15.2
Hispanic or Latino (of any race)	3,234	25.9
Mexican	2,590	25.9

Foreign-Born Naturalized U.S. Citizens

Group	Number	%
Total Population	3,745	53.1
Hispanic or Latino (of any race)	1,135	35.1
Mexican	831	32.1

Language Spoken at Home: English Only
(Universe: Population 5 Years and Over)

Group	Number	%
Total Population	32,306	75.7
Hispanic or Latino (of any race)	4,855	43.8
Mexican	3,726	42.1

Language Spoken at Home: Spanish
(Universe: Population 5 Years and Over)

Group	Number	%
Total Population	6,746	15.8
Hispanic or Latino (of any race)	6,214	56.0

Notes: (1) Percent of total population; (2) Percent of Hispanic/Latino population; Profiles include places with an overall population of at least 125,000, OR an overall population of at least 25,000 where the Hispanic/Latino population is at least 20% of the overall population. In states where less than five places meet either of these criteria, we have included places with at least 10,000 total population with the highest percentage of Hispanic/Latino population. These places are identified with an asterisk (*); Please refer to the User's Guide for a full explanation of data.

Mexican	5,123	57.8

Unemployment Rate
(Universe: Population 16 Years and Over)

Group		%
Total Population		7.4
Hispanic or Latino (of any race)		7.1
Mexican		8.5

Class of Worker: Private Wage and Salary
(Universe: Civilian Employed Population 16 Years and Over)

Group	Number	%
Total Population	14,544	75.0
Hispanic or Latino (of any race)	3,889	76.5
Mexican	2,954	76.5

Class of Worker: Government
(Universe: Civilian Employed Population 16 Years and Over)

Group	Number	%
Total Population	3,325	17.2
Hispanic or Latino (of any race)	714	14.0
Mexican	529	13.7

Means of Transportation to Work: Car, Truck or Van
(Universe: Workers 16 Years and Over)

Group	Number	%
Total Population	16,913	90.3
Hispanic or Latino (of any race)	4,434	90.6
Mexican	3,379	91.0

Means of Transportation to Work: Public Transportation (ex. Taxicab)
(Universe: Workers 16 Years and Over)

Group	Number	%
Total Population	531	2.8
Hispanic or Latino (of any race)	97	2.0
Mexican	83	2.2

Homeownership Rate
(Universe: Occupied Housing Units)

Group	%
Total Population	76.3
Hispanic or Latino (of any race)	65.0
Central American, ex. Mexican	69.6
Guatemalan	65.3
Nicaraguan	69.5
Salvadoran	69.4
Mexican	62.5
Puerto Rican	63.9
South American	79.1
Peruvian	81.5
Spaniard	80.3

Median Home Value

Group	Dollars
Total Population	471,600
Hispanic or Latino (of any race)	439,500
Mexican	428,200

Median Gross Rent

Group	Dollars
Total Population	1,567
Hispanic or Latino (of any race)	1,051
Mexican	1,143

Median Household Income
(2010 Inflation-Adjusted Dollars)

Group	Dollars
Total Population	89,515
Hispanic or Latino (of any race)	68,894
Mexican	67,873

Per Capita Income
(2010 Inflation-Adjusted Dollars)

Group	Dollars
Total Population	32,374
Hispanic or Latino (of any race)	21,747
Mexican	20,108

Households with $100,000+ Income

Group	Number	%
Total Population	6,459	43.6
Hispanic or Latino (of any race)	1,065	34.1
Mexican	826	34.5

Households with Food Stamps/SNAP Benefits During Past 12 Months

Group	Number	%
Total Population	425	2.9
Hispanic or Latino (of any race)	164	5.2
Mexican	107	4.5

Poverty Rate
(Income in Past 12 Months Below Poverty Level)

Group	%
Total Population	5.4
Hispanic or Latino (of any race)	7.7
Mexican	8.8

Buena Park

Population

Group	Number	%TP[1]	%HP[2]
Total Population	80,530	100.0	–
Hispanic or Latino (of any race)	31,638	39.3	100.0
Central American, ex. Mexican	1,700	2.1	5.4
Guatemalan	592	0.7	1.9
Honduran	119	0.1	0.4
Nicaraguan	206	0.3	0.7
Salvadoran	679	0.8	2.1
Cuban	261	0.3	0.8
Mexican	26,549	33.0	83.9
Puerto Rican	422	0.5	1.3
South American	930	1.2	2.9
Argentinean	112	0.1	0.4
Colombian	209	0.3	0.7
Ecuadorian	146	0.2	0.5
Peruvian	374	0.5	1.2
Spaniard	229	0.3	0.7

Population Growth: 2000–2010

Group	%
Total Population	2.9
Hispanic or Latino (of any race)	20.7
Central American, ex. Mexican	93.0
Guatemalan	128.6
Nicaraguan	56.1
Salvadoran	134.9
Cuban	-11.2
Mexican	27.1
Puerto Rican	0.5
South American	73.5
Colombian	106.9
Peruvian	105.5

Males per 100 Females

Group	Number
Total Population	97.4
Hispanic or Latino (of any race)	100.2
Central American, ex. Mexican	89.9
Guatemalan	108.5
Honduran	72.5
Nicaraguan	96.2
Salvadoran	76.4
Cuban	87.8
Mexican	101.6
Puerto Rican	89.2
South American	90.6
Argentinean	89.8
Colombian	102.9
Ecuadorian	97.3
Peruvian	82.4
Spaniard	94.1

Average Household Size

Group	People
Total Population	3.37
Hispanic or Latino (of any race)	4.21
Central American, ex. Mexican	4.40
Guatemalan	4.79
Honduran	3.77
Nicaraguan	4.02
Salvadoran	4.46
Cuban	3.09
Mexican	4.32
Puerto Rican	2.95
South American	3.55
Argentinean	3.28
Colombian	3.59
Ecuadorian	3.59
Peruvian	3.73
Spaniard	3.35

Median Age

Group	Years
Total Population	35.1
Hispanic or Latino (of any race)	27.2
Central American, ex. Mexican	32.9
Guatemalan	31.0
Honduran	32.4
Nicaraguan	40.0
Salvadoran	32.9
Cuban	37.5
Mexican	26.3
Puerto Rican	30.8
South American	37.7
Argentinean	35.5
Colombian	37.9
Ecuadorian	41.5
Peruvian	37.5
Spaniard	38.8

High School Graduates
(Universe: Population 25 Years and Over)

Group	Number	%
Total Population	40,506	81.1
Hispanic or Latino (of any race)	8,519	56.3
Central American, ex. Mexican	453	66.6
Mexican	6,965	53.4

Four-Year College Graduates
(Universe: Population 25 Years and Over)

Group	Number	%
Total Population	13,279	26.6
Hispanic or Latino (of any race)	1,297	8.6
Central American, ex. Mexican	165	24.3
Mexican	885	6.8

Population Age 3–17 Enrolled in Public School
(Universe: Population Age 3–17 Enrolled in School)

Group	Number	%
Total Population	14,980	88.5
Hispanic or Latino (of any race)	7,537	93.5
Central American, ex. Mexican	123	87.2
Mexican	7,037	93.6

Population Age 3–17 Enrolled in Private School
(Universe: Population Age 3–17 Enrolled in School)

Group	Number	%
Total Population	1,943	11.5
Hispanic or Latino (of any race)	527	6.5
Central American, ex. Mexican	18	12.8
Mexican	482	6.4

Foreign-Born Population

Group	Number	%
Total Population	29,517	37.0
Hispanic or Latino (of any race)	11,877	40.8
Central American, ex. Mexican	610	52.0
Mexican	10,473	40.6

Foreign-Born Naturalized U.S. Citizens

Group	Number	%
Total Population	13,535	45.9
Hispanic or Latino (of any race)	3,421	28.8
Central American, ex. Mexican	232	38.0
Mexican	2,647	25.3

Language Spoken at Home: English Only
(Universe: Population 5 Years and Over)

Group	Number	%
Total Population	34,599	46.7
Hispanic or Latino (of any race)	6,636	25.6
Central American, ex. Mexican	104	10.7
Mexican	5,767	25.1

Language Spoken at Home: Spanish
(Universe: Population 5 Years and Over)

Group	Number	%
Total Population	19,705	26.6
Hispanic or Latino (of any race)	19,108	73.7
Central American, ex. Mexican	872	89.3
Mexican	17,053	74.3

Notes: (1) Percent of total population; (2) Percent of Hispanic/Latino population; Profiles include places with an overall population of at least 125,000, OR an overall population of at least 25,000 where the Hispanic/Latino population is at least 20% of the overall population. In states where less than five places meet either of these criteria, we have included places with at least 10,000 total population with the highest percentage of Hispanic/Latino population. These places are identified with an asterisk (*); Please refer to the User's Guide for a full explanation of data.

Unemployment Rate
(Universe: Population 16 Years and Over)

Group	%
Total Population	7.0
Hispanic or Latino (of any race)	7.4
Central American, ex. Mexican	13.0
Mexican	7.1

Class of Worker: Private Wage and Salary
(Universe: Civilian Employed Population 16 Years and Over)

Group	Number	%
Total Population	30,366	82.0
Hispanic or Latino (of any race)	11,013	88.8
Central American, ex. Mexican	502	85.1
Mexican	9,687	89.6

Class of Worker: Government
(Universe: Civilian Employed Population 16 Years and Over)

Group	Number	%
Total Population	3,964	10.7
Hispanic or Latino (of any race)	729	5.9
Central American, ex. Mexican	28	4.7
Mexican	593	5.5

Means of Transportation to Work: Car, Truck or Van
(Universe: Workers 16 Years and Over)

Group	Number	%
Total Population	32,405	89.3
Hispanic or Latino (of any race)	10,493	86.7
Central American, ex. Mexican	456	79.0
Mexican	9,176	86.8

Means of Transportation to Work: Public Transportation (ex. Taxicab)
(Universe: Workers 16 Years and Over)

Group	Number	%
Total Population	1,011	2.8
Hispanic or Latino (of any race)	386	3.2
Central American, ex. Mexican	56	9.7
Mexican	273	2.6

Homeownership Rate
(Universe: Occupied Housing Units)

Group	%
Total Population	56.7
Hispanic or Latino (of any race)	44.4
Central American, ex. Mexican	36.9
Guatemalan	29.5
Honduran	37.1
Nicaraguan	44.9
Salvadoran	41.5
Cuban	54.4
Mexican	44.1
Puerto Rican	42.4
South American	63.1
Argentinean	62.5
Colombian	66.1
Ecuadorian	65.3
Peruvian	59.6
Spaniard	61.7

Median Home Value

Group	Dollars
Total Population	485,000
Hispanic or Latino (of any race)	477,100
Central American, ex. Mexican	408,300
Mexican	477,000

Median Gross Rent

Group	Dollars
Total Population	1,341
Hispanic or Latino (of any race)	1,246
Central American, ex. Mexican	1,318
Mexican	1,239

Median Household Income
(2010 Inflation-Adjusted Dollars)

Group	Dollars
Total Population	63,295
Hispanic or Latino (of any race)	50,662
Central American, ex. Mexican	63,942
Mexican	50,311

Per Capita Income
(2010 Inflation-Adjusted Dollars)

Group	Dollars
Total Population	22,966
Hispanic or Latino (of any race)	14,988
Central American, ex. Mexican	17,393
Mexican	14,411

Households with $100,000+ Income

Group	Number	%
Total Population	6,152	26.7
Hispanic or Latino (of any race)	1,074	16.6
Central American, ex. Mexican	68	20.9
Mexican	863	16.0

Households with Food Stamps/SNAP Benefits During Past 12 Months

Group	Number	%
Total Population	1,345	5.8
Hispanic or Latino (of any race)	734	11.3
Central American, ex. Mexican	10	3.1
Mexican	716	13.3

Poverty Rate
(Income in Past 12 Months Below Poverty Level)

Group	%
Total Population	9.8
Hispanic or Latino (of any race)	14.6
Central American, ex. Mexican	15.9
Mexican	15.1

Burbank

Population

Group	Number	%TP[1]	%HP[2]
Total Population	103,340	100.0	–
Hispanic or Latino (of any race)	25,310	24.5	100.0
Central American, ex. Mexican	4,331	4.2	17.1
Costa Rican	199	0.2	0.8
Guatemalan	1,238	1.2	4.9
Honduran	165	0.2	0.7
Nicaraguan	406	0.4	1.6
Salvadoran	2,231	2.2	8.8
Cuban	1,087	1.1	4.3
Mexican	14,706	14.2	58.1
Puerto Rican	601	0.6	2.4
South American	2,548	2.5	10.1
Argentinean	406	0.4	1.6
Bolivian	208	0.2	0.8
Chilean	165	0.2	0.7
Colombian	677	0.7	2.7
Ecuadorian	376	0.4	1.5
Peruvian	589	0.6	2.3
Spaniard	478	0.5	1.9

Population Growth: 2000–2010

Group	%
Total Population	3.0
Hispanic or Latino (of any race)	1.4
Central American, ex. Mexican	52.9
Costa Rican	33.6
Guatemalan	56.3
Nicaraguan	67.8
Salvadoran	76.8
Cuban	0.5
Mexican	3.4
Puerto Rican	18.8
South American	38.9
Argentinean	88.8
Bolivian	30.8
Colombian	34.9
Ecuadorian	37.2
Peruvian	53.0

Males per 100 Females

Group	Number
Total Population	93.6
Hispanic or Latino (of any race)	88.5
Central American, ex. Mexican	82.0
Costa Rican	73.0
Guatemalan	93.4
Honduran	63.4
Nicaraguan	86.2
Salvadoran	78.3
Cuban	79.7
Mexican	91.6
Puerto Rican	105.1
South American	84.5
Argentinean	120.7
Bolivian	77.8
Chilean	77.4
Colombian	78.6
Ecuadorian	80.8
Peruvian	80.1
Spaniard	79.0

Average Household Size

Group	People
Total Population	2.45
Hispanic or Latino (of any race)	2.96
Central American, ex. Mexican	3.21
Costa Rican	2.80
Guatemalan	3.32
Honduran	3.32
Nicaraguan	2.93
Salvadoran	3.29
Cuban	2.54
Mexican	3.05
Puerto Rican	2.36
South American	2.76
Argentinean	2.45
Bolivian	2.97
Chilean	2.83
Colombian	2.72
Ecuadorian	3.01
Peruvian	2.84
Spaniard	2.16

Median Age

Group	Years
Total Population	38.9
Hispanic or Latino (of any race)	33.0
Central American, ex. Mexican	35.7
Costa Rican	45.1
Guatemalan	36.9
Honduran	32.7
Nicaraguan	38.7
Salvadoran	34.1
Cuban	38.8
Mexican	30.9
Puerto Rican	34.8
South American	39.9
Argentinean	36.6
Bolivian	39.0
Chilean	37.1
Colombian	41.0
Ecuadorian	40.7
Peruvian	42.1
Spaniard	38.3

High School Graduates
(Universe: Population 25 Years and Over)

Group	Number	%
Total Population	64,622	87.7
Hispanic or Latino (of any race)	12,128	75.9
Central American, ex. Mexican	1,951	74.4
Guatemalan	709	79.9
Salvadoran	851	71.9
Cuban	524	86.6
Mexican	7,137	72.2
South American	1,789	87.8
Colombian	752	91.5

Four-Year College Graduates
(Universe: Population 25 Years and Over)

Group	Number	%
Total Population	25,847	35.1
Hispanic or Latino (of any race)	2,834	17.7
Central American, ex. Mexican	385	14.7
Guatemalan	142	16.0
Salvadoran	119	10.1
Cuban	175	28.9
Mexican	1,362	13.8
South American	622	30.5
Colombian	310	37.7

Notes: (1) Percent of total population; (2) Percent of Hispanic/Latino population; Profiles include places with an overall population of at least 125,000, OR an overall population of at least 25,000 where the Hispanic/Latino population is at least 20% of the overall population. In states where less than five places meet either of these criteria, we have included places with at least 10,000 total population with the highest percentage of Hispanic/Latino population. These places are identified with an asterisk (*); Please refer to the User's Guide for a full explanation of data.

Population Age 3–17 Enrolled in Public School
(Universe: Population Age 3–17 Enrolled in School)

Group	Number	%
Total Population	13,135	83.1
Hispanic or Latino (of any race)	4,514	87.6
Central American, ex. Mexican	448	96.6
Guatemalan	128	100.0
Salvadoran	142	89.9
Cuban	182	91.0
Mexican	3,142	87.7
South American	263	95.6
Colombian	221	100.0

Population Age 3–17 Enrolled in Private School
(Universe: Population Age 3–17 Enrolled in School)

Group	Number	%
Total Population	2,669	16.9
Hispanic or Latino (of any race)	639	12.4
Central American, ex. Mexican	16	3.4
Guatemalan	0	0.0
Salvadoran	16	10.1
Cuban	18	9.0
Mexican	440	12.3
South American	12	4.4
Colombian	0	0.0

Foreign-Born Population

Group	Number	%
Total Population	33,303	32.4
Hispanic or Latino (of any race)	10,050	39.6
Central American, ex. Mexican	2,119	58.3
Guatemalan	738	63.6
Salvadoran	1,005	65.6
Cuban	490	51.3
Mexican	5,614	34.4
South American	1,610	61.1
Colombian	619	50.2

Foreign-Born Naturalized U.S. Citizens

Group	Number	%
Total Population	20,804	62.5
Hispanic or Latino (of any race)	5,786	57.6
Central American, ex. Mexican	1,430	67.5
Guatemalan	510	69.1
Salvadoran	769	76.5
Cuban	490	100.0
Mexican	2,882	51.3
South American	841	52.2
Colombian	341	55.1

Language Spoken at Home: English Only
(Universe: Population 5 Years and Over)

Group	Number	%
Total Population	54,100	55.5
Hispanic or Latino (of any race)	6,273	26.6
Central American, ex. Mexican	679	19.2
Guatemalan	124	10.9
Salvadoran	318	20.7
Cuban	337	35.8
Mexican	4,248	28.7
South American	234	9.1
Colombian	135	11.0

Language Spoken at Home: Spanish
(Universe: Population 5 Years and Over)

Group	Number	%
Total Population	18,796	19.3
Hispanic or Latino (of any race)	17,197	73.1
Central American, ex. Mexican	2,843	80.4
Guatemalan	999	87.9
Salvadoran	1,215	79.3
Cuban	604	64.2
Mexican	10,529	71.2
South American	2,350	90.9
Colombian	1,097	89.0

Unemployment Rate
(Universe: Population 16 Years and Over)

Group	%
Total Population	6.8
Hispanic or Latino (of any race)	6.9
Central American, ex. Mexican	4.6
Guatemalan	6.3
Salvadoran	5.3
Cuban	9.2
Mexican	8.3
South American	3.2
Colombian	3.1

Class of Worker: Private Wage and Salary
(Universe: Civilian Employed Population 16 Years and Over)

Group	Number	%
Total Population	41,776	77.6
Hispanic or Latino (of any race)	9,504	73.8
Central American, ex. Mexican	1,519	69.0
Guatemalan	420	59.8
Salvadoran	819	78.0
Cuban	336	83.4
Mexican	5,868	75.1
South American	1,140	67.9
Colombian	605	73.2

Class of Worker: Government
(Universe: Civilian Employed Population 16 Years and Over)

Group	Number	%
Total Population	6,311	11.7
Hispanic or Latino (of any race)	1,976	15.4
Central American, ex. Mexican	491	22.3
Guatemalan	234	33.3
Salvadoran	143	13.6
Cuban	36	8.9
Mexican	1,036	13.3
South American	306	18.2
Colombian	100	12.1

Means of Transportation to Work: Car, Truck or Van
(Universe: Workers 16 Years and Over)

Group	Number	%
Total Population	46,009	87.5
Hispanic or Latino (of any race)	10,697	85.4
Central American, ex. Mexican	1,920	89.1
Guatemalan	503	76.7
Salvadoran	969	92.3
Cuban	355	88.1
Mexican	6,283	82.6
South American	1,449	90.5
Colombian	719	89.4

Means of Transportation to Work: Public Transportation (ex. Taxicab)
(Universe: Workers 16 Years and Over)

Group	Number	%
Total Population	1,707	3.2
Hispanic or Latino (of any race)	656	5.2
Central American, ex. Mexican	94	4.4
Guatemalan	80	12.2
Salvadoran	14	1.3
Cuban	0	0.0
Mexican	509	6.7
South American	19	1.2
Colombian	19	2.4

Homeownership Rate
(Universe: Occupied Housing Units)

Group	%
Total Population	44.0
Hispanic or Latino (of any race)	34.4
Central American, ex. Mexican	29.6
Costa Rican	35.5
Guatemalan	30.4
Honduran	25.5
Nicaraguan	30.6
Salvadoran	28.8
Cuban	49.0
Mexican	32.7
Puerto Rican	32.5
South American	43.3
Argentinean	50.0
Bolivian	42.1
Chilean	41.7
Colombian	43.5
Ecuadorian	52.3
Peruvian	38.7
Spaniard	45.5

Median Home Value

Group	Dollars
Total Population	608,800
Hispanic or Latino (of any race)	596,100
Central American, ex. Mexican	412,300
Guatemalan	394,700
Salvadoran	434,600
Cuban	575,200
Mexican	625,000
South American	595,400
Colombian	632,600

Median Gross Rent

Group	Dollars
Total Population	1,299
Hispanic or Latino (of any race)	1,177
Central American, ex. Mexican	1,241
Guatemalan	1,315
Salvadoran	1,255
Cuban	1,118
Mexican	1,159
South American	1,156
Colombian	1,195

Median Household Income
(2010 Inflation-Adjusted Dollars)

Group	Dollars
Total Population	63,356
Hispanic or Latino (of any race)	55,364
Central American, ex. Mexican	56,989
Guatemalan	54,335
Salvadoran	62,036
Cuban	58,125
Mexican	54,653
South American	59,180
Colombian	72,500

Per Capita Income
(2010 Inflation-Adjusted Dollars)

Group	Dollars
Total Population	33,320
Hispanic or Latino (of any race)	23,939
Central American, ex. Mexican	25,002
Guatemalan	24,386
Salvadoran	30,640
Cuban	36,645
Mexican	22,558
South American	26,529
Colombian	25,065

Households with $100,000+ Income

Group	Number	%
Total Population	11,528	27.9
Hispanic or Latino (of any race)	1,929	24.7
Central American, ex. Mexican	314	26.3
Guatemalan	102	20.8
Salvadoran	147	29.8
Cuban	152	37.6
Mexican	1,112	23.2
South American	268	25.8
Colombian	144	33.8

Households with Food Stamps/SNAP Benefits During Past 12 Months

Group	Number	%
Total Population	621	1.5
Hispanic or Latino (of any race)	94	1.2
Central American, ex. Mexican	36	3.0
Guatemalan	12	2.4
Salvadoran	24	4.9
Cuban	8	2.0
Mexican	34	0.7
South American	16	1.5
Colombian	0	0.0

Poverty Rate
(Income in Past 12 Months Below Poverty Level)

Group	%
Total Population	8.2
Hispanic or Latino (of any race)	10.7
Central American, ex. Mexican	5.5
Guatemalan	4.3
Salvadoran	6.9
Cuban	8.3
Mexican	12.6
South American	5.0
Colombian	3.4

STATE & PLACE PROFILES

Notes: (1) Percent of total population; (2) Percent of Hispanic/Latino population; Profiles include places with an overall population of at least 125,000, OR an overall population of at least 25,000 where the Hispanic/Latino population is at least 20% of the overall population. In states where less than five places meet either of these criteria, we have included places with at least 10,000 total population with the highest percentage of Hispanic/Latino population. These places are identified with an asterisk (*); Please refer to the User's Guide for a full explanation of data.

Calexico

Population

Group	Number	%TP[1]	%HP[2]
Total Population	38,572	100.0	–
Hispanic or Latino (of any race)	37,354	96.8	100.0
Mexican	36,443	94.5	97.6

Population Growth: 2000–2010

Group	%
Total Population	42.3
Hispanic or Latino (of any race)	44.6
Mexican	53.2

Males per 100 Females

Group	Number
Total Population	89.6
Hispanic or Latino (of any race)	88.5
Mexican	88.4

Average Household Size

Group	People
Total Population	3.80
Hispanic or Latino (of any race)	3.84
Mexican	3.84

Median Age

Group	Years
Total Population	31.8
Hispanic or Latino (of any race)	31.5
Mexican	31.4

High School Graduates
(Universe: Population 25 Years and Over)

Group	Number	%
Total Population	11,155	54.4
Hispanic or Latino (of any race)	10,418	53.1
Mexican	10,345	53.1

Four-Year College Graduates
(Universe: Population 25 Years and Over)

Group	Number	%
Total Population	2,577	12.6
Hispanic or Latino (of any race)	2,299	11.7
Mexican	2,256	11.6

Population Age 3–17 Enrolled in Public School
(Universe: Population Age 3–17 Enrolled in School)

Group	Number	%
Total Population	8,757	95.6
Hispanic or Latino (of any race)	8,409	95.6
Mexican	8,373	95.6

Population Age 3–17 Enrolled in Private School
(Universe: Population Age 3–17 Enrolled in School)

Group	Number	%
Total Population	401	4.4
Hispanic or Latino (of any race)	389	4.4
Mexican	389	4.4

Foreign-Born Population

Group	Number	%
Total Population	16,304	44.9
Hispanic or Latino (of any race)	15,747	45.3
Mexican	15,662	45.3

Foreign-Born Naturalized U.S. Citizens

Group	Number	%
Total Population	6,021	36.9
Hispanic or Latino (of any race)	5,554	35.3
Mexican	5,500	35.1

Language Spoken at Home: English Only
(Universe: Population 5 Years and Over)

Group	Number	%
Total Population	2,035	6.1
Hispanic or Latino (of any race)	1,554	4.8
Mexican	1,532	4.8

Language Spoken at Home: Spanish
(Universe: Population 5 Years and Over)

Group	Number	%
Total Population	30,845	92.0
Hispanic or Latino (of any race)	30,522	95.1
Mexican	30,362	95.2

Unemployment Rate
(Universe: Population 16 Years and Over)

Group	%
Total Population	16.1
Hispanic or Latino (of any race)	16.4
Mexican	16.5

Class of Worker: Private Wage and Salary
(Universe: Civilian Employed Population 16 Years and Over)

Group	Number	%
Total Population	8,441	66.3
Hispanic or Latino (of any race)	8,192	67.9
Mexican	8,111	67.8

Class of Worker: Government
(Universe: Civilian Employed Population 16 Years and Over)

Group	Number	%
Total Population	2,988	23.5
Hispanic or Latino (of any race)	2,903	24.1
Mexican	2,883	24.1

Means of Transportation to Work: Car, Truck or Van
(Universe: Workers 16 Years and Over)

Group	Number	%
Total Population	10,646	88.2
Hispanic or Latino (of any race)	10,004	87.7
Mexican	9,903	87.6

Means of Transportation to Work: Public Transportation (ex. Taxicab)
(Universe: Workers 16 Years and Over)

Group	Number	%
Total Population	233	1.9
Hispanic or Latino (of any race)	233	2.0
Mexican	233	2.1

Homeownership Rate
(Universe: Occupied Housing Units)

Group	%
Total Population	53.7
Hispanic or Latino (of any race)	53.1
Mexican	53.3

Median Home Value

Group	Dollars
Total Population	209,900
Hispanic or Latino (of any race)	207,600
Mexican	206,300

Median Gross Rent

Group	Dollars
Total Population	736
Hispanic or Latino (of any race)	735
Mexican	739

Median Household Income
(2010 Inflation-Adjusted Dollars)

Group	Dollars
Total Population	34,848
Hispanic or Latino (of any race)	33,847
Mexican	33,754

Per Capita Income
(2010 Inflation-Adjusted Dollars)

Group	Dollars
Total Population	14,472
Hispanic or Latino (of any race)	13,342
Mexican	13,255

Households with $100,000+ Income

Group	Number	%
Total Population	1,065	11.1
Hispanic or Latino (of any race)	874	9.6
Mexican	852	9.5

Households with Food Stamps/SNAP Benefits During Past 12 Months

Group	Number	%
Total Population	1,410	14.7
Hispanic or Latino (of any race)	1,390	15.3
Mexican	1,390	15.4

Poverty Rate
(Income in Past 12 Months Below Poverty Level)

Group	%
Total Population	22.1
Hispanic or Latino (of any race)	22.9
Mexican	22.9

Camarillo

Population

Group	Number	%TP[1]	%HP[2]
Total Population	65,201	100.0	–
Hispanic or Latino (of any race)	14,958	22.9	100.0
Central American, ex. Mexican	502	0.8	3.4
Guatemalan	156	0.2	1.0
Salvadoran	183	0.3	1.2
Cuban	100	0.2	0.7
Mexican	12,613	19.3	84.3
Puerto Rican	271	0.4	1.8
South American	487	0.7	3.3
Peruvian	116	0.2	0.8
Spaniard	277	0.4	1.9

Population Growth: 2000–2010

Group	%
Total Population	14.2
Hispanic or Latino (of any race)	68.7
Central American, ex. Mexican	186.9
Mexican	78.9
Puerto Rican	44.1
South American	166.1

Males per 100 Females

Group	Number
Total Population	93.7
Hispanic or Latino (of any race)	99.3
Central American, ex. Mexican	81.9
Guatemalan	85.7
Salvadoran	84.8
Cuban	117.4
Mexican	100.4
Puerto Rican	97.8
South American	82.4
Peruvian	87.1
Spaniard	103.7

Average Household Size

Group	People
Total Population	2.64
Hispanic or Latino (of any race)	3.55
Central American, ex. Mexican	3.66
Guatemalan	3.97
Salvadoran	3.79
Cuban	2.62
Mexican	3.66
Puerto Rican	3.13
South American	2.89
Peruvian	3.29
Spaniard	2.69

Median Age

Group	Years
Total Population	40.8
Hispanic or Latino (of any race)	28.5
Central American, ex. Mexican	32.4
Guatemalan	30.7
Salvadoran	32.2
Cuban	40.8
Mexican	27.5
Puerto Rican	29.3
South American	38.9
Peruvian	37.5
Spaniard	37.6

High School Graduates
(Universe: Population 25 Years and Over)

Group	Number	%
Total Population	39,967	91.7
Hispanic or Latino (of any race)	6,433	75.0
Mexican	4,976	71.5

Notes: (1) Percent of total population; (2) Percent of Hispanic/Latino population; Profiles include places with an overall population of at least 125,000, OR an overall population of at least 25,000 where the Hispanic/Latino population is at least 20% of the overall population. In states where less than five places meet either of these criteria, we have included places with at least 10,000 total population with the highest percentage of Hispanic/Latino population. These places are identified with an asterisk (*); Please refer to the User's Guide for a full explanation of data.

Four-Year College Graduates (Universe: Population 25 Years and Over)		
Group	Number	%
Total Population	16,687	38.3
Hispanic or Latino (of any race)	1,470	17.1
Mexican	985	14.2

Population Age 3–17 Enrolled in Public School (Universe: Population Age 3–17 Enrolled in School)		
Group	Number	%
Total Population	9,868	82.2
Hispanic or Latino (of any race)	3,033	82.8
Mexican	2,642	87.1

Population Age 3–17 Enrolled in Private School (Universe: Population Age 3–17 Enrolled in School)		
Group	Number	%
Total Population	2,142	17.8
Hispanic or Latino (of any race)	628	17.2
Mexican	392	12.9

Foreign-Born Population		
Group	Number	%
Total Population	10,104	15.9
Hispanic or Latino (of any race)	4,048	27.1
Mexican	3,192	26.3

Foreign-Born Naturalized U.S. Citizens		
Group	Number	%
Total Population	5,584	55.3
Hispanic or Latino (of any race)	1,571	38.8
Mexican	1,182	37.0

Language Spoken at Home: English Only (Universe: Population 5 Years and Over)		
Group	Number	%
Total Population	44,874	74.9
Hispanic or Latino (of any race)	5,340	39.6
Mexican	4,188	38.6

Language Spoken at Home: Spanish (Universe: Population 5 Years and Over)		
Group	Number	%
Total Population	8,904	14.9
Hispanic or Latino (of any race)	8,039	59.6
Mexican	6,645	61.2

Unemployment Rate (Universe: Population 16 Years and Over)	
Group	%
Total Population	6.9
Hispanic or Latino (of any race)	8.5
Mexican	8.8

Class of Worker: Private Wage and Salary (Universe: Civilian Employed Population 16 Years and Over)		
Group	Number	%
Total Population	22,517	74.4
Hispanic or Latino (of any race)	5,947	84.5
Mexican	4,931	87.0

Class of Worker: Government (Universe: Civilian Employed Population 16 Years and Over)		
Group	Number	%
Total Population	5,096	16.8
Hispanic or Latino (of any race)	775	11.0
Mexican	492	8.7

Means of Transportation to Work: Car, Truck or Van (Universe: Workers 16 Years and Over)		
Group	Number	%
Total Population	27,264	91.2
Hispanic or Latino (of any race)	6,244	90.6
Mexican	5,102	92.1

Means of Transportation to Work: Public Transportation (ex. Taxicab) (Universe: Workers 16 Years and Over)		
Group	Number	%
Total Population	199	0.7
Hispanic or Latino (of any race)	34	0.5
Mexican	0	0.0

Homeownership Rate (Universe: Occupied Housing Units)	
Group	%
Total Population	69.6
Hispanic or Latino (of any race)	56.6
Central American, ex. Mexican	54.7
Guatemalan	41.7
Salvadoran	51.9
Cuban	67.6
Mexican	56.4
Puerto Rican	58.9
South American	61.1
Peruvian	51.6
Spaniard	64.8

Median Home Value	
Group	Dollars
Total Population	558,200
Hispanic or Latino (of any race)	584,800
Mexican	566,000

Median Gross Rent	
Group	Dollars
Total Population	1,507
Hispanic or Latino (of any race)	1,380
Mexican	1,370

Median Household Income (2010 Inflation-Adjusted Dollars)	
Group	Dollars
Total Population	81,518
Hispanic or Latino (of any race)	71,939
Mexican	67,361

Per Capita Income (2010 Inflation-Adjusted Dollars)	
Group	Dollars
Total Population	37,470
Hispanic or Latino (of any race)	24,304
Mexican	23,010

Households with $100,000+ Income		
Group	Number	%
Total Population	9,288	39.2
Hispanic or Latino (of any race)	1,455	37.7
Mexican	1,064	34.7

Households with Food Stamps/SNAP Benefits During Past 12 Months		
Group	Number	%
Total Population	505	2.1
Hispanic or Latino (of any race)	295	7.6
Mexican	234	7.6

Poverty Rate (Income in Past 12 Months Below Poverty Level)	
Group	%
Total Population	4.7
Hispanic or Latino (of any race)	7.5
Mexican	8.5

Carson

Population			
Group	Number	%TP[1]	%HP[2]
Total Population	91,714	100.0	–
Hispanic or Latino (of any race)	35,417	38.6	100.0
Central American, ex. Mexican	2,402	2.6	6.8
Guatemalan	896	1.0	2.5
Honduran	170	0.2	0.5
Nicaraguan	113	0.1	0.3
Salvadoran	1,033	1.1	2.9
Cuban	274	0.3	0.8
Mexican	29,896	32.6	84.4
Puerto Rican	576	0.6	1.6
South American	627	0.7	1.8
Colombian	110	0.1	0.3
Ecuadorian	139	0.2	0.4
Peruvian	204	0.2	0.6
Spaniard	188	0.2	0.5

Population Growth: 2000–2010	
Group	%
Total Population	2.2
Hispanic or Latino (of any race)	13.0
Central American, ex. Mexican	113.7
Guatemalan	150.3
Salvadoran	132.7
Cuban	21.2
Mexican	18.3
Puerto Rican	0.9
South American	78.6
Peruvian	94.3

Males per 100 Females	
Group	Number
Total Population	91.9
Hispanic or Latino (of any race)	97.6
Central American, ex. Mexican	88.4
Guatemalan	90.6
Honduran	78.9
Nicaraguan	63.8
Salvadoran	93.8
Cuban	91.6
Mexican	98.2
Puerto Rican	105.7
South American	104.2
Colombian	89.7
Ecuadorian	104.4
Peruvian	117.0
Spaniard	84.3

Average Household Size	
Group	People
Total Population	3.56
Hispanic or Latino (of any race)	4.27
Central American, ex. Mexican	4.27
Guatemalan	4.41
Honduran	4.44
Nicaraguan	3.41
Salvadoran	4.39
Cuban	2.86
Mexican	4.36
Puerto Rican	3.33
South American	3.73
Colombian	3.63
Ecuadorian	3.93
Peruvian	4.06
Spaniard	3.10

Median Age	
Group	Years
Total Population	37.6
Hispanic or Latino (of any race)	29.7
Central American, ex. Mexican	35.5
Guatemalan	34.5
Honduran	34.0
Nicaraguan	37.5
Salvadoran	35.1
Cuban	47.3
Mexican	29.0
Puerto Rican	33.0
South American	41.9
Colombian	36.0
Ecuadorian	38.5
Peruvian	43.6
Spaniard	42.5

High School Graduates (Universe: Population 25 Years and Over)		
Group	Number	%
Total Population	46,451	79.1
Hispanic or Latino (of any race)	10,993	58.7
Central American, ex. Mexican	1,075	64.9
Salvadoran	304	50.8
Mexican	8,428	55.2

Four-Year College Graduates (Universe: Population 25 Years and Over)		
Group	Number	%
Total Population	14,298	24.3
Hispanic or Latino (of any race)	1,672	8.9
Central American, ex. Mexican	102	6.2
Salvadoran	33	5.5
Mexican	1,361	8.9

STATE & PLACE PROFILES

Notes: (1) Percent of total population; (2) Percent of Hispanic/Latino population; Profiles include places with an overall population of at least 125,000, OR an overall population of at least 25,000 where the Hispanic/Latino population is at least 20% of the overall population. In states where less than five places meet either of these criteria, we have included places with at least 10,000 total population with the highest percentage of Hispanic/Latino population. These places are identified with an asterisk (*); Please refer to the User's Guide for a full explanation of data.

Population Age 3–17 Enrolled in Public School
(Universe: Population Age 3–17 Enrolled in School)

Group	Number	%
Total Population	15,801	88.9
Hispanic or Latino (of any race)	7,962	93.5
Central American, ex. Mexican	505	86.9
Salvadoran	158	100.0
Mexican	6,848	94.1

Population Age 3–17 Enrolled in Private School
(Universe: Population Age 3–17 Enrolled in School)

Group	Number	%
Total Population	1,972	11.1
Hispanic or Latino (of any race)	551	6.5
Central American, ex. Mexican	76	13.1
Salvadoran	0	0.0
Mexican	430	5.9

Foreign-Born Population

Group	Number	%
Total Population	30,748	33.7
Hispanic or Latino (of any race)	12,648	37.0
Central American, ex. Mexican	1,571	56.5
Salvadoran	572	57.1
Mexican	10,229	35.9

Foreign-Born Naturalized U.S. Citizens

Group	Number	%
Total Population	18,042	58.7
Hispanic or Latino (of any race)	5,880	46.5
Central American, ex. Mexican	850	54.1
Salvadoran	385	67.3
Mexican	4,340	42.4

Language Spoken at Home: English Only
(Universe: Population 5 Years and Over)

Group	Number	%
Total Population	41,059	47.7
Hispanic or Latino (of any race)	7,282	23.2
Central American, ex. Mexican	545	20.0
Salvadoran	50	5.1
Mexican	5,934	23.0

Language Spoken at Home: Spanish
(Universe: Population 5 Years and Over)

Group	Number	%
Total Population	24,532	28.5
Hispanic or Latino (of any race)	23,899	76.2
Central American, ex. Mexican	2,169	79.6
Salvadoran	909	93.6
Mexican	19,842	76.8

Unemployment Rate
(Universe: Population 16 Years and Over)

Group	%
Total Population	9.3
Hispanic or Latino (of any race)	8.5
Central American, ex. Mexican	13.4
Salvadoran	14.0
Mexican	6.9

Class of Worker: Private Wage and Salary
(Universe: Civilian Employed Population 16 Years and Over)

Group	Number	%
Total Population	31,750	74.9
Hispanic or Latino (of any race)	11,737	78.2
Central American, ex. Mexican	1,132	78.3
Salvadoran	472	85.2
Mexican	9,649	78.8

Class of Worker: Government
(Universe: Civilian Employed Population 16 Years and Over)

Group	Number	%
Total Population	7,945	18.8
Hispanic or Latino (of any race)	1,890	12.6
Central American, ex. Mexican	149	10.3
Salvadoran	59	10.6
Mexican	1,522	12.4

Means of Transportation to Work: Car, Truck or Van
(Universe: Workers 16 Years and Over)

Group	Number	%
Total Population	37,050	90.6
Hispanic or Latino (of any race)	13,053	89.9
Central American, ex. Mexican	1,312	92.1
Salvadoran	488	90.0
Mexican	10,599	89.8

Means of Transportation to Work: Public Transportation (ex. Taxicab)
(Universe: Workers 16 Years and Over)

Group	Number	%
Total Population	1,279	3.1
Hispanic or Latino (of any race)	597	4.1
Central American, ex. Mexican	92	6.5
Salvadoran	54	10.0
Mexican	483	4.1

Homeownership Rate
(Universe: Occupied Housing Units)

Group	%
Total Population	76.8
Hispanic or Latino (of any race)	73.7
Central American, ex. Mexican	69.6
Guatemalan	69.8
Honduran	62.5
Nicaraguan	59.3
Salvadoran	68.9
Cuban	70.2
Mexican	74.2
Puerto Rican	70.3
South American	77.2
Colombian	80.0
Ecuadorian	65.9
Peruvian	88.7
Spaniard	75.0

Median Home Value

Group	Dollars
Total Population	422,100
Hispanic or Latino (of any race)	370,600
Central American, ex. Mexican	373,800
Salvadoran	406,100
Mexican	370,100

Median Gross Rent

Group	Dollars
Total Population	1,190
Hispanic or Latino (of any race)	1,135
Central American, ex. Mexican	1,217
Salvadoran	1,282
Mexican	1,101

Median Household Income
(2010 Inflation-Adjusted Dollars)

Group	Dollars
Total Population	68,425
Hispanic or Latino (of any race)	57,551
Central American, ex. Mexican	58,171
Salvadoran	44,500
Mexican	55,989

Per Capita Income
(2010 Inflation-Adjusted Dollars)

Group	Dollars
Total Population	23,318
Hispanic or Latino (of any race)	17,177
Central American, ex. Mexican	20,744
Salvadoran	18,345
Mexican	16,385

Households with $100,000+ Income

Group	Number	%
Total Population	7,421	29.8
Hispanic or Latino (of any race)	1,683	21.4
Central American, ex. Mexican	95	12.7
Salvadoran	58	20.4
Mexican	1,396	22.4

Households with Food Stamps/SNAP Benefits During Past 12 Months

Group	Number	%
Total Population	1,026	4.1
Hispanic or Latino (of any race)	462	5.9
Central American, ex. Mexican	17	2.3
Salvadoran	0	0.0
Mexican	408	6.5

Poverty Rate
(Income in Past 12 Months Below Poverty Level)

Group	%
Total Population	8.0
Hispanic or Latino (of any race)	10.5
Central American, ex. Mexican	11.3
Salvadoran	9.2
Mexican	10.2

Cathedral City

Population

Group	Number	%TP[1]	%HP[2]
Total Population	51,200	100.0	–
Hispanic or Latino (of any race)	30,085	58.8	100.0
Central American, ex. Mexican	1,927	3.8	6.4
Guatemalan	994	1.9	3.3
Nicaraguan	122	0.2	0.4
Salvadoran	704	1.4	2.3
Mexican	26,165	51.1	87.0
Puerto Rican	222	0.4	0.7
South American	390	0.8	1.3
Peruvian	159	0.3	0.5
Spaniard	166	0.3	0.6

Population Growth: 2000–2010

Group	%
Total Population	20.1
Hispanic or Latino (of any race)	41.2
Central American, ex. Mexican	160.4
Guatemalan	193.2
Salvadoran	164.7
Mexican	47.1
Puerto Rican	25.4
South American	156.6

Males per 100 Females

Group	Number
Total Population	105.9
Hispanic or Latino (of any race)	104.3
Central American, ex. Mexican	105.4
Guatemalan	124.4
Nicaraguan	74.3
Salvadoran	86.2
Mexican	104.2
Puerto Rican	111.4
South American	106.3
Peruvian	117.8
Spaniard	97.6

Average Household Size

Group	People
Total Population	2.99
Hispanic or Latino (of any race)	4.14
Central American, ex. Mexican	4.42
Guatemalan	4.55
Nicaraguan	4.22
Salvadoran	4.37
Mexican	4.19
Puerto Rican	2.79
South American	3.48
Peruvian	3.68
Spaniard	2.57

Median Age

Group	Years
Total Population	36.0
Hispanic or Latino (of any race)	26.3
Central American, ex. Mexican	32.2
Guatemalan	31.6
Nicaraguan	34.3
Salvadoran	32.1
Mexican	25.5
Puerto Rican	40.0
South American	40.3
Peruvian	39.8
Spaniard	40.5

High School Graduates
(Universe: Population 25 Years and Over)

Group	Number	%
Total Population	23,852	73.7
Hispanic or Latino (of any race)	7,967	53.8

Notes: (1) Percent of total population; (2) Percent of Hispanic/Latino population; Profiles include places with an overall population of at least 125,000, OR an overall population of at least 25,000 where the Hispanic/Latino population is at least 20% of the overall population. In states where less than five places meet either of these criteria, we have included places with at least 10,000 total population with the highest percentage of Hispanic/Latino population. These places are identified with an asterisk (*); Please refer to the User's Guide for a full explanation of data.

Central American, ex. Mexican	450	40.7
Guatemalan	171	26.6
Mexican	7,076	54.6

Four-Year College Graduates
(Universe: Population 25 Years and Over)

Group	Number	%
Total Population	5,363	16.6
Hispanic or Latino (of any race)	485	3.3
Central American, ex. Mexican	25	2.3
Guatemalan	0	0.0
Mexican	424	3.3

Population Age 3–17 Enrolled in Public School
(Universe: Population Age 3–17 Enrolled in School)

Group	Number	%
Total Population	9,338	92.3
Hispanic or Latino (of any race)	6,944	97.8
Central American, ex. Mexican	341	100.0
Guatemalan	196	100.0
Mexican	6,359	97.6

Population Age 3–17 Enrolled in Private School
(Universe: Population Age 3–17 Enrolled in School)

Group	Number	%
Total Population	782	7.7
Hispanic or Latino (of any race)	156	2.2
Central American, ex. Mexican	0	0.0
Guatemalan	0	0.0
Mexican	155	2.4

Foreign-Born Population

Group	Number	%
Total Population	16,112	31.8
Hispanic or Latino (of any race)	12,668	44.3
Central American, ex. Mexican	1,267	67.9
Guatemalan	794	69.2
Mexican	11,013	43.3

Foreign-Born Naturalized U.S. Citizens

Group	Number	%
Total Population	5,443	33.8
Hispanic or Latino (of any race)	3,719	29.4
Central American, ex. Mexican	377	29.8
Guatemalan	130	16.4
Mexican	3,117	28.3

Language Spoken at Home: English Only
(Universe: Population 5 Years and Over)

Group	Number	%
Total Population	21,573	45.9
Hispanic or Latino (of any race)	3,130	12.2
Central American, ex. Mexican	76	4.4
Guatemalan	0	0.0
Mexican	2,735	12.1

Language Spoken at Home: Spanish
(Universe: Population 5 Years and Over)

Group	Number	%
Total Population	23,365	49.7
Hispanic or Latino (of any race)	22,496	87.6
Central American, ex. Mexican	1,667	95.6
Guatemalan	1,041	100.0
Mexican	19,923	87.8

Unemployment Rate
(Universe: Population 16 Years and Over)

Group	%
Total Population	9.0
Hispanic or Latino (of any race)	9.3
Central American, ex. Mexican	0.0
Guatemalan	0.0
Mexican	10.2

Class of Worker: Private Wage and Salary
(Universe: Civilian Employed Population 16 Years and Over)

Group	Number	%
Total Population	17,525	78.1
Hispanic or Latino (of any race)	10,357	82.3
Central American, ex. Mexican	916	74.1
Guatemalan	635	79.5
Mexican	8,951	83.7

Class of Worker: Government
(Universe: Civilian Employed Population 16 Years and Over)

Group	Number	%
Total Population	2,162	9.6
Hispanic or Latino (of any race)	863	6.9
Central American, ex. Mexican	62	5.0
Guatemalan	18	2.3
Mexican	733	6.9

Means of Transportation to Work: Car, Truck or Van
(Universe: Workers 16 Years and Over)

Group	Number	%
Total Population	19,558	89.1
Hispanic or Latino (of any race)	11,318	91.5
Central American, ex. Mexican	947	77.5
Guatemalan	557	70.1
Mexican	9,837	93.5

Means of Transportation to Work: Public Transportation (ex. Taxicab)
(Universe: Workers 16 Years and Over)

Group	Number	%
Total Population	400	1.8
Hispanic or Latino (of any race)	326	2.6
Central American, ex. Mexican	136	11.1
Guatemalan	126	15.8
Mexican	172	1.6

Homeownership Rate
(Universe: Occupied Housing Units)

Group	%
Total Population	63.2
Hispanic or Latino (of any race)	49.3
Central American, ex. Mexican	43.8
Guatemalan	47.9
Nicaraguan	46.9
Salvadoran	38.9
Mexican	49.6
Puerto Rican	52.6
South American	58.5
Peruvian	54.0
Spaniard	43.3

Median Home Value

Group	Dollars
Total Population	294,500
Hispanic or Latino (of any race)	289,900
Central American, ex. Mexican	244,400
Guatemalan	261,600
Mexican	293,500

Median Gross Rent

Group	Dollars
Total Population	1,046
Hispanic or Latino (of any race)	1,030
Central American, ex. Mexican	1,198
Guatemalan	1,236
Mexican	1,016

Median Household Income
(2010 Inflation-Adjusted Dollars)

Group	Dollars
Total Population	45,693
Hispanic or Latino (of any race)	40,560
Central American, ex. Mexican	52,333
Guatemalan	52,167
Mexican	40,341

Per Capita Income
(2010 Inflation-Adjusted Dollars)

Group	Dollars
Total Population	22,374
Hispanic or Latino (of any race)	13,125
Central American, ex. Mexican	16,733
Guatemalan	14,600
Mexican	12,711

Households with $100,000+ Income

Group	Number	%
Total Population	2,915	16.3
Hispanic or Latino (of any race)	571	7.9
Central American, ex. Mexican	42	7.9
Guatemalan	7	2.3
Mexican	479	7.6

Households with Food Stamps/SNAP Benefits During Past 12 Months

Group	Number	%
Total Population	796	4.5
Hispanic or Latino (of any race)	564	7.8
Central American, ex. Mexican	35	6.6
Guatemalan	35	11.7
Mexican	520	8.3

Poverty Rate
(Income in Past 12 Months Below Poverty Level)

Group	%
Total Population	16.3
Hispanic or Latino (of any race)	21.1
Central American, ex. Mexican	8.3
Guatemalan	11.5
Mexican	22.5

Ceres

Population

Group	Number	%TP[1]	%HP[2]
Total Population	45,417	100.0	–
Hispanic or Latino (of any race)	25,436	56.0	100.0
Central American, ex. Mexican	572	1.3	2.2
Guatemalan	105	0.2	0.4
Nicaraguan	137	0.3	0.5
Salvadoran	256	0.6	1.0
Mexican	23,232	51.2	91.3
Puerto Rican	278	0.6	1.1
South American	115	0.3	0.5
Spaniard	143	0.3	0.6

Population Growth: 2000–2010

Group	%
Total Population	31.2
Hispanic or Latino (of any race)	93.9
Central American, ex. Mexican	281.3
Mexican	107.7
Puerto Rican	65.5

Males per 100 Females

Group	Number
Total Population	97.9
Hispanic or Latino (of any race)	100.2
Central American, ex. Mexican	88.2
Guatemalan	105.9
Nicaraguan	90.3
Salvadoran	84.2
Mexican	101.1
Puerto Rican	89.1
South American	82.5
Spaniard	107.2

Average Household Size

Group	People
Total Population	3.55
Hispanic or Latino (of any race)	4.20
Central American, ex. Mexican	4.21
Guatemalan	4.90
Nicaraguan	3.94
Salvadoran	4.17
Mexican	4.24
Puerto Rican	3.48
South American	3.86
Spaniard	3.25

Median Age

Group	Years
Total Population	29.4
Hispanic or Latino (of any race)	24.0
Central American, ex. Mexican	32.0
Guatemalan	24.9
Nicaraguan	34.8
Salvadoran	34.0
Mexican	23.8
Puerto Rican	27.5
South American	36.5
Spaniard	26.2

High School Graduates
(Universe: Population 25 Years and Over)

Group	Number	%
Total Population	17,312	66.5

STATE & PLACE PROFILES

Notes: (1) Percent of total population; (2) Percent of Hispanic/Latino population; Profiles include places with an overall population of at least 125,000, OR an overall population of at least 25,000 where the Hispanic/Latino population is at least 20% of the overall population. In states where less than five places meet either of these criteria, we have included places with at least 10,000 total population with the highest percentage of Hispanic/Latino population. These places are identified with an asterisk (*); Please refer to the User's Guide for a full explanation of data.

Hispanic or Latino (of any race)	5,936	51.5
Mexican	5,273	49.5

Four-Year College Graduates
(Universe: Population 25 Years and Over)

Group	Number	%
Total Population	2,444	9.4
Hispanic or Latino (of any race)	668	5.8
Mexican	635	6.0

Population Age 3–17 Enrolled in Public School
(Universe: Population Age 3–17 Enrolled in School)

Group	Number	%
Total Population	9,347	94.0
Hispanic or Latino (of any race)	6,062	99.1
Mexican	5,637	99.0

Population Age 3–17 Enrolled in Private School
(Universe: Population Age 3–17 Enrolled in School)

Group	Number	%
Total Population	592	6.0
Hispanic or Latino (of any race)	57	0.9
Mexican	57	1.0

Foreign-Born Population

Group	Number	%
Total Population	11,771	26.7
Hispanic or Latino (of any race)	8,364	36.1
Mexican	7,881	36.8

Foreign-Born Naturalized U.S. Citizens

Group	Number	%
Total Population	4,762	40.5
Hispanic or Latino (of any race)	2,620	31.3
Mexican	2,372	30.1

Language Spoken at Home: English Only
(Universe: Population 5 Years and Over)

Group	Number	%
Total Population	19,283	47.7
Hispanic or Latino (of any race)	3,931	19.3
Mexican	3,352	17.8

Language Spoken at Home: Spanish
(Universe: Population 5 Years and Over)

Group	Number	%
Total Population	16,786	41.5
Hispanic or Latino (of any race)	16,442	80.7
Mexican	15,433	82.2

Unemployment Rate
(Universe: Population 16 Years and Over)

Group	%
Total Population	13.8
Hispanic or Latino (of any race)	15.8
Mexican	15.7

Class of Worker: Private Wage and Salary
(Universe: Civilian Employed Population 16 Years and Over)

Group	Number	%
Total Population	14,570	79.3
Hispanic or Latino (of any race)	7,757	83.7
Mexican	7,224	83.8

Class of Worker: Government
(Universe: Civilian Employed Population 16 Years and Over)

Group	Number	%
Total Population	2,221	12.1
Hispanic or Latino (of any race)	739	8.0
Mexican	650	7.5

Means of Transportation to Work: Car, Truck or Van
(Universe: Workers 16 Years and Over)

Group	Number	%
Total Population	16,082	92.2
Hispanic or Latino (of any race)	8,237	94.2
Mexican	7,685	94.4

Means of Transportation to Work: Public Transportation (ex. Taxicab)
(Universe: Workers 16 Years and Over)

Group	Number	%
Total Population	190	1.1
Hispanic or Latino (of any race)	127	1.5
Mexican	111	1.4

Homeownership Rate
(Universe: Occupied Housing Units)

Group	%
Total Population	63.1
Hispanic or Latino (of any race)	57.9
Central American, ex. Mexican	61.1
Guatemalan	57.1
Nicaraguan	58.8
Salvadoran	62.7
Mexican	58.1
Puerto Rican	48.8
South American	71.4
Spaniard	68.2

Median Home Value

Group	Dollars
Total Population	256,200
Hispanic or Latino (of any race)	246,900
Mexican	244,600

Median Gross Rent

Group	Dollars
Total Population	887
Hispanic or Latino (of any race)	940
Mexican	981

Median Household Income
(2010 Inflation-Adjusted Dollars)

Group	Dollars
Total Population	50,124
Hispanic or Latino (of any race)	50,116
Mexican	50,083

Per Capita Income
(2010 Inflation-Adjusted Dollars)

Group	Dollars
Total Population	18,154
Hispanic or Latino (of any race)	14,091
Mexican	14,102

Households with $100,000+ Income

Group	Number	%
Total Population	1,886	14.6
Hispanic or Latino (of any race)	718	12.8
Mexican	687	13.5

Households with Food Stamps/SNAP Benefits During Past 12 Months

Group	Number	%
Total Population	1,372	10.6
Hispanic or Latino (of any race)	584	10.4
Mexican	494	9.7

Poverty Rate
(Income in Past 12 Months Below Poverty Level)

Group	%
Total Population	16.9
Hispanic or Latino (of any race)	20.6
Mexican	19.7

Chino

Population

Group	Number	%TP[1]	%HP[2]
Total Population	77,983	100.0	–
Hispanic or Latino (of any race)	41,993	53.8	100.0
Central American, ex. Mexican	1,792	2.3	4.3
Costa Rican	106	0.1	0.3
Guatemalan	432	0.6	1.0
Honduran	145	0.2	0.3
Nicaraguan	221	0.3	0.5
Salvadoran	849	1.1	2.0
Cuban	355	0.5	0.8
Mexican	36,069	46.3	85.9
Puerto Rican	490	0.6	1.2
South American	874	1.1	2.1
Argentinean	229	0.3	0.5
Colombian	182	0.2	0.4
Ecuadorian	151	0.2	0.4
Peruvian	213	0.3	0.5
Spaniard	388	0.5	0.9

Population Growth: 2000–2010

Group	%
Total Population	16.1
Hispanic or Latino (of any race)	31.9
Central American, ex. Mexican	146.5
Guatemalan	127.4
Nicaraguan	92.2
Salvadoran	207.6
Cuban	49.8
Mexican	37.5
Puerto Rican	98.4
South American	88.0
Argentinean	52.7
Colombian	52.9

Males per 100 Females

Group	Number
Total Population	105.7
Hispanic or Latino (of any race)	104.3
Central American, ex. Mexican	88.4
Costa Rican	79.7
Guatemalan	77.8
Honduran	98.6
Nicaraguan	93.9
Salvadoran	93.0
Cuban	81.1
Mexican	104.0
Puerto Rican	78.8
South American	83.6
Argentinean	80.3
Colombian	95.7
Ecuadorian	77.6
Peruvian	83.6
Spaniard	86.5

Average Household Size

Group	People
Total Population	3.41
Hispanic or Latino (of any race)	3.97
Central American, ex. Mexican	4.01
Costa Rican	3.75
Guatemalan	4.16
Honduran	4.47
Nicaraguan	3.98
Salvadoran	4.00
Cuban	3.38
Mexican	4.04
Puerto Rican	3.00
South American	3.52
Argentinean	3.20
Colombian	3.41
Ecuadorian	3.46
Peruvian	3.94
Spaniard	3.25

Median Age

Group	Years
Total Population	33.2
Hispanic or Latino (of any race)	28.7
Central American, ex. Mexican	32.0
Costa Rican	30.5
Guatemalan	31.7
Honduran	29.8
Nicaraguan	36.8
Salvadoran	32.0
Cuban	33.5
Mexican	28.2
Puerto Rican	30.4
South American	38.1
Argentinean	39.1
Colombian	38.6
Ecuadorian	36.9
Peruvian	38.2
Spaniard	34.2

High School Graduates
(Universe: Population 25 Years and Over)

Group	Number	%
Total Population	37,227	74.8
Hispanic or Latino (of any race)	14,911	63.2
Central American, ex. Mexican	977	62.9
Salvadoran	388	45.3
Mexican	12,409	61.6
South American	482	84.7

Notes: (1) Percent of total population; (2) Percent of Hispanic/Latino population; Profiles include places with an overall population of at least 125,000, OR an overall population of at least 25,000 where the Hispanic/Latino population is at least 20% of the overall population. In states where less than five places meet either of these criteria, we have included places with at least 10,000 total population with the highest percentage of Hispanic/Latino population. These places are identified with an asterisk (*); Please refer to the User's Guide for a full explanation of data.

Four-Year College Graduates
(Universe: Population 25 Years and Over)

Group	Number	%
Total Population	8,861	17.8
Hispanic or Latino (of any race)	2,206	9.4
Central American, ex. Mexican	147	9.5
Salvadoran	79	9.2
Mexican	1,703	8.4
South American	162	28.5

Population Age 3–17 Enrolled in Public School
(Universe: Population Age 3–17 Enrolled in School)

Group	Number	%
Total Population	13,005	89.0
Hispanic or Latino (of any race)	8,484	91.7
Central American, ex. Mexican	243	92.7
Salvadoran	93	83.0
Mexican	7,558	91.8
South American	233	82.3

Population Age 3–17 Enrolled in Private School
(Universe: Population Age 3–17 Enrolled in School)

Group	Number	%
Total Population	1,614	11.0
Hispanic or Latino (of any race)	772	8.3
Central American, ex. Mexican	19	7.3
Salvadoran	19	17.0
Mexican	672	8.2
South American	50	17.7

Foreign-Born Population

Group	Number	%
Total Population	19,234	24.7
Hispanic or Latino (of any race)	12,848	31.1
Central American, ex. Mexican	1,455	57.5
Salvadoran	873	57.5
Mexican	10,682	30.1
South American	456	48.7

Foreign-Born Naturalized U.S. Citizens

Group	Number	%
Total Population	9,101	47.3
Hispanic or Latino (of any race)	5,027	39.1
Central American, ex. Mexican	478	32.9
Salvadoran	229	26.2
Mexican	4,165	39.0
South American	310	68.0

Language Spoken at Home: English Only
(Universe: Population 5 Years and Over)

Group	Number	%
Total Population	38,008	52.2
Hispanic or Latino (of any race)	11,179	29.4
Central American, ex. Mexican	205	9.1
Salvadoran	74	5.4
Mexican	9,583	29.2
South American	184	21.4

Language Spoken at Home: Spanish
(Universe: Population 5 Years and Over)

Group	Number	%
Total Population	28,015	38.5
Hispanic or Latino (of any race)	26,841	70.6
Central American, ex. Mexican	2,059	90.9
Salvadoran	1,288	94.6
Mexican	23,189	70.7
South American	677	78.6

Unemployment Rate
(Universe: Population 16 Years and Over)

Group	%
Total Population	9.4
Hispanic or Latino (of any race)	11.3
Central American, ex. Mexican	9.2
Salvadoran	7.6
Mexican	11.6
South American	4.9

Class of Worker: Private Wage and Salary
(Universe: Civilian Employed Population 16 Years and Over)

Group	Number	%
Total Population	26,015	78.7
Hispanic or Latino (of any race)	14,182	80.4
Central American, ex. Mexican	1,051	76.4
Salvadoran	758	85.6
Mexican	12,108	81.2
South American	360	74.5

Class of Worker: Government
(Universe: Civilian Employed Population 16 Years and Over)

Group	Number	%
Total Population	5,171	15.6
Hispanic or Latino (of any race)	2,527	14.3
Central American, ex. Mexican	231	16.8
Salvadoran	66	7.5
Mexican	2,101	14.1
South American	39	8.1

Means of Transportation to Work: Car, Truck or Van
(Universe: Workers 16 Years and Over)

Group	Number	%
Total Population	29,478	93.0
Hispanic or Latino (of any race)	15,791	93.8
Central American, ex. Mexican	1,273	95.1
Salvadoran	793	93.6
Mexican	13,326	93.5
South American	470	98.7

Means of Transportation to Work: Public Transportation (ex. Taxicab)
(Universe: Workers 16 Years and Over)

Group	Number	%
Total Population	399	1.3
Hispanic or Latino (of any race)	195	1.2
Central American, ex. Mexican	21	1.6
Salvadoran	21	2.5
Mexican	174	1.2
South American	0	0.0

Homeownership Rate
(Universe: Occupied Housing Units)

Group	%
Total Population	68.9
Hispanic or Latino (of any race)	61.4
Central American, ex. Mexican	56.3
Costa Rican	67.9
Guatemalan	54.4
Honduran	50.0
Nicaraguan	75.0
Salvadoran	52.3
Cuban	57.1
Mexican	62.0
Puerto Rican	52.2
South American	63.2
Argentinean	68.4
Colombian	67.2
Ecuadorian	62.5
Peruvian	59.4
Spaniard	74.2

Median Home Value

Group	Dollars
Total Population	425,000
Hispanic or Latino (of any race)	419,500
Central American, ex. Mexican	438,400
Salvadoran	433,800
Mexican	410,900
South American	494,800

Median Gross Rent

Group	Dollars
Total Population	1,200
Hispanic or Latino (of any race)	1,227
Central American, ex. Mexican	1,243
Salvadoran	1,216
Mexican	1,238
South American	854

Median Household Income
(2010 Inflation-Adjusted Dollars)

Group	Dollars
Total Population	71,659
Hispanic or Latino (of any race)	66,559
Central American, ex. Mexican	79,813
Salvadoran	79,875
Mexican	65,233
South American	56,250

Per Capita Income
(2010 Inflation-Adjusted Dollars)

Group	Dollars
Total Population	22,580
Hispanic or Latino (of any race)	18,377
Central American, ex. Mexican	20,447
Salvadoran	21,899
Mexican	18,078
South American	19,765

Households with $100,000+ Income

Group	Number	%
Total Population	6,336	31.6
Hispanic or Latino (of any race)	2,503	27.5
Central American, ex. Mexican	267	45.4
Salvadoran	159	43.1
Mexican	2,046	26.2
South American	37	16.7

Households with Food Stamps/SNAP Benefits During Past 12 Months

Group	Number	%
Total Population	786	3.9
Hispanic or Latino (of any race)	431	4.7
Central American, ex. Mexican	85	14.5
Salvadoran	71	19.2
Mexican	346	4.4
South American	0	0.0

Poverty Rate
(Income in Past 12 Months Below Poverty Level)

Group	%
Total Population	6.2
Hispanic or Latino (of any race)	6.1
Central American, ex. Mexican	6.4
Salvadoran	9.8
Mexican	6.0
South American	3.6

Chino Hills

Population

Group	Number	%TP[1]	%HP[2]
Total Population	74,799	100.0	–
Hispanic or Latino (of any race)	21,802	29.1	100.0
Central American, ex. Mexican	1,180	1.6	5.4
Guatemalan	278	0.4	1.3
Nicaraguan	169	0.2	0.8
Salvadoran	547	0.7	2.5
Cuban	383	0.5	1.8
Mexican	17,678	23.6	81.1
Puerto Rican	389	0.5	1.8
South American	965	1.3	4.4
Argentinean	167	0.2	0.8
Colombian	273	0.4	1.3
Ecuadorian	191	0.3	0.9
Peruvian	171	0.2	0.8
Spaniard	342	0.5	1.6

Population Growth: 2000–2010

Group	%
Total Population	12.0
Hispanic or Latino (of any race)	27.1
Central American, ex. Mexican	114.2
Guatemalan	148.2
Salvadoran	159.2
Cuban	24.4
Mexican	36.8
Puerto Rican	27.5
South American	69.9
Argentinean	59.0
Colombian	99.3

Males per 100 Females

Group	Number
Total Population	97.7
Hispanic or Latino (of any race)	95.8
Central American, ex. Mexican	102.1
Guatemalan	109.0
Nicaraguan	79.8
Salvadoran	99.6
Cuban	95.4
Mexican	96.5

Notes: (1) Percent of total population; (2) Percent of Hispanic/Latino population; Profiles include places with an overall population of at least 125,000, OR an overall population of at least 25,000 where the Hispanic/Latino population is at least 20% of the overall population. In states where less than five places meet either of these criteria, we have included places with at least 10,000 total population with the highest percentage of Hispanic/Latino population. These places are identified with an asterisk (*); Please refer to the User's Guide for a full explanation of data.

Group	
Puerto Rican	95.5
South American	84.5
Argentinean	79.6
Colombian	89.6
Ecuadorian	85.4
Peruvian	76.3
Spaniard	84.9

Average Household Size

Group	People
Total Population	3.25
Hispanic or Latino (of any race)	3.67
Central American, ex. Mexican	3.92
Guatemalan	4.15
Nicaraguan	4.08
Salvadoran	3.89
Cuban	3.45
Mexican	3.74
Puerto Rican	3.41
South American	3.29
Argentinean	3.23
Colombian	3.15
Ecuadorian	3.63
Peruvian	3.38
Spaniard	3.02

Median Age

Group	Years
Total Population	36.6
Hispanic or Latino (of any race)	29.3
Central American, ex. Mexican	35.0
Guatemalan	36.3
Nicaraguan	39.4
Salvadoran	33.1
Cuban	34.3
Mexican	28.4
Puerto Rican	33.4
South American	38.5
Argentinean	39.4
Colombian	37.9
Ecuadorian	36.1
Peruvian	38.8
Spaniard	30.5

High School Graduates
(Universe: Population 25 Years and Over)

Group	Number	%
Total Population	42,767	92.3
Hispanic or Latino (of any race)	9,356	82.9
Central American, ex. Mexican	511	82.3
Mexican	7,299	81.5
South American	606	90.4

Four-Year College Graduates
(Universe: Population 25 Years and Over)

Group	Number	%
Total Population	19,688	42.5
Hispanic or Latino (of any race)	2,534	22.5
Central American, ex. Mexican	243	39.1
Mexican	1,812	20.2
South American	210	31.3

Population Age 3–17 Enrolled in Public School
(Universe: Population Age 3–17 Enrolled in School)

Group	Number	%
Total Population	14,127	86.4
Hispanic or Latino (of any race)	4,950	88.7
Central American, ex. Mexican	219	66.2
Mexican	4,227	91.6
South American	209	82.6

Population Age 3–17 Enrolled in Private School
(Universe: Population Age 3–17 Enrolled in School)

Group	Number	%
Total Population	2,229	13.6
Hispanic or Latino (of any race)	633	11.3
Central American, ex. Mexican	112	33.8
Mexican	388	8.4
South American	44	17.4

Foreign-Born Population

Group	Number	%
Total Population	20,052	26.9
Hispanic or Latino (of any race)	4,595	21.8
Central American, ex. Mexican	563	42.0
Mexican	3,427	20.4
South American	449	40.3

Foreign-Born Naturalized U.S. Citizens

Group	Number	%
Total Population	13,422	66.9
Hispanic or Latino (of any race)	2,836	61.7
Central American, ex. Mexican	474	84.2
Mexican	1,875	54.7
South American	338	75.3

Language Spoken at Home: English Only
(Universe: Population 5 Years and Over)

Group	Number	%
Total Population	41,305	59.7
Hispanic or Latino (of any race)	9,103	48.0
Central American, ex. Mexican	363	33.3
Mexican	7,491	49.1
South American	215	21.0

Language Spoken at Home: Spanish
(Universe: Population 5 Years and Over)

Group	Number	%
Total Population	10,763	15.5
Hispanic or Latino (of any race)	9,839	51.9
Central American, ex. Mexican	728	66.7
Mexican	7,761	50.8
South American	811	79.0

Unemployment Rate
(Universe: Population 16 Years and Over)

Group	%
Total Population	7.9
Hispanic or Latino (of any race)	10.4
Central American, ex. Mexican	9.2
Mexican	9.4
South American	10.6

Class of Worker: Private Wage and Salary
(Universe: Civilian Employed Population 16 Years and Over)

Group	Number	%
Total Population	28,468	75.6
Hispanic or Latino (of any race)	7,365	74.5
Central American, ex. Mexican	418	71.6
Mexican	5,872	74.2
South American	507	84.5

Class of Worker: Government
(Universe: Civilian Employed Population 16 Years and Over)

Group	Number	%
Total Population	6,511	17.3
Hispanic or Latino (of any race)	1,787	18.1
Central American, ex. Mexican	61	10.4
Mexican	1,494	18.9
South American	42	7.0

Means of Transportation to Work: Car, Truck or Van
(Universe: Workers 16 Years and Over)

Group	Number	%
Total Population	33,559	92.2
Hispanic or Latino (of any race)	8,853	93.1
Central American, ex. Mexican	433	89.1
Mexican	7,165	93.9
South American	522	87.0

Means of Transportation to Work: Public Transportation (ex. Taxicab)
(Universe: Workers 16 Years and Over)

Group	Number	%
Total Population	613	1.7
Hispanic or Latino (of any race)	106	1.1
Central American, ex. Mexican	11	2.3
Mexican	88	1.2
South American	7	1.2

Homeownership Rate
(Universe: Occupied Housing Units)

Group	%
Total Population	80.3
Hispanic or Latino (of any race)	76.2
Central American, ex. Mexican	75.0
Guatemalan	75.3
Nicaraguan	90.0
Salvadoran	73.5
Cuban	85.5
Mexican	76.6
Puerto Rican	76.2
South American	77.4
Argentinean	80.4
Colombian	74.1
Ecuadorian	84.3
Peruvian	79.2
Spaniard	79.6

Median Home Value

Group	Dollars
Total Population	567,100
Hispanic or Latino (of any race)	514,500
Central American, ex. Mexican	554,800
Mexican	518,500
South American	429,400

Median Gross Rent

Group	Dollars
Total Population	1,760
Hispanic or Latino (of any race)	1,804
Central American, ex. Mexican	1,965
Mexican	1,797
South American	1,910

Median Household Income
(2010 Inflation-Adjusted Dollars)

Group	Dollars
Total Population	103,891
Hispanic or Latino (of any race)	91,556
Central American, ex. Mexican	71,509
Mexican	90,193
South American	92,419

Per Capita Income
(2010 Inflation-Adjusted Dollars)

Group	Dollars
Total Population	35,392
Hispanic or Latino (of any race)	25,789
Central American, ex. Mexican	19,246
Mexican	25,283
South American	31,318

Households with $100,000+ Income

Group	Number	%
Total Population	11,741	52.8
Hispanic or Latino (of any race)	2,400	45.6
Central American, ex. Mexican	112	36.5
Mexican	1,856	45.1
South American	133	38.2

Households with Food Stamps/SNAP Benefits During Past 12 Months

Group	Number	%
Total Population	155	0.7
Hispanic or Latino (of any race)	72	1.4
Central American, ex. Mexican	0	0.0
Mexican	72	1.7
South American	0	0.0

Poverty Rate
(Income in Past 12 Months Below Poverty Level)

Group	%
Total Population	4.1
Hispanic or Latino (of any race)	5.8
Central American, ex. Mexican	10.2
Mexican	6.3
South American	0.0

Chula Vista

Population

Group	Number	%TP[1]	%HP[2]
Total Population	243,916	100.0	–
Hispanic or Latino (of any race)	142,066	58.2	100.0
Central American, ex. Mexican	1,619	0.7	1.1
Costa Rican	181	0.1	0.1
Guatemalan	320	0.1	0.2
Honduran	176	0.1	0.1
Nicaraguan	236	0.1	0.2
Panamanian	203	0.1	0.1
Salvadoran	489	0.2	0.3
Cuban	532	0.2	0.4
Dominican Republic	193	0.1	0.1

Notes: (1) Percent of total population; (2) Percent of Hispanic/Latino population; Profiles include places with an overall population of at least 125,000, OR an overall population of at least 25,000 where the Hispanic/Latino population is at least 20% of the overall population. In states where less than five places meet either of these criteria, we have included places with at least 10,000 total population with the highest percentage of Hispanic/Latino population. These places are identified with an asterisk (*); Please refer to the User's Guide for a full explanation of data.

Mexican	130,413	53.5	91.8
Puerto Rican	2,282	0.9	1.6
South American	1,763	0.7	1.2
Argentinean	202	0.1	0.1
Bolivian	113	<0.1	0.1
Chilean	168	0.1	0.1
Colombian	572	0.2	0.4
Ecuadorian	176	0.1	0.1
Peruvian	408	0.2	0.3
Spaniard	1,015	0.4	0.7

Population Growth: 2000–2010

Group	%
Total Population	40.5
Hispanic or Latino (of any race)	65.1
Central American, ex. Mexican	116.4
Guatemalan	131.9
Panamanian	67.8
Salvadoran	145.7
Cuban	73.9
Mexican	74.2
Puerto Rican	60.6
South American	125.7
Argentinean	64.2
Colombian	156.5
Peruvian	135.8
Spaniard	559.1

Males per 100 Females

Group	Number
Total Population	93.9
Hispanic or Latino (of any race)	89.8
Central American, ex. Mexican	81.9
Costa Rican	72.4
Guatemalan	91.6
Honduran	85.3
Nicaraguan	93.4
Panamanian	72.0
Salvadoran	76.5
Cuban	105.4
Dominican Republic	119.3
Mexican	89.6
Puerto Rican	102.1
South American	93.9
Argentinean	92.4
Bolivian	88.3
Chilean	78.7
Colombian	90.0
Ecuadorian	102.3
Peruvian	109.2
Spaniard	86.6

Average Household Size

Group	People
Total Population	3.21
Hispanic or Latino (of any race)	3.58
Central American, ex. Mexican	3.29
Costa Rican	3.24
Guatemalan	3.50
Honduran	3.34
Nicaraguan	3.26
Panamanian	3.12
Salvadoran	3.26
Cuban	2.89
Dominican Republic	2.92
Mexican	3.62
Puerto Rican	3.10
South American	3.21
Argentinean	3.04
Bolivian	3.59
Chilean	3.76
Colombian	3.14
Ecuadorian	3.25
Peruvian	3.20
Spaniard	2.98

Median Age

Group	Years
Total Population	33.7
Hispanic or Latino (of any race)	29.4
Central American, ex. Mexican	33.3
Costa Rican	37.8
Guatemalan	30.3
Honduran	34.3
Nicaraguan	32.0
Panamanian	37.8
Salvadoran	32.6
Cuban	36.3
Dominican Republic	29.3
Mexican	29.2
Puerto Rican	28.0
South American	37.5
Argentinean	43.5
Bolivian	41.5
Chilean	37.7
Colombian	35.4
Ecuadorian	34.0
Peruvian	38.5
Spaniard	35.4

High School Graduates
(Universe: Population 25 Years and Over)

Group	Number	%
Total Population	113,792	81.5
Hispanic or Latino (of any race)	48,897	70.0
Central American, ex. Mexican	980	74.0
Mexican	44,293	69.0
Puerto Rican	931	88.2
South American	1,068	84.8

Four-Year College Graduates
(Universe: Population 25 Years and Over)

Group	Number	%
Total Population	36,826	26.4
Hispanic or Latino (of any race)	12,338	17.7
Central American, ex. Mexican	245	18.5
Mexican	10,743	16.7
Puerto Rican	359	34.0
South American	425	33.7

Population Age 3–17 Enrolled in Public School
(Universe: Population Age 3–17 Enrolled in School)

Group	Number	%
Total Population	45,567	88.6
Hispanic or Latino (of any race)	29,992	89.3
Central American, ex. Mexican	244	100.0
Mexican	28,349	89.3
Puerto Rican	503	93.5
South American	155	74.5

Population Age 3–17 Enrolled in Private School
(Universe: Population Age 3–17 Enrolled in School)

Group	Number	%
Total Population	5,886	11.4
Hispanic or Latino (of any race)	3,581	10.7
Central American, ex. Mexican	0	0.0
Mexican	3,383	10.7
Puerto Rican	35	6.5
South American	53	25.5

Foreign-Born Population

Group	Number	%
Total Population	70,660	30.8
Hispanic or Latino (of any race)	46,922	36.6
Central American, ex. Mexican	1,142	63.1
Mexican	43,819	36.8
Puerto Rican	23	1.2
South American	1,200	71.0

Foreign-Born Naturalized U.S. Citizens

Group	Number	%
Total Population	38,214	54.1
Hispanic or Latino (of any race)	21,886	46.6
Central American, ex. Mexican	557	48.8
Mexican	20,322	46.4
Puerto Rican	23	100.0
South American	646	53.8

Language Spoken at Home: English Only
(Universe: Population 5 Years and Over)

Group	Number	%
Total Population	91,299	42.9
Hispanic or Latino (of any race)	21,701	18.6
Central American, ex. Mexican	202	11.8
Mexican	19,246	17.7
Puerto Rican	797	43.1
South American	110	7.1

Language Spoken at Home: Spanish
(Universe: Population 5 Years and Over)

Group	Number	%
Total Population	97,958	46.0
Hispanic or Latino (of any race)	94,626	81.0
Central American, ex. Mexican	1,507	88.2
Mexican	88,833	81.9
Puerto Rican	1,054	56.9
South American	1,427	91.8

Unemployment Rate
(Universe: Population 16 Years and Over)

Group	%
Total Population	8.8
Hispanic or Latino (of any race)	10.3
Central American, ex. Mexican	6.4
Mexican	10.5
Puerto Rican	6.3
South American	6.5

Class of Worker: Private Wage and Salary
(Universe: Civilian Employed Population 16 Years and Over)

Group	Number	%
Total Population	71,748	71.4
Hispanic or Latino (of any race)	39,984	74.3
Central American, ex. Mexican	645	71.0
Mexican	37,015	74.6
Puerto Rican	514	62.4
South American	718	74.3

Class of Worker: Government
(Universe: Civilian Employed Population 16 Years and Over)

Group	Number	%
Total Population	21,911	21.8
Hispanic or Latino (of any race)	9,994	18.6
Central American, ex. Mexican	213	23.4
Mexican	9,046	18.2
Puerto Rican	282	34.2
South American	152	15.7

Means of Transportation to Work: Car, Truck or Van
(Universe: Workers 16 Years and Over)

Group	Number	%
Total Population	90,776	90.0
Hispanic or Latino (of any race)	46,929	89.3
Central American, ex. Mexican	922	100.0
Mexican	43,056	89.1
Puerto Rican	779	91.3
South American	788	80.7

Means of Transportation to Work: Public Transportation (ex. Taxicab)
(Universe: Workers 16 Years and Over)

Group	Number	%
Total Population	3,378	3.3
Hispanic or Latino (of any race)	2,141	4.1
Central American, ex. Mexican	0	0.0
Mexican	2,042	4.2
Puerto Rican	41	4.8
South American	58	5.9

Homeownership Rate
(Universe: Occupied Housing Units)

Group	%
Total Population	58.1
Hispanic or Latino (of any race)	49.5
Central American, ex. Mexican	51.6
Costa Rican	55.9
Guatemalan	52.6
Honduran	45.2
Nicaraguan	54.5
Panamanian	59.2
Salvadoran	47.8
Cuban	59.6
Dominican Republic	39.7
Mexican	49.4
Puerto Rican	47.4
South American	58.7
Argentinean	61.9
Bolivian	76.9
Chilean	57.8
Colombian	55.7
Ecuadorian	54.0
Peruvian	59.7

Notes: (1) Percent of total population; (2) Percent of Hispanic/Latino population; Profiles include places with an overall population of at least 125,000, OR an overall population of at least 25,000 where the Hispanic/Latino population is at least 20% of the overall population. In states where less than five places meet either of these criteria, we have included places with at least 10,000 total population with the highest percentage of Hispanic/Latino population. These places are identified with an asterisk (*); Please refer to the User's Guide for a full explanation of data.

Spaniard	64.4

Median Home Value

Group	Dollars
Total Population	445,000
Hispanic or Latino (of any race)	413,600
Central American, ex. Mexican	331,700
Mexican	415,600
Puerto Rican	400,000
South American	458,100

Median Gross Rent

Group	Dollars
Total Population	1,201
Hispanic or Latino (of any race)	1,134
Central American, ex. Mexican	1,316
Mexican	1,140
Puerto Rican	982
South American	1,076

Median Household Income
(2010 Inflation-Adjusted Dollars)

Group	Dollars
Total Population	63,779
Hispanic or Latino (of any race)	54,077
Central American, ex. Mexican	72,806
Mexican	53,222
Puerto Rican	89,667
South American	55,716

Per Capita Income
(2010 Inflation-Adjusted Dollars)

Group	Dollars
Total Population	24,646
Hispanic or Latino (of any race)	18,703
Central American, ex. Mexican	20,871
Mexican	18,241
Puerto Rican	28,589
South American	31,196

Households with $100,000+ Income

Group	Number	%
Total Population	19,228	26.8
Hispanic or Latino (of any race)	6,715	19.3
Central American, ex. Mexican	190	27.7
Mexican	5,883	18.4
Puerto Rican	294	49.7
South American	155	26.3

Households with Food Stamps/SNAP Benefits During Past 12 Months

Group	Number	%
Total Population	2,546	3.5
Hispanic or Latino (of any race)	1,872	5.4
Central American, ex. Mexican	18	2.6
Mexican	1,721	5.4
Puerto Rican	66	11.1
South American	0	0.0

Poverty Rate
(Income in Past 12 Months Below Poverty Level)

Group	%
Total Population	9.6
Hispanic or Latino (of any race)	13.1
Central American, ex. Mexican	8.5
Mexican	13.4
Puerto Rican	8.2
South American	6.6

Clovis

Population

Group	Number	%TP[1]	%HP[2]
Total Population	95,631	100.0	–
Hispanic or Latino (of any race)	24,514	25.6	100.0
Central American, ex. Mexican	556	0.6	2.3
Salvadoran	230	0.2	0.9
Mexican	21,360	22.3	87.1
Puerto Rican	307	0.3	1.3
South American	275	0.3	1.1
Spaniard	430	0.4	1.8

Population Growth: 2000–2010

Group	%
Total Population	39.7
Hispanic or Latino (of any race)	76.7
Central American, ex. Mexican	288.8
Mexican	86.7
Puerto Rican	98.1
South American	137.1

Males per 100 Females

Group	Number
Total Population	93.2
Hispanic or Latino (of any race)	95.3
Central American, ex. Mexican	85.3
Salvadoran	101.8
Mexican	96.3
Puerto Rican	107.4
South American	76.3
Spaniard	92.8

Average Household Size

Group	People
Total Population	2.85
Hispanic or Latino (of any race)	3.25
Central American, ex. Mexican	3.73
Salvadoran	3.89
Mexican	3.26
Puerto Rican	2.77
South American	3.33
Spaniard	3.05

Median Age

Group	Years
Total Population	34.1
Hispanic or Latino (of any race)	25.8
Central American, ex. Mexican	30.3
Salvadoran	28.0
Mexican	25.7
Puerto Rican	26.1
South American	39.1
Spaniard	30.1

High School Graduates
(Universe: Population 25 Years and Over)

Group	Number	%
Total Population	50,309	89.6
Hispanic or Latino (of any race)	9,195	79.7
Central American, ex. Mexican	211	47.2
Mexican	7,738	80.3

Four-Year College Graduates
(Universe: Population 25 Years and Over)

Group	Number	%
Total Population	16,866	30.0
Hispanic or Latino (of any race)	1,960	17.0
Central American, ex. Mexican	63	14.1
Mexican	1,621	16.8

Population Age 3–17 Enrolled in Public School
(Universe: Population Age 3–17 Enrolled in School)

Group	Number	%
Total Population	18,042	92.4
Hispanic or Latino (of any race)	5,770	94.9
Central American, ex. Mexican	121	71.6
Mexican	5,162	96.9

Population Age 3–17 Enrolled in Private School
(Universe: Population Age 3–17 Enrolled in School)

Group	Number	%
Total Population	1,478	7.6
Hispanic or Latino (of any race)	310	5.1
Central American, ex. Mexican	48	28.4
Mexican	165	3.1

Foreign-Born Population

Group	Number	%
Total Population	10,619	11.6
Hispanic or Latino (of any race)	3,818	17.1
Central American, ex. Mexican	339	39.6
Mexican	2,878	15.0

Foreign-Born Naturalized U.S. Citizens

Group	Number	%
Total Population	6,523	61.4
Hispanic or Latino (of any race)	1,794	47.0
Central American, ex. Mexican	193	56.9
Mexican	1,300	45.2

Language Spoken at Home: English Only
(Universe: Population 5 Years and Over)

Group	Number	%
Total Population	66,676	78.7
Hispanic or Latino (of any race)	11,003	54.4
Central American, ex. Mexican	226	31.3
Mexican	9,654	56.2

Language Spoken at Home: Spanish
(Universe: Population 5 Years and Over)

Group	Number	%
Total Population	9,720	11.5
Hispanic or Latino (of any race)	9,106	45.0
Central American, ex. Mexican	496	68.7
Mexican	7,475	43.5

Unemployment Rate
(Universe: Population 16 Years and Over)

Group	%
Total Population	9.1
Hispanic or Latino (of any race)	11.2
Central American, ex. Mexican	10.5
Mexican	11.1

Class of Worker: Private Wage and Salary
(Universe: Civilian Employed Population 16 Years and Over)

Group	Number	%
Total Population	30,213	71.9
Hispanic or Latino (of any race)	6,882	72.0
Central American, ex. Mexican	272	72.5
Mexican	5,927	72.5

Class of Worker: Government
(Universe: Civilian Employed Population 16 Years and Over)

Group	Number	%
Total Population	9,052	21.5
Hispanic or Latino (of any race)	1,950	20.4
Central American, ex. Mexican	52	13.9
Mexican	1,723	21.1

Means of Transportation to Work: Car, Truck or Van
(Universe: Workers 16 Years and Over)

Group	Number	%
Total Population	38,547	93.5
Hispanic or Latino (of any race)	8,719	93.5
Central American, ex. Mexican	375	100.0
Mexican	7,473	94.0

Means of Transportation to Work: Public Transportation (ex. Taxicab)
(Universe: Workers 16 Years and Over)

Group	Number	%
Total Population	394	1.0
Hispanic or Latino (of any race)	117	1.3
Central American, ex. Mexican	0	0.0
Mexican	117	1.5

Homeownership Rate
(Universe: Occupied Housing Units)

Group	%
Total Population	62.3
Hispanic or Latino (of any race)	50.9
Central American, ex. Mexican	55.9
Salvadoran	51.4
Mexican	51.1
Puerto Rican	63.3
South American	71.3
Spaniard	53.9

Median Home Value

Group	Dollars
Total Population	314,700
Hispanic or Latino (of any race)	293,400
Central American, ex. Mexican	276,500
Mexican	292,800

Median Gross Rent

Group	Dollars
Total Population	951
Hispanic or Latino (of any race)	894
Central American, ex. Mexican	1,011
Mexican	890

Notes: (1) Percent of total population; (2) Percent of Hispanic/Latino population; Profiles include places with an overall population of at least 125,000, OR an overall population of at least 25,000 where the Hispanic/Latino population is at least 20% of the overall population. In states where less than five places meet either of these criteria, we have included places with at least 10,000 total population with the highest percentage of Hispanic/Latino population. These places are identified with an asterisk (*); Please refer to the User's Guide for a full explanation of data.

Median Household Income (2010 Inflation-Adjusted Dollars)	
Group	Dollars
Total Population	63,229
Hispanic or Latino (of any race)	54,307
Central American, ex. Mexican	59,659
Mexican	56,179

Per Capita Income (2010 Inflation-Adjusted Dollars)	
Group	Dollars
Total Population	27,375
Hispanic or Latino (of any race)	18,664
Central American, ex. Mexican	17,545
Mexican	18,771

Households with $100,000+ Income		
Group	Number	%
Total Population	8,433	26.5
Hispanic or Latino (of any race)	1,117	17.1
Central American, ex. Mexican	72	36.2
Mexican	891	16.2

Households with Food Stamps/SNAP Benefits During Past 12 Months		
Group	Number	%
Total Population	1,729	5.4
Hispanic or Latino (of any race)	641	9.8
Central American, ex. Mexican	23	11.6
Mexican	478	8.7

Poverty Rate (Income in Past 12 Months Below Poverty Level)	
Group	%
Total Population	10.2
Hispanic or Latino (of any race)	14.7
Central American, ex. Mexican	11.8
Mexican	15.2

Coachella

Population			
Group	Number	%TP[1]	%HP[2]
Total Population	40,704	100.0	–
Hispanic or Latino (of any race)	39,254	96.4	100.0
Central American, ex. Mexican	522	1.3	1.3
Salvadoran	351	0.9	0.9
Mexican	37,265	91.6	94.9

Population Growth: 2000–2010	
Group	%
Total Population	79.1
Hispanic or Latino (of any race)	77.4
Central American, ex. Mexican	342.4
Mexican	88.0

Males per 100 Females	
Group	Number
Total Population	99.3
Hispanic or Latino (of any race)	99.2
Central American, ex. Mexican	113.1
Salvadoran	119.4
Mexican	99.1

Average Household Size	
Group	People
Total Population	4.52
Hispanic or Latino (of any race)	4.58
Central American, ex. Mexican	4.84
Salvadoran	4.93
Mexican	4.57

Median Age	
Group	Years
Total Population	24.5
Hispanic or Latino (of any race)	24.2
Central American, ex. Mexican	30.9
Salvadoran	30.9
Mexican	24.2

High School Graduates (Universe: Population 25 Years and Over)		
Group	Number	%
Total Population	8,384	45.3
Hispanic or Latino (of any race)	7,636	43.6
Mexican	7,424	43.7

Four-Year College Graduates (Universe: Population 25 Years and Over)		
Group	Number	%
Total Population	868	4.7
Hispanic or Latino (of any race)	714	4.1
Mexican	704	4.1

Population Age 3–17 Enrolled in Public School (Universe: Population Age 3–17 Enrolled in School)		
Group	Number	%
Total Population	11,316	99.0
Hispanic or Latino (of any race)	10,906	99.1
Mexican	10,794	99.1

Population Age 3–17 Enrolled in Private School (Universe: Population Age 3–17 Enrolled in School)		
Group	Number	%
Total Population	111	1.0
Hispanic or Latino (of any race)	101	0.9
Mexican	101	0.9

Foreign-Born Population		
Group	Number	%
Total Population	15,654	41.0
Hispanic or Latino (of any race)	15,279	42.1
Mexican	14,827	41.8

Foreign-Born Naturalized U.S. Citizens		
Group	Number	%
Total Population	3,639	23.2
Hispanic or Latino (of any race)	3,370	22.1
Mexican	3,313	22.3

Language Spoken at Home: English Only (Universe: Population 5 Years and Over)		
Group	Number	%
Total Population	4,232	12.3
Hispanic or Latino (of any race)	3,032	9.3
Mexican	2,925	9.2

Language Spoken at Home: Spanish (Universe: Population 5 Years and Over)		
Group	Number	%
Total Population	29,972	87.4
Hispanic or Latino (of any race)	29,620	90.7
Mexican	28,958	90.8

Unemployment Rate (Universe: Population 16 Years and Over)	
Group	%
Total Population	14.9
Hispanic or Latino (of any race)	15.4
Mexican	15.0

Class of Worker: Private Wage and Salary (Universe: Civilian Employed Population 16 Years and Over)		
Group	Number	%
Total Population	12,420	85.6
Hispanic or Latino (of any race)	11,800	86.1
Mexican	11,448	86.1

Class of Worker: Government (Universe: Civilian Employed Population 16 Years and Over)		
Group	Number	%
Total Population	1,483	10.2
Hispanic or Latino (of any race)	1,339	9.8
Mexican	1,319	9.9

Means of Transportation to Work: Car, Truck or Van (Universe: Workers 16 Years and Over)		
Group	Number	%
Total Population	13,314	94.6
Hispanic or Latino (of any race)	12,556	94.5
Mexican	12,179	94.5

Means of Transportation to Work: Public Transportation (ex. Taxicab) (Universe: Workers 16 Years and Over)		
Group	Number	%
Total Population	135	1.0
Hispanic or Latino (of any race)	128	1.0
Mexican	116	0.9

Homeownership Rate (Universe: Occupied Housing Units)	
Group	%
Total Population	62.1
Hispanic or Latino (of any race)	61.5
Central American, ex. Mexican	61.4
Salvadoran	66.7
Mexican	61.6

Median Home Value	
Group	Dollars
Total Population	204,200
Hispanic or Latino (of any race)	201,300
Mexican	203,200

Median Gross Rent	
Group	Dollars
Total Population	833
Hispanic or Latino (of any race)	832
Mexican	831

Median Household Income (2010 Inflation-Adjusted Dollars)	
Group	Dollars
Total Population	43,018
Hispanic or Latino (of any race)	42,234
Mexican	42,315

Per Capita Income (2010 Inflation-Adjusted Dollars)	
Group	Dollars
Total Population	12,019
Hispanic or Latino (of any race)	11,616
Mexican	11,564

Households with $100,000+ Income		
Group	Number	%
Total Population	698	8.0
Hispanic or Latino (of any race)	572	7.0
Mexican	561	7.0

Households with Food Stamps/SNAP Benefits During Past 12 Months		
Group	Number	%
Total Population	1,097	12.6
Hispanic or Latino (of any race)	1,088	13.3
Mexican	1,038	13.0

Poverty Rate (Income in Past 12 Months Below Poverty Level)	
Group	%
Total Population	23.7
Hispanic or Latino (of any race)	24.4
Mexican	24.5

Colton

Population			
Group	Number	%TP[1]	%HP[2]
Total Population	52,154	100.0	–
Hispanic or Latino (of any race)	37,039	71.0	100.0
Central American, ex. Mexican	1,397	2.7	3.8
Guatemalan	406	0.8	1.1
Nicaraguan	157	0.3	0.4
Salvadoran	656	1.3	1.8
Cuban	119	0.2	0.3
Mexican	32,985	63.2	89.1
Puerto Rican	397	0.8	1.1
South American	289	0.6	0.8
Spaniard	170	0.3	0.5

Population Growth: 2000–2010	
Group	%
Total Population	9.4
Hispanic or Latino (of any race)	28.0
Central American, ex. Mexican	138.8
Guatemalan	160.3
Salvadoran	203.7
Cuban	19.0
Mexican	38.5
Puerto Rican	24.8
South American	55.4

STATE & PLACE PROFILES

Notes: (1) Percent of total population; (2) Percent of Hispanic/Latino population; Profiles include places with an overall population of at least 125,000, OR an overall population of at least 25,000 where the Hispanic/Latino population is at least 20% of the overall population. In states where less than five places meet either of these criteria, we have included places with at least 10,000 total population with the highest percentage of Hispanic/Latino population. These places are identified with an asterisk (*); Please refer to the User's Guide for a full explanation of data.

Males per 100 Females	
Group	Number
Total Population	96.0
Hispanic or Latino (of any race)	97.8
Central American, ex. Mexican	97.0
Guatemalan	105.1
Nicaraguan	96.3
Salvadoran	97.6
Cuban	98.3
Mexican	97.9
Puerto Rican	101.5
South American	105.0
Spaniard	107.3

Average Household Size	
Group	People
Total Population	3.46
Hispanic or Latino (of any race)	3.97
Central American, ex. Mexican	4.17
Guatemalan	4.39
Nicaraguan	4.00
Salvadoran	4.29
Cuban	3.66
Mexican	4.00
Puerto Rican	3.37
South American	3.42
Spaniard	3.13

Median Age	
Group	Years
Total Population	28.4
Hispanic or Latino (of any race)	25.9
Central American, ex. Mexican	33.0
Guatemalan	33.2
Nicaraguan	35.8
Salvadoran	32.4
Cuban	35.3
Mexican	25.6
Puerto Rican	26.3
South American	35.5
Spaniard	33.3

High School Graduates (Universe: Population 25 Years and Over)		
Group	Number	%
Total Population	21,260	72.7
Hispanic or Latino (of any race)	11,503	62.0
Central American, ex. Mexican	322	50.5
Mexican	10,529	62.5

Four-Year College Graduates (Universe: Population 25 Years and Over)		
Group	Number	%
Total Population	3,500	12.0
Hispanic or Latino (of any race)	1,205	6.5
Central American, ex. Mexican	14	2.2
Mexican	1,134	6.7

Population Age 3–17 Enrolled in Public School (Universe: Population Age 3–17 Enrolled in School)		
Group	Number	%
Total Population	12,350	94.1
Hispanic or Latino (of any race)	9,578	97.3
Central American, ex. Mexican	294	100.0
Mexican	8,844	97.6

Population Age 3–17 Enrolled in Private School (Universe: Population Age 3–17 Enrolled in School)		
Group	Number	%
Total Population	773	5.9
Hispanic or Latino (of any race)	263	2.7
Central American, ex. Mexican	0	0.0
Mexican	222	2.4

Foreign-Born Population		
Group	Number	%
Total Population	13,877	26.6
Hispanic or Latino (of any race)	10,787	30.3
Central American, ex. Mexican	596	57.1
Mexican	9,857	30.1

Foreign-Born Naturalized U.S. Citizens		
Group	Number	%
Total Population	5,302	38.2
Hispanic or Latino (of any race)	3,366	31.2
Central American, ex. Mexican	169	28.4
Mexican	3,061	31.1

Language Spoken at Home: English Only (Universe: Population 5 Years and Over)		
Group	Number	%
Total Population	22,391	46.8
Hispanic or Latino (of any race)	9,779	30.4
Central American, ex. Mexican	147	15.5
Mexican	9,136	30.9

Language Spoken at Home: Spanish (Universe: Population 5 Years and Over)		
Group	Number	%
Total Population	22,735	47.5
Hispanic or Latino (of any race)	22,416	69.6
Central American, ex. Mexican	799	84.5
Mexican	20,386	69.0

Unemployment Rate (Universe: Population 16 Years and Over)	
Group	%
Total Population	10.7
Hispanic or Latino (of any race)	12.3
Central American, ex. Mexican	14.7
Mexican	12.6

Class of Worker: Private Wage and Salary (Universe: Civilian Employed Population 16 Years and Over)		
Group	Number	%
Total Population	17,162	79.2
Hispanic or Latino (of any race)	11,086	82.6
Central American, ex. Mexican	411	88.6
Mexican	10,238	83.4

Class of Worker: Government (Universe: Civilian Employed Population 16 Years and Over)		
Group	Number	%
Total Population	3,306	15.3
Hispanic or Latino (of any race)	1,637	12.2
Central American, ex. Mexican	48	10.3
Mexican	1,429	11.6

Means of Transportation to Work: Car, Truck or Van (Universe: Workers 16 Years and Over)		
Group	Number	%
Total Population	19,367	92.2
Hispanic or Latino (of any race)	12,122	93.5
Central American, ex. Mexican	385	92.1
Mexican	11,214	93.9

Means of Transportation to Work: Public Transportation (ex. Taxicab) (Universe: Workers 16 Years and Over)		
Group	Number	%
Total Population	570	2.7
Hispanic or Latino (of any race)	322	2.5
Central American, ex. Mexican	33	7.9
Mexican	289	2.4

Homeownership Rate (Universe: Occupied Housing Units)	
Group	%
Total Population	51.9
Hispanic or Latino (of any race)	53.5
Central American, ex. Mexican	56.7
Guatemalan	55.2
Nicaraguan	56.5
Salvadoran	56.7
Cuban	55.2
Mexican	54.2
Puerto Rican	31.5
South American	61.9
Spaniard	51.7

Median Home Value	
Group	Dollars
Total Population	255,100
Hispanic or Latino (of any race)	238,600
Central American, ex. Mexican	298,900
Mexican	233,300

Median Gross Rent	
Group	Dollars
Total Population	993
Hispanic or Latino (of any race)	963
Central American, ex. Mexican	1,047
Mexican	957

Median Household Income (2010 Inflation-Adjusted Dollars)	
Group	Dollars
Total Population	43,373
Hispanic or Latino (of any race)	41,223
Central American, ex. Mexican	51,429
Mexican	41,733

Per Capita Income (2010 Inflation-Adjusted Dollars)	
Group	Dollars
Total Population	16,496
Hispanic or Latino (of any race)	13,214
Central American, ex. Mexican	14,984
Mexican	13,126

Households with $100,000+ Income		
Group	Number	%
Total Population	1,939	12.8
Hispanic or Latino (of any race)	829	9.2
Central American, ex. Mexican	0	0.0
Mexican	767	9.5

Households with Food Stamps/SNAP Benefits During Past 12 Months		
Group	Number	%
Total Population	1,700	11.2
Hispanic or Latino (of any race)	1,163	12.8
Central American, ex. Mexican	46	13.8
Mexican	991	12.3

Poverty Rate (Income in Past 12 Months Below Poverty Level)	
Group	%
Total Population	17.9
Hispanic or Latino (of any race)	21.4
Central American, ex. Mexican	27.9
Mexican	20.7

Compton

Population			
Group	Number	%TP[1]	%HP[2]
Total Population	96,455	100.0	–
Hispanic or Latino (of any race)	62,669	65.0	100.0
Central American, ex. Mexican	4,910	5.1	7.8
Guatemalan	1,471	1.5	2.3
Honduran	571	0.6	0.9
Nicaraguan	215	0.2	0.3
Salvadoran	2,470	2.6	3.9
Mexican	54,084	56.1	86.3
Puerto Rican	218	0.2	0.3
South American	209	0.2	0.3
Spaniard	114	0.1	0.2

Population Growth: 2000–2010	
Group	%
Total Population	3.2
Hispanic or Latino (of any race)	17.9
Central American, ex. Mexican	124.1
Guatemalan	138.4
Honduran	112.3
Salvadoran	141.2
Mexican	23.4
Puerto Rican	35.4
South American	101.0

Males per 100 Females	
Group	Number
Total Population	94.8
Hispanic or Latino (of any race)	102.6
Central American, ex. Mexican	106.1
Guatemalan	109.8
Honduran	107.6
Nicaraguan	92.0
Salvadoran	105.8
Mexican	102.5
Puerto Rican	115.8
South American	106.9
Spaniard	123.5

Notes: (1) Percent of total population; (2) Percent of Hispanic/Latino population; Profiles include places with an overall population of at least 125,000, OR an overall population of at least 25,000 where the Hispanic/Latino population is at least 20% of the overall population. In states where less than five places meet either of these criteria, we have included places with at least 10,000 total population with the highest percentage of Hispanic/Latino population. These places are identified with an asterisk (*); Please refer to the User's Guide for a full explanation of data.

Average Household Size

Group	People
Total Population	4.15
Hispanic or Latino (of any race)	5.30
Central American, ex. Mexican	5.09
Guatemalan	5.14
Honduran	5.25
Nicaraguan	5.21
Salvadoran	5.03
Mexican	5.35
Puerto Rican	3.79
South American	4.54
Spaniard	4.05

Median Age

Group	Years
Total Population	28.0
Hispanic or Latino (of any race)	24.5
Central American, ex. Mexican	32.3
Guatemalan	32.4
Honduran	29.8
Nicaraguan	32.2
Salvadoran	32.9
Mexican	24.0
Puerto Rican	29.0
South American	34.6
Spaniard	34.0

High School Graduates
(Universe: Population 25 Years and Over)

Group	Number	%
Total Population	29,335	58.8
Hispanic or Latino (of any race)	11,249	39.4
Central American, ex. Mexican	1,614	44.5
Guatemalan	556	46.1
Salvadoran	726	37.5
Mexican	9,252	37.9

Four-Year College Graduates
(Universe: Population 25 Years and Over)

Group	Number	%
Total Population	3,543	7.1
Hispanic or Latino (of any race)	810	2.8
Central American, ex. Mexican	210	5.8
Guatemalan	42	3.5
Salvadoran	132	6.8
Mexican	551	2.3

Population Age 3–17 Enrolled in Public School
(Universe: Population Age 3–17 Enrolled in School)

Group	Number	%
Total Population	24,819	96.1
Hispanic or Latino (of any race)	17,987	97.6
Central American, ex. Mexican	1,282	94.9
Guatemalan	304	90.5
Salvadoran	806	95.6
Mexican	16,226	97.9

Population Age 3–17 Enrolled in Private School
(Universe: Population Age 3–17 Enrolled in School)

Group	Number	%
Total Population	1,020	3.9
Hispanic or Latino (of any race)	437	2.4
Central American, ex. Mexican	69	5.1
Guatemalan	32	9.5
Salvadoran	37	4.4
Mexican	348	2.1

Foreign-Born Population

Group	Number	%
Total Population	28,616	29.9
Hispanic or Latino (of any race)	27,729	45.5
Central American, ex. Mexican	4,446	66.9
Guatemalan	1,532	72.4
Salvadoran	2,233	62.4
Mexican	23,037	43.5

Foreign-Born Naturalized U.S. Citizens

Group	Number	%
Total Population	7,055	24.7
Hispanic or Latino (of any race)	6,481	23.4
Central American, ex. Mexican	1,025	23.1
Guatemalan	313	20.4
Salvadoran	508	22.7
Mexican	5,294	23.0

Language Spoken at Home: English Only
(Universe: Population 5 Years and Over)

Group	Number	%
Total Population	34,424	39.9
Hispanic or Latino (of any race)	2,989	5.6
Central American, ex. Mexican	147	2.4
Guatemalan	35	1.8
Salvadoran	64	2.0
Mexican	2,321	5.0

Language Spoken at Home: Spanish
(Universe: Population 5 Years and Over)

Group	Number	%
Total Population	51,184	59.3
Hispanic or Latino (of any race)	50,613	94.4
Central American, ex. Mexican	5,845	97.4
Guatemalan	1,940	98.2
Salvadoran	3,065	98.0
Mexican	44,201	95.0

Unemployment Rate
(Universe: Population 16 Years and Over)

Group	%
Total Population	13.0
Hispanic or Latino (of any race)	11.2
Central American, ex. Mexican	13.0
Guatemalan	8.0
Salvadoran	19.1
Mexican	10.9

Class of Worker: Private Wage and Salary
(Universe: Civilian Employed Population 16 Years and Over)

Group	Number	%
Total Population	27,292	78.1
Hispanic or Latino (of any race)	19,487	85.7
Central American, ex. Mexican	2,633	87.6
Guatemalan	883	84.7
Salvadoran	1,254	88.6
Mexican	16,555	85.5

Class of Worker: Government
(Universe: Civilian Employed Population 16 Years and Over)

Group	Number	%
Total Population	5,149	14.7
Hispanic or Latino (of any race)	1,327	5.8
Central American, ex. Mexican	138	4.6
Guatemalan	33	3.2
Salvadoran	76	5.4
Mexican	1,112	5.7

Means of Transportation to Work: Car, Truck or Van
(Universe: Workers 16 Years and Over)

Group	Number	%
Total Population	29,747	88.2
Hispanic or Latino (of any race)	19,494	87.7
Central American, ex. Mexican	2,682	91.5
Guatemalan	920	89.8
Salvadoran	1,226	90.2
Mexican	16,453	87.0

Means of Transportation to Work: Public Transportation (ex. Taxicab)
(Universe: Workers 16 Years and Over)

Group	Number	%
Total Population	2,046	6.1
Hispanic or Latino (of any race)	1,391	6.3
Central American, ex. Mexican	174	5.9
Guatemalan	74	7.2
Salvadoran	100	7.4
Mexican	1,190	6.3

Homeownership Rate
(Universe: Occupied Housing Units)

Group	%
Total Population	55.2
Hispanic or Latino (of any race)	49.7
Central American, ex. Mexican	56.5
Guatemalan	51.2
Honduran	43.1
Nicaraguan	60.4
Salvadoran	61.1
Mexican	49.4
Puerto Rican	48.2
South American	62.5
Spaniard	48.6

Median Home Value

Group	Dollars
Total Population	330,100
Hispanic or Latino (of any race)	327,600
Central American, ex. Mexican	331,200
Guatemalan	342,600
Salvadoran	295,400
Mexican	327,800

Median Gross Rent

Group	Dollars
Total Population	929
Hispanic or Latino (of any race)	938
Central American, ex. Mexican	1,015
Guatemalan	891
Salvadoran	1,065
Mexican	935

Median Household Income
(2010 Inflation-Adjusted Dollars)

Group	Dollars
Total Population	43,201
Hispanic or Latino (of any race)	42,879
Central American, ex. Mexican	45,521
Guatemalan	47,955
Salvadoran	42,813
Mexican	42,781

Per Capita Income
(2010 Inflation-Adjusted Dollars)

Group	Dollars
Total Population	13,542
Hispanic or Latino (of any race)	10,361
Central American, ex. Mexican	12,494
Guatemalan	12,908
Salvadoran	11,319
Mexican	10,148

Households with $100,000+ Income

Group	Number	%
Total Population	2,713	11.6
Hispanic or Latino (of any race)	970	8.2
Central American, ex. Mexican	152	11.1
Guatemalan	76	15.6
Salvadoran	52	7.4
Mexican	818	7.9

Households with Food Stamps/SNAP Benefits During Past 12 Months

Group	Number	%
Total Population	3,919	16.7
Hispanic or Latino (of any race)	2,354	19.8
Central American, ex. Mexican	265	19.4
Guatemalan	98	20.1
Salvadoran	159	22.5
Mexican	2,077	20.2

Poverty Rate
(Income in Past 12 Months Below Poverty Level)

Group	%
Total Population	22.8
Hispanic or Latino (of any race)	26.6
Central American, ex. Mexican	19.5
Guatemalan	15.3
Salvadoran	23.8
Mexican	27.5

Concord

Population

Group	Number	%TP[1]	%HP[2]
Total Population	122,067	100.0	–
Hispanic or Latino (of any race)	37,311	30.6	100.0
Central American, ex. Mexican	4,761	3.9	12.8
Costa Rican	118	0.1	0.3
Guatemalan	592	0.5	1.6
Honduran	116	0.1	0.3
Nicaraguan	886	0.7	2.4
Panamanian	119	0.1	0.3
Salvadoran	2,904	2.4	7.8
Cuban	214	0.2	0.6
Mexican	26,779	21.9	71.8

Notes: (1) Percent of total population; (2) Percent of Hispanic/Latino population; Profiles include places with an overall population of at least 125,000, OR an overall population of at least 25,000 where the Hispanic/Latino population is at least 20% of the overall population. In states where less than five places meet either of these criteria, we have included places with at least 10,000 total population with the highest percentage of Hispanic/Latino population. These places are identified with an asterisk (*); Please refer to the User's Guide for a full explanation of data.

Puerto Rican	892	0.7	2.4
South American	1,845	1.5	4.9
Argentinean	146	0.1	0.4
Chilean	101	0.1	0.3
Colombian	279	0.2	0.7
Ecuadorian	111	0.1	0.3
Peruvian	1,056	0.9	2.8
Spaniard	708	0.6	1.9

Population Growth: 2000–2010

Group	%
Total Population	0.2
Hispanic or Latino (of any race)	40.5
Central American, ex. Mexican	87.2
Guatemalan	102.7
Nicaraguan	93.9
Salvadoran	102.9
Cuban	19.6
Mexican	53.5
Puerto Rican	33.9
South American	79.6
Colombian	128.7
Peruvian	86.6
Spaniard	537.8

Males per 100 Females

Group	Number
Total Population	98.8
Hispanic or Latino (of any race)	109.3
Central American, ex. Mexican	95.8
Costa Rican	87.3
Guatemalan	107.0
Honduran	123.1
Nicaraguan	93.0
Panamanian	80.3
Salvadoran	94.8
Cuban	107.8
Mexican	116.0
Puerto Rican	87.0
South American	85.6
Argentinean	114.7
Chilean	65.6
Colombian	83.6
Ecuadorian	76.2
Peruvian	85.3
Spaniard	86.3

Average Household Size

Group	People
Total Population	2.73
Hispanic or Latino (of any race)	3.81
Central American, ex. Mexican	3.59
Costa Rican	3.14
Guatemalan	3.65
Honduran	2.93
Nicaraguan	3.31
Panamanian	2.65
Salvadoran	3.78
Cuban	2.76
Mexican	4.07
Puerto Rican	2.96
South American	3.05
Argentinean	2.68
Chilean	2.55
Colombian	2.74
Ecuadorian	2.78
Peruvian	3.31
Spaniard	2.55

Median Age

Group	Years
Total Population	37.0
Hispanic or Latino (of any race)	27.4
Central American, ex. Mexican	32.2
Costa Rican	37.0
Guatemalan	32.1
Honduran	31.0
Nicaraguan	32.9
Panamanian	32.1
Salvadoran	31.9
Cuban	36.3
Mexican	25.9
Puerto Rican	27.3
South American	38.5
Argentinean	44.5
Chilean	38.5
Colombian	34.6
Ecuadorian	36.3
Peruvian	38.8
Spaniard	38.2

High School Graduates
(Universe: Population 25 Years and Over)

Group	Number	%
Total Population	70,798	86.1
Hispanic or Latino (of any race)	11,665	63.0
Central American, ex. Mexican	2,036	70.8
Salvadoran	794	61.4
Mexican	6,737	53.9
South American	1,133	94.6
Peruvian	558	89.6

Four-Year College Graduates
(Universe: Population 25 Years and Over)

Group	Number	%
Total Population	24,993	30.4
Hispanic or Latino (of any race)	2,809	15.2
Central American, ex. Mexican	607	21.1
Salvadoran	134	10.4
Mexican	1,350	10.8
South American	395	33.0
Peruvian	116	18.6

Population Age 3–17 Enrolled in Public School
(Universe: Population Age 3–17 Enrolled in School)

Group	Number	%
Total Population	17,271	82.6
Hispanic or Latino (of any race)	7,471	89.1
Central American, ex. Mexican	795	83.9
Salvadoran	338	73.5
Mexican	5,733	91.4
South American	342	77.2
Peruvian	129	56.1

Population Age 3–17 Enrolled in Private School
(Universe: Population Age 3–17 Enrolled in School)

Group	Number	%
Total Population	3,645	17.4
Hispanic or Latino (of any race)	915	10.9
Central American, ex. Mexican	153	16.1
Salvadoran	122	26.5
Mexican	542	8.6
South American	101	22.8
Peruvian	101	43.9

Foreign-Born Population

Group	Number	%
Total Population	32,554	26.8
Hispanic or Latino (of any race)	16,028	46.4
Central American, ex. Mexican	2,671	57.0
Salvadoran	1,353	65.9
Mexican	11,315	45.6
South American	1,283	65.1
Peruvian	648	61.8

Foreign-Born Naturalized U.S. Citizens

Group	Number	%
Total Population	13,017	40.0
Hispanic or Latino (of any race)	3,063	19.1
Central American, ex. Mexican	708	26.5
Salvadoran	397	29.3
Mexican	1,482	13.1
South American	521	40.6
Peruvian	234	36.1

Language Spoken at Home: English Only
(Universe: Population 5 Years and Over)

Group	Number	%
Total Population	72,965	64.5
Hispanic or Latino (of any race)	8,201	26.5
Central American, ex. Mexican	890	20.5
Salvadoran	129	6.5
Mexican	5,649	25.7
South American	317	17.3
Peruvian	268	28.2

Language Spoken at Home: Spanish
(Universe: Population 5 Years and Over)

Group	Number	%
Total Population	24,037	21.2
Hispanic or Latino (of any race)	22,713	73.3
Central American, ex. Mexican	3,431	79.2
Salvadoran	1,847	93.0
Mexican	16,278	74.1
South American	1,513	82.7
Peruvian	684	71.8

Unemployment Rate
(Universe: Population 16 Years and Over)

Group	%
Total Population	8.3
Hispanic or Latino (of any race)	7.7
Central American, ex. Mexican	8.9
Salvadoran	5.7
Mexican	7.4
South American	6.5
Peruvian	4.0

Class of Worker: Private Wage and Salary
(Universe: Civilian Employed Population 16 Years and Over)

Group	Number	%
Total Population	50,091	80.6
Hispanic or Latino (of any race)	14,680	85.0
Central American, ex. Mexican	2,259	80.7
Salvadoran	1,073	89.3
Mexican	10,265	85.9
South American	761	75.3
Peruvian	466	77.3

Class of Worker: Government
(Universe: Civilian Employed Population 16 Years and Over)

Group	Number	%
Total Population	7,320	11.8
Hispanic or Latino (of any race)	1,167	6.8
Central American, ex. Mexican	243	8.7
Salvadoran	23	1.9
Mexican	761	6.4
South American	100	9.9
Peruvian	58	9.6

Means of Transportation to Work: Car, Truck or Van
(Universe: Workers 16 Years and Over)

Group	Number	%
Total Population	49,058	81.1
Hispanic or Latino (of any race)	13,453	80.7
Central American, ex. Mexican	1,965	74.4
Salvadoran	849	72.8
Mexican	9,486	81.7
South American	883	88.0
Peruvian	585	97.0

Means of Transportation to Work: Public Transportation (ex. Taxicab)
(Universe: Workers 16 Years and Over)

Group	Number	%
Total Population	6,060	10.0
Hispanic or Latino (of any race)	1,717	10.3
Central American, ex. Mexican	467	17.7
Salvadoran	227	19.5
Mexican	973	8.4
South American	97	9.7
Peruvian	18	3.0

Homeownership Rate
(Universe: Occupied Housing Units)

Group	%
Total Population	61.1
Hispanic or Latino (of any race)	38.9
Central American, ex. Mexican	46.3
Costa Rican	48.6
Guatemalan	44.2
Honduran	41.4
Nicaraguan	53.6
Panamanian	48.8
Salvadoran	43.9
Cuban	64.8
Mexican	33.9
Puerto Rican	49.8
South American	53.4
Argentinean	66.1
Chilean	58.1
Colombian	52.2
Ecuadorian	55.0
Peruvian	49.5
Spaniard	68.9

Notes: (1) Percent of total population; (2) Percent of Hispanic/Latino population; Profiles include places with an overall population of at least 125,000, OR an overall population of at least 25,000 where the Hispanic/Latino population is at least 20% of the overall population. In states where less than five places meet either of these criteria, we have included places with at least 10,000 total population with the highest percentage of Hispanic/Latino population. These places are identified with an asterisk (*); Please refer to the User's Guide for a full explanation of data.

Median Home Value

Group	Dollars
Total Population	470,200
Hispanic or Latino (of any race)	445,900
Central American, ex. Mexican	432,700
Salvadoran	348,800
Mexican	437,200
South American	539,400
Peruvian	584,000

Median Gross Rent

Group	Dollars
Total Population	1,188
Hispanic or Latino (of any race)	1,158
Central American, ex. Mexican	973
Salvadoran	999
Mexican	1,181
South American	1,217
Peruvian	1,397

Median Household Income
(2010 Inflation-Adjusted Dollars)

Group	Dollars
Total Population	65,123
Hispanic or Latino (of any race)	54,164
Central American, ex. Mexican	62,702
Salvadoran	57,929
Mexican	52,599
South American	50,699
Peruvian	37,008

Per Capita Income
(2010 Inflation-Adjusted Dollars)

Group	Dollars
Total Population	31,029
Hispanic or Latino (of any race)	18,187
Central American, ex. Mexican	24,271
Salvadoran	20,710
Mexican	16,401
South American	16,386
Peruvian	15,662

Households with $100,000+ Income

Group	Number	%
Total Population	13,118	29.2
Hispanic or Latino (of any race)	1,579	17.4
Central American, ex. Mexican	492	30.9
Salvadoran	124	17.3
Mexican	860	14.2
South American	33	6.9
Peruvian	24	12.3

Households with Food Stamps/SNAP Benefits During Past 12 Months

Group	Number	%
Total Population	1,440	3.2
Hispanic or Latino (of any race)	510	5.6
Central American, ex. Mexican	0	0.0
Salvadoran	0	0.0
Mexican	437	7.2
South American	0	0.0
Peruvian	0	0.0

Poverty Rate
(Income in Past 12 Months Below Poverty Level)

Group	%
Total Population	9.6
Hispanic or Latino (of any race)	14.4
Central American, ex. Mexican	9.0
Salvadoran	9.4
Mexican	17.1
South American	7.1
Peruvian	12.5

Corona

Population

Group	Number	%TP[1]	%HP[2]
Total Population	152,374	100.0	–
Hispanic or Latino (of any race)	66,447	43.6	100.0
Central American, ex. Mexican	3,118	2.0	4.7
Costa Rican	173	0.1	0.3
Guatemalan	934	0.6	1.4
Honduran	215	0.1	0.3
Nicaraguan	296	0.2	0.4
Panamanian	111	0.1	0.2
Salvadoran	1,350	0.9	2.0
Cuban	651	0.4	1.0
Mexican	56,979	37.4	85.8
Puerto Rican	899	0.6	1.4
South American	1,740	1.1	2.6
Argentinean	244	0.2	0.4
Chilean	140	0.1	0.2
Colombian	396	0.3	0.6
Ecuadorian	239	0.2	0.4
Peruvian	513	0.3	0.8
Spaniard	548	0.4	0.8

Population Growth: 2000–2010

Group	%
Total Population	21.9
Hispanic or Latino (of any race)	49.1
Central American, ex. Mexican	167.6
Guatemalan	210.3
Honduran	102.8
Salvadoran	230.9
Cuban	46.0
Mexican	57.3
Puerto Rican	49.1
South American	117.2
Argentinean	106.8
Colombian	117.6
Ecuadorian	132.0
Peruvian	150.2

Males per 100 Females

Group	Number
Total Population	97.0
Hispanic or Latino (of any race)	99.0
Central American, ex. Mexican	95.7
Costa Rican	86.0
Guatemalan	103.0
Honduran	82.2
Nicaraguan	86.2
Panamanian	91.4
Salvadoran	95.9
Cuban	93.8
Mexican	99.8
Puerto Rican	96.3
South American	88.5
Argentinean	105.0
Chilean	72.8
Colombian	85.9
Ecuadorian	100.8
Peruvian	85.9
Spaniard	89.0

Average Household Size

Group	People
Total Population	3.38
Hispanic or Latino (of any race)	4.15
Central American, ex. Mexican	4.20
Costa Rican	3.53
Guatemalan	4.26
Honduran	4.00
Nicaraguan	3.86
Panamanian	3.13
Salvadoran	4.45
Cuban	3.07
Mexican	4.25
Puerto Rican	3.40
South American	3.41
Argentinean	3.12
Chilean	3.48
Colombian	3.42
Ecuadorian	3.36
Peruvian	3.70
Spaniard	3.13

Median Age

Group	Years
Total Population	32.5
Hispanic or Latino (of any race)	26.1
Central American, ex. Mexican	32.5
Costa Rican	33.1
Guatemalan	32.6
Honduran	35.9
Nicaraguan	33.3
Panamanian	38.8
Salvadoran	31.1
Cuban	37.3
Mexican	25.4
Puerto Rican	26.7
South American	35.9
Argentinean	37.4
Chilean	38.0
Colombian	34.8
Ecuadorian	38.5
Peruvian	35.4
Spaniard	34.8

High School Graduates
(Universe: Population 25 Years and Over)

Group	Number	%
Total Population	72,182	81.2
Hispanic or Latino (of any race)	20,556	61.9
Central American, ex. Mexican	1,273	73.3
Guatemalan	436	66.1
Salvadoran	493	75.0
Mexican	16,715	58.7
South American	1,227	97.8

Four-Year College Graduates
(Universe: Population 25 Years and Over)

Group	Number	%
Total Population	21,579	24.3
Hispanic or Latino (of any race)	3,739	11.3
Central American, ex. Mexican	269	15.5
Guatemalan	58	8.8
Salvadoran	136	20.7
Mexican	2,634	9.2
South American	500	39.8

Population Age 3–17 Enrolled in Public School
(Universe: Population Age 3–17 Enrolled in School)

Group	Number	%
Total Population	31,336	87.8
Hispanic or Latino (of any race)	16,077	92.2
Central American, ex. Mexican	525	90.8
Guatemalan	190	80.5
Salvadoran	99	100.0
Mexican	14,511	93.1
South American	333	74.0

Population Age 3–17 Enrolled in Private School
(Universe: Population Age 3–17 Enrolled in School)

Group	Number	%
Total Population	4,361	12.2
Hispanic or Latino (of any race)	1,364	7.8
Central American, ex. Mexican	53	9.2
Guatemalan	46	19.5
Salvadoran	0	0.0
Mexican	1,068	6.9
South American	117	26.0

Foreign-Born Population

Group	Number	%
Total Population	38,611	25.7
Hispanic or Latino (of any race)	24,022	37.3
Central American, ex. Mexican	1,631	59.6
Guatemalan	649	56.5
Salvadoran	589	67.5
Mexican	20,984	37.2
South American	1,066	55.4

Foreign-Born Naturalized U.S. Citizens

Group	Number	%
Total Population	17,442	45.2
Hispanic or Latino (of any race)	7,809	32.5
Central American, ex. Mexican	962	59.0
Guatemalan	376	57.9
Salvadoran	324	55.0
Mexican	6,141	29.3
South American	477	44.7

Language Spoken at Home: English Only
(Universe: Population 5 Years and Over)

Group	Number	%
Total Population	79,467	57.2
Hispanic or Latino (of any race)	15,546	26.8
Central American, ex. Mexican	461	18.1
Guatemalan	155	15.4
Salvadoran	183	22.1
Mexican	13,173	25.9

Notes: (1) Percent of total population; (2) Percent of Hispanic/Latino population; Profiles include places with an overall population of at least 125,000, OR an overall population of at least 25,000 where the Hispanic/Latino population is at least 20% of the overall population. In states where less than five places meet either of these criteria, we have included places with at least 10,000 total population with the highest percentage of Hispanic/Latino population. These places are identified with an asterisk (*); Please refer to the User's Guide for a full explanation of data.

South American	254	14.5

Language Spoken at Home: Spanish
(Universe: Population 5 Years and Over)

Group	Number	%
Total Population	44,050	31.7
Hispanic or Latino (of any race)	42,230	72.8
Central American, ex. Mexican	2,089	81.9
Guatemalan	853	84.6
Salvadoran	644	77.9
Mexican	37,486	73.8
South American	1,492	85.5

Unemployment Rate
(Universe: Population 16 Years and Over)

Group	%
Total Population	10.4
Hispanic or Latino (of any race)	11.7
Central American, ex. Mexican	11.0
Guatemalan	17.6
Salvadoran	4.1
Mexican	12.7
South American	3.4

Class of Worker: Private Wage and Salary
(Universe: Civilian Employed Population 16 Years and Over)

Group	Number	%
Total Population	54,692	78.2
Hispanic or Latino (of any race)	22,217	81.8
Central American, ex. Mexican	1,190	88.9
Guatemalan	431	95.8
Salvadoran	518	91.8
Mexican	19,089	82.4
South American	635	57.5

Class of Worker: Government
(Universe: Civilian Employed Population 16 Years and Over)

Group	Number	%
Total Population	9,852	14.1
Hispanic or Latino (of any race)	2,961	10.9
Central American, ex. Mexican	128	9.6
Guatemalan	10	2.2
Salvadoran	46	8.2
Mexican	2,499	10.8
South American	103	9.3

Means of Transportation to Work: Car, Truck or Van
(Universe: Workers 16 Years and Over)

Group	Number	%
Total Population	61,120	90.7
Hispanic or Latino (of any race)	23,145	89.5
Central American, ex. Mexican	1,228	94.9
Guatemalan	450	100.0
Salvadoran	472	87.7
Mexican	19,600	89.0
South American	889	85.0

Means of Transportation to Work: Public Transportation (ex. Taxicab)
(Universe: Workers 16 Years and Over)

Group	Number	%
Total Population	1,186	1.8
Hispanic or Latino (of any race)	533	2.1
Central American, ex. Mexican	66	5.1
Guatemalan	0	0.0
Salvadoran	66	12.3
Mexican	420	1.9
South American	28	2.7

Homeownership Rate
(Universe: Occupied Housing Units)

Group	%
Total Population	67.2
Hispanic or Latino (of any race)	55.7
Central American, ex. Mexican	57.5
Costa Rican	63.8
Guatemalan	47.7
Honduran	64.4
Nicaraguan	60.9
Panamanian	80.6
Salvadoran	60.8
Cuban	70.0
Mexican	54.9
Puerto Rican	56.3
South American	67.7
Argentinean	67.9
Chilean	55.0
Colombian	68.5
Ecuadorian	77.9
Peruvian	65.1
Spaniard	67.6

Median Home Value

Group	Dollars
Total Population	435,500
Hispanic or Latino (of any race)	409,600
Central American, ex. Mexican	422,300
Guatemalan	421,900
Salvadoran	410,500
Mexican	402,200
South American	504,100

Median Gross Rent

Group	Dollars
Total Population	1,280
Hispanic or Latino (of any race)	1,151
Central American, ex. Mexican	1,247
Guatemalan	1,128
Salvadoran	1,295
Mexican	1,138
South American	1,308

Median Household Income
(2010 Inflation-Adjusted Dollars)

Group	Dollars
Total Population	79,180
Hispanic or Latino (of any race)	57,382
Central American, ex. Mexican	57,226
Guatemalan	43,077
Salvadoran	60,040
Mexican	56,305
South American	81,250

Per Capita Income
(2010 Inflation-Adjusted Dollars)

Group	Dollars
Total Population	27,409
Hispanic or Latino (of any race)	17,571
Central American, ex. Mexican	21,698
Guatemalan	17,932
Salvadoran	23,767
Mexican	16,403
South American	33,945

Households with $100,000+ Income

Group	Number	%
Total Population	16,016	37.0
Hispanic or Latino (of any race)	3,614	24.2
Central American, ex. Mexican	314	36.3
Guatemalan	46	20.2
Salvadoran	147	37.4
Mexican	2,734	21.6
South American	237	38.6

Households with Food Stamps/SNAP Benefits During Past 12 Months

Group	Number	%
Total Population	1,656	3.8
Hispanic or Latino (of any race)	1,003	6.7
Central American, ex. Mexican	14	1.6
Guatemalan	0	0.0
Salvadoran	0	0.0
Mexican	989	7.8
South American	0	0.0

Poverty Rate
(Income in Past 12 Months Below Poverty Level)

Group	%
Total Population	8.9
Hispanic or Latino (of any race)	13.6
Central American, ex. Mexican	11.1
Guatemalan	19.5
Salvadoran	1.3
Mexican	14.8
South American	0.0

Costa Mesa

Population

Group	Number	%TP[1]	%HP[2]
Total Population	109,960	100.0	–
Hispanic or Latino (of any race)	39,403	35.8	100.0
Central American, ex. Mexican	3,497	3.2	8.9
Guatemalan	1,134	1.0	2.9
Honduran	174	0.2	0.4
Nicaraguan	108	0.1	0.3
Salvadoran	1,983	1.8	5.0
Cuban	233	0.2	0.6
Mexican	31,646	28.8	80.3
Puerto Rican	433	0.4	1.1
South American	1,146	1.0	2.9
Argentinean	239	0.2	0.6
Colombian	299	0.3	0.8
Ecuadorian	153	0.1	0.4
Peruvian	251	0.2	0.6
Spaniard	378	0.3	1.0

Population Growth: 2000–2010

Group	%
Total Population	1.1
Hispanic or Latino (of any race)	14.1
Central American, ex. Mexican	61.9
Guatemalan	83.5
Honduran	65.7
Salvadoran	73.3
Cuban	33.9
Mexican	21.1
Puerto Rican	39.2
South American	62.8
Argentinean	62.6
Colombian	43.8
Peruvian	94.6

Males per 100 Females

Group	Number
Total Population	103.7
Hispanic or Latino (of any race)	105.5
Central American, ex. Mexican	102.1
Guatemalan	105.8
Honduran	100.0
Nicaraguan	116.0
Salvadoran	101.1
Cuban	115.7
Mexican	107.4
Puerto Rican	101.4
South American	85.7
Argentinean	99.2
Colombian	78.0
Ecuadorian	70.0
Peruvian	76.8
Spaniard	81.7

Average Household Size

Group	People
Total Population	2.68
Hispanic or Latino (of any race)	4.10
Central American, ex. Mexican	4.23
Guatemalan	4.28
Honduran	3.78
Nicaraguan	3.00
Salvadoran	4.46
Cuban	2.29
Mexican	4.32
Puerto Rican	2.24
South American	2.74
Argentinean	2.61
Colombian	2.76
Ecuadorian	2.93
Peruvian	2.96
Spaniard	2.42

Median Age

Group	Years
Total Population	33.6
Hispanic or Latino (of any race)	27.0
Central American, ex. Mexican	31.5
Guatemalan	31.0
Honduran	32.0
Nicaraguan	36.8
Salvadoran	31.4

Notes: (1) Percent of total population; (2) Percent of Hispanic/Latino population; Profiles include places with an overall population of at least 125,000, OR an overall population of at least 25,000 where the Hispanic/Latino population is at least 20% of the overall population. In states where less than five places meet either of these criteria, we have included places with at least 10,000 total population with the highest percentage of Hispanic/Latino population. These places are identified with an asterisk (*); Please refer to the User's Guide for a full explanation of data.

Cuban		34.3
Mexican		26.1
Puerto Rican		29.7
South American		35.9
Argentinean		36.6
Colombian		39.4
Ecuadorian		34.2
Peruvian		35.2
Spaniard		32.8

High School Graduates
(Universe: Population 25 Years and Over)

Group	Number	%
Total Population	62,831	85.7
Hispanic or Latino (of any race)	12,220	61.2
Central American, ex. Mexican	860	63.3
Salvadoran	488	59.4
Mexican	9,405	57.0
South American	946	93.8

Four-Year College Graduates
(Universe: Population 25 Years and Over)

Group	Number	%
Total Population	24,839	33.9
Hispanic or Latino (of any race)	2,329	11.7
Central American, ex. Mexican	141	10.4
Salvadoran	53	6.4
Mexican	1,636	9.9
South American	309	30.6

Population Age 3–17 Enrolled in Public School
(Universe: Population Age 3–17 Enrolled in School)

Group	Number	%
Total Population	14,178	84.0
Hispanic or Latino (of any race)	7,763	95.1
Central American, ex. Mexican	343	100.0
Salvadoran	305	100.0
Mexican	6,978	95.5
South American	168	88.4

Population Age 3–17 Enrolled in Private School
(Universe: Population Age 3–17 Enrolled in School)

Group	Number	%
Total Population	2,708	16.0
Hispanic or Latino (of any race)	399	4.9
Central American, ex. Mexican	0	0.0
Salvadoran	0	0.0
Mexican	330	4.5
South American	22	11.6

Foreign-Born Population

Group	Number	%
Total Population	29,573	27.1
Hispanic or Latino (of any race)	18,521	49.6
Central American, ex. Mexican	1,451	65.6
Salvadoran	845	57.8
Mexican	15,952	50.4
South American	931	59.1

Foreign-Born Naturalized U.S. Citizens

Group	Number	%
Total Population	10,431	35.3
Hispanic or Latino (of any race)	4,211	22.7
Central American, ex. Mexican	502	34.6
Salvadoran	289	34.2
Mexican	3,167	19.9
South American	405	43.5

Language Spoken at Home: English Only
(Universe: Population 5 Years and Over)

Group	Number	%
Total Population	62,374	61.3
Hispanic or Latino (of any race)	5,468	16.5
Central American, ex. Mexican	182	8.7
Salvadoran	92	6.7
Mexican	3,913	14.1
South American	176	11.9

Language Spoken at Home: Spanish
(Universe: Population 5 Years and Over)

Group	Number	%
Total Population	29,624	29.1
Hispanic or Latino (of any race)	27,629	83.2
Central American, ex. Mexican	1,901	91.3
Salvadoran	1,278	93.3
Mexican	23,870	85.7
South American	1,304	88.1

Unemployment Rate
(Universe: Population 16 Years and Over)

Group	%
Total Population	7.3
Hispanic or Latino (of any race)	6.3
Central American, ex. Mexican	4.3
Salvadoran	4.4
Mexican	6.1
South American	8.0

Class of Worker: Private Wage and Salary
(Universe: Civilian Employed Population 16 Years and Over)

Group	Number	%
Total Population	48,172	80.4
Hispanic or Latino (of any race)	15,799	85.3
Central American, ex. Mexican	1,163	84.0
Salvadoran	660	77.2
Mexican	13,129	86.3
South American	758	74.5

Class of Worker: Government
(Universe: Civilian Employed Population 16 Years and Over)

Group	Number	%
Total Population	5,312	8.9
Hispanic or Latino (of any race)	1,019	5.5
Central American, ex. Mexican	103	7.4
Salvadoran	103	12.0
Mexican	619	4.1
South American	189	18.6

Means of Transportation to Work: Car, Truck or Van
(Universe: Workers 16 Years and Over)

Group	Number	%
Total Population	49,211	84.3
Hispanic or Latino (of any race)	14,436	78.9
Central American, ex. Mexican	1,142	84.0
Salvadoran	743	89.4
Mexican	11,545	77.1
South American	819	80.5

Means of Transportation to Work: Public Transportation (ex. Taxicab)
(Universe: Workers 16 Years and Over)

Group	Number	%
Total Population	1,960	3.4
Hispanic or Latino (of any race)	1,481	8.1
Central American, ex. Mexican	176	12.9
Salvadoran	62	7.5
Mexican	1,236	8.3
South American	69	6.8

Homeownership Rate
(Universe: Occupied Housing Units)

Group	%
Total Population	39.6
Hispanic or Latino (of any race)	20.6
Central American, ex. Mexican	14.6
Guatemalan	16.3
Honduran	13.0
Nicaraguan	32.5
Salvadoran	12.5
Cuban	39.4
Mexican	20.0
Puerto Rican	20.6
South American	32.2
Argentinean	39.8
Colombian	29.5
Ecuadorian	29.1
Peruvian	30.8
Spaniard	36.5

Median Home Value

Group	Dollars
Total Population	644,900
Hispanic or Latino (of any race)	586,200
Central American, ex. Mexican	626,300
Salvadoran	–
Mexican	582,900
South American	580,600

Median Gross Rent

Group	Dollars
Total Population	1,422
Hispanic or Latino (of any race)	1,386
Central American, ex. Mexican	1,399
Salvadoran	1,392
Mexican	1,359
South American	1,621

Median Household Income
(2010 Inflation-Adjusted Dollars)

Group	Dollars
Total Population	64,864
Hispanic or Latino (of any race)	50,100
Central American, ex. Mexican	53,036
Salvadoran	53,143
Mexican	48,094
South American	55,000

Per Capita Income
(2010 Inflation-Adjusted Dollars)

Group	Dollars
Total Population	33,338
Hispanic or Latino (of any race)	16,434
Central American, ex. Mexican	22,095
Salvadoran	18,908
Mexican	14,880
South American	24,847

Households with $100,000+ Income

Group	Number	%
Total Population	11,459	28.6
Hispanic or Latino (of any race)	1,436	16.0
Central American, ex. Mexican	100	17.3
Salvadoran	65	16.8
Mexican	963	13.4
South American	96	18.7

Households with Food Stamps/SNAP Benefits During Past 12 Months

Group	Number	%
Total Population	813	2.0
Hispanic or Latino (of any race)	546	6.1
Central American, ex. Mexican	24	4.1
Salvadoran	24	6.2
Mexican	498	7.0
South American	12	2.3

Poverty Rate
(Income in Past 12 Months Below Poverty Level)

Group	%
Total Population	13.3
Hispanic or Latino (of any race)	22.6
Central American, ex. Mexican	19.0
Salvadoran	26.1
Mexican	24.4
South American	5.9

Covina

Population

Group	Number	%TP[1]	%HP[2]
Total Population	47,796	100.0	–
Hispanic or Latino (of any race)	25,030	52.4	100.0
Central American, ex. Mexican	1,680	3.5	6.7
Guatemalan	424	0.9	1.7
Nicaraguan	256	0.5	1.0
Salvadoran	779	1.6	3.1
Cuban	281	0.6	1.1
Mexican	20,430	42.7	81.6
Puerto Rican	431	0.9	1.7
South American	880	1.8	3.5
Argentinean	145	0.3	0.6
Colombian	184	0.4	0.7
Ecuadorian	186	0.4	0.7
Peruvian	279	0.6	1.1
Spaniard	246	0.5	1.0

Population Growth: 2000–2010

Group	%
Total Population	2.0
Hispanic or Latino (of any race)	32.6
Central American, ex. Mexican	119.9
Guatemalan	124.3
Nicaraguan	103.2
Salvadoran	170.5
Cuban	19.1

Notes: (1) Percent of total population; (2) Percent of Hispanic/Latino population; Profiles include places with an overall population of at least 125,000, OR an overall population of at least 25,000 where the Hispanic/Latino population is at least 20% of the overall population. In states where less than five places meet either of these criteria, we have included places with at least 10,000 total population with the highest percentage of Hispanic/Latino population. These places are identified with an asterisk (*); Please refer to the User's Guide for a full explanation of data.

Mexican	42.1
Puerto Rican	33.4
South American	70.2
Argentinean	33.0
Peruvian	95.1

Males per 100 Females

Group	Number
Total Population	93.3
Hispanic or Latino (of any race)	93.0
Central American, ex. Mexican	88.8
Guatemalan	101.9
Nicaraguan	84.2
Salvadoran	79.1
Cuban	95.1
Mexican	93.5
Puerto Rican	88.2
South American	100.5
Argentinean	126.6
Colombian	85.9
Ecuadorian	95.8
Peruvian	93.8
Spaniard	80.9

Average Household Size

Group	People
Total Population	2.99
Hispanic or Latino (of any race)	3.49
Central American, ex. Mexican	3.57
Guatemalan	3.50
Nicaraguan	3.63
Salvadoran	3.64
Cuban	3.20
Mexican	3.54
Puerto Rican	2.98
South American	3.33
Argentinean	3.10
Colombian	3.12
Ecuadorian	3.79
Peruvian	3.52
Spaniard	2.71

Median Age

Group	Years
Total Population	35.7
Hispanic or Latino (of any race)	29.1
Central American, ex. Mexican	34.7
Guatemalan	34.1
Nicaraguan	35.2
Salvadoran	34.6
Cuban	39.5
Mexican	28.2
Puerto Rican	29.3
South American	36.4
Argentinean	37.6
Colombian	40.0
Ecuadorian	33.5
Peruvian	33.7
Spaniard	40.3

High School Graduates
(Universe: Population 25 Years and Over)

Group	Number	%
Total Population	24,981	84.1
Hispanic or Latino (of any race)	9,660	76.7
Central American, ex. Mexican	707	64.6
Mexican	7,515	76.5
South American	674	89.7

Four-Year College Graduates
(Universe: Population 25 Years and Over)

Group	Number	%
Total Population	6,827	23.0
Hispanic or Latino (of any race)	1,921	15.3
Central American, ex. Mexican	201	18.4
Mexican	1,408	14.3
South American	193	25.7

Population Age 3–17 Enrolled in Public School
(Universe: Population Age 3–17 Enrolled in School)

Group	Number	%
Total Population	8,159	84.1
Hispanic or Latino (of any race)	5,082	88.3
Central American, ex. Mexican	423	97.7
Mexican	4,231	87.9
South American	226	90.0

Population Age 3–17 Enrolled in Private School
(Universe: Population Age 3–17 Enrolled in School)

Group	Number	%
Total Population	1,543	15.9
Hispanic or Latino (of any race)	673	11.7
Central American, ex. Mexican	10	2.3
Mexican	580	12.1
South American	25	10.0

Foreign-Born Population

Group	Number	%
Total Population	10,014	21.1
Hispanic or Latino (of any race)	5,336	22.9
Central American, ex. Mexican	1,110	57.7
Mexican	3,302	17.5
South American	776	70.7

Foreign-Born Naturalized U.S. Citizens

Group	Number	%
Total Population	5,933	59.2
Hispanic or Latino (of any race)	2,638	49.4
Central American, ex. Mexican	432	38.9
Mexican	1,742	52.8
South American	345	44.5

Language Spoken at Home: English Only
(Universe: Population 5 Years and Over)

Group	Number	%
Total Population	26,408	60.2
Hispanic or Latino (of any race)	8,884	42.5
Central American, ex. Mexican	269	15.3
Mexican	7,764	46.3
South American	128	12.0

Language Spoken at Home: Spanish
(Universe: Population 5 Years and Over)

Group	Number	%
Total Population	12,740	29.0
Hispanic or Latino (of any race)	11,983	57.3
Central American, ex. Mexican	1,484	84.2
Mexican	8,989	53.6
South American	942	88.0

Unemployment Rate
(Universe: Population 16 Years and Over)

Group	%
Total Population	11.0
Hispanic or Latino (of any race)	13.4
Central American, ex. Mexican	14.7
Mexican	14.0
South American	1.8

Class of Worker: Private Wage and Salary
(Universe: Civilian Employed Population 16 Years and Over)

Group	Number	%
Total Population	16,467	74.8
Hispanic or Latino (of any race)	7,472	73.0
Central American, ex. Mexican	442	65.0
Mexican	6,205	73.6
South American	283	64.5

Class of Worker: Government
(Universe: Civilian Employed Population 16 Years and Over)

Group	Number	%
Total Population	3,908	17.7
Hispanic or Latino (of any race)	1,906	18.6
Central American, ex. Mexican	110	16.2
Mexican	1,607	19.1
South American	69	15.7

Means of Transportation to Work: Car, Truck or Van
(Universe: Workers 16 Years and Over)

Group	Number	%
Total Population	19,581	91.7
Hispanic or Latino (of any race)	9,059	92.3
Central American, ex. Mexican	603	95.4
Mexican	7,423	92.0
South American	414	96.5

Means of Transportation to Work: Public Transportation (ex. Taxicab)
(Universe: Workers 16 Years and Over)

Group	Number	%
Total Population	812	3.8
Hispanic or Latino (of any race)	274	2.8
Central American, ex. Mexican	0	0.0
Mexican	256	3.2
South American	6	1.4

Homeownership Rate
(Universe: Occupied Housing Units)

Group	%
Total Population	58.4
Hispanic or Latino (of any race)	50.8
Central American, ex. Mexican	51.8
Guatemalan	52.9
Nicaraguan	47.4
Salvadoran	51.0
Cuban	57.1
Mexican	50.7
Puerto Rican	42.0
South American	50.5
Argentinean	38.3
Colombian	61.0
Ecuadorian	74.1
Peruvian	35.8
Spaniard	60.8

Median Home Value

Group	Dollars
Total Population	446,600
Hispanic or Latino (of any race)	428,400
Central American, ex. Mexican	383,500
Mexican	438,100
South American	495,600

Median Gross Rent

Group	Dollars
Total Population	1,176
Hispanic or Latino (of any race)	1,169
Central American, ex. Mexican	1,699
Mexican	1,152
South American	1,372

Median Household Income
(2010 Inflation-Adjusted Dollars)

Group	Dollars
Total Population	64,141
Hispanic or Latino (of any race)	63,993
Central American, ex. Mexican	76,500
Mexican	64,881
South American	49,148

Per Capita Income
(2010 Inflation-Adjusted Dollars)

Group	Dollars
Total Population	24,713
Hispanic or Latino (of any race)	20,207
Central American, ex. Mexican	16,826
Mexican	20,419
South American	19,677

Households with $100,000+ Income

Group	Number	%
Total Population	3,948	25.9
Hispanic or Latino (of any race)	1,512	24.1
Central American, ex. Mexican	67	14.6
Mexican	1,306	25.8
South American	74	20.4

Households with Food Stamps/SNAP Benefits During Past 12 Months

Group	Number	%
Total Population	429	2.8
Hispanic or Latino (of any race)	307	4.9
Central American, ex. Mexican	0	0.0
Mexican	282	5.6
South American	0	0.0

Poverty Rate
(Income in Past 12 Months Below Poverty Level)

Group	%
Total Population	10.7
Hispanic or Latino (of any race)	12.3

Notes: (1) Percent of total population; (2) Percent of Hispanic/Latino population; Profiles include places with an overall population of at least 125,000, OR an overall population of at least 25,000 where the Hispanic/Latino population is at least 20% of the overall population. In states where less than five places meet either of these criteria, we have included places with at least 10,000 total population with the highest percentage of Hispanic/Latino population. These places are identified with an asterisk (*); Please refer to the User's Guide for a full explanation of data.

Central American, ex. Mexican	8.8
Mexican	12.9
South American	20.3

Culver City

Population

Group	Number	%TP[1]	%HP[2]
Total Population	38,883	100.0	–
Hispanic or Latino (of any race)	9,025	23.2	100.0
Central American, ex. Mexican	1,047	2.7	11.6
Guatemalan	276	0.7	3.1
Honduran	100	0.3	1.1
Salvadoran	479	1.2	5.3
Cuban	414	1.1	4.6
Mexican	6,004	15.4	66.5
Puerto Rican	159	0.4	1.8
South American	699	1.8	7.7
Argentinean	190	0.5	2.1
Colombian	150	0.4	1.7
Peruvian	112	0.3	1.2
Spaniard	200	0.5	2.2

Population Growth: 2000–2010

Group	%
Total Population	0.2
Hispanic or Latino (of any race)	-1.9
Central American, ex. Mexican	26.4
Guatemalan	17.4
Salvadoran	30.5
Cuban	-6.8
Mexican	4.6
Puerto Rican	19.5
South American	50.6
Argentinean	46.2

Males per 100 Females

Group	Number
Total Population	89.1
Hispanic or Latino (of any race)	91.4
Central American, ex. Mexican	80.5
Guatemalan	79.2
Honduran	75.4
Salvadoran	84.2
Cuban	81.6
Mexican	95.7
Puerto Rican	93.9
South American	83.0
Argentinean	79.2
Colombian	56.3
Peruvian	86.7
Spaniard	75.4

Average Household Size

Group	People
Total Population	2.30
Hispanic or Latino (of any race)	3.01
Central American, ex. Mexican	2.99
Guatemalan	3.20
Honduran	3.13
Salvadoran	3.02
Cuban	2.31
Mexican	3.24
Puerto Rican	2.44
South American	2.56
Argentinean	2.36
Colombian	2.55
Peruvian	2.67
Spaniard	2.36

Median Age

Group	Years
Total Population	40.5
Hispanic or Latino (of any race)	34.1
Central American, ex. Mexican	38.2
Guatemalan	37.8
Honduran	38.0
Salvadoran	39.6
Cuban	48.1
Mexican	32.1
Puerto Rican	33.2
South American	40.7
Argentinean	45.8
Colombian	42.5
Peruvian	42.0
Spaniard	43.3

High School Graduates

(Universe: Population 25 Years and Over)

Group	Number	%
Total Population	26,030	90.8
Hispanic or Latino (of any race)	3,923	71.5
Central American, ex. Mexican	445	65.5
Mexican	2,263	64.0

Four-Year College Graduates

(Universe: Population 25 Years and Over)

Group	Number	%
Total Population	14,852	51.8
Hispanic or Latino (of any race)	1,496	27.3
Central American, ex. Mexican	193	28.4
Mexican	817	23.1

Population Age 3–17 Enrolled in Public School

(Universe: Population Age 3–17 Enrolled in School)

Group	Number	%
Total Population	4,944	82.2
Hispanic or Latino (of any race)	1,886	88.0
Central American, ex. Mexican	158	75.6
Mexican	1,365	89.3

Population Age 3–17 Enrolled in Private School

(Universe: Population Age 3–17 Enrolled in School)

Group	Number	%
Total Population	1,071	17.8
Hispanic or Latino (of any race)	258	12.0
Central American, ex. Mexican	51	24.4
Mexican	164	10.7

Foreign-Born Population

Group	Number	%
Total Population	9,988	25.7
Hispanic or Latino (of any race)	3,560	39.0
Central American, ex. Mexican	517	51.3
Mexican	2,247	36.0

Foreign-Born Naturalized U.S. Citizens

Group	Number	%
Total Population	6,260	62.7
Hispanic or Latino (of any race)	1,986	55.8
Central American, ex. Mexican	297	57.4
Mexican	919	40.9

Language Spoken at Home: English Only

(Universe: Population 5 Years and Over)

Group	Number	%
Total Population	23,089	63.1
Hispanic or Latino (of any race)	1,663	20.1
Central American, ex. Mexican	69	6.9
Mexican	1,185	21.5

Language Spoken at Home: Spanish

(Universe: Population 5 Years and Over)

Group	Number	%
Total Population	7,577	20.7
Hispanic or Latino (of any race)	6,446	77.8
Central American, ex. Mexican	925	93.1
Mexican	4,196	76.3

Unemployment Rate

(Universe: Population 16 Years and Over)

Group	%
Total Population	6.4
Hispanic or Latino (of any race)	6.4
Central American, ex. Mexican	0.0
Mexican	7.9

Class of Worker: Private Wage and Salary

(Universe: Civilian Employed Population 16 Years and Over)

Group	Number	%
Total Population	15,064	71.8
Hispanic or Latino (of any race)	3,075	73.5
Central American, ex. Mexican	481	81.0
Mexican	2,094	75.7

Class of Worker: Government

(Universe: Civilian Employed Population 16 Years and Over)

Group	Number	%
Total Population	3,156	15.0
Hispanic or Latino (of any race)	651	15.6
Central American, ex. Mexican	93	15.7
Mexican	327	11.8

Means of Transportation to Work: Car, Truck or Van

(Universe: Workers 16 Years and Over)

Group	Number	%
Total Population	17,602	86.1
Hispanic or Latino (of any race)	3,322	83.5
Central American, ex. Mexican	431	79.1
Mexican	2,181	82.3

Means of Transportation to Work: Public Transportation (ex. Taxicab)

(Universe: Workers 16 Years and Over)

Group	Number	%
Total Population	714	3.5
Hispanic or Latino (of any race)	303	7.6
Central American, ex. Mexican	21	3.9
Mexican	282	10.6

Homeownership Rate

(Universe: Occupied Housing Units)

Group	%
Total Population	54.3
Hispanic or Latino (of any race)	40.4
Central American, ex. Mexican	35.5
Guatemalan	34.8
Honduran	22.6
Salvadoran	37.7
Cuban	46.2
Mexican	38.2
Puerto Rican	47.1
South American	48.4
Argentinean	52.9
Colombian	54.7
Peruvian	44.2
Spaniard	64.0

Median Home Value

Group	Dollars
Total Population	618,600
Hispanic or Latino (of any race)	564,400
Central American, ex. Mexican	531,300
Mexican	567,800

Median Gross Rent

Group	Dollars
Total Population	1,394
Hispanic or Latino (of any race)	1,146
Central American, ex. Mexican	1,074
Mexican	1,160

Median Household Income

(2010 Inflation-Adjusted Dollars)

Group	Dollars
Total Population	72,199
Hispanic or Latino (of any race)	54,308
Central American, ex. Mexican	61,691
Mexican	44,121

Per Capita Income

(2010 Inflation-Adjusted Dollars)

Group	Dollars
Total Population	40,523
Hispanic or Latino (of any race)	21,504
Central American, ex. Mexican	26,205
Mexican	18,635

Households with $100,000+ Income

Group	Number	%
Total Population	5,863	34.8
Hispanic or Latino (of any race)	545	18.1
Central American, ex. Mexican	68	21.4
Mexican	249	13.5

Households with Food Stamps/SNAP Benefits During Past 12 Months

Group	Number	%
Total Population	158	0.9
Hispanic or Latino (of any race)	86	2.9
Central American, ex. Mexican	0	0.0
Mexican	86	4.7

Notes: (1) Percent of total population; (2) Percent of Hispanic/Latino population; Profiles include places with an overall population of at least 125,000, OR an overall population of at least 25,000 where the Hispanic/Latino population is at least 20% of the overall population. In states where less than five places meet either of these criteria, we have included places with at least 10,000 total population with the highest percentage of Hispanic/Latino population. These places are identified with an asterisk (*); Please refer to the User's Guide for a full explanation of data.

Poverty Rate
(Income in Past 12 Months Below Poverty Level)

Group	%
Total Population	7.2
Hispanic or Latino (of any race)	13.3
Central American, ex. Mexican	1.9
Mexican	17.6

Daly City

Population

Group	Number	%TP[1]	%HP[2]
Total Population	101,123	100.0	–
Hispanic or Latino (of any race)	23,929	23.7	100.0
Central American, ex. Mexican	9,813	9.7	41.0
Guatemalan	1,363	1.3	5.7
Honduran	479	0.5	2.0
Nicaraguan	2,764	2.7	11.6
Salvadoran	5,000	4.9	20.9
Cuban	131	0.1	0.5
Mexican	9,535	9.4	39.8
Puerto Rican	684	0.7	2.9
South American	1,233	1.2	5.2
Colombian	143	0.1	0.6
Peruvian	738	0.7	3.1
Spaniard	382	0.4	1.6

Population Growth: 2000–2010

Group	%
Total Population	2.4
Hispanic or Latino (of any race)	3.7
Central American, ex. Mexican	52.7
Guatemalan	155.7
Honduran	365.0
Nicaraguan	34.7
Salvadoran	72.7
Cuban	12.9
Mexican	10.2
Puerto Rican	3.3
South American	34.3
Colombian	32.4
Peruvian	48.8

Males per 100 Females

Group	Number
Total Population	97.5
Hispanic or Latino (of any race)	101.1
Central American, ex. Mexican	96.6
Guatemalan	114.3
Honduran	109.2
Nicaraguan	85.9
Salvadoran	97.5
Cuban	79.5
Mexican	108.7
Puerto Rican	98.8
South American	89.7
Colombian	83.3
Peruvian	85.4
Spaniard	96.9

Average Household Size

Group	People
Total Population	3.23
Hispanic or Latino (of any race)	3.59
Central American, ex. Mexican	3.81
Guatemalan	4.30
Honduran	4.41
Nicaraguan	3.58
Salvadoran	3.83
Cuban	2.60
Mexican	3.69
Puerto Rican	2.86
South American	3.15
Colombian	2.72
Peruvian	3.32
Spaniard	2.40

Median Age

Group	Years
Total Population	38.3
Hispanic or Latino (of any race)	31.7
Central American, ex. Mexican	34.3
Guatemalan	32.5
Honduran	30.0
Nicaraguan	36.3
Salvadoran	34.7
Cuban	37.5
Mexican	28.8
Puerto Rican	30.4
South American	37.4
Colombian	40.3
Peruvian	37.4
Spaniard	47.8

High School Graduates
(Universe: Population 25 Years and Over)

Group	Number	%
Total Population	60,238	86.3
Hispanic or Latino (of any race)	11,390	75.6
Central American, ex. Mexican	4,784	78.4
Nicaraguan	2,445	86.3
Salvadoran	1,589	72.2
Mexican	3,992	66.4
South American	1,132	85.2

Four-Year College Graduates
(Universe: Population 25 Years and Over)

Group	Number	%
Total Population	23,725	34.0
Hispanic or Latino (of any race)	2,064	13.7
Central American, ex. Mexican	820	13.4
Nicaraguan	530	18.7
Salvadoran	224	10.2
Mexican	701	11.7
South American	334	25.2

Population Age 3–17 Enrolled in Public School
(Universe: Population Age 3–17 Enrolled in School)

Group	Number	%
Total Population	11,227	76.6
Hispanic or Latino (of any race)	3,368	81.5
Central American, ex. Mexican	1,201	84.3
Nicaraguan	600	85.7
Salvadoran	433	80.3
Mexican	1,384	77.7
South American	307	100.0

Population Age 3–17 Enrolled in Private School
(Universe: Population Age 3–17 Enrolled in School)

Group	Number	%
Total Population	3,430	23.4
Hispanic or Latino (of any race)	766	18.5
Central American, ex. Mexican	224	15.7
Nicaraguan	100	14.3
Salvadoran	106	19.7
Mexican	398	22.3
South American	0	0.0

Foreign-Born Population

Group	Number	%
Total Population	52,800	52.9
Hispanic or Latino (of any race)	11,854	49.3
Central American, ex. Mexican	5,650	62.1
Nicaraguan	2,402	58.6
Salvadoran	2,229	62.8
Mexican	4,453	43.7
South American	1,241	67.4

Foreign-Born Naturalized U.S. Citizens

Group	Number	%
Total Population	34,201	64.8
Hispanic or Latino (of any race)	5,507	46.5
Central American, ex. Mexican	3,328	58.9
Nicaraguan	1,618	67.4
Salvadoran	1,204	54.0
Mexican	1,126	25.3
South American	686	55.3

Language Spoken at Home: English Only
(Universe: Population 5 Years and Over)

Group	Number	%
Total Population	29,576	31.3
Hispanic or Latino (of any race)	4,693	21.1
Central American, ex. Mexican	796	9.5
Nicaraguan	397	10.3
Salvadoran	296	9.3
Mexican	2,182	23.4
South American	213	11.9

Language Spoken at Home: Spanish
(Universe: Population 5 Years and Over)

Group	Number	%
Total Population	17,905	19.0
Hispanic or Latino (of any race)	17,158	77.0
Central American, ex. Mexican	7,508	89.7
Nicaraguan	3,393	88.5
Salvadoran	2,888	90.4
Mexican	6,891	74.0
South American	1,570	87.4

Unemployment Rate
(Universe: Population 16 Years and Over)

Group	%
Total Population	8.7
Hispanic or Latino (of any race)	8.5
Central American, ex. Mexican	8.2
Nicaraguan	9.7
Salvadoran	8.3
Mexican	9.4
South American	1.7

Class of Worker: Private Wage and Salary
(Universe: Civilian Employed Population 16 Years and Over)

Group	Number	%
Total Population	39,834	77.4
Hispanic or Latino (of any race)	9,601	79.4
Central American, ex. Mexican	3,703	78.4
Nicaraguan	1,572	74.5
Salvadoran	1,548	83.8
Mexican	4,200	83.2
South American	752	68.2

Class of Worker: Government
(Universe: Civilian Employed Population 16 Years and Over)

Group	Number	%
Total Population	8,583	16.7
Hispanic or Latino (of any race)	1,492	12.3
Central American, ex. Mexican	718	15.2
Nicaraguan	424	20.1
Salvadoran	217	11.7
Mexican	488	9.7
South American	100	9.1

Means of Transportation to Work: Car, Truck or Van
(Universe: Workers 16 Years and Over)

Group	Number	%
Total Population	37,091	74.6
Hispanic or Latino (of any race)	7,801	67.1
Central American, ex. Mexican	3,382	72.6
Nicaraguan	1,582	75.1
Salvadoran	1,360	76.1
Mexican	2,948	60.6
South American	618	63.4

Means of Transportation to Work: Public Transportation (ex. Taxicab)
(Universe: Workers 16 Years and Over)

Group	Number	%
Total Population	9,813	19.7
Hispanic or Latino (of any race)	2,775	23.9
Central American, ex. Mexican	1,055	22.7
Nicaraguan	432	20.5
Salvadoran	324	18.1
Mexican	1,230	25.3
South American	251	25.7

Homeownership Rate
(Universe: Occupied Housing Units)

Group	%
Total Population	56.5
Hispanic or Latino (of any race)	39.2
Central American, ex. Mexican	35.8
Guatemalan	32.1
Honduran	17.5
Nicaraguan	37.4
Salvadoran	37.2
Cuban	45.5
Mexican	41.8
Puerto Rican	40.3
South American	42.5
Colombian	40.4
Peruvian	38.8
Spaniard	63.1

Notes: (1) Percent of total population; (2) Percent of Hispanic/Latino population; Profiles include places with an overall population of at least 125,000, OR an overall population of at least 25,000 where the Hispanic/Latino population is at least 20% of the overall population. In states where less than five places meet either of these criteria, we have included places with at least 10,000 total population with the highest percentage of Hispanic/Latino population. These places are identified with an asterisk (*); Please refer to the User's Guide for a full explanation of data.

Median Home Value	
Group	Dollars
Total Population	611,200
Hispanic or Latino (of any race)	600,400
Central American, ex. Mexican	625,500
Nicaraguan	660,300
Salvadoran	653,300
Mexican	571,600
South American	686,500

Median Gross Rent	
Group	Dollars
Total Population	1,396
Hispanic or Latino (of any race)	1,434
Central American, ex. Mexican	1,458
Nicaraguan	1,424
Salvadoran	1,608
Mexican	1,292
South American	1,581

Median Household Income (2010 Inflation-Adjusted Dollars)	
Group	Dollars
Total Population	74,987
Hispanic or Latino (of any race)	65,549
Central American, ex. Mexican	64,612
Nicaraguan	69,250
Salvadoran	57,759
Mexican	65,395
South American	72,833

Per Capita Income (2010 Inflation-Adjusted Dollars)	
Group	Dollars
Total Population	27,731
Hispanic or Latino (of any race)	21,818
Central American, ex. Mexican	23,025
Nicaraguan	24,086
Salvadoran	22,094
Mexican	20,282
South American	22,907

Households with $100,000+ Income		
Group	Number	%
Total Population	10,516	34.3
Hispanic or Latino (of any race)	1,762	25.9
Central American, ex. Mexican	617	21.1
Nicaraguan	272	21.5
Salvadoran	243	23.0
Mexican	673	26.7
South American	177	34.8

Households with Food Stamps/SNAP Benefits During Past 12 Months		
Group	Number	%
Total Population	675	2.2
Hispanic or Latino (of any race)	155	2.3
Central American, ex. Mexican	37	1.3
Nicaraguan	32	2.5
Salvadoran	5	0.5
Mexican	81	3.2
South American	0	0.0

Poverty Rate (Income in Past 12 Months Below Poverty Level)	
Group	%
Total Population	7.0
Hispanic or Latino (of any race)	8.3
Central American, ex. Mexican	4.7
Nicaraguan	2.3
Salvadoran	2.6
Mexican	10.0
South American	14.3

Delano

Population			
Group	Number	%TP[1]	%HP[2]
Total Population	53,041	100.0	–
Hispanic or Latino (of any race)	37,913	71.5	100.0
Central American, ex. Mexican	427	0.8	1.1
Guatemalan	121	0.2	0.3
Salvadoran	238	0.4	0.6
Mexican	34,658	65.3	91.4
Puerto Rican	197	0.4	0.5
Spaniard	109	0.2	0.3

Population Growth: 2000–2010	
Group	%
Total Population	36.6
Hispanic or Latino (of any race)	42.6
Central American, ex. Mexican	113.5
Salvadoran	108.8
Mexican	47.9
Puerto Rican	18.7

Males per 100 Females	
Group	Number
Total Population	149.1
Hispanic or Latino (of any race)	128.1
Central American, ex. Mexican	109.3
Guatemalan	120.0
Salvadoran	88.9
Mexican	125.5
Puerto Rican	116.5
Spaniard	127.1

Average Household Size	
Group	People
Total Population	4.11
Hispanic or Latino (of any race)	4.28
Central American, ex. Mexican	4.42
Guatemalan	5.03
Salvadoran	4.23
Mexican	4.29
Puerto Rican	3.46
Spaniard	4.66

Median Age	
Group	Years
Total Population	28.5
Hispanic or Latino (of any race)	25.8
Central American, ex. Mexican	32.1
Guatemalan	27.5
Salvadoran	33.0
Mexican	25.6
Puerto Rican	32.8
Spaniard	36.3

High School Graduates (Universe: Population 25 Years and Over)		
Group	Number	%
Total Population	15,075	50.6
Hispanic or Latino (of any race)	8,106	42.2
Central American, ex. Mexican	227	65.6
Mexican	7,536	41.4

Four-Year College Graduates (Universe: Population 25 Years and Over)		
Group	Number	%
Total Population	1,728	5.8
Hispanic or Latino (of any race)	526	2.7
Central American, ex. Mexican	44	12.7
Mexican	468	2.6

Population Age 3–17 Enrolled in Public School (Universe: Population Age 3–17 Enrolled in School)		
Group	Number	%
Total Population	11,284	98.4
Hispanic or Latino (of any race)	9,344	98.8
Central American, ex. Mexican	97	100.0
Mexican	8,959	99.1

Population Age 3–17 Enrolled in Private School (Universe: Population Age 3–17 Enrolled in School)		
Group	Number	%
Total Population	178	1.6
Hispanic or Latino (of any race)	113	1.2
Central American, ex. Mexican	0	0.0
Mexican	84	0.9

Foreign-Born Population		
Group	Number	%
Total Population	19,176	37.4
Hispanic or Latino (of any race)	14,044	38.4
Central American, ex. Mexican	434	61.9
Mexican	13,469	38.8

Foreign-Born Naturalized U.S. Citizens		
Group	Number	%
Total Population	5,510	28.7
Hispanic or Latino (of any race)	2,933	20.9
Central American, ex. Mexican	43	9.9
Mexican	2,856	21.2

Language Spoken at Home: English Only (Universe: Population 5 Years and Over)		
Group	Number	%
Total Population	13,173	27.9
Hispanic or Latino (of any race)	5,447	16.5
Central American, ex. Mexican	10	1.5
Mexican	5,059	16.2

Language Spoken at Home: Spanish (Universe: Population 5 Years and Over)		
Group	Number	%
Total Population	27,942	59.3
Hispanic or Latino (of any race)	27,564	83.4
Central American, ex. Mexican	648	98.5
Mexican	26,200	83.7

Unemployment Rate (Universe: Population 16 Years and Over)	
Group	%
Total Population	13.3
Hispanic or Latino (of any race)	11.5
Central American, ex. Mexican	19.0
Mexican	11.4

Class of Worker: Private Wage and Salary (Universe: Civilian Employed Population 16 Years and Over)		
Group	Number	%
Total Population	12,392	80.8
Hispanic or Latino (of any race)	9,933	82.2
Central American, ex. Mexican	152	88.9
Mexican	9,496	81.9

Class of Worker: Government (Universe: Civilian Employed Population 16 Years and Over)		
Group	Number	%
Total Population	2,321	15.1
Hispanic or Latino (of any race)	1,681	13.9
Central American, ex. Mexican	0	0.0
Mexican	1,646	14.2

Means of Transportation to Work: Car, Truck or Van (Universe: Workers 16 Years and Over)		
Group	Number	%
Total Population	14,014	94.4
Hispanic or Latino (of any race)	11,072	94.1
Central American, ex. Mexican	149	90.3
Mexican	10,613	94.1

Means of Transportation to Work: Public Transportation (ex. Taxicab) (Universe: Workers 16 Years and Over)		
Group	Number	%
Total Population	95	0.6
Hispanic or Latino (of any race)	95	0.8
Central American, ex. Mexican	0	0.0
Mexican	95	0.8

Homeownership Rate (Universe: Occupied Housing Units)	
Group	%
Total Population	56.2
Hispanic or Latino (of any race)	53.2
Central American, ex. Mexican	44.1
Guatemalan	50.0
Salvadoran	40.6
Mexican	54.7
Puerto Rican	33.8
Spaniard	63.2

Median Home Value	
Group	Dollars
Total Population	184,300
Hispanic or Latino (of any race)	177,100
Central American, ex. Mexican	221,400
Mexican	174,800

Notes: (1) Percent of total population; (2) Percent of Hispanic/Latino population; Profiles include places with an overall population of at least 125,000, OR an overall population of at least 25,000 where the Hispanic/Latino population is at least 20% of the overall population. In states where less than five places meet either of these criteria, we have included places with at least 10,000 total population with the highest percentage of Hispanic/Latino population. These places are identified with an asterisk (*); Please refer to the User's Guide for a full explanation of data.

Median Gross Rent

Group	Dollars
Total Population	690
Hispanic or Latino (of any race)	674
Central American, ex. Mexican	957
Mexican	664

Median Household Income
(2010 Inflation-Adjusted Dollars)

Group	Dollars
Total Population	35,673
Hispanic or Latino (of any race)	33,686
Central American, ex. Mexican	31,773
Mexican	33,462

Per Capita Income
(2010 Inflation-Adjusted Dollars)

Group	Dollars
Total Population	10,739
Hispanic or Latino (of any race)	10,223
Central American, ex. Mexican	9,156
Mexican	10,255

Households with $100,000+ Income

Group	Number	%
Total Population	839	8.3
Hispanic or Latino (of any race)	441	5.8
Central American, ex. Mexican	0	0.0
Mexican	410	5.7

Households with Food Stamps/SNAP Benefits During Past 12 Months

Group	Number	%
Total Population	1,512	14.9
Hispanic or Latino (of any race)	1,242	16.4
Central American, ex. Mexican	50	28.6
Mexican	1,165	16.1

Poverty Rate
(Income in Past 12 Months Below Poverty Level)

Group	%
Total Population	27.7
Hispanic or Latino (of any race)	29.9
Central American, ex. Mexican	23.0
Mexican	30.5

Desert Hot Springs

Population

Group	Number	%TP[1]	%HP[2]
Total Population	25,938	100.0	–
Hispanic or Latino (of any race)	13,646	52.6	100.0
Central American, ex. Mexican	789	3.0	5.8
Guatemalan	303	1.2	2.2
Salvadoran	373	1.4	2.7
Mexican	11,775	45.4	86.3
Puerto Rican	161	0.6	1.2

Population Growth: 2000–2010

Group	%
Total Population	56.4
Hispanic or Latino (of any race)	103.7
Central American, ex. Mexican	277.5
Mexican	112.7

Males per 100 Females

Group	Number
Total Population	100.3
Hispanic or Latino (of any race)	99.5
Central American, ex. Mexican	100.8
Guatemalan	116.4
Salvadoran	97.4
Mexican	99.1
Puerto Rican	109.1

Average Household Size

Group	People
Total Population	2.98
Hispanic or Latino (of any race)	3.92
Central American, ex. Mexican	4.18
Guatemalan	4.25
Salvadoran	4.42
Mexican	3.99
Puerto Rican	2.76

Median Age

Group	Years
Total Population	31.0
Hispanic or Latino (of any race)	23.2
Central American, ex. Mexican	30.2
Guatemalan	28.7
Salvadoran	31.1
Mexican	22.3
Puerto Rican	28.6

High School Graduates
(Universe: Population 25 Years and Over)

Group	Number	%
Total Population	10,021	72.6
Hispanic or Latino (of any race)	2,747	50.5
Central American, ex. Mexican	353	51.5
Mexican	2,133	48.3

Four-Year College Graduates
(Universe: Population 25 Years and Over)

Group	Number	%
Total Population	1,748	12.7
Hispanic or Latino (of any race)	258	4.7
Central American, ex. Mexican	121	17.7
Mexican	88	2.0

Population Age 3–17 Enrolled in Public School
(Universe: Population Age 3–17 Enrolled in School)

Group	Number	%
Total Population	5,694	97.8
Hispanic or Latino (of any race)	3,789	98.2
Central American, ex. Mexican	420	100.0
Mexican	3,243	97.9

Population Age 3–17 Enrolled in Private School
(Universe: Population Age 3–17 Enrolled in School)

Group	Number	%
Total Population	130	2.2
Hispanic or Latino (of any race)	70	1.8
Central American, ex. Mexican	0	0.0
Mexican	70	2.1

Foreign-Born Population

Group	Number	%
Total Population	5,596	22.7
Hispanic or Latino (of any race)	4,639	37.3
Central American, ex. Mexican	893	63.0
Mexican	3,663	35.0

Foreign-Born Naturalized U.S. Citizens

Group	Number	%
Total Population	2,144	38.3
Hispanic or Latino (of any race)	1,511	32.6
Central American, ex. Mexican	158	17.7
Mexican	1,307	35.7

Language Spoken at Home: English Only
(Universe: Population 5 Years and Over)

Group	Number	%
Total Population	12,907	57.4
Hispanic or Latino (of any race)	2,549	23.2
Central American, ex. Mexican	50	4.0
Mexican	2,275	24.7

Language Spoken at Home: Spanish
(Universe: Population 5 Years and Over)

Group	Number	%
Total Population	8,751	38.9
Hispanic or Latino (of any race)	8,448	76.8
Central American, ex. Mexican	1,202	96.0
Mexican	6,927	75.3

Unemployment Rate
(Universe: Population 16 Years and Over)

Group	%
Total Population	16.1
Hispanic or Latino (of any race)	16.1
Central American, ex. Mexican	9.9
Mexican	16.8

Class of Worker: Private Wage and Salary
(Universe: Civilian Employed Population 16 Years and Over)

Group	Number	%
Total Population	6,997	77.8
Hispanic or Latino (of any race)	3,555	80.4
Central American, ex. Mexican	563	88.7
Mexican	2,843	79.0

Class of Worker: Government
(Universe: Civilian Employed Population 16 Years and Over)

Group	Number	%
Total Population	816	9.1
Hispanic or Latino (of any race)	240	5.4
Central American, ex. Mexican	0	0.0
Mexican	221	6.1

Means of Transportation to Work: Car, Truck or Van
(Universe: Workers 16 Years and Over)

Group	Number	%
Total Population	7,937	90.4
Hispanic or Latino (of any race)	3,973	92.0
Central American, ex. Mexican	520	83.2
Mexican	3,276	93.4

Means of Transportation to Work: Public Transportation (ex. Taxicab)
(Universe: Workers 16 Years and Over)

Group	Number	%
Total Population	133	1.5
Hispanic or Latino (of any race)	45	1.0
Central American, ex. Mexican	0	0.0
Mexican	45	1.3

Homeownership Rate
(Universe: Occupied Housing Units)

Group	%
Total Population	48.2
Hispanic or Latino (of any race)	40.8
Central American, ex. Mexican	52.6
Guatemalan	42.4
Salvadoran	65.1
Mexican	40.0
Puerto Rican	32.3

Median Home Value

Group	Dollars
Total Population	202,000
Hispanic or Latino (of any race)	182,900
Central American, ex. Mexican	79,100
Mexican	185,300

Median Gross Rent

Group	Dollars
Total Population	870
Hispanic or Latino (of any race)	930
Central American, ex. Mexican	946
Mexican	917

Median Household Income
(2010 Inflation-Adjusted Dollars)

Group	Dollars
Total Population	36,326
Hispanic or Latino (of any race)	36,414
Central American, ex. Mexican	38,125
Mexican	36,689

Per Capita Income
(2010 Inflation-Adjusted Dollars)

Group	Dollars
Total Population	15,901
Hispanic or Latino (of any race)	11,553
Central American, ex. Mexican	10,115
Mexican	11,280

Households with $100,000+ Income

Group	Number	%
Total Population	841	10.4
Hispanic or Latino (of any race)	156	5.2
Central American, ex. Mexican	12	3.5
Mexican	113	4.7

Households with Food Stamps/SNAP Benefits During Past 12 Months

Group	Number	%
Total Population	804	9.9
Hispanic or Latino (of any race)	436	14.5
Central American, ex. Mexican	11	3.2
Mexican	388	16.0

Notes: (1) Percent of total population; (2) Percent of Hispanic/Latino population; Profiles include places with an overall population of at least 125,000, OR an overall population of at least 25,000 where the Hispanic/Latino population is at least 20% of the overall population. In states where less than five places meet either of these criteria, we have included places with at least 10,000 total population with the highest percentage of Hispanic/Latino population. These places are identified with an asterisk (*); Please refer to the User's Guide for a full explanation of data.

Poverty Rate
(Income in Past 12 Months Below Poverty Level)

Group	%
Total Population	24.9
Hispanic or Latino (of any race)	23.0
Central American, ex. Mexican	11.4
Mexican	25.1

Diamond Bar

Population

Group	Number	%TP[1]	%HP[2]
Total Population	55,544	100.0	–
Hispanic or Latino (of any race)	11,138	20.1	100.0
Central American, ex. Mexican	675	1.2	6.1
Guatemalan	174	0.3	1.6
Nicaraguan	118	0.2	1.1
Salvadoran	255	0.5	2.3
Cuban	193	0.3	1.7
Mexican	8,766	15.8	78.7
Puerto Rican	185	0.3	1.7
South American	640	1.2	5.7
Colombian	163	0.3	1.5
Ecuadorian	120	0.2	1.1
Peruvian	174	0.3	1.6
Spaniard	133	0.2	1.2

Population Growth: 2000–2010

Group	%
Total Population	-1.3
Hispanic or Latino (of any race)	7.2
Central American, ex. Mexican	87.0
Salvadoran	110.7
Cuban	-15.4
Mexican	15.6
Puerto Rican	-6.1
South American	30.3
Colombian	17.3

Males per 100 Females

Group	Number
Total Population	95.2
Hispanic or Latino (of any race)	92.8
Central American, ex. Mexican	102.1
Guatemalan	102.3
Nicaraguan	96.7
Salvadoran	97.7
Cuban	87.4
Mexican	92.3
Puerto Rican	120.2
South American	81.8
Colombian	91.8
Ecuadorian	87.5
Peruvian	70.6
Spaniard	82.2

Average Household Size

Group	People
Total Population	3.10
Hispanic or Latino (of any race)	3.41
Central American, ex. Mexican	3.72
Guatemalan	4.13
Nicaraguan	3.47
Salvadoran	3.85
Cuban	2.85
Mexican	3.44
Puerto Rican	3.29
South American	3.28
Colombian	3.35
Ecuadorian	3.53
Peruvian	3.28
Spaniard	2.62

Median Age

Group	Years
Total Population	41.0
Hispanic or Latino (of any race)	33.7
Central American, ex. Mexican	38.0
Guatemalan	38.3
Nicaraguan	38.3
Salvadoran	35.3
Cuban	39.9
Mexican	32.6
Puerto Rican	34.5
South American	40.9
Colombian	44.3
Ecuadorian	39.0
Peruvian	39.7
Spaniard	49.5

High School Graduates
(Universe: Population 25 Years and Over)

Group	Number	%
Total Population	35,526	92.5
Hispanic or Latino (of any race)	5,748	85.6
Mexican	4,593	85.9

Four-Year College Graduates
(Universe: Population 25 Years and Over)

Group	Number	%
Total Population	18,364	47.8
Hispanic or Latino (of any race)	1,582	23.6
Mexican	1,196	22.4

Population Age 3–17 Enrolled in Public School
(Universe: Population Age 3–17 Enrolled in School)

Group	Number	%
Total Population	9,160	89.0
Hispanic or Latino (of any race)	1,986	85.2
Mexican	1,681	84.7

Population Age 3–17 Enrolled in Private School
(Universe: Population Age 3–17 Enrolled in School)

Group	Number	%
Total Population	1,134	11.0
Hispanic or Latino (of any race)	346	14.8
Mexican	304	15.3

Foreign-Born Population

Group	Number	%
Total Population	23,371	42.0
Hispanic or Latino (of any race)	2,186	20.5
Mexican	1,505	17.5

Foreign-Born Naturalized U.S. Citizens

Group	Number	%
Total Population	15,829	67.7
Hispanic or Latino (of any race)	1,698	77.7
Mexican	1,206	80.1

Language Spoken at Home: English Only
(Universe: Population 5 Years and Over)

Group	Number	%
Total Population	23,250	43.8
Hispanic or Latino (of any race)	5,208	51.5
Mexican	4,216	52.3

Language Spoken at Home: Spanish
(Universe: Population 5 Years and Over)

Group	Number	%
Total Population	5,152	9.7
Hispanic or Latino (of any race)	4,764	47.1
Mexican	3,720	46.1

Unemployment Rate
(Universe: Population 16 Years and Over)

Group	%
Total Population	5.2
Hispanic or Latino (of any race)	7.3
Mexican	5.6

Class of Worker: Private Wage and Salary
(Universe: Civilian Employed Population 16 Years and Over)

Group	Number	%
Total Population	20,705	74.9
Hispanic or Latino (of any race)	4,026	75.6
Mexican	3,210	74.0

Class of Worker: Government
(Universe: Civilian Employed Population 16 Years and Over)

Group	Number	%
Total Population	4,496	16.3
Hispanic or Latino (of any race)	958	18.0
Mexican	853	19.7

Means of Transportation to Work: Car, Truck or Van
(Universe: Workers 16 Years and Over)

Group	Number	%
Total Population	24,419	90.2
Hispanic or Latino (of any race)	4,841	93.6
Mexican	3,901	93.0

Means of Transportation to Work: Public Transportation (ex. Taxicab)
(Universe: Workers 16 Years and Over)

Group	Number	%
Total Population	444	1.6
Hispanic or Latino (of any race)	89	1.7
Mexican	69	1.6

Homeownership Rate
(Universe: Occupied Housing Units)

Group	%
Total Population	81.2
Hispanic or Latino (of any race)	80.3
Central American, ex. Mexican	76.9
Guatemalan	75.0
Nicaraguan	76.7
Salvadoran	78.8
Cuban	74.2
Mexican	80.7
Puerto Rican	85.5
South American	82.8
Colombian	75.0
Ecuadorian	85.3
Peruvian	84.0
Spaniard	84.6

Median Home Value

Group	Dollars
Total Population	574,900
Hispanic or Latino (of any race)	523,500
Mexican	518,400

Median Gross Rent

Group	Dollars
Total Population	1,666
Hispanic or Latino (of any race)	1,714
Mexican	1,699

Median Household Income
(2010 Inflation-Adjusted Dollars)

Group	Dollars
Total Population	87,216
Hispanic or Latino (of any race)	88,659
Mexican	91,736

Per Capita Income
(2010 Inflation-Adjusted Dollars)

Group	Dollars
Total Population	33,145
Hispanic or Latino (of any race)	25,861
Mexican	26,076

Households with $100,000+ Income

Group	Number	%
Total Population	7,754	43.5
Hispanic or Latino (of any race)	1,228	44.5
Mexican	987	46.0

Households with Food Stamps/SNAP Benefits During Past 12 Months

Group	Number	%
Total Population	140	0.8
Hispanic or Latino (of any race)	65	2.4
Mexican	50	2.3

Poverty Rate
(Income in Past 12 Months Below Poverty Level)

Group	%
Total Population	4.6
Hispanic or Latino (of any race)	5.1
Mexican	4.7

Notes: (1) Percent of total population; (2) Percent of Hispanic/Latino population; Profiles include places with an overall population of at least 125,000, OR an overall population of at least 25,000 where the Hispanic/Latino population is at least 20% of the overall population. In states where less than five places meet either of these criteria, we have included places with at least 10,000 total population with the highest percentage of Hispanic/Latino population. These places are identified with an asterisk (*); Please refer to the User's Guide for a full explanation of data.

Downey

Population

Group	Number	%TP[1]	%HP[2]
Total Population	111,772	100.0	–
Hispanic or Latino (of any race)	78,996	70.7	100.0
Central American, ex. Mexican	8,546	7.6	10.8
Costa Rican	263	0.2	0.3
Guatemalan	2,180	2.0	2.8
Honduran	505	0.5	0.6
Nicaraguan	1,092	1.0	1.4
Salvadoran	4,356	3.9	5.5
Cuban	2,283	2.0	2.9
Mexican	60,331	54.0	76.4
Puerto Rican	745	0.7	0.9
South American	3,506	3.1	4.4
Argentinean	429	0.4	0.5
Bolivian	134	0.1	0.2
Chilean	120	0.1	0.2
Colombian	733	0.7	0.9
Ecuadorian	678	0.6	0.9
Peruvian	1,277	1.1	1.6
Spaniard	428	0.4	0.5

Population Growth: 2000–2010

Group	%
Total Population	4.1
Hispanic or Latino (of any race)	27.2
Central American, ex. Mexican	99.9
Costa Rican	33.5
Guatemalan	116.5
Honduran	167.2
Nicaraguan	71.7
Salvadoran	137.5
Cuban	8.7
Mexican	39.5
Puerto Rican	12.7
South American	41.5
Argentinean	22.6
Colombian	55.3
Ecuadorian	87.3
Peruvian	43.3

Males per 100 Females

Group	Number
Total Population	94.1
Hispanic or Latino (of any race)	94.0
Central American, ex. Mexican	89.3
Costa Rican	75.3
Guatemalan	92.7
Honduran	87.0
Nicaraguan	97.5
Salvadoran	87.3
Cuban	91.7
Mexican	94.9
Puerto Rican	101.4
South American	89.5
Argentinean	104.3
Bolivian	83.6
Chilean	84.6
Colombian	84.6
Ecuadorian	83.2
Peruvian	88.6
Spaniard	91.1

Average Household Size

Group	People
Total Population	3.27
Hispanic or Latino (of any race)	3.73
Central American, ex. Mexican	3.94
Costa Rican	3.65
Guatemalan	3.98
Honduran	3.91
Nicaraguan	4.11
Salvadoran	3.94
Cuban	3.01
Mexican	3.80
Puerto Rican	2.81
South American	3.47
Argentinean	3.28
Bolivian	3.49
Chilean	3.53
Colombian	3.41
Ecuadorian	3.56
Peruvian	3.58
Spaniard	2.72

Median Age

Group	Years
Total Population	33.3
Hispanic or Latino (of any race)	29.4
Central American, ex. Mexican	34.6
Costa Rican	38.5
Guatemalan	35.8
Honduran	32.3
Nicaraguan	36.9
Salvadoran	33.8
Cuban	42.1
Mexican	28.0
Puerto Rican	33.2
South American	38.8
Argentinean	40.2
Bolivian	37.0
Chilean	35.5
Colombian	36.9
Ecuadorian	40.1
Peruvian	39.2
Spaniard	39.5

High School Graduates
(Universe: Population 25 Years and Over)

Group	Number	%
Total Population	51,396	75.2
Hispanic or Latino (of any race)	28,170	66.3
Central American, ex. Mexican	3,342	74.3
Guatemalan	984	79.1
Salvadoran	1,479	68.8
Cuban	1,091	76.1
Mexican	20,313	62.6
South American	2,107	90.7
Colombian	844	96.7
Ecuadorian	293	69.8
Peruvian	571	100.0

Four-Year College Graduates
(Universe: Population 25 Years and Over)

Group	Number	%
Total Population	13,289	19.4
Hispanic or Latino (of any race)	5,112	12.0
Central American, ex. Mexican	480	10.7
Guatemalan	115	9.2
Salvadoran	147	6.8
Cuban	221	15.4
Mexican	3,603	11.1
South American	554	23.8
Colombian	180	20.6
Ecuadorian	103	24.5
Peruvian	82	14.4

Population Age 3–17 Enrolled in Public School
(Universe: Population Age 3–17 Enrolled in School)

Group	Number	%
Total Population	22,178	89.9
Hispanic or Latino (of any race)	18,498	91.4
Central American, ex. Mexican	1,072	88.5
Guatemalan	161	65.2
Salvadoran	740	95.0
Cuban	211	98.1
Mexican	15,647	92.5
South American	613	85.6
Colombian	127	62.3
Ecuadorian	46	63.9
Peruvian	197	100.0

Population Age 3–17 Enrolled in Private School
(Universe: Population Age 3–17 Enrolled in School)

Group	Number	%
Total Population	2,478	10.1
Hispanic or Latino (of any race)	1,745	8.6
Central American, ex. Mexican	139	11.5
Guatemalan	86	34.8
Salvadoran	39	5.0
Cuban	4	1.9
Mexican	1,267	7.5
South American	103	14.4
Colombian	77	37.7
Ecuadorian	26	36.1
Peruvian	0	0.0

Foreign-Born Population

Group	Number	%
Total Population	39,672	35.8
Hispanic or Latino (of any race)	30,201	39.2
Central American, ex. Mexican	3,871	55.2
Guatemalan	1,047	56.4
Salvadoran	1,951	53.6
Cuban	1,412	69.1
Mexican	21,934	36.2
South American	2,566	68.2
Colombian	858	66.5
Ecuadorian	452	72.7
Peruvian	713	78.4

Foreign-Born Naturalized U.S. Citizens

Group	Number	%
Total Population	19,800	49.9
Hispanic or Latino (of any race)	13,703	45.4
Central American, ex. Mexican	2,297	59.3
Guatemalan	657	62.8
Salvadoran	1,202	61.6
Cuban	854	60.5
Mexican	8,949	40.8
South American	1,321	51.5
Colombian	582	67.8
Ecuadorian	265	58.6
Peruvian	285	40.0

Language Spoken at Home: English Only
(Universe: Population 5 Years and Over)

Group	Number	%
Total Population	33,427	32.4
Hispanic or Latino (of any race)	12,170	17.2
Central American, ex. Mexican	492	7.6
Guatemalan	162	9.8
Salvadoran	266	7.8
Cuban	158	7.9
Mexican	10,306	18.5
South American	185	5.6
Colombian	80	7.2
Ecuadorian	31	5.8
Peruvian	46	5.1

Language Spoken at Home: Spanish
(Universe: Population 5 Years and Over)

Group	Number	%
Total Population	59,657	57.8
Hispanic or Latino (of any race)	58,364	82.7
Central American, ex. Mexican	5,964	92.4
Guatemalan	1,485	90.2
Salvadoran	3,135	92.2
Cuban	1,844	92.1
Mexican	45,321	81.4
South American	3,113	94.1
Colombian	1,020	92.1
Ecuadorian	505	93.7
Peruvian	852	94.9

Unemployment Rate
(Universe: Population 16 Years and Over)

Group	%
Total Population	9.7
Hispanic or Latino (of any race)	10.2
Central American, ex. Mexican	14.2
Guatemalan	7.2
Salvadoran	22.9
Cuban	5.3
Mexican	10.3
South American	5.4
Colombian	8.5
Ecuadorian	0.7
Peruvian	0.0

Class of Worker: Private Wage and Salary
(Universe: Civilian Employed Population 16 Years and Over)

Group	Number	%
Total Population	38,480	77.6
Hispanic or Latino (of any race)	27,056	80.0
Central American, ex. Mexican	2,639	81.8
Guatemalan	701	82.9
Salvadoran	1,290	86.3
Cuban	808	81.5
Mexican	21,176	80.5
South American	1,294	71.2
Colombian	341	56.9

Notes: (1) Percent of total population; (2) Percent of Hispanic/Latino population; Profiles include places with an overall population of at least 125,000, OR an overall population of at least 25,000 where the Hispanic/Latino population is at least 20% of the overall population. In states where less than five places meet either of these criteria, we have included places with at least 10,000 total population with the highest percentage of Hispanic/Latino population. These places are identified with an asterisk (*); Please refer to the User's Guide for a full explanation of data.

Ecuadorian	229	77.9
Peruvian	435	78.7

Class of Worker: Government
(Universe: Civilian Employed Population 16 Years and Over)

Group	Number	%
Total Population	7,310	14.8
Hispanic or Latino (of any race)	4,442	13.1
Central American, ex. Mexican	368	11.4
Guatemalan	88	10.4
Salvadoran	128	8.6
Cuban	162	16.3
Mexican	3,434	13.0
South American	249	13.7
Colombian	136	22.7
Ecuadorian	24	8.2
Peruvian	68	12.3

Means of Transportation to Work: Car, Truck or Van
(Universe: Workers 16 Years and Over)

Group	Number	%
Total Population	44,464	92.7
Hispanic or Latino (of any race)	30,129	92.2
Central American, ex. Mexican	2,831	88.4
Guatemalan	753	92.3
Salvadoran	1,318	89.4
Cuban	918	96.7
Mexican	23,431	92.6
South American	1,567	89.9
Colombian	531	91.2
Ecuadorian	281	95.6
Peruvian	424	83.8

Means of Transportation to Work: Public Transportation (ex. Taxicab)
(Universe: Workers 16 Years and Over)

Group	Number	%
Total Population	1,138	2.4
Hispanic or Latino (of any race)	767	2.3
Central American, ex. Mexican	99	3.1
Guatemalan	0	0.0
Salvadoran	47	3.2
Cuban	3	0.3
Mexican	646	2.6
South American	7	0.4
Colombian	0	0.0
Ecuadorian	0	0.0
Peruvian	7	1.4

Homeownership Rate
(Universe: Occupied Housing Units)

Group	%
Total Population	50.5
Hispanic or Latino (of any race)	44.8
Central American, ex. Mexican	42.9
Costa Rican	53.5
Guatemalan	40.7
Honduran	32.2
Nicaraguan	41.9
Salvadoran	45.2
Cuban	52.3
Mexican	45.5
Puerto Rican	36.7
South American	41.2
Argentinean	51.3
Bolivian	53.8
Chilean	41.7
Colombian	35.0
Ecuadorian	49.6
Peruvian	36.2
Spaniard	52.3

Median Home Value

Group	Dollars
Total Population	522,800
Hispanic or Latino (of any race)	514,800
Central American, ex. Mexican	504,200
Guatemalan	530,500
Salvadoran	533,100
Cuban	597,000
Mexican	515,200
South American	499,700
Colombian	458,100
Ecuadorian	621,600
Peruvian	414,000

Median Gross Rent

Group	Dollars
Total Population	1,139
Hispanic or Latino (of any race)	1,131
Central American, ex. Mexican	1,194
Guatemalan	1,204
Salvadoran	1,190
Cuban	1,040
Mexican	1,124
South American	1,270
Colombian	1,178
Ecuadorian	1,146
Peruvian	1,312

Median Household Income
(2010 Inflation-Adjusted Dollars)

Group	Dollars
Total Population	59,674
Hispanic or Latino (of any race)	56,646
Central American, ex. Mexican	64,824
Guatemalan	47,528
Salvadoran	67,794
Cuban	52,833
Mexican	56,396
South American	52,393
Colombian	51,493
Ecuadorian	57,115
Peruvian	60,132

Per Capita Income
(2010 Inflation-Adjusted Dollars)

Group	Dollars
Total Population	22,731
Hispanic or Latino (of any race)	18,026
Central American, ex. Mexican	19,963
Guatemalan	15,345
Salvadoran	19,634
Cuban	23,248
Mexican	17,572
South American	20,102
Colombian	19,282
Ecuadorian	20,641
Peruvian	21,162

Households with $100,000+ Income

Group	Number	%
Total Population	7,695	23.0
Hispanic or Latino (of any race)	4,141	20.7
Central American, ex. Mexican	474	21.2
Guatemalan	98	17.4
Salvadoran	260	24.0
Cuban	146	21.7
Mexican	3,095	20.6
South American	257	24.2
Colombian	116	37.5
Ecuadorian	38	19.6
Peruvian	53	20.2

Households with Food Stamps/SNAP Benefits During Past 12 Months

Group	Number	%
Total Population	1,434	4.3
Hispanic or Latino (of any race)	1,165	5.8
Central American, ex. Mexican	52	2.3
Guatemalan	22	3.9
Salvadoran	8	0.7
Cuban	33	4.9
Mexican	953	6.3
South American	85	8.0
Colombian	24	7.8
Ecuadorian	46	23.7
Peruvian	15	5.7

Poverty Rate
(Income in Past 12 Months Below Poverty Level)

Group	%
Total Population	10.0
Hispanic or Latino (of any race)	11.9
Central American, ex. Mexican	7.2
Guatemalan	6.2
Salvadoran	7.4
Cuban	4.1
Mexican	12.9
South American	7.5
Colombian	2.6
Ecuadorian	28.3
Peruvian	6.6

East Los Angeles

Population

Group	Number	%TP[1]	%HP[2]
Total Population	126,496	100.0	–
Hispanic or Latino (of any race)	122,784	97.1	100.0
Central American, ex. Mexican	5,994	4.7	4.9
Guatemalan	1,825	1.4	1.5
Honduran	494	0.4	0.4
Nicaraguan	283	0.2	0.2
Salvadoran	3,274	2.6	2.7
Cuban	132	0.1	0.1
Mexican	111,441	88.1	90.8
Puerto Rican	264	0.2	0.2
South American	458	0.4	0.4
Ecuadorian	163	0.1	0.1
Peruvian	100	0.1	0.1
Spaniard	244	0.2	0.2

Population Growth: 2000–2010

Group	%
Total Population	1.8
Hispanic or Latino (of any race)	2.1
Central American, ex. Mexican	98.5
Guatemalan	160.3
Honduran	133.0
Nicaraguan	102.1
Salvadoran	103.7
Cuban	-5.7
Mexican	6.9
Puerto Rican	38.9
South American	61.3

Males per 100 Females

Group	Number
Total Population	98.9
Hispanic or Latino (of any race)	98.9
Central American, ex. Mexican	96.3
Guatemalan	113.0
Honduran	85.0
Nicaraguan	66.5
Salvadoran	92.7
Cuban	94.1
Mexican	99.2
Puerto Rican	107.9
South American	92.4
Ecuadorian	66.3
Peruvian	92.3
Spaniard	87.7

Average Household Size

Group	People
Total Population	4.09
Hispanic or Latino (of any race)	4.16
Central American, ex. Mexican	4.18
Guatemalan	4.48
Honduran	4.29
Nicaraguan	3.52
Salvadoran	4.09
Cuban	2.55
Mexican	4.18
Puerto Rican	2.82
South American	3.08
Ecuadorian	3.13
Peruvian	3.82
Spaniard	3.26

Median Age

Group	Years
Total Population	29.1
Hispanic or Latino (of any race)	28.9
Central American, ex. Mexican	34.5
Guatemalan	32.5
Honduran	33.2
Nicaraguan	38.7
Salvadoran	36.1
Cuban	41.5
Mexican	28.7
Puerto Rican	34.0

Notes: (1) Percent of total population; (2) Percent of Hispanic/Latino population; Profiles include places with an overall population of at least 125,000, OR an overall population of at least 25,000 where the Hispanic/Latino population is at least 20% of the overall population. In states where less than five places meet either of these criteria, we have included places with at least 10,000 total population with the highest percentage of Hispanic/Latino population. These places are identified with an asterisk (*); Please refer to the User's Guide for a full explanation of data.

Group		%
South American		43.7
Ecuadorian		45.5
Peruvian		41.8
Spaniard		40.0

High School Graduates
(Universe: Population 25 Years and Over)

Group	Number	%
Total Population	30,902	44.3
Hispanic or Latino (of any race)	29,064	43.0
Central American, ex. Mexican	1,800	40.5
Guatemalan	483	34.8
Salvadoran	760	40.4
Mexican	26,252	42.8

Four-Year College Graduates
(Universe: Population 25 Years and Over)

Group	Number	%
Total Population	3,779	5.4
Hispanic or Latino (of any race)	3,105	4.6
Central American, ex. Mexican	273	6.1
Guatemalan	90	6.5
Salvadoran	108	5.7
Mexican	2,681	4.4

Population Age 3–17 Enrolled in Public School
(Universe: Population Age 3–17 Enrolled in School)

Group	Number	%
Total Population	27,870	96.1
Hispanic or Latino (of any race)	27,638	96.3
Central American, ex. Mexican	1,035	93.1
Guatemalan	346	95.1
Salvadoran	487	89.2
Mexican	25,553	96.7

Population Age 3–17 Enrolled in Private School
(Universe: Population Age 3–17 Enrolled in School)

Group	Number	%
Total Population	1,132	3.9
Hispanic or Latino (of any race)	1,068	3.7
Central American, ex. Mexican	77	6.9
Guatemalan	18	4.9
Salvadoran	59	10.8
Mexican	879	3.3

Foreign-Born Population

Group	Number	%
Total Population	54,778	44.5
Hispanic or Latino (of any race)	53,897	44.8
Central American, ex. Mexican	4,821	70.6
Guatemalan	1,552	68.9
Salvadoran	2,068	69.9
Mexican	48,187	43.8

Foreign-Born Naturalized U.S. Citizens

Group	Number	%
Total Population	15,725	28.7
Hispanic or Latino (of any race)	15,189	28.2
Central American, ex. Mexican	1,227	25.5
Guatemalan	329	21.2
Salvadoran	588	28.4
Mexican	13,603	28.2

Language Spoken at Home: English Only
(Universe: Population 5 Years and Over)

Group	Number	%
Total Population	12,095	10.7
Hispanic or Latino (of any race)	10,765	9.8
Central American, ex. Mexican	132	2.0
Guatemalan	57	2.8
Salvadoran	52	1.8
Mexican	9,876	9.8

Language Spoken at Home: Spanish
(Universe: Population 5 Years and Over)

Group	Number	%
Total Population	99,586	88.3
Hispanic or Latino (of any race)	99,219	90.1
Central American, ex. Mexican	6,328	98.0
Guatemalan	2,014	97.2
Salvadoran	2,805	98.2
Mexican	90,532	90.0

Unemployment Rate
(Universe: Population 16 Years and Over)

Group	%
Total Population	9.9
Hispanic or Latino (of any race)	9.9
Central American, ex. Mexican	10.2
Guatemalan	11.0
Salvadoran	8.7
Mexican	9.8

Class of Worker: Private Wage and Salary
(Universe: Civilian Employed Population 16 Years and Over)

Group	Number	%
Total Population	40,232	82.3
Hispanic or Latino (of any race)	39,363	82.5
Central American, ex. Mexican	2,948	87.9
Guatemalan	803	82.4
Salvadoran	1,414	90.7
Mexican	35,638	82.3

Class of Worker: Government
(Universe: Civilian Employed Population 16 Years and Over)

Group	Number	%
Total Population	5,066	10.4
Hispanic or Latino (of any race)	4,876	10.2
Central American, ex. Mexican	148	4.4
Guatemalan	57	5.8
Salvadoran	64	4.1
Mexican	4,527	10.5

Means of Transportation to Work: Car, Truck or Van
(Universe: Workers 16 Years and Over)

Group	Number	%
Total Population	36,627	76.8
Hispanic or Latino (of any race)	35,663	76.6
Central American, ex. Mexican	2,204	66.4
Guatemalan	648	66.5
Salvadoran	1,031	66.6
Mexican	32,680	77.4

Means of Transportation to Work: Public Transportation (ex. Taxicab)
(Universe: Workers 16 Years and Over)

Group	Number	%
Total Population	6,578	13.8
Hispanic or Latino (of any race)	6,565	14.1
Central American, ex. Mexican	744	22.4
Guatemalan	256	26.3
Salvadoran	299	19.3
Mexican	5,730	13.6

Homeownership Rate
(Universe: Occupied Housing Units)

Group	%
Total Population	35.7
Hispanic or Latino (of any race)	35.4
Central American, ex. Mexican	25.3
Guatemalan	22.7
Honduran	22.1
Nicaraguan	23.3
Salvadoran	27.1
Cuban	31.0
Mexican	36.3
Puerto Rican	26.5
South American	28.1
Ecuadorian	26.7
Peruvian	17.9
Spaniard	39.1

Median Home Value

Group	Dollars
Total Population	369,200
Hispanic or Latino (of any race)	371,400
Central American, ex. Mexican	387,600
Guatemalan	360,700
Salvadoran	403,100
Mexican	369,800

Median Gross Rent

Group	Dollars
Total Population	873
Hispanic or Latino (of any race)	875
Central American, ex. Mexican	872
Guatemalan	938
Salvadoran	855
Mexican	876

Median Household Income
(2010 Inflation-Adjusted Dollars)

Group	Dollars
Total Population	37,128
Hispanic or Latino (of any race)	37,303
Central American, ex. Mexican	36,880
Guatemalan	38,833
Salvadoran	34,088
Mexican	37,480

Per Capita Income
(2010 Inflation-Adjusted Dollars)

Group	Dollars
Total Population	12,633
Hispanic or Latino (of any race)	12,433
Central American, ex. Mexican	12,946
Guatemalan	10,565
Salvadoran	13,550
Mexican	12,472

Households with $100,000+ Income

Group	Number	%
Total Population	2,606	8.4
Hispanic or Latino (of any race)	2,475	8.3
Central American, ex. Mexican	123	5.7
Guatemalan	22	3.3
Salvadoran	69	7.0
Mexican	2,311	8.6

Households with Food Stamps/SNAP Benefits During Past 12 Months

Group	Number	%
Total Population	3,263	10.5
Hispanic or Latino (of any race)	3,256	10.9
Central American, ex. Mexican	187	8.7
Guatemalan	82	12.3
Salvadoran	61	6.2
Mexican	3,014	11.2

Poverty Rate
(Income in Past 12 Months Below Poverty Level)

Group	%
Total Population	24.1
Hispanic or Latino (of any race)	24.2
Central American, ex. Mexican	22.7
Guatemalan	24.4
Salvadoran	26.9
Mexican	24.0

East Palo Alto

Population

Group	Number	%TP[1]	%HP[2]
Total Population	28,155	100.0	–
Hispanic or Latino (of any race)	18,147	64.5	100.0
Central American, ex. Mexican	1,877	6.7	10.3
Guatemalan	431	1.5	2.4
Nicaraguan	151	0.5	0.8
Salvadoran	1,202	4.3	6.6
Mexican	15,319	54.4	84.4
South American	127	0.5	0.7

Population Growth: 2000–2010

Group	%
Total Population	-4.6
Hispanic or Latino (of any race)	4.6
Central American, ex. Mexican	81.0
Guatemalan	133.0
Salvadoran	86.9
Mexican	5.3

Males per 100 Females

Group	Number
Total Population	102.7
Hispanic or Latino (of any race)	107.2
Central American, ex. Mexican	112.3
Guatemalan	155.0
Nicaraguan	75.6
Salvadoran	105.1
Mexican	106.4
South American	101.6

Notes: (1) Percent of total population; (2) Percent of Hispanic/Latino population; Profiles include places with an overall population of at least 125,000, OR an overall population of at least 25,000 where the Hispanic/Latino population is at least 20% of the overall population. In states where less than five places meet either of these criteria, we have included places with at least 10,000 total population with the highest percentage of Hispanic/Latino population. These places are identified with an asterisk (*); Please refer to the User's Guide for a full explanation of data.

Average Household Size

Group	People
Total Population	4.03
Hispanic or Latino (of any race)	5.21
Central American, ex. Mexican	5.02
Guatemalan	5.09
Nicaraguan	4.13
Salvadoran	5.15
Mexican	5.31
South American	3.21

Median Age

Group	Years
Total Population	28.1
Hispanic or Latino (of any race)	24.5
Central American, ex. Mexican	29.6
Guatemalan	29.0
Nicaraguan	29.5
Salvadoran	29.9
Mexican	23.8
South American	31.6

High School Graduates
(Universe: Population 25 Years and Over)

Group	Number	%
Total Population	10,143	65.0
Hispanic or Latino (of any race)	4,224	49.2
Central American, ex. Mexican	484	34.8
Salvadoran	300	39.4
Mexican	3,466	51.2

Four-Year College Graduates
(Universe: Population 25 Years and Over)

Group	Number	%
Total Population	2,499	16.0
Hispanic or Latino (of any race)	626	7.3
Central American, ex. Mexican	174	12.5
Salvadoran	77	10.1
Mexican	357	5.3

Population Age 3–17 Enrolled in Public School
(Universe: Population Age 3–17 Enrolled in School)

Group	Number	%
Total Population	5,904	91.2
Hispanic or Latino (of any race)	4,212	91.2
Central American, ex. Mexican	388	96.5
Salvadoran	262	100.0
Mexican	3,690	90.6

Population Age 3–17 Enrolled in Private School
(Universe: Population Age 3–17 Enrolled in School)

Group	Number	%
Total Population	573	8.8
Hispanic or Latino (of any race)	406	8.8
Central American, ex. Mexican	14	3.5
Salvadoran	0	0.0
Mexican	384	9.4

Foreign-Born Population

Group	Number	%
Total Population	11,496	41.2
Hispanic or Latino (of any race)	8,810	51.2
Central American, ex. Mexican	1,573	73.6
Salvadoran	695	58.7
Mexican	7,027	49.0

Foreign-Born Naturalized U.S. Citizens

Group	Number	%
Total Population	2,770	24.1
Hispanic or Latino (of any race)	1,598	18.1
Central American, ex. Mexican	224	14.2
Salvadoran	206	29.6
Mexican	1,259	17.9

Language Spoken at Home: English Only
(Universe: Population 5 Years and Over)

Group	Number	%
Total Population	7,631	29.9
Hispanic or Latino (of any race)	845	5.5
Central American, ex. Mexican	50	2.5
Salvadoran	33	3.1
Mexican	556	4.4

Language Spoken at Home: Spanish
(Universe: Population 5 Years and Over)

Group	Number	%
Total Population	14,860	58.3
Hispanic or Latino (of any race)	14,618	94.4
Central American, ex. Mexican	1,963	96.6
Salvadoran	1,046	96.9
Mexican	12,217	95.6

Unemployment Rate
(Universe: Population 16 Years and Over)

Group	%
Total Population	9.6
Hispanic or Latino (of any race)	8.5
Central American, ex. Mexican	3.8
Salvadoran	0.0
Mexican	9.9

Class of Worker: Private Wage and Salary
(Universe: Civilian Employed Population 16 Years and Over)

Group	Number	%
Total Population	10,094	80.9
Hispanic or Latino (of any race)	6,643	84.8
Central American, ex. Mexican	1,072	79.5
Salvadoran	381	60.4
Mexican	5,381	87.3

Class of Worker: Government
(Universe: Civilian Employed Population 16 Years and Over)

Group	Number	%
Total Population	1,150	9.2
Hispanic or Latino (of any race)	471	6.0
Central American, ex. Mexican	82	6.1
Salvadoran	68	10.8
Mexican	311	5.0

Means of Transportation to Work: Car, Truck or Van
(Universe: Workers 16 Years and Over)

Group	Number	%
Total Population	10,194	83.5
Hispanic or Latino (of any race)	6,281	81.8
Central American, ex. Mexican	829	61.5
Salvadoran	575	91.1
Mexican	5,131	85.3

Means of Transportation to Work: Public Transportation (ex. Taxicab)
(Universe: Workers 16 Years and Over)

Group	Number	%
Total Population	635	5.2
Hispanic or Latino (of any race)	361	4.7
Central American, ex. Mexican	86	6.4
Salvadoran	0	0.0
Mexican	275	4.6

Homeownership Rate
(Universe: Occupied Housing Units)

Group	%
Total Population	42.8
Hispanic or Latino (of any race)	36.0
Central American, ex. Mexican	36.6
Guatemalan	32.6
Nicaraguan	25.0
Salvadoran	38.5
Mexican	36.3
South American	38.5

Median Home Value

Group	Dollars
Total Population	525,600
Hispanic or Latino (of any race)	517,700
Central American, ex. Mexican	487,500
Salvadoran	437,500
Mexican	522,900

Median Gross Rent

Group	Dollars
Total Population	1,154
Hispanic or Latino (of any race)	1,163
Central American, ex. Mexican	1,057
Salvadoran	1,526
Mexican	1,214

Median Household Income
(2010 Inflation-Adjusted Dollars)

Group	Dollars
Total Population	48,734
Hispanic or Latino (of any race)	49,921
Central American, ex. Mexican	51,563
Salvadoran	50,813
Mexican	47,452

Per Capita Income
(2010 Inflation-Adjusted Dollars)

Group	Dollars
Total Population	17,942
Hispanic or Latino (of any race)	12,301
Central American, ex. Mexican	14,334
Salvadoran	15,340
Mexican	11,938

Households with $100,000+ Income

Group	Number	%
Total Population	1,389	18.8
Hispanic or Latino (of any race)	413	11.6
Central American, ex. Mexican	32	6.8
Salvadoran	12	4.6
Mexican	309	10.9

Households with Food Stamps/SNAP Benefits During Past 12 Months

Group	Number	%
Total Population	566	7.6
Hispanic or Latino (of any race)	314	8.8
Central American, ex. Mexican	19	4.1
Salvadoran	19	7.3
Mexican	264	9.4

Poverty Rate
(Income in Past 12 Months Below Poverty Level)

Group	%
Total Population	16.6
Hispanic or Latino (of any race)	18.4
Central American, ex. Mexican	12.7
Salvadoran	16.8
Mexican	19.4

Eastvale

Population

Group	Number	%TP[1]	%HP[2]
Total Population	53,668	100.0	–
Hispanic or Latino (of any race)	21,445	40.0	100.0
Central American, ex. Mexican	1,198	2.2	5.6
Guatemalan	311	0.6	1.5
Nicaraguan	149	0.3	0.7
Salvadoran	561	1.0	2.6
Cuban	277	0.5	1.3
Mexican	17,575	32.7	82.0
Puerto Rican	356	0.7	1.7
South American	739	1.4	3.4
Colombian	200	0.4	0.9
Ecuadorian	145	0.3	0.7
Peruvian	199	0.4	0.9
Spaniard	169	0.3	0.8

Population Growth: 2000–2010

Group	%
Total Population	n/a

Males per 100 Females

Group	Number
Total Population	98.1
Hispanic or Latino (of any race)	95.8
Central American, ex. Mexican	94.8
Guatemalan	85.1
Nicaraguan	93.5
Salvadoran	104.7
Cuban	84.7
Mexican	95.6
Puerto Rican	96.7
South American	98.1
Colombian	86.9
Ecuadorian	119.7
Peruvian	101.0
Spaniard	85.7

STATE & PLACE PROFILES

Notes: (1) Percent of total population; (2) Percent of Hispanic/Latino population; Profiles include places with an overall population of at least 125,000, OR an overall population of at least 25,000 where the Hispanic/Latino population is at least 20% of the overall population. In states where less than five places meet either of these criteria, we have included places with at least 10,000 total population with the highest percentage of Hispanic/Latino population. These places are identified with an asterisk (*); Please refer to the User's Guide for a full explanation of data.

Average Household Size

Group	People
Total Population	3.93
Hispanic or Latino (of any race)	4.56
Central American, ex. Mexican	4.85
Guatemalan	4.94
Nicaraguan	4.72
Salvadoran	4.95
Cuban	4.03
Mexican	4.62
Puerto Rican	3.83
South American	4.13
Colombian	4.06
Ecuadorian	4.36
Peruvian	4.06
Spaniard	3.63

Median Age

Group	Years
Total Population	30.9
Hispanic or Latino (of any race)	26.0
Central American, ex. Mexican	31.7
Guatemalan	32.5
Nicaraguan	30.7
Salvadoran	31.0
Cuban	28.1
Mexican	25.3
Puerto Rican	24.8
South American	33.3
Colombian	30.7
Ecuadorian	33.5
Peruvian	35.8
Spaniard	33.3

High School Graduates
(Universe: Population 25 Years and Over)

Group	Number	%
Total Population	24,546	87.3
Hispanic or Latino (of any race)	7,761	76.3
Central American, ex. Mexican	595	82.6
Mexican	6,002	73.9

Four-Year College Graduates
(Universe: Population 25 Years and Over)

Group	Number	%
Total Population	8,947	31.8
Hispanic or Latino (of any race)	1,543	15.2
Central American, ex. Mexican	136	18.9
Mexican	1,085	13.4

Population Age 3–17 Enrolled in Public School
(Universe: Population Age 3–17 Enrolled in School)

Group	Number	%
Total Population	10,514	85.8
Hispanic or Latino (of any race)	5,251	89.0
Central American, ex. Mexican	266	100.0
Mexican	4,223	89.2

Population Age 3–17 Enrolled in Private School
(Universe: Population Age 3–17 Enrolled in School)

Group	Number	%
Total Population	1,735	14.2
Hispanic or Latino (of any race)	647	11.0
Central American, ex. Mexican	0	0.0
Mexican	511	10.8

Foreign-Born Population

Group	Number	%
Total Population	13,820	28.1
Hispanic or Latino (of any race)	5,992	29.1
Central American, ex. Mexican	668	54.0
Mexican	4,725	28.3

Foreign-Born Naturalized U.S. Citizens

Group	Number	%
Total Population	7,549	54.6
Hispanic or Latino (of any race)	2,834	47.3
Central American, ex. Mexican	534	79.9
Mexican	1,927	40.8

Language Spoken at Home: English Only
(Universe: Population 5 Years and Over)

Group	Number	%
Total Population	23,472	52.7
Hispanic or Latino (of any race)	5,982	32.3
Central American, ex. Mexican	84	7.5
Mexican	5,023	33.6

Language Spoken at Home: Spanish
(Universe: Population 5 Years and Over)

Group	Number	%
Total Population	12,722	28.6
Hispanic or Latino (of any race)	12,437	67.2
Central American, ex. Mexican	1,030	92.5
Mexican	9,874	66.0

Unemployment Rate
(Universe: Population 16 Years and Over)

Group	%
Total Population	6.9
Hispanic or Latino (of any race)	8.6
Central American, ex. Mexican	1.7
Mexican	8.7

Class of Worker: Private Wage and Salary
(Universe: Civilian Employed Population 16 Years and Over)

Group	Number	%
Total Population	17,517	74.9
Hispanic or Latino (of any race)	7,447	82.4
Central American, ex. Mexican	584	85.4
Mexican	6,039	82.9

Class of Worker: Government
(Universe: Civilian Employed Population 16 Years and Over)

Group	Number	%
Total Population	3,899	16.7
Hispanic or Latino (of any race)	1,045	11.6
Central American, ex. Mexican	85	12.4
Mexican	774	10.6

Means of Transportation to Work: Car, Truck or Van
(Universe: Workers 16 Years and Over)

Group	Number	%
Total Population	20,024	90.2
Hispanic or Latino (of any race)	7,849	91.7
Central American, ex. Mexican	637	100.0
Mexican	6,318	91.2

Means of Transportation to Work: Public Transportation (ex. Taxicab)
(Universe: Workers 16 Years and Over)

Group	Number	%
Total Population	291	1.3
Hispanic or Latino (of any race)	170	2.0
Central American, ex. Mexican	0	0.0
Mexican	157	2.3

Homeownership Rate
(Universe: Occupied Housing Units)

Group	%
Total Population	82.7
Hispanic or Latino (of any race)	80.3
Central American, ex. Mexican	83.2
Guatemalan	81.7
Nicaraguan	77.8
Salvadoran	85.9
Cuban	86.2
Mexican	80.5
Puerto Rican	71.6
South American	84.8
Colombian	80.9
Ecuadorian	89.4
Peruvian	82.7
Spaniard	71.2

Median Home Value

Group	Dollars
Total Population	472,200
Hispanic or Latino (of any race)	458,500
Central American, ex. Mexican	410,400
Mexican	448,300

Median Gross Rent

Group	Dollars
Total Population	2,000+
Hispanic or Latino (of any race)	2,000+
Central American, ex. Mexican	2,000+
Mexican	2,000+

Median Household Income
(2010 Inflation-Adjusted Dollars)

Group	Dollars
Total Population	105,894
Hispanic or Latino (of any race)	99,893
Central American, ex. Mexican	127,750
Mexican	98,329

Per Capita Income
(2010 Inflation-Adjusted Dollars)

Group	Dollars
Total Population	30,821
Hispanic or Latino (of any race)	22,491
Central American, ex. Mexican	27,555
Mexican	21,629

Households with $100,000+ Income

Group	Number	%
Total Population	6,568	53.6
Hispanic or Latino (of any race)	2,171	49.9
Central American, ex. Mexican	255	70.8
Mexican	1,619	48.2

Households with Food Stamps/SNAP Benefits During Past 12 Months

Group	Number	%
Total Population	224	1.8
Hispanic or Latino (of any race)	152	3.5
Central American, ex. Mexican	0	0.0
Mexican	124	3.7

Poverty Rate
(Income in Past 12 Months Below Poverty Level)

Group	%
Total Population	3.8
Hispanic or Latino (of any race)	5.2
Central American, ex. Mexican	3.8
Mexican	6.1

El Cajon

Population

Group	Number	%TP[1]	%HP[2]
Total Population	99,478	100.0	–
Hispanic or Latino (of any race)	28,036	28.2	100.0
Central American, ex. Mexican	694	0.7	2.5
Guatemalan	225	0.2	0.8
Salvadoran	219	0.2	0.8
Mexican	24,534	24.7	87.5
Puerto Rican	646	0.6	2.3
South American	339	0.3	1.2
Spaniard	320	0.3	1.1

Population Growth: 2000–2010

Group	%
Total Population	4.9
Hispanic or Latino (of any race)	31.5
Central American, ex. Mexican	98.3
Guatemalan	94.0
Mexican	42.1
Puerto Rican	14.3
South American	76.6

Males per 100 Females

Group	Number
Total Population	95.6
Hispanic or Latino (of any race)	94.8
Central American, ex. Mexican	88.1
Guatemalan	112.3
Salvadoran	82.5
Mexican	96.4
Puerto Rican	82.5
South American	75.6
Spaniard	79.8

Average Household Size

Group	People
Total Population	2.84
Hispanic or Latino (of any race)	3.55
Central American, ex. Mexican	3.36
Guatemalan	3.35
Salvadoran	3.75
Mexican	3.64
Puerto Rican	2.59

Notes: (1) Percent of total population; (2) Percent of Hispanic/Latino population; Profiles include places with an overall population of at least 125,000, OR an overall population of at least 25,000 where the Hispanic/Latino population is at least 20% of the overall population. In states where less than five places meet either of these criteria, we have included places with at least 10,000 total population with the highest percentage of Hispanic/Latino population. These places are identified with an asterisk (*); Please refer to the User's Guide for a full explanation of data.

South American	2.85
Spaniard	2.65

Median Age

Group	Years
Total Population	33.7
Hispanic or Latino (of any race)	25.7
Central American, ex. Mexican	29.2
Guatemalan	27.8
Salvadoran	31.4
Mexican	25.4
Puerto Rican	24.7
South American	34.9
Spaniard	31.3

High School Graduates
(Universe: Population 25 Years and Over)

Group	Number	%
Total Population	48,688	79.6
Hispanic or Latino (of any race)	9,358	62.8
Mexican	7,771	60.2

Four-Year College Graduates
(Universe: Population 25 Years and Over)

Group	Number	%
Total Population	9,910	16.2
Hispanic or Latino (of any race)	933	6.3
Mexican	761	5.9

Population Age 3–17 Enrolled in Public School
(Universe: Population Age 3–17 Enrolled in School)

Group	Number	%
Total Population	17,899	92.0
Hispanic or Latino (of any race)	7,866	94.8
Mexican	6,874	95.6

Population Age 3–17 Enrolled in Private School
(Universe: Population Age 3–17 Enrolled in School)

Group	Number	%
Total Population	1,566	8.0
Hispanic or Latino (of any race)	432	5.2
Mexican	320	4.4

Foreign-Born Population

Group	Number	%
Total Population	24,527	25.0
Hispanic or Latino (of any race)	11,650	38.2
Mexican	10,838	40.5

Foreign-Born Naturalized U.S. Citizens

Group	Number	%
Total Population	9,271	37.8
Hispanic or Latino (of any race)	3,260	28.0
Mexican	2,831	26.1

Language Spoken at Home: English Only
(Universe: Population 5 Years and Over)

Group	Number	%
Total Population	57,875	64.4
Hispanic or Latino (of any race)	8,371	31.3
Mexican	6,443	27.5

Language Spoken at Home: Spanish
(Universe: Population 5 Years and Over)

Group	Number	%
Total Population	19,289	21.5
Hispanic or Latino (of any race)	18,338	68.5
Mexican	16,909	72.3

Unemployment Rate
(Universe: Population 16 Years and Over)

Group	%
Total Population	11.0
Hispanic or Latino (of any race)	9.7
Mexican	8.8

Class of Worker: Private Wage and Salary
(Universe: Civilian Employed Population 16 Years and Over)

Group	Number	%
Total Population	32,193	77.2
Hispanic or Latino (of any race)	10,124	79.0
Mexican	9,183	79.3

Class of Worker: Government
(Universe: Civilian Employed Population 16 Years and Over)

Group	Number	%
Total Population	6,102	14.6
Hispanic or Latino (of any race)	1,821	14.2
Mexican	1,555	13.4

Means of Transportation to Work: Car, Truck or Van
(Universe: Workers 16 Years and Over)

Group	Number	%
Total Population	35,684	87.4
Hispanic or Latino (of any race)	10,841	86.5
Mexican	9,798	86.7

Means of Transportation to Work: Public Transportation (ex. Taxicab)
(Universe: Workers 16 Years and Over)

Group	Number	%
Total Population	1,689	4.1
Hispanic or Latino (of any race)	657	5.2
Mexican	510	4.5

Homeownership Rate
(Universe: Occupied Housing Units)

Group	%
Total Population	41.3
Hispanic or Latino (of any race)	29.4
Central American, ex. Mexican	30.1
Guatemalan	26.5
Salvadoran	31.3
Mexican	29.2
Puerto Rican	24.5
South American	39.6
Spaniard	30.6

Median Home Value

Group	Dollars
Total Population	388,900
Hispanic or Latino (of any race)	324,800
Mexican	303,800

Median Gross Rent

Group	Dollars
Total Population	1,017
Hispanic or Latino (of any race)	988
Mexican	992

Median Household Income
(2010 Inflation-Adjusted Dollars)

Group	Dollars
Total Population	47,048
Hispanic or Latino (of any race)	43,643
Mexican	43,628

Per Capita Income
(2010 Inflation-Adjusted Dollars)

Group	Dollars
Total Population	21,150
Hispanic or Latino (of any race)	13,843
Mexican	13,614

Households with $100,000+ Income

Group	Number	%
Total Population	5,303	16.1
Hispanic or Latino (of any race)	868	10.9
Mexican	740	11.0

Households with Food Stamps/SNAP Benefits During Past 12 Months

Group	Number	%
Total Population	3,152	9.6
Hispanic or Latino (of any race)	860	10.8
Mexican	751	11.1

Poverty Rate
(Income in Past 12 Months Below Poverty Level)

Group	%
Total Population	21.3
Hispanic or Latino (of any race)	25.2
Mexican	26.8

El Centro

Population

Group	Number	%TP[1]	%HP[2]
Total Population	42,598	100.0	–
Hispanic or Latino (of any race)	34,751	81.6	100.0
Central American, ex. Mexican	143	0.3	0.4
Mexican	33,206	78.0	95.6
Puerto Rican	138	0.3	0.4

Population Growth: 2000–2010

Group	%
Total Population	12.6
Hispanic or Latino (of any race)	23.1
Central American, ex. Mexican	-13.3
Mexican	31.5

Males per 100 Females

Group	Number
Total Population	94.7
Hispanic or Latino (of any race)	90.8
Central American, ex. Mexican	197.9
Mexican	90.2
Puerto Rican	170.6

Average Household Size

Group	People
Total Population	3.19
Hispanic or Latino (of any race)	3.45
Central American, ex. Mexican	3.10
Mexican	3.47
Puerto Rican	3.17

Median Age

Group	Years
Total Population	31.8
Hispanic or Latino (of any race)	29.0
Central American, ex. Mexican	33.9
Mexican	28.9
Puerto Rican	31.2

High School Graduates
(Universe: Population 25 Years and Over)

Group	Number	%
Total Population	16,666	68.3
Hispanic or Latino (of any race)	10,588	59.6
Mexican	10,214	59.1

Four-Year College Graduates
(Universe: Population 25 Years and Over)

Group	Number	%
Total Population	3,761	15.4
Hispanic or Latino (of any race)	1,825	10.3
Mexican	1,673	9.7

Population Age 3–17 Enrolled in Public School
(Universe: Population Age 3–17 Enrolled in School)

Group	Number	%
Total Population	9,701	94.9
Hispanic or Latino (of any race)	8,434	95.5
Mexican	8,162	95.4

Population Age 3–17 Enrolled in Private School
(Universe: Population Age 3–17 Enrolled in School)

Group	Number	%
Total Population	520	5.1
Hispanic or Latino (of any race)	395	4.5
Mexican	391	4.6

Foreign-Born Population

Group	Number	%
Total Population	12,877	31.0
Hispanic or Latino (of any race)	11,986	37.1
Mexican	11,814	37.7

Foreign-Born Naturalized U.S. Citizens

Group	Number	%
Total Population	5,419	42.1
Hispanic or Latino (of any race)	5,074	42.3
Mexican	4,964	42.0

Language Spoken at Home: English Only
(Universe: Population 5 Years and Over)

Group	Number	%
Total Population	10,884	28.5

STATE & PLACE PROFILES

Notes: (1) Percent of total population; (2) Percent of Hispanic/Latino population; Profiles include places with an overall population of at least 125,000, OR an overall population of at least 25,000 where the Hispanic/Latino population is at least 20% of the overall population. In states where less than five places meet either of these criteria, we have included places with at least 10,000 total population with the highest percentage of Hispanic/Latino population. These places are identified with an asterisk (*); Please refer to the User's Guide for a full explanation of data.

Hispanic or Latino (of any race)	3,989	13.5
Mexican	3,806	13.3

Language Spoken at Home: Spanish
(Universe: Population 5 Years and Over)

Group	Number	%
Total Population	26,313	68.8
Hispanic or Latino (of any race)	25,440	86.4
Mexican	24,737	86.6

Unemployment Rate
(Universe: Population 16 Years and Over)

Group	%
Total Population	14.2
Hispanic or Latino (of any race)	16.7
Mexican	16.5

Class of Worker: Private Wage and Salary
(Universe: Civilian Employed Population 16 Years and Over)

Group	Number	%
Total Population	10,017	63.2
Hispanic or Latino (of any race)	7,401	65.6
Mexican	7,142	65.6

Class of Worker: Government
(Universe: Civilian Employed Population 16 Years and Over)

Group	Number	%
Total Population	4,654	29.4
Hispanic or Latino (of any race)	3,080	27.3
Mexican	2,983	27.4

Means of Transportation to Work: Car, Truck or Van
(Universe: Workers 16 Years and Over)

Group	Number	%
Total Population	13,944	90.4
Hispanic or Latino (of any race)	9,963	90.4
Mexican	9,563	90.1

Means of Transportation to Work: Public Transportation (ex. Taxicab)
(Universe: Workers 16 Years and Over)

Group	Number	%
Total Population	76	0.5
Hispanic or Latino (of any race)	49	0.4
Mexican	49	0.5

Homeownership Rate
(Universe: Occupied Housing Units)

Group	%
Total Population	49.5
Hispanic or Latino (of any race)	44.6
Central American, ex. Mexican	46.0
Mexican	44.9
Puerto Rican	30.4

Median Home Value

Group	Dollars
Total Population	211,300
Hispanic or Latino (of any race)	195,200
Mexican	195,800

Median Gross Rent

Group	Dollars
Total Population	692
Hispanic or Latino (of any race)	681
Mexican	682

Median Household Income
(2010 Inflation-Adjusted Dollars)

Group	Dollars
Total Population	38,481
Hispanic or Latino (of any race)	33,678
Mexican	33,320

Per Capita Income
(2010 Inflation-Adjusted Dollars)

Group	Dollars
Total Population	18,830
Hispanic or Latino (of any race)	14,364
Mexican	14,209

Households with $100,000+ Income

Group	Number	%
Total Population	2,183	16.3
Hispanic or Latino (of any race)	1,029	11.2
Mexican	961	10.7

Households with Food Stamps/SNAP Benefits During Past 12 Months

Group	Number	%
Total Population	1,921	14.3
Hispanic or Latino (of any race)	1,763	19.1
Mexican	1,697	19.0

Poverty Rate
(Income in Past 12 Months Below Poverty Level)

Group	%
Total Population	20.9
Hispanic or Latino (of any race)	22.8
Mexican	23.1

El Monte

Population

Group	Number	%TP[1]	%HP[2]
Total Population	113,475	100.0	–
Hispanic or Latino (of any race)	78,317	69.0	100.0
Central American, ex. Mexican	4,961	4.4	6.3
Guatemalan	1,393	1.2	1.8
Honduran	388	0.3	0.5
Nicaraguan	450	0.4	0.6
Salvadoran	2,570	2.3	3.3
Cuban	350	0.3	0.4
Mexican	69,053	60.9	88.2
Puerto Rican	232	0.2	0.3
South American	565	0.5	0.7
Argentinean	103	0.1	0.1
Ecuadorian	102	0.1	0.1
Peruvian	209	0.2	0.3
Spaniard	265	0.2	0.3

Population Growth: 2000–2010

Group	%
Total Population	-2.1
Hispanic or Latino (of any race)	-6.7
Central American, ex. Mexican	63.7
Guatemalan	108.8
Honduran	92.1
Nicaraguan	52.5
Salvadoran	70.9
Cuban	-18.8
Mexican	-1.2
Puerto Rican	-18.0
South American	35.2
Argentinean	-1.9
Peruvian	75.6

Males per 100 Females

Group	Number
Total Population	100.9
Hispanic or Latino (of any race)	102.7
Central American, ex. Mexican	104.0
Guatemalan	144.8
Honduran	89.3
Nicaraguan	89.9
Salvadoran	92.1
Cuban	104.7
Mexican	103.3
Puerto Rican	127.5
South American	82.3
Argentinean	87.3
Ecuadorian	78.9
Peruvian	86.6
Spaniard	105.4

Average Household Size

Group	People
Total Population	4.04
Hispanic or Latino (of any race)	4.49
Central American, ex. Mexican	4.53
Guatemalan	4.75
Honduran	4.43
Nicaraguan	4.20
Salvadoran	4.55
Cuban	2.99
Mexican	4.53
Puerto Rican	3.43
South American	3.36
Argentinean	2.90
Ecuadorian	3.29
Peruvian	3.88
Spaniard	3.85

Median Age

Group	Years
Total Population	31.6
Hispanic or Latino (of any race)	27.4
Central American, ex. Mexican	33.4
Guatemalan	31.5
Honduran	31.2
Nicaraguan	34.7
Salvadoran	34.8
Cuban	46.4
Mexican	26.8
Puerto Rican	34.3
South American	41.5
Argentinean	44.1
Ecuadorian	46.5
Peruvian	38.5
Spaniard	34.9

High School Graduates
(Universe: Population 25 Years and Over)

Group	Number	%
Total Population	36,020	52.3
Hispanic or Latino (of any race)	19,157	44.6
Central American, ex. Mexican	1,661	46.2
Guatemalan	251	26.3
Salvadoran	1,018	54.9
Mexican	16,342	43.5

Four-Year College Graduates
(Universe: Population 25 Years and Over)

Group	Number	%
Total Population	7,400	10.7
Hispanic or Latino (of any race)	2,024	4.7
Central American, ex. Mexican	144	4.0
Guatemalan	18	1.9
Salvadoran	112	6.0
Mexican	1,654	4.4

Population Age 3–17 Enrolled in Public School
(Universe: Population Age 3–17 Enrolled in School)

Group	Number	%
Total Population	22,863	97.3
Hispanic or Latino (of any race)	17,976	98.1
Central American, ex. Mexican	1,016	91.7
Guatemalan	150	96.8
Salvadoran	667	94.7
Mexican	16,630	98.6

Population Age 3–17 Enrolled in Private School
(Universe: Population Age 3–17 Enrolled in School)

Group	Number	%
Total Population	642	2.7
Hispanic or Latino (of any race)	354	1.9
Central American, ex. Mexican	92	8.3
Guatemalan	5	3.2
Salvadoran	37	5.3
Mexican	242	1.4

Foreign-Born Population

Group	Number	%
Total Population	60,243	52.9
Hispanic or Latino (of any race)	37,948	48.5
Central American, ex. Mexican	3,814	68.1
Guatemalan	996	73.3
Salvadoran	2,090	66.9
Mexican	33,167	47.4

Foreign-Born Naturalized U.S. Citizens

Group	Number	%
Total Population	24,590	40.8
Hispanic or Latino (of any race)	10,305	27.2
Central American, ex. Mexican	1,387	36.4
Guatemalan	209	21.0
Salvadoran	717	34.3
Mexican	8,516	25.7

Language Spoken at Home: English Only
(Universe: Population 5 Years and Over)

Group	Number	%
Total Population	16,424	15.6
Hispanic or Latino (of any race)	8,999	12.7
Central American, ex. Mexican	221	4.2

Notes: (1) Percent of total population; (2) Percent of Hispanic/Latino population; Profiles include places with an overall population of at least 125,000, OR an overall population of at least 25,000 where the Hispanic/Latino population is at least 20% of the overall population. In states where less than five places meet either of these criteria, we have included places with at least 10,000 total population with the highest percentage of Hispanic/Latino population. These places are identified with an asterisk (*); Please refer to the User's Guide for a full explanation of data.

Guatemalan	43	3.3
Salvadoran	146	5.0
Mexican	8,109	12.8

Language Spoken at Home: Spanish
(Universe: Population 5 Years and Over)

Group	Number	%
Total Population	62,534	59.5
Hispanic or Latino (of any race)	62,116	87.3
Central American, ex. Mexican	5,060	95.8
Guatemalan	1,243	96.7
Salvadoran	2,776	95.0
Mexican	55,232	87.2

Unemployment Rate
(Universe: Population 16 Years and Over)

Group	%
Total Population	9.5
Hispanic or Latino (of any race)	9.6
Central American, ex. Mexican	8.9
Guatemalan	3.8
Salvadoran	9.4
Mexican	9.5

Class of Worker: Private Wage and Salary
(Universe: Civilian Employed Population 16 Years and Over)

Group	Number	%
Total Population	41,223	84.9
Hispanic or Latino (of any race)	28,803	86.1
Central American, ex. Mexican	2,429	90.4
Guatemalan	579	90.8
Salvadoran	1,418	94.6
Mexican	25,325	85.8

Class of Worker: Government
(Universe: Civilian Employed Population 16 Years and Over)

Group	Number	%
Total Population	4,048	8.3
Hispanic or Latino (of any race)	2,583	7.7
Central American, ex. Mexican	158	5.9
Guatemalan	19	3.0
Salvadoran	51	3.4
Mexican	2,305	7.8

Means of Transportation to Work: Car, Truck or Van
(Universe: Workers 16 Years and Over)

Group	Number	%
Total Population	39,633	83.3
Hispanic or Latino (of any race)	26,810	81.4
Central American, ex. Mexican	2,152	81.8
Guatemalan	538	85.5
Salvadoran	1,124	77.4
Mexican	23,686	81.5

Means of Transportation to Work: Public Transportation (ex. Taxicab)
(Universe: Workers 16 Years and Over)

Group	Number	%
Total Population	2,940	6.2
Hispanic or Latino (of any race)	2,417	7.3
Central American, ex. Mexican	312	11.9
Guatemalan	65	10.3
Salvadoran	224	15.4
Mexican	1,887	6.5

Homeownership Rate
(Universe: Occupied Housing Units)

Group	%
Total Population	42.2
Hispanic or Latino (of any race)	31.9
Central American, ex. Mexican	31.5
Guatemalan	27.5
Honduran	26.4
Nicaraguan	29.4
Salvadoran	34.0
Cuban	45.8
Mexican	31.8
Puerto Rican	30.7
South American	40.6
Argentinean	37.5
Ecuadorian	47.4
Peruvian	36.4
Spaniard	43.6

Median Home Value

Group	Dollars
Total Population	396,600
Hispanic or Latino (of any race)	410,800
Central American, ex. Mexican	396,100
Guatemalan	445,100
Salvadoran	377,400
Mexican	410,000

Median Gross Rent

Group	Dollars
Total Population	1,037
Hispanic or Latino (of any race)	1,039
Central American, ex. Mexican	1,048
Guatemalan	1,110
Salvadoran	1,028
Mexican	1,044

Median Household Income
(2010 Inflation-Adjusted Dollars)

Group	Dollars
Total Population	42,750
Hispanic or Latino (of any race)	41,116
Central American, ex. Mexican	44,978
Guatemalan	49,286
Salvadoran	39,318
Mexican	40,736

Per Capita Income
(2010 Inflation-Adjusted Dollars)

Group	Dollars
Total Population	14,303
Hispanic or Latino (of any race)	12,588
Central American, ex. Mexican	13,780
Guatemalan	14,241
Salvadoran	13,269
Mexican	12,227

Households with $100,000+ Income

Group	Number	%
Total Population	3,403	12.3
Hispanic or Latino (of any race)	1,848	10.5
Central American, ex. Mexican	184	14.9
Guatemalan	52	18.7
Salvadoran	102	13.3
Mexican	1,534	9.8

Households with Food Stamps/SNAP Benefits During Past 12 Months

Group	Number	%
Total Population	3,158	11.4
Hispanic or Latino (of any race)	2,394	13.6
Central American, ex. Mexican	125	10.1
Guatemalan	26	9.4
Salvadoran	99	12.9
Mexican	2,229	14.2

Poverty Rate
(Income in Past 12 Months Below Poverty Level)

Group	%
Total Population	20.7
Hispanic or Latino (of any race)	22.1
Central American, ex. Mexican	18.7
Guatemalan	28.2
Salvadoran	18.4
Mexican	22.8

El Paso de Robles (Paso Robles)

Population

Group	Number	%TP[1]	%HP[2]
Total Population	29,793	100.0	–
Hispanic or Latino (of any race)	10,275	34.5	100.0
Central American, ex. Mexican	217	0.7	2.1
Mexican	9,131	30.6	88.9
Puerto Rican	109	0.4	1.1
Spaniard	152	0.5	1.5

Population Growth: 2000–2010

Group	%
Total Population	22.6
Hispanic or Latino (of any race)	52.6
Central American, ex. Mexican	85.5
Mexican	59.9

Males per 100 Females

Group	Number
Total Population	94.9
Hispanic or Latino (of any race)	102.1
Central American, ex. Mexican	100.9
Mexican	103.7
Puerto Rican	118.0
Spaniard	78.8

Average Household Size

Group	People
Total Population	2.73
Hispanic or Latino (of any race)	3.78
Central American, ex. Mexican	3.59
Mexican	3.89
Puerto Rican	2.70
Spaniard	2.67

Median Age

Group	Years
Total Population	35.3
Hispanic or Latino (of any race)	24.6
Central American, ex. Mexican	32.5
Mexican	24.0
Puerto Rican	30.5
Spaniard	36.0

High School Graduates
(Universe: Population 25 Years and Over)

Group	Number	%
Total Population	15,052	83.6
Hispanic or Latino (of any race)	2,889	58.0
Mexican	2,439	57.7

Four-Year College Graduates
(Universe: Population 25 Years and Over)

Group	Number	%
Total Population	3,923	21.8
Hispanic or Latino (of any race)	399	8.0
Mexican	334	7.9

Population Age 3–17 Enrolled in Public School
(Universe: Population Age 3–17 Enrolled in School)

Group	Number	%
Total Population	5,436	91.1
Hispanic or Latino (of any race)	2,789	96.1
Mexican	2,438	98.4

Population Age 3–17 Enrolled in Private School
(Universe: Population Age 3–17 Enrolled in School)

Group	Number	%
Total Population	530	8.9
Hispanic or Latino (of any race)	114	3.9
Mexican	39	1.6

Foreign-Born Population

Group	Number	%
Total Population	4,424	15.4
Hispanic or Latino (of any race)	3,588	35.8
Mexican	3,312	39.0

Foreign-Born Naturalized U.S. Citizens

Group	Number	%
Total Population	1,524	34.4
Hispanic or Latino (of any race)	990	27.6
Mexican	898	27.1

Language Spoken at Home: English Only
(Universe: Population 5 Years and Over)

Group	Number	%
Total Population	19,851	75.8
Hispanic or Latino (of any race)	3,170	37.0
Mexican	2,242	30.9

Language Spoken at Home: Spanish
(Universe: Population 5 Years and Over)

Group	Number	%
Total Population	5,668	21.6
Hispanic or Latino (of any race)	5,374	62.8
Mexican	4,997	68.9

Unemployment Rate
(Universe: Population 16 Years and Over)

Group	%
Total Population	7.6
Hispanic or Latino (of any race)	9.1

STATE & PLACE PROFILES

Notes: (1) Percent of total population; (2) Percent of Hispanic/Latino population; Profiles include places with an overall population of at least 125,000, OR an overall population of at least 25,000 where the Hispanic/Latino population is at least 20% of the overall population. In states where less than five places meet either of these criteria, we have included places with at least 10,000 total population with the highest percentage of Hispanic/Latino population. These places are identified with an asterisk (*); Please refer to the User's Guide for a full explanation of data.

Mexican	10.3

Class of Worker: Private Wage and Salary
(Universe: Civilian Employed Population 16 Years and Over)

Group	Number	%
Total Population	8,713	67.9
Hispanic or Latino (of any race)	3,107	79.1
Mexican	2,616	78.3

Class of Worker: Government
(Universe: Civilian Employed Population 16 Years and Over)

Group	Number	%
Total Population	2,868	22.3
Hispanic or Latino (of any race)	567	14.4
Mexican	480	14.4

Means of Transportation to Work: Car, Truck or Van
(Universe: Workers 16 Years and Over)

Group	Number	%
Total Population	11,184	88.5
Hispanic or Latino (of any race)	3,457	90.5
Mexican	2,942	90.1

Means of Transportation to Work: Public Transportation (ex. Taxicab)
(Universe: Workers 16 Years and Over)

Group	Number	%
Total Population	112	0.9
Hispanic or Latino (of any race)	65	1.7
Mexican	65	2.0

Homeownership Rate
(Universe: Occupied Housing Units)

Group	%
Total Population	59.2
Hispanic or Latino (of any race)	34.4
Central American, ex. Mexican	40.6
Mexican	33.2
Puerto Rican	34.1
Spaniard	57.1

Median Home Value

Group	Dollars
Total Population	417,200
Hispanic or Latino (of any race)	412,100
Mexican	395,500

Median Gross Rent

Group	Dollars
Total Population	987
Hispanic or Latino (of any race)	905
Mexican	837

Median Household Income
(2010 Inflation-Adjusted Dollars)

Group	Dollars
Total Population	57,459
Hispanic or Latino (of any race)	48,790
Mexican	44,433

Per Capita Income
(2010 Inflation-Adjusted Dollars)

Group	Dollars
Total Population	25,839
Hispanic or Latino (of any race)	13,587
Mexican	13,101

Households with $100,000+ Income

Group	Number	%
Total Population	2,183	20.3
Hispanic or Latino (of any race)	348	13.4
Mexican	227	10.7

Households with Food Stamps/SNAP Benefits During Past 12 Months

Group	Number	%
Total Population	697	6.5
Hispanic or Latino (of any race)	348	13.4
Mexican	287	13.5

Poverty Rate
(Income in Past 12 Months Below Poverty Level)

Group	%
Total Population	10.0
Hispanic or Latino (of any race)	17.4
Mexican	20.0

Elk Grove

Population

Group	Number	%TP[1]	%HP[2]
Total Population	153,015	100.0	–
Hispanic or Latino (of any race)	27,581	18.0	100.0
Central American, ex. Mexican	1,882	1.2	6.8
Guatemalan	255	0.2	0.9
Nicaraguan	453	0.3	1.6
Panamanian	175	0.1	0.6
Salvadoran	831	0.5	3.0
Cuban	222	0.1	0.8
Mexican	21,186	13.8	76.8
Puerto Rican	1,064	0.7	3.9
South American	699	0.5	2.5
Colombian	140	0.1	0.5
Peruvian	275	0.2	1.0
Spaniard	773	0.5	2.8

Population Growth: 2000–2010

Group	%
Total Population	155.1
Hispanic or Latino (of any race)	228.4
Central American, ex. Mexican	591.9
Mexican	236.3
Puerto Rican	350.8

Males per 100 Females

Group	Number
Total Population	93.9
Hispanic or Latino (of any race)	95.3
Central American, ex. Mexican	84.0
Guatemalan	84.8
Nicaraguan	91.9
Panamanian	68.3
Salvadoran	91.5
Cuban	88.1
Mexican	98.2
Puerto Rican	97.0
South American	75.6
Colombian	66.7
Peruvian	80.9
Spaniard	83.6

Average Household Size

Group	People
Total Population	3.18
Hispanic or Latino (of any race)	3.58
Central American, ex. Mexican	3.74
Guatemalan	4.10
Nicaraguan	3.80
Panamanian	3.17
Salvadoran	3.79
Cuban	2.86
Mexican	3.66
Puerto Rican	3.11
South American	3.32
Colombian	3.44
Peruvian	3.39
Spaniard	2.92

Median Age

Group	Years
Total Population	34.3
Hispanic or Latino (of any race)	25.4
Central American, ex. Mexican	31.6
Guatemalan	33.2
Nicaraguan	29.3
Panamanian	33.1
Salvadoran	32.3
Cuban	31.8
Mexican	24.4
Puerto Rican	25.8
South American	33.7
Colombian	31.5
Peruvian	36.3
Spaniard	34.8

High School Graduates
(Universe: Population 25 Years and Over)

Group	Number	%
Total Population	76,406	89.3
Hispanic or Latino (of any race)	9,398	76.2
Central American, ex. Mexican	866	80.3
Mexican	6,607	72.3
Puerto Rican	527	89.0

Four-Year College Graduates
(Universe: Population 25 Years and Over)

Group	Number	%
Total Population	28,509	33.3
Hispanic or Latino (of any race)	2,574	20.9
Central American, ex. Mexican	267	24.8
Mexican	1,722	18.8
Puerto Rican	140	23.6

Population Age 3–17 Enrolled in Public School
(Universe: Population Age 3–17 Enrolled in School)

Group	Number	%
Total Population	30,661	87.6
Hispanic or Latino (of any race)	7,662	88.4
Central American, ex. Mexican	526	83.1
Mexican	6,156	89.4
Puerto Rican	366	83.6

Population Age 3–17 Enrolled in Private School
(Universe: Population Age 3–17 Enrolled in School)

Group	Number	%
Total Population	4,331	12.4
Hispanic or Latino (of any race)	1,010	11.6
Central American, ex. Mexican	107	16.9
Mexican	731	10.6
Puerto Rican	72	16.4

Foreign-Born Population

Group	Number	%
Total Population	31,931	22.6
Hispanic or Latino (of any race)	5,368	21.2
Central American, ex. Mexican	863	40.5
Mexican	3,905	19.9
Puerto Rican	77	6.7

Foreign-Born Naturalized U.S. Citizens

Group	Number	%
Total Population	22,007	68.9
Hispanic or Latino (of any race)	2,643	49.2
Central American, ex. Mexican	524	60.7
Mexican	1,684	43.1
Puerto Rican	9	11.7

Language Spoken at Home: English Only
(Universe: Population 5 Years and Over)

Group	Number	%
Total Population	87,814	67.3
Hispanic or Latino (of any race)	12,021	52.6
Central American, ex. Mexican	478	26.4
Mexican	9,313	52.6
Puerto Rican	695	63.4

Language Spoken at Home: Spanish
(Universe: Population 5 Years and Over)

Group	Number	%
Total Population	12,053	9.2
Hispanic or Latino (of any race)	10,729	46.9
Central American, ex. Mexican	1,334	73.6
Mexican	8,345	47.2
Puerto Rican	393	35.8

Unemployment Rate
(Universe: Population 16 Years and Over)

Group	%
Total Population	8.1
Hispanic or Latino (of any race)	9.2
Central American, ex. Mexican	7.3
Mexican	9.1
Puerto Rican	18.1

Class of Worker: Private Wage and Salary
(Universe: Civilian Employed Population 16 Years and Over)

Group	Number	%
Total Population	42,760	63.8
Hispanic or Latino (of any race)	6,586	62.5
Central American, ex. Mexican	582	69.0
Mexican	5,021	60.9
Puerto Rican	414	81.5

Notes: (1) Percent of total population; (2) Percent of Hispanic/Latino population; Profiles include places with an overall population of at least 125,000, OR an overall population of at least 25,000 where the Hispanic/Latino population is at least 20% of the overall population. In states where less than five places meet either of these criteria, we have included places with at least 10,000 total population with the highest percentage of Hispanic/Latino population. These places are identified with an asterisk (*); Please refer to the User's Guide for a full explanation of data.

Class of Worker: Government
(Universe: Civilian Employed Population 16 Years and Over)

Group	Number	%
Total Population	18,819	28.1
Hispanic or Latino (of any race)	2,885	27.4
Central American, ex. Mexican	111	13.2
Mexican	2,410	29.2
Puerto Rican	62	12.2

Means of Transportation to Work: Car, Truck or Van
(Universe: Workers 16 Years and Over)

Group	Number	%
Total Population	58,521	89.9
Hispanic or Latino (of any race)	8,968	86.4
Central American, ex. Mexican	799	94.8
Mexican	6,930	85.6
Puerto Rican	417	82.1

Means of Transportation to Work: Public Transportation (ex. Taxicab)
(Universe: Workers 16 Years and Over)

Group	Number	%
Total Population	1,926	3.0
Hispanic or Latino (of any race)	483	4.7
Central American, ex. Mexican	0	0.0
Mexican	396	4.9
Puerto Rican	69	13.6

Homeownership Rate
(Universe: Occupied Housing Units)

Group	%
Total Population	74.6
Hispanic or Latino (of any race)	69.0
Central American, ex. Mexican	70.2
Guatemalan	69.6
Nicaraguan	75.8
Panamanian	73.1
Salvadoran	69.6
Cuban	67.1
Mexican	69.2
Puerto Rican	66.1
South American	78.6
Colombian	82.1
Peruvian	75.9
Spaniard	76.8

Median Home Value

Group	Dollars
Total Population	360,900
Hispanic or Latino (of any race)	345,600
Central American, ex. Mexican	357,600
Mexican	359,400
Puerto Rican	299,000

Median Gross Rent

Group	Dollars
Total Population	1,410
Hispanic or Latino (of any race)	1,428
Central American, ex. Mexican	1,282
Mexican	1,411
Puerto Rican	1,488

Median Household Income
(2010 Inflation-Adjusted Dollars)

Group	Dollars
Total Population	79,457
Hispanic or Latino (of any race)	73,731
Central American, ex. Mexican	54,450
Mexican	72,731
Puerto Rican	95,117

Per Capita Income
(2010 Inflation-Adjusted Dollars)

Group	Dollars
Total Population	29,164
Hispanic or Latino (of any race)	20,983
Central American, ex. Mexican	18,816
Mexican	20,900
Puerto Rican	23,822

Households with $100,000+ Income

Group	Number	%
Total Population	16,026	36.1
Hispanic or Latino (of any race)	1,846	29.5
Central American, ex. Mexican	130	22.8
Mexican	1,308	28.0
Puerto Rican	89	37.2

Households with Food Stamps/SNAP Benefits During Past 12 Months

Group	Number	%
Total Population	1,637	3.7
Hispanic or Latino (of any race)	340	5.4
Central American, ex. Mexican	28	4.9
Mexican	244	5.2
Puerto Rican	20	8.4

Poverty Rate
(Income in Past 12 Months Below Poverty Level)

Group	%
Total Population	8.0
Hispanic or Latino (of any race)	12.3
Central American, ex. Mexican	23.7
Mexican	10.9
Puerto Rican	22.9

Escondido

Population

Group	Number	%TP[1]	%HP[2]
Total Population	143,911	100.0	–
Hispanic or Latino (of any race)	70,326	48.9	100.0
Central American, ex. Mexican	1,816	1.3	2.6
Guatemalan	872	0.6	1.2
Honduran	101	0.1	0.1
Salvadoran	616	0.4	0.9
Cuban	173	0.1	0.2
Mexican	63,552	44.2	90.4
Puerto Rican	863	0.6	1.2
South American	535	0.4	0.8
Colombian	155	0.1	0.2
Peruvian	126	0.1	0.2
Spaniard	476	0.3	0.7

Population Growth: 2000–2010

Group	%
Total Population	7.8
Hispanic or Latino (of any race)	36.0
Central American, ex. Mexican	115.7
Guatemalan	136.3
Salvadoran	147.4
Cuban	46.6
Mexican	42.1
Puerto Rican	33.4
South American	82.0
Colombian	55.0
Spaniard	344.9

Males per 100 Females

Group	Number
Total Population	98.2
Hispanic or Latino (of any race)	103.0
Central American, ex. Mexican	135.5
Guatemalan	199.7
Honduran	114.9
Salvadoran	100.0
Cuban	94.4
Mexican	102.7
Puerto Rican	95.2
South American	76.0
Colombian	72.2
Peruvian	85.3
Spaniard	83.8

Average Household Size

Group	People
Total Population	3.12
Hispanic or Latino (of any race)	4.39
Central American, ex. Mexican	4.27
Guatemalan	4.69
Honduran	4.59
Salvadoran	4.10
Cuban	2.85
Mexican	4.50
Puerto Rican	2.83
South American	2.67
Colombian	2.29
Peruvian	3.22
Spaniard	2.93

Median Age

Group	Years
Total Population	32.5
Hispanic or Latino (of any race)	24.9
Central American, ex. Mexican	29.1
Guatemalan	26.9
Honduran	32.8
Salvadoran	32.1
Cuban	37.3
Mexican	24.5
Puerto Rican	27.1
South American	39.9
Colombian	40.3
Peruvian	38.8
Spaniard	32.8

High School Graduates
(Universe: Population 25 Years and Over)

Group	Number	%
Total Population	65,733	75.0
Hispanic or Latino (of any race)	15,395	46.5
Central American, ex. Mexican	481	48.9
Mexican	13,436	44.4

Four-Year College Graduates
(Universe: Population 25 Years and Over)

Group	Number	%
Total Population	19,373	22.1
Hispanic or Latino (of any race)	2,257	6.8
Central American, ex. Mexican	66	6.7
Mexican	1,766	5.8

Population Age 3–17 Enrolled in Public School
(Universe: Population Age 3–17 Enrolled in School)

Group	Number	%
Total Population	25,752	92.9
Hispanic or Latino (of any race)	16,136	98.3
Central American, ex. Mexican	434	100.0
Mexican	15,345	98.6

Population Age 3–17 Enrolled in Private School
(Universe: Population Age 3–17 Enrolled in School)

Group	Number	%
Total Population	1,966	7.1
Hispanic or Latino (of any race)	282	1.7
Central American, ex. Mexican	0	0.0
Mexican	224	1.4

Foreign-Born Population

Group	Number	%
Total Population	40,650	28.8
Hispanic or Latino (of any race)	31,337	48.1
Central American, ex. Mexican	919	54.2
Mexican	29,732	48.8

Foreign-Born Naturalized U.S. Citizens

Group	Number	%
Total Population	10,900	26.8
Hispanic or Latino (of any race)	4,934	15.7
Central American, ex. Mexican	126	13.7
Mexican	4,435	14.9

Language Spoken at Home: English Only
(Universe: Population 5 Years and Over)

Group	Number	%
Total Population	68,552	52.9
Hispanic or Latino (of any race)	7,519	13.0
Central American, ex. Mexican	210	13.2
Mexican	6,162	11.4

Language Spoken at Home: Spanish
(Universe: Population 5 Years and Over)

Group	Number	%
Total Population	52,224	40.3
Hispanic or Latino (of any race)	50,449	87.0
Central American, ex. Mexican	1,376	86.8
Mexican	47,891	88.6

Unemployment Rate
(Universe: Population 16 Years and Over)

Group	%
Total Population	8.1
Hispanic or Latino (of any race)	9.2
Central American, ex. Mexican	13.8

STATE & PLACE PROFILES

Notes: (1) Percent of total population; (2) Percent of Hispanic/Latino population; Profiles include places with an overall population of at least 125,000, OR an overall population of at least 25,000 where the Hispanic/Latino population is at least 20% of the overall population. In states where less than five places meet either of these criteria, we have included places with at least 10,000 total population with the highest percentage of Hispanic/Latino population. These places are identified with an asterisk (*); Please refer to the User's Guide for a full explanation of data.

Mexican	9.2

Class of Worker: Private Wage and Salary
(Universe: Civilian Employed Population 16 Years and Over)

Group	Number	%
Total Population	50,893	80.4
Hispanic or Latino (of any race)	23,585	84.2
Central American, ex. Mexican	626	76.1
Mexican	21,877	84.6

Class of Worker: Government
(Universe: Civilian Employed Population 16 Years and Over)

Group	Number	%
Total Population	6,694	10.6
Hispanic or Latino (of any race)	1,871	6.7
Central American, ex. Mexican	50	6.1
Mexican	1,691	6.5

Means of Transportation to Work: Car, Truck or Van
(Universe: Workers 16 Years and Over)

Group	Number	%
Total Population	56,314	89.5
Hispanic or Latino (of any race)	24,747	88.9
Central American, ex. Mexican	713	85.1
Mexican	22,774	89.1

Means of Transportation to Work: Public Transportation (ex. Taxicab)
(Universe: Workers 16 Years and Over)

Group	Number	%
Total Population	1,668	2.7
Hispanic or Latino (of any race)	1,020	3.7
Central American, ex. Mexican	62	7.4
Mexican	931	3.6

Homeownership Rate
(Universe: Occupied Housing Units)

Group	%
Total Population	52.2
Hispanic or Latino (of any race)	35.2
Central American, ex. Mexican	30.5
Guatemalan	19.6
Honduran	50.0
Salvadoran	34.1
Cuban	55.7
Mexican	35.0
Puerto Rican	34.9
South American	52.2
Colombian	63.5
Peruvian	35.1
Spaniard	58.0

Median Home Value

Group	Dollars
Total Population	404,900
Hispanic or Latino (of any race)	357,300
Central American, ex. Mexican	324,100
Mexican	356,200

Median Gross Rent

Group	Dollars
Total Population	1,116
Hispanic or Latino (of any race)	1,107
Central American, ex. Mexican	1,228
Mexican	1,106

Median Household Income
(2010 Inflation-Adjusted Dollars)

Group	Dollars
Total Population	51,675
Hispanic or Latino (of any race)	42,050
Central American, ex. Mexican	48,147
Mexican	41,359

Per Capita Income
(2010 Inflation-Adjusted Dollars)

Group	Dollars
Total Population	23,182
Hispanic or Latino (of any race)	13,142
Central American, ex. Mexican	16,344
Mexican	12,567

Households with $100,000+ Income

Group	Number	%
Total Population	9,505	21.3
Hispanic or Latino (of any race)	1,706	11.1
Central American, ex. Mexican	97	19.1
Mexican	1,373	9.9

Households with Food Stamps/SNAP Benefits During Past 12 Months

Group	Number	%
Total Population	1,509	3.4
Hispanic or Latino (of any race)	925	6.0
Central American, ex. Mexican	29	5.7
Mexican	866	6.3

Poverty Rate
(Income in Past 12 Months Below Poverty Level)

Group	%
Total Population	15.6
Hispanic or Latino (of any race)	22.0
Central American, ex. Mexican	18.9
Mexican	22.5

Fairfield

Population

Group	Number	%TP[1]	%HP[2]
Total Population	105,321	100.0	–
Hispanic or Latino (of any race)	28,789	27.3	100.0
Central American, ex. Mexican	2,099	2.0	7.3
Guatemalan	275	0.3	1.0
Honduran	106	0.1	0.4
Nicaraguan	478	0.5	1.7
Salvadoran	1,068	1.0	3.7
Cuban	179	0.2	0.6
Mexican	22,360	21.2	77.7
Puerto Rican	1,184	1.1	4.1
South American	566	0.5	2.0
Colombian	136	0.1	0.5
Peruvian	254	0.2	0.9
Spaniard	682	0.6	2.4

Population Growth: 2000–2010

Group	%
Total Population	9.5
Hispanic or Latino (of any race)	59.5
Central American, ex. Mexican	144.6
Guatemalan	133.1
Nicaraguan	157.0
Salvadoran	206.0
Cuban	54.3
Mexican	73.4
Puerto Rican	39.3
South American	101.4

Males per 100 Females

Group	Number
Total Population	97.0
Hispanic or Latino (of any race)	102.6
Central American, ex. Mexican	86.6
Guatemalan	84.6
Honduran	76.7
Nicaraguan	90.4
Salvadoran	88.4
Cuban	98.9
Mexican	105.7
Puerto Rican	92.2
South American	87.4
Colombian	72.2
Peruvian	80.1
Spaniard	86.8

Average Household Size

Group	People
Total Population	2.98
Hispanic or Latino (of any race)	3.89
Central American, ex. Mexican	3.68
Guatemalan	3.77
Honduran	3.50
Nicaraguan	3.52
Salvadoran	3.82
Cuban	2.86
Mexican	4.11
Puerto Rican	2.91
South American	3.07
Colombian	3.09
Peruvian	3.36
Spaniard	3.06

Median Age

Group	Years
Total Population	33.7
Hispanic or Latino (of any race)	25.1
Central American, ex. Mexican	32.0
Guatemalan	33.3
Honduran	34.3
Nicaraguan	34.1
Salvadoran	31.1
Cuban	27.8
Mexican	24.0
Puerto Rican	26.5
South American	37.0
Colombian	30.4
Peruvian	37.3
Spaniard	33.6

High School Graduates
(Universe: Population 25 Years and Over)

Group	Number	%
Total Population	53,855	84.8
Hispanic or Latino (of any race)	8,428	61.8
Central American, ex. Mexican	886	74.1
Salvadoran	642	95.0
Mexican	6,160	58.3
Puerto Rican	401	64.1

Four-Year College Graduates
(Universe: Population 25 Years and Over)

Group	Number	%
Total Population	14,062	22.2
Hispanic or Latino (of any race)	1,316	9.6
Central American, ex. Mexican	124	10.4
Salvadoran	100	14.8
Mexican	874	8.3
Puerto Rican	90	14.4

Population Age 3–17 Enrolled in Public School
(Universe: Population Age 3–17 Enrolled in School)

Group	Number	%
Total Population	20,895	93.5
Hispanic or Latino (of any race)	6,780	96.1
Central American, ex. Mexican	474	100.0
Salvadoran	259	100.0
Mexican	5,484	96.0
Puerto Rican	281	100.0

Population Age 3–17 Enrolled in Private School
(Universe: Population Age 3–17 Enrolled in School)

Group	Number	%
Total Population	1,454	6.5
Hispanic or Latino (of any race)	273	3.9
Central American, ex. Mexican	0	0.0
Salvadoran	0	0.0
Mexican	229	4.0
Puerto Rican	0	0.0

Foreign-Born Population

Group	Number	%
Total Population	22,861	22.0
Hispanic or Latino (of any race)	10,296	38.4
Central American, ex. Mexican	1,073	54.9
Salvadoran	563	51.0
Mexican	8,636	40.5
Puerto Rican	24	1.9

Foreign-Born Naturalized U.S. Citizens

Group	Number	%
Total Population	10,884	47.6
Hispanic or Latino (of any race)	2,396	23.3
Central American, ex. Mexican	460	42.9
Salvadoran	234	41.6
Mexican	1,622	18.8
Puerto Rican	24	100.0

Language Spoken at Home: English Only
(Universe: Population 5 Years and Over)

Group	Number	%
Total Population	64,485	67.1
Hispanic or Latino (of any race)	6,556	27.3
Central American, ex. Mexican	410	21.8
Salvadoran	243	22.6
Mexican	4,594	24.1
Puerto Rican	518	48.3

Notes: (1) Percent of total population; (2) Percent of Hispanic/Latino population; Profiles include places with an overall population of at least 125,000, OR an overall population of at least 25,000 where the Hispanic/Latino population is at least 20% of the overall population. In states where less than five places meet either of these criteria, we have included places with at least 10,000 total population with the highest percentage of Hispanic/Latino population. These places are identified with an asterisk (*); Please refer to the User's Guide for a full explanation of data.

Language Spoken at Home: Spanish
(Universe: Population 5 Years and Over)

Group	Number	%
Total Population	18,244	19.0
Hispanic or Latino (of any race)	17,208	71.7
Central American, ex. Mexican	1,448	76.9
Salvadoran	832	77.4
Mexican	14,363	75.2
Puerto Rican	520	48.5

Unemployment Rate
(Universe: Population 16 Years and Over)

Group	%
Total Population	9.5
Hispanic or Latino (of any race)	11.3
Central American, ex. Mexican	6.5
Salvadoran	9.2
Mexican	11.3
Puerto Rican	17.1

Class of Worker: Private Wage and Salary
(Universe: Civilian Employed Population 16 Years and Over)

Group	Number	%
Total Population	34,350	74.7
Hispanic or Latino (of any race)	9,332	84.5
Central American, ex. Mexican	780	84.6
Salvadoran	433	88.2
Mexican	7,571	86.3
Puerto Rican	357	83.0

Class of Worker: Government
(Universe: Civilian Employed Population 16 Years and Over)

Group	Number	%
Total Population	9,265	20.2
Hispanic or Latino (of any race)	1,427	12.9
Central American, ex. Mexican	105	11.4
Salvadoran	58	11.8
Mexican	986	11.2
Puerto Rican	73	17.0

Means of Transportation to Work: Car, Truck or Van
(Universe: Workers 16 Years and Over)

Group	Number	%
Total Population	43,054	92.6
Hispanic or Latino (of any race)	10,412	94.9
Central American, ex. Mexican	873	94.1
Salvadoran	492	95.2
Mexican	8,179	94.4
Puerto Rican	443	96.3

Means of Transportation to Work: Public Transportation (ex. Taxicab)
(Universe: Workers 16 Years and Over)

Group	Number	%
Total Population	956	2.1
Hispanic or Latino (of any race)	118	1.1
Central American, ex. Mexican	17	1.8
Salvadoran	17	3.3
Mexican	101	1.2
Puerto Rican	0	0.0

Homeownership Rate
(Universe: Occupied Housing Units)

Group	%
Total Population	60.4
Hispanic or Latino (of any race)	50.3
Central American, ex. Mexican	61.7
Guatemalan	61.0
Honduran	43.8
Nicaraguan	66.9
Salvadoran	60.3
Cuban	43.1
Mexican	48.1
Puerto Rican	46.4
South American	65.4
Colombian	55.8
Peruvian	67.1
Spaniard	68.2

Median Home Value

Group	Dollars
Total Population	392,700
Hispanic or Latino (of any race)	364,800
Central American, ex. Mexican	427,900
Salvadoran	327,300
Mexican	349,900
Puerto Rican	343,900

Median Gross Rent

Group	Dollars
Total Population	1,172
Hispanic or Latino (of any race)	1,056
Central American, ex. Mexican	1,270
Salvadoran	792
Mexican	1,041
Puerto Rican	866

Median Household Income
(2010 Inflation-Adjusted Dollars)

Group	Dollars
Total Population	68,009
Hispanic or Latino (of any race)	55,138
Central American, ex. Mexican	57,950
Salvadoran	51,458
Mexican	51,406
Puerto Rican	56,563

Per Capita Income
(2010 Inflation-Adjusted Dollars)

Group	Dollars
Total Population	26,647
Hispanic or Latino (of any race)	17,978
Central American, ex. Mexican	27,328
Salvadoran	33,393
Mexican	16,438
Puerto Rican	17,469

Households with $100,000+ Income

Group	Number	%
Total Population	9,321	28.0
Hispanic or Latino (of any race)	1,303	19.9
Central American, ex. Mexican	162	33.1
Salvadoran	77	32.5
Mexican	808	16.0
Puerto Rican	113	30.2

Households with Food Stamps/SNAP Benefits During Past 12 Months

Group	Number	%
Total Population	1,852	5.6
Hispanic or Latino (of any race)	564	8.6
Central American, ex. Mexican	58	11.9
Salvadoran	36	15.2
Mexican	464	9.2
Puerto Rican	11	2.9

Poverty Rate
(Income in Past 12 Months Below Poverty Level)

Group	%
Total Population	11.0
Hispanic or Latino (of any race)	17.6
Central American, ex. Mexican	15.3
Salvadoran	4.4
Mexican	19.1
Puerto Rican	19.9

Fallbrook

Population

Group	Number	%TP[1]	%HP[2]
Total Population	30,534	100.0	–
Hispanic or Latino (of any race)	13,800	45.2	100.0
Central American, ex. Mexican	911	3.0	6.6
Guatemalan	815	2.7	5.9
Mexican	12,033	39.4	87.2
Puerto Rican	148	0.5	1.1
South American	104	0.3	0.8
Spaniard	100	0.3	0.7

Population Growth: 2000–2010

Group	%
Total Population	4.9
Hispanic or Latino (of any race)	27.2
Central American, ex. Mexican	127.8
Guatemalan	140.4
Mexican	31.1
Puerto Rican	34.5

Males per 100 Females

Group	Number
Total Population	99.5
Hispanic or Latino (of any race)	105.6
Central American, ex. Mexican	156.6
Guatemalan	164.6
Mexican	103.1
Puerto Rican	85.0
South American	76.3
Spaniard	108.3

Average Household Size

Group	People
Total Population	3.04
Hispanic or Latino (of any race)	4.33
Central American, ex. Mexican	4.86
Guatemalan	5.19
Mexican	4.39
Puerto Rican	2.61
South American	2.62
Spaniard	3.24

Median Age

Group	Years
Total Population	34.7
Hispanic or Latino (of any race)	24.3
Central American, ex. Mexican	23.8
Guatemalan	24.0
Mexican	24.2
Puerto Rican	23.7
South American	33.5
Spaniard	40.3

High School Graduates
(Universe: Population 25 Years and Over)

Group	Number	%
Total Population	14,394	77.6
Hispanic or Latino (of any race)	2,640	44.1
Mexican	2,256	43.5

Four-Year College Graduates
(Universe: Population 25 Years and Over)

Group	Number	%
Total Population	4,230	22.8
Hispanic or Latino (of any race)	352	5.9
Mexican	276	5.3

Population Age 3–17 Enrolled in Public School
(Universe: Population Age 3–17 Enrolled in School)

Group	Number	%
Total Population	5,411	88.9
Hispanic or Latino (of any race)	3,261	96.1
Mexican	3,037	95.9

Population Age 3–17 Enrolled in Private School
(Universe: Population Age 3–17 Enrolled in School)

Group	Number	%
Total Population	675	11.1
Hispanic or Latino (of any race)	131	3.9
Mexican	129	4.1

Foreign-Born Population

Group	Number	%
Total Population	6,736	22.5
Hispanic or Latino (of any race)	5,555	46.0
Mexican	4,968	46.8

Foreign-Born Naturalized U.S. Citizens

Group	Number	%
Total Population	2,104	31.2
Hispanic or Latino (of any race)	1,449	26.1
Mexican	1,256	25.3

Language Spoken at Home: English Only
(Universe: Population 5 Years and Over)

Group	Number	%
Total Population	17,560	63.1
Hispanic or Latino (of any race)	1,779	16.3
Mexican	1,302	13.6

Language Spoken at Home: Spanish
(Universe: Population 5 Years and Over)

Group	Number	%
Total Population	9,574	34.4
Hispanic or Latino (of any race)	9,073	83.3
Mexican	8,248	86.3

STATE & PLACE PROFILES

Notes: (1) Percent of total population; (2) Percent of Hispanic/Latino population; Profiles include places with an overall population of at least 125,000, OR an overall population of at least 25,000 where the Hispanic/Latino population is at least 20% of the overall population. In states where less than five places meet either of these criteria, we have included places with at least 10,000 total population with the highest percentage of Hispanic/Latino population. These places are identified with an asterisk (*); Please refer to the User's Guide for a full explanation of data.

Unemployment Rate
(Universe: Population 16 Years and Over)

Group	%
Total Population	10.1
Hispanic or Latino (of any race)	12.5
Mexican	12.6

Class of Worker: Private Wage and Salary
(Universe: Civilian Employed Population 16 Years and Over)

Group	Number	%
Total Population	9,008	72.4
Hispanic or Latino (of any race)	3,825	79.4
Mexican	3,303	79.0

Class of Worker: Government
(Universe: Civilian Employed Population 16 Years and Over)

Group	Number	%
Total Population	2,067	16.6
Hispanic or Latino (of any race)	508	10.6
Mexican	448	10.7

Means of Transportation to Work: Car, Truck or Van
(Universe: Workers 16 Years and Over)

Group	Number	%
Total Population	11,205	87.9
Hispanic or Latino (of any race)	4,574	93.2
Mexican	3,940	93.4

Means of Transportation to Work: Public Transportation (ex. Taxicab)
(Universe: Workers 16 Years and Over)

Group	Number	%
Total Population	178	1.4
Hispanic or Latino (of any race)	46	0.9
Mexican	46	1.1

Homeownership Rate
(Universe: Occupied Housing Units)

Group	%
Total Population	59.2
Hispanic or Latino (of any race)	38.3
Central American, ex. Mexican	19.2
Guatemalan	18.8
Mexican	39.0
Puerto Rican	25.9
South American	41.2
Spaniard	61.0

Median Home Value

Group	Dollars
Total Population	512,500
Hispanic or Latino (of any race)	366,000
Mexican	373,800

Median Gross Rent

Group	Dollars
Total Population	1,072
Hispanic or Latino (of any race)	1,022
Mexican	987

Median Household Income
(2010 Inflation-Adjusted Dollars)

Group	Dollars
Total Population	58,864
Hispanic or Latino (of any race)	44,844
Mexican	44,688

Per Capita Income
(2010 Inflation-Adjusted Dollars)

Group	Dollars
Total Population	27,601
Hispanic or Latino (of any race)	14,879
Mexican	14,074

Households with $100,000+ Income

Group	Number	%
Total Population	2,593	25.4
Hispanic or Latino (of any race)	416	14.0
Mexican	356	14.5

Households with Food Stamps/SNAP Benefits During Past 12 Months

Group	Number	%
Total Population	278	2.7
Hispanic or Latino (of any race)	163	5.5
Mexican	126	5.1

Poverty Rate
(Income in Past 12 Months Below Poverty Level)

Group	%
Total Population	10.5
Hispanic or Latino (of any race)	15.2
Mexican	15.4

Florence-Graham

Population

Group	Number	%TP[1]	%HP[2]
Total Population	63,387	100.0	–
Hispanic or Latino (of any race)	57,066	90.0	100.0
Central American, ex. Mexican	5,736	9.0	10.1
Guatemalan	1,685	2.7	3.0
Honduran	505	0.8	0.9
Nicaraguan	196	0.3	0.3
Salvadoran	3,239	5.1	5.7
Mexican	47,862	75.5	83.9
Puerto Rican	143	0.2	0.3
South American	120	0.2	0.2
Spaniard	127	0.2	0.2

Population Growth: 2000–2010

Group	%
Total Population	5.3
Hispanic or Latino (of any race)	10.4
Central American, ex. Mexican	144.6
Guatemalan	241.8
Honduran	274.1
Nicaraguan	67.5
Salvadoran	142.6
Mexican	14.2
Puerto Rican	-11.7

Males per 100 Females

Group	Number
Total Population	100.2
Hispanic or Latino (of any race)	102.4
Central American, ex. Mexican	101.6
Guatemalan	116.6
Honduran	94.2
Nicaraguan	88.5
Salvadoran	97.0
Mexican	102.9
Puerto Rican	104.3
South American	114.3
Spaniard	76.4

Average Household Size

Group	People
Total Population	4.56
Hispanic or Latino (of any race)	4.87
Central American, ex. Mexican	4.79
Guatemalan	4.93
Honduran	4.66
Nicaraguan	4.46
Salvadoran	4.73
Mexican	4.89
Puerto Rican	4.09
South American	4.09
Spaniard	4.31

Median Age

Group	Years
Total Population	26.3
Hispanic or Latino (of any race)	25.7
Central American, ex. Mexican	32.1
Guatemalan	30.3
Honduran	27.7
Nicaraguan	34.7
Salvadoran	33.8
Mexican	25.1
Puerto Rican	28.2
South American	43.5
Spaniard	34.3

High School Graduates
(Universe: Population 25 Years and Over)

Group	Number	%
Total Population	12,875	40.5
Hispanic or Latino (of any race)	9,444	34.3
Central American, ex. Mexican	960	29.6
Guatemalan	487	31.1
Salvadoran	381	30.2
Mexican	8,361	34.9

Four-Year College Graduates
(Universe: Population 25 Years and Over)

Group	Number	%
Total Population	1,219	3.8
Hispanic or Latino (of any race)	840	3.0
Central American, ex. Mexican	115	3.5
Guatemalan	73	4.7
Salvadoran	13	1.0
Mexican	719	3.0

Population Age 3–17 Enrolled in Public School
(Universe: Population Age 3–17 Enrolled in School)

Group	Number	%
Total Population	15,568	96.1
Hispanic or Latino (of any race)	14,080	96.6
Central American, ex. Mexican	953	98.0
Guatemalan	454	96.0
Salvadoran	411	100.0
Mexican	12,954	96.5

Population Age 3–17 Enrolled in Private School
(Universe: Population Age 3–17 Enrolled in School)

Group	Number	%
Total Population	633	3.9
Hispanic or Latino (of any race)	497	3.4
Central American, ex. Mexican	19	2.0
Guatemalan	19	4.0
Salvadoran	0	0.0
Mexican	468	3.5

Foreign-Born Population

Group	Number	%
Total Population	26,323	43.3
Hispanic or Latino (of any race)	26,040	48.5
Central American, ex. Mexican	3,685	72.6
Guatemalan	1,803	75.0
Salvadoran	1,372	66.6
Mexican	22,119	46.1

Foreign-Born Naturalized U.S. Citizens

Group	Number	%
Total Population	6,068	23.1
Hispanic or Latino (of any race)	5,918	22.7
Central American, ex. Mexican	634	17.2
Guatemalan	198	11.0
Salvadoran	311	22.7
Mexican	5,203	23.5

Language Spoken at Home: English Only
(Universe: Population 5 Years and Over)

Group	Number	%
Total Population	7,824	14.3
Hispanic or Latino (of any race)	1,794	3.7
Central American, ex. Mexican	143	3.0
Guatemalan	22	1.0
Salvadoran	121	6.2
Mexican	1,554	3.6

Language Spoken at Home: Spanish
(Universe: Population 5 Years and Over)

Group	Number	%
Total Population	46,855	85.5
Hispanic or Latino (of any race)	46,365	96.2
Central American, ex. Mexican	4,656	97.0
Guatemalan	2,230	99.0
Salvadoran	1,821	93.8
Mexican	41,199	96.4

Unemployment Rate
(Universe: Population 16 Years and Over)

Group	%
Total Population	9.4
Hispanic or Latino (of any race)	8.6
Central American, ex. Mexican	9.1
Guatemalan	6.5
Salvadoran	11.2
Mexican	8.5

Notes: (1) Percent of total population; (2) Percent of Hispanic/Latino population; Profiles include places with an overall population of at least 125,000, OR an overall population of at least 25,000 where the Hispanic/Latino population is at least 20% of the overall population. In states where less than five places meet either of these criteria, we have included places with at least 10,000 total population with the highest percentage of Hispanic/Latino population. These places are identified with an asterisk (*); Please refer to the User's Guide for a full explanation of data.

Class of Worker: Private Wage and Salary
(Universe: Civilian Employed Population 16 Years and Over)

Group	Number	%
Total Population	20,104	86.1
Hispanic or Latino (of any race)	18,319	87.8
Central American, ex. Mexican	2,054	87.5
Guatemalan	882	86.6
Salvadoran	911	86.6
Mexican	16,049	87.9

Class of Worker: Government
(Universe: Civilian Employed Population 16 Years and Over)

Group	Number	%
Total Population	1,967	8.4
Hispanic or Latino (of any race)	1,309	6.3
Central American, ex. Mexican	85	3.6
Guatemalan	35	3.4
Salvadoran	50	4.8
Mexican	1,210	6.6

Means of Transportation to Work: Car, Truck or Van
(Universe: Workers 16 Years and Over)

Group	Number	%
Total Population	18,625	81.1
Hispanic or Latino (of any race)	16,623	80.9
Central American, ex. Mexican	1,803	78.5
Guatemalan	791	78.6
Salvadoran	869	86.0
Mexican	14,705	81.6

Means of Transportation to Work: Public Transportation (ex. Taxicab)
(Universe: Workers 16 Years and Over)

Group	Number	%
Total Population	2,687	11.7
Hispanic or Latino (of any race)	2,349	11.4
Central American, ex. Mexican	344	15.0
Guatemalan	156	15.5
Salvadoran	89	8.8
Mexican	1,934	10.7

Homeownership Rate
(Universe: Occupied Housing Units)

Group	%
Total Population	36.7
Hispanic or Latino (of any race)	35.8
Central American, ex. Mexican	35.3
Guatemalan	30.0
Honduran	23.4
Nicaraguan	42.3
Salvadoran	38.8
Mexican	36.2
Puerto Rican	32.4
South American	52.9
Spaniard	20.0

Median Home Value

Group	Dollars
Total Population	339,400
Hispanic or Latino (of any race)	343,900
Central American, ex. Mexican	359,400
Guatemalan	337,400
Salvadoran	359,800
Mexican	338,800

Median Gross Rent

Group	Dollars
Total Population	904
Hispanic or Latino (of any race)	906
Central American, ex. Mexican	882
Guatemalan	1,015
Salvadoran	799
Mexican	909

Median Household Income
(2010 Inflation-Adjusted Dollars)

Group	Dollars
Total Population	35,851
Hispanic or Latino (of any race)	36,947
Central American, ex. Mexican	40,398
Guatemalan	41,553
Salvadoran	42,652
Mexican	36,830

Per Capita Income
(2010 Inflation-Adjusted Dollars)

Group	Dollars
Total Population	11,236
Hispanic or Latino (of any race)	10,533
Central American, ex. Mexican	11,261
Guatemalan	11,644
Salvadoran	11,629
Mexican	10,422

Households with $100,000+ Income

Group	Number	%
Total Population	947	6.8
Hispanic or Latino (of any race)	743	6.5
Central American, ex. Mexican	77	6.0
Guatemalan	42	7.6
Salvadoran	35	6.1
Mexican	666	6.6

Households with Food Stamps/SNAP Benefits During Past 12 Months

Group	Number	%
Total Population	2,733	19.7
Hispanic or Latino (of any race)	2,355	20.5
Central American, ex. Mexican	205	15.9
Guatemalan	110	20.0
Salvadoran	81	14.1
Mexican	2,132	21.2

Poverty Rate
(Income in Past 12 Months Below Poverty Level)

Group	%
Total Population	28.7
Hispanic or Latino (of any race)	28.7
Central American, ex. Mexican	25.0
Guatemalan	28.6
Salvadoran	19.5
Mexican	29.0

Florin

Population

Group	Number	%TP[1]	%HP[2]
Total Population	47,513	100.0	–
Hispanic or Latino (of any race)	13,048	27.5	100.0
Central American, ex. Mexican	616	1.3	4.7
Guatemalan	134	0.3	1.0
Nicaraguan	140	0.3	1.1
Salvadoran	246	0.5	1.9
Mexican	11,196	23.6	85.8
Puerto Rican	337	0.7	2.6
Spaniard	108	0.2	0.8

Population Growth: 2000–2010

Group	%
Total Population	71.8
Hispanic or Latino (of any race)	126.5
Central American, ex. Mexican	381.3
Mexican	151.0
Puerto Rican	94.8

Males per 100 Females

Group	Number
Total Population	96.2
Hispanic or Latino (of any race)	104.1
Central American, ex. Mexican	100.7
Guatemalan	139.3
Nicaraguan	91.8
Salvadoran	98.4
Mexican	104.8
Puerto Rican	87.2
Spaniard	61.2

Average Household Size

Group	People
Total Population	3.19
Hispanic or Latino (of any race)	3.90
Central American, ex. Mexican	3.89
Guatemalan	4.20
Nicaraguan	4.10
Salvadoran	3.72
Mexican	4.01
Puerto Rican	3.08
Spaniard	2.81

Median Age

Group	Years
Total Population	32.1
Hispanic or Latino (of any race)	25.2
Central American, ex. Mexican	32.5
Guatemalan	33.2
Nicaraguan	30.3
Salvadoran	32.7
Mexican	24.5
Puerto Rican	26.9
Spaniard	42.0

High School Graduates
(Universe: Population 25 Years and Over)

Group	Number	%
Total Population	20,188	72.5
Hispanic or Latino (of any race)	3,758	53.4
Mexican	3,041	50.5

Four-Year College Graduates
(Universe: Population 25 Years and Over)

Group	Number	%
Total Population	3,240	11.6
Hispanic or Latino (of any race)	355	5.0
Mexican	197	3.3

Population Age 3–17 Enrolled in Public School
(Universe: Population Age 3–17 Enrolled in School)

Group	Number	%
Total Population	10,184	94.6
Hispanic or Latino (of any race)	4,186	95.5
Mexican	3,505	95.4

Population Age 3–17 Enrolled in Private School
(Universe: Population Age 3–17 Enrolled in School)

Group	Number	%
Total Population	584	5.4
Hispanic or Latino (of any race)	195	4.5
Mexican	168	4.6

Foreign-Born Population

Group	Number	%
Total Population	13,144	27.5
Hispanic or Latino (of any race)	4,852	31.9
Mexican	4,416	33.3

Foreign-Born Naturalized U.S. Citizens

Group	Number	%
Total Population	6,803	51.8
Hispanic or Latino (of any race)	1,432	29.5
Mexican	1,124	25.5

Language Spoken at Home: English Only
(Universe: Population 5 Years and Over)

Group	Number	%
Total Population	23,284	52.7
Hispanic or Latino (of any race)	4,141	30.6
Mexican	3,317	28.3

Language Spoken at Home: Spanish
(Universe: Population 5 Years and Over)

Group	Number	%
Total Population	9,663	21.9
Hispanic or Latino (of any race)	9,366	69.2
Mexican	8,402	71.7

Unemployment Rate
(Universe: Population 16 Years and Over)

Group	%
Total Population	14.2
Hispanic or Latino (of any race)	14.7
Mexican	15.0

Class of Worker: Private Wage and Salary
(Universe: Civilian Employed Population 16 Years and Over)

Group	Number	%
Total Population	12,845	72.3
Hispanic or Latino (of any race)	4,301	81.2
Mexican	3,922	82.8

Class of Worker: Government
(Universe: Civilian Employed Population 16 Years and Over)

Group	Number	%
Total Population	3,856	21.7
Hispanic or Latino (of any race)	699	13.2
Mexican	533	11.2

STATE & PLACE PROFILES

Notes: (1) Percent of total population; (2) Percent of Hispanic/Latino population; Profiles include places with an overall population of at least 125,000, OR an overall population of at least 25,000 where the Hispanic/Latino population is at least 20% of the overall population. In states where less than five places meet either of these criteria, we have included places with at least 10,000 total population with the highest percentage of Hispanic/Latino population. These places are identified with an asterisk (*); Please refer to the User's Guide for a full explanation of data.

Means of Transportation to Work: Car, Truck or Van
(Universe: Workers 16 Years and Over)

Group	Number	%
Total Population	15,396	90.2
Hispanic or Latino (of any race)	4,457	89.7
Mexican	3,945	89.1

Means of Transportation to Work: Public Transportation (ex. Taxicab)
(Universe: Workers 16 Years and Over)

Group	Number	%
Total Population	562	3.3
Hispanic or Latino (of any race)	182	3.7
Mexican	182	4.1

Homeownership Rate
(Universe: Occupied Housing Units)

Group	%
Total Population	55.2
Hispanic or Latino (of any race)	48.7
Central American, ex. Mexican	56.4
Guatemalan	52.2
Nicaraguan	64.5
Salvadoran	54.2
Mexican	48.0
Puerto Rican	49.1
Spaniard	69.8

Median Home Value

Group	Dollars
Total Population	208,000
Hispanic or Latino (of any race)	217,400
Mexican	225,400

Median Gross Rent

Group	Dollars
Total Population	995
Hispanic or Latino (of any race)	1,035
Mexican	1,027

Median Household Income
(2010 Inflation-Adjusted Dollars)

Group	Dollars
Total Population	46,561
Hispanic or Latino (of any race)	51,891
Mexican	54,155

Per Capita Income
(2010 Inflation-Adjusted Dollars)

Group	Dollars
Total Population	17,408
Hispanic or Latino (of any race)	13,136
Mexican	13,033

Households with $100,000+ Income

Group	Number	%
Total Population	1,639	10.6
Hispanic or Latino (of any race)	403	11.1
Mexican	383	12.5

Households with Food Stamps/SNAP Benefits During Past 12 Months

Group	Number	%
Total Population	1,942	12.5
Hispanic or Latino (of any race)	532	14.7
Mexican	446	14.6

Poverty Rate
(Income in Past 12 Months Below Poverty Level)

Group	%
Total Population	18.1
Hispanic or Latino (of any race)	17.3
Mexican	17.1

Fontana

Population

Group	Number	%TP[1]	%HP[2]
Total Population	196,069	100.0	–
Hispanic or Latino (of any race)	130,957	66.8	100.0
Central American, ex. Mexican	8,860	4.5	6.8
Costa Rican	187	0.1	0.1
Guatemalan	2,230	1.1	1.7
Honduran	636	0.3	0.5
Nicaraguan	1,152	0.6	0.9
Panamanian	179	0.1	0.1
Salvadoran	4,382	2.2	3.3
Cuban	617	0.3	0.5
Mexican	111,818	57.0	85.4
Puerto Rican	1,344	0.7	1.0
South American	2,245	1.1	1.7
Argentinean	323	0.2	0.2
Chilean	134	0.1	0.1
Colombian	545	0.3	0.4
Ecuadorian	415	0.2	0.3
Peruvian	646	0.3	0.5
Spaniard	616	0.3	0.5

Population Growth: 2000–2010

Group	%
Total Population	52.1
Hispanic or Latino (of any race)	76.0
Central American, ex. Mexican	182.1
Guatemalan	249.5
Honduran	226.2
Nicaraguan	164.2
Salvadoran	234.5
Cuban	95.9
Mexican	88.3
Puerto Rican	57.2
South American	148.1
Argentinean	94.6
Colombian	193.0
Ecuadorian	254.7
Peruvian	218.2
Spaniard	445.1

Males per 100 Females

Group	Number
Total Population	98.7
Hispanic or Latino (of any race)	99.6
Central American, ex. Mexican	94.6
Costa Rican	105.5
Guatemalan	100.9
Honduran	82.8
Nicaraguan	88.9
Panamanian	90.4
Salvadoran	94.8
Cuban	94.0
Mexican	100.6
Puerto Rican	97.4
South American	95.0
Argentinean	91.1
Chilean	100.0
Colombian	98.2
Ecuadorian	88.6
Peruvian	93.4
Spaniard	104.7

Average Household Size

Group	People
Total Population	3.98
Hispanic or Latino (of any race)	4.55
Central American, ex. Mexican	4.54
Costa Rican	4.09
Guatemalan	4.56
Honduran	4.79
Nicaraguan	4.54
Panamanian	3.78
Salvadoran	4.55
Cuban	3.34
Mexican	4.62
Puerto Rican	3.64
South American	3.78
Argentinean	3.27
Chilean	3.70
Colombian	4.08
Ecuadorian	3.62
Peruvian	4.03
Spaniard	3.66

Median Age

Group	Years
Total Population	28.7
Hispanic or Latino (of any race)	25.3
Central American, ex. Mexican	34.1
Costa Rican	35.3
Guatemalan	35.7
Honduran	31.2
Nicaraguan	35.8
Panamanian	38.1
Salvadoran	33.3
Cuban	35.6
Mexican	24.5
Puerto Rican	26.1
South American	36.9
Argentinean	39.0
Chilean	26.5
Colombian	34.0
Ecuadorian	41.4
Peruvian	36.6
Spaniard	31.5

High School Graduates
(Universe: Population 25 Years and Over)

Group	Number	%
Total Population	74,239	70.9
Hispanic or Latino (of any race)	35,742	57.4
Central American, ex. Mexican	3,346	59.2
Guatemalan	914	61.7
Nicaraguan	497	62.4
Salvadoran	1,500	53.9
Mexican	29,524	55.6
Puerto Rican	429	76.2
South American	963	86.9

Four-Year College Graduates
(Universe: Population 25 Years and Over)

Group	Number	%
Total Population	15,079	14.4
Hispanic or Latino (of any race)	3,894	6.3
Central American, ex. Mexican	426	7.5
Guatemalan	70	4.7
Nicaraguan	55	6.9
Salvadoran	227	8.2
Mexican	2,847	5.4
Puerto Rican	72	12.8
South American	272	24.5

Population Age 3–17 Enrolled in Public School
(Universe: Population Age 3–17 Enrolled in School)

Group	Number	%
Total Population	45,396	94.9
Hispanic or Latino (of any race)	33,958	96.7
Central American, ex. Mexican	1,773	96.7
Guatemalan	391	97.5
Nicaraguan	105	100.0
Salvadoran	1,054	98.7
Mexican	30,391	97.4
Puerto Rican	372	74.0
South American	288	77.8

Population Age 3–17 Enrolled in Private School
(Universe: Population Age 3–17 Enrolled in School)

Group	Number	%
Total Population	2,437	5.1
Hispanic or Latino (of any race)	1,160	3.3
Central American, ex. Mexican	61	3.3
Guatemalan	10	2.5
Nicaraguan	0	0.0
Salvadoran	14	1.3
Mexican	824	2.6
Puerto Rican	131	26.0
South American	82	22.2

Foreign-Born Population

Group	Number	%
Total Population	59,559	31.4
Hispanic or Latino (of any race)	48,357	38.8
Central American, ex. Mexican	5,944	65.4
Guatemalan	1,655	70.4
Nicaraguan	857	81.6
Salvadoran	2,880	61.4
Mexican	40,276	37.2
Puerto Rican	0	0.0
South American	1,187	63.0

Foreign-Born Naturalized U.S. Citizens

Group	Number	%
Total Population	22,817	38.3
Hispanic or Latino (of any race)	15,774	32.6
Central American, ex. Mexican	2,455	41.3
Guatemalan	844	51.0

Notes: (1) Percent of total population; (2) Percent of Hispanic/Latino population; Profiles include places with an overall population of at least 125,000, OR an overall population of at least 25,000 where the Hispanic/Latino population is at least 20% of the overall population. In states where less than five places meet either of these criteria, we have included places with at least 10,000 total population with the highest percentage of Hispanic/Latino population. These places are identified with an asterisk (*); Please refer to the User's Guide for a full explanation of data.

Nicaraguan	258	30.1
Salvadoran	1,177	40.9
Mexican	11,977	29.7
Puerto Rican	0	0.0
South American	606	51.1

Language Spoken at Home: English Only
(Universe: Population 5 Years and Over)

Group	Number	%
Total Population	70,692	40.9
Hispanic or Latino (of any race)	24,206	21.7
Central American, ex. Mexican	617	7.2
Guatemalan	124	5.4
Nicaraguan	41	4.1
Salvadoran	317	7.3
Mexican	21,631	22.4
Puerto Rican	499	39.7
South American	169	9.6

Language Spoken at Home: Spanish
(Universe: Population 5 Years and Over)

Group	Number	%
Total Population	89,475	51.8
Hispanic or Latino (of any race)	87,348	78.2
Central American, ex. Mexican	7,892	92.6
Guatemalan	2,149	93.8
Nicaraguan	948	95.9
Salvadoran	4,004	92.7
Mexican	74,977	77.6
Puerto Rican	750	59.7
South American	1,572	89.3

Unemployment Rate
(Universe: Population 16 Years and Over)

Group	%
Total Population	10.3
Hispanic or Latino (of any race)	10.6
Central American, ex. Mexican	6.0
Guatemalan	3.1
Nicaraguan	4.8
Salvadoran	5.7
Mexican	10.8
Puerto Rican	12.9
South American	12.4

Class of Worker: Private Wage and Salary
(Universe: Civilian Employed Population 16 Years and Over)

Group	Number	%
Total Population	66,003	80.5
Hispanic or Latino (of any race)	41,881	83.8
Central American, ex. Mexican	3,714	82.8
Guatemalan	1,080	80.5
Nicaraguan	536	91.0
Salvadoran	1,804	82.3
Mexican	35,962	84.5
Puerto Rican	299	64.9
South American	769	81.6

Class of Worker: Government
(Universe: Civilian Employed Population 16 Years and Over)

Group	Number	%
Total Population	11,060	13.5
Hispanic or Latino (of any race)	4,726	9.5
Central American, ex. Mexican	434	9.7
Guatemalan	151	11.3
Nicaraguan	30	5.1
Salvadoran	213	9.7
Mexican	3,828	9.0
Puerto Rican	123	26.7
South American	80	8.5

Means of Transportation to Work: Car, Truck or Van
(Universe: Workers 16 Years and Over)

Group	Number	%
Total Population	73,608	92.8
Hispanic or Latino (of any race)	45,217	93.4
Central American, ex. Mexican	3,942	90.1
Guatemalan	1,282	95.6
Nicaraguan	501	87.7
Salvadoran	1,879	89.3
Mexican	38,674	93.7
Puerto Rican	402	87.2
South American	858	95.8

Means of Transportation to Work: Public Transportation (ex. Taxicab)
(Universe: Workers 16 Years and Over)

Group	Number	%
Total Population	1,678	2.1
Hispanic or Latino (of any race)	934	1.9
Central American, ex. Mexican	123	2.8
Guatemalan	0	0.0
Nicaraguan	27	4.7
Salvadoran	25	1.2
Mexican	787	1.9
Puerto Rican	10	2.2
South American	0	0.0

Homeownership Rate
(Universe: Occupied Housing Units)

Group	%
Total Population	68.9
Hispanic or Latino (of any race)	64.4
Central American, ex. Mexican	66.3
Costa Rican	69.0
Guatemalan	66.1
Honduran	57.0
Nicaraguan	70.2
Panamanian	72.2
Salvadoran	66.2
Cuban	72.0
Mexican	64.5
Puerto Rican	61.0
South American	70.5
Argentinean	70.5
Chilean	66.7
Colombian	72.4
Ecuadorian	73.9
Peruvian	67.2
Spaniard	69.3

Median Home Value

Group	Dollars
Total Population	346,700
Hispanic or Latino (of any race)	333,100
Central American, ex. Mexican	333,100
Guatemalan	327,300
Nicaraguan	334,500
Salvadoran	336,300
Mexican	329,000
Puerto Rican	347,000
South American	356,900

Median Gross Rent

Group	Dollars
Total Population	1,083
Hispanic or Latino (of any race)	1,064
Central American, ex. Mexican	1,121
Guatemalan	1,136
Nicaraguan	1,359
Salvadoran	1,078
Mexican	1,052
Puerto Rican	1,722
South American	1,324

Median Household Income
(2010 Inflation-Adjusted Dollars)

Group	Dollars
Total Population	63,252
Hispanic or Latino (of any race)	56,080
Central American, ex. Mexican	56,138
Guatemalan	68,553
Nicaraguan	53,191
Salvadoran	54,337
Mexican	54,650
Puerto Rican	81,801
South American	70,446

Per Capita Income
(2010 Inflation-Adjusted Dollars)

Group	Dollars
Total Population	19,272
Hispanic or Latino (of any race)	14,495
Central American, ex. Mexican	17,347
Guatemalan	17,772
Nicaraguan	28,436
Salvadoran	15,108
Mexican	13,943
Puerto Rican	16,592
South American	22,556

Households with $100,000+ Income

Group	Number	%
Total Population	11,263	24.1
Hispanic or Latino (of any race)	4,399	16.7
Central American, ex. Mexican	325	13.7
Guatemalan	138	20.7
Nicaraguan	27	7.7
Salvadoran	133	12.0
Mexican	3,509	15.8
Puerto Rican	121	39.9
South American	175	31.5

Households with Food Stamps/SNAP Benefits During Past 12 Months

Group	Number	%
Total Population	3,756	8.0
Hispanic or Latino (of any race)	2,514	9.6
Central American, ex. Mexican	297	12.5
Guatemalan	76	11.4
Nicaraguan	8	2.3
Salvadoran	157	14.2
Mexican	2,129	9.6
Puerto Rican	7	2.3
South American	30	5.4

Poverty Rate
(Income in Past 12 Months Below Poverty Level)

Group	%
Total Population	12.5
Hispanic or Latino (of any race)	15.1
Central American, ex. Mexican	10.5
Guatemalan	8.2
Nicaraguan	3.0
Salvadoran	11.3
Mexican	16.0
Puerto Rican	1.6
South American	7.5

STATE & PLACE PROFILES

Foothill Farms

Population

Group	Number	%TP[1]	%HP[2]
Total Population	33,121	100.0	–
Hispanic or Latino (of any race)	7,579	22.9	100.0
Central American, ex. Mexican	513	1.5	6.8
Salvadoran	315	1.0	4.2
Mexican	6,006	18.1	79.2
Puerto Rican	314	0.9	4.1
South American	122	0.4	1.6

Population Growth: 2000–2010

Group	%
Total Population	90.1
Hispanic or Latino (of any race)	200.4
Mexican	241.1

Males per 100 Females

Group	Number
Total Population	95.3
Hispanic or Latino (of any race)	98.8
Central American, ex. Mexican	106.9
Salvadoran	101.9
Mexican	99.0
Puerto Rican	98.7
South American	93.7

Average Household Size

Group	People
Total Population	2.82
Hispanic or Latino (of any race)	3.54
Central American, ex. Mexican	3.89
Salvadoran	4.20
Mexican	3.62
Puerto Rican	2.95
South American	3.11

Median Age

Group	Years
Total Population	31.1
Hispanic or Latino (of any race)	23.9
Central American, ex. Mexican	28.3
Salvadoran	29.4

Notes: (1) Percent of total population; (2) Percent of Hispanic/Latino population; Profiles include places with an overall population of at least 125,000, OR an overall population of at least 25,000 where the Hispanic/Latino population is at least 20% of the overall population. In states where less than five places meet either of these criteria, we have included places with at least 10,000 total population with the highest percentage of Hispanic/Latino population. These places are identified with an asterisk (*); Please refer to the User's Guide for a full explanation of data.

Mexican	23.1
Puerto Rican	23.1
South American	36.7

High School Graduates
(Universe: Population 25 Years and Over)

Group	Number	%
Total Population	16,597	85.2
Hispanic or Latino (of any race)	1,905	63.1
Mexican	1,320	57.5

Four-Year College Graduates
(Universe: Population 25 Years and Over)

Group	Number	%
Total Population	3,146	16.1
Hispanic or Latino (of any race)	245	8.1
Mexican	182	7.9

Population Age 3–17 Enrolled in Public School
(Universe: Population Age 3–17 Enrolled in School)

Group	Number	%
Total Population	6,778	94.1
Hispanic or Latino (of any race)	1,830	95.2
Mexican	1,373	96.7

Population Age 3–17 Enrolled in Private School
(Universe: Population Age 3–17 Enrolled in School)

Group	Number	%
Total Population	423	5.9
Hispanic or Latino (of any race)	92	4.8
Mexican	47	3.3

Foreign-Born Population

Group	Number	%
Total Population	5,344	16.3
Hispanic or Latino (of any race)	1,926	30.0
Mexican	1,480	29.6

Foreign-Born Naturalized U.S. Citizens

Group	Number	%
Total Population	1,743	32.6
Hispanic or Latino (of any race)	353	18.3
Mexican	172	11.6

Language Spoken at Home: English Only
(Universe: Population 5 Years and Over)

Group	Number	%
Total Population	22,260	74.0
Hispanic or Latino (of any race)	2,178	39.3
Mexican	1,548	36.7

Language Spoken at Home: Spanish
(Universe: Population 5 Years and Over)

Group	Number	%
Total Population	3,715	12.3
Hispanic or Latino (of any race)	3,360	60.7
Mexican	2,675	63.3

Unemployment Rate
(Universe: Population 16 Years and Over)

Group	%
Total Population	12.4
Hispanic or Latino (of any race)	14.7
Mexican	13.4

Class of Worker: Private Wage and Salary
(Universe: Civilian Employed Population 16 Years and Over)

Group	Number	%
Total Population	10,632	77.2
Hispanic or Latino (of any race)	2,117	87.2
Mexican	1,603	86.9

Class of Worker: Government
(Universe: Civilian Employed Population 16 Years and Over)

Group	Number	%
Total Population	2,339	17.0
Hispanic or Latino (of any race)	241	9.9
Mexican	182	9.9

Means of Transportation to Work: Car, Truck or Van
(Universe: Workers 16 Years and Over)

Group	Number	%
Total Population	12,081	90.6
Hispanic or Latino (of any race)	2,205	94.2
Mexican	1,707	94.7

Means of Transportation to Work: Public Transportation (ex. Taxicab)
(Universe: Workers 16 Years and Over)

Group	Number	%
Total Population	570	4.3
Hispanic or Latino (of any race)	10	0.4
Mexican	10	0.6

Homeownership Rate
(Universe: Occupied Housing Units)

Group	%
Total Population	53.7
Hispanic or Latino (of any race)	32.8
Central American, ex. Mexican	37.3
Salvadoran	35.3
Mexican	30.8
Puerto Rican	32.3
South American	54.1

Median Home Value

Group	Dollars
Total Population	227,300
Hispanic or Latino (of any race)	222,700
Mexican	221,600

Median Gross Rent

Group	Dollars
Total Population	940
Hispanic or Latino (of any race)	893
Mexican	917

Median Household Income
(2010 Inflation-Adjusted Dollars)

Group	Dollars
Total Population	46,289
Hispanic or Latino (of any race)	43,891
Mexican	46,657

Per Capita Income
(2010 Inflation-Adjusted Dollars)

Group	Dollars
Total Population	20,086
Hispanic or Latino (of any race)	13,137
Mexican	12,909

Households with $100,000+ Income

Group	Number	%
Total Population	1,693	14.5
Hispanic or Latino (of any race)	123	7.1
Mexican	123	9.9

Households with Food Stamps/SNAP Benefits During Past 12 Months

Group	Number	%
Total Population	1,927	16.5
Hispanic or Latino (of any race)	231	13.3
Mexican	201	16.1

Poverty Rate
(Income in Past 12 Months Below Poverty Level)

Group	%
Total Population	20.4
Hispanic or Latino (of any race)	28.8
Mexican	27.5

Fremont

Population

Group	Number	%TP[1]	%HP[2]
Total Population	214,089	100.0	–
Hispanic or Latino (of any race)	31,698	14.8	100.0
Central American, ex. Mexican	2,429	1.1	7.7
Guatemalan	430	0.2	1.4
Nicaraguan	645	0.3	2.0
Salvadoran	1,102	0.5	3.5
Cuban	165	0.1	0.5
Mexican	23,600	11.0	74.5
Puerto Rican	1,241	0.6	3.9
South American	1,344	0.6	4.2
Argentinean	103	<0.1	0.3
Chilean	124	0.1	0.4
Colombian	228	0.1	0.7
Peruvian	616	0.3	1.9
Spaniard	924	0.4	2.9

Population Growth: 2000–2010

Group	%
Total Population	5.2
Hispanic or Latino (of any race)	15.6
Central American, ex. Mexican	89.9
Guatemalan	188.6
Nicaraguan	104.8
Salvadoran	101.5
Cuban	-4.1
Mexican	25.2
Puerto Rican	0.6
South American	59.2
Chilean	22.8
Colombian	54.1
Peruvian	110.2
Spaniard	574.5

Males per 100 Females

Group	Number
Total Population	98.9
Hispanic or Latino (of any race)	101.8
Central American, ex. Mexican	86.8
Guatemalan	110.8
Nicaraguan	72.5
Salvadoran	92.0
Cuban	85.4
Mexican	105.4
Puerto Rican	98.9
South American	93.1
Argentinean	114.6
Chilean	90.8
Colombian	83.9
Peruvian	91.9
Spaniard	87.8

Average Household Size

Group	People
Total Population	2.99
Hispanic or Latino (of any race)	3.54
Central American, ex. Mexican	3.60
Guatemalan	4.21
Nicaraguan	3.23
Salvadoran	3.73
Cuban	2.42
Mexican	3.72
Puerto Rican	2.95
South American	3.18
Argentinean	3.05
Chilean	2.78
Colombian	2.87
Peruvian	3.43
Spaniard	2.59

Median Age

Group	Years
Total Population	36.8
Hispanic or Latino (of any race)	29.5
Central American, ex. Mexican	31.8
Guatemalan	27.8
Nicaraguan	34.5
Salvadoran	32.0
Cuban	38.3
Mexican	28.3
Puerto Rican	32.3
South American	38.4
Argentinean	49.4
Chilean	39.3
Colombian	37.4
Peruvian	38.4
Spaniard	42.8

High School Graduates
(Universe: Population 25 Years and Over)

Group	Number	%
Total Population	130,562	91.1
Hispanic or Latino (of any race)	13,104	75.1
Central American, ex. Mexican	1,271	80.3
Salvadoran	705	79.9
Mexican	8,884	70.3
Puerto Rican	539	83.7
South American	735	94.0

Notes: (1) Percent of total population; (2) Percent of Hispanic/Latino population; Profiles include places with an overall population of at least 125,000, OR an overall population of at least 25,000 where the Hispanic/Latino population is at least 20% of the overall population. In states where less than five places meet either of these criteria, we have included places with at least 10,000 total population with the highest percentage of Hispanic/Latino population. These places are identified with an asterisk (*); Please refer to the User's Guide for a full explanation of data.

Four-Year College Graduates
(Universe: Population 25 Years and Over)

Group	Number	%
Total Population	71,713	50.1
Hispanic or Latino (of any race)	2,698	15.5
Central American, ex. Mexican	403	25.5
Salvadoran	185	21.0
Mexican	1,457	11.5
Puerto Rican	188	29.2
South American	129	16.5

Population Age 3–17 Enrolled in Public School
(Universe: Population Age 3–17 Enrolled in School)

Group	Number	%
Total Population	33,128	82.1
Hispanic or Latino (of any race)	5,900	90.3
Central American, ex. Mexican	456	86.7
Salvadoran	329	97.1
Mexican	4,519	90.7
Puerto Rican	268	97.1
South American	180	100.0

Population Age 3–17 Enrolled in Private School
(Universe: Population Age 3–17 Enrolled in School)

Group	Number	%
Total Population	7,240	17.9
Hispanic or Latino (of any race)	636	9.7
Central American, ex. Mexican	70	13.3
Salvadoran	10	2.9
Mexican	462	9.3
Puerto Rican	8	2.9
South American	0	0.0

Foreign-Born Population

Group	Number	%
Total Population	90,196	43.1
Hispanic or Latino (of any race)	9,955	33.8
Central American, ex. Mexican	1,144	45.1
Salvadoran	542	36.8
Mexican	7,736	35.3
Puerto Rican	0	0.0
South American	699	61.1

Foreign-Born Naturalized U.S. Citizens

Group	Number	%
Total Population	50,171	55.6
Hispanic or Latino (of any race)	4,255	42.7
Central American, ex. Mexican	643	56.2
Salvadoran	410	75.6
Mexican	3,054	39.5
Puerto Rican	0	0.0
South American	334	47.8

Language Spoken at Home: English Only
(Universe: Population 5 Years and Over)

Group	Number	%
Total Population	84,687	43.5
Hispanic or Latino (of any race)	9,082	33.9
Central American, ex. Mexican	262	11.5
Salvadoran	104	7.8
Mexican	6,216	31.3
Puerto Rican	703	69.3
South American	118	11.0

Language Spoken at Home: Spanish
(Universe: Population 5 Years and Over)

Group	Number	%
Total Population	18,758	9.6
Hispanic or Latino (of any race)	17,481	65.3
Central American, ex. Mexican	2,017	88.5
Salvadoran	1,222	92.2
Mexican	13,568	68.3
Puerto Rican	311	30.7
South American	946	87.8

Unemployment Rate
(Universe: Population 16 Years and Over)

Group	%
Total Population	6.5
Hispanic or Latino (of any race)	8.9
Central American, ex. Mexican	4.0
Salvadoran	0.0
Mexican	9.7
Puerto Rican	8.3
South American	6.2

Class of Worker: Private Wage and Salary
(Universe: Civilian Employed Population 16 Years and Over)

Group	Number	%
Total Population	86,938	84.2
Hispanic or Latino (of any race)	11,546	84.0
Central American, ex. Mexican	1,203	88.3
Salvadoran	655	82.6
Mexican	8,610	86.2
Puerto Rican	385	79.4
South American	502	73.4

Class of Worker: Government
(Universe: Civilian Employed Population 16 Years and Over)

Group	Number	%
Total Population	10,494	10.2
Hispanic or Latino (of any race)	1,214	8.8
Central American, ex. Mexican	34	2.5
Salvadoran	26	3.3
Mexican	850	8.5
Puerto Rican	100	20.6
South American	28	4.1

Means of Transportation to Work: Car, Truck or Van
(Universe: Workers 16 Years and Over)

Group	Number	%
Total Population	85,811	86.1
Hispanic or Latino (of any race)	11,587	87.2
Central American, ex. Mexican	1,073	81.6
Salvadoran	594	78.8
Mexican	8,487	87.9
Puerto Rican	341	77.9
South American	635	92.8

Means of Transportation to Work: Public Transportation (ex. Taxicab)
(Universe: Workers 16 Years and Over)

Group	Number	%
Total Population	7,240	7.3
Hispanic or Latino (of any race)	540	4.1
Central American, ex. Mexican	68	5.2
Salvadoran	39	5.2
Mexican	406	4.2
Puerto Rican	46	10.5
South American	10	1.5

Homeownership Rate
(Universe: Occupied Housing Units)

Group	%
Total Population	62.6
Hispanic or Latino (of any race)	50.0
Central American, ex. Mexican	50.4
Guatemalan	32.7
Nicaraguan	46.6
Salvadoran	58.1
Cuban	57.8
Mexican	48.3
Puerto Rican	51.7
South American	54.1
Argentinean	60.0
Chilean	67.5
Colombian	48.4
Peruvian	52.4
Spaniard	68.6

Median Home Value

Group	Dollars
Total Population	641,900
Hispanic or Latino (of any race)	551,400
Central American, ex. Mexican	587,500
Salvadoran	586,300
Mexican	528,900
Puerto Rican	602,300
South American	610,200

Median Gross Rent

Group	Dollars
Total Population	1,456
Hispanic or Latino (of any race)	1,330
Central American, ex. Mexican	1,636
Salvadoran	1,761
Mexican	1,262
Puerto Rican	1,244
South American	1,646

Median Household Income
(2010 Inflation-Adjusted Dollars)

Group	Dollars
Total Population	96,287
Hispanic or Latino (of any race)	70,490
Central American, ex. Mexican	68,445
Salvadoran	59,563
Mexican	66,110
Puerto Rican	108,641
South American	86,932

Per Capita Income
(2010 Inflation-Adjusted Dollars)

Group	Dollars
Total Population	37,844
Hispanic or Latino (of any race)	23,376
Central American, ex. Mexican	26,763
Salvadoran	23,279
Mexican	21,200
Puerto Rican	29,239
South American	25,686

Households with $100,000+ Income

Group	Number	%
Total Population	33,225	48.2
Hispanic or Latino (of any race)	2,165	28.1
Central American, ex. Mexican	211	34.1
Salvadoran	56	17.0
Mexican	1,261	22.9
Puerto Rican	217	57.7
South American	155	45.3

Households with Food Stamps/SNAP Benefits During Past 12 Months

Group	Number	%
Total Population	1,274	1.8
Hispanic or Latino (of any race)	191	2.5
Central American, ex. Mexican	13	2.1
Salvadoran	8	2.4
Mexican	150	2.7
Puerto Rican	0	0.0
South American	8	2.3

Poverty Rate
(Income in Past 12 Months Below Poverty Level)

Group	%
Total Population	5.2
Hispanic or Latino (of any race)	5.2
Central American, ex. Mexican	2.3
Salvadoran	1.0
Mexican	5.9
Puerto Rican	1.7
South American	3.1

Fresno

Population

Group	Number	%TP[1]	%HP[2]
Total Population	494,665	100.0	–
Hispanic or Latino (of any race)	232,055	46.9	100.0
Central American, ex. Mexican	3,381	0.7	1.5
Guatemalan	678	0.1	0.3
Honduran	318	0.1	0.1
Nicaraguan	320	0.1	0.1
Panamanian	107	<0.1	<0.1
Salvadoran	1,833	0.4	0.8
Cuban	406	0.1	0.2
Mexican	211,431	42.7	91.1
Puerto Rican	1,825	0.4	0.8
South American	1,084	0.2	0.5
Argentinean	148	<0.1	0.1
Chilean	113	<0.1	<0.1
Colombian	318	0.1	0.1
Peruvian	283	0.1	0.1
Spaniard	1,752	0.4	0.8

Population Growth: 2000–2010

Group	%
Total Population	15.7
Hispanic or Latino (of any race)	36.1
Central American, ex. Mexican	115.2
Guatemalan	202.7
Honduran	205.8

STATE & PLACE PROFILES

Notes: (1) Percent of total population; (2) Percent of Hispanic/Latino population; Profiles include places with an overall population of at least 125,000, OR an overall population of at least 25,000 where the Hispanic/Latino population is at least 20% of the overall population. In states where less than five places meet either of these criteria, we have included places with at least 10,000 total population with the highest percentage of Hispanic/Latino population. These places are identified with an asterisk (*); Please refer to the User's Guide for a full explanation of data.

Nicaraguan	86.0
Salvadoran	129.4
Cuban	41.0
Mexican	46.0
Puerto Rican	65.2
South American	98.5
Colombian	139.1
Peruvian	164.5
Spaniard	532.5

Males per 100 Females

Group	Number
Total Population	96.7
Hispanic or Latino (of any race)	100.5
Central American, ex. Mexican	94.8
Guatemalan	111.2
Honduran	119.3
Nicaraguan	71.1
Panamanian	64.6
Salvadoran	92.3
Cuban	108.2
Mexican	101.2
Puerto Rican	103.0
South American	87.5
Argentinean	82.7
Chilean	91.5
Colombian	86.0
Peruvian	85.0
Spaniard	86.0

Average Household Size

Group	People
Total Population	3.07
Hispanic or Latino (of any race)	3.68
Central American, ex. Mexican	3.83
Guatemalan	4.05
Honduran	3.88
Nicaraguan	3.26
Panamanian	3.15
Salvadoran	3.92
Cuban	2.77
Mexican	3.71
Puerto Rican	3.04
South American	2.85
Argentinean	2.94
Chilean	2.48
Colombian	2.79
Peruvian	2.97
Spaniard	2.83

Median Age

Group	Years
Total Population	29.3
Hispanic or Latino (of any race)	24.6
Central American, ex. Mexican	31.4
Guatemalan	31.0
Honduran	29.0
Nicaraguan	33.6
Panamanian	28.6
Salvadoran	32.0
Cuban	29.0
Mexican	24.4
Puerto Rican	25.9
South American	34.1
Argentinean	34.0
Chilean	36.8
Colombian	34.6
Peruvian	33.7
Spaniard	33.7

High School Graduates
(Universe: Population 25 Years and Over)

Group	Number	%
Total Population	206,658	74.7
Hispanic or Latino (of any race)	62,400	57.3
Central American, ex. Mexican	1,092	52.8
Salvadoran	461	43.0
Mexican	57,185	56.6
Puerto Rican	537	75.5
South American	873	79.1
Spaniard	483	63.6

Four-Year College Graduates
(Universe: Population 25 Years and Over)

Group	Number	%
Total Population	56,734	20.5
Hispanic or Latino (of any race)	9,624	8.8
Central American, ex. Mexican	225	10.9
Salvadoran	64	6.0
Mexican	8,187	8.1
Puerto Rican	195	27.4
South American	383	34.7
Spaniard	157	20.7

Population Age 3–17 Enrolled in Public School
(Universe: Population Age 3–17 Enrolled in School)

Group	Number	%
Total Population	102,875	95.1
Hispanic or Latino (of any race)	58,216	97.0
Central American, ex. Mexican	507	86.5
Salvadoran	261	86.7
Mexican	55,302	97.2
Puerto Rican	298	100.0
South American	143	78.1
Spaniard	89	91.8

Population Age 3–17 Enrolled in Private School
(Universe: Population Age 3–17 Enrolled in School)

Group	Number	%
Total Population	5,314	4.9
Hispanic or Latino (of any race)	1,806	3.0
Central American, ex. Mexican	79	13.5
Salvadoran	40	13.3
Mexican	1,587	2.8
Puerto Rican	0	0.0
South American	40	21.9
Spaniard	8	8.2

Foreign-Born Population

Group	Number	%
Total Population	101,178	20.9
Hispanic or Latino (of any race)	58,843	26.6
Central American, ex. Mexican	1,887	56.4
Salvadoran	921	55.5
Mexican	55,448	26.7
Puerto Rican	1	0.1
South American	804	47.3
Spaniard	78	7.4

Foreign-Born Naturalized U.S. Citizens

Group	Number	%
Total Population	35,330	34.9
Hispanic or Latino (of any race)	13,859	23.6
Central American, ex. Mexican	782	41.4
Salvadoran	347	37.7
Mexican	12,353	22.3
Puerto Rican	1	100.0
South American	355	44.2
Spaniard	36	46.2

Language Spoken at Home: English Only
(Universe: Population 5 Years and Over)

Group	Number	%
Total Population	254,505	57.6
Hispanic or Latino (of any race)	72,299	36.9
Central American, ex. Mexican	485	15.2
Salvadoran	115	7.2
Mexican	66,311	36.1
Puerto Rican	783	66.6
South American	457	32.1
Spaniard	807	76.9

Language Spoken at Home: Spanish
(Universe: Population 5 Years and Over)

Group	Number	%
Total Population	127,898	29.0
Hispanic or Latino (of any race)	123,417	62.9
Central American, ex. Mexican	2,705	84.8
Salvadoran	1,493	92.8
Mexican	116,892	63.7
Puerto Rican	374	31.8
South American	959	67.4
Spaniard	227	21.6

Unemployment Rate
(Universe: Population 16 Years and Over)

Group	%
Total Population	12.4
Hispanic or Latino (of any race)	14.1
Central American, ex. Mexican	8.8
Salvadoran	4.1
Mexican	14.4
Puerto Rican	10.8
South American	8.5
Spaniard	9.2

Class of Worker: Private Wage and Salary
(Universe: Civilian Employed Population 16 Years and Over)

Group	Number	%
Total Population	147,012	74.8
Hispanic or Latino (of any race)	66,901	79.1
Central American, ex. Mexican	1,438	82.7
Salvadoran	678	79.7
Mexican	62,395	79.3
Puerto Rican	379	73.2
South American	556	68.1
Spaniard	491	88.6

Class of Worker: Government
(Universe: Civilian Employed Population 16 Years and Over)

Group	Number	%
Total Population	36,048	18.3
Hispanic or Latino (of any race)	12,924	15.3
Central American, ex. Mexican	136	7.8
Salvadoran	81	9.5
Mexican	11,982	15.2
Puerto Rican	139	26.8
South American	174	21.3
Spaniard	63	11.4

Means of Transportation to Work: Car, Truck or Van
(Universe: Workers 16 Years and Over)

Group	Number	%
Total Population	167,564	89.2
Hispanic or Latino (of any race)	70,190	88.2
Central American, ex. Mexican	1,554	92.6
Salvadoran	738	88.5
Mexican	65,199	88.2
Puerto Rican	445	89.7
South American	616	84.2
Spaniard	426	83.5

Means of Transportation to Work: Public Transportation (ex. Taxicab)
(Universe: Workers 16 Years and Over)

Group	Number	%
Total Population	4,263	2.3
Hispanic or Latino (of any race)	2,228	2.8
Central American, ex. Mexican	42	2.5
Salvadoran	35	4.2
Mexican	2,004	2.7
Puerto Rican	0	0.0
South American	74	10.1
Spaniard	51	10.0

Homeownership Rate
(Universe: Occupied Housing Units)

Group	%
Total Population	49.1
Hispanic or Latino (of any race)	40.5
Central American, ex. Mexican	46.0
Guatemalan	42.5
Honduran	29.9
Nicaraguan	46.4
Panamanian	40.0
Salvadoran	51.3
Cuban	39.6
Mexican	40.7
Puerto Rican	38.1
South American	54.4
Argentinean	54.9
Chilean	52.4
Colombian	64.1
Peruvian	44.9
Spaniard	51.7

Notes: (1) Percent of total population; (2) Percent of Hispanic/Latino population; Profiles include places with an overall population of at least 125,000, OR an overall population of at least 25,000 where the Hispanic/Latino population is at least 20% of the overall population. In states where less than five places meet either of these criteria, we have included places with at least 10,000 total population with the highest percentage of Hispanic/Latino population. These places are identified with an asterisk (*); Please refer to the User's Guide for a full explanation of data.

Median Home Value	
Group	Dollars
Total Population	244,200
Hispanic or Latino (of any race)	211,000
Central American, ex. Mexican	249,100
Salvadoran	235,000
Mexican	205,900
Puerto Rican	202,100
South American	395,300
Spaniard	342,500

Median Gross Rent	
Group	Dollars
Total Population	832
Hispanic or Latino (of any race)	797
Central American, ex. Mexican	767
Salvadoran	735
Mexican	795
Puerto Rican	850
South American	851
Spaniard	812

Median Household Income (2010 Inflation-Adjusted Dollars)	
Group	Dollars
Total Population	43,124
Hispanic or Latino (of any race)	35,919
Central American, ex. Mexican	47,583
Salvadoran	39,490
Mexican	35,386
Puerto Rican	61,563
South American	53,633
Spaniard	24,983

Per Capita Income (2010 Inflation-Adjusted Dollars)	
Group	Dollars
Total Population	19,709
Hispanic or Latino (of any race)	13,156
Central American, ex. Mexican	22,607
Salvadoran	18,674
Mexican	12,710
Puerto Rican	18,235
South American	30,800
Spaniard	27,974

Households with $100,000+ Income		
Group	Number	%
Total Population	24,085	15.4
Hispanic or Latino (of any race)	5,088	8.8
Central American, ex. Mexican	158	14.7
Salvadoran	70	13.9
Mexican	4,442	8.3
Puerto Rican	51	15.8
South American	194	32.2
Spaniard	41	6.9

Households with Food Stamps/SNAP Benefits During Past 12 Months		
Group	Number	%
Total Population	24,230	15.5
Hispanic or Latino (of any race)	13,286	23.0
Central American, ex. Mexican	127	11.8
Salvadoran	58	11.6
Mexican	12,780	24.0
Puerto Rican	10	3.1
South American	28	4.6
Spaniard	56	9.4

Poverty Rate (Income in Past 12 Months Below Poverty Level)	
Group	%
Total Population	24.9
Hispanic or Latino (of any race)	31.0
Central American, ex. Mexican	14.8
Salvadoran	16.0
Mexican	31.6
Puerto Rican	21.9
South American	14.7
Spaniard	12.3

Fullerton

Population			
Group	Number	%TP[1]	%HP[2]
Total Population	135,161	100.0	–
Hispanic or Latino (of any race)	46,501	34.4	100.0
Central American, ex. Mexican	2,039	1.5	4.4
Costa Rican	117	0.1	0.3
Guatemalan	594	0.4	1.3
Honduran	163	0.1	0.4
Nicaraguan	274	0.2	0.6
Salvadoran	800	0.6	1.7
Cuban	413	0.3	0.9
Mexican	39,718	29.4	85.4
Puerto Rican	594	0.4	1.3
South American	1,291	1.0	2.8
Argentinean	244	0.2	0.5
Colombian	269	0.2	0.6
Ecuadorian	161	0.1	0.3
Peruvian	423	0.3	0.9
Spaniard	452	0.3	1.0

Population Growth: 2000–2010	
Group	%
Total Population	7.3
Hispanic or Latino (of any race)	22.3
Central American, ex. Mexican	113.5
Guatemalan	132.9
Nicaraguan	103.0
Salvadoran	144.6
Cuban	18.3
Mexican	27.1
Puerto Rican	40.8
South American	74.2
Argentinean	110.3
Colombian	70.3
Peruvian	94.9

Males per 100 Females	
Group	Number
Total Population	96.6
Hispanic or Latino (of any race)	99.2
Central American, ex. Mexican	88.6
Costa Rican	72.1
Guatemalan	89.8
Honduran	77.2
Nicaraguan	87.7
Salvadoran	90.9
Cuban	102.5
Mexican	100.5
Puerto Rican	95.4
South American	95.3
Argentinean	105.0
Colombian	78.1
Ecuadorian	101.3
Peruvian	108.4
Spaniard	84.5

Average Household Size	
Group	People
Total Population	2.91
Hispanic or Latino (of any race)	3.90
Central American, ex. Mexican	3.73
Costa Rican	3.33
Guatemalan	3.83
Honduran	3.78
Nicaraguan	3.71
Salvadoran	3.75
Cuban	2.83
Mexican	4.05
Puerto Rican	2.60
South American	2.95
Argentinean	2.67
Colombian	2.89
Ecuadorian	3.00
Peruvian	3.26
Spaniard	2.77

Median Age	
Group	Years
Total Population	34.8
Hispanic or Latino (of any race)	26.4
Central American, ex. Mexican	29.7
Costa Rican	35.8
Guatemalan	28.9
Honduran	29.1
Nicaraguan	30.5
Salvadoran	29.6
Cuban	37.3
Mexican	25.8
Puerto Rican	27.3
South American	35.8
Argentinean	40.2
Colombian	33.8
Ecuadorian	31.5
Peruvian	36.4
Spaniard	35.0

High School Graduates (Universe: Population 25 Years and Over)		
Group	Number	%
Total Population	73,115	85.8
Hispanic or Latino (of any race)	14,333	61.5
Central American, ex. Mexican	1,077	71.1
Salvadoran	599	64.8
Mexican	11,349	57.4
South American	620	96.0

Four-Year College Graduates (Universe: Population 25 Years and Over)		
Group	Number	%
Total Population	31,913	37.4
Hispanic or Latino (of any race)	2,657	11.4
Central American, ex. Mexican	164	10.8
Salvadoran	79	8.5
Mexican	1,894	9.6
South American	328	50.8

Population Age 3–17 Enrolled in Public School (Universe: Population Age 3–17 Enrolled in School)		
Group	Number	%
Total Population	20,914	87.3
Hispanic or Latino (of any race)	10,271	93.5
Central American, ex. Mexican	290	81.9
Salvadoran	62	49.2
Mexican	9,517	94.2
South American	73	88.0

Population Age 3–17 Enrolled in Private School (Universe: Population Age 3–17 Enrolled in School)		
Group	Number	%
Total Population	3,041	12.7
Hispanic or Latino (of any race)	709	6.5
Central American, ex. Mexican	64	18.1
Salvadoran	64	50.8
Mexican	584	5.8
South American	10	12.0

Foreign-Born Population		
Group	Number	%
Total Population	41,548	31.3
Hispanic or Latino (of any race)	17,129	39.3
Central American, ex. Mexican	1,484	61.7
Salvadoran	942	67.3
Mexican	14,730	38.9
South American	630	61.8

Foreign-Born Naturalized U.S. Citizens		
Group	Number	%
Total Population	19,507	47.0
Hispanic or Latino (of any race)	4,707	27.5
Central American, ex. Mexican	459	30.9
Salvadoran	211	22.4
Mexican	3,734	25.3
South American	290	46.0

Language Spoken at Home: English Only (Universe: Population 5 Years and Over)		
Group	Number	%
Total Population	66,502	53.8
Hispanic or Latino (of any race)	9,712	24.9
Central American, ex. Mexican	358	16.9
Salvadoran	137	12.0
Mexican	7,712	22.9
South American	283	28.8

Language Spoken at Home: Spanish (Universe: Population 5 Years and Over)		
Group	Number	%
Total Population	30,270	24.5

STATE & PLACE PROFILES

Notes: (1) Percent of total population; (2) Percent of Hispanic/Latino population; Profiles include places with an overall population of at least 125,000, OR an overall population of at least 25,000 where the Hispanic/Latino population is at least 20% of the overall population. In states where less than five places meet either of these criteria, we have included places with at least 10,000 total population with the highest percentage of Hispanic/Latino population. These places are identified with an asterisk (*); Please refer to the User's Guide for a full explanation of data.

Hispanic or Latino (of any race)	29,038	74.6
Central American, ex. Mexican	1,762	83.1
Salvadoran	1,008	88.0
Mexican	25,992	77.0
South American	641	65.3

Unemployment Rate
(Universe: Population 16 Years and Over)

Group	%
Total Population	7.5
Hispanic or Latino (of any race)	8.5
Central American, ex. Mexican	3.4
Salvadoran	4.8
Mexican	9.2
South American	7.1

Class of Worker: Private Wage and Salary
(Universe: Civilian Employed Population 16 Years and Over)

Group	Number	%
Total Population	51,760	80.2
Hispanic or Latino (of any race)	17,745	87.1
Central American, ex. Mexican	1,043	88.3
Salvadoran	565	95.4
Mexican	15,175	87.8
South American	465	73.8

Class of Worker: Government
(Universe: Civilian Employed Population 16 Years and Over)

Group	Number	%
Total Population	7,574	11.7
Hispanic or Latino (of any race)	1,632	8.0
Central American, ex. Mexican	75	6.4
Salvadoran	0	0.0
Mexican	1,292	7.5
South American	139	22.1

Means of Transportation to Work: Car, Truck or Van
(Universe: Workers 16 Years and Over)

Group	Number	%
Total Population	55,769	88.8
Hispanic or Latino (of any race)	17,446	87.6
Central American, ex. Mexican	990	85.4
Salvadoran	579	97.8
Mexican	14,697	87.0
South American	535	94.0

Means of Transportation to Work: Public Transportation (ex. Taxicab)
(Universe: Workers 16 Years and Over)

Group	Number	%
Total Population	2,109	3.4
Hispanic or Latino (of any race)	1,084	5.4
Central American, ex. Mexican	89	7.7
Salvadoran	13	2.2
Mexican	967	5.7
South American	0	0.0

Homeownership Rate
(Universe: Occupied Housing Units)

Group	%
Total Population	54.2
Hispanic or Latino (of any race)	36.9
Central American, ex. Mexican	30.3
Costa Rican	52.4
Guatemalan	24.8
Honduran	32.7
Nicaraguan	35.9
Salvadoran	28.9
Cuban	57.2
Mexican	36.6
Puerto Rican	35.4
South American	43.0
Argentinean	55.3
Colombian	38.7
Ecuadorian	44.2
Peruvian	38.9
Spaniard	47.1

Median Home Value

Group	Dollars
Total Population	582,600
Hispanic or Latino (of any race)	460,600
Central American, ex. Mexican	589,300
Salvadoran	665,500
Mexican	434,100
South American	750,000

Median Gross Rent

Group	Dollars
Total Population	1,275
Hispanic or Latino (of any race)	1,226
Central American, ex. Mexican	1,294
Salvadoran	1,396
Mexican	1,215
South American	1,245

Median Household Income
(2010 Inflation-Adjusted Dollars)

Group	Dollars
Total Population	67,179
Hispanic or Latino (of any race)	52,331
Central American, ex. Mexican	72,976
Salvadoran	68,750
Mexican	51,393
South American	75,050

Per Capita Income
(2010 Inflation-Adjusted Dollars)

Group	Dollars
Total Population	30,580
Hispanic or Latino (of any race)	17,441
Central American, ex. Mexican	20,112
Salvadoran	19,754
Mexican	16,398
South American	28,908

Households with $100,000+ Income

Group	Number	%
Total Population	14,253	31.3
Hispanic or Latino (of any race)	2,161	19.4
Central American, ex. Mexican	149	30.3
Salvadoran	66	23.9
Mexican	1,632	17.4
South American	123	34.8

Households with Food Stamps/SNAP Benefits During Past 12 Months

Group	Number	%
Total Population	1,077	2.4
Hispanic or Latino (of any race)	510	4.6
Central American, ex. Mexican	43	8.7
Salvadoran	43	15.6
Mexican	452	4.8
South American	0	0.0

Poverty Rate
(Income in Past 12 Months Below Poverty Level)

Group	%
Total Population	11.3
Hispanic or Latino (of any race)	14.8
Central American, ex. Mexican	13.8
Salvadoran	18.0
Mexican	15.5
South American	4.9

Garden Grove

Population

Group	Number	%TP[1]	%HP[2]
Total Population	170,883	100.0	–
Hispanic or Latino (of any race)	63,079	36.9	100.0
Central American, ex. Mexican	2,968	1.7	4.7
Guatemalan	841	0.5	1.3
Honduran	210	0.1	0.3
Nicaraguan	156	0.1	0.2
Salvadoran	1,609	0.9	2.6
Cuban	341	0.2	0.5
Mexican	54,565	31.9	86.5
Puerto Rican	524	0.3	0.8
South American	1,465	0.9	2.3
Argentinean	169	0.1	0.3
Bolivian	110	0.1	0.2
Colombian	327	0.2	0.5
Ecuadorian	149	0.1	0.2
Peruvian	569	0.3	0.9
Spaniard	415	0.2	0.7

Population Growth: 2000–2010

Group	%
Total Population	3.4
Hispanic or Latino (of any race)	17.7
Central American, ex. Mexican	47.4
Guatemalan	72.3
Honduran	69.4
Salvadoran	59.1
Cuban	-5.3
Mexican	25.2
Puerto Rican	-9.3
South American	48.1
Argentinean	50.9
Colombian	44.7
Peruvian	57.2

Males per 100 Females

Group	Number
Total Population	99.6
Hispanic or Latino (of any race)	102.4
Central American, ex. Mexican	94.8
Guatemalan	95.6
Honduran	92.7
Nicaraguan	81.4
Salvadoran	97.4
Cuban	93.8
Mexican	103.6
Puerto Rican	85.2
South American	87.1
Argentinean	108.6
Bolivian	83.3
Colombian	71.2
Ecuadorian	86.3
Peruvian	93.5
Spaniard	99.5

Average Household Size

Group	People
Total Population	3.67
Hispanic or Latino (of any race)	4.75
Central American, ex. Mexican	4.69
Guatemalan	4.85
Honduran	4.28
Nicaraguan	3.98
Salvadoran	4.84
Cuban	3.05
Mexican	4.91
Puerto Rican	2.84
South American	3.59
Argentinean	3.52
Bolivian	3.72
Colombian	3.37
Ecuadorian	3.62
Peruvian	3.99
Spaniard	3.29

Median Age

Group	Years
Total Population	35.6
Hispanic or Latino (of any race)	26.6
Central American, ex. Mexican	34.4
Guatemalan	36.5
Honduran	34.0
Nicaraguan	31.7
Salvadoran	33.7
Cuban	40.9
Mexican	25.8
Puerto Rican	35.0
South American	38.2
Argentinean	36.8
Bolivian	31.7
Colombian	36.9
Ecuadorian	38.5
Peruvian	40.8
Spaniard	37.1

High School Graduates
(Universe: Population 25 Years and Over)

Group	Number	%
Total Population	78,168	72.2
Hispanic or Latino (of any race)	18,135	54.2
Central American, ex. Mexican	1,265	58.7
Guatemalan	572	75.9
Salvadoran	636	48.9
Mexican	14,958	51.7

Notes: (1) Percent of total population; (2) Percent of Hispanic/Latino population; Profiles include places with an overall population of at least 125,000, OR an overall population of at least 25,000 where the Hispanic/Latino population is at least 20% of the overall population. In states where less than five places meet either of these criteria, we have included places with at least 10,000 total population with the highest percentage of Hispanic/Latino population. These places are identified with an asterisk (*); Please refer to the User's Guide for a full explanation of data.

South American	984	81.4

Four-Year College Graduates
(Universe: Population 25 Years and Over)

Group	Number	%
Total Population	21,310	19.7
Hispanic or Latino (of any race)	2,558	7.7
Central American, ex. Mexican	214	9.9
Guatemalan	191	25.3
Salvadoran	3	0.2
Mexican	1,902	6.6
South American	237	19.6

Population Age 3–17 Enrolled in Public School
(Universe: Population Age 3–17 Enrolled in School)

Group	Number	%
Total Population	30,630	91.7
Hispanic or Latino (of any race)	16,463	94.6
Central American, ex. Mexican	640	90.5
Guatemalan	133	91.1
Salvadoran	496	90.2
Mexican	15,029	94.6
South American	217	96.9

Population Age 3–17 Enrolled in Private School
(Universe: Population Age 3–17 Enrolled in School)

Group	Number	%
Total Population	2,781	8.3
Hispanic or Latino (of any race)	941	5.4
Central American, ex. Mexican	67	9.5
Guatemalan	13	8.9
Salvadoran	54	9.8
Mexican	855	5.4
South American	7	3.1

Foreign-Born Population

Group	Number	%
Total Population	73,857	43.7
Hispanic or Latino (of any race)	28,216	44.0
Central American, ex. Mexican	2,179	60.3
Guatemalan	768	77.0
Salvadoran	1,331	53.1
Mexican	24,399	43.0
South American	1,172	74.6

Foreign-Born Naturalized U.S. Citizens

Group	Number	%
Total Population	40,473	54.8
Hispanic or Latino (of any race)	7,448	26.4
Central American, ex. Mexican	719	33.0
Guatemalan	146	19.0
Salvadoran	546	41.0
Mexican	5,853	24.0
South American	515	43.9

Language Spoken at Home: English Only
(Universe: Population 5 Years and Over)

Group	Number	%
Total Population	53,063	33.6
Hispanic or Latino (of any race)	9,842	16.9
Central American, ex. Mexican	86	2.5
Guatemalan	38	3.9
Salvadoran	27	1.2
Mexican	8,479	16.5
South American	205	13.3

Language Spoken at Home: Spanish
(Universe: Population 5 Years and Over)

Group	Number	%
Total Population	49,216	31.2
Hispanic or Latino (of any race)	48,116	82.6
Central American, ex. Mexican	3,311	97.5
Guatemalan	942	96.1
Salvadoran	2,279	98.8
Mexican	42,565	83.1
South American	1,335	86.7

Unemployment Rate
(Universe: Population 16 Years and Over)

Group	%
Total Population	9.7
Hispanic or Latino (of any race)	10.4
Central American, ex. Mexican	9.9
Guatemalan	4.3
Salvadoran	12.0
Mexican	10.2
South American	14.2

Class of Worker: Private Wage and Salary
(Universe: Civilian Employed Population 16 Years and Over)

Group	Number	%
Total Population	61,995	81.3
Hispanic or Latino (of any race)	23,589	85.0
Central American, ex. Mexican	1,769	90.3
Guatemalan	680	93.3
Salvadoran	1,047	89.4
Mexican	20,466	84.9
South American	618	79.6

Class of Worker: Government
(Universe: Civilian Employed Population 16 Years and Over)

Group	Number	%
Total Population	8,848	11.6
Hispanic or Latino (of any race)	2,565	9.2
Central American, ex. Mexican	131	6.7
Guatemalan	35	4.8
Salvadoran	78	6.7
Mexican	2,181	9.0
South American	122	15.7

Means of Transportation to Work: Car, Truck or Van
(Universe: Workers 16 Years and Over)

Group	Number	%
Total Population	67,365	90.8
Hispanic or Latino (of any race)	23,994	88.4
Central American, ex. Mexican	1,663	88.3
Guatemalan	613	85.7
Salvadoran	1,022	92.2
Mexican	20,713	88.0
South American	731	94.2

Means of Transportation to Work: Public Transportation (ex. Taxicab)
(Universe: Workers 16 Years and Over)

Group	Number	%
Total Population	3,211	4.3
Hispanic or Latino (of any race)	1,833	6.8
Central American, ex. Mexican	148	7.9
Guatemalan	70	9.8
Salvadoran	78	7.0
Mexican	1,656	7.0
South American	29	3.7

Homeownership Rate
(Universe: Occupied Housing Units)

Group	%
Total Population	57.0
Hispanic or Latino (of any race)	45.5
Central American, ex. Mexican	45.8
Guatemalan	42.7
Honduran	35.2
Nicaraguan	54.3
Salvadoran	46.3
Cuban	61.8
Mexican	45.2
Puerto Rican	50.9
South American	47.8
Argentinean	48.5
Bolivian	62.1
Colombian	37.9
Ecuadorian	54.0
Peruvian	47.3
Spaniard	66.4

Median Home Value

Group	Dollars
Total Population	472,900
Hispanic or Latino (of any race)	467,400
Central American, ex. Mexican	459,900
Guatemalan	380,000
Salvadoran	512,500
Mexican	464,100
South American	533,900

Median Gross Rent

Group	Dollars
Total Population	1,284
Hispanic or Latino (of any race)	1,296
Central American, ex. Mexican	1,246
Guatemalan	1,180
Salvadoran	1,260
Mexican	1,284
South American	1,481

Median Household Income
(2010 Inflation-Adjusted Dollars)

Group	Dollars
Total Population	61,026
Hispanic or Latino (of any race)	56,565
Central American, ex. Mexican	61,106
Guatemalan	62,269
Salvadoran	58,688
Mexican	55,975
South American	72,286

Per Capita Income
(2010 Inflation-Adjusted Dollars)

Group	Dollars
Total Population	20,971
Hispanic or Latino (of any race)	14,782
Central American, ex. Mexican	16,009
Guatemalan	19,650
Salvadoran	14,132
Mexican	14,310
South American	21,656

Households with $100,000+ Income

Group	Number	%
Total Population	11,403	25.0
Hispanic or Latino (of any race)	2,627	19.6
Central American, ex. Mexican	165	22.0
Guatemalan	23	11.4
Salvadoran	133	27.4
Mexican	2,159	18.7
South American	114	26.0

Households with Food Stamps/SNAP Benefits During Past 12 Months

Group	Number	%
Total Population	2,704	5.9
Hispanic or Latino (of any race)	1,186	8.9
Central American, ex. Mexican	54	7.2
Guatemalan	0	0.0
Salvadoran	54	11.1
Mexican	1,091	9.4
South American	23	5.3

Poverty Rate
(Income in Past 12 Months Below Poverty Level)

Group	%
Total Population	12.9
Hispanic or Latino (of any race)	16.2
Central American, ex. Mexican	5.4
Guatemalan	0.0
Salvadoran	6.4
Mexican	17.3
South American	9.6

Gardena

Population

Group	Number	%TP[1]	%HP[2]
Total Population	58,829	100.0	–
Hispanic or Latino (of any race)	22,151	37.7	100.0
Central American, ex. Mexican	2,934	5.0	13.2
Guatemalan	1,080	1.8	4.9
Honduran	170	0.3	0.8
Nicaraguan	190	0.3	0.9
Salvadoran	1,341	2.3	6.1
Cuban	225	0.4	1.0
Mexican	16,462	28.0	74.3
Puerto Rican	356	0.6	1.6
South American	867	1.5	3.9
Colombian	122	0.2	0.6
Ecuadorian	176	0.3	0.8
Peruvian	439	0.7	2.0
Spaniard	143	0.2	0.6

Population Growth: 2000–2010

Group	%
Total Population	1.9
Hispanic or Latino (of any race)	20.6
Central American, ex. Mexican	120.6
Guatemalan	178.4

Notes: (1) Percent of total population; (2) Percent of Hispanic/Latino population; Profiles include places with an overall population of at least 125,000, OR an overall population of at least 25,000 where the Hispanic/Latino population is at least 20% of the overall population. In states where less than five places meet either of these criteria, we have included places with at least 10,000 total population with the highest percentage of Hispanic/Latino population. These places are identified with an asterisk (*); Please refer to the User's Guide for a full explanation of data.

Nicaraguan	77.6
Salvadoran	137.3
Cuban	14.8
Mexican	25.3
Puerto Rican	-11.2
South American	89.3
Ecuadorian	74.3
Peruvian	132.3

Males per 100 Females

Group	Number
Total Population	92.6
Hispanic or Latino (of any race)	100.7
Central American, ex. Mexican	93.3
Guatemalan	103.0
Honduran	84.8
Nicaraguan	75.9
Salvadoran	91.3
Cuban	63.0
Mexican	103.5
Puerto Rican	90.4
South American	90.5
Colombian	62.7
Ecuadorian	91.3
Peruvian	98.6
Spaniard	90.7

Average Household Size

Group	People
Total Population	2.82
Hispanic or Latino (of any race)	3.78
Central American, ex. Mexican	3.87
Guatemalan	3.99
Honduran	3.95
Nicaraguan	3.41
Salvadoran	3.93
Cuban	2.82
Mexican	3.89
Puerto Rican	2.70
South American	3.25
Colombian	2.51
Ecuadorian	3.96
Peruvian	3.37
Spaniard	2.56

Median Age

Group	Years
Total Population	37.9
Hispanic or Latino (of any race)	29.3
Central American, ex. Mexican	34.0
Guatemalan	32.8
Honduran	30.9
Nicaraguan	38.0
Salvadoran	34.1
Cuban	46.4
Mexican	28.0
Puerto Rican	32.8
South American	38.7
Colombian	39.0
Ecuadorian	40.0
Peruvian	38.3
Spaniard	43.8

High School Graduates
(Universe: Population 25 Years and Over)

Group	Number	%
Total Population	32,100	80.3
Hispanic or Latino (of any race)	6,792	57.9
Central American, ex. Mexican	848	48.3
Guatemalan	398	60.5
Salvadoran	293	37.6
Mexican	4,954	56.8

Four-Year College Graduates
(Universe: Population 25 Years and Over)

Group	Number	%
Total Population	8,732	21.8
Hispanic or Latino (of any race)	697	5.9
Central American, ex. Mexican	92	5.2
Guatemalan	0	0.0
Salvadoran	69	8.9
Mexican	480	5.5

Population Age 3–17 Enrolled in Public School
(Universe: Population Age 3–17 Enrolled in School)

Group	Number	%
Total Population	9,274	87.3
Hispanic or Latino (of any race)	5,205	92.4
Central American, ex. Mexican	662	100.0
Guatemalan	308	100.0
Salvadoran	232	100.0
Mexican	4,295	92.1

Population Age 3–17 Enrolled in Private School
(Universe: Population Age 3–17 Enrolled in School)

Group	Number	%
Total Population	1,348	12.7
Hispanic or Latino (of any race)	430	7.6
Central American, ex. Mexican	0	0.0
Guatemalan	0	0.0
Salvadoran	0	0.0
Mexican	366	7.9

Foreign-Born Population

Group	Number	%
Total Population	19,944	34.0
Hispanic or Latino (of any race)	9,529	44.3
Central American, ex. Mexican	1,735	57.1
Guatemalan	721	63.7
Salvadoran	740	55.7
Mexican	7,042	42.5

Foreign-Born Naturalized U.S. Citizens

Group	Number	%
Total Population	9,891	49.6
Hispanic or Latino (of any race)	3,247	34.1
Central American, ex. Mexican	831	47.9
Guatemalan	429	59.5
Salvadoran	294	39.7
Mexican	1,978	28.1

Language Spoken at Home: English Only
(Universe: Population 5 Years and Over)

Group	Number	%
Total Population	26,056	47.3
Hispanic or Latino (of any race)	2,527	13.1
Central American, ex. Mexican	153	5.3
Guatemalan	84	7.6
Salvadoran	25	2.1
Mexican	1,975	13.5

Language Spoken at Home: Spanish
(Universe: Population 5 Years and Over)

Group	Number	%
Total Population	17,479	31.7
Hispanic or Latino (of any race)	16,669	86.7
Central American, ex. Mexican	2,748	94.7
Guatemalan	1,025	92.4
Salvadoran	1,191	97.9
Mexican	12,676	86.5

Unemployment Rate
(Universe: Population 16 Years and Over)

Group	%
Total Population	9.4
Hispanic or Latino (of any race)	10.3
Central American, ex. Mexican	10.0
Guatemalan	10.7
Salvadoran	9.9
Mexican	10.5

Class of Worker: Private Wage and Salary
(Universe: Civilian Employed Population 16 Years and Over)

Group	Number	%
Total Population	20,652	79.0
Hispanic or Latino (of any race)	7,461	88.3
Central American, ex. Mexican	1,372	94.0
Guatemalan	473	94.0
Salvadoran	632	97.8
Mexican	5,483	87.2

Class of Worker: Government
(Universe: Civilian Employed Population 16 Years and Over)

Group	Number	%
Total Population	3,835	14.7
Hispanic or Latino (of any race)	602	7.1
Central American, ex. Mexican	58	4.0
Guatemalan	30	6.0
Salvadoran	0	0.0
Mexican	484	7.7

Means of Transportation to Work: Car, Truck or Van
(Universe: Workers 16 Years and Over)

Group	Number	%
Total Population	22,600	89.0
Hispanic or Latino (of any race)	7,082	85.8
Central American, ex. Mexican	1,182	84.1
Guatemalan	457	93.1
Salvadoran	480	77.8
Mexican	5,289	85.6

Means of Transportation to Work: Public Transportation (ex. Taxicab)
(Universe: Workers 16 Years and Over)

Group	Number	%
Total Population	1,100	4.3
Hispanic or Latino (of any race)	515	6.2
Central American, ex. Mexican	133	9.5
Guatemalan	21	4.3
Salvadoran	60	9.7
Mexican	382	6.2

Homeownership Rate
(Universe: Occupied Housing Units)

Group	%
Total Population	47.9
Hispanic or Latino (of any race)	40.5
Central American, ex. Mexican	42.7
Guatemalan	40.9
Honduran	30.0
Nicaraguan	40.6
Salvadoran	43.9
Cuban	53.3
Mexican	39.3
Puerto Rican	48.0
South American	43.7
Colombian	48.9
Ecuadorian	60.7
Peruvian	40.6
Spaniard	66.0

Median Home Value

Group	Dollars
Total Population	417,800
Hispanic or Latino (of any race)	374,900
Central American, ex. Mexican	341,500
Guatemalan	282,500
Salvadoran	447,700
Mexican	394,700

Median Gross Rent

Group	Dollars
Total Population	998
Hispanic or Latino (of any race)	963
Central American, ex. Mexican	961
Guatemalan	1,009
Salvadoran	853
Mexican	976

Median Household Income
(2010 Inflation-Adjusted Dollars)

Group	Dollars
Total Population	46,837
Hispanic or Latino (of any race)	35,775
Central American, ex. Mexican	41,419
Guatemalan	43,375
Salvadoran	32,008
Mexican	36,395

Per Capita Income
(2010 Inflation-Adjusted Dollars)

Group	Dollars
Total Population	21,636
Hispanic or Latino (of any race)	13,201
Central American, ex. Mexican	13,558
Guatemalan	14,213
Salvadoran	12,068
Mexican	13,002

Households with $100,000+ Income

Group	Number	%
Total Population	3,080	14.6
Hispanic or Latino (of any race)	362	6.3

Notes: (1) Percent of total population; (2) Percent of Hispanic/Latino population; Profiles include places with an overall population of at least 125,000, OR an overall population of at least 25,000 where the Hispanic/Latino population is at least 20% of the overall population. In states where less than five places meet either of these criteria, we have included places with at least 10,000 total population with the highest percentage of Hispanic/Latino population. These places are identified with an asterisk (*); Please refer to the User's Guide for a full explanation of data.

Central American, ex. Mexican	49	6.0
Guatemalan	10	2.7
Salvadoran	11	3.3
Mexican	276	6.5

Households with Food Stamps/SNAP Benefits During Past 12 Months

Group	Number	%
Total Population	1,060	5.0
Hispanic or Latino (of any race)	610	10.6
Central American, ex. Mexican	132	16.1
Guatemalan	64	17.0
Salvadoran	41	12.3
Mexican	469	11.0

Poverty Rate
(Income in Past 12 Months Below Poverty Level)

Group	%
Total Population	15.9
Hispanic or Latino (of any race)	24.5
Central American, ex. Mexican	14.9
Guatemalan	18.5
Salvadoran	15.4
Mexican	26.8

Gilroy

Population

Group	Number	%TP[1]	%HP[2]
Total Population	48,821	100.0	–
Hispanic or Latino (of any race)	28,214	57.8	100.0
Central American, ex. Mexican	577	1.2	2.0
Guatemalan	120	0.2	0.4
Salvadoran	265	0.5	0.9
Mexican	25,617	52.5	90.8
Puerto Rican	258	0.5	0.9
South American	213	0.4	0.8
Spaniard	329	0.7	1.2

Population Growth: 2000–2010

Group	%
Total Population	17.7
Hispanic or Latino (of any race)	26.5
Central American, ex. Mexican	140.4
Mexican	33.2
Puerto Rican	47.4
South American	100.9

Males per 100 Females

Group	Number
Total Population	98.5
Hispanic or Latino (of any race)	100.2
Central American, ex. Mexican	89.2
Guatemalan	122.2
Salvadoran	92.0
Mexican	100.1
Puerto Rican	109.8
South American	106.8
Spaniard	93.5

Average Household Size

Group	People
Total Population	3.39
Hispanic or Latino (of any race)	4.10
Central American, ex. Mexican	3.97
Guatemalan	4.06
Salvadoran	3.88
Mexican	4.16
Puerto Rican	3.00
South American	3.57
Spaniard	2.94

Median Age

Group	Years
Total Population	32.4
Hispanic or Latino (of any race)	26.7
Central American, ex. Mexican	31.6
Guatemalan	30.3
Salvadoran	31.3
Mexican	26.3
Puerto Rican	29.4
South American	34.9
Spaniard	35.1

High School Graduates
(Universe: Population 25 Years and Over)

Group	Number	%
Total Population	21,197	75.9
Hispanic or Latino (of any race)	8,100	58.5
Mexican	7,261	57.2

Four-Year College Graduates
(Universe: Population 25 Years and Over)

Group	Number	%
Total Population	6,878	24.6
Hispanic or Latino (of any race)	1,544	11.2
Mexican	1,159	9.1

Population Age 3–17 Enrolled in Public School
(Universe: Population Age 3–17 Enrolled in School)

Group	Number	%
Total Population	9,277	85.2
Hispanic or Latino (of any race)	6,614	90.5
Mexican	6,395	91.0

Population Age 3–17 Enrolled in Private School
(Universe: Population Age 3–17 Enrolled in School)

Group	Number	%
Total Population	1,614	14.8
Hispanic or Latino (of any race)	694	9.5
Mexican	630	9.0

Foreign-Born Population

Group	Number	%
Total Population	11,886	25.4
Hispanic or Latino (of any race)	8,887	33.1
Mexican	8,302	33.0

Foreign-Born Naturalized U.S. Citizens

Group	Number	%
Total Population	4,854	40.8
Hispanic or Latino (of any race)	2,682	30.2
Mexican	2,366	28.5

Language Spoken at Home: English Only
(Universe: Population 5 Years and Over)

Group	Number	%
Total Population	23,104	53.9
Hispanic or Latino (of any race)	7,170	30.0
Mexican	6,480	29.0

Language Spoken at Home: Spanish
(Universe: Population 5 Years and Over)

Group	Number	%
Total Population	17,084	39.8
Hispanic or Latino (of any race)	16,716	70.0
Mexican	15,847	71.0

Unemployment Rate
(Universe: Population 16 Years and Over)

Group	%
Total Population	8.9
Hispanic or Latino (of any race)	10.2
Mexican	10.5

Class of Worker: Private Wage and Salary
(Universe: Civilian Employed Population 16 Years and Over)

Group	Number	%
Total Population	16,660	78.3
Hispanic or Latino (of any race)	9,451	83.0
Mexican	8,861	83.3

Class of Worker: Government
(Universe: Civilian Employed Population 16 Years and Over)

Group	Number	%
Total Population	3,077	14.5
Hispanic or Latino (of any race)	1,289	11.3
Mexican	1,210	11.4

Means of Transportation to Work: Car, Truck or Van
(Universe: Workers 16 Years and Over)

Group	Number	%
Total Population	18,464	88.5
Hispanic or Latino (of any race)	9,651	87.1
Mexican	8,952	86.6

Means of Transportation to Work: Public Transportation (ex. Taxicab)
(Universe: Workers 16 Years and Over)

Group	Number	%
Total Population	562	2.7
Hispanic or Latino (of any race)	361	3.3
Mexican	361	3.5

Homeownership Rate
(Universe: Occupied Housing Units)

Group	%
Total Population	60.8
Hispanic or Latino (of any race)	42.6
Central American, ex. Mexican	49.0
Guatemalan	41.9
Salvadoran	51.3
Mexican	41.5
Puerto Rican	53.8
South American	73.8
Spaniard	71.3

Median Home Value

Group	Dollars
Total Population	592,300
Hispanic or Latino (of any race)	569,200
Mexican	554,700

Median Gross Rent

Group	Dollars
Total Population	1,167
Hispanic or Latino (of any race)	1,137
Mexican	1,121

Median Household Income
(2010 Inflation-Adjusted Dollars)

Group	Dollars
Total Population	71,340
Hispanic or Latino (of any race)	46,868
Mexican	44,726

Per Capita Income
(2010 Inflation-Adjusted Dollars)

Group	Dollars
Total Population	28,527
Hispanic or Latino (of any race)	16,462
Mexican	16,015

Households with $100,000+ Income

Group	Number	%
Total Population	5,329	37.7
Hispanic or Latino (of any race)	1,340	19.7
Mexican	1,102	17.7

Households with Food Stamps/SNAP Benefits During Past 12 Months

Group	Number	%
Total Population	1,140	8.1
Hispanic or Latino (of any race)	942	13.9
Mexican	879	14.1

Poverty Rate
(Income in Past 12 Months Below Poverty Level)

Group	%
Total Population	8.7
Hispanic or Latino (of any race)	12.5
Mexican	12.9

Glendale

Population

Group	Number	%TP[1]	%HP[2]
Total Population	191,719	100.0	–
Hispanic or Latino (of any race)	33,414	17.4	100.0
Central American, ex. Mexican	6,392	3.3	19.1
Costa Rican	145	0.1	0.4
Guatemalan	1,723	0.9	5.2
Honduran	367	0.2	1.1
Nicaraguan	526	0.3	1.6
Salvadoran	3,481	1.8	10.4
Cuban	1,513	0.8	4.5
Mexican	19,126	10.0	57.2
Puerto Rican	575	0.3	1.7
South American	3,287	1.7	9.8
Argentinean	539	0.3	1.6

Notes: (1) Percent of total population; (2) Percent of Hispanic/Latino population; Profiles include places with an overall population of at least 125,000, OR an overall population of at least 25,000 where the Hispanic/Latino population is at least 20% of the overall population. In states where less than five places meet either of these criteria, we have included places with at least 10,000 total population with the highest percentage of Hispanic/Latino population. These places are identified with an asterisk (*); Please refer to the User's Guide for a full explanation of data.

STATE & PLACE PROFILES

Bolivian	150	0.1	0.4
Chilean	230	0.1	0.7
Colombian	841	0.4	2.5
Ecuadorian	542	0.3	1.6
Peruvian	803	0.4	2.4
Spaniard	452	0.2	1.4

Population Growth: 2000–2010

Group	%
Total Population	-1.7
Hispanic or Latino (of any race)	-13.1
Central American, ex. Mexican	26.4
Costa Rican	3.6
Guatemalan	50.9
Honduran	41.7
Nicaraguan	37.3
Salvadoran	35.8
Cuban	-17.7
Mexican	-8.1
Puerto Rican	-7.9
South American	22.1
Argentinean	32.1
Chilean	39.4
Colombian	33.1
Ecuadorian	31.9
Peruvian	27.5
Spaniard	205.4

Males per 100 Females

Group	Number
Total Population	91.1
Hispanic or Latino (of any race)	89.1
Central American, ex. Mexican	77.4
Costa Rican	85.9
Guatemalan	82.3
Honduran	61.7
Nicaraguan	70.2
Salvadoran	78.4
Cuban	81.4
Mexican	95.3
Puerto Rican	86.7
South American	77.9
Argentinean	88.5
Bolivian	66.7
Chilean	76.9
Colombian	66.2
Ecuadorian	78.9
Peruvian	84.2
Spaniard	81.5

Average Household Size

Group	People
Total Population	2.63
Hispanic or Latino (of any race)	2.93
Central American, ex. Mexican	3.17
Costa Rican	2.89
Guatemalan	3.35
Honduran	3.14
Nicaraguan	2.94
Salvadoran	3.19
Cuban	2.31
Mexican	3.08
Puerto Rican	2.37
South American	2.59
Argentinean	2.36
Bolivian	2.82
Chilean	2.47
Colombian	2.57
Ecuadorian	2.84
Peruvian	2.70
Spaniard	2.35

Median Age

Group	Years
Total Population	41.0
Hispanic or Latino (of any race)	33.8
Central American, ex. Mexican	36.1
Costa Rican	38.5
Guatemalan	35.0
Honduran	36.8
Nicaraguan	42.2
Salvadoran	35.6
Cuban	48.4
Mexican	31.3
Puerto Rican	34.3
South American	42.6
Argentinean	46.8
Bolivian	43.5
Chilean	39.8
Colombian	41.7
Ecuadorian	41.3
Peruvian	43.3
Spaniard	42.0

High School Graduates
(Universe: Population 25 Years and Over)

Group	Number	%
Total Population	117,634	85.2
Hispanic or Latino (of any race)	14,865	71.6
Central American, ex. Mexican	2,910	65.8
Guatemalan	554	62.9
Salvadoran	1,577	62.1
Cuban	976	85.2
Mexican	7,466	67.8
South American	2,167	82.3
Colombian	527	78.9

Four-Year College Graduates
(Universe: Population 25 Years and Over)

Group	Number	%
Total Population	53,500	38.8
Hispanic or Latino (of any race)	4,512	21.7
Central American, ex. Mexican	705	15.9
Guatemalan	84	9.5
Salvadoran	242	9.5
Cuban	303	26.4
Mexican	2,247	20.4
South American	927	35.2
Colombian	216	32.3

Population Age 3–17 Enrolled in Public School
(Universe: Population Age 3–17 Enrolled in School)

Group	Number	%
Total Population	25,178	82.7
Hispanic or Latino (of any race)	6,043	86.3
Central American, ex. Mexican	1,229	85.0
Guatemalan	228	78.6
Salvadoran	792	96.7
Cuban	58	27.4
Mexican	3,885	89.5
South American	484	81.2
Colombian	46	66.7

Population Age 3–17 Enrolled in Private School
(Universe: Population Age 3–17 Enrolled in School)

Group	Number	%
Total Population	5,251	17.3
Hispanic or Latino (of any race)	958	13.7
Central American, ex. Mexican	217	15.0
Guatemalan	62	21.4
Salvadoran	27	3.3
Cuban	154	72.6
Mexican	457	10.5
South American	112	18.8
Colombian	23	33.3

Foreign-Born Population

Group	Number	%
Total Population	105,034	54.7
Hispanic or Latino (of any race)	15,590	48.3
Central American, ex. Mexican	4,258	64.5
Guatemalan	872	64.8
Salvadoran	2,611	69.1
Cuban	975	69.4
Mexican	7,264	39.7
South American	2,368	65.7
Colombian	548	66.3

Foreign-Born Naturalized U.S. Citizens

Group	Number	%
Total Population	62,167	59.2
Hispanic or Latino (of any race)	8,053	51.7
Central American, ex. Mexican	2,225	52.3
Guatemalan	445	51.0
Salvadoran	1,352	51.8
Cuban	865	88.7
Mexican	3,095	42.6
South American	1,358	57.3
Colombian	373	68.1

Language Spoken at Home: English Only
(Universe: Population 5 Years and Over)

Group	Number	%
Total Population	58,485	31.9
Hispanic or Latino (of any race)	5,965	19.6
Central American, ex. Mexican	450	7.1
Guatemalan	83	6.4
Salvadoran	151	4.1
Cuban	82	5.8
Mexican	4,274	24.9
South American	349	10.4
Colombian	90	11.2

Language Spoken at Home: Spanish
(Universe: Population 5 Years and Over)

Group	Number	%
Total Population	25,764	14.0
Hispanic or Latino (of any race)	24,121	79.3
Central American, ex. Mexican	5,898	92.9
Guatemalan	1,223	93.6
Salvadoran	3,491	95.9
Cuban	1,293	92.1
Mexican	12,687	74.0
South American	2,944	87.4
Colombian	712	88.8

Unemployment Rate
(Universe: Population 16 Years and Over)

Group	%
Total Population	8.0
Hispanic or Latino (of any race)	5.8
Central American, ex. Mexican	6.4
Guatemalan	9.6
Salvadoran	5.8
Cuban	2.9
Mexican	5.2
South American	6.6
Colombian	2.2

Class of Worker: Private Wage and Salary
(Universe: Civilian Employed Population 16 Years and Over)

Group	Number	%
Total Population	71,701	76.7
Hispanic or Latino (of any race)	13,282	79.2
Central American, ex. Mexican	2,642	72.2
Guatemalan	668	83.1
Salvadoran	1,377	67.4
Cuban	421	74.1
Mexican	7,734	82.0
South American	1,594	81.5
Colombian	523	85.3

Class of Worker: Government
(Universe: Civilian Employed Population 16 Years and Over)

Group	Number	%
Total Population	10,884	11.6
Hispanic or Latino (of any race)	2,029	12.1
Central American, ex. Mexican	425	11.6
Guatemalan	45	5.6
Salvadoran	208	10.2
Cuban	109	19.2
Mexican	1,167	12.4
South American	199	10.2
Colombian	26	4.2

Means of Transportation to Work: Car, Truck or Van
(Universe: Workers 16 Years and Over)

Group	Number	%
Total Population	78,365	85.9
Hispanic or Latino (of any race)	12,716	77.6
Central American, ex. Mexican	2,918	81.1
Guatemalan	664	83.8
Salvadoran	1,583	79.2
Cuban	515	90.7
Mexican	6,762	74.0
South American	1,594	82.6
Colombian	398	66.0

Means of Transportation to Work: Public Transportation (ex. Taxicab)
(Universe: Workers 16 Years and Over)

Group	Number	%
Total Population	3,724	4.1
Hispanic or Latino (of any race)	1,867	11.4

Notes: (1) Percent of total population; (2) Percent of Hispanic/Latino population; Profiles include places with an overall population of at least 125,000, OR an overall population of at least 25,000 where the Hispanic/Latino population is at least 20% of the overall population. In states where less than five places meet either of these criteria, we have included places with at least 10,000 total population with the highest percentage of Hispanic/Latino population. These places are identified with an asterisk (*); Please refer to the User's Guide for a full explanation of data.

Central American, ex. Mexican	476	13.2
Guatemalan	50	6.3
Salvadoran	308	15.4
Cuban	31	5.5
Mexican	1,082	11.8
South American	173	9.0
Colombian	145	24.0

Homeownership Rate
(Universe: Occupied Housing Units)

Group	%
Total Population	38.1
Hispanic or Latino (of any race)	26.7
Central American, ex. Mexican	18.7
Costa Rican	34.5
Guatemalan	18.0
Honduran	21.6
Nicaraguan	28.8
Salvadoran	15.9
Cuban	42.4
Mexican	25.5
Puerto Rican	26.6
South American	34.8
Argentinean	47.9
Bolivian	44.3
Chilean	37.5
Colombian	32.1
Ecuadorian	39.1
Peruvian	24.6
Spaniard	43.5

Median Home Value

Group	Dollars
Total Population	635,100
Hispanic or Latino (of any race)	616,300
Central American, ex. Mexican	622,000
Guatemalan	603,600
Salvadoran	697,800
Cuban	684,200
Mexican	611,100
South American	597,500
Colombian	628,400

Median Gross Rent

Group	Dollars
Total Population	1,220
Hispanic or Latino (of any race)	1,114
Central American, ex. Mexican	1,098
Guatemalan	998
Salvadoran	1,117
Cuban	918
Mexican	1,117
South American	1,114
Colombian	1,137

Median Household Income
(2010 Inflation-Adjusted Dollars)

Group	Dollars
Total Population	54,677
Hispanic or Latino (of any race)	45,968
Central American, ex. Mexican	45,111
Guatemalan	42,577
Salvadoran	41,545
Cuban	46,801
Mexican	46,436
South American	45,871
Colombian	52,000

Per Capita Income
(2010 Inflation-Adjusted Dollars)

Group	Dollars
Total Population	29,823
Hispanic or Latino (of any race)	22,232
Central American, ex. Mexican	19,009
Guatemalan	21,553
Salvadoran	15,167
Cuban	26,533
Mexican	22,174
South American	24,975
Colombian	28,655

Households with $100,000+ Income

Group	Number	%
Total Population	18,110	25.3
Hispanic or Latino (of any race)	1,775	16.6
Central American, ex. Mexican	199	9.2
Guatemalan	76	16.7
Salvadoran	52	4.2
Cuban	82	12.1
Mexican	1,056	18.9
South American	270	18.7
Colombian	83	22.2

Households with Food Stamps/SNAP Benefits During Past 12 Months

Group	Number	%
Total Population	3,273	4.6
Hispanic or Latino (of any race)	562	5.3
Central American, ex. Mexican	154	7.1
Guatemalan	28	6.2
Salvadoran	106	8.6
Cuban	0	0.0
Mexican	367	6.6
South American	0	0.0
Colombian	0	0.0

Poverty Rate
(Income in Past 12 Months Below Poverty Level)

Group	%
Total Population	13.0
Hispanic or Latino (of any race)	15.4
Central American, ex. Mexican	18.4
Guatemalan	15.6
Salvadoran	23.4
Cuban	6.7
Mexican	15.7
South American	8.4
Colombian	11.4

Glendora

Population

Group	Number	%TP[1]	%HP[2]
Total Population	50,073	100.0	–
Hispanic or Latino (of any race)	15,348	30.7	100.0
Central American, ex. Mexican	898	1.8	5.9
Guatemalan	205	0.4	1.3
Nicaraguan	175	0.3	1.1
Salvadoran	401	0.8	2.6
Cuban	259	0.5	1.7
Mexican	12,151	24.3	79.2
Puerto Rican	274	0.5	1.8
South American	622	1.2	4.1
Argentinean	142	0.3	0.9
Colombian	148	0.3	1.0
Peruvian	148	0.3	1.0
Spaniard	261	0.5	1.7

Population Growth: 2000–2010

Group	%
Total Population	1.3
Hispanic or Latino (of any race)	42.9
Central American, ex. Mexican	153.0
Salvadoran	220.8
Cuban	30.2
Mexican	54.4
Puerto Rican	58.4
South American	65.9
Argentinean	42.0

Males per 100 Females

Group	Number
Total Population	93.7
Hispanic or Latino (of any race)	90.2
Central American, ex. Mexican	93.1
Guatemalan	93.4
Nicaraguan	92.3
Salvadoran	90.0
Cuban	89.1
Mexican	90.8
Puerto Rican	79.1
South American	80.3
Argentinean	84.4
Colombian	85.0
Peruvian	78.3
Spaniard	97.7

Average Household Size

Group	People
Total Population	2.88
Hispanic or Latino (of any race)	3.41
Central American, ex. Mexican	3.50
Guatemalan	3.61
Nicaraguan	3.77
Salvadoran	3.49
Cuban	3.34
Mexican	3.47
Puerto Rican	2.76
South American	3.35
Argentinean	3.28
Colombian	2.93
Peruvian	3.56
Spaniard	2.64

Median Age

Group	Years
Total Population	40.2
Hispanic or Latino (of any race)	29.8
Central American, ex. Mexican	36.1
Guatemalan	37.8
Nicaraguan	32.8
Salvadoran	35.6
Cuban	34.6
Mexican	28.6
Puerto Rican	31.4
South American	41.8
Argentinean	42.6
Colombian	40.5
Peruvian	43.3
Spaniard	33.8

High School Graduates
(Universe: Population 25 Years and Over)

Group	Number	%
Total Population	28,901	89.3
Hispanic or Latino (of any race)	6,516	81.7
Mexican	4,940	80.6
South American	470	86.7

Four-Year College Graduates
(Universe: Population 25 Years and Over)

Group	Number	%
Total Population	9,590	29.6
Hispanic or Latino (of any race)	1,395	17.5
Mexican	979	16.0
South American	114	21.0

Population Age 3–17 Enrolled in Public School
(Universe: Population Age 3–17 Enrolled in School)

Group	Number	%
Total Population	8,508	87.0
Hispanic or Latino (of any race)	3,002	90.1
Mexican	2,422	93.5
South American	98	64.5

Population Age 3–17 Enrolled in Private School
(Universe: Population Age 3–17 Enrolled in School)

Group	Number	%
Total Population	1,272	13.0
Hispanic or Latino (of any race)	331	9.9
Mexican	167	6.5
South American	54	35.5

Foreign-Born Population

Group	Number	%
Total Population	7,344	14.7
Hispanic or Latino (of any race)	2,928	20.8
Mexican	1,933	17.8
South American	428	52.6

Foreign-Born Naturalized U.S. Citizens

Group	Number	%
Total Population	4,587	62.5
Hispanic or Latino (of any race)	1,466	50.1
Mexican	889	46.0
South American	202	47.2

Language Spoken at Home: English Only
(Universe: Population 5 Years and Over)

Group	Number	%
Total Population	35,540	75.7
Hispanic or Latino (of any race)	6,282	49.0

Notes: (1) Percent of total population; (2) Percent of Hispanic/Latino population; Profiles include places with an overall population of at least 125,000, OR an overall population of at least 25,000 where the Hispanic/Latino population is at least 20% of the overall population. In states where less than five places meet either of these criteria, we have included places with at least 10,000 total population with the highest percentage of Hispanic/Latino population. These places are identified with an asterisk (*); Please refer to the User's Guide for a full explanation of data.

Mexican	5,061	51.2
South American	257	36.1

Language Spoken at Home: Spanish
(Universe: Population 5 Years and Over)

Group	Number	%
Total Population	7,133	15.2
Hispanic or Latino (of any race)	6,492	50.7
Mexican	4,808	48.6
South American	441	61.9

Unemployment Rate
(Universe: Population 16 Years and Over)

Group	%
Total Population	7.7
Hispanic or Latino (of any race)	8.1
Mexican	8.3
South American	13.1

Class of Worker: Private Wage and Salary
(Universe: Civilian Employed Population 16 Years and Over)

Group	Number	%
Total Population	16,931	73.6
Hispanic or Latino (of any race)	4,510	74.8
Mexican	3,547	74.9
South American	293	75.1

Class of Worker: Government
(Universe: Civilian Employed Population 16 Years and Over)

Group	Number	%
Total Population	4,095	17.8
Hispanic or Latino (of any race)	1,130	18.7
Mexican	859	18.1
South American	66	16.9

Means of Transportation to Work: Car, Truck or Van
(Universe: Workers 16 Years and Over)

Group	Number	%
Total Population	19,770	89.0
Hispanic or Latino (of any race)	5,349	91.3
Mexican	4,200	91.4
South American	306	78.5

Means of Transportation to Work: Public Transportation (ex. Taxicab)
(Universe: Workers 16 Years and Over)

Group	Number	%
Total Population	690	3.1
Hispanic or Latino (of any race)	171	2.9
Mexican	99	2.2
South American	43	11.0

Homeownership Rate
(Universe: Occupied Housing Units)

Group	%
Total Population	72.3
Hispanic or Latino (of any race)	62.9
Central American, ex. Mexican	61.1
Guatemalan	60.9
Nicaraguan	61.5
Salvadoran	58.4
Cuban	75.9
Mexican	62.8
Puerto Rican	61.0
South American	66.2
Argentinean	67.4
Colombian	59.6
Peruvian	64.4
Spaniard	68.0

Median Home Value

Group	Dollars
Total Population	529,200
Hispanic or Latino (of any race)	486,500
Mexican	474,300
South American	515,800

Median Gross Rent

Group	Dollars
Total Population	1,300
Hispanic or Latino (of any race)	1,399
Mexican	1,446
South American	–

Median Household Income
(2010 Inflation-Adjusted Dollars)

Group	Dollars
Total Population	75,954
Hispanic or Latino (of any race)	69,620
Mexican	69,921
South American	74,848

Per Capita Income
(2010 Inflation-Adjusted Dollars)

Group	Dollars
Total Population	32,951
Hispanic or Latino (of any race)	23,502
Mexican	23,541
South American	26,434

Households with $100,000+ Income

Group	Number	%
Total Population	5,619	34.2
Hispanic or Latino (of any race)	1,157	30.5
Mexican	864	30.7
South American	109	49.1

Households with Food Stamps/SNAP Benefits During Past 12 Months

Group	Number	%
Total Population	411	2.5
Hispanic or Latino (of any race)	267	7.0
Mexican	241	8.6
South American	0	0.0

Poverty Rate
(Income in Past 12 Months Below Poverty Level)

Group	%
Total Population	6.5
Hispanic or Latino (of any race)	10.0
Mexican	11.1
South American	0.0

Goleta

Population

Group	Number	%TP[1]	%HP[2]
Total Population	29,888	100.0	–
Hispanic or Latino (of any race)	9,824	32.9	100.0
Central American, ex. Mexican	292	1.0	3.0
Guatemalan	152	0.5	1.5
Mexican	8,690	29.1	88.5
South American	200	0.7	2.0
Spaniard	117	0.4	1.2

Population Growth: 2000–2010

Group	%
Total Population	-45.9
Hispanic or Latino (of any race)	-20.3
Central American, ex. Mexican	9.8
Guatemalan	7.8
Mexican	-16.0
South American	3.6

Males per 100 Females

Group	Number
Total Population	101.3
Hispanic or Latino (of any race)	101.1
Central American, ex. Mexican	97.3
Guatemalan	108.2
Mexican	102.3
South American	94.2
Spaniard	101.7

Average Household Size

Group	People
Total Population	2.72
Hispanic or Latino (of any race)	3.87
Central American, ex. Mexican	3.73
Guatemalan	4.06
Mexican	4.00
South American	2.85
Spaniard	2.40

Median Age

Group	Years
Total Population	36.5
Hispanic or Latino (of any race)	27.4
Central American, ex. Mexican	28.7
Guatemalan	31.8
Mexican	27.0
South American	35.6
Spaniard	34.8

High School Graduates
(Universe: Population 25 Years and Over)

Group	Number	%
Total Population	16,343	86.8
Hispanic or Latino (of any race)	2,611	58.9
Mexican	2,062	54.3

Four-Year College Graduates
(Universe: Population 25 Years and Over)

Group	Number	%
Total Population	7,946	42.2
Hispanic or Latino (of any race)	699	15.8
Mexican	485	12.8

Population Age 3–17 Enrolled in Public School
(Universe: Population Age 3–17 Enrolled in School)

Group	Number	%
Total Population	4,132	85.0
Hispanic or Latino (of any race)	1,792	90.8
Mexican	1,537	92.6

Population Age 3–17 Enrolled in Private School
(Universe: Population Age 3–17 Enrolled in School)

Group	Number	%
Total Population	727	15.0
Hispanic or Latino (of any race)	181	9.2
Mexican	122	7.4

Foreign-Born Population

Group	Number	%
Total Population	7,620	25.9
Hispanic or Latino (of any race)	4,074	45.3
Mexican	3,611	46.9

Foreign-Born Naturalized U.S. Citizens

Group	Number	%
Total Population	3,491	45.8
Hispanic or Latino (of any race)	1,529	37.5
Mexican	1,342	37.2

Language Spoken at Home: English Only
(Universe: Population 5 Years and Over)

Group	Number	%
Total Population	16,969	62.7
Hispanic or Latino (of any race)	1,649	21.1
Mexican	1,283	19.1

Language Spoken at Home: Spanish
(Universe: Population 5 Years and Over)

Group	Number	%
Total Population	6,642	24.5
Hispanic or Latino (of any race)	6,159	78.6
Mexican	5,443	80.9

Unemployment Rate
(Universe: Population 16 Years and Over)

Group	%
Total Population	4.2
Hispanic or Latino (of any race)	4.8
Mexican	4.4

Class of Worker: Private Wage and Salary
(Universe: Civilian Employed Population 16 Years and Over)

Group	Number	%
Total Population	11,118	71.7
Hispanic or Latino (of any race)	3,355	74.8
Mexican	3,070	78.8

Class of Worker: Government
(Universe: Civilian Employed Population 16 Years and Over)

Group	Number	%
Total Population	3,141	20.3
Hispanic or Latino (of any race)	839	18.7
Mexican	620	15.9

Means of Transportation to Work: Car, Truck or Van
(Universe: Workers 16 Years and Over)

Group	Number	%
Total Population	12,018	80.5

Notes: (1) Percent of total population; (2) Percent of Hispanic/Latino population; Profiles include places with an overall population of at least 125,000, OR an overall population of at least 25,000 where the Hispanic/Latino population is at least 20% of the overall population. In states where less than five places meet either of these criteria, we have included places with at least 10,000 total population with the highest percentage of Hispanic/Latino population. These places are identified with an asterisk (*); Please refer to the User's Guide for a full explanation of data.

Hispanic or Latino (of any race)	3,618	83.3
Mexican	3,129	83.8

Means of Transportation to Work: Public Transportation (ex. Taxicab)
(Universe: Workers 16 Years and Over)

Group	Number	%
Total Population	720	4.8
Hispanic or Latino (of any race)	328	7.6
Mexican	328	8.8

Homeownership Rate
(Universe: Occupied Housing Units)

Group	%
Total Population	53.6
Hispanic or Latino (of any race)	42.0
Central American, ex. Mexican	25.6
Guatemalan	31.3
Mexican	42.0
South American	55.7
Spaniard	60.0

Median Home Value

Group	Dollars
Total Population	767,100
Hispanic or Latino (of any race)	759,100
Mexican	757,000

Median Gross Rent

Group	Dollars
Total Population	1,495
Hispanic or Latino (of any race)	1,338
Mexican	1,363

Median Household Income
(2010 Inflation-Adjusted Dollars)

Group	Dollars
Total Population	67,895
Hispanic or Latino (of any race)	60,907
Mexican	60,268

Per Capita Income
(2010 Inflation-Adjusted Dollars)

Group	Dollars
Total Population	32,073
Hispanic or Latino (of any race)	17,769
Mexican	16,535

Households with $100,000+ Income

Group	Number	%
Total Population	3,472	32.1
Hispanic or Latino (of any race)	407	17.6
Mexican	291	15.1

Households with Food Stamps/SNAP Benefits During Past 12 Months

Group	Number	%
Total Population	163	1.5
Hispanic or Latino (of any race)	74	3.2
Mexican	74	3.8

Poverty Rate
(Income in Past 12 Months Below Poverty Level)

Group	%
Total Population	9.1
Hispanic or Latino (of any race)	11.4
Mexican	12.1

Hacienda Heights

Population

Group	Number	%TP[1]	%HP[2]
Total Population	54,038	100.0	–
Hispanic or Latino (of any race)	24,608	45.5	100.0
Central American, ex. Mexican	1,511	2.8	6.1
Guatemalan	378	0.7	1.5
Nicaraguan	157	0.3	0.6
Salvadoran	807	1.5	3.3
Cuban	157	0.3	0.6
Mexican	20,994	38.9	85.3
Puerto Rican	215	0.4	0.9
South American	660	1.2	2.7
Argentinean	117	0.2	0.5
Colombian	142	0.3	0.6
Ecuadorian	135	0.2	0.5
Peruvian	182	0.3	0.7
Spaniard	187	0.3	0.8

Population Growth: 2000–2010

Group	%
Total Population	1.7
Hispanic or Latino (of any race)	21.1
Central American, ex. Mexican	127.6
Guatemalan	164.3
Salvadoran	181.2
Cuban	17.2
Mexican	28.2
Puerto Rican	25.0
South American	68.4
Peruvian	78.4

Males per 100 Females

Group	Number
Total Population	94.8
Hispanic or Latino (of any race)	95.6
Central American, ex. Mexican	84.0
Guatemalan	80.0
Nicaraguan	58.6
Salvadoran	92.6
Cuban	89.2
Mexican	96.3
Puerto Rican	112.9
South American	97.6
Argentinean	105.3
Colombian	100.0
Ecuadorian	98.5
Peruvian	91.6
Spaniard	103.3

Average Household Size

Group	People
Total Population	3.33
Hispanic or Latino (of any race)	4.06
Central American, ex. Mexican	4.73
Guatemalan	5.00
Nicaraguan	4.09
Salvadoran	4.84
Cuban	2.76
Mexican	4.07
Puerto Rican	3.41
South American	3.78
Argentinean	2.60
Colombian	4.28
Ecuadorian	4.27
Peruvian	4.02
Spaniard	3.09

Median Age

Group	Years
Total Population	40.1
Hispanic or Latino (of any race)	32.1
Central American, ex. Mexican	36.0
Guatemalan	35.0
Nicaraguan	41.1
Salvadoran	35.3
Cuban	39.1
Mexican	31.4
Puerto Rican	41.1
South American	42.6
Argentinean	51.8
Colombian	42.4
Ecuadorian	37.9
Peruvian	41.8
Spaniard	46.2

High School Graduates
(Universe: Population 25 Years and Over)

Group	Number	%
Total Population	31,124	84.8
Hispanic or Latino (of any race)	9,706	73.3
Central American, ex. Mexican	594	66.3
Mexican	8,043	72.8

Four-Year College Graduates
(Universe: Population 25 Years and Over)

Group	Number	%
Total Population	12,459	33.9
Hispanic or Latino (of any race)	2,128	16.1
Central American, ex. Mexican	235	26.2
Mexican	1,588	14.4

Population Age 3–17 Enrolled in Public School
(Universe: Population Age 3–17 Enrolled in School)

Group	Number	%
Total Population	8,185	86.2
Hispanic or Latino (of any race)	4,682	87.8
Central American, ex. Mexican	127	100.0
Mexican	4,139	87.9

Population Age 3–17 Enrolled in Private School
(Universe: Population Age 3–17 Enrolled in School)

Group	Number	%
Total Population	1,310	13.8
Hispanic or Latino (of any race)	650	12.2
Central American, ex. Mexican	0	0.0
Mexican	569	12.1

Foreign-Born Population

Group	Number	%
Total Population	22,147	41.3
Hispanic or Latino (of any race)	6,399	28.6
Central American, ex. Mexican	870	74.2
Mexican	4,723	24.8

Foreign-Born Naturalized U.S. Citizens

Group	Number	%
Total Population	14,601	65.9
Hispanic or Latino (of any race)	3,591	56.1
Central American, ex. Mexican	445	51.1
Mexican	2,682	56.8

Language Spoken at Home: English Only
(Universe: Population 5 Years and Over)

Group	Number	%
Total Population	18,259	35.8
Hispanic or Latino (of any race)	6,458	31.2
Central American, ex. Mexican	145	12.8
Mexican	5,686	32.6

Language Spoken at Home: Spanish
(Universe: Population 5 Years and Over)

Group	Number	%
Total Population	14,688	28.8
Hispanic or Latino (of any race)	14,187	68.5
Central American, ex. Mexican	988	87.2
Mexican	11,690	67.0

Unemployment Rate
(Universe: Population 16 Years and Over)

Group	%
Total Population	6.5
Hispanic or Latino (of any race)	7.5
Central American, ex. Mexican	5.9
Mexican	7.9

Class of Worker: Private Wage and Salary
(Universe: Civilian Employed Population 16 Years and Over)

Group	Number	%
Total Population	18,712	76.7
Hispanic or Latino (of any race)	7,736	78.2
Central American, ex. Mexican	632	86.1
Mexican	6,233	76.4

Class of Worker: Government
(Universe: Civilian Employed Population 16 Years and Over)

Group	Number	%
Total Population	3,624	14.9
Hispanic or Latino (of any race)	1,421	14.4
Central American, ex. Mexican	37	5.0
Mexican	1,263	15.5

Means of Transportation to Work: Car, Truck or Van
(Universe: Workers 16 Years and Over)

Group	Number	%
Total Population	21,685	91.4
Hispanic or Latino (of any race)	8,906	92.9
Central American, ex. Mexican	734	100.0
Mexican	7,304	92.7

Means of Transportation to Work: Public Transportation (ex. Taxicab)
(Universe: Workers 16 Years and Over)

Group	Number	%
Total Population	643	2.7

Notes: (1) Percent of total population; (2) Percent of Hispanic/Latino population; Profiles include places with an overall population of at least 125,000, OR an overall population of at least 25,000 where the Hispanic/Latino population is at least 20% of the overall population. In states where less than five places meet either of these criteria, we have included places with at least 10,000 total population with the highest percentage of Hispanic/Latino population. These places are identified with an asterisk (*); Please refer to the User's Guide for a full explanation of data.

Hispanic or Latino (of any race)	236	2.5
Central American, ex. Mexican	0	0.0
Mexican	149	1.9

Homeownership Rate
(Universe: Occupied Housing Units)

Group	%
Total Population	78.6
Hispanic or Latino (of any race)	75.9
Central American, ex. Mexican	77.8
Guatemalan	75.0
Nicaraguan	94.1
Salvadoran	75.5
Cuban	83.7
Mexican	75.9
Puerto Rican	74.6
South American	76.3
Argentinean	88.1
Colombian	84.6
Ecuadorian	68.9
Peruvian	70.8
Spaniard	76.5

Median Home Value

Group	Dollars
Total Population	513,200
Hispanic or Latino (of any race)	476,500
Central American, ex. Mexican	375,000
Mexican	481,400

Median Gross Rent

Group	Dollars
Total Population	1,445
Hispanic or Latino (of any race)	1,470
Central American, ex. Mexican	2,000+
Mexican	1,463

Median Household Income
(2010 Inflation-Adjusted Dollars)

Group	Dollars
Total Population	69,501
Hispanic or Latino (of any race)	71,418
Central American, ex. Mexican	84,318
Mexican	73,226

Per Capita Income
(2010 Inflation-Adjusted Dollars)

Group	Dollars
Total Population	28,084
Hispanic or Latino (of any race)	23,839
Central American, ex. Mexican	26,904
Mexican	23,889

Households with $100,000+ Income

Group	Number	%
Total Population	5,294	32.3
Hispanic or Latino (of any race)	1,786	31.6
Central American, ex. Mexican	110	48.7
Mexican	1,560	31.7

Households with Food Stamps/SNAP Benefits During Past 12 Months

Group	Number	%
Total Population	170	1.0
Hispanic or Latino (of any race)	112	2.0
Central American, ex. Mexican	0	0.0
Mexican	104	2.1

Poverty Rate
(Income in Past 12 Months Below Poverty Level)

Group	%
Total Population	7.7
Hispanic or Latino (of any race)	8.6
Central American, ex. Mexican	1.6
Mexican	8.2

Hanford

Population

Group	Number	%TP[1]	%HP[2]
Total Population	53,967	100.0	–
Hispanic or Latino (of any race)	25,419	47.1	100.0
Central American, ex. Mexican	282	0.5	1.1
Salvadoran	117	0.2	0.5
Mexican	23,269	43.1	91.5
Puerto Rican	180	0.3	0.7
Spaniard	196	0.4	0.8

Population Growth: 2000–2010

Group	%
Total Population	29.5
Hispanic or Latino (of any race)	57.7
Mexican	67.2
Puerto Rican	65.1

Males per 100 Females

Group	Number
Total Population	96.3
Hispanic or Latino (of any race)	99.0
Central American, ex. Mexican	66.9
Salvadoran	80.0
Mexican	99.4
Puerto Rican	97.8
Spaniard	88.5

Average Household Size

Group	People
Total Population	3.03
Hispanic or Latino (of any race)	3.71
Central American, ex. Mexican	3.93
Salvadoran	3.97
Mexican	3.74
Puerto Rican	2.89
Spaniard	2.79

Median Age

Group	Years
Total Population	30.9
Hispanic or Latino (of any race)	24.3
Central American, ex. Mexican	32.0
Salvadoran	35.8
Mexican	24.0
Puerto Rican	26.3
Spaniard	30.3

High School Graduates
(Universe: Population 25 Years and Over)

Group	Number	%
Total Population	25,916	80.1
Hispanic or Latino (of any race)	7,201	63.1
Mexican	6,468	62.7

Four-Year College Graduates
(Universe: Population 25 Years and Over)

Group	Number	%
Total Population	5,368	16.6
Hispanic or Latino (of any race)	728	6.4
Mexican	528	5.1

Population Age 3–17 Enrolled in Public School
(Universe: Population Age 3–17 Enrolled in School)

Group	Number	%
Total Population	10,193	91.3
Hispanic or Latino (of any race)	5,753	94.8
Mexican	5,436	95.0

Population Age 3–17 Enrolled in Private School
(Universe: Population Age 3–17 Enrolled in School)

Group	Number	%
Total Population	974	8.7
Hispanic or Latino (of any race)	318	5.2
Mexican	284	5.0

Foreign-Born Population

Group	Number	%
Total Population	8,621	16.5
Hispanic or Latino (of any race)	6,263	28.2
Mexican	5,775	28.0

Foreign-Born Naturalized U.S. Citizens

Group	Number	%
Total Population	3,107	36.0
Hispanic or Latino (of any race)	1,379	22.0
Mexican	1,106	19.2

Language Spoken at Home: English Only
(Universe: Population 5 Years and Over)

Group	Number	%
Total Population	32,072	66.5
Hispanic or Latino (of any race)	7,426	37.3
Mexican	6,770	37.0

Language Spoken at Home: Spanish
(Universe: Population 5 Years and Over)

Group	Number	%
Total Population	13,267	27.5
Hispanic or Latino (of any race)	12,448	62.6
Mexican	11,551	63.0

Unemployment Rate
(Universe: Population 16 Years and Over)

Group	%
Total Population	10.7
Hispanic or Latino (of any race)	12.9
Mexican	13.1

Class of Worker: Private Wage and Salary
(Universe: Civilian Employed Population 16 Years and Over)

Group	Number	%
Total Population	14,512	66.5
Hispanic or Latino (of any race)	6,213	77.8
Mexican	5,848	77.8

Class of Worker: Government
(Universe: Civilian Employed Population 16 Years and Over)

Group	Number	%
Total Population	6,034	27.6
Hispanic or Latino (of any race)	1,422	17.8
Mexican	1,350	18.0

Means of Transportation to Work: Car, Truck or Van
(Universe: Workers 16 Years and Over)

Group	Number	%
Total Population	20,093	92.2
Hispanic or Latino (of any race)	7,284	92.3
Mexican	6,831	92.7

Means of Transportation to Work: Public Transportation (ex. Taxicab)
(Universe: Workers 16 Years and Over)

Group	Number	%
Total Population	104	0.5
Hispanic or Latino (of any race)	49	0.6
Mexican	24	0.3

Homeownership Rate
(Universe: Occupied Housing Units)

Group	%
Total Population	58.4
Hispanic or Latino (of any race)	49.6
Central American, ex. Mexican	40.5
Salvadoran	44.4
Mexican	50.3
Puerto Rican	43.4
Spaniard	54.4

Median Home Value

Group	Dollars
Total Population	231,200
Hispanic or Latino (of any race)	203,500
Mexican	202,600

Median Gross Rent

Group	Dollars
Total Population	846
Hispanic or Latino (of any race)	779
Mexican	777

Median Household Income
(2010 Inflation-Adjusted Dollars)

Group	Dollars
Total Population	54,742
Hispanic or Latino (of any race)	38,487
Mexican	38,350

Per Capita Income
(2010 Inflation-Adjusted Dollars)

Group	Dollars
Total Population	22,008
Hispanic or Latino (of any race)	13,086
Mexican	13,019

Households with $100,000+ Income

Group	Number	%
Total Population	3,449	20.5

Notes: (1) Percent of total population; (2) Percent of Hispanic/Latino population; Profiles include places with an overall population of at least 125,000, OR an overall population of at least 25,000 where the Hispanic/Latino population is at least 20% of the overall population. In states where less than five places meet either of these criteria, we have included places with at least 10,000 total population with the highest percentage of Hispanic/Latino population. These places are identified with an asterisk (*); Please refer to the User's Guide for a full explanation of data.

Hispanic or Latino (of any race)	541	9.9
Mexican	527	10.3

Households with Food Stamps/SNAP Benefits During Past 12 Months

Group	Number	%
Total Population	1,493	8.9
Hispanic or Latino (of any race)	745	13.6
Mexican	735	14.4

Poverty Rate
(Income in Past 12 Months Below Poverty Level)

Group	%
Total Population	16.5
Hispanic or Latino (of any race)	27.2
Mexican	28.6

Hawthorne

Population

Group	Number	%TP[1]	%HP[2]
Total Population	84,293	100.0	–
Hispanic or Latino (of any race)	44,572	52.9	100.0
Central American, ex. Mexican	8,547	10.1	19.2
Costa Rican	169	0.2	0.4
Guatemalan	3,669	4.4	8.2
Honduran	584	0.7	1.3
Nicaraguan	556	0.7	1.2
Panamanian	130	0.2	0.3
Salvadoran	3,335	4.0	7.5
Cuban	752	0.9	1.7
Mexican	29,371	34.8	65.9
Puerto Rican	689	0.8	1.5
South American	1,826	2.2	4.1
Argentinean	123	0.1	0.3
Colombian	487	0.6	1.1
Ecuadorian	280	0.3	0.6
Peruvian	768	0.9	1.7
Spaniard	215	0.3	0.5

Population Growth: 2000–2010

Group	%
Total Population	0.2
Hispanic or Latino (of any race)	19.7
Central American, ex. Mexican	82.6
Costa Rican	59.4
Guatemalan	95.3
Honduran	243.5
Nicaraguan	59.3
Salvadoran	99.3
Cuban	-21.2
Mexican	31.2
Puerto Rican	0.3
South American	48.5
Colombian	65.1
Ecuadorian	48.9
Peruvian	71.8

Males per 100 Females

Group	Number
Total Population	93.2
Hispanic or Latino (of any race)	97.8
Central American, ex. Mexican	91.9
Costa Rican	108.6
Guatemalan	102.1
Honduran	78.6
Nicaraguan	77.6
Panamanian	75.7
Salvadoran	86.0
Cuban	96.9
Mexican	99.9
Puerto Rican	100.3
South American	96.6
Argentinean	95.2
Colombian	91.7
Ecuadorian	90.5
Peruvian	96.4
Spaniard	97.2

Average Household Size

Group	People
Total Population	2.94
Hispanic or Latino (of any race)	3.72
Central American, ex. Mexican	3.84
Costa Rican	2.99
Guatemalan	4.02
Honduran	3.59
Nicaraguan	3.83
Panamanian	2.37
Salvadoran	3.81
Cuban	2.44
Mexican	3.85
Puerto Rican	2.76
South American	3.26
Argentinean	2.90
Colombian	3.10
Ecuadorian	3.11
Peruvian	3.68
Spaniard	2.75

Median Age

Group	Years
Total Population	31.5
Hispanic or Latino (of any race)	28.2
Central American, ex. Mexican	33.0
Costa Rican	38.8
Guatemalan	33.1
Honduran	31.6
Nicaraguan	33.3
Panamanian	36.0
Salvadoran	32.8
Cuban	46.2
Mexican	26.6
Puerto Rican	29.4
South American	39.0
Argentinean	42.7
Colombian	38.1
Ecuadorian	42.2
Peruvian	38.1
Spaniard	37.1

High School Graduates
(Universe: Population 25 Years and Over)

Group	Number	%
Total Population	38,447	75.0
Hispanic or Latino (of any race)	13,594	57.5
Central American, ex. Mexican	4,126	63.8
Guatemalan	1,529	57.1
Salvadoran	1,732	67.6
Mexican	7,399	51.2
South American	903	77.6

Four-Year College Graduates
(Universe: Population 25 Years and Over)

Group	Number	%
Total Population	8,610	16.8
Hispanic or Latino (of any race)	1,522	6.4
Central American, ex. Mexican	400	6.2
Guatemalan	106	4.0
Salvadoran	190	7.4
Mexican	723	5.0
South American	163	14.0

Population Age 3–17 Enrolled in Public School
(Universe: Population Age 3–17 Enrolled in School)

Group	Number	%
Total Population	16,302	90.0
Hispanic or Latino (of any race)	9,897	91.6
Central American, ex. Mexican	1,996	91.9
Guatemalan	857	98.4
Salvadoran	774	85.2
Mexican	6,951	91.7
South American	243	80.2

Population Age 3–17 Enrolled in Private School
(Universe: Population Age 3–17 Enrolled in School)

Group	Number	%
Total Population	1,804	10.0
Hispanic or Latino (of any race)	913	8.4
Central American, ex. Mexican	175	8.1
Guatemalan	14	1.6
Salvadoran	134	14.8
Mexican	633	8.3
South American	60	19.8

Foreign-Born Population

Group	Number	%
Total Population	28,926	34.4
Hispanic or Latino (of any race)	20,929	48.6
Central American, ex. Mexican	7,005	65.4
Guatemalan	3,231	68.5
Salvadoran	2,613	66.7
Mexican	11,715	42.0
South American	1,233	72.7

Foreign-Born Naturalized U.S. Citizens

Group	Number	%
Total Population	11,624	40.2
Hispanic or Latino (of any race)	7,261	34.7
Central American, ex. Mexican	2,196	31.3
Guatemalan	621	19.2
Salvadoran	1,178	45.1
Mexican	3,721	31.8
South American	823	66.7

Language Spoken at Home: English Only
(Universe: Population 5 Years and Over)

Group	Number	%
Total Population	34,509	44.9
Hispanic or Latino (of any race)	4,818	12.6
Central American, ex. Mexican	531	5.4
Guatemalan	299	6.9
Salvadoran	175	4.7
Mexican	3,429	14.1
South American	158	9.7

Language Spoken at Home: Spanish
(Universe: Population 5 Years and Over)

Group	Number	%
Total Population	34,501	44.9
Hispanic or Latino (of any race)	33,399	87.3
Central American, ex. Mexican	9,220	94.6
Guatemalan	4,025	93.1
Salvadoran	3,519	95.3
Mexican	20,877	85.7
South American	1,476	90.3

Unemployment Rate
(Universe: Population 16 Years and Over)

Group	%
Total Population	7.1
Hispanic or Latino (of any race)	6.4
Central American, ex. Mexican	5.4
Guatemalan	10.2
Salvadoran	1.2
Mexican	6.9
South American	2.5

Class of Worker: Private Wage and Salary
(Universe: Civilian Employed Population 16 Years and Over)

Group	Number	%
Total Population	30,172	77.8
Hispanic or Latino (of any race)	15,448	84.0
Central American, ex. Mexican	4,510	87.9
Guatemalan	1,935	86.3
Salvadoran	1,814	91.8
Mexican	9,383	84.1
South American	529	64.4

Class of Worker: Government
(Universe: Civilian Employed Population 16 Years and Over)

Group	Number	%
Total Population	5,995	15.5
Hispanic or Latino (of any race)	1,552	8.4
Central American, ex. Mexican	163	3.2
Guatemalan	106	4.7
Salvadoran	22	1.1
Mexican	906	8.1
South American	259	31.5

Means of Transportation to Work: Car, Truck or Van
(Universe: Workers 16 Years and Over)

Group	Number	%
Total Population	32,573	85.4
Hispanic or Latino (of any race)	15,273	84.5
Central American, ex. Mexican	4,293	83.8
Guatemalan	1,830	82.5
Salvadoran	1,693	85.7
Mexican	9,211	84.8
South American	676	82.3

STATE & PLACE PROFILES

Notes: (1) Percent of total population; (2) Percent of Hispanic/Latino population; Profiles include places with an overall population of at least 125,000, OR an overall population of at least 25,000 where the Hispanic/Latino population is at least 20% of the overall population. In states where less than five places meet either of these criteria, we have included places with at least 10,000 total population with the highest percentage of Hispanic/Latino population. These places are identified with an asterisk (*); Please refer to the User's Guide for a full explanation of data.

Means of Transportation to Work: Public Transportation (ex. Taxicab)
(Universe: Workers 16 Years and Over)

Group	Number	%
Total Population	3,009	7.9
Hispanic or Latino (of any race)	1,244	6.9
Central American, ex. Mexican	530	10.3
Guatemalan	280	12.6
Salvadoran	197	10.0
Mexican	574	5.3
South American	71	8.6

Homeownership Rate
(Universe: Occupied Housing Units)

Group	%
Total Population	26.8
Hispanic or Latino (of any race)	26.0
Central American, ex. Mexican	23.1
Costa Rican	31.0
Guatemalan	22.6
Honduran	13.8
Nicaraguan	22.5
Panamanian	13.0
Salvadoran	25.0
Cuban	30.3
Mexican	27.4
Puerto Rican	20.7
South American	28.3
Argentinean	33.3
Colombian	23.9
Ecuadorian	42.4
Peruvian	25.0
Spaniard	43.4

Median Home Value

Group	Dollars
Total Population	501,400
Hispanic or Latino (of any race)	500,800
Central American, ex. Mexican	470,800
Guatemalan	405,100
Salvadoran	509,400
Mexican	478,500
South American	526,700

Median Gross Rent

Group	Dollars
Total Population	972
Hispanic or Latino (of any race)	966
Central American, ex. Mexican	912
Guatemalan	930
Salvadoran	886
Mexican	984
South American	1,084

Median Household Income
(2010 Inflation-Adjusted Dollars)

Group	Dollars
Total Population	44,469
Hispanic or Latino (of any race)	43,685
Central American, ex. Mexican	44,107
Guatemalan	44,322
Salvadoran	45,978
Mexican	42,959
South American	44,355

Per Capita Income
(2010 Inflation-Adjusted Dollars)

Group	Dollars
Total Population	19,616
Hispanic or Latino (of any race)	14,931
Central American, ex. Mexican	16,894
Guatemalan	14,444
Salvadoran	19,718
Mexican	13,523
South American	17,736

Households with $100,000+ Income

Group	Number	%
Total Population	3,627	12.7
Hispanic or Latino (of any race)	1,161	10.2
Central American, ex. Mexican	289	9.7
Guatemalan	55	4.5
Salvadoran	144	12.6
Mexican	705	10.0
South American	43	8.0

Households with Food Stamps/SNAP Benefits During Past 12 Months

Group	Number	%
Total Population	1,858	6.5
Hispanic or Latino (of any race)	956	8.4
Central American, ex. Mexican	218	7.3
Guatemalan	41	3.4
Salvadoran	67	5.9
Mexican	690	9.8
South American	11	2.0

Poverty Rate
(Income in Past 12 Months Below Poverty Level)

Group	%
Total Population	16.1
Hispanic or Latino (of any race)	18.0
Central American, ex. Mexican	15.1
Guatemalan	16.6
Salvadoran	6.4
Mexican	20.1
South American	18.7

Hayward

Population

Group	Number	%TP[1]	%HP[2]
Total Population	144,186	100.0	–
Hispanic or Latino (of any race)	58,730	40.7	100.0
Central American, ex. Mexican	7,505	5.2	12.8
Guatemalan	1,504	1.0	2.6
Honduran	329	0.2	0.6
Nicaraguan	1,745	1.2	3.0
Panamanian	100	0.1	0.2
Salvadoran	3,676	2.5	6.3
Cuban	217	0.2	0.4
Mexican	43,597	30.2	74.2
Puerto Rican	2,232	1.5	3.8
South American	1,300	0.9	2.2
Colombian	196	0.1	0.3
Peruvian	761	0.5	1.3
Spaniard	740	0.5	1.3

Population Growth: 2000–2010

Group	%
Total Population	3.0
Hispanic or Latino (of any race)	22.7
Central American, ex. Mexican	120.7
Guatemalan	209.5
Nicaraguan	67.0
Salvadoran	172.5
Cuban	1.9
Mexican	28.1
Puerto Rican	2.5
South American	47.4
Colombian	69.0
Peruvian	80.8
Spaniard	421.1

Males per 100 Females

Group	Number
Total Population	97.4
Hispanic or Latino (of any race)	106.0
Central American, ex. Mexican	111.7
Guatemalan	156.2
Honduran	161.1
Nicaraguan	89.5
Panamanian	61.3
Salvadoran	107.1
Cuban	97.3
Mexican	106.8
Puerto Rican	96.5
South American	96.4
Colombian	92.2
Peruvian	91.2
Spaniard	81.4

Average Household Size

Group	People
Total Population	3.12
Hispanic or Latino (of any race)	4.03
Central American, ex. Mexican	4.18
Guatemalan	4.69
Honduran	4.16
Nicaraguan	3.90
Panamanian	3.27
Salvadoran	4.20
Cuban	2.59
Mexican	4.22
Puerto Rican	3.00
South American	3.36
Colombian	3.20
Peruvian	3.48
Spaniard	2.63

Median Age

Group	Years
Total Population	33.5
Hispanic or Latino (of any race)	27.6
Central American, ex. Mexican	30.8
Guatemalan	29.6
Honduran	29.0
Nicaraguan	33.5
Panamanian	39.8
Salvadoran	30.3
Cuban	33.6
Mexican	26.3
Puerto Rican	31.3
South American	36.2
Colombian	36.7
Peruvian	36.3
Spaniard	43.7

High School Graduates
(Universe: Population 25 Years and Over)

Group	Number	%
Total Population	72,279	79.2
Hispanic or Latino (of any race)	18,591	61.8
Central American, ex. Mexican	2,769	62.8
Guatemalan	495	46.0
Nicaraguan	767	79.1
Salvadoran	1,200	59.6
Mexican	13,123	59.2
Puerto Rican	1,205	71.9
South American	581	96.5

Four-Year College Graduates
(Universe: Population 25 Years and Over)

Group	Number	%
Total Population	21,058	23.1
Hispanic or Latino (of any race)	2,532	8.4
Central American, ex. Mexican	567	12.9
Guatemalan	34	3.2
Nicaraguan	203	20.9
Salvadoran	255	12.7
Mexican	1,397	6.3
Puerto Rican	263	15.7
South American	174	28.9

Population Age 3–17 Enrolled in Public School
(Universe: Population Age 3–17 Enrolled in School)

Group	Number	%
Total Population	23,226	90.4
Hispanic or Latino (of any race)	13,022	96.3
Central American, ex. Mexican	1,028	98.7
Guatemalan	152	100.0
Nicaraguan	165	100.0
Salvadoran	631	97.8
Mexican	10,831	96.4
Puerto Rican	369	100.0
South American	122	74.4

Population Age 3–17 Enrolled in Private School
(Universe: Population Age 3–17 Enrolled in School)

Group	Number	%
Total Population	2,472	9.6
Hispanic or Latino (of any race)	500	3.7
Central American, ex. Mexican	14	1.3
Guatemalan	0	0.0
Nicaraguan	0	0.0
Salvadoran	14	2.2
Mexican	407	3.6
Puerto Rican	0	0.0
South American	42	25.6

Foreign-Born Population

Group	Number	%
Total Population	52,386	37.0
Hispanic or Latino (of any race)	24,122	43.4

Notes: (1) Percent of total population; (2) Percent of Hispanic/Latino population; Profiles include places with an overall population of at least 125,000, OR an overall population of at least 25,000 where the Hispanic/Latino population is at least 20% of the overall population. In states where less than five places meet either of these criteria, we have included places with at least 10,000 total population with the highest percentage of Hispanic/Latino population. These places are identified with an asterisk (*); Please refer to the User's Guide for a full explanation of data.

Group	Number	%
Central American, ex. Mexican	4,545	62.8
Guatemalan	1,362	73.4
Nicaraguan	970	70.7
Salvadoran	1,958	56.7
Mexican	18,677	44.0
Puerto Rican	0	0.0
South American	615	67.9

Foreign-Born Naturalized U.S. Citizens

Group	Number	%
Total Population	24,898	47.5
Hispanic or Latino (of any race)	7,153	29.7
Central American, ex. Mexican	1,810	39.8
Guatemalan	344	25.3
Nicaraguan	472	48.7
Salvadoran	842	43.0
Mexican	4,777	25.6
Puerto Rican	0	0.0
South American	420	68.3

Language Spoken at Home: English Only
(Universe: Population 5 Years and Over)

Group	Number	%
Total Population	59,313	45.1
Hispanic or Latino (of any race)	10,252	20.4
Central American, ex. Mexican	389	6.0
Guatemalan	11	0.7
Nicaraguan	130	10.2
Salvadoran	199	6.6
Mexican	7,189	18.8
Puerto Rican	1,306	55.2
South American	151	17.6

Language Spoken at Home: Spanish
(Universe: Population 5 Years and Over)

Group	Number	%
Total Population	41,071	31.3
Hispanic or Latino (of any race)	39,941	79.5
Central American, ex. Mexican	6,082	94.0
Guatemalan	1,626	99.3
Nicaraguan	1,149	89.8
Salvadoran	2,839	93.4
Mexican	31,085	81.2
Puerto Rican	1,059	44.8
South American	694	81.1

Unemployment Rate
(Universe: Population 16 Years and Over)

Group	%
Total Population	11.5
Hispanic or Latino (of any race)	13.0
Central American, ex. Mexican	11.3
Guatemalan	8.4
Nicaraguan	14.6
Salvadoran	10.8
Mexican	13.4
Puerto Rican	15.1
South American	11.3

Class of Worker: Private Wage and Salary
(Universe: Civilian Employed Population 16 Years and Over)

Group	Number	%
Total Population	54,692	81.8
Hispanic or Latino (of any race)	20,321	82.7
Central American, ex. Mexican	3,372	82.0
Guatemalan	993	87.7
Nicaraguan	630	83.2
Salvadoran	1,470	80.5
Mexican	14,871	83.5
Puerto Rican	1,034	82.2
South American	371	73.8

Class of Worker: Government
(Universe: Civilian Employed Population 16 Years and Over)

Group	Number	%
Total Population	8,076	12.1
Hispanic or Latino (of any race)	2,305	9.4
Central American, ex. Mexican	311	7.6
Guatemalan	40	3.5
Nicaraguan	67	8.9
Salvadoran	170	9.3
Mexican	1,580	8.9
Puerto Rican	168	13.4
South American	111	22.1

Means of Transportation to Work: Car, Truck or Van
(Universe: Workers 16 Years and Over)

Group	Number	%
Total Population	55,695	86.2
Hispanic or Latino (of any race)	20,222	86.8
Central American, ex. Mexican	3,326	84.1
Guatemalan	796	73.0
Nicaraguan	693	91.5
Salvadoran	1,537	88.9
Mexican	14,882	87.5
Puerto Rican	914	91.0
South American	437	90.1

Means of Transportation to Work: Public Transportation (ex. Taxicab)
(Universe: Workers 16 Years and Over)

Group	Number	%
Total Population	4,876	7.5
Hispanic or Latino (of any race)	1,429	6.1
Central American, ex. Mexican	156	3.9
Guatemalan	13	1.2
Nicaraguan	10	1.3
Salvadoran	133	7.7
Mexican	1,114	6.6
Puerto Rican	78	7.8
South American	27	5.6

Homeownership Rate
(Universe: Occupied Housing Units)

Group	%
Total Population	52.8
Hispanic or Latino (of any race)	44.4
Central American, ex. Mexican	43.4
Guatemalan	36.3
Honduran	20.5
Nicaraguan	45.0
Panamanian	53.3
Salvadoran	46.5
Cuban	52.1
Mexican	43.8
Puerto Rican	49.7
South American	45.7
Colombian	41.5
Peruvian	37.8
Spaniard	67.8

Median Home Value

Group	Dollars
Total Population	434,000
Hispanic or Latino (of any race)	414,100
Central American, ex. Mexican	388,600
Guatemalan	374,100
Nicaraguan	498,500
Salvadoran	372,200
Mexican	419,700
Puerto Rican	468,800
South American	275,700

Median Gross Rent

Group	Dollars
Total Population	1,224
Hispanic or Latino (of any race)	1,209
Central American, ex. Mexican	1,209
Guatemalan	1,159
Nicaraguan	1,358
Salvadoran	1,214
Mexican	1,204
Puerto Rican	1,214
South American	951

Median Household Income
(2010 Inflation-Adjusted Dollars)

Group	Dollars
Total Population	61,268
Hispanic or Latino (of any race)	55,397
Central American, ex. Mexican	64,431
Guatemalan	52,472
Nicaraguan	75,326
Salvadoran	65,795
Mexican	55,252
Puerto Rican	50,759
South American	55,217

Per Capita Income
(2010 Inflation-Adjusted Dollars)

Group	Dollars
Total Population	24,868
Hispanic or Latino (of any race)	16,344
Central American, ex. Mexican	19,417
Guatemalan	13,799
Nicaraguan	26,095
Salvadoran	19,572
Mexican	15,273
Puerto Rican	22,280
South American	26,089

Households with $100,000+ Income

Group	Number	%
Total Population	11,354	25.6
Hispanic or Latino (of any race)	2,306	17.6
Central American, ex. Mexican	431	25.2
Guatemalan	34	10.2
Nicaraguan	148	38.1
Salvadoran	237	28.9
Mexican	1,617	17.1
Puerto Rican	150	15.9
South American	33	12.4

Households with Food Stamps/SNAP Benefits During Past 12 Months

Group	Number	%
Total Population	2,631	5.9
Hispanic or Latino (of any race)	994	7.6
Central American, ex. Mexican	93	5.4
Guatemalan	35	10.5
Nicaraguan	18	4.6
Salvadoran	40	4.9
Mexican	782	8.3
Puerto Rican	113	12.0
South American	0	0.0

Poverty Rate
(Income in Past 12 Months Below Poverty Level)

Group	%
Total Population	12.5
Hispanic or Latino (of any race)	17.2
Central American, ex. Mexican	17.2
Guatemalan	25.3
Nicaraguan	3.0
Salvadoran	21.0
Mexican	17.8
Puerto Rican	16.5
South American	10.2

Hemet

Population

Group	Number	%TP[1]	%HP[2]
Total Population	78,657	100.0	–
Hispanic or Latino (of any race)	28,150	35.8	100.0
Central American, ex. Mexican	788	1.0	2.8
Guatemalan	235	0.3	0.8
Nicaraguan	102	0.1	0.4
Salvadoran	330	0.4	1.2
Cuban	203	0.3	0.7
Mexican	24,271	30.9	86.2
Puerto Rican	627	0.8	2.2
South American	357	0.5	1.3
Colombian	101	0.1	0.4
Spaniard	353	0.4	1.3

Population Growth: 2000–2010

Group	%
Total Population	33.7
Hispanic or Latino (of any race)	107.2
Central American, ex. Mexican	251.8
Mexican	121.4
Puerto Rican	130.5
South American	240.0

Males per 100 Females

Group	Number
Total Population	88.9
Hispanic or Latino (of any race)	95.2
Central American, ex. Mexican	91.7
Guatemalan	117.6

Notes: (1) Percent of total population; (2) Percent of Hispanic/Latino population; Profiles include places with an overall population of at least 125,000, OR an overall population of at least 25,000 where the Hispanic/Latino population is at least 20% of the overall population. In states where less than five places meet either of these criteria, we have included places with at least 10,000 total population with the highest percentage of Hispanic/Latino population. These places are identified with an asterisk (*); Please refer to the User's Guide for a full explanation of data.

Group	Number
Nicaraguan	96.2
Salvadoran	81.3
Cuban	105.1
Mexican	96.2
Puerto Rican	92.9
South American	83.1
Colombian	74.1
Spaniard	100.6

Average Household Size

Group	People
Total Population	2.59
Hispanic or Latino (of any race)	3.67
Central American, ex. Mexican	3.66
Guatemalan	3.78
Nicaraguan	3.48
Salvadoran	3.63
Cuban	3.26
Mexican	3.77
Puerto Rican	2.82
South American	2.94
Colombian	2.94
Spaniard	2.67

Median Age

Group	Years
Total Population	39.0
Hispanic or Latino (of any race)	24.8
Central American, ex. Mexican	31.3
Guatemalan	29.9
Nicaraguan	30.3
Salvadoran	33.1
Cuban	29.9
Mexican	24.1
Puerto Rican	29.1
South American	42.3
Colombian	40.3
Spaniard	34.3

High School Graduates
(Universe: Population 25 Years and Over)

Group	Number	%
Total Population	38,248	77.0
Hispanic or Latino (of any race)	6,922	52.5
Mexican	5,931	50.5

Four-Year College Graduates
(Universe: Population 25 Years and Over)

Group	Number	%
Total Population	6,381	12.8
Hispanic or Latino (of any race)	712	5.4
Mexican	591	5.0

Population Age 3–17 Enrolled in Public School
(Universe: Population Age 3–17 Enrolled in School)

Group	Number	%
Total Population	13,771	93.0
Hispanic or Latino (of any race)	8,017	97.2
Mexican	7,390	97.2

Population Age 3–17 Enrolled in Private School
(Universe: Population Age 3–17 Enrolled in School)

Group	Number	%
Total Population	1,029	7.0
Hispanic or Latino (of any race)	228	2.8
Mexican	216	2.8

Foreign-Born Population

Group	Number	%
Total Population	11,493	15.0
Hispanic or Latino (of any race)	7,858	28.3
Mexican	7,303	28.9

Foreign-Born Naturalized U.S. Citizens

Group	Number	%
Total Population	5,011	43.6
Hispanic or Latino (of any race)	2,710	34.5
Mexican	2,422	33.2

Language Spoken at Home: English Only
(Universe: Population 5 Years and Over)

Group	Number	%
Total Population	51,495	73.2
Hispanic or Latino (of any race)	8,591	35.5
Mexican	7,472	34.1

Language Spoken at Home: Spanish
(Universe: Population 5 Years and Over)

Group	Number	%
Total Population	16,104	22.9
Hispanic or Latino (of any race)	15,506	64.2
Mexican	14,361	65.6

Unemployment Rate
(Universe: Population 16 Years and Over)

Group	%
Total Population	15.7
Hispanic or Latino (of any race)	19.2
Mexican	19.5

Class of Worker: Private Wage and Salary
(Universe: Civilian Employed Population 16 Years and Over)

Group	Number	%
Total Population	18,049	75.7
Hispanic or Latino (of any race)	7,098	79.9
Mexican	6,579	81.5

Class of Worker: Government
(Universe: Civilian Employed Population 16 Years and Over)

Group	Number	%
Total Population	3,855	16.2
Hispanic or Latino (of any race)	1,143	12.9
Mexican	917	11.4

Means of Transportation to Work: Car, Truck or Van
(Universe: Workers 16 Years and Over)

Group	Number	%
Total Population	21,132	90.9
Hispanic or Latino (of any race)	8,038	93.2
Mexican	7,276	93.2

Means of Transportation to Work: Public Transportation (ex. Taxicab)
(Universe: Workers 16 Years and Over)

Group	Number	%
Total Population	343	1.5
Hispanic or Latino (of any race)	74	0.9
Mexican	57	0.7

Homeownership Rate
(Universe: Occupied Housing Units)

Group	%
Total Population	61.7
Hispanic or Latino (of any race)	50.9
Central American, ex. Mexican	57.1
Guatemalan	50.0
Nicaraguan	62.1
Salvadoran	62.5
Cuban	47.7
Mexican	51.1
Puerto Rican	39.1
South American	68.3
Colombian	60.0
Spaniard	57.6

Median Home Value

Group	Dollars
Total Population	156,600
Hispanic or Latino (of any race)	173,300
Mexican	178,000

Median Gross Rent

Group	Dollars
Total Population	949
Hispanic or Latino (of any race)	950
Mexican	952

Median Household Income
(2010 Inflation-Adjusted Dollars)

Group	Dollars
Total Population	35,306
Hispanic or Latino (of any race)	36,899
Mexican	37,274

Per Capita Income
(2010 Inflation-Adjusted Dollars)

Group	Dollars
Total Population	18,897
Hispanic or Latino (of any race)	12,339
Mexican	11,934

Households with $100,000+ Income

Group	Number	%
Total Population	2,560	8.6
Hispanic or Latino (of any race)	327	4.6
Mexican	238	3.8

Households with Food Stamps/SNAP Benefits During Past 12 Months

Group	Number	%
Total Population	2,416	8.1
Hispanic or Latino (of any race)	1,085	15.3
Mexican	1,054	16.8

Poverty Rate
(Income in Past 12 Months Below Poverty Level)

Group	%
Total Population	18.0
Hispanic or Latino (of any race)	27.3
Mexican	28.2

Hesperia

Population

Group	Number	%TP[1]	%HP[2]
Total Population	90,173	100.0	–
Hispanic or Latino (of any race)	44,091	48.9	100.0
Central American, ex. Mexican	2,847	3.2	6.5
Guatemalan	863	1.0	2.0
Honduran	183	0.2	0.4
Nicaraguan	202	0.2	0.5
Salvadoran	1,450	1.6	3.3
Cuban	237	0.3	0.5
Mexican	36,486	40.5	82.8
Puerto Rican	626	0.7	1.4
South American	454	0.5	1.0
Colombian	107	0.1	0.2
Peruvian	128	0.1	0.3
Spaniard	438	0.5	1.0

Population Growth: 2000–2010

Group	%
Total Population	44.1
Hispanic or Latino (of any race)	139.6
Central American, ex. Mexican	452.8
Guatemalan	371.6
Salvadoran	728.6
Cuban	25.4
Mexican	157.2
Puerto Rican	81.4
South American	281.5

Males per 100 Females

Group	Number
Total Population	98.5
Hispanic or Latino (of any race)	99.6
Central American, ex. Mexican	95.8
Guatemalan	104.0
Honduran	90.6
Nicaraguan	94.2
Salvadoran	94.1
Cuban	102.6
Mexican	100.8
Puerto Rican	92.6
South American	104.5
Colombian	114.0
Peruvian	128.6
Spaniard	72.4

Average Household Size

Group	People
Total Population	3.41
Hispanic or Latino (of any race)	4.26
Central American, ex. Mexican	4.44
Guatemalan	4.49
Honduran	4.71
Nicaraguan	4.28
Salvadoran	4.49
Cuban	3.29
Mexican	4.32
Puerto Rican	3.39
South American	3.46
Colombian	3.77
Peruvian	3.64

Notes: (1) Percent of total population; (2) Percent of Hispanic/Latino population; Profiles include places with an overall population of at least 125,000, OR an overall population of at least 25,000 where the Hispanic/Latino population is at least 20% of the overall population. In states where less than five places meet either of these criteria, we have included places with at least 10,000 total population with the highest percentage of Hispanic/Latino population. These places are identified with an asterisk (*); Please refer to the User's Guide for a full explanation of data.

Group		
Spaniard		3.23

Median Age

Group	Years
Total Population	30.5
Hispanic or Latino (of any race)	23.8
Central American, ex. Mexican	32.6
Guatemalan	33.0
Honduran	29.5
Nicaraguan	33.2
Salvadoran	32.8
Cuban	34.6
Mexican	23.3
Puerto Rican	26.2
South American	36.1
Colombian	38.3
Peruvian	31.0
Spaniard	29.9

High School Graduates
(Universe: Population 25 Years and Over)

Group	Number	%
Total Population	36,416	75.7
Hispanic or Latino (of any race)	11,246	59.6
Central American, ex. Mexican	909	60.1
Guatemalan	292	44.0
Salvadoran	357	67.9
Mexican	9,094	58.4

Four-Year College Graduates
(Universe: Population 25 Years and Over)

Group	Number	%
Total Population	4,587	9.5
Hispanic or Latino (of any race)	814	4.3
Central American, ex. Mexican	200	13.2
Guatemalan	71	10.7
Salvadoran	20	3.8
Mexican	384	2.5

Population Age 3–17 Enrolled in Public School
(Universe: Population Age 3–17 Enrolled in School)

Group	Number	%
Total Population	19,745	94.9
Hispanic or Latino (of any race)	12,296	98.2
Central American, ex. Mexican	521	96.5
Guatemalan	241	100.0
Salvadoran	198	100.0
Mexican	10,998	98.7

Population Age 3–17 Enrolled in Private School
(Universe: Population Age 3–17 Enrolled in School)

Group	Number	%
Total Population	1,057	5.1
Hispanic or Latino (of any race)	231	1.8
Central American, ex. Mexican	19	3.5
Guatemalan	0	0.0
Salvadoran	0	0.0
Mexican	144	1.3

Foreign-Born Population

Group	Number	%
Total Population	13,407	15.5
Hispanic or Latino (of any race)	11,172	27.4
Central American, ex. Mexican	1,453	58.3
Guatemalan	615	58.1
Salvadoran	579	62.7
Mexican	8,963	25.6

Foreign-Born Naturalized U.S. Citizens

Group	Number	%
Total Population	5,027	37.5
Hispanic or Latino (of any race)	3,669	32.8
Central American, ex. Mexican	649	44.7
Guatemalan	304	49.4
Salvadoran	193	33.3
Mexican	2,695	30.1

Language Spoken at Home: English Only
(Universe: Population 5 Years and Over)

Group	Number	%
Total Population	51,787	65.9
Hispanic or Latino (of any race)	12,331	34.2
Central American, ex. Mexican	301	13.4
Guatemalan	102	10.7
Salvadoran	63	7.4
Mexican	10,325	33.5

Language Spoken at Home: Spanish
(Universe: Population 5 Years and Over)

Group	Number	%
Total Population	24,585	31.3
Hispanic or Latino (of any race)	23,582	65.4
Central American, ex. Mexican	1,940	86.6
Guatemalan	850	89.3
Salvadoran	792	92.6
Mexican	20,352	66.1

Unemployment Rate
(Universe: Population 16 Years and Over)

Group	%
Total Population	15.4
Hispanic or Latino (of any race)	18.5
Central American, ex. Mexican	19.7
Guatemalan	22.6
Salvadoran	19.7
Mexican	18.1

Class of Worker: Private Wage and Salary
(Universe: Civilian Employed Population 16 Years and Over)

Group	Number	%
Total Population	24,194	77.3
Hispanic or Latino (of any race)	11,133	82.9
Central American, ex. Mexican	822	77.5
Guatemalan	378	83.8
Salvadoran	320	81.8
Mexican	9,362	84.3

Class of Worker: Government
(Universe: Civilian Employed Population 16 Years and Over)

Group	Number	%
Total Population	4,954	15.8
Hispanic or Latino (of any race)	1,349	10.0
Central American, ex. Mexican	96	9.1
Guatemalan	20	4.4
Salvadoran	48	12.3
Mexican	1,038	9.3

Means of Transportation to Work: Car, Truck or Van
(Universe: Workers 16 Years and Over)

Group	Number	%
Total Population	27,528	91.3
Hispanic or Latino (of any race)	11,974	92.7
Central American, ex. Mexican	969	96.6
Guatemalan	440	97.6
Salvadoran	355	93.9
Mexican	9,874	92.5

Means of Transportation to Work: Public Transportation (ex. Taxicab)
(Universe: Workers 16 Years and Over)

Group	Number	%
Total Population	253	0.8
Hispanic or Latino (of any race)	115	0.9
Central American, ex. Mexican	14	1.4
Guatemalan	0	0.0
Salvadoran	14	3.7
Mexican	101	0.9

Homeownership Rate
(Universe: Occupied Housing Units)

Group	%
Total Population	66.9
Hispanic or Latino (of any race)	62.1
Central American, ex. Mexican	63.3
Guatemalan	59.3
Honduran	48.9
Nicaraguan	67.7
Salvadoran	67.8
Cuban	65.3
Mexican	62.4
Puerto Rican	53.7
South American	65.0
Colombian	64.5
Peruvian	69.4
Spaniard	66.1

Median Home Value

Group	Dollars
Total Population	250,900
Hispanic or Latino (of any race)	275,900
Central American, ex. Mexican	307,100
Guatemalan	350,000
Salvadoran	256,300
Mexican	264,600

Median Gross Rent

Group	Dollars
Total Population	1,033
Hispanic or Latino (of any race)	1,063
Central American, ex. Mexican	1,302
Guatemalan	1,261
Salvadoran	1,153
Mexican	1,032

Median Household Income
(2010 Inflation-Adjusted Dollars)

Group	Dollars
Total Population	48,386
Hispanic or Latino (of any race)	43,961
Central American, ex. Mexican	51,250
Guatemalan	50,727
Salvadoran	54,474
Mexican	43,410

Per Capita Income
(2010 Inflation-Adjusted Dollars)

Group	Dollars
Total Population	17,815
Hispanic or Latino (of any race)	12,114
Central American, ex. Mexican	14,614
Guatemalan	14,868
Salvadoran	13,079
Mexican	11,670

Households with $100,000+ Income

Group	Number	%
Total Population	4,032	16.2
Hispanic or Latino (of any race)	929	10.9
Central American, ex. Mexican	62	7.8
Guatemalan	33	10.9
Salvadoran	6	2.0
Mexican	792	11.1

Households with Food Stamps/SNAP Benefits During Past 12 Months

Group	Number	%
Total Population	2,643	10.6
Hispanic or Latino (of any race)	1,328	15.5
Central American, ex. Mexican	112	14.2
Guatemalan	71	23.4
Salvadoran	41	13.8
Mexican	1,070	15.1

Poverty Rate
(Income in Past 12 Months Below Poverty Level)

Group	%
Total Population	19.2
Hispanic or Latino (of any race)	23.7
Central American, ex. Mexican	27.7
Guatemalan	35.6
Salvadoran	22.9
Mexican	24.0

Highland

Population

Group	Number	%TP[1]	%HP[2]
Total Population	53,104	100.0	–
Hispanic or Latino (of any race)	25,556	48.1	100.0
Central American, ex. Mexican	911	1.7	3.6
Guatemalan	278	0.5	1.1
Nicaraguan	113	0.2	0.4
Salvadoran	352	0.7	1.4
Cuban	156	0.3	0.6
Mexican	22,430	42.2	87.8
Puerto Rican	294	0.6	1.2
South American	252	0.5	1.0
Spaniard	227	0.4	0.9

Population Growth: 2000–2010

Group	%
Total Population	19.1
Hispanic or Latino (of any race)	56.4
Central American, ex. Mexican	186.5
Salvadoran	225.9

Notes: (1) Percent of total population; (2) Percent of Hispanic/Latino population; Profiles include places with an overall population of at least 125,000, OR an overall population of at least 25,000 where the Hispanic/Latino population is at least 20% of the overall population. In states where less than five places meet either of these criteria, we have included places with at least 10,000 total population with the highest percentage of Hispanic/Latino population. These places are identified with an asterisk (*); Please refer to the User's Guide for a full explanation of data.

Mexican	67.4
Puerto Rican	20.0

Males per 100 Females

Group	Number
Total Population	95.1
Hispanic or Latino (of any race)	98.1
Central American, ex. Mexican	102.9
Guatemalan	112.2
Nicaraguan	76.6
Salvadoran	100.0
Cuban	105.3
Mexican	98.2
Puerto Rican	96.0
South American	81.3
Spaniard	78.7

Average Household Size

Group	People
Total Population	3.42
Hispanic or Latino (of any race)	4.22
Central American, ex. Mexican	4.43
Guatemalan	4.83
Nicaraguan	4.23
Salvadoran	4.36
Cuban	3.89
Mexican	4.28
Puerto Rican	3.36
South American	3.61
Spaniard	3.25

Median Age

Group	Years
Total Population	30.6
Hispanic or Latino (of any race)	24.0
Central American, ex. Mexican	32.8
Guatemalan	32.3
Nicaraguan	39.8
Salvadoran	33.5
Cuban	19.5
Mexican	23.6
Puerto Rican	25.0
South American	35.0
Spaniard	34.4

High School Graduates
(Universe: Population 25 Years and Over)

Group	Number	%
Total Population	21,747	74.9
Hispanic or Latino (of any race)	6,579	56.8
Mexican	5,381	52.8

Four-Year College Graduates
(Universe: Population 25 Years and Over)

Group	Number	%
Total Population	5,520	19.0
Hispanic or Latino (of any race)	1,037	9.0
Mexican	795	7.8

Population Age 3–17 Enrolled in Public School
(Universe: Population Age 3–17 Enrolled in School)

Group	Number	%
Total Population	13,496	93.8
Hispanic or Latino (of any race)	8,022	95.9
Mexican	7,306	96.0

Population Age 3–17 Enrolled in Private School
(Universe: Population Age 3–17 Enrolled in School)

Group	Number	%
Total Population	895	6.2
Hispanic or Latino (of any race)	343	4.1
Mexican	306	4.0

Foreign-Born Population

Group	Number	%
Total Population	11,694	22.3
Hispanic or Latino (of any race)	8,109	32.0
Mexican	7,234	32.1

Foreign-Born Naturalized U.S. Citizens

Group	Number	%
Total Population	4,520	38.7
Hispanic or Latino (of any race)	2,343	28.9
Mexican	1,954	27.0

Language Spoken at Home: English Only
(Universe: Population 5 Years and Over)

Group	Number	%
Total Population	28,098	58.8
Hispanic or Latino (of any race)	6,966	31.3
Mexican	5,932	30.0

Language Spoken at Home: Spanish
(Universe: Population 5 Years and Over)

Group	Number	%
Total Population	15,714	32.9
Hispanic or Latino (of any race)	15,259	68.6
Mexican	13,832	69.9

Unemployment Rate
(Universe: Population 16 Years and Over)

Group	%
Total Population	10.7
Hispanic or Latino (of any race)	11.3
Mexican	11.2

Class of Worker: Private Wage and Salary
(Universe: Civilian Employed Population 16 Years and Over)

Group	Number	%
Total Population	15,254	71.5
Hispanic or Latino (of any race)	7,077	78.9
Mexican	6,356	80.3

Class of Worker: Government
(Universe: Civilian Employed Population 16 Years and Over)

Group	Number	%
Total Population	4,389	20.6
Hispanic or Latino (of any race)	1,129	12.6
Mexican	909	11.5

Means of Transportation to Work: Car, Truck or Van
(Universe: Workers 16 Years and Over)

Group	Number	%
Total Population	18,779	91.7
Hispanic or Latino (of any race)	8,008	92.6
Mexican	6,996	92.1

Means of Transportation to Work: Public Transportation (ex. Taxicab)
(Universe: Workers 16 Years and Over)

Group	Number	%
Total Population	332	1.6
Hispanic or Latino (of any race)	116	1.3
Mexican	116	1.5

Homeownership Rate
(Universe: Occupied Housing Units)

Group	%
Total Population	65.3
Hispanic or Latino (of any race)	56.9
Central American, ex. Mexican	56.9
Guatemalan	55.6
Nicaraguan	71.4
Salvadoran	55.2
Cuban	70.3
Mexican	57.3
Puerto Rican	52.6
South American	72.7
Spaniard	74.6

Median Home Value

Group	Dollars
Total Population	334,200
Hispanic or Latino (of any race)	313,500
Mexican	308,600

Median Gross Rent

Group	Dollars
Total Population	967
Hispanic or Latino (of any race)	941
Mexican	947

Median Household Income
(2010 Inflation-Adjusted Dollars)

Group	Dollars
Total Population	59,549
Hispanic or Latino (of any race)	49,433
Mexican	49,246

Per Capita Income
(2010 Inflation-Adjusted Dollars)

Group	Dollars
Total Population	22,479
Hispanic or Latino (of any race)	14,143
Mexican	14,012

Households with $100,000+ Income

Group	Number	%
Total Population	4,009	27.3
Hispanic or Latino (of any race)	1,058	20.0
Mexican	869	18.5

Households with Food Stamps/SNAP Benefits During Past 12 Months

Group	Number	%
Total Population	1,549	10.5
Hispanic or Latino (of any race)	994	18.7
Mexican	911	19.4

Poverty Rate
(Income in Past 12 Months Below Poverty Level)

Group	%
Total Population	17.3
Hispanic or Latino (of any race)	24.5
Mexican	25.0

Hollister

Population

Group	Number	%TP[1]	%HP[2]
Total Population	34,928	100.0	–
Hispanic or Latino (of any race)	22,965	65.7	100.0
Central American, ex. Mexican	310	0.9	1.3
Salvadoran	137	0.4	0.6
Mexican	21,304	61.0	92.8
Puerto Rican	171	0.5	0.7
Spaniard	264	0.8	1.1

Population Growth: 2000–2010

Group	%
Total Population	1.5
Hispanic or Latino (of any race)	21.2
Central American, ex. Mexican	96.2
Mexican	30.1
Puerto Rican	41.3

Males per 100 Females

Group	Number
Total Population	98.7
Hispanic or Latino (of any race)	100.0
Central American, ex. Mexican	106.7
Salvadoran	104.5
Mexican	100.1
Puerto Rican	90.0
Spaniard	84.6

Average Household Size

Group	People
Total Population	3.53
Hispanic or Latino (of any race)	4.13
Central American, ex. Mexican	4.10
Salvadoran	4.03
Mexican	4.19
Puerto Rican	3.57
Spaniard	2.91

Median Age

Group	Years
Total Population	30.8
Hispanic or Latino (of any race)	26.6
Central American, ex. Mexican	32.2
Salvadoran	30.8
Mexican	26.3
Puerto Rican	24.8
Spaniard	39.0

High School Graduates
(Universe: Population 25 Years and Over)

Group	Number	%
Total Population	14,388	70.7
Hispanic or Latino (of any race)	6,025	54.0
Mexican	5,446	52.6

Notes: (1) Percent of total population; (2) Percent of Hispanic/Latino population; Profiles include places with an overall population of at least 125,000, OR an overall population of at least 25,000 where the Hispanic/Latino population is at least 20% of the overall population. In states where less than five places meet either of these criteria, we have included places with at least 10,000 total population with the highest percentage of Hispanic/Latino population. These places are identified with an asterisk (*); Please refer to the User's Guide for a full explanation of data.

Four-Year College Graduates (Universe: Population 25 Years and Over)		
Group	Number	%
Total Population	3,212	15.8
Hispanic or Latino (of any race)	899	8.1
Mexican	801	7.7

Population Age 3–17 Enrolled in Public School (Universe: Population Age 3–17 Enrolled in School)		
Group	Number	%
Total Population	7,900	91.5
Hispanic or Latino (of any race)	5,925	93.6
Mexican	5,641	96.6

Population Age 3–17 Enrolled in Private School (Universe: Population Age 3–17 Enrolled in School)		
Group	Number	%
Total Population	730	8.5
Hispanic or Latino (of any race)	407	6.4
Mexican	196	3.4

Foreign-Born Population		
Group	Number	%
Total Population	7,742	22.4
Hispanic or Latino (of any race)	6,637	30.8
Mexican	6,298	31.4

Foreign-Born Naturalized U.S. Citizens		
Group	Number	%
Total Population	2,524	32.6
Hispanic or Latino (of any race)	2,019	30.4
Mexican	1,825	29.0

Language Spoken at Home: English Only (Universe: Population 5 Years and Over)		
Group	Number	%
Total Population	17,409	54.8
Hispanic or Latino (of any race)	6,173	31.9
Mexican	5,443	30.2

Language Spoken at Home: Spanish (Universe: Population 5 Years and Over)		
Group	Number	%
Total Population	13,485	42.5
Hispanic or Latino (of any race)	13,159	68.1
Mexican	12,560	69.7

Unemployment Rate (Universe: Population 16 Years and Over)	
Group	%
Total Population	12.0
Hispanic or Latino (of any race)	14.4
Mexican	14.8

Class of Worker: Private Wage and Salary (Universe: Civilian Employed Population 16 Years and Over)		
Group	Number	%
Total Population	12,152	80.5
Hispanic or Latino (of any race)	6,977	82.6
Mexican	6,528	83.0

Class of Worker: Government (Universe: Civilian Employed Population 16 Years and Over)		
Group	Number	%
Total Population	2,246	14.9
Hispanic or Latino (of any race)	1,173	13.9
Mexican	1,086	13.8

Means of Transportation to Work: Car, Truck or Van (Universe: Workers 16 Years and Over)		
Group	Number	%
Total Population	13,590	93.2
Hispanic or Latino (of any race)	7,384	92.4
Mexican	6,928	93.0

Means of Transportation to Work: Public Transportation (ex. Taxicab) (Universe: Workers 16 Years and Over)		
Group	Number	%
Total Population	64	0.4
Hispanic or Latino (of any race)	64	0.8
Mexican	64	0.9

Homeownership Rate (Universe: Occupied Housing Units)	
Group	%
Total Population	61.2
Hispanic or Latino (of any race)	52.0
Central American, ex. Mexican	57.0
Salvadoran	54.1
Mexican	51.9
Puerto Rican	54.8
Spaniard	69.1

Median Home Value	
Group	Dollars
Total Population	443,900
Hispanic or Latino (of any race)	396,200
Mexican	391,400

Median Gross Rent	
Group	Dollars
Total Population	1,138
Hispanic or Latino (of any race)	1,077
Mexican	1,057

Median Household Income (2010 Inflation-Adjusted Dollars)	
Group	Dollars
Total Population	63,289
Hispanic or Latino (of any race)	51,392
Mexican	50,853

Per Capita Income (2010 Inflation-Adjusted Dollars)	
Group	Dollars
Total Population	22,339
Hispanic or Latino (of any race)	16,016
Mexican	15,858

Households with $100,000+ Income		
Group	Number	%
Total Population	2,734	25.8
Hispanic or Latino (of any race)	838	15.5
Mexican	691	14.0

Households with Food Stamps/SNAP Benefits During Past 12 Months		
Group	Number	%
Total Population	944	8.9
Hispanic or Latino (of any race)	774	14.3
Mexican	688	13.9

Poverty Rate (Income in Past 12 Months Below Poverty Level)	
Group	%
Total Population	12.5
Hispanic or Latino (of any race)	15.1
Mexican	14.6

Huntington Beach

Population			
Group	Number	%TP[1]	%HP[2]
Total Population	189,992	100.0	–
Hispanic or Latino (of any race)	32,411	17.1	100.0
Central American, ex. Mexican	1,216	0.6	3.8
Costa Rican	118	0.1	0.4
Guatemalan	373	0.2	1.2
Honduran	107	0.1	0.3
Nicaraguan	137	0.1	0.4
Salvadoran	397	0.2	1.2
Cuban	633	0.3	2.0
Mexican	25,139	13.2	77.6
Puerto Rican	844	0.4	2.6
South American	1,805	1.0	5.6
Argentinean	394	0.2	1.2
Chilean	159	0.1	0.5
Colombian	418	0.2	1.3
Ecuadorian	216	0.1	0.7
Peruvian	411	0.2	1.3
Spaniard	827	0.4	2.6

Population Growth: 2000–2010	
Group	%
Total Population	0.2
Hispanic or Latino (of any race)	16.6
Central American, ex. Mexican	89.7
Guatemalan	102.7
Salvadoran	161.2
Cuban	30.5
Mexican	20.3
Puerto Rican	34.2
South American	70.0
Argentinean	77.5
Colombian	108.0
Peruvian	69.8
Spaniard	490.7

Males per 100 Females	
Group	Number
Total Population	98.5
Hispanic or Latino (of any race)	98.5
Central American, ex. Mexican	87.1
Costa Rican	76.1
Guatemalan	104.9
Honduran	55.1
Nicaraguan	93.0
Salvadoran	84.7
Cuban	96.6
Mexican	100.6
Puerto Rican	91.4
South American	84.0
Argentinean	85.8
Chilean	109.2
Colombian	77.9
Ecuadorian	78.5
Peruvian	73.4
Spaniard	90.1

Average Household Size	
Group	People
Total Population	2.55
Hispanic or Latino (of any race)	3.36
Central American, ex. Mexican	3.19
Costa Rican	2.54
Guatemalan	3.80
Honduran	2.67
Nicaraguan	3.02
Salvadoran	3.28
Cuban	2.35
Mexican	3.60
Puerto Rican	2.63
South American	2.72
Argentinean	2.52
Chilean	2.75
Colombian	2.73
Ecuadorian	2.88
Peruvian	2.79
Spaniard	2.53

Median Age	
Group	Years
Total Population	40.2
Hispanic or Latino (of any race)	28.9
Central American, ex. Mexican	32.3
Costa Rican	34.5
Guatemalan	30.2
Honduran	34.5
Nicaraguan	35.1
Salvadoran	31.5
Cuban	39.3
Mexican	27.5
Puerto Rican	31.4
South American	37.7
Argentinean	40.0
Chilean	41.8
Colombian	35.4
Ecuadorian	33.8
Peruvian	37.4
Spaniard	37.7

High School Graduates (Universe: Population 25 Years and Over)		
Group	Number	%
Total Population	124,542	92.8
Hispanic or Latino (of any race)	14,644	77.2
Central American, ex. Mexican	709	69.1
Mexican	10,231	73.1
Puerto Rican	716	96.5
South American	1,136	99.0

STATE & PLACE PROFILES

Notes: (1) Percent of total population; (2) Percent of Hispanic/Latino population; Profiles include places with an overall population of at least 125,000, OR an overall population of at least 25,000 where the Hispanic/Latino population is at least 20% of the overall population. In states where less than five places meet either of these criteria, we have included places with at least 10,000 total population with the highest percentage of Hispanic/Latino population. These places are identified with an asterisk (*); Please refer to the User's Guide for a full explanation of data.

Four-Year College Graduates
(Universe: Population 25 Years and Over)

Group	Number	%
Total Population	53,864	40.1
Hispanic or Latino (of any race)	4,312	22.7
Central American, ex. Mexican	216	21.1
Mexican	2,458	17.6
Puerto Rican	261	35.2
South American	657	57.2

Population Age 3–17 Enrolled in Public School
(Universe: Population Age 3–17 Enrolled in School)

Group	Number	%
Total Population	25,371	83.5
Hispanic or Latino (of any race)	6,581	88.7
Central American, ex. Mexican	218	71.9
Mexican	5,573	91.2
Puerto Rican	192	79.7
South American	134	61.8

Population Age 3–17 Enrolled in Private School
(Universe: Population Age 3–17 Enrolled in School)

Group	Number	%
Total Population	5,011	16.5
Hispanic or Latino (of any race)	839	11.3
Central American, ex. Mexican	85	28.1
Mexican	540	8.8
Puerto Rican	49	20.3
South American	83	38.2

Foreign-Born Population

Group	Number	%
Total Population	30,631	16.2
Hispanic or Latino (of any race)	9,818	30.2
Central American, ex. Mexican	829	51.5
Mexican	7,301	29.0
Puerto Rican	32	2.9
South American	972	65.0

Foreign-Born Naturalized U.S. Citizens

Group	Number	%
Total Population	17,724	57.9
Hispanic or Latino (of any race)	3,054	31.1
Central American, ex. Mexican	456	55.0
Mexican	1,437	19.7
Puerto Rican	32	100.0
South American	605	62.2

Language Spoken at Home: English Only
(Universe: Population 5 Years and Over)

Group	Number	%
Total Population	138,712	77.7
Hispanic or Latino (of any race)	12,933	43.9
Central American, ex. Mexican	483	31.7
Mexican	9,775	43.1
Puerto Rican	587	58.3
South American	296	20.8

Language Spoken at Home: Spanish
(Universe: Population 5 Years and Over)

Group	Number	%
Total Population	18,276	10.2
Hispanic or Latino (of any race)	16,340	55.4
Central American, ex. Mexican	1,039	68.3
Mexican	12,800	56.4
Puerto Rican	355	35.3
South American	1,127	79.2

Unemployment Rate
(Universe: Population 16 Years and Over)

Group	%
Total Population	7.0
Hispanic or Latino (of any race)	8.5
Central American, ex. Mexican	10.0
Mexican	8.0
Puerto Rican	8.3
South American	14.8

Class of Worker: Private Wage and Salary
(Universe: Civilian Employed Population 16 Years and Over)

Group	Number	%
Total Population	78,273	78.7
Hispanic or Latino (of any race)	13,160	83.3
Central American, ex. Mexican	747	95.4
Mexican	10,203	83.8
Puerto Rican	547	84.3
South American	518	72.0

Class of Worker: Government
(Universe: Civilian Employed Population 16 Years and Over)

Group	Number	%
Total Population	12,009	12.1
Hispanic or Latino (of any race)	1,483	9.4
Central American, ex. Mexican	4	0.5
Mexican	1,136	9.3
Puerto Rican	82	12.6
South American	141	19.6

Means of Transportation to Work: Car, Truck or Van
(Universe: Workers 16 Years and Over)

Group	Number	%
Total Population	87,853	90.2
Hispanic or Latino (of any race)	13,507	87.7
Central American, ex. Mexican	632	80.7
Mexican	10,356	87.5
Puerto Rican	649	100.0
South American	632	89.9

Means of Transportation to Work: Public Transportation (ex. Taxicab)
(Universe: Workers 16 Years and Over)

Group	Number	%
Total Population	1,143	1.2
Hispanic or Latino (of any race)	467	3.0
Central American, ex. Mexican	93	11.9
Mexican	349	2.9
Puerto Rican	0	0.0
South American	16	2.3

Homeownership Rate
(Universe: Occupied Housing Units)

Group	%
Total Population	60.5
Hispanic or Latino (of any race)	39.5
Central American, ex. Mexican	34.0
Costa Rican	53.8
Guatemalan	25.3
Honduran	36.4
Nicaraguan	49.0
Salvadoran	21.3
Cuban	62.3
Mexican	36.4
Puerto Rican	44.4
South American	52.4
Argentinean	63.0
Chilean	50.8
Colombian	44.2
Ecuadorian	43.4
Peruvian	55.0
Spaniard	56.7

Median Home Value

Group	Dollars
Total Population	689,400
Hispanic or Latino (of any race)	567,000
Central American, ex. Mexican	632,400
Mexican	577,300
Puerto Rican	677,800
South American	491,900

Median Gross Rent

Group	Dollars
Total Population	1,464
Hispanic or Latino (of any race)	1,407
Central American, ex. Mexican	1,419
Mexican	1,378
Puerto Rican	1,541
South American	1,711

Median Household Income
(2010 Inflation-Adjusted Dollars)

Group	Dollars
Total Population	80,280
Hispanic or Latino (of any race)	64,527
Central American, ex. Mexican	62,165
Mexican	60,815
Puerto Rican	75,333
South American	73,594

Per Capita Income
(2010 Inflation-Adjusted Dollars)

Group	Dollars
Total Population	41,552
Hispanic or Latino (of any race)	23,071
Central American, ex. Mexican	23,433
Mexican	21,757
Puerto Rican	40,793
South American	29,122

Households with $100,000+ Income

Group	Number	%
Total Population	29,640	39.4
Hispanic or Latino (of any race)	2,560	27.6
Central American, ex. Mexican	119	23.8
Mexican	1,876	27.3
Puerto Rican	182	42.7
South American	134	28.3

Households with Food Stamps/SNAP Benefits During Past 12 Months

Group	Number	%
Total Population	1,094	1.5
Hispanic or Latino (of any race)	394	4.2
Central American, ex. Mexican	40	8.0
Mexican	334	4.9
Puerto Rican	7	1.6
South American	0	0.0

Poverty Rate
(Income in Past 12 Months Below Poverty Level)

Group	%
Total Population	7.0
Hispanic or Latino (of any race)	14.8
Central American, ex. Mexican	12.1
Mexican	16.9
Puerto Rican	2.5
South American	5.8

Huntington Park

Population

Group	Number	%TP[1]	%HP[2]
Total Population	58,114	100.0	–
Hispanic or Latino (of any race)	56,445	97.1	100.0
Central American, ex. Mexican	6,404	11.0	11.3
Guatemalan	1,822	3.1	3.2
Honduran	487	0.8	0.9
Nicaraguan	546	0.9	1.0
Salvadoran	3,381	5.8	6.0
Cuban	442	0.8	0.8
Mexican	46,467	80.0	82.3
Puerto Rican	188	0.3	0.3
South American	447	0.8	0.8
Colombian	115	0.2	0.2
Ecuadorian	142	0.2	0.3
Peruvian	112	0.2	0.2
Spaniard	114	0.2	0.2

Population Growth: 2000–2010

Group	%
Total Population	-5.3
Hispanic or Latino (of any race)	-3.7
Central American, ex. Mexican	47.8
Guatemalan	83.1
Honduran	111.7
Nicaraguan	63.5
Salvadoran	49.7
Cuban	-35.8
Mexican	3.4
Puerto Rican	-19.7
South American	6.7
Colombian	0.0
Ecuadorian	19.3

Males per 100 Females

Group	Number
Total Population	99.6
Hispanic or Latino (of any race)	99.3
Central American, ex. Mexican	96.0
Guatemalan	116.4
Honduran	85.2
Nicaraguan	101.5

Notes: (1) Percent of total population; (2) Percent of Hispanic/Latino population; Profiles include places with an overall population of at least 125,000, OR an overall population of at least 25,000 where the Hispanic/Latino population is at least 20% of the overall population. In states where less than five places meet either of these criteria, we have included places with at least 10,000 total population with the highest percentage of Hispanic/Latino population. These places are identified with an asterisk (*); Please refer to the User's Guide for a full explanation of data.

Group	
Salvadoran	87.3
Cuban	100.0
Mexican	100.3
Puerto Rican	88.0
South American	95.2
Colombian	71.6
Ecuadorian	97.2
Peruvian	111.3
Spaniard	86.9

Average Household Size

Group	People
Total Population	3.96
Hispanic or Latino (of any race)	4.03
Central American, ex. Mexican	3.90
Guatemalan	4.03
Honduran	3.90
Nicaraguan	3.90
Salvadoran	3.87
Cuban	2.21
Mexican	4.13
Puerto Rican	2.39
South American	2.93
Colombian	2.67
Ecuadorian	3.16
Peruvian	3.56
Spaniard	3.05

Median Age

Group	Years
Total Population	28.9
Hispanic or Latino (of any race)	28.6
Central American, ex. Mexican	35.7
Guatemalan	34.2
Honduran	33.2
Nicaraguan	40.0
Salvadoran	36.5
Cuban	60.7
Mexican	27.6
Puerto Rican	37.5
South American	48.3
Colombian	49.1
Ecuadorian	51.0
Peruvian	46.5
Spaniard	42.0

High School Graduates
(Universe: Population 25 Years and Over)

Group	Number	%
Total Population	13,926	42.2
Hispanic or Latino (of any race)	12,867	40.6
Central American, ex. Mexican	2,533	50.5
Guatemalan	580	38.3
Salvadoran	1,613	61.4
Mexican	9,557	38.0

Four-Year College Graduates
(Universe: Population 25 Years and Over)

Group	Number	%
Total Population	2,165	6.6
Hispanic or Latino (of any race)	1,865	5.9
Central American, ex. Mexican	604	12.0
Guatemalan	85	5.6
Salvadoran	465	17.7
Mexican	1,106	4.4

Population Age 3–17 Enrolled in Public School
(Universe: Population Age 3–17 Enrolled in School)

Group	Number	%
Total Population	13,420	97.4
Hispanic or Latino (of any race)	13,313	97.5
Central American, ex. Mexican	1,478	99.3
Guatemalan	382	97.4
Salvadoran	732	100.0
Mexican	11,528	97.4

Population Age 3–17 Enrolled in Private School
(Universe: Population Age 3–17 Enrolled in School)

Group	Number	%
Total Population	357	2.6
Hispanic or Latino (of any race)	345	2.5
Central American, ex. Mexican	10	0.7
Guatemalan	10	2.6
Salvadoran	0	0.0
Mexican	305	2.6

Foreign-Born Population

Group	Number	%
Total Population	30,060	51.3
Hispanic or Latino (of any race)	29,590	51.8
Central American, ex. Mexican	4,940	64.1
Guatemalan	1,492	63.7
Salvadoran	2,562	64.7
Mexican	23,480	49.7

Foreign-Born Naturalized U.S. Citizens

Group	Number	%
Total Population	8,625	28.7
Hispanic or Latino (of any race)	8,294	28.0
Central American, ex. Mexican	1,997	40.4
Guatemalan	448	30.0
Salvadoran	1,248	48.7
Mexican	5,700	24.3

Language Spoken at Home: English Only
(Universe: Population 5 Years and Over)

Group	Number	%
Total Population	3,094	5.8
Hispanic or Latino (of any race)	2,298	4.4
Central American, ex. Mexican	211	2.9
Guatemalan	22	1.0
Salvadoran	189	5.1
Mexican	1,926	4.5

Language Spoken at Home: Spanish
(Universe: Population 5 Years and Over)

Group	Number	%
Total Population	49,629	93.1
Hispanic or Latino (of any race)	49,496	95.5
Central American, ex. Mexican	6,985	97.1
Guatemalan	2,153	99.0
Salvadoran	3,545	94.9
Mexican	40,594	95.4

Unemployment Rate
(Universe: Population 16 Years and Over)

Group	%
Total Population	8.1
Hispanic or Latino (of any race)	8.2
Central American, ex. Mexican	9.4
Guatemalan	7.1
Salvadoran	11.2
Mexican	7.8

Class of Worker: Private Wage and Salary
(Universe: Civilian Employed Population 16 Years and Over)

Group	Number	%
Total Population	21,013	84.5
Hispanic or Latino (of any race)	20,516	84.7
Central American, ex. Mexican	3,205	82.4
Guatemalan	828	75.0
Salvadoran	1,695	83.5
Mexican	16,729	86.0

Class of Worker: Government
(Universe: Civilian Employed Population 16 Years and Over)

Group	Number	%
Total Population	2,197	8.8
Hispanic or Latino (of any race)	2,086	8.6
Central American, ex. Mexican	286	7.4
Guatemalan	89	8.1
Salvadoran	188	9.3
Mexican	1,572	8.1

Means of Transportation to Work: Car, Truck or Van
(Universe: Workers 16 Years and Over)

Group	Number	%
Total Population	18,792	76.7
Hispanic or Latino (of any race)	18,341	76.8
Central American, ex. Mexican	3,181	83.4
Guatemalan	935	84.7
Salvadoran	1,638	83.6
Mexican	14,467	75.3

Means of Transportation to Work: Public Transportation (ex. Taxicab)
(Universe: Workers 16 Years and Over)

Group	Number	%
Total Population	3,243	13.2
Hispanic or Latino (of any race)	3,165	13.3

Group	Number	%
Central American, ex. Mexican	408	10.7
Guatemalan	149	13.5
Salvadoran	194	9.9
Mexican	2,705	14.1

Homeownership Rate
(Universe: Occupied Housing Units)

Group	%
Total Population	27.0
Hispanic or Latino (of any race)	26.2
Central American, ex. Mexican	24.5
Guatemalan	24.5
Honduran	15.2
Nicaraguan	25.6
Salvadoran	25.6
Cuban	29.5
Mexican	26.6
Puerto Rican	9.9
South American	33.3
Colombian	23.3
Ecuadorian	50.9
Peruvian	27.8
Spaniard	35.7

Median Home Value

Group	Dollars
Total Population	397,700
Hispanic or Latino (of any race)	396,600
Central American, ex. Mexican	460,100
Guatemalan	351,700
Salvadoran	488,100
Mexican	383,500

Median Gross Rent

Group	Dollars
Total Population	852
Hispanic or Latino (of any race)	854
Central American, ex. Mexican	867
Guatemalan	966
Salvadoran	843
Mexican	854

Median Household Income
(2010 Inflation-Adjusted Dollars)

Group	Dollars
Total Population	37,224
Hispanic or Latino (of any race)	37,092
Central American, ex. Mexican	39,913
Guatemalan	44,191
Salvadoran	39,275
Mexican	36,697

Per Capita Income
(2010 Inflation-Adjusted Dollars)

Group	Dollars
Total Population	12,563
Hispanic or Latino (of any race)	12,221
Central American, ex. Mexican	14,330
Guatemalan	14,454
Salvadoran	14,768
Mexican	11,750

Households with $100,000+ Income

Group	Number	%
Total Population	1,366	9.5
Hispanic or Latino (of any race)	1,280	9.2
Central American, ex. Mexican	214	9.7
Guatemalan	83	15.2
Salvadoran	107	8.6
Mexican	1,007	9.2

Households with Food Stamps/SNAP Benefits During Past 12 Months

Group	Number	%
Total Population	2,004	13.9
Hispanic or Latino (of any race)	2,004	14.5
Central American, ex. Mexican	266	12.0
Guatemalan	85	15.6
Salvadoran	115	9.3
Mexican	1,701	15.5

Poverty Rate
(Income in Past 12 Months Below Poverty Level)

Group	%
Total Population	24.0
Hispanic or Latino (of any race)	24.2

Notes: (1) Percent of total population; (2) Percent of Hispanic/Latino population; Profiles include places with an overall population of at least 125,000, OR an overall population of at least 25,000 where the Hispanic/Latino population is at least 20% of the overall population. In states where less than five places meet either of these criteria, we have included places with at least 10,000 total population with the highest percentage of Hispanic/Latino population. These places are identified with an asterisk (*); Please refer to the User's Guide for a full explanation of data.

Central American, ex. Mexican	18.2
Guatemalan	15.6
Salvadoran	18.7
Mexican	25.5

Imperial Beach

Population

Group	Number	%TP[1]	%HP[2]
Total Population	26,324	100.0	–
Hispanic or Latino (of any race)	12,893	49.0	100.0
Central American, ex. Mexican	131	0.5	1.0
Mexican	11,732	44.6	91.0
Puerto Rican	314	1.2	2.4
Spaniard	111	0.4	0.9

Population Growth: 2000–2010

Group	%
Total Population	-2.5
Hispanic or Latino (of any race)	19.2
Mexican	29.2
Puerto Rican	28.2

Males per 100 Females

Group	Number
Total Population	101.1
Hispanic or Latino (of any race)	92.7
Central American, ex. Mexican	87.1
Mexican	92.0
Puerto Rican	105.2
Spaniard	91.4

Average Household Size

Group	People
Total Population	2.82
Hispanic or Latino (of any race)	3.47
Central American, ex. Mexican	2.96
Mexican	3.55
Puerto Rican	2.86
Spaniard	2.73

Median Age

Group	Years
Total Population	31.0
Hispanic or Latino (of any race)	25.9
Central American, ex. Mexican	30.9
Mexican	25.5
Puerto Rican	26.0
Spaniard	27.5

High School Graduates
(Universe: Population 25 Years and Over)

Group	Number	%
Total Population	12,606	81.0
Hispanic or Latino (of any race)	4,097	66.4
Mexican	3,718	64.9

Four-Year College Graduates
(Universe: Population 25 Years and Over)

Group	Number	%
Total Population	2,463	15.8
Hispanic or Latino (of any race)	621	10.1
Mexican	585	10.2

Population Age 3–17 Enrolled in Public School
(Universe: Population Age 3–17 Enrolled in School)

Group	Number	%
Total Population	4,836	95.7
Hispanic or Latino (of any race)	3,523	97.0
Mexican	3,334	97.3

Population Age 3–17 Enrolled in Private School
(Universe: Population Age 3–17 Enrolled in School)

Group	Number	%
Total Population	216	4.3
Hispanic or Latino (of any race)	109	3.0
Mexican	93	2.7

Foreign-Born Population

Group	Number	%
Total Population	5,339	20.3
Hispanic or Latino (of any race)	3,888	30.0
Mexican	3,622	30.0

Foreign-Born Naturalized U.S. Citizens

Group	Number	%
Total Population	2,245	42.0
Hispanic or Latino (of any race)	1,359	35.0
Mexican	1,313	36.3

Language Spoken at Home: English Only
(Universe: Population 5 Years and Over)

Group	Number	%
Total Population	12,959	53.7
Hispanic or Latino (of any race)	2,060	18.0
Mexican	1,858	17.2

Language Spoken at Home: Spanish
(Universe: Population 5 Years and Over)

Group	Number	%
Total Population	9,821	40.7
Hispanic or Latino (of any race)	9,367	81.9
Mexican	8,931	82.8

Unemployment Rate
(Universe: Population 16 Years and Over)

Group	%
Total Population	9.7
Hispanic or Latino (of any race)	10.2
Mexican	9.3

Class of Worker: Private Wage and Salary
(Universe: Civilian Employed Population 16 Years and Over)

Group	Number	%
Total Population	8,099	73.4
Hispanic or Latino (of any race)	3,928	79.1
Mexican	3,798	79.5

Class of Worker: Government
(Universe: Civilian Employed Population 16 Years and Over)

Group	Number	%
Total Population	2,227	20.2
Hispanic or Latino (of any race)	684	13.8
Mexican	626	13.1

Means of Transportation to Work: Car, Truck or Van
(Universe: Workers 16 Years and Over)

Group	Number	%
Total Population	9,967	84.6
Hispanic or Latino (of any race)	4,290	85.3
Mexican	4,136	85.7

Means of Transportation to Work: Public Transportation (ex. Taxicab)
(Universe: Workers 16 Years and Over)

Group	Number	%
Total Population	783	6.6
Hispanic or Latino (of any race)	389	7.7
Mexican	339	7.0

Homeownership Rate
(Universe: Occupied Housing Units)

Group	%
Total Population	30.2
Hispanic or Latino (of any race)	19.7
Central American, ex. Mexican	18.8
Mexican	19.9
Puerto Rican	14.4
Spaniard	32.5

Median Home Value

Group	Dollars
Total Population	405,600
Hispanic or Latino (of any race)	465,600
Mexican	485,900

Median Gross Rent

Group	Dollars
Total Population	1,073
Hispanic or Latino (of any race)	1,075
Mexican	1,076

Median Household Income
(2010 Inflation-Adjusted Dollars)

Group	Dollars
Total Population	45,418
Hispanic or Latino (of any race)	40,974
Mexican	40,148

Per Capita Income
(2010 Inflation-Adjusted Dollars)

Group	Dollars
Total Population	20,374
Hispanic or Latino (of any race)	14,168
Mexican	14,302

Households with $100,000+ Income

Group	Number	%
Total Population	1,125	12.3
Hispanic or Latino (of any race)	338	9.8
Mexican	338	10.5

Households with Food Stamps/SNAP Benefits During Past 12 Months

Group	Number	%
Total Population	533	5.8
Hispanic or Latino (of any race)	377	10.9
Mexican	340	10.5

Poverty Rate
(Income in Past 12 Months Below Poverty Level)

Group	%
Total Population	19.5
Hispanic or Latino (of any race)	26.3
Mexican	25.9

Indio

Population

Group	Number	%TP[1]	%HP[2]
Total Population	76,036	100.0	–
Hispanic or Latino (of any race)	51,540	67.8	100.0
Central American, ex. Mexican	876	1.2	1.7
Guatemalan	180	0.2	0.3
Salvadoran	492	0.6	1.0
Mexican	48,095	63.3	93.3
Puerto Rican	232	0.3	0.5
South American	289	0.4	0.6
Spaniard	199	0.3	0.4

Population Growth: 2000–2010

Group	%
Total Population	54.8
Hispanic or Latino (of any race)	39.2
Central American, ex. Mexican	168.7
Salvadoran	148.5
Mexican	45.8

Males per 100 Females

Group	Number
Total Population	97.3
Hispanic or Latino (of any race)	97.9
Central American, ex. Mexican	104.2
Guatemalan	116.9
Salvadoran	102.5
Mexican	98.0
Puerto Rican	114.8
South American	91.4
Spaniard	99.0

Average Household Size

Group	People
Total Population	3.21
Hispanic or Latino (of any race)	3.93
Central American, ex. Mexican	3.82
Guatemalan	4.34
Salvadoran	3.77
Mexican	3.96
Puerto Rican	2.90
South American	2.92
Spaniard	2.94

Median Age

Group	Years
Total Population	32.2
Hispanic or Latino (of any race)	26.0
Central American, ex. Mexican	32.1
Guatemalan	33.3
Salvadoran	32.8
Mexican	25.8
Puerto Rican	32.2
South American	37.3
Spaniard	40.6

Notes: (1) Percent of total population; (2) Percent of Hispanic/Latino population; Profiles include places with an overall population of at least 125,000, OR an overall population of at least 25,000 where the Hispanic/Latino population is at least 20% of the overall population. In states where less than five places meet either of these criteria, we have included places with at least 10,000 total population with the highest percentage of Hispanic/Latino population. These places are identified with an asterisk (*); Please refer to the User's Guide for a full explanation of data.

High School Graduates
(Universe: Population 25 Years and Over)

Group	Number	%
Total Population	30,397	71.0
Hispanic or Latino (of any race)	13,792	57.7
Central American, ex. Mexican	314	50.5
Mexican	12,603	57.1

Four-Year College Graduates
(Universe: Population 25 Years and Over)

Group	Number	%
Total Population	7,452	17.4
Hispanic or Latino (of any race)	1,983	8.3
Central American, ex. Mexican	12	1.9
Mexican	1,773	8.0

Population Age 3–17 Enrolled in Public School
(Universe: Population Age 3–17 Enrolled in School)

Group	Number	%
Total Population	15,563	93.8
Hispanic or Latino (of any race)	12,753	96.0
Central American, ex. Mexican	162	100.0
Mexican	12,296	96.1

Population Age 3–17 Enrolled in Private School
(Universe: Population Age 3–17 Enrolled in School)

Group	Number	%
Total Population	1,024	6.2
Hispanic or Latino (of any race)	535	4.0
Central American, ex. Mexican	0	0.0
Mexican	499	3.9

Foreign-Born Population

Group	Number	%
Total Population	20,205	27.9
Hispanic or Latino (of any race)	16,825	35.3
Central American, ex. Mexican	773	65.2
Mexican	15,638	35.1

Foreign-Born Naturalized U.S. Citizens

Group	Number	%
Total Population	6,951	34.4
Hispanic or Latino (of any race)	5,450	32.4
Central American, ex. Mexican	169	21.9
Mexican	4,960	31.7

Language Spoken at Home: English Only
(Universe: Population 5 Years and Over)

Group	Number	%
Total Population	28,828	43.6
Hispanic or Latino (of any race)	9,287	21.9
Central American, ex. Mexican	39	4.1
Mexican	8,506	21.4

Language Spoken at Home: Spanish
(Universe: Population 5 Years and Over)

Group	Number	%
Total Population	35,971	54.4
Hispanic or Latino (of any race)	33,030	78.0
Central American, ex. Mexican	916	95.9
Mexican	31,204	78.5

Unemployment Rate
(Universe: Population 16 Years and Over)

Group	%
Total Population	10.7
Hispanic or Latino (of any race)	13.2
Central American, ex. Mexican	5.2
Mexican	13.8

Class of Worker: Private Wage and Salary
(Universe: Civilian Employed Population 16 Years and Over)

Group	Number	%
Total Population	23,298	76.7
Hispanic or Latino (of any race)	15,167	79.8
Central American, ex. Mexican	611	90.8
Mexican	13,838	79.5

Class of Worker: Government
(Universe: Civilian Employed Population 16 Years and Over)

Group	Number	%
Total Population	4,650	15.3
Hispanic or Latino (of any race)	2,477	13.0
Central American, ex. Mexican	27	4.0
Mexican	2,283	13.1

Means of Transportation to Work: Car, Truck or Van
(Universe: Workers 16 Years and Over)

Group	Number	%
Total Population	27,061	91.8
Hispanic or Latino (of any race)	17,151	93.3
Central American, ex. Mexican	625	92.9
Mexican	15,673	93.1

Means of Transportation to Work: Public Transportation (ex. Taxicab)
(Universe: Workers 16 Years and Over)

Group	Number	%
Total Population	519	1.8
Hispanic or Latino (of any race)	383	2.1
Central American, ex. Mexican	13	1.9
Mexican	351	2.1

Homeownership Rate
(Universe: Occupied Housing Units)

Group	%
Total Population	65.3
Hispanic or Latino (of any race)	53.1
Central American, ex. Mexican	54.0
Guatemalan	50.0
Salvadoran	56.6
Mexican	53.1
Puerto Rican	52.2
South American	63.5
Spaniard	71.8

Median Home Value

Group	Dollars
Total Population	286,400
Hispanic or Latino (of any race)	245,100
Central American, ex. Mexican	152,700
Mexican	240,400

Median Gross Rent

Group	Dollars
Total Population	926
Hispanic or Latino (of any race)	864
Central American, ex. Mexican	798
Mexican	859

Median Household Income
(2010 Inflation-Adjusted Dollars)

Group	Dollars
Total Population	51,921
Hispanic or Latino (of any race)	39,777
Central American, ex. Mexican	65,625
Mexican	38,717

Per Capita Income
(2010 Inflation-Adjusted Dollars)

Group	Dollars
Total Population	21,333
Hispanic or Latino (of any race)	13,932
Central American, ex. Mexican	19,604
Mexican	13,284

Households with $100,000+ Income

Group	Number	%
Total Population	4,527	19.7
Hispanic or Latino (of any race)	1,517	12.4
Central American, ex. Mexican	56	17.8
Mexican	1,206	10.8

Households with Food Stamps/SNAP Benefits During Past 12 Months

Group	Number	%
Total Population	1,508	6.6
Hispanic or Latino (of any race)	1,372	11.2
Central American, ex. Mexican	42	13.4
Mexican	1,321	11.8

Poverty Rate
(Income in Past 12 Months Below Poverty Level)

Group	%
Total Population	19.7
Hispanic or Latino (of any race)	25.3
Central American, ex. Mexican	24.5
Mexican	26.2

Inglewood

Population

Group	Number	%TP[1]	%HP[2]
Total Population	109,673	100.0	–
Hispanic or Latino (of any race)	55,449	50.6	100.0
Central American, ex. Mexican	8,697	7.9	15.7
Guatemalan	3,593	3.3	6.5
Honduran	649	0.6	1.2
Nicaraguan	337	0.3	0.6
Panamanian	119	0.1	0.2
Salvadoran	3,869	3.5	7.0
Cuban	362	0.3	0.7
Mexican	41,983	38.3	75.7
Puerto Rican	578	0.5	1.0
South American	505	0.5	0.9
Colombian	140	0.1	0.3
Ecuadorian	105	0.1	0.2
Peruvian	161	0.1	0.3
Spaniard	181	0.2	0.3

Population Growth: 2000–2010

Group	%
Total Population	-2.6
Hispanic or Latino (of any race)	7.0
Central American, ex. Mexican	71.1
Guatemalan	98.9
Honduran	111.4
Nicaraguan	52.5
Panamanian	19.0
Salvadoran	85.0
Cuban	-15.0
Mexican	12.6
Puerto Rican	27.3
South American	34.0
Colombian	38.6

Males per 100 Females

Group	Number
Total Population	90.6
Hispanic or Latino (of any race)	102.3
Central American, ex. Mexican	96.2
Guatemalan	104.8
Honduran	102.2
Nicaraguan	93.7
Panamanian	88.9
Salvadoran	88.6
Cuban	81.0
Mexican	104.4
Puerto Rican	88.3
South American	102.8
Colombian	91.8
Ecuadorian	110.0
Peruvian	106.4
Spaniard	79.2

Average Household Size

Group	People
Total Population	2.97
Hispanic or Latino (of any race)	4.12
Central American, ex. Mexican	3.98
Guatemalan	4.14
Honduran	3.87
Nicaraguan	3.35
Panamanian	2.54
Salvadoran	4.05
Cuban	2.58
Mexican	4.25
Puerto Rican	2.80
South American	3.17
Colombian	3.39
Ecuadorian	3.23
Peruvian	3.51
Spaniard	3.20

Median Age

Group	Years
Total Population	33.4
Hispanic or Latino (of any race)	28.0
Central American, ex. Mexican	33.7
Guatemalan	32.9
Honduran	31.6
Nicaraguan	37.9
Panamanian	46.5

Notes: (1) Percent of total population; (2) Percent of Hispanic/Latino population; Profiles include places with an overall population of at least 125,000, OR an overall population of at least 25,000 where the Hispanic/Latino population is at least 20% of the overall population. In states where less than five places meet either of these criteria, we have included places with at least 10,000 total population with the highest percentage of Hispanic/Latino population. These places are identified with an asterisk (*); Please refer to the User's Guide for a full explanation of data.

Salvadoran	34.3
Cuban	48.3
Mexican	27.1
Puerto Rican	29.3
South American	41.2
Colombian	36.2
Ecuadorian	42.1
Peruvian	43.1
Spaniard	26.4

High School Graduates
(Universe: Population 25 Years and Over)

Group	Number	%
Total Population	48,176	71.3
Hispanic or Latino (of any race)	14,185	48.3
Central American, ex. Mexican	2,885	47.9
Guatemalan	1,127	46.7
Salvadoran	1,272	44.6
Mexican	10,005	46.4
South American	518	74.4

Four-Year College Graduates
(Universe: Population 25 Years and Over)

Group	Number	%
Total Population	11,603	17.2
Hispanic or Latino (of any race)	1,565	5.3
Central American, ex. Mexican	315	5.2
Guatemalan	78	3.2
Salvadoran	157	5.5
Mexican	945	4.4
South American	205	29.5

Population Age 3–17 Enrolled in Public School
(Universe: Population Age 3–17 Enrolled in School)

Group	Number	%
Total Population	20,697	90.9
Hispanic or Latino (of any race)	13,220	96.1
Central American, ex. Mexican	1,960	98.7
Guatemalan	901	97.3
Salvadoran	769	100.0
Mexican	10,661	95.9
South American	219	100.0

Population Age 3–17 Enrolled in Private School
(Universe: Population Age 3–17 Enrolled in School)

Group	Number	%
Total Population	2,078	9.1
Hispanic or Latino (of any race)	535	3.9
Central American, ex. Mexican	25	1.3
Guatemalan	25	2.7
Salvadoran	0	0.0
Mexican	455	4.1
South American	0	0.0

Foreign-Born Population

Group	Number	%
Total Population	31,237	28.4
Hispanic or Latino (of any race)	26,997	49.4
Central American, ex. Mexican	6,183	63.5
Guatemalan	2,288	58.8
Salvadoran	3,121	69.2
Mexican	19,447	46.4
South American	727	69.3

Foreign-Born Naturalized U.S. Citizens

Group	Number	%
Total Population	10,693	34.2
Hispanic or Latino (of any race)	8,255	30.6
Central American, ex. Mexican	2,010	32.5
Guatemalan	712	31.1
Salvadoran	989	31.7
Mexican	5,607	28.8
South American	295	40.6

Language Spoken at Home: English Only
(Universe: Population 5 Years and Over)

Group	Number	%
Total Population	50,401	50.1
Hispanic or Latino (of any race)	3,877	8.0
Central American, ex. Mexican	494	5.5
Guatemalan	146	4.1
Salvadoran	196	4.8
Mexican	2,912	7.8
South American	60	6.5

Language Spoken at Home: Spanish
(Universe: Population 5 Years and Over)

Group	Number	%
Total Population	46,336	46.0
Hispanic or Latino (of any race)	44,746	91.9
Central American, ex. Mexican	8,389	94.1
Guatemalan	3,414	95.4
Salvadoran	3,921	95.2
Mexican	34,199	92.1
South American	857	93.5

Unemployment Rate
(Universe: Population 16 Years and Over)

Group	%
Total Population	9.6
Hispanic or Latino (of any race)	7.8
Central American, ex. Mexican	7.3
Guatemalan	8.7
Salvadoran	8.1
Mexican	8.2
South American	0.0

Class of Worker: Private Wage and Salary
(Universe: Civilian Employed Population 16 Years and Over)

Group	Number	%
Total Population	36,407	74.3
Hispanic or Latino (of any race)	19,113	80.7
Central American, ex. Mexican	4,006	83.0
Guatemalan	1,446	79.2
Salvadoran	1,908	85.4
Mexican	14,195	80.4
South American	261	61.4

Class of Worker: Government
(Universe: Civilian Employed Population 16 Years and Over)

Group	Number	%
Total Population	8,456	17.3
Hispanic or Latino (of any race)	1,721	7.3
Central American, ex. Mexican	243	5.0
Guatemalan	172	9.4
Salvadoran	43	1.9
Mexican	1,365	7.7
South American	59	13.9

Means of Transportation to Work: Car, Truck or Van
(Universe: Workers 16 Years and Over)

Group	Number	%
Total Population	40,504	85.6
Hispanic or Latino (of any race)	19,476	84.2
Central American, ex. Mexican	4,062	86.2
Guatemalan	1,471	83.4
Salvadoran	1,937	87.9
Mexican	14,397	83.7
South American	362	85.2

Means of Transportation to Work: Public Transportation (ex. Taxicab)
(Universe: Workers 16 Years and Over)

Group	Number	%
Total Population	3,578	7.6
Hispanic or Latino (of any race)	2,015	8.7
Central American, ex. Mexican	429	9.1
Guatemalan	139	7.9
Salvadoran	219	9.9
Mexican	1,432	8.3
South American	44	10.4

Homeownership Rate
(Universe: Occupied Housing Units)

Group	%
Total Population	37.0
Hispanic or Latino (of any race)	34.4
Central American, ex. Mexican	27.4
Guatemalan	27.1
Honduran	20.5
Nicaraguan	22.6
Panamanian	40.4
Salvadoran	27.8
Cuban	47.7
Mexican	36.8
Puerto Rican	20.2
South American	34.5
Colombian	31.7
Ecuadorian	46.7
Peruvian	23.7
Spaniard	36.6

Median Home Value

Group	Dollars
Total Population	419,300
Hispanic or Latino (of any race)	407,300
Central American, ex. Mexican	368,000
Guatemalan	411,400
Salvadoran	331,300
Mexican	412,600
South American	400,000

Median Gross Rent

Group	Dollars
Total Population	985
Hispanic or Latino (of any race)	946
Central American, ex. Mexican	983
Guatemalan	969
Salvadoran	979
Mexican	929
South American	1,031

Median Household Income
(2010 Inflation-Adjusted Dollars)

Group	Dollars
Total Population	43,460
Hispanic or Latino (of any race)	38,835
Central American, ex. Mexican	37,414
Guatemalan	35,829
Salvadoran	41,154
Mexican	39,794
South American	31,858

Per Capita Income
(2010 Inflation-Adjusted Dollars)

Group	Dollars
Total Population	19,508
Hispanic or Latino (of any race)	12,347
Central American, ex. Mexican	12,943
Guatemalan	12,778
Salvadoran	12,342
Mexican	12,081
South American	15,094

Households with $100,000+ Income

Group	Number	%
Total Population	4,924	13.5
Hispanic or Latino (of any race)	1,132	8.5
Central American, ex. Mexican	197	7.1
Guatemalan	79	6.9
Salvadoran	63	4.9
Mexican	861	9.0
South American	25	8.3

Households with Food Stamps/SNAP Benefits During Past 12 Months

Group	Number	%
Total Population	3,197	8.8
Hispanic or Latino (of any race)	1,412	10.6
Central American, ex. Mexican	323	11.7
Guatemalan	130	11.4
Salvadoran	158	12.4
Mexican	1,030	10.7
South American	11	3.7

Poverty Rate
(Income in Past 12 Months Below Poverty Level)

Group	%
Total Population	19.8
Hispanic or Latino (of any race)	26.3
Central American, ex. Mexican	26.1
Guatemalan	30.4
Salvadoran	26.2
Mexican	26.7
South American	20.5

Irvine

Population

Group	Number	%TP[1]	%HP[2]
Total Population	212,375	100.0	–
Hispanic or Latino (of any race)	19,621	9.2	100.0
Central American, ex. Mexican	1,461	0.7	7.4

Notes: (1) Percent of total population; (2) Percent of Hispanic/Latino population; Profiles include places with an overall population of at least 125,000, OR an overall population of at least 25,000 where the Hispanic/Latino population is at least 20% of the overall population. In states where less than five places meet either of these criteria, we have included places with at least 10,000 total population with the highest percentage of Hispanic/Latino population. These places are identified with an asterisk (*); Please refer to the User's Guide for a full explanation of data.

Costa Rican	172	0.1	0.9
Guatemalan	334	0.2	1.7
Nicaraguan	176	0.1	0.9
Salvadoran	585	0.3	3.0
Cuban	467	0.2	2.4
Mexican	12,807	6.0	65.3
Puerto Rican	641	0.3	3.3
South American	2,418	1.1	12.3
Argentinean	440	0.2	2.2
Bolivian	123	0.1	0.6
Chilean	198	0.1	1.0
Colombian	662	0.3	3.4
Ecuadorian	249	0.1	1.3
Peruvian	557	0.3	2.8
Venezuelan	115	0.1	0.6
Spaniard	609	0.3	3.1

Population Growth: 2000–2010

Group	%
Total Population	48.4
Hispanic or Latino (of any race)	86.2
Central American, ex. Mexican	208.2
Guatemalan	193.0
Salvadoran	290.0
Cuban	46.4
Mexican	99.8
Puerto Rican	82.6
South American	127.7
Argentinean	132.8
Colombian	189.1
Peruvian	108.6
Spaniard	469.2

Males per 100 Females

Group	Number
Total Population	94.9
Hispanic or Latino (of any race)	90.0
Central American, ex. Mexican	77.7
Costa Rican	77.3
Guatemalan	76.7
Nicaraguan	97.8
Salvadoran	72.1
Cuban	85.3
Mexican	91.3
Puerto Rican	96.6
South American	87.2
Argentinean	99.1
Bolivian	92.2
Chilean	88.6
Colombian	78.4
Ecuadorian	81.8
Peruvian	81.4
Venezuelan	109.1
Spaniard	91.5

Average Household Size

Group	People
Total Population	2.61
Hispanic or Latino (of any race)	2.82
Central American, ex. Mexican	2.93
Costa Rican	2.94
Guatemalan	3.33
Nicaraguan	2.56
Salvadoran	2.98
Cuban	2.37
Mexican	2.90
Puerto Rican	2.65
South American	2.74
Argentinean	2.58
Bolivian	2.77
Chilean	2.74
Colombian	2.78
Ecuadorian	2.92
Peruvian	2.85
Venezuelan	2.69
Spaniard	2.44

Median Age

Group	Years
Total Population	33.9
Hispanic or Latino (of any race)	27.4
Central American, ex. Mexican	26.9
Costa Rican	32.0
Guatemalan	26.4
Nicaraguan	27.0
Salvadoran	25.4
Cuban	35.8
Mexican	25.5
Puerto Rican	29.6
South American	35.3
Argentinean	38.5
Bolivian	39.8
Chilean	35.5
Colombian	35.3
Ecuadorian	32.8
Peruvian	34.4
Venezuelan	32.6
Spaniard	31.5

High School Graduates

(Universe: Population 25 Years and Over)

Group	Number	%
Total Population	120,115	96.4
Hispanic or Latino (of any race)	8,137	88.6
Central American, ex. Mexican	533	85.6
Mexican	4,994	85.4
South American	1,170	95.4

Four-Year College Graduates

(Universe: Population 25 Years and Over)

Group	Number	%
Total Population	81,535	65.5
Hispanic or Latino (of any race)	3,739	40.7
Central American, ex. Mexican	291	46.7
Mexican	2,017	34.5
South American	709	57.8

Population Age 3–17 Enrolled in Public School

(Universe: Population Age 3–17 Enrolled in School)

Group	Number	%
Total Population	28,738	85.2
Hispanic or Latino (of any race)	3,422	87.9
Central American, ex. Mexican	92	86.8
Mexican	2,214	90.7
South American	352	91.9

Population Age 3–17 Enrolled in Private School

(Universe: Population Age 3–17 Enrolled in School)

Group	Number	%
Total Population	4,985	14.8
Hispanic or Latino (of any race)	472	12.1
Central American, ex. Mexican	14	13.2
Mexican	227	9.3
South American	31	8.1

Foreign-Born Population

Group	Number	%
Total Population	67,973	34.1
Hispanic or Latino (of any race)	4,786	26.6
Central American, ex. Mexican	548	45.7
Mexican	2,509	21.1
South American	1,193	62.6

Foreign-Born Naturalized U.S. Citizens

Group	Number	%
Total Population	37,757	55.5
Hispanic or Latino (of any race)	2,263	47.3
Central American, ex. Mexican	283	51.6
Mexican	1,033	41.2
South American	597	50.0

Language Spoken at Home: English Only

(Universe: Population 5 Years and Over)

Group	Number	%
Total Population	108,997	57.8
Hispanic or Latino (of any race)	7,778	45.2
Central American, ex. Mexican	464	39.4
Mexican	5,141	45.1
South American	284	15.5

Language Spoken at Home: Spanish

(Universe: Population 5 Years and Over)

Group	Number	%
Total Population	10,556	5.6
Hispanic or Latino (of any race)	9,261	53.8
Central American, ex. Mexican	715	60.6
Mexican	6,223	54.6
South American	1,504	82.2

Unemployment Rate

(Universe: Population 16 Years and Over)

Group	%
Total Population	5.5
Hispanic or Latino (of any race)	6.3
Central American, ex. Mexican	2.1
Mexican	6.0
South American	13.1

Class of Worker: Private Wage and Salary

(Universe: Civilian Employed Population 16 Years and Over)

Group	Number	%
Total Population	77,106	77.9
Hispanic or Latino (of any race)	6,585	77.3
Central American, ex. Mexican	383	67.1
Mexican	4,639	79.4
South American	769	83.6

Class of Worker: Government

(Universe: Civilian Employed Population 16 Years and Over)

Group	Number	%
Total Population	14,657	14.8
Hispanic or Latino (of any race)	1,440	16.9
Central American, ex. Mexican	115	20.1
Mexican	933	16.0
South American	84	9.1

Means of Transportation to Work: Car, Truck or Van

(Universe: Workers 16 Years and Over)

Group	Number	%
Total Population	82,065	84.5
Hispanic or Latino (of any race)	6,950	83.6
Central American, ex. Mexican	462	80.9
Mexican	4,722	82.4
South American	795	89.9

Means of Transportation to Work: Public Transportation (ex. Taxicab)

(Universe: Workers 16 Years and Over)

Group	Number	%
Total Population	1,321	1.4
Hispanic or Latino (of any race)	257	3.1
Central American, ex. Mexican	0	0.0
Mexican	220	3.8
South American	10	1.1

Homeownership Rate

(Universe: Occupied Housing Units)

Group	%
Total Population	50.2
Hispanic or Latino (of any race)	34.7
Central American, ex. Mexican	27.6
Costa Rican	30.6
Guatemalan	28.9
Nicaraguan	28.1
Salvadoran	23.4
Cuban	45.5
Mexican	31.9
Puerto Rican	29.5
South American	43.2
Argentinean	51.4
Bolivian	57.4
Chilean	44.9
Colombian	39.0
Ecuadorian	44.8
Peruvian	41.0
Venezuelan	25.6
Spaniard	46.8

Median Home Value

Group	Dollars
Total Population	677,100
Hispanic or Latino (of any race)	597,200
Central American, ex. Mexican	379,000
Mexican	532,600
South American	657,600

Median Gross Rent

Group	Dollars
Total Population	1,788
Hispanic or Latino (of any race)	1,655
Central American, ex. Mexican	1,533
Mexican	1,670
South American	1,766

Notes: (1) Percent of total population; (2) Percent of Hispanic/Latino population; Profiles include places with an overall population of at least 125,000, OR an overall population of at least 25,000 where the Hispanic/Latino population is at least 20% of the overall population. In states where less than five places meet either of these criteria, we have included places with at least 10,000 total population with the highest percentage of Hispanic/Latino population. These places are identified with an asterisk (*); Please refer to the User's Guide for a full explanation of data.

Median Household Income
(2010 Inflation-Adjusted Dollars)

Group	Dollars
Total Population	90,939
Hispanic or Latino (of any race)	65,447
Central American, ex. Mexican	52,452
Mexican	64,167
South American	63,380

Per Capita Income
(2010 Inflation-Adjusted Dollars)

Group	Dollars
Total Population	41,898
Hispanic or Latino (of any race)	26,681
Central American, ex. Mexican	23,994
Mexican	24,800
South American	32,550

Households with $100,000+ Income

Group	Number	%
Total Population	32,816	45.8
Hispanic or Latino (of any race)	1,652	31.9
Central American, ex. Mexican	77	22.2
Mexican	911	27.5
South American	236	32.5

Households with Food Stamps/SNAP Benefits During Past 12 Months

Group	Number	%
Total Population	1,015	1.4
Hispanic or Latino (of any race)	89	1.7
Central American, ex. Mexican	0	0.0
Mexican	44	1.3
South American	45	6.2

Poverty Rate
(Income in Past 12 Months Below Poverty Level)

Group	%
Total Population	10.2
Hispanic or Latino (of any race)	13.6
Central American, ex. Mexican	23.1
Mexican	15.5
South American	5.4

La Habra

Population

Group	Number	%TP[1]	%HP[2]
Total Population	60,239	100.0	–
Hispanic or Latino (of any race)	34,449	57.2	100.0
Central American, ex. Mexican	1,283	2.1	3.7
Guatemalan	418	0.7	1.2
Nicaraguan	119	0.2	0.3
Salvadoran	577	1.0	1.7
Cuban	279	0.5	0.8
Mexican	30,316	50.3	88.0
Puerto Rican	313	0.5	0.9
South American	634	1.1	1.8
Argentinean	123	0.2	0.4
Colombian	162	0.3	0.5
Ecuadorian	101	0.2	0.3
Peruvian	151	0.3	0.4
Spaniard	290	0.5	0.8

Population Growth: 2000–2010

Group	%
Total Population	2.1
Hispanic or Latino (of any race)	19.1
Central American, ex. Mexican	115.6
Guatemalan	132.2
Salvadoran	137.4
Cuban	54.1
Mexican	25.3
Puerto Rican	11.4
South American	70.9

Males per 100 Females

Group	Number
Total Population	97.0
Hispanic or Latino (of any race)	99.5
Central American, ex. Mexican	92.4
Guatemalan	96.2
Nicaraguan	77.6
Salvadoran	92.3
Cuban	87.2
Mexican	100.7
Puerto Rican	117.4
South American	84.8
Argentinean	92.2
Colombian	88.4
Ecuadorian	119.6
Peruvian	62.4
Spaniard	82.4

Average Household Size

Group	People
Total Population	3.16
Hispanic or Latino (of any race)	3.96
Central American, ex. Mexican	3.85
Guatemalan	4.08
Nicaraguan	3.40
Salvadoran	3.99
Cuban	2.90
Mexican	4.05
Puerto Rican	3.02
South American	3.20
Argentinean	3.22
Colombian	2.92
Ecuadorian	3.25
Peruvian	3.61
Spaniard	2.96

Median Age

Group	Years
Total Population	33.6
Hispanic or Latino (of any race)	27.5
Central American, ex. Mexican	32.4
Guatemalan	31.4
Nicaraguan	32.1
Salvadoran	33.2
Cuban	36.1
Mexican	26.9
Puerto Rican	32.9
South American	35.1
Argentinean	35.5
Colombian	34.5
Ecuadorian	40.3
Peruvian	34.4
Spaniard	37.6

High School Graduates
(Universe: Population 25 Years and Over)

Group	Number	%
Total Population	29,851	80.3
Hispanic or Latino (of any race)	11,973	65.6
Central American, ex. Mexican	556	55.3
Mexican	10,408	64.6

Four-Year College Graduates
(Universe: Population 25 Years and Over)

Group	Number	%
Total Population	8,080	21.7
Hispanic or Latino (of any race)	1,877	10.3
Central American, ex. Mexican	67	6.7
Mexican	1,388	8.6

Population Age 3–17 Enrolled in Public School
(Universe: Population Age 3–17 Enrolled in School)

Group	Number	%
Total Population	11,432	89.9
Hispanic or Latino (of any race)	8,565	94.3
Central American, ex. Mexican	408	84.8
Mexican	7,618	94.9

Population Age 3–17 Enrolled in Private School
(Universe: Population Age 3–17 Enrolled in School)

Group	Number	%
Total Population	1,281	10.1
Hispanic or Latino (of any race)	517	5.7
Central American, ex. Mexican	73	15.2
Mexican	409	5.1

Foreign-Born Population

Group	Number	%
Total Population	16,643	27.8
Hispanic or Latino (of any race)	12,730	37.6
Central American, ex. Mexican	1,017	58.1
Mexican	11,345	37.8

Foreign-Born Naturalized U.S. Citizens

Group	Number	%
Total Population	5,654	34.0
Hispanic or Latino (of any race)	3,062	24.1
Central American, ex. Mexican	361	35.5
Mexican	2,488	21.9

Language Spoken at Home: English Only
(Universe: Population 5 Years and Over)

Group	Number	%
Total Population	28,020	50.6
Hispanic or Latino (of any race)	7,766	25.5
Central American, ex. Mexican	99	6.2
Mexican	6,955	25.8

Language Spoken at Home: Spanish
(Universe: Population 5 Years and Over)

Group	Number	%
Total Population	22,995	41.5
Hispanic or Latino (of any race)	22,576	74.3
Central American, ex. Mexican	1,508	93.8
Mexican	20,027	74.2

Unemployment Rate
(Universe: Population 16 Years and Over)

Group	%
Total Population	7.3
Hispanic or Latino (of any race)	7.3
Central American, ex. Mexican	0.8
Mexican	7.6

Class of Worker: Private Wage and Salary
(Universe: Civilian Employed Population 16 Years and Over)

Group	Number	%
Total Population	23,504	80.4
Hispanic or Latino (of any race)	12,988	82.7
Central American, ex. Mexican	707	76.8
Mexican	11,683	84.3

Class of Worker: Government
(Universe: Civilian Employed Population 16 Years and Over)

Group	Number	%
Total Population	3,799	13.0
Hispanic or Latino (of any race)	1,840	11.7
Central American, ex. Mexican	121	13.1
Mexican	1,459	10.5

Means of Transportation to Work: Car, Truck or Van
(Universe: Workers 16 Years and Over)

Group	Number	%
Total Population	25,710	90.4
Hispanic or Latino (of any race)	13,514	87.9
Central American, ex. Mexican	658	74.3
Mexican	12,037	88.8

Means of Transportation to Work: Public Transportation (ex. Taxicab)
(Universe: Workers 16 Years and Over)

Group	Number	%
Total Population	1,005	3.5
Hispanic or Latino (of any race)	775	5.0
Central American, ex. Mexican	82	9.3
Mexican	645	4.8

Homeownership Rate
(Universe: Occupied Housing Units)

Group	%
Total Population	57.7
Hispanic or Latino (of any race)	46.6
Central American, ex. Mexican	39.8
Guatemalan	34.2
Nicaraguan	44.2
Salvadoran	40.8
Cuban	58.0
Mexican	46.6
Puerto Rican	52.6
South American	52.2
Argentinean	51.2
Colombian	41.5
Ecuadorian	66.7
Peruvian	39.5
Spaniard	65.4

Notes: (1) Percent of total population; (2) Percent of Hispanic/Latino population; Profiles include places with an overall population of at least 125,000, OR an overall population of at least 25,000 where the Hispanic/Latino population is at least 20% of the overall population. In states where less than five places meet either of these criteria, we have included places with at least 10,000 total population with the highest percentage of Hispanic/Latino population. These places are identified with an asterisk (*); Please refer to the User's Guide for a full explanation of data.

Median Home Value

Group	Dollars
Total Population	472,400
Hispanic or Latino (of any race)	452,500
Central American, ex. Mexican	434,400
Mexican	445,200

Median Gross Rent

Group	Dollars
Total Population	1,242
Hispanic or Latino (of any race)	1,217
Central American, ex. Mexican	1,178
Mexican	1,215

Median Household Income
(2010 Inflation-Adjusted Dollars)

Group	Dollars
Total Population	62,078
Hispanic or Latino (of any race)	56,611
Central American, ex. Mexican	37,772
Mexican	56,148

Per Capita Income
(2010 Inflation-Adjusted Dollars)

Group	Dollars
Total Population	25,060
Hispanic or Latino (of any race)	17,778
Central American, ex. Mexican	14,240
Mexican	17,506

Households with $100,000+ Income

Group	Number	%
Total Population	4,563	24.5
Hispanic or Latino (of any race)	1,660	20.5
Central American, ex. Mexican	23	5.3
Mexican	1,427	20.3

Households with Food Stamps/SNAP Benefits During Past 12 Months

Group	Number	%
Total Population	710	3.8
Hispanic or Latino (of any race)	479	5.9
Central American, ex. Mexican	54	12.4
Mexican	400	5.7

Poverty Rate
(Income in Past 12 Months Below Poverty Level)

Group	%
Total Population	10.8
Hispanic or Latino (of any race)	15.0
Central American, ex. Mexican	16.9
Mexican	15.4

La Mesa

Population

Group	Number	%TP[1]	%HP[2]
Total Population	57,065	100.0	–
Hispanic or Latino (of any race)	11,696	20.5	100.0
Central American, ex. Mexican	339	0.6	2.9
Cuban	124	0.2	1.1
Mexican	9,496	16.6	81.2
Puerto Rican	402	0.7	3.4
South American	349	0.6	3.0
Colombian	114	0.2	1.0
Peruvian	108	0.2	0.9
Spaniard	275	0.5	2.4

Population Growth: 2000–2010

Group	%
Total Population	4.2
Hispanic or Latino (of any race)	58.0
Central American, ex. Mexican	130.6
Mexican	68.5
Puerto Rican	51.1
South American	88.6
Puerto Rican	88.7
South American	91.8
Colombian	100.0
Peruvian	66.2
Spaniard	95.0

Males per 100 Females

Group	Number
Total Population	90.8
Hispanic or Latino (of any race)	89.8
Central American, ex. Mexican	80.3
Cuban	125.5
Mexican	90.2
Puerto Rican	88.7
South American	91.8
Colombian	100.0
Peruvian	66.2
Spaniard	95.0

Average Household Size

Group	People
Total Population	2.30
Hispanic or Latino (of any race)	2.85
Central American, ex. Mexican	2.85
Cuban	2.42
Mexican	2.92
Puerto Rican	2.38
South American	2.52
Colombian	2.94
Peruvian	2.69
Spaniard	2.74

Median Age

Group	Years
Total Population	37.1
Hispanic or Latino (of any race)	27.5
Central American, ex. Mexican	28.1
Cuban	24.8
Mexican	27.2
Puerto Rican	26.3
South American	32.7
Colombian	30.0
Peruvian	35.0
Spaniard	33.7

High School Graduates
(Universe: Population 25 Years and Over)

Group	Number	%
Total Population	35,480	91.0
Hispanic or Latino (of any race)	4,046	75.8
Mexican	3,337	73.7

Four-Year College Graduates
(Universe: Population 25 Years and Over)

Group	Number	%
Total Population	12,765	32.8
Hispanic or Latino (of any race)	1,157	21.7
Mexican	923	20.4

Population Age 3–17 Enrolled in Public School
(Universe: Population Age 3–17 Enrolled in School)

Group	Number	%
Total Population	6,522	85.7
Hispanic or Latino (of any race)	1,870	91.0
Mexican	1,718	90.3

Population Age 3–17 Enrolled in Private School
(Universe: Population Age 3–17 Enrolled in School)

Group	Number	%
Total Population	1,090	14.3
Hispanic or Latino (of any race)	184	9.0
Mexican	184	9.7

Foreign-Born Population

Group	Number	%
Total Population	7,618	13.5
Hispanic or Latino (of any race)	2,304	23.7
Mexican	1,969	23.5

Foreign-Born Naturalized U.S. Citizens

Group	Number	%
Total Population	4,006	52.6
Hispanic or Latino (of any race)	1,161	50.4
Mexican	912	46.3

Language Spoken at Home: English Only
(Universe: Population 5 Years and Over)

Group	Number	%
Total Population	42,576	80.9
Hispanic or Latino (of any race)	4,163	47.0
Mexican	3,510	46.2

Language Spoken at Home: Spanish
(Universe: Population 5 Years and Over)

Group	Number	%
Total Population	5,266	10.0
Hispanic or Latino (of any race)	4,680	52.8
Mexican	4,083	53.8

Unemployment Rate
(Universe: Population 16 Years and Over)

Group	%
Total Population	8.7
Hispanic or Latino (of any race)	12.2
Mexican	11.2

Class of Worker: Private Wage and Salary
(Universe: Civilian Employed Population 16 Years and Over)

Group	Number	%
Total Population	20,448	73.7
Hispanic or Latino (of any race)	3,573	74.9
Mexican	3,019	74.6

Class of Worker: Government
(Universe: Civilian Employed Population 16 Years and Over)

Group	Number	%
Total Population	5,213	18.8
Hispanic or Latino (of any race)	961	20.1
Mexican	800	19.8

Means of Transportation to Work: Car, Truck or Van
(Universe: Workers 16 Years and Over)

Group	Number	%
Total Population	24,768	87.9
Hispanic or Latino (of any race)	4,111	87.3
Mexican	3,485	86.7

Means of Transportation to Work: Public Transportation (ex. Taxicab)
(Universe: Workers 16 Years and Over)

Group	Number	%
Total Population	1,030	3.7
Hispanic or Latino (of any race)	300	6.4
Mexican	246	6.1

Homeownership Rate
(Universe: Occupied Housing Units)

Group	%
Total Population	45.8
Hispanic or Latino (of any race)	31.2
Central American, ex. Mexican	29.0
Cuban	34.9
Mexican	31.0
Puerto Rican	19.8
South American	47.6
Colombian	61.8
Peruvian	37.1
Spaniard	56.2

Median Home Value

Group	Dollars
Total Population	437,000
Hispanic or Latino (of any race)	443,600
Mexican	441,600

Median Gross Rent

Group	Dollars
Total Population	1,137
Hispanic or Latino (of any race)	1,103
Mexican	1,072

Median Household Income
(2010 Inflation-Adjusted Dollars)

Group	Dollars
Total Population	52,932
Hispanic or Latino (of any race)	48,778
Mexican	51,964

Per Capita Income
(2010 Inflation-Adjusted Dollars)

Group	Dollars
Total Population	29,255
Hispanic or Latino (of any race)	21,094
Mexican	21,139

Households with $100,000+ Income

Group	Number	%
Total Population	4,516	18.7
Hispanic or Latino (of any race)	522	16.4
Mexican	411	16.4

Notes: (1) Percent of total population; (2) Percent of Hispanic/Latino population; Profiles include places with an overall population of at least 125,000, OR an overall population of at least 25,000 where the Hispanic/Latino population is at least 20% of the overall population. In states where less than five places meet either of these criteria, we have included places with at least 10,000 total population with the highest percentage of Hispanic/Latino population. These places are identified with an asterisk (*); Please refer to the User's Guide for a full explanation of data.

Households with Food Stamps/SNAP Benefits During Past 12 Months

Group	Number	%
Total Population	994	4.1
Hispanic or Latino (of any race)	286	9.0
Mexican	271	10.8

Poverty Rate
(Income in Past 12 Months Below Poverty Level)

Group	%
Total Population	11.7
Hispanic or Latino (of any race)	14.4
Mexican	13.4

La Mirada

Population

Group	Number	%TP[1]	%HP[2]
Total Population	48,527	100.0	–
Hispanic or Latino (of any race)	19,272	39.7	100.0
Central American, ex. Mexican	1,067	2.2	5.5
Guatemalan	258	0.5	1.3
Nicaraguan	153	0.3	0.8
Salvadoran	498	1.0	2.6
Cuban	352	0.7	1.8
Mexican	15,796	32.6	82.0
Puerto Rican	321	0.7	1.7
South American	635	1.3	3.3
Colombian	133	0.3	0.7
Ecuadorian	119	0.2	0.6
Peruvian	204	0.4	1.1
Spaniard	249	0.5	1.3

Population Growth: 2000–2010

Group	%
Total Population	3.7
Hispanic or Latino (of any race)	23.1
Central American, ex. Mexican	99.8
Guatemalan	75.5
Salvadoran	136.0
Cuban	27.1
Mexican	32.2
Puerto Rican	43.9
South American	54.1
Peruvian	59.4

Males per 100 Females

Group	Number
Total Population	92.2
Hispanic or Latino (of any race)	92.8
Central American, ex. Mexican	87.5
Guatemalan	91.1
Nicaraguan	86.6
Salvadoran	88.6
Cuban	101.1
Mexican	93.6
Puerto Rican	73.5
South American	90.1
Colombian	68.4
Ecuadorian	105.2
Peruvian	98.1
Spaniard	91.5

Average Household Size

Group	People
Total Population	3.11
Hispanic or Latino (of any race)	3.81
Central American, ex. Mexican	4.08
Guatemalan	4.16
Nicaraguan	4.23
Salvadoran	4.22
Cuban	3.49
Mexican	3.88
Puerto Rican	3.26
South American	3.47
Colombian	3.06
Ecuadorian	4.43
Peruvian	3.73
Spaniard	2.91

Median Age

Group	Years
Total Population	37.9
Hispanic or Latino (of any race)	31.7
Central American, ex. Mexican	35.7
Guatemalan	35.4
Nicaraguan	38.3
Salvadoran	33.8
Cuban	42.0
Mexican	30.8
Puerto Rican	34.2
South American	40.5
Colombian	39.2
Ecuadorian	32.3
Peruvian	41.7
Spaniard	39.1

High School Graduates
(Universe: Population 25 Years and Over)

Group	Number	%
Total Population	26,095	86.4
Hispanic or Latino (of any race)	8,110	74.4
Central American, ex. Mexican	494	79.4
Mexican	6,588	72.2

Four-Year College Graduates
(Universe: Population 25 Years and Over)

Group	Number	%
Total Population	8,299	27.5
Hispanic or Latino (of any race)	1,729	15.9
Central American, ex. Mexican	155	24.9
Mexican	1,299	14.2

Population Age 3–17 Enrolled in Public School
(Universe: Population Age 3–17 Enrolled in School)

Group	Number	%
Total Population	7,598	84.2
Hispanic or Latino (of any race)	3,966	84.6
Central American, ex. Mexican	113	73.4
Mexican	3,460	85.8

Population Age 3–17 Enrolled in Private School
(Universe: Population Age 3–17 Enrolled in School)

Group	Number	%
Total Population	1,428	15.8
Hispanic or Latino (of any race)	724	15.4
Central American, ex. Mexican	41	26.6
Mexican	572	14.2

Foreign-Born Population

Group	Number	%
Total Population	10,946	22.7
Hispanic or Latino (of any race)	4,898	25.5
Central American, ex. Mexican	609	62.5
Mexican	3,832	23.8

Foreign-Born Naturalized U.S. Citizens

Group	Number	%
Total Population	7,082	64.7
Hispanic or Latino (of any race)	2,808	57.3
Central American, ex. Mexican	361	59.3
Mexican	2,078	54.2

Language Spoken at Home: English Only
(Universe: Population 5 Years and Over)

Group	Number	%
Total Population	27,931	61.1
Hispanic or Latino (of any race)	7,675	42.5
Central American, ex. Mexican	135	14.6
Mexican	6,479	42.9

Language Spoken at Home: Spanish
(Universe: Population 5 Years and Over)

Group	Number	%
Total Population	10,807	23.7
Hispanic or Latino (of any race)	10,351	57.3
Central American, ex. Mexican	774	83.9
Mexican	8,623	57.1

Unemployment Rate
(Universe: Population 16 Years and Over)

Group	%
Total Population	7.2
Hispanic or Latino (of any race)	7.1
Central American, ex. Mexican	7.2
Mexican	7.2

Class of Worker: Private Wage and Salary
(Universe: Civilian Employed Population 16 Years and Over)

Group	Number	%
Total Population	17,017	77.8
Hispanic or Latino (of any race)	6,098	76.7
Central American, ex. Mexican	231	52.9
Mexican	5,086	76.5

Class of Worker: Government
(Universe: Civilian Employed Population 16 Years and Over)

Group	Number	%
Total Population	3,215	14.7
Hispanic or Latino (of any race)	1,308	16.4
Central American, ex. Mexican	131	30.0
Mexican	1,101	16.6

Means of Transportation to Work: Car, Truck or Van
(Universe: Workers 16 Years and Over)

Group	Number	%
Total Population	19,144	90.5
Hispanic or Latino (of any race)	7,267	92.8
Central American, ex. Mexican	419	95.9
Mexican	6,043	92.6

Means of Transportation to Work: Public Transportation (ex. Taxicab)
(Universe: Workers 16 Years and Over)

Group	Number	%
Total Population	434	2.1
Hispanic or Latino (of any race)	130	1.7
Central American, ex. Mexican	10	2.3
Mexican	120	1.8

Homeownership Rate
(Universe: Occupied Housing Units)

Group	%
Total Population	79.1
Hispanic or Latino (of any race)	78.5
Central American, ex. Mexican	76.5
Guatemalan	77.9
Nicaraguan	82.1
Salvadoran	74.3
Cuban	68.3
Mexican	79.7
Puerto Rican	68.3
South American	76.3
Colombian	81.8
Ecuadorian	80.0
Peruvian	74.2
Spaniard	77.4

Median Home Value

Group	Dollars
Total Population	508,100
Hispanic or Latino (of any race)	520,200
Central American, ex. Mexican	504,300
Mexican	517,900

Median Gross Rent

Group	Dollars
Total Population	1,338
Hispanic or Latino (of any race)	1,360
Central American, ex. Mexican	1,500
Mexican	1,302

Median Household Income
(2010 Inflation-Adjusted Dollars)

Group	Dollars
Total Population	79,347
Hispanic or Latino (of any race)	75,304
Central American, ex. Mexican	120,272
Mexican	74,682

Per Capita Income
(2010 Inflation-Adjusted Dollars)

Group	Dollars
Total Population	28,367
Hispanic or Latino (of any race)	21,101
Central American, ex. Mexican	28,925
Mexican	20,436

Households with $100,000+ Income

Group	Number	%
Total Population	5,439	37.6

Notes: (1) Percent of total population; (2) Percent of Hispanic/Latino population; Profiles include places with an overall population of at least 125,000, OR an overall population of at least 25,000 where the Hispanic/Latino population is at least 20% of the overall population. In states where less than five places meet either of these criteria, we have included places with at least 10,000 total population with the highest percentage of Hispanic/Latino population. These places are identified with an asterisk (*); Please refer to the User's Guide for a full explanation of data.

Group	Number	%
Hispanic or Latino (of any race)	1,683	35.7
Central American, ex. Mexican	146	58.2
Mexican	1,306	33.9

Households with Food Stamps/SNAP Benefits During Past 12 Months

Group	Number	%
Total Population	365	2.5
Hispanic or Latino (of any race)	209	4.4
Central American, ex. Mexican	8	3.2
Mexican	160	4.2

Poverty Rate
(Income in Past 12 Months Below Poverty Level)

Group	%
Total Population	5.2
Hispanic or Latino (of any race)	5.5
Central American, ex. Mexican	4.8
Mexican	5.0

La Presa

Population

Group	Number	%TP[1]	%HP[2]
Total Population	34,169	100.0	–
Hispanic or Latino (of any race)	16,150	47.3	100.0
Central American, ex. Mexican	253	0.7	1.6
Mexican	14,443	42.3	89.4
Puerto Rican	314	0.9	1.9
South American	151	0.4	0.9

Population Growth: 2000–2010

Group	%
Total Population	4.4
Hispanic or Latino (of any race)	49.4
Central American, ex. Mexican	93.1
Mexican	58.2
Puerto Rican	11.3

Males per 100 Females

Group	Number
Total Population	95.9
Hispanic or Latino (of any race)	95.1
Central American, ex. Mexican	88.8
Mexican	95.0
Puerto Rican	124.3
South American	79.8

Average Household Size

Group	People
Total Population	3.33
Hispanic or Latino (of any race)	4.11
Central American, ex. Mexican	3.79
Mexican	4.17
Puerto Rican	3.48
South American	3.72

Median Age

Group	Years
Total Population	32.7
Hispanic or Latino (of any race)	26.1
Central American, ex. Mexican	30.8
Mexican	25.9
Puerto Rican	30.0
South American	33.1

High School Graduates
(Universe: Population 25 Years and Over)

Group	Number	%
Total Population	16,185	77.7
Hispanic or Latino (of any race)	5,000	60.9
Mexican	4,393	58.4

Four-Year College Graduates
(Universe: Population 25 Years and Over)

Group	Number	%
Total Population	3,669	17.6
Hispanic or Latino (of any race)	720	8.8
Mexican	514	6.8

Population Age 3–17 Enrolled in Public School
(Universe: Population Age 3–17 Enrolled in School)

Group	Number	%
Total Population	6,960	92.2
Hispanic or Latino (of any race)	4,394	92.7
Mexican	4,240	94.3

Population Age 3–17 Enrolled in Private School
(Universe: Population Age 3–17 Enrolled in School)

Group	Number	%
Total Population	585	7.8
Hispanic or Latino (of any race)	348	7.3
Mexican	256	5.7

Foreign-Born Population

Group	Number	%
Total Population	9,240	26.5
Hispanic or Latino (of any race)	5,766	35.1
Mexican	5,309	34.7

Foreign-Born Naturalized U.S. Citizens

Group	Number	%
Total Population	5,009	54.2
Hispanic or Latino (of any race)	2,455	42.6
Mexican	2,240	42.2

Language Spoken at Home: English Only
(Universe: Population 5 Years and Over)

Group	Number	%
Total Population	18,779	58.1
Hispanic or Latino (of any race)	5,030	33.8
Mexican	4,687	33.7

Language Spoken at Home: Spanish
(Universe: Population 5 Years and Over)

Group	Number	%
Total Population	10,142	31.4
Hispanic or Latino (of any race)	9,822	66.1
Mexican	9,192	66.2

Unemployment Rate
(Universe: Population 16 Years and Over)

Group	%
Total Population	12.6
Hispanic or Latino (of any race)	9.8
Mexican	10.0

Class of Worker: Private Wage and Salary
(Universe: Civilian Employed Population 16 Years and Over)

Group	Number	%
Total Population	11,482	76.7
Hispanic or Latino (of any race)	5,117	81.1
Mexican	4,790	82.4

Class of Worker: Government
(Universe: Civilian Employed Population 16 Years and Over)

Group	Number	%
Total Population	2,684	17.9
Hispanic or Latino (of any race)	771	12.2
Mexican	639	11.0

Means of Transportation to Work: Car, Truck or Van
(Universe: Workers 16 Years and Over)

Group	Number	%
Total Population	13,631	90.8
Hispanic or Latino (of any race)	5,605	88.9
Mexican	5,117	88.2

Means of Transportation to Work: Public Transportation (ex. Taxicab)
(Universe: Workers 16 Years and Over)

Group	Number	%
Total Population	371	2.5
Hispanic or Latino (of any race)	204	3.2
Mexican	196	3.4

Homeownership Rate
(Universe: Occupied Housing Units)

Group	%
Total Population	62.3
Hispanic or Latino (of any race)	57.4
Central American, ex. Mexican	58.5
Mexican	57.5
Puerto Rican	55.4
South American	79.3

Median Home Value

Group	Dollars
Total Population	373,300
Hispanic or Latino (of any race)	369,500
Mexican	361,900

Median Gross Rent

Group	Dollars
Total Population	1,129
Hispanic or Latino (of any race)	1,045
Mexican	1,029

Median Household Income
(2010 Inflation-Adjusted Dollars)

Group	Dollars
Total Population	59,946
Hispanic or Latino (of any race)	50,441
Mexican	49,915

Per Capita Income
(2010 Inflation-Adjusted Dollars)

Group	Dollars
Total Population	22,195
Hispanic or Latino (of any race)	15,763
Mexican	15,384

Households with $100,000+ Income

Group	Number	%
Total Population	2,239	21.2
Hispanic or Latino (of any race)	612	15.9
Mexican	554	16.0

Households with Food Stamps/SNAP Benefits During Past 12 Months

Group	Number	%
Total Population	662	6.3
Hispanic or Latino (of any race)	414	10.8
Mexican	378	10.9

Poverty Rate
(Income in Past 12 Months Below Poverty Level)

Group	%
Total Population	13.9
Hispanic or Latino (of any race)	21.1
Mexican	22.3

La Puente

Population

Group	Number	%TP[1]	%HP[2]
Total Population	39,816	100.0	–
Hispanic or Latino (of any race)	33,896	85.1	100.0
Central American, ex. Mexican	2,362	5.9	7.0
Guatemalan	683	1.7	2.0
Nicaraguan	250	0.6	0.7
Salvadoran	1,292	3.2	3.8
Mexican	29,607	74.4	87.3
Puerto Rican	167	0.4	0.5
South American	358	0.9	1.1
Ecuadorian	107	0.3	0.3
Spaniard	116	0.3	0.3

Population Growth: 2000–2010

Group	%
Total Population	-3.0
Hispanic or Latino (of any race)	-0.7
Central American, ex. Mexican	61.1
Guatemalan	145.7
Nicaraguan	60.3
Salvadoran	63.5
Mexican	5.3
Puerto Rican	-23.0
South American	46.7

Males per 100 Females

Group	Number
Total Population	99.7
Hispanic or Latino (of any race)	100.7
Central American, ex. Mexican	96.7
Guatemalan	125.4
Nicaraguan	70.1
Salvadoran	89.7
Mexican	101.0
Puerto Rican	131.9
South American	87.4
Ecuadorian	81.4
Spaniard	93.3

Notes: (1) Percent of total population; (2) Percent of Hispanic/Latino population; Profiles include places with an overall population of at least 125,000, OR an overall population of at least 25,000 where the Hispanic/Latino population is at least 20% of the overall population. In states where less than five places meet either of these criteria, we have included places with at least 10,000 total population with the highest percentage of Hispanic/Latino population. These places are identified with an asterisk (*); Please refer to the User's Guide for a full explanation of data.

Average Household Size	
Group	People
Total Population	4.21
Hispanic or Latino (of any race)	4.56
Central American, ex. Mexican	4.56
Guatemalan	4.86
Nicaraguan	3.84
Salvadoran	4.61
Mexican	4.62
Puerto Rican	3.58
South American	3.74
Ecuadorian	4.34
Spaniard	3.28

Median Age	
Group	Years
Total Population	31.5
Hispanic or Latino (of any race)	29.5
Central American, ex. Mexican	34.9
Guatemalan	31.5
Nicaraguan	42.0
Salvadoran	35.9
Mexican	28.9
Puerto Rican	31.6
South American	43.3
Ecuadorian	47.5
Spaniard	47.0

High School Graduates (Universe: Population 25 Years and Over)		
Group	Number	%
Total Population	12,893	56.0
Hispanic or Latino (of any race)	10,127	52.7
Central American, ex. Mexican	1,094	54.4
Guatemalan	218	32.4
Salvadoran	580	64.6
Mexican	8,276	50.8

Four-Year College Graduates (Universe: Population 25 Years and Over)		
Group	Number	%
Total Population	2,373	10.3
Hispanic or Latino (of any race)	1,411	7.3
Central American, ex. Mexican	335	16.7
Guatemalan	12	1.8
Salvadoran	167	18.6
Mexican	979	6.0

Population Age 3–17 Enrolled in Public School (Universe: Population Age 3–17 Enrolled in School)		
Group	Number	%
Total Population	9,605	96.3
Hispanic or Latino (of any race)	8,966	97.8
Central American, ex. Mexican	711	98.6
Guatemalan	173	100.0
Salvadoran	366	97.3
Mexican	7,996	97.9

Population Age 3–17 Enrolled in Private School (Universe: Population Age 3–17 Enrolled in School)		
Group	Number	%
Total Population	367	3.7
Hispanic or Latino (of any race)	199	2.2
Central American, ex. Mexican	10	1.4
Guatemalan	0	0.0
Salvadoran	10	2.7
Mexican	168	2.1

Foreign-Born Population		
Group	Number	%
Total Population	16,851	42.0
Hispanic or Latino (of any race)	14,491	41.7
Central American, ex. Mexican	2,245	68.1
Guatemalan	922	79.3
Salvadoran	790	58.0
Mexican	11,886	39.6

Foreign-Born Naturalized U.S. Citizens		
Group	Number	%
Total Population	6,370	37.8
Hispanic or Latino (of any race)	4,825	33.3
Central American, ex. Mexican	1,072	47.8
Guatemalan	160	17.4
Salvadoran	551	69.7
Mexican	3,489	29.4

Language Spoken at Home: English Only (Universe: Population 5 Years and Over)		
Group	Number	%
Total Population	8,994	24.3
Hispanic or Latino (of any race)	6,923	21.6
Central American, ex. Mexican	254	8.3
Guatemalan	240	22.0
Salvadoran	14	1.1
Mexican	6,072	22.0

Language Spoken at Home: Spanish (Universe: Population 5 Years and Over)		
Group	Number	%
Total Population	25,557	68.9
Hispanic or Latino (of any race)	25,058	78.3
Central American, ex. Mexican	2,820	91.7
Guatemalan	853	78.0
Salvadoran	1,244	98.9
Mexican	21,469	77.9

Unemployment Rate (Universe: Population 16 Years and Over)	
Group	%
Total Population	7.8
Hispanic or Latino (of any race)	7.5
Central American, ex. Mexican	5.4
Guatemalan	3.1
Salvadoran	8.6
Mexican	7.5

Class of Worker: Private Wage and Salary (Universe: Civilian Employed Population 16 Years and Over)		
Group	Number	%
Total Population	14,432	82.7
Hispanic or Latino (of any race)	12,733	84.0
Central American, ex. Mexican	1,187	75.6
Guatemalan	433	67.0
Salvadoran	530	80.3
Mexican	11,138	85.3

Class of Worker: Government (Universe: Civilian Employed Population 16 Years and Over)		
Group	Number	%
Total Population	1,693	9.7
Hispanic or Latino (of any race)	1,371	9.0
Central American, ex. Mexican	185	11.8
Guatemalan	60	9.3
Salvadoran	95	14.4
Mexican	1,114	8.5

Means of Transportation to Work: Car, Truck or Van (Universe: Workers 16 Years and Over)		
Group	Number	%
Total Population	15,469	90.1
Hispanic or Latino (of any race)	13,285	89.4
Central American, ex. Mexican	1,378	90.7
Guatemalan	523	81.0
Salvadoran	590	97.0
Mexican	11,403	88.9

Means of Transportation to Work: Public Transportation (ex. Taxicab) (Universe: Workers 16 Years and Over)		
Group	Number	%
Total Population	450	2.6
Hispanic or Latino (of any race)	408	2.7
Central American, ex. Mexican	36	2.4
Guatemalan	36	5.6
Salvadoran	0	0.0
Mexican	361	2.8

Homeownership Rate (Universe: Occupied Housing Units)	
Group	%
Total Population	60.2
Hispanic or Latino (of any race)	59.9
Central American, ex. Mexican	59.2
Guatemalan	52.5
Nicaraguan	59.7
Salvadoran	63.9
Mexican	60.2
Puerto Rican	57.8
South American	58.9
Ecuadorian	77.1
Spaniard	76.1

Median Home Value	
Group	Dollars
Total Population	372,300
Hispanic or Latino (of any race)	373,000
Central American, ex. Mexican	435,900
Guatemalan	406,300
Salvadoran	437,000
Mexican	363,700

Median Gross Rent	
Group	Dollars
Total Population	1,057
Hispanic or Latino (of any race)	1,060
Central American, ex. Mexican	883
Guatemalan	1,260
Salvadoran	548
Mexican	1,060

Median Household Income (2010 Inflation-Adjusted Dollars)	
Group	Dollars
Total Population	51,023
Hispanic or Latino (of any race)	50,782
Central American, ex. Mexican	50,721
Guatemalan	49,375
Salvadoran	47,115
Mexican	50,753

Per Capita Income (2010 Inflation-Adjusted Dollars)	
Group	Dollars
Total Population	15,006
Hispanic or Latino (of any race)	13,902
Central American, ex. Mexican	15,433
Guatemalan	13,067
Salvadoran	17,984
Mexican	13,714

Households with $100,000+ Income		
Group	Number	%
Total Population	1,326	14.0
Hispanic or Latino (of any race)	956	12.3
Central American, ex. Mexican	111	15.4
Guatemalan	38	15.2
Salvadoran	59	19.5
Mexican	761	11.4

Households with Food Stamps/SNAP Benefits During Past 12 Months		
Group	Number	%
Total Population	662	7.0
Hispanic or Latino (of any race)	633	8.1
Central American, ex. Mexican	46	6.4
Guatemalan	0	0.0
Salvadoran	0	0.0
Mexican	565	8.5

Poverty Rate (Income in Past 12 Months Below Poverty Level)	
Group	%
Total Population	12.0
Hispanic or Latino (of any race)	12.2
Central American, ex. Mexican	9.3
Guatemalan	12.7
Salvadoran	6.0
Mexican	12.4

La Quinta

Population			
Group	Number	%TP[1]	%HP[2]
Total Population	37,467	100.0	–
Hispanic or Latino (of any race)	11,339	30.3	100.0
Central American, ex. Mexican	244	0.7	2.2
Salvadoran	134	0.4	1.2
Mexican	10,122	27.0	89.3
Puerto Rican	134	0.4	1.2
South American	195	0.5	1.7
Spaniard	132	0.4	1.2

Notes: (1) Percent of total population; (2) Percent of Hispanic/Latino population; Profiles include places with an overall population of at least 125,000, OR an overall population of at least 25,000 where the Hispanic/Latino population is at least 20% of the overall population. In states where less than five places meet either of these criteria, we have included places with at least 10,000 total population with the highest percentage of Hispanic/Latino population. These places are identified with an asterisk (*); Please refer to the User's Guide for a full explanation of data.

Population Growth: 2000–2010	
Group	%
Total Population	58.1
Hispanic or Latino (of any race)	49.5
Mexican	56.3

Males per 100 Females	
Group	Number
Total Population	93.5
Hispanic or Latino (of any race)	94.9
Central American, ex. Mexican	82.1
Salvadoran	88.7
Mexican	95.7
Puerto Rican	83.6
South American	95.0
Spaniard	112.9

Average Household Size	
Group	People
Total Population	2.52
Hispanic or Latino (of any race)	3.61
Central American, ex. Mexican	4.04
Salvadoran	3.71
Mexican	3.68
Puerto Rican	2.50
South American	2.92
Spaniard	2.49

Median Age	
Group	Years
Total Population	45.6
Hispanic or Latino (of any race)	27.0
Central American, ex. Mexican	27.9
Salvadoran	29.0
Mexican	26.8
Puerto Rican	33.3
South American	32.5
Spaniard	42.0

High School Graduates (Universe: Population 25 Years and Over)		
Group	Number	%
Total Population	22,712	90.7
Hispanic or Latino (of any race)	3,985	70.3
Mexican	3,291	66.9

Four-Year College Graduates (Universe: Population 25 Years and Over)		
Group	Number	%
Total Population	8,452	33.8
Hispanic or Latino (of any race)	675	11.9
Mexican	495	10.1

Population Age 3–17 Enrolled in Public School (Universe: Population Age 3–17 Enrolled in School)		
Group	Number	%
Total Population	5,599	79.3
Hispanic or Latino (of any race)	2,758	89.1
Mexican	2,573	88.4

Population Age 3–17 Enrolled in Private School (Universe: Population Age 3–17 Enrolled in School)		
Group	Number	%
Total Population	1,459	20.7
Hispanic or Latino (of any race)	337	10.9
Mexican	337	11.6

Foreign-Born Population		
Group	Number	%
Total Population	5,334	15.0
Hispanic or Latino (of any race)	3,292	30.7
Mexican	2,929	30.2

Foreign-Born Naturalized U.S. Citizens		
Group	Number	%
Total Population	2,972	55.7
Hispanic or Latino (of any race)	1,796	54.6
Mexican	1,569	53.6

Language Spoken at Home: English Only (Universe: Population 5 Years and Over)		
Group	Number	%
Total Population	25,344	74.8
Hispanic or Latino (of any race)	3,511	35.2
Mexican	3,032	33.7

Language Spoken at Home: Spanish (Universe: Population 5 Years and Over)		
Group	Number	%
Total Population	6,984	20.6
Hispanic or Latino (of any race)	6,431	64.5
Mexican	5,956	66.3

Unemployment Rate (Universe: Population 16 Years and Over)	
Group	%
Total Population	5.8
Hispanic or Latino (of any race)	7.7
Mexican	8.5

Class of Worker: Private Wage and Salary (Universe: Civilian Employed Population 16 Years and Over)		
Group	Number	%
Total Population	11,699	73.8
Hispanic or Latino (of any race)	3,513	76.3
Mexican	3,084	77.4

Class of Worker: Government (Universe: Civilian Employed Population 16 Years and Over)		
Group	Number	%
Total Population	2,022	12.8
Hispanic or Latino (of any race)	639	13.9
Mexican	551	13.8

Means of Transportation to Work: Car, Truck or Van (Universe: Workers 16 Years and Over)		
Group	Number	%
Total Population	13,319	87.2
Hispanic or Latino (of any race)	3,946	88.6
Mexican	3,461	89.9

Means of Transportation to Work: Public Transportation (ex. Taxicab) (Universe: Workers 16 Years and Over)		
Group	Number	%
Total Population	289	1.9
Hispanic or Latino (of any race)	152	3.4
Mexican	99	2.6

Homeownership Rate (Universe: Occupied Housing Units)	
Group	%
Total Population	75.2
Hispanic or Latino (of any race)	60.4
Central American, ex. Mexican	42.6
Salvadoran	42.1
Mexican	60.5
Puerto Rican	73.7
South American	64.2
Spaniard	70.9

Median Home Value	
Group	Dollars
Total Population	448,600
Hispanic or Latino (of any race)	324,800
Mexican	315,100

Median Gross Rent	
Group	Dollars
Total Population	1,412
Hispanic or Latino (of any race)	1,345
Mexican	1,303

Median Household Income (2010 Inflation-Adjusted Dollars)	
Group	Dollars
Total Population	75,358
Hispanic or Latino (of any race)	55,870
Mexican	55,145

Per Capita Income (2010 Inflation-Adjusted Dollars)	
Group	Dollars
Total Population	43,479
Hispanic or Latino (of any race)	19,541
Mexican	17,067

Households with $100,000+ Income		
Group	Number	%
Total Population	4,783	35.0
Hispanic or Latino (of any race)	539	19.1
Mexican	416	16.8

Households with Food Stamps/SNAP Benefits During Past 12 Months		
Group	Number	%
Total Population	234	1.7
Hispanic or Latino (of any race)	128	4.5
Mexican	119	4.8

Poverty Rate (Income in Past 12 Months Below Poverty Level)	
Group	%
Total Population	9.3
Hispanic or Latino (of any race)	13.4
Mexican	12.8

La Verne

Population			
Group	Number	%TP[1]	%HP[2]
Total Population	31,063	100.0	–
Hispanic or Latino (of any race)	9,635	31.0	100.0
Central American, ex. Mexican	519	1.7	5.4
Guatemalan	145	0.5	1.5
Nicaraguan	113	0.4	1.2
Salvadoran	178	0.6	1.8
Cuban	182	0.6	1.9
Mexican	7,627	24.6	79.2
Puerto Rican	180	0.6	1.9
South American	425	1.4	4.4
Argentinean	121	0.4	1.3
Spaniard	149	0.5	1.5

Population Growth: 2000–2010	
Group	%
Total Population	-1.8
Hispanic or Latino (of any race)	31.7
Central American, ex. Mexican	177.5
Cuban	25.5
Mexican	37.3
Puerto Rican	52.5
South American	76.3

Males per 100 Females	
Group	Number
Total Population	89.9
Hispanic or Latino (of any race)	89.2
Central American, ex. Mexican	90.8
Guatemalan	85.9
Nicaraguan	94.8
Salvadoran	79.8
Cuban	95.7
Mexican	90.0
Puerto Rican	91.5
South American	90.6
Argentinean	89.1
Spaniard	88.6

Average Household Size	
Group	People
Total Population	2.70
Hispanic or Latino (of any race)	3.20
Central American, ex. Mexican	3.67
Guatemalan	3.78
Nicaraguan	3.96
Salvadoran	3.73
Cuban	2.98
Mexican	3.25
Puerto Rican	2.51
South American	3.04
Argentinean	2.75
Spaniard	2.68

Median Age	
Group	Years
Total Population	42.9
Hispanic or Latino (of any race)	32.0
Central American, ex. Mexican	33.2
Guatemalan	34.3
Nicaraguan	33.3
Salvadoran	30.0
Cuban	42.5
Mexican	31.1
Puerto Rican	34.7

STATE & PLACE PROFILES

Notes: (1) Percent of total population; (2) Percent of Hispanic/Latino population; Profiles include places with an overall population of at least 125,000, OR an overall population of at least 25,000 where the Hispanic/Latino population is at least 20% of the overall population. In states where less than five places meet either of these criteria, we have included places with at least 10,000 total population with the highest percentage of Hispanic/Latino population. These places are identified with an asterisk (*); Please refer to the User's Guide for a full explanation of data.

South American	40.6
Argentinean	48.5
Spaniard	40.2

High School Graduates
(Universe: Population 25 Years and Over)

Group	Number	%
Total Population	19,349	91.9
Hispanic or Latino (of any race)	4,188	82.9
Mexican	3,123	83.1

Four-Year College Graduates
(Universe: Population 25 Years and Over)

Group	Number	%
Total Population	6,652	31.6
Hispanic or Latino (of any race)	877	17.4
Mexican	675	18.0

Population Age 3–17 Enrolled in Public School
(Universe: Population Age 3–17 Enrolled in School)

Group	Number	%
Total Population	4,789	79.4
Hispanic or Latino (of any race)	1,930	85.6
Mexican	1,486	87.0

Population Age 3–17 Enrolled in Private School
(Universe: Population Age 3–17 Enrolled in School)

Group	Number	%
Total Population	1,240	20.6
Hispanic or Latino (of any race)	324	14.4
Mexican	223	13.0

Foreign-Born Population

Group	Number	%
Total Population	3,832	12.3
Hispanic or Latino (of any race)	1,013	11.7
Mexican	591	9.1

Foreign-Born Naturalized U.S. Citizens

Group	Number	%
Total Population	2,503	65.3
Hispanic or Latino (of any race)	653	64.5
Mexican	366	61.9

Language Spoken at Home: English Only
(Universe: Population 5 Years and Over)

Group	Number	%
Total Population	23,065	77.8
Hispanic or Latino (of any race)	4,832	59.8
Mexican	3,580	59.8

Language Spoken at Home: Spanish
(Universe: Population 5 Years and Over)

Group	Number	%
Total Population	3,564	12.0
Hispanic or Latino (of any race)	3,162	39.1
Mexican	2,345	39.2

Unemployment Rate
(Universe: Population 16 Years and Over)

Group	%
Total Population	7.8
Hispanic or Latino (of any race)	9.0
Mexican	8.2

Class of Worker: Private Wage and Salary
(Universe: Civilian Employed Population 16 Years and Over)

Group	Number	%
Total Population	10,456	71.9
Hispanic or Latino (of any race)	2,888	73.5
Mexican	2,256	75.3

Class of Worker: Government
(Universe: Civilian Employed Population 16 Years and Over)

Group	Number	%
Total Population	2,751	18.9
Hispanic or Latino (of any race)	694	17.7
Mexican	527	17.6

Means of Transportation to Work: Car, Truck or Van
(Universe: Workers 16 Years and Over)

Group	Number	%
Total Population	12,788	90.0
Hispanic or Latino (of any race)	3,451	89.7
Mexican	2,607	89.5

Means of Transportation to Work: Public Transportation (ex. Taxicab)
(Universe: Workers 16 Years and Over)

Group	Number	%
Total Population	359	2.5
Hispanic or Latino (of any race)	68	1.8
Mexican	51	1.8

Homeownership Rate
(Universe: Occupied Housing Units)

Group	%
Total Population	74.5
Hispanic or Latino (of any race)	66.1
Central American, ex. Mexican	64.8
Guatemalan	62.5
Nicaraguan	70.4
Salvadoran	63.3
Cuban	66.1
Mexican	65.9
Puerto Rican	68.6
South American	73.2
Argentinean	72.7
Spaniard	77.4

Median Home Value

Group	Dollars
Total Population	512,400
Hispanic or Latino (of any race)	449,400
Mexican	452,200

Median Gross Rent

Group	Dollars
Total Population	1,171
Hispanic or Latino (of any race)	1,102
Mexican	1,104

Median Household Income
(2010 Inflation-Adjusted Dollars)

Group	Dollars
Total Population	77,227
Hispanic or Latino (of any race)	68,684
Mexican	67,150

Per Capita Income
(2010 Inflation-Adjusted Dollars)

Group	Dollars
Total Population	32,343
Hispanic or Latino (of any race)	21,956
Mexican	21,962

Households with $100,000+ Income

Group	Number	%
Total Population	3,848	35.1
Hispanic or Latino (of any race)	582	23.5
Mexican	409	22.2

Households with Food Stamps/SNAP Benefits During Past 12 Months

Group	Number	%
Total Population	179	1.6
Hispanic or Latino (of any race)	35	1.4
Mexican	35	1.9

Poverty Rate
(Income in Past 12 Months Below Poverty Level)

Group	%
Total Population	6.8
Hispanic or Latino (of any race)	4.3
Mexican	4.9

Laguna Hills

Population

Group	Number	%TP[1]	%HP[2]
Total Population	30,344	100.0	–
Hispanic or Latino (of any race)	6,242	20.6	100.0
Central American, ex. Mexican	292	1.0	4.7
Guatemalan	106	0.3	1.7
Salvadoran	114	0.4	1.8
Mexican	4,822	15.9	77.3
Puerto Rican	119	0.4	1.9
South American	487	1.6	7.8
Colombian	160	0.5	2.6
Peruvian	139	0.5	2.2

Population Growth: 2000–2010

Group	%
Total Population	-2.7
Hispanic or Latino (of any race)	22.1
Central American, ex. Mexican	51.3
Mexican	30.6
South American	73.3

Males per 100 Females

Group	Number
Total Population	95.5
Hispanic or Latino (of any race)	102.5
Central American, ex. Mexican	83.6
Guatemalan	107.8
Salvadoran	72.7
Mexican	107.3
Puerto Rican	77.6
South American	79.0
Colombian	73.9
Peruvian	82.9

Average Household Size

Group	People
Total Population	2.86
Hispanic or Latino (of any race)	4.04
Central American, ex. Mexican	4.29
Guatemalan	4.03
Salvadoran	5.21
Mexican	4.32
Puerto Rican	3.25
South American	3.38
Colombian	3.21
Peruvian	3.91

Median Age

Group	Years
Total Population	40.8
Hispanic or Latino (of any race)	29.2
Central American, ex. Mexican	33.1
Guatemalan	31.0
Salvadoran	32.5
Mexican	27.6
Puerto Rican	32.5
South American	41.2
Colombian	45.4
Peruvian	35.9

High School Graduates
(Universe: Population 25 Years and Over)

Group	Number	%
Total Population	18,789	91.4
Hispanic or Latino (of any race)	2,602	69.2
Mexican	1,974	65.7

Four-Year College Graduates
(Universe: Population 25 Years and Over)

Group	Number	%
Total Population	8,832	43.0
Hispanic or Latino (of any race)	584	15.5
Mexican	389	13.0

Population Age 3–17 Enrolled in Public School
(Universe: Population Age 3–17 Enrolled in School)

Group	Number	%
Total Population	4,314	81.6
Hispanic or Latino (of any race)	1,429	92.3
Mexican	1,322	94.1

Population Age 3–17 Enrolled in Private School
(Universe: Population Age 3–17 Enrolled in School)

Group	Number	%
Total Population	974	18.4
Hispanic or Latino (of any race)	119	7.7
Mexican	83	5.9

Foreign-Born Population

Group	Number	%
Total Population	7,390	24.3
Hispanic or Latino (of any race)	3,391	50.8
Mexican	2,803	49.6

Foreign-Born Naturalized U.S. Citizens

Group	Number	%
Total Population	3,575	48.4
Hispanic or Latino (of any race)	729	21.5

Notes: (1) Percent of total population; (2) Percent of Hispanic/Latino population; Profiles include places with an overall population of at least 125,000, OR an overall population of at least 25,000 where the Hispanic/Latino population is at least 20% of the overall population. In states where less than five places meet either of these criteria, we have included places with at least 10,000 total population with the highest percentage of Hispanic/Latino population. These places are identified with an asterisk (*); Please refer to the User's Guide for a full explanation of data.

Group	Number	%
Mexican	405	14.4

Language Spoken at Home: English Only
(Universe: Population 5 Years and Over)

Group	Number	%
Total Population	19,909	69.2
Hispanic or Latino (of any race)	1,576	25.9
Mexican	1,226	24.1

Language Spoken at Home: Spanish
(Universe: Population 5 Years and Over)

Group	Number	%
Total Population	5,033	17.5
Hispanic or Latino (of any race)	4,510	74.1
Mexican	3,859	75.9

Unemployment Rate
(Universe: Population 16 Years and Over)

Group	%
Total Population	7.5
Hispanic or Latino (of any race)	3.3
Mexican	3.6

Class of Worker: Private Wage and Salary
(Universe: Civilian Employed Population 16 Years and Over)

Group	Number	%
Total Population	12,529	79.8
Hispanic or Latino (of any race)	3,369	89.7
Mexican	2,821	92.0

Class of Worker: Government
(Universe: Civilian Employed Population 16 Years and Over)

Group	Number	%
Total Population	1,673	10.7
Hispanic or Latino (of any race)	145	3.9
Mexican	64	2.1

Means of Transportation to Work: Car, Truck or Van
(Universe: Workers 16 Years and Over)

Group	Number	%
Total Population	13,435	87.5
Hispanic or Latino (of any race)	3,230	86.8
Mexican	2,634	86.8

Means of Transportation to Work: Public Transportation (ex. Taxicab)
(Universe: Workers 16 Years and Over)

Group	Number	%
Total Population	393	2.6
Hispanic or Latino (of any race)	208	5.6
Mexican	208	6.9

Homeownership Rate
(Universe: Occupied Housing Units)

Group	%
Total Population	74.7
Hispanic or Latino (of any race)	54.4
Central American, ex. Mexican	46.8
Guatemalan	27.6
Salvadoran	51.7
Mexican	50.0
Puerto Rican	72.2
South American	73.8
Colombian	66.7
Peruvian	58.8

Median Home Value

Group	Dollars
Total Population	627,600
Hispanic or Latino (of any race)	455,600
Mexican	432,300

Median Gross Rent

Group	Dollars
Total Population	1,727
Hispanic or Latino (of any race)	1,607
Mexican	1,579

Median Household Income
(2010 Inflation-Adjusted Dollars)

Group	Dollars
Total Population	87,337
Hispanic or Latino (of any race)	62,133
Mexican	60,711

Per Capita Income
(2010 Inflation-Adjusted Dollars)

Group	Dollars
Total Population	47,542
Hispanic or Latino (of any race)	18,573
Mexican	15,922

Households with $100,000+ Income

Group	Number	%
Total Population	4,737	45.4
Hispanic or Latino (of any race)	532	36.0
Mexican	357	32.1

Households with Food Stamps/SNAP Benefits During Past 12 Months

Group	Number	%
Total Population	53	0.5
Hispanic or Latino (of any race)	23	1.6
Mexican	23	2.1

Poverty Rate
(Income in Past 12 Months Below Poverty Level)

Group	%
Total Population	8.5
Hispanic or Latino (of any race)	15.4
Mexican	17.9

Lake Elsinore

Population

Group	Number	%TP[1]	%HP[2]
Total Population	51,821	100.0	–
Hispanic or Latino (of any race)	25,073	48.4	100.0
Central American, ex. Mexican	1,935	3.7	7.7
Guatemalan	1,268	2.4	5.1
Salvadoran	433	0.8	1.7
Cuban	150	0.3	0.6
Mexican	20,497	39.6	81.7
Puerto Rican	319	0.6	1.3
South American	558	1.1	2.2
Argentinean	142	0.3	0.6
Colombian	136	0.3	0.5
Peruvian	130	0.3	0.5
Spaniard	210	0.4	0.8

Population Growth: 2000–2010

Group	%
Total Population	79.1
Hispanic or Latino (of any race)	127.8
Central American, ex. Mexican	336.8
Guatemalan	415.4
Mexican	138.8
Puerto Rican	73.4
South American	398.2

Males per 100 Females

Group	Number
Total Population	100.4
Hispanic or Latino (of any race)	101.9
Central American, ex. Mexican	111.7
Guatemalan	126.4
Salvadoran	91.6
Cuban	114.3
Mexican	101.2
Puerto Rican	101.9
South American	93.8
Argentinean	100.0
Colombian	76.6
Peruvian	103.1
Spaniard	100.0

Average Household Size

Group	People
Total Population	3.48
Hispanic or Latino (of any race)	4.28
Central American, ex. Mexican	4.62
Guatemalan	5.01
Salvadoran	4.20
Cuban	3.46
Mexican	4.34
Puerto Rican	3.44
South American	3.56
Argentinean	3.33
Colombian	3.57
Peruvian	3.76
Spaniard	3.52

Median Age

Group	Years
Total Population	29.8
Hispanic or Latino (of any race)	24.4
Central American, ex. Mexican	28.6
Guatemalan	27.6
Salvadoran	32.6
Cuban	32.0
Mexican	23.4
Puerto Rican	25.0
South American	36.3
Argentinean	37.6
Colombian	35.2
Peruvian	36.3
Spaniard	25.3

High School Graduates
(Universe: Population 25 Years and Over)

Group	Number	%
Total Population	21,602	80.2
Hispanic or Latino (of any race)	7,189	66.5
Central American, ex. Mexican	573	57.2
Guatemalan	226	41.1
Mexican	5,779	65.3

Four-Year College Graduates
(Universe: Population 25 Years and Over)

Group	Number	%
Total Population	4,783	17.8
Hispanic or Latino (of any race)	1,062	9.8
Central American, ex. Mexican	61	6.1
Guatemalan	11	2.0
Mexican	885	10.0

Population Age 3–17 Enrolled in Public School
(Universe: Population Age 3–17 Enrolled in School)

Group	Number	%
Total Population	11,712	94.3
Hispanic or Latino (of any race)	6,699	97.4
Central American, ex. Mexican	364	100.0
Guatemalan	160	100.0
Mexican	5,926	97.8

Population Age 3–17 Enrolled in Private School
(Universe: Population Age 3–17 Enrolled in School)

Group	Number	%
Total Population	706	5.7
Hispanic or Latino (of any race)	181	2.6
Central American, ex. Mexican	0	0.0
Guatemalan	0	0.0
Mexican	133	2.2

Foreign-Born Population

Group	Number	%
Total Population	10,213	21.0
Hispanic or Latino (of any race)	7,766	34.3
Central American, ex. Mexican	1,084	63.1
Guatemalan	642	67.8
Mexican	6,332	32.8

Foreign-Born Naturalized U.S. Citizens

Group	Number	%
Total Population	4,229	41.4
Hispanic or Latino (of any race)	2,848	36.7
Central American, ex. Mexican	403	37.2
Guatemalan	157	24.5
Mexican	2,203	34.8

Language Spoken at Home: English Only
(Universe: Population 5 Years and Over)

Group	Number	%
Total Population	27,316	61.7
Hispanic or Latino (of any race)	6,677	33.0
Central American, ex. Mexican	227	14.2
Guatemalan	62	7.0
Mexican	5,579	32.5

Language Spoken at Home: Spanish
(Universe: Population 5 Years and Over)

Group	Number	%
Total Population	14,486	32.7
Hispanic or Latino (of any race)	13,535	66.8
Central American, ex. Mexican	1,364	85.0

Notes: (1) Percent of total population; (2) Percent of Hispanic/Latino population; Profiles include places with an overall population of at least 125,000, OR an overall population of at least 25,000 where the Hispanic/Latino population is at least 20% of the overall population. In states where less than five places meet either of these criteria, we have included places with at least 10,000 total population with the highest percentage of Hispanic/Latino population. These places are identified with an asterisk (*); Please refer to the User's Guide for a full explanation of data.

Group	Number	%
Guatemalan	830	93.0
Mexican	11,535	67.3

Unemployment Rate
(Universe: Population 16 Years and Over)

Group	%
Total Population	10.9
Hispanic or Latino (of any race)	9.5
Central American, ex. Mexican	16.4
Guatemalan	10.1
Mexican	8.4

Class of Worker: Private Wage and Salary
(Universe: Civilian Employed Population 16 Years and Over)

Group	Number	%
Total Population	16,507	77.6
Hispanic or Latino (of any race)	7,235	78.7
Central American, ex. Mexican	686	83.3
Guatemalan	465	82.0
Mexican	6,006	78.7

Class of Worker: Government
(Universe: Civilian Employed Population 16 Years and Over)

Group	Number	%
Total Population	2,993	14.1
Hispanic or Latino (of any race)	983	10.7
Central American, ex. Mexican	27	3.3
Guatemalan	16	2.8
Mexican	850	11.1

Means of Transportation to Work: Car, Truck or Van
(Universe: Workers 16 Years and Over)

Group	Number	%
Total Population	18,732	91.3
Hispanic or Latino (of any race)	7,941	90.1
Central American, ex. Mexican	599	74.0
Guatemalan	355	64.3
Mexican	6,720	92.0

Means of Transportation to Work: Public Transportation (ex. Taxicab)
(Universe: Workers 16 Years and Over)

Group	Number	%
Total Population	170	0.8
Hispanic or Latino (of any race)	107	1.2
Central American, ex. Mexican	22	2.7
Guatemalan	9	1.6
Mexican	74	1.0

Homeownership Rate
(Universe: Occupied Housing Units)

Group	%
Total Population	66.0
Hispanic or Latino (of any race)	58.3
Central American, ex. Mexican	44.3
Guatemalan	26.6
Salvadoran	70.0
Cuban	75.6
Mexican	59.5
Puerto Rican	58.4
South American	76.2
Argentinean	83.7
Colombian	65.7
Peruvian	68.3
Spaniard	60.7

Median Home Value

Group	Dollars
Total Population	293,700
Hispanic or Latino (of any race)	282,500
Central American, ex. Mexican	233,300
Guatemalan	256,800
Mexican	292,800

Median Gross Rent

Group	Dollars
Total Population	1,149
Hispanic or Latino (of any race)	1,064
Central American, ex. Mexican	998
Guatemalan	998
Mexican	1,061

Median Household Income
(2010 Inflation-Adjusted Dollars)

Group	Dollars
Total Population	63,726
Hispanic or Latino (of any race)	52,870
Central American, ex. Mexican	41,538
Guatemalan	43,750
Mexican	52,758

Per Capita Income
(2010 Inflation-Adjusted Dollars)

Group	Dollars
Total Population	22,108
Hispanic or Latino (of any race)	14,123
Central American, ex. Mexican	16,128
Guatemalan	16,048
Mexican	13,377

Households with $100,000+ Income

Group	Number	%
Total Population	3,403	24.2
Hispanic or Latino (of any race)	760	14.1
Central American, ex. Mexican	79	15.6
Guatemalan	32	9.8
Mexican	556	12.5

Households with Food Stamps/SNAP Benefits During Past 12 Months

Group	Number	%
Total Population	632	4.5
Hispanic or Latino (of any race)	373	6.9
Central American, ex. Mexican	36	7.1
Guatemalan	10	3.1
Mexican	328	7.4

Poverty Rate
(Income in Past 12 Months Below Poverty Level)

Group	%
Total Population	12.4
Hispanic or Latino (of any race)	17.6
Central American, ex. Mexican	24.0
Guatemalan	25.2
Mexican	17.1

Lake Forest

Population

Group	Number	%TP[1]	%HP[2]
Total Population	77,264	100.0	–
Hispanic or Latino (of any race)	19,024	24.6	100.0
Central American, ex. Mexican	1,595	2.1	8.4
Guatemalan	855	1.1	4.5
Salvadoran	474	0.6	2.5
Cuban	200	0.3	1.1
Mexican	14,299	18.5	75.2
Puerto Rican	354	0.5	1.9
South American	1,430	1.9	7.5
Argentinean	261	0.3	1.4
Colombian	454	0.6	2.4
Ecuadorian	120	0.2	0.6
Peruvian	371	0.5	2.0
Spaniard	247	0.3	1.3

Population Growth: 2000–2010

Group	%
Total Population	31.6
Hispanic or Latino (of any race)	74.3
Central American, ex. Mexican	197.6
Guatemalan	270.1
Salvadoran	166.3
Cuban	35.1
Mexican	83.6
Puerto Rican	70.2
South American	132.1
Colombian	114.2

Males per 100 Females

Group	Number
Total Population	98.7
Hispanic or Latino (of any race)	100.1
Central American, ex. Mexican	101.4
Guatemalan	115.9
Salvadoran	116.4
Cuban	81.8
Mexican	101.8
Puerto Rican	102.3
South American	89.4
Argentinean	94.8
Colombian	94.8
Ecuadorian	93.5
Peruvian	81.0
Spaniard	85.7

Average Household Size

Group	People
Total Population	2.93
Hispanic or Latino (of any race)	4.12
Central American, ex. Mexican	4.99
Guatemalan	5.74
Salvadoran	4.68
Cuban	2.87
Mexican	4.27
Puerto Rican	2.70
South American	3.47
Argentinean	3.18
Colombian	3.45
Ecuadorian	3.39
Peruvian	3.62
Spaniard	2.84

Median Age

Group	Years
Total Population	37.2
Hispanic or Latino (of any race)	28.1
Central American, ex. Mexican	29.5
Guatemalan	27.6
Salvadoran	31.8
Cuban	33.0
Mexican	27.0
Puerto Rican	32.2
South American	37.8
Argentinean	37.4
Colombian	40.1
Ecuadorian	37.5
Peruvian	38.0
Spaniard	40.5

High School Graduates
(Universe: Population 25 Years and Over)

Group	Number	%
Total Population	47,568	92.3
Hispanic or Latino (of any race)	7,029	73.7
Central American, ex. Mexican	307	73.4
Mexican	5,253	69.8
South American	786	93.0

Four-Year College Graduates
(Universe: Population 25 Years and Over)

Group	Number	%
Total Population	21,601	41.9
Hispanic or Latino (of any race)	1,461	15.3
Central American, ex. Mexican	142	34.0
Mexican	834	11.1
South American	249	29.5

Population Age 3–17 Enrolled in Public School
(Universe: Population Age 3–17 Enrolled in School)

Group	Number	%
Total Population	12,996	84.1
Hispanic or Latino (of any race)	4,009	90.0
Central American, ex. Mexican	365	96.3
Mexican	3,066	91.4
South American	75	83.3

Population Age 3–17 Enrolled in Private School
(Universe: Population Age 3–17 Enrolled in School)

Group	Number	%
Total Population	2,461	15.9
Hispanic or Latino (of any race)	443	10.0
Central American, ex. Mexican	14	3.7
Mexican	287	8.6
South American	15	16.7

Foreign-Born Population

Group	Number	%
Total Population	17,825	23.2
Hispanic or Latino (of any race)	7,146	41.6
Central American, ex. Mexican	408	42.7
Mexican	5,501	41.1

Notes: (1) Percent of total population; (2) Percent of Hispanic/Latino population; Profiles include places with an overall population of at least 125,000, OR an overall population of at least 25,000 where the Hispanic/Latino population is at least 20% of the overall population. In states where less than five places meet either of these criteria, we have included places with at least 10,000 total population with the highest percentage of Hispanic/Latino population. These places are identified with an asterisk (*); Please refer to the User's Guide for a full explanation of data.

South American	894	79.6

Foreign-Born Naturalized U.S. Citizens

Group	Number	%
Total Population	8,953	50.2
Hispanic or Latino (of any race)	2,301	32.2
Central American, ex. Mexican	135	33.1
Mexican	1,531	27.8
South American	432	48.3

Language Spoken at Home: English Only
(Universe: Population 5 Years and Over)

Group	Number	%
Total Population	49,528	69.1
Hispanic or Latino (of any race)	4,226	27.0
Central American, ex. Mexican	221	26.6
Mexican	2,989	24.5
South American	138	12.9

Language Spoken at Home: Spanish
(Universe: Population 5 Years and Over)

Group	Number	%
Total Population	12,287	17.1
Hispanic or Latino (of any race)	11,245	71.8
Central American, ex. Mexican	611	73.4
Mexican	9,057	74.1
South American	918	85.9

Unemployment Rate
(Universe: Population 16 Years and Over)

Group	%
Total Population	5.6
Hispanic or Latino (of any race)	5.3
Central American, ex. Mexican	4.9
Mexican	5.8
South American	1.6

Class of Worker: Private Wage and Salary
(Universe: Civilian Employed Population 16 Years and Over)

Group	Number	%
Total Population	34,074	82.4
Hispanic or Latino (of any race)	7,452	86.9
Central American, ex. Mexican	355	96.7
Mexican	5,802	86.4
South American	638	87.5

Class of Worker: Government
(Universe: Civilian Employed Population 16 Years and Over)

Group	Number	%
Total Population	4,054	9.8
Hispanic or Latino (of any race)	553	6.4
Central American, ex. Mexican	12	3.3
Mexican	452	6.7
South American	21	2.9

Means of Transportation to Work: Car, Truck or Van
(Universe: Workers 16 Years and Over)

Group	Number	%
Total Population	36,766	91.1
Hispanic or Latino (of any race)	7,479	88.3
Central American, ex. Mexican	348	94.8
Mexican	5,789	87.5
South American	649	91.0

Means of Transportation to Work: Public Transportation (ex. Taxicab)
(Universe: Workers 16 Years and Over)

Group	Number	%
Total Population	457	1.1
Hispanic or Latino (of any race)	142	1.7
Central American, ex. Mexican	19	5.2
Mexican	123	1.9
South American	0	0.0

Homeownership Rate
(Universe: Occupied Housing Units)

Group	%
Total Population	70.8
Hispanic or Latino (of any race)	53.5
Central American, ex. Mexican	37.7
Guatemalan	27.5
Salvadoran	44.4
Cuban	70.5
Mexican	52.5
Puerto Rican	62.6
South American	63.2
Argentinean	71.9
Colombian	61.0
Ecuadorian	78.0
Peruvian	55.9
Spaniard	72.2

Median Home Value

Group	Dollars
Total Population	579,000
Hispanic or Latino (of any race)	516,600
Central American, ex. Mexican	446,200
Mexican	506,600
South American	470,500

Median Gross Rent

Group	Dollars
Total Population	1,664
Hispanic or Latino (of any race)	1,613
Central American, ex. Mexican	1,200
Mexican	1,612
South American	1,640

Median Household Income
(2010 Inflation-Adjusted Dollars)

Group	Dollars
Total Population	91,040
Hispanic or Latino (of any race)	71,808
Central American, ex. Mexican	88,669
Mexican	68,958
South American	71,809

Per Capita Income
(2010 Inflation-Adjusted Dollars)

Group	Dollars
Total Population	38,844
Hispanic or Latino (of any race)	21,813
Central American, ex. Mexican	18,533
Mexican	20,337
South American	34,515

Households with $100,000+ Income

Group	Number	%
Total Population	12,356	45.9
Hispanic or Latino (of any race)	1,268	32.8
Central American, ex. Mexican	86	42.0
Mexican	874	30.1
South American	92	27.2

Households with Food Stamps/SNAP Benefits During Past 12 Months

Group	Number	%
Total Population	456	1.7
Hispanic or Latino (of any race)	216	5.6
Central American, ex. Mexican	0	0.0
Mexican	204	7.0
South American	12	3.6

Poverty Rate
(Income in Past 12 Months Below Poverty Level)

Group	%
Total Population	5.3
Hispanic or Latino (of any race)	10.8
Central American, ex. Mexican	2.0
Mexican	13.0
South American	0.0

Lakewood

Population

Group	Number	%TP[1]	%HP[2]
Total Population	80,048	100.0	–
Hispanic or Latino (of any race)	24,101	30.1	100.0
Central American, ex. Mexican	1,566	2.0	6.5
Costa Rican	106	0.1	0.4
Guatemalan	394	0.5	1.6
Honduran	153	0.2	0.6
Nicaraguan	170	0.2	0.7
Salvadoran	662	0.8	2.7
Cuban	315	0.4	1.3
Mexican	19,252	24.1	79.9
Puerto Rican	537	0.7	2.2
South American	824	1.0	3.4
Argentinean	151	0.2	0.6
Colombian	193	0.2	0.8
Ecuadorian	136	0.2	0.6
Peruvian	227	0.3	0.9
Spaniard	367	0.5	1.5

Population Growth: 2000–2010

Group	%
Total Population	0.9
Hispanic or Latino (of any race)	33.4
Central American, ex. Mexican	145.8
Guatemalan	191.9
Salvadoran	213.7
Cuban	1.3
Mexican	42.5
Puerto Rican	15.2
South American	69.9
Colombian	87.4
Peruvian	63.3

Males per 100 Females

Group	Number
Total Population	94.3
Hispanic or Latino (of any race)	96.0
Central American, ex. Mexican	88.7
Costa Rican	89.3
Guatemalan	97.0
Honduran	80.0
Nicaraguan	88.9
Salvadoran	90.8
Cuban	99.4
Mexican	97.1
Puerto Rican	93.2
South American	85.6
Argentinean	91.1
Colombian	73.9
Ecuadorian	97.1
Peruvian	84.6
Spaniard	82.6

Average Household Size

Group	People
Total Population	3.01
Hispanic or Latino (of any race)	3.68
Central American, ex. Mexican	3.82
Costa Rican	3.10
Guatemalan	3.92
Honduran	3.85
Nicaraguan	4.00
Salvadoran	4.09
Cuban	3.07
Mexican	3.78
Puerto Rican	3.11
South American	3.14
Argentinean	2.83
Colombian	2.89
Ecuadorian	3.85
Peruvian	3.23
Spaniard	2.76

Median Age

Group	Years
Total Population	37.5
Hispanic or Latino (of any race)	29.0
Central American, ex. Mexican	33.5
Costa Rican	40.2
Guatemalan	33.6
Honduran	30.9
Nicaraguan	35.2
Salvadoran	33.3
Cuban	35.5
Mexican	27.9
Puerto Rican	30.3
South American	37.0
Argentinean	41.2
Colombian	38.2
Ecuadorian	40.5
Peruvian	34.9
Spaniard	35.9

High School Graduates
(Universe: Population 25 Years and Over)

Group	Number	%
Total Population	45,922	88.5
Hispanic or Latino (of any race)	9,790	77.5
Central American, ex. Mexican	623	82.6

Notes: (1) Percent of total population; (2) Percent of Hispanic/Latino population; Profiles include places with an overall population of at least 125,000, OR an overall population of at least 25,000 where the Hispanic/Latino population is at least 20% of the overall population. In states where less than five places meet either of these criteria, we have included places with at least 10,000 total population with the highest percentage of Hispanic/Latino population. These places are identified with an asterisk (*); Please refer to the User's Guide for a full explanation of data.

Mexican	7,751	75.4

Four-Year College Graduates
(Universe: Population 25 Years and Over)

Group	Number	%
Total Population	14,289	27.5
Hispanic or Latino (of any race)	2,167	17.2
Central American, ex. Mexican	160	21.2
Mexican	1,666	16.2

Population Age 3–17 Enrolled in Public School
(Universe: Population Age 3–17 Enrolled in School)

Group	Number	%
Total Population	13,225	83.5
Hispanic or Latino (of any race)	4,923	89.1
Central American, ex. Mexican	123	87.2
Mexican	4,370	90.8

Population Age 3–17 Enrolled in Private School
(Universe: Population Age 3–17 Enrolled in School)

Group	Number	%
Total Population	2,613	16.5
Hispanic or Latino (of any race)	602	10.9
Central American, ex. Mexican	18	12.8
Mexican	442	9.2

Foreign-Born Population

Group	Number	%
Total Population	17,002	21.3
Hispanic or Latino (of any race)	5,487	23.6
Central American, ex. Mexican	534	45.6
Mexican	4,359	22.6

Foreign-Born Naturalized U.S. Citizens

Group	Number	%
Total Population	10,754	63.3
Hispanic or Latino (of any race)	2,723	49.6
Central American, ex. Mexican	247	46.3
Mexican	2,030	46.6

Language Spoken at Home: English Only
(Universe: Population 5 Years and Over)

Group	Number	%
Total Population	49,447	66.3
Hispanic or Latino (of any race)	8,698	41.2
Central American, ex. Mexican	250	22.0
Mexican	7,188	41.2

Language Spoken at Home: Spanish
(Universe: Population 5 Years and Over)

Group	Number	%
Total Population	13,095	17.6
Hispanic or Latino (of any race)	12,315	58.3
Central American, ex. Mexican	886	78.0
Mexican	10,176	58.4

Unemployment Rate
(Universe: Population 16 Years and Over)

Group	%
Total Population	6.4
Hispanic or Latino (of any race)	5.7
Central American, ex. Mexican	4.6
Mexican	5.9

Class of Worker: Private Wage and Salary
(Universe: Civilian Employed Population 16 Years and Over)

Group	Number	%
Total Population	31,113	78.1
Hispanic or Latino (of any race)	9,203	80.8
Central American, ex. Mexican	570	76.4
Mexican	7,436	80.7

Class of Worker: Government
(Universe: Civilian Employed Population 16 Years and Over)

Group	Number	%
Total Population	6,631	16.6
Hispanic or Latino (of any race)	1,456	12.8
Central American, ex. Mexican	30	4.0
Mexican	1,211	13.1

Means of Transportation to Work: Car, Truck or Van
(Universe: Workers 16 Years and Over)

Group	Number	%
Total Population	35,593	92.2
Hispanic or Latino (of any race)	10,025	91.0
Central American, ex. Mexican	684	91.7
Mexican	8,099	91.2

Means of Transportation to Work: Public Transportation (ex. Taxicab)
(Universe: Workers 16 Years and Over)

Group	Number	%
Total Population	651	1.7
Hispanic or Latino (of any race)	214	1.9
Central American, ex. Mexican	22	2.9
Mexican	139	1.6

Homeownership Rate
(Universe: Occupied Housing Units)

Group	%
Total Population	72.1
Hispanic or Latino (of any race)	67.2
Central American, ex. Mexican	64.1
Costa Rican	79.3
Guatemalan	68.9
Honduran	55.0
Nicaraguan	69.8
Salvadoran	60.0
Cuban	65.7
Mexican	67.0
Puerto Rican	65.6
South American	74.3
Argentinean	68.3
Colombian	77.0
Ecuadorian	82.9
Peruvian	73.2
Spaniard	69.4

Median Home Value

Group	Dollars
Total Population	499,100
Hispanic or Latino (of any race)	512,900
Central American, ex. Mexican	500,000
Mexican	505,700

Median Gross Rent

Group	Dollars
Total Population	1,388
Hispanic or Latino (of any race)	1,311
Central American, ex. Mexican	1,023
Mexican	1,351

Median Household Income
(2010 Inflation-Adjusted Dollars)

Group	Dollars
Total Population	77,380
Hispanic or Latino (of any race)	78,624
Central American, ex. Mexican	70,446
Mexican	79,729

Per Capita Income
(2010 Inflation-Adjusted Dollars)

Group	Dollars
Total Population	28,764
Hispanic or Latino (of any race)	22,434
Central American, ex. Mexican	26,203
Mexican	21,873

Households with $100,000+ Income

Group	Number	%
Total Population	8,662	33.6
Hispanic or Latino (of any race)	2,018	33.5
Central American, ex. Mexican	128	31.4
Mexican	1,558	33.6

Households with Food Stamps/SNAP Benefits During Past 12 Months

Group	Number	%
Total Population	371	1.4
Hispanic or Latino (of any race)	89	1.5
Central American, ex. Mexican	11	2.7
Mexican	78	1.7

Poverty Rate
(Income in Past 12 Months Below Poverty Level)

Group	%
Total Population	5.2
Hispanic or Latino (of any race)	7.6
Central American, ex. Mexican	6.8
Mexican	7.2

Lancaster

Population

Group	Number	%TP[1]	%HP[2]
Total Population	156,633	100.0	–
Hispanic or Latino (of any race)	59,596	38.0	100.0
Central American, ex. Mexican	8,114	5.2	13.6
Costa Rican	156	0.1	0.3
Guatemalan	2,075	1.3	3.5
Honduran	474	0.3	0.8
Nicaraguan	442	0.3	0.7
Panamanian	170	0.1	0.3
Salvadoran	4,713	3.0	7.9
Cuban	514	0.3	0.9
Mexican	42,115	26.9	70.7
Puerto Rican	1,105	0.7	1.9
South American	1,345	0.9	2.3
Argentinean	204	0.1	0.3
Chilean	162	0.1	0.3
Colombian	227	0.1	0.4
Ecuadorian	181	0.1	0.3
Peruvian	457	0.3	0.8
Spaniard	486	0.3	0.8

Population Growth: 2000–2010

Group	%
Total Population	31.9
Hispanic or Latino (of any race)	108.1
Central American, ex. Mexican	425.2
Guatemalan	510.3
Salvadoran	535.2
Cuban	95.4
Mexican	109.3
Puerto Rican	53.9
South American	113.8
Chilean	12.5
Colombian	102.7
Peruvian	139.3

Males per 100 Females

Group	Number
Total Population	100.6
Hispanic or Latino (of any race)	106.7
Central American, ex. Mexican	100.0
Costa Rican	66.0
Guatemalan	107.1
Honduran	93.5
Nicaraguan	93.9
Panamanian	65.0
Salvadoran	101.2
Cuban	91.1
Mexican	105.1
Puerto Rican	99.8
South American	91.3
Argentinean	96.2
Chilean	105.1
Colombian	77.3
Ecuadorian	98.9
Peruvian	90.4
Spaniard	107.7

Average Household Size

Group	People
Total Population	3.16
Hispanic or Latino (of any race)	4.01
Central American, ex. Mexican	4.22
Costa Rican	2.86
Guatemalan	4.37
Honduran	4.27
Nicaraguan	4.02
Panamanian	3.23
Salvadoran	4.27
Cuban	2.95
Mexican	4.10
Puerto Rican	3.39
South American	3.38
Argentinean	3.19
Chilean	3.11
Colombian	3.25
Ecuadorian	3.88
Peruvian	3.47
Spaniard	2.95

Notes: (1) Percent of total population; (2) Percent of Hispanic/Latino population; Profiles include places with an overall population of at least 125,000, OR an overall population of at least 25,000 where the Hispanic/Latino population is at least 20% of the overall population. In states where less than five places meet either of these criteria, we have included places with at least 10,000 total population with the highest percentage of Hispanic/Latino population. These places are identified with an asterisk (*); Please refer to the User's Guide for a full explanation of data.

Median Age	
Group	Years
Total Population	30.4
Hispanic or Latino (of any race)	24.9
Central American, ex. Mexican	31.5
Costa Rican	34.7
Guatemalan	31.4
Honduran	31.1
Nicaraguan	35.3
Panamanian	32.5
Salvadoran	31.2
Cuban	28.6
Mexican	23.8
Puerto Rican	25.8
South American	37.6
Argentinean	41.0
Chilean	41.7
Colombian	35.3
Ecuadorian	39.3
Peruvian	35.5
Spaniard	30.1

High School Graduates
(Universe: Population 25 Years and Over)

Group	Number	%
Total Population	70,408	80.4
Hispanic or Latino (of any race)	17,442	63.4
Central American, ex. Mexican	2,397	66.1
Guatemalan	486	53.9
Salvadoran	1,433	69.5
Mexican	12,384	60.1
Puerto Rican	478	77.5
South American	642	85.8

Four-Year College Graduates
(Universe: Population 25 Years and Over)

Group	Number	%
Total Population	14,681	16.8
Hispanic or Latino (of any race)	1,878	6.8
Central American, ex. Mexican	184	5.1
Guatemalan	85	9.4
Salvadoran	78	3.8
Mexican	1,184	5.8
Puerto Rican	71	11.5
South American	125	16.7

Population Age 3–17 Enrolled in Public School
(Universe: Population Age 3–17 Enrolled in School)

Group	Number	%
Total Population	31,445	89.2
Hispanic or Latino (of any race)	14,044	91.7
Central American, ex. Mexican	1,482	91.5
Guatemalan	311	95.7
Salvadoran	956	95.7
Mexican	11,170	93.7
Puerto Rican	232	65.5
South American	168	90.8

Population Age 3–17 Enrolled in Private School
(Universe: Population Age 3–17 Enrolled in School)

Group	Number	%
Total Population	3,802	10.8
Hispanic or Latino (of any race)	1,272	8.3
Central American, ex. Mexican	138	8.5
Guatemalan	14	4.3
Salvadoran	43	4.3
Mexican	754	6.3
Puerto Rican	122	34.5
South American	17	9.2

Foreign-Born Population

Group	Number	%
Total Population	20,235	13.5
Hispanic or Latino (of any race)	12,559	23.2
Central American, ex. Mexican	2,927	47.6
Guatemalan	853	60.2
Salvadoran	1,665	47.2
Mexican	8,529	20.3
Puerto Rican	59	4.9
South American	368	33.3

Foreign-Born Naturalized U.S. Citizens

Group	Number	%
Total Population	9,409	46.5
Hispanic or Latino (of any race)	4,761	37.9
Central American, ex. Mexican	1,523	52.0
Guatemalan	306	35.9
Salvadoran	962	57.8
Mexican	2,734	32.1
Puerto Rican	14	23.7
South American	184	50.0

Language Spoken at Home: English Only
(Universe: Population 5 Years and Over)

Group	Number	%
Total Population	100,321	73.1
Hispanic or Latino (of any race)	20,784	42.8
Central American, ex. Mexican	1,684	28.1
Guatemalan	323	23.6
Salvadoran	816	23.9
Mexican	15,867	42.9
Puerto Rican	627	55.1
South American	662	60.6

Language Spoken at Home: Spanish
(Universe: Population 5 Years and Over)

Group	Number	%
Total Population	29,822	21.7
Hispanic or Latino (of any race)	27,778	57.2
Central American, ex. Mexican	4,300	71.9
Guatemalan	1,044	76.4
Salvadoran	2,595	76.1
Mexican	21,108	57.1
Puerto Rican	502	44.1
South American	418	38.3

Unemployment Rate
(Universe: Population 16 Years and Over)

Group	%
Total Population	10.0
Hispanic or Latino (of any race)	10.1
Central American, ex. Mexican	16.1
Guatemalan	10.5
Salvadoran	16.2
Mexican	8.8
Puerto Rican	16.6
South American	5.2

Class of Worker: Private Wage and Salary
(Universe: Civilian Employed Population 16 Years and Over)

Group	Number	%
Total Population	40,571	72.6
Hispanic or Latino (of any race)	14,976	79.2
Central American, ex. Mexican	1,777	78.7
Guatemalan	527	81.5
Salvadoran	1,023	77.6
Mexican	11,680	81.4
Puerto Rican	307	66.5
South American	499	80.1

Class of Worker: Government
(Universe: Civilian Employed Population 16 Years and Over)

Group	Number	%
Total Population	11,963	21.4
Hispanic or Latino (of any race)	2,558	13.5
Central American, ex. Mexican	224	9.9
Guatemalan	72	11.1
Salvadoran	115	8.7
Mexican	1,759	12.3
Puerto Rican	130	28.1
South American	106	17.0

Means of Transportation to Work: Car, Truck or Van
(Universe: Workers 16 Years and Over)

Group	Number	%
Total Population	50,616	93.6
Hispanic or Latino (of any race)	17,430	95.5
Central American, ex. Mexican	2,065	93.7
Guatemalan	554	91.3
Salvadoran	1,241	95.2
Mexican	13,288	95.9
Puerto Rican	403	91.0
South American	608	97.6

Means of Transportation to Work: Public Transportation (ex. Taxicab)
(Universe: Workers 16 Years and Over)

Group	Number	%
Total Population	880	1.6
Hispanic or Latino (of any race)	177	1.0
Central American, ex. Mexican	26	1.2
Guatemalan	15	2.5
Salvadoran	11	0.8
Mexican	140	1.0
Puerto Rican	0	0.0
South American	0	0.0

Homeownership Rate
(Universe: Occupied Housing Units)

Group	%
Total Population	60.4
Hispanic or Latino (of any race)	60.9
Central American, ex. Mexican	68.3
Costa Rican	75.5
Guatemalan	70.9
Honduran	62.6
Nicaraguan	60.0
Panamanian	58.5
Salvadoran	69.0
Cuban	47.9
Mexican	60.6
Puerto Rican	48.6
South American	67.9
Argentinean	64.0
Chilean	75.4
Colombian	66.7
Ecuadorian	74.1
Peruvian	62.8
Spaniard	66.3

Median Home Value

Group	Dollars
Total Population	252,100
Hispanic or Latino (of any race)	247,500
Central American, ex. Mexican	261,900
Guatemalan	267,900
Salvadoran	251,200
Mexican	230,300
Puerto Rican	278,100
South American	268,300

Median Gross Rent

Group	Dollars
Total Population	1,081
Hispanic or Latino (of any race)	1,030
Central American, ex. Mexican	810
Guatemalan	631
Salvadoran	817
Mexican	1,066
Puerto Rican	1,086
South American	1,068

Median Household Income
(2010 Inflation-Adjusted Dollars)

Group	Dollars
Total Population	51,192
Hispanic or Latino (of any race)	46,331
Central American, ex. Mexican	46,189
Guatemalan	50,732
Salvadoran	47,176
Mexican	45,583
Puerto Rican	54,323
South American	65,833

Per Capita Income
(2010 Inflation-Adjusted Dollars)

Group	Dollars
Total Population	20,256
Hispanic or Latino (of any race)	13,807
Central American, ex. Mexican	14,906
Guatemalan	16,843
Salvadoran	14,546
Mexican	13,007
Puerto Rican	15,185
South American	20,326

Households with $100,000+ Income

Group	Number	%
Total Population	8,552	18.8
Hispanic or Latino (of any race)	1,634	12.7
Central American, ex. Mexican	212	10.8
Guatemalan	36	7.9
Salvadoran	145	13.3
Mexican	899	9.8

STATE & PLACE PROFILES

Notes: (1) Percent of total population; (2) Percent of Hispanic/Latino population; Profiles include places with an overall population of at least 125,000, OR an overall population of at least 25,000 where the Hispanic/Latino population is at least 20% of the overall population. In states where less than five places meet either of these criteria, we have included places with at least 10,000 total population with the highest percentage of Hispanic/Latino population. These places are identified with an asterisk (*); Please refer to the User's Guide for a full explanation of data.

Puerto Rican	77	26.5
South American	92	28.2

Households with Food Stamps/SNAP Benefits During Past 12 Months

Group	Number	%
Total Population	3,609	7.9
Hispanic or Latino (of any race)	1,021	7.9
Central American, ex. Mexican	169	8.6
Guatemalan	22	4.8
Salvadoran	128	11.7
Mexican	716	7.8
Puerto Rican	14	4.8
South American	34	10.4

Poverty Rate
(Income in Past 12 Months Below Poverty Level)

Group	%
Total Population	20.2
Hispanic or Latino (of any race)	22.7
Central American, ex. Mexican	17.2
Guatemalan	11.8
Salvadoran	11.2
Mexican	24.5
Puerto Rican	21.2
South American	1.9

Lawndale

Population

Group	Number	%TP[1]	%HP[2]
Total Population	32,769	100.0	–
Hispanic or Latino (of any race)	20,002	61.0	100.0
Central American, ex. Mexican	3,568	10.9	17.8
Guatemalan	1,953	6.0	9.8
Honduran	200	0.6	1.0
Nicaraguan	264	0.8	1.3
Salvadoran	1,005	3.1	5.0
Cuban	276	0.8	1.4
Mexican	13,300	40.6	66.5
Puerto Rican	302	0.9	1.5
South American	1,092	3.3	5.5
Colombian	191	0.6	1.0
Ecuadorian	191	0.6	1.0
Peruvian	525	1.6	2.6

Population Growth: 2000–2010

Group	%
Total Population	3.3
Hispanic or Latino (of any race)	21.1
Central American, ex. Mexican	99.9
Guatemalan	146.9
Nicaraguan	61.0
Salvadoran	90.7
Cuban	-21.6
Mexican	27.6
Puerto Rican	-11.4
South American	88.3
Colombian	29.1
Peruvian	122.5

Males per 100 Females

Group	Number
Total Population	101.3
Hispanic or Latino (of any race)	102.6
Central American, ex. Mexican	100.4
Guatemalan	124.7
Honduran	50.4
Nicaraguan	77.2
Salvadoran	83.1
Cuban	94.4
Mexican	104.9
Puerto Rican	88.8
South American	91.6
Colombian	69.0
Ecuadorian	85.4
Peruvian	96.6

Average Household Size

Group	People
Total Population	3.37
Hispanic or Latino (of any race)	4.03
Central American, ex. Mexican	4.32
Guatemalan	4.64
Honduran	4.31
Nicaraguan	3.74
Salvadoran	4.10
Cuban	2.65
Mexican	4.14
Puerto Rican	2.96
South American	3.40
Colombian	2.95
Ecuadorian	3.53
Peruvian	3.74

Median Age

Group	Years
Total Population	31.9
Hispanic or Latino (of any race)	28.6
Central American, ex. Mexican	32.8
Guatemalan	32.1
Honduran	31.4
Nicaraguan	33.7
Salvadoran	33.3
Cuban	45.7
Mexican	26.6
Puerto Rican	30.0
South American	38.6
Colombian	41.3
Ecuadorian	43.7
Peruvian	36.6

High School Graduates
(Universe: Population 25 Years and Over)

Group	Number	%
Total Population	14,220	73.9
Hispanic or Latino (of any race)	6,710	63.4
Central American, ex. Mexican	1,491	64.5
Guatemalan	619	55.4
Mexican	3,994	57.9

Four-Year College Graduates
(Universe: Population 25 Years and Over)

Group	Number	%
Total Population	3,102	16.1
Hispanic or Latino (of any race)	889	8.4
Central American, ex. Mexican	193	8.3
Guatemalan	51	4.6
Mexican	393	5.7

Population Age 3–17 Enrolled in Public School
(Universe: Population Age 3–17 Enrolled in School)

Group	Number	%
Total Population	6,426	94.3
Hispanic or Latino (of any race)	5,025	98.3
Central American, ex. Mexican	765	97.5
Guatemalan	436	100.0
Mexican	3,923	99.0

Population Age 3–17 Enrolled in Private School
(Universe: Population Age 3–17 Enrolled in School)

Group	Number	%
Total Population	388	5.7
Hispanic or Latino (of any race)	87	1.7
Central American, ex. Mexican	20	2.5
Guatemalan	0	0.0
Mexican	41	1.0

Foreign-Born Population

Group	Number	%
Total Population	12,607	38.7
Hispanic or Latino (of any race)	9,292	46.1
Central American, ex. Mexican	2,527	63.5
Guatemalan	1,205	58.4
Mexican	5,650	40.3

Foreign-Born Naturalized U.S. Citizens

Group	Number	%
Total Population	5,111	40.5
Hispanic or Latino (of any race)	3,179	34.2
Central American, ex. Mexican	797	31.5
Guatemalan	142	11.8
Mexican	1,995	35.3

Language Spoken at Home: English Only
(Universe: Population 5 Years and Over)

Group	Number	%
Total Population	9,864	33.6
Hispanic or Latino (of any race)	2,524	13.8
Central American, ex. Mexican	200	5.6
Guatemalan	118	6.5
Mexican	1,917	15.2

Language Spoken at Home: Spanish
(Universe: Population 5 Years and Over)

Group	Number	%
Total Population	15,975	54.4
Hispanic or Latino (of any race)	15,736	86.2
Central American, ex. Mexican	3,363	94.4
Guatemalan	1,696	93.5
Mexican	10,682	84.8

Unemployment Rate
(Universe: Population 16 Years and Over)

Group	%
Total Population	11.3
Hispanic or Latino (of any race)	12.2
Central American, ex. Mexican	12.0
Guatemalan	13.3
Mexican	13.3

Class of Worker: Private Wage and Salary
(Universe: Civilian Employed Population 16 Years and Over)

Group	Number	%
Total Population	11,819	83.6
Hispanic or Latino (of any race)	7,568	87.9
Central American, ex. Mexican	1,628	90.4
Guatemalan	826	86.9
Mexican	4,890	86.1

Class of Worker: Government
(Universe: Civilian Employed Population 16 Years and Over)

Group	Number	%
Total Population	1,114	7.9
Hispanic or Latino (of any race)	336	3.9
Central American, ex. Mexican	10	0.6
Guatemalan	0	0.0
Mexican	304	5.4

Means of Transportation to Work: Car, Truck or Van
(Universe: Workers 16 Years and Over)

Group	Number	%
Total Population	12,431	89.3
Hispanic or Latino (of any race)	7,458	88.2
Central American, ex. Mexican	1,509	87.3
Guatemalan	764	84.2
Mexican	4,940	87.6

Means of Transportation to Work: Public Transportation (ex. Taxicab)
(Universe: Workers 16 Years and Over)

Group	Number	%
Total Population	471	3.4
Hispanic or Latino (of any race)	379	4.5
Central American, ex. Mexican	102	5.9
Guatemalan	91	10.0
Mexican	241	4.3

Homeownership Rate
(Universe: Occupied Housing Units)

Group	%
Total Population	34.4
Hispanic or Latino (of any race)	31.8
Central American, ex. Mexican	26.2
Guatemalan	23.7
Honduran	33.3
Nicaraguan	21.4
Salvadoran	31.5
Cuban	42.1
Mexican	33.5
Puerto Rican	28.6
South American	30.7
Colombian	35.5
Ecuadorian	48.3
Peruvian	25.2

Median Home Value

Group	Dollars
Total Population	439,500
Hispanic or Latino (of any race)	459,400
Central American, ex. Mexican	411,200
Guatemalan	391,300
Mexican	465,400

Notes: (1) Percent of total population; (2) Percent of Hispanic/Latino population; Profiles include places with an overall population of at least 125,000, OR an overall population of at least 25,000 where the Hispanic/Latino population is at least 20% of the overall population. In states where less than five places meet either of these criteria, we have included places with at least 10,000 total population with the highest percentage of Hispanic/Latino population. These places are identified with an asterisk (*); Please refer to the User's Guide for a full explanation of data.

Median Gross Rent	
Group	Dollars
Total Population	1,264
Hispanic or Latino (of any race)	1,245
Central American, ex. Mexican	1,215
Guatemalan	1,341
Mexican	1,291

Median Household Income
(2010 Inflation-Adjusted Dollars)

Group	Dollars
Total Population	48,357
Hispanic or Latino (of any race)	46,152
Central American, ex. Mexican	46,454
Guatemalan	45,146
Mexican	47,038

Per Capita Income
(2010 Inflation-Adjusted Dollars)

Group	Dollars
Total Population	18,948
Hispanic or Latino (of any race)	14,782
Central American, ex. Mexican	15,674
Guatemalan	12,561
Mexican	13,638

Households with $100,000+ Income

Group	Number	%
Total Population	1,436	14.6
Hispanic or Latino (of any race)	550	11.4
Central American, ex. Mexican	117	12.7
Guatemalan	39	8.0
Mexican	348	10.9

Households with Food Stamps/SNAP Benefits During Past 12 Months

Group	Number	%
Total Population	417	4.2
Hispanic or Latino (of any race)	250	5.2
Central American, ex. Mexican	18	2.0
Guatemalan	18	3.7
Mexican	204	6.4

Poverty Rate
(Income in Past 12 Months Below Poverty Level)

Group	%
Total Population	15.8
Hispanic or Latino (of any race)	17.8
Central American, ex. Mexican	19.2
Guatemalan	29.1
Mexican	17.2

Lemon Grove

Population

Group	Number	%TP[1]	%HP[2]
Total Population	25,320	100.0	–
Hispanic or Latino (of any race)	10,435	41.2	100.0
Central American, ex. Mexican	194	0.8	1.9
Mexican	9,395	37.1	90.0
Puerto Rican	240	0.9	2.3
South American	123	0.5	1.2
Spaniard	117	0.5	1.1

Population Growth: 2000–2010

Group	%
Total Population	1.6
Hispanic or Latino (of any race)	46.8
Mexican	63.9
Puerto Rican	28.3

Males per 100 Females

Group	Number
Total Population	95.3
Hispanic or Latino (of any race)	94.0
Central American, ex. Mexican	92.1
Mexican	94.8
Puerto Rican	98.3
South American	75.7
Spaniard	95.0

Average Household Size

Group	People
Total Population	2.96
Hispanic or Latino (of any race)	3.79
Central American, ex. Mexican	3.62
Mexican	3.85
Puerto Rican	3.03
South American	3.72
Spaniard	3.15

Median Age

Group	Years
Total Population	35.0
Hispanic or Latino (of any race)	27.5
Central American, ex. Mexican	33.0
Mexican	27.3
Puerto Rican	24.5
South American	35.2
Spaniard	28.5

High School Graduates
(Universe: Population 25 Years and Over)

Group	Number	%
Total Population	13,580	85.3
Hispanic or Latino (of any race)	3,865	77.9
Mexican	3,522	77.3

Four-Year College Graduates
(Universe: Population 25 Years and Over)

Group	Number	%
Total Population	2,657	16.7
Hispanic or Latino (of any race)	541	10.9
Mexican	407	8.9

Population Age 3–17 Enrolled in Public School
(Universe: Population Age 3–17 Enrolled in School)

Group	Number	%
Total Population	4,708	93.1
Hispanic or Latino (of any race)	2,656	96.1
Mexican	2,619	97.1

Population Age 3–17 Enrolled in Private School
(Universe: Population Age 3–17 Enrolled in School)

Group	Number	%
Total Population	347	6.9
Hispanic or Latino (of any race)	107	3.9
Mexican	78	2.9

Foreign-Born Population

Group	Number	%
Total Population	4,439	17.7
Hispanic or Latino (of any race)	2,708	27.1
Mexican	2,530	27.1

Foreign-Born Naturalized U.S. Citizens

Group	Number	%
Total Population	2,344	52.8
Hispanic or Latino (of any race)	1,184	43.7
Mexican	1,084	42.8

Language Spoken at Home: English Only
(Universe: Population 5 Years and Over)

Group	Number	%
Total Population	15,387	66.4
Hispanic or Latino (of any race)	2,745	31.7
Mexican	2,412	29.9

Language Spoken at Home: Spanish
(Universe: Population 5 Years and Over)

Group	Number	%
Total Population	6,047	26.1
Hispanic or Latino (of any race)	5,895	68.1
Mexican	5,649	70.0

Unemployment Rate
(Universe: Population 16 Years and Over)

Group	%
Total Population	7.0
Hispanic or Latino (of any race)	4.1
Mexican	4.2

Class of Worker: Private Wage and Salary
(Universe: Civilian Employed Population 16 Years and Over)

Group	Number	%
Total Population	8,017	74.8
Hispanic or Latino (of any race)	3,048	79.1
Mexican	2,847	81.5

Class of Worker: Government
(Universe: Civilian Employed Population 16 Years and Over)

Group	Number	%
Total Population	1,959	18.3
Hispanic or Latino (of any race)	505	13.1
Mexican	429	12.3

Means of Transportation to Work: Car, Truck or Van
(Universe: Workers 16 Years and Over)

Group	Number	%
Total Population	9,652	90.4
Hispanic or Latino (of any race)	3,438	89.1
Mexican	3,140	89.4

Means of Transportation to Work: Public Transportation (ex. Taxicab)
(Universe: Workers 16 Years and Over)

Group	Number	%
Total Population	473	4.4
Hispanic or Latino (of any race)	282	7.3
Mexican	271	7.7

Homeownership Rate
(Universe: Occupied Housing Units)

Group	%
Total Population	54.6
Hispanic or Latino (of any race)	51.1
Central American, ex. Mexican	47.6
Mexican	51.0
Puerto Rican	52.9
South American	66.7
Spaniard	64.7

Median Home Value

Group	Dollars
Total Population	378,000
Hispanic or Latino (of any race)	355,400
Mexican	354,200

Median Gross Rent

Group	Dollars
Total Population	1,089
Hispanic or Latino (of any race)	1,175
Mexican	1,227

Median Household Income
(2010 Inflation-Adjusted Dollars)

Group	Dollars
Total Population	50,839
Hispanic or Latino (of any race)	52,669
Mexican	55,145

Per Capita Income
(2010 Inflation-Adjusted Dollars)

Group	Dollars
Total Population	21,965
Hispanic or Latino (of any race)	16,565
Mexican	15,930

Households with $100,000+ Income

Group	Number	%
Total Population	1,414	16.3
Hispanic or Latino (of any race)	484	19.1
Mexican	430	19.3

Households with Food Stamps/SNAP Benefits During Past 12 Months

Group	Number	%
Total Population	581	6.7
Hispanic or Latino (of any race)	306	12.1
Mexican	245	11.0

Poverty Rate
(Income in Past 12 Months Below Poverty Level)

Group	%
Total Population	16.4
Hispanic or Latino (of any race)	19.7
Mexican	20.5

STATE & PLACE PROFILES

Notes: (1) Percent of total population; (2) Percent of Hispanic/Latino population; Profiles include places with an overall population of at least 125,000, OR an overall population of at least 25,000 where the Hispanic/Latino population is at least 20% of the overall population. In states where less than five places meet either of these criteria, we have included places with at least 10,000 total population with the highest percentage of Hispanic/Latino population. These places are identified with an asterisk (*); Please refer to the User's Guide for a full explanation of data.

Livermore

Population

Group	Number	%TP[1]	%HP[2]
Total Population	80,968	100.0	–
Hispanic or Latino (of any race)	16,920	20.9	100.0
Central American, ex. Mexican	730	0.9	4.3
Nicaraguan	174	0.2	1.0
Salvadoran	385	0.5	2.3
Cuban	105	0.1	0.6
Mexican	13,296	16.4	78.6
Puerto Rican	586	0.7	3.5
South American	499	0.6	2.9
Colombian	109	0.1	0.6
Peruvian	195	0.2	1.2
Spaniard	629	0.8	3.7

Population Growth: 2000–2010

Group	%
Total Population	10.4
Hispanic or Latino (of any race)	60.5
Central American, ex. Mexican	171.4
Salvadoran	240.7
Mexican	75.6
Puerto Rican	51.8
South American	130.0

Males per 100 Females

Group	Number
Total Population	98.6
Hispanic or Latino (of any race)	101.3
Central American, ex. Mexican	99.5
Nicaraguan	95.5
Salvadoran	103.7
Cuban	156.1
Mexican	103.7
Puerto Rican	100.7
South American	88.3
Colombian	101.9
Peruvian	75.7
Spaniard	84.5

Average Household Size

Group	People
Total Population	2.76
Hispanic or Latino (of any race)	3.67
Central American, ex. Mexican	3.38
Nicaraguan	3.11
Salvadoran	3.58
Cuban	2.74
Mexican	3.92
Puerto Rican	2.79
South American	2.96
Colombian	2.84
Peruvian	3.26
Spaniard	2.65

Median Age

Group	Years
Total Population	38.3
Hispanic or Latino (of any race)	27.3
Central American, ex. Mexican	31.7
Nicaraguan	35.0
Salvadoran	30.4
Cuban	34.5
Mexican	25.9
Puerto Rican	31.4
South American	39.6
Colombian	33.5
Peruvian	39.8
Spaniard	37.1

High School Graduates
(Universe: Population 25 Years and Over)

Group	Number	%
Total Population	48,174	92.3
Hispanic or Latino (of any race)	5,679	69.8
Mexican	4,625	67.0

Four-Year College Graduates
(Universe: Population 25 Years and Over)

Group	Number	%
Total Population	19,272	36.9
Hispanic or Latino (of any race)	1,009	12.4
Mexican	727	10.5

Population Age 3–17 Enrolled in Public School
(Universe: Population Age 3–17 Enrolled in School)

Group	Number	%
Total Population	13,662	84.7
Hispanic or Latino (of any race)	3,248	88.2
Mexican	2,976	89.6

Population Age 3–17 Enrolled in Private School
(Universe: Population Age 3–17 Enrolled in School)

Group	Number	%
Total Population	2,471	15.3
Hispanic or Latino (of any race)	435	11.8
Mexican	346	10.4

Foreign-Born Population

Group	Number	%
Total Population	12,560	16.0
Hispanic or Latino (of any race)	5,641	37.3
Mexican	5,106	39.2

Foreign-Born Naturalized U.S. Citizens

Group	Number	%
Total Population	6,064	48.3
Hispanic or Latino (of any race)	1,257	22.3
Mexican	991	19.4

Language Spoken at Home: English Only
(Universe: Population 5 Years and Over)

Group	Number	%
Total Population	57,120	78.1
Hispanic or Latino (of any race)	4,955	36.3
Mexican	3,884	33.0

Language Spoken at Home: Spanish
(Universe: Population 5 Years and Over)

Group	Number	%
Total Population	9,372	12.8
Hispanic or Latino (of any race)	8,673	63.6
Mexican	7,876	66.9

Unemployment Rate
(Universe: Population 16 Years and Over)

Group	%
Total Population	6.8
Hispanic or Latino (of any race)	9.4
Mexican	9.1

Class of Worker: Private Wage and Salary
(Universe: Civilian Employed Population 16 Years and Over)

Group	Number	%
Total Population	30,860	76.1
Hispanic or Latino (of any race)	6,186	83.6
Mexican	5,381	85.6

Class of Worker: Government
(Universe: Civilian Employed Population 16 Years and Over)

Group	Number	%
Total Population	7,224	17.8
Hispanic or Latino (of any race)	777	10.5
Mexican	561	8.9

Means of Transportation to Work: Car, Truck or Van
(Universe: Workers 16 Years and Over)

Group	Number	%
Total Population	35,123	89.0
Hispanic or Latino (of any race)	6,556	90.3
Mexican	5,560	89.9

Means of Transportation to Work: Public Transportation (ex. Taxicab)
(Universe: Workers 16 Years and Over)

Group	Number	%
Total Population	1,335	3.4
Hispanic or Latino (of any race)	326	4.5
Mexican	326	5.3

Homeownership Rate
(Universe: Occupied Housing Units)

Group	%
Total Population	70.0
Hispanic or Latino (of any race)	50.1
Central American, ex. Mexican	60.1
Nicaraguan	63.0
Salvadoran	54.4
Cuban	61.8
Mexican	46.2
Puerto Rican	49.7
South American	66.3
Colombian	68.8
Peruvian	51.9
Spaniard	78.2

Median Home Value

Group	Dollars
Total Population	592,500
Hispanic or Latino (of any race)	515,200
Mexican	513,600

Median Gross Rent

Group	Dollars
Total Population	1,314
Hispanic or Latino (of any race)	1,291
Mexican	1,271

Median Household Income
(2010 Inflation-Adjusted Dollars)

Group	Dollars
Total Population	93,988
Hispanic or Latino (of any race)	63,295
Mexican	61,088

Per Capita Income
(2010 Inflation-Adjusted Dollars)

Group	Dollars
Total Population	41,072
Hispanic or Latino (of any race)	23,145
Mexican	21,356

Households with $100,000+ Income

Group	Number	%
Total Population	13,445	47.3
Hispanic or Latino (of any race)	1,072	26.8
Mexican	779	24.2

Households with Food Stamps/SNAP Benefits During Past 12 Months

Group	Number	%
Total Population	591	2.1
Hispanic or Latino (of any race)	120	3.0
Mexican	75	2.3

Poverty Rate
(Income in Past 12 Months Below Poverty Level)

Group	%
Total Population	5.6
Hispanic or Latino (of any race)	13.9
Mexican	14.9

Lodi

Population

Group	Number	%TP[1]	%HP[2]
Total Population	62,134	100.0	–
Hispanic or Latino (of any race)	22,613	36.4	100.0
Central American, ex. Mexican	285	0.5	1.3
Salvadoran	115	0.2	0.5
Mexican	20,579	33.1	91.0
Puerto Rican	246	0.4	1.1
Spaniard	254	0.4	1.1

Population Growth: 2000–2010

Group	%
Total Population	9.0
Hispanic or Latino (of any race)	46.2
Central American, ex. Mexican	65.7
Mexican	55.7
Puerto Rican	39.8

Males per 100 Females

Group	Number
Total Population	95.5
Hispanic or Latino (of any race)	103.6
Central American, ex. Mexican	88.7
Salvadoran	91.7
Mexican	104.4
Puerto Rican	100.0
Spaniard	95.4

Notes: (1) Percent of total population; (2) Percent of Hispanic/Latino population; Profiles include places with an overall population of at least 125,000, OR an overall population of at least 25,000 where the Hispanic/Latino population is at least 20% of the overall population. In states where less than five places meet either of these criteria, we have included places with at least 10,000 total population with the highest percentage of Hispanic/Latino population. These places are identified with an asterisk (*); Please refer to the User's Guide for a full explanation of data.

Average Household Size

Group	People
Total Population	2.78
Hispanic or Latino (of any race)	3.91
Central American, ex. Mexican	3.23
Salvadoran	3.26
Mexican	3.98
Puerto Rican	3.04
Spaniard	2.91

Median Age

Group	Years
Total Population	34.3
Hispanic or Latino (of any race)	23.7
Central American, ex. Mexican	32.6
Salvadoran	34.5
Mexican	23.3
Puerto Rican	26.8
Spaniard	34.3

High School Graduates
(Universe: Population 25 Years and Over)

Group	Number	%
Total Population	30,361	78.1
Hispanic or Latino (of any race)	4,919	50.5
Mexican	4,339	48.6

Four-Year College Graduates
(Universe: Population 25 Years and Over)

Group	Number	%
Total Population	7,047	18.1
Hispanic or Latino (of any race)	489	5.0
Mexican	261	2.9

Population Age 3–17 Enrolled in Public School
(Universe: Population Age 3–17 Enrolled in School)

Group	Number	%
Total Population	11,455	90.0
Hispanic or Latino (of any race)	5,956	98.3
Mexican	5,595	98.2

Population Age 3–17 Enrolled in Private School
(Universe: Population Age 3–17 Enrolled in School)

Group	Number	%
Total Population	1,279	10.0
Hispanic or Latino (of any race)	105	1.7
Mexican	105	1.8

Foreign-Born Population

Group	Number	%
Total Population	11,980	19.3
Hispanic or Latino (of any race)	8,649	41.9
Mexican	8,351	43.3

Foreign-Born Naturalized U.S. Citizens

Group	Number	%
Total Population	3,574	29.8
Hispanic or Latino (of any race)	1,639	19.0
Mexican	1,538	18.4

Language Spoken at Home: English Only
(Universe: Population 5 Years and Over)

Group	Number	%
Total Population	39,343	68.7
Hispanic or Latino (of any race)	4,705	25.9
Mexican	3,857	22.9

Language Spoken at Home: Spanish
(Universe: Population 5 Years and Over)

Group	Number	%
Total Population	14,010	24.5
Hispanic or Latino (of any race)	13,421	74.0
Mexican	12,951	77.0

Unemployment Rate
(Universe: Population 16 Years and Over)

Group	%
Total Population	9.5
Hispanic or Latino (of any race)	13.4
Mexican	14.2

Class of Worker: Private Wage and Salary
(Universe: Civilian Employed Population 16 Years and Over)

Group	Number	%
Total Population	19,652	76.7
Hispanic or Latino (of any race)	6,775	87.4
Mexican	6,310	88.5

Class of Worker: Government
(Universe: Civilian Employed Population 16 Years and Over)

Group	Number	%
Total Population	3,952	15.4
Hispanic or Latino (of any race)	580	7.5
Mexican	439	6.2

Means of Transportation to Work: Car, Truck or Van
(Universe: Workers 16 Years and Over)

Group	Number	%
Total Population	22,226	90.0
Hispanic or Latino (of any race)	6,759	90.2
Mexican	6,166	89.7

Means of Transportation to Work: Public Transportation (ex. Taxicab)
(Universe: Workers 16 Years and Over)

Group	Number	%
Total Population	247	1.0
Hispanic or Latino (of any race)	84	1.1
Mexican	84	1.2

Homeownership Rate
(Universe: Occupied Housing Units)

Group	%
Total Population	54.7
Hispanic or Latino (of any race)	34.1
Central American, ex. Mexican	31.1
Salvadoran	33.3
Mexican	33.6
Puerto Rican	48.1
Spaniard	57.6

Median Home Value

Group	Dollars
Total Population	334,000
Hispanic or Latino (of any race)	305,400
Mexican	301,200

Median Gross Rent

Group	Dollars
Total Population	986
Hispanic or Latino (of any race)	928
Mexican	917

Median Household Income
(2010 Inflation-Adjusted Dollars)

Group	Dollars
Total Population	48,695
Hispanic or Latino (of any race)	37,175
Mexican	36,742

Per Capita Income
(2010 Inflation-Adjusted Dollars)

Group	Dollars
Total Population	23,748
Hispanic or Latino (of any race)	13,410
Mexican	12,802

Households with $100,000+ Income

Group	Number	%
Total Population	4,410	20.5
Hispanic or Latino (of any race)	362	6.9
Mexican	274	5.7

Households with Food Stamps/SNAP Benefits During Past 12 Months

Group	Number	%
Total Population	1,738	8.1
Hispanic or Latino (of any race)	807	15.4
Mexican	765	16.0

Poverty Rate
(Income in Past 12 Months Below Poverty Level)

Group	%
Total Population	15.8
Hispanic or Latino (of any race)	26.6
Mexican	26.7

Lompoc

Population

Group	Number	%TP[1]	%HP[2]
Total Population	42,434	100.0	–
Hispanic or Latino (of any race)	21,557	50.8	100.0
Central American, ex. Mexican	531	1.3	2.5
Guatemalan	214	0.5	1.0
Salvadoran	183	0.4	0.8
Mexican	19,252	45.4	89.3
Puerto Rican	262	0.6	1.2
South American	127	0.3	0.6
Spaniard	184	0.4	0.9

Population Growth: 2000–2010

Group	%
Total Population	3.2
Hispanic or Latino (of any race)	40.6
Central American, ex. Mexican	126.0
Mexican	48.3
Puerto Rican	50.6

Males per 100 Females

Group	Number
Total Population	114.9
Hispanic or Latino (of any race)	119.2
Central American, ex. Mexican	157.8
Guatemalan	143.2
Salvadoran	154.2
Mexican	119.2
Puerto Rican	129.8
South American	84.1
Spaniard	95.7

Average Household Size

Group	People
Total Population	2.90
Hispanic or Latino (of any race)	3.83
Central American, ex. Mexican	3.68
Guatemalan	3.74
Salvadoran	3.59
Mexican	3.89
Puerto Rican	3.00
South American	3.05
Spaniard	2.49

Median Age

Group	Years
Total Population	33.9
Hispanic or Latino (of any race)	26.7
Central American, ex. Mexican	34.5
Guatemalan	35.7
Salvadoran	35.4
Mexican	26.5
Puerto Rican	28.0
South American	40.5
Spaniard	40.0

High School Graduates
(Universe: Population 25 Years and Over)

Group	Number	%
Total Population	18,803	74.3
Hispanic or Latino (of any race)	5,017	48.5
Mexican	4,329	46.0

Four-Year College Graduates
(Universe: Population 25 Years and Over)

Group	Number	%
Total Population	3,574	14.1
Hispanic or Latino (of any race)	476	4.6
Mexican	320	3.4

Population Age 3–17 Enrolled in Public School
(Universe: Population Age 3–17 Enrolled in School)

Group	Number	%
Total Population	8,598	96.3
Hispanic or Latino (of any race)	5,737	98.7
Mexican	5,546	99.0

Population Age 3–17 Enrolled in Private School
(Universe: Population Age 3–17 Enrolled in School)

Group	Number	%
Total Population	332	3.7
Hispanic or Latino (of any race)	75	1.3
Mexican	58	1.0

Notes: (1) Percent of total population; (2) Percent of Hispanic/Latino population; Profiles include places with an overall population of at least 125,000, OR an overall population of at least 25,000 where the Hispanic/Latino population is at least 20% of the overall population. In states where less than five places meet either of these criteria, we have included places with at least 10,000 total population with the highest percentage of Hispanic/Latino population. These places are identified with an asterisk (*); Please refer to the User's Guide for a full explanation of data.

Foreign-Born Population

Group	Number	%
Total Population	11,011	26.3
Hispanic or Latino (of any race)	8,970	43.7
Mexican	8,405	44.3

Foreign-Born Naturalized U.S. Citizens

Group	Number	%
Total Population	3,017	27.4
Hispanic or Latino (of any race)	1,750	19.5
Mexican	1,500	17.8

Language Spoken at Home: English Only
(Universe: Population 5 Years and Over)

Group	Number	%
Total Population	21,601	56.0
Hispanic or Latino (of any race)	3,652	20.0
Mexican	3,253	19.3

Language Spoken at Home: Spanish
(Universe: Population 5 Years and Over)

Group	Number	%
Total Population	15,043	39.0
Hispanic or Latino (of any race)	14,607	79.9
Mexican	13,620	80.6

Unemployment Rate
(Universe: Population 16 Years and Over)

Group	%
Total Population	9.7
Hispanic or Latino (of any race)	10.9
Mexican	10.3

Class of Worker: Private Wage and Salary
(Universe: Civilian Employed Population 16 Years and Over)

Group	Number	%
Total Population	12,643	75.0
Hispanic or Latino (of any race)	6,042	81.8
Mexican	5,651	83.3

Class of Worker: Government
(Universe: Civilian Employed Population 16 Years and Over)

Group	Number	%
Total Population	3,312	19.6
Hispanic or Latino (of any race)	968	13.1
Mexican	808	11.9

Means of Transportation to Work: Car, Truck or Van
(Universe: Workers 16 Years and Over)

Group	Number	%
Total Population	14,353	85.7
Hispanic or Latino (of any race)	5,956	85.3
Mexican	5,538	86.5

Means of Transportation to Work: Public Transportation (ex. Taxicab)
(Universe: Workers 16 Years and Over)

Group	Number	%
Total Population	904	5.4
Hispanic or Latino (of any race)	397	5.7
Mexican	283	4.4

Homeownership Rate
(Universe: Occupied Housing Units)

Group	%
Total Population	48.6
Hispanic or Latino (of any race)	38.4
Central American, ex. Mexican	35.9
Guatemalan	45.9
Salvadoran	31.5
Mexican	39.1
Puerto Rican	33.8
South American	43.2
Spaniard	37.3

Median Home Value

Group	Dollars
Total Population	330,600
Hispanic or Latino (of any race)	313,800
Mexican	306,600

Median Gross Rent

Group	Dollars
Total Population	917
Hispanic or Latino (of any race)	842
Mexican	851

Median Household Income
(2010 Inflation-Adjusted Dollars)

Group	Dollars
Total Population	46,932
Hispanic or Latino (of any race)	41,465
Mexican	41,660

Per Capita Income
(2010 Inflation-Adjusted Dollars)

Group	Dollars
Total Population	19,746
Hispanic or Latino (of any race)	11,876
Mexican	11,388

Households with $100,000+ Income

Group	Number	%
Total Population	2,142	16.0
Hispanic or Latino (of any race)	370	7.6
Mexican	288	6.7

Households with Food Stamps/SNAP Benefits During Past 12 Months

Group	Number	%
Total Population	1,284	9.6
Hispanic or Latino (of any race)	640	13.2
Mexican	610	14.1

Poverty Rate
(Income in Past 12 Months Below Poverty Level)

Group	%
Total Population	18.9
Hispanic or Latino (of any race)	26.4
Mexican	26.2

Long Beach

Population

Group	Number	%TP[1]	%HP[2]
Total Population	462,257	100.0	–
Hispanic or Latino (of any race)	188,412	40.8	100.0
Central American, ex. Mexican	16,486	3.6	8.7
Costa Rican	467	0.1	0.2
Guatemalan	5,134	1.1	2.7
Honduran	2,696	0.6	1.4
Nicaraguan	1,007	0.2	0.5
Panamanian	313	0.1	0.2
Salvadoran	6,657	1.4	3.5
Cuban	1,264	0.3	0.7
Dominican Republic	194	<0.1	0.1
Mexican	151,983	32.9	80.7
Puerto Rican	3,025	0.7	1.6
South American	4,123	0.9	2.2
Argentinean	650	0.1	0.3
Bolivian	125	<0.1	0.1
Chilean	288	0.1	0.2
Colombian	1,037	0.2	0.6
Ecuadorian	679	0.1	0.4
Peruvian	1,109	0.2	0.6
Venezuelan	123	<0.1	0.1
Spaniard	1,630	0.4	0.9

Population Growth: 2000–2010

Group	%
Total Population	0.2
Hispanic or Latino (of any race)	14.1
Central American, ex. Mexican	84.7
Costa Rican	68.0
Guatemalan	110.2
Honduran	119.2
Nicaraguan	97.8
Panamanian	41.6
Salvadoran	94.8
Cuban	18.5
Mexican	19.6
Puerto Rican	29.3
South American	85.1
Argentinean	136.4
Chilean	58.2
Colombian	74.6
Ecuadorian	100.3
Peruvian	99.5
Spaniard	462.1

Males per 100 Females

Group	Number
Total Population	96.1
Hispanic or Latino (of any race)	100.2
Central American, ex. Mexican	94.9
Costa Rican	87.6
Guatemalan	100.2
Honduran	86.2
Nicaraguan	91.1
Panamanian	68.3
Salvadoran	96.9
Cuban	100.3
Dominican Republic	81.3
Mexican	101.5
Puerto Rican	101.0
South American	91.0
Argentinean	94.0
Bolivian	104.9
Chilean	98.6
Colombian	89.9
Ecuadorian	84.5
Peruvian	88.6
Venezuelan	95.2
Spaniard	86.9

Average Household Size

Group	People
Total Population	2.78
Hispanic or Latino (of any race)	3.73
Central American, ex. Mexican	3.81
Costa Rican	2.60
Guatemalan	3.92
Honduran	4.24
Nicaraguan	3.36
Panamanian	2.45
Salvadoran	3.82
Cuban	2.30
Dominican Republic	2.69
Mexican	3.87
Puerto Rican	2.59
South American	2.67
Argentinean	2.38
Bolivian	2.49
Chilean	2.46
Colombian	2.55
Ecuadorian	2.92
Peruvian	2.91
Venezuelan	3.05
Spaniard	2.44

Median Age

Group	Years
Total Population	33.2
Hispanic or Latino (of any race)	26.5
Central American, ex. Mexican	31.1
Costa Rican	34.0
Guatemalan	31.2
Honduran	29.0
Nicaraguan	33.1
Panamanian	33.7
Salvadoran	31.5
Cuban	36.5
Dominican Republic	30.5
Mexican	25.6
Puerto Rican	28.8
South American	35.9
Argentinean	37.9
Bolivian	31.7
Chilean	39.3
Colombian	36.1
Ecuadorian	34.4
Peruvian	35.6
Venezuelan	33.4
Spaniard	35.7

High School Graduates
(Universe: Population 25 Years and Over)

Group	Number	%
Total Population	225,318	78.5
Hispanic or Latino (of any race)	54,104	56.6
Central American, ex. Mexican	6,270	57.1
Guatemalan	1,229	46.2
Honduran	1,090	52.1
Salvadoran	2,989	61.5
Cuban	738	87.4

Notes: (1) Percent of total population; (2) Percent of Hispanic/Latino population; Profiles include places with an overall population of at least 125,000, OR an overall population of at least 25,000 where the Hispanic/Latino population is at least 20% of the overall population. In states where less than five places meet either of these criteria, we have included places with at least 10,000 total population with the highest percentage of Hispanic/Latino population. These places are identified with an asterisk (*); Please refer to the User's Guide for a full explanation of data.

Mexican	41,335	54.3
Puerto Rican	1,415	69.6
South American	2,039	82.5
Colombian	366	72.8
Peruvian	588	85.8
Spaniard	849	86.2

Four-Year College Graduates
(Universe: Population 25 Years and Over)

Group	Number	%
Total Population	80,429	28.0
Hispanic or Latino (of any race)	10,946	11.4
Central American, ex. Mexican	1,241	11.3
Guatemalan	319	12.0
Honduran	47	2.2
Salvadoran	601	12.4
Cuban	286	33.9
Mexican	7,413	9.7
Puerto Rican	395	19.4
South American	829	33.5
Colombian	178	35.4
Peruvian	259	37.8
Spaniard	325	33.0

Population Age 3–17 Enrolled in Public School
(Universe: Population Age 3–17 Enrolled in School)

Group	Number	%
Total Population	84,896	91.5
Hispanic or Latino (of any race)	47,321	93.9
Central American, ex. Mexican	4,036	96.4
Guatemalan	1,114	96.5
Honduran	827	96.3
Salvadoran	1,602	97.7
Cuban	94	59.9
Mexican	40,600	94.4
Puerto Rican	625	84.5
South American	702	95.0
Colombian	150	100.0
Peruvian	183	92.9
Spaniard	111	57.8

Population Age 3–17 Enrolled in Private School
(Universe: Population Age 3–17 Enrolled in School)

Group	Number	%
Total Population	7,899	8.5
Hispanic or Latino (of any race)	3,062	6.1
Central American, ex. Mexican	152	3.6
Guatemalan	40	3.5
Honduran	32	3.7
Salvadoran	37	2.3
Cuban	63	40.1
Mexican	2,422	5.6
Puerto Rican	115	15.5
South American	37	5.0
Colombian	0	0.0
Peruvian	14	7.1
Spaniard	81	42.2

Foreign-Born Population

Group	Number	%
Total Population	126,384	27.4
Hispanic or Latino (of any race)	76,071	40.8
Central American, ex. Mexican	11,565	62.7
Guatemalan	2,997	65.4
Honduran	2,367	65.1
Salvadoran	4,790	60.3
Cuban	420	34.4
Mexican	60,802	39.7
Puerto Rican	61	1.8
South American	2,143	55.1
Colombian	431	54.6
Peruvian	610	61.1
Spaniard	282	17.8

Foreign-Born Naturalized U.S. Citizens

Group	Number	%
Total Population	51,192	40.5
Hispanic or Latino (of any race)	20,590	27.1
Central American, ex. Mexican	3,620	31.3
Guatemalan	697	23.3
Honduran	408	17.2
Salvadoran	1,888	39.4
Cuban	241	57.4
Mexican	15,330	25.2
Puerto Rican	40	65.6

South American	831	38.8
Colombian	123	28.5
Peruvian	339	55.6
Spaniard	221	78.4

Language Spoken at Home: English Only
(Universe: Population 5 Years and Over)

Group	Number	%
Total Population	230,885	54.1
Hispanic or Latino (of any race)	31,195	18.9
Central American, ex. Mexican	1,359	8.0
Guatemalan	215	5.1
Honduran	117	3.6
Salvadoran	548	7.6
Cuban	376	34.1
Mexican	24,777	18.3
Puerto Rican	1,442	46.1
South American	718	19.3
Colombian	147	19.3
Peruvian	86	8.6
Spaniard	929	63.2

Language Spoken at Home: Spanish
(Universe: Population 5 Years and Over)

Group	Number	%
Total Population	139,416	32.6
Hispanic or Latino (of any race)	133,471	80.8
Central American, ex. Mexican	15,521	91.8
Guatemalan	4,039	94.9
Honduran	3,081	96.1
Salvadoran	6,644	92.2
Cuban	675	61.3
Mexican	110,116	81.5
Puerto Rican	1,687	53.9
South American	2,914	78.4
Colombian	598	78.4
Peruvian	901	90.2
Spaniard	453	30.8

Unemployment Rate
(Universe: Population 16 Years and Over)

Group	%
Total Population	10.1
Hispanic or Latino (of any race)	11.4
Central American, ex. Mexican	12.3
Guatemalan	9.8
Honduran	19.9
Salvadoran	11.7
Cuban	10.5
Mexican	11.3
Puerto Rican	12.6
South American	6.1
Colombian	10.5
Peruvian	0.0
Spaniard	17.6

Class of Worker: Private Wage and Salary
(Universe: Civilian Employed Population 16 Years and Over)

Group	Number	%
Total Population	167,694	77.8
Hispanic or Latino (of any race)	65,142	82.9
Central American, ex. Mexican	7,215	81.0
Guatemalan	1,817	79.2
Honduran	1,377	88.4
Salvadoran	3,090	80.0
Cuban	479	70.2
Mexican	52,844	83.8
Puerto Rican	1,435	85.5
South American	1,422	76.1
Colombian	292	78.1
Peruvian	415	83.8
Spaniard	425	65.0

Class of Worker: Government
(Universe: Civilian Employed Population 16 Years and Over)

Group	Number	%
Total Population	31,754	14.7
Hispanic or Latino (of any race)	7,411	9.4
Central American, ex. Mexican	740	8.3
Guatemalan	166	7.2
Honduran	52	3.3
Salvadoran	326	8.4
Cuban	166	24.3
Mexican	5,665	9.0
Puerto Rican	193	11.5

South American	268	14.3
Colombian	37	9.9
Peruvian	56	11.3
Spaniard	170	26.0

Means of Transportation to Work: Car, Truck or Van
(Universe: Workers 16 Years and Over)

Group	Number	%
Total Population	174,811	83.8
Hispanic or Latino (of any race)	61,495	80.8
Central American, ex. Mexican	7,204	83.3
Guatemalan	1,756	80.3
Honduran	1,166	75.5
Salvadoran	3,430	91.0
Cuban	571	85.1
Mexican	48,884	80.1
Puerto Rican	1,396	84.0
South American	1,540	84.2
Colombian	327	95.1
Peruvian	366	75.3
Spaniard	562	89.3

Means of Transportation to Work: Public Transportation (ex. Taxicab)
(Universe: Workers 16 Years and Over)

Group	Number	%
Total Population	14,827	7.1
Hispanic or Latino (of any race)	7,948	10.4
Central American, ex. Mexican	917	10.6
Guatemalan	311	14.2
Honduran	286	18.5
Salvadoran	119	3.2
Cuban	11	1.6
Mexican	6,619	10.8
Puerto Rican	157	9.4
South American	105	5.7
Colombian	8	2.3
Peruvian	30	6.2
Spaniard	15	2.4

Homeownership Rate
(Universe: Occupied Housing Units)

Group	%
Total Population	41.6
Hispanic or Latino (of any race)	31.5
Central American, ex. Mexican	28.4
Costa Rican	37.3
Guatemalan	27.1
Honduran	17.9
Nicaraguan	28.3
Panamanian	27.4
Salvadoran	32.7
Cuban	38.5
Dominican Republic	24.0
Mexican	31.7
Puerto Rican	30.7
South American	41.5
Argentinean	45.0
Bolivian	44.7
Chilean	45.1
Colombian	40.9
Ecuadorian	42.2
Peruvian	39.9
Venezuelan	22.0
Spaniard	40.7

Median Home Value

Group	Dollars
Total Population	508,900
Hispanic or Latino (of any race)	417,800
Central American, ex. Mexican	384,900
Guatemalan	395,200
Honduran	343,600
Salvadoran	365,900
Cuban	480,800
Mexican	411,700
Puerto Rican	507,900
South American	522,300
Colombian	378,600
Peruvian	472,200
Spaniard	470,500

STATE & PLACE PROFILES

Notes: (1) Percent of total population; (2) Percent of Hispanic/Latino population; Profiles include places with an overall population of at least 125,000, OR an overall population of at least 25,000 where the Hispanic/Latino population is at least 20% of the overall population. In states where less than five places meet either of these criteria, we have included places with at least 10,000 total population with the highest percentage of Hispanic/Latino population. These places are identified with an asterisk (*); Please refer to the User's Guide for a full explanation of data.

Median Gross Rent

Group	Dollars
Total Population	1,033
Hispanic or Latino (of any race)	956
Central American, ex. Mexican	968
Guatemalan	964
Honduran	1,038
Salvadoran	942
Cuban	1,059
Mexican	946
Puerto Rican	1,048
South American	1,069
Colombian	1,002
Peruvian	980
Spaniard	1,028

Median Household Income
(2010 Inflation-Adjusted Dollars)

Group	Dollars
Total Population	51,173
Hispanic or Latino (of any race)	41,567
Central American, ex. Mexican	43,094
Guatemalan	45,318
Honduran	38,625
Salvadoran	38,889
Cuban	62,598
Mexican	40,876
Puerto Rican	53,269
South American	51,802
Colombian	44,821
Peruvian	44,063
Spaniard	26,419

Per Capita Income
(2010 Inflation-Adjusted Dollars)

Group	Dollars
Total Population	25,929
Hispanic or Latino (of any race)	15,051
Central American, ex. Mexican	15,284
Guatemalan	15,289
Honduran	11,327
Salvadoran	15,066
Cuban	25,441
Mexican	14,413
Puerto Rican	21,721
South American	22,934
Colombian	17,850
Peruvian	23,511
Spaniard	22,099

Households with $100,000+ Income

Group	Number	%
Total Population	35,355	21.8
Hispanic or Latino (of any race)	5,928	12.4
Central American, ex. Mexican	603	12.3
Guatemalan	66	5.2
Honduran	94	11.1
Salvadoran	268	11.9
Cuban	77	14.3
Mexican	4,501	11.9
Puerto Rican	244	19.9
South American	193	15.5
Colombian	9	2.9
Peruvian	48	16.9
Spaniard	51	6.8

Households with Food Stamps/SNAP Benefits During Past 12 Months

Group	Number	%
Total Population	13,882	8.6
Hispanic or Latino (of any race)	6,623	13.9
Central American, ex. Mexican	624	12.7
Guatemalan	62	4.9
Honduran	260	30.6
Salvadoran	288	12.8
Cuban	0	0.0
Mexican	5,702	15.1
Puerto Rican	164	13.4
South American	33	2.7
Colombian	17	5.5
Peruvian	7	2.5
Spaniard	16	2.1

Poverty Rate
(Income in Past 12 Months Below Poverty Level)

Group	%
Total Population	19.1
Hispanic or Latino (of any race)	25.8
Central American, ex. Mexican	25.7
Guatemalan	25.0
Honduran	37.2
Salvadoran	23.0
Cuban	15.9
Mexican	26.6
Puerto Rican	20.7
South American	13.8
Colombian	26.1
Peruvian	1.5
Spaniard	23.1

Los Angeles

Population

Group	Number	%TP[1]	%HP[2]
Total Population	3,792,621	100.0	–
Hispanic or Latino (of any race)	1,838,822	48.5	100.0
Central American, ex. Mexican	415,913	11.0	22.6
Costa Rican	3,182	0.1	0.2
Guatemalan	138,139	3.6	7.5
Honduran	23,919	0.6	1.3
Nicaraguan	15,572	0.4	0.8
Panamanian	2,131	0.1	0.1
Salvadoran	228,990	6.0	12.5
Cuban	13,494	0.4	0.7
Dominican Republic	1,602	<0.1	0.1
Mexican	1,209,573	31.9	65.8
Puerto Rican	15,565	0.4	0.8
South American	49,352	1.3	2.7
Argentinean	8,570	0.2	0.5
Bolivian	2,561	0.1	0.1
Chilean	4,112	0.1	0.2
Colombian	9,766	0.3	0.5
Ecuadorian	7,314	0.2	0.4
Paraguayan	180	<0.1	<0.1
Peruvian	14,033	0.4	0.8
Uruguayan	697	<0.1	<0.1
Venezuelan	1,490	<0.1	0.1
Spaniard	11,211	0.3	0.6

Population Growth: 2000–2010

Group	%
Total Population	2.6
Hispanic or Latino (of any race)	7.0
Central American, ex. Mexican	74.6
Costa Rican	49.7
Guatemalan	109.5
Honduran	98.8
Nicaraguan	77.1
Panamanian	50.6
Salvadoran	81.5
Cuban	8.6
Dominican Republic	126.9
Mexican	10.8
Puerto Rican	15.9
South American	56.6
Argentinean	67.2
Bolivian	96.8
Chilean	50.3
Colombian	67.8
Ecuadorian	55.9
Paraguayan	71.4
Peruvian	85.5
Uruguayan	117.8
Venezuelan	88.6
Spaniard	280.9

Males per 100 Females

Group	Number
Total Population	99.2
Hispanic or Latino (of any race)	102.5
Central American, ex. Mexican	98.8
Costa Rican	86.2
Guatemalan	114.0
Honduran	88.8
Nicaraguan	87.2
Panamanian	78.5
Salvadoran	92.8
Cuban	104.0
Dominican Republic	94.7
Mexican	104.4
Puerto Rican	101.2
South American	91.3
Argentinean	104.5
Bolivian	88.3
Chilean	88.9
Colombian	82.7
Ecuadorian	86.8
Paraguayan	59.3
Peruvian	92.7
Uruguayan	100.9
Venezuelan	95.8
Spaniard	93.6

Average Household Size

Group	People
Total Population	2.81
Hispanic or Latino (of any race)	3.89
Central American, ex. Mexican	3.94
Costa Rican	2.77
Guatemalan	4.09
Honduran	3.83
Nicaraguan	3.54
Panamanian	2.35
Salvadoran	3.94
Cuban	2.29
Dominican Republic	2.35
Mexican	4.06
Puerto Rican	2.35
South American	2.79
Argentinean	2.43
Bolivian	3.19
Chilean	2.67
Colombian	2.65
Ecuadorian	3.04
Paraguayan	2.74
Peruvian	3.07
Uruguayan	2.54
Venezuelan	2.39
Spaniard	2.58

Median Age

Group	Years
Total Population	34.1
Hispanic or Latino (of any race)	28.6
Central American, ex. Mexican	33.2
Costa Rican	39.5
Guatemalan	31.7
Honduran	32.1
Nicaraguan	36.8
Panamanian	40.7
Salvadoran	34.1
Cuban	40.7
Dominican Republic	31.6
Mexican	27.0
Puerto Rican	31.9
South American	38.7
Argentinean	39.4
Bolivian	39.5
Chilean	39.5
Colombian	36.1
Ecuadorian	41.2
Paraguayan	35.7
Peruvian	39.4
Uruguayan	40.3
Venezuelan	33.1
Spaniard	34.9

High School Graduates
(Universe: Population 25 Years and Over)

Group	Number	%
Total Population	1,809,429	73.7
Hispanic or Latino (of any race)	493,910	49.0
Central American, ex. Mexican	117,139	44.5
Costa Rican	1,650	83.8
Guatemalan	34,064	40.0
Honduran	6,028	44.1
Nicaraguan	7,804	67.3
Panamanian	1,306	91.6
Salvadoran	63,380	44.1
Cuban	7,384	75.8
Dominican Republic	676	83.5

Notes: (1) Percent of total population; (2) Percent of Hispanic/Latino population; Profiles include places with an overall population of at least 125,000, OR an overall population of at least 25,000 where the Hispanic/Latino population is at least 20% of the overall population. In states where less than five places meet either of these criteria, we have included places with at least 10,000 total population with the highest percentage of Hispanic/Latino population. These places are identified with an asterisk (*); Please refer to the User's Guide for a full explanation of data.

Mexican	309,521	47.0
Puerto Rican	7,884	80.2
South American	31,585	85.9
Argentinean	5,440	86.4
Bolivian	2,279	91.6
Chilean	2,846	86.7
Colombian	5,792	84.4
Ecuadorian	4,173	79.9
Peruvian	8,664	87.2
Venezuelan	888	88.7
Spaniard	4,624	87.7

Four-Year College Graduates
(Universe: Population 25 Years and Over)

Group	Number	%
Total Population	742,172	30.2
Hispanic or Latino (of any race)	92,069	9.1
Central American, ex. Mexican	19,863	7.5
Costa Rican	458	23.3
Guatemalan	6,163	7.2
Honduran	1,102	8.1
Nicaraguan	1,435	12.4
Panamanian	514	36.0
Salvadoran	9,646	6.7
Cuban	2,793	28.7
Dominican Republic	173	21.4
Mexican	49,079	7.4
Puerto Rican	2,707	27.5
South American	11,822	32.2
Argentinean	2,294	36.4
Bolivian	737	29.6
Chilean	878	26.8
Colombian	2,187	31.9
Ecuadorian	1,602	30.7
Peruvian	3,088	31.1
Venezuelan	355	35.5
Spaniard	1,850	35.1

Population Age 3–17 Enrolled in Public School
(Universe: Population Age 3–17 Enrolled in School)

Group	Number	%
Total Population	589,068	86.1
Hispanic or Latino (of any race)	411,269	94.4
Central American, ex. Mexican	77,465	95.0
Costa Rican	445	77.3
Guatemalan	24,804	95.7
Honduran	4,463	95.1
Nicaraguan	2,452	89.5
Panamanian	77	71.3
Salvadoran	44,067	95.3
Cuban	1,347	74.5
Dominican Republic	125	94.0
Mexican	311,583	95.0
Puerto Rican	2,180	82.9
South American	6,117	83.9
Argentinean	960	81.4
Bolivian	538	92.4
Chilean	520	95.1
Colombian	1,058	82.7
Ecuadorian	686	83.8
Peruvian	1,985	86.3
Venezuelan	103	72.0
Spaniard	604	67.7

Population Age 3–17 Enrolled in Private School
(Universe: Population Age 3–17 Enrolled in School)

Group	Number	%
Total Population	94,921	13.9
Hispanic or Latino (of any race)	24,443	5.6
Central American, ex. Mexican	4,073	5.0
Costa Rican	131	22.7
Guatemalan	1,102	4.3
Honduran	231	4.9
Nicaraguan	289	10.5
Panamanian	31	28.7
Salvadoran	2,169	4.7
Cuban	460	25.5
Dominican Republic	8	6.0
Mexican	16,393	5.0
Puerto Rican	449	17.1
South American	1,171	16.1
Argentinean	220	18.6
Bolivian	44	7.6
Chilean	27	4.9
Colombian	221	17.3

Ecuadorian	133	16.2
Peruvian	314	13.7
Venezuelan	40	28.0
Spaniard	288	32.3

Foreign-Born Population

Group	Number	%
Total Population	1,494,946	39.6
Hispanic or Latino (of any race)	922,507	50.9
Central American, ex. Mexican	285,693	67.0
Costa Rican	1,615	53.7
Guatemalan	98,505	69.5
Honduran	15,802	67.6
Nicaraguan	11,404	67.6
Panamanian	911	56.3
Salvadoran	151,631	65.5
Cuban	7,051	51.2
Dominican Republic	308	26.2
Mexican	579,073	46.2
Puerto Rican	539	3.7
South American	33,578	65.9
Argentinean	5,757	66.9
Bolivian	2,395	66.9
Chilean	2,663	59.2
Colombian	5,889	63.1
Ecuadorian	4,449	65.3
Peruvian	9,988	69.6
Venezuelan	1,060	81.9
Spaniard	1,502	20.9

Foreign-Born Naturalized U.S. Citizens

Group	Number	%
Total Population	592,483	39.6
Hispanic or Latino (of any race)	256,256	27.8
Central American, ex. Mexican	85,881	30.1
Costa Rican	885	54.8
Guatemalan	21,360	21.7
Honduran	3,600	22.8
Nicaraguan	4,899	43.0
Panamanian	714	78.4
Salvadoran	52,085	34.3
Cuban	5,048	71.6
Dominican Republic	189	61.4
Mexican	141,307	24.4
Puerto Rican	265	49.2
South American	16,684	49.7
Argentinean	2,855	49.6
Bolivian	1,377	57.5
Chilean	1,485	55.8
Colombian	2,688	45.6
Ecuadorian	2,882	64.8
Peruvian	4,182	41.9
Venezuelan	298	28.1
Spaniard	675	44.9

Language Spoken at Home: English Only
(Universe: Population 5 Years and Over)

Group	Number	%
Total Population	1,415,116	40.3
Hispanic or Latino (of any race)	180,050	10.9
Central American, ex. Mexican	15,256	3.8
Costa Rican	767	26.2
Guatemalan	3,718	2.8
Honduran	590	2.8
Nicaraguan	1,358	8.4
Panamanian	399	25.4
Salvadoran	7,989	3.7
Cuban	2,606	20.3
Dominican Republic	323	28.6
Mexican	135,186	12.0
Puerto Rican	5,804	41.9
South American	6,614	13.8
Argentinean	1,136	14.1
Bolivian	195	5.6
Chilean	734	17.6
Colombian	1,198	13.9
Ecuadorian	833	12.9
Peruvian	1,744	13.0
Venezuelan	141	11.1
Spaniard	3,564	52.1

Language Spoken at Home: Spanish
(Universe: Population 5 Years and Over)

Group	Number	%
Total Population	1,515,409	43.1
Hispanic or Latino (of any race)	1,465,019	88.8
Central American, ex. Mexican	380,800	96.0
Costa Rican	2,114	72.1
Guatemalan	126,587	96.9
Honduran	20,561	97.2
Nicaraguan	14,751	91.5
Panamanian	1,153	73.4
Salvadoran	208,046	96.2
Cuban	10,109	78.6
Dominican Republic	763	67.5
Mexican	991,579	87.9
Puerto Rican	7,817	56.5
South American	40,710	85.2
Argentinean	6,722	83.5
Bolivian	3,257	94.2
Chilean	3,391	81.3
Colombian	7,363	85.1
Ecuadorian	5,608	86.7
Peruvian	11,626	86.4
Venezuelan	1,134	88.9
Spaniard	3,072	44.9

Unemployment Rate
(Universe: Population 16 Years and Over)

Group	%
Total Population	9.1
Hispanic or Latino (of any race)	9.3
Central American, ex. Mexican	9.4
Costa Rican	6.3
Guatemalan	9.3
Honduran	9.7
Nicaraguan	9.5
Panamanian	12.5
Salvadoran	9.5
Cuban	7.1
Dominican Republic	11.9
Mexican	9.3
Puerto Rican	11.1
South American	7.8
Argentinean	3.3
Bolivian	14.2
Chilean	9.0
Colombian	9.5
Ecuadorian	5.8
Peruvian	7.5
Venezuelan	14.0
Spaniard	10.1

Class of Worker: Private Wage and Salary
(Universe: Civilian Employed Population 16 Years and Over)

Group	Number	%
Total Population	1,414,430	78.7
Hispanic or Latino (of any race)	665,476	81.9
Central American, ex. Mexican	181,928	81.1
Costa Rican	1,033	67.2
Guatemalan	61,246	80.8
Honduran	9,597	81.4
Nicaraguan	6,905	80.3
Panamanian	672	74.5
Salvadoran	98,612	81.6
Cuban	5,139	80.1
Dominican Republic	485	78.9
Mexican	433,709	82.8
Puerto Rican	5,441	76.2
South American	21,538	77.3
Argentinean	3,768	75.5
Bolivian	1,340	72.7
Chilean	1,710	74.2
Colombian	4,000	80.8
Ecuadorian	2,898	76.6
Peruvian	6,478	79.4
Venezuelan	446	71.4
Spaniard	2,808	73.8

Class of Worker: Government
(Universe: Civilian Employed Population 16 Years and Over)

Group	Number	%
Total Population	180,342	10.0
Hispanic or Latino (of any race)	59,643	7.3
Central American, ex. Mexican	12,259	5.5
Costa Rican	217	14.1
Guatemalan	3,022	4.0
Honduran	525	4.5
Nicaraguan	824	9.6
Panamanian	102	11.3

STATE & PLACE PROFILES

Notes: (1) Percent of total population; (2) Percent of Hispanic/Latino population; Profiles include places with an overall population of at least 125,000, OR an overall population of at least 25,000 where the Hispanic/Latino population is at least 20% of the overall population. In states where less than five places meet either of these criteria, we have included places with at least 10,000 total population with the highest percentage of Hispanic/Latino population. These places are identified with an asterisk (*); Please refer to the User's Guide for a full explanation of data.

Group	Number	%
Salvadoran	7,268	6.0
Cuban	819	12.8
Dominican Republic	33	5.4
Mexican	40,703	7.8
Puerto Rican	922	12.9
South American	2,450	8.8
Argentinean	437	8.8
Bolivian	173	9.4
Chilean	220	9.5
Colombian	317	6.4
Ecuadorian	502	13.3
Peruvian	558	6.8
Venezuelan	45	7.2
Spaniard	595	15.6

Means of Transportation to Work: Car, Truck or Van

(Universe: Workers 16 Years and Over)

Group	Number	%
Total Population	1,364,484	78.1
Hispanic or Latino (of any race)	582,673	73.5
Central American, ex. Mexican	151,658	69.1
Costa Rican	1,323	87.4
Guatemalan	44,727	60.2
Honduran	7,879	68.6
Nicaraguan	5,984	71.6
Panamanian	527	60.4
Salvadoran	87,916	74.3
Cuban	5,142	82.1
Dominican Republic	439	76.3
Mexican	381,413	74.6
Puerto Rican	5,544	79.2
South American	21,400	78.6
Argentinean	4,022	81.6
Bolivian	1,358	73.7
Chilean	1,685	75.6
Colombian	3,482	71.9
Ecuadorian	2,960	80.6
Peruvian	6,352	80.7
Venezuelan	433	69.3
Spaniard	3,089	82.0

Means of Transportation to Work: Public Transportation (ex. Taxicab)

(Universe: Workers 16 Years and Over)

Group	Number	%
Total Population	192,261	11.0
Hispanic or Latino (of any race)	139,486	17.6
Central American, ex. Mexican	49,746	22.7
Costa Rican	18	1.2
Guatemalan	22,504	30.3
Honduran	2,631	22.9
Nicaraguan	1,598	19.1
Panamanian	122	14.0
Salvadoran	21,876	18.5
Cuban	435	6.9
Dominican Republic	36	6.3
Mexican	83,927	16.4
Puerto Rican	643	9.2
South American	2,511	9.2
Argentinean	314	6.4
Bolivian	315	17.1
Chilean	141	6.3
Colombian	556	11.5
Ecuadorian	366	10.0
Peruvian	760	9.7
Venezuelan	24	3.8
Spaniard	188	5.0

Homeownership Rate

(Universe: Occupied Housing Units)

Group	%
Total Population	38.2
Hispanic or Latino (of any race)	29.4
Central American, ex. Mexican	23.8
Costa Rican	39.4
Guatemalan	19.2
Honduran	16.9
Nicaraguan	25.8
Panamanian	31.6
Salvadoran	26.7
Cuban	37.8
Dominican Republic	26.1
Mexican	31.5
Puerto Rican	26.6
South American	37.2
Argentinean	42.4
Bolivian	44.1
Chilean	41.3
Colombian	33.1
Ecuadorian	40.7
Paraguayan	31.5
Peruvian	33.3
Uruguayan	39.2
Venezuelan	26.3
Spaniard	39.8

Median Home Value

Group	Dollars
Total Population	553,900
Hispanic or Latino (of any race)	431,800
Central American, ex. Mexican	421,100
Costa Rican	527,200
Guatemalan	424,100
Honduran	439,100
Nicaraguan	468,500
Panamanian	687,500
Salvadoran	409,400
Cuban	569,300
Dominican Republic	523,300
Mexican	423,800
Puerto Rican	537,800
South American	509,300
Argentinean	561,000
Bolivian	486,900
Chilean	505,800
Colombian	523,900
Ecuadorian	538,800
Peruvian	459,000
Venezuelan	292,300
Spaniard	533,200

Median Gross Rent

Group	Dollars
Total Population	1,077
Hispanic or Latino (of any race)	947
Central American, ex. Mexican	909
Costa Rican	991
Guatemalan	905
Honduran	908
Nicaraguan	909
Panamanian	961
Salvadoran	908
Cuban	999
Dominican Republic	1,383
Mexican	949
Puerto Rican	1,073
South American	1,138
Argentinean	1,197
Bolivian	1,063
Chilean	1,256
Colombian	1,217
Ecuadorian	1,017
Peruvian	1,048
Venezuelan	1,341
Spaniard	1,287

Median Household Income

(2010 Inflation-Adjusted Dollars)

Group	Dollars
Total Population	49,138
Hispanic or Latino (of any race)	38,617
Central American, ex. Mexican	36,976
Costa Rican	48,734
Guatemalan	35,135
Honduran	31,665
Nicaraguan	48,625
Panamanian	39,174
Salvadoran	37,381
Cuban	50,390
Dominican Republic	41,303
Mexican	38,235
Puerto Rican	41,092
South American	49,538
Argentinean	61,048
Bolivian	41,735
Chilean	59,259
Colombian	46,241
Ecuadorian	50,199
Peruvian	44,700
Venezuelan	31,550
Spaniard	57,774

Per Capita Income

(2010 Inflation-Adjusted Dollars)

Group	Dollars
Total Population	27,620
Hispanic or Latino (of any race)	13,977
Central American, ex. Mexican	13,818
Costa Rican	21,143
Guatemalan	12,750
Honduran	13,175
Nicaraguan	17,390
Panamanian	32,361
Salvadoran	13,985
Cuban	35,090
Dominican Republic	27,303
Mexican	13,014
Puerto Rican	24,620
South American	25,891
Argentinean	31,683
Bolivian	20,830
Chilean	29,133
Colombian	23,192
Ecuadorian	25,363
Peruvian	21,591
Venezuelan	22,046
Spaniard	32,352

Households with $100,000+ Income

Group	Number	%
Total Population	290,386	22.1
Hispanic or Latino (of any race)	50,371	10.8
Central American, ex. Mexican	9,543	8.0
Costa Rican	177	17.0
Guatemalan	2,581	6.8
Honduran	475	7.4
Nicaraguan	826	16.7
Panamanian	147	18.1
Salvadoran	5,059	7.8
Cuban	1,212	22.1
Dominican Republic	72	13.2
Mexican	32,211	10.7
Puerto Rican	1,196	19.7
South American	3,679	19.4
Argentinean	971	28.5
Bolivian	258	23.9
Chilean	460	25.6
Colombian	558	15.7
Ecuadorian	590	21.6
Peruvian	436	9.0
Venezuelan	104	17.1
Spaniard	937	28.0

Households with Food Stamps/SNAP Benefits During Past 12 Months

Group	Number	%
Total Population	80,046	6.1
Hispanic or Latino (of any race)	48,036	10.3
Central American, ex. Mexican	10,067	8.5
Costa Rican	73	7.0
Guatemalan	3,417	9.0
Honduran	732	11.5
Nicaraguan	435	8.8
Panamanian	15	1.9
Salvadoran	5,192	8.0
Cuban	206	3.8
Dominican Republic	53	9.7
Mexican	35,911	11.9
Puerto Rican	317	5.2
South American	585	3.1
Argentinean	87	2.6
Bolivian	0	0.0
Chilean	68	3.8
Colombian	33	0.9
Ecuadorian	156	5.7
Peruvian	182	3.8
Venezuelan	0	0.0
Spaniard	120	3.6

Poverty Rate

(Income in Past 12 Months Below Poverty Level)

Group	%
Total Population	19.5
Hispanic or Latino (of any race)	25.4

Notes: (1) Percent of total population; (2) Percent of Hispanic/Latino population; Profiles include places with an overall population of at least 125,000, OR an overall population of at least 25,000 where the Hispanic/Latino population is at least 20% of the overall population. In states where less than five places meet either of these criteria, we have included places with at least 10,000 total population with the highest percentage of Hispanic/Latino population. These places are identified with an asterisk (*); Please refer to the User's Guide for a full explanation of data.

Central American, ex. Mexican	23.1
Costa Rican	17.3
Guatemalan	27.2
Honduran	32.3
Nicaraguan	17.6
Panamanian	4.7
Salvadoran	20.3
Cuban	9.0
Dominican Republic	19.3
Mexican	27.2
Puerto Rican	21.4
South American	14.6
Argentinean	10.4
Bolivian	7.9
Chilean	8.3
Colombian	15.9
Ecuadorian	15.0
Peruvian	18.8
Venezuelan	15.7
Spaniard	14.2

Los Banos

Population

Group	Number	%TP[1]	%HP[2]
Total Population	35,972	100.0	–
Hispanic or Latino (of any race)	23,346	64.9	100.0
Central American, ex. Mexican	531	1.5	2.3
Salvadoran	312	0.9	1.3
Mexican	21,344	59.3	91.4
Puerto Rican	226	0.6	1.0
South American	160	0.4	0.7
Spaniard	123	0.3	0.5

Population Growth: 2000–2010

Group	%
Total Population	39.1
Hispanic or Latino (of any race)	78.9
Central American, ex. Mexican	156.5
Mexican	98.5
Puerto Rican	59.2

Males per 100 Females

Group	Number
Total Population	99.2
Hispanic or Latino (of any race)	102.0
Central American, ex. Mexican	103.4
Salvadoran	98.7
Mexican	102.3
Puerto Rican	86.8
South American	113.3
Spaniard	75.7

Average Household Size

Group	People
Total Population	3.49
Hispanic or Latino (of any race)	4.13
Central American, ex. Mexican	4.03
Salvadoran	3.80
Mexican	4.16
Puerto Rican	3.41
South American	3.68
Spaniard	2.79

Median Age

Group	Years
Total Population	29.8
Hispanic or Latino (of any race)	24.3
Central American, ex. Mexican	30.2
Salvadoran	29.2
Mexican	24.1
Puerto Rican	22.3
South American	33.4
Spaniard	37.8

High School Graduates
(Universe: Population 25 Years and Over)

Group	Number	%
Total Population	12,222	65.1
Hispanic or Latino (of any race)	5,960	53.2
Mexican	5,526	52.7

Four-Year College Graduates
(Universe: Population 25 Years and Over)

Group	Number	%
Total Population	1,745	9.3
Hispanic or Latino (of any race)	603	5.4
Mexican	530	5.1

Population Age 3–17 Enrolled in Public School
(Universe: Population Age 3–17 Enrolled in School)

Group	Number	%
Total Population	8,468	96.6
Hispanic or Latino (of any race)	6,644	97.5
Mexican	6,294	97.3

Population Age 3–17 Enrolled in Private School
(Universe: Population Age 3–17 Enrolled in School)

Group	Number	%
Total Population	296	3.4
Hispanic or Latino (of any race)	172	2.5
Mexican	172	2.7

Foreign-Born Population

Group	Number	%
Total Population	8,613	24.9
Hispanic or Latino (of any race)	7,057	30.0
Mexican	6,622	29.8

Foreign-Born Naturalized U.S. Citizens

Group	Number	%
Total Population	2,982	34.6
Hispanic or Latino (of any race)	2,072	29.4
Mexican	1,938	29.3

Language Spoken at Home: English Only
(Universe: Population 5 Years and Over)

Group	Number	%
Total Population	13,894	44.3
Hispanic or Latino (of any race)	5,691	27.3
Mexican	5,285	26.8

Language Spoken at Home: Spanish
(Universe: Population 5 Years and Over)

Group	Number	%
Total Population	15,503	49.4
Hispanic or Latino (of any race)	15,134	72.6
Mexican	14,418	73.0

Unemployment Rate
(Universe: Population 16 Years and Over)

Group	%
Total Population	14.7
Hispanic or Latino (of any race)	14.0
Mexican	14.2

Class of Worker: Private Wage and Salary
(Universe: Civilian Employed Population 16 Years and Over)

Group	Number	%
Total Population	11,200	84.0
Hispanic or Latino (of any race)	7,745	91.6
Mexican	7,428	92.1

Class of Worker: Government
(Universe: Civilian Employed Population 16 Years and Over)

Group	Number	%
Total Population	1,537	11.5
Hispanic or Latino (of any race)	474	5.6
Mexican	460	5.7

Means of Transportation to Work: Car, Truck or Van
(Universe: Workers 16 Years and Over)

Group	Number	%
Total Population	12,084	94.8
Hispanic or Latino (of any race)	7,708	95.4
Mexican	7,366	95.5

Means of Transportation to Work: Public Transportation (ex. Taxicab)
(Universe: Workers 16 Years and Over)

Group	Number	%
Total Population	25	0.2
Hispanic or Latino (of any race)	25	0.3
Mexican	25	0.3

Homeownership Rate
(Universe: Occupied Housing Units)

Group	%
Total Population	60.4
Hispanic or Latino (of any race)	53.2
Central American, ex. Mexican	58.0
Salvadoran	59.0
Mexican	53.2
Puerto Rican	57.1
South American	77.3
Spaniard	63.5

Median Home Value

Group	Dollars
Total Population	248,900
Hispanic or Latino (of any race)	253,700
Mexican	247,700

Median Gross Rent

Group	Dollars
Total Population	972
Hispanic or Latino (of any race)	1,018
Mexican	1,005

Median Household Income
(2010 Inflation-Adjusted Dollars)

Group	Dollars
Total Population	54,375
Hispanic or Latino (of any race)	51,508
Mexican	51,548

Per Capita Income
(2010 Inflation-Adjusted Dollars)

Group	Dollars
Total Population	18,437
Hispanic or Latino (of any race)	13,697
Mexican	13,368

Households with $100,000+ Income

Group	Number	%
Total Population	1,557	16.1
Hispanic or Latino (of any race)	670	12.1
Mexican	617	12.3

Households with Food Stamps/SNAP Benefits During Past 12 Months

Group	Number	%
Total Population	906	9.4
Hispanic or Latino (of any race)	599	10.9
Mexican	517	10.3

Poverty Rate
(Income in Past 12 Months Below Poverty Level)

Group	%
Total Population	18.7
Hispanic or Latino (of any race)	21.5
Mexican	21.3

Lynwood

Population

Group	Number	%TP[1]	%HP[2]
Total Population	69,772	100.0	–
Hispanic or Latino (of any race)	60,452	86.6	100.0
Central American, ex. Mexican	5,761	8.3	9.5
Guatemalan	1,754	2.5	2.9
Honduran	420	0.6	0.7
Nicaraguan	315	0.5	0.5
Salvadoran	3,154	4.5	5.2
Cuban	110	0.2	0.2
Mexican	51,021	73.1	84.4
Puerto Rican	192	0.3	0.3
South American	349	0.5	0.6
Ecuadorian	128	0.2	0.2
Peruvian	137	0.2	0.2

Population Growth: 2000–2010

Group	%
Total Population	-0.1
Hispanic or Latino (of any race)	5.1
Central American, ex. Mexican	67.4
Guatemalan	82.9
Honduran	122.2
Nicaraguan	80.0

Notes: (1) Percent of total population; (2) Percent of Hispanic/Latino population; Profiles include places with an overall population of at least 125,000, OR an overall population of at least 25,000 where the Hispanic/Latino population is at least 20% of the overall population. In states where less than five places meet either of these criteria, we have included places with at least 10,000 total population with the highest percentage of Hispanic/Latino population. These places are identified with an asterisk (*); Please refer to the User's Guide for a full explanation of data.

Salvadoran	77.7
Mexican	9.7
Puerto Rican	11.0
South American	51.1

Males per 100 Females

Group	Number
Total Population	94.7
Hispanic or Latino (of any race)	98.7
Central American, ex. Mexican	96.3
Guatemalan	106.1
Honduran	89.2
Nicaraguan	81.0
Salvadoran	93.6
Cuban	120.0
Mexican	100.2
Puerto Rican	92.0
South American	96.1
Ecuadorian	80.3
Peruvian	132.2

Average Household Size

Group	People
Total Population	4.57
Hispanic or Latino (of any race)	4.93
Central American, ex. Mexican	4.79
Guatemalan	4.90
Honduran	4.69
Nicaraguan	4.51
Salvadoran	4.82
Cuban	3.68
Mexican	4.98
Puerto Rican	3.43
South American	4.53
Ecuadorian	4.45
Peruvian	5.13

Median Age

Group	Years
Total Population	27.8
Hispanic or Latino (of any race)	26.4
Central American, ex. Mexican	33.9
Guatemalan	34.5
Honduran	31.4
Nicaraguan	35.8
Salvadoran	33.9
Cuban	39.0
Mexican	25.6
Puerto Rican	26.5
South American	39.8
Ecuadorian	41.5
Peruvian	32.8

High School Graduates
(Universe: Population 25 Years and Over)

Group	Number	%
Total Population	19,113	49.7
Hispanic or Latino (of any race)	12,882	42.7
Central American, ex. Mexican	1,765	44.0
Guatemalan	403	39.9
Salvadoran	1,104	46.0
Mexican	10,595	42.0

Four-Year College Graduates
(Universe: Population 25 Years and Over)

Group	Number	%
Total Population	1,798	4.7
Hispanic or Latino (of any race)	1,030	3.4
Central American, ex. Mexican	153	3.8
Guatemalan	29	2.9
Salvadoran	102	4.3
Mexican	856	3.4

Population Age 3–17 Enrolled in Public School
(Universe: Population Age 3–17 Enrolled in School)

Group	Number	%
Total Population	17,135	97.5
Hispanic or Latino (of any race)	15,673	97.6
Central American, ex. Mexican	1,344	94.6
Guatemalan	262	100.0
Salvadoran	895	94.2
Mexican	13,961	98.0

Population Age 3–17 Enrolled in Private School
(Universe: Population Age 3–17 Enrolled in School)

Group	Number	%
Total Population	445	2.5
Hispanic or Latino (of any race)	379	2.4
Central American, ex. Mexican	77	5.4
Guatemalan	0	0.0
Salvadoran	55	5.8
Mexican	292	2.0

Foreign-Born Population

Group	Number	%
Total Population	27,995	40.1
Hispanic or Latino (of any race)	27,505	47.0
Central American, ex. Mexican	4,040	60.4
Guatemalan	892	56.2
Salvadoran	2,462	60.5
Mexican	22,892	45.6

Foreign-Born Naturalized U.S. Citizens

Group	Number	%
Total Population	8,724	31.2
Hispanic or Latino (of any race)	8,511	30.9
Central American, ex. Mexican	1,584	39.2
Guatemalan	331	37.1
Salvadoran	1,017	41.3
Mexican	6,494	28.4

Language Spoken at Home: English Only
(Universe: Population 5 Years and Over)

Group	Number	%
Total Population	12,755	19.8
Hispanic or Latino (of any race)	2,927	5.5
Central American, ex. Mexican	189	3.1
Guatemalan	0	0.0
Salvadoran	128	3.5
Mexican	2,433	5.3

Language Spoken at Home: Spanish
(Universe: Population 5 Years and Over)

Group	Number	%
Total Population	51,017	79.3
Hispanic or Latino (of any race)	50,529	94.5
Central American, ex. Mexican	5,963	96.9
Guatemalan	1,548	100.0
Salvadoran	3,559	96.5
Mexican	43,339	94.7

Unemployment Rate
(Universe: Population 16 Years and Over)

Group	%
Total Population	10.5
Hispanic or Latino (of any race)	10.3
Central American, ex. Mexican	11.0
Guatemalan	8.1
Salvadoran	11.6
Mexican	10.0

Class of Worker: Private Wage and Salary
(Universe: Civilian Employed Population 16 Years and Over)

Group	Number	%
Total Population	21,376	83.9
Hispanic or Latino (of any race)	19,711	86.5
Central American, ex. Mexican	2,605	86.9
Guatemalan	805	93.2
Salvadoran	1,548	86.6
Mexican	16,619	86.6

Class of Worker: Government
(Universe: Civilian Employed Population 16 Years and Over)

Group	Number	%
Total Population	2,650	10.4
Hispanic or Latino (of any race)	1,774	7.8
Central American, ex. Mexican	177	5.9
Guatemalan	51	5.9
Salvadoran	95	5.3
Mexican	1,559	8.1

Means of Transportation to Work: Car, Truck or Van
(Universe: Workers 16 Years and Over)

Group	Number	%
Total Population	21,821	87.0
Hispanic or Latino (of any race)	19,629	87.3
Central American, ex. Mexican	2,400	80.4
Guatemalan	578	67.8
Salvadoran	1,538	86.1
Mexican	16,692	88.4

Means of Transportation to Work: Public Transportation (ex. Taxicab)
(Universe: Workers 16 Years and Over)

Group	Number	%
Total Population	1,508	6.0
Hispanic or Latino (of any race)	1,371	6.1
Central American, ex. Mexican	340	11.4
Guatemalan	160	18.8
Salvadoran	118	6.6
Mexican	978	5.2

Homeownership Rate
(Universe: Occupied Housing Units)

Group	%
Total Population	46.5
Hispanic or Latino (of any race)	45.1
Central American, ex. Mexican	49.5
Guatemalan	50.8
Honduran	34.3
Nicaraguan	37.9
Salvadoran	52.3
Cuban	41.9
Mexican	45.1
Puerto Rican	20.5
South American	46.9
Ecuadorian	65.0
Peruvian	32.3

Median Home Value

Group	Dollars
Total Population	406,500
Hispanic or Latino (of any race)	409,200
Central American, ex. Mexican	350,000
Guatemalan	304,700
Salvadoran	351,100
Mexican	413,000

Median Gross Rent

Group	Dollars
Total Population	955
Hispanic or Latino (of any race)	963
Central American, ex. Mexican	943
Guatemalan	1,005
Salvadoran	919
Mexican	962

Median Household Income
(2010 Inflation-Adjusted Dollars)

Group	Dollars
Total Population	43,654
Hispanic or Latino (of any race)	44,029
Central American, ex. Mexican	50,799
Guatemalan	55,521
Salvadoran	47,863
Mexican	43,099

Per Capita Income
(2010 Inflation-Adjusted Dollars)

Group	Dollars
Total Population	12,674
Hispanic or Latino (of any race)	12,011
Central American, ex. Mexican	13,661
Guatemalan	14,403
Salvadoran	13,530
Mexican	11,745

Households with $100,000+ Income

Group	Number	%
Total Population	1,510	10.0
Hispanic or Latino (of any race)	1,235	9.9
Central American, ex. Mexican	197	12.9
Guatemalan	18	5.3
Salvadoran	142	14.3
Mexican	1,028	9.7

Households with Food Stamps/SNAP Benefits During Past 12 Months

Group	Number	%
Total Population	1,522	10.1
Hispanic or Latino (of any race)	1,315	10.5
Central American, ex. Mexican	173	11.3
Guatemalan	23	6.7

Notes: (1) Percent of total population; (2) Percent of Hispanic/Latino population; Profiles include places with an overall population of at least 125,000, OR an overall population of at least 25,000 where the Hispanic/Latino population is at least 20% of the overall population. In states where less than five places meet either of these criteria, we have included places with at least 10,000 total population with the highest percentage of Hispanic/Latino population. These places are identified with an asterisk (*); Please refer to the User's Guide for a full explanation of data.

Group	Number	%
Salvadoran	105	10.6
Mexican	1,107	10.5

Poverty Rate
(Income in Past 12 Months Below Poverty Level)

Group	%
Total Population	20.1
Hispanic or Latino (of any race)	20.4
Central American, ex. Mexican	15.6
Guatemalan	15.4
Salvadoran	16.1
Mexican	21.2

Madera

Population

Group	Number	%TP[1]	%HP[2]
Total Population	61,416	100.0	–
Hispanic or Latino (of any race)	47,103	76.7	100.0
Central American, ex. Mexican	491	0.8	1.0
Guatemalan	104	0.2	0.2
Salvadoran	287	0.5	0.6
Mexican	44,444	72.4	94.4
Puerto Rican	227	0.4	0.5
Spaniard	235	0.4	0.5

Population Growth: 2000–2010

Group	%
Total Population	42.1
Hispanic or Latino (of any race)	60.9
Central American, ex. Mexican	149.2
Mexican	73.9
Puerto Rican	112.1

Males per 100 Females

Group	Number
Total Population	104.0
Hispanic or Latino (of any race)	108.4
Central American, ex. Mexican	91.1
Guatemalan	96.2
Salvadoran	90.1
Mexican	109.5
Puerto Rican	94.0
Spaniard	97.5

Average Household Size

Group	People
Total Population	3.82
Hispanic or Latino (of any race)	4.47
Central American, ex. Mexican	4.02
Guatemalan	5.06
Salvadoran	3.83
Mexican	4.50
Puerto Rican	3.12
Spaniard	4.06

Median Age

Group	Years
Total Population	26.6
Hispanic or Latino (of any race)	23.6
Central American, ex. Mexican	34.9
Guatemalan	32.0
Salvadoran	35.2
Mexican	23.4
Puerto Rican	29.3
Spaniard	29.8

High School Graduates
(Universe: Population 25 Years and Over)

Group	Number	%
Total Population	17,444	55.8
Hispanic or Latino (of any race)	8,222	41.1
Mexican	7,637	40.6

Four-Year College Graduates
(Universe: Population 25 Years and Over)

Group	Number	%
Total Population	3,129	10.0
Hispanic or Latino (of any race)	1,097	5.5
Mexican	1,011	5.4

Population Age 3–17 Enrolled in Public School
(Universe: Population Age 3–17 Enrolled in School)

Group	Number	%
Total Population	14,811	97.6
Hispanic or Latino (of any race)	12,252	97.7
Mexican	11,906	97.8

Population Age 3–17 Enrolled in Private School
(Universe: Population Age 3–17 Enrolled in School)

Group	Number	%
Total Population	370	2.4
Hispanic or Latino (of any race)	286	2.3
Mexican	274	2.2

Foreign-Born Population

Group	Number	%
Total Population	17,392	29.5
Hispanic or Latino (of any race)	15,981	36.7
Mexican	15,284	36.6

Foreign-Born Naturalized U.S. Citizens

Group	Number	%
Total Population	3,290	18.9
Hispanic or Latino (of any race)	2,570	16.1
Mexican	2,342	15.3

Language Spoken at Home: English Only
(Universe: Population 5 Years and Over)

Group	Number	%
Total Population	20,997	39.7
Hispanic or Latino (of any race)	8,629	22.6
Mexican	8,023	22.1

Language Spoken at Home: Spanish
(Universe: Population 5 Years and Over)

Group	Number	%
Total Population	29,896	56.6
Hispanic or Latino (of any race)	29,274	76.8
Mexican	28,173	77.5

Unemployment Rate
(Universe: Population 16 Years and Over)

Group	%
Total Population	12.6
Hispanic or Latino (of any race)	14.4
Mexican	13.8

Class of Worker: Private Wage and Salary
(Universe: Civilian Employed Population 16 Years and Over)

Group	Number	%
Total Population	16,436	77.3
Hispanic or Latino (of any race)	12,471	83.9
Mexican	12,049	84.5

Class of Worker: Government
(Universe: Civilian Employed Population 16 Years and Over)

Group	Number	%
Total Population	3,345	15.7
Hispanic or Latino (of any race)	1,733	11.7
Mexican	1,589	11.1

Means of Transportation to Work: Car, Truck or Van
(Universe: Workers 16 Years and Over)

Group	Number	%
Total Population	16,691	91.6
Hispanic or Latino (of any race)	11,336	92.5
Mexican	10,903	92.5

Means of Transportation to Work: Public Transportation (ex. Taxicab)
(Universe: Workers 16 Years and Over)

Group	Number	%
Total Population	36	0.2
Hispanic or Latino (of any race)	36	0.3
Mexican	36	0.3

Homeownership Rate
(Universe: Occupied Housing Units)

Group	%
Total Population	50.8
Hispanic or Latino (of any race)	44.1
Central American, ex. Mexican	50.0
Guatemalan	29.4
Salvadoran	55.4
Mexican	44.0

Group	%
Puerto Rican	43.2
Spaniard	52.8

Median Home Value

Group	Dollars
Total Population	230,300
Hispanic or Latino (of any race)	219,000
Mexican	221,500

Median Gross Rent

Group	Dollars
Total Population	841
Hispanic or Latino (of any race)	825
Mexican	822

Median Household Income
(2010 Inflation-Adjusted Dollars)

Group	Dollars
Total Population	40,889
Hispanic or Latino (of any race)	37,139
Mexican	36,687

Per Capita Income
(2010 Inflation-Adjusted Dollars)

Group	Dollars
Total Population	14,784
Hispanic or Latino (of any race)	10,859
Mexican	10,686

Households with $100,000+ Income

Group	Number	%
Total Population	1,624	10.2
Hispanic or Latino (of any race)	414	4.4
Mexican	361	4.1

Households with Food Stamps/SNAP Benefits During Past 12 Months

Group	Number	%
Total Population	2,783	17.6
Hispanic or Latino (of any race)	2,191	23.2
Mexican	2,123	23.9

Poverty Rate
(Income in Past 12 Months Below Poverty Level)

Group	%
Total Population	25.7
Hispanic or Latino (of any race)	29.3
Mexican	29.6

Manteca

Population

Group	Number	%TP[1]	%HP[2]
Total Population	67,096	100.0	–
Hispanic or Latino (of any race)	25,317	37.7	100.0
Central American, ex. Mexican	882	1.3	3.5
Guatemalan	175	0.3	0.7
Nicaraguan	210	0.3	0.8
Salvadoran	396	0.6	1.6
Mexican	20,962	31.2	82.8
Puerto Rican	844	1.3	3.3
South American	315	0.5	1.2
Peruvian	173	0.3	0.7
Spaniard	433	0.6	1.7

Population Growth: 2000–2010

Group	%
Total Population	36.2
Hispanic or Latino (of any race)	104.8
Central American, ex. Mexican	628.9
Mexican	115.4
Puerto Rican	87.1

Males per 100 Females

Group	Number
Total Population	96.8
Hispanic or Latino (of any race)	100.1
Central American, ex. Mexican	90.5
Guatemalan	108.3
Nicaraguan	94.4
Salvadoran	88.6
Mexican	102.1
Puerto Rican	89.7
South American	104.5

STATE & PLACE PROFILES

Notes: (1) Percent of total population; (2) Percent of Hispanic/Latino population; Profiles include places with an overall population of at least 125,000, OR an overall population of at least 25,000 where the Hispanic/Latino population is at least 20% of the overall population. In states where less than five places meet either of these criteria, we have included places with at least 10,000 total population with the highest percentage of Hispanic/Latino population. These places are identified with an asterisk (*); Please refer to the User's Guide for a full explanation of data.

Peruvian	98.9
Spaniard	78.2

Average Household Size

Group	People
Total Population	3.08
Hispanic or Latino (of any race)	3.80
Central American, ex. Mexican	3.81
Guatemalan	4.62
Nicaraguan	3.45
Salvadoran	3.97
Mexican	3.90
Puerto Rican	3.23
South American	3.17
Peruvian	3.26
Spaniard	2.75

Median Age

Group	Years
Total Population	33.6
Hispanic or Latino (of any race)	25.1
Central American, ex. Mexican	32.3
Guatemalan	33.1
Nicaraguan	27.5
Salvadoran	32.4
Mexican	24.3
Puerto Rican	25.3
South American	37.1
Peruvian	37.8
Spaniard	37.8

High School Graduates
(Universe: Population 25 Years and Over)

Group	Number	%
Total Population	32,228	82.5
Hispanic or Latino (of any race)	7,499	65.4
Mexican	6,055	62.8

Four-Year College Graduates
(Universe: Population 25 Years and Over)

Group	Number	%
Total Population	6,097	15.6
Hispanic or Latino (of any race)	662	5.8
Mexican	539	5.6

Population Age 3–17 Enrolled in Public School
(Universe: Population Age 3–17 Enrolled in School)

Group	Number	%
Total Population	13,984	93.4
Hispanic or Latino (of any race)	6,845	95.0
Mexican	5,801	94.7

Population Age 3–17 Enrolled in Private School
(Universe: Population Age 3–17 Enrolled in School)

Group	Number	%
Total Population	992	6.6
Hispanic or Latino (of any race)	358	5.0
Mexican	323	5.3

Foreign-Born Population

Group	Number	%
Total Population	10,864	16.7
Hispanic or Latino (of any race)	6,200	25.9
Mexican	5,459	26.7

Foreign-Born Naturalized U.S. Citizens

Group	Number	%
Total Population	5,621	51.7
Hispanic or Latino (of any race)	2,233	36.0
Mexican	1,677	30.7

Language Spoken at Home: English Only
(Universe: Population 5 Years and Over)

Group	Number	%
Total Population	42,178	70.8
Hispanic or Latino (of any race)	8,998	43.3
Mexican	6,858	39.2

Language Spoken at Home: Spanish
(Universe: Population 5 Years and Over)

Group	Number	%
Total Population	12,083	20.3
Hispanic or Latino (of any race)	11,615	55.9
Mexican	10,580	60.4

Unemployment Rate
(Universe: Population 16 Years and Over)

Group	%
Total Population	11.8
Hispanic or Latino (of any race)	11.7
Mexican	11.4

Class of Worker: Private Wage and Salary
(Universe: Civilian Employed Population 16 Years and Over)

Group	Number	%
Total Population	22,719	78.6
Hispanic or Latino (of any race)	8,223	86.3
Mexican	7,243	88.2

Class of Worker: Government
(Universe: Civilian Employed Population 16 Years and Over)

Group	Number	%
Total Population	4,432	15.3
Hispanic or Latino (of any race)	925	9.7
Mexican	721	8.8

Means of Transportation to Work: Car, Truck or Van
(Universe: Workers 16 Years and Over)

Group	Number	%
Total Population	26,190	93.4
Hispanic or Latino (of any race)	8,882	96.1
Mexican	7,645	96.2

Means of Transportation to Work: Public Transportation (ex. Taxicab)
(Universe: Workers 16 Years and Over)

Group	Number	%
Total Population	379	1.4
Hispanic or Latino (of any race)	60	0.6
Mexican	47	0.6

Homeownership Rate
(Universe: Occupied Housing Units)

Group	%
Total Population	62.5
Hispanic or Latino (of any race)	52.2
Central American, ex. Mexican	56.1
Guatemalan	47.6
Nicaraguan	67.9
Salvadoran	52.8
Mexican	51.9
Puerto Rican	49.0
South American	60.2
Peruvian	53.4
Spaniard	65.1

Median Home Value

Group	Dollars
Total Population	324,900
Hispanic or Latino (of any race)	327,200
Mexican	333,000

Median Gross Rent

Group	Dollars
Total Population	1,077
Hispanic or Latino (of any race)	1,054
Mexican	1,044

Median Household Income
(2010 Inflation-Adjusted Dollars)

Group	Dollars
Total Population	60,944
Hispanic or Latino (of any race)	53,960
Mexican	52,695

Per Capita Income
(2010 Inflation-Adjusted Dollars)

Group	Dollars
Total Population	24,434
Hispanic or Latino (of any race)	16,432
Mexican	16,180

Households with $100,000+ Income

Group	Number	%
Total Population	5,066	23.4
Hispanic or Latino (of any race)	1,071	17.3
Mexican	873	17.2

Households with Food Stamps/SNAP Benefits During Past 12 Months

Group	Number	%
Total Population	1,182	5.5
Hispanic or Latino (of any race)	572	9.2
Mexican	572	11.2

Poverty Rate
(Income in Past 12 Months Below Poverty Level)

Group	%
Total Population	9.1
Hispanic or Latino (of any race)	13.3
Mexican	14.1

Maywood

Population

Group	Number	%TP[1]	%HP[2]
Total Population	27,395	100.0	–
Hispanic or Latino (of any race)	26,696	97.4	100.0
Central American, ex. Mexican	2,460	9.0	9.2
Guatemalan	609	2.2	2.3
Honduran	178	0.6	0.7
Nicaraguan	263	1.0	1.0
Salvadoran	1,354	4.9	5.1
Cuban	193	0.7	0.7
Mexican	22,719	82.9	85.1
South American	162	0.6	0.6

Population Growth: 2000–2010

Group	%
Total Population	-2.4
Hispanic or Latino (of any race)	-1.3
Central American, ex. Mexican	62.2
Guatemalan	97.1
Nicaraguan	34.9
Salvadoran	76.3
Cuban	-7.7
Mexican	5.4
South American	24.6

Males per 100 Females

Group	Number
Total Population	104.5
Hispanic or Latino (of any race)	104.6
Central American, ex. Mexican	105.3
Guatemalan	112.2
Honduran	97.8
Nicaraguan	110.4
Salvadoran	100.0
Cuban	114.4
Mexican	104.2
South American	121.9

Average Household Size

Group	People
Total Population	4.16
Hispanic or Latino (of any race)	4.23
Central American, ex. Mexican	3.98
Guatemalan	4.03
Honduran	4.51
Nicaraguan	4.16
Salvadoran	3.90
Cuban	2.44
Mexican	4.31
South American	3.12

Median Age

Group	Years
Total Population	27.9
Hispanic or Latino (of any race)	27.7
Central American, ex. Mexican	33.7
Guatemalan	33.5
Honduran	32.0
Nicaraguan	32.2
Salvadoran	34.5
Cuban	54.5
Mexican	26.9
South American	42.8

High School Graduates
(Universe: Population 25 Years and Over)

Group	Number	%
Total Population	6,069	40.9

Notes: (1) Percent of total population; (2) Percent of Hispanic/Latino population; Profiles include places with an overall population of at least 125,000, OR an overall population of at least 25,000 where the Hispanic/Latino population is at least 20% of the overall population. In states where less than five places meet either of these criteria, we have included places with at least 10,000 total population with the highest percentage of Hispanic/Latino population. These places are identified with an asterisk (*); Please refer to the User's Guide for a full explanation of data.

Hispanic or Latino (of any race)	5,645	39.6
Central American, ex. Mexican	604	35.3
Salvadoran	425	41.0
Mexican	4,691	39.2

Four-Year College Graduates
(Universe: Population 25 Years and Over)

Group	Number	%
Total Population	539	3.6
Hispanic or Latino (of any race)	453	3.2
Central American, ex. Mexican	55	3.2
Salvadoran	10	1.0
Mexican	365	3.0

Population Age 3–17 Enrolled in Public School
(Universe: Population Age 3–17 Enrolled in School)

Group	Number	%
Total Population	6,811	98.2
Hispanic or Latino (of any race)	6,766	98.2
Central American, ex. Mexican	601	93.8
Salvadoran	273	87.2
Mexican	5,980	98.6

Population Age 3–17 Enrolled in Private School
(Universe: Population Age 3–17 Enrolled in School)

Group	Number	%
Total Population	124	1.8
Hispanic or Latino (of any race)	124	1.8
Central American, ex. Mexican	40	6.2
Salvadoran	40	12.8
Mexican	84	1.4

Foreign-Born Population

Group	Number	%
Total Population	13,354	48.5
Hispanic or Latino (of any race)	13,195	49.2
Central American, ex. Mexican	1,738	66.0
Salvadoran	939	61.5
Mexican	11,158	47.9

Foreign-Born Naturalized U.S. Citizens

Group	Number	%
Total Population	3,551	26.6
Hispanic or Latino (of any race)	3,517	26.7
Central American, ex. Mexican	447	25.7
Salvadoran	238	25.3
Mexican	2,912	26.1

Language Spoken at Home: English Only
(Universe: Population 5 Years and Over)

Group	Number	%
Total Population	2,017	8.1
Hispanic or Latino (of any race)	1,595	6.6
Central American, ex. Mexican	66	2.7
Salvadoran	44	3.2
Mexican	1,463	7.0

Language Spoken at Home: Spanish
(Universe: Population 5 Years and Over)

Group	Number	%
Total Population	22,677	91.1
Hispanic or Latino (of any race)	22,664	93.4
Central American, ex. Mexican	2,366	97.3
Salvadoran	1,335	96.8
Mexican	19,502	93.0

Unemployment Rate
(Universe: Population 16 Years and Over)

Group	%
Total Population	12.1
Hispanic or Latino (of any race)	12.1
Central American, ex. Mexican	10.2
Salvadoran	10.3
Mexican	12.1

Class of Worker: Private Wage and Salary
(Universe: Civilian Employed Population 16 Years and Over)

Group	Number	%
Total Population	9,835	89.0
Hispanic or Latino (of any race)	9,644	89.1
Central American, ex. Mexican	829	79.2
Salvadoran	516	82.4
Mexican	8,432	89.8

Class of Worker: Government
(Universe: Civilian Employed Population 16 Years and Over)

Group	Number	%
Total Population	685	6.2
Hispanic or Latino (of any race)	642	5.9
Central American, ex. Mexican	144	13.8
Salvadoran	72	11.5
Mexican	498	5.3

Means of Transportation to Work: Car, Truck or Van
(Universe: Workers 16 Years and Over)

Group	Number	%
Total Population	8,597	78.7
Hispanic or Latino (of any race)	8,481	79.3
Central American, ex. Mexican	770	77.2
Salvadoran	455	75.2
Mexican	7,371	79.2

Means of Transportation to Work: Public Transportation (ex. Taxicab)
(Universe: Workers 16 Years and Over)

Group	Number	%
Total Population	819	7.5
Hispanic or Latino (of any race)	766	7.2
Central American, ex. Mexican	20	2.0
Salvadoran	11	1.8
Mexican	734	7.9

Homeownership Rate
(Universe: Occupied Housing Units)

Group	%
Total Population	30.2
Hispanic or Latino (of any race)	29.8
Central American, ex. Mexican	24.0
Guatemalan	25.0
Honduran	20.0
Nicaraguan	21.7
Salvadoran	24.9
Cuban	29.5
Mexican	30.5
South American	44.1

Median Home Value

Group	Dollars
Total Population	360,200
Hispanic or Latino (of any race)	364,300
Central American, ex. Mexican	502,800
Salvadoran	550,000
Mexican	358,900

Median Gross Rent

Group	Dollars
Total Population	941
Hispanic or Latino (of any race)	942
Central American, ex. Mexican	962
Salvadoran	930
Mexican	941

Median Household Income
(2010 Inflation-Adjusted Dollars)

Group	Dollars
Total Population	38,740
Hispanic or Latino (of any race)	39,106
Central American, ex. Mexican	27,346
Salvadoran	33,952
Mexican	41,061

Per Capita Income
(2010 Inflation-Adjusted Dollars)

Group	Dollars
Total Population	12,164
Hispanic or Latino (of any race)	11,987
Central American, ex. Mexican	11,549
Salvadoran	10,897
Mexican	11,871

Households with $100,000+ Income

Group	Number	%
Total Population	568	8.6
Hispanic or Latino (of any race)	545	8.6
Central American, ex. Mexican	10	1.5
Salvadoran	0	0.0
Mexican	519	9.6

Households with Food Stamps/SNAP Benefits During Past 12 Months

Group	Number	%
Total Population	726	11.0
Hispanic or Latino (of any race)	717	11.3
Central American, ex. Mexican	75	11.2
Salvadoran	63	15.9
Mexican	632	11.6

Poverty Rate
(Income in Past 12 Months Below Poverty Level)

Group	%
Total Population	22.5
Hispanic or Latino (of any race)	22.7
Central American, ex. Mexican	36.2
Salvadoran	42.4
Mexican	21.6

Menifee

Population

Group	Number	%TP[1]	%HP[2]
Total Population	77,519	100.0	–
Hispanic or Latino (of any race)	25,551	33.0	100.0
Central American, ex. Mexican	730	0.9	2.9
Guatemalan	194	0.3	0.8
Nicaraguan	117	0.2	0.5
Salvadoran	284	0.4	1.1
Cuban	212	0.3	0.8
Mexican	21,690	28.0	84.9
Puerto Rican	591	0.8	2.3
South American	488	0.6	1.9
Colombian	163	0.2	0.6
Spaniard	293	0.4	1.1

Population Growth: 2000–2010

Group	%
Total Population	n/a

Males per 100 Females

Group	Number
Total Population	92.8
Hispanic or Latino (of any race)	97.2
Central American, ex. Mexican	86.7
Guatemalan	73.2
Nicaraguan	80.0
Salvadoran	104.3
Cuban	107.8
Mexican	97.7
Puerto Rican	94.4
South American	100.0
Colombian	96.4
Spaniard	80.9

Average Household Size

Group	People
Total Population	2.82
Hispanic or Latino (of any race)	3.86
Central American, ex. Mexican	3.81
Guatemalan	3.90
Nicaraguan	3.03
Salvadoran	4.18
Cuban	2.87
Mexican	3.99
Puerto Rican	2.96
South American	2.96
Colombian	3.53
Spaniard	2.84

Median Age

Group	Years
Total Population	38.1
Hispanic or Latino (of any race)	26.7
Central American, ex. Mexican	33.8
Guatemalan	32.7
Nicaraguan	37.1
Salvadoran	33.1
Cuban	37.8
Mexican	25.8
Puerto Rican	30.8
South American	41.5
Colombian	33.9
Spaniard	39.3

Notes: (1) Percent of total population; (2) Percent of Hispanic/Latino population; Profiles include places with an overall population of at least 125,000, OR an overall population of at least 25,000 where the Hispanic/Latino population is at least 20% of the overall population. In states where less than five places meet either of these criteria, we have included places with at least 10,000 total population with the highest percentage of Hispanic/Latino population. These places are identified with an asterisk (*); Please refer to the User's Guide for a full explanation of data.

High School Graduates
(Universe: Population 25 Years and Over)

Group	Number	%
Total Population	40,086	83.3
Hispanic or Latino (of any race)	7,114	61.2
Mexican	5,827	58.9

Four-Year College Graduates
(Universe: Population 25 Years and Over)

Group	Number	%
Total Population	8,281	17.2
Hispanic or Latino (of any race)	1,048	9.0
Mexican	780	7.9

Population Age 3–17 Enrolled in Public School
(Universe: Population Age 3–17 Enrolled in School)

Group	Number	%
Total Population	12,859	89.4
Hispanic or Latino (of any race)	6,007	96.1
Mexican	5,476	96.5

Population Age 3–17 Enrolled in Private School
(Universe: Population Age 3–17 Enrolled in School)

Group	Number	%
Total Population	1,529	10.6
Hispanic or Latino (of any race)	242	3.9
Mexican	198	3.5

Foreign-Born Population

Group	Number	%
Total Population	11,658	16.1
Hispanic or Latino (of any race)	6,826	29.9
Mexican	5,900	29.2

Foreign-Born Naturalized U.S. Citizens

Group	Number	%
Total Population	6,299	54.0
Hispanic or Latino (of any race)	2,995	43.9
Mexican	2,424	41.1

Language Spoken at Home: English Only
(Universe: Population 5 Years and Over)

Group	Number	%
Total Population	49,135	72.8
Hispanic or Latino (of any race)	6,611	32.8
Mexican	5,528	31.2

Language Spoken at Home: Spanish
(Universe: Population 5 Years and Over)

Group	Number	%
Total Population	14,200	21.0
Hispanic or Latino (of any race)	13,509	67.0
Mexican	12,139	68.5

Unemployment Rate
(Universe: Population 16 Years and Over)

Group	%
Total Population	12.0
Hispanic or Latino (of any race)	13.9
Mexican	13.5

Class of Worker: Private Wage and Salary
(Universe: Civilian Employed Population 16 Years and Over)

Group	Number	%
Total Population	20,921	75.5
Hispanic or Latino (of any race)	6,824	79.5
Mexican	6,002	79.0

Class of Worker: Government
(Universe: Civilian Employed Population 16 Years and Over)

Group	Number	%
Total Population	4,501	16.2
Hispanic or Latino (of any race)	1,064	12.4
Mexican	977	12.9

Means of Transportation to Work: Car, Truck or Van
(Universe: Workers 16 Years and Over)

Group	Number	%
Total Population	24,703	91.5
Hispanic or Latino (of any race)	7,822	93.2
Mexican	6,959	93.8

Means of Transportation to Work: Public Transportation (ex. Taxicab)
(Universe: Workers 16 Years and Over)

Group	Number	%
Total Population	139	0.5
Hispanic or Latino (of any race)	60	0.7
Mexican	34	0.5

Homeownership Rate
(Universe: Occupied Housing Units)

Group	%
Total Population	76.9
Hispanic or Latino (of any race)	72.1
Central American, ex. Mexican	75.0
Guatemalan	73.1
Nicaraguan	80.6
Salvadoran	70.7
Cuban	68.4
Mexican	72.5
Puerto Rican	69.7
South American	73.8
Colombian	65.0
Spaniard	71.2

Median Home Value

Group	Dollars
Total Population	252,900
Hispanic or Latino (of any race)	252,600
Mexican	252,600

Median Gross Rent

Group	Dollars
Total Population	1,175
Hispanic or Latino (of any race)	1,106
Mexican	1,102

Median Household Income
(2010 Inflation-Adjusted Dollars)

Group	Dollars
Total Population	52,246
Hispanic or Latino (of any race)	50,772
Mexican	50,182

Per Capita Income
(2010 Inflation-Adjusted Dollars)

Group	Dollars
Total Population	23,984
Hispanic or Latino (of any race)	16,633
Mexican	15,910

Households with $100,000+ Income

Group	Number	%
Total Population	5,061	19.4
Hispanic or Latino (of any race)	954	17.1
Mexican	779	16.4

Households with Food Stamps/SNAP Benefits During Past 12 Months

Group	Number	%
Total Population	610	2.3
Hispanic or Latino (of any race)	182	3.3
Mexican	175	3.7

Poverty Rate
(Income in Past 12 Months Below Poverty Level)

Group	%
Total Population	9.0
Hispanic or Latino (of any race)	12.0
Mexican	13.1

Merced

Population

Group	Number	%TP[1]	%HP[2]
Total Population	78,958	100.0	–
Hispanic or Latino (of any race)	39,140	49.6	100.0
Central American, ex. Mexican	502	0.6	1.3
Nicaraguan	120	0.2	0.3
Salvadoran	248	0.3	0.6
Mexican	35,593	45.1	90.9
Puerto Rican	384	0.5	1.0
South American	152	0.2	0.4
Spaniard	274	0.3	0.7

Population Growth: 2000–2010

Group	%
Total Population	23.6
Hispanic or Latino (of any race)	48.1
Central American, ex. Mexican	132.4
Mexican	57.4
Puerto Rican	92.0

Males per 100 Females

Group	Number
Total Population	96.3
Hispanic or Latino (of any race)	99.1
Central American, ex. Mexican	85.9
Nicaraguan	84.6
Salvadoran	83.7
Mexican	99.8
Puerto Rican	100.0
South American	111.1
Spaniard	100.0

Average Household Size

Group	People
Total Population	3.13
Hispanic or Latino (of any race)	3.67
Central American, ex. Mexican	3.44
Nicaraguan	3.33
Salvadoran	3.71
Mexican	3.73
Puerto Rican	2.72
South American	2.56
Spaniard	2.94

Median Age

Group	Years
Total Population	28.1
Hispanic or Latino (of any race)	23.9
Central American, ex. Mexican	29.0
Nicaraguan	37.0
Salvadoran	27.4
Mexican	23.8
Puerto Rican	26.2
South American	37.0
Spaniard	33.0

High School Graduates
(Universe: Population 25 Years and Over)

Group	Number	%
Total Population	29,641	70.7
Hispanic or Latino (of any race)	9,472	53.6
Mexican	8,594	53.0

Four-Year College Graduates
(Universe: Population 25 Years and Over)

Group	Number	%
Total Population	6,461	15.4
Hispanic or Latino (of any race)	987	5.6
Mexican	769	4.7

Population Age 3–17 Enrolled in Public School
(Universe: Population Age 3–17 Enrolled in School)

Group	Number	%
Total Population	17,572	97.4
Hispanic or Latino (of any race)	10,272	99.0
Mexican	9,607	99.1

Population Age 3–17 Enrolled in Private School
(Universe: Population Age 3–17 Enrolled in School)

Group	Number	%
Total Population	463	2.6
Hispanic or Latino (of any race)	101	1.0
Mexican	91	0.9

Foreign-Born Population

Group	Number	%
Total Population	16,509	21.4
Hispanic or Latino (of any race)	10,608	28.2
Mexican	9,790	28.5

Foreign-Born Naturalized U.S. Citizens

Group	Number	%
Total Population	5,641	34.2
Hispanic or Latino (of any race)	2,812	26.5
Mexican	2,475	25.3

Notes: (1) Percent of total population; (2) Percent of Hispanic/Latino population; Profiles include places with an overall population of at least 125,000, OR an overall population of at least 25,000 where the Hispanic/Latino population is at least 20% of the overall population. In states where less than five places meet either of these criteria, we have included places with at least 10,000 total population with the highest percentage of Hispanic/Latino population. These places are identified with an asterisk (*); Please refer to the User's Guide for a full explanation of data.

Language Spoken at Home: English Only
(Universe: Population 5 Years and Over)

Group	Number	%
Total Population	37,742	54.3
Hispanic or Latino (of any race)	10,359	31.3
Mexican	9,155	30.1

Language Spoken at Home: Spanish
(Universe: Population 5 Years and Over)

Group	Number	%
Total Population	23,394	33.6
Hispanic or Latino (of any race)	22,575	68.3
Mexican	21,129	69.5

Unemployment Rate
(Universe: Population 16 Years and Over)

Group	%
Total Population	13.1
Hispanic or Latino (of any race)	15.5
Mexican	15.2

Class of Worker: Private Wage and Salary
(Universe: Civilian Employed Population 16 Years and Over)

Group	Number	%
Total Population	22,606	78.2
Hispanic or Latino (of any race)	11,443	84.9
Mexican	10,724	86.5

Class of Worker: Government
(Universe: Civilian Employed Population 16 Years and Over)

Group	Number	%
Total Population	4,817	16.7
Hispanic or Latino (of any race)	1,399	10.4
Mexican	1,131	9.1

Means of Transportation to Work: Car, Truck or Van
(Universe: Workers 16 Years and Over)

Group	Number	%
Total Population	23,998	86.1
Hispanic or Latino (of any race)	10,855	84.1
Mexican	10,002	84.4

Means of Transportation to Work: Public Transportation (ex. Taxicab)
(Universe: Workers 16 Years and Over)

Group	Number	%
Total Population	257	0.9
Hispanic or Latino (of any race)	120	0.9
Mexican	98	0.8

Homeownership Rate
(Universe: Occupied Housing Units)

Group	%
Total Population	42.7
Hispanic or Latino (of any race)	35.7
Central American, ex. Mexican	48.4
Nicaraguan	52.5
Salvadoran	55.6
Mexican	36.0
Puerto Rican	28.0
South American	54.1
Spaniard	45.0

Median Home Value

Group	Dollars
Total Population	223,500
Hispanic or Latino (of any race)	198,200
Mexican	188,900

Median Gross Rent

Group	Dollars
Total Population	775
Hispanic or Latino (of any race)	720
Mexican	699

Median Household Income
(2010 Inflation-Adjusted Dollars)

Group	Dollars
Total Population	36,269
Hispanic or Latino (of any race)	29,773
Mexican	29,785

Per Capita Income
(2010 Inflation-Adjusted Dollars)

Group	Dollars
Total Population	16,887
Hispanic or Latino (of any race)	11,600
Mexican	11,255

Households with $100,000+ Income

Group	Number	%
Total Population	3,015	12.7
Hispanic or Latino (of any race)	643	6.6
Mexican	519	5.9

Households with Food Stamps/SNAP Benefits During Past 12 Months

Group	Number	%
Total Population	4,058	17.1
Hispanic or Latino (of any race)	2,219	22.9
Mexican	2,101	23.9

Poverty Rate
(Income in Past 12 Months Below Poverty Level)

Group	%
Total Population	26.2
Hispanic or Latino (of any race)	31.4
Mexican	31.6

Modesto

Population

Group	Number	%TP[1]	%HP[2]
Total Population	201,165	100.0	–
Hispanic or Latino (of any race)	71,381	35.5	100.0
Central American, ex. Mexican	2,341	1.2	3.3
Guatemalan	421	0.2	0.6
Honduran	126	0.1	0.2
Nicaraguan	510	0.3	0.7
Salvadoran	1,134	0.6	1.6
Cuban	196	0.1	0.3
Mexican	62,010	30.8	86.9
Puerto Rican	1,447	0.7	2.0
South American	749	0.4	1.0
Colombian	239	0.1	0.3
Peruvian	230	0.1	0.3
Spaniard	971	0.5	1.4

Population Growth: 2000–2010

Group	%
Total Population	6.5
Hispanic or Latino (of any race)	47.8
Central American, ex. Mexican	160.1
Guatemalan	180.7
Nicaraguan	107.3
Salvadoran	306.5
Cuban	28.1
Mexican	59.7
Puerto Rican	37.9
South American	153.0
Spaniard	774.8

Males per 100 Females

Group	Number
Total Population	95.0
Hispanic or Latino (of any race)	99.9
Central American, ex. Mexican	98.2
Guatemalan	84.6
Honduran	103.2
Nicaraguan	93.2
Salvadoran	107.7
Cuban	117.8
Mexican	100.8
Puerto Rican	99.6
South American	87.3
Colombian	78.4
Peruvian	100.0
Spaniard	81.8

Average Household Size

Group	People
Total Population	2.87
Hispanic or Latino (of any race)	3.72
Central American, ex. Mexican	3.77
Guatemalan	3.80
Honduran	3.48
Nicaraguan	3.65
Salvadoran	3.94
Cuban	3.07
Mexican	3.80
Puerto Rican	3.07
South American	2.92
Colombian	3.36
Peruvian	3.19
Spaniard	2.67

Median Age

Group	Years
Total Population	34.2
Hispanic or Latino (of any race)	25.1
Central American, ex. Mexican	31.8
Guatemalan	33.9
Honduran	28.0
Nicaraguan	34.1
Salvadoran	31.2
Cuban	30.0
Mexican	24.6
Puerto Rican	26.5
South American	36.8
Colombian	38.3
Peruvian	36.3
Spaniard	30.9

High School Graduates
(Universe: Population 25 Years and Over)

Group	Number	%
Total Population	98,216	79.3
Hispanic or Latino (of any race)	20,421	59.4
Central American, ex. Mexican	1,039	69.6
Salvadoran	475	70.0
Mexican	17,409	57.1
Puerto Rican	581	86.6
South American	370	80.8

Four-Year College Graduates
(Universe: Population 25 Years and Over)

Group	Number	%
Total Population	22,727	18.3
Hispanic or Latino (of any race)	2,366	6.9
Central American, ex. Mexican	269	18.0
Salvadoran	59	8.7
Mexican	1,670	5.5
Puerto Rican	140	20.9
South American	108	23.6

Population Age 3–17 Enrolled in Public School
(Universe: Population Age 3–17 Enrolled in School)

Group	Number	%
Total Population	41,203	94.0
Hispanic or Latino (of any race)	20,478	97.3
Central American, ex. Mexican	379	98.7
Salvadoran	232	97.9
Mexican	18,764	97.7
Puerto Rican	499	92.8
South American	167	93.3

Population Age 3–17 Enrolled in Private School
(Universe: Population Age 3–17 Enrolled in School)

Group	Number	%
Total Population	2,642	6.0
Hispanic or Latino (of any race)	559	2.7
Central American, ex. Mexican	5	1.3
Salvadoran	5	2.1
Mexican	441	2.3
Puerto Rican	39	7.2
South American	12	6.7

Foreign-Born Population

Group	Number	%
Total Population	32,883	16.3
Hispanic or Latino (of any race)	19,014	26.8
Central American, ex. Mexican	1,430	61.9
Salvadoran	579	50.9
Mexican	16,850	26.3
Puerto Rican	0	0.0
South American	439	53.1

Foreign-Born Naturalized U.S. Citizens

Group	Number	%
Total Population	13,622	41.4
Hispanic or Latino (of any race)	5,037	26.5

Notes: (1) Percent of total population; (2) Percent of Hispanic/Latino population; Profiles include places with an overall population of at least 125,000, OR an overall population of at least 25,000 where the Hispanic/Latino population is at least 20% of the overall population. In states where less than five places meet either of these criteria, we have included places with at least 10,000 total population with the highest percentage of Hispanic/Latino population. These places are identified with an asterisk (*); Please refer to the User's Guide for a full explanation of data.

Central American, ex. Mexican	527	36.9
Salvadoran	230	39.7
Mexican	4,212	25.0
Puerto Rican	0	0.0
South American	176	40.1

Language Spoken at Home: English Only
(Universe: Population 5 Years and Over)

Group	Number	%
Total Population	119,815	64.5
Hispanic or Latino (of any race)	19,150	30.7
Central American, ex. Mexican	291	13.8
Salvadoran	192	18.6
Mexican	16,390	29.2
Puerto Rican	910	72.3
South American	141	18.4

Language Spoken at Home: Spanish
(Universe: Population 5 Years and Over)

Group	Number	%
Total Population	45,827	24.7
Hispanic or Latino (of any race)	43,088	69.0
Central American, ex. Mexican	1,819	86.2
Salvadoran	841	81.4
Mexican	39,640	70.6
Puerto Rican	348	27.7
South American	627	81.6

Unemployment Rate
(Universe: Population 16 Years and Over)

Group	%
Total Population	12.7
Hispanic or Latino (of any race)	18.6
Central American, ex. Mexican	15.8
Salvadoran	18.2
Mexican	19.0
Puerto Rican	22.1
South American	10.6

Class of Worker: Private Wage and Salary
(Universe: Civilian Employed Population 16 Years and Over)

Group	Number	%
Total Population	63,100	77.8
Hispanic or Latino (of any race)	19,971	83.7
Central American, ex. Mexican	1,004	86.6
Salvadoran	437	87.4
Mexican	17,656	83.9
Puerto Rican	252	61.0
South American	375	84.3

Class of Worker: Government
(Universe: Civilian Employed Population 16 Years and Over)

Group	Number	%
Total Population	12,455	15.4
Hispanic or Latino (of any race)	2,661	11.2
Central American, ex. Mexican	100	8.6
Salvadoran	34	6.8
Mexican	2,366	11.2
Puerto Rican	121	29.3
South American	27	6.1

Means of Transportation to Work: Car, Truck or Van
(Universe: Workers 16 Years and Over)

Group	Number	%
Total Population	72,194	91.1
Hispanic or Latino (of any race)	21,440	92.3
Central American, ex. Mexican	958	88.2
Salvadoran	440	90.5
Mexican	19,079	93.0
Puerto Rican	362	87.7
South American	389	90.0

Means of Transportation to Work: Public Transportation (ex. Taxicab)
(Universe: Workers 16 Years and Over)

Group	Number	%
Total Population	1,059	1.3
Hispanic or Latino (of any race)	362	1.6
Central American, ex. Mexican	0	0.0
Salvadoran	0	0.0
Mexican	288	1.4
Puerto Rican	45	10.9
South American	13	3.0

Homeownership Rate
(Universe: Occupied Housing Units)

Group	%
Total Population	57.0
Hispanic or Latino (of any race)	47.6
Central American, ex. Mexican	54.5
Guatemalan	52.3
Honduran	48.5
Nicaraguan	54.1
Salvadoran	54.5
Cuban	62.9
Mexican	47.3
Puerto Rican	43.2
South American	54.8
Colombian	53.0
Peruvian	55.8
Spaniard	59.0

Median Home Value

Group	Dollars
Total Population	282,500
Hispanic or Latino (of any race)	267,000
Central American, ex. Mexican	267,600
Salvadoran	242,700
Mexican	263,900
Puerto Rican	271,200
South American	251,600

Median Gross Rent

Group	Dollars
Total Population	974
Hispanic or Latino (of any race)	960
Central American, ex. Mexican	908
Salvadoran	866
Mexican	965
Puerto Rican	945
South American	1,075

Median Household Income
(2010 Inflation-Adjusted Dollars)

Group	Dollars
Total Population	50,550
Hispanic or Latino (of any race)	43,152
Central American, ex. Mexican	66,000
Salvadoran	69,423
Mexican	42,349
Puerto Rican	25,893
South American	85,167

Per Capita Income
(2010 Inflation-Adjusted Dollars)

Group	Dollars
Total Population	23,383
Hispanic or Latino (of any race)	13,474
Central American, ex. Mexican	25,512
Salvadoran	23,686
Mexican	12,734
Puerto Rican	15,110
South American	25,133

Households with $100,000+ Income

Group	Number	%
Total Population	13,060	19.1
Hispanic or Latino (of any race)	2,039	11.6
Central American, ex. Mexican	218	33.5
Salvadoran	93	35.8
Mexican	1,628	10.4
Puerto Rican	27	8.6
South American	97	43.7

Households with Food Stamps/SNAP Benefits During Past 12 Months

Group	Number	%
Total Population	6,057	8.9
Hispanic or Latino (of any race)	2,468	14.1
Central American, ex. Mexican	17	2.6
Salvadoran	0	0.0
Mexican	2,323	14.9
Puerto Rican	0	0.0
South American	0	0.0

Poverty Rate
(Income in Past 12 Months Below Poverty Level)

Group	%
Total Population	16.8
Hispanic or Latino (of any race)	24.6
Central American, ex. Mexican	9.9
Salvadoran	13.3
Mexican	25.7
Puerto Rican	24.3
South American	20.9

Monrovia

Population

Group	Number	%TP[1]	%HP[2]
Total Population	36,590	100.0	–
Hispanic or Latino (of any race)	14,043	38.4	100.0
Central American, ex. Mexican	986	2.7	7.0
Guatemalan	245	0.7	1.7
Honduran	109	0.3	0.8
Nicaraguan	113	0.3	0.8
Salvadoran	446	1.2	3.2
Cuban	287	0.8	2.0
Mexican	11,123	30.4	79.2
Puerto Rican	196	0.5	1.4
South American	561	1.5	4.0
Argentinean	139	0.4	1.0
Colombian	126	0.3	0.9
Peruvian	141	0.4	1.0
Spaniard	166	0.5	1.2

Population Growth: 2000–2010

Group	%
Total Population	-0.9
Hispanic or Latino (of any race)	7.9
Central American, ex. Mexican	78.9
Salvadoran	102.7
Cuban	40.0
Mexican	12.9
Puerto Rican	-15.9
South American	62.6

Males per 100 Females

Group	Number
Total Population	91.6
Hispanic or Latino (of any race)	92.9
Central American, ex. Mexican	84.3
Guatemalan	89.9
Honduran	98.2
Nicaraguan	105.5
Salvadoran	73.5
Cuban	90.1
Mexican	94.0
Puerto Rican	100.0
South American	90.8
Argentinean	117.2
Colombian	93.8
Peruvian	74.1
Spaniard	84.4

Average Household Size

Group	People
Total Population	2.65
Hispanic or Latino (of any race)	3.35
Central American, ex. Mexican	3.57
Guatemalan	3.43
Honduran	3.76
Nicaraguan	3.74
Salvadoran	3.68
Cuban	2.53
Mexican	3.45
Puerto Rican	2.42
South American	2.60
Argentinean	2.67
Colombian	2.42
Peruvian	2.83
Spaniard	2.70

Median Age

Group	Years
Total Population	37.9
Hispanic or Latino (of any race)	29.6
Central American, ex. Mexican	34.3
Guatemalan	36.4
Honduran	30.3
Nicaraguan	32.8
Salvadoran	34.0
Cuban	38.8

Notes: (1) Percent of total population; (2) Percent of Hispanic/Latino population; Profiles include places with an overall population of at least 125,000, OR an overall population of at least 25,000 where the Hispanic/Latino population is at least 20% of the overall population. In states where less than five places meet either of these criteria, we have included places with at least 10,000 total population with the highest percentage of Hispanic/Latino population. These places are identified with an asterisk (*); Please refer to the User's Guide for a full explanation of data.

Mexican	28.5
Puerto Rican	30.5
South American	39.1
Argentinean	38.6
Colombian	35.3
Peruvian	41.5
Spaniard	39.7

High School Graduates
(Universe: Population 25 Years and Over)

Group	Number	%
Total Population	21,623	86.1
Hispanic or Latino (of any race)	5,549	70.3
Central American, ex. Mexican	759	79.7
Mexican	3,834	67.5

Four-Year College Graduates
(Universe: Population 25 Years and Over)

Group	Number	%
Total Population	8,403	33.5
Hispanic or Latino (of any race)	1,468	18.6
Central American, ex. Mexican	220	23.1
Mexican	902	15.9

Population Age 3–17 Enrolled in Public School
(Universe: Population Age 3–17 Enrolled in School)

Group	Number	%
Total Population	4,908	78.5
Hispanic or Latino (of any race)	2,780	81.9
Central American, ex. Mexican	226	95.0
Mexican	2,193	82.9

Population Age 3–17 Enrolled in Private School
(Universe: Population Age 3–17 Enrolled in School)

Group	Number	%
Total Population	1,341	21.5
Hispanic or Latino (of any race)	613	18.1
Central American, ex. Mexican	12	5.0
Mexican	451	17.1

Foreign-Born Population

Group	Number	%
Total Population	8,971	24.5
Hispanic or Latino (of any race)	4,885	35.6
Central American, ex. Mexican	993	62.5
Mexican	3,069	30.5

Foreign-Born Naturalized U.S. Citizens

Group	Number	%
Total Population	4,349	48.5
Hispanic or Latino (of any race)	2,050	42.0
Central American, ex. Mexican	452	45.5
Mexican	1,042	34.0

Language Spoken at Home: English Only
(Universe: Population 5 Years and Over)

Group	Number	%
Total Population	21,703	63.2
Hispanic or Latino (of any race)	4,525	36.0
Central American, ex. Mexican	131	8.8
Mexican	3,523	38.5

Language Spoken at Home: Spanish
(Universe: Population 5 Years and Over)

Group	Number	%
Total Population	8,601	25.0
Hispanic or Latino (of any race)	8,023	63.8
Central American, ex. Mexican	1,358	91.2
Mexican	5,617	61.3

Unemployment Rate
(Universe: Population 16 Years and Over)

Group	%
Total Population	6.0
Hispanic or Latino (of any race)	6.9
Central American, ex. Mexican	5.9
Mexican	6.5

Class of Worker: Private Wage and Salary
(Universe: Civilian Employed Population 16 Years and Over)

Group	Number	%
Total Population	14,910	77.7
Hispanic or Latino (of any race)	5,039	78.7
Central American, ex. Mexican	844	92.0
Mexican	3,469	75.7

Class of Worker: Government
(Universe: Civilian Employed Population 16 Years and Over)

Group	Number	%
Total Population	2,797	14.6
Hispanic or Latino (of any race)	887	13.8
Central American, ex. Mexican	0	0.0
Mexican	796	17.4

Means of Transportation to Work: Car, Truck or Van
(Universe: Workers 16 Years and Over)

Group	Number	%
Total Population	15,779	84.9
Hispanic or Latino (of any race)	4,982	79.5
Central American, ex. Mexican	818	90.3
Mexican	3,424	76.6

Means of Transportation to Work: Public Transportation (ex. Taxicab)
(Universe: Workers 16 Years and Over)

Group	Number	%
Total Population	935	5.0
Hispanic or Latino (of any race)	471	7.5
Central American, ex. Mexican	22	2.4
Mexican	368	8.2

Homeownership Rate
(Universe: Occupied Housing Units)

Group	%
Total Population	49.5
Hispanic or Latino (of any race)	34.7
Central American, ex. Mexican	32.3
Guatemalan	36.0
Honduran	20.7
Nicaraguan	31.6
Salvadoran	29.2
Cuban	40.6
Mexican	33.6
Puerto Rican	38.5
South American	44.0
Argentinean	61.4
Colombian	37.8
Peruvian	34.5
Spaniard	45.9

Median Home Value

Group	Dollars
Total Population	561,000
Hispanic or Latino (of any race)	557,500
Central American, ex. Mexican	535,300
Mexican	555,300

Median Gross Rent

Group	Dollars
Total Population	1,220
Hispanic or Latino (of any race)	1,157
Central American, ex. Mexican	1,309
Mexican	1,107

Median Household Income
(2010 Inflation-Adjusted Dollars)

Group	Dollars
Total Population	65,477
Hispanic or Latino (of any race)	57,033
Central American, ex. Mexican	56,375
Mexican	56,830

Per Capita Income
(2010 Inflation-Adjusted Dollars)

Group	Dollars
Total Population	31,582
Hispanic or Latino (of any race)	19,465
Central American, ex. Mexican	19,977
Mexican	18,218

Households with $100,000+ Income

Group	Number	%
Total Population	4,278	31.1
Hispanic or Latino (of any race)	815	23.0
Central American, ex. Mexican	66	16.9
Mexican	634	25.6

Households with Food Stamps/SNAP Benefits During Past 12 Months

Group	Number	%
Total Population	367	2.7
Hispanic or Latino (of any race)	176	5.0
Central American, ex. Mexican	0	0.0
Mexican	147	5.9

Poverty Rate
(Income in Past 12 Months Below Poverty Level)

Group	%
Total Population	9.8
Hispanic or Latino (of any race)	13.7
Central American, ex. Mexican	14.1
Mexican	15.3

Montclair

Population

Group	Number	%TP[1]	%HP[2]
Total Population	36,664	100.0	–
Hispanic or Latino (of any race)	25,744	70.2	100.0
Central American, ex. Mexican	1,764	4.8	6.9
Guatemalan	513	1.4	2.0
Honduran	159	0.4	0.6
Nicaraguan	182	0.5	0.7
Salvadoran	834	2.3	3.2
Cuban	147	0.4	0.6
Mexican	21,893	59.7	85.0
Puerto Rican	176	0.5	0.7
South American	382	1.0	1.5
Colombian	100	0.3	0.4
Peruvian	110	0.3	0.4

Population Growth: 2000–2010

Group	%
Total Population	10.9
Hispanic or Latino (of any race)	29.9
Central American, ex. Mexican	89.9
Guatemalan	157.8
Nicaraguan	28.2
Salvadoran	114.4
Cuban	-3.9
Mexican	38.1
Puerto Rican	21.4
South American	97.9

Males per 100 Females

Group	Number
Total Population	99.1
Hispanic or Latino (of any race)	102.0
Central American, ex. Mexican	101.1
Guatemalan	110.2
Honduran	127.1
Nicaraguan	76.7
Salvadoran	98.1
Cuban	77.1
Mexican	102.9
Puerto Rican	102.3
South American	89.1
Colombian	88.7
Peruvian	83.3

Average Household Size

Group	People
Total Population	3.81
Hispanic or Latino (of any race)	4.42
Central American, ex. Mexican	4.60
Guatemalan	4.65
Honduran	5.11
Nicaraguan	4.44
Salvadoran	4.61
Cuban	3.11
Mexican	4.48
Puerto Rican	3.88
South American	3.47
Colombian	3.96
Peruvian	3.59

Median Age

Group	Years
Total Population	30.7
Hispanic or Latino (of any race)	26.8

Notes: (1) Percent of total population; (2) Percent of Hispanic/Latino population; Profiles include places with an overall population of at least 125,000, OR an overall population of at least 25,000 where the Hispanic/Latino population is at least 20% of the overall population. In states where less than five places meet either of these criteria, we have included places with at least 10,000 total population with the highest percentage of Hispanic/Latino population. These places are identified with an asterisk (*); Please refer to the User's Guide for a full explanation of data.

Central American, ex. Mexican	34.5
Guatemalan	34.1
Honduran	29.8
Nicaraguan	39.8
Salvadoran	34.6
Cuban	45.5
Mexican	26.0
Puerto Rican	34.0
South American	38.5
Colombian	39.0
Peruvian	34.5

High School Graduates
(Universe: Population 25 Years and Over)

Group	Number	%
Total Population	15,345	70.1
Hispanic or Latino (of any race)	7,935	59.2
Central American, ex. Mexican	645	57.4
Mexican	6,659	57.8

Four-Year College Graduates
(Universe: Population 25 Years and Over)

Group	Number	%
Total Population	2,883	13.2
Hispanic or Latino (of any race)	817	6.1
Central American, ex. Mexican	98	8.7
Mexican	670	5.8

Population Age 3–17 Enrolled in Public School
(Universe: Population Age 3–17 Enrolled in School)

Group	Number	%
Total Population	7,079	92.6
Hispanic or Latino (of any race)	5,752	93.5
Central American, ex. Mexican	239	96.0
Mexican	5,369	93.3

Population Age 3–17 Enrolled in Private School
(Universe: Population Age 3–17 Enrolled in School)

Group	Number	%
Total Population	563	7.4
Hispanic or Latino (of any race)	402	6.5
Central American, ex. Mexican	10	4.0
Mexican	385	6.7

Foreign-Born Population

Group	Number	%
Total Population	13,519	36.8
Hispanic or Latino (of any race)	10,388	42.0
Central American, ex. Mexican	1,081	60.0
Mexican	8,960	41.1

Foreign-Born Naturalized U.S. Citizens

Group	Number	%
Total Population	4,961	36.7
Hispanic or Latino (of any race)	3,227	31.1
Central American, ex. Mexican	499	46.2
Mexican	2,553	28.5

Language Spoken at Home: English Only
(Universe: Population 5 Years and Over)

Group	Number	%
Total Population	11,468	34.3
Hispanic or Latino (of any race)	4,100	18.5
Central American, ex. Mexican	167	10.2
Mexican	3,747	19.2

Language Spoken at Home: Spanish
(Universe: Population 5 Years and Over)

Group	Number	%
Total Population	18,524	55.4
Hispanic or Latino (of any race)	18,089	81.5
Central American, ex. Mexican	1,469	89.8
Mexican	15,750	80.8

Unemployment Rate
(Universe: Population 16 Years and Over)

Group	%
Total Population	15.6
Hispanic or Latino (of any race)	15.3
Central American, ex. Mexican	19.8
Mexican	14.3

Class of Worker: Private Wage and Salary
(Universe: Civilian Employed Population 16 Years and Over)

Group	Number	%
Total Population	12,381	79.3
Hispanic or Latino (of any race)	8,494	81.6
Central American, ex. Mexican	666	79.0
Mexican	7,524	81.8

Class of Worker: Government
(Universe: Civilian Employed Population 16 Years and Over)

Group	Number	%
Total Population	2,060	13.2
Hispanic or Latino (of any race)	1,242	11.9
Central American, ex. Mexican	108	12.8
Mexican	1,104	12.0

Means of Transportation to Work: Car, Truck or Van
(Universe: Workers 16 Years and Over)

Group	Number	%
Total Population	13,414	88.8
Hispanic or Latino (of any race)	8,866	88.2
Central American, ex. Mexican	755	89.6
Mexican	7,817	88.1

Means of Transportation to Work: Public Transportation (ex. Taxicab)
(Universe: Workers 16 Years and Over)

Group	Number	%
Total Population	456	3.0
Hispanic or Latino (of any race)	331	3.3
Central American, ex. Mexican	20	2.4
Mexican	283	3.2

Homeownership Rate
(Universe: Occupied Housing Units)

Group	%
Total Population	59.7
Hispanic or Latino (of any race)	54.6
Central American, ex. Mexican	58.5
Guatemalan	57.9
Honduran	34.3
Nicaraguan	58.0
Salvadoran	64.5
Cuban	75.9
Mexican	54.0
Puerto Rican	52.1
South American	62.6
Colombian	60.7
Peruvian	53.7

Median Home Value

Group	Dollars
Total Population	330,900
Hispanic or Latino (of any race)	319,400
Central American, ex. Mexican	343,900
Mexican	315,600

Median Gross Rent

Group	Dollars
Total Population	1,040
Hispanic or Latino (of any race)	1,041
Central American, ex. Mexican	1,465
Mexican	1,002

Median Household Income
(2010 Inflation-Adjusted Dollars)

Group	Dollars
Total Population	53,870
Hispanic or Latino (of any race)	54,571
Central American, ex. Mexican	90,417
Mexican	50,407

Per Capita Income
(2010 Inflation-Adjusted Dollars)

Group	Dollars
Total Population	17,471
Hispanic or Latino (of any race)	14,142
Central American, ex. Mexican	18,289
Mexican	13,858

Households with $100,000+ Income

Group	Number	%
Total Population	1,497	16.4
Hispanic or Latino (of any race)	728	14.0
Central American, ex. Mexican	94	16.8
Mexican	585	13.5

Households with Food Stamps/SNAP Benefits During Past 12 Months

Group	Number	%
Total Population	693	7.6
Hispanic or Latino (of any race)	518	9.9
Central American, ex. Mexican	0	0.0
Mexican	518	11.9

Poverty Rate
(Income in Past 12 Months Below Poverty Level)

Group	%
Total Population	15.2
Hispanic or Latino (of any race)	16.4
Central American, ex. Mexican	11.6
Mexican	16.7

Montebello

Population

Group	Number	%TP[1]	%HP[2]
Total Population	62,500	100.0	–
Hispanic or Latino (of any race)	49,578	79.3	100.0
Central American, ex. Mexican	3,219	5.2	6.5
Guatemalan	789	1.3	1.6
Honduran	210	0.3	0.4
Nicaraguan	341	0.5	0.7
Salvadoran	1,780	2.8	3.6
Cuban	127	0.2	0.3
Mexican	43,662	69.9	88.1
Puerto Rican	212	0.3	0.4
South American	654	1.0	1.3
Argentinean	106	0.2	0.2
Colombian	128	0.2	0.3
Ecuadorian	124	0.2	0.3
Peruvian	194	0.3	0.4
Spaniard	197	0.3	0.4

Population Growth: 2000–2010

Group	%
Total Population	0.6
Hispanic or Latino (of any race)	7.0
Central American, ex. Mexican	87.7
Guatemalan	128.0
Nicaraguan	91.6
Salvadoran	106.0
Cuban	-6.6
Mexican	12.3
Puerto Rican	-7.8
South American	35.1
Colombian	4.1
Peruvian	51.6

Males per 100 Females

Group	Number
Total Population	93.3
Hispanic or Latino (of any race)	93.9
Central American, ex. Mexican	91.4
Guatemalan	102.8
Honduran	78.0
Nicaraguan	70.5
Salvadoran	93.9
Cuban	130.9
Mexican	93.9
Puerto Rican	109.9
South American	94.6
Argentinean	125.5
Colombian	88.2
Ecuadorian	85.1
Peruvian	96.0
Spaniard	82.4

Average Household Size

Group	People
Total Population	3.27
Hispanic or Latino (of any race)	3.54
Central American, ex. Mexican	3.85
Guatemalan	4.00
Honduran	3.57
Nicaraguan	4.01
Salvadoran	3.85
Cuban	3.54
Mexican	3.54
Puerto Rican	2.59

Notes: (1) Percent of total population; (2) Percent of Hispanic/Latino population; Profiles include places with an overall population of at least 125,000, OR an overall population of at least 25,000 where the Hispanic/Latino population is at least 20% of the overall population. In states where less than five places meet either of these criteria, we have included places with at least 10,000 total population with the highest percentage of Hispanic/Latino population. These places are identified with an asterisk (*); Please refer to the User's Guide for a full explanation of data.

Group	
South American	3.32
Argentinean	3.25
Colombian	3.37
Ecuadorian	3.41
Peruvian	3.53
Spaniard	2.94

Median Age

Group	Years
Total Population	34.7
Hispanic or Latino (of any race)	31.5
Central American, ex. Mexican	35.2
Guatemalan	33.4
Honduran	33.9
Nicaraguan	36.6
Salvadoran	35.5
Cuban	38.5
Mexican	31.1
Puerto Rican	37.0
South American	39.1
Argentinean	41.5
Colombian	31.0
Ecuadorian	37.7
Peruvian	40.3
Spaniard	50.5

High School Graduates
(Universe: Population 25 Years and Over)

Group	Number	%
Total Population	27,817	69.2
Hispanic or Latino (of any race)	18,889	63.6
Central American, ex. Mexican	1,475	63.9
Guatemalan	485	62.4
Salvadoran	609	56.6
Mexican	16,471	63.2
South American	443	73.6

Four-Year College Graduates
(Universe: Population 25 Years and Over)

Group	Number	%
Total Population	6,567	16.3
Hispanic or Latino (of any race)	3,220	10.8
Central American, ex. Mexican	228	9.9
Guatemalan	71	9.1
Salvadoran	105	9.8
Mexican	2,787	10.7
South American	123	20.4

Population Age 3–17 Enrolled in Public School
(Universe: Population Age 3–17 Enrolled in School)

Group	Number	%
Total Population	11,487	89.3
Hispanic or Latino (of any race)	10,338	90.3
Central American, ex. Mexican	348	82.9
Guatemalan	104	83.2
Salvadoran	207	95.4
Mexican	9,502	90.6
South American	142	92.2

Population Age 3–17 Enrolled in Private School
(Universe: Population Age 3–17 Enrolled in School)

Group	Number	%
Total Population	1,373	10.7
Hispanic or Latino (of any race)	1,113	9.7
Central American, ex. Mexican	72	17.1
Guatemalan	21	16.8
Salvadoran	10	4.6
Mexican	986	9.4
South American	12	7.8

Foreign-Born Population

Group	Number	%
Total Population	23,768	38.1
Hispanic or Latino (of any race)	17,531	35.7
Central American, ex. Mexican	2,270	67.8
Guatemalan	714	75.0
Salvadoran	1,109	63.9
Mexican	14,383	33.0
South American	641	76.7

Foreign-Born Naturalized U.S. Citizens

Group	Number	%
Total Population	11,906	50.1
Hispanic or Latino (of any race)	7,355	42.0
Central American, ex. Mexican	1,068	47.0
Guatemalan	389	54.5
Salvadoran	438	39.5
Mexican	5,965	41.5
South American	218	34.0

Language Spoken at Home: English Only
(Universe: Population 5 Years and Over)

Group	Number	%
Total Population	14,848	25.8
Hispanic or Latino (of any race)	9,814	21.9
Central American, ex. Mexican	93	3.0
Guatemalan	0	0.0
Salvadoran	44	2.8
Mexican	9,426	23.7
South American	21	2.6

Language Spoken at Home: Spanish
(Universe: Population 5 Years and Over)

Group	Number	%
Total Population	35,319	61.3
Hispanic or Latino (of any race)	34,902	78.0
Central American, ex. Mexican	2,978	97.0
Guatemalan	889	100.0
Salvadoran	1,547	97.2
Mexican	30,337	76.2
South American	782	97.4

Unemployment Rate
(Universe: Population 16 Years and Over)

Group	%
Total Population	8.4
Hispanic or Latino (of any race)	8.6
Central American, ex. Mexican	5.5
Guatemalan	9.1
Salvadoran	6.0
Mexican	9.1
South American	6.0

Class of Worker: Private Wage and Salary
(Universe: Civilian Employed Population 16 Years and Over)

Group	Number	%
Total Population	20,038	75.8
Hispanic or Latino (of any race)	15,673	76.3
Central American, ex. Mexican	1,450	78.4
Guatemalan	368	87.2
Salvadoran	802	77.0
Mexican	13,498	75.9
South American	347	73.4

Class of Worker: Government
(Universe: Civilian Employed Population 16 Years and Over)

Group	Number	%
Total Population	4,769	18.0
Hispanic or Latino (of any race)	3,703	18.0
Central American, ex. Mexican	303	16.4
Guatemalan	54	12.8
Salvadoran	157	15.1
Mexican	3,253	18.3
South American	102	21.6

Means of Transportation to Work: Car, Truck or Van
(Universe: Workers 16 Years and Over)

Group	Number	%
Total Population	22,774	88.1
Hispanic or Latino (of any race)	17,538	87.3
Central American, ex. Mexican	1,575	88.3
Guatemalan	413	97.9
Salvadoran	813	81.8
Mexican	15,141	87.0
South American	433	91.5

Means of Transportation to Work: Public Transportation (ex. Taxicab)
(Universe: Workers 16 Years and Over)

Group	Number	%
Total Population	1,623	6.3
Hispanic or Latino (of any race)	1,352	6.7
Central American, ex. Mexican	161	9.0
Guatemalan	0	0.0
Salvadoran	153	15.4
Mexican	1,128	6.5
South American	31	6.6

Homeownership Rate
(Universe: Occupied Housing Units)

Group	%
Total Population	46.1
Hispanic or Latino (of any race)	40.5
Central American, ex. Mexican	26.7
Guatemalan	27.7
Honduran	20.7
Nicaraguan	24.5
Salvadoran	26.7
Cuban	63.4
Mexican	41.7
Puerto Rican	39.2
South American	37.9
Argentinean	40.0
Colombian	26.7
Ecuadorian	53.8
Peruvian	25.7
Spaniard	57.8

Median Home Value

Group	Dollars
Total Population	456,500
Hispanic or Latino (of any race)	441,800
Central American, ex. Mexican	391,200
Guatemalan	396,900
Salvadoran	383,300
Mexican	449,300
South American	367,600

Median Gross Rent

Group	Dollars
Total Population	1,045
Hispanic or Latino (of any race)	1,037
Central American, ex. Mexican	911
Guatemalan	1,065
Salvadoran	823
Mexican	1,049
South American	1,125

Median Household Income
(2010 Inflation-Adjusted Dollars)

Group	Dollars
Total Population	50,881
Hispanic or Latino (of any race)	48,801
Central American, ex. Mexican	47,303
Guatemalan	51,500
Salvadoran	40,694
Mexican	48,574
South American	56,071

Per Capita Income
(2010 Inflation-Adjusted Dollars)

Group	Dollars
Total Population	20,373
Hispanic or Latino (of any race)	17,732
Central American, ex. Mexican	18,164
Guatemalan	15,969
Salvadoran	17,976
Mexican	17,705
South American	20,012

Households with $100,000+ Income

Group	Number	%
Total Population	3,436	18.1
Hispanic or Latino (of any race)	2,183	15.8
Central American, ex. Mexican	123	11.6
Guatemalan	35	12.0
Salvadoran	75	14.0
Mexican	1,980	16.3
South American	33	12.5

Households with Food Stamps/SNAP Benefits During Past 12 Months

Group	Number	%
Total Population	1,371	7.2
Hispanic or Latino (of any race)	1,181	8.5
Central American, ex. Mexican	87	8.2
Guatemalan	24	8.2
Salvadoran	63	11.7
Mexican	1,049	8.6
South American	0	0.0

Notes: (1) Percent of total population; (2) Percent of Hispanic/Latino population; Profiles include places with an overall population of at least 125,000, OR an overall population of at least 25,000 where the Hispanic/Latino population is at least 20% of the overall population. In states where less than five places meet either of these criteria, we have included places with at least 10,000 total population with the highest percentage of Hispanic/Latino population. These places are identified with an asterisk (*); Please refer to the User's Guide for a full explanation of data.

Poverty Rate
(Income in Past 12 Months Below Poverty Level)

Group	%
Total Population	14.9
Hispanic or Latino (of any race)	15.8
Central American, ex. Mexican	18.1
Guatemalan	9.9
Salvadoran	23.3
Mexican	15.9
South American	24.3

Monterey Park

Population

Group	Number	%TP[1]	%HP[2]
Total Population	60,269	100.0	–
Hispanic or Latino (of any race)	16,218	26.9	100.0
Central American, ex. Mexican	1,183	2.0	7.3
Guatemalan	275	0.5	1.7
Nicaraguan	164	0.3	1.0
Salvadoran	641	1.1	4.0
Cuban	108	0.2	0.7
Mexican	13,659	22.7	84.2
Puerto Rican	124	0.2	0.8
South American	326	0.5	2.0
Ecuadorian	103	0.2	0.6
Spaniard	144	0.2	0.9

Population Growth: 2000–2010

Group	%
Total Population	0.4
Hispanic or Latino (of any race)	-6.6
Central American, ex. Mexican	70.0
Guatemalan	91.0
Nicaraguan	54.7
Salvadoran	121.8
Cuban	-11.5
Mexican	-3.3
Puerto Rican	-18.4
South American	34.7

Males per 100 Females

Group	Number
Total Population	92.2
Hispanic or Latino (of any race)	93.2
Central American, ex. Mexican	89.9
Guatemalan	84.6
Nicaraguan	92.9
Salvadoran	91.9
Cuban	100.0
Mexican	93.2
Puerto Rican	100.0
South American	97.6
Ecuadorian	119.1
Spaniard	100.0

Average Household Size

Group	People
Total Population	3.01
Hispanic or Latino (of any race)	3.24
Central American, ex. Mexican	3.91
Guatemalan	4.15
Nicaraguan	3.40
Salvadoran	4.06
Cuban	2.46
Mexican	3.21
Puerto Rican	2.40
South American	3.33
Ecuadorian	3.48
Spaniard	2.67

Median Age

Group	Years
Total Population	43.1
Hispanic or Latino (of any race)	34.8
Central American, ex. Mexican	35.0
Guatemalan	35.5
Nicaraguan	45.5
Salvadoran	33.5
Cuban	45.3
Mexican	34.8
Puerto Rican	42.0
South American	40.8
Ecuadorian	40.2
Spaniard	49.0

High School Graduates
(Universe: Population 25 Years and Over)

Group	Number	%
Total Population	32,619	75.3
Hispanic or Latino (of any race)	7,885	74.5
Central American, ex. Mexican	705	84.7
Mexican	6,374	72.4

Four-Year College Graduates
(Universe: Population 25 Years and Over)

Group	Number	%
Total Population	12,165	28.1
Hispanic or Latino (of any race)	1,591	15.0
Central American, ex. Mexican	161	19.4
Mexican	1,194	13.6

Population Age 3–17 Enrolled in Public School
(Universe: Population Age 3–17 Enrolled in School)

Group	Number	%
Total Population	7,723	86.8
Hispanic or Latino (of any race)	3,247	85.9
Central American, ex. Mexican	282	86.8
Mexican	2,834	85.6

Population Age 3–17 Enrolled in Private School
(Universe: Population Age 3–17 Enrolled in School)

Group	Number	%
Total Population	1,178	13.2
Hispanic or Latino (of any race)	531	14.1
Central American, ex. Mexican	43	13.2
Mexican	477	14.4

Foreign-Born Population

Group	Number	%
Total Population	32,741	54.4
Hispanic or Latino (of any race)	4,524	27.4
Central American, ex. Mexican	642	52.2
Mexican	3,370	23.9

Foreign-Born Naturalized U.S. Citizens

Group	Number	%
Total Population	21,392	65.3
Hispanic or Latino (of any race)	2,693	59.5
Central American, ex. Mexican	466	72.6
Mexican	1,798	53.4

Language Spoken at Home: English Only
(Universe: Population 5 Years and Over)

Group	Number	%
Total Population	13,403	23.4
Hispanic or Latino (of any race)	4,844	31.3
Central American, ex. Mexican	220	18.9
Mexican	4,198	32.0

Language Spoken at Home: Spanish
(Universe: Population 5 Years and Over)

Group	Number	%
Total Population	10,902	19.0
Hispanic or Latino (of any race)	10,451	67.4
Central American, ex. Mexican	898	77.1
Mexican	8,818	67.3

Unemployment Rate
(Universe: Population 16 Years and Over)

Group	%
Total Population	6.9
Hispanic or Latino (of any race)	7.6
Central American, ex. Mexican	7.2
Mexican	7.3

Class of Worker: Private Wage and Salary
(Universe: Civilian Employed Population 16 Years and Over)

Group	Number	%
Total Population	20,487	76.3
Hispanic or Latino (of any race)	4,933	73.2
Central American, ex. Mexican	432	75.7
Mexican	4,071	71.6

Class of Worker: Government
(Universe: Civilian Employed Population 16 Years and Over)

Group	Number	%
Total Population	4,502	16.8
Hispanic or Latino (of any race)	1,368	20.3
Central American, ex. Mexican	66	11.6
Mexican	1,257	22.1

Means of Transportation to Work: Car, Truck or Van
(Universe: Workers 16 Years and Over)

Group	Number	%
Total Population	23,507	89.0
Hispanic or Latino (of any race)	5,908	88.5
Central American, ex. Mexican	514	90.8
Mexican	4,988	88.3

Means of Transportation to Work: Public Transportation (ex. Taxicab)
(Universe: Workers 16 Years and Over)

Group	Number	%
Total Population	906	3.4
Hispanic or Latino (of any race)	301	4.5
Central American, ex. Mexican	9	1.6
Mexican	271	4.8

Homeownership Rate
(Universe: Occupied Housing Units)

Group	%
Total Population	55.4
Hispanic or Latino (of any race)	48.5
Central American, ex. Mexican	31.4
Guatemalan	28.0
Nicaraguan	31.9
Salvadoran	31.3
Cuban	46.3
Mexican	50.2
Puerto Rican	35.6
South American	50.5
Ecuadorian	48.4
Spaniard	58.3

Median Home Value

Group	Dollars
Total Population	495,600
Hispanic or Latino (of any race)	489,900
Central American, ex. Mexican	479,700
Mexican	491,700

Median Gross Rent

Group	Dollars
Total Population	1,111
Hispanic or Latino (of any race)	1,084
Central American, ex. Mexican	1,041
Mexican	1,131

Median Household Income
(2010 Inflation-Adjusted Dollars)

Group	Dollars
Total Population	52,159
Hispanic or Latino (of any race)	53,157
Central American, ex. Mexican	60,875
Mexican	52,884

Per Capita Income
(2010 Inflation-Adjusted Dollars)

Group	Dollars
Total Population	23,860
Hispanic or Latino (of any race)	20,566
Central American, ex. Mexican	19,818
Mexican	19,764

Households with $100,000+ Income

Group	Number	%
Total Population	4,666	23.7
Hispanic or Latino (of any race)	1,017	20.8
Central American, ex. Mexican	102	29.1
Mexican	800	19.8

Households with Food Stamps/SNAP Benefits During Past 12 Months

Group	Number	%
Total Population	793	4.0
Hispanic or Latino (of any race)	302	6.2
Central American, ex. Mexican	19	5.4
Mexican	241	6.0

Poverty Rate
(Income in Past 12 Months Below Poverty Level)

Group	%
Total Population	12.6

Notes: (1) Percent of total population; (2) Percent of Hispanic/Latino population; Profiles include places with an overall population of at least 125,000, OR an overall population of at least 25,000 where the Hispanic/Latino population is at least 20% of the overall population. In states where less than five places meet either of these criteria, we have included places with at least 10,000 total population with the highest percentage of Hispanic/Latino population. These places are identified with an asterisk (*); Please refer to the User's Guide for a full explanation of data.

Hispanic or Latino (of any race)		12.4
Central American, ex. Mexican		2.4
Mexican		13.9

Moorpark

Population

Group	Number	%TP[1]	%HP[2]
Total Population	34,421	100.0	–
Hispanic or Latino (of any race)	10,813	31.4	100.0
Central American, ex. Mexican	424	1.2	3.9
Guatemalan	148	0.4	1.4
Salvadoran	160	0.5	1.5
Cuban	108	0.3	1.0
Mexican	9,244	26.9	85.5
Puerto Rican	126	0.4	1.2
South American	327	1.0	3.0
Colombian	102	0.3	0.9
Spaniard	114	0.3	1.1

Population Growth: 2000–2010

Group	%
Total Population	9.6
Hispanic or Latino (of any race)	23.8
Central American, ex. Mexican	117.4
Mexican	27.4
Puerto Rican	17.8
South American	99.4

Males per 100 Females

Group	Number
Total Population	98.6
Hispanic or Latino (of any race)	98.5
Central American, ex. Mexican	98.1
Guatemalan	92.2
Salvadoran	88.2
Cuban	74.2
Mexican	100.0
Puerto Rican	103.2
South American	75.8
Colombian	88.9
Spaniard	86.9

Average Household Size

Group	People
Total Population	3.28
Hispanic or Latino (of any race)	4.58
Central American, ex. Mexican	3.96
Guatemalan	3.94
Salvadoran	4.16
Cuban	2.86
Mexican	4.81
Puerto Rican	3.09
South American	3.20
Colombian	3.31
Spaniard	3.15

Median Age

Group	Years
Total Population	34.7
Hispanic or Latino (of any race)	27.3
Central American, ex. Mexican	31.8
Guatemalan	31.3
Salvadoran	31.0
Cuban	34.5
Mexican	26.6
Puerto Rican	27.3
South American	36.6
Colombian	32.0
Spaniard	40.0

High School Graduates
(Universe: Population 25 Years and Over)

Group	Number	%
Total Population	18,084	86.6
Hispanic or Latino (of any race)	3,341	59.4
Mexican	2,724	56.8

Four-Year College Graduates
(Universe: Population 25 Years and Over)

Group	Number	%
Total Population	7,821	37.5
Hispanic or Latino (of any race)	793	14.1
Mexican	616	12.8

Population Age 3–17 Enrolled in Public School
(Universe: Population Age 3–17 Enrolled in School)

Group	Number	%
Total Population	6,590	87.6
Hispanic or Latino (of any race)	2,496	95.9
Mexican	2,177	95.3

Population Age 3–17 Enrolled in Private School
(Universe: Population Age 3–17 Enrolled in School)

Group	Number	%
Total Population	933	12.4
Hispanic or Latino (of any race)	108	4.1
Mexican	108	4.7

Foreign-Born Population

Group	Number	%
Total Population	6,687	19.8
Hispanic or Latino (of any race)	4,196	39.5
Mexican	3,640	39.2

Foreign-Born Naturalized U.S. Citizens

Group	Number	%
Total Population	2,783	41.6
Hispanic or Latino (of any race)	1,006	24.0
Mexican	820	22.5

Language Spoken at Home: English Only
(Universe: Population 5 Years and Over)

Group	Number	%
Total Population	21,486	68.4
Hispanic or Latino (of any race)	2,460	25.7
Mexican	2,069	24.9

Language Spoken at Home: Spanish
(Universe: Population 5 Years and Over)

Group	Number	%
Total Population	7,495	23.8
Hispanic or Latino (of any race)	7,084	73.9
Mexican	6,185	74.6

Unemployment Rate
(Universe: Population 16 Years and Over)

Group	%
Total Population	5.1
Hispanic or Latino (of any race)	5.4
Mexican	4.7

Class of Worker: Private Wage and Salary
(Universe: Civilian Employed Population 16 Years and Over)

Group	Number	%
Total Population	14,053	78.3
Hispanic or Latino (of any race)	4,137	79.3
Mexican	3,658	80.2

Class of Worker: Government
(Universe: Civilian Employed Population 16 Years and Over)

Group	Number	%
Total Population	2,150	12.0
Hispanic or Latino (of any race)	454	8.7
Mexican	401	8.8

Means of Transportation to Work: Car, Truck or Van
(Universe: Workers 16 Years and Over)

Group	Number	%
Total Population	16,035	91.3
Hispanic or Latino (of any race)	4,681	92.9
Mexican	4,073	92.3

Means of Transportation to Work: Public Transportation (ex. Taxicab)
(Universe: Workers 16 Years and Over)

Group	Number	%
Total Population	267	1.5
Hispanic or Latino (of any race)	146	2.9
Mexican	128	2.9

Homeownership Rate
(Universe: Occupied Housing Units)

Group	%
Total Population	78.0
Hispanic or Latino (of any race)	63.9
Central American, ex. Mexican	55.3
Guatemalan	48.5
Salvadoran	54.8
Cuban	73.0
Mexican	62.6
Puerto Rican	69.7
South American	75.0
Colombian	71.4
Spaniard	87.8

Median Home Value

Group	Dollars
Total Population	609,000
Hispanic or Latino (of any race)	526,100
Mexican	517,200

Median Gross Rent

Group	Dollars
Total Population	1,672
Hispanic or Latino (of any race)	1,655
Mexican	1,657

Median Household Income
(2010 Inflation-Adjusted Dollars)

Group	Dollars
Total Population	101,962
Hispanic or Latino (of any race)	83,854
Mexican	73,681

Per Capita Income
(2010 Inflation-Adjusted Dollars)

Group	Dollars
Total Population	37,121
Hispanic or Latino (of any race)	19,337
Mexican	18,506

Households with $100,000+ Income

Group	Number	%
Total Population	5,352	51.4
Hispanic or Latino (of any race)	906	39.2
Mexican	707	36.5

Households with Food Stamps/SNAP Benefits During Past 12 Months

Group	Number	%
Total Population	164	1.6
Hispanic or Latino (of any race)	75	3.2
Mexican	75	3.9

Poverty Rate
(Income in Past 12 Months Below Poverty Level)

Group	%
Total Population	3.5
Hispanic or Latino (of any race)	7.7
Mexican	8.2

Moreno Valley

Population

Group	Number	%TP[1]	%HP[2]
Total Population	193,365	100.0	–
Hispanic or Latino (of any race)	105,169	54.4	100.0
Central American, ex. Mexican	5,710	3.0	5.4
Costa Rican	185	0.1	0.2
Guatemalan	1,562	0.8	1.5
Honduran	386	0.2	0.4
Nicaraguan	528	0.3	0.5
Panamanian	186	0.1	0.2
Salvadoran	2,794	1.4	2.7
Cuban	606	0.3	0.6
Mexican	90,054	46.6	85.6
Puerto Rican	1,636	0.8	1.6
South American	1,587	0.8	1.5
Argentinean	233	0.1	0.2
Colombian	355	0.2	0.3
Ecuadorian	296	0.2	0.3
Peruvian	463	0.2	0.4
Spaniard	727	0.4	0.7

Population Growth: 2000–2010

Group	%
Total Population	35.8
Hispanic or Latino (of any race)	92.3
Central American, ex. Mexican	260.0
Costa Rican	63.7
Guatemalan	389.7
Nicaraguan	166.7
Salvadoran	344.9

Notes: (1) Percent of total population; (2) Percent of Hispanic/Latino population; Profiles include places with an overall population of at least 125,000, OR an overall population of at least 25,000 where the Hispanic/Latino population is at least 20% of the overall population. In states where less than five places meet either of these criteria, we have included places with at least 10,000 total population with the highest percentage of Hispanic/Latino population. These places are identified with an asterisk (*); Please refer to the User's Guide for a full explanation of data.

Cuban	45.3
Mexican	107.1
Puerto Rican	39.0
South American	118.3
Colombian	155.4
Ecuadorian	107.0
Peruvian	138.7

Males per 100 Females

Group	Number
Total Population	95.1
Hispanic or Latino (of any race)	97.7
Central American, ex. Mexican	97.3
Costa Rican	72.9
Guatemalan	107.4
Honduran	99.0
Nicaraguan	97.8
Panamanian	84.2
Salvadoran	94.6
Cuban	88.2
Mexican	98.4
Puerto Rican	96.9
South American	92.6
Argentinean	102.6
Colombian	79.3
Ecuadorian	89.7
Peruvian	97.0
Spaniard	93.4

Average Household Size

Group	People
Total Population	3.74
Hispanic or Latino (of any race)	4.49
Central American, ex. Mexican	4.52
Costa Rican	4.12
Guatemalan	4.76
Honduran	4.54
Nicaraguan	4.12
Panamanian	3.49
Salvadoran	4.60
Cuban	3.50
Mexican	4.57
Puerto Rican	3.42
South American	3.74
Argentinean	3.69
Colombian	3.74
Ecuadorian	3.82
Peruvian	3.69
Spaniard	3.70

Median Age

Group	Years
Total Population	28.6
Hispanic or Latino (of any race)	24.5
Central American, ex. Mexican	32.7
Costa Rican	32.8
Guatemalan	31.9
Honduran	31.0
Nicaraguan	36.0
Panamanian	46.3
Salvadoran	32.8
Cuban	30.0
Mexican	23.8
Puerto Rican	27.3
South American	35.5
Argentinean	32.3
Colombian	33.7
Ecuadorian	35.8
Peruvian	39.7
Spaniard	29.7

High School Graduates
(Universe: Population 25 Years and Over)

Group	Number	%
Total Population	76,533	75.5
Hispanic or Latino (of any race)	26,541	57.3
Central American, ex. Mexican	1,717	66.7
Guatemalan	488	65.1
Salvadoran	597	54.0
Mexican	21,863	54.7
Puerto Rican	530	76.6
South American	707	85.8

Four-Year College Graduates
(Universe: Population 25 Years and Over)

Group	Number	%
Total Population	15,096	14.9
Hispanic or Latino (of any race)	3,165	6.8
Central American, ex. Mexican	291	11.3
Guatemalan	141	18.8
Salvadoran	68	6.2
Mexican	2,406	6.0
Puerto Rican	27	3.9
South American	97	11.8

Population Age 3–17 Enrolled in Public School
(Universe: Population Age 3–17 Enrolled in School)

Group	Number	%
Total Population	44,704	94.1
Hispanic or Latino (of any race)	27,419	96.6
Central American, ex. Mexican	875	96.9
Guatemalan	394	100.0
Salvadoran	381	93.2
Mexican	24,587	97.1
Puerto Rican	340	95.8
South American	177	76.6

Population Age 3–17 Enrolled in Private School
(Universe: Population Age 3–17 Enrolled in School)

Group	Number	%
Total Population	2,828	5.9
Hispanic or Latino (of any race)	969	3.4
Central American, ex. Mexican	28	3.1
Guatemalan	0	0.0
Salvadoran	28	6.8
Mexican	736	2.9
Puerto Rican	15	4.2
South American	54	23.4

Foreign-Born Population

Group	Number	%
Total Population	46,427	24.8
Hispanic or Latino (of any race)	34,686	36.0
Central American, ex. Mexican	2,429	60.5
Guatemalan	751	60.3
Salvadoran	1,020	56.2
Mexican	30,127	35.6
Puerto Rican	11	0.9
South American	754	56.9

Foreign-Born Naturalized U.S. Citizens

Group	Number	%
Total Population	18,521	39.9
Hispanic or Latino (of any race)	11,331	32.7
Central American, ex. Mexican	1,056	43.5
Guatemalan	361	48.1
Salvadoran	393	38.5
Mexican	9,194	30.5
Puerto Rican	0	0.0
South American	349	46.3

Language Spoken at Home: English Only
(Universe: Population 5 Years and Over)

Group	Number	%
Total Population	93,282	54.3
Hispanic or Latino (of any race)	20,764	24.1
Central American, ex. Mexican	400	10.7
Guatemalan	75	6.2
Salvadoran	190	11.7
Mexican	17,824	23.6
Puerto Rican	620	50.2
South American	263	20.3

Language Spoken at Home: Spanish
(Universe: Population 5 Years and Over)

Group	Number	%
Total Population	68,102	39.7
Hispanic or Latino (of any race)	65,460	75.8
Central American, ex. Mexican	3,352	89.3
Guatemalan	1,129	93.8
Salvadoran	1,438	88.3
Mexican	57,793	76.4
Puerto Rican	614	49.8
South American	987	76.1

Unemployment Rate
(Universe: Population 16 Years and Over)

Group	%
Total Population	11.4
Hispanic or Latino (of any race)	12.3
Central American, ex. Mexican	13.2
Guatemalan	7.6
Salvadoran	18.2
Mexican	12.7
Puerto Rican	16.3
South American	4.6

Class of Worker: Private Wage and Salary
(Universe: Civilian Employed Population 16 Years and Over)

Group	Number	%
Total Population	57,006	75.0
Hispanic or Latino (of any race)	28,696	81.0
Central American, ex. Mexican	1,558	81.7
Guatemalan	463	75.8
Salvadoran	622	82.8
Mexican	24,940	81.8
Puerto Rican	305	62.4
South American	477	65.5

Class of Worker: Government
(Universe: Civilian Employed Population 16 Years and Over)

Group	Number	%
Total Population	13,943	18.3
Hispanic or Latino (of any race)	4,311	12.2
Central American, ex. Mexican	126	6.6
Guatemalan	10	1.6
Salvadoran	73	9.7
Mexican	3,714	12.2
Puerto Rican	140	28.6
South American	35	4.8

Means of Transportation to Work: Car, Truck or Van
(Universe: Workers 16 Years and Over)

Group	Number	%
Total Population	68,387	92.4
Hispanic or Latino (of any race)	32,047	93.9
Central American, ex. Mexican	1,690	95.2
Guatemalan	475	91.9
Salvadoran	698	96.1
Mexican	27,531	93.6
Puerto Rican	451	95.3
South American	715	98.2

Means of Transportation to Work: Public Transportation (ex. Taxicab)
(Universe: Workers 16 Years and Over)

Group	Number	%
Total Population	1,264	1.7
Hispanic or Latino (of any race)	435	1.3
Central American, ex. Mexican	32	1.8
Guatemalan	4	0.8
Salvadoran	28	3.9
Mexican	355	1.2
Puerto Rican	22	4.7
South American	0	0.0

Homeownership Rate
(Universe: Occupied Housing Units)

Group	%
Total Population	64.7
Hispanic or Latino (of any race)	64.0
Central American, ex. Mexican	69.0
Costa Rican	72.5
Guatemalan	64.9
Honduran	71.3
Nicaraguan	75.5
Panamanian	77.6
Salvadoran	68.9
Cuban	66.5
Mexican	64.2
Puerto Rican	59.3
South American	70.5
Argentinean	68.9
Colombian	64.4
Ecuadorian	68.9
Peruvian	72.6
Spaniard	66.1

Notes: (1) Percent of total population; (2) Percent of Hispanic/Latino population; Profiles include places with an overall population of at least 125,000, OR an overall population of at least 25,000 where the Hispanic/Latino population is at least 20% of the overall population. In states where less than five places meet either of these criteria, we have included places with at least 10,000 total population with the highest percentage of Hispanic/Latino population. These places are identified with an asterisk (*); Please refer to the User's Guide for a full explanation of data.

Median Home Value

Group	Dollars
Total Population	296,400
Hispanic or Latino (of any race)	281,800
Central American, ex. Mexican	288,500
Guatemalan	321,900
Salvadoran	298,200
Mexican	273,700
Puerto Rican	290,300
South American	342,700

Median Gross Rent

Group	Dollars
Total Population	1,271
Hispanic or Latino (of any race)	1,248
Central American, ex. Mexican	1,248
Guatemalan	1,040
Salvadoran	1,323
Mexican	1,246
Puerto Rican	1,366
South American	1,143

Median Household Income
(2010 Inflation-Adjusted Dollars)

Group	Dollars
Total Population	56,507
Hispanic or Latino (of any race)	51,805
Central American, ex. Mexican	54,675
Guatemalan	85,927
Salvadoran	55,370
Mexican	50,430
Puerto Rican	36,000
South American	55,417

Per Capita Income
(2010 Inflation-Adjusted Dollars)

Group	Dollars
Total Population	18,440
Hispanic or Latino (of any race)	13,525
Central American, ex. Mexican	20,871
Guatemalan	19,580
Salvadoran	16,733
Mexican	12,943
Puerto Rican	14,634
South American	18,394

Households with $100,000+ Income

Group	Number	%
Total Population	9,801	19.7
Hispanic or Latino (of any race)	2,945	14.1
Central American, ex. Mexican	253	22.3
Guatemalan	129	38.5
Salvadoran	79	13.9
Mexican	2,342	13.1
Puerto Rican	18	4.1
South American	73	17.8

Households with Food Stamps/SNAP Benefits During Past 12 Months

Group	Number	%
Total Population	3,588	7.2
Hispanic or Latino (of any race)	1,634	7.8
Central American, ex. Mexican	76	6.7
Guatemalan	14	4.2
Salvadoran	59	10.4
Mexican	1,401	7.8
Puerto Rican	67	15.4
South American	11	2.7

Poverty Rate
(Income in Past 12 Months Below Poverty Level)

Group	%
Total Population	16.2
Hispanic or Latino (of any race)	18.7
Central American, ex. Mexican	18.7
Guatemalan	9.5
Salvadoran	30.2
Mexican	18.8
Puerto Rican	26.2
South American	14.9

Morgan Hill

Population

Group	Number	%TP[1]	%HP[2]
Total Population	37,882	100.0	–
Hispanic or Latino (of any race)	12,863	34.0	100.0
Central American, ex. Mexican	411	1.1	3.2
Salvadoran	199	0.5	1.5
Mexican	10,821	28.6	84.1
Puerto Rican	206	0.5	1.6
South American	311	0.8	2.4
Spaniard	292	0.8	2.3

Population Growth: 2000–2010

Group	%
Total Population	12.9
Hispanic or Latino (of any race)	39.4
Central American, ex. Mexican	161.8
Mexican	44.3
Puerto Rican	90.7
South American	185.3

Males per 100 Females

Group	Number
Total Population	97.9
Hispanic or Latino (of any race)	98.5
Central American, ex. Mexican	87.7
Salvadoran	91.3
Mexican	99.0
Puerto Rican	98.1
South American	104.6
Spaniard	92.1

Average Household Size

Group	People
Total Population	3.04
Hispanic or Latino (of any race)	3.77
Central American, ex. Mexican	3.66
Salvadoran	3.87
Mexican	3.90
Puerto Rican	2.92
South American	3.15
Spaniard	2.94

Median Age

Group	Years
Total Population	36.8
Hispanic or Latino (of any race)	26.7
Central American, ex. Mexican	32.7
Salvadoran	31.3
Mexican	25.9
Puerto Rican	29.3
South American	40.3
Spaniard	32.4

High School Graduates
(Universe: Population 25 Years and Over)

Group	Number	%
Total Population	19,615	85.2
Hispanic or Latino (of any race)	4,001	62.7
Mexican	3,340	58.8

Four-Year College Graduates
(Universe: Population 25 Years and Over)

Group	Number	%
Total Population	8,783	38.2
Hispanic or Latino (of any race)	954	15.0
Mexican	773	13.6

Population Age 3–17 Enrolled in Public School
(Universe: Population Age 3–17 Enrolled in School)

Group	Number	%
Total Population	6,647	80.7
Hispanic or Latino (of any race)	3,330	93.4
Mexican	2,965	94.2

Population Age 3–17 Enrolled in Private School
(Universe: Population Age 3–17 Enrolled in School)

Group	Number	%
Total Population	1,591	19.3
Hispanic or Latino (of any race)	234	6.6
Mexican	184	5.8

Foreign-Born Population

Group	Number	%
Total Population	7,494	20.5
Hispanic or Latino (of any race)	3,800	29.6
Mexican	3,609	31.0

Foreign-Born Naturalized U.S. Citizens

Group	Number	%
Total Population	4,087	54.5
Hispanic or Latino (of any race)	1,430	37.6
Mexican	1,311	36.3

Language Spoken at Home: English Only
(Universe: Population 5 Years and Over)

Group	Number	%
Total Population	21,927	64.9
Hispanic or Latino (of any race)	4,036	35.5
Mexican	3,444	33.4

Language Spoken at Home: Spanish
(Universe: Population 5 Years and Over)

Group	Number	%
Total Population	7,863	23.3
Hispanic or Latino (of any race)	7,298	64.1
Mexican	6,848	66.4

Unemployment Rate
(Universe: Population 16 Years and Over)

Group	%
Total Population	7.2
Hispanic or Latino (of any race)	8.5
Mexican	8.3

Class of Worker: Private Wage and Salary
(Universe: Civilian Employed Population 16 Years and Over)

Group	Number	%
Total Population	13,264	75.8
Hispanic or Latino (of any race)	4,422	79.0
Mexican	4,023	79.1

Class of Worker: Government
(Universe: Civilian Employed Population 16 Years and Over)

Group	Number	%
Total Population	2,548	14.6
Hispanic or Latino (of any race)	645	11.5
Mexican	534	10.5

Means of Transportation to Work: Car, Truck or Van
(Universe: Workers 16 Years and Over)

Group	Number	%
Total Population	14,733	86.5
Hispanic or Latino (of any race)	4,740	85.8
Mexican	4,259	84.9

Means of Transportation to Work: Public Transportation (ex. Taxicab)
(Universe: Workers 16 Years and Over)

Group	Number	%
Total Population	393	2.3
Hispanic or Latino (of any race)	161	2.9
Mexican	161	3.2

Homeownership Rate
(Universe: Occupied Housing Units)

Group	%
Total Population	71.3
Hispanic or Latino (of any race)	48.2
Central American, ex. Mexican	56.8
Salvadoran	59.3
Mexican	46.4
Puerto Rican	50.0
South American	75.0
Spaniard	73.7

Median Home Value

Group	Dollars
Total Population	673,400
Hispanic or Latino (of any race)	588,100
Mexican	579,100

Median Gross Rent

Group	Dollars
Total Population	1,401
Hispanic or Latino (of any race)	1,378
Mexican	1,348

Notes: (1) Percent of total population; (2) Percent of Hispanic/Latino population; Profiles include places with an overall population of at least 125,000, OR an overall population of at least 25,000 where the Hispanic/Latino population is at least 20% of the overall population. In states where less than five places meet either of these criteria, we have included places with at least 10,000 total population with the highest percentage of Hispanic/Latino population. These places are identified with an asterisk (*); Please refer to the User's Guide for a full explanation of data.

Median Household Income
(2010 Inflation-Adjusted Dollars)

Group	Dollars
Total Population	92,771
Hispanic or Latino (of any race)	62,604
Mexican	58,693

Per Capita Income
(2010 Inflation-Adjusted Dollars)

Group	Dollars
Total Population	38,695
Hispanic or Latino (of any race)	20,051
Mexican	18,692

Households with $100,000+ Income

Group	Number	%
Total Population	5,506	45.7
Hispanic or Latino (of any race)	836	25.1
Mexican	684	22.9

Households with Food Stamps/SNAP Benefits During Past 12 Months

Group	Number	%
Total Population	398	3.3
Hispanic or Latino (of any race)	146	4.4
Mexican	146	4.9

Poverty Rate
(Income in Past 12 Months Below Poverty Level)

Group	%
Total Population	10.0
Hispanic or Latino (of any race)	20.1
Mexican	21.5

Mountain View

Population

Group	Number	%TP[1]	%HP[2]
Total Population	74,066	100.0	–
Hispanic or Latino (of any race)	16,071	21.7	100.0
Central American, ex. Mexican	1,910	2.6	11.9
Guatemalan	474	0.6	2.9
Nicaraguan	109	0.1	0.7
Salvadoran	1,155	1.6	7.2
Mexican	11,523	15.6	71.7
Puerto Rican	338	0.5	2.1
South American	874	1.2	5.4
Colombian	137	0.2	0.9
Peruvian	395	0.5	2.5
Spaniard	370	0.5	2.3

Population Growth: 2000–2010

Group	%
Total Population	4.7
Hispanic or Latino (of any race)	24.5
Central American, ex. Mexican	99.8
Guatemalan	120.5
Salvadoran	121.7
Mexican	24.7
Puerto Rican	19.9
South American	96.4
Peruvian	178.2

Males per 100 Females

Group	Number
Total Population	103.6
Hispanic or Latino (of any race)	108.7
Central American, ex. Mexican	107.4
Guatemalan	135.8
Nicaraguan	87.9
Salvadoran	102.6
Mexican	110.7
Puerto Rican	115.3
South American	93.4
Colombian	104.5
Peruvian	94.6
Spaniard	90.7

Average Household Size

Group	People
Total Population	2.31
Hispanic or Latino (of any race)	3.39
Central American, ex. Mexican	3.54
Guatemalan	3.94
Nicaraguan	2.78
Salvadoran	3.57
Mexican	3.64
Puerto Rican	2.40
South American	2.55
Colombian	2.35
Peruvian	2.96
Spaniard	2.21

Median Age

Group	Years
Total Population	35.9
Hispanic or Latino (of any race)	29.2
Central American, ex. Mexican	31.5
Guatemalan	30.7
Nicaraguan	37.1
Salvadoran	31.5
Mexican	27.8
Puerto Rican	34.0
South American	37.0
Colombian	36.1
Peruvian	37.0
Spaniard	37.8

High School Graduates
(Universe: Population 25 Years and Over)

Group	Number	%
Total Population	48,011	90.4
Hispanic or Latino (of any race)	5,146	58.6
Central American, ex. Mexican	671	57.0
Mexican	3,061	50.9
South American	751	93.1

Four-Year College Graduates
(Universe: Population 25 Years and Over)

Group	Number	%
Total Population	31,162	58.7
Hispanic or Latino (of any race)	1,836	20.9
Central American, ex. Mexican	423	35.9
Mexican	702	11.7
South American	361	44.7

Population Age 3–17 Enrolled in Public School
(Universe: Population Age 3–17 Enrolled in School)

Group	Number	%
Total Population	7,890	78.6
Hispanic or Latino (of any race)	2,850	92.3
Central American, ex. Mexican	248	96.1
Mexican	2,432	94.1
South American	115	100.0

Population Age 3–17 Enrolled in Private School
(Universe: Population Age 3–17 Enrolled in School)

Group	Number	%
Total Population	2,154	21.4
Hispanic or Latino (of any race)	239	7.7
Central American, ex. Mexican	10	3.9
Mexican	153	5.9
South American	0	0.0

Foreign-Born Population

Group	Number	%
Total Population	28,767	39.7
Hispanic or Latino (of any race)	8,521	58.0
Central American, ex. Mexican	1,274	76.1
Mexican	6,063	55.8
South American	911	79.8

Foreign-Born Naturalized U.S. Citizens

Group	Number	%
Total Population	11,071	38.5
Hispanic or Latino (of any race)	1,656	19.4
Central American, ex. Mexican	220	17.3
Mexican	1,189	19.6
South American	171	18.8

Language Spoken at Home: English Only
(Universe: Population 5 Years and Over)

Group	Number	%
Total Population	36,105	53.4
Hispanic or Latino (of any race)	2,258	16.7
Central American, ex. Mexican	113	7.6
Mexican	1,481	14.9
South American	70	6.5

Language Spoken at Home: Spanish
(Universe: Population 5 Years and Over)

Group	Number	%
Total Population	11,899	17.6
Hispanic or Latino (of any race)	11,116	82.4
Central American, ex. Mexican	1,305	87.3
Mexican	8,441	85.0
South American	1,002	93.5

Unemployment Rate
(Universe: Population 16 Years and Over)

Group	%
Total Population	6.1
Hispanic or Latino (of any race)	6.8
Central American, ex. Mexican	24.8
Mexican	4.3
South American	4.9

Class of Worker: Private Wage and Salary
(Universe: Civilian Employed Population 16 Years and Over)

Group	Number	%
Total Population	34,558	85.2
Hispanic or Latino (of any race)	6,528	84.5
Central American, ex. Mexican	632	89.1
Mexican	4,761	84.7
South American	670	84.9

Class of Worker: Government
(Universe: Civilian Employed Population 16 Years and Over)

Group	Number	%
Total Population	3,127	7.7
Hispanic or Latino (of any race)	527	6.8
Central American, ex. Mexican	29	4.1
Mexican	351	6.2
South American	46	5.8

Means of Transportation to Work: Car, Truck or Van
(Universe: Workers 16 Years and Over)

Group	Number	%
Total Population	32,485	82.0
Hispanic or Latino (of any race)	5,735	75.7
Central American, ex. Mexican	582	82.1
Mexican	4,056	73.1
South American	629	84.8

Means of Transportation to Work: Public Transportation (ex. Taxicab)
(Universe: Workers 16 Years and Over)

Group	Number	%
Total Population	1,842	4.7
Hispanic or Latino (of any race)	654	8.6
Central American, ex. Mexican	41	5.8
Mexican	503	9.1
South American	50	6.7

Homeownership Rate
(Universe: Occupied Housing Units)

Group	%
Total Population	41.7
Hispanic or Latino (of any race)	20.7
Central American, ex. Mexican	17.5
Guatemalan	13.5
Nicaraguan	19.5
Salvadoran	18.3
Mexican	18.1
Puerto Rican	34.6
South American	29.8
Colombian	37.5
Peruvian	21.3
Spaniard	44.5

Median Home Value

Group	Dollars
Total Population	779,500
Hispanic or Latino (of any race)	687,200
Central American, ex. Mexican	1,000,000+
Mexican	636,700
South American	764,100

Median Gross Rent

Group	Dollars
Total Population	1,427
Hispanic or Latino (of any race)	1,284
Central American, ex. Mexican	1,315

Notes: (1) Percent of total population; (2) Percent of Hispanic/Latino population; Profiles include places with an overall population of at least 125,000, OR an overall population of at least 25,000 where the Hispanic/Latino population is at least 20% of the overall population. In states where less than five places meet either of these criteria, we have included places with at least 10,000 total population with the highest percentage of Hispanic/Latino population. These places are identified with an asterisk (*); Please refer to the User's Guide for a full explanation of data.

Mexican	1,251
South American	1,606

Median Household Income
(2010 Inflation-Adjusted Dollars)

Group	Dollars
Total Population	88,244
Hispanic or Latino (of any race)	52,654
Central American, ex. Mexican	53,403
Mexican	48,433
South American	54,906

Per Capita Income
(2010 Inflation-Adjusted Dollars)

Group	Dollars
Total Population	49,403
Hispanic or Latino (of any race)	20,281
Central American, ex. Mexican	21,093
Mexican	17,318
South American	24,012

Households with $100,000+ Income

Group	Number	%
Total Population	13,981	45.0
Hispanic or Latino (of any race)	797	18.2
Central American, ex. Mexican	80	14.8
Mexican	401	13.9
South American	102	25.9

Households with Food Stamps/SNAP Benefits During Past 12 Months

Group	Number	%
Total Population	318	1.0
Hispanic or Latino (of any race)	213	4.9
Central American, ex. Mexican	48	8.9
Mexican	90	3.1
South American	75	19.0

Poverty Rate
(Income in Past 12 Months Below Poverty Level)

Group	%
Total Population	6.8
Hispanic or Latino (of any race)	12.3
Central American, ex. Mexican	14.6
Mexican	10.6
South American	21.6

Murrieta

Population

Group	Number	%TP[1]	%HP[2]
Total Population	103,466	100.0	–
Hispanic or Latino (of any race)	26,792	25.9	100.0
Central American, ex. Mexican	1,151	1.1	4.3
Guatemalan	273	0.3	1.0
Nicaraguan	123	0.1	0.5
Panamanian	121	0.1	0.5
Salvadoran	445	0.4	1.7
Cuban	375	0.4	1.4
Mexican	21,400	20.7	79.9
Puerto Rican	1,025	1.0	3.8
South American	905	0.9	3.4
Argentinean	144	0.1	0.5
Colombian	228	0.2	0.9
Ecuadorian	137	0.1	0.5
Peruvian	240	0.2	0.9
Spaniard	546	0.5	2.0

Population Growth: 2000–2010

Group	%
Total Population	133.7
Hispanic or Latino (of any race)	246.2
Central American, ex. Mexican	428.0
Cuban	193.0
Mexican	269.6
Puerto Rican	306.7
South American	381.4

Males per 100 Females

Group	Number
Total Population	95.2
Hispanic or Latino (of any race)	96.5
Central American, ex. Mexican	94.1
Guatemalan	92.3
Nicaraguan	75.7
Panamanian	89.1
Salvadoran	117.1
Cuban	89.4
Mexican	96.9
Puerto Rican	102.6
South American	89.3
Argentinean	105.7
Colombian	76.7
Ecuadorian	95.7
Peruvian	83.2
Spaniard	85.7

Average Household Size

Group	People
Total Population	3.15
Hispanic or Latino (of any race)	3.76
Central American, ex. Mexican	3.86
Guatemalan	4.46
Nicaraguan	3.63
Panamanian	3.22
Salvadoran	4.22
Cuban	3.22
Mexican	3.84
Puerto Rican	3.58
South American	3.57
Argentinean	3.08
Colombian	3.98
Ecuadorian	3.38
Peruvian	4.06
Spaniard	2.99

Median Age

Group	Years
Total Population	33.4
Hispanic or Latino (of any race)	24.9
Central American, ex. Mexican	30.4
Guatemalan	30.3
Nicaraguan	34.7
Panamanian	33.6
Salvadoran	28.4
Cuban	25.6
Mexican	24.2
Puerto Rican	24.2
South American	34.5
Argentinean	39.5
Colombian	32.3
Ecuadorian	30.5
Peruvian	33.4
Spaniard	33.0

High School Graduates
(Universe: Population 25 Years and Over)

Group	Number	%
Total Population	51,261	91.2
Hispanic or Latino (of any race)	9,946	79.5
Central American, ex. Mexican	454	92.1
Mexican	7,701	77.1
Puerto Rican	440	81.5

Four-Year College Graduates
(Universe: Population 25 Years and Over)

Group	Number	%
Total Population	16,291	29.0
Hispanic or Latino (of any race)	1,949	15.6
Central American, ex. Mexican	150	30.4
Mexican	1,446	14.5
Puerto Rican	78	14.4

Population Age 3–17 Enrolled in Public School
(Universe: Population Age 3–17 Enrolled in School)

Group	Number	%
Total Population	20,730	88.1
Hispanic or Latino (of any race)	7,394	90.7
Central American, ex. Mexican	197	59.9
Mexican	6,039	92.9
Puerto Rican	479	77.3

Population Age 3–17 Enrolled in Private School
(Universe: Population Age 3–17 Enrolled in School)

Group	Number	%
Total Population	2,803	11.9
Hispanic or Latino (of any race)	760	9.3
Central American, ex. Mexican	132	40.1
Mexican	464	7.1
Puerto Rican	141	22.7

Foreign-Born Population

Group	Number	%
Total Population	13,702	14.3
Hispanic or Latino (of any race)	5,620	21.6
Central American, ex. Mexican	293	26.3
Mexican	4,516	21.4
Puerto Rican	0	0.0

Foreign-Born Naturalized U.S. Citizens

Group	Number	%
Total Population	7,671	56.0
Hispanic or Latino (of any race)	2,762	49.1
Central American, ex. Mexican	185	63.1
Mexican	2,018	44.7
Puerto Rican	0	0.0

Language Spoken at Home: English Only
(Universe: Population 5 Years and Over)

Group	Number	%
Total Population	66,697	75.4
Hispanic or Latino (of any race)	10,887	47.0
Central American, ex. Mexican	342	38.2
Mexican	8,764	46.7
Puerto Rican	542	47.0

Language Spoken at Home: Spanish
(Universe: Population 5 Years and Over)

Group	Number	%
Total Population	13,010	14.7
Hispanic or Latino (of any race)	12,010	51.8
Central American, ex. Mexican	517	57.7
Mexican	9,908	52.9
Puerto Rican	497	43.1

Unemployment Rate
(Universe: Population 16 Years and Over)

Group	%
Total Population	9.5
Hispanic or Latino (of any race)	13.0
Central American, ex. Mexican	15.0
Mexican	13.8
Puerto Rican	7.7

Class of Worker: Private Wage and Salary
(Universe: Civilian Employed Population 16 Years and Over)

Group	Number	%
Total Population	30,748	75.3
Hispanic or Latino (of any race)	7,390	76.4
Central American, ex. Mexican	200	51.8
Mexican	5,991	78.0
Puerto Rican	399	78.7

Class of Worker: Government
(Universe: Civilian Employed Population 16 Years and Over)

Group	Number	%
Total Population	6,880	16.8
Hispanic or Latino (of any race)	1,544	16.0
Central American, ex. Mexican	88	22.8
Mexican	1,308	17.0
Puerto Rican	12	2.4

Means of Transportation to Work: Car, Truck or Van
(Universe: Workers 16 Years and Over)

Group	Number	%
Total Population	36,417	90.6
Hispanic or Latino (of any race)	8,765	94.7
Central American, ex. Mexican	339	89.2
Mexican	7,073	95.8
Puerto Rican	415	85.6

Means of Transportation to Work: Public Transportation (ex. Taxicab)
(Universe: Workers 16 Years and Over)

Group	Number	%
Total Population	86	0.2
Hispanic or Latino (of any race)	0	0.0
Central American, ex. Mexican	0	0.0
Mexican	0	0.0
Puerto Rican	0	0.0

Notes: (1) Percent of total population; (2) Percent of Hispanic/Latino population; Profiles include places with an overall population of at least 125,000, OR an overall population of at least 25,000 where the Hispanic/Latino population is at least 20% of the overall population. In states where less than five places meet either of these criteria, we have included places with at least 10,000 total population with the highest percentage of Hispanic/Latino population. These places are identified with an asterisk (*); Please refer to the User's Guide for a full explanation of data.

Homeownership Rate
(Universe: Occupied Housing Units)

Group	%
Total Population	70.6
Hispanic or Latino (of any race)	63.0
Central American, ex. Mexican	63.5
Guatemalan	71.0
Nicaraguan	60.0
Panamanian	63.9
Salvadoran	63.3
Cuban	61.3
Mexican	62.9
Puerto Rican	63.1
South American	71.8
Argentinean	76.0
Colombian	74.5
Ecuadorian	74.4
Peruvian	59.6
Spaniard	66.5

Median Home Value

Group	Dollars
Total Population	369,600
Hispanic or Latino (of any race)	344,200
Central American, ex. Mexican	312,200
Mexican	333,700
Puerto Rican	432,100

Median Gross Rent

Group	Dollars
Total Population	1,365
Hispanic or Latino (of any race)	1,369
Central American, ex. Mexican	–
Mexican	1,378
Puerto Rican	1,792

Median Household Income
(2010 Inflation-Adjusted Dollars)

Group	Dollars
Total Population	78,739
Hispanic or Latino (of any race)	74,298
Central American, ex. Mexican	93,074
Mexican	75,331
Puerto Rican	72,222

Per Capita Income
(2010 Inflation-Adjusted Dollars)

Group	Dollars
Total Population	28,876
Hispanic or Latino (of any race)	19,236
Central American, ex. Mexican	19,869
Mexican	18,571
Puerto Rican	20,711

Households with $100,000+ Income

Group	Number	%
Total Population	10,735	36.3
Hispanic or Latino (of any race)	1,570	26.4
Central American, ex. Mexican	89	33.1
Mexican	1,194	26.2
Puerto Rican	85	29.9

Households with Food Stamps/SNAP Benefits During Past 12 Months

Group	Number	%
Total Population	633	2.1
Hispanic or Latino (of any race)	198	3.3
Central American, ex. Mexican	28	10.4
Mexican	144	3.2
Puerto Rican	0	0.0

Poverty Rate
(Income in Past 12 Months Below Poverty Level)

Group	%
Total Population	6.2
Hispanic or Latino (of any race)	9.0
Central American, ex. Mexican	3.6
Mexican	9.7
Puerto Rican	18.0

Napa

Population

Group	Number	%TP[1]	%HP[2]
Total Population	76,915	100.0	–
Hispanic or Latino (of any race)	28,923	37.6	100.0
Central American, ex. Mexican	693	0.9	2.4
Guatemalan	258	0.3	0.9
Salvadoran	248	0.3	0.9
Mexican	26,246	34.1	90.7
Puerto Rican	220	0.3	0.8
South American	268	0.3	0.9
Spaniard	341	0.4	1.2

Population Growth: 2000–2010

Group	%
Total Population	6.0
Hispanic or Latino (of any race)	48.5
Central American, ex. Mexican	122.1
Guatemalan	128.3
Mexican	55.4
Puerto Rican	24.3
South American	125.2

Males per 100 Females

Group	Number
Total Population	97.4
Hispanic or Latino (of any race)	109.4
Central American, ex. Mexican	87.3
Guatemalan	103.1
Salvadoran	85.1
Mexican	110.8
Puerto Rican	91.3
South American	84.8
Spaniard	100.6

Average Household Size

Group	People
Total Population	2.69
Hispanic or Latino (of any race)	4.15
Central American, ex. Mexican	3.63
Guatemalan	4.20
Salvadoran	3.60
Mexican	4.27
Puerto Rican	2.59
South American	2.75
Spaniard	2.70

Median Age

Group	Years
Total Population	37.4
Hispanic or Latino (of any race)	26.0
Central American, ex. Mexican	30.8
Guatemalan	28.9
Salvadoran	34.0
Mexican	25.6
Puerto Rican	31.0
South American	32.3
Spaniard	38.8

High School Graduates
(Universe: Population 25 Years and Over)

Group	Number	%
Total Population	39,922	78.3
Hispanic or Latino (of any race)	6,447	43.6
Mexican	5,202	39.4

Four-Year College Graduates
(Universe: Population 25 Years and Over)

Group	Number	%
Total Population	13,387	26.3
Hispanic or Latino (of any race)	881	6.0
Mexican	473	3.6

Population Age 3–17 Enrolled in Public School
(Universe: Population Age 3–17 Enrolled in School)

Group	Number	%
Total Population	12,370	88.1
Hispanic or Latino (of any race)	6,952	96.0
Mexican	6,550	96.6

Population Age 3–17 Enrolled in Private School
(Universe: Population Age 3–17 Enrolled in School)

Group	Number	%
Total Population	1,672	11.9
Hispanic or Latino (of any race)	289	4.0
Mexican	230	3.4

Foreign-Born Population

Group	Number	%
Total Population	18,078	23.8
Hispanic or Latino (of any race)	14,618	51.9
Mexican	13,722	53.0

Foreign-Born Naturalized U.S. Citizens

Group	Number	%
Total Population	5,581	30.9
Hispanic or Latino (of any race)	3,856	26.4
Mexican	3,415	24.9

Language Spoken at Home: English Only
(Universe: Population 5 Years and Over)

Group	Number	%
Total Population	45,050	63.4
Hispanic or Latino (of any race)	4,062	16.1
Mexican	2,933	12.7

Language Spoken at Home: Spanish
(Universe: Population 5 Years and Over)

Group	Number	%
Total Population	23,253	32.7
Hispanic or Latino (of any race)	21,105	83.7
Mexican	20,036	87.1

Unemployment Rate
(Universe: Population 16 Years and Over)

Group	%
Total Population	7.7
Hispanic or Latino (of any race)	9.4
Mexican	9.8

Class of Worker: Private Wage and Salary
(Universe: Civilian Employed Population 16 Years and Over)

Group	Number	%
Total Population	28,725	78.6
Hispanic or Latino (of any race)	11,354	87.8
Mexican	10,457	89.5

Class of Worker: Government
(Universe: Civilian Employed Population 16 Years and Over)

Group	Number	%
Total Population	4,543	12.4
Hispanic or Latino (of any race)	835	6.5
Mexican	639	5.5

Means of Transportation to Work: Car, Truck or Van
(Universe: Workers 16 Years and Over)

Group	Number	%
Total Population	32,142	89.6
Hispanic or Latino (of any race)	11,510	91.3
Mexican	10,335	91.1

Means of Transportation to Work: Public Transportation (ex. Taxicab)
(Universe: Workers 16 Years and Over)

Group	Number	%
Total Population	841	2.3
Hispanic or Latino (of any race)	185	1.5
Mexican	185	1.6

Homeownership Rate
(Universe: Occupied Housing Units)

Group	%
Total Population	57.3
Hispanic or Latino (of any race)	35.4
Central American, ex. Mexican	27.6
Guatemalan	15.0
Salvadoran	41.8
Mexican	34.7
Puerto Rican	53.5
South American	50.0
Spaniard	53.8

Median Home Value

Group	Dollars
Total Population	528,000
Hispanic or Latino (of any race)	448,300
Mexican	443,200

Notes: (1) Percent of total population; (2) Percent of Hispanic/Latino population; Profiles include places with an overall population of at least 125,000, OR an overall population of at least 25,000 where the Hispanic/Latino population is at least 20% of the overall population. In states where less than five places meet either of these criteria, we have included places with at least 10,000 total population with the highest percentage of Hispanic/Latino population. These places are identified with an asterisk (*); Please refer to the User's Guide for a full explanation of data.

Median Gross Rent	
Group	Dollars
Total Population	1,177
Hispanic or Latino (of any race)	1,150
Mexican	1,141

Median Household Income (2010 Inflation-Adjusted Dollars)	
Group	Dollars
Total Population	62,767
Hispanic or Latino (of any race)	46,975
Mexican	45,425

Per Capita Income (2010 Inflation-Adjusted Dollars)	
Group	Dollars
Total Population	30,108
Hispanic or Latino (of any race)	15,163
Mexican	14,244

Households with $100,000+ Income		
Group	Number	%
Total Population	8,136	28.4
Hispanic or Latino (of any race)	1,075	15.4
Mexican	880	14.1

Households with Food Stamps/SNAP Benefits During Past 12 Months		
Group	Number	%
Total Population	1,031	3.6
Hispanic or Latino (of any race)	495	7.1
Mexican	481	7.7

Poverty Rate (Income in Past 12 Months Below Poverty Level)	
Group	%
Total Population	11.7
Hispanic or Latino (of any race)	17.2
Mexican	17.8

National City

Population			
Group	Number	%TP[1]	%HP[2]
Total Population	58,582	100.0	–
Hispanic or Latino (of any race)	36,911	63.0	100.0
Central American, ex. Mexican	504	0.9	1.4
Guatemalan	101	0.2	0.3
Salvadoran	141	0.2	0.4
Cuban	109	0.2	0.3
Mexican	34,473	58.8	93.4
Puerto Rican	489	0.8	1.3
South American	206	0.4	0.6
Spaniard	151	0.3	0.4

Population Growth: 2000–2010	
Group	%
Total Population	8.0
Hispanic or Latino (of any race)	15.2
Central American, ex. Mexican	85.3
Mexican	20.8
Puerto Rican	36.6
South American	52.6

Males per 100 Females	
Group	Number
Total Population	105.5
Hispanic or Latino (of any race)	95.5
Central American, ex. Mexican	100.0
Guatemalan	110.4
Salvadoran	88.0
Cuban	137.0
Mexican	94.1
Puerto Rican	191.1
South American	148.2
Spaniard	101.3

Average Household Size	
Group	People
Total Population	3.41
Hispanic or Latino (of any race)	3.82
Central American, ex. Mexican	3.63
Guatemalan	3.55
Salvadoran	3.94
Cuban	2.54
Mexican	3.86
Puerto Rican	3.08
South American	3.47
Spaniard	3.14

Median Age	
Group	Years
Total Population	30.2
Hispanic or Latino (of any race)	27.5
Central American, ex. Mexican	30.9
Guatemalan	37.8
Salvadoran	26.8
Cuban	34.8
Mexican	27.5
Puerto Rican	24.1
South American	28.8
Spaniard	29.9

High School Graduates (Universe: Population 25 Years and Over)		
Group	Number	%
Total Population	22,509	65.1
Hispanic or Latino (of any race)	10,534	52.5
Mexican	9,857	51.9

Four-Year College Graduates (Universe: Population 25 Years and Over)		
Group	Number	%
Total Population	4,362	12.6
Hispanic or Latino (of any race)	1,522	7.6
Mexican	1,371	7.2

Population Age 3–17 Enrolled in Public School (Universe: Population Age 3–17 Enrolled in School)		
Group	Number	%
Total Population	11,567	96.7
Hispanic or Latino (of any race)	9,170	97.9
Mexican	9,081	98.1

Population Age 3–17 Enrolled in Private School (Universe: Population Age 3–17 Enrolled in School)		
Group	Number	%
Total Population	398	3.3
Hispanic or Latino (of any race)	200	2.1
Mexican	179	1.9

Foreign-Born Population		
Group	Number	%
Total Population	25,054	43.7
Hispanic or Latino (of any race)	16,153	43.9
Mexican	15,418	43.6

Foreign-Born Naturalized U.S. Citizens		
Group	Number	%
Total Population	10,715	42.8
Hispanic or Latino (of any race)	5,523	34.2
Mexican	5,130	33.3

Language Spoken at Home: English Only (Universe: Population 5 Years and Over)		
Group	Number	%
Total Population	14,716	27.7
Hispanic or Latino (of any race)	4,636	13.9
Mexican	4,321	13.5

Language Spoken at Home: Spanish (Universe: Population 5 Years and Over)		
Group	Number	%
Total Population	29,289	55.2
Hispanic or Latino (of any race)	28,645	85.8
Mexican	27,551	86.3

Unemployment Rate (Universe: Population 16 Years and Over)	
Group	%
Total Population	10.4
Hispanic or Latino (of any race)	10.8
Mexican	10.8

Class of Worker: Private Wage and Salary (Universe: Civilian Employed Population 16 Years and Over)		
Group	Number	%
Total Population	16,399	78.4
Hispanic or Latino (of any race)	10,725	79.1
Mexican	10,222	79.6

Class of Worker: Government (Universe: Civilian Employed Population 16 Years and Over)		
Group	Number	%
Total Population	3,142	15.0
Hispanic or Latino (of any race)	1,743	12.8
Mexican	1,564	12.2

Means of Transportation to Work: Car, Truck or Van (Universe: Workers 16 Years and Over)		
Group	Number	%
Total Population	18,473	78.9
Hispanic or Latino (of any race)	11,168	80.3
Mexican	10,604	81.0

Means of Transportation to Work: Public Transportation (ex. Taxicab) (Universe: Workers 16 Years and Over)		
Group	Number	%
Total Population	1,801	7.7
Hispanic or Latino (of any race)	1,109	8.0
Mexican	1,043	8.0

Homeownership Rate (Universe: Occupied Housing Units)	
Group	%
Total Population	33.5
Hispanic or Latino (of any race)	32.0
Central American, ex. Mexican	30.7
Guatemalan	32.3
Salvadoran	27.8
Cuban	11.4
Mexican	32.5
Puerto Rican	16.7
South American	36.8
Spaniard	37.2

Median Home Value	
Group	Dollars
Total Population	351,900
Hispanic or Latino (of any race)	338,600
Mexican	337,000

Median Gross Rent	
Group	Dollars
Total Population	893
Hispanic or Latino (of any race)	876
Mexican	880

Median Household Income (2010 Inflation-Adjusted Dollars)	
Group	Dollars
Total Population	36,280
Hispanic or Latino (of any race)	32,328
Mexican	32,495

Per Capita Income (2010 Inflation-Adjusted Dollars)	
Group	Dollars
Total Population	16,277
Hispanic or Latino (of any race)	12,551
Mexican	12,199

Households with $100,000+ Income		
Group	Number	%
Total Population	1,572	9.6
Hispanic or Latino (of any race)	662	6.6
Mexican	636	6.7

Households with Food Stamps/SNAP Benefits During Past 12 Months		
Group	Number	%
Total Population	1,502	9.2
Hispanic or Latino (of any race)	1,154	11.5
Mexican	1,102	11.5

Poverty Rate (Income in Past 12 Months Below Poverty Level)	
Group	%
Total Population	22.6
Hispanic or Latino (of any race)	27.5
Mexican	27.9

Notes: (1) Percent of total population; (2) Percent of Hispanic/Latino population; Profiles include places with an overall population of at least 125,000, OR an overall population of at least 25,000 where the Hispanic/Latino population is at least 20% of the overall population. In states where less than five places meet either of these criteria, we have included places with at least 10,000 total population with the highest percentage of Hispanic/Latino population. These places are identified with an asterisk (*); Please refer to the User's Guide for a full explanation of data.

Newark

Population

Group	Number	%TP[1]	%HP[2]
Total Population	42,573	100.0	–
Hispanic or Latino (of any race)	14,994	35.2	100.0
Central American, ex. Mexican	992	2.3	6.6
Guatemalan	186	0.4	1.2
Nicaraguan	221	0.5	1.5
Salvadoran	504	1.2	3.4
Mexican	12,221	28.7	81.5
Puerto Rican	352	0.8	2.3
South American	363	0.9	2.4
Peruvian	147	0.3	1.0
Spaniard	224	0.5	1.5

Population Growth: 2000–2010

Group	%
Total Population	0.2
Hispanic or Latino (of any race)	23.5
Central American, ex. Mexican	94.5
Nicaraguan	44.4
Salvadoran	189.7
Mexican	32.3
Puerto Rican	-5.6
South American	59.9

Males per 100 Females

Group	Number
Total Population	99.3
Hispanic or Latino (of any race)	101.4
Central American, ex. Mexican	96.8
Guatemalan	111.4
Nicaraguan	88.9
Salvadoran	96.9
Mexican	102.6
Puerto Rican	102.3
South American	85.2
Peruvian	90.9
Spaniard	83.6

Average Household Size

Group	People
Total Population	3.27
Hispanic or Latino (of any race)	4.13
Central American, ex. Mexican	3.95
Guatemalan	4.41
Nicaraguan	3.33
Salvadoran	4.11
Mexican	4.27
Puerto Rican	3.13
South American	3.36
Peruvian	3.70
Spaniard	3.06

Median Age

Group	Years
Total Population	35.4
Hispanic or Latino (of any race)	28.2
Central American, ex. Mexican	33.6
Guatemalan	35.0
Nicaraguan	36.3
Salvadoran	33.4
Mexican	27.3
Puerto Rican	31.7
South American	37.4
Peruvian	34.8
Spaniard	36.0

High School Graduates

(Universe: Population 25 Years and Over)

Group	Number	%
Total Population	23,680	84.7
Hispanic or Latino (of any race)	5,551	68.6
Mexican	4,128	64.7

Four-Year College Graduates

(Universe: Population 25 Years and Over)

Group	Number	%
Total Population	7,910	28.3
Hispanic or Latino (of any race)	1,173	14.5
Mexican	651	10.2

Population Age 3–17 Enrolled in Public School

(Universe: Population Age 3–17 Enrolled in School)

Group	Number	%
Total Population	6,812	87.8
Hispanic or Latino (of any race)	3,122	96.2
Mexican	2,708	96.5

Population Age 3–17 Enrolled in Private School

(Universe: Population Age 3–17 Enrolled in School)

Group	Number	%
Total Population	943	12.2
Hispanic or Latino (of any race)	125	3.8
Mexican	99	3.5

Foreign-Born Population

Group	Number	%
Total Population	15,597	37.2
Hispanic or Latino (of any race)	5,207	37.0
Mexican	4,391	37.9

Foreign-Born Naturalized U.S. Citizens

Group	Number	%
Total Population	9,434	60.5
Hispanic or Latino (of any race)	2,458	47.2
Mexican	1,849	42.1

Language Spoken at Home: English Only

(Universe: Population 5 Years and Over)

Group	Number	%
Total Population	18,366	47.0
Hispanic or Latino (of any race)	3,335	25.9
Mexican	2,308	21.9

Language Spoken at Home: Spanish

(Universe: Population 5 Years and Over)

Group	Number	%
Total Population	9,700	24.8
Hispanic or Latino (of any race)	9,420	73.2
Mexican	8,165	77.5

Unemployment Rate

(Universe: Population 16 Years and Over)

Group	%
Total Population	7.9
Hispanic or Latino (of any race)	7.7
Mexican	8.8

Class of Worker: Private Wage and Salary

(Universe: Civilian Employed Population 16 Years and Over)

Group	Number	%
Total Population	17,568	83.9
Hispanic or Latino (of any race)	5,625	84.0
Mexican	4,503	85.5

Class of Worker: Government

(Universe: Civilian Employed Population 16 Years and Over)

Group	Number	%
Total Population	2,199	10.5
Hispanic or Latino (of any race)	530	7.9
Mexican	347	6.6

Means of Transportation to Work: Car, Truck or Van

(Universe: Workers 16 Years and Over)

Group	Number	%
Total Population	18,607	91.4
Hispanic or Latino (of any race)	5,981	91.0
Mexican	4,663	90.0

Means of Transportation to Work: Public Transportation (ex. Taxicab)

(Universe: Workers 16 Years and Over)

Group	Number	%
Total Population	697	3.4
Hispanic or Latino (of any race)	296	4.5
Mexican	274	5.3

Homeownership Rate

(Universe: Occupied Housing Units)

Group	%
Total Population	68.9
Hispanic or Latino (of any race)	57.4
Central American, ex. Mexican	65.6
Guatemalan	66.7
Nicaraguan	73.1
Salvadoran	62.0
Mexican	56.0
Puerto Rican	55.1
South American	67.7
Peruvian	73.0
Spaniard	76.8

Median Home Value

Group	Dollars
Total Population	551,900
Hispanic or Latino (of any race)	531,100
Mexican	536,300

Median Gross Rent

Group	Dollars
Total Population	1,387
Hispanic or Latino (of any race)	1,293
Mexican	1,244

Median Household Income

(2010 Inflation-Adjusted Dollars)

Group	Dollars
Total Population	81,352
Hispanic or Latino (of any race)	66,331
Mexican	62,486

Per Capita Income

(2010 Inflation-Adjusted Dollars)

Group	Dollars
Total Population	29,186
Hispanic or Latino (of any race)	21,764
Mexican	19,611

Households with $100,000+ Income

Group	Number	%
Total Population	4,898	38.1
Hispanic or Latino (of any race)	1,057	30.4
Mexican	702	26.6

Households with Food Stamps/SNAP Benefits During Past 12 Months

Group	Number	%
Total Population	548	4.3
Hispanic or Latino (of any race)	268	7.7
Mexican	176	6.7

Poverty Rate

(Income in Past 12 Months Below Poverty Level)

Group	%
Total Population	7.6
Hispanic or Latino (of any race)	11.6
Mexican	13.5

Norco

Population

Group	Number	%TP[1]	%HP[2]
Total Population	27,063	100.0	–
Hispanic or Latino (of any race)	8,405	31.1	100.0
Central American, ex. Mexican	195	0.7	2.3
Mexican	7,354	27.2	87.5
Puerto Rican	103	0.4	1.2
South American	135	0.5	1.6

Population Growth: 2000–2010

Group	%
Total Population	12.0
Hispanic or Latino (of any race)	52.7
Mexican	52.3

Males per 100 Females

Group	Number
Total Population	136.8
Hispanic or Latino (of any race)	150.3
Central American, ex. Mexican	93.1
Mexican	158.7
Puerto Rican	110.2
South American	87.5

Average Household Size

Group	People
Total Population	3.23
Hispanic or Latino (of any race)	4.25
Central American, ex. Mexican	4.22
Mexican	4.38

Notes: (1) Percent of total population; (2) Percent of Hispanic/Latino population; Profiles include places with an overall population of at least 125,000, OR an overall population of at least 25,000 where the Hispanic/Latino population is at least 20% of the overall population. In states where less than five places meet either of these criteria, we have included places with at least 10,000 total population with the highest percentage of Hispanic/Latino population. These places are identified with an asterisk (*); Please refer to the User's Guide for a full explanation of data.

Puerto Rican	3.47
South American	3.62

Median Age

Group	Years
Total Population	39.5
Hispanic or Latino (of any race)	31.1
Central American, ex. Mexican	36.3
Mexican	31.0
Puerto Rican	29.5
South American	33.5

High School Graduates
(Universe: Population 25 Years and Over)

Group	Number	%
Total Population	14,846	80.3
Hispanic or Latino (of any race)	2,546	59.6
Mexican	2,243	57.9

Four-Year College Graduates
(Universe: Population 25 Years and Over)

Group	Number	%
Total Population	2,867	15.5
Hispanic or Latino (of any race)	356	8.3
Mexican	318	8.2

Population Age 3–17 Enrolled in Public School
(Universe: Population Age 3–17 Enrolled in School)

Group	Number	%
Total Population	4,198	87.4
Hispanic or Latino (of any race)	1,401	87.9
Mexican	1,279	88.3

Population Age 3–17 Enrolled in Private School
(Universe: Population Age 3–17 Enrolled in School)

Group	Number	%
Total Population	603	12.6
Hispanic or Latino (of any race)	192	12.1
Mexican	170	11.7

Foreign-Born Population

Group	Number	%
Total Population	2,894	10.7
Hispanic or Latino (of any race)	1,920	26.3
Mexican	1,792	26.8

Foreign-Born Naturalized U.S. Citizens

Group	Number	%
Total Population	1,496	51.7
Hispanic or Latino (of any race)	726	37.8
Mexican	662	36.9

Language Spoken at Home: English Only
(Universe: Population 5 Years and Over)

Group	Number	%
Total Population	20,273	77.9
Hispanic or Latino (of any race)	2,675	38.3
Mexican	2,348	36.7

Language Spoken at Home: Spanish
(Universe: Population 5 Years and Over)

Group	Number	%
Total Population	4,613	17.7
Hispanic or Latino (of any race)	4,312	61.7
Mexican	4,046	63.3

Unemployment Rate
(Universe: Population 16 Years and Over)

Group	%
Total Population	7.8
Hispanic or Latino (of any race)	10.7
Mexican	11.3

Class of Worker: Private Wage and Salary
(Universe: Civilian Employed Population 16 Years and Over)

Group	Number	%
Total Population	8,283	73.6
Hispanic or Latino (of any race)	1,925	73.8
Mexican	1,824	74.4

Class of Worker: Government
(Universe: Civilian Employed Population 16 Years and Over)

Group	Number	%
Total Population	1,626	14.5
Hispanic or Latino (of any race)	478	18.3
Mexican	447	18.2

Means of Transportation to Work: Car, Truck or Van
(Universe: Workers 16 Years and Over)

Group	Number	%
Total Population	9,776	89.5
Hispanic or Latino (of any race)	2,351	93.5
Mexican	2,197	93.1

Means of Transportation to Work: Public Transportation (ex. Taxicab)
(Universe: Workers 16 Years and Over)

Group	Number	%
Total Population	184	1.7
Hispanic or Latino (of any race)	0	0.0
Mexican	0	0.0

Homeownership Rate
(Universe: Occupied Housing Units)

Group	%
Total Population	81.2
Hispanic or Latino (of any race)	76.2
Central American, ex. Mexican	67.3
Mexican	76.8
Puerto Rican	89.5
South American	81.1

Median Home Value

Group	Dollars
Total Population	524,600
Hispanic or Latino (of any race)	476,700
Mexican	470,500

Median Gross Rent

Group	Dollars
Total Population	1,417
Hispanic or Latino (of any race)	1,355
Mexican	1,355

Median Household Income
(2010 Inflation-Adjusted Dollars)

Group	Dollars
Total Population	80,426
Hispanic or Latino (of any race)	60,602
Mexican	60,949

Per Capita Income
(2010 Inflation-Adjusted Dollars)

Group	Dollars
Total Population	27,005
Hispanic or Latino (of any race)	19,469
Mexican	19,598

Households with $100,000+ Income

Group	Number	%
Total Population	2,580	36.4
Hispanic or Latino (of any race)	373	26.5
Mexican	351	26.6

Households with Food Stamps/SNAP Benefits During Past 12 Months

Group	Number	%
Total Population	203	2.9
Hispanic or Latino (of any race)	151	10.7
Mexican	151	11.4

Poverty Rate
(Income in Past 12 Months Below Poverty Level)

Group	%
Total Population	9.4
Hispanic or Latino (of any race)	18.9
Mexican	20.0

North Highlands

Population

Group	Number	%TP[1]	%HP[2]
Total Population	42,694	100.0	–
Hispanic or Latino (of any race)	10,077	23.6	100.0
Central American, ex. Mexican	516	1.2	5.1
Guatemalan	106	0.2	1.1
Salvadoran	252	0.6	2.5
Cuban	116	0.3	1.2
Mexican	8,147	19.1	80.8
Puerto Rican	377	0.9	3.7
Spaniard	188	0.4	1.9

Population Growth: 2000–2010

Group	%
Total Population	-3.4
Hispanic or Latino (of any race)	50.5
Central American, ex. Mexican	232.9
Mexican	62.5
Puerto Rican	55.8

Males per 100 Females

Group	Number
Total Population	96.0
Hispanic or Latino (of any race)	103.8
Central American, ex. Mexican	122.4
Guatemalan	112.0
Salvadoran	129.1
Cuban	63.4
Mexican	105.3
Puerto Rican	104.9
Spaniard	64.9

Average Household Size

Group	People
Total Population	2.92
Hispanic or Latino (of any race)	3.84
Central American, ex. Mexican	3.76
Guatemalan	3.91
Salvadoran	4.25
Cuban	3.31
Mexican	4.04
Puerto Rican	3.22
Spaniard	2.73

Median Age

Group	Years
Total Population	32.1
Hispanic or Latino (of any race)	24.0
Central American, ex. Mexican	30.3
Guatemalan	28.5
Salvadoran	30.5
Cuban	24.0
Mexican	23.2
Puerto Rican	22.3
Spaniard	31.6

High School Graduates
(Universe: Population 25 Years and Over)

Group	Number	%
Total Population	20,573	81.0
Hispanic or Latino (of any race)	3,242	64.0
Mexican	2,594	63.7

Four-Year College Graduates
(Universe: Population 25 Years and Over)

Group	Number	%
Total Population	3,202	12.6
Hispanic or Latino (of any race)	272	5.4
Mexican	217	5.3

Population Age 3–17 Enrolled in Public School
(Universe: Population Age 3–17 Enrolled in School)

Group	Number	%
Total Population	7,931	91.8
Hispanic or Latino (of any race)	2,485	93.5
Mexican	2,090	94.0

Population Age 3–17 Enrolled in Private School
(Universe: Population Age 3–17 Enrolled in School)

Group	Number	%
Total Population	707	8.2
Hispanic or Latino (of any race)	174	6.5
Mexican	133	6.0

Foreign-Born Population

Group	Number	%
Total Population	9,317	21.8
Hispanic or Latino (of any race)	3,639	36.1
Mexican	2,949	35.2

Foreign-Born Naturalized U.S. Citizens

Group	Number	%
Total Population	2,734	29.3
Hispanic or Latino (of any race)	636	17.5
Mexican	318	10.8

Notes: (1) Percent of total population; (2) Percent of Hispanic/Latino population; Profiles include places with an overall population of at least 125,000, OR an overall population of at least 25,000 where the Hispanic/Latino population is at least 20% of the overall population. In states where less than five places meet either of these criteria, we have included places with at least 10,000 total population with the highest percentage of Hispanic/Latino population. These places are identified with an asterisk (*); Please refer to the User's Guide for a full explanation of data.

Language Spoken at Home: English Only
(Universe: Population 5 Years and Over)

Group	Number	%
Total Population	25,671	66.7
Hispanic or Latino (of any race)	2,885	33.0
Mexican	2,345	33.1

Language Spoken at Home: Spanish
(Universe: Population 5 Years and Over)

Group	Number	%
Total Population	6,568	17.1
Hispanic or Latino (of any race)	5,784	66.2
Mexican	4,693	66.2

Unemployment Rate
(Universe: Population 16 Years and Over)

Group	%
Total Population	10.5
Hispanic or Latino (of any race)	12.5
Mexican	14.1

Class of Worker: Private Wage and Salary
(Universe: Civilian Employed Population 16 Years and Over)

Group	Number	%
Total Population	12,323	73.9
Hispanic or Latino (of any race)	2,915	79.4
Mexican	2,325	78.6

Class of Worker: Government
(Universe: Civilian Employed Population 16 Years and Over)

Group	Number	%
Total Population	3,072	18.4
Hispanic or Latino (of any race)	438	11.9
Mexican	393	13.3

Means of Transportation to Work: Car, Truck or Van
(Universe: Workers 16 Years and Over)

Group	Number	%
Total Population	13,911	85.7
Hispanic or Latino (of any race)	3,048	85.1
Mexican	2,417	83.8

Means of Transportation to Work: Public Transportation (ex. Taxicab)
(Universe: Workers 16 Years and Over)

Group	Number	%
Total Population	832	5.1
Hispanic or Latino (of any race)	84	2.3
Mexican	55	1.9

Homeownership Rate
(Universe: Occupied Housing Units)

Group	%
Total Population	48.9
Hispanic or Latino (of any race)	41.4
Central American, ex. Mexican	44.2
Guatemalan	26.1
Salvadoran	42.7
Cuban	45.7
Mexican	41.7
Puerto Rican	26.0
Spaniard	54.0

Median Home Value

Group	Dollars
Total Population	222,800
Hispanic or Latino (of any race)	235,900
Mexican	242,100

Median Gross Rent

Group	Dollars
Total Population	938
Hispanic or Latino (of any race)	1,063
Mexican	1,063

Median Household Income
(2010 Inflation-Adjusted Dollars)

Group	Dollars
Total Population	40,873
Hispanic or Latino (of any race)	41,376
Mexican	44,713

Per Capita Income
(2010 Inflation-Adjusted Dollars)

Group	Dollars
Total Population	17,243
Hispanic or Latino (of any race)	12,686
Mexican	12,793

Households with $100,000+ Income

Group	Number	%
Total Population	1,212	8.2
Hispanic or Latino (of any race)	198	7.3
Mexican	198	9.4

Households with Food Stamps/SNAP Benefits During Past 12 Months

Group	Number	%
Total Population	1,881	12.7
Hispanic or Latino (of any race)	375	13.8
Mexican	265	12.5

Poverty Rate
(Income in Past 12 Months Below Poverty Level)

Group	%
Total Population	21.6
Hispanic or Latino (of any race)	23.4
Mexican	24.0

Norwalk

Population

Group	Number	%TP[1]	%HP[2]
Total Population	105,549	100.0	–
Hispanic or Latino (of any race)	74,041	70.1	100.0
Central American, ex. Mexican	5,460	5.2	7.4
Costa Rican	158	0.1	0.2
Guatemalan	1,411	1.3	1.9
Honduran	330	0.3	0.4
Nicaraguan	603	0.6	0.8
Salvadoran	2,871	2.7	3.9
Cuban	386	0.4	0.5
Mexican	63,299	60.0	85.5
Puerto Rican	488	0.5	0.7
South American	1,333	1.3	1.8
Argentinean	120	0.1	0.2
Colombian	303	0.3	0.4
Ecuadorian	325	0.3	0.4
Peruvian	453	0.4	0.6
Spaniard	345	0.3	0.5

Population Growth: 2000–2010

Group	%
Total Population	2.2
Hispanic or Latino (of any race)	14.0
Central American, ex. Mexican	100.1
Costa Rican	21.5
Guatemalan	154.2
Honduran	223.5
Nicaraguan	92.0
Salvadoran	113.3
Cuban	16.3
Mexican	20.2
Puerto Rican	1.7
South American	84.6
Colombian	79.3
Ecuadorian	85.7
Peruvian	99.6

Males per 100 Females

Group	Number
Total Population	98.5
Hispanic or Latino (of any race)	99.4
Central American, ex. Mexican	95.5
Costa Rican	113.5
Guatemalan	108.1
Honduran	89.7
Nicaraguan	80.5
Salvadoran	92.8
Cuban	94.0
Mexican	100.1
Puerto Rican	95.2
South American	100.5
Argentinean	126.4
Colombian	90.6
Ecuadorian	105.7
Peruvian	94.4
Spaniard	92.7

Average Household Size

Group	People
Total Population	3.83
Hispanic or Latino (of any race)	4.40
Central American, ex. Mexican	4.51
Costa Rican	3.77
Guatemalan	4.54
Honduran	4.87
Nicaraguan	4.38
Salvadoran	4.59
Cuban	3.34
Mexican	4.45
Puerto Rican	3.55
South American	3.94
Argentinean	3.87
Colombian	3.45
Ecuadorian	4.04
Peruvian	4.36
Spaniard	3.20

Median Age

Group	Years
Total Population	32.5
Hispanic or Latino (of any race)	28.7
Central American, ex. Mexican	34.8
Costa Rican	38.5
Guatemalan	34.6
Honduran	35.6
Nicaraguan	35.8
Salvadoran	34.5
Cuban	37.0
Mexican	27.9
Puerto Rican	34.6
South American	39.6
Argentinean	35.0
Colombian	37.4
Ecuadorian	42.3
Peruvian	40.6
Spaniard	43.5

High School Graduates
(Universe: Population 25 Years and Over)

Group	Number	%
Total Population	46,563	71.8
Hispanic or Latino (of any race)	24,054	61.2
Central American, ex. Mexican	3,213	65.7
Guatemalan	979	71.5
Salvadoran	1,513	63.2
Mexican	18,919	59.3
South American	724	92.1

Four-Year College Graduates
(Universe: Population 25 Years and Over)

Group	Number	%
Total Population	9,741	15.0
Hispanic or Latino (of any race)	2,650	6.7
Central American, ex. Mexican	541	11.1
Guatemalan	109	8.0
Salvadoran	251	10.5
Mexican	1,815	5.7
South American	138	17.6

Population Age 3–17 Enrolled in Public School
(Universe: Population Age 3–17 Enrolled in School)

Group	Number	%
Total Population	20,962	91.7
Hispanic or Latino (of any race)	16,708	93.5
Central American, ex. Mexican	1,184	88.8
Guatemalan	332	100.0
Salvadoran	557	85.3
Mexican	14,630	93.7
South American	130	100.0

Population Age 3–17 Enrolled in Private School
(Universe: Population Age 3–17 Enrolled in School)

Group	Number	%
Total Population	1,900	8.3
Hispanic or Latino (of any race)	1,163	6.5
Central American, ex. Mexican	149	11.2
Guatemalan	0	0.0
Salvadoran	96	14.7

Notes: (1) Percent of total population; (2) Percent of Hispanic/Latino population; Profiles include places with an overall population of at least 125,000, OR an overall population of at least 25,000 where the Hispanic/Latino population is at least 20% of the overall population. In states where less than five places meet either of these criteria, we have included places with at least 10,000 total population with the highest percentage of Hispanic/Latino population. These places are identified with an asterisk (*); Please refer to the User's Guide for a full explanation of data.

Mexican	978	6.3
South American	0	0.0

Foreign-Born Population

Group	Number	%
Total Population	38,361	36.5
Hispanic or Latino (of any race)	26,348	37.2
Central American, ex. Mexican	4,601	61.4
Guatemalan	1,197	58.4
Salvadoran	2,267	62.7
Mexican	20,347	34.3
South American	694	65.1

Foreign-Born Naturalized U.S. Citizens

Group	Number	%
Total Population	20,022	52.2
Hispanic or Latino (of any race)	12,391	47.0
Central American, ex. Mexican	2,435	52.9
Guatemalan	689	57.6
Salvadoran	1,266	55.8
Mexican	9,093	44.7
South American	315	45.4

Language Spoken at Home: English Only
(Universe: Population 5 Years and Over)

Group	Number	%
Total Population	32,763	33.3
Hispanic or Latino (of any race)	13,818	21.1
Central American, ex. Mexican	200	2.9
Guatemalan	111	5.7
Salvadoran	21	0.6
Mexican	12,576	23.0
South American	65	6.3

Language Spoken at Home: Spanish
(Universe: Population 5 Years and Over)

Group	Number	%
Total Population	52,274	53.1
Hispanic or Latino (of any race)	51,632	78.7
Central American, ex. Mexican	6,786	97.0
Guatemalan	1,828	93.9
Salvadoran	3,363	99.4
Mexican	42,107	76.9
South American	973	93.7

Unemployment Rate
(Universe: Population 16 Years and Over)

Group	%
Total Population	9.8
Hispanic or Latino (of any race)	10.3
Central American, ex. Mexican	9.1
Guatemalan	10.1
Salvadoran	7.5
Mexican	10.7
South American	2.4

Class of Worker: Private Wage and Salary
(Universe: Civilian Employed Population 16 Years and Over)

Group	Number	%
Total Population	36,867	80.7
Hispanic or Latino (of any race)	25,035	83.2
Central American, ex. Mexican	2,998	78.3
Guatemalan	799	70.9
Salvadoran	1,604	85.5
Mexican	20,547	83.5
South American	499	89.4

Class of Worker: Government
(Universe: Civilian Employed Population 16 Years and Over)

Group	Number	%
Total Population	6,495	14.2
Hispanic or Latino (of any race)	3,573	11.9
Central American, ex. Mexican	357	9.3
Guatemalan	164	14.6
Salvadoran	97	5.2
Mexican	3,097	12.6
South American	49	8.8

Means of Transportation to Work: Car, Truck or Van
(Universe: Workers 16 Years and Over)

Group	Number	%
Total Population	39,795	90.1
Hispanic or Latino (of any race)	26,123	89.6
Central American, ex. Mexican	3,287	87.0
Guatemalan	1,018	92.0
Salvadoran	1,611	87.2
Mexican	21,522	89.8
South American	360	93.0

Means of Transportation to Work: Public Transportation (ex. Taxicab)
(Universe: Workers 16 Years and Over)

Group	Number	%
Total Population	1,741	3.9
Hispanic or Latino (of any race)	1,208	4.1
Central American, ex. Mexican	115	3.0
Guatemalan	19	1.7
Salvadoran	64	3.5
Mexican	1,034	4.3
South American	12	3.1

Homeownership Rate
(Universe: Occupied Housing Units)

Group	%
Total Population	65.1
Hispanic or Latino (of any race)	65.0
Central American, ex. Mexican	67.2
Costa Rican	66.7
Guatemalan	71.2
Honduran	59.8
Nicaraguan	56.1
Salvadoran	68.6
Cuban	58.3
Mexican	65.0
Puerto Rican	57.4
South American	64.0
Argentinean	59.0
Colombian	56.6
Ecuadorian	73.3
Peruvian	64.5
Spaniard	71.4

Median Home Value

Group	Dollars
Total Population	398,300
Hispanic or Latino (of any race)	396,800
Central American, ex. Mexican	417,500
Guatemalan	441,000
Salvadoran	409,600
Mexican	396,600
South American	348,000

Median Gross Rent

Group	Dollars
Total Population	1,207
Hispanic or Latino (of any race)	1,179
Central American, ex. Mexican	1,216
Guatemalan	1,288
Salvadoran	1,089
Mexican	1,188
South American	890

Median Household Income
(2010 Inflation-Adjusted Dollars)

Group	Dollars
Total Population	60,488
Hispanic or Latino (of any race)	58,530
Central American, ex. Mexican	56,292
Guatemalan	49,167
Salvadoran	52,068
Mexican	59,384
South American	44,488

Per Capita Income
(2010 Inflation-Adjusted Dollars)

Group	Dollars
Total Population	19,302
Hispanic or Latino (of any race)	15,992
Central American, ex. Mexican	17,427
Guatemalan	18,241
Salvadoran	17,537
Mexican	15,678
South American	18,297

Households with $100,000+ Income

Group	Number	%
Total Population	5,981	21.6
Hispanic or Latino (of any race)	2,946	18.1
Central American, ex. Mexican	401	23.2
Guatemalan	59	11.4
Salvadoran	249	30.2
Mexican	2,410	18.0
South American	37	10.2

Households with Food Stamps/SNAP Benefits During Past 12 Months

Group	Number	%
Total Population	1,673	6.0
Hispanic or Latino (of any race)	1,176	7.2
Central American, ex. Mexican	134	7.8
Guatemalan	38	7.4
Salvadoran	80	9.7
Mexican	981	7.3
South American	0	0.0

Poverty Rate
(Income in Past 12 Months Below Poverty Level)

Group	%
Total Population	11.1
Hispanic or Latino (of any race)	11.6
Central American, ex. Mexican	6.0
Guatemalan	7.3
Salvadoran	6.8
Mexican	12.7
South American	7.5

Novato

Population

Group	Number	%TP[1]	%HP[2]
Total Population	51,904	100.0	–
Hispanic or Latino (of any race)	11,046	21.3	100.0
Central American, ex. Mexican	2,892	5.6	26.2
Guatemalan	1,412	2.7	12.8
Nicaraguan	206	0.4	1.9
Salvadoran	1,156	2.2	10.5
Mexican	5,941	11.4	53.8
Puerto Rican	239	0.5	2.2
South American	829	1.6	7.5
Colombian	103	0.2	0.9
Peruvian	496	1.0	4.5
Spaniard	258	0.5	2.3

Population Growth: 2000–2010

Group	%
Total Population	9.0
Hispanic or Latino (of any race)	77.3
Central American, ex. Mexican	254.0
Guatemalan	359.9
Salvadoran	265.8
Mexican	64.1
Puerto Rican	113.4
South American	102.2
Peruvian	161.1

Males per 100 Females

Group	Number
Total Population	93.6
Hispanic or Latino (of any race)	102.4
Central American, ex. Mexican	104.5
Guatemalan	119.6
Nicaraguan	74.6
Salvadoran	95.3
Mexican	105.1
Puerto Rican	94.3
South American	85.0
Colombian	71.7
Peruvian	90.0
Spaniard	87.0

Average Household Size

Group	People
Total Population	2.53
Hispanic or Latino (of any race)	3.80
Central American, ex. Mexican	4.17
Guatemalan	4.68
Nicaraguan	2.77
Salvadoran	4.03
Mexican	3.97
Puerto Rican	2.51
South American	3.16
Colombian	2.78
Peruvian	3.61
Spaniard	2.34

Notes: (1) Percent of total population; (2) Percent of Hispanic/Latino population; Profiles include places with an overall population of at least 125,000, OR an overall population of at least 25,000 where the Hispanic/Latino population is at least 20% of the overall population. In states where less than five places meet either of these criteria, we have included places with at least 10,000 total population with the highest percentage of Hispanic/Latino population. These places are identified with an asterisk (*); Please refer to the User's Guide for a full explanation of data.

Median Age

Group	Years
Total Population	42.6
Hispanic or Latino (of any race)	28.3
Central American, ex. Mexican	29.0
Guatemalan	26.6
Nicaraguan	35.0
Salvadoran	31.0
Mexican	26.9
Puerto Rican	28.4
South American	37.3
Colombian	36.3
Peruvian	36.2
Spaniard	45.7

High School Graduates
(Universe: Population 25 Years and Over)

Group	Number	%
Total Population	32,618	91.2
Hispanic or Latino (of any race)	3,029	63.3
Central American, ex. Mexican	671	54.4
Mexican	1,439	57.0

Four-Year College Graduates
(Universe: Population 25 Years and Over)

Group	Number	%
Total Population	15,304	42.8
Hispanic or Latino (of any race)	657	13.7
Central American, ex. Mexican	106	8.6
Mexican	320	12.7

Population Age 3–17 Enrolled in Public School
(Universe: Population Age 3–17 Enrolled in School)

Group	Number	%
Total Population	7,048	74.7
Hispanic or Latino (of any race)	1,732	86.6
Central American, ex. Mexican	387	73.6
Mexican	1,078	90.5

Population Age 3–17 Enrolled in Private School
(Universe: Population Age 3–17 Enrolled in School)

Group	Number	%
Total Population	2,383	25.3
Hispanic or Latino (of any race)	269	13.4
Central American, ex. Mexican	139	26.4
Mexican	113	9.5

Foreign-Born Population

Group	Number	%
Total Population	10,614	21.0
Hispanic or Latino (of any race)	4,317	51.6
Central American, ex. Mexican	1,295	54.9
Mexican	2,353	52.4

Foreign-Born Naturalized U.S. Citizens

Group	Number	%
Total Population	5,381	50.7
Hispanic or Latino (of any race)	1,581	36.6
Central American, ex. Mexican	425	32.8
Mexican	799	34.0

Language Spoken at Home: English Only
(Universe: Population 5 Years and Over)

Group	Number	%
Total Population	35,567	74.5
Hispanic or Latino (of any race)	1,839	24.1
Central American, ex. Mexican	368	18.2
Mexican	942	22.7

Language Spoken at Home: Spanish
(Universe: Population 5 Years and Over)

Group	Number	%
Total Population	6,249	13.1
Hispanic or Latino (of any race)	5,697	74.7
Central American, ex. Mexican	1,655	81.8
Mexican	3,196	77.0

Unemployment Rate
(Universe: Population 16 Years and Over)

Group	%
Total Population	5.8
Hispanic or Latino (of any race)	7.2
Central American, ex. Mexican	8.3
Mexican	7.5

Class of Worker: Private Wage and Salary
(Universe: Civilian Employed Population 16 Years and Over)

Group	Number	%
Total Population	18,035	71.3
Hispanic or Latino (of any race)	3,026	72.7
Central American, ex. Mexican	1,005	82.2
Mexican	1,542	71.5

Class of Worker: Government
(Universe: Civilian Employed Population 16 Years and Over)

Group	Number	%
Total Population	3,366	13.3
Hispanic or Latino (of any race)	378	9.1
Central American, ex. Mexican	58	4.7
Mexican	264	12.2

Means of Transportation to Work: Car, Truck or Van
(Universe: Workers 16 Years and Over)

Group	Number	%
Total Population	20,726	84.2
Hispanic or Latino (of any race)	3,288	81.6
Central American, ex. Mexican	854	73.3
Mexican	1,778	85.4

Means of Transportation to Work: Public Transportation (ex. Taxicab)
(Universe: Workers 16 Years and Over)

Group	Number	%
Total Population	1,193	4.8
Hispanic or Latino (of any race)	263	6.5
Central American, ex. Mexican	169	14.5
Mexican	70	3.4

Homeownership Rate
(Universe: Occupied Housing Units)

Group	%
Total Population	67.0
Hispanic or Latino (of any race)	35.1
Central American, ex. Mexican	28.1
Guatemalan	18.4
Nicaraguan	45.5
Salvadoran	32.6
Mexican	32.5
Puerto Rican	46.8
South American	42.0
Colombian	48.1
Peruvian	33.1
Spaniard	75.0

Median Home Value

Group	Dollars
Total Population	686,400
Hispanic or Latino (of any race)	661,000
Central American, ex. Mexican	788,200
Mexican	630,000

Median Gross Rent

Group	Dollars
Total Population	1,455
Hispanic or Latino (of any race)	1,451
Central American, ex. Mexican	1,370
Mexican	1,504

Median Household Income
(2010 Inflation-Adjusted Dollars)

Group	Dollars
Total Population	80,250
Hispanic or Latino (of any race)	59,702
Central American, ex. Mexican	37,656
Mexican	69,517

Per Capita Income
(2010 Inflation-Adjusted Dollars)

Group	Dollars
Total Population	41,573
Hispanic or Latino (of any race)	18,686
Central American, ex. Mexican	17,063
Mexican	17,514

Households with $100,000+ Income

Group	Number	%
Total Population	7,841	39.4
Hispanic or Latino (of any race)	426	19.7
Central American, ex. Mexican	150	24.2
Mexican	171	17.2

Households with Food Stamps/SNAP Benefits During Past 12 Months

Group	Number	%
Total Population	567	2.8
Hispanic or Latino (of any race)	88	4.1
Central American, ex. Mexican	50	8.1
Mexican	0	0.0

Poverty Rate
(Income in Past 12 Months Below Poverty Level)

Group	%
Total Population	7.4
Hispanic or Latino (of any race)	12.2
Central American, ex. Mexican	22.0
Mexican	8.4

Oakland

Population

Group	Number	%TP[1]	%HP[2]
Total Population	390,724	100.0	–
Hispanic or Latino (of any race)	99,068	25.4	100.0
Central American, ex. Mexican	15,387	3.9	15.5
Costa Rican	145	<0.1	0.1
Guatemalan	5,223	1.3	5.3
Honduran	1,160	0.3	1.2
Nicaraguan	1,156	0.3	1.2
Panamanian	301	0.1	0.3
Salvadoran	7,246	1.9	7.3
Cuban	862	0.2	0.9
Dominican Republic	183	<0.1	0.2
Mexican	70,799	18.1	71.5
Puerto Rican	2,737	0.7	2.8
South American	2,371	0.6	2.4
Argentinean	334	0.1	0.3
Chilean	297	0.1	0.3
Colombian	493	0.1	0.5
Ecuadorian	193	<0.1	0.2
Peruvian	690	0.2	0.7
Venezuelan	176	<0.1	0.2
Spaniard	1,141	0.3	1.2

Population Growth: 2000–2010

Group	%
Total Population	-2.2
Hispanic or Latino (of any race)	13.3
Central American, ex. Mexican	127.7
Guatemalan	237.2
Honduran	152.7
Nicaraguan	77.3
Panamanian	96.7
Salvadoran	125.9
Cuban	48.4
Mexican	8.8
Puerto Rican	17.7
South American	101.3
Argentinean	127.2
Chilean	110.6
Colombian	131.5
Peruvian	96.6
Spaniard	506.9

Males per 100 Females

Group	Number
Total Population	94.2
Hispanic or Latino (of any race)	110.3
Central American, ex. Mexican	124.8
Costa Rican	95.9
Guatemalan	156.0
Honduran	134.3
Nicaraguan	88.9
Panamanian	88.1
Salvadoran	113.1
Cuban	107.7
Dominican Republic	86.7
Mexican	109.9
Puerto Rican	96.1
South American	96.1
Argentinean	115.5
Chilean	99.3
Colombian	91.8
Ecuadorian	103.2

Notes: (1) Percent of total population; (2) Percent of Hispanic/Latino population; Profiles include places with an overall population of at least 125,000, OR an overall population of at least 25,000 where the Hispanic/Latino population is at least 20% of the overall population. In states where less than five places meet either of these criteria, we have included places with at least 10,000 total population with the highest percentage of Hispanic/Latino population. These places are identified with an asterisk (*); Please refer to the User's Guide for a full explanation of data.

Peruvian	88.5
Venezuelan	104.7
Spaniard	81.1

Average Household Size

Group	People
Total Population	2.49
Hispanic or Latino (of any race)	3.76
Central American, ex. Mexican	4.12
Costa Rican	2.39
Guatemalan	4.68
Honduran	4.11
Nicaraguan	3.14
Panamanian	2.13
Salvadoran	4.19
Cuban	2.38
Dominican Republic	2.27
Mexican	3.95
Puerto Rican	2.51
South American	2.36
Argentinean	2.36
Chilean	2.50
Colombian	2.24
Ecuadorian	2.38
Peruvian	2.37
Venezuelan	2.45
Spaniard	2.40

Median Age

Group	Years
Total Population	36.2
Hispanic or Latino (of any race)	27.8
Central American, ex. Mexican	29.5
Costa Rican	33.1
Guatemalan	28.0
Honduran	28.9
Nicaraguan	32.3
Panamanian	33.9
Salvadoran	30.5
Cuban	33.0
Dominican Republic	28.4
Mexican	26.8
Puerto Rican	30.5
South American	34.2
Argentinean	36.2
Chilean	35.3
Colombian	32.8
Ecuadorian	30.9
Peruvian	34.7
Venezuelan	33.4
Spaniard	34.8

High School Graduates
(Universe: Population 25 Years and Over)

Group	Number	%
Total Population	209,537	78.9
Hispanic or Latino (of any race)	27,360	51.3
Central American, ex. Mexican	3,664	44.4
Guatemalan	811	30.9
Honduran	422	47.2
Nicaraguan	487	71.9
Salvadoran	1,653	44.4
Mexican	18,623	47.4
Puerto Rican	977	90.6
South American	1,775	93.9

Four-Year College Graduates
(Universe: Population 25 Years and Over)

Group	Number	%
Total Population	96,327	36.3
Hispanic or Latino (of any race)	7,581	14.2
Central American, ex. Mexican	937	11.4
Guatemalan	183	7.0
Honduran	71	7.9
Nicaraguan	169	25.0
Salvadoran	321	8.6
Mexican	3,937	10.0
Puerto Rican	491	45.5
South American	1,106	58.5

Population Age 3–17 Enrolled in Public School
(Universe: Population Age 3–17 Enrolled in School)

Group	Number	%
Total Population	53,359	83.8
Hispanic or Latino (of any race)	21,209	91.4
Central American, ex. Mexican	1,688	88.7
Guatemalan	391	89.3
Honduran	243	85.0
Nicaraguan	338	100.0
Salvadoran	598	88.3
Mexican	18,317	92.9
Puerto Rican	343	80.7
South American	190	61.3

Population Age 3–17 Enrolled in Private School
(Universe: Population Age 3–17 Enrolled in School)

Group	Number	%
Total Population	10,349	16.2
Hispanic or Latino (of any race)	1,984	8.6
Central American, ex. Mexican	216	11.3
Guatemalan	47	10.7
Honduran	43	15.0
Nicaraguan	0	0.0
Salvadoran	79	11.7
Mexican	1,393	7.1
Puerto Rican	82	19.3
South American	120	38.7

Foreign-Born Population

Group	Number	%
Total Population	109,990	28.4
Hispanic or Latino (of any race)	51,085	52.5
Central American, ex. Mexican	9,523	70.7
Guatemalan	3,463	82.7
Honduran	846	63.0
Nicaraguan	737	54.0
Salvadoran	4,280	71.3
Mexican	39,061	52.0
Puerto Rican	0	0.0
South American	1,398	52.9

Foreign-Born Naturalized U.S. Citizens

Group	Number	%
Total Population	44,254	40.2
Hispanic or Latino (of any race)	8,779	17.2
Central American, ex. Mexican	1,489	15.6
Guatemalan	169	4.9
Honduran	170	20.1
Nicaraguan	290	39.3
Salvadoran	764	17.9
Mexican	5,955	15.2
Puerto Rican	0	0.0
South American	762	54.5

Language Spoken at Home: English Only
(Universe: Population 5 Years and Over)

Group	Number	%
Total Population	215,290	59.8
Hispanic or Latino (of any race)	11,364	13.2
Central American, ex. Mexican	841	7.0
Guatemalan	75	2.0
Honduran	76	6.4
Nicaraguan	30	2.3
Salvadoran	479	9.1
Mexican	7,290	11.0
Puerto Rican	1,008	58.9
South American	620	26.4

Language Spoken at Home: Spanish
(Universe: Population 5 Years and Over)

Group	Number	%
Total Population	79,959	22.2
Hispanic or Latino (of any race)	74,613	86.6
Central American, ex. Mexican	11,098	92.9
Guatemalan	3,670	97.8
Honduran	1,118	93.6
Nicaraguan	1,255	97.7
Salvadoran	4,763	90.9
Mexican	58,936	88.9
Puerto Rican	704	41.1
South American	1,705	72.6

Unemployment Rate
(Universe: Population 16 Years and Over)

Group	%
Total Population	10.1
Hispanic or Latino (of any race)	10.1
Central American, ex. Mexican	10.8
Guatemalan	9.7
Honduran	11.6
Nicaraguan	5.1
Salvadoran	13.3
Mexican	10.3
Puerto Rican	6.8
South American	4.2

Class of Worker: Private Wage and Salary
(Universe: Civilian Employed Population 16 Years and Over)

Group	Number	%
Total Population	136,179	74.3
Hispanic or Latino (of any race)	35,660	83.5
Central American, ex. Mexican	5,917	82.0
Guatemalan	1,926	75.9
Honduran	604	84.2
Nicaraguan	520	82.8
Salvadoran	2,649	86.7
Mexican	26,724	85.2
Puerto Rican	828	77.3
South American	1,107	71.9

Class of Worker: Government
(Universe: Civilian Employed Population 16 Years and Over)

Group	Number	%
Total Population	27,717	15.1
Hispanic or Latino (of any race)	3,121	7.3
Central American, ex. Mexican	331	4.6
Guatemalan	39	1.5
Honduran	25	3.5
Nicaraguan	53	8.4
Salvadoran	190	6.2
Mexican	2,133	6.8
Puerto Rican	183	17.1
South American	244	15.9

Means of Transportation to Work: Car, Truck or Van
(Universe: Workers 16 Years and Over)

Group	Number	%
Total Population	121,007	67.9
Hispanic or Latino (of any race)	29,992	71.7
Central American, ex. Mexican	4,784	67.4
Guatemalan	1,132	45.2
Honduran	601	85.5
Nicaraguan	547	87.1
Salvadoran	2,324	77.6
Mexican	22,567	73.7
Puerto Rican	739	69.6
South American	941	61.6

Means of Transportation to Work: Public Transportation (ex. Taxicab)
(Universe: Workers 16 Years and Over)

Group	Number	%
Total Population	29,741	16.7
Hispanic or Latino (of any race)	6,556	15.7
Central American, ex. Mexican	1,284	18.1
Guatemalan	741	29.6
Honduran	84	11.9
Nicaraguan	61	9.7
Salvadoran	398	13.3
Mexican	4,520	14.8
Puerto Rican	173	16.3
South American	346	22.7

Homeownership Rate
(Universe: Occupied Housing Units)

Group	%
Total Population	41.1
Hispanic or Latino (of any race)	32.6
Central American, ex. Mexican	28.8
Costa Rican	40.4
Guatemalan	21.5
Honduran	18.1
Nicaraguan	32.4
Panamanian	34.5
Salvadoran	33.4
Cuban	35.4
Dominican Republic	19.0
Mexican	33.5
Puerto Rican	28.1
South American	38.4
Argentinean	41.9
Chilean	44.5
Colombian	34.8
Ecuadorian	41.1

Notes: (1) Percent of total population; (2) Percent of Hispanic/Latino population; Profiles include places with an overall population of at least 125,000, OR an overall population of at least 25,000 where the Hispanic/Latino population is at least 20% of the overall population. In states where less than five places meet either of these criteria, we have included places with at least 10,000 total population with the highest percentage of Hispanic/Latino population. These places are identified with an asterisk (*); Please refer to the User's Guide for a full explanation of data.

Peruvian	35.8
Venezuelan	36.1
Spaniard	41.2

Median Home Value

Group	Dollars
Total Population	528,600
Hispanic or Latino (of any race)	400,900
Central American, ex. Mexican	416,200
Guatemalan	397,200
Honduran	386,400
Nicaraguan	431,300
Salvadoran	355,100
Mexican	375,200
Puerto Rican	481,300
South American	597,400

Median Gross Rent

Group	Dollars
Total Population	1,000
Hispanic or Latino (of any race)	976
Central American, ex. Mexican	945
Guatemalan	977
Honduran	888
Nicaraguan	1,114
Salvadoran	894
Mexican	974
Puerto Rican	1,158
South American	996

Median Household Income
(2010 Inflation-Adjusted Dollars)

Group	Dollars
Total Population	49,721
Hispanic or Latino (of any race)	43,445
Central American, ex. Mexican	41,042
Guatemalan	32,160
Honduran	33,074
Nicaraguan	28,406
Salvadoran	46,442
Mexican	43,033
Puerto Rican	61,250
South American	46,506

Per Capita Income
(2010 Inflation-Adjusted Dollars)

Group	Dollars
Total Population	30,671
Hispanic or Latino (of any race)	15,981
Central American, ex. Mexican	15,658
Guatemalan	13,362
Honduran	14,091
Nicaraguan	17,913
Salvadoran	14,746
Mexican	14,273
Puerto Rican	30,407
South American	35,598

Households with $100,000+ Income

Group	Number	%
Total Population	35,817	23.1
Hispanic or Latino (of any race)	3,465	14.1
Central American, ex. Mexican	437	12.1
Guatemalan	144	14.9
Honduran	34	9.9
Nicaraguan	60	13.9
Salvadoran	67	4.3
Mexican	2,177	12.2
Puerto Rican	240	38.5
South American	210	21.0

Households with Food Stamps/SNAP Benefits During Past 12 Months

Group	Number	%
Total Population	10,959	7.1
Hispanic or Latino (of any race)	2,300	9.3
Central American, ex. Mexican	286	7.9
Guatemalan	46	4.8
Honduran	0	0.0
Nicaraguan	43	10.0
Salvadoran	170	10.9
Mexican	1,770	9.9
Puerto Rican	57	9.1
South American	86	8.6

Poverty Rate
(Income in Past 12 Months Below Poverty Level)

Group	%
Total Population	18.7
Hispanic or Latino (of any race)	23.7
Central American, ex. Mexican	24.4
Guatemalan	38.7
Honduran	15.8
Nicaraguan	28.0
Salvadoran	15.5
Mexican	25.0
Puerto Rican	12.1
South American	8.0

Oakley

Population

Group	Number	%TP[1]	%HP[2]
Total Population	35,432	100.0	–
Hispanic or Latino (of any race)	12,364	34.9	100.0
Central American, ex. Mexican	835	2.4	6.8
Guatemalan	110	0.3	0.9
Nicaraguan	194	0.5	1.6
Salvadoran	449	1.3	3.6
Mexican	9,960	28.1	80.6
Puerto Rican	469	1.3	3.8
South American	157	0.4	1.3
Spaniard	238	0.7	1.9

Population Growth: 2000–2010

Group	%
Total Population	38.3
Hispanic or Latino (of any race)	93.2
Central American, ex. Mexican	313.4
Mexican	109.6
Puerto Rican	107.5

Males per 100 Females

Group	Number
Total Population	98.8
Hispanic or Latino (of any race)	101.9
Central American, ex. Mexican	100.2
Guatemalan	96.4
Nicaraguan	110.9
Salvadoran	96.1
Mexican	102.3
Puerto Rican	93.8
South American	109.3
Spaniard	105.2

Average Household Size

Group	People
Total Population	3.29
Hispanic or Latino (of any race)	3.98
Central American, ex. Mexican	4.15
Guatemalan	4.04
Nicaraguan	4.23
Salvadoran	4.16
Mexican	4.07
Puerto Rican	3.41
South American	3.54
Spaniard	3.14

Median Age

Group	Years
Total Population	32.0
Hispanic or Latino (of any race)	25.2
Central American, ex. Mexican	29.0
Guatemalan	28.8
Nicaraguan	30.5
Salvadoran	29.0
Mexican	24.8
Puerto Rican	22.7
South American	35.5
Spaniard	35.5

High School Graduates
(Universe: Population 25 Years and Over)

Group	Number	%
Total Population	16,307	83.2
Hispanic or Latino (of any race)	4,324	68.7
Mexican	3,009	63.1

Four-Year College Graduates
(Universe: Population 25 Years and Over)

Group	Number	%
Total Population	2,586	13.2
Hispanic or Latino (of any race)	437	6.9
Mexican	298	6.2

Population Age 3–17 Enrolled in Public School
(Universe: Population Age 3–17 Enrolled in School)

Group	Number	%
Total Population	8,270	94.4
Hispanic or Latino (of any race)	3,821	96.2
Mexican	3,233	99.5

Population Age 3–17 Enrolled in Private School
(Universe: Population Age 3–17 Enrolled in School)

Group	Number	%
Total Population	493	5.6
Hispanic or Latino (of any race)	150	3.8
Mexican	16	0.5

Foreign-Born Population

Group	Number	%
Total Population	5,938	17.7
Hispanic or Latino (of any race)	4,312	33.3
Mexican	3,431	33.5

Foreign-Born Naturalized U.S. Citizens

Group	Number	%
Total Population	2,811	47.3
Hispanic or Latino (of any race)	1,582	36.7
Mexican	1,179	34.4

Language Spoken at Home: English Only
(Universe: Population 5 Years and Over)

Group	Number	%
Total Population	21,821	69.8
Hispanic or Latino (of any race)	4,658	39.5
Mexican	3,397	36.9

Language Spoken at Home: Spanish
(Universe: Population 5 Years and Over)

Group	Number	%
Total Population	7,518	24.0
Hispanic or Latino (of any race)	7,094	60.2
Mexican	5,809	63.1

Unemployment Rate
(Universe: Population 16 Years and Over)

Group	%
Total Population	10.7
Hispanic or Latino (of any race)	12.9
Mexican	13.6

Class of Worker: Private Wage and Salary
(Universe: Civilian Employed Population 16 Years and Over)

Group	Number	%
Total Population	11,264	78.0
Hispanic or Latino (of any race)	4,172	84.7
Mexican	3,305	85.7

Class of Worker: Government
(Universe: Civilian Employed Population 16 Years and Over)

Group	Number	%
Total Population	2,327	16.1
Hispanic or Latino (of any race)	504	10.2
Mexican	330	8.6

Means of Transportation to Work: Car, Truck or Van
(Universe: Workers 16 Years and Over)

Group	Number	%
Total Population	12,415	88.9
Hispanic or Latino (of any race)	4,386	91.0
Mexican	3,472	91.4

Means of Transportation to Work: Public Transportation (ex. Taxicab)
(Universe: Workers 16 Years and Over)

Group	Number	%
Total Population	430	3.1
Hispanic or Latino (of any race)	148	3.1
Mexican	116	3.1

Notes: (1) Percent of total population; (2) Percent of Hispanic/Latino population; Profiles include places with an overall population of at least 125,000, OR an overall population of at least 25,000 where the Hispanic/Latino population is at least 20% of the overall population. In states where less than five places meet either of these criteria, we have included places with at least 10,000 total population with the highest percentage of Hispanic/Latino population. These places are identified with an asterisk (*); Please refer to the User's Guide for a full explanation of data.

Homeownership Rate (Universe: Occupied Housing Units)	
Group	%
Total Population	76.1
Hispanic or Latino (of any race)	69.9
Central American, ex. Mexican	76.6
Guatemalan	82.1
Nicaraguan	78.8
Salvadoran	73.9
Mexican	69.2
Puerto Rican	57.8
South American	76.0
Spaniard	81.1

Median Home Value	
Group	Dollars
Total Population	384,300
Hispanic or Latino (of any race)	369,800
Mexican	348,000

Median Gross Rent	
Group	Dollars
Total Population	1,423
Hispanic or Latino (of any race)	1,528
Mexican	1,318

Median Household Income (2010 Inflation-Adjusted Dollars)	
Group	Dollars
Total Population	76,583
Hispanic or Latino (of any race)	61,313
Mexican	57,059

Per Capita Income (2010 Inflation-Adjusted Dollars)	
Group	Dollars
Total Population	27,069
Hispanic or Latino (of any race)	18,050
Mexican	16,744

Households with $100,000+ Income		
Group	Number	%
Total Population	3,624	35.4
Hispanic or Latino (of any race)	882	26.7
Mexican	678	26.4

Households with Food Stamps/SNAP Benefits During Past 12 Months		
Group	Number	%
Total Population	303	3.0
Hispanic or Latino (of any race)	141	4.3
Mexican	141	5.5

Poverty Rate (Income in Past 12 Months Below Poverty Level)	
Group	%
Total Population	7.4
Hispanic or Latino (of any race)	7.4
Mexican	8.6

Oceanside

Population			
Group	Number	%TP[1]	%HP[2]
Total Population	167,086	100.0	–
Hispanic or Latino (of any race)	59,947	35.9	100.0
Central American, ex. Mexican	1,547	0.9	2.6
Costa Rican	131	0.1	0.2
Guatemalan	371	0.2	0.6
Honduran	138	0.1	0.2
Nicaraguan	127	0.1	0.2
Panamanian	175	0.1	0.3
Salvadoran	589	0.4	1.0
Cuban	288	0.2	0.5
Dominican Republic	154	0.1	0.3
Mexican	52,217	31.3	87.1
Puerto Rican	1,602	1.0	2.7
South American	1,084	0.6	1.8
Argentinean	116	0.1	0.2
Colombian	316	0.2	0.5
Ecuadorian	130	0.1	0.2
Peruvian	301	0.2	0.5
Spaniard	671	0.4	1.1

Population Growth: 2000–2010	
Group	%
Total Population	3.8
Hispanic or Latino (of any race)	23.1
Central American, ex. Mexican	85.9
Guatemalan	123.5
Panamanian	16.7
Salvadoran	126.5
Cuban	39.8
Mexican	28.2
Puerto Rican	22.7
South American	129.2
Colombian	154.8
Peruvian	171.2

Males per 100 Females	
Group	Number
Total Population	97.4
Hispanic or Latino (of any race)	99.1
Central American, ex. Mexican	87.7
Costa Rican	74.7
Guatemalan	110.8
Honduran	89.0
Nicaraguan	76.4
Panamanian	75.0
Salvadoran	85.8
Cuban	100.0
Dominican Republic	105.3
Mexican	99.7
Puerto Rican	111.1
South American	87.2
Argentinean	110.9
Colombian	79.5
Ecuadorian	106.3
Peruvian	82.4
Spaniard	79.4

Average Household Size	
Group	People
Total Population	2.80
Hispanic or Latino (of any race)	4.08
Central American, ex. Mexican	3.46
Costa Rican	3.27
Guatemalan	4.03
Honduran	3.25
Nicaraguan	2.98
Panamanian	2.38
Salvadoran	3.86
Cuban	2.64
Dominican Republic	2.73
Mexican	4.30
Puerto Rican	2.84
South American	2.79
Argentinean	2.36
Colombian	2.94
Ecuadorian	2.57
Peruvian	3.08
Spaniard	2.64

Median Age	
Group	Years
Total Population	35.2
Hispanic or Latino (of any race)	25.9
Central American, ex. Mexican	30.9
Costa Rican	30.5
Guatemalan	28.9
Honduran	28.8
Nicaraguan	31.7
Panamanian	39.1
Salvadoran	30.4
Cuban	31.8
Dominican Republic	24.4
Mexican	25.4
Puerto Rican	26.4
South American	35.7
Argentinean	42.0
Colombian	36.4
Ecuadorian	33.8
Peruvian	33.8
Spaniard	35.6

High School Graduates (Universe: Population 25 Years and Over)		
Group	Number	%
Total Population	87,927	82.6
Hispanic or Latino (of any race)	17,426	56.6
Central American, ex. Mexican	623	64.6
Mexican	12,854	52.1
Puerto Rican	461	98.1
South American	622	89.5

Four-Year College Graduates (Universe: Population 25 Years and Over)		
Group	Number	%
Total Population	26,465	24.9
Hispanic or Latino (of any race)	2,875	9.3
Central American, ex. Mexican	140	14.5
Mexican	2,019	8.2
Puerto Rican	51	10.9
South American	242	34.8

Population Age 3–17 Enrolled in Public School (Universe: Population Age 3–17 Enrolled in School)		
Group	Number	%
Total Population	27,226	91.4
Hispanic or Latino (of any race)	14,365	97.4
Central American, ex. Mexican	222	96.1
Mexican	12,132	97.7
Puerto Rican	192	75.9
South American	125	88.0

Population Age 3–17 Enrolled in Private School (Universe: Population Age 3–17 Enrolled in School)		
Group	Number	%
Total Population	2,558	8.6
Hispanic or Latino (of any race)	389	2.6
Central American, ex. Mexican	9	3.9
Mexican	291	2.3
Puerto Rican	61	24.1
South American	17	12.0

Foreign-Born Population		
Group	Number	%
Total Population	36,221	22.0
Hispanic or Latino (of any race)	23,645	40.0
Central American, ex. Mexican	858	59.5
Mexican	19,505	40.4
Puerto Rican	25	2.9
South American	624	66.6

Foreign-Born Naturalized U.S. Citizens		
Group	Number	%
Total Population	14,385	39.7
Hispanic or Latino (of any race)	6,318	26.7
Central American, ex. Mexican	365	42.5
Mexican	4,199	21.5
Puerto Rican	11	44.0
South American	411	65.9

Language Spoken at Home: English Only (Universe: Population 5 Years and Over)		
Group	Number	%
Total Population	98,804	64.6
Hispanic or Latino (of any race)	12,450	23.7
Central American, ex. Mexican	262	20.2
Mexican	9,660	22.5
Puerto Rican	462	58.1
South American	232	26.3

Language Spoken at Home: Spanish (Universe: Population 5 Years and Over)		
Group	Number	%
Total Population	42,065	27.5
Hispanic or Latino (of any race)	40,001	76.1
Central American, ex. Mexican	1,028	79.3
Mexican	33,208	77.3
Puerto Rican	296	37.2
South American	650	73.7

Unemployment Rate (Universe: Population 16 Years and Over)	
Group	%
Total Population	8.8
Hispanic or Latino (of any race)	8.3
Central American, ex. Mexican	3.6
Mexican	9.1
Puerto Rican	6.6
South American	4.5

Notes: (1) Percent of total population; (2) Percent of Hispanic/Latino population; Profiles include places with an overall population of at least 125,000, OR an overall population of at least 25,000 where the Hispanic/Latino population is at least 20% of the overall population. In states where less than five places meet either of these criteria, we have included places with at least 10,000 total population with the highest percentage of Hispanic/Latino population. These places are identified with an asterisk (*); Please refer to the User's Guide for a full explanation of data.

Class of Worker: Private Wage and Salary
(Universe: Civilian Employed Population 16 Years and Over)

Group	Number	%
Total Population	58,192	78.2
Hispanic or Latino (of any race)	21,932	84.8
Central American, ex. Mexican	574	84.8
Mexican	17,337	84.2
Puerto Rican	335	79.0
South American	455	80.0

Class of Worker: Government
(Universe: Civilian Employed Population 16 Years and Over)

Group	Number	%
Total Population	10,559	14.2
Hispanic or Latino (of any race)	2,351	9.1
Central American, ex. Mexican	68	10.0
Mexican	1,914	9.3
Puerto Rican	80	18.9
South American	0	0.0

Means of Transportation to Work: Car, Truck or Van
(Universe: Workers 16 Years and Over)

Group	Number	%
Total Population	67,233	88.1
Hispanic or Latino (of any race)	23,007	88.2
Central American, ex. Mexican	658	91.6
Mexican	18,289	88.3
Puerto Rican	415	91.0
South American	518	88.2

Means of Transportation to Work: Public Transportation (ex. Taxicab)
(Universe: Workers 16 Years and Over)

Group	Number	%
Total Population	3,305	4.3
Hispanic or Latino (of any race)	1,346	5.2
Central American, ex. Mexican	10	1.4
Mexican	1,108	5.4
Puerto Rican	9	2.0
South American	38	6.5

Homeownership Rate
(Universe: Occupied Housing Units)

Group	%
Total Population	59.1
Hispanic or Latino (of any race)	46.8
Central American, ex. Mexican	47.1
Costa Rican	68.3
Guatemalan	36.6
Honduran	52.5
Nicaraguan	56.1
Panamanian	52.1
Salvadoran	42.9
Cuban	50.0
Dominican Republic	30.8
Mexican	46.7
Puerto Rican	40.2
South American	61.4
Argentinean	62.2
Colombian	63.3
Ecuadorian	62.5
Peruvian	60.9
Spaniard	57.6

Median Home Value

Group	Dollars
Total Population	429,700
Hispanic or Latino (of any race)	401,200
Central American, ex. Mexican	388,700
Mexican	391,000
Puerto Rican	472,200
South American	491,100

Median Gross Rent

Group	Dollars
Total Population	1,299
Hispanic or Latino (of any race)	1,257
Central American, ex. Mexican	1,368
Mexican	1,230
Puerto Rican	1,064
South American	2,000+

Median Household Income
(2010 Inflation-Adjusted Dollars)

Group	Dollars
Total Population	63,577
Hispanic or Latino (of any race)	54,478
Central American, ex. Mexican	60,559
Mexican	53,381
Puerto Rican	69,519
South American	61,538

Per Capita Income
(2010 Inflation-Adjusted Dollars)

Group	Dollars
Total Population	27,639
Hispanic or Latino (of any race)	16,609
Central American, ex. Mexican	21,007
Mexican	15,414
Puerto Rican	29,707
South American	37,615

Households with $100,000+ Income

Group	Number	%
Total Population	14,873	25.5
Hispanic or Latino (of any race)	2,609	18.3
Central American, ex. Mexican	76	17.4
Mexican	1,923	17.5
Puerto Rican	93	37.1
South American	70	24.1

Households with Food Stamps/SNAP Benefits During Past 12 Months

Group	Number	%
Total Population	1,416	2.4
Hispanic or Latino (of any race)	519	3.6
Central American, ex. Mexican	12	2.7
Mexican	423	3.8
Puerto Rican	0	0.0
South American	26	9.0

Poverty Rate
(Income in Past 12 Months Below Poverty Level)

Group	%
Total Population	10.1
Hispanic or Latino (of any race)	15.7
Central American, ex. Mexican	6.8
Mexican	16.4
Puerto Rican	5.6
South American	1.5

Ontario

Population

Group	Number	%TP[1]	%HP[2]
Total Population	163,924	100.0	–
Hispanic or Latino (of any race)	113,085	69.0	100.0
Central American, ex. Mexican	6,264	3.8	5.5
Costa Rican	175	0.1	0.2
Guatemalan	1,676	1.0	1.5
Honduran	793	0.5	0.7
Nicaraguan	658	0.4	0.6
Panamanian	102	0.1	0.1
Salvadoran	2,791	1.7	2.5
Cuban	592	0.4	0.5
Mexican	98,596	60.1	87.2
Puerto Rican	1,001	0.6	0.9
South American	1,519	0.9	1.3
Argentinean	243	0.1	0.2
Colombian	376	0.2	0.3
Ecuadorian	270	0.2	0.2
Peruvian	404	0.2	0.4
Spaniard	576	0.4	0.5

Population Growth: 2000–2010

Group	%
Total Population	3.7
Hispanic or Latino (of any race)	19.5
Central American, ex. Mexican	111.8
Costa Rican	44.6
Guatemalan	125.6
Honduran	172.5
Nicaraguan	108.9
Salvadoran	152.8
Cuban	47.6
Mexican	27.3
Puerto Rican	39.6
South American	60.1
Argentinean	53.8
Colombian	48.6
Ecuadorian	98.5
Peruvian	92.4
Spaniard	400.9

Males per 100 Females

Group	Number
Total Population	99.0
Hispanic or Latino (of any race)	101.2
Central American, ex. Mexican	95.8
Costa Rican	80.4
Guatemalan	110.0
Honduran	90.2
Nicaraguan	85.4
Panamanian	67.2
Salvadoran	94.2
Cuban	94.7
Mexican	102.1
Puerto Rican	99.4
South American	92.5
Argentinean	105.9
Colombian	84.3
Ecuadorian	84.9
Peruvian	97.1
Spaniard	104.3

Average Household Size

Group	People
Total Population	3.63
Hispanic or Latino (of any race)	4.33
Central American, ex. Mexican	4.39
Costa Rican	3.77
Guatemalan	4.53
Honduran	4.74
Nicaraguan	4.22
Panamanian	3.33
Salvadoran	4.38
Cuban	3.13
Mexican	4.38
Puerto Rican	3.46
South American	3.46
Argentinean	2.87
Colombian	3.36
Ecuadorian	3.73
Peruvian	3.79
Spaniard	3.09

Median Age

Group	Years
Total Population	29.9
Hispanic or Latino (of any race)	26.4
Central American, ex. Mexican	31.9
Costa Rican	37.3
Guatemalan	31.9
Honduran	28.2
Nicaraguan	33.3
Panamanian	32.7
Salvadoran	32.5
Cuban	34.9
Mexican	25.9
Puerto Rican	27.1
South American	37.3
Argentinean	37.1
Colombian	40.7
Ecuadorian	37.2
Peruvian	36.0
Spaniard	34.1

High School Graduates
(Universe: Population 25 Years and Over)

Group	Number	%
Total Population	67,458	70.1
Hispanic or Latino (of any race)	31,845	56.2
Central American, ex. Mexican	2,071	53.2
Guatemalan	617	56.7
Salvadoran	917	53.8
Mexican	27,027	55.2
South American	834	74.7

Notes: (1) Percent of total population; (2) Percent of Hispanic/Latino population; Profiles include places with an overall population of at least 125,000, OR an overall population of at least 25,000 where the Hispanic/Latino population is at least 20% of the overall population. In states where less than five places meet either of these criteria, we have included places with at least 10,000 total population with the highest percentage of Hispanic/Latino population. These places are identified with an asterisk (*); Please refer to the User's Guide for a full explanation of data.

Four-Year College Graduates
(Universe: Population 25 Years and Over)

Group	Number	%
Total Population	14,786	15.4
Hispanic or Latino (of any race)	4,148	7.3
Central American, ex. Mexican	331	8.5
Guatemalan	182	16.7
Salvadoran	75	4.4
Mexican	3,257	6.7
South American	276	24.7

Population Age 3–17 Enrolled in Public School
(Universe: Population Age 3–17 Enrolled in School)

Group	Number	%
Total Population	35,599	94.1
Hispanic or Latino (of any race)	27,639	96.2
Central American, ex. Mexican	799	97.8
Guatemalan	79	100.0
Salvadoran	416	100.0
Mexican	25,444	96.6
South American	313	80.1

Population Age 3–17 Enrolled in Private School
(Universe: Population Age 3–17 Enrolled in School)

Group	Number	%
Total Population	2,221	5.9
Hispanic or Latino (of any race)	1,100	3.8
Central American, ex. Mexican	18	2.2
Guatemalan	0	0.0
Salvadoran	0	0.0
Mexican	892	3.4
South American	78	19.9

Foreign-Born Population

Group	Number	%
Total Population	48,915	29.6
Hispanic or Latino (of any race)	41,763	38.7
Central American, ex. Mexican	4,106	70.4
Guatemalan	1,163	81.6
Salvadoran	1,746	63.9
Mexican	35,557	37.3
South American	1,204	65.4

Foreign-Born Naturalized U.S. Citizens

Group	Number	%
Total Population	18,196	37.2
Hispanic or Latino (of any race)	13,801	33.0
Central American, ex. Mexican	1,226	29.9
Guatemalan	227	19.5
Salvadoran	572	32.8
Mexican	11,727	33.0
South American	422	35.0

Language Spoken at Home: English Only
(Universe: Population 5 Years and Over)

Group	Number	%
Total Population	67,475	44.1
Hispanic or Latino (of any race)	22,302	22.6
Central American, ex. Mexican	188	3.4
Guatemalan	15	1.1
Salvadoran	86	3.2
Mexican	20,187	23.2
South American	193	11.1

Language Spoken at Home: Spanish
(Universe: Population 5 Years and Over)

Group	Number	%
Total Population	78,232	51.1
Hispanic or Latino (of any race)	76,337	77.3
Central American, ex. Mexican	5,352	96.3
Guatemalan	1,365	98.9
Salvadoran	2,605	96.3
Mexican	66,693	76.7
South American	1,547	88.9

Unemployment Rate
(Universe: Population 16 Years and Over)

Group	%
Total Population	11.6
Hispanic or Latino (of any race)	13.3
Central American, ex. Mexican	19.6
Guatemalan	26.1
Salvadoran	20.0
Mexican	12.9
South American	9.1

Class of Worker: Private Wage and Salary
(Universe: Civilian Employed Population 16 Years and Over)

Group	Number	%
Total Population	60,573	80.9
Hispanic or Latino (of any race)	38,799	85.1
Central American, ex. Mexican	2,654	84.8
Guatemalan	625	80.6
Salvadoran	1,302	83.4
Mexican	33,770	85.6
South American	739	84.5

Class of Worker: Government
(Universe: Civilian Employed Population 16 Years and Over)

Group	Number	%
Total Population	9,845	13.1
Hispanic or Latino (of any race)	4,299	9.4
Central American, ex. Mexican	217	6.9
Guatemalan	23	3.0
Salvadoran	167	10.7
Mexican	3,534	9.0
South American	122	13.9

Means of Transportation to Work: Car, Truck or Van
(Universe: Workers 16 Years and Over)

Group	Number	%
Total Population	66,373	91.7
Hispanic or Latino (of any race)	40,222	90.7
Central American, ex. Mexican	2,662	87.3
Guatemalan	634	82.9
Salvadoran	1,323	86.0
Mexican	34,879	90.8
South American	773	92.5

Means of Transportation to Work: Public Transportation (ex. Taxicab)
(Universe: Workers 16 Years and Over)

Group	Number	%
Total Population	1,587	2.2
Hispanic or Latino (of any race)	1,204	2.7
Central American, ex. Mexican	161	5.3
Guatemalan	0	0.0
Salvadoran	161	10.5
Mexican	946	2.5
South American	19	2.3

Homeownership Rate
(Universe: Occupied Housing Units)

Group	%
Total Population	55.3
Hispanic or Latino (of any race)	51.2
Central American, ex. Mexican	46.0
Costa Rican	50.0
Guatemalan	45.8
Honduran	30.2
Nicaraguan	46.7
Panamanian	41.0
Salvadoran	50.3
Cuban	50.0
Mexican	51.8
Puerto Rican	48.1
South American	59.9
Argentinean	51.6
Colombian	62.9
Ecuadorian	64.1
Peruvian	55.0
Spaniard	60.2

Median Home Value

Group	Dollars
Total Population	346,800
Hispanic or Latino (of any race)	345,700
Central American, ex. Mexican	351,900
Guatemalan	385,200
Salvadoran	353,500
Mexican	343,600
South American	373,800

Median Gross Rent

Group	Dollars
Total Population	1,198
Hispanic or Latino (of any race)	1,133
Central American, ex. Mexican	1,052
Guatemalan	955
Salvadoran	1,089
Mexican	1,130
South American	1,409

Median Household Income
(2010 Inflation-Adjusted Dollars)

Group	Dollars
Total Population	57,771
Hispanic or Latino (of any race)	53,875
Central American, ex. Mexican	43,882
Guatemalan	38,646
Salvadoran	53,264
Mexican	55,445
South American	37,896

Per Capita Income
(2010 Inflation-Adjusted Dollars)

Group	Dollars
Total Population	19,534
Hispanic or Latino (of any race)	15,009
Central American, ex. Mexican	17,530
Guatemalan	23,508
Salvadoran	17,982
Mexican	14,541
South American	22,938

Households with $100,000+ Income

Group	Number	%
Total Population	9,134	20.1
Hispanic or Latino (of any race)	3,833	15.6
Central American, ex. Mexican	315	19.4
Guatemalan	175	31.2
Salvadoran	101	14.5
Mexican	3,235	15.4
South American	81	15.9

Households with Food Stamps/SNAP Benefits During Past 12 Months

Group	Number	%
Total Population	3,077	6.8
Hispanic or Latino (of any race)	2,104	8.6
Central American, ex. Mexican	224	13.8
Guatemalan	68	12.1
Salvadoran	37	5.3
Mexican	1,736	8.3
South American	78	15.4

Poverty Rate
(Income in Past 12 Months Below Poverty Level)

Group	%
Total Population	12.7
Hispanic or Latino (of any race)	15.5
Central American, ex. Mexican	19.0
Guatemalan	23.3
Salvadoran	10.3
Mexican	14.9
South American	36.0

Orange

Population

Group	Number	%TP[1]	%HP[2]
Total Population	136,416	100.0	–
Hispanic or Latino (of any race)	52,014	38.1	100.0
Central American, ex. Mexican	2,152	1.6	4.1
Guatemalan	790	0.6	1.5
Honduran	163	0.1	0.3
Nicaraguan	163	0.1	0.3
Salvadoran	851	0.6	1.6
Cuban	414	0.3	0.8
Mexican	45,074	33.0	86.7
Puerto Rican	488	0.4	0.9
South American	1,349	1.0	2.6
Argentinean	257	0.2	0.5
Bolivian	157	0.1	0.3
Colombian	257	0.2	0.5
Ecuadorian	158	0.1	0.3
Peruvian	371	0.3	0.7
Spaniard	471	0.3	0.9

Population Growth: 2000–2010

Group	%
Total Population	5.9
Hispanic or Latino (of any race)	25.5
Central American, ex. Mexican	80.2

Notes: (1) Percent of total population; (2) Percent of Hispanic/Latino population; Profiles include places with an overall population of at least 125,000, OR an overall population of at least 25,000 where the Hispanic/Latino population is at least 20% of the overall population. In states where less than five places meet either of these criteria, we have included places with at least 10,000 total population with the highest percentage of Hispanic/Latino population. These places are identified with an asterisk (*); Please refer to the User's Guide for a full explanation of data.

Guatemalan	104.7
Salvadoran	100.2
Cuban	52.2
Mexican	31.3
Puerto Rican	44.4
South American	106.0
Argentinean	121.6
Colombian	138.0
Peruvian	81.9

Males per 100 Females

Group	Number
Total Population	101.5
Hispanic or Latino (of any race)	109.0
Central American, ex. Mexican	91.3
Guatemalan	101.0
Honduran	83.1
Nicaraguan	85.2
Salvadoran	86.2
Cuban	100.0
Mexican	111.9
Puerto Rican	73.7
South American	84.0
Argentinean	83.6
Bolivian	91.5
Colombian	86.2
Ecuadorian	73.6
Peruvian	80.1
Spaniard	93.8

Average Household Size

Group	People
Total Population	3.00
Hispanic or Latino (of any race)	4.15
Central American, ex. Mexican	3.91
Guatemalan	4.18
Honduran	3.95
Nicaraguan	3.15
Salvadoran	4.10
Cuban	2.82
Mexican	4.31
Puerto Rican	2.77
South American	3.18
Argentinean	2.89
Bolivian	4.11
Colombian	3.01
Ecuadorian	3.11
Peruvian	3.32
Spaniard	2.74

Median Age

Group	Years
Total Population	34.8
Hispanic or Latino (of any race)	27.0
Central American, ex. Mexican	32.4
Guatemalan	32.8
Honduran	28.5
Nicaraguan	32.4
Salvadoran	32.5
Cuban	33.2
Mexican	26.4
Puerto Rican	28.8
South American	34.7
Argentinean	35.4
Bolivian	33.2
Colombian	33.1
Ecuadorian	33.8
Peruvian	35.6
Spaniard	37.4

High School Graduates
(Universe: Population 25 Years and Over)

Group	Number	%
Total Population	70,941	82.4
Hispanic or Latino (of any race)	15,186	56.9
Central American, ex. Mexican	740	58.2
Mexican	12,897	54.8
South American	546	87.5

Four-Year College Graduates
(Universe: Population 25 Years and Over)

Group	Number	%
Total Population	27,892	32.4
Hispanic or Latino (of any race)	3,763	14.1
Central American, ex. Mexican	208	16.4
Mexican	2,980	12.7
South American	272	43.6

Population Age 3–17 Enrolled in Public School
(Universe: Population Age 3–17 Enrolled in School)

Group	Number	%
Total Population	20,540	78.8
Hispanic or Latino (of any race)	11,174	90.2
Central American, ex. Mexican	397	77.2
Mexican	10,498	91.9
South American	147	79.0

Population Age 3–17 Enrolled in Private School
(Universe: Population Age 3–17 Enrolled in School)

Group	Number	%
Total Population	5,541	21.2
Hispanic or Latino (of any race)	1,220	9.8
Central American, ex. Mexican	117	22.8
Mexican	929	8.1
South American	39	21.0

Foreign-Born Population

Group	Number	%
Total Population	35,876	26.7
Hispanic or Latino (of any race)	21,029	41.7
Central American, ex. Mexican	1,128	53.3
Mexican	18,886	41.5
South American	491	50.2

Foreign-Born Naturalized U.S. Citizens

Group	Number	%
Total Population	15,708	43.8
Hispanic or Latino (of any race)	5,280	25.1
Central American, ex. Mexican	579	51.3
Mexican	4,092	21.7
South American	314	64.0

Language Spoken at Home: English Only
(Universe: Population 5 Years and Over)

Group	Number	%
Total Population	72,675	57.9
Hispanic or Latino (of any race)	9,796	21.4
Central American, ex. Mexican	453	22.0
Mexican	8,284	20.1
South American	200	22.8

Language Spoken at Home: Spanish
(Universe: Population 5 Years and Over)

Group	Number	%
Total Population	37,322	29.8
Hispanic or Latino (of any race)	35,855	78.3
Central American, ex. Mexican	1,607	78.0
Mexican	32,752	79.6
South American	677	77.2

Unemployment Rate
(Universe: Population 16 Years and Over)

Group	%
Total Population	7.7
Hispanic or Latino (of any race)	9.4
Central American, ex. Mexican	11.6
Mexican	9.3
South American	1.1

Class of Worker: Private Wage and Salary
(Universe: Civilian Employed Population 16 Years and Over)

Group	Number	%
Total Population	53,769	81.1
Hispanic or Latino (of any race)	19,477	84.4
Central American, ex. Mexican	1,004	93.2
Mexican	17,471	84.2
South American	332	70.9

Class of Worker: Government
(Universe: Civilian Employed Population 16 Years and Over)

Group	Number	%
Total Population	7,502	11.3
Hispanic or Latino (of any race)	2,028	8.8
Central American, ex. Mexican	52	4.8
Mexican	1,790	8.6
South American	99	21.2

Means of Transportation to Work: Car, Truck or Van
(Universe: Workers 16 Years and Over)

Group	Number	%
Total Population	58,141	89.2
Hispanic or Latino (of any race)	19,660	86.0
Central American, ex. Mexican	1,007	94.9
Mexican	17,549	85.4
South American	419	89.5

Means of Transportation to Work: Public Transportation (ex. Taxicab)
(Universe: Workers 16 Years and Over)

Group	Number	%
Total Population	2,114	3.2
Hispanic or Latino (of any race)	1,614	7.1
Central American, ex. Mexican	31	2.9
Mexican	1,563	7.6
South American	0	0.0

Homeownership Rate
(Universe: Occupied Housing Units)

Group	%
Total Population	60.7
Hispanic or Latino (of any race)	39.4
Central American, ex. Mexican	34.2
Guatemalan	35.5
Honduran	25.0
Nicaraguan	37.5
Salvadoran	32.0
Cuban	62.7
Mexican	38.7
Puerto Rican	43.5
South American	47.9
Argentinean	58.0
Bolivian	59.1
Colombian	40.0
Ecuadorian	41.3
Peruvian	42.0
Spaniard	61.6

Median Home Value

Group	Dollars
Total Population	598,000
Hispanic or Latino (of any race)	561,500
Central American, ex. Mexican	417,300
Mexican	566,100
South American	458,000

Median Gross Rent

Group	Dollars
Total Population	1,385
Hispanic or Latino (of any race)	1,338
Central American, ex. Mexican	1,300
Mexican	1,340
South American	1,490

Median Household Income
(2010 Inflation-Adjusted Dollars)

Group	Dollars
Total Population	76,742
Hispanic or Latino (of any race)	60,549
Central American, ex. Mexican	75,469
Mexican	60,469
South American	59,231

Per Capita Income
(2010 Inflation-Adjusted Dollars)

Group	Dollars
Total Population	31,653
Hispanic or Latino (of any race)	17,743
Central American, ex. Mexican	18,311
Mexican	17,246
South American	25,384

Households with $100,000+ Income

Group	Number	%
Total Population	15,425	36.6
Hispanic or Latino (of any race)	2,562	23.4
Central American, ex. Mexican	102	17.2
Mexican	2,246	23.7
South American	76	27.5

Notes: (1) Percent of total population; (2) Percent of Hispanic/Latino population; Profiles include places with an overall population of at least 125,000, OR an overall population of at least 25,000 where the Hispanic/Latino population is at least 20% of the overall population. In states where less than five places meet either of these criteria, we have included places with at least 10,000 total population with the highest percentage of Hispanic/Latino population. These places are identified with an asterisk (*); Please refer to the User's Guide for a full explanation of data.

Households with Food Stamps/SNAP Benefits During Past 12 Months

Group	Number	%
Total Population	1,131	2.7
Hispanic or Latino (of any race)	780	7.1
Central American, ex. Mexican	0	0.0
Mexican	755	8.0
South American	25	9.1

Poverty Rate
(Income in Past 12 Months Below Poverty Level)

Group	%
Total Population	9.1
Hispanic or Latino (of any race)	13.5
Central American, ex. Mexican	12.7
Mexican	13.8
South American	14.9

Orcutt

Population

Group	Number	%TP[1]	%HP[2]
Total Population	28,905	100.0	–
Hispanic or Latino (of any race)	6,870	23.8	100.0
Central American, ex. Mexican	141	0.5	2.1
Mexican	6,023	20.8	87.7
Puerto Rican	130	0.4	1.9
South American	107	0.4	1.6
Spaniard	165	0.6	2.4

Population Growth: 2000–2010

Group	%
Total Population	0.3
Hispanic or Latino (of any race)	64.9
Mexican	77.5

Males per 100 Females

Group	Number
Total Population	96.1
Hispanic or Latino (of any race)	98.6
Central American, ex. Mexican	95.8
Mexican	98.9
Puerto Rican	116.7
South American	91.1
Spaniard	87.5

Average Household Size

Group	People
Total Population	2.71
Hispanic or Latino (of any race)	3.51
Central American, ex. Mexican	3.39
Mexican	3.62
Puerto Rican	2.74
South American	2.49
Spaniard	2.82

Median Age

Group	Years
Total Population	42.3
Hispanic or Latino (of any race)	27.3
Central American, ex. Mexican	30.3
Mexican	26.3
Puerto Rican	29.4
South American	42.2
Spaniard	39.2

High School Graduates
(Universe: Population 25 Years and Over)

Group	Number	%
Total Population	18,238	92.9
Hispanic or Latino (of any race)	2,177	74.9
Mexican	1,865	71.9

Four-Year College Graduates
(Universe: Population 25 Years and Over)

Group	Number	%
Total Population	5,197	26.5
Hispanic or Latino (of any race)	333	11.5
Mexican	305	11.8

Population Age 3–17 Enrolled in Public School
(Universe: Population Age 3–17 Enrolled in School)

Group	Number	%
Total Population	4,714	78.5
Hispanic or Latino (of any race)	1,748	88.5
Mexican	1,580	89.4

Population Age 3–17 Enrolled in Private School
(Universe: Population Age 3–17 Enrolled in School)

Group	Number	%
Total Population	1,292	21.5
Hispanic or Latino (of any race)	228	11.5
Mexican	188	10.6

Foreign-Born Population

Group	Number	%
Total Population	2,338	8.1
Hispanic or Latino (of any race)	1,019	17.3
Mexican	955	18.1

Foreign-Born Naturalized U.S. Citizens

Group	Number	%
Total Population	1,156	49.4
Hispanic or Latino (of any race)	284	27.9
Mexican	246	25.8

Language Spoken at Home: English Only
(Universe: Population 5 Years and Over)

Group	Number	%
Total Population	23,475	86.8
Hispanic or Latino (of any race)	3,209	62.6
Mexican	2,745	60.5

Language Spoken at Home: Spanish
(Universe: Population 5 Years and Over)

Group	Number	%
Total Population	2,189	8.1
Hispanic or Latino (of any race)	1,867	36.4
Mexican	1,746	38.5

Unemployment Rate
(Universe: Population 16 Years and Over)

Group	%
Total Population	6.6
Hispanic or Latino (of any race)	8.2
Mexican	7.4

Class of Worker: Private Wage and Salary
(Universe: Civilian Employed Population 16 Years and Over)

Group	Number	%
Total Population	8,558	68.1
Hispanic or Latino (of any race)	1,488	71.1
Mexican	1,338	73.0

Class of Worker: Government
(Universe: Civilian Employed Population 16 Years and Over)

Group	Number	%
Total Population	2,598	20.7
Hispanic or Latino (of any race)	433	20.7
Mexican	384	20.9

Means of Transportation to Work: Car, Truck or Van
(Universe: Workers 16 Years and Over)

Group	Number	%
Total Population	11,078	91.6
Hispanic or Latino (of any race)	1,834	92.2
Mexican	1,631	92.9

Means of Transportation to Work: Public Transportation (ex. Taxicab)
(Universe: Workers 16 Years and Over)

Group	Number	%
Total Population	284	2.3
Hispanic or Latino (of any race)	91	4.6
Mexican	61	3.5

Homeownership Rate
(Universe: Occupied Housing Units)

Group	%
Total Population	78.1
Hispanic or Latino (of any race)	67.5
Central American, ex. Mexican	75.8
Mexican	67.0
Puerto Rican	61.5
South American	66.7
Spaniard	72.1

Median Home Value

Group	Dollars
Total Population	406,900
Hispanic or Latino (of any race)	382,900
Mexican	370,200

Median Gross Rent

Group	Dollars
Total Population	1,432
Hispanic or Latino (of any race)	1,471
Mexican	1,536

Median Household Income
(2010 Inflation-Adjusted Dollars)

Group	Dollars
Total Population	65,425
Hispanic or Latino (of any race)	64,861
Mexican	67,615

Per Capita Income
(2010 Inflation-Adjusted Dollars)

Group	Dollars
Total Population	29,246
Hispanic or Latino (of any race)	17,026
Mexican	16,831

Households with $100,000+ Income

Group	Number	%
Total Population	3,191	30.2
Hispanic or Latino (of any race)	319	23.0
Mexican	288	23.4

Households with Food Stamps/SNAP Benefits During Past 12 Months

Group	Number	%
Total Population	301	2.8
Hispanic or Latino (of any race)	102	7.4
Mexican	77	6.3

Poverty Rate
(Income in Past 12 Months Below Poverty Level)

Group	%
Total Population	5.5
Hispanic or Latino (of any race)	5.7
Mexican	5.2

Oxnard

Population

Group	Number	%TP[1]	%HP[2]
Total Population	197,899	100.0	–
Hispanic or Latino (of any race)	145,551	73.5	100.0
Central American, ex. Mexican	2,288	1.2	1.6
Guatemalan	630	0.3	0.4
Honduran	204	0.1	0.1
Nicaraguan	138	0.1	0.1
Salvadoran	1,172	0.6	0.8
Cuban	166	0.1	0.1
Mexican	136,991	69.2	94.1
Puerto Rican	678	0.3	0.5
South American	686	0.3	0.5
Argentinean	105	0.1	0.1
Colombian	183	0.1	0.1
Peruvian	185	0.1	0.1
Spaniard	586	0.3	0.4

Population Growth: 2000–2010

Group	%
Total Population	16.2
Hispanic or Latino (of any race)	29.0
Central American, ex. Mexican	137.6
Guatemalan	187.7
Salvadoran	192.3
Cuban	32.8
Mexican	35.3
Puerto Rican	28.2
South American	61.4
Colombian	76.0

Males per 100 Females

Group	Number
Total Population	103.0
Hispanic or Latino (of any race)	104.8
Central American, ex. Mexican	103.2

STATE & PLACE PROFILES

Notes: (1) Percent of total population; (2) Percent of Hispanic/Latino population; Profiles include places with an overall population of at least 125,000, OR an overall population of at least 25,000 where the Hispanic/Latino population is at least 20% of the overall population. In states where less than five places meet either of these criteria, we have included places with at least 10,000 total population with the highest percentage of Hispanic/Latino population. These places are identified with an asterisk (*); Please refer to the User's Guide for a full explanation of data.

Group	People
Guatemalan	97.5
Honduran	119.4
Nicaraguan	81.6
Salvadoran	107.1
Cuban	93.0
Mexican	105.3
Puerto Rican	97.1
South American	90.0
Argentinean	144.2
Colombian	67.9
Peruvian	88.8
Spaniard	83.1

Average Household Size

Group	People
Total Population	3.95
Hispanic or Latino (of any race)	4.80
Central American, ex. Mexican	4.51
Guatemalan	4.70
Honduran	5.00
Nicaraguan	4.00
Salvadoran	4.70
Cuban	2.94
Mexican	4.85
Puerto Rican	3.17
South American	3.08
Argentinean	2.63
Colombian	3.28
Peruvian	3.62
Spaniard	3.59

Median Age

Group	Years
Total Population	29.9
Hispanic or Latino (of any race)	26.1
Central American, ex. Mexican	31.4
Guatemalan	31.3
Honduran	29.8
Nicaraguan	37.8
Salvadoran	30.6
Cuban	33.0
Mexican	25.9
Puerto Rican	29.0
South American	36.4
Argentinean	38.5
Colombian	33.5
Peruvian	36.8
Spaniard	34.4

High School Graduates
(Universe: Population 25 Years and Over)

Group	Number	%
Total Population	71,280	63.0
Hispanic or Latino (of any race)	32,989	46.7
Central American, ex. Mexican	741	50.0
Mexican	30,609	45.7

Four-Year College Graduates
(Universe: Population 25 Years and Over)

Group	Number	%
Total Population	17,431	15.4
Hispanic or Latino (of any race)	4,253	6.0
Central American, ex. Mexican	126	8.5
Mexican	3,772	5.6

Population Age 3–17 Enrolled in Public School
(Universe: Population Age 3–17 Enrolled in School)

Group	Number	%
Total Population	39,229	94.0
Hispanic or Latino (of any race)	33,016	96.2
Central American, ex. Mexican	479	99.2
Mexican	31,846	96.3

Population Age 3–17 Enrolled in Private School
(Universe: Population Age 3–17 Enrolled in School)

Group	Number	%
Total Population	2,509	6.0
Hispanic or Latino (of any race)	1,290	3.8
Central American, ex. Mexican	4	0.8
Mexican	1,226	3.7

Foreign-Born Population

Group	Number	%
Total Population	73,154	38.0
Hispanic or Latino (of any race)	59,746	44.2
Central American, ex. Mexican	1,759	73.3
Mexican	57,094	44.3

Foreign-Born Naturalized U.S. Citizens

Group	Number	%
Total Population	26,136	35.7
Hispanic or Latino (of any race)	16,716	28.0
Central American, ex. Mexican	448	25.5
Mexican	15,821	27.7

Language Spoken at Home: English Only
(Universe: Population 5 Years and Over)

Group	Number	%
Total Population	56,605	32.1
Hispanic or Latino (of any race)	17,398	14.3
Central American, ex. Mexican	74	3.3
Mexican	16,096	13.9

Language Spoken at Home: Spanish
(Universe: Population 5 Years and Over)

Group	Number	%
Total Population	105,400	59.8
Hispanic or Latino (of any race)	103,646	85.3
Central American, ex. Mexican	2,195	96.7
Mexican	99,231	85.7

Unemployment Rate
(Universe: Population 16 Years and Over)

Group	%
Total Population	8.2
Hispanic or Latino (of any race)	9.6
Central American, ex. Mexican	17.7
Mexican	9.5

Class of Worker: Private Wage and Salary
(Universe: Civilian Employed Population 16 Years and Over)

Group	Number	%
Total Population	66,975	77.5
Hispanic or Latino (of any race)	48,359	82.3
Central American, ex. Mexican	1,162	92.6
Mexican	45,935	82.4

Class of Worker: Government
(Universe: Civilian Employed Population 16 Years and Over)

Group	Number	%
Total Population	13,453	15.6
Hispanic or Latino (of any race)	6,664	11.3
Central American, ex. Mexican	65	5.2
Mexican	6,256	11.2

Means of Transportation to Work: Car, Truck or Van
(Universe: Workers 16 Years and Over)

Group	Number	%
Total Population	77,781	91.7
Hispanic or Latino (of any race)	52,533	92.4
Central American, ex. Mexican	1,134	88.2
Mexican	49,805	92.5

Means of Transportation to Work: Public Transportation (ex. Taxicab)
(Universe: Workers 16 Years and Over)

Group	Number	%
Total Population	1,318	1.6
Hispanic or Latino (of any race)	1,002	1.8
Central American, ex. Mexican	43	3.3
Mexican	959	1.8

Homeownership Rate
(Universe: Occupied Housing Units)

Group	%
Total Population	55.7
Hispanic or Latino (of any race)	49.4
Central American, ex. Mexican	35.4
Guatemalan	38.7
Honduran	33.3
Nicaraguan	40.4
Salvadoran	30.4
Cuban	52.1
Mexican	49.9
Puerto Rican	46.9
South American	49.3
Argentinean	46.9
Colombian	65.1
Peruvian	44.4
Spaniard	61.6

Median Home Value

Group	Dollars
Total Population	454,700
Hispanic or Latino (of any race)	422,700
Central American, ex. Mexican	356,900
Mexican	423,100

Median Gross Rent

Group	Dollars
Total Population	1,219
Hispanic or Latino (of any race)	1,173
Central American, ex. Mexican	1,377
Mexican	1,154

Median Household Income
(2010 Inflation-Adjusted Dollars)

Group	Dollars
Total Population	59,015
Hispanic or Latino (of any race)	51,961
Central American, ex. Mexican	58,799
Mexican	51,529

Per Capita Income
(2010 Inflation-Adjusted Dollars)

Group	Dollars
Total Population	20,613
Hispanic or Latino (of any race)	14,877
Central American, ex. Mexican	18,411
Mexican	14,649

Households with $100,000+ Income

Group	Number	%
Total Population	12,364	24.1
Hispanic or Latino (of any race)	5,394	18.1
Central American, ex. Mexican	69	9.8
Mexican	5,170	18.4

Households with Food Stamps/SNAP Benefits During Past 12 Months

Group	Number	%
Total Population	4,223	8.2
Hispanic or Latino (of any race)	3,294	11.1
Central American, ex. Mexican	25	3.5
Mexican	3,162	11.3

Poverty Rate
(Income in Past 12 Months Below Poverty Level)

Group	%
Total Population	15.1
Hispanic or Latino (of any race)	18.0
Central American, ex. Mexican	19.4
Mexican	17.7

Palm Desert

Population

Group	Number	%TP[1]	%HP[2]
Total Population	48,445	100.0	–
Hispanic or Latino (of any race)	11,038	22.8	100.0
Central American, ex. Mexican	542	1.1	4.9
Guatemalan	108	0.2	1.0
Salvadoran	267	0.6	2.4
Cuban	111	0.2	1.0
Mexican	9,147	18.9	82.9
Puerto Rican	152	0.3	1.4
South American	330	0.7	3.0
Colombian	106	0.2	1.0
Peruvian	110	0.2	1.0
Spaniard	141	0.3	1.3

Population Growth: 2000–2010

Group	%
Total Population	17.7
Hispanic or Latino (of any race)	57.0
Central American, ex. Mexican	191.4
Mexican	65.3
Puerto Rican	46.2
South American	123.0

Males per 100 Females

Group	Number
Total Population	88.7
Hispanic or Latino (of any race)	95.3
Central American, ex. Mexican	106.1

Notes: (1) Percent of total population; (2) Percent of Hispanic/Latino population; Profiles include places with an overall population of at least 125,000, OR an overall population of at least 25,000 where the Hispanic/Latino population is at least 20% of the overall population. In states where less than five places meet either of these criteria, we have included places with at least 10,000 total population with the highest percentage of Hispanic/Latino population. These places are identified with an asterisk (*); Please refer to the User's Guide for a full explanation of data.

Group	
Guatemalan	107.7
Salvadoran	103.8
Cuban	94.7
Mexican	96.2
Puerto Rican	81.0
South American	85.4
Colombian	65.6
Peruvian	100.0
Spaniard	98.6

Average Household Size

Group	People
Total Population	2.08
Hispanic or Latino (of any race)	3.10
Central American, ex. Mexican	3.45
Guatemalan	3.16
Salvadoran	3.51
Cuban	2.39
Mexican	3.19
Puerto Rican	2.22
South American	2.51
Colombian	2.57
Peruvian	2.79
Spaniard	1.95

Median Age

Group	Years
Total Population	53.0
Hispanic or Latino (of any race)	27.2
Central American, ex. Mexican	30.4
Guatemalan	31.7
Salvadoran	29.9
Cuban	38.5
Mexican	26.3
Puerto Rican	36.0
South American	41.0
Colombian	46.5
Peruvian	35.0
Spaniard	46.8

High School Graduates
(Universe: Population 25 Years and Over)

Group	Number	%
Total Population	34,070	90.3
Hispanic or Latino (of any race)	3,778	66.9
Mexican	3,078	69.0

Four-Year College Graduates
(Universe: Population 25 Years and Over)

Group	Number	%
Total Population	12,662	33.6
Hispanic or Latino (of any race)	686	12.1
Mexican	468	10.5

Population Age 3–17 Enrolled in Public School
(Universe: Population Age 3–17 Enrolled in School)

Group	Number	%
Total Population	4,739	76.5
Hispanic or Latino (of any race)	2,122	87.6
Mexican	1,600	84.2

Population Age 3–17 Enrolled in Private School
(Universe: Population Age 3–17 Enrolled in School)

Group	Number	%
Total Population	1,457	23.5
Hispanic or Latino (of any race)	300	12.4
Mexican	300	15.8

Foreign-Born Population

Group	Number	%
Total Population	8,971	18.5
Hispanic or Latino (of any race)	4,200	40.6
Mexican	3,328	39.8

Foreign-Born Naturalized U.S. Citizens

Group	Number	%
Total Population	3,931	43.8
Hispanic or Latino (of any race)	919	21.9
Mexican	568	17.1

Language Spoken at Home: English Only
(Universe: Population 5 Years and Over)

Group	Number	%
Total Population	36,527	78.5
Hispanic or Latino (of any race)	2,756	29.4
Mexican	2,168	29.0

Language Spoken at Home: Spanish
(Universe: Population 5 Years and Over)

Group	Number	%
Total Population	7,256	15.6
Hispanic or Latino (of any race)	6,603	70.6
Mexican	5,313	71.0

Unemployment Rate
(Universe: Population 16 Years and Over)

Group	%
Total Population	8.0
Hispanic or Latino (of any race)	8.9
Mexican	10.3

Class of Worker: Private Wage and Salary
(Universe: Civilian Employed Population 16 Years and Over)

Group	Number	%
Total Population	15,557	78.7
Hispanic or Latino (of any race)	4,267	86.7
Mexican	3,323	85.9

Class of Worker: Government
(Universe: Civilian Employed Population 16 Years and Over)

Group	Number	%
Total Population	1,764	8.9
Hispanic or Latino (of any race)	276	5.6
Mexican	233	6.0

Means of Transportation to Work: Car, Truck or Van
(Universe: Workers 16 Years and Over)

Group	Number	%
Total Population	16,628	87.0
Hispanic or Latino (of any race)	4,385	89.6
Mexican	3,474	90.4

Means of Transportation to Work: Public Transportation (ex. Taxicab)
(Universe: Workers 16 Years and Over)

Group	Number	%
Total Population	228	1.2
Hispanic or Latino (of any race)	100	2.0
Mexican	60	1.6

Homeownership Rate
(Universe: Occupied Housing Units)

Group	%
Total Population	65.6
Hispanic or Latino (of any race)	35.7
Central American, ex. Mexican	28.9
Guatemalan	28.1
Salvadoran	33.3
Cuban	50.0
Mexican	35.3
Puerto Rican	41.7
South American	41.5
Colombian	29.8
Peruvian	30.8
Spaniard	46.9

Median Home Value

Group	Dollars
Total Population	384,300
Hispanic or Latino (of any race)	328,400
Mexican	306,900

Median Gross Rent

Group	Dollars
Total Population	1,160
Hispanic or Latino (of any race)	1,007
Mexican	1,030

Median Household Income
(2010 Inflation-Adjusted Dollars)

Group	Dollars
Total Population	56,897
Hispanic or Latino (of any race)	42,368
Mexican	38,432

Per Capita Income
(2010 Inflation-Adjusted Dollars)

Group	Dollars
Total Population	41,237
Hispanic or Latino (of any race)	17,576
Mexican	15,156

Households with $100,000+ Income

Group	Number	%
Total Population	6,407	27.8
Hispanic or Latino (of any race)	407	13.7
Mexican	278	12.4

Households with Food Stamps/SNAP Benefits During Past 12 Months

Group	Number	%
Total Population	279	1.2
Hispanic or Latino (of any race)	87	2.9
Mexican	87	3.9

Poverty Rate
(Income in Past 12 Months Below Poverty Level)

Group	%
Total Population	8.8
Hispanic or Latino (of any race)	11.6
Mexican	14.0

Palm Springs

Population

Group	Number	%TP[1]	%HP[2]
Total Population	44,552	100.0	–
Hispanic or Latino (of any race)	11,286	25.3	100.0
Central American, ex. Mexican	634	1.4	5.6
Guatemalan	299	0.7	2.6
Salvadoran	220	0.5	1.9
Cuban	127	0.3	1.1
Mexican	9,144	20.5	81.0
Puerto Rican	214	0.5	1.9
South American	347	0.8	3.1
Peruvian	168	0.4	1.5
Spaniard	177	0.4	1.6

Population Growth: 2000–2010

Group	%
Total Population	4.1
Hispanic or Latino (of any race)	11.1
Central American, ex. Mexican	53.1
Guatemalan	56.5
Mexican	15.6
Puerto Rican	103.8
South American	84.6

Males per 100 Females

Group	Number
Total Population	129.3
Hispanic or Latino (of any race)	108.3
Central American, ex. Mexican	105.2
Guatemalan	109.1
Salvadoran	103.7
Cuban	182.2
Mexican	107.8
Puerto Rican	135.2
South American	96.0
Peruvian	102.4
Spaniard	126.9

Average Household Size

Group	People
Total Population	1.93
Hispanic or Latino (of any race)	2.98
Central American, ex. Mexican	3.10
Guatemalan	3.20
Salvadoran	3.15
Cuban	1.67
Mexican	3.14
Puerto Rican	1.79
South American	2.38
Peruvian	2.66
Spaniard	2.10

Median Age

Group	Years
Total Population	51.6
Hispanic or Latino (of any race)	29.1
Central American, ex. Mexican	35.2
Guatemalan	33.3
Salvadoran	37.4
Cuban	46.3
Mexican	27.5
Puerto Rican	45.0

Notes: (1) Percent of total population; (2) Percent of Hispanic/Latino population; Profiles include places with an overall population of at least 125,000, OR an overall population of at least 25,000 where the Hispanic/Latino population is at least 20% of the overall population. In states where less than five places meet either of these criteria, we have included places with at least 10,000 total population with the highest percentage of Hispanic/Latino population. These places are identified with an asterisk (*); Please refer to the User's Guide for a full explanation of data.

Group	Number	%
South American		46.3
Peruvian		46.3
Spaniard		43.8

High School Graduates
(Universe: Population 25 Years and Over)

Group	Number	%
Total Population	32,083	88.7
Hispanic or Latino (of any race)	3,733	63.2
Central American, ex. Mexican	172	55.1
Mexican	2,924	60.4
South American	255	91.1

Four-Year College Graduates
(Universe: Population 25 Years and Over)

Group	Number	%
Total Population	11,886	32.9
Hispanic or Latino (of any race)	665	11.3
Central American, ex. Mexican	31	9.9
Mexican	384	7.9
South American	121	43.2

Population Age 3–17 Enrolled in Public School
(Universe: Population Age 3–17 Enrolled in School)

Group	Number	%
Total Population	4,180	88.1
Hispanic or Latino (of any race)	2,400	94.9
Central American, ex. Mexican	55	79.7
Mexican	2,162	94.9
South American	127	100.0

Population Age 3–17 Enrolled in Private School
(Universe: Population Age 3–17 Enrolled in School)

Group	Number	%
Total Population	562	11.9
Hispanic or Latino (of any race)	129	5.1
Central American, ex. Mexican	14	20.3
Mexican	115	5.1
South American	0	0.0

Foreign-Born Population

Group	Number	%
Total Population	8,939	19.9
Hispanic or Latino (of any race)	4,558	43.5
Central American, ex. Mexican	305	66.3
Mexican	3,750	42.4
South American	359	71.2

Foreign-Born Naturalized U.S. Citizens

Group	Number	%
Total Population	3,640	40.7
Hispanic or Latino (of any race)	1,279	28.1
Central American, ex. Mexican	130	42.6
Mexican	851	22.7
South American	242	67.4

Language Spoken at Home: English Only
(Universe: Population 5 Years and Over)

Group	Number	%
Total Population	31,160	72.1
Hispanic or Latino (of any race)	1,791	18.9
Central American, ex. Mexican	75	16.6
Mexican	1,415	17.8
South American	61	12.3

Language Spoken at Home: Spanish
(Universe: Population 5 Years and Over)

Group	Number	%
Total Population	8,689	20.1
Hispanic or Latino (of any race)	7,657	80.8
Central American, ex. Mexican	378	83.4
Mexican	6,531	82.2
South American	432	86.9

Unemployment Rate
(Universe: Population 16 Years and Over)

Group	%
Total Population	8.6
Hispanic or Latino (of any race)	8.6
Central American, ex. Mexican	2.9
Mexican	9.3
South American	0.8

Class of Worker: Private Wage and Salary
(Universe: Civilian Employed Population 16 Years and Over)

Group	Number	%
Total Population	15,029	74.9
Hispanic or Latino (of any race)	3,835	84.2
Central American, ex. Mexican	239	89.2
Mexican	3,094	83.2
South American	224	88.2

Class of Worker: Government
(Universe: Civilian Employed Population 16 Years and Over)

Group	Number	%
Total Population	1,667	8.3
Hispanic or Latino (of any race)	154	3.4
Central American, ex. Mexican	16	6.0
Mexican	107	2.9
South American	9	3.5

Means of Transportation to Work: Car, Truck or Van
(Universe: Workers 16 Years and Over)

Group	Number	%
Total Population	16,592	84.4
Hispanic or Latino (of any race)	3,981	89.0
Central American, ex. Mexican	219	94.8
Mexican	3,285	89.4
South American	241	95.6

Means of Transportation to Work: Public Transportation (ex. Taxicab)
(Universe: Workers 16 Years and Over)

Group	Number	%
Total Population	319	1.6
Hispanic or Latino (of any race)	101	2.3
Central American, ex. Mexican	3	1.3
Mexican	66	1.8
South American	0	0.0

Homeownership Rate
(Universe: Occupied Housing Units)

Group	%
Total Population	58.7
Hispanic or Latino (of any race)	32.3
Central American, ex. Mexican	22.3
Guatemalan	21.2
Salvadoran	19.1
Cuban	51.9
Mexican	31.3
Puerto Rican	40.4
South American	39.7
Peruvian	38.5
Spaniard	50.0

Median Home Value

Group	Dollars
Total Population	352,700
Hispanic or Latino (of any race)	338,500
Central American, ex. Mexican	404,500
Mexican	319,300
South American	350,900

Median Gross Rent

Group	Dollars
Total Population	933
Hispanic or Latino (of any race)	837
Central American, ex. Mexican	820
Mexican	831
South American	897

Median Household Income
(2010 Inflation-Adjusted Dollars)

Group	Dollars
Total Population	44,728
Hispanic or Latino (of any race)	35,477
Central American, ex. Mexican	28,800
Mexican	35,070
South American	42,019

Per Capita Income
(2010 Inflation-Adjusted Dollars)

Group	Dollars
Total Population	37,094
Hispanic or Latino (of any race)	17,120
Central American, ex. Mexican	20,485
Mexican	15,282
South American	15,392

Households with $100,000+ Income

Group	Number	%
Total Population	4,438	19.0
Hispanic or Latino (of any race)	272	7.4
Central American, ex. Mexican	6	2.5
Mexican	160	5.5
South American	4	2.2

Households with Food Stamps/SNAP Benefits During Past 12 Months

Group	Number	%
Total Population	432	1.8
Hispanic or Latino (of any race)	187	5.1
Central American, ex. Mexican	7	2.9
Mexican	139	4.8
South American	26	14.1

Poverty Rate
(Income in Past 12 Months Below Poverty Level)

Group	%
Total Population	11.9
Hispanic or Latino (of any race)	15.8
Central American, ex. Mexican	17.6
Mexican	16.2
South American	9.3

Palmdale

Population

Group	Number	%TP[1]	%HP[2]
Total Population	152,750	100.0	–
Hispanic or Latino (of any race)	83,097	54.4	100.0
Central American, ex. Mexican	14,815	9.7	17.8
Costa Rican	176	0.1	0.2
Guatemalan	3,618	2.4	4.4
Honduran	656	0.4	0.8
Nicaraguan	650	0.4	0.8
Panamanian	124	0.1	0.1
Salvadoran	9,488	6.2	11.4
Cuban	705	0.5	0.8
Mexican	58,207	38.1	70.0
Puerto Rican	1,138	0.7	1.4
South American	1,951	1.3	2.3
Argentinean	307	0.2	0.4
Chilean	172	0.1	0.2
Colombian	385	0.3	0.5
Ecuadorian	385	0.3	0.5
Peruvian	573	0.4	0.7
Spaniard	603	0.4	0.7

Population Growth: 2000–2010

Group	%
Total Population	30.9
Hispanic or Latino (of any race)	88.9
Central American, ex. Mexican	313.9
Guatemalan	371.7
Nicaraguan	205.2
Salvadoran	359.0
Cuban	20.3
Mexican	93.3
Puerto Rican	32.6
South American	147.0
Argentinean	91.9
Colombian	156.7
Ecuadorian	277.5
Peruvian	258.1

Males per 100 Females

Group	Number
Total Population	95.3
Hispanic or Latino (of any race)	96.7
Central American, ex. Mexican	90.9
Costa Rican	91.3
Guatemalan	97.0
Honduran	85.8
Nicaraguan	78.1
Panamanian	55.0
Salvadoran	90.4
Cuban	85.0
Mexican	98.6
Puerto Rican	95.9
South American	90.5

Notes: (1) Percent of total population; (2) Percent of Hispanic/Latino population; Profiles include places with an overall population of at least 125,000, OR an overall population of at least 25,000 where the Hispanic/Latino population is at least 20% of the overall population. In states where less than five places meet either of these criteria, we have included places with at least 10,000 total population with the highest percentage of Hispanic/Latino population. These places are identified with an asterisk (*); Please refer to the User's Guide for a full explanation of data.

Argentinean	104.7
Chilean	117.7
Colombian	73.4
Ecuadorian	86.0
Peruvian	94.2
Spaniard	94.5

Average Household Size

Group	People
Total Population	3.55
Hispanic or Latino (of any race)	4.31
Central American, ex. Mexican	4.40
Costa Rican	4.20
Guatemalan	4.38
Honduran	4.58
Nicaraguan	4.53
Panamanian	2.94
Salvadoran	4.42
Cuban	3.38
Mexican	4.39
Puerto Rican	3.39
South American	3.66
Argentinean	3.38
Chilean	4.00
Colombian	3.55
Ecuadorian	3.82
Peruvian	3.76
Spaniard	3.72

Median Age

Group	Years
Total Population	29.7
Hispanic or Latino (of any race)	24.8
Central American, ex. Mexican	33.1
Costa Rican	30.8
Guatemalan	34.5
Honduran	32.3
Nicaraguan	34.8
Panamanian	35.0
Salvadoran	32.5
Cuban	35.1
Mexican	23.2
Puerto Rican	24.8
South American	38.4
Argentinean	39.9
Chilean	34.0
Colombian	36.9
Ecuadorian	37.4
Peruvian	39.0
Spaniard	27.4

High School Graduates
(Universe: Population 25 Years and Over)

Group	Number	%
Total Population	58,577	73.4
Hispanic or Latino (of any race)	20,324	54.8
Central American, ex. Mexican	5,228	58.6
Guatemalan	1,270	53.2
Salvadoran	3,266	58.8
Mexican	12,597	50.9
Puerto Rican	364	66.7
South American	970	84.9

Four-Year College Graduates
(Universe: Population 25 Years and Over)

Group	Number	%
Total Population	12,087	15.2
Hispanic or Latino (of any race)	2,465	6.6
Central American, ex. Mexican	773	8.7
Guatemalan	139	5.8
Salvadoran	590	10.6
Mexican	1,221	4.9
Puerto Rican	0	0.0
South American	166	14.5

Population Age 3–17 Enrolled in Public School
(Universe: Population Age 3–17 Enrolled in School)

Group	Number	%
Total Population	37,364	92.9
Hispanic or Latino (of any race)	23,348	95.5
Central American, ex. Mexican	4,154	97.3
Guatemalan	954	96.8
Salvadoran	2,878	97.2
Mexican	17,433	95.5
Puerto Rican	138	78.0
South American	237	92.2

Population Age 3–17 Enrolled in Private School
(Universe: Population Age 3–17 Enrolled in School)

Group	Number	%
Total Population	2,871	7.1
Hispanic or Latino (of any race)	1,101	4.5
Central American, ex. Mexican	116	2.7
Guatemalan	32	3.2
Salvadoran	84	2.8
Mexican	830	4.5
Puerto Rican	39	22.0
South American	20	7.8

Foreign-Born Population

Group	Number	%
Total Population	36,828	25.2
Hispanic or Latino (of any race)	29,226	37.8
Central American, ex. Mexican	8,934	56.0
Guatemalan	2,577	62.9
Salvadoran	5,424	52.5
Mexican	18,149	33.3
Puerto Rican	13	1.3
South American	1,208	73.7

Foreign-Born Naturalized U.S. Citizens

Group	Number	%
Total Population	16,126	43.8
Hispanic or Latino (of any race)	11,095	38.0
Central American, ex. Mexican	3,689	41.3
Guatemalan	852	33.1
Salvadoran	2,347	43.3
Mexican	6,314	34.8
Puerto Rican	13	100.0
South American	592	49.0

Language Spoken at Home: English Only
(Universe: Population 5 Years and Over)

Group	Number	%
Total Population	71,973	53.5
Hispanic or Latino (of any race)	15,327	22.0
Central American, ex. Mexican	1,290	8.8
Guatemalan	310	8.2
Salvadoran	880	9.3
Mexican	11,846	24.4
Puerto Rican	515	55.9
South American	154	9.8

Language Spoken at Home: Spanish
(Universe: Population 5 Years and Over)

Group	Number	%
Total Population	55,581	41.3
Hispanic or Latino (of any race)	54,251	77.9
Central American, ex. Mexican	13,345	91.2
Guatemalan	3,451	91.8
Salvadoran	8,564	90.7
Mexican	36,800	75.6
Puerto Rican	407	44.1
South American	1,397	88.8

Unemployment Rate
(Universe: Population 16 Years and Over)

Group	%
Total Population	12.0
Hispanic or Latino (of any race)	12.4
Central American, ex. Mexican	13.6
Guatemalan	10.5
Salvadoran	15.3
Mexican	11.8
Puerto Rican	8.4
South American	9.5

Class of Worker: Private Wage and Salary
(Universe: Civilian Employed Population 16 Years and Over)

Group	Number	%
Total Population	43,249	76.4
Hispanic or Latino (of any race)	22,661	80.7
Central American, ex. Mexican	5,356	83.8
Guatemalan	1,552	88.3
Salvadoran	3,217	81.5
Mexican	15,585	81.1
Puerto Rican	323	80.0
South American	620	69.5

Class of Worker: Government
(Universe: Civilian Employed Population 16 Years and Over)

Group	Number	%
Total Population	9,199	16.3
Hispanic or Latino (of any race)	2,857	10.2
Central American, ex. Mexican	311	4.9
Guatemalan	53	3.0
Salvadoran	232	5.9
Mexican	2,069	10.8
Puerto Rican	81	20.0
South American	166	18.6

Means of Transportation to Work: Car, Truck or Van
(Universe: Workers 16 Years and Over)

Group	Number	%
Total Population	50,740	92.0
Hispanic or Latino (of any race)	25,613	93.7
Central American, ex. Mexican	5,838	93.2
Guatemalan	1,588	93.1
Salvadoran	3,642	94.0
Mexican	17,762	95.1
Puerto Rican	332	82.2
South American	754	91.0

Means of Transportation to Work: Public Transportation (ex. Taxicab)
(Universe: Workers 16 Years and Over)

Group	Number	%
Total Population	1,632	3.0
Hispanic or Latino (of any race)	675	2.5
Central American, ex. Mexican	210	3.4
Guatemalan	58	3.4
Salvadoran	106	2.7
Mexican	353	1.9
Puerto Rican	26	6.4
South American	71	8.6

Homeownership Rate
(Universe: Occupied Housing Units)

Group	%
Total Population	67.9
Hispanic or Latino (of any race)	66.0
Central American, ex. Mexican	70.7
Costa Rican	76.1
Guatemalan	71.4
Honduran	62.2
Nicaraguan	65.0
Panamanian	61.7
Salvadoran	71.4
Cuban	69.6
Mexican	64.5
Puerto Rican	61.8
South American	76.1
Argentinean	79.6
Chilean	66.7
Colombian	71.6
Ecuadorian	76.1
Peruvian	78.0
Spaniard	67.1

Median Home Value

Group	Dollars
Total Population	277,700
Hispanic or Latino (of any race)	243,300
Central American, ex. Mexican	223,500
Guatemalan	197,500
Salvadoran	221,600
Mexican	239,200
Puerto Rican	270,200
South American	321,800

Median Gross Rent

Group	Dollars
Total Population	1,078
Hispanic or Latino (of any race)	1,048
Central American, ex. Mexican	1,088
Guatemalan	1,004
Salvadoran	1,098
Mexican	1,024
Puerto Rican	906
South American	1,144

STATE & PLACE PROFILES

Notes: (1) Percent of total population; (2) Percent of Hispanic/Latino population; Profiles include places with an overall population of at least 125,000, OR an overall population of at least 25,000 where the Hispanic/Latino population is at least 20% of the overall population. In states where less than five places meet either of these criteria, we have included places with at least 10,000 total population with the highest percentage of Hispanic/Latino population. These places are identified with an asterisk (*); Please refer to the User's Guide for a full explanation of data.

Median Household Income
(2010 Inflation-Adjusted Dollars)

Group	Dollars
Total Population	55,696
Hispanic or Latino (of any race)	49,302
Central American, ex. Mexican	46,985
Guatemalan	51,425
Salvadoran	42,460
Mexican	50,076
Puerto Rican	69,091
South American	59,375

Per Capita Income
(2010 Inflation-Adjusted Dollars)

Group	Dollars
Total Population	19,410
Hispanic or Latino (of any race)	13,302
Central American, ex. Mexican	13,237
Guatemalan	13,433
Salvadoran	12,796
Mexican	12,822
Puerto Rican	20,360
South American	22,860

Households with $100,000+ Income

Group	Number	%
Total Population	8,491	21.1
Hispanic or Latino (of any race)	2,286	13.3
Central American, ex. Mexican	366	9.4
Guatemalan	128	13.5
Salvadoran	194	7.9
Mexican	1,488	13.0
Puerto Rican	92	31.7
South American	153	24.0

Households with Food Stamps/SNAP Benefits During Past 12 Months

Group	Number	%
Total Population	3,892	9.7
Hispanic or Latino (of any race)	2,089	12.2
Central American, ex. Mexican	484	12.5
Guatemalan	108	11.4
Salvadoran	318	12.9
Mexican	1,514	13.2
Puerto Rican	33	11.4
South American	39	6.1

Poverty Rate
(Income in Past 12 Months Below Poverty Level)

Group	%
Total Population	17.7
Hispanic or Latino (of any race)	21.1
Central American, ex. Mexican	19.7
Guatemalan	11.5
Salvadoran	21.3
Mexican	22.1
Puerto Rican	13.5
South American	5.1

Paramount

Population

Group	Number	%TP[1]	%HP[2]
Total Population	54,098	100.0	–
Hispanic or Latino (of any race)	42,547	78.6	100.0
Central American, ex. Mexican	2,962	5.5	7.0
Guatemalan	943	1.7	2.2
Honduran	206	0.4	0.5
Nicaraguan	249	0.5	0.6
Salvadoran	1,463	2.7	3.4
Cuban	133	0.2	0.3
Mexican	37,077	68.5	87.1
Puerto Rican	234	0.4	0.5
South American	426	0.8	1.0
Peruvian	169	0.3	0.4

Population Growth: 2000–2010

Group	%
Total Population	-2.1
Hispanic or Latino (of any race)	6.5
Central American, ex. Mexican	77.9
Guatemalan	89.7
Honduran	102.0
Nicaraguan	94.5
Salvadoran	101.8
Cuban	6.4
Mexican	11.9
Puerto Rican	10.4
South American	73.2

Males per 100 Females

Group	Number
Total Population	94.7
Hispanic or Latino (of any race)	98.4
Central American, ex. Mexican	89.5
Guatemalan	92.1
Honduran	80.7
Nicaraguan	91.5
Salvadoran	87.6
Cuban	75.0
Mexican	99.4
Puerto Rican	112.7
South American	106.8
Peruvian	116.7

Average Household Size

Group	People
Total Population	3.87
Hispanic or Latino (of any race)	4.45
Central American, ex. Mexican	4.27
Guatemalan	4.62
Honduran	4.04
Nicaraguan	3.89
Salvadoran	4.20
Cuban	2.70
Mexican	4.52
Puerto Rican	3.66
South American	3.26
Peruvian	3.48

Median Age

Group	Years
Total Population	28.6
Hispanic or Latino (of any race)	26.5
Central American, ex. Mexican	34.8
Guatemalan	36.0
Honduran	34.7
Nicaraguan	35.8
Salvadoran	33.6
Cuban	36.8
Mexican	25.9
Puerto Rican	27.6
South American	36.9
Peruvian	33.5

High School Graduates
(Universe: Population 25 Years and Over)

Group	Number	%
Total Population	17,236	57.5
Hispanic or Latino (of any race)	10,345	47.0
Central American, ex. Mexican	836	39.7
Guatemalan	242	27.3
Salvadoran	421	50.4
Mexican	8,930	46.9

Four-Year College Graduates
(Universe: Population 25 Years and Over)

Group	Number	%
Total Population	2,912	9.7
Hispanic or Latino (of any race)	1,086	4.9
Central American, ex. Mexican	66	3.1
Guatemalan	0	0.0
Salvadoran	56	6.7
Mexican	968	5.1

Population Age 3–17 Enrolled in Public School
(Universe: Population Age 3–17 Enrolled in School)

Group	Number	%
Total Population	13,305	95.1
Hispanic or Latino (of any race)	11,585	97.0
Central American, ex. Mexican	428	88.8
Guatemalan	76	75.2
Salvadoran	254	89.8
Mexican	10,674	97.3

Population Age 3–17 Enrolled in Private School
(Universe: Population Age 3–17 Enrolled in School)

Group	Number	%
Total Population	680	4.9
Hispanic or Latino (of any race)	354	3.0
Central American, ex. Mexican	54	11.2
Guatemalan	25	24.8
Salvadoran	29	10.2
Mexican	300	2.7

Foreign-Born Population

Group	Number	%
Total Population	21,325	39.4
Hispanic or Latino (of any race)	19,356	45.9
Central American, ex. Mexican	2,222	67.9
Guatemalan	971	70.2
Salvadoran	868	65.6
Mexican	16,653	44.6

Foreign-Born Naturalized U.S. Citizens

Group	Number	%
Total Population	7,529	35.3
Hispanic or Latino (of any race)	6,225	32.2
Central American, ex. Mexican	776	34.9
Guatemalan	340	35.0
Salvadoran	349	40.2
Mexican	5,221	31.4

Language Spoken at Home: English Only
(Universe: Population 5 Years and Over)

Group	Number	%
Total Population	12,399	25.0
Hispanic or Latino (of any race)	3,855	10.0
Central American, ex. Mexican	131	4.2
Guatemalan	40	3.0
Salvadoran	36	2.8
Mexican	3,425	10.1

Language Spoken at Home: Spanish
(Universe: Population 5 Years and Over)

Group	Number	%
Total Population	34,989	70.5
Hispanic or Latino (of any race)	34,612	90.0
Central American, ex. Mexican	2,999	95.8
Guatemalan	1,278	97.0
Salvadoran	1,259	97.2
Mexican	30,444	89.9

Unemployment Rate
(Universe: Population 16 Years and Over)

Group	%
Total Population	10.2
Hispanic or Latino (of any race)	10.1
Central American, ex. Mexican	8.3
Guatemalan	9.1
Salvadoran	9.6
Mexican	10.4

Class of Worker: Private Wage and Salary
(Universe: Civilian Employed Population 16 Years and Over)

Group	Number	%
Total Population	17,812	81.1
Hispanic or Latino (of any race)	14,282	84.6
Central American, ex. Mexican	1,377	83.4
Guatemalan	643	86.7
Salvadoran	456	76.0
Mexican	12,363	84.6

Class of Worker: Government
(Universe: Civilian Employed Population 16 Years and Over)

Group	Number	%
Total Population	2,657	12.1
Hispanic or Latino (of any race)	1,463	8.7
Central American, ex. Mexican	177	10.7
Guatemalan	60	8.1
Salvadoran	107	17.8
Mexican	1,236	8.5

Means of Transportation to Work: Car, Truck or Van
(Universe: Workers 16 Years and Over)

Group	Number	%
Total Population	18,803	87.5
Hispanic or Latino (of any race)	14,555	88.0
Central American, ex. Mexican	1,423	88.4

Notes: (1) Percent of total population; (2) Percent of Hispanic/Latino population; Profiles include places with an overall population of at least 125,000, OR an overall population of at least 25,000 where the Hispanic/Latino population is at least 20% of the overall population. In states where less than five places meet either of these criteria, we have included places with at least 10,000 total population with the highest percentage of Hispanic/Latino population. These places are identified with an asterisk (*); Please refer to the User's Guide for a full explanation of data.

Guatemalan	617	86.3
Salvadoran	559	93.2
Mexican	12,636	88.3

Means of Transportation to Work: Public Transportation (ex. Taxicab)
(Universe: Workers 16 Years and Over)

Group	Number	%
Total Population	996	4.6
Hispanic or Latino (of any race)	632	3.8
Central American, ex. Mexican	55	3.4
Guatemalan	28	3.9
Salvadoran	27	4.5
Mexican	554	3.9

Homeownership Rate
(Universe: Occupied Housing Units)

Group	%
Total Population	43.4
Hispanic or Latino (of any race)	42.7
Central American, ex. Mexican	43.7
Guatemalan	42.1
Honduran	27.9
Nicaraguan	45.1
Salvadoran	45.6
Cuban	45.5
Mexican	42.9
Puerto Rican	42.6
South American	43.4
Peruvian	41.7

Median Home Value

Group	Dollars
Total Population	336,300
Hispanic or Latino (of any race)	347,300
Central American, ex. Mexican	341,900
Guatemalan	325,800
Salvadoran	325,700
Mexican	351,300

Median Gross Rent

Group	Dollars
Total Population	1,107
Hispanic or Latino (of any race)	1,109
Central American, ex. Mexican	1,094
Guatemalan	970
Salvadoran	1,166
Mexican	1,109

Median Household Income
(2010 Inflation-Adjusted Dollars)

Group	Dollars
Total Population	41,333
Hispanic or Latino (of any race)	41,025
Central American, ex. Mexican	49,057
Guatemalan	44,375
Salvadoran	47,847
Mexican	40,857

Per Capita Income
(2010 Inflation-Adjusted Dollars)

Group	Dollars
Total Population	13,936
Hispanic or Latino (of any race)	12,012
Central American, ex. Mexican	14,093
Guatemalan	13,697
Salvadoran	15,379
Mexican	11,740

Households with $100,000+ Income

Group	Number	%
Total Population	1,335	9.2
Hispanic or Latino (of any race)	764	7.7
Central American, ex. Mexican	84	9.1
Guatemalan	11	2.9
Salvadoran	27	6.9
Mexican	672	7.9

Households with Food Stamps/SNAP Benefits During Past 12 Months

Group	Number	%
Total Population	1,442	9.9
Hispanic or Latino (of any race)	1,036	10.4
Central American, ex. Mexican	91	9.8
Guatemalan	54	14.5
Salvadoran	18	4.6

Mexican	911	10.7

Poverty Rate
(Income in Past 12 Months Below Poverty Level)

Group	%
Total Population	19.2
Hispanic or Latino (of any race)	21.0
Central American, ex. Mexican	14.2
Guatemalan	9.1
Salvadoran	19.1
Mexican	21.3

Pasadena

Population

Group	Number	%TP[1]	%HP[2]
Total Population	137,122	100.0	–
Hispanic or Latino (of any race)	46,174	33.7	100.0
Central American, ex. Mexican	5,724	4.2	12.4
Costa Rican	178	0.1	0.4
Guatemalan	1,367	1.0	3.0
Honduran	897	0.7	1.9
Nicaraguan	357	0.3	0.8
Panamanian	170	0.1	0.4
Salvadoran	2,689	2.0	5.8
Cuban	627	0.5	1.4
Mexican	34,168	24.9	74.0
Puerto Rican	624	0.5	1.4
South American	2,283	1.7	4.9
Argentinean	404	0.3	0.9
Bolivian	101	0.1	0.2
Chilean	171	0.1	0.4
Colombian	540	0.4	1.2
Ecuadorian	334	0.2	0.7
Peruvian	584	0.4	1.3
Venezuelan	100	0.1	0.2
Spaniard	474	0.3	1.0

Population Growth: 2000–2010

Group	%
Total Population	2.4
Hispanic or Latino (of any race)	3.2
Central American, ex. Mexican	55.2
Costa Rican	49.6
Guatemalan	92.0
Honduran	93.7
Nicaraguan	90.9
Panamanian	54.5
Salvadoran	59.5
Cuban	24.4
Mexican	5.9
Puerto Rican	45.5
South American	54.9
Argentinean	51.3
Chilean	61.3
Colombian	49.2
Ecuadorian	127.2
Peruvian	71.8
Spaniard	312.2

Males per 100 Females

Group	Number
Total Population	95.1
Hispanic or Latino (of any race)	99.6
Central American, ex. Mexican	94.8
Costa Rican	93.5
Guatemalan	112.9
Honduran	95.0
Nicaraguan	97.2
Panamanian	73.5
Salvadoran	88.3
Cuban	91.2
Mexican	101.8
Puerto Rican	104.6
South American	82.6
Argentinean	82.0
Bolivian	90.6
Chilean	90.0
Colombian	74.8
Ecuadorian	84.5
Peruvian	90.2
Venezuelan	72.4
Spaniard	99.2

Average Household Size

Group	People
Total Population	2.42
Hispanic or Latino (of any race)	3.41
Central American, ex. Mexican	3.66
Costa Rican	2.65
Guatemalan	3.77
Honduran	4.20
Nicaraguan	3.21
Panamanian	2.39
Salvadoran	3.78
Cuban	2.23
Mexican	3.58
Puerto Rican	2.36
South American	2.52
Argentinean	2.12
Bolivian	2.75
Chilean	2.23
Colombian	2.48
Ecuadorian	2.92
Peruvian	2.83
Venezuelan	2.22
Spaniard	2.27

Median Age

Group	Years
Total Population	37.2
Hispanic or Latino (of any race)	30.6
Central American, ex. Mexican	33.3
Costa Rican	44.0
Guatemalan	31.5
Honduran	31.6
Nicaraguan	35.1
Panamanian	41.0
Salvadoran	34.0
Cuban	37.6
Mexican	29.6
Puerto Rican	31.7
South American	40.1
Argentinean	43.2
Bolivian	42.3
Chilean	38.8
Colombian	39.9
Ecuadorian	39.0
Peruvian	40.9
Venezuelan	33.0
Spaniard	38.3

High School Graduates
(Universe: Population 25 Years and Over)

Group	Number	%
Total Population	81,018	83.4
Hispanic or Latino (of any race)	17,014	59.8
Central American, ex. Mexican	1,894	49.9
Guatemalan	472	48.1
Honduran	283	35.0
Salvadoran	836	50.4
Mexican	11,882	56.4
South American	1,711	93.4

Four-Year College Graduates
(Universe: Population 25 Years and Over)

Group	Number	%
Total Population	44,463	45.7
Hispanic or Latino (of any race)	4,882	17.2
Central American, ex. Mexican	539	14.2
Guatemalan	162	16.5
Honduran	32	4.0
Salvadoran	233	14.1
Mexican	3,233	15.3
South American	598	32.6

Population Age 3–17 Enrolled in Public School
(Universe: Population Age 3–17 Enrolled in School)

Group	Number	%
Total Population	14,320	72.0
Hispanic or Latino (of any race)	9,184	87.1
Central American, ex. Mexican	924	91.4
Guatemalan	431	85.9
Honduran	183	100.0
Salvadoran	291	94.8
Mexican	7,740	89.8
South American	150	39.6

Notes: (1) Percent of total population; (2) Percent of Hispanic/Latino population; Profiles include places with an overall population of at least 125,000, OR an overall population of at least 25,000 where the Hispanic/Latino population is at least 20% of the overall population. In states where less than five places meet either of these criteria, we have included places with at least 10,000 total population with the highest percentage of Hispanic/Latino population. These places are identified with an asterisk (*); Please refer to the User's Guide for a full explanation of data.

Population Age 3–17 Enrolled in Private School
(Universe: Population Age 3–17 Enrolled in School)

Group	Number	%
Total Population	5,569	28.0
Hispanic or Latino (of any race)	1,356	12.9
Central American, ex. Mexican	87	8.6
Guatemalan	71	14.1
Honduran	0	0.0
Salvadoran	16	5.2
Mexican	882	10.2
South American	229	60.4

Foreign-Born Population

Group	Number	%
Total Population	40,589	29.7
Hispanic or Latino (of any race)	19,672	42.1
Central American, ex. Mexican	3,236	57.5
Guatemalan	800	45.0
Honduran	770	65.8
Salvadoran	1,472	64.1
Mexican	14,071	39.0
South American	1,675	68.1

Foreign-Born Naturalized U.S. Citizens

Group	Number	%
Total Population	19,513	48.1
Hispanic or Latino (of any race)	7,514	38.2
Central American, ex. Mexican	1,105	34.1
Guatemalan	214	26.8
Honduran	185	24.0
Salvadoran	554	37.6
Mexican	4,921	35.0
South American	982	58.6

Language Spoken at Home: English Only
(Universe: Population 5 Years and Over)

Group	Number	%
Total Population	69,139	53.8
Hispanic or Latino (of any race)	7,692	17.8
Central American, ex. Mexican	316	6.0
Guatemalan	167	10.3
Honduran	0	0.0
Salvadoran	79	3.6
Mexican	6,136	18.5
South American	247	10.6

Language Spoken at Home: Spanish
(Universe: Population 5 Years and Over)

Group	Number	%
Total Population	37,443	29.1
Hispanic or Latino (of any race)	35,416	82.1
Central American, ex. Mexican	4,961	93.8
Guatemalan	1,448	89.7
Honduran	1,105	100.0
Salvadoran	2,109	95.8
Mexican	26,921	81.4
South American	2,093	89.4

Unemployment Rate
(Universe: Population 16 Years and Over)

Group	%
Total Population	8.0
Hispanic or Latino (of any race)	7.8
Central American, ex. Mexican	8.0
Guatemalan	0.0
Honduran	11.2
Salvadoran	10.2
Mexican	7.8
South American	5.3

Class of Worker: Private Wage and Salary
(Universe: Civilian Employed Population 16 Years and Over)

Group	Number	%
Total Population	52,850	77.7
Hispanic or Latino (of any race)	18,000	80.6
Central American, ex. Mexican	2,441	76.6
Guatemalan	765	81.6
Honduran	407	59.2
Salvadoran	1,063	79.2
Mexican	13,560	81.9
South American	1,051	73.1

Class of Worker: Government
(Universe: Civilian Employed Population 16 Years and Over)

Group	Number	%
Total Population	8,926	13.1
Hispanic or Latino (of any race)	2,264	10.1
Central American, ex. Mexican	214	6.7
Guatemalan	97	10.4
Honduran	63	9.2
Salvadoran	54	4.0
Mexican	1,707	10.3
South American	211	14.7

Means of Transportation to Work: Car, Truck or Van
(Universe: Workers 16 Years and Over)

Group	Number	%
Total Population	52,177	79.7
Hispanic or Latino (of any race)	16,752	78.0
Central American, ex. Mexican	2,067	67.7
Guatemalan	523	55.8
Honduran	347	52.2
Salvadoran	1,049	82.3
Mexican	12,524	78.9
South American	1,130	81.0

Means of Transportation to Work: Public Transportation (ex. Taxicab)
(Universe: Workers 16 Years and Over)

Group	Number	%
Total Population	4,345	6.6
Hispanic or Latino (of any race)	1,756	8.2
Central American, ex. Mexican	430	14.1
Guatemalan	172	18.4
Honduran	173	26.0
Salvadoran	85	6.7
Mexican	1,274	8.0
South American	5	0.4

Homeownership Rate
(Universe: Occupied Housing Units)

Group	%
Total Population	45.0
Hispanic or Latino (of any race)	35.7
Central American, ex. Mexican	28.2
Costa Rican	53.2
Guatemalan	23.6
Honduran	23.1
Nicaraguan	29.8
Panamanian	31.7
Salvadoran	29.0
Cuban	47.0
Mexican	36.0
Puerto Rican	33.8
South American	45.0
Argentinean	50.3
Bolivian	53.1
Chilean	47.1
Colombian	46.6
Ecuadorian	54.8
Peruvian	33.6
Venezuelan	37.8
Spaniard	44.7

Median Home Value

Group	Dollars
Total Population	657,300
Hispanic or Latino (of any race)	549,700
Central American, ex. Mexican	441,800
Guatemalan	373,900
Honduran	643,400
Salvadoran	486,400
Mexican	570,200
South American	491,400

Median Gross Rent

Group	Dollars
Total Population	1,260
Hispanic or Latino (of any race)	1,164
Central American, ex. Mexican	1,256
Guatemalan	1,511
Honduran	1,185
Salvadoran	1,115
Mexican	1,144
South American	1,139

Median Household Income
(2010 Inflation-Adjusted Dollars)

Group	Dollars
Total Population	65,422
Hispanic or Latino (of any race)	49,561
Central American, ex. Mexican	48,145
Guatemalan	48,598
Honduran	35,417
Salvadoran	50,152
Mexican	47,821
South American	71,071

Per Capita Income
(2010 Inflation-Adjusted Dollars)

Group	Dollars
Total Population	38,650
Hispanic or Latino (of any race)	19,020
Central American, ex. Mexican	18,126
Guatemalan	17,378
Honduran	14,154
Salvadoran	17,463
Mexican	17,776
South American	28,220

Households with $100,000+ Income

Group	Number	%
Total Population	16,530	31.2
Hispanic or Latino (of any race)	2,101	16.2
Central American, ex. Mexican	196	12.7
Guatemalan	41	10.0
Honduran	50	13.4
Salvadoran	60	10.2
Mexican	1,408	14.6
South American	290	34.2

Households with Food Stamps/SNAP Benefits During Past 12 Months

Group	Number	%
Total Population	2,213	4.2
Hispanic or Latino (of any race)	1,206	9.3
Central American, ex. Mexican	146	9.4
Guatemalan	30	7.3
Honduran	69	18.4
Salvadoran	37	6.3
Mexican	985	10.2
South American	26	3.1

Poverty Rate
(Income in Past 12 Months Below Poverty Level)

Group	%
Total Population	13.5
Hispanic or Latino (of any race)	18.1
Central American, ex. Mexican	23.6
Guatemalan	24.5
Honduran	44.7
Salvadoran	14.8
Mexican	17.8
South American	11.8

Perris

Population

Group	Number	%TP[1]	%HP[2]
Total Population	68,386	100.0	–
Hispanic or Latino (of any race)	49,079	71.8	100.0
Central American, ex. Mexican	2,089	3.1	4.3
Guatemalan	704	1.0	1.4
Honduran	102	0.1	0.2
Nicaraguan	195	0.3	0.4
Salvadoran	997	1.5	2.0
Cuban	211	0.3	0.4
Mexican	43,641	63.8	88.9
Puerto Rican	410	0.6	0.8
South American	403	0.6	0.8
Peruvian	119	0.2	0.2
Spaniard	217	0.3	0.4

Population Growth: 2000–2010

Group	%
Total Population	89.0
Hispanic or Latino (of any race)	141.5
Central American, ex. Mexican	341.6
Guatemalan	506.9

Notes: (1) Percent of total population; (2) Percent of Hispanic/Latino population; Profiles include places with an overall population of at least 125,000, OR an overall population of at least 25,000 where the Hispanic/Latino population is at least 20% of the overall population. In states where less than five places meet either of these criteria, we have included places with at least 10,000 total population with the highest percentage of Hispanic/Latino population. These places are identified with an asterisk (*); Please refer to the User's Guide for a full explanation of data.

Group	%
Salvadoran	347.1
Cuban	93.6
Mexican	160.0
Puerto Rican	63.3
South American	214.8

Males per 100 Females

Group	Number
Total Population	98.3
Hispanic or Latino (of any race)	100.4
Central American, ex. Mexican	102.0
Guatemalan	111.4
Honduran	78.9
Nicaraguan	112.0
Salvadoran	98.6
Cuban	104.9
Mexican	100.5
Puerto Rican	102.0
South American	86.6
Peruvian	70.0
Spaniard	73.6

Average Household Size

Group	People
Total Population	4.16
Hispanic or Latino (of any race)	4.69
Central American, ex. Mexican	4.70
Guatemalan	4.97
Honduran	4.30
Nicaraguan	4.94
Salvadoran	4.61
Cuban	3.63
Mexican	4.73
Puerto Rican	3.64
South American	3.67
Peruvian	4.09
Spaniard	4.18

Median Age

Group	Years
Total Population	25.9
Hispanic or Latino (of any race)	23.6
Central American, ex. Mexican	33.7
Guatemalan	31.8
Honduran	32.3
Nicaraguan	33.7
Salvadoran	34.9
Cuban	36.2
Mexican	23.1
Puerto Rican	25.4
South American	38.1
Peruvian	41.6
Spaniard	28.6

High School Graduates
(Universe: Population 25 Years and Over)

Group	Number	%
Total Population	20,211	62.2
Hispanic or Latino (of any race)	10,816	50.2
Central American, ex. Mexican	608	58.5
Mexican	9,413	48.6

Four-Year College Graduates
(Universe: Population 25 Years and Over)

Group	Number	%
Total Population	2,935	9.0
Hispanic or Latino (of any race)	1,343	6.2
Central American, ex. Mexican	163	15.7
Mexican	1,082	5.6

Population Age 3–17 Enrolled in Public School
(Universe: Population Age 3–17 Enrolled in School)

Group	Number	%
Total Population	17,801	96.3
Hispanic or Latino (of any race)	13,710	97.2
Central American, ex. Mexican	546	100.0
Mexican	12,571	97.4

Population Age 3–17 Enrolled in Private School
(Universe: Population Age 3–17 Enrolled in School)

Group	Number	%
Total Population	675	3.7
Hispanic or Latino (of any race)	397	2.8
Central American, ex. Mexican	0	0.0
Mexican	335	2.6

Foreign-Born Population

Group	Number	%
Total Population	19,306	30.3
Hispanic or Latino (of any race)	17,134	38.2
Central American, ex. Mexican	956	51.0
Mexican	15,622	38.2

Foreign-Born Naturalized U.S. Citizens

Group	Number	%
Total Population	7,159	37.1
Hispanic or Latino (of any race)	5,818	34.0
Central American, ex. Mexican	442	46.2
Mexican	5,010	32.1

Language Spoken at Home: English Only
(Universe: Population 5 Years and Over)

Group	Number	%
Total Population	21,839	38.1
Hispanic or Latino (of any race)	7,260	18.2
Central American, ex. Mexican	115	6.8
Mexican	6,549	18.0

Language Spoken at Home: Spanish
(Universe: Population 5 Years and Over)

Group	Number	%
Total Population	33,445	58.3
Hispanic or Latino (of any race)	32,644	81.7
Central American, ex. Mexican	1,586	93.2
Mexican	29,812	81.9

Unemployment Rate
(Universe: Population 16 Years and Over)

Group	%
Total Population	16.1
Hispanic or Latino (of any race)	15.8
Central American, ex. Mexican	10.0
Mexican	16.6

Class of Worker: Private Wage and Salary
(Universe: Civilian Employed Population 16 Years and Over)

Group	Number	%
Total Population	18,456	79.6
Hispanic or Latino (of any race)	13,093	81.4
Central American, ex. Mexican	589	69.4
Mexican	11,778	81.5

Class of Worker: Government
(Universe: Civilian Employed Population 16 Years and Over)

Group	Number	%
Total Population	3,097	13.4
Hispanic or Latino (of any race)	1,678	10.4
Central American, ex. Mexican	150	17.7
Mexican	1,463	10.1

Means of Transportation to Work: Car, Truck or Van
(Universe: Workers 16 Years and Over)

Group	Number	%
Total Population	21,168	93.5
Hispanic or Latino (of any race)	14,769	94.3
Central American, ex. Mexican	766	91.8
Mexican	13,313	94.6

Means of Transportation to Work: Public Transportation (ex. Taxicab)
(Universe: Workers 16 Years and Over)

Group	Number	%
Total Population	416	1.8
Hispanic or Latino (of any race)	179	1.1
Central American, ex. Mexican	0	0.0
Mexican	146	1.0

Homeownership Rate
(Universe: Occupied Housing Units)

Group	%
Total Population	66.3
Hispanic or Latino (of any race)	66.2
Central American, ex. Mexican	71.1
Guatemalan	71.4
Honduran	48.6
Nicaraguan	80.4
Salvadoran	70.9
Cuban	65.8
Mexican	66.3
Puerto Rican	68.8
South American	73.1
Peruvian	75.0
Spaniard	62.0

Median Home Value

Group	Dollars
Total Population	239,100
Hispanic or Latino (of any race)	232,200
Central American, ex. Mexican	212,100
Mexican	225,700

Median Gross Rent

Group	Dollars
Total Population	1,153
Hispanic or Latino (of any race)	1,152
Central American, ex. Mexican	1,605
Mexican	1,145

Median Household Income
(2010 Inflation-Adjusted Dollars)

Group	Dollars
Total Population	50,471
Hispanic or Latino (of any race)	49,343
Central American, ex. Mexican	30,595
Mexican	49,499

Per Capita Income
(2010 Inflation-Adjusted Dollars)

Group	Dollars
Total Population	14,472
Hispanic or Latino (of any race)	12,481
Central American, ex. Mexican	13,630
Mexican	12,186

Households with $100,000+ Income

Group	Number	%
Total Population	1,779	11.6
Hispanic or Latino (of any race)	921	9.4
Central American, ex. Mexican	26	5.4
Mexican	803	9.3

Households with Food Stamps/SNAP Benefits During Past 12 Months

Group	Number	%
Total Population	1,767	11.5
Hispanic or Latino (of any race)	1,113	11.4
Central American, ex. Mexican	72	14.9
Mexican	985	11.4

Poverty Rate
(Income in Past 12 Months Below Poverty Level)

Group	%
Total Population	22.3
Hispanic or Latino (of any race)	24.0
Central American, ex. Mexican	40.7
Mexican	23.6

Petaluma

Population

Group	Number	%TP[1]	%HP[2]
Total Population	57,941	100.0	–
Hispanic or Latino (of any race)	12,453	21.5	100.0
Central American, ex. Mexican	1,342	2.3	10.8
Guatemalan	375	0.6	3.0
Nicaraguan	178	0.3	1.4
Salvadoran	688	1.2	5.5
Mexican	9,378	16.2	75.3
Puerto Rican	164	0.3	1.3
South American	472	0.8	3.8
Colombian	135	0.2	1.1
Peruvian	200	0.3	1.6
Spaniard	251	0.4	2.0

Population Growth: 2000–2010

Group	%
Total Population	6.2
Hispanic or Latino (of any race)	56.0
Central American, ex. Mexican	134.2
Guatemalan	264.1
Salvadoran	156.7
Mexican	69.1
Puerto Rican	7.9
South American	101.7

Notes: (1) Percent of total population; (2) Percent of Hispanic/Latino population; Profiles include places with an overall population of at least 125,000, OR an overall population of at least 25,000 where the Hispanic/Latino population is at least 20% of the overall population. In states where less than five places meet either of these criteria, we have included places with at least 10,000 total population with the highest percentage of Hispanic/Latino population. These places are identified with an asterisk (*); Please refer to the User's Guide for a full explanation of data.

Peruvian	68.1

Males per 100 Females

Group	Number
Total Population	96.3
Hispanic or Latino (of any race)	109.4
Central American, ex. Mexican	96.8
Guatemalan	113.1
Nicaraguan	76.2
Salvadoran	94.4
Mexican	115.0
Puerto Rican	70.8
South American	82.2
Colombian	62.7
Peruvian	94.2
Spaniard	83.2

Average Household Size

Group	People
Total Population	2.63
Hispanic or Latino (of any race)	4.02
Central American, ex. Mexican	3.77
Guatemalan	4.48
Nicaraguan	3.02
Salvadoran	3.79
Mexican	4.29
Puerto Rican	2.65
South American	3.20
Colombian	3.29
Peruvian	3.23
Spaniard	2.63

Median Age

Group	Years
Total Population	40.3
Hispanic or Latino (of any race)	27.5
Central American, ex. Mexican	32.7
Guatemalan	28.2
Nicaraguan	39.3
Salvadoran	34.3
Mexican	26.0
Puerto Rican	35.0
South American	38.1
Colombian	34.5
Peruvian	40.0
Spaniard	39.4

High School Graduates
(Universe: Population 25 Years and Over)

Group	Number	%
Total Population	34,193	87.6
Hispanic or Latino (of any race)	3,570	53.3
Central American, ex. Mexican	566	74.2
Mexican	2,447	46.0

Four-Year College Graduates
(Universe: Population 25 Years and Over)

Group	Number	%
Total Population	13,006	33.3
Hispanic or Latino (of any race)	566	8.5
Central American, ex. Mexican	90	11.8
Mexican	310	5.8

Population Age 3–17 Enrolled in Public School
(Universe: Population Age 3–17 Enrolled in School)

Group	Number	%
Total Population	8,858	85.5
Hispanic or Latino (of any race)	3,394	90.6
Central American, ex. Mexican	172	78.9
Mexican	3,036	92.5

Population Age 3–17 Enrolled in Private School
(Universe: Population Age 3–17 Enrolled in School)

Group	Number	%
Total Population	1,507	14.5
Hispanic or Latino (of any race)	351	9.4
Central American, ex. Mexican	46	21.1
Mexican	245	7.5

Foreign-Born Population

Group	Number	%
Total Population	10,789	19.0
Hispanic or Latino (of any race)	6,662	50.5
Central American, ex. Mexican	716	58.7
Mexican	5,725	51.8

Foreign-Born Naturalized U.S. Citizens

Group	Number	%
Total Population	4,312	40.0
Hispanic or Latino (of any race)	1,533	23.0
Central American, ex. Mexican	393	54.9
Mexican	985	17.2

Language Spoken at Home: English Only
(Universe: Population 5 Years and Over)

Group	Number	%
Total Population	38,908	73.2
Hispanic or Latino (of any race)	2,460	20.9
Central American, ex. Mexican	175	16.1
Mexican	1,811	18.5

Language Spoken at Home: Spanish
(Universe: Population 5 Years and Over)

Group	Number	%
Total Population	10,007	18.8
Hispanic or Latino (of any race)	9,258	78.7
Central American, ex. Mexican	912	83.9
Mexican	7,942	81.1

Unemployment Rate
(Universe: Population 16 Years and Over)

Group	%
Total Population	6.8
Hispanic or Latino (of any race)	9.3
Central American, ex. Mexican	3.3
Mexican	9.4

Class of Worker: Private Wage and Salary
(Universe: Civilian Employed Population 16 Years and Over)

Group	Number	%
Total Population	22,795	77.3
Hispanic or Latino (of any race)	4,623	83.6
Central American, ex. Mexican	464	73.1
Mexican	3,798	84.8

Class of Worker: Government
(Universe: Civilian Employed Population 16 Years and Over)

Group	Number	%
Total Population	3,466	11.8
Hispanic or Latino (of any race)	198	3.6
Central American, ex. Mexican	23	3.6
Mexican	162	3.6

Means of Transportation to Work: Car, Truck or Van
(Universe: Workers 16 Years and Over)

Group	Number	%
Total Population	24,427	85.4
Hispanic or Latino (of any race)	4,362	81.4
Central American, ex. Mexican	509	83.9
Mexican	3,545	80.8

Means of Transportation to Work: Public Transportation (ex. Taxicab)
(Universe: Workers 16 Years and Over)

Group	Number	%
Total Population	1,059	3.7
Hispanic or Latino (of any race)	353	6.6
Central American, ex. Mexican	66	10.9
Mexican	276	6.3

Homeownership Rate
(Universe: Occupied Housing Units)

Group	%
Total Population	65.1
Hispanic or Latino (of any race)	44.3
Central American, ex. Mexican	56.7
Guatemalan	52.8
Nicaraguan	66.7
Salvadoran	57.5
Mexican	39.0
Puerto Rican	65.4
South American	59.2
Colombian	60.0
Peruvian	59.4
Spaniard	65.3

Median Home Value

Group	Dollars
Total Population	541,100
Hispanic or Latino (of any race)	554,900
Central American, ex. Mexican	483,600
Mexican	565,800

Median Gross Rent

Group	Dollars
Total Population	1,347
Hispanic or Latino (of any race)	1,273
Central American, ex. Mexican	1,685
Mexican	1,250

Median Household Income
(2010 Inflation-Adjusted Dollars)

Group	Dollars
Total Population	73,284
Hispanic or Latino (of any race)	53,440
Central American, ex. Mexican	63,304
Mexican	51,779

Per Capita Income
(2010 Inflation-Adjusted Dollars)

Group	Dollars
Total Population	34,159
Hispanic or Latino (of any race)	15,118
Central American, ex. Mexican	18,781
Mexican	13,828

Households with $100,000+ Income

Group	Number	%
Total Population	7,498	35.3
Hispanic or Latino (of any race)	543	18.7
Central American, ex. Mexican	39	14.3
Mexican	399	17.6

Households with Food Stamps/SNAP Benefits During Past 12 Months

Group	Number	%
Total Population	417	2.0
Hispanic or Latino (of any race)	92	3.2
Central American, ex. Mexican	23	8.4
Mexican	30	1.3

Poverty Rate
(Income in Past 12 Months Below Poverty Level)

Group	%
Total Population	7.5
Hispanic or Latino (of any race)	15.8
Central American, ex. Mexican	17.1
Mexican	16.1

Pico Rivera

Population

Group	Number	%TP[1]	%HP[2]
Total Population	62,942	100.0	–
Hispanic or Latino (of any race)	57,400	91.2	100.0
Central American, ex. Mexican	3,059	4.9	5.3
Guatemalan	761	1.2	1.3
Honduran	154	0.2	0.3
Nicaraguan	281	0.4	0.5
Salvadoran	1,733	2.8	3.0
Cuban	166	0.3	0.3
Mexican	51,337	81.6	89.4
Puerto Rican	268	0.4	0.5
South American	530	0.8	0.9
Colombian	154	0.2	0.3
Ecuadorian	114	0.2	0.2
Peruvian	155	0.2	0.3
Spaniard	226	0.4	0.4

Population Growth: 2000–2010

Group	%
Total Population	-0.8
Hispanic or Latino (of any race)	2.5
Central American, ex. Mexican	96.3
Guatemalan	143.1
Nicaraguan	83.7
Salvadoran	110.3
Cuban	23.9
Mexican	6.9
Puerto Rican	13.6
South American	44.8

Notes: (1) Percent of total population; (2) Percent of Hispanic/Latino population; Profiles include places with an overall population of at least 125,000, OR an overall population of at least 25,000 where the Hispanic/Latino population is at least 20% of the overall population. In states where less than five places meet either of these criteria, we have included places with at least 10,000 total population with the highest percentage of Hispanic/Latino population. These places are identified with an asterisk (*); Please refer to the User's Guide for a full explanation of data.

Males per 100 Females

Group	Number
Total Population	95.5
Hispanic or Latino (of any race)	95.4
Central American, ex. Mexican	90.6
Guatemalan	113.2
Honduran	85.5
Nicaraguan	82.5
Salvadoran	85.0
Cuban	97.6
Mexican	95.6
Puerto Rican	97.1
South American	97.8
Colombian	87.8
Ecuadorian	103.6
Peruvian	86.7
Spaniard	83.7

Average Household Size

Group	People
Total Population	3.77
Hispanic or Latino (of any race)	3.96
Central American, ex. Mexican	4.32
Guatemalan	4.30
Honduran	4.58
Nicaraguan	3.89
Salvadoran	4.40
Cuban	3.10
Mexican	3.98
Puerto Rican	3.27
South American	3.68
Colombian	3.40
Ecuadorian	3.95
Peruvian	3.83
Spaniard	2.89

Median Age

Group	Years
Total Population	34.0
Hispanic or Latino (of any race)	32.7
Central American, ex. Mexican	37.1
Guatemalan	38.8
Honduran	33.9
Nicaraguan	42.9
Salvadoran	36.3
Cuban	43.0
Mexican	32.3
Puerto Rican	34.3
South American	40.1
Colombian	40.7
Ecuadorian	40.7
Peruvian	41.5
Spaniard	48.3

High School Graduates
(Universe: Population 25 Years and Over)

Group	Number	%
Total Population	25,958	65.9
Hispanic or Latino (of any race)	22,160	63.6
Central American, ex. Mexican	1,640	70.1
Salvadoran	1,059	70.7
Mexican	19,314	62.3

Four-Year College Graduates
(Universe: Population 25 Years and Over)

Group	Number	%
Total Population	4,000	10.2
Hispanic or Latino (of any race)	2,892	8.3
Central American, ex. Mexican	318	13.6
Salvadoran	227	15.2
Mexican	2,426	7.8

Population Age 3–17 Enrolled in Public School
(Universe: Population Age 3–17 Enrolled in School)

Group	Number	%
Total Population	12,266	93.6
Hispanic or Latino (of any race)	11,755	94.1
Central American, ex. Mexican	414	90.6
Salvadoran	203	82.5
Mexican	10,896	94.1

Population Age 3–17 Enrolled in Private School
(Universe: Population Age 3–17 Enrolled in School)

Group	Number	%
Total Population	843	6.4
Hispanic or Latino (of any race)	741	5.9
Central American, ex. Mexican	43	9.4
Salvadoran	43	17.5
Mexican	688	5.9

Foreign-Born Population

Group	Number	%
Total Population	20,613	32.7
Hispanic or Latino (of any race)	19,056	33.3
Central American, ex. Mexican	2,236	63.2
Salvadoran	1,484	67.3
Mexican	16,193	31.5

Foreign-Born Naturalized U.S. Citizens

Group	Number	%
Total Population	10,156	49.3
Hispanic or Latino (of any race)	9,165	48.1
Central American, ex. Mexican	1,138	50.9
Salvadoran	752	50.7
Mexican	7,755	47.9

Language Spoken at Home: English Only
(Universe: Population 5 Years and Over)

Group	Number	%
Total Population	16,788	28.4
Hispanic or Latino (of any race)	13,416	25.0
Central American, ex. Mexican	171	5.2
Salvadoran	81	4.0
Mexican	12,495	25.9

Language Spoken at Home: Spanish
(Universe: Population 5 Years and Over)

Group	Number	%
Total Population	40,631	68.7
Hispanic or Latino (of any race)	40,227	74.9
Central American, ex. Mexican	3,122	94.8
Salvadoran	1,921	96.0
Mexican	35,637	74.0

Unemployment Rate
(Universe: Population 16 Years and Over)

Group	%
Total Population	6.9
Hispanic or Latino (of any race)	7.0
Central American, ex. Mexican	3.4
Salvadoran	3.8
Mexican	7.3

Class of Worker: Private Wage and Salary
(Universe: Civilian Employed Population 16 Years and Over)

Group	Number	%
Total Population	21,555	78.4
Hispanic or Latino (of any race)	19,862	78.9
Central American, ex. Mexican	1,516	82.7
Salvadoran	884	81.4
Mexican	17,536	78.8

Class of Worker: Government
(Universe: Civilian Employed Population 16 Years and Over)

Group	Number	%
Total Population	3,939	14.3
Hispanic or Latino (of any race)	3,635	14.4
Central American, ex. Mexican	198	10.8
Salvadoran	123	11.3
Mexican	3,222	14.5

Means of Transportation to Work: Car, Truck or Van
(Universe: Workers 16 Years and Over)

Group	Number	%
Total Population	23,828	88.6
Hispanic or Latino (of any race)	22,021	89.3
Central American, ex. Mexican	1,467	80.4
Salvadoran	777	72.1
Mexican	19,631	90.2

Means of Transportation to Work: Public Transportation (ex. Taxicab)
(Universe: Workers 16 Years and Over)

Group	Number	%
Total Population	854	3.2
Hispanic or Latino (of any race)	793	3.2
Central American, ex. Mexican	193	10.6
Salvadoran	176	16.3
Mexican	530	2.4

Homeownership Rate
(Universe: Occupied Housing Units)

Group	%
Total Population	69.1
Hispanic or Latino (of any race)	68.9
Central American, ex. Mexican	65.7
Guatemalan	64.3
Honduran	51.5
Nicaraguan	69.4
Salvadoran	66.5
Cuban	64.6
Mexican	69.6
Puerto Rican	63.9
South American	60.3
Colombian	73.6
Ecuadorian	62.2
Peruvian	50.0
Spaniard	75.8

Median Home Value

Group	Dollars
Total Population	414,200
Hispanic or Latino (of any race)	415,800
Central American, ex. Mexican	387,000
Salvadoran	360,500
Mexican	415,600

Median Gross Rent

Group	Dollars
Total Population	1,123
Hispanic or Latino (of any race)	1,132
Central American, ex. Mexican	1,046
Salvadoran	1,292
Mexican	1,137

Median Household Income
(2010 Inflation-Adjusted Dollars)

Group	Dollars
Total Population	57,594
Hispanic or Latino (of any race)	58,546
Central American, ex. Mexican	54,665
Salvadoran	58,571
Mexican	58,926

Per Capita Income
(2010 Inflation-Adjusted Dollars)

Group	Dollars
Total Population	18,118
Hispanic or Latino (of any race)	17,350
Central American, ex. Mexican	18,529
Salvadoran	17,266
Mexican	17,140

Households with $100,000+ Income

Group	Number	%
Total Population	3,027	18.4
Hispanic or Latino (of any race)	2,507	17.4
Central American, ex. Mexican	195	21.7
Salvadoran	128	23.7
Mexican	2,180	17.0

Households with Food Stamps/SNAP Benefits During Past 12 Months

Group	Number	%
Total Population	703	4.3
Hispanic or Latino (of any race)	660	4.6
Central American, ex. Mexican	72	8.0
Salvadoran	53	9.8
Mexican	576	4.5

Poverty Rate
(Income in Past 12 Months Below Poverty Level)

Group	%
Total Population	11.0
Hispanic or Latino (of any race)	11.4
Central American, ex. Mexican	10.2
Salvadoran	14.9
Mexican	11.9

Pittsburg

Population

Group	Number	%TP[1]	%HP[2]
Total Population	63,264	100.0	–

Notes: (1) Percent of total population; (2) Percent of Hispanic/Latino population; Profiles include places with an overall population of at least 125,000, OR an overall population of at least 25,000 where the Hispanic/Latino population is at least 20% of the overall population. In states where less than five places meet either of these criteria, we have included places with at least 10,000 total population with the highest percentage of Hispanic/Latino population. These places are identified with an asterisk (*); Please refer to the User's Guide for a full explanation of data.

Hispanic or Latino (of any race)	26,841	42.4	100.0
Central American, ex. Mexican	3,513	5.6	13.1
Guatemalan	354	0.6	1.3
Nicaraguan	879	1.4	3.3
Salvadoran	2,076	3.3	7.7
Mexican	20,109	31.8	74.9
Puerto Rican	890	1.4	3.3
South American	610	1.0	2.3
Colombian	112	0.2	0.4
Peruvian	348	0.6	1.3
Spaniard	288	0.5	1.1

Population Growth: 2000–2010

Group	%
Total Population	11.4
Hispanic or Latino (of any race)	46.8
Central American, ex. Mexican	136.2
Guatemalan	178.7
Nicaraguan	130.7
Salvadoran	173.9
Mexican	53.7
Puerto Rican	26.6
South American	93.7
Peruvian	113.5

Males per 100 Females

Group	Number
Total Population	94.9
Hispanic or Latino (of any race)	101.1
Central American, ex. Mexican	94.2
Guatemalan	117.2
Nicaraguan	92.3
Salvadoran	90.8
Mexican	103.0
Puerto Rican	91.8
South American	91.2
Colombian	89.8
Peruvian	94.4
Spaniard	108.7

Average Household Size

Group	People
Total Population	3.22
Hispanic or Latino (of any race)	4.06
Central American, ex. Mexican	3.85
Guatemalan	3.86
Nicaraguan	3.76
Salvadoran	3.95
Mexican	4.24
Puerto Rican	3.17
South American	3.61
Colombian	3.80
Peruvian	3.75
Spaniard	3.15

Median Age

Group	Years
Total Population	32.5
Hispanic or Latino (of any race)	26.3
Central American, ex. Mexican	32.8
Guatemalan	32.4
Nicaraguan	34.2
Salvadoran	32.8
Mexican	25.1
Puerto Rican	27.1
South American	37.6
Colombian	37.3
Peruvian	37.1
Spaniard	31.4

High School Graduates
(Universe: Population 25 Years and Over)

Group	Number	%
Total Population	28,511	77.3
Hispanic or Latino (of any race)	7,858	58.3
Central American, ex. Mexican	1,056	64.7
Salvadoran	621	65.3
Mexican	5,765	54.1

Four-Year College Graduates
(Universe: Population 25 Years and Over)

Group	Number	%
Total Population	5,841	15.8
Hispanic or Latino (of any race)	706	5.2
Central American, ex. Mexican	70	4.3
Salvadoran	32	3.4
Mexican	526	4.9

Population Age 3–17 Enrolled in Public School
(Universe: Population Age 3–17 Enrolled in School)

Group	Number	%
Total Population	11,840	89.8
Hispanic or Latino (of any race)	5,928	95.4
Central American, ex. Mexican	415	89.6
Salvadoran	246	93.9
Mexican	5,248	96.0

Population Age 3–17 Enrolled in Private School
(Universe: Population Age 3–17 Enrolled in School)

Group	Number	%
Total Population	1,350	10.2
Hispanic or Latino (of any race)	283	4.6
Central American, ex. Mexican	48	10.4
Salvadoran	16	6.1
Mexican	218	4.0

Foreign-Born Population

Group	Number	%
Total Population	19,714	31.9
Hispanic or Latino (of any race)	11,979	46.5
Central American, ex. Mexican	1,524	57.2
Salvadoran	853	55.4
Mexican	9,889	46.4

Foreign-Born Naturalized U.S. Citizens

Group	Number	%
Total Population	8,700	44.1
Hispanic or Latino (of any race)	3,255	27.2
Central American, ex. Mexican	1,018	66.8
Salvadoran	633	74.2
Mexican	1,961	19.8

Language Spoken at Home: English Only
(Universe: Population 5 Years and Over)

Group	Number	%
Total Population	29,849	52.7
Hispanic or Latino (of any race)	4,346	19.0
Central American, ex. Mexican	375	15.3
Salvadoran	174	12.5
Mexican	3,303	17.7

Language Spoken at Home: Spanish
(Universe: Population 5 Years and Over)

Group	Number	%
Total Population	19,130	33.8
Hispanic or Latino (of any race)	18,458	80.9
Central American, ex. Mexican	2,072	84.3
Salvadoran	1,210	86.7
Mexican	15,348	82.3

Unemployment Rate
(Universe: Population 16 Years and Over)

Group	%
Total Population	8.9
Hispanic or Latino (of any race)	9.5
Central American, ex. Mexican	9.1
Salvadoran	9.3
Mexican	9.0

Class of Worker: Private Wage and Salary
(Universe: Civilian Employed Population 16 Years and Over)

Group	Number	%
Total Population	21,818	80.0
Hispanic or Latino (of any race)	8,488	81.6
Central American, ex. Mexican	995	69.9
Salvadoran	645	75.1
Mexican	6,850	83.6

Class of Worker: Government
(Universe: Civilian Employed Population 16 Years and Over)

Group	Number	%
Total Population	3,509	12.9
Hispanic or Latino (of any race)	968	9.3
Central American, ex. Mexican	197	13.8
Salvadoran	139	16.2
Mexican	673	8.2

Means of Transportation to Work: Car, Truck or Van
(Universe: Workers 16 Years and Over)

Group	Number	%
Total Population	22,511	85.5
Hispanic or Latino (of any race)	8,730	88.7
Central American, ex. Mexican	1,197	87.6
Salvadoran	784	91.3
Mexican	6,892	88.7

Means of Transportation to Work: Public Transportation (ex. Taxicab)
(Universe: Workers 16 Years and Over)

Group	Number	%
Total Population	2,070	7.9
Hispanic or Latino (of any race)	510	5.2
Central American, ex. Mexican	121	8.9
Salvadoran	75	8.7
Mexican	364	4.7

Homeownership Rate
(Universe: Occupied Housing Units)

Group	%
Total Population	58.8
Hispanic or Latino (of any race)	53.1
Central American, ex. Mexican	61.1
Guatemalan	56.2
Nicaraguan	62.7
Salvadoran	62.2
Mexican	51.8
Puerto Rican	46.8
South American	61.4
Colombian	56.7
Peruvian	58.6
Spaniard	68.0

Median Home Value

Group	Dollars
Total Population	361,100
Hispanic or Latino (of any race)	363,800
Central American, ex. Mexican	414,200
Salvadoran	432,500
Mexican	360,900

Median Gross Rent

Group	Dollars
Total Population	1,229
Hispanic or Latino (of any race)	1,332
Central American, ex. Mexican	1,066
Salvadoran	1,161
Mexican	1,356

Median Household Income
(2010 Inflation-Adjusted Dollars)

Group	Dollars
Total Population	57,828
Hispanic or Latino (of any race)	52,534
Central American, ex. Mexican	60,000
Salvadoran	60,909
Mexican	51,094

Per Capita Income
(2010 Inflation-Adjusted Dollars)

Group	Dollars
Total Population	22,200
Hispanic or Latino (of any race)	15,310
Central American, ex. Mexican	19,119
Salvadoran	21,671
Mexican	14,433

Households with $100,000+ Income

Group	Number	%
Total Population	4,564	24.4
Hispanic or Latino (of any race)	852	14.5
Central American, ex. Mexican	121	16.0
Salvadoran	82	15.5
Mexican	643	13.7

Households with Food Stamps/SNAP Benefits During Past 12 Months

Group	Number	%
Total Population	1,187	6.3
Hispanic or Latino (of any race)	449	7.6
Central American, ex. Mexican	39	5.1
Salvadoran	0	0.0

Notes: (1) Percent of total population; (2) Percent of Hispanic/Latino population; Profiles include places with an overall population of at least 125,000, OR an overall population of at least 25,000 where the Hispanic/Latino population is at least 20% of the overall population. In states where less than five places meet either of these criteria, we have included places with at least 10,000 total population with the highest percentage of Hispanic/Latino population. These places are identified with an asterisk (*); Please refer to the User's Guide for a full explanation of data.

Mexican	387	8.3

Poverty Rate
(Income in Past 12 Months Below Poverty Level)

Group	%
Total Population	13.6
Hispanic or Latino (of any race)	17.8
Central American, ex. Mexican	5.0
Salvadoran	2.7
Mexican	19.8

Placentia

Population

Group	Number	%TP[1]	%HP[2]
Total Population	50,533	100.0	–
Hispanic or Latino (of any race)	18,416	36.4	100.0
Central American, ex. Mexican	934	1.8	5.1
Guatemalan	492	1.0	2.7
Salvadoran	272	0.5	1.5
Cuban	172	0.3	0.9
Mexican	15,464	30.6	84.0
Puerto Rican	163	0.3	0.9
South American	554	1.1	3.0
Colombian	129	0.3	0.7
Peruvian	179	0.4	1.0
Spaniard	165	0.3	0.9

Population Growth: 2000–2010

Group	%
Total Population	8.7
Hispanic or Latino (of any race)	27.4
Central American, ex. Mexican	137.1
Guatemalan	143.6
Cuban	27.4
Mexican	28.6
South American	124.3

Males per 100 Females

Group	Number
Total Population	97.0
Hispanic or Latino (of any race)	103.3
Central American, ex. Mexican	125.1
Guatemalan	160.3
Salvadoran	106.1
Cuban	73.7
Mexican	104.2
Puerto Rican	89.5
South American	69.9
Colombian	72.0
Peruvian	58.4
Spaniard	103.7

Average Household Size

Group	People
Total Population	3.07
Hispanic or Latino (of any race)	4.18
Central American, ex. Mexican	4.52
Guatemalan	4.91
Salvadoran	4.37
Cuban	2.89
Mexican	4.31
Puerto Rican	3.02
South American	3.16
Colombian	2.70
Peruvian	3.64
Spaniard	2.82

Median Age

Group	Years
Total Population	36.0
Hispanic or Latino (of any race)	27.1
Central American, ex. Mexican	28.8
Guatemalan	28.4
Salvadoran	29.7
Cuban	39.3
Mexican	26.6
Puerto Rican	25.8
South American	38.3
Colombian	40.5
Peruvian	33.8
Spaniard	36.4

High School Graduates
(Universe: Population 25 Years and Over)

Group	Number	%
Total Population	26,690	85.5
Hispanic or Latino (of any race)	5,350	59.4
Central American, ex. Mexican	267	58.4
Mexican	3,864	53.8
South American	474	87.5

Four-Year College Graduates
(Universe: Population 25 Years and Over)

Group	Number	%
Total Population	11,327	36.3
Hispanic or Latino (of any race)	1,435	15.9
Central American, ex. Mexican	10	2.2
Mexican	962	13.4
South American	249	45.9

Population Age 3–17 Enrolled in Public School
(Universe: Population Age 3–17 Enrolled in School)

Group	Number	%
Total Population	8,245	84.8
Hispanic or Latino (of any race)	4,208	88.9
Central American, ex. Mexican	167	100.0
Mexican	3,593	89.0
South American	224	90.3

Population Age 3–17 Enrolled in Private School
(Universe: Population Age 3–17 Enrolled in School)

Group	Number	%
Total Population	1,474	15.2
Hispanic or Latino (of any race)	524	11.1
Central American, ex. Mexican	0	0.0
Mexican	443	11.0
South American	24	9.7

Foreign-Born Population

Group	Number	%
Total Population	12,459	25.1
Hispanic or Latino (of any race)	6,529	36.6
Central American, ex. Mexican	613	64.1
Mexican	5,418	37.2
South American	307	34.4

Foreign-Born Naturalized U.S. Citizens

Group	Number	%
Total Population	6,432	51.6
Hispanic or Latino (of any race)	1,887	28.9
Central American, ex. Mexican	176	28.7
Mexican	1,386	25.6
South American	147	47.9

Language Spoken at Home: English Only
(Universe: Population 5 Years and Over)

Group	Number	%
Total Population	29,083	63.2
Hispanic or Latino (of any race)	5,415	33.8
Central American, ex. Mexican	153	18.4
Mexican	4,006	30.7
South American	288	33.7

Language Spoken at Home: Spanish
(Universe: Population 5 Years and Over)

Group	Number	%
Total Population	11,014	23.9
Hispanic or Latino (of any race)	10,615	66.2
Central American, ex. Mexican	678	81.6
Mexican	9,023	69.3
South American	567	66.3

Unemployment Rate
(Universe: Population 16 Years and Over)

Group	%
Total Population	6.6
Hispanic or Latino (of any race)	10.1
Central American, ex. Mexican	6.7
Mexican	11.0
South American	3.9

Class of Worker: Private Wage and Salary
(Universe: Civilian Employed Population 16 Years and Over)

Group	Number	%
Total Population	18,750	77.7
Hispanic or Latino (of any race)	6,023	80.8
Central American, ex. Mexican	481	85.7
Mexican	4,728	81.3
South American	259	58.2

Class of Worker: Government
(Universe: Civilian Employed Population 16 Years and Over)

Group	Number	%
Total Population	3,422	14.2
Hispanic or Latino (of any race)	809	10.8
Central American, ex. Mexican	49	8.7
Mexican	611	10.5
South American	102	22.9

Means of Transportation to Work: Car, Truck or Van
(Universe: Workers 16 Years and Over)

Group	Number	%
Total Population	21,526	90.9
Hispanic or Latino (of any race)	6,453	87.9
Central American, ex. Mexican	534	95.2
Mexican	4,915	86.0
South American	400	89.9

Means of Transportation to Work: Public Transportation (ex. Taxicab)
(Universe: Workers 16 Years and Over)

Group	Number	%
Total Population	437	1.8
Hispanic or Latino (of any race)	272	3.7
Central American, ex. Mexican	0	0.0
Mexican	272	4.8
South American	0	0.0

Homeownership Rate
(Universe: Occupied Housing Units)

Group	%
Total Population	65.3
Hispanic or Latino (of any race)	44.6
Central American, ex. Mexican	30.8
Guatemalan	24.3
Salvadoran	33.8
Cuban	57.8
Mexican	44.6
Puerto Rican	45.3
South American	57.2
Colombian	51.2
Peruvian	61.9
Spaniard	52.8

Median Home Value

Group	Dollars
Total Population	576,400
Hispanic or Latino (of any race)	548,900
Central American, ex. Mexican	514,400
Mexican	541,300
South American	597,700

Median Gross Rent

Group	Dollars
Total Population	1,386
Hispanic or Latino (of any race)	1,318
Central American, ex. Mexican	1,420
Mexican	1,287
South American	1,688

Median Household Income
(2010 Inflation-Adjusted Dollars)

Group	Dollars
Total Population	76,678
Hispanic or Latino (of any race)	55,286
Central American, ex. Mexican	60,952
Mexican	50,127
South American	109,469

Per Capita Income
(2010 Inflation-Adjusted Dollars)

Group	Dollars
Total Population	30,800
Hispanic or Latino (of any race)	17,755
Central American, ex. Mexican	15,960
Mexican	16,280
South American	31,405

Households with $100,000+ Income

Group	Number	%
Total Population	5,925	36.8
Hispanic or Latino (of any race)	1,075	25.1

Notes: (1) Percent of total population; (2) Percent of Hispanic/Latino population; Profiles include places with an overall population of at least 125,000, OR an overall population of at least 25,000 where the Hispanic/Latino population is at least 20% of the overall population. In states where less than five places meet either of these criteria, we have included places with at least 10,000 total population with the highest percentage of Hispanic/Latino population. These places are identified with an asterisk (*); Please refer to the User's Guide for a full explanation of data.

Central American, ex. Mexican	55	30.9
Mexican	733	21.3
South American	151	63.2

Households with Food Stamps/SNAP Benefits During Past 12 Months

Group	Number	%
Total Population	416	2.6
Hispanic or Latino (of any race)	301	7.0
Central American, ex. Mexican	0	0.0
Mexican	301	8.8
South American	0	0.0

Poverty Rate
(Income in Past 12 Months Below Poverty Level)

Group	%
Total Population	10.9
Hispanic or Latino (of any race)	20.2
Central American, ex. Mexican	16.3
Mexican	21.8
South American	1.9

Pomona

Population

Group	Number	%TP[1]	%HP[2]
Total Population	149,058	100.0	–
Hispanic or Latino (of any race)	105,135	70.5	100.0
Central American, ex. Mexican	6,907	4.6	6.6
Guatemalan	1,885	1.3	1.8
Honduran	632	0.4	0.6
Nicaraguan	625	0.4	0.6
Salvadoran	3,518	2.4	3.3
Cuban	404	0.3	0.4
Mexican	90,988	61.0	86.5
Puerto Rican	725	0.5	0.7
South American	1,007	0.7	1.0
Argentinean	154	0.1	0.1
Colombian	200	0.1	0.2
Ecuadorian	219	0.1	0.2
Peruvian	288	0.2	0.3
Spaniard	408	0.3	0.4

Population Growth: 2000–2010

Group	%
Total Population	-0.3
Hispanic or Latino (of any race)	9.1
Central American, ex. Mexican	80.7
Guatemalan	113.5
Honduran	84.8
Nicaraguan	73.6
Salvadoran	108.4
Cuban	9.2
Mexican	14.1
Puerto Rican	20.4
South American	37.2
Colombian	13.0
Ecuadorian	84.0
Peruvian	48.5
Spaniard	206.8

Males per 100 Females

Group	Number
Total Population	100.0
Hispanic or Latino (of any race)	101.1
Central American, ex. Mexican	102.7
Guatemalan	121.8
Honduran	103.2
Nicaraguan	92.9
Salvadoran	97.0
Cuban	130.9
Mexican	101.2
Puerto Rican	94.4
South American	98.2
Argentinean	94.9
Colombian	83.5
Ecuadorian	100.9
Peruvian	97.3
Spaniard	99.0

Average Household Size

Group	People
Total Population	3.77
Hispanic or Latino (of any race)	4.51
Central American, ex. Mexican	4.56
Guatemalan	4.60
Honduran	4.90
Nicaraguan	4.28
Salvadoran	4.65
Cuban	2.99
Mexican	4.57
Puerto Rican	3.22
South American	3.33
Argentinean	2.87
Colombian	3.41
Ecuadorian	3.74
Peruvian	3.43
Spaniard	3.45

Median Age

Group	Years
Total Population	29.5
Hispanic or Latino (of any race)	26.2
Central American, ex. Mexican	33.6
Guatemalan	33.6
Honduran	31.1
Nicaraguan	35.7
Salvadoran	33.7
Cuban	40.3
Mexican	25.6
Puerto Rican	28.8
South American	36.8
Argentinean	38.0
Colombian	36.5
Ecuadorian	34.7
Peruvian	38.8
Spaniard	32.8

High School Graduates
(Universe: Population 25 Years and Over)

Group	Number	%
Total Population	52,804	63.2
Hispanic or Latino (of any race)	26,770	50.5
Central American, ex. Mexican	2,649	51.7
Guatemalan	463	31.8
Salvadoran	1,428	56.4
Mexican	22,400	49.2
South American	588	95.0

Four-Year College Graduates
(Universe: Population 25 Years and Over)

Group	Number	%
Total Population	11,866	14.2
Hispanic or Latino (of any race)	3,288	6.2
Central American, ex. Mexican	385	7.5
Guatemalan	109	7.5
Salvadoran	135	5.3
Mexican	2,509	5.5
South American	173	27.9

Population Age 3–17 Enrolled in Public School
(Universe: Population Age 3–17 Enrolled in School)

Group	Number	%
Total Population	32,996	95.2
Hispanic or Latino (of any race)	27,073	96.1
Central American, ex. Mexican	2,315	98.3
Guatemalan	602	100.0
Salvadoran	1,191	96.7
Mexican	23,650	96.2
South American	247	78.9

Population Age 3–17 Enrolled in Private School
(Universe: Population Age 3–17 Enrolled in School)

Group	Number	%
Total Population	1,665	4.8
Hispanic or Latino (of any race)	1,105	3.9
Central American, ex. Mexican	41	1.7
Guatemalan	0	0.0
Salvadoran	41	3.3
Mexican	943	3.8
South American	66	21.1

Foreign-Born Population

Group	Number	%
Total Population	52,647	35.4
Hispanic or Latino (of any race)	42,149	40.2
Central American, ex. Mexican	5,480	60.5
Guatemalan	1,657	64.5
Salvadoran	2,637	57.8
Mexican	35,482	38.9
South American	448	42.3

Foreign-Born Naturalized U.S. Citizens

Group	Number	%
Total Population	18,323	34.8
Hispanic or Latino (of any race)	11,872	28.2
Central American, ex. Mexican	1,733	31.6
Guatemalan	289	17.4
Salvadoran	972	36.9
Mexican	9,611	27.1
South American	213	47.5

Language Spoken at Home: English Only
(Universe: Population 5 Years and Over)

Group	Number	%
Total Population	46,034	33.9
Hispanic or Latino (of any race)	17,000	18.1
Central American, ex. Mexican	699	8.4
Guatemalan	91	3.9
Salvadoran	302	7.4
Mexican	14,788	18.1
South American	305	31.0

Language Spoken at Home: Spanish
(Universe: Population 5 Years and Over)

Group	Number	%
Total Population	78,284	57.6
Hispanic or Latino (of any race)	76,973	81.8
Central American, ex. Mexican	7,569	91.3
Guatemalan	2,268	96.1
Salvadoran	3,796	92.6
Mexican	66,752	81.8
South American	680	69.0

Unemployment Rate
(Universe: Population 16 Years and Over)

Group	%
Total Population	10.7
Hispanic or Latino (of any race)	11.2
Central American, ex. Mexican	10.5
Guatemalan	8.3
Salvadoran	13.5
Mexican	11.3
South American	9.1

Class of Worker: Private Wage and Salary
(Universe: Civilian Employed Population 16 Years and Over)

Group	Number	%
Total Population	51,721	82.6
Hispanic or Latino (of any race)	37,430	86.9
Central American, ex. Mexican	3,714	90.4
Guatemalan	1,038	88.0
Salvadoran	1,712	90.7
Mexican	32,169	86.9
South American	341	67.1

Class of Worker: Government
(Universe: Civilian Employed Population 16 Years and Over)

Group	Number	%
Total Population	7,202	11.5
Hispanic or Latino (of any race)	3,349	7.8
Central American, ex. Mexican	193	4.7
Guatemalan	75	6.4
Salvadoran	49	2.6
Mexican	2,966	8.0
South American	97	19.1

Means of Transportation to Work: Car, Truck or Van
(Universe: Workers 16 Years and Over)

Group	Number	%
Total Population	53,928	88.8
Hispanic or Latino (of any race)	37,031	88.5
Central American, ex. Mexican	3,503	88.1
Guatemalan	948	82.4
Salvadoran	1,636	90.4
Mexican	31,928	88.6
South American	377	82.1

Means of Transportation to Work: Public Transportation (ex. Taxicab)
(Universe: Workers 16 Years and Over)

Group	Number	%
Total Population	2,594	4.3
Hispanic or Latino (of any race)	1,904	4.6

Notes: (1) Percent of total population; (2) Percent of Hispanic/Latino population; Profiles include places with an overall population of at least 125,000, OR an overall population of at least 25,000 where the Hispanic/Latino population is at least 20% of the overall population. In states where less than five places meet either of these criteria, we have included places with at least 10,000 total population with the highest percentage of Hispanic/Latino population. These places are identified with an asterisk (*); Please refer to the User's Guide for a full explanation of data.

Group	Number	%
Central American, ex. Mexican	271	6.8
Guatemalan	173	15.0
Salvadoran	19	1.0
Mexican	1,595	4.4
South American	0	0.0

Homeownership Rate
(Universe: Occupied Housing Units)

Group	%
Total Population	55.1
Hispanic or Latino (of any race)	52.3
Central American, ex. Mexican	53.7
Guatemalan	50.0
Honduran	41.8
Nicaraguan	56.5
Salvadoran	57.1
Cuban	56.9
Mexican	52.5
Puerto Rican	50.2
South American	58.5
Argentinean	57.1
Colombian	55.7
Ecuadorian	69.4
Peruvian	54.5
Spaniard	61.6

Median Home Value

Group	Dollars
Total Population	355,900
Hispanic or Latino (of any race)	344,200
Central American, ex. Mexican	323,500
Guatemalan	323,500
Salvadoran	342,500
Mexican	346,400
South American	368,900

Median Gross Rent

Group	Dollars
Total Population	1,040
Hispanic or Latino (of any race)	1,006
Central American, ex. Mexican	1,061
Guatemalan	1,125
Salvadoran	1,031
Mexican	996
South American	1,164

Median Household Income
(2010 Inflation-Adjusted Dollars)

Group	Dollars
Total Population	50,497
Hispanic or Latino (of any race)	50,278
Central American, ex. Mexican	53,375
Guatemalan	45,192
Salvadoran	57,279
Mexican	50,066
South American	70,370

Per Capita Income
(2010 Inflation-Adjusted Dollars)

Group	Dollars
Total Population	16,682
Hispanic or Latino (of any race)	13,547
Central American, ex. Mexican	13,060
Guatemalan	13,508
Salvadoran	12,380
Mexican	13,473
South American	19,157

Households with $100,000+ Income

Group	Number	%
Total Population	5,819	15.1
Hispanic or Latino (of any race)	2,867	12.7
Central American, ex. Mexican	230	10.7
Guatemalan	38	6.3
Salvadoran	169	15.7
Mexican	2,382	12.5
South American	108	35.5

Households with Food Stamps/SNAP Benefits During Past 12 Months

Group	Number	%
Total Population	3,785	9.8
Hispanic or Latino (of any race)	2,657	11.8
Central American, ex. Mexican	352	16.3
Guatemalan	162	26.8
Salvadoran	155	14.4
Mexican	2,158	11.3
South American	20	6.6

Poverty Rate
(Income in Past 12 Months Below Poverty Level)

Group	%
Total Population	17.2
Hispanic or Latino (of any race)	18.3
Central American, ex. Mexican	17.5
Guatemalan	18.1
Salvadoran	17.0
Mexican	18.4
South American	6.5

Porterville

Population

Group	Number	%TP[1]	%HP[2]
Total Population	54,165	100.0	-
Hispanic or Latino (of any race)	33,549	61.9	100.0
Central American, ex. Mexican	236	0.4	0.7
Salvadoran	104	0.2	0.3
Mexican	31,421	58.0	93.7
Puerto Rican	173	0.3	0.5
Spaniard	139	0.3	0.4

Population Growth: 2000–2010

Group	%
Total Population	36.7
Hispanic or Latino (of any race)	71.3
Mexican	83.2

Males per 100 Females

Group	Number
Total Population	97.9
Hispanic or Latino (of any race)	102.4
Central American, ex. Mexican	96.7
Salvadoran	89.1
Mexican	102.4
Puerto Rican	119.0
Spaniard	104.4

Average Household Size

Group	People
Total Population	3.39
Hispanic or Latino (of any race)	4.08
Central American, ex. Mexican	4.18
Salvadoran	3.69
Mexican	4.08
Puerto Rican	3.33
Spaniard	3.22

Median Age

Group	Years
Total Population	28.8
Hispanic or Latino (of any race)	23.2
Central American, ex. Mexican	33.0
Salvadoran	32.7
Mexican	23.2
Puerto Rican	25.8
Spaniard	32.2

High School Graduates
(Universe: Population 25 Years and Over)

Group	Number	%
Total Population	20,199	68.3
Hispanic or Latino (of any race)	8,073	52.8
Mexican	7,518	52.4

Four-Year College Graduates
(Universe: Population 25 Years and Over)

Group	Number	%
Total Population	3,264	11.0
Hispanic or Latino (of any race)	835	5.5
Mexican	701	4.9

Population Age 3–17 Enrolled in Public School
(Universe: Population Age 3–17 Enrolled in School)

Group	Number	%
Total Population	13,103	97.2
Hispanic or Latino (of any race)	9,372	98.0
Mexican	8,951	97.9

Population Age 3–17 Enrolled in Private School
(Universe: Population Age 3–17 Enrolled in School)

Group	Number	%
Total Population	375	2.8
Hispanic or Latino (of any race)	191	2.0
Mexican	191	2.1

Foreign-Born Population

Group	Number	%
Total Population	10,415	19.7
Hispanic or Latino (of any race)	9,010	28.3
Mexican	8,542	28.2

Foreign-Born Naturalized U.S. Citizens

Group	Number	%
Total Population	3,432	33.0
Hispanic or Latino (of any race)	2,667	29.6
Mexican	2,494	29.2

Language Spoken at Home: English Only
(Universe: Population 5 Years and Over)

Group	Number	%
Total Population	25,875	54.1
Hispanic or Latino (of any race)	7,989	28.6
Mexican	7,690	29.1

Language Spoken at Home: Spanish
(Universe: Population 5 Years and Over)

Group	Number	%
Total Population	20,119	42.1
Hispanic or Latino (of any race)	19,834	71.1
Mexican	18,745	70.8

Unemployment Rate
(Universe: Population 16 Years and Over)

Group	%
Total Population	12.5
Hispanic or Latino (of any race)	15.4
Mexican	15.3

Class of Worker: Private Wage and Salary
(Universe: Civilian Employed Population 16 Years and Over)

Group	Number	%
Total Population	13,327	65.9
Hispanic or Latino (of any race)	8,225	73.5
Mexican	7,861	73.9

Class of Worker: Government
(Universe: Civilian Employed Population 16 Years and Over)

Group	Number	%
Total Population	5,684	28.1
Hispanic or Latino (of any race)	2,368	21.2
Mexican	2,268	21.3

Means of Transportation to Work: Car, Truck or Van
(Universe: Workers 16 Years and Over)

Group	Number	%
Total Population	17,791	90.7
Hispanic or Latino (of any race)	9,932	90.6
Mexican	9,448	90.8

Means of Transportation to Work: Public Transportation (ex. Taxicab)
(Universe: Workers 16 Years and Over)

Group	Number	%
Total Population	274	1.4
Hispanic or Latino (of any race)	134	1.2
Mexican	134	1.3

Homeownership Rate
(Universe: Occupied Housing Units)

Group	%
Total Population	57.3
Hispanic or Latino (of any race)	52.3
Central American, ex. Mexican	51.4
Salvadoran	58.6
Mexican	52.7
Puerto Rican	60.0
Spaniard	52.5

Median Home Value

Group	Dollars
Total Population	183,200
Hispanic or Latino (of any race)	176,100
Mexican	177,600

Notes: (1) Percent of total population; (2) Percent of Hispanic/Latino population; Profiles include places with an overall population of at least 125,000, OR an overall population of at least 25,000 where the Hispanic/Latino population is at least 20% of the overall population. In states where less than five places meet either of these criteria, we have included places with at least 10,000 total population with the highest percentage of Hispanic/Latino population. These places are identified with an asterisk (*); Please refer to the User's Guide for a full explanation of data.

Median Gross Rent

Group	Dollars
Total Population	693
Hispanic or Latino (of any race)	636
Mexican	641

Median Household Income
(2010 Inflation-Adjusted Dollars)

Group	Dollars
Total Population	39,838
Hispanic or Latino (of any race)	32,917
Mexican	34,140

Per Capita Income
(2010 Inflation-Adjusted Dollars)

Group	Dollars
Total Population	16,322
Hispanic or Latino (of any race)	11,605
Mexican	11,504

Households with $100,000+ Income

Group	Number	%
Total Population	1,824	11.5
Hispanic or Latino (of any race)	526	6.6
Mexican	486	6.6

Households with Food Stamps/SNAP Benefits During Past 12 Months

Group	Number	%
Total Population	2,612	16.5
Hispanic or Latino (of any race)	1,799	22.7
Mexican	1,618	22.0

Poverty Rate
(Income in Past 12 Months Below Poverty Level)

Group	%
Total Population	25.9
Hispanic or Latino (of any race)	32.7
Mexican	34.0

Males per 100 Females

Group	Number
Total Population	97.6
Hispanic or Latino (of any race)	96.5
Central American, ex. Mexican	88.5
Costa Rican	75.0
Guatemalan	101.1
Honduran	66.1
Nicaraguan	84.6
Panamanian	78.6
Salvadoran	89.9
Cuban	93.4
Mexican	97.4
Puerto Rican	92.7
South American	89.7
Argentinean	96.8
Chilean	89.6
Colombian	77.5
Ecuadorian	85.6
Peruvian	94.6
Spaniard	83.2

Average Household Size

Group	People
Total Population	2.98
Hispanic or Latino (of any race)	3.46
Central American, ex. Mexican	3.69
Costa Rican	3.23
Guatemalan	3.96
Honduran	3.26
Nicaraguan	3.72
Panamanian	2.66
Salvadoran	3.78
Cuban	3.03
Mexican	3.50
Puerto Rican	2.97
South American	3.33
Argentinean	2.88
Chilean	3.32
Colombian	3.34
Ecuadorian	3.60
Peruvian	3.63
Spaniard	2.92

Rancho Cucamonga

Population

Group	Number	%TP[1]	%HP[2]
Total Population	165,269	100.0	–
Hispanic or Latino (of any race)	57,688	34.9	100.0
Central American, ex. Mexican	3,487	2.1	6.0
Costa Rican	245	0.1	0.4
Guatemalan	907	0.5	1.6
Honduran	211	0.1	0.4
Nicaraguan	598	0.4	1.0
Panamanian	100	0.1	0.2
Salvadoran	1,396	0.8	2.4
Cuban	820	0.5	1.4
Mexican	45,369	27.5	78.6
Puerto Rican	1,214	0.7	2.1
South American	2,823	1.7	4.9
Argentinean	561	0.3	1.0
Chilean	146	0.1	0.3
Colombian	694	0.4	1.2
Ecuadorian	399	0.2	0.7
Peruvian	800	0.5	1.4
Spaniard	722	0.4	1.3

Population Growth: 2000–2010

Group	%
Total Population	29.4
Hispanic or Latino (of any race)	62.5
Central American, ex. Mexican	186.5
Costa Rican	133.3
Guatemalan	181.7
Nicaraguan	234.1
Salvadoran	286.7
Cuban	79.4
Mexican	71.0
Puerto Rican	44.4
South American	145.5
Argentinean	124.4
Colombian	179.8
Ecuadorian	202.3
Peruvian	181.7

Median Age

Group	Years
Total Population	34.5
Hispanic or Latino (of any race)	28.5
Central American, ex. Mexican	33.9
Costa Rican	35.3
Guatemalan	34.0
Honduran	29.9
Nicaraguan	34.8
Panamanian	39.0
Salvadoran	33.1
Cuban	34.1
Mexican	27.7
Puerto Rican	29.3
South American	35.8
Argentinean	39.3
Chilean	35.0
Colombian	33.6
Ecuadorian	34.4
Peruvian	36.8
Spaniard	34.7

High School Graduates
(Universe: Population 25 Years and Over)

Group	Number	%
Total Population	90,899	90.6
Hispanic or Latino (of any race)	24,200	81.4
Central American, ex. Mexican	1,791	78.2
Salvadoran	761	74.8
Mexican	18,325	80.4
Puerto Rican	551	88.6
South American	1,429	86.4

Four-Year College Graduates
(Universe: Population 25 Years and Over)

Group	Number	%
Total Population	29,226	29.1
Hispanic or Latino (of any race)	5,168	17.4
Central American, ex. Mexican	540	23.6
Salvadoran	247	24.3
Mexican	3,496	15.3

Puerto Rican	101	16.2
South American	510	30.8

Population Age 3–17 Enrolled in Public School
(Universe: Population Age 3–17 Enrolled in School)

Group	Number	%
Total Population	30,413	89.6
Hispanic or Latino (of any race)	13,644	91.0
Central American, ex. Mexican	709	94.0
Salvadoran	339	88.3
Mexican	11,077	92.0
Puerto Rican	224	100.0
South American	486	79.9

Population Age 3–17 Enrolled in Private School
(Universe: Population Age 3–17 Enrolled in School)

Group	Number	%
Total Population	3,522	10.4
Hispanic or Latino (of any race)	1,346	9.0
Central American, ex. Mexican	45	6.0
Salvadoran	45	11.7
Mexican	962	8.0
Puerto Rican	0	0.0
South American	122	20.1

Foreign-Born Population

Group	Number	%
Total Population	27,254	17.0
Hispanic or Latino (of any race)	11,842	21.4
Central American, ex. Mexican	2,258	60.6
Salvadoran	871	51.1
Mexican	7,472	17.3
Puerto Rican	0	0.0
South American	1,400	54.0

Foreign-Born Naturalized U.S. Citizens

Group	Number	%
Total Population	15,836	58.1
Hispanic or Latino (of any race)	6,518	55.0
Central American, ex. Mexican	1,217	53.9
Salvadoran	674	77.4
Mexican	4,059	54.3
Puerto Rican	0	0.0
South American	737	52.6

Language Spoken at Home: English Only
(Universe: Population 5 Years and Over)

Group	Number	%
Total Population	105,075	70.0
Hispanic or Latino (of any race)	23,145	45.9
Central American, ex. Mexican	311	9.4
Salvadoran	135	8.9
Mexican	19,471	49.5
Puerto Rican	529	53.2
South American	541	21.4

Language Spoken at Home: Spanish
(Universe: Population 5 Years and Over)

Group	Number	%
Total Population	29,110	19.4
Hispanic or Latino (of any race)	27,146	53.8
Central American, ex. Mexican	3,010	90.6
Salvadoran	1,379	91.1
Mexican	19,813	50.4
Puerto Rican	465	46.8
South American	1,984	78.6

Unemployment Rate
(Universe: Population 16 Years and Over)

Group	%
Total Population	8.5
Hispanic or Latino (of any race)	9.8
Central American, ex. Mexican	10.5
Salvadoran	14.9
Mexican	10.0
Puerto Rican	4.3
South American	11.2

Class of Worker: Private Wage and Salary
(Universe: Civilian Employed Population 16 Years and Over)

Group	Number	%
Total Population	60,456	75.6
Hispanic or Latino (of any race)	19,268	78.8
Central American, ex. Mexican	1,412	76.3
Salvadoran	603	79.8
Mexican	15,167	79.9

Notes: (1) Percent of total population; (2) Percent of Hispanic/Latino population; Profiles include places with an overall population of at least 125,000, OR an overall population of at least 25,000 where the Hispanic/Latino population is at least 20% of the overall population. In states where less than five places meet either of these criteria, we have included places with at least 10,000 total population with the highest percentage of Hispanic/Latino population. These places are identified with an asterisk (*); Please refer to the User's Guide for a full explanation of data.

Puerto Rican	312	74.3
South American	871	70.2

Class of Worker: Government
(Universe: Civilian Employed Population 16 Years and Over)

Group	Number	%
Total Population	14,032	17.5
Hispanic or Latino (of any race)	3,729	15.2
Central American, ex. Mexican	308	16.6
Salvadoran	139	18.4
Mexican	2,802	14.8
Puerto Rican	78	18.6
South American	221	17.8

Means of Transportation to Work: Car, Truck or Van
(Universe: Workers 16 Years and Over)

Group	Number	%
Total Population	71,499	92.5
Hispanic or Latino (of any race)	21,659	93.0
Central American, ex. Mexican	1,536	89.9
Salvadoran	567	86.3
Mexican	16,987	93.6
Puerto Rican	327	86.5
South American	1,156	96.1

Means of Transportation to Work: Public Transportation (ex. Taxicab)
(Universe: Workers 16 Years and Over)

Group	Number	%
Total Population	1,357	1.8
Hispanic or Latino (of any race)	387	1.7
Central American, ex. Mexican	53	3.1
Salvadoran	53	8.1
Mexican	260	1.4
Puerto Rican	0	0.0
South American	31	2.6

Homeownership Rate
(Universe: Occupied Housing Units)

Group	%
Total Population	64.8
Hispanic or Latino (of any race)	58.8
Central American, ex. Mexican	56.2
Costa Rican	64.4
Guatemalan	55.9
Honduran	37.7
Nicaraguan	55.8
Panamanian	47.7
Salvadoran	59.5
Cuban	68.8
Mexican	59.4
Puerto Rican	50.8
South American	59.4
Argentinean	58.3
Chilean	52.3
Colombian	61.2
Ecuadorian	62.3
Peruvian	57.4
Spaniard	64.5

Median Home Value

Group	Dollars
Total Population	449,800
Hispanic or Latino (of any race)	445,900
Central American, ex. Mexican	445,600
Salvadoran	472,000
Mexican	437,200
Puerto Rican	561,400
South American	527,200

Median Gross Rent

Group	Dollars
Total Population	1,409
Hispanic or Latino (of any race)	1,328
Central American, ex. Mexican	1,172
Salvadoran	1,352
Mexican	1,366
Puerto Rican	1,288
South American	1,413

Median Household Income
(2010 Inflation-Adjusted Dollars)

Group	Dollars
Total Population	78,572
Hispanic or Latino (of any race)	71,125
Central American, ex. Mexican	65,484
Salvadoran	61,389
Mexican	74,157
Puerto Rican	84,044
South American	65,496

Per Capita Income
(2010 Inflation-Adjusted Dollars)

Group	Dollars
Total Population	32,285
Hispanic or Latino (of any race)	23,179
Central American, ex. Mexican	22,765
Salvadoran	18,339
Mexican	22,791
Puerto Rican	20,721
South American	29,294

Households with $100,000+ Income

Group	Number	%
Total Population	19,730	37.4
Hispanic or Latino (of any race)	4,477	31.0
Central American, ex. Mexican	271	27.5
Salvadoran	73	18.3
Mexican	3,420	32.0
Puerto Rican	105	29.4
South American	279	26.7

Households with Food Stamps/SNAP Benefits During Past 12 Months

Group	Number	%
Total Population	1,253	2.4
Hispanic or Latino (of any race)	474	3.3
Central American, ex. Mexican	17	1.7
Salvadoran	5	1.3
Mexican	390	3.7
Puerto Rican	0	0.0
South American	0	0.0

Poverty Rate
(Income in Past 12 Months Below Poverty Level)

Group	%
Total Population	4.8
Hispanic or Latino (of any race)	5.0
Central American, ex. Mexican	3.8
Salvadoran	7.5
Mexican	4.5
Puerto Rican	23.1
South American	6.5

Redlands

Population

Group	Number	%TP[1]	%HP[2]
Total Population	68,747	100.0	–
Hispanic or Latino (of any race)	20,810	30.3	100.0
Central American, ex. Mexican	611	0.9	2.9
Guatemalan	127	0.2	0.6
Salvadoran	255	0.4	1.2
Cuban	137	0.2	0.7
Mexican	17,460	25.4	83.9
Puerto Rican	477	0.7	2.3
South American	462	0.7	2.2
Colombian	141	0.2	0.7
Peruvian	106	0.2	0.5
Spaniard	343	0.5	1.6

Population Growth: 2000–2010

Group	%
Total Population	8.1
Hispanic or Latino (of any race)	36.0
Central American, ex. Mexican	191.0
Cuban	14.2
Mexican	43.2
Puerto Rican	67.4
South American	126.5

Males per 100 Females

Group	Number
Total Population	90.9
Hispanic or Latino (of any race)	94.0
Central American, ex. Mexican	107.8
Guatemalan	130.9
Salvadoran	104.0
Cuban	144.6
Mexican	94.6
Puerto Rican	86.3
South American	83.3
Colombian	69.9
Peruvian	71.0
Spaniard	85.4

Average Household Size

Group	People
Total Population	2.68
Hispanic or Latino (of any race)	3.39
Central American, ex. Mexican	3.47
Guatemalan	3.71
Salvadoran	4.12
Cuban	2.56
Mexican	3.47
Puerto Rican	2.92
South American	2.88
Colombian	2.74
Peruvian	3.28
Spaniard	2.71

Median Age

Group	Years
Total Population	36.2
Hispanic or Latino (of any race)	26.8
Central American, ex. Mexican	32.1
Guatemalan	32.3
Salvadoran	30.9
Cuban	44.3
Mexican	26.4
Puerto Rican	27.3
South American	32.6
Colombian	29.4
Peruvian	32.0
Spaniard	33.2

High School Graduates
(Universe: Population 25 Years and Over)

Group	Number	%
Total Population	38,412	89.2
Hispanic or Latino (of any race)	7,848	74.2
Mexican	6,315	71.5

Four-Year College Graduates
(Universe: Population 25 Years and Over)

Group	Number	%
Total Population	15,978	37.1
Hispanic or Latino (of any race)	1,788	16.9
Mexican	1,148	13.0

Population Age 3–17 Enrolled in Public School
(Universe: Population Age 3–17 Enrolled in School)

Group	Number	%
Total Population	12,021	84.4
Hispanic or Latino (of any race)	5,287	90.1
Mexican	4,674	90.6

Population Age 3–17 Enrolled in Private School
(Universe: Population Age 3–17 Enrolled in School)

Group	Number	%
Total Population	2,227	15.6
Hispanic or Latino (of any race)	584	9.9
Mexican	483	9.4

Foreign-Born Population

Group	Number	%
Total Population	10,346	15.0
Hispanic or Latino (of any race)	4,364	21.5
Mexican	3,458	20.0

Foreign-Born Naturalized U.S. Citizens

Group	Number	%
Total Population	5,561	53.8
Hispanic or Latino (of any race)	1,937	44.4
Mexican	1,442	41.7

Language Spoken at Home: English Only
(Universe: Population 5 Years and Over)

Group	Number	%
Total Population	49,621	76.7
Hispanic or Latino (of any race)	9,321	50.7
Mexican	7,979	50.9

STATE & PLACE PROFILES

Notes: (1) Percent of total population; (2) Percent of Hispanic/Latino population; Profiles include places with an overall population of at least 125,000, OR an overall population of at least 25,000 where the Hispanic/Latino population is at least 20% of the overall population. In states where less than five places meet either of these criteria, we have included places with at least 10,000 total population with the highest percentage of Hispanic/Latino population. These places are identified with an asterisk (*); Please refer to the User's Guide for a full explanation of data.

Language Spoken at Home: Spanish
(Universe: Population 5 Years and Over)

Group	Number	%
Total Population	9,659	14.9
Hispanic or Latino (of any race)	9,037	49.1
Mexican	7,660	48.9

Unemployment Rate
(Universe: Population 16 Years and Over)

Group	%
Total Population	8.3
Hispanic or Latino (of any race)	11.1
Mexican	11.6

Class of Worker: Private Wage and Salary
(Universe: Civilian Employed Population 16 Years and Over)

Group	Number	%
Total Population	22,711	70.8
Hispanic or Latino (of any race)	6,183	75.2
Mexican	5,069	74.4

Class of Worker: Government
(Universe: Civilian Employed Population 16 Years and Over)

Group	Number	%
Total Population	7,066	22.0
Hispanic or Latino (of any race)	1,710	20.8
Mexican	1,438	21.1

Means of Transportation to Work: Car, Truck or Van
(Universe: Workers 16 Years and Over)

Group	Number	%
Total Population	27,733	89.3
Hispanic or Latino (of any race)	7,462	92.1
Mexican	6,241	92.6

Means of Transportation to Work: Public Transportation (ex. Taxicab)
(Universe: Workers 16 Years and Over)

Group	Number	%
Total Population	300	1.0
Hispanic or Latino (of any race)	67	0.8
Mexican	67	1.0

Homeownership Rate
(Universe: Occupied Housing Units)

Group	%
Total Population	60.8
Hispanic or Latino (of any race)	50.1
Central American, ex. Mexican	50.3
Guatemalan	48.8
Salvadoran	50.8
Cuban	64.6
Mexican	51.1
Puerto Rican	38.9
South American	57.5
Colombian	61.7
Peruvian	44.8
Spaniard	60.6

Median Home Value

Group	Dollars
Total Population	370,600
Hispanic or Latino (of any race)	316,700
Mexican	313,800

Median Gross Rent

Group	Dollars
Total Population	1,067
Hispanic or Latino (of any race)	997
Mexican	1,002

Median Household Income
(2010 Inflation-Adjusted Dollars)

Group	Dollars
Total Population	67,651
Hispanic or Latino (of any race)	55,874
Mexican	55,586

Per Capita Income
(2010 Inflation-Adjusted Dollars)

Group	Dollars
Total Population	31,488
Hispanic or Latino (of any race)	20,542
Mexican	19,724

Households with $100,000+ Income

Group	Number	%
Total Population	7,225	29.9
Hispanic or Latino (of any race)	1,121	20.4
Mexican	885	19.6

Households with Food Stamps/SNAP Benefits During Past 12 Months

Group	Number	%
Total Population	1,297	5.4
Hispanic or Latino (of any race)	610	11.1
Mexican	532	11.8

Poverty Rate
(Income in Past 12 Months Below Poverty Level)

Group	%
Total Population	10.1
Hispanic or Latino (of any race)	15.0
Mexican	15.8

Redwood City

Population

Group	Number	%TP[1]	%HP[2]
Total Population	76,815	100.0	–
Hispanic or Latino (of any race)	29,810	38.8	100.0
Central American, ex. Mexican	5,032	6.6	16.9
Guatemalan	1,756	2.3	5.9
Honduran	135	0.2	0.5
Nicaraguan	565	0.7	1.9
Salvadoran	2,432	3.2	8.2
Cuban	167	0.2	0.6
Mexican	21,132	27.5	70.9
Puerto Rican	384	0.5	1.3
South American	1,166	1.5	3.9
Argentinean	149	0.2	0.5
Colombian	133	0.2	0.4
Peruvian	578	0.8	1.9
Spaniard	405	0.5	1.4

Population Growth: 2000–2010

Group	%
Total Population	1.9
Hispanic or Latino (of any race)	26.5
Central American, ex. Mexican	111.3
Guatemalan	245.7
Nicaraguan	98.2
Salvadoran	93.0
Cuban	6.4
Mexican	28.5
Puerto Rican	45.5
South American	54.2
Peruvian	77.8

Males per 100 Females

Group	Number
Total Population	99.2
Hispanic or Latino (of any race)	105.8
Central American, ex. Mexican	113.7
Guatemalan	178.3
Honduran	110.9
Nicaraguan	87.1
Salvadoran	89.0
Cuban	108.8
Mexican	106.2
Puerto Rican	97.9
South American	80.8
Argentinean	104.1
Colombian	44.6
Peruvian	85.3
Spaniard	93.8

Average Household Size

Group	People
Total Population	2.69
Hispanic or Latino (of any race)	3.80
Central American, ex. Mexican	3.94
Guatemalan	4.43
Honduran	4.00
Nicaraguan	3.31
Salvadoran	3.85
Cuban	2.60
Mexican	3.98
Puerto Rican	2.28
South American	2.83
Argentinean	2.67
Colombian	2.38
Peruvian	3.18
Spaniard	2.54

Median Age

Group	Years
Total Population	36.7
Hispanic or Latino (of any race)	28.5
Central American, ex. Mexican	30.6
Guatemalan	28.8
Honduran	37.8
Nicaraguan	32.1
Salvadoran	31.7
Cuban	35.8
Mexican	27.2
Puerto Rican	33.5
South American	38.4
Argentinean	35.8
Colombian	37.5
Peruvian	38.3
Spaniard	38.9

High School Graduates
(Universe: Population 25 Years and Over)

Group	Number	%
Total Population	43,593	85.3
Hispanic or Latino (of any race)	9,683	63.5
Central American, ex. Mexican	1,540	67.2
Salvadoran	815	61.5
Mexican	6,838	59.9
South American	586	86.0

Four-Year College Graduates
(Universe: Population 25 Years and Over)

Group	Number	%
Total Population	20,281	39.7
Hispanic or Latino (of any race)	1,801	11.8
Central American, ex. Mexican	357	15.6
Salvadoran	152	11.5
Mexican	935	8.2
South American	243	35.7

Population Age 3–17 Enrolled in Public School
(Universe: Population Age 3–17 Enrolled in School)

Group	Number	%
Total Population	10,740	78.5
Hispanic or Latino (of any race)	6,599	93.7
Central American, ex. Mexican	577	100.0
Salvadoran	452	100.0
Mexican	5,613	95.5
South American	171	71.8

Population Age 3–17 Enrolled in Private School
(Universe: Population Age 3–17 Enrolled in School)

Group	Number	%
Total Population	2,949	21.5
Hispanic or Latino (of any race)	441	6.3
Central American, ex. Mexican	0	0.0
Salvadoran	0	0.0
Mexican	265	4.5
South American	67	28.2

Foreign-Born Population

Group	Number	%
Total Population	24,226	32.2
Hispanic or Latino (of any race)	14,447	52.3
Central American, ex. Mexican	2,470	76.2
Salvadoran	1,494	73.2
Mexican	10,928	49.4
South American	770	79.9

Foreign-Born Naturalized U.S. Citizens

Group	Number	%
Total Population	9,227	38.1
Hispanic or Latino (of any race)	3,296	22.8
Central American, ex. Mexican	722	29.2
Salvadoran	463	31.0
Mexican	2,157	19.7
South American	274	35.6

Notes: (1) Percent of total population; (2) Percent of Hispanic/Latino population; Profiles include places with an overall population of at least 125,000, OR an overall population of at least 25,000 where the Hispanic/Latino population is at least 20% of the overall population. In states where less than five places meet either of these criteria, we have included places with at least 10,000 total population with the highest percentage of Hispanic/Latino population. These places are identified with an asterisk (*); Please refer to the User's Guide for a full explanation of data.

Language Spoken at Home: English Only
(Universe: Population 5 Years and Over)

Group	Number	%
Total Population	37,391	54.6
Hispanic or Latino (of any race)	3,339	13.7
Central American, ex. Mexican	182	5.8
Salvadoran	60	3.1
Mexican	2,559	13.3
South American	125	13.6

Language Spoken at Home: Spanish
(Universe: Population 5 Years and Over)

Group	Number	%
Total Population	21,811	31.9
Hispanic or Latino (of any race)	20,970	85.8
Central American, ex. Mexican	2,957	94.2
Salvadoran	1,900	96.9
Mexican	16,608	86.4
South American	797	86.4

Unemployment Rate
(Universe: Population 16 Years and Over)

Group	%
Total Population	6.4
Hispanic or Latino (of any race)	8.0
Central American, ex. Mexican	13.5
Salvadoran	13.8
Mexican	7.1
South American	10.6

Class of Worker: Private Wage and Salary
(Universe: Civilian Employed Population 16 Years and Over)

Group	Number	%
Total Population	29,237	77.2
Hispanic or Latino (of any race)	9,621	76.4
Central American, ex. Mexican	1,274	74.3
Salvadoran	664	70.9
Mexican	7,710	77.6
South American	372	78.5

Class of Worker: Government
(Universe: Civilian Employed Population 16 Years and Over)

Group	Number	%
Total Population	3,600	9.5
Hispanic or Latino (of any race)	1,037	8.2
Central American, ex. Mexican	242	14.1
Salvadoran	129	13.8
Mexican	649	6.5
South American	11	2.3

Means of Transportation to Work: Car, Truck or Van
(Universe: Workers 16 Years and Over)

Group	Number	%
Total Population	31,570	84.9
Hispanic or Latino (of any race)	10,349	83.8
Central American, ex. Mexican	1,439	85.3
Salvadoran	745	82.0
Mexican	8,020	82.3
South American	456	96.2

Means of Transportation to Work: Public Transportation (ex. Taxicab)
(Universe: Workers 16 Years and Over)

Group	Number	%
Total Population	1,290	3.5
Hispanic or Latino (of any race)	627	5.1
Central American, ex. Mexican	134	7.9
Salvadoran	81	8.9
Mexican	478	4.9
South American	7	1.5

Homeownership Rate
(Universe: Occupied Housing Units)

Group	%
Total Population	50.6
Hispanic or Latino (of any race)	26.8
Central American, ex. Mexican	21.1
Guatemalan	17.6
Honduran	15.2
Nicaraguan	20.4
Salvadoran	22.9
Cuban	39.7
Mexican	25.6
Puerto Rican	32.5
South American	39.3
Argentinean	38.9
Colombian	51.3
Peruvian	33.1
Spaniard	60.4

Median Home Value

Group	Dollars
Total Population	808,600
Hispanic or Latino (of any race)	724,300
Central American, ex. Mexican	615,900
Salvadoran	551,500
Mexican	738,700
South American	661,800

Median Gross Rent

Group	Dollars
Total Population	1,340
Hispanic or Latino (of any race)	1,275
Central American, ex. Mexican	1,268
Salvadoran	1,202
Mexican	1,276
South American	1,144

Median Household Income
(2010 Inflation-Adjusted Dollars)

Group	Dollars
Total Population	75,231
Hispanic or Latino (of any race)	54,229
Central American, ex. Mexican	53,932
Salvadoran	57,736
Mexican	54,691
South American	41,950

Per Capita Income
(2010 Inflation-Adjusted Dollars)

Group	Dollars
Total Population	39,245
Hispanic or Latino (of any race)	16,793
Central American, ex. Mexican	18,947
Salvadoran	15,320
Mexican	15,580
South American	21,703

Households with $100,000+ Income

Group	Number	%
Total Population	10,608	38.2
Hispanic or Latino (of any race)	1,021	14.3
Central American, ex. Mexican	125	12.4
Salvadoran	77	12.3
Mexican	725	13.4
South American	27	7.5

Households with Food Stamps/SNAP Benefits During Past 12 Months

Group	Number	%
Total Population	695	2.5
Hispanic or Latino (of any race)	395	5.5
Central American, ex. Mexican	0	0.0
Salvadoran	0	0.0
Mexican	395	7.3
South American	0	0.0

Poverty Rate
(Income in Past 12 Months Below Poverty Level)

Group	%
Total Population	9.6
Hispanic or Latino (of any race)	16.2
Central American, ex. Mexican	13.4
Salvadoran	10.8
Mexican	17.2
South American	7.9

Rialto

Population

Group	Number	%TP[1]	%HP[2]
Total Population	99,171	100.0	–
Hispanic or Latino (of any race)	67,038	67.6	100.0
Central American, ex. Mexican	4,402	4.4	6.6
Costa Rican	102	0.1	0.2
Guatemalan	1,111	1.1	1.7
Honduran	324	0.3	0.5
Nicaraguan	482	0.5	0.7
Salvadoran	2,246	2.3	3.4
Cuban	251	0.3	0.4
Mexican	57,699	58.2	86.1
Puerto Rican	687	0.7	1.0
South American	747	0.8	1.1
Colombian	201	0.2	0.3
Ecuadorian	127	0.1	0.2
Peruvian	207	0.2	0.3
Spaniard	220	0.2	0.3

Population Growth: 2000–2010

Group	%
Total Population	7.9
Hispanic or Latino (of any race)	42.5
Central American, ex. Mexican	139.9
Guatemalan	187.1
Nicaraguan	95.1
Salvadoran	187.6
Cuban	-2.7
Mexican	53.5
Puerto Rican	1.5
South American	103.0

Males per 100 Females

Group	Number
Total Population	94.7
Hispanic or Latino (of any race)	97.0
Central American, ex. Mexican	94.3
Costa Rican	96.2
Guatemalan	109.2
Honduran	88.4
Nicaraguan	93.6
Salvadoran	89.4
Cuban	93.1
Mexican	97.3
Puerto Rican	103.3
South American	93.0
Colombian	99.0
Ecuadorian	81.4
Peruvian	93.5
Spaniard	96.4

Average Household Size

Group	People
Total Population	3.92
Hispanic or Latino (of any race)	4.61
Central American, ex. Mexican	4.53
Costa Rican	3.36
Guatemalan	4.77
Honduran	4.39
Nicaraguan	4.34
Salvadoran	4.61
Cuban	3.39
Mexican	4.67
Puerto Rican	3.36
South American	4.04
Colombian	3.89
Ecuadorian	4.27
Peruvian	3.98
Spaniard	3.86

Median Age

Group	Years
Total Population	28.3
Hispanic or Latino (of any race)	25.0
Central American, ex. Mexican	33.3
Costa Rican	41.5
Guatemalan	33.0
Honduran	30.6
Nicaraguan	35.8
Salvadoran	32.7
Cuban	34.8
Mexican	24.3
Puerto Rican	28.2
South American	34.5
Colombian	32.3
Ecuadorian	37.5
Peruvian	38.3
Spaniard	36.3

High School Graduates
(Universe: Population 25 Years and Over)

Group	Number	%
Total Population	35,401	65.2
Hispanic or Latino (of any race)	16,666	51.6

Notes: (1) Percent of total population; (2) Percent of Hispanic/Latino population; Profiles include places with an overall population of at least 125,000, OR an overall population of at least 25,000 where the Hispanic/Latino population is at least 20% of the overall population. In states where less than five places meet either of these criteria, we have included places with at least 10,000 total population with the highest percentage of Hispanic/Latino population. These places are identified with an asterisk (*); Please refer to the User's Guide for a full explanation of data.

Central American, ex. Mexican	1,289	55.0
Salvadoran	510	50.6
Mexican	13,826	49.7

Four-Year College Graduates
(Universe: Population 25 Years and Over)

Group	Number	%
Total Population	4,693	8.6
Hispanic or Latino (of any race)	1,335	4.1
Central American, ex. Mexican	242	10.3
Salvadoran	44	4.4
Mexican	841	3.0

Population Age 3–17 Enrolled in Public School
(Universe: Population Age 3–17 Enrolled in School)

Group	Number	%
Total Population	24,042	95.5
Hispanic or Latino (of any race)	17,896	97.1
Central American, ex. Mexican	955	95.6
Salvadoran	373	100.0
Mexican	16,069	97.3

Population Age 3–17 Enrolled in Private School
(Universe: Population Age 3–17 Enrolled in School)

Group	Number	%
Total Population	1,133	4.5
Hispanic or Latino (of any race)	527	2.9
Central American, ex. Mexican	44	4.4
Salvadoran	0	0.0
Mexican	448	2.7

Foreign-Born Population

Group	Number	%
Total Population	27,906	28.1
Hispanic or Latino (of any race)	25,386	38.6
Central American, ex. Mexican	2,211	56.7
Salvadoran	992	59.7
Mexican	22,147	38.3

Foreign-Born Naturalized U.S. Citizens

Group	Number	%
Total Population	9,761	35.0
Hispanic or Latino (of any race)	8,076	31.8
Central American, ex. Mexican	859	38.9
Salvadoran	312	31.5
Mexican	6,694	30.2

Language Spoken at Home: English Only
(Universe: Population 5 Years and Over)

Group	Number	%
Total Population	38,770	42.9
Hispanic or Latino (of any race)	10,606	18.1
Central American, ex. Mexican	149	4.0
Salvadoran	138	8.5
Mexican	9,158	17.8

Language Spoken at Home: Spanish
(Universe: Population 5 Years and Over)

Group	Number	%
Total Population	49,111	54.3
Hispanic or Latino (of any race)	47,936	81.8
Central American, ex. Mexican	3,552	94.8
Salvadoran	1,483	91.5
Mexican	42,192	82.2

Unemployment Rate
(Universe: Population 16 Years and Over)

Group	%
Total Population	10.9
Hispanic or Latino (of any race)	10.4
Central American, ex. Mexican	8.0
Salvadoran	11.7
Mexican	10.5

Class of Worker: Private Wage and Salary
(Universe: Civilian Employed Population 16 Years and Over)

Group	Number	%
Total Population	30,929	78.6
Hispanic or Latino (of any race)	21,019	83.1
Central American, ex. Mexican	1,604	81.6
Salvadoran	749	92.1
Mexican	18,252	83.1

Class of Worker: Government
(Universe: Civilian Employed Population 16 Years and Over)

Group	Number	%
Total Population	5,180	13.2
Hispanic or Latino (of any race)	2,047	8.1
Central American, ex. Mexican	208	10.6
Salvadoran	0	0.0
Mexican	1,742	7.9

Means of Transportation to Work: Car, Truck or Van
(Universe: Workers 16 Years and Over)

Group	Number	%
Total Population	35,497	93.6
Hispanic or Latino (of any race)	23,172	94.8
Central American, ex. Mexican	1,662	88.7
Salvadoran	610	81.4
Mexican	20,387	95.7

Means of Transportation to Work: Public Transportation (ex. Taxicab)
(Universe: Workers 16 Years and Over)

Group	Number	%
Total Population	746	2.0
Hispanic or Latino (of any race)	364	1.5
Central American, ex. Mexican	37	2.0
Salvadoran	15	2.0
Mexican	313	1.5

Homeownership Rate
(Universe: Occupied Housing Units)

Group	%
Total Population	64.7
Hispanic or Latino (of any race)	63.9
Central American, ex. Mexican	65.4
Costa Rican	78.8
Guatemalan	66.9
Honduran	59.0
Nicaraguan	63.6
Salvadoran	64.6
Cuban	61.3
Mexican	64.5
Puerto Rican	47.7
South American	66.8
Colombian	62.5
Ecuadorian	56.8
Peruvian	75.4
Spaniard	78.6

Median Home Value

Group	Dollars
Total Population	301,100
Hispanic or Latino (of any race)	284,000
Central American, ex. Mexican	321,000
Salvadoran	319,200
Mexican	277,700

Median Gross Rent

Group	Dollars
Total Population	1,069
Hispanic or Latino (of any race)	1,085
Central American, ex. Mexican	1,088
Salvadoran	778
Mexican	1,117

Median Household Income
(2010 Inflation-Adjusted Dollars)

Group	Dollars
Total Population	50,555
Hispanic or Latino (of any race)	51,053
Central American, ex. Mexican	63,229
Salvadoran	43,922
Mexican	50,664

Per Capita Income
(2010 Inflation-Adjusted Dollars)

Group	Dollars
Total Population	16,040
Hispanic or Latino (of any race)	12,918
Central American, ex. Mexican	19,087
Salvadoran	15,559
Mexican	12,491

Households with $100,000+ Income

Group	Number	%
Total Population	4,026	16.3
Hispanic or Latino (of any race)	2,043	15.3
Central American, ex. Mexican	258	24.0
Salvadoran	45	12.4
Mexican	1,572	14.0

Households with Food Stamps/SNAP Benefits During Past 12 Months

Group	Number	%
Total Population	2,718	11.0
Hispanic or Latino (of any race)	1,596	12.0
Central American, ex. Mexican	136	12.6
Salvadoran	15	4.1
Mexican	1,354	12.1

Poverty Rate
(Income in Past 12 Months Below Poverty Level)

Group	%
Total Population	14.7
Hispanic or Latino (of any race)	15.9
Central American, ex. Mexican	9.9
Salvadoran	5.9
Mexican	16.3

Richmond

Population

Group	Number	%TP[1]	%HP[2]
Total Population	103,701	100.0	–
Hispanic or Latino (of any race)	40,921	39.5	100.0
Central American, ex. Mexican	8,329	8.0	20.4
Guatemalan	1,717	1.7	4.2
Honduran	319	0.3	0.8
Nicaraguan	1,209	1.2	3.0
Salvadoran	4,888	4.7	11.9
Cuban	141	0.1	0.3
Mexican	28,275	27.3	69.1
Puerto Rican	534	0.5	1.3
South American	942	0.9	2.3
Chilean	136	0.1	0.3
Colombian	107	0.1	0.3
Peruvian	548	0.5	1.3
Spaniard	254	0.2	0.6

Population Growth: 2000–2010

Group	%
Total Population	4.5
Hispanic or Latino (of any race)	55.5
Central American, ex. Mexican	229.5
Guatemalan	366.6
Nicaraguan	190.6
Salvadoran	264.8
Cuban	18.5
Mexican	53.7
Puerto Rican	16.6
South American	95.4
Peruvian	119.2

Males per 100 Females

Group	Number
Total Population	94.8
Hispanic or Latino (of any race)	107.0
Central American, ex. Mexican	104.3
Guatemalan	127.1
Honduran	98.1
Nicaraguan	92.2
Salvadoran	101.1
Cuban	104.3
Mexican	109.2
Puerto Rican	95.6
South American	86.5
Chilean	88.9
Colombian	84.5
Peruvian	80.9
Spaniard	77.6

Average Household Size

Group	People
Total Population	2.83
Hispanic or Latino (of any race)	4.06
Central American, ex. Mexican	4.11

Notes: (1) Percent of total population; (2) Percent of Hispanic/Latino population; Profiles include places with an overall population of at least 125,000, OR an overall population of at least 25,000 where the Hispanic/Latino population is at least 20% of the overall population. In states where less than five places meet either of these criteria, we have included places with at least 10,000 total population with the highest percentage of Hispanic/Latino population. These places are identified with an asterisk (*); Please refer to the User's Guide for a full explanation of data.

Group	
Guatemalan	4.26
Honduran	4.41
Nicaraguan	4.06
Salvadoran	4.11
Cuban	2.51
Mexican	4.21
Puerto Rican	2.78
South American	2.95
Chilean	3.02
Colombian	2.32
Peruvian	3.26
Spaniard	2.59

Median Age

Group	Years
Total Population	34.8
Hispanic or Latino (of any race)	27.1
Central American, ex. Mexican	31.4
Guatemalan	29.9
Honduran	31.3
Nicaraguan	33.1
Salvadoran	31.7
Cuban	32.5
Mexican	25.5
Puerto Rican	27.1
South American	37.2
Chilean	39.5
Colombian	33.7
Peruvian	36.0
Spaniard	37.4

High School Graduates

(Universe: Population 25 Years and Over)

Group	Number	%
Total Population	52,738	79.6
Hispanic or Latino (of any race)	11,568	59.8
Central American, ex. Mexican	2,821	58.1
Guatemalan	659	47.9
Nicaraguan	570	79.9
Salvadoran	1,439	56.6
Mexican	7,081	56.0
South American	741	89.0

Four-Year College Graduates

(Universe: Population 25 Years and Over)

Group	Number	%
Total Population	17,755	26.8
Hispanic or Latino (of any race)	2,049	10.6
Central American, ex. Mexican	437	9.0
Guatemalan	90	6.5
Nicaraguan	91	12.8
Salvadoran	215	8.5
Mexican	1,163	9.2
South American	205	24.6

Population Age 3–17 Enrolled in Public School

(Universe: Population Age 3–17 Enrolled in School)

Group	Number	%
Total Population	17,276	87.9
Hispanic or Latino (of any race)	8,792	93.2
Central American, ex. Mexican	1,934	95.7
Guatemalan	409	96.9
Nicaraguan	137	77.8
Salvadoran	1,299	97.4
Mexican	6,303	94.2
South American	193	65.4

Population Age 3–17 Enrolled in Private School

(Universe: Population Age 3–17 Enrolled in School)

Group	Number	%
Total Population	2,378	12.1
Hispanic or Latino (of any race)	639	6.8
Central American, ex. Mexican	87	4.3
Guatemalan	13	3.1
Nicaraguan	39	22.2
Salvadoran	35	2.6
Mexican	390	5.8
South American	102	34.6

Foreign-Born Population

Group	Number	%
Total Population	32,885	32.2
Hispanic or Latino (of any race)	18,633	51.2
Central American, ex. Mexican	5,034	59.5
Guatemalan	1,523	70.7
Nicaraguan	680	64.8
Salvadoran	2,687	54.5
Mexican	12,216	49.6
South American	1,095	77.1

Foreign-Born Naturalized U.S. Citizens

Group	Number	%
Total Population	13,102	39.8
Hispanic or Latino (of any race)	5,032	27.0
Central American, ex. Mexican	1,938	38.5
Guatemalan	315	20.7
Nicaraguan	441	64.9
Salvadoran	1,099	40.9
Mexican	2,454	20.1
South American	490	44.7

Language Spoken at Home: English Only

(Universe: Population 5 Years and Over)

Group	Number	%
Total Population	49,961	52.7
Hispanic or Latino (of any race)	4,108	12.8
Central American, ex. Mexican	748	9.6
Guatemalan	139	7.1
Nicaraguan	133	13.7
Salvadoran	279	6.2
Mexican	2,462	11.5
South American	13	1.0

Language Spoken at Home: Spanish

(Universe: Population 5 Years and Over)

Group	Number	%
Total Population	28,754	30.3
Hispanic or Latino (of any race)	28,005	87.2
Central American, ex. Mexican	7,013	90.4
Guatemalan	1,824	92.9
Nicaraguan	839	86.3
Salvadoran	4,218	93.8
Mexican	18,978	88.4
South American	1,255	99.0

Unemployment Rate

(Universe: Population 16 Years and Over)

Group	%
Total Population	12.3
Hispanic or Latino (of any race)	10.4
Central American, ex. Mexican	6.6
Guatemalan	6.2
Nicaraguan	10.3
Salvadoran	6.4
Mexican	12.3
South American	10.4

Class of Worker: Private Wage and Salary

(Universe: Civilian Employed Population 16 Years and Over)

Group	Number	%
Total Population	33,138	72.6
Hispanic or Latino (of any race)	12,804	82.2
Central American, ex. Mexican	3,642	80.2
Guatemalan	1,059	81.1
Nicaraguan	459	76.8
Salvadoran	1,969	80.6
Mexican	8,095	84.4
South American	565	81.6

Class of Worker: Government

(Universe: Civilian Employed Population 16 Years and Over)

Group	Number	%
Total Population	8,249	18.1
Hispanic or Latino (of any race)	1,387	8.9
Central American, ex. Mexican	440	9.7
Guatemalan	64	4.9
Nicaraguan	130	21.7
Salvadoran	208	8.5
Mexican	637	6.6
South American	112	16.2

Means of Transportation to Work: Car, Truck or Van

(Universe: Workers 16 Years and Over)

Group	Number	%
Total Population	34,233	78.3
Hispanic or Latino (of any race)	12,094	80.7
Central American, ex. Mexican	3,423	78.3
Guatemalan	877	71.8
Nicaraguan	470	84.5
Salvadoran	1,924	80.1
Mexican	7,589	82.5
South American	487	73.6

Means of Transportation to Work: Public Transportation (ex. Taxicab)

(Universe: Workers 16 Years and Over)

Group	Number	%
Total Population	6,470	14.8
Hispanic or Latino (of any race)	2,201	14.7
Central American, ex. Mexican	808	18.5
Guatemalan	329	26.9
Nicaraguan	69	12.4
Salvadoran	369	15.4
Mexican	1,105	12.0
South American	175	26.4

Homeownership Rate

(Universe: Occupied Housing Units)

Group	%
Total Population	51.7
Hispanic or Latino (of any race)	43.8
Central American, ex. Mexican	48.2
Guatemalan	37.5
Honduran	34.1
Nicaraguan	51.6
Salvadoran	52.0
Cuban	44.7
Mexican	42.1
Puerto Rican	37.9
South American	54.6
Chilean	58.5
Colombian	55.3
Peruvian	50.0
Spaniard	57.7

Median Home Value

Group	Dollars
Total Population	408,200
Hispanic or Latino (of any race)	360,800
Central American, ex. Mexican	383,800
Guatemalan	421,300
Nicaraguan	437,200
Salvadoran	334,700
Mexican	346,600
South American	318,600

Median Gross Rent

Group	Dollars
Total Population	1,133
Hispanic or Latino (of any race)	1,141
Central American, ex. Mexican	1,173
Guatemalan	1,160
Nicaraguan	1,769
Salvadoran	1,134
Mexican	1,110
South American	1,403

Median Household Income

(2010 Inflation-Adjusted Dollars)

Group	Dollars
Total Population	54,012
Hispanic or Latino (of any race)	48,913
Central American, ex. Mexican	57,054
Guatemalan	42,823
Nicaraguan	99,412
Salvadoran	58,684
Mexican	45,142
South American	80,272

Per Capita Income

(2010 Inflation-Adjusted Dollars)

Group	Dollars
Total Population	24,847
Hispanic or Latino (of any race)	15,509
Central American, ex. Mexican	19,324
Guatemalan	17,371
Nicaraguan	24,435
Salvadoran	18,903
Mexican	13,593
South American	19,056

Households with $100,000+ Income

Group	Number	%
Total Population	7,943	22.3

Notes: (1) Percent of total population; (2) Percent of Hispanic/Latino population; Profiles include places with an overall population of at least 125,000, OR an overall population of at least 25,000 where the Hispanic/Latino population is at least 20% of the overall population. In states where less than five places meet either of these criteria, we have included places with at least 10,000 total population with the highest percentage of Hispanic/Latino population. These places are identified with an asterisk (*); Please refer to the User's Guide for a full explanation of data.

Hispanic or Latino (of any race)	1,382	15.5
Central American, ex. Mexican	436	20.9
Guatemalan	92	16.0
Nicaraguan	133	48.5
Salvadoran	199	18.0
Mexican	723	12.3
South American	99	29.7

Households with Food Stamps/SNAP Benefits During Past 12 Months

Group	Number	%
Total Population	2,471	6.9
Hispanic or Latino (of any race)	766	8.6
Central American, ex. Mexican	89	4.3
Guatemalan	19	3.3
Nicaraguan	0	0.0
Salvadoran	70	6.3
Mexican	635	10.8
South American	0	0.0

Poverty Rate
(Income in Past 12 Months Below Poverty Level)

Group	%
Total Population	16.4
Hispanic or Latino (of any race)	21.0
Central American, ex. Mexican	15.5
Guatemalan	28.2
Nicaraguan	7.1
Salvadoran	12.5
Mexican	24.5
South American	5.4

Riverside

Population

Group	Number	%TP[1]	%HP[2]
Total Population	303,871	100.0	–
Hispanic or Latino (of any race)	148,953	49.0	100.0
Central American, ex. Mexican	7,792	2.6	5.2
Costa Rican	249	0.1	0.2
Guatemalan	3,338	1.1	2.2
Honduran	367	0.1	0.2
Nicaraguan	600	0.2	0.4
Panamanian	144	<0.1	0.1
Salvadoran	2,995	1.0	2.0
Cuban	912	0.3	0.6
Mexican	127,165	41.8	85.4
Puerto Rican	2,115	0.7	1.4
South American	2,540	0.8	1.7
Argentinean	379	0.1	0.3
Bolivian	102	<0.1	0.1
Chilean	236	0.1	0.2
Colombian	660	0.2	0.4
Ecuadorian	317	0.1	0.2
Peruvian	702	0.2	0.5
Spaniard	1,146	0.4	0.8

Population Growth: 2000–2010

Group	%
Total Population	19.1
Hispanic or Latino (of any race)	53.1
Central American, ex. Mexican	219.6
Costa Rican	75.4
Guatemalan	241.3
Nicaraguan	226.1
Panamanian	20.0
Salvadoran	292.5
Cuban	50.0
Mexican	60.9
Puerto Rican	35.4
South American	127.4
Argentinean	124.3
Colombian	137.4
Ecuadorian	157.7
Peruvian	158.1
Spaniard	879.5

Males per 100 Females

Group	Number
Total Population	97.6
Hispanic or Latino (of any race)	99.1
Central American, ex. Mexican	112.5
Costa Rican	87.2
Guatemalan	146.3
Honduran	81.7
Nicaraguan	85.8
Panamanian	84.6
Salvadoran	95.6
Cuban	89.2
Mexican	99.2
Puerto Rican	93.5
South American	85.8
Argentinean	90.5
Bolivian	78.9
Chilean	103.4
Colombian	76.0
Ecuadorian	96.9
Peruvian	88.2
Spaniard	92.0

Average Household Size

Group	People
Total Population	3.18
Hispanic or Latino (of any race)	4.16
Central American, ex. Mexican	4.31
Costa Rican	3.38
Guatemalan	4.87
Honduran	3.78
Nicaraguan	3.80
Panamanian	2.49
Salvadoran	4.20
Cuban	2.82
Mexican	4.26
Puerto Rican	3.05
South American	3.18
Argentinean	3.05
Bolivian	2.89
Chilean	3.10
Colombian	3.11
Ecuadorian	3.47
Peruvian	3.30
Spaniard	3.05

Median Age

Group	Years
Total Population	30.0
Hispanic or Latino (of any race)	24.8
Central American, ex. Mexican	28.1
Costa Rican	32.1
Guatemalan	26.9
Honduran	30.7
Nicaraguan	28.7
Panamanian	36.3
Salvadoran	29.0
Cuban	33.0
Mexican	24.4
Puerto Rican	27.7
South American	33.5
Argentinean	30.9
Bolivian	37.5
Chilean	34.0
Colombian	32.9
Ecuadorian	32.1
Peruvian	37.1
Spaniard	31.4

High School Graduates
(Universe: Population 25 Years and Over)

Group	Number	%
Total Population	134,782	77.6
Hispanic or Latino (of any race)	42,302	58.7
Central American, ex. Mexican	1,918	50.0
Guatemalan	706	52.4
Salvadoran	699	45.1
Cuban	436	77.0
Mexican	35,395	57.0
Puerto Rican	787	73.8
South American	1,490	90.3
Spaniard	462	81.2

Four-Year College Graduates
(Universe: Population 25 Years and Over)

Group	Number	%
Total Population	38,204	22.0
Hispanic or Latino (of any race)	6,343	8.8
Central American, ex. Mexican	297	7.7
Guatemalan	81	6.0
Salvadoran	39	2.5
Cuban	144	25.4
Mexican	4,614	7.4
Puerto Rican	221	20.7
South American	654	39.6
Spaniard	112	19.7

Population Age 3–17 Enrolled in Public School
(Universe: Population Age 3–17 Enrolled in School)

Group	Number	%
Total Population	57,824	91.3
Hispanic or Latino (of any race)	37,511	95.7
Central American, ex. Mexican	1,032	94.7
Guatemalan	211	87.6
Salvadoran	669	96.0
Cuban	181	88.3
Mexican	34,369	96.1
Puerto Rican	259	90.6
South American	433	88.4
Spaniard	43	100.0

Population Age 3–17 Enrolled in Private School
(Universe: Population Age 3–17 Enrolled in School)

Group	Number	%
Total Population	5,509	8.7
Hispanic or Latino (of any race)	1,701	4.3
Central American, ex. Mexican	58	5.3
Guatemalan	30	12.4
Salvadoran	28	4.0
Cuban	24	11.7
Mexican	1,390	3.9
Puerto Rican	27	9.4
South American	57	11.6
Spaniard	0	0.0

Foreign-Born Population

Group	Number	%
Total Population	73,817	24.6
Hispanic or Latino (of any race)	54,149	37.0
Central American, ex. Mexican	4,324	64.0
Guatemalan	1,612	75.2
Salvadoran	1,745	58.3
Cuban	389	42.1
Mexican	46,959	36.4
Puerto Rican	19	1.2
South American	1,542	59.4
Spaniard	121	13.8

Foreign-Born Naturalized U.S. Citizens

Group	Number	%
Total Population	26,776	36.3
Hispanic or Latino (of any race)	15,997	29.5
Central American, ex. Mexican	1,230	28.4
Guatemalan	394	24.4
Salvadoran	455	26.1
Cuban	297	76.3
Mexican	13,234	28.2
Puerto Rican	19	100.0
South American	717	46.5
Spaniard	65	53.7

Language Spoken at Home: English Only
(Universe: Population 5 Years and Over)

Group	Number	%
Total Population	157,274	56.8
Hispanic or Latino (of any race)	34,307	26.3
Central American, ex. Mexican	588	9.6
Guatemalan	83	4.3
Salvadoran	190	6.7
Cuban	438	47.8
Mexican	29,362	25.7
Puerto Rican	763	47.9
South American	583	24.1
Spaniard	595	70.7

Language Spoken at Home: Spanish
(Universe: Population 5 Years and Over)

Group	Number	%
Total Population	98,663	35.6
Hispanic or Latino (of any race)	95,917	73.5
Central American, ex. Mexican	5,527	89.8
Guatemalan	1,784	93.5
Salvadoran	2,625	93.3
Cuban	450	49.1
Mexican	84,985	74.3
Puerto Rican	813	51.0
South American	1,823	75.3

Notes: (1) Percent of total population; (2) Percent of Hispanic/Latino population; Profiles include places with an overall population of at least 125,000, OR an overall population of at least 25,000 where the Hispanic/Latino population is at least 20% of the overall population. In states where less than five places meet either of these criteria, we have included places with at least 10,000 total population with the highest percentage of Hispanic/Latino population. These places are identified with an asterisk (*); Please refer to the User's Guide for a full explanation of data.

Spaniard	222	26.4

Unemployment Rate
(Universe: Population 16 Years and Over)

Group	%
Total Population	10.6
Hispanic or Latino (of any race)	11.9
Central American, ex. Mexican	11.9
Guatemalan	14.4
Salvadoran	13.0
Cuban	19.0
Mexican	11.7
Puerto Rican	13.4
South American	9.9
Spaniard	4.2

Class of Worker: Private Wage and Salary
(Universe: Civilian Employed Population 16 Years and Over)

Group	Number	%
Total Population	98,821	75.5
Hispanic or Latino (of any race)	48,649	82.9
Central American, ex. Mexican	2,867	85.4
Guatemalan	882	85.5
Salvadoran	1,271	88.3
Cuban	212	67.1
Mexican	42,343	83.4
Puerto Rican	543	66.9
South American	1,131	79.0
Spaniard	384	70.1

Class of Worker: Government
(Universe: Civilian Employed Population 16 Years and Over)

Group	Number	%
Total Population	22,369	17.1
Hispanic or Latino (of any race)	6,257	10.7
Central American, ex. Mexican	262	7.8
Guatemalan	26	2.5
Salvadoran	114	7.9
Cuban	85	26.9
Mexican	5,211	10.3
Puerto Rican	175	21.6
South American	153	10.7
Spaniard	122	22.3

Means of Transportation to Work: Car, Truck or Van
(Universe: Workers 16 Years and Over)

Group	Number	%
Total Population	113,324	89.2
Hispanic or Latino (of any race)	52,133	91.1
Central American, ex. Mexican	3,015	92.0
Guatemalan	964	93.4
Salvadoran	1,261	89.1
Cuban	304	96.2
Mexican	45,252	91.6
Puerto Rican	675	83.1
South American	1,190	85.1
Spaniard	447	87.3

Means of Transportation to Work: Public Transportation (ex. Taxicab)
(Universe: Workers 16 Years and Over)

Group	Number	%
Total Population	3,166	2.5
Hispanic or Latino (of any race)	1,606	2.8
Central American, ex. Mexican	144	4.4
Guatemalan	7	0.7
Salvadoran	113	8.0
Cuban	0	0.0
Mexican	1,258	2.5
Puerto Rican	26	3.2
South American	73	5.2
Spaniard	25	4.9

Homeownership Rate
(Universe: Occupied Housing Units)

Group	%
Total Population	55.7
Hispanic or Latino (of any race)	50.7
Central American, ex. Mexican	43.6
Costa Rican	55.8
Guatemalan	36.9
Honduran	41.7
Nicaraguan	43.7
Panamanian	59.6
Salvadoran	48.0
Cuban	55.6
Mexican	52.0
Puerto Rican	43.3
South American	51.0
Argentinean	53.0
Bolivian	63.2
Chilean	44.3
Colombian	42.8
Ecuadorian	58.8
Peruvian	55.6
Spaniard	54.0

Median Home Value

Group	Dollars
Total Population	345,400
Hispanic or Latino (of any race)	322,100
Central American, ex. Mexican	343,200
Guatemalan	268,400
Salvadoran	342,900
Cuban	480,300
Mexican	316,800
Puerto Rican	304,200
South American	321,100
Spaniard	433,500

Median Gross Rent

Group	Dollars
Total Population	1,092
Hispanic or Latino (of any race)	1,065
Central American, ex. Mexican	1,105
Guatemalan	1,190
Salvadoran	1,006
Cuban	1,040
Mexican	1,059
Puerto Rican	968
South American	1,258
Spaniard	934

Median Household Income
(2010 Inflation-Adjusted Dollars)

Group	Dollars
Total Population	56,991
Hispanic or Latino (of any race)	51,985
Central American, ex. Mexican	53,704
Guatemalan	44,148
Salvadoran	62,250
Cuban	62,833
Mexican	51,827
Puerto Rican	53,917
South American	56,362
Spaniard	47,074

Per Capita Income
(2010 Inflation-Adjusted Dollars)

Group	Dollars
Total Population	22,665
Hispanic or Latino (of any race)	14,550
Central American, ex. Mexican	15,363
Guatemalan	13,346
Salvadoran	14,521
Cuban	41,527
Mexican	13,911
Puerto Rican	22,122
South American	20,688
Spaniard	36,896

Households with $100,000+ Income

Group	Number	%
Total Population	19,861	21.9
Hispanic or Latino (of any race)	4,368	13.2
Central American, ex. Mexican	308	19.7
Guatemalan	22	4.0
Salvadoran	190	32.5
Cuban	82	28.1
Mexican	3,466	12.1
Puerto Rican	65	14.5
South American	130	16.4
Spaniard	133	38.4

Households with Food Stamps/SNAP Benefits During Past 12 Months

Group	Number	%
Total Population	4,771	5.3
Hispanic or Latino (of any race)	2,570	7.7
Central American, ex. Mexican	105	6.7
Guatemalan	61	11.2
Salvadoran	44	7.5
Cuban	10	3.4
Mexican	2,285	8.0
Puerto Rican	0	0.0
South American	23	2.9
Spaniard	59	17.1

Poverty Rate
(Income in Past 12 Months Below Poverty Level)

Group	%
Total Population	14.9
Hispanic or Latino (of any race)	17.6
Central American, ex. Mexican	15.6
Guatemalan	19.1
Salvadoran	19.0
Cuban	18.0
Mexican	18.0
Puerto Rican	14.1
South American	8.7
Spaniard	14.9

Rohnert Park

Population

Group	Number	%TP[1]	%HP[2]
Total Population	40,971	100.0	–
Hispanic or Latino (of any race)	9,068	22.1	100.0
Central American, ex. Mexican	721	1.8	8.0
Guatemalan	147	0.4	1.6
Nicaraguan	107	0.3	1.2
Salvadoran	394	1.0	4.3
Mexican	7,093	17.3	78.2
Puerto Rican	241	0.6	2.7
South American	268	0.7	3.0
Peruvian	115	0.3	1.3
Spaniard	202	0.5	2.2

Population Growth: 2000–2010

Group	%
Total Population	-3.0
Hispanic or Latino (of any race)	58.2
Central American, ex. Mexican	87.3
Salvadoran	88.5
Mexican	76.9
Puerto Rican	26.8
South American	94.2

Males per 100 Females

Group	Number
Total Population	95.3
Hispanic or Latino (of any race)	97.8
Central American, ex. Mexican	87.3
Guatemalan	104.2
Nicaraguan	75.4
Salvadoran	87.6
Mexican	102.0
Puerto Rican	88.3
South American	81.1
Peruvian	79.7
Spaniard	75.7

Average Household Size

Group	People
Total Population	2.57
Hispanic or Latino (of any race)	3.55
Central American, ex. Mexican	3.31
Guatemalan	3.35
Nicaraguan	2.74
Salvadoran	3.53
Mexican	3.80
Puerto Rican	2.50
South American	2.74
Peruvian	2.89
Spaniard	2.35

Median Age

Group	Years
Total Population	33.0
Hispanic or Latino (of any race)	25.9
Central American, ex. Mexican	31.3
Guatemalan	35.4
Nicaraguan	28.2

Notes: (1) Percent of total population; (2) Percent of Hispanic/Latino population; Profiles include places with an overall population of at least 125,000, OR an overall population of at least 25,000 where the Hispanic/Latino population is at least 20% of the overall population. In states where less than five places meet either of these criteria, we have included places with at least 10,000 total population with the highest percentage of Hispanic/Latino population. These places are identified with an asterisk (*); Please refer to the User's Guide for a full explanation of data.

Salvadoran		31.3
Mexican		24.7
Puerto Rican		27.9
South American		37.0
Peruvian		33.3
Spaniard		36.0

High School Graduates
(Universe: Population 25 Years and Over)

Group	Number	%
Total Population	22,696	89.5
Hispanic or Latino (of any race)	3,145	70.2
Central American, ex. Mexican	396	83.4
Mexican	2,472	67.4

Four-Year College Graduates
(Universe: Population 25 Years and Over)

Group	Number	%
Total Population	6,362	25.1
Hispanic or Latino (of any race)	580	12.9
Central American, ex. Mexican	111	23.4
Mexican	431	11.8

Population Age 3–17 Enrolled in Public School
(Universe: Population Age 3–17 Enrolled in School)

Group	Number	%
Total Population	6,070	86.5
Hispanic or Latino (of any race)	1,863	95.1
Central American, ex. Mexican	70	61.4
Mexican	1,656	97.9

Population Age 3–17 Enrolled in Private School
(Universe: Population Age 3–17 Enrolled in School)

Group	Number	%
Total Population	949	13.5
Hispanic or Latino (of any race)	95	4.9
Central American, ex. Mexican	44	38.6
Mexican	36	2.1

Foreign-Born Population

Group	Number	%
Total Population	6,118	15.1
Hispanic or Latino (of any race)	3,259	39.6
Central American, ex. Mexican	423	60.4
Mexican	2,635	38.6

Foreign-Born Naturalized U.S. Citizens

Group	Number	%
Total Population	3,156	51.6
Hispanic or Latino (of any race)	1,354	41.5
Central American, ex. Mexican	196	46.3
Mexican	1,083	41.1

Language Spoken at Home: English Only
(Universe: Population 5 Years and Over)

Group	Number	%
Total Population	30,048	78.3
Hispanic or Latino (of any race)	2,498	34.1
Central American, ex. Mexican	149	25.9
Mexican	2,032	33.0

Language Spoken at Home: Spanish
(Universe: Population 5 Years and Over)

Group	Number	%
Total Population	5,131	13.4
Hispanic or Latino (of any race)	4,815	65.8
Central American, ex. Mexican	426	74.1
Mexican	4,125	67.0

Unemployment Rate
(Universe: Population 16 Years and Over)

Group	%
Total Population	7.5
Hispanic or Latino (of any race)	8.2
Central American, ex. Mexican	10.5
Mexican	7.5

Class of Worker: Private Wage and Salary
(Universe: Civilian Employed Population 16 Years and Over)

Group	Number	%
Total Population	16,712	78.6
Hispanic or Latino (of any race)	3,359	81.7
Central American, ex. Mexican	346	86.7
Mexican	2,826	82.3

Class of Worker: Government
(Universe: Civilian Employed Population 16 Years and Over)

Group	Number	%
Total Population	3,140	14.8
Hispanic or Latino (of any race)	560	13.6
Central American, ex. Mexican	45	11.3
Mexican	421	12.3

Means of Transportation to Work: Car, Truck or Van
(Universe: Workers 16 Years and Over)

Group	Number	%
Total Population	18,476	88.9
Hispanic or Latino (of any race)	3,668	91.6
Central American, ex. Mexican	367	92.0
Mexican	3,117	93.6

Means of Transportation to Work: Public Transportation (ex. Taxicab)
(Universe: Workers 16 Years and Over)

Group	Number	%
Total Population	510	2.5
Hispanic or Latino (of any race)	35	0.9
Central American, ex. Mexican	0	0.0
Mexican	35	1.1

Homeownership Rate
(Universe: Occupied Housing Units)

Group	%
Total Population	54.0
Hispanic or Latino (of any race)	40.6
Central American, ex. Mexican	46.1
Guatemalan	53.5
Nicaraguan	39.5
Salvadoran	50.0
Mexican	39.5
Puerto Rican	37.8
South American	51.6
Peruvian	52.3
Spaniard	49.4

Median Home Value

Group	Dollars
Total Population	399,200
Hispanic or Latino (of any race)	349,600
Central American, ex. Mexican	318,200
Mexican	356,600

Median Gross Rent

Group	Dollars
Total Population	1,253
Hispanic or Latino (of any race)	1,142
Central American, ex. Mexican	965
Mexican	1,193

Median Household Income
(2010 Inflation-Adjusted Dollars)

Group	Dollars
Total Population	57,387
Hispanic or Latino (of any race)	49,226
Central American, ex. Mexican	64,444
Mexican	48,785

Per Capita Income
(2010 Inflation-Adjusted Dollars)

Group	Dollars
Total Population	28,263
Hispanic or Latino (of any race)	17,673
Central American, ex. Mexican	20,666
Mexican	17,669

Households with $100,000+ Income

Group	Number	%
Total Population	3,454	21.5
Hispanic or Latino (of any race)	288	12.4
Central American, ex. Mexican	24	9.4
Mexican	225	12.2

Households with Food Stamps/SNAP Benefits During Past 12 Months

Group	Number	%
Total Population	404	2.5
Hispanic or Latino (of any race)	48	2.1
Central American, ex. Mexican	0	0.0
Mexican	36	2.0

Poverty Rate
(Income in Past 12 Months Below Poverty Level)

Group	%
Total Population	11.3
Hispanic or Latino (of any race)	13.8
Central American, ex. Mexican	1.3
Mexican	14.2

Rosemead

Population

Group	Number	%TP[1]	%HP[2]
Total Population	53,764	100.0	–
Hispanic or Latino (of any race)	18,147	33.8	100.0
Central American, ex. Mexican	1,188	2.2	6.5
Guatemalan	306	0.6	1.7
Nicaraguan	143	0.3	0.8
Salvadoran	594	1.1	3.3
Cuban	153	0.3	0.8
Mexican	15,469	28.8	85.2
Puerto Rican	113	0.2	0.6
South American	251	0.5	1.4

Population Growth: 2000–2010

Group	%
Total Population	0.5
Hispanic or Latino (of any race)	-17.9
Central American, ex. Mexican	37.7
Guatemalan	70.0
Nicaraguan	10.0
Salvadoran	47.0
Cuban	-20.7
Mexican	-13.4
Puerto Rican	-8.9
South American	21.3

Males per 100 Females

Group	Number
Total Population	97.3
Hispanic or Latino (of any race)	97.1
Central American, ex. Mexican	94.4
Guatemalan	102.6
Nicaraguan	93.2
Salvadoran	96.0
Cuban	101.3
Mexican	97.5
Puerto Rican	82.3
South American	88.7

Average Household Size

Group	People
Total Population	3.74
Hispanic or Latino (of any race)	3.83
Central American, ex. Mexican	4.00
Guatemalan	3.98
Nicaraguan	3.20
Salvadoran	4.30
Cuban	2.81
Mexican	3.88
Puerto Rican	2.68
South American	3.31

Median Age

Group	Years
Total Population	38.1
Hispanic or Latino (of any race)	31.6
Central American, ex. Mexican	37.3
Guatemalan	38.0
Nicaraguan	45.1
Salvadoran	34.9
Cuban	55.8
Mexican	30.8
Puerto Rican	35.3
South American	40.5

High School Graduates
(Universe: Population 25 Years and Over)

Group	Number	%
Total Population	22,281	60.9
Hispanic or Latino (of any race)	6,698	63.7
Mexican	5,819	62.0

Notes: (1) Percent of total population; (2) Percent of Hispanic/Latino population; Profiles include places with an overall population of at least 125,000, OR an overall population of at least 25,000 where the Hispanic/Latino population is at least 20% of the overall population. In states where less than five places meet either of these criteria, we have included places with at least 10,000 total population with the highest percentage of Hispanic/Latino population. These places are identified with an asterisk (*); Please refer to the User's Guide for a full explanation of data.

Four-Year College Graduates
(Universe: Population 25 Years and Over)

Group	Number	%
Total Population	5,291	14.5
Hispanic or Latino (of any race)	587	5.6
Mexican	498	5.3

Population Age 3–17 Enrolled in Public School
(Universe: Population Age 3–17 Enrolled in School)

Group	Number	%
Total Population	8,633	92.2
Hispanic or Latino (of any race)	3,680	91.3
Mexican	3,412	91.4

Population Age 3–17 Enrolled in Private School
(Universe: Population Age 3–17 Enrolled in School)

Group	Number	%
Total Population	730	7.8
Hispanic or Latino (of any race)	349	8.7
Mexican	320	8.6

Foreign-Born Population

Group	Number	%
Total Population	30,808	57.4
Hispanic or Latino (of any race)	6,073	34.5
Mexican	5,394	33.9

Foreign-Born Naturalized U.S. Citizens

Group	Number	%
Total Population	18,701	60.7
Hispanic or Latino (of any race)	2,318	38.2
Mexican	1,958	36.3

Language Spoken at Home: English Only
(Universe: Population 5 Years and Over)

Group	Number	%
Total Population	9,912	19.4
Hispanic or Latino (of any race)	4,335	26.4
Mexican	3,737	25.3

Language Spoken at Home: Spanish
(Universe: Population 5 Years and Over)

Group	Number	%
Total Population	12,483	24.5
Hispanic or Latino (of any race)	12,064	73.5
Mexican	11,006	74.6

Unemployment Rate
(Universe: Population 16 Years and Over)

Group	%
Total Population	8.3
Hispanic or Latino (of any race)	8.7
Mexican	7.8

Class of Worker: Private Wage and Salary
(Universe: Civilian Employed Population 16 Years and Over)

Group	Number	%
Total Population	18,860	82.2
Hispanic or Latino (of any race)	5,628	78.5
Mexican	5,012	77.8

Class of Worker: Government
(Universe: Civilian Employed Population 16 Years and Over)

Group	Number	%
Total Population	2,635	11.5
Hispanic or Latino (of any race)	982	13.7
Mexican	891	13.8

Means of Transportation to Work: Car, Truck or Van
(Universe: Workers 16 Years and Over)

Group	Number	%
Total Population	19,769	87.6
Hispanic or Latino (of any race)	5,852	83.4
Mexican	5,243	83.1

Means of Transportation to Work: Public Transportation (ex. Taxicab)
(Universe: Workers 16 Years and Over)

Group	Number	%
Total Population	1,294	5.7
Hispanic or Latino (of any race)	645	9.2
Mexican	581	9.2

Homeownership Rate
(Universe: Occupied Housing Units)

Group	%
Total Population	48.9
Hispanic or Latino (of any race)	41.4
Central American, ex. Mexican	35.0
Guatemalan	33.0
Nicaraguan	25.5
Salvadoran	40.0
Cuban	51.6
Mexican	41.6
Puerto Rican	55.0
South American	47.1

Median Home Value

Group	Dollars
Total Population	470,700
Hispanic or Latino (of any race)	460,000
Mexican	454,400

Median Gross Rent

Group	Dollars
Total Population	1,110
Hispanic or Latino (of any race)	1,036
Mexican	1,042

Median Household Income
(2010 Inflation-Adjusted Dollars)

Group	Dollars
Total Population	46,706
Hispanic or Latino (of any race)	44,051
Mexican	43,509

Per Capita Income
(2010 Inflation-Adjusted Dollars)

Group	Dollars
Total Population	17,749
Hispanic or Latino (of any race)	16,159
Mexican	15,026

Households with $100,000+ Income

Group	Number	%
Total Population	2,239	15.5
Hispanic or Latino (of any race)	581	12.5
Mexican	474	11.7

Households with Food Stamps/SNAP Benefits During Past 12 Months

Group	Number	%
Total Population	838	5.8
Hispanic or Latino (of any race)	223	4.8
Mexican	200	4.9

Poverty Rate
(Income in Past 12 Months Below Poverty Level)

Group	%
Total Population	14.2
Hispanic or Latino (of any race)	14.0
Mexican	13.7

Rowland Heights

Population

Group	Number	%TP[1]	%HP[2]
Total Population	48,993	100.0	–
Hispanic or Latino (of any race)	13,229	27.0	100.0
Central American, ex. Mexican	926	1.9	7.0
Guatemalan	327	0.7	2.5
Nicaraguan	112	0.2	0.8
Salvadoran	419	0.9	3.2
Mexican	10,976	22.4	83.0
Puerto Rican	161	0.3	1.2
South American	484	1.0	3.7
Ecuadorian	114	0.2	0.9
Peruvian	154	0.3	1.2
Spaniard	102	0.2	0.8

Population Growth: 2000–2010

Group	%
Total Population	0.9
Hispanic or Latino (of any race)	-3.8
Central American, ex. Mexican	74.4
Guatemalan	127.1
Salvadoran	86.2
Mexican	2.1
Puerto Rican	15.0
South American	23.5

Males per 100 Females

Group	Number
Total Population	96.6
Hispanic or Latino (of any race)	102.2
Central American, ex. Mexican	101.3
Guatemalan	122.4
Nicaraguan	93.1
Salvadoran	94.0
Mexican	103.3
Puerto Rican	78.9
South American	98.4
Ecuadorian	78.1
Peruvian	111.0
Spaniard	92.5

Average Household Size

Group	People
Total Population	3.36
Hispanic or Latino (of any race)	4.02
Central American, ex. Mexican	4.51
Guatemalan	4.87
Nicaraguan	4.03
Salvadoran	4.70
Mexican	4.04
Puerto Rican	3.12
South American	3.49
Ecuadorian	3.48
Peruvian	3.80
Spaniard	3.03

Median Age

Group	Years
Total Population	40.2
Hispanic or Latino (of any race)	30.2
Central American, ex. Mexican	33.1
Guatemalan	31.6
Nicaraguan	36.5
Salvadoran	32.5
Mexican	29.6
Puerto Rican	37.8
South American	42.7
Ecuadorian	45.5
Peruvian	40.1
Spaniard	39.0

High School Graduates
(Universe: Population 25 Years and Over)

Group	Number	%
Total Population	30,231	85.7
Hispanic or Latino (of any race)	6,418	70.4
Mexican	5,400	70.1

Four-Year College Graduates
(Universe: Population 25 Years and Over)

Group	Number	%
Total Population	12,230	34.7
Hispanic or Latino (of any race)	869	9.5
Mexican	626	8.1

Population Age 3–17 Enrolled in Public School
(Universe: Population Age 3–17 Enrolled in School)

Group	Number	%
Total Population	8,306	91.2
Hispanic or Latino (of any race)	3,420	95.5
Mexican	2,792	96.1

Population Age 3–17 Enrolled in Private School
(Universe: Population Age 3–17 Enrolled in School)

Group	Number	%
Total Population	806	8.8
Hispanic or Latino (of any race)	161	4.5
Mexican	113	3.9

Foreign-Born Population

Group	Number	%
Total Population	28,840	55.9
Hispanic or Latino (of any race)	5,750	37.5
Mexican	4,803	36.8

Foreign-Born Naturalized U.S. Citizens

Group	Number	%
Total Population	15,819	54.9

STATE & PLACE PROFILES

Notes: (1) Percent of total population; (2) Percent of Hispanic/Latino population; Profiles include places with an overall population of at least 125,000, OR an overall population of at least 25,000 where the Hispanic/Latino population is at least 20% of the overall population. In states where less than five places meet either of these criteria, we have included places with at least 10,000 total population with the highest percentage of Hispanic/Latino population. These places are identified with an asterisk (*); Please refer to the User's Guide for a full explanation of data.

Hispanic or Latino (of any race)	2,244	39.0
Mexican	1,726	35.9

Language Spoken at Home: English Only
(Universe: Population 5 Years and Over)

Group	Number	%
Total Population	13,425	27.5
Hispanic or Latino (of any race)	4,472	31.8
Mexican	3,679	31.0

Language Spoken at Home: Spanish
(Universe: Population 5 Years and Over)

Group	Number	%
Total Population	9,794	20.1
Hispanic or Latino (of any race)	9,565	67.9
Mexican	8,168	68.9

Unemployment Rate
(Universe: Population 16 Years and Over)

Group	%
Total Population	6.0
Hispanic or Latino (of any race)	5.6
Mexican	5.4

Class of Worker: Private Wage and Salary
(Universe: Civilian Employed Population 16 Years and Over)

Group	Number	%
Total Population	18,704	77.3
Hispanic or Latino (of any race)	5,727	80.2
Mexican	4,972	79.8

Class of Worker: Government
(Universe: Civilian Employed Population 16 Years and Over)

Group	Number	%
Total Population	2,964	12.2
Hispanic or Latino (of any race)	911	12.8
Mexican	823	13.2

Means of Transportation to Work: Car, Truck or Van
(Universe: Workers 16 Years and Over)

Group	Number	%
Total Population	20,505	86.9
Hispanic or Latino (of any race)	5,898	84.2
Mexican	5,097	83.7

Means of Transportation to Work: Public Transportation (ex. Taxicab)
(Universe: Workers 16 Years and Over)

Group	Number	%
Total Population	668	2.8
Hispanic or Latino (of any race)	260	3.7
Mexican	260	4.3

Homeownership Rate
(Universe: Occupied Housing Units)

Group	%
Total Population	67.6
Hispanic or Latino (of any race)	57.2
Central American, ex. Mexican	54.4
Guatemalan	44.9
Nicaraguan	51.4
Salvadoran	61.9
Mexican	56.8
Puerto Rican	61.0
South American	70.5
Ecuadorian	82.5
Peruvian	52.3
Spaniard	63.6

Median Home Value

Group	Dollars
Total Population	550,400
Hispanic or Latino (of any race)	451,900
Mexican	446,400

Median Gross Rent

Group	Dollars
Total Population	1,309
Hispanic or Latino (of any race)	1,353
Mexican	1,346

Median Household Income
(2010 Inflation-Adjusted Dollars)

Group	Dollars
Total Population	68,645
Hispanic or Latino (of any race)	72,170
Mexican	75,381

Per Capita Income
(2010 Inflation-Adjusted Dollars)

Group	Dollars
Total Population	25,261
Hispanic or Latino (of any race)	19,575
Mexican	19,691

Households with $100,000+ Income

Group	Number	%
Total Population	4,780	32.1
Hispanic or Latino (of any race)	967	27.0
Mexican	853	28.6

Households with Food Stamps/SNAP Benefits During Past 12 Months

Group	Number	%
Total Population	371	2.5
Hispanic or Latino (of any race)	232	6.5
Mexican	150	5.0

Poverty Rate
(Income in Past 12 Months Below Poverty Level)

Group	%
Total Population	10.5
Hispanic or Latino (of any race)	10.8
Mexican	10.2

Rubidoux

Population

Group	Number	%TP[1]	%HP[2]
Total Population	34,280	100.0	–
Hispanic or Latino (of any race)	23,322	68.0	100.0
Central American, ex. Mexican	835	2.4	3.6
Guatemalan	250	0.7	1.1
Honduran	101	0.3	0.4
Salvadoran	371	1.1	1.6
Mexican	21,173	61.8	90.8
Puerto Rican	186	0.5	0.8
South American	149	0.4	0.6
Spaniard	109	0.3	0.5

Population Growth: 2000–2010

Group	%
Total Population	17.5
Hispanic or Latino (of any race)	47.2
Central American, ex. Mexican	166.8
Guatemalan	127.3
Salvadoran	209.2
Mexican	59.5
Puerto Rican	5.7

Males per 100 Females

Group	Number
Total Population	100.4
Hispanic or Latino (of any race)	102.0
Central American, ex. Mexican	118.0
Guatemalan	152.5
Honduran	83.6
Salvadoran	113.2
Mexican	102.1
Puerto Rican	82.4
South American	88.6
Spaniard	78.7

Average Household Size

Group	People
Total Population	3.80
Hispanic or Latino (of any race)	4.64
Central American, ex. Mexican	4.44
Guatemalan	4.36
Honduran	5.33
Salvadoran	4.64
Mexican	4.71
Puerto Rican	3.30
South American	3.25
Spaniard	3.29

Median Age

Group	Years
Total Population	29.2
Hispanic or Latino (of any race)	24.4
Central American, ex. Mexican	32.6
Guatemalan	31.0
Honduran	26.8
Salvadoran	34.6
Mexican	24.0
Puerto Rican	27.6
South American	34.8
Spaniard	33.5

High School Graduates
(Universe: Population 25 Years and Over)

Group	Number	%
Total Population	13,127	62.7
Hispanic or Latino (of any race)	6,045	48.6
Central American, ex. Mexican	366	53.0
Mexican	5,121	45.9

Four-Year College Graduates
(Universe: Population 25 Years and Over)

Group	Number	%
Total Population	2,009	9.6
Hispanic or Latino (of any race)	553	4.4
Central American, ex. Mexican	32	4.6
Mexican	359	3.2

Population Age 3–17 Enrolled in Public School
(Universe: Population Age 3–17 Enrolled in School)

Group	Number	%
Total Population	8,660	96.5
Hispanic or Latino (of any race)	7,105	97.6
Central American, ex. Mexican	556	100.0
Mexican	6,334	97.7

Population Age 3–17 Enrolled in Private School
(Universe: Population Age 3–17 Enrolled in School)

Group	Number	%
Total Population	310	3.5
Hispanic or Latino (of any race)	175	2.4
Central American, ex. Mexican	0	0.0
Mexican	146	2.3

Foreign-Born Population

Group	Number	%
Total Population	11,731	31.5
Hispanic or Latino (of any race)	10,957	43.5
Central American, ex. Mexican	754	45.3
Mexican	9,977	44.3

Foreign-Born Naturalized U.S. Citizens

Group	Number	%
Total Population	3,573	30.5
Hispanic or Latino (of any race)	2,977	27.2
Central American, ex. Mexican	469	62.2
Mexican	2,385	23.9

Language Spoken at Home: English Only
(Universe: Population 5 Years and Over)

Group	Number	%
Total Population	13,975	41.0
Hispanic or Latino (of any race)	3,710	16.3
Central American, ex. Mexican	57	3.7
Mexican	3,240	15.9

Language Spoken at Home: Spanish
(Universe: Population 5 Years and Over)

Group	Number	%
Total Population	19,270	56.5
Hispanic or Latino (of any race)	19,032	83.6
Central American, ex. Mexican	1,467	96.3
Mexican	17,128	84.1

Unemployment Rate
(Universe: Population 16 Years and Over)

Group	%
Total Population	15.7
Hispanic or Latino (of any race)	16.6
Central American, ex. Mexican	16.4
Mexican	16.9

Class of Worker: Private Wage and Salary
(Universe: Civilian Employed Population 16 Years and Over)

Group	Number	%
Total Population	12,087	81.2
Hispanic or Latino (of any race)	7,926	86.5
Central American, ex. Mexican	531	88.8

Notes: (1) Percent of total population; (2) Percent of Hispanic/Latino population; Profiles include places with an overall population of at least 125,000, OR an overall population of at least 25,000 where the Hispanic/Latino population is at least 20% of the overall population. In states where less than five places meet either of these criteria, we have included places with at least 10,000 total population with the highest percentage of Hispanic/Latino population. These places are identified with an asterisk (*); Please refer to the User's Guide for a full explanation of data.

Group	Number	%
Mexican	7,139	87.0

Class of Worker: Government
(Universe: Civilian Employed Population 16 Years and Over)

Group	Number	%
Total Population	1,834	12.3
Hispanic or Latino (of any race)	613	6.7
Central American, ex. Mexican	67	11.2
Mexican	445	5.4

Means of Transportation to Work: Car, Truck or Van
(Universe: Workers 16 Years and Over)

Group	Number	%
Total Population	13,678	94.9
Hispanic or Latino (of any race)	8,480	95.5
Central American, ex. Mexican	581	98.8
Mexican	7,615	95.5

Means of Transportation to Work: Public Transportation (ex. Taxicab)
(Universe: Workers 16 Years and Over)

Group	Number	%
Total Population	109	0.8
Hispanic or Latino (of any race)	45	0.5
Central American, ex. Mexican	0	0.0
Mexican	45	0.6

Homeownership Rate
(Universe: Occupied Housing Units)

Group	%
Total Population	65.3
Hispanic or Latino (of any race)	59.4
Central American, ex. Mexican	58.8
Guatemalan	52.2
Honduran	57.1
Salvadoran	64.9
Mexican	59.5
Puerto Rican	57.5
South American	72.7
Spaniard	61.3

Median Home Value

Group	Dollars
Total Population	286,600
Hispanic or Latino (of any race)	267,400
Central American, ex. Mexican	224,600
Mexican	271,600

Median Gross Rent

Group	Dollars
Total Population	947
Hispanic or Latino (of any race)	935
Central American, ex. Mexican	338
Mexican	938

Median Household Income
(2010 Inflation-Adjusted Dollars)

Group	Dollars
Total Population	51,545
Hispanic or Latino (of any race)	43,644
Central American, ex. Mexican	34,662
Mexican	43,245

Per Capita Income
(2010 Inflation-Adjusted Dollars)

Group	Dollars
Total Population	17,094
Hispanic or Latino (of any race)	12,927
Central American, ex. Mexican	16,617
Mexican	12,474

Households with $100,000+ Income

Group	Number	%
Total Population	1,746	18.3
Hispanic or Latino (of any race)	676	12.8
Central American, ex. Mexican	68	19.3
Mexican	518	11.2

Households with Food Stamps/SNAP Benefits During Past 12 Months

Group	Number	%
Total Population	829	8.7
Hispanic or Latino (of any race)	658	12.4
Central American, ex. Mexican	53	15.1
Mexican	605	13.1

Poverty Rate
(Income in Past 12 Months Below Poverty Level)

Group	%
Total Population	17.4
Hispanic or Latino (of any race)	19.5
Central American, ex. Mexican	55.0
Mexican	16.9

Sacramento

Population

Group	Number	%TP[1]	%HP[2]
Total Population	466,488	100.0	–
Hispanic or Latino (of any race)	125,276	26.9	100.0
Central American, ex. Mexican	5,184	1.1	4.1
Costa Rican	162	<0.1	0.1
Guatemalan	977	0.2	0.8
Honduran	357	0.1	0.3
Nicaraguan	895	0.2	0.7
Panamanian	325	0.1	0.3
Salvadoran	2,425	0.5	1.9
Cuban	640	0.1	0.5
Dominican Republic	190	<0.1	0.2
Mexican	105,467	22.6	84.2
Puerto Rican	3,344	0.7	2.7
South American	1,777	0.4	1.4
Argentinean	179	<0.1	0.1
Chilean	205	<0.1	0.2
Colombian	400	0.1	0.3
Ecuadorian	116	<0.1	0.1
Peruvian	614	0.1	0.5
Venezuelan	118	<0.1	0.1
Spaniard	1,979	0.4	1.6

Population Growth: 2000–2010

Group	%
Total Population	14.6
Hispanic or Latino (of any race)	42.4
Central American, ex. Mexican	174.1
Guatemalan	185.7
Nicaraguan	178.8
Panamanian	112.4
Salvadoran	218.2
Cuban	35.0
Mexican	49.1
Puerto Rican	62.9
South American	161.3
Chilean	95.2
Colombian	154.8
Peruvian	216.5
Spaniard	698.0

Males per 100 Females

Group	Number
Total Population	94.9
Hispanic or Latino (of any race)	100.8
Central American, ex. Mexican	97.9
Costa Rican	107.7
Guatemalan	107.0
Honduran	98.3
Nicaraguan	90.4
Panamanian	60.9
Salvadoran	102.1
Cuban	96.9
Dominican Republic	93.9
Mexican	102.0
Puerto Rican	92.3
South American	87.4
Argentinean	92.5
Chilean	81.4
Colombian	93.2
Ecuadorian	100.0
Peruvian	90.1
Venezuelan	78.8
Spaniard	79.6

Average Household Size

Group	People
Total Population	2.62
Hispanic or Latino (of any race)	3.37
Central American, ex. Mexican	3.52
Costa Rican	3.24
Guatemalan	3.98
Honduran	3.54
Nicaraguan	3.23
Panamanian	2.59
Salvadoran	3.64
Cuban	2.24
Dominican Republic	2.93
Mexican	3.47
Puerto Rican	2.78
South American	2.66
Argentinean	2.55
Chilean	2.56
Colombian	2.68
Ecuadorian	2.42
Peruvian	2.82
Venezuelan	2.78
Spaniard	2.33

Median Age

Group	Years
Total Population	33.0
Hispanic or Latino (of any race)	26.2
Central American, ex. Mexican	30.3
Costa Rican	30.0
Guatemalan	29.4
Honduran	29.2
Nicaraguan	29.9
Panamanian	36.2
Salvadoran	30.5
Cuban	29.8
Dominican Republic	24.2
Mexican	25.6
Puerto Rican	25.3
South American	34.0
Argentinean	32.2
Chilean	34.2
Colombian	32.6
Ecuadorian	33.3
Peruvian	36.5
Venezuelan	33.3
Spaniard	34.4

High School Graduates
(Universe: Population 25 Years and Over)

Group	Number	%
Total Population	238,717	81.4
Hispanic or Latino (of any race)	37,314	61.7
Central American, ex. Mexican	1,823	60.8
Guatemalan	328	54.8
Nicaraguan	483	80.6
Salvadoran	692	50.8
Mexican	29,657	58.9
Puerto Rican	1,526	88.1
South American	885	84.7
Spaniard	1,056	93.0

Four-Year College Graduates
(Universe: Population 25 Years and Over)

Group	Number	%
Total Population	86,885	29.6
Hispanic or Latino (of any race)	8,481	14.0
Central American, ex. Mexican	626	20.9
Guatemalan	138	23.0
Nicaraguan	59	9.8
Salvadoran	302	22.2
Mexican	5,836	11.6
Puerto Rican	283	16.3
South American	388	37.1
Spaniard	393	34.6

Population Age 3–17 Enrolled in Public School
(Universe: Population Age 3–17 Enrolled in School)

Group	Number	%
Total Population	76,053	88.9
Hispanic or Latino (of any race)	27,744	92.7
Central American, ex. Mexican	1,184	97.0
Guatemalan	454	94.8
Nicaraguan	169	93.4
Salvadoran	439	100.0
Mexican	24,209	92.8
Puerto Rican	497	88.1
South American	269	79.1
Spaniard	366	96.1

Notes: (1) Percent of total population; (2) Percent of Hispanic/Latino population; Profiles include places with an overall population of at least 125,000, OR an overall population of at least 25,000 where the Hispanic/Latino population is at least 20% of the overall population. In states where less than five places meet either of these criteria, we have included places with at least 10,000 total population with the highest percentage of Hispanic/Latino population. These places are identified with an asterisk (*); Please refer to the User's Guide for a full explanation of data.

Population Age 3–17 Enrolled in Private School
(Universe: Population Age 3–17 Enrolled in School)

Group	Number	%
Total Population	9,493	11.1
Hispanic or Latino (of any race)	2,175	7.3
Central American, ex. Mexican	37	3.0
Guatemalan	25	5.2
Nicaraguan	12	6.6
Salvadoran	0	0.0
Mexican	1,882	7.2
Puerto Rican	67	11.9
South American	71	20.9
Spaniard	15	3.9

Foreign-Born Population

Group	Number	%
Total Population	102,113	22.2
Hispanic or Latino (of any race)	36,654	31.4
Central American, ex. Mexican	2,661	49.6
Guatemalan	582	46.6
Nicaraguan	376	34.8
Salvadoran	1,303	55.4
Mexican	32,313	32.5
Puerto Rican	41	1.5
South American	819	52.2
Spaniard	71	3.7

Foreign-Born Naturalized U.S. Citizens

Group	Number	%
Total Population	47,811	46.8
Hispanic or Latino (of any race)	10,083	27.5
Central American, ex. Mexican	763	28.7
Guatemalan	126	21.6
Nicaraguan	141	37.5
Salvadoran	301	23.1
Mexican	8,519	26.4
Puerto Rican	27	65.9
South American	376	45.9
Spaniard	19	26.8

Language Spoken at Home: English Only
(Universe: Population 5 Years and Over)

Group	Number	%
Total Population	269,326	63.4
Hispanic or Latino (of any race)	34,467	33.5
Central American, ex. Mexican	1,086	22.5
Guatemalan	244	21.7
Nicaraguan	319	34.4
Salvadoran	272	12.7
Mexican	27,453	31.5
Puerto Rican	1,199	45.8
South American	457	31.3
Spaniard	1,285	74.1

Language Spoken at Home: Spanish
(Universe: Population 5 Years and Over)

Group	Number	%
Total Population	72,961	17.2
Hispanic or Latino (of any race)	67,899	66.0
Central American, ex. Mexican	3,748	77.5
Guatemalan	878	78.3
Nicaraguan	607	65.6
Salvadoran	1,867	87.3
Mexican	59,520	68.2
Puerto Rican	1,354	51.7
South American	1,003	68.7
Spaniard	393	22.7

Unemployment Rate
(Universe: Population 16 Years and Over)

Group	%
Total Population	11.4
Hispanic or Latino (of any race)	13.9
Central American, ex. Mexican	12.4
Guatemalan	5.7
Nicaraguan	17.5
Salvadoran	11.8
Mexican	14.4
Puerto Rican	10.3
South American	6.4
Spaniard	9.7

Class of Worker: Private Wage and Salary
(Universe: Civilian Employed Population 16 Years and Over)

Group	Number	%
Total Population	140,085	68.5
Hispanic or Latino (of any race)	35,003	75.9
Central American, ex. Mexican	2,155	87.1
Guatemalan	504	94.6
Nicaraguan	338	79.0
Salvadoran	1,039	87.5
Mexican	29,394	76.5
Puerto Rican	816	64.2
South American	664	78.2
Spaniard	576	61.5

Class of Worker: Government
(Universe: Civilian Employed Population 16 Years and Over)

Group	Number	%
Total Population	51,472	25.2
Hispanic or Latino (of any race)	8,386	18.2
Central American, ex. Mexican	233	9.4
Guatemalan	29	5.4
Nicaraguan	75	17.5
Salvadoran	77	6.5
Mexican	6,845	17.8
Puerto Rican	254	20.0
South American	163	19.2
Spaniard	335	35.8

Means of Transportation to Work: Car, Truck or Van
(Universe: Workers 16 Years and Over)

Group	Number	%
Total Population	170,996	86.3
Hispanic or Latino (of any race)	39,036	88.2
Central American, ex. Mexican	2,177	91.0
Guatemalan	506	96.0
Nicaraguan	406	97.1
Salvadoran	981	87.6
Mexican	32,660	88.5
Puerto Rican	850	71.1
South American	722	86.1
Spaniard	866	96.7

Means of Transportation to Work: Public Transportation (ex. Taxicab)
(Universe: Workers 16 Years and Over)

Group	Number	%
Total Population	7,612	3.8
Hispanic or Latino (of any race)	1,826	4.1
Central American, ex. Mexican	21	0.9
Guatemalan	0	0.0
Nicaraguan	0	0.0
Salvadoran	21	1.9
Mexican	1,653	4.5
Puerto Rican	8	0.7
South American	25	3.0
Spaniard	13	1.5

Homeownership Rate
(Universe: Occupied Housing Units)

Group	%
Total Population	49.4
Hispanic or Latino (of any race)	42.8
Central American, ex. Mexican	44.8
Costa Rican	41.2
Guatemalan	41.9
Honduran	35.6
Nicaraguan	42.6
Panamanian	46.2
Salvadoran	47.9
Cuban	32.7
Dominican Republic	39.7
Mexican	43.3
Puerto Rican	30.4
South American	52.5
Argentinean	57.3
Chilean	44.4
Colombian	51.0
Ecuadorian	57.9
Peruvian	52.5
Venezuelan	51.2
Spaniard	50.9

Median Home Value

Group	Dollars
Total Population	311,900
Hispanic or Latino (of any race)	266,300
Central American, ex. Mexican	256,100
Guatemalan	139,900
Nicaraguan	262,500
Salvadoran	263,600
Mexican	258,000
Puerto Rican	349,600
South American	274,400
Spaniard	285,400

Median Gross Rent

Group	Dollars
Total Population	959
Hispanic or Latino (of any race)	940
Central American, ex. Mexican	967
Guatemalan	1,026
Nicaraguan	1,103
Salvadoran	877
Mexican	936
Puerto Rican	913
South American	1,015
Spaniard	990

Median Household Income
(2010 Inflation-Adjusted Dollars)

Group	Dollars
Total Population	50,267
Hispanic or Latino (of any race)	44,018
Central American, ex. Mexican	45,137
Guatemalan	42,656
Nicaraguan	37,813
Salvadoran	48,681
Mexican	42,784
Puerto Rican	50,379
South American	60,821
Spaniard	52,821

Per Capita Income
(2010 Inflation-Adjusted Dollars)

Group	Dollars
Total Population	25,427
Hispanic or Latino (of any race)	16,281
Central American, ex. Mexican	16,354
Guatemalan	13,665
Nicaraguan	14,245
Salvadoran	17,363
Mexican	15,083
Puerto Rican	23,843
South American	25,794
Spaniard	29,037

Households with $100,000+ Income

Group	Number	%
Total Population	33,726	19.4
Hispanic or Latino (of any race)	4,050	12.3
Central American, ex. Mexican	149	8.7
Guatemalan	37	10.9
Nicaraguan	7	1.9
Salvadoran	63	8.9
Mexican	3,072	11.6
Puerto Rican	224	20.2
South American	103	19.3
Spaniard	84	10.8

Households with Food Stamps/SNAP Benefits During Past 12 Months

Group	Number	%
Total Population	16,220	9.3
Hispanic or Latino (of any race)	4,602	13.9
Central American, ex. Mexican	256	14.9
Guatemalan	35	10.3
Nicaraguan	129	34.4
Salvadoran	78	11.0
Mexican	3,829	14.4
Puerto Rican	168	15.2
South American	0	0.0
Spaniard	142	18.3

Poverty Rate
(Income in Past 12 Months Below Poverty Level)

Group	%
Total Population	17.3

Notes: (1) Percent of total population; (2) Percent of Hispanic/Latino population; Profiles include places with an overall population of at least 125,000, OR an overall population of at least 25,000 where the Hispanic/Latino population is at least 20% of the overall population. In states where less than five places meet either of these criteria, we have included places with at least 10,000 total population with the highest percentage of Hispanic/Latino population. These places are identified with an asterisk (*); Please refer to the User's Guide for a full explanation of data.

Hispanic or Latino (of any race)	20.5
Central American, ex. Mexican	15.0
Guatemalan	10.1
Nicaraguan	25.9
Salvadoran	14.5
Mexican	21.8
Puerto Rican	19.4
South American	3.3
Spaniard	11.9

Salinas

Population

Group	Number	%TP[1]	%HP[2]
Total Population	150,441	100.0	–
Hispanic or Latino (of any race)	112,799	75.0	100.0
Central American, ex. Mexican	1,800	1.2	1.6
Guatemalan	177	0.1	0.2
Honduran	136	0.1	0.1
Salvadoran	1,302	0.9	1.2
Mexican	104,237	69.3	92.4
Puerto Rican	715	0.5	0.6
South American	420	0.3	0.4
Peruvian	179	0.1	0.2
Spaniard	607	0.4	0.5

Population Growth: 2000–2010

Group	%
Total Population	-0.4
Hispanic or Latino (of any race)	16.4
Central American, ex. Mexican	172.3
Guatemalan	52.6
Salvadoran	249.1
Mexican	22.9
Puerto Rican	22.6
South American	52.7
Peruvian	47.9
Spaniard	437.2

Males per 100 Females

Group	Number
Total Population	102.1
Hispanic or Latino (of any race)	104.7
Central American, ex. Mexican	115.3
Guatemalan	142.5
Honduran	83.8
Salvadoran	127.2
Mexican	103.7
Puerto Rican	105.5
South American	94.4
Peruvian	103.4
Spaniard	90.3

Average Household Size

Group	People
Total Population	3.66
Hispanic or Latino (of any race)	4.40
Central American, ex. Mexican	4.36
Guatemalan	3.89
Honduran	4.09
Salvadoran	4.76
Mexican	4.46
Puerto Rican	2.79
South American	3.07
Peruvian	3.25
Spaniard	3.22

Median Age

Group	Years
Total Population	28.8
Hispanic or Latino (of any race)	25.4
Central American, ex. Mexican	28.7
Guatemalan	30.3
Honduran	31.6
Salvadoran	27.7
Mexican	25.2
Puerto Rican	29.0
South American	38.4
Peruvian	44.1
Spaniard	35.3

High School Graduates
(Universe: Population 25 Years and Over)

Group	Number	%
Total Population	49,615	59.5
Hispanic or Latino (of any race)	24,189	43.9
Central American, ex. Mexican	550	50.4
Salvadoran	207	30.5
Mexican	22,111	42.5

Four-Year College Graduates
(Universe: Population 25 Years and Over)

Group	Number	%
Total Population	11,249	13.5
Hispanic or Latino (of any race)	2,772	5.0
Central American, ex. Mexican	94	8.6
Salvadoran	8	1.2
Mexican	2,382	4.6

Population Age 3–17 Enrolled in Public School
(Universe: Population Age 3–17 Enrolled in School)

Group	Number	%
Total Population	32,623	95.5
Hispanic or Latino (of any race)	28,041	97.5
Central American, ex. Mexican	264	95.3
Salvadoran	157	92.4
Mexican	26,827	97.7

Population Age 3–17 Enrolled in Private School
(Universe: Population Age 3–17 Enrolled in School)

Group	Number	%
Total Population	1,550	4.5
Hispanic or Latino (of any race)	715	2.5
Central American, ex. Mexican	13	4.7
Salvadoran	13	7.6
Mexican	634	2.3

Foreign-Born Population

Group	Number	%
Total Population	55,022	37.4
Hispanic or Latino (of any race)	47,812	43.9
Central American, ex. Mexican	1,272	71.1
Salvadoran	831	77.3
Mexican	45,689	44.4

Foreign-Born Naturalized U.S. Citizens

Group	Number	%
Total Population	13,062	23.7
Hispanic or Latino (of any race)	8,755	18.3
Central American, ex. Mexican	340	26.7
Salvadoran	88	10.6
Mexican	8,172	17.9

Language Spoken at Home: English Only
(Universe: Population 5 Years and Over)

Group	Number	%
Total Population	43,135	32.4
Hispanic or Latino (of any race)	15,196	15.7
Central American, ex. Mexican	203	12.9
Salvadoran	51	5.3
Mexican	13,053	14.3

Language Spoken at Home: Spanish
(Universe: Population 5 Years and Over)

Group	Number	%
Total Population	82,557	62.1
Hispanic or Latino (of any race)	81,363	84.2
Central American, ex. Mexican	1,369	87.1
Salvadoran	912	94.7
Mexican	78,297	85.7

Unemployment Rate
(Universe: Population 16 Years and Over)

Group	%
Total Population	11.3
Hispanic or Latino (of any race)	13.2
Central American, ex. Mexican	6.1
Salvadoran	5.0
Mexican	13.6

Class of Worker: Private Wage and Salary
(Universe: Civilian Employed Population 16 Years and Over)

Group	Number	%
Total Population	49,766	78.5
Hispanic or Latino (of any race)	37,098	83.7
Central American, ex. Mexican	981	93.7
Salvadoran	666	100.0
Mexican	34,753	83.7

Class of Worker: Government
(Universe: Civilian Employed Population 16 Years and Over)

Group	Number	%
Total Population	9,624	15.2
Hispanic or Latino (of any race)	4,941	11.2
Central American, ex. Mexican	66	6.3
Salvadoran	0	0.0
Mexican	4,589	11.1

Means of Transportation to Work: Car, Truck or Van
(Universe: Workers 16 Years and Over)

Group	Number	%
Total Population	53,630	86.6
Hispanic or Latino (of any race)	36,155	83.9
Central American, ex. Mexican	791	77.2
Salvadoran	432	69.3
Mexican	33,860	83.8

Means of Transportation to Work: Public Transportation (ex. Taxicab)
(Universe: Workers 16 Years and Over)

Group	Number	%
Total Population	1,466	2.4
Hispanic or Latino (of any race)	1,334	3.1
Central American, ex. Mexican	100	9.8
Salvadoran	100	16.1
Mexican	1,225	3.0

Homeownership Rate
(Universe: Occupied Housing Units)

Group	%
Total Population	45.1
Hispanic or Latino (of any race)	36.5
Central American, ex. Mexican	25.6
Guatemalan	24.1
Honduran	25.7
Salvadoran	21.2
Mexican	36.8
Puerto Rican	38.5
South American	57.7
Peruvian	64.3
Spaniard	42.7

Median Home Value

Group	Dollars
Total Population	417,400
Hispanic or Latino (of any race)	376,100
Central American, ex. Mexican	401,900
Salvadoran	262,500
Mexican	366,300

Median Gross Rent

Group	Dollars
Total Population	998
Hispanic or Latino (of any race)	976
Central American, ex. Mexican	923
Salvadoran	923
Mexican	971

Median Household Income
(2010 Inflation-Adjusted Dollars)

Group	Dollars
Total Population	50,808
Hispanic or Latino (of any race)	44,172
Central American, ex. Mexican	49,000
Salvadoran	49,712
Mexican	43,650

Per Capita Income
(2010 Inflation-Adjusted Dollars)

Group	Dollars
Total Population	18,474
Hispanic or Latino (of any race)	13,485
Central American, ex. Mexican	18,971
Salvadoran	16,867
Mexican	13,192

Households with $100,000+ Income

Group	Number	%
Total Population	7,136	17.4
Hispanic or Latino (of any race)	2,921	11.5
Central American, ex. Mexican	87	15.0

Notes: (1) Percent of total population; (2) Percent of Hispanic/Latino population; Profiles include places with an overall population of at least 125,000, OR an overall population of at least 25,000 where the Hispanic/Latino population is at least 20% of the overall population. In states where less than five places meet either of these criteria, we have included places with at least 10,000 total population with the highest percentage of Hispanic/Latino population. These places are identified with an asterisk (*); Please refer to the User's Guide for a full explanation of data.

Salvadoran	15	5.5
Mexican	2,599	11.1

Households with Food Stamps/SNAP Benefits During Past 12 Months

Group	Number	%
Total Population	2,925	7.1
Hispanic or Latino (of any race)	2,433	9.6
Central American, ex. Mexican	41	7.1
Salvadoran	33	12.1
Mexican	2,301	9.8

Poverty Rate
(Income in Past 12 Months Below Poverty Level)

Group	%
Total Population	18.1
Hispanic or Latino (of any race)	21.6
Central American, ex. Mexican	21.7
Salvadoran	31.9
Mexican	21.8

San Bernardino

Population

Group	Number	%TP[1]	%HP[2]
Total Population	209,924	100.0	–
Hispanic or Latino (of any race)	125,994	60.0	100.0
Central American, ex. Mexican	5,616	2.7	4.5
Costa Rican	159	0.1	0.1
Guatemalan	1,509	0.7	1.2
Honduran	528	0.3	0.4
Nicaraguan	559	0.3	0.4
Panamanian	152	0.1	0.1
Salvadoran	2,641	1.3	2.1
Cuban	412	0.2	0.3
Mexican	109,448	52.1	86.9
Puerto Rican	1,495	0.7	1.2
South American	764	0.4	0.6
Argentinean	132	0.1	0.1
Colombian	203	0.1	0.2
Ecuadorian	106	0.1	0.1
Peruvian	205	0.1	0.2
Spaniard	710	0.3	0.6

Population Growth: 2000–2010

Group	%
Total Population	13.2
Hispanic or Latino (of any race)	43.1
Central American, ex. Mexican	206.6
Guatemalan	250.9
Honduran	236.3
Nicaraguan	191.1
Salvadoran	277.3
Cuban	64.1
Mexican	52.2
Puerto Rican	38.8
South American	78.5
Colombian	61.1

Males per 100 Females

Group	Number
Total Population	97.2
Hispanic or Latino (of any race)	99.3
Central American, ex. Mexican	97.7
Costa Rican	65.6
Guatemalan	116.2
Honduran	102.3
Nicaraguan	91.4
Panamanian	74.7
Salvadoran	92.5
Cuban	114.6
Mexican	99.2
Puerto Rican	99.1
South American	95.4
Argentinean	140.0
Colombian	86.2
Ecuadorian	103.8
Peruvian	93.4
Spaniard	78.4

Average Household Size

Group	People
Total Population	3.42
Hispanic or Latino (of any race)	4.17
Central American, ex. Mexican	4.27
Costa Rican	3.69
Guatemalan	4.48
Honduran	4.31
Nicaraguan	3.91
Panamanian	2.78
Salvadoran	4.35
Cuban	2.85
Mexican	4.22
Puerto Rican	3.21
South American	3.58
Argentinean	3.67
Colombian	3.58
Ecuadorian	3.47
Peruvian	3.66
Spaniard	3.14

Median Age

Group	Years
Total Population	28.5
Hispanic or Latino (of any race)	24.1
Central American, ex. Mexican	31.7
Costa Rican	36.9
Guatemalan	32.1
Honduran	31.4
Nicaraguan	34.0
Panamanian	31.0
Salvadoran	31.2
Cuban	32.2
Mexican	23.7
Puerto Rican	25.2
South American	35.4
Argentinean	29.5
Colombian	36.1
Ecuadorian	36.0
Peruvian	41.3
Spaniard	30.5

High School Graduates
(Universe: Population 25 Years and Over)

Group	Number	%
Total Population	76,989	66.7
Hispanic or Latino (of any race)	29,547	50.5
Central American, ex. Mexican	1,677	51.6
Guatemalan	269	46.1
Salvadoran	637	43.9
Mexican	25,135	48.8
Puerto Rican	682	78.6
Spaniard	370	79.2

Four-Year College Graduates
(Universe: Population 25 Years and Over)

Group	Number	%
Total Population	14,016	12.1
Hispanic or Latino (of any race)	3,393	5.8
Central American, ex. Mexican	202	6.2
Guatemalan	74	12.7
Salvadoran	36	2.5
Mexican	2,745	5.3
Puerto Rican	76	8.8
Spaniard	36	7.7

Population Age 3–17 Enrolled in Public School
(Universe: Population Age 3–17 Enrolled in School)

Group	Number	%
Total Population	48,104	94.9
Hispanic or Latino (of any race)	33,175	95.4
Central American, ex. Mexican	1,313	98.1
Guatemalan	428	94.5
Salvadoran	683	100.0
Mexican	30,349	95.5
Puerto Rican	201	89.3
Spaniard	225	100.0

Population Age 3–17 Enrolled in Private School
(Universe: Population Age 3–17 Enrolled in School)

Group	Number	%
Total Population	2,565	5.1
Hispanic or Latino (of any race)	1,587	4.6
Central American, ex. Mexican	25	1.9
Guatemalan	25	5.5
Salvadoran	0	0.0
Mexican	1,421	4.5
Puerto Rican	24	10.7
Spaniard	0	0.0

Foreign-Born Population

Group	Number	%
Total Population	49,804	23.8
Hispanic or Latino (of any race)	39,599	32.6
Central American, ex. Mexican	3,504	57.2
Guatemalan	766	58.5
Salvadoran	1,473	49.7
Mexican	35,075	32.3
Puerto Rican	68	4.4
Spaniard	49	5.7

Foreign-Born Naturalized U.S. Citizens

Group	Number	%
Total Population	16,320	32.8
Hispanic or Latino (of any race)	11,094	28.0
Central American, ex. Mexican	1,637	46.7
Guatemalan	278	36.3
Salvadoran	657	44.6
Mexican	9,025	25.7
Puerto Rican	0	0.0
Spaniard	9	18.4

Language Spoken at Home: English Only
(Universe: Population 5 Years and Over)

Group	Number	%
Total Population	101,299	53.3
Hispanic or Latino (of any race)	31,518	29.1
Central American, ex. Mexican	643	11.7
Guatemalan	128	12.3
Salvadoran	284	10.3
Mexican	27,901	28.9
Puerto Rican	468	36.0
Spaniard	463	64.8

Language Spoken at Home: Spanish
(Universe: Population 5 Years and Over)

Group	Number	%
Total Population	78,669	41.4
Hispanic or Latino (of any race)	76,459	70.7
Central American, ex. Mexican	4,700	85.9
Guatemalan	913	87.7
Salvadoran	2,462	89.3
Mexican	68,793	71.1
Puerto Rican	831	64.0
Spaniard	252	35.2

Unemployment Rate
(Universe: Population 16 Years and Over)

Group	%
Total Population	13.0
Hispanic or Latino (of any race)	14.0
Central American, ex. Mexican	14.2
Guatemalan	20.6
Salvadoran	12.0
Mexican	14.0
Puerto Rican	20.6
Spaniard	8.9

Class of Worker: Private Wage and Salary
(Universe: Civilian Employed Population 16 Years and Over)

Group	Number	%
Total Population	57,545	75.6
Hispanic or Latino (of any race)	33,577	80.7
Central American, ex. Mexican	2,262	89.4
Guatemalan	408	95.6
Salvadoran	1,206	91.2
Mexican	29,983	80.8
Puerto Rican	197	53.7
Spaniard	181	83.8

Class of Worker: Government
(Universe: Civilian Employed Population 16 Years and Over)

Group	Number	%
Total Population	13,671	18.0
Hispanic or Latino (of any race)	5,400	13.0
Central American, ex. Mexican	67	2.6
Guatemalan	0	0.0
Salvadoran	14	1.1
Mexican	4,785	12.9
Puerto Rican	119	32.4
Spaniard	35	16.2

Notes: (1) Percent of total population; (2) Percent of Hispanic/Latino population; Profiles include places with an overall population of at least 125,000, OR an overall population of at least 25,000 where the Hispanic/Latino population is at least 20% of the overall population. In states where less than five places meet either of these criteria, we have included places with at least 10,000 total population with the highest percentage of Hispanic/Latino population. These places are identified with an asterisk (*); Please refer to the User's Guide for a full explanation of data.

Means of Transportation to Work: Car, Truck or Van
(Universe: Workers 16 Years and Over)

Group	Number	%
Total Population	66,114	89.8
Hispanic or Latino (of any race)	36,009	89.6
Central American, ex. Mexican	2,237	93.1
Guatemalan	427	100.0
Salvadoran	1,210	95.3
Mexican	32,143	89.6
Puerto Rican	303	84.9
Spaniard	120	80.0

Means of Transportation to Work: Public Transportation (ex. Taxicab)
(Universe: Workers 16 Years and Over)

Group	Number	%
Total Population	2,240	3.0
Hispanic or Latino (of any race)	1,377	3.4
Central American, ex. Mexican	100	4.2
Guatemalan	0	0.0
Salvadoran	33	2.6
Mexican	1,220	3.4
Puerto Rican	0	0.0
Spaniard	23	15.3

Homeownership Rate
(Universe: Occupied Housing Units)

Group	%
Total Population	50.3
Hispanic or Latino (of any race)	49.7
Central American, ex. Mexican	52.3
Costa Rican	64.4
Guatemalan	48.1
Honduran	38.9
Nicaraguan	49.1
Panamanian	51.0
Salvadoran	58.0
Cuban	46.2
Mexican	50.5
Puerto Rican	37.4
South American	59.4
Argentinean	59.0
Colombian	59.5
Ecuadorian	69.4
Peruvian	55.4
Spaniard	54.9

Median Home Value

Group	Dollars
Total Population	243,800
Hispanic or Latino (of any race)	230,000
Central American, ex. Mexican	243,600
Guatemalan	290,900
Salvadoran	242,600
Mexican	231,200
Puerto Rican	205,900
Spaniard	115,200

Median Gross Rent

Group	Dollars
Total Population	905
Hispanic or Latino (of any race)	890
Central American, ex. Mexican	1,063
Guatemalan	988
Salvadoran	1,007
Mexican	881
Puerto Rican	1,324
Spaniard	1,045

Median Household Income
(2010 Inflation-Adjusted Dollars)

Group	Dollars
Total Population	39,895
Hispanic or Latino (of any race)	37,737
Central American, ex. Mexican	41,729
Guatemalan	29,861
Salvadoran	39,891
Mexican	37,376
Puerto Rican	43,083
Spaniard	30,507

Per Capita Income
(2010 Inflation-Adjusted Dollars)

Group	Dollars
Total Population	15,616
Hispanic or Latino (of any race)	11,689
Central American, ex. Mexican	13,012
Guatemalan	11,860
Salvadoran	12,657
Mexican	11,500
Puerto Rican	11,132
Spaniard	14,310

Households with $100,000+ Income

Group	Number	%
Total Population	6,669	10.9
Hispanic or Latino (of any race)	2,364	8.2
Central American, ex. Mexican	97	6.1
Guatemalan	16	4.7
Salvadoran	31	4.2
Mexican	2,066	8.1
Puerto Rican	28	7.0
Spaniard	24	8.7

Households with Food Stamps/SNAP Benefits During Past 12 Months

Group	Number	%
Total Population	8,231	13.5
Hispanic or Latino (of any race)	4,699	16.3
Central American, ex. Mexican	265	16.6
Guatemalan	118	34.8
Salvadoran	78	10.6
Mexican	4,125	16.1
Puerto Rican	129	32.1
Spaniard	25	9.0

Poverty Rate
(Income in Past 12 Months Below Poverty Level)

Group	%
Total Population	27.4
Hispanic or Latino (of any race)	29.7
Central American, ex. Mexican	28.0
Guatemalan	52.3
Salvadoran	25.1
Mexican	29.6
Puerto Rican	43.2
Spaniard	19.0

San Bruno

Population

Group	Number	%TP[1]	%HP[2]
Total Population	41,114	100.0	–
Hispanic or Latino (of any race)	12,016	29.2	100.0
Central American, ex. Mexican	2,800	6.8	23.3
Guatemalan	341	0.8	2.8
Honduran	114	0.3	0.9
Nicaraguan	824	2.0	6.9
Salvadoran	1,418	3.4	11.8
Mexican	6,990	17.0	58.2
Puerto Rican	369	0.9	3.1
South American	564	1.4	4.7
Peruvian	308	0.7	2.6
Spaniard	334	0.8	2.8

Population Growth: 2000–2010

Group	%
Total Population	2.4
Hispanic or Latino (of any race)	24.1
Central American, ex. Mexican	79.3
Guatemalan	105.4
Nicaraguan	62.2
Salvadoran	121.9
Mexican	38.4
Puerto Rican	22.2
South American	52.8
Peruvian	51.0

Males per 100 Females

Group	Number
Total Population	97.1
Hispanic or Latino (of any race)	99.7
Central American, ex. Mexican	90.9
Guatemalan	103.0
Honduran	100.0
Nicaraguan	87.7
Salvadoran	88.6
Mexican	107.0
Puerto Rican	87.3
South American	77.4
Peruvian	86.7
Spaniard	79.6

Average Household Size

Group	People
Total Population	2.77
Hispanic or Latino (of any race)	3.50
Central American, ex. Mexican	3.32
Guatemalan	3.11
Honduran	3.78
Nicaraguan	3.20
Salvadoran	3.46
Mexican	3.82
Puerto Rican	2.69
South American	3.10
Peruvian	3.34
Spaniard	2.62

Median Age

Group	Years
Total Population	38.8
Hispanic or Latino (of any race)	30.4
Central American, ex. Mexican	34.3
Guatemalan	32.9
Honduran	26.9
Nicaraguan	35.8
Salvadoran	35.0
Mexican	27.8
Puerto Rican	30.6
South American	36.7
Peruvian	37.4
Spaniard	45.7

High School Graduates
(Universe: Population 25 Years and Over)

Group	Number	%
Total Population	25,613	90.6
Hispanic or Latino (of any race)	5,273	79.9
Central American, ex. Mexican	1,508	84.5
Salvadoran	844	86.3
Mexican	2,765	75.8

Four-Year College Graduates
(Universe: Population 25 Years and Over)

Group	Number	%
Total Population	9,548	33.8
Hispanic or Latino (of any race)	1,102	16.7
Central American, ex. Mexican	275	15.4
Salvadoran	133	13.6
Mexican	606	16.6

Population Age 3–17 Enrolled in Public School
(Universe: Population Age 3–17 Enrolled in School)

Group	Number	%
Total Population	5,066	79.5
Hispanic or Latino (of any race)	1,945	85.6
Central American, ex. Mexican	162	88.0
Salvadoran	90	90.0
Mexican	1,347	83.5

Population Age 3–17 Enrolled in Private School
(Universe: Population Age 3–17 Enrolled in School)

Group	Number	%
Total Population	1,305	20.5
Hispanic or Latino (of any race)	328	14.4
Central American, ex. Mexican	22	12.0
Salvadoran	10	10.0
Mexican	267	16.5

Foreign-Born Population

Group	Number	%
Total Population	15,072	37.5
Hispanic or Latino (of any race)	4,463	40.9
Central American, ex. Mexican	1,483	60.1
Salvadoran	805	60.4
Mexican	2,341	35.2

Foreign-Born Naturalized U.S. Citizens

Group	Number	%
Total Population	9,430	62.6

Notes: (1) Percent of total population; (2) Percent of Hispanic/Latino population; Profiles include places with an overall population of at least 125,000, OR an overall population of at least 25,000 where the Hispanic/Latino population is at least 20% of the overall population. In states where less than five places meet either of these criteria, we have included places with at least 10,000 total population with the highest percentage of Hispanic/Latino population. These places are identified with an asterisk (*); Please refer to the User's Guide for a full explanation of data.

Group	Number	%
Hispanic or Latino (of any race)	2,505	56.1
Central American, ex. Mexican	1,066	71.9
Salvadoran	539	67.0
Mexican	1,117	47.7

Language Spoken at Home: English Only
(Universe: Population 5 Years and Over)

Group	Number	%
Total Population	19,082	50.6
Hispanic or Latino (of any race)	3,028	30.4
Central American, ex. Mexican	356	15.5
Salvadoran	129	10.7
Mexican	1,906	32.0

Language Spoken at Home: Spanish
(Universe: Population 5 Years and Over)

Group	Number	%
Total Population	7,345	19.5
Hispanic or Latino (of any race)	6,833	68.7
Central American, ex. Mexican	1,921	83.6
Salvadoran	1,055	87.6
Mexican	4,027	67.7

Unemployment Rate
(Universe: Population 16 Years and Over)

Group	%
Total Population	6.7
Hispanic or Latino (of any race)	8.9
Central American, ex. Mexican	6.3
Salvadoran	1.0
Mexican	9.0

Class of Worker: Private Wage and Salary
(Universe: Civilian Employed Population 16 Years and Over)

Group	Number	%
Total Population	17,109	78.6
Hispanic or Latino (of any race)	4,663	82.8
Central American, ex. Mexican	1,370	83.7
Salvadoran	779	80.2
Mexican	2,738	84.1

Class of Worker: Government
(Universe: Civilian Employed Population 16 Years and Over)

Group	Number	%
Total Population	3,186	14.6
Hispanic or Latino (of any race)	731	13.0
Central American, ex. Mexican	201	12.3
Salvadoran	126	13.0
Mexican	411	12.6

Means of Transportation to Work: Car, Truck or Van
(Universe: Workers 16 Years and Over)

Group	Number	%
Total Population	17,717	84.9
Hispanic or Latino (of any race)	4,756	85.8
Central American, ex. Mexican	1,388	87.3
Salvadoran	872	91.8
Mexican	2,729	84.4

Means of Transportation to Work: Public Transportation (ex. Taxicab)
(Universe: Workers 16 Years and Over)

Group	Number	%
Total Population	1,716	8.2
Hispanic or Latino (of any race)	493	8.9
Central American, ex. Mexican	202	12.7
Salvadoran	78	8.2
Mexican	222	6.9

Homeownership Rate
(Universe: Occupied Housing Units)

Group	%
Total Population	60.8
Hispanic or Latino (of any race)	44.7
Central American, ex. Mexican	42.1
Guatemalan	50.9
Honduran	29.6
Nicaraguan	39.5
Salvadoran	42.3
Mexican	43.4
Puerto Rican	50.0
South American	50.0
Peruvian	50.0
Spaniard	70.1

Median Home Value

Group	Dollars
Total Population	648,400
Hispanic or Latino (of any race)	660,100
Central American, ex. Mexican	564,000
Salvadoran	628,000
Mexican	716,200

Median Gross Rent

Group	Dollars
Total Population	1,455
Hispanic or Latino (of any race)	1,412
Central American, ex. Mexican	1,256
Salvadoran	1,059
Mexican	1,514

Median Household Income
(2010 Inflation-Adjusted Dollars)

Group	Dollars
Total Population	75,576
Hispanic or Latino (of any race)	61,393
Central American, ex. Mexican	46,331
Salvadoran	47,093
Mexican	68,672

Per Capita Income
(2010 Inflation-Adjusted Dollars)

Group	Dollars
Total Population	33,496
Hispanic or Latino (of any race)	22,288
Central American, ex. Mexican	23,884
Salvadoran	25,426
Mexican	21,708

Households with $100,000+ Income

Group	Number	%
Total Population	5,116	34.3
Hispanic or Latino (of any race)	738	23.8
Central American, ex. Mexican	119	16.1
Salvadoran	78	18.3
Mexican	514	30.1

Households with Food Stamps/SNAP Benefits During Past 12 Months

Group	Number	%
Total Population	292	2.0
Hispanic or Latino (of any race)	154	5.0
Central American, ex. Mexican	47	6.4
Salvadoran	28	6.6
Mexican	43	2.5

Poverty Rate
(Income in Past 12 Months Below Poverty Level)

Group	%
Total Population	7.2
Hispanic or Latino (of any race)	11.1
Central American, ex. Mexican	11.1
Salvadoran	8.8
Mexican	12.1

San Buenaventura (Ventura)

Population

Group	Number	%TP[1]	%HP[2]
Total Population	106,433	100.0	–
Hispanic or Latino (of any race)	33,874	31.8	100.0
Central American, ex. Mexican	758	0.7	2.2
Guatemalan	277	0.3	0.8
Salvadoran	262	0.2	0.8
Cuban	144	0.1	0.4
Mexican	29,837	28.0	88.1
Puerto Rican	396	0.4	1.2
South American	674	0.6	2.0
Argentinean	111	0.1	0.3
Colombian	149	0.1	0.4
Peruvian	183	0.2	0.5
Spaniard	524	0.5	1.5

Population Growth: 2000–2010

Group	%
Total Population	5.5
Hispanic or Latino (of any race)	37.9
Central American, ex. Mexican	133.2
Cuban	44.0
Mexican	49.4
Puerto Rican	34.7
South American	95.4
Peruvian	83.0

Males per 100 Females

Group	Number
Total Population	97.7
Hispanic or Latino (of any race)	101.8
Central American, ex. Mexican	83.5
Guatemalan	78.7
Salvadoran	103.1
Cuban	77.8
Mexican	103.8
Puerto Rican	78.4
South American	82.2
Argentinean	113.5
Colombian	63.7
Peruvian	64.9
Spaniard	94.8

Average Household Size

Group	People
Total Population	2.57
Hispanic or Latino (of any race)	3.51
Central American, ex. Mexican	3.30
Guatemalan	3.97
Salvadoran	3.03
Cuban	2.24
Mexican	3.62
Puerto Rican	2.60
South American	2.76
Argentinean	2.63
Colombian	2.88
Peruvian	2.67
Spaniard	2.52

Median Age

Group	Years
Total Population	39.0
Hispanic or Latino (of any race)	28.0
Central American, ex. Mexican	31.9
Guatemalan	32.2
Salvadoran	30.5
Cuban	32.7
Mexican	27.6
Puerto Rican	28.8
South American	36.6
Argentinean	41.8
Colombian	39.8
Peruvian	33.1
Spaniard	38.4

High School Graduates
(Universe: Population 25 Years and Over)

Group	Number	%
Total Population	61,645	87.1
Hispanic or Latino (of any race)	11,976	65.8
Mexican	10,270	62.9

Four-Year College Graduates
(Universe: Population 25 Years and Over)

Group	Number	%
Total Population	22,310	31.5
Hispanic or Latino (of any race)	2,217	12.2
Mexican	1,767	10.8

Population Age 3–17 Enrolled in Public School
(Universe: Population Age 3–17 Enrolled in School)

Group	Number	%
Total Population	16,889	87.4
Hispanic or Latino (of any race)	7,964	92.3
Mexican	7,557	93.2

Population Age 3–17 Enrolled in Private School
(Universe: Population Age 3–17 Enrolled in School)

Group	Number	%
Total Population	2,437	12.6
Hispanic or Latino (of any race)	661	7.7
Mexican	553	6.8

Foreign-Born Population

Group	Number	%
Total Population	14,843	14.1
Hispanic or Latino (of any race)	10,153	30.1
Mexican	9,531	31.2

Notes: (1) Percent of total population; (2) Percent of Hispanic/Latino population; Profiles include places with an overall population of at least 125,000, OR an overall population of at least 25,000 where the Hispanic/Latino population is at least 20% of the overall population. In states where less than five places meet either of these criteria, we have included places with at least 10,000 total population with the highest percentage of Hispanic/Latino population. These places are identified with an asterisk (*); Please refer to the User's Guide for a full explanation of data.

Foreign-Born Naturalized U.S. Citizens

Group	Number	%
Total Population	6,264	42.2
Hispanic or Latino (of any race)	3,403	33.5
Mexican	3,084	32.4

Language Spoken at Home: English Only
(Universe: Population 5 Years and Over)

Group	Number	%
Total Population	74,155	75.5
Hispanic or Latino (of any race)	11,840	39.1
Mexican	10,100	36.8

Language Spoken at Home: Spanish
(Universe: Population 5 Years and Over)

Group	Number	%
Total Population	19,337	19.7
Hispanic or Latino (of any race)	18,347	60.6
Mexican	17,268	63.0

Unemployment Rate
(Universe: Population 16 Years and Over)

Group	%
Total Population	7.5
Hispanic or Latino (of any race)	9.3
Mexican	9.3

Class of Worker: Private Wage and Salary
(Universe: Civilian Employed Population 16 Years and Over)

Group	Number	%
Total Population	37,888	73.2
Hispanic or Latino (of any race)	11,802	79.7
Mexican	10,724	80.9

Class of Worker: Government
(Universe: Civilian Employed Population 16 Years and Over)

Group	Number	%
Total Population	9,038	17.5
Hispanic or Latino (of any race)	1,811	12.2
Mexican	1,466	11.1

Means of Transportation to Work: Car, Truck or Van
(Universe: Workers 16 Years and Over)

Group	Number	%
Total Population	45,446	90.1
Hispanic or Latino (of any race)	12,967	89.7
Mexican	11,502	89.1

Means of Transportation to Work: Public Transportation (ex. Taxicab)
(Universe: Workers 16 Years and Over)

Group	Number	%
Total Population	891	1.8
Hispanic or Latino (of any race)	429	3.0
Mexican	415	3.2

Homeownership Rate
(Universe: Occupied Housing Units)

Group	%
Total Population	55.9
Hispanic or Latino (of any race)	42.3
Central American, ex. Mexican	43.6
Guatemalan	39.2
Salvadoran	45.1
Cuban	56.0
Mexican	41.8
Puerto Rican	50.7
South American	55.3
Argentinean	63.4
Colombian	65.9
Peruvian	52.6
Spaniard	50.4

Median Home Value

Group	Dollars
Total Population	532,300
Hispanic or Latino (of any race)	474,300
Mexican	463,500

Median Gross Rent

Group	Dollars
Total Population	1,321
Hispanic or Latino (of any race)	1,315
Mexican	1,310

Median Household Income
(2010 Inflation-Adjusted Dollars)

Group	Dollars
Total Population	65,782
Hispanic or Latino (of any race)	55,054
Mexican	54,920

Per Capita Income
(2010 Inflation-Adjusted Dollars)

Group	Dollars
Total Population	31,864
Hispanic or Latino (of any race)	18,340
Mexican	17,401

Households with $100,000+ Income

Group	Number	%
Total Population	11,719	29.1
Hispanic or Latino (of any race)	1,761	19.8
Mexican	1,468	18.9

Households with Food Stamps/SNAP Benefits During Past 12 Months

Group	Number	%
Total Population	1,714	4.3
Hispanic or Latino (of any race)	771	8.7
Mexican	723	9.3

Poverty Rate
(Income in Past 12 Months Below Poverty Level)

Group	%
Total Population	9.4
Hispanic or Latino (of any race)	13.5
Mexican	13.4

San Diego

Population

Group	Number	%TP[1]	%HP[2]
Total Population	1,307,402	100.0	–
Hispanic or Latino (of any race)	376,020	28.8	100.0
Central American, ex. Mexican	9,188	0.7	2.4
Costa Rican	723	0.1	0.2
Guatemalan	2,696	0.2	0.7
Honduran	1,293	0.1	0.3
Nicaraguan	895	0.1	0.2
Panamanian	1,018	0.1	0.3
Salvadoran	2,415	0.2	0.6
Cuban	2,694	0.2	0.7
Dominican Republic	903	0.1	0.2
Mexican	325,812	24.9	86.6
Puerto Rican	8,220	0.6	2.2
South American	8,220	0.6	2.2
Argentinean	1,322	0.1	0.4
Bolivian	345	<0.1	0.1
Chilean	876	0.1	0.2
Colombian	2,214	0.2	0.6
Ecuadorian	737	0.1	0.2
Peruvian	1,901	0.1	0.5
Uruguayan	141	<0.1	<0.1
Venezuelan	525	<0.1	0.1
Spaniard	4,921	0.4	1.3

Population Growth: 2000–2010

Group	%
Total Population	6.9
Hispanic or Latino (of any race)	21.0
Central American, ex. Mexican	81.0
Costa Rican	56.5
Guatemalan	104.2
Honduran	88.8
Nicaraguan	89.2
Panamanian	49.3
Salvadoran	133.6
Cuban	40.2
Dominican Republic	130.4
Mexican	25.7
Puerto Rican	38.4
South American	86.4
Argentinean	105.9
Bolivian	124.0
Chilean	95.1
Colombian	92.2
Ecuadorian	92.4
Peruvian	92.6
Venezuelan	95.9
Spaniard	561.4

Males per 100 Females

Group	Number
Total Population	102.1
Hispanic or Latino (of any race)	97.5
Central American, ex. Mexican	100.5
Costa Rican	79.9
Guatemalan	115.2
Honduran	88.5
Nicaraguan	88.8
Panamanian	83.8
Salvadoran	110.5
Cuban	115.3
Dominican Republic	121.9
Mexican	96.9
Puerto Rican	118.2
South American	89.5
Argentinean	100.0
Bolivian	94.9
Chilean	86.8
Colombian	85.1
Ecuadorian	85.2
Peruvian	93.0
Uruguayan	113.6
Venezuelan	82.3
Spaniard	88.8

Average Household Size

Group	People
Total Population	2.60
Hispanic or Latino (of any race)	3.51
Central American, ex. Mexican	3.29
Costa Rican	2.66
Guatemalan	3.89
Honduran	3.44
Nicaraguan	2.98
Panamanian	2.53
Salvadoran	3.31
Cuban	2.46
Dominican Republic	2.48
Mexican	3.66
Puerto Rican	2.58
South American	2.53
Argentinean	2.43
Bolivian	2.85
Chilean	2.48
Colombian	2.49
Ecuadorian	2.56
Peruvian	2.71
Uruguayan	2.46
Venezuelan	2.29
Spaniard	2.46

Median Age

Group	Years
Total Population	33.6
Hispanic or Latino (of any race)	27.3
Central American, ex. Mexican	29.8
Costa Rican	31.7
Guatemalan	29.0
Honduran	30.6
Nicaraguan	30.1
Panamanian	33.1
Salvadoran	28.6
Cuban	29.0
Dominican Republic	26.7
Mexican	26.9
Puerto Rican	27.2
South American	33.6
Argentinean	36.3
Bolivian	32.9
Chilean	34.4
Colombian	31.9
Ecuadorian	31.5
Peruvian	33.7
Uruguayan	35.6
Venezuelan	34.1
Spaniard	34.0

Notes: (1) Percent of total population; (2) Percent of Hispanic/Latino population; Profiles include places with an overall population of at least 125,000, OR an overall population of at least 25,000 where the Hispanic/Latino population is at least 20% of the overall population. In states where less than five places meet either of these criteria, we have included places with at least 10,000 total population with the highest percentage of Hispanic/Latino population. These places are identified with an asterisk (*); Please refer to the User's Guide for a full explanation of data.

High School Graduates
(Universe: Population 25 Years and Over)

Group	Number	%
Total Population	721,897	86.4
Hispanic or Latino (of any race)	119,219	62.3
Central American, ex. Mexican	3,506	64.2
Guatemalan	644	50.0
Honduran	426	42.5
Nicaraguan	432	75.1
Panamanian	688	84.2
Salvadoran	924	77.4
Cuban	920	84.0
Mexican	99,171	59.2
Puerto Rican	3,451	90.2
South American	4,564	91.7
Argentinean	551	93.5
Colombian	1,341	90.9
Peruvian	933	94.6
Spaniard	2,916	92.5

Four-Year College Graduates
(Universe: Population 25 Years and Over)

Group	Number	%
Total Population	340,907	40.8
Hispanic or Latino (of any race)	31,724	16.6
Central American, ex. Mexican	1,362	24.9
Guatemalan	323	25.1
Honduran	109	10.9
Nicaraguan	146	25.4
Panamanian	333	40.8
Salvadoran	300	25.1
Cuban	591	54.0
Mexican	23,145	13.8
Puerto Rican	1,239	32.4
South American	2,394	48.1
Argentinean	326	55.3
Colombian	667	45.2
Peruvian	427	43.3
Spaniard	1,371	43.5

Population Age 3–17 Enrolled in Public School
(Universe: Population Age 3–17 Enrolled in School)

Group	Number	%
Total Population	186,711	88.5
Hispanic or Latino (of any race)	83,168	94.6
Central American, ex. Mexican	1,380	91.2
Guatemalan	239	83.9
Honduran	246	100.0
Nicaraguan	145	100.0
Panamanian	354	98.3
Salvadoran	226	73.6
Cuban	328	89.9
Mexican	77,245	95.1
Puerto Rican	811	91.1
South American	1,274	87.9
Argentinean	38	69.1
Colombian	630	95.5
Peruvian	135	74.6
Spaniard	448	90.5

Population Age 3–17 Enrolled in Private School
(Universe: Population Age 3–17 Enrolled in School)

Group	Number	%
Total Population	24,266	11.5
Hispanic or Latino (of any race)	4,710	5.4
Central American, ex. Mexican	133	8.8
Guatemalan	46	16.1
Honduran	0	0.0
Nicaraguan	0	0.0
Panamanian	6	1.7
Salvadoran	81	26.4
Cuban	37	10.1
Mexican	3,986	4.9
Puerto Rican	79	8.9
South American	175	12.1
Argentinean	17	30.9
Colombian	30	4.5
Peruvian	46	25.4
Spaniard	47	9.5

Foreign-Born Population

Group	Number	%
Total Population	332,084	25.9
Hispanic or Latino (of any race)	137,497	38.4
Central American, ex. Mexican	5,287	56.0
Guatemalan	1,442	64.1
Honduran	1,186	73.6
Nicaraguan	423	42.7
Panamanian	766	51.8
Salvadoran	1,049	46.8
Cuban	464	22.0
Mexican	124,528	39.0
Puerto Rican	236	3.8
South American	4,515	57.9
Argentinean	560	65.3
Colombian	1,174	46.4
Peruvian	937	67.5
Spaniard	689	16.4

Foreign-Born Naturalized U.S. Citizens

Group	Number	%
Total Population	161,050	48.5
Hispanic or Latino (of any race)	44,653	32.5
Central American, ex. Mexican	2,180	41.2
Guatemalan	449	31.1
Honduran	335	28.2
Nicaraguan	206	48.7
Panamanian	361	47.1
Salvadoran	604	57.6
Cuban	293	63.1
Mexican	38,196	30.7
Puerto Rican	130	55.1
South American	2,639	58.4
Argentinean	308	55.0
Colombian	634	54.0
Peruvian	631	67.3
Spaniard	276	40.1

Language Spoken at Home: English Only
(Universe: Population 5 Years and Over)

Group	Number	%
Total Population	736,035	61.2
Hispanic or Latino (of any race)	74,786	23.0
Central American, ex. Mexican	1,897	22.0
Guatemalan	191	9.4
Honduran	142	9.4
Nicaraguan	327	36.3
Panamanian	426	31.3
Salvadoran	565	28.5
Cuban	963	51.6
Mexican	59,397	20.6
Puerto Rican	3,152	54.5
South American	2,269	30.2
Argentinean	277	33.3
Colombian	809	34.3
Peruvian	427	31.5
Spaniard	2,492	62.0

Language Spoken at Home: Spanish
(Universe: Population 5 Years and Over)

Group	Number	%
Total Population	266,883	22.2
Hispanic or Latino (of any race)	248,643	76.5
Central American, ex. Mexican	6,705	77.8
Guatemalan	1,838	90.6
Honduran	1,365	90.6
Nicaraguan	575	63.7
Panamanian	921	67.7
Salvadoran	1,419	71.5
Cuban	894	47.9
Mexican	228,478	79.1
Puerto Rican	2,558	44.2
South American	5,139	68.4
Argentinean	555	66.7
Colombian	1,475	62.6
Peruvian	903	66.5
Spaniard	1,347	33.5

Unemployment Rate
(Universe: Population 16 Years and Over)

Group	%
Total Population	7.3
Hispanic or Latino (of any race)	9.0
Central American, ex. Mexican	13.2
Guatemalan	5.5
Honduran	15.5
Nicaraguan	23.9
Panamanian	7.2
Salvadoran	19.5
Cuban	9.0
Mexican	8.9
Puerto Rican	8.9
South American	8.1
Argentinean	14.7
Colombian	8.7
Peruvian	14.0
Spaniard	8.6

Class of Worker: Private Wage and Salary
(Universe: Civilian Employed Population 16 Years and Over)

Group	Number	%
Total Population	472,754	77.0
Hispanic or Latino (of any race)	118,560	80.0
Central American, ex. Mexican	3,482	81.3
Guatemalan	926	78.6
Honduran	611	85.7
Nicaraguan	315	74.5
Panamanian	446	84.0
Salvadoran	866	83.7
Cuban	723	75.4
Mexican	105,128	80.6
Puerto Rican	1,972	67.7
South American	3,037	77.2
Argentinean	390	87.2
Colombian	824	75.8
Peruvian	544	79.6
Spaniard	1,440	69.4

Class of Worker: Government
(Universe: Civilian Employed Population 16 Years and Over)

Group	Number	%
Total Population	93,883	15.3
Hispanic or Latino (of any race)	18,830	12.7
Central American, ex. Mexican	514	12.0
Guatemalan	108	9.2
Honduran	75	10.5
Nicaraguan	65	15.4
Panamanian	70	13.2
Salvadoran	124	12.0
Cuban	119	12.4
Mexican	15,701	12.0
Puerto Rican	762	26.1
South American	577	14.7
Argentinean	57	12.8
Colombian	145	13.3
Peruvian	53	7.8
Spaniard	480	23.1

Means of Transportation to Work: Car, Truck or Van
(Universe: Workers 16 Years and Over)

Group	Number	%
Total Population	530,301	84.5
Hispanic or Latino (of any race)	125,971	83.7
Central American, ex. Mexican	3,448	78.6
Guatemalan	871	69.7
Honduran	543	79.0
Nicaraguan	389	88.0
Panamanian	474	84.3
Salvadoran	802	78.8
Cuban	815	80.8
Mexican	110,599	84.0
Puerto Rican	2,818	81.4
South American	3,541	87.3
Argentinean	423	94.0
Colombian	917	82.3
Peruvian	562	78.4
Spaniard	1,640	83.7

Means of Transportation to Work: Public Transportation (ex. Taxicab)
(Universe: Workers 16 Years and Over)

Group	Number	%
Total Population	25,410	4.1
Hispanic or Latino (of any race)	10,801	7.2
Central American, ex. Mexican	410	9.4
Guatemalan	267	21.4
Honduran	73	10.6
Nicaraguan	0	0.0
Panamanian	0	0.0
Salvadoran	40	3.9
Cuban	11	1.1
Mexican	9,593	7.3
Puerto Rican	261	7.5
South American	214	5.3

Notes: (1) Percent of total population; (2) Percent of Hispanic/Latino population; Profiles include places with an overall population of at least 125,000, OR an overall population of at least 25,000 where the Hispanic/Latino population is at least 20% of the overall population. In states where less than five places meet either of these criteria, we have included places with at least 10,000 total population with the highest percentage of Hispanic/Latino population. These places are identified with an asterisk (*); Please refer to the User's Guide for a full explanation of data.

Group	Number	%
Argentinean	14	3.1
Colombian	78	7.0
Peruvian	95	13.2
Spaniard	135	6.9

Homeownership Rate
(Universe: Occupied Housing Units)

Group	%
Total Population	48.3
Hispanic or Latino (of any race)	35.9
Central American, ex. Mexican	30.4
Costa Rican	41.7
Guatemalan	23.6
Honduran	27.5
Nicaraguan	35.1
Panamanian	40.9
Salvadoran	28.4
Cuban	33.9
Dominican Republic	24.8
Mexican	36.0
Puerto Rican	30.4
South American	42.9
Argentinean	47.9
Bolivian	54.6
Chilean	45.6
Colombian	41.0
Ecuadorian	43.3
Peruvian	39.4
Uruguayan	53.6
Venezuelan	36.8
Spaniard	47.6

Median Home Value

Group	Dollars
Total Population	503,700
Hispanic or Latino (of any race)	400,500
Central American, ex. Mexican	446,200
Guatemalan	544,600
Honduran	492,200
Nicaraguan	401,000
Panamanian	422,200
Salvadoran	455,300
Cuban	533,300
Mexican	390,800
Puerto Rican	513,200
South American	432,900
Argentinean	378,100
Colombian	398,600
Peruvian	437,300
Spaniard	506,200

Median Gross Rent

Group	Dollars
Total Population	1,259
Hispanic or Latino (of any race)	1,065
Central American, ex. Mexican	1,096
Guatemalan	1,036
Honduran	1,115
Nicaraguan	888
Panamanian	1,752
Salvadoran	960
Cuban	1,395
Mexican	1,038
Puerto Rican	1,244
South American	1,272
Argentinean	1,611
Colombian	1,210
Peruvian	1,167
Spaniard	1,461

Median Household Income
(2010 Inflation-Adjusted Dollars)

Group	Dollars
Total Population	62,480
Hispanic or Latino (of any race)	43,267
Central American, ex. Mexican	43,423
Guatemalan	43,696
Honduran	42,448
Nicaraguan	19,960
Panamanian	66,593
Salvadoran	37,937
Cuban	56,290
Mexican	42,275
Puerto Rican	52,576
South American	60,152
Argentinean	49,188
Colombian	60,205
Peruvian	69,750
Spaniard	50,648

Per Capita Income
(2010 Inflation-Adjusted Dollars)

Group	Dollars
Total Population	32,553
Hispanic or Latino (of any race)	16,613
Central American, ex. Mexican	20,719
Guatemalan	21,485
Honduran	14,043
Nicaraguan	20,149
Panamanian	23,436
Salvadoran	21,332
Cuban	28,729
Mexican	15,388
Puerto Rican	29,921
South American	31,837
Argentinean	38,402
Colombian	33,968
Peruvian	31,122
Spaniard	30,310

Households with $100,000+ Income

Group	Number	%
Total Population	135,967	28.6
Hispanic or Latino (of any race)	13,581	14.0
Central American, ex. Mexican	515	16.1
Guatemalan	120	17.5
Honduran	60	11.7
Nicaraguan	11	4.1
Panamanian	153	28.0
Salvadoran	113	14.5
Cuban	161	23.2
Mexican	10,978	13.2
Puerto Rican	542	24.4
South American	607	22.9
Argentinean	70	26.8
Colombian	245	32.8
Peruvian	88	17.6
Spaniard	422	21.9

Households with Food Stamps/SNAP Benefits During Past 12 Months

Group	Number	%
Total Population	15,202	3.2
Hispanic or Latino (of any race)	6,967	7.2
Central American, ex. Mexican	244	7.6
Guatemalan	12	1.8
Honduran	63	12.3
Nicaraguan	49	18.1
Panamanian	25	4.6
Salvadoran	95	12.2
Cuban	18	2.6
Mexican	6,283	7.5
Puerto Rican	124	5.6
South American	114	4.3
Argentinean	0	0.0
Colombian	48	6.4
Peruvian	0	0.0
Spaniard	52	2.7

Poverty Rate
(Income in Past 12 Months Below Poverty Level)

Group	%
Total Population	14.1
Hispanic or Latino (of any race)	21.9
Central American, ex. Mexican	20.4
Guatemalan	29.5
Honduran	14.9
Nicaraguan	37.0
Panamanian	13.6
Salvadoran	17.3
Cuban	15.9
Mexican	22.6
Puerto Rican	13.5
South American	11.3
Argentinean	3.8
Colombian	22.8
Peruvian	7.5
Spaniard	11.2

San Dimas

Population

Group	Number	%TP[1]	%HP[2]
Total Population	33,371	100.0	–
Hispanic or Latino (of any race)	10,491	31.4	100.0
Central American, ex. Mexican	587	1.8	5.6
Guatemalan	161	0.5	1.5
Salvadoran	245	0.7	2.3
Cuban	267	0.8	2.5
Mexican	8,085	24.2	77.1
Puerto Rican	223	0.7	2.1
South American	543	1.6	5.2
Argentinean	117	0.4	1.1
Colombian	151	0.5	1.4
Peruvian	112	0.3	1.1
Spaniard	187	0.6	1.8

Population Growth: 2000–2010

Group	%
Total Population	-4.6
Hispanic or Latino (of any race)	28.5
Central American, ex. Mexican	138.6
Salvadoran	137.9
Cuban	28.4
Mexican	34.1
Puerto Rican	17.4
South American	61.6
Colombian	36.0

Males per 100 Females

Group	Number
Total Population	90.5
Hispanic or Latino (of any race)	88.7
Central American, ex. Mexican	80.1
Guatemalan	89.4
Salvadoran	64.4
Cuban	90.7
Mexican	89.8
Puerto Rican	95.6
South American	76.9
Argentinean	108.9
Colombian	65.9
Peruvian	62.3
Spaniard	83.3

Average Household Size

Group	People
Total Population	2.73
Hispanic or Latino (of any race)	3.20
Central American, ex. Mexican	3.51
Guatemalan	4.02
Salvadoran	3.67
Cuban	3.28
Mexican	3.23
Puerto Rican	2.78
South American	2.95
Argentinean	2.55
Colombian	2.78
Peruvian	3.08
Spaniard	2.82

Median Age

Group	Years
Total Population	42.6
Hispanic or Latino (of any race)	32.5
Central American, ex. Mexican	37.0
Guatemalan	32.5
Salvadoran	38.6
Cuban	44.4
Mexican	31.4
Puerto Rican	29.5
South American	43.8
Argentinean	48.5
Colombian	42.5
Peruvian	45.0
Spaniard	40.6

High School Graduates
(Universe: Population 25 Years and Over)

Group	Number	%
Total Population	21,210	92.9
Hispanic or Latino (of any race)	4,840	87.9
Mexican	3,366	87.0

Notes: (1) Percent of total population; (2) Percent of Hispanic/Latino population; Profiles include places with an overall population of at least 125,000, OR an overall population of at least 25,000 where the Hispanic/Latino population is at least 20% of the overall population. In states where less than five places meet either of these criteria, we have included places with at least 10,000 total population with the highest percentage of Hispanic/Latino population. These places are identified with an asterisk (*); Please refer to the User's Guide for a full explanation of data.

Four-Year College Graduates
(Universe: Population 25 Years and Over)

Group	Number	%
Total Population	7,303	32.0
Hispanic or Latino (of any race)	1,277	23.2
Mexican	618	16.0

Population Age 3–17 Enrolled in Public School
(Universe: Population Age 3–17 Enrolled in School)

Group	Number	%
Total Population	4,786	80.4
Hispanic or Latino (of any race)	1,633	81.5
Mexican	1,173	81.9

Population Age 3–17 Enrolled in Private School
(Universe: Population Age 3–17 Enrolled in School)

Group	Number	%
Total Population	1,168	19.6
Hispanic or Latino (of any race)	371	18.5
Mexican	259	18.1

Foreign-Born Population

Group	Number	%
Total Population	6,696	19.9
Hispanic or Latino (of any race)	2,159	23.7
Mexican	976	14.8

Foreign-Born Naturalized U.S. Citizens

Group	Number	%
Total Population	4,667	69.7
Hispanic or Latino (of any race)	1,595	73.9
Mexican	627	64.2

Language Spoken at Home: English Only
(Universe: Population 5 Years and Over)

Group	Number	%
Total Population	23,071	72.7
Hispanic or Latino (of any race)	4,382	51.6
Mexican	3,467	57.4

Language Spoken at Home: Spanish
(Universe: Population 5 Years and Over)

Group	Number	%
Total Population	4,359	13.7
Hispanic or Latino (of any race)	4,096	48.2
Mexican	2,566	42.4

Unemployment Rate
(Universe: Population 16 Years and Over)

Group	%
Total Population	5.8
Hispanic or Latino (of any race)	3.9
Mexican	3.9

Class of Worker: Private Wage and Salary
(Universe: Civilian Employed Population 16 Years and Over)

Group	Number	%
Total Population	12,444	75.0
Hispanic or Latino (of any race)	3,589	81.8
Mexican	2,574	84.1

Class of Worker: Government
(Universe: Civilian Employed Population 16 Years and Over)

Group	Number	%
Total Population	2,821	17.0
Hispanic or Latino (of any race)	615	14.0
Mexican	425	13.9

Means of Transportation to Work: Car, Truck or Van
(Universe: Workers 16 Years and Over)

Group	Number	%
Total Population	14,673	90.5
Hispanic or Latino (of any race)	4,096	95.4
Mexican	2,815	94.3

Means of Transportation to Work: Public Transportation (ex. Taxicab)
(Universe: Workers 16 Years and Over)

Group	Number	%
Total Population	287	1.8
Hispanic or Latino (of any race)	59	1.4
Mexican	45	1.5

Homeownership Rate
(Universe: Occupied Housing Units)

Group	%
Total Population	72.8
Hispanic or Latino (of any race)	67.5
Central American, ex. Mexican	63.5
Guatemalan	66.7
Salvadoran	59.7
Cuban	71.7
Mexican	67.8
Puerto Rican	68.3
South American	68.4
Argentinean	66.0
Colombian	62.2
Peruvian	62.2
Spaniard	73.8

Median Home Value

Group	Dollars
Total Population	488,300
Hispanic or Latino (of any race)	460,100
Mexican	460,900

Median Gross Rent

Group	Dollars
Total Population	1,423
Hispanic or Latino (of any race)	1,373
Mexican	1,241

Median Household Income
(2010 Inflation-Adjusted Dollars)

Group	Dollars
Total Population	74,150
Hispanic or Latino (of any race)	69,675
Mexican	69,266

Per Capita Income
(2010 Inflation-Adjusted Dollars)

Group	Dollars
Total Population	32,345
Hispanic or Latino (of any race)	27,202
Mexican	24,533

Households with $100,000+ Income

Group	Number	%
Total Population	4,076	35.2
Hispanic or Latino (of any race)	882	33.9
Mexican	545	30.0

Households with Food Stamps/SNAP Benefits During Past 12 Months

Group	Number	%
Total Population	95	0.8
Hispanic or Latino (of any race)	35	1.3
Mexican	35	1.9

Poverty Rate
(Income in Past 12 Months Below Poverty Level)

Group	%
Total Population	5.4
Hispanic or Latino (of any race)	2.1
Mexican	2.1

San Francisco

Population

Group	Number	%TP[1]	%HP[2]
Total Population	805,235	100.0	–
Hispanic or Latino (of any race)	121,774	15.1	100.0
Central American, ex. Mexican	33,834	4.2	27.8
Costa Rican	487	0.1	0.4
Guatemalan	6,154	0.8	5.1
Honduran	2,611	0.3	2.1
Nicaraguan	7,604	0.9	6.2
Panamanian	399	<0.1	0.3
Salvadoran	16,165	2.0	13.3
Cuban	1,992	0.2	1.6
Dominican Republic	289	<0.1	0.2
Mexican	59,675	7.4	49.0
Puerto Rican	4,204	0.5	3.5
South American	8,618	1.1	7.1
Argentinean	1,100	0.1	0.9
Bolivian	416	0.1	0.3
Chilean	754	0.1	0.6
Colombian	1,717	0.2	1.4
Ecuadorian	577	0.1	0.5
Peruvian	3,260	0.4	2.7
Uruguayan	118	<0.1	0.1
Venezuelan	496	0.1	0.4
Spaniard	3,306	0.4	2.7

Population Growth: 2000–2010

Group	%
Total Population	3.7
Hispanic or Latino (of any race)	11.2
Central American, ex. Mexican	44.8
Costa Rican	49.4
Guatemalan	92.6
Honduran	179.6
Nicaraguan	39.3
Panamanian	52.9
Salvadoran	51.7
Cuban	22.1
Dominican Republic	95.3
Mexican	21.9
Puerto Rican	11.9
South American	72.1
Argentinean	103.7
Bolivian	61.2
Chilean	86.2
Colombian	110.2
Ecuadorian	75.4
Peruvian	84.3
Venezuelan	112.0
Spaniard	370.3

Males per 100 Females

Group	Number
Total Population	102.9
Hispanic or Latino (of any race)	113.4
Central American, ex. Mexican	97.3
Costa Rican	101.2
Guatemalan	115.9
Honduran	123.5
Nicaraguan	84.3
Panamanian	98.5
Salvadoran	93.7
Cuban	137.1
Dominican Republic	120.6
Mexican	126.8
Puerto Rican	110.1
South American	98.0
Argentinean	101.5
Bolivian	84.9
Chilean	97.4
Colombian	89.9
Ecuadorian	88.6
Peruvian	100.6
Uruguayan	122.6
Venezuelan	125.5
Spaniard	103.1

Average Household Size

Group	People
Total Population	2.26
Hispanic or Latino (of any race)	2.94
Central American, ex. Mexican	3.51
Costa Rican	2.43
Guatemalan	4.11
Honduran	4.45
Nicaraguan	3.10
Panamanian	2.02
Salvadoran	3.53
Cuban	2.09
Dominican Republic	2.06
Mexican	3.03
Puerto Rican	2.06
South American	2.39
Argentinean	2.07
Bolivian	2.37
Chilean	2.11
Colombian	2.12
Ecuadorian	2.42
Peruvian	2.86
Uruguayan	1.89
Venezuelan	2.02
Spaniard	2.00

Notes: (1) Percent of total population; (2) Percent of Hispanic/Latino population; Profiles include places with an overall population of at least 125,000, OR an overall population of at least 25,000 where the Hispanic/Latino population is at least 20% of the overall population. In states where less than five places meet either of these criteria, we have included places with at least 10,000 total population with the highest percentage of Hispanic/Latino population. These places are identified with an asterisk (*); Please refer to the User's Guide for a full explanation of data.

Median Age

Group	Years
Total Population	38.5
Hispanic or Latino (of any race)	32.2
Central American, ex. Mexican	35.0
Costa Rican	37.7
Guatemalan	30.9
Honduran	29.7
Nicaraguan	40.5
Panamanian	38.3
Salvadoran	36.3
Cuban	38.9
Dominican Republic	31.6
Mexican	30.1
Puerto Rican	34.9
South American	35.7
Argentinean	35.0
Bolivian	37.4
Chilean	35.8
Colombian	33.7
Ecuadorian	35.7
Peruvian	38.0
Uruguayan	36.0
Venezuelan	33.5
Spaniard	37.7

High School Graduates
(Universe: Population 25 Years and Over)

Group	Number	%
Total Population	521,610	85.7
Hispanic or Latino (of any race)	57,129	73.5
Central American, ex. Mexican	13,429	62.1
Guatemalan	2,136	55.4
Honduran	821	52.3
Nicaraguan	3,221	69.4
Salvadoran	6,146	59.9
Cuban	1,078	82.0
Mexican	28,824	73.7
Puerto Rican	2,415	83.9
South American	5,437	89.5
Argentinean	973	93.1
Colombian	957	83.9
Peruvian	1,761	91.1
Spaniard	1,948	95.8

Four-Year College Graduates
(Universe: Population 25 Years and Over)

Group	Number	%
Total Population	311,713	51.2
Hispanic or Latino (of any race)	21,521	27.7
Central American, ex. Mexican	3,119	14.4
Guatemalan	561	14.5
Honduran	161	10.3
Nicaraguan	701	15.1
Salvadoran	1,240	12.1
Cuban	579	44.1
Mexican	10,917	27.9
Puerto Rican	1,174	40.8
South American	2,937	48.4
Argentinean	673	64.4
Colombian	737	64.6
Peruvian	643	33.2
Spaniard	1,105	54.4

Population Age 3–17 Enrolled in Public School
(Universe: Population Age 3–17 Enrolled in School)

Group	Number	%
Total Population	55,212	71.0
Hispanic or Latino (of any race)	13,094	81.6
Central American, ex. Mexican	4,018	82.8
Guatemalan	631	76.2
Honduran	334	75.7
Nicaraguan	758	86.5
Salvadoran	2,072	85.6
Cuban	91	89.2
Mexican	7,520	83.6
Puerto Rican	231	96.7
South American	597	77.3
Argentinean	67	78.8
Colombian	74	63.8
Peruvian	321	79.9
Spaniard	92	35.0

Population Age 3–17 Enrolled in Private School
(Universe: Population Age 3–17 Enrolled in School)

Group	Number	%
Total Population	22,595	29.0
Hispanic or Latino (of any race)	2,958	18.4
Central American, ex. Mexican	836	17.2
Guatemalan	197	23.8
Honduran	107	24.3
Nicaraguan	118	13.5
Salvadoran	348	14.4
Cuban	11	10.8
Mexican	1,471	16.4
Puerto Rican	8	3.3
South American	175	22.7
Argentinean	18	21.2
Colombian	42	36.2
Peruvian	81	20.1
Spaniard	171	65.0

Foreign-Born Population

Group	Number	%
Total Population	281,062	35.6
Hispanic or Latino (of any race)	53,269	45.9
Central American, ex. Mexican	20,397	63.9
Guatemalan	4,025	71.2
Honduran	1,676	66.5
Nicaraguan	3,799	58.8
Salvadoran	10,068	65.2
Cuban	698	42.4
Mexican	24,912	40.3
Puerto Rican	81	2.3
South American	4,599	58.4
Argentinean	737	55.7
Colombian	833	56.4
Peruvian	1,671	63.3
Spaniard	486	18.8

Foreign-Born Naturalized U.S. Citizens

Group	Number	%
Total Population	173,639	61.8
Hispanic or Latino (of any race)	19,833	37.2
Central American, ex. Mexican	8,937	43.8
Guatemalan	1,415	35.2
Honduran	181	10.8
Nicaraguan	2,292	60.3
Salvadoran	4,546	45.2
Cuban	345	49.4
Mexican	6,340	25.4
Puerto Rican	45	55.6
South American	2,589	56.3
Argentinean	399	54.1
Colombian	457	54.9
Peruvian	917	54.9
Spaniard	187	38.5

Language Spoken at Home: English Only
(Universe: Population 5 Years and Over)

Group	Number	%
Total Population	411,728	54.6
Hispanic or Latino (of any race)	28,803	26.5
Central American, ex. Mexican	3,430	11.4
Guatemalan	407	7.5
Honduran	231	9.5
Nicaraguan	921	15.0
Salvadoran	1,353	9.3
Cuban	480	29.8
Mexican	17,052	29.9
Puerto Rican	1,842	53.0
South American	1,791	23.7
Argentinean	234	18.6
Colombian	313	23.3
Peruvian	500	19.7
Spaniard	1,622	66.1

Language Spoken at Home: Spanish
(Universe: Population 5 Years and Over)

Group	Number	%
Total Population	88,147	11.7
Hispanic or Latino (of any race)	78,679	72.5
Central American, ex. Mexican	26,689	88.3
Guatemalan	4,980	92.0
Honduran	2,163	89.4
Nicaraguan	5,206	84.8
Salvadoran	13,133	90.5
Cuban	1,076	66.7

Group	Number	%
Mexican	39,516	69.3
Puerto Rican	1,592	45.8
South American	5,562	73.7
Argentinean	997	79.3
Colombian	1,001	74.4
Peruvian	1,980	77.9
Spaniard	816	33.2

Unemployment Rate
(Universe: Population 16 Years and Over)

Group	%
Total Population	7.1
Hispanic or Latino (of any race)	8.2
Central American, ex. Mexican	9.8
Guatemalan	13.8
Honduran	8.9
Nicaraguan	10.3
Salvadoran	7.7
Cuban	8.7
Mexican	7.4
Puerto Rican	14.6
South American	4.9
Argentinean	0.0
Colombian	5.0
Peruvian	9.4
Spaniard	10.5

Class of Worker: Private Wage and Salary
(Universe: Civilian Employed Population 16 Years and Over)

Group	Number	%
Total Population	346,801	78.0
Hispanic or Latino (of any race)	51,143	80.9
Central American, ex. Mexican	13,449	80.2
Guatemalan	2,732	83.7
Honduran	1,292	83.4
Nicaraguan	2,561	78.3
Salvadoran	6,090	78.9
Cuban	964	86.3
Mexican	27,892	82.2
Puerto Rican	1,599	81.9
South American	3,510	72.6
Argentinean	462	58.7
Colombian	640	67.4
Peruvian	1,187	82.5
Spaniard	986	71.1

Class of Worker: Government
(Universe: Civilian Employed Population 16 Years and Over)

Group	Number	%
Total Population	58,166	13.1
Hispanic or Latino (of any race)	7,623	12.1
Central American, ex. Mexican	1,904	11.4
Guatemalan	127	3.9
Honduran	84	5.4
Nicaraguan	517	15.8
Salvadoran	1,037	13.4
Cuban	93	8.3
Mexican	3,947	11.6
Puerto Rican	268	13.7
South American	817	16.9
Argentinean	219	27.8
Colombian	162	17.1
Peruvian	119	8.3
Spaniard	276	19.9

Means of Transportation to Work: Car, Truck or Van
(Universe: Workers 16 Years and Over)

Group	Number	%
Total Population	199,818	46.1
Hispanic or Latino (of any race)	26,349	42.4
Central American, ex. Mexican	7,792	46.9
Guatemalan	1,251	39.4
Honduran	624	40.3
Nicaraguan	1,631	50.2
Salvadoran	3,845	50.3
Cuban	453	41.1
Mexican	13,054	39.2
Puerto Rican	751	39.1
South American	1,889	39.9
Argentinean	367	46.6
Colombian	285	30.0
Peruvian	602	42.8
Spaniard	728	53.6

Notes: (1) Percent of total population; (2) Percent of Hispanic/Latino population; Profiles include places with an overall population of at least 125,000, OR an overall population of at least 25,000 where the Hispanic/Latino population is at least 20% of the overall population. In states where less than five places meet either of these criteria, we have included places with at least 10,000 total population with the highest percentage of Hispanic/Latino population. These places are identified with an asterisk (*); Please refer to the User's Guide for a full explanation of data.

Means of Transportation to Work: Public Transportation (ex. Taxicab)
(Universe: Workers 16 Years and Over)

Group	Number	%
Total Population	141,169	32.6
Hispanic or Latino (of any race)	23,773	38.3
Central American, ex. Mexican	6,703	40.4
Guatemalan	1,446	45.5
Honduran	686	44.3
Nicaraguan	1,288	39.6
Salvadoran	2,796	36.5
Cuban	527	47.9
Mexican	12,573	37.7
Puerto Rican	688	35.9
South American	1,969	41.6
Argentinean	279	35.5
Colombian	405	42.7
Peruvian	691	49.1
Spaniard	290	21.3

Homeownership Rate
(Universe: Occupied Housing Units)

Group	%
Total Population	35.8
Hispanic or Latino (of any race)	26.1
Central American, ex. Mexican	28.8
Costa Rican	36.5
Guatemalan	21.7
Honduran	14.5
Nicaraguan	34.3
Panamanian	27.1
Salvadoran	29.6
Cuban	25.3
Dominican Republic	14.4
Mexican	24.0
Puerto Rican	24.3
South American	27.2
Argentinean	29.7
Bolivian	33.1
Chilean	25.1
Colombian	26.4
Ecuadorian	35.0
Peruvian	26.2
Uruguayan	20.8
Venezuelan	23.6
Spaniard	35.5

Median Home Value

Group	Dollars
Total Population	785,200
Hispanic or Latino (of any race)	700,000
Central American, ex. Mexican	673,400
Guatemalan	610,700
Honduran	595,900
Nicaraguan	641,500
Salvadoran	707,800
Cuban	731,100
Mexican	682,300
Puerto Rican	690,800
South American	710,100
Argentinean	650,600
Colombian	814,500
Peruvian	787,600
Spaniard	869,300

Median Gross Rent

Group	Dollars
Total Population	1,328
Hispanic or Latino (of any race)	1,219
Central American, ex. Mexican	1,073
Guatemalan	1,210
Honduran	987
Nicaraguan	1,114
Salvadoran	1,007
Cuban	990
Mexican	1,250
Puerto Rican	1,331
South American	1,375
Argentinean	1,947
Colombian	1,337
Peruvian	1,330
Spaniard	1,492

Median Household Income
(2010 Inflation-Adjusted Dollars)

Group	Dollars
Total Population	71,304
Hispanic or Latino (of any race)	55,985
Central American, ex. Mexican	52,816
Guatemalan	51,178
Honduran	64,330
Nicaraguan	52,167
Salvadoran	49,467
Cuban	51,739
Mexican	54,080
Puerto Rican	64,921
South American	60,720
Argentinean	83,295
Colombian	51,027
Peruvian	55,519
Spaniard	79,833

Per Capita Income
(2010 Inflation-Adjusted Dollars)

Group	Dollars
Total Population	45,478
Hispanic or Latino (of any race)	26,042
Central American, ex. Mexican	19,662
Guatemalan	16,291
Honduran	17,548
Nicaraguan	20,977
Salvadoran	19,746
Cuban	41,126
Mexican	25,170
Puerto Rican	36,766
South American	37,256
Argentinean	52,111
Colombian	34,495
Peruvian	32,177
Spaniard	54,164

Households with $100,000+ Income

Group	Number	%
Total Population	122,778	36.5
Hispanic or Latino (of any race)	9,228	25.0
Central American, ex. Mexican	1,855	20.8
Guatemalan	261	17.9
Honduran	107	20.5
Nicaraguan	379	20.2
Salvadoran	912	20.8
Cuban	143	17.6
Mexican	4,348	23.6
Puerto Rican	629	39.7
South American	999	29.3
Argentinean	254	44.7
Colombian	183	25.4
Peruvian	273	23.7
Spaniard	627	41.6

Households with Food Stamps/SNAP Benefits During Past 12 Months

Group	Number	%
Total Population	10,354	3.1
Hispanic or Latino (of any race)	2,079	5.6
Central American, ex. Mexican	707	7.9
Guatemalan	143	9.8
Honduran	86	16.4
Nicaraguan	148	7.9
Salvadoran	292	6.6
Cuban	16	2.0
Mexican	1,085	5.9
Puerto Rican	129	8.1
South American	63	1.9
Argentinean	0	0.0
Colombian	33	4.6
Peruvian	18	1.6
Spaniard	21	1.4

Poverty Rate
(Income in Past 12 Months Below Poverty Level)

Group	%
Total Population	11.9
Hispanic or Latino (of any race)	14.4
Central American, ex. Mexican	11.5
Guatemalan	12.5
Honduran	17.3
Nicaraguan	8.2
Salvadoran	12.0
Cuban	7.5
Mexican	17.0
Puerto Rican	19.1
South American	7.9
Argentinean	12.6
Colombian	11.0
Peruvian	6.8
Spaniard	13.8

San Gabriel

Population

Group	Number	%TP[1]	%HP[2]
Total Population	39,718	100.0	–
Hispanic or Latino (of any race)	10,189	25.7	100.0
Central American, ex. Mexican	739	1.9	7.3
Guatemalan	142	0.4	1.4
Nicaraguan	124	0.3	1.2
Salvadoran	374	0.9	3.7
Cuban	119	0.3	1.2
Mexican	8,433	21.2	82.8
Puerto Rican	121	0.3	1.2
South American	231	0.6	2.3

Population Growth: 2000–2010

Group	%
Total Population	-0.2
Hispanic or Latino (of any race)	-16.6
Central American, ex. Mexican	30.3
Nicaraguan	-3.9
Salvadoran	49.0
Cuban	-14.4
Mexican	-11.8
Puerto Rican	-1.6
South American	17.9

Males per 100 Females

Group	Number
Total Population	93.2
Hispanic or Latino (of any race)	90.7
Central American, ex. Mexican	80.7
Guatemalan	73.2
Nicaraguan	69.9
Salvadoran	82.4
Cuban	105.2
Mexican	90.9
Puerto Rican	92.1
South American	104.4

Average Household Size

Group	People
Total Population	3.13
Hispanic or Latino (of any race)	3.28
Central American, ex. Mexican	3.30
Guatemalan	3.35
Nicaraguan	3.16
Salvadoran	3.41
Cuban	2.57
Mexican	3.33
Puerto Rican	2.77
South American	2.88

Median Age

Group	Years
Total Population	40.3
Hispanic or Latino (of any race)	34.2
Central American, ex. Mexican	37.6
Guatemalan	36.8
Nicaraguan	45.0
Salvadoran	36.9
Cuban	51.3
Mexican	33.3
Puerto Rican	32.3
South American	44.8

High School Graduates
(Universe: Population 25 Years and Over)

Group	Number	%
Total Population	21,892	76.8
Hispanic or Latino (of any race)	5,231	75.6
Mexican	4,065	73.4

Notes: (1) Percent of total population; (2) Percent of Hispanic/Latino population; Profiles include places with an overall population of at least 125,000, OR an overall population of at least 25,000 where the Hispanic/Latino population is at least 20% of the overall population. In states where less than five places meet either of these criteria, we have included places with at least 10,000 total population with the highest percentage of Hispanic/Latino population. These places are identified with an asterisk (*); Please refer to the User's Guide for a full explanation of data.

Four-Year College Graduates *(Universe: Population 25 Years and Over)*

Group	Number	%
Total Population	8,308	29.2
Hispanic or Latino (of any race)	803	11.6
Mexican	607	11.0

Population Age 3–17 Enrolled in Public School *(Universe: Population Age 3–17 Enrolled in School)*

Group	Number	%
Total Population	5,142	82.9
Hispanic or Latino (of any race)	1,694	81.5
Mexican	1,509	83.2

Population Age 3–17 Enrolled in Private School *(Universe: Population Age 3–17 Enrolled in School)*

Group	Number	%
Total Population	1,063	17.1
Hispanic or Latino (of any race)	385	18.5
Mexican	304	16.8

Foreign-Born Population

Group	Number	%
Total Population	21,949	55.3
Hispanic or Latino (of any race)	3,640	34.5
Mexican	2,841	33.0

Foreign-Born Naturalized U.S. Citizens

Group	Number	%
Total Population	12,795	58.3
Hispanic or Latino (of any race)	1,622	44.6
Mexican	1,173	41.3

Language Spoken at Home: English Only *(Universe: Population 5 Years and Over)*

Group	Number	%
Total Population	9,975	26.5
Hispanic or Latino (of any race)	2,830	29.2
Mexican	2,218	28.1

Language Spoken at Home: Spanish *(Universe: Population 5 Years and Over)*

Group	Number	%
Total Population	7,042	18.7
Hispanic or Latino (of any race)	6,716	69.2
Mexican	5,628	71.3

Unemployment Rate *(Universe: Population 16 Years and Over)*

Group	%
Total Population	5.9
Hispanic or Latino (of any race)	7.4
Mexican	7.2

Class of Worker: Private Wage and Salary *(Universe: Civilian Employed Population 16 Years and Over)*

Group	Number	%
Total Population	15,665	81.1
Hispanic or Latino (of any race)	3,834	78.2
Mexican	3,074	79.8

Class of Worker: Government *(Universe: Civilian Employed Population 16 Years and Over)*

Group	Number	%
Total Population	2,626	13.6
Hispanic or Latino (of any race)	775	15.8
Mexican	582	15.1

Means of Transportation to Work: Car, Truck or Van *(Universe: Workers 16 Years and Over)*

Group	Number	%
Total Population	16,218	87.2
Hispanic or Latino (of any race)	3,813	84.3
Mexican	3,015	85.1

Means of Transportation to Work: Public Transportation (ex. Taxicab) *(Universe: Workers 16 Years and Over)*

Group	Number	%
Total Population	799	4.3
Hispanic or Latino (of any race)	247	5.5
Mexican	125	3.5

Homeownership Rate *(Universe: Occupied Housing Units)*

Group	%
Total Population	49.2
Hispanic or Latino (of any race)	41.5
Central American, ex. Mexican	24.3
Guatemalan	25.6
Nicaraguan	22.2
Salvadoran	20.7
Cuban	54.3
Mexican	43.1
Puerto Rican	37.1
South American	44.9

Median Home Value

Group	Dollars
Total Population	569,100
Hispanic or Latino (of any race)	551,400
Mexican	551,600

Median Gross Rent

Group	Dollars
Total Population	1,188
Hispanic or Latino (of any race)	1,101
Mexican	1,081

Median Household Income *(2010 Inflation-Adjusted Dollars)*

Group	Dollars
Total Population	56,720
Hispanic or Latino (of any race)	52,397
Mexican	53,510

Per Capita Income *(2010 Inflation-Adjusted Dollars)*

Group	Dollars
Total Population	24,816
Hispanic or Latino (of any race)	20,886
Mexican	20,422

Households with $100,000+ Income

Group	Number	%
Total Population	3,153	25.4
Hispanic or Latino (of any race)	584	19.4
Mexican	459	18.6

Households with Food Stamps/SNAP Benefits During Past 12 Months

Group	Number	%
Total Population	700	5.6
Hispanic or Latino (of any race)	255	8.5
Mexican	191	7.7

Poverty Rate *(Income in Past 12 Months Below Poverty Level)*

Group	%
Total Population	13.7
Hispanic or Latino (of any race)	16.3
Mexican	17.6

San Jacinto

Population

Group	Number	%TP[1]	%HP[2]
Total Population	44,199	100.0	–
Hispanic or Latino (of any race)	23,109	52.3	100.0
Central American, ex. Mexican	936	2.1	4.1
Guatemalan	319	0.7	1.4
Nicaraguan	128	0.3	0.6
Salvadoran	340	0.8	1.5
Mexican	20,322	46.0	87.9
Puerto Rican	386	0.9	1.7
South American	226	0.5	1.0
Spaniard	185	0.4	0.8

Population Growth: 2000–2010

Group	%
Total Population	85.9
Hispanic or Latino (of any race)	141.1
Central American, ex. Mexican	422.9
Mexican	155.8
Puerto Rican	185.9

Males per 100 Females

Group	Number
Total Population	95.6
Hispanic or Latino (of any race)	99.8
Central American, ex. Mexican	94.6
Guatemalan	92.2
Nicaraguan	106.5
Salvadoran	96.5
Mexican	100.9
Puerto Rican	91.1
South American	113.2
Spaniard	81.4

Average Household Size

Group	People
Total Population	3.34
Hispanic or Latino (of any race)	4.17
Central American, ex. Mexican	4.18
Guatemalan	4.63
Nicaraguan	3.58
Salvadoran	4.22
Mexican	4.21
Puerto Rican	3.92
South American	3.68
Spaniard	3.46

Median Age

Group	Years
Total Population	30.3
Hispanic or Latino (of any race)	24.2
Central American, ex. Mexican	32.7
Guatemalan	31.9
Nicaraguan	37.2
Salvadoran	33.9
Mexican	23.6
Puerto Rican	25.1
South American	34.5
Spaniard	33.5

High School Graduates *(Universe: Population 25 Years and Over)*

Group	Number	%
Total Population	18,089	73.1
Hispanic or Latino (of any race)	6,150	55.2
Central American, ex. Mexican	332	43.3
Mexican	5,248	55.7

Four-Year College Graduates *(Universe: Population 25 Years and Over)*

Group	Number	%
Total Population	2,893	11.7
Hispanic or Latino (of any race)	659	5.9
Central American, ex. Mexican	24	3.1
Mexican	550	5.8

Population Age 3–17 Enrolled in Public School *(Universe: Population Age 3–17 Enrolled in School)*

Group	Number	%
Total Population	8,493	91.9
Hispanic or Latino (of any race)	5,774	93.5
Central American, ex. Mexican	227	100.0
Mexican	4,926	92.4

Population Age 3–17 Enrolled in Private School *(Universe: Population Age 3–17 Enrolled in School)*

Group	Number	%
Total Population	750	8.1
Hispanic or Latino (of any race)	403	6.5
Central American, ex. Mexican	0	0.0
Mexican	403	7.6

Foreign-Born Population

Group	Number	%
Total Population	9,603	23.3
Hispanic or Latino (of any race)	7,937	36.2
Central American, ex. Mexican	750	66.7
Mexican	6,643	35.2

Foreign-Born Naturalized U.S. Citizens

Group	Number	%
Total Population	3,533	36.8
Hispanic or Latino (of any race)	2,539	32.0
Central American, ex. Mexican	396	52.8
Mexican	1,714	25.8

Notes: (1) Percent of total population; (2) Percent of Hispanic/Latino population; Profiles include places with an overall population of at least 125,000, OR an overall population of at least 25,000 where the Hispanic/Latino population is at least 20% of the overall population. In states where less than five places meet either of these criteria, we have included places with at least 10,000 total population with the highest percentage of Hispanic/Latino population. These places are identified with an asterisk (*); Please refer to the User's Guide for a full explanation of data.

Language Spoken at Home: English Only
(Universe: Population 5 Years and Over)

Group	Number	%
Total Population	21,538	57.4
Hispanic or Latino (of any race)	5,473	27.9
Central American, ex. Mexican	28	2.6
Mexican	4,698	28.0

Language Spoken at Home: Spanish
(Universe: Population 5 Years and Over)

Group	Number	%
Total Population	14,377	38.3
Hispanic or Latino (of any race)	14,111	72.1
Central American, ex. Mexican	1,032	97.4
Mexican	12,098	72.0

Unemployment Rate
(Universe: Population 16 Years and Over)

Group	%
Total Population	16.9
Hispanic or Latino (of any race)	17.4
Central American, ex. Mexican	11.5
Mexican	17.8

Class of Worker: Private Wage and Salary
(Universe: Civilian Employed Population 16 Years and Over)

Group	Number	%
Total Population	10,637	75.1
Hispanic or Latino (of any race)	5,907	82.2
Central American, ex. Mexican	366	75.3
Mexican	5,063	83.0

Class of Worker: Government
(Universe: Civilian Employed Population 16 Years and Over)

Group	Number	%
Total Population	2,231	15.8
Hispanic or Latino (of any race)	703	9.8
Central American, ex. Mexican	42	8.6
Mexican	604	9.9

Means of Transportation to Work: Car, Truck or Van
(Universe: Workers 16 Years and Over)

Group	Number	%
Total Population	12,679	91.3
Hispanic or Latino (of any race)	6,451	91.6
Central American, ex. Mexican	391	80.5
Mexican	5,480	91.9

Means of Transportation to Work: Public Transportation (ex. Taxicab)
(Universe: Workers 16 Years and Over)

Group	Number	%
Total Population	84	0.6
Hispanic or Latino (of any race)	18	0.3
Central American, ex. Mexican	0	0.0
Mexican	0	0.0

Homeownership Rate
(Universe: Occupied Housing Units)

Group	%
Total Population	68.0
Hispanic or Latino (of any race)	63.0
Central American, ex. Mexican	69.8
Guatemalan	65.0
Nicaraguan	75.6
Salvadoran	72.9
Mexican	62.9
Puerto Rican	55.7
South American	77.0
Spaniard	69.2

Median Home Value

Group	Dollars
Total Population	184,000
Hispanic or Latino (of any race)	180,400
Central American, ex. Mexican	188,100
Mexican	190,700

Median Gross Rent

Group	Dollars
Total Population	1,000
Hispanic or Latino (of any race)	1,076
Central American, ex. Mexican	535
Mexican	1,086

Median Household Income
(2010 Inflation-Adjusted Dollars)

Group	Dollars
Total Population	45,567
Hispanic or Latino (of any race)	47,083
Central American, ex. Mexican	44,000
Mexican	48,420

Per Capita Income
(2010 Inflation-Adjusted Dollars)

Group	Dollars
Total Population	18,154
Hispanic or Latino (of any race)	13,793
Central American, ex. Mexican	19,006
Mexican	13,578

Households with $100,000+ Income

Group	Number	%
Total Population	1,879	14.5
Hispanic or Latino (of any race)	723	13.7
Central American, ex. Mexican	59	16.5
Mexican	619	14.3

Households with Food Stamps/SNAP Benefits During Past 12 Months

Group	Number	%
Total Population	1,324	10.2
Hispanic or Latino (of any race)	496	9.4
Central American, ex. Mexican	12	3.4
Mexican	433	10.0

Poverty Rate
(Income in Past 12 Months Below Poverty Level)

Group	%
Total Population	17.2
Hispanic or Latino (of any race)	20.0
Central American, ex. Mexican	15.1
Mexican	20.5

San Jose

Population

Group	Number	%TP[1]	%HP[2]
Total Population	945,942	100.0	–
Hispanic or Latino (of any race)	313,636	33.2	100.0
Central American, ex. Mexican	14,697	1.6	4.7
Costa Rican	258	<0.1	0.1
Guatemalan	2,294	0.2	0.7
Honduran	1,890	0.2	0.6
Nicaraguan	2,917	0.3	0.9
Panamanian	371	<0.1	0.1
Salvadoran	6,829	0.7	2.2
Cuban	1,194	0.1	0.4
Dominican Republic	235	<0.1	0.1
Mexican	268,538	28.4	85.6
Puerto Rican	4,763	0.5	1.5
South American	6,035	0.6	1.9
Argentinean	666	0.1	0.2
Bolivian	459	<0.1	0.1
Chilean	632	0.1	0.2
Colombian	1,266	0.1	0.4
Ecuadorian	368	<0.1	0.1
Peruvian	2,128	0.2	0.7
Venezuelan	350	<0.1	0.1
Spaniard	4,011	0.4	1.3

Population Growth: 2000–2010

Group	%
Total Population	5.7
Hispanic or Latino (of any race)	16.2
Central American, ex. Mexican	98.9
Costa Rican	37.2
Guatemalan	150.2
Honduran	157.8
Nicaraguan	71.1
Panamanian	98.4
Salvadoran	130.5
Cuban	19.3
Mexican	21.4
Puerto Rican	17.0
South American	78.7
Argentinean	103.7
Bolivian	84.3
Chilean	53.4
Colombian	112.1
Ecuadorian	92.7
Peruvian	99.3
Venezuelan	83.2
Spaniard	590.4

Males per 100 Females

Group	Number
Total Population	101.1
Hispanic or Latino (of any race)	104.6
Central American, ex. Mexican	101.4
Costa Rican	81.7
Guatemalan	118.5
Honduran	114.3
Nicaraguan	91.5
Panamanian	74.2
Salvadoran	100.1
Cuban	103.8
Dominican Republic	109.8
Mexican	105.9
Puerto Rican	94.8
South American	87.8
Argentinean	103.7
Bolivian	78.6
Chilean	92.7
Colombian	82.2
Ecuadorian	76.9
Peruvian	87.5
Venezuelan	88.2
Spaniard	89.5

Average Household Size

Group	People
Total Population	3.09
Hispanic or Latino (of any race)	4.06
Central American, ex. Mexican	3.96
Costa Rican	2.63
Guatemalan	4.20
Honduran	4.70
Nicaraguan	3.56
Panamanian	2.68
Salvadoran	4.07
Cuban	2.69
Dominican Republic	2.90
Mexican	4.21
Puerto Rican	2.99
South American	3.05
Argentinean	2.75
Bolivian	3.21
Chilean	2.97
Colombian	2.96
Ecuadorian	2.91
Peruvian	3.38
Venezuelan	2.73
Spaniard	2.77

Median Age

Group	Years
Total Population	35.2
Hispanic or Latino (of any race)	27.6
Central American, ex. Mexican	31.9
Costa Rican	43.2
Guatemalan	30.3
Honduran	30.4
Nicaraguan	33.8
Panamanian	38.4
Salvadoran	31.9
Cuban	33.0
Dominican Republic	28.1
Mexican	26.9
Puerto Rican	29.5
South American	36.5
Argentinean	38.3
Bolivian	36.7
Chilean	37.5
Colombian	35.1
Ecuadorian	35.4
Peruvian	36.6
Venezuelan	34.7
Spaniard	36.9

Notes: (1) Percent of total population; (2) Percent of Hispanic/Latino population; Profiles include places with an overall population of at least 125,000, OR an overall population of at least 25,000 where the Hispanic/Latino population is at least 20% of the overall population. In states where less than five places meet either of these criteria, we have included places with at least 10,000 total population with the highest percentage of Hispanic/Latino population. These places are identified with an asterisk (*); Please refer to the User's Guide for a full explanation of data.

High School Graduates
(Universe: Population 25 Years and Over)

Group	Number	%
Total Population	498,217	82.4
Hispanic or Latino (of any race)	102,992	62.7
Central American, ex. Mexican	5,865	64.6
Guatemalan	627	45.0
Honduran	523	42.5
Nicaraguan	933	72.7
Salvadoran	3,320	72.8
Cuban	686	86.7
Mexican	84,633	60.4
Puerto Rican	2,394	86.7
South American	3,522	87.1
Argentinean	462	77.6
Colombian	536	92.3
Peruvian	1,055	85.1
Spaniard	1,599	83.7

Four-Year College Graduates
(Universe: Population 25 Years and Over)

Group	Number	%
Total Population	221,217	36.6
Hispanic or Latino (of any race)	20,295	12.4
Central American, ex. Mexican	1,441	15.9
Guatemalan	310	22.2
Honduran	34	2.8
Nicaraguan	245	19.1
Salvadoran	680	14.9
Cuban	327	41.3
Mexican	14,385	10.3
Puerto Rican	673	24.4
South American	1,642	40.6
Argentinean	248	41.7
Colombian	228	39.2
Peruvian	567	45.7
Spaniard	696	36.4

Population Age 3–17 Enrolled in Public School
(Universe: Population Age 3–17 Enrolled in School)

Group	Number	%
Total Population	145,817	84.7
Hispanic or Latino (of any race)	67,102	93.5
Central American, ex. Mexican	2,739	93.9
Guatemalan	403	95.7
Honduran	409	97.6
Nicaraguan	423	91.4
Salvadoran	1,466	93.9
Cuban	276	88.2
Mexican	60,399	94.1
Puerto Rican	839	92.2
South American	797	82.3
Argentinean	99	77.3
Colombian	30	81.1
Peruvian	278	74.1
Spaniard	248	71.1

Population Age 3–17 Enrolled in Private School
(Universe: Population Age 3–17 Enrolled in School)

Group	Number	%
Total Population	26,436	15.3
Hispanic or Latino (of any race)	4,639	6.5
Central American, ex. Mexican	177	6.1
Guatemalan	18	4.3
Honduran	10	2.4
Nicaraguan	40	8.6
Salvadoran	95	6.1
Cuban	37	11.8
Mexican	3,763	5.9
Puerto Rican	71	7.8
South American	171	17.7
Argentinean	29	22.7
Colombian	7	18.9
Peruvian	97	25.9
Spaniard	101	28.9

Foreign-Born Population

Group	Number	%
Total Population	357,333	38.6
Hispanic or Latino (of any race)	116,491	38.7
Central American, ex. Mexican	9,505	61.7
Guatemalan	1,487	63.4
Honduran	1,714	77.0
Nicaraguan	1,054	51.8
Salvadoran	4,803	60.2
Cuban	376	27.0
Mexican	100,586	38.4
Puerto Rican	133	2.9
South American	4,058	67.3
Argentinean	582	68.2
Colombian	506	66.4
Peruvian	1,463	72.8
Spaniard	325	13.0

Foreign-Born Naturalized U.S. Citizens

Group	Number	%
Total Population	183,707	51.4
Hispanic or Latino (of any race)	29,627	25.4
Central American, ex. Mexican	2,869	30.2
Guatemalan	524	35.2
Honduran	162	9.5
Nicaraguan	566	53.7
Salvadoran	1,461	30.4
Cuban	289	76.9
Mexican	23,489	23.4
Puerto Rican	82	61.7
South American	2,108	51.9
Argentinean	180	30.9
Colombian	281	55.5
Peruvian	656	44.8
Spaniard	192	59.1

Language Spoken at Home: English Only
(Universe: Population 5 Years and Over)

Group	Number	%
Total Population	381,683	44.6
Hispanic or Latino (of any race)	71,439	26.5
Central American, ex. Mexican	1,644	11.7
Guatemalan	239	11.4
Honduran	53	2.6
Nicaraguan	483	25.4
Salvadoran	753	10.5
Cuban	647	55.2
Mexican	58,922	25.2
Puerto Rican	2,621	62.4
South American	743	13.0
Argentinean	123	14.9
Colombian	26	3.8
Peruvian	157	8.4
Spaniard	1,577	68.0

Language Spoken at Home: Spanish
(Universe: Population 5 Years and Over)

Group	Number	%
Total Population	204,393	23.9
Hispanic or Latino (of any race)	197,597	73.2
Central American, ex. Mexican	12,304	87.9
Guatemalan	1,855	88.6
Honduran	1,998	97.0
Nicaraguan	1,397	73.6
Salvadoran	6,393	89.3
Cuban	512	43.6
Mexican	174,265	74.5
Puerto Rican	1,547	36.8
South American	4,896	86.0
Argentinean	704	85.1
Colombian	654	96.2
Peruvian	1,680	89.6
Spaniard	732	31.6

Unemployment Rate
(Universe: Population 16 Years and Over)

Group	%
Total Population	8.7
Hispanic or Latino (of any race)	10.0
Central American, ex. Mexican	9.5
Guatemalan	7.0
Honduran	15.7
Nicaraguan	6.6
Salvadoran	6.8
Cuban	8.5
Mexican	10.0
Puerto Rican	9.0
South American	8.7
Argentinean	4.9
Colombian	3.9
Peruvian	12.8
Spaniard	16.9

Class of Worker: Private Wage and Salary
(Universe: Civilian Employed Population 16 Years and Over)

Group	Number	%
Total Population	367,713	82.3
Hispanic or Latino (of any race)	113,211	84.1
Central American, ex. Mexican	6,728	82.0
Guatemalan	977	81.6
Honduran	948	84.6
Nicaraguan	880	87.0
Salvadoran	3,483	79.9
Cuban	519	83.6
Mexican	97,717	84.8
Puerto Rican	1,990	84.5
South American	2,524	79.5
Argentinean	413	82.3
Colombian	378	85.1
Peruvian	728	70.3
Spaniard	726	71.0

Class of Worker: Government
(Universe: Civilian Employed Population 16 Years and Over)

Group	Number	%
Total Population	49,758	11.1
Hispanic or Latino (of any race)	13,487	10.0
Central American, ex. Mexican	842	10.3
Guatemalan	138	11.5
Honduran	12	1.1
Nicaraguan	106	10.5
Salvadoran	523	12.0
Cuban	56	9.0
Mexican	11,174	9.7
Puerto Rican	276	11.7
South American	411	12.9
Argentinean	89	17.7
Colombian	41	9.2
Peruvian	219	21.1
Spaniard	187	18.3

Means of Transportation to Work: Car, Truck or Van
(Universe: Workers 16 Years and Over)

Group	Number	%
Total Population	384,601	88.5
Hispanic or Latino (of any race)	111,222	85.4
Central American, ex. Mexican	6,667	84.1
Guatemalan	945	82.9
Honduran	863	80.7
Nicaraguan	933	92.2
Salvadoran	3,484	83.1
Cuban	517	87.8
Mexican	95,275	85.4
Puerto Rican	2,008	87.4
South American	2,753	90.6
Argentinean	360	75.5
Colombian	424	100.0
Peruvian	880	88.1
Spaniard	775	76.6

Means of Transportation to Work: Public Transportation (ex. Taxicab)
(Universe: Workers 16 Years and Over)

Group	Number	%
Total Population	15,299	3.5
Hispanic or Latino (of any race)	6,817	5.2
Central American, ex. Mexican	543	6.8
Guatemalan	116	10.2
Honduran	136	12.7
Nicaraguan	25	2.5
Salvadoran	228	5.4
Cuban	45	7.6
Mexican	5,917	5.3
Puerto Rican	83	3.6
South American	67	2.2
Argentinean	35	7.3
Colombian	0	0.0
Peruvian	32	3.2
Spaniard	47	4.6

Homeownership Rate
(Universe: Occupied Housing Units)

Group	%
Total Population	58.5
Hispanic or Latino (of any race)	41.5
Central American, ex. Mexican	38.5
Costa Rican	52.7

Notes: (1) Percent of total population; (2) Percent of Hispanic/Latino population; Profiles include places with an overall population of at least 125,000, OR an overall population of at least 25,000 where the Hispanic/Latino population is at least 20% of the overall population. In states where less than five places meet either of these criteria, we have included places with at least 10,000 total population with the highest percentage of Hispanic/Latino population. These places are identified with an asterisk (*); Please refer to the User's Guide for a full explanation of data.

Guatemalan	32.6
Honduran	26.6
Nicaraguan	41.0
Panamanian	44.1
Salvadoran	40.7
Cuban	53.3
Dominican Republic	34.3
Mexican	40.9
Puerto Rican	44.0
South American	51.9
Argentinean	60.9
Bolivian	61.7
Chilean	56.1
Colombian	50.4
Ecuadorian	50.0
Peruvian	47.7
Venezuelan	46.7
Spaniard	62.0

Median Home Value

Group	Dollars
Total Population	633,800
Hispanic or Latino (of any race)	554,900
Central American, ex. Mexican	533,500
Guatemalan	544,200
Honduran	517,500
Nicaraguan	542,900
Salvadoran	516,600
Cuban	712,000
Mexican	551,100
Puerto Rican	496,800
South American	571,900
Argentinean	475,800
Colombian	470,800
Peruvian	647,100
Spaniard	668,500

Median Gross Rent

Group	Dollars
Total Population	1,339
Hispanic or Latino (of any race)	1,264
Central American, ex. Mexican	1,257
Guatemalan	1,036
Honduran	1,440
Nicaraguan	1,078
Salvadoran	1,363
Cuban	1,931
Mexican	1,257
Puerto Rican	1,275
South American	1,552
Argentinean	2,000+
Colombian	1,411
Peruvian	1,361
Spaniard	1,626

Median Household Income
(2010 Inflation-Adjusted Dollars)

Group	Dollars
Total Population	79,405
Hispanic or Latino (of any race)	57,921
Central American, ex. Mexican	60,175
Guatemalan	58,730
Honduran	65,750
Nicaraguan	77,971
Salvadoran	60,035
Cuban	66,458
Mexican	57,240
Puerto Rican	61,080
South American	71,375
Argentinean	51,563
Colombian	73,417
Peruvian	90,417
Spaniard	73,095

Per Capita Income
(2010 Inflation-Adjusted Dollars)

Group	Dollars
Total Population	33,233
Hispanic or Latino (of any race)	18,565
Central American, ex. Mexican	19,842
Guatemalan	18,425
Honduran	18,081
Nicaraguan	24,528
Salvadoran	19,084
Cuban	30,499
Mexican	17,769
Puerto Rican	25,995
South American	28,002
Argentinean	26,994
Colombian	36,323
Peruvian	23,951
Spaniard	36,318

Households with $100,000+ Income

Group	Number	%
Total Population	117,807	39.3
Hispanic or Latino (of any race)	16,570	22.2
Central American, ex. Mexican	924	22.4
Guatemalan	110	20.0
Honduran	68	12.9
Nicaraguan	197	31.5
Salvadoran	484	23.0
Cuban	184	37.2
Mexican	13,516	21.5
Puerto Rican	365	25.7
South American	569	30.9
Argentinean	46	17.2
Colombian	54	21.7
Peruvian	170	41.3
Spaniard	357	33.9

Households with Food Stamps/SNAP Benefits During Past 12 Months

Group	Number	%
Total Population	12,650	4.2
Hispanic or Latino (of any race)	6,340	8.5
Central American, ex. Mexican	257	6.2
Guatemalan	43	7.8
Honduran	20	3.8
Nicaraguan	39	6.2
Salvadoran	155	7.4
Cuban	0	0.0
Mexican	5,550	8.8
Puerto Rican	113	8.0
South American	107	5.8
Argentinean	30	11.2
Colombian	0	0.0
Peruvian	38	9.2
Spaniard	14	1.3

Poverty Rate
(Income in Past 12 Months Below Poverty Level)

Group	%
Total Population	10.8
Hispanic or Latino (of any race)	17.2
Central American, ex. Mexican	13.6
Guatemalan	10.7
Honduran	14.9
Nicaraguan	14.0
Salvadoran	13.8
Cuban	15.0
Mexican	17.9
Puerto Rican	8.7
South American	9.3
Argentinean	15.7
Colombian	2.6
Peruvian	8.4
Spaniard	6.9

San Juan Capistrano

Population

Group	Number	%TP[1]	%HP[2]
Total Population	34,593	100.0	–
Hispanic or Latino (of any race)	13,388	38.7	100.0
Central American, ex. Mexican	273	0.8	2.0
Guatemalan	111	0.3	0.8
Salvadoran	113	0.3	0.8
Mexican	12,122	35.0	90.5
South American	314	0.9	2.3
Spaniard	109	0.3	0.8

Population Growth: 2000–2010

Group	%
Total Population	2.3
Hispanic or Latino (of any race)	19.5
Central American, ex. Mexican	96.4
Mexican	25.4
South American	72.5

Males per 100 Females

Group	Number
Total Population	98.3
Hispanic or Latino (of any race)	104.8
Central American, ex. Mexican	75.0
Guatemalan	91.4
Salvadoran	63.8
Mexican	106.7
South American	84.7
Spaniard	98.2

Average Household Size

Group	People
Total Population	3.03
Hispanic or Latino (of any race)	5.02
Central American, ex. Mexican	4.85
Guatemalan	4.66
Salvadoran	5.70
Mexican	5.26
South American	3.32
Spaniard	2.45

Median Age

Group	Years
Total Population	40.2
Hispanic or Latino (of any race)	26.5
Central American, ex. Mexican	35.8
Guatemalan	34.5
Salvadoran	35.8
Mexican	25.7
South American	44.4
Spaniard	46.3

High School Graduates
(Universe: Population 25 Years and Over)

Group	Number	%
Total Population	18,456	82.9
Hispanic or Latino (of any race)	3,154	51.4
Mexican	2,465	45.6

Four-Year College Graduates
(Universe: Population 25 Years and Over)

Group	Number	%
Total Population	8,162	36.7
Hispanic or Latino (of any race)	701	11.4
Mexican	421	7.8

Population Age 3–17 Enrolled in Public School
(Universe: Population Age 3–17 Enrolled in School)

Group	Number	%
Total Population	5,296	76.7
Hispanic or Latino (of any race)	2,921	89.5
Mexican	2,792	90.8

Population Age 3–17 Enrolled in Private School
(Universe: Population Age 3–17 Enrolled in School)

Group	Number	%
Total Population	1,612	23.3
Hispanic or Latino (of any race)	343	10.5
Mexican	283	9.2

Foreign-Born Population

Group	Number	%
Total Population	8,051	23.5
Hispanic or Latino (of any race)	5,727	46.7
Mexican	5,362	48.1

Foreign-Born Naturalized U.S. Citizens

Group	Number	%
Total Population	2,786	34.6
Hispanic or Latino (of any race)	1,210	21.1
Mexican	1,025	19.1

Language Spoken at Home: English Only
(Universe: Population 5 Years and Over)

Group	Number	%
Total Population	21,007	66.2
Hispanic or Latino (of any race)	2,174	20.3
Mexican	1,427	14.8

Language Spoken at Home: Spanish
(Universe: Population 5 Years and Over)

Group	Number	%
Total Population	9,104	28.7
Hispanic or Latino (of any race)	8,501	79.4
Mexican	8,180	84.9

Notes: (1) Percent of total population; (2) Percent of Hispanic/Latino population; Profiles include places with an overall population of at least 125,000, OR an overall population of at least 25,000 where the Hispanic/Latino population is at least 20% of the overall population. In states where less than five places meet either of these criteria, we have included places with at least 10,000 total population with the highest percentage of Hispanic/Latino population. These places are identified with an asterisk (*); Please refer to the User's Guide for a full explanation of data.

Unemployment Rate
(Universe: Population 16 Years and Over)

Group	%
Total Population	5.8
Hispanic or Latino (of any race)	5.7
Mexican	5.5

Class of Worker: Private Wage and Salary
(Universe: Civilian Employed Population 16 Years and Over)

Group	Number	%
Total Population	12,298	80.1
Hispanic or Latino (of any race)	4,213	83.5
Mexican	3,843	85.0

Class of Worker: Government
(Universe: Civilian Employed Population 16 Years and Over)

Group	Number	%
Total Population	1,203	7.8
Hispanic or Latino (of any race)	237	4.7
Mexican	189	4.2

Means of Transportation to Work: Car, Truck or Van
(Universe: Workers 16 Years and Over)

Group	Number	%
Total Population	12,916	85.6
Hispanic or Latino (of any race)	3,980	79.7
Mexican	3,679	82.2

Means of Transportation to Work: Public Transportation (ex. Taxicab)
(Universe: Workers 16 Years and Over)

Group	Number	%
Total Population	342	2.3
Hispanic or Latino (of any race)	286	5.7
Mexican	265	5.9

Homeownership Rate
(Universe: Occupied Housing Units)

Group	%
Total Population	74.3
Hispanic or Latino (of any race)	55.1
Central American, ex. Mexican	52.8
Guatemalan	50.0
Salvadoran	48.1
Mexican	53.1
South American	76.9
Spaniard	77.5

Median Home Value

Group	Dollars
Total Population	654,900
Hispanic or Latino (of any race)	486,400
Mexican	439,500

Median Gross Rent

Group	Dollars
Total Population	1,637
Hispanic or Latino (of any race)	1,480
Mexican	1,503

Median Household Income
(2010 Inflation-Adjusted Dollars)

Group	Dollars
Total Population	76,686
Hispanic or Latino (of any race)	50,893
Mexican	48,985

Per Capita Income
(2010 Inflation-Adjusted Dollars)

Group	Dollars
Total Population	41,632
Hispanic or Latino (of any race)	16,912
Mexican	16,037

Households with $100,000+ Income

Group	Number	%
Total Population	4,762	41.5
Hispanic or Latino (of any race)	504	20.8
Mexican	364	17.1

Households with Food Stamps/SNAP Benefits During Past 12 Months

Group	Number	%
Total Population	202	1.8
Hispanic or Latino (of any race)	119	4.9
Mexican	119	5.6

Poverty Rate
(Income in Past 12 Months Below Poverty Level)

Group	%
Total Population	11.4
Hispanic or Latino (of any race)	21.3
Mexican	23.1

San Leandro

Population

Group	Number	%TP[1]	%HP[2]
Total Population	84,950	100.0	–
Hispanic or Latino (of any race)	23,237	27.4	100.0
Central American, ex. Mexican	2,371	2.8	10.2
Guatemalan	455	0.5	2.0
Honduran	118	0.1	0.5
Nicaraguan	444	0.5	1.9
Salvadoran	1,229	1.4	5.3
Cuban	121	0.1	0.5
Mexican	17,102	20.1	73.6
Puerto Rican	831	1.0	3.6
South American	668	0.8	2.9
Colombian	135	0.2	0.6
Peruvian	298	0.4	1.3
Spaniard	582	0.7	2.5

Population Growth: 2000–2010

Group	%
Total Population	6.9
Hispanic or Latino (of any race)	45.8
Central American, ex. Mexican	185.3
Guatemalan	269.9
Nicaraguan	130.1
Salvadoran	259.4
Mexican	59.5
Puerto Rican	19.4
South American	70.8
Peruvian	96.1

Males per 100 Females

Group	Number
Total Population	92.3
Hispanic or Latino (of any race)	97.7
Central American, ex. Mexican	93.1
Guatemalan	97.0
Honduran	87.3
Nicaraguan	87.3
Salvadoran	92.0
Cuban	120.0
Mexican	100.7
Puerto Rican	91.0
South American	83.0
Colombian	68.8
Peruvian	93.5
Spaniard	78.0

Average Household Size

Group	People
Total Population	2.74
Hispanic or Latino (of any race)	3.50
Central American, ex. Mexican	3.71
Guatemalan	3.92
Honduran	3.87
Nicaraguan	3.51
Salvadoran	3.87
Cuban	2.65
Mexican	3.71
Puerto Rican	2.62
South American	3.15
Colombian	3.00
Peruvian	3.62
Spaniard	2.35

Median Age

Group	Years
Total Population	39.3
Hispanic or Latino (of any race)	29.2
Central American, ex. Mexican	31.6
Guatemalan	30.5
Honduran	29.4
Nicaraguan	33.4
Salvadoran	31.2
Cuban	36.8
Mexican	27.8
Puerto Rican	30.3
South American	40.2
Colombian	38.3
Peruvian	38.7
Spaniard	45.9

High School Graduates
(Universe: Population 25 Years and Over)

Group	Number	%
Total Population	47,681	83.3
Hispanic or Latino (of any race)	7,846	67.0
Central American, ex. Mexican	739	65.1
Mexican	6,159	66.5

Four-Year College Graduates
(Universe: Population 25 Years and Over)

Group	Number	%
Total Population	15,418	26.9
Hispanic or Latino (of any race)	1,949	16.6
Central American, ex. Mexican	215	18.9
Mexican	1,450	15.6

Population Age 3–17 Enrolled in Public School
(Universe: Population Age 3–17 Enrolled in School)

Group	Number	%
Total Population	12,283	83.1
Hispanic or Latino (of any race)	5,225	92.5
Central American, ex. Mexican	443	94.7
Mexican	4,407	92.1

Population Age 3–17 Enrolled in Private School
(Universe: Population Age 3–17 Enrolled in School)

Group	Number	%
Total Population	2,497	16.9
Hispanic or Latino (of any race)	423	7.5
Central American, ex. Mexican	25	5.3
Mexican	379	7.9

Foreign-Born Population

Group	Number	%
Total Population	27,982	33.8
Hispanic or Latino (of any race)	7,973	37.4
Central American, ex. Mexican	1,074	56.0
Mexican	6,493	37.3

Foreign-Born Naturalized U.S. Citizens

Group	Number	%
Total Population	15,690	56.1
Hispanic or Latino (of any race)	2,754	34.5
Central American, ex. Mexican	309	28.8
Mexican	2,222	34.2

Language Spoken at Home: English Only
(Universe: Population 5 Years and Over)

Group	Number	%
Total Population	40,807	52.4
Hispanic or Latino (of any race)	5,604	29.1
Central American, ex. Mexican	250	14.2
Mexican	4,134	26.4

Language Spoken at Home: Spanish
(Universe: Population 5 Years and Over)

Group	Number	%
Total Population	14,331	18.4
Hispanic or Latino (of any race)	13,560	70.3
Central American, ex. Mexican	1,507	85.8
Mexican	11,441	73.1

Unemployment Rate
(Universe: Population 16 Years and Over)

Group	%
Total Population	9.3
Hispanic or Latino (of any race)	11.9
Central American, ex. Mexican	15.0
Mexican	12.1

Class of Worker: Private Wage and Salary
(Universe: Civilian Employed Population 16 Years and Over)

Group	Number	%
Total Population	31,798	78.9
Hispanic or Latino (of any race)	7,508	81.6
Central American, ex. Mexican	693	79.7
Mexican	6,007	82.1

Notes: (1) Percent of total population; (2) Percent of Hispanic/Latino population; Profiles include places with an overall population of at least 125,000, OR an overall population of at least 25,000 where the Hispanic/Latino population is at least 20% of the overall population. In states where less than five places meet either of these criteria, we have included places with at least 10,000 total population with the highest percentage of Hispanic/Latino population. These places are identified with an asterisk (*); Please refer to the User's Guide for a full explanation of data.

Class of Worker: Government
(Universe: Civilian Employed Population 16 Years and Over)

Group	Number	%
Total Population	5,913	14.7
Hispanic or Latino (of any race)	1,120	12.2
Central American, ex. Mexican	149	17.1
Mexican	854	11.7

Means of Transportation to Work: Car, Truck or Van
(Universe: Workers 16 Years and Over)

Group	Number	%
Total Population	31,656	80.6
Hispanic or Latino (of any race)	7,446	82.7
Central American, ex. Mexican	756	90.5
Mexican	5,875	82.0

Means of Transportation to Work: Public Transportation (ex. Taxicab)
(Universe: Workers 16 Years and Over)

Group	Number	%
Total Population	4,792	12.2
Hispanic or Latino (of any race)	837	9.3
Central American, ex. Mexican	19	2.3
Mexican	772	10.8

Homeownership Rate
(Universe: Occupied Housing Units)

Group	%
Total Population	57.5
Hispanic or Latino (of any race)	45.8
Central American, ex. Mexican	39.7
Guatemalan	35.7
Honduran	16.7
Nicaraguan	46.9
Salvadoran	40.2
Cuban	50.0
Mexican	45.5
Puerto Rican	35.4
South American	51.2
Colombian	41.0
Peruvian	50.0
Spaniard	65.1

Median Home Value

Group	Dollars
Total Population	493,300
Hispanic or Latino (of any race)	522,800
Central American, ex. Mexican	548,400
Mexican	511,800

Median Gross Rent

Group	Dollars
Total Population	1,135
Hispanic or Latino (of any race)	1,135
Central American, ex. Mexican	996
Mexican	1,150

Median Household Income
(2010 Inflation-Adjusted Dollars)

Group	Dollars
Total Population	62,609
Hispanic or Latino (of any race)	60,966
Central American, ex. Mexican	88,160
Mexican	56,956

Per Capita Income
(2010 Inflation-Adjusted Dollars)

Group	Dollars
Total Population	27,831
Hispanic or Latino (of any race)	19,870
Central American, ex. Mexican	21,794
Mexican	18,549

Households with $100,000+ Income

Group	Number	%
Total Population	7,474	25.5
Hispanic or Latino (of any race)	1,244	22.5
Central American, ex. Mexican	169	37.6
Mexican	822	19.4

Households with Food Stamps/SNAP Benefits During Past 12 Months

Group	Number	%
Total Population	990	3.4
Hispanic or Latino (of any race)	236	4.3
Central American, ex. Mexican	0	0.0
Mexican	198	4.7

Poverty Rate
(Income in Past 12 Months Below Poverty Level)

Group	%
Total Population	8.6
Hispanic or Latino (of any race)	9.5
Central American, ex. Mexican	10.6
Mexican	9.8

San Marcos

Population

Group	Number	%TP[1]	%HP[2]
Total Population	83,781	100.0	–
Hispanic or Latino (of any race)	30,697	36.6	100.0
Central American, ex. Mexican	634	0.8	2.1
Guatemalan	203	0.2	0.7
Salvadoran	231	0.3	0.8
Cuban	170	0.2	0.6
Mexican	27,350	32.6	89.1
Puerto Rican	455	0.5	1.5
South American	544	0.6	1.8
Colombian	156	0.2	0.5
Peruvian	155	0.2	0.5
Spaniard	319	0.4	1.0

Population Growth: 2000–2010

Group	%
Total Population	52.4
Hispanic or Latino (of any race)	51.4
Central American, ex. Mexican	142.0
Mexican	55.3
Puerto Rican	76.4
South American	168.0

Males per 100 Females

Group	Number
Total Population	95.6
Hispanic or Latino (of any race)	99.5
Central American, ex. Mexican	93.9
Guatemalan	113.7
Salvadoran	94.1
Cuban	117.9
Mexican	100.8
Puerto Rican	92.0
South American	79.5
Colombian	67.7
Peruvian	61.5
Spaniard	77.2

Average Household Size

Group	People
Total Population	3.05
Hispanic or Latino (of any race)	4.23
Central American, ex. Mexican	3.93
Guatemalan	4.13
Salvadoran	4.02
Cuban	3.14
Mexican	4.38
Puerto Rican	2.91
South American	2.89
Colombian	2.87
Peruvian	2.85
Spaniard	2.74

Median Age

Group	Years
Total Population	32.9
Hispanic or Latino (of any race)	25.3
Central American, ex. Mexican	29.8
Guatemalan	27.4
Salvadoran	30.9
Cuban	31.0
Mexican	24.7
Puerto Rican	29.9
South American	37.4
Colombian	35.0
Peruvian	37.9
Spaniard	33.9

High School Graduates
(Universe: Population 25 Years and Over)

Group	Number	%
Total Population	39,259	81.5
Hispanic or Latino (of any race)	7,660	52.6
Mexican	6,406	48.9

Four-Year College Graduates
(Universe: Population 25 Years and Over)

Group	Number	%
Total Population	14,254	29.6
Hispanic or Latino (of any race)	1,791	12.3
Mexican	1,168	8.9

Population Age 3–17 Enrolled in Public School
(Universe: Population Age 3–17 Enrolled in School)

Group	Number	%
Total Population	13,635	88.7
Hispanic or Latino (of any race)	6,988	92.4
Mexican	6,477	96.9

Population Age 3–17 Enrolled in Private School
(Universe: Population Age 3–17 Enrolled in School)

Group	Number	%
Total Population	1,734	11.3
Hispanic or Latino (of any race)	577	7.6
Mexican	204	3.1

Foreign-Born Population

Group	Number	%
Total Population	18,823	24.1
Hispanic or Latino (of any race)	11,748	40.6
Mexican	10,851	41.9

Foreign-Born Naturalized U.S. Citizens

Group	Number	%
Total Population	6,707	35.6
Hispanic or Latino (of any race)	2,613	22.2
Mexican	2,089	19.3

Language Spoken at Home: English Only
(Universe: Population 5 Years and Over)

Group	Number	%
Total Population	42,644	60.4
Hispanic or Latino (of any race)	4,911	19.2
Mexican	3,698	16.2

Language Spoken at Home: Spanish
(Universe: Population 5 Years and Over)

Group	Number	%
Total Population	21,537	30.5
Hispanic or Latino (of any race)	20,600	80.5
Mexican	19,142	83.6

Unemployment Rate
(Universe: Population 16 Years and Over)

Group	%
Total Population	7.9
Hispanic or Latino (of any race)	8.1
Mexican	8.0

Class of Worker: Private Wage and Salary
(Universe: Civilian Employed Population 16 Years and Over)

Group	Number	%
Total Population	27,472	80.8
Hispanic or Latino (of any race)	9,893	84.1
Mexican	9,127	85.3

Class of Worker: Government
(Universe: Civilian Employed Population 16 Years and Over)

Group	Number	%
Total Population	3,948	11.6
Hispanic or Latino (of any race)	996	8.5
Mexican	772	7.2

Means of Transportation to Work: Car, Truck or Van
(Universe: Workers 16 Years and Over)

Group	Number	%
Total Population	30,713	90.5
Hispanic or Latino (of any race)	10,724	92.2
Mexican	9,708	91.7

Notes: (1) Percent of total population; (2) Percent of Hispanic/Latino population; Profiles include places with an overall population of at least 125,000, OR an overall population of at least 25,000 where the Hispanic/Latino population is at least 20% of the overall population. In states where less than five places meet either of these criteria, we have included places with at least 10,000 total population with the highest percentage of Hispanic/Latino population. These places are identified with an asterisk (*); Please refer to the User's Guide for a full explanation of data.

Means of Transportation to Work: Public Transportation (ex. Taxicab)
(Universe: Workers 16 Years and Over)

Group	Number	%
Total Population	696	2.1
Hispanic or Latino (of any race)	323	2.8
Mexican	323	3.1

Homeownership Rate
(Universe: Occupied Housing Units)

Group	%
Total Population	62.8
Hispanic or Latino (of any race)	41.0
Central American, ex. Mexican	46.3
Guatemalan	42.6
Salvadoran	47.5
Cuban	55.1
Mexican	40.0
Puerto Rican	46.6
South American	61.5
Colombian	59.6
Peruvian	73.2
Spaniard	60.0

Median Home Value

Group	Dollars
Total Population	441,400
Hispanic or Latino (of any race)	420,800
Mexican	406,900

Median Gross Rent

Group	Dollars
Total Population	1,237
Hispanic or Latino (of any race)	1,152
Mexican	1,142

Median Household Income
(2010 Inflation-Adjusted Dollars)

Group	Dollars
Total Population	58,897
Hispanic or Latino (of any race)	42,470
Mexican	40,397

Per Capita Income
(2010 Inflation-Adjusted Dollars)

Group	Dollars
Total Population	26,091
Hispanic or Latino (of any race)	14,079
Mexican	13,393

Households with $100,000+ Income

Group	Number	%
Total Population	6,979	27.2
Hispanic or Latino (of any race)	1,010	14.8
Mexican	794	13.1

Households with Food Stamps/SNAP Benefits During Past 12 Months

Group	Number	%
Total Population	592	2.3
Hispanic or Latino (of any race)	389	5.7
Mexican	340	5.6

Poverty Rate
(Income in Past 12 Months Below Poverty Level)

Group	%
Total Population	11.3
Hispanic or Latino (of any race)	17.5
Mexican	17.6

San Mateo

Population

Group	Number	%TP[1]	%HP[2]
Total Population	97,207	100.0	–
Hispanic or Latino (of any race)	25,815	26.6	100.0
Central American, ex. Mexican	6,575	6.8	25.5
Guatemalan	2,755	2.8	10.7
Honduran	189	0.2	0.7
Nicaraguan	910	0.9	3.5
Salvadoran	2,571	2.6	10.0
Cuban	189	0.2	0.7
Mexican	13,959	14.4	54.1
Puerto Rican	519	0.5	2.0
South American	2,228	2.3	8.6
Argentinean	225	0.2	0.9
Bolivian	131	0.1	0.5
Chilean	258	0.3	1.0
Colombian	244	0.3	0.9
Peruvian	1,163	1.2	4.5
Spaniard	502	0.5	1.9

Population Growth: 2000–2010

Group	%
Total Population	5.1
Hispanic or Latino (of any race)	36.1
Central American, ex. Mexican	132.7
Guatemalan	201.8
Nicaraguan	150.7
Salvadoran	122.4
Cuban	26.0
Mexican	34.9
Puerto Rican	40.7
South American	69.7
Chilean	74.3
Colombian	60.5
Peruvian	86.7

Males per 100 Females

Group	Number
Total Population	95.4
Hispanic or Latino (of any race)	105.8
Central American, ex. Mexican	112.8
Guatemalan	143.4
Honduran	89.0
Nicaraguan	86.9
Salvadoran	100.4
Cuban	101.1
Mexican	108.3
Puerto Rican	80.8
South American	86.4
Argentinean	102.7
Bolivian	67.9
Chilean	91.1
Colombian	71.8
Peruvian	88.8
Spaniard	82.5

Average Household Size

Group	People
Total Population	2.51
Hispanic or Latino (of any race)	3.66
Central American, ex. Mexican	3.92
Guatemalan	4.67
Honduran	3.50
Nicaraguan	3.27
Salvadoran	3.69
Cuban	2.43
Mexican	3.94
Puerto Rican	2.47
South American	2.97
Argentinean	2.76
Bolivian	3.53
Chilean	2.52
Colombian	2.87
Peruvian	3.12
Spaniard	2.26

Median Age

Group	Years
Total Population	38.9
Hispanic or Latino (of any race)	29.3
Central American, ex. Mexican	30.7
Guatemalan	28.7
Honduran	33.6
Nicaraguan	34.2
Salvadoran	32.5
Cuban	36.3
Mexican	27.1
Puerto Rican	30.8
South American	38.3
Argentinean	36.6
Bolivian	34.3
Chilean	46.5
Colombian	37.4
Peruvian	38.4
Spaniard	40.2

High School Graduates
(Universe: Population 25 Years and Over)

Group	Number	%
Total Population	60,132	88.6
Hispanic or Latino (of any race)	8,680	66.1
Central American, ex. Mexican	2,447	60.2
Guatemalan	520	42.7
Salvadoran	1,421	63.6
Mexican	3,638	59.0
South American	1,232	94.0
Peruvian	811	100.0

Four-Year College Graduates
(Universe: Population 25 Years and Over)

Group	Number	%
Total Population	29,502	43.4
Hispanic or Latino (of any race)	2,336	17.8
Central American, ex. Mexican	726	17.9
Guatemalan	114	9.4
Salvadoran	375	16.8
Mexican	850	13.8
South American	305	23.3
Peruvian	187	23.1

Population Age 3–17 Enrolled in Public School
(Universe: Population Age 3–17 Enrolled in School)

Group	Number	%
Total Population	10,546	71.5
Hispanic or Latino (of any race)	4,285	85.3
Central American, ex. Mexican	995	86.3
Guatemalan	369	93.7
Salvadoran	411	78.0
Mexican	2,641	88.4
South American	205	87.2
Peruvian	109	87.2

Population Age 3–17 Enrolled in Private School
(Universe: Population Age 3–17 Enrolled in School)

Group	Number	%
Total Population	4,209	28.5
Hispanic or Latino (of any race)	737	14.7
Central American, ex. Mexican	158	13.7
Guatemalan	25	6.3
Salvadoran	116	22.0
Mexican	348	11.6
South American	30	12.8
Peruvian	16	12.8

Foreign-Born Population

Group	Number	%
Total Population	31,428	33.2
Hispanic or Latino (of any race)	11,794	51.6
Central American, ex. Mexican	4,744	73.0
Guatemalan	1,672	79.2
Salvadoran	2,616	75.5
Mexican	5,199	43.9
South American	1,315	71.4
Peruvian	853	76.5

Foreign-Born Naturalized U.S. Citizens

Group	Number	%
Total Population	15,816	50.3
Hispanic or Latino (of any race)	3,527	29.9
Central American, ex. Mexican	1,498	31.6
Guatemalan	355	21.2
Salvadoran	863	33.0
Mexican	1,128	21.7
South American	601	45.7
Peruvian	332	38.9

Language Spoken at Home: English Only
(Universe: Population 5 Years and Over)

Group	Number	%
Total Population	51,550	58.5
Hispanic or Latino (of any race)	4,217	20.5
Central American, ex. Mexican	398	6.7
Guatemalan	83	4.4
Salvadoran	191	6.0
Mexican	2,131	20.7
South American	280	15.8
Peruvian	138	13.1

Notes: (1) Percent of total population; (2) Percent of Hispanic/Latino population; Profiles include places with an overall population of at least 125,000, OR an overall population of at least 25,000 where the Hispanic/Latino population is at least 20% of the overall population. In states where less than five places meet either of these criteria, we have included places with at least 10,000 total population with the highest percentage of Hispanic/Latino population. These places are identified with an asterisk (*); Please refer to the User's Guide for a full explanation of data.

Language Spoken at Home: Spanish
(Universe: Population 5 Years and Over)

Group	Number	%
Total Population	17,395	19.7
Hispanic or Latino (of any race)	16,178	78.7
Central American, ex. Mexican	5,567	93.2
Guatemalan	1,817	95.6
Salvadoran	2,979	94.0
Mexican	8,104	78.7
South American	1,477	83.4
Peruvian	904	85.6

Unemployment Rate
(Universe: Population 16 Years and Over)

Group	%
Total Population	5.5
Hispanic or Latino (of any race)	6.7
Central American, ex. Mexican	8.5
Guatemalan	15.7
Salvadoran	4.2
Mexican	6.2
South American	2.5
Peruvian	0.0

Class of Worker: Private Wage and Salary
(Universe: Civilian Employed Population 16 Years and Over)

Group	Number	%
Total Population	39,867	77.8
Hispanic or Latino (of any race)	9,849	78.0
Central American, ex. Mexican	3,040	76.8
Guatemalan	935	72.9
Salvadoran	1,693	77.3
Mexican	4,796	77.7
South American	945	85.2
Peruvian	580	85.8

Class of Worker: Government
(Universe: Civilian Employed Population 16 Years and Over)

Group	Number	%
Total Population	5,809	11.3
Hispanic or Latino (of any race)	1,034	8.2
Central American, ex. Mexican	258	6.5
Guatemalan	28	2.2
Salvadoran	170	7.8
Mexican	517	8.4
South American	22	2.0
Peruvian	0	0.0

Means of Transportation to Work: Car, Truck or Van
(Universe: Workers 16 Years and Over)

Group	Number	%
Total Population	41,177	82.8
Hispanic or Latino (of any race)	9,831	80.5
Central American, ex. Mexican	3,057	80.3
Guatemalan	902	74.3
Salvadoran	1,718	81.5
Mexican	5,036	83.2
South American	888	83.1
Peruvian	554	87.1

Means of Transportation to Work: Public Transportation (ex. Taxicab)
(Universe: Workers 16 Years and Over)

Group	Number	%
Total Population	3,869	7.8
Hispanic or Latino (of any race)	1,168	9.6
Central American, ex. Mexican	365	9.6
Guatemalan	142	11.7
Salvadoran	188	8.9
Mexican	439	7.3
South American	64	6.0
Peruvian	29	4.6

Homeownership Rate
(Universe: Occupied Housing Units)

Group	%
Total Population	52.2
Hispanic or Latino (of any race)	30.6
Central American, ex. Mexican	26.5
Guatemalan	18.3
Honduran	33.3
Nicaraguan	32.7
Salvadoran	29.7
Cuban	45.8
Mexican	28.3
Puerto Rican	37.4
South American	40.7
Argentinean	45.8
Bolivian	61.1
Chilean	47.1
Colombian	44.3
Peruvian	34.0
Spaniard	51.8

Median Home Value

Group	Dollars
Total Population	769,000
Hispanic or Latino (of any race)	705,100
Central American, ex. Mexican	700,800
Guatemalan	713,700
Salvadoran	698,300
Mexican	673,400
South American	609,600
Peruvian	622,600

Median Gross Rent

Group	Dollars
Total Population	1,472
Hispanic or Latino (of any race)	1,415
Central American, ex. Mexican	1,288
Guatemalan	1,165
Salvadoran	1,403
Mexican	1,446
South American	1,433
Peruvian	1,409

Median Household Income
(2010 Inflation-Adjusted Dollars)

Group	Dollars
Total Population	83,850
Hispanic or Latino (of any race)	70,539
Central American, ex. Mexican	63,750
Guatemalan	46,161
Salvadoran	70,000
Mexican	75,838
South American	67,125
Peruvian	83,929

Per Capita Income
(2010 Inflation-Adjusted Dollars)

Group	Dollars
Total Population	44,949
Hispanic or Latino (of any race)	22,902
Central American, ex. Mexican	20,918
Guatemalan	15,369
Salvadoran	23,703
Mexican	20,059
South American	29,305
Peruvian	28,558

Households with $100,000+ Income

Group	Number	%
Total Population	15,918	42.2
Hispanic or Latino (of any race)	1,783	29.9
Central American, ex. Mexican	402	22.6
Guatemalan	93	15.9
Salvadoran	197	21.5
Mexican	950	35.3
South American	145	26.6
Peruvian	86	28.1

Households with Food Stamps/SNAP Benefits During Past 12 Months

Group	Number	%
Total Population	377	1.0
Hispanic or Latino (of any race)	208	3.5
Central American, ex. Mexican	37	2.1
Guatemalan	37	6.3
Salvadoran	0	0.0
Mexican	165	6.1
South American	6	1.1
Peruvian	0	0.0

Poverty Rate
(Income in Past 12 Months Below Poverty Level)

Group	%
Total Population	5.9
Hispanic or Latino (of any race)	8.0
Central American, ex. Mexican	6.6
Guatemalan	19.0
Salvadoran	0.0
Mexican	10.6
South American	1.6
Peruvian	0.0

San Pablo

Population

Group	Number	%TP[1]	%HP[2]
Total Population	29,139	100.0	–
Hispanic or Latino (of any race)	16,462	56.5	100.0
Central American, ex. Mexican	3,235	11.1	19.7
Guatemalan	667	2.3	4.1
Honduran	102	0.4	0.6
Nicaraguan	517	1.8	3.1
Salvadoran	1,908	6.5	11.6
Mexican	11,960	41.0	72.7
Puerto Rican	120	0.4	0.7
South American	278	1.0	1.7
Peruvian	198	0.7	1.2

Population Growth: 2000–2010

Group	%
Total Population	-3.6
Hispanic or Latino (of any race)	22.0
Central American, ex. Mexican	120.5
Guatemalan	206.0
Nicaraguan	101.2
Salvadoran	132.7
Mexican	25.0
Puerto Rican	-27.7
South American	73.8

Males per 100 Females

Group	Number
Total Population	98.8
Hispanic or Latino (of any race)	105.2
Central American, ex. Mexican	99.6
Guatemalan	111.1
Honduran	96.2
Nicaraguan	85.3
Salvadoran	100.4
Mexican	107.3
Puerto Rican	96.7
South American	97.2
Peruvian	112.9

Average Household Size

Group	People
Total Population	3.28
Hispanic or Latino (of any race)	4.22
Central American, ex. Mexican	4.06
Guatemalan	4.37
Honduran	4.48
Nicaraguan	3.81
Salvadoran	4.06
Mexican	4.38
Puerto Rican	2.85
South American	3.19
Peruvian	3.58

Median Age

Group	Years
Total Population	31.6
Hispanic or Latino (of any race)	26.6
Central American, ex. Mexican	32.2
Guatemalan	30.9
Honduran	33.0
Nicaraguan	33.4
Salvadoran	32.4
Mexican	24.9
Puerto Rican	28.3
South American	40.5
Peruvian	39.0

High School Graduates
(Universe: Population 25 Years and Over)

Group	Number	%
Total Population	11,447	64.6
Hispanic or Latino (of any race)	4,108	48.3
Central American, ex. Mexican	835	54.6
Salvadoran	598	52.2
Mexican	2,978	45.3

Notes: (1) Percent of total population; (2) Percent of Hispanic/Latino population; Profiles include places with an overall population of at least 125,000, OR an overall population of at least 25,000 where the Hispanic/Latino population is at least 20% of the overall population. In states where less than five places meet either of these criteria, we have included places with at least 10,000 total population with the highest percentage of Hispanic/Latino population. These places are identified with an asterisk (*); Please refer to the User's Guide for a full explanation of data.

Four-Year College Graduates
(Universe: Population 25 Years and Over)

Group	Number	%
Total Population	2,206	12.4
Hispanic or Latino (of any race)	320	3.8
Central American, ex. Mexican	92	6.0
Salvadoran	53	4.6
Mexican	124	1.9

Population Age 3–17 Enrolled in Public School
(Universe: Population Age 3–17 Enrolled in School)

Group	Number	%
Total Population	5,602	92.3
Hispanic or Latino (of any race)	4,161	92.8
Central American, ex. Mexican	456	83.4
Salvadoran	358	93.7
Mexican	3,537	97.1

Population Age 3–17 Enrolled in Private School
(Universe: Population Age 3–17 Enrolled in School)

Group	Number	%
Total Population	469	7.7
Hispanic or Latino (of any race)	323	7.2
Central American, ex. Mexican	91	16.6
Salvadoran	24	6.3
Mexican	104	2.9

Foreign-Born Population

Group	Number	%
Total Population	13,138	45.1
Hispanic or Latino (of any race)	8,743	53.1
Central American, ex. Mexican	1,571	59.8
Salvadoran	1,148	62.4
Mexican	6,829	52.5

Foreign-Born Naturalized U.S. Citizens

Group	Number	%
Total Population	4,977	37.9
Hispanic or Latino (of any race)	2,067	23.6
Central American, ex. Mexican	559	35.6
Salvadoran	370	32.2
Mexican	1,455	21.3

Language Spoken at Home: English Only
(Universe: Population 5 Years and Over)

Group	Number	%
Total Population	8,284	30.9
Hispanic or Latino (of any race)	1,093	7.4
Central American, ex. Mexican	91	3.7
Salvadoran	91	5.1
Mexican	825	7.2

Language Spoken at Home: Spanish
(Universe: Population 5 Years and Over)

Group	Number	%
Total Population	13,919	51.9
Hispanic or Latino (of any race)	13,622	92.6
Central American, ex. Mexican	2,379	96.3
Salvadoran	1,685	94.9
Mexican	10,663	92.8

Unemployment Rate
(Universe: Population 16 Years and Over)

Group	%
Total Population	12.7
Hispanic or Latino (of any race)	12.0
Central American, ex. Mexican	20.6
Salvadoran	20.0
Mexican	9.5

Class of Worker: Private Wage and Salary
(Universe: Civilian Employed Population 16 Years and Over)

Group	Number	%
Total Population	9,430	77.0
Hispanic or Latino (of any race)	5,634	82.9
Central American, ex. Mexican	980	75.7
Salvadoran	810	82.1
Mexican	4,482	85.1

Class of Worker: Government
(Universe: Civilian Employed Population 16 Years and Over)

Group	Number	%
Total Population	1,825	14.9
Hispanic or Latino (of any race)	551	8.1
Central American, ex. Mexican	249	19.2
Salvadoran	129	13.1
Mexican	302	5.7

Means of Transportation to Work: Car, Truck or Van
(Universe: Workers 16 Years and Over)

Group	Number	%
Total Population	9,718	82.6
Hispanic or Latino (of any race)	5,685	86.0
Central American, ex. Mexican	1,090	86.0
Salvadoran	842	87.8
Mexican	4,469	87.3

Means of Transportation to Work: Public Transportation (ex. Taxicab)
(Universe: Workers 16 Years and Over)

Group	Number	%
Total Population	1,230	10.5
Hispanic or Latino (of any race)	447	6.8
Central American, ex. Mexican	132	10.4
Salvadoran	106	11.1
Mexican	221	4.3

Homeownership Rate
(Universe: Occupied Housing Units)

Group	%
Total Population	46.9
Hispanic or Latino (of any race)	46.3
Central American, ex. Mexican	52.7
Guatemalan	44.2
Honduran	60.0
Nicaraguan	52.1
Salvadoran	55.1
Mexican	43.5
Puerto Rican	52.9
South American	67.8
Peruvian	63.2

Median Home Value

Group	Dollars
Total Population	298,800
Hispanic or Latino (of any race)	269,200
Central American, ex. Mexican	312,600
Salvadoran	303,300
Mexican	241,600

Median Gross Rent

Group	Dollars
Total Population	1,022
Hispanic or Latino (of any race)	1,117
Central American, ex. Mexican	1,190
Salvadoran	1,329
Mexican	1,100

Median Household Income
(2010 Inflation-Adjusted Dollars)

Group	Dollars
Total Population	43,872
Hispanic or Latino (of any race)	46,282
Central American, ex. Mexican	61,329
Salvadoran	61,687
Mexican	41,750

Per Capita Income
(2010 Inflation-Adjusted Dollars)

Group	Dollars
Total Population	17,286
Hispanic or Latino (of any race)	14,121
Central American, ex. Mexican	18,809
Salvadoran	21,064
Mexican	13,092

Households with $100,000+ Income

Group	Number	%
Total Population	1,149	13.1
Hispanic or Latino (of any race)	535	13.4
Central American, ex. Mexican	102	13.6
Salvadoran	80	14.6
Mexican	396	13.2

Households with Food Stamps/SNAP Benefits During Past 12 Months

Group	Number	%
Total Population	803	9.1
Hispanic or Latino (of any race)	348	8.7
Central American, ex. Mexican	18	2.4
Salvadoran	0	0.0
Mexican	318	10.6

Poverty Rate
(Income in Past 12 Months Below Poverty Level)

Group	%
Total Population	18.3
Hispanic or Latino (of any race)	18.1
Central American, ex. Mexican	2.9
Salvadoran	0.9
Mexican	20.2

San Rafael

Population

Group	Number	%TP[1]	%HP[2]
Total Population	57,713	100.0	–
Hispanic or Latino (of any race)	17,302	30.0	100.0
Central American, ex. Mexican	7,740	13.4	44.7
Guatemalan	5,895	10.2	34.1
Nicaraguan	175	0.3	1.0
Salvadoran	1,478	2.6	8.5
Mexican	7,011	12.1	40.5
Puerto Rican	173	0.3	1.0
South American	586	1.0	3.4
Colombian	112	0.2	0.6
Peruvian	251	0.4	1.5
Spaniard	276	0.5	1.6

Population Growth: 2000–2010

Group	%
Total Population	2.9
Hispanic or Latino (of any race)	32.4
Central American, ex. Mexican	123.0
Guatemalan	182.1
Nicaraguan	49.6
Salvadoran	37.9
Mexican	16.7
Puerto Rican	24.5
South American	23.9
Peruvian	23.0

Males per 100 Females

Group	Number
Total Population	99.7
Hispanic or Latino (of any race)	129.7
Central American, ex. Mexican	133.9
Guatemalan	149.3
Nicaraguan	82.3
Salvadoran	96.3
Mexican	138.8
Puerto Rican	88.0
South American	77.6
Colombian	53.4
Peruvian	87.3
Spaniard	85.2

Average Household Size

Group	People
Total Population	2.44
Hispanic or Latino (of any race)	4.05
Central American, ex. Mexican	4.64
Guatemalan	5.11
Nicaraguan	3.13
Salvadoran	3.69
Mexican	3.93
Puerto Rican	2.25
South American	2.36
Colombian	2.00
Peruvian	2.55
Spaniard	2.43

Median Age

Group	Years
Total Population	40.2
Hispanic or Latino (of any race)	27.6
Central American, ex. Mexican	27.8
Guatemalan	27.0
Nicaraguan	35.4
Salvadoran	31.8
Mexican	27.1
Puerto Rican	30.4
South American	41.5
Colombian	43.8

STATE & PLACE PROFILES

Notes: (1) Percent of total population; (2) Percent of Hispanic/Latino population; Profiles include places with an overall population of at least 125,000, OR an overall population of at least 25,000 where the Hispanic/Latino population is at least 20% of the overall population. In states where less than five places meet either of these criteria, we have included places with at least 10,000 total population with the highest percentage of Hispanic/Latino population. These places are identified with an asterisk (*); Please refer to the User's Guide for a full explanation of data.

Peruvian		40.8
Spaniard		36.0

High School Graduates
(Universe: Population 25 Years and Over)

Group	Number	%
Total Population	34,865	84.4
Hispanic or Latino (of any race)	4,321	47.8
Central American, ex. Mexican	1,127	32.4
Guatemalan	794	33.2
Salvadoran	264	28.7
Mexican	2,321	54.1

Four-Year College Graduates
(Universe: Population 25 Years and Over)

Group	Number	%
Total Population	18,917	45.8
Hispanic or Latino (of any race)	1,242	13.7
Central American, ex. Mexican	141	4.1
Guatemalan	90	3.8
Salvadoran	32	3.5
Mexican	647	15.1

Population Age 3–17 Enrolled in Public School
(Universe: Population Age 3–17 Enrolled in School)

Group	Number	%
Total Population	6,359	79.3
Hispanic or Latino (of any race)	2,808	94.7
Central American, ex. Mexican	1,021	97.7
Guatemalan	626	100.0
Salvadoran	340	93.4
Mexican	1,319	90.8

Population Age 3–17 Enrolled in Private School
(Universe: Population Age 3–17 Enrolled in School)

Group	Number	%
Total Population	1,659	20.7
Hispanic or Latino (of any race)	157	5.3
Central American, ex. Mexican	24	2.3
Guatemalan	0	0.0
Salvadoran	24	6.6
Mexican	133	9.2

Foreign-Born Population

Group	Number	%
Total Population	15,582	27.4
Hispanic or Latino (of any race)	9,714	61.6
Central American, ex. Mexican	4,698	78.4
Guatemalan	3,093	76.6
Salvadoran	1,399	81.5
Mexican	4,266	55.7

Foreign-Born Naturalized U.S. Citizens

Group	Number	%
Total Population	4,539	29.1
Hispanic or Latino (of any race)	1,233	12.7
Central American, ex. Mexican	429	9.1
Guatemalan	213	6.9
Salvadoran	131	9.4
Mexican	401	9.4

Language Spoken at Home: English Only
(Universe: Population 5 Years and Over)

Group	Number	%
Total Population	34,770	65.4
Hispanic or Latino (of any race)	1,488	10.7
Central American, ex. Mexican	63	1.2
Guatemalan	0	0.0
Salvadoran	63	4.1
Mexican	773	11.8

Language Spoken at Home: Spanish
(Universe: Population 5 Years and Over)

Group	Number	%
Total Population	13,048	24.5
Hispanic or Latino (of any race)	12,324	89.0
Central American, ex. Mexican	5,394	98.8
Guatemalan	3,724	100.0
Salvadoran	1,456	95.9
Mexican	5,782	88.2

Unemployment Rate
(Universe: Population 16 Years and Over)

Group	%
Total Population	6.0
Hispanic or Latino (of any race)	7.0
Central American, ex. Mexican	10.3
Guatemalan	4.2
Salvadoran	22.5
Mexican	4.8

Class of Worker: Private Wage and Salary
(Universe: Civilian Employed Population 16 Years and Over)

Group	Number	%
Total Population	22,184	74.2
Hispanic or Latino (of any race)	6,848	81.4
Central American, ex. Mexican	2,887	81.0
Guatemalan	2,091	80.0
Salvadoran	759	89.0
Mexican	3,366	83.1

Class of Worker: Government
(Universe: Civilian Employed Population 16 Years and Over)

Group	Number	%
Total Population	2,911	9.7
Hispanic or Latino (of any race)	403	4.8
Central American, ex. Mexican	62	1.7
Guatemalan	39	1.5
Salvadoran	23	2.7
Mexican	210	5.2

Means of Transportation to Work: Car, Truck or Van
(Universe: Workers 16 Years and Over)

Group	Number	%
Total Population	21,802	74.4
Hispanic or Latino (of any race)	5,591	67.1
Central American, ex. Mexican	2,375	67.2
Guatemalan	1,702	65.8
Salvadoran	587	68.8
Mexican	2,621	65.6

Means of Transportation to Work: Public Transportation (ex. Taxicab)
(Universe: Workers 16 Years and Over)

Group	Number	%
Total Population	3,282	11.2
Hispanic or Latino (of any race)	1,744	20.9
Central American, ex. Mexican	615	17.4
Guatemalan	519	20.1
Salvadoran	85	10.0
Mexican	1,039	26.0

Homeownership Rate
(Universe: Occupied Housing Units)

Group	%
Total Population	52.3
Hispanic or Latino (of any race)	13.6
Central American, ex. Mexican	6.7
Guatemalan	4.4
Nicaraguan	19.6
Salvadoran	10.6
Mexican	13.1
Puerto Rican	27.5
South American	37.5
Colombian	38.6
Peruvian	32.7
Spaniard	51.5

Median Home Value

Group	Dollars
Total Population	811,000
Hispanic or Latino (of any race)	643,400
Central American, ex. Mexican	790,900
Guatemalan	809,400
Salvadoran	–
Mexican	553,300

Median Gross Rent

Group	Dollars
Total Population	1,362
Hispanic or Latino (of any race)	1,318
Central American, ex. Mexican	1,329
Guatemalan	1,366
Salvadoran	1,194
Mexican	1,309

Median Household Income
(2010 Inflation-Adjusted Dollars)

Group	Dollars
Total Population	72,326
Hispanic or Latino (of any race)	34,672
Central American, ex. Mexican	33,270
Guatemalan	33,214
Salvadoran	33,513
Mexican	39,111

Per Capita Income
(2010 Inflation-Adjusted Dollars)

Group	Dollars
Total Population	41,968
Hispanic or Latino (of any race)	15,277
Central American, ex. Mexican	12,985
Guatemalan	13,828
Salvadoran	10,637
Mexican	15,049

Households with $100,000+ Income

Group	Number	%
Total Population	8,462	36.2
Hispanic or Latino (of any race)	468	10.9
Central American, ex. Mexican	131	8.5
Guatemalan	97	9.2
Salvadoran	16	3.8
Mexican	202	9.6

Households with Food Stamps/SNAP Benefits During Past 12 Months

Group	Number	%
Total Population	708	3.0
Hispanic or Latino (of any race)	494	11.5
Central American, ex. Mexican	169	11.0
Guatemalan	98	9.3
Salvadoran	39	9.2
Mexican	286	13.6

Poverty Rate
(Income in Past 12 Months Below Poverty Level)

Group	%
Total Population	10.3
Hispanic or Latino (of any race)	19.6
Central American, ex. Mexican	19.4
Guatemalan	18.3
Salvadoran	19.6
Mexican	20.0

Santa Ana

Population

Group	Number	%TP[1]	%HP[2]
Total Population	324,528	100.0	–
Hispanic or Latino (of any race)	253,928	78.2	100.0
Central American, ex. Mexican	11,011	3.4	4.3
Costa Rican	117	<0.1	<0.1
Guatemalan	3,300	1.0	1.3
Honduran	663	0.2	0.3
Nicaraguan	375	0.1	0.1
Salvadoran	6,389	2.0	2.5
Cuban	506	0.2	0.2
Mexican	230,381	71.0	90.7
Puerto Rican	667	0.2	0.3
South American	2,303	0.7	0.9
Argentinean	276	0.1	0.1
Bolivian	398	0.1	0.2
Colombian	532	0.2	0.2
Ecuadorian	224	0.1	0.1
Peruvian	651	0.2	0.3
Spaniard	564	0.2	0.2

Population Growth: 2000–2010

Group	%
Total Population	-4.0
Hispanic or Latino (of any race)	-1.2
Central American, ex. Mexican	45.7
Guatemalan	70.9
Honduran	136.8
Nicaraguan	97.4
Salvadoran	54.7
Cuban	-8.2
Mexican	3.4
Puerto Rican	-8.6
South American	32.2
Argentinean	40.8
Bolivian	48.0
Colombian	34.0
Ecuadorian	60.0

Notes: (1) Percent of total population; (2) Percent of Hispanic/Latino population; Profiles include places with an overall population of at least 125,000, OR an overall population of at least 25,000 where the Hispanic/Latino population is at least 20% of the overall population. In states where less than five places meet either of these criteria, we have included places with at least 10,000 total population with the highest percentage of Hispanic/Latino population. These places are identified with an asterisk (*); Please refer to the User's Guide for a full explanation of data.

Group	Number
Peruvian	55.0
Spaniard	243.9

Males per 100 Females

Group	Number
Total Population	104.4
Hispanic or Latino (of any race)	105.8
Central American, ex. Mexican	103.3
Costa Rican	95.0
Guatemalan	112.4
Honduran	92.7
Nicaraguan	87.5
Salvadoran	101.0
Cuban	104.0
Mexican	106.2
Puerto Rican	88.4
South American	87.8
Argentinean	107.5
Bolivian	86.0
Colombian	80.3
Ecuadorian	82.1
Peruvian	83.9
Spaniard	99.3

Average Household Size

Group	People
Total Population	4.37
Hispanic or Latino (of any race)	5.19
Central American, ex. Mexican	4.98
Costa Rican	3.39
Guatemalan	4.94
Honduran	4.88
Nicaraguan	4.17
Salvadoran	5.13
Cuban	2.65
Mexican	5.28
Puerto Rican	3.10
South American	3.36
Argentinean	2.76
Bolivian	3.87
Colombian	3.17
Ecuadorian	3.51
Peruvian	3.65
Spaniard	3.48

Median Age

Group	Years
Total Population	29.1
Hispanic or Latino (of any race)	26.3
Central American, ex. Mexican	33.0
Costa Rican	36.3
Guatemalan	32.1
Honduran	32.1
Nicaraguan	32.6
Salvadoran	33.5
Cuban	45.8
Mexican	25.8
Puerto Rican	33.2
South American	40.4
Argentinean	41.5
Bolivian	37.7
Colombian	38.6
Ecuadorian	44.6
Peruvian	41.2
Spaniard	34.3

High School Graduates

(Universe: Population 25 Years and Over)

Group	Number	%
Total Population	94,533	51.4
Hispanic or Latino (of any race)	50,737	38.6
Central American, ex. Mexican	3,104	39.9
Guatemalan	897	40.9
Salvadoran	1,856	39.0
Mexican	44,672	37.4
South American	1,250	75.7
Peruvian	465	83.5

Four-Year College Graduates

(Universe: Population 25 Years and Over)

Group	Number	%
Total Population	22,008	12.0
Hispanic or Latino (of any race)	6,600	5.0
Central American, ex. Mexican	442	5.7
Guatemalan	105	4.8

Group	Number	%
Salvadoran	278	5.8
Mexican	5,378	4.5
South American	381	23.1
Peruvian	117	21.0

Population Age 3–17 Enrolled in Public School

(Universe: Population Age 3–17 Enrolled in School)

Group	Number	%
Total Population	70,124	96.0
Hispanic or Latino (of any race)	63,065	97.4
Central American, ex. Mexican	1,989	98.3
Guatemalan	630	100.0
Salvadoran	1,150	98.2
Mexican	60,098	97.5
South American	297	95.2
Peruvian	107	100.0

Population Age 3–17 Enrolled in Private School

(Universe: Population Age 3–17 Enrolled in School)

Group	Number	%
Total Population	2,907	4.0
Hispanic or Latino (of any race)	1,690	2.6
Central American, ex. Mexican	34	1.7
Guatemalan	0	0.0
Salvadoran	21	1.8
Mexican	1,550	2.5
South American	15	4.8
Peruvian	0	0.0

Foreign-Born Population

Group	Number	%
Total Population	160,779	49.4
Hispanic or Latino (of any race)	134,623	53.0
Central American, ex. Mexican	8,656	71.5
Guatemalan	2,493	71.0
Salvadoran	5,313	72.7
Mexican	122,934	52.1
South American	1,794	77.3
Peruvian	587	75.6

Foreign-Born Naturalized U.S. Citizens

Group	Number	%
Total Population	46,804	29.1
Hispanic or Latino (of any race)	28,241	21.0
Central American, ex. Mexican	2,365	27.3
Guatemalan	625	25.1
Salvadoran	1,435	27.0
Mexican	24,841	20.2
South American	623	34.7
Peruvian	295	50.3

Language Spoken at Home: English Only

(Universe: Population 5 Years and Over)

Group	Number	%
Total Population	51,469	17.4
Hispanic or Latino (of any race)	15,774	6.9
Central American, ex. Mexican	233	2.0
Guatemalan	89	2.7
Salvadoran	111	1.6
Mexican	14,147	6.7
South American	129	5.9
Peruvian	32	4.2

Language Spoken at Home: Spanish

(Universe: Population 5 Years and Over)

Group	Number	%
Total Population	213,182	72.2
Hispanic or Latino (of any race)	211,411	93.0
Central American, ex. Mexican	11,205	98.0
Guatemalan	3,216	97.3
Salvadoran	6,780	98.4
Mexican	195,855	93.2
South American	2,043	93.5
Peruvian	714	94.1

Unemployment Rate

(Universe: Population 16 Years and Over)

Group	%
Total Population	9.3
Hispanic or Latino (of any race)	9.5
Central American, ex. Mexican	10.6
Guatemalan	14.5
Salvadoran	8.8
Mexican	9.5
South American	5.1

Group	%
Peruvian	3.8

Class of Worker: Private Wage and Salary

(Universe: Civilian Employed Population 16 Years and Over)

Group	Number	%
Total Population	127,606	87.1
Hispanic or Latino (of any race)	99,880	88.7
Central American, ex. Mexican	5,660	86.0
Guatemalan	1,538	89.9
Salvadoran	3,577	86.6
Mexican	91,735	89.1
South American	1,124	85.4
Peruvian	378	92.4

Class of Worker: Government

(Universe: Civilian Employed Population 16 Years and Over)

Group	Number	%
Total Population	10,304	7.0
Hispanic or Latino (of any race)	6,343	5.6
Central American, ex. Mexican	275	4.2
Guatemalan	65	3.8
Salvadoran	149	3.6
Mexican	5,790	5.6
South American	67	5.1
Peruvian	19	4.6

Means of Transportation to Work: Car, Truck or Van

(Universe: Workers 16 Years and Over)

Group	Number	%
Total Population	125,816	87.2
Hispanic or Latino (of any race)	95,302	85.9
Central American, ex. Mexican	5,479	84.3
Guatemalan	1,426	85.7
Salvadoran	3,449	84.2
Mexican	87,266	85.9
South American	1,105	85.6
Peruvian	370	90.5

Means of Transportation to Work: Public Transportation (ex. Taxicab)

(Universe: Workers 16 Years and Over)

Group	Number	%
Total Population	10,988	7.6
Hispanic or Latino (of any race)	10,214	9.2
Central American, ex. Mexican	511	7.9
Guatemalan	165	9.9
Salvadoran	276	6.7
Mexican	9,463	9.3
South American	126	9.8
Peruvian	29	7.1

Homeownership Rate

(Universe: Occupied Housing Units)

Group	%
Total Population	47.5
Hispanic or Latino (of any race)	42.3
Central American, ex. Mexican	38.9
Costa Rican	54.5
Guatemalan	33.2
Honduran	35.9
Nicaraguan	30.7
Salvadoran	42.7
Cuban	46.5
Mexican	42.8
Puerto Rican	40.0
South American	49.1
Argentinean	47.9
Bolivian	62.2
Colombian	42.7
Ecuadorian	53.4
Peruvian	46.4
Spaniard	49.8

Median Home Value

Group	Dollars
Total Population	417,400
Hispanic or Latino (of any race)	407,500
Central American, ex. Mexican	387,800
Guatemalan	442,500
Salvadoran	347,500
Mexican	409,900
South American	336,000
Peruvian	305,400

STATE & PLACE PROFILES

Notes: (1) Percent of total population; (2) Percent of Hispanic/Latino population; Profiles include places with an overall population of at least 125,000, OR an overall population of at least 25,000 where the Hispanic/Latino population is at least 20% of the overall population. In states where less than five places meet either of these criteria, we have included places with at least 10,000 total population with the highest percentage of Hispanic/Latino population. These places are identified with an asterisk (*); Please refer to the User's Guide for a full explanation of data.

Median Gross Rent

Group	Dollars
Total Population	1,231
Hispanic or Latino (of any race)	1,191
Central American, ex. Mexican	1,182
Guatemalan	993
Salvadoran	1,202
Mexican	1,184
South American	1,402
Peruvian	1,363

Median Household Income
(2010 Inflation-Adjusted Dollars)

Group	Dollars
Total Population	54,877
Hispanic or Latino (of any race)	52,963
Central American, ex. Mexican	47,234
Guatemalan	42,609
Salvadoran	49,483
Mexican	53,422
South American	44,900
Peruvian	61,792

Per Capita Income
(2010 Inflation-Adjusted Dollars)

Group	Dollars
Total Population	16,613
Hispanic or Latino (of any race)	13,040
Central American, ex. Mexican	14,549
Guatemalan	13,514
Salvadoran	14,698
Mexican	12,781
South American	18,222
Peruvian	19,796

Households with $100,000+ Income

Group	Number	%
Total Population	14,378	19.3
Hispanic or Latino (of any race)	8,029	16.3
Central American, ex. Mexican	377	13.4
Guatemalan	144	20.1
Salvadoran	216	12.6
Mexican	7,303	16.4
South American	111	17.5
Peruvian	51	21.2

Households with Food Stamps/SNAP Benefits During Past 12 Months

Group	Number	%
Total Population	5,959	8.0
Hispanic or Latino (of any race)	4,955	10.1
Central American, ex. Mexican	219	7.8
Guatemalan	43	6.0
Salvadoran	159	9.3
Mexican	4,649	10.4
South American	21	3.3
Peruvian	21	8.7

Poverty Rate
(Income in Past 12 Months Below Poverty Level)

Group	%
Total Population	17.9
Hispanic or Latino (of any race)	19.6
Central American, ex. Mexican	12.9
Guatemalan	15.6
Salvadoran	11.5
Mexican	20.1
South American	21.7
Peruvian	23.8

Santa Barbara

Population

Group	Number	%TP[1]	%HP[2]
Total Population	88,410	100.0	–
Hispanic or Latino (of any race)	33,591	38.0	100.0
Central American, ex. Mexican	1,013	1.1	3.0
Guatemalan	546	0.6	1.6
Salvadoran	244	0.3	0.7
Cuban	106	0.1	0.3
Mexican	29,502	33.4	87.8
Puerto Rican	197	0.2	0.6
South American	651	0.7	1.9
Argentinean	121	0.1	0.4
Colombian	151	0.2	0.4
Peruvian	176	0.2	0.5
Spaniard	374	0.4	1.1

Population Growth: 2000–2010

Group	%
Total Population	-4.2
Hispanic or Latino (of any race)	3.9
Central American, ex. Mexican	58.5
Guatemalan	66.0
Salvadoran	93.7
Cuban	-1.9
Mexican	7.2
Puerto Rican	-0.5
South American	64.8

Males per 100 Females

Group	Number
Total Population	98.5
Hispanic or Latino (of any race)	105.2
Central American, ex. Mexican	103.0
Guatemalan	130.4
Salvadoran	78.1
Cuban	51.4
Mexican	106.9
Puerto Rican	109.6
South American	88.2
Argentinean	83.3
Colombian	79.8
Peruvian	85.3
Spaniard	71.6

Average Household Size

Group	People
Total Population	2.45
Hispanic or Latino (of any race)	3.64
Central American, ex. Mexican	3.52
Guatemalan	4.00
Salvadoran	3.90
Cuban	1.98
Mexican	3.77
Puerto Rican	2.39
South American	2.50
Argentinean	2.22
Colombian	2.41
Peruvian	3.04
Spaniard	2.26

Median Age

Group	Years
Total Population	36.8
Hispanic or Latino (of any race)	28.7
Central American, ex. Mexican	31.1
Guatemalan	31.6
Salvadoran	29.0
Cuban	36.0
Mexican	28.4
Puerto Rican	32.7
South American	33.2
Argentinean	34.4
Colombian	33.8
Peruvian	33.8
Spaniard	37.2

High School Graduates
(Universe: Population 25 Years and Over)

Group	Number	%
Total Population	51,481	84.5
Hispanic or Latino (of any race)	10,535	57.6
Mexican	8,821	54.5

Four-Year College Graduates
(Universe: Population 25 Years and Over)

Group	Number	%
Total Population	25,793	42.3
Hispanic or Latino (of any race)	2,362	12.9
Mexican	1,554	9.6

Population Age 3–17 Enrolled in Public School
(Universe: Population Age 3–17 Enrolled in School)

Group	Number	%
Total Population	10,113	84.0
Hispanic or Latino (of any race)	6,002	93.4
Mexican	5,566	93.8

Population Age 3–17 Enrolled in Private School
(Universe: Population Age 3–17 Enrolled in School)

Group	Number	%
Total Population	1,927	16.0
Hispanic or Latino (of any race)	427	6.6
Mexican	371	6.2

Foreign-Born Population

Group	Number	%
Total Population	21,026	23.9
Hispanic or Latino (of any race)	14,281	45.5
Mexican	13,037	46.4

Foreign-Born Naturalized U.S. Citizens

Group	Number	%
Total Population	7,524	35.8
Hispanic or Latino (of any race)	3,939	27.6
Mexican	3,449	26.5

Language Spoken at Home: English Only
(Universe: Population 5 Years and Over)

Group	Number	%
Total Population	53,479	64.0
Hispanic or Latino (of any race)	6,320	21.8
Mexican	5,105	19.7

Language Spoken at Home: Spanish
(Universe: Population 5 Years and Over)

Group	Number	%
Total Population	23,977	28.7
Hispanic or Latino (of any race)	22,482	77.6
Mexican	20,626	79.7

Unemployment Rate
(Universe: Population 16 Years and Over)

Group	%
Total Population	5.9
Hispanic or Latino (of any race)	8.2
Mexican	8.4

Class of Worker: Private Wage and Salary
(Universe: Civilian Employed Population 16 Years and Over)

Group	Number	%
Total Population	34,979	75.2
Hispanic or Latino (of any race)	12,833	82.6
Mexican	11,845	84.7

Class of Worker: Government
(Universe: Civilian Employed Population 16 Years and Over)

Group	Number	%
Total Population	6,293	13.5
Hispanic or Latino (of any race)	1,387	8.9
Mexican	1,182	8.5

Means of Transportation to Work: Car, Truck or Van
(Universe: Workers 16 Years and Over)

Group	Number	%
Total Population	33,397	74.6
Hispanic or Latino (of any race)	10,454	70.5
Mexican	9,190	69.1

Means of Transportation to Work: Public Transportation (ex. Taxicab)
(Universe: Workers 16 Years and Over)

Group	Number	%
Total Population	2,487	5.6
Hispanic or Latino (of any race)	1,663	11.2
Mexican	1,564	11.8

Homeownership Rate
(Universe: Occupied Housing Units)

Group	%
Total Population	38.9
Hispanic or Latino (of any race)	23.4
Central American, ex. Mexican	11.4
Guatemalan	10.1
Salvadoran	6.9
Cuban	25.0
Mexican	23.7
Puerto Rican	26.0
South American	25.3
Argentinean	40.7
Colombian	23.2
Peruvian	18.8
Spaniard	33.9

Notes: (1) Percent of total population; (2) Percent of Hispanic/Latino population; Profiles include places with an overall population of at least 125,000, OR an overall population of at least 25,000 where the Hispanic/Latino population is at least 20% of the overall population. In states where less than five places meet either of these criteria, we have included places with at least 10,000 total population with the highest percentage of Hispanic/Latino population. These places are identified with an asterisk (*); Please refer to the User's Guide for a full explanation of data.

Median Home Value	
Group	Dollars
Total Population	969,200
Hispanic or Latino (of any race)	876,200
Mexican	868,400

Median Gross Rent	
Group	Dollars
Total Population	1,373
Hispanic or Latino (of any race)	1,256
Mexican	1,229

Median Household Income (2010 Inflation-Adjusted Dollars)	
Group	Dollars
Total Population	61,665
Hispanic or Latino (of any race)	48,778
Mexican	49,568

Per Capita Income (2010 Inflation-Adjusted Dollars)	
Group	Dollars
Total Population	36,601
Hispanic or Latino (of any race)	17,829
Mexican	17,256

Households with $100,000+ Income		
Group	Number	%
Total Population	10,332	29.2
Hispanic or Latino (of any race)	1,398	15.8
Mexican	1,242	16.4

Households with Food Stamps/SNAP Benefits During Past 12 Months		
Group	Number	%
Total Population	1,186	3.4
Hispanic or Latino (of any race)	861	9.7
Mexican	798	10.5

Poverty Rate (Income in Past 12 Months Below Poverty Level)	
Group	%
Total Population	14.1
Hispanic or Latino (of any race)	19.7
Mexican	19.9

Santa Clarita

Population			
Group	Number	%TP[1]	%HP[2]
Total Population	176,320	100.0	–
Hispanic or Latino (of any race)	51,941	29.5	100.0
Central American, ex. Mexican	5,657	3.2	10.9
Costa Rican	185	0.1	0.4
Guatemalan	2,410	1.4	4.6
Honduran	276	0.2	0.5
Nicaraguan	324	0.2	0.6
Salvadoran	2,272	1.3	4.4
Cuban	1,053	0.6	2.0
Mexican	36,666	20.8	70.6
Puerto Rican	1,004	0.6	1.9
South American	3,311	1.9	6.4
Argentinean	621	0.4	1.2
Bolivian	124	0.1	0.2
Chilean	284	0.2	0.5
Colombian	773	0.4	1.5
Ecuadorian	509	0.3	1.0
Peruvian	831	0.5	1.6
Spaniard	672	0.4	1.3

Population Growth: 2000–2010	
Group	%
Total Population	16.7
Hispanic or Latino (of any race)	67.7
Central American, ex. Mexican	194.3
Guatemalan	174.2
Salvadoran	299.3
Cuban	49.6
Mexican	69.7
Puerto Rican	58.4
South American	128.2
Argentinean	145.5
Chilean	158.2
Colombian	158.5
Ecuadorian	239.3
Peruvian	131.5

Males per 100 Females	
Group	Number
Total Population	97.1
Hispanic or Latino (of any race)	99.6
Central American, ex. Mexican	90.5
Costa Rican	92.7
Guatemalan	102.4
Honduran	79.2
Nicaraguan	80.0
Salvadoran	81.9
Cuban	97.6
Mexican	102.4
Puerto Rican	100.0
South American	88.1
Argentinean	89.9
Bolivian	100.0
Chilean	101.4
Colombian	78.9
Ecuadorian	88.5
Peruvian	89.7
Spaniard	92.0

Average Household Size	
Group	People
Total Population	2.94
Hispanic or Latino (of any race)	3.87
Central American, ex. Mexican	4.03
Costa Rican	3.04
Guatemalan	4.41
Honduran	4.17
Nicaraguan	3.22
Salvadoran	3.93
Cuban	2.97
Mexican	4.05
Puerto Rican	2.89
South American	3.21
Argentinean	2.99
Bolivian	3.23
Chilean	3.18
Colombian	3.20
Ecuadorian	3.27
Peruvian	3.47
Spaniard	2.98

Median Age	
Group	Years
Total Population	36.2
Hispanic or Latino (of any race)	27.5
Central American, ex. Mexican	31.7
Costa Rican	31.9
Guatemalan	30.8
Honduran	34.3
Nicaraguan	36.3
Salvadoran	31.9
Cuban	35.1
Mexican	26.1
Puerto Rican	29.7
South American	37.6
Argentinean	38.7
Bolivian	45.2
Chilean	37.0
Colombian	37.1
Ecuadorian	36.8
Peruvian	36.5
Spaniard	34.2

High School Graduates (Universe: Population 25 Years and Over)		
Group	Number	%
Total Population	95,701	88.0
Hispanic or Latino (of any race)	17,254	67.8
Central American, ex. Mexican	2,400	61.8
Guatemalan	891	51.3
Salvadoran	968	66.9
Cuban	466	92.5
Mexican	10,463	62.6
South American	2,126	88.4
Peruvian	642	79.1

Four-Year College Graduates (Universe: Population 25 Years and Over)		
Group	Number	%
Total Population	35,002	32.2
Hispanic or Latino (of any race)	3,982	15.6
Central American, ex. Mexican	594	15.3
Guatemalan	208	12.0
Salvadoran	156	10.8
Cuban	201	39.9
Mexican	2,127	12.7
South American	673	28.0
Peruvian	224	27.6

Population Age 3–17 Enrolled in Public School (Universe: Population Age 3–17 Enrolled in School)		
Group	Number	%
Total Population	32,750	87.3
Hispanic or Latino (of any race)	12,260	92.4
Central American, ex. Mexican	968	94.5
Guatemalan	454	92.7
Salvadoran	335	97.4
Cuban	285	93.1
Mexican	9,419	92.6
South American	732	91.7
Peruvian	298	88.7

Population Age 3–17 Enrolled in Private School (Universe: Population Age 3–17 Enrolled in School)		
Group	Number	%
Total Population	4,774	12.7
Hispanic or Latino (of any race)	1,011	7.6
Central American, ex. Mexican	56	5.5
Guatemalan	36	7.3
Salvadoran	9	2.6
Cuban	21	6.9
Mexican	755	7.4
South American	66	8.3
Peruvian	38	11.3

Foreign-Born Population		
Group	Number	%
Total Population	35,414	20.6
Hispanic or Latino (of any race)	18,508	38.7
Central American, ex. Mexican	3,801	63.0
Guatemalan	1,818	66.4
Salvadoran	1,428	65.7
Cuban	385	43.3
Mexican	11,404	34.0
South American	2,280	59.2
Peruvian	997	64.1

Foreign-Born Naturalized U.S. Citizens		
Group	Number	%
Total Population	17,493	49.4
Hispanic or Latino (of any race)	6,419	34.7
Central American, ex. Mexican	1,501	39.5
Guatemalan	491	27.0
Salvadoran	734	51.4
Cuban	331	86.0
Mexican	2,969	26.0
South American	1,371	60.1
Peruvian	487	48.8

Language Spoken at Home: English Only (Universe: Population 5 Years and Over)		
Group	Number	%
Total Population	113,183	70.4
Hispanic or Latino (of any race)	13,824	32.1
Central American, ex. Mexican	1,050	19.3
Guatemalan	397	16.3
Salvadoran	483	23.7
Cuban	426	52.2
Mexican	9,737	32.3
South American	702	20.1
Peruvian	124	8.8

Language Spoken at Home: Spanish (Universe: Population 5 Years and Over)		
Group	Number	%
Total Population	31,054	19.3
Hispanic or Latino (of any race)	29,164	67.7
Central American, ex. Mexican	4,378	80.5
Guatemalan	2,037	83.7
Salvadoran	1,550	75.9
Cuban	390	47.8

Notes: (1) Percent of total population; (2) Percent of Hispanic/Latino population; Profiles include places with an overall population of at least 125,000, OR an overall population of at least 25,000 where the Hispanic/Latino population is at least 20% of the overall population. In states where less than five places meet either of these criteria, we have included places with at least 10,000 total population with the highest percentage of Hispanic/Latino population. These places are identified with an asterisk (*); Please refer to the User's Guide for a full explanation of data.

Mexican	20,345	67.6
South American	2,754	78.8
Peruvian	1,288	91.2

Unemployment Rate
(Universe: Population 16 Years and Over)

Group	%
Total Population	7.7
Hispanic or Latino (of any race)	9.1
Central American, ex. Mexican	6.0
Guatemalan	6.2
Salvadoran	5.6
Cuban	0.9
Mexican	10.2
South American	7.3
Peruvian	3.9

Class of Worker: Private Wage and Salary
(Universe: Civilian Employed Population 16 Years and Over)

Group	Number	%
Total Population	66,047	76.3
Hispanic or Latino (of any race)	17,290	78.4
Central American, ex. Mexican	2,524	78.6
Guatemalan	1,322	88.7
Salvadoran	857	74.1
Cuban	257	79.1
Mexican	11,536	77.8
South American	1,634	82.7
Peruvian	747	81.7

Class of Worker: Government
(Universe: Civilian Employed Population 16 Years and Over)

Group	Number	%
Total Population	12,902	14.9
Hispanic or Latino (of any race)	2,728	12.4
Central American, ex. Mexican	339	10.6
Guatemalan	59	4.0
Salvadoran	124	10.7
Cuban	51	15.7
Mexican	1,920	12.9
South American	106	5.4
Peruvian	29	3.2

Means of Transportation to Work: Car, Truck or Van
(Universe: Workers 16 Years and Over)

Group	Number	%
Total Population	73,914	88.0
Hispanic or Latino (of any race)	18,701	86.8
Central American, ex. Mexican	2,787	87.0
Guatemalan	1,267	85.0
Salvadoran	1,030	89.8
Cuban	220	85.6
Mexican	12,678	87.7
South American	1,689	86.5
Peruvian	844	94.7

Means of Transportation to Work: Public Transportation (ex. Taxicab)
(Universe: Workers 16 Years and Over)

Group	Number	%
Total Population	3,448	4.1
Hispanic or Latino (of any race)	1,430	6.6
Central American, ex. Mexican	226	7.1
Guatemalan	117	7.8
Salvadoran	102	8.9
Cuban	29	11.3
Mexican	845	5.8
South American	51	2.6
Peruvian	10	1.1

Homeownership Rate
(Universe: Occupied Housing Units)

Group	%
Total Population	71.1
Hispanic or Latino (of any race)	58.0
Central American, ex. Mexican	56.7
Costa Rican	64.9
Guatemalan	49.3
Honduran	49.2
Nicaraguan	65.3
Salvadoran	62.2
Cuban	73.2
Mexican	55.9
Puerto Rican	62.4

South American	68.0
Argentinean	70.2
Bolivian	89.7
Chilean	67.3
Colombian	64.3
Ecuadorian	68.4
Peruvian	67.1
Spaniard	69.4

Median Home Value

Group	Dollars
Total Population	465,700
Hispanic or Latino (of any race)	429,000
Central American, ex. Mexican	416,300
Guatemalan	372,000
Salvadoran	414,000
Cuban	389,600
Mexican	415,300
South American	484,300
Peruvian	494,700

Median Gross Rent

Group	Dollars
Total Population	1,474
Hispanic or Latino (of any race)	1,381
Central American, ex. Mexican	1,271
Guatemalan	1,156
Salvadoran	1,403
Cuban	1,464
Mexican	1,360
South American	1,696
Peruvian	1,530

Median Household Income
(2010 Inflation-Adjusted Dollars)

Group	Dollars
Total Population	82,642
Hispanic or Latino (of any race)	70,668
Central American, ex. Mexican	67,969
Guatemalan	71,410
Salvadoran	61,596
Cuban	102,702
Mexican	67,914
South American	79,837
Peruvian	63,938

Per Capita Income
(2010 Inflation-Adjusted Dollars)

Group	Dollars
Total Population	32,862
Hispanic or Latino (of any race)	19,091
Central American, ex. Mexican	20,459
Guatemalan	16,511
Salvadoran	24,829
Cuban	28,492
Mexican	17,720
South American	23,349
Peruvian	18,575

Households with $100,000+ Income

Group	Number	%
Total Population	22,344	39.0
Hispanic or Latino (of any race)	3,143	27.8
Central American, ex. Mexican	394	26.0
Guatemalan	102	18.8
Salvadoran	195	31.6
Cuban	140	50.9
Mexican	1,872	25.2
South American	393	35.3
Peruvian	72	19.9

Households with Food Stamps/SNAP Benefits During Past 12 Months

Group	Number	%
Total Population	1,289	2.2
Hispanic or Latino (of any race)	522	4.6
Central American, ex. Mexican	39	2.6
Guatemalan	0	0.0
Salvadoran	39	6.3
Cuban	0	0.0
Mexican	473	6.4
South American	0	0.0
Peruvian	0	0.0

Poverty Rate
(Income in Past 12 Months Below Poverty Level)

Group	%
Total Population	7.6
Hispanic or Latino (of any race)	15.1
Central American, ex. Mexican	12.1
Guatemalan	8.9
Salvadoran	7.8
Cuban	0.9
Mexican	17.3
South American	4.1
Peruvian	0.0

Santa Maria

Population

Group	Number	%TP[1]	%HP[2]
Total Population	99,553	100.0	–
Hispanic or Latino (of any race)	70,114	70.4	100.0
Central American, ex. Mexican	962	1.0	1.4
Guatemalan	225	0.2	0.3
Honduran	115	0.1	0.2
Salvadoran	536	0.5	0.8
Mexican	65,188	65.5	93.0
Puerto Rican	362	0.4	0.5
South American	178	0.2	0.3
Spaniard	381	0.4	0.5

Population Growth: 2000–2010

Group	%
Total Population	28.6
Hispanic or Latino (of any race)	51.8
Central American, ex. Mexican	192.4
Salvadoran	176.3
Mexican	60.1
Puerto Rican	54.0
South American	61.8

Males per 100 Females

Group	Number
Total Population	102.2
Hispanic or Latino (of any race)	107.9
Central American, ex. Mexican	121.7
Guatemalan	87.5
Honduran	210.8
Salvadoran	132.0
Mexican	108.3
Puerto Rican	94.6
South American	81.6
Spaniard	85.9

Average Household Size

Group	People
Total Population	3.66
Hispanic or Latino (of any race)	4.71
Central American, ex. Mexican	4.34
Guatemalan	4.12
Honduran	4.46
Salvadoran	4.72
Mexican	4.79
Puerto Rican	3.21
South American	2.79
Spaniard	3.40

Median Age

Group	Years
Total Population	28.6
Hispanic or Latino (of any race)	24.3
Central American, ex. Mexican	28.9
Guatemalan	33.5
Honduran	26.5
Salvadoran	28.0
Mexican	24.1
Puerto Rican	27.3
South American	43.0
Spaniard	31.7

High School Graduates
(Universe: Population 25 Years and Over)

Group	Number	%
Total Population	33,087	62.6
Hispanic or Latino (of any race)	13,584	43.4
Central American, ex. Mexican	169	33.9

Notes: (1) Percent of total population; (2) Percent of Hispanic/Latino population; Profiles include places with an overall population of at least 125,000, OR an overall population of at least 25,000 where the Hispanic/Latino population is at least 20% of the overall population. In states where less than five places meet either of these criteria, we have included places with at least 10,000 total population with the highest percentage of Hispanic/Latino population. These places are identified with an asterisk (*); Please refer to the User's Guide for a full explanation of data.

Mexican	12,761	42.8

Four-Year College Graduates
(Universe: Population 25 Years and Over)

Group	Number	%
Total Population	6,797	12.9
Hispanic or Latino (of any race)	1,638	5.2
Central American, ex. Mexican	32	6.4
Mexican	1,452	4.9

Population Age 3–17 Enrolled in Public School
(Universe: Population Age 3–17 Enrolled in School)

Group	Number	%
Total Population	20,021	92.5
Hispanic or Latino (of any race)	16,812	95.4
Central American, ex. Mexican	144	94.1
Mexican	16,155	95.4

Population Age 3–17 Enrolled in Private School
(Universe: Population Age 3–17 Enrolled in School)

Group	Number	%
Total Population	1,623	7.5
Hispanic or Latino (of any race)	819	4.6
Central American, ex. Mexican	9	5.9
Mexican	785	4.6

Foreign-Born Population

Group	Number	%
Total Population	33,292	35.2
Hispanic or Latino (of any race)	29,089	44.3
Central American, ex. Mexican	584	63.5
Mexican	28,132	44.6

Foreign-Born Naturalized U.S. Citizens

Group	Number	%
Total Population	7,271	21.8
Hispanic or Latino (of any race)	4,737	16.3
Central American, ex. Mexican	87	14.9
Mexican	4,523	16.1

Language Spoken at Home: English Only
(Universe: Population 5 Years and Over)

Group	Number	%
Total Population	32,797	38.5
Hispanic or Latino (of any race)	9,808	17.1
Central American, ex. Mexican	47	6.5
Mexican	9,023	16.4

Language Spoken at Home: Spanish
(Universe: Population 5 Years and Over)

Group	Number	%
Total Population	48,150	56.5
Hispanic or Latino (of any race)	47,568	82.7
Central American, ex. Mexican	674	93.5
Mexican	46,009	83.4

Unemployment Rate
(Universe: Population 16 Years and Over)

Group	%
Total Population	9.2
Hispanic or Latino (of any race)	10.1
Central American, ex. Mexican	9.0
Mexican	10.3

Class of Worker: Private Wage and Salary
(Universe: Civilian Employed Population 16 Years and Over)

Group	Number	%
Total Population	33,250	83.2
Hispanic or Latino (of any race)	23,486	87.2
Central American, ex. Mexican	441	92.8
Mexican	22,488	87.1

Class of Worker: Government
(Universe: Civilian Employed Population 16 Years and Over)

Group	Number	%
Total Population	4,588	11.5
Hispanic or Latino (of any race)	2,216	8.2
Central American, ex. Mexican	13	2.7
Mexican	2,119	8.2

Means of Transportation to Work: Car, Truck or Van
(Universe: Workers 16 Years and Over)

Group	Number	%
Total Population	36,020	91.9
Hispanic or Latino (of any race)	24,497	93.2
Central American, ex. Mexican	453	95.4
Mexican	23,414	93.0

Means of Transportation to Work: Public Transportation (ex. Taxicab)
(Universe: Workers 16 Years and Over)

Group	Number	%
Total Population	940	2.4
Hispanic or Latino (of any race)	392	1.5
Central American, ex. Mexican	0	0.0
Mexican	392	1.6

Homeownership Rate
(Universe: Occupied Housing Units)

Group	%
Total Population	51.6
Hispanic or Latino (of any race)	41.4
Central American, ex. Mexican	34.9
Guatemalan	42.3
Honduran	25.0
Salvadoran	29.3
Mexican	41.5
Puerto Rican	28.3
South American	60.0
Spaniard	52.9

Median Home Value

Group	Dollars
Total Population	338,800
Hispanic or Latino (of any race)	329,400
Central American, ex. Mexican	196,900
Mexican	329,000

Median Gross Rent

Group	Dollars
Total Population	1,085
Hispanic or Latino (of any race)	1,075
Central American, ex. Mexican	1,177
Mexican	1,070

Median Household Income
(2010 Inflation-Adjusted Dollars)

Group	Dollars
Total Population	50,208
Hispanic or Latino (of any race)	47,039
Central American, ex. Mexican	55,517
Mexican	46,873

Per Capita Income
(2010 Inflation-Adjusted Dollars)

Group	Dollars
Total Population	18,301
Hispanic or Latino (of any race)	13,027
Central American, ex. Mexican	13,007
Mexican	12,806

Households with $100,000+ Income

Group	Number	%
Total Population	4,207	15.9
Hispanic or Latino (of any race)	1,695	11.9
Central American, ex. Mexican	0	0.0
Mexican	1,587	11.9

Households with Food Stamps/SNAP Benefits During Past 12 Months

Group	Number	%
Total Population	2,687	10.1
Hispanic or Latino (of any race)	2,187	15.4
Central American, ex. Mexican	33	14.3
Mexican	2,109	15.8

Poverty Rate
(Income in Past 12 Months Below Poverty Level)

Group	%
Total Population	17.7
Hispanic or Latino (of any race)	21.0
Central American, ex. Mexican	28.4
Mexican	21.0

Santa Paula

Population

Group	Number	%TP[1]	%HP[2]
Total Population	29,321	100.0	–
Hispanic or Latino (of any race)	23,299	79.5	100.0
Central American, ex. Mexican	271	0.9	1.2
Salvadoran	120	0.4	0.5
Mexican	22,077	75.3	94.8

Population Growth: 2000–2010

Group	%
Total Population	2.5
Hispanic or Latino (of any race)	14.4
Central American, ex. Mexican	56.6
Mexican	22.2

Males per 100 Females

Group	Number
Total Population	101.9
Hispanic or Latino (of any race)	105.5
Central American, ex. Mexican	79.5
Salvadoran	64.4
Mexican	105.9

Average Household Size

Group	People
Total Population	3.50
Hispanic or Latino (of any race)	4.03
Central American, ex. Mexican	4.05
Salvadoran	4.25
Mexican	4.06

Median Age

Group	Years
Total Population	31.1
Hispanic or Latino (of any race)	27.6
Central American, ex. Mexican	32.2
Salvadoran	31.8
Mexican	27.5

High School Graduates
(Universe: Population 25 Years and Over)

Group	Number	%
Total Population	10,928	63.7
Hispanic or Latino (of any race)	6,470	53.1
Mexican	6,154	52.7

Four-Year College Graduates
(Universe: Population 25 Years and Over)

Group	Number	%
Total Population	1,882	11.0
Hispanic or Latino (of any race)	698	5.7
Mexican	617	5.3

Population Age 3–17 Enrolled in Public School
(Universe: Population Age 3–17 Enrolled in School)

Group	Number	%
Total Population	5,862	92.3
Hispanic or Latino (of any race)	5,543	94.8
Mexican	5,329	94.6

Population Age 3–17 Enrolled in Private School
(Universe: Population Age 3–17 Enrolled in School)

Group	Number	%
Total Population	490	7.7
Hispanic or Latino (of any race)	304	5.2
Mexican	304	5.4

Foreign-Born Population

Group	Number	%
Total Population	8,593	29.5
Hispanic or Latino (of any race)	8,223	35.7
Mexican	7,977	35.8

Foreign-Born Naturalized U.S. Citizens

Group	Number	%
Total Population	2,646	30.8
Hispanic or Latino (of any race)	2,456	29.9
Mexican	2,333	29.2

Language Spoken at Home: English Only
(Universe: Population 5 Years and Over)

Group	Number	%
Total Population	10,745	41.0
Hispanic or Latino (of any race)	5,384	26.4
Mexican	5,024	25.5

Notes: (1) Percent of total population; (2) Percent of Hispanic/Latino population; Profiles include places with an overall population of at least 125,000, OR an overall population of at least 25,000 where the Hispanic/Latino population is at least 20% of the overall population. In states where less than five places meet either of these criteria, we have included places with at least 10,000 total population with the highest percentage of Hispanic/Latino population. These places are identified with an asterisk (*); Please refer to the User's Guide for a full explanation of data.

Language Spoken at Home: Spanish
(Universe: Population 5 Years and Over)

Group	Number	%
Total Population	15,105	57.6
Hispanic or Latino (of any race)	15,000	73.5
Mexican	14,629	74.4

Unemployment Rate
(Universe: Population 16 Years and Over)

Group	%
Total Population	13.0
Hispanic or Latino (of any race)	14.9
Mexican	14.8

Class of Worker: Private Wage and Salary
(Universe: Civilian Employed Population 16 Years and Over)

Group	Number	%
Total Population	9,629	81.3
Hispanic or Latino (of any race)	7,610	84.6
Mexican	7,406	84.5

Class of Worker: Government
(Universe: Civilian Employed Population 16 Years and Over)

Group	Number	%
Total Population	1,490	12.6
Hispanic or Latino (of any race)	911	10.1
Mexican	891	10.2

Means of Transportation to Work: Car, Truck or Van
(Universe: Workers 16 Years and Over)

Group	Number	%
Total Population	10,866	95.6
Hispanic or Latino (of any race)	8,363	96.5
Mexican	8,138	96.5

Means of Transportation to Work: Public Transportation (ex. Taxicab)
(Universe: Workers 16 Years and Over)

Group	Number	%
Total Population	72	0.6
Hispanic or Latino (of any race)	44	0.5
Mexican	44	0.5

Homeownership Rate
(Universe: Occupied Housing Units)

Group	%
Total Population	56.2
Hispanic or Latino (of any race)	49.0
Central American, ex. Mexican	32.5
Salvadoran	44.4
Mexican	49.4

Median Home Value

Group	Dollars
Total Population	415,900
Hispanic or Latino (of any race)	429,000
Mexican	436,400

Median Gross Rent

Group	Dollars
Total Population	1,080
Hispanic or Latino (of any race)	1,096
Mexican	1,106

Median Household Income
(2010 Inflation-Adjusted Dollars)

Group	Dollars
Total Population	51,233
Hispanic or Latino (of any race)	50,823
Mexican	51,415

Per Capita Income
(2010 Inflation-Adjusted Dollars)

Group	Dollars
Total Population	19,552
Hispanic or Latino (of any race)	15,649
Mexican	15,577

Households with $100,000+ Income

Group	Number	%
Total Population	1,619	19.2
Hispanic or Latino (of any race)	874	15.6
Mexican	822	15.6

Households with Food Stamps/SNAP Benefits During Past 12 Months

Group	Number	%
Total Population	692	8.2
Hispanic or Latino (of any race)	620	11.1
Mexican	593	11.3

Poverty Rate
(Income in Past 12 Months Below Poverty Level)

Group	%
Total Population	18.1
Hispanic or Latino (of any race)	20.3
Mexican	20.6

Santa Rosa

Population

Group	Number	%TP[1]	%HP[2]
Total Population	167,815	100.0	–
Hispanic or Latino (of any race)	47,970	28.6	100.0
Central American, ex. Mexican	2,239	1.3	4.7
Guatemalan	348	0.2	0.7
Honduran	132	0.1	0.3
Nicaraguan	325	0.2	0.7
Salvadoran	1,311	0.8	2.7
Cuban	178	0.1	0.4
Mexican	40,889	24.4	85.2
Puerto Rican	661	0.4	1.4
South American	845	0.5	1.8
Colombian	207	0.1	0.4
Peruvian	290	0.2	0.6
Spaniard	744	0.4	1.6

Population Growth: 2000–2010

Group	%
Total Population	13.7
Hispanic or Latino (of any race)	69.4
Central American, ex. Mexican	143.6
Guatemalan	187.6
Nicaraguan	140.7
Salvadoran	177.8
Cuban	60.4
Mexican	79.5
Puerto Rican	31.7
South American	135.4
Colombian	105.0
Spaniard	588.9

Males per 100 Females

Group	Number
Total Population	95.2
Hispanic or Latino (of any race)	108.4
Central American, ex. Mexican	102.8
Guatemalan	113.5
Honduran	106.3
Nicaraguan	84.7
Salvadoran	109.8
Cuban	79.8
Mexican	110.5
Puerto Rican	91.0
South American	94.7
Colombian	89.9
Peruvian	101.4
Spaniard	83.3

Average Household Size

Group	People
Total Population	2.59
Hispanic or Latino (of any race)	4.03
Central American, ex. Mexican	3.69
Guatemalan	3.80
Honduran	3.44
Nicaraguan	3.04
Salvadoran	4.03
Cuban	2.43
Mexican	4.22
Puerto Rican	2.62
South American	2.83
Colombian	3.13
Peruvian	3.10
Spaniard	2.58

Median Age

Group	Years
Total Population	36.7
Hispanic or Latino (of any race)	25.1
Central American, ex. Mexican	30.5
Guatemalan	28.1
Honduran	30.0
Nicaraguan	33.7
Salvadoran	30.3
Cuban	30.0
Mexican	24.3
Puerto Rican	27.2
South American	35.5
Colombian	29.3
Peruvian	34.5
Spaniard	36.4

High School Graduates
(Universe: Population 25 Years and Over)

Group	Number	%
Total Population	91,323	84.6
Hispanic or Latino (of any race)	12,294	53.9
Central American, ex. Mexican	770	67.3
Salvadoran	331	58.5
Mexican	10,150	50.7

Four-Year College Graduates
(Universe: Population 25 Years and Over)

Group	Number	%
Total Population	31,549	29.2
Hispanic or Latino (of any race)	1,920	8.4
Central American, ex. Mexican	149	13.0
Salvadoran	56	9.9
Mexican	1,385	6.9

Population Age 3–17 Enrolled in Public School
(Universe: Population Age 3–17 Enrolled in School)

Group	Number	%
Total Population	26,081	90.8
Hispanic or Latino (of any race)	11,380	96.4
Central American, ex. Mexican	424	90.0
Salvadoran	235	83.3
Mexican	10,646	96.9

Population Age 3–17 Enrolled in Private School
(Universe: Population Age 3–17 Enrolled in School)

Group	Number	%
Total Population	2,641	9.2
Hispanic or Latino (of any race)	421	3.6
Central American, ex. Mexican	47	10.0
Salvadoran	47	16.7
Mexican	344	3.1

Foreign-Born Population

Group	Number	%
Total Population	31,862	19.6
Hispanic or Latino (of any race)	21,317	47.1
Central American, ex. Mexican	1,060	55.5
Salvadoran	548	54.7
Mexican	19,532	47.9

Foreign-Born Naturalized U.S. Citizens

Group	Number	%
Total Population	10,722	33.7
Hispanic or Latino (of any race)	4,197	19.7
Central American, ex. Mexican	493	46.5
Salvadoran	197	35.9
Mexican	3,418	17.5

Language Spoken at Home: English Only
(Universe: Population 5 Years and Over)

Group	Number	%
Total Population	108,347	71.6
Hispanic or Latino (of any race)	8,324	21.0
Central American, ex. Mexican	398	22.8
Salvadoran	134	15.2
Mexican	6,689	18.7

Language Spoken at Home: Spanish
(Universe: Population 5 Years and Over)

Group	Number	%
Total Population	33,189	21.9
Hispanic or Latino (of any race)	31,312	78.8
Central American, ex. Mexican	1,323	75.7
Salvadoran	737	83.6

Notes: (1) Percent of total population; (2) Percent of Hispanic/Latino population; Profiles include places with an overall population of at least 125,000, OR an overall population of at least 25,000 where the Hispanic/Latino population is at least 20% of the overall population. In states where less than five places meet either of these criteria, we have included places with at least 10,000 total population with the highest percentage of Hispanic/Latino population. These places are identified with an asterisk (*); Please refer to the User's Guide for a full explanation of data.

Mexican	29,023	81.2

Unemployment Rate
(Universe: Population 16 Years and Over)

Group	%
Total Population	9.2
Hispanic or Latino (of any race)	8.8
Central American, ex. Mexican	10.8
Salvadoran	12.5
Mexican	8.5

Class of Worker: Private Wage and Salary
(Universe: Civilian Employed Population 16 Years and Over)

Group	Number	%
Total Population	59,760	77.1
Hispanic or Latino (of any race)	17,665	86.2
Central American, ex. Mexican	764	79.3
Salvadoran	319	72.5
Mexican	15,926	87.3

Class of Worker: Government
(Universe: Civilian Employed Population 16 Years and Over)

Group	Number	%
Total Population	9,930	12.8
Hispanic or Latino (of any race)	1,446	7.1
Central American, ex. Mexican	150	15.6
Salvadoran	95	21.6
Mexican	1,102	6.0

Means of Transportation to Work: Car, Truck or Van
(Universe: Workers 16 Years and Over)

Group	Number	%
Total Population	65,047	86.5
Hispanic or Latino (of any race)	17,478	87.8
Central American, ex. Mexican	837	89.4
Salvadoran	372	87.5
Mexican	15,492	87.5

Means of Transportation to Work: Public Transportation (ex. Taxicab)
(Universe: Workers 16 Years and Over)

Group	Number	%
Total Population	1,658	2.2
Hispanic or Latino (of any race)	623	3.1
Central American, ex. Mexican	45	4.8
Salvadoran	10	2.4
Mexican	536	3.0

Homeownership Rate
(Universe: Occupied Housing Units)

Group	%
Total Population	54.1
Hispanic or Latino (of any race)	32.4
Central American, ex. Mexican	37.3
Guatemalan	38.9
Honduran	52.8
Nicaraguan	36.4
Salvadoran	36.0
Cuban	42.6
Mexican	30.9
Puerto Rican	34.5
South American	45.7
Colombian	38.1
Peruvian	43.0
Spaniard	53.8

Median Home Value

Group	Dollars
Total Population	468,600
Hispanic or Latino (of any race)	423,700
Central American, ex. Mexican	433,300
Salvadoran	408,700
Mexican	427,000

Median Gross Rent

Group	Dollars
Total Population	1,141
Hispanic or Latino (of any race)	1,098
Central American, ex. Mexican	961
Salvadoran	1,132
Mexican	1,101

Median Household Income
(2010 Inflation-Adjusted Dollars)

Group	Dollars
Total Population	59,326
Hispanic or Latino (of any race)	47,609
Central American, ex. Mexican	48,125
Salvadoran	61,354
Mexican	47,963

Per Capita Income
(2010 Inflation-Adjusted Dollars)

Group	Dollars
Total Population	29,794
Hispanic or Latino (of any race)	15,091
Central American, ex. Mexican	17,669
Salvadoran	14,994
Mexican	14,552

Households with $100,000+ Income

Group	Number	%
Total Population	15,428	24.7
Hispanic or Latino (of any race)	1,537	14.0
Central American, ex. Mexican	148	33.3
Salvadoran	60	29.3
Mexican	1,302	13.5

Households with Food Stamps/SNAP Benefits During Past 12 Months

Group	Number	%
Total Population	3,098	5.0
Hispanic or Latino (of any race)	1,235	11.3
Central American, ex. Mexican	60	13.5
Salvadoran	48	23.4
Mexican	1,078	11.2

Poverty Rate
(Income in Past 12 Months Below Poverty Level)

Group	%
Total Population	12.2
Hispanic or Latino (of any race)	16.9
Central American, ex. Mexican	8.5
Salvadoran	5.6
Mexican	17.6

Seaside

Population

Group	Number	%TP[1]	%HP[2]
Total Population	33,025	100.0	–
Hispanic or Latino (of any race)	14,347	43.4	100.0
Central American, ex. Mexican	1,193	3.6	8.3
Salvadoran	971	2.9	6.8
Mexican	11,629	35.2	81.1
Puerto Rican	312	0.9	2.2
South American	202	0.6	1.4
Spaniard	180	0.5	1.3

Population Growth: 2000–2010

Group	%
Total Population	4.2
Hispanic or Latino (of any race)	31.3
Central American, ex. Mexican	56.4
Salvadoran	71.6
Mexican	39.2
Puerto Rican	11.0

Males per 100 Females

Group	Number
Total Population	100.5
Hispanic or Latino (of any race)	109.2
Central American, ex. Mexican	105.0
Salvadoran	110.2
Mexican	111.6
Puerto Rican	103.9
South American	98.0
Spaniard	76.5

Average Household Size

Group	People
Total Population	3.16
Hispanic or Latino (of any race)	4.45
Central American, ex. Mexican	4.43
Salvadoran	4.70
Mexican	4.62

Group	Number
Puerto Rican	3.38
South American	3.13
Spaniard	2.69

Median Age

Group	Years
Total Population	30.6
Hispanic or Latino (of any race)	25.3
Central American, ex. Mexican	30.0
Salvadoran	29.2
Mexican	24.7
Puerto Rican	25.7
South American	29.0
Spaniard	29.7

High School Graduates
(Universe: Population 25 Years and Over)

Group	Number	%
Total Population	13,902	71.9
Hispanic or Latino (of any race)	2,582	39.2
Mexican	1,752	32.9

Four-Year College Graduates
(Universe: Population 25 Years and Over)

Group	Number	%
Total Population	3,501	18.1
Hispanic or Latino (of any race)	342	5.2
Mexican	163	3.1

Population Age 3–17 Enrolled in Public School
(Universe: Population Age 3–17 Enrolled in School)

Group	Number	%
Total Population	5,510	91.1
Hispanic or Latino (of any race)	3,235	96.8
Mexican	2,752	96.9

Population Age 3–17 Enrolled in Private School
(Universe: Population Age 3–17 Enrolled in School)

Group	Number	%
Total Population	538	8.9
Hispanic or Latino (of any race)	107	3.2
Mexican	89	3.1

Foreign-Born Population

Group	Number	%
Total Population	10,408	32.1
Hispanic or Latino (of any race)	7,105	53.0
Mexican	6,218	55.9

Foreign-Born Naturalized U.S. Citizens

Group	Number	%
Total Population	3,539	34.0
Hispanic or Latino (of any race)	1,521	21.4
Mexican	1,093	17.6

Language Spoken at Home: English Only
(Universe: Population 5 Years and Over)

Group	Number	%
Total Population	15,739	53.0
Hispanic or Latino (of any race)	1,647	14.0
Mexican	1,056	10.8

Language Spoken at Home: Spanish
(Universe: Population 5 Years and Over)

Group	Number	%
Total Population	10,685	36.0
Hispanic or Latino (of any race)	10,084	85.6
Mexican	8,651	88.8

Unemployment Rate
(Universe: Population 16 Years and Over)

Group	%
Total Population	8.4
Hispanic or Latino (of any race)	7.0
Mexican	7.0

Class of Worker: Private Wage and Salary
(Universe: Civilian Employed Population 16 Years and Over)

Group	Number	%
Total Population	11,659	76.1
Hispanic or Latino (of any race)	5,700	86.5
Mexican	4,626	87.0

STATE & PLACE PROFILES

Notes: (1) Percent of total population; (2) Percent of Hispanic/Latino population; Profiles include places with an overall population of at least 125,000, OR an overall population of at least 25,000 where the Hispanic/Latino population is at least 20% of the overall population. In states where less than five places meet either of these criteria, we have included places with at least 10,000 total population with the highest percentage of Hispanic/Latino population. These places are identified with an asterisk (*); Please refer to the User's Guide for a full explanation of data.

Class of Worker: Government
(Universe: Civilian Employed Population 16 Years and Over)

Group	Number	%
Total Population	2,203	14.4
Hispanic or Latino (of any race)	356	5.4
Mexican	257	4.8

Means of Transportation to Work: Car, Truck or Van
(Universe: Workers 16 Years and Over)

Group	Number	%
Total Population	13,283	82.7
Hispanic or Latino (of any race)	4,922	75.3
Mexican	3,948	75.7

Means of Transportation to Work: Public Transportation (ex. Taxicab)
(Universe: Workers 16 Years and Over)

Group	Number	%
Total Population	984	6.1
Hispanic or Latino (of any race)	745	11.4
Mexican	639	12.3

Homeownership Rate
(Universe: Occupied Housing Units)

Group	%
Total Population	41.4
Hispanic or Latino (of any race)	24.9
Central American, ex. Mexican	30.8
Salvadoran	29.6
Mexican	23.2
Puerto Rican	31.3
South American	35.5
Spaniard	50.0

Median Home Value

Group	Dollars
Total Population	556,700
Hispanic or Latino (of any race)	559,100
Mexican	563,100

Median Gross Rent

Group	Dollars
Total Population	1,381
Hispanic or Latino (of any race)	1,088
Mexican	1,076

Median Household Income
(2010 Inflation-Adjusted Dollars)

Group	Dollars
Total Population	57,713
Hispanic or Latino (of any race)	47,023
Mexican	46,887

Per Capita Income
(2010 Inflation-Adjusted Dollars)

Group	Dollars
Total Population	21,961
Hispanic or Latino (of any race)	13,019
Mexican	11,835

Households with $100,000+ Income

Group	Number	%
Total Population	1,987	19.6
Hispanic or Latino (of any race)	222	8.1
Mexican	177	8.1

Households with Food Stamps/SNAP Benefits During Past 12 Months

Group	Number	%
Total Population	560	5.5
Hispanic or Latino (of any race)	209	7.6
Mexican	209	9.6

Poverty Rate
(Income in Past 12 Months Below Poverty Level)

Group	%
Total Population	11.6
Hispanic or Latino (of any race)	17.1
Mexican	20.1

Simi Valley

Population

Group	Number	%TP[1]	%HP[2]
Total Population	124,237	100.0	–
Hispanic or Latino (of any race)	28,938	23.3	100.0
Central American, ex. Mexican	3,370	2.7	11.6
Costa Rican	164	0.1	0.6
Guatemalan	1,082	0.9	3.7
Honduran	265	0.2	0.9
Nicaraguan	234	0.2	0.8
Salvadoran	1,520	1.2	5.3
Cuban	431	0.3	1.5
Mexican	20,165	16.2	69.7
Puerto Rican	698	0.6	2.4
South American	2,077	1.7	7.2
Argentinean	351	0.3	1.2
Chilean	132	0.1	0.5
Colombian	502	0.4	1.7
Ecuadorian	226	0.2	0.8
Peruvian	716	0.6	2.5
Spaniard	490	0.4	1.7

Population Growth: 2000–2010

Group	%
Total Population	11.6
Hispanic or Latino (of any race)	54.5
Central American, ex. Mexican	202.8
Guatemalan	213.6
Salvadoran	264.5
Cuban	42.7
Mexican	61.3
Puerto Rican	55.5
South American	111.9
Argentinean	101.7
Colombian	104.1
Ecuadorian	101.8
Peruvian	180.8

Males per 100 Females

Group	Number
Total Population	96.6
Hispanic or Latino (of any race)	97.4
Central American, ex. Mexican	89.5
Costa Rican	64.0
Guatemalan	92.2
Honduran	84.0
Nicaraguan	80.0
Salvadoran	93.4
Cuban	87.4
Mexican	100.5
Puerto Rican	100.6
South American	85.0
Argentinean	78.2
Chilean	85.9
Colombian	87.3
Ecuadorian	85.2
Peruvian	83.1
Spaniard	95.2

Average Household Size

Group	People
Total Population	3.00
Hispanic or Latino (of any race)	4.00
Central American, ex. Mexican	4.49
Costa Rican	3.16
Guatemalan	4.80
Honduran	4.66
Nicaraguan	3.81
Salvadoran	4.58
Cuban	3.22
Mexican	4.18
Puerto Rican	3.19
South American	3.23
Argentinean	2.89
Chilean	2.60
Colombian	3.33
Ecuadorian	3.24
Peruvian	3.56
Spaniard	2.95

Median Age

Group	Years
Total Population	37.8
Hispanic or Latino (of any race)	28.7
Central American, ex. Mexican	31.5
Costa Rican	34.8
Guatemalan	31.1
Honduran	33.1
Nicaraguan	34.3
Salvadoran	31.2
Cuban	39.5
Mexican	27.2
Puerto Rican	31.2
South American	38.3
Argentinean	42.3
Chilean	39.0
Colombian	36.9
Ecuadorian	36.3
Peruvian	37.5
Spaniard	37.7

High School Graduates
(Universe: Population 25 Years and Over)

Group	Number	%
Total Population	71,824	90.0
Hispanic or Latino (of any race)	11,316	73.7
Central American, ex. Mexican	1,368	70.6
Salvadoran	636	73.6
Mexican	7,289	69.3
South American	1,409	91.1

Four-Year College Graduates
(Universe: Population 25 Years and Over)

Group	Number	%
Total Population	25,010	31.3
Hispanic or Latino (of any race)	2,634	17.2
Central American, ex. Mexican	255	13.2
Salvadoran	132	15.3
Mexican	1,447	13.8
South American	505	32.7

Population Age 3–17 Enrolled in Public School
(Universe: Population Age 3–17 Enrolled in School)

Group	Number	%
Total Population	20,364	82.8
Hispanic or Latino (of any race)	6,527	90.6
Central American, ex. Mexican	704	95.9
Salvadoran	479	100.0
Mexican	5,133	91.8
South American	265	75.3

Population Age 3–17 Enrolled in Private School
(Universe: Population Age 3–17 Enrolled in School)

Group	Number	%
Total Population	4,217	17.2
Hispanic or Latino (of any race)	680	9.4
Central American, ex. Mexican	30	4.1
Salvadoran	0	0.0
Mexican	460	8.2
South American	87	24.7

Foreign-Born Population

Group	Number	%
Total Population	22,978	18.9
Hispanic or Latino (of any race)	10,654	37.3
Central American, ex. Mexican	2,076	64.7
Salvadoran	956	63.3
Mexican	6,696	32.2
South American	1,510	67.7

Foreign-Born Naturalized U.S. Citizens

Group	Number	%
Total Population	11,736	51.1
Hispanic or Latino (of any race)	3,549	33.3
Central American, ex. Mexican	749	36.1
Salvadoran	462	48.3
Mexican	1,605	24.0
South American	903	59.8

Language Spoken at Home: English Only
(Universe: Population 5 Years and Over)

Group	Number	%
Total Population	84,665	74.1
Hispanic or Latino (of any race)	8,869	34.7
Central American, ex. Mexican	441	15.0
Salvadoran	281	19.3
Mexican	7,066	38.4
South American	221	10.2

Notes: (1) Percent of total population; (2) Percent of Hispanic/Latino population; Profiles include places with an overall population of at least 125,000, OR an overall population of at least 25,000 where the Hispanic/Latino population is at least 20% of the overall population. In states where less than five places meet either of these criteria, we have included places with at least 10,000 total population with the highest percentage of Hispanic/Latino population. These places are identified with an asterisk (*); Please refer to the User's Guide for a full explanation of data.

Language Spoken at Home: Spanish (Universe: Population 5 Years and Over)		
Group	Number	%
Total Population	18,034	15.8
Hispanic or Latino (of any race)	16,660	65.1
Central American, ex. Mexican	2,496	85.0
Salvadoran	1,173	80.7
Mexican	11,334	61.6
South American	1,939	89.8

Unemployment Rate (Universe: Population 16 Years and Over)	
Group	%
Total Population	5.6
Hispanic or Latino (of any race)	6.3
Central American, ex. Mexican	10.7
Salvadoran	15.8
Mexican	5.6
South American	7.5

Class of Worker: Private Wage and Salary (Universe: Civilian Employed Population 16 Years and Over)		
Group	Number	%
Total Population	50,280	78.9
Hispanic or Latino (of any race)	11,284	83.0
Central American, ex. Mexican	1,334	84.1
Salvadoran	621	85.2
Mexican	8,143	83.0
South American	865	78.6

Class of Worker: Government (Universe: Civilian Employed Population 16 Years and Over)		
Group	Number	%
Total Population	7,833	12.3
Hispanic or Latino (of any race)	1,036	7.6
Central American, ex. Mexican	84	5.3
Salvadoran	27	3.7
Mexican	837	8.5
South American	62	5.6

Means of Transportation to Work: Car, Truck or Van (Universe: Workers 16 Years and Over)		
Group	Number	%
Total Population	56,946	91.0
Hispanic or Latino (of any race)	12,156	91.1
Central American, ex. Mexican	1,459	94.3
Salvadoran	705	96.7
Mexican	8,805	91.2
South American	981	92.5

Means of Transportation to Work: Public Transportation (ex. Taxicab) (Universe: Workers 16 Years and Over)		
Group	Number	%
Total Population	759	1.2
Hispanic or Latino (of any race)	139	1.0
Central American, ex. Mexican	21	1.4
Salvadoran	7	1.0
Mexican	53	0.5
South American	34	3.2

Homeownership Rate (Universe: Occupied Housing Units)	
Group	%
Total Population	74.1
Hispanic or Latino (of any race)	63.4
Central American, ex. Mexican	60.5
Costa Rican	72.1
Guatemalan	53.8
Honduran	64.2
Nicaraguan	58.5
Salvadoran	62.0
Cuban	72.2
Mexican	62.6
Puerto Rican	67.7
South American	69.6
Argentinean	78.0
Chilean	67.3
Colombian	68.9
Ecuadorian	75.6
Peruvian	64.2
Spaniard	73.1

Median Home Value	
Group	Dollars
Total Population	553,400
Hispanic or Latino (of any race)	527,300
Central American, ex. Mexican	462,000
Salvadoran	453,300
Mexican	537,200
South American	565,300

Median Gross Rent	
Group	Dollars
Total Population	1,607
Hispanic or Latino (of any race)	1,604
Central American, ex. Mexican	1,445
Salvadoran	1,635
Mexican	1,613
South American	1,672

Median Household Income (2010 Inflation-Adjusted Dollars)	
Group	Dollars
Total Population	88,675
Hispanic or Latino (of any race)	71,197
Central American, ex. Mexican	66,994
Salvadoran	72,333
Mexican	70,775
South American	81,641

Per Capita Income (2010 Inflation-Adjusted Dollars)	
Group	Dollars
Total Population	35,159
Hispanic or Latino (of any race)	20,797
Central American, ex. Mexican	16,327
Salvadoran	18,653
Mexican	19,837
South American	31,226

Households with $100,000+ Income		
Group	Number	%
Total Population	17,114	42.5
Hispanic or Latino (of any race)	1,818	27.3
Central American, ex. Mexican	215	26.3
Salvadoran	125	30.5
Mexican	1,216	26.5
South American	210	29.2

Households with Food Stamps/SNAP Benefits During Past 12 Months		
Group	Number	%
Total Population	997	2.5
Hispanic or Latino (of any race)	439	6.6
Central American, ex. Mexican	95	11.6
Salvadoran	35	8.5
Mexican	252	5.5
South American	0	0.0

Poverty Rate (Income in Past 12 Months Below Poverty Level)	
Group	%
Total Population	5.8
Hispanic or Latino (of any race)	11.0
Central American, ex. Mexican	17.8
Salvadoran	8.2
Mexican	10.7
South American	2.3

Soledad

Population			
Group	Number	%TP[1]	%HP[2]
Total Population	25,738	100.0	–
Hispanic or Latino (of any race)	18,308	71.1	100.0
Central American, ex. Mexican	125	0.5	0.7
Mexican	16,261	63.2	88.8

Population Growth: 2000–2010	
Group	%
Total Population	128.5
Hispanic or Latino (of any race)	87.2
Mexican	84.8

Males per 100 Females	
Group	Number
Total Population	235.5
Hispanic or Latino (of any race)	169.8
Central American, ex. Mexican	111.9
Mexican	156.0

Average Household Size	
Group	People
Total Population	4.27
Hispanic or Latino (of any race)	4.53
Central American, ex. Mexican	4.32
Mexican	4.53

Median Age	
Group	Years
Total Population	34.9
Hispanic or Latino (of any race)	30.9
Central American, ex. Mexican	27.9
Mexican	30.6

High School Graduates (Universe: Population 25 Years and Over)		
Group	Number	%
Total Population	9,446	54.0
Hispanic or Latino (of any race)	4,716	43.3
Mexican	4,314	42.7

Four-Year College Graduates (Universe: Population 25 Years and Over)		
Group	Number	%
Total Population	922	5.3
Hispanic or Latino (of any race)	476	4.4
Mexican	372	3.7

Population Age 3–17 Enrolled in Public School (Universe: Population Age 3–17 Enrolled in School)		
Group	Number	%
Total Population	3,468	95.6
Hispanic or Latino (of any race)	3,280	96.1
Mexican	3,171	96.7

Population Age 3–17 Enrolled in Private School (Universe: Population Age 3–17 Enrolled in School)		
Group	Number	%
Total Population	160	4.4
Hispanic or Latino (of any race)	134	3.9
Mexican	107	3.3

Foreign-Born Population		
Group	Number	%
Total Population	7,893	31.1
Hispanic or Latino (of any race)	7,350	41.3
Mexican	6,847	40.8

Foreign-Born Naturalized U.S. Citizens		
Group	Number	%
Total Population	1,602	20.3
Hispanic or Latino (of any race)	1,456	19.8
Mexican	1,350	19.7

Language Spoken at Home: English Only (Universe: Population 5 Years and Over)		
Group	Number	%
Total Population	8,505	35.8
Hispanic or Latino (of any race)	2,173	13.3
Mexican	1,998	13.0

Language Spoken at Home: Spanish (Universe: Population 5 Years and Over)		
Group	Number	%
Total Population	14,514	61.1
Hispanic or Latino (of any race)	14,112	86.5
Mexican	13,320	86.9

Unemployment Rate (Universe: Population 16 Years and Over)	
Group	%
Total Population	12.8
Hispanic or Latino (of any race)	13.5
Mexican	13.8

Class of Worker: Private Wage and Salary (Universe: Civilian Employed Population 16 Years and Over)		
Group	Number	%
Total Population	4,623	74.2

STATE & PLACE PROFILES

Notes: (1) Percent of total population; (2) Percent of Hispanic/Latino population; Profiles include places with an overall population of at least 125,000, OR an overall population of at least 25,000 where the Hispanic/Latino population is at least 20% of the overall population. In states where less than five places meet either of these criteria, we have included places with at least 10,000 total population with the highest percentage of Hispanic/Latino population. These places are identified with an asterisk (*); Please refer to the User's Guide for a full explanation of data.

Hispanic or Latino (of any race)	4,107	75.5
Mexican	3,962	76.0

Class of Worker: Government
(Universe: Civilian Employed Population 16 Years and Over)

Group	Number	%
Total Population	1,384	22.2
Hispanic or Latino (of any race)	1,128	20.7
Mexican	1,080	20.7

Means of Transportation to Work: Car, Truck or Van
(Universe: Workers 16 Years and Over)

Group	Number	%
Total Population	5,589	93.1
Hispanic or Latino (of any race)	4,887	93.0
Mexican	4,719	93.9

Means of Transportation to Work: Public Transportation (ex. Taxicab)
(Universe: Workers 16 Years and Over)

Group	Number	%
Total Population	139	2.3
Hispanic or Latino (of any race)	139	2.6
Mexican	77	1.5

Homeownership Rate
(Universe: Occupied Housing Units)

Group	%
Total Population	57.1
Hispanic or Latino (of any race)	53.7
Central American, ex. Mexican	54.8
Mexican	54.2

Median Home Value

Group	Dollars
Total Population	396,600
Hispanic or Latino (of any race)	398,500
Mexican	393,100

Median Gross Rent

Group	Dollars
Total Population	1,013
Hispanic or Latino (of any race)	993
Mexican	984

Median Household Income
(2010 Inflation-Adjusted Dollars)

Group	Dollars
Total Population	50,912
Hispanic or Latino (of any race)	48,077
Mexican	46,937

Per Capita Income
(2010 Inflation-Adjusted Dollars)

Group	Dollars
Total Population	10,118
Hispanic or Latino (of any race)	11,129
Mexican	11,257

Households with $100,000+ Income

Group	Number	%
Total Population	716	18.9
Hispanic or Latino (of any race)	495	15.6
Mexican	484	15.9

Households with Food Stamps/SNAP Benefits During Past 12 Months

Group	Number	%
Total Population	429	11.3
Hispanic or Latino (of any race)	365	11.5
Mexican	340	11.2

Poverty Rate
(Income in Past 12 Months Below Poverty Level)

Group	%
Total Population	15.5
Hispanic or Latino (of any race)	16.1
Mexican	16.5

South Gate

Population

Group	Number	%TP[1]	%HP[2]
Total Population	94,396	100.0	–
Hispanic or Latino (of any race)	89,442	94.8	100.0
Central American, ex. Mexican	9,777	10.4	10.9
Guatemalan	2,629	2.8	2.9
Honduran	507	0.5	0.6
Nicaraguan	983	1.0	1.1
Salvadoran	5,407	5.7	6.0
Cuban	754	0.8	0.8
Mexican	73,677	78.1	82.4
Puerto Rican	464	0.5	0.5
South American	1,216	1.3	1.4
Argentinean	112	0.1	0.1
Colombian	237	0.3	0.3
Ecuadorian	348	0.4	0.4
Peruvian	431	0.5	0.5
Spaniard	164	0.2	0.2

Population Growth: 2000–2010

Group	%
Total Population	-2.1
Hispanic or Latino (of any race)	0.9
Central American, ex. Mexican	58.6
Guatemalan	76.7
Honduran	92.0
Nicaraguan	69.2
Salvadoran	77.9
Cuban	-0.9
Mexican	8.1
Puerto Rican	-19.4
South American	12.3
Argentinean	6.7
Colombian	19.7
Ecuadorian	60.4
Peruvian	13.4

Males per 100 Females

Group	Number
Total Population	96.4
Hispanic or Latino (of any race)	96.4
Central American, ex. Mexican	91.9
Guatemalan	94.5
Honduran	68.4
Nicaraguan	86.9
Salvadoran	93.8
Cuban	94.3
Mexican	97.2
Puerto Rican	107.1
South American	93.9
Argentinean	133.3
Colombian	79.5
Ecuadorian	89.1
Peruvian	95.0
Spaniard	74.5

Average Household Size

Group	People
Total Population	4.05
Hispanic or Latino (of any race)	4.21
Central American, ex. Mexican	4.16
Guatemalan	4.28
Honduran	3.97
Nicaraguan	3.99
Salvadoran	4.19
Cuban	2.59
Mexican	4.29
Puerto Rican	2.92
South American	3.46
Argentinean	2.69
Colombian	3.74
Ecuadorian	3.50
Peruvian	3.54
Spaniard	3.55

Median Age

Group	Years
Total Population	29.4
Hispanic or Latino (of any race)	28.7
Central American, ex. Mexican	37.2
Guatemalan	37.8
Honduran	33.0
Nicaraguan	39.4
Salvadoran	37.1
Cuban	49.3
Mexican	27.5
Puerto Rican	37.4
South American	43.5
Argentinean	45.5
Colombian	41.1
Ecuadorian	44.2
Peruvian	44.3
Spaniard	44.4

High School Graduates
(Universe: Population 25 Years and Over)

Group	Number	%
Total Population	27,275	51.1
Hispanic or Latino (of any race)	24,204	48.7
Central American, ex. Mexican	3,147	46.4
Guatemalan	1,019	50.8
Nicaraguan	347	60.6
Salvadoran	1,484	40.7
Mexican	19,251	47.8
South American	654	67.2

Four-Year College Graduates
(Universe: Population 25 Years and Over)

Group	Number	%
Total Population	3,600	6.7
Hispanic or Latino (of any race)	2,841	5.7
Central American, ex. Mexican	514	7.6
Guatemalan	146	7.3
Nicaraguan	88	15.4
Salvadoran	262	7.2
Mexican	1,881	4.7
South American	166	17.1

Population Age 3–17 Enrolled in Public School
(Universe: Population Age 3–17 Enrolled in School)

Group	Number	%
Total Population	21,091	95.7
Hispanic or Latino (of any race)	20,604	96.2
Central American, ex. Mexican	1,410	97.6
Guatemalan	517	100.0
Nicaraguan	99	90.0
Salvadoran	638	96.5
Mexican	18,461	96.4
South American	232	83.2

Population Age 3–17 Enrolled in Private School
(Universe: Population Age 3–17 Enrolled in School)

Group	Number	%
Total Population	947	4.3
Hispanic or Latino (of any race)	817	3.8
Central American, ex. Mexican	34	2.4
Guatemalan	0	0.0
Nicaraguan	11	10.0
Salvadoran	23	3.5
Mexican	690	3.6
South American	47	16.8

Foreign-Born Population

Group	Number	%
Total Population	43,168	45.6
Hispanic or Latino (of any race)	42,052	46.7
Central American, ex. Mexican	6,652	64.6
Guatemalan	1,833	61.3
Nicaraguan	597	60.0
Salvadoran	3,609	66.5
Mexican	33,382	44.3
South American	1,000	66.1

Foreign-Born Naturalized U.S. Citizens

Group	Number	%
Total Population	15,566	36.1
Hispanic or Latino (of any race)	14,887	35.4
Central American, ex. Mexican	2,753	41.4
Guatemalan	848	46.3
Nicaraguan	287	48.1
Salvadoran	1,410	39.1
Mexican	11,128	33.3
South American	533	53.3

Notes: (1) Percent of total population; (2) Percent of Hispanic/Latino population; Profiles include places with an overall population of at least 125,000, OR an overall population of at least 25,000 where the Hispanic/Latino population is at least 20% of the overall population. In states where less than five places meet either of these criteria, we have included places with at least 10,000 total population with the highest percentage of Hispanic/Latino population. These places are identified with an asterisk (*); Please refer to the User's Guide for a full explanation of data.

Language Spoken at Home: English Only
(Universe: Population 5 Years and Over)

Group	Number	%
Total Population	9,921	11.5
Hispanic or Latino (of any race)	6,746	8.2
Central American, ex. Mexican	463	4.8
Guatemalan	93	3.2
Nicaraguan	8	0.9
Salvadoran	311	6.2
Mexican	5,882	8.6
South American	0	0.0

Language Spoken at Home: Spanish
(Universe: Population 5 Years and Over)

Group	Number	%
Total Population	75,527	87.3
Hispanic or Latino (of any race)	75,148	91.6
Central American, ex. Mexican	9,207	95.1
Guatemalan	2,807	96.4
Nicaraguan	859	99.1
Salvadoran	4,733	93.8
Mexican	62,448	91.4
South American	1,407	100.0

Unemployment Rate
(Universe: Population 16 Years and Over)

Group	%
Total Population	11.0
Hispanic or Latino (of any race)	11.0
Central American, ex. Mexican	6.8
Guatemalan	4.5
Nicaraguan	19.3
Salvadoran	4.9
Mexican	11.9
South American	5.3

Class of Worker: Private Wage and Salary
(Universe: Civilian Employed Population 16 Years and Over)

Group	Number	%
Total Population	32,786	85.7
Hispanic or Latino (of any race)	31,350	86.1
Central American, ex. Mexican	4,765	90.4
Guatemalan	1,481	87.4
Nicaraguan	252	83.7
Salvadoran	2,673	92.3
Mexican	25,264	85.8
South American	542	85.9

Class of Worker: Government
(Universe: Civilian Employed Population 16 Years and Over)

Group	Number	%
Total Population	3,810	10.0
Hispanic or Latino (of any race)	3,523	9.7
Central American, ex. Mexican	261	5.0
Guatemalan	106	6.3
Nicaraguan	20	6.6
Salvadoran	135	4.7
Mexican	3,050	10.4
South American	26	4.1

Means of Transportation to Work: Car, Truck or Van
(Universe: Workers 16 Years and Over)

Group	Number	%
Total Population	32,871	87.7
Hispanic or Latino (of any race)	31,336	87.8
Central American, ex. Mexican	4,770	91.5
Guatemalan	1,556	94.2
Nicaraguan	252	82.6
Salvadoran	2,609	90.3
Mexican	25,190	87.4
South American	479	79.6

Means of Transportation to Work: Public Transportation (ex. Taxicab)
(Universe: Workers 16 Years and Over)

Group	Number	%
Total Population	2,669	7.1
Hispanic or Latino (of any race)	2,529	7.1
Central American, ex. Mexican	205	3.9
Guatemalan	13	0.8
Nicaraguan	46	15.1
Salvadoran	132	4.6
Mexican	2,140	7.4
South American	71	11.8

Homeownership Rate
(Universe: Occupied Housing Units)

Group	%
Total Population	45.8
Hispanic or Latino (of any race)	44.0
Central American, ex. Mexican	43.5
Guatemalan	45.1
Honduran	20.5
Nicaraguan	41.7
Salvadoran	45.9
Cuban	48.9
Mexican	44.2
Puerto Rican	40.6
South American	48.4
Argentinean	73.8
Colombian	49.3
Ecuadorian	46.3
Peruvian	41.5
Spaniard	47.8

Median Home Value

Group	Dollars
Total Population	376,700
Hispanic or Latino (of any race)	380,000
Central American, ex. Mexican	367,100
Guatemalan	358,900
Nicaraguan	366,500
Salvadoran	355,400
Mexican	380,200
South American	431,300

Median Gross Rent

Group	Dollars
Total Population	938
Hispanic or Latino (of any race)	937
Central American, ex. Mexican	887
Guatemalan	912
Nicaraguan	937
Salvadoran	879
Mexican	944
South American	977

Median Household Income
(2010 Inflation-Adjusted Dollars)

Group	Dollars
Total Population	43,268
Hispanic or Latino (of any race)	42,797
Central American, ex. Mexican	40,188
Guatemalan	40,000
Nicaraguan	38,182
Salvadoran	41,250
Mexican	43,176
South American	51,546

Per Capita Income
(2010 Inflation-Adjusted Dollars)

Group	Dollars
Total Population	13,913
Hispanic or Latino (of any race)	13,203
Central American, ex. Mexican	15,437
Guatemalan	15,859
Nicaraguan	11,636
Salvadoran	15,700
Mexican	12,803
South American	15,342

Households with $100,000+ Income

Group	Number	%
Total Population	2,496	10.5
Hispanic or Latino (of any race)	2,260	10.4
Central American, ex. Mexican	322	10.8
Guatemalan	157	21.0
Nicaraguan	17	6.0
Salvadoran	118	7.2
Mexican	1,824	10.4
South American	37	8.1

Households with Food Stamps/SNAP Benefits During Past 12 Months

Group	Number	%
Total Population	1,875	7.9
Hispanic or Latino (of any race)	1,826	8.4
Central American, ex. Mexican	141	4.7
Guatemalan	4	0.5
Nicaraguan	12	4.3
Salvadoran	106	6.4
Mexican	1,633	9.4
South American	9	2.0

Poverty Rate
(Income in Past 12 Months Below Poverty Level)

Group	%
Total Population	18.5
Hispanic or Latino (of any race)	19.0
Central American, ex. Mexican	12.2
Guatemalan	15.2
Nicaraguan	22.7
Salvadoran	9.4
Mexican	20.3
South American	15.5

South San Francisco

Population

Group	Number	%TP[1]	%HP[2]
Total Population	63,632	100.0	–
Hispanic or Latino (of any race)	21,645	34.0	100.0
Central American, ex. Mexican	5,381	8.5	24.9
Guatemalan	576	0.9	2.7
Honduran	140	0.2	0.6
Nicaraguan	1,639	2.6	7.6
Salvadoran	2,897	4.6	13.4
Mexican	13,194	20.7	61.0
Puerto Rican	571	0.9	2.6
South American	815	1.3	3.8
Colombian	152	0.2	0.7
Peruvian	424	0.7	2.0
Spaniard	396	0.6	1.8

Population Growth: 2000–2010

Group	%
Total Population	5.1
Hispanic or Latino (of any race)	12.3
Central American, ex. Mexican	71.1
Guatemalan	113.3
Nicaraguan	73.4
Salvadoran	91.3
Mexican	19.0
Puerto Rican	13.3
South American	69.4
Peruvian	97.2

Males per 100 Females

Group	Number
Total Population	97.6
Hispanic or Latino (of any race)	102.9
Central American, ex. Mexican	88.7
Guatemalan	95.9
Honduran	91.8
Nicaraguan	82.3
Salvadoran	91.0
Mexican	111.3
Puerto Rican	105.4
South American	85.6
Colombian	74.7
Peruvian	93.6
Spaniard	85.0

Average Household Size

Group	People
Total Population	3.01
Hispanic or Latino (of any race)	3.69
Central American, ex. Mexican	3.50
Guatemalan	3.47
Honduran	3.91
Nicaraguan	3.42
Salvadoran	3.57
Mexican	4.02
Puerto Rican	2.93
South American	3.12
Colombian	3.36
Peruvian	3.29
Spaniard	2.71

Median Age

Group	Years
Total Population	38.1
Hispanic or Latino (of any race)	30.7
Central American, ex. Mexican	35.4

Notes: (1) Percent of total population; (2) Percent of Hispanic/Latino population; Profiles include places with an overall population of at least 125,000, OR an overall population of at least 25,000 where the Hispanic/Latino population is at least 20% of the overall population. In states where less than five places meet either of these criteria, we have included places with at least 10,000 total population with the highest percentage of Hispanic/Latino population. These places are identified with an asterisk (*); Please refer to the User's Guide for a full explanation of data.

Guatemalan		34.5
Honduran		32.8
Nicaraguan		36.5
Salvadoran		35.2
Mexican		29.0
Puerto Rican		33.2
South American		37.1
Colombian		36.0
Peruvian		38.4
Spaniard		42.7

High School Graduates
(Universe: Population 25 Years and Over)

Group	Number	%
Total Population	36,208	84.8
Hispanic or Latino (of any race)	8,133	67.7
Central American, ex. Mexican	1,985	70.8
Nicaraguan	530	69.1
Salvadoran	1,215	72.8
Mexican	4,900	64.0

Four-Year College Graduates
(Universe: Population 25 Years and Over)

Group	Number	%
Total Population	13,440	31.5
Hispanic or Latino (of any race)	1,447	12.0
Central American, ex. Mexican	325	11.6
Nicaraguan	88	11.5
Salvadoran	237	14.2
Mexican	791	10.3

Population Age 3–17 Enrolled in Public School
(Universe: Population Age 3–17 Enrolled in School)

Group	Number	%
Total Population	8,242	77.9
Hispanic or Latino (of any race)	3,879	88.9
Central American, ex. Mexican	582	88.2
Nicaraguan	168	81.6
Salvadoran	349	94.6
Mexican	2,991	89.4

Population Age 3–17 Enrolled in Private School
(Universe: Population Age 3–17 Enrolled in School)

Group	Number	%
Total Population	2,342	22.1
Hispanic or Latino (of any race)	486	11.1
Central American, ex. Mexican	78	11.8
Nicaraguan	38	18.4
Salvadoran	20	5.4
Mexican	353	10.6

Foreign-Born Population

Group	Number	%
Total Population	25,666	41.4
Hispanic or Latino (of any race)	8,919	44.0
Central American, ex. Mexican	2,611	63.1
Nicaraguan	907	73.1
Salvadoran	1,384	59.6
Mexican	5,599	40.3

Foreign-Born Naturalized U.S. Citizens

Group	Number	%
Total Population	16,679	65.0
Hispanic or Latino (of any race)	3,536	39.6
Central American, ex. Mexican	1,334	51.1
Nicaraguan	428	47.2
Salvadoran	774	55.9
Mexican	1,727	30.8

Language Spoken at Home: English Only
(Universe: Population 5 Years and Over)

Group	Number	%
Total Population	23,618	40.6
Hispanic or Latino (of any race)	4,254	23.0
Central American, ex. Mexican	506	13.0
Nicaraguan	164	14.0
Salvadoran	272	12.2
Mexican	2,627	21.0

Language Spoken at Home: Spanish
(Universe: Population 5 Years and Over)

Group	Number	%
Total Population	14,546	25.0
Hispanic or Latino (of any race)	14,126	76.2
Central American, ex. Mexican	3,371	86.7
Nicaraguan	1,009	86.0
Salvadoran	1,944	87.4
Mexican	9,792	78.4

Unemployment Rate
(Universe: Population 16 Years and Over)

Group	%
Total Population	5.8
Hispanic or Latino (of any race)	7.6
Central American, ex. Mexican	8.2
Nicaraguan	13.6
Salvadoran	6.4
Mexican	7.1

Class of Worker: Private Wage and Salary
(Universe: Civilian Employed Population 16 Years and Over)

Group	Number	%
Total Population	25,219	79.1
Hispanic or Latino (of any race)	8,432	85.5
Central American, ex. Mexican	1,902	85.1
Nicaraguan	472	75.5
Salvadoran	1,165	89.8
Mexican	5,716	86.1

Class of Worker: Government
(Universe: Civilian Employed Population 16 Years and Over)

Group	Number	%
Total Population	4,613	14.5
Hispanic or Latino (of any race)	913	9.3
Central American, ex. Mexican	200	8.9
Nicaraguan	97	15.5
Salvadoran	68	5.2
Mexican	562	8.5

Means of Transportation to Work: Car, Truck or Van
(Universe: Workers 16 Years and Over)

Group	Number	%
Total Population	25,147	81.5
Hispanic or Latino (of any race)	7,305	76.8
Central American, ex. Mexican	1,555	73.7
Nicaraguan	373	63.7
Salvadoran	1,023	84.5
Mexican	4,974	77.6

Means of Transportation to Work: Public Transportation (ex. Taxicab)
(Universe: Workers 16 Years and Over)

Group	Number	%
Total Population	3,286	10.7
Hispanic or Latino (of any race)	1,030	10.8
Central American, ex. Mexican	335	15.9
Nicaraguan	130	22.2
Salvadoran	149	12.3
Mexican	521	8.1

Homeownership Rate
(Universe: Occupied Housing Units)

Group	%
Total Population	60.2
Hispanic or Latino (of any race)	41.7
Central American, ex. Mexican	36.1
Guatemalan	35.4
Honduran	26.5
Nicaraguan	32.5
Salvadoran	38.8
Mexican	42.7
Puerto Rican	44.5
South American	42.3
Colombian	36.4
Peruvian	44.4
Spaniard	68.3

Median Home Value

Group	Dollars
Total Population	648,500
Hispanic or Latino (of any race)	622,100
Central American, ex. Mexican	612,400
Nicaraguan	638,600
Salvadoran	584,500
Mexican	640,000

Median Gross Rent

Group	Dollars
Total Population	1,423
Hispanic or Latino (of any race)	1,345
Central American, ex. Mexican	1,467
Nicaraguan	1,394
Salvadoran	1,302
Mexican	1,345

Median Household Income
(2010 Inflation-Adjusted Dollars)

Group	Dollars
Total Population	74,158
Hispanic or Latino (of any race)	59,978
Central American, ex. Mexican	71,771
Nicaraguan	100,263
Salvadoran	62,004
Mexican	58,230

Per Capita Income
(2010 Inflation-Adjusted Dollars)

Group	Dollars
Total Population	31,163
Hispanic or Latino (of any race)	20,301
Central American, ex. Mexican	22,544
Nicaraguan	23,810
Salvadoran	21,366
Mexican	19,356

Households with $100,000+ Income

Group	Number	%
Total Population	7,192	34.5
Hispanic or Latino (of any race)	1,207	22.2
Central American, ex. Mexican	382	31.8
Nicaraguan	145	50.7
Salvadoran	198	29.1
Mexican	687	19.7

Households with Food Stamps/SNAP Benefits During Past 12 Months

Group	Number	%
Total Population	373	1.8
Hispanic or Latino (of any race)	245	4.5
Central American, ex. Mexican	78	6.5
Nicaraguan	0	0.0
Salvadoran	43	6.3
Mexican	87	2.5

Poverty Rate
(Income in Past 12 Months Below Poverty Level)

Group	%
Total Population	6.3
Hispanic or Latino (of any race)	9.7
Central American, ex. Mexican	5.6
Nicaraguan	3.6
Salvadoran	8.0
Mexican	9.3

South Whittier

Population

Group	Number	%TP[1]	%HP[2]
Total Population	57,156	100.0	–
Hispanic or Latino (of any race)	44,094	77.1	100.0
Central American, ex. Mexican	2,217	3.9	5.0
Guatemalan	612	1.1	1.4
Honduran	103	0.2	0.2
Nicaraguan	299	0.5	0.7
Salvadoran	1,110	1.9	2.5
Cuban	206	0.4	0.5
Mexican	38,766	67.8	87.9
Puerto Rican	354	0.6	0.8
South American	548	1.0	1.2
Colombian	136	0.2	0.3
Ecuadorian	108	0.2	0.2
Peruvian	170	0.3	0.4
Spaniard	284	0.5	0.6

Population Growth: 2000–2010

Group	%
Total Population	3.6
Hispanic or Latino (of any race)	15.3
Central American, ex. Mexican	109.0
Guatemalan	180.7
Nicaraguan	160.0
Salvadoran	122.4
Cuban	4.0
Mexican	22.3
Puerto Rican	41.0

Notes: (1) Percent of total population; (2) Percent of Hispanic/Latino population; Profiles include places with an overall population of at least 125,000, OR an overall population of at least 25,000 where the Hispanic/Latino population is at least 20% of the overall population. In states where less than five places meet either of these criteria, we have included places with at least 10,000 total population with the highest percentage of Hispanic/Latino population. These places are identified with an asterisk (*); Please refer to the User's Guide for a full explanation of data.

Group	%
South American	56.6
Peruvian	63.5

Males per 100 Females

Group	Number
Total Population	98.5
Hispanic or Latino (of any race)	99.4
Central American, ex. Mexican	86.6
Guatemalan	90.7
Honduran	80.7
Nicaraguan	83.4
Salvadoran	86.6
Cuban	94.3
Mexican	100.8
Puerto Rican	95.6
South American	87.0
Colombian	94.3
Ecuadorian	68.8
Peruvian	84.8
Spaniard	83.2

Average Household Size

Group	People
Total Population	3.77
Hispanic or Latino (of any race)	4.29
Central American, ex. Mexican	4.38
Guatemalan	4.13
Honduran	4.40
Nicaraguan	4.38
Salvadoran	4.61
Cuban	3.24
Mexican	4.34
Puerto Rican	3.55
South American	3.61
Colombian	3.63
Ecuadorian	3.37
Peruvian	4.04
Spaniard	3.31

Median Age

Group	Years
Total Population	32.0
Hispanic or Latino (of any race)	28.7
Central American, ex. Mexican	34.3
Guatemalan	35.9
Honduran	33.6
Nicaraguan	35.1
Salvadoran	32.3
Cuban	42.7
Mexican	28.3
Puerto Rican	31.6
South American	40.9
Colombian	42.5
Ecuadorian	43.5
Peruvian	40.3
Spaniard	35.5

High School Graduates
(Universe: Population 25 Years and Over)

Group	Number	%
Total Population	23,221	68.2
Hispanic or Latino (of any race)	14,559	60.6
Central American, ex. Mexican	930	64.4
Mexican	12,573	59.4

Four-Year College Graduates
(Universe: Population 25 Years and Over)

Group	Number	%
Total Population	4,011	11.8
Hispanic or Latino (of any race)	2,035	8.5
Central American, ex. Mexican	136	9.4
Mexican	1,713	8.1

Population Age 3–17 Enrolled in Public School
(Universe: Population Age 3–17 Enrolled in School)

Group	Number	%
Total Population	12,205	92.4
Hispanic or Latino (of any race)	10,961	93.3
Central American, ex. Mexican	519	91.1
Mexican	9,825	94.4

Population Age 3–17 Enrolled in Private School
(Universe: Population Age 3–17 Enrolled in School)

Group	Number	%
Total Population	999	7.6
Hispanic or Latino (of any race)	784	6.7
Central American, ex. Mexican	51	8.9
Mexican	586	5.6

Foreign-Born Population

Group	Number	%
Total Population	16,564	29.1
Hispanic or Latino (of any race)	14,202	32.3
Central American, ex. Mexican	1,483	62.3
Mexican	12,004	30.7

Foreign-Born Naturalized U.S. Citizens

Group	Number	%
Total Population	6,342	38.3
Hispanic or Latino (of any race)	4,964	35.0
Central American, ex. Mexican	802	54.1
Mexican	3,768	31.4

Language Spoken at Home: English Only
(Universe: Population 5 Years and Over)

Group	Number	%
Total Population	21,070	40.1
Hispanic or Latino (of any race)	11,201	28.0
Central American, ex. Mexican	212	9.5
Mexican	10,024	28.3

Language Spoken at Home: Spanish
(Universe: Population 5 Years and Over)

Group	Number	%
Total Population	29,221	55.7
Hispanic or Latino (of any race)	28,805	71.9
Central American, ex. Mexican	2,014	90.5
Mexican	25,369	71.6

Unemployment Rate
(Universe: Population 16 Years and Over)

Group	%
Total Population	8.0
Hispanic or Latino (of any race)	8.4
Central American, ex. Mexican	5.1
Mexican	8.0

Class of Worker: Private Wage and Salary
(Universe: Civilian Employed Population 16 Years and Over)

Group	Number	%
Total Population	20,479	78.7
Hispanic or Latino (of any race)	15,458	79.6
Central American, ex. Mexican	886	84.3
Mexican	13,857	80.0

Class of Worker: Government
(Universe: Civilian Employed Population 16 Years and Over)

Group	Number	%
Total Population	3,606	13.9
Hispanic or Latino (of any race)	2,570	13.2
Central American, ex. Mexican	110	10.5
Mexican	2,260	13.1

Means of Transportation to Work: Car, Truck or Van
(Universe: Workers 16 Years and Over)

Group	Number	%
Total Population	23,110	91.6
Hispanic or Latino (of any race)	16,971	90.3
Central American, ex. Mexican	953	93.6
Mexican	15,112	90.1

Means of Transportation to Work: Public Transportation (ex. Taxicab)
(Universe: Workers 16 Years and Over)

Group	Number	%
Total Population	623	2.5
Hispanic or Latino (of any race)	544	2.9
Central American, ex. Mexican	0	0.0
Mexican	457	2.7

Homeownership Rate
(Universe: Occupied Housing Units)

Group	%
Total Population	63.5
Hispanic or Latino (of any race)	59.8
Central American, ex. Mexican	56.2
Guatemalan	57.8
Honduran	35.0
Nicaraguan	40.0
Salvadoran	60.1
Cuban	72.7
Mexican	60.0
Puerto Rican	64.2
South American	62.4
Colombian	48.8
Ecuadorian	62.9
Peruvian	65.2
Spaniard	62.1

Median Home Value

Group	Dollars
Total Population	421,000
Hispanic or Latino (of any race)	419,500
Central American, ex. Mexican	357,100
Mexican	420,900

Median Gross Rent

Group	Dollars
Total Population	1,154
Hispanic or Latino (of any race)	1,144
Central American, ex. Mexican	1,367
Mexican	1,114

Median Household Income
(2010 Inflation-Adjusted Dollars)

Group	Dollars
Total Population	65,043
Hispanic or Latino (of any race)	63,139
Central American, ex. Mexican	58,671
Mexican	65,125

Per Capita Income
(2010 Inflation-Adjusted Dollars)

Group	Dollars
Total Population	20,754
Hispanic or Latino (of any race)	17,731
Central American, ex. Mexican	17,896
Mexican	17,570

Households with $100,000+ Income

Group	Number	%
Total Population	3,270	21.2
Hispanic or Latino (of any race)	2,072	19.9
Central American, ex. Mexican	52	10.0
Mexican	1,900	20.6

Households with Food Stamps/SNAP Benefits During Past 12 Months

Group	Number	%
Total Population	830	5.4
Hispanic or Latino (of any race)	738	7.1
Central American, ex. Mexican	53	10.2
Mexican	673	7.3

Poverty Rate
(Income in Past 12 Months Below Poverty Level)

Group	%
Total Population	10.8
Hispanic or Latino (of any race)	12.4
Central American, ex. Mexican	11.1
Mexican	12.4

Spring Valley

Population

Group	Number	%TP[1]	%HP[2]
Total Population	28,205	100.0	–
Hispanic or Latino (of any race)	9,196	32.6	100.0
Central American, ex. Mexican	163	0.6	1.8
Mexican	8,231	29.2	89.5
Puerto Rican	236	0.8	2.6
South American	126	0.4	1.4
Spaniard	122	0.4	1.3

Population Growth: 2000–2010

Group	%
Total Population	5.8
Hispanic or Latino (of any race)	60.6
Mexican	74.9
Puerto Rican	10.3

Males per 100 Females

Group	Number
Total Population	95.2

STATE & PLACE PROFILES

Notes: (1) Percent of total population; (2) Percent of Hispanic/Latino population; Profiles include places with an overall population of at least 125,000, OR an overall population of at least 25,000 where the Hispanic/Latino population is at least 20% of the overall population. In states where less than five places meet either of these criteria, we have included places with at least 10,000 total population with the highest percentage of Hispanic/Latino population. These places are identified with an asterisk (*); Please refer to the User's Guide for a full explanation of data.

Hispanic or Latino (of any race)	96.3
Central American, ex. Mexican	96.4
Mexican	96.8
Puerto Rican	96.7
South American	82.6
Spaniard	93.7

Average Household Size

Group	People
Total Population	3.01
Hispanic or Latino (of any race)	3.80
Central American, ex. Mexican	3.52
Mexican	3.89
Puerto Rican	2.87
South American	3.25
Spaniard	2.95

Median Age

Group	Years
Total Population	35.0
Hispanic or Latino (of any race)	25.9
Central American, ex. Mexican	34.5
Mexican	25.5
Puerto Rican	27.0
South American	31.0
Spaniard	31.0

High School Graduates
(Universe: Population 25 Years and Over)

Group	Number	%
Total Population	15,290	87.5
Hispanic or Latino (of any race)	2,750	69.0
Mexican	2,386	67.4

Four-Year College Graduates
(Universe: Population 25 Years and Over)

Group	Number	%
Total Population	4,305	24.6
Hispanic or Latino (of any race)	438	11.0
Mexican	333	9.4

Population Age 3–17 Enrolled in Public School
(Universe: Population Age 3–17 Enrolled in School)

Group	Number	%
Total Population	4,740	88.3
Hispanic or Latino (of any race)	1,938	96.9
Mexican	1,800	97.8

Population Age 3–17 Enrolled in Private School
(Universe: Population Age 3–17 Enrolled in School)

Group	Number	%
Total Population	630	11.7
Hispanic or Latino (of any race)	62	3.1
Mexican	40	2.2

Foreign-Born Population

Group	Number	%
Total Population	4,261	15.6
Hispanic or Latino (of any race)	2,104	28.4
Mexican	1,901	28.7

Foreign-Born Naturalized U.S. Citizens

Group	Number	%
Total Population	2,525	59.3
Hispanic or Latino (of any race)	906	43.1
Mexican	854	44.9

Language Spoken at Home: English Only
(Universe: Population 5 Years and Over)

Group	Number	%
Total Population	18,408	72.5
Hispanic or Latino (of any race)	2,127	31.8
Mexican	1,778	29.8

Language Spoken at Home: Spanish
(Universe: Population 5 Years and Over)

Group	Number	%
Total Population	4,961	19.5
Hispanic or Latino (of any race)	4,554	68.2
Mexican	4,180	70.2

Unemployment Rate
(Universe: Population 16 Years and Over)

Group	%
Total Population	8.7
Hispanic or Latino (of any race)	5.1
Mexican	5.8

Class of Worker: Private Wage and Salary
(Universe: Civilian Employed Population 16 Years and Over)

Group	Number	%
Total Population	9,970	76.4
Hispanic or Latino (of any race)	2,654	77.2
Mexican	2,357	77.8

Class of Worker: Government
(Universe: Civilian Employed Population 16 Years and Over)

Group	Number	%
Total Population	2,268	17.4
Hispanic or Latino (of any race)	572	16.6
Mexican	477	15.7

Means of Transportation to Work: Car, Truck or Van
(Universe: Workers 16 Years and Over)

Group	Number	%
Total Population	11,793	91.6
Hispanic or Latino (of any race)	3,011	88.9
Mexican	2,699	90.2

Means of Transportation to Work: Public Transportation (ex. Taxicab)
(Universe: Workers 16 Years and Over)

Group	Number	%
Total Population	366	2.8
Hispanic or Latino (of any race)	196	5.8
Mexican	127	4.2

Homeownership Rate
(Universe: Occupied Housing Units)

Group	%
Total Population	63.6
Hispanic or Latino (of any race)	51.2
Central American, ex. Mexican	61.7
Mexican	51.1
Puerto Rican	46.7
South American	65.0
Spaniard	51.4

Median Home Value

Group	Dollars
Total Population	406,000
Hispanic or Latino (of any race)	343,300
Mexican	353,400

Median Gross Rent

Group	Dollars
Total Population	1,314
Hispanic or Latino (of any race)	1,316
Mexican	1,342

Median Household Income
(2010 Inflation-Adjusted Dollars)

Group	Dollars
Total Population	64,796
Hispanic or Latino (of any race)	58,299
Mexican	57,762

Per Capita Income
(2010 Inflation-Adjusted Dollars)

Group	Dollars
Total Population	26,109
Hispanic or Latino (of any race)	18,883
Mexican	18,508

Households with $100,000+ Income

Group	Number	%
Total Population	2,243	23.9
Hispanic or Latino (of any race)	376	19.4
Mexican	342	20.3

Households with Food Stamps/SNAP Benefits During Past 12 Months

Group	Number	%
Total Population	525	5.6
Hispanic or Latino (of any race)	128	6.6
Mexican	128	7.6

Poverty Rate
(Income in Past 12 Months Below Poverty Level)

Group	%
Total Population	9.8
Hispanic or Latino (of any race)	13.6
Mexican	14.8

Stanton

Population

Group	Number	%TP[1]	%HP[2]
Total Population	38,186	100.0	–
Hispanic or Latino (of any race)	19,417	50.8	100.0
Central American, ex. Mexican	871	2.3	4.5
Guatemalan	302	0.8	1.6
Salvadoran	396	1.0	2.0
Cuban	100	0.3	0.5
Mexican	16,878	44.2	86.9
Puerto Rican	139	0.4	0.7
South American	327	0.9	1.7
Peruvian	143	0.4	0.7
Spaniard	108	0.3	0.6

Population Growth: 2000–2010

Group	%
Total Population	2.1
Hispanic or Latino (of any race)	6.2
Central American, ex. Mexican	106.4
Guatemalan	149.6
Salvadoran	155.5
Mexican	8.9
Puerto Rican	-22.8
South American	50.0

Males per 100 Females

Group	Number
Total Population	98.0
Hispanic or Latino (of any race)	105.5
Central American, ex. Mexican	100.7
Guatemalan	104.1
Salvadoran	104.1
Cuban	88.7
Mexican	106.9
Puerto Rican	110.6
South American	79.7
Peruvian	68.2
Spaniard	129.8

Average Household Size

Group	People
Total Population	3.50
Hispanic or Latino (of any race)	4.72
Central American, ex. Mexican	4.50
Guatemalan	5.14
Salvadoran	4.39
Cuban	2.85
Mexican	4.84
Puerto Rican	3.21
South American	3.58
Peruvian	4.36
Spaniard	3.05

Median Age

Group	Years
Total Population	33.0
Hispanic or Latino (of any race)	25.6
Central American, ex. Mexican	31.5
Guatemalan	31.5
Salvadoran	31.4
Cuban	29.5
Mexican	25.0
Puerto Rican	27.8
South American	38.7
Peruvian	37.6
Spaniard	38.0

High School Graduates
(Universe: Population 25 Years and Over)

Group	Number	%
Total Population	16,109	67.1
Hispanic or Latino (of any race)	3,663	39.6
Mexican	3,043	36.7

Four-Year College Graduates
(Universe: Population 25 Years and Over)

Group	Number	%
Total Population	3,976	16.6
Hispanic or Latino (of any race)	557	6.0

Notes: (1) Percent of total population; (2) Percent of Hispanic/Latino population; Profiles include places with an overall population of at least 125,000, OR an overall population of at least 25,000 where the Hispanic/Latino population is at least 20% of the overall population. In states where less than five places meet either of these criteria, we have included places with at least 10,000 total population with the highest percentage of Hispanic/Latino population. These places are identified with an asterisk (*); Please refer to the User's Guide for a full explanation of data.

Group	Number	%
Mexican	459	5.5

Population Age 3–17 Enrolled in Public School
(Universe: Population Age 3–17 Enrolled in School)

Group	Number	%
Total Population	7,409	94.5
Hispanic or Latino (of any race)	4,860	99.8
Mexican	4,596	99.8

Population Age 3–17 Enrolled in Private School
(Universe: Population Age 3–17 Enrolled in School)

Group	Number	%
Total Population	431	5.5
Hispanic or Latino (of any race)	10	0.2
Mexican	10	0.2

Foreign-Born Population

Group	Number	%
Total Population	16,305	42.9
Hispanic or Latino (of any race)	8,639	48.6
Mexican	7,919	48.9

Foreign-Born Naturalized U.S. Citizens

Group	Number	%
Total Population	6,784	41.6
Hispanic or Latino (of any race)	1,631	18.9
Mexican	1,394	17.6

Language Spoken at Home: English Only
(Universe: Population 5 Years and Over)

Group	Number	%
Total Population	12,747	36.0
Hispanic or Latino (of any race)	2,070	12.9
Mexican	1,717	11.8

Language Spoken at Home: Spanish
(Universe: Population 5 Years and Over)

Group	Number	%
Total Population	14,393	40.7
Hispanic or Latino (of any race)	13,924	86.7
Mexican	12,789	87.8

Unemployment Rate
(Universe: Population 16 Years and Over)

Group	%
Total Population	9.9
Hispanic or Latino (of any race)	10.4
Mexican	10.6

Class of Worker: Private Wage and Salary
(Universe: Civilian Employed Population 16 Years and Over)

Group	Number	%
Total Population	14,716	82.8
Hispanic or Latino (of any race)	6,453	83.6
Mexican	5,735	82.9

Class of Worker: Government
(Universe: Civilian Employed Population 16 Years and Over)

Group	Number	%
Total Population	1,635	9.2
Hispanic or Latino (of any race)	481	6.2
Mexican	440	6.4

Means of Transportation to Work: Car, Truck or Van
(Universe: Workers 16 Years and Over)

Group	Number	%
Total Population	15,232	87.4
Hispanic or Latino (of any race)	6,336	83.4
Mexican	5,675	83.1

Means of Transportation to Work: Public Transportation (ex. Taxicab)
(Universe: Workers 16 Years and Over)

Group	Number	%
Total Population	1,030	5.9
Hispanic or Latino (of any race)	615	8.1
Mexican	586	8.6

Homeownership Rate
(Universe: Occupied Housing Units)

Group	%
Total Population	50.1
Hispanic or Latino (of any race)	37.4
Central American, ex. Mexican	42.3
Guatemalan	32.4
Salvadoran	43.9
Cuban	60.6
Mexican	36.1
Puerto Rican	51.3
South American	52.9
Peruvian	41.0
Spaniard	58.5

Median Home Value

Group	Dollars
Total Population	331,300
Hispanic or Latino (of any race)	375,200
Mexican	395,100

Median Gross Rent

Group	Dollars
Total Population	1,227
Hispanic or Latino (of any race)	1,260
Mexican	1,264

Median Household Income
(2010 Inflation-Adjusted Dollars)

Group	Dollars
Total Population	51,539
Hispanic or Latino (of any race)	47,628
Mexican	46,369

Per Capita Income
(2010 Inflation-Adjusted Dollars)

Group	Dollars
Total Population	20,444
Hispanic or Latino (of any race)	13,883
Mexican	13,225

Households with $100,000+ Income

Group	Number	%
Total Population	2,109	18.3
Hispanic or Latino (of any race)	507	12.9
Mexican	374	10.8

Households with Food Stamps/SNAP Benefits During Past 12 Months

Group	Number	%
Total Population	826	7.2
Hispanic or Latino (of any race)	495	12.6
Mexican	451	13.0

Poverty Rate
(Income in Past 12 Months Below Poverty Level)

Group	%
Total Population	15.7
Hispanic or Latino (of any race)	23.3
Mexican	24.2

Stockton

Population

Group	Number	%TP[1]	%HP[2]
Total Population	291,707	100.0	–
Hispanic or Latino (of any race)	117,590	40.3	100.0
Central American, ex. Mexican	3,302	1.1	2.8
Guatemalan	793	0.3	0.7
Honduran	205	0.1	0.2
Nicaraguan	786	0.3	0.7
Panamanian	131	<0.1	0.1
Salvadoran	1,296	0.4	1.1
Cuban	245	0.1	0.2
Mexican	104,172	35.7	88.6
Puerto Rican	1,831	0.6	1.6
South American	962	0.3	0.8
Chilean	207	0.1	0.2
Colombian	211	0.1	0.2
Peruvian	273	0.1	0.2
Spaniard	1,181	0.4	1.0

Population Growth: 2000–2010

Group	%
Total Population	19.7
Hispanic or Latino (of any race)	48.4
Central American, ex. Mexican	207.7
Guatemalan	174.4
Nicaraguan	238.8
Salvadoran	281.2
Cuban	40.0
Mexican	55.7
Puerto Rican	73.4
South American	119.1
Chilean	61.7
Spaniard	594.7

Males per 100 Females

Group	Number
Total Population	96.1
Hispanic or Latino (of any race)	102.0
Central American, ex. Mexican	103.5
Guatemalan	144.8
Honduran	88.1
Nicaraguan	89.4
Panamanian	81.9
Salvadoran	96.4
Cuban	147.5
Mexican	102.7
Puerto Rican	93.3
South American	92.4
Chilean	83.2
Colombian	106.9
Peruvian	89.6
Spaniard	90.5

Average Household Size

Group	People
Total Population	3.16
Hispanic or Latino (of any race)	3.78
Central American, ex. Mexican	3.95
Guatemalan	4.44
Honduran	3.63
Nicaraguan	3.79
Panamanian	3.20
Salvadoran	3.95
Cuban	3.53
Mexican	3.83
Puerto Rican	3.09
South American	3.02
Chilean	2.99
Colombian	3.00
Peruvian	3.49
Spaniard	2.71

Median Age

Group	Years
Total Population	30.8
Hispanic or Latino (of any race)	25.0
Central American, ex. Mexican	30.1
Guatemalan	28.1
Honduran	32.8
Nicaraguan	29.4
Panamanian	30.7
Salvadoran	31.4
Cuban	25.8
Mexican	24.7
Puerto Rican	23.5
South American	37.2
Chilean	41.6
Colombian	34.3
Peruvian	35.1
Spaniard	35.4

High School Graduates
(Universe: Population 25 Years and Over)

Group	Number	%
Total Population	122,738	73.7
Hispanic or Latino (of any race)	31,303	56.7
Central American, ex. Mexican	1,299	58.7
Salvadoran	651	54.1
Mexican	27,147	55.0
Puerto Rican	445	79.9
South American	503	96.0
Spaniard	700	77.5

Four-Year College Graduates
(Universe: Population 25 Years and Over)

Group	Number	%
Total Population	29,458	17.7
Hispanic or Latino (of any race)	3,721	6.7
Central American, ex. Mexican	238	10.8
Salvadoran	64	5.3
Mexican	2,935	5.9
Puerto Rican	104	18.7
South American	112	21.4

Notes: (1) Percent of total population; (2) Percent of Hispanic/Latino population; Profiles include places with an overall population of at least 125,000, OR an overall population of at least 25,000 where the Hispanic/Latino population is at least 20% of the overall population. In states where less than five places meet either of these criteria, we have included places with at least 10,000 total population with the highest percentage of Hispanic/Latino population. These places are identified with an asterisk (*); Please refer to the User's Guide for a full explanation of data.

Group	Number	%
Spaniard	144	15.9

Population Age 3–17 Enrolled in Public School
(Universe: Population Age 3–17 Enrolled in School)

Group	Number	%
Total Population	59,951	91.9
Hispanic or Latino (of any race)	28,991	93.7
Central American, ex. Mexican	805	82.1
Salvadoran	467	88.4
Mexican	26,123	94.2
Puerto Rican	282	84.9
South American	187	100.0
Spaniard	234	85.4

Population Age 3–17 Enrolled in Private School
(Universe: Population Age 3–17 Enrolled in School)

Group	Number	%
Total Population	5,255	8.1
Hispanic or Latino (of any race)	1,950	6.3
Central American, ex. Mexican	176	17.9
Salvadoran	61	11.6
Mexican	1,612	5.8
Puerto Rican	50	15.1
South American	0	0.0
Spaniard	40	14.6

Foreign-Born Population

Group	Number	%
Total Population	77,736	27.1
Hispanic or Latino (of any race)	37,229	33.4
Central American, ex. Mexican	2,193	58.7
Salvadoran	1,210	59.2
Mexican	33,887	33.8
Puerto Rican	0	0.0
South American	518	54.9
Spaniard	153	10.8

Foreign-Born Naturalized U.S. Citizens

Group	Number	%
Total Population	33,377	42.9
Hispanic or Latino (of any race)	9,555	25.7
Central American, ex. Mexican	862	39.3
Salvadoran	402	33.2
Mexican	8,130	24.0
Puerto Rican	0	0.0
South American	306	59.1
Spaniard	75	49.0

Language Spoken at Home: English Only
(Universe: Population 5 Years and Over)

Group	Number	%
Total Population	144,880	55.3
Hispanic or Latino (of any race)	33,277	33.7
Central American, ex. Mexican	387	11.2
Salvadoran	188	9.9
Mexican	28,750	32.5
Puerto Rican	743	67.3
South American	128	15.8
Spaniard	1,056	80.9

Language Spoken at Home: Spanish
(Universe: Population 5 Years and Over)

Group	Number	%
Total Population	67,074	25.6
Hispanic or Latino (of any race)	65,002	65.9
Central American, ex. Mexican	3,075	88.8
Salvadoran	1,703	90.1
Mexican	59,601	67.3
Puerto Rican	354	32.1
South American	684	84.2
Spaniard	167	12.8

Unemployment Rate
(Universe: Population 16 Years and Over)

Group	%
Total Population	13.9
Hispanic or Latino (of any race)	15.5
Central American, ex. Mexican	13.7
Salvadoran	5.9
Mexican	15.7
Puerto Rican	8.3
South American	8.1
Spaniard	21.8

Class of Worker: Private Wage and Salary
(Universe: Civilian Employed Population 16 Years and Over)

Group	Number	%
Total Population	85,051	76.3
Hispanic or Latino (of any race)	34,259	81.3
Central American, ex. Mexican	1,472	82.4
Salvadoran	885	84.8
Mexican	30,828	81.9
Puerto Rican	426	81.9
South American	292	82.5
Spaniard	326	56.9

Class of Worker: Government
(Universe: Civilian Employed Population 16 Years and Over)

Group	Number	%
Total Population	18,978	17.0
Hispanic or Latino (of any race)	5,468	13.0
Central American, ex. Mexican	163	9.1
Salvadoran	105	10.1
Mexican	4,672	12.4
Puerto Rican	85	16.3
South American	44	12.4
Spaniard	218	38.0

Means of Transportation to Work: Car, Truck or Van
(Universe: Workers 16 Years and Over)

Group	Number	%
Total Population	98,176	91.5
Hispanic or Latino (of any race)	37,467	92.2
Central American, ex. Mexican	1,592	90.8
Salvadoran	944	91.3
Mexican	33,498	92.3
Puerto Rican	459	91.4
South American	307	89.5
Spaniard	561	94.8

Means of Transportation to Work: Public Transportation (ex. Taxicab)
(Universe: Workers 16 Years and Over)

Group	Number	%
Total Population	1,426	1.3
Hispanic or Latino (of any race)	578	1.4
Central American, ex. Mexican	20	1.1
Salvadoran	20	1.9
Mexican	479	1.3
Puerto Rican	8	1.6
South American	12	3.5
Spaniard	19	3.2

Homeownership Rate
(Universe: Occupied Housing Units)

Group	%
Total Population	51.6
Hispanic or Latino (of any race)	45.3
Central American, ex. Mexican	47.6
Guatemalan	34.4
Honduran	39.7
Nicaraguan	51.9
Panamanian	61.0
Salvadoran	52.2
Cuban	41.4
Mexican	45.4
Puerto Rican	38.7
South American	59.7
Chilean	54.7
Colombian	56.3
Peruvian	61.8
Spaniard	57.0

Median Home Value

Group	Dollars
Total Population	276,600
Hispanic or Latino (of any race)	245,000
Central American, ex. Mexican	203,800
Salvadoran	231,100
Mexican	242,700
Puerto Rican	183,400
South American	235,000
Spaniard	328,800

Median Gross Rent

Group	Dollars
Total Population	917
Hispanic or Latino (of any race)	870
Central American, ex. Mexican	972
Salvadoran	1,280
Mexican	862
Puerto Rican	936
South American	1,276
Spaniard	877

Median Household Income
(2010 Inflation-Adjusted Dollars)

Group	Dollars
Total Population	47,946
Hispanic or Latino (of any race)	42,182
Central American, ex. Mexican	50,403
Salvadoran	60,042
Mexican	41,171
Puerto Rican	57,750
South American	47,500
Spaniard	57,000

Per Capita Income
(2010 Inflation-Adjusted Dollars)

Group	Dollars
Total Population	20,176
Hispanic or Latino (of any race)	13,917
Central American, ex. Mexican	18,042
Salvadoran	17,296
Mexican	13,553
Puerto Rican	24,182
South American	15,221
Spaniard	23,328

Households with $100,000+ Income

Group	Number	%
Total Population	15,365	17.0
Hispanic or Latino (of any race)	3,052	10.6
Central American, ex. Mexican	194	17.3
Salvadoran	136	22.5
Mexican	2,461	9.7
Puerto Rican	85	18.8
South American	9	3.0
Spaniard	160	26.4

Households with Food Stamps/SNAP Benefits During Past 12 Months

Group	Number	%
Total Population	10,131	11.2
Hispanic or Latino (of any race)	3,700	12.9
Central American, ex. Mexican	72	6.4
Salvadoran	20	3.3
Mexican	3,186	12.6
Puerto Rican	77	17.1
South American	25	8.3
Spaniard	21	3.5

Poverty Rate
(Income in Past 12 Months Below Poverty Level)

Group	%
Total Population	19.8
Hispanic or Latino (of any race)	23.3
Central American, ex. Mexican	17.7
Salvadoran	13.4
Mexican	23.6
Puerto Rican	20.0
South American	28.7
Spaniard	12.9

Suisun City

Population

Group	Number	%TP[1]	%HP[2]
Total Population	28,111	100.0	–
Hispanic or Latino (of any race)	6,753	24.0	100.0
Central American, ex. Mexican	600	2.1	8.9
Nicaraguan	156	0.6	2.3
Salvadoran	302	1.1	4.5
Mexican	5,040	17.9	74.6
Puerto Rican	344	1.2	5.1
South American	132	0.5	2.0
Spaniard	164	0.6	2.4

Population Growth: 2000–2010

Group	%
Total Population	7.6
Hispanic or Latino (of any race)	45.2

Notes: (1) Percent of total population; (2) Percent of Hispanic/Latino population; Profiles include places with an overall population of at least 125,000, OR an overall population of at least 25,000 where the Hispanic/Latino population is at least 20% of the overall population. In states where less than five places meet either of these criteria, we have included places with at least 10,000 total population with the highest percentage of Hispanic/Latino population. These places are identified with an asterisk (*); Please refer to the User's Guide for a full explanation of data.

Central American, ex. Mexican		94.2
Mexican		65.7
Puerto Rican		39.8

Males per 100 Females

Group	Number
Total Population	96.9
Hispanic or Latino (of any race)	100.0
Central American, ex. Mexican	92.3
Nicaraguan	85.7
Salvadoran	100.0
Mexican	104.9
Puerto Rican	102.4
South American	65.0
Spaniard	69.1

Average Household Size

Group	People
Total Population	3.15
Hispanic or Latino (of any race)	3.87
Central American, ex. Mexican	3.57
Nicaraguan	3.59
Salvadoran	3.60
Mexican	4.08
Puerto Rican	3.28
South American	3.33
Spaniard	2.88

Median Age

Group	Years
Total Population	33.0
Hispanic or Latino (of any race)	25.1
Central American, ex. Mexican	33.5
Nicaraguan	30.0
Salvadoran	32.0
Mexican	23.8
Puerto Rican	25.7
South American	29.5
Spaniard	33.5

High School Graduates
(Universe: Population 25 Years and Over)

Group	Number	%
Total Population	14,709	86.1
Hispanic or Latino (of any race)	2,100	64.5
Mexican	1,536	59.9

Four-Year College Graduates
(Universe: Population 25 Years and Over)

Group	Number	%
Total Population	3,298	19.3
Hispanic or Latino (of any race)	276	8.5
Mexican	199	7.8

Population Age 3–17 Enrolled in Public School
(Universe: Population Age 3–17 Enrolled in School)

Group	Number	%
Total Population	5,361	89.7
Hispanic or Latino (of any race)	1,847	94.4
Mexican	1,255	93.6

Population Age 3–17 Enrolled in Private School
(Universe: Population Age 3–17 Enrolled in School)

Group	Number	%
Total Population	613	10.3
Hispanic or Latino (of any race)	109	5.6
Mexican	86	6.4

Foreign-Born Population

Group	Number	%
Total Population	6,336	22.8
Hispanic or Latino (of any race)	2,383	34.1
Mexican	2,016	36.6

Foreign-Born Naturalized U.S. Citizens

Group	Number	%
Total Population	3,533	55.8
Hispanic or Latino (of any race)	718	30.1
Mexican	435	21.6

Language Spoken at Home: English Only
(Universe: Population 5 Years and Over)

Group	Number	%
Total Population	16,913	65.5
Hispanic or Latino (of any race)	1,728	27.7
Mexican	1,021	21.3

Language Spoken at Home: Spanish
(Universe: Population 5 Years and Over)

Group	Number	%
Total Population	4,675	18.1
Hispanic or Latino (of any race)	4,510	72.3
Mexican	3,762	78.7

Unemployment Rate
(Universe: Population 16 Years and Over)

Group	%
Total Population	9.3
Hispanic or Latino (of any race)	10.7
Mexican	9.3

Class of Worker: Private Wage and Salary
(Universe: Civilian Employed Population 16 Years and Over)

Group	Number	%
Total Population	9,693	73.7
Hispanic or Latino (of any race)	2,552	84.7
Mexican	2,243	89.3

Class of Worker: Government
(Universe: Civilian Employed Population 16 Years and Over)

Group	Number	%
Total Population	2,919	22.2
Hispanic or Latino (of any race)	373	12.4
Mexican	230	9.2

Means of Transportation to Work: Car, Truck or Van
(Universe: Workers 16 Years and Over)

Group	Number	%
Total Population	12,271	93.4
Hispanic or Latino (of any race)	2,931	97.1
Mexican	2,528	98.4

Means of Transportation to Work: Public Transportation (ex. Taxicab)
(Universe: Workers 16 Years and Over)

Group	Number	%
Total Population	347	2.6
Hispanic or Latino (of any race)	20	0.7
Mexican	0	0.0

Homeownership Rate
(Universe: Occupied Housing Units)

Group	%
Total Population	69.3
Hispanic or Latino (of any race)	66.4
Central American, ex. Mexican	82.2
Nicaraguan	78.4
Salvadoran	80.2
Mexican	66.2
Puerto Rican	54.1
South American	89.7
Spaniard	67.9

Median Home Value

Group	Dollars
Total Population	341,400
Hispanic or Latino (of any race)	345,200
Mexican	335,500

Median Gross Rent

Group	Dollars
Total Population	1,320
Hispanic or Latino (of any race)	1,459
Mexican	1,384

Median Household Income
(2010 Inflation-Adjusted Dollars)

Group	Dollars
Total Population	71,795
Hispanic or Latino (of any race)	64,355
Mexican	75,640

Per Capita Income
(2010 Inflation-Adjusted Dollars)

Group	Dollars
Total Population	25,166
Hispanic or Latino (of any race)	17,413
Mexican	17,988

Households with $100,000+ Income

Group	Number	%
Total Population	2,194	25.3
Hispanic or Latino (of any race)	377	25.0
Mexican	346	29.6

Households with Food Stamps/SNAP Benefits During Past 12 Months

Group	Number	%
Total Population	456	5.3
Hispanic or Latino (of any race)	134	8.9
Mexican	106	9.1

Poverty Rate
(Income in Past 12 Months Below Poverty Level)

Group	%
Total Population	8.9
Hispanic or Latino (of any race)	4.3
Mexican	5.0

Sunnyvale

Population

Group	Number	%TP[1]	%HP[2]
Total Population	140,081	100.0	–
Hispanic or Latino (of any race)	26,517	18.9	100.0
Central American, ex. Mexican	2,609	1.9	9.8
Guatemalan	684	0.5	2.6
Nicaraguan	289	0.2	1.1
Salvadoran	1,460	1.0	5.5
Cuban	116	0.1	0.4
Mexican	19,939	14.2	75.2
Puerto Rican	559	0.4	2.1
South American	1,241	0.9	4.7
Argentinean	125	0.1	0.5
Colombian	207	0.1	0.8
Peruvian	607	0.4	2.3
Spaniard	672	0.5	2.5

Population Growth: 2000–2010

Group	%
Total Population	6.3
Hispanic or Latino (of any race)	30.0
Central American, ex. Mexican	138.7
Guatemalan	168.2
Nicaraguan	167.6
Salvadoran	177.0
Cuban	-10.1
Mexican	38.4
Puerto Rican	23.7
South American	72.8
Colombian	81.6
Peruvian	105.8
Spaniard	373.2

Males per 100 Females

Group	Number
Total Population	101.5
Hispanic or Latino (of any race)	105.1
Central American, ex. Mexican	110.2
Guatemalan	129.5
Nicaraguan	79.5
Salvadoran	111.6
Cuban	110.9
Mexican	106.0
Puerto Rican	104.0
South American	91.8
Argentinean	98.4
Colombian	78.4
Peruvian	98.4
Spaniard	89.8

Average Household Size

Group	People
Total Population	2.61
Hispanic or Latino (of any race)	3.58
Central American, ex. Mexican	3.91
Guatemalan	4.19
Nicaraguan	3.55
Salvadoran	4.03
Cuban	2.38
Mexican	3.81
Puerto Rican	2.35
South American	2.82
Argentinean	2.94
Colombian	2.57
Peruvian	3.14

Notes: (1) Percent of total population; (2) Percent of Hispanic/Latino population; Profiles include places with an overall population of at least 125,000, OR an overall population of at least 25,000 where the Hispanic/Latino population is at least 20% of the overall population. In states where less than five places meet either of these criteria, we have included places with at least 10,000 total population with the highest percentage of Hispanic/Latino population. These places are identified with an asterisk (*); Please refer to the User's Guide for a full explanation of data.

Group	Years
Spaniard	2.25

Median Age

Group	Years
Total Population	35.6
Hispanic or Latino (of any race)	28.8
Central American, ex. Mexican	31.2
Guatemalan	30.1
Nicaraguan	34.5
Salvadoran	31.1
Cuban	41.5
Mexican	27.3
Puerto Rican	31.6
South American	37.3
Argentinean	38.5
Colombian	33.6
Peruvian	36.8
Spaniard	46.3

High School Graduates
(Universe: Population 25 Years and Over)

Group	Number	%
Total Population	88,846	90.9
Hispanic or Latino (of any race)	7,814	60.5
Central American, ex. Mexican	1,183	65.8
Salvadoran	615	51.7
Mexican	4,765	54.2
South American	804	79.5

Four-Year College Graduates
(Universe: Population 25 Years and Over)

Group	Number	%
Total Population	54,868	56.1
Hispanic or Latino (of any race)	1,917	14.9
Central American, ex. Mexican	333	18.5
Salvadoran	92	7.7
Mexican	777	8.8
South American	470	46.5

Population Age 3–17 Enrolled in Public School
(Universe: Population Age 3–17 Enrolled in School)

Group	Number	%
Total Population	15,998	76.1
Hispanic or Latino (of any race)	5,211	93.5
Central American, ex. Mexican	507	89.9
Salvadoran	229	83.3
Mexican	4,221	95.7
South American	199	78.0

Population Age 3–17 Enrolled in Private School
(Universe: Population Age 3–17 Enrolled in School)

Group	Number	%
Total Population	5,021	23.9
Hispanic or Latino (of any race)	365	6.5
Central American, ex. Mexican	57	10.1
Salvadoran	46	16.7
Mexican	188	4.3
South American	56	22.0

Foreign-Born Population

Group	Number	%
Total Population	59,957	43.9
Hispanic or Latino (of any race)	11,131	48.4
Central American, ex. Mexican	1,965	62.3
Salvadoran	1,294	68.5
Mexican	7,844	47.7
South American	900	63.0

Foreign-Born Naturalized U.S. Citizens

Group	Number	%
Total Population	23,789	39.7
Hispanic or Latino (of any race)	2,858	25.7
Central American, ex. Mexican	879	44.7
Salvadoran	434	33.5
Mexican	1,172	14.9
South American	518	57.6

Language Spoken at Home: English Only
(Universe: Population 5 Years and Over)

Group	Number	%
Total Population	58,928	47.1
Hispanic or Latino (of any race)	4,498	21.8
Central American, ex. Mexican	385	13.2
Salvadoran	131	7.6
Mexican	2,826	19.3
South American	258	19.7

Language Spoken at Home: Spanish
(Universe: Population 5 Years and Over)

Group	Number	%
Total Population	17,096	13.7
Hispanic or Latino (of any race)	15,874	76.9
Central American, ex. Mexican	2,535	86.8
Salvadoran	1,587	92.4
Mexican	11,728	80.1
South American	1,047	79.9

Unemployment Rate
(Universe: Population 16 Years and Over)

Group	%
Total Population	6.6
Hispanic or Latino (of any race)	6.4
Central American, ex. Mexican	5.5
Salvadoran	3.6
Mexican	5.1
South American	8.9

Class of Worker: Private Wage and Salary
(Universe: Civilian Employed Population 16 Years and Over)

Group	Number	%
Total Population	61,699	87.0
Hispanic or Latino (of any race)	9,379	87.2
Central American, ex. Mexican	1,454	88.7
Salvadoran	928	86.2
Mexican	6,615	87.0
South American	578	79.7

Class of Worker: Government
(Universe: Civilian Employed Population 16 Years and Over)

Group	Number	%
Total Population	4,903	6.9
Hispanic or Latino (of any race)	557	5.2
Central American, ex. Mexican	67	4.1
Salvadoran	43	4.0
Mexican	343	4.5
South American	111	15.3

Means of Transportation to Work: Car, Truck or Van
(Universe: Workers 16 Years and Over)

Group	Number	%
Total Population	60,483	87.3
Hispanic or Latino (of any race)	8,686	82.6
Central American, ex. Mexican	1,347	83.1
Salvadoran	882	82.7
Mexican	5,999	80.7
South American	655	91.7

Means of Transportation to Work: Public Transportation (ex. Taxicab)
(Universe: Workers 16 Years and Over)

Group	Number	%
Total Population	3,182	4.6
Hispanic or Latino (of any race)	808	7.7
Central American, ex. Mexican	179	11.0
Salvadoran	168	15.8
Mexican	599	8.1
South American	17	2.4

Homeownership Rate
(Universe: Occupied Housing Units)

Group	%
Total Population	48.0
Hispanic or Latino (of any race)	31.7
Central American, ex. Mexican	29.7
Guatemalan	24.6
Nicaraguan	40.2
Salvadoran	31.1
Cuban	58.2
Mexican	28.2
Puerto Rican	35.4
South American	39.2
Argentinean	46.0
Colombian	32.4
Peruvian	35.8
Spaniard	66.6

Median Home Value

Group	Dollars
Total Population	707,900
Hispanic or Latino (of any race)	608,100
Central American, ex. Mexican	582,500
Salvadoran	617,300
Mexican	623,200
South American	636,700

Median Gross Rent

Group	Dollars
Total Population	1,429
Hispanic or Latino (of any race)	1,211
Central American, ex. Mexican	1,147
Salvadoran	1,211
Mexican	1,170
South American	1,682

Median Household Income
(2010 Inflation-Adjusted Dollars)

Group	Dollars
Total Population	90,174
Hispanic or Latino (of any race)	58,327
Central American, ex. Mexican	64,975
Salvadoran	64,976
Mexican	54,085
South American	71,370

Per Capita Income
(2010 Inflation-Adjusted Dollars)

Group	Dollars
Total Population	43,828
Hispanic or Latino (of any race)	20,184
Central American, ex. Mexican	19,051
Salvadoran	19,470
Mexican	17,243
South American	34,323

Households with $100,000+ Income

Group	Number	%
Total Population	23,997	44.9
Hispanic or Latino (of any race)	1,421	23.5
Central American, ex. Mexican	108	15.3
Salvadoran	27	5.7
Mexican	960	23.1
South American	160	34.4

Households with Food Stamps/SNAP Benefits During Past 12 Months

Group	Number	%
Total Population	1,235	2.3
Hispanic or Latino (of any race)	462	7.6
Central American, ex. Mexican	38	5.4
Salvadoran	22	4.7
Mexican	390	9.4
South American	0	0.0

Poverty Rate
(Income in Past 12 Months Below Poverty Level)

Group	%
Total Population	6.2
Hispanic or Latino (of any race)	11.3
Central American, ex. Mexican	2.8
Salvadoran	0.6
Mexican	14.7
South American	3.2

Temecula

Population

Group	Number	%TP[1]	%HP[2]
Total Population	100,097	100.0	–
Hispanic or Latino (of any race)	24,727	24.7	100.0
Central American, ex. Mexican	1,027	1.0	4.2
Guatemalan	334	0.3	1.4
Salvadoran	368	0.4	1.5
Cuban	249	0.2	1.0
Mexican	19,928	19.9	80.6
Puerto Rican	970	1.0	3.9
South American	848	0.8	3.4
Argentinean	131	0.1	0.5
Colombian	219	0.2	0.9
Ecuadorian	109	0.1	0.4
Peruvian	205	0.2	0.8
Spaniard	462	0.5	1.9

Population Growth: 2000–2010

Group	%
Total Population	73.4

Notes: (1) Percent of total population; (2) Percent of Hispanic/Latino population; Profiles include places with an overall population of at least 125,000, OR an overall population of at least 25,000 where the Hispanic/Latino population is at least 20% of the overall population. In states where less than five places meet either of these criteria, we have included places with at least 10,000 total population with the highest percentage of Hispanic/Latino population. These places are identified with an asterisk (*); Please refer to the User's Guide for a full explanation of data.

Hispanic or Latino (of any race)	125.3
Central American, ex. Mexican	261.6
Cuban	100.8
Mexican	136.1
Puerto Rican	117.0
South American	363.4

Males per 100 Females

Group	Number
Total Population	95.9
Hispanic or Latino (of any race)	94.5
Central American, ex. Mexican	92.0
Guatemalan	125.7
Salvadoran	101.1
Cuban	85.8
Mexican	95.9
Puerto Rican	89.5
South American	83.5
Argentinean	95.5
Colombian	58.7
Ecuadorian	84.7
Peruvian	109.2
Spaniard	89.3

Average Household Size

Group	People
Total Population	3.15
Hispanic or Latino (of any race)	3.66
Central American, ex. Mexican	3.90
Guatemalan	4.29
Salvadoran	3.98
Cuban	3.06
Mexican	3.74
Puerto Rican	3.22
South American	3.28
Argentinean	3.10
Colombian	3.16
Ecuadorian	3.59
Peruvian	3.30
Spaniard	3.08

Median Age

Group	Years
Total Population	33.4
Hispanic or Latino (of any race)	25.6
Central American, ex. Mexican	30.0
Guatemalan	28.7
Salvadoran	31.0
Cuban	31.9
Mexican	24.9
Puerto Rican	25.9
South American	35.8
Argentinean	41.8
Colombian	31.5
Ecuadorian	39.3
Peruvian	34.8
Spaniard	30.3

High School Graduates
(Universe: Population 25 Years and Over)

Group	Number	%
Total Population	52,051	91.9
Hispanic or Latino (of any race)	8,483	78.2
Mexican	6,345	73.8
Puerto Rican	457	100.0

Four-Year College Graduates
(Universe: Population 25 Years and Over)

Group	Number	%
Total Population	17,563	31.0
Hispanic or Latino (of any race)	2,078	19.2
Mexican	1,308	15.2
Puerto Rican	201	44.0

Population Age 3–17 Enrolled in Public School
(Universe: Population Age 3–17 Enrolled in School)

Group	Number	%
Total Population	20,090	85.8
Hispanic or Latino (of any race)	6,545	90.7
Mexican	5,441	89.7
Puerto Rican	333	97.1

Population Age 3–17 Enrolled in Private School
(Universe: Population Age 3–17 Enrolled in School)

Group	Number	%
Total Population	3,328	14.2
Hispanic or Latino (of any race)	673	9.3
Mexican	622	10.3
Puerto Rican	10	2.9

Foreign-Born Population

Group	Number	%
Total Population	14,506	15.1
Hispanic or Latino (of any race)	5,836	25.5
Mexican	4,862	25.8
Puerto Rican	0	0.0

Foreign-Born Naturalized U.S. Citizens

Group	Number	%
Total Population	7,149	49.3
Hispanic or Latino (of any race)	2,217	38.0
Mexican	1,686	34.7
Puerto Rican	0	0.0

Language Spoken at Home: English Only
(Universe: Population 5 Years and Over)

Group	Number	%
Total Population	68,218	77.5
Hispanic or Latino (of any race)	9,680	47.2
Mexican	7,768	46.3
Puerto Rican	511	58.1

Language Spoken at Home: Spanish
(Universe: Population 5 Years and Over)

Group	Number	%
Total Population	11,651	13.2
Hispanic or Latino (of any race)	10,688	52.1
Mexican	8,871	52.8
Puerto Rican	368	41.9

Unemployment Rate
(Universe: Population 16 Years and Over)

Group	%
Total Population	8.7
Hispanic or Latino (of any race)	8.1
Mexican	6.6
Puerto Rican	14.6

Class of Worker: Private Wage and Salary
(Universe: Civilian Employed Population 16 Years and Over)

Group	Number	%
Total Population	33,305	75.5
Hispanic or Latino (of any race)	7,440	78.8
Mexican	6,134	78.5
Puerto Rican	248	66.5

Class of Worker: Government
(Universe: Civilian Employed Population 16 Years and Over)

Group	Number	%
Total Population	7,325	16.6
Hispanic or Latino (of any race)	1,508	16.0
Mexican	1,245	15.9
Puerto Rican	113	30.3

Means of Transportation to Work: Car, Truck or Van
(Universe: Workers 16 Years and Over)

Group	Number	%
Total Population	39,721	90.4
Hispanic or Latino (of any race)	8,456	91.5
Mexican	6,974	90.8
Puerto Rican	392	97.0

Means of Transportation to Work: Public Transportation (ex. Taxicab)
(Universe: Workers 16 Years and Over)

Group	Number	%
Total Population	166	0.4
Hispanic or Latino (of any race)	37	0.4
Mexican	37	0.5
Puerto Rican	0	0.0

Homeownership Rate
(Universe: Occupied Housing Units)

Group	%
Total Population	69.2
Hispanic or Latino (of any race)	58.7
Central American, ex. Mexican	50.4
Guatemalan	48.2
Salvadoran	47.6
Cuban	70.4
Mexican	58.3
Puerto Rican	58.2
South American	66.5
Argentinean	72.5
Colombian	51.7
Ecuadorian	79.3
Peruvian	61.4
Spaniard	69.9

Median Home Value

Group	Dollars
Total Population	384,200
Hispanic or Latino (of any race)	378,700
Mexican	365,000
Puerto Rican	450,000

Median Gross Rent

Group	Dollars
Total Population	1,398
Hispanic or Latino (of any race)	1,318
Mexican	1,239
Puerto Rican	1,571

Median Household Income
(2010 Inflation-Adjusted Dollars)

Group	Dollars
Total Population	77,850
Hispanic or Latino (of any race)	62,269
Mexican	60,655
Puerto Rican	86,458

Per Capita Income
(2010 Inflation-Adjusted Dollars)

Group	Dollars
Total Population	29,089
Hispanic or Latino (of any race)	18,405
Mexican	16,773
Puerto Rican	29,458

Households with $100,000+ Income

Group	Number	%
Total Population	10,603	34.9
Hispanic or Latino (of any race)	1,345	25.3
Mexican	946	23.4
Puerto Rican	115	43.9

Households with Food Stamps/SNAP Benefits During Past 12 Months

Group	Number	%
Total Population	517	1.7
Hispanic or Latino (of any race)	163	3.1
Mexican	163	4.0
Puerto Rican	0	0.0

Poverty Rate
(Income in Past 12 Months Below Poverty Level)

Group	%
Total Population	8.2
Hispanic or Latino (of any race)	11.6
Mexican	13.0
Puerto Rican	1.2

Thousand Oaks

Population

Group	Number	%TP[1]	%HP[2]
Total Population	126,683	100.0	–
Hispanic or Latino (of any race)	21,341	16.8	100.0
Central American, ex. Mexican	2,441	1.9	11.4
Guatemalan	1,173	0.9	5.5
Honduran	102	0.1	0.5
Nicaraguan	231	0.2	1.1
Salvadoran	793	0.6	3.7
Cuban	280	0.2	1.3
Mexican	14,671	11.6	68.7
Puerto Rican	466	0.4	2.2
South American	1,325	1.0	6.2
Argentinean	278	0.2	1.3
Chilean	112	0.1	0.5
Colombian	285	0.2	1.3
Ecuadorian	145	0.1	0.7

Notes: (1) Percent of total population; (2) Percent of Hispanic/Latino population; Profiles include places with an overall population of at least 125,000, OR an overall population of at least 25,000 where the Hispanic/Latino population is at least 20% of the overall population. In states where less than five places meet either of these criteria, we have included places with at least 10,000 total population with the highest percentage of Hispanic/Latino population. These places are identified with an asterisk (*); Please refer to the User's Guide for a full explanation of data.

Peruvian	390	0.3	1.8
Spaniard	489	0.4	2.3

Population Growth: 2000–2010

Group	%
Total Population	8.3
Hispanic or Latino (of any race)	39.2
Central American, ex. Mexican	96.2
Guatemalan	132.7
Nicaraguan	79.1
Salvadoran	112.6
Cuban	25.0
Mexican	45.3
Puerto Rican	43.8
South American	105.4
Argentinean	89.1
Colombian	108.0
Peruvian	121.6

Males per 100 Females

Group	Number
Total Population	95.8
Hispanic or Latino (of any race)	102.0
Central American, ex. Mexican	101.1
Guatemalan	115.6
Honduran	112.5
Nicaraguan	97.4
Salvadoran	92.9
Cuban	102.9
Mexican	105.0
Puerto Rican	82.0
South American	80.0
Argentinean	89.1
Chilean	89.8
Colombian	70.7
Ecuadorian	72.6
Peruvian	81.4
Spaniard	88.8

Average Household Size

Group	People
Total Population	2.73
Hispanic or Latino (of any race)	3.90
Central American, ex. Mexican	4.32
Guatemalan	4.70
Honduran	4.33
Nicaraguan	4.09
Salvadoran	4.11
Cuban	2.44
Mexican	4.14
Puerto Rican	2.99
South American	3.03
Argentinean	3.08
Chilean	2.49
Colombian	2.81
Ecuadorian	3.17
Peruvian	3.36
Spaniard	2.83

Median Age

Group	Years
Total Population	41.5
Hispanic or Latino (of any race)	28.6
Central American, ex. Mexican	31.9
Guatemalan	30.2
Honduran	31.0
Nicaraguan	32.8
Salvadoran	33.9
Cuban	43.4
Mexican	27.1
Puerto Rican	34.4
South American	40.6
Argentinean	41.2
Chilean	43.7
Colombian	42.1
Ecuadorian	40.2
Peruvian	38.7
Spaniard	39.1

High School Graduates
(Universe: Population 25 Years and Over)

Group	Number	%
Total Population	77,684	93.7
Hispanic or Latino (of any race)	7,778	71.5
Central American, ex. Mexican	826	56.7
Mexican	5,115	68.9
South American	875	89.6

Four-Year College Graduates
(Universe: Population 25 Years and Over)

Group	Number	%
Total Population	40,007	48.2
Hispanic or Latino (of any race)	2,635	24.2
Central American, ex. Mexican	227	15.6
Mexican	1,415	19.1
South American	494	50.6

Population Age 3–17 Enrolled in Public School
(Universe: Population Age 3–17 Enrolled in School)

Group	Number	%
Total Population	21,542	81.8
Hispanic or Latino (of any race)	5,232	89.2
Central American, ex. Mexican	523	94.9
Mexican	4,152	89.6
South American	207	81.8

Population Age 3–17 Enrolled in Private School
(Universe: Population Age 3–17 Enrolled in School)

Group	Number	%
Total Population	4,801	18.2
Hispanic or Latino (of any race)	635	10.8
Central American, ex. Mexican	28	5.1
Mexican	481	10.4
South American	46	18.2

Foreign-Born Population

Group	Number	%
Total Population	23,815	19.1
Hispanic or Latino (of any race)	8,136	39.6
Central American, ex. Mexican	1,422	55.8
Mexican	5,481	36.9
South American	841	57.8

Foreign-Born Naturalized U.S. Citizens

Group	Number	%
Total Population	12,079	50.7
Hispanic or Latino (of any race)	2,432	29.9
Central American, ex. Mexican	569	40.0
Mexican	1,199	21.9
South American	459	54.6

Language Spoken at Home: English Only
(Universe: Population 5 Years and Over)

Group	Number	%
Total Population	90,531	76.9
Hispanic or Latino (of any race)	6,293	33.4
Central American, ex. Mexican	328	14.2
Mexican	4,559	33.4
South American	453	34.3

Language Spoken at Home: Spanish
(Universe: Population 5 Years and Over)

Group	Number	%
Total Population	14,187	12.1
Hispanic or Latino (of any race)	12,510	66.3
Central American, ex. Mexican	1,979	85.8
Mexican	9,080	66.5
South American	866	65.7

Unemployment Rate
(Universe: Population 16 Years and Over)

Group	%
Total Population	6.3
Hispanic or Latino (of any race)	7.7
Central American, ex. Mexican	11.9
Mexican	6.3
South American	8.8

Class of Worker: Private Wage and Salary
(Universe: Civilian Employed Population 16 Years and Over)

Group	Number	%
Total Population	48,496	78.4
Hispanic or Latino (of any race)	8,113	83.5
Central American, ex. Mexican	1,090	85.8
Mexican	5,776	83.3
South American	730	90.2

Class of Worker: Government
(Universe: Civilian Employed Population 16 Years and Over)

Group	Number	%
Total Population	6,584	10.6
Hispanic or Latino (of any race)	803	8.3
Central American, ex. Mexican	40	3.1
Mexican	587	8.5
South American	43	5.3

Means of Transportation to Work: Car, Truck or Van
(Universe: Workers 16 Years and Over)

Group	Number	%
Total Population	53,479	88.9
Hispanic or Latino (of any race)	8,168	86.6
Central American, ex. Mexican	1,004	82.6
Mexican	5,954	87.1
South American	682	90.1

Means of Transportation to Work: Public Transportation (ex. Taxicab)
(Universe: Workers 16 Years and Over)

Group	Number	%
Total Population	396	0.7
Hispanic or Latino (of any race)	120	1.3
Central American, ex. Mexican	17	1.4
Mexican	103	1.5
South American	0	0.0

Homeownership Rate
(Universe: Occupied Housing Units)

Group	%
Total Population	73.1
Hispanic or Latino (of any race)	52.5
Central American, ex. Mexican	41.1
Guatemalan	37.0
Honduran	38.1
Nicaraguan	34.5
Salvadoran	44.3
Cuban	62.2
Mexican	51.7
Puerto Rican	61.2
South American	62.8
Argentinean	67.4
Chilean	65.9
Colombian	64.7
Ecuadorian	66.7
Peruvian	56.7
Spaniard	76.7

Median Home Value

Group	Dollars
Total Population	673,500
Hispanic or Latino (of any race)	597,300
Central American, ex. Mexican	510,700
Mexican	601,500
South American	587,500

Median Gross Rent

Group	Dollars
Total Population	1,731
Hispanic or Latino (of any race)	1,578
Central American, ex. Mexican	1,586
Mexican	1,517
South American	2,000+

Median Household Income
(2010 Inflation-Adjusted Dollars)

Group	Dollars
Total Population	98,713
Hispanic or Latino (of any race)	75,306
Central American, ex. Mexican	44,833
Mexican	72,003
South American	99,755

Per Capita Income
(2010 Inflation-Adjusted Dollars)

Group	Dollars
Total Population	44,775
Hispanic or Latino (of any race)	23,975
Central American, ex. Mexican	17,293
Mexican	20,485
South American	36,014

Households with $100,000+ Income

Group	Number	%
Total Population	21,933	49.4
Hispanic or Latino (of any race)	1,624	34.4
Central American, ex. Mexican	155	21.8
Mexican	949	32.1

Notes: (1) Percent of total population; (2) Percent of Hispanic/Latino population; Profiles include places with an overall population of at least 125,000, OR an overall population of at least 25,000 where the Hispanic/Latino population is at least 20% of the overall population. In states where less than five places meet either of these criteria, we have included places with at least 10,000 total population with the highest percentage of Hispanic/Latino population. These places are identified with an asterisk (*); Please refer to the User's Guide for a full explanation of data.

South American	243	49.0

Households with Food Stamps/SNAP Benefits During Past 12 Months

Group	Number	%
Total Population	648	1.5
Hispanic or Latino (of any race)	234	5.0
Central American, ex. Mexican	70	9.9
Mexican	152	5.1
South American	0	0.0

Poverty Rate
(Income in Past 12 Months Below Poverty Level)

Group	%
Total Population	5.1
Hispanic or Latino (of any race)	12.6
Central American, ex. Mexican	11.0
Mexican	14.7
South American	2.3

Torrance

Population

Group	Number	%TP[1]	%HP[2]
Total Population	145,438	100.0	–
Hispanic or Latino (of any race)	23,440	16.1	100.0
Central American, ex. Mexican	2,147	1.5	9.2
Costa Rican	218	0.1	0.9
Guatemalan	630	0.4	2.7
Honduran	168	0.1	0.7
Nicaraguan	342	0.2	1.5
Salvadoran	723	0.5	3.1
Cuban	882	0.6	3.8
Mexican	14,880	10.2	63.5
Puerto Rican	731	0.5	3.1
South American	2,540	1.7	10.8
Argentinean	371	0.3	1.6
Chilean	221	0.2	0.9
Colombian	498	0.3	2.1
Ecuadorian	295	0.2	1.3
Peruvian	955	0.7	4.1
Spaniard	568	0.4	2.4

Population Growth: 2000–2010

Group	%
Total Population	5.4
Hispanic or Latino (of any race)	32.9
Central American, ex. Mexican	102.7
Costa Rican	77.2
Guatemalan	129.9
Nicaraguan	87.9
Salvadoran	134.7
Cuban	19.2
Mexican	43.1
Puerto Rican	33.2
South American	67.0
Argentinean	96.3
Chilean	57.9
Colombian	72.3
Ecuadorian	81.0
Peruvian	85.8

Males per 100 Females

Group	Number
Total Population	94.7
Hispanic or Latino (of any race)	92.0
Central American, ex. Mexican	78.0
Costa Rican	83.2
Guatemalan	91.5
Honduran	78.7
Nicaraguan	71.0
Salvadoran	74.6
Cuban	82.6
Mexican	96.3
Puerto Rican	92.4
South American	83.4
Argentinean	95.3
Chilean	93.9
Colombian	72.3
Ecuadorian	95.4
Peruvian	79.8
Spaniard	78.6

Average Household Size

Group	People
Total Population	2.58
Hispanic or Latino (of any race)	3.00
Central American, ex. Mexican	3.26
Costa Rican	2.83
Guatemalan	3.59
Honduran	3.31
Nicaraguan	3.24
Salvadoran	3.23
Cuban	2.67
Mexican	3.08
Puerto Rican	2.61
South American	2.93
Argentinean	2.61
Chilean	2.70
Colombian	2.81
Ecuadorian	2.79
Peruvian	3.25
Spaniard	2.46

Median Age

Group	Years
Total Population	41.3
Hispanic or Latino (of any race)	31.6
Central American, ex. Mexican	33.4
Costa Rican	35.0
Guatemalan	33.4
Honduran	34.0
Nicaraguan	37.8
Salvadoran	31.3
Cuban	38.5
Mexican	29.6
Puerto Rican	35.0
South American	38.5
Argentinean	40.6
Chilean	44.8
Colombian	37.7
Ecuadorian	38.2
Peruvian	37.2
Spaniard	39.6

High School Graduates
(Universe: Population 25 Years and Over)

Group	Number	%
Total Population	94,115	92.4
Hispanic or Latino (of any race)	11,060	80.2
Central American, ex. Mexican	1,007	67.4
Mexican	6,440	77.8
Puerto Rican	556	86.2
South American	1,411	93.5
Peruvian	450	92.6

Four-Year College Graduates
(Universe: Population 25 Years and Over)

Group	Number	%
Total Population	45,453	44.6
Hispanic or Latino (of any race)	3,554	25.8
Central American, ex. Mexican	202	13.5
Mexican	1,873	22.6
Puerto Rican	207	32.1
South American	665	44.1
Peruvian	185	38.1

Population Age 3–17 Enrolled in Public School
(Universe: Population Age 3–17 Enrolled in School)

Group	Number	%
Total Population	21,094	82.3
Hispanic or Latino (of any race)	4,067	83.8
Central American, ex. Mexican	329	96.8
Mexican	2,469	85.5
Puerto Rican	229	94.6
South American	574	73.1
Peruvian	257	87.4

Population Age 3–17 Enrolled in Private School
(Universe: Population Age 3–17 Enrolled in School)

Group	Number	%
Total Population	4,550	17.7
Hispanic or Latino (of any race)	788	16.2
Central American, ex. Mexican	11	3.2
Mexican	420	14.5
Puerto Rican	13	5.4
South American	211	26.9
Peruvian	37	12.6

Foreign-Born Population

Group	Number	%
Total Population	43,960	30.5
Hispanic or Latino (of any race)	5,931	26.4
Central American, ex. Mexican	1,130	49.5
Mexican	2,838	20.5
Puerto Rican	14	1.5
South American	1,259	47.0
Peruvian	487	55.1

Foreign-Born Naturalized U.S. Citizens

Group	Number	%
Total Population	24,287	55.2
Hispanic or Latino (of any race)	3,593	60.6
Central American, ex. Mexican	779	68.9
Mexican	1,501	52.9
Puerto Rican	14	100.0
South American	820	65.1
Peruvian	229	47.0

Language Spoken at Home: English Only
(Universe: Population 5 Years and Over)

Group	Number	%
Total Population	83,043	60.9
Hispanic or Latino (of any race)	9,596	45.9
Central American, ex. Mexican	596	27.9
Mexican	6,882	54.1
Puerto Rican	441	48.3
South American	524	20.4
Peruvian	58	6.7

Language Spoken at Home: Spanish
(Universe: Population 5 Years and Over)

Group	Number	%
Total Population	12,583	9.2
Hispanic or Latino (of any race)	11,091	53.0
Central American, ex. Mexican	1,543	72.1
Mexican	5,796	45.6
Puerto Rican	379	41.5
South American	2,017	78.4
Peruvian	802	93.3

Unemployment Rate
(Universe: Population 16 Years and Over)

Group	%
Total Population	6.3
Hispanic or Latino (of any race)	7.4
Central American, ex. Mexican	7.0
Mexican	7.6
Puerto Rican	0.0
South American	10.7
Peruvian	20.0

Class of Worker: Private Wage and Salary
(Universe: Civilian Employed Population 16 Years and Over)

Group	Number	%
Total Population	56,341	77.6
Hispanic or Latino (of any race)	9,095	79.7
Central American, ex. Mexican	1,204	89.5
Mexican	5,545	78.2
Puerto Rican	285	92.2
South American	952	77.7
Peruvian	250	72.5

Class of Worker: Government
(Universe: Civilian Employed Population 16 Years and Over)

Group	Number	%
Total Population	9,104	12.5
Hispanic or Latino (of any race)	1,519	13.3
Central American, ex. Mexican	81	6.0
Mexican	969	13.7
Puerto Rican	24	7.8
South American	177	14.4
Peruvian	34	9.9

Means of Transportation to Work: Car, Truck or Van
(Universe: Workers 16 Years and Over)

Group	Number	%
Total Population	63,062	89.8
Hispanic or Latino (of any race)	9,898	89.2
Central American, ex. Mexican	1,208	89.8
Mexican	6,230	89.1
Puerto Rican	298	96.4
South American	1,005	87.6

Notes: (1) Percent of total population; (2) Percent of Hispanic/Latino population; Profiles include places with an overall population of at least 125,000, OR an overall population of at least 25,000 where the Hispanic/Latino population is at least 20% of the overall population. In states where less than five places meet either of these criteria, we have included places with at least 10,000 total population with the highest percentage of Hispanic/Latino population. These places are identified with an asterisk (*); Please refer to the User's Guide for a full explanation of data.

Peruvian	298	100.0

Means of Transportation to Work: Public Transportation (ex. Taxicab)
(Universe: Workers 16 Years and Over)

Group	Number	%
Total Population	1,407	2.0
Hispanic or Latino (of any race)	366	3.3
Central American, ex. Mexican	10	0.7
Mexican	289	4.1
Puerto Rican	0	0.0
South American	0	0.0
Peruvian	0	0.0

Homeownership Rate
(Universe: Occupied Housing Units)

Group	%
Total Population	56.5
Hispanic or Latino (of any race)	42.1
Central American, ex. Mexican	33.0
Costa Rican	38.2
Guatemalan	24.7
Honduran	33.3
Nicaraguan	50.0
Salvadoran	30.6
Cuban	53.0
Mexican	42.7
Puerto Rican	42.3
South American	39.5
Argentinean	48.9
Chilean	37.6
Colombian	42.4
Ecuadorian	40.4
Peruvian	34.2
Spaniard	55.1

Median Home Value

Group	Dollars
Total Population	657,700
Hispanic or Latino (of any race)	584,500
Central American, ex. Mexican	502,700
Mexican	588,500
Puerto Rican	526,300
South American	558,000
Peruvian	488,700

Median Gross Rent

Group	Dollars
Total Population	1,358
Hispanic or Latino (of any race)	1,245
Central American, ex. Mexican	1,298
Mexican	1,192
Puerto Rican	1,226
South American	1,459
Peruvian	1,202

Median Household Income
(2010 Inflation-Adjusted Dollars)

Group	Dollars
Total Population	74,163
Hispanic or Latino (of any race)	59,948
Central American, ex. Mexican	63,421
Mexican	66,211
Puerto Rican	29,864
South American	55,854
Peruvian	37,075

Per Capita Income
(2010 Inflation-Adjusted Dollars)

Group	Dollars
Total Population	36,007
Hispanic or Latino (of any race)	25,245
Central American, ex. Mexican	20,776
Mexican	24,743
Puerto Rican	21,796
South American	26,537
Peruvian	18,917

Households with $100,000+ Income

Group	Number	%
Total Population	19,373	34.9
Hispanic or Latino (of any race)	1,614	22.4
Central American, ex. Mexican	132	20.6
Mexican	983	23.5
Puerto Rican	43	9.6
South American	244	25.5
Peruvian	60	23.5

Households with Food Stamps/SNAP Benefits During Past 12 Months

Group	Number	%
Total Population	576	1.0
Hispanic or Latino (of any race)	79	1.1
Central American, ex. Mexican	0	0.0
Mexican	20	0.5
Puerto Rican	43	9.6
South American	0	0.0
Peruvian	0	0.0

Poverty Rate
(Income in Past 12 Months Below Poverty Level)

Group	%
Total Population	6.3
Hispanic or Latino (of any race)	7.3
Central American, ex. Mexican	8.4
Mexican	8.5
Puerto Rican	13.5
South American	2.0
Peruvian	1.5

Tracy

Population

Group	Number	%TP[1]	%HP[2]
Total Population	82,922	100.0	–
Hispanic or Latino (of any race)	30,557	36.9	100.0
Central American, ex. Mexican	1,690	2.0	5.5
Guatemalan	260	0.3	0.9
Nicaraguan	427	0.5	1.4
Salvadoran	835	1.0	2.7
Cuban	136	0.2	0.4
Mexican	25,099	30.3	82.1
Puerto Rican	906	1.1	3.0
South American	632	0.8	2.1
Peruvian	337	0.4	1.1
Spaniard	565	0.7	1.8

Population Growth: 2000–2010

Group	%
Total Population	45.7
Hispanic or Latino (of any race)	93.8
Central American, ex. Mexican	439.9
Salvadoran	537.4
Mexican	102.1
Puerto Rican	77.3
South American	324.2

Males per 100 Females

Group	Number
Total Population	98.3
Hispanic or Latino (of any race)	101.1
Central American, ex. Mexican	98.4
Guatemalan	108.0
Nicaraguan	92.3
Salvadoran	99.3
Cuban	78.9
Mexican	102.5
Puerto Rican	93.2
South American	84.3
Peruvian	86.2
Spaniard	89.0

Average Household Size

Group	People
Total Population	3.40
Hispanic or Latino (of any race)	4.01
Central American, ex. Mexican	4.16
Guatemalan	4.14
Nicaraguan	3.87
Salvadoran	4.43
Cuban	3.50
Mexican	4.08
Puerto Rican	3.25
South American	3.90
Peruvian	3.91
Spaniard	3.16

Median Age

Group	Years
Total Population	32.3
Hispanic or Latino (of any race)	25.3
Central American, ex. Mexican	31.6
Guatemalan	31.0
Nicaraguan	32.0
Salvadoran	31.5
Cuban	27.0
Mexican	24.6
Puerto Rican	27.7
South American	33.6
Peruvian	33.6
Spaniard	35.1

High School Graduates
(Universe: Population 25 Years and Over)

Group	Number	%
Total Population	39,153	85.5
Hispanic or Latino (of any race)	10,991	73.5
Central American, ex. Mexican	773	88.0
Mexican	8,093	68.8

Four-Year College Graduates
(Universe: Population 25 Years and Over)

Group	Number	%
Total Population	9,940	21.7
Hispanic or Latino (of any race)	1,320	8.8
Central American, ex. Mexican	138	15.7
Mexican	916	7.8

Population Age 3–17 Enrolled in Public School
(Universe: Population Age 3–17 Enrolled in School)

Group	Number	%
Total Population	18,636	90.4
Hispanic or Latino (of any race)	8,406	92.9
Central American, ex. Mexican	158	92.9
Mexican	6,971	93.0

Population Age 3–17 Enrolled in Private School
(Universe: Population Age 3–17 Enrolled in School)

Group	Number	%
Total Population	1,970	9.6
Hispanic or Latino (of any race)	639	7.1
Central American, ex. Mexican	12	7.1
Mexican	527	7.0

Foreign-Born Population

Group	Number	%
Total Population	19,691	24.8
Hispanic or Latino (of any race)	9,920	33.0
Central American, ex. Mexican	847	62.5
Mexican	8,456	34.9

Foreign-Born Naturalized U.S. Citizens

Group	Number	%
Total Population	9,915	50.4
Hispanic or Latino (of any race)	3,437	34.6
Central American, ex. Mexican	571	67.4
Mexican	2,430	28.7

Language Spoken at Home: English Only
(Universe: Population 5 Years and Over)

Group	Number	%
Total Population	43,777	60.5
Hispanic or Latino (of any race)	9,103	34.3
Central American, ex. Mexican	124	9.8
Mexican	6,321	29.7

Language Spoken at Home: Spanish
(Universe: Population 5 Years and Over)

Group	Number	%
Total Population	17,897	24.7
Hispanic or Latino (of any race)	17,391	65.5
Central American, ex. Mexican	1,145	90.2
Mexican	14,882	70.0

Unemployment Rate
(Universe: Population 16 Years and Over)

Group	%
Total Population	11.0
Hispanic or Latino (of any race)	12.9
Central American, ex. Mexican	6.5
Mexican	12.8

Notes: (1) Percent of total population; (2) Percent of Hispanic/Latino population; Profiles include places with an overall population of at least 125,000, OR an overall population of at least 25,000 where the Hispanic/Latino population is at least 20% of the overall population. In states where less than five places meet either of these criteria, we have included places with at least 10,000 total population with the highest percentage of Hispanic/Latino population. These places are identified with an asterisk (*); Please refer to the User's Guide for a full explanation of data.

Class of Worker: Private Wage and Salary (Universe: Civilian Employed Population 16 Years and Over)		
Group	Number	%
Total Population	28,408	80.2
Hispanic or Latino (of any race)	10,321	86.3
Central American, ex. Mexican	682	92.7
Mexican	8,327	87.4

Class of Worker: Government (Universe: Civilian Employed Population 16 Years and Over)		
Group	Number	%
Total Population	4,808	13.6
Hispanic or Latino (of any race)	988	8.3
Central American, ex. Mexican	38	5.2
Mexican	662	6.9

Means of Transportation to Work: Car, Truck or Van (Universe: Workers 16 Years and Over)		
Group	Number	%
Total Population	31,027	90.4
Hispanic or Latino (of any race)	10,571	92.1
Central American, ex. Mexican	611	88.7
Mexican	8,390	91.8

Means of Transportation to Work: Public Transportation (ex. Taxicab) (Universe: Workers 16 Years and Over)		
Group	Number	%
Total Population	881	2.6
Hispanic or Latino (of any race)	167	1.5
Central American, ex. Mexican	54	7.8
Mexican	70	0.8

Homeownership Rate (Universe: Occupied Housing Units)	
Group	%
Total Population	66.4
Hispanic or Latino (of any race)	55.0
Central American, ex. Mexican	62.8
Guatemalan	59.1
Nicaraguan	64.2
Salvadoran	63.2
Cuban	73.7
Mexican	53.3
Puerto Rican	56.5
South American	65.2
Peruvian	60.8
Spaniard	74.3

Median Home Value	
Group	Dollars
Total Population	386,800
Hispanic or Latino (of any race)	398,100
Central American, ex. Mexican	416,900
Mexican	383,400

Median Gross Rent	
Group	Dollars
Total Population	1,290
Hispanic or Latino (of any race)	1,200
Central American, ex. Mexican	980
Mexican	1,138

Median Household Income (2010 Inflation-Adjusted Dollars)	
Group	Dollars
Total Population	76,753
Hispanic or Latino (of any race)	62,422
Central American, ex. Mexican	73,194
Mexican	53,878

Per Capita Income (2010 Inflation-Adjusted Dollars)	
Group	Dollars
Total Population	26,956
Hispanic or Latino (of any race)	19,356
Central American, ex. Mexican	24,662
Mexican	18,653

Households with $100,000+ Income		
Group	Number	%
Total Population	8,344	35.3
Hispanic or Latino (of any race)	1,741	24.0
Central American, ex. Mexican	136	29.1
Mexican	1,047	18.8

Households with Food Stamps/SNAP Benefits During Past 12 Months		
Group	Number	%
Total Population	1,218	5.2
Hispanic or Latino (of any race)	492	6.8
Central American, ex. Mexican	27	5.8
Mexican	386	6.9

Poverty Rate (Income in Past 12 Months Below Poverty Level)	
Group	%
Total Population	10.4
Hispanic or Latino (of any race)	15.4
Central American, ex. Mexican	13.3
Mexican	15.6

Tulare

Population			
Group	Number	%TP[1]	%HP[2]
Total Population	59,278	100.0	–
Hispanic or Latino (of any race)	34,062	57.5	100.0
Central American, ex. Mexican	364	0.6	1.1
Salvadoran	194	0.3	0.6
Mexican	31,539	53.2	92.6
Puerto Rican	210	0.4	0.6
Spaniard	170	0.3	0.5

Population Growth: 2000–2010	
Group	%
Total Population	34.7
Hispanic or Latino (of any race)	69.8
Mexican	85.5
Puerto Rican	72.1

Males per 100 Females	
Group	Number
Total Population	96.6
Hispanic or Latino (of any race)	100.8
Central American, ex. Mexican	88.6
Salvadoran	79.6
Mexican	101.2
Puerto Rican	103.9
Spaniard	100.0

Average Household Size	
Group	People
Total Population	3.33
Hispanic or Latino (of any race)	4.01
Central American, ex. Mexican	3.99
Salvadoran	3.67
Mexican	4.04
Puerto Rican	3.22
Spaniard	3.90

Median Age	
Group	Years
Total Population	29.1
Hispanic or Latino (of any race)	23.4
Central American, ex. Mexican	33.9
Salvadoran	32.0
Mexican	23.2
Puerto Rican	27.0
Spaniard	32.8

High School Graduates (Universe: Population 25 Years and Over)		
Group	Number	%
Total Population	22,867	71.8
Hispanic or Latino (of any race)	8,438	57.2
Mexican	7,981	56.6

Four-Year College Graduates (Universe: Population 25 Years and Over)		
Group	Number	%
Total Population	3,549	11.1
Hispanic or Latino (of any race)	819	5.5
Mexican	740	5.3

Population Age 3–17 Enrolled in Public School (Universe: Population Age 3–17 Enrolled in School)		
Group	Number	%
Total Population	13,454	95.7
Hispanic or Latino (of any race)	9,139	97.3
Mexican	8,860	97.8

Population Age 3–17 Enrolled in Private School (Universe: Population Age 3–17 Enrolled in School)		
Group	Number	%
Total Population	610	4.3
Hispanic or Latino (of any race)	251	2.7
Mexican	201	2.2

Foreign-Born Population		
Group	Number	%
Total Population	12,304	21.6
Hispanic or Latino (of any race)	9,615	30.8
Mexican	9,150	30.5

Foreign-Born Naturalized U.S. Citizens		
Group	Number	%
Total Population	4,240	34.5
Hispanic or Latino (of any race)	2,289	23.8
Mexican	2,070	22.6

Language Spoken at Home: English Only (Universe: Population 5 Years and Over)		
Group	Number	%
Total Population	29,174	56.6
Hispanic or Latino (of any race)	8,803	32.0
Mexican	8,413	31.9

Language Spoken at Home: Spanish (Universe: Population 5 Years and Over)		
Group	Number	%
Total Population	19,020	36.9
Hispanic or Latino (of any race)	18,703	67.9
Mexican	17,898	68.0

Unemployment Rate (Universe: Population 16 Years and Over)	
Group	%
Total Population	9.8
Hispanic or Latino (of any race)	10.3
Mexican	10.3

Class of Worker: Private Wage and Salary (Universe: Civilian Employed Population 16 Years and Over)		
Group	Number	%
Total Population	16,824	76.0
Hispanic or Latino (of any race)	9,220	81.7
Mexican	8,887	82.0

Class of Worker: Government (Universe: Civilian Employed Population 16 Years and Over)		
Group	Number	%
Total Population	4,015	18.1
Hispanic or Latino (of any race)	1,717	15.2
Mexican	1,646	15.2

Means of Transportation to Work: Car, Truck or Van (Universe: Workers 16 Years and Over)		
Group	Number	%
Total Population	20,109	93.0
Hispanic or Latino (of any race)	10,195	92.2
Mexican	9,840	92.5

Means of Transportation to Work: Public Transportation (ex. Taxicab) (Universe: Workers 16 Years and Over)		
Group	Number	%
Total Population	189	0.9
Hispanic or Latino (of any race)	126	1.1
Mexican	108	1.0

Homeownership Rate (Universe: Occupied Housing Units)	
Group	%
Total Population	58.6
Hispanic or Latino (of any race)	51.2
Central American, ex. Mexican	53.7
Salvadoran	51.4
Mexican	51.5
Puerto Rican	53.3

STATE & PLACE PROFILES

Notes: (1) Percent of total population; (2) Percent of Hispanic/Latino population; Profiles include places with an overall population of at least 125,000, OR an overall population of at least 25,000 where the Hispanic/Latino population is at least 20% of the overall population. In states where less than five places meet either of these criteria, we have included places with at least 10,000 total population with the highest percentage of Hispanic/Latino population. These places are identified with an asterisk (*); Please refer to the User's Guide for a full explanation of data.

Spaniard	52.9

Median Home Value

Group	Dollars
Total Population	208,500
Hispanic or Latino (of any race)	195,000
Mexican	194,600

Median Gross Rent

Group	Dollars
Total Population	884
Hispanic or Latino (of any race)	900
Mexican	912

Median Household Income
(2010 Inflation-Adjusted Dollars)

Group	Dollars
Total Population	46,647
Hispanic or Latino (of any race)	40,962
Mexican	42,509

Per Capita Income
(2010 Inflation-Adjusted Dollars)

Group	Dollars
Total Population	17,734
Hispanic or Latino (of any race)	12,208
Mexican	12,236

Households with $100,000+ Income

Group	Number	%
Total Population	2,374	13.9
Hispanic or Latino (of any race)	595	8.2
Mexican	546	7.9

Households with Food Stamps/SNAP Benefits During Past 12 Months

Group	Number	%
Total Population	2,420	14.2
Hispanic or Latino (of any race)	1,665	22.9
Mexican	1,605	23.3

Poverty Rate
(Income in Past 12 Months Below Poverty Level)

Group	%
Total Population	19.1
Hispanic or Latino (of any race)	23.9
Mexican	23.7

Turlock

Population

Group	Number	%TP[1]	%HP[2]
Total Population	68,549	100.0	–
Hispanic or Latino (of any race)	24,957	36.4	100.0
Central American, ex. Mexican	482	0.7	1.9
Guatemalan	162	0.2	0.6
Salvadoran	164	0.2	0.7
Mexican	22,605	33.0	90.6
Puerto Rican	324	0.5	1.3
South American	240	0.4	1.0
Colombian	112	0.2	0.4
Spaniard	202	0.3	0.8

Population Growth: 2000–2010

Group	%
Total Population	22.8
Hispanic or Latino (of any race)	52.0
Central American, ex. Mexican	175.4
Mexican	61.9
Puerto Rican	125.0
South American	130.8

Males per 100 Females

Group	Number
Total Population	94.8
Hispanic or Latino (of any race)	100.3
Central American, ex. Mexican	112.3
Guatemalan	138.2
Salvadoran	110.3
Mexican	101.3
Puerto Rican	96.4
South American	81.8
Colombian	86.7
Spaniard	98.0

Average Household Size

Group	People
Total Population	2.96
Hispanic or Latino (of any race)	3.80
Central American, ex. Mexican	3.81
Guatemalan	3.98
Salvadoran	3.81
Mexican	3.86
Puerto Rican	2.91
South American	3.33
Colombian	3.72
Spaniard	2.90

Median Age

Group	Years
Total Population	32.5
Hispanic or Latino (of any race)	23.9
Central American, ex. Mexican	32.3
Guatemalan	33.0
Salvadoran	31.0
Mexican	23.7
Puerto Rican	23.5
South American	34.0
Colombian	32.0
Spaniard	33.7

High School Graduates
(Universe: Population 25 Years and Over)

Group	Number	%
Total Population	32,504	78.9
Hispanic or Latino (of any race)	6,698	60.4
Mexican	5,787	58.9

Four-Year College Graduates
(Universe: Population 25 Years and Over)

Group	Number	%
Total Population	9,827	23.9
Hispanic or Latino (of any race)	1,426	12.9
Mexican	1,266	12.9

Population Age 3–17 Enrolled in Public School
(Universe: Population Age 3–17 Enrolled in School)

Group	Number	%
Total Population	12,386	91.1
Hispanic or Latino (of any race)	6,133	93.8
Mexican	5,695	93.3

Population Age 3–17 Enrolled in Private School
(Universe: Population Age 3–17 Enrolled in School)

Group	Number	%
Total Population	1,216	8.9
Hispanic or Latino (of any race)	407	6.2
Mexican	407	6.7

Foreign-Born Population

Group	Number	%
Total Population	16,752	24.9
Hispanic or Latino (of any race)	7,039	30.8
Mexican	6,482	31.3

Foreign-Born Naturalized U.S. Citizens

Group	Number	%
Total Population	7,357	43.9
Hispanic or Latino (of any race)	2,256	32.1
Mexican	2,001	30.9

Language Spoken at Home: English Only
(Universe: Population 5 Years and Over)

Group	Number	%
Total Population	36,427	57.9
Hispanic or Latino (of any race)	6,166	29.9
Mexican	5,246	28.2

Language Spoken at Home: Spanish
(Universe: Population 5 Years and Over)

Group	Number	%
Total Population	15,215	24.2
Hispanic or Latino (of any race)	14,385	69.9
Mexican	13,320	71.6

Unemployment Rate
(Universe: Population 16 Years and Over)

Group	%
Total Population	10.6
Hispanic or Latino (of any race)	12.1
Mexican	12.7

Class of Worker: Private Wage and Salary
(Universe: Civilian Employed Population 16 Years and Over)

Group	Number	%
Total Population	22,717	75.7
Hispanic or Latino (of any race)	7,542	79.8
Mexican	6,739	80.2

Class of Worker: Government
(Universe: Civilian Employed Population 16 Years and Over)

Group	Number	%
Total Population	5,189	17.3
Hispanic or Latino (of any race)	1,274	13.5
Mexican	1,056	12.6

Means of Transportation to Work: Car, Truck or Van
(Universe: Workers 16 Years and Over)

Group	Number	%
Total Population	26,649	92.2
Hispanic or Latino (of any race)	8,577	93.2
Mexican	7,583	92.7

Means of Transportation to Work: Public Transportation (ex. Taxicab)
(Universe: Workers 16 Years and Over)

Group	Number	%
Total Population	40	0.1
Hispanic or Latino (of any race)	19	0.2
Mexican	19	0.2

Homeownership Rate
(Universe: Occupied Housing Units)

Group	%
Total Population	55.4
Hispanic or Latino (of any race)	44.5
Central American, ex. Mexican	52.1
Guatemalan	40.0
Salvadoran	56.3
Mexican	44.4
Puerto Rican	36.8
South American	61.8
Colombian	59.4
Spaniard	63.8

Median Home Value

Group	Dollars
Total Population	294,100
Hispanic or Latino (of any race)	288,400
Mexican	275,500

Median Gross Rent

Group	Dollars
Total Population	898
Hispanic or Latino (of any race)	860
Mexican	865

Median Household Income
(2010 Inflation-Adjusted Dollars)

Group	Dollars
Total Population	50,573
Hispanic or Latino (of any race)	42,096
Mexican	40,675

Per Capita Income
(2010 Inflation-Adjusted Dollars)

Group	Dollars
Total Population	22,444
Hispanic or Latino (of any race)	14,105
Mexican	13,589

Households with $100,000+ Income

Group	Number	%
Total Population	4,606	20.1
Hispanic or Latino (of any race)	699	11.6
Mexican	628	12.0

Households with Food Stamps/SNAP Benefits During Past 12 Months

Group	Number	%
Total Population	1,829	8.0
Hispanic or Latino (of any race)	715	11.9
Mexican	653	12.4

Notes: (1) Percent of total population; (2) Percent of Hispanic/Latino population; Profiles include places with an overall population of at least 125,000, OR an overall population of at least 25,000 where the Hispanic/Latino population is at least 20% of the overall population. In states where less than five places meet either of these criteria, we have included places with at least 10,000 total population with the highest percentage of Hispanic/Latino population. These places are identified with an asterisk (*); Please refer to the User's Guide for a full explanation of data.

Poverty Rate
(Income in Past 12 Months Below Poverty Level)

Group	%
Total Population	14.1
Hispanic or Latino (of any race)	19.8
Mexican	19.9

Tustin

Population

Group	Number	%TP[1]	%HP[2]
Total Population	75,540	100.0	–
Hispanic or Latino (of any race)	30,024	39.7	100.0
Central American, ex. Mexican	1,738	2.3	5.8
Guatemalan	577	0.8	1.9
Honduran	114	0.2	0.4
Nicaraguan	100	0.1	0.3
Salvadoran	871	1.2	2.9
Cuban	169	0.2	0.6
Mexican	24,715	32.7	82.3
Puerto Rican	233	0.3	0.8
South American	1,443	1.9	4.8
Argentinean	150	0.2	0.5
Bolivian	285	0.4	0.9
Colombian	298	0.4	1.0
Ecuadorian	113	0.1	0.4
Peruvian	463	0.6	1.5
Spaniard	227	0.3	0.8

Population Growth: 2000–2010

Group	%
Total Population	11.9
Hispanic or Latino (of any race)	29.9
Central American, ex. Mexican	79.9
Guatemalan	126.3
Salvadoran	94.0
Cuban	-0.6
Mexican	37.6
Puerto Rican	8.9
South American	80.4
Bolivian	71.7
Colombian	87.4
Peruvian	114.4

Males per 100 Females

Group	Number
Total Population	94.7
Hispanic or Latino (of any race)	96.9
Central American, ex. Mexican	99.3
Guatemalan	124.5
Honduran	67.6
Nicaraguan	88.7
Salvadoran	95.3
Cuban	89.9
Mexican	97.6
Puerto Rican	80.6
South American	86.7
Argentinean	94.8
Bolivian	83.9
Colombian	86.3
Ecuadorian	76.6
Peruvian	94.5
Spaniard	86.1

Average Household Size

Group	People
Total Population	2.98
Hispanic or Latino (of any race)	4.04
Central American, ex. Mexican	4.06
Guatemalan	4.23
Honduran	4.39
Nicaraguan	3.50
Salvadoran	4.09
Cuban	2.57
Mexican	4.19
Puerto Rican	2.75
South American	3.23
Argentinean	2.77
Bolivian	3.69
Colombian	3.05
Ecuadorian	3.05
Peruvian	3.45
Spaniard	2.93

Median Age

Group	Years
Total Population	33.4
Hispanic or Latino (of any race)	26.4
Central American, ex. Mexican	32.0
Guatemalan	31.6
Honduran	31.0
Nicaraguan	34.5
Salvadoran	31.8
Cuban	39.4
Mexican	25.3
Puerto Rican	29.9
South American	37.2
Argentinean	37.4
Bolivian	35.9
Colombian	36.4
Ecuadorian	30.8
Peruvian	41.0
Spaniard	34.3

High School Graduates
(Universe: Population 25 Years and Over)

Group	Number	%
Total Population	39,761	84.5
Hispanic or Latino (of any race)	8,573	60.4
Central American, ex. Mexican	683	64.6
Mexican	6,278	55.0
South American	959	93.6

Four-Year College Graduates
(Universe: Population 25 Years and Over)

Group	Number	%
Total Population	18,170	38.6
Hispanic or Latino (of any race)	2,019	14.2
Central American, ex. Mexican	71	6.7
Mexican	1,393	12.2
South American	346	33.8

Population Age 3–17 Enrolled in Public School
(Universe: Population Age 3–17 Enrolled in School)

Group	Number	%
Total Population	13,679	88.8
Hispanic or Latino (of any race)	7,547	95.3
Central American, ex. Mexican	393	100.0
Mexican	6,763	95.9
South American	149	81.0

Population Age 3–17 Enrolled in Private School
(Universe: Population Age 3–17 Enrolled in School)

Group	Number	%
Total Population	1,730	11.2
Hispanic or Latino (of any race)	370	4.7
Central American, ex. Mexican	0	0.0
Mexican	289	4.1
South American	35	19.0

Foreign-Born Population

Group	Number	%
Total Population	25,569	34.7
Hispanic or Latino (of any race)	12,357	44.9
Central American, ex. Mexican	1,236	70.5
Mexican	9,776	42.0
South American	1,064	76.5

Foreign-Born Naturalized U.S. Citizens

Group	Number	%
Total Population	11,889	46.5
Hispanic or Latino (of any race)	3,474	28.1
Central American, ex. Mexican	342	27.7
Mexican	2,600	26.6
South American	380	35.7

Language Spoken at Home: English Only
(Universe: Population 5 Years and Over)

Group	Number	%
Total Population	32,981	48.5
Hispanic or Latino (of any race)	4,593	18.6
Central American, ex. Mexican	76	4.5
Mexican	3,779	18.3
South American	80	6.2

Language Spoken at Home: Spanish
(Universe: Population 5 Years and Over)

Group	Number	%
Total Population	20,784	30.6
Hispanic or Latino (of any race)	20,027	81.0
Central American, ex. Mexican	1,603	94.7
Mexican	16,870	81.6
South American	1,213	93.8

Unemployment Rate
(Universe: Population 16 Years and Over)

Group	%
Total Population	7.9
Hispanic or Latino (of any race)	7.7
Central American, ex. Mexican	3.0
Mexican	8.6
South American	6.6

Class of Worker: Private Wage and Salary
(Universe: Civilian Employed Population 16 Years and Over)

Group	Number	%
Total Population	31,547	83.9
Hispanic or Latino (of any race)	11,252	86.9
Central American, ex. Mexican	879	83.7
Mexican	9,096	87.8
South American	790	86.0

Class of Worker: Government
(Universe: Civilian Employed Population 16 Years and Over)

Group	Number	%
Total Population	3,482	9.3
Hispanic or Latino (of any race)	879	6.8
Central American, ex. Mexican	42	4.0
Mexican	699	6.7
South American	68	7.4

Means of Transportation to Work: Car, Truck or Van
(Universe: Workers 16 Years and Over)

Group	Number	%
Total Population	33,156	89.7
Hispanic or Latino (of any race)	11,121	86.6
Central American, ex. Mexican	972	92.6
Mexican	8,842	86.2
South American	868	94.5

Means of Transportation to Work: Public Transportation (ex. Taxicab)
(Universe: Workers 16 Years and Over)

Group	Number	%
Total Population	1,076	2.9
Hispanic or Latino (of any race)	715	5.6
Central American, ex. Mexican	78	7.4
Mexican	606	5.9
South American	31	3.4

Homeownership Rate
(Universe: Occupied Housing Units)

Group	%
Total Population	50.8
Hispanic or Latino (of any race)	27.9
Central American, ex. Mexican	23.7
Guatemalan	24.7
Honduran	15.2
Nicaraguan	33.3
Salvadoran	22.1
Cuban	63.3
Mexican	26.6
Puerto Rican	32.9
South American	39.4
Argentinean	54.8
Bolivian	37.9
Colombian	34.0
Ecuadorian	52.6
Peruvian	33.8
Spaniard	53.1

Median Home Value

Group	Dollars
Total Population	573,100
Hispanic or Latino (of any race)	446,800
Central American, ex. Mexican	357,600
Mexican	444,500
South American	555,100

Median Gross Rent

Group	Dollars
Total Population	1,424
Hispanic or Latino (of any race)	1,376
Central American, ex. Mexican	1,378

Notes: (1) Percent of total population; (2) Percent of Hispanic/Latino population; Profiles include places with an overall population of at least 125,000, OR an overall population of at least 25,000 where the Hispanic/Latino population is at least 20% of the overall population. In states where less than five places meet either of these criteria, we have included places with at least 10,000 total population with the highest percentage of Hispanic/Latino population. These places are identified with an asterisk (*); Please refer to the User's Guide for a full explanation of data.

Mexican	1,355
South American	1,750

Median Household Income
(2010 Inflation-Adjusted Dollars)

Group	Dollars
Total Population	73,170
Hispanic or Latino (of any race)	54,752
Central American, ex. Mexican	63,995
Mexican	54,082
South American	75,764

Per Capita Income
(2010 Inflation-Adjusted Dollars)

Group	Dollars
Total Population	32,949
Hispanic or Latino (of any race)	17,260
Central American, ex. Mexican	14,622
Mexican	16,403
South American	24,794

Households with $100,000+ Income

Group	Number	%
Total Population	8,559	34.5
Hispanic or Latino (of any race)	1,267	18.9
Central American, ex. Mexican	51	13.5
Mexican	920	16.7
South American	170	37.2

Households with Food Stamps/SNAP Benefits During Past 12 Months

Group	Number	%
Total Population	807	3.2
Hispanic or Latino (of any race)	451	6.7
Central American, ex. Mexican	44	11.7
Mexican	379	6.9
South American	28	6.1

Poverty Rate
(Income in Past 12 Months Below Poverty Level)

Group	%
Total Population	9.6
Hispanic or Latino (of any race)	14.7
Central American, ex. Mexican	22.5
Mexican	15.2
South American	1.6

Twentynine Palms

Population

Group	Number	%TP[1]	%HP[2]
Total Population	25,048	100.0	–
Hispanic or Latino (of any race)	5,212	20.8	100.0
Central American, ex. Mexican	272	1.1	5.2
Mexican	3,803	15.2	73.0
Puerto Rican	453	1.8	8.7
South American	126	0.5	2.4

Population Growth: 2000–2010

Group	%
Total Population	69.7
Hispanic or Latino (of any race)	136.7
Mexican	151.5
Puerto Rican	216.8

Males per 100 Females

Group	Number
Total Population	129.0
Hispanic or Latino (of any race)	123.0
Central American, ex. Mexican	130.5
Mexican	119.7
Puerto Rican	133.5
South American	106.6

Average Household Size

Group	People
Total Population	2.68
Hispanic or Latino (of any race)	3.04
Central American, ex. Mexican	2.91
Mexican	3.11
Puerto Rican	2.93
South American	2.89

Median Age

Group	Years
Total Population	23.5
Hispanic or Latino (of any race)	21.5
Central American, ex. Mexican	23.1
Mexican	21.3
Puerto Rican	21.4
South American	22.5

High School Graduates
(Universe: Population 25 Years and Over)

Group	Number	%
Total Population	10,323	88.4
Hispanic or Latino (of any race)	1,444	84.6
Mexican	977	81.3

Four-Year College Graduates
(Universe: Population 25 Years and Over)

Group	Number	%
Total Population	1,931	16.5
Hispanic or Latino (of any race)	119	7.0
Mexican	57	4.7

Population Age 3–17 Enrolled in Public School
(Universe: Population Age 3–17 Enrolled in School)

Group	Number	%
Total Population	3,488	91.6
Hispanic or Latino (of any race)	1,069	94.8
Mexican	955	99.3

Population Age 3–17 Enrolled in Private School
(Universe: Population Age 3–17 Enrolled in School)

Group	Number	%
Total Population	321	8.4
Hispanic or Latino (of any race)	59	5.2
Mexican	7	0.7

Foreign-Born Population

Group	Number	%
Total Population	1,591	6.1
Hispanic or Latino (of any race)	512	11.0
Mexican	351	10.3

Foreign-Born Naturalized U.S. Citizens

Group	Number	%
Total Population	935	58.8
Hispanic or Latino (of any race)	284	55.5
Mexican	155	44.2

Language Spoken at Home: English Only
(Universe: Population 5 Years and Over)

Group	Number	%
Total Population	19,918	85.4
Hispanic or Latino (of any race)	2,019	49.3
Mexican	1,509	51.0

Language Spoken at Home: Spanish
(Universe: Population 5 Years and Over)

Group	Number	%
Total Population	2,194	9.4
Hispanic or Latino (of any race)	2,054	50.1
Mexican	1,449	49.0

Unemployment Rate
(Universe: Population 16 Years and Over)

Group	%
Total Population	13.9
Hispanic or Latino (of any race)	10.5
Mexican	8.5

Class of Worker: Private Wage and Salary
(Universe: Civilian Employed Population 16 Years and Over)

Group	Number	%
Total Population	2,826	46.2
Hispanic or Latino (of any race)	577	59.7
Mexican	351	51.6

Class of Worker: Government
(Universe: Civilian Employed Population 16 Years and Over)

Group	Number	%
Total Population	2,933	48.0
Hispanic or Latino (of any race)	358	37.0
Mexican	305	44.9

Means of Transportation to Work: Car, Truck or Van
(Universe: Workers 16 Years and Over)

Group	Number	%
Total Population	10,097	74.6
Hispanic or Latino (of any race)	1,603	75.5
Mexican	1,035	74.2

Means of Transportation to Work: Public Transportation (ex. Taxicab)
(Universe: Workers 16 Years and Over)

Group	Number	%
Total Population	305	2.3
Hispanic or Latino (of any race)	29	1.4
Mexican	14	1.0

Homeownership Rate
(Universe: Occupied Housing Units)

Group	%
Total Population	33.9
Hispanic or Latino (of any race)	26.3
Central American, ex. Mexican	24.3
Mexican	27.8
Puerto Rican	22.3
South American	17.1

Median Home Value

Group	Dollars
Total Population	173,100
Hispanic or Latino (of any race)	208,600
Mexican	200,000

Median Gross Rent

Group	Dollars
Total Population	885
Hispanic or Latino (of any race)	865
Mexican	884

Median Household Income
(2010 Inflation-Adjusted Dollars)

Group	Dollars
Total Population	42,027
Hispanic or Latino (of any race)	35,909
Mexican	33,426

Per Capita Income
(2010 Inflation-Adjusted Dollars)

Group	Dollars
Total Population	20,693
Hispanic or Latino (of any race)	15,532
Mexican	13,813

Households with $100,000+ Income

Group	Number	%
Total Population	954	12.1
Hispanic or Latino (of any race)	112	10.0
Mexican	49	6.3

Households with Food Stamps/SNAP Benefits During Past 12 Months

Group	Number	%
Total Population	726	9.2
Hispanic or Latino (of any race)	102	9.1
Mexican	102	13.1

Poverty Rate
(Income in Past 12 Months Below Poverty Level)

Group	%
Total Population	14.2
Hispanic or Latino (of any race)	15.5
Mexican	20.0

Union City

Population

Group	Number	%TP[1]	%HP[2]
Total Population	69,516	100.0	–
Hispanic or Latino (of any race)	15,895	22.9	100.0
Central American, ex. Mexican	1,208	1.7	7.6
Guatemalan	137	0.2	0.9
Nicaraguan	299	0.4	1.9
Salvadoran	605	0.9	3.8
Mexican	12,652	18.2	79.6
Puerto Rican	611	0.9	3.8

Notes: (1) Percent of total population; (2) Percent of Hispanic/Latino population; Profiles include places with an overall population of at least 125,000, OR an overall population of at least 25,000 where the Hispanic/Latino population is at least 20% of the overall population. In states where less than five places meet either of these criteria, we have included places with at least 10,000 total population with the highest percentage of Hispanic/Latino population. These places are identified with an asterisk (*); Please refer to the User's Guide for a full explanation of data.

South American	372	0.5	2.3
Peruvian	184	0.3	1.2
Spaniard	275	0.4	1.7

Population Growth: 2000–2010

Group	%
Total Population	4.0
Hispanic or Latino (of any race)	-0.8
Central American, ex. Mexican	65.5
Guatemalan	28.0
Nicaraguan	76.9
Salvadoran	103.0
Mexican	5.8
Puerto Rican	19.8
South American	42.5
Peruvian	64.3

Males per 100 Females

Group	Number
Total Population	97.5
Hispanic or Latino (of any race)	101.5
Central American, ex. Mexican	93.3
Guatemalan	117.5
Nicaraguan	88.1
Salvadoran	86.7
Mexican	104.6
Puerto Rican	95.2
South American	86.9
Peruvian	95.7
Spaniard	87.1

Average Household Size

Group	People
Total Population	3.38
Hispanic or Latino (of any race)	3.81
Central American, ex. Mexican	3.90
Guatemalan	4.50
Nicaraguan	3.60
Salvadoran	3.97
Mexican	3.94
Puerto Rican	2.99
South American	3.14
Peruvian	3.46
Spaniard	2.84

Median Age

Group	Years
Total Population	36.2
Hispanic or Latino (of any race)	29.7
Central American, ex. Mexican	33.4
Guatemalan	33.8
Nicaraguan	33.8
Salvadoran	33.9
Mexican	28.9
Puerto Rican	31.4
South American	39.5
Peruvian	40.5
Spaniard	40.6

High School Graduates
(Universe: Population 25 Years and Over)

Group	Number	%
Total Population	38,914	85.7
Hispanic or Latino (of any race)	6,169	71.6
Central American, ex. Mexican	513	61.4
Mexican	4,624	70.4

Four-Year College Graduates
(Universe: Population 25 Years and Over)

Group	Number	%
Total Population	17,024	37.5
Hispanic or Latino (of any race)	867	10.1
Central American, ex. Mexican	98	11.7
Mexican	608	9.3

Population Age 3–17 Enrolled in Public School
(Universe: Population Age 3–17 Enrolled in School)

Group	Number	%
Total Population	10,736	86.2
Hispanic or Latino (of any race)	2,969	93.2
Central American, ex. Mexican	145	100.0
Mexican	2,380	93.4

Population Age 3–17 Enrolled in Private School
(Universe: Population Age 3–17 Enrolled in School)

Group	Number	%
Total Population	1,713	13.8
Hispanic or Latino (of any race)	217	6.8
Central American, ex. Mexican	0	0.0
Mexican	167	6.6

Foreign-Born Population

Group	Number	%
Total Population	31,497	46.3
Hispanic or Latino (of any race)	5,742	38.5
Central American, ex. Mexican	1,073	83.7
Mexican	4,005	35.0

Foreign-Born Naturalized U.S. Citizens

Group	Number	%
Total Population	19,777	62.8
Hispanic or Latino (of any race)	2,191	38.2
Central American, ex. Mexican	321	29.9
Mexican	1,583	39.5

Language Spoken at Home: English Only
(Universe: Population 5 Years and Over)

Group	Number	%
Total Population	23,728	37.6
Hispanic or Latino (of any race)	4,297	31.4
Central American, ex. Mexican	48	4.1
Mexican	3,301	31.2

Language Spoken at Home: Spanish
(Universe: Population 5 Years and Over)

Group	Number	%
Total Population	9,713	15.4
Hispanic or Latino (of any race)	9,253	67.6
Central American, ex. Mexican	1,114	95.9
Mexican	7,258	68.6

Unemployment Rate
(Universe: Population 16 Years and Over)

Group	%
Total Population	7.5
Hispanic or Latino (of any race)	8.8
Central American, ex. Mexican	10.9
Mexican	8.7

Class of Worker: Private Wage and Salary
(Universe: Civilian Employed Population 16 Years and Over)

Group	Number	%
Total Population	27,127	82.2
Hispanic or Latino (of any race)	5,546	83.1
Central American, ex. Mexican	679	92.3
Mexican	4,068	82.7

Class of Worker: Government
(Universe: Civilian Employed Population 16 Years and Over)

Group	Number	%
Total Population	4,357	13.2
Hispanic or Latino (of any race)	830	12.4
Central American, ex. Mexican	34	4.6
Mexican	637	13.0

Means of Transportation to Work: Car, Truck or Van
(Universe: Workers 16 Years and Over)

Group	Number	%
Total Population	26,768	83.7
Hispanic or Latino (of any race)	5,375	83.6
Central American, ex. Mexican	467	65.3
Mexican	4,150	87.6

Means of Transportation to Work: Public Transportation (ex. Taxicab)
(Universe: Workers 16 Years and Over)

Group	Number	%
Total Population	3,178	9.9
Hispanic or Latino (of any race)	464	7.2
Central American, ex. Mexican	101	14.1
Mexican	308	6.5

Homeownership Rate
(Universe: Occupied Housing Units)

Group	%
Total Population	66.5
Hispanic or Latino (of any race)	58.2
Central American, ex. Mexican	61.7
Guatemalan	70.0
Nicaraguan	61.6
Salvadoran	62.8
Mexican	57.3
Puerto Rican	57.6
South American	58.3
Peruvian	56.1
Spaniard	77.2

Median Home Value

Group	Dollars
Total Population	569,300
Hispanic or Latino (of any race)	513,200
Central American, ex. Mexican	474,000
Mexican	511,700

Median Gross Rent

Group	Dollars
Total Population	1,321
Hispanic or Latino (of any race)	1,241
Central American, ex. Mexican	1,693
Mexican	1,238

Median Household Income
(2010 Inflation-Adjusted Dollars)

Group	Dollars
Total Population	83,629
Hispanic or Latino (of any race)	56,463
Central American, ex. Mexican	52,336
Mexican	56,580

Per Capita Income
(2010 Inflation-Adjusted Dollars)

Group	Dollars
Total Population	29,767
Hispanic or Latino (of any race)	19,950
Central American, ex. Mexican	18,074
Mexican	19,547

Households with $100,000+ Income

Group	Number	%
Total Population	8,262	41.7
Hispanic or Latino (of any race)	865	23.5
Central American, ex. Mexican	76	32.3
Mexican	606	22.1

Households with Food Stamps/SNAP Benefits During Past 12 Months

Group	Number	%
Total Population	701	3.5
Hispanic or Latino (of any race)	120	3.3
Central American, ex. Mexican	0	0.0
Mexican	120	4.4

Poverty Rate
(Income in Past 12 Months Below Poverty Level)

Group	%
Total Population	7.3
Hispanic or Latino (of any race)	9.5
Central American, ex. Mexican	1.3
Mexican	11.2

Upland

Population

Group	Number	%TP[1]	%HP[2]
Total Population	73,732	100.0	–
Hispanic or Latino (of any race)	28,035	38.0	100.0
Central American, ex. Mexican	1,628	2.2	5.8
Guatemalan	402	0.5	1.4
Honduran	115	0.2	0.4
Nicaraguan	250	0.3	0.9
Salvadoran	719	1.0	2.6
Cuban	363	0.5	1.3
Mexican	22,727	30.8	81.1
Puerto Rican	443	0.6	1.6
South American	1,040	1.4	3.7
Argentinean	222	0.3	0.8
Colombian	193	0.3	0.7
Ecuadorian	161	0.2	0.6
Peruvian	299	0.4	1.1
Spaniard	373	0.5	1.3

Notes: (1) Percent of total population; (2) Percent of Hispanic/Latino population; Profiles include places with an overall population of at least 125,000, OR an overall population of at least 25,000 where the Hispanic/Latino population is at least 20% of the overall population. In states where less than five places meet either of these criteria, we have included places with at least 10,000 total population with the highest percentage of Hispanic/Latino population. These places are identified with an asterisk (*); Please refer to the User's Guide for a full explanation of data.

Population Growth: 2000–2010

Group	%
Total Population	7.8
Hispanic or Latino (of any race)	48.9
Central American, ex. Mexican	129.9
Guatemalan	173.5
Nicaraguan	79.9
Salvadoran	189.9
Cuban	39.6
Mexican	60.3
Puerto Rican	37.2
South American	101.9
Argentinean	80.5
Colombian	77.1
Peruvian	174.3

Males per 100 Females

Group	Number
Total Population	93.1
Hispanic or Latino (of any race)	92.5
Central American, ex. Mexican	88.4
Guatemalan	86.1
Honduran	57.5
Nicaraguan	100.0
Salvadoran	92.2
Cuban	86.2
Mexican	93.6
Puerto Rican	88.5
South American	81.5
Argentinean	93.0
Colombian	80.4
Ecuadorian	78.9
Peruvian	81.2
Spaniard	109.6

Average Household Size

Group	People
Total Population	2.83
Hispanic or Latino (of any race)	3.40
Central American, ex. Mexican	3.67
Guatemalan	3.85
Honduran	3.42
Nicaraguan	3.94
Salvadoran	3.69
Cuban	2.98
Mexican	3.44
Puerto Rican	2.86
South American	3.22
Argentinean	3.47
Colombian	2.95
Ecuadorian	3.09
Peruvian	3.30
Spaniard	2.82

Median Age

Group	Years
Total Population	36.1
Hispanic or Latino (of any race)	27.6
Central American, ex. Mexican	31.8
Guatemalan	29.6
Honduran	31.5
Nicaraguan	34.7
Salvadoran	31.3
Cuban	35.4
Mexican	27.0
Puerto Rican	27.7
South American	35.9
Argentinean	35.2
Colombian	37.5
Ecuadorian	31.2
Peruvian	37.9
Spaniard	37.5

High School Graduates
(Universe: Population 25 Years and Over)

Group	Number	%
Total Population	41,610	88.2
Hispanic or Latino (of any race)	10,333	73.8
Central American, ex. Mexican	814	80.4
Mexican	7,604	71.1
South American	808	80.7

Four-Year College Graduates
(Universe: Population 25 Years and Over)

Group	Number	%
Total Population	13,632	28.9
Hispanic or Latino (of any race)	2,033	14.5
Central American, ex. Mexican	223	22.0
Mexican	1,420	13.3
South American	175	17.5

Population Age 3–17 Enrolled in Public School
(Universe: Population Age 3–17 Enrolled in School)

Group	Number	%
Total Population	12,920	84.6
Hispanic or Latino (of any race)	6,977	90.8
Central American, ex. Mexican	465	94.7
Mexican	5,305	90.7
South American	522	96.1

Population Age 3–17 Enrolled in Private School
(Universe: Population Age 3–17 Enrolled in School)

Group	Number	%
Total Population	2,343	15.4
Hispanic or Latino (of any race)	703	9.2
Central American, ex. Mexican	26	5.3
Mexican	546	9.3
South American	21	3.9

Foreign-Born Population

Group	Number	%
Total Population	14,278	19.3
Hispanic or Latino (of any race)	7,008	25.3
Central American, ex. Mexican	1,030	59.3
Mexican	4,866	22.5
South American	855	50.2

Foreign-Born Naturalized U.S. Citizens

Group	Number	%
Total Population	7,420	52.0
Hispanic or Latino (of any race)	2,976	42.5
Central American, ex. Mexican	586	56.9
Mexican	1,931	39.7
South American	246	28.8

Language Spoken at Home: English Only
(Universe: Population 5 Years and Over)

Group	Number	%
Total Population	46,323	67.2
Hispanic or Latino (of any race)	10,954	43.8
Central American, ex. Mexican	148	9.3
Mexican	8,737	44.9
South American	486	30.6

Language Spoken at Home: Spanish
(Universe: Population 5 Years and Over)

Group	Number	%
Total Population	14,810	21.5
Hispanic or Latino (of any race)	14,011	56.0
Central American, ex. Mexican	1,445	90.7
Mexican	10,683	55.0
South American	1,102	69.4

Unemployment Rate
(Universe: Population 16 Years and Over)

Group	%
Total Population	10.0
Hispanic or Latino (of any race)	14.4
Central American, ex. Mexican	16.0
Mexican	14.9
South American	3.1

Class of Worker: Private Wage and Salary
(Universe: Civilian Employed Population 16 Years and Over)

Group	Number	%
Total Population	26,184	75.6
Hispanic or Latino (of any race)	9,132	80.3
Central American, ex. Mexican	634	85.7
Mexican	7,133	79.7
South American	561	80.5

Class of Worker: Government
(Universe: Civilian Employed Population 16 Years and Over)

Group	Number	%
Total Population	5,652	16.3
Hispanic or Latino (of any race)	1,713	15.1
Central American, ex. Mexican	72	9.7
Mexican	1,390	15.5
South American	103	14.8

Means of Transportation to Work: Car, Truck or Van
(Universe: Workers 16 Years and Over)

Group	Number	%
Total Population	30,638	91.1
Hispanic or Latino (of any race)	10,298	92.7
Central American, ex. Mexican	706	98.3
Mexican	8,156	92.6
South American	627	91.8

Means of Transportation to Work: Public Transportation (ex. Taxicab)
(Universe: Workers 16 Years and Over)

Group	Number	%
Total Population	1,030	3.1
Hispanic or Latino (of any race)	410	3.7
Central American, ex. Mexican	0	0.0
Mexican	289	3.3
South American	56	8.2

Homeownership Rate
(Universe: Occupied Housing Units)

Group	%
Total Population	57.9
Hispanic or Latino (of any race)	43.0
Central American, ex. Mexican	37.0
Guatemalan	42.1
Honduran	22.6
Nicaraguan	41.4
Salvadoran	33.3
Cuban	55.0
Mexican	42.8
Puerto Rican	39.0
South American	50.0
Argentinean	47.3
Colombian	46.9
Ecuadorian	62.9
Peruvian	46.2
Spaniard	65.0

Median Home Value

Group	Dollars
Total Population	479,500
Hispanic or Latino (of any race)	461,100
Central American, ex. Mexican	507,900
Mexican	442,500
South American	398,300

Median Gross Rent

Group	Dollars
Total Population	1,151
Hispanic or Latino (of any race)	1,150
Central American, ex. Mexican	1,187
Mexican	1,159
South American	1,159

Median Household Income
(2010 Inflation-Adjusted Dollars)

Group	Dollars
Total Population	67,567
Hispanic or Latino (of any race)	58,770
Central American, ex. Mexican	62,885
Mexican	58,818
South American	48,006

Per Capita Income
(2010 Inflation-Adjusted Dollars)

Group	Dollars
Total Population	29,694
Hispanic or Latino (of any race)	19,795
Central American, ex. Mexican	19,061
Mexican	19,514
South American	21,654

Households with $100,000+ Income

Group	Number	%
Total Population	7,540	29.9
Hispanic or Latino (of any race)	1,647	23.0
Central American, ex. Mexican	66	11.4
Mexican	1,248	23.2
South American	92	18.3

Notes: (1) Percent of total population; (2) Percent of Hispanic/Latino population; Profiles include places with an overall population of at least 125,000, OR an overall population of at least 25,000 where the Hispanic/Latino population is at least 20% of the overall population. In states where less than five places meet either of these criteria, we have included places with at least 10,000 total population with the highest percentage of Hispanic/Latino population. These places are identified with an asterisk (*); Please refer to the User's Guide for a full explanation of data.

Households with Food Stamps/SNAP Benefits During Past 12 Months

Group	Number	%
Total Population	952	3.8
Hispanic or Latino (of any race)	544	7.6
Central American, ex. Mexican	30	5.2
Mexican	374	7.0
South American	30	6.0

Poverty Rate
(Income in Past 12 Months Below Poverty Level)

Group	%
Total Population	8.9
Hispanic or Latino (of any race)	11.2
Central American, ex. Mexican	7.6
Mexican	11.9
South American	10.3

Vacaville

Population

Group	Number	%TP[1]	%HP[2]
Total Population	92,428	100.0	–
Hispanic or Latino (of any race)	21,121	22.9	100.0
Central American, ex. Mexican	1,176	1.3	5.6
Guatemalan	229	0.2	1.1
Nicaraguan	317	0.3	1.5
Salvadoran	424	0.5	2.0
Cuban	164	0.2	0.8
Mexican	15,753	17.0	74.6
Puerto Rican	846	0.9	4.0
South American	374	0.4	1.8
Peruvian	175	0.2	0.8
Spaniard	761	0.8	3.6

Population Growth: 2000–2010

Group	%
Total Population	4.3
Hispanic or Latino (of any race)	33.3
Central American, ex. Mexican	167.3
Nicaraguan	173.3
Salvadoran	194.4
Cuban	12.3
Mexican	42.0
Puerto Rican	39.1
South American	128.0
Spaniard	480.9

Males per 100 Females

Group	Number
Total Population	112.5
Hispanic or Latino (of any race)	115.1
Central American, ex. Mexican	97.3
Guatemalan	112.0
Nicaraguan	94.5
Salvadoran	102.9
Cuban	102.5
Mexican	114.3
Puerto Rican	100.0
South American	87.9
Peruvian	80.4
Spaniard	86.1

Average Household Size

Group	People
Total Population	2.71
Hispanic or Latino (of any race)	3.43
Central American, ex. Mexican	3.47
Guatemalan	4.18
Nicaraguan	3.42
Salvadoran	3.45
Cuban	3.26
Mexican	3.62
Puerto Rican	2.86
South American	3.17
Peruvian	2.87
Spaniard	2.54

Median Age

Group	Years
Total Population	37.2
Hispanic or Latino (of any race)	26.8
Central American, ex. Mexican	28.7
Guatemalan	26.5
Nicaraguan	29.2
Salvadoran	31.9
Cuban	31.7
Mexican	26.2
Puerto Rican	25.6
South American	32.0
Peruvian	35.4
Spaniard	41.2

High School Graduates
(Universe: Population 25 Years and Over)

Group	Number	%
Total Population	51,810	85.4
Hispanic or Latino (of any race)	6,849	66.3
Mexican	4,965	61.5

Four-Year College Graduates
(Universe: Population 25 Years and Over)

Group	Number	%
Total Population	12,761	21.0
Hispanic or Latino (of any race)	1,023	9.9
Mexican	593	7.4

Population Age 3–17 Enrolled in Public School
(Universe: Population Age 3–17 Enrolled in School)

Group	Number	%
Total Population	14,757	88.6
Hispanic or Latino (of any race)	4,984	90.3
Mexican	4,046	89.9

Population Age 3–17 Enrolled in Private School
(Universe: Population Age 3–17 Enrolled in School)

Group	Number	%
Total Population	1,904	11.4
Hispanic or Latino (of any race)	536	9.7
Mexican	453	10.1

Foreign-Born Population

Group	Number	%
Total Population	10,846	11.8
Hispanic or Latino (of any race)	5,063	26.0
Mexican	4,094	26.6

Foreign-Born Naturalized U.S. Citizens

Group	Number	%
Total Population	5,361	49.4
Hispanic or Latino (of any race)	1,705	33.7
Mexican	1,281	31.3

Language Spoken at Home: English Only
(Universe: Population 5 Years and Over)

Group	Number	%
Total Population	69,582	80.4
Hispanic or Latino (of any race)	7,789	43.9
Mexican	5,779	40.6

Language Spoken at Home: Spanish
(Universe: Population 5 Years and Over)

Group	Number	%
Total Population	11,123	12.9
Hispanic or Latino (of any race)	9,890	55.7
Mexican	8,432	59.3

Unemployment Rate
(Universe: Population 16 Years and Over)

Group	%
Total Population	6.7
Hispanic or Latino (of any race)	5.3
Mexican	5.6

Class of Worker: Private Wage and Salary
(Universe: Civilian Employed Population 16 Years and Over)

Group	Number	%
Total Population	29,302	73.1
Hispanic or Latino (of any race)	5,998	77.9
Mexican	4,753	79.4

Class of Worker: Government
(Universe: Civilian Employed Population 16 Years and Over)

Group	Number	%
Total Population	8,199	20.5
Hispanic or Latino (of any race)	1,231	16.0
Mexican	941	15.7

Means of Transportation to Work: Car, Truck or Van
(Universe: Workers 16 Years and Over)

Group	Number	%
Total Population	38,230	93.8
Hispanic or Latino (of any race)	7,098	94.5
Mexican	5,453	94.3

Means of Transportation to Work: Public Transportation (ex. Taxicab)
(Universe: Workers 16 Years and Over)

Group	Number	%
Total Population	301	0.7
Hispanic or Latino (of any race)	50	0.7
Mexican	33	0.6

Homeownership Rate
(Universe: Occupied Housing Units)

Group	%
Total Population	63.4
Hispanic or Latino (of any race)	51.6
Central American, ex. Mexican	56.1
Guatemalan	37.5
Nicaraguan	67.3
Salvadoran	53.0
Cuban	60.0
Mexican	49.7
Puerto Rican	46.5
South American	55.8
Peruvian	57.4
Spaniard	69.9

Median Home Value

Group	Dollars
Total Population	377,900
Hispanic or Latino (of any race)	393,300
Mexican	385,100

Median Gross Rent

Group	Dollars
Total Population	1,256
Hispanic or Latino (of any race)	1,230
Mexican	1,248

Median Household Income
(2010 Inflation-Adjusted Dollars)

Group	Dollars
Total Population	70,838
Hispanic or Latino (of any race)	62,726
Mexican	64,409

Per Capita Income
(2010 Inflation-Adjusted Dollars)

Group	Dollars
Total Population	28,512
Hispanic or Latino (of any race)	16,557
Mexican	15,544

Households with $100,000+ Income

Group	Number	%
Total Population	10,099	33.7
Hispanic or Latino (of any race)	1,061	25.1
Mexican	826	26.6

Households with Food Stamps/SNAP Benefits During Past 12 Months

Group	Number	%
Total Population	1,088	3.6
Hispanic or Latino (of any race)	227	5.4
Mexican	178	5.7

Poverty Rate
(Income in Past 12 Months Below Poverty Level)

Group	%
Total Population	7.0
Hispanic or Latino (of any race)	10.5
Mexican	9.7

Vallejo

Population

Group	Number	%TP[1]	%HP[2]
Total Population	115,942	100.0	–
Hispanic or Latino (of any race)	26,165	22.6	100.0

STATE & PLACE PROFILES

Notes: (1) Percent of total population; (2) Percent of Hispanic/Latino population; Profiles include places with an overall population of at least 125,000, OR an overall population of at least 25,000 where the Hispanic/Latino population is at least 20% of the overall population. In states where less than five places meet either of these criteria, we have included places with at least 10,000 total population with the highest percentage of Hispanic/Latino population. These places are identified with an asterisk (*); Please refer to the User's Guide for a full explanation of data.

Group	Number	% (1)	% (2)
Central American, ex. Mexican	3,861	3.3	14.8
Guatemalan	787	0.7	3.0
Honduran	159	0.1	0.6
Nicaraguan	629	0.5	2.4
Salvadoran	2,135	1.8	8.2
Cuban	186	0.2	0.7
Mexican	18,611	16.1	71.1
Puerto Rican	906	0.8	3.5
South American	507	0.4	1.9
Colombian	110	0.1	0.4
Peruvian	215	0.2	0.8
Spaniard	485	0.4	1.9

Population Growth: 2000–2010

Group	%
Total Population	-0.7
Hispanic or Latino (of any race)	40.7
Central American, ex. Mexican	132.9
Guatemalan	257.7
Nicaraguan	133.0
Salvadoran	139.1
Mexican	51.9
Puerto Rican	11.3
South American	74.2
Peruvian	115.0

Males per 100 Females

Group	Number
Total Population	94.3
Hispanic or Latino (of any race)	105.0
Central American, ex. Mexican	100.9
Guatemalan	120.4
Honduran	76.7
Nicaraguan	90.0
Salvadoran	101.0
Cuban	97.9
Mexican	108.4
Puerto Rican	85.3
South American	83.7
Colombian	100.0
Peruvian	74.8
Spaniard	94.0

Average Household Size

Group	People
Total Population	2.82
Hispanic or Latino (of any race)	3.77
Central American, ex. Mexican	3.78
Guatemalan	4.33
Honduran	3.85
Nicaraguan	3.49
Salvadoran	3.79
Cuban	2.74
Mexican	3.99
Puerto Rican	2.79
South American	2.86
Colombian	3.06
Peruvian	3.05
Spaniard	2.47

Median Age

Group	Years
Total Population	37.9
Hispanic or Latino (of any race)	27.2
Central American, ex. Mexican	32.2
Guatemalan	29.8
Honduran	29.6
Nicaraguan	33.5
Salvadoran	33.0
Cuban	26.0
Mexican	25.4
Puerto Rican	28.4
South American	38.0
Colombian	40.4
Peruvian	35.6
Spaniard	40.0

High School Graduates
(Universe: Population 25 Years and Over)

Group	Number	%
Total Population	65,347	84.7
Hispanic or Latino (of any race)	8,048	60.2
Central American, ex. Mexican	1,297	64.6
Salvadoran	752	59.7
Mexican	5,504	56.2
Puerto Rican	476	84.8

Four-Year College Graduates
(Universe: Population 25 Years and Over)

Group	Number	%
Total Population	19,083	24.7
Hispanic or Latino (of any race)	1,350	10.1
Central American, ex. Mexican	231	11.5
Salvadoran	89	7.1
Mexican	822	8.4
Puerto Rican	71	12.7

Population Age 3–17 Enrolled in Public School
(Universe: Population Age 3–17 Enrolled in School)

Group	Number	%
Total Population	17,133	84.9
Hispanic or Latino (of any race)	5,347	92.6
Central American, ex. Mexican	513	87.8
Salvadoran	279	88.9
Mexican	4,354	94.1
Puerto Rican	238	81.5

Population Age 3–17 Enrolled in Private School
(Universe: Population Age 3–17 Enrolled in School)

Group	Number	%
Total Population	3,052	15.1
Hispanic or Latino (of any race)	430	7.4
Central American, ex. Mexican	71	12.2
Salvadoran	35	11.1
Mexican	273	5.9
Puerto Rican	54	18.5

Foreign-Born Population

Group	Number	%
Total Population	31,402	27.1
Hispanic or Latino (of any race)	10,287	41.5
Central American, ex. Mexican	1,975	65.6
Salvadoran	1,172	66.3
Mexican	7,719	40.1
Puerto Rican	68	6.7

Foreign-Born Naturalized U.S. Citizens

Group	Number	%
Total Population	16,611	52.9
Hispanic or Latino (of any race)	2,546	24.7
Central American, ex. Mexican	609	30.8
Salvadoran	368	31.4
Mexican	1,580	20.5
Puerto Rican	10	14.7

Language Spoken at Home: English Only
(Universe: Population 5 Years and Over)

Group	Number	%
Total Population	66,470	61.7
Hispanic or Latino (of any race)	5,823	26.7
Central American, ex. Mexican	270	9.8
Salvadoran	115	7.1
Mexican	4,192	25.2
Puerto Rican	687	75.7

Language Spoken at Home: Spanish
(Universe: Population 5 Years and Over)

Group	Number	%
Total Population	16,729	15.5
Hispanic or Latino (of any race)	15,857	72.7
Central American, ex. Mexican	2,499	90.2
Salvadoran	1,512	92.9
Mexican	12,404	74.6
Puerto Rican	193	21.3

Unemployment Rate
(Universe: Population 16 Years and Over)

Group	%
Total Population	12.0
Hispanic or Latino (of any race)	14.3
Central American, ex. Mexican	7.7
Salvadoran	1.7
Mexican	15.2
Puerto Rican	24.8

Class of Worker: Private Wage and Salary
(Universe: Civilian Employed Population 16 Years and Over)

Group	Number	%
Total Population	39,315	75.0
Hispanic or Latino (of any race)	8,050	78.2
Central American, ex. Mexican	1,223	72.8
Salvadoran	796	72.6
Mexican	6,142	82.1
Puerto Rican	242	68.4

Class of Worker: Government
(Universe: Civilian Employed Population 16 Years and Over)

Group	Number	%
Total Population	9,411	18.0
Hispanic or Latino (of any race)	1,115	10.8
Central American, ex. Mexican	224	13.3
Salvadoran	156	14.2
Mexican	649	8.7
Puerto Rican	99	28.0

Means of Transportation to Work: Car, Truck or Van
(Universe: Workers 16 Years and Over)

Group	Number	%
Total Population	44,567	88.0
Hispanic or Latino (of any race)	8,842	90.9
Central American, ex. Mexican	1,425	92.4
Salvadoran	928	92.2
Mexican	6,445	89.9
Puerto Rican	302	96.5

Means of Transportation to Work: Public Transportation (ex. Taxicab)
(Universe: Workers 16 Years and Over)

Group	Number	%
Total Population	2,446	4.8
Hispanic or Latino (of any race)	356	3.7
Central American, ex. Mexican	0	0.0
Salvadoran	0	0.0
Mexican	330	4.6
Puerto Rican	11	3.5

Homeownership Rate
(Universe: Occupied Housing Units)

Group	%
Total Population	59.6
Hispanic or Latino (of any race)	52.9
Central American, ex. Mexican	63.1
Guatemalan	56.3
Honduran	56.5
Nicaraguan	69.5
Salvadoran	65.4
Cuban	52.3
Mexican	50.0
Puerto Rican	47.1
South American	64.7
Colombian	52.9
Peruvian	63.1
Spaniard	63.4

Median Home Value

Group	Dollars
Total Population	355,300
Hispanic or Latino (of any race)	316,400
Central American, ex. Mexican	306,500
Salvadoran	371,600
Mexican	303,800
Puerto Rican	426,300

Median Gross Rent

Group	Dollars
Total Population	1,144
Hispanic or Latino (of any race)	1,125
Central American, ex. Mexican	1,193
Salvadoran	1,183
Mexican	1,124
Puerto Rican	858

Median Household Income
(2010 Inflation-Adjusted Dollars)

Group	Dollars
Total Population	61,481
Hispanic or Latino (of any race)	54,714
Central American, ex. Mexican	50,625
Salvadoran	48,333
Mexican	55,432
Puerto Rican	39,833

Per Capita Income
(2010 Inflation-Adjusted Dollars)

Group	Dollars
Total Population	26,575

Notes: (1) Percent of total population; (2) Percent of Hispanic/Latino population; Profiles include places with an overall population of at least 125,000, OR an overall population of at least 25,000 where the Hispanic/Latino population is at least 20% of the overall population. In states where less than five places meet either of these criteria, we have included places with at least 10,000 total population with the highest percentage of Hispanic/Latino population. These places are identified with an asterisk (*); Please refer to the User's Guide for a full explanation of data.

Hispanic or Latino (of any race)	16,600
Central American, ex. Mexican	17,865
Salvadoran	18,457
Mexican	15,340
Puerto Rican	19,618

Households with $100,000+ Income

Group	Number	%
Total Population	10,025	24.9
Hispanic or Latino (of any race)	1,116	17.8
Central American, ex. Mexican	143	17.5
Salvadoran	99	21.3
Mexican	733	15.9
Puerto Rican	86	31.6

Households with Food Stamps/SNAP Benefits During Past 12 Months

Group	Number	%
Total Population	2,917	7.2
Hispanic or Latino (of any race)	470	7.5
Central American, ex. Mexican	38	4.7
Salvadoran	27	5.8
Mexican	380	8.2
Puerto Rican	20	7.4

Poverty Rate
(Income in Past 12 Months Below Poverty Level)

Group	%
Total Population	13.9
Hispanic or Latino (of any race)	18.3
Central American, ex. Mexican	13.6
Salvadoran	7.0
Mexican	19.8
Puerto Rican	4.4

Victorville

Population

Group	Number	%TP[1]	%HP[2]
Total Population	115,903	100.0	–
Hispanic or Latino (of any race)	55,359	47.8	100.0
Central American, ex. Mexican	3,702	3.2	6.7
Costa Rican	115	0.1	0.2
Guatemalan	1,045	0.9	1.9
Honduran	245	0.2	0.4
Nicaraguan	311	0.3	0.6
Panamanian	106	0.1	0.2
Salvadoran	1,801	1.6	3.3
Cuban	399	0.3	0.7
Mexican	45,246	39.0	81.7
Puerto Rican	1,218	1.1	2.2
South American	745	0.6	1.3
Colombian	232	0.2	0.4
Ecuadorian	106	0.1	0.2
Peruvian	172	0.1	0.3
Spaniard	557	0.5	1.0

Population Growth: 2000–2010

Group	%
Total Population	81.0
Hispanic or Latino (of any race)	158.4
Central American, ex. Mexican	529.6
Guatemalan	610.9
Salvadoran	689.9
Cuban	115.7
Mexican	181.2
Puerto Rican	95.5
South American	290.1

Males per 100 Females

Group	Number
Total Population	100.4
Hispanic or Latino (of any race)	100.8
Central American, ex. Mexican	97.0
Costa Rican	74.2
Guatemalan	101.7
Honduran	105.9
Nicaraguan	84.0
Panamanian	112.0
Salvadoran	98.1
Cuban	116.8
Mexican	101.5
Puerto Rican	112.6
South American	90.5

Colombian	84.1
Ecuadorian	89.3
Peruvian	77.3
Spaniard	82.0

Average Household Size

Group	People
Total Population	3.40
Hispanic or Latino (of any race)	4.04
Central American, ex. Mexican	4.24
Costa Rican	3.80
Guatemalan	4.44
Honduran	4.24
Nicaraguan	4.01
Panamanian	3.38
Salvadoran	4.23
Cuban	3.28
Mexican	4.11
Puerto Rican	3.32
South American	3.48
Colombian	3.50
Ecuadorian	3.79
Peruvian	3.21
Spaniard	2.99

Median Age

Group	Years
Total Population	29.5
Hispanic or Latino (of any race)	25.0
Central American, ex. Mexican	31.9
Costa Rican	31.5
Guatemalan	31.5
Honduran	33.9
Nicaraguan	32.2
Panamanian	30.5
Salvadoran	32.3
Cuban	30.8
Mexican	24.2
Puerto Rican	26.3
South American	36.0
Colombian	37.3
Ecuadorian	48.3
Peruvian	32.3
Spaniard	31.7

High School Graduates
(Universe: Population 25 Years and Over)

Group	Number	%
Total Population	46,881	78.9
Hispanic or Latino (of any race)	15,559	64.7
Central American, ex. Mexican	1,030	62.6
Guatemalan	298	60.7
Salvadoran	305	45.1
Mexican	12,909	63.0

Four-Year College Graduates
(Universe: Population 25 Years and Over)

Group	Number	%
Total Population	7,424	12.5
Hispanic or Latino (of any race)	1,796	7.5
Central American, ex. Mexican	220	13.4
Guatemalan	52	10.6
Salvadoran	97	14.3
Mexican	1,322	6.5

Population Age 3–17 Enrolled in Public School
(Universe: Population Age 3–17 Enrolled in School)

Group	Number	%
Total Population	26,604	94.6
Hispanic or Latino (of any race)	14,784	96.3
Central American, ex. Mexican	767	95.9
Guatemalan	278	92.7
Salvadoran	391	100.0
Mexican	12,995	96.1

Population Age 3–17 Enrolled in Private School
(Universe: Population Age 3–17 Enrolled in School)

Group	Number	%
Total Population	1,525	5.4
Hispanic or Latino (of any race)	572	3.7
Central American, ex. Mexican	33	4.1
Guatemalan	22	7.3
Salvadoran	0	0.0
Mexican	529	3.9

Foreign-Born Population

Group	Number	%
Total Population	18,049	16.7
Hispanic or Latino (of any race)	13,550	27.0
Central American, ex. Mexican	1,839	63.4
Guatemalan	488	47.8
Salvadoran	844	73.3
Mexican	11,083	25.4

Foreign-Born Naturalized U.S. Citizens

Group	Number	%
Total Population	6,625	36.7
Hispanic or Latino (of any race)	4,038	29.8
Central American, ex. Mexican	718	39.0
Guatemalan	104	21.3
Salvadoran	333	39.5
Mexican	2,967	26.8

Language Spoken at Home: English Only
(Universe: Population 5 Years and Over)

Group	Number	%
Total Population	64,020	65.5
Hispanic or Latino (of any race)	16,409	36.9
Central American, ex. Mexican	269	10.3
Guatemalan	109	12.1
Salvadoran	72	7.0
Mexican	14,320	37.2

Language Spoken at Home: Spanish
(Universe: Population 5 Years and Over)

Group	Number	%
Total Population	29,086	29.8
Hispanic or Latino (of any race)	27,951	62.9
Central American, ex. Mexican	2,334	89.3
Guatemalan	792	87.9
Salvadoran	957	93.0
Mexican	24,099	62.7

Unemployment Rate
(Universe: Population 16 Years and Over)

Group	%
Total Population	14.1
Hispanic or Latino (of any race)	13.5
Central American, ex. Mexican	8.5
Guatemalan	8.1
Salvadoran	10.6
Mexican	13.1

Class of Worker: Private Wage and Salary
(Universe: Civilian Employed Population 16 Years and Over)

Group	Number	%
Total Population	27,588	74.8
Hispanic or Latino (of any race)	13,131	80.0
Central American, ex. Mexican	971	82.7
Guatemalan	308	84.4
Salvadoran	350	83.3
Mexican	11,122	80.3

Class of Worker: Government
(Universe: Civilian Employed Population 16 Years and Over)

Group	Number	%
Total Population	6,914	18.8
Hispanic or Latino (of any race)	2,307	14.0
Central American, ex. Mexican	127	10.8
Guatemalan	28	7.7
Salvadoran	23	5.5
Mexican	1,901	13.7

Means of Transportation to Work: Car, Truck or Van
(Universe: Workers 16 Years and Over)

Group	Number	%
Total Population	33,525	93.5
Hispanic or Latino (of any race)	15,061	93.8
Central American, ex. Mexican	1,109	97.0
Guatemalan	325	96.7
Salvadoran	395	94.5
Mexican	12,694	93.7

Means of Transportation to Work: Public Transportation (ex. Taxicab)
(Universe: Workers 16 Years and Over)

Group	Number	%
Total Population	178	0.5
Hispanic or Latino (of any race)	57	0.4

Notes: (1) Percent of total population; (2) Percent of Hispanic/Latino population; Profiles include places with an overall population of at least 125,000, OR an overall population of at least 25,000 where the Hispanic/Latino population is at least 20% of the overall population. In states where less than five places meet either of these criteria, we have included places with at least 10,000 total population with the highest percentage of Hispanic/Latino population. These places are identified with an asterisk (*); Please refer to the User's Guide for a full explanation of data.

Group	Number	%
Central American, ex. Mexican	0	0.0
Guatemalan	0	0.0
Salvadoran	0	0.0
Mexican	57	0.4

Homeownership Rate
(Universe: Occupied Housing Units)

Group	%
Total Population	61.8
Hispanic or Latino (of any race)	61.7
Central American, ex. Mexican	65.8
Costa Rican	56.7
Guatemalan	62.3
Honduran	66.1
Nicaraguan	72.8
Panamanian	65.6
Salvadoran	68.0
Cuban	66.7
Mexican	61.5
Puerto Rican	61.4
South American	69.6
Colombian	65.2
Ecuadorian	70.6
Peruvian	71.7
Spaniard	64.9

Median Home Value

Group	Dollars
Total Population	227,300
Hispanic or Latino (of any race)	240,400
Central American, ex. Mexican	246,200
Guatemalan	274,700
Salvadoran	198,000
Mexican	239,500

Median Gross Rent

Group	Dollars
Total Population	1,069
Hispanic or Latino (of any race)	1,037
Central American, ex. Mexican	984
Guatemalan	1,295
Salvadoran	909
Mexican	1,053

Median Household Income
(2010 Inflation-Adjusted Dollars)

Group	Dollars
Total Population	53,566
Hispanic or Latino (of any race)	53,816
Central American, ex. Mexican	54,221
Guatemalan	53,879
Salvadoran	49,716
Mexican	52,834

Per Capita Income
(2010 Inflation-Adjusted Dollars)

Group	Dollars
Total Population	17,907
Hispanic or Latino (of any race)	14,148
Central American, ex. Mexican	14,595
Guatemalan	12,770
Salvadoran	14,307
Mexican	13,625

Households with $100,000+ Income

Group	Number	%
Total Population	4,468	14.7
Hispanic or Latino (of any race)	1,444	12.8
Central American, ex. Mexican	73	10.4
Guatemalan	65	23.6
Salvadoran	8	3.1
Mexican	1,195	12.5

Households with Food Stamps/SNAP Benefits During Past 12 Months

Group	Number	%
Total Population	3,551	11.7
Hispanic or Latino (of any race)	1,473	13.0
Central American, ex. Mexican	106	15.2
Guatemalan	43	15.6
Salvadoran	35	13.6
Mexican	1,246	13.0

Poverty Rate
(Income in Past 12 Months Below Poverty Level)

Group	%
Total Population	19.4
Hispanic or Latino (of any race)	19.3
Central American, ex. Mexican	18.6
Guatemalan	15.5
Salvadoran	32.6
Mexican	19.4

Visalia

Population

Group	Number	%TP[1]	%HP[2]
Total Population	124,442	100.0	–
Hispanic or Latino (of any race)	57,262	46.0	100.0
Central American, ex. Mexican	857	0.7	1.5
Guatemalan	190	0.2	0.3
Salvadoran	472	0.4	0.8
Cuban	117	0.1	0.2
Mexican	52,121	41.9	91.0
Puerto Rican	542	0.4	0.9
South American	336	0.3	0.6
Spaniard	375	0.3	0.7

Population Growth: 2000–2010

Group	%
Total Population	35.9
Hispanic or Latino (of any race)	75.5
Central American, ex. Mexican	320.1
Mexican	86.7
Puerto Rican	100.7
South American	184.7

Males per 100 Females

Group	Number
Total Population	95.2
Hispanic or Latino (of any race)	98.8
Central American, ex. Mexican	98.4
Guatemalan	100.0
Salvadoran	104.3
Cuban	85.7
Mexican	99.5
Puerto Rican	106.1
South American	80.6
Spaniard	70.5

Average Household Size

Group	People
Total Population	2.98
Hispanic or Latino (of any race)	3.65
Central American, ex. Mexican	3.73
Guatemalan	3.73
Salvadoran	4.05
Cuban	3.30
Mexican	3.68
Puerto Rican	3.23
South American	2.97
Spaniard	2.99

Median Age

Group	Years
Total Population	31.6
Hispanic or Latino (of any race)	24.6
Central American, ex. Mexican	34.4
Guatemalan	35.4
Salvadoran	33.8
Cuban	27.1
Mexican	24.3
Puerto Rican	22.6
South American	35.3
Spaniard	31.6

High School Graduates
(Universe: Population 25 Years and Over)

Group	Number	%
Total Population	57,199	80.5
Hispanic or Latino (of any race)	16,494	65.6
Mexican	15,503	65.3

Four-Year College Graduates
(Universe: Population 25 Years and Over)

Group	Number	%
Total Population	14,842	20.9
Hispanic or Latino (of any race)	2,485	9.9
Mexican	2,299	9.7

Population Age 3–17 Enrolled in Public School
(Universe: Population Age 3–17 Enrolled in School)

Group	Number	%
Total Population	24,537	91.9
Hispanic or Latino (of any race)	14,327	96.2
Mexican	13,640	96.5

Population Age 3–17 Enrolled in Private School
(Universe: Population Age 3–17 Enrolled in School)

Group	Number	%
Total Population	2,172	8.1
Hispanic or Latino (of any race)	559	3.8
Mexican	489	3.5

Foreign-Born Population

Group	Number	%
Total Population	16,438	13.8
Hispanic or Latino (of any race)	10,944	21.2
Mexican	10,143	20.7

Foreign-Born Naturalized U.S. Citizens

Group	Number	%
Total Population	6,494	39.5
Hispanic or Latino (of any race)	3,371	30.8
Mexican	2,927	28.9

Language Spoken at Home: English Only
(Universe: Population 5 Years and Over)

Group	Number	%
Total Population	77,757	71.9
Hispanic or Latino (of any race)	21,847	48.4
Mexican	20,711	48.4

Language Spoken at Home: Spanish
(Universe: Population 5 Years and Over)

Group	Number	%
Total Population	24,158	22.3
Hispanic or Latino (of any race)	23,180	51.4
Mexican	22,037	51.5

Unemployment Rate
(Universe: Population 16 Years and Over)

Group	%
Total Population	8.4
Hispanic or Latino (of any race)	11.1
Mexican	11.2

Class of Worker: Private Wage and Salary
(Universe: Civilian Employed Population 16 Years and Over)

Group	Number	%
Total Population	35,069	71.0
Hispanic or Latino (of any race)	14,147	73.9
Mexican	13,442	74.4

Class of Worker: Government
(Universe: Civilian Employed Population 16 Years and Over)

Group	Number	%
Total Population	10,660	21.6
Hispanic or Latino (of any race)	4,114	21.5
Mexican	3,847	21.3

Means of Transportation to Work: Car, Truck or Van
(Universe: Workers 16 Years and Over)

Group	Number	%
Total Population	44,654	92.5
Hispanic or Latino (of any race)	17,407	92.5
Mexican	16,488	92.9

Means of Transportation to Work: Public Transportation (ex. Taxicab)
(Universe: Workers 16 Years and Over)

Group	Number	%
Total Population	523	1.1
Hispanic or Latino (of any race)	247	1.3
Mexican	247	1.4

Homeownership Rate
(Universe: Occupied Housing Units)

Group	%
Total Population	61.4
Hispanic or Latino (of any race)	51.1
Central American, ex. Mexican	55.2

Notes: (1) Percent of total population; (2) Percent of Hispanic/Latino population; Profiles include places with an overall population of at least 125,000, OR an overall population of at least 25,000 where the Hispanic/Latino population is at least 20% of the overall population. In states where less than five places meet either of these criteria, we have included places with at least 10,000 total population with the highest percentage of Hispanic/Latino population. These places are identified with an asterisk (*); Please refer to the User's Guide for a full explanation of data.

Group	Number
Guatemalan	50.0
Salvadoran	63.3
Cuban	50.0
Mexican	51.5
Puerto Rican	50.7
South American	57.8
Spaniard	56.9

Median Home Value

Group	Dollars
Total Population	231,900
Hispanic or Latino (of any race)	215,800
Mexican	213,200

Median Gross Rent

Group	Dollars
Total Population	894
Hispanic or Latino (of any race)	847
Mexican	851

Median Household Income
(2010 Inflation-Adjusted Dollars)

Group	Dollars
Total Population	53,606
Hispanic or Latino (of any race)	43,561
Mexican	43,739

Per Capita Income
(2010 Inflation-Adjusted Dollars)

Group	Dollars
Total Population	23,458
Hispanic or Latino (of any race)	14,905
Mexican	14,660

Households with $100,000+ Income

Group	Number	%
Total Population	8,700	22.3
Hispanic or Latino (of any race)	2,028	15.5
Mexican	1,934	15.7

Households with Food Stamps/SNAP Benefits During Past 12 Months

Group	Number	%
Total Population	4,578	11.7
Hispanic or Latino (of any race)	2,858	21.8
Mexican	2,777	22.5

Poverty Rate
(Income in Past 12 Months Below Poverty Level)

Group	%
Total Population	15.6
Hispanic or Latino (of any race)	22.1
Mexican	22.4

Vista

Population

Group	Number	%TP[1]	%HP[2]
Total Population	93,834	100.0	–
Hispanic or Latino (of any race)	45,380	48.4	100.0
Central American, ex. Mexican	768	0.8	1.7
Guatemalan	269	0.3	0.6
Salvadoran	245	0.3	0.5
Cuban	131	0.1	0.3
Mexican	40,799	43.5	89.9
Puerto Rican	657	0.7	1.4
South American	442	0.5	1.0
Colombian	134	0.1	0.3
Spaniard	373	0.4	0.8

Population Growth: 2000–2010

Group	%
Total Population	4.4
Hispanic or Latino (of any race)	29.7
Central American, ex. Mexican	66.2
Guatemalan	108.5
Salvadoran	62.3
Mexican	36.9
Puerto Rican	18.2
South American	131.4

Males per 100 Females

Group	Number
Total Population	100.7
Hispanic or Latino (of any race)	103.6
Central American, ex. Mexican	107.6
Guatemalan	113.5
Salvadoran	107.6
Cuban	151.9
Mexican	103.9
Puerto Rican	110.6
South American	88.9
Colombian	78.7
Spaniard	101.6

Average Household Size

Group	People
Total Population	3.13
Hispanic or Latino (of any race)	4.46
Central American, ex. Mexican	3.89
Guatemalan	4.38
Salvadoran	3.81
Cuban	2.56
Mexican	4.63
Puerto Rican	2.71
South American	2.62
Colombian	2.49
Spaniard	3.21

Median Age

Group	Years
Total Population	31.1
Hispanic or Latino (of any race)	24.8
Central American, ex. Mexican	28.3
Guatemalan	28.2
Salvadoran	30.3
Cuban	28.3
Mexican	24.6
Puerto Rican	26.6
South American	33.9
Colombian	31.0
Spaniard	30.6

High School Graduates
(Universe: Population 25 Years and Over)

Group	Number	%
Total Population	42,018	74.5
Hispanic or Latino (of any race)	9,809	46.2
Mexican	8,693	44.4

Four-Year College Graduates
(Universe: Population 25 Years and Over)

Group	Number	%
Total Population	11,539	20.5
Hispanic or Latino (of any race)	1,434	6.8
Mexican	1,087	5.6

Population Age 3–17 Enrolled in Public School
(Universe: Population Age 3–17 Enrolled in School)

Group	Number	%
Total Population	16,049	92.7
Hispanic or Latino (of any race)	10,588	97.1
Mexican	10,132	97.0

Population Age 3–17 Enrolled in Private School
(Universe: Population Age 3–17 Enrolled in School)

Group	Number	%
Total Population	1,261	7.3
Hispanic or Latino (of any race)	317	2.9
Mexican	317	3.0

Foreign-Born Population

Group	Number	%
Total Population	24,398	26.4
Hispanic or Latino (of any race)	19,369	45.6
Mexican	18,475	46.4

Foreign-Born Naturalized U.S. Citizens

Group	Number	%
Total Population	6,553	26.9
Hispanic or Latino (of any race)	3,530	18.2
Mexican	3,021	16.4

Language Spoken at Home: English Only
(Universe: Population 5 Years and Over)

Group	Number	%
Total Population	47,546	55.9
Hispanic or Latino (of any race)	6,079	16.1
Mexican	5,161	14.6

Language Spoken at Home: Spanish
(Universe: Population 5 Years and Over)

Group	Number	%
Total Population	32,684	38.4
Hispanic or Latino (of any race)	31,669	83.8
Mexican	30,130	85.3

Unemployment Rate
(Universe: Population 16 Years and Over)

Group	%
Total Population	8.8
Hispanic or Latino (of any race)	9.3
Mexican	9.7

Class of Worker: Private Wage and Salary
(Universe: Civilian Employed Population 16 Years and Over)

Group	Number	%
Total Population	32,711	79.9
Hispanic or Latino (of any race)	15,245	86.5
Mexican	14,127	86.8

Class of Worker: Government
(Universe: Civilian Employed Population 16 Years and Over)

Group	Number	%
Total Population	4,652	11.4
Hispanic or Latino (of any race)	1,053	6.0
Mexican	921	5.7

Means of Transportation to Work: Car, Truck or Van
(Universe: Workers 16 Years and Over)

Group	Number	%
Total Population	36,978	88.9
Hispanic or Latino (of any race)	16,008	90.4
Mexican	14,825	91.0

Means of Transportation to Work: Public Transportation (ex. Taxicab)
(Universe: Workers 16 Years and Over)

Group	Number	%
Total Population	1,177	2.8
Hispanic or Latino (of any race)	649	3.7
Mexican	583	3.6

Homeownership Rate
(Universe: Occupied Housing Units)

Group	%
Total Population	51.8
Hispanic or Latino (of any race)	35.6
Central American, ex. Mexican	34.5
Guatemalan	25.6
Salvadoran	37.5
Cuban	52.0
Mexican	35.8
Puerto Rican	36.8
South American	44.1
Colombian	35.6
Spaniard	40.7

Median Home Value

Group	Dollars
Total Population	421,700
Hispanic or Latino (of any race)	383,800
Mexican	383,000

Median Gross Rent

Group	Dollars
Total Population	1,217
Hispanic or Latino (of any race)	1,204
Mexican	1,203

Median Household Income
(2010 Inflation-Adjusted Dollars)

Group	Dollars
Total Population	52,602
Hispanic or Latino (of any race)	45,808
Mexican	45,627

Per Capita Income
(2010 Inflation-Adjusted Dollars)

Group	Dollars
Total Population	21,645
Hispanic or Latino (of any race)	12,674
Mexican	12,127

Notes: (1) Percent of total population; (2) Percent of Hispanic/Latino population; Profiles include places with an overall population of at least 125,000, OR an overall population of at least 25,000 where the Hispanic/Latino population is at least 20% of the overall population. In states where less than five places meet either of these criteria, we have included places with at least 10,000 total population with the highest percentage of Hispanic/Latino population. These places are identified with an asterisk (*); Please refer to the User's Guide for a full explanation of data.

Households with $100,000+ Income

Group	Number	%
Total Population	5,608	19.8
Hispanic or Latino (of any race)	921	10.4
Mexican	842	10.5

Households with Food Stamps/SNAP Benefits During Past 12 Months

Group	Number	%
Total Population	946	3.3
Hispanic or Latino (of any race)	600	6.8
Mexican	561	7.0

Poverty Rate
(Income in Past 12 Months Below Poverty Level)

Group	%
Total Population	13.8
Hispanic or Latino (of any race)	19.6
Mexican	19.7

Wasco

Population

Group	Number	%TP[1]	%HP[2]
Total Population	25,545	100.0	–
Hispanic or Latino (of any race)	19,585	76.7	100.0
Central American, ex. Mexican	285	1.1	1.5
Salvadoran	206	0.8	1.1
Mexican	17,814	69.7	91.0
Puerto Rican	158	0.6	0.8

Population Growth: 2000–2010

Group	%
Total Population	20.1
Hispanic or Latino (of any race)	38.0
Mexican	42.1
Puerto Rican	42.3

Males per 100 Females

Group	Number
Total Population	160.3
Hispanic or Latino (of any race)	135.3
Central American, ex. Mexican	93.9
Salvadoran	79.1
Mexican	131.5
Puerto Rican	113.5

Average Household Size

Group	People
Total Population	3.86
Hispanic or Latino (of any race)	4.19
Central American, ex. Mexican	3.91
Salvadoran	3.85
Mexican	4.20
Puerto Rican	4.11

Median Age

Group	Years
Total Population	28.3
Hispanic or Latino (of any race)	25.6
Central American, ex. Mexican	31.3
Salvadoran	31.7
Mexican	25.4
Puerto Rican	20.7

High School Graduates
(Universe: Population 25 Years and Over)

Group	Number	%
Total Population	7,915	56.9
Hispanic or Latino (of any race)	4,651	50.3
Mexican	4,288	49.9

Four-Year College Graduates
(Universe: Population 25 Years and Over)

Group	Number	%
Total Population	634	4.6
Hispanic or Latino (of any race)	281	3.0
Mexican	210	2.4

Population Age 3–17 Enrolled in Public School
(Universe: Population Age 3–17 Enrolled in School)

Group	Number	%
Total Population	5,323	97.0
Hispanic or Latino (of any race)	4,809	96.9
Mexican	4,684	96.8

Population Age 3–17 Enrolled in Private School
(Universe: Population Age 3–17 Enrolled in School)

Group	Number	%
Total Population	165	3.0
Hispanic or Latino (of any race)	155	3.1
Mexican	155	3.2

Foreign-Born Population

Group	Number	%
Total Population	7,197	28.6
Hispanic or Latino (of any race)	6,687	35.5
Mexican	6,283	35.2

Foreign-Born Naturalized U.S. Citizens

Group	Number	%
Total Population	1,917	26.6
Hispanic or Latino (of any race)	1,637	24.5
Mexican	1,478	23.5

Language Spoken at Home: English Only
(Universe: Population 5 Years and Over)

Group	Number	%
Total Population	7,622	33.1
Hispanic or Latino (of any race)	2,454	14.5
Mexican	2,298	14.3

Language Spoken at Home: Spanish
(Universe: Population 5 Years and Over)

Group	Number	%
Total Population	14,735	64.0
Hispanic or Latino (of any race)	14,490	85.5
Mexican	13,752	85.7

Unemployment Rate
(Universe: Population 16 Years and Over)

Group	%
Total Population	12.6
Hispanic or Latino (of any race)	12.8
Mexican	12.7

Class of Worker: Private Wage and Salary
(Universe: Civilian Employed Population 16 Years and Over)

Group	Number	%
Total Population	6,000	82.0
Hispanic or Latino (of any race)	5,365	85.7
Mexican	5,033	85.8

Class of Worker: Government
(Universe: Civilian Employed Population 16 Years and Over)

Group	Number	%
Total Population	868	11.9
Hispanic or Latino (of any race)	557	8.9
Mexican	544	9.3

Means of Transportation to Work: Car, Truck or Van
(Universe: Workers 16 Years and Over)

Group	Number	%
Total Population	6,784	94.6
Hispanic or Latino (of any race)	5,816	94.6
Mexican	5,569	96.6

Means of Transportation to Work: Public Transportation (ex. Taxicab)
(Universe: Workers 16 Years and Over)

Group	Number	%
Total Population	9	0.1
Hispanic or Latino (of any race)	9	0.1
Mexican	9	0.2

Homeownership Rate
(Universe: Occupied Housing Units)

Group	%
Total Population	52.2
Hispanic or Latino (of any race)	48.2
Central American, ex. Mexican	37.8
Salvadoran	40.3
Mexican	48.8
Puerto Rican	41.7

Median Home Value

Group	Dollars
Total Population	174,000
Hispanic or Latino (of any race)	169,500
Mexican	165,800

Median Gross Rent

Group	Dollars
Total Population	568
Hispanic or Latino (of any race)	568
Mexican	563

Median Household Income
(2010 Inflation-Adjusted Dollars)

Group	Dollars
Total Population	40,054
Hispanic or Latino (of any race)	39,109
Mexican	38,910

Per Capita Income
(2010 Inflation-Adjusted Dollars)

Group	Dollars
Total Population	11,799
Hispanic or Latino (of any race)	10,749
Mexican	10,508

Households with $100,000+ Income

Group	Number	%
Total Population	424	8.3
Hispanic or Latino (of any race)	302	7.6
Mexican	296	8.0

Households with Food Stamps/SNAP Benefits During Past 12 Months

Group	Number	%
Total Population	987	19.2
Hispanic or Latino (of any race)	846	21.3
Mexican	777	21.0

Poverty Rate
(Income in Past 12 Months Below Poverty Level)

Group	%
Total Population	26.3
Hispanic or Latino (of any race)	28.0
Mexican	28.4

Watsonville

Population

Group	Number	%TP[1]	%HP[2]
Total Population	51,199	100.0	–
Hispanic or Latino (of any race)	41,656	81.4	100.0
Central American, ex. Mexican	361	0.7	0.9
Salvadoran	256	0.5	0.6
Mexican	39,083	76.3	93.8
South American	113	0.2	0.3
Spaniard	147	0.3	0.4

Population Growth: 2000–2010

Group	%
Total Population	15.7
Hispanic or Latino (of any race)	25.3
Central American, ex. Mexican	72.7
Salvadoran	134.9
Mexican	30.5

Males per 100 Females

Group	Number
Total Population	99.2
Hispanic or Latino (of any race)	103.0
Central American, ex. Mexican	106.3
Salvadoran	109.8
Mexican	103.3
South American	88.3
Spaniard	101.4

Average Household Size

Group	People
Total Population	3.75
Hispanic or Latino (of any race)	4.44
Central American, ex. Mexican	3.51
Salvadoran	3.77
Mexican	4.49
South American	2.86
Spaniard	2.88

Notes: (1) Percent of total population; (2) Percent of Hispanic/Latino population; Profiles include places with an overall population of at least 125,000, OR an overall population of at least 25,000 where the Hispanic/Latino population is at least 20% of the overall population. In states where less than five places meet either of these criteria, we have included places with at least 10,000 total population with the highest percentage of Hispanic/Latino population. These places are identified with an asterisk (*); Please refer to the User's Guide for a full explanation of data.

Median Age	
Group	Years
Total Population	29.2
Hispanic or Latino (of any race)	26.1
Central American, ex. Mexican	32.9
Salvadoran	33.3
Mexican	26.0
South American	40.3
Spaniard	43.5

High School Graduates
(Universe: Population 25 Years and Over)

Group	Number	%
Total Population	14,656	52.5
Hispanic or Latino (of any race)	7,786	39.0
Mexican	7,251	37.8

Four-Year College Graduates
(Universe: Population 25 Years and Over)

Group	Number	%
Total Population	2,838	10.2
Hispanic or Latino (of any race)	1,018	5.1
Mexican	885	4.6

Population Age 3–17 Enrolled in Public School
(Universe: Population Age 3–17 Enrolled in School)

Group	Number	%
Total Population	11,028	94.1
Hispanic or Latino (of any race)	9,939	96.4
Mexican	9,681	96.4

Population Age 3–17 Enrolled in Private School
(Universe: Population Age 3–17 Enrolled in School)

Group	Number	%
Total Population	690	5.9
Hispanic or Latino (of any race)	371	3.6
Mexican	360	3.6

Foreign-Born Population

Group	Number	%
Total Population	20,798	41.9
Hispanic or Latino (of any race)	19,300	49.5
Mexican	18,627	49.3

Foreign-Born Naturalized U.S. Citizens

Group	Number	%
Total Population	5,256	25.3
Hispanic or Latino (of any race)	4,220	21.9
Mexican	3,897	20.9

Language Spoken at Home: English Only
(Universe: Population 5 Years and Over)

Group	Number	%
Total Population	11,737	26.0
Hispanic or Latino (of any race)	3,665	10.5
Mexican	3,464	10.2

Language Spoken at Home: Spanish
(Universe: Population 5 Years and Over)

Group	Number	%
Total Population	31,578	69.9
Hispanic or Latino (of any race)	31,180	89.1
Mexican	30,209	89.3

Unemployment Rate
(Universe: Population 16 Years and Over)

Group	%
Total Population	11.0
Hispanic or Latino (of any race)	11.4
Mexican	11.4

Class of Worker: Private Wage and Salary
(Universe: Civilian Employed Population 16 Years and Over)

Group	Number	%
Total Population	17,642	82.4
Hispanic or Latino (of any race)	14,149	85.3
Mexican	13,783	85.5

Class of Worker: Government
(Universe: Civilian Employed Population 16 Years and Over)

Group	Number	%
Total Population	2,291	10.7
Hispanic or Latino (of any race)	1,613	9.7
Mexican	1,554	9.6

Means of Transportation to Work: Car, Truck or Van
(Universe: Workers 16 Years and Over)

Group	Number	%
Total Population	18,351	89.4
Hispanic or Latino (of any race)	14,280	89.1
Mexican	13,874	89.0

Means of Transportation to Work: Public Transportation (ex. Taxicab)
(Universe: Workers 16 Years and Over)

Group	Number	%
Total Population	268	1.3
Hispanic or Latino (of any race)	219	1.4
Mexican	210	1.3

Homeownership Rate
(Universe: Occupied Housing Units)

Group	%
Total Population	44.0
Hispanic or Latino (of any race)	35.2
Central American, ex. Mexican	24.6
Salvadoran	26.9
Mexican	35.7
South American	65.7
Spaniard	56.9

Median Home Value

Group	Dollars
Total Population	445,900
Hispanic or Latino (of any race)	444,300
Mexican	440,100

Median Gross Rent

Group	Dollars
Total Population	1,016
Hispanic or Latino (of any race)	985
Mexican	986

Median Household Income
(2010 Inflation-Adjusted Dollars)

Group	Dollars
Total Population	46,675
Hispanic or Latino (of any race)	44,305
Mexican	44,704

Per Capita Income
(2010 Inflation-Adjusted Dollars)

Group	Dollars
Total Population	16,227
Hispanic or Latino (of any race)	13,146
Mexican	12,970

Households with $100,000+ Income

Group	Number	%
Total Population	1,982	14.4
Hispanic or Latino (of any race)	1,151	12.6
Mexican	1,095	12.5

Households with Food Stamps/SNAP Benefits During Past 12 Months

Group	Number	%
Total Population	1,563	11.3
Hispanic or Latino (of any race)	1,391	15.2
Mexican	1,344	15.4

Poverty Rate
(Income in Past 12 Months Below Poverty Level)

Group	%
Total Population	18.7
Hispanic or Latino (of any race)	21.4
Mexican	21.4

West Covina

Population

Group	Number	%TP[1]	%HP[2]
Total Population	106,098	100.0	–
Hispanic or Latino (of any race)	56,471	53.2	100.0
Central American, ex. Mexican	4,091	3.9	7.2
Costa Rican	145	0.1	0.3
Guatemalan	946	0.9	1.7
Honduran	235	0.2	0.4
Nicaraguan	611	0.6	1.1
Salvadoran	2,019	1.9	3.6
Cuban	517	0.5	0.9
Mexican	46,505	43.8	82.4
Puerto Rican	615	0.6	1.1
South American	1,506	1.4	2.7
Argentinean	219	0.2	0.4
Colombian	331	0.3	0.6
Ecuadorian	302	0.3	0.5
Peruvian	437	0.4	0.8
Spaniard	440	0.4	0.8

Population Growth: 2000–2010

Group	%
Total Population	1.0
Hispanic or Latino (of any race)	17.5
Central American, ex. Mexican	84.9
Costa Rican	38.1
Guatemalan	106.1
Nicaraguan	59.5
Salvadoran	115.7
Cuban	7.3
Mexican	25.0
Puerto Rican	9.8
South American	33.2
Argentinean	18.4
Colombian	37.9
Ecuadorian	39.2
Peruvian	70.7

Males per 100 Females

Group	Number
Total Population	93.1
Hispanic or Latino (of any race)	93.2
Central American, ex. Mexican	84.4
Costa Rican	72.6
Guatemalan	97.9
Honduran	75.4
Nicaraguan	79.2
Salvadoran	82.1
Cuban	99.6
Mexican	94.4
Puerto Rican	81.4
South American	83.7
Argentinean	106.6
Colombian	65.5
Ecuadorian	81.9
Peruvian	90.8
Spaniard	97.3

Average Household Size

Group	People
Total Population	3.34
Hispanic or Latino (of any race)	3.82
Central American, ex. Mexican	4.00
Costa Rican	3.37
Guatemalan	3.96
Honduran	4.00
Nicaraguan	3.81
Salvadoran	4.22
Cuban	3.51
Mexican	3.86
Puerto Rican	3.10
South American	3.29
Argentinean	3.00
Colombian	3.20
Ecuadorian	3.23
Peruvian	3.55
Spaniard	3.12

Median Age

Group	Years
Total Population	36.0
Hispanic or Latino (of any race)	29.6
Central American, ex. Mexican	35.8
Costa Rican	37.3
Guatemalan	35.9
Honduran	35.6
Nicaraguan	38.6
Salvadoran	35.0
Cuban	37.6
Mexican	28.8
Puerto Rican	33.2
South American	40.0
Argentinean	39.5
Colombian	35.3

Notes: (1) Percent of total population; (2) Percent of Hispanic/Latino population; Profiles include places with an overall population of at least 125,000, OR an overall population of at least 25,000 where the Hispanic/Latino population is at least 20% of the overall population. In states where less than five places meet either of these criteria, we have included places with at least 10,000 total population with the highest percentage of Hispanic/Latino population. These places are identified with an asterisk (*); Please refer to the User's Guide for a full explanation of data.

STATE & PLACE PROFILES

Ecuadorian		41.6
Peruvian		40.9
Spaniard		39.5

High School Graduates
(Universe: Population 25 Years and Over)

Group	Number	%
Total Population	55,407	82.7
Hispanic or Latino (of any race)	22,452	74.5
Central American, ex. Mexican	2,132	75.8
Guatemalan	356	70.6
Salvadoran	1,123	75.8
Mexican	17,973	73.6
Puerto Rican	283	89.0
South American	919	84.2

Four-Year College Graduates
(Universe: Population 25 Years and Over)

Group	Number	%
Total Population	17,379	25.9
Hispanic or Latino (of any race)	4,044	13.4
Central American, ex. Mexican	522	18.6
Guatemalan	138	27.4
Salvadoran	165	11.1
Mexican	2,715	11.1
Puerto Rican	73	23.0
South American	252	23.1

Population Age 3–17 Enrolled in Public School
(Universe: Population Age 3–17 Enrolled in School)

Group	Number	%
Total Population	18,457	87.3
Hispanic or Latino (of any race)	12,291	88.2
Central American, ex. Mexican	924	89.2
Guatemalan	390	90.5
Salvadoran	344	82.9
Mexican	10,190	87.7
Puerto Rican	145	89.0
South American	212	100.0

Population Age 3–17 Enrolled in Private School
(Universe: Population Age 3–17 Enrolled in School)

Group	Number	%
Total Population	2,687	12.7
Hispanic or Latino (of any race)	1,647	11.8
Central American, ex. Mexican	112	10.8
Guatemalan	41	9.5
Salvadoran	71	17.1
Mexican	1,424	12.3
Puerto Rican	18	11.0
South American	0	0.0

Foreign-Born Population

Group	Number	%
Total Population	36,379	34.5
Hispanic or Latino (of any race)	15,161	27.6
Central American, ex. Mexican	2,569	55.4
Guatemalan	488	39.7
Salvadoran	1,306	59.1
Mexican	10,880	23.9
Puerto Rican	7	1.1
South American	1,100	75.1

Foreign-Born Naturalized U.S. Citizens

Group	Number	%
Total Population	22,900	62.9
Hispanic or Latino (of any race)	8,485	56.0
Central American, ex. Mexican	1,932	75.2
Guatemalan	327	67.0
Salvadoran	991	75.9
Mexican	5,291	48.6
Puerto Rican	0	0.0
South American	775	70.5

Language Spoken at Home: English Only
(Universe: Population 5 Years and Over)

Group	Number	%
Total Population	43,093	43.7
Hispanic or Latino (of any race)	17,709	35.5
Central American, ex. Mexican	395	9.2
Guatemalan	106	9.5
Salvadoran	159	7.5
Mexican	15,550	37.8
Puerto Rican	300	55.0
South American	237	16.7

Language Spoken at Home: Spanish
(Universe: Population 5 Years and Over)

Group	Number	%
Total Population	32,868	33.3
Hispanic or Latino (of any race)	31,922	64.0
Central American, ex. Mexican	3,896	90.8
Guatemalan	1,009	90.5
Salvadoran	1,959	92.5
Mexican	25,480	61.9
Puerto Rican	245	45.0
South American	1,096	77.3

Unemployment Rate
(Universe: Population 16 Years and Over)

Group	%
Total Population	8.8
Hispanic or Latino (of any race)	9.7
Central American, ex. Mexican	9.1
Guatemalan	19.4
Salvadoran	8.3
Mexican	9.9
Puerto Rican	6.4
South American	5.7

Class of Worker: Private Wage and Salary
(Universe: Civilian Employed Population 16 Years and Over)

Group	Number	%
Total Population	37,420	75.8
Hispanic or Latino (of any race)	18,451	75.1
Central American, ex. Mexican	1,761	75.7
Guatemalan	369	77.4
Salvadoran	993	76.9
Mexican	15,107	75.0
Puerto Rican	202	81.1
South American	621	77.8

Class of Worker: Government
(Universe: Civilian Employed Population 16 Years and Over)

Group	Number	%
Total Population	8,192	16.6
Hispanic or Latino (of any race)	4,249	17.3
Central American, ex. Mexican	441	19.0
Guatemalan	101	21.2
Salvadoran	256	19.8
Mexican	3,425	17.0
Puerto Rican	21	8.4
South American	123	15.4

Means of Transportation to Work: Car, Truck or Van
(Universe: Workers 16 Years and Over)

Group	Number	%
Total Population	43,694	91.3
Hispanic or Latino (of any race)	21,933	91.7
Central American, ex. Mexican	1,992	86.5
Guatemalan	390	81.8
Salvadoran	1,097	86.4
Mexican	18,122	92.6
Puerto Rican	189	75.9
South American	712	89.2

Means of Transportation to Work: Public Transportation (ex. Taxicab)
(Universe: Workers 16 Years and Over)

Group	Number	%
Total Population	1,586	3.3
Hispanic or Latino (of any race)	695	2.9
Central American, ex. Mexican	85	3.7
Guatemalan	40	8.4
Salvadoran	39	3.1
Mexican	522	2.7
Puerto Rican	0	0.0
South American	46	5.8

Homeownership Rate
(Universe: Occupied Housing Units)

Group	%
Total Population	65.5
Hispanic or Latino (of any race)	59.2
Central American, ex. Mexican	59.4
Costa Rican	65.4
Guatemalan	59.8
Honduran	50.0
Nicaraguan	60.3
Salvadoran	59.6

Cuban	69.2
Mexican	59.8
Puerto Rican	52.9
South American	57.3
Argentinean	66.3
Colombian	60.6
Ecuadorian	63.5
Peruvian	51.0
Spaniard	69.3

Median Home Value

Group	Dollars
Total Population	465,400
Hispanic or Latino (of any race)	467,800
Central American, ex. Mexican	454,500
Guatemalan	432,000
Salvadoran	502,700
Mexican	464,700
Puerto Rican	437,500
South American	497,600

Median Gross Rent

Group	Dollars
Total Population	1,281
Hispanic or Latino (of any race)	1,180
Central American, ex. Mexican	989
Guatemalan	995
Salvadoran	971
Mexican	1,198
Puerto Rican	1,338
South American	843

Median Household Income
(2010 Inflation-Adjusted Dollars)

Group	Dollars
Total Population	69,587
Hispanic or Latino (of any race)	69,887
Central American, ex. Mexican	75,110
Guatemalan	68,707
Salvadoran	73,482
Mexican	69,450
Puerto Rican	97,813
South American	68,860

Per Capita Income
(2010 Inflation-Adjusted Dollars)

Group	Dollars
Total Population	25,303
Hispanic or Latino (of any race)	21,116
Central American, ex. Mexican	20,945
Guatemalan	15,962
Salvadoran	22,614
Mexican	20,953
Puerto Rican	18,897
South American	24,196

Households with $100,000+ Income

Group	Number	%
Total Population	9,565	30.8
Hispanic or Latino (of any race)	4,012	29.2
Central American, ex. Mexican	398	34.0
Guatemalan	93	29.6
Salvadoran	154	31.0
Mexican	3,244	28.8
Puerto Rican	56	42.1
South American	125	24.3

Households with Food Stamps/SNAP Benefits During Past 12 Months

Group	Number	%
Total Population	1,118	3.6
Hispanic or Latino (of any race)	718	5.2
Central American, ex. Mexican	43	3.7
Guatemalan	0	0.0
Salvadoran	43	8.7
Mexican	628	5.6
Puerto Rican	9	6.8
South American	18	3.5

Poverty Rate
(Income in Past 12 Months Below Poverty Level)

Group	%
Total Population	8.7
Hispanic or Latino (of any race)	9.7
Central American, ex. Mexican	7.9

Notes: (1) Percent of total population; (2) Percent of Hispanic/Latino population; Profiles include places with an overall population of at least 125,000, OR an overall population of at least 25,000 where the Hispanic/Latino population is at least 20% of the overall population. In states where less than five places meet either of these criteria, we have included places with at least 10,000 total population with the highest percentage of Hispanic/Latino population. These places are identified with an asterisk (*); Please refer to the User's Guide for a full explanation of data.

Guatemalan	20.7
Salvadoran	3.1
Mexican	9.8
Puerto Rican	15.8
South American	15.7

West Sacramento

Population

Group	Number	%TP[1]	%HP[2]
Total Population	48,744	100.0	–
Hispanic or Latino (of any race)	15,282	31.4	100.0
Central American, ex. Mexican	419	0.9	2.7
Guatemalan	108	0.2	0.7
Salvadoran	175	0.4	1.1
Mexican	13,276	27.2	86.9
Puerto Rican	257	0.5	1.7
South American	198	0.4	1.3
Spaniard	259	0.5	1.7

Population Growth: 2000–2010

Group	%
Total Population	54.2
Hispanic or Latino (of any race)	61.4
Central American, ex. Mexican	199.3
Mexican	64.5
Puerto Rican	133.6

Males per 100 Females

Group	Number
Total Population	97.7
Hispanic or Latino (of any race)	101.7
Central American, ex. Mexican	91.3
Guatemalan	116.0
Salvadoran	88.2
Mexican	103.4
Puerto Rican	91.8
South American	90.4
Spaniard	87.7

Average Household Size

Group	People
Total Population	2.78
Hispanic or Latino (of any race)	3.38
Central American, ex. Mexican	3.24
Guatemalan	3.12
Salvadoran	3.66
Mexican	3.46
Puerto Rican	2.79
South American	3.06
Spaniard	2.77

Median Age

Group	Years
Total Population	33.6
Hispanic or Latino (of any race)	27.1
Central American, ex. Mexican	31.7
Guatemalan	32.0
Salvadoran	33.3
Mexican	26.6
Puerto Rican	27.4
South American	32.1
Spaniard	33.6

High School Graduates
(Universe: Population 25 Years and Over)

Group	Number	%
Total Population	23,680	81.8
Hispanic or Latino (of any race)	4,967	61.7
Mexican	3,924	59.0

Four-Year College Graduates
(Universe: Population 25 Years and Over)

Group	Number	%
Total Population	6,808	23.5
Hispanic or Latino (of any race)	996	12.4
Mexican	818	12.3

Population Age 3–17 Enrolled in Public School
(Universe: Population Age 3–17 Enrolled in School)

Group	Number	%
Total Population	8,259	89.2
Hispanic or Latino (of any race)	4,346	93.7
Mexican	3,638	94.3

Population Age 3–17 Enrolled in Private School
(Universe: Population Age 3–17 Enrolled in School)

Group	Number	%
Total Population	999	10.8
Hispanic or Latino (of any race)	292	6.3
Mexican	218	5.7

Foreign-Born Population

Group	Number	%
Total Population	10,080	21.9
Hispanic or Latino (of any race)	4,426	27.7
Mexican	3,773	28.5

Foreign-Born Naturalized U.S. Citizens

Group	Number	%
Total Population	4,704	46.7
Hispanic or Latino (of any race)	1,377	31.1
Mexican	1,053	27.9

Language Spoken at Home: English Only
(Universe: Population 5 Years and Over)

Group	Number	%
Total Population	26,732	63.6
Hispanic or Latino (of any race)	6,456	44.8
Mexican	5,328	45.1

Language Spoken at Home: Spanish
(Universe: Population 5 Years and Over)

Group	Number	%
Total Population	8,395	20.0
Hispanic or Latino (of any race)	7,914	55.0
Mexican	6,463	54.7

Unemployment Rate
(Universe: Population 16 Years and Over)

Group	%
Total Population	9.6
Hispanic or Latino (of any race)	12.7
Mexican	12.7

Class of Worker: Private Wage and Salary
(Universe: Civilian Employed Population 16 Years and Over)

Group	Number	%
Total Population	14,553	68.3
Hispanic or Latino (of any race)	4,767	72.6
Mexican	3,656	71.3

Class of Worker: Government
(Universe: Civilian Employed Population 16 Years and Over)

Group	Number	%
Total Population	5,494	25.8
Hispanic or Latino (of any race)	1,370	20.9
Mexican	1,082	21.1

Means of Transportation to Work: Car, Truck or Van
(Universe: Workers 16 Years and Over)

Group	Number	%
Total Population	18,830	92.0
Hispanic or Latino (of any race)	5,653	89.8
Mexican	4,379	89.9

Means of Transportation to Work: Public Transportation (ex. Taxicab)
(Universe: Workers 16 Years and Over)

Group	Number	%
Total Population	317	1.5
Hispanic or Latino (of any race)	98	1.6
Mexican	90	1.8

Homeownership Rate
(Universe: Occupied Housing Units)

Group	%
Total Population	58.7
Hispanic or Latino (of any race)	49.5
Central American, ex. Mexican	52.0
Guatemalan	58.5
Salvadoran	51.1
Mexican	49.6
Puerto Rican	35.9
South American	59.4
Spaniard	62.7

Median Home Value

Group	Dollars
Total Population	293,900
Hispanic or Latino (of any race)	239,900
Mexican	247,800

Median Gross Rent

Group	Dollars
Total Population	853
Hispanic or Latino (of any race)	861
Mexican	837

Median Household Income
(2010 Inflation-Adjusted Dollars)

Group	Dollars
Total Population	53,559
Hispanic or Latino (of any race)	45,291
Mexican	43,244

Per Capita Income
(2010 Inflation-Adjusted Dollars)

Group	Dollars
Total Population	24,695
Hispanic or Latino (of any race)	16,430
Mexican	15,973

Households with $100,000+ Income

Group	Number	%
Total Population	3,859	22.8
Hispanic or Latino (of any race)	637	13.8
Mexican	557	15.2

Households with Food Stamps/SNAP Benefits During Past 12 Months

Group	Number	%
Total Population	1,703	10.1
Hispanic or Latino (of any race)	705	15.3
Mexican	596	16.3

Poverty Rate
(Income in Past 12 Months Below Poverty Level)

Group	%
Total Population	16.6
Hispanic or Latino (of any race)	26.2
Mexican	27.4

West Whittier-Los Nietos

Population

Group	Number	%TP[1]	%HP[2]
Total Population	25,540	100.0	–
Hispanic or Latino (of any race)	22,369	87.6	100.0
Central American, ex. Mexican	1,107	4.3	4.9
Guatemalan	224	0.9	1.0
Nicaraguan	122	0.5	0.5
Salvadoran	621	2.4	2.8
Mexican	19,824	77.6	88.6
Puerto Rican	129	0.5	0.6
South American	226	0.9	1.0
Spaniard	105	0.4	0.5

Population Growth: 2000–2010

Group	%
Total Population	1.6
Hispanic or Latino (of any race)	7.2
Central American, ex. Mexican	93.2
Guatemalan	94.8
Salvadoran	121.8
Mexican	11.5
Puerto Rican	-8.5
South American	107.3

Males per 100 Females

Group	Number
Total Population	97.0
Hispanic or Latino (of any race)	97.5
Central American, ex. Mexican	93.5
Guatemalan	121.8
Nicaraguan	71.8
Salvadoran	93.5
Mexican	98.6
Puerto Rican	95.5
South American	85.2
Spaniard	87.5

Notes: (1) Percent of total population; (2) Percent of Hispanic/Latino population; Profiles include places with an overall population of at least 125,000, OR an overall population of at least 25,000 where the Hispanic/Latino population is at least 20% of the overall population. In states where less than five places meet either of these criteria, we have included places with at least 10,000 total population with the highest percentage of Hispanic/Latino population. These places are identified with an asterisk (*); Please refer to the User's Guide for a full explanation of data.

Average Household Size

Group	People
Total Population	3.80
Hispanic or Latino (of any race)	4.08
Central American, ex. Mexican	4.69
Guatemalan	4.87
Nicaraguan	4.00
Salvadoran	4.87
Mexican	4.09
Puerto Rican	3.33
South American	3.49
Spaniard	3.21

Median Age

Group	Years
Total Population	33.7
Hispanic or Latino (of any race)	31.7
Central American, ex. Mexican	35.9
Guatemalan	39.0
Nicaraguan	37.7
Salvadoran	35.4
Mexican	31.5
Puerto Rican	33.2
South American	40.0
Spaniard	41.1

High School Graduates
(Universe: Population 25 Years and Over)

Group	Number	%
Total Population	10,680	66.6
Hispanic or Latino (of any race)	8,671	63.3
Central American, ex. Mexican	508	69.3
Mexican	7,615	62.2

Four-Year College Graduates
(Universe: Population 25 Years and Over)

Group	Number	%
Total Population	1,292	8.1
Hispanic or Latino (of any race)	904	6.6
Central American, ex. Mexican	107	14.6
Mexican	705	5.8

Population Age 3–17 Enrolled in Public School
(Universe: Population Age 3–17 Enrolled in School)

Group	Number	%
Total Population	4,435	84.1
Hispanic or Latino (of any race)	4,158	84.3
Central American, ex. Mexican	204	88.3
Mexican	3,793	84.2

Population Age 3–17 Enrolled in Private School
(Universe: Population Age 3–17 Enrolled in School)

Group	Number	%
Total Population	840	15.9
Hispanic or Latino (of any race)	776	15.7
Central American, ex. Mexican	27	11.7
Mexican	712	15.8

Foreign-Born Population

Group	Number	%
Total Population	6,814	27.1
Hispanic or Latino (of any race)	6,479	29.1
Central American, ex. Mexican	638	55.5
Mexican	5,694	28.5

Foreign-Born Naturalized U.S. Citizens

Group	Number	%
Total Population	3,329	48.9
Hispanic or Latino (of any race)	3,099	47.8
Central American, ex. Mexican	370	58.0
Mexican	2,612	45.9

Language Spoken at Home: English Only
(Universe: Population 5 Years and Over)

Group	Number	%
Total Population	8,526	36.3
Hispanic or Latino (of any race)	6,131	29.7
Central American, ex. Mexican	33	3.2
Mexican	5,646	30.3

Language Spoken at Home: Spanish
(Universe: Population 5 Years and Over)

Group	Number	%
Total Population	14,693	62.6
Hispanic or Latino (of any race)	14,497	70.1
Central American, ex. Mexican	974	95.7
Mexican	12,973	69.6

Unemployment Rate
(Universe: Population 16 Years and Over)

Group	%
Total Population	10.6
Hispanic or Latino (of any race)	10.6
Central American, ex. Mexican	1.8
Mexican	11.2

Class of Worker: Private Wage and Salary
(Universe: Civilian Employed Population 16 Years and Over)

Group	Number	%
Total Population	8,265	79.8
Hispanic or Latino (of any race)	7,466	81.0
Central American, ex. Mexican	456	74.8
Mexican	6,689	80.9

Class of Worker: Government
(Universe: Civilian Employed Population 16 Years and Over)

Group	Number	%
Total Population	1,390	13.4
Hispanic or Latino (of any race)	1,198	13.0
Central American, ex. Mexican	52	8.5
Mexican	1,126	13.6

Means of Transportation to Work: Car, Truck or Van
(Universe: Workers 16 Years and Over)

Group	Number	%
Total Population	9,049	88.6
Hispanic or Latino (of any race)	8,110	89.1
Central American, ex. Mexican	609	96.7
Mexican	7,203	88.6

Means of Transportation to Work: Public Transportation (ex. Taxicab)
(Universe: Workers 16 Years and Over)

Group	Number	%
Total Population	406	4.0
Hispanic or Latino (of any race)	356	3.9
Central American, ex. Mexican	0	0.0
Mexican	349	4.3

Homeownership Rate
(Universe: Occupied Housing Units)

Group	%
Total Population	73.1
Hispanic or Latino (of any race)	71.5
Central American, ex. Mexican	69.9
Guatemalan	77.4
Nicaraguan	62.5
Salvadoran	67.3
Mexican	71.7
Puerto Rican	83.3
South American	67.6
Spaniard	76.9

Median Home Value

Group	Dollars
Total Population	411,900
Hispanic or Latino (of any race)	406,900
Central American, ex. Mexican	394,700
Mexican	405,900

Median Gross Rent

Group	Dollars
Total Population	1,166
Hispanic or Latino (of any race)	1,161
Central American, ex. Mexican	991
Mexican	1,154

Median Household Income
(2010 Inflation-Adjusted Dollars)

Group	Dollars
Total Population	55,879
Hispanic or Latino (of any race)	56,233
Central American, ex. Mexican	70,962
Mexican	56,573

Per Capita Income
(2010 Inflation-Adjusted Dollars)

Group	Dollars
Total Population	19,600
Hispanic or Latino (of any race)	17,899
Central American, ex. Mexican	20,486
Mexican	17,711

Households with $100,000+ Income

Group	Number	%
Total Population	1,638	24.4
Hispanic or Latino (of any race)	1,346	24.4
Central American, ex. Mexican	92	28.9
Mexican	1,141	23.8

Households with Food Stamps/SNAP Benefits During Past 12 Months

Group	Number	%
Total Population	416	6.2
Hispanic or Latino (of any race)	378	6.8
Central American, ex. Mexican	12	3.8
Mexican	353	7.4

Poverty Rate
(Income in Past 12 Months Below Poverty Level)

Group	%
Total Population	10.0
Hispanic or Latino (of any race)	10.1
Central American, ex. Mexican	10.0
Mexican	10.5

Westminster

Population

Group	Number	%TP[1]	%HP[2]
Total Population	89,701	100.0	–
Hispanic or Latino (of any race)	21,176	23.6	100.0
Central American, ex. Mexican	867	1.0	4.1
Guatemalan	249	0.3	1.2
Salvadoran	374	0.4	1.8
Cuban	213	0.2	1.0
Mexican	18,037	20.1	85.2
Puerto Rican	257	0.3	1.2
South American	579	0.6	2.7
Colombian	122	0.1	0.6
Peruvian	229	0.3	1.1
Spaniard	185	0.2	0.9

Population Growth: 2000–2010

Group	%
Total Population	1.7
Hispanic or Latino (of any race)	10.6
Central American, ex. Mexican	67.7
Guatemalan	85.8
Salvadoran	89.8
Cuban	2.4
Mexican	17.2
Puerto Rican	-4.5
South American	53.2
Peruvian	112.0

Males per 100 Females

Group	Number
Total Population	97.8
Hispanic or Latino (of any race)	103.1
Central American, ex. Mexican	109.4
Guatemalan	120.4
Salvadoran	110.1
Cuban	76.0
Mexican	103.9
Puerto Rican	127.4
South American	100.3
Colombian	100.0
Peruvian	104.5
Spaniard	76.2

Average Household Size

Group	People
Total Population	3.40
Hispanic or Latino (of any race)	4.39
Central American, ex. Mexican	3.95
Guatemalan	4.42
Salvadoran	4.17
Cuban	2.60
Mexican	4.57
Puerto Rican	3.16
South American	3.31
Colombian	3.38
Peruvian	3.77

Notes: (1) Percent of total population; (2) Percent of Hispanic/Latino population; Profiles include places with an overall population of at least 125,000, OR an overall population of at least 25,000 where the Hispanic/Latino population is at least 20% of the overall population. In states where less than five places meet either of these criteria, we have included places with at least 10,000 total population with the highest percentage of Hispanic/Latino population. These places are identified with an asterisk (*); Please refer to the User's Guide for a full explanation of data.

Spaniard	2.94

Median Age

Group	Years
Total Population	38.7
Hispanic or Latino (of any race)	27.2
Central American, ex. Mexican	34.5
Guatemalan	31.8
Salvadoran	34.0
Cuban	45.9
Mexican	26.3
Puerto Rican	31.1
South American	43.2
Colombian	41.0
Peruvian	43.2
Spaniard	37.6

High School Graduates
(Universe: Population 25 Years and Over)

Group	Number	%
Total Population	43,918	74.2
Hispanic or Latino (of any race)	6,532	62.2
Central American, ex. Mexican	620	59.1
Mexican	4,981	59.4

Four-Year College Graduates
(Universe: Population 25 Years and Over)

Group	Number	%
Total Population	11,775	19.9
Hispanic or Latino (of any race)	892	8.5
Central American, ex. Mexican	127	12.1
Mexican	562	6.7

Population Age 3–17 Enrolled in Public School
(Universe: Population Age 3–17 Enrolled in School)

Group	Number	%
Total Population	15,762	89.6
Hispanic or Latino (of any race)	5,144	96.0
Central American, ex. Mexican	199	100.0
Mexican	4,580	95.8

Population Age 3–17 Enrolled in Private School
(Universe: Population Age 3–17 Enrolled in School)

Group	Number	%
Total Population	1,834	10.4
Hispanic or Latino (of any race)	215	4.0
Central American, ex. Mexican	0	0.0
Mexican	199	4.2

Foreign-Born Population

Group	Number	%
Total Population	40,627	45.7
Hispanic or Latino (of any race)	8,429	42.5
Central American, ex. Mexican	1,049	71.1
Mexican	6,874	41.5

Foreign-Born Naturalized U.S. Citizens

Group	Number	%
Total Population	27,367	67.4
Hispanic or Latino (of any race)	2,704	32.1
Central American, ex. Mexican	353	33.7
Mexican	1,967	28.6

Language Spoken at Home: English Only
(Universe: Population 5 Years and Over)

Group	Number	%
Total Population	30,348	36.2
Hispanic or Latino (of any race)	4,227	23.3
Central American, ex. Mexican	139	9.8
Mexican	3,336	22.1

Language Spoken at Home: Spanish
(Universe: Population 5 Years and Over)

Group	Number	%
Total Population	14,301	17.0
Hispanic or Latino (of any race)	13,830	76.2
Central American, ex. Mexican	1,283	90.2
Mexican	11,686	77.6

Unemployment Rate
(Universe: Population 16 Years and Over)

Group	%
Total Population	9.4
Hispanic or Latino (of any race)	6.9
Central American, ex. Mexican	4.5
Mexican	7.4

Class of Worker: Private Wage and Salary
(Universe: Civilian Employed Population 16 Years and Over)

Group	Number	%
Total Population	31,965	80.8
Hispanic or Latino (of any race)	8,045	85.7
Central American, ex. Mexican	711	80.2
Mexican	6,602	86.4

Class of Worker: Government
(Universe: Civilian Employed Population 16 Years and Over)

Group	Number	%
Total Population	4,414	11.2
Hispanic or Latino (of any race)	756	8.1
Central American, ex. Mexican	37	4.2
Mexican	627	8.2

Means of Transportation to Work: Car, Truck or Van
(Universe: Workers 16 Years and Over)

Group	Number	%
Total Population	34,726	90.0
Hispanic or Latino (of any race)	7,112	78.3
Central American, ex. Mexican	598	67.4
Mexican	5,745	78.2

Means of Transportation to Work: Public Transportation (ex. Taxicab)
(Universe: Workers 16 Years and Over)

Group	Number	%
Total Population	1,277	3.3
Hispanic or Latino (of any race)	913	10.0
Central American, ex. Mexican	88	9.9
Mexican	777	10.6

Homeownership Rate
(Universe: Occupied Housing Units)

Group	%
Total Population	57.8
Hispanic or Latino (of any race)	40.1
Central American, ex. Mexican	42.3
Guatemalan	41.5
Salvadoran	35.1
Cuban	47.6
Mexican	38.8
Puerto Rican	49.3
South American	48.3
Colombian	46.2
Peruvian	38.5
Spaniard	57.1

Median Home Value

Group	Dollars
Total Population	529,900
Hispanic or Latino (of any race)	515,800
Central American, ex. Mexican	594,000
Mexican	496,300

Median Gross Rent

Group	Dollars
Total Population	1,263
Hispanic or Latino (of any race)	1,270
Central American, ex. Mexican	1,466
Mexican	1,246

Median Household Income
(2010 Inflation-Adjusted Dollars)

Group	Dollars
Total Population	57,892
Hispanic or Latino (of any race)	53,877
Central American, ex. Mexican	66,250
Mexican	52,748

Per Capita Income
(2010 Inflation-Adjusted Dollars)

Group	Dollars
Total Population	22,518
Hispanic or Latino (of any race)	16,462
Central American, ex. Mexican	19,702
Mexican	14,719

Households with $100,000+ Income

Group	Number	%
Total Population	6,230	23.4
Hispanic or Latino (of any race)	729	15.0
Central American, ex. Mexican	35	9.4

Mexican	489	12.5

Households with Food Stamps/SNAP Benefits During Past 12 Months

Group	Number	%
Total Population	1,721	6.5
Hispanic or Latino (of any race)	308	6.4
Central American, ex. Mexican	5	1.3
Mexican	292	7.5

Poverty Rate
(Income in Past 12 Months Below Poverty Level)

Group	%
Total Population	12.9
Hispanic or Latino (of any race)	14.7
Central American, ex. Mexican	17.8
Mexican	15.4

Westmont

Population

Group	Number	%TP[1]	%HP[2]
Total Population	31,853	100.0	–
Hispanic or Latino (of any race)	14,871	46.7	100.0
Central American, ex. Mexican	4,034	12.7	27.1
Guatemalan	1,440	4.5	9.7
Honduran	298	0.9	2.0
Nicaraguan	135	0.4	0.9
Salvadoran	2,044	6.4	13.7
Mexican	9,357	29.4	62.9
Puerto Rican	138	0.4	0.9

Population Growth: 2000–2010

Group	%
Total Population	0.7
Hispanic or Latino (of any race)	19.0
Central American, ex. Mexican	120.9
Guatemalan	179.6
Honduran	154.7
Salvadoran	119.3
Mexican	25.4
Puerto Rican	26.6

Males per 100 Females

Group	Number
Total Population	86.8
Hispanic or Latino (of any race)	101.1
Central American, ex. Mexican	98.1
Guatemalan	102.8
Honduran	96.1
Nicaraguan	101.5
Salvadoran	95.8
Mexican	103.9
Puerto Rican	74.7

Average Household Size

Group	People
Total Population	3.27
Hispanic or Latino (of any race)	4.58
Central American, ex. Mexican	4.58
Guatemalan	4.66
Honduran	4.77
Nicaraguan	4.06
Salvadoran	4.59
Mexican	4.66
Puerto Rican	3.54

Median Age

Group	Years
Total Population	29.9
Hispanic or Latino (of any race)	25.7
Central American, ex. Mexican	32.5
Guatemalan	32.3
Honduran	30.3
Nicaraguan	35.6
Salvadoran	32.7
Mexican	23.6
Puerto Rican	23.0

High School Graduates
(Universe: Population 25 Years and Over)

Group	Number	%
Total Population	11,151	64.1
Hispanic or Latino (of any race)	2,588	37.9

Notes: (1) Percent of total population; (2) Percent of Hispanic/Latino population; Profiles include places with an overall population of at least 125,000, OR an overall population of at least 25,000 where the Hispanic/Latino population is at least 20% of the overall population. In states where less than five places meet either of these criteria, we have included places with at least 10,000 total population with the highest percentage of Hispanic/Latino population. These places are identified with an asterisk (*); Please refer to the User's Guide for a full explanation of data.

Group	Number	%
Central American, ex. Mexican	845	35.2
Guatemalan	150	22.1
Salvadoran	504	37.6
Mexican	1,608	38.0

Four-Year College Graduates
(Universe: Population 25 Years and Over)

Group	Number	%
Total Population	1,399	8.0
Hispanic or Latino (of any race)	290	4.2
Central American, ex. Mexican	112	4.7
Guatemalan	20	2.9
Salvadoran	79	5.9
Mexican	178	4.2

Population Age 3–17 Enrolled in Public School
(Universe: Population Age 3–17 Enrolled in School)

Group	Number	%
Total Population	7,249	94.9
Hispanic or Latino (of any race)	3,898	98.3
Central American, ex. Mexican	1,088	96.5
Guatemalan	275	90.2
Salvadoran	683	98.6
Mexican	2,787	99.0

Population Age 3–17 Enrolled in Private School
(Universe: Population Age 3–17 Enrolled in School)

Group	Number	%
Total Population	388	5.1
Hispanic or Latino (of any race)	68	1.7
Central American, ex. Mexican	40	3.5
Guatemalan	30	9.8
Salvadoran	10	1.4
Mexican	28	1.0

Foreign-Born Population

Group	Number	%
Total Population	7,417	23.7
Hispanic or Latino (of any race)	6,508	45.7
Central American, ex. Mexican	2,617	57.7
Guatemalan	682	53.6
Salvadoran	1,534	59.6
Mexican	3,814	40.5

Foreign-Born Naturalized U.S. Citizens

Group	Number	%
Total Population	1,953	26.3
Hispanic or Latino (of any race)	1,451	22.3
Central American, ex. Mexican	683	26.1
Guatemalan	238	34.9
Salvadoran	317	20.7
Mexican	735	19.3

Language Spoken at Home: English Only
(Universe: Population 5 Years and Over)

Group	Number	%
Total Population	15,554	55.0
Hispanic or Latino (of any race)	673	5.4
Central American, ex. Mexican	45	1.1
Guatemalan	16	1.5
Salvadoran	17	0.7
Mexican	528	6.6

Language Spoken at Home: Spanish
(Universe: Population 5 Years and Over)

Group	Number	%
Total Population	12,168	43.0
Hispanic or Latino (of any race)	11,693	94.5
Central American, ex. Mexican	4,110	98.9
Guatemalan	1,066	98.5
Salvadoran	2,426	99.3
Mexican	7,467	93.3

Unemployment Rate
(Universe: Population 16 Years and Over)

Group	%
Total Population	12.9
Hispanic or Latino (of any race)	10.0
Central American, ex. Mexican	8.0
Guatemalan	15.7
Salvadoran	5.5
Mexican	10.5

Class of Worker: Private Wage and Salary
(Universe: Civilian Employed Population 16 Years and Over)

Group	Number	%
Total Population	8,898	77.7
Hispanic or Latino (of any race)	4,717	86.0
Central American, ex. Mexican	1,804	85.1
Guatemalan	439	85.2
Salvadoran	1,105	85.9
Mexican	2,851	86.5

Class of Worker: Government
(Universe: Civilian Employed Population 16 Years and Over)

Group	Number	%
Total Population	1,742	15.2
Hispanic or Latino (of any race)	307	5.6
Central American, ex. Mexican	102	4.8
Guatemalan	25	4.9
Salvadoran	33	2.6
Mexican	195	5.9

Means of Transportation to Work: Car, Truck or Van
(Universe: Workers 16 Years and Over)

Group	Number	%
Total Population	9,025	83.0
Hispanic or Latino (of any race)	4,210	80.6
Central American, ex. Mexican	1,468	74.4
Guatemalan	333	69.8
Salvadoran	848	72.1
Mexican	2,670	84.0

Means of Transportation to Work: Public Transportation (ex. Taxicab)
(Universe: Workers 16 Years and Over)

Group	Number	%
Total Population	1,221	11.2
Hispanic or Latino (of any race)	700	13.4
Central American, ex. Mexican	338	17.1
Guatemalan	57	11.9
Salvadoran	259	22.0
Mexican	362	11.4

Homeownership Rate
(Universe: Occupied Housing Units)

Group	%
Total Population	31.1
Hispanic or Latino (of any race)	31.3
Central American, ex. Mexican	35.9
Guatemalan	35.1
Honduran	27.5
Nicaraguan	30.6
Salvadoran	37.6
Mexican	29.9
Puerto Rican	31.7

Median Home Value

Group	Dollars
Total Population	395,000
Hispanic or Latino (of any race)	338,700
Central American, ex. Mexican	292,400
Guatemalan	481,300
Salvadoran	305,600
Mexican	361,500

Median Gross Rent

Group	Dollars
Total Population	900
Hispanic or Latino (of any race)	892
Central American, ex. Mexican	864
Guatemalan	1,228
Salvadoran	866
Mexican	918

Median Household Income
(2010 Inflation-Adjusted Dollars)

Group	Dollars
Total Population	32,973
Hispanic or Latino (of any race)	34,289
Central American, ex. Mexican	36,130
Guatemalan	23,611
Salvadoran	38,750
Mexican	31,818

Per Capita Income
(2010 Inflation-Adjusted Dollars)

Group	Dollars
Total Population	14,349
Hispanic or Latino (of any race)	10,370
Central American, ex. Mexican	11,717
Guatemalan	9,555
Salvadoran	12,495
Mexican	9,636

Households with $100,000+ Income

Group	Number	%
Total Population	797	8.1
Hispanic or Latino (of any race)	277	9.3
Central American, ex. Mexican	123	10.9
Guatemalan	40	16.1
Salvadoran	50	7.4
Mexican	154	8.6

Households with Food Stamps/SNAP Benefits During Past 12 Months

Group	Number	%
Total Population	1,616	16.4
Hispanic or Latino (of any race)	578	19.3
Central American, ex. Mexican	151	13.4
Guatemalan	49	19.8
Salvadoran	51	7.5
Mexican	427	23.9

Poverty Rate
(Income in Past 12 Months Below Poverty Level)

Group	%
Total Population	29.6
Hispanic or Latino (of any race)	34.5
Central American, ex. Mexican	28.9
Guatemalan	35.5
Salvadoran	23.0
Mexican	36.6

Whittier

Population

Group	Number	%TP[1]	%HP[2]
Total Population	85,331	100.0	–
Hispanic or Latino (of any race)	56,081	65.7	100.0
Central American, ex. Mexican	2,758	3.2	4.9
Costa Rican	152	0.2	0.3
Guatemalan	684	0.8	1.2
Honduran	125	0.1	0.2
Nicaraguan	313	0.4	0.6
Salvadoran	1,390	1.6	2.5
Cuban	410	0.5	0.7
Mexican	48,567	56.9	86.6
Puerto Rican	555	0.7	1.0
South American	904	1.1	1.6
Argentinean	188	0.2	0.3
Colombian	192	0.2	0.3
Ecuadorian	156	0.2	0.3
Peruvian	191	0.2	0.3
Spaniard	449	0.5	0.8

Population Growth: 2000–2010

Group	%
Total Population	2.0
Hispanic or Latino (of any race)	19.9
Central American, ex. Mexican	96.9
Guatemalan	131.1
Nicaraguan	130.1
Salvadoran	112.9
Cuban	19.5
Mexican	25.9
Puerto Rican	41.2
South American	78.0
Peruvian	69.0

Males per 100 Females

Group	Number
Total Population	94.0
Hispanic or Latino (of any race)	93.4
Central American, ex. Mexican	91.4
Costa Rican	76.7
Guatemalan	96.0
Honduran	92.3

Notes: (1) Percent of total population; (2) Percent of Hispanic/Latino population; Profiles include places with an overall population of at least 125,000, OR an overall population of at least 25,000 where the Hispanic/Latino population is at least 20% of the overall population. In states where less than five places meet either of these criteria, we have included places with at least 10,000 total population with the highest percentage of Hispanic/Latino population. These places are identified with an asterisk (*); Please refer to the User's Guide for a full explanation of data.

Nicaraguan	79.9
Salvadoran	95.8
Cuban	110.3
Mexican	93.8
Puerto Rican	94.1
South American	93.6
Argentinean	86.1
Colombian	86.4
Ecuadorian	102.6
Peruvian	96.9
Spaniard	83.3

Average Household Size

Group	People
Total Population	2.96
Hispanic or Latino (of any race)	3.38
Central American, ex. Mexican	3.64
Costa Rican	3.00
Guatemalan	3.84
Honduran	3.62
Nicaraguan	3.40
Salvadoran	3.75
Cuban	2.75
Mexican	3.40
Puerto Rican	3.07
South American	3.11
Argentinean	3.09
Colombian	2.98
Ecuadorian	2.66
Peruvian	3.41
Spaniard	2.85

Median Age

Group	Years
Total Population	35.4
Hispanic or Latino (of any race)	30.4
Central American, ex. Mexican	33.9
Costa Rican	36.5
Guatemalan	33.9
Honduran	33.5
Nicaraguan	35.9
Salvadoran	33.5
Cuban	36.0
Mexican	30.0
Puerto Rican	33.1
South American	36.1
Argentinean	37.7
Colombian	35.7
Ecuadorian	39.0
Peruvian	37.2
Spaniard	39.3

High School Graduates
(Universe: Population 25 Years and Over)

Group	Number	%
Total Population	43,790	82.2
Hispanic or Latino (of any race)	23,667	75.6
Central American, ex. Mexican	1,533	75.9
Salvadoran	814	87.0
Mexican	20,255	75.2

Four-Year College Graduates
(Universe: Population 25 Years and Over)

Group	Number	%
Total Population	12,296	23.1
Hispanic or Latino (of any race)	4,948	15.8
Central American, ex. Mexican	365	18.1
Salvadoran	144	15.4
Mexican	4,215	15.7

Population Age 3–17 Enrolled in Public School
(Universe: Population Age 3–17 Enrolled in School)

Group	Number	%
Total Population	14,372	82.5
Hispanic or Latino (of any race)	11,339	83.2
Central American, ex. Mexican	318	80.3
Salvadoran	118	79.7
Mexican	10,272	83.0

Population Age 3–17 Enrolled in Private School
(Universe: Population Age 3–17 Enrolled in School)

Group	Number	%
Total Population	3,055	17.5
Hispanic or Latino (of any race)	2,285	16.8
Central American, ex. Mexican	78	19.7
Salvadoran	30	20.3
Mexican	2,106	17.0

Foreign-Born Population

Group	Number	%
Total Population	17,355	20.4
Hispanic or Latino (of any race)	13,891	25.0
Central American, ex. Mexican	1,782	60.6
Salvadoran	767	61.0
Mexican	11,296	23.3

Foreign-Born Naturalized U.S. Citizens

Group	Number	%
Total Population	8,929	51.4
Hispanic or Latino (of any race)	6,310	45.4
Central American, ex. Mexican	1,024	57.5
Salvadoran	509	66.4
Mexican	4,881	43.2

Language Spoken at Home: English Only
(Universe: Population 5 Years and Over)

Group	Number	%
Total Population	44,843	56.6
Hispanic or Latino (of any race)	20,319	40.1
Central American, ex. Mexican	230	8.3
Salvadoran	108	8.9
Mexican	18,025	40.7

Language Spoken at Home: Spanish
(Universe: Population 5 Years and Over)

Group	Number	%
Total Population	31,217	39.4
Hispanic or Latino (of any race)	30,349	59.9
Central American, ex. Mexican	2,532	91.7
Salvadoran	1,104	91.1
Mexican	26,229	59.2

Unemployment Rate
(Universe: Population 16 Years and Over)

Group	%
Total Population	7.7
Hispanic or Latino (of any race)	8.4
Central American, ex. Mexican	9.3
Salvadoran	12.9
Mexican	8.2

Class of Worker: Private Wage and Salary
(Universe: Civilian Employed Population 16 Years and Over)

Group	Number	%
Total Population	29,931	75.0
Hispanic or Latino (of any race)	20,068	76.7
Central American, ex. Mexican	1,217	73.7
Salvadoran	528	74.2
Mexican	17,437	76.7

Class of Worker: Government
(Universe: Civilian Employed Population 16 Years and Over)

Group	Number	%
Total Population	7,211	18.1
Hispanic or Latino (of any race)	4,367	16.7
Central American, ex. Mexican	274	16.6
Salvadoran	149	20.9
Mexican	3,800	16.7

Means of Transportation to Work: Car, Truck or Van
(Universe: Workers 16 Years and Over)

Group	Number	%
Total Population	34,794	89.6
Hispanic or Latino (of any race)	22,860	89.7
Central American, ex. Mexican	1,321	81.4
Salvadoran	579	83.3
Mexican	19,990	90.2

Means of Transportation to Work: Public Transportation (ex. Taxicab)
(Universe: Workers 16 Years and Over)

Group	Number	%
Total Population	956	2.5
Hispanic or Latino (of any race)	653	2.6
Central American, ex. Mexican	73	4.5
Salvadoran	52	7.5
Mexican	558	2.5

Homeownership Rate
(Universe: Occupied Housing Units)

Group	%
Total Population	57.3
Hispanic or Latino (of any race)	48.4
Central American, ex. Mexican	41.5
Costa Rican	54.0
Guatemalan	38.9
Honduran	34.5
Nicaraguan	52.7
Salvadoran	37.8
Cuban	53.0
Mexican	49.4
Puerto Rican	40.2
South American	53.7
Argentinean	56.9
Colombian	60.4
Ecuadorian	54.8
Peruvian	42.2
Spaniard	50.6

Median Home Value

Group	Dollars
Total Population	512,400
Hispanic or Latino (of any race)	499,100
Central American, ex. Mexican	529,200
Salvadoran	784,400
Mexican	497,200

Median Gross Rent

Group	Dollars
Total Population	1,091
Hispanic or Latino (of any race)	1,099
Central American, ex. Mexican	1,110
Salvadoran	1,151
Mexican	1,085

Median Household Income
(2010 Inflation-Adjusted Dollars)

Group	Dollars
Total Population	65,308
Hispanic or Latino (of any race)	63,206
Central American, ex. Mexican	65,483
Salvadoran	60,769
Mexican	63,742

Per Capita Income
(2010 Inflation-Adjusted Dollars)

Group	Dollars
Total Population	26,943
Hispanic or Latino (of any race)	22,549
Central American, ex. Mexican	22,336
Salvadoran	26,421
Mexican	22,706

Households with $100,000+ Income

Group	Number	%
Total Population	8,062	29.2
Hispanic or Latino (of any race)	4,267	27.3
Central American, ex. Mexican	254	31.8
Salvadoran	112	28.0
Mexican	3,735	27.6

Households with Food Stamps/SNAP Benefits During Past 12 Months

Group	Number	%
Total Population	1,312	4.8
Hispanic or Latino (of any race)	1,135	7.3
Central American, ex. Mexican	62	7.8
Salvadoran	33	8.3
Mexican	1,029	7.6

Poverty Rate
(Income in Past 12 Months Below Poverty Level)

Group	%
Total Population	9.2
Hispanic or Latino (of any race)	10.0
Central American, ex. Mexican	12.8
Salvadoran	6.1
Mexican	9.6

Notes: (1) Percent of total population; (2) Percent of Hispanic/Latino population; Profiles include places with an overall population of at least 125,000, OR an overall population of at least 25,000 where the Hispanic/Latino population is at least 20% of the overall population. In states where less than five places meet either of these criteria, we have included places with at least 10,000 total population with the highest percentage of Hispanic/Latino population. These places are identified with an asterisk (*); Please refer to the User's Guide for a full explanation of data.

Wildomar

Population

Group	Number	%TP[1]	%HP[2]
Total Population	32,176	100.0	–
Hispanic or Latino (of any race)	11,363	35.3	100.0
Central American, ex. Mexican	500	1.6	4.4
Guatemalan	136	0.4	1.2
Salvadoran	250	0.8	2.2
Mexican	9,642	30.0	84.9
Puerto Rican	249	0.8	2.2
South American	193	0.6	1.7
Spaniard	161	0.5	1.4

Population Growth: 2000–2010

Group	%
Total Population	128.8
Hispanic or Latino (of any race)	274.4
Mexican	281.9

Males per 100 Females

Group	Number
Total Population	97.6
Hispanic or Latino (of any race)	97.9
Central American, ex. Mexican	88.0
Guatemalan	86.3
Salvadoran	93.8
Mexican	98.9
Puerto Rican	100.8
South American	82.1
Spaniard	75.0

Average Household Size

Group	People
Total Population	3.22
Hispanic or Latino (of any race)	4.14
Central American, ex. Mexican	4.63
Guatemalan	5.30
Salvadoran	4.44
Mexican	4.20
Puerto Rican	3.83
South American	3.42
Spaniard	3.71

Median Age

Group	Years
Total Population	34.6
Hispanic or Latino (of any race)	25.9
Central American, ex. Mexican	29.8
Guatemalan	29.4
Salvadoran	29.5
Mexican	25.3
Puerto Rican	25.4
South American	38.5
Spaniard	28.1

High School Graduates
(Universe: Population 25 Years and Over)

Group	Number	%
Total Population	15,662	82.9
Hispanic or Latino (of any race)	3,589	64.7
Mexican	3,086	63.5

Four-Year College Graduates
(Universe: Population 25 Years and Over)

Group	Number	%
Total Population	3,345	17.7
Hispanic or Latino (of any race)	369	6.7
Mexican	277	5.7

Population Age 3–17 Enrolled in Public School
(Universe: Population Age 3–17 Enrolled in School)

Group	Number	%
Total Population	5,830	89.1
Hispanic or Latino (of any race)	2,987	97.5
Mexican	2,538	99.5

Population Age 3–17 Enrolled in Private School
(Universe: Population Age 3–17 Enrolled in School)

Group	Number	%
Total Population	712	10.9
Hispanic or Latino (of any race)	77	2.5
Mexican	12	0.5

Foreign-Born Population

Group	Number	%
Total Population	5,551	18.1
Hispanic or Latino (of any race)	3,939	35.6
Mexican	3,533	36.7

Foreign-Born Naturalized U.S. Citizens

Group	Number	%
Total Population	2,724	49.1
Hispanic or Latino (of any race)	1,408	35.7
Mexican	1,208	34.2

Language Spoken at Home: English Only
(Universe: Population 5 Years and Over)

Group	Number	%
Total Population	19,553	69.4
Hispanic or Latino (of any race)	3,002	30.5
Mexican	2,427	28.5

Language Spoken at Home: Spanish
(Universe: Population 5 Years and Over)

Group	Number	%
Total Population	7,236	25.7
Hispanic or Latino (of any race)	6,846	69.5
Mexican	6,082	71.5

Unemployment Rate
(Universe: Population 16 Years and Over)

Group	%
Total Population	9.3
Hispanic or Latino (of any race)	10.0
Mexican	9.7

Class of Worker: Private Wage and Salary
(Universe: Civilian Employed Population 16 Years and Over)

Group	Number	%
Total Population	10,787	78.0
Hispanic or Latino (of any race)	3,457	79.9
Mexican	2,944	78.7

Class of Worker: Government
(Universe: Civilian Employed Population 16 Years and Over)

Group	Number	%
Total Population	1,693	12.2
Hispanic or Latino (of any race)	418	9.7
Mexican	366	9.8

Means of Transportation to Work: Car, Truck or Van
(Universe: Workers 16 Years and Over)

Group	Number	%
Total Population	12,231	91.4
Hispanic or Latino (of any race)	3,897	92.7
Mexican	3,358	92.9

Means of Transportation to Work: Public Transportation (ex. Taxicab)
(Universe: Workers 16 Years and Over)

Group	Number	%
Total Population	31	0.2
Hispanic or Latino (of any race)	18	0.4
Mexican	18	0.5

Homeownership Rate
(Universe: Occupied Housing Units)

Group	%
Total Population	73.3
Hispanic or Latino (of any race)	66.9
Central American, ex. Mexican	61.8
Guatemalan	63.6
Salvadoran	58.7
Mexican	67.1
Puerto Rican	71.2
South American	76.9
Spaniard	70.7

Median Home Value

Group	Dollars
Total Population	313,400
Hispanic or Latino (of any race)	318,700
Mexican	316,900

Median Gross Rent

Group	Dollars
Total Population	1,329
Hispanic or Latino (of any race)	1,322
Mexican	1,272

Median Household Income
(2010 Inflation-Adjusted Dollars)

Group	Dollars
Total Population	63,699
Hispanic or Latino (of any race)	56,052
Mexican	55,162

Per Capita Income
(2010 Inflation-Adjusted Dollars)

Group	Dollars
Total Population	24,292
Hispanic or Latino (of any race)	15,427
Mexican	14,778

Households with $100,000+ Income

Group	Number	%
Total Population	2,488	26.2
Hispanic or Latino (of any race)	518	19.8
Mexican	380	16.8

Households with Food Stamps/SNAP Benefits During Past 12 Months

Group	Number	%
Total Population	282	3.0
Hispanic or Latino (of any race)	152	5.8
Mexican	88	3.9

Poverty Rate
(Income in Past 12 Months Below Poverty Level)

Group	%
Total Population	10.8
Hispanic or Latino (of any race)	15.8
Mexican	14.5

Willowbrook

Population

Group	Number	%TP[1]	%HP[2]
Total Population	35,983	100.0	–
Hispanic or Latino (of any race)	22,979	63.9	100.0
Central American, ex. Mexican	2,344	6.5	10.2
Guatemalan	690	1.9	3.0
Honduran	168	0.5	0.7
Salvadoran	1,333	3.7	5.8
Mexican	19,293	53.6	84.0

Population Growth: 2000–2010

Group	%
Total Population	5.4
Hispanic or Latino (of any race)	25.6
Central American, ex. Mexican	184.5
Guatemalan	243.3
Salvadoran	200.2
Mexican	30.1

Males per 100 Females

Group	Number
Total Population	92.1
Hispanic or Latino (of any race)	101.3
Central American, ex. Mexican	100.7
Guatemalan	98.3
Honduran	95.3
Salvadoran	105.7
Mexican	101.9

Average Household Size

Group	People
Total Population	4.08
Hispanic or Latino (of any race)	5.40
Central American, ex. Mexican	5.28
Guatemalan	5.27
Honduran	5.68
Salvadoran	5.33
Mexican	5.46

Median Age

Group	Years
Total Population	28.2
Hispanic or Latino (of any race)	24.9
Central American, ex. Mexican	32.2
Guatemalan	31.5
Honduran	30.8

Notes: (1) Percent of total population; (2) Percent of Hispanic/Latino population; Profiles include places with an overall population of at least 125,000, OR an overall population of at least 25,000 where the Hispanic/Latino population is at least 20% of the overall population. In states where less than five places meet either of these criteria, we have included places with at least 10,000 total population with the highest percentage of Hispanic/Latino population. These places are identified with an asterisk (*); Please refer to the User's Guide for a full explanation of data.

Salvadoran		32.7
Mexican		24.3

High School Graduates
(Universe: Population 25 Years and Over)

Group	Number	%
Total Population	11,640	60.6
Hispanic or Latino (of any race)	3,593	37.6
Central American, ex. Mexican	401	39.2
Salvadoran	203	35.6
Mexican	3,106	37.6

Four-Year College Graduates
(Universe: Population 25 Years and Over)

Group	Number	%
Total Population	1,465	7.6
Hispanic or Latino (of any race)	162	1.7
Central American, ex. Mexican	0	0.0
Salvadoran	0	0.0
Mexican	154	1.9

Population Age 3–17 Enrolled in Public School
(Universe: Population Age 3–17 Enrolled in School)

Group	Number	%
Total Population	8,678	95.7
Hispanic or Latino (of any race)	5,649	97.4
Central American, ex. Mexican	346	90.3
Salvadoran	216	85.4
Mexican	5,038	97.8

Population Age 3–17 Enrolled in Private School
(Universe: Population Age 3–17 Enrolled in School)

Group	Number	%
Total Population	390	4.3
Hispanic or Latino (of any race)	152	2.6
Central American, ex. Mexican	37	9.7
Salvadoran	37	14.6
Mexican	115	2.2

Foreign-Born Population

Group	Number	%
Total Population	9,659	27.5
Hispanic or Latino (of any race)	9,414	47.0
Central American, ex. Mexican	1,066	61.3
Salvadoran	537	54.2
Mexican	8,166	46.4

Foreign-Born Naturalized U.S. Citizens

Group	Number	%
Total Population	2,672	27.7
Hispanic or Latino (of any race)	2,538	27.0
Central American, ex. Mexican	460	43.2
Salvadoran	191	35.6
Mexican	1,994	24.4

Language Spoken at Home: English Only
(Universe: Population 5 Years and Over)

Group	Number	%
Total Population	14,867	46.6
Hispanic or Latino (of any race)	1,103	6.2
Central American, ex. Mexican	61	4.0
Salvadoran	51	6.3
Mexican	891	5.7

Language Spoken at Home: Spanish
(Universe: Population 5 Years and Over)

Group	Number	%
Total Population	16,796	52.6
Hispanic or Latino (of any race)	16,610	93.7
Central American, ex. Mexican	1,456	96.0
Salvadoran	755	93.7
Mexican	14,720	94.3

Unemployment Rate
(Universe: Population 16 Years and Over)

Group	%
Total Population	15.0
Hispanic or Latino (of any race)	12.2
Central American, ex. Mexican	12.7
Salvadoran	3.6
Mexican	12.2

Class of Worker: Private Wage and Salary
(Universe: Civilian Employed Population 16 Years and Over)

Group	Number	%
Total Population	9,063	74.4
Hispanic or Latino (of any race)	6,244	82.5
Central American, ex. Mexican	705	81.2
Salvadoran	400	83.2
Mexican	5,354	82.4

Class of Worker: Government
(Universe: Civilian Employed Population 16 Years and Over)

Group	Number	%
Total Population	2,033	16.7
Hispanic or Latino (of any race)	546	7.2
Central American, ex. Mexican	51	5.9
Salvadoran	17	3.5
Mexican	487	7.5

Means of Transportation to Work: Car, Truck or Van
(Universe: Workers 16 Years and Over)

Group	Number	%
Total Population	9,943	84.3
Hispanic or Latino (of any race)	6,175	84.8
Central American, ex. Mexican	797	93.3
Salvadoran	446	92.7
Mexican	5,226	84.0

Means of Transportation to Work: Public Transportation (ex. Taxicab)
(Universe: Workers 16 Years and Over)

Group	Number	%
Total Population	956	8.1
Hispanic or Latino (of any race)	665	9.1
Central American, ex. Mexican	38	4.4
Salvadoran	16	3.3
Mexican	574	9.2

Homeownership Rate
(Universe: Occupied Housing Units)

Group	%
Total Population	51.9
Hispanic or Latino (of any race)	50.6
Central American, ex. Mexican	59.5
Guatemalan	53.7
Honduran	50.0
Salvadoran	65.1
Mexican	50.1

Median Home Value

Group	Dollars
Total Population	328,900
Hispanic or Latino (of any race)	295,900
Central American, ex. Mexican	332,600
Salvadoran	242,300
Mexican	288,800

Median Gross Rent

Group	Dollars
Total Population	898
Hispanic or Latino (of any race)	953
Central American, ex. Mexican	852
Salvadoran	835
Mexican	948

Median Household Income
(2010 Inflation-Adjusted Dollars)

Group	Dollars
Total Population	37,465
Hispanic or Latino (of any race)	41,258
Central American, ex. Mexican	44,340
Salvadoran	43,819
Mexican	41,621

Per Capita Income
(2010 Inflation-Adjusted Dollars)

Group	Dollars
Total Population	13,579
Hispanic or Latino (of any race)	10,294
Central American, ex. Mexican	13,335
Salvadoran	11,768
Mexican	10,062

Households with $100,000+ Income

Group	Number	%
Total Population	924	10.3
Hispanic or Latino (of any race)	271	6.9
Central American, ex. Mexican	22	5.1
Salvadoran	0	0.0
Mexican	249	7.4

Households with Food Stamps/SNAP Benefits During Past 12 Months

Group	Number	%
Total Population	1,559	17.3
Hispanic or Latino (of any race)	687	17.4
Central American, ex. Mexican	24	5.6
Salvadoran	18	7.8
Mexican	654	19.4

Poverty Rate
(Income in Past 12 Months Below Poverty Level)

Group	%
Total Population	25.4
Hispanic or Latino (of any race)	27.8
Central American, ex. Mexican	22.4
Salvadoran	18.8
Mexican	28.8

Windsor

Population

Group	Number	%TP[1]	%HP[2]
Total Population	26,801	100.0	–
Hispanic or Latino (of any race)	8,511	31.8	100.0
Central American, ex. Mexican	187	0.7	2.2
Mexican	7,646	28.5	89.8
Puerto Rican	100	0.4	1.2
South American	105	0.4	1.2
Spaniard	105	0.4	1.2

Population Growth: 2000–2010

Group	%
Total Population	17.8
Hispanic or Latino (of any race)	58.7
Mexican	68.4

Males per 100 Females

Group	Number
Total Population	96.6
Hispanic or Latino (of any race)	107.8
Central American, ex. Mexican	81.6
Mexican	110.4
Puerto Rican	92.3
South American	87.5
Spaniard	84.2

Average Household Size

Group	People
Total Population	2.98
Hispanic or Latino (of any race)	4.33
Central American, ex. Mexican	3.47
Mexican	4.45
Puerto Rican	3.30
South American	3.17
Spaniard	2.82

Median Age

Group	Years
Total Population	37.0
Hispanic or Latino (of any race)	25.5
Central American, ex. Mexican	30.9
Mexican	25.1
Puerto Rican	27.0
South American	38.1
Spaniard	41.2

High School Graduates
(Universe: Population 25 Years and Over)

Group	Number	%
Total Population	13,466	82.6
Hispanic or Latino (of any race)	2,676	59.0
Mexican	2,053	53.0

Four-Year College Graduates
(Universe: Population 25 Years and Over)

Group	Number	%
Total Population	4,083	25.0
Hispanic or Latino (of any race)	412	9.1
Mexican	286	7.4

Population Age 3–17 Enrolled in Public School
(Universe: Population Age 3–17 Enrolled in School)

Group	Number	%
Total Population	4,912	85.8

STATE & PLACE PROFILES

Notes: (1) Percent of total population; (2) Percent of Hispanic/Latino population; Profiles include places with an overall population of at least 125,000, OR an overall population of at least 25,000 where the Hispanic/Latino population is at least 20% of the overall population. In states where less than five places meet either of these criteria, we have included places with at least 10,000 total population with the highest percentage of Hispanic/Latino population. These places are identified with an asterisk (*); Please refer to the User's Guide for a full explanation of data.

Group	Number	%
Hispanic or Latino (of any race)	2,241	91.2
Mexican	1,961	93.9

Population Age 3–17 Enrolled in Private School
(Universe: Population Age 3–17 Enrolled in School)

Group	Number	%
Total Population	812	14.2
Hispanic or Latino (of any race)	216	8.8
Mexican	127	6.1

Foreign-Born Population

Group	Number	%
Total Population	3,917	15.2
Hispanic or Latino (of any race)	3,037	35.7
Mexican	2,747	38.4

Foreign-Born Naturalized U.S. Citizens

Group	Number	%
Total Population	1,793	45.8
Hispanic or Latino (of any race)	1,184	39.0
Mexican	1,065	38.8

Language Spoken at Home: English Only
(Universe: Population 5 Years and Over)

Group	Number	%
Total Population	17,539	72.8
Hispanic or Latino (of any race)	2,374	30.5
Mexican	1,509	22.8

Language Spoken at Home: Spanish
(Universe: Population 5 Years and Over)

Group	Number	%
Total Population	5,582	23.2
Hispanic or Latino (of any race)	5,308	68.1
Mexican	5,121	77.2

Unemployment Rate
(Universe: Population 16 Years and Over)

Group	%
Total Population	5.9
Hispanic or Latino (of any race)	7.8
Mexican	8.3

Class of Worker: Private Wage and Salary
(Universe: Civilian Employed Population 16 Years and Over)

Group	Number	%
Total Population	9,972	76.7
Hispanic or Latino (of any race)	3,375	82.6
Mexican	2,800	81.9

Class of Worker: Government
(Universe: Civilian Employed Population 16 Years and Over)

Group	Number	%
Total Population	1,767	13.6
Hispanic or Latino (of any race)	369	9.0
Mexican	307	9.0

Means of Transportation to Work: Car, Truck or Van
(Universe: Workers 16 Years and Over)

Group	Number	%
Total Population	11,787	93.0
Hispanic or Latino (of any race)	3,853	95.4
Mexican	3,227	95.8

Means of Transportation to Work: Public Transportation (ex. Taxicab)
(Universe: Workers 16 Years and Over)

Group	Number	%
Total Population	40	0.3
Hispanic or Latino (of any race)	0	0.0
Mexican	0	0.0

Homeownership Rate
(Universe: Occupied Housing Units)

Group	%
Total Population	75.8
Hispanic or Latino (of any race)	62.1
Central American, ex. Mexican	71.1
Mexican	61.8
Puerto Rican	63.0
South American	82.9
Spaniard	78.9

Median Home Value

Group	Dollars
Total Population	468,800
Hispanic or Latino (of any race)	417,300
Mexican	398,900

Median Gross Rent

Group	Dollars
Total Population	1,621
Hispanic or Latino (of any race)	1,459
Mexican	1,573

Median Household Income
(2010 Inflation-Adjusted Dollars)

Group	Dollars
Total Population	73,709
Hispanic or Latino (of any race)	64,306
Mexican	67,845

Per Capita Income
(2010 Inflation-Adjusted Dollars)

Group	Dollars
Total Population	29,349
Hispanic or Latino (of any race)	18,942
Mexican	17,821

Households with $100,000+ Income

Group	Number	%
Total Population	2,984	33.7
Hispanic or Latino (of any race)	636	28.5
Mexican	532	31.1

Households with Food Stamps/SNAP Benefits During Past 12 Months

Group	Number	%
Total Population	224	2.5
Hispanic or Latino (of any race)	96	4.3
Mexican	86	5.0

Poverty Rate
(Income in Past 12 Months Below Poverty Level)

Group	%
Total Population	5.0
Hispanic or Latino (of any race)	6.1
Mexican	6.9

Woodland

Population

Group	Number	%TP[1]	%HP[2]
Total Population	55,468	100.0	–
Hispanic or Latino (of any race)	26,289	47.4	100.0
Central American, ex. Mexican	367	0.7	1.4
Honduran	109	0.2	0.4
Salvadoran	127	0.2	0.5
Mexican	24,330	43.9	92.5
Puerto Rican	183	0.3	0.7
South American	157	0.3	0.6
Spaniard	292	0.5	1.1

Population Growth: 2000–2010

Group	%
Total Population	12.9
Hispanic or Latino (of any race)	37.8
Central American, ex. Mexican	230.6
Mexican	46.2
Puerto Rican	45.2

Males per 100 Females

Group	Number
Total Population	97.0
Hispanic or Latino (of any race)	103.4
Central American, ex. Mexican	108.5
Honduran	142.2
Salvadoran	98.4
Mexican	104.1
Puerto Rican	110.3
South American	65.3
Spaniard	74.9

Average Household Size

Group	People
Total Population	2.91
Hispanic or Latino (of any race)	3.70
Central American, ex. Mexican	3.60
Honduran	4.92
Salvadoran	3.57
Mexican	3.76
Puerto Rican	2.78
South American	2.70
Spaniard	2.57

Median Age

Group	Years
Total Population	33.7
Hispanic or Latino (of any race)	26.5
Central American, ex. Mexican	27.8
Honduran	26.5
Salvadoran	30.5
Mexican	26.3
Puerto Rican	28.9
South American	37.3
Spaniard	42.0

High School Graduates
(Universe: Population 25 Years and Over)

Group	Number	%
Total Population	26,645	77.8
Hispanic or Latino (of any race)	7,239	58.9
Central American, ex. Mexican	289	55.6
Mexican	6,177	57.2

Four-Year College Graduates
(Universe: Population 25 Years and Over)

Group	Number	%
Total Population	7,751	22.6
Hispanic or Latino (of any race)	888	7.2
Central American, ex. Mexican	11	2.1
Mexican	679	6.3

Population Age 3–17 Enrolled in Public School
(Universe: Population Age 3–17 Enrolled in School)

Group	Number	%
Total Population	10,511	92.3
Hispanic or Latino (of any race)	5,906	94.6
Central American, ex. Mexican	371	100.0
Mexican	5,093	93.9

Population Age 3–17 Enrolled in Private School
(Universe: Population Age 3–17 Enrolled in School)

Group	Number	%
Total Population	871	7.7
Hispanic or Latino (of any race)	339	5.4
Central American, ex. Mexican	0	0.0
Mexican	328	6.1

Foreign-Born Population

Group	Number	%
Total Population	11,630	21.2
Hispanic or Latino (of any race)	8,604	36.0
Central American, ex. Mexican	475	48.4
Mexican	7,844	37.0

Foreign-Born Naturalized U.S. Citizens

Group	Number	%
Total Population	4,285	36.8
Hispanic or Latino (of any race)	2,541	29.5
Central American, ex. Mexican	164	34.5
Mexican	2,253	28.7

Language Spoken at Home: English Only
(Universe: Population 5 Years and Over)

Group	Number	%
Total Population	30,968	60.9
Hispanic or Latino (of any race)	5,727	26.8
Central American, ex. Mexican	245	26.8
Mexican	4,498	23.9

Language Spoken at Home: Spanish
(Universe: Population 5 Years and Over)

Group	Number	%
Total Population	16,247	32.0
Hispanic or Latino (of any race)	15,592	73.0
Central American, ex. Mexican	669	73.2
Mexican	14,338	76.1

Unemployment Rate
(Universe: Population 16 Years and Over)

Group	%
Total Population	8.9

Notes: (1) Percent of total population; (2) Percent of Hispanic/Latino population; Profiles include places with an overall population of at least 125,000, OR an overall population of at least 25,000 where the Hispanic/Latino population is at least 20% of the overall population. In states where less than five places meet either of these criteria, we have included places with at least 10,000 total population with the highest percentage of Hispanic/Latino population. These places are identified with an asterisk (*); Please refer to the User's Guide for a full explanation of data.

Hispanic or Latino (of any race)		11.5
Central American, ex. Mexican		6.9
Mexican		11.5

Class of Worker: Private Wage and Salary
(Universe: Civilian Employed Population 16 Years and Over)

Group	Number	%
Total Population	17,866	70.6
Hispanic or Latino (of any race)	7,813	77.9
Central American, ex. Mexican	338	86.0
Mexican	6,925	77.6

Class of Worker: Government
(Universe: Civilian Employed Population 16 Years and Over)

Group	Number	%
Total Population	5,580	22.1
Hispanic or Latino (of any race)	1,588	15.8
Central American, ex. Mexican	41	10.4
Mexican	1,426	16.0

Means of Transportation to Work: Car, Truck or Van
(Universe: Workers 16 Years and Over)

Group	Number	%
Total Population	21,614	88.9
Hispanic or Latino (of any race)	8,481	88.4
Central American, ex. Mexican	356	90.6
Mexican	7,577	88.7

Means of Transportation to Work: Public Transportation (ex. Taxicab)
(Universe: Workers 16 Years and Over)

Group	Number	%
Total Population	433	1.8
Hispanic or Latino (of any race)	170	1.8
Central American, ex. Mexican	0	0.0
Mexican	170	2.0

Homeownership Rate
(Universe: Occupied Housing Units)

Group	%
Total Population	55.9
Hispanic or Latino (of any race)	44.3
Central American, ex. Mexican	36.5
Honduran	41.7
Salvadoran	31.4
Mexican	44.3
Puerto Rican	40.0
South American	61.4
Spaniard	65.9

Median Home Value

Group	Dollars
Total Population	352,100
Hispanic or Latino (of any race)	347,500
Central American, ex. Mexican	327,500
Mexican	347,100

Median Gross Rent

Group	Dollars
Total Population	935
Hispanic or Latino (of any race)	909
Central American, ex. Mexican	842
Mexican	910

Median Household Income
(2010 Inflation-Adjusted Dollars)

Group	Dollars
Total Population	55,406
Hispanic or Latino (of any race)	46,812
Central American, ex. Mexican	63,417
Mexican	47,197

Per Capita Income
(2010 Inflation-Adjusted Dollars)

Group	Dollars
Total Population	25,616
Hispanic or Latino (of any race)	16,177
Central American, ex. Mexican	14,320
Mexican	15,931

Households with $100,000+ Income

Group	Number	%
Total Population	4,209	21.8
Hispanic or Latino (of any race)	860	13.3
Central American, ex. Mexican	11	6.7
Mexican	716	12.6

Households with Food Stamps/SNAP Benefits During Past 12 Months

Group	Number	%
Total Population	1,034	5.4
Hispanic or Latino (of any race)	416	6.4
Central American, ex. Mexican	49	29.9
Mexican	323	5.7

Poverty Rate
(Income in Past 12 Months Below Poverty Level)

Group	%
Total Population	11.2
Hispanic or Latino (of any race)	13.4
Central American, ex. Mexican	12.6
Mexican	13.3

Yuba City

Population

Group	Number	%TP[1]	%HP[2]
Total Population	64,925	100.0	–
Hispanic or Latino (of any race)	18,413	28.4	100.0
Central American, ex. Mexican	271	0.4	1.5
Mexican	16,488	25.4	89.5
Puerto Rican	262	0.4	1.4
South American	116	0.2	0.6
Spaniard	240	0.4	1.3

Population Growth: 2000–2010

Group	%
Total Population	76.6
Hispanic or Latino (of any race)	103.9
Mexican	114.7
Puerto Rican	100.0

Males per 100 Females

Group	Number
Total Population	97.9
Hispanic or Latino (of any race)	107.7
Central American, ex. Mexican	92.2
Mexican	108.8
Puerto Rican	125.9
South American	90.2
Spaniard	87.5

Average Household Size

Group	People
Total Population	2.99
Hispanic or Latino (of any race)	3.83
Central American, ex. Mexican	3.41
Mexican	3.91
Puerto Rican	2.90
South American	3.05
Spaniard	2.84

Median Age

Group	Years
Total Population	33.0
Hispanic or Latino (of any race)	23.9
Central American, ex. Mexican	32.8
Mexican	23.6
Puerto Rican	24.3
South American	34.2
Spaniard	35.0

High School Graduates
(Universe: Population 25 Years and Over)

Group	Number	%
Total Population	30,590	78.5
Hispanic or Latino (of any race)	4,451	52.6
Mexican	3,875	50.5

Four-Year College Graduates
(Universe: Population 25 Years and Over)

Group	Number	%
Total Population	7,436	19.1
Hispanic or Latino (of any race)	591	7.0
Mexican	492	6.4

Population Age 3–17 Enrolled in Public School
(Universe: Population Age 3–17 Enrolled in School)

Group	Number	%
Total Population	12,201	93.3
Hispanic or Latino (of any race)	4,676	96.5
Mexican	4,277	96.4

Population Age 3–17 Enrolled in Private School
(Universe: Population Age 3–17 Enrolled in School)

Group	Number	%
Total Population	874	6.7
Hispanic or Latino (of any race)	168	3.5
Mexican	161	3.6

Foreign-Born Population

Group	Number	%
Total Population	15,374	24.2
Hispanic or Latino (of any race)	6,823	38.7
Mexican	6,355	39.5

Foreign-Born Naturalized U.S. Citizens

Group	Number	%
Total Population	5,964	38.8
Hispanic or Latino (of any race)	1,740	25.5
Mexican	1,470	23.1

Language Spoken at Home: English Only
(Universe: Population 5 Years and Over)

Group	Number	%
Total Population	36,008	62.0
Hispanic or Latino (of any race)	4,105	26.7
Mexican	3,394	24.2

Language Spoken at Home: Spanish
(Universe: Population 5 Years and Over)

Group	Number	%
Total Population	11,776	20.3
Hispanic or Latino (of any race)	11,214	73.0
Mexican	10,620	75.6

Unemployment Rate
(Universe: Population 16 Years and Over)

Group	%
Total Population	14.1
Hispanic or Latino (of any race)	16.3
Mexican	16.0

Class of Worker: Private Wage and Salary
(Universe: Civilian Employed Population 16 Years and Over)

Group	Number	%
Total Population	19,291	74.6
Hispanic or Latino (of any race)	5,303	81.9
Mexican	5,036	83.2

Class of Worker: Government
(Universe: Civilian Employed Population 16 Years and Over)

Group	Number	%
Total Population	4,595	17.8
Hispanic or Latino (of any race)	791	12.2
Mexican	674	11.1

Means of Transportation to Work: Car, Truck or Van
(Universe: Workers 16 Years and Over)

Group	Number	%
Total Population	23,564	91.5
Hispanic or Latino (of any race)	5,576	88.9
Mexican	5,240	88.9

Means of Transportation to Work: Public Transportation (ex. Taxicab)
(Universe: Workers 16 Years and Over)

Group	Number	%
Total Population	412	1.6
Hispanic or Latino (of any race)	132	2.1
Mexican	114	1.9

Homeownership Rate
(Universe: Occupied Housing Units)

Group	%
Total Population	56.9
Hispanic or Latino (of any race)	39.8
Central American, ex. Mexican	47.5
Mexican	39.3
Puerto Rican	37.5
South American	60.5

STATE & PLACE PROFILES

Notes: (1) Percent of total population; (2) Percent of Hispanic/Latino population; Profiles include places with an overall population of at least 125,000, OR an overall population of at least 25,000 where the Hispanic/Latino population is at least 20% of the overall population. In states where less than five places meet either of these criteria, we have included places with at least 10,000 total population with the highest percentage of Hispanic/Latino population. These places are identified with an asterisk (*); Please refer to the User's Guide for a full explanation of data.

Spaniard	61.2

Median Home Value

Group	Dollars
Total Population	254,300
Hispanic or Latino (of any race)	253,800
Mexican	255,600

Median Gross Rent

Group	Dollars
Total Population	857
Hispanic or Latino (of any race)	787
Mexican	792

Median Household Income
(2010 Inflation-Adjusted Dollars)

Group	Dollars
Total Population	49,500
Hispanic or Latino (of any race)	36,650
Mexican	36,844

Per Capita Income
(2010 Inflation-Adjusted Dollars)

Group	Dollars
Total Population	21,389
Hispanic or Latino (of any race)	13,215
Mexican	12,625

Households with $100,000+ Income

Group	Number	%
Total Population	3,634	17.0
Hispanic or Latino (of any race)	443	10.1
Mexican	384	9.7

Households with Food Stamps/SNAP Benefits During Past 12 Months

Group	Number	%
Total Population	1,754	8.2
Hispanic or Latino (of any race)	678	15.5
Mexican	609	15.4

Poverty Rate
(Income in Past 12 Months Below Poverty Level)

Group	%
Total Population	14.3
Hispanic or Latino (of any race)	26.2
Mexican	27.9

Yucaipa

Population

Group	Number	%TP[1]	%HP[2]
Total Population	51,367	100.0	–
Hispanic or Latino (of any race)	13,943	27.1	100.0
Central American, ex. Mexican	374	0.7	2.7
Guatemalan	151	0.3	1.1
Mexican	11,979	23.3	85.9
Puerto Rican	244	0.5	1.7
South American	184	0.4	1.3
Spaniard	210	0.4	1.5

Population Growth: 2000–2010

Group	%
Total Population	24.7
Hispanic or Latino (of any race)	84.4
Mexican	93.0

Males per 100 Females

Group	Number
Total Population	96.8
Hispanic or Latino (of any race)	99.6
Central American, ex. Mexican	92.8
Guatemalan	88.8
Mexican	100.0
Puerto Rican	98.4
South American	89.7
Spaniard	128.3

Average Household Size

Group	People
Total Population	2.79
Hispanic or Latino (of any race)	3.59
Central American, ex. Mexican	3.85
Guatemalan	4.21
Mexican	3.66
Puerto Rican	3.21
South American	2.72
Spaniard	2.86

Median Age

Group	Years
Total Population	37.8
Hispanic or Latino (of any race)	26.9
Central American, ex. Mexican	31.9
Guatemalan	33.3
Mexican	26.3
Puerto Rican	22.5
South American	43.6
Spaniard	33.7

High School Graduates
(Universe: Population 25 Years and Over)

Group	Number	%
Total Population	28,597	87.8
Hispanic or Latino (of any race)	4,709	73.4
Mexican	4,081	72.8

Four-Year College Graduates
(Universe: Population 25 Years and Over)

Group	Number	%
Total Population	6,971	21.4
Hispanic or Latino (of any race)	678	10.6
Mexican	479	8.5

Population Age 3–17 Enrolled in Public School
(Universe: Population Age 3–17 Enrolled in School)

Group	Number	%
Total Population	8,945	84.1
Hispanic or Latino (of any race)	3,694	92.7
Mexican	3,281	92.7

Population Age 3–17 Enrolled in Private School
(Universe: Population Age 3–17 Enrolled in School)

Group	Number	%
Total Population	1,697	15.9
Hispanic or Latino (of any race)	289	7.3
Mexican	257	7.3

Foreign-Born Population

Group	Number	%
Total Population	5,415	10.8
Hispanic or Latino (of any race)	3,172	24.6
Mexican	2,612	22.8

Foreign-Born Naturalized U.S. Citizens

Group	Number	%
Total Population	2,560	47.3
Hispanic or Latino (of any race)	1,063	33.5
Mexican	778	29.8

Language Spoken at Home: English Only
(Universe: Population 5 Years and Over)

Group	Number	%
Total Population	38,891	82.4
Hispanic or Latino (of any race)	5,790	48.6
Mexican	5,154	48.9

Language Spoken at Home: Spanish
(Universe: Population 5 Years and Over)

Group	Number	%
Total Population	6,553	13.9
Hispanic or Latino (of any race)	6,063	50.9
Mexican	5,382	51.1

Unemployment Rate
(Universe: Population 16 Years and Over)

Group	%
Total Population	10.1
Hispanic or Latino (of any race)	9.5
Mexican	9.6

Class of Worker: Private Wage and Salary
(Universe: Civilian Employed Population 16 Years and Over)

Group	Number	%
Total Population	15,639	70.6
Hispanic or Latino (of any race)	3,993	76.8
Mexican	3,574	77.0

Class of Worker: Government
(Universe: Civilian Employed Population 16 Years and Over)

Group	Number	%
Total Population	4,743	21.4
Hispanic or Latino (of any race)	931	17.9
Mexican	812	17.5

Means of Transportation to Work: Car, Truck or Van
(Universe: Workers 16 Years and Over)

Group	Number	%
Total Population	20,089	92.7
Hispanic or Latino (of any race)	4,866	94.7
Mexican	4,380	96.4

Means of Transportation to Work: Public Transportation (ex. Taxicab)
(Universe: Workers 16 Years and Over)

Group	Number	%
Total Population	221	1.0
Hispanic or Latino (of any race)	39	0.8
Mexican	39	0.9

Homeownership Rate
(Universe: Occupied Housing Units)

Group	%
Total Population	74.1
Hispanic or Latino (of any race)	65.7
Central American, ex. Mexican	57.7
Guatemalan	53.5
Mexican	66.1
Puerto Rican	62.0
South American	86.9
Spaniard	78.4

Median Home Value

Group	Dollars
Total Population	299,400
Hispanic or Latino (of any race)	291,800
Mexican	283,400

Median Gross Rent

Group	Dollars
Total Population	966
Hispanic or Latino (of any race)	919
Mexican	885

Median Household Income
(2010 Inflation-Adjusted Dollars)

Group	Dollars
Total Population	57,492
Hispanic or Latino (of any race)	54,728
Mexican	54,362

Per Capita Income
(2010 Inflation-Adjusted Dollars)

Group	Dollars
Total Population	26,750
Hispanic or Latino (of any race)	17,781
Mexican	17,158

Households with $100,000+ Income

Group	Number	%
Total Population	4,706	27.1
Hispanic or Latino (of any race)	775	23.4
Mexican	639	22.1

Households with Food Stamps/SNAP Benefits During Past 12 Months

Group	Number	%
Total Population	817	4.7
Hispanic or Latino (of any race)	239	7.2
Mexican	227	7.8

Poverty Rate
(Income in Past 12 Months Below Poverty Level)

Group	%
Total Population	10.4
Hispanic or Latino (of any race)	14.9
Mexican	15.7

Notes: (1) Percent of total population; (2) Percent of Hispanic/Latino population; Profiles include places with an overall population of at least 125,000, OR an overall population of at least 25,000 where the Hispanic/Latino population is at least 20% of the overall population. In states where less than five places meet either of these criteria, we have included places with at least 10,000 total population with the highest percentage of Hispanic/Latino population. These places are identified with an asterisk (*); Please refer to the User's Guide for a full explanation of data.

Colorado

EDITOR'S NOTE: For a place to be included in this edition, it must meet one of two criteria. Either its overall population is at least 125,000, OR its overall population is at least 25,000 and its Hispanic/Latino population is at least 20% of the overall population. For the state of Colorado, the following locations are included:

- Aurora
- Brighton
- Colorado Springs
- Commerce City
- Denver
- Fort Collins
- Greeley
- Lakewood
- Longmont
- Northglenn
- Pueblo
- Pueblo West
- Thornton
- Westminster
- Wheat Ridge

Section Two: State & Place Profiles starts with the state profile, followed by place profiles that meet the criteria above. Places are listed alphabetically within each state. All states, all counties and places that meet the above criteria are ranked and compared in *Section Three: Rankings & Comparisons*, on page 1055.

For a more detailed look at the Hispanic/Latino population in Colorado, a companion web site is available at no additional charge with purchase of this print edition. Visit http://gold.greyhouse.com/page/info_hispanic for more information.

The web site includes data for all counties and places in Colorado with Hispanic/Latino population, plus ten additional topics: Self Employed Worker; Walked to Work; Worked from Home; Mean Travel Time to Work; Mean Household Income; Households with Cash Public Assistance; Mean Cash Pubic Assistance; Poverty Rates for 18 and Under, 18 to 64, and 65 and Over.

Population

Group	Number	%TP[1]	%HP[2]
Total Population	5,029,196	100.0	–
Hispanic or Latino (of any race)	1,038,687	20.7	100.0
Central American, ex. Mexican	29,386	0.6	2.8
Costa Rican	1,104	<0.1	0.1
Guatemalan	7,488	0.1	0.7
Honduran	4,356	0.1	0.4
Nicaraguan	1,364	<0.1	0.1
Panamanian	2,414	<0.1	0.2
Salvadoran	12,329	0.2	1.2
Cuban	6,253	0.1	0.6
Dominican Republic	1,744	<0.1	0.2
Mexican	757,181	15.1	72.9
Puerto Rican	22,995	0.5	2.2
South American	19,117	0.4	1.8
Argentinean	2,165	<0.1	0.2
Bolivian	775	<0.1	0.1
Chilean	1,678	<0.1	0.2
Colombian	4,858	0.1	0.5
Ecuadorian	1,375	<0.1	0.1
Paraguayan	214	<0.1	<0.1
Peruvian	5,835	0.1	0.6
Uruguayan	224	<0.1	<0.1
Venezuelan	1,802	<0.1	0.2
Spaniard	41,960	0.8	4.0

Population Growth: 2000–2010

Group	%
Total Population	16.9
Hispanic or Latino (of any race)	41.2
Central American, ex. Mexican	206.5
Costa Rican	135.4
Guatemalan	217.0
Honduran	236.4
Nicaraguan	231.1
Panamanian	109.9
Salvadoran	267.2
Cuban	69.0
Dominican Republic	204.4
Mexican	68.0
Puerto Rican	77.0
South American	165.9
Argentinean	173.4
Bolivian	162.7
Chilean	126.8
Colombian	181.8
Ecuadorian	214.6
Peruvian	197.4
Venezuelan	163.1
Spaniard	1,754.2

Males per 100 Females

Group	Number
Total Population	100.5
Hispanic or Latino (of any race)	104.1
Central American, ex. Mexican	110.7
Costa Rican	79.5
Guatemalan	123.5
Honduran	121.3
Nicaraguan	101.8
Panamanian	71.7
Salvadoran	113.7
Cuban	108.2
Dominican Republic	100.5
Mexican	107.5
Puerto Rican	104.7
South American	86.5
Argentinean	88.8
Bolivian	98.2
Chilean	90.0
Colombian	79.0
Ecuadorian	84.3
Paraguayan	69.8
Peruvian	90.1
Uruguayan	80.6
Venezuelan	89.3
Spaniard	91.4

Average Household Size

Group	People
Total Population	2.49
Hispanic or Latino (of any race)	3.24
Central American, ex. Mexican	3.70
Costa Rican	2.66
Guatemalan	3.91
Honduran	3.72
Nicaraguan	3.06
Panamanian	2.71
Salvadoran	3.99
Cuban	2.56
Dominican Republic	2.89
Mexican	3.44
Puerto Rican	2.73
South American	2.76
Argentinean	2.70
Bolivian	2.80
Chilean	2.53
Colombian	2.57
Ecuadorian	2.78
Paraguayan	3.53
Peruvian	3.05
Uruguayan	2.75
Venezuelan	2.64
Spaniard	2.64

Median Age

Group	Years
Total Population	36.1
Hispanic or Latino (of any race)	26.5
Central American, ex. Mexican	29.0
Costa Rican	29.2
Guatemalan	27.5
Honduran	28.8
Nicaraguan	31.5
Panamanian	30.4
Salvadoran	29.5
Cuban	30.4
Dominican Republic	26.9
Mexican	25.4
Puerto Rican	25.5
South American	32.8
Argentinean	34.8
Bolivian	33.1
Chilean	33.3
Colombian	31.9
Ecuadorian	31.3
Paraguayan	23.8
Peruvian	33.5
Uruguayan	38.3
Venezuelan	31.9
Spaniard	34.3

High School Graduates

(Universe: Population 25 Years and Over)

Group	Number	%
Total Population	2,858,883	89.3
Hispanic or Latino (of any race)	331,389	64.6
Central American, ex. Mexican	8,035	53.1
Costa Rican	544	85.1
Guatemalan	1,589	48.9
Honduran	1,244	45.6
Nicaraguan	644	74.6
Panamanian	1,101	94.0
Salvadoran	2,717	43.6
Cuban	2,858	89.2
Dominican Republic	674	80.0
Mexican	218,728	59.6
Puerto Rican	9,090	89.3
South American	9,217	92.0
Argentinean	1,066	96.6
Chilean	662	78.1
Colombian	2,732	93.3
Ecuadorian	565	95.4
Peruvian	2,585	89.4
Venezuelan	941	100.0
Spaniard	22,418	85.4

Four-Year College Graduates

(Universe: Population 25 Years and Over)

Group	Number	%
Total Population	1,148,749	35.9
Hispanic or Latino (of any race)	61,984	12.1
Central American, ex. Mexican	1,839	12.1
Costa Rican	353	55.2
Guatemalan	276	8.5
Honduran	241	8.8
Nicaraguan	153	17.7
Panamanian	333	28.4
Salvadoran	392	6.3
Cuban	1,437	44.9
Dominican Republic	193	22.9
Mexican	36,138	9.8
Puerto Rican	2,876	28.2
South American	4,780	47.7
Argentinean	641	58.1
Chilean	291	34.3
Colombian	1,492	50.9
Ecuadorian	358	60.5
Peruvian	1,064	36.8
Venezuelan	569	60.5
Spaniard	4,739	18.0

Population Age 3–17 Enrolled in Public School

(Universe: Population Age 3–17 Enrolled in School)

Group	Number	%
Total Population	786,961	88.2
Hispanic or Latino (of any race)	232,114	94.1
Central American, ex. Mexican	5,389	90.2
Costa Rican	371	92.5
Guatemalan	1,221	92.4
Honduran	763	88.2

Notes: (1) Percent of total population; (2) Percent of Hispanic/Latino population; Profiles include places with an overall population of at least 125,000, OR an overall population of at least 25,000 where the Hispanic/Latino population is at least 20% of the overall population. In states where less than five places meet either of these criteria, we have included places with at least 10,000 total population with the highest percentage of Hispanic/Latino population. These places are identified with an asterisk (*); Please refer to the User's Guide for a full explanation of data.

Group	Number	%
Nicaraguan	200	70.2
Panamanian	446	78.2
Salvadoran	2,314	94.2
Cuban	992	75.8
Dominican Republic	318	91.6
Mexican	182,908	95.2
Puerto Rican	4,430	91.8
South American	2,739	84.9
Argentinean	197	78.8
Chilean	269	83.8
Colombian	978	84.7
Ecuadorian	266	100.0
Peruvian	710	90.7
Venezuelan	117	74.5
Spaniard	8,306	88.6

Population Age 3–17 Enrolled in Private School
(Universe: Population Age 3–17 Enrolled in School)

Group	Number	%
Total Population	105,771	11.8
Hispanic or Latino (of any race)	14,463	5.9
Central American, ex. Mexican	583	9.8
Costa Rican	30	7.5
Guatemalan	100	7.6
Honduran	102	11.8
Nicaraguan	85	29.8
Panamanian	124	21.8
Salvadoran	142	5.8
Cuban	317	24.2
Dominican Republic	29	8.4
Mexican	9,321	4.8
Puerto Rican	397	8.2
South American	488	15.1
Argentinean	53	21.2
Chilean	52	16.2
Colombian	177	15.3
Ecuadorian	0	0.0
Peruvian	73	9.3
Venezuelan	40	25.5
Spaniard	1,067	11.4

Foreign-Born Population

Group	Number	%
Total Population	479,769	9.8
Hispanic or Latino (of any race)	265,179	27.0
Central American, ex. Mexican	17,143	60.7
Costa Rican	521	43.0
Guatemalan	4,209	65.3
Honduran	3,246	67.4
Nicaraguan	662	48.8
Panamanian	811	38.0
Salvadoran	7,494	63.2
Cuban	1,304	24.2
Dominican Republic	664	45.0
Mexican	230,622	31.3
Puerto Rican	178	0.9
South American	9,302	58.3
Argentinean	872	59.5
Chilean	880	63.3
Colombian	2,679	55.6
Ecuadorian	408	40.0
Peruvian	3,063	69.4
Venezuelan	837	53.7
Spaniard	1,028	2.4

Foreign-Born Naturalized U.S. Citizens

Group	Number	%
Total Population	158,669	33.1
Hispanic or Latino (of any race)	45,927	17.3
Central American, ex. Mexican	3,426	20.0
Costa Rican	192	36.9
Guatemalan	906	21.5
Honduran	470	14.5
Nicaraguan	217	32.8
Panamanian	582	71.8
Salvadoran	981	13.1
Cuban	995	76.3
Dominican Republic	431	64.9
Mexican	35,073	15.2
Puerto Rican	68	38.2
South American	4,065	43.7
Argentinean	465	53.3
Chilean	298	33.9
Colombian	1,330	49.6
Ecuadorian	211	51.7
Peruvian	1,188	38.8
Venezuelan	261	31.2
Spaniard	386	37.5

Language Spoken at Home: English Only
(Universe: Population 5 Years and Over)

Group	Number	%
Total Population	3,783,688	83.2
Hispanic or Latino (of any race)	386,966	44.3
Central American, ex. Mexican	4,322	17.6
Costa Rican	619	53.1
Guatemalan	864	15.8
Honduran	519	12.5
Nicaraguan	438	34.8
Panamanian	782	41.0
Salvadoran	1,000	9.9
Cuban	3,193	62.1
Dominican Republic	310	22.7
Mexican	249,112	38.5
Puerto Rican	10,187	58.9
South American	3,535	24.1
Argentinean	224	16.7
Chilean	312	24.2
Colombian	1,203	26.9
Ecuadorian	437	44.8
Peruvian	708	17.5
Venezuelan	345	25.6
Spaniard	30,428	76.3

Language Spoken at Home: Spanish
(Universe: Population 5 Years and Over)

Group	Number	%
Total Population	542,257	11.9
Hispanic or Latino (of any race)	482,912	55.3
Central American, ex. Mexican	19,884	81.1
Costa Rican	518	44.5
Guatemalan	4,461	81.5
Honduran	3,637	87.3
Nicaraguan	792	63.0
Panamanian	1,083	56.9
Salvadoran	9,137	90.1
Cuban	1,926	37.5
Dominican Republic	1,053	77.3
Mexican	397,122	61.3
Puerto Rican	6,973	40.3
South American	11,049	75.4
Argentinean	1,118	83.3
Chilean	977	75.8
Colombian	3,274	73.1
Ecuadorian	523	53.6
Peruvian	3,336	82.2
Venezuelan	977	72.6
Spaniard	9,162	23.0

Unemployment Rate
(Universe: Population 16 Years and Over)

Group	%
Total Population	6.8
Hispanic or Latino (of any race)	9.7
Central American, ex. Mexican	6.3
Costa Rican	5.7
Guatemalan	5.4
Honduran	3.9
Nicaraguan	9.9
Panamanian	11.7
Salvadoran	6.1
Cuban	4.9
Dominican Republic	12.4
Mexican	9.7
Puerto Rican	9.7
South American	5.6
Argentinean	4.3
Chilean	4.9
Colombian	4.1
Ecuadorian	5.7
Peruvian	8.1
Venezuelan	3.6
Spaniard	10.9

Class of Worker: Private Wage and Salary
(Universe: Civilian Employed Population 16 Years and Over)

Group	Number	%
Total Population	1,923,666	78.3
Hispanic or Latino (of any race)	342,940	83.5
Central American, ex. Mexican	12,334	88.5
Costa Rican	606	89.1
Guatemalan	2,816	93.2
Honduran	2,223	87.5
Nicaraguan	586	84.0
Panamanian	586	70.3
Salvadoran	5,283	89.5
Cuban	2,237	77.1
Dominican Republic	574	77.2
Mexican	259,064	85.4
Puerto Rican	6,950	79.3
South American	6,619	79.8
Argentinean	580	74.6
Chilean	631	82.1
Colombian	1,851	76.7
Ecuadorian	460	77.1
Peruvian	1,844	82.9
Venezuelan	763	88.2
Spaniard	14,692	74.6

Class of Worker: Government
(Universe: Civilian Employed Population 16 Years and Over)

Group	Number	%
Total Population	349,593	14.2
Hispanic or Latino (of any race)	46,861	11.4
Central American, ex. Mexican	867	6.2
Costa Rican	35	5.1
Guatemalan	89	2.9
Honduran	219	8.6
Nicaraguan	51	7.3
Panamanian	170	20.4
Salvadoran	278	4.7
Cuban	406	14.0
Dominican Republic	116	15.6
Mexican	29,701	9.8
Puerto Rican	1,400	16.0
South American	1,262	15.2
Argentinean	177	22.8
Chilean	99	12.9
Colombian	444	18.4
Ecuadorian	102	17.1
Peruvian	233	10.5
Venezuelan	87	10.1
Spaniard	3,584	18.2

Means of Transportation to Work: Car, Truck or Van
(Universe: Workers 16 Years and Over)

Group	Number	%
Total Population	2,064,661	85.0
Hispanic or Latino (of any race)	354,205	87.6
Central American, ex. Mexican	11,769	84.8
Costa Rican	496	72.9
Guatemalan	2,465	82.3
Honduran	2,083	81.7
Nicaraguan	577	79.1
Panamanian	803	88.0
Salvadoran	5,150	89.4
Cuban	2,273	79.0
Dominican Republic	668	84.2
Mexican	262,955	88.0
Puerto Rican	7,630	85.1
South American	6,637	80.9
Argentinean	598	77.0
Chilean	627	83.8
Colombian	2,020	84.4
Ecuadorian	395	66.5
Peruvian	1,673	76.3
Venezuelan	719	85.2
Spaniard	16,739	87.1

Means of Transportation to Work: Public Transportation (ex. Taxicab)
(Universe: Workers 16 Years and Over)

Group	Number	%
Total Population	79,899	3.3
Hispanic or Latino (of any race)	20,668	5.1
Central American, ex. Mexican	1,341	9.7
Costa Rican	131	19.3
Guatemalan	244	8.1
Honduran	440	17.3
Nicaraguan	129	17.7
Panamanian	26	2.9
Salvadoran	371	6.4
Cuban	135	4.7
Dominican Republic	58	7.3

Notes: (1) Percent of total population; (2) Percent of Hispanic/Latino population; Profiles include places with an overall population of at least 125,000, OR an overall population of at least 25,000 where the Hispanic/Latino population is at least 20% of the overall population. In states where less than five places meet either of these criteria, we have included places with at least 10,000 total population with the highest percentage of Hispanic/Latino population. These places are identified with an asterisk (*); Please refer to the User's Guide for a full explanation of data.

Group	Number	%
Mexican	15,443	5.2
Puerto Rican	430	4.8
South American	520	6.3
Argentinean	31	4.0
Chilean	14	1.9
Colombian	161	6.7
Ecuadorian	55	9.3
Peruvian	203	9.3
Venezuelan	47	5.6
Spaniard	961	5.0

Homeownership Rate
(Universe: Occupied Housing Units)

Group	%
Total Population	65.5
Hispanic or Latino (of any race)	49.6
Central American, ex. Mexican	42.5
Costa Rican	52.9
Guatemalan	38.6
Honduran	31.2
Nicaraguan	48.5
Panamanian	52.3
Salvadoran	44.7
Cuban	53.6
Dominican Republic	42.5
Mexican	48.4
Puerto Rican	47.0
South American	55.2
Argentinean	58.2
Bolivian	62.6
Chilean	54.6
Colombian	56.4
Ecuadorian	58.3
Paraguayan	57.5
Peruvian	52.9
Uruguayan	61.9
Venezuelan	51.3
Spaniard	64.3

Median Home Value

Group	Dollars
Total Population	236,600
Hispanic or Latino (of any race)	175,400
Central American, ex. Mexican	189,700
Costa Rican	225,600
Guatemalan	167,800
Honduran	188,800
Nicaraguan	185,500
Panamanian	217,300
Salvadoran	167,600
Cuban	278,000
Dominican Republic	171,900
Mexican	170,400
Puerto Rican	202,200
South American	235,900
Argentinean	365,000
Chilean	225,000
Colombian	177,500
Ecuadorian	297,700
Peruvian	259,100
Venezuelan	220,500
Spaniard	193,800

Median Gross Rent

Group	Dollars
Total Population	852
Hispanic or Latino (of any race)	784
Central American, ex. Mexican	795
Costa Rican	678
Guatemalan	794
Honduran	707
Nicaraguan	1,077
Panamanian	676
Salvadoran	833
Cuban	854
Dominican Republic	910
Mexican	780
Puerto Rican	850
South American	814
Argentinean	872
Chilean	1,096
Colombian	837
Ecuadorian	780
Peruvian	732
Venezuelan	855
Spaniard	847

Median Household Income
(2010 Inflation-Adjusted Dollars)

Group	Dollars
Total Population	56,456
Hispanic or Latino (of any race)	38,450
Central American, ex. Mexican	43,227
Costa Rican	64,821
Guatemalan	39,055
Honduran	40,082
Nicaraguan	41,705
Panamanian	32,131
Salvadoran	45,531
Cuban	53,847
Dominican Republic	46,182
Mexican	37,073
Puerto Rican	43,830
South American	50,040
Argentinean	91,250
Chilean	56,944
Colombian	43,581
Ecuadorian	49,875
Peruvian	47,139
Venezuelan	45,605
Spaniard	49,055

Per Capita Income
(2010 Inflation-Adjusted Dollars)

Group	Dollars
Total Population	30,151
Hispanic or Latino (of any race)	15,113
Central American, ex. Mexican	15,264
Costa Rican	29,658
Guatemalan	13,126
Honduran	14,506
Nicaraguan	17,401
Panamanian	16,344
Salvadoran	14,230
Cuban	29,059
Dominican Republic	21,887
Mexican	13,829
Puerto Rican	20,123
South American	23,672
Argentinean	31,424
Chilean	19,057
Colombian	20,080
Ecuadorian	28,716
Peruvian	21,798
Venezuelan	31,068
Spaniard	21,984

Households with $100,000+ Income

Group	Number	%
Total Population	452,445	23.6
Hispanic or Latino (of any race)	28,544	10.0
Central American, ex. Mexican	728	9.7
Costa Rican	98	21.9
Guatemalan	100	7.0
Honduran	184	13.3
Nicaraguan	20	4.2
Panamanian	59	12.1
Salvadoran	208	6.7
Cuban	526	26.9
Dominican Republic	28	5.8
Mexican	18,191	9.0
Puerto Rican	1,218	18.6
South American	990	19.8
Argentinean	256	48.5
Chilean	26	7.1
Colombian	245	17.6
Ecuadorian	75	24.8
Peruvian	163	12.1
Venezuelan	172	26.3
Spaniard	2,036	12.6

Households with Food Stamps/SNAP Benefits During Past 12 Months

Group	Number	%
Total Population	109,816	5.7
Hispanic or Latino (of any race)	39,626	13.9
Central American, ex. Mexican	592	7.9
Costa Rican	13	2.9
Guatemalan	183	12.8
Honduran	93	6.7
Nicaraguan	49	10.4
Panamanian	11	2.3
Salvadoran	236	7.6
Cuban	170	8.7
Dominican Republic	84	17.4
Mexican	28,693	14.2
Puerto Rican	1,144	17.5
South American	253	5.1
Argentinean	9	1.7
Chilean	0	0.0
Colombian	81	5.8
Ecuadorian	0	0.0
Peruvian	66	4.9
Venezuelan	82	12.6
Spaniard	1,941	12.0

Poverty Rate
(Income in Past 12 Months Below Poverty Level)

Group	%
Total Population	12.2
Hispanic or Latino (of any race)	24.3
Central American, ex. Mexican	19.8
Costa Rican	12.8
Guatemalan	24.0
Honduran	26.3
Nicaraguan	16.2
Panamanian	13.5
Salvadoran	17.6
Cuban	11.9
Dominican Republic	28.1
Mexican	26.4
Puerto Rican	22.0
South American	13.5
Argentinean	5.9
Chilean	21.7
Colombian	12.4
Ecuadorian	9.1
Peruvian	17.6
Venezuelan	12.1
Spaniard	12.8

Aurora

Population

Group	Number	%TP[1]	%HP[2]
Total Population	325,078	100.0	–
Hispanic or Latino (of any race)	93,263	28.7	100.0
Central American, ex. Mexican	6,031	1.9	6.5
Guatemalan	1,300	0.4	1.4
Honduran	970	0.3	1.0
Nicaraguan	142	<0.1	0.2
Panamanian	321	0.1	0.3
Salvadoran	3,128	1.0	3.4
Cuban	578	0.2	0.6
Dominican Republic	284	0.1	0.3
Mexican	71,225	21.9	76.4
Puerto Rican	2,324	0.7	2.5
South American	2,277	0.7	2.4
Argentinean	154	<0.1	0.2
Chilean	171	0.1	0.2
Colombian	483	0.1	0.5
Ecuadorian	133	<0.1	0.1
Peruvian	1,058	0.3	1.1
Venezuelan	150	<0.1	0.2
Spaniard	2,038	0.6	2.2

Population Growth: 2000–2010

Group	%
Total Population	17.6
Hispanic or Latino (of any race)	70.3
Central American, ex. Mexican	219.4
Guatemalan	234.2
Honduran	210.9
Panamanian	111.2
Salvadoran	266.7
Cuban	77.8
Mexican	86.1
Puerto Rican	45.6
South American	166.3
Colombian	180.8
Peruvian	167.8
Spaniard	1,019.8

Notes: (1) Percent of total population; (2) Percent of Hispanic/Latino population; Profiles include places with an overall population of at least 125,000, OR an overall population of at least 25,000 where the Hispanic/Latino population is at least 20% of the overall population. In states where less than five places meet either of these criteria, we have included places with at least 10,000 total population with the highest percentage of Hispanic/Latino population. These places are identified with an asterisk (*); Please refer to the User's Guide for a full explanation of data.

Males per 100 Females

Group	Number
Total Population	97.0
Hispanic or Latino (of any race)	106.4
Central American, ex. Mexican	116.2
Guatemalan	124.9
Honduran	136.6
Nicaraguan	108.8
Panamanian	71.7
Salvadoran	115.1
Cuban	106.4
Dominican Republic	89.3
Mexican	108.2
Puerto Rican	103.9
South American	92.2
Argentinean	92.5
Chilean	96.6
Colombian	81.6
Ecuadorian	104.6
Peruvian	97.0
Venezuelan	70.5
Spaniard	84.3

Average Household Size

Group	People
Total Population	2.65
Hispanic or Latino (of any race)	3.69
Central American, ex. Mexican	3.81
Guatemalan	3.84
Honduran	3.96
Nicaraguan	2.51
Panamanian	2.81
Salvadoran	3.96
Cuban	2.64
Dominican Republic	3.10
Mexican	3.89
Puerto Rican	2.72
South American	3.16
Argentinean	2.83
Chilean	2.86
Colombian	3.09
Ecuadorian	3.30
Peruvian	3.39
Venezuelan	3.13
Spaniard	2.61

Median Age

Group	Years
Total Population	33.2
Hispanic or Latino (of any race)	24.7
Central American, ex. Mexican	30.4
Guatemalan	30.7
Honduran	28.5
Nicaraguan	34.6
Panamanian	29.4
Salvadoran	30.6
Cuban	32.4
Dominican Republic	29.0
Mexican	23.5
Puerto Rican	26.1
South American	36.2
Argentinean	37.8
Chilean	34.5
Colombian	36.1
Ecuadorian	34.2
Peruvian	37.0
Venezuelan	33.5
Spaniard	33.3

High School Graduates
(Universe: Population 25 Years and Over)

Group	Number	%
Total Population	167,414	84.7
Hispanic or Latino (of any race)	24,577	57.3
Central American, ex. Mexican	1,805	47.3
Guatemalan	423	47.3
Honduran	214	23.9
Salvadoran	1,002	55.6
Mexican	17,735	53.1
Puerto Rican	802	95.6
South American	1,138	91.9
Peruvian	566	93.7
Spaniard	1,131	94.1

Four-Year College Graduates
(Universe: Population 25 Years and Over)

Group	Number	%
Total Population	50,153	25.4
Hispanic or Latino (of any race)	3,897	9.1
Central American, ex. Mexican	193	5.1
Guatemalan	16	1.8
Honduran	33	3.7
Salvadoran	104	5.8
Mexican	2,312	6.9
Puerto Rican	236	28.1
South American	488	39.4
Peruvian	225	37.3
Spaniard	353	29.4

Population Age 3–17 Enrolled in Public School
(Universe: Population Age 3–17 Enrolled in School)

Group	Number	%
Total Population	53,636	91.2
Hispanic or Latino (of any race)	20,451	94.8
Central American, ex. Mexican	1,039	86.4
Guatemalan	212	85.1
Honduran	215	67.8
Salvadoran	539	95.7
Mexican	17,684	96.6
Puerto Rican	480	88.9
South American	275	87.0
Peruvian	164	93.7
Spaniard	92	76.0

Population Age 3–17 Enrolled in Private School
(Universe: Population Age 3–17 Enrolled in School)

Group	Number	%
Total Population	5,168	8.8
Hispanic or Latino (of any race)	1,125	5.2
Central American, ex. Mexican	163	13.6
Guatemalan	37	14.9
Honduran	102	32.2
Salvadoran	24	4.3
Mexican	627	3.4
Puerto Rican	60	11.1
South American	41	13.0
Peruvian	11	6.3
Spaniard	29	24.0

Foreign-Born Population

Group	Number	%
Total Population	64,734	20.6
Hispanic or Latino (of any race)	39,903	45.3
Central American, ex. Mexican	4,591	69.0
Guatemalan	1,089	71.3
Honduran	1,127	73.6
Salvadoran	2,164	68.5
Mexican	33,425	46.4
Puerto Rican	0	0.0
South American	1,306	71.6
Peruvian	761	78.3
Spaniard	95	5.8

Foreign-Born Naturalized U.S. Citizens

Group	Number	%
Total Population	16,593	25.6
Hispanic or Latino (of any race)	4,190	10.5
Central American, ex. Mexican	603	13.1
Guatemalan	203	18.6
Honduran	36	3.2
Salvadoran	263	12.2
Mexican	2,936	8.8
Puerto Rican	0	0.0
South American	394	30.2
Peruvian	269	35.3
Spaniard	51	53.7

Language Spoken at Home: English Only
(Universe: Population 5 Years and Over)

Group	Number	%
Total Population	198,363	69.3
Hispanic or Latino (of any race)	17,623	23.1
Central American, ex. Mexican	299	5.0
Guatemalan	99	7.3
Honduran	0	0.0
Salvadoran	101	3.7
Mexican	12,082	19.6
Puerto Rican	1,070	65.8
South American	346	19.7
Peruvian	67	7.2
Spaniard	1,229	78.5

Language Spoken at Home: Spanish
(Universe: Population 5 Years and Over)

Group	Number	%
Total Population	61,314	21.4
Hispanic or Latino (of any race)	58,386	76.6
Central American, ex. Mexican	5,569	93.9
Guatemalan	1,236	91.4
Honduran	1,429	100.0
Salvadoran	2,646	96.3
Mexican	49,473	80.2
Puerto Rican	557	34.2
South American	1,401	79.7
Peruvian	861	92.8
Spaniard	336	21.5

Unemployment Rate
(Universe: Population 16 Years and Over)

Group	%
Total Population	7.7
Hispanic or Latino (of any race)	8.7
Central American, ex. Mexican	6.3
Guatemalan	7.5
Honduran	4.4
Salvadoran	5.1
Mexican	9.1
Puerto Rican	13.4
South American	0.9
Peruvian	0.0
Spaniard	10.2

Class of Worker: Private Wage and Salary
(Universe: Civilian Employed Population 16 Years and Over)

Group	Number	%
Total Population	128,397	82.7
Hispanic or Latino (of any race)	34,243	89.1
Central American, ex. Mexican	3,335	89.5
Guatemalan	793	96.8
Honduran	728	83.0
Salvadoran	1,618	91.2
Mexican	27,011	90.0
Puerto Rican	616	73.9
South American	956	91.4
Peruvian	534	93.4
Spaniard	668	75.2

Class of Worker: Government
(Universe: Civilian Employed Population 16 Years and Over)

Group	Number	%
Total Population	18,545	12.0
Hispanic or Latino (of any race)	2,180	5.7
Central American, ex. Mexican	190	5.1
Guatemalan	5	0.6
Honduran	74	8.4
Salvadoran	63	3.5
Mexican	1,469	4.9
Puerto Rican	148	17.7
South American	58	5.5
Peruvian	19	3.3
Spaniard	126	14.2

Means of Transportation to Work: Car, Truck or Van
(Universe: Workers 16 Years and Over)

Group	Number	%
Total Population	135,682	88.4
Hispanic or Latino (of any race)	33,357	88.5
Central American, ex. Mexican	3,240	89.9
Guatemalan	634	80.2
Honduran	775	90.4
Salvadoran	1,601	94.1
Mexican	26,065	88.4
Puerto Rican	758	92.1
South American	870	85.4
Peruvian	456	82.2
Spaniard	798	92.6

Means of Transportation to Work: Public Transportation (ex. Taxicab)
(Universe: Workers 16 Years and Over)

Group	Number	%
Total Population	8,265	5.4
Hispanic or Latino (of any race)	2,499	6.6

Notes: (1) Percent of total population; (2) Percent of Hispanic/Latino population; Profiles include places with an overall population of at least 125,000, OR an overall population of at least 25,000 where the Hispanic/Latino population is at least 20% of the overall population. In states where less than five places meet either of these criteria, we have included places with at least 10,000 total population with the highest percentage of Hispanic/Latino population. These places are identified with an asterisk (*); Please refer to the User's Guide for a full explanation of data.

Group	Number	%
Central American, ex. Mexican	255	7.1
Guatemalan	88	11.1
Honduran	82	9.6
Salvadoran	85	5.0
Mexican	1,999	6.8
Puerto Rican	33	4.0
South American	55	5.4
Peruvian	41	7.4
Spaniard	30	3.5

Homeownership Rate
(Universe: Occupied Housing Units)

Group	%
Total Population	59.9
Hispanic or Latino (of any race)	40.0
Central American, ex. Mexican	36.3
Guatemalan	33.8
Honduran	20.1
Nicaraguan	41.5
Panamanian	48.6
Salvadoran	39.8
Cuban	49.3
Dominican Republic	47.8
Mexican	37.8
Puerto Rican	48.4
South American	60.1
Argentinean	65.1
Chilean	60.7
Colombian	66.9
Ecuadorian	65.0
Peruvian	56.8
Venezuelan	51.8
Spaniard	64.1

Median Home Value

Group	Dollars
Total Population	187,800
Hispanic or Latino (of any race)	171,800
Central American, ex. Mexican	162,600
Guatemalan	144,300
Honduran	179,000
Salvadoran	148,300
Mexican	168,700
Puerto Rican	186,900
South American	172,200
Peruvian	208,300
Spaniard	190,700

Median Gross Rent

Group	Dollars
Total Population	853
Hispanic or Latino (of any race)	806
Central American, ex. Mexican	781
Guatemalan	770
Honduran	674
Salvadoran	938
Mexican	810
Puerto Rican	814
South American	804
Peruvian	681
Spaniard	799

Median Household Income
(2010 Inflation-Adjusted Dollars)

Group	Dollars
Total Population	49,515
Hispanic or Latino (of any race)	36,614
Central American, ex. Mexican	42,147
Guatemalan	42,177
Honduran	29,868
Salvadoran	45,550
Mexican	33,916
Puerto Rican	48,390
South American	41,116
Peruvian	41,638
Spaniard	52,699

Per Capita Income
(2010 Inflation-Adjusted Dollars)

Group	Dollars
Total Population	23,862
Hispanic or Latino (of any race)	12,622
Central American, ex. Mexican	14,742
Guatemalan	13,476
Honduran	11,517
Salvadoran	15,337
Mexican	11,295
Puerto Rican	16,754
South American	21,263
Peruvian	18,669
Spaniard	29,647

Households with $100,000+ Income

Group	Number	%
Total Population	19,719	16.3
Hispanic or Latino (of any race)	1,806	7.6
Central American, ex. Mexican	151	8.1
Guatemalan	49	14.1
Honduran	69	13.9
Salvadoran	18	2.1
Mexican	1,319	7.2
Puerto Rican	66	10.8
South American	48	7.1
Peruvian	32	11.8
Spaniard	113	11.6

Households with Food Stamps/SNAP Benefits During Past 12 Months

Group	Number	%
Total Population	7,996	6.6
Hispanic or Latino (of any race)	2,302	9.7
Central American, ex. Mexican	157	8.4
Guatemalan	0	0.0
Honduran	47	9.5
Salvadoran	110	12.9
Mexican	1,855	10.1
Puerto Rican	93	15.2
South American	29	4.3
Peruvian	0	0.0
Spaniard	20	2.1

Poverty Rate
(Income in Past 12 Months Below Poverty Level)

Group	%
Total Population	16.7
Hispanic or Latino (of any race)	29.0
Central American, ex. Mexican	20.9
Guatemalan	24.5
Honduran	43.3
Salvadoran	10.9
Mexican	31.3
Puerto Rican	27.9
South American	7.2
Peruvian	8.2
Spaniard	13.4

Brighton

Population

Group	Number	%TP[1]	%HP[2]
Total Population	33,352	100.0	–
Hispanic or Latino (of any race)	13,505	40.5	100.0
Central American, ex. Mexican	105	0.3	0.8
Mexican	10,620	31.8	78.6
Puerto Rican	103	0.3	0.8
Spaniard	487	1.5	3.6

Population Growth: 2000–2010

Group	%
Total Population	59.5
Hispanic or Latino (of any race)	69.0
Mexican	95.3

Males per 100 Females

Group	Number
Total Population	102.4
Hispanic or Latino (of any race)	108.1
Central American, ex. Mexican	98.1
Mexican	110.2
Puerto Rican	134.1
Spaniard	107.2

Average Household Size

Group	People
Total Population	2.95
Hispanic or Latino (of any race)	3.62
Central American, ex. Mexican	3.68
Mexican	3.76
Puerto Rican	3.43
Spaniard	3.09

Median Age

Group	Years
Total Population	32.2
Hispanic or Latino (of any race)	26.1
Central American, ex. Mexican	30.5
Mexican	25.5
Puerto Rican	26.5
Spaniard	32.1

High School Graduates
(Universe: Population 25 Years and Over)

Group	Number	%
Total Population	16,079	83.3
Hispanic or Latino (of any race)	4,153	64.6
Mexican	3,177	61.1

Four-Year College Graduates
(Universe: Population 25 Years and Over)

Group	Number	%
Total Population	3,553	18.4
Hispanic or Latino (of any race)	510	7.9
Mexican	376	7.2

Population Age 3–17 Enrolled in Public School
(Universe: Population Age 3–17 Enrolled in School)

Group	Number	%
Total Population	5,557	88.1
Hispanic or Latino (of any race)	2,744	95.6
Mexican	2,299	96.4

Population Age 3–17 Enrolled in Private School
(Universe: Population Age 3–17 Enrolled in School)

Group	Number	%
Total Population	754	11.9
Hispanic or Latino (of any race)	127	4.4
Mexican	85	3.6

Foreign-Born Population

Group	Number	%
Total Population	3,352	10.8
Hispanic or Latino (of any race)	2,931	23.9
Mexican	2,853	28.6

Foreign-Born Naturalized U.S. Citizens

Group	Number	%
Total Population	697	20.8
Hispanic or Latino (of any race)	471	16.1
Mexican	426	14.9

Language Spoken at Home: English Only
(Universe: Population 5 Years and Over)

Group	Number	%
Total Population	21,531	76.2
Hispanic or Latino (of any race)	4,688	44.2
Mexican	3,238	37.5

Language Spoken at Home: Spanish
(Universe: Population 5 Years and Over)

Group	Number	%
Total Population	6,095	21.6
Hispanic or Latino (of any race)	5,929	55.8
Mexican	5,403	62.5

Unemployment Rate
(Universe: Population 16 Years and Over)

Group	%
Total Population	6.1
Hispanic or Latino (of any race)	8.9
Mexican	9.9

Class of Worker: Private Wage and Salary
(Universe: Civilian Employed Population 16 Years and Over)

Group	Number	%
Total Population	12,088	81.8
Hispanic or Latino (of any race)	4,310	86.3
Mexican	3,513	88.2

Class of Worker: Government
(Universe: Civilian Employed Population 16 Years and Over)

Group	Number	%
Total Population	2,126	14.4
Hispanic or Latino (of any race)	559	11.2
Mexican	382	9.6

Notes: (1) Percent of total population; (2) Percent of Hispanic/Latino population; Profiles include places with an overall population of at least 125,000, OR an overall population of at least 25,000 where the Hispanic/Latino population is at least 20% of the overall population. In states where less than five places meet either of these criteria, we have included places with at least 10,000 total population with the highest percentage of Hispanic/Latino population. These places are identified with an asterisk (*); Please refer to the User's Guide for a full explanation of data.

Means of Transportation to Work: Car, Truck or Van
(Universe: Workers 16 Years and Over)

Group	Number	%
Total Population	13,598	93.5
Hispanic or Latino (of any race)	4,540	92.8
Mexican	3,621	92.3

Means of Transportation to Work: Public Transportation (ex. Taxicab)
(Universe: Workers 16 Years and Over)

Group	Number	%
Total Population	205	1.4
Hispanic or Latino (of any race)	66	1.3
Mexican	66	1.7

Homeownership Rate
(Universe: Occupied Housing Units)

Group	%
Total Population	69.6
Hispanic or Latino (of any race)	56.3
Central American, ex. Mexican	67.9
Mexican	56.0
Puerto Rican	71.4
Spaniard	64.9

Median Home Value

Group	Dollars
Total Population	200,300
Hispanic or Latino (of any race)	172,700
Mexican	169,100

Median Gross Rent

Group	Dollars
Total Population	886
Hispanic or Latino (of any race)	822
Mexican	804

Median Household Income
(2010 Inflation-Adjusted Dollars)

Group	Dollars
Total Population	65,788
Hispanic or Latino (of any race)	49,388
Mexican	46,462

Per Capita Income
(2010 Inflation-Adjusted Dollars)

Group	Dollars
Total Population	23,771
Hispanic or Latino (of any race)	15,206
Mexican	14,349

Households with $100,000+ Income

Group	Number	%
Total Population	2,039	20.1
Hispanic or Latino (of any race)	282	9.5
Mexican	190	8.0

Households with Food Stamps/SNAP Benefits During Past 12 Months

Group	Number	%
Total Population	561	5.5
Hispanic or Latino (of any race)	352	11.8
Mexican	282	11.9

Poverty Rate
(Income in Past 12 Months Below Poverty Level)

Group	%
Total Population	9.6
Hispanic or Latino (of any race)	17.6
Mexican	21.5

Colorado Springs

Population

Group	Number	%TP[1]	%HP[2]
Total Population	416,427	100.0	–
Hispanic or Latino (of any race)	66,866	16.1	100.0
Central American, ex. Mexican	2,456	0.6	3.7
Costa Rican	104	<0.1	0.2
Guatemalan	565	0.1	0.8
Honduran	385	0.1	0.6
Nicaraguan	204	<0.1	0.3
Panamanian	642	0.2	1.0
Salvadoran	521	0.1	0.8
Cuban	802	0.2	1.2
Dominican Republic	271	0.1	0.4
Mexican	44,135	10.6	66.0
Puerto Rican	4,759	1.1	7.1
South American	1,599	0.4	2.4
Argentinean	134	<0.1	0.2
Chilean	105	<0.1	0.2
Colombian	444	0.1	0.7
Ecuadorian	176	<0.1	0.3
Peruvian	487	0.1	0.7
Venezuelan	146	<0.1	0.2
Spaniard	3,319	0.8	5.0

Population Growth: 2000–2010

Group	%
Total Population	15.4
Hispanic or Latino (of any race)	54.3
Central American, ex. Mexican	158.3
Guatemalan	281.8
Panamanian	49.7
Salvadoran	196.0
Cuban	131.8
Dominican Republic	155.7
Mexican	92.0
Puerto Rican	77.2
South American	169.6
Colombian	142.6
Peruvian	283.5
Spaniard	1,495.7

Males per 100 Females

Group	Number
Total Population	96.0
Hispanic or Latino (of any race)	99.4
Central American, ex. Mexican	106.0
Costa Rican	100.0
Guatemalan	134.4
Honduran	125.1
Nicaraguan	100.0
Panamanian	68.5
Salvadoran	124.6
Cuban	109.9
Dominican Republic	85.6
Mexican	102.5
Puerto Rican	107.3
South American	82.1
Argentinean	86.1
Chilean	78.0
Colombian	100.0
Ecuadorian	72.5
Peruvian	77.1
Venezuelan	92.1
Spaniard	84.8

Average Household Size

Group	People
Total Population	2.44
Hispanic or Latino (of any race)	2.96
Central American, ex. Mexican	3.07
Costa Rican	2.75
Guatemalan	3.47
Honduran	3.38
Nicaraguan	2.92
Panamanian	2.52
Salvadoran	3.35
Cuban	2.84
Dominican Republic	2.98
Mexican	3.13
Puerto Rican	2.76
South American	2.68
Argentinean	2.44
Chilean	2.37
Colombian	2.43
Ecuadorian	2.91
Peruvian	3.10
Venezuelan	2.71
Spaniard	2.60

Median Age

Group	Years
Total Population	34.9
Hispanic or Latino (of any race)	25.1
Central American, ex. Mexican	27.6
Costa Rican	25.4
Guatemalan	24.3
Honduran	29.0
Nicaraguan	33.7
Panamanian	28.6
Salvadoran	28.4
Cuban	26.6
Dominican Republic	26.3
Mexican	24.1
Puerto Rican	24.5
South American	30.8
Argentinean	38.2
Chilean	30.3
Colombian	28.7
Ecuadorian	29.8
Peruvian	32.9
Venezuelan	27.9
Spaniard	31.7

High School Graduates
(Universe: Population 25 Years and Over)

Group	Number	%
Total Population	239,352	91.9
Hispanic or Latino (of any race)	23,532	74.0
Central American, ex. Mexican	962	70.6
Mexican	13,373	67.7
Puerto Rican	2,015	90.4
South American	755	89.8
Spaniard	1,273	87.6

Four-Year College Graduates
(Universe: Population 25 Years and Over)

Group	Number	%
Total Population	93,608	35.9
Hispanic or Latino (of any race)	4,410	13.9
Central American, ex. Mexican	284	20.8
Mexican	2,227	11.3
Puerto Rican	402	18.0
South American	295	35.1
Spaniard	426	29.3

Population Age 3–17 Enrolled in Public School
(Universe: Population Age 3–17 Enrolled in School)

Group	Number	%
Total Population	68,956	89.5
Hispanic or Latino (of any race)	15,169	94.0
Central American, ex. Mexican	586	92.4
Mexican	10,600	94.8
Puerto Rican	1,159	96.2
South American	247	94.6
Spaniard	299	94.3

Population Age 3–17 Enrolled in Private School
(Universe: Population Age 3–17 Enrolled in School)

Group	Number	%
Total Population	8,092	10.5
Hispanic or Latino (of any race)	969	6.0
Central American, ex. Mexican	48	7.6
Mexican	577	5.2
Puerto Rican	46	3.8
South American	14	5.4
Spaniard	18	5.7

Foreign-Born Population

Group	Number	%
Total Population	32,315	8.0
Hispanic or Latino (of any race)	12,523	20.0
Central American, ex. Mexican	1,549	56.7
Mexican	9,643	23.6
Puerto Rican	59	1.3
South American	763	60.5
Spaniard	54	2.5

Foreign-Born Naturalized U.S. Citizens

Group	Number	%
Total Population	13,664	42.3
Hispanic or Latino (of any race)	2,572	20.5
Central American, ex. Mexican	506	32.7
Mexican	1,475	15.3
Puerto Rican	0	0.0
South American	392	51.4
Spaniard	24	44.4

Notes: (1) Percent of total population; (2) Percent of Hispanic/Latino population; Profiles include places with an overall population of at least 125,000, OR an overall population of at least 25,000 where the Hispanic/Latino population is at least 20% of the overall population. In states where less than five places meet either of these criteria, we have included places with at least 10,000 total population with the highest percentage of Hispanic/Latino population. These places are identified with an asterisk (*); Please refer to the User's Guide for a full explanation of data.

Language Spoken at Home: English Only
(Universe: Population 5 Years and Over)

Group	Number	%
Total Population	329,183	87.6
Hispanic or Latino (of any race)	30,720	55.5
Central American, ex. Mexican	919	39.4
Mexican	18,146	50.9
Puerto Rican	2,206	54.3
South American	256	22.1
Spaniard	1,459	73.9

Language Spoken at Home: Spanish
(Universe: Population 5 Years and Over)

Group	Number	%
Total Population	27,944	7.4
Hispanic or Latino (of any race)	24,334	44.0
Central American, ex. Mexican	1,389	59.5
Mexican	17,446	48.9
Puerto Rican	1,817	44.7
South American	885	76.5
Spaniard	473	24.0

Unemployment Rate
(Universe: Population 16 Years and Over)

Group	%
Total Population	7.6
Hispanic or Latino (of any race)	10.2
Central American, ex. Mexican	10.2
Mexican	10.3
Puerto Rican	10.1
South American	2.3
Spaniard	8.2

Class of Worker: Private Wage and Salary
(Universe: Civilian Employed Population 16 Years and Over)

Group	Number	%
Total Population	153,587	78.8
Hispanic or Latino (of any race)	22,141	83.0
Central American, ex. Mexican	1,020	86.8
Mexican	14,002	83.3
Puerto Rican	1,715	84.2
South American	529	83.0
Spaniard	757	71.4

Class of Worker: Government
(Universe: Civilian Employed Population 16 Years and Over)

Group	Number	%
Total Population	29,037	14.9
Hispanic or Latino (of any race)	3,282	12.3
Central American, ex. Mexican	128	10.9
Mexican	1,933	11.5
Puerto Rican	256	12.6
South American	75	11.8
Spaniard	243	22.9

Means of Transportation to Work: Car, Truck or Van
(Universe: Workers 16 Years and Over)

Group	Number	%
Total Population	177,418	89.4
Hispanic or Latino (of any race)	24,609	91.3
Central American, ex. Mexican	1,018	81.7
Mexican	15,568	91.4
Puerto Rican	1,895	89.0
South American	599	90.6
Spaniard	985	91.3

Means of Transportation to Work: Public Transportation (ex. Taxicab)
(Universe: Workers 16 Years and Over)

Group	Number	%
Total Population	3,080	1.6
Hispanic or Latino (of any race)	575	2.1
Central American, ex. Mexican	129	10.4
Mexican	389	2.3
Puerto Rican	22	1.0
South American	19	2.9
Spaniard	9	0.8

Homeownership Rate
(Universe: Occupied Housing Units)

Group	%
Total Population	60.1
Hispanic or Latino (of any race)	43.9
Central American, ex. Mexican	35.9
Costa Rican	68.8
Guatemalan	19.6
Honduran	23.3
Nicaraguan	42.3
Panamanian	43.0
Salvadoran	42.0
Cuban	45.6
Dominican Republic	41.0
Mexican	42.7
Puerto Rican	40.6
South American	49.2
Argentinean	55.8
Chilean	55.3
Colombian	47.5
Ecuadorian	55.2
Peruvian	47.0
Venezuelan	40.0
Spaniard	58.1

Median Home Value

Group	Dollars
Total Population	213,200
Hispanic or Latino (of any race)	176,000
Central American, ex. Mexican	217,600
Mexican	176,300
Puerto Rican	168,100
South American	195,200
Spaniard	175,700

Median Gross Rent

Group	Dollars
Total Population	781
Hispanic or Latino (of any race)	691
Central American, ex. Mexican	553
Mexican	686
Puerto Rican	823
South American	761
Spaniard	687

Median Household Income
(2010 Inflation-Adjusted Dollars)

Group	Dollars
Total Population	53,074
Hispanic or Latino (of any race)	36,014
Central American, ex. Mexican	26,664
Mexican	35,412
Puerto Rican	34,419
South American	40,481
Spaniard	51,538

Per Capita Income
(2010 Inflation-Adjusted Dollars)

Group	Dollars
Total Population	28,402
Hispanic or Latino (of any race)	15,475
Central American, ex. Mexican	14,733
Mexican	14,027
Puerto Rican	16,389
South American	19,219
Spaniard	24,351

Households with $100,000+ Income

Group	Number	%
Total Population	33,627	20.7
Hispanic or Latino (of any race)	1,696	8.5
Central American, ex. Mexican	41	5.4
Mexican	932	7.7
Puerto Rican	159	9.5
South American	25	8.3
Spaniard	68	6.7

Households with Food Stamps/SNAP Benefits During Past 12 Months

Group	Number	%
Total Population	11,197	6.9
Hispanic or Latino (of any race)	3,217	16.2
Central American, ex. Mexican	127	16.7
Mexican	1,974	16.2
Puerto Rican	429	25.7
South American	15	5.0
Spaniard	152	14.9

Poverty Rate
(Income in Past 12 Months Below Poverty Level)

Group	%
Total Population	11.8
Hispanic or Latino (of any race)	25.4
Central American, ex. Mexican	28.6
Mexican	28.4
Puerto Rican	28.5
South American	15.9
Spaniard	12.9

Commerce City

Population

Group	Number	%TP[1]	%HP[2]
Total Population	45,913	100.0	–
Hispanic or Latino (of any race)	21,509	46.8	100.0
Central American, ex. Mexican	222	0.5	1.0
Salvadoran	101	0.2	0.5
Mexican	17,004	37.0	79.1
Puerto Rican	221	0.5	1.0
South American	100	0.2	0.5
Spaniard	754	1.6	3.5

Population Growth: 2000–2010

Group	%
Total Population	118.7
Hispanic or Latino (of any race)	93.8
Mexican	125.0

Males per 100 Females

Group	Number
Total Population	101.8
Hispanic or Latino (of any race)	102.1
Central American, ex. Mexican	126.5
Salvadoran	124.4
Mexican	104.2
Puerto Rican	93.9
South American	108.3
Spaniard	97.9

Average Household Size

Group	People
Total Population	3.15
Hispanic or Latino (of any race)	3.78
Central American, ex. Mexican	3.69
Salvadoran	3.59
Mexican	3.95
Puerto Rican	3.04
South American	3.23
Spaniard	3.06

Median Age

Group	Years
Total Population	30.4
Hispanic or Latino (of any race)	25.1
Central American, ex. Mexican	32.4
Salvadoran	30.6
Mexican	24.6
Puerto Rican	21.2
South American	32.5
Spaniard	31.1

High School Graduates
(Universe: Population 25 Years and Over)

Group	Number	%
Total Population	18,840	75.3
Hispanic or Latino (of any race)	5,379	54.9
Mexican	4,349	53.3

Four-Year College Graduates
(Universe: Population 25 Years and Over)

Group	Number	%
Total Population	4,950	19.8
Hispanic or Latino (of any race)	685	7.0
Mexican	565	6.9

Population Age 3–17 Enrolled in Public School
(Universe: Population Age 3–17 Enrolled in School)

Group	Number	%
Total Population	8,115	91.8
Hispanic or Latino (of any race)	5,384	96.1
Mexican	4,705	96.0

Notes: (1) Percent of total population; (2) Percent of Hispanic/Latino population; Profiles include places with an overall population of at least 125,000, OR an overall population of at least 25,000 where the Hispanic/Latino population is at least 20% of the overall population. In states where less than five places meet either of these criteria, we have included places with at least 10,000 total population with the highest percentage of Hispanic/Latino population. These places are identified with an asterisk (*); Please refer to the User's Guide for a full explanation of data.

Population Age 3–17 Enrolled in Private School
(Universe: Population Age 3–17 Enrolled in School)

Group	Number	%
Total Population	727	8.2
Hispanic or Latino (of any race)	220	3.9
Mexican	197	4.0

Foreign-Born Population

Group	Number	%
Total Population	7,236	17.4
Hispanic or Latino (of any race)	6,086	31.2
Mexican	6,004	35.9

Foreign-Born Naturalized U.S. Citizens

Group	Number	%
Total Population	1,784	24.7
Hispanic or Latino (of any race)	1,169	19.2
Mexican	1,153	19.2

Language Spoken at Home: English Only
(Universe: Population 5 Years and Over)

Group	Number	%
Total Population	24,294	66.9
Hispanic or Latino (of any race)	6,607	38.9
Mexican	4,909	34.0

Language Spoken at Home: Spanish
(Universe: Population 5 Years and Over)

Group	Number	%
Total Population	10,708	29.5
Hispanic or Latino (of any race)	10,387	61.1
Mexican	9,527	66.0

Unemployment Rate
(Universe: Population 16 Years and Over)

Group	%
Total Population	7.0
Hispanic or Latino (of any race)	8.2
Mexican	7.4

Class of Worker: Private Wage and Salary
(Universe: Civilian Employed Population 16 Years and Over)

Group	Number	%
Total Population	17,086	85.2
Hispanic or Latino (of any race)	6,949	86.6
Mexican	6,106	87.4

Class of Worker: Government
(Universe: Civilian Employed Population 16 Years and Over)

Group	Number	%
Total Population	2,035	10.2
Hispanic or Latino (of any race)	589	7.3
Mexican	431	6.2

Means of Transportation to Work: Car, Truck or Van
(Universe: Workers 16 Years and Over)

Group	Number	%
Total Population	18,222	92.9
Hispanic or Latino (of any race)	7,367	93.5
Mexican	6,447	94.0

Means of Transportation to Work: Public Transportation (ex. Taxicab)
(Universe: Workers 16 Years and Over)

Group	Number	%
Total Population	425	2.2
Hispanic or Latino (of any race)	196	2.5
Mexican	130	1.9

Homeownership Rate
(Universe: Occupied Housing Units)

Group	%
Total Population	69.8
Hispanic or Latino (of any race)	55.7
Central American, ex. Mexican	56.9
Salvadoran	48.3
Mexican	55.3
Puerto Rican	49.1
South American	80.6
Spaniard	69.9

Median Home Value

Group	Dollars
Total Population	206,600
Hispanic or Latino (of any race)	174,500
Mexican	169,400

Median Gross Rent

Group	Dollars
Total Population	870
Hispanic or Latino (of any race)	877
Mexican	885

Median Household Income
(2010 Inflation-Adjusted Dollars)

Group	Dollars
Total Population	56,635
Hispanic or Latino (of any race)	44,824
Mexican	44,464

Per Capita Income
(2010 Inflation-Adjusted Dollars)

Group	Dollars
Total Population	22,112
Hispanic or Latino (of any race)	13,850
Mexican	13,024

Households with $100,000+ Income

Group	Number	%
Total Population	2,783	20.7
Hispanic or Latino (of any race)	554	11.4
Mexican	415	10.6

Households with Food Stamps/SNAP Benefits During Past 12 Months

Group	Number	%
Total Population	1,341	10.0
Hispanic or Latino (of any race)	678	14.0
Mexican	482	12.3

Poverty Rate
(Income in Past 12 Months Below Poverty Level)

Group	%
Total Population	14.8
Hispanic or Latino (of any race)	22.7
Mexican	24.1

Denver

Population

Group	Number	%TP[1]	%HP[2]
Total Population	600,158	100.0	–
Hispanic or Latino (of any race)	190,965	31.8	100.0
Central American, ex. Mexican	5,114	0.9	2.7
Costa Rican	147	<0.1	0.1
Guatemalan	1,324	0.2	0.7
Honduran	799	0.1	0.4
Nicaraguan	200	<0.1	0.1
Panamanian	216	<0.1	0.1
Salvadoran	2,372	0.4	1.2
Cuban	909	0.2	0.5
Dominican Republic	257	<0.1	0.1
Mexican	149,366	24.9	78.2
Puerto Rican	2,561	0.4	1.3
South American	2,739	0.5	1.4
Argentinean	269	<0.1	0.1
Bolivian	130	<0.1	0.1
Chilean	249	<0.1	0.1
Colombian	730	0.1	0.4
Ecuadorian	162	<0.1	0.1
Peruvian	835	0.1	0.4
Venezuelan	284	<0.1	0.1
Spaniard	5,269	0.9	2.8

Population Growth: 2000–2010

Group	%
Total Population	8.2
Hispanic or Latino (of any race)	8.7
Central American, ex. Mexican	156.1
Guatemalan	182.3
Honduran	176.5
Panamanian	60.0
Salvadoran	192.5
Cuban	35.9
Mexican	23.8
Puerto Rican	56.9
South American	116.5
Argentinean	111.8
Chilean	87.2
Colombian	134.7
Peruvian	123.9
Venezuelan	163.0
Spaniard	1,312.6

Males per 100 Females

Group	Number
Total Population	100.0
Hispanic or Latino (of any race)	104.2
Central American, ex. Mexican	114.3
Costa Rican	107.0
Guatemalan	107.5
Honduran	128.3
Nicaraguan	102.0
Panamanian	80.0
Salvadoran	119.2
Cuban	95.5
Dominican Republic	89.0
Mexican	107.1
Puerto Rican	103.9
South American	91.4
Argentinean	111.8
Bolivian	97.0
Chilean	90.1
Colombian	75.1
Ecuadorian	67.0
Peruvian	95.6
Venezuelan	130.9
Spaniard	92.4

Average Household Size

Group	People
Total Population	2.22
Hispanic or Latino (of any race)	3.27
Central American, ex. Mexican	3.63
Costa Rican	2.12
Guatemalan	3.64
Honduran	3.63
Nicaraguan	2.96
Panamanian	2.18
Salvadoran	4.05
Cuban	2.16
Dominican Republic	2.60
Mexican	3.50
Puerto Rican	2.22
South American	2.32
Argentinean	2.19
Bolivian	2.48
Chilean	2.01
Colombian	2.08
Ecuadorian	2.49
Peruvian	2.64
Venezuelan	2.12
Spaniard	2.41

Median Age

Group	Years
Total Population	33.7
Hispanic or Latino (of any race)	27.3
Central American, ex. Mexican	30.1
Costa Rican	30.1
Guatemalan	29.9
Honduran	28.7
Nicaraguan	35.1
Panamanian	32.9
Salvadoran	30.0
Cuban	32.7
Dominican Republic	28.6
Mexican	26.3
Puerto Rican	27.8
South American	32.7
Argentinean	33.3
Bolivian	32.2
Chilean	32.9
Colombian	31.3
Ecuadorian	31.0
Peruvian	36.0
Venezuelan	31.6
Spaniard	35.3

High School Graduates
(Universe: Population 25 Years and Over)

Group	Number	%
Total Population	330,222	84.0
Hispanic or Latino (of any race)	55,977	56.2

Notes: (1) Percent of total population; (2) Percent of Hispanic/Latino population; Profiles include places with an overall population of at least 125,000, OR an overall population of at least 25,000 where the Hispanic/Latino population is at least 20% of the overall population. In states where less than five places meet either of these criteria, we have included places with at least 10,000 total population with the highest percentage of Hispanic/Latino population. These places are identified with an asterisk (*); Please refer to the User's Guide for a full explanation of data.

Group	Number	%
Central American, ex. Mexican	900	41.6
Salvadoran	308	33.6
Mexican	41,265	52.1
Puerto Rican	1,285	90.5
South American	1,445	91.7
Peruvian	314	87.0
Spaniard	3,015	85.6

Four-Year College Graduates
(Universe: Population 25 Years and Over)

Group	Number	%
Total Population	157,718	40.1
Hispanic or Latino (of any race)	10,236	10.3
Central American, ex. Mexican	154	7.1
Salvadoran	19	2.1
Mexican	6,552	8.3
Puerto Rican	399	28.1
South American	780	49.5
Peruvian	110	30.5
Spaniard	721	20.5

Population Age 3–17 Enrolled in Public School
(Universe: Population Age 3–17 Enrolled in School)

Group	Number	%
Total Population	72,592	85.5
Hispanic or Latino (of any race)	40,264	94.0
Central American, ex. Mexican	601	92.7
Salvadoran	369	88.7
Mexican	34,628	94.4
Puerto Rican	422	98.1
South American	270	72.8
Peruvian	102	100.0
Spaniard	1,032	85.7

Population Age 3–17 Enrolled in Private School
(Universe: Population Age 3–17 Enrolled in School)

Group	Number	%
Total Population	12,296	14.5
Hispanic or Latino (of any race)	2,582	6.0
Central American, ex. Mexican	47	7.3
Salvadoran	47	11.3
Mexican	2,037	5.6
Puerto Rican	8	1.9
South American	101	27.2
Peruvian	0	0.0
Spaniard	172	14.3

Foreign-Born Population

Group	Number	%
Total Population	96,230	16.6
Hispanic or Latino (of any race)	62,131	33.5
Central American, ex. Mexican	2,367	63.6
Salvadoran	1,035	60.5
Mexican	57,421	37.4
Puerto Rican	28	1.2
South American	1,278	57.6
Peruvian	349	66.0
Spaniard	137	2.4

Foreign-Born Naturalized U.S. Citizens

Group	Number	%
Total Population	27,161	28.2
Hispanic or Latino (of any race)	10,314	16.6
Central American, ex. Mexican	394	16.6
Salvadoran	94	9.1
Mexican	8,879	15.5
Puerto Rican	17	60.7
South American	592	46.3
Peruvian	112	32.1
Spaniard	22	16.1

Language Spoken at Home: English Only
(Universe: Population 5 Years and Over)

Group	Number	%
Total Population	386,815	72.3
Hispanic or Latino (of any race)	58,659	35.7
Central American, ex. Mexican	298	9.1
Salvadoran	191	12.1
Mexican	40,125	29.8
Puerto Rican	1,309	60.4
South American	490	24.5
Peruvian	112	21.9
Spaniard	4,234	80.9

Language Spoken at Home: Spanish
(Universe: Population 5 Years and Over)

Group	Number	%
Total Population	114,635	21.4
Hispanic or Latino (of any race)	105,436	64.1
Central American, ex. Mexican	2,985	90.9
Salvadoran	1,386	87.9
Mexican	94,499	70.1
Puerto Rican	828	38.2
South American	1,501	74.9
Peruvian	399	78.1
Spaniard	991	18.9

Unemployment Rate
(Universe: Population 16 Years and Over)

Group	%
Total Population	7.8
Hispanic or Latino (of any race)	11.1
Central American, ex. Mexican	7.0
Salvadoran	8.4
Mexican	11.1
Puerto Rican	5.8
South American	4.2
Peruvian	14.5
Spaniard	12.7

Class of Worker: Private Wage and Salary
(Universe: Civilian Employed Population 16 Years and Over)

Group	Number	%
Total Population	245,331	81.4
Hispanic or Latino (of any race)	66,100	85.0
Central American, ex. Mexican	1,841	94.7
Salvadoran	841	97.3
Mexican	54,770	86.7
Puerto Rican	1,196	86.9
South American	1,059	86.3
Peruvian	213	88.4
Spaniard	1,629	66.9

Class of Worker: Government
(Universe: Civilian Employed Population 16 Years and Over)

Group	Number	%
Total Population	35,504	11.8
Hispanic or Latino (of any race)	7,255	9.3
Central American, ex. Mexican	78	4.0
Salvadoran	23	2.7
Mexican	5,034	8.0
Puerto Rican	133	9.7
South American	135	11.0
Peruvian	19	7.9
Spaniard	568	23.3

Means of Transportation to Work: Car, Truck or Van
(Universe: Workers 16 Years and Over)

Group	Number	%
Total Population	234,610	79.4
Hispanic or Latino (of any race)	62,963	82.5
Central American, ex. Mexican	1,469	75.8
Salvadoran	727	84.1
Mexican	51,742	83.5
Puerto Rican	1,104	79.0
South American	949	78.7
Peruvian	199	92.6
Spaniard	1,938	81.0

Means of Transportation to Work: Public Transportation (ex. Taxicab)
(Universe: Workers 16 Years and Over)

Group	Number	%
Total Population	22,968	7.8
Hispanic or Latino (of any race)	7,456	9.8
Central American, ex. Mexican	351	18.1
Salvadoran	92	10.6
Mexican	5,844	9.4
Puerto Rican	126	9.0
South American	125	10.4
Peruvian	1	0.5
Spaniard	232	9.7

Homeownership Rate
(Universe: Occupied Housing Units)

Group	%
Total Population	50.0
Hispanic or Latino (of any race)	41.7
Central American, ex. Mexican	39.8
Costa Rican	45.0
Guatemalan	37.3
Honduran	29.3
Nicaraguan	40.3
Panamanian	43.3
Salvadoran	44.2
Cuban	40.4
Dominican Republic	23.3
Mexican	41.4
Puerto Rican	31.3
South American	43.6
Argentinean	49.6
Bolivian	53.8
Chilean	42.0
Colombian	41.4
Ecuadorian	41.8
Peruvian	43.5
Venezuelan	41.4
Spaniard	53.8

Median Home Value

Group	Dollars
Total Population	240,900
Hispanic or Latino (of any race)	183,000
Central American, ex. Mexican	193,200
Salvadoran	177,500
Mexican	178,500
Puerto Rican	209,700
South American	161,700
Peruvian	401,400
Spaniard	218,400

Median Gross Rent

Group	Dollars
Total Population	798
Hispanic or Latino (of any race)	773
Central American, ex. Mexican	834
Salvadoran	920
Mexican	773
Puerto Rican	730
South American	717
Peruvian	578
Spaniard	771

Median Household Income
(2010 Inflation-Adjusted Dollars)

Group	Dollars
Total Population	45,501
Hispanic or Latino (of any race)	33,669
Central American, ex. Mexican	38,884
Salvadoran	49,226
Mexican	33,066
Puerto Rican	35,212
South American	43,464
Peruvian	46,500
Spaniard	39,718

Per Capita Income
(2010 Inflation-Adjusted Dollars)

Group	Dollars
Total Population	30,806
Hispanic or Latino (of any race)	14,198
Central American, ex. Mexican	13,361
Salvadoran	12,689
Mexican	13,046
Puerto Rican	26,449
South American	27,662
Peruvian	34,323
Spaniard	23,095

Households with $100,000+ Income

Group	Number	%
Total Population	48,361	19.0
Hispanic or Latino (of any race)	4,056	7.3
Central American, ex. Mexican	55	5.5
Salvadoran	9	2.3
Mexican	2,918	6.8
Puerto Rican	144	14.7
South American	36	4.6
Peruvian	16	9.8
Spaniard	247	10.0

Notes: (1) Percent of total population; (2) Percent of Hispanic/Latino population; Profiles include places with an overall population of at least 125,000, OR an overall population of at least 25,000 where the Hispanic/Latino population is at least 20% of the overall population. In states where less than five places meet either of these criteria, we have included places with at least 10,000 total population with the highest percentage of Hispanic/Latino population. These places are identified with an asterisk (*); Please refer to the User's Guide for a full explanation of data.

Households with Food Stamps/SNAP Benefits During Past 12 Months

Group	Number	%
Total Population	19,755	7.8
Hispanic or Latino (of any race)	8,569	15.5
Central American, ex. Mexican	54	5.4
Salvadoran	39	10.1
Mexican	6,886	16.1
Puerto Rican	154	15.8
South American	57	7.2
Peruvian	41	25.0
Spaniard	192	7.8

Poverty Rate
(Income in Past 12 Months Below Poverty Level)

Group	%
Total Population	19.2
Hispanic or Latino (of any race)	29.5
Central American, ex. Mexican	20.2
Salvadoran	24.1
Mexican	31.1
Puerto Rican	17.7
South American	11.6
Peruvian	17.4
Spaniard	16.7

Fort Collins

Population

Group	Number	%TP[1]	%HP[2]
Total Population	143,986	100.0	–
Hispanic or Latino (of any race)	14,572	10.1	100.0
Central American, ex. Mexican	458	0.3	3.1
Guatemalan	129	0.1	0.9
Cuban	177	0.1	1.2
Mexican	9,902	6.9	68.0
Puerto Rican	446	0.3	3.1
South American	581	0.4	4.0
Argentinean	108	0.1	0.7
Colombian	155	0.1	1.1
Spaniard	790	0.5	5.4

Population Growth: 2000–2010

Group	%
Total Population	21.4
Hispanic or Latino (of any race)	40.1
Central American, ex. Mexican	181.0
Mexican	59.1
Puerto Rican	88.2
South American	128.7

Males per 100 Females

Group	Number
Total Population	99.8
Hispanic or Latino (of any race)	103.5
Central American, ex. Mexican	103.6
Guatemalan	108.1
Cuban	92.4
Mexican	105.2
Puerto Rican	87.4
South American	89.9
Argentinean	89.5
Colombian	91.4
Spaniard	93.2

Average Household Size

Group	People
Total Population	2.37
Hispanic or Latino (of any race)	2.90
Central American, ex. Mexican	3.23
Guatemalan	3.61
Cuban	2.29
Mexican	3.05
Puerto Rican	2.52
South American	2.37
Argentinean	2.63
Colombian	2.19
Spaniard	2.39

Median Age

Group	Years
Total Population	29.6
Hispanic or Latino (of any race)	24.0
Central American, ex. Mexican	26.9
Guatemalan	26.8
Cuban	25.2
Mexican	23.4
Puerto Rican	22.5
South American	28.4
Argentinean	32.5
Colombian	28.3
Spaniard	26.5

High School Graduates
(Universe: Population 25 Years and Over)

Group	Number	%
Total Population	76,708	94.6
Hispanic or Latino (of any race)	5,196	75.5
Mexican	3,185	69.9
Spaniard	395	89.2

Four-Year College Graduates
(Universe: Population 25 Years and Over)

Group	Number	%
Total Population	40,634	50.1
Hispanic or Latino (of any race)	1,537	22.3
Mexican	778	17.1
Spaniard	128	28.9

Population Age 3–17 Enrolled in Public School
(Universe: Population Age 3–17 Enrolled in School)

Group	Number	%
Total Population	19,115	88.2
Hispanic or Latino (of any race)	3,026	93.2
Mexican	2,247	94.0
Spaniard	219	100.0

Population Age 3–17 Enrolled in Private School
(Universe: Population Age 3–17 Enrolled in School)

Group	Number	%
Total Population	2,560	11.8
Hispanic or Latino (of any race)	221	6.8
Mexican	144	6.0
Spaniard	0	0.0

Foreign-Born Population

Group	Number	%
Total Population	8,354	6.0
Hispanic or Latino (of any race)	2,590	18.6
Mexican	2,093	21.9
Spaniard	23	2.6

Foreign-Born Naturalized U.S. Citizens

Group	Number	%
Total Population	3,076	36.8
Hispanic or Latino (of any race)	594	22.9
Mexican	307	14.7
Spaniard	12	52.2

Language Spoken at Home: English Only
(Universe: Population 5 Years and Over)

Group	Number	%
Total Population	120,347	91.0
Hispanic or Latino (of any race)	7,749	61.2
Mexican	4,582	53.4
Spaniard	773	92.1

Language Spoken at Home: Spanish
(Universe: Population 5 Years and Over)

Group	Number	%
Total Population	6,387	4.8
Hispanic or Latino (of any race)	4,897	38.6
Mexican	3,985	46.4
Spaniard	66	7.9

Unemployment Rate
(Universe: Population 16 Years and Over)

Group	%
Total Population	7.4
Hispanic or Latino (of any race)	10.7
Mexican	11.8
Spaniard	15.3

Class of Worker: Private Wage and Salary
(Universe: Civilian Employed Population 16 Years and Over)

Group	Number	%
Total Population	56,108	74.1
Hispanic or Latino (of any race)	5,089	77.1
Mexican	3,627	81.9
Spaniard	310	85.9

Class of Worker: Government
(Universe: Civilian Employed Population 16 Years and Over)

Group	Number	%
Total Population	15,159	20.0
Hispanic or Latino (of any race)	1,235	18.7
Mexican	675	15.2
Spaniard	20	5.5

Means of Transportation to Work: Car, Truck or Van
(Universe: Workers 16 Years and Over)

Group	Number	%
Total Population	60,602	82.1
Hispanic or Latino (of any race)	5,420	84.0
Mexican	3,716	85.9
Spaniard	301	83.4

Means of Transportation to Work: Public Transportation (ex. Taxicab)
(Universe: Workers 16 Years and Over)

Group	Number	%
Total Population	755	1.0
Hispanic or Latino (of any race)	50	0.8
Mexican	37	0.9
Spaniard	13	3.6

Homeownership Rate
(Universe: Occupied Housing Units)

Group	%
Total Population	55.1
Hispanic or Latino (of any race)	42.7
Central American, ex. Mexican	39.2
Guatemalan	45.2
Cuban	46.4
Mexican	42.9
Puerto Rican	37.7
South American	52.4
Argentinean	65.9
Colombian	54.7
Spaniard	48.0

Median Home Value

Group	Dollars
Total Population	241,600
Hispanic or Latino (of any race)	191,600
Mexican	190,400
Spaniard	333,800

Median Gross Rent

Group	Dollars
Total Population	853
Hispanic or Latino (of any race)	799
Mexican	756
Spaniard	1,255

Median Household Income
(2010 Inflation-Adjusted Dollars)

Group	Dollars
Total Population	49,589
Hispanic or Latino (of any race)	35,989
Mexican	32,326
Spaniard	61,083

Per Capita Income
(2010 Inflation-Adjusted Dollars)

Group	Dollars
Total Population	27,771
Hispanic or Latino (of any race)	15,662
Mexican	13,610
Spaniard	24,445

Households with $100,000+ Income

Group	Number	%
Total Population	11,820	21.1
Hispanic or Latino (of any race)	348	8.3
Mexican	164	5.9
Spaniard	44	15.3

Households with Food Stamps/SNAP Benefits During Past 12 Months

Group	Number	%
Total Population	2,610	4.7
Hispanic or Latino (of any race)	633	15.0
Mexican	429	15.3

Notes: (1) Percent of total population; (2) Percent of Hispanic/Latino population; Profiles include places with an overall population of at least 125,000, OR an overall population of at least 25,000 where the Hispanic/Latino population is at least 20% of the overall population. In states where less than five places meet either of these criteria, we have included places with at least 10,000 total population with the highest percentage of Hispanic/Latino population. These places are identified with an asterisk (*); Please refer to the User's Guide for a full explanation of data.

Spaniard	46	16.0

Poverty Rate
(Income in Past 12 Months Below Poverty Level)

Group	%
Total Population	18.0
Hispanic or Latino (of any race)	27.1
Mexican	28.6
Spaniard	37.1

Greeley

Population

Group	Number	%TP[1]	%HP[2]
Total Population	92,889	100.0	–
Hispanic or Latino (of any race)	33,440	36.0	100.0
Central American, ex. Mexican	969	1.0	2.9
Guatemalan	479	0.5	1.4
Salvadoran	358	0.4	1.1
Cuban	103	0.1	0.3
Mexican	27,171	29.3	81.3
Puerto Rican	265	0.3	0.8
South American	191	0.2	0.6
Spaniard	599	0.6	1.8

Population Growth: 2000–2010

Group	%
Total Population	20.7
Hispanic or Latino (of any race)	47.4
Central American, ex. Mexican	210.6
Guatemalan	207.1
Salvadoran	247.6
Mexican	66.3

Males per 100 Females

Group	Number
Total Population	96.6
Hispanic or Latino (of any race)	104.3
Central American, ex. Mexican	119.2
Guatemalan	166.1
Salvadoran	95.6
Cuban	134.1
Mexican	105.9
Puerto Rican	90.6
South American	101.1
Spaniard	88.4

Average Household Size

Group	People
Total Population	2.63
Hispanic or Latino (of any race)	3.46
Central American, ex. Mexican	4.25
Guatemalan	4.72
Salvadoran	3.85
Cuban	2.32
Mexican	3.53
Puerto Rican	2.93
South American	2.72
Spaniard	2.76

Median Age

Group	Years
Total Population	29.8
Hispanic or Latino (of any race)	23.6
Central American, ex. Mexican	27.2
Guatemalan	25.7
Salvadoran	29.0
Cuban	34.5
Mexican	23.2
Puerto Rican	22.3
South American	30.8
Spaniard	28.1

High School Graduates
(Universe: Population 25 Years and Over)

Group	Number	%
Total Population	42,543	81.4
Hispanic or Latino (of any race)	8,439	54.6
Mexican	6,947	52.3

Four-Year College Graduates
(Universe: Population 25 Years and Over)

Group	Number	%
Total Population	13,707	26.2
Hispanic or Latino (of any race)	1,073	6.9
Mexican	791	6.0

Population Age 3–17 Enrolled in Public School
(Universe: Population Age 3–17 Enrolled in School)

Group	Number	%
Total Population	14,705	88.3
Hispanic or Latino (of any race)	8,150	95.4
Mexican	7,260	96.7

Population Age 3–17 Enrolled in Private School
(Universe: Population Age 3–17 Enrolled in School)

Group	Number	%
Total Population	1,940	11.7
Hispanic or Latino (of any race)	397	4.6
Mexican	245	3.3

Foreign-Born Population

Group	Number	%
Total Population	10,900	12.0
Hispanic or Latino (of any race)	9,075	28.0
Mexican	8,455	29.9

Foreign-Born Naturalized U.S. Citizens

Group	Number	%
Total Population	2,648	24.3
Hispanic or Latino (of any race)	1,760	19.4
Mexican	1,623	19.2

Language Spoken at Home: English Only
(Universe: Population 5 Years and Over)

Group	Number	%
Total Population	63,841	75.8
Hispanic or Latino (of any race)	10,632	37.0
Mexican	8,472	34.0

Language Spoken at Home: Spanish
(Universe: Population 5 Years and Over)

Group	Number	%
Total Population	18,765	22.3
Hispanic or Latino (of any race)	18,089	63.0
Mexican	16,428	65.9

Unemployment Rate
(Universe: Population 16 Years and Over)

Group	%
Total Population	8.6
Hispanic or Latino (of any race)	11.2
Mexican	11.8

Class of Worker: Private Wage and Salary
(Universe: Civilian Employed Population 16 Years and Over)

Group	Number	%
Total Population	33,787	79.8
Hispanic or Latino (of any race)	10,628	87.1
Mexican	9,292	88.7

Class of Worker: Government
(Universe: Civilian Employed Population 16 Years and Over)

Group	Number	%
Total Population	6,488	15.3
Hispanic or Latino (of any race)	1,034	8.5
Mexican	794	7.6

Means of Transportation to Work: Car, Truck or Van
(Universe: Workers 16 Years and Over)

Group	Number	%
Total Population	37,760	91.3
Hispanic or Latino (of any race)	11,032	92.6
Mexican	9,470	92.5

Means of Transportation to Work: Public Transportation (ex. Taxicab)
(Universe: Workers 16 Years and Over)

Group	Number	%
Total Population	294	0.7
Hispanic or Latino (of any race)	110	0.9
Mexican	110	1.1

Homeownership Rate
(Universe: Occupied Housing Units)

Group	%
Total Population	56.6
Hispanic or Latino (of any race)	43.2
Central American, ex. Mexican	39.4
Guatemalan	34.2
Salvadoran	48.1
Cuban	22.0
Mexican	44.8
Puerto Rican	35.1
South American	32.8
Spaniard	55.7

Median Home Value

Group	Dollars
Total Population	172,200
Hispanic or Latino (of any race)	134,700
Mexican	128,800

Median Gross Rent

Group	Dollars
Total Population	687
Hispanic or Latino (of any race)	638
Mexican	636

Median Household Income
(2010 Inflation-Adjusted Dollars)

Group	Dollars
Total Population	41,845
Hispanic or Latino (of any race)	32,409
Mexican	32,414

Per Capita Income
(2010 Inflation-Adjusted Dollars)

Group	Dollars
Total Population	21,408
Hispanic or Latino (of any race)	11,443
Mexican	11,214

Households with $100,000+ Income

Group	Number	%
Total Population	4,964	15.0
Hispanic or Latino (of any race)	655	7.4
Mexican	616	8.2

Households with Food Stamps/SNAP Benefits During Past 12 Months

Group	Number	%
Total Population	2,722	8.2
Hispanic or Latino (of any race)	1,503	17.1
Mexican	1,127	15.0

Poverty Rate
(Income in Past 12 Months Below Poverty Level)

Group	%
Total Population	22.3
Hispanic or Latino (of any race)	34.7
Mexican	35.0

Lakewood

Population

Group	Number	%TP[1]	%HP[2]
Total Population	142,980	100.0	–
Hispanic or Latino (of any race)	31,467	22.0	100.0
Central American, ex. Mexican	649	0.5	2.1
Guatemalan	186	0.1	0.6
Salvadoran	299	0.2	1.0
Cuban	163	0.1	0.5
Mexican	22,026	15.4	70.0
Puerto Rican	522	0.4	1.7
South American	609	0.4	1.9
Colombian	146	0.1	0.5
Peruvian	207	0.1	0.7
Spaniard	1,703	1.2	5.4

Population Growth: 2000–2010

Group	%
Total Population	-0.8
Hispanic or Latino (of any race)	50.2
Central American, ex. Mexican	213.5
Cuban	-8.4
Mexican	87.3
Puerto Rican	47.0
South American	115.2

Males per 100 Females

Group	Number
Total Population	95.7

Notes: (1) Percent of total population; (2) Percent of Hispanic/Latino population; Profiles include places with an overall population of at least 125,000, OR an overall population of at least 25,000 where the Hispanic/Latino population is at least 20% of the overall population. In states where less than five places meet either of these criteria, we have included places with at least 10,000 total population with the highest percentage of Hispanic/Latino population. These places are identified with an asterisk (*); Please refer to the User's Guide for a full explanation of data.

Group	
Hispanic or Latino (of any race)	96.4
Central American, ex. Mexican	110.7
Guatemalan	121.4
Salvadoran	106.2
Cuban	120.3
Mexican	100.0
Puerto Rican	97.7
South American	82.9
Colombian	67.8
Peruvian	80.0
Spaniard	85.5

Average Household Size

Group	People
Total Population	2.27
Hispanic or Latino (of any race)	2.98
Central American, ex. Mexican	3.41
Guatemalan	3.60
Salvadoran	3.74
Cuban	2.37
Mexican	3.14
Puerto Rican	2.45
South American	2.58
Colombian	2.44
Peruvian	2.33
Spaniard	2.57

Median Age

Group	Years
Total Population	39.2
Hispanic or Latino (of any race)	27.1
Central American, ex. Mexican	29.1
Guatemalan	28.3
Salvadoran	28.4
Cuban	34.4
Mexican	26.2
Puerto Rican	27.4
South American	35.0
Colombian	32.5
Peruvian	33.9
Spaniard	35.3

High School Graduates
(Universe: Population 25 Years and Over)

Group	Number	%
Total Population	88,508	89.8
Hispanic or Latino (of any race)	10,579	69.0
Mexican	6,788	64.3
Spaniard	737	91.8

Four-Year College Graduates
(Universe: Population 25 Years and Over)

Group	Number	%
Total Population	33,959	34.5
Hispanic or Latino (of any race)	2,118	13.8
Mexican	1,372	13.0
Spaniard	179	22.3

Population Age 3–17 Enrolled in Public School
(Universe: Population Age 3–17 Enrolled in School)

Group	Number	%
Total Population	19,195	89.4
Hispanic or Latino (of any race)	7,110	95.6
Mexican	5,310	96.7
Spaniard	243	93.5

Population Age 3–17 Enrolled in Private School
(Universe: Population Age 3–17 Enrolled in School)

Group	Number	%
Total Population	2,275	10.6
Hispanic or Latino (of any race)	329	4.4
Mexican	181	3.3
Spaniard	17	6.5

Foreign-Born Population

Group	Number	%
Total Population	13,284	9.4
Hispanic or Latino (of any race)	6,520	22.3
Mexican	5,510	25.9
Spaniard	0	0.0

Foreign-Born Naturalized U.S. Citizens

Group	Number	%
Total Population	4,898	36.9
Hispanic or Latino (of any race)	1,128	17.3
Mexican	851	15.4
Spaniard	0	0.0

Language Spoken at Home: English Only
(Universe: Population 5 Years and Over)

Group	Number	%
Total Population	112,614	84.1
Hispanic or Latino (of any race)	13,631	51.6
Mexican	8,123	42.8
Spaniard	1,022	83.6

Language Spoken at Home: Spanish
(Universe: Population 5 Years and Over)

Group	Number	%
Total Population	14,145	10.6
Hispanic or Latino (of any race)	12,690	48.0
Mexican	10,781	56.8
Spaniard	201	16.4

Unemployment Rate
(Universe: Population 16 Years and Over)

Group	%
Total Population	7.8
Hispanic or Latino (of any race)	9.7
Mexican	8.4
Spaniard	17.5

Class of Worker: Private Wage and Salary
(Universe: Civilian Employed Population 16 Years and Over)

Group	Number	%
Total Population	57,269	78.3
Hispanic or Latino (of any race)	10,545	84.3
Mexican	7,949	87.1
Spaniard	369	67.7

Class of Worker: Government
(Universe: Civilian Employed Population 16 Years and Over)

Group	Number	%
Total Population	10,836	14.8
Hispanic or Latino (of any race)	1,421	11.4
Mexican	882	9.7
Spaniard	135	24.8

Means of Transportation to Work: Car, Truck or Van
(Universe: Workers 16 Years and Over)

Group	Number	%
Total Population	62,133	86.5
Hispanic or Latino (of any race)	10,767	87.1
Mexican	7,871	87.4
Spaniard	438	80.4

Means of Transportation to Work: Public Transportation (ex. Taxicab)
(Universe: Workers 16 Years and Over)

Group	Number	%
Total Population	3,468	4.8
Hispanic or Latino (of any race)	1,049	8.5
Mexican	839	9.3
Spaniard	44	8.1

Homeownership Rate
(Universe: Occupied Housing Units)

Group	%
Total Population	58.9
Hispanic or Latino (of any race)	37.6
Central American, ex. Mexican	28.0
Guatemalan	23.3
Salvadoran	28.6
Cuban	55.4
Mexican	35.5
Puerto Rican	43.2
South American	46.7
Colombian	44.2
Peruvian	45.3
Spaniard	53.2

Median Home Value

Group	Dollars
Total Population	237,300
Hispanic or Latino (of any race)	220,300
Mexican	221,300
Spaniard	226,200

Median Gross Rent

Group	Dollars
Total Population	876
Hispanic or Latino (of any race)	847
Mexican	849
Spaniard	826

Median Household Income
(2010 Inflation-Adjusted Dollars)

Group	Dollars
Total Population	52,960
Hispanic or Latino (of any race)	35,150
Mexican	34,987
Spaniard	30,765

Per Capita Income
(2010 Inflation-Adjusted Dollars)

Group	Dollars
Total Population	30,027
Hispanic or Latino (of any race)	15,490
Mexican	14,839
Spaniard	20,463

Households with $100,000+ Income

Group	Number	%
Total Population	12,264	20.0
Hispanic or Latino (of any race)	858	9.1
Mexican	622	9.6
Spaniard	55	9.1

Households with Food Stamps/SNAP Benefits During Past 12 Months

Group	Number	%
Total Population	3,876	6.3
Hispanic or Latino (of any race)	1,723	18.3
Mexican	1,285	19.8
Spaniard	105	17.4

Poverty Rate
(Income in Past 12 Months Below Poverty Level)

Group	%
Total Population	11.7
Hispanic or Latino (of any race)	25.0
Mexican	28.0
Spaniard	19.9

Longmont

Population

Group	Number	%TP[1]	%HP[2]
Total Population	86,270	100.0	–
Hispanic or Latino (of any race)	21,191	24.6	100.0
Central American, ex. Mexican	522	0.6	2.5
Guatemalan	209	0.2	1.0
Salvadoran	207	0.2	1.0
Mexican	17,630	20.4	83.2
Puerto Rican	288	0.3	1.4
South American	361	0.4	1.7
Peruvian	145	0.2	0.7
Spaniard	452	0.5	2.1

Population Growth: 2000–2010

Group	%
Total Population	21.3
Hispanic or Latino (of any race)	56.3
Central American, ex. Mexican	321.0
Mexican	71.9
Puerto Rican	83.4
South American	203.4

Males per 100 Females

Group	Number
Total Population	97.1
Hispanic or Latino (of any race)	103.9
Central American, ex. Mexican	113.1
Guatemalan	132.2
Salvadoran	107.0
Mexican	105.4
Puerto Rican	85.8
South American	108.7
Peruvian	141.7
Spaniard	90.7

Average Household Size

Group	People
Total Population	2.58
Hispanic or Latino (of any race)	3.72

Notes: (1) Percent of total population; (2) Percent of Hispanic/Latino population; Profiles include places with an overall population of at least 125,000, OR an overall population of at least 25,000 where the Hispanic/Latino population is at least 20% of the overall population. In states where less than five places meet either of these criteria, we have included places with at least 10,000 total population with the highest percentage of Hispanic/Latino population. These places are identified with an asterisk (*); Please refer to the User's Guide for a full explanation of data.

Group	%
Central American, ex. Mexican	3.64
Guatemalan	4.06
Salvadoran	3.56
Mexican	3.90
Puerto Rican	2.96
South American	3.10
Peruvian	3.50
Spaniard	2.85

Median Age

Group	Years
Total Population	36.6
Hispanic or Latino (of any race)	24.8
Central American, ex. Mexican	29.4
Guatemalan	26.6
Salvadoran	30.3
Mexican	24.0
Puerto Rican	27.2
South American	36.5
Peruvian	34.5
Spaniard	33.0

High School Graduates
(Universe: Population 25 Years and Over)

Group	Number	%
Total Population	47,348	88.1
Hispanic or Latino (of any race)	5,807	58.0
Mexican	4,199	52.8

Four-Year College Graduates
(Universe: Population 25 Years and Over)

Group	Number	%
Total Population	20,225	37.6
Hispanic or Latino (of any race)	1,315	13.1
Mexican	816	10.3

Population Age 3–17 Enrolled in Public School
(Universe: Population Age 3–17 Enrolled in School)

Group	Number	%
Total Population	14,831	87.8
Hispanic or Latino (of any race)	5,260	96.1
Mexican	4,399	95.4

Population Age 3–17 Enrolled in Private School
(Universe: Population Age 3–17 Enrolled in School)

Group	Number	%
Total Population	2,064	12.2
Hispanic or Latino (of any race)	213	3.9
Mexican	213	4.6

Foreign-Born Population

Group	Number	%
Total Population	11,512	13.8
Hispanic or Latino (of any race)	7,837	38.9
Mexican	7,062	43.3

Foreign-Born Naturalized U.S. Citizens

Group	Number	%
Total Population	2,819	24.5
Hispanic or Latino (of any race)	1,465	18.7
Mexican	1,280	18.1

Language Spoken at Home: English Only
(Universe: Population 5 Years and Over)

Group	Number	%
Total Population	59,186	76.8
Hispanic or Latino (of any race)	4,871	27.4
Mexican	3,203	22.2

Language Spoken at Home: Spanish
(Universe: Population 5 Years and Over)

Group	Number	%
Total Population	14,415	18.7
Hispanic or Latino (of any race)	12,849	72.2
Mexican	11,153	77.2

Unemployment Rate
(Universe: Population 16 Years and Over)

Group	%
Total Population	7.0
Hispanic or Latino (of any race)	11.7
Mexican	8.7

Class of Worker: Private Wage and Salary
(Universe: Civilian Employed Population 16 Years and Over)

Group	Number	%
Total Population	33,635	80.8
Hispanic or Latino (of any race)	7,269	87.3
Mexican	5,988	88.4

Class of Worker: Government
(Universe: Civilian Employed Population 16 Years and Over)

Group	Number	%
Total Population	5,173	12.4
Hispanic or Latino (of any race)	663	8.0
Mexican	505	7.5

Means of Transportation to Work: Car, Truck or Van
(Universe: Workers 16 Years and Over)

Group	Number	%
Total Population	35,730	87.3
Hispanic or Latino (of any race)	7,283	89.7
Mexican	5,848	89.1

Means of Transportation to Work: Public Transportation (ex. Taxicab)
(Universe: Workers 16 Years and Over)

Group	Number	%
Total Population	1,199	2.9
Hispanic or Latino (of any race)	391	4.8
Mexican	359	5.5

Homeownership Rate
(Universe: Occupied Housing Units)

Group	%
Total Population	63.5
Hispanic or Latino (of any race)	40.4
Central American, ex. Mexican	36.2
Guatemalan	20.8
Salvadoran	45.3
Mexican	39.2
Puerto Rican	49.4
South American	58.4
Peruvian	50.0
Spaniard	54.2

Median Home Value

Group	Dollars
Total Population	238,400
Hispanic or Latino (of any race)	197,600
Mexican	197,800

Median Gross Rent

Group	Dollars
Total Population	902
Hispanic or Latino (of any race)	812
Mexican	792

Median Household Income
(2010 Inflation-Adjusted Dollars)

Group	Dollars
Total Population	56,025
Hispanic or Latino (of any race)	36,072
Mexican	38,910

Per Capita Income
(2010 Inflation-Adjusted Dollars)

Group	Dollars
Total Population	28,290
Hispanic or Latino (of any race)	13,675
Mexican	13,226

Households with $100,000+ Income

Group	Number	%
Total Population	7,871	24.5
Hispanic or Latino (of any race)	558	10.6
Mexican	432	10.5

Households with Food Stamps/SNAP Benefits During Past 12 Months

Group	Number	%
Total Population	2,095	6.5
Hispanic or Latino (of any race)	754	14.4
Mexican	459	11.2

Poverty Rate
(Income in Past 12 Months Below Poverty Level)

Group	%
Total Population	12.5
Hispanic or Latino (of any race)	26.2
Mexican	25.3

Northglenn

Population

Group	Number	%TP[1]	%HP[2]
Total Population	35,789	100.0	–
Hispanic or Latino (of any race)	10,957	30.6	100.0
Central American, ex. Mexican	216	0.6	2.0
Mexican	7,820	21.9	71.4
Puerto Rican	139	0.4	1.3
South American	139	0.4	1.3
Spaniard	592	1.7	5.4

Population Growth: 2000–2010

Group	%
Total Population	13.3
Hispanic or Latino (of any race)	71.2
Mexican	133.0
Puerto Rican	32.4

Males per 100 Females

Group	Number
Total Population	99.2
Hispanic or Latino (of any race)	99.1
Central American, ex. Mexican	98.2
Mexican	102.9
Puerto Rican	120.6
South American	117.2
Spaniard	88.5

Average Household Size

Group	People
Total Population	2.64
Hispanic or Latino (of any race)	3.30
Central American, ex. Mexican	3.69
Mexican	3.46
Puerto Rican	2.89
South American	3.43
Spaniard	2.91

Median Age

Group	Years
Total Population	33.1
Hispanic or Latino (of any race)	26.0
Central American, ex. Mexican	26.7
Mexican	25.2
Puerto Rican	27.5
South American	30.7
Spaniard	30.4

High School Graduates
(Universe: Population 25 Years and Over)

Group	Number	%
Total Population	18,348	83.3
Hispanic or Latino (of any race)	3,647	66.7
Mexican	2,775	62.1

Four-Year College Graduates
(Universe: Population 25 Years and Over)

Group	Number	%
Total Population	3,558	16.2
Hispanic or Latino (of any race)	475	8.7
Mexican	316	7.1

Population Age 3–17 Enrolled in Public School
(Universe: Population Age 3–17 Enrolled in School)

Group	Number	%
Total Population	5,660	91.3
Hispanic or Latino (of any race)	2,665	95.9
Mexican	2,371	95.5

Population Age 3–17 Enrolled in Private School
(Universe: Population Age 3–17 Enrolled in School)

Group	Number	%
Total Population	537	8.7
Hispanic or Latino (of any race)	113	4.1
Mexican	113	4.5

STATE & PLACE PROFILES

Notes: (1) Percent of total population; (2) Percent of Hispanic/Latino population; Profiles include places with an overall population of at least 125,000, OR an overall population of at least 25,000 where the Hispanic/Latino population is at least 20% of the overall population. In states where less than five places meet either of these criteria, we have included places with at least 10,000 total population with the highest percentage of Hispanic/Latino population. These places are identified with an asterisk (*); Please refer to the User's Guide for a full explanation of data.

Foreign-Born Population

Group	Number	%
Total Population	3,797	10.8
Hispanic or Latino (of any race)	1,908	17.3
Mexican	1,732	18.7

Foreign-Born Naturalized U.S. Citizens

Group	Number	%
Total Population	1,414	37.2
Hispanic or Latino (of any race)	393	20.6
Mexican	381	22.0

Language Spoken at Home: English Only
(Universe: Population 5 Years and Over)

Group	Number	%
Total Population	25,177	78.2
Hispanic or Latino (of any race)	5,116	52.7
Mexican	4,194	51.4

Language Spoken at Home: Spanish
(Universe: Population 5 Years and Over)

Group	Number	%
Total Population	4,724	14.7
Hispanic or Latino (of any race)	4,457	45.9
Mexican	3,888	47.6

Unemployment Rate
(Universe: Population 16 Years and Over)

Group	%
Total Population	10.5
Hispanic or Latino (of any race)	10.0
Mexican	8.5

Class of Worker: Private Wage and Salary
(Universe: Civilian Employed Population 16 Years and Over)

Group	Number	%
Total Population	14,468	82.4
Hispanic or Latino (of any race)	3,621	77.9
Mexican	3,079	77.3

Class of Worker: Government
(Universe: Civilian Employed Population 16 Years and Over)

Group	Number	%
Total Population	2,243	12.8
Hispanic or Latino (of any race)	899	19.3
Mexican	796	20.0

Means of Transportation to Work: Car, Truck or Van
(Universe: Workers 16 Years and Over)

Group	Number	%
Total Population	15,222	88.0
Hispanic or Latino (of any race)	4,006	86.4
Mexican	3,538	89.2

Means of Transportation to Work: Public Transportation (ex. Taxicab)
(Universe: Workers 16 Years and Over)

Group	Number	%
Total Population	732	4.2
Hispanic or Latino (of any race)	254	5.5
Mexican	136	3.4

Homeownership Rate
(Universe: Occupied Housing Units)

Group	%
Total Population	58.5
Hispanic or Latino (of any race)	50.2
Central American, ex. Mexican	37.3
Mexican	50.2
Puerto Rican	52.7
South American	59.5
Spaniard	64.6

Median Home Value

Group	Dollars
Total Population	194,800
Hispanic or Latino (of any race)	192,800
Mexican	195,500

Median Gross Rent

Group	Dollars
Total Population	852
Hispanic or Latino (of any race)	818
Mexican	803

Median Household Income
(2010 Inflation-Adjusted Dollars)

Group	Dollars
Total Population	52,093
Hispanic or Latino (of any race)	43,459
Mexican	43,073

Per Capita Income
(2010 Inflation-Adjusted Dollars)

Group	Dollars
Total Population	22,904
Hispanic or Latino (of any race)	15,884
Mexican	15,462

Households with $100,000+ Income

Group	Number	%
Total Population	1,863	14.8
Hispanic or Latino (of any race)	255	8.3
Mexican	230	9.3

Households with Food Stamps/SNAP Benefits During Past 12 Months

Group	Number	%
Total Population	506	4.0
Hispanic or Latino (of any race)	203	6.6
Mexican	162	6.5

Poverty Rate
(Income in Past 12 Months Below Poverty Level)

Group	%
Total Population	12.3
Hispanic or Latino (of any race)	19.9
Mexican	20.0

Pueblo

Population

Group	Number	%TP[1]	%HP[2]
Total Population	106,595	100.0	–
Hispanic or Latino (of any race)	53,098	49.8	100.0
Central American, ex. Mexican	198	0.2	0.4
Mexican	32,847	30.8	61.9
Puerto Rican	614	0.6	1.2
South American	124	0.1	0.2
Spaniard	2,708	2.5	5.1

Population Growth: 2000–2010

Group	%
Total Population	4.4
Hispanic or Latino (of any race)	17.8
Mexican	68.2
Puerto Rican	75.4
Spaniard	2,581.2

Males per 100 Females

Group	Number
Total Population	95.4
Hispanic or Latino (of any race)	98.1
Central American, ex. Mexican	90.4
Mexican	102.8
Puerto Rican	131.7
South American	85.1
Spaniard	93.3

Average Household Size

Group	People
Total Population	2.37
Hispanic or Latino (of any race)	2.68
Central American, ex. Mexican	3.36
Mexican	2.76
Puerto Rican	2.72
South American	2.62
Spaniard	2.39

Median Age

Group	Years
Total Population	37.5
Hispanic or Latino (of any race)	30.3
Central American, ex. Mexican	26.5
Mexican	29.9
Puerto Rican	26.1
South American	30.3
Spaniard	40.1

High School Graduates
(Universe: Population 25 Years and Over)

Group	Number	%
Total Population	57,316	83.1
Hispanic or Latino (of any race)	22,094	74.8
Mexican	14,369	73.9
Spaniard	1,556	74.8

Four-Year College Graduates
(Universe: Population 25 Years and Over)

Group	Number	%
Total Population	12,693	18.4
Hispanic or Latino (of any race)	2,711	9.2
Mexican	1,847	9.5
Spaniard	176	8.5

Population Age 3–17 Enrolled in Public School
(Universe: Population Age 3–17 Enrolled in School)

Group	Number	%
Total Population	17,314	92.2
Hispanic or Latino (of any race)	11,265	95.9
Mexican	7,991	97.3
Spaniard	785	88.5

Population Age 3–17 Enrolled in Private School
(Universe: Population Age 3–17 Enrolled in School)

Group	Number	%
Total Population	1,471	7.8
Hispanic or Latino (of any race)	482	4.1
Mexican	220	2.7
Spaniard	102	11.5

Foreign-Born Population

Group	Number	%
Total Population	4,012	3.8
Hispanic or Latino (of any race)	2,544	5.0
Mexican	2,240	6.5
Spaniard	11	0.3

Foreign-Born Naturalized U.S. Citizens

Group	Number	%
Total Population	1,491	37.2
Hispanic or Latino (of any race)	685	26.9
Mexican	573	25.6
Spaniard	11	100.0

Language Spoken at Home: English Only
(Universe: Population 5 Years and Over)

Group	Number	%
Total Population	82,633	83.9
Hispanic or Latino (of any race)	33,358	71.5
Mexican	22,130	70.6
Spaniard	2,586	81.2

Language Spoken at Home: Spanish
(Universe: Population 5 Years and Over)

Group	Number	%
Total Population	14,143	14.4
Hispanic or Latino (of any race)	13,266	28.5
Mexican	9,204	29.4
Spaniard	599	18.8

Unemployment Rate
(Universe: Population 16 Years and Over)

Group	%
Total Population	11.1
Hispanic or Latino (of any race)	12.0
Mexican	13.1
Spaniard	14.2

Class of Worker: Private Wage and Salary
(Universe: Civilian Employed Population 16 Years and Over)

Group	Number	%
Total Population	32,562	76.8
Hispanic or Latino (of any race)	15,393	79.8
Mexican	10,762	81.5
Spaniard	794	66.6

Class of Worker: Government
(Universe: Civilian Employed Population 16 Years and Over)

Group	Number	%
Total Population	7,333	17.3
Hispanic or Latino (of any race)	3,046	15.8
Mexican	1,877	14.2
Spaniard	252	21.1

Notes: (1) Percent of total population; (2) Percent of Hispanic/Latino population; Profiles include places with an overall population of at least 125,000, OR an overall population of at least 25,000 where the Hispanic/Latino population is at least 20% of the overall population. In states where less than five places meet either of these criteria, we have included places with at least 10,000 total population with the highest percentage of Hispanic/Latino population. These places are identified with an asterisk (*); Please refer to the User's Guide for a full explanation of data.

Means of Transportation to Work: Car, Truck or Van
(Universe: Workers 16 Years and Over)

Group	Number	%
Total Population	38,162	91.6
Hispanic or Latino (of any race)	17,582	93.2
Mexican	12,025	92.7
Spaniard	1,138	96.6

Means of Transportation to Work: Public Transportation (ex. Taxicab)
(Universe: Workers 16 Years and Over)

Group	Number	%
Total Population	383	0.9
Hispanic or Latino (of any race)	227	1.2
Mexican	194	1.5
Spaniard	0	0.0

Homeownership Rate
(Universe: Occupied Housing Units)

Group	%
Total Population	60.2
Hispanic or Latino (of any race)	54.0
Central American, ex. Mexican	47.3
Mexican	55.7
Puerto Rican	47.9
South American	48.7
Spaniard	66.5

Median Home Value

Group	Dollars
Total Population	120,600
Hispanic or Latino (of any race)	107,500
Mexican	105,100
Spaniard	122,100

Median Gross Rent

Group	Dollars
Total Population	626
Hispanic or Latino (of any race)	640
Mexican	653
Spaniard	635

Median Household Income
(2010 Inflation-Adjusted Dollars)

Group	Dollars
Total Population	34,323
Hispanic or Latino (of any race)	31,467
Mexican	32,508
Spaniard	35,739

Per Capita Income
(2010 Inflation-Adjusted Dollars)

Group	Dollars
Total Population	19,620
Hispanic or Latino (of any race)	14,675
Mexican	14,549
Spaniard	17,069

Households with $100,000+ Income

Group	Number	%
Total Population	3,631	8.6
Hispanic or Latino (of any race)	889	4.9
Mexican	571	4.9
Spaniard	69	5.0

Households with Food Stamps/SNAP Benefits During Past 12 Months

Group	Number	%
Total Population	7,341	17.3
Hispanic or Latino (of any race)	4,236	23.6
Mexican	2,740	23.6
Spaniard	282	20.5

Poverty Rate
(Income in Past 12 Months Below Poverty Level)

Group	%
Total Population	21.2
Hispanic or Latino (of any race)	26.0
Mexican	25.2
Spaniard	19.9

Pueblo West

Population

Group	Number	%TP[1]	%HP[2]
Total Population	29,637	100.0	–
Hispanic or Latino (of any race)	6,787	22.9	100.0
Mexican	4,218	14.2	62.1
Puerto Rican	107	0.4	1.6
Spaniard	565	1.9	8.3

Population Growth: 2000–2010

Group	%
Total Population	75.4
Hispanic or Latino (of any race)	119.5
Mexican	229.0

Males per 100 Females

Group	Number
Total Population	99.4
Hispanic or Latino (of any race)	97.2
Mexican	100.0
Puerto Rican	109.8
Spaniard	100.4

Average Household Size

Group	People
Total Population	2.76
Hispanic or Latino (of any race)	3.17
Mexican	3.27
Puerto Rican	3.36
Spaniard	2.94

Median Age

Group	Years
Total Population	37.6
Hispanic or Latino (of any race)	27.4
Mexican	26.1
Puerto Rican	27.5
Spaniard	32.8

High School Graduates
(Universe: Population 25 Years and Over)

Group	Number	%
Total Population	16,624	92.9
Hispanic or Latino (of any race)	2,948	90.9
Mexican	1,741	87.3

Four-Year College Graduates
(Universe: Population 25 Years and Over)

Group	Number	%
Total Population	5,183	29.0
Hispanic or Latino (of any race)	609	18.8
Mexican	370	18.5

Population Age 3–17 Enrolled in Public School
(Universe: Population Age 3–17 Enrolled in School)

Group	Number	%
Total Population	5,453	90.4
Hispanic or Latino (of any race)	1,638	91.9
Mexican	950	94.3

Population Age 3–17 Enrolled in Private School
(Universe: Population Age 3–17 Enrolled in School)

Group	Number	%
Total Population	579	9.6
Hispanic or Latino (of any race)	144	8.1
Mexican	57	5.7

Foreign-Born Population

Group	Number	%
Total Population	622	2.2
Hispanic or Latino (of any race)	60	1.0
Mexican	52	1.4

Foreign-Born Naturalized U.S. Citizens

Group	Number	%
Total Population	353	56.8
Hispanic or Latino (of any race)	3	5.0
Mexican	3	5.8

Language Spoken at Home: English Only
(Universe: Population 5 Years and Over)

Group	Number	%
Total Population	24,077	92.4
Hispanic or Latino (of any race)	4,504	79.5
Mexican	2,499	73.2

Language Spoken at Home: Spanish
(Universe: Population 5 Years and Over)

Group	Number	%
Total Population	1,314	5.0
Hispanic or Latino (of any race)	1,112	19.6
Mexican	894	26.2

Unemployment Rate
(Universe: Population 16 Years and Over)

Group	%
Total Population	6.3
Hispanic or Latino (of any race)	8.6
Mexican	10.2

Class of Worker: Private Wage and Salary
(Universe: Civilian Employed Population 16 Years and Over)

Group	Number	%
Total Population	9,324	72.7
Hispanic or Latino (of any race)	1,862	70.9
Mexican	1,194	77.4

Class of Worker: Government
(Universe: Civilian Employed Population 16 Years and Over)

Group	Number	%
Total Population	2,887	22.5
Hispanic or Latino (of any race)	682	26.0
Mexican	332	21.5

Means of Transportation to Work: Car, Truck or Van
(Universe: Workers 16 Years and Over)

Group	Number	%
Total Population	11,795	93.5
Hispanic or Latino (of any race)	2,503	97.4
Mexican	1,447	96.9

Means of Transportation to Work: Public Transportation (ex. Taxicab)
(Universe: Workers 16 Years and Over)

Group	Number	%
Total Population	11	0.1
Hispanic or Latino (of any race)	0	0.0
Mexican	0	0.0

Homeownership Rate
(Universe: Occupied Housing Units)

Group	%
Total Population	81.8
Hispanic or Latino (of any race)	77.4
Mexican	77.9
Puerto Rican	85.7
Spaniard	86.0

Median Home Value

Group	Dollars
Total Population	179,800
Hispanic or Latino (of any race)	174,200
Mexican	161,700

Median Gross Rent

Group	Dollars
Total Population	864
Hispanic or Latino (of any race)	938
Mexican	935

Median Household Income
(2010 Inflation-Adjusted Dollars)

Group	Dollars
Total Population	59,086
Hispanic or Latino (of any race)	63,216
Mexican	62,197

Per Capita Income
(2010 Inflation-Adjusted Dollars)

Group	Dollars
Total Population	25,293
Hispanic or Latino (of any race)	18,560
Mexican	18,185

Households with $100,000+ Income

Group	Number	%
Total Population	1,805	17.6
Hispanic or Latino (of any race)	273	14.7
Mexican	119	10.1

Notes: (1) Percent of total population; (2) Percent of Hispanic/Latino population; Profiles include places with an overall population of at least 125,000, OR an overall population of at least 25,000 where the Hispanic/Latino population is at least 20% of the overall population. In states where less than five places meet either of these criteria, we have included places with at least 10,000 total population with the highest percentage of Hispanic/Latino population. These places are identified with an asterisk (*); Please refer to the User's Guide for a full explanation of data.

Households with Food Stamps/SNAP Benefits During Past 12 Months

Group	Number	%
Total Population	611	6.0
Hispanic or Latino (of any race)	188	10.2
Mexican	84	7.2

Poverty Rate
(Income in Past 12 Months Below Poverty Level)

Group	%
Total Population	8.7
Hispanic or Latino (of any race)	10.7
Mexican	11.0

Thornton

Population

Group	Number	%TP[1]	%HP[2]
Total Population	118,772	100.0	–
Hispanic or Latino (of any race)	37,602	31.7	100.0
Central American, ex. Mexican	588	0.5	1.6
Guatemalan	150	0.1	0.4
Salvadoran	281	0.2	0.7
Cuban	157	0.1	0.4
Mexican	28,054	23.6	74.6
Puerto Rican	449	0.4	1.2
South American	464	0.4	1.2
Colombian	114	0.1	0.3
Peruvian	157	0.1	0.4
Spaniard	1,639	1.4	4.4

Population Growth: 2000–2010

Group	%
Total Population	44.2
Hispanic or Latino (of any race)	113.9
Central American, ex. Mexican	370.4
Mexican	193.4
Puerto Rican	98.7
South American	254.2

Males per 100 Females

Group	Number
Total Population	97.9
Hispanic or Latino (of any race)	99.9
Central American, ex. Mexican	102.8
Guatemalan	80.7
Salvadoran	102.2
Cuban	121.1
Mexican	102.6
Puerto Rican	96.1
South American	90.2
Colombian	78.1
Peruvian	78.4
Spaniard	89.0

Average Household Size

Group	People
Total Population	2.86
Hispanic or Latino (of any race)	3.43
Central American, ex. Mexican	4.21
Guatemalan	3.85
Salvadoran	4.63
Cuban	3.12
Mexican	3.58
Puerto Rican	2.89
South American	3.21
Colombian	2.97
Peruvian	3.42
Spaniard	2.94

Median Age

Group	Years
Total Population	32.0
Hispanic or Latino (of any race)	25.5
Central American, ex. Mexican	30.1
Guatemalan	31.0
Salvadoran	29.4
Cuban	28.6
Mexican	24.8
Puerto Rican	27.5
South American	32.4
Colombian	31.7
Peruvian	32.8
Spaniard	32.2

High School Graduates
(Universe: Population 25 Years and Over)

Group	Number	%
Total Population	59,972	86.1
Hispanic or Latino (of any race)	12,265	69.7
Mexican	8,716	65.5
Spaniard	660	93.2

Four-Year College Graduates
(Universe: Population 25 Years and Over)

Group	Number	%
Total Population	18,041	25.9
Hispanic or Latino (of any race)	2,280	13.0
Mexican	1,559	11.7
Spaniard	47	6.6

Population Age 3–17 Enrolled in Public School
(Universe: Population Age 3–17 Enrolled in School)

Group	Number	%
Total Population	21,083	88.9
Hispanic or Latino (of any race)	7,971	91.7
Mexican	6,497	93.3
Spaniard	180	70.6

Population Age 3–17 Enrolled in Private School
(Universe: Population Age 3–17 Enrolled in School)

Group	Number	%
Total Population	2,621	11.1
Hispanic or Latino (of any race)	719	8.3
Mexican	468	6.7
Spaniard	75	29.4

Foreign-Born Population

Group	Number	%
Total Population	12,871	11.5
Hispanic or Latino (of any race)	7,752	23.1
Mexican	6,895	26.3
Spaniard	31	2.7

Foreign-Born Naturalized U.S. Citizens

Group	Number	%
Total Population	4,879	37.9
Hispanic or Latino (of any race)	1,730	22.3
Mexican	1,446	21.0
Spaniard	0	0.0

Language Spoken at Home: English Only
(Universe: Population 5 Years and Over)

Group	Number	%
Total Population	80,065	77.9
Hispanic or Latino (of any race)	14,949	50.2
Mexican	10,511	45.4
Spaniard	961	87.2

Language Spoken at Home: Spanish
(Universe: Population 5 Years and Over)

Group	Number	%
Total Population	15,838	15.4
Hispanic or Latino (of any race)	14,761	49.6
Mexican	12,582	54.4
Spaniard	141	12.8

Unemployment Rate
(Universe: Population 16 Years and Over)

Group	%
Total Population	5.7
Hispanic or Latino (of any race)	7.7
Mexican	7.1
Spaniard	10.0

Class of Worker: Private Wage and Salary
(Universe: Civilian Employed Population 16 Years and Over)

Group	Number	%
Total Population	48,238	82.7
Hispanic or Latino (of any race)	12,447	85.4
Mexican	9,488	85.6
Spaniard	581	93.4

Class of Worker: Government
(Universe: Civilian Employed Population 16 Years and Over)

Group	Number	%
Total Population	7,633	13.1
Hispanic or Latino (of any race)	1,494	10.2
Mexican	1,079	9.7
Spaniard	41	6.6

Means of Transportation to Work: Car, Truck or Van
(Universe: Workers 16 Years and Over)

Group	Number	%
Total Population	51,509	89.9
Hispanic or Latino (of any race)	13,196	91.6
Mexican	10,131	92.3
Spaniard	511	84.3

Means of Transportation to Work: Public Transportation (ex. Taxicab)
(Universe: Workers 16 Years and Over)

Group	Number	%
Total Population	2,312	4.0
Hispanic or Latino (of any race)	705	4.9
Mexican	480	4.4
Spaniard	68	11.2

Homeownership Rate
(Universe: Occupied Housing Units)

Group	%
Total Population	70.3
Hispanic or Latino (of any race)	57.3
Central American, ex. Mexican	54.8
Guatemalan	50.0
Salvadoran	54.2
Cuban	58.8
Mexican	57.4
Puerto Rican	57.7
South American	72.8
Colombian	77.4
Peruvian	81.4
Spaniard	73.8

Median Home Value

Group	Dollars
Total Population	214,200
Hispanic or Latino (of any race)	201,300
Mexican	188,400
Spaniard	264,500

Median Gross Rent

Group	Dollars
Total Population	982
Hispanic or Latino (of any race)	948
Mexican	951
Spaniard	955

Median Household Income
(2010 Inflation-Adjusted Dollars)

Group	Dollars
Total Population	65,578
Hispanic or Latino (of any race)	51,057
Mexican	44,059
Spaniard	54,583

Per Capita Income
(2010 Inflation-Adjusted Dollars)

Group	Dollars
Total Population	26,100
Hispanic or Latino (of any race)	16,729
Mexican	14,969
Spaniard	21,921

Households with $100,000+ Income

Group	Number	%
Total Population	9,801	25.4
Hispanic or Latino (of any race)	1,618	17.6
Mexican	990	14.2
Spaniard	55	13.0

Households with Food Stamps/SNAP Benefits During Past 12 Months

Group	Number	%
Total Population	1,729	4.5
Hispanic or Latino (of any race)	803	8.8
Mexican	664	9.5
Spaniard	65	15.4

Poverty Rate
(Income in Past 12 Months Below Poverty Level)

Group	%
Total Population	9.9
Hispanic or Latino (of any race)	20.0

Notes: (1) Percent of total population; (2) Percent of Hispanic/Latino population; Profiles include places with an overall population of at least 125,000, OR an overall population of at least 25,000 where the Hispanic/Latino population is at least 20% of the overall population. In states where less than five places meet either of these criteria, we have included places with at least 10,000 total population with the highest percentage of Hispanic/Latino population. These places are identified with an asterisk (*); Please refer to the User's Guide for a full explanation of data.

Mexican	24.2
Spaniard	9.8

Westminster

Population

Group	Number	%TP[1]	%HP[2]
Total Population	106,114	100.0	–
Hispanic or Latino (of any race)	22,006	20.7	100.0
Central American, ex. Mexican	450	0.4	2.0
Guatemalan	175	0.2	0.8
Salvadoran	177	0.2	0.8
Cuban	139	0.1	0.6
Mexican	15,374	14.5	69.9
Puerto Rican	380	0.4	1.7
South American	436	0.4	2.0
Peruvian	127	0.1	0.6
Spaniard	1,197	1.1	5.4

Population Growth: 2000–2010

Group	%
Total Population	5.1
Hispanic or Latino (of any race)	43.2
Central American, ex. Mexican	294.7
Cuban	-2.1
Mexican	75.5
Puerto Rican	64.5
South American	186.8

Males per 100 Females

Group	Number
Total Population	98.2
Hispanic or Latino (of any race)	100.9
Central American, ex. Mexican	111.3
Guatemalan	150.0
Salvadoran	94.5
Cuban	104.4
Mexican	103.2
Puerto Rican	119.7
South American	91.2
Peruvian	92.4
Spaniard	88.2

Average Household Size

Group	People
Total Population	2.51
Hispanic or Latino (of any race)	3.08
Central American, ex. Mexican	3.55
Guatemalan	3.78
Salvadoran	3.71
Cuban	2.56
Mexican	3.21
Puerto Rican	2.68
South American	2.70
Peruvian	2.98
Spaniard	2.61

Median Age

Group	Years
Total Population	35.1
Hispanic or Latino (of any race)	26.8
Central American, ex. Mexican	29.5
Guatemalan	28.8
Salvadoran	28.4
Cuban	31.3
Mexican	26.0
Puerto Rican	24.8
South American	32.7
Peruvian	35.1
Spaniard	34.0

High School Graduates
(Universe: Population 25 Years and Over)

Group	Number	%
Total Population	60,770	90.2
Hispanic or Latino (of any race)	7,712	70.6
Mexican	4,819	64.2
Spaniard	655	91.2

Four-Year College Graduates
(Universe: Population 25 Years and Over)

Group	Number	%
Total Population	22,419	33.3
Hispanic or Latino (of any race)	1,623	14.9
Mexican	919	12.2
Spaniard	102	14.2

Population Age 3–17 Enrolled in Public School
(Universe: Population Age 3–17 Enrolled in School)

Group	Number	%
Total Population	17,497	86.0
Hispanic or Latino (of any race)	4,991	93.2
Mexican	3,788	94.4
Spaniard	290	80.3

Population Age 3–17 Enrolled in Private School
(Universe: Population Age 3–17 Enrolled in School)

Group	Number	%
Total Population	2,848	14.0
Hispanic or Latino (of any race)	365	6.8
Mexican	226	5.6
Spaniard	71	19.7

Foreign-Born Population

Group	Number	%
Total Population	10,046	9.6
Hispanic or Latino (of any race)	4,596	21.5
Mexican	3,945	25.2
Spaniard	0	0.0

Foreign-Born Naturalized U.S. Citizens

Group	Number	%
Total Population	4,190	41.7
Hispanic or Latino (of any race)	585	12.7
Mexican	424	10.7
Spaniard	0	0.0

Language Spoken at Home: English Only
(Universe: Population 5 Years and Over)

Group	Number	%
Total Population	81,547	83.9
Hispanic or Latino (of any race)	10,718	56.4
Mexican	7,022	50.7
Spaniard	1,013	87.9

Language Spoken at Home: Spanish
(Universe: Population 5 Years and Over)

Group	Number	%
Total Population	9,165	9.4
Hispanic or Latino (of any race)	8,243	43.4
Mexican	6,820	49.2
Spaniard	140	12.1

Unemployment Rate
(Universe: Population 16 Years and Over)

Group	%
Total Population	6.9
Hispanic or Latino (of any race)	10.9
Mexican	11.9
Spaniard	16.1

Class of Worker: Private Wage and Salary
(Universe: Civilian Employed Population 16 Years and Over)

Group	Number	%
Total Population	46,809	82.6
Hispanic or Latino (of any race)	8,225	84.7
Mexican	5,869	84.9
Spaniard	551	86.2

Class of Worker: Government
(Universe: Civilian Employed Population 16 Years and Over)

Group	Number	%
Total Population	7,008	12.4
Hispanic or Latino (of any race)	1,038	10.7
Mexican	749	10.8
Spaniard	76	11.9

Means of Transportation to Work: Car, Truck or Van
(Universe: Workers 16 Years and Over)

Group	Number	%
Total Population	49,308	88.7
Hispanic or Latino (of any race)	8,546	89.7
Mexican	6,240	90.7
Spaniard	417	71.2

Means of Transportation to Work: Public Transportation (ex. Taxicab)
(Universe: Workers 16 Years and Over)

Group	Number	%
Total Population	2,351	4.2
Hispanic or Latino (of any race)	465	4.9
Mexican	292	4.2
Spaniard	66	11.3

Homeownership Rate
(Universe: Occupied Housing Units)

Group	%
Total Population	65.4
Hispanic or Latino (of any race)	48.0
Central American, ex. Mexican	43.3
Guatemalan	36.0
Salvadoran	49.0
Cuban	61.4
Mexican	46.3
Puerto Rican	48.9
South American	60.7
Peruvian	60.5
Spaniard	64.8

Median Home Value

Group	Dollars
Total Population	226,500
Hispanic or Latino (of any race)	200,500
Mexican	194,100
Spaniard	221,100

Median Gross Rent

Group	Dollars
Total Population	929
Hispanic or Latino (of any race)	843
Mexican	793
Spaniard	990

Median Household Income
(2010 Inflation-Adjusted Dollars)

Group	Dollars
Total Population	61,936
Hispanic or Latino (of any race)	45,284
Mexican	42,798
Spaniard	60,059

Per Capita Income
(2010 Inflation-Adjusted Dollars)

Group	Dollars
Total Population	30,061
Hispanic or Latino (of any race)	16,907
Mexican	14,790
Spaniard	21,830

Households with $100,000+ Income

Group	Number	%
Total Population	10,296	25.3
Hispanic or Latino (of any race)	825	13.0
Mexican	405	9.2
Spaniard	69	15.9

Households with Food Stamps/SNAP Benefits During Past 12 Months

Group	Number	%
Total Population	1,661	4.1
Hispanic or Latino (of any race)	669	10.5
Mexican	513	11.6
Spaniard	41	9.4

Poverty Rate
(Income in Past 12 Months Below Poverty Level)

Group	%
Total Population	10.3
Hispanic or Latino (of any race)	21.1
Mexican	23.5
Spaniard	23.1

Wheat Ridge

Population

Group	Number	%TP[1]	%HP[2]
Total Population	30,166	100.0	–
Hispanic or Latino (of any race)	6,309	20.9	100.0
Mexican	4,435	14.7	70.3

Notes: (1) Percent of total population; (2) Percent of Hispanic/Latino population; Profiles include places with an overall population of at least 125,000, OR an overall population of at least 25,000 where the Hispanic/Latino population is at least 20% of the overall population. In states where less than five places meet either of these criteria, we have included places with at least 10,000 total population with the highest percentage of Hispanic/Latino population. These places are identified with an asterisk (*); Please refer to the User's Guide for a full explanation of data.

STATE & PLACE PROFILES

Spaniard	332	1.1	5.3

Population Growth: 2000–2010

Group	%
Total Population	-8.3
Hispanic or Latino (of any race)	42.3
Mexican	72.6

Males per 100 Females

Group	Number
Total Population	94.4
Hispanic or Latino (of any race)	94.4
Mexican	97.5
Spaniard	82.4

Average Household Size

Group	People
Total Population	2.12
Hispanic or Latino (of any race)	2.72
Mexican	2.84
Spaniard	2.35

Median Age

Group	Years
Total Population	43.7
Hispanic or Latino (of any race)	28.9
Mexican	27.8
Spaniard	38.7

High School Graduates
(Universe: Population 25 Years and Over)

Group	Number	%
Total Population	19,315	87.0
Hispanic or Latino (of any race)	2,217	64.8
Mexican	1,307	63.5

Four-Year College Graduates
(Universe: Population 25 Years and Over)

Group	Number	%
Total Population	6,095	27.4
Hispanic or Latino (of any race)	233	6.8
Mexican	132	6.4

Population Age 3–17 Enrolled in Public School
(Universe: Population Age 3–17 Enrolled in School)

Group	Number	%
Total Population	3,762	90.5
Hispanic or Latino (of any race)	1,199	94.8
Mexican	814	92.5

Population Age 3–17 Enrolled in Private School
(Universe: Population Age 3–17 Enrolled in School)

Group	Number	%
Total Population	397	9.5
Hispanic or Latino (of any race)	66	5.2
Mexican	66	7.5

Foreign-Born Population

Group	Number	%
Total Population	2,083	6.9
Hispanic or Latino (of any race)	1,150	18.7
Mexican	926	23.2

Foreign-Born Naturalized U.S. Citizens

Group	Number	%
Total Population	846	40.6
Hispanic or Latino (of any race)	293	25.5
Mexican	216	23.3

Language Spoken at Home: English Only
(Universe: Population 5 Years and Over)

Group	Number	%
Total Population	25,509	88.2
Hispanic or Latino (of any race)	3,422	61.9
Mexican	1,809	52.1

Language Spoken at Home: Spanish
(Universe: Population 5 Years and Over)

Group	Number	%
Total Population	2,399	8.3
Hispanic or Latino (of any race)	2,093	37.9
Mexican	1,662	47.9

Unemployment Rate
(Universe: Population 16 Years and Over)

Group	%
Total Population	6.4
Hispanic or Latino (of any race)	10.1
Mexican	11.6

Class of Worker: Private Wage and Salary
(Universe: Civilian Employed Population 16 Years and Over)

Group	Number	%
Total Population	12,386	80.4
Hispanic or Latino (of any race)	2,375	87.6
Mexican	1,517	89.3

Class of Worker: Government
(Universe: Civilian Employed Population 16 Years and Over)

Group	Number	%
Total Population	1,913	12.4
Hispanic or Latino (of any race)	251	9.3
Mexican	114	6.7

Means of Transportation to Work: Car, Truck or Van
(Universe: Workers 16 Years and Over)

Group	Number	%
Total Population	13,028	86.4
Hispanic or Latino (of any race)	2,332	86.7
Mexican	1,456	87.4

Means of Transportation to Work: Public Transportation (ex. Taxicab)
(Universe: Workers 16 Years and Over)

Group	Number	%
Total Population	469	3.1
Hispanic or Latino (of any race)	158	5.9
Mexican	119	7.1

Homeownership Rate
(Universe: Occupied Housing Units)

Group	%
Total Population	54.6
Hispanic or Latino (of any race)	32.5
Mexican	30.8
Spaniard	45.5

Median Home Value

Group	Dollars
Total Population	232,200
Hispanic or Latino (of any race)	216,900
Mexican	219,800

Median Gross Rent

Group	Dollars
Total Population	791
Hispanic or Latino (of any race)	758
Mexican	723

Median Household Income
(2010 Inflation-Adjusted Dollars)

Group	Dollars
Total Population	47,014
Hispanic or Latino (of any race)	38,600
Mexican	38,898

Per Capita Income
(2010 Inflation-Adjusted Dollars)

Group	Dollars
Total Population	28,372
Hispanic or Latino (of any race)	16,764
Mexican	15,551

Households with $100,000+ Income

Group	Number	%
Total Population	2,058	14.4
Hispanic or Latino (of any race)	133	5.8
Mexican	88	6.8

Households with Food Stamps/SNAP Benefits During Past 12 Months

Group	Number	%
Total Population	1,086	7.6
Hispanic or Latino (of any race)	391	17.2
Mexican	195	15.1

Poverty Rate
(Income in Past 12 Months Below Poverty Level)

Group	%
Total Population	10.9
Hispanic or Latino (of any race)	18.6
Mexican	24.7

Notes: (1) Percent of total population; (2) Percent of Hispanic/Latino population; Profiles include places with an overall population of at least 125,000, OR an overall population of at least 25,000 where the Hispanic/Latino population is at least 20% of the overall population. In states where less than five places meet either of these criteria, we have included places with at least 10,000 total population with the highest percentage of Hispanic/Latino population. These places are identified with an asterisk (*); Please refer to the User's Guide for a full explanation of data.

Connecticut

EDITOR'S NOTE: For a place to be included in this edition, it must meet one of two criteria. Either its overall population is at least 125,000, OR its overall population is at least 25,000 and its Hispanic/Latino population is at least 20% of the overall population. For the state of Connecticut, the following locations are included:

- Bridgeport
- Danbury
- East Hartford
- Hartford
- Meriden
- New Britain
- New Haven
- New London
- Norwalk
- Stamford
- Waterbury
- Windham

Section Two: State & Place Profiles starts with the state profile, followed by place profiles that meet the criteria above. Places are listed alphabetically within each state. All states, all counties and places that meet the above criteria are ranked and compared in *Section Three: Rankings & Comparisons*, on page 1055.

For a more detailed look at the Hispanic/Latino population in Connecticut, a companion web site is available at no additional charge with purchase of this print edition. Visit http://gold.greyhouse.com/page/info_hispanic for more information.

The web site includes data for all counties and places in Connecticut with Hispanic/Latino population, plus ten additional topics: Self Employed Worker; Walked to Work; Worked from Home; Mean Travel Time to Work; Mean Household Income; Households with Cash Public Assistance; Mean Cash Pubic Assistance; Poverty Rates for 18 and Under, 18 to 64, and 65 and Over.

Population

Group	Number	%TP[1]	%HP[2]
Total Population	3,574,097	100.0	–
Hispanic or Latino (of any race)	479,087	13.4	100.0
Central American, ex. Mexican	35,023	1.0	7.3
Costa Rican	2,767	0.1	0.6
Guatemalan	16,715	0.5	3.5
Honduran	6,242	0.2	1.3
Nicaraguan	1,538	<0.1	0.3
Panamanian	1,304	<0.1	0.3
Salvadoran	6,223	0.2	1.3
Cuban	9,490	0.3	2.0
Dominican Republic	26,093	0.7	5.4
Mexican	50,658	1.4	10.6
Puerto Rican	252,972	7.1	52.8
South American	71,355	2.0	14.9
Argentinean	3,609	0.1	0.8
Bolivian	781	<0.1	0.2
Chilean	2,356	0.1	0.5
Colombian	20,048	0.6	4.2
Ecuadorian	23,677	0.7	4.9
Paraguayan	494	<0.1	0.1
Peruvian	16,424	0.5	3.4
Uruguayan	1,294	<0.1	0.3
Venezuelan	2,129	0.1	0.4
Spaniard	5,371	0.2	1.1

Population Growth: 2000–2010

Group	%
Total Population	4.9
Hispanic or Latino (of any race)	49.6
Central American, ex. Mexican	169.7
Costa Rican	74.4
Guatemalan	217.0
Honduran	216.4
Nicaraguan	113.3
Panamanian	79.6
Salvadoran	202.1
Cuban	33.6
Dominican Republic	173.3
Mexican	115.7
Puerto Rican	30.1
South American	127.9
Argentinean	134.4
Bolivian	118.2
Chilean	86.4
Colombian	82.7
Ecuadorian	207.4
Paraguayan	91.5
Peruvian	148.2
Uruguayan	230.9
Venezuelan	98.0
Spaniard	300.2

Males per 100 Females

Group	Number
Total Population	94.8
Hispanic or Latino (of any race)	99.9
Central American, ex. Mexican	132.1
Costa Rican	111.5
Guatemalan	158.9
Honduran	123.3
Nicaraguan	98.5
Panamanian	81.4
Salvadoran	112.2
Cuban	97.5
Dominican Republic	85.2
Mexican	125.8
Puerto Rican	90.2
South American	100.0
Argentinean	96.2
Bolivian	89.1
Chilean	93.6
Colombian	81.9
Ecuadorian	128.0
Paraguayan	84.3
Peruvian	93.5
Uruguayan	109.0
Venezuelan	84.2
Spaniard	97.1

Average Household Size

Group	People
Total Population	2.52
Hispanic or Latino (of any race)	3.20
Central American, ex. Mexican	3.96
Costa Rican	3.02
Guatemalan	4.35
Honduran	4.03
Nicaraguan	3.67
Panamanian	2.76
Salvadoran	3.89
Cuban	2.64
Dominican Republic	3.45
Mexican	3.93
Puerto Rican	2.98
South American	3.38
Argentinean	2.94
Bolivian	3.35
Chilean	2.92
Colombian	3.06
Ecuadorian	3.96
Paraguayan	3.17
Peruvian	3.34
Uruguayan	2.99
Venezuelan	3.05
Spaniard	2.54

Median Age

Group	Years
Total Population	40.0
Hispanic or Latino (of any race)	27.4
Central American, ex. Mexican	29.1
Costa Rican	32.9
Guatemalan	28.1
Honduran	29.5
Nicaraguan	31.0
Panamanian	32.0
Salvadoran	29.7
Cuban	33.3
Dominican Republic	26.8
Mexican	25.7
Puerto Rican	25.6
South American	33.0
Argentinean	36.1
Bolivian	30.4
Chilean	36.0
Colombian	34.6
Ecuadorian	30.3
Paraguayan	28.3
Peruvian	35.8
Uruguayan	36.1
Venezuelan	32.2
Spaniard	35.8

High School Graduates
(Universe: Population 25 Years and Over)

Group	Number	%
Total Population	2,118,884	88.4
Hispanic or Latino (of any race)	162,821	67.8
Central American, ex. Mexican	10,294	54.5
Costa Rican	977	74.0
Guatemalan	4,535	49.3
Honduran	1,736	56.9
Nicaraguan	469	96.7
Panamanian	650	98.0
Salvadoran	1,803	45.5
Cuban	4,745	86.1
Dominican Republic	7,871	66.1
Mexican	13,945	60.6
Puerto Rican	81,699	65.0
South American	34,231	79.7
Argentinean	2,446	93.4
Chilean	862	82.2
Colombian	10,671	83.9
Ecuadorian	9,045	64.5
Peruvian	8,657	89.4
Venezuelan	1,311	94.2
Spaniard	3,312	94.9

Four-Year College Graduates
(Universe: Population 25 Years and Over)

Group	Number	%
Total Population	843,575	35.2
Hispanic or Latino (of any race)	34,140	14.2
Central American, ex. Mexican	2,119	11.2
Costa Rican	199	15.1
Guatemalan	532	5.8
Honduran	435	14.3
Nicaraguan	190	39.2
Panamanian	270	40.7
Salvadoran	472	11.9
Cuban	2,013	36.5
Dominican Republic	1,458	12.2
Mexican	3,594	15.6
Puerto Rican	10,906	8.7
South American	10,457	24.4
Argentinean	1,335	51.0
Chilean	314	29.9
Colombian	3,124	24.5
Ecuadorian	1,788	12.8
Peruvian	2,587	26.7
Venezuelan	762	54.8
Spaniard	1,624	46.5

Population Age 3–17 Enrolled in Public School
(Universe: Population Age 3–17 Enrolled in School)

Group	Number	%
Total Population	564,853	85.6
Hispanic or Latino (of any race)	104,324	92.7
Central American, ex. Mexican	4,900	91.2
Costa Rican	313	85.8
Guatemalan	2,304	92.7
Honduran	873	94.3
Nicaraguan	203	87.5

Notes: (1) Percent of total population; (2) Percent of Hispanic/Latino population; Profiles include places with an overall population of at least 125,000, OR an overall population of at least 25,000 where the Hispanic/Latino population is at least 20% of the overall population. In states where less than five places meet either of these criteria, we have included places with at least 10,000 total population with the highest percentage of Hispanic/Latino population. These places are identified with an asterisk (*); Please refer to the User's Guide for a full explanation of data.

Panamanian	242	93.1
Salvadoran	927	87.2
Cuban	1,529	79.1
Dominican Republic	5,666	93.3
Mexican	9,965	92.6
Puerto Rican	65,958	94.5
South American	10,960	86.8
Argentinean	618	86.2
Chilean	284	91.9
Colombian	3,288	87.5
Ecuadorian	3,537	90.5
Peruvian	2,313	83.2
Venezuelan	386	68.2
Spaniard	986	86.9

Population Age 3–17 Enrolled in Private School
(Universe: Population Age 3–17 Enrolled in School)

Group	Number	%
Total Population	95,264	14.4
Hispanic or Latino (of any race)	8,217	7.3
Central American, ex. Mexican	470	8.8
Costa Rican	52	14.2
Guatemalan	182	7.3
Honduran	53	5.7
Nicaraguan	29	12.5
Panamanian	18	6.9
Salvadoran	136	12.8
Cuban	403	20.9
Dominican Republic	410	6.7
Mexican	791	7.4
Puerto Rican	3,829	5.5
South American	1,661	13.2
Argentinean	99	13.8
Chilean	25	8.1
Colombian	470	12.5
Ecuadorian	370	9.5
Peruvian	467	16.8
Venezuelan	180	31.8
Spaniard	149	13.1

Foreign-Born Population

Group	Number	%
Total Population	469,180	13.2
Hispanic or Latino (of any race)	118,049	26.4
Central American, ex. Mexican	23,067	72.7
Costa Rican	1,240	52.4
Guatemalan	12,127	79.3
Honduran	3,739	72.3
Nicaraguan	476	50.5
Panamanian	448	40.2
Salvadoran	4,772	73.6
Cuban	3,453	37.4
Dominican Republic	12,570	55.5
Mexican	23,573	52.0
Puerto Rican	1,635	0.7
South American	46,908	69.7
Argentinean	2,348	63.4
Chilean	1,120	72.5
Colombian	13,434	68.3
Ecuadorian	16,378	71.5
Peruvian	10,488	70.7
Venezuelan	1,354	60.6
Spaniard	1,444	26.5

Foreign-Born Naturalized U.S. Citizens

Group	Number	%
Total Population	217,613	46.4
Hispanic or Latino (of any race)	34,989	29.6
Central American, ex. Mexican	4,297	18.6
Costa Rican	270	21.8
Guatemalan	1,613	13.3
Honduran	513	13.7
Nicaraguan	204	42.9
Panamanian	279	62.3
Salvadoran	1,311	27.5
Cuban	2,585	74.9
Dominican Republic	5,269	41.9
Mexican	2,578	10.9
Puerto Rican	969	59.3
South American	16,620	35.4
Argentinean	1,097	46.7
Chilean	495	44.2
Colombian	6,351	47.3
Ecuadorian	3,628	22.2
Peruvian	3,840	36.6

Venezuelan	500	36.9
Spaniard	699	48.4

Language Spoken at Home: English Only
(Universe: Population 5 Years and Over)

Group	Number	%
Total Population	2,652,446	79.4
Hispanic or Latino (of any race)	93,150	23.1
Central American, ex. Mexican	3,096	10.7
Costa Rican	529	26.8
Guatemalan	1,032	7.4
Honduran	510	10.9
Nicaraguan	184	22.2
Panamanian	456	44.7
Salvadoran	385	6.4
Cuban	4,101	47.9
Dominican Republic	2,750	13.4
Mexican	8,946	22.4
Puerto Rican	59,045	26.5
South American	7,172	11.7
Argentinean	811	23.5
Chilean	251	16.8
Colombian	2,116	11.5
Ecuadorian	1,717	8.4
Peruvian	1,479	11.0
Venezuelan	435	21.2
Spaniard	3,031	59.4

Language Spoken at Home: Spanish
(Universe: Population 5 Years and Over)

Group	Number	%
Total Population	339,414	10.2
Hispanic or Latino (of any race)	307,432	76.3
Central American, ex. Mexican	25,664	89.1
Costa Rican	1,443	73.2
Guatemalan	12,941	92.4
Honduran	4,157	89.1
Nicaraguan	644	77.8
Panamanian	565	55.3
Salvadoran	5,611	93.4
Cuban	4,346	50.7
Dominican Republic	17,749	86.3
Mexican	30,698	76.8
Puerto Rican	163,422	73.2
South American	53,927	87.6
Argentinean	2,635	76.2
Chilean	1,239	83.2
Colombian	16,289	88.2
Ecuadorian	18,631	91.5
Peruvian	11,803	87.5
Venezuelan	1,525	74.2
Spaniard	1,911	37.4

Unemployment Rate
(Universe: Population 16 Years and Over)

Group	%
Total Population	7.6
Hispanic or Latino (of any race)	13.2
Central American, ex. Mexican	12.8
Costa Rican	9.9
Guatemalan	12.6
Honduran	20.7
Nicaraguan	4.9
Panamanian	11.7
Salvadoran	10.0
Cuban	9.8
Dominican Republic	15.2
Mexican	9.7
Puerto Rican	16.2
South American	8.5
Argentinean	4.6
Chilean	2.9
Colombian	9.4
Ecuadorian	9.0
Peruvian	7.4
Venezuelan	9.0
Spaniard	7.4

Class of Worker: Private Wage and Salary
(Universe: Civilian Employed Population 16 Years and Over)

Group	Number	%
Total Population	1,407,377	79.7
Hispanic or Latino (of any race)	160,374	83.9
Central American, ex. Mexican	14,758	83.2
Costa Rican	915	82.8

Guatemalan	7,271	80.9
Honduran	2,062	82.0
Nicaraguan	333	75.3
Panamanian	388	68.3
Salvadoran	3,582	92.2
Cuban	3,512	83.0
Dominican Republic	8,673	87.5
Mexican	17,991	87.2
Puerto Rican	76,263	83.6
South American	30,940	83.5
Argentinean	1,558	79.9
Chilean	708	78.9
Colombian	8,754	80.2
Ecuadorian	10,964	86.6
Peruvian	7,260	85.1
Venezuelan	816	79.8
Spaniard	2,293	82.3

Class of Worker: Government
(Universe: Civilian Employed Population 16 Years and Over)

Group	Number	%
Total Population	236,804	13.4
Hispanic or Latino (of any race)	19,619	10.3
Central American, ex. Mexican	661	3.7
Costa Rican	79	7.1
Guatemalan	188	2.1
Honduran	82	3.3
Nicaraguan	64	14.5
Panamanian	157	27.6
Salvadoran	78	2.0
Cuban	562	13.3
Dominican Republic	743	7.5
Mexican	1,104	5.4
Puerto Rican	13,141	14.4
South American	2,278	6.1
Argentinean	184	9.4
Chilean	50	5.6
Colombian	937	8.6
Ecuadorian	328	2.6
Peruvian	516	6.0
Venezuelan	136	13.3
Spaniard	397	14.3

Means of Transportation to Work: Car, Truck or Van
(Universe: Workers 16 Years and Over)

Group	Number	%
Total Population	1,508,300	87.4
Hispanic or Latino (of any race)	152,243	81.8
Central American, ex. Mexican	12,862	74.1
Costa Rican	1,031	93.3
Guatemalan	6,249	71.3
Honduran	1,902	78.3
Nicaraguan	396	89.6
Panamanian	543	90.0
Salvadoran	2,520	66.5
Cuban	3,571	85.8
Dominican Republic	7,445	78.3
Mexican	14,456	71.8
Puerto Rican	74,938	84.5
South American	30,438	84.3
Argentinean	1,569	84.0
Chilean	763	86.2
Colombian	9,144	86.5
Ecuadorian	10,065	80.4
Peruvian	7,070	86.0
Venezuelan	875	90.4
Spaniard	2,331	84.1

Means of Transportation to Work: Public Transportation (ex. Taxicab)
(Universe: Workers 16 Years and Over)

Group	Number	%
Total Population	76,305	4.4
Hispanic or Latino (of any race)	15,357	8.3
Central American, ex. Mexican	1,990	11.5
Costa Rican	9	0.8
Guatemalan	1,232	14.1
Honduran	197	8.1
Nicaraguan	14	3.2
Panamanian	30	5.0
Salvadoran	492	13.0
Cuban	225	5.4
Dominican Republic	651	6.8
Mexican	2,690	13.4

Notes: (1) Percent of total population; (2) Percent of Hispanic/Latino population; Profiles include places with an overall population of at least 125,000, OR an overall population of at least 25,000 where the Hispanic/Latino population is at least 20% of the overall population. In states where less than five places meet either of these criteria, we have included places with at least 10,000 total population with the highest percentage of Hispanic/Latino population. These places are identified with an asterisk (*); Please refer to the User's Guide for a full explanation of data.

Puerto Rican	6,530	7.4
South American	2,614	7.2
Argentinean	114	6.1
Chilean	40	4.5
Colombian	749	7.1
Ecuadorian	1,009	8.1
Peruvian	617	7.5
Venezuelan	60	6.2
Spaniard	225	8.1

Homeownership Rate
(Universe: Occupied Housing Units)

Group	%
Total Population	67.5
Hispanic or Latino (of any race)	33.2
Central American, ex. Mexican	31.9
Costa Rican	42.7
Guatemalan	25.1
Honduran	28.6
Nicaraguan	37.0
Panamanian	50.7
Salvadoran	38.5
Cuban	58.8
Dominican Republic	33.0
Mexican	28.3
Puerto Rican	28.3
South American	47.0
Argentinean	63.2
Bolivian	50.5
Chilean	53.0
Colombian	49.3
Ecuadorian	39.5
Paraguayan	50.4
Peruvian	48.5
Uruguayan	44.7
Venezuelan	47.7
Spaniard	69.3

Median Home Value

Group	Dollars
Total Population	296,500
Hispanic or Latino (of any race)	245,400
Central American, ex. Mexican	297,500
Costa Rican	318,800
Guatemalan	346,600
Honduran	219,500
Nicaraguan	352,400
Panamanian	327,000
Salvadoran	253,600
Cuban	346,100
Dominican Republic	245,400
Mexican	250,600
Puerto Rican	215,400
South American	294,700
Argentinean	355,900
Chilean	392,900
Colombian	292,400
Ecuadorian	291,100
Peruvian	282,300
Venezuelan	264,000
Spaniard	328,300

Median Gross Rent

Group	Dollars
Total Population	982
Hispanic or Latino (of any race)	948
Central American, ex. Mexican	1,223
Costa Rican	1,197
Guatemalan	1,398
Honduran	1,139
Nicaraguan	1,194
Panamanian	767
Salvadoran	966
Cuban	961
Dominican Republic	988
Mexican	1,121
Puerto Rican	863
South American	1,136
Argentinean	1,180
Chilean	923
Colombian	1,034
Ecuadorian	1,218
Peruvian	1,098
Venezuelan	1,301
Spaniard	1,099

Median Household Income
(2010 Inflation-Adjusted Dollars)

Group	Dollars
Total Population	67,740
Hispanic or Latino (of any race)	39,536
Central American, ex. Mexican	50,771
Costa Rican	62,500
Guatemalan	47,048
Honduran	44,222
Nicaraguan	70,000
Panamanian	74,485
Salvadoran	56,198
Cuban	65,476
Dominican Republic	36,160
Mexican	44,940
Puerto Rican	31,486
South American	53,615
Argentinean	102,386
Chilean	76,903
Colombian	50,401
Ecuadorian	49,903
Peruvian	49,931
Venezuelan	60,724
Spaniard	71,250

Per Capita Income
(2010 Inflation-Adjusted Dollars)

Group	Dollars
Total Population	36,775
Hispanic or Latino (of any race)	17,752
Central American, ex. Mexican	17,779
Costa Rican	19,474
Guatemalan	15,412
Honduran	16,859
Nicaraguan	32,240
Panamanian	33,343
Salvadoran	18,654
Cuban	32,117
Dominican Republic	16,557
Mexican	17,190
Puerto Rican	15,229
South American	22,800
Argentinean	49,985
Chilean	41,280
Colombian	22,311
Ecuadorian	17,765
Peruvian	21,568
Venezuelan	24,073
Spaniard	43,980

Households with $100,000+ Income

Group	Number	%
Total Population	429,842	31.6
Hispanic or Latino (of any race)	18,689	14.0
Central American, ex. Mexican	1,260	15.5
Costa Rican	63	8.9
Guatemalan	485	12.8
Honduran	229	16.0
Nicaraguan	85	40.9
Panamanian	134	39.3
Salvadoran	250	16.7
Cuban	1,078	35.6
Dominican Republic	816	12.0
Mexican	1,659	14.7
Puerto Rican	7,764	9.9
South American	3,973	20.3
Argentinean	685	51.6
Chilean	146	34.4
Colombian	1,069	17.7
Ecuadorian	812	13.4
Peruvian	828	18.9
Venezuelan	191	29.5
Spaniard	917	39.7

Households with Food Stamps/SNAP Benefits During Past 12 Months

Group	Number	%
Total Population	98,180	7.2
Hispanic or Latino (of any race)	34,169	25.5
Central American, ex. Mexican	782	9.6
Costa Rican	58	8.2
Guatemalan	294	7.7
Honduran	210	14.7
Nicaraguan	0	0.0
Panamanian	24	7.0
Salvadoran	184	12.3
Cuban	326	10.8
Dominican Republic	1,783	26.2
Mexican	1,080	9.6
Puerto Rican	28,065	35.9
South American	1,460	7.5
Argentinean	42	3.2
Chilean	0	0.0
Colombian	603	10.0
Ecuadorian	463	7.7
Peruvian	315	7.2
Venezuelan	15	2.3
Spaniard	183	7.9

Poverty Rate
(Income in Past 12 Months Below Poverty Level)

Group	%
Total Population	9.2
Hispanic or Latino (of any race)	24.4
Central American, ex. Mexican	20.5
Costa Rican	14.3
Guatemalan	23.1
Honduran	27.1
Nicaraguan	2.5
Panamanian	11.6
Salvadoran	15.6
Cuban	8.3
Dominican Republic	24.9
Mexican	23.8
Puerto Rican	30.5
South American	10.3
Argentinean	6.1
Chilean	3.9
Colombian	8.1
Ecuadorian	13.9
Peruvian	10.5
Venezuelan	3.6
Spaniard	5.8

Bridgeport

Population

Group	Number	%TP[1]	%HP[2]
Total Population	144,229	100.0	–
Hispanic or Latino (of any race)	55,100	38.2	100.0
Central American, ex. Mexican	4,451	3.1	8.1
Costa Rican	478	0.3	0.9
Guatemalan	1,310	0.9	2.4
Honduran	999	0.7	1.8
Nicaraguan	305	0.2	0.6
Salvadoran	1,230	0.9	2.2
Cuban	935	0.6	1.7
Dominican Republic	2,429	1.7	4.4
Mexican	7,205	5.0	13.1
Puerto Rican	31,881	22.1	57.9
South American	5,531	3.8	10.0
Argentinean	117	0.1	0.2
Chilean	107	0.1	0.2
Colombian	1,948	1.4	3.5
Ecuadorian	1,950	1.4	3.5
Peruvian	1,017	0.7	1.8
Uruguayan	110	0.1	0.2
Venezuelan	172	0.1	0.3
Spaniard	183	0.1	0.3

Population Growth: 2000–2010

Group	%
Total Population	3.4
Hispanic or Latino (of any race)	23.9
Central American, ex. Mexican	208.5
Costa Rican	94.3
Guatemalan	356.4
Honduran	200.9
Salvadoran	222.0
Cuban	-5.9
Dominican Republic	174.2
Mexican	168.1
Puerto Rican	-0.9
South American	177.1
Colombian	129.2
Ecuadorian	333.3
Peruvian	211.0

Notes: (1) Percent of total population; (2) Percent of Hispanic/Latino population; Profiles include places with an overall population of at least 125,000, OR an overall population of at least 25,000 where the Hispanic/Latino population is at least 20% of the overall population. In states where less than five places meet either of these criteria, we have included places with at least 10,000 total population with the highest percentage of Hispanic/Latino population. These places are identified with an asterisk (*); Please refer to the User's Guide for a full explanation of data.

Males per 100 Females

Group	Number
Total Population	94.3
Hispanic or Latino (of any race)	100.1
Central American, ex. Mexican	127.6
Costa Rican	118.3
Guatemalan	149.5
Honduran	120.0
Nicaraguan	156.3
Salvadoran	113.2
Cuban	94.4
Dominican Republic	83.3
Mexican	142.3
Puerto Rican	88.6
South American	107.1
Argentinean	108.9
Chilean	143.2
Colombian	91.7
Ecuadorian	128.9
Peruvian	96.3
Uruguayan	161.9
Venezuelan	100.0
Spaniard	105.6

Average Household Size

Group	People
Total Population	2.72
Hispanic or Latino (of any race)	3.24
Central American, ex. Mexican	3.95
Costa Rican	3.04
Guatemalan	4.14
Honduran	4.13
Nicaraguan	4.47
Salvadoran	4.01
Cuban	2.57
Dominican Republic	3.55
Mexican	4.78
Puerto Rican	2.91
South American	3.57
Argentinean	2.38
Chilean	3.28
Colombian	3.33
Ecuadorian	4.02
Peruvian	3.65
Uruguayan	3.03
Venezuelan	3.27
Spaniard	2.26

Median Age

Group	Years
Total Population	32.6
Hispanic or Latino (of any race)	28.6
Central American, ex. Mexican	30.5
Costa Rican	34.1
Guatemalan	29.5
Honduran	31.6
Nicaraguan	29.2
Salvadoran	29.7
Cuban	40.5
Dominican Republic	28.1
Mexican	25.5
Puerto Rican	28.6
South American	33.8
Argentinean	36.5
Chilean	38.6
Colombian	36.5
Ecuadorian	31.1
Peruvian	34.2
Uruguayan	35.7
Venezuelan	31.6
Spaniard	36.9

High School Graduates
(Universe: Population 25 Years and Over)

Group	Number	%
Total Population	64,657	73.5
Hispanic or Latino (of any race)	17,245	60.7
Central American, ex. Mexican	971	50.4
Salvadoran	182	37.2
Cuban	562	65.9
Dominican Republic	661	60.9
Mexican	1,317	46.0
Puerto Rican	10,431	59.3
South American	2,754	79.8
Colombian	1,000	77.2
Ecuadorian	871	74.6
Peruvian	506	88.8

Four-Year College Graduates
(Universe: Population 25 Years and Over)

Group	Number	%
Total Population	13,936	15.8
Hispanic or Latino (of any race)	1,975	6.9
Central American, ex. Mexican	144	7.5
Salvadoran	30	6.1
Cuban	205	24.0
Dominican Republic	89	8.2
Mexican	221	7.7
Puerto Rican	705	4.0
South American	437	12.7
Colombian	141	10.9
Ecuadorian	27	2.3
Peruvian	155	27.2

Population Age 3–17 Enrolled in Public School
(Universe: Population Age 3–17 Enrolled in School)

Group	Number	%
Total Population	24,676	87.3
Hispanic or Latino (of any race)	11,094	91.3
Central American, ex. Mexican	456	100.0
Salvadoran	42	100.0
Cuban	131	86.2
Dominican Republic	400	93.2
Mexican	1,330	96.0
Puerto Rican	7,220	89.6
South American	1,142	96.4
Colombian	317	92.4
Ecuadorian	434	98.4
Peruvian	184	94.8

Population Age 3–17 Enrolled in Private School
(Universe: Population Age 3–17 Enrolled in School)

Group	Number	%
Total Population	3,583	12.7
Hispanic or Latino (of any race)	1,058	8.7
Central American, ex. Mexican	0	0.0
Salvadoran	0	0.0
Cuban	21	13.8
Dominican Republic	29	6.8
Mexican	56	4.0
Puerto Rican	840	10.4
South American	43	3.6
Colombian	26	7.6
Ecuadorian	7	1.6
Peruvian	10	5.2

Foreign-Born Population

Group	Number	%
Total Population	37,874	26.6
Hispanic or Latino (of any race)	12,620	25.0
Central American, ex. Mexican	2,553	75.2
Salvadoran	692	86.5
Cuban	624	52.2
Dominican Republic	1,001	53.0
Mexican	3,814	67.6
Puerto Rican	469	1.5
South American	3,768	68.6
Colombian	1,368	65.8
Ecuadorian	1,314	69.9
Peruvian	579	65.1

Foreign-Born Naturalized U.S. Citizens

Group	Number	%
Total Population	13,560	35.8
Hispanic or Latino (of any race)	3,119	24.7
Central American, ex. Mexican	407	15.9
Salvadoran	158	22.8
Cuban	452	72.4
Dominican Republic	439	43.9
Mexican	331	8.7
Puerto Rican	237	50.5
South American	1,086	28.8
Colombian	514	37.6
Ecuadorian	312	23.7
Peruvian	167	28.8

Language Spoken at Home: English Only
(Universe: Population 5 Years and Over)

Group	Number	%
Total Population	72,135	54.4
Hispanic or Latino (of any race)	7,680	16.6
Central American, ex. Mexican	197	6.5
Salvadoran	19	2.6
Cuban	278	24.2
Dominican Republic	163	9.8
Mexican	318	6.2
Puerto Rican	6,088	21.0
South American	320	6.4
Colombian	61	3.2
Ecuadorian	81	4.8
Peruvian	54	6.9

Language Spoken at Home: Spanish
(Universe: Population 5 Years and Over)

Group	Number	%
Total Population	39,766	30.0
Hispanic or Latino (of any race)	38,010	82.3
Central American, ex. Mexican	2,819	93.0
Salvadoran	713	97.4
Cuban	807	70.2
Dominican Republic	1,502	90.2
Mexican	4,746	93.2
Puerto Rican	22,767	78.6
South American	4,556	90.5
Colombian	1,871	96.8
Ecuadorian	1,614	95.2
Peruvian	577	73.4

Unemployment Rate
(Universe: Population 16 Years and Over)

Group	%
Total Population	12.4
Hispanic or Latino (of any race)	12.8
Central American, ex. Mexican	11.4
Salvadoran	7.6
Cuban	11.9
Dominican Republic	17.8
Mexican	9.7
Puerto Rican	14.8
South American	7.4
Colombian	3.8
Ecuadorian	12.3
Peruvian	6.7

Class of Worker: Private Wage and Salary
(Universe: Civilian Employed Population 16 Years and Over)

Group	Number	%
Total Population	53,058	83.3
Hispanic or Latino (of any race)	17,117	84.2
Central American, ex. Mexican	1,386	80.8
Salvadoran	387	85.8
Cuban	416	87.6
Dominican Republic	719	84.9
Mexican	2,079	81.2
Puerto Rican	10,014	86.6
South American	2,189	83.0
Colombian	797	75.8
Ecuadorian	762	89.2
Peruvian	370	85.1

Class of Worker: Government
(Universe: Civilian Employed Population 16 Years and Over)

Group	Number	%
Total Population	6,345	10.0
Hispanic or Latino (of any race)	1,818	8.9
Central American, ex. Mexican	34	2.0
Salvadoran	0	0.0
Cuban	59	12.4
Dominican Republic	109	12.9
Mexican	69	2.7
Puerto Rican	1,343	11.6
South American	111	4.2
Colombian	27	2.6
Ecuadorian	46	5.4
Peruvian	38	8.7

Means of Transportation to Work: Car, Truck or Van
(Universe: Workers 16 Years and Over)

Group	Number	%
Total Population	49,497	79.7
Hispanic or Latino (of any race)	15,794	79.9
Central American, ex. Mexican	1,355	81.0
Salvadoran	355	82.6
Cuban	435	95.8

Notes: (1) Percent of total population; (2) Percent of Hispanic/Latino population; Profiles include places with an overall population of at least 125,000, OR an overall population of at least 25,000 where the Hispanic/Latino population is at least 20% of the overall population. In states where less than five places meet either of these criteria, we have included places with at least 10,000 total population with the highest percentage of Hispanic/Latino population. These places are identified with an asterisk (*); Please refer to the User's Guide for a full explanation of data.

Dominican Republic	391	53.7
Mexican	1,241	51.8
Puerto Rican	9,646	84.4
South American	2,345	90.7
Colombian	936	90.6
Ecuadorian	750	89.5
Peruvian	379	87.1

Means of Transportation to Work: Public Transportation (ex. Taxicab)
(Universe: Workers 16 Years and Over)

Group	Number	%
Total Population	7,749	12.5
Hispanic or Latino (of any race)	2,423	12.3
Central American, ex. Mexican	132	7.9
Salvadoran	29	6.7
Cuban	19	4.2
Dominican Republic	194	26.6
Mexican	859	35.9
Puerto Rican	1,039	9.1
South American	136	5.3
Colombian	40	3.9
Ecuadorian	69	8.2
Peruvian	27	6.2

Homeownership Rate
(Universe: Occupied Housing Units)

Group	%
Total Population	42.6
Hispanic or Latino (of any race)	30.9
Central American, ex. Mexican	39.8
Costa Rican	51.7
Guatemalan	41.8
Honduran	34.6
Nicaraguan	28.8
Salvadoran	38.7
Cuban	46.6
Dominican Republic	33.0
Mexican	20.3
Puerto Rican	27.3
South American	51.8
Argentinean	50.0
Chilean	62.5
Colombian	56.3
Ecuadorian	45.3
Peruvian	57.3
Uruguayan	39.5
Venezuelan	31.1
Spaniard	54.3

Median Home Value

Group	Dollars
Total Population	236,000
Hispanic or Latino (of any race)	235,800
Central American, ex. Mexican	257,900
Salvadoran	205,300
Cuban	191,000
Dominican Republic	269,400
Mexican	262,500
Puerto Rican	222,200
South American	286,000
Colombian	275,000
Ecuadorian	320,100
Peruvian	319,600

Median Gross Rent

Group	Dollars
Total Population	996
Hispanic or Latino (of any race)	1,003
Central American, ex. Mexican	1,002
Salvadoran	810
Cuban	1,256
Dominican Republic	1,094
Mexican	1,208
Puerto Rican	934
South American	1,144
Colombian	839
Ecuadorian	1,183
Peruvian	1,182

Median Household Income
(2010 Inflation-Adjusted Dollars)

Group	Dollars
Total Population	41,047
Hispanic or Latino (of any race)	33,455
Central American, ex. Mexican	41,216
Salvadoran	50,875
Cuban	36,875
Dominican Republic	51,250
Mexican	42,565
Puerto Rican	27,342
South American	44,212
Colombian	45,721
Ecuadorian	46,250
Peruvian	43,492

Per Capita Income
(2010 Inflation-Adjusted Dollars)

Group	Dollars
Total Population	19,854
Hispanic or Latino (of any race)	15,189
Central American, ex. Mexican	14,901
Salvadoran	15,582
Cuban	22,221
Dominican Republic	18,494
Mexican	12,382
Puerto Rican	14,648
South American	17,860
Colombian	16,188
Ecuadorian	17,111
Peruvian	22,099

Households with $100,000+ Income

Group	Number	%
Total Population	6,734	12.9
Hispanic or Latino (of any race)	1,638	9.9
Central American, ex. Mexican	107	11.3
Salvadoran	60	25.5
Cuban	73	15.1
Dominican Republic	160	28.5
Mexican	64	5.0
Puerto Rican	1,041	9.0
South American	113	7.5
Colombian	54	9.7
Ecuadorian	9	1.8
Peruvian	24	7.8

Households with Food Stamps/SNAP Benefits During Past 12 Months

Group	Number	%
Total Population	9,320	17.8
Hispanic or Latino (of any race)	4,477	26.9
Central American, ex. Mexican	144	15.2
Salvadoran	44	18.7
Cuban	60	12.4
Dominican Republic	174	31.0
Mexican	93	7.2
Puerto Rican	3,921	34.0
South American	52	3.5
Colombian	6	1.1
Ecuadorian	23	4.7
Peruvian	23	7.4

Poverty Rate
(Income in Past 12 Months Below Poverty Level)

Group	%
Total Population	20.8
Hispanic or Latino (of any race)	25.8
Central American, ex. Mexican	32.3
Salvadoran	36.9
Cuban	17.7
Dominican Republic	34.3
Mexican	24.0
Puerto Rican	28.9
South American	6.4
Colombian	8.1
Ecuadorian	3.5
Peruvian	13.3

Danbury

Population

Group	Number	%TP[1]	%HP[2]
Total Population	80,893	100.0	–
Hispanic or Latino (of any race)	20,185	25.0	100.0
Central American, ex. Mexican	1,840	2.3	9.1
Guatemalan	1,036	1.3	5.1
Honduran	168	0.2	0.8
Nicaraguan	239	0.3	1.2
Salvadoran	259	0.3	1.3
Cuban	167	0.2	0.8
Dominican Republic	3,852	4.8	19.1
Mexican	2,102	2.6	10.4
Puerto Rican	2,513	3.1	12.4
South American	7,674	9.5	38.0
Colombian	736	0.9	3.6
Ecuadorian	6,125	7.6	30.3
Peruvian	510	0.6	2.5
Spaniard	142	0.2	0.7

Population Growth: 2000–2010

Group	%
Total Population	8.1
Hispanic or Latino (of any race)	71.2
Central American, ex. Mexican	131.4
Guatemalan	224.8
Nicaraguan	35.0
Salvadoran	99.2
Cuban	21.0
Dominican Republic	89.5
Mexican	62.4
Puerto Rican	38.2
South American	151.7
Colombian	49.9
Ecuadorian	180.6
Peruvian	115.2

Males per 100 Females

Group	Number
Total Population	96.4
Hispanic or Latino (of any race)	111.5
Central American, ex. Mexican	135.0
Guatemalan	174.8
Honduran	104.9
Nicaraguan	81.1
Salvadoran	110.6
Cuban	77.7
Dominican Republic	88.4
Mexican	94.8
Puerto Rican	92.3
South American	132.6
Colombian	74.4
Ecuadorian	151.4
Peruvian	75.3
Spaniard	108.8

Average Household Size

Group	People
Total Population	2.66
Hispanic or Latino (of any race)	3.83
Central American, ex. Mexican	4.02
Guatemalan	4.27
Honduran	4.25
Nicaraguan	3.80
Salvadoran	3.88
Cuban	2.31
Dominican Republic	3.74
Mexican	3.88
Puerto Rican	2.86
South American	4.31
Colombian	3.17
Ecuadorian	4.62
Peruvian	3.47
Spaniard	2.52

Median Age

Group	Years
Total Population	36.2
Hispanic or Latino (of any race)	29.1
Central American, ex. Mexican	29.0
Guatemalan	28.5
Honduran	29.1
Nicaraguan	30.1
Salvadoran	31.9
Cuban	35.5
Dominican Republic	29.1
Mexican	30.5
Puerto Rican	28.0
South American	30.4
Colombian	36.4
Ecuadorian	29.6
Peruvian	36.4
Spaniard	32.7

STATE & PLACE PROFILES

Notes: (1) Percent of total population; (2) Percent of Hispanic/Latino population; Profiles include places with an overall population of at least 125,000, OR an overall population of at least 25,000 where the Hispanic/Latino population is at least 20% of the overall population. In states where less than five places meet either of these criteria, we have included places with at least 10,000 total population with the highest percentage of Hispanic/Latino population. These places are identified with an asterisk (*); Please refer to the User's Guide for a full explanation of data.

High School Graduates
(Universe: Population 25 Years and Over)

Group	Number	%
Total Population	44,829	82.4
Hispanic or Latino (of any race)	6,810	61.5
Central American, ex. Mexican	358	62.2
Dominican Republic	962	57.1
Mexican	686	66.5
Puerto Rican	1,391	70.5
South American	2,907	58.0
Ecuadorian	2,373	54.6

Four-Year College Graduates
(Universe: Population 25 Years and Over)

Group	Number	%
Total Population	16,698	30.7
Hispanic or Latino (of any race)	1,353	12.2
Central American, ex. Mexican	35	6.1
Dominican Republic	205	12.2
Mexican	91	8.8
Puerto Rican	204	10.3
South American	652	13.0
Ecuadorian	416	9.6

Population Age 3–17 Enrolled in Public School
(Universe: Population Age 3–17 Enrolled in School)

Group	Number	%
Total Population	10,609	85.7
Hispanic or Latino (of any race)	3,052	91.7
Central American, ex. Mexican	63	100.0
Dominican Republic	722	90.1
Mexican	206	92.4
Puerto Rican	705	98.7
South American	984	85.2
Ecuadorian	746	83.8

Population Age 3–17 Enrolled in Private School
(Universe: Population Age 3–17 Enrolled in School)

Group	Number	%
Total Population	1,768	14.3
Hispanic or Latino (of any race)	276	8.3
Central American, ex. Mexican	0	0.0
Dominican Republic	79	9.9
Mexican	17	7.6
Puerto Rican	9	1.3
South American	171	14.8
Ecuadorian	144	16.2

Foreign-Born Population

Group	Number	%
Total Population	23,764	29.9
Hispanic or Latino (of any race)	10,489	56.1
Central American, ex. Mexican	740	80.8
Dominican Republic	2,045	62.8
Mexican	1,005	63.3
Puerto Rican	46	1.3
South American	5,917	74.8
Ecuadorian	5,288	78.0

Foreign-Born Naturalized U.S. Citizens

Group	Number	%
Total Population	7,495	31.5
Hispanic or Latino (of any race)	1,918	18.3
Central American, ex. Mexican	111	15.0
Dominican Republic	772	37.8
Mexican	47	4.7
Puerto Rican	0	0.0
South American	796	13.5
Ecuadorian	635	12.0

Language Spoken at Home: English Only
(Universe: Population 5 Years and Over)

Group	Number	%
Total Population	45,164	61.3
Hispanic or Latino (of any race)	2,398	14.4
Central American, ex. Mexican	32	3.9
Dominican Republic	55	1.9
Mexican	255	17.7
Puerto Rican	1,220	38.8
South American	493	7.1
Ecuadorian	264	4.4

Language Spoken at Home: Spanish
(Universe: Population 5 Years and Over)

Group	Number	%
Total Population	14,682	19.9
Hispanic or Latino (of any race)	13,919	83.9
Central American, ex. Mexican	794	96.1
Dominican Republic	2,786	98.1
Mexican	1,155	80.3
Puerto Rican	1,899	60.4
South American	6,476	92.9
Ecuadorian	5,750	95.6

Unemployment Rate
(Universe: Population 16 Years and Over)

Group	%
Total Population	6.9
Hispanic or Latino (of any race)	7.9
Central American, ex. Mexican	2.0
Dominican Republic	7.1
Mexican	3.6
Puerto Rican	13.8
South American	5.4
Ecuadorian	5.8

Class of Worker: Private Wage and Salary
(Universe: Civilian Employed Population 16 Years and Over)

Group	Number	%
Total Population	34,695	82.0
Hispanic or Latino (of any race)	8,340	87.0
Central American, ex. Mexican	552	87.5
Dominican Republic	1,269	91.0
Mexican	746	92.6
Puerto Rican	1,328	82.5
South American	3,994	87.6
Ecuadorian	3,534	86.5

Class of Worker: Government
(Universe: Civilian Employed Population 16 Years and Over)

Group	Number	%
Total Population	4,143	9.8
Hispanic or Latino (of any race)	452	4.7
Central American, ex. Mexican	0	0.0
Dominican Republic	86	6.2
Mexican	0	0.0
Puerto Rican	228	14.2
South American	68	1.5
Ecuadorian	55	1.3

Means of Transportation to Work: Car, Truck or Van
(Universe: Workers 16 Years and Over)

Group	Number	%
Total Population	35,450	86.0
Hispanic or Latino (of any race)	7,330	77.8
Central American, ex. Mexican	345	58.7
Dominican Republic	1,155	83.9
Mexican	587	74.5
Puerto Rican	1,340	84.0
South American	3,386	74.8
Ecuadorian	2,973	73.1

Means of Transportation to Work: Public Transportation (ex. Taxicab)
(Universe: Workers 16 Years and Over)

Group	Number	%
Total Population	1,405	3.4
Hispanic or Latino (of any race)	648	6.9
Central American, ex. Mexican	0	0.0
Dominican Republic	8	0.6
Mexican	129	16.4
Puerto Rican	180	11.3
South American	331	7.3
Ecuadorian	294	7.2

Homeownership Rate
(Universe: Occupied Housing Units)

Group	%
Total Population	60.7
Hispanic or Latino (of any race)	34.3
Central American, ex. Mexican	29.0
Guatemalan	21.3
Honduran	30.0
Nicaraguan	23.7
Salvadoran	50.7
Cuban	59.0
Dominican Republic	33.9
Mexican	27.0
Puerto Rican	39.7
South American	33.9
Colombian	51.5
Ecuadorian	29.2
Peruvian	44.0
Spaniard	63.0

Median Home Value

Group	Dollars
Total Population	342,200
Hispanic or Latino (of any race)	306,900
Central American, ex. Mexican	458,800
Dominican Republic	317,900
Mexican	279,600
Puerto Rican	260,900
South American	300,500
Ecuadorian	317,200

Median Gross Rent

Group	Dollars
Total Population	1,195
Hispanic or Latino (of any race)	1,284
Central American, ex. Mexican	1,236
Dominican Republic	934
Mexican	1,409
Puerto Rican	1,074
South American	1,376
Ecuadorian	1,400

Median Household Income
(2010 Inflation-Adjusted Dollars)

Group	Dollars
Total Population	65,275
Hispanic or Latino (of any race)	48,707
Central American, ex. Mexican	22,176
Dominican Republic	42,228
Mexican	51,290
Puerto Rican	37,689
South American	58,273
Ecuadorian	58,647

Per Capita Income
(2010 Inflation-Adjusted Dollars)

Group	Dollars
Total Population	31,461
Hispanic or Latino (of any race)	17,805
Central American, ex. Mexican	16,191
Dominican Republic	22,779
Mexican	13,011
Puerto Rican	17,339
South American	17,161
Ecuadorian	17,369

Households with $100,000+ Income

Group	Number	%
Total Population	8,196	27.7
Hispanic or Latino (of any race)	641	12.3
Central American, ex. Mexican	24	7.7
Dominican Republic	79	8.0
Mexican	60	16.9
Puerto Rican	73	6.1
South American	342	17.6
Ecuadorian	299	18.7

Households with Food Stamps/SNAP Benefits During Past 12 Months

Group	Number	%
Total Population	1,621	5.5
Hispanic or Latino (of any race)	501	9.6
Central American, ex. Mexican	12	3.9
Dominican Republic	139	14.1
Mexican	19	5.4
Puerto Rican	203	16.9
South American	42	2.2
Ecuadorian	42	2.6

Poverty Rate
(Income in Past 12 Months Below Poverty Level)

Group	%
Total Population	8.4
Hispanic or Latino (of any race)	15.9
Central American, ex. Mexican	25.5
Dominican Republic	25.0

Notes: (1) Percent of total population; (2) Percent of Hispanic/Latino population; Profiles include places with an overall population of at least 125,000, OR an overall population of at least 25,000 where the Hispanic/Latino population is at least 20% of the overall population. In states where less than five places meet either of these criteria, we have included places with at least 10,000 total population with the highest percentage of Hispanic/Latino population. These places are identified with an asterisk (*); Please refer to the User's Guide for a full explanation of data.

Mexican	10.0
Puerto Rican	12.6
South American	13.3
Ecuadorian	14.1

East Hartford

Population

Group	Number	%TP[1]	%HP[2]
Total Population	51,252	100.0	–
Hispanic or Latino (of any race)	13,232	25.8	100.0
Central American, ex. Mexican	809	1.6	6.1
Honduran	185	0.4	1.4
Salvadoran	504	1.0	3.8
Cuban	156	0.3	1.2
Dominican Republic	418	0.8	3.2
Mexican	568	1.1	4.3
Puerto Rican	8,903	17.4	67.3
South American	1,675	3.3	12.7
Colombian	410	0.8	3.1
Peruvian	962	1.9	7.3

Population Growth: 2000–2010

Group	%
Total Population	3.4
Hispanic or Latino (of any race)	75.2
Central American, ex. Mexican	266.1
Salvadoran	281.8
Cuban	41.8
Dominican Republic	205.1
Mexican	119.3
Puerto Rican	73.9
South American	121.3
Colombian	67.3
Peruvian	154.5

Males per 100 Females

Group	Number
Total Population	92.0
Hispanic or Latino (of any race)	93.1
Central American, ex. Mexican	141.5
Honduran	137.2
Salvadoran	150.7
Cuban	113.7
Dominican Republic	74.9
Mexican	125.4
Puerto Rican	88.5
South American	90.8
Colombian	82.2
Peruvian	93.2

Average Household Size

Group	People
Total Population	2.50
Hispanic or Latino (of any race)	3.21
Central American, ex. Mexican	4.13
Honduran	4.64
Salvadoran	4.19
Cuban	2.60
Dominican Republic	3.44
Mexican	3.79
Puerto Rican	3.09
South American	3.32
Colombian	2.91
Peruvian	3.47

Median Age

Group	Years
Total Population	37.8
Hispanic or Latino (of any race)	27.0
Central American, ex. Mexican	27.4
Honduran	28.1
Salvadoran	27.1
Cuban	35.8
Dominican Republic	27.3
Mexican	26.4
Puerto Rican	25.4
South American	36.7
Colombian	37.0
Peruvian	37.6

High School Graduates
(Universe: Population 25 Years and Over)

Group	Number	%
Total Population	28,564	82.6
Hispanic or Latino (of any race)	4,743	69.9
Puerto Rican	3,393	71.9
South American	768	81.1

Four-Year College Graduates
(Universe: Population 25 Years and Over)

Group	Number	%
Total Population	6,206	18.0
Hispanic or Latino (of any race)	497	7.3
Puerto Rican	303	6.4
South American	72	7.6

Population Age 3–17 Enrolled in Public School
(Universe: Population Age 3–17 Enrolled in School)

Group	Number	%
Total Population	8,840	91.0
Hispanic or Latino (of any race)	3,981	96.9
Puerto Rican	3,244	98.8
South American	282	91.9

Population Age 3–17 Enrolled in Private School
(Universe: Population Age 3–17 Enrolled in School)

Group	Number	%
Total Population	874	9.0
Hispanic or Latino (of any race)	127	3.1
Puerto Rican	41	1.2
South American	25	8.1

Foreign-Born Population

Group	Number	%
Total Population	9,764	19.2
Hispanic or Latino (of any race)	2,275	17.1
Puerto Rican	59	0.6
South American	986	72.9

Foreign-Born Naturalized U.S. Citizens

Group	Number	%
Total Population	4,429	45.4
Hispanic or Latino (of any race)	693	30.5
Puerto Rican	11	18.6
South American	417	42.3

Language Spoken at Home: English Only
(Universe: Population 5 Years and Over)

Group	Number	%
Total Population	31,745	66.4
Hispanic or Latino (of any race)	2,846	23.6
Puerto Rican	2,594	28.9
South American	111	8.6

Language Spoken at Home: Spanish
(Universe: Population 5 Years and Over)

Group	Number	%
Total Population	9,697	20.3
Hispanic or Latino (of any race)	9,093	75.3
Puerto Rican	6,326	70.5
South American	1,180	91.4

Unemployment Rate
(Universe: Population 16 Years and Over)

Group	%
Total Population	10.7
Hispanic or Latino (of any race)	15.9
Puerto Rican	16.8
South American	7.3

Class of Worker: Private Wage and Salary
(Universe: Civilian Employed Population 16 Years and Over)

Group	Number	%
Total Population	20,658	84.8
Hispanic or Latino (of any race)	4,887	86.6
Puerto Rican	3,340	84.9
South American	736	90.9

Class of Worker: Government
(Universe: Civilian Employed Population 16 Years and Over)

Group	Number	%
Total Population	2,611	10.7
Hispanic or Latino (of any race)	542	9.6
Puerto Rican	458	11.6
South American	53	6.5

Means of Transportation to Work: Car, Truck or Van
(Universe: Workers 16 Years and Over)

Group	Number	%
Total Population	21,368	89.6
Hispanic or Latino (of any race)	4,821	87.3
Puerto Rican	3,452	88.7
South American	707	89.5

Means of Transportation to Work: Public Transportation (ex. Taxicab)
(Universe: Workers 16 Years and Over)

Group	Number	%
Total Population	1,414	5.9
Hispanic or Latino (of any race)	379	6.9
Puerto Rican	212	5.4
South American	61	7.7

Homeownership Rate
(Universe: Occupied Housing Units)

Group	%
Total Population	58.5
Hispanic or Latino (of any race)	39.6
Central American, ex. Mexican	30.5
Honduran	34.1
Salvadoran	26.9
Cuban	77.2
Dominican Republic	41.9
Mexican	33.3
Puerto Rican	36.6
South American	57.7
Colombian	65.0
Peruvian	57.4

Median Home Value

Group	Dollars
Total Population	193,000
Hispanic or Latino (of any race)	190,600
Puerto Rican	186,300
South American	215,700

Median Gross Rent

Group	Dollars
Total Population	865
Hispanic or Latino (of any race)	889
Puerto Rican	897
South American	665

Median Household Income
(2010 Inflation-Adjusted Dollars)

Group	Dollars
Total Population	48,613
Hispanic or Latino (of any race)	38,538
Puerto Rican	32,767
South American	47,500

Per Capita Income
(2010 Inflation-Adjusted Dollars)

Group	Dollars
Total Population	24,373
Hispanic or Latino (of any race)	14,854
Puerto Rican	13,569
South American	23,252

Households with $100,000+ Income

Group	Number	%
Total Population	2,988	14.8
Hispanic or Latino (of any race)	336	8.1
Puerto Rican	228	7.4
South American	76	17.2

Households with Food Stamps/SNAP Benefits During Past 12 Months

Group	Number	%
Total Population	2,694	13.3
Hispanic or Latino (of any race)	1,102	26.6
Puerto Rican	952	30.9
South American	0	0.0

Poverty Rate
(Income in Past 12 Months Below Poverty Level)

Group	%
Total Population	14.8
Hispanic or Latino (of any race)	24.0
Puerto Rican	26.6

Notes: (1) Percent of total population; (2) Percent of Hispanic/Latino population; Profiles include places with an overall population of at least 125,000, OR an overall population of at least 25,000 where the Hispanic/Latino population is at least 20% of the overall population. In states where less than five places meet either of these criteria, we have included places with at least 10,000 total population with the highest percentage of Hispanic/Latino population. These places are identified with an asterisk (*); Please refer to the User's Guide for a full explanation of data.

South American	13.6

Hartford

Population

Group	Number	%TP[1]	%HP[2]
Total Population	124,775	100.0	–
Hispanic or Latino (of any race)	54,185	43.4	100.0
Central American, ex. Mexican	1,124	0.9	2.1
Guatemalan	354	0.3	0.7
Honduran	307	0.2	0.6
Salvadoran	315	0.3	0.6
Cuban	661	0.5	1.2
Dominican Republic	2,191	1.8	4.0
Mexican	2,272	1.8	4.2
Puerto Rican	41,995	33.7	77.5
South American	3,773	3.0	7.0
Colombian	1,074	0.9	2.0
Ecuadorian	287	0.2	0.5
Peruvian	2,119	1.7	3.9
Spaniard	117	0.1	0.2

Population Growth: 2000–2010

Group	%
Total Population	2.6
Hispanic or Latino (of any race)	10.0
Central American, ex. Mexican	166.4
Honduran	160.2
Cuban	8.4
Dominican Republic	116.3
Mexican	128.8
Puerto Rican	6.1
South American	55.3
Colombian	29.6
Ecuadorian	87.6
Peruvian	79.0

Males per 100 Females

Group	Number
Total Population	93.4
Hispanic or Latino (of any race)	93.7
Central American, ex. Mexican	141.2
Guatemalan	170.2
Honduran	139.8
Salvadoran	126.6
Cuban	124.1
Dominican Republic	90.9
Mexican	152.7
Puerto Rican	87.8
South American	99.7
Colombian	79.6
Ecuadorian	143.2
Peruvian	104.9
Spaniard	101.7

Average Household Size

Group	People
Total Population	2.57
Hispanic or Latino (of any race)	2.95
Central American, ex. Mexican	3.54
Guatemalan	4.22
Honduran	3.59
Salvadoran	3.36
Cuban	2.19
Dominican Republic	3.11
Mexican	3.83
Puerto Rican	2.91
South American	2.97
Colombian	2.66
Ecuadorian	3.39
Peruvian	3.15
Spaniard	2.06

Median Age

Group	Years
Total Population	30.2
Hispanic or Latino (of any race)	27.7
Central American, ex. Mexican	27.7
Guatemalan	27.3
Honduran	27.2
Salvadoran	28.2
Cuban	40.1
Dominican Republic	28.9
Mexican	25.2
Puerto Rican	27.1
South American	36.7
Colombian	38.2
Ecuadorian	30.6
Peruvian	38.0
Spaniard	31.5

High School Graduates
(Universe: Population 25 Years and Over)

Group	Number	%
Total Population	49,547	67.9
Hispanic or Latino (of any race)	15,507	54.7
Central American, ex. Mexican	371	42.2
Dominican Republic	705	52.7
Mexican	403	42.3
Puerto Rican	11,300	52.0
South American	2,232	81.0
Colombian	729	70.5
Peruvian	1,421	88.0

Four-Year College Graduates
(Universe: Population 25 Years and Over)

Group	Number	%
Total Population	9,708	13.3
Hispanic or Latino (of any race)	1,963	6.9
Central American, ex. Mexican	47	5.3
Dominican Republic	129	9.6
Mexican	166	17.4
Puerto Rican	978	4.5
South American	536	19.4
Colombian	234	22.6
Peruvian	243	15.0

Population Age 3–17 Enrolled in Public School
(Universe: Population Age 3–17 Enrolled in School)

Group	Number	%
Total Population	24,710	93.0
Hispanic or Latino (of any race)	12,868	95.9
Central American, ex. Mexican	134	100.0
Dominican Republic	472	89.4
Mexican	330	94.3
Puerto Rican	11,069	96.5
South American	545	89.1
Colombian	225	100.0
Peruvian	282	80.8

Population Age 3–17 Enrolled in Private School
(Universe: Population Age 3–17 Enrolled in School)

Group	Number	%
Total Population	1,856	7.0
Hispanic or Latino (of any race)	552	4.1
Central American, ex. Mexican	0	0.0
Dominican Republic	56	10.6
Mexican	20	5.7
Puerto Rican	399	3.5
South American	67	10.9
Colombian	0	0.0
Peruvian	67	19.2

Foreign-Born Population

Group	Number	%
Total Population	26,774	21.5
Hispanic or Latino (of any race)	7,318	14.0
Central American, ex. Mexican	1,274	79.1
Dominican Republic	1,524	69.3
Mexican	1,013	50.1
Puerto Rican	222	0.5
South American	2,982	77.2
Colombian	1,024	73.4
Peruvian	1,789	81.2

Foreign-Born Naturalized U.S. Citizens

Group	Number	%
Total Population	9,985	37.3
Hispanic or Latino (of any race)	1,764	24.1
Central American, ex. Mexican	91	7.1
Dominican Republic	427	28.0
Mexican	216	21.3
Puerto Rican	140	63.1
South American	788	26.4
Colombian	211	20.6
Peruvian	510	28.5

Language Spoken at Home: English Only
(Universe: Population 5 Years and Over)

Group	Number	%
Total Population	60,545	52.3
Hispanic or Latino (of any race)	5,893	12.3
Central American, ex. Mexican	61	4.2
Dominican Republic	201	9.6
Mexican	429	24.1
Puerto Rican	4,562	12.1
South American	190	5.2
Colombian	125	9.1
Peruvian	65	3.2

Language Spoken at Home: Spanish
(Universe: Population 5 Years and Over)

Group	Number	%
Total Population	44,136	38.1
Hispanic or Latino (of any race)	41,838	87.4
Central American, ex. Mexican	1,376	95.8
Dominican Republic	1,900	90.4
Mexican	1,298	73.0
Puerto Rican	33,165	87.9
South American	3,414	93.9
Colombian	1,245	90.9
Peruvian	1,950	96.8

Unemployment Rate
(Universe: Population 16 Years and Over)

Group	%
Total Population	17.3
Hispanic or Latino (of any race)	21.2
Central American, ex. Mexican	18.0
Dominican Republic	18.4
Mexican	12.6
Puerto Rican	24.8
South American	4.8
Colombian	3.4
Peruvian	6.1

Class of Worker: Private Wage and Salary
(Universe: Civilian Employed Population 16 Years and Over)

Group	Number	%
Total Population	41,273	85.1
Hispanic or Latino (of any race)	16,444	88.5
Central American, ex. Mexican	937	93.8
Dominican Republic	1,043	97.1
Mexican	862	89.5
Puerto Rican	11,086	87.5
South American	2,025	87.5
Colombian	694	82.4
Peruvian	1,214	90.1

Class of Worker: Government
(Universe: Civilian Employed Population 16 Years and Over)

Group	Number	%
Total Population	5,532	11.4
Hispanic or Latino (of any race)	1,679	9.0
Central American, ex. Mexican	55	5.5
Dominican Republic	31	2.9
Mexican	35	3.6
Puerto Rican	1,361	10.7
South American	176	7.6
Colombian	109	12.9
Peruvian	59	4.4

Means of Transportation to Work: Car, Truck or Van
(Universe: Workers 16 Years and Over)

Group	Number	%
Total Population	32,649	70.0
Hispanic or Latino (of any race)	12,732	71.8
Central American, ex. Mexican	453	46.5
Dominican Republic	739	73.9
Mexican	686	74.2
Puerto Rican	8,650	71.7
South American	1,812	80.6
Colombian	614	73.8
Peruvian	1,100	85.2

Means of Transportation to Work: Public Transportation (ex. Taxicab)
(Universe: Workers 16 Years and Over)

Group	Number	%
Total Population	7,872	16.9
Hispanic or Latino (of any race)	2,820	15.9

Notes: (1) Percent of total population; (2) Percent of Hispanic/Latino population; Profiles include places with an overall population of at least 125,000, OR an overall population of at least 25,000 where the Hispanic/Latino population is at least 20% of the overall population. In states where less than five places meet either of these criteria, we have included places with at least 10,000 total population with the highest percentage of Hispanic/Latino population. These places are identified with an asterisk (*); Please refer to the User's Guide for a full explanation of data.

Central American, ex. Mexican	192	19.7
Dominican Republic	202	20.2
Mexican	99	10.7
Puerto Rican	2,021	16.8
South American	230	10.2
Colombian	92	11.1
Peruvian	111	8.6

Homeownership Rate
(Universe: Occupied Housing Units)

Group	%
Total Population	24.4
Hispanic or Latino (of any race)	15.5
Central American, ex. Mexican	19.5
Guatemalan	18.6
Honduran	20.0
Salvadoran	14.4
Cuban	21.4
Dominican Republic	19.3
Mexican	9.7
Puerto Rican	14.0
South American	29.9
Colombian	30.1
Ecuadorian	19.7
Peruvian	31.2
Spaniard	29.2

Median Home Value

Group	Dollars
Total Population	188,000
Hispanic or Latino (of any race)	187,400
Central American, ex. Mexican	142,100
Dominican Republic	208,500
Mexican	242,600
Puerto Rican	179,500
South American	218,500
Colombian	193,300
Peruvian	221,900

Median Gross Rent

Group	Dollars
Total Population	805
Hispanic or Latino (of any race)	760
Central American, ex. Mexican	945
Dominican Republic	830
Mexican	1,024
Puerto Rican	732
South American	897
Colombian	820
Peruvian	919

Median Household Income
(2010 Inflation-Adjusted Dollars)

Group	Dollars
Total Population	28,970
Hispanic or Latino (of any race)	22,885
Central American, ex. Mexican	50,463
Dominican Republic	22,981
Mexican	44,828
Puerto Rican	20,913
South American	37,663
Colombian	33,781
Peruvian	39,682

Per Capita Income
(2010 Inflation-Adjusted Dollars)

Group	Dollars
Total Population	16,798
Hispanic or Latino (of any race)	11,862
Central American, ex. Mexican	14,456
Dominican Republic	13,788
Mexican	14,455
Puerto Rican	10,897
South American	17,697
Colombian	18,031
Peruvian	17,203

Households with $100,000+ Income

Group	Number	%
Total Population	3,546	7.7
Hispanic or Latino (of any race)	764	4.3
Central American, ex. Mexican	63	18.9
Dominican Republic	64	8.5
Mexican	45	8.9
Puerto Rican	466	3.3
South American	65	4.8
Colombian	0	0.0
Peruvian	45	6.5

Households with Food Stamps/SNAP Benefits During Past 12 Months

Group	Number	%
Total Population	14,945	32.4
Hispanic or Latino (of any race)	8,344	47.3
Central American, ex. Mexican	135	40.4
Dominican Republic	182	24.1
Mexican	80	15.7
Puerto Rican	7,669	53.6
South American	160	11.8
Colombian	79	13.9
Peruvian	81	11.8

Poverty Rate
(Income in Past 12 Months Below Poverty Level)

Group	%
Total Population	32.1
Hispanic or Latino (of any race)	40.0
Central American, ex. Mexican	27.3
Dominican Republic	26.5
Mexican	27.8
Puerto Rican	44.4
South American	14.1
Colombian	6.7
Peruvian	19.5

Meriden

Population

Group	Number	%TP[1]	%HP[2]
Total Population	60,868	100.0	–
Hispanic or Latino (of any race)	17,590	28.9	100.0
Central American, ex. Mexican	303	0.5	1.7
Cuban	190	0.3	1.1
Dominican Republic	562	0.9	3.2
Mexican	2,385	3.9	13.6
Puerto Rican	12,572	20.7	71.5
South American	858	1.4	4.9
Colombian	191	0.3	1.1
Ecuadorian	470	0.8	2.7

Population Growth: 2000–2010

Group	%
Total Population	4.5
Hispanic or Latino (of any race)	43.1
Central American, ex. Mexican	116.4
Cuban	15.2
Dominican Republic	277.2
Mexican	151.6
Puerto Rican	30.5
South American	196.9
Ecuadorian	238.1

Males per 100 Females

Group	Number
Total Population	93.7
Hispanic or Latino (of any race)	94.3
Central American, ex. Mexican	96.8
Cuban	102.1
Dominican Republic	96.5
Mexican	112.0
Puerto Rican	90.1
South American	105.3
Colombian	80.2
Ecuadorian	124.9

Average Household Size

Group	People
Total Population	2.50
Hispanic or Latino (of any race)	3.11
Central American, ex. Mexican	3.46
Cuban	2.57
Dominican Republic	3.47
Mexican	4.26
Puerto Rican	2.94
South American	3.23
Colombian	2.88
Ecuadorian	3.56

Median Age

Group	Years
Total Population	37.7
Hispanic or Latino (of any race)	26.0
Central American, ex. Mexican	29.4
Cuban	30.5
Dominican Republic	25.6
Mexican	23.5
Puerto Rican	26.0
South American	31.5
Colombian	38.1
Ecuadorian	29.8

High School Graduates
(Universe: Population 25 Years and Over)

Group	Number	%
Total Population	33,313	81.5
Hispanic or Latino (of any race)	5,509	63.7
Mexican	346	33.9
Puerto Rican	3,987	68.2
South American	499	62.3

Four-Year College Graduates
(Universe: Population 25 Years and Over)

Group	Number	%
Total Population	7,912	19.4
Hispanic or Latino (of any race)	736	8.5
Mexican	14	1.4
Puerto Rican	474	8.1
South American	76	9.5

Population Age 3–17 Enrolled in Public School
(Universe: Population Age 3–17 Enrolled in School)

Group	Number	%
Total Population	10,446	89.7
Hispanic or Latino (of any race)	4,776	95.0
Mexican	646	97.1
Puerto Rican	3,537	95.0
South American	179	94.7

Population Age 3–17 Enrolled in Private School
(Universe: Population Age 3–17 Enrolled in School)

Group	Number	%
Total Population	1,203	10.3
Hispanic or Latino (of any race)	249	5.0
Mexican	19	2.9
Puerto Rican	186	5.0
South American	10	5.3

Foreign-Born Population

Group	Number	%
Total Population	6,583	10.9
Hispanic or Latino (of any race)	2,872	16.8
Mexican	1,061	44.5
Puerto Rican	89	0.8
South American	891	75.2

Foreign-Born Naturalized U.S. Citizens

Group	Number	%
Total Population	3,135	47.6
Hispanic or Latino (of any race)	1,202	41.9
Mexican	244	23.0
Puerto Rican	89	100.0
South American	338	37.9

Language Spoken at Home: English Only
(Universe: Population 5 Years and Over)

Group	Number	%
Total Population	40,023	70.1
Hispanic or Latino (of any race)	3,209	20.7
Mexican	243	12.4
Puerto Rican	2,401	22.2
South American	194	17.3

Language Spoken at Home: Spanish
(Universe: Population 5 Years and Over)

Group	Number	%
Total Population	12,764	22.4
Hispanic or Latino (of any race)	12,250	79.0
Mexican	1,722	87.6
Puerto Rican	8,373	77.4
South American	926	82.7

Notes: (1) Percent of total population; (2) Percent of Hispanic/Latino population; Profiles include places with an overall population of at least 125,000, OR an overall population of at least 25,000 where the Hispanic/Latino population is at least 20% of the overall population. In states where less than five places meet either of these criteria, we have included places with at least 10,000 total population with the highest percentage of Hispanic/Latino population. These places are identified with an asterisk (*); Please refer to the User's Guide for a full explanation of data.

Unemployment Rate
(Universe: Population 16 Years and Over)

Group	%
Total Population	9.7
Hispanic or Latino (of any race)	15.1
Mexican	12.3
Puerto Rican	15.2
South American	12.8

Class of Worker: Private Wage and Salary
(Universe: Civilian Employed Population 16 Years and Over)

Group	Number	%
Total Population	25,027	83.1
Hispanic or Latino (of any race)	6,187	87.7
Mexican	901	93.5
Puerto Rican	3,943	85.6
South American	590	91.8

Class of Worker: Government
(Universe: Civilian Employed Population 16 Years and Over)

Group	Number	%
Total Population	3,689	12.3
Hispanic or Latino (of any race)	681	9.7
Mexican	23	2.4
Puerto Rican	559	12.1
South American	39	6.1

Means of Transportation to Work: Car, Truck or Van
(Universe: Workers 16 Years and Over)

Group	Number	%
Total Population	26,633	90.2
Hispanic or Latino (of any race)	5,653	81.1
Mexican	707	74.2
Puerto Rican	3,812	83.7
South American	567	90.4

Means of Transportation to Work: Public Transportation (ex. Taxicab)
(Universe: Workers 16 Years and Over)

Group	Number	%
Total Population	439	1.5
Hispanic or Latino (of any race)	139	2.0
Mexican	11	1.2
Puerto Rican	49	1.1
South American	0	0.0

Homeownership Rate
(Universe: Occupied Housing Units)

Group	%
Total Population	60.9
Hispanic or Latino (of any race)	33.4
Central American, ex. Mexican	35.8
Cuban	57.1
Dominican Republic	38.1
Mexican	28.9
Puerto Rican	32.4
South American	47.1
Colombian	53.0
Ecuadorian	40.5

Median Home Value

Group	Dollars
Total Population	208,200
Hispanic or Latino (of any race)	196,600
Mexican	174,200
Puerto Rican	205,600
South American	175,000

Median Gross Rent

Group	Dollars
Total Population	880
Hispanic or Latino (of any race)	869
Mexican	1,024
Puerto Rican	834
South American	885

Median Household Income
(2010 Inflation-Adjusted Dollars)

Group	Dollars
Total Population	53,873
Hispanic or Latino (of any race)	34,544
Mexican	32,434
Puerto Rican	33,735
South American	33,875

Per Capita Income
(2010 Inflation-Adjusted Dollars)

Group	Dollars
Total Population	27,625
Hispanic or Latino (of any race)	15,859
Mexican	13,163
Puerto Rican	15,014
South American	19,813

Households with $100,000+ Income

Group	Number	%
Total Population	4,996	20.9
Hispanic or Latino (of any race)	528	10.1
Mexican	17	2.7
Puerto Rican	383	10.0
South American	16	4.5

Households with Food Stamps/SNAP Benefits During Past 12 Months

Group	Number	%
Total Population	2,806	11.8
Hispanic or Latino (of any race)	1,572	29.9
Mexican	80	12.6
Puerto Rican	1,377	35.9
South American	40	11.2

Poverty Rate
(Income in Past 12 Months Below Poverty Level)

Group	%
Total Population	13.8
Hispanic or Latino (of any race)	28.3
Mexican	41.5
Puerto Rican	29.4
South American	15.3

New Britain

Population

Group	Number	%TP[1]	%HP[2]
Total Population	73,206	100.0	–
Hispanic or Latino (of any race)	26,934	36.8	100.0
Central American, ex. Mexican	388	0.5	1.4
Guatemalan	116	0.2	0.4
Cuban	233	0.3	0.9
Dominican Republic	1,055	1.4	3.9
Mexican	1,257	1.7	4.7
Puerto Rican	21,914	29.9	81.4
South American	1,199	1.6	4.5
Colombian	333	0.5	1.2
Ecuadorian	285	0.4	1.1
Peruvian	409	0.6	1.5
Spaniard	133	0.2	0.5

Population Growth: 2000–2010

Group	%
Total Population	2.3
Hispanic or Latino (of any race)	40.7
Central American, ex. Mexican	183.2
Cuban	3.1
Dominican Republic	223.6
Mexican	101.1
Puerto Rican	39.6
South American	146.7
Colombian	150.4
Peruvian	152.5

Males per 100 Females

Group	Number
Total Population	94.3
Hispanic or Latino (of any race)	90.7
Central American, ex. Mexican	114.4
Guatemalan	141.7
Cuban	83.5
Dominican Republic	84.8
Mexican	121.3
Puerto Rican	88.4
South American	104.6
Colombian	103.0
Ecuadorian	124.4
Peruvian	99.5
Spaniard	82.2

Average Household Size

Group	People
Total Population	2.49
Hispanic or Latino (of any race)	3.13
Central American, ex. Mexican	3.47
Guatemalan	3.92
Cuban	2.43
Dominican Republic	3.46
Mexican	4.01
Puerto Rican	3.10
South American	3.15
Colombian	3.20
Ecuadorian	3.55
Peruvian	3.08
Spaniard	2.11

Median Age

Group	Years
Total Population	32.6
Hispanic or Latino (of any race)	25.0
Central American, ex. Mexican	31.2
Guatemalan	31.3
Cuban	29.2
Dominican Republic	26.4
Mexican	24.3
Puerto Rican	24.4
South American	32.0
Colombian	30.6
Ecuadorian	27.2
Peruvian	36.1
Spaniard	50.8

High School Graduates
(Universe: Population 25 Years and Over)

Group	Number	%
Total Population	35,543	75.7
Hispanic or Latino (of any race)	7,630	60.5
Puerto Rican	5,913	58.2
South American	615	85.5

Four-Year College Graduates
(Universe: Population 25 Years and Over)

Group	Number	%
Total Population	8,393	17.9
Hispanic or Latino (of any race)	1,012	8.0
Puerto Rican	579	5.7
South American	157	21.8

Population Age 3–17 Enrolled in Public School
(Universe: Population Age 3–17 Enrolled in School)

Group	Number	%
Total Population	10,313	90.3
Hispanic or Latino (of any race)	5,573	96.4
Puerto Rican	5,071	97.0
South American	144	85.7

Population Age 3–17 Enrolled in Private School
(Universe: Population Age 3–17 Enrolled in School)

Group	Number	%
Total Population	1,114	9.7
Hispanic or Latino (of any race)	209	3.6
Puerto Rican	157	3.0
South American	24	14.3

Foreign-Born Population

Group	Number	%
Total Population	15,572	21.3
Hispanic or Latino (of any race)	2,192	9.2
Puerto Rican	15	0.1
South American	731	71.1

Foreign-Born Naturalized U.S. Citizens

Group	Number	%
Total Population	6,634	42.6
Hispanic or Latino (of any race)	778	35.5
Puerto Rican	15	100.0
South American	356	48.7

Language Spoken at Home: English Only
(Universe: Population 5 Years and Over)

Group	Number	%
Total Population	34,527	51.3
Hispanic or Latino (of any race)	3,949	18.9
Puerto Rican	3,496	19.9
South American	116	11.6

Notes: (1) Percent of total population; (2) Percent of Hispanic/Latino population; Profiles include places with an overall population of at least 125,000, OR an overall population of at least 25,000 where the Hispanic/Latino population is at least 20% of the overall population. In states where less than five places meet either of these criteria, we have included places with at least 10,000 total population with the highest percentage of Hispanic/Latino population. These places are identified with an asterisk (*); Please refer to the User's Guide for a full explanation of data.

Language Spoken at Home: Spanish
(Universe: Population 5 Years and Over)

Group	Number	%
Total Population	17,541	26.1
Hispanic or Latino (of any race)	16,847	80.5
Puerto Rican	14,064	80.0
South American	855	85.7

Unemployment Rate
(Universe: Population 16 Years and Over)

Group	%
Total Population	10.9
Hispanic or Latino (of any race)	15.8
Puerto Rican	17.6
South American	3.1

Class of Worker: Private Wage and Salary
(Universe: Civilian Employed Population 16 Years and Over)

Group	Number	%
Total Population	28,914	83.9
Hispanic or Latino (of any race)	8,479	86.3
Puerto Rican	6,805	86.6
South American	537	85.5

Class of Worker: Government
(Universe: Civilian Employed Population 16 Years and Over)

Group	Number	%
Total Population	4,325	12.5
Hispanic or Latino (of any race)	1,192	12.1
Puerto Rican	986	12.5
South American	53	8.4

Means of Transportation to Work: Car, Truck or Van
(Universe: Workers 16 Years and Over)

Group	Number	%
Total Population	29,402	88.0
Hispanic or Latino (of any race)	8,129	85.9
Puerto Rican	6,433	85.7
South American	533	84.9

Means of Transportation to Work: Public Transportation (ex. Taxicab)
(Universe: Workers 16 Years and Over)

Group	Number	%
Total Population	903	2.7
Hispanic or Latino (of any race)	482	5.1
Puerto Rican	397	5.3
South American	40	6.4

Homeownership Rate
(Universe: Occupied Housing Units)

Group	%
Total Population	42.9
Hispanic or Latino (of any race)	24.3
Central American, ex. Mexican	49.5
Guatemalan	46.2
Cuban	31.9
Dominican Republic	34.1
Mexican	21.2
Puerto Rican	21.9
South American	46.3
Colombian	47.5
Ecuadorian	43.8
Peruvian	46.7
Spaniard	65.2

Median Home Value

Group	Dollars
Total Population	175,800
Hispanic or Latino (of any race)	185,200
Puerto Rican	180,600
South American	193,100

Median Gross Rent

Group	Dollars
Total Population	832
Hispanic or Latino (of any race)	836
Puerto Rican	823
South American	858

Median Household Income
(2010 Inflation-Adjusted Dollars)

Group	Dollars
Total Population	39,706
Hispanic or Latino (of any race)	30,666
Puerto Rican	28,497
South American	42,500

Per Capita Income
(2010 Inflation-Adjusted Dollars)

Group	Dollars
Total Population	21,056
Hispanic or Latino (of any race)	14,402
Puerto Rican	13,495
South American	19,544

Households with $100,000+ Income

Group	Number	%
Total Population	2,896	9.8
Hispanic or Latino (of any race)	448	5.6
Puerto Rican	272	4.0
South American	25	7.4

Households with Food Stamps/SNAP Benefits During Past 12 Months

Group	Number	%
Total Population	4,727	16.0
Hispanic or Latino (of any race)	2,720	33.7
Puerto Rican	2,480	36.3
South American	44	13.0

Poverty Rate
(Income in Past 12 Months Below Poverty Level)

Group	%
Total Population	20.5
Hispanic or Latino (of any race)	33.6
Puerto Rican	35.9
South American	13.2

New Haven

Population

Group	Number	%TP[1]	%HP[2]
Total Population	129,779	100.0	–
Hispanic or Latino (of any race)	35,591	27.4	100.0
Central American, ex. Mexican	1,373	1.1	3.9
Guatemalan	728	0.6	2.0
Honduran	209	0.2	0.6
Salvadoran	243	0.2	0.7
Cuban	485	0.4	1.4
Dominican Republic	1,097	0.8	3.1
Mexican	6,907	5.3	19.4
Puerto Rican	20,505	15.8	57.6
South American	3,426	2.6	9.6
Argentinean	182	0.1	0.5
Chilean	164	0.1	0.5
Colombian	469	0.4	1.3
Ecuadorian	1,978	1.5	5.6
Peruvian	448	0.3	1.3
Venezuelan	127	0.1	0.4
Spaniard	203	0.2	0.6

Population Growth: 2000–2010

Group	%
Total Population	5.0
Hispanic or Latino (of any race)	34.6
Central American, ex. Mexican	134.3
Guatemalan	203.3
Cuban	30.7
Dominican Republic	138.5
Mexican	98.3
Puerto Rican	16.0
South American	110.2
Argentinean	59.6
Chilean	46.4
Colombian	21.5
Ecuadorian	199.7
Peruvian	90.6

Males per 100 Females

Group	Number
Total Population	92.9
Hispanic or Latino (of any race)	102.5
Central American, ex. Mexican	122.9
Guatemalan	139.5
Honduran	102.9
Salvadoran	122.9
Cuban	98.8
Dominican Republic	77.2
Mexican	142.0
Puerto Rican	87.6
South American	122.9
Argentinean	82.0
Chilean	105.0
Colombian	75.0
Ecuadorian	157.2
Peruvian	105.5
Venezuelan	78.9
Spaniard	99.0

Average Household Size

Group	People
Total Population	2.43
Hispanic or Latino (of any race)	3.27
Central American, ex. Mexican	3.96
Guatemalan	4.44
Honduran	4.59
Salvadoran	3.78
Cuban	2.46
Dominican Republic	3.29
Mexican	4.13
Puerto Rican	3.06
South American	3.27
Argentinean	2.45
Chilean	2.76
Colombian	2.31
Ecuadorian	3.88
Peruvian	2.93
Venezuelan	2.57
Spaniard	1.99

Median Age

Group	Years
Total Population	29.9
Hispanic or Latino (of any race)	26.3
Central American, ex. Mexican	27.3
Guatemalan	26.3
Honduran	27.7
Salvadoran	30.8
Cuban	26.2
Dominican Republic	25.8
Mexican	26.1
Puerto Rican	25.5
South American	30.6
Argentinean	31.6
Chilean	28.9
Colombian	30.3
Ecuadorian	30.6
Peruvian	33.6
Venezuelan	28.1
Spaniard	28.6

High School Graduates
(Universe: Population 25 Years and Over)

Group	Number	%
Total Population	61,419	80.5
Hispanic or Latino (of any race)	10,751	61.9
Central American, ex. Mexican	526	46.5
Dominican Republic	337	53.3
Mexican	2,252	66.7
Puerto Rican	5,779	59.3
South American	1,414	73.9
Ecuadorian	562	60.2

Four-Year College Graduates
(Universe: Population 25 Years and Over)

Group	Number	%
Total Population	23,981	31.4
Hispanic or Latino (of any race)	1,783	10.3
Central American, ex. Mexican	102	9.0
Dominican Republic	0	0.0
Mexican	618	18.3
Puerto Rican	402	4.1
South American	436	22.8
Ecuadorian	77	8.3

Population Age 3–17 Enrolled in Public School
(Universe: Population Age 3–17 Enrolled in School)

Group	Number	%
Total Population	19,134	87.5
Hispanic or Latino (of any race)	7,280	95.5
Central American, ex. Mexican	328	87.9
Dominican Republic	301	95.3

Notes: (1) Percent of total population; (2) Percent of Hispanic/Latino population; Profiles include places with an overall population of at least 125,000, OR an overall population of at least 25,000 where the Hispanic/Latino population is at least 20% of the overall population. In states where less than five places meet either of these criteria, we have included places with at least 10,000 total population with the highest percentage of Hispanic/Latino population. These places are identified with an asterisk (*); Please refer to the User's Guide for a full explanation of data.

Mexican	1,010	100.0
Puerto Rican	5,226	96.4
South American	323	80.5
Ecuadorian	238	100.0

Population Age 3–17 Enrolled in Private School
(Universe: Population Age 3–17 Enrolled in School)

Group	Number	%
Total Population	2,732	12.5
Hispanic or Latino (of any race)	344	4.5
Central American, ex. Mexican	45	12.1
Dominican Republic	15	4.7
Mexican	0	0.0
Puerto Rican	197	3.6
South American	78	19.5
Ecuadorian	0	0.0

Foreign-Born Population

Group	Number	%
Total Population	20,920	16.2
Hispanic or Latino (of any race)	8,480	25.6
Central American, ex. Mexican	1,479	70.7
Dominican Republic	694	54.8
Mexican	3,762	65.3
Puerto Rican	107	0.5
South American	2,195	76.1
Ecuadorian	1,161	75.6

Foreign-Born Naturalized U.S. Citizens

Group	Number	%
Total Population	5,899	28.2
Hispanic or Latino (of any race)	1,427	16.8
Central American, ex. Mexican	406	27.5
Dominican Republic	255	36.7
Mexican	106	2.8
Puerto Rican	36	33.6
South American	500	22.8
Ecuadorian	184	15.8

Language Spoken at Home: English Only
(Universe: Population 5 Years and Over)

Group	Number	%
Total Population	81,273	67.3
Hispanic or Latino (of any race)	3,817	12.8
Central American, ex. Mexican	163	8.6
Dominican Republic	53	4.7
Mexican	265	5.2
Puerto Rican	2,830	15.8
South American	102	3.8
Ecuadorian	9	0.7

Language Spoken at Home: Spanish
(Universe: Population 5 Years and Over)

Group	Number	%
Total Population	27,932	23.1
Hispanic or Latino (of any race)	25,825	86.9
Central American, ex. Mexican	1,741	91.4
Dominican Republic	1,081	95.3
Mexican	4,820	94.4
Puerto Rican	15,078	84.0
South American	2,551	96.2
Ecuadorian	1,369	99.3

Unemployment Rate
(Universe: Population 16 Years and Over)

Group	%
Total Population	10.8
Hispanic or Latino (of any race)	14.5
Central American, ex. Mexican	5.0
Dominican Republic	19.6
Mexican	7.4
Puerto Rican	19.0
South American	15.1
Ecuadorian	20.2

Class of Worker: Private Wage and Salary
(Universe: Civilian Employed Population 16 Years and Over)

Group	Number	%
Total Population	49,409	82.6
Hispanic or Latino (of any race)	12,041	87.7
Central American, ex. Mexican	1,168	93.9
Dominican Republic	354	77.1
Mexican	2,913	92.7
Puerto Rican	5,584	82.4
South American	1,536	97.6
Ecuadorian	807	97.1

Class of Worker: Government
(Universe: Civilian Employed Population 16 Years and Over)

Group	Number	%
Total Population	7,774	13.0
Hispanic or Latino (of any race)	1,261	9.2
Central American, ex. Mexican	14	1.1
Dominican Republic	77	16.8
Mexican	34	1.1
Puerto Rican	1,069	15.8
South American	27	1.7
Ecuadorian	14	1.7

Means of Transportation to Work: Car, Truck or Van
(Universe: Workers 16 Years and Over)

Group	Number	%
Total Population	39,532	68.2
Hispanic or Latino (of any race)	10,037	76.0
Central American, ex. Mexican	1,115	91.9
Dominican Republic	295	68.8
Mexican	1,866	60.8
Puerto Rican	5,227	81.5
South American	1,252	80.1
Ecuadorian	777	94.5

Means of Transportation to Work: Public Transportation (ex. Taxicab)
(Universe: Workers 16 Years and Over)

Group	Number	%
Total Population	6,402	11.0
Hispanic or Latino (of any race)	1,373	10.4
Central American, ex. Mexican	0	0.0
Dominican Republic	92	21.4
Mexican	591	19.3
Puerto Rican	555	8.7
South American	25	1.6
Ecuadorian	0	0.0

Homeownership Rate
(Universe: Occupied Housing Units)

Group	%
Total Population	29.5
Hispanic or Latino (of any race)	20.2
Central American, ex. Mexican	25.8
Guatemalan	22.0
Honduran	28.2
Salvadoran	33.3
Cuban	24.3
Dominican Republic	24.3
Mexican	11.3
Puerto Rican	20.7
South American	25.3
Argentinean	22.7
Chilean	24.4
Colombian	28.1
Ecuadorian	23.6
Peruvian	30.5
Venezuelan	25.5
Spaniard	22.2

Median Home Value

Group	Dollars
Total Population	227,800
Hispanic or Latino (of any race)	213,200
Central American, ex. Mexican	207,400
Dominican Republic	–
Mexican	225,900
Puerto Rican	206,000
South American	229,000
Ecuadorian	203,700

Median Gross Rent

Group	Dollars
Total Population	1,024
Hispanic or Latino (of any race)	1,054
Central American, ex. Mexican	1,178
Dominican Republic	1,036
Mexican	1,134
Puerto Rican	1,027
South American	993
Ecuadorian	993

Median Household Income
(2010 Inflation-Adjusted Dollars)

Group	Dollars
Total Population	38,963
Hispanic or Latino (of any race)	30,757
Central American, ex. Mexican	77,604
Dominican Republic	24,231
Mexican	43,109
Puerto Rican	23,369
South American	47,066
Ecuadorian	45,245

Per Capita Income
(2010 Inflation-Adjusted Dollars)

Group	Dollars
Total Population	21,789
Hispanic or Latino (of any race)	13,751
Central American, ex. Mexican	16,888
Dominican Republic	11,063
Mexican	16,426
Puerto Rican	11,149
South American	22,084
Ecuadorian	19,908

Households with $100,000+ Income

Group	Number	%
Total Population	7,103	14.7
Hispanic or Latino (of any race)	952	9.6
Central American, ex. Mexican	144	30.3
Dominican Republic	0	0.0
Mexican	197	12.4
Puerto Rican	375	6.1
South American	155	16.6
Ecuadorian	30	6.3

Households with Food Stamps/SNAP Benefits During Past 12 Months

Group	Number	%
Total Population	9,117	18.8
Hispanic or Latino (of any race)	3,351	33.8
Central American, ex. Mexican	100	21.1
Dominican Republic	131	39.7
Mexican	180	11.4
Puerto Rican	2,848	46.7
South American	32	3.4
Ecuadorian	21	4.4

Poverty Rate
(Income in Past 12 Months Below Poverty Level)

Group	%
Total Population	25.2
Hispanic or Latino (of any race)	36.7
Central American, ex. Mexican	15.8
Dominican Republic	29.8
Mexican	32.5
Puerto Rican	44.7
South American	10.9
Ecuadorian	15.1

New London

Population

Group	Number	%TP[1]	%HP[2]
Total Population	27,620	100.0	–
Hispanic or Latino (of any race)	7,815	28.3	100.0
Central American, ex. Mexican	533	1.9	6.8
Honduran	108	0.4	1.4
Salvadoran	234	0.8	3.0
Dominican Republic	1,230	4.5	15.7
Mexican	366	1.3	4.7
Puerto Rican	4,264	15.4	54.6
South American	975	3.5	12.5
Colombian	134	0.5	1.7
Ecuadorian	241	0.9	3.1
Peruvian	513	1.9	6.6

Population Growth: 2000–2010

Group	%
Total Population	7.6
Hispanic or Latino (of any race)	54.4
Central American, ex. Mexican	134.8
Salvadoran	105.3
Dominican Republic	339.3

Notes: (1) Percent of total population; (2) Percent of Hispanic/Latino population; Profiles include places with an overall population of at least 125,000, OR an overall population of at least 25,000 where the Hispanic/Latino population is at least 20% of the overall population. In states where less than five places meet either of these criteria, we have included places with at least 10,000 total population with the highest percentage of Hispanic/Latino population. These places are identified with an asterisk (*); Please refer to the User's Guide for a full explanation of data.

Mexican	108.0
Puerto Rican	26.1
South American	222.8
Peruvian	203.6

Males per 100 Females

Group	Number
Total Population	97.6
Hispanic or Latino (of any race)	96.2
Central American, ex. Mexican	116.7
Honduran	125.0
Salvadoran	96.6
Dominican Republic	88.1
Mexican	106.8
Puerto Rican	91.0
South American	111.0
Colombian	100.0
Ecuadorian	167.8
Peruvian	98.1

Average Household Size

Group	People
Total Population	2.30
Hispanic or Latino (of any race)	3.04
Central American, ex. Mexican	3.59
Honduran	3.81
Salvadoran	3.85
Dominican Republic	3.52
Mexican	2.78
Puerto Rican	2.88
South American	3.23
Colombian	2.64
Ecuadorian	3.70
Peruvian	3.19

Median Age

Group	Years
Total Population	30.3
Hispanic or Latino (of any race)	25.4
Central American, ex. Mexican	27.9
Honduran	27.7
Salvadoran	30.5
Dominican Republic	24.8
Mexican	22.6
Puerto Rican	25.0
South American	30.2
Colombian	28.8
Ecuadorian	29.0
Peruvian	33.4

High School Graduates
(Universe: Population 25 Years and Over)

Group	Number	%
Total Population	13,223	83.1
Hispanic or Latino (of any race)	2,569	66.3
Dominican Republic	383	66.8
Puerto Rican	1,338	62.8
South American	440	81.0

Four-Year College Graduates
(Universe: Population 25 Years and Over)

Group	Number	%
Total Population	3,556	22.3
Hispanic or Latino (of any race)	439	11.3
Dominican Republic	11	1.9
Puerto Rican	113	5.3
South American	146	26.9

Population Age 3–17 Enrolled in Public School
(Universe: Population Age 3–17 Enrolled in School)

Group	Number	%
Total Population	3,708	86.4
Hispanic or Latino (of any race)	1,777	92.0
Dominican Republic	338	100.0
Puerto Rican	1,173	93.3
South American	164	85.9

Population Age 3–17 Enrolled in Private School
(Universe: Population Age 3–17 Enrolled in School)

Group	Number	%
Total Population	584	13.6
Hispanic or Latino (of any race)	154	8.0
Dominican Republic	0	0.0
Puerto Rican	84	6.7
South American	27	14.1

Foreign-Born Population

Group	Number	%
Total Population	4,078	14.8
Hispanic or Latino (of any race)	2,048	28.0
Dominican Republic	687	70.2
Puerto Rican	54	1.3
South American	739	78.3

Foreign-Born Naturalized U.S. Citizens

Group	Number	%
Total Population	1,318	32.3
Hispanic or Latino (of any race)	540	26.4
Dominican Republic	316	46.0
Puerto Rican	54	100.0
South American	118	16.0

Language Spoken at Home: English Only
(Universe: Population 5 Years and Over)

Group	Number	%
Total Population	18,247	70.5
Hispanic or Latino (of any race)	1,378	20.9
Dominican Republic	54	5.7
Puerto Rican	947	24.9
South American	79	9.1

Language Spoken at Home: Spanish
(Universe: Population 5 Years and Over)

Group	Number	%
Total Population	5,442	21.0
Hispanic or Latino (of any race)	5,149	78.2
Dominican Republic	889	94.3
Puerto Rican	2,841	74.8
South American	789	90.9

Unemployment Rate
(Universe: Population 16 Years and Over)

Group	%
Total Population	12.2
Hispanic or Latino (of any race)	20.2
Dominican Republic	27.3
Puerto Rican	25.4
South American	2.6

Class of Worker: Private Wage and Salary
(Universe: Civilian Employed Population 16 Years and Over)

Group	Number	%
Total Population	9,787	82.7
Hispanic or Latino (of any race)	2,556	91.5
Dominican Republic	399	100.0
Puerto Rican	1,071	83.4
South American	590	100.0

Class of Worker: Government
(Universe: Civilian Employed Population 16 Years and Over)

Group	Number	%
Total Population	1,491	12.6
Hispanic or Latino (of any race)	222	7.9
Dominican Republic	0	0.0
Puerto Rican	210	16.4
South American	0	0.0

Means of Transportation to Work: Car, Truck or Van
(Universe: Workers 16 Years and Over)

Group	Number	%
Total Population	9,249	70.4
Hispanic or Latino (of any race)	2,351	83.7
Dominican Republic	348	87.2
Puerto Rican	1,099	89.0
South American	530	89.8

Means of Transportation to Work: Public Transportation (ex. Taxicab)
(Universe: Workers 16 Years and Over)

Group	Number	%
Total Population	784	6.0
Hispanic or Latino (of any race)	178	6.3
Dominican Republic	10	2.5
Puerto Rican	54	4.4
South American	38	6.4

Homeownership Rate
(Universe: Occupied Housing Units)

Group	%
Total Population	37.7
Hispanic or Latino (of any race)	22.9
Central American, ex. Mexican	37.8
Honduran	38.5
Salvadoran	38.5
Dominican Republic	28.9
Mexican	15.1
Puerto Rican	19.9
South American	24.4
Colombian	19.0
Ecuadorian	14.8
Peruvian	26.9

Median Home Value

Group	Dollars
Total Population	206,600
Hispanic or Latino (of any race)	195,300
Dominican Republic	–
Puerto Rican	192,200
South American	183,100

Median Gross Rent

Group	Dollars
Total Population	894
Hispanic or Latino (of any race)	879
Dominican Republic	870
Puerto Rican	831
South American	956

Median Household Income
(2010 Inflation-Adjusted Dollars)

Group	Dollars
Total Population	43,551
Hispanic or Latino (of any race)	39,110
Dominican Republic	37,775
Puerto Rican	39,583
South American	37,614

Per Capita Income
(2010 Inflation-Adjusted Dollars)

Group	Dollars
Total Population	21,110
Hispanic or Latino (of any race)	14,401
Dominican Republic	14,155
Puerto Rican	12,651
South American	16,035

Households with $100,000+ Income

Group	Number	%
Total Population	1,251	12.2
Hispanic or Latino (of any race)	130	5.3
Dominican Republic	0	0.0
Puerto Rican	70	5.2
South American	0	0.0

Households with Food Stamps/SNAP Benefits During Past 12 Months

Group	Number	%
Total Population	1,908	18.7
Hispanic or Latino (of any race)	847	34.7
Dominican Republic	164	42.8
Puerto Rican	556	41.4
South American	99	23.5

Poverty Rate
(Income in Past 12 Months Below Poverty Level)

Group	%
Total Population	17.3
Hispanic or Latino (of any race)	24.4
Dominican Republic	21.1
Puerto Rican	32.4
South American	15.1

Norwalk

Population

Group	Number	%TP[1]	%HP[2]
Total Population	85,603	100.0	–
Hispanic or Latino (of any race)	20,770	24.3	100.0
Central American, ex. Mexican	5,186	6.1	25.0
Costa Rican	1,024	1.2	4.9
Guatemalan	1,619	1.9	7.8
Honduran	1,506	1.8	7.3
Nicaraguan	231	0.3	1.1
Salvadoran	754	0.9	3.6

Notes: (1) Percent of total population; (2) Percent of Hispanic/Latino population; Profiles include places with an overall population of at least 125,000, OR an overall population of at least 25,000 where the Hispanic/Latino population is at least 20% of the overall population. In states where less than five places meet either of these criteria, we have included places with at least 10,000 total population with the highest percentage of Hispanic/Latino population. These places are identified with an asterisk (*); Please refer to the User's Guide for a full explanation of data.

Cuban	244	0.3	1.2
Dominican Republic	824	1.0	4.0
Mexican	3,962	4.6	19.1
Puerto Rican	3,190	3.7	15.4
South American	5,799	6.8	27.9
Argentinean	126	0.1	0.6
Chilean	128	0.1	0.6
Colombian	3,084	3.6	14.8
Ecuadorian	1,027	1.2	4.9
Peruvian	859	1.0	4.1
Uruguayan	128	0.1	0.6
Venezuelan	319	0.4	1.5
Spaniard	138	0.2	0.7

Population Growth: 2000–2010

Group	%
Total Population	3.2
Hispanic or Latino (of any race)	60.2
Central American, ex. Mexican	145.0
Costa Rican	47.6
Guatemalan	425.6
Honduran	261.2
Nicaraguan	28.3
Salvadoran	144.8
Cuban	27.7
Dominican Republic	281.5
Mexican	108.9
Puerto Rican	7.1
South American	96.0
Colombian	56.6
Ecuadorian	211.2
Peruvian	331.7
Venezuelan	74.3

Males per 100 Females

Group	Number
Total Population	96.2
Hispanic or Latino (of any race)	109.5
Central American, ex. Mexican	138.3
Costa Rican	124.6
Guatemalan	164.1
Honduran	148.1
Nicaraguan	89.3
Salvadoran	114.2
Cuban	93.7
Dominican Republic	77.2
Mexican	133.5
Puerto Rican	89.5
South American	93.0
Argentinean	80.0
Chilean	100.0
Colombian	86.6
Ecuadorian	110.5
Peruvian	96.1
Uruguayan	116.9
Venezuelan	94.5
Spaniard	97.1

Average Household Size

Group	People
Total Population	2.55
Hispanic or Latino (of any race)	3.54
Central American, ex. Mexican	4.06
Costa Rican	3.23
Guatemalan	4.59
Honduran	4.24
Nicaraguan	4.02
Salvadoran	4.24
Cuban	2.51
Dominican Republic	3.25
Mexican	4.32
Puerto Rican	2.91
South American	3.30
Argentinean	2.35
Chilean	2.83
Colombian	3.09
Ecuadorian	3.78
Peruvian	3.83
Uruguayan	3.24
Venezuelan	3.50
Spaniard	2.43

Median Age

Group	Years
Total Population	38.2
Hispanic or Latino (of any race)	30.0
Central American, ex. Mexican	30.3
Costa Rican	33.3
Guatemalan	28.0
Honduran	29.8
Nicaraguan	34.1
Salvadoran	33.0
Cuban	37.3
Dominican Republic	27.9
Mexican	26.9
Puerto Rican	27.6
South American	35.0
Argentinean	39.2
Chilean	39.5
Colombian	37.3
Ecuadorian	30.8
Peruvian	34.2
Uruguayan	37.5
Venezuelan	33.2
Spaniard	41.0

High School Graduates
(Universe: Population 25 Years and Over)

Group	Number	%
Total Population	53,659	87.7
Hispanic or Latino (of any race)	7,706	72.3
Central American, ex. Mexican	1,407	76.1
Mexican	903	45.6
Puerto Rican	1,511	80.7
South American	2,891	78.8
Colombian	1,814	86.6
Ecuadorian	377	48.5

Four-Year College Graduates
(Universe: Population 25 Years and Over)

Group	Number	%
Total Population	23,901	39.1
Hispanic or Latino (of any race)	1,978	18.6
Central American, ex. Mexican	191	10.3
Mexican	259	13.1
Puerto Rican	325	17.4
South American	886	24.1
Colombian	439	21.0
Ecuadorian	121	15.6

Population Age 3–17 Enrolled in Public School
(Universe: Population Age 3–17 Enrolled in School)

Group	Number	%
Total Population	11,118	81.5
Hispanic or Latino (of any race)	3,177	93.6
Central American, ex. Mexican	447	95.1
Mexican	825	95.4
Puerto Rican	583	100.0
South American	729	85.0
Colombian	440	86.1
Ecuadorian	169	84.1

Population Age 3–17 Enrolled in Private School
(Universe: Population Age 3–17 Enrolled in School)

Group	Number	%
Total Population	2,524	18.5
Hispanic or Latino (of any race)	216	6.4
Central American, ex. Mexican	23	4.9
Mexican	40	4.6
Puerto Rican	0	0.0
South American	129	15.0
Colombian	71	13.9
Ecuadorian	32	15.9

Foreign-Born Population

Group	Number	%
Total Population	19,066	22.5
Hispanic or Latino (of any race)	8,949	51.8
Central American, ex. Mexican	1,960	69.7
Mexican	2,247	63.2
Puerto Rican	45	1.5
South American	3,684	65.6
Colombian	2,124	69.0
Ecuadorian	904	66.5

Foreign-Born Naturalized U.S. Citizens

Group	Number	%
Total Population	8,176	42.9
Hispanic or Latino (of any race)	2,580	28.8
Central American, ex. Mexican	383	19.5
Mexican	313	13.9
Puerto Rican	12	26.7
South American	1,402	38.1
Colombian	976	46.0
Ecuadorian	185	20.5

Language Spoken at Home: English Only
(Universe: Population 5 Years and Over)

Group	Number	%
Total Population	54,787	69.4
Hispanic or Latino (of any race)	2,351	15.2
Central American, ex. Mexican	196	7.5
Mexican	437	13.6
Puerto Rican	813	30.7
South American	437	8.7
Colombian	208	7.1
Ecuadorian	105	9.1

Language Spoken at Home: Spanish
(Universe: Population 5 Years and Over)

Group	Number	%
Total Population	14,095	17.9
Hispanic or Latino (of any race)	13,032	84.3
Central American, ex. Mexican	2,406	92.5
Mexican	2,770	86.4
Puerto Rican	1,839	69.3
South American	4,560	90.4
Colombian	2,691	91.4
Ecuadorian	1,053	90.9

Unemployment Rate
(Universe: Population 16 Years and Over)

Group	%
Total Population	6.3
Hispanic or Latino (of any race)	6.7
Central American, ex. Mexican	6.1
Mexican	17.7
Puerto Rican	4.5
South American	3.6
Colombian	4.2
Ecuadorian	1.8

Class of Worker: Private Wage and Salary
(Universe: Civilian Employed Population 16 Years and Over)

Group	Number	%
Total Population	37,300	81.3
Hispanic or Latino (of any race)	7,632	83.1
Central American, ex. Mexican	1,290	78.4
Mexican	1,272	87.6
Puerto Rican	1,468	92.2
South American	2,781	81.4
Colombian	1,510	77.4
Ecuadorian	727	91.0

Class of Worker: Government
(Universe: Civilian Employed Population 16 Years and Over)

Group	Number	%
Total Population	4,081	8.9
Hispanic or Latino (of any race)	374	4.1
Central American, ex. Mexican	23	1.4
Mexican	6	0.4
Puerto Rican	100	6.3
South American	90	2.6
Colombian	90	4.6
Ecuadorian	0	0.0

Means of Transportation to Work: Car, Truck or Van
(Universe: Workers 16 Years and Over)

Group	Number	%
Total Population	37,394	83.5
Hispanic or Latino (of any race)	7,178	80.8
Central American, ex. Mexican	1,327	81.4
Mexican	1,027	73.8
Puerto Rican	1,333	83.7
South American	2,593	81.0
Colombian	1,593	88.1
Ecuadorian	451	56.4

Means of Transportation to Work: Public Transportation (ex. Taxicab)
(Universe: Workers 16 Years and Over)

Group	Number	%
Total Population	4,293	9.6
Hispanic or Latino (of any race)	1,121	12.6

Notes: (1) Percent of total population; (2) Percent of Hispanic/Latino population; Profiles include places with an overall population of at least 125,000, OR an overall population of at least 25,000 where the Hispanic/Latino population is at least 20% of the overall population. In states where less than five places meet either of these criteria, we have included places with at least 10,000 total population with the highest percentage of Hispanic/Latino population. These places are identified with an asterisk (*); Please refer to the User's Guide for a full explanation of data.

Group	Number	%
Central American, ex. Mexican	190	11.7
Mexican	251	18.0
Puerto Rican	169	10.6
South American	419	13.1
Colombian	202	11.2
Ecuadorian	187	23.4

Homeownership Rate
(Universe: Occupied Housing Units)

Group	%
Total Population	62.4
Hispanic or Latino (of any race)	33.7
Central American, ex. Mexican	25.5
Costa Rican	25.0
Guatemalan	28.8
Honduran	18.5
Nicaraguan	26.2
Salvadoran	32.5
Cuban	60.2
Dominican Republic	23.8
Mexican	24.2
Puerto Rican	32.5
South American	44.5
Argentinean	57.1
Chilean	52.8
Colombian	42.8
Ecuadorian	47.3
Peruvian	49.2
Uruguayan	48.0
Venezuelan	28.1
Spaniard	64.7

Median Home Value

Group	Dollars
Total Population	479,400
Hispanic or Latino (of any race)	449,500
Central American, ex. Mexican	464,500
Mexican	433,500
Puerto Rican	419,400
South American	446,800
Colombian	421,400
Ecuadorian	367,900

Median Gross Rent

Group	Dollars
Total Population	1,231
Hispanic or Latino (of any race)	1,250
Central American, ex. Mexican	1,346
Mexican	1,303
Puerto Rican	1,039
South American	1,265
Colombian	1,119
Ecuadorian	1,435

Median Household Income
(2010 Inflation-Adjusted Dollars)

Group	Dollars
Total Population	76,161
Hispanic or Latino (of any race)	52,703
Central American, ex. Mexican	63,223
Mexican	43,958
Puerto Rican	46,831
South American	56,265
Colombian	49,063
Ecuadorian	54,676

Per Capita Income
(2010 Inflation-Adjusted Dollars)

Group	Dollars
Total Population	43,303
Hispanic or Latino (of any race)	21,055
Central American, ex. Mexican	20,733
Mexican	16,882
Puerto Rican	22,553
South American	23,459
Colombian	21,868
Ecuadorian	12,751

Households with $100,000+ Income

Group	Number	%
Total Population	12,732	36.2
Hispanic or Latino (of any race)	997	18.8
Central American, ex. Mexican	105	12.6
Mexican	125	12.4
Puerto Rican	159	14.4
South American	424	24.7
Colombian	138	14.4
Ecuadorian	49	15.0

Households with Food Stamps/SNAP Benefits During Past 12 Months

Group	Number	%
Total Population	1,765	5.0
Hispanic or Latino (of any race)	409	7.7
Central American, ex. Mexican	17	2.0
Mexican	84	8.3
Puerto Rican	109	9.8
South American	152	8.9
Colombian	108	11.3
Ecuadorian	44	13.5

Poverty Rate
(Income in Past 12 Months Below Poverty Level)

Group	%
Total Population	8.2
Hispanic or Latino (of any race)	14.0
Central American, ex. Mexican	16.0
Mexican	24.8
Puerto Rican	11.2
South American	6.6
Colombian	6.6
Ecuadorian	10.8

Stamford

Population

Group	Number	%TP[1]	%HP[2]
Total Population	122,643	100.0	–
Hispanic or Latino (of any race)	29,188	23.8	100.0
Central American, ex. Mexican	9,866	8.0	33.8
Costa Rican	133	0.1	0.5
Guatemalan	7,707	6.3	26.4
Honduran	1,279	1.0	4.4
Salvadoran	584	0.5	2.0
Cuban	403	0.3	1.4
Dominican Republic	1,476	1.2	5.1
Mexican	2,478	2.0	8.5
Puerto Rican	3,458	2.8	11.8
South American	8,807	7.2	30.2
Argentinean	278	0.2	1.0
Bolivian	112	0.1	0.4
Chilean	282	0.2	1.0
Colombian	2,679	2.2	9.2
Ecuadorian	2,313	1.9	7.9
Peruvian	2,560	2.1	8.8
Uruguayan	371	0.3	1.3
Venezuelan	142	0.1	0.5
Spaniard	239	0.2	0.8

Population Growth: 2000–2010

Group	%
Total Population	4.7
Hispanic or Latino (of any race)	48.7
Central American, ex. Mexican	140.8
Guatemalan	151.3
Honduran	142.7
Salvadoran	175.5
Cuban	12.6
Dominican Republic	125.0
Mexican	75.2
Puerto Rican	9.2
South American	70.7
Argentinean	141.7
Chilean	45.4
Colombian	38.3
Ecuadorian	97.7
Peruvian	101.9
Uruguayan	168.8

Males per 100 Females

Group	Number
Total Population	97.0
Hispanic or Latino (of any race)	115.5
Central American, ex. Mexican	164.2
Costa Rican	114.5
Guatemalan	177.3
Honduran	141.8
Salvadoran	107.8
Cuban	104.6
Dominican Republic	76.1
Mexican	113.4
Puerto Rican	87.2
South American	95.0
Argentinean	93.1
Bolivian	83.6
Chilean	90.5
Colombian	85.1
Ecuadorian	103.8
Peruvian	100.2
Uruguayan	108.4
Venezuelan	79.7
Spaniard	113.4

Average Household Size

Group	People
Total Population	2.56
Hispanic or Latino (of any race)	3.62
Central American, ex. Mexican	4.49
Costa Rican	2.75
Guatemalan	4.66
Honduran	4.43
Salvadoran	3.89
Cuban	2.37
Dominican Republic	3.61
Mexican	4.07
Puerto Rican	2.79
South American	3.32
Argentinean	2.75
Bolivian	3.22
Chilean	2.73
Colombian	3.06
Ecuadorian	3.64
Peruvian	3.62
Uruguayan	3.02
Venezuelan	2.67
Spaniard	2.53

Median Age

Group	Years
Total Population	37.1
Hispanic or Latino (of any race)	30.4
Central American, ex. Mexican	29.2
Costa Rican	34.2
Guatemalan	28.9
Honduran	29.1
Salvadoran	32.3
Cuban	41.8
Dominican Republic	27.9
Mexican	27.4
Puerto Rican	29.4
South American	36.0
Argentinean	37.2
Bolivian	36.7
Chilean	43.3
Colombian	37.2
Ecuadorian	33.9
Peruvian	36.5
Uruguayan	34.7
Venezuelan	34.3
Spaniard	35.3

High School Graduates
(Universe: Population 25 Years and Over)

Group	Number	%
Total Population	73,601	86.2
Hispanic or Latino (of any race)	11,405	64.1
Central American, ex. Mexican	3,202	44.8
Guatemalan	2,464	43.5
Dominican Republic	484	71.0
Mexican	761	63.2
Puerto Rican	1,178	79.5
South American	4,619	78.8
Colombian	1,411	79.7
Ecuadorian	1,083	67.1
Peruvian	1,410	83.6

Four-Year College Graduates
(Universe: Population 25 Years and Over)

Group	Number	%
Total Population	36,366	42.6
Hispanic or Latino (of any race)	2,871	16.1
Central American, ex. Mexican	660	9.2
Guatemalan	317	5.6
Dominican Republic	52	7.6

Notes: (1) Percent of total population; (2) Percent of Hispanic/Latino population; Profiles include places with an overall population of at least 125,000, OR an overall population of at least 25,000 where the Hispanic/Latino population is at least 20% of the overall population. In states where less than five places meet either of these criteria, we have included places with at least 10,000 total population with the highest percentage of Hispanic/Latino population. These places are identified with an asterisk (*); Please refer to the User's Guide for a full explanation of data.

Group	Number	%
Mexican	161	13.4
Puerto Rican	295	19.9
South American	1,261	21.5
Colombian	285	16.1
Ecuadorian	361	22.4
Peruvian	304	18.0

Population Age 3–17 Enrolled in Public School
(Universe: Population Age 3–17 Enrolled in School)

Group	Number	%
Total Population	14,428	75.0
Hispanic or Latino (of any race)	4,672	87.0
Central American, ex. Mexican	1,315	92.2
Guatemalan	953	91.2
Dominican Republic	485	88.0
Mexican	478	79.4
Puerto Rican	313	96.3
South American	1,589	83.8
Colombian	468	89.7
Ecuadorian	467	93.0
Peruvian	531	91.1

Population Age 3–17 Enrolled in Private School
(Universe: Population Age 3–17 Enrolled in School)

Group	Number	%
Total Population	4,812	25.0
Hispanic or Latino (of any race)	697	13.0
Central American, ex. Mexican	112	7.8
Guatemalan	92	8.8
Dominican Republic	66	12.0
Mexican	124	20.6
Puerto Rican	12	3.7
South American	308	16.2
Colombian	54	10.3
Ecuadorian	35	7.0
Peruvian	52	8.9

Foreign-Born Population

Group	Number	%
Total Population	45,620	37.7
Hispanic or Latino (of any race)	19,410	67.2
Central American, ex. Mexican	8,866	80.1
Guatemalan	7,314	81.9
Dominican Republic	831	51.2
Mexican	1,522	60.7
Puerto Rican	28	1.3
South American	7,024	76.0
Colombian	2,172	77.6
Ecuadorian	1,964	78.3
Peruvian	2,128	78.3

Foreign-Born Naturalized U.S. Citizens

Group	Number	%
Total Population	15,292	33.5
Hispanic or Latino (of any race)	3,877	20.0
Central American, ex. Mexican	900	10.2
Guatemalan	388	5.3
Dominican Republic	316	38.0
Mexican	224	14.7
Puerto Rican	28	100.0
South American	1,879	26.8
Colombian	740	34.1
Ecuadorian	532	27.1
Peruvian	344	16.2

Language Spoken at Home: English Only
(Universe: Population 5 Years and Over)

Group	Number	%
Total Population	62,566	55.6
Hispanic or Latino (of any race)	1,834	6.9
Central American, ex. Mexican	179	1.7
Guatemalan	153	1.9
Dominican Republic	62	4.3
Mexican	192	9.0
Puerto Rican	600	28.1
South American	358	4.2
Colombian	37	1.4
Ecuadorian	193	8.3
Peruvian	58	2.4

Language Spoken at Home: Spanish
(Universe: Population 5 Years and Over)

Group	Number	%
Total Population	25,836	23.0
Hispanic or Latino (of any race)	24,715	92.7
Central American, ex. Mexican	10,120	98.3
Guatemalan	8,083	98.1
Dominican Republic	1,395	95.7
Mexican	1,910	89.8
Puerto Rican	1,516	70.9
South American	8,110	95.0
Colombian	2,570	98.6
Ecuadorian	2,142	91.7
Peruvian	2,370	96.3

Unemployment Rate
(Universe: Population 16 Years and Over)

Group	%
Total Population	9.0
Hispanic or Latino (of any race)	13.2
Central American, ex. Mexican	16.6
Guatemalan	16.2
Dominican Republic	3.3
Mexican	12.5
Puerto Rican	13.3
South American	10.1
Colombian	15.4
Ecuadorian	3.4
Peruvian	10.9

Class of Worker: Private Wage and Salary
(Universe: Civilian Employed Population 16 Years and Over)

Group	Number	%
Total Population	53,026	82.4
Hispanic or Latino (of any race)	12,968	81.8
Central American, ex. Mexican	5,541	82.1
Guatemalan	4,441	80.5
Dominican Republic	774	100.0
Mexican	958	83.7
Puerto Rican	1,159	91.5
South American	3,694	75.9
Colombian	1,167	78.4
Ecuadorian	1,031	71.7
Peruvian	1,103	75.2

Class of Worker: Government
(Universe: Civilian Employed Population 16 Years and Over)

Group	Number	%
Total Population	4,797	7.5
Hispanic or Latino (of any race)	360	2.3
Central American, ex. Mexican	62	0.9
Guatemalan	25	0.5
Dominican Republic	0	0.0
Mexican	10	0.9
Puerto Rican	101	8.0
South American	125	2.6
Colombian	63	4.2
Ecuadorian	28	1.9
Peruvian	0	0.0

Means of Transportation to Work: Car, Truck or Van
(Universe: Workers 16 Years and Over)

Group	Number	%
Total Population	48,337	77.2
Hispanic or Latino (of any race)	10,913	70.7
Central American, ex. Mexican	4,279	65.1
Guatemalan	3,470	64.7
Dominican Republic	475	63.1
Mexican	721	64.9
Puerto Rican	842	69.4
South American	3,784	79.8
Colombian	1,218	83.6
Ecuadorian	1,132	81.8
Peruvian	1,068	72.8

Means of Transportation to Work: Public Transportation (ex. Taxicab)
(Universe: Workers 16 Years and Over)

Group	Number	%
Total Population	7,476	11.9
Hispanic or Latino (of any race)	2,197	14.2
Central American, ex. Mexican	1,220	18.6
Guatemalan	1,012	18.9
Dominican Republic	29	3.9
Mexican	165	14.9
Puerto Rican	181	14.9
South American	571	12.0
Colombian	139	9.5
Ecuadorian	115	8.3
Peruvian	275	18.7

Homeownership Rate
(Universe: Occupied Housing Units)

Group	%
Total Population	55.3
Hispanic or Latino (of any race)	30.5
Central American, ex. Mexican	18.5
Costa Rican	39.6
Guatemalan	16.3
Honduran	20.3
Salvadoran	27.6
Cuban	52.1
Dominican Republic	22.6
Mexican	25.8
Puerto Rican	28.1
South American	41.9
Argentinean	51.3
Bolivian	47.2
Chilean	46.7
Colombian	44.6
Ecuadorian	41.7
Peruvian	38.8
Uruguayan	29.4
Venezuelan	36.7
Spaniard	54.8

Median Home Value

Group	Dollars
Total Population	574,900
Hispanic or Latino (of any race)	477,500
Central American, ex. Mexican	408,700
Guatemalan	415,300
Dominican Republic	592,300
Mexican	508,200
Puerto Rican	438,900
South American	530,900
Colombian	554,400
Ecuadorian	562,000
Peruvian	512,100

Median Gross Rent

Group	Dollars
Total Population	1,445
Hispanic or Latino (of any race)	1,438
Central American, ex. Mexican	1,471
Guatemalan	1,486
Dominican Republic	1,407
Mexican	1,538
Puerto Rican	1,423
South American	1,385
Colombian	1,554
Ecuadorian	1,132
Peruvian	1,355

Median Household Income
(2010 Inflation-Adjusted Dollars)

Group	Dollars
Total Population	75,579
Hispanic or Latino (of any race)	51,419
Central American, ex. Mexican	51,513
Guatemalan	50,295
Dominican Republic	36,017
Mexican	39,813
Puerto Rican	45,795
South American	55,331
Colombian	68,056
Ecuadorian	47,266
Peruvian	47,607

Per Capita Income
(2010 Inflation-Adjusted Dollars)

Group	Dollars
Total Population	44,667
Hispanic or Latino (of any race)	19,803
Central American, ex. Mexican	16,507
Guatemalan	15,186
Dominican Republic	13,902
Mexican	16,787
Puerto Rican	37,280
South American	20,444
Colombian	21,891
Ecuadorian	18,822
Peruvian	17,887

Notes: (1) Percent of total population; (2) Percent of Hispanic/Latino population; Profiles include places with an overall population of at least 125,000, OR an overall population of at least 25,000 where the Hispanic/Latino population is at least 20% of the overall population. In states where less than five places meet either of these criteria, we have included places with at least 10,000 total population with the highest percentage of Hispanic/Latino population. These places are identified with an asterisk (*); Please refer to the User's Guide for a full explanation of data.

Households with $100,000+ Income

Group	Number	%
Total Population	16,995	36.6
Hispanic or Latino (of any race)	1,354	17.2
Central American, ex. Mexican	381	14.6
Guatemalan	255	12.2
Dominican Republic	98	17.9
Mexican	82	13.8
Puerto Rican	128	15.1
South American	536	20.8
Colombian	207	25.8
Ecuadorian	82	12.3
Peruvian	149	19.3

Households with Food Stamps/SNAP Benefits During Past 12 Months

Group	Number	%
Total Population	2,503	5.4
Hispanic or Latino (of any race)	901	11.4
Central American, ex. Mexican	182	7.0
Guatemalan	141	6.8
Dominican Republic	143	26.1
Mexican	93	15.6
Puerto Rican	219	25.9
South American	264	10.2
Colombian	150	18.7
Ecuadorian	32	4.8
Peruvian	69	8.9

Poverty Rate
(Income in Past 12 Months Below Poverty Level)

Group	%
Total Population	11.1
Hispanic or Latino (of any race)	20.7
Central American, ex. Mexican	25.2
Guatemalan	28.2
Dominican Republic	31.1
Mexican	32.8
Puerto Rican	24.4
South American	12.6
Colombian	11.2
Ecuadorian	11.0
Peruvian	15.1

Waterbury

Population

Group	Number	%TP[1]	%HP[2]
Total Population	110,366	100.0	–
Hispanic or Latino (of any race)	34,446	31.2	100.0
Central American, ex. Mexican	824	0.7	2.4
Guatemalan	166	0.2	0.5
Honduran	346	0.3	1.0
Salvadoran	139	0.1	0.4
Cuban	277	0.3	0.8
Dominican Republic	3,743	3.4	10.9
Mexican	1,572	1.4	4.6
Puerto Rican	24,947	22.6	72.4
South American	1,823	1.7	5.3
Colombian	458	0.4	1.3
Ecuadorian	972	0.9	2.8
Peruvian	162	0.1	0.5
Spaniard	104	0.1	0.3

Population Growth: 2000–2010

Group	%
Total Population	2.9
Hispanic or Latino (of any race)	47.5
Central American, ex. Mexican	343.0
Cuban	34.5
Dominican Republic	180.2
Mexican	167.3
Puerto Rican	37.5
South American	221.0
Colombian	153.0
Ecuadorian	308.4

Males per 100 Females

Group	Number
Total Population	90.8
Hispanic or Latino (of any race)	91.6
Central American, ex. Mexican	111.3
Guatemalan	181.4
Honduran	111.0
Salvadoran	78.2
Cuban	106.7
Dominican Republic	86.3
Mexican	130.5
Puerto Rican	88.8
South American	101.2
Colombian	83.9
Ecuadorian	117.4
Peruvian	95.2
Spaniard	73.3

Average Household Size

Group	People
Total Population	2.54
Hispanic or Latino (of any race)	3.09
Central American, ex. Mexican	3.52
Guatemalan	3.02
Honduran	3.68
Salvadoran	4.00
Cuban	2.83
Dominican Republic	3.42
Mexican	3.53
Puerto Rican	3.01
South American	3.26
Colombian	2.89
Ecuadorian	3.73
Peruvian	3.00
Spaniard	2.50

Median Age

Group	Years
Total Population	35.2
Hispanic or Latino (of any race)	25.4
Central American, ex. Mexican	28.3
Guatemalan	28.5
Honduran	28.1
Salvadoran	27.4
Cuban	25.1
Dominican Republic	26.8
Mexican	25.7
Puerto Rican	24.7
South American	30.8
Colombian	32.2
Ecuadorian	28.8
Peruvian	38.5
Spaniard	39.5

High School Graduates
(Universe: Population 25 Years and Over)

Group	Number	%
Total Population	55,073	78.5
Hispanic or Latino (of any race)	10,716	65.9
Central American, ex. Mexican	368	59.8
Dominican Republic	853	58.5
Mexican	364	47.9
Puerto Rican	7,467	64.9
South American	955	83.0

Four-Year College Graduates
(Universe: Population 25 Years and Over)

Group	Number	%
Total Population	11,848	16.9
Hispanic or Latino (of any race)	1,508	9.3
Central American, ex. Mexican	65	10.6
Dominican Republic	141	9.7
Mexican	12	1.6
Puerto Rican	909	7.9
South American	214	18.6

Population Age 3–17 Enrolled in Public School
(Universe: Population Age 3–17 Enrolled in School)

Group	Number	%
Total Population	18,754	85.6
Hispanic or Latino (of any race)	8,653	95.0
Central American, ex. Mexican	272	93.2
Dominican Republic	891	97.5
Mexican	257	79.6
Puerto Rican	6,784	96.9
South American	194	62.8

Population Age 3–17 Enrolled in Private School
(Universe: Population Age 3–17 Enrolled in School)

Group	Number	%
Total Population	3,165	14.4
Hispanic or Latino (of any race)	454	5.0
Central American, ex. Mexican	20	6.8
Dominican Republic	23	2.5
Mexican	66	20.4
Puerto Rican	216	3.1
South American	115	37.2

Foreign-Born Population

Group	Number	%
Total Population	15,480	14.1
Hispanic or Latino (of any race)	4,473	13.6
Central American, ex. Mexican	708	65.4
Dominican Republic	1,392	48.6
Mexican	736	46.4
Puerto Rican	186	0.8
South American	1,138	65.4

Foreign-Born Naturalized U.S. Citizens

Group	Number	%
Total Population	7,328	47.3
Hispanic or Latino (of any race)	1,590	35.5
Central American, ex. Mexican	223	31.5
Dominican Republic	614	44.1
Mexican	0	0.0
Puerto Rican	140	75.3
South American	536	47.1

Language Spoken at Home: English Only
(Universe: Population 5 Years and Over)

Group	Number	%
Total Population	70,274	69.3
Hispanic or Latino (of any race)	8,678	30.1
Central American, ex. Mexican	148	15.1
Dominican Republic	547	21.5
Mexican	259	19.9
Puerto Rican	7,003	32.8
South American	210	13.9

Language Spoken at Home: Spanish
(Universe: Population 5 Years and Over)

Group	Number	%
Total Population	20,854	20.6
Hispanic or Latino (of any race)	20,129	69.8
Central American, ex. Mexican	812	82.9
Dominican Republic	2,000	78.5
Mexican	1,043	80.1
Puerto Rican	14,335	67.2
South American	1,299	86.1

Unemployment Rate
(Universe: Population 16 Years and Over)

Group	%
Total Population	12.1
Hispanic or Latino (of any race)	14.5
Central American, ex. Mexican	23.2
Dominican Republic	18.4
Mexican	10.2
Puerto Rican	15.1
South American	11.1

Class of Worker: Private Wage and Salary
(Universe: Civilian Employed Population 16 Years and Over)

Group	Number	%
Total Population	38,362	81.4
Hispanic or Latino (of any race)	9,945	85.9
Central American, ex. Mexican	360	78.1
Dominican Republic	958	87.9
Mexican	641	93.7
Puerto Rican	6,800	86.5
South American	727	81.6

Class of Worker: Government
(Universe: Civilian Employed Population 16 Years and Over)

Group	Number	%
Total Population	6,722	14.3
Hispanic or Latino (of any race)	1,106	9.5
Central American, ex. Mexican	15	3.3
Dominican Republic	61	5.6
Mexican	32	4.7
Puerto Rican	874	11.1
South American	65	7.3

STATE & PLACE PROFILES

Notes: (1) Percent of total population; (2) Percent of Hispanic/Latino population; Profiles include places with an overall population of at least 125,000, OR an overall population of at least 25,000 where the Hispanic/Latino population is at least 20% of the overall population. In states where less than five places meet either of these criteria, we have included places with at least 10,000 total population with the highest percentage of Hispanic/Latino population. These places are identified with an asterisk (*); Please refer to the User's Guide for a full explanation of data.

Means of Transportation to Work: Car, Truck or Van
(Universe: Workers 16 Years and Over)

Group	Number	%
Total Population	41,065	90.5
Hispanic or Latino (of any race)	9,370	83.2
Central American, ex. Mexican	326	73.9
Dominican Republic	817	77.4
Mexican	542	81.7
Puerto Rican	6,404	83.6
South American	796	90.6

Means of Transportation to Work: Public Transportation (ex. Taxicab)
(Universe: Workers 16 Years and Over)

Group	Number	%
Total Population	1,953	4.3
Hispanic or Latino (of any race)	864	7.7
Central American, ex. Mexican	50	11.3
Dominican Republic	21	2.0
Mexican	35	5.3
Puerto Rican	690	9.0
South American	41	4.7

Homeownership Rate
(Universe: Occupied Housing Units)

Group	%
Total Population	47.0
Hispanic or Latino (of any race)	24.6
Central American, ex. Mexican	35.3
Guatemalan	34.6
Honduran	27.8
Salvadoran	39.5
Cuban	33.3
Dominican Republic	31.5
Mexican	17.6
Puerto Rican	21.9
South American	44.0
Colombian	39.1
Ecuadorian	42.5
Peruvian	44.8
Spaniard	56.8

Median Home Value

Group	Dollars
Total Population	165,200
Hispanic or Latino (of any race)	154,500
Central American, ex. Mexican	188,000
Dominican Republic	143,200
Mexican	118,900
Puerto Rican	149,700
South American	169,100

Median Gross Rent

Group	Dollars
Total Population	853
Hispanic or Latino (of any race)	856
Central American, ex. Mexican	917
Dominican Republic	918
Mexican	935
Puerto Rican	841
South American	908

Median Household Income
(2010 Inflation-Adjusted Dollars)

Group	Dollars
Total Population	40,254
Hispanic or Latino (of any race)	27,146
Central American, ex. Mexican	28,958
Dominican Republic	30,139
Mexican	21,728
Puerto Rican	26,019
South American	37,411

Per Capita Income
(2010 Inflation-Adjusted Dollars)

Group	Dollars
Total Population	21,545
Hispanic or Latino (of any race)	12,984
Central American, ex. Mexican	16,007
Dominican Republic	11,537
Mexican	11,879
Puerto Rican	12,379
South American	17,455

Households with $100,000+ Income

Group	Number	%
Total Population	5,241	12.0
Hispanic or Latino (of any race)	735	6.7
Central American, ex. Mexican	50	12.3
Dominican Republic	27	2.9
Mexican	12	2.7
Puerto Rican	504	6.2
South American	30	5.8

Households with Food Stamps/SNAP Benefits During Past 12 Months

Group	Number	%
Total Population	8,659	19.8
Hispanic or Latino (of any race)	4,330	39.2
Central American, ex. Mexican	109	26.8
Dominican Republic	346	37.1
Mexican	89	19.8
Puerto Rican	3,605	44.0
South American	67	12.9

Poverty Rate
(Income in Past 12 Months Below Poverty Level)

Group	%
Total Population	20.9
Hispanic or Latino (of any race)	37.5
Central American, ex. Mexican	26.4
Dominican Republic	28.6
Mexican	43.0
Puerto Rican	40.4
South American	20.7

Windham

Population

Group	Number	%TP[1]	%HP[2]
Total Population	25,268	100.0	–
Hispanic or Latino (of any race)	8,653	34.2	100.0
Central American, ex. Mexican	249	1.0	2.9
Guatemalan	178	0.7	2.1
Dominican Republic	196	0.8	2.3
Mexican	1,704	6.7	19.7
Puerto Rican	6,061	24.0	70.0
South American	216	0.9	2.5

Population Growth: 2000–2010

Group	%
Total Population	10.5
Hispanic or Latino (of any race)	41.0
Mexican	74.4
Puerto Rican	35.8
South American	103.8

Males per 100 Females

Group	Number
Total Population	95.1
Hispanic or Latino (of any race)	101.5
Central American, ex. Mexican	255.7
Guatemalan	456.3
Dominican Republic	94.1
Mexican	136.3
Puerto Rican	90.6
South American	92.9

Average Household Size

Group	People
Total Population	2.50
Hispanic or Latino (of any race)	3.22
Central American, ex. Mexican	3.82
Guatemalan	3.86
Dominican Republic	3.26
Mexican	4.61
Puerto Rican	2.99
South American	2.63

Median Age

Group	Years
Total Population	30.3
Hispanic or Latino (of any race)	23.5
Central American, ex. Mexican	25.5
Guatemalan	24.6
Dominican Republic	24.7
Mexican	24.0
Puerto Rican	23.1
South American	28.3

High School Graduates
(Universe: Population 25 Years and Over)

Group	Number	%
Total Population	10,824	75.8
Hispanic or Latino (of any race)	1,904	51.7
Mexican	234	36.2
Puerto Rican	1,401	52.5

Four-Year College Graduates
(Universe: Population 25 Years and Over)

Group	Number	%
Total Population	2,842	19.9
Hispanic or Latino (of any race)	272	7.4
Mexican	25	3.9
Puerto Rican	140	5.2

Population Age 3–17 Enrolled in Public School
(Universe: Population Age 3–17 Enrolled in School)

Group	Number	%
Total Population	3,726	95.5
Hispanic or Latino (of any race)	2,401	98.5
Mexican	429	100.0
Puerto Rican	1,935	98.1

Population Age 3–17 Enrolled in Private School
(Universe: Population Age 3–17 Enrolled in School)

Group	Number	%
Total Population	176	4.5
Hispanic or Latino (of any race)	37	1.5
Mexican	0	0.0
Puerto Rican	37	1.9

Foreign-Born Population

Group	Number	%
Total Population	2,656	10.6
Hispanic or Latino (of any race)	1,547	19.0
Mexican	1,188	67.3
Puerto Rican	46	0.8

Foreign-Born Naturalized U.S. Citizens

Group	Number	%
Total Population	595	22.4
Hispanic or Latino (of any race)	156	10.1
Mexican	41	3.5
Puerto Rican	46	100.0

Language Spoken at Home: English Only
(Universe: Population 5 Years and Over)

Group	Number	%
Total Population	15,766	67.3
Hispanic or Latino (of any race)	982	13.5
Mexican	11	0.7
Puerto Rican	840	16.1

Language Spoken at Home: Spanish
(Universe: Population 5 Years and Over)

Group	Number	%
Total Population	6,530	27.9
Hispanic or Latino (of any race)	6,285	86.5
Mexican	1,522	99.3
Puerto Rican	4,379	83.9

Unemployment Rate
(Universe: Population 16 Years and Over)

Group	%
Total Population	13.6
Hispanic or Latino (of any race)	16.3
Mexican	11.0
Puerto Rican	18.2

Class of Worker: Private Wage and Salary
(Universe: Civilian Employed Population 16 Years and Over)

Group	Number	%
Total Population	8,436	70.0
Hispanic or Latino (of any race)	2,530	77.6
Mexican	831	95.2
Puerto Rican	1,516	70.5

Class of Worker: Government
(Universe: Civilian Employed Population 16 Years and Over)

Group	Number	%
Total Population	3,075	25.5
Hispanic or Latino (of any race)	712	21.8
Mexican	31	3.6

Notes: (1) Percent of total population; (2) Percent of Hispanic/Latino population; Profiles include places with an overall population of at least 125,000, OR an overall population of at least 25,000 where the Hispanic/Latino population is at least 20% of the overall population. In states where less than five places meet either of these criteria, we have included places with at least 10,000 total population with the highest percentage of Hispanic/Latino population. These places are identified with an asterisk (*); Please refer to the User's Guide for a full explanation of data.

Puerto Rican	624	29.0

Means of Transportation to Work: Car, Truck or Van
(Universe: Workers 16 Years and Over)

Group	Number	%
Total Population	9,914	85.1
Hispanic or Latino (of any race)	2,733	88.2
Mexican	638	76.4
Puerto Rican	1,870	92.3

Means of Transportation to Work: Public Transportation (ex. Taxicab)
(Universe: Workers 16 Years and Over)

Group	Number	%
Total Population	213	1.8
Hispanic or Latino (of any race)	60	1.9
Mexican	46	5.5
Puerto Rican	14	0.7

Homeownership Rate
(Universe: Occupied Housing Units)

Group	%
Total Population	48.7
Hispanic or Latino (of any race)	22.2
Central American, ex. Mexican	24.6
Guatemalan	7.1
Dominican Republic	25.9
Mexican	20.2
Puerto Rican	20.9
South American	53.7

Median Home Value

Group	Dollars
Total Population	173,000
Hispanic or Latino (of any race)	171,100
Mexican	232,900
Puerto Rican	159,900

Median Gross Rent

Group	Dollars
Total Population	794
Hispanic or Latino (of any race)	770
Mexican	882
Puerto Rican	586

Median Household Income
(2010 Inflation-Adjusted Dollars)

Group	Dollars
Total Population	40,063
Hispanic or Latino (of any race)	29,239
Mexican	45,379
Puerto Rican	23,750

Per Capita Income
(2010 Inflation-Adjusted Dollars)

Group	Dollars
Total Population	20,272
Hispanic or Latino (of any race)	13,383
Mexican	12,740
Puerto Rican	12,592

Households with $100,000+ Income

Group	Number	%
Total Population	1,059	11.8
Hispanic or Latino (of any race)	178	7.2
Mexican	34	7.3
Puerto Rican	104	5.6

Households with Food Stamps/SNAP Benefits During Past 12 Months

Group	Number	%
Total Population	1,907	21.3
Hispanic or Latino (of any race)	1,058	42.7
Mexican	130	28.1
Puerto Rican	922	49.5

Poverty Rate
(Income in Past 12 Months Below Poverty Level)

Group	%
Total Population	22.8
Hispanic or Latino (of any race)	36.2
Mexican	39.6
Puerto Rican	36.0

Notes: (1) Percent of total population; (2) Percent of Hispanic/Latino population; Profiles include places with an overall population of at least 125,000, OR an overall population of at least 25,000 where the Hispanic/Latino population is at least 20% of the overall population. In states where less than five places meet either of these criteria, we have included places with at least 10,000 total population with the highest percentage of Hispanic/Latino population. These places are identified with an asterisk (*); Please refer to the User's Guide for a full explanation of data.

STATE & PLACE PROFILES

Delaware

EDITOR'S NOTE: For a place to be included in this edition, it must meet one of two criteria. Either its overall population is at least 125,000, OR its overall population is at least 25,000 and its Hispanic/Latino population is at least 20% of the overall population. In Delaware, less than five places meet either of these criteria. In an effort to include at least five places for each state, we have included places with at least 10,000 total population with the highest percentage of Hispanic/Latino population. These places are identified with an asterisk (*). For the state of Delaware, the following locations are included:

Bear*
Brookside*
Dover*
Middle*
Wilmington*

Section Two: State & Place Profiles starts with the state profile, followed by place profiles that meet the criteria above. Places are listed alphabetically within each state. All states, all counties and places that meet the above criteria are ranked and compared in *Section Three: Rankings & Comparisons*, on page 1055.

For a more detailed look at the Hispanic/Latino population in Delaware, a companion web site is available at no additional charge with purchase of this print edition. Visit http://gold.greyhouse.com/page/info_hispanic for more information.

The web site includes data for all counties and places in Delaware with Hispanic/Latino population, plus ten additional topics: Self Employed Worker; Walked to Work; Worked from Home; Mean Travel Time to Work; Mean Household Income; Households with Cash Public Assistance; Mean Cash Pubic Assistance; Poverty Rates for 18 and Under, 18 to 64, and 65 and Over.

Population

Group	Number	%TP[1]	%HP[2]
Total Population	897,934	100.0	–
Hispanic or Latino (of any race)	73,221	8.2	100.0
Central American, ex. Mexican	8,112	0.9	11.1
Costa Rican	243	<0.1	0.3
Guatemalan	5,202	0.6	7.1
Honduran	675	0.1	0.9
Nicaraguan	225	<0.1	0.3
Panamanian	501	0.1	0.7
Salvadoran	1,231	0.1	1.7
Cuban	1,443	0.2	2.0
Dominican Republic	2,035	0.2	2.8
Mexican	30,283	3.4	41.4
Puerto Rican	22,533	2.5	30.8
South American	3,849	0.4	5.3
Argentinean	360	<0.1	0.5
Bolivian	112	<0.1	0.2
Chilean	335	<0.1	0.5
Colombian	1,248	0.1	1.7
Ecuadorian	545	0.1	0.7
Peruvian	704	0.1	1.0
Venezuelan	389	<0.1	0.5
Spaniard	850	0.1	1.2

Population Growth: 2000–2010

Group	%
Total Population	14.6
Hispanic or Latino (of any race)	96.4
Central American, ex. Mexican	229.5
Guatemalan	218.6
Honduran	440.0
Panamanian	111.4
Salvadoran	423.8
Cuban	54.8
Dominican Republic	203.3
Mexican	133.2
Puerto Rican	60.9
South American	142.7
Argentinean	146.6
Chilean	131.0
Colombian	124.9
Ecuadorian	157.1
Peruvian	240.1
Venezuelan	92.6
Spaniard	507.1

Males per 100 Females

Group	Number
Total Population	93.9
Hispanic or Latino (of any race)	107.5
Central American, ex. Mexican	121.2
Costa Rican	88.4
Guatemalan	136.8
Honduran	116.3
Nicaraguan	92.3
Panamanian	59.6
Salvadoran	110.4
Cuban	87.4
Dominican Republic	86.2
Mexican	119.4
Puerto Rican	96.8
South American	91.4
Argentinean	103.4
Bolivian	124.0
Chilean	108.1
Colombian	82.2
Ecuadorian	87.3
Peruvian	98.3
Venezuelan	80.1
Spaniard	90.6

Average Household Size

Group	People
Total Population	2.55
Hispanic or Latino (of any race)	3.70
Central American, ex. Mexican	4.78
Costa Rican	3.05
Guatemalan	5.79
Honduran	3.77
Nicaraguan	3.44
Panamanian	2.48
Salvadoran	4.21
Cuban	2.60
Dominican Republic	3.49
Mexican	4.36
Puerto Rican	3.12
South American	2.99
Argentinean	2.66
Bolivian	3.33
Chilean	2.68
Colombian	3.03
Ecuadorian	3.37
Peruvian	3.21
Venezuelan	2.82
Spaniard	2.52

Median Age

Group	Years
Total Population	38.8
Hispanic or Latino (of any race)	24.8
Central American, ex. Mexican	25.8
Costa Rican	28.9
Guatemalan	24.6
Honduran	27.7
Nicaraguan	29.5
Panamanian	35.2
Salvadoran	28.5
Cuban	31.3
Dominican Republic	25.5
Mexican	23.8
Puerto Rican	24.8
South American	32.4
Argentinean	35.2
Bolivian	31.7
Chilean	32.1
Colombian	30.9
Ecuadorian	29.4
Peruvian	35.6
Venezuelan	34.1
Spaniard	31.8

High School Graduates
(Universe: Population 25 Years and Over)

Group	Number	%
Total Population	511,757	87.0
Hispanic or Latino (of any race)	19,189	57.7
Central American, ex. Mexican	1,431	38.1
Guatemalan	721	27.4
Cuban	777	91.4
Dominican Republic	409	57.7
Mexican	5,727	42.9
Puerto Rican	7,299	70.5
South American	2,549	84.0
Colombian	608	88.2
Peruvian	678	68.8

Four-Year College Graduates
(Universe: Population 25 Years and Over)

Group	Number	%
Total Population	162,651	27.7
Hispanic or Latino (of any race)	4,163	12.5
Central American, ex. Mexican	392	10.4
Guatemalan	168	6.4
Cuban	335	39.4
Dominican Republic	91	12.8
Mexican	929	7.0
Puerto Rican	1,193	11.5
South American	922	30.4
Colombian	231	33.5
Peruvian	217	22.0

Population Age 3–17 Enrolled in Public School
(Universe: Population Age 3–17 Enrolled in School)

Group	Number	%
Total Population	122,713	79.5
Hispanic or Latino (of any race)	15,426	92.9
Central American, ex. Mexican	1,558	94.3
Guatemalan	1,035	92.7
Cuban	167	46.9
Dominican Republic	235	95.9
Mexican	6,949	95.5
Puerto Rican	5,179	92.6
South American	908	88.6
Colombian	134	100.0
Peruvian	479	100.0

Population Age 3–17 Enrolled in Private School
(Universe: Population Age 3–17 Enrolled in School)

Group	Number	%
Total Population	31,547	20.5
Hispanic or Latino (of any race)	1,187	7.1
Central American, ex. Mexican	95	5.7
Guatemalan	81	7.3
Cuban	189	53.1
Dominican Republic	10	4.1
Mexican	328	4.5
Puerto Rican	411	7.4
South American	117	11.4
Colombian	0	0.0
Peruvian	0	0.0

Foreign-Born Population

Group	Number	%
Total Population	72,531	8.2
Hispanic or Latino (of any race)	26,170	39.1
Central American, ex. Mexican	4,640	64.0
Guatemalan	3,450	67.2
Cuban	425	29.4
Dominican Republic	805	54.6
Mexican	16,047	56.3
Puerto Rican	122	0.6
South American	3,212	65.2
Colombian	811	74.1
Peruvian	1,123	69.4

Notes: (1) Percent of total population; (2) Percent of Hispanic/Latino population; Profiles include places with an overall population of at least 125,000, OR an overall population of at least 25,000 where the Hispanic/Latino population is at least 20% of the overall population. In states where less than five places meet either of these criteria, we have included places with at least 10,000 total population with the highest percentage of Hispanic/Latino population. These places are identified with an asterisk (*); Please refer to the User's Guide for a full explanation of data.

Foreign-Born Naturalized U.S. Citizens

Group	Number	%
Total Population	29,935	41.3
Hispanic or Latino (of any race)	5,244	20.0
Central American, ex. Mexican	443	9.5
Guatemalan	181	5.2
Cuban	398	93.6
Dominican Republic	428	53.2
Mexican	1,969	12.3
Puerto Rican	113	92.6
South American	1,468	45.7
Colombian	227	28.0
Peruvian	482	42.9

Language Spoken at Home: English Only
(Universe: Population 5 Years and Over)

Group	Number	%
Total Population	724,189	87.8
Hispanic or Latino (of any race)	14,807	25.4
Central American, ex. Mexican	907	14.6
Guatemalan	225	5.2
Cuban	756	57.4
Dominican Republic	207	15.8
Mexican	4,175	17.0
Puerto Rican	6,960	38.2
South American	849	18.4
Colombian	87	8.4
Peruvian	105	6.8

Language Spoken at Home: Spanish
(Universe: Population 5 Years and Over)

Group	Number	%
Total Population	54,227	6.6
Hispanic or Latino (of any race)	43,236	74.0
Central American, ex. Mexican	5,209	83.7
Guatemalan	4,017	92.3
Cuban	562	42.6
Dominican Republic	1,103	84.2
Mexican	20,331	82.8
Puerto Rican	11,219	61.6
South American	3,734	81.0
Colombian	946	91.6
Peruvian	1,448	93.2

Unemployment Rate
(Universe: Population 16 Years and Over)

Group	%
Total Population	7.1
Hispanic or Latino (of any race)	8.9
Central American, ex. Mexican	9.2
Guatemalan	11.7
Cuban	11.5
Dominican Republic	15.7
Mexican	6.8
Puerto Rican	10.0
South American	10.1
Colombian	5.9
Peruvian	21.4

Class of Worker: Private Wage and Salary
(Universe: Civilian Employed Population 16 Years and Over)

Group	Number	%
Total Population	339,582	81.0
Hispanic or Latino (of any race)	25,118	89.8
Central American, ex. Mexican	3,259	94.3
Guatemalan	2,364	96.7
Cuban	411	78.9
Dominican Republic	531	81.9
Mexican	11,308	92.9
Puerto Rican	6,906	87.1
South American	1,897	84.0
Colombian	512	95.0
Peruvian	452	74.8

Class of Worker: Government
(Universe: Civilian Employed Population 16 Years and Over)

Group	Number	%
Total Population	60,859	14.5
Hispanic or Latino (of any race)	2,055	7.4
Central American, ex. Mexican	108	3.1
Guatemalan	7	0.3
Cuban	81	15.5
Dominican Republic	62	9.6
Mexican	410	3.4
Puerto Rican	958	12.1
South American	301	13.3
Colombian	27	5.0
Peruvian	124	20.5

Means of Transportation to Work: Car, Truck or Van
(Universe: Workers 16 Years and Over)

Group	Number	%
Total Population	369,627	89.7
Hispanic or Latino (of any race)	23,573	86.1
Central American, ex. Mexican	2,688	80.9
Guatemalan	1,752	75.8
Cuban	416	82.2
Dominican Republic	555	83.6
Mexican	10,193	85.7
Puerto Rican	6,971	88.5
South American	1,852	87.4
Colombian	493	94.3
Peruvian	407	74.4

Means of Transportation to Work: Public Transportation (ex. Taxicab)
(Universe: Workers 16 Years and Over)

Group	Number	%
Total Population	13,062	3.2
Hispanic or Latino (of any race)	1,450	5.3
Central American, ex. Mexican	30	0.9
Guatemalan	18	0.8
Cuban	25	4.9
Dominican Republic	0	0.0
Mexican	948	8.0
Puerto Rican	322	4.1
South American	125	5.9
Colombian	0	0.0
Peruvian	83	15.2

Homeownership Rate
(Universe: Occupied Housing Units)

Group	%
Total Population	72.1
Hispanic or Latino (of any race)	46.1
Central American, ex. Mexican	36.6
Costa Rican	62.1
Guatemalan	26.1
Honduran	35.0
Nicaraguan	50.0
Panamanian	59.7
Salvadoran	47.8
Cuban	66.6
Dominican Republic	49.3
Mexican	39.6
Puerto Rican	49.7
South American	61.1
Argentinean	70.0
Bolivian	70.0
Chilean	54.2
Colombian	63.7
Ecuadorian	59.3
Peruvian	56.2
Venezuelan	62.3
Spaniard	74.8

Median Home Value

Group	Dollars
Total Population	242,300
Hispanic or Latino (of any race)	190,900
Central American, ex. Mexican	179,100
Guatemalan	151,300
Cuban	286,400
Dominican Republic	196,900
Mexican	167,300
Puerto Rican	188,700
South American	254,300
Colombian	220,800
Peruvian	264,400

Median Gross Rent

Group	Dollars
Total Population	938
Hispanic or Latino (of any race)	913
Central American, ex. Mexican	1,038
Guatemalan	1,088
Cuban	839
Dominican Republic	944
Mexican	923
Puerto Rican	806
South American	880
Colombian	748
Peruvian	846

Median Household Income
(2010 Inflation-Adjusted Dollars)

Group	Dollars
Total Population	57,599
Hispanic or Latino (of any race)	41,530
Central American, ex. Mexican	50,315
Guatemalan	50,650
Cuban	36,875
Dominican Republic	36,219
Mexican	39,714
Puerto Rican	41,429
South American	43,977
Colombian	48,636
Peruvian	39,225

Per Capita Income
(2010 Inflation-Adjusted Dollars)

Group	Dollars
Total Population	29,007
Hispanic or Latino (of any race)	14,946
Central American, ex. Mexican	13,747
Guatemalan	13,088
Cuban	31,686
Dominican Republic	21,147
Mexican	13,055
Puerto Rican	14,765
South American	21,163
Colombian	13,879
Peruvian	11,992

Households with $100,000+ Income

Group	Number	%
Total Population	77,739	23.4
Hispanic or Latino (of any race)	2,182	13.2
Central American, ex. Mexican	324	20.7
Guatemalan	275	30.4
Cuban	182	33.9
Dominican Republic	52	11.7
Mexican	741	11.8
Puerto Rican	523	9.1
South American	222	16.6
Colombian	16	6.3
Peruvian	21	5.2

Households with Food Stamps/SNAP Benefits During Past 12 Months

Group	Number	%
Total Population	27,718	8.4
Hispanic or Latino (of any race)	3,058	18.5
Central American, ex. Mexican	327	20.9
Guatemalan	221	24.4
Cuban	58	10.8
Dominican Republic	115	26.0
Mexican	785	12.5
Puerto Rican	1,551	27.1
South American	161	12.0
Colombian	29	11.5
Peruvian	76	18.8

Poverty Rate
(Income in Past 12 Months Below Poverty Level)

Group	%
Total Population	11.0
Hispanic or Latino (of any race)	23.2
Central American, ex. Mexican	22.3
Guatemalan	26.4
Cuban	18.5
Dominican Republic	20.9
Mexican	24.8
Puerto Rican	23.9
South American	16.4
Colombian	15.2
Peruvian	12.2

Bear*

Population

Group	Number	%TP[1]	%HP[2]
Total Population	19,371	100.0	–

Notes: (1) Percent of total population; (2) Percent of Hispanic/Latino population; Profiles include places with an overall population of at least 125,000, OR an overall population of at least 25,000 where the Hispanic/Latino population is at least 20% of the overall population. In states where less than five places meet either of these criteria, we have included places with at least 10,000 total population with the highest percentage of Hispanic/Latino population. These places are identified with an asterisk (*); Please refer to the User's Guide for a full explanation of data.

Hispanic or Latino (of any race)	2,750	14.2	100.0
Mexican	1,673	8.6	60.8
Puerto Rican	658	3.4	23.9
South American	135	0.7	4.9

Population Growth: 2000–2010

Group	%
Total Population	10.1
Hispanic or Latino (of any race)	184.1
Mexican	708.2
Puerto Rican	40.3

Males per 100 Females

Group	Number
Total Population	93.4
Hispanic or Latino (of any race)	113.7
Mexican	124.6
Puerto Rican	95.8
South American	101.5

Average Household Size

Group	People
Total Population	2.80
Hispanic or Latino (of any race)	4.01
Mexican	4.94
Puerto Rican	3.05
South American	3.20

Median Age

Group	Years
Total Population	33.1
Hispanic or Latino (of any race)	24.5
Mexican	23.6
Puerto Rican	25.3
South American	33.8

High School Graduates
(Universe: Population 25 Years and Over)

Group	Number	%
Total Population	9,853	86.9
Hispanic or Latino (of any race)	1,013	66.0
Mexican	370	45.2

Four-Year College Graduates
(Universe: Population 25 Years and Over)

Group	Number	%
Total Population	2,300	20.3
Hispanic or Latino (of any race)	260	16.9
Mexican	85	10.4

Population Age 3–17 Enrolled in Public School
(Universe: Population Age 3–17 Enrolled in School)

Group	Number	%
Total Population	3,771	87.5
Hispanic or Latino (of any race)	799	98.4
Mexican	407	96.9

Population Age 3–17 Enrolled in Private School
(Universe: Population Age 3–17 Enrolled in School)

Group	Number	%
Total Population	538	12.5
Hispanic or Latino (of any race)	13	1.6
Mexican	13	3.1

Foreign-Born Population

Group	Number	%
Total Population	2,449	13.1
Hispanic or Latino (of any race)	1,554	47.1
Mexican	1,172	58.0

Foreign-Born Naturalized U.S. Citizens

Group	Number	%
Total Population	849	34.7
Hispanic or Latino (of any race)	363	23.4
Mexican	99	8.4

Language Spoken at Home: English Only
(Universe: Population 5 Years and Over)

Group	Number	%
Total Population	13,950	80.0
Hispanic or Latino (of any race)	251	8.8
Mexican	106	6.5

Language Spoken at Home: Spanish
(Universe: Population 5 Years and Over)

Group	Number	%
Total Population	2,750	15.8
Hispanic or Latino (of any race)	2,610	91.2
Mexican	1,532	93.5

Unemployment Rate
(Universe: Population 16 Years and Over)

Group	%
Total Population	7.8
Hispanic or Latino (of any race)	8.2
Mexican	2.4

Class of Worker: Private Wage and Salary
(Universe: Civilian Employed Population 16 Years and Over)

Group	Number	%
Total Population	8,108	85.8
Hispanic or Latino (of any race)	1,430	94.0
Mexican	921	96.3

Class of Worker: Government
(Universe: Civilian Employed Population 16 Years and Over)

Group	Number	%
Total Population	942	10.0
Hispanic or Latino (of any race)	69	4.5
Mexican	13	1.4

Means of Transportation to Work: Car, Truck or Van
(Universe: Workers 16 Years and Over)

Group	Number	%
Total Population	8,524	91.8
Hispanic or Latino (of any race)	1,348	88.6
Mexican	800	83.7

Means of Transportation to Work: Public Transportation (ex. Taxicab)
(Universe: Workers 16 Years and Over)

Group	Number	%
Total Population	407	4.4
Hispanic or Latino (of any race)	113	7.4
Mexican	96	10.0

Homeownership Rate
(Universe: Occupied Housing Units)

Group	%
Total Population	67.8
Hispanic or Latino (of any race)	52.7
Mexican	49.7
Puerto Rican	55.2
South American	65.0

Median Home Value

Group	Dollars
Total Population	196,300
Hispanic or Latino (of any race)	214,300
Mexican	107,600

Median Gross Rent

Group	Dollars
Total Population	1,280
Hispanic or Latino (of any race)	1,239
Mexican	1,214

Median Household Income
(2010 Inflation-Adjusted Dollars)

Group	Dollars
Total Population	60,970
Hispanic or Latino (of any race)	48,438
Mexican	39,955

Per Capita Income
(2010 Inflation-Adjusted Dollars)

Group	Dollars
Total Population	23,618
Hispanic or Latino (of any race)	13,947
Mexican	12,381

Households with $100,000+ Income

Group	Number	%
Total Population	1,198	18.8
Hispanic or Latino (of any race)	85	11.3
Mexican	54	14.5

Households with Food Stamps/SNAP Benefits During Past 12 Months

Group	Number	%
Total Population	540	8.5
Hispanic or Latino (of any race)	93	12.3
Mexican	42	11.3

Poverty Rate
(Income in Past 12 Months Below Poverty Level)

Group	%
Total Population	11.9
Hispanic or Latino (of any race)	23.1
Mexican	20.7

Brookside*

Population

Group	Number	%TP[1]	%HP[2]
Total Population	14,353	100.0	–
Hispanic or Latino (of any race)	1,601	11.2	100.0
Mexican	806	5.6	50.3
Puerto Rican	472	3.3	29.5
South American	112	0.8	7.0

Population Growth: 2000–2010

Group	%
Total Population	-3.1
Hispanic or Latino (of any race)	93.6
Mexican	164.3
Puerto Rican	63.9

Males per 100 Females

Group	Number
Total Population	91.6
Hispanic or Latino (of any race)	107.1
Mexican	125.8
Puerto Rican	86.6
South American	96.5

Average Household Size

Group	People
Total Population	2.72
Hispanic or Latino (of any race)	3.96
Mexican	5.02
Puerto Rican	3.35
South American	3.81

Median Age

Group	Years
Total Population	34.9
Hispanic or Latino (of any race)	24.5
Mexican	24.2
Puerto Rican	23.0
South American	31.8

High School Graduates
(Universe: Population 25 Years and Over)

Group	Number	%
Total Population	7,947	87.8
Hispanic or Latino (of any race)	315	53.9

Four-Year College Graduates
(Universe: Population 25 Years and Over)

Group	Number	%
Total Population	1,744	19.3
Hispanic or Latino (of any race)	39	6.7

Population Age 3–17 Enrolled in Public School
(Universe: Population Age 3–17 Enrolled in School)

Group	Number	%
Total Population	2,479	91.3
Hispanic or Latino (of any race)	416	98.1

Population Age 3–17 Enrolled in Private School
(Universe: Population Age 3–17 Enrolled in School)

Group	Number	%
Total Population	237	8.7
Hispanic or Latino (of any race)	8	1.9

Foreign-Born Population

Group	Number	%
Total Population	1,282	8.9
Hispanic or Latino (of any race)	678	55.6

Notes: (1) Percent of total population; (2) Percent of Hispanic/Latino population; Profiles include places with an overall population of at least 125,000, OR an overall population of at least 25,000 where the Hispanic/Latino population is at least 20% of the overall population. In states where less than five places meet either of these criteria, we have included places with at least 10,000 total population with the highest percentage of Hispanic/Latino population. These places are identified with an asterisk (*); Please refer to the User's Guide for a full explanation of data.

Foreign-Born Naturalized U.S. Citizens

Group	Number	%
Total Population	746	58.2
Hispanic or Latino (of any race)	376	55.5

Language Spoken at Home: English Only
(Universe: Population 5 Years and Over)

Group	Number	%
Total Population	11,437	85.7
Hispanic or Latino (of any race)	273	23.9

Language Spoken at Home: Spanish
(Universe: Population 5 Years and Over)

Group	Number	%
Total Population	924	6.9
Hispanic or Latino (of any race)	870	76.1

Unemployment Rate
(Universe: Population 16 Years and Over)

Group	%
Total Population	6.7
Hispanic or Latino (of any race)	10.0

Class of Worker: Private Wage and Salary
(Universe: Civilian Employed Population 16 Years and Over)

Group	Number	%
Total Population	6,581	87.7
Hispanic or Latino (of any race)	512	100.0

Class of Worker: Government
(Universe: Civilian Employed Population 16 Years and Over)

Group	Number	%
Total Population	775	10.3
Hispanic or Latino (of any race)	0	0.0

Means of Transportation to Work: Car, Truck or Van
(Universe: Workers 16 Years and Over)

Group	Number	%
Total Population	6,911	93.4
Hispanic or Latino (of any race)	416	93.9

Means of Transportation to Work: Public Transportation (ex. Taxicab)
(Universe: Workers 16 Years and Over)

Group	Number	%
Total Population	191	2.6
Hispanic or Latino (of any race)	27	6.1

Homeownership Rate
(Universe: Occupied Housing Units)

Group	%
Total Population	68.6
Hispanic or Latino (of any race)	56.3
Mexican	62.3
Puerto Rican	51.6
South American	68.8

Median Home Value

Group	Dollars
Total Population	198,700
Hispanic or Latino (of any race)	206,400

Median Gross Rent

Group	Dollars
Total Population	972
Hispanic or Latino (of any race)	786

Median Household Income
(2010 Inflation-Adjusted Dollars)

Group	Dollars
Total Population	53,470
Hispanic or Latino (of any race)	49,774

Per Capita Income
(2010 Inflation-Adjusted Dollars)

Group	Dollars
Total Population	23,945
Hispanic or Latino (of any race)	13,311

Households with $100,000+ Income

Group	Number	%
Total Population	882	16.6
Hispanic or Latino (of any race)	21	7.2

Households with Food Stamps/SNAP Benefits During Past 12 Months

Group	Number	%
Total Population	256	4.8
Hispanic or Latino (of any race)	13	4.4

Poverty Rate
(Income in Past 12 Months Below Poverty Level)

Group	%
Total Population	6.2
Hispanic or Latino (of any race)	7.1

Dover*

Population

Group	Number	%TP[1]	%HP[2]
Total Population	36,047	100.0	–
Hispanic or Latino (of any race)	2,362	6.6	100.0
Central American, ex. Mexican	190	0.5	8.0
Mexican	584	1.6	24.7
Puerto Rican	1,091	3.0	46.2
South American	126	0.3	5.3

Population Growth: 2000–2010

Group	%
Total Population	12.2
Hispanic or Latino (of any race)	78.0
Mexican	105.6
Puerto Rican	77.1

Males per 100 Females

Group	Number
Total Population	86.7
Hispanic or Latino (of any race)	93.6
Central American, ex. Mexican	108.8
Mexican	111.6
Puerto Rican	88.4
South American	88.1

Average Household Size

Group	People
Total Population	2.35
Hispanic or Latino (of any race)	2.86
Central American, ex. Mexican	3.29
Mexican	3.20
Puerto Rican	2.80
South American	2.40

Median Age

Group	Years
Total Population	31.3
Hispanic or Latino (of any race)	23.8
Central American, ex. Mexican	25.5
Mexican	23.6
Puerto Rican	22.7
South American	30.0

High School Graduates
(Universe: Population 25 Years and Over)

Group	Number	%
Total Population	17,654	86.3
Hispanic or Latino (of any race)	503	59.6

Four-Year College Graduates
(Universe: Population 25 Years and Over)

Group	Number	%
Total Population	5,662	27.7
Hispanic or Latino (of any race)	64	7.6

Population Age 3–17 Enrolled in Public School
(Universe: Population Age 3–17 Enrolled in School)

Group	Number	%
Total Population	5,402	87.5
Hispanic or Latino (of any race)	452	96.4

Population Age 3–17 Enrolled in Private School
(Universe: Population Age 3–17 Enrolled in School)

Group	Number	%
Total Population	772	12.5
Hispanic or Latino (of any race)	17	3.6

Foreign-Born Population

Group	Number	%
Total Population	2,366	6.7
Hispanic or Latino (of any race)	372	20.4

Foreign-Born Naturalized U.S. Citizens

Group	Number	%
Total Population	1,192	50.4
Hispanic or Latino (of any race)	157	42.2

Language Spoken at Home: English Only
(Universe: Population 5 Years and Over)

Group	Number	%
Total Population	29,829	90.9
Hispanic or Latino (of any race)	443	29.9

Language Spoken at Home: Spanish
(Universe: Population 5 Years and Over)

Group	Number	%
Total Population	1,277	3.9
Hispanic or Latino (of any race)	998	67.4

Unemployment Rate
(Universe: Population 16 Years and Over)

Group	%
Total Population	8.5
Hispanic or Latino (of any race)	10.5

Class of Worker: Private Wage and Salary
(Universe: Civilian Employed Population 16 Years and Over)

Group	Number	%
Total Population	10,846	72.4
Hispanic or Latino (of any race)	639	87.5

Class of Worker: Government
(Universe: Civilian Employed Population 16 Years and Over)

Group	Number	%
Total Population	3,719	24.8
Hispanic or Latino (of any race)	91	12.5

Means of Transportation to Work: Car, Truck or Van
(Universe: Workers 16 Years and Over)

Group	Number	%
Total Population	14,500	90.5
Hispanic or Latino (of any race)	726	96.0

Means of Transportation to Work: Public Transportation (ex. Taxicab)
(Universe: Workers 16 Years and Over)

Group	Number	%
Total Population	423	2.6
Hispanic or Latino (of any race)	0	0.0

Homeownership Rate
(Universe: Occupied Housing Units)

Group	%
Total Population	51.9
Hispanic or Latino (of any race)	39.1
Central American, ex. Mexican	37.5
Mexican	37.2
Puerto Rican	38.0
South American	45.2

Median Home Value

Group	Dollars
Total Population	192,400
Hispanic or Latino (of any race)	177,200

Median Gross Rent

Group	Dollars
Total Population	891
Hispanic or Latino (of any race)	1,026

Median Household Income
(2010 Inflation-Adjusted Dollars)

Group	Dollars
Total Population	46,195
Hispanic or Latino (of any race)	42,520

Per Capita Income
(2010 Inflation-Adjusted Dollars)

Group	Dollars
Total Population	22,697
Hispanic or Latino (of any race)	14,298

Households with $100,000+ Income

Group	Number	%
Total Population	1,611	12.3

Notes: (1) Percent of total population; (2) Percent of Hispanic/Latino population; Profiles include places with an overall population of at least 125,000, OR an overall population of at least 25,000 where the Hispanic/Latino population is at least 20% of the overall population. In states where less than five places meet either of these criteria, we have included places with at least 10,000 total population with the highest percentage of Hispanic/Latino population. These places are identified with an asterisk (*); Please refer to the User's Guide for a full explanation of data.

Hispanic or Latino (of any race)	44	8.7

Households with Food Stamps/SNAP Benefits During Past 12 Months

Group	Number	%
Total Population	1,492	11.4
Hispanic or Latino (of any race)	82	16.2

Poverty Rate
(Income in Past 12 Months Below Poverty Level)

Group	%
Total Population	17.2
Hispanic or Latino (of any race)	35.2

Middle*

Population

Group	Number	%TP[1]	%HP[2]
Total Population	18,871	100.0	–
Hispanic or Latino (of any race)	1,396	7.4	100.0
Central American, ex. Mexican	108	0.6	7.7
Mexican	487	2.6	34.9
Puerto Rican	513	2.7	36.7

Population Growth: 2000–2010

Group	%
Total Population	206.3
Hispanic or Latino (of any race)	328.2
Mexican	206.3

Males per 100 Females

Group	Number
Total Population	88.9
Hispanic or Latino (of any race)	97.2
Central American, ex. Mexican	103.8
Mexican	117.4
Puerto Rican	92.9

Average Household Size

Group	People
Total Population	2.90
Hispanic or Latino (of any race)	3.60
Central American, ex. Mexican	4.07
Mexican	3.97
Puerto Rican	3.38

Median Age

Group	Years
Total Population	33.0
Hispanic or Latino (of any race)	25.5
Central American, ex. Mexican	28.7
Mexican	26.0
Puerto Rican	21.9

High School Graduates
(Universe: Population 25 Years and Over)

Group	Number	%
Total Population	9,350	92.1
Hispanic or Latino (of any race)	404	86.9

Four-Year College Graduates
(Universe: Population 25 Years and Over)

Group	Number	%
Total Population	3,158	31.1
Hispanic or Latino (of any race)	37	8.0

Population Age 3–17 Enrolled in Public School
(Universe: Population Age 3–17 Enrolled in School)

Group	Number	%
Total Population	3,257	81.2
Hispanic or Latino (of any race)	408	85.5

Population Age 3–17 Enrolled in Private School
(Universe: Population Age 3–17 Enrolled in School)

Group	Number	%
Total Population	755	18.8
Hispanic or Latino (of any race)	69	14.5

Foreign-Born Population

Group	Number	%
Total Population	1,209	7.3
Hispanic or Latino (of any race)	334	27.9

Foreign-Born Naturalized U.S. Citizens

Group	Number	%
Total Population	532	44.0
Hispanic or Latino (of any race)	10	3.0

Language Spoken at Home: English Only
(Universe: Population 5 Years and Over)

Group	Number	%
Total Population	13,345	89.2
Hispanic or Latino (of any race)	505	46.8

Language Spoken at Home: Spanish
(Universe: Population 5 Years and Over)

Group	Number	%
Total Population	763	5.1
Hispanic or Latino (of any race)	573	53.2

Unemployment Rate
(Universe: Population 16 Years and Over)

Group	%
Total Population	8.1
Hispanic or Latino (of any race)	24.2

Class of Worker: Private Wage and Salary
(Universe: Civilian Employed Population 16 Years and Over)

Group	Number	%
Total Population	6,292	79.2
Hispanic or Latino (of any race)	318	75.4

Class of Worker: Government
(Universe: Civilian Employed Population 16 Years and Over)

Group	Number	%
Total Population	1,377	17.3
Hispanic or Latino (of any race)	72	17.1

Means of Transportation to Work: Car, Truck or Van
(Universe: Workers 16 Years and Over)

Group	Number	%
Total Population	7,253	92.6
Hispanic or Latino (of any race)	376	89.1

Means of Transportation to Work: Public Transportation (ex. Taxicab)
(Universe: Workers 16 Years and Over)

Group	Number	%
Total Population	57	0.7
Hispanic or Latino (of any race)	0	0.0

Homeownership Rate
(Universe: Occupied Housing Units)

Group	%
Total Population	77.5
Hispanic or Latino (of any race)	60.3
Central American, ex. Mexican	65.5
Mexican	42.9
Puerto Rican	65.1

Median Home Value

Group	Dollars
Total Population	269,200
Hispanic or Latino (of any race)	321,500

Median Gross Rent

Group	Dollars
Total Population	832
Hispanic or Latino (of any race)	814

Median Household Income
(2010 Inflation-Adjusted Dollars)

Group	Dollars
Total Population	67,500
Hispanic or Latino (of any race)	52,904

Per Capita Income
(2010 Inflation-Adjusted Dollars)

Group	Dollars
Total Population	27,834
Hispanic or Latino (of any race)	14,983

Households with $100,000+ Income

Group	Number	%
Total Population	1,646	28.1
Hispanic or Latino (of any race)	109	35.5

Households with Food Stamps/SNAP Benefits During Past 12 Months

Group	Number	%
Total Population	485	8.3
Hispanic or Latino (of any race)	16	5.2

Poverty Rate
(Income in Past 12 Months Below Poverty Level)

Group	%
Total Population	8.7
Hispanic or Latino (of any race)	24.4

Wilmington*

Population

Group	Number	%TP[1]	%HP[2]
Total Population	70,851	100.0	–
Hispanic or Latino (of any race)	8,788	12.4	100.0
Central American, ex. Mexican	217	0.3	2.5
Cuban	116	0.2	1.3
Dominican Republic	371	0.5	4.2
Mexican	3,060	4.3	34.8
Puerto Rican	4,404	6.2	50.1
South American	224	0.3	2.5

Population Growth: 2000–2010

Group	%
Total Population	-2.5
Hispanic or Latino (of any race)	22.9
Dominican Republic	126.2
Mexican	75.3
Puerto Rican	1.8
South American	96.5

Males per 100 Females

Group	Number
Total Population	90.5
Hispanic or Latino (of any race)	105.2
Central American, ex. Mexican	99.1
Cuban	73.1
Dominican Republic	76.7
Mexican	129.9
Puerto Rican	95.9
South American	96.5

Average Household Size

Group	People
Total Population	2.36
Hispanic or Latino (of any race)	3.42
Central American, ex. Mexican	3.34
Cuban	1.92
Dominican Republic	3.47
Mexican	4.55
Puerto Rican	3.09
South American	2.15

Median Age

Group	Years
Total Population	34.3
Hispanic or Latino (of any race)	26.3
Central American, ex. Mexican	28.4
Cuban	38.0
Dominican Republic	25.3
Mexican	25.1
Puerto Rican	26.5
South American	34.8

High School Graduates
(Universe: Population 25 Years and Over)

Group	Number	%
Total Population	38,537	80.5
Hispanic or Latino (of any race)	2,108	48.1
Mexican	468	31.5
Puerto Rican	1,253	54.0

Four-Year College Graduates
(Universe: Population 25 Years and Over)

Group	Number	%
Total Population	12,014	25.1
Hispanic or Latino (of any race)	417	9.5
Mexican	107	7.2
Puerto Rican	137	5.9

Notes: (1) Percent of total population; (2) Percent of Hispanic/Latino population; Profiles include places with an overall population of at least 125,000, OR an overall population of at least 25,000 where the Hispanic/Latino population is at least 20% of the overall population. In states where less than five places meet either of these criteria, we have included places with at least 10,000 total population with the highest percentage of Hispanic/Latino population. These places are identified with an asterisk (*); Please refer to the User's Guide for a full explanation of data.

Population Age 3–17 Enrolled in Public School
(Universe: Population Age 3–17 Enrolled in School)

Group	Number	%
Total Population	11,147	87.0
Hispanic or Latino (of any race)	1,663	94.9
Mexican	608	100.0
Puerto Rican	717	92.6

Population Age 3–17 Enrolled in Private School
(Universe: Population Age 3–17 Enrolled in School)

Group	Number	%
Total Population	1,666	13.0
Hispanic or Latino (of any race)	89	5.1
Mexican	0	0.0
Puerto Rican	57	7.4

Foreign-Born Population

Group	Number	%
Total Population	4,535	6.3
Hispanic or Latino (of any race)	2,455	29.8
Mexican	1,948	62.9
Puerto Rican	11	0.3

Foreign-Born Naturalized U.S. Citizens

Group	Number	%
Total Population	1,413	31.2
Hispanic or Latino (of any race)	379	15.4
Mexican	128	6.6
Puerto Rican	11	100.0

Language Spoken at Home: English Only
(Universe: Population 5 Years and Over)

Group	Number	%
Total Population	57,133	85.7
Hispanic or Latino (of any race)	1,731	23.5
Mexican	406	14.5
Puerto Rican	923	26.1

Language Spoken at Home: Spanish
(Universe: Population 5 Years and Over)

Group	Number	%
Total Population	7,499	11.3
Hispanic or Latino (of any race)	5,635	76.5
Mexican	2,392	85.5
Puerto Rican	2,619	73.9

Unemployment Rate
(Universe: Population 16 Years and Over)

Group	%
Total Population	10.8
Hispanic or Latino (of any race)	8.7
Mexican	5.8
Puerto Rican	10.9

Class of Worker: Private Wage and Salary
(Universe: Civilian Employed Population 16 Years and Over)

Group	Number	%
Total Population	25,907	81.5
Hispanic or Latino (of any race)	3,201	88.4
Mexican	1,544	93.5
Puerto Rican	1,359	90.7

Class of Worker: Government
(Universe: Civilian Employed Population 16 Years and Over)

Group	Number	%
Total Population	4,559	14.3
Hispanic or Latino (of any race)	320	8.8
Mexican	79	4.8
Puerto Rican	133	8.9

Means of Transportation to Work: Car, Truck or Van
(Universe: Workers 16 Years and Over)

Group	Number	%
Total Population	23,507	75.8
Hispanic or Latino (of any race)	2,565	72.7
Mexican	1,162	70.9
Puerto Rican	1,179	81.4

Means of Transportation to Work: Public Transportation (ex. Taxicab)
(Universe: Workers 16 Years and Over)

Group	Number	%
Total Population	4,177	13.5
Hispanic or Latino (of any race)	718	20.4
Mexican	414	25.3
Puerto Rican	196	13.5

Homeownership Rate
(Universe: Occupied Housing Units)

Group	%
Total Population	47.7
Hispanic or Latino (of any race)	33.6
Central American, ex. Mexican	44.8
Cuban	34.0
Dominican Republic	37.1
Mexican	24.5
Puerto Rican	36.1
South American	48.8

Median Home Value

Group	Dollars
Total Population	179,200
Hispanic or Latino (of any race)	139,800
Mexican	130,300
Puerto Rican	128,400

Median Gross Rent

Group	Dollars
Total Population	858
Hispanic or Latino (of any race)	908
Mexican	991
Puerto Rican	726

Median Household Income
(2010 Inflation-Adjusted Dollars)

Group	Dollars
Total Population	38,386
Hispanic or Latino (of any race)	28,996
Mexican	41,027
Puerto Rican	24,405

Per Capita Income
(2010 Inflation-Adjusted Dollars)

Group	Dollars
Total Population	25,228
Hispanic or Latino (of any race)	14,863
Mexican	12,526
Puerto Rican	12,859

Households with $100,000+ Income

Group	Number	%
Total Population	4,424	15.0
Hispanic or Latino (of any race)	170	7.0
Mexican	59	9.1
Puerto Rican	44	3.1

Households with Food Stamps/SNAP Benefits During Past 12 Months

Group	Number	%
Total Population	6,127	20.8
Hispanic or Latino (of any race)	714	29.5
Mexican	119	18.4
Puerto Rican	484	33.7

Poverty Rate
(Income in Past 12 Months Below Poverty Level)

Group	%
Total Population	23.9
Hispanic or Latino (of any race)	30.3
Mexican	29.5
Puerto Rican	38.0

STATE & PLACE PROFILES

Notes: (1) Percent of total population; (2) Percent of Hispanic/Latino population; Profiles include places with an overall population of at least 125,000, OR an overall population of at least 25,000 where the Hispanic/Latino population is at least 20% of the overall population. In states where less than five places meet either of these criteria, we have included places with at least 10,000 total population with the highest percentage of Hispanic/Latino population. These places are identified with an asterisk (*); Please refer to the User's Guide for a full explanation of data.

District of Columbia

EDITOR'S NOTE: For a place to be included in this edition, it must meet one of two criteria. Either its overall population is at least 125,000, OR its overall population is at least 25,000 and its Hispanic/Latino population is at least 20% of the overall population. The District of Columbia meets this criteria.

All states, all counties and places that meet the above criteria are ranked and compared in *Section Three: Rankings & Comparisons*, on page 1055.

For a more detailed look at the Hispanic/Latino population in America, a companion web site is available at no additional charge with purchase of this print edition. Visit http://gold.greyhouse.com/page/info_hispanic for more information.

The web site includes data for all counties and places in America with Hispanic/Latino population, plus ten additional topics: Self Employed Worker; Walked to Work; Worked from Home; Mean Travel Time to Work; Mean Household Income; Households with Cash Public Assistance; Mean Cash Pubic Assistance; Poverty Rates for 18 and Under, 18 to 64, and 65 and Over.

Population

Group	Number	%TP[1]	%HP[2]
Total Population	601,723	100.0	–
Hispanic or Latino (of any race)	54,749	9.1	100.0
Central American, ex. Mexican	23,354	3.9	42.7
Costa Rican	258	<0.1	0.5
Guatemalan	2,635	0.4	4.8
Honduran	2,139	0.4	3.9
Nicaraguan	859	0.1	1.6
Panamanian	742	0.1	1.4
Salvadoran	16,611	2.8	30.3
Cuban	1,789	0.3	3.3
Dominican Republic	2,508	0.4	4.6
Mexican	8,507	1.4	15.5
Puerto Rican	3,129	0.5	5.7
South American	7,639	1.3	14.0
Argentinean	1,134	0.2	2.1
Bolivian	591	0.1	1.1
Chilean	697	0.1	1.3
Colombian	1,982	0.3	3.6
Ecuadorian	707	0.1	1.3
Paraguayan	161	<0.1	0.3
Peruvian	1,482	0.2	2.7
Uruguayan	216	<0.1	0.4
Venezuelan	596	0.1	1.1
Spaniard	1,421	0.2	2.6

Population Growth: 2000–2010

Group	%
Total Population	5.2
Hispanic or Latino (of any race)	21.8
Central American, ex. Mexican	47.8
Costa Rican	54.5
Guatemalan	95.2
Honduran	150.8
Nicaraguan	44.6
Panamanian	69.8
Salvadoran	41.5
Cuban	62.5
Dominican Republic	67.6
Mexican	66.9
Puerto Rican	34.4
South American	105.3
Argentinean	122.4
Bolivian	90.6
Chilean	94.2
Colombian	130.7
Ecuadorian	103.2
Peruvian	109.3
Uruguayan	116.0
Venezuelan	141.3
Spaniard	234.4

Males per 100 Females

Group	Number
Total Population	89.5
Hispanic or Latino (of any race)	106.7
Central American, ex. Mexican	117.4
Costa Rican	91.1
Guatemalan	159.1
Honduran	155.6
Nicaraguan	83.2
Panamanian	66.7
Salvadoran	113.0
Cuban	95.3
Dominican Republic	79.7
Mexican	117.5
Puerto Rican	99.8
South American	83.1
Argentinean	96.9
Bolivian	89.4
Chilean	80.6
Colombian	77.4
Ecuadorian	70.4
Paraguayan	76.9
Peruvian	87.4
Uruguayan	83.1
Venezuelan	82.8
Spaniard	98.7

Average Household Size

Group	People
Total Population	2.11
Hispanic or Latino (of any race)	2.79
Central American, ex. Mexican	3.78
Costa Rican	1.94
Guatemalan	3.58
Honduran	3.68
Nicaraguan	2.68
Panamanian	2.09
Salvadoran	4.10
Cuban	1.92
Dominican Republic	2.97
Mexican	2.42
Puerto Rican	1.87
South American	2.03
Argentinean	1.97
Bolivian	2.03
Chilean	1.94
Colombian	2.00
Ecuadorian	2.05
Paraguayan	2.23
Peruvian	2.24
Uruguayan	1.89
Venezuelan	1.84
Spaniard	1.96

Median Age

Group	Years
Total Population	33.8
Hispanic or Latino (of any race)	30.1
Central American, ex. Mexican	30.1
Costa Rican	34.3
Guatemalan	29.0
Honduran	28.7
Nicaraguan	36.6
Panamanian	35.0
Salvadoran	30.2
Cuban	31.1
Dominican Republic	30.7
Mexican	28.6
Puerto Rican	30.0
South American	34.1
Argentinean	34.7
Bolivian	35.3
Chilean	35.2
Colombian	32.2
Ecuadorian	32.4
Paraguayan	33.1
Peruvian	36.4
Uruguayan	37.0
Venezuelan	32.8
Spaniard	34.5

High School Graduates

(Universe: Population 25 Years and Over)

Group	Number	%
Total Population	345,504	86.5
Hispanic or Latino (of any race)	19,593	60.9
Central American, ex. Mexican	5,511	38.6
Guatemalan	543	50.7
Honduran	433	36.8
Nicaraguan	428	58.6
Salvadoran	3,372	32.4
Cuban	1,123	95.1
Dominican Republic	1,068	72.7
Mexican	3,168	62.2
Puerto Rican	2,097	96.1
South American	4,497	89.9
Argentinean	830	96.7
Colombian	1,300	91.3
Peruvian	697	79.2
Spaniard	841	88.3

Four-Year College Graduates

(Universe: Population 25 Years and Over)

Group	Number	%
Total Population	196,513	49.2
Hispanic or Latino (of any race)	11,550	35.9
Central American, ex. Mexican	1,867	13.1
Guatemalan	183	17.1
Honduran	179	15.2
Nicaraguan	139	19.0
Salvadoran	821	7.9
Cuban	686	58.1
Dominican Republic	416	28.3
Mexican	2,251	44.2
Puerto Rican	1,335	61.2
South American	3,434	68.7
Argentinean	732	85.3
Colombian	956	67.1
Peruvian	421	47.8
Spaniard	725	76.2

Population Age 3–17 Enrolled in Public School

(Universe: Population Age 3–17 Enrolled in School)

Group	Number	%
Total Population	60,279	78.8
Hispanic or Latino (of any race)	6,884	85.5
Central American, ex. Mexican	3,908	90.6
Guatemalan	142	38.4
Honduran	312	92.3
Nicaraguan	118	100.0
Salvadoran	3,224	95.8
Cuban	116	56.0
Dominican Republic	495	88.6
Mexican	1,139	83.1
Puerto Rican	293	78.3
South American	486	75.7
Argentinean	21	23.9
Colombian	145	76.3
Peruvian	121	86.4
Spaniard	11	100.0

Population Age 3–17 Enrolled in Private School

(Universe: Population Age 3–17 Enrolled in School)

Group	Number	%
Total Population	16,239	21.2
Hispanic or Latino (of any race)	1,169	14.5
Central American, ex. Mexican	405	9.4
Guatemalan	228	61.6
Honduran	26	7.7
Nicaraguan	0	0.0
Salvadoran	141	4.2
Cuban	91	44.0
Dominican Republic	64	11.4
Mexican	232	16.9
Puerto Rican	81	21.7
South American	156	24.3
Argentinean	67	76.1
Colombian	45	23.7
Peruvian	19	13.6
Spaniard	0	0.0

Notes: (1) Percent of total population; (2) Percent of Hispanic/Latino population; Profiles include places with an overall population of at least 125,000, OR an overall population of at least 25,000 where the Hispanic/Latino population is at least 20% of the overall population. In states where less than five places meet either of these criteria, we have included places with at least 10,000 total population with the highest percentage of Hispanic/Latino population. These places are identified with an asterisk (*); Please refer to the User's Guide for a full explanation of data.

Foreign-Born Population

Group	Number	%
Total Population	76,058	13.0
Hispanic or Latino (of any race)	28,270	55.1
Central American, ex. Mexican	16,570	69.5
Guatemalan	1,553	82.7
Honduran	1,319	68.5
Nicaraguan	630	63.4
Salvadoran	12,305	68.8
Cuban	576	28.2
Dominican Republic	1,258	47.5
Mexican	3,697	44.1
Puerto Rican	193	5.7
South American	4,207	63.5
Argentinean	685	67.0
Colombian	1,150	60.0
Peruvian	800	65.0
Spaniard	509	48.9

Foreign-Born Naturalized U.S. Citizens

Group	Number	%
Total Population	27,350	36.0
Hispanic or Latino (of any race)	7,023	24.8
Central American, ex. Mexican	3,369	20.3
Guatemalan	273	17.6
Honduran	208	15.8
Nicaraguan	289	45.9
Salvadoran	2,262	18.4
Cuban	459	79.7
Dominican Republic	591	47.0
Mexican	470	12.7
Puerto Rican	17	8.8
South American	1,494	35.5
Argentinean	232	33.9
Colombian	347	30.2
Peruvian	371	46.4
Spaniard	203	39.9

Language Spoken at Home: English Only
(Universe: Population 5 Years and Over)

Group	Number	%
Total Population	471,292	85.4
Hispanic or Latino (of any race)	15,718	33.4
Central American, ex. Mexican	6,814	31.7
Guatemalan	510	29.7
Honduran	886	50.1
Nicaraguan	102	11.8
Salvadoran	5,116	32.0
Cuban	874	43.9
Dominican Republic	457	18.8
Mexican	3,725	48.8
Puerto Rican	1,391	45.0
South American	1,189	19.0
Argentinean	165	17.4
Colombian	257	14.2
Peruvian	287	24.8
Spaniard	296	29.4

Language Spoken at Home: Spanish
(Universe: Population 5 Years and Over)

Group	Number	%
Total Population	40,324	7.3
Hispanic or Latino (of any race)	30,920	65.8
Central American, ex. Mexican	14,614	68.1
Guatemalan	1,207	70.3
Honduran	882	49.9
Nicaraguan	761	88.2
Salvadoran	10,857	67.8
Cuban	1,080	54.3
Dominican Republic	1,977	81.2
Mexican	3,835	50.2
Puerto Rican	1,669	54.0
South American	4,961	79.2
Argentinean	786	82.6
Colombian	1,517	83.8
Peruvian	851	73.6
Spaniard	680	67.6

Unemployment Rate
(Universe: Population 16 Years and Over)

Group	%
Total Population	9.4
Hispanic or Latino (of any race)	7.1
Central American, ex. Mexican	7.8
Guatemalan	9.3
Honduran	2.1
Nicaraguan	12.3
Salvadoran	7.6
Cuban	4.9
Dominican Republic	13.1
Mexican	6.0
Puerto Rican	7.3
South American	4.1
Argentinean	3.4
Colombian	1.4
Peruvian	6.8
Spaniard	0.0

Class of Worker: Private Wage and Salary
(Universe: Civilian Employed Population 16 Years and Over)

Group	Number	%
Total Population	203,846	68.6
Hispanic or Latino (of any race)	23,614	81.8
Central American, ex. Mexican	12,097	91.8
Guatemalan	890	87.6
Honduran	1,180	95.0
Nicaraguan	477	85.6
Salvadoran	9,103	92.8
Cuban	652	65.1
Dominican Republic	1,183	88.8
Mexican	3,682	76.5
Puerto Rican	1,348	65.7
South American	2,820	67.9
Argentinean	451	64.2
Colombian	758	65.0
Peruvian	574	75.6
Spaniard	442	71.1

Class of Worker: Government
(Universe: Civilian Employed Population 16 Years and Over)

Group	Number	%
Total Population	78,192	26.3
Hispanic or Latino (of any race)	4,190	14.5
Central American, ex. Mexican	654	5.0
Guatemalan	101	9.9
Honduran	62	5.0
Nicaraguan	63	11.3
Salvadoran	347	3.5
Cuban	299	29.9
Dominican Republic	70	5.3
Mexican	1,008	20.9
Puerto Rican	644	31.4
South American	1,076	25.9
Argentinean	215	30.6
Colombian	383	32.8
Peruvian	153	20.2
Spaniard	169	27.2

Means of Transportation to Work: Car, Truck or Van
(Universe: Workers 16 Years and Over)

Group	Number	%
Total Population	124,251	42.4
Hispanic or Latino (of any race)	10,025	35.5
Central American, ex. Mexican	4,528	35.2
Guatemalan	314	30.9
Honduran	382	31.5
Nicaraguan	213	42.3
Salvadoran	3,355	35.1
Cuban	315	32.0
Dominican Republic	558	43.4
Mexican	1,612	34.3
Puerto Rican	891	44.5
South American	1,419	35.0
Argentinean	185	28.7
Colombian	497	41.1
Peruvian	335	43.5
Spaniard	88	13.7

Means of Transportation to Work: Public Transportation (ex. Taxicab)
(Universe: Workers 16 Years and Over)

Group	Number	%
Total Population	110,108	37.6
Hispanic or Latino (of any race)	12,832	45.5
Central American, ex. Mexican	6,566	51.1
Guatemalan	490	48.2
Honduran	632	52.1
Nicaraguan	99	19.7
Salvadoran	5,135	53.8
Cuban	405	41.2
Dominican Republic	632	49.2
Mexican	1,746	37.1
Puerto Rican	753	37.6
South American	1,621	40.0
Argentinean	297	46.1
Colombian	475	39.3
Peruvian	238	30.9
Spaniard	329	51.3

Homeownership Rate
(Universe: Occupied Housing Units)

Group	%
Total Population	42.0
Hispanic or Latino (of any race)	31.5
Central American, ex. Mexican	27.4
Costa Rican	47.6
Guatemalan	22.1
Honduran	18.0
Nicaraguan	33.8
Panamanian	38.5
Salvadoran	27.4
Cuban	39.7
Dominican Republic	32.1
Mexican	28.2
Puerto Rican	34.2
South American	38.8
Argentinean	44.8
Bolivian	41.2
Chilean	38.9
Colombian	34.6
Ecuadorian	37.5
Paraguayan	41.9
Peruvian	34.4
Uruguayan	47.4
Venezuelan	44.3
Spaniard	43.0

Median Home Value

Group	Dollars
Total Population	443,300
Hispanic or Latino (of any race)	462,200
Central American, ex. Mexican	395,300
Guatemalan	548,600
Honduran	318,400
Nicaraguan	679,300
Salvadoran	391,900
Cuban	675,800
Dominican Republic	337,100
Mexican	540,100
Puerto Rican	388,900
South American	550,900
Argentinean	575,400
Colombian	598,000
Peruvian	614,700
Spaniard	761,000

Median Gross Rent

Group	Dollars
Total Population	1,063
Hispanic or Latino (of any race)	1,118
Central American, ex. Mexican	942
Guatemalan	1,037
Honduran	925
Nicaraguan	1,130
Salvadoran	927
Cuban	1,406
Dominican Republic	1,261
Mexican	1,175
Puerto Rican	1,442
South American	1,306
Argentinean	1,480
Colombian	1,430
Peruvian	1,147
Spaniard	1,399

Median Household Income
(2010 Inflation-Adjusted Dollars)

Group	Dollars
Total Population	58,526
Hispanic or Latino (of any race)	51,569
Central American, ex. Mexican	42,901
Guatemalan	40,144
Honduran	28,707
Nicaraguan	37,713

Notes: (1) Percent of total population; (2) Percent of Hispanic/Latino population; Profiles include places with an overall population of at least 125,000, OR an overall population of at least 25,000 where the Hispanic/Latino population is at least 20% of the overall population. In states where less than five places meet either of these criteria, we have included places with at least 10,000 total population with the highest percentage of Hispanic/Latino population. These places are identified with an asterisk (*); Please refer to the User's Guide for a full explanation of data.

Salvadoran	43,820
Cuban	78,417
Dominican Republic	37,951
Mexican	49,912
Puerto Rican	72,500
South American	72,271
Argentinean	84,583
Colombian	84,406
Peruvian	52,463
Spaniard	58,250

Per Capita Income
(2010 Inflation-Adjusted Dollars)

Group	Dollars
Total Population	42,078
Hispanic or Latino (of any race)	29,285
Central American, ex. Mexican	19,215
Guatemalan	19,551
Honduran	18,851
Nicaraguan	31,282
Salvadoran	17,996
Cuban	55,976
Dominican Republic	19,652
Mexican	31,032
Puerto Rican	40,879
South American	48,046
Argentinean	65,629
Colombian	46,951
Peruvian	46,300
Spaniard	59,812

Households with $100,000+ Income

Group	Number	%
Total Population	76,064	29.6
Hispanic or Latino (of any race)	4,234	22.9
Central American, ex. Mexican	1,006	14.5
Guatemalan	73	15.6
Honduran	45	7.8
Nicaraguan	49	13.4
Salvadoran	760	15.0
Cuban	351	36.6
Dominican Republic	201	20.8
Mexican	696	21.8
Puerto Rican	486	31.7
South American	1,029	34.3
Argentinean	224	44.7
Colombian	285	32.9
Peruvian	127	23.5
Spaniard	162	38.1

Households with Food Stamps/SNAP Benefits During Past 12 Months

Group	Number	%
Total Population	27,437	10.7
Hispanic or Latino (of any race)	1,342	7.3
Central American, ex. Mexican	770	11.1
Guatemalan	63	13.4
Honduran	40	6.9
Nicaraguan	13	3.5
Salvadoran	579	11.4
Cuban	59	6.2
Dominican Republic	138	14.3
Mexican	206	6.4
Puerto Rican	60	3.9
South American	78	2.6
Argentinean	0	0.0
Colombian	23	2.7
Peruvian	55	10.2
Spaniard	0	0.0

Poverty Rate
(Income in Past 12 Months Below Poverty Level)

Group	%
Total Population	18.5
Hispanic or Latino (of any race)	13.8
Central American, ex. Mexican	12.6
Guatemalan	14.1
Honduran	23.3
Nicaraguan	7.5
Salvadoran	11.8
Cuban	31.0
Dominican Republic	15.2
Mexican	19.4
Puerto Rican	9.2
South American	10.8
Argentinean	6.9
Colombian	12.3
Peruvian	10.2
Spaniard	14.0

Notes: (1) Percent of total population; (2) Percent of Hispanic/Latino population; Profiles include places with an overall population of at least 125,000, OR an overall population of at least 25,000 where the Hispanic/Latino population is at least 20% of the overall population. In states where less than five places meet either of these criteria, we have included places with at least 10,000 total population with the highest percentage of Hispanic/Latino population. These places are identified with an asterisk (*); Please refer to the User's Guide for a full explanation of data.

Florida

EDITOR'S NOTE: For a place to be included in this edition, it must meet one of two criteria. Either its overall population is at least 125,000, OR its overall population is at least 25,000 and its Hispanic/Latino population is at least 20% of the overall population. For the state of Florida, the following locations are included:

- Alafaya
- Altamonte Springs
- Apopka
- Aventura
- Bonita Springs
- Brandon
- Buenaventura Lakes
- Cape Coral
- Carrollwood
- Casselberry
- Coconut Creek
- Cooper City
- Coral Gables
- Coral Springs
- Country Club
- Cutler Bay
- Dania Beach
- Davie
- Deltona
- Doral
- Egypt Lake-Leto
- Fort Lauderdale
- Fort Pierce
- Fountainebleau
- Four Corners
- Greenacres
- Hallandale Beach
- Hialeah
- Hollywood
- Homestead
- Jacksonville
- Kendale Lakes
- Kendall
- Kendall West
- Kissimmee
- Lake Magdalene
- Lake Worth
- Lehigh Acres
- Margate
- Meadow Woods
- Miami
- Miami Beach
- Miami Gardens
- Miami Lakes
- Miramar
- North Lauderdale
- North Miami
- North Miami Beach
- Oakland Park
- Ocoee
- Orlando
- Pembroke Pines
- Plant City
- Plantation
- Poinciana
- Port Saint Lucie
- Richmond West
- Riverview
- Royal Palm Beach
- Saint Cloud
- Saint Petersburg
- Sanford
- South Miami Heights
- Sunrise
- Tallahassee
- Tamarac
- Tamiami
- Tampa
- The Hammocks
- Town 'n' Country
- University (Hillsborough County)
- University (Orange County)
- University Park
- Wesley Chapel
- West Little River
- West Palm Beach
- Westchester
- Weston
- Winter Garden

Section Two: State & Place Profiles starts with the state profile, followed by place profiles that meet the criteria above. Places are listed alphabetically within each state. All states, all counties and places that meet the above criteria are ranked and compared in *Section Three: Rankings & Comparisons*, on page 1055.

For a more detailed look at the Hispanic/Latino population in Florida, a companion web site is available at no additional charge with purchase of this print edition. Visit http://gold.greyhouse.com/page/info_hispanic for more information.

The web site includes data for all counties and places in Florida with Hispanic/Latino population, plus ten additional topics: Self Employed Worker; Walked to Work; Worked from Home; Mean Travel Time to Work; Mean Household Income; Households with Cash Public Assistance; Mean Cash Pubic Assistance; Poverty Rates for 18 and Under, 18 to 64, and 65 and Over.

Population

Group	Number	%TP[1]	%HP[2]
Total Population	18,801,310	100.0	–
Hispanic or Latino (of any race)	4,223,806	22.5	100.0
Central American, ex. Mexican	432,665	2.3	10.2
Costa Rican	20,761	0.1	0.5
Guatemalan	83,882	0.4	2.0
Honduran	107,302	0.6	2.5
Nicaraguan	135,143	0.7	3.2
Panamanian	28,741	0.2	0.7
Salvadoran	55,144	0.3	1.3
Cuban	1,213,438	6.5	28.7
Dominican Republic	172,451	0.9	4.1
Mexican	629,718	3.3	14.9
Puerto Rican	847,550	4.5	20.1
South American	674,542	3.6	16.0
Argentinean	56,260	0.3	1.3
Bolivian	10,938	0.1	0.3
Chilean	23,549	0.1	0.6
Colombian	300,414	1.6	7.1
Ecuadorian	60,574	0.3	1.4
Paraguayan	2,222	<0.1	0.1
Peruvian	100,965	0.5	2.4
Uruguayan	14,542	0.1	0.3
Venezuelan	102,116	0.5	2.4
Spaniard	48,815	0.3	1.2

Population Growth: 2000–2010

Group	%
Total Population	17.6
Hispanic or Latino (of any race)	57.4
Central American, ex. Mexican	113.4
Costa Rican	84.6
Guatemalan	192.8
Honduran	160.3
Nicaraguan	69.9
Panamanian	90.1
Salvadoran	166.4
Cuban	45.6
Dominican Republic	143.0
Mexican	73.0
Puerto Rican	75.8
South American	123.9
Argentinean	145.9
Bolivian	134.8
Chilean	75.7
Colombian	116.5
Ecuadorian	153.0
Paraguayan	144.4
Peruvian	129.3
Uruguayan	259.5
Venezuelan	150.4
Spaniard	246.0

Males per 100 Females

Group	Number
Total Population	95.6
Hispanic or Latino (of any race)	97.7
Central American, ex. Mexican	101.9
Costa Rican	80.9
Guatemalan	159.0
Honduran	97.4
Nicaraguan	88.4
Panamanian	71.0
Salvadoran	106.3
Cuban	97.4
Dominican Republic	84.2
Mexican	122.2
Puerto Rican	94.5
South American	82.7
Argentinean	102.0
Bolivian	85.8
Chilean	94.2
Colombian	77.5
Ecuadorian	82.9
Paraguayan	72.8
Peruvian	82.0
Uruguayan	103.6
Venezuelan	84.1
Spaniard	93.1

Average Household Size

Group	People
Total Population	2.48
Hispanic or Latino (of any race)	3.07
Central American, ex. Mexican	3.61
Costa Rican	2.89
Guatemalan	4.18
Honduran	3.60
Nicaraguan	3.61
Panamanian	2.74
Salvadoran	3.70
Cuban	2.87
Dominican Republic	3.25
Mexican	3.89
Puerto Rican	2.91
South American	2.94
Argentinean	2.72
Bolivian	3.04
Chilean	2.80
Colombian	2.95
Ecuadorian	3.12
Paraguayan	2.80
Peruvian	3.02
Uruguayan	2.83
Venezuelan	2.93
Spaniard	2.43

Median Age

Group	Years
Total Population	40.7
Hispanic or Latino (of any race)	33.6
Central American, ex. Mexican	31.8
Costa Rican	34.8
Guatemalan	27.8
Honduran	31.4
Nicaraguan	35.0
Panamanian	38.0
Salvadoran	31.1
Cuban	42.0
Dominican Republic	32.3
Mexican	24.6
Puerto Rican	30.9

Notes: (1) Percent of total population; (2) Percent of Hispanic/Latino population; Profiles include places with an overall population of at least 125,000, OR an overall population of at least 25,000 where the Hispanic/Latino population is at least 20% of the overall population. In states where less than five places meet either of these criteria, we have included places with at least 10,000 total population with the highest percentage of Hispanic/Latino population. These places are identified with an asterisk (*); Please refer to the User's Guide for a full explanation of data.

STATE & PLACE PROFILES

South American	37.2
Argentinean	37.1
Bolivian	35.2
Chilean	40.3
Colombian	37.7
Ecuadorian	37.4
Paraguayan	34.9
Peruvian	38.7
Uruguayan	37.3
Venezuelan	34.5
Spaniard	41.6

High School Graduates
(Universe: Population 25 Years and Over)

Group	Number	%
Total Population	10,908,069	85.3
Hispanic or Latino (of any race)	1,853,026	73.9
Central American, ex. Mexican	171,797	62.1
Costa Rican	10,447	80.0
Guatemalan	20,888	43.2
Honduran	38,858	56.6
Nicaraguan	68,327	72.4
Panamanian	15,244	89.9
Salvadoran	16,296	49.7
Cuban	612,769	73.9
Dominican Republic	73,772	76.4
Mexican	145,292	49.7
Puerto Rican	371,118	79.6
South American	392,267	88.5
Argentinean	32,662	86.3
Bolivian	5,830	91.5
Chilean	15,216	89.8
Colombian	169,402	87.1
Ecuadorian	34,652	85.8
Paraguayan	882	83.4
Peruvian	62,583	91.9
Uruguayan	7,810	77.9
Venezuelan	59,352	93.8
Spaniard	26,133	88.4

Four-Year College Graduates
(Universe: Population 25 Years and Over)

Group	Number	%
Total Population	3,313,411	25.9
Hispanic or Latino (of any race)	532,242	21.2
Central American, ex. Mexican	41,173	14.9
Costa Rican	3,142	24.1
Guatemalan	4,295	8.9
Honduran	7,496	10.9
Nicaraguan	16,845	17.8
Panamanian	5,339	31.5
Salvadoran	3,581	10.9
Cuban	185,277	22.3
Dominican Republic	19,808	20.5
Mexican	26,766	9.2
Puerto Rican	84,335	18.1
South American	145,912	32.9
Argentinean	11,879	31.4
Bolivian	2,334	36.6
Chilean	5,646	33.3
Colombian	59,383	30.5
Ecuadorian	10,254	25.4
Paraguayan	421	39.8
Peruvian	22,300	32.8
Uruguayan	1,942	19.4
Venezuelan	30,191	47.7
Spaniard	10,995	37.2

Population Age 3–17 Enrolled in Public School
(Universe: Population Age 3–17 Enrolled in School)

Group	Number	%
Total Population	2,575,757	84.5
Hispanic or Latino (of any race)	674,661	88.0
Central American, ex. Mexican	67,854	92.5
Costa Rican	3,227	87.6
Guatemalan	12,110	88.6
Honduran	17,916	95.4
Nicaraguan	21,488	93.0
Panamanian	3,981	89.9
Salvadoran	8,435	94.8
Cuban	139,006	81.0
Dominican Republic	30,110	92.4
Mexican	134,304	94.6
Puerto Rican	162,696	90.4
South American	101,499	85.8
Argentinean	6,712	81.6
Bolivian	1,635	88.6
Chilean	2,664	82.8
Colombian	47,135	87.0
Ecuadorian	9,793	90.2
Paraguayan	133	47.7
Peruvian	13,819	85.2
Uruguayan	2,204	94.2
Venezuelan	16,411	82.6
Spaniard	5,225	73.1

Population Age 3–17 Enrolled in Private School
(Universe: Population Age 3–17 Enrolled in School)

Group	Number	%
Total Population	471,003	15.5
Hispanic or Latino (of any race)	92,190	12.0
Central American, ex. Mexican	5,478	7.5
Costa Rican	456	12.4
Guatemalan	1,556	11.4
Honduran	863	4.6
Nicaraguan	1,623	7.0
Panamanian	446	10.1
Salvadoran	460	5.2
Cuban	32,539	19.0
Dominican Republic	2,461	7.6
Mexican	7,718	5.4
Puerto Rican	17,370	9.6
South American	16,816	14.2
Argentinean	1,511	18.4
Bolivian	211	11.4
Chilean	552	17.2
Colombian	7,037	13.0
Ecuadorian	1,067	9.8
Paraguayan	146	52.3
Peruvian	2,397	14.8
Uruguayan	135	5.8
Venezuelan	3,460	17.4
Spaniard	1,920	26.9

Foreign-Born Population

Group	Number	%
Total Population	3,549,510	19.2
Hispanic or Latino (of any race)	2,007,233	50.2
Central American, ex. Mexican	312,198	70.4
Costa Rican	13,246	65.9
Guatemalan	62,889	73.1
Honduran	80,349	72.0
Nicaraguan	101,602	71.5
Panamanian	14,859	56.7
Salvadoran	36,518	68.7
Cuban	761,873	66.0
Dominican Republic	91,878	57.9
Mexican	284,472	48.0
Puerto Rican	8,908	1.1
South American	487,765	73.5
Argentinean	41,829	78.1
Bolivian	6,890	68.3
Chilean	17,172	74.7
Colombian	209,877	71.5
Ecuadorian	40,792	67.1
Paraguayan	1,196	70.6
Peruvian	76,605	76.6
Uruguayan	11,512	78.8
Venezuelan	77,464	77.2
Spaniard	13,997	33.0

Foreign-Born Naturalized U.S. Citizens

Group	Number	%
Total Population	1,667,068	47.0
Hispanic or Latino (of any race)	850,115	42.4
Central American, ex. Mexican	100,490	32.2
Costa Rican	5,682	42.9
Guatemalan	11,910	18.9
Honduran	19,483	24.2
Nicaraguan	42,772	42.1
Panamanian	9,372	63.1
Salvadoran	10,143	27.8
Cuban	424,455	55.7
Dominican Republic	52,088	56.7
Mexican	43,750	15.4
Puerto Rican	4,667	52.4
South American	193,942	39.8
Argentinean	13,253	31.7
Bolivian	3,159	45.8
Chilean	8,310	48.4
Colombian	90,541	43.1
Ecuadorian	21,522	52.8
Paraguayan	695	58.1
Peruvian	31,754	41.5
Uruguayan	3,202	27.8
Venezuelan	19,191	24.8
Spaniard	7,678	54.9

Language Spoken at Home: English Only
(Universe: Population 5 Years and Over)

Group	Number	%
Total Population	12,786,704	73.4
Hispanic or Latino (of any race)	516,481	14.0
Central American, ex. Mexican	28,089	6.9
Costa Rican	2,671	14.2
Guatemalan	4,223	5.4
Honduran	5,345	5.2
Nicaraguan	6,479	4.8
Panamanian	4,830	19.6
Salvadoran	4,036	8.3
Cuban	99,353	9.1
Dominican Republic	14,625	9.9
Mexican	95,279	18.4
Puerto Rican	178,395	24.5
South American	45,654	7.3
Argentinean	3,454	6.9
Bolivian	680	7.4
Chilean	1,979	9.0
Colombian	19,067	6.9
Ecuadorian	5,489	9.6
Paraguayan	214	14.2
Peruvian	6,916	7.4
Uruguayan	754	5.6
Venezuelan	6,273	6.7
Spaniard	17,938	44.7

Language Spoken at Home: Spanish
(Universe: Population 5 Years and Over)

Group	Number	%
Total Population	3,408,312	19.6
Hispanic or Latino (of any race)	3,154,843	85.5
Central American, ex. Mexican	378,865	92.6
Costa Rican	15,998	85.3
Guatemalan	72,017	92.7
Honduran	96,470	94.7
Nicaraguan	127,100	95.0
Panamanian	19,667	80.0
Salvadoran	44,454	91.5
Cuban	990,912	90.7
Dominican Republic	132,272	89.6
Mexican	421,502	81.2
Puerto Rican	546,296	75.2
South American	574,071	92.0
Argentinean	45,838	91.4
Bolivian	8,373	90.6
Chilean	19,696	89.5
Colombian	257,524	92.8
Ecuadorian	51,104	89.7
Paraguayan	1,280	84.9
Peruvian	86,611	92.2
Uruguayan	12,449	93.1
Venezuelan	86,173	92.3
Spaniard	21,571	53.7

Unemployment Rate
(Universe: Population 16 Years and Over)

Group	%
Total Population	8.9
Hispanic or Latino (of any race)	9.2
Central American, ex. Mexican	9.5
Costa Rican	9.0
Guatemalan	7.9
Honduran	11.4
Nicaraguan	8.8
Panamanian	9.5
Salvadoran	10.2
Cuban	8.3
Dominican Republic	11.1
Mexican	9.0
Puerto Rican	11.2
South American	8.3
Argentinean	7.1
Bolivian	9.8
Chilean	6.4
Colombian	8.4

Notes: (1) Percent of total population; (2) Percent of Hispanic/Latino population; Profiles include places with an overall population of at least 125,000, OR an overall population of at least 25,000 where the Hispanic/Latino population is at least 20% of the overall population. In states where less than five places meet either of these criteria, we have included places with at least 10,000 total population with the highest percentage of Hispanic/Latino population. These places are identified with an asterisk (*); Please refer to the User's Guide for a full explanation of data.

Group	%
Ecuadorian	9.0
Paraguayan	8.2
Peruvian	8.9
Uruguayan	9.9
Venezuelan	7.7
Spaniard	8.5

Class of Worker: Private Wage and Salary
(Universe: Civilian Employed Population 16 Years and Over)

Group	Number	%
Total Population	6,703,300	80.6
Hispanic or Latino (of any race)	1,561,438	84.1
Central American, ex. Mexican	197,680	84.2
Costa Rican	8,326	83.7
Guatemalan	42,259	89.1
Honduran	46,172	79.4
Nicaraguan	63,882	85.4
Panamanian	10,353	76.3
Salvadoran	25,024	86.9
Cuban	435,092	81.2
Dominican Republic	63,927	84.8
Mexican	235,105	90.6
Puerto Rican	275,879	83.6
South American	292,915	84.5
Argentinean	24,346	82.7
Bolivian	4,530	84.0
Chilean	10,566	84.7
Colombian	130,006	85.1
Ecuadorian	26,088	84.6
Paraguayan	689	77.8
Peruvian	45,134	83.3
Uruguayan	5,888	77.7
Venezuelan	43,032	86.0
Spaniard	14,889	76.7

Class of Worker: Government
(Universe: Civilian Employed Population 16 Years and Over)

Group	Number	%
Total Population	1,098,322	13.2
Hispanic or Latino (of any race)	161,482	8.7
Central American, ex. Mexican	11,561	4.9
Costa Rican	884	8.9
Guatemalan	1,453	3.1
Honduran	2,065	3.6
Nicaraguan	3,418	4.6
Panamanian	2,488	18.3
Salvadoran	948	3.3
Cuban	58,500	10.9
Dominican Republic	6,544	8.7
Mexican	11,704	4.5
Puerto Rican	42,344	12.8
South American	21,696	6.3
Argentinean	1,490	5.1
Bolivian	361	6.7
Chilean	1,140	9.1
Colombian	10,392	6.8
Ecuadorian	2,232	7.2
Paraguayan	36	4.1
Peruvian	3,040	5.6
Uruguayan	309	4.1
Venezuelan	2,454	4.9
Spaniard	3,250	16.7

Means of Transportation to Work: Car, Truck or Van
(Universe: Workers 16 Years and Over)

Group	Number	%
Total Population	7,334,876	89.8
Hispanic or Latino (of any race)	1,617,886	88.7
Central American, ex. Mexican	191,898	83.2
Costa Rican	8,547	88.6
Guatemalan	37,147	79.7
Honduran	45,180	78.8
Nicaraguan	62,540	85.1
Panamanian	12,070	90.4
Salvadoran	24,540	86.8
Cuban	480,493	91.4
Dominican Republic	67,218	90.7
Mexican	215,701	83.9
Puerto Rican	296,182	91.3
South American	301,004	88.7
Argentinean	24,104	83.6
Bolivian	4,847	92.7
Chilean	11,075	90.1
Colombian	133,818	89.8
Ecuadorian	27,485	90.3
Paraguayan	676	79.2
Peruvian	46,777	88.1
Uruguayan	5,792	79.5
Venezuelan	43,787	89.1
Spaniard	17,253	90.9

Means of Transportation to Work: Public Transportation (ex. Taxicab)
(Universe: Workers 16 Years and Over)

Group	Number	%
Total Population	160,236	2.0
Hispanic or Latino (of any race)	62,006	3.4
Central American, ex. Mexican	16,228	7.0
Costa Rican	377	3.9
Guatemalan	2,980	6.4
Honduran	5,465	9.5
Nicaraguan	5,512	7.5
Panamanian	362	2.7
Salvadoran	1,497	5.3
Cuban	9,559	1.8
Dominican Republic	2,292	3.1
Mexican	13,724	5.3
Puerto Rican	7,290	2.2
South American	11,384	3.4
Argentinean	1,343	4.7
Bolivian	76	1.5
Chilean	427	3.5
Colombian	4,271	2.9
Ecuadorian	837	2.7
Paraguayan	105	12.3
Peruvian	2,446	4.6
Uruguayan	443	6.1
Venezuelan	1,381	2.8
Spaniard	116	0.6

Homeownership Rate
(Universe: Occupied Housing Units)

Group	%
Total Population	67.4
Hispanic or Latino (of any race)	54.4
Central American, ex. Mexican	45.1
Costa Rican	54.7
Guatemalan	35.0
Honduran	38.2
Nicaraguan	48.6
Panamanian	57.2
Salvadoran	51.1
Cuban	60.6
Dominican Republic	52.5
Mexican	43.3
Puerto Rican	52.1
South American	56.8
Argentinean	54.6
Bolivian	57.1
Chilean	58.1
Colombian	58.4
Ecuadorian	61.7
Paraguayan	56.1
Peruvian	54.3
Uruguayan	45.6
Venezuelan	54.5
Spaniard	71.9

Median Home Value

Group	Dollars
Total Population	205,600
Hispanic or Latino (of any race)	225,900
Central American, ex. Mexican	212,400
Costa Rican	209,400
Guatemalan	195,700
Honduran	211,200
Nicaraguan	222,200
Panamanian	204,900
Salvadoran	196,600
Cuban	260,500
Dominican Republic	216,900
Mexican	152,400
Puerto Rican	197,800
South American	238,000
Argentinean	243,700
Bolivian	227,600
Chilean	237,100
Colombian	235,000
Ecuadorian	238,200
Paraguayan	240,800
Peruvian	220,000
Uruguayan	202,400
Venezuelan	272,800
Spaniard	243,600

Median Gross Rent

Group	Dollars
Total Population	957
Hispanic or Latino (of any race)	977
Central American, ex. Mexican	986
Costa Rican	1,031
Guatemalan	1,019
Honduran	957
Nicaraguan	1,006
Panamanian	1,019
Salvadoran	944
Cuban	940
Dominican Republic	1,018
Mexican	872
Puerto Rican	973
South American	1,128
Argentinean	1,091
Bolivian	1,099
Chilean	1,144
Colombian	1,144
Ecuadorian	1,075
Paraguayan	986
Peruvian	1,092
Uruguayan	1,044
Venezuelan	1,212
Spaniard	966

Median Household Income
(2010 Inflation-Adjusted Dollars)

Group	Dollars
Total Population	47,661
Hispanic or Latino (of any race)	41,758
Central American, ex. Mexican	40,264
Costa Rican	43,967
Guatemalan	39,772
Honduran	34,310
Nicaraguan	43,103
Panamanian	45,433
Salvadoran	40,184
Cuban	41,249
Dominican Republic	41,814
Mexican	37,006
Puerto Rican	41,198
South American	46,319
Argentinean	44,445
Bolivian	47,038
Chilean	51,681
Colombian	46,411
Ecuadorian	48,685
Paraguayan	53,261
Peruvian	44,237
Uruguayan	37,978
Venezuelan	48,036
Spaniard	52,364

Per Capita Income
(2010 Inflation-Adjusted Dollars)

Group	Dollars
Total Population	26,551
Hispanic or Latino (of any race)	18,749
Central American, ex. Mexican	15,663
Costa Rican	18,790
Guatemalan	14,179
Honduran	13,316
Nicaraguan	16,563
Panamanian	22,620
Salvadoran	15,835
Cuban	22,130
Dominican Republic	17,438
Mexican	12,945
Puerto Rican	17,812
South American	20,998
Argentinean	25,845
Bolivian	21,657
Chilean	25,034
Colombian	19,823
Ecuadorian	20,673
Paraguayan	22,271
Peruvian	19,911

Notes: (1) Percent of total population; (2) Percent of Hispanic/Latino population; Profiles include places with an overall population of at least 125,000, OR an overall population of at least 25,000 where the Hispanic/Latino population is at least 20% of the overall population. In states where less than five places meet either of these criteria, we have included places with at least 10,000 total population with the highest percentage of Hispanic/Latino population. These places are identified with an asterisk (*); Please refer to the User's Guide for a full explanation of data.

Uruguayan	19,246
Venezuelan	22,055
Spaniard	31,036

Households with $100,000+ Income

Group	Number	%
Total Population	1,253,066	17.5
Hispanic or Latino (of any race)	163,881	13.2
Central American, ex. Mexican	11,987	10.0
Costa Rican	809	12.4
Guatemalan	2,029	10.3
Honduran	1,748	5.8
Nicaraguan	4,397	11.3
Panamanian	1,457	16.7
Salvadoran	1,374	9.1
Cuban	65,553	16.0
Dominican Republic	5,770	11.6
Mexican	11,664	8.5
Puerto Rican	28,072	11.0
South American	30,556	14.1
Argentinean	3,606	17.8
Bolivian	500	15.3
Chilean	1,292	15.4
Colombian	11,854	12.8
Ecuadorian	2,779	14.3
Paraguayan	64	12.6
Peruvian	4,001	12.4
Uruguayan	472	8.9
Venezuelan	5,533	16.9
Spaniard	4,123	22.4

Households with Food Stamps/SNAP Benefits During Past 12 Months

Group	Number	%
Total Population	605,727	8.5
Hispanic or Latino (of any race)	192,784	15.5
Central American, ex. Mexican	17,090	14.2
Costa Rican	669	10.2
Guatemalan	2,645	13.4
Honduran	4,160	13.9
Nicaraguan	6,561	16.9
Panamanian	861	9.9
Salvadoran	2,045	13.5
Cuban	84,019	20.6
Dominican Republic	8,787	17.7
Mexican	21,026	15.2
Puerto Rican	39,253	15.4
South American	18,420	8.5
Argentinean	1,466	7.2
Bolivian	177	5.4
Chilean	608	7.2
Colombian	8,555	9.2
Ecuadorian	2,184	11.2
Paraguayan	22	4.3
Peruvian	2,854	8.9
Uruguayan	491	9.3
Venezuelan	2,014	6.2
Spaniard	1,048	5.7

Poverty Rate
(Income in Past 12 Months Below Poverty Level)

Group	%
Total Population	13.8
Hispanic or Latino (of any race)	18.3
Central American, ex. Mexican	21.6
Costa Rican	19.1
Guatemalan	28.6
Honduran	25.9
Nicaraguan	15.7
Panamanian	16.0
Salvadoran	21.5
Cuban	15.7
Dominican Republic	17.3
Mexican	29.0
Puerto Rican	18.3
South American	12.8
Argentinean	13.5
Bolivian	10.5
Chilean	9.8
Colombian	12.7
Ecuadorian	12.9
Paraguayan	6.6
Peruvian	12.3
Uruguayan	14.9
Venezuelan	14.2
Spaniard	11.1

Alafaya

Population

Group	Number	%TP[1]	%HP[2]
Total Population	78,113	100.0	–
Hispanic or Latino (of any race)	25,448	32.6	100.0
Central American, ex. Mexican	1,089	1.4	4.3
Costa Rican	136	0.2	0.5
Guatemalan	156	0.2	0.6
Honduran	232	0.3	0.9
Nicaraguan	124	0.2	0.5
Panamanian	230	0.3	0.9
Salvadoran	205	0.3	0.8
Cuban	1,861	2.4	7.3
Dominican Republic	1,878	2.4	7.4
Mexican	1,280	1.6	5.0
Puerto Rican	14,044	18.0	55.2
South American	4,114	5.3	16.2
Argentinean	130	0.2	0.5
Colombian	2,251	2.9	8.8
Ecuadorian	489	0.6	1.9
Peruvian	413	0.5	1.6
Venezuelan	653	0.8	2.6
Spaniard	210	0.3	0.8

Population Growth: 2000–2010

Group	%
Total Population	n/a

Males per 100 Females

Group	Number
Total Population	96.5
Hispanic or Latino (of any race)	89.2
Central American, ex. Mexican	84.6
Costa Rican	109.2
Guatemalan	77.3
Honduran	79.8
Nicaraguan	103.3
Panamanian	69.1
Salvadoran	88.1
Cuban	102.9
Dominican Republic	85.0
Mexican	96.6
Puerto Rican	89.5
South American	83.9
Argentinean	160.0
Colombian	83.8
Ecuadorian	74.0
Peruvian	79.6
Venezuelan	84.5
Spaniard	69.4

Average Household Size

Group	People
Total Population	2.86
Hispanic or Latino (of any race)	3.18
Central American, ex. Mexican	3.30
Costa Rican	2.90
Guatemalan	3.37
Honduran	3.56
Nicaraguan	3.35
Panamanian	2.94
Salvadoran	3.70
Cuban	3.04
Dominican Republic	3.44
Mexican	3.45
Puerto Rican	3.15
South American	3.23
Argentinean	3.06
Colombian	3.27
Ecuadorian	3.54
Peruvian	3.18
Venezuelan	2.99
Spaniard	2.63

Median Age

Group	Years
Total Population	30.2
Hispanic or Latino (of any race)	29.6
Central American, ex. Mexican	31.3
Costa Rican	30.7
Guatemalan	27.0
Honduran	32.0
Nicaraguan	30.5
Panamanian	32.0
Salvadoran	34.8
Cuban	28.4
Dominican Republic	29.2
Mexican	24.4
Puerto Rican	30.0
South American	32.9
Argentinean	31.0
Colombian	34.2
Ecuadorian	32.3
Peruvian	33.1
Venezuelan	30.7
Spaniard	29.9

High School Graduates
(Universe: Population 25 Years and Over)

Group	Number	%
Total Population	41,143	94.2
Hispanic or Latino (of any race)	12,797	90.4
Central American, ex. Mexican	479	86.8
Cuban	614	90.6
Dominican Republic	794	95.8
Mexican	610	97.9
Puerto Rican	6,718	88.3
South American	3,037	93.6
Colombian	1,801	92.4

Four-Year College Graduates
(Universe: Population 25 Years and Over)

Group	Number	%
Total Population	19,027	43.6
Hispanic or Latino (of any race)	4,350	30.7
Central American, ex. Mexican	153	27.7
Cuban	199	29.4
Dominican Republic	210	25.3
Mexican	207	33.2
Puerto Rican	2,330	30.6
South American	1,067	32.9
Colombian	466	23.9

Population Age 3–17 Enrolled in Public School
(Universe: Population Age 3–17 Enrolled in School)

Group	Number	%
Total Population	14,554	84.1
Hispanic or Latino (of any race)	6,162	86.9
Central American, ex. Mexican	226	86.6
Cuban	63	65.6
Dominican Republic	485	100.0
Mexican	218	84.2
Puerto Rican	3,483	85.6
South American	1,475	90.3
Colombian	1,004	98.5

Population Age 3–17 Enrolled in Private School
(Universe: Population Age 3–17 Enrolled in School)

Group	Number	%
Total Population	2,749	15.9
Hispanic or Latino (of any race)	932	13.1
Central American, ex. Mexican	35	13.4
Cuban	33	34.4
Dominican Republic	0	0.0
Mexican	41	15.8
Puerto Rican	585	14.4
South American	159	9.7
Colombian	15	1.5

Foreign-Born Population

Group	Number	%
Total Population	15,272	19.8
Hispanic or Latino (of any race)	7,116	27.3
Central American, ex. Mexican	583	54.4
Cuban	619	49.7
Dominican Republic	645	44.3
Mexican	323	30.9
Puerto Rican	468	3.3
South American	4,132	69.6
Colombian	2,482	70.1

Foreign-Born Naturalized U.S. Citizens

Group	Number	%
Total Population	8,017	52.5
Hispanic or Latino (of any race)	3,232	45.4
Central American, ex. Mexican	498	85.4

Notes: (1) Percent of total population; (2) Percent of Hispanic/Latino population; Profiles include places with an overall population of at least 125,000, OR an overall population of at least 25,000 where the Hispanic/Latino population is at least 20% of the overall population. In states where less than five places meet either of these criteria, we have included places with at least 10,000 total population with the highest percentage of Hispanic/Latino population. These places are identified with an asterisk (*); Please refer to the User's Guide for a full explanation of data.

Group	Number	%
Cuban	344	55.6
Dominican Republic	380	58.9
Mexican	135	41.8
Puerto Rican	0	0.0
South American	1,626	39.4
Colombian	989	39.8

Language Spoken at Home: English Only
(Universe: Population 5 Years and Over)

Group	Number	%
Total Population	44,345	62.0
Hispanic or Latino (of any race)	4,982	20.5
Central American, ex. Mexican	151	15.6
Cuban	490	40.7
Dominican Republic	499	35.9
Mexican	309	32.1
Puerto Rican	2,679	20.3
South American	538	9.6
Colombian	306	8.9

Language Spoken at Home: Spanish
(Universe: Population 5 Years and Over)

Group	Number	%
Total Population	20,357	28.5
Hispanic or Latino (of any race)	19,241	79.1
Central American, ex. Mexican	818	84.4
Cuban	713	59.3
Dominican Republic	890	64.1
Mexican	653	67.9
Puerto Rican	10,467	79.3
South American	5,015	89.9
Colombian	3,141	91.1

Unemployment Rate
(Universe: Population 16 Years and Over)

Group	%
Total Population	8.4
Hispanic or Latino (of any race)	11.2
Central American, ex. Mexican	7.6
Cuban	9.0
Dominican Republic	22.4
Mexican	21.3
Puerto Rican	10.5
South American	9.6
Colombian	11.1

Class of Worker: Private Wage and Salary
(Universe: Civilian Employed Population 16 Years and Over)

Group	Number	%
Total Population	32,832	84.1
Hispanic or Latino (of any race)	9,541	83.2
Central American, ex. Mexican	399	89.1
Cuban	479	81.6
Dominican Republic	494	79.9
Mexican	414	92.4
Puerto Rican	4,969	81.0
South American	2,362	87.0
Colombian	1,394	87.6

Class of Worker: Government
(Universe: Civilian Employed Population 16 Years and Over)

Group	Number	%
Total Population	5,038	12.9
Hispanic or Latino (of any race)	1,604	14.0
Central American, ex. Mexican	49	10.9
Cuban	96	16.4
Dominican Republic	72	11.7
Mexican	25	5.6
Puerto Rican	1,028	16.8
South American	243	9.0
Colombian	131	8.2

Means of Transportation to Work: Car, Truck or Van
(Universe: Workers 16 Years and Over)

Group	Number	%
Total Population	35,398	93.0
Hispanic or Latino (of any race)	10,642	95.4
Central American, ex. Mexican	448	100.0
Cuban	537	97.6
Dominican Republic	564	95.6
Mexican	419	95.4
Puerto Rican	5,718	95.4
South American	2,481	94.9
Colombian	1,493	97.9

Means of Transportation to Work: Public Transportation (ex. Taxicab)
(Universe: Workers 16 Years and Over)

Group	Number	%
Total Population	22	0.1
Hispanic or Latino (of any race)	20	0.2
Central American, ex. Mexican	0	0.0
Cuban	0	0.0
Dominican Republic	0	0.0
Mexican	20	4.6
Puerto Rican	0	0.0
South American	0	0.0
Colombian	0	0.0

Homeownership Rate
(Universe: Occupied Housing Units)

Group	%
Total Population	63.3
Hispanic or Latino (of any race)	58.7
Central American, ex. Mexican	64.5
Costa Rican	71.4
Guatemalan	68.6
Honduran	56.8
Nicaraguan	74.2
Panamanian	54.4
Salvadoran	72.5
Cuban	61.3
Dominican Republic	54.5
Mexican	54.4
Puerto Rican	57.5
South American	64.7
Argentinean	59.3
Colombian	65.6
Ecuadorian	69.5
Peruvian	63.7
Venezuelan	61.0
Spaniard	55.6

Median Home Value

Group	Dollars
Total Population	278,400
Hispanic or Latino (of any race)	268,000
Central American, ex. Mexican	274,000
Cuban	246,300
Dominican Republic	261,300
Mexican	230,700
Puerto Rican	260,300
South American	289,400
Colombian	256,700

Median Gross Rent

Group	Dollars
Total Population	1,128
Hispanic or Latino (of any race)	1,061
Central American, ex. Mexican	1,111
Cuban	1,325
Dominican Republic	906
Mexican	1,168
Puerto Rican	1,020
South American	1,083
Colombian	1,110

Median Household Income
(2010 Inflation-Adjusted Dollars)

Group	Dollars
Total Population	65,639
Hispanic or Latino (of any race)	50,438
Central American, ex. Mexican	65,568
Cuban	82,218
Dominican Republic	46,985
Mexican	46,167
Puerto Rican	45,892
South American	53,582
Colombian	45,179

Per Capita Income
(2010 Inflation-Adjusted Dollars)

Group	Dollars
Total Population	25,655
Hispanic or Latino (of any race)	18,856
Central American, ex. Mexican	16,775
Cuban	29,958
Dominican Republic	13,428
Mexican	16,835
Puerto Rican	18,912
South American	18,596
Colombian	16,820

Households with $100,000+ Income

Group	Number	%
Total Population	7,033	27.7
Hispanic or Latino (of any race)	1,209	15.7
Central American, ex. Mexican	66	22.5
Cuban	153	30.4
Dominican Republic	46	10.7
Mexican	33	11.0
Puerto Rican	549	13.6
South American	289	16.2
Colombian	137	13.6

Households with Food Stamps/SNAP Benefits During Past 12 Months

Group	Number	%
Total Population	1,079	4.2
Hispanic or Latino (of any race)	601	7.8
Central American, ex. Mexican	41	14.0
Cuban	9	1.8
Dominican Republic	44	10.3
Mexican	13	4.3
Puerto Rican	407	10.1
South American	61	3.4
Colombian	61	6.1

Poverty Rate
(Income in Past 12 Months Below Poverty Level)

Group	%
Total Population	10.6
Hispanic or Latino (of any race)	12.8
Central American, ex. Mexican	15.4
Cuban	24.5
Dominican Republic	14.5
Mexican	10.0
Puerto Rican	12.6
South American	12.5
Colombian	15.9

Altamonte Springs

Population

Group	Number	%TP[1]	%HP[2]
Total Population	41,496	100.0	–
Hispanic or Latino (of any race)	10,067	24.3	100.0
Central American, ex. Mexican	602	1.5	6.0
Honduran	103	0.2	1.0
Nicaraguan	142	0.3	1.4
Panamanian	114	0.3	1.1
Cuban	786	1.9	7.8
Dominican Republic	616	1.5	6.1
Mexican	932	2.2	9.3
Puerto Rican	4,738	11.4	47.1
South American	1,860	4.5	18.5
Argentinean	134	0.3	1.3
Colombian	908	2.2	9.0
Ecuadorian	203	0.5	2.0
Peruvian	262	0.6	2.6
Venezuelan	269	0.6	2.7
Spaniard	133	0.3	1.3

Population Growth: 2000–2010

Group	%
Total Population	0.7
Hispanic or Latino (of any race)	53.4
Central American, ex. Mexican	129.8
Cuban	68.3
Dominican Republic	106.0
Mexican	92.2
Puerto Rican	57.6
South American	94.2
Colombian	97.8
Peruvian	127.8
Venezuelan	83.0

Males per 100 Females

Group	Number
Total Population	88.7
Hispanic or Latino (of any race)	87.5
Central American, ex. Mexican	84.7
Honduran	80.7
Nicaraguan	89.3

STATE & PLACE PROFILES

Notes: (1) Percent of total population; (2) Percent of Hispanic/Latino population; Profiles include places with an overall population of at least 125,000, OR an overall population of at least 25,000 where the Hispanic/Latino population is at least 20% of the overall population. In states where less than five places meet either of these criteria, we have included places with at least 10,000 total population with the highest percentage of Hispanic/Latino population. These places are identified with an asterisk (*); Please refer to the User's Guide for a full explanation of data.

Panamanian	67.6
Cuban	88.9
Dominican Republic	75.5
Mexican	114.3
Puerto Rican	86.8
South American	80.8
Argentinean	76.3
Colombian	73.0
Ecuadorian	105.1
Peruvian	91.2
Venezuelan	81.8
Spaniard	98.5

Average Household Size

Group	People
Total Population	2.15
Hispanic or Latino (of any race)	2.58
Central American, ex. Mexican	2.97
Honduran	3.09
Nicaraguan	3.20
Panamanian	2.56
Cuban	2.43
Dominican Republic	2.69
Mexican	3.04
Puerto Rican	2.53
South American	2.59
Argentinean	2.26
Colombian	2.59
Ecuadorian	2.71
Peruvian	2.65
Venezuelan	2.73
Spaniard	2.13

Median Age

Group	Years
Total Population	35.5
Hispanic or Latino (of any race)	30.2
Central American, ex. Mexican	31.2
Honduran	30.2
Nicaraguan	32.3
Panamanian	37.7
Cuban	34.8
Dominican Republic	28.4
Mexican	26.7
Puerto Rican	29.6
South American	34.3
Argentinean	35.8
Colombian	34.5
Ecuadorian	34.6
Peruvian	35.2
Venezuelan	32.7
Spaniard	35.1

High School Graduates
(Universe: Population 25 Years and Over)

Group	Number	%
Total Population	27,463	91.7
Hispanic or Latino (of any race)	4,619	82.6
Puerto Rican	2,324	85.6
South American	760	67.8

Four-Year College Graduates
(Universe: Population 25 Years and Over)

Group	Number	%
Total Population	9,815	32.8
Hispanic or Latino (of any race)	1,532	27.4
Puerto Rican	718	26.5
South American	453	40.4

Population Age 3–17 Enrolled in Public School
(Universe: Population Age 3–17 Enrolled in School)

Group	Number	%
Total Population	5,089	82.7
Hispanic or Latino (of any race)	1,727	85.1
Puerto Rican	840	78.3
South American	355	91.3

Population Age 3–17 Enrolled in Private School
(Universe: Population Age 3–17 Enrolled in School)

Group	Number	%
Total Population	1,062	17.3
Hispanic or Latino (of any race)	303	14.9
Puerto Rican	233	21.7
South American	34	8.7

Foreign-Born Population

Group	Number	%
Total Population	5,963	14.2
Hispanic or Latino (of any race)	2,378	25.7
Puerto Rican	0	0.0
South American	1,122	67.5

Foreign-Born Naturalized U.S. Citizens

Group	Number	%
Total Population	2,916	48.9
Hispanic or Latino (of any race)	924	38.9
Puerto Rican	0	0.0
South American	356	31.7

Language Spoken at Home: English Only
(Universe: Population 5 Years and Over)

Group	Number	%
Total Population	29,803	75.0
Hispanic or Latino (of any race)	1,528	18.2
Puerto Rican	902	22.0
South American	98	6.4

Language Spoken at Home: Spanish
(Universe: Population 5 Years and Over)

Group	Number	%
Total Population	7,722	19.4
Hispanic or Latino (of any race)	6,864	81.7
Puerto Rican	3,195	78.0
South American	1,421	92.8

Unemployment Rate
(Universe: Population 16 Years and Over)

Group	%
Total Population	7.2
Hispanic or Latino (of any race)	11.8
Puerto Rican	12.6
South American	14.2

Class of Worker: Private Wage and Salary
(Universe: Civilian Employed Population 16 Years and Over)

Group	Number	%
Total Population	21,054	89.1
Hispanic or Latino (of any race)	4,221	88.2
Puerto Rican	2,078	91.0
South American	644	79.2

Class of Worker: Government
(Universe: Civilian Employed Population 16 Years and Over)

Group	Number	%
Total Population	1,797	7.6
Hispanic or Latino (of any race)	291	6.1
Puerto Rican	187	8.2
South American	55	6.8

Means of Transportation to Work: Car, Truck or Van
(Universe: Workers 16 Years and Over)

Group	Number	%
Total Population	20,966	89.9
Hispanic or Latino (of any race)	4,036	86.8
Puerto Rican	1,792	81.2
South American	719	91.7

Means of Transportation to Work: Public Transportation (ex. Taxicab)
(Universe: Workers 16 Years and Over)

Group	Number	%
Total Population	280	1.2
Hispanic or Latino (of any race)	49	1.1
Puerto Rican	49	2.2
South American	0	0.0

Homeownership Rate
(Universe: Occupied Housing Units)

Group	%
Total Population	42.3
Hispanic or Latino (of any race)	31.7
Central American, ex. Mexican	35.8
Honduran	28.1
Nicaraguan	31.7
Panamanian	36.0
Cuban	40.7
Dominican Republic	26.8
Mexican	19.4
Puerto Rican	28.9
South American	39.8
Argentinean	46.8
Colombian	42.4
Ecuadorian	36.1
Peruvian	36.4
Venezuelan	36.8
Spaniard	37.1

Median Home Value

Group	Dollars
Total Population	201,500
Hispanic or Latino (of any race)	197,100
Puerto Rican	203,500
South American	197,400

Median Gross Rent

Group	Dollars
Total Population	973
Hispanic or Latino (of any race)	946
Puerto Rican	904
South American	1,053

Median Household Income
(2010 Inflation-Adjusted Dollars)

Group	Dollars
Total Population	50,484
Hispanic or Latino (of any race)	43,012
Puerto Rican	43,138
South American	40,594

Per Capita Income
(2010 Inflation-Adjusted Dollars)

Group	Dollars
Total Population	27,786
Hispanic or Latino (of any race)	19,594
Puerto Rican	18,864
South American	19,592

Households with $100,000+ Income

Group	Number	%
Total Population	2,429	13.5
Hispanic or Latino (of any race)	306	9.6
Puerto Rican	72	4.7
South American	68	11.1

Households with Food Stamps/SNAP Benefits During Past 12 Months

Group	Number	%
Total Population	763	4.2
Hispanic or Latino (of any race)	229	7.2
Puerto Rican	202	13.2
South American	14	2.3

Poverty Rate
(Income in Past 12 Months Below Poverty Level)

Group	%
Total Population	7.5
Hispanic or Latino (of any race)	10.5
Puerto Rican	10.2
South American	15.4

Apopka

Population

Group	Number	%TP[1]	%HP[2]
Total Population	41,542	100.0	–
Hispanic or Latino (of any race)	10,548	25.4	100.0
Central American, ex. Mexican	901	2.2	8.5
Guatemalan	346	0.8	3.3
Honduran	224	0.5	2.1
Nicaraguan	105	0.3	1.0
Salvadoran	113	0.3	1.1
Cuban	625	1.5	5.9
Dominican Republic	528	1.3	5.0
Mexican	3,695	8.9	35.0
Puerto Rican	3,400	8.2	32.2
South American	888	2.1	8.4
Colombian	412	1.0	3.9
Ecuadorian	109	0.3	1.0
Peruvian	124	0.3	1.2
Venezuelan	144	0.3	1.4

Notes: (1) Percent of total population; (2) Percent of Hispanic/Latino population; Profiles include places with an overall population of at least 125,000, OR an overall population of at least 25,000 where the Hispanic/Latino population is at least 20% of the overall population. In states where less than five places meet either of these criteria, we have included places with at least 10,000 total population with the highest percentage of Hispanic/Latino population. These places are identified with an asterisk (*); Please refer to the User's Guide for a full explanation of data.

Population Growth: 2000–2010	
Group	%
Total Population	55.9
Hispanic or Latino (of any race)	119.0
Central American, ex. Mexican	530.1
Cuban	288.2
Dominican Republic	363.2
Mexican	96.2
Puerto Rican	99.5
South American	225.3
Colombian	212.1

Males per 100 Females	
Group	Number
Total Population	94.2
Hispanic or Latino (of any race)	102.6
Central American, ex. Mexican	128.7
Guatemalan	170.3
Honduran	146.2
Nicaraguan	87.5
Salvadoran	130.6
Cuban	92.3
Dominican Republic	79.0
Mexican	123.5
Puerto Rican	87.8
South American	91.8
Colombian	87.3
Ecuadorian	75.8
Peruvian	100.0
Venezuelan	105.7

Average Household Size	
Group	People
Total Population	2.88
Hispanic or Latino (of any race)	3.63
Central American, ex. Mexican	4.14
Guatemalan	4.99
Honduran	3.93
Nicaraguan	3.82
Salvadoran	3.89
Cuban	3.09
Dominican Republic	3.62
Mexican	4.51
Puerto Rican	3.16
South American	3.19
Colombian	3.07
Ecuadorian	3.75
Peruvian	3.26
Venezuelan	3.30

Median Age	
Group	Years
Total Population	35.4
Hispanic or Latino (of any race)	28.1
Central American, ex. Mexican	28.3
Guatemalan	25.7
Honduran	29.5
Nicaraguan	30.1
Salvadoran	31.5
Cuban	35.7
Dominican Republic	31.7
Mexican	23.5
Puerto Rican	31.6
South American	36.2
Colombian	36.6
Ecuadorian	35.4
Peruvian	38.0
Venezuelan	35.5

High School Graduates (Universe: Population 25 Years and Over)		
Group	Number	%
Total Population	23,462	88.5
Hispanic or Latino (of any race)	4,020	80.0
Mexican	704	70.0
Puerto Rican	1,639	88.5
South American	571	87.0

Four-Year College Graduates (Universe: Population 25 Years and Over)		
Group	Number	%
Total Population	7,635	28.8
Hispanic or Latino (of any race)	1,155	23.0
Mexican	146	14.5
Puerto Rican	483	26.1
South American	255	38.9

Population Age 3–17 Enrolled in Public School (Universe: Population Age 3–17 Enrolled in School)		
Group	Number	%
Total Population	5,399	81.2
Hispanic or Latino (of any race)	1,310	94.9
Mexican	268	100.0
Puerto Rican	491	93.9
South American	222	96.5

Population Age 3–17 Enrolled in Private School (Universe: Population Age 3–17 Enrolled in School)		
Group	Number	%
Total Population	1,246	18.8
Hispanic or Latino (of any race)	70	5.1
Mexican	0	0.0
Puerto Rican	32	6.1
South American	8	3.5

Foreign-Born Population		
Group	Number	%
Total Population	6,542	16.6
Hispanic or Latino (of any race)	3,314	37.7
Mexican	1,074	53.0
Puerto Rican	98	3.3
South American	495	48.9

Foreign-Born Naturalized U.S. Citizens		
Group	Number	%
Total Population	3,167	48.4
Hispanic or Latino (of any race)	1,289	38.9
Mexican	150	14.0
Puerto Rican	45	45.9
South American	324	65.5

Language Spoken at Home: English Only (Universe: Population 5 Years and Over)		
Group	Number	%
Total Population	26,729	73.0
Hispanic or Latino (of any race)	1,345	17.1
Mexican	320	19.0
Puerto Rican	549	20.5
South American	253	26.1

Language Spoken at Home: Spanish (Universe: Population 5 Years and Over)		
Group	Number	%
Total Population	7,187	19.6
Hispanic or Latino (of any race)	6,449	82.2
Mexican	1,368	81.0
Puerto Rican	2,128	79.5
South American	682	70.3

Unemployment Rate (Universe: Population 16 Years and Over)	
Group	%
Total Population	6.4
Hispanic or Latino (of any race)	8.6
Mexican	5.1
Puerto Rican	9.9
South American	6.5

Class of Worker: Private Wage and Salary (Universe: Civilian Employed Population 16 Years and Over)		
Group	Number	%
Total Population	17,281	83.3
Hispanic or Latino (of any race)	3,985	89.8
Mexican	1,111	92.4
Puerto Rican	1,209	83.8
South American	457	90.1

Class of Worker: Government (Universe: Civilian Employed Population 16 Years and Over)		
Group	Number	%
Total Population	2,398	11.6
Hispanic or Latino (of any race)	356	8.0
Mexican	82	6.8
Puerto Rican	205	14.2
South American	25	4.9

Means of Transportation to Work: Car, Truck or Van (Universe: Workers 16 Years and Over)		
Group	Number	%
Total Population	18,623	91.2
Hispanic or Latino (of any race)	3,789	86.6
Mexican	939	80.9
Puerto Rican	1,265	89.0
South American	456	89.9

Means of Transportation to Work: Public Transportation (ex. Taxicab) (Universe: Workers 16 Years and Over)		
Group	Number	%
Total Population	225	1.1
Hispanic or Latino (of any race)	101	2.3
Mexican	26	2.2
Puerto Rican	75	5.3
South American	0	0.0

Homeownership Rate (Universe: Occupied Housing Units)	
Group	%
Total Population	77.6
Hispanic or Latino (of any race)	63.3
Central American, ex. Mexican	46.3
Guatemalan	23.7
Honduran	47.4
Nicaraguan	53.6
Salvadoran	61.1
Cuban	74.4
Dominican Republic	64.1
Mexican	50.3
Puerto Rican	69.9
South American	77.6
Colombian	80.8
Ecuadorian	75.0
Peruvian	70.6
Venezuelan	73.9

Median Home Value	
Group	Dollars
Total Population	222,100
Hispanic or Latino (of any race)	193,400
Mexican	114,700
Puerto Rican	193,900
South American	192,100

Median Gross Rent	
Group	Dollars
Total Population	929
Hispanic or Latino (of any race)	891
Mexican	897
Puerto Rican	858
South American	854

Median Household Income (2010 Inflation-Adjusted Dollars)	
Group	Dollars
Total Population	59,688
Hispanic or Latino (of any race)	47,099
Mexican	36,250
Puerto Rican	55,673
South American	48,500

Per Capita Income (2010 Inflation-Adjusted Dollars)	
Group	Dollars
Total Population	27,379
Hispanic or Latino (of any race)	18,176
Mexican	15,595
Puerto Rican	18,906
South American	20,532

Households with $100,000+ Income		
Group	Number	%
Total Population	3,080	20.9
Hispanic or Latino (of any race)	261	9.7
Mexican	29	4.3
Puerto Rican	62	6.7
South American	46	14.5

Households with Food Stamps/SNAP Benefits During Past 12 Months		
Group	Number	%
Total Population	644	4.4
Hispanic or Latino (of any race)	176	6.5
Mexican	51	7.5
Puerto Rican	83	9.0
South American	16	5.0

STATE & PLACE PROFILES

Notes: (1) Percent of total population; (2) Percent of Hispanic/Latino population; Profiles include places with an overall population of at least 125,000, OR an overall population of at least 25,000 where the Hispanic/Latino population is at least 20% of the overall population. In states where less than five places meet either of these criteria, we have included places with at least 10,000 total population with the highest percentage of Hispanic/Latino population. These places are identified with an asterisk (*); Please refer to the User's Guide for a full explanation of data.

Poverty Rate
(Income in Past 12 Months Below Poverty Level)

Group	%
Total Population	7.9
Hispanic or Latino (of any race)	11.7
Mexican	16.1
Puerto Rican	3.7
South American	9.0

Aventura

Population

Group	Number	%TP[1]	%HP[2]
Total Population	35,762	100.0	–
Hispanic or Latino (of any race)	12,798	35.8	100.0
Central American, ex. Mexican	531	1.5	4.1
Nicaraguan	153	0.4	1.2
Cuban	1,408	3.9	11.0
Dominican Republic	374	1.0	2.9
Mexican	831	2.3	6.5
Puerto Rican	695	1.9	5.4
South American	8,112	22.7	63.4
Argentinean	1,579	4.4	12.3
Chilean	176	0.5	1.4
Colombian	3,285	9.2	25.7
Ecuadorian	330	0.9	2.6
Peruvian	713	2.0	5.6
Uruguayan	148	0.4	1.2
Venezuelan	1,765	4.9	13.8
Spaniard	195	0.5	1.5

Population Growth: 2000–2010

Group	%
Total Population	41.5
Hispanic or Latino (of any race)	145.3
Central American, ex. Mexican	104.2
Cuban	92.6
Dominican Republic	266.7
Mexican	155.7
Puerto Rican	119.9
South American	254.4
Argentinean	272.4
Colombian	205.6
Peruvian	202.1
Venezuelan	433.2

Males per 100 Females

Group	Number
Total Population	84.6
Hispanic or Latino (of any race)	80.6
Central American, ex. Mexican	72.4
Nicaraguan	75.9
Cuban	87.5
Dominican Republic	65.5
Mexican	92.4
Puerto Rican	76.8
South American	79.4
Argentinean	104.8
Chilean	63.0
Colombian	68.8
Ecuadorian	70.1
Peruvian	75.6
Uruguayan	97.3
Venezuelan	84.4
Spaniard	97.0

Average Household Size

Group	People
Total Population	1.99
Hispanic or Latino (of any race)	2.34
Central American, ex. Mexican	2.21
Nicaraguan	2.20
Cuban	1.97
Dominican Republic	2.43
Mexican	2.64
Puerto Rican	1.99
South American	2.45
Argentinean	2.49
Chilean	2.18
Colombian	2.43
Ecuadorian	2.56
Peruvian	2.52
Uruguayan	2.44
Venezuelan	2.45
Spaniard	2.23

Median Age

Group	Years
Total Population	46.1
Hispanic or Latino (of any race)	39.3
Central American, ex. Mexican	39.1
Nicaraguan	38.4
Cuban	51.8
Dominican Republic	33.0
Mexican	34.4
Puerto Rican	39.8
South American	38.9
Argentinean	39.9
Chilean	44.8
Colombian	39.2
Ecuadorian	40.5
Peruvian	39.4
Uruguayan	42.0
Venezuelan	35.9
Spaniard	41.4

High School Graduates
(Universe: Population 25 Years and Over)

Group	Number	%
Total Population	25,250	93.2
Hispanic or Latino (of any race)	7,956	92.2
South American	5,148	95.2
Argentinean	902	95.6
Colombian	2,512	96.7
Venezuelan	877	93.2

Four-Year College Graduates
(Universe: Population 25 Years and Over)

Group	Number	%
Total Population	12,873	47.5
Hispanic or Latino (of any race)	4,586	53.2
South American	2,870	53.1
Argentinean	434	46.0
Colombian	1,249	48.1
Venezuelan	720	76.5

Population Age 3–17 Enrolled in Public School
(Universe: Population Age 3–17 Enrolled in School)

Group	Number	%
Total Population	2,411	75.7
Hispanic or Latino (of any race)	1,046	70.7
South American	737	71.3
Argentinean	236	78.7
Colombian	304	72.7
Venezuelan	153	67.7

Population Age 3–17 Enrolled in Private School
(Universe: Population Age 3–17 Enrolled in School)

Group	Number	%
Total Population	776	24.3
Hispanic or Latino (of any race)	434	29.3
South American	297	28.7
Argentinean	64	21.3
Colombian	114	27.3
Venezuelan	73	32.3

Foreign-Born Population

Group	Number	%
Total Population	14,838	43.9
Hispanic or Latino (of any race)	8,200	72.6
South American	5,688	81.5
Argentinean	1,120	86.4
Colombian	2,688	80.0
Venezuelan	910	74.3

Foreign-Born Naturalized U.S. Citizens

Group	Number	%
Total Population	7,661	51.6
Hispanic or Latino (of any race)	3,676	44.8
South American	2,320	40.8
Argentinean	435	38.8
Colombian	1,180	43.9
Venezuelan	196	21.5

Language Spoken at Home: English Only
(Universe: Population 5 Years and Over)

Group	Number	%
Total Population	15,295	47.9
Hispanic or Latino (of any race)	516	4.9
South American	70	1.1
Argentinean	0	0.0
Colombian	27	0.9
Venezuelan	0	0.0

Language Spoken at Home: Spanish
(Universe: Population 5 Years and Over)

Group	Number	%
Total Population	11,145	34.9
Hispanic or Latino (of any race)	9,777	93.1
South American	6,380	98.4
Argentinean	1,237	100.0
Colombian	3,016	99.1
Venezuelan	1,127	98.9

Unemployment Rate
(Universe: Population 16 Years and Over)

Group	%
Total Population	6.9
Hispanic or Latino (of any race)	7.6
South American	8.1
Argentinean	7.4
Colombian	10.8
Venezuelan	4.5

Class of Worker: Private Wage and Salary
(Universe: Civilian Employed Population 16 Years and Over)

Group	Number	%
Total Population	11,973	82.2
Hispanic or Latino (of any race)	4,499	82.6
South American	2,577	83.8
Argentinean	675	93.4
Colombian	1,092	75.5
Venezuelan	325	96.7

Class of Worker: Government
(Universe: Civilian Employed Population 16 Years and Over)

Group	Number	%
Total Population	1,381	9.5
Hispanic or Latino (of any race)	467	8.6
South American	229	7.4
Argentinean	11	1.5
Colombian	149	10.3
Venezuelan	0	0.0

Means of Transportation to Work: Car, Truck or Van
(Universe: Workers 16 Years and Over)

Group	Number	%
Total Population	12,407	88.0
Hispanic or Latino (of any race)	4,614	86.7
South American	2,522	84.0
Argentinean	705	97.5
Colombian	1,134	79.4
Venezuelan	261	77.7

Means of Transportation to Work: Public Transportation (ex. Taxicab)
(Universe: Workers 16 Years and Over)

Group	Number	%
Total Population	111	0.8
Hispanic or Latino (of any race)	67	1.3
South American	0	0.0
Argentinean	0	0.0
Colombian	0	0.0
Venezuelan	0	0.0

Homeownership Rate
(Universe: Occupied Housing Units)

Group	%
Total Population	65.7
Hispanic or Latino (of any race)	58.9
Central American, ex. Mexican	53.4
Nicaraguan	54.1
Cuban	65.6
Dominican Republic	40.4
Mexican	59.3
Puerto Rican	49.6
South American	59.8
Argentinean	68.0
Chilean	71.8
Colombian	56.0
Ecuadorian	60.7
Peruvian	49.3
Uruguayan	60.9

Notes: (1) Percent of total population; (2) Percent of Hispanic/Latino population; Profiles include places with an overall population of at least 125,000, OR an overall population of at least 25,000 where the Hispanic/Latino population is at least 20% of the overall population. In states where less than five places meet either of these criteria, we have included places with at least 10,000 total population with the highest percentage of Hispanic/Latino population. These places are identified with an asterisk (*); Please refer to the User's Guide for a full explanation of data.

Venezuelan	61.0
Spaniard	66.0

Median Home Value

Group	Dollars
Total Population	344,400
Hispanic or Latino (of any race)	325,900
South American	298,000
Argentinean	259,400
Colombian	324,400
Venezuelan	301,200

Median Gross Rent

Group	Dollars
Total Population	1,610
Hispanic or Latino (of any race)	1,502
South American	1,501
Argentinean	1,305
Colombian	1,486
Venezuelan	1,774

Median Household Income
(2010 Inflation-Adjusted Dollars)

Group	Dollars
Total Population	56,046
Hispanic or Latino (of any race)	58,119
South American	58,016
Argentinean	118,438
Colombian	59,662
Venezuelan	33,167

Per Capita Income
(2010 Inflation-Adjusted Dollars)

Group	Dollars
Total Population	47,462
Hispanic or Latino (of any race)	36,267
South American	34,533
Argentinean	46,099
Colombian	32,714
Venezuelan	30,987

Households with $100,000+ Income

Group	Number	%
Total Population	4,724	28.1
Hispanic or Latino (of any race)	1,318	27.9
South American	711	25.9
Argentinean	269	54.2
Colombian	227	20.5
Venezuelan	165	29.6

Households with Food Stamps/SNAP Benefits During Past 12 Months

Group	Number	%
Total Population	264	1.6
Hispanic or Latino (of any race)	116	2.5
South American	100	3.6
Argentinean	0	0.0
Colombian	100	9.0
Venezuelan	0	0.0

Poverty Rate
(Income in Past 12 Months Below Poverty Level)

Group	%
Total Population	10.8
Hispanic or Latino (of any race)	11.7
South American	10.5
Argentinean	4.9
Colombian	11.6
Venezuelan	8.8

Bonita Springs

Population

Group	Number	%TP[1]	%HP[2]
Total Population	43,914	100.0	–
Hispanic or Latino (of any race)	9,877	22.5	100.0
Central American, ex. Mexican	2,152	4.9	21.8
Guatemalan	1,539	3.5	15.6
Honduran	198	0.5	2.0
Salvadoran	266	0.6	2.7
Cuban	371	0.8	3.8
Mexican	5,846	13.3	59.2
Puerto Rican	389	0.9	3.9
South American	561	1.3	5.7
Colombian	237	0.5	2.4

Population Growth: 2000–2010

Group	%
Total Population	33.9
Hispanic or Latino (of any race)	75.9
Central American, ex. Mexican	224.6
Guatemalan	291.6
Salvadoran	107.8
Cuban	127.6
Mexican	47.8
Puerto Rican	188.1
South American	292.3

Males per 100 Females

Group	Number
Total Population	101.8
Hispanic or Latino (of any race)	133.3
Central American, ex. Mexican	185.0
Guatemalan	221.3
Honduran	130.2
Salvadoran	121.7
Cuban	103.8
Mexican	129.9
Puerto Rican	114.9
South American	81.6
Colombian	75.6

Average Household Size

Group	People
Total Population	2.19
Hispanic or Latino (of any race)	4.08
Central American, ex. Mexican	4.64
Guatemalan	5.09
Honduran	3.96
Salvadoran	3.89
Cuban	2.78
Mexican	4.40
Puerto Rican	2.89
South American	2.91
Colombian	2.71

Median Age

Group	Years
Total Population	55.2
Hispanic or Latino (of any race)	26.5
Central American, ex. Mexican	27.4
Guatemalan	26.2
Honduran	32.7
Salvadoran	30.6
Cuban	39.6
Mexican	24.8
Puerto Rican	30.3
South American	35.2
Colombian	37.3

High School Graduates
(Universe: Population 25 Years and Over)

Group	Number	%
Total Population	30,468	87.0
Hispanic or Latino (of any race)	2,233	46.2
Central American, ex. Mexican	368	30.7
Guatemalan	233	26.9
Mexican	1,083	44.1

Four-Year College Graduates
(Universe: Population 25 Years and Over)

Group	Number	%
Total Population	10,495	30.0
Hispanic or Latino (of any race)	409	8.5
Central American, ex. Mexican	166	13.8
Guatemalan	72	8.3
Mexican	87	3.5

Population Age 3–17 Enrolled in Public School
(Universe: Population Age 3–17 Enrolled in School)

Group	Number	%
Total Population	3,587	88.4
Hispanic or Latino (of any race)	1,974	95.3
Central American, ex. Mexican	292	86.4
Guatemalan	143	75.7
Mexican	1,324	100.0

Population Age 3–17 Enrolled in Private School
(Universe: Population Age 3–17 Enrolled in School)

Group	Number	%
Total Population	472	11.6
Hispanic or Latino (of any race)	97	4.7
Central American, ex. Mexican	46	13.6
Guatemalan	46	24.3
Mexican	0	0.0

Foreign-Born Population

Group	Number	%
Total Population	8,229	19.0
Hispanic or Latino (of any race)	5,182	55.9
Central American, ex. Mexican	1,725	75.6
Guatemalan	1,369	86.2
Mexican	2,640	51.5

Foreign-Born Naturalized U.S. Citizens

Group	Number	%
Total Population	2,047	24.9
Hispanic or Latino (of any race)	788	15.2
Central American, ex. Mexican	81	4.7
Guatemalan	68	5.0
Mexican	381	14.4

Language Spoken at Home: English Only
(Universe: Population 5 Years and Over)

Group	Number	%
Total Population	31,296	75.5
Hispanic or Latino (of any race)	504	6.1
Central American, ex. Mexican	0	0.0
Guatemalan	0	0.0
Mexican	231	5.1

Language Spoken at Home: Spanish
(Universe: Population 5 Years and Over)

Group	Number	%
Total Population	7,997	19.3
Hispanic or Latino (of any race)	7,719	93.7
Central American, ex. Mexican	1,996	99.4
Guatemalan	1,470	99.1
Mexican	4,295	94.9

Unemployment Rate
(Universe: Population 16 Years and Over)

Group	%
Total Population	8.3
Hispanic or Latino (of any race)	10.1
Central American, ex. Mexican	6.2
Guatemalan	1.8
Mexican	9.5

Class of Worker: Private Wage and Salary
(Universe: Civilian Employed Population 16 Years and Over)

Group	Number	%
Total Population	14,414	86.6
Hispanic or Latino (of any race)	3,449	93.0
Central American, ex. Mexican	1,027	100.0
Guatemalan	840	100.0
Mexican	1,722	87.9

Class of Worker: Government
(Universe: Civilian Employed Population 16 Years and Over)

Group	Number	%
Total Population	1,033	6.2
Hispanic or Latino (of any race)	62	1.7
Central American, ex. Mexican	0	0.0
Guatemalan	0	0.0
Mexican	54	2.8

Means of Transportation to Work: Car, Truck or Van
(Universe: Workers 16 Years and Over)

Group	Number	%
Total Population	14,075	86.3
Hispanic or Latino (of any race)	2,942	81.0
Central American, ex. Mexican	639	66.1
Guatemalan	452	58.0
Mexican	1,635	84.1

Means of Transportation to Work: Public Transportation (ex. Taxicab)
(Universe: Workers 16 Years and Over)

Group	Number	%
Total Population	266	1.6

Notes: (1) Percent of total population; (2) Percent of Hispanic/Latino population; Profiles include places with an overall population of at least 125,000, OR an overall population of at least 25,000 where the Hispanic/Latino population is at least 20% of the overall population. In states where less than five places meet either of these criteria, we have included places with at least 10,000 total population with the highest percentage of Hispanic/Latino population. These places are identified with an asterisk (*); Please refer to the User's Guide for a full explanation of data.

Group	Number	%
Hispanic or Latino (of any race)	266	7.3
Central American, ex. Mexican	64	6.6
Guatemalan	64	8.2
Mexican	188	9.7

Homeownership Rate
(Universe: Occupied Housing Units)

Group	%
Total Population	77.5
Hispanic or Latino (of any race)	41.2
Central American, ex. Mexican	24.0
Guatemalan	14.6
Honduran	35.4
Salvadoran	46.3
Cuban	62.1
Mexican	42.0
Puerto Rican	53.0
South American	52.6
Colombian	52.5

Median Home Value

Group	Dollars
Total Population	292,800
Hispanic or Latino (of any race)	168,600
Central American, ex. Mexican	337,000
Guatemalan	162,500
Mexican	142,800

Median Gross Rent

Group	Dollars
Total Population	994
Hispanic or Latino (of any race)	967
Central American, ex. Mexican	1,049
Guatemalan	1,018
Mexican	903

Median Household Income
(2010 Inflation-Adjusted Dollars)

Group	Dollars
Total Population	54,814
Hispanic or Latino (of any race)	37,065
Central American, ex. Mexican	39,741
Guatemalan	38,987
Mexican	35,411

Per Capita Income
(2010 Inflation-Adjusted Dollars)

Group	Dollars
Total Population	41,037
Hispanic or Latino (of any race)	11,412
Central American, ex. Mexican	11,154
Guatemalan	10,364
Mexican	9,253

Households with $100,000+ Income

Group	Number	%
Total Population	4,805	25.1
Hispanic or Latino (of any race)	129	6.1
Central American, ex. Mexican	57	14.5
Guatemalan	34	15.4
Mexican	33	2.9

Households with Food Stamps/SNAP Benefits During Past 12 Months

Group	Number	%
Total Population	569	3.0
Hispanic or Latino (of any race)	351	16.6
Central American, ex. Mexican	87	22.1
Guatemalan	0	0.0
Mexican	151	13.4

Poverty Rate
(Income in Past 12 Months Below Poverty Level)

Group	%
Total Population	11.0
Hispanic or Latino (of any race)	26.0
Central American, ex. Mexican	34.8
Guatemalan	28.0
Mexican	25.6

Brandon

Population

Group	Number	%TP[1]	%HP[2]
Total Population	103,483	100.0	–
Hispanic or Latino (of any race)	21,687	21.0	100.0
Central American, ex. Mexican	1,388	1.3	6.4
Costa Rican	128	0.1	0.6
Guatemalan	227	0.2	1.0
Honduran	352	0.3	1.6
Nicaraguan	185	0.2	0.9
Panamanian	294	0.3	1.4
Salvadoran	187	0.2	0.9
Cuban	2,690	2.6	12.4
Dominican Republic	1,335	1.3	6.2
Mexican	2,413	2.3	11.1
Puerto Rican	9,574	9.3	44.1
South American	2,194	2.1	10.1
Argentinean	105	0.1	0.5
Colombian	1,139	1.1	5.3
Ecuadorian	233	0.2	1.1
Peruvian	357	0.3	1.6
Venezuelan	191	0.2	0.9
Spaniard	519	0.5	2.4

Population Growth: 2000–2010

Group	%
Total Population	32.8
Hispanic or Latino (of any race)	119.5
Central American, ex. Mexican	267.2
Panamanian	141.0
Cuban	149.5
Dominican Republic	475.4
Mexican	161.4
Puerto Rican	108.2
South American	233.4
Colombian	267.4

Males per 100 Females

Group	Number
Total Population	95.2
Hispanic or Latino (of any race)	96.6
Central American, ex. Mexican	90.7
Costa Rican	96.9
Guatemalan	114.2
Honduran	110.8
Nicaraguan	86.9
Panamanian	63.3
Salvadoran	83.3
Cuban	95.6
Dominican Republic	89.4
Mexican	110.4
Puerto Rican	92.6
South American	81.5
Argentinean	128.3
Colombian	76.6
Ecuadorian	72.6
Peruvian	87.9
Venezuelan	85.4
Spaniard	88.0

Average Household Size

Group	People
Total Population	2.52
Hispanic or Latino (of any race)	2.91
Central American, ex. Mexican	3.03
Costa Rican	3.20
Guatemalan	3.67
Honduran	3.11
Nicaraguan	3.17
Panamanian	2.41
Salvadoran	3.35
Cuban	2.86
Dominican Republic	3.13
Mexican	3.31
Puerto Rican	2.86
South American	2.87
Argentinean	2.63
Colombian	2.97
Ecuadorian	3.18
Peruvian	2.62
Venezuelan	2.78
Spaniard	2.65

Median Age

Group	Years
Total Population	34.6
Hispanic or Latino (of any race)	29.3
Central American, ex. Mexican	30.7
Costa Rican	29.0
Guatemalan	28.4
Honduran	30.2
Nicaraguan	31.1
Panamanian	34.8
Salvadoran	27.6
Cuban	31.9
Dominican Republic	28.9
Mexican	24.3
Puerto Rican	29.2
South American	33.3
Argentinean	30.3
Colombian	33.6
Ecuadorian	31.3
Peruvian	34.8
Venezuelan	32.2
Spaniard	38.2

High School Graduates
(Universe: Population 25 Years and Over)

Group	Number	%
Total Population	57,819	89.6
Hispanic or Latino (of any race)	9,384	79.0
Central American, ex. Mexican	632	84.9
Cuban	1,672	88.6
Mexican	631	67.4
Puerto Rican	4,434	78.6
South American	1,125	78.2
Colombian	564	67.9

Four-Year College Graduates
(Universe: Population 25 Years and Over)

Group	Number	%
Total Population	17,472	27.1
Hispanic or Latino (of any race)	2,526	21.3
Central American, ex. Mexican	213	28.6
Cuban	516	27.3
Mexican	140	15.0
Puerto Rican	949	16.8
South American	408	28.4
Colombian	180	21.7

Population Age 3–17 Enrolled in Public School
(Universe: Population Age 3–17 Enrolled in School)

Group	Number	%
Total Population	15,495	85.1
Hispanic or Latino (of any race)	4,226	89.7
Central American, ex. Mexican	302	91.8
Cuban	524	82.3
Mexican	476	87.5
Puerto Rican	2,142	97.2
South American	241	100.0
Colombian	101	100.0

Population Age 3–17 Enrolled in Private School
(Universe: Population Age 3–17 Enrolled in School)

Group	Number	%
Total Population	2,717	14.9
Hispanic or Latino (of any race)	484	10.3
Central American, ex. Mexican	27	8.2
Cuban	113	17.7
Mexican	68	12.5
Puerto Rican	62	2.8
South American	0	0.0
Colombian	0	0.0

Foreign-Born Population

Group	Number	%
Total Population	11,634	11.7
Hispanic or Latino (of any race)	5,167	24.3
Central American, ex. Mexican	681	55.2
Cuban	1,266	42.0
Mexican	741	35.5
Puerto Rican	84	0.8
South American	1,734	72.5
Colombian	866	74.7

Foreign-Born Naturalized U.S. Citizens

Group	Number	%
Total Population	5,925	50.9

Notes: (1) Percent of total population; (2) Percent of Hispanic/Latino population; Profiles include places with an overall population of at least 125,000, OR an overall population of at least 25,000 where the Hispanic/Latino population is at least 20% of the overall population. In states where less than five places meet either of these criteria, we have included places with at least 10,000 total population with the highest percentage of Hispanic/Latino population. These places are identified with an asterisk (*); Please refer to the User's Guide for a full explanation of data.

Hispanic or Latino (of any race)	2,205	42.7
Central American, ex. Mexican	325	47.7
Cuban	816	64.5
Mexican	172	23.2
Puerto Rican	26	31.0
South American	436	25.1
Colombian	152	17.6

Language Spoken at Home: English Only
(Universe: Population 5 Years and Over)

Group	Number	%
Total Population	72,077	77.9
Hispanic or Latino (of any race)	4,443	23.2
Central American, ex. Mexican	335	28.6
Cuban	738	26.9
Mexican	621	32.5
Puerto Rican	1,586	17.8
South American	328	14.9
Colombian	88	8.5

Language Spoken at Home: Spanish
(Universe: Population 5 Years and Over)

Group	Number	%
Total Population	15,524	16.8
Hispanic or Latino (of any race)	14,661	76.4
Central American, ex. Mexican	791	67.5
Cuban	2,001	73.1
Mexican	1,291	67.5
Puerto Rican	7,292	81.9
South American	1,875	85.1
Colombian	946	91.5

Unemployment Rate
(Universe: Population 16 Years and Over)

Group	%
Total Population	5.8
Hispanic or Latino (of any race)	7.4
Central American, ex. Mexican	0.0
Cuban	7.4
Mexican	4.7
Puerto Rican	9.5
South American	7.9
Colombian	2.7

Class of Worker: Private Wage and Salary
(Universe: Civilian Employed Population 16 Years and Over)

Group	Number	%
Total Population	43,102	83.0
Hispanic or Latino (of any race)	8,147	84.8
Central American, ex. Mexican	579	85.8
Cuban	1,174	81.8
Mexican	862	90.6
Puerto Rican	3,475	83.9
South American	1,015	87.8
Colombian	456	90.8

Class of Worker: Government
(Universe: Civilian Employed Population 16 Years and Over)

Group	Number	%
Total Population	6,426	12.4
Hispanic or Latino (of any race)	873	9.1
Central American, ex. Mexican	38	5.6
Cuban	237	16.5
Mexican	62	6.5
Puerto Rican	405	9.8
South American	32	2.8
Colombian	16	3.2

Means of Transportation to Work: Car, Truck or Van
(Universe: Workers 16 Years and Over)

Group	Number	%
Total Population	47,800	93.0
Hispanic or Latino (of any race)	8,848	92.2
Central American, ex. Mexican	675	100.0
Cuban	1,356	94.6
Mexican	804	88.5
Puerto Rican	3,858	91.9
South American	1,032	92.6
Colombian	467	97.7

Means of Transportation to Work: Public Transportation (ex. Taxicab)
(Universe: Workers 16 Years and Over)

Group	Number	%
Total Population	262	0.5
Hispanic or Latino (of any race)	15	0.2
Central American, ex. Mexican	0	0.0
Cuban	0	0.0
Mexican	0	0.0
Puerto Rican	0	0.0
South American	8	0.7
Colombian	0	0.0

Homeownership Rate
(Universe: Occupied Housing Units)

Group	%
Total Population	57.5
Hispanic or Latino (of any race)	47.6
Central American, ex. Mexican	46.9
Costa Rican	40.9
Guatemalan	44.4
Honduran	38.9
Nicaraguan	57.7
Panamanian	52.1
Salvadoran	44.9
Cuban	57.8
Dominican Republic	42.2
Mexican	35.5
Puerto Rican	45.6
South American	51.5
Argentinean	42.5
Colombian	53.3
Ecuadorian	56.9
Peruvian	45.1
Venezuelan	52.8
Spaniard	70.1

Median Home Value

Group	Dollars
Total Population	190,700
Hispanic or Latino (of any race)	189,700
Central American, ex. Mexican	212,900
Cuban	173,500
Mexican	173,400
Puerto Rican	187,400
South American	227,800
Colombian	235,900

Median Gross Rent

Group	Dollars
Total Population	997
Hispanic or Latino (of any race)	942
Central American, ex. Mexican	993
Cuban	904
Mexican	1,054
Puerto Rican	956
South American	843
Colombian	647

Median Household Income
(2010 Inflation-Adjusted Dollars)

Group	Dollars
Total Population	55,881
Hispanic or Latino (of any race)	48,408
Central American, ex. Mexican	48,750
Cuban	51,950
Mexican	48,356
Puerto Rican	47,649
South American	40,192
Colombian	47,564

Per Capita Income
(2010 Inflation-Adjusted Dollars)

Group	Dollars
Total Population	25,890
Hispanic or Latino (of any race)	18,464
Central American, ex. Mexican	19,529
Cuban	25,997
Mexican	16,532
Puerto Rican	18,017
South American	15,313
Colombian	15,278

Households with $100,000+ Income

Group	Number	%
Total Population	6,528	17.2
Hispanic or Latino (of any race)	714	10.4
Central American, ex. Mexican	0	0.0
Cuban	238	21.1
Mexican	44	7.4
Puerto Rican	345	10.2
South American	75	9.4
Colombian	36	9.9

Households with Food Stamps/SNAP Benefits During Past 12 Months

Group	Number	%
Total Population	1,853	4.9
Hispanic or Latino (of any race)	570	8.3
Central American, ex. Mexican	24	6.4
Cuban	69	6.1
Mexican	18	3.0
Puerto Rican	345	10.2
South American	38	4.8
Colombian	14	3.9

Poverty Rate
(Income in Past 12 Months Below Poverty Level)

Group	%
Total Population	9.2
Hispanic or Latino (of any race)	13.9
Central American, ex. Mexican	3.9
Cuban	4.9
Mexican	13.9
Puerto Rican	19.6
South American	9.2
Colombian	12.8

Buenaventura Lakes

Population

Group	Number	%TP[1]	%HP[2]
Total Population	26,079	100.0	–
Hispanic or Latino (of any race)	18,160	69.6	100.0
Central American, ex. Mexican	731	2.8	4.0
Honduran	143	0.5	0.8
Nicaraguan	143	0.5	0.8
Salvadoran	239	0.9	1.3
Cuban	799	3.1	4.4
Dominican Republic	1,687	6.5	9.3
Mexican	585	2.2	3.2
Puerto Rican	11,618	44.5	64.0
South American	2,108	8.1	11.6
Argentinean	154	0.6	0.8
Colombian	1,198	4.6	6.6
Ecuadorian	246	0.9	1.4
Peruvian	234	0.9	1.3
Venezuelan	177	0.7	1.0

Population Growth: 2000–2010

Group	%
Total Population	n/a

Males per 100 Females

Group	Number
Total Population	93.7
Hispanic or Latino (of any race)	93.7
Central American, ex. Mexican	112.5
Honduran	120.0
Nicaraguan	83.3
Salvadoran	141.4
Cuban	98.8
Dominican Republic	84.8
Mexican	114.3
Puerto Rican	94.3
South American	86.7
Argentinean	90.1
Colombian	85.2
Ecuadorian	92.2
Peruvian	85.7
Venezuelan	82.5

Average Household Size

Group	People
Total Population	3.19
Hispanic or Latino (of any race)	3.37

Notes: (1) Percent of total population; (2) Percent of Hispanic/Latino population; Profiles include places with an overall population of at least 125,000, OR an overall population of at least 25,000 where the Hispanic/Latino population is at least 20% of the overall population. In states where less than five places meet either of these criteria, we have included places with at least 10,000 total population with the highest percentage of Hispanic/Latino population. These places are identified with an asterisk (*); Please refer to the User's Guide for a full explanation of data.

Group	
Central American, ex. Mexican	3.89
Honduran	3.56
Nicaraguan	4.22
Salvadoran	4.17
Cuban	3.25
Dominican Republic	3.67
Mexican	3.98
Puerto Rican	3.29
South American	3.35
Argentinean	2.98
Colombian	3.42
Ecuadorian	3.19
Peruvian	3.62
Venezuelan	3.16

Median Age

Group	Years
Total Population	34.7
Hispanic or Latino (of any race)	33.0
Central American, ex. Mexican	32.7
Honduran	31.4
Nicaraguan	31.8
Salvadoran	31.6
Cuban	38.6
Dominican Republic	34.8
Mexican	25.7
Puerto Rican	32.6
South American	38.5
Argentinean	33.5
Colombian	39.0
Ecuadorian	42.7
Peruvian	36.7
Venezuelan	35.2

High School Graduates
(Universe: Population 25 Years and Over)

Group	Number	%
Total Population	13,017	79.2
Hispanic or Latino (of any race)	8,015	74.6
Central American, ex. Mexican	293	46.6
Dominican Republic	609	64.1
Puerto Rican	5,093	78.2
South American	1,089	75.5
Colombian	598	75.0

Four-Year College Graduates
(Universe: Population 25 Years and Over)

Group	Number	%
Total Population	2,184	13.3
Hispanic or Latino (of any race)	1,166	10.9
Central American, ex. Mexican	39	6.2
Dominican Republic	16	1.7
Puerto Rican	707	10.9
South American	314	21.8
Colombian	122	15.3

Population Age 3–17 Enrolled in Public School
(Universe: Population Age 3–17 Enrolled in School)

Group	Number	%
Total Population	5,598	91.4
Hispanic or Latino (of any race)	3,884	91.2
Central American, ex. Mexican	121	100.0
Dominican Republic	346	100.0
Puerto Rican	2,280	92.5
South American	778	94.8
Colombian	471	93.8

Population Age 3–17 Enrolled in Private School
(Universe: Population Age 3–17 Enrolled in School)

Group	Number	%
Total Population	528	8.6
Hispanic or Latino (of any race)	377	8.8
Central American, ex. Mexican	0	0.0
Dominican Republic	0	0.0
Puerto Rican	185	7.5
South American	43	5.2
Colombian	31	6.2

Foreign-Born Population

Group	Number	%
Total Population	6,845	25.5
Hispanic or Latino (of any race)	4,583	25.5
Central American, ex. Mexican	682	65.8
Dominican Republic	1,058	64.5
Puerto Rican	59	0.6
South American	1,817	65.7
Colombian	958	64.4

Foreign-Born Naturalized U.S. Citizens

Group	Number	%
Total Population	3,284	48.0
Hispanic or Latino (of any race)	1,907	41.6
Central American, ex. Mexican	297	43.5
Dominican Republic	447	42.2
Puerto Rican	22	37.3
South American	746	41.1
Colombian	449	46.9

Language Spoken at Home: English Only
(Universe: Population 5 Years and Over)

Group	Number	%
Total Population	8,116	32.0
Hispanic or Latino (of any race)	1,503	8.9
Central American, ex. Mexican	60	6.2
Dominican Republic	63	4.1
Puerto Rican	938	9.4
South American	49	1.9
Colombian	33	2.4

Language Spoken at Home: Spanish
(Universe: Population 5 Years and Over)

Group	Number	%
Total Population	15,646	61.6
Hispanic or Latino (of any race)	15,389	90.9
Central American, ex. Mexican	905	93.8
Dominican Republic	1,474	95.9
Puerto Rican	9,038	90.6
South American	2,488	97.6
Colombian	1,335	97.6

Unemployment Rate
(Universe: Population 16 Years and Over)

Group	%
Total Population	9.7
Hispanic or Latino (of any race)	8.1
Central American, ex. Mexican	12.8
Dominican Republic	2.8
Puerto Rican	7.7
South American	11.5
Colombian	10.1

Class of Worker: Private Wage and Salary
(Universe: Civilian Employed Population 16 Years and Over)

Group	Number	%
Total Population	10,979	88.3
Hispanic or Latino (of any race)	7,109	87.9
Central American, ex. Mexican	535	87.6
Dominican Republic	748	85.4
Puerto Rican	3,806	85.1
South American	1,193	96.7
Colombian	667	95.7

Class of Worker: Government
(Universe: Civilian Employed Population 16 Years and Over)

Group	Number	%
Total Population	1,088	8.8
Hispanic or Latino (of any race)	790	9.8
Central American, ex. Mexican	36	5.9
Dominican Republic	89	10.2
Puerto Rican	570	12.7
South American	41	3.3
Colombian	30	4.3

Means of Transportation to Work: Car, Truck or Van
(Universe: Workers 16 Years and Over)

Group	Number	%
Total Population	11,366	92.7
Hispanic or Latino (of any race)	7,536	93.7
Central American, ex. Mexican	497	81.3
Dominican Republic	781	90.7
Puerto Rican	4,198	94.5
South American	1,175	95.2
Colombian	697	100.0

Means of Transportation to Work: Public Transportation (ex. Taxicab)
(Universe: Workers 16 Years and Over)

Group	Number	%
Total Population	176	1.4
Hispanic or Latino (of any race)	157	2.0
Central American, ex. Mexican	14	2.3
Dominican Republic	46	5.3
Puerto Rican	64	1.4
South American	21	1.7
Colombian	0	0.0

Homeownership Rate
(Universe: Occupied Housing Units)

Group	%
Total Population	71.1
Hispanic or Latino (of any race)	67.3
Central American, ex. Mexican	69.8
Honduran	70.7
Nicaraguan	66.7
Salvadoran	73.3
Cuban	64.7
Dominican Republic	70.3
Mexican	62.5
Puerto Rican	66.0
South American	73.3
Argentinean	70.8
Colombian	74.2
Ecuadorian	78.0
Peruvian	67.6
Venezuelan	68.8

Median Home Value

Group	Dollars
Total Population	189,000
Hispanic or Latino (of any race)	196,100
Central American, ex. Mexican	156,100
Dominican Republic	250,200
Puerto Rican	193,800
South American	219,100
Colombian	219,900

Median Gross Rent

Group	Dollars
Total Population	1,168
Hispanic or Latino (of any race)	1,178
Central American, ex. Mexican	1,333
Dominican Republic	1,478
Puerto Rican	1,150
South American	1,272
Colombian	1,154

Median Household Income
(2010 Inflation-Adjusted Dollars)

Group	Dollars
Total Population	43,252
Hispanic or Latino (of any race)	42,601
Central American, ex. Mexican	53,250
Dominican Republic	40,811
Puerto Rican	42,984
South American	39,919
Colombian	39,778

Per Capita Income
(2010 Inflation-Adjusted Dollars)

Group	Dollars
Total Population	16,526
Hispanic or Latino (of any race)	14,977
Central American, ex. Mexican	16,431
Dominican Republic	11,627
Puerto Rican	16,487
South American	12,666
Colombian	13,034

Households with $100,000+ Income

Group	Number	%
Total Population	709	8.0
Hispanic or Latino (of any race)	331	5.9
Central American, ex. Mexican	10	3.3
Dominican Republic	15	3.0
Puerto Rican	254	7.4
South American	17	2.2
Colombian	17	4.1

Households with Food Stamps/SNAP Benefits During Past 12 Months

Group	Number	%
Total Population	1,041	11.8
Hispanic or Latino (of any race)	786	14.0
Central American, ex. Mexican	0	0.0
Dominican Republic	115	23.1

Notes: (1) Percent of total population; (2) Percent of Hispanic/Latino population; Profiles include places with an overall population of at least 125,000, OR an overall population of at least 25,000 where the Hispanic/Latino population is at least 20% of the overall population. In states where less than five places meet either of these criteria, we have included places with at least 10,000 total population with the highest percentage of Hispanic/Latino population. These places are identified with an asterisk (*); Please refer to the User's Guide for a full explanation of data.

Group	Number	%
Puerto Rican	457	13.3
South American	103	13.1
Colombian	86	20.8

Poverty Rate
(Income in Past 12 Months Below Poverty Level)

Group	%
Total Population	11.3
Hispanic or Latino (of any race)	12.2
Central American, ex. Mexican	4.1
Dominican Republic	22.1
Puerto Rican	13.8
South American	4.5
Colombian	0.0

Cape Coral

Population

Group	Number	%TP[1]	%HP[2]
Total Population	154,305	100.0	–
Hispanic or Latino (of any race)	30,017	19.5	100.0
Central American, ex. Mexican	2,127	1.4	7.1
Costa Rican	207	0.1	0.7
Guatemalan	322	0.2	1.1
Honduran	625	0.4	2.1
Nicaraguan	410	0.3	1.4
Panamanian	119	0.1	0.4
Salvadoran	440	0.3	1.5
Cuban	9,843	6.4	32.8
Dominican Republic	1,631	1.1	5.4
Mexican	2,710	1.8	9.0
Puerto Rican	7,261	4.7	24.2
South American	4,657	3.0	15.5
Argentinean	313	0.2	1.0
Colombian	2,313	1.5	7.7
Ecuadorian	540	0.3	1.8
Peruvian	749	0.5	2.5
Uruguayan	121	0.1	0.4
Venezuelan	411	0.3	1.4
Spaniard	305	0.2	1.0

Population Growth: 2000–2010

Group	%
Total Population	50.9
Hispanic or Latino (of any race)	252.3
Central American, ex. Mexican	392.4
Cuban	599.1
Dominican Republic	329.2
Mexican	229.7
Puerto Rican	167.4
South American	319.9
Colombian	301.6
Ecuadorian	239.6
Peruvian	402.7

Males per 100 Females

Group	Number
Total Population	95.5
Hispanic or Latino (of any race)	95.2
Central American, ex. Mexican	88.2
Costa Rican	102.9
Guatemalan	113.2
Honduran	77.6
Nicaraguan	81.4
Panamanian	67.6
Salvadoran	95.6
Cuban	101.0
Dominican Republic	83.5
Mexican	108.5
Puerto Rican	94.5
South American	84.7
Argentinean	107.3
Colombian	82.7
Ecuadorian	76.5
Peruvian	82.7
Uruguayan	128.3
Venezuelan	87.7
Spaniard	91.8

Average Household Size

Group	People
Total Population	2.53
Hispanic or Latino (of any race)	3.22
Central American, ex. Mexican	3.51
Costa Rican	3.57
Guatemalan	3.60
Honduran	3.61
Nicaraguan	3.56
Panamanian	2.92
Salvadoran	3.45
Cuban	3.21
Dominican Republic	3.30
Mexican	3.53
Puerto Rican	3.12
South American	3.22
Argentinean	3.15
Colombian	3.24
Ecuadorian	3.26
Peruvian	3.28
Uruguayan	3.17
Venezuelan	3.25
Spaniard	2.39

Median Age

Group	Years
Total Population	42.4
Hispanic or Latino (of any race)	32.6
Central American, ex. Mexican	33.0
Costa Rican	31.8
Guatemalan	31.3
Honduran	32.9
Nicaraguan	33.6
Panamanian	38.5
Salvadoran	33.1
Cuban	37.0
Dominican Republic	33.5
Mexican	24.6
Puerto Rican	29.2
South American	37.2
Argentinean	38.5
Colombian	37.1
Ecuadorian	38.8
Peruvian	37.0
Uruguayan	38.9
Venezuelan	33.5
Spaniard	39.9

High School Graduates
(Universe: Population 25 Years and Over)

Group	Number	%
Total Population	92,748	89.0
Hispanic or Latino (of any race)	13,790	79.7
Central American, ex. Mexican	1,192	74.3
Cuban	4,484	78.0
Dominican Republic	693	79.3
Mexican	871	60.2
Puerto Rican	2,909	79.7
South American	3,268	92.9
Colombian	1,565	88.3
Peruvian	398	95.7

Four-Year College Graduates
(Universe: Population 25 Years and Over)

Group	Number	%
Total Population	21,292	20.4
Hispanic or Latino (of any race)	3,160	18.3
Central American, ex. Mexican	299	18.6
Cuban	1,014	17.6
Dominican Republic	73	8.4
Mexican	116	8.0
Puerto Rican	410	11.2
South American	1,183	33.6
Colombian	539	30.4
Peruvian	141	33.9

Population Age 3–17 Enrolled in Public School
(Universe: Population Age 3–17 Enrolled in School)

Group	Number	%
Total Population	24,803	90.5
Hispanic or Latino (of any race)	7,245	91.7
Central American, ex. Mexican	514	92.9
Cuban	1,683	91.2
Dominican Republic	409	100.0
Mexican	1,179	92.9
Puerto Rican	1,882	87.9
South American	1,317	95.0
Colombian	482	92.5
Peruvian	235	100.0

Population Age 3–17 Enrolled in Private School
(Universe: Population Age 3–17 Enrolled in School)

Group	Number	%
Total Population	2,609	9.5
Hispanic or Latino (of any race)	652	8.3
Central American, ex. Mexican	39	7.1
Cuban	162	8.8
Dominican Republic	0	0.0
Mexican	90	7.1
Puerto Rican	259	12.1
South American	69	5.0
Colombian	39	7.5
Peruvian	0	0.0

Foreign-Born Population

Group	Number	%
Total Population	22,876	15.3
Hispanic or Latino (of any race)	14,154	47.0
Central American, ex. Mexican	1,896	71.5
Cuban	6,233	67.6
Dominican Republic	606	41.0
Mexican	831	26.1
Puerto Rican	28	0.4
South American	4,298	72.5
Colombian	1,953	70.5
Peruvian	665	83.5

Foreign-Born Naturalized U.S. Citizens

Group	Number	%
Total Population	11,054	48.3
Hispanic or Latino (of any race)	5,768	40.8
Central American, ex. Mexican	974	51.4
Cuban	2,707	43.4
Dominican Republic	403	66.5
Mexican	265	31.9
Puerto Rican	18	64.3
South American	1,247	29.0
Colombian	752	38.5
Peruvian	205	30.8

Language Spoken at Home: English Only
(Universe: Population 5 Years and Over)

Group	Number	%
Total Population	109,567	77.6
Hispanic or Latino (of any race)	5,230	19.0
Central American, ex. Mexican	209	8.4
Cuban	627	7.6
Dominican Republic	79	5.8
Mexican	1,146	40.4
Puerto Rican	2,377	38.3
South American	525	9.4
Colombian	282	11.1
Peruvian	33	4.2

Language Spoken at Home: Spanish
(Universe: Population 5 Years and Over)

Group	Number	%
Total Population	24,301	17.2
Hispanic or Latino (of any race)	22,256	80.7
Central American, ex. Mexican	2,267	91.6
Cuban	7,635	92.2
Dominican Republic	1,283	94.2
Mexican	1,689	59.6
Puerto Rican	3,798	61.3
South American	5,006	90.0
Colombian	2,252	88.9
Peruvian	747	95.8

Unemployment Rate
(Universe: Population 16 Years and Over)

Group	%
Total Population	10.4
Hispanic or Latino (of any race)	14.1
Central American, ex. Mexican	13.2
Cuban	20.8
Dominican Republic	14.3
Mexican	9.3
Puerto Rican	10.7
South American	9.0
Colombian	9.9
Peruvian	9.6

Notes: (1) Percent of total population; (2) Percent of Hispanic/Latino population; Profiles include places with an overall population of at least 125,000, OR an overall population of at least 25,000 where the Hispanic/Latino population is at least 20% of the overall population. In states where less than five places meet either of these criteria, we have included places with at least 10,000 total population with the highest percentage of Hispanic/Latino population. These places are identified with an asterisk (*); Please refer to the User's Guide for a full explanation of data.

Class of Worker: Private Wage and Salary
(Universe: Civilian Employed Population 16 Years and Over)

Group	Number	%
Total Population	55,223	79.6
Hispanic or Latino (of any race)	9,852	80.4
Central American, ex. Mexican	911	80.7
Cuban	2,938	85.6
Dominican Republic	444	76.6
Mexican	1,103	84.3
Puerto Rican	1,970	73.4
South American	2,204	79.1
Colombian	886	70.2
Peruvian	305	90.2

Class of Worker: Government
(Universe: Civilian Employed Population 16 Years and Over)

Group	Number	%
Total Population	8,920	12.9
Hispanic or Latino (of any race)	1,331	10.9
Central American, ex. Mexican	107	9.5
Cuban	243	7.1
Dominican Republic	61	10.5
Mexican	114	8.7
Puerto Rican	493	18.4
South American	286	10.3
Colombian	227	18.0
Peruvian	33	9.8

Means of Transportation to Work: Car, Truck or Van
(Universe: Workers 16 Years and Over)

Group	Number	%
Total Population	62,143	91.8
Hispanic or Latino (of any race)	10,930	91.5
Central American, ex. Mexican	854	75.6
Cuban	3,126	93.7
Dominican Republic	448	77.2
Mexican	1,145	88.1
Puerto Rican	2,496	97.2
South American	2,554	93.8
Colombian	1,144	93.3
Peruvian	296	92.5

Means of Transportation to Work: Public Transportation (ex. Taxicab)
(Universe: Workers 16 Years and Over)

Group	Number	%
Total Population	396	0.6
Hispanic or Latino (of any race)	122	1.0
Central American, ex. Mexican	8	0.7
Cuban	0	0.0
Dominican Republic	0	0.0
Mexican	108	8.3
Puerto Rican	6	0.2
South American	0	0.0
Colombian	0	0.0
Peruvian	0	0.0

Homeownership Rate
(Universe: Occupied Housing Units)

Group	%
Total Population	72.5
Hispanic or Latino (of any race)	57.5
Central American, ex. Mexican	56.3
Costa Rican	50.9
Guatemalan	53.6
Honduran	57.9
Nicaraguan	62.1
Panamanian	55.6
Salvadoran	52.6
Cuban	59.4
Dominican Republic	61.2
Mexican	49.5
Puerto Rican	54.2
South American	62.5
Argentinean	61.3
Colombian	63.0
Ecuadorian	70.1
Peruvian	55.5
Uruguayan	59.6
Venezuelan	62.9
Spaniard	69.6

Median Home Value

Group	Dollars
Total Population	222,700
Hispanic or Latino (of any race)	204,700
Central American, ex. Mexican	239,300
Cuban	199,800
Dominican Republic	213,700
Mexican	226,100
Puerto Rican	199,900
South American	180,700
Colombian	181,300
Peruvian	200,300

Median Gross Rent

Group	Dollars
Total Population	1,063
Hispanic or Latino (of any race)	1,052
Central American, ex. Mexican	1,199
Cuban	1,020
Dominican Republic	895
Mexican	1,271
Puerto Rican	1,081
South American	896
Colombian	1,018
Peruvian	883

Median Household Income
(2010 Inflation-Adjusted Dollars)

Group	Dollars
Total Population	52,761
Hispanic or Latino (of any race)	44,340
Central American, ex. Mexican	51,944
Cuban	36,733
Dominican Republic	48,148
Mexican	56,745
Puerto Rican	51,250
South American	44,946
Colombian	48,417
Peruvian	39,801

Per Capita Income
(2010 Inflation-Adjusted Dollars)

Group	Dollars
Total Population	25,090
Hispanic or Latino (of any race)	14,994
Central American, ex. Mexican	15,823
Cuban	14,017
Dominican Republic	12,647
Mexican	13,586
Puerto Rican	14,766
South American	17,115
Colombian	16,289
Peruvian	14,993

Households with $100,000+ Income

Group	Number	%
Total Population	9,017	16.0
Hispanic or Latino (of any race)	544	6.4
Central American, ex. Mexican	35	5.2
Cuban	91	3.2
Dominican Republic	13	3.0
Mexican	34	5.3
Puerto Rican	140	8.7
South American	219	11.0
Colombian	75	8.3
Peruvian	18	6.6

Households with Food Stamps/SNAP Benefits During Past 12 Months

Group	Number	%
Total Population	3,027	5.4
Hispanic or Latino (of any race)	972	11.5
Central American, ex. Mexican	62	9.2
Cuban	577	20.1
Dominican Republic	86	20.0
Mexican	35	5.5
Puerto Rican	100	6.2
South American	100	5.0
Colombian	62	6.8
Peruvian	0	0.0

Poverty Rate
(Income in Past 12 Months Below Poverty Level)

Group	%
Total Population	9.7
Hispanic or Latino (of any race)	15.0
Central American, ex. Mexican	15.1
Cuban	20.5
Dominican Republic	12.1
Mexican	6.7
Puerto Rican	15.0
South American	12.1
Colombian	10.4
Peruvian	23.4

Carrollwood

Population

Group	Number	%TP[1]	%HP[2]
Total Population	33,365	100.0	–
Hispanic or Latino (of any race)	9,155	27.4	100.0
Central American, ex. Mexican	461	1.4	5.0
Honduran	128	0.4	1.4
Cuban	2,108	6.3	23.0
Dominican Republic	359	1.1	3.9
Mexican	469	1.4	5.1
Puerto Rican	2,782	8.3	30.4
South American	1,820	5.5	19.9
Colombian	1,090	3.3	11.9
Ecuadorian	188	0.6	2.1
Peruvian	212	0.6	2.3
Venezuelan	197	0.6	2.2
Spaniard	527	1.6	5.8

Population Growth: 2000–2010

Group	%
Total Population	n/a

Males per 100 Females

Group	Number
Total Population	90.2
Hispanic or Latino (of any race)	89.6
Central American, ex. Mexican	88.9
Honduran	88.2
Cuban	90.4
Dominican Republic	102.8
Mexican	98.7
Puerto Rican	91.6
South American	82.7
Colombian	81.1
Ecuadorian	86.1
Peruvian	91.0
Venezuelan	72.8
Spaniard	84.9

Average Household Size

Group	People
Total Population	2.36
Hispanic or Latino (of any race)	2.73
Central American, ex. Mexican	3.11
Honduran	3.21
Cuban	2.68
Dominican Republic	2.98
Mexican	3.01
Puerto Rican	2.75
South American	2.84
Colombian	2.91
Ecuadorian	2.86
Peruvian	2.89
Venezuelan	2.69
Spaniard	2.34

Median Age

Group	Years
Total Population	41.3
Hispanic or Latino (of any race)	34.0
Central American, ex. Mexican	35.1
Honduran	36.3
Cuban	37.3
Dominican Republic	30.4
Mexican	24.7
Puerto Rican	31.0
South American	38.5
Colombian	37.6
Ecuadorian	40.6
Peruvian	43.0
Venezuelan	33.8
Spaniard	43.9

Notes: (1) Percent of total population; (2) Percent of Hispanic/Latino population; Profiles include places with an overall population of at least 125,000, OR an overall population of at least 25,000 where the Hispanic/Latino population is at least 20% of the overall population. In states where less than five places meet either of these criteria, we have included places with at least 10,000 total population with the highest percentage of Hispanic/Latino population. These places are identified with an asterisk (*); Please refer to the User's Guide for a full explanation of data.

High School Graduates
(Universe: Population 25 Years and Over)

Group	Number	%
Total Population	21,756	92.7
Hispanic or Latino (of any race)	4,061	85.6
Cuban	969	92.6
Puerto Rican	851	72.1
South American	1,179	90.8
Colombian	857	89.0

Four-Year College Graduates
(Universe: Population 25 Years and Over)

Group	Number	%
Total Population	9,199	39.2
Hispanic or Latino (of any race)	1,333	28.1
Cuban	466	44.5
Puerto Rican	202	17.1
South American	374	28.8
Colombian	276	28.7

Population Age 3–17 Enrolled in Public School
(Universe: Population Age 3–17 Enrolled in School)

Group	Number	%
Total Population	4,305	75.3
Hispanic or Latino (of any race)	954	70.1
Cuban	84	29.5
Puerto Rican	183	83.2
South American	497	80.8
Colombian	253	77.4

Population Age 3–17 Enrolled in Private School
(Universe: Population Age 3–17 Enrolled in School)

Group	Number	%
Total Population	1,415	24.7
Hispanic or Latino (of any race)	406	29.9
Cuban	201	70.5
Puerto Rican	37	16.8
South American	118	19.2
Colombian	74	22.6

Foreign-Born Population

Group	Number	%
Total Population	5,895	17.2
Hispanic or Latino (of any race)	3,000	37.7
Cuban	959	49.8
Puerto Rican	9	0.5
South American	1,456	63.1
Colombian	1,042	68.0

Foreign-Born Naturalized U.S. Citizens

Group	Number	%
Total Population	3,585	60.8
Hispanic or Latino (of any race)	1,903	63.4
Cuban	677	70.6
Puerto Rican	9	100.0
South American	915	62.8
Colombian	593	56.9

Language Spoken at Home: English Only
(Universe: Population 5 Years and Over)

Group	Number	%
Total Population	23,991	74.3
Hispanic or Latino (of any race)	1,931	26.2
Cuban	502	29.5
Puerto Rican	470	27.4
South American	364	16.4
Colombian	175	11.6

Language Spoken at Home: Spanish
(Universe: Population 5 Years and Over)

Group	Number	%
Total Population	5,989	18.6
Hispanic or Latino (of any race)	5,423	73.5
Cuban	1,200	70.5
Puerto Rican	1,222	71.3
South American	1,862	83.6
Colombian	1,328	88.4

Unemployment Rate
(Universe: Population 16 Years and Over)

Group	%
Total Population	7.7
Hispanic or Latino (of any race)	12.7
Cuban	21.3
Puerto Rican	20.3
South American	8.0
Colombian	10.2

Class of Worker: Private Wage and Salary
(Universe: Civilian Employed Population 16 Years and Over)

Group	Number	%
Total Population	15,110	83.5
Hispanic or Latino (of any race)	3,022	78.3
Cuban	509	59.2
Puerto Rican	728	87.8
South American	992	80.3
Colombian	644	76.8

Class of Worker: Government
(Universe: Civilian Employed Population 16 Years and Over)

Group	Number	%
Total Population	1,975	10.9
Hispanic or Latino (of any race)	527	13.7
Cuban	158	18.4
Puerto Rican	67	8.1
South American	231	18.7
Colombian	181	21.6

Means of Transportation to Work: Car, Truck or Van
(Universe: Workers 16 Years and Over)

Group	Number	%
Total Population	16,004	90.1
Hispanic or Latino (of any race)	3,482	90.7
Cuban	739	91.0
Puerto Rican	753	89.4
South American	1,149	93.0
Colombian	773	92.2

Means of Transportation to Work: Public Transportation (ex. Taxicab)
(Universe: Workers 16 Years and Over)

Group	Number	%
Total Population	214	1.2
Hispanic or Latino (of any race)	42	1.1
Cuban	0	0.0
Puerto Rican	0	0.0
South American	42	3.4
Colombian	42	5.0

Homeownership Rate
(Universe: Occupied Housing Units)

Group	%
Total Population	69.1
Hispanic or Latino (of any race)	62.0
Central American, ex. Mexican	61.7
Honduran	51.3
Cuban	69.9
Dominican Republic	53.4
Mexican	38.6
Puerto Rican	52.1
South American	63.5
Colombian	60.8
Ecuadorian	74.0
Peruvian	61.4
Venezuelan	59.7
Spaniard	80.8

Median Home Value

Group	Dollars
Total Population	229,600
Hispanic or Latino (of any race)	189,800
Cuban	226,100
Puerto Rican	186,400
South American	170,100
Colombian	159,900

Median Gross Rent

Group	Dollars
Total Population	1,003
Hispanic or Latino (of any race)	1,013
Cuban	817
Puerto Rican	978
South American	1,350
Colombian	793

Median Household Income
(2010 Inflation-Adjusted Dollars)

Group	Dollars
Total Population	58,286
Hispanic or Latino (of any race)	38,761
Cuban	43,737
Puerto Rican	35,081
South American	38,834
Colombian	35,000

Per Capita Income
(2010 Inflation-Adjusted Dollars)

Group	Dollars
Total Population	34,131
Hispanic or Latino (of any race)	21,747
Cuban	23,684
Puerto Rican	18,912
South American	16,596
Colombian	14,927

Households with $100,000+ Income

Group	Number	%
Total Population	3,578	25.1
Hispanic or Latino (of any race)	458	15.9
Cuban	133	20.6
Puerto Rican	48	5.8
South American	130	17.6
Colombian	71	14.8

Households with Food Stamps/SNAP Benefits During Past 12 Months

Group	Number	%
Total Population	701	4.9
Hispanic or Latino (of any race)	233	8.1
Cuban	48	7.4
Puerto Rican	156	18.7
South American	12	1.6
Colombian	12	2.5

Poverty Rate
(Income in Past 12 Months Below Poverty Level)

Group	%
Total Population	7.7
Hispanic or Latino (of any race)	10.1
Cuban	19.3
Puerto Rican	12.5
South American	2.6
Colombian	3.9

Casselberry

Population

Group	Number	%TP[1]	%HP[2]
Total Population	26,241	100.0	–
Hispanic or Latino (of any race)	5,923	22.6	100.0
Central American, ex. Mexican	273	1.0	4.6
Cuban	479	1.8	8.1
Dominican Republic	322	1.2	5.4
Mexican	438	1.7	7.4
Puerto Rican	3,159	12.0	53.3
South American	949	3.6	16.0
Colombian	533	2.0	9.0
Ecuadorian	111	0.4	1.9
Peruvian	102	0.4	1.7

Population Growth: 2000–2010

Group	%
Total Population	16.0
Hispanic or Latino (of any race)	73.0
Central American, ex. Mexican	148.2
Cuban	97.1
Dominican Republic	203.8
Mexican	57.6
Puerto Rican	69.0
South American	171.1
Colombian	239.5

Males per 100 Females

Group	Number
Total Population	93.9
Hispanic or Latino (of any race)	92.2
Central American, ex. Mexican	89.6
Cuban	97.9
Dominican Republic	75.0
Mexican	125.8
Puerto Rican	90.4
South American	87.9
Colombian	89.0
Ecuadorian	101.8

Notes: (1) Percent of total population; (2) Percent of Hispanic/Latino population; Profiles include places with an overall population of at least 125,000, OR an overall population of at least 25,000 where the Hispanic/Latino population is at least 20% of the overall population. In states where less than five places meet either of these criteria, we have included places with at least 10,000 total population with the highest percentage of Hispanic/Latino population. These places are identified with an asterisk (*); Please refer to the User's Guide for a full explanation of data.

Peruvian	82.1

Average Household Size

Group	People
Total Population	2.29
Hispanic or Latino (of any race)	2.74
Central American, ex. Mexican	2.95
Cuban	2.66
Dominican Republic	3.13
Mexican	2.97
Puerto Rican	2.64
South American	2.95
Colombian	2.91
Ecuadorian	3.46
Peruvian	2.85

Median Age

Group	Years
Total Population	37.5
Hispanic or Latino (of any race)	31.7
Central American, ex. Mexican	29.2
Cuban	37.1
Dominican Republic	29.1
Mexican	27.0
Puerto Rican	32.0
South American	34.5
Colombian	32.9
Ecuadorian	33.5
Peruvian	40.7

High School Graduates
(Universe: Population 25 Years and Over)

Group	Number	%
Total Population	16,488	87.9
Hispanic or Latino (of any race)	2,841	74.6
Puerto Rican	1,183	62.0

Four-Year College Graduates
(Universe: Population 25 Years and Over)

Group	Number	%
Total Population	3,984	21.2
Hispanic or Latino (of any race)	504	13.2
Puerto Rican	171	9.0

Population Age 3–17 Enrolled in Public School
(Universe: Population Age 3–17 Enrolled in School)

Group	Number	%
Total Population	3,156	84.2
Hispanic or Latino (of any race)	906	90.2
Puerto Rican	263	83.2

Population Age 3–17 Enrolled in Private School
(Universe: Population Age 3–17 Enrolled in School)

Group	Number	%
Total Population	592	15.8
Hispanic or Latino (of any race)	98	9.8
Puerto Rican	53	16.8

Foreign-Born Population

Group	Number	%
Total Population	2,827	10.8
Hispanic or Latino (of any race)	1,485	27.7
Puerto Rican	48	2.0

Foreign-Born Naturalized U.S. Citizens

Group	Number	%
Total Population	1,579	55.9
Hispanic or Latino (of any race)	629	42.4
Puerto Rican	10	20.8

Language Spoken at Home: English Only
(Universe: Population 5 Years and Over)

Group	Number	%
Total Population	19,586	79.1
Hispanic or Latino (of any race)	1,286	25.0
Puerto Rican	514	21.9

Language Spoken at Home: Spanish
(Universe: Population 5 Years and Over)

Group	Number	%
Total Population	4,217	17.0
Hispanic or Latino (of any race)	3,858	75.0
Puerto Rican	1,834	78.1

Unemployment Rate
(Universe: Population 16 Years and Over)

Group	%
Total Population	8.3
Hispanic or Latino (of any race)	14.5
Puerto Rican	26.2

Class of Worker: Private Wage and Salary
(Universe: Civilian Employed Population 16 Years and Over)

Group	Number	%
Total Population	12,160	86.1
Hispanic or Latino (of any race)	2,224	89.8
Puerto Rican	828	94.6

Class of Worker: Government
(Universe: Civilian Employed Population 16 Years and Over)

Group	Number	%
Total Population	1,091	7.7
Hispanic or Latino (of any race)	117	4.7
Puerto Rican	17	1.9

Means of Transportation to Work: Car, Truck or Van
(Universe: Workers 16 Years and Over)

Group	Number	%
Total Population	12,719	91.5
Hispanic or Latino (of any race)	2,223	90.3
Puerto Rican	794	90.7

Means of Transportation to Work: Public Transportation (ex. Taxicab)
(Universe: Workers 16 Years and Over)

Group	Number	%
Total Population	208	1.5
Hispanic or Latino (of any race)	60	2.4
Puerto Rican	9	1.0

Homeownership Rate
(Universe: Occupied Housing Units)

Group	%
Total Population	57.3
Hispanic or Latino (of any race)	46.6
Central American, ex. Mexican	36.0
Cuban	54.5
Dominican Republic	37.3
Mexican	35.2
Puerto Rican	46.3
South American	51.1
Colombian	53.1
Ecuadorian	57.1
Peruvian	38.5

Median Home Value

Group	Dollars
Total Population	178,800
Hispanic or Latino (of any race)	170,100
Puerto Rican	175,700

Median Gross Rent

Group	Dollars
Total Population	961
Hispanic or Latino (of any race)	893
Puerto Rican	932

Median Household Income
(2010 Inflation-Adjusted Dollars)

Group	Dollars
Total Population	44,807
Hispanic or Latino (of any race)	36,639
Puerto Rican	40,055

Per Capita Income
(2010 Inflation-Adjusted Dollars)

Group	Dollars
Total Population	24,184
Hispanic or Latino (of any race)	17,569
Puerto Rican	15,190

Households with $100,000+ Income

Group	Number	%
Total Population	1,032	9.3
Hispanic or Latino (of any race)	123	6.0
Puerto Rican	14	1.6

Households with Food Stamps/SNAP Benefits During Past 12 Months

Group	Number	%
Total Population	610	5.5
Hispanic or Latino (of any race)	187	9.1
Puerto Rican	90	10.0

Poverty Rate
(Income in Past 12 Months Below Poverty Level)

Group	%
Total Population	14.7
Hispanic or Latino (of any race)	22.0
Puerto Rican	29.9

Coconut Creek

Population

Group	Number	%TP[1]	%HP[2]
Total Population	52,909	100.0	–
Hispanic or Latino (of any race)	10,800	20.4	100.0
Central American, ex. Mexican	821	1.6	7.6
Guatemalan	170	0.3	1.6
Honduran	190	0.4	1.8
Nicaraguan	169	0.3	1.6
Salvadoran	124	0.2	1.1
Cuban	979	1.9	9.1
Dominican Republic	736	1.4	6.8
Mexican	1,120	2.1	10.4
Puerto Rican	2,196	4.2	20.3
South American	4,166	7.9	38.6
Argentinean	309	0.6	2.9
Colombian	1,857	3.5	17.2
Ecuadorian	380	0.7	3.5
Peruvian	859	1.6	8.0
Venezuelan	531	1.0	4.9

Population Growth: 2000–2010

Group	%
Total Population	21.4
Hispanic or Latino (of any race)	112.8
Central American, ex. Mexican	211.0
Cuban	125.1
Dominican Republic	304.4
Mexican	62.8
Puerto Rican	96.1
South American	197.1
Colombian	233.4
Ecuadorian	258.5
Peruvian	207.9
Venezuelan	145.8

Males per 100 Females

Group	Number
Total Population	87.3
Hispanic or Latino (of any race)	89.9
Central American, ex. Mexican	95.9
Guatemalan	139.4
Honduran	72.7
Nicaraguan	89.9
Salvadoran	100.0
Cuban	100.2
Dominican Republic	86.3
Mexican	110.1
Puerto Rican	90.8
South American	82.6
Argentinean	100.6
Colombian	72.4
Ecuadorian	87.2
Peruvian	93.5
Venezuelan	91.0

Average Household Size

Group	People
Total Population	2.32
Hispanic or Latino (of any race)	2.96
Central American, ex. Mexican	3.48
Guatemalan	3.98
Honduran	3.46
Nicaraguan	3.64
Salvadoran	3.60
Cuban	2.69
Dominican Republic	3.28
Mexican	3.58

Notes: (1) Percent of total population; (2) Percent of Hispanic/Latino population; Profiles include places with an overall population of at least 125,000, OR an overall population of at least 25,000 where the Hispanic/Latino population is at least 20% of the overall population. In states where less than five places meet either of these criteria, we have included places with at least 10,000 total population with the highest percentage of Hispanic/Latino population. These places are identified with an asterisk (*); Please refer to the User's Guide for a full explanation of data.

Puerto Rican	2.69
South American	2.96
Argentinean	2.68
Colombian	2.99
Ecuadorian	3.02
Peruvian	3.06
Venezuelan	2.80

Median Age

Group	Years
Total Population	40.3
Hispanic or Latino (of any race)	32.3
Central American, ex. Mexican	29.4
Guatemalan	29.0
Honduran	28.6
Nicaraguan	29.1
Salvadoran	30.3
Cuban	35.8
Dominican Republic	30.3
Mexican	27.0
Puerto Rican	31.6
South American	35.5
Argentinean	36.6
Colombian	34.8
Ecuadorian	34.8
Peruvian	36.6
Venezuelan	34.6

High School Graduates
(Universe: Population 25 Years and Over)

Group	Number	%
Total Population	34,493	92.4
Hispanic or Latino (of any race)	5,586	93.5
Cuban	546	96.8
Puerto Rican	1,223	92.7
South American	2,721	95.6
Colombian	936	100.0

Four-Year College Graduates
(Universe: Population 25 Years and Over)

Group	Number	%
Total Population	11,607	31.1
Hispanic or Latino (of any race)	1,903	31.8
Cuban	275	48.8
Puerto Rican	296	22.4
South American	956	33.6
Colombian	326	34.8

Population Age 3–17 Enrolled in Public School
(Universe: Population Age 3–17 Enrolled in School)

Group	Number	%
Total Population	7,494	85.0
Hispanic or Latino (of any race)	1,948	92.2
Cuban	292	94.8
Puerto Rican	510	94.4
South American	620	88.8
Colombian	267	91.8

Population Age 3–17 Enrolled in Private School
(Universe: Population Age 3–17 Enrolled in School)

Group	Number	%
Total Population	1,327	15.0
Hispanic or Latino (of any race)	164	7.8
Cuban	16	5.2
Puerto Rican	30	5.6
South American	78	11.2
Colombian	24	8.2

Foreign-Born Population

Group	Number	%
Total Population	13,624	26.4
Hispanic or Latino (of any race)	4,907	51.7
Cuban	309	33.1
Puerto Rican	0	0.0
South American	3,379	82.3
Colombian	1,071	75.2

Foreign-Born Naturalized U.S. Citizens

Group	Number	%
Total Population	6,198	45.5
Hispanic or Latino (of any race)	2,079	42.4
Cuban	260	84.1
Puerto Rican	0	0.0
South American	1,366	40.4
Colombian	614	57.3

Language Spoken at Home: English Only
(Universe: Population 5 Years and Over)

Group	Number	%
Total Population	32,853	67.5
Hispanic or Latino (of any race)	1,406	15.8
Cuban	207	22.9
Puerto Rican	581	30.8
South American	166	4.3
Colombian	37	2.6

Language Spoken at Home: Spanish
(Universe: Population 5 Years and Over)

Group	Number	%
Total Population	8,258	17.0
Hispanic or Latino (of any race)	7,300	82.1
Cuban	687	76.0
Puerto Rican	1,307	69.2
South American	3,619	92.9
Colombian	1,361	97.4

Unemployment Rate
(Universe: Population 16 Years and Over)

Group	%
Total Population	5.8
Hispanic or Latino (of any race)	7.1
Cuban	0.0
Puerto Rican	3.7
South American	10.8
Colombian	10.1

Class of Worker: Private Wage and Salary
(Universe: Civilian Employed Population 16 Years and Over)

Group	Number	%
Total Population	20,866	82.7
Hispanic or Latino (of any race)	4,429	90.1
Cuban	498	93.1
Puerto Rican	985	96.5
South American	1,876	85.4
Colombian	702	96.4

Class of Worker: Government
(Universe: Civilian Employed Population 16 Years and Over)

Group	Number	%
Total Population	2,552	10.1
Hispanic or Latino (of any race)	200	4.1
Cuban	37	6.9
Puerto Rican	24	2.4
South American	78	3.5
Colombian	15	2.1

Means of Transportation to Work: Car, Truck or Van
(Universe: Workers 16 Years and Over)

Group	Number	%
Total Population	23,045	92.7
Hispanic or Latino (of any race)	4,442	91.4
Cuban	514	98.3
Puerto Rican	1,010	98.9
South American	1,873	86.0
Colombian	665	91.3

Means of Transportation to Work: Public Transportation (ex. Taxicab)
(Universe: Workers 16 Years and Over)

Group	Number	%
Total Population	460	1.8
Hispanic or Latino (of any race)	170	3.5
Cuban	0	0.0
Puerto Rican	0	0.0
South American	142	6.5
Colombian	0	0.0

Homeownership Rate
(Universe: Occupied Housing Units)

Group	%
Total Population	70.9
Hispanic or Latino (of any race)	58.2
Central American, ex. Mexican	58.1
Guatemalan	65.3
Honduran	48.1
Nicaraguan	56.8
Salvadoran	57.1
Cuban	65.9
Dominican Republic	57.3
Mexican	53.4
Puerto Rican	57.2
South American	58.5
Argentinean	66.2
Colombian	57.2
Ecuadorian	59.6
Peruvian	53.0
Venezuelan	62.9

Median Home Value

Group	Dollars
Total Population	203,700
Hispanic or Latino (of any race)	218,500
Cuban	224,500
Puerto Rican	209,200
South American	198,600
Colombian	289,500

Median Gross Rent

Group	Dollars
Total Population	1,338
Hispanic or Latino (of any race)	1,397
Cuban	1,340
Puerto Rican	1,394
South American	1,447
Colombian	1,346

Median Household Income
(2010 Inflation-Adjusted Dollars)

Group	Dollars
Total Population	49,427
Hispanic or Latino (of any race)	50,379
Cuban	78,214
Puerto Rican	55,417
South American	45,357
Colombian	50,167

Per Capita Income
(2010 Inflation-Adjusted Dollars)

Group	Dollars
Total Population	27,876
Hispanic or Latino (of any race)	19,674
Cuban	33,660
Puerto Rican	24,332
South American	16,989
Colombian	19,402

Households with $100,000+ Income

Group	Number	%
Total Population	4,136	18.8
Hispanic or Latino (of any race)	443	14.8
Cuban	76	18.8
Puerto Rican	162	23.2
South American	142	11.5
Colombian	60	13.9

Households with Food Stamps/SNAP Benefits During Past 12 Months

Group	Number	%
Total Population	764	3.5
Hispanic or Latino (of any race)	174	5.8
Cuban	0	0.0
Puerto Rican	23	3.3
South American	111	9.0
Colombian	25	5.8

Poverty Rate
(Income in Past 12 Months Below Poverty Level)

Group	%
Total Population	8.0
Hispanic or Latino (of any race)	13.0
Cuban	4.2
Puerto Rican	3.1
South American	12.6
Colombian	5.1

Cooper City

Population

Group	Number	%TP[1]	%HP[2]
Total Population	28,547	100.0	–
Hispanic or Latino (of any race)	6,520	22.8	100.0
Central American, ex. Mexican	452	1.6	6.9
Nicaraguan	115	0.4	1.8
Cuban	2,246	7.9	34.4

Notes: (1) Percent of total population; (2) Percent of Hispanic/Latino population; Profiles include places with an overall population of at least 125,000, OR an overall population of at least 25,000 where the Hispanic/Latino population is at least 20% of the overall population. In states where less than five places meet either of these criteria, we have included places with at least 10,000 total population with the highest percentage of Hispanic/Latino population. These places are identified with an asterisk (*); Please refer to the User's Guide for a full explanation of data.

Group	Number	% (1)	% (2)
Dominican Republic	315	1.1	4.8
Mexican	212	0.7	3.3
Puerto Rican	1,040	3.6	16.0
South American	1,881	6.6	28.8
Argentinean	145	0.5	2.2
Colombian	923	3.2	14.2
Ecuadorian	190	0.7	2.9
Peruvian	303	1.1	4.6
Venezuelan	185	0.6	2.8
Spaniard	127	0.4	1.9

Population Growth: 2000–2010

Group	%
Total Population	2.2
Hispanic or Latino (of any race)	49.9
Central American, ex. Mexican	167.5
Cuban	52.1
Dominican Republic	173.9
Mexican	52.5
Puerto Rican	45.7
South American	104.0
Colombian	86.1
Peruvian	131.3

Males per 100 Females

Group	Number
Total Population	93.7
Hispanic or Latino (of any race)	85.2
Central American, ex. Mexican	75.2
Nicaraguan	76.9
Cuban	91.6
Dominican Republic	78.0
Mexican	75.2
Puerto Rican	87.7
South American	82.1
Argentinean	104.2
Colombian	82.1
Ecuadorian	75.9
Peruvian	68.3
Venezuelan	83.2
Spaniard	76.4

Average Household Size

Group	People
Total Population	2.96
Hispanic or Latino (of any race)	3.34
Central American, ex. Mexican	3.40
Nicaraguan	3.04
Cuban	3.26
Dominican Republic	3.59
Mexican	3.09
Puerto Rican	3.28
South American	3.48
Argentinean	3.44
Colombian	3.51
Ecuadorian	3.43
Peruvian	3.57
Venezuelan	3.34
Spaniard	2.89

Median Age

Group	Years
Total Population	41.0
Hispanic or Latino (of any race)	36.0
Central American, ex. Mexican	35.4
Nicaraguan	31.6
Cuban	38.9
Dominican Republic	31.2
Mexican	27.0
Puerto Rican	33.2
South American	37.9
Argentinean	42.5
Colombian	35.6
Ecuadorian	39.4
Peruvian	41.7
Venezuelan	37.1
Spaniard	43.5

High School Graduates
(Universe: Population 25 Years and Over)

Group	Number	%
Total Population	17,046	94.2
Hispanic or Latino (of any race)	3,216	88.2
Cuban	1,216	89.7
Puerto Rican	331	89.7
South American	1,052	83.9
Colombian	513	88.1

Four-Year College Graduates
(Universe: Population 25 Years and Over)

Group	Number	%
Total Population	7,027	38.8
Hispanic or Latino (of any race)	1,090	29.9
Cuban	418	30.8
Puerto Rican	57	15.4
South American	398	31.7
Colombian	149	25.6

Population Age 3–17 Enrolled in Public School
(Universe: Population Age 3–17 Enrolled in School)

Group	Number	%
Total Population	5,095	75.1
Hispanic or Latino (of any race)	1,245	70.9
Cuban	355	64.2
Puerto Rican	225	72.6
South American	394	69.2
Colombian	162	76.1

Population Age 3–17 Enrolled in Private School
(Universe: Population Age 3–17 Enrolled in School)

Group	Number	%
Total Population	1,690	24.9
Hispanic or Latino (of any race)	512	29.1
Cuban	198	35.8
Puerto Rican	85	27.4
South American	175	30.8
Colombian	51	23.9

Foreign-Born Population

Group	Number	%
Total Population	6,504	22.7
Hispanic or Latino (of any race)	2,792	45.3
Cuban	918	41.8
Puerto Rican	0	0.0
South American	1,373	67.6
Colombian	578	68.0

Foreign-Born Naturalized U.S. Citizens

Group	Number	%
Total Population	4,427	68.1
Hispanic or Latino (of any race)	2,153	77.1
Cuban	859	93.6
Puerto Rican	0	0.0
South American	917	66.8
Colombian	373	64.5

Language Spoken at Home: English Only
(Universe: Population 5 Years and Over)

Group	Number	%
Total Population	19,197	70.9
Hispanic or Latino (of any race)	1,497	25.8
Cuban	550	26.9
Puerto Rican	302	41.7
South American	426	21.2
Colombian	235	27.6

Language Spoken at Home: Spanish
(Universe: Population 5 Years and Over)

Group	Number	%
Total Population	5,049	18.6
Hispanic or Latino (of any race)	4,309	74.1
Cuban	1,492	73.1
Puerto Rican	422	58.3
South American	1,577	78.5
Colombian	615	72.4

Unemployment Rate
(Universe: Population 16 Years and Over)

Group	%
Total Population	5.8
Hispanic or Latino (of any race)	5.8
Cuban	2.7
Puerto Rican	0.0
South American	11.0
Colombian	6.0

Class of Worker: Private Wage and Salary
(Universe: Civilian Employed Population 16 Years and Over)

Group	Number	%
Total Population	11,630	77.8
Hispanic or Latino (of any race)	2,343	77.9
Cuban	854	73.9
Puerto Rican	238	74.6
South American	852	84.5
Colombian	428	93.4

Class of Worker: Government
(Universe: Civilian Employed Population 16 Years and Over)

Group	Number	%
Total Population	2,754	18.4
Hispanic or Latino (of any race)	550	18.3
Cuban	261	22.6
Puerto Rican	81	25.4
South American	80	7.9
Colombian	30	6.6

Means of Transportation to Work: Car, Truck or Van
(Universe: Workers 16 Years and Over)

Group	Number	%
Total Population	13,454	93.2
Hispanic or Latino (of any race)	2,672	93.3
Cuban	1,057	94.0
Puerto Rican	265	86.0
South American	928	95.1
Colombian	421	94.2

Means of Transportation to Work: Public Transportation (ex. Taxicab)
(Universe: Workers 16 Years and Over)

Group	Number	%
Total Population	54	0.4
Hispanic or Latino (of any race)	22	0.8
Cuban	0	0.0
Puerto Rican	0	0.0
South American	22	2.3
Colombian	0	0.0

Homeownership Rate
(Universe: Occupied Housing Units)

Group	%
Total Population	89.2
Hispanic or Latino (of any race)	86.0
Central American, ex. Mexican	85.0
Nicaraguan	76.0
Cuban	90.2
Dominican Republic	84.1
Mexican	78.3
Puerto Rican	82.8
South American	82.5
Argentinean	86.0
Colombian	81.6
Ecuadorian	86.8
Peruvian	86.1
Venezuelan	80.4
Spaniard	91.3

Median Home Value

Group	Dollars
Total Population	372,100
Hispanic or Latino (of any race)	360,600
Cuban	360,400
Puerto Rican	384,800
South American	363,900
Colombian	347,900

Median Gross Rent

Group	Dollars
Total Population	1,673
Hispanic or Latino (of any race)	1,523
Cuban	1,217
Puerto Rican	994
South American	1,694
Colombian	–

Median Household Income
(2010 Inflation-Adjusted Dollars)

Group	Dollars
Total Population	91,315
Hispanic or Latino (of any race)	79,444
Cuban	84,821
Puerto Rican	92,614
South American	66,895
Colombian	66,736

Notes: (1) Percent of total population; (2) Percent of Hispanic/Latino population; Profiles include places with an overall population of at least 125,000, OR an overall population of at least 25,000 where the Hispanic/Latino population is at least 20% of the overall population. In states where less than five places meet either of these criteria, we have included places with at least 10,000 total population with the highest percentage of Hispanic/Latino population. These places are identified with an asterisk (*); Please refer to the User's Guide for a full explanation of data.

Per Capita Income
(2010 Inflation-Adjusted Dollars)

Group	Dollars
Total Population	35,061
Hispanic or Latino (of any race)	26,964
Cuban	34,784
Puerto Rican	20,664
South American	22,777
Colombian	23,219

Households with $100,000+ Income

Group	Number	%
Total Population	4,123	44.2
Hispanic or Latino (of any race)	638	39.8
Cuban	258	47.5
Puerto Rican	102	45.3
South American	177	29.2
Colombian	102	32.8

Households with Food Stamps/SNAP Benefits During Past 12 Months

Group	Number	%
Total Population	393	4.2
Hispanic or Latino (of any race)	132	8.2
Cuban	74	13.6
Puerto Rican	27	12.0
South American	17	2.8
Colombian	10	3.2

Poverty Rate
(Income in Past 12 Months Below Poverty Level)

Group	%
Total Population	4.4
Hispanic or Latino (of any race)	5.4
Cuban	1.1
Puerto Rican	11.7
South American	10.1
Colombian	1.2

Coral Gables

Population

Group	Number	%TP[1]	%HP[2]
Total Population	46,780	100.0	–
Hispanic or Latino (of any race)	25,062	53.6	100.0
Central American, ex. Mexican	1,489	3.2	5.9
Guatemalan	122	0.3	0.5
Honduran	291	0.6	1.2
Nicaraguan	651	1.4	2.6
Panamanian	151	0.3	0.6
Salvadoran	169	0.4	0.7
Cuban	14,657	31.3	58.5
Dominican Republic	480	1.0	1.9
Mexican	829	1.8	3.3
Puerto Rican	1,144	2.4	4.6
South American	4,941	10.6	19.7
Argentinean	557	1.2	2.2
Chilean	230	0.5	0.9
Colombian	1,678	3.6	6.7
Ecuadorian	351	0.8	1.4
Peruvian	651	1.4	2.6
Uruguayan	147	0.3	0.6
Venezuelan	1,201	2.6	4.8
Spaniard	649	1.4	2.6

Population Growth: 2000–2010

Group	%
Total Population	10.7
Hispanic or Latino (of any race)	27.2
Central American, ex. Mexican	59.1
Honduran	110.9
Nicaraguan	62.8
Panamanian	33.6
Cuban	20.8
Dominican Republic	111.5
Mexican	72.0
Puerto Rican	29.0
South American	91.1
Argentinean	87.5
Chilean	48.4
Colombian	74.6
Ecuadorian	70.4
Peruvian	127.6
Venezuelan	142.1
Spaniard	118.5

Males per 100 Females

Group	Number
Total Population	89.7
Hispanic or Latino (of any race)	82.5
Central American, ex. Mexican	63.8
Guatemalan	74.3
Honduran	46.2
Nicaraguan	67.4
Panamanian	65.9
Salvadoran	76.0
Cuban	86.5
Dominican Republic	65.5
Mexican	93.7
Puerto Rican	77.6
South American	75.5
Argentinean	94.1
Chilean	100.0
Colombian	69.0
Ecuadorian	65.6
Peruvian	65.6
Uruguayan	83.8
Venezuelan	79.3
Spaniard	100.3

Average Household Size

Group	People
Total Population	2.35
Hispanic or Latino (of any race)	2.47
Central American, ex. Mexican	2.52
Guatemalan	2.50
Honduran	2.64
Nicaraguan	2.51
Panamanian	2.32
Salvadoran	2.66
Cuban	2.46
Dominican Republic	2.37
Mexican	2.75
Puerto Rican	2.29
South American	2.51
Argentinean	2.46
Chilean	2.27
Colombian	2.47
Ecuadorian	2.51
Peruvian	2.36
Uruguayan	2.90
Venezuelan	2.70
Spaniard	2.51

Median Age

Group	Years
Total Population	38.8
Hispanic or Latino (of any race)	41.3
Central American, ex. Mexican	38.5
Guatemalan	35.3
Honduran	38.6
Nicaraguan	38.8
Panamanian	39.5
Salvadoran	40.1
Cuban	45.4
Dominican Republic	36.4
Mexican	32.8
Puerto Rican	36.0
South American	37.6
Argentinean	37.7
Chilean	41.0
Colombian	37.9
Ecuadorian	34.4
Peruvian	40.1
Uruguayan	38.2
Venezuelan	36.7
Spaniard	40.4

High School Graduates
(Universe: Population 25 Years and Over)

Group	Number	%
Total Population	27,411	94.7
Hispanic or Latino (of any race)	15,807	92.9
Central American, ex. Mexican	706	90.4
Cuban	9,783	92.3
Mexican	558	93.6
Puerto Rican	1,065	93.0
South American	2,763	94.7
Colombian	878	87.1

Four-Year College Graduates
(Universe: Population 25 Years and Over)

Group	Number	%
Total Population	18,427	63.7
Hispanic or Latino (of any race)	10,102	59.4
Central American, ex. Mexican	386	49.4
Cuban	6,072	57.3
Mexican	355	59.6
Puerto Rican	776	67.8
South American	1,946	66.7
Colombian	630	62.5

Population Age 3–17 Enrolled in Public School
(Universe: Population Age 3–17 Enrolled in School)

Group	Number	%
Total Population	2,544	35.1
Hispanic or Latino (of any race)	1,483	34.9
Central American, ex. Mexican	61	55.5
Cuban	878	35.5
Mexican	45	27.6
Puerto Rican	117	42.5
South American	290	37.1
Colombian	88	28.8

Population Age 3–17 Enrolled in Private School
(Universe: Population Age 3–17 Enrolled in School)

Group	Number	%
Total Population	4,704	64.9
Hispanic or Latino (of any race)	2,762	65.1
Central American, ex. Mexican	49	44.5
Cuban	1,592	64.5
Mexican	118	72.4
Puerto Rican	158	57.5
South American	491	62.9
Colombian	218	71.2

Foreign-Born Population

Group	Number	%
Total Population	16,670	36.3
Hispanic or Latino (of any race)	13,347	55.6
Central American, ex. Mexican	738	70.5
Cuban	8,291	56.8
Mexican	535	56.6
Puerto Rican	0	0.0
South American	3,032	72.3
Colombian	1,087	71.5

Foreign-Born Naturalized U.S. Citizens

Group	Number	%
Total Population	11,415	68.5
Hispanic or Latino (of any race)	9,734	72.9
Central American, ex. Mexican	432	58.5
Cuban	7,431	89.6
Mexican	95	17.8
Puerto Rican	0	0.0
South American	1,305	43.0
Colombian	473	43.5

Language Spoken at Home: English Only
(Universe: Population 5 Years and Over)

Group	Number	%
Total Population	18,745	42.5
Hispanic or Latino (of any race)	1,790	7.8
Central American, ex. Mexican	20	2.1
Cuban	881	6.3
Mexican	148	16.6
Puerto Rican	397	25.7
South American	265	6.5
Colombian	104	7.2

Language Spoken at Home: Spanish
(Universe: Population 5 Years and Over)

Group	Number	%
Total Population	22,877	51.9
Hispanic or Latino (of any race)	21,012	91.4
Central American, ex. Mexican	925	94.9
Cuban	13,122	93.6
Mexican	742	83.4
Puerto Rican	1,150	74.3
South American	3,691	90.8
Colombian	1,278	88.4

Notes: (1) Percent of total population; (2) Percent of Hispanic/Latino population; Profiles include places with an overall population of at least 125,000, OR an overall population of at least 25,000 where the Hispanic/Latino population is at least 20% of the overall population. In states where less than five places meet either of these criteria, we have included places with at least 10,000 total population with the highest percentage of Hispanic/Latino population. These places are identified with an asterisk (*); Please refer to the User's Guide for a full explanation of data.

Unemployment Rate
(Universe: Population 16 Years and Over)

Group	%
Total Population	5.9
Hispanic or Latino (of any race)	6.2
Central American, ex. Mexican	2.5
Cuban	5.3
Mexican	0.0
Puerto Rican	14.6
South American	10.2
Colombian	4.3

Class of Worker: Private Wage and Salary
(Universe: Civilian Employed Population 16 Years and Over)

Group	Number	%
Total Population	16,257	78.7
Hispanic or Latino (of any race)	8,653	77.3
Central American, ex. Mexican	547	82.6
Cuban	5,111	76.7
Mexican	311	77.2
Puerto Rican	607	84.8
South American	1,462	74.1
Colombian	588	78.0

Class of Worker: Government
(Universe: Civilian Employed Population 16 Years and Over)

Group	Number	%
Total Population	2,327	11.3
Hispanic or Latino (of any race)	1,182	10.6
Central American, ex. Mexican	11	1.7
Cuban	791	11.9
Mexican	80	19.9
Puerto Rican	62	8.7
South American	170	8.6
Colombian	16	2.1

Means of Transportation to Work: Car, Truck or Van
(Universe: Workers 16 Years and Over)

Group	Number	%
Total Population	16,395	81.3
Hispanic or Latino (of any race)	9,357	86.0
Central American, ex. Mexican	494	83.3
Cuban	5,757	88.5
Mexican	250	65.4
Puerto Rican	601	83.9
South American	1,646	86.1
Colombian	630	83.6

Means of Transportation to Work: Public Transportation (ex. Taxicab)
(Universe: Workers 16 Years and Over)

Group	Number	%
Total Population	949	4.7
Hispanic or Latino (of any race)	422	3.9
Central American, ex. Mexican	35	5.9
Cuban	177	2.7
Mexican	52	13.6
Puerto Rican	50	7.0
South American	108	5.7
Colombian	40	5.3

Homeownership Rate
(Universe: Occupied Housing Units)

Group	%
Total Population	63.8
Hispanic or Latino (of any race)	61.5
Central American, ex. Mexican	40.6
Guatemalan	34.1
Honduran	27.9
Nicaraguan	38.6
Panamanian	45.2
Salvadoran	60.7
Cuban	70.1
Dominican Republic	38.3
Mexican	50.2
Puerto Rican	47.8
South American	47.5
Argentinean	48.5
Chilean	49.1
Colombian	45.9
Ecuadorian	55.5
Peruvian	36.4
Uruguayan	48.0
Venezuelan	52.8
Spaniard	63.5

Median Home Value

Group	Dollars
Total Population	690,100
Hispanic or Latino (of any race)	636,700
Central American, ex. Mexican	541,100
Cuban	642,300
Mexican	1,000,000+
Puerto Rican	587,000
South American	616,100
Colombian	477,000

Median Gross Rent

Group	Dollars
Total Population	1,174
Hispanic or Latino (of any race)	1,077
Central American, ex. Mexican	1,024
Cuban	1,062
Mexican	888
Puerto Rican	1,107
South American	1,134
Colombian	989

Median Household Income
(2010 Inflation-Adjusted Dollars)

Group	Dollars
Total Population	84,027
Hispanic or Latino (of any race)	65,616
Central American, ex. Mexican	54,375
Cuban	63,819
Mexican	104,940
Puerto Rican	111,629
South American	56,818
Colombian	55,881

Per Capita Income
(2010 Inflation-Adjusted Dollars)

Group	Dollars
Total Population	53,264
Hispanic or Latino (of any race)	44,849
Central American, ex. Mexican	36,919
Cuban	48,407
Mexican	50,452
Puerto Rican	37,886
South American	38,753
Colombian	34,020

Households with $100,000+ Income

Group	Number	%
Total Population	7,408	45.0
Hispanic or Latino (of any race)	3,361	37.4
Central American, ex. Mexican	77	17.0
Cuban	2,172	37.5
Mexican	151	57.9
Puerto Rican	253	57.6
South American	524	34.5
Colombian	128	22.8

Households with Food Stamps/SNAP Benefits During Past 12 Months

Group	Number	%
Total Population	371	2.3
Hispanic or Latino (of any race)	308	3.4
Central American, ex. Mexican	0	0.0
Cuban	251	4.3
Mexican	0	0.0
Puerto Rican	0	0.0
South American	31	2.0
Colombian	0	0.0

Poverty Rate
(Income in Past 12 Months Below Poverty Level)

Group	%
Total Population	9.0
Hispanic or Latino (of any race)	9.8
Central American, ex. Mexican	11.5
Cuban	10.1
Mexican	12.9
Puerto Rican	2.0
South American	11.5
Colombian	17.3

Coral Springs

Population

Group	Number	%TP[1]	%HP[2]
Total Population	121,096	100.0	–
Hispanic or Latino (of any race)	28,442	23.5	100.0
Central American, ex. Mexican	1,865	1.5	6.6
Costa Rican	165	0.1	0.6
Guatemalan	324	0.3	1.1
Honduran	395	0.3	1.4
Nicaraguan	341	0.3	1.2
Panamanian	290	0.2	1.0
Salvadoran	337	0.3	1.2
Cuban	2,853	2.4	10.0
Dominican Republic	1,938	1.6	6.8
Mexican	2,199	1.8	7.7
Puerto Rican	5,910	4.9	20.8
South American	11,749	9.7	41.3
Argentinean	832	0.7	2.9
Bolivian	146	0.1	0.5
Chilean	342	0.3	1.2
Colombian	5,521	4.6	19.4
Ecuadorian	956	0.8	3.4
Peruvian	2,226	1.8	7.8
Uruguayan	224	0.2	0.8
Venezuelan	1,414	1.2	5.0
Spaniard	309	0.3	1.1

Population Growth: 2000–2010

Group	%
Total Population	3.0
Hispanic or Latino (of any race)	56.0
Central American, ex. Mexican	132.0
Costa Rican	39.8
Guatemalan	167.8
Honduran	234.7
Nicaraguan	175.0
Panamanian	102.8
Salvadoran	114.6
Cuban	41.4
Dominican Republic	207.6
Mexican	37.2
Puerto Rican	42.0
South American	123.3
Argentinean	67.1
Chilean	111.1
Colombian	129.3
Ecuadorian	116.8
Peruvian	156.2
Venezuelan	148.9
Spaniard	90.7

Males per 100 Females

Group	Number
Total Population	92.7
Hispanic or Latino (of any race)	90.1
Central American, ex. Mexican	88.0
Costa Rican	94.1
Guatemalan	105.1
Honduran	89.0
Nicaraguan	81.4
Panamanian	70.6
Salvadoran	93.7
Cuban	97.2
Dominican Republic	90.4
Mexican	104.0
Puerto Rican	88.5
South American	86.3
Argentinean	96.7
Bolivian	87.2
Chilean	103.6
Colombian	85.5
Ecuadorian	86.7
Peruvian	85.0
Uruguayan	107.4
Venezuelan	78.1
Spaniard	95.6

Average Household Size

Group	People
Total Population	2.89
Hispanic or Latino (of any race)	3.22
Central American, ex. Mexican	3.51
Costa Rican	3.40

Notes: (1) Percent of total population; (2) Percent of Hispanic/Latino population; Profiles include places with an overall population of at least 125,000, OR an overall population of at least 25,000 where the Hispanic/Latino population is at least 20% of the overall population. In states where less than five places meet either of these criteria, we have included places with at least 10,000 total population with the highest percentage of Hispanic/Latino population. These places are identified with an asterisk (*); Please refer to the User's Guide for a full explanation of data.

Group	
Guatemalan	3.98
Honduran	3.57
Nicaraguan	3.31
Panamanian	3.22
Salvadoran	3.64
Cuban	2.93
Dominican Republic	3.42
Mexican	3.77
Puerto Rican	3.09
South American	3.26
Argentinean	3.30
Bolivian	3.38
Chilean	3.34
Colombian	3.20
Ecuadorian	3.44
Peruvian	3.34
Uruguayan	3.01
Venezuelan	3.24
Spaniard	3.00

Median Age

Group	Years
Total Population	36.5
Hispanic or Latino (of any race)	31.6
Central American, ex. Mexican	32.1
Costa Rican	32.9
Guatemalan	30.2
Honduran	32.4
Nicaraguan	34.1
Panamanian	36.5
Salvadoran	30.4
Cuban	36.1
Dominican Republic	29.6
Mexican	25.7
Puerto Rican	28.2
South American	35.4
Argentinean	36.1
Bolivian	35.8
Chilean	37.6
Colombian	35.5
Ecuadorian	35.7
Peruvian	36.1
Uruguayan	34.4
Venezuelan	33.0
Spaniard	34.9

High School Graduates

(Universe: Population 25 Years and Over)

Group	Number	%
Total Population	70,989	92.1
Hispanic or Latino (of any race)	14,342	88.7
Central American, ex. Mexican	1,031	90.9
Cuban	1,569	87.4
Dominican Republic	794	79.1
Mexican	878	74.9
Puerto Rican	2,683	88.4
South American	6,602	93.5
Argentinean	685	93.1
Colombian	2,975	91.1
Ecuadorian	623	91.2
Peruvian	1,380	97.1
Venezuelan	622	98.0

Four-Year College Graduates

(Universe: Population 25 Years and Over)

Group	Number	%
Total Population	27,780	36.1
Hispanic or Latino (of any race)	5,003	30.9
Central American, ex. Mexican	333	29.4
Cuban	573	31.9
Dominican Republic	255	25.4
Mexican	338	28.8
Puerto Rican	689	22.7
South American	2,559	36.3
Argentinean	380	51.6
Colombian	1,011	31.0
Ecuadorian	261	38.2
Peruvian	479	33.7
Venezuelan	286	45.0

Population Age 3–17 Enrolled in Public School

(Universe: Population Age 3–17 Enrolled in School)

Group	Number	%
Total Population	22,862	85.4
Hispanic or Latino (of any race)	5,906	89.4
Central American, ex. Mexican	373	91.2
Cuban	499	75.8
Dominican Republic	397	92.1
Mexican	439	100.0
Puerto Rican	1,132	85.6
South American	2,375	89.6
Argentinean	226	100.0
Colombian	1,130	86.0
Ecuadorian	207	94.5
Peruvian	377	85.1
Venezuelan	300	95.2

Population Age 3–17 Enrolled in Private School

(Universe: Population Age 3–17 Enrolled in School)

Group	Number	%
Total Population	3,922	14.6
Hispanic or Latino (of any race)	699	10.6
Central American, ex. Mexican	36	8.8
Cuban	159	24.2
Dominican Republic	34	7.9
Mexican	0	0.0
Puerto Rican	190	14.4
South American	277	10.4
Argentinean	0	0.0
Colombian	184	14.0
Ecuadorian	12	5.5
Peruvian	66	14.9
Venezuelan	15	4.8

Foreign-Born Population

Group	Number	%
Total Population	31,790	26.2
Hispanic or Latino (of any race)	13,345	48.8
Central American, ex. Mexican	1,160	59.8
Cuban	1,272	43.8
Dominican Republic	726	37.5
Mexican	1,122	50.9
Puerto Rican	44	0.8
South American	8,023	72.0
Argentinean	730	72.2
Colombian	3,798	71.7
Ecuadorian	657	60.5
Peruvian	1,592	78.1
Venezuelan	877	77.9

Foreign-Born Naturalized U.S. Citizens

Group	Number	%
Total Population	15,336	48.2
Hispanic or Latino (of any race)	5,579	41.8
Central American, ex. Mexican	569	49.1
Cuban	792	62.3
Dominican Republic	525	72.3
Mexican	395	35.2
Puerto Rican	37	84.1
South American	2,768	34.5
Argentinean	221	30.3
Colombian	1,284	33.8
Ecuadorian	175	26.6
Peruvian	635	39.9
Venezuelan	296	33.8

Language Spoken at Home: English Only

(Universe: Population 5 Years and Over)

Group	Number	%
Total Population	77,565	67.8
Hispanic or Latino (of any race)	4,424	17.4
Central American, ex. Mexican	166	9.2
Cuban	747	27.4
Dominican Republic	373	20.8
Mexican	541	26.6
Puerto Rican	1,394	28.8
South American	858	8.2
Argentinean	190	18.8
Colombian	277	5.5
Ecuadorian	64	7.1
Peruvian	160	8.1
Venezuelan	132	12.0

Language Spoken at Home: Spanish

(Universe: Population 5 Years and Over)

Group	Number	%
Total Population	22,967	20.1
Hispanic or Latino (of any race)	20,723	81.4
Central American, ex. Mexican	1,620	90.2
Cuban	1,938	71.1
Dominican Republic	1,349	75.2
Mexican	1,491	73.4
Puerto Rican	3,454	71.2
South American	9,516	90.7
Argentinean	782	77.3
Colombian	4,749	94.5
Ecuadorian	810	90.4
Peruvian	1,788	90.9
Venezuelan	964	88.0

Unemployment Rate

(Universe: Population 16 Years and Over)

Group	%
Total Population	8.5
Hispanic or Latino (of any race)	8.4
Central American, ex. Mexican	9.0
Cuban	5.4
Dominican Republic	15.0
Mexican	7.6
Puerto Rican	10.0
South American	6.9
Argentinean	16.9
Colombian	4.3
Ecuadorian	12.2
Peruvian	7.3
Venezuelan	3.2

Class of Worker: Private Wage and Salary

(Universe: Civilian Employed Population 16 Years and Over)

Group	Number	%
Total Population	53,046	84.0
Hispanic or Latino (of any race)	11,668	86.1
Central American, ex. Mexican	839	87.9
Cuban	1,288	87.1
Dominican Republic	702	82.3
Mexican	1,089	91.3
Puerto Rican	2,152	85.2
South American	5,067	85.0
Argentinean	353	74.8
Colombian	2,501	86.5
Ecuadorian	393	84.2
Peruvian	1,065	89.9
Venezuelan	538	80.4

Class of Worker: Government

(Universe: Civilian Employed Population 16 Years and Over)

Group	Number	%
Total Population	7,194	11.4
Hispanic or Latino (of any race)	999	7.4
Central American, ex. Mexican	65	6.8
Cuban	153	10.4
Dominican Republic	71	8.3
Mexican	63	5.3
Puerto Rican	266	10.5
South American	342	5.7
Argentinean	25	5.3
Colombian	256	8.9
Ecuadorian	11	2.4
Peruvian	24	2.0
Venezuelan	9	1.3

Means of Transportation to Work: Car, Truck or Van

(Universe: Workers 16 Years and Over)

Group	Number	%
Total Population	56,081	90.6
Hispanic or Latino (of any race)	11,879	89.4
Central American, ex. Mexican	897	94.3
Cuban	1,347	91.8
Dominican Republic	812	95.2
Mexican	842	71.4
Puerto Rican	2,341	94.2
South American	5,139	89.0
Argentinean	400	84.7
Colombian	2,376	86.1
Ecuadorian	489	100.0
Peruvian	1,011	88.6
Venezuelan	638	97.7

Means of Transportation to Work: Public Transportation (ex. Taxicab)

(Universe: Workers 16 Years and Over)

Group	Number	%
Total Population	942	1.5
Hispanic or Latino (of any race)	213	1.6

Notes: (1) Percent of total population; (2) Percent of Hispanic/Latino population; Profiles include places with an overall population of at least 125,000, OR an overall population of at least 25,000 where the Hispanic/Latino population is at least 20% of the overall population. In states where less than five places meet either of these criteria, we have included places with at least 10,000 total population with the highest percentage of Hispanic/Latino population. These places are identified with an asterisk (*); Please refer to the User's Guide for a full explanation of data.

Central American, ex. Mexican	15	1.6
Cuban	0	0.0
Dominican Republic	0	0.0
Mexican	59	5.0
Puerto Rican	34	1.4
South American	105	1.8
Argentinean	12	2.5
Colombian	62	2.2
Ecuadorian	0	0.0
Peruvian	31	2.7
Venezuelan	0	0.0

Homeownership Rate
(Universe: Occupied Housing Units)

Group	%
Total Population	65.3
Hispanic or Latino (of any race)	51.9
Central American, ex. Mexican	49.8
Costa Rican	61.4
Guatemalan	39.3
Honduran	48.3
Nicaraguan	47.6
Panamanian	54.6
Salvadoran	50.5
Cuban	65.5
Dominican Republic	46.7
Mexican	38.2
Puerto Rican	45.0
South American	54.3
Argentinean	58.8
Bolivian	66.7
Chilean	54.8
Colombian	54.6
Ecuadorian	58.2
Peruvian	48.5
Uruguayan	54.2
Venezuelan	53.7
Spaniard	73.4

Median Home Value

Group	Dollars
Total Population	346,700
Hispanic or Latino (of any race)	289,700
Central American, ex. Mexican	309,400
Cuban	362,600
Dominican Republic	242,500
Mexican	386,700
Puerto Rican	252,300
South American	269,900
Argentinean	292,100
Colombian	246,100
Ecuadorian	271,000
Peruvian	311,400
Venezuelan	231,500

Median Gross Rent

Group	Dollars
Total Population	1,275
Hispanic or Latino (of any race)	1,225
Central American, ex. Mexican	1,324
Cuban	1,378
Dominican Republic	1,308
Mexican	1,110
Puerto Rican	1,199
South American	1,223
Argentinean	1,192
Colombian	1,233
Ecuadorian	1,063
Peruvian	1,191
Venezuelan	1,434

Median Household Income
(2010 Inflation-Adjusted Dollars)

Group	Dollars
Total Population	71,456
Hispanic or Latino (of any race)	54,003
Central American, ex. Mexican	47,481
Cuban	77,500
Dominican Republic	44,704
Mexican	63,365
Puerto Rican	51,550
South American	52,245
Argentinean	59,224
Colombian	50,995
Ecuadorian	61,591
Peruvian	57,778
Venezuelan	46,765

Per Capita Income
(2010 Inflation-Adjusted Dollars)

Group	Dollars
Total Population	31,405
Hispanic or Latino (of any race)	20,659
Central American, ex. Mexican	17,648
Cuban	26,271
Dominican Republic	15,168
Mexican	23,685
Puerto Rican	22,395
South American	20,522
Argentinean	23,851
Colombian	20,940
Ecuadorian	19,454
Peruvian	19,068
Venezuelan	17,265

Households with $100,000+ Income

Group	Number	%
Total Population	13,395	32.7
Hispanic or Latino (of any race)	1,441	18.4
Central American, ex. Mexican	67	13.4
Cuban	239	33.5
Dominican Republic	68	15.2
Mexican	97	15.4
Puerto Rican	406	23.3
South American	527	16.1
Argentinean	60	17.0
Colombian	292	18.4
Ecuadorian	41	16.9
Peruvian	57	8.6
Venezuelan	39	12.9

Households with Food Stamps/SNAP Benefits During Past 12 Months

Group	Number	%
Total Population	2,458	6.0
Hispanic or Latino (of any race)	730	9.3
Central American, ex. Mexican	21	4.2
Cuban	27	3.8
Dominican Republic	60	13.4
Mexican	17	2.7
Puerto Rican	189	10.8
South American	348	10.7
Argentinean	86	24.4
Colombian	168	10.6
Ecuadorian	0	0.0
Peruvian	86	13.0
Venezuelan	8	2.6

Poverty Rate
(Income in Past 12 Months Below Poverty Level)

Group	%
Total Population	7.6
Hispanic or Latino (of any race)	10.9
Central American, ex. Mexican	13.8
Cuban	7.8
Dominican Republic	6.1
Mexican	15.4
Puerto Rican	13.3
South American	9.8
Argentinean	15.6
Colombian	8.8
Ecuadorian	22.4
Peruvian	4.7
Venezuelan	8.0

Country Club

Population

Group	Number	%TP[1]	%HP[2]
Total Population	47,105	100.0	–
Hispanic or Latino (of any race)	37,133	78.8	100.0
Central American, ex. Mexican	3,509	7.4	9.4
Costa Rican	206	0.4	0.6
Guatemalan	294	0.6	0.8
Honduran	748	1.6	2.0
Nicaraguan	1,772	3.8	4.8
Panamanian	249	0.5	0.7
Salvadoran	240	0.5	0.6
Cuban	15,509	32.9	41.8
Dominican Republic	2,999	6.4	8.1
Mexican	466	1.0	1.3
Puerto Rican	2,786	5.9	7.5
South American	10,161	21.6	27.4
Argentinean	366	0.8	1.0
Chilean	233	0.5	0.6
Colombian	6,439	13.7	17.3
Ecuadorian	768	1.6	2.1
Peruvian	1,033	2.2	2.8
Uruguayan	100	0.2	0.3
Venezuelan	1,161	2.5	3.1
Spaniard	137	0.3	0.4

Population Growth: 2000–2010

Group	%
Total Population	29.7
Hispanic or Latino (of any race)	69.5
Central American, ex. Mexican	151.0
Guatemalan	117.8
Honduran	241.6
Nicaraguan	202.9
Panamanian	3.8
Cuban	113.9
Dominican Republic	129.1
Mexican	20.4
Puerto Rican	29.5
South American	109.8
Argentinean	109.1
Chilean	68.8
Colombian	105.5
Ecuadorian	135.6
Peruvian	127.5
Venezuelan	154.6

Males per 100 Females

Group	Number
Total Population	86.6
Hispanic or Latino (of any race)	86.1
Central American, ex. Mexican	80.0
Costa Rican	54.9
Guatemalan	96.0
Honduran	74.4
Nicaraguan	81.9
Panamanian	77.9
Salvadoran	95.1
Cuban	90.8
Dominican Republic	82.5
Mexican	109.9
Puerto Rican	82.4
South American	80.7
Argentinean	110.3
Chilean	126.2
Colombian	78.3
Ecuadorian	79.0
Peruvian	81.5
Uruguayan	117.4
Venezuelan	75.6
Spaniard	107.6

Average Household Size

Group	People
Total Population	2.90
Hispanic or Latino (of any race)	3.00
Central American, ex. Mexican	3.24
Costa Rican	2.79
Guatemalan	3.02
Honduran	3.28
Nicaraguan	3.42
Panamanian	2.76
Salvadoran	3.26
Cuban	2.89
Dominican Republic	3.14
Mexican	3.28
Puerto Rican	2.92
South American	3.09
Argentinean	2.79
Chilean	3.09
Colombian	3.09
Ecuadorian	3.30
Peruvian	3.16
Uruguayan	2.62
Venezuelan	3.08
Spaniard	2.73

Notes: (1) Percent of total population; (2) Percent of Hispanic/Latino population; Profiles include places with an overall population of at least 125,000, OR an overall population of at least 25,000 where the Hispanic/Latino population is at least 20% of the overall population. In states where less than five places meet either of these criteria, we have included places with at least 10,000 total population with the highest percentage of Hispanic/Latino population. These places are identified with an asterisk (*); Please refer to the User's Guide for a full explanation of data.

Median Age

Group	Years
Total Population	33.7
Hispanic or Latino (of any race)	34.1
Central American, ex. Mexican	32.3
Costa Rican	35.5
Guatemalan	33.8
Honduran	30.1
Nicaraguan	31.0
Panamanian	39.0
Salvadoran	37.2
Cuban	36.4
Dominican Republic	30.9
Mexican	27.4
Puerto Rican	30.3
South American	35.8
Argentinean	34.1
Chilean	38.8
Colombian	35.8
Ecuadorian	35.8
Peruvian	39.0
Uruguayan	37.7
Venezuelan	33.6
Spaniard	38.3

High School Graduates
(Universe: Population 25 Years and Over)

Group	Number	%
Total Population	21,307	83.7
Hispanic or Latino (of any race)	16,078	81.3
Central American, ex. Mexican	1,470	71.2
Nicaraguan	771	70.5
Cuban	5,952	76.8
Dominican Republic	982	80.6
Puerto Rican	1,177	79.3
South American	5,808	89.7
Colombian	3,308	89.7
Ecuadorian	487	88.2
Venezuelan	891	85.8

Four-Year College Graduates
(Universe: Population 25 Years and Over)

Group	Number	%
Total Population	6,276	24.6
Hispanic or Latino (of any race)	4,278	21.6
Central American, ex. Mexican	304	14.7
Nicaraguan	122	11.2
Cuban	1,466	18.9
Dominican Republic	367	30.1
Puerto Rican	128	8.6
South American	1,847	28.5
Colombian	1,035	28.1
Ecuadorian	191	34.6
Venezuelan	337	32.4

Population Age 3–17 Enrolled in Public School
(Universe: Population Age 3–17 Enrolled in School)

Group	Number	%
Total Population	6,580	89.3
Hispanic or Latino (of any race)	5,035	90.1
Central American, ex. Mexican	469	92.0
Nicaraguan	273	95.5
Cuban	1,566	88.2
Dominican Republic	350	100.0
Puerto Rican	565	98.1
South American	1,645	89.1
Colombian	936	87.4
Ecuadorian	167	86.5
Venezuelan	307	100.0

Population Age 3–17 Enrolled in Private School
(Universe: Population Age 3–17 Enrolled in School)

Group	Number	%
Total Population	789	10.7
Hispanic or Latino (of any race)	555	9.9
Central American, ex. Mexican	41	8.0
Nicaraguan	13	4.5
Cuban	210	11.8
Dominican Republic	0	0.0
Puerto Rican	11	1.9
South American	201	10.9
Colombian	135	12.6
Ecuadorian	26	13.5
Venezuelan	0	0.0

Foreign-Born Population

Group	Number	%
Total Population	19,624	49.4
Hispanic or Latino (of any race)	17,182	56.0
Central American, ex. Mexican	2,013	63.4
Nicaraguan	1,194	71.6
Cuban	6,510	57.3
Dominican Republic	1,081	59.0
Puerto Rican	74	2.9
South American	6,729	67.3
Colombian	3,732	64.7
Ecuadorian	510	57.0
Venezuelan	1,224	76.7

Foreign-Born Naturalized U.S. Citizens

Group	Number	%
Total Population	8,733	44.5
Hispanic or Latino (of any race)	7,422	43.2
Central American, ex. Mexican	815	40.5
Nicaraguan	523	43.8
Cuban	3,547	54.5
Dominican Republic	589	54.5
Puerto Rican	48	64.9
South American	2,126	31.6
Colombian	1,173	31.4
Ecuadorian	378	74.1
Venezuelan	105	8.6

Language Spoken at Home: English Only
(Universe: Population 5 Years and Over)

Group	Number	%
Total Population	7,138	19.7
Hispanic or Latino (of any race)	1,327	4.7
Central American, ex. Mexican	130	4.4
Nicaraguan	44	2.7
Cuban	651	6.1
Dominican Republic	34	2.0
Puerto Rican	283	12.6
South American	181	2.0
Colombian	136	2.6
Ecuadorian	24	2.9
Venezuelan	8	0.5

Language Spoken at Home: Spanish
(Universe: Population 5 Years and Over)

Group	Number	%
Total Population	27,458	75.8
Hispanic or Latino (of any race)	26,690	95.0
Central American, ex. Mexican	2,856	95.6
Nicaraguan	1,585	97.3
Cuban	10,013	93.7
Dominican Republic	1,658	98.0
Puerto Rican	1,971	87.4
South American	8,922	97.8
Colombian	5,087	97.4
Ecuadorian	774	95.0
Venezuelan	1,487	99.5

Unemployment Rate
(Universe: Population 16 Years and Over)

Group	%
Total Population	6.4
Hispanic or Latino (of any race)	6.3
Central American, ex. Mexican	4.7
Nicaraguan	6.2
Cuban	5.7
Dominican Republic	10.0
Puerto Rican	0.6
South American	8.3
Colombian	8.6
Ecuadorian	17.0
Venezuelan	3.8

Class of Worker: Private Wage and Salary
(Universe: Civilian Employed Population 16 Years and Over)

Group	Number	%
Total Population	17,422	85.8
Hispanic or Latino (of any race)	14,446	89.3
Central American, ex. Mexican	1,724	92.3
Nicaraguan	922	93.8
Cuban	5,410	87.9
Dominican Republic	922	91.7
Puerto Rican	1,160	84.7
South American	4,649	90.4
Colombian	2,728	90.9
Ecuadorian	381	95.0
Venezuelan	839	90.1

Class of Worker: Government
(Universe: Civilian Employed Population 16 Years and Over)

Group	Number	%
Total Population	2,190	10.8
Hispanic or Latino (of any race)	1,242	7.7
Central American, ex. Mexican	88	4.7
Nicaraguan	25	2.5
Cuban	566	9.2
Dominican Republic	62	6.2
Puerto Rican	209	15.3
South American	281	5.5
Colombian	159	5.3
Ecuadorian	11	2.7
Venezuelan	21	2.3

Means of Transportation to Work: Car, Truck or Van
(Universe: Workers 16 Years and Over)

Group	Number	%
Total Population	19,223	95.6
Hispanic or Latino (of any race)	15,374	95.8
Central American, ex. Mexican	1,812	97.1
Nicaraguan	928	94.4
Cuban	5,913	97.1
Dominican Republic	975	96.9
Puerto Rican	1,225	91.8
South American	4,826	94.4
Colombian	2,782	93.2
Ecuadorian	387	96.5
Venezuelan	891	95.7

Means of Transportation to Work: Public Transportation (ex. Taxicab)
(Universe: Workers 16 Years and Over)

Group	Number	%
Total Population	314	1.6
Hispanic or Latino (of any race)	248	1.5
Central American, ex. Mexican	14	0.7
Nicaraguan	14	1.4
Cuban	77	1.3
Dominican Republic	22	2.2
Puerto Rican	55	4.1
South American	80	1.6
Colombian	35	1.2
Ecuadorian	14	3.5
Venezuelan	0	0.0

Homeownership Rate
(Universe: Occupied Housing Units)

Group	%
Total Population	51.8
Hispanic or Latino (of any race)	50.4
Central American, ex. Mexican	50.5
Costa Rican	50.7
Guatemalan	56.5
Honduran	47.7
Nicaraguan	49.2
Panamanian	48.1
Salvadoran	63.6
Cuban	54.8
Dominican Republic	39.9
Mexican	35.7
Puerto Rican	44.0
South American	48.3
Argentinean	51.4
Chilean	62.1
Colombian	47.9
Ecuadorian	49.1
Peruvian	50.6
Uruguayan	28.6
Venezuelan	45.2
Spaniard	67.8

Median Home Value

Group	Dollars
Total Population	228,500
Hispanic or Latino (of any race)	217,100
Central American, ex. Mexican	212,600
Nicaraguan	227,200
Cuban	221,400
Dominican Republic	219,900
Puerto Rican	215,600

STATE & PLACE PROFILES

Notes: (1) Percent of total population; (2) Percent of Hispanic/Latino population; Profiles include places with an overall population of at least 125,000, OR an overall population of at least 25,000 where the Hispanic/Latino population is at least 20% of the overall population. In states where less than five places meet either of these criteria, we have included places with at least 10,000 total population with the highest percentage of Hispanic/Latino population. These places are identified with an asterisk (*); Please refer to the User's Guide for a full explanation of data.

Group	
South American	211,600
Colombian	196,500
Ecuadorian	215,400
Venezuelan	224,400

Median Gross Rent

Group	Dollars
Total Population	1,095
Hispanic or Latino (of any race)	1,074
Central American, ex. Mexican	1,112
Nicaraguan	1,182
Cuban	1,062
Dominican Republic	926
Puerto Rican	1,056
South American	1,107
Colombian	1,162
Ecuadorian	1,003
Venezuelan	985

Median Household Income
(2010 Inflation-Adjusted Dollars)

Group	Dollars
Total Population	47,154
Hispanic or Latino (of any race)	45,330
Central American, ex. Mexican	46,717
Nicaraguan	65,093
Cuban	53,698
Dominican Republic	55,270
Puerto Rican	32,600
South American	39,906
Colombian	38,974
Ecuadorian	42,634
Venezuelan	35,588

Per Capita Income
(2010 Inflation-Adjusted Dollars)

Group	Dollars
Total Population	20,471
Hispanic or Latino (of any race)	19,676
Central American, ex. Mexican	19,255
Nicaraguan	19,145
Cuban	22,124
Dominican Republic	19,304
Puerto Rican	18,519
South American	17,719
Colombian	16,582
Ecuadorian	16,503
Venezuelan	19,850

Households with $100,000+ Income

Group	Number	%
Total Population	1,621	11.6
Hispanic or Latino (of any race)	1,065	9.9
Central American, ex. Mexican	71	6.6
Nicaraguan	38	8.0
Cuban	471	10.9
Dominican Republic	94	15.9
Puerto Rican	93	9.1
South American	257	7.7
Colombian	122	6.4
Ecuadorian	9	2.6
Venezuelan	56	11.6

Households with Food Stamps/SNAP Benefits During Past 12 Months

Group	Number	%
Total Population	1,863	13.3
Hispanic or Latino (of any race)	1,773	16.4
Central American, ex. Mexican	117	11.0
Nicaraguan	98	20.6
Cuban	679	15.7
Dominican Republic	89	15.1
Puerto Rican	179	17.6
South American	687	20.5
Colombian	365	19.1
Ecuadorian	67	19.6
Venezuelan	90	18.6

Poverty Rate
(Income in Past 12 Months Below Poverty Level)

Group	%
Total Population	13.5
Hispanic or Latino (of any race)	12.1
Central American, ex. Mexican	12.4
Nicaraguan	3.5
Cuban	9.5
Dominican Republic	14.1
Puerto Rican	21.3
South American	11.9
Colombian	17.4
Ecuadorian	4.6
Venezuelan	5.1

Cutler Bay

Population

Group	Number	%TP[1]	%HP[2]
Total Population	40,286	100.0	–
Hispanic or Latino (of any race)	21,936	54.5	100.0
Central American, ex. Mexican	2,566	6.4	11.7
Costa Rican	122	0.3	0.6
Guatemalan	199	0.5	0.9
Honduran	528	1.3	2.4
Nicaraguan	1,266	3.1	5.8
Panamanian	187	0.5	0.9
Salvadoran	258	0.6	1.2
Cuban	9,858	24.5	44.9
Dominican Republic	1,057	2.6	4.8
Mexican	732	1.8	3.3
Puerto Rican	2,669	6.6	12.2
South American	3,989	9.9	18.2
Argentinean	343	0.9	1.6
Chilean	194	0.5	0.9
Colombian	1,731	4.3	7.9
Ecuadorian	290	0.7	1.3
Peruvian	643	1.6	2.9
Venezuelan	597	1.5	2.7
Spaniard	176	0.4	0.8

Population Growth: 2000–2010

Group	%
Total Population	n/a

Males per 100 Females

Group	Number
Total Population	93.3
Hispanic or Latino (of any race)	91.0
Central American, ex. Mexican	84.3
Costa Rican	100.0
Guatemalan	93.2
Honduran	69.8
Nicaraguan	84.3
Panamanian	85.1
Salvadoran	108.1
Cuban	99.5
Dominican Republic	73.8
Mexican	96.8
Puerto Rican	89.0
South American	81.6
Argentinean	99.4
Chilean	90.2
Colombian	75.9
Ecuadorian	79.0
Peruvian	81.6
Venezuelan	82.0
Spaniard	91.3

Average Household Size

Group	People
Total Population	3.00
Hispanic or Latino (of any race)	3.20
Central American, ex. Mexican	3.71
Costa Rican	3.48
Guatemalan	3.51
Honduran	3.95
Nicaraguan	3.78
Panamanian	2.97
Salvadoran	3.79
Cuban	3.07
Dominican Republic	3.40
Mexican	3.52
Puerto Rican	3.13
South American	3.29
Argentinean	3.15
Chilean	3.39
Colombian	3.14
Ecuadorian	3.99
Peruvian	3.22
Venezuelan	3.48
Spaniard	2.62

Median Age

Group	Years
Total Population	36.3
Hispanic or Latino (of any race)	35.1
Central American, ex. Mexican	33.9
Costa Rican	32.0
Guatemalan	35.1
Honduran	32.7
Nicaraguan	33.0
Panamanian	41.8
Salvadoran	35.3
Cuban	37.4
Dominican Republic	32.6
Mexican	26.5
Puerto Rican	32.1
South American	36.2
Argentinean	36.8
Chilean	38.2
Colombian	36.4
Ecuadorian	38.3
Peruvian	37.7
Venezuelan	33.0
Spaniard	40.6

High School Graduates
(Universe: Population 25 Years and Over)

Group	Number	%
Total Population	21,150	88.1
Hispanic or Latino (of any race)	10,285	83.0
Central American, ex. Mexican	1,343	78.1
Cuban	4,590	80.7
Puerto Rican	1,390	89.3
South American	2,007	86.7
Colombian	932	79.2

Four-Year College Graduates
(Universe: Population 25 Years and Over)

Group	Number	%
Total Population	7,436	31.0
Hispanic or Latino (of any race)	3,373	27.2
Central American, ex. Mexican	244	14.2
Cuban	1,573	27.7
Puerto Rican	368	23.7
South American	698	30.1
Colombian	316	26.8

Population Age 3–17 Enrolled in Public School
(Universe: Population Age 3–17 Enrolled in School)

Group	Number	%
Total Population	7,385	83.5
Hispanic or Latino (of any race)	3,521	86.2
Central American, ex. Mexican	817	96.6
Cuban	1,318	84.9
Puerto Rican	206	73.6
South American	615	78.7
Colombian	319	83.1

Population Age 3–17 Enrolled in Private School
(Universe: Population Age 3–17 Enrolled in School)

Group	Number	%
Total Population	1,458	16.5
Hispanic or Latino (of any race)	562	13.8
Central American, ex. Mexican	29	3.4
Cuban	235	15.1
Puerto Rican	74	26.4
South American	166	21.3
Colombian	65	16.9

Foreign-Born Population

Group	Number	%
Total Population	12,790	33.3
Hispanic or Latino (of any race)	9,630	49.8
Central American, ex. Mexican	1,671	60.4
Cuban	4,787	58.1
Puerto Rican	0	0.0
South American	2,394	61.8
Colombian	1,329	62.1

Foreign-Born Naturalized U.S. Citizens

Group	Number	%
Total Population	7,082	55.4
Hispanic or Latino (of any race)	4,936	51.3

Notes: (1) Percent of total population; (2) Percent of Hispanic/Latino population; Profiles include places with an overall population of at least 125,000, OR an overall population of at least 25,000 where the Hispanic/Latino population is at least 20% of the overall population. In states where less than five places meet either of these criteria, we have included places with at least 10,000 total population with the highest percentage of Hispanic/Latino population. These places are identified with an asterisk (*); Please refer to the User's Guide for a full explanation of data.

Central American, ex. Mexican	948	56.7
Cuban	2,571	53.7
Puerto Rican	0	0.0
South American	957	40.0
Colombian	564	42.4

Language Spoken at Home: English Only
(Universe: Population 5 Years and Over)

Group	Number	%
Total Population	16,285	46.0
Hispanic or Latino (of any race)	1,749	9.9
Central American, ex. Mexican	144	5.7
Cuban	592	7.8
Puerto Rican	403	18.9
South American	299	8.6
Colombian	180	9.5

Language Spoken at Home: Spanish
(Universe: Population 5 Years and Over)

Group	Number	%
Total Population	17,308	48.9
Hispanic or Latino (of any race)	15,860	89.8
Central American, ex. Mexican	2,401	94.3
Cuban	6,957	92.2
Puerto Rican	1,728	81.1
South American	3,117	89.9
Colombian	1,705	90.5

Unemployment Rate
(Universe: Population 16 Years and Over)

Group	%
Total Population	7.4
Hispanic or Latino (of any race)	9.3
Central American, ex. Mexican	8.9
Cuban	6.6
Puerto Rican	12.2
South American	12.9
Colombian	17.4

Class of Worker: Private Wage and Salary
(Universe: Civilian Employed Population 16 Years and Over)

Group	Number	%
Total Population	13,748	77.0
Hispanic or Latino (of any race)	7,343	79.9
Central American, ex. Mexican	1,106	80.6
Cuban	3,101	78.2
Puerto Rican	918	75.6
South American	1,588	87.6
Colombian	788	84.6

Class of Worker: Government
(Universe: Civilian Employed Population 16 Years and Over)

Group	Number	%
Total Population	3,446	19.3
Hispanic or Latino (of any race)	1,510	16.4
Central American, ex. Mexican	171	12.5
Cuban	692	17.4
Puerto Rican	263	21.7
South American	200	11.0
Colombian	118	12.7

Means of Transportation to Work: Car, Truck or Van
(Universe: Workers 16 Years and Over)

Group	Number	%
Total Population	16,096	92.3
Hispanic or Latino (of any race)	8,442	93.2
Central American, ex. Mexican	1,273	95.1
Cuban	3,659	92.7
Puerto Rican	1,082	89.9
South American	1,662	94.0
Colombian	850	92.0

Means of Transportation to Work: Public Transportation (ex. Taxicab)
(Universe: Workers 16 Years and Over)

Group	Number	%
Total Population	562	3.2
Hispanic or Latino (of any race)	277	3.1
Central American, ex. Mexican	34	2.5
Cuban	94	2.4
Puerto Rican	60	5.0
South American	79	4.5
Colombian	47	5.1

Homeownership Rate
(Universe: Occupied Housing Units)

Group	%
Total Population	72.8
Hispanic or Latino (of any race)	67.8
Central American, ex. Mexican	72.8
Costa Rican	58.1
Guatemalan	81.1
Honduran	65.4
Nicaraguan	73.2
Panamanian	79.7
Salvadoran	77.6
Cuban	67.3
Dominican Republic	56.0
Mexican	67.4
Puerto Rican	65.1
South American	70.7
Argentinean	62.4
Chilean	76.8
Colombian	71.4
Ecuadorian	79.3
Peruvian	68.5
Venezuelan	70.1
Spaniard	77.9

Median Home Value

Group	Dollars
Total Population	270,500
Hispanic or Latino (of any race)	270,400
Central American, ex. Mexican	237,300
Cuban	284,400
Puerto Rican	275,900
South American	287,000
Colombian	293,900

Median Gross Rent

Group	Dollars
Total Population	1,333
Hispanic or Latino (of any race)	1,220
Central American, ex. Mexican	1,328
Cuban	388
Puerto Rican	1,260
South American	1,484
Colombian	1,295

Median Household Income
(2010 Inflation-Adjusted Dollars)

Group	Dollars
Total Population	61,370
Hispanic or Latino (of any race)	57,172
Central American, ex. Mexican	60,449
Cuban	54,864
Puerto Rican	56,625
South American	56,760
Colombian	55,884

Per Capita Income
(2010 Inflation-Adjusted Dollars)

Group	Dollars
Total Population	25,193
Hispanic or Latino (of any race)	22,875
Central American, ex. Mexican	19,487
Cuban	24,835
Puerto Rican	26,230
South American	19,589
Colombian	16,332

Households with $100,000+ Income

Group	Number	%
Total Population	3,271	26.4
Hispanic or Latino (of any race)	1,433	24.4
Central American, ex. Mexican	185	20.7
Cuban	717	26.4
Puerto Rican	135	19.6
South American	212	20.7
Colombian	118	24.2

Households with Food Stamps/SNAP Benefits During Past 12 Months

Group	Number	%
Total Population	1,443	11.7
Hispanic or Latino (of any race)	1,025	17.4
Central American, ex. Mexican	123	13.8
Cuban	653	24.0
Puerto Rican	68	9.9
South American	87	8.5
Colombian	59	12.1

Poverty Rate
(Income in Past 12 Months Below Poverty Level)

Group	%
Total Population	10.5
Hispanic or Latino (of any race)	12.4
Central American, ex. Mexican	16.2
Cuban	12.8
Puerto Rican	11.4
South American	5.6
Colombian	8.1

Dania Beach

Population

Group	Number	%TP[1]	%HP[2]
Total Population	29,639	100.0	–
Hispanic or Latino (of any race)	6,652	22.4	100.0
Central American, ex. Mexican	599	2.0	9.0
Honduran	163	0.5	2.5
Nicaraguan	133	0.4	2.0
Salvadoran	118	0.4	1.8
Cuban	1,160	3.9	17.4
Dominican Republic	422	1.4	6.3
Mexican	324	1.1	4.9
Puerto Rican	1,433	4.8	21.5
South American	2,135	7.2	32.1
Argentinean	266	0.9	4.0
Colombian	877	3.0	13.2
Ecuadorian	189	0.6	2.8
Peruvian	411	1.4	6.2
Venezuelan	255	0.9	3.8
Spaniard	135	0.5	2.0

Population Growth: 2000–2010

Group	%
Total Population	n/a

Males per 100 Females

Group	Number
Total Population	97.3
Hispanic or Latino (of any race)	92.0
Central American, ex. Mexican	93.9
Honduran	89.5
Nicaraguan	64.2
Salvadoran	100.0
Cuban	100.7
Dominican Republic	94.5
Mexican	102.5
Puerto Rican	95.5
South American	84.1
Argentinean	97.0
Colombian	84.6
Ecuadorian	71.8
Peruvian	81.9
Venezuelan	91.7
Spaniard	98.5

Average Household Size

Group	People
Total Population	2.28
Hispanic or Latino (of any race)	2.73
Central American, ex. Mexican	3.00
Honduran	2.98
Nicaraguan	3.02
Salvadoran	2.90
Cuban	2.54
Dominican Republic	2.87
Mexican	2.57
Puerto Rican	2.74
South American	2.85
Argentinean	2.83
Colombian	2.81
Ecuadorian	3.07
Peruvian	2.87
Venezuelan	2.88
Spaniard	2.36

Median Age

Group	Years
Total Population	41.0
Hispanic or Latino (of any race)	33.6

STATE & PLACE PROFILES

Notes: (1) Percent of total population; (2) Percent of Hispanic/Latino population; Profiles include places with an overall population of at least 125,000, OR an overall population of at least 25,000 where the Hispanic/Latino population is at least 20% of the overall population. In states where less than five places meet either of these criteria, we have included places with at least 10,000 total population with the highest percentage of Hispanic/Latino population. These places are identified with an asterisk (*); Please refer to the User's Guide for a full explanation of data.

Group	%
Central American, ex. Mexican	33.3
Honduran	33.1
Nicaraguan	31.2
Salvadoran	34.3
Cuban	38.4
Dominican Republic	30.3
Mexican	29.9
Puerto Rican	31.1
South American	35.6
Argentinean	36.7
Colombian	36.9
Ecuadorian	32.8
Peruvian	35.2
Venezuelan	33.1
Spaniard	38.5

High School Graduates
(Universe: Population 25 Years and Over)

Group	Number	%
Total Population	18,557	85.7
Hispanic or Latino (of any race)	3,929	83.6
Cuban	1,051	81.0
Puerto Rican	720	68.1
South American	1,621	92.9

Four-Year College Graduates
(Universe: Population 25 Years and Over)

Group	Number	%
Total Population	5,130	23.7
Hispanic or Latino (of any race)	1,063	22.6
Cuban	226	17.4
Puerto Rican	77	7.3
South American	593	34.0

Population Age 3–17 Enrolled in Public School
(Universe: Population Age 3–17 Enrolled in School)

Group	Number	%
Total Population	2,811	71.1
Hispanic or Latino (of any race)	860	73.7
Cuban	184	72.4
Puerto Rican	295	61.3
South American	247	82.9

Population Age 3–17 Enrolled in Private School
(Universe: Population Age 3–17 Enrolled in School)

Group	Number	%
Total Population	1,145	28.9
Hispanic or Latino (of any race)	307	26.3
Cuban	70	27.6
Puerto Rican	186	38.7
South American	51	17.1

Foreign-Born Population

Group	Number	%
Total Population	8,021	27.3
Hispanic or Latino (of any race)	3,430	50.4
Cuban	1,060	64.1
Puerto Rican	0	0.0
South American	1,897	80.9

Foreign-Born Naturalized U.S. Citizens

Group	Number	%
Total Population	3,776	47.1
Hispanic or Latino (of any race)	1,795	52.3
Cuban	770	72.6
Puerto Rican	0	0.0
South American	771	40.6

Language Spoken at Home: English Only
(Universe: Population 5 Years and Over)

Group	Number	%
Total Population	18,576	67.3
Hispanic or Latino (of any race)	1,165	18.5
Cuban	416	25.9
Puerto Rican	324	19.9
South American	269	12.3

Language Spoken at Home: Spanish
(Universe: Population 5 Years and Over)

Group	Number	%
Total Population	5,702	20.7
Hispanic or Latino (of any race)	5,007	79.5
Cuban	1,192	74.1
Puerto Rican	1,308	80.1
South American	1,782	81.7

Unemployment Rate
(Universe: Population 16 Years and Over)

Group	%
Total Population	9.0
Hispanic or Latino (of any race)	7.7
Cuban	10.9
Puerto Rican	14.4
South American	4.4

Class of Worker: Private Wage and Salary
(Universe: Civilian Employed Population 16 Years and Over)

Group	Number	%
Total Population	12,041	81.2
Hispanic or Latino (of any race)	3,143	84.9
Cuban	729	80.3
Puerto Rican	591	73.8
South American	1,320	94.3

Class of Worker: Government
(Universe: Civilian Employed Population 16 Years and Over)

Group	Number	%
Total Population	1,640	11.1
Hispanic or Latino (of any race)	224	6.1
Cuban	69	7.6
Puerto Rican	115	14.4
South American	0	0.0

Means of Transportation to Work: Car, Truck or Van
(Universe: Workers 16 Years and Over)

Group	Number	%
Total Population	12,742	88.2
Hispanic or Latino (of any race)	3,232	88.0
Cuban	738	82.7
Puerto Rican	735	91.8
South American	1,228	88.7

Means of Transportation to Work: Public Transportation (ex. Taxicab)
(Universe: Workers 16 Years and Over)

Group	Number	%
Total Population	426	2.9
Hispanic or Latino (of any race)	65	1.8
Cuban	20	2.2
Puerto Rican	0	0.0
South American	15	1.1

Homeownership Rate
(Universe: Occupied Housing Units)

Group	%
Total Population	55.7
Hispanic or Latino (of any race)	43.9
Central American, ex. Mexican	35.8
Honduran	40.8
Nicaraguan	37.5
Salvadoran	39.0
Cuban	51.5
Dominican Republic	34.5
Mexican	35.1
Puerto Rican	38.0
South American	46.0
Argentinean	50.5
Colombian	48.8
Ecuadorian	50.7
Peruvian	34.5
Venezuelan	48.9
Spaniard	65.6

Median Home Value

Group	Dollars
Total Population	207,100
Hispanic or Latino (of any race)	212,700
Cuban	238,500
Puerto Rican	172,600
South American	256,300

Median Gross Rent

Group	Dollars
Total Population	1,069
Hispanic or Latino (of any race)	1,111
Cuban	992
Puerto Rican	1,190
South American	1,151

Median Household Income
(2010 Inflation-Adjusted Dollars)

Group	Dollars
Total Population	44,569
Hispanic or Latino (of any race)	41,589
Cuban	39,375
Puerto Rican	46,193
South American	42,368

Per Capita Income
(2010 Inflation-Adjusted Dollars)

Group	Dollars
Total Population	24,739
Hispanic or Latino (of any race)	20,681
Cuban	25,212
Puerto Rican	14,085
South American	20,834

Households with $100,000+ Income

Group	Number	%
Total Population	1,587	12.4
Hispanic or Latino (of any race)	174	6.8
Cuban	93	13.1
Puerto Rican	14	2.5
South American	47	5.3

Households with Food Stamps/SNAP Benefits During Past 12 Months

Group	Number	%
Total Population	1,147	9.0
Hispanic or Latino (of any race)	370	14.6
Cuban	170	23.9
Puerto Rican	74	13.4
South American	54	6.1

Poverty Rate
(Income in Past 12 Months Below Poverty Level)

Group	%
Total Population	15.3
Hispanic or Latino (of any race)	18.6
Cuban	24.0
Puerto Rican	21.4
South American	15.9

Davie

Population

Group	Number	%TP[1]	%HP[2]
Total Population	91,992	100.0	–
Hispanic or Latino (of any race)	26,809	29.1	100.0
Central American, ex. Mexican	2,693	2.9	10.0
Costa Rican	203	0.2	0.8
Guatemalan	552	0.6	2.1
Honduran	612	0.7	2.3
Nicaraguan	542	0.6	2.0
Panamanian	231	0.3	0.9
Salvadoran	547	0.6	2.0
Cuban	6,071	6.6	22.6
Dominican Republic	1,479	1.6	5.5
Mexican	1,600	1.7	6.0
Puerto Rican	5,006	5.4	18.7
South American	8,321	9.0	31.0
Argentinean	566	0.6	2.1
Chilean	268	0.3	1.0
Colombian	3,715	4.0	13.9
Ecuadorian	774	0.8	2.9
Peruvian	1,533	1.7	5.7
Uruguayan	121	0.1	0.5
Venezuelan	1,231	1.3	4.6
Spaniard	328	0.4	1.2

Population Growth: 2000–2010

Group	%
Total Population	21.5
Hispanic or Latino (of any race)	87.9
Central American, ex. Mexican	209.2
Guatemalan	283.3
Honduran	305.3
Nicaraguan	185.3
Salvadoran	209.0
Cuban	85.4
Dominican Republic	235.4
Mexican	104.6

Notes: (1) Percent of total population; (2) Percent of Hispanic/Latino population; Profiles include places with an overall population of at least 125,000, OR an overall population of at least 25,000 where the Hispanic/Latino population is at least 20% of the overall population. In states where less than five places meet either of these criteria, we have included places with at least 10,000 total population with the highest percentage of Hispanic/Latino population. These places are identified with an asterisk (*); Please refer to the User's Guide for a full explanation of data.

Puerto Rican	52.4
South American	178.9
Argentinean	197.9
Chilean	129.1
Colombian	184.9
Ecuadorian	152.1
Peruvian	218.0
Venezuelan	216.5
Spaniard	228.0

Males per 100 Females

Group	Number
Total Population	94.0
Hispanic or Latino (of any race)	92.1
Central American, ex. Mexican	103.7
Costa Rican	105.1
Guatemalan	134.9
Honduran	98.1
Nicaraguan	86.3
Panamanian	77.7
Salvadoran	112.8
Cuban	99.6
Dominican Republic	75.4
Mexican	114.2
Puerto Rican	91.5
South American	82.1
Argentinean	110.4
Chilean	82.3
Colombian	77.6
Ecuadorian	76.3
Peruvian	82.9
Uruguayan	95.2
Venezuelan	86.0
Spaniard	113.0

Average Household Size

Group	People
Total Population	2.64
Hispanic or Latino (of any race)	3.10
Central American, ex. Mexican	3.39
Costa Rican	2.90
Guatemalan	3.57
Honduran	3.60
Nicaraguan	3.29
Panamanian	2.78
Salvadoran	3.63
Cuban	3.04
Dominican Republic	3.16
Mexican	3.54
Puerto Rican	2.94
South American	3.15
Argentinean	3.03
Chilean	3.06
Colombian	3.18
Ecuadorian	3.15
Peruvian	3.18
Uruguayan	3.17
Venezuelan	3.12
Spaniard	2.57

Median Age

Group	Years
Total Population	37.5
Hispanic or Latino (of any race)	32.3
Central American, ex. Mexican	31.2
Costa Rican	37.8
Guatemalan	30.0
Honduran	30.9
Nicaraguan	31.2
Panamanian	30.8
Salvadoran	30.8
Cuban	36.4
Dominican Republic	29.1
Mexican	27.3
Puerto Rican	30.1
South American	35.4
Argentinean	37.1
Chilean	39.0
Colombian	34.9
Ecuadorian	36.5
Peruvian	36.5
Uruguayan	37.3
Venezuelan	33.9
Spaniard	38.5

High School Graduates
(Universe: Population 25 Years and Over)

Group	Number	%
Total Population	53,206	89.7
Hispanic or Latino (of any race)	12,988	85.1
Central American, ex. Mexican	1,019	69.2
Cuban	2,797	87.5
Dominican Republic	1,081	92.6
Mexican	413	59.4
Puerto Rican	2,213	83.5
South American	4,816	91.1
Colombian	2,102	88.7
Peruvian	651	97.3
Venezuelan	783	98.4

Four-Year College Graduates
(Universe: Population 25 Years and Over)

Group	Number	%
Total Population	17,918	30.2
Hispanic or Latino (of any race)	3,417	22.4
Central American, ex. Mexican	192	13.0
Cuban	990	31.0
Dominican Republic	166	14.2
Mexican	67	9.6
Puerto Rican	373	14.1
South American	1,445	27.3
Colombian	579	24.4
Peruvian	160	23.9
Venezuelan	433	54.4

Population Age 3–17 Enrolled in Public School
(Universe: Population Age 3–17 Enrolled in School)

Group	Number	%
Total Population	13,923	78.6
Hispanic or Latino (of any race)	5,154	82.6
Central American, ex. Mexican	319	100.0
Cuban	1,126	77.1
Dominican Republic	530	86.0
Mexican	236	97.1
Puerto Rican	999	81.3
South American	1,646	82.8
Colombian	737	82.6
Peruvian	176	64.2
Venezuelan	322	91.0

Population Age 3–17 Enrolled in Private School
(Universe: Population Age 3–17 Enrolled in School)

Group	Number	%
Total Population	3,782	21.4
Hispanic or Latino (of any race)	1,088	17.4
Central American, ex. Mexican	0	0.0
Cuban	334	22.9
Dominican Republic	86	14.0
Mexican	7	2.9
Puerto Rican	230	18.7
South American	342	17.2
Colombian	155	17.4
Peruvian	98	35.8
Venezuelan	32	9.0

Foreign-Born Population

Group	Number	%
Total Population	21,857	24.1
Hispanic or Latino (of any race)	12,297	46.6
Central American, ex. Mexican	1,596	73.4
Cuban	2,376	42.1
Dominican Republic	1,166	56.1
Mexican	402	29.7
Puerto Rican	14	0.3
South American	6,270	70.8
Colombian	2,883	70.1
Peruvian	749	67.6
Venezuelan	1,176	82.6

Foreign-Born Naturalized U.S. Citizens

Group	Number	%
Total Population	11,756	53.8
Hispanic or Latino (of any race)	6,156	50.1
Central American, ex. Mexican	731	45.8
Cuban	1,650	69.4
Dominican Republic	817	70.1
Mexican	113	28.1
Puerto Rican	14	100.0
South American	2,619	41.8
Colombian	1,310	45.4

Peruvian	310	41.4
Venezuelan	253	21.5

Language Spoken at Home: English Only
(Universe: Population 5 Years and Over)

Group	Number	%
Total Population	56,284	65.9
Hispanic or Latino (of any race)	4,486	18.5
Central American, ex. Mexican	113	5.6
Cuban	1,230	24.1
Dominican Republic	321	16.6
Mexican	476	40.6
Puerto Rican	1,272	28.4
South American	413	5.0
Colombian	229	6.1
Peruvian	95	9.6
Venezuelan	24	1.7

Language Spoken at Home: Spanish
(Universe: Population 5 Years and Over)

Group	Number	%
Total Population	21,377	25.0
Hispanic or Latino (of any race)	19,644	80.9
Central American, ex. Mexican	1,913	94.4
Cuban	3,853	75.4
Dominican Republic	1,608	83.4
Mexican	696	59.4
Puerto Rican	3,186	71.0
South American	7,736	94.0
Colombian	3,512	93.1
Peruvian	863	87.0
Venezuelan	1,374	97.3

Unemployment Rate
(Universe: Population 16 Years and Over)

Group	%
Total Population	6.5
Hispanic or Latino (of any race)	7.4
Central American, ex. Mexican	4.7
Cuban	10.4
Dominican Republic	0.0
Mexican	4.0
Puerto Rican	8.5
South American	7.7
Colombian	11.4
Peruvian	8.2
Venezuelan	3.6

Class of Worker: Private Wage and Salary
(Universe: Civilian Employed Population 16 Years and Over)

Group	Number	%
Total Population	38,277	83.1
Hispanic or Latino (of any race)	11,238	87.3
Central American, ex. Mexican	1,118	94.7
Cuban	2,111	83.5
Dominican Republic	976	93.8
Mexican	688	94.9
Puerto Rican	1,817	83.3
South American	3,968	86.7
Colombian	1,625	84.6
Peruvian	492	91.6
Venezuelan	643	83.6

Class of Worker: Government
(Universe: Civilian Employed Population 16 Years and Over)

Group	Number	%
Total Population	5,872	12.8
Hispanic or Latino (of any race)	1,025	8.0
Central American, ex. Mexican	62	5.3
Cuban	344	13.6
Dominican Republic	52	5.0
Mexican	10	1.4
Puerto Rican	334	15.3
South American	168	3.7
Colombian	95	4.9
Peruvian	0	0.0
Venezuelan	22	2.9

Means of Transportation to Work: Car, Truck or Van
(Universe: Workers 16 Years and Over)

Group	Number	%
Total Population	40,917	90.9
Hispanic or Latino (of any race)	11,560	91.8
Central American, ex. Mexican	1,095	92.8

STATE & PLACE PROFILES

Notes: (1) Percent of total population; (2) Percent of Hispanic/Latino population; Profiles include places with an overall population of at least 125,000, OR an overall population of at least 25,000 where the Hispanic/Latino population is at least 20% of the overall population. In states where less than five places meet either of these criteria, we have included places with at least 10,000 total population with the highest percentage of Hispanic/Latino population. These places are identified with an asterisk (*); Please refer to the User's Guide for a full explanation of data.

Cuban	2,281	93.1
Dominican Republic	955	95.0
Mexican	688	94.9
Puerto Rican	1,947	92.1
South American	3,998	89.3
Colombian	1,771	94.1
Peruvian	496	94.8
Venezuelan	590	76.7

Means of Transportation to Work: Public Transportation (ex. Taxicab)
(Universe: Workers 16 Years and Over)

Group	Number	%
Total Population	644	1.4
Hispanic or Latino (of any race)	190	1.5
Central American, ex. Mexican	15	1.3
Cuban	6	0.2
Dominican Republic	35	3.5
Mexican	0	0.0
Puerto Rican	85	4.0
South American	49	1.1
Colombian	0	0.0
Peruvian	0	0.0
Venezuelan	9	1.2

Homeownership Rate
(Universe: Occupied Housing Units)

Group	%
Total Population	73.7
Hispanic or Latino (of any race)	64.4
Central American, ex. Mexican	52.3
Costa Rican	61.4
Guatemalan	55.3
Honduran	47.5
Nicaraguan	51.2
Panamanian	44.4
Salvadoran	57.0
Cuban	76.4
Dominican Republic	52.2
Mexican	51.6
Puerto Rican	58.8
South American	66.4
Argentinean	71.7
Chilean	72.9
Colombian	67.7
Ecuadorian	64.5
Peruvian	62.7
Uruguayan	63.0
Venezuelan	62.6
Spaniard	81.2

Median Home Value

Group	Dollars
Total Population	267,800
Hispanic or Latino (of any race)	235,500
Central American, ex. Mexican	118,200
Cuban	261,900
Dominican Republic	389,300
Mexican	191,700
Puerto Rican	200,800
South American	236,200
Colombian	243,800
Peruvian	179,200
Venezuelan	197,300

Median Gross Rent

Group	Dollars
Total Population	1,120
Hispanic or Latino (of any race)	1,109
Central American, ex. Mexican	902
Cuban	1,114
Dominican Republic	1,275
Mexican	1,071
Puerto Rican	1,156
South American	1,118
Colombian	1,215
Peruvian	1,005
Venezuelan	1,164

Median Household Income
(2010 Inflation-Adjusted Dollars)

Group	Dollars
Total Population	58,796
Hispanic or Latino (of any race)	53,983
Central American, ex. Mexican	52,054
Cuban	51,875
Dominican Republic	78,606
Mexican	37,439
Puerto Rican	51,685
South American	51,406
Colombian	53,425
Peruvian	33,500
Venezuelan	53,616

Per Capita Income
(2010 Inflation-Adjusted Dollars)

Group	Dollars
Total Population	30,981
Hispanic or Latino (of any race)	22,302
Central American, ex. Mexican	20,984
Cuban	25,120
Dominican Republic	21,155
Mexican	16,359
Puerto Rican	21,898
South American	21,334
Colombian	19,564
Peruvian	15,502
Venezuelan	22,790

Households with $100,000+ Income

Group	Number	%
Total Population	9,393	28.3
Hispanic or Latino (of any race)	1,803	23.4
Central American, ex. Mexican	100	14.9
Cuban	496	30.7
Dominican Republic	213	31.9
Mexican	24	8.8
Puerto Rican	389	25.7
South American	475	18.4
Colombian	144	12.1
Peruvian	17	5.4
Venezuelan	97	23.6

Households with Food Stamps/SNAP Benefits During Past 12 Months

Group	Number	%
Total Population	1,965	5.9
Hispanic or Latino (of any race)	630	8.2
Central American, ex. Mexican	42	6.3
Cuban	61	3.8
Dominican Republic	44	6.6
Mexican	50	18.4
Puerto Rican	108	7.1
South American	312	12.1
Colombian	126	10.6
Peruvian	0	0.0
Venezuelan	71	17.3

Poverty Rate
(Income in Past 12 Months Below Poverty Level)

Group	%
Total Population	10.8
Hispanic or Latino (of any race)	10.8
Central American, ex. Mexican	13.5
Cuban	12.1
Dominican Republic	5.9
Mexican	8.7
Puerto Rican	11.8
South American	11.4
Colombian	11.6
Peruvian	9.5
Venezuelan	18.8

Deltona

Population

Group	Number	%TP[1]	%HP[2]
Total Population	85,182	100.0	–
Hispanic or Latino (of any race)	25,734	30.2	100.0
Central American, ex. Mexican	1,173	1.4	4.6
Guatemalan	160	0.2	0.6
Honduran	267	0.3	1.0
Nicaraguan	150	0.2	0.6
Panamanian	213	0.3	0.8
Salvadoran	288	0.3	1.1
Cuban	1,548	1.8	6.0
Dominican Republic	1,240	1.5	4.8
Mexican	1,340	1.6	5.2
Puerto Rican	17,661	20.7	68.6
South American	1,755	2.1	6.8
Argentinean	128	0.2	0.5
Colombian	776	0.9	3.0
Ecuadorian	391	0.5	1.5
Peruvian	212	0.2	0.8
Venezuelan	119	0.1	0.5
Spaniard	134	0.2	0.5

Population Growth: 2000–2010

Group	%
Total Population	22.5
Hispanic or Latino (of any race)	101.9
Central American, ex. Mexican	212.0
Panamanian	110.9
Cuban	185.1
Dominican Republic	341.3
Mexican	145.4
Puerto Rican	93.3
South American	230.5
Colombian	218.0

Males per 100 Females

Group	Number
Total Population	95.0
Hispanic or Latino (of any race)	95.0
Central American, ex. Mexican	84.4
Guatemalan	113.3
Honduran	80.4
Nicaraguan	85.2
Panamanian	65.1
Salvadoran	98.6
Cuban	107.0
Dominican Republic	95.0
Mexican	100.3
Puerto Rican	96.0
South American	81.5
Argentinean	96.9
Colombian	76.0
Ecuadorian	85.3
Peruvian	82.8
Venezuelan	85.9
Spaniard	97.1

Average Household Size

Group	People
Total Population	2.81
Hispanic or Latino (of any race)	3.23
Central American, ex. Mexican	3.36
Guatemalan	3.98
Honduran	3.58
Nicaraguan	3.21
Panamanian	3.05
Salvadoran	3.27
Cuban	3.18
Dominican Republic	3.62
Mexican	3.77
Puerto Rican	3.19
South American	3.18
Argentinean	2.77
Colombian	3.09
Ecuadorian	3.45
Peruvian	3.31
Venezuelan	3.00
Spaniard	2.85

Median Age

Group	Years
Total Population	37.8
Hispanic or Latino (of any race)	32.7
Central American, ex. Mexican	33.2
Guatemalan	31.6
Honduran	31.4
Nicaraguan	30.0
Panamanian	36.9
Salvadoran	37.3
Cuban	35.5
Dominican Republic	31.6
Mexican	24.0
Puerto Rican	33.3
South American	38.0
Argentinean	36.2
Colombian	38.6
Ecuadorian	39.8
Peruvian	38.3
Venezuelan	34.1

Notes: (1) Percent of total population; (2) Percent of Hispanic/Latino population; Profiles include places with an overall population of at least 125,000, OR an overall population of at least 25,000 where the Hispanic/Latino population is at least 20% of the overall population. In states where less than five places meet either of these criteria, we have included places with at least 10,000 total population with the highest percentage of Hispanic/Latino population. These places are identified with an asterisk (*); Please refer to the User's Guide for a full explanation of data.

Group	Number	%
Spaniard		37.0

High School Graduates
(Universe: Population 25 Years and Over)

Group	Number	%
Total Population	47,366	84.7
Hispanic or Latino (of any race)	11,077	75.3
Central American, ex. Mexican	499	74.1
Cuban	893	65.5
Dominican Republic	425	53.1
Mexican	466	56.3
Puerto Rican	7,039	77.9
South American	1,129	90.2
Colombian	593	87.0

Four-Year College Graduates
(Universe: Population 25 Years and Over)

Group	Number	%
Total Population	7,929	14.2
Hispanic or Latino (of any race)	1,926	13.1
Central American, ex. Mexican	71	10.5
Cuban	98	7.2
Dominican Republic	132	16.5
Mexican	46	5.6
Puerto Rican	1,129	12.5
South American	280	22.4
Colombian	121	17.7

Population Age 3–17 Enrolled in Public School
(Universe: Population Age 3–17 Enrolled in School)

Group	Number	%
Total Population	15,173	91.1
Hispanic or Latino (of any race)	5,421	93.6
Central American, ex. Mexican	445	100.0
Cuban	187	78.2
Dominican Republic	142	91.6
Mexican	672	95.6
Puerto Rican	3,331	93.5
South American	433	100.0
Colombian	244	100.0

Population Age 3–17 Enrolled in Private School
(Universe: Population Age 3–17 Enrolled in School)

Group	Number	%
Total Population	1,481	8.9
Hispanic or Latino (of any race)	369	6.4
Central American, ex. Mexican	0	0.0
Cuban	52	21.8
Dominican Republic	13	8.4
Mexican	31	4.4
Puerto Rican	231	6.5
South American	0	0.0
Colombian	0	0.0

Foreign-Born Population

Group	Number	%
Total Population	7,724	9.2
Hispanic or Latino (of any race)	4,338	17.8
Central American, ex. Mexican	566	47.2
Cuban	1,259	56.6
Dominican Republic	613	56.7
Mexican	483	27.4
Puerto Rican	85	0.6
South American	1,035	53.7
Colombian	542	50.1

Foreign-Born Naturalized U.S. Citizens

Group	Number	%
Total Population	4,560	59.0
Hispanic or Latino (of any race)	2,423	55.9
Central American, ex. Mexican	258	45.6
Cuban	745	59.2
Dominican Republic	454	74.1
Mexican	213	44.1
Puerto Rican	80	94.1
South American	575	55.6
Colombian	323	59.6

Language Spoken at Home: English Only
(Universe: Population 5 Years and Over)

Group	Number	%
Total Population	60,012	75.8
Hispanic or Latino (of any race)	6,403	28.5
Central American, ex. Mexican	158	13.7
Cuban	444	22.0
Dominican Republic	243	23.2
Mexican	464	29.3
Puerto Rican	4,434	32.2
South American	393	21.1
Colombian	225	21.9

Language Spoken at Home: Spanish
(Universe: Population 5 Years and Over)

Group	Number	%
Total Population	16,757	21.2
Hispanic or Latino (of any race)	15,934	71.0
Central American, ex. Mexican	992	86.3
Cuban	1,573	78.0
Dominican Republic	784	74.8
Mexican	1,101	69.6
Puerto Rican	9,320	67.6
South American	1,467	78.9
Colombian	804	78.1

Unemployment Rate
(Universe: Population 16 Years and Over)

Group	%
Total Population	8.1
Hispanic or Latino (of any race)	8.9
Central American, ex. Mexican	6.4
Cuban	8.7
Dominican Republic	8.5
Mexican	7.6
Puerto Rican	10.2
South American	5.5
Colombian	5.7

Class of Worker: Private Wage and Salary
(Universe: Civilian Employed Population 16 Years and Over)

Group	Number	%
Total Population	31,835	82.3
Hispanic or Latino (of any race)	7,708	81.5
Central American, ex. Mexican	398	80.4
Cuban	516	76.0
Dominican Republic	277	68.1
Mexican	505	89.9
Puerto Rican	4,640	82.5
South American	899	75.5
Colombian	497	72.7

Class of Worker: Government
(Universe: Civilian Employed Population 16 Years and Over)

Group	Number	%
Total Population	4,649	12.0
Hispanic or Latino (of any race)	938	9.9
Central American, ex. Mexican	37	7.5
Cuban	106	15.6
Dominican Republic	0	0.0
Mexican	51	9.1
Puerto Rican	590	10.5
South American	140	11.8
Colombian	91	13.3

Means of Transportation to Work: Car, Truck or Van
(Universe: Workers 16 Years and Over)

Group	Number	%
Total Population	35,504	93.4
Hispanic or Latino (of any race)	8,689	93.6
Central American, ex. Mexican	449	90.7
Cuban	679	100.0
Dominican Republic	407	100.0
Mexican	548	97.5
Puerto Rican	5,057	91.4
South American	1,050	94.3
Colombian	608	95.0

Means of Transportation to Work: Public Transportation (ex. Taxicab)
(Universe: Workers 16 Years and Over)

Group	Number	%
Total Population	211	0.6
Hispanic or Latino (of any race)	79	0.9
Central American, ex. Mexican	0	0.0
Cuban	0	0.0
Dominican Republic	0	0.0
Mexican	0	0.0
Puerto Rican	79	1.4
South American	0	0.0
Colombian	0	0.0

Homeownership Rate
(Universe: Occupied Housing Units)

Group	%
Total Population	81.5
Hispanic or Latino (of any race)	76.6
Central American, ex. Mexican	78.9
Guatemalan	84.0
Honduran	74.0
Nicaraguan	78.6
Panamanian	78.1
Salvadoran	81.1
Cuban	76.3
Dominican Republic	76.0
Mexican	66.3
Puerto Rican	76.5
South American	81.3
Argentinean	83.3
Colombian	81.8
Ecuadorian	84.9
Peruvian	77.6
Venezuelan	75.0
Spaniard	86.5

Median Home Value

Group	Dollars
Total Population	178,500
Hispanic or Latino (of any race)	187,800
Central American, ex. Mexican	179,900
Cuban	214,900
Dominican Republic	231,100
Mexican	115,800
Puerto Rican	184,200
South American	174,000
Colombian	178,100

Median Gross Rent

Group	Dollars
Total Population	1,127
Hispanic or Latino (of any race)	1,104
Central American, ex. Mexican	–
Cuban	–
Dominican Republic	–
Mexican	1,027
Puerto Rican	1,091
South American	1,173
Colombian	–

Median Household Income
(2010 Inflation-Adjusted Dollars)

Group	Dollars
Total Population	50,058
Hispanic or Latino (of any race)	42,508
Central American, ex. Mexican	49,048
Cuban	31,947
Dominican Republic	53,636
Mexican	57,984
Puerto Rican	39,702
South American	49,167
Colombian	43,000

Per Capita Income
(2010 Inflation-Adjusted Dollars)

Group	Dollars
Total Population	21,019
Hispanic or Latino (of any race)	15,537
Central American, ex. Mexican	11,224
Cuban	13,507
Dominican Republic	28,326
Mexican	10,302
Puerto Rican	15,214
South American	21,874
Colombian	21,378

Households with $100,000+ Income

Group	Number	%
Total Population	3,531	12.0
Hispanic or Latino (of any race)	668	9.1
Central American, ex. Mexican	0	0.0
Cuban	60	8.4
Dominican Republic	113	30.2
Mexican	0	0.0
Puerto Rican	293	6.5
South American	109	14.8
Colombian	68	16.7

Notes: (1) Percent of total population; (2) Percent of Hispanic/Latino population; Profiles include places with an overall population of at least 125,000, OR an overall population of at least 25,000 where the Hispanic/Latino population is at least 20% of the overall population. In states where less than five places meet either of these criteria, we have included places with at least 10,000 total population with the highest percentage of Hispanic/Latino population. These places are identified with an asterisk (*); Please refer to the User's Guide for a full explanation of data.

Households with Food Stamps/SNAP Benefits During Past 12 Months

Group	Number	%
Total Population	2,406	8.2
Hispanic or Latino (of any race)	1,011	13.8
Central American, ex. Mexican	28	6.7
Cuban	140	19.5
Dominican Republic	69	18.4
Mexican	50	18.7
Puerto Rican	646	14.3
South American	51	6.9
Colombian	0	0.0

Poverty Rate
(Income in Past 12 Months Below Poverty Level)

Group	%
Total Population	11.1
Hispanic or Latino (of any race)	16.9
Central American, ex. Mexican	5.0
Cuban	21.8
Dominican Republic	20.5
Mexican	31.6
Puerto Rican	16.9
South American	8.7
Colombian	6.2

Doral

Population

Group	Number	%TP[1]	%HP[2]
Total Population	45,704	100.0	–
Hispanic or Latino (of any race)	36,344	79.5	100.0
Central American, ex. Mexican	2,402	5.3	6.6
Costa Rican	184	0.4	0.5
Guatemalan	263	0.6	0.7
Honduran	462	1.0	1.3
Nicaraguan	871	1.9	2.4
Panamanian	387	0.8	1.1
Salvadoran	234	0.5	0.6
Cuban	5,806	12.7	16.0
Dominican Republic	1,751	3.8	4.8
Mexican	1,152	2.5	3.2
Puerto Rican	2,238	4.9	6.2
South American	21,078	46.1	58.0
Argentinean	1,082	2.4	3.0
Bolivian	192	0.4	0.5
Chilean	622	1.4	1.7
Colombian	6,731	14.7	18.5
Ecuadorian	1,248	2.7	3.4
Peruvian	1,535	3.4	4.2
Uruguayan	180	0.4	0.5
Venezuelan	9,423	20.6	25.9
Spaniard	509	1.1	1.4

Population Growth: 2000–2010

Group	%
Total Population	123.6
Hispanic or Latino (of any race)	163.7
Central American, ex. Mexican	142.6
Guatemalan	102.3
Honduran	242.2
Nicaraguan	151.7
Panamanian	101.6
Cuban	86.9
Dominican Republic	224.3
Mexican	119.4
Puerto Rican	146.7
South American	322.5
Argentinean	313.0
Chilean	177.7
Colombian	278.1
Ecuadorian	417.8
Peruvian	155.0
Venezuelan	460.9
Spaniard	131.4

Males per 100 Females

Group	Number
Total Population	92.5
Hispanic or Latino (of any race)	88.8
Central American, ex. Mexican	83.9
Costa Rican	87.8
Guatemalan	89.2
Honduran	79.8
Nicaraguan	86.9
Panamanian	71.2
Salvadoran	95.0
Cuban	95.7
Dominican Republic	84.9
Mexican	99.7
Puerto Rican	93.3
South American	86.2
Argentinean	116.0
Bolivian	93.9
Chilean	101.9
Colombian	78.6
Ecuadorian	90.2
Peruvian	87.2
Uruguayan	127.8
Venezuelan	86.7
Spaniard	119.4

Average Household Size

Group	People
Total Population	3.00
Hispanic or Latino (of any race)	3.08
Central American, ex. Mexican	3.21
Costa Rican	2.96
Guatemalan	3.38
Honduran	3.26
Nicaraguan	3.34
Panamanian	2.99
Salvadoran	3.05
Cuban	2.74
Dominican Republic	3.36
Mexican	3.23
Puerto Rican	2.86
South American	3.18
Argentinean	3.26
Bolivian	3.29
Chilean	3.31
Colombian	3.16
Ecuadorian	3.54
Peruvian	3.20
Uruguayan	2.95
Venezuelan	3.14
Spaniard	2.94

Median Age

Group	Years
Total Population	34.0
Hispanic or Latino (of any race)	34.5
Central American, ex. Mexican	34.5
Costa Rican	33.0
Guatemalan	35.3
Honduran	29.9
Nicaraguan	34.6
Panamanian	38.1
Salvadoran	35.4
Cuban	38.9
Dominican Republic	33.1
Mexican	32.5
Puerto Rican	33.4
South American	34.4
Argentinean	36.4
Bolivian	32.8
Chilean	36.3
Colombian	34.5
Ecuadorian	34.0
Peruvian	37.5
Uruguayan	40.0
Venezuelan	33.3
Spaniard	39.7

High School Graduates
(Universe: Population 25 Years and Over)

Group	Number	%
Total Population	23,988	94.6
Hispanic or Latino (of any race)	18,632	95.0
Central American, ex. Mexican	1,044	94.9
Cuban	3,452	91.6
Dominican Republic	703	93.9
Mexican	595	92.8
Puerto Rican	1,714	91.2
South American	10,043	97.0
Argentinean	674	97.8
Colombian	3,088	97.0
Ecuadorian	802	97.9
Peruvian	581	100.0
Venezuelan	4,260	96.6

Four-Year College Graduates
(Universe: Population 25 Years and Over)

Group	Number	%
Total Population	14,064	55.4
Hispanic or Latino (of any race)	10,661	54.3
Central American, ex. Mexican	590	53.6
Cuban	1,440	38.2
Dominican Republic	394	52.6
Mexican	451	70.4
Puerto Rican	1,009	53.7
South American	6,088	58.8
Argentinean	446	64.7
Colombian	1,623	51.0
Ecuadorian	438	53.5
Peruvian	405	69.7
Venezuelan	2,797	63.4

Population Age 3–17 Enrolled in Public School
(Universe: Population Age 3–17 Enrolled in School)

Group	Number	%
Total Population	6,781	74.0
Hispanic or Latino (of any race)	5,292	76.4
Central American, ex. Mexican	195	78.6
Cuban	667	71.6
Dominican Republic	236	88.1
Mexican	225	79.2
Puerto Rican	527	69.9
South American	3,062	79.2
Argentinean	238	82.6
Colombian	866	76.0
Ecuadorian	321	96.7
Peruvian	131	69.3
Venezuelan	1,375	79.5

Population Age 3–17 Enrolled in Private School
(Universe: Population Age 3–17 Enrolled in School)

Group	Number	%
Total Population	2,381	26.0
Hispanic or Latino (of any race)	1,632	23.6
Central American, ex. Mexican	53	21.4
Cuban	264	28.4
Dominican Republic	32	11.9
Mexican	59	20.8
Puerto Rican	227	30.1
South American	806	20.8
Argentinean	50	17.4
Colombian	273	24.0
Ecuadorian	11	3.3
Peruvian	58	30.7
Venezuelan	355	20.5

Foreign-Born Population

Group	Number	%
Total Population	24,886	60.5
Hispanic or Latino (of any race)	20,133	63.7
Central American, ex. Mexican	1,200	68.3
Cuban	3,169	58.5
Dominican Republic	752	56.6
Mexican	798	72.0
Puerto Rican	20	0.7
South American	12,989	76.6
Argentinean	858	85.0
Colombian	3,818	75.0
Ecuadorian	1,247	85.5
Peruvian	656	72.3
Venezuelan	5,576	75.4

Foreign-Born Naturalized U.S. Citizens

Group	Number	%
Total Population	8,398	33.7
Hispanic or Latino (of any race)	6,839	34.0
Central American, ex. Mexican	670	55.8
Cuban	2,317	73.1
Dominican Republic	279	37.1
Mexican	136	17.0
Puerto Rican	20	100.0
South American	3,040	23.4
Argentinean	167	19.5
Colombian	1,203	31.5
Ecuadorian	316	25.3
Peruvian	170	25.9
Venezuelan	1,033	18.5

Notes: (1) Percent of total population; (2) Percent of Hispanic/Latino population; Profiles include places with an overall population of at least 125,000, OR an overall population of at least 25,000 where the Hispanic/Latino population is at least 20% of the overall population. In states where less than five places meet either of these criteria, we have included places with at least 10,000 total population with the highest percentage of Hispanic/Latino population. These places are identified with an asterisk (*); Please refer to the User's Guide for a full explanation of data.

Language Spoken at Home: English Only
(Universe: Population 5 Years and Over)

Group	Number	%
Total Population	4,134	11.2
Hispanic or Latino (of any race)	1,089	3.8
Central American, ex. Mexican	101	6.4
Cuban	364	7.2
Dominican Republic	0	0.0
Mexican	83	8.6
Puerto Rican	236	8.5
South American	196	1.3
Argentinean	12	1.2
Colombian	81	1.7
Ecuadorian	17	1.3
Peruvian	5	0.6
Venezuelan	40	0.6

Language Spoken at Home: Spanish
(Universe: Population 5 Years and Over)

Group	Number	%
Total Population	28,740	77.9
Hispanic or Latino (of any race)	27,392	95.8
Central American, ex. Mexican	1,461	92.8
Cuban	4,673	92.8
Dominican Republic	1,167	99.5
Mexican	877	91.4
Puerto Rican	2,554	91.5
South American	15,047	98.5
Argentinean	973	97.5
Colombian	4,643	98.3
Ecuadorian	1,313	98.7
Peruvian	768	97.1
Venezuelan	6,458	99.4

Unemployment Rate
(Universe: Population 16 Years and Over)

Group	%
Total Population	5.4
Hispanic or Latino (of any race)	6.2
Central American, ex. Mexican	2.5
Cuban	8.2
Dominican Republic	5.3
Mexican	9.9
Puerto Rican	6.4
South American	5.8
Argentinean	0.0
Colombian	6.4
Ecuadorian	3.8
Peruvian	0.9
Venezuelan	7.3

Class of Worker: Private Wage and Salary
(Universe: Civilian Employed Population 16 Years and Over)

Group	Number	%
Total Population	16,835	85.3
Hispanic or Latino (of any race)	13,308	85.2
Central American, ex. Mexican	864	83.1
Cuban	2,329	81.8
Dominican Republic	544	82.5
Mexican	355	81.1
Puerto Rican	1,204	82.6
South American	7,249	87.6
Argentinean	566	91.7
Colombian	2,452	89.5
Ecuadorian	575	90.0
Peruvian	397	94.7
Venezuelan	2,831	84.7

Class of Worker: Government
(Universe: Civilian Employed Population 16 Years and Over)

Group	Number	%
Total Population	1,668	8.5
Hispanic or Latino (of any race)	1,252	8.0
Central American, ex. Mexican	147	14.1
Cuban	363	12.8
Dominican Republic	68	10.3
Mexican	46	10.5
Puerto Rican	207	14.2
South American	367	4.4
Argentinean	18	2.9
Colombian	99	3.6
Ecuadorian	51	8.0
Peruvian	12	2.9
Venezuelan	165	4.9

Means of Transportation to Work: Car, Truck or Van
(Universe: Workers 16 Years and Over)

Group	Number	%
Total Population	18,022	92.8
Hispanic or Latino (of any race)	14,304	93.1
Central American, ex. Mexican	945	90.9
Cuban	2,786	99.6
Dominican Republic	622	94.4
Mexican	401	91.6
Puerto Rican	1,368	94.7
South American	7,396	90.9
Argentinean	549	94.3
Colombian	2,465	91.3
Ecuadorian	511	80.0
Peruvian	409	97.6
Venezuelan	2,995	91.1

Means of Transportation to Work: Public Transportation (ex. Taxicab)
(Universe: Workers 16 Years and Over)

Group	Number	%
Total Population	156	0.8
Hispanic or Latino (of any race)	129	0.8
Central American, ex. Mexican	67	6.4
Cuban	0	0.0
Dominican Republic	0	0.0
Mexican	13	3.0
Puerto Rican	0	0.0
South American	49	0.6
Argentinean	0	0.0
Colombian	49	1.8
Ecuadorian	0	0.0
Peruvian	0	0.0
Venezuelan	0	0.0

Homeownership Rate
(Universe: Occupied Housing Units)

Group	%
Total Population	55.1
Hispanic or Latino (of any race)	55.1
Central American, ex. Mexican	55.1
Costa Rican	57.4
Guatemalan	68.4
Honduran	46.7
Nicaraguan	52.3
Panamanian	58.0
Salvadoran	60.7
Cuban	64.0
Dominican Republic	51.4
Mexican	59.0
Puerto Rican	54.3
South American	51.8
Argentinean	57.8
Bolivian	42.9
Chilean	49.8
Colombian	48.9
Ecuadorian	54.4
Peruvian	50.7
Uruguayan	50.0
Venezuelan	53.3
Spaniard	77.0

Median Home Value

Group	Dollars
Total Population	361,500
Hispanic or Latino (of any race)	353,800
Central American, ex. Mexican	331,900
Cuban	367,900
Dominican Republic	214,100
Mexican	588,000
Puerto Rican	392,500
South American	342,700
Argentinean	357,200
Colombian	304,400
Ecuadorian	297,100
Peruvian	354,500
Venezuelan	373,600

Median Gross Rent

Group	Dollars
Total Population	1,672
Hispanic or Latino (of any race)	1,673
Central American, ex. Mexican	1,576
Cuban	1,508
Dominican Republic	1,607
Mexican	1,559
Puerto Rican	1,822
South American	1,689
Argentinean	2,000+
Colombian	1,531
Ecuadorian	1,395
Peruvian	1,814
Venezuelan	1,707

Median Household Income
(2010 Inflation-Adjusted Dollars)

Group	Dollars
Total Population	69,300
Hispanic or Latino (of any race)	67,233
Central American, ex. Mexican	63,438
Cuban	77,327
Dominican Republic	46,397
Mexican	88,333
Puerto Rican	83,977
South American	59,375
Argentinean	114,808
Colombian	51,476
Ecuadorian	57,768
Peruvian	86,111
Venezuelan	60,231

Per Capita Income
(2010 Inflation-Adjusted Dollars)

Group	Dollars
Total Population	30,048
Hispanic or Latino (of any race)	28,229
Central American, ex. Mexican	26,751
Cuban	35,721
Dominican Republic	20,530
Mexican	33,653
Puerto Rican	28,154
South American	27,011
Argentinean	51,818
Colombian	23,310
Ecuadorian	24,566
Peruvian	32,804
Venezuelan	25,258

Households with $100,000+ Income

Group	Number	%
Total Population	4,074	30.3
Hispanic or Latino (of any race)	2,949	28.5
Central American, ex. Mexican	181	28.1
Cuban	655	33.0
Dominican Republic	57	13.7
Mexican	152	44.4
Puerto Rican	338	32.7
South American	1,429	26.5
Argentinean	217	57.1
Colombian	314	17.9
Ecuadorian	139	39.4
Peruvian	104	31.9
Venezuelan	534	23.8

Households with Food Stamps/SNAP Benefits During Past 12 Months

Group	Number	%
Total Population	406	3.0
Hispanic or Latino (of any race)	352	3.4
Central American, ex. Mexican	11	1.7
Cuban	47	2.4
Dominican Republic	46	11.1
Mexican	12	3.5
Puerto Rican	93	9.0
South American	109	2.0
Argentinean	12	3.2
Colombian	39	2.2
Ecuadorian	15	4.2
Peruvian	0	0.0
Venezuelan	43	1.9

Poverty Rate
(Income in Past 12 Months Below Poverty Level)

Group	%
Total Population	9.8
Hispanic or Latino (of any race)	11.1
Central American, ex. Mexican	0.0
Cuban	12.9
Dominican Republic	1.1

Notes: (1) Percent of total population; (2) Percent of Hispanic/Latino population; Profiles include places with an overall population of at least 125,000, OR an overall population of at least 25,000 where the Hispanic/Latino population is at least 20% of the overall population. In states where less than five places meet either of these criteria, we have included places with at least 10,000 total population with the highest percentage of Hispanic/Latino population. These places are identified with an asterisk (*); Please refer to the User's Guide for a full explanation of data.

Mexican	5.0
Puerto Rican	8.8
South American	13.4
Argentinean	1.6
Colombian	10.4
Ecuadorian	28.3
Peruvian	3.6
Venezuelan	16.1

Egypt Lake-Leto

Population

Group	Number	%TP[1]	%HP[2]
Total Population	35,282	100.0	–
Hispanic or Latino (of any race)	21,157	60.0	100.0
Central American, ex. Mexican	943	2.7	4.5
Guatemalan	173	0.5	0.8
Honduran	335	0.9	1.6
Nicaraguan	115	0.3	0.5
Salvadoran	144	0.4	0.7
Cuban	9,697	27.5	45.8
Dominican Republic	1,042	3.0	4.9
Mexican	1,288	3.7	6.1
Puerto Rican	4,902	13.9	23.2
South American	1,910	5.4	9.0
Colombian	1,027	2.9	4.9
Ecuadorian	170	0.5	0.8
Peruvian	254	0.7	1.2
Venezuelan	236	0.7	1.1
Spaniard	401	1.1	1.9

Population Growth: 2000–2010

Group	%
Total Population	7.6
Hispanic or Latino (of any race)	40.9
Central American, ex. Mexican	115.8
Cuban	62.2
Dominican Republic	121.2
Mexican	101.6
Puerto Rican	37.7
South American	75.7
Colombian	68.9
Peruvian	98.4
Venezuelan	48.4
Spaniard	215.7

Males per 100 Females

Group	Number
Total Population	94.2
Hispanic or Latino (of any race)	94.8
Central American, ex. Mexican	98.1
Guatemalan	116.3
Honduran	105.5
Nicaraguan	94.9
Salvadoran	92.0
Cuban	97.0
Dominican Republic	80.6
Mexican	117.6
Puerto Rican	94.7
South American	78.5
Colombian	74.7
Ecuadorian	91.0
Peruvian	77.6
Venezuelan	81.5
Spaniard	77.4

Average Household Size

Group	People
Total Population	2.55
Hispanic or Latino (of any race)	2.94
Central American, ex. Mexican	3.24
Guatemalan	3.39
Honduran	3.40
Nicaraguan	3.38
Salvadoran	3.60
Cuban	3.02
Dominican Republic	3.35
Mexican	3.68
Puerto Rican	2.81
South American	2.75
Colombian	2.72
Ecuadorian	2.84
Peruvian	2.73
Venezuelan	2.86
Spaniard	2.15

Median Age

Group	Years
Total Population	34.9
Hispanic or Latino (of any race)	33.9
Central American, ex. Mexican	31.1
Guatemalan	31.8
Honduran	29.4
Nicaraguan	31.9
Salvadoran	32.0
Cuban	39.2
Dominican Republic	27.8
Mexican	24.7
Puerto Rican	28.9
South American	35.6
Colombian	36.1
Ecuadorian	39.3
Peruvian	35.4
Venezuelan	29.6
Spaniard	53.7

High School Graduates
(Universe: Population 25 Years and Over)

Group	Number	%
Total Population	18,862	80.4
Hispanic or Latino (of any race)	9,787	74.3
Cuban	4,548	74.0
Puerto Rican	2,417	74.3
South American	1,216	88.1
Colombian	671	94.8

Four-Year College Graduates
(Universe: Population 25 Years and Over)

Group	Number	%
Total Population	4,327	18.4
Hispanic or Latino (of any race)	2,087	15.9
Cuban	1,060	17.2
Puerto Rican	400	12.3
South American	260	18.8
Colombian	136	19.2

Population Age 3–17 Enrolled in Public School
(Universe: Population Age 3–17 Enrolled in School)

Group	Number	%
Total Population	5,223	92.6
Hispanic or Latino (of any race)	3,773	93.8
Cuban	1,200	91.2
Puerto Rican	1,529	98.6
South American	256	94.1
Colombian	123	100.0

Population Age 3–17 Enrolled in Private School
(Universe: Population Age 3–17 Enrolled in School)

Group	Number	%
Total Population	417	7.4
Hispanic or Latino (of any race)	251	6.2
Cuban	116	8.8
Puerto Rican	22	1.4
South American	16	5.9
Colombian	0	0.0

Foreign-Born Population

Group	Number	%
Total Population	12,140	34.7
Hispanic or Latino (of any race)	10,032	48.3
Cuban	6,472	75.8
Puerto Rican	247	4.1
South American	1,511	76.4
Colombian	753	78.2

Foreign-Born Naturalized U.S. Citizens

Group	Number	%
Total Population	5,128	42.2
Hispanic or Latino (of any race)	3,682	36.7
Cuban	2,416	37.3
Puerto Rican	112	45.3
South American	637	42.2
Colombian	306	40.6

Language Spoken at Home: English Only
(Universe: Population 5 Years and Over)

Group	Number	%
Total Population	13,567	41.5
Hispanic or Latino (of any race)	2,637	13.6
Cuban	897	10.9
Puerto Rican	972	17.4
South American	107	5.7
Colombian	38	4.2

Language Spoken at Home: Spanish
(Universe: Population 5 Years and Over)

Group	Number	%
Total Population	17,180	52.5
Hispanic or Latino (of any race)	16,655	86.0
Cuban	7,264	88.6
Puerto Rican	4,624	82.6
South American	1,767	94.3
Colombian	858	95.8

Unemployment Rate
(Universe: Population 16 Years and Over)

Group	%
Total Population	10.5
Hispanic or Latino (of any race)	10.4
Cuban	7.9
Puerto Rican	17.1
South American	9.8
Colombian	8.8

Class of Worker: Private Wage and Salary
(Universe: Civilian Employed Population 16 Years and Over)

Group	Number	%
Total Population	14,763	84.9
Hispanic or Latino (of any race)	8,273	85.8
Cuban	3,469	83.3
Puerto Rican	2,289	86.2
South American	894	94.1
Colombian	528	94.6

Class of Worker: Government
(Universe: Civilian Employed Population 16 Years and Over)

Group	Number	%
Total Population	1,967	11.3
Hispanic or Latino (of any race)	1,029	10.7
Cuban	538	12.9
Puerto Rican	347	13.1
South American	10	1.1
Colombian	0	0.0

Means of Transportation to Work: Car, Truck or Van
(Universe: Workers 16 Years and Over)

Group	Number	%
Total Population	15,614	92.1
Hispanic or Latino (of any race)	8,668	91.5
Cuban	3,719	91.9
Puerto Rican	2,368	89.0
South American	893	94.0
Colombian	509	91.2

Means of Transportation to Work: Public Transportation (ex. Taxicab)
(Universe: Workers 16 Years and Over)

Group	Number	%
Total Population	126	0.7
Hispanic or Latino (of any race)	63	0.7
Cuban	0	0.0
Puerto Rican	38	1.4
South American	0	0.0
Colombian	0	0.0

Homeownership Rate
(Universe: Occupied Housing Units)

Group	%
Total Population	44.9
Hispanic or Latino (of any race)	43.9
Central American, ex. Mexican	34.0
Guatemalan	46.3
Honduran	22.9
Nicaraguan	43.6
Salvadoran	39.5
Cuban	56.1
Dominican Republic	29.2
Mexican	24.8
Puerto Rican	26.0
South American	34.8
Colombian	35.0
Ecuadorian	57.4
Peruvian	26.7

Notes: (1) Percent of total population; (2) Percent of Hispanic/Latino population; Profiles include places with an overall population of at least 125,000, OR an overall population of at least 25,000 where the Hispanic/Latino population is at least 20% of the overall population. In states where less than five places meet either of these criteria, we have included places with at least 10,000 total population with the highest percentage of Hispanic/Latino population. These places are identified with an asterisk (*); Please refer to the User's Guide for a full explanation of data.

Venezuelan	29.7
Spaniard	82.0

Median Home Value

Group	Dollars
Total Population	160,100
Hispanic or Latino (of any race)	164,200
Cuban	168,600
Puerto Rican	143,600
South American	150,700
Colombian	169,500

Median Gross Rent

Group	Dollars
Total Population	854
Hispanic or Latino (of any race)	867
Cuban	867
Puerto Rican	894
South American	824
Colombian	791

Median Household Income
(2010 Inflation-Adjusted Dollars)

Group	Dollars
Total Population	37,822
Hispanic or Latino (of any race)	35,546
Cuban	40,482
Puerto Rican	35,207
South American	26,782
Colombian	28,458

Per Capita Income
(2010 Inflation-Adjusted Dollars)

Group	Dollars
Total Population	19,090
Hispanic or Latino (of any race)	15,516
Cuban	16,158
Puerto Rican	14,607
South American	15,558
Colombian	16,439

Households with $100,000+ Income

Group	Number	%
Total Population	996	7.3
Hispanic or Latino (of any race)	443	6.1
Cuban	224	7.6
Puerto Rican	113	5.7
South American	33	3.7
Colombian	24	6.1

Households with Food Stamps/SNAP Benefits During Past 12 Months

Group	Number	%
Total Population	1,688	12.4
Hispanic or Latino (of any race)	1,337	18.5
Cuban	539	18.3
Puerto Rican	399	20.1
South American	104	11.7
Colombian	15	3.8

Poverty Rate
(Income in Past 12 Months Below Poverty Level)

Group	%
Total Population	15.0
Hispanic or Latino (of any race)	16.7
Cuban	16.9
Puerto Rican	16.5
South American	13.4
Colombian	11.4

Fort Lauderdale

Population

Group	Number	%TP[1]	%HP[2]
Total Population	165,521	100.0	–
Hispanic or Latino (of any race)	22,752	13.7	100.0
Central American, ex. Mexican	4,424	2.7	19.4
Costa Rican	143	0.1	0.6
Guatemalan	1,413	0.9	6.2
Honduran	1,002	0.6	4.4
Nicaraguan	354	0.2	1.6
Panamanian	198	0.1	0.9
Salvadoran	1,284	0.8	5.6
Cuban	4,093	2.5	18.0
Dominican Republic	692	0.4	3.0
Mexican	2,742	1.7	12.1
Puerto Rican	3,821	2.3	16.8
South American	4,939	3.0	21.7
Argentinean	616	0.4	2.7
Chilean	180	0.1	0.8
Colombian	1,768	1.1	7.8
Ecuadorian	380	0.2	1.7
Peruvian	962	0.6	4.2
Uruguayan	218	0.1	1.0
Venezuelan	661	0.4	2.9
Spaniard	376	0.2	1.7

Population Growth: 2000–2010

Group	%
Total Population	8.6
Hispanic or Latino (of any race)	57.9
Central American, ex. Mexican	129.6
Guatemalan	196.2
Honduran	163.0
Nicaraguan	154.7
Salvadoran	90.5
Cuban	58.9
Dominican Republic	154.4
Mexican	95.3
Puerto Rican	36.4
South American	101.7
Argentinean	113.1
Colombian	78.9
Ecuadorian	204.0
Peruvian	102.1
Venezuelan	109.8
Spaniard	229.8

Males per 100 Females

Group	Number
Total Population	111.8
Hispanic or Latino (of any race)	113.9
Central American, ex. Mexican	130.4
Costa Rican	88.2
Guatemalan	179.8
Honduran	103.2
Nicaraguan	108.2
Panamanian	83.3
Salvadoran	131.8
Cuban	117.0
Dominican Republic	90.1
Mexican	133.8
Puerto Rican	118.0
South American	89.3
Argentinean	109.5
Chilean	106.9
Colombian	81.7
Ecuadorian	87.2
Peruvian	99.2
Uruguayan	83.2
Venezuelan	82.6
Spaniard	110.1

Average Household Size

Group	People
Total Population	2.17
Hispanic or Latino (of any race)	2.57
Central American, ex. Mexican	3.53
Costa Rican	2.34
Guatemalan	3.89
Honduran	3.50
Nicaraguan	2.79
Panamanian	2.27
Salvadoran	3.92
Cuban	2.42
Dominican Republic	2.64
Mexican	3.00
Puerto Rican	2.22
South American	2.29
Argentinean	2.27
Chilean	2.14
Colombian	2.26
Ecuadorian	2.28
Peruvian	2.39
Uruguayan	2.50
Venezuelan	2.24
Spaniard	2.03

Median Age

Group	Years
Total Population	42.2
Hispanic or Latino (of any race)	33.7
Central American, ex. Mexican	30.0
Costa Rican	34.4
Guatemalan	29.1
Honduran	30.7
Nicaraguan	30.2
Panamanian	39.0
Salvadoran	29.3
Cuban	41.3
Dominican Republic	30.7
Mexican	28.9
Puerto Rican	33.8
South American	38.0
Argentinean	39.5
Chilean	39.3
Colombian	37.0
Ecuadorian	39.3
Peruvian	39.0
Uruguayan	38.4
Venezuelan	35.9
Spaniard	45.8

High School Graduates
(Universe: Population 25 Years and Over)

Group	Number	%
Total Population	103,861	84.8
Hispanic or Latino (of any race)	11,657	76.1
Central American, ex. Mexican	1,076	52.0
Cuban	2,274	76.5
Mexican	965	56.0
Puerto Rican	2,533	83.7
South American	3,654	87.7
Colombian	1,343	84.9
Peruvian	740	96.9

Four-Year College Graduates
(Universe: Population 25 Years and Over)

Group	Number	%
Total Population	39,854	32.5
Hispanic or Latino (of any race)	3,753	24.5
Central American, ex. Mexican	243	11.7
Cuban	557	18.7
Mexican	269	15.6
Puerto Rican	841	27.8
South American	1,388	33.3
Colombian	448	28.3
Peruvian	342	44.8

Population Age 3–17 Enrolled in Public School
(Universe: Population Age 3–17 Enrolled in School)

Group	Number	%
Total Population	18,485	78.5
Hispanic or Latino (of any race)	2,233	77.4
Central American, ex. Mexican	228	84.4
Cuban	550	71.1
Mexican	433	96.4
Puerto Rican	238	64.7
South American	584	80.9
Colombian	313	69.4
Peruvian	87	100.0

Population Age 3–17 Enrolled in Private School
(Universe: Population Age 3–17 Enrolled in School)

Group	Number	%
Total Population	5,055	21.5
Hispanic or Latino (of any race)	651	22.6
Central American, ex. Mexican	42	15.6
Cuban	224	28.9
Mexican	16	3.6
Puerto Rican	130	35.3
South American	138	19.1
Colombian	138	30.6
Peruvian	0	0.0

Foreign-Born Population

Group	Number	%
Total Population	35,644	21.3
Hispanic or Latino (of any race)	11,186	52.4
Central American, ex. Mexican	2,347	77.8
Cuban	2,383	58.7
Mexican	1,246	48.6
Puerto Rican	139	3.5

Notes: (1) Percent of total population; (2) Percent of Hispanic/Latino population; Profiles include places with an overall population of at least 125,000, OR an overall population of at least 25,000 where the Hispanic/Latino population is at least 20% of the overall population. In states where less than five places meet either of these criteria, we have included places with at least 10,000 total population with the highest percentage of Hispanic/Latino population. These places are identified with an asterisk (*); Please refer to the User's Guide for a full explanation of data.

South American	4,243	74.9
Colombian	1,402	59.3
Peruvian	781	80.0

Foreign-Born Naturalized U.S. Citizens

Group	Number	%
Total Population	15,330	43.0
Hispanic or Latino (of any race)	4,077	36.4
Central American, ex. Mexican	356	15.2
Cuban	1,056	44.3
Mexican	319	25.6
Puerto Rican	59	42.4
South American	1,699	40.0
Colombian	768	54.8
Peruvian	309	39.6

Language Spoken at Home: English Only
(Universe: Population 5 Years and Over)

Group	Number	%
Total Population	118,341	74.9
Hispanic or Latino (of any race)	3,113	15.7
Central American, ex. Mexican	192	6.9
Cuban	611	15.9
Mexican	440	18.8
Puerto Rican	1,000	26.7
South American	517	9.8
Colombian	217	10.2
Peruvian	199	22.2

Language Spoken at Home: Spanish
(Universe: Population 5 Years and Over)

Group	Number	%
Total Population	18,945	12.0
Hispanic or Latino (of any race)	16,407	82.9
Central American, ex. Mexican	2,575	93.1
Cuban	3,226	84.1
Mexican	1,833	78.5
Puerto Rican	2,724	72.6
South American	4,708	89.3
Colombian	1,898	88.9
Peruvian	699	77.8

Unemployment Rate
(Universe: Population 16 Years and Over)

Group	%
Total Population	9.1
Hispanic or Latino (of any race)	7.8
Central American, ex. Mexican	13.6
Cuban	8.7
Mexican	3.8
Puerto Rican	6.1
South American	4.0
Colombian	7.5
Peruvian	0.0

Class of Worker: Private Wage and Salary
(Universe: Civilian Employed Population 16 Years and Over)

Group	Number	%
Total Population	68,373	82.0
Hispanic or Latino (of any race)	10,246	86.0
Central American, ex. Mexican	1,685	85.5
Cuban	1,658	87.4
Mexican	1,298	88.7
Puerto Rican	2,213	89.9
South American	2,602	80.9
Colombian	940	77.0
Peruvian	433	80.3

Class of Worker: Government
(Universe: Civilian Employed Population 16 Years and Over)

Group	Number	%
Total Population	9,130	10.9
Hispanic or Latino (of any race)	550	4.6
Central American, ex. Mexican	38	1.9
Cuban	147	7.7
Mexican	79	5.4
Puerto Rican	77	3.1
South American	139	4.3
Colombian	87	7.1
Peruvian	22	4.1

Means of Transportation to Work: Car, Truck or Van
(Universe: Workers 16 Years and Over)

Group	Number	%
Total Population	68,313	83.8
Hispanic or Latino (of any race)	9,810	83.4
Central American, ex. Mexican	1,634	82.9
Cuban	1,669	88.7
Mexican	1,282	88.4
Puerto Rican	1,987	81.7
South American	2,511	79.5
Colombian	1,041	86.0
Peruvian	419	82.6

Means of Transportation to Work: Public Transportation (ex. Taxicab)
(Universe: Workers 16 Years and Over)

Group	Number	%
Total Population	3,770	4.6
Hispanic or Latino (of any race)	465	4.0
Central American, ex. Mexican	74	3.8
Cuban	0	0.0
Mexican	114	7.9
Puerto Rican	128	5.3
South American	131	4.1
Colombian	37	3.1
Peruvian	0	0.0

Homeownership Rate
(Universe: Occupied Housing Units)

Group	%
Total Population	54.9
Hispanic or Latino (of any race)	40.5
Central American, ex. Mexican	31.7
Costa Rican	41.5
Guatemalan	25.4
Honduran	29.9
Nicaraguan	35.0
Panamanian	37.5
Salvadoran	35.7
Cuban	51.6
Dominican Republic	38.2
Mexican	34.3
Puerto Rican	31.9
South American	46.6
Argentinean	54.2
Chilean	44.3
Colombian	48.2
Ecuadorian	48.1
Peruvian	42.8
Uruguayan	44.2
Venezuelan	43.3
Spaniard	60.7

Median Home Value

Group	Dollars
Total Population	316,100
Hispanic or Latino (of any race)	249,400
Central American, ex. Mexican	260,300
Cuban	238,800
Mexican	111,100
Puerto Rican	258,700
South American	257,500
Colombian	233,500
Peruvian	241,700

Median Gross Rent

Group	Dollars
Total Population	1,009
Hispanic or Latino (of any race)	1,074
Central American, ex. Mexican	1,093
Cuban	940
Mexican	943
Puerto Rican	1,023
South American	1,243
Colombian	1,293
Peruvian	1,197

Median Household Income
(2010 Inflation-Adjusted Dollars)

Group	Dollars
Total Population	49,818
Hispanic or Latino (of any race)	48,000
Central American, ex. Mexican	52,813
Cuban	39,922
Mexican	52,975
Puerto Rican	44,566
South American	49,009
Colombian	43,177
Peruvian	41,928

Per Capita Income
(2010 Inflation-Adjusted Dollars)

Group	Dollars
Total Population	35,828
Hispanic or Latino (of any race)	25,767
Central American, ex. Mexican	24,010
Cuban	26,772
Mexican	26,699
Puerto Rican	30,903
South American	22,340
Colombian	17,519
Peruvian	20,499

Households with $100,000+ Income

Group	Number	%
Total Population	16,957	23.3
Hispanic or Latino (of any race)	1,181	15.7
Central American, ex. Mexican	168	20.9
Cuban	228	14.3
Mexican	95	12.3
Puerto Rican	272	18.3
South American	235	11.6
Colombian	31	3.8
Peruvian	17	5.0

Households with Food Stamps/SNAP Benefits During Past 12 Months

Group	Number	%
Total Population	6,867	9.4
Hispanic or Latino (of any race)	700	9.3
Central American, ex. Mexican	64	8.0
Cuban	219	13.7
Mexican	111	14.4
Puerto Rican	140	9.4
South American	122	6.0
Colombian	84	10.2
Peruvian	0	0.0

Poverty Rate
(Income in Past 12 Months Below Poverty Level)

Group	%
Total Population	18.2
Hispanic or Latino (of any race)	18.0
Central American, ex. Mexican	14.7
Cuban	18.2
Mexican	23.6
Puerto Rican	10.1
South American	22.8
Colombian	37.4
Peruvian	11.8

Fort Pierce

Population

Group	Number	%TP[1]	%HP[2]
Total Population	41,590	100.0	–
Hispanic or Latino (of any race)	9,004	21.6	100.0
Central American, ex. Mexican	963	2.3	10.7
Guatemalan	444	1.1	4.9
Honduran	335	0.8	3.7
Salvadoran	131	0.3	1.5
Cuban	233	0.6	2.6
Mexican	6,431	15.5	71.4
Puerto Rican	670	1.6	7.4
South American	216	0.5	2.4

Population Growth: 2000–2010

Group	%
Total Population	10.9
Hispanic or Latino (of any race)	60.0
Central American, ex. Mexican	360.8
Cuban	79.2
Mexican	49.2
Puerto Rican	83.1

Males per 100 Females

Group	Number
Total Population	97.3

Notes: (1) Percent of total population; (2) Percent of Hispanic/Latino population; Profiles include places with an overall population of at least 125,000, OR an overall population of at least 25,000 where the Hispanic/Latino population is at least 20% of the overall population. In states where less than five places meet either of these criteria, we have included places with at least 10,000 total population with the highest percentage of Hispanic/Latino population. These places are identified with an asterisk (*); Please refer to the User's Guide for a full explanation of data.

Group	Years
Hispanic or Latino (of any race)	127.4
Central American, ex. Mexican	165.3
Guatemalan	141.3
Honduran	235.0
Salvadoran	147.2
Cuban	147.9
Mexican	130.2
Puerto Rican	97.1
South American	81.5

Average Household Size

Group	People
Total Population	2.59
Hispanic or Latino (of any race)	3.94
Central American, ex. Mexican	4.41
Guatemalan	4.60
Honduran	4.38
Salvadoran	4.95
Cuban	2.55
Mexican	4.41
Puerto Rican	2.50
South American	2.41

Median Age

Group	Years
Total Population	35.7
Hispanic or Latino (of any race)	25.4
Central American, ex. Mexican	28.1
Guatemalan	27.8
Honduran	26.9
Salvadoran	30.4
Cuban	43.1
Mexican	24.1
Puerto Rican	29.2
South American	38.5

High School Graduates
(Universe: Population 25 Years and Over)

Group	Number	%
Total Population	18,146	67.6
Hispanic or Latino (of any race)	1,901	41.8
Mexican	1,056	32.7

Four-Year College Graduates
(Universe: Population 25 Years and Over)

Group	Number	%
Total Population	3,498	13.0
Hispanic or Latino (of any race)	365	8.0
Mexican	201	6.2

Population Age 3–17 Enrolled in Public School
(Universe: Population Age 3–17 Enrolled in School)

Group	Number	%
Total Population	7,884	96.4
Hispanic or Latino (of any race)	2,073	98.1
Mexican	1,811	98.5

Population Age 3–17 Enrolled in Private School
(Universe: Population Age 3–17 Enrolled in School)

Group	Number	%
Total Population	294	3.6
Hispanic or Latino (of any race)	40	1.9
Mexican	27	1.5

Foreign-Born Population

Group	Number	%
Total Population	8,353	19.7
Hispanic or Latino (of any race)	4,968	57.7
Mexican	4,031	60.4

Foreign-Born Naturalized U.S. Citizens

Group	Number	%
Total Population	1,508	18.1
Hispanic or Latino (of any race)	568	11.4
Mexican	388	9.6

Language Spoken at Home: English Only
(Universe: Population 5 Years and Over)

Group	Number	%
Total Population	29,317	74.9
Hispanic or Latino (of any race)	595	7.8
Mexican	392	6.8

Language Spoken at Home: Spanish
(Universe: Population 5 Years and Over)

Group	Number	%
Total Population	7,355	18.8
Hispanic or Latino (of any race)	6,995	92.2
Mexican	5,396	93.2

Unemployment Rate
(Universe: Population 16 Years and Over)

Group	%
Total Population	15.0
Hispanic or Latino (of any race)	13.3
Mexican	12.5

Class of Worker: Private Wage and Salary
(Universe: Civilian Employed Population 16 Years and Over)

Group	Number	%
Total Population	13,223	81.5
Hispanic or Latino (of any race)	3,266	94.2
Mexican	2,467	94.1

Class of Worker: Government
(Universe: Civilian Employed Population 16 Years and Over)

Group	Number	%
Total Population	2,187	13.5
Hispanic or Latino (of any race)	75	2.2
Mexican	55	2.1

Means of Transportation to Work: Car, Truck or Van
(Universe: Workers 16 Years and Over)

Group	Number	%
Total Population	14,717	94.7
Hispanic or Latino (of any race)	3,112	93.0
Mexican	2,427	94.7

Means of Transportation to Work: Public Transportation (ex. Taxicab)
(Universe: Workers 16 Years and Over)

Group	Number	%
Total Population	126	0.8
Hispanic or Latino (of any race)	83	2.5
Mexican	0	0.0

Homeownership Rate
(Universe: Occupied Housing Units)

Group	%
Total Population	48.3
Hispanic or Latino (of any race)	40.1
Central American, ex. Mexican	20.9
Guatemalan	21.5
Honduran	7.2
Salvadoran	37.8
Cuban	50.9
Mexican	45.7
Puerto Rican	25.5
South American	36.3

Median Home Value

Group	Dollars
Total Population	134,300
Hispanic or Latino (of any race)	117,700
Mexican	116,300

Median Gross Rent

Group	Dollars
Total Population	846
Hispanic or Latino (of any race)	915
Mexican	875

Median Household Income
(2010 Inflation-Adjusted Dollars)

Group	Dollars
Total Population	31,598
Hispanic or Latino (of any race)	32,190
Mexican	31,637

Per Capita Income
(2010 Inflation-Adjusted Dollars)

Group	Dollars
Total Population	16,961
Hispanic or Latino (of any race)	10,382
Mexican	8,763

Households with $100,000+ Income

Group	Number	%
Total Population	1,145	7.5
Hispanic or Latino (of any race)	74	3.9
Mexican	0	0.0

Households with Food Stamps/SNAP Benefits During Past 12 Months

Group	Number	%
Total Population	2,563	16.9
Hispanic or Latino (of any race)	233	12.3
Mexican	132	9.8

Poverty Rate
(Income in Past 12 Months Below Poverty Level)

Group	%
Total Population	28.1
Hispanic or Latino (of any race)	25.8
Mexican	27.5

Fountainebleau

Population

Group	Number	%TP[1]	%HP[2]
Total Population	59,764	100.0	–
Hispanic or Latino (of any race)	54,727	91.6	100.0
Central American, ex. Mexican	9,106	15.2	16.6
Costa Rican	255	0.4	0.5
Guatemalan	338	0.6	0.6
Honduran	1,117	1.9	2.0
Nicaraguan	6,738	11.3	12.3
Panamanian	272	0.5	0.5
Salvadoran	383	0.6	0.7
Cuban	27,798	46.5	50.8
Dominican Republic	2,063	3.5	3.8
Mexican	557	0.9	1.0
Puerto Rican	1,837	3.1	3.4
South American	11,183	18.7	20.4
Argentinean	780	1.3	1.4
Bolivian	215	0.4	0.4
Chilean	549	0.9	1.0
Colombian	4,714	7.9	8.6
Ecuadorian	914	1.5	1.7
Peruvian	1,408	2.4	2.6
Uruguayan	209	0.3	0.4
Venezuelan	2,334	3.9	4.3
Spaniard	276	0.5	0.5

Population Growth: 2000–2010

Group	%
Total Population	0.4
Hispanic or Latino (of any race)	5.3
Central American, ex. Mexican	24.0
Costa Rican	66.7
Guatemalan	43.8
Honduran	71.8
Nicaraguan	19.8
Panamanian	-7.2
Salvadoran	57.0
Cuban	25.2
Dominican Republic	16.0
Mexican	2.4
Puerto Rican	-8.8
South American	38.1
Argentinean	50.6
Bolivian	40.5
Chilean	-0.2
Colombian	49.5
Ecuadorian	62.1
Peruvian	34.9
Venezuelan	24.9
Spaniard	6.6

Males per 100 Females

Group	Number
Total Population	86.2
Hispanic or Latino (of any race)	84.1
Central American, ex. Mexican	81.7
Costa Rican	79.6
Guatemalan	79.8
Honduran	70.0
Nicaraguan	84.2
Panamanian	74.4

STATE & PLACE PROFILES

Notes: (1) Percent of total population; (2) Percent of Hispanic/Latino population; Profiles include places with an overall population of at least 125,000, OR an overall population of at least 25,000 where the Hispanic/Latino population is at least 20% of the overall population. In states where less than five places meet either of these criteria, we have included places with at least 10,000 total population with the highest percentage of Hispanic/Latino population. These places are identified with an asterisk (*); Please refer to the User's Guide for a full explanation of data.

Group	
Salvadoran	82.4
Cuban	86.6
Dominican Republic	73.2
Mexican	105.5
Puerto Rican	83.7
South American	79.4
Argentinean	105.3
Bolivian	70.6
Chilean	94.0
Colombian	72.2
Ecuadorian	82.8
Peruvian	85.0
Uruguayan	97.2
Venezuelan	79.7
Spaniard	89.0

Average Household Size

Group	People
Total Population	2.76
Hispanic or Latino (of any race)	2.79
Central American, ex. Mexican	3.46
Costa Rican	2.97
Guatemalan	3.09
Honduran	3.37
Nicaraguan	3.55
Panamanian	2.77
Salvadoran	3.55
Cuban	2.59
Dominican Republic	2.99
Mexican	2.72
Puerto Rican	2.51
South American	2.91
Argentinean	2.92
Bolivian	3.10
Chilean	2.88
Colombian	2.86
Ecuadorian	2.99
Peruvian	3.03
Uruguayan	3.19
Venezuelan	2.86
Spaniard	2.19

Median Age

Group	Years
Total Population	39.5
Hispanic or Latino (of any race)	40.8
Central American, ex. Mexican	37.0
Costa Rican	33.1
Guatemalan	37.1
Honduran	33.6
Nicaraguan	37.8
Panamanian	41.0
Salvadoran	35.4
Cuban	45.4
Dominican Republic	35.5
Mexican	31.5
Puerto Rican	35.3
South American	37.7
Argentinean	38.4
Bolivian	39.6
Chilean	45.0
Colombian	38.4
Ecuadorian	36.7
Peruvian	41.4
Uruguayan	37.3
Venezuelan	34.3
Spaniard	53.2

High School Graduates

(Universe: Population 25 Years and Over)

Group	Number	%
Total Population	34,119	80.3
Hispanic or Latino (of any race)	31,256	79.4
Central American, ex. Mexican	5,340	80.5
Nicaraguan	4,177	78.8
Cuban	13,979	73.0
Dominican Republic	1,227	78.9
Puerto Rican	1,197	86.9
South American	8,110	90.1
Colombian	3,361	85.9
Peruvian	987	91.4
Venezuelan	2,234	97.0

Four-Year College Graduates

(Universe: Population 25 Years and Over)

Group	Number	%
Total Population	11,780	27.7
Hispanic or Latino (of any race)	10,419	26.5
Central American, ex. Mexican	1,375	20.7
Nicaraguan	1,007	19.0
Cuban	5,164	27.0
Dominican Republic	429	27.6
Puerto Rican	269	19.5
South American	2,651	29.5
Colombian	903	23.1
Peruvian	406	37.6
Venezuelan	927	40.3

Population Age 3–17 Enrolled in Public School

(Universe: Population Age 3–17 Enrolled in School)

Group	Number	%
Total Population	7,048	89.1
Hispanic or Latino (of any race)	6,562	90.6
Central American, ex. Mexican	1,160	93.9
Nicaraguan	926	92.4
Cuban	2,471	90.0
Dominican Republic	152	84.9
Puerto Rican	473	100.0
South American	1,880	88.1
Colombian	688	85.7
Peruvian	272	91.3
Venezuelan	599	86.8

Population Age 3–17 Enrolled in Private School

(Universe: Population Age 3–17 Enrolled in School)

Group	Number	%
Total Population	864	10.9
Hispanic or Latino (of any race)	678	9.4
Central American, ex. Mexican	76	6.1
Nicaraguan	76	7.6
Cuban	276	10.0
Dominican Republic	27	15.1
Puerto Rican	0	0.0
South American	254	11.9
Colombian	115	14.3
Peruvian	26	8.7
Venezuelan	91	13.2

Foreign-Born Population

Group	Number	%
Total Population	43,714	74.1
Hispanic or Latino (of any race)	41,665	76.4
Central American, ex. Mexican	7,282	75.4
Nicaraguan	5,785	74.6
Cuban	19,915	81.1
Dominican Republic	1,891	84.6
Puerto Rican	39	1.8
South American	10,857	83.0
Colombian	4,644	81.7
Peruvian	1,224	83.2
Venezuelan	2,983	87.5

Foreign-Born Naturalized U.S. Citizens

Group	Number	%
Total Population	20,076	45.9
Hispanic or Latino (of any race)	19,378	46.5
Central American, ex. Mexican	3,474	47.7
Nicaraguan	2,623	45.3
Cuban	11,242	56.4
Dominican Republic	765	40.5
Puerto Rican	14	35.9
South American	3,141	28.9
Colombian	1,682	36.2
Peruvian	435	35.5
Venezuelan	484	16.2

Language Spoken at Home: English Only

(Universe: Population 5 Years and Over)

Group	Number	%
Total Population	2,399	4.3
Hispanic or Latino (of any race)	837	1.6
Central American, ex. Mexican	94	1.1
Nicaraguan	79	1.1
Cuban	357	1.5
Dominican Republic	31	1.4
Puerto Rican	21	1.1
South American	155	1.2
Colombian	77	1.4
Peruvian	0	0.0
Venezuelan	22	0.7

Language Spoken at Home: Spanish

(Universe: Population 5 Years and Over)

Group	Number	%
Total Population	51,832	92.9
Hispanic or Latino (of any race)	50,837	98.2
Central American, ex. Mexican	8,836	98.8
Nicaraguan	7,020	98.7
Cuban	23,229	98.2
Dominican Republic	2,151	98.6
Puerto Rican	1,957	98.9
South American	12,257	98.8
Colombian	5,327	98.6
Peruvian	1,417	100.0
Venezuelan	3,237	99.3

Unemployment Rate

(Universe: Population 16 Years and Over)

Group	%
Total Population	8.9
Hispanic or Latino (of any race)	9.1
Central American, ex. Mexican	10.2
Nicaraguan	9.2
Cuban	8.4
Dominican Republic	10.1
Puerto Rican	14.0
South American	8.5
Colombian	8.3
Peruvian	16.4
Venezuelan	2.4

Class of Worker: Private Wage and Salary

(Universe: Civilian Employed Population 16 Years and Over)

Group	Number	%
Total Population	25,481	85.3
Hispanic or Latino (of any race)	23,345	85.2
Central American, ex. Mexican	4,323	84.5
Nicaraguan	3,270	83.0
Cuban	10,316	84.7
Dominican Republic	1,163	89.9
Puerto Rican	764	76.0
South American	5,782	87.6
Colombian	2,393	82.8
Peruvian	570	83.5
Venezuelan	1,719	95.9

Class of Worker: Government

(Universe: Civilian Employed Population 16 Years and Over)

Group	Number	%
Total Population	2,379	8.0
Hispanic or Latino (of any race)	2,167	7.9
Central American, ex. Mexican	241	4.7
Nicaraguan	204	5.2
Cuban	1,182	9.7
Dominican Republic	52	4.0
Puerto Rican	227	22.6
South American	382	5.8
Colombian	272	9.4
Peruvian	41	6.0
Venezuelan	24	1.3

Means of Transportation to Work: Car, Truck or Van

(Universe: Workers 16 Years and Over)

Group	Number	%
Total Population	27,281	92.2
Hispanic or Latino (of any race)	24,974	92.0
Central American, ex. Mexican	4,447	88.2
Nicaraguan	3,409	87.0
Cuban	11,232	93.4
Dominican Republic	1,231	95.2
Puerto Rican	950	94.7
South American	5,984	91.2
Colombian	2,654	92.2
Peruvian	560	84.5
Venezuelan	1,656	92.6

Means of Transportation to Work: Public Transportation (ex. Taxicab)

(Universe: Workers 16 Years and Over)

Group	Number	%
Total Population	919	3.1
Hispanic or Latino (of any race)	849	3.1

Notes: (1) Percent of total population; (2) Percent of Hispanic/Latino population; Profiles include places with an overall population of at least 125,000, OR an overall population of at least 25,000 where the Hispanic/Latino population is at least 20% of the overall population. In states where less than five places meet either of these criteria, we have included places with at least 10,000 total population with the highest percentage of Hispanic/Latino population. These places are identified with an asterisk (*); Please refer to the User's Guide for a full explanation of data.

Central American, ex. Mexican	353	7.0
Nicaraguan	296	7.6
Cuban	242	2.0
Dominican Republic	22	1.7
Puerto Rican	21	2.1
South American	179	2.7
Colombian	77	2.7
Peruvian	43	6.5
Venezuelan	50	2.8

Homeownership Rate
(Universe: Occupied Housing Units)

Group	%
Total Population	54.8
Hispanic or Latino (of any race)	55.3
Central American, ex. Mexican	52.9
Costa Rican	40.5
Guatemalan	49.6
Honduran	48.3
Nicaraguan	53.9
Panamanian	55.0
Salvadoran	59.3
Cuban	58.7
Dominican Republic	49.0
Mexican	51.4
Puerto Rican	50.4
South American	48.7
Argentinean	44.2
Bolivian	65.4
Chilean	51.1
Colombian	48.4
Ecuadorian	50.5
Peruvian	53.5
Uruguayan	36.5
Venezuelan	45.9
Spaniard	79.3

Median Home Value

Group	Dollars
Total Population	195,500
Hispanic or Latino (of any race)	194,800
Central American, ex. Mexican	204,500
Nicaraguan	201,600
Cuban	188,700
Dominican Republic	217,900
Puerto Rican	192,200
South American	198,400
Colombian	199,500
Peruvian	227,100
Venezuelan	198,600

Median Gross Rent

Group	Dollars
Total Population	1,188
Hispanic or Latino (of any race)	1,182
Central American, ex. Mexican	1,257
Nicaraguan	1,254
Cuban	1,097
Dominican Republic	1,220
Puerto Rican	1,166
South American	1,263
Colombian	1,285
Peruvian	1,176
Venezuelan	1,308

Median Household Income
(2010 Inflation-Adjusted Dollars)

Group	Dollars
Total Population	42,127
Hispanic or Latino (of any race)	41,564
Central American, ex. Mexican	43,564
Nicaraguan	44,315
Cuban	38,102
Dominican Republic	43,000
Puerto Rican	42,297
South American	46,337
Colombian	45,795
Peruvian	34,618
Venezuelan	47,063

Per Capita Income
(2010 Inflation-Adjusted Dollars)

Group	Dollars
Total Population	18,418
Hispanic or Latino (of any race)	17,978
Central American, ex. Mexican	15,598
Nicaraguan	15,008
Cuban	19,560
Dominican Republic	19,099
Puerto Rican	19,884
South American	16,940
Colombian	16,578
Peruvian	15,183
Venezuelan	16,734

Households with $100,000+ Income

Group	Number	%
Total Population	1,893	9.1
Hispanic or Latino (of any race)	1,669	8.8
Central American, ex. Mexican	239	8.9
Nicaraguan	173	8.6
Cuban	839	8.5
Dominican Republic	80	10.7
Puerto Rican	135	19.5
South American	296	6.9
Colombian	124	6.7
Peruvian	90	18.9
Venezuelan	55	5.5

Households with Food Stamps/SNAP Benefits During Past 12 Months

Group	Number	%
Total Population	3,315	16.0
Hispanic or Latino (of any race)	3,177	16.7
Central American, ex. Mexican	447	16.6
Nicaraguan	429	21.4
Cuban	2,172	22.0
Dominican Republic	61	8.2
Puerto Rican	94	13.6
South American	283	6.6
Colombian	75	4.0
Peruvian	53	11.2
Venezuelan	43	4.3

Poverty Rate
(Income in Past 12 Months Below Poverty Level)

Group	%
Total Population	14.8
Hispanic or Latino (of any race)	14.9
Central American, ex. Mexican	8.6
Nicaraguan	8.9
Cuban	15.4
Dominican Republic	15.2
Puerto Rican	22.7
South American	16.7
Colombian	13.5
Peruvian	25.5
Venezuelan	13.1

Four Corners

Population

Group	Number	%TP[1]	%HP[2]
Total Population	26,116	100.0	–
Hispanic or Latino (of any race)	7,859	30.1	100.0
Central American, ex. Mexican	353	1.4	4.5
Cuban	438	1.7	5.6
Dominican Republic	490	1.9	6.2
Mexican	534	2.0	6.8
Puerto Rican	4,375	16.8	55.7
South American	1,230	4.7	15.7
Colombian	540	2.1	6.9
Ecuadorian	210	0.8	2.7
Peruvian	191	0.7	2.4
Venezuelan	176	0.7	2.2

Population Growth: 2000–2010

Group	%
Total Population	n/a

Males per 100 Females

Group	Number
Total Population	94.6
Hispanic or Latino (of any race)	90.8
Central American, ex. Mexican	91.8
Cuban	96.4
Dominican Republic	77.5
Mexican	97.0
Puerto Rican	92.0
South American	83.9
Colombian	85.6
Ecuadorian	78.0
Peruvian	89.1
Venezuelan	76.0

Average Household Size

Group	People
Total Population	2.64
Hispanic or Latino (of any race)	3.20
Central American, ex. Mexican	3.43
Cuban	3.01
Dominican Republic	3.65
Mexican	3.62
Puerto Rican	3.13
South American	3.28
Colombian	3.12
Ecuadorian	4.05
Peruvian	3.03
Venezuelan	3.24

Median Age

Group	Years
Total Population	36.7
Hispanic or Latino (of any race)	29.3
Central American, ex. Mexican	33.2
Cuban	34.3
Dominican Republic	27.4
Mexican	24.8
Puerto Rican	28.1
South American	36.8
Colombian	37.1
Ecuadorian	34.8
Peruvian	38.8
Venezuelan	36.0

High School Graduates
(Universe: Population 25 Years and Over)

Group	Number	%
Total Population	15,459	91.6
Hispanic or Latino (of any race)	3,692	88.8
Puerto Rican	1,798	89.5
South American	863	91.7

Four-Year College Graduates
(Universe: Population 25 Years and Over)

Group	Number	%
Total Population	3,913	23.2
Hispanic or Latino (of any race)	750	18.0
Puerto Rican	378	18.8
South American	198	21.0

Population Age 3–17 Enrolled in Public School
(Universe: Population Age 3–17 Enrolled in School)

Group	Number	%
Total Population	4,014	89.8
Hispanic or Latino (of any race)	1,719	95.2
Puerto Rican	718	96.9
South American	395	92.5

Population Age 3–17 Enrolled in Private School
(Universe: Population Age 3–17 Enrolled in School)

Group	Number	%
Total Population	458	10.2
Hispanic or Latino (of any race)	86	4.8
Puerto Rican	23	3.1
South American	32	7.5

Foreign-Born Population

Group	Number	%
Total Population	4,884	19.1
Hispanic or Latino (of any race)	2,094	27.4
Puerto Rican	0	0.0
South American	1,036	59.6

Foreign-Born Naturalized U.S. Citizens

Group	Number	%
Total Population	1,884	38.6
Hispanic or Latino (of any race)	826	39.4
Puerto Rican	0	0.0
South American	342	33.0

Language Spoken at Home: English Only
(Universe: Population 5 Years and Over)

Group	Number	%
Total Population	16,680	71.1

STATE & PLACE PROFILES

Notes: (1) Percent of total population; (2) Percent of Hispanic/Latino population; Profiles include places with an overall population of at least 125,000, OR an overall population of at least 25,000 where the Hispanic/Latino population is at least 20% of the overall population. In states where less than five places meet either of these criteria, we have included places with at least 10,000 total population with the highest percentage of Hispanic/Latino population. These places are identified with an asterisk (*); Please refer to the User's Guide for a full explanation of data.

Hispanic or Latino (of any race)	1,459	21.8
Puerto Rican	542	17.5
South American	305	20.7

Language Spoken at Home: Spanish
(Universe: Population 5 Years and Over)

Group	Number	%
Total Population	5,413	23.1
Hispanic or Latino (of any race)	5,140	77.0
Puerto Rican	2,548	82.5
South American	1,166	79.3

Unemployment Rate
(Universe: Population 16 Years and Over)

Group	%
Total Population	6.8
Hispanic or Latino (of any race)	8.0
Puerto Rican	8.9
South American	3.2

Class of Worker: Private Wage and Salary
(Universe: Civilian Employed Population 16 Years and Over)

Group	Number	%
Total Population	11,703	91.0
Hispanic or Latino (of any race)	3,348	92.7
Puerto Rican	1,571	94.4
South American	743	92.3

Class of Worker: Government
(Universe: Civilian Employed Population 16 Years and Over)

Group	Number	%
Total Population	702	5.5
Hispanic or Latino (of any race)	149	4.1
Puerto Rican	63	3.8
South American	10	1.2

Means of Transportation to Work: Car, Truck or Van
(Universe: Workers 16 Years and Over)

Group	Number	%
Total Population	11,741	94.1
Hispanic or Latino (of any race)	3,354	93.1
Puerto Rican	1,551	93.7
South American	744	92.4

Means of Transportation to Work: Public Transportation (ex. Taxicab)
(Universe: Workers 16 Years and Over)

Group	Number	%
Total Population	133	1.1
Hispanic or Latino (of any race)	0	0.0
Puerto Rican	0	0.0
South American	0	0.0

Homeownership Rate
(Universe: Occupied Housing Units)

Group	%
Total Population	58.7
Hispanic or Latino (of any race)	41.3
Central American, ex. Mexican	58.6
Cuban	54.2
Dominican Republic	41.1
Mexican	49.2
Puerto Rican	34.2
South American	52.6
Colombian	54.3
Ecuadorian	47.5
Peruvian	48.3
Venezuelan	60.3

Median Home Value

Group	Dollars
Total Population	186,300
Hispanic or Latino (of any race)	227,600
Puerto Rican	236,400
South American	221,700

Median Gross Rent

Group	Dollars
Total Population	988
Hispanic or Latino (of any race)	927
Puerto Rican	946
South American	736

Median Household Income
(2010 Inflation-Adjusted Dollars)

Group	Dollars
Total Population	49,108
Hispanic or Latino (of any race)	39,180
Puerto Rican	38,531
South American	33,893

Per Capita Income
(2010 Inflation-Adjusted Dollars)

Group	Dollars
Total Population	22,337
Hispanic or Latino (of any race)	13,946
Puerto Rican	13,451
South American	14,256

Households with $100,000+ Income

Group	Number	%
Total Population	1,077	11.1
Hispanic or Latino (of any race)	101	4.6
Puerto Rican	68	6.2
South American	33	7.9

Households with Food Stamps/SNAP Benefits During Past 12 Months

Group	Number	%
Total Population	690	7.1
Hispanic or Latino (of any race)	488	22.1
Puerto Rican	273	24.7
South American	116	27.9

Poverty Rate
(Income in Past 12 Months Below Poverty Level)

Group	%
Total Population	13.3
Hispanic or Latino (of any race)	26.5
Puerto Rican	28.5
South American	34.8

Greenacres

Population

Group	Number	%TP[1]	%HP[2]
Total Population	37,573	100.0	–
Hispanic or Latino (of any race)	14,390	38.3	100.0
Central American, ex. Mexican	2,244	6.0	15.6
Guatemalan	624	1.7	4.3
Honduran	836	2.2	5.8
Nicaraguan	294	0.8	2.0
Salvadoran	342	0.9	2.4
Cuban	1,593	4.2	11.1
Dominican Republic	757	2.0	5.3
Mexican	3,360	8.9	23.3
Puerto Rican	2,475	6.6	17.2
South American	3,241	8.6	22.5
Argentinean	246	0.7	1.7
Chilean	101	0.3	0.7
Colombian	1,707	4.5	11.9
Ecuadorian	271	0.7	1.9
Peruvian	435	1.2	3.0
Uruguayan	130	0.3	0.9
Venezuelan	266	0.7	1.8

Population Growth: 2000–2010

Group	%
Total Population	36.3
Hispanic or Latino (of any race)	145.6
Central American, ex. Mexican	334.0
Guatemalan	462.2
Honduran	364.4
Nicaraguan	162.5
Cuban	139.5
Dominican Republic	282.3
Mexican	133.5
Puerto Rican	111.7
South American	262.9
Colombian	270.3

Males per 100 Females

Group	Number
Total Population	90.6
Hispanic or Latino (of any race)	99.5
Central American, ex. Mexican	127.6
Guatemalan	197.1
Honduran	116.0
Nicaraguan	87.3
Salvadoran	128.0
Cuban	96.2
Dominican Republic	81.1
Mexican	118.8
Puerto Rican	92.0
South American	80.5
Argentinean	95.2
Chilean	90.6
Colombian	76.7
Ecuadorian	76.0
Peruvian	78.3
Uruguayan	116.7
Venezuelan	76.2

Average Household Size

Group	People
Total Population	2.61
Hispanic or Latino (of any race)	3.41
Central American, ex. Mexican	4.06
Guatemalan	4.47
Honduran	4.16
Nicaraguan	3.41
Salvadoran	4.17
Cuban	2.76
Dominican Republic	3.20
Mexican	4.33
Puerto Rican	3.04
South American	3.13
Argentinean	3.08
Chilean	3.25
Colombian	3.06
Ecuadorian	3.33
Peruvian	3.23
Uruguayan	3.05
Venezuelan	3.31

Median Age

Group	Years
Total Population	36.3
Hispanic or Latino (of any race)	29.5
Central American, ex. Mexican	29.4
Guatemalan	28.2
Honduran	29.2
Nicaraguan	33.7
Salvadoran	26.8
Cuban	37.5
Dominican Republic	31.9
Mexican	23.3
Puerto Rican	28.7
South American	35.7
Argentinean	35.6
Chilean	38.5
Colombian	36.2
Ecuadorian	37.1
Peruvian	37.0
Uruguayan	36.0
Venezuelan	32.0

High School Graduates
(Universe: Population 25 Years and Over)

Group	Number	%
Total Population	20,863	83.0
Hispanic or Latino (of any race)	6,097	71.2
Central American, ex. Mexican	735	44.4
Cuban	925	83.0
Mexican	673	63.0
Puerto Rican	950	70.3
South American	2,073	83.2
Colombian	932	87.6

Four-Year College Graduates
(Universe: Population 25 Years and Over)

Group	Number	%
Total Population	5,404	21.5
Hispanic or Latino (of any race)	1,427	16.7
Central American, ex. Mexican	181	10.9
Cuban	327	29.4
Mexican	32	3.0
Puerto Rican	154	11.4
South American	539	21.6
Colombian	275	25.8

Notes: (1) Percent of total population; (2) Percent of Hispanic/Latino population; Profiles include places with an overall population of at least 125,000, OR an overall population of at least 25,000 where the Hispanic/Latino population is at least 20% of the overall population. In states where less than five places meet either of these criteria, we have included places with at least 10,000 total population with the highest percentage of Hispanic/Latino population. These places are identified with an asterisk (*); Please refer to the User's Guide for a full explanation of data.

Population Age 3–17 Enrolled in Public School
(Universe: Population Age 3–17 Enrolled in School)

Group	Number	%
Total Population	5,446	89.2
Hispanic or Latino (of any race)	2,832	92.5
Central American, ex. Mexican	295	92.2
Cuban	152	100.0
Mexican	728	100.0
Puerto Rican	341	83.8
South American	871	87.7
Colombian	369	84.8

Population Age 3–17 Enrolled in Private School
(Universe: Population Age 3–17 Enrolled in School)

Group	Number	%
Total Population	659	10.8
Hispanic or Latino (of any race)	229	7.5
Central American, ex. Mexican	25	7.8
Cuban	0	0.0
Mexican	0	0.0
Puerto Rican	66	16.2
South American	122	12.3
Colombian	66	15.2

Foreign-Born Population

Group	Number	%
Total Population	12,585	34.7
Hispanic or Latino (of any race)	7,937	56.3
Central American, ex. Mexican	1,930	79.7
Cuban	974	62.7
Mexican	1,350	54.6
Puerto Rican	49	2.5
South American	2,777	69.2
Colombian	1,133	66.8

Foreign-Born Naturalized U.S. Citizens

Group	Number	%
Total Population	4,725	37.5
Hispanic or Latino (of any race)	2,315	29.2
Central American, ex. Mexican	394	20.4
Cuban	539	55.3
Mexican	321	23.8
Puerto Rican	24	49.0
South American	676	24.3
Colombian	376	33.2

Language Spoken at Home: English Only
(Universe: Population 5 Years and Over)

Group	Number	%
Total Population	18,644	55.1
Hispanic or Latino (of any race)	1,827	14.2
Central American, ex. Mexican	10	0.4
Cuban	354	24.9
Mexican	438	19.1
Puerto Rican	507	27.6
South American	361	10.2
Colombian	92	6.0

Language Spoken at Home: Spanish
(Universe: Population 5 Years and Over)

Group	Number	%
Total Population	11,235	33.2
Hispanic or Latino (of any race)	10,955	85.1
Central American, ex. Mexican	2,261	99.6
Cuban	1,066	75.1
Mexican	1,856	80.9
Puerto Rican	1,333	72.4
South American	3,153	89.0
Colombian	1,430	94.0

Unemployment Rate
(Universe: Population 16 Years and Over)

Group	%
Total Population	8.7
Hispanic or Latino (of any race)	9.3
Central American, ex. Mexican	12.4
Cuban	5.6
Mexican	8.3
Puerto Rican	1.4
South American	11.6
Colombian	8.3

Class of Worker: Private Wage and Salary
(Universe: Civilian Employed Population 16 Years and Over)

Group	Number	%
Total Population	14,829	82.3
Hispanic or Latino (of any race)	5,692	81.6
Central American, ex. Mexican	1,422	96.2
Cuban	494	63.7
Mexican	1,015	89.6
Puerto Rican	770	86.1
South American	1,350	72.0
Colombian	651	78.2

Class of Worker: Government
(Universe: Civilian Employed Population 16 Years and Over)

Group	Number	%
Total Population	2,001	11.1
Hispanic or Latino (of any race)	586	8.4
Central American, ex. Mexican	14	0.9
Cuban	174	22.5
Mexican	52	4.6
Puerto Rican	124	13.9
South American	169	9.0
Colombian	31	3.7

Means of Transportation to Work: Car, Truck or Van
(Universe: Workers 16 Years and Over)

Group	Number	%
Total Population	16,502	94.1
Hispanic or Latino (of any race)	6,287	91.7
Central American, ex. Mexican	1,343	93.4
Cuban	763	98.5
Mexican	1,008	89.0
Puerto Rican	825	92.3
South American	1,626	89.2
Colombian	735	91.9

Means of Transportation to Work: Public Transportation (ex. Taxicab)
(Universe: Workers 16 Years and Over)

Group	Number	%
Total Population	35	0.2
Hispanic or Latino (of any race)	18	0.3
Central American, ex. Mexican	5	0.3
Cuban	0	0.0
Mexican	13	1.1
Puerto Rican	0	0.0
South American	0	0.0
Colombian	0	0.0

Homeownership Rate
(Universe: Occupied Housing Units)

Group	%
Total Population	67.9
Hispanic or Latino (of any race)	55.1
Central American, ex. Mexican	50.2
Guatemalan	37.1
Honduran	47.0
Nicaraguan	63.2
Salvadoran	62.0
Cuban	65.5
Dominican Republic	63.7
Mexican	49.2
Puerto Rican	48.0
South American	58.6
Argentinean	47.7
Chilean	65.6
Colombian	61.0
Ecuadorian	66.7
Peruvian	55.7
Uruguayan	48.8
Venezuelan	50.7

Median Home Value

Group	Dollars
Total Population	175,600
Hispanic or Latino (of any race)	165,300
Central American, ex. Mexican	169,300
Cuban	165,300
Mexican	77,300
Puerto Rican	202,500
South American	150,800
Colombian	170,700

Median Gross Rent

Group	Dollars
Total Population	1,095
Hispanic or Latino (of any race)	1,115
Central American, ex. Mexican	1,246
Cuban	825
Mexican	791
Puerto Rican	1,114
South American	1,235
Colombian	1,275

Median Household Income
(2010 Inflation-Adjusted Dollars)

Group	Dollars
Total Population	43,722
Hispanic or Latino (of any race)	39,787
Central American, ex. Mexican	39,306
Cuban	48,528
Mexican	24,421
Puerto Rican	41,138
South American	38,895
Colombian	39,918

Per Capita Income
(2010 Inflation-Adjusted Dollars)

Group	Dollars
Total Population	22,591
Hispanic or Latino (of any race)	14,761
Central American, ex. Mexican	14,394
Cuban	22,364
Mexican	9,965
Puerto Rican	20,196
South American	12,512
Colombian	13,697

Households with $100,000+ Income

Group	Number	%
Total Population	1,644	11.5
Hispanic or Latino (of any race)	251	5.9
Central American, ex. Mexican	46	7.9
Cuban	80	11.0
Mexican	13	2.4
Puerto Rican	61	8.2
South American	42	3.7
Colombian	42	8.2

Households with Food Stamps/SNAP Benefits During Past 12 Months

Group	Number	%
Total Population	1,065	7.5
Hispanic or Latino (of any race)	531	12.5
Central American, ex. Mexican	36	6.2
Cuban	133	18.3
Mexican	58	10.5
Puerto Rican	111	14.9
South American	116	10.3
Colombian	65	12.7

Poverty Rate
(Income in Past 12 Months Below Poverty Level)

Group	%
Total Population	14.4
Hispanic or Latino (of any race)	22.4
Central American, ex. Mexican	26.8
Cuban	9.8
Mexican	34.7
Puerto Rican	13.4
South American	25.8
Colombian	24.3

Hallandale Beach

Population

Group	Number	%TP[1]	%HP[2]
Total Population	37,113	100.0	–
Hispanic or Latino (of any race)	11,809	31.8	100.0
Central American, ex. Mexican	1,171	3.2	9.9
Costa Rican	112	0.3	0.9
Guatemalan	122	0.3	1.0
Honduran	460	1.2	3.9
Nicaraguan	265	0.7	2.2
Salvadoran	120	0.3	1.0
Cuban	2,251	6.1	19.1

Notes: (1) Percent of total population; (2) Percent of Hispanic/Latino population; Profiles include places with an overall population of at least 125,000, OR an overall population of at least 25,000 where the Hispanic/Latino population is at least 20% of the overall population. In states where less than five places meet either of these criteria, we have included places with at least 10,000 total population with the highest percentage of Hispanic/Latino population. These places are identified with an asterisk (*); Please refer to the User's Guide for a full explanation of data.

Dominican Republic	583	1.6	4.9
Mexican	603	1.6	5.1
Puerto Rican	1,416	3.8	12.0
South American	4,912	13.2	41.6
Argentinean	724	2.0	6.1
Chilean	140	0.4	1.2
Colombian	1,874	5.0	15.9
Ecuadorian	346	0.9	2.9
Peruvian	1,053	2.8	8.9
Uruguayan	213	0.6	1.8
Venezuelan	500	1.3	4.2
Spaniard	126	0.3	1.1

Population Growth: 2000–2010

Group	%
Total Population	n/a

Males per 100 Females

Group	Number
Total Population	90.4
Hispanic or Latino (of any race)	90.7
Central American, ex. Mexican	94.2
Costa Rican	93.1
Guatemalan	117.9
Honduran	101.8
Nicaraguan	81.5
Salvadoran	110.5
Cuban	116.7
Dominican Republic	83.3
Mexican	120.9
Puerto Rican	94.8
South American	77.3
Argentinean	91.5
Chilean	100.0
Colombian	67.9
Ecuadorian	81.2
Peruvian	82.5
Uruguayan	88.5
Venezuelan	70.6
Spaniard	72.6

Average Household Size

Group	People
Total Population	2.02
Hispanic or Latino (of any race)	2.35
Central American, ex. Mexican	2.87
Costa Rican	2.65
Guatemalan	2.39
Honduran	3.40
Nicaraguan	2.73
Salvadoran	2.46
Cuban	2.09
Dominican Republic	2.54
Mexican	2.76
Puerto Rican	2.31
South American	2.38
Argentinean	2.25
Chilean	2.26
Colombian	2.28
Ecuadorian	2.55
Peruvian	2.60
Uruguayan	2.78
Venezuelan	2.36
Spaniard	2.05

Median Age

Group	Years
Total Population	46.7
Hispanic or Latino (of any race)	39.8
Central American, ex. Mexican	35.1
Costa Rican	35.2
Guatemalan	36.4
Honduran	33.9
Nicaraguan	33.6
Salvadoran	35.4
Cuban	48.8
Dominican Republic	36.2
Mexican	30.2
Puerto Rican	36.1
South American	40.3
Argentinean	39.7
Chilean	50.3
Colombian	40.3
Ecuadorian	41.3
Peruvian	41.6

Uruguayan	38.1
Venezuelan	38.1
Spaniard	54.0

High School Graduates
(Universe: Population 25 Years and Over)

Group	Number	%
Total Population	22,944	81.9
Hispanic or Latino (of any race)	6,329	79.6
Central American, ex. Mexican	768	72.0
Cuban	1,292	76.5
Puerto Rican	521	78.6
South American	2,895	86.4
Colombian	1,176	82.0

Four-Year College Graduates
(Universe: Population 25 Years and Over)

Group	Number	%
Total Population	7,034	25.1
Hispanic or Latino (of any race)	2,136	26.9
Central American, ex. Mexican	210	19.7
Cuban	245	14.5
Puerto Rican	139	21.0
South American	1,307	39.0
Colombian	380	26.5

Population Age 3–17 Enrolled in Public School
(Universe: Population Age 3–17 Enrolled in School)

Group	Number	%
Total Population	3,553	88.7
Hispanic or Latino (of any race)	1,334	89.7
Central American, ex. Mexican	288	100.0
Cuban	113	70.2
Puerto Rican	227	87.3
South American	403	91.2
Colombian	227	100.0

Population Age 3–17 Enrolled in Private School
(Universe: Population Age 3–17 Enrolled in School)

Group	Number	%
Total Population	453	11.3
Hispanic or Latino (of any race)	153	10.3
Central American, ex. Mexican	0	0.0
Cuban	48	29.8
Puerto Rican	33	12.7
South American	39	8.8
Colombian	0	0.0

Foreign-Born Population

Group	Number	%
Total Population	15,578	42.4
Hispanic or Latino (of any race)	7,824	71.0
Central American, ex. Mexican	1,442	82.2
Cuban	1,583	78.4
Puerto Rican	0	0.0
South American	3,863	91.0
Colombian	1,721	94.0

Foreign-Born Naturalized U.S. Citizens

Group	Number	%
Total Population	7,890	50.6
Hispanic or Latino (of any race)	3,504	44.8
Central American, ex. Mexican	397	27.5
Cuban	997	63.0
Puerto Rican	0	0.0
South American	1,657	42.9
Colombian	769	44.7

Language Spoken at Home: English Only
(Universe: Population 5 Years and Over)

Group	Number	%
Total Population	17,440	50.5
Hispanic or Latino (of any race)	662	6.5
Central American, ex. Mexican	6	0.4
Cuban	179	9.2
Puerto Rican	199	21.7
South American	80	2.0
Colombian	10	0.6

Language Spoken at Home: Spanish
(Universe: Population 5 Years and Over)

Group	Number	%
Total Population	10,711	31.0
Hispanic or Latino (of any race)	9,393	92.2
Central American, ex. Mexican	1,626	99.6
Cuban	1,743	89.2
Puerto Rican	719	78.3
South American	3,972	96.9
Colombian	1,802	99.4

Unemployment Rate
(Universe: Population 16 Years and Over)

Group	%
Total Population	10.8
Hispanic or Latino (of any race)	10.6
Central American, ex. Mexican	11.9
Cuban	12.6
Puerto Rican	10.8
South American	8.9
Colombian	2.2

Class of Worker: Private Wage and Salary
(Universe: Civilian Employed Population 16 Years and Over)

Group	Number	%
Total Population	13,138	84.2
Hispanic or Latino (of any race)	4,549	87.0
Central American, ex. Mexican	684	88.8
Cuban	879	92.2
Puerto Rican	351	85.4
South American	2,041	84.5
Colombian	867	85.0

Class of Worker: Government
(Universe: Civilian Employed Population 16 Years and Over)

Group	Number	%
Total Population	1,565	10.0
Hispanic or Latino (of any race)	330	6.3
Central American, ex. Mexican	44	5.7
Cuban	44	4.6
Puerto Rican	60	14.6
South American	125	5.2
Colombian	73	7.2

Means of Transportation to Work: Car, Truck or Van
(Universe: Workers 16 Years and Over)

Group	Number	%
Total Population	12,510	82.6
Hispanic or Latino (of any race)	4,124	79.4
Central American, ex. Mexican	476	61.8
Cuban	757	80.4
Puerto Rican	411	95.6
South American	1,862	77.9
Colombian	751	75.0

Means of Transportation to Work: Public Transportation (ex. Taxicab)
(Universe: Workers 16 Years and Over)

Group	Number	%
Total Population	985	6.5
Hispanic or Latino (of any race)	345	6.6
Central American, ex. Mexican	119	15.5
Cuban	59	6.3
Puerto Rican	0	0.0
South American	135	5.6
Colombian	86	8.6

Homeownership Rate
(Universe: Occupied Housing Units)

Group	%
Total Population	58.2
Hispanic or Latino (of any race)	48.9
Central American, ex. Mexican	34.3
Costa Rican	34.7
Guatemalan	35.3
Honduran	27.3
Nicaraguan	36.1
Salvadoran	32.6
Cuban	64.4
Dominican Republic	36.0
Mexican	30.9
Puerto Rican	39.8
South American	49.0
Argentinean	54.6
Chilean	63.0
Colombian	50.3
Ecuadorian	55.4
Peruvian	43.8
Uruguayan	35.6
Venezuelan	43.1
Spaniard	69.7

Notes: (1) Percent of total population; (2) Percent of Hispanic/Latino population; Profiles include places with an overall population of at least 125,000, OR an overall population of at least 25,000 where the Hispanic/Latino population is at least 20% of the overall population. In states where less than five places meet either of these criteria, we have included places with at least 10,000 total population with the highest percentage of Hispanic/Latino population. These places are identified with an asterisk (*); Please refer to the User's Guide for a full explanation of data.

Median Home Value

Group	Dollars
Total Population	189,200
Hispanic or Latino (of any race)	194,300
Central American, ex. Mexican	221,900
Cuban	241,400
Puerto Rican	190,900
South American	182,500
Colombian	157,500

Median Gross Rent

Group	Dollars
Total Population	991
Hispanic or Latino (of any race)	1,026
Central American, ex. Mexican	942
Cuban	866
Puerto Rican	1,153
South American	1,005
Colombian	998

Median Household Income
(2010 Inflation-Adjusted Dollars)

Group	Dollars
Total Population	34,953
Hispanic or Latino (of any race)	34,226
Central American, ex. Mexican	38,125
Cuban	28,864
Puerto Rican	32,972
South American	37,063
Colombian	33,409

Per Capita Income
(2010 Inflation-Adjusted Dollars)

Group	Dollars
Total Population	24,770
Hispanic or Latino (of any race)	17,454
Central American, ex. Mexican	12,780
Cuban	21,709
Puerto Rican	15,812
South American	20,961
Colombian	16,283

Households with $100,000+ Income

Group	Number	%
Total Population	1,709	9.7
Hispanic or Latino (of any race)	147	3.3
Central American, ex. Mexican	0	0.0
Cuban	24	2.6
Puerto Rican	17	4.4
South American	97	4.9
Colombian	44	5.5

Households with Food Stamps/SNAP Benefits During Past 12 Months

Group	Number	%
Total Population	2,065	11.7
Hispanic or Latino (of any race)	595	13.5
Central American, ex. Mexican	89	16.5
Cuban	90	9.7
Puerto Rican	42	11.0
South American	313	15.8
Colombian	183	22.8

Poverty Rate
(Income in Past 12 Months Below Poverty Level)

Group	%
Total Population	20.3
Hispanic or Latino (of any race)	21.1
Central American, ex. Mexican	23.9
Cuban	19.8
Puerto Rican	27.4
South American	16.7
Colombian	26.1

Hialeah

Population

Group	Number	%TP[1]	%HP[2]
Total Population	224,669	100.0	–
Hispanic or Latino (of any race)	212,805	94.7	100.0
Central American, ex. Mexican	17,305	7.7	8.1
Costa Rican	476	0.2	0.2
Guatemalan	1,120	0.5	0.5
Honduran	3,744	1.7	1.8
Nicaraguan	10,410	4.6	4.9
Panamanian	391	0.2	0.2
Salvadoran	1,151	0.5	0.5
Cuban	164,717	73.3	77.4
Dominican Republic	4,206	1.9	2.0
Mexican	1,825	0.8	0.9
Puerto Rican	5,027	2.2	2.4
South American	13,835	6.2	6.5
Argentinean	1,087	0.5	0.5
Chilean	602	0.3	0.3
Colombian	6,800	3.0	3.2
Ecuadorian	1,606	0.7	0.8
Peruvian	1,920	0.9	0.9
Uruguayan	291	0.1	0.1
Venezuelan	1,405	0.6	0.7
Spaniard	639	0.3	0.3

Population Growth: 2000–2010

Group	%
Total Population	-0.8
Hispanic or Latino (of any race)	4.0
Central American, ex. Mexican	18.0
Costa Rican	0.6
Guatemalan	36.1
Honduran	44.4
Nicaraguan	13.0
Panamanian	3.2
Salvadoran	50.9
Cuban	17.1
Dominican Republic	2.4
Mexican	6.2
Puerto Rican	-23.6
South American	10.6
Argentinean	72.0
Chilean	-1.5
Colombian	-4.9
Ecuadorian	38.6
Peruvian	35.4
Uruguayan	146.6
Venezuelan	25.8
Spaniard	37.7

Males per 100 Females

Group	Number
Total Population	93.2
Hispanic or Latino (of any race)	92.7
Central American, ex. Mexican	87.2
Costa Rican	62.5
Guatemalan	94.8
Honduran	82.1
Nicaraguan	87.8
Panamanian	67.8
Salvadoran	113.9
Cuban	94.6
Dominican Republic	75.2
Mexican	105.5
Puerto Rican	88.4
South American	80.7
Argentinean	111.9
Chilean	96.1
Colombian	74.0
Ecuadorian	85.9
Peruvian	83.4
Uruguayan	96.6
Venezuelan	75.2
Spaniard	100.3

Average Household Size

Group	People
Total Population	3.13
Hispanic or Latino (of any race)	3.16
Central American, ex. Mexican	3.77
Costa Rican	3.17
Guatemalan	3.67
Honduran	3.72
Nicaraguan	3.83
Panamanian	3.05
Salvadoran	3.95
Cuban	3.09
Dominican Republic	3.44
Mexican	3.69
Puerto Rican	3.06
South American	3.32
Argentinean	3.30
Chilean	3.16
Colombian	3.29
Ecuadorian	3.48
Peruvian	3.40
Uruguayan	3.20
Venezuelan	3.28
Spaniard	2.64

Median Age

Group	Years
Total Population	42.2
Hispanic or Latino (of any race)	42.8
Central American, ex. Mexican	35.6
Costa Rican	39.7
Guatemalan	35.5
Honduran	34.0
Nicaraguan	36.4
Panamanian	40.8
Salvadoran	33.4
Cuban	44.7
Dominican Republic	36.6
Mexican	26.2
Puerto Rican	36.9
South American	41.3
Argentinean	34.8
Chilean	44.7
Colombian	44.3
Ecuadorian	43.1
Peruvian	41.6
Uruguayan	38.4
Venezuelan	33.2
Spaniard	52.8

High School Graduates
(Universe: Population 25 Years and Over)

Group	Number	%
Total Population	109,278	66.7
Hispanic or Latino (of any race)	104,413	66.3
Central American, ex. Mexican	9,301	68.3
Guatemalan	721	50.6
Honduran	2,120	67.5
Nicaraguan	5,710	73.4
Salvadoran	385	46.9
Cuban	78,697	64.9
Dominican Republic	2,077	75.8
Mexican	951	49.8
Puerto Rican	2,632	62.7
South American	9,191	79.8
Argentinean	685	74.9
Colombian	4,295	75.5
Ecuadorian	1,139	80.7
Peruvian	1,362	87.8
Venezuelan	747	83.8

Four-Year College Graduates
(Universe: Population 25 Years and Over)

Group	Number	%
Total Population	22,138	13.5
Hispanic or Latino (of any race)	20,910	13.3
Central American, ex. Mexican	1,235	9.1
Guatemalan	58	4.1
Honduran	174	5.5
Nicaraguan	895	11.5
Salvadoran	0	0.0
Cuban	16,643	13.7
Dominican Republic	478	17.4
Mexican	93	4.9
Puerto Rican	413	9.8
South American	1,757	15.3
Argentinean	154	16.8
Colombian	691	12.1
Ecuadorian	173	12.3
Peruvian	225	14.5
Venezuelan	285	32.0

Population Age 3–17 Enrolled in Public School
(Universe: Population Age 3–17 Enrolled in School)

Group	Number	%
Total Population	27,575	92.1
Hispanic or Latino (of any race)	25,950	92.7
Central American, ex. Mexican	3,132	94.9
Guatemalan	275	100.0
Honduran	781	98.1
Nicaraguan	1,733	93.7
Salvadoran	221	100.0
Cuban	17,734	92.8

STATE & PLACE PROFILES

Notes: (1) Percent of total population; (2) Percent of Hispanic/Latino population; Profiles include places with an overall population of at least 125,000, OR an overall population of at least 25,000 where the Hispanic/Latino population is at least 20% of the overall population. In states where less than five places meet either of these criteria, we have included places with at least 10,000 total population with the highest percentage of Hispanic/Latino population. These places are identified with an asterisk (*); Please refer to the User's Guide for a full explanation of data.

Group	Number	%
Dominican Republic	779	95.8
Mexican	303	81.2
Puerto Rican	837	100.0
South American	2,441	94.5
Argentinean	140	100.0
Colombian	1,145	95.5
Ecuadorian	329	95.6
Peruvian	372	92.5
Venezuelan	264	86.0

Population Age 3–17 Enrolled in Private School
(Universe: Population Age 3–17 Enrolled in School)

Group	Number	%
Total Population	2,381	7.9
Hispanic or Latino (of any race)	2,038	7.3
Central American, ex. Mexican	170	5.1
Guatemalan	0	0.0
Honduran	15	1.9
Nicaraguan	116	6.3
Salvadoran	0	0.0
Cuban	1,386	7.2
Dominican Republic	34	4.2
Mexican	70	18.8
Puerto Rican	0	0.0
South American	142	5.5
Argentinean	0	0.0
Colombian	54	4.5
Ecuadorian	15	4.4
Peruvian	30	7.5
Venezuelan	43	14.0

Foreign-Born Population

Group	Number	%
Total Population	164,066	73.2
Hispanic or Latino (of any race)	161,926	75.6
Central American, ex. Mexican	14,926	73.9
Guatemalan	1,654	73.2
Honduran	3,415	76.1
Nicaraguan	8,292	73.6
Salvadoran	1,050	72.9
Cuban	127,836	79.8
Dominican Republic	2,937	72.0
Mexican	1,828	57.7
Puerto Rican	247	4.3
South American	12,548	74.9
Argentinean	1,121	81.7
Colombian	6,096	75.8
Ecuadorian	1,537	76.5
Peruvian	1,821	71.1
Venezuelan	1,028	72.4

Foreign-Born Naturalized U.S. Citizens

Group	Number	%
Total Population	72,409	44.1
Hispanic or Latino (of any race)	71,449	44.1
Central American, ex. Mexican	5,146	34.5
Guatemalan	645	39.0
Honduran	986	28.9
Nicaraguan	3,151	38.0
Salvadoran	103	9.8
Cuban	58,060	45.4
Dominican Republic	1,710	58.2
Mexican	434	23.7
Puerto Rican	150	60.7
South American	4,982	39.7
Argentinean	299	26.7
Colombian	2,281	37.4
Ecuadorian	1,015	66.0
Peruvian	810	44.5
Venezuelan	215	20.9

Language Spoken at Home: English Only
(Universe: Population 5 Years and Over)

Group	Number	%
Total Population	12,484	5.8
Hispanic or Latino (of any race)	7,371	3.6
Central American, ex. Mexican	317	1.7
Guatemalan	65	3.1
Honduran	56	1.3
Nicaraguan	145	1.4
Salvadoran	38	2.9
Cuban	5,236	3.4
Dominican Republic	127	3.1
Mexican	185	6.7
Puerto Rican	594	10.8
South American	395	2.5
Argentinean	0	0.0
Colombian	228	3.0
Ecuadorian	53	2.9
Peruvian	46	1.9
Venezuelan	35	2.6

Language Spoken at Home: Spanish
(Universe: Population 5 Years and Over)

Group	Number	%
Total Population	200,558	93.8
Hispanic or Latino (of any race)	196,932	96.3
Central American, ex. Mexican	18,737	98.3
Guatemalan	2,020	96.9
Honduran	4,291	98.7
Nicaraguan	10,566	98.6
Salvadoran	1,291	97.1
Cuban	148,189	96.6
Dominican Republic	3,911	96.9
Mexican	2,589	93.3
Puerto Rican	4,862	88.6
South American	15,405	97.3
Argentinean	1,239	98.2
Colombian	7,472	97.0
Ecuadorian	1,787	97.1
Peruvian	2,355	98.1
Venezuelan	1,325	97.4

Unemployment Rate
(Universe: Population 16 Years and Over)

Group	%
Total Population	8.7
Hispanic or Latino (of any race)	8.7
Central American, ex. Mexican	7.0
Guatemalan	5.7
Honduran	5.4
Nicaraguan	6.9
Salvadoran	13.8
Cuban	9.1
Dominican Republic	12.7
Mexican	7.8
Puerto Rican	12.7
South American	6.4
Argentinean	2.2
Colombian	8.3
Ecuadorian	7.1
Peruvian	0.0
Venezuelan	2.6

Class of Worker: Private Wage and Salary
(Universe: Civilian Employed Population 16 Years and Over)

Group	Number	%
Total Population	82,699	82.7
Hispanic or Latino (of any race)	80,095	82.8
Central American, ex. Mexican	9,198	83.5
Guatemalan	1,130	83.0
Honduran	2,037	76.1
Nicaraguan	5,241	88.0
Salvadoran	594	77.2
Cuban	58,490	83.0
Dominican Republic	1,658	86.8
Mexican	1,163	73.7
Puerto Rican	1,754	83.5
South American	6,547	81.1
Argentinean	420	68.0
Colombian	3,173	82.4
Ecuadorian	506	63.0
Peruvian	1,237	87.9
Venezuelan	709	90.4

Class of Worker: Government
(Universe: Civilian Employed Population 16 Years and Over)

Group	Number	%
Total Population	6,130	6.1
Hispanic or Latino (of any race)	5,691	5.9
Central American, ex. Mexican	263	2.4
Guatemalan	9	0.7
Honduran	22	0.8
Nicaraguan	200	3.4
Salvadoran	15	2.0
Cuban	4,424	6.3
Dominican Republic	104	5.4
Mexican	69	4.4
Puerto Rican	279	13.3
South American	390	4.8
Argentinean	43	7.0
Colombian	225	5.8
Ecuadorian	65	8.1
Peruvian	7	0.5
Venezuelan	39	5.0

Means of Transportation to Work: Car, Truck or Van
(Universe: Workers 16 Years and Over)

Group	Number	%
Total Population	84,980	86.3
Hispanic or Latino (of any race)	82,151	86.2
Central American, ex. Mexican	8,343	76.6
Guatemalan	1,195	88.8
Honduran	1,498	56.9
Nicaraguan	4,906	82.8
Salvadoran	501	69.2
Cuban	61,022	88.0
Dominican Republic	1,683	90.7
Mexican	959	60.9
Puerto Rican	1,861	89.8
South American	6,868	86.3
Argentinean	471	76.2
Colombian	3,492	92.3
Ecuadorian	646	82.4
Peruvian	1,119	80.9
Venezuelan	743	94.8

Means of Transportation to Work: Public Transportation (ex. Taxicab)
(Universe: Workers 16 Years and Over)

Group	Number	%
Total Population	2,894	2.9
Hispanic or Latino (of any race)	2,815	3.0
Central American, ex. Mexican	666	6.1
Guatemalan	0	0.0
Honduran	361	13.7
Nicaraguan	235	4.0
Salvadoran	70	9.7
Cuban	1,397	2.0
Dominican Republic	103	5.6
Mexican	152	9.7
Puerto Rican	139	6.7
South American	322	4.0
Argentinean	50	8.1
Colombian	99	2.6
Ecuadorian	17	2.2
Peruvian	105	7.6
Venezuelan	0	0.0

Homeownership Rate
(Universe: Occupied Housing Units)

Group	%
Total Population	50.6
Hispanic or Latino (of any race)	50.1
Central American, ex. Mexican	44.1
Costa Rican	49.2
Guatemalan	54.5
Honduran	39.3
Nicaraguan	44.2
Panamanian	50.4
Salvadoran	43.8
Cuban	50.4
Dominican Republic	50.5
Mexican	37.4
Puerto Rican	48.4
South American	54.6
Argentinean	40.3
Chilean	55.5
Colombian	58.6
Ecuadorian	59.1
Peruvian	52.6
Uruguayan	26.1
Venezuelan	46.8
Spaniard	69.8

Median Home Value

Group	Dollars
Total Population	219,900
Hispanic or Latino (of any race)	219,400
Central American, ex. Mexican	208,900
Guatemalan	229,300
Honduran	224,100
Nicaraguan	194,000
Salvadoran	240,000

Notes: (1) Percent of total population; (2) Percent of Hispanic/Latino population; Profiles include places with an overall population of at least 125,000, OR an overall population of at least 25,000 where the Hispanic/Latino population is at least 20% of the overall population. In states where less than five places meet either of these criteria, we have included places with at least 10,000 total population with the highest percentage of Hispanic/Latino population. These places are identified with an asterisk (*); Please refer to the User's Guide for a full explanation of data.

Group	Dollars
Cuban	224,800
Dominican Republic	222,500
Mexican	165,500
Puerto Rican	205,100
South American	193,200
Argentinean	256,300
Colombian	201,500
Ecuadorian	183,800
Peruvian	187,800
Venezuelan	162,400

Median Gross Rent

Group	Dollars
Total Population	937
Hispanic or Latino (of any race)	938
Central American, ex. Mexican	999
Guatemalan	1,111
Honduran	1,029
Nicaraguan	973
Salvadoran	840
Cuban	898
Dominican Republic	1,102
Mexican	987
Puerto Rican	1,041
South American	1,068
Argentinean	1,082
Colombian	1,078
Ecuadorian	954
Peruvian	1,070
Venezuelan	1,154

Median Household Income
(2010 Inflation-Adjusted Dollars)

Group	Dollars
Total Population	31,648
Hispanic or Latino (of any race)	31,560
Central American, ex. Mexican	33,690
Guatemalan	40,417
Honduran	33,557
Nicaraguan	32,620
Salvadoran	34,432
Cuban	30,886
Dominican Republic	27,739
Mexican	36,310
Puerto Rican	31,951
South American	34,254
Argentinean	33,603
Colombian	33,342
Ecuadorian	30,227
Peruvian	37,875
Venezuelan	40,240

Per Capita Income
(2010 Inflation-Adjusted Dollars)

Group	Dollars
Total Population	15,080
Hispanic or Latino (of any race)	15,000
Central American, ex. Mexican	14,007
Guatemalan	26,120
Honduran	11,922
Nicaraguan	13,097
Salvadoran	10,846
Cuban	15,214
Dominican Republic	14,192
Mexican	14,148
Puerto Rican	16,790
South American	14,251
Argentinean	14,002
Colombian	12,996
Ecuadorian	13,399
Peruvian	16,120
Venezuelan	16,014

Households with $100,000+ Income

Group	Number	%
Total Population	4,606	6.2
Hispanic or Latino (of any race)	4,264	6.0
Central American, ex. Mexican	215	3.7
Guatemalan	79	12.3
Honduran	0	0.0
Nicaraguan	114	3.5
Salvadoran	0	0.0
Cuban	3,495	6.3
Dominican Republic	61	4.2
Mexican	50	5.0
Puerto Rican	110	5.6
South American	226	4.6
Argentinean	0	0.0
Colombian	103	4.9
Ecuadorian	36	6.0
Peruvian	27	3.6
Venezuelan	6	1.4

Households with Food Stamps/SNAP Benefits During Past 12 Months

Group	Number	%
Total Population	20,809	28.2
Hispanic or Latino (of any race)	20,416	28.6
Central American, ex. Mexican	1,099	18.9
Guatemalan	160	25.0
Honduran	208	15.3
Nicaraguan	618	19.1
Salvadoran	61	16.5
Cuban	17,158	30.9
Dominican Republic	310	21.3
Mexican	146	14.7
Puerto Rican	575	29.4
South American	902	18.5
Argentinean	0	0.0
Colombian	433	20.5
Ecuadorian	137	22.8
Peruvian	147	19.4
Venezuelan	113	26.3

Poverty Rate
(Income in Past 12 Months Below Poverty Level)

Group	%
Total Population	20.1
Hispanic or Latino (of any race)	20.0
Central American, ex. Mexican	19.7
Guatemalan	11.1
Honduran	23.7
Nicaraguan	19.1
Salvadoran	11.1
Cuban	20.4
Dominican Republic	23.7
Mexican	11.3
Puerto Rican	21.6
South American	19.2
Argentinean	26.3
Colombian	18.6
Ecuadorian	33.0
Peruvian	18.0
Venezuelan	5.2

Hollywood

Population

Group	Number	%TP[1]	%HP[2]
Total Population	140,768	100.0	–
Hispanic or Latino (of any race)	45,825	32.6	100.0
Central American, ex. Mexican	4,896	3.5	10.7
Costa Rican	349	0.2	0.8
Guatemalan	712	0.5	1.6
Honduran	1,283	0.9	2.8
Nicaraguan	1,321	0.9	2.9
Panamanian	398	0.3	0.9
Salvadoran	822	0.6	1.8
Cuban	9,258	6.6	20.2
Dominican Republic	3,481	2.5	7.6
Mexican	1,970	1.4	4.3
Puerto Rican	8,818	6.3	19.2
South American	14,020	10.0	30.6
Argentinean	1,626	1.2	3.5
Bolivian	130	0.1	0.3
Chilean	542	0.4	1.2
Colombian	5,583	4.0	12.2
Ecuadorian	1,203	0.9	2.6
Peruvian	2,995	2.1	6.5
Uruguayan	498	0.4	1.1
Venezuelan	1,334	0.9	2.9
Spaniard	388	0.3	0.8

Population Growth: 2000–2010

Group	%
Total Population	1.0
Hispanic or Latino (of any race)	46.0
Central American, ex. Mexican	142.3
Costa Rican	36.3
Guatemalan	161.8
Honduran	206.9
Nicaraguan	163.7
Panamanian	65.1
Salvadoran	202.2
Cuban	57.2
Dominican Republic	107.1
Mexican	53.0
Puerto Rican	18.2
South American	101.7
Argentinean	256.6
Bolivian	30.0
Chilean	79.5
Colombian	77.1
Ecuadorian	103.2
Peruvian	104.3
Uruguayan	340.7
Venezuelan	134.9
Spaniard	207.9

Males per 100 Females

Group	Number
Total Population	96.1
Hispanic or Latino (of any race)	94.6
Central American, ex. Mexican	96.5
Costa Rican	69.4
Guatemalan	135.0
Honduran	83.3
Nicaraguan	98.3
Panamanian	70.8
Salvadoran	116.3
Cuban	105.6
Dominican Republic	85.0
Mexican	115.8
Puerto Rican	98.6
South American	84.4
Argentinean	104.3
Bolivian	66.7
Chilean	97.8
Colombian	79.1
Ecuadorian	85.9
Peruvian	81.7
Uruguayan	111.9
Venezuelan	80.5
Spaniard	99.0

Average Household Size

Group	People
Total Population	2.39
Hispanic or Latino (of any race)	2.83
Central American, ex. Mexican	3.30
Costa Rican	2.85
Guatemalan	3.50
Honduran	3.30
Nicaraguan	3.35
Panamanian	2.65
Salvadoran	3.74
Cuban	2.69
Dominican Republic	3.02
Mexican	3.09
Puerto Rican	2.68
South American	2.85
Argentinean	2.76
Bolivian	2.55
Chilean	2.59
Colombian	2.87
Ecuadorian	3.03
Peruvian	3.01
Uruguayan	2.61
Venezuelan	2.66
Spaniard	2.25

Median Age

Group	Years
Total Population	41.1
Hispanic or Latino (of any race)	35.9
Central American, ex. Mexican	33.5
Costa Rican	37.1
Guatemalan	31.2
Honduran	32.6
Nicaraguan	34.2
Panamanian	40.0
Salvadoran	31.5
Cuban	39.8

Notes: (1) Percent of total population; (2) Percent of Hispanic/Latino population; Profiles include places with an overall population of at least 125,000, OR an overall population of at least 25,000 where the Hispanic/Latino population is at least 20% of the overall population. In states where less than five places meet either of these criteria, we have included places with at least 10,000 total population with the highest percentage of Hispanic/Latino population. These places are identified with an asterisk (*); Please refer to the User's Guide for a full explanation of data.

Group	Number	%
Dominican Republic		33.8
Mexican		29.7
Puerto Rican		33.2
South American		38.8
Argentinean		36.2
Bolivian		38.8
Chilean		39.8
Colombian		39.6
Ecuadorian		40.8
Peruvian		40.3
Uruguayan		37.4
Venezuelan		35.7
Spaniard		44.8

High School Graduates
(Universe: Population 25 Years and Over)

Group	Number	%
Total Population	87,269	86.0
Hispanic or Latino (of any race)	22,822	81.6
Central American, ex. Mexican	2,727	76.7
Nicaraguan	820	88.4
Cuban	5,182	83.4
Dominican Republic	1,359	73.4
Mexican	725	59.9
Puerto Rican	3,408	79.8
South American	8,584	87.8
Argentinean	829	78.1
Colombian	3,162	91.8
Ecuadorian	573	83.3
Peruvian	2,370	91.9
Venezuelan	921	94.9

Four-Year College Graduates
(Universe: Population 25 Years and Over)

Group	Number	%
Total Population	27,948	27.5
Hispanic or Latino (of any race)	6,508	23.3
Central American, ex. Mexican	567	15.9
Nicaraguan	97	10.5
Cuban	1,597	25.7
Dominican Republic	424	22.9
Mexican	102	8.4
Puerto Rican	674	15.8
South American	2,909	29.8
Argentinean	268	25.2
Colombian	1,199	34.8
Ecuadorian	154	22.4
Peruvian	592	23.0
Venezuelan	464	47.8

Population Age 3–17 Enrolled in Public School
(Universe: Population Age 3–17 Enrolled in School)

Group	Number	%
Total Population	16,581	77.3
Hispanic or Latino (of any race)	5,278	85.0
Central American, ex. Mexican	464	85.0
Nicaraguan	179	81.4
Cuban	824	75.9
Dominican Republic	482	96.4
Mexican	436	90.6
Puerto Rican	1,078	93.8
South American	1,512	80.6
Argentinean	180	82.9
Colombian	523	78.2
Ecuadorian	77	51.0
Peruvian	532	91.7
Venezuelan	95	92.2

Population Age 3–17 Enrolled in Private School
(Universe: Population Age 3–17 Enrolled in School)

Group	Number	%
Total Population	4,871	22.7
Hispanic or Latino (of any race)	933	15.0
Central American, ex. Mexican	82	15.0
Nicaraguan	41	18.6
Cuban	262	24.1
Dominican Republic	18	3.6
Mexican	45	9.4
Puerto Rican	71	6.2
South American	365	19.4
Argentinean	37	17.1
Colombian	146	21.8
Ecuadorian	74	49.0
Peruvian	48	8.3
Venezuelan	8	7.8

Foreign-Born Population

Group	Number	%
Total Population	47,150	33.4
Hispanic or Latino (of any race)	24,524	60.6
Central American, ex. Mexican	3,886	76.8
Nicaraguan	1,090	71.8
Cuban	5,426	64.3
Dominican Republic	1,936	68.4
Mexican	1,146	56.7
Puerto Rican	123	1.9
South American	11,242	82.0
Argentinean	1,380	85.4
Colombian	3,919	82.6
Ecuadorian	619	63.3
Peruvian	3,124	85.6
Venezuelan	959	75.2

Foreign-Born Naturalized U.S. Citizens

Group	Number	%
Total Population	23,034	48.9
Hispanic or Latino (of any race)	11,102	45.3
Central American, ex. Mexican	1,591	40.9
Nicaraguan	589	54.0
Cuban	3,035	55.9
Dominican Republic	1,109	57.3
Mexican	307	26.8
Puerto Rican	88	71.5
South American	4,523	40.2
Argentinean	379	27.5
Colombian	1,753	44.7
Ecuadorian	489	79.0
Peruvian	1,395	44.7
Venezuelan	259	27.0

Language Spoken at Home: English Only
(Universe: Population 5 Years and Over)

Group	Number	%
Total Population	75,918	57.0
Hispanic or Latino (of any race)	4,560	11.9
Central American, ex. Mexican	363	7.9
Nicaraguan	57	4.4
Cuban	1,257	15.7
Dominican Republic	170	6.4
Mexican	458	22.9
Puerto Rican	1,471	24.0
South American	490	3.7
Argentinean	106	6.9
Colombian	121	2.7
Ecuadorian	75	7.7
Peruvian	116	3.2
Venezuelan	43	3.8

Language Spoken at Home: Spanish
(Universe: Population 5 Years and Over)

Group	Number	%
Total Population	39,352	29.5
Hispanic or Latino (of any race)	33,401	87.3
Central American, ex. Mexican	4,221	91.8
Nicaraguan	1,232	95.6
Cuban	6,680	83.7
Dominican Republic	2,464	93.3
Mexican	1,541	77.1
Puerto Rican	4,639	75.8
South American	12,410	94.9
Argentinean	1,412	91.6
Colombian	4,359	96.1
Ecuadorian	877	89.7
Peruvian	3,427	95.9
Venezuelan	1,042	92.4

Unemployment Rate
(Universe: Population 16 Years and Over)

Group	%
Total Population	9.5
Hispanic or Latino (of any race)	10.8
Central American, ex. Mexican	12.1
Nicaraguan	17.8
Cuban	7.8
Dominican Republic	12.9
Mexican	8.0
Puerto Rican	9.9
South American	12.8
Argentinean	6.0
Colombian	10.6
Ecuadorian	10.9

Group	Number	%
Peruvian		19.1
Venezuelan		17.6

Class of Worker: Private Wage and Salary
(Universe: Civilian Employed Population 16 Years and Over)

Group	Number	%
Total Population	58,007	82.8
Hispanic or Latino (of any race)	18,191	83.5
Central American, ex. Mexican	2,278	81.3
Nicaraguan	601	81.5
Cuban	4,028	83.9
Dominican Republic	1,072	80.3
Mexican	1,024	84.1
Puerto Rican	3,077	91.2
South American	6,154	81.1
Argentinean	746	76.0
Colombian	2,174	81.1
Ecuadorian	546	90.0
Peruvian	1,613	85.8
Venezuelan	630	94.9

Class of Worker: Government
(Universe: Civilian Employed Population 16 Years and Over)

Group	Number	%
Total Population	7,103	10.1
Hispanic or Latino (of any race)	1,544	7.1
Central American, ex. Mexican	216	7.7
Nicaraguan	68	9.2
Cuban	493	10.3
Dominican Republic	156	11.7
Mexican	54	4.4
Puerto Rican	268	7.9
South American	333	4.4
Argentinean	61	6.2
Colombian	123	4.6
Ecuadorian	45	7.4
Peruvian	104	5.5
Venezuelan	0	0.0

Means of Transportation to Work: Car, Truck or Van
(Universe: Workers 16 Years and Over)

Group	Number	%
Total Population	59,229	86.8
Hispanic or Latino (of any race)	18,310	86.2
Central American, ex. Mexican	2,372	87.8
Nicaraguan	724	98.2
Cuban	3,995	84.4
Dominican Republic	1,212	94.7
Mexican	709	58.6
Puerto Rican	2,798	85.1
South American	6,619	90.2
Argentinean	819	90.3
Colombian	2,432	91.9
Ecuadorian	531	88.6
Peruvian	1,521	85.4
Venezuelan	621	94.8

Means of Transportation to Work: Public Transportation (ex. Taxicab)
(Universe: Workers 16 Years and Over)

Group	Number	%
Total Population	3,003	4.4
Hispanic or Latino (of any race)	1,081	5.1
Central American, ex. Mexican	210	7.8
Nicaraguan	13	1.8
Cuban	203	4.3
Dominican Republic	21	1.6
Mexican	43	3.6
Puerto Rican	351	10.7
South American	205	2.8
Argentinean	0	0.0
Colombian	37	1.4
Ecuadorian	13	2.2
Peruvian	155	8.7
Venezuelan	0	0.0

Homeownership Rate
(Universe: Occupied Housing Units)

Group	%
Total Population	59.6
Hispanic or Latino (of any race)	52.3
Central American, ex. Mexican	49.6
Costa Rican	52.0
Guatemalan	43.5

Notes: (1) Percent of total population; (2) Percent of Hispanic/Latino population; Profiles include places with an overall population of at least 125,000, OR an overall population of at least 25,000 where the Hispanic/Latino population is at least 20% of the overall population. In states where less than five places meet either of these criteria, we have included places with at least 10,000 total population with the highest percentage of Hispanic/Latino population. These places are identified with an asterisk (*); Please refer to the User's Guide for a full explanation of data.

Honduran	45.8
Nicaraguan	53.1
Panamanian	49.1
Salvadoran	55.0
Cuban	64.0
Dominican Republic	49.6
Mexican	41.3
Puerto Rican	44.9
South American	52.3
Argentinean	52.0
Bolivian	56.9
Chilean	47.9
Colombian	55.9
Ecuadorian	62.4
Peruvian	47.2
Uruguayan	29.7
Venezuelan	50.3
Spaniard	65.3

Median Home Value

Group	Dollars
Total Population	243,700
Hispanic or Latino (of any race)	214,300
Central American, ex. Mexican	172,800
Nicaraguan	169,900
Cuban	248,500
Dominican Republic	207,600
Mexican	161,600
Puerto Rican	210,600
South American	199,900
Argentinean	269,100
Colombian	210,100
Ecuadorian	276,000
Peruvian	151,000
Venezuelan	351,400

Median Gross Rent

Group	Dollars
Total Population	963
Hispanic or Latino (of any race)	999
Central American, ex. Mexican	1,161
Nicaraguan	1,040
Cuban	882
Dominican Republic	858
Mexican	849
Puerto Rican	1,069
South American	1,000
Argentinean	970
Colombian	1,094
Ecuadorian	773
Peruvian	944
Venezuelan	1,293

Median Household Income
(2010 Inflation-Adjusted Dollars)

Group	Dollars
Total Population	45,699
Hispanic or Latino (of any race)	44,075
Central American, ex. Mexican	39,238
Nicaraguan	44,231
Cuban	50,877
Dominican Republic	35,435
Mexican	40,619
Puerto Rican	42,527
South American	43,989
Argentinean	38,338
Colombian	47,388
Ecuadorian	43,359
Peruvian	42,949
Venezuelan	89,018

Per Capita Income
(2010 Inflation-Adjusted Dollars)

Group	Dollars
Total Population	27,315
Hispanic or Latino (of any race)	21,866
Central American, ex. Mexican	17,803
Nicaraguan	17,734
Cuban	25,050
Dominican Republic	17,516
Mexican	29,296
Puerto Rican	20,920
South American	21,098
Argentinean	21,098
Colombian	21,284
Ecuadorian	21,645
Peruvian	14,803
Venezuelan	38,939

Households with $100,000+ Income

Group	Number	%
Total Population	9,874	16.9
Hispanic or Latino (of any race)	1,765	12.2
Central American, ex. Mexican	160	9.2
Nicaraguan	45	8.7
Cuban	560	17.1
Dominican Republic	47	5.0
Mexican	60	9.3
Puerto Rican	182	7.4
South American	658	13.6
Argentinean	68	9.8
Colombian	201	11.8
Ecuadorian	71	20.9
Peruvian	12	1.1
Venezuelan	217	48.8

Households with Food Stamps/SNAP Benefits During Past 12 Months

Group	Number	%
Total Population	4,796	8.2
Hispanic or Latino (of any race)	1,602	11.0
Central American, ex. Mexican	150	8.7
Nicaraguan	28	5.4
Cuban	432	13.2
Dominican Republic	175	18.6
Mexican	100	15.5
Puerto Rican	320	13.0
South American	357	7.4
Argentinean	15	2.2
Colombian	82	4.8
Ecuadorian	33	9.7
Peruvian	174	15.6
Venezuelan	0	0.0

Poverty Rate
(Income in Past 12 Months Below Poverty Level)

Group	%
Total Population	13.7
Hispanic or Latino (of any race)	13.9
Central American, ex. Mexican	11.2
Nicaraguan	5.1
Cuban	12.0
Dominican Republic	29.7
Mexican	5.6
Puerto Rican	12.0
South American	15.1
Argentinean	17.0
Colombian	13.6
Ecuadorian	3.7
Peruvian	12.7
Venezuelan	21.6

Homestead

Population

Group	Number	%TP[1]	%HP[2]
Total Population	60,512	100.0	–
Hispanic or Latino (of any race)	38,078	62.9	100.0
Central American, ex. Mexican	7,477	12.4	19.6
Costa Rican	181	0.3	0.5
Guatemalan	3,275	5.4	8.6
Honduran	936	1.5	2.5
Nicaraguan	1,354	2.2	3.6
Panamanian	200	0.3	0.5
Salvadoran	1,507	2.5	4.0
Cuban	9,524	15.7	25.0
Dominican Republic	1,259	2.1	3.3
Mexican	9,311	15.4	24.5
Puerto Rican	5,186	8.6	13.6
South American	3,564	5.9	9.4
Argentinean	210	0.3	0.6
Chilean	131	0.2	0.3
Colombian	1,540	2.5	4.0
Ecuadorian	338	0.6	0.9
Peruvian	560	0.9	1.5
Venezuelan	667	1.1	1.8
Spaniard	133	0.2	0.3

Population Growth: 2000–2010

Group	%
Total Population	89.6
Hispanic or Latino (of any race)	130.3
Central American, ex. Mexican	188.1
Guatemalan	209.3
Honduran	172.9
Nicaraguan	493.9
Salvadoran	75.4
Cuban	338.7
Dominican Republic	378.7
Mexican	27.9
Puerto Rican	148.8
South American	738.6
Colombian	689.7

Males per 100 Females

Group	Number
Total Population	101.5
Hispanic or Latino (of any race)	107.3
Central American, ex. Mexican	141.0
Costa Rican	63.1
Guatemalan	242.9
Honduran	98.7
Nicaraguan	77.0
Panamanian	78.6
Salvadoran	121.6
Cuban	100.7
Dominican Republic	81.9
Mexican	118.8
Puerto Rican	90.4
South American	82.4
Argentinean	101.9
Chilean	129.8
Colombian	75.2
Ecuadorian	92.0
Peruvian	85.4
Venezuelan	74.2
Spaniard	75.0

Average Household Size

Group	People
Total Population	3.16
Hispanic or Latino (of any race)	3.51
Central American, ex. Mexican	4.24
Costa Rican	2.89
Guatemalan	4.95
Honduran	3.98
Nicaraguan	3.60
Panamanian	3.26
Salvadoran	4.18
Cuban	2.98
Dominican Republic	3.32
Mexican	4.24
Puerto Rican	3.11
South American	3.24
Argentinean	3.27
Chilean	2.96
Colombian	3.35
Ecuadorian	3.11
Peruvian	3.31
Venezuelan	3.26
Spaniard	2.58

Median Age

Group	Years
Total Population	29.1
Hispanic or Latino (of any race)	28.2
Central American, ex. Mexican	28.0
Costa Rican	31.5
Guatemalan	26.5
Honduran	28.9
Nicaraguan	30.8
Panamanian	34.6
Salvadoran	29.6
Cuban	33.4
Dominican Republic	29.3
Mexican	23.8
Puerto Rican	28.3
South American	33.7
Argentinean	33.3
Chilean	38.3
Colombian	32.5
Ecuadorian	34.2
Peruvian	35.8

Notes: (1) Percent of total population; (2) Percent of Hispanic/Latino population; Profiles include places with an overall population of at least 125,000, OR an overall population of at least 25,000 where the Hispanic/Latino population is at least 20% of the overall population. In states where less than five places meet either of these criteria, we have included places with at least 10,000 total population with the highest percentage of Hispanic/Latino population. These places are identified with an asterisk (*); Please refer to the User's Guide for a full explanation of data.

Venezuelan		33.8
Spaniard		36.2

High School Graduates

(Universe: Population 25 Years and Over)

Group	Number	%
Total Population	22,555	72.1
Hispanic or Latino (of any race)	13,033	65.3
Central American, ex. Mexican	1,772	43.9
Guatemalan	278	17.5
Nicaraguan	659	88.0
Salvadoran	252	25.0
Cuban	3,945	74.8
Dominican Republic	550	85.9
Mexican	1,255	34.3
Puerto Rican	2,615	81.9
South American	2,549	92.9
Colombian	1,047	93.9

Four-Year College Graduates

(Universe: Population 25 Years and Over)

Group	Number	%
Total Population	5,822	18.6
Hispanic or Latino (of any race)	3,333	16.7
Central American, ex. Mexican	634	15.7
Guatemalan	169	10.6
Nicaraguan	144	19.2
Salvadoran	116	11.5
Cuban	697	13.2
Dominican Republic	111	17.3
Mexican	192	5.2
Puerto Rican	606	19.0
South American	1,033	37.6
Colombian	372	33.4

Population Age 3–17 Enrolled in Public School

(Universe: Population Age 3–17 Enrolled in School)

Group	Number	%
Total Population	9,983	86.2
Hispanic or Latino (of any race)	5,997	90.7
Central American, ex. Mexican	1,275	94.9
Guatemalan	394	100.0
Nicaraguan	205	86.1
Salvadoran	458	92.7
Cuban	1,046	89.2
Dominican Republic	206	96.3
Mexican	1,451	96.5
Puerto Rican	1,231	91.7
South American	509	71.1
Colombian	203	86.8

Population Age 3–17 Enrolled in Private School

(Universe: Population Age 3–17 Enrolled in School)

Group	Number	%
Total Population	1,600	13.8
Hispanic or Latino (of any race)	612	9.3
Central American, ex. Mexican	69	5.1
Guatemalan	0	0.0
Nicaraguan	33	13.9
Salvadoran	36	7.3
Cuban	126	10.8
Dominican Republic	8	3.7
Mexican	52	3.5
Puerto Rican	112	8.3
South American	207	28.9
Colombian	31	13.2

Foreign-Born Population

Group	Number	%
Total Population	20,383	37.0
Hispanic or Latino (of any race)	17,404	50.2
Central American, ex. Mexican	5,333	72.1
Guatemalan	2,448	78.3
Nicaraguan	815	67.0
Salvadoran	1,387	67.2
Cuban	4,644	58.0
Dominican Republic	522	39.9
Mexican	3,883	55.0
Puerto Rican	25	0.4
South American	2,736	67.1
Colombian	1,064	71.1

Foreign-Born Naturalized U.S. Citizens

Group	Number	%
Total Population	5,365	26.3
Hispanic or Latino (of any race)	4,296	24.7
Central American, ex. Mexican	821	15.4
Guatemalan	159	6.5
Nicaraguan	346	42.5
Salvadoran	104	7.5
Cuban	1,663	35.8
Dominican Republic	292	55.9
Mexican	456	11.7
Puerto Rican	0	0.0
South American	923	33.7
Colombian	444	41.7

Language Spoken at Home: English Only

(Universe: Population 5 Years and Over)

Group	Number	%
Total Population	19,360	40.0
Hispanic or Latino (of any race)	4,548	15.0
Central American, ex. Mexican	659	9.9
Guatemalan	177	6.2
Nicaraguan	142	13.5
Salvadoran	167	9.1
Cuban	1,355	19.5
Dominican Republic	237	21.3
Mexican	594	9.6
Puerto Rican	1,107	21.4
South American	425	12.2
Colombian	44	3.2

Language Spoken at Home: Spanish

(Universe: Population 5 Years and Over)

Group	Number	%
Total Population	26,806	55.4
Hispanic or Latino (of any race)	25,619	84.6
Central American, ex. Mexican	5,946	89.3
Guatemalan	2,627	92.3
Nicaraguan	912	86.5
Salvadoran	1,662	90.2
Cuban	5,576	80.5
Dominican Republic	874	78.7
Mexican	5,616	90.4
Puerto Rican	4,075	78.6
South American	2,979	85.7
Colombian	1,327	95.7

Unemployment Rate

(Universe: Population 16 Years and Over)

Group	%
Total Population	9.0
Hispanic or Latino (of any race)	8.6
Central American, ex. Mexican	7.5
Guatemalan	1.4
Nicaraguan	20.0
Salvadoran	9.7
Cuban	7.6
Dominican Republic	10.8
Mexican	7.8
Puerto Rican	13.5
South American	6.7
Colombian	3.4

Class of Worker: Private Wage and Salary

(Universe: Civilian Employed Population 16 Years and Over)

Group	Number	%
Total Population	19,327	80.9
Hispanic or Latino (of any race)	13,390	84.0
Central American, ex. Mexican	3,308	78.8
Guatemalan	1,673	84.6
Nicaraguan	526	92.1
Salvadoran	774	72.0
Cuban	2,716	82.0
Dominican Republic	458	90.7
Mexican	3,273	94.6
Puerto Rican	1,613	74.6
South American	1,747	88.1
Colombian	796	90.9

Class of Worker: Government

(Universe: Civilian Employed Population 16 Years and Over)

Group	Number	%
Total Population	3,219	13.5
Hispanic or Latino (of any race)	1,397	8.8
Central American, ex. Mexican	300	7.1
Guatemalan	29	1.5
Nicaraguan	34	6.0
Salvadoran	137	12.7
Cuban	289	8.7
Dominican Republic	47	9.3
Mexican	106	3.1
Puerto Rican	493	22.8
South American	131	6.6
Colombian	29	3.3

Means of Transportation to Work: Car, Truck or Van

(Universe: Workers 16 Years and Over)

Group	Number	%
Total Population	19,148	81.1
Hispanic or Latino (of any race)	12,098	76.7
Central American, ex. Mexican	2,421	58.2
Guatemalan	690	35.3
Nicaraguan	496	89.5
Salvadoran	733	68.2
Cuban	2,986	90.5
Dominican Republic	322	65.3
Mexican	2,405	70.7
Puerto Rican	1,877	86.7
South American	1,839	95.0
Colombian	844	97.5

Means of Transportation to Work: Public Transportation (ex. Taxicab)

(Universe: Workers 16 Years and Over)

Group	Number	%
Total Population	1,576	6.7
Hispanic or Latino (of any race)	1,298	8.2
Central American, ex. Mexican	779	18.7
Guatemalan	539	27.5
Nicaraguan	21	3.8
Salvadoran	187	17.4
Cuban	34	1.0
Dominican Republic	0	0.0
Mexican	317	9.3
Puerto Rican	127	5.9
South American	0	0.0
Colombian	0	0.0

Homeownership Rate

(Universe: Occupied Housing Units)

Group	%
Total Population	41.0
Hispanic or Latino (of any race)	37.5
Central American, ex. Mexican	26.4
Costa Rican	50.9
Guatemalan	8.7
Honduran	30.9
Nicaraguan	53.2
Panamanian	39.7
Salvadoran	21.6
Cuban	44.0
Dominican Republic	38.8
Mexican	23.2
Puerto Rican	39.3
South American	57.7
Argentinean	53.7
Chilean	65.5
Colombian	58.9
Ecuadorian	55.0
Peruvian	58.6
Venezuelan	56.4
Spaniard	72.1

Median Home Value

Group	Dollars
Total Population	209,100
Hispanic or Latino (of any race)	199,900
Central American, ex. Mexican	243,800
Guatemalan	89,000
Nicaraguan	264,900
Salvadoran	237,500
Cuban	186,300
Dominican Republic	210,300
Mexican	171,100
Puerto Rican	200,400
South American	197,100
Colombian	295,500

Median Gross Rent

Group	Dollars
Total Population	976
Hispanic or Latino (of any race)	964

Notes: (1) Percent of total population; (2) Percent of Hispanic/Latino population; Profiles include places with an overall population of at least 125,000, OR an overall population of at least 25,000 where the Hispanic/Latino population is at least 20% of the overall population. In states where less than five places meet either of these criteria, we have included places with at least 10,000 total population with the highest percentage of Hispanic/Latino population. These places are identified with an asterisk (*); Please refer to the User's Guide for a full explanation of data.

Central American, ex. Mexican	934
Guatemalan	992
Nicaraguan	1,067
Salvadoran	807
Cuban	967
Dominican Republic	1,598
Mexican	857
Puerto Rican	1,022
South American	1,108
Colombian	1,663

Median Household Income
(2010 Inflation-Adjusted Dollars)

Group	Dollars
Total Population	37,901
Hispanic or Latino (of any race)	34,340
Central American, ex. Mexican	28,837
Guatemalan	26,842
Nicaraguan	38,647
Salvadoran	27,035
Cuban	31,540
Dominican Republic	36,167
Mexican	32,605
Puerto Rican	38,559
South American	57,880
Colombian	84,635

Per Capita Income
(2010 Inflation-Adjusted Dollars)

Group	Dollars
Total Population	16,663
Hispanic or Latino (of any race)	15,178
Central American, ex. Mexican	12,952
Guatemalan	10,734
Nicaraguan	18,699
Salvadoran	9,394
Cuban	15,230
Dominican Republic	17,969
Mexican	11,702
Puerto Rican	17,441
South American	21,565
Colombian	26,985

Households with $100,000+ Income

Group	Number	%
Total Population	1,975	11.4
Hispanic or Latino (of any race)	992	9.5
Central American, ex. Mexican	183	9.5
Guatemalan	37	4.9
Nicaraguan	90	23.4
Salvadoran	10	2.1
Cuban	155	5.6
Dominican Republic	40	11.8
Mexican	209	11.7
Puerto Rican	245	12.6
South American	148	10.2
Colombian	116	24.3

Households with Food Stamps/SNAP Benefits During Past 12 Months

Group	Number	%
Total Population	3,764	21.6
Hispanic or Latino (of any race)	2,582	24.7
Central American, ex. Mexican	576	29.8
Guatemalan	223	29.4
Nicaraguan	68	17.7
Salvadoran	195	41.7
Cuban	787	28.3
Dominican Republic	121	35.6
Mexican	404	22.5
Puerto Rican	500	25.7
South American	168	11.6
Colombian	40	8.4

Poverty Rate
(Income in Past 12 Months Below Poverty Level)

Group	%
Total Population	28.4
Hispanic or Latino (of any race)	30.2
Central American, ex. Mexican	36.3
Guatemalan	43.6
Nicaraguan	13.3
Salvadoran	44.3
Cuban	28.1
Dominican Republic	23.9
Mexican	34.7
Puerto Rican	33.7
South American	14.5
Colombian	7.3

Jacksonville

Population

Group	Number	%TP[1]	%HP[2]
Total Population	821,784	100.0	–
Hispanic or Latino (of any race)	63,485	7.7	100.0
Central American, ex. Mexican	6,594	0.8	10.4
Costa Rican	542	0.1	0.9
Guatemalan	914	0.1	1.4
Honduran	1,983	0.2	3.1
Nicaraguan	902	0.1	1.4
Panamanian	1,165	0.1	1.8
Salvadoran	1,039	0.1	1.6
Cuban	7,006	0.9	11.0
Dominican Republic	2,172	0.3	3.4
Mexican	13,838	1.7	21.8
Puerto Rican	21,128	2.6	33.3
South American	7,152	0.9	11.3
Argentinean	387	<0.1	0.6
Bolivian	231	<0.1	0.4
Chilean	287	<0.1	0.5
Colombian	3,197	0.4	5.0
Ecuadorian	808	0.1	1.3
Peruvian	1,282	0.2	2.0
Uruguayan	129	<0.1	0.2
Venezuelan	751	0.1	1.2
Spaniard	1,412	0.2	2.2

Population Growth: 2000–2010

Group	%
Total Population	11.7
Hispanic or Latino (of any race)	107.5
Central American, ex. Mexican	299.4
Costa Rican	109.3
Guatemalan	431.4
Honduran	642.7
Nicaraguan	243.0
Panamanian	152.7
Salvadoran	514.8
Cuban	117.0
Dominican Republic	261.4
Mexican	127.7
Puerto Rican	90.9
South American	251.1
Argentinean	230.8
Chilean	145.3
Colombian	246.0
Ecuadorian	302.0
Peruvian	323.1
Venezuelan	259.3
Spaniard	395.4

Males per 100 Females

Group	Number
Total Population	94.1
Hispanic or Latino (of any race)	103.0
Central American, ex. Mexican	105.5
Costa Rican	87.5
Guatemalan	147.0
Honduran	133.6
Nicaraguan	87.9
Panamanian	68.1
Salvadoran	104.5
Cuban	101.8
Dominican Republic	93.6
Mexican	124.8
Puerto Rican	96.5
South American	91.0
Argentinean	111.5
Bolivian	92.5
Chilean	111.0
Colombian	84.5
Ecuadorian	92.8
Peruvian	95.4
Uruguayan	158.0
Venezuelan	85.4
Spaniard	82.9

Average Household Size

Group	People
Total Population	2.48
Hispanic or Latino (of any race)	2.92
Central American, ex. Mexican	3.22
Costa Rican	2.67
Guatemalan	3.52
Honduran	3.48
Nicaraguan	3.00
Panamanian	2.74
Salvadoran	3.69
Cuban	2.75
Dominican Republic	3.03
Mexican	3.26
Puerto Rican	2.84
South American	2.81
Argentinean	2.69
Bolivian	3.04
Chilean	2.64
Colombian	2.77
Ecuadorian	3.16
Peruvian	2.84
Uruguayan	2.54
Venezuelan	2.85
Spaniard	2.41

Median Age

Group	Years
Total Population	35.5
Hispanic or Latino (of any race)	28.0
Central American, ex. Mexican	28.8
Costa Rican	33.3
Guatemalan	27.0
Honduran	28.4
Nicaraguan	30.4
Panamanian	29.8
Salvadoran	27.9
Cuban	34.2
Dominican Republic	27.2
Mexican	24.9
Puerto Rican	27.2
South American	33.0
Argentinean	32.9
Bolivian	30.1
Chilean	38.2
Colombian	32.7
Ecuadorian	31.1
Peruvian	34.8
Uruguayan	33.3
Venezuelan	31.3
Spaniard	35.6

High School Graduates
(Universe: Population 25 Years and Over)

Group	Number	%
Total Population	458,352	86.9
Hispanic or Latino (of any race)	25,109	77.5
Central American, ex. Mexican	2,325	68.2
Nicaraguan	660	82.7
Panamanian	664	92.7
Salvadoran	253	45.4
Cuban	4,151	85.5
Dominican Republic	653	62.5
Mexican	4,374	64.0
Puerto Rican	8,127	83.2
South American	3,468	83.3
Colombian	1,745	83.6
Peruvian	589	86.2
Spaniard	675	93.5

Four-Year College Graduates
(Universe: Population 25 Years and Over)

Group	Number	%
Total Population	126,784	24.0
Hispanic or Latino (of any race)	6,330	19.5
Central American, ex. Mexican	526	15.4
Nicaraguan	115	14.4
Panamanian	241	33.7
Salvadoran	32	5.7
Cuban	1,188	24.5
Dominican Republic	183	17.5
Mexican	892	13.1
Puerto Rican	1,767	18.1
South American	1,189	28.6
Colombian	628	30.1

Notes: (1) Percent of total population; (2) Percent of Hispanic/Latino population; Profiles include places with an overall population of at least 125,000, OR an overall population of at least 25,000 where the Hispanic/Latino population is at least 20% of the overall population. In states where less than five places meet either of these criteria, we have included places with at least 10,000 total population with the highest percentage of Hispanic/Latino population. These places are identified with an asterisk (*); Please refer to the User's Guide for a full explanation of data.

Group	Number	%
Peruvian	128	18.7
Spaniard	217	30.1

Population Age 3–17 Enrolled in Public School
(Universe: Population Age 3–17 Enrolled in School)

Group	Number	%
Total Population	118,161	80.1
Hispanic or Latino (of any race)	10,706	84.2
Central American, ex. Mexican	1,028	92.5
Nicaraguan	151	86.3
Panamanian	191	100.0
Salvadoran	155	88.1
Cuban	1,155	72.4
Dominican Republic	311	79.7
Mexican	2,434	85.2
Puerto Rican	4,002	87.5
South American	869	72.3
Colombian	531	76.6
Peruvian	20	27.4
Spaniard	33	62.3

Population Age 3–17 Enrolled in Private School
(Universe: Population Age 3–17 Enrolled in School)

Group	Number	%
Total Population	29,315	19.9
Hispanic or Latino (of any race)	2,016	15.8
Central American, ex. Mexican	83	7.5
Nicaraguan	24	13.7
Panamanian	0	0.0
Salvadoran	21	11.9
Cuban	440	27.6
Dominican Republic	79	20.3
Mexican	423	14.8
Puerto Rican	570	12.5
South American	333	27.7
Colombian	162	23.4
Peruvian	53	72.6
Spaniard	20	37.7

Foreign-Born Population

Group	Number	%
Total Population	74,806	9.2
Hispanic or Latino (of any race)	19,564	33.4
Central American, ex. Mexican	3,291	60.7
Nicaraguan	745	62.4
Panamanian	607	51.9
Salvadoran	541	60.7
Cuban	3,859	50.2
Dominican Republic	936	45.1
Mexican	6,014	42.4
Puerto Rican	109	0.6
South American	4,344	67.6
Colombian	2,313	70.8
Peruvian	703	73.4
Spaniard	141	13.3

Foreign-Born Naturalized U.S. Citizens

Group	Number	%
Total Population	37,092	49.6
Hispanic or Latino (of any race)	7,183	36.7
Central American, ex. Mexican	1,430	43.5
Nicaraguan	297	39.9
Panamanian	455	75.0
Salvadoran	137	25.3
Cuban	1,798	46.6
Dominican Republic	464	49.6
Mexican	981	16.3
Puerto Rican	52	47.7
South American	1,979	45.6
Colombian	942	40.7
Peruvian	324	46.1
Spaniard	94	66.7

Language Spoken at Home: English Only
(Universe: Population 5 Years and Over)

Group	Number	%
Total Population	657,169	87.1
Hispanic or Latino (of any race)	15,280	29.3
Central American, ex. Mexican	1,080	21.6
Nicaraguan	249	22.9
Panamanian	338	31.2
Salvadoran	270	34.3
Cuban	2,195	31.0
Dominican Republic	177	10.4
Mexican	3,712	30.4
Puerto Rican	5,326	32.4
South American	724	12.3
Colombian	287	9.3
Peruvian	81	9.8
Spaniard	555	57.7

Language Spoken at Home: Spanish
(Universe: Population 5 Years and Over)

Group	Number	%
Total Population	43,880	5.8
Hispanic or Latino (of any race)	36,309	69.5
Central American, ex. Mexican	3,862	77.3
Nicaraguan	839	77.1
Panamanian	744	68.8
Salvadoran	518	65.7
Cuban	4,861	68.6
Dominican Republic	1,487	87.6
Mexican	8,319	68.2
Puerto Rican	10,984	66.9
South American	5,133	87.0
Colombian	2,770	90.2
Peruvian	738	89.1
Spaniard	367	38.1

Unemployment Rate
(Universe: Population 16 Years and Over)

Group	%
Total Population	8.8
Hispanic or Latino (of any race)	8.1
Central American, ex. Mexican	7.4
Nicaraguan	11.9
Panamanian	6.2
Salvadoran	15.1
Cuban	7.6
Dominican Republic	10.1
Mexican	9.4
Puerto Rican	7.5
South American	7.5
Colombian	4.5
Peruvian	7.5
Spaniard	16.5

Class of Worker: Private Wage and Salary
(Universe: Civilian Employed Population 16 Years and Over)

Group	Number	%
Total Population	320,458	82.9
Hispanic or Latino (of any race)	23,521	85.7
Central American, ex. Mexican	2,431	81.1
Nicaraguan	463	75.7
Panamanian	549	75.2
Salvadoran	352	83.6
Cuban	2,986	83.8
Dominican Republic	827	76.4
Mexican	5,836	88.5
Puerto Rican	7,170	85.7
South American	2,808	90.3
Colombian	1,501	90.7
Peruvian	467	97.5
Spaniard	426	89.3

Class of Worker: Government
(Universe: Civilian Employed Population 16 Years and Over)

Group	Number	%
Total Population	49,015	12.7
Hispanic or Latino (of any race)	2,343	8.5
Central American, ex. Mexican	295	9.8
Nicaraguan	76	12.4
Panamanian	138	18.9
Salvadoran	25	5.9
Cuban	445	12.5
Dominican Republic	29	2.7
Mexican	404	6.1
Puerto Rican	789	9.4
South American	188	6.0
Colombian	75	4.5
Peruvian	12	2.5
Spaniard	18	3.8

Means of Transportation to Work: Car, Truck or Van
(Universe: Workers 16 Years and Over)

Group	Number	%
Total Population	356,460	91.9
Hispanic or Latino (of any race)	25,717	91.9
Central American, ex. Mexican	2,734	93.6
Nicaraguan	554	93.9
Panamanian	649	93.1
Salvadoran	368	92.2
Cuban	3,427	95.2
Dominican Republic	924	85.1
Mexican	6,212	91.5
Puerto Rican	7,904	92.9
South American	2,859	87.3
Colombian	1,546	89.2
Peruvian	373	73.6
Spaniard	462	96.9

Means of Transportation to Work: Public Transportation (ex. Taxicab)
(Universe: Workers 16 Years and Over)

Group	Number	%
Total Population	6,066	1.6
Hispanic or Latino (of any race)	490	1.8
Central American, ex. Mexican	17	0.6
Nicaraguan	0	0.0
Panamanian	0	0.0
Salvadoran	17	4.3
Cuban	54	1.5
Dominican Republic	15	1.4
Mexican	201	3.0
Puerto Rican	116	1.4
South American	49	1.5
Colombian	0	0.0
Peruvian	20	3.9
Spaniard	0	0.0

Homeownership Rate
(Universe: Occupied Housing Units)

Group	%
Total Population	61.7
Hispanic or Latino (of any race)	48.8
Central American, ex. Mexican	43.0
Costa Rican	56.1
Guatemalan	37.8
Honduran	29.9
Nicaraguan	46.9
Panamanian	52.1
Salvadoran	46.4
Cuban	56.5
Dominican Republic	49.4
Mexican	40.7
Puerto Rican	48.1
South American	55.8
Argentinean	51.6
Bolivian	57.3
Chilean	64.5
Colombian	57.2
Ecuadorian	63.5
Peruvian	53.4
Uruguayan	46.4
Venezuelan	48.7
Spaniard	67.4

Median Home Value

Group	Dollars
Total Population	171,500
Hispanic or Latino (of any race)	170,600
Central American, ex. Mexican	166,700
Nicaraguan	206,600
Panamanian	141,100
Salvadoran	151,900
Cuban	173,400
Dominican Republic	167,900
Mexican	163,100
Puerto Rican	168,600
South American	177,200
Colombian	186,600
Peruvian	166,600
Spaniard	184,600

Median Gross Rent

Group	Dollars
Total Population	872
Hispanic or Latino (of any race)	884
Central American, ex. Mexican	916
Nicaraguan	781
Panamanian	740
Salvadoran	643
Cuban	965
Dominican Republic	881

Notes: (1) Percent of total population; (2) Percent of Hispanic/Latino population; Profiles include places with an overall population of at least 125,000, OR an overall population of at least 25,000 where the Hispanic/Latino population is at least 20% of the overall population. In states where less than five places meet either of these criteria, we have included places with at least 10,000 total population with the highest percentage of Hispanic/Latino population. These places are identified with an asterisk (*); Please refer to the User's Guide for a full explanation of data.

Mexican	864
Puerto Rican	843
South American	946
Colombian	1,039
Peruvian	766
Spaniard	758

Median Household Income
(2010 Inflation-Adjusted Dollars)

Group	Dollars
Total Population	48,829
Hispanic or Latino (of any race)	42,495
Central American, ex. Mexican	37,775
Nicaraguan	27,061
Panamanian	40,625
Salvadoran	46,111
Cuban	54,134
Dominican Republic	41,952
Mexican	40,031
Puerto Rican	44,664
South American	41,453
Colombian	41,622
Peruvian	41,207
Spaniard	54,333

Per Capita Income
(2010 Inflation-Adjusted Dollars)

Group	Dollars
Total Population	25,227
Hispanic or Latino (of any race)	17,989
Central American, ex. Mexican	17,321
Nicaraguan	17,777
Panamanian	21,699
Salvadoran	11,612
Cuban	23,227
Dominican Republic	14,221
Mexican	14,505
Puerto Rican	18,150
South American	20,002
Colombian	22,776
Peruvian	18,019
Spaniard	25,762

Households with $100,000+ Income

Group	Number	%
Total Population	50,205	16.1
Hispanic or Latino (of any race)	1,932	10.9
Central American, ex. Mexican	193	12.4
Nicaraguan	51	13.1
Panamanian	36	9.7
Salvadoran	0	0.0
Cuban	452	17.1
Dominican Republic	18	2.6
Mexican	341	9.6
Puerto Rican	476	8.6
South American	283	12.5
Colombian	227	19.4
Peruvian	31	8.1
Spaniard	66	13.6

Households with Food Stamps/SNAP Benefits During Past 12 Months

Group	Number	%
Total Population	28,163	9.1
Hispanic or Latino (of any race)	1,489	8.4
Central American, ex. Mexican	171	11.0
Nicaraguan	56	14.4
Panamanian	46	12.4
Salvadoran	29	12.2
Cuban	290	10.9
Dominican Republic	41	6.0
Mexican	223	6.3
Puerto Rican	580	10.5
South American	135	6.0
Colombian	61	5.2
Peruvian	33	8.6
Spaniard	0	0.0

Poverty Rate
(Income in Past 12 Months Below Poverty Level)

Group	%
Total Population	14.3
Hispanic or Latino (of any race)	17.5
Central American, ex. Mexican	16.6
Nicaraguan	14.2

Panamanian	8.4
Salvadoran	26.9
Cuban	8.5
Dominican Republic	10.8
Mexican	30.1
Puerto Rican	14.2
South American	16.6
Colombian	18.2
Peruvian	4.2
Spaniard	7.1

Kendale Lakes

Population

Group	Number	%TP[1]	%HP[2]
Total Population	56,148	100.0	–
Hispanic or Latino (of any race)	48,584	86.5	100.0
Central American, ex. Mexican	5,076	9.0	10.4
Costa Rican	153	0.3	0.3
Guatemalan	238	0.4	0.5
Honduran	569	1.0	1.2
Nicaraguan	3,560	6.3	7.3
Panamanian	201	0.4	0.4
Salvadoran	349	0.6	0.7
Cuban	29,095	51.8	59.9
Dominican Republic	1,197	2.1	2.5
Mexican	765	1.4	1.6
Puerto Rican	1,805	3.2	3.7
South American	8,687	15.5	17.9
Argentinean	509	0.9	1.0
Bolivian	167	0.3	0.3
Chilean	469	0.8	1.0
Colombian	4,281	7.6	8.8
Ecuadorian	527	0.9	1.1
Peruvian	1,473	2.6	3.0
Uruguayan	161	0.3	0.3
Venezuelan	1,082	1.9	2.2
Spaniard	287	0.5	0.6

Population Growth: 2000–2010

Group	%
Total Population	-1.3
Hispanic or Latino (of any race)	11.5
Central American, ex. Mexican	39.5
Costa Rican	41.7
Guatemalan	66.4
Honduran	100.4
Nicaraguan	36.3
Panamanian	-9.0
Salvadoran	91.8
Cuban	32.5
Dominican Republic	39.5
Mexican	33.5
Puerto Rican	-9.5
South American	22.8
Argentinean	47.1
Chilean	23.1
Colombian	18.3
Ecuadorian	41.7
Peruvian	27.3
Uruguayan	61.0
Venezuelan	23.7
Spaniard	56.0

Males per 100 Females

Group	Number
Total Population	87.4
Hispanic or Latino (of any race)	85.6
Central American, ex. Mexican	82.0
Costa Rican	54.5
Guatemalan	91.9
Honduran	82.4
Nicaraguan	84.0
Panamanian	76.3
Salvadoran	72.8
Cuban	89.0
Dominican Republic	74.7
Mexican	120.5
Puerto Rican	85.9
South American	74.5
Argentinean	89.2
Bolivian	81.5
Chilean	80.4

Colombian	69.6
Ecuadorian	83.0
Peruvian	72.1
Uruguayan	96.3
Venezuelan	80.9
Spaniard	106.5

Average Household Size

Group	People
Total Population	3.06
Hispanic or Latino (of any race)	3.16
Central American, ex. Mexican	3.65
Costa Rican	3.62
Guatemalan	3.71
Honduran	3.76
Nicaraguan	3.67
Panamanian	3.26
Salvadoran	3.59
Cuban	3.10
Dominican Republic	3.32
Mexican	3.75
Puerto Rican	2.95
South American	3.15
Argentinean	2.92
Bolivian	3.50
Chilean	3.12
Colombian	3.09
Ecuadorian	3.41
Peruvian	3.33
Uruguayan	2.88
Venezuelan	3.14
Spaniard	2.50

Median Age

Group	Years
Total Population	40.7
Hispanic or Latino (of any race)	41.0
Central American, ex. Mexican	39.0
Costa Rican	34.2
Guatemalan	39.7
Honduran	34.3
Nicaraguan	39.8
Panamanian	45.1
Salvadoran	38.7
Cuban	42.9
Dominican Republic	36.6
Mexican	27.4
Puerto Rican	37.5
South American	41.3
Argentinean	39.3
Bolivian	38.8
Chilean	47.8
Colombian	42.8
Ecuadorian	40.8
Peruvian	40.7
Uruguayan	39.2
Venezuelan	35.6
Spaniard	49.6

High School Graduates
(Universe: Population 25 Years and Over)

Group	Number	%
Total Population	30,783	80.7
Hispanic or Latino (of any race)	25,838	79.8
Central American, ex. Mexican	2,670	75.5
Nicaraguan	1,815	76.5
Cuban	15,138	77.3
Dominican Republic	580	88.5
Puerto Rican	1,081	90.4
South American	5,356	87.8
Colombian	3,249	88.4
Peruvian	674	95.5

Four-Year College Graduates
(Universe: Population 25 Years and Over)

Group	Number	%
Total Population	10,287	27.0
Hispanic or Latino (of any race)	8,690	26.9
Central American, ex. Mexican	728	20.6
Nicaraguan	645	27.2
Cuban	5,489	28.0
Dominican Republic	137	20.9
Puerto Rican	289	24.2
South American	1,787	29.3
Colombian	1,202	32.7

Notes: (1) Percent of total population; (2) Percent of Hispanic/Latino population; Profiles include places with an overall population of at least 125,000, OR an overall population of at least 25,000 where the Hispanic/Latino population is at least 20% of the overall population. In states where less than five places meet either of these criteria, we have included places with at least 10,000 total population with the highest percentage of Hispanic/Latino population. These places are identified with an asterisk (*); Please refer to the User's Guide for a full explanation of data.

Group	Number	%
Peruvian	205	29.0

Population Age 3–17 Enrolled in Public School
(Universe: Population Age 3–17 Enrolled in School)

Group	Number	%
Total Population	7,250	81.7
Hispanic or Latino (of any race)	6,146	81.5
Central American, ex. Mexican	906	85.1
Nicaraguan	601	93.5
Cuban	3,098	80.2
Dominican Republic	84	87.5
Puerto Rican	168	56.9
South American	1,241	91.9
Colombian	809	92.9
Peruvian	165	91.2

Population Age 3–17 Enrolled in Private School
(Universe: Population Age 3–17 Enrolled in School)

Group	Number	%
Total Population	1,629	18.3
Hispanic or Latino (of any race)	1,391	18.5
Central American, ex. Mexican	159	14.9
Nicaraguan	42	6.5
Cuban	763	19.8
Dominican Republic	12	12.5
Puerto Rican	127	43.1
South American	109	8.1
Colombian	62	7.1
Peruvian	16	8.8

Foreign-Born Population

Group	Number	%
Total Population	31,570	56.7
Hispanic or Latino (of any race)	30,026	63.7
Central American, ex. Mexican	3,535	64.6
Nicaraguan	2,475	70.2
Cuban	18,745	68.0
Dominican Republic	617	56.2
Puerto Rican	18	1.1
South American	6,034	69.1
Colombian	3,655	69.6
Peruvian	782	78.0

Foreign-Born Naturalized U.S. Citizens

Group	Number	%
Total Population	18,034	57.1
Hispanic or Latino (of any race)	17,088	56.9
Central American, ex. Mexican	1,752	49.6
Nicaraguan	1,289	52.1
Cuban	11,758	62.7
Dominican Republic	422	68.4
Puerto Rican	15	83.3
South American	2,632	43.6
Colombian	1,426	39.0
Peruvian	482	61.6

Language Spoken at Home: English Only
(Universe: Population 5 Years and Over)

Group	Number	%
Total Population	7,273	13.9
Hispanic or Latino (of any race)	1,880	4.2
Central American, ex. Mexican	107	2.0
Nicaraguan	0	0.0
Cuban	1,106	4.3
Dominican Republic	20	1.9
Puerto Rican	239	15.7
South American	251	3.0
Colombian	122	2.4
Peruvian	44	4.5

Language Spoken at Home: Spanish
(Universe: Population 5 Years and Over)

Group	Number	%
Total Population	44,124	84.1
Hispanic or Latino (of any race)	42,491	95.7
Central American, ex. Mexican	5,125	98.0
Nicaraguan	3,401	100.0
Cuban	24,774	95.7
Dominican Republic	1,025	98.1
Puerto Rican	1,280	84.3
South American	8,069	96.8
Colombian	4,872	97.6
Peruvian	929	95.5

Unemployment Rate
(Universe: Population 16 Years and Over)

Group	%
Total Population	8.3
Hispanic or Latino (of any race)	8.3
Central American, ex. Mexican	3.2
Nicaraguan	3.7
Cuban	7.9
Dominican Republic	6.8
Puerto Rican	9.0
South American	10.9
Colombian	9.9
Peruvian	18.7

Class of Worker: Private Wage and Salary
(Universe: Civilian Employed Population 16 Years and Over)

Group	Number	%
Total Population	22,887	82.2
Hispanic or Latino (of any race)	19,825	82.5
Central American, ex. Mexican	2,586	86.7
Nicaraguan	1,910	91.0
Cuban	11,167	81.6
Dominican Republic	463	85.1
Puerto Rican	733	81.0
South American	4,147	83.5
Colombian	2,425	84.1
Peruvian	415	76.3

Class of Worker: Government
(Universe: Civilian Employed Population 16 Years and Over)

Group	Number	%
Total Population	3,099	11.1
Hispanic or Latino (of any race)	2,523	10.5
Central American, ex. Mexican	147	4.9
Nicaraguan	88	4.2
Cuban	1,635	12.0
Dominican Republic	81	14.9
Puerto Rican	131	14.5
South American	453	9.1
Colombian	211	7.3
Peruvian	61	11.2

Means of Transportation to Work: Car, Truck or Van
(Universe: Workers 16 Years and Over)

Group	Number	%
Total Population	25,933	94.9
Hispanic or Latino (of any race)	22,514	95.5
Central American, ex. Mexican	2,762	93.5
Nicaraguan	1,967	95.0
Cuban	12,945	96.1
Dominican Republic	544	100.0
Puerto Rican	871	99.0
South American	4,528	93.6
Colombian	2,613	92.9
Peruvian	513	100.0

Means of Transportation to Work: Public Transportation (ex. Taxicab)
(Universe: Workers 16 Years and Over)

Group	Number	%
Total Population	382	1.4
Hispanic or Latino (of any race)	251	1.1
Central American, ex. Mexican	86	2.9
Nicaraguan	68	3.3
Cuban	28	0.2
Dominican Republic	0	0.0
Puerto Rican	9	1.0
South American	119	2.5
Colombian	103	3.7
Peruvian	0	0.0

Homeownership Rate
(Universe: Occupied Housing Units)

Group	%
Total Population	74.9
Hispanic or Latino (of any race)	73.2
Central American, ex. Mexican	71.1
Costa Rican	61.8
Guatemalan	73.9
Honduran	59.2
Nicaraguan	72.9
Panamanian	67.6
Salvadoran	74.8
Cuban	76.1
Dominican Republic	63.8
Mexican	51.9
Puerto Rican	68.7
South American	67.2
Argentinean	74.7
Bolivian	72.0
Chilean	73.3
Colombian	68.8
Ecuadorian	68.4
Peruvian	67.6
Uruguayan	55.4
Venezuelan	54.0
Spaniard	85.5

Median Home Value

Group	Dollars
Total Population	235,700
Hispanic or Latino (of any race)	232,300
Central American, ex. Mexican	177,000
Nicaraguan	173,300
Cuban	246,700
Dominican Republic	219,600
Puerto Rican	226,600
South American	212,400
Colombian	214,500
Peruvian	230,000

Median Gross Rent

Group	Dollars
Total Population	1,310
Hispanic or Latino (of any race)	1,324
Central American, ex. Mexican	1,378
Nicaraguan	1,350
Cuban	1,326
Dominican Republic	1,172
Puerto Rican	1,479
South American	1,239
Colombian	1,205
Peruvian	1,100

Median Household Income
(2010 Inflation-Adjusted Dollars)

Group	Dollars
Total Population	53,284
Hispanic or Latino (of any race)	52,480
Central American, ex. Mexican	51,214
Nicaraguan	60,304
Cuban	53,572
Dominican Republic	52,917
Puerto Rican	71,316
South American	50,618
Colombian	50,296
Peruvian	63,750

Per Capita Income
(2010 Inflation-Adjusted Dollars)

Group	Dollars
Total Population	22,463
Hispanic or Latino (of any race)	21,876
Central American, ex. Mexican	16,427
Nicaraguan	18,537
Cuban	23,975
Dominican Republic	24,150
Puerto Rican	22,040
South American	20,057
Colombian	16,777
Peruvian	21,351

Households with $100,000+ Income

Group	Number	%
Total Population	3,271	18.2
Hispanic or Latino (of any race)	2,601	17.0
Central American, ex. Mexican	111	7.2
Nicaraguan	47	5.1
Cuban	1,858	20.0
Dominican Republic	29	8.5
Puerto Rican	165	27.2
South American	350	12.4
Colombian	203	12.7
Peruvian	17	5.3

Households with Food Stamps/SNAP Benefits During Past 12 Months

Group	Number	%
Total Population	2,163	12.0

Notes: (1) Percent of total population; (2) Percent of Hispanic/Latino population; Profiles include places with an overall population of at least 125,000, OR an overall population of at least 25,000 where the Hispanic/Latino population is at least 20% of the overall population. In states where less than five places meet either of these criteria, we have included places with at least 10,000 total population with the highest percentage of Hispanic/Latino population. These places are identified with an asterisk (*); Please refer to the User's Guide for a full explanation of data.

Hispanic or Latino (of any race)	2,014	13.2
Central American, ex. Mexican	169	10.9
Nicaraguan	112	12.2
Cuban	1,486	16.0
Dominican Republic	39	11.5
Puerto Rican	53	8.7
South American	243	8.6
Colombian	152	9.5
Peruvian	28	8.8

Poverty Rate
(Income in Past 12 Months Below Poverty Level)

Group	%
Total Population	11.8
Hispanic or Latino (of any race)	11.9
Central American, ex. Mexican	8.1
Nicaraguan	6.2
Cuban	12.4
Dominican Republic	4.6
Puerto Rican	6.1
South American	13.1
Colombian	13.8
Peruvian	4.3

Kendall

Population

Group	Number	%TP[1]	%HP[2]
Total Population	75,371	100.0	–
Hispanic or Latino (of any race)	48,038	63.7	100.0
Central American, ex. Mexican	4,668	6.2	9.7
Costa Rican	260	0.3	0.5
Guatemalan	289	0.4	0.6
Honduran	705	0.9	1.5
Nicaraguan	2,629	3.5	5.5
Panamanian	336	0.4	0.7
Salvadoran	426	0.6	0.9
Cuban	24,533	32.5	51.1
Dominican Republic	1,383	1.8	2.9
Mexican	796	1.1	1.7
Puerto Rican	2,461	3.3	5.1
South American	11,514	15.3	24.0
Argentinean	840	1.1	1.7
Bolivian	274	0.4	0.6
Chilean	613	0.8	1.3
Colombian	4,870	6.5	10.1
Ecuadorian	766	1.0	1.6
Peruvian	2,280	3.0	4.7
Uruguayan	188	0.2	0.4
Venezuelan	1,611	2.1	3.4
Spaniard	548	0.7	1.1

Population Growth: 2000–2010

Group	%
Total Population	0.2
Hispanic or Latino (of any race)	27.9
Central American, ex. Mexican	41.0
Costa Rican	52.0
Guatemalan	45.2
Honduran	82.2
Nicaraguan	40.7
Panamanian	25.4
Salvadoran	26.4
Cuban	53.1
Dominican Republic	68.5
Mexican	36.8
Puerto Rican	7.1
South American	44.6
Argentinean	38.8
Bolivian	61.2
Chilean	28.0
Colombian	42.0
Ecuadorian	84.6
Peruvian	50.8
Venezuelan	45.4
Spaniard	109.2

Males per 100 Females

Group	Number
Total Population	86.6
Hispanic or Latino (of any race)	83.0
Central American, ex. Mexican	79.6
Costa Rican	85.7
Guatemalan	94.0
Honduran	74.9
Nicaraguan	77.2
Panamanian	73.2
Salvadoran	91.9
Cuban	88.0
Dominican Republic	73.3
Mexican	90.9
Puerto Rican	87.0
South American	74.6
Argentinean	92.2
Bolivian	103.0
Chilean	91.0
Colombian	69.1
Ecuadorian	72.1
Peruvian	71.8
Uruguayan	95.8
Venezuelan	76.6
Spaniard	83.9

Average Household Size

Group	People
Total Population	2.58
Hispanic or Latino (of any race)	2.77
Central American, ex. Mexican	3.09
Costa Rican	3.11
Guatemalan	2.73
Honduran	3.31
Nicaraguan	3.16
Panamanian	2.61
Salvadoran	3.01
Cuban	2.73
Dominican Republic	2.90
Mexican	2.67
Puerto Rican	2.54
South American	2.80
Argentinean	2.70
Bolivian	2.99
Chilean	2.83
Colombian	2.75
Ecuadorian	2.84
Peruvian	2.92
Uruguayan	2.87
Venezuelan	2.81
Spaniard	2.59

Median Age

Group	Years
Total Population	40.7
Hispanic or Latino (of any race)	38.8
Central American, ex. Mexican	36.7
Costa Rican	34.0
Guatemalan	34.8
Honduran	34.0
Nicaraguan	37.5
Panamanian	41.4
Salvadoran	39.5
Cuban	39.9
Dominican Republic	34.9
Mexican	33.4
Puerto Rican	36.2
South American	39.7
Argentinean	39.5
Bolivian	36.7
Chilean	43.7
Colombian	39.7
Ecuadorian	40.2
Peruvian	40.8
Uruguayan	37.7
Venezuelan	37.4
Spaniard	42.4

High School Graduates
(Universe: Population 25 Years and Over)

Group	Number	%
Total Population	47,385	88.6
Hispanic or Latino (of any race)	28,752	85.8
Central American, ex. Mexican	3,163	82.2
Nicaraguan	1,696	83.1
Cuban	14,297	83.6
Dominican Republic	1,037	91.0
Mexican	851	82.3
Puerto Rican	1,589	88.7
South American	6,738	90.5
Chilean	471	88.2
Colombian	2,854	88.8
Peruvian	1,278	93.4
Venezuelan	920	91.9

Four-Year College Graduates
(Universe: Population 25 Years and Over)

Group	Number	%
Total Population	22,176	41.5
Hispanic or Latino (of any race)	12,287	36.6
Central American, ex. Mexican	921	23.9
Nicaraguan	443	21.7
Cuban	6,385	37.4
Dominican Republic	449	39.4
Mexican	216	20.9
Puerto Rican	627	35.0
South American	3,141	42.2
Chilean	214	40.1
Colombian	1,260	39.2
Peruvian	596	43.5
Venezuelan	585	58.4

Population Age 3–17 Enrolled in Public School
(Universe: Population Age 3–17 Enrolled in School)

Group	Number	%
Total Population	9,064	71.4
Hispanic or Latino (of any race)	5,454	69.9
Central American, ex. Mexican	708	90.5
Nicaraguan	416	90.4
Cuban	2,274	57.4
Dominican Republic	167	86.1
Mexican	175	82.2
Puerto Rican	287	86.2
South American	1,546	84.5
Chilean	238	93.7
Colombian	624	80.6
Peruvian	213	93.8
Venezuelan	216	78.3

Population Age 3–17 Enrolled in Private School
(Universe: Population Age 3–17 Enrolled in School)

Group	Number	%
Total Population	3,625	28.6
Hispanic or Latino (of any race)	2,351	30.1
Central American, ex. Mexican	74	9.5
Nicaraguan	44	9.6
Cuban	1,690	42.6
Dominican Republic	27	13.9
Mexican	38	17.8
Puerto Rican	46	13.8
South American	283	15.5
Chilean	16	6.3
Colombian	150	19.4
Peruvian	14	6.2
Venezuelan	60	21.7

Foreign-Born Population

Group	Number	%
Total Population	34,313	44.8
Hispanic or Latino (of any race)	29,015	60.2
Central American, ex. Mexican	4,267	74.6
Nicaraguan	2,412	79.1
Cuban	13,384	55.4
Dominican Republic	976	63.6
Mexican	847	64.8
Puerto Rican	54	2.5
South American	8,479	75.4
Chilean	599	61.7
Colombian	3,597	73.7
Peruvian	1,419	79.9
Venezuelan	1,294	76.5

Foreign-Born Naturalized U.S. Citizens

Group	Number	%
Total Population	20,297	59.2
Hispanic or Latino (of any race)	17,055	58.8
Central American, ex. Mexican	2,191	51.3
Nicaraguan	1,266	52.5
Cuban	9,695	72.4
Dominican Republic	365	37.4
Mexican	321	37.9
Puerto Rican	54	100.0
South American	3,790	44.7
Chilean	405	67.6
Colombian	1,843	51.2
Peruvian	695	49.0

Notes: (1) Percent of total population; (2) Percent of Hispanic/Latino population; Profiles include places with an overall population of at least 125,000, OR an overall population of at least 25,000 where the Hispanic/Latino population is at least 20% of the overall population. In states where less than five places meet either of these criteria, we have included places with at least 10,000 total population with the highest percentage of Hispanic/Latino population. These places are identified with an asterisk (*); Please refer to the User's Guide for a full explanation of data.

Venezuelan	373	28.8

Language Spoken at Home: English Only
(Universe: Population 5 Years and Over)

Group	Number	%
Total Population	22,269	30.5
Hispanic or Latino (of any race)	2,667	5.8
Central American, ex. Mexican	214	3.9
Nicaraguan	57	1.9
Cuban	1,445	6.4
Dominican Republic	40	2.9
Mexican	161	12.6
Puerto Rican	272	12.8
South American	405	3.8
Chilean	91	9.5
Colombian	158	3.4
Peruvian	6	0.3
Venezuelan	62	4.1

Language Spoken at Home: Spanish
(Universe: Population 5 Years and Over)

Group	Number	%
Total Population	46,522	63.7
Hispanic or Latino (of any race)	42,906	93.9
Central American, ex. Mexican	5,312	96.1
Nicaraguan	2,875	98.1
Cuban	21,254	93.4
Dominican Republic	1,342	95.9
Mexican	1,118	87.4
Puerto Rican	1,850	87.2
South American	10,304	96.0
Chilean	862	90.5
Colombian	4,525	96.4
Peruvian	1,732	99.7
Venezuelan	1,430	95.2

Unemployment Rate
(Universe: Population 16 Years and Over)

Group	%
Total Population	7.2
Hispanic or Latino (of any race)	8.2
Central American, ex. Mexican	7.7
Nicaraguan	5.2
Cuban	8.6
Dominican Republic	3.8
Mexican	9.7
Puerto Rican	3.3
South American	9.1
Chilean	3.5
Colombian	9.4
Peruvian	10.7
Venezuelan	7.2

Class of Worker: Private Wage and Salary
(Universe: Civilian Employed Population 16 Years and Over)

Group	Number	%
Total Population	31,212	80.5
Hispanic or Latino (of any race)	20,879	83.7
Central American, ex. Mexican	2,706	82.6
Nicaraguan	1,358	77.7
Cuban	9,679	81.3
Dominican Republic	783	88.0
Mexican	840	100.0
Puerto Rican	805	76.1
South American	5,216	86.3
Chilean	453	85.3
Colombian	2,193	87.3
Peruvian	906	83.8
Venezuelan	647	86.7

Class of Worker: Government
(Universe: Civilian Employed Population 16 Years and Over)

Group	Number	%
Total Population	4,759	12.3
Hispanic or Latino (of any race)	2,174	8.7
Central American, ex. Mexican	230	7.0
Nicaraguan	103	5.9
Cuban	1,371	11.5
Dominican Republic	22	2.5
Mexican	0	0.0
Puerto Rican	155	14.7
South American	343	5.7
Chilean	78	14.7
Colombian	138	5.5
Peruvian	62	5.7

Venezuelan	23	3.1

Means of Transportation to Work: Car, Truck or Van
(Universe: Workers 16 Years and Over)

Group	Number	%
Total Population	33,619	88.8
Hispanic or Latino (of any race)	21,589	88.9
Central American, ex. Mexican	2,773	87.3
Nicaraguan	1,395	83.8
Cuban	10,475	90.6
Dominican Republic	801	90.0
Mexican	744	88.6
Puerto Rican	874	82.6
South American	5,067	86.7
Chilean	445	83.8
Colombian	2,203	90.0
Peruvian	890	86.1
Venezuelan	624	86.0

Means of Transportation to Work: Public Transportation (ex. Taxicab)
(Universe: Workers 16 Years and Over)

Group	Number	%
Total Population	1,308	3.5
Hispanic or Latino (of any race)	805	3.3
Central American, ex. Mexican	177	5.6
Nicaraguan	73	4.4
Cuban	228	2.0
Dominican Republic	56	6.3
Mexican	10	1.2
Puerto Rican	62	5.9
South American	245	4.2
Chilean	79	14.9
Colombian	35	1.4
Peruvian	20	1.9
Venezuelan	87	12.0

Homeownership Rate
(Universe: Occupied Housing Units)

Group	%
Total Population	66.2
Hispanic or Latino (of any race)	60.6
Central American, ex. Mexican	49.1
Costa Rican	51.3
Guatemalan	47.9
Honduran	40.4
Nicaraguan	47.3
Panamanian	58.3
Salvadoran	63.3
Cuban	66.2
Dominican Republic	51.0
Mexican	52.2
Puerto Rican	57.7
South American	54.7
Argentinean	57.4
Bolivian	60.8
Chilean	65.1
Colombian	55.0
Ecuadorian	53.5
Peruvian	50.1
Uruguayan	51.7
Venezuelan	54.9
Spaniard	76.7

Median Home Value

Group	Dollars
Total Population	335,600
Hispanic or Latino (of any race)	321,100
Central American, ex. Mexican	271,400
Nicaraguan	254,200
Cuban	353,000
Dominican Republic	225,000
Mexican	336,100
Puerto Rican	249,600
South American	264,400
Chilean	187,800
Colombian	241,700
Peruvian	243,100
Venezuelan	369,100

Median Gross Rent

Group	Dollars
Total Population	1,244
Hispanic or Latino (of any race)	1,216
Central American, ex. Mexican	1,308
Nicaraguan	1,352
Cuban	1,180
Dominican Republic	1,118
Mexican	1,342
Puerto Rican	1,127
South American	1,259
Chilean	1,357
Colombian	1,221
Peruvian	1,127
Venezuelan	1,232

Median Household Income
(2010 Inflation-Adjusted Dollars)

Group	Dollars
Total Population	61,266
Hispanic or Latino (of any race)	54,781
Central American, ex. Mexican	53,071
Nicaraguan	58,554
Cuban	59,031
Dominican Republic	54,464
Mexican	81,964
Puerto Rican	44,764
South American	49,432
Chilean	40,100
Colombian	45,750
Peruvian	53,409
Venezuelan	52,216

Per Capita Income
(2010 Inflation-Adjusted Dollars)

Group	Dollars
Total Population	32,520
Hispanic or Latino (of any race)	28,289
Central American, ex. Mexican	23,276
Nicaraguan	25,405
Cuban	31,998
Dominican Republic	22,139
Mexican	26,231
Puerto Rican	26,493
South American	23,454
Chilean	14,331
Colombian	21,683
Peruvian	29,558
Venezuelan	21,572

Households with $100,000+ Income

Group	Number	%
Total Population	8,228	30.2
Hispanic or Latino (of any race)	4,464	27.1
Central American, ex. Mexican	346	21.5
Nicaraguan	232	28.7
Cuban	2,850	32.7
Dominican Republic	96	13.4
Mexican	96	27.0
Puerto Rican	186	21.3
South American	649	17.9
Chilean	23	10.6
Colombian	242	14.2
Peruvian	116	17.3
Venezuelan	97	24.7

Households with Food Stamps/SNAP Benefits During Past 12 Months

Group	Number	%
Total Population	2,453	9.0
Hispanic or Latino (of any race)	2,159	13.1
Central American, ex. Mexican	147	9.1
Nicaraguan	89	11.0
Cuban	1,366	15.7
Dominican Republic	84	11.7
Mexican	0	0.0
Puerto Rican	72	8.2
South American	430	11.9
Chilean	0	0.0
Colombian	242	14.2
Peruvian	24	3.6
Venezuelan	83	21.1

Poverty Rate
(Income in Past 12 Months Below Poverty Level)

Group	%
Total Population	9.2
Hispanic or Latino (of any race)	9.9
Central American, ex. Mexican	12.3

Notes: (1) Percent of total population; (2) Percent of Hispanic/Latino population; Profiles include places with an overall population of at least 125,000, OR an overall population of at least 25,000 where the Hispanic/Latino population is at least 20% of the overall population. In states where less than five places meet either of these criteria, we have included places with at least 10,000 total population with the highest percentage of Hispanic/Latino population. These places are identified with an asterisk (*); Please refer to the User's Guide for a full explanation of data.

Nicaraguan	8.7
Cuban	9.7
Dominican Republic	10.4
Mexican	4.7
Puerto Rican	5.7
South American	11.6
Chilean	14.8
Colombian	16.7
Peruvian	10.1
Venezuelan	8.1

Kendall West

Population

Group	Number	%TP[1]	%HP[2]
Total Population	36,154	100.0	–
Hispanic or Latino (of any race)	31,912	88.3	100.0
Central American, ex. Mexican	3,435	9.5	10.8
Costa Rican	100	0.3	0.3
Guatemalan	167	0.5	0.5
Honduran	469	1.3	1.5
Nicaraguan	2,265	6.3	7.1
Panamanian	162	0.4	0.5
Salvadoran	253	0.7	0.8
Cuban	16,109	44.6	50.5
Dominican Republic	1,064	2.9	3.3
Mexican	392	1.1	1.2
Puerto Rican	1,621	4.5	5.1
South American	7,715	21.3	24.2
Argentinean	432	1.2	1.4
Bolivian	100	0.3	0.3
Chilean	276	0.8	0.9
Colombian	3,772	10.4	11.8
Ecuadorian	487	1.3	1.5
Peruvian	1,369	3.8	4.3
Uruguayan	145	0.4	0.5
Venezuelan	1,118	3.1	3.5
Spaniard	173	0.5	0.5

Population Growth: 2000–2010

Group	%
Total Population	-4.9
Hispanic or Latino (of any race)	6.2
Central American, ex. Mexican	36.8
Costa Rican	-4.8
Honduran	81.1
Nicaraguan	35.6
Panamanian	13.3
Salvadoran	26.5
Cuban	45.2
Dominican Republic	8.4
Mexican	-11.9
Puerto Rican	-24.3
South American	9.1
Argentinean	46.9
Chilean	10.8
Colombian	-0.2
Ecuadorian	16.8
Peruvian	26.3
Venezuelan	10.1
Spaniard	44.2

Males per 100 Females

Group	Number
Total Population	88.2
Hispanic or Latino (of any race)	86.5
Central American, ex. Mexican	83.4
Costa Rican	81.8
Guatemalan	131.9
Honduran	76.3
Nicaraguan	83.8
Panamanian	70.5
Salvadoran	75.7
Cuban	92.4
Dominican Republic	73.6
Mexican	96.0
Puerto Rican	83.2
South American	78.6
Argentinean	102.8
Bolivian	75.4
Chilean	102.9
Colombian	74.1
Ecuadorian	77.1
Peruvian	80.8
Uruguayan	79.0
Venezuelan	79.5
Spaniard	96.6

Average Household Size

Group	People
Total Population	3.13
Hispanic or Latino (of any race)	3.18
Central American, ex. Mexican	3.62
Costa Rican	3.15
Guatemalan	3.72
Honduran	3.52
Nicaraguan	3.69
Panamanian	3.16
Salvadoran	3.67
Cuban	3.12
Dominican Republic	3.22
Mexican	3.47
Puerto Rican	2.97
South American	3.23
Argentinean	3.34
Bolivian	3.03
Chilean	2.97
Colombian	3.15
Ecuadorian	3.24
Peruvian	3.55
Uruguayan	3.33
Venezuelan	3.12
Spaniard	2.83

Median Age

Group	Years
Total Population	37.5
Hispanic or Latino (of any race)	38.4
Central American, ex. Mexican	36.1
Costa Rican	36.7
Guatemalan	33.1
Honduran	33.3
Nicaraguan	37.4
Panamanian	34.3
Salvadoran	37.1
Cuban	40.5
Dominican Republic	35.3
Mexican	28.3
Puerto Rican	34.7
South American	38.7
Argentinean	36.2
Bolivian	41.5
Chilean	42.0
Colombian	39.5
Ecuadorian	38.6
Peruvian	40.8
Uruguayan	35.2
Venezuelan	34.6
Spaniard	45.5

High School Graduates
(Universe: Population 25 Years and Over)

Group	Number	%
Total Population	18,888	82.6
Hispanic or Latino (of any race)	16,373	81.3
Central American, ex. Mexican	1,597	73.5
Nicaraguan	1,141	80.5
Cuban	6,881	76.9
Dominican Republic	928	87.7
Puerto Rican	883	86.1
South American	5,326	88.5
Colombian	2,648	83.4
Peruvian	1,204	93.8
Venezuelan	700	95.6

Four-Year College Graduates
(Universe: Population 25 Years and Over)

Group	Number	%
Total Population	5,948	26.0
Hispanic or Latino (of any race)	5,103	25.4
Central American, ex. Mexican	522	24.0
Nicaraguan	461	32.5
Cuban	2,141	23.9
Dominican Republic	251	23.7
Puerto Rican	211	20.6
South American	1,809	30.1
Colombian	919	29.0
Peruvian	431	33.6
Venezuelan	280	38.3

Population Age 3–17 Enrolled in Public School
(Universe: Population Age 3–17 Enrolled in School)

Group	Number	%
Total Population	5,471	87.3
Hispanic or Latino (of any race)	4,345	89.4
Central American, ex. Mexican	505	91.5
Nicaraguan	145	86.3
Cuban	1,466	85.6
Dominican Republic	239	100.0
Puerto Rican	391	90.9
South American	1,508	93.2
Colombian	691	89.9
Peruvian	297	100.0
Venezuelan	291	92.7

Population Age 3–17 Enrolled in Private School
(Universe: Population Age 3–17 Enrolled in School)

Group	Number	%
Total Population	796	12.7
Hispanic or Latino (of any race)	516	10.6
Central American, ex. Mexican	47	8.5
Nicaraguan	23	13.7
Cuban	247	14.4
Dominican Republic	0	0.0
Puerto Rican	39	9.1
South American	110	6.8
Colombian	78	10.1
Peruvian	0	0.0
Venezuelan	23	7.3

Foreign-Born Population

Group	Number	%
Total Population	21,081	59.7
Hispanic or Latino (of any race)	19,351	64.2
Central American, ex. Mexican	2,247	68.2
Nicaraguan	1,451	74.8
Cuban	8,639	68.5
Dominican Republic	824	55.5
Puerto Rican	14	0.7
South American	6,775	73.4
Colombian	3,516	75.0
Peruvian	1,612	80.2
Venezuelan	852	67.5

Foreign-Born Naturalized U.S. Citizens

Group	Number	%
Total Population	10,231	48.5
Hispanic or Latino (of any race)	9,341	48.3
Central American, ex. Mexican	1,022	45.5
Nicaraguan	717	49.4
Cuban	4,930	57.1
Dominican Republic	506	61.4
Puerto Rican	14	100.0
South American	2,573	38.0
Colombian	1,583	45.0
Peruvian	338	21.0
Venezuelan	254	29.8

Language Spoken at Home: English Only
(Universe: Population 5 Years and Over)

Group	Number	%
Total Population	3,337	10.2
Hispanic or Latino (of any race)	1,009	3.6
Central American, ex. Mexican	62	2.0
Nicaraguan	62	3.5
Cuban	361	3.0
Dominican Republic	24	1.7
Puerto Rican	268	15.9
South American	130	1.5
Colombian	93	2.1
Peruvian	0	0.0
Venezuelan	0	0.0

Language Spoken at Home: Spanish
(Universe: Population 5 Years and Over)

Group	Number	%
Total Population	28,118	85.9
Hispanic or Latino (of any race)	26,964	96.3
Central American, ex. Mexican	2,989	98.0
Nicaraguan	1,721	96.5
Cuban	11,641	97.0
Dominican Republic	1,360	98.3
Puerto Rican	1,413	83.7

Notes: (1) Percent of total population; (2) Percent of Hispanic/Latino population; Profiles include places with an overall population of at least 125,000, OR an overall population of at least 25,000 where the Hispanic/Latino population is at least 20% of the overall population. In states where less than five places meet either of these criteria, we have included places with at least 10,000 total population with the highest percentage of Hispanic/Latino population. These places are identified with an asterisk (*); Please refer to the User's Guide for a full explanation of data.

South American	8,264	98.3
Colombian	4,278	97.9
Peruvian	1,724	100.0
Venezuelan	1,103	98.7

Unemployment Rate
(Universe: Population 16 Years and Over)

Group	%
Total Population	7.2
Hispanic or Latino (of any race)	7.0
Central American, ex. Mexican	3.1
Nicaraguan	2.7
Cuban	6.5
Dominican Republic	0.0
Puerto Rican	15.7
South American	8.8
Colombian	8.5
Peruvian	10.0
Venezuelan	11.8

Class of Worker: Private Wage and Salary
(Universe: Civilian Employed Population 16 Years and Over)

Group	Number	%
Total Population	14,515	82.4
Hispanic or Latino (of any race)	12,417	81.7
Central American, ex. Mexican	1,616	89.0
Nicaraguan	1,031	92.7
Cuban	5,085	78.2
Dominican Republic	536	87.3
Puerto Rican	609	78.0
South American	4,044	85.5
Colombian	2,031	85.6
Peruvian	836	83.2
Venezuelan	532	92.4

Class of Worker: Government
(Universe: Civilian Employed Population 16 Years and Over)

Group	Number	%
Total Population	1,705	9.7
Hispanic or Latino (of any race)	1,419	9.3
Central American, ex. Mexican	105	5.8
Nicaraguan	47	4.2
Cuban	895	13.8
Dominican Republic	0	0.0
Puerto Rican	143	18.3
South American	159	3.4
Colombian	103	4.3
Peruvian	17	1.7
Venezuelan	20	3.5

Means of Transportation to Work: Car, Truck or Van
(Universe: Workers 16 Years and Over)

Group	Number	%
Total Population	15,953	93.4
Hispanic or Latino (of any race)	13,773	93.1
Central American, ex. Mexican	1,602	91.6
Nicaraguan	949	89.4
Cuban	6,007	94.7
Dominican Republic	578	100.0
Puerto Rican	674	86.3
South American	4,213	91.8
Colombian	2,031	89.2
Peruvian	939	93.4
Venezuelan	526	97.0

Means of Transportation to Work: Public Transportation (ex. Taxicab)
(Universe: Workers 16 Years and Over)

Group	Number	%
Total Population	481	2.8
Hispanic or Latino (of any race)	436	2.9
Central American, ex. Mexican	72	4.1
Nicaraguan	52	4.9
Cuban	153	2.4
Dominican Republic	0	0.0
Puerto Rican	70	9.0
South American	106	2.3
Colombian	61	2.7
Peruvian	45	4.5
Venezuelan	0	0.0

Homeownership Rate
(Universe: Occupied Housing Units)

Group	%
Total Population	63.4
Hispanic or Latino (of any race)	62.5
Central American, ex. Mexican	64.1
Costa Rican	64.7
Guatemalan	56.6
Honduran	54.7
Nicaraguan	67.2
Panamanian	45.5
Salvadoran	75.0
Cuban	65.0
Dominican Republic	58.7
Mexican	60.9
Puerto Rican	58.8
South American	57.9
Argentinean	62.9
Bolivian	74.4
Chilean	71.9
Colombian	56.6
Ecuadorian	65.9
Peruvian	54.8
Uruguayan	56.3
Venezuelan	54.6
Spaniard	83.1

Median Home Value

Group	Dollars
Total Population	229,500
Hispanic or Latino (of any race)	230,900
Central American, ex. Mexican	215,500
Nicaraguan	235,500
Cuban	232,700
Dominican Republic	209,100
Puerto Rican	210,400
South American	243,300
Colombian	232,200
Peruvian	289,700
Venezuelan	220,700

Median Gross Rent

Group	Dollars
Total Population	1,181
Hispanic or Latino (of any race)	1,174
Central American, ex. Mexican	1,287
Nicaraguan	1,326
Cuban	1,096
Dominican Republic	1,247
Puerto Rican	1,227
South American	1,183
Colombian	1,152
Peruvian	1,233
Venezuelan	1,046

Median Household Income
(2010 Inflation-Adjusted Dollars)

Group	Dollars
Total Population	45,431
Hispanic or Latino (of any race)	43,962
Central American, ex. Mexican	44,292
Nicaraguan	48,095
Cuban	42,493
Dominican Republic	52,108
Puerto Rican	43,781
South American	42,561
Colombian	42,258
Peruvian	50,703
Venezuelan	38,640

Per Capita Income
(2010 Inflation-Adjusted Dollars)

Group	Dollars
Total Population	18,941
Hispanic or Latino (of any race)	18,398
Central American, ex. Mexican	16,588
Nicaraguan	17,604
Cuban	21,324
Dominican Republic	16,860
Puerto Rican	16,505
South American	16,389
Colombian	17,223
Peruvian	14,301
Venezuelan	14,198

Households with $100,000+ Income

Group	Number	%
Total Population	1,368	12.4
Hispanic or Latino (of any race)	1,098	11.6
Central American, ex. Mexican	25	2.9
Nicaraguan	25	5.0
Cuban	587	13.3
Dominican Republic	65	15.0
Puerto Rican	61	10.5
South American	283	9.8
Colombian	185	13.1
Peruvian	45	7.7
Venezuelan	15	3.3

Households with Food Stamps/SNAP Benefits During Past 12 Months

Group	Number	%
Total Population	1,359	12.3
Hispanic or Latino (of any race)	1,259	13.3
Central American, ex. Mexican	134	15.7
Nicaraguan	92	18.4
Cuban	621	14.1
Dominican Republic	68	15.7
Puerto Rican	29	5.0
South American	321	11.2
Colombian	115	8.1
Peruvian	111	18.9
Venezuelan	87	19.0

Poverty Rate
(Income in Past 12 Months Below Poverty Level)

Group	%
Total Population	10.4
Hispanic or Latino (of any race)	11.4
Central American, ex. Mexican	4.7
Nicaraguan	2.3
Cuban	9.5
Dominican Republic	6.9
Puerto Rican	10.5
South American	16.0
Colombian	12.3
Peruvian	27.3
Venezuelan	21.2

Kissimmee

Population

Group	Number	%TP[1]	%HP[2]
Total Population	59,682	100.0	–
Hispanic or Latino (of any race)	35,170	58.9	100.0
Central American, ex. Mexican	2,036	3.4	5.8
Costa Rican	115	0.2	0.3
Guatemalan	274	0.5	0.8
Honduran	387	0.6	1.1
Nicaraguan	339	0.6	1.0
Panamanian	167	0.3	0.5
Salvadoran	753	1.3	2.1
Cuban	1,524	2.6	4.3
Dominican Republic	3,061	5.1	8.7
Mexican	2,351	3.9	6.7
Puerto Rican	19,728	33.1	56.1
South American	5,135	8.6	14.6
Argentinean	283	0.5	0.8
Chilean	127	0.2	0.4
Colombian	2,370	4.0	6.7
Ecuadorian	533	0.9	1.5
Peruvian	750	1.3	2.1
Uruguayan	164	0.3	0.5
Venezuelan	848	1.4	2.4
Spaniard	111	0.2	0.3

Population Growth: 2000–2010

Group	%
Total Population	24.8
Hispanic or Latino (of any race)	76.3
Central American, ex. Mexican	138.7
Honduran	174.5
Nicaraguan	129.1
Salvadoran	172.8
Cuban	86.5
Dominican Republic	217.5
Mexican	49.5
Puerto Rican	74.4

Notes: (1) Percent of total population; (2) Percent of Hispanic/Latino population; Profiles include places with an overall population of at least 125,000, OR an overall population of at least 25,000 where the Hispanic/Latino population is at least 20% of the overall population. In states where less than five places meet either of these criteria, we have included places with at least 10,000 total population with the highest percentage of Hispanic/Latino population. These places are identified with an asterisk (*); Please refer to the User's Guide for a full explanation of data.

South American	150.9
Colombian	146.9
Ecuadorian	197.8
Peruvian	200.0
Venezuelan	86.8

Males per 100 Females

Group	Number
Total Population	94.6
Hispanic or Latino (of any race)	93.4
Central American, ex. Mexican	108.2
Costa Rican	113.0
Guatemalan	121.0
Honduran	107.0
Nicaraguan	86.3
Panamanian	65.3
Salvadoran	128.9
Cuban	100.5
Dominican Republic	85.6
Mexican	121.2
Puerto Rican	92.9
South American	83.0
Argentinean	100.7
Chilean	98.4
Colombian	77.3
Ecuadorian	83.2
Peruvian	96.3
Uruguayan	82.2
Venezuelan	80.8
Spaniard	82.0

Average Household Size

Group	People
Total Population	2.85
Hispanic or Latino (of any race)	3.13
Central American, ex. Mexican	3.70
Costa Rican	3.26
Guatemalan	3.88
Honduran	3.67
Nicaraguan	3.86
Panamanian	2.97
Salvadoran	3.88
Cuban	2.91
Dominican Republic	3.26
Mexican	3.89
Puerto Rican	3.01
South American	3.17
Argentinean	2.78
Chilean	3.21
Colombian	3.18
Ecuadorian	3.14
Peruvian	3.19
Uruguayan	3.74
Venezuelan	3.21
Spaniard	2.50

Median Age

Group	Years
Total Population	33.5
Hispanic or Latino (of any race)	30.6
Central American, ex. Mexican	29.9
Costa Rican	33.3
Guatemalan	30.6
Honduran	30.5
Nicaraguan	31.1
Panamanian	36.5
Salvadoran	28.5
Cuban	37.8
Dominican Republic	31.8
Mexican	25.8
Puerto Rican	30.2
South American	35.9
Argentinean	33.8
Chilean	38.9
Colombian	38.0
Ecuadorian	35.7
Peruvian	37.3
Uruguayan	34.1
Venezuelan	32.1
Spaniard	31.5

High School Graduates
(Universe: Population 25 Years and Over)

Group	Number	%
Total Population	29,811	81.3
Hispanic or Latino (of any race)	14,502	76.6
Central American, ex. Mexican	733	67.8
Cuban	806	80.5
Dominican Republic	1,448	73.8
Mexican	457	43.9
Puerto Rican	7,769	76.9
South American	2,869	90.3
Colombian	1,306	89.2

Four-Year College Graduates
(Universe: Population 25 Years and Over)

Group	Number	%
Total Population	5,679	15.5
Hispanic or Latino (of any race)	2,274	12.0
Central American, ex. Mexican	67	6.2
Cuban	279	27.9
Dominican Republic	249	12.7
Mexican	59	5.7
Puerto Rican	943	9.3
South American	609	19.2
Colombian	343	23.4

Population Age 3–17 Enrolled in Public School
(Universe: Population Age 3–17 Enrolled in School)

Group	Number	%
Total Population	9,985	90.2
Hispanic or Latino (of any race)	6,008	91.0
Central American, ex. Mexican	258	100.0
Cuban	176	78.6
Dominican Republic	698	98.0
Mexican	681	100.0
Puerto Rican	3,342	89.1
South American	747	91.7
Colombian	434	97.1

Population Age 3–17 Enrolled in Private School
(Universe: Population Age 3–17 Enrolled in School)

Group	Number	%
Total Population	1,080	9.8
Hispanic or Latino (of any race)	595	9.0
Central American, ex. Mexican	0	0.0
Cuban	48	21.4
Dominican Republic	14	2.0
Mexican	0	0.0
Puerto Rican	410	10.9
South American	68	8.3
Colombian	13	2.9

Foreign-Born Population

Group	Number	%
Total Population	15,163	25.6
Hispanic or Latino (of any race)	9,950	30.1
Central American, ex. Mexican	1,395	66.8
Cuban	900	56.3
Dominican Republic	2,015	58.2
Mexican	1,124	48.3
Puerto Rican	110	0.6
South American	3,896	78.8
Colombian	1,696	73.4

Foreign-Born Naturalized U.S. Citizens

Group	Number	%
Total Population	5,241	34.6
Hispanic or Latino (of any race)	2,544	25.6
Central American, ex. Mexican	183	13.1
Cuban	288	32.0
Dominican Republic	940	46.7
Mexican	55	4.9
Puerto Rican	110	100.0
South American	799	20.5
Colombian	338	19.9

Language Spoken at Home: English Only
(Universe: Population 5 Years and Over)

Group	Number	%
Total Population	23,222	42.8
Hispanic or Latino (of any race)	3,103	10.5
Central American, ex. Mexican	86	4.7
Cuban	137	9.5
Dominican Republic	126	4.0
Mexican	361	17.1
Puerto Rican	1,959	12.6
South American	327	7.1
Colombian	166	7.8

Language Spoken at Home: Spanish
(Universe: Population 5 Years and Over)

Group	Number	%
Total Population	27,233	50.1
Hispanic or Latino (of any race)	26,292	89.0
Central American, ex. Mexican	1,732	95.3
Cuban	1,287	89.1
Dominican Republic	2,976	95.4
Mexican	1,725	81.8
Puerto Rican	13,631	87.4
South American	4,173	90.8
Colombian	1,929	90.8

Unemployment Rate
(Universe: Population 16 Years and Over)

Group	%
Total Population	9.7
Hispanic or Latino (of any race)	10.1
Central American, ex. Mexican	5.7
Cuban	15.3
Dominican Republic	9.2
Mexican	7.8
Puerto Rican	10.8
South American	10.6
Colombian	1.8

Class of Worker: Private Wage and Salary
(Universe: Civilian Employed Population 16 Years and Over)

Group	Number	%
Total Population	25,187	87.9
Hispanic or Latino (of any race)	13,619	89.5
Central American, ex. Mexican	1,081	94.0
Cuban	760	89.6
Dominican Republic	1,558	93.0
Mexican	836	92.0
Puerto Rican	6,717	89.1
South American	2,285	85.4
Colombian	1,029	80.3

Class of Worker: Government
(Universe: Civilian Employed Population 16 Years and Over)

Group	Number	%
Total Population	2,321	8.1
Hispanic or Latino (of any race)	981	6.4
Central American, ex. Mexican	11	1.0
Cuban	53	6.3
Dominican Republic	63	3.8
Mexican	0	0.0
Puerto Rican	726	9.6
South American	89	3.3
Colombian	62	4.8

Means of Transportation to Work: Car, Truck or Van
(Universe: Workers 16 Years and Over)

Group	Number	%
Total Population	24,781	88.4
Hispanic or Latino (of any race)	13,342	89.6
Central American, ex. Mexican	860	81.5
Cuban	806	98.7
Dominican Republic	1,514	92.7
Mexican	529	58.8
Puerto Rican	6,940	93.1
South American	2,272	86.8
Colombian	1,097	85.6

Means of Transportation to Work: Public Transportation (ex. Taxicab)
(Universe: Workers 16 Years and Over)

Group	Number	%
Total Population	791	2.8
Hispanic or Latino (of any race)	377	2.5
Central American, ex. Mexican	71	6.7
Cuban	0	0.0
Dominican Republic	37	2.3
Mexican	70	7.8
Puerto Rican	143	1.9
South American	56	2.1
Colombian	0	0.0

Homeownership Rate
(Universe: Occupied Housing Units)

Group	%
Total Population	45.7
Hispanic or Latino (of any race)	37.0

Notes: (1) Percent of total population; (2) Percent of Hispanic/Latino population; Profiles include places with an overall population of at least 125,000, OR an overall population of at least 25,000 where the Hispanic/Latino population is at least 20% of the overall population. In states where less than five places meet either of these criteria, we have included places with at least 10,000 total population with the highest percentage of Hispanic/Latino population. These places are identified with an asterisk (*); Please refer to the User's Guide for a full explanation of data.

Central American, ex. Mexican	37.6
Costa Rican	39.5
Guatemalan	54.9
Honduran	37.2
Nicaraguan	32.0
Panamanian	30.3
Salvadoran	35.2
Cuban	44.0
Dominican Republic	42.4
Mexican	30.0
Puerto Rican	34.1
South American	44.6
Argentinean	41.6
Chilean	47.6
Colombian	49.5
Ecuadorian	43.2
Peruvian	39.5
Uruguayan	32.0
Venezuelan	36.8
Spaniard	35.0

Median Home Value

Group	Dollars
Total Population	181,100
Hispanic or Latino (of any race)	183,300
Central American, ex. Mexican	120,300
Cuban	229,500
Dominican Republic	190,500
Mexican	159,600
Puerto Rican	179,500
South American	200,700
Colombian	197,300

Median Gross Rent

Group	Dollars
Total Population	961
Hispanic or Latino (of any race)	976
Central American, ex. Mexican	951
Cuban	945
Dominican Republic	1,059
Mexican	948
Puerto Rican	988
South American	972
Colombian	1,132

Median Household Income
(2010 Inflation-Adjusted Dollars)

Group	Dollars
Total Population	37,995
Hispanic or Latino (of any race)	34,714
Central American, ex. Mexican	40,625
Cuban	38,787
Dominican Republic	37,650
Mexican	35,909
Puerto Rican	33,898
South American	32,931
Colombian	35,221

Per Capita Income
(2010 Inflation-Adjusted Dollars)

Group	Dollars
Total Population	17,501
Hispanic or Latino (of any race)	14,385
Central American, ex. Mexican	13,632
Cuban	15,892
Dominican Republic	12,841
Mexican	9,957
Puerto Rican	14,736
South American	16,403
Colombian	16,753

Households with $100,000+ Income

Group	Number	%
Total Population	1,799	8.2
Hispanic or Latino (of any race)	693	6.2
Central American, ex. Mexican	16	2.7
Cuban	107	19.6
Dominican Republic	12	1.2
Mexican	32	5.5
Puerto Rican	375	5.9
South American	140	7.7
Colombian	36	4.4

Households with Food Stamps/SNAP Benefits During Past 12 Months

Group	Number	%
Total Population	3,329	15.1
Hispanic or Latino (of any race)	2,376	21.3
Central American, ex. Mexican	77	13.1
Cuban	16	2.9
Dominican Republic	123	12.2
Mexican	128	22.0
Puerto Rican	1,710	27.0
South American	240	13.2
Colombian	47	5.8

Poverty Rate
(Income in Past 12 Months Below Poverty Level)

Group	%
Total Population	17.0
Hispanic or Latino (of any race)	20.1
Central American, ex. Mexican	22.9
Cuban	18.6
Dominican Republic	29.3
Mexican	43.2
Puerto Rican	18.9
South American	8.9
Colombian	9.0

Lake Magdalene

Population

Group	Number	%TP[1]	%HP[2]
Total Population	28,509	100.0	–
Hispanic or Latino (of any race)	6,019	21.1	100.0
Central American, ex. Mexican	377	1.3	6.3
Honduran	144	0.5	2.4
Cuban	1,344	4.7	22.3
Dominican Republic	216	0.8	3.6
Mexican	490	1.7	8.1
Puerto Rican	2,003	7.0	33.3
South American	830	2.9	13.8
Colombian	402	1.4	6.7
Peruvian	156	0.5	2.6
Venezuelan	116	0.4	1.9
Spaniard	283	1.0	4.7

Population Growth: 2000–2010

Group	%
Total Population	-0.9
Hispanic or Latino (of any race)	54.9
Central American, ex. Mexican	110.6
Cuban	102.1
Mexican	125.8
Puerto Rican	52.6
South American	168.6
Colombian	175.3

Males per 100 Females

Group	Number
Total Population	90.6
Hispanic or Latino (of any race)	93.2
Central American, ex. Mexican	88.5
Honduran	108.7
Cuban	97.4
Dominican Republic	92.9
Mexican	103.3
Puerto Rican	91.3
South American	81.2
Colombian	85.3
Peruvian	83.5
Venezuelan	78.5
Spaniard	97.9

Average Household Size

Group	People
Total Population	2.30
Hispanic or Latino (of any race)	2.70
Central American, ex. Mexican	3.13
Honduran	3.20
Cuban	2.70
Dominican Republic	2.86
Mexican	3.01
Puerto Rican	2.64
South American	2.74
Colombian	2.63
Peruvian	2.77
Venezuelan	2.83
Spaniard	2.46

Median Age

Group	Years
Total Population	43.9
Hispanic or Latino (of any race)	33.9
Central American, ex. Mexican	32.6
Honduran	31.3
Cuban	37.6
Dominican Republic	30.0
Mexican	25.4
Puerto Rican	32.1
South American	38.0
Colombian	38.4
Peruvian	39.9
Venezuelan	35.0
Spaniard	48.4

High School Graduates
(Universe: Population 25 Years and Over)

Group	Number	%
Total Population	18,839	89.1
Hispanic or Latino (of any race)	3,407	82.9
Cuban	595	83.5
Puerto Rican	1,104	79.8

Four-Year College Graduates
(Universe: Population 25 Years and Over)

Group	Number	%
Total Population	7,015	33.2
Hispanic or Latino (of any race)	879	21.4
Cuban	110	15.4
Puerto Rican	266	19.2

Population Age 3–17 Enrolled in Public School
(Universe: Population Age 3–17 Enrolled in School)

Group	Number	%
Total Population	3,279	72.2
Hispanic or Latino (of any race)	1,001	78.7
Cuban	216	75.0
Puerto Rican	271	91.9

Population Age 3–17 Enrolled in Private School
(Universe: Population Age 3–17 Enrolled in School)

Group	Number	%
Total Population	1,264	27.8
Hispanic or Latino (of any race)	271	21.3
Cuban	72	25.0
Puerto Rican	24	8.1

Foreign-Born Population

Group	Number	%
Total Population	3,846	13.0
Hispanic or Latino (of any race)	2,071	32.3
Cuban	520	42.9
Puerto Rican	12	0.6

Foreign-Born Naturalized U.S. Citizens

Group	Number	%
Total Population	1,952	50.8
Hispanic or Latino (of any race)	1,021	49.3
Cuban	425	81.7
Puerto Rican	12	100.0

Language Spoken at Home: English Only
(Universe: Population 5 Years and Over)

Group	Number	%
Total Population	21,492	76.0
Hispanic or Latino (of any race)	1,384	23.2
Cuban	321	27.5
Puerto Rican	356	18.4

Language Spoken at Home: Spanish
(Universe: Population 5 Years and Over)

Group	Number	%
Total Population	5,064	17.9
Hispanic or Latino (of any race)	4,546	76.1
Cuban	846	72.5
Puerto Rican	1,578	81.6

Unemployment Rate
(Universe: Population 16 Years and Over)

Group	%
Total Population	9.1

Notes: (1) Percent of total population; (2) Percent of Hispanic/Latino population; Profiles include places with an overall population of at least 125,000, OR an overall population of at least 25,000 where the Hispanic/Latino population is at least 20% of the overall population. In states where less than five places meet either of these criteria, we have included places with at least 10,000 total population with the highest percentage of Hispanic/Latino population. These places are identified with an asterisk (*); Please refer to the User's Guide for a full explanation of data.

Hispanic or Latino (of any race)	11.9
Cuban	17.0
Puerto Rican	15.4

Class of Worker: Private Wage and Salary
(Universe: Civilian Employed Population 16 Years and Over)

Group	Number	%
Total Population	12,531	83.1
Hispanic or Latino (of any race)	2,653	86.8
Cuban	542	92.0
Puerto Rican	855	94.2

Class of Worker: Government
(Universe: Civilian Employed Population 16 Years and Over)

Group	Number	%
Total Population	1,771	11.7
Hispanic or Latino (of any race)	263	8.6
Cuban	35	5.9
Puerto Rican	0	0.0

Means of Transportation to Work: Car, Truck or Van
(Universe: Workers 16 Years and Over)

Group	Number	%
Total Population	13,416	90.7
Hispanic or Latino (of any race)	2,666	89.3
Cuban	552	98.0
Puerto Rican	873	98.0

Means of Transportation to Work: Public Transportation (ex. Taxicab)
(Universe: Workers 16 Years and Over)

Group	Number	%
Total Population	203	1.4
Hispanic or Latino (of any race)	105	3.5
Cuban	0	0.0
Puerto Rican	0	0.0

Homeownership Rate
(Universe: Occupied Housing Units)

Group	%
Total Population	67.0
Hispanic or Latino (of any race)	54.8
Central American, ex. Mexican	52.4
Honduran	46.9
Cuban	66.6
Dominican Republic	46.6
Mexican	37.3
Puerto Rican	42.7
South American	58.6
Colombian	57.3
Peruvian	56.6
Venezuelan	51.2
Spaniard	89.4

Median Home Value

Group	Dollars
Total Population	212,900
Hispanic or Latino (of any race)	205,900
Cuban	242,300
Puerto Rican	187,700

Median Gross Rent

Group	Dollars
Total Population	896
Hispanic or Latino (of any race)	928
Cuban	1,135
Puerto Rican	892

Median Household Income
(2010 Inflation-Adjusted Dollars)

Group	Dollars
Total Population	51,842
Hispanic or Latino (of any race)	39,493
Cuban	68,274
Puerto Rican	32,000

Per Capita Income
(2010 Inflation-Adjusted Dollars)

Group	Dollars
Total Population	33,363
Hispanic or Latino (of any race)	23,427
Cuban	24,771
Puerto Rican	19,956

Households with $100,000+ Income

Group	Number	%
Total Population	2,771	22.6
Hispanic or Latino (of any race)	446	20.0
Cuban	106	26.2
Puerto Rican	72	8.6

Households with Food Stamps/SNAP Benefits During Past 12 Months

Group	Number	%
Total Population	595	4.9
Hispanic or Latino (of any race)	208	9.3
Cuban	42	10.4
Puerto Rican	80	9.5

Poverty Rate
(Income in Past 12 Months Below Poverty Level)

Group	%
Total Population	11.5
Hispanic or Latino (of any race)	12.3
Cuban	9.5
Puerto Rican	14.7

Lake Worth

Population

Group	Number	%TP[1]	%HP[2]
Total Population	34,910	100.0	–
Hispanic or Latino (of any race)	13,834	39.6	100.0
Central American, ex. Mexican	6,320	18.1	45.7
Guatemalan	4,432	12.7	32.0
Honduran	906	2.6	6.5
Nicaraguan	180	0.5	1.3
Salvadoran	687	2.0	5.0
Cuban	1,438	4.1	10.4
Dominican Republic	314	0.9	2.3
Mexican	2,765	7.9	20.0
Puerto Rican	1,413	4.0	10.2
South American	726	2.1	5.2
Colombian	285	0.8	2.1
Peruvian	100	0.3	0.7

Population Growth: 2000–2010

Group	%
Total Population	-0.6
Hispanic or Latino (of any race)	32.5
Central American, ex. Mexican	113.2
Guatemalan	159.0
Honduran	62.1
Nicaraguan	47.5
Salvadoran	58.7
Cuban	18.1
Dominican Republic	82.6
Mexican	15.2
Puerto Rican	-14.5
South American	39.1
Colombian	85.1

Males per 100 Females

Group	Number
Total Population	117.5
Hispanic or Latino (of any race)	145.2
Central American, ex. Mexican	185.6
Guatemalan	232.0
Honduran	107.8
Nicaraguan	83.7
Salvadoran	133.7
Cuban	106.0
Dominican Republic	102.6
Mexican	146.4
Puerto Rican	98.2
South American	96.7
Colombian	83.9
Peruvian	104.1

Average Household Size

Group	People
Total Population	2.65
Hispanic or Latino (of any race)	3.79
Central American, ex. Mexican	4.85
Guatemalan	5.33
Honduran	3.93
Nicaraguan	3.25
Salvadoran	4.28
Cuban	2.69
Dominican Republic	2.99
Mexican	4.02
Puerto Rican	2.63
South American	2.75
Colombian	2.70
Peruvian	3.27

Median Age

Group	Years
Total Population	35.0
Hispanic or Latino (of any race)	27.8
Central American, ex. Mexican	26.6
Guatemalan	25.8
Honduran	29.1
Nicaraguan	38.5
Salvadoran	29.0
Cuban	41.4
Dominican Republic	31.5
Mexican	25.4
Puerto Rican	33.4
South American	37.9
Colombian	37.1
Peruvian	37.3

High School Graduates
(Universe: Population 25 Years and Over)

Group	Number	%
Total Population	15,818	66.0
Hispanic or Latino (of any race)	3,974	45.4
Central American, ex. Mexican	1,263	27.9
Guatemalan	907	28.9
Salvadoran	136	25.1
Cuban	908	76.6
Mexican	601	43.2
Puerto Rican	467	78.1

Four-Year College Graduates
(Universe: Population 25 Years and Over)

Group	Number	%
Total Population	4,533	18.9
Hispanic or Latino (of any race)	802	9.2
Central American, ex. Mexican	235	5.2
Guatemalan	141	4.5
Salvadoran	0	0.0
Cuban	242	20.4
Mexican	53	3.8
Puerto Rican	82	13.7

Population Age 3–17 Enrolled in Public School
(Universe: Population Age 3–17 Enrolled in School)

Group	Number	%
Total Population	4,447	88.6
Hispanic or Latino (of any race)	2,694	94.0
Central American, ex. Mexican	1,522	97.8
Guatemalan	1,058	100.0
Salvadoran	140	80.5
Cuban	212	85.8
Mexican	312	100.0
Puerto Rican	260	88.4

Population Age 3–17 Enrolled in Private School
(Universe: Population Age 3–17 Enrolled in School)

Group	Number	%
Total Population	572	11.4
Hispanic or Latino (of any race)	171	6.0
Central American, ex. Mexican	34	2.2
Guatemalan	0	0.0
Salvadoran	34	19.5
Cuban	35	14.2
Mexican	0	0.0
Puerto Rican	34	11.6

Foreign-Born Population

Group	Number	%
Total Population	15,697	44.3
Hispanic or Latino (of any race)	10,120	65.1
Central American, ex. Mexican	5,842	72.5
Guatemalan	4,142	73.5
Salvadoran	611	66.5
Cuban	1,199	74.1
Mexican	2,042	68.0
Puerto Rican	0	0.0

Notes: (1) Percent of total population; (2) Percent of Hispanic/Latino population; Profiles include places with an overall population of at least 125,000, OR an overall population of at least 25,000 where the Hispanic/Latino population is at least 20% of the overall population. In states where less than five places meet either of these criteria, we have included places with at least 10,000 total population with the highest percentage of Hispanic/Latino population. These places are identified with an asterisk (*); Please refer to the User's Guide for a full explanation of data.

Foreign-Born Naturalized U.S. Citizens

Group	Number	%
Total Population	3,301	21.0
Hispanic or Latino (of any race)	1,164	11.5
Central American, ex. Mexican	211	3.6
Guatemalan	70	1.7
Salvadoran	116	19.0
Cuban	530	44.2
Mexican	119	5.8
Puerto Rican	0	0.0

Language Spoken at Home: English Only
(Universe: Population 5 Years and Over)

Group	Number	%
Total Population	14,598	44.4
Hispanic or Latino (of any race)	1,001	7.1
Central American, ex. Mexican	77	1.0
Guatemalan	17	0.3
Salvadoran	0	0.0
Cuban	202	12.6
Mexican	136	5.3
Puerto Rican	322	34.4

Language Spoken at Home: Spanish
(Universe: Population 5 Years and Over)

Group	Number	%
Total Population	13,033	39.6
Hispanic or Latino (of any race)	12,791	90.7
Central American, ex. Mexican	7,088	96.0
Guatemalan	5,117	97.8
Salvadoran	787	95.7
Cuban	1,407	87.4
Mexican	2,446	94.7
Puerto Rican	615	65.6

Unemployment Rate
(Universe: Population 16 Years and Over)

Group	%
Total Population	15.8
Hispanic or Latino (of any race)	17.8
Central American, ex. Mexican	19.1
Guatemalan	19.8
Salvadoran	20.9
Cuban	22.3
Mexican	11.7
Puerto Rican	26.0

Class of Worker: Private Wage and Salary
(Universe: Civilian Employed Population 16 Years and Over)

Group	Number	%
Total Population	14,779	86.4
Hispanic or Latino (of any race)	7,019	94.4
Central American, ex. Mexican	4,013	96.7
Guatemalan	2,904	98.1
Salvadoran	485	95.7
Cuban	392	78.2
Mexican	1,468	93.7
Puerto Rican	383	91.4

Class of Worker: Government
(Universe: Civilian Employed Population 16 Years and Over)

Group	Number	%
Total Population	1,536	9.0
Hispanic or Latino (of any race)	220	3.0
Central American, ex. Mexican	24	0.6
Guatemalan	24	0.8
Salvadoran	0	0.0
Cuban	109	21.8
Mexican	12	0.8
Puerto Rican	36	8.6

Means of Transportation to Work: Car, Truck or Van
(Universe: Workers 16 Years and Over)

Group	Number	%
Total Population	14,550	88.3
Hispanic or Latino (of any race)	6,618	92.1
Central American, ex. Mexican	3,771	93.9
Guatemalan	2,776	94.8
Salvadoran	507	100.0
Cuban	470	93.8
Mexican	1,313	87.4
Puerto Rican	332	79.2

Means of Transportation to Work: Public Transportation (ex. Taxicab)
(Universe: Workers 16 Years and Over)

Group	Number	%
Total Population	792	4.8
Hispanic or Latino (of any race)	392	5.5
Central American, ex. Mexican	222	5.5
Guatemalan	130	4.4
Salvadoran	0	0.0
Cuban	14	2.8
Mexican	148	9.9
Puerto Rican	8	1.9

Homeownership Rate
(Universe: Occupied Housing Units)

Group	%
Total Population	49.6
Hispanic or Latino (of any race)	34.0
Central American, ex. Mexican	19.8
Guatemalan	12.6
Honduran	21.9
Nicaraguan	51.0
Salvadoran	40.8
Cuban	58.7
Dominican Republic	45.7
Mexican	28.2
Puerto Rican	42.3
South American	52.1
Colombian	53.6
Peruvian	39.4

Median Home Value

Group	Dollars
Total Population	186,200
Hispanic or Latino (of any race)	176,800
Central American, ex. Mexican	207,300
Guatemalan	203,800
Salvadoran	232,100
Cuban	192,500
Mexican	200,000
Puerto Rican	120,300

Median Gross Rent

Group	Dollars
Total Population	925
Hispanic or Latino (of any race)	947
Central American, ex. Mexican	974
Guatemalan	1,042
Salvadoran	870
Cuban	880
Mexican	849
Puerto Rican	816

Median Household Income
(2010 Inflation-Adjusted Dollars)

Group	Dollars
Total Population	38,492
Hispanic or Latino (of any race)	37,681
Central American, ex. Mexican	38,929
Guatemalan	43,103
Salvadoran	39,226
Cuban	24,911
Mexican	35,000
Puerto Rican	24,354

Per Capita Income
(2010 Inflation-Adjusted Dollars)

Group	Dollars
Total Population	18,918
Hispanic or Latino (of any race)	12,582
Central American, ex. Mexican	10,750
Guatemalan	10,460
Salvadoran	14,105
Cuban	14,078
Mexican	12,772
Puerto Rican	15,212

Households with $100,000+ Income

Group	Number	%
Total Population	1,246	10.0
Hispanic or Latino (of any race)	211	5.5
Central American, ex. Mexican	87	5.5
Guatemalan	65	7.0
Salvadoran	22	7.1
Cuban	46	8.2
Mexican	17	2.5
Puerto Rican	0	0.0

Households with Food Stamps/SNAP Benefits During Past 12 Months

Group	Number	%
Total Population	1,397	11.2
Hispanic or Latino (of any race)	665	17.4
Central American, ex. Mexican	283	18.0
Guatemalan	199	21.4
Salvadoran	13	4.2
Cuban	141	25.0
Mexican	127	18.8
Puerto Rican	66	14.9

Poverty Rate
(Income in Past 12 Months Below Poverty Level)

Group	%
Total Population	25.3
Hispanic or Latino (of any race)	31.1
Central American, ex. Mexican	33.3
Guatemalan	35.0
Salvadoran	17.6
Cuban	36.9
Mexican	27.8
Puerto Rican	38.0

Lehigh Acres

Population

Group	Number	%TP[1]	%HP[2]
Total Population	86,784	100.0	–
Hispanic or Latino (of any race)	29,797	34.3	100.0
Central American, ex. Mexican	2,598	3.0	8.7
Costa Rican	122	0.1	0.4
Guatemalan	652	0.8	2.2
Honduran	901	1.0	3.0
Nicaraguan	424	0.5	1.4
Salvadoran	393	0.5	1.3
Cuban	6,506	7.5	21.8
Dominican Republic	861	1.0	2.9
Mexican	9,005	10.4	30.2
Puerto Rican	7,864	9.1	26.4
South American	1,653	1.9	5.5
Argentinean	127	0.1	0.4
Colombian	743	0.9	2.5
Ecuadorian	172	0.2	0.6
Peruvian	273	0.3	0.9
Venezuelan	152	0.2	0.5
Spaniard	127	0.1	0.4

Population Growth: 2000–2010

Group	%
Total Population	159.6
Hispanic or Latino (of any race)	567.2
Central American, ex. Mexican	1,824.4
Cuban	2,622.2
Mexican	670.3
Puerto Rican	274.8
South American	907.9

Males per 100 Females

Group	Number
Total Population	97.0
Hispanic or Latino (of any race)	101.9
Central American, ex. Mexican	102.3
Costa Rican	125.9
Guatemalan	125.6
Honduran	98.5
Nicaraguan	87.6
Salvadoran	101.5
Cuban	106.1
Dominican Republic	81.3
Mexican	110.3
Puerto Rican	96.2
South American	80.3
Argentinean	64.9
Colombian	79.5
Ecuadorian	91.1
Peruvian	80.8
Venezuelan	85.4
Spaniard	81.4

Notes: (1) Percent of total population; (2) Percent of Hispanic/Latino population; Profiles include places with an overall population of at least 125,000, OR an overall population of at least 25,000 where the Hispanic/Latino population is at least 20% of the overall population. In states where less than five places meet either of these criteria, we have included places with at least 10,000 total population with the highest percentage of Hispanic/Latino population. These places are identified with an asterisk (*); Please refer to the User's Guide for a full explanation of data.

Average Household Size

Group	People
Total Population	2.97
Hispanic or Latino (of any race)	3.60
Central American, ex. Mexican	4.13
Costa Rican	3.74
Guatemalan	4.59
Honduran	4.18
Nicaraguan	3.97
Salvadoran	4.09
Cuban	3.29
Dominican Republic	3.57
Mexican	4.35
Puerto Rican	3.22
South American	3.32
Argentinean	3.21
Colombian	3.06
Ecuadorian	3.57
Peruvian	3.74
Venezuelan	3.29
Spaniard	3.23

Median Age

Group	Years
Total Population	32.3
Hispanic or Latino (of any race)	27.0
Central American, ex. Mexican	27.9
Costa Rican	27.0
Guatemalan	24.7
Honduran	27.9
Nicaraguan	30.4
Salvadoran	29.2
Cuban	35.8
Dominican Republic	33.7
Mexican	21.9
Puerto Rican	26.9
South American	35.8
Argentinean	37.4
Colombian	37.9
Ecuadorian	36.5
Peruvian	35.6
Venezuelan	30.3
Spaniard	32.8

High School Graduates
(Universe: Population 25 Years and Over)

Group	Number	%
Total Population	41,527	80.3
Hispanic or Latino (of any race)	9,212	65.4
Central American, ex. Mexican	797	64.4
Cuban	2,769	75.2
Mexican	1,580	45.1
Puerto Rican	2,694	71.6
South American	840	83.1

Four-Year College Graduates
(Universe: Population 25 Years and Over)

Group	Number	%
Total Population	7,497	14.5
Hispanic or Latino (of any race)	1,302	9.2
Central American, ex. Mexican	132	10.7
Cuban	597	16.2
Mexican	110	3.1
Puerto Rican	250	6.6
South American	172	17.0

Population Age 3–17 Enrolled in Public School
(Universe: Population Age 3–17 Enrolled in School)

Group	Number	%
Total Population	17,233	92.2
Hispanic or Latino (of any race)	6,271	95.1
Central American, ex. Mexican	305	100.0
Cuban	1,358	98.7
Mexican	2,008	96.8
Puerto Rican	1,644	94.9
South American	288	100.0

Population Age 3–17 Enrolled in Private School
(Universe: Population Age 3–17 Enrolled in School)

Group	Number	%
Total Population	1,465	7.8
Hispanic or Latino (of any race)	326	4.9
Central American, ex. Mexican	0	0.0
Cuban	18	1.3
Mexican	66	3.2
Puerto Rican	89	5.1
South American	0	0.0

Foreign-Born Population

Group	Number	%
Total Population	19,109	22.6
Hispanic or Latino (of any race)	10,330	40.1
Central American, ex. Mexican	1,191	62.3
Cuban	4,272	70.3
Mexican	3,330	44.8
Puerto Rican	41	0.6
South American	1,032	70.8

Foreign-Born Naturalized U.S. Citizens

Group	Number	%
Total Population	7,233	37.9
Hispanic or Latino (of any race)	2,833	27.4
Central American, ex. Mexican	427	35.9
Cuban	1,048	24.5
Mexican	482	14.5
Puerto Rican	41	100.0
South American	515	49.9

Language Spoken at Home: English Only
(Universe: Population 5 Years and Over)

Group	Number	%
Total Population	50,985	65.8
Hispanic or Latino (of any race)	3,747	16.1
Central American, ex. Mexican	122	7.1
Cuban	130	2.3
Mexican	1,040	16.1
Puerto Rican	1,658	26.9
South American	191	14.0

Language Spoken at Home: Spanish
(Universe: Population 5 Years and Over)

Group	Number	%
Total Population	20,904	27.0
Hispanic or Latino (of any race)	19,458	83.8
Central American, ex. Mexican	1,605	92.9
Cuban	5,550	97.7
Mexican	5,427	83.9
Puerto Rican	4,514	73.1
South American	1,173	86.0

Unemployment Rate
(Universe: Population 16 Years and Over)

Group	%
Total Population	12.0
Hispanic or Latino (of any race)	11.7
Central American, ex. Mexican	8.2
Cuban	18.3
Mexican	8.3
Puerto Rican	11.2
South American	4.4

Class of Worker: Private Wage and Salary
(Universe: Civilian Employed Population 16 Years and Over)

Group	Number	%
Total Population	29,856	80.5
Hispanic or Latino (of any race)	9,174	83.9
Central American, ex. Mexican	666	89.8
Cuban	1,975	83.4
Mexican	2,728	84.5
Puerto Rican	2,608	83.0
South American	600	78.5

Class of Worker: Government
(Universe: Civilian Employed Population 16 Years and Over)

Group	Number	%
Total Population	5,597	15.1
Hispanic or Latino (of any race)	1,035	9.5
Central American, ex. Mexican	59	8.0
Cuban	195	8.2
Mexican	169	5.2
Puerto Rican	430	13.7
South American	129	16.9

Means of Transportation to Work: Car, Truck or Van
(Universe: Workers 16 Years and Over)

Group	Number	%
Total Population	34,376	95.0
Hispanic or Latino (of any race)	9,958	93.2
Central American, ex. Mexican	725	97.7
Cuban	2,267	98.5
Mexican	2,751	87.2
Puerto Rican	2,835	91.9
South American	734	98.9

Means of Transportation to Work: Public Transportation (ex. Taxicab)
(Universe: Workers 16 Years and Over)

Group	Number	%
Total Population	350	1.0
Hispanic or Latino (of any race)	211	2.0
Central American, ex. Mexican	0	0.0
Cuban	0	0.0
Mexican	96	3.0
Puerto Rican	115	3.7
South American	0	0.0

Homeownership Rate
(Universe: Occupied Housing Units)

Group	%
Total Population	64.3
Hispanic or Latino (of any race)	53.7
Central American, ex. Mexican	50.5
Costa Rican	64.7
Guatemalan	39.1
Honduran	45.2
Nicaraguan	64.2
Salvadoran	49.1
Cuban	62.0
Dominican Republic	52.7
Mexican	46.4
Puerto Rican	50.9
South American	66.4
Argentinean	60.5
Colombian	70.9
Ecuadorian	71.4
Peruvian	51.9
Venezuelan	68.9
Spaniard	62.8

Median Home Value

Group	Dollars
Total Population	158,600
Hispanic or Latino (of any race)	158,100
Central American, ex. Mexican	205,600
Cuban	185,100
Mexican	143,800
Puerto Rican	140,300
South American	179,500

Median Gross Rent

Group	Dollars
Total Population	975
Hispanic or Latino (of any race)	987
Central American, ex. Mexican	803
Cuban	1,059
Mexican	1,060
Puerto Rican	944
South American	789

Median Household Income
(2010 Inflation-Adjusted Dollars)

Group	Dollars
Total Population	47,277
Hispanic or Latino (of any race)	43,584
Central American, ex. Mexican	34,730
Cuban	29,877
Mexican	46,875
Puerto Rican	45,349
South American	46,566

Per Capita Income
(2010 Inflation-Adjusted Dollars)

Group	Dollars
Total Population	19,008
Hispanic or Latino (of any race)	13,299
Central American, ex. Mexican	9,856
Cuban	11,915
Mexican	12,092
Puerto Rican	15,945
South American	16,150

Households with $100,000+ Income

Group	Number	%
Total Population	2,785	10.3
Hispanic or Latino (of any race)	282	4.1

Notes: (1) Percent of total population; (2) Percent of Hispanic/Latino population; Profiles include places with an overall population of at least 125,000, OR an overall population of at least 25,000 where the Hispanic/Latino population is at least 20% of the overall population. In states where less than five places meet either of these criteria, we have included places with at least 10,000 total population with the highest percentage of Hispanic/Latino population. These places are identified with an asterisk (*); Please refer to the User's Guide for a full explanation of data.

Central American, ex. Mexican	16	3.0
Cuban	28	1.6
Mexican	57	3.5
Puerto Rican	170	8.7
South American	11	2.1

Households with Food Stamps/SNAP Benefits During Past 12 Months

Group	Number	%
Total Population	3,130	11.6
Hispanic or Latino (of any race)	1,313	19.0
Central American, ex. Mexican	134	24.8
Cuban	519	30.0
Mexican	235	14.6
Puerto Rican	255	13.0
South American	54	10.4

Poverty Rate
(Income in Past 12 Months Below Poverty Level)

Group	%
Total Population	15.7
Hispanic or Latino (of any race)	20.0
Central American, ex. Mexican	25.1
Cuban	45.0
Mexican	8.2
Puerto Rican	15.3
South American	13.0

Margate

Population

Group	Number	%TP[1]	%HP[2]
Total Population	53,284	100.0	–
Hispanic or Latino (of any race)	11,846	22.2	100.0
Central American, ex. Mexican	1,451	2.7	12.2
Costa Rican	108	0.2	0.9
Guatemalan	257	0.5	2.2
Honduran	384	0.7	3.2
Nicaraguan	151	0.3	1.3
Salvadoran	458	0.9	3.9
Cuban	970	1.8	8.2
Dominican Republic	615	1.2	5.2
Mexican	1,033	1.9	8.7
Puerto Rican	2,841	5.3	24.0
South American	4,158	7.8	35.1
Argentinean	263	0.5	2.2
Colombian	2,220	4.2	18.7
Ecuadorian	365	0.7	3.1
Peruvian	772	1.4	6.5
Venezuelan	341	0.6	2.9

Population Growth: 2000–2010

Group	%
Total Population	-1.2
Hispanic or Latino (of any race)	43.8
Central American, ex. Mexican	173.8
Honduran	269.2
Salvadoran	114.0
Cuban	21.9
Dominican Republic	149.0
Mexican	26.0
Puerto Rican	31.9
South American	104.9
Colombian	85.2
Ecuadorian	170.4
Peruvian	145.1
Venezuelan	150.7

Males per 100 Females

Group	Number
Total Population	87.9
Hispanic or Latino (of any race)	93.1
Central American, ex. Mexican	115.3
Costa Rican	83.1
Guatemalan	238.2
Honduran	94.9
Nicaraguan	91.1
Salvadoran	117.1
Cuban	96.0
Dominican Republic	75.7
Mexican	104.6
Puerto Rican	94.3
South American	83.6
Argentinean	94.8
Colombian	82.3
Ecuadorian	90.1
Peruvian	84.7
Venezuelan	74.9

Average Household Size

Group	People
Total Population	2.47
Hispanic or Latino (of any race)	2.90
Central American, ex. Mexican	3.75
Costa Rican	2.97
Guatemalan	3.81
Honduran	3.86
Nicaraguan	3.33
Salvadoran	4.34
Cuban	2.43
Dominican Republic	3.09
Mexican	3.76
Puerto Rican	2.61
South American	2.86
Argentinean	2.36
Colombian	2.87
Ecuadorian	3.17
Peruvian	2.85
Venezuelan	3.03

Median Age

Group	Years
Total Population	42.3
Hispanic or Latino (of any race)	36.5
Central American, ex. Mexican	30.1
Costa Rican	33.7
Guatemalan	26.8
Honduran	31.1
Nicaraguan	33.8
Salvadoran	29.6
Cuban	44.8
Dominican Republic	35.3
Mexican	28.7
Puerto Rican	37.8
South American	42.1
Argentinean	46.9
Colombian	42.6
Ecuadorian	41.8
Peruvian	43.3
Venezuelan	36.1

High School Graduates
(Universe: Population 25 Years and Over)

Group	Number	%
Total Population	32,576	83.6
Hispanic or Latino (of any race)	5,724	72.9
Central American, ex. Mexican	477	51.0
Puerto Rican	2,043	74.4
South American	2,048	87.2
Colombian	947	80.9

Four-Year College Graduates
(Universe: Population 25 Years and Over)

Group	Number	%
Total Population	8,419	21.6
Hispanic or Latino (of any race)	1,391	17.7
Central American, ex. Mexican	38	4.1
Puerto Rican	468	17.0
South American	711	30.3
Colombian	190	16.2

Population Age 3–17 Enrolled in Public School
(Universe: Population Age 3–17 Enrolled in School)

Group	Number	%
Total Population	6,722	86.9
Hispanic or Latino (of any race)	2,211	94.1
Central American, ex. Mexican	286	100.0
Puerto Rican	421	89.6
South American	772	94.7
Colombian	419	96.8

Population Age 3–17 Enrolled in Private School
(Universe: Population Age 3–17 Enrolled in School)

Group	Number	%
Total Population	1,013	13.1
Hispanic or Latino (of any race)	139	5.9
Central American, ex. Mexican	0	0.0
Puerto Rican	49	10.4
South American	43	5.3
Colombian	14	3.2

Foreign-Born Population

Group	Number	%
Total Population	15,940	29.7
Hispanic or Latino (of any race)	5,794	48.1
Central American, ex. Mexican	1,268	81.6
Puerto Rican	78	2.0
South American	2,773	75.1
Colombian	1,367	77.1

Foreign-Born Naturalized U.S. Citizens

Group	Number	%
Total Population	8,064	50.6
Hispanic or Latino (of any race)	2,418	41.7
Central American, ex. Mexican	358	28.2
Puerto Rican	22	28.2
South American	1,096	39.5
Colombian	691	50.5

Language Spoken at Home: English Only
(Universe: Population 5 Years and Over)

Group	Number	%
Total Population	33,118	65.4
Hispanic or Latino (of any race)	1,677	14.7
Central American, ex. Mexican	83	5.4
Puerto Rican	1,002	28.0
South American	241	7.0
Colombian	141	8.3

Language Spoken at Home: Spanish
(Universe: Population 5 Years and Over)

Group	Number	%
Total Population	10,471	20.7
Hispanic or Latino (of any race)	9,606	84.5
Central American, ex. Mexican	1,425	93.6
Puerto Rican	2,576	72.0
South American	3,218	93.0
Colombian	1,554	91.7

Unemployment Rate
(Universe: Population 16 Years and Over)

Group	%
Total Population	9.4
Hispanic or Latino (of any race)	11.1
Central American, ex. Mexican	11.5
Puerto Rican	15.0
South American	12.1
Colombian	21.1

Class of Worker: Private Wage and Salary
(Universe: Civilian Employed Population 16 Years and Over)

Group	Number	%
Total Population	22,262	83.7
Hispanic or Latino (of any race)	5,003	84.1
Central American, ex. Mexican	885	87.0
Puerto Rican	1,464	78.5
South American	1,387	82.1
Colombian	705	89.7

Class of Worker: Government
(Universe: Civilian Employed Population 16 Years and Over)

Group	Number	%
Total Population	3,032	11.4
Hispanic or Latino (of any race)	546	9.2
Central American, ex. Mexican	67	6.6
Puerto Rican	359	19.3
South American	78	4.6
Colombian	38	4.8

Means of Transportation to Work: Car, Truck or Van
(Universe: Workers 16 Years and Over)

Group	Number	%
Total Population	23,965	92.9
Hispanic or Latino (of any race)	5,293	92.2
Central American, ex. Mexican	887	92.4
Puerto Rican	1,631	91.5
South American	1,527	90.9
Colombian	748	95.2

Means of Transportation to Work: Public Transportation (ex. Taxicab)
(Universe: Workers 16 Years and Over)

Group	Number	%
Total Population	594	2.3

Notes: (1) Percent of total population; (2) Percent of Hispanic/Latino population; Profiles include places with an overall population of at least 125,000, OR an overall population of at least 25,000 where the Hispanic/Latino population is at least 20% of the overall population. In states where less than five places meet either of these criteria, we have included places with at least 10,000 total population with the highest percentage of Hispanic/Latino population. These places are identified with an asterisk (*); Please refer to the User's Guide for a full explanation of data.

Hispanic or Latino (of any race)	221	3.8
Central American, ex. Mexican	62	6.5
Puerto Rican	44	2.5
South American	67	4.0
Colombian	8	1.0

Homeownership Rate
(Universe: Occupied Housing Units)

Group	%
Total Population	76.2
Hispanic or Latino (of any race)	69.4
Central American, ex. Mexican	55.3
Costa Rican	77.8
Guatemalan	32.4
Honduran	57.0
Nicaraguan	55.6
Salvadoran	52.9
Cuban	77.0
Dominican Republic	70.1
Mexican	55.5
Puerto Rican	72.3
South American	71.9
Argentinean	72.6
Colombian	73.5
Ecuadorian	75.2
Peruvian	68.8
Venezuelan	67.0

Median Home Value

Group	Dollars
Total Population	169,100
Hispanic or Latino (of any race)	179,600
Central American, ex. Mexican	209,200
Puerto Rican	176,200
South American	173,100
Colombian	183,900

Median Gross Rent

Group	Dollars
Total Population	1,224
Hispanic or Latino (of any race)	1,274
Central American, ex. Mexican	1,152
Puerto Rican	1,313
South American	1,352
Colombian	1,449

Median Household Income
(2010 Inflation-Adjusted Dollars)

Group	Dollars
Total Population	45,815
Hispanic or Latino (of any race)	40,175
Central American, ex. Mexican	55,900
Puerto Rican	48,750
South American	29,772
Colombian	37,984

Per Capita Income
(2010 Inflation-Adjusted Dollars)

Group	Dollars
Total Population	24,238
Hispanic or Latino (of any race)	17,710
Central American, ex. Mexican	16,855
Puerto Rican	21,858
South American	15,141
Colombian	15,994

Households with $100,000+ Income

Group	Number	%
Total Population	3,164	14.5
Hispanic or Latino (of any race)	495	12.9
Central American, ex. Mexican	65	18.7
Puerto Rican	219	15.6
South American	111	9.0
Colombian	91	16.2

Households with Food Stamps/SNAP Benefits During Past 12 Months

Group	Number	%
Total Population	1,155	5.3
Hispanic or Latino (of any race)	258	6.7
Central American, ex. Mexican	34	9.8
Puerto Rican	108	7.7
South American	63	5.1
Colombian	63	11.2

Poverty Rate
(Income in Past 12 Months Below Poverty Level)

Group	%
Total Population	11.0
Hispanic or Latino (of any race)	15.8
Central American, ex. Mexican	23.8
Puerto Rican	8.5
South American	22.8
Colombian	26.3

Meadow Woods

Population

Group	Number	%TP[1]	%HP[2]
Total Population	25,558	100.0	–
Hispanic or Latino (of any race)	17,185	67.2	100.0
Central American, ex. Mexican	696	2.7	4.1
Honduran	129	0.5	0.8
Nicaraguan	118	0.5	0.7
Panamanian	100	0.4	0.6
Salvadoran	179	0.7	1.0
Cuban	657	2.6	3.8
Dominican Republic	1,651	6.5	9.6
Mexican	469	1.8	2.7
Puerto Rican	8,974	35.1	52.2
South American	3,989	15.6	23.2
Argentinean	122	0.5	0.7
Colombian	2,226	8.7	13.0
Ecuadorian	526	2.1	3.1
Peruvian	351	1.4	2.0
Venezuelan	660	2.6	3.8

Population Growth: 2000–2010

Group	%
Total Population	126.5
Hispanic or Latino (of any race)	188.1
Central American, ex. Mexican	367.1
Cuban	192.0
Dominican Republic	624.1
Mexican	191.3
Puerto Rican	137.9
South American	458.7
Colombian	445.6

Males per 100 Females

Group	Number
Total Population	92.4
Hispanic or Latino (of any race)	89.4
Central American, ex. Mexican	90.2
Honduran	118.6
Nicaraguan	93.4
Panamanian	63.9
Salvadoran	103.4
Cuban	106.0
Dominican Republic	83.2
Mexican	100.4
Puerto Rican	89.4
South American	86.4
Argentinean	100.0
Colombian	79.1
Ecuadorian	99.2
Peruvian	87.7
Venezuelan	99.4

Average Household Size

Group	People
Total Population	3.29
Hispanic or Latino (of any race)	3.45
Central American, ex. Mexican	3.68
Honduran	3.26
Nicaraguan	4.43
Panamanian	3.46
Salvadoran	4.06
Cuban	3.30
Dominican Republic	3.89
Mexican	3.76
Puerto Rican	3.32
South American	3.57
Argentinean	3.27
Colombian	3.65
Ecuadorian	3.95
Peruvian	3.28
Venezuelan	3.35

Median Age

Group	Years
Total Population	31.7
Hispanic or Latino (of any race)	31.2
Central American, ex. Mexican	31.6
Honduran	31.5
Nicaraguan	28.5
Panamanian	38.0
Salvadoran	32.2
Cuban	35.6
Dominican Republic	30.1
Mexican	26.5
Puerto Rican	30.9
South American	35.0
Argentinean	33.8
Colombian	34.6
Ecuadorian	35.8
Peruvian	36.2
Venezuelan	34.4

High School Graduates
(Universe: Population 25 Years and Over)

Group	Number	%
Total Population	11,826	85.4
Hispanic or Latino (of any race)	7,338	83.7
Puerto Rican	4,328	84.2
South American	2,082	89.1
Colombian	1,403	94.3

Four-Year College Graduates
(Universe: Population 25 Years and Over)

Group	Number	%
Total Population	3,332	24.1
Hispanic or Latino (of any race)	2,057	23.5
Puerto Rican	1,322	25.7
South American	557	23.8
Colombian	220	14.8

Population Age 3–17 Enrolled in Public School
(Universe: Population Age 3–17 Enrolled in School)

Group	Number	%
Total Population	5,216	93.8
Hispanic or Latino (of any race)	3,852	94.5
Puerto Rican	2,370	93.6
South American	758	93.9
Colombian	593	92.4

Population Age 3–17 Enrolled in Private School
(Universe: Population Age 3–17 Enrolled in School)

Group	Number	%
Total Population	342	6.2
Hispanic or Latino (of any race)	223	5.5
Puerto Rican	162	6.4
South American	49	6.1
Colombian	49	7.6

Foreign-Born Population

Group	Number	%
Total Population	6,318	26.6
Hispanic or Latino (of any race)	4,159	25.8
Puerto Rican	182	1.9
South American	2,726	66.3
Colombian	1,811	66.6

Foreign-Born Naturalized U.S. Citizens

Group	Number	%
Total Population	2,927	46.3
Hispanic or Latino (of any race)	1,659	39.9
Puerto Rican	143	78.6
South American	959	35.2
Colombian	664	36.7

Language Spoken at Home: English Only
(Universe: Population 5 Years and Over)

Group	Number	%
Total Population	6,496	29.3
Hispanic or Latino (of any race)	1,176	7.9
Puerto Rican	803	9.2
South American	120	3.2
Colombian	14	0.6

Language Spoken at Home: Spanish
(Universe: Population 5 Years and Over)

Group	Number	%
Total Population	13,768	62.2

Notes: (1) Percent of total population; (2) Percent of Hispanic/Latino population; Profiles include places with an overall population of at least 125,000, OR an overall population of at least 25,000 where the Hispanic/Latino population is at least 20% of the overall population. In states where less than five places meet either of these criteria, we have included places with at least 10,000 total population with the highest percentage of Hispanic/Latino population. These places are identified with an asterisk (*); Please refer to the User's Guide for a full explanation of data.

Group	Number	%
Hispanic or Latino (of any race)	13,518	91.3
Puerto Rican	7,905	90.4
South American	3,518	94.9
Colombian	2,353	97.1

Unemployment Rate
(Universe: Population 16 Years and Over)

Group	%
Total Population	10.6
Hispanic or Latino (of any race)	12.3
Puerto Rican	14.0
South American	9.3
Colombian	5.4

Class of Worker: Private Wage and Salary
(Universe: Civilian Employed Population 16 Years and Over)

Group	Number	%
Total Population	9,445	84.3
Hispanic or Latino (of any race)	5,862	84.3
Puerto Rican	2,978	79.9
South American	1,892	89.9
Colombian	1,253	91.2

Class of Worker: Government
(Universe: Civilian Employed Population 16 Years and Over)

Group	Number	%
Total Population	1,024	9.1
Hispanic or Latino (of any race)	786	11.3
Puerto Rican	607	16.3
South American	97	4.6
Colombian	27	2.0

Means of Transportation to Work: Car, Truck or Van
(Universe: Workers 16 Years and Over)

Group	Number	%
Total Population	10,381	93.8
Hispanic or Latino (of any race)	6,337	92.7
Puerto Rican	3,323	90.5
South American	1,921	93.4
Colombian	1,292	96.4

Means of Transportation to Work: Public Transportation (ex. Taxicab)
(Universe: Workers 16 Years and Over)

Group	Number	%
Total Population	64	0.6
Hispanic or Latino (of any race)	62	0.9
Puerto Rican	10	0.3
South American	52	2.5
Colombian	0	0.0

Homeownership Rate
(Universe: Occupied Housing Units)

Group	%
Total Population	65.6
Hispanic or Latino (of any race)	60.1
Central American, ex. Mexican	65.7
Honduran	55.9
Nicaraguan	71.4
Panamanian	67.9
Salvadoran	73.5
Cuban	62.4
Dominican Republic	59.7
Mexican	62.9
Puerto Rican	60.0
South American	58.1
Argentinean	68.2
Colombian	57.9
Ecuadorian	59.9
Peruvian	66.4
Venezuelan	50.5

Median Home Value

Group	Dollars
Total Population	221,800
Hispanic or Latino (of any race)	228,300
Puerto Rican	212,000
South American	261,900
Colombian	269,600

Median Gross Rent

Group	Dollars
Total Population	1,249
Hispanic or Latino (of any race)	1,214
Puerto Rican	1,257
South American	1,258
Colombian	1,295

Median Household Income
(2010 Inflation-Adjusted Dollars)

Group	Dollars
Total Population	46,725
Hispanic or Latino (of any race)	42,199
Puerto Rican	44,068
South American	46,630
Colombian	45,927

Per Capita Income
(2010 Inflation-Adjusted Dollars)

Group	Dollars
Total Population	17,371
Hispanic or Latino (of any race)	14,362
Puerto Rican	15,007
South American	14,149
Colombian	14,764

Households with $100,000+ Income

Group	Number	%
Total Population	744	10.5
Hispanic or Latino (of any race)	328	7.1
Puerto Rican	236	8.7
South American	37	3.2
Colombian	20	2.6

Households with Food Stamps/SNAP Benefits During Past 12 Months

Group	Number	%
Total Population	947	13.3
Hispanic or Latino (of any race)	880	19.2
Puerto Rican	446	16.4
South American	296	25.8
Colombian	187	23.9

Poverty Rate
(Income in Past 12 Months Below Poverty Level)

Group	%
Total Population	12.4
Hispanic or Latino (of any race)	15.3
Puerto Rican	15.5
South American	16.9
Colombian	12.1

Miami

Population

Group	Number	%TP[1]	%HP[2]
Total Population	399,457	100.0	–
Hispanic or Latino (of any race)	279,456	70.0	100.0
Central American, ex. Mexican	62,995	15.8	22.5
Costa Rican	1,197	0.3	0.4
Guatemalan	4,135	1.0	1.5
Honduran	23,209	5.8	8.3
Nicaraguan	28,618	7.2	10.2
Panamanian	1,113	0.3	0.4
Salvadoran	4,610	1.2	1.6
Cuban	137,301	34.4	49.1
Dominican Republic	9,668	2.4	3.5
Mexican	5,830	1.5	2.1
Puerto Rican	12,789	3.2	4.6
South American	34,718	8.7	12.4
Argentinean	4,891	1.2	1.8
Bolivian	709	0.2	0.3
Chilean	1,427	0.4	0.5
Colombian	12,966	3.2	4.6
Ecuadorian	2,777	0.7	1.0
Paraguayan	131	<0.1	<0.1
Peruvian	4,946	1.2	1.8
Uruguayan	1,040	0.3	0.4
Venezuelan	5,770	1.4	2.1
Spaniard	2,104	0.5	0.8

Population Growth: 2000–2010

Group	%
Total Population	10.2
Hispanic or Latino (of any race)	17.2
Central American, ex. Mexican	56.9
Costa Rican	54.5
Guatemalan	67.1
Honduran	91.5
Nicaraguan	39.3
Panamanian	69.4
Salvadoran	85.7
Cuban	10.9
Dominican Republic	51.8
Mexican	58.9
Puerto Rican	24.7
South American	130.3
Argentinean	193.0
Bolivian	99.7
Chilean	52.0
Colombian	124.2
Ecuadorian	97.2
Peruvian	102.1
Uruguayan	370.6
Venezuelan	194.5
Spaniard	114.7

Males per 100 Females

Group	Number
Total Population	99.2
Hispanic or Latino (of any race)	97.2
Central American, ex. Mexican	99.4
Costa Rican	79.7
Guatemalan	119.8
Honduran	103.3
Nicaraguan	94.3
Panamanian	74.7
Salvadoran	108.7
Cuban	98.7
Dominican Republic	83.7
Mexican	123.3
Puerto Rican	99.4
South American	85.1
Argentinean	108.7
Bolivian	86.1
Chilean	98.7
Colombian	74.9
Ecuadorian	85.4
Paraguayan	81.9
Peruvian	80.0
Uruguayan	116.2
Venezuelan	87.9
Spaniard	114.3

Average Household Size

Group	People
Total Population	2.47
Hispanic or Latino (of any race)	2.57
Central American, ex. Mexican	3.40
Costa Rican	2.54
Guatemalan	3.26
Honduran	3.43
Nicaraguan	3.50
Panamanian	2.26
Salvadoran	3.40
Cuban	2.38
Dominican Republic	2.80
Mexican	2.54
Puerto Rican	2.39
South American	2.33
Argentinean	2.44
Bolivian	2.60
Chilean	2.38
Colombian	2.22
Ecuadorian	2.53
Paraguayan	2.28
Peruvian	2.55
Uruguayan	2.51
Venezuelan	2.15
Spaniard	2.02

Median Age

Group	Years
Total Population	38.8
Hispanic or Latino (of any race)	40.6
Central American, ex. Mexican	34.2
Costa Rican	37.6
Guatemalan	34.9
Honduran	32.5
Nicaraguan	35.6
Panamanian	39.8
Salvadoran	33.7
Cuban	49.1
Dominican Republic	36.3

Notes: (1) Percent of total population; (2) Percent of Hispanic/Latino population; Profiles include places with an overall population of at least 125,000, OR an overall population of at least 25,000 where the Hispanic/Latino population is at least 20% of the overall population. In states where less than five places meet either of these criteria, we have included places with at least 10,000 total population with the highest percentage of Hispanic/Latino population. These places are identified with an asterisk (*); Please refer to the User's Guide for a full explanation of data.

Mexican		30.2
Puerto Rican		33.9
South American		36.4
Argentinean		35.8
Bolivian		36.8
Chilean		40.8
Colombian		36.7
Ecuadorian		37.5
Paraguayan		32.9
Peruvian		39.6
Uruguayan		34.4
Venezuelan		33.9
Spaniard		41.6

High School Graduates
(Universe: Population 25 Years and Over)

Group	Number	%
Total Population	187,231	67.4
Hispanic or Latino (of any race)	128,987	64.0
Central American, ex. Mexican	24,251	52.3
Costa Rican	830	81.5
Guatemalan	1,805	54.4
Honduran	6,986	41.1
Nicaraguan	12,823	59.8
Panamanian	537	73.5
Salvadoran	1,148	42.9
Cuban	70,004	64.1
Dominican Republic	3,700	60.4
Mexican	2,621	63.9
Puerto Rican	5,831	69.8
South American	19,085	83.4
Argentinean	3,236	82.6
Chilean	842	90.2
Colombian	6,471	78.6
Ecuadorian	1,245	80.6
Peruvian	2,736	84.3
Venezuelan	3,558	94.9
Spaniard	789	86.3

Four-Year College Graduates
(Universe: Population 25 Years and Over)

Group	Number	%
Total Population	61,651	22.2
Hispanic or Latino (of any race)	38,521	19.1
Central American, ex. Mexican	4,876	10.5
Costa Rican	176	17.3
Guatemalan	331	10.0
Honduran	1,093	6.4
Nicaraguan	2,947	13.7
Panamanian	111	15.2
Salvadoran	204	7.6
Cuban	20,224	18.5
Dominican Republic	936	15.3
Mexican	1,144	27.9
Puerto Rican	1,737	20.8
South American	8,074	35.3
Argentinean	1,202	30.7
Chilean	403	43.2
Colombian	2,707	32.9
Ecuadorian	551	35.7
Peruvian	854	26.3
Venezuelan	1,870	49.9
Spaniard	421	46.1

Population Age 3–17 Enrolled in Public School
(Universe: Population Age 3–17 Enrolled in School)

Group	Number	%
Total Population	46,900	88.2
Hispanic or Latino (of any race)	30,065	89.5
Central American, ex. Mexican	9,987	95.9
Costa Rican	109	83.8
Guatemalan	786	100.0
Honduran	4,010	97.2
Nicaraguan	4,567	95.0
Panamanian	127	100.0
Salvadoran	376	87.9
Cuban	11,256	84.9
Dominican Republic	1,339	93.5
Mexican	720	91.7
Puerto Rican	2,677	90.9
South American	3,087	89.2
Argentinean	822	93.1
Chilean	114	82.6
Colombian	867	88.4
Ecuadorian	142	100.0
Peruvian	367	85.0
Venezuelan	472	81.0
Spaniard	28	100.0

Population Age 3–17 Enrolled in Private School
(Universe: Population Age 3–17 Enrolled in School)

Group	Number	%
Total Population	6,304	11.8
Hispanic or Latino (of any race)	3,519	10.5
Central American, ex. Mexican	431	4.1
Costa Rican	21	16.2
Guatemalan	0	0.0
Honduran	116	2.8
Nicaraguan	242	5.0
Panamanian	0	0.0
Salvadoran	52	12.1
Cuban	2,002	15.1
Dominican Republic	93	6.5
Mexican	65	8.3
Puerto Rican	268	9.1
South American	375	10.8
Argentinean	61	6.9
Chilean	24	17.4
Colombian	114	11.6
Ecuadorian	0	0.0
Peruvian	65	15.0
Venezuelan	111	19.0
Spaniard	0	0.0

Foreign-Born Population

Group	Number	%
Total Population	227,605	58.1
Hispanic or Latino (of any race)	201,058	73.0
Central American, ex. Mexican	53,612	74.5
Costa Rican	1,167	73.7
Guatemalan	3,889	75.8
Honduran	20,934	75.5
Nicaraguan	24,045	74.4
Panamanian	563	49.1
Salvadoran	2,845	74.2
Cuban	107,047	79.2
Dominican Republic	6,343	67.0
Mexican	4,424	66.0
Puerto Rican	403	3.0
South American	25,437	80.5
Argentinean	4,708	81.1
Chilean	896	76.0
Colombian	8,512	79.8
Ecuadorian	1,539	77.5
Peruvian	3,807	80.5
Venezuelan	4,408	82.9
Spaniard	806	74.3

Foreign-Born Naturalized U.S. Citizens

Group	Number	%
Total Population	93,626	41.1
Hispanic or Latino (of any race)	83,296	41.4
Central American, ex. Mexican	10,363	19.3
Costa Rican	280	24.0
Guatemalan	807	20.8
Honduran	2,916	13.9
Nicaraguan	5,657	23.5
Panamanian	314	55.8
Salvadoran	365	12.8
Cuban	59,628	55.7
Dominican Republic	3,057	48.2
Mexican	652	14.7
Puerto Rican	158	39.2
South American	7,634	30.0
Argentinean	827	17.6
Chilean	539	60.2
Colombian	3,386	39.8
Ecuadorian	783	50.9
Peruvian	989	26.0
Venezuelan	733	16.6
Spaniard	328	40.7

Language Spoken at Home: English Only
(Universe: Population 5 Years and Over)

Group	Number	%
Total Population	83,501	22.7
Hispanic or Latino (of any race)	9,438	3.6
Central American, ex. Mexican	1,357	2.1
Costa Rican	42	3.1
Guatemalan	30	0.6
Honduran	459	1.9
Nicaraguan	700	2.3
Panamanian	16	1.5
Salvadoran	89	2.5
Cuban	3,799	2.9
Dominican Republic	337	3.8
Mexican	604	9.9
Puerto Rican	1,834	14.8
South American	922	3.1
Argentinean	191	3.6
Chilean	139	12.0
Colombian	224	2.2
Ecuadorian	107	5.7
Peruvian	209	5.0
Venezuelan	52	1.1
Spaniard	72	6.8

Language Spoken at Home: Spanish
(Universe: Population 5 Years and Over)

Group	Number	%
Total Population	257,822	70.2
Hispanic or Latino (of any race)	250,215	96.1
Central American, ex. Mexican	64,627	97.8
Costa Rican	1,315	96.9
Guatemalan	4,744	98.2
Honduran	24,330	98.1
Nicaraguan	29,513	97.6
Panamanian	1,055	98.5
Salvadoran	3,494	97.5
Cuban	126,813	97.0
Dominican Republic	8,630	96.2
Mexican	5,481	89.9
Puerto Rican	10,478	84.6
South American	28,252	96.0
Argentinean	5,174	96.2
Chilean	1,024	88.0
Colombian	9,783	96.6
Ecuadorian	1,772	94.3
Peruvian	3,977	94.3
Venezuelan	4,808	97.2
Spaniard	994	93.2

Unemployment Rate
(Universe: Population 16 Years and Over)

Group		%
Total Population		8.9
Hispanic or Latino (of any race)		8.1
Central American, ex. Mexican		9.1
Costa Rican		2.6
Guatemalan		7.1
Honduran		10.9
Nicaraguan		8.8
Panamanian		7.8
Salvadoran		4.8
Cuban		8.3
Dominican Republic		7.0
Mexican		5.5
Puerto Rican		10.6
South American		4.9
Argentinean		4.5
Chilean		0.0
Colombian		4.3
Ecuadorian		5.3
Peruvian		6.3
Venezuelan		6.0
Spaniard		18.0

Class of Worker: Private Wage and Salary
(Universe: Civilian Employed Population 16 Years and Over)

Group	Number	%
Total Population	137,383	78.0
Hispanic or Latino (of any race)	100,017	77.2
Central American, ex. Mexican	26,462	72.0
Costa Rican	512	70.9
Guatemalan	1,856	70.9
Honduran	9,566	65.4
Nicaraguan	12,392	77.9
Panamanian	318	68.8
Salvadoran	1,692	75.2
Cuban	45,421	78.8
Dominican Republic	3,712	79.5
Mexican	3,013	78.5
Puerto Rican	4,274	82.4
South American	14,718	79.7
Argentinean	2,510	75.8

Notes: (1) Percent of total population; (2) Percent of Hispanic/Latino population; Profiles include places with an overall population of at least 125,000, OR an overall population of at least 25,000 where the Hispanic/Latino population is at least 20% of the overall population. In states where less than five places meet either of these criteria, we have included places with at least 10,000 total population with the highest percentage of Hispanic/Latino population. These places are identified with an asterisk (*); Please refer to the User's Guide for a full explanation of data.

Group	Number	%
Chilean	613	79.3
Colombian	5,446	84.1
Ecuadorian	882	78.3
Peruvian	1,781	68.2
Venezuelan	2,671	85.7
Spaniard	408	84.0

Class of Worker: Government
(Universe: Civilian Employed Population 16 Years and Over)

Group	Number	%
Total Population	15,006	8.5
Hispanic or Latino (of any race)	8,770	6.8
Central American, ex. Mexican	818	2.2
Costa Rican	17	2.4
Guatemalan	137	5.2
Honduran	184	1.3
Nicaraguan	378	2.4
Panamanian	29	6.3
Salvadoran	73	3.2
Cuban	6,006	10.4
Dominican Republic	215	4.6
Mexican	84	2.2
Puerto Rican	543	10.5
South American	877	4.8
Argentinean	167	5.0
Chilean	121	15.7
Colombian	325	5.0
Ecuadorian	48	4.3
Peruvian	61	2.3
Venezuelan	132	4.2
Spaniard	45	9.3

Means of Transportation to Work: Car, Truck or Van
(Universe: Workers 16 Years and Over)

Group	Number	%
Total Population	138,013	79.7
Hispanic or Latino (of any race)	104,604	82.0
Central American, ex. Mexican	27,070	74.7
Costa Rican	470	67.1
Guatemalan	1,809	71.0
Honduran	10,555	72.9
Nicaraguan	11,964	76.3
Panamanian	315	68.2
Salvadoran	1,806	81.4
Cuban	50,465	89.1
Dominican Republic	3,546	76.2
Mexican	2,826	75.0
Puerto Rican	4,089	78.9
South American	14,093	77.7
Argentinean	2,412	74.1
Chilean	682	90.0
Colombian	4,871	77.3
Ecuadorian	979	89.1
Peruvian	1,702	66.1
Venezuelan	2,533	81.8
Spaniard	420	86.4

Means of Transportation to Work: Public Transportation (ex. Taxicab)
(Universe: Workers 16 Years and Over)

Group	Number	%
Total Population	20,250	11.7
Hispanic or Latino (of any race)	13,314	10.4
Central American, ex. Mexican	6,547	18.1
Costa Rican	63	9.0
Guatemalan	524	20.6
Honduran	2,794	19.3
Nicaraguan	2,770	17.7
Panamanian	35	7.6
Salvadoran	361	16.3
Cuban	2,604	4.6
Dominican Republic	816	17.5
Mexican	480	12.7
Puerto Rican	464	9.0
South American	2,315	12.8
Argentinean	449	13.8
Chilean	54	7.1
Colombian	756	12.0
Ecuadorian	74	6.7
Peruvian	601	23.4
Venezuelan	304	9.8
Spaniard	0	0.0

Homeownership Rate
(Universe: Occupied Housing Units)

Group	%
Total Population	32.3
Hispanic or Latino (of any race)	31.4
Central American, ex. Mexican	18.8
Costa Rican	30.1
Guatemalan	23.2
Honduran	15.6
Nicaraguan	18.6
Panamanian	30.5
Salvadoran	23.8
Cuban	36.3
Dominican Republic	26.6
Mexican	24.9
Puerto Rican	25.8
South American	31.8
Argentinean	32.9
Bolivian	34.2
Chilean	33.5
Colombian	32.2
Ecuadorian	36.4
Paraguayan	40.0
Peruvian	25.5
Uruguayan	16.6
Venezuelan	34.7
Spaniard	49.8

Median Home Value

Group	Dollars
Total Population	278,600
Hispanic or Latino (of any race)	269,100
Central American, ex. Mexican	259,300
Costa Rican	315,800
Guatemalan	300,800
Honduran	232,800
Nicaraguan	271,700
Panamanian	334,400
Salvadoran	263,300
Cuban	266,700
Dominican Republic	231,500
Mexican	315,400
Puerto Rican	227,500
South American	321,400
Argentinean	337,000
Chilean	266,400
Colombian	306,600
Ecuadorian	332,400
Peruvian	273,500
Venezuelan	368,300
Spaniard	337,700

Median Gross Rent

Group	Dollars
Total Population	875
Hispanic or Latino (of any race)	874
Central American, ex. Mexican	907
Costa Rican	995
Guatemalan	867
Honduran	894
Nicaraguan	922
Panamanian	1,043
Salvadoran	885
Cuban	783
Dominican Republic	912
Mexican	1,015
Puerto Rican	974
South American	1,043
Argentinean	1,067
Chilean	908
Colombian	1,054
Ecuadorian	886
Peruvian	975
Venezuelan	1,183
Spaniard	1,125

Median Household Income
(2010 Inflation-Adjusted Dollars)

Group	Dollars
Total Population	29,621
Hispanic or Latino (of any race)	27,217
Central American, ex. Mexican	28,314
Costa Rican	24,375
Guatemalan	31,837
Honduran	26,325
Nicaraguan	29,282
Panamanian	35,144
Salvadoran	34,472
Cuban	23,960
Dominican Republic	24,215
Mexican	36,226
Puerto Rican	31,848
South American	38,358
Argentinean	38,314
Chilean	60,915
Colombian	40,594
Ecuadorian	35,152
Peruvian	30,703
Venezuelan	35,725
Spaniard	37,092

Per Capita Income
(2010 Inflation-Adjusted Dollars)

Group	Dollars
Total Population	19,745
Hispanic or Latino (of any race)	17,456
Central American, ex. Mexican	11,908
Costa Rican	9,650
Guatemalan	11,782
Honduran	10,977
Nicaraguan	11,875
Panamanian	19,513
Salvadoran	17,378
Cuban	18,749
Dominican Republic	12,846
Mexican	18,232
Puerto Rican	17,745
South American	23,988
Argentinean	23,185
Chilean	32,319
Colombian	25,201
Ecuadorian	37,845
Peruvian	17,415
Venezuelan	22,591
Spaniard	46,309

Households with $100,000+ Income

Group	Number	%
Total Population	15,762	10.6
Hispanic or Latino (of any race)	8,557	8.2
Central American, ex. Mexican	882	4.5
Costa Rican	27	5.6
Guatemalan	68	4.9
Honduran	188	2.4
Nicaraguan	414	4.8
Panamanian	43	11.3
Salvadoran	130	11.5
Cuban	4,647	7.8
Dominican Republic	107	3.1
Mexican	230	9.8
Puerto Rican	435	8.5
South American	1,820	14.7
Argentinean	368	16.5
Chilean	121	26.3
Colombian	574	13.3
Ecuadorian	190	19.3
Peruvian	219	14.0
Venezuelan	258	12.6
Spaniard	104	16.7

Households with Food Stamps/SNAP Benefits During Past 12 Months

Group	Number	%
Total Population	35,468	23.8
Hispanic or Latino (of any race)	28,032	26.7
Central American, ex. Mexican	4,124	20.8
Costa Rican	77	15.9
Guatemalan	299	21.7
Honduran	1,328	17.1
Nicaraguan	2,130	24.8
Panamanian	101	26.6
Salvadoran	178	15.7
Cuban	19,762	33.4
Dominican Republic	1,040	30.0
Mexican	270	11.5
Puerto Rican	1,287	25.1
South American	1,197	9.7
Argentinean	183	8.2
Chilean	38	8.3
Colombian	575	13.3

Notes: (1) Percent of total population; (2) Percent of Hispanic/Latino population; Profiles include places with an overall population of at least 125,000, OR an overall population of at least 25,000 where the Hispanic/Latino population is at least 20% of the overall population. In states where less than five places meet either of these criteria, we have included places with at least 10,000 total population with the highest percentage of Hispanic/Latino population. These places are identified with an asterisk (*); Please refer to the User's Guide for a full explanation of data.

Group	Number	%
Ecuadorian	92	9.3
Peruvian	140	8.9
Venezuelan	140	6.9
Spaniard	25	4.0

Poverty Rate
(Income in Past 12 Months Below Poverty Level)

Group	%
Total Population	27.3
Hispanic or Latino (of any race)	25.7
Central American, ex. Mexican	29.8
Costa Rican	40.4
Guatemalan	36.6
Honduran	33.8
Nicaraguan	25.2
Panamanian	31.4
Salvadoran	27.3
Cuban	25.1
Dominican Republic	31.6
Mexican	22.7
Puerto Rican	30.0
South American	19.1
Argentinean	28.1
Chilean	17.8
Colombian	13.7
Ecuadorian	20.5
Peruvian	17.8
Venezuelan	21.0
Spaniard	17.4

Miami Beach

Population

Group	Number	%TP[1]	%HP[2]
Total Population	87,779	100.0	–
Hispanic or Latino (of any race)	46,564	53.0	100.0
Central American, ex. Mexican	4,661	5.3	10.0
Costa Rican	298	0.3	0.6
Guatemalan	1,432	1.6	3.1
Honduran	1,483	1.7	3.2
Nicaraguan	912	1.0	2.0
Panamanian	240	0.3	0.5
Salvadoran	274	0.3	0.6
Cuban	17,599	20.0	37.8
Dominican Republic	1,212	1.4	2.6
Mexican	1,548	1.8	3.3
Puerto Rican	3,242	3.7	7.0
South American	15,106	17.2	32.4
Argentinean	4,030	4.6	8.7
Bolivian	211	0.2	0.5
Chilean	739	0.8	1.6
Colombian	4,327	4.9	9.3
Ecuadorian	830	0.9	1.8
Peruvian	2,091	2.4	4.5
Uruguayan	958	1.1	2.1
Venezuelan	1,802	2.1	3.9
Spaniard	956	1.1	2.1

Population Growth: 2000–2010

Group	%
Total Population	-0.2
Hispanic or Latino (of any race)	-0.9
Central American, ex. Mexican	50.5
Costa Rican	1.7
Guatemalan	336.6
Honduran	39.6
Nicaraguan	0.8
Panamanian	7.1
Salvadoran	36.3
Cuban	-2.4
Dominican Republic	11.8
Mexican	30.9
Puerto Rican	-9.8
South American	30.3
Argentinean	50.4
Bolivian	19.9
Chilean	18.6
Colombian	11.8
Ecuadorian	68.4
Peruvian	28.3
Uruguayan	331.5
Venezuelan	14.6
Spaniard	105.2

Males per 100 Females

Group	Number
Total Population	109.9
Hispanic or Latino (of any race)	100.7
Central American, ex. Mexican	138.7
Costa Rican	82.8
Guatemalan	388.7
Honduran	103.4
Nicaraguan	88.8
Panamanian	80.5
Salvadoran	95.7
Cuban	100.4
Dominican Republic	81.2
Mexican	125.7
Puerto Rican	106.9
South American	89.0
Argentinean	105.1
Bolivian	81.9
Chilean	95.5
Colombian	75.5
Ecuadorian	85.3
Peruvian	82.5
Uruguayan	97.9
Venezuelan	95.0
Spaniard	108.3

Average Household Size

Group	People
Total Population	1.84
Hispanic or Latino (of any race)	1.94
Central American, ex. Mexican	2.52
Costa Rican	2.18
Guatemalan	3.02
Honduran	2.68
Nicaraguan	2.28
Panamanian	1.77
Salvadoran	2.01
Cuban	1.81
Dominican Republic	2.05
Mexican	1.92
Puerto Rican	1.81
South American	2.04
Argentinean	2.04
Bolivian	2.14
Chilean	1.92
Colombian	1.98
Ecuadorian	2.18
Peruvian	2.09
Uruguayan	2.31
Venezuelan	1.97
Spaniard	1.92

Median Age

Group	Years
Total Population	40.3
Hispanic or Latino (of any race)	41.5
Central American, ex. Mexican	32.5
Costa Rican	39.8
Guatemalan	27.6
Honduran	32.6
Nicaraguan	39.3
Panamanian	42.3
Salvadoran	34.5
Cuban	52.5
Dominican Republic	38.2
Mexican	33.4
Puerto Rican	37.9
South American	38.5
Argentinean	36.9
Bolivian	37.1
Chilean	42.0
Colombian	40.9
Ecuadorian	38.8
Peruvian	40.9
Uruguayan	35.6
Venezuelan	37.6
Spaniard	39.9

High School Graduates
(Universe: Population 25 Years and Over)

Group	Number	%
Total Population	57,782	84.2
Hispanic or Latino (of any race)	27,824	76.5
Central American, ex. Mexican	1,849	50.6
Honduran	536	40.6
Cuban	10,535	73.1
Mexican	896	82.8
Puerto Rican	2,210	76.9
South American	10,270	86.8
Argentinean	2,975	88.1
Colombian	2,987	89.9
Peruvian	1,176	91.4
Venezuelan	1,279	95.4

Four-Year College Graduates
(Universe: Population 25 Years and Over)

Group	Number	%
Total Population	29,589	43.1
Hispanic or Latino (of any race)	10,891	29.9
Central American, ex. Mexican	389	10.6
Honduran	98	7.4
Cuban	4,238	29.4
Mexican	348	32.2
Puerto Rican	877	30.5
South American	4,038	34.1
Argentinean	1,058	31.3
Colombian	1,384	41.6
Peruvian	475	36.9
Venezuelan	590	44.0

Population Age 3–17 Enrolled in Public School
(Universe: Population Age 3–17 Enrolled in School)

Group	Number	%
Total Population	5,688	61.8
Hispanic or Latino (of any race)	3,362	79.5
Central American, ex. Mexican	241	87.3
Honduran	87	71.3
Cuban	666	65.9
Mexican	175	100.0
Puerto Rican	516	75.1
South American	1,267	84.9
Argentinean	536	97.5
Colombian	215	93.1
Peruvian	136	69.0
Venezuelan	107	44.4

Population Age 3–17 Enrolled in Private School
(Universe: Population Age 3–17 Enrolled in School)

Group	Number	%
Total Population	3,515	38.2
Hispanic or Latino (of any race)	865	20.5
Central American, ex. Mexican	35	12.7
Honduran	35	28.7
Cuban	344	34.1
Mexican	0	0.0
Puerto Rican	171	24.9
South American	225	15.1
Argentinean	14	2.5
Colombian	16	6.9
Peruvian	61	31.0
Venezuelan	134	55.6

Foreign-Born Population

Group	Number	%
Total Population	45,255	51.7
Hispanic or Latino (of any race)	32,982	72.5
Central American, ex. Mexican	4,300	87.8
Honduran	1,455	90.6
Cuban	12,742	77.2
Mexican	1,043	72.7
Puerto Rican	101	2.6
South American	12,679	85.0
Argentinean	3,821	87.8
Colombian	3,275	83.4
Peruvian	1,432	85.6
Venezuelan	1,475	80.2

Foreign-Born Naturalized U.S. Citizens

Group	Number	%
Total Population	20,642	45.6
Hispanic or Latino (of any race)	15,352	46.5
Central American, ex. Mexican	885	20.6
Honduran	75	5.2
Cuban	9,241	72.5
Mexican	190	18.2
Puerto Rican	13	12.9
South American	4,025	31.7
Argentinean	495	13.0
Colombian	1,633	49.9
Peruvian	695	48.5

Notes: (1) Percent of total population; (2) Percent of Hispanic/Latino population; Profiles include places with an overall population of at least 125,000, OR an overall population of at least 25,000 where the Hispanic/Latino population is at least 20% of the overall population. In states where less than five places meet either of these criteria, we have included places with at least 10,000 total population with the highest percentage of Hispanic/Latino population. These places are identified with an asterisk (*); Please refer to the User's Guide for a full explanation of data.

Group	Number	%
Venezuelan	601	40.7

Language Spoken at Home: English Only
(Universe: Population 5 Years and Over)

Group	Number	%
Total Population	27,635	33.1
Hispanic or Latino (of any race)	2,689	6.1
Central American, ex. Mexican	132	2.8
Honduran	12	0.8
Cuban	726	4.5
Mexican	142	10.1
Puerto Rican	661	17.6
South American	522	3.6
Argentinean	24	0.6
Colombian	145	3.8
Peruvian	105	6.3
Venezuelan	130	7.2

Language Spoken at Home: Spanish
(Universe: Population 5 Years and Over)

Group	Number	%
Total Population	45,424	54.5
Hispanic or Latino (of any race)	40,844	93.0
Central American, ex. Mexican	4,597	97.2
Honduran	1,546	99.2
Cuban	15,375	95.2
Mexican	1,230	87.8
Puerto Rican	3,074	81.7
South American	13,799	95.8
Argentinean	4,046	98.6
Colombian	3,669	95.4
Peruvian	1,558	93.2
Venezuelan	1,673	92.2

Unemployment Rate
(Universe: Population 16 Years and Over)

Group	%
Total Population	5.3
Hispanic or Latino (of any race)	5.8
Central American, ex. Mexican	4.1
Honduran	4.3
Cuban	5.6
Mexican	2.9
Puerto Rican	6.7
South American	6.9
Argentinean	11.8
Colombian	4.9
Peruvian	7.0
Venezuelan	3.0

Class of Worker: Private Wage and Salary
(Universe: Civilian Employed Population 16 Years and Over)

Group	Number	%
Total Population	41,079	83.6
Hispanic or Latino (of any race)	22,357	85.8
Central American, ex. Mexican	3,583	89.3
Honduran	1,224	89.9
Cuban	6,272	82.4
Mexican	953	91.2
Puerto Rican	1,973	94.7
South American	7,894	83.6
Argentinean	2,197	83.6
Colombian	2,187	83.5
Peruvian	811	73.6
Venezuelan	1,125	96.0

Class of Worker: Government
(Universe: Civilian Employed Population 16 Years and Over)

Group	Number	%
Total Population	3,088	6.3
Hispanic or Latino (of any race)	1,512	5.8
Central American, ex. Mexican	155	3.9
Honduran	22	1.6
Cuban	835	11.0
Mexican	44	4.2
Puerto Rican	111	5.3
South American	304	3.2
Argentinean	31	1.2
Colombian	157	6.0
Peruvian	68	6.2
Venezuelan	38	3.2

Means of Transportation to Work: Car, Truck or Van
(Universe: Workers 16 Years and Over)

Group	Number	%
Total Population	30,925	65.0
Hispanic or Latino (of any race)	15,590	62.2
Central American, ex. Mexican	899	22.5
Honduran	199	14.6
Cuban	5,705	78.0
Mexican	625	61.8
Puerto Rican	1,576	77.5
South American	5,573	62.4
Argentinean	1,452	58.9
Colombian	1,821	72.6
Peruvian	612	56.3
Venezuelan	966	82.4

Means of Transportation to Work: Public Transportation (ex. Taxicab)
(Universe: Workers 16 Years and Over)

Group	Number	%
Total Population	4,027	8.5
Hispanic or Latino (of any race)	2,894	11.5
Central American, ex. Mexican	540	13.5
Honduran	174	12.8
Cuban	385	5.3
Mexican	108	10.7
Puerto Rican	228	11.2
South American	1,373	15.4
Argentinean	264	10.7
Colombian	292	11.6
Peruvian	298	27.4
Venezuelan	73	6.2

Homeownership Rate
(Universe: Occupied Housing Units)

Group	%
Total Population	38.6
Hispanic or Latino (of any race)	32.9
Central American, ex. Mexican	14.3
Costa Rican	23.1
Guatemalan	8.0
Honduran	9.8
Nicaraguan	18.3
Panamanian	25.6
Salvadoran	22.4
Cuban	42.9
Dominican Republic	18.0
Mexican	23.3
Puerto Rican	25.9
South American	27.7
Argentinean	26.4
Bolivian	41.2
Chilean	32.0
Colombian	29.8
Ecuadorian	32.0
Peruvian	22.8
Uruguayan	16.6
Venezuelan	32.0
Spaniard	46.5

Median Home Value

Group	Dollars
Total Population	358,400
Hispanic or Latino (of any race)	302,400
Central American, ex. Mexican	309,100
Honduran	565,000
Cuban	302,200
Mexican	540,500
Puerto Rican	317,500
South American	286,300
Argentinean	230,300
Colombian	277,100
Peruvian	263,400
Venezuelan	475,900

Median Gross Rent

Group	Dollars
Total Population	1,025
Hispanic or Latino (of any race)	925
Central American, ex. Mexican	1,013
Honduran	991
Cuban	800
Mexican	1,167
Puerto Rican	982

Group	Dollars
South American	966
Argentinean	1,076
Colombian	897
Peruvian	852
Venezuelan	1,013

Median Household Income
(2010 Inflation-Adjusted Dollars)

Group	Dollars
Total Population	43,538
Hispanic or Latino (of any race)	33,261
Central American, ex. Mexican	37,447
Honduran	32,139
Cuban	27,753
Mexican	54,500
Puerto Rican	33,268
South American	33,588
Argentinean	35,766
Colombian	30,288
Peruvian	29,667
Venezuelan	45,376

Per Capita Income
(2010 Inflation-Adjusted Dollars)

Group	Dollars
Total Population	40,515
Hispanic or Latino (of any race)	29,043
Central American, ex. Mexican	18,130
Honduran	16,113
Cuban	35,979
Mexican	28,105
Puerto Rican	26,450
South American	25,694
Argentinean	24,321
Colombian	27,900
Peruvian	22,501
Venezuelan	29,829

Households with $100,000+ Income

Group	Number	%
Total Population	9,971	22.4
Hispanic or Latino (of any race)	2,905	12.7
Central American, ex. Mexican	115	6.3
Honduran	0	0.0
Cuban	1,456	15.4
Mexican	159	28.3
Puerto Rican	251	12.5
South American	681	9.2
Argentinean	181	8.4
Colombian	139	7.1
Peruvian	54	6.8
Venezuelan	95	9.8

Households with Food Stamps/SNAP Benefits During Past 12 Months

Group	Number	%
Total Population	5,379	12.1
Hispanic or Latino (of any race)	4,442	19.4
Central American, ex. Mexican	316	17.2
Honduran	82	16.6
Cuban	2,284	24.2
Mexican	69	12.3
Puerto Rican	366	18.2
South American	1,128	15.3
Argentinean	227	10.5
Colombian	386	19.7
Peruvian	165	20.8
Venezuelan	41	4.2

Poverty Rate
(Income in Past 12 Months Below Poverty Level)

Group	%
Total Population	15.6
Hispanic or Latino (of any race)	18.6
Central American, ex. Mexican	19.7
Honduran	21.3
Cuban	20.6
Mexican	1.5
Puerto Rican	15.8
South American	16.8
Argentinean	13.4
Colombian	17.5
Peruvian	18.0
Venezuelan	16.6

Notes: (1) Percent of total population; (2) Percent of Hispanic/Latino population; Profiles include places with an overall population of at least 125,000, OR an overall population of at least 25,000 where the Hispanic/Latino population is at least 20% of the overall population. In states where less than five places meet either of these criteria, we have included places with at least 10,000 total population with the highest percentage of Hispanic/Latino population. These places are identified with an asterisk (*); Please refer to the User's Guide for a full explanation of data.

Miami Gardens

Population

Group	Number	%TP[1]	%HP[2]
Total Population	107,167	100.0	–
Hispanic or Latino (of any race)	23,606	22.0	100.0
Central American, ex. Mexican	4,338	4.0	18.4
Costa Rican	140	0.1	0.6
Guatemalan	315	0.3	1.3
Honduran	1,068	1.0	4.5
Nicaraguan	2,134	2.0	9.0
Panamanian	361	0.3	1.5
Salvadoran	292	0.3	1.2
Cuban	9,587	8.9	40.6
Dominican Republic	2,521	2.4	10.7
Mexican	474	0.4	2.0
Puerto Rican	2,745	2.6	11.6
South American	2,291	2.1	9.7
Argentinean	136	0.1	0.6
Colombian	1,127	1.1	4.8
Ecuadorian	300	0.3	1.3
Peruvian	371	0.3	1.6
Venezuelan	240	0.2	1.0

Population Growth: 2000–2010

Group	%
Total Population	n/a

Males per 100 Females

Group	Number
Total Population	87.9
Hispanic or Latino (of any race)	95.6
Central American, ex. Mexican	85.8
Costa Rican	53.8
Guatemalan	92.1
Honduran	89.7
Nicaraguan	86.9
Panamanian	80.5
Salvadoran	87.2
Cuban	108.1
Dominican Republic	83.5
Mexican	122.5
Puerto Rican	91.4
South American	81.3
Argentinean	94.3
Colombian	73.7
Ecuadorian	78.6
Peruvian	89.3
Venezuelan	86.0

Average Household Size

Group	People
Total Population	3.28
Hispanic or Latino (of any race)	3.44
Central American, ex. Mexican	3.96
Costa Rican	3.74
Guatemalan	3.78
Honduran	4.05
Nicaraguan	4.10
Panamanian	3.13
Salvadoran	4.41
Cuban	3.35
Dominican Republic	3.52
Mexican	2.96
Puerto Rican	3.27
South American	3.26
Argentinean	2.70
Colombian	3.36
Ecuadorian	3.46
Peruvian	3.08
Venezuelan	3.23

Median Age

Group	Years
Total Population	33.5
Hispanic or Latino (of any race)	36.8
Central American, ex. Mexican	34.9
Costa Rican	39.0
Guatemalan	36.8
Honduran	32.8
Nicaraguan	34.3
Panamanian	42.4
Salvadoran	34.9
Cuban	41.8
Dominican Republic	34.5
Mexican	27.8
Puerto Rican	30.8
South American	40.2
Argentinean	39.5
Colombian	42.1
Ecuadorian	40.0
Peruvian	42.6
Venezuelan	33.0

High School Graduates
(Universe: Population 25 Years and Over)

Group	Number	%
Total Population	50,179	77.4
Hispanic or Latino (of any race)	9,826	64.8
Central American, ex. Mexican	1,751	68.6
Nicaraguan	916	67.1
Cuban	4,276	63.7
Dominican Republic	901	67.3
Puerto Rican	1,252	57.2
South American	1,198	78.2
Colombian	622	82.2

Four-Year College Graduates
(Universe: Population 25 Years and Over)

Group	Number	%
Total Population	10,659	16.4
Hispanic or Latino (of any race)	1,787	11.8
Central American, ex. Mexican	223	8.7
Nicaraguan	185	13.6
Cuban	1,028	15.3
Dominican Republic	161	12.0
Puerto Rican	145	6.6
South American	213	13.9
Colombian	62	8.2

Population Age 3–17 Enrolled in Public School
(Universe: Population Age 3–17 Enrolled in School)

Group	Number	%
Total Population	20,161	94.0
Hispanic or Latino (of any race)	3,209	93.2
Central American, ex. Mexican	704	97.5
Nicaraguan	479	96.4
Cuban	989	85.4
Dominican Republic	620	95.7
Puerto Rican	302	97.4
South American	309	100.0
Colombian	148	100.0

Population Age 3–17 Enrolled in Private School
(Universe: Population Age 3–17 Enrolled in School)

Group	Number	%
Total Population	1,279	6.0
Hispanic or Latino (of any race)	235	6.8
Central American, ex. Mexican	18	2.5
Nicaraguan	18	3.6
Cuban	169	14.6
Dominican Republic	28	4.3
Puerto Rican	8	2.6
South American	0	0.0
Colombian	0	0.0

Foreign-Born Population

Group	Number	%
Total Population	30,522	28.9
Hispanic or Latino (of any race)	12,650	56.1
Central American, ex. Mexican	2,367	63.3
Nicaraguan	1,519	69.5
Cuban	6,550	72.9
Dominican Republic	1,417	57.6
Puerto Rican	162	4.8
South American	1,699	71.6
Colombian	803	73.1

Foreign-Born Naturalized U.S. Citizens

Group	Number	%
Total Population	16,488	54.0
Hispanic or Latino (of any race)	5,697	45.0
Central American, ex. Mexican	1,011	42.7
Nicaraguan	638	42.0
Cuban	2,956	45.1
Dominican Republic	746	52.6
Puerto Rican	58	35.8
South American	772	45.4
Colombian	476	59.3

Language Spoken at Home: English Only
(Universe: Population 5 Years and Over)

Group	Number	%
Total Population	68,270	69.7
Hispanic or Latino (of any race)	1,811	8.6
Central American, ex. Mexican	260	7.1
Nicaraguan	166	7.7
Cuban	394	4.7
Dominican Republic	198	9.1
Puerto Rican	629	20.5
South American	78	3.5
Colombian	16	1.5

Language Spoken at Home: Spanish
(Universe: Population 5 Years and Over)

Group	Number	%
Total Population	20,370	20.8
Hispanic or Latino (of any race)	19,029	90.9
Central American, ex. Mexican	3,389	92.9
Nicaraguan	1,999	92.3
Cuban	8,040	95.0
Dominican Republic	1,933	88.8
Puerto Rican	2,440	79.5
South American	2,145	96.5
Colombian	1,032	98.5

Unemployment Rate
(Universe: Population 16 Years and Over)

Group	%
Total Population	13.0
Hispanic or Latino (of any race)	10.3
Central American, ex. Mexican	14.5
Nicaraguan	11.8
Cuban	7.6
Dominican Republic	10.3
Puerto Rican	13.4
South American	9.9
Colombian	4.5

Class of Worker: Private Wage and Salary
(Universe: Civilian Employed Population 16 Years and Over)

Group	Number	%
Total Population	33,339	73.9
Hispanic or Latino (of any race)	8,572	87.7
Central American, ex. Mexican	1,675	88.0
Nicaraguan	1,055	90.2
Cuban	3,618	87.5
Dominican Republic	826	85.2
Puerto Rican	1,185	92.5
South American	776	80.1
Colombian	306	75.7

Class of Worker: Government
(Universe: Civilian Employed Population 16 Years and Over)

Group	Number	%
Total Population	9,858	21.8
Hispanic or Latino (of any race)	523	5.4
Central American, ex. Mexican	78	4.1
Nicaraguan	36	3.1
Cuban	183	4.4
Dominican Republic	62	6.4
Puerto Rican	63	4.9
South American	115	11.9
Colombian	80	19.8

Means of Transportation to Work: Car, Truck or Van
(Universe: Workers 16 Years and Over)

Group	Number	%
Total Population	40,037	90.5
Hispanic or Latino (of any race)	8,973	94.0
Central American, ex. Mexican	1,832	98.5
Nicaraguan	1,125	100.0
Cuban	3,812	93.0
Dominican Republic	926	98.0
Puerto Rican	1,102	87.2
South American	916	98.0
Colombian	370	100.0

Means of Transportation to Work: Public Transportation (ex. Taxicab)
(Universe: Workers 16 Years and Over)

Group	Number	%
Total Population	2,861	6.5
Hispanic or Latino (of any race)	263	2.8

Notes: (1) Percent of total population; (2) Percent of Hispanic/Latino population; Profiles include places with an overall population of at least 125,000, OR an overall population of at least 25,000 where the Hispanic/Latino population is at least 20% of the overall population. In states where less than five places meet either of these criteria, we have included places with at least 10,000 total population with the highest percentage of Hispanic/Latino population. These places are identified with an asterisk (*); Please refer to the User's Guide for a full explanation of data.

Central American, ex. Mexican	27	1.5
Nicaraguan	0	0.0
Cuban	82	2.0
Dominican Republic	12	1.3
Puerto Rican	106	8.4
South American	9	1.0
Colombian	0	0.0

Homeownership Rate
(Universe: Occupied Housing Units)

Group	%
Total Population	68.4
Hispanic or Latino (of any race)	67.1
Central American, ex. Mexican	73.1
Costa Rican	83.9
Guatemalan	69.8
Honduran	73.6
Nicaraguan	74.7
Panamanian	63.2
Salvadoran	74.7
Cuban	73.2
Dominican Republic	53.5
Mexican	41.6
Puerto Rican	57.7
South American	62.1
Argentinean	57.4
Colombian	65.0
Ecuadorian	74.4
Peruvian	54.5
Venezuelan	39.1

Median Home Value

Group	Dollars
Total Population	203,100
Hispanic or Latino (of any race)	193,900
Central American, ex. Mexican	199,500
Nicaraguan	199,000
Cuban	206,700
Dominican Republic	201,000
Puerto Rican	186,800
South American	151,600
Colombian	145,800

Median Gross Rent

Group	Dollars
Total Population	960
Hispanic or Latino (of any race)	950
Central American, ex. Mexican	941
Nicaraguan	1,040
Cuban	957
Dominican Republic	954
Puerto Rican	897
South American	997
Colombian	931

Median Household Income
(2010 Inflation-Adjusted Dollars)

Group	Dollars
Total Population	43,147
Hispanic or Latino (of any race)	35,062
Central American, ex. Mexican	41,154
Nicaraguan	48,621
Cuban	35,383
Dominican Republic	35,099
Puerto Rican	36,639
South American	30,852
Colombian	47,992

Per Capita Income
(2010 Inflation-Adjusted Dollars)

Group	Dollars
Total Population	16,533
Hispanic or Latino (of any race)	14,050
Central American, ex. Mexican	15,371
Nicaraguan	16,361
Cuban	15,583
Dominican Republic	12,031
Puerto Rican	13,242
South American	13,160
Colombian	14,444

Households with $100,000+ Income

Group	Number	%
Total Population	3,255	10.2
Hispanic or Latino (of any race)	409	5.8
Central American, ex. Mexican	91	7.7
Nicaraguan	71	13.9
Cuban	211	7.4
Dominican Republic	83	10.5
Puerto Rican	10	0.9
South American	14	1.8
Colombian	0	0.0

Households with Food Stamps/SNAP Benefits During Past 12 Months

Group	Number	%
Total Population	6,135	19.2
Hispanic or Latino (of any race)	1,512	21.3
Central American, ex. Mexican	217	18.4
Nicaraguan	80	15.6
Cuban	532	18.6
Dominican Republic	274	34.8
Puerto Rican	282	25.3
South American	178	23.1
Colombian	84	20.6

Poverty Rate
(Income in Past 12 Months Below Poverty Level)

Group	%
Total Population	18.7
Hispanic or Latino (of any race)	22.2
Central American, ex. Mexican	19.1
Nicaraguan	22.1
Cuban	18.3
Dominican Republic	26.5
Puerto Rican	29.2
South American	28.8
Colombian	16.5

Miami Lakes

Population

Group	Number	%TP[1]	%HP[2]
Total Population	29,361	100.0	–
Hispanic or Latino (of any race)	23,826	81.1	100.0
Central American, ex. Mexican	1,165	4.0	4.9
Honduran	230	0.8	1.0
Nicaraguan	574	2.0	2.4
Panamanian	115	0.4	0.5
Cuban	16,752	57.1	70.3
Dominican Republic	691	2.4	2.9
Mexican	232	0.8	1.0
Puerto Rican	1,176	4.0	4.9
South American	2,968	10.1	12.5
Argentinean	220	0.7	0.9
Chilean	120	0.4	0.5
Colombian	1,548	5.3	6.5
Ecuadorian	280	1.0	1.2
Peruvian	371	1.3	1.6
Venezuelan	337	1.1	1.4
Spaniard	190	0.6	0.8

Population Growth: 2000–2010

Group	%
Total Population	29.5
Hispanic or Latino (of any race)	58.0
Central American, ex. Mexican	140.2
Nicaraguan	136.2
Cuban	74.7
Dominican Republic	84.3
Mexican	44.1
Puerto Rican	67.8
South American	58.0
Argentinean	120.0
Colombian	54.0
Ecuadorian	64.7
Peruvian	72.6
Venezuelan	40.4

Males per 100 Females

Group	Number
Total Population	89.4
Hispanic or Latino (of any race)	86.9
Central American, ex. Mexican	70.1
Honduran	67.9
Nicaraguan	67.8
Panamanian	71.6
Cuban	89.9
Dominican Republic	86.3
Mexican	109.0
Puerto Rican	79.3
South American	79.1
Argentinean	107.5
Chilean	100.0
Colombian	75.7
Ecuadorian	78.3
Peruvian	80.1
Venezuelan	74.6
Spaniard	82.7

Average Household Size

Group	People
Total Population	2.86
Hispanic or Latino (of any race)	3.04
Central American, ex. Mexican	3.31
Honduran	3.22
Nicaraguan	3.56
Panamanian	3.12
Cuban	3.06
Dominican Republic	3.39
Mexican	2.74
Puerto Rican	2.61
South American	3.03
Argentinean	3.21
Chilean	3.26
Colombian	3.14
Ecuadorian	2.81
Peruvian	2.85
Venezuelan	2.81
Spaniard	2.81

Median Age

Group	Years
Total Population	38.9
Hispanic or Latino (of any race)	38.9
Central American, ex. Mexican	34.2
Honduran	34.3
Nicaraguan	32.9
Panamanian	35.8
Cuban	40.3
Dominican Republic	33.3
Mexican	29.7
Puerto Rican	35.0
South American	38.3
Argentinean	37.9
Chilean	44.0
Colombian	37.6
Ecuadorian	39.5
Peruvian	40.4
Venezuelan	35.4
Spaniard	46.0

High School Graduates
(Universe: Population 25 Years and Over)

Group	Number	%
Total Population	16,566	88.5
Hispanic or Latino (of any race)	12,906	86.7
Central American, ex. Mexican	906	94.0
Cuban	9,072	84.5
South American	1,536	94.3
Colombian	687	91.5

Four-Year College Graduates
(Universe: Population 25 Years and Over)

Group	Number	%
Total Population	6,438	34.4
Hispanic or Latino (of any race)	4,626	31.1
Central American, ex. Mexican	239	24.8
Cuban	3,105	28.9
South American	563	34.6
Colombian	259	34.5

Population Age 3–17 Enrolled in Public School
(Universe: Population Age 3–17 Enrolled in School)

Group	Number	%
Total Population	3,803	76.7
Hispanic or Latino (of any race)	3,157	80.9
Central American, ex. Mexican	165	83.3
Cuban	2,034	76.9
South American	424	93.6
Colombian	132	82.0

Notes: (1) Percent of total population; (2) Percent of Hispanic/Latino population; Profiles include places with an overall population of at least 125,000, OR an overall population of at least 25,000 where the Hispanic/Latino population is at least 20% of the overall population. In states where less than five places meet either of these criteria, we have included places with at least 10,000 total population with the highest percentage of Hispanic/Latino population. These places are identified with an asterisk (*); Please refer to the User's Guide for a full explanation of data.

Population Age 3–17 Enrolled in Private School
(Universe: Population Age 3–17 Enrolled in School)

Group	Number	%
Total Population	1,158	23.3
Hispanic or Latino (of any race)	743	19.1
Central American, ex. Mexican	33	16.7
Cuban	612	23.1
South American	29	6.4
Colombian	29	18.0

Foreign-Born Population

Group	Number	%
Total Population	13,403	47.7
Hispanic or Latino (of any race)	12,320	55.2
Central American, ex. Mexican	879	63.1
Cuban	8,981	57.0
South American	1,682	65.9
Colombian	728	66.4

Foreign-Born Naturalized U.S. Citizens

Group	Number	%
Total Population	9,163	68.4
Hispanic or Latino (of any race)	8,526	69.2
Central American, ex. Mexican	532	60.5
Cuban	6,603	73.5
South American	773	46.0
Colombian	456	62.6

Language Spoken at Home: English Only
(Universe: Population 5 Years and Over)

Group	Number	%
Total Population	4,795	18.2
Hispanic or Latino (of any race)	1,347	6.5
Central American, ex. Mexican	84	6.1
Cuban	1,024	6.9
South American	58	2.5
Colombian	58	5.6

Language Spoken at Home: Spanish
(Universe: Population 5 Years and Over)

Group	Number	%
Total Population	20,376	77.4
Hispanic or Latino (of any race)	19,504	93.5
Central American, ex. Mexican	1,283	93.9
Cuban	13,713	93.1
South American	2,260	97.5
Colombian	970	94.4

Unemployment Rate
(Universe: Population 16 Years and Over)

Group	%
Total Population	4.6
Hispanic or Latino (of any race)	4.7
Central American, ex. Mexican	8.8
Cuban	4.9
South American	3.1
Colombian	0.0

Class of Worker: Private Wage and Salary
(Universe: Civilian Employed Population 16 Years and Over)

Group	Number	%
Total Population	11,648	80.4
Hispanic or Latino (of any race)	9,521	81.7
Central American, ex. Mexican	632	73.5
Cuban	6,649	81.9
South American	1,183	86.9
Colombian	544	81.7

Class of Worker: Government
(Universe: Civilian Employed Population 16 Years and Over)

Group	Number	%
Total Population	1,879	13.0
Hispanic or Latino (of any race)	1,343	11.5
Central American, ex. Mexican	51	5.9
Cuban	1,002	12.3
South American	73	5.4
Colombian	37	5.6

Means of Transportation to Work: Car, Truck or Van
(Universe: Workers 16 Years and Over)

Group	Number	%
Total Population	12,666	89.9
Hispanic or Latino (of any race)	10,154	89.9
Central American, ex. Mexican	799	92.9
Cuban	7,003	87.9
South American	1,269	97.2
Colombian	606	94.8

Means of Transportation to Work: Public Transportation (ex. Taxicab)
(Universe: Workers 16 Years and Over)

Group	Number	%
Total Population	242	1.7
Hispanic or Latino (of any race)	131	1.2
Central American, ex. Mexican	0	0.0
Cuban	126	1.6
South American	5	0.4
Colombian	5	0.8

Homeownership Rate
(Universe: Occupied Housing Units)

Group	%
Total Population	69.4
Hispanic or Latino (of any race)	70.6
Central American, ex. Mexican	57.3
Honduran	65.3
Nicaraguan	55.0
Panamanian	57.1
Cuban	76.2
Dominican Republic	55.2
Mexican	39.2
Puerto Rican	48.4
South American	57.9
Argentinean	61.5
Chilean	64.3
Colombian	57.5
Ecuadorian	54.4
Peruvian	56.7
Venezuelan	55.7
Spaniard	80.0

Median Home Value

Group	Dollars
Total Population	380,000
Hispanic or Latino (of any race)	383,800
Central American, ex. Mexican	310,000
Cuban	387,900
South American	275,300
Colombian	333,300

Median Gross Rent

Group	Dollars
Total Population	1,318
Hispanic or Latino (of any race)	1,319
Central American, ex. Mexican	1,249
Cuban	1,325
South American	1,516
Colombian	1,292

Median Household Income
(2010 Inflation-Adjusted Dollars)

Group	Dollars
Total Population	66,369
Hispanic or Latino (of any race)	66,602
Central American, ex. Mexican	69,423
Cuban	70,298
South American	59,904
Colombian	55,395

Per Capita Income
(2010 Inflation-Adjusted Dollars)

Group	Dollars
Total Population	30,518
Hispanic or Latino (of any race)	29,355
Central American, ex. Mexican	37,150
Cuban	28,334
South American	21,784
Colombian	22,632

Households with $100,000+ Income

Group	Number	%
Total Population	2,704	28.4
Hispanic or Latino (of any race)	2,071	28.3
Central American, ex. Mexican	126	30.1
Cuban	1,518	28.6
South American	207	27.5
Colombian	80	24.4

Households with Food Stamps/SNAP Benefits During Past 12 Months

Group	Number	%
Total Population	688	7.2
Hispanic or Latino (of any race)	638	8.7
Central American, ex. Mexican	0	0.0
Cuban	556	10.5
South American	34	4.5
Colombian	34	10.4

Poverty Rate
(Income in Past 12 Months Below Poverty Level)

Group	%
Total Population	5.9
Hispanic or Latino (of any race)	4.9
Central American, ex. Mexican	8.0
Cuban	4.9
South American	1.1
Colombian	0.5

Miramar

Population

Group	Number	%TP[1]	%HP[2]
Total Population	122,041	100.0	–
Hispanic or Latino (of any race)	45,039	36.9	100.0
Central American, ex. Mexican	4,460	3.7	9.9
Costa Rican	315	0.3	0.7
Guatemalan	409	0.3	0.9
Honduran	1,011	0.8	2.2
Nicaraguan	1,691	1.4	3.8
Panamanian	700	0.6	1.6
Salvadoran	314	0.3	0.7
Cuban	12,924	10.6	28.7
Dominican Republic	4,529	3.7	10.1
Mexican	1,230	1.0	2.7
Puerto Rican	6,658	5.5	14.8
South American	12,551	10.3	27.9
Argentinean	558	0.5	1.2
Bolivian	116	0.1	0.3
Chilean	340	0.3	0.8
Colombian	6,230	5.1	13.8
Ecuadorian	1,132	0.9	2.5
Peruvian	1,401	1.1	3.1
Uruguayan	142	0.1	0.3
Venezuelan	2,594	2.1	5.8
Spaniard	326	0.3	0.7

Population Growth: 2000–2010

Group	%
Total Population	67.8
Hispanic or Latino (of any race)	110.7
Central American, ex. Mexican	175.0
Costa Rican	158.2
Guatemalan	214.6
Honduran	252.3
Nicaraguan	187.1
Panamanian	108.3
Cuban	102.7
Dominican Republic	214.7
Mexican	162.3
Puerto Rican	75.2
South American	239.6
Argentinean	274.5
Chilean	137.8
Colombian	241.0
Ecuadorian	281.1
Peruvian	128.2
Venezuelan	419.8

Males per 100 Females

Group	Number
Total Population	89.3
Hispanic or Latino (of any race)	91.8
Central American, ex. Mexican	82.1
Costa Rican	74.0
Guatemalan	96.6
Honduran	80.9
Nicaraguan	80.7
Panamanian	79.5
Salvadoran	90.3
Cuban	101.6
Dominican Republic	85.4

STATE & PLACE PROFILES

Notes: (1) Percent of total population; (2) Percent of Hispanic/Latino population; Profiles include places with an overall population of at least 125,000, OR an overall population of at least 25,000 where the Hispanic/Latino population is at least 20% of the overall population. In states where less than five places meet either of these criteria, we have included places with at least 10,000 total population with the highest percentage of Hispanic/Latino population. These places are identified with an asterisk (*); Please refer to the User's Guide for a full explanation of data.

Mexican	103.3
Puerto Rican	91.7
South American	86.0
Argentinean	113.0
Bolivian	75.8
Chilean	101.2
Colombian	84.0
Ecuadorian	80.5
Peruvian	81.7
Uruguayan	102.9
Venezuelan	88.0
Spaniard	92.9

Average Household Size

Group	People
Total Population	3.26
Hispanic or Latino (of any race)	3.42
Central American, ex. Mexican	3.66
Costa Rican	3.19
Guatemalan	3.60
Honduran	3.88
Nicaraguan	3.83
Panamanian	3.35
Salvadoran	3.61
Cuban	3.30
Dominican Republic	3.77
Mexican	3.45
Puerto Rican	3.26
South American	3.48
Argentinean	3.45
Bolivian	3.83
Chilean	3.13
Colombian	3.51
Ecuadorian	3.60
Peruvian	3.58
Uruguayan	3.16
Venezuelan	3.40
Spaniard	3.09

Median Age

Group	Years
Total Population	33.6
Hispanic or Latino (of any race)	34.4
Central American, ex. Mexican	34.0
Costa Rican	34.6
Guatemalan	32.3
Honduran	32.5
Nicaraguan	33.4
Panamanian	39.3
Salvadoran	34.8
Cuban	36.5
Dominican Republic	32.4
Mexican	29.0
Puerto Rican	32.9
South American	36.2
Argentinean	35.3
Bolivian	35.0
Chilean	41.6
Colombian	36.2
Ecuadorian	35.8
Peruvian	38.0
Uruguayan	38.3
Venezuelan	35.2
Spaniard	39.8

High School Graduates
(Universe: Population 25 Years and Over)

Group	Number	%
Total Population	60,927	88.6
Hispanic or Latino (of any race)	22,553	87.1
Central American, ex. Mexican	1,885	73.7
Honduran	379	60.8
Nicaraguan	810	80.3
Cuban	6,807	87.6
Dominican Republic	1,966	84.2
Mexican	435	89.0
Puerto Rican	3,808	88.7
South American	6,555	90.4
Colombian	3,866	93.3
Ecuadorian	440	72.2
Peruvian	685	91.2
Venezuelan	911	92.6

Four-Year College Graduates
(Universe: Population 25 Years and Over)

Group	Number	%
Total Population	22,294	32.4
Hispanic or Latino (of any race)	8,347	32.2
Central American, ex. Mexican	394	15.4
Honduran	105	16.9
Nicaraguan	146	14.5
Cuban	2,400	30.9
Dominican Republic	660	28.3
Mexican	237	48.5
Puerto Rican	1,318	30.7
South American	2,993	41.3
Colombian	1,841	44.4
Ecuadorian	167	27.4
Peruvian	241	32.1
Venezuelan	521	52.9

Population Age 3–17 Enrolled in Public School
(Universe: Population Age 3–17 Enrolled in School)

Group	Number	%
Total Population	21,879	83.5
Hispanic or Latino (of any race)	8,062	83.7
Central American, ex. Mexican	603	95.9
Honduran	205	100.0
Nicaraguan	258	97.7
Cuban	2,309	79.4
Dominican Republic	1,033	93.6
Mexican	217	80.4
Puerto Rican	1,160	85.4
South American	2,038	85.6
Colombian	1,068	80.8
Ecuadorian	229	100.0
Peruvian	263	84.8
Venezuelan	282	92.5

Population Age 3–17 Enrolled in Private School
(Universe: Population Age 3–17 Enrolled in School)

Group	Number	%
Total Population	4,322	16.5
Hispanic or Latino (of any race)	1,569	16.3
Central American, ex. Mexican	26	4.1
Honduran	0	0.0
Nicaraguan	6	2.3
Cuban	600	20.6
Dominican Republic	71	6.4
Mexican	53	19.6
Puerto Rican	199	14.6
South American	343	14.4
Colombian	253	19.2
Ecuadorian	0	0.0
Peruvian	47	15.2
Venezuelan	23	7.5

Foreign-Born Population

Group	Number	%
Total Population	46,771	41.1
Hispanic or Latino (of any race)	20,292	47.9
Central American, ex. Mexican	2,503	67.9
Honduran	612	65.7
Nicaraguan	1,000	70.1
Cuban	5,840	47.9
Dominican Republic	2,063	49.3
Mexican	423	45.5
Puerto Rican	202	3.0
South American	8,469	73.7
Colombian	4,606	70.0
Ecuadorian	597	65.0
Peruvian	993	81.1
Venezuelan	1,399	89.2

Foreign-Born Naturalized U.S. Citizens

Group	Number	%
Total Population	26,949	57.6
Hispanic or Latino (of any race)	10,648	52.5
Central American, ex. Mexican	1,484	59.3
Honduran	383	62.6
Nicaraguan	490	49.0
Cuban	3,748	64.2
Dominican Republic	1,361	66.0
Mexican	171	40.4
Puerto Rican	128	63.4
South American	3,327	39.3
Colombian	1,874	40.7
Ecuadorian	379	63.5
Peruvian	637	64.1
Venezuelan	178	12.7

Language Spoken at Home: English Only
(Universe: Population 5 Years and Over)

Group	Number	%
Total Population	51,726	49.5
Hispanic or Latino (of any race)	4,277	11.1
Central American, ex. Mexican	252	7.2
Honduran	93	10.0
Nicaraguan	100	7.3
Cuban	1,495	13.4
Dominican Republic	256	6.7
Mexican	188	23.5
Puerto Rican	1,151	18.9
South American	507	4.7
Colombian	274	4.4
Ecuadorian	63	7.1
Peruvian	60	5.2
Venezuelan	69	4.5

Language Spoken at Home: Spanish
(Universe: Population 5 Years and Over)

Group	Number	%
Total Population	37,098	35.5
Hispanic or Latino (of any race)	34,246	88.6
Central American, ex. Mexican	3,267	92.8
Honduran	839	90.0
Nicaraguan	1,265	92.7
Cuban	9,649	86.2
Dominican Republic	3,573	93.3
Mexican	612	76.5
Puerto Rican	4,919	80.9
South American	10,260	94.8
Colombian	5,874	95.2
Ecuadorian	822	92.9
Peruvian	1,097	94.8
Venezuelan	1,440	94.1

Unemployment Rate
(Universe: Population 16 Years and Over)

Group	%
Total Population	9.7
Hispanic or Latino (of any race)	10.0
Central American, ex. Mexican	7.7
Honduran	13.5
Nicaraguan	10.6
Cuban	7.9
Dominican Republic	11.9
Mexican	3.6
Puerto Rican	12.5
South American	11.0
Colombian	12.1
Ecuadorian	15.9
Peruvian	3.6
Venezuelan	7.8

Class of Worker: Private Wage and Salary
(Universe: Civilian Employed Population 16 Years and Over)

Group	Number	%
Total Population	43,885	78.3
Hispanic or Latino (of any race)	16,841	82.2
Central American, ex. Mexican	1,810	84.9
Honduran	337	74.2
Nicaraguan	715	84.6
Cuban	4,962	80.4
Dominican Republic	1,652	83.9
Mexican	293	78.6
Puerto Rican	2,729	81.0
South American	4,550	82.7
Colombian	2,540	82.6
Ecuadorian	309	91.4
Peruvian	453	67.0
Venezuelan	698	90.6

Class of Worker: Government
(Universe: Civilian Employed Population 16 Years and Over)

Group	Number	%
Total Population	9,436	16.8
Hispanic or Latino (of any race)	2,471	12.1
Central American, ex. Mexican	180	8.4
Honduran	102	22.5
Nicaraguan	27	3.2
Cuban	975	15.8
Dominican Republic	215	10.9

Notes: (1) Percent of total population; (2) Percent of Hispanic/Latino population; Profiles include places with an overall population of at least 125,000, OR an overall population of at least 25,000 where the Hispanic/Latino population is at least 20% of the overall population. In states where less than five places meet either of these criteria, we have included places with at least 10,000 total population with the highest percentage of Hispanic/Latino population. These places are identified with an asterisk (*); Please refer to the User's Guide for a full explanation of data.

Mexican	56	15.0
Puerto Rican	544	16.1
South American	381	6.9
Colombian	208	6.8
Ecuadorian	29	8.6
Peruvian	81	12.0
Venezuelan	20	2.6

Means of Transportation to Work: Car, Truck or Van
(Universe: Workers 16 Years and Over)

Group	Number	%
Total Population	50,647	93.9
Hispanic or Latino (of any race)	18,375	93.7
Central American, ex. Mexican	2,016	97.6
Honduran	437	96.3
Nicaraguan	775	98.4
Cuban	5,645	96.5
Dominican Republic	1,871	95.2
Mexican	376	97.9
Puerto Rican	2,961	92.2
South American	4,729	90.4
Colombian	2,517	88.9
Ecuadorian	288	85.2
Peruvian	629	94.9
Venezuelan	678	89.4

Means of Transportation to Work: Public Transportation (ex. Taxicab)
(Universe: Workers 16 Years and Over)

Group	Number	%
Total Population	790	1.5
Hispanic or Latino (of any race)	232	1.2
Central American, ex. Mexican	19	0.9
Honduran	0	0.0
Nicaraguan	0	0.0
Cuban	58	1.0
Dominican Republic	0	0.0
Mexican	0	0.0
Puerto Rican	16	0.5
South American	110	2.1
Colombian	38	1.3
Ecuadorian	50	14.8
Peruvian	9	1.4
Venezuelan	13	1.7

Homeownership Rate
(Universe: Occupied Housing Units)

Group	%
Total Population	75.0
Hispanic or Latino (of any race)	77.3
Central American, ex. Mexican	77.7
Costa Rican	74.0
Guatemalan	72.3
Honduran	78.5
Nicaraguan	78.9
Panamanian	78.1
Salvadoran	79.3
Cuban	82.7
Dominican Republic	73.0
Mexican	71.2
Puerto Rican	75.0
South American	75.1
Argentinean	80.1
Bolivian	90.0
Chilean	76.2
Colombian	74.8
Ecuadorian	77.3
Peruvian	76.7
Uruguayan	80.0
Venezuelan	72.3
Spaniard	85.5

Median Home Value

Group	Dollars
Total Population	297,000
Hispanic or Latino (of any race)	315,600
Central American, ex. Mexican	235,300
Honduran	295,800
Nicaraguan	212,600
Cuban	330,200
Dominican Republic	293,800
Mexican	317,700
Puerto Rican	337,800
South American	308,600
Colombian	326,300
Ecuadorian	258,200
Peruvian	260,500
Venezuelan	314,300

Median Gross Rent

Group	Dollars
Total Population	1,416
Hispanic or Latino (of any race)	1,495
Central American, ex. Mexican	1,256
Honduran	1,269
Nicaraguan	685
Cuban	1,791
Dominican Republic	1,419
Mexican	1,325
Puerto Rican	1,356
South American	1,511
Colombian	1,477
Ecuadorian	1,188
Peruvian	1,421
Venezuelan	1,635

Median Household Income
(2010 Inflation-Adjusted Dollars)

Group	Dollars
Total Population	64,928
Hispanic or Latino (of any race)	66,888
Central American, ex. Mexican	55,650
Honduran	39,491
Nicaraguan	59,286
Cuban	75,339
Dominican Republic	61,275
Mexican	110,061
Puerto Rican	72,013
South American	60,404
Colombian	54,395
Ecuadorian	62,167
Peruvian	49,565
Venezuelan	54,830

Per Capita Income
(2010 Inflation-Adjusted Dollars)

Group	Dollars
Total Population	24,582
Hispanic or Latino (of any race)	23,714
Central American, ex. Mexican	21,307
Honduran	20,941
Nicaraguan	20,749
Cuban	30,443
Dominican Republic	20,438
Mexican	25,909
Puerto Rican	24,863
South American	19,779
Colombian	18,818
Ecuadorian	17,334
Peruvian	20,679
Venezuelan	20,814

Households with $100,000+ Income

Group	Number	%
Total Population	9,150	26.7
Hispanic or Latino (of any race)	3,541	29.4
Central American, ex. Mexican	214	21.1
Honduran	28	11.2
Nicaraguan	94	21.7
Cuban	1,403	37.1
Dominican Republic	244	19.7
Mexican	139	50.4
Puerto Rican	643	32.1
South American	705	22.1
Colombian	445	24.8
Ecuadorian	49	22.7
Peruvian	78	23.1
Venezuelan	75	15.7

Households with Food Stamps/SNAP Benefits During Past 12 Months

Group	Number	%
Total Population	3,423	10.0
Hispanic or Latino (of any race)	1,338	11.1
Central American, ex. Mexican	125	12.3
Honduran	66	26.5
Nicaraguan	9	2.1
Cuban	384	10.2
Dominican Republic	220	17.8
Mexican	14	5.1
Puerto Rican	346	17.3
South American	249	7.8
Colombian	139	7.7
Ecuadorian	31	14.4
Peruvian	46	13.6
Venezuelan	0	0.0

Poverty Rate
(Income in Past 12 Months Below Poverty Level)

Group	%
Total Population	8.4
Hispanic or Latino (of any race)	9.0
Central American, ex. Mexican	7.6
Honduran	5.5
Nicaraguan	11.8
Cuban	7.3
Dominican Republic	10.1
Mexican	19.4
Puerto Rican	11.0
South American	9.3
Colombian	8.5
Ecuadorian	2.2
Peruvian	24.1
Venezuelan	7.5

North Lauderdale

Population

Group	Number	%TP[1]	%HP[2]
Total Population	41,023	100.0	–
Hispanic or Latino (of any race)	10,578	25.8	100.0
Central American, ex. Mexican	2,104	5.1	19.9
Guatemalan	149	0.4	1.4
Honduran	560	1.4	5.3
Nicaraguan	236	0.6	2.2
Salvadoran	1,037	2.5	9.8
Cuban	602	1.5	5.7
Dominican Republic	660	1.6	6.2
Mexican	2,043	5.0	19.3
Puerto Rican	1,948	4.7	18.4
South American	2,572	6.3	24.3
Argentinean	127	0.3	1.2
Colombian	1,481	3.6	14.0
Ecuadorian	219	0.5	2.1
Peruvian	444	1.1	4.2
Venezuelan	158	0.4	1.5

Population Growth: 2000–2010

Group	%
Total Population	27.1
Hispanic or Latino (of any race)	55.2
Central American, ex. Mexican	191.8
Honduran	286.2
Salvadoran	208.6
Cuban	80.2
Dominican Republic	168.3
Mexican	151.9
Puerto Rican	25.5
South American	50.1
Colombian	38.3
Ecuadorian	90.4
Peruvian	85.0
Venezuelan	54.9

Males per 100 Females

Group	Number
Total Population	91.4
Hispanic or Latino (of any race)	104.2
Central American, ex. Mexican	119.6
Guatemalan	166.1
Honduran	118.8
Nicaraguan	88.8
Salvadoran	131.0
Cuban	98.7
Dominican Republic	72.3
Mexican	125.2
Puerto Rican	93.3
South American	96.9
Argentinean	98.4
Colombian	90.4
Ecuadorian	100.9
Peruvian	111.4

STATE & PLACE PROFILES

Notes: (1) Percent of total population; (2) Percent of Hispanic/Latino population; Profiles include places with an overall population of at least 125,000, OR an overall population of at least 25,000 where the Hispanic/Latino population is at least 20% of the overall population. In states where less than five places meet either of these criteria, we have included places with at least 10,000 total population with the highest percentage of Hispanic/Latino population. These places are identified with an asterisk (*); Please refer to the User's Guide for a full explanation of data.

Group	%
Venezuelan	95.1

Average Household Size

Group	People
Total Population	3.16
Hispanic or Latino (of any race)	3.63
Central American, ex. Mexican	4.41
Guatemalan	4.19
Honduran	4.44
Nicaraguan	4.29
Salvadoran	4.69
Cuban	2.76
Dominican Republic	3.55
Mexican	4.66
Puerto Rican	3.13
South American	3.30
Argentinean	2.96
Colombian	3.26
Ecuadorian	3.63
Peruvian	3.53
Venezuelan	2.96

Median Age

Group	Years
Total Population	30.9
Hispanic or Latino (of any race)	30.1
Central American, ex. Mexican	29.5
Guatemalan	31.9
Honduran	29.7
Nicaraguan	29.6
Salvadoran	28.9
Cuban	35.7
Dominican Republic	31.5
Mexican	25.4
Puerto Rican	29.4
South American	38.1
Argentinean	38.8
Colombian	39.4
Ecuadorian	38.3
Peruvian	37.0
Venezuelan	32.7

High School Graduates
(Universe: Population 25 Years and Over)

Group	Number	%
Total Population	19,677	78.7
Hispanic or Latino (of any race)	4,494	70.7
Central American, ex. Mexican	683	57.2
Mexican	440	48.9
Puerto Rican	1,143	75.4
South American	1,534	84.8
Colombian	755	76.9

Four-Year College Graduates
(Universe: Population 25 Years and Over)

Group	Number	%
Total Population	3,707	14.8
Hispanic or Latino (of any race)	1,003	15.8
Central American, ex. Mexican	349	29.2
Mexican	33	3.7
Puerto Rican	240	15.8
South American	279	15.4
Colombian	106	10.8

Population Age 3–17 Enrolled in Public School
(Universe: Population Age 3–17 Enrolled in School)

Group	Number	%
Total Population	8,153	93.1
Hispanic or Latino (of any race)	2,122	94.6
Central American, ex. Mexican	221	100.0
Mexican	728	95.3
Puerto Rican	357	85.0
South American	504	98.8
Colombian	306	98.1

Population Age 3–17 Enrolled in Private School
(Universe: Population Age 3–17 Enrolled in School)

Group	Number	%
Total Population	603	6.9
Hispanic or Latino (of any race)	121	5.4
Central American, ex. Mexican	0	0.0
Mexican	36	4.7
Puerto Rican	63	15.0
South American	6	1.2
Colombian	6	1.9

Foreign-Born Population

Group	Number	%
Total Population	17,675	43.3
Hispanic or Latino (of any race)	5,503	51.5
Central American, ex. Mexican	1,405	73.7
Mexican	1,130	53.1
Puerto Rican	24	1.0
South American	1,893	70.1
Colombian	1,036	69.5

Foreign-Born Naturalized U.S. Citizens

Group	Number	%
Total Population	7,041	39.8
Hispanic or Latino (of any race)	2,010	36.5
Central American, ex. Mexican	174	12.4
Mexican	142	12.6
Puerto Rican	0	0.0
South American	1,022	54.0
Colombian	527	50.9

Language Spoken at Home: English Only
(Universe: Population 5 Years and Over)

Group	Number	%
Total Population	19,151	50.9
Hispanic or Latino (of any race)	902	9.3
Central American, ex. Mexican	72	4.3
Mexican	135	6.9
Puerto Rican	397	19.0
South American	226	8.7
Colombian	113	7.8

Language Spoken at Home: Spanish
(Universe: Population 5 Years and Over)

Group	Number	%
Total Population	8,973	23.9
Hispanic or Latino (of any race)	8,663	88.9
Central American, ex. Mexican	1,601	95.7
Mexican	1,827	93.1
Puerto Rican	1,677	80.2
South American	2,374	91.3
Colombian	1,342	92.2

Unemployment Rate
(Universe: Population 16 Years and Over)

Group	%
Total Population	9.2
Hispanic or Latino (of any race)	12.2
Central American, ex. Mexican	10.8
Mexican	15.4
Puerto Rican	16.2
South American	8.1
Colombian	8.5

Class of Worker: Private Wage and Salary
(Universe: Civilian Employed Population 16 Years and Over)

Group	Number	%
Total Population	16,441	82.0
Hispanic or Latino (of any race)	4,155	82.6
Central American, ex. Mexican	1,050	94.8
Mexican	497	72.9
Puerto Rican	854	89.5
South American	1,216	74.9
Colombian	737	80.3

Class of Worker: Government
(Universe: Civilian Employed Population 16 Years and Over)

Group	Number	%
Total Population	2,037	10.2
Hispanic or Latino (of any race)	293	5.8
Central American, ex. Mexican	0	0.0
Mexican	7	1.0
Puerto Rican	57	6.0
South American	160	9.9
Colombian	92	10.0

Means of Transportation to Work: Car, Truck or Van
(Universe: Workers 16 Years and Over)

Group	Number	%
Total Population	17,954	92.0
Hispanic or Latino (of any race)	4,577	93.9
Central American, ex. Mexican	945	85.3
Mexican	648	98.3
Puerto Rican	794	90.5
South American	1,553	99.2
Colombian	882	98.7

Means of Transportation to Work: Public Transportation (ex. Taxicab)
(Universe: Workers 16 Years and Over)

Group	Number	%
Total Population	568	2.9
Hispanic or Latino (of any race)	158	3.2
Central American, ex. Mexican	115	10.4
Mexican	0	0.0
Puerto Rican	33	3.8
South American	0	0.0
Colombian	0	0.0

Homeownership Rate
(Universe: Occupied Housing Units)

Group	%
Total Population	58.8
Hispanic or Latino (of any race)	55.3
Central American, ex. Mexican	46.8
Guatemalan	64.9
Honduran	39.4
Nicaraguan	57.6
Salvadoran	42.8
Cuban	67.3
Dominican Republic	61.5
Mexican	43.5
Puerto Rican	54.0
South American	62.5
Argentinean	67.3
Colombian	67.2
Ecuadorian	64.4
Peruvian	56.5
Venezuelan	44.4

Median Home Value

Group	Dollars
Total Population	188,100
Hispanic or Latino (of any race)	173,300
Central American, ex. Mexican	212,500
Mexican	188,200
Puerto Rican	172,000
South American	123,200
Colombian	124,000

Median Gross Rent

Group	Dollars
Total Population	1,181
Hispanic or Latino (of any race)	1,171
Central American, ex. Mexican	1,228
Mexican	1,072
Puerto Rican	1,385
South American	1,084
Colombian	1,137

Median Household Income
(2010 Inflation-Adjusted Dollars)

Group	Dollars
Total Population	43,146
Hispanic or Latino (of any race)	38,367
Central American, ex. Mexican	40,993
Mexican	23,438
Puerto Rican	58,173
South American	48,036
Colombian	31,545

Per Capita Income
(2010 Inflation-Adjusted Dollars)

Group	Dollars
Total Population	16,761
Hispanic or Latino (of any race)	13,971
Central American, ex. Mexican	13,452
Mexican	6,344
Puerto Rican	19,594
South American	15,659
Colombian	15,151

Households with $100,000+ Income

Group	Number	%
Total Population	1,173	9.3
Hispanic or Latino (of any race)	231	7.9
Central American, ex. Mexican	38	7.5
Mexican	14	2.9
Puerto Rican	136	18.9
South American	43	5.7

Notes: (1) Percent of total population; (2) Percent of Hispanic/Latino population; Profiles include places with an overall population of at least 125,000, OR an overall population of at least 25,000 where the Hispanic/Latino population is at least 20% of the overall population. In states where less than five places meet either of these criteria, we have included places with at least 10,000 total population with the highest percentage of Hispanic/Latino population. These places are identified with an asterisk (*); Please refer to the User's Guide for a full explanation of data.

Colombian	41	9.3

Households with Food Stamps/SNAP Benefits During Past 12 Months

Group	Number	%
Total Population	1,582	12.6
Hispanic or Latino (of any race)	475	16.2
Central American, ex. Mexican	74	14.7
Mexican	96	19.9
Puerto Rican	108	15.0
South American	122	16.2
Colombian	95	21.6

Poverty Rate
(Income in Past 12 Months Below Poverty Level)

Group	%
Total Population	19.9
Hispanic or Latino (of any race)	27.4
Central American, ex. Mexican	24.1
Mexican	62.3
Puerto Rican	25.1
South American	9.2
Colombian	16.6

North Miami

Population

Group	Number	%TP[1]	%HP[2]
Total Population	58,786	100.0	–
Hispanic or Latino (of any race)	15,959	27.1	100.0
Central American, ex. Mexican	3,137	5.3	19.7
Guatemalan	349	0.6	2.2
Honduran	1,342	2.3	8.4
Nicaraguan	999	1.7	6.3
Panamanian	154	0.3	1.0
Salvadoran	187	0.3	1.2
Cuban	3,762	6.4	23.6
Dominican Republic	1,391	2.4	8.7
Mexican	441	0.8	2.8
Puerto Rican	2,274	3.9	14.2
South American	3,560	6.1	22.3
Argentinean	627	1.1	3.9
Chilean	150	0.3	0.9
Colombian	1,363	2.3	8.5
Ecuadorian	257	0.4	1.6
Peruvian	565	1.0	3.5
Uruguayan	122	0.2	0.8
Venezuelan	390	0.7	2.4
Spaniard	117	0.2	0.7

Population Growth: 2000–2010

Group	%
Total Population	-1.8
Hispanic or Latino (of any race)	15.1
Central American, ex. Mexican	83.6
Guatemalan	60.8
Honduran	137.5
Nicaraguan	80.7
Salvadoran	73.1
Cuban	41.7
Dominican Republic	34.8
Mexican	20.2
Puerto Rican	-14.5
South American	77.2
Argentinean	181.2
Colombian	58.9
Ecuadorian	117.8
Peruvian	47.1
Venezuelan	81.4

Males per 100 Females

Group	Number
Total Population	92.7
Hispanic or Latino (of any race)	97.2
Central American, ex. Mexican	87.4
Guatemalan	106.5
Honduran	89.3
Nicaraguan	83.0
Panamanian	71.1
Salvadoran	68.5
Cuban	118.6
Dominican Republic	89.8
Mexican	121.6
Puerto Rican	99.0
South American	84.7
Argentinean	96.6
Chilean	111.3
Colombian	76.3
Ecuadorian	86.2
Peruvian	79.9
Uruguayan	121.8
Venezuelan	83.1
Spaniard	143.8

Average Household Size

Group	People
Total Population	2.96
Hispanic or Latino (of any race)	2.81
Central American, ex. Mexican	3.60
Guatemalan	3.42
Honduran	3.83
Nicaraguan	3.74
Panamanian	2.86
Salvadoran	3.25
Cuban	2.58
Dominican Republic	3.28
Mexican	2.73
Puerto Rican	2.65
South American	2.54
Argentinean	2.52
Chilean	2.62
Colombian	2.49
Ecuadorian	2.58
Peruvian	2.69
Uruguayan	2.59
Venezuelan	2.46
Spaniard	2.54

Median Age

Group	Years
Total Population	34.4
Hispanic or Latino (of any race)	37.1
Central American, ex. Mexican	36.0
Guatemalan	38.8
Honduran	34.5
Nicaraguan	35.5
Panamanian	35.8
Salvadoran	39.3
Cuban	42.3
Dominican Republic	34.2
Mexican	31.7
Puerto Rican	35.4
South American	38.8
Argentinean	36.7
Chilean	43.0
Colombian	40.3
Ecuadorian	42.2
Peruvian	43.2
Uruguayan	36.2
Venezuelan	36.1
Spaniard	39.9

High School Graduates
(Universe: Population 25 Years and Over)

Group	Number	%
Total Population	26,836	74.2
Hispanic or Latino (of any race)	8,346	76.4
Central American, ex. Mexican	1,942	72.1
Honduran	946	75.9
Nicaraguan	671	65.0
Cuban	2,225	76.0
Dominican Republic	446	66.5
Puerto Rican	1,131	67.8
South American	2,002	89.1
Colombian	740	84.7

Four-Year College Graduates
(Universe: Population 25 Years and Over)

Group	Number	%
Total Population	6,019	16.6
Hispanic or Latino (of any race)	1,756	16.1
Central American, ex. Mexican	143	5.3
Honduran	48	3.8
Nicaraguan	46	4.5
Cuban	557	19.0
Dominican Republic	174	25.9
Puerto Rican	263	15.8
South American	443	19.7
Colombian	126	14.4

Population Age 3–17 Enrolled in Public School
(Universe: Population Age 3–17 Enrolled in School)

Group	Number	%
Total Population	10,124	87.8
Hispanic or Latino (of any race)	2,400	86.4
Central American, ex. Mexican	891	86.9
Honduran	469	84.2
Nicaraguan	362	97.3
Cuban	303	72.8
Dominican Republic	79	100.0
Puerto Rican	480	98.0
South American	307	100.0
Colombian	158	100.0

Population Age 3–17 Enrolled in Private School
(Universe: Population Age 3–17 Enrolled in School)

Group	Number	%
Total Population	1,412	12.2
Hispanic or Latino (of any race)	379	13.6
Central American, ex. Mexican	134	13.1
Honduran	88	15.8
Nicaraguan	10	2.7
Cuban	113	27.2
Dominican Republic	0	0.0
Puerto Rican	10	2.0
South American	0	0.0
Colombian	0	0.0

Foreign-Born Population

Group	Number	%
Total Population	29,647	50.4
Hispanic or Latino (of any race)	9,114	56.2
Central American, ex. Mexican	2,720	62.1
Honduran	1,182	57.6
Nicaraguan	1,093	64.0
Cuban	2,637	69.9
Dominican Republic	653	67.5
Puerto Rican	8	0.3
South American	2,465	80.7
Colombian	996	76.0

Foreign-Born Naturalized U.S. Citizens

Group	Number	%
Total Population	13,469	45.4
Hispanic or Latino (of any race)	4,707	51.6
Central American, ex. Mexican	1,133	41.7
Honduran	420	35.5
Nicaraguan	474	43.4
Cuban	1,656	62.8
Dominican Republic	348	53.3
Puerto Rican	8	100.0
South American	1,197	48.6
Colombian	397	39.9

Language Spoken at Home: English Only
(Universe: Population 5 Years and Over)

Group	Number	%
Total Population	16,056	29.7
Hispanic or Latino (of any race)	1,036	6.9
Central American, ex. Mexican	341	8.5
Honduran	155	8.2
Nicaraguan	127	8.0
Cuban	109	3.1
Dominican Republic	39	4.5
Puerto Rican	334	13.7
South American	32	1.1
Colombian	13	1.0

Language Spoken at Home: Spanish
(Universe: Population 5 Years and Over)

Group	Number	%
Total Population	14,837	27.5
Hispanic or Latino (of any race)	13,969	92.6
Central American, ex. Mexican	3,688	91.5
Honduran	1,728	91.8
Nicaraguan	1,460	92.0
Cuban	3,374	96.9
Dominican Republic	802	93.1
Puerto Rican	2,106	86.3
South American	2,892	97.2
Colombian	1,237	99.0

Notes: (1) Percent of total population; (2) Percent of Hispanic/Latino population; Profiles include places with an overall population of at least 125,000, OR an overall population of at least 25,000 where the Hispanic/Latino population is at least 20% of the overall population. In states where less than five places meet either of these criteria, we have included places with at least 10,000 total population with the highest percentage of Hispanic/Latino population. These places are identified with an asterisk (*); Please refer to the User's Guide for a full explanation of data.

Unemployment Rate
(Universe: Population 16 Years and Over)

Group	%
Total Population	11.1
Hispanic or Latino (of any race)	8.9
Central American, ex. Mexican	9.2
Honduran	6.8
Nicaraguan	15.6
Cuban	10.2
Dominican Republic	7.1
Puerto Rican	7.9
South American	8.3
Colombian	9.6

Class of Worker: Private Wage and Salary
(Universe: Civilian Employed Population 16 Years and Over)

Group	Number	%
Total Population	22,027	82.2
Hispanic or Latino (of any race)	6,677	83.2
Central American, ex. Mexican	1,938	90.4
Honduran	930	86.3
Nicaraguan	637	94.7
Cuban	1,557	85.6
Dominican Republic	281	59.5
Puerto Rican	1,001	82.9
South American	1,442	78.1
Colombian	715	84.1

Class of Worker: Government
(Universe: Civilian Employed Population 16 Years and Over)

Group	Number	%
Total Population	3,158	11.8
Hispanic or Latino (of any race)	747	9.3
Central American, ex. Mexican	50	2.3
Honduran	10	0.9
Nicaraguan	19	2.8
Cuban	168	9.2
Dominican Republic	191	40.5
Puerto Rican	157	13.0
South American	132	7.1
Colombian	35	4.1

Means of Transportation to Work: Car, Truck or Van
(Universe: Workers 16 Years and Over)

Group	Number	%
Total Population	21,837	83.4
Hispanic or Latino (of any race)	7,009	91.4
Central American, ex. Mexican	1,793	90.0
Honduran	911	88.4
Nicaraguan	563	94.5
Cuban	1,628	91.6
Dominican Republic	416	88.1
Puerto Rican	1,069	91.0
South American	1,610	92.7
Colombian	678	89.9

Means of Transportation to Work: Public Transportation (ex. Taxicab)
(Universe: Workers 16 Years and Over)

Group	Number	%
Total Population	3,005	11.5
Hispanic or Latino (of any race)	345	4.5
Central American, ex. Mexican	132	6.6
Honduran	79	7.7
Nicaraguan	33	5.5
Cuban	88	5.0
Dominican Republic	9	1.9
Puerto Rican	57	4.9
South American	59	3.4
Colombian	18	2.4

Homeownership Rate
(Universe: Occupied Housing Units)

Group	%
Total Population	51.0
Hispanic or Latino (of any race)	58.4
Central American, ex. Mexican	62.5
Guatemalan	67.6
Honduran	61.4
Nicaraguan	59.9
Panamanian	67.2
Salvadoran	70.5
Cuban	66.6
Dominican Republic	53.1
Mexican	36.4
Puerto Rican	49.7
South American	55.8
Argentinean	52.4
Chilean	60.6
Colombian	59.1
Ecuadorian	62.6
Peruvian	53.3
Uruguayan	46.9
Venezuelan	51.7
Spaniard	78.0

Median Home Value

Group	Dollars
Total Population	220,700
Hispanic or Latino (of any race)	213,500
Central American, ex. Mexican	241,300
Honduran	216,000
Nicaraguan	276,000
Cuban	218,700
Dominican Republic	232,600
Puerto Rican	217,900
South American	172,800
Colombian	200,000

Median Gross Rent

Group	Dollars
Total Population	947
Hispanic or Latino (of any race)	1,040
Central American, ex. Mexican	988
Honduran	911
Nicaraguan	1,117
Cuban	921
Dominican Republic	781
Puerto Rican	1,067
South American	1,150
Colombian	1,091

Median Household Income
(2010 Inflation-Adjusted Dollars)

Group	Dollars
Total Population	36,808
Hispanic or Latino (of any race)	39,087
Central American, ex. Mexican	44,549
Honduran	43,722
Nicaraguan	43,529
Cuban	40,822
Dominican Republic	38,324
Puerto Rican	44,559
South American	33,594
Colombian	34,276

Per Capita Income
(2010 Inflation-Adjusted Dollars)

Group	Dollars
Total Population	17,264
Hispanic or Latino (of any race)	19,012
Central American, ex. Mexican	13,822
Honduran	14,798
Nicaraguan	10,384
Cuban	24,051
Dominican Republic	16,516
Puerto Rican	20,848
South American	22,939
Colombian	19,648

Households with $100,000+ Income

Group	Number	%
Total Population	1,883	10.1
Hispanic or Latino (of any race)	568	10.3
Central American, ex. Mexican	40	3.1
Honduran	0	0.0
Nicaraguan	0	0.0
Cuban	192	14.2
Dominican Republic	21	7.4
Puerto Rican	179	17.6
South American	78	6.9
Colombian	35	7.9

Households with Food Stamps/SNAP Benefits During Past 12 Months

Group	Number	%
Total Population	3,046	16.4
Hispanic or Latino (of any race)	1,035	18.8
Central American, ex. Mexican	265	20.7
Honduran	56	10.5
Nicaraguan	174	34.1
Cuban	343	25.4
Dominican Republic	67	23.5
Puerto Rican	151	14.9
South American	79	7.0
Colombian	45	10.2

Poverty Rate
(Income in Past 12 Months Below Poverty Level)

Group	%
Total Population	21.2
Hispanic or Latino (of any race)	15.3
Central American, ex. Mexican	8.3
Honduran	6.0
Nicaraguan	14.0
Cuban	16.8
Dominican Republic	11.8
Puerto Rican	28.0
South American	11.2
Colombian	6.6

North Miami Beach

Population

Group	Number	%TP[1]	%HP[2]
Total Population	41,523	100.0	–
Hispanic or Latino (of any race)	15,213	36.6	100.0
Central American, ex. Mexican	2,569	6.2	16.9
Costa Rican	115	0.3	0.8
Guatemalan	391	0.9	2.6
Honduran	1,088	2.6	7.2
Nicaraguan	699	1.7	4.6
Panamanian	101	0.2	0.7
Salvadoran	167	0.4	1.1
Cuban	2,909	7.0	19.1
Dominican Republic	1,336	3.2	8.8
Mexican	411	1.0	2.7
Puerto Rican	1,844	4.4	12.1
South American	4,830	11.6	31.7
Argentinean	704	1.7	4.6
Chilean	160	0.4	1.1
Colombian	1,687	4.1	11.1
Ecuadorian	278	0.7	1.8
Peruvian	1,325	3.2	8.7
Uruguayan	186	0.4	1.2
Venezuelan	377	0.9	2.5

Population Growth: 2000–2010

Group	%
Total Population	1.8
Hispanic or Latino (of any race)	24.2
Central American, ex. Mexican	105.0
Guatemalan	93.6
Honduran	176.1
Nicaraguan	86.9
Cuban	44.9
Dominican Republic	36.9
Mexican	98.6
Puerto Rican	3.1
South American	64.5
Argentinean	131.6
Chilean	-14.0
Colombian	46.2
Ecuadorian	62.6
Peruvian	80.8
Venezuelan	69.8

Males per 100 Females

Group	Number
Total Population	92.0
Hispanic or Latino (of any race)	95.6
Central American, ex. Mexican	100.9
Costa Rican	74.2
Guatemalan	126.0
Honduran	96.4
Nicaraguan	106.8
Panamanian	87.0
Salvadoran	81.5
Cuban	109.7
Dominican Republic	85.8
Mexican	127.1
Puerto Rican	96.0

Notes: (1) Percent of total population; (2) Percent of Hispanic/Latino population; Profiles include places with an overall population of at least 125,000, OR an overall population of at least 25,000 where the Hispanic/Latino population is at least 20% of the overall population. In states where less than five places meet either of these criteria, we have included places with at least 10,000 total population with the highest percentage of Hispanic/Latino population. These places are identified with an asterisk (*); Please refer to the User's Guide for a full explanation of data.

Group	
South American	85.5
Argentinean	105.8
Chilean	107.8
Colombian	79.9
Ecuadorian	87.8
Peruvian	85.6
Uruguayan	91.8
Venezuelan	75.3

Average Household Size

Group	People
Total Population	2.86
Hispanic or Latino (of any race)	2.88
Central American, ex. Mexican	3.49
Costa Rican	3.10
Guatemalan	3.88
Honduran	3.63
Nicaraguan	3.42
Panamanian	2.92
Salvadoran	3.00
Cuban	2.53
Dominican Republic	3.30
Mexican	3.20
Puerto Rican	2.71
South American	2.81
Argentinean	2.63
Chilean	2.62
Colombian	2.69
Ecuadorian	2.99
Peruvian	3.08
Uruguayan	2.67
Venezuelan	2.75

Median Age

Group	Years
Total Population	36.4
Hispanic or Latino (of any race)	37.4
Central American, ex. Mexican	33.4
Costa Rican	34.5
Guatemalan	32.2
Honduran	31.6
Nicaraguan	37.3
Panamanian	41.8
Salvadoran	35.5
Cuban	44.4
Dominican Republic	36.2
Mexican	29.1
Puerto Rican	34.5
South American	40.0
Argentinean	38.1
Chilean	47.4
Colombian	42.1
Ecuadorian	38.1
Peruvian	40.6
Uruguayan	37.3
Venezuelan	36.5

High School Graduates
(Universe: Population 25 Years and Over)

Group	Number	%
Total Population	22,037	81.7
Hispanic or Latino (of any race)	8,040	82.2
Central American, ex. Mexican	1,410	72.8
Honduran	477	71.6
Cuban	1,497	87.0
Dominican Republic	652	81.7
Puerto Rican	756	77.6
South American	2,908	84.1
Colombian	1,045	82.0

Four-Year College Graduates
(Universe: Population 25 Years and Over)

Group	Number	%
Total Population	6,323	23.4
Hispanic or Latino (of any race)	2,181	22.3
Central American, ex. Mexican	279	14.4
Honduran	101	15.2
Cuban	475	27.6
Dominican Republic	102	12.8
Puerto Rican	193	19.8
South American	819	23.7
Colombian	334	26.2

Population Age 3–17 Enrolled in Public School
(Universe: Population Age 3–17 Enrolled in School)

Group	Number	%
Total Population	7,353	91.1
Hispanic or Latino (of any race)	1,752	91.9
Central American, ex. Mexican	367	94.8
Honduran	223	100.0
Cuban	263	90.4
Dominican Republic	210	82.0
Puerto Rican	235	89.7
South American	381	91.8
Colombian	7	43.8

Population Age 3–17 Enrolled in Private School
(Universe: Population Age 3–17 Enrolled in School)

Group	Number	%
Total Population	718	8.9
Hispanic or Latino (of any race)	155	8.1
Central American, ex. Mexican	20	5.2
Honduran	0	0.0
Cuban	28	9.6
Dominican Republic	46	18.0
Puerto Rican	27	10.3
South American	34	8.2
Colombian	9	56.3

Foreign-Born Population

Group	Number	%
Total Population	21,219	51.3
Hispanic or Latino (of any race)	9,102	66.6
Central American, ex. Mexican	2,020	77.6
Honduran	687	64.2
Cuban	1,724	75.5
Dominican Republic	811	57.2
Puerto Rican	17	1.0
South American	3,764	89.6
Colombian	1,360	94.1

Foreign-Born Naturalized U.S. Citizens

Group	Number	%
Total Population	10,231	48.2
Hispanic or Latino (of any race)	4,724	51.9
Central American, ex. Mexican	1,067	52.8
Honduran	297	43.2
Cuban	1,195	69.3
Dominican Republic	584	72.0
Puerto Rican	0	0.0
South American	1,459	38.8
Colombian	695	51.1

Language Spoken at Home: English Only
(Universe: Population 5 Years and Over)

Group	Number	%
Total Population	13,552	34.6
Hispanic or Latino (of any race)	1,066	8.1
Central American, ex. Mexican	90	3.5
Honduran	13	1.2
Cuban	214	9.9
Dominican Republic	60	4.7
Puerto Rican	420	26.7
South American	82	2.0
Colombian	31	2.2

Language Spoken at Home: Spanish
(Universe: Population 5 Years and Over)

Group	Number	%
Total Population	12,645	32.3
Hispanic or Latino (of any race)	12,006	91.5
Central American, ex. Mexican	2,489	96.5
Honduran	1,033	98.8
Cuban	1,914	88.6
Dominican Republic	1,206	95.3
Puerto Rican	1,153	73.3
South American	3,991	97.7
Colombian	1,365	97.8

Unemployment Rate
(Universe: Population 16 Years and Over)

Group	%
Total Population	11.1
Hispanic or Latino (of any race)	10.6
Central American, ex. Mexican	13.8
Honduran	0.0
Cuban	7.7
Dominican Republic	2.0
Puerto Rican	25.6
South American	7.0
Colombian	9.2

Class of Worker: Private Wage and Salary
(Universe: Civilian Employed Population 16 Years and Over)

Group	Number	%
Total Population	16,651	83.1
Hispanic or Latino (of any race)	6,197	85.1
Central American, ex. Mexican	1,273	85.9
Honduran	469	72.3
Cuban	972	83.7
Dominican Republic	523	90.3
Puerto Rican	651	81.2
South American	2,318	86.8
Colombian	862	92.4

Class of Worker: Government
(Universe: Civilian Employed Population 16 Years and Over)

Group	Number	%
Total Population	1,779	8.9
Hispanic or Latino (of any race)	370	5.1
Central American, ex. Mexican	62	4.2
Honduran	33	5.1
Cuban	55	4.7
Dominican Republic	0	0.0
Puerto Rican	106	13.2
South American	87	3.3
Colombian	31	3.3

Means of Transportation to Work: Car, Truck or Van
(Universe: Workers 16 Years and Over)

Group	Number	%
Total Population	17,251	87.2
Hispanic or Latino (of any race)	6,516	89.8
Central American, ex. Mexican	1,142	77.1
Honduran	492	75.8
Cuban	1,116	96.1
Dominican Republic	576	94.6
Puerto Rican	763	100.0
South American	2,357	88.7
Colombian	849	91.0

Means of Transportation to Work: Public Transportation (ex. Taxicab)
(Universe: Workers 16 Years and Over)

Group	Number	%
Total Population	1,625	8.2
Hispanic or Latino (of any race)	456	6.3
Central American, ex. Mexican	240	16.2
Honduran	57	8.8
Cuban	11	0.9
Dominican Republic	14	2.3
Puerto Rican	0	0.0
South American	168	6.3
Colombian	13	1.4

Homeownership Rate
(Universe: Occupied Housing Units)

Group	%
Total Population	55.3
Hispanic or Latino (of any race)	53.2
Central American, ex. Mexican	48.3
Costa Rican	48.8
Guatemalan	51.4
Honduran	38.4
Nicaraguan	56.0
Panamanian	60.5
Salvadoran	60.3
Cuban	63.3
Dominican Republic	51.4
Mexican	40.3
Puerto Rican	42.3
South American	53.7
Argentinean	51.1
Chilean	57.6
Colombian	55.7
Ecuadorian	58.4
Peruvian	53.6
Uruguayan	37.3
Venezuelan	50.0

STATE & PLACE PROFILES

Notes: (1) Percent of total population; (2) Percent of Hispanic/Latino population; Profiles include places with an overall population of at least 125,000, OR an overall population of at least 25,000 where the Hispanic/Latino population is at least 20% of the overall population. In states where less than five places meet either of these criteria, we have included places with at least 10,000 total population with the highest percentage of Hispanic/Latino population. These places are identified with an asterisk (*); Please refer to the User's Guide for a full explanation of data.

Median Home Value

Group	Dollars
Total Population	231,300
Hispanic or Latino (of any race)	221,800
Central American, ex. Mexican	191,200
Honduran	165,900
Cuban	226,100
Dominican Republic	294,600
Puerto Rican	210,800
South American	214,800
Colombian	231,300

Median Gross Rent

Group	Dollars
Total Population	974
Hispanic or Latino (of any race)	919
Central American, ex. Mexican	985
Honduran	1,018
Cuban	1,061
Dominican Republic	855
Puerto Rican	875
South American	866
Colombian	804

Median Household Income
(2010 Inflation-Adjusted Dollars)

Group	Dollars
Total Population	44,034
Hispanic or Latino (of any race)	46,646
Central American, ex. Mexican	52,563
Honduran	41,815
Cuban	42,411
Dominican Republic	55,288
Puerto Rican	48,125
South American	48,026
Colombian	43,920

Per Capita Income
(2010 Inflation-Adjusted Dollars)

Group	Dollars
Total Population	20,189
Hispanic or Latino (of any race)	18,159
Central American, ex. Mexican	17,646
Honduran	17,493
Cuban	20,327
Dominican Republic	12,822
Puerto Rican	19,159
South American	20,171
Colombian	20,969

Households with $100,000+ Income

Group	Number	%
Total Population	1,622	11.9
Hispanic or Latino (of any race)	500	11.1
Central American, ex. Mexican	115	16.2
Honduran	72	24.4
Cuban	133	14.9
Dominican Republic	0	0.0
Puerto Rican	72	11.8
South American	119	8.0
Colombian	50	9.9

Households with Food Stamps/SNAP Benefits During Past 12 Months

Group	Number	%
Total Population	1,588	11.6
Hispanic or Latino (of any race)	525	11.6
Central American, ex. Mexican	72	10.1
Honduran	16	5.4
Cuban	193	21.6
Dominican Republic	18	4.8
Puerto Rican	31	5.1
South American	202	13.6
Colombian	91	17.9

Poverty Rate
(Income in Past 12 Months Below Poverty Level)

Group	%
Total Population	16.4
Hispanic or Latino (of any race)	13.9
Central American, ex. Mexican	10.7
Honduran	11.2
Cuban	10.3
Dominican Republic	18.4
Puerto Rican	23.4

South American	11.7
Colombian	10.8

Oakland Park

Population

Group	Number	%TP[1]	%HP[2]
Total Population	41,363	100.0	–
Hispanic or Latino (of any race)	10,584	25.6	100.0
Central American, ex. Mexican	2,915	7.0	27.5
Guatemalan	649	1.6	6.1
Honduran	491	1.2	4.6
Nicaraguan	169	0.4	1.6
Salvadoran	1,460	3.5	13.8
Cuban	1,319	3.2	12.5
Dominican Republic	354	0.9	3.3
Mexican	1,430	3.5	13.5
Puerto Rican	1,496	3.6	14.1
South American	2,195	5.3	20.7
Argentinean	191	0.5	1.8
Colombian	660	1.6	6.2
Ecuadorian	186	0.4	1.8
Peruvian	514	1.2	4.9
Uruguayan	218	0.5	2.1
Venezuelan	260	0.6	2.5

Population Growth: 2000–2010

Group	%
Total Population	33.6
Hispanic or Latino (of any race)	90.5
Central American, ex. Mexican	244.6
Guatemalan	432.0
Honduran	201.2
Salvadoran	243.5
Cuban	109.7
Dominican Republic	152.9
Mexican	66.1
Puerto Rican	44.1
South American	136.0
Colombian	90.2
Peruvian	162.2
Venezuelan	150.0

Males per 100 Females

Group	Number
Total Population	115.1
Hispanic or Latino (of any race)	114.4
Central American, ex. Mexican	125.6
Guatemalan	184.6
Honduran	100.4
Nicaraguan	83.7
Salvadoran	122.6
Cuban	114.1
Dominican Republic	78.8
Mexican	134.8
Puerto Rican	117.1
South American	93.1
Argentinean	124.7
Colombian	81.3
Ecuadorian	97.9
Peruvian	83.6
Uruguayan	98.2
Venezuelan	111.4

Average Household Size

Group	People
Total Population	2.35
Hispanic or Latino (of any race)	3.00
Central American, ex. Mexican	3.81
Guatemalan	3.95
Honduran	3.78
Nicaraguan	3.56
Salvadoran	3.97
Cuban	2.58
Dominican Republic	2.69
Mexican	3.53
Puerto Rican	2.48
South American	2.72
Argentinean	2.50
Colombian	2.67
Ecuadorian	2.98
Peruvian	3.07
Uruguayan	3.10
Venezuelan	2.18

Median Age

Group	Years
Total Population	38.8
Hispanic or Latino (of any race)	32.6
Central American, ex. Mexican	30.5
Guatemalan	29.1
Honduran	31.6
Nicaraguan	34.1
Salvadoran	30.2
Cuban	42.2
Dominican Republic	29.8
Mexican	27.6
Puerto Rican	34.0
South American	39.0
Argentinean	38.4
Colombian	38.6
Ecuadorian	38.2
Peruvian	39.0
Uruguayan	38.5
Venezuelan	39.6

High School Graduates
(Universe: Population 25 Years and Over)

Group	Number	%
Total Population	25,865	83.9
Hispanic or Latino (of any race)	4,524	64.4
Central American, ex. Mexican	736	43.2
Cuban	621	65.1
Puerto Rican	884	83.0
South American	1,400	85.4

Four-Year College Graduates
(Universe: Population 25 Years and Over)

Group	Number	%
Total Population	7,371	23.9
Hispanic or Latino (of any race)	754	10.7
Central American, ex. Mexican	85	5.0
Cuban	68	7.1
Puerto Rican	81	7.6
South American	320	19.5

Population Age 3–17 Enrolled in Public School
(Universe: Population Age 3–17 Enrolled in School)

Group	Number	%
Total Population	4,432	82.9
Hispanic or Latino (of any race)	1,155	81.1
Central American, ex. Mexican	208	80.0
Cuban	187	57.9
Puerto Rican	217	88.2
South American	208	79.7

Population Age 3–17 Enrolled in Private School
(Universe: Population Age 3–17 Enrolled in School)

Group	Number	%
Total Population	912	17.1
Hispanic or Latino (of any race)	270	18.9
Central American, ex. Mexican	52	20.0
Cuban	136	42.1
Puerto Rican	29	11.8
South American	53	20.3

Foreign-Born Population

Group	Number	%
Total Population	13,251	31.8
Hispanic or Latino (of any race)	6,309	60.4
Central American, ex. Mexican	2,272	88.9
Cuban	891	63.2
Puerto Rican	0	0.0
South American	1,814	77.1

Foreign-Born Naturalized U.S. Citizens

Group	Number	%
Total Population	4,291	32.4
Hispanic or Latino (of any race)	1,941	30.8
Central American, ex. Mexican	267	11.8
Cuban	565	63.4
Puerto Rican	0	0.0
South American	629	34.7

Language Spoken at Home: English Only
(Universe: Population 5 Years and Over)

Group	Number	%
Total Population	23,811	60.8
Hispanic or Latino (of any race)	1,168	11.9

Notes: (1) Percent of total population; (2) Percent of Hispanic/Latino population; Profiles include places with an overall population of at least 125,000, OR an overall population of at least 25,000 where the Hispanic/Latino population is at least 20% of the overall population. In states where less than five places meet either of these criteria, we have included places with at least 10,000 total population with the highest percentage of Hispanic/Latino population. These places are identified with an asterisk (*); Please refer to the User's Guide for a full explanation of data.

Central American, ex. Mexican	34	1.4
Cuban	86	6.4
Puerto Rican	274	19.1
South American	201	8.9

Language Spoken at Home: Spanish
(Universe: Population 5 Years and Over)

Group	Number	%
Total Population	9,005	23.0
Hispanic or Latino (of any race)	8,539	86.7
Central American, ex. Mexican	2,454	98.6
Cuban	1,187	88.7
Puerto Rican	1,163	80.9
South American	2,014	89.6

Unemployment Rate
(Universe: Population 16 Years and Over)

Group	%
Total Population	11.1
Hispanic or Latino (of any race)	9.8
Central American, ex. Mexican	1.4
Cuban	16.6
Puerto Rican	7.6
South American	13.0

Class of Worker: Private Wage and Salary
(Universe: Civilian Employed Population 16 Years and Over)

Group	Number	%
Total Population	19,441	82.4
Hispanic or Latino (of any race)	5,233	85.0
Central American, ex. Mexican	1,448	72.9
Cuban	661	97.6
Puerto Rican	729	90.6
South American	1,092	83.4

Class of Worker: Government
(Universe: Civilian Employed Population 16 Years and Over)

Group	Number	%
Total Population	2,418	10.2
Hispanic or Latino (of any race)	218	3.5
Central American, ex. Mexican	33	1.7
Cuban	0	0.0
Puerto Rican	76	9.4
South American	48	3.7

Means of Transportation to Work: Car, Truck or Van
(Universe: Workers 16 Years and Over)

Group	Number	%
Total Population	20,058	87.8
Hispanic or Latino (of any race)	5,126	86.8
Central American, ex. Mexican	1,620	84.0
Cuban	598	91.7
Puerto Rican	523	73.5
South American	1,144	92.5

Means of Transportation to Work: Public Transportation (ex. Taxicab)
(Universe: Workers 16 Years and Over)

Group	Number	%
Total Population	1,051	4.6
Hispanic or Latino (of any race)	423	7.2
Central American, ex. Mexican	243	12.6
Cuban	0	0.0
Puerto Rican	80	11.2
South American	0	0.0

Homeownership Rate
(Universe: Occupied Housing Units)

Group	%
Total Population	58.3
Hispanic or Latino (of any race)	47.2
Central American, ex. Mexican	39.7
Guatemalan	28.1
Honduran	35.5
Nicaraguan	46.7
Salvadoran	43.6
Cuban	67.2
Dominican Republic	44.1
Mexican	29.1
Puerto Rican	44.2
South American	54.2
Argentinean	56.6
Colombian	56.8
Ecuadorian	52.4
Peruvian	49.7
Uruguayan	50.7
Venezuelan	51.9

Median Home Value

Group	Dollars
Total Population	207,500
Hispanic or Latino (of any race)	187,900
Central American, ex. Mexican	168,600
Cuban	227,900
Puerto Rican	232,000
South American	156,300

Median Gross Rent

Group	Dollars
Total Population	1,022
Hispanic or Latino (of any race)	1,098
Central American, ex. Mexican	1,126
Cuban	1,057
Puerto Rican	1,110
South American	1,090

Median Household Income
(2010 Inflation-Adjusted Dollars)

Group	Dollars
Total Population	45,233
Hispanic or Latino (of any race)	40,614
Central American, ex. Mexican	34,726
Cuban	42,273
Puerto Rican	50,786
South American	34,595

Per Capita Income
(2010 Inflation-Adjusted Dollars)

Group	Dollars
Total Population	25,274
Hispanic or Latino (of any race)	16,953
Central American, ex. Mexican	15,415
Cuban	17,631
Puerto Rican	16,825
South American	15,915

Households with $100,000+ Income

Group	Number	%
Total Population	2,410	13.4
Hispanic or Latino (of any race)	376	10.5
Central American, ex. Mexican	25	2.9
Cuban	73	13.9
Puerto Rican	71	11.6
South American	34	4.4

Households with Food Stamps/SNAP Benefits During Past 12 Months

Group	Number	%
Total Population	1,394	7.7
Hispanic or Latino (of any race)	407	11.4
Central American, ex. Mexican	21	2.4
Cuban	82	15.6
Puerto Rican	94	15.4
South American	118	15.2

Poverty Rate
(Income in Past 12 Months Below Poverty Level)

Group	%
Total Population	13.3
Hispanic or Latino (of any race)	14.2
Central American, ex. Mexican	17.9
Cuban	1.1
Puerto Rican	18.4
South American	8.2

Ocoee

Population

Group	Number	%TP[1]	%HP[2]
Total Population	35,579	100.0	–
Hispanic or Latino (of any race)	7,394	20.8	100.0
Central American, ex. Mexican	729	2.0	9.9
Guatemalan	487	1.4	6.6
Cuban	367	1.0	5.0
Dominican Republic	256	0.7	3.5
Mexican	3,040	8.5	41.1
Puerto Rican	2,051	5.8	27.7
South American	608	1.7	8.2
Colombian	290	0.8	3.9
Venezuelan	105	0.3	1.4

Population Growth: 2000–2010

Group	%
Total Population	45.9
Hispanic or Latino (of any race)	99.5
Central American, ex. Mexican	460.8
Cuban	126.5
Mexican	73.4
Puerto Rican	102.5
South American	159.8
Colombian	128.3

Males per 100 Females

Group	Number
Total Population	95.3
Hispanic or Latino (of any race)	105.4
Central American, ex. Mexican	135.9
Guatemalan	175.1
Cuban	96.3
Dominican Republic	95.4
Mexican	120.4
Puerto Rican	87.3
South American	84.8
Colombian	81.3
Venezuelan	72.1

Average Household Size

Group	People
Total Population	2.99
Hispanic or Latino (of any race)	3.65
Central American, ex. Mexican	4.32
Guatemalan	4.82
Cuban	3.02
Dominican Republic	3.48
Mexican	4.33
Puerto Rican	3.11
South American	3.14
Colombian	3.14
Venezuelan	3.25

Median Age

Group	Years
Total Population	35.4
Hispanic or Latino (of any race)	28.2
Central American, ex. Mexican	26.8
Guatemalan	26.3
Cuban	34.9
Dominican Republic	34.2
Mexican	24.3
Puerto Rican	32.7
South American	37.5
Colombian	35.9
Venezuelan	37.3

High School Graduates
(Universe: Population 25 Years and Over)

Group	Number	%
Total Population	18,440	84.6
Hispanic or Latino (of any race)	1,981	65.1
Mexican	444	42.7
Puerto Rican	942	82.3

Four-Year College Graduates
(Universe: Population 25 Years and Over)

Group	Number	%
Total Population	5,705	26.2
Hispanic or Latino (of any race)	263	8.6
Mexican	27	2.6
Puerto Rican	92	8.0

Population Age 3–17 Enrolled in Public School
(Universe: Population Age 3–17 Enrolled in School)

Group	Number	%
Total Population	5,634	82.8
Hispanic or Latino (of any race)	1,355	94.8
Mexican	572	100.0
Puerto Rican	564	88.4

Population Age 3–17 Enrolled in Private School
(Universe: Population Age 3–17 Enrolled in School)

Group	Number	%
Total Population	1,173	17.2
Hispanic or Latino (of any race)	74	5.2
Mexican	0	0.0

Notes: (1) Percent of total population; (2) Percent of Hispanic/Latino population; Profiles include places with an overall population of at least 125,000, OR an overall population of at least 25,000 where the Hispanic/Latino population is at least 20% of the overall population. In states where less than five places meet either of these criteria, we have included places with at least 10,000 total population with the highest percentage of Hispanic/Latino population. These places are identified with an asterisk (*); Please refer to the User's Guide for a full explanation of data.

Puerto Rican	74	11.6

Foreign-Born Population

Group	Number	%
Total Population	5,656	16.6
Hispanic or Latino (of any race)	2,008	33.4
Mexican	1,247	52.0
Puerto Rican	24	1.0

Foreign-Born Naturalized U.S. Citizens

Group	Number	%
Total Population	2,830	50.0
Hispanic or Latino (of any race)	561	27.9
Mexican	146	11.7
Puerto Rican	0	0.0

Language Spoken at Home: English Only
(Universe: Population 5 Years and Over)

Group	Number	%
Total Population	24,726	78.4
Hispanic or Latino (of any race)	1,035	19.6
Mexican	168	8.3
Puerto Rican	657	32.1

Language Spoken at Home: Spanish
(Universe: Population 5 Years and Over)

Group	Number	%
Total Population	4,602	14.6
Hispanic or Latino (of any race)	4,248	80.4
Mexican	1,855	91.7
Puerto Rican	1,389	67.9

Unemployment Rate
(Universe: Population 16 Years and Over)

Group	%
Total Population	6.5
Hispanic or Latino (of any race)	8.3
Mexican	3.4
Puerto Rican	5.3

Class of Worker: Private Wage and Salary
(Universe: Civilian Employed Population 16 Years and Over)

Group	Number	%
Total Population	15,230	84.1
Hispanic or Latino (of any race)	2,321	90.3
Mexican	969	100.0
Puerto Rican	731	75.3

Class of Worker: Government
(Universe: Civilian Employed Population 16 Years and Over)

Group	Number	%
Total Population	2,073	11.4
Hispanic or Latino (of any race)	190	7.4
Mexican	0	0.0
Puerto Rican	190	19.6

Means of Transportation to Work: Car, Truck or Van
(Universe: Workers 16 Years and Over)

Group	Number	%
Total Population	16,742	93.8
Hispanic or Latino (of any race)	2,409	93.5
Mexican	920	94.9
Puerto Rican	860	87.9

Means of Transportation to Work: Public Transportation (ex. Taxicab)
(Universe: Workers 16 Years and Over)

Group	Number	%
Total Population	124	0.7
Hispanic or Latino (of any race)	47	1.8
Mexican	0	0.0
Puerto Rican	47	4.8

Homeownership Rate
(Universe: Occupied Housing Units)

Group	%
Total Population	76.1
Hispanic or Latino (of any race)	64.7
Central American, ex. Mexican	42.3
Guatemalan	26.2
Cuban	77.9
Dominican Republic	80.5
Mexican	57.5
Puerto Rican	69.6
South American	77.2
Colombian	77.8
Venezuelan	75.0

Median Home Value

Group	Dollars
Total Population	230,400
Hispanic or Latino (of any race)	183,800
Mexican	117,100
Puerto Rican	171,900

Median Gross Rent

Group	Dollars
Total Population	1,196
Hispanic or Latino (of any race)	941
Mexican	747
Puerto Rican	945

Median Household Income
(2010 Inflation-Adjusted Dollars)

Group	Dollars
Total Population	60,135
Hispanic or Latino (of any race)	41,708
Mexican	34,271
Puerto Rican	37,821

Per Capita Income
(2010 Inflation-Adjusted Dollars)

Group	Dollars
Total Population	25,994
Hispanic or Latino (of any race)	13,371
Mexican	7,960
Puerto Rican	15,553

Households with $100,000+ Income

Group	Number	%
Total Population	2,611	22.5
Hispanic or Latino (of any race)	84	5.2
Mexican	17	3.2
Puerto Rican	21	3.0

Households with Food Stamps/SNAP Benefits During Past 12 Months

Group	Number	%
Total Population	419	3.6
Hispanic or Latino (of any race)	152	9.5
Mexican	86	16.0
Puerto Rican	43	6.1

Poverty Rate
(Income in Past 12 Months Below Poverty Level)

Group	%
Total Population	8.3
Hispanic or Latino (of any race)	21.9
Mexican	38.8
Puerto Rican	12.2

Orlando

Population

Group	Number	%TP[1]	%HP[2]
Total Population	238,300	100.0	–
Hispanic or Latino (of any race)	60,483	25.4	100.0
Central American, ex. Mexican	3,306	1.4	5.5
Costa Rican	245	0.1	0.4
Guatemalan	597	0.3	1.0
Honduran	956	0.4	1.6
Nicaraguan	377	0.2	0.6
Panamanian	596	0.3	1.0
Salvadoran	521	0.2	0.9
Cuban	4,299	1.8	7.1
Dominican Republic	4,278	1.8	7.1
Mexican	4,262	1.8	7.0
Puerto Rican	31,201	13.1	51.6
South American	9,977	4.2	16.5
Argentinean	421	0.2	0.7
Bolivian	108	<0.1	0.2
Chilean	290	0.1	0.5
Colombian	4,688	2.0	7.8
Ecuadorian	1,039	0.4	1.7
Peruvian	1,144	0.5	1.9
Uruguayan	129	0.1	0.2
Venezuelan	2,076	0.9	3.4
Spaniard	460	0.2	0.8

Population Growth: 2000–2010

Group	%
Total Population	28.2
Hispanic or Latino (of any race)	86.0
Central American, ex. Mexican	179.5
Costa Rican	105.9
Guatemalan	233.5
Honduran	190.6
Nicaraguan	206.5
Panamanian	159.1
Salvadoran	294.7
Cuban	59.5
Dominican Republic	259.2
Mexican	87.0
Puerto Rican	83.2
South American	185.5
Argentinean	135.2
Colombian	181.9
Ecuadorian	176.3
Peruvian	240.5
Venezuelan	208.0
Spaniard	233.3

Males per 100 Females

Group	Number
Total Population	94.7
Hispanic or Latino (of any race)	93.2
Central American, ex. Mexican	105.5
Costa Rican	102.5
Guatemalan	149.8
Honduran	116.3
Nicaraguan	99.5
Panamanian	70.3
Salvadoran	99.6
Cuban	101.3
Dominican Republic	78.5
Mexican	123.4
Puerto Rican	92.3
South American	83.8
Argentinean	95.8
Bolivian	77.0
Chilean	104.2
Colombian	81.4
Ecuadorian	78.5
Peruvian	90.7
Uruguayan	115.0
Venezuelan	80.5
Spaniard	82.5

Average Household Size

Group	People
Total Population	2.29
Hispanic or Latino (of any race)	2.62
Central American, ex. Mexican	2.93
Costa Rican	2.45
Guatemalan	3.24
Honduran	3.35
Nicaraguan	3.00
Panamanian	2.24
Salvadoran	3.07
Cuban	2.40
Dominican Republic	2.87
Mexican	2.78
Puerto Rican	2.59
South American	2.64
Argentinean	2.33
Bolivian	2.86
Chilean	2.63
Colombian	2.60
Ecuadorian	2.83
Peruvian	2.70
Uruguayan	2.83
Venezuelan	2.65
Spaniard	2.15

Median Age

Group	Years
Total Population	32.8
Hispanic or Latino (of any race)	30.2
Central American, ex. Mexican	29.9
Costa Rican	31.9
Guatemalan	28.2
Honduran	29.6
Nicaraguan	30.5
Panamanian	31.4

Notes: (1) Percent of total population; (2) Percent of Hispanic/Latino population; Profiles include places with an overall population of at least 125,000, OR an overall population of at least 25,000 where the Hispanic/Latino population is at least 20% of the overall population. In states where less than five places meet either of these criteria, we have included places with at least 10,000 total population with the highest percentage of Hispanic/Latino population. These places are identified with an asterisk (*); Please refer to the User's Guide for a full explanation of data.

Salvadoran	29.4
Cuban	35.8
Dominican Republic	29.7
Mexican	27.5
Puerto Rican	29.4
South American	33.5
Argentinean	34.3
Bolivian	33.3
Chilean	37.7
Colombian	33.3
Ecuadorian	34.8
Peruvian	32.9
Uruguayan	33.3
Venezuelan	32.8
Spaniard	33.3

High School Graduates
(Universe: Population 25 Years and Over)

Group	Number	%
Total Population	133,090	86.6
Hispanic or Latino (of any race)	25,685	77.6
Central American, ex. Mexican	909	54.9
Cuban	2,492	84.8
Dominican Republic	2,323	80.2
Mexican	1,768	56.5
Puerto Rican	11,559	78.4
South American	5,806	85.8
Colombian	2,588	87.3
Ecuadorian	689	67.9
Peruvian	709	91.2
Venezuelan	1,196	98.4

Four-Year College Graduates
(Universe: Population 25 Years and Over)

Group	Number	%
Total Population	49,622	32.3
Hispanic or Latino (of any race)	7,158	21.6
Central American, ex. Mexican	137	8.3
Cuban	913	31.1
Dominican Republic	590	20.4
Mexican	597	19.1
Puerto Rican	2,718	18.4
South American	1,948	28.8
Colombian	889	30.0
Ecuadorian	115	11.3
Peruvian	258	33.2
Venezuelan	491	40.4

Population Age 3–17 Enrolled in Public School
(Universe: Population Age 3–17 Enrolled in School)

Group	Number	%
Total Population	30,855	82.8
Hispanic or Latino (of any race)	9,546	88.0
Central American, ex. Mexican	295	89.9
Cuban	197	58.5
Dominican Republic	949	91.7
Mexican	1,060	92.5
Puerto Rican	5,063	89.5
South American	1,483	81.4
Colombian	627	77.8
Ecuadorian	304	95.6
Peruvian	61	40.4
Venezuelan	274	83.3

Population Age 3–17 Enrolled in Private School
(Universe: Population Age 3–17 Enrolled in School)

Group	Number	%
Total Population	6,421	17.2
Hispanic or Latino (of any race)	1,305	12.0
Central American, ex. Mexican	33	10.1
Cuban	140	41.5
Dominican Republic	86	8.3
Mexican	86	7.5
Puerto Rican	591	10.5
South American	338	18.6
Colombian	179	22.2
Ecuadorian	14	4.4
Peruvian	90	59.6
Venezuelan	55	16.7

Foreign-Born Population

Group	Number	%
Total Population	43,533	18.6
Hispanic or Latino (of any race)	17,661	32.3
Central American, ex. Mexican	1,951	68.8
Cuban	2,128	51.2
Dominican Republic	2,658	54.4
Mexican	2,635	46.5
Puerto Rican	340	1.4
South American	7,233	70.3
Colombian	3,167	70.7
Ecuadorian	952	56.6
Peruvian	724	57.1
Venezuelan	1,409	77.5

Foreign-Born Naturalized U.S. Citizens

Group	Number	%
Total Population	15,408	35.4
Hispanic or Latino (of any race)	5,774	32.7
Central American, ex. Mexican	384	19.7
Cuban	1,236	58.1
Dominican Republic	1,278	48.1
Mexican	530	20.1
Puerto Rican	138	40.6
South American	1,963	27.1
Colombian	1,185	37.4
Ecuadorian	220	23.1
Peruvian	241	33.3
Venezuelan	87	6.2

Language Spoken at Home: English Only
(Universe: Population 5 Years and Over)

Group	Number	%
Total Population	149,595	68.7
Hispanic or Latino (of any race)	7,599	15.3
Central American, ex. Mexican	491	18.7
Cuban	697	17.9
Dominican Republic	318	7.2
Mexican	1,001	19.5
Puerto Rican	3,828	17.0
South American	993	10.5
Colombian	449	10.6
Ecuadorian	104	7.0
Peruvian	133	12.9
Venezuelan	291	17.0

Language Spoken at Home: Spanish
(Universe: Population 5 Years and Over)

Group	Number	%
Total Population	44,271	20.3
Hispanic or Latino (of any race)	41,640	83.6
Central American, ex. Mexican	2,134	81.3
Cuban	3,191	82.1
Dominican Republic	4,102	92.8
Mexican	3,946	76.9
Puerto Rican	18,611	82.6
South American	8,416	88.9
Colombian	3,774	89.4
Ecuadorian	1,386	93.0
Peruvian	870	84.1
Venezuelan	1,400	82.0

Unemployment Rate
(Universe: Population 16 Years and Over)

Group	%
Total Population	9.8
Hispanic or Latino (of any race)	10.3
Central American, ex. Mexican	8.4
Cuban	12.3
Dominican Republic	14.2
Mexican	10.6
Puerto Rican	10.8
South American	7.8
Colombian	6.8
Ecuadorian	12.9
Peruvian	4.3
Venezuelan	6.2

Class of Worker: Private Wage and Salary
(Universe: Civilian Employed Population 16 Years and Over)

Group	Number	%
Total Population	107,534	86.0
Hispanic or Latino (of any race)	24,510	89.1
Central American, ex. Mexican	1,794	96.2
Cuban	2,005	88.5
Dominican Republic	2,252	90.0
Mexican	2,591	85.0
Puerto Rican	10,153	89.1
South American	4,994	89.3
Colombian	2,345	93.4
Ecuadorian	672	91.2
Peruvian	559	81.4
Venezuelan	918	87.8

Class of Worker: Government
(Universe: Civilian Employed Population 16 Years and Over)

Group	Number	%
Total Population	11,605	9.3
Hispanic or Latino (of any race)	1,690	6.1
Central American, ex. Mexican	62	3.3
Cuban	160	7.1
Dominican Republic	105	4.2
Mexican	241	7.9
Puerto Rican	827	7.3
South American	250	4.5
Colombian	93	3.7
Ecuadorian	23	3.1
Peruvian	72	10.5
Venezuelan	20	1.9

Means of Transportation to Work: Car, Truck or Van
(Universe: Workers 16 Years and Over)

Group	Number	%
Total Population	107,644	88.4
Hispanic or Latino (of any race)	23,726	88.9
Central American, ex. Mexican	1,516	82.1
Cuban	2,009	93.9
Dominican Republic	2,078	88.5
Mexican	2,644	88.6
Puerto Rican	9,835	88.5
South American	4,938	90.7
Colombian	2,295	94.3
Ecuadorian	687	93.2
Peruvian	526	80.3
Venezuelan	961	92.8

Means of Transportation to Work: Public Transportation (ex. Taxicab)
(Universe: Workers 16 Years and Over)

Group	Number	%
Total Population	5,281	4.3
Hispanic or Latino (of any race)	1,388	5.2
Central American, ex. Mexican	223	12.1
Cuban	47	2.2
Dominican Republic	135	5.8
Mexican	133	4.5
Puerto Rican	685	6.2
South American	165	3.0
Colombian	19	0.8
Ecuadorian	18	2.4
Peruvian	11	1.7
Venezuelan	30	2.9

Homeownership Rate
(Universe: Occupied Housing Units)

Group	%
Total Population	39.5
Hispanic or Latino (of any race)	28.8
Central American, ex. Mexican	24.8
Costa Rican	22.8
Guatemalan	25.9
Honduran	18.8
Nicaraguan	28.2
Panamanian	27.4
Salvadoran	29.1
Cuban	42.4
Dominican Republic	31.9
Mexican	23.0
Puerto Rican	25.9
South American	33.9
Argentinean	31.0
Bolivian	32.4
Chilean	27.2
Colombian	34.9
Ecuadorian	34.6
Peruvian	30.4
Uruguayan	27.7
Venezuelan	35.8
Spaniard	41.0

Median Home Value

Group	Dollars
Total Population	217,500
Hispanic or Latino (of any race)	198,300

Notes: (1) Percent of total population; (2) Percent of Hispanic/Latino population; Profiles include places with an overall population of at least 125,000, OR an overall population of at least 25,000 where the Hispanic/Latino population is at least 20% of the overall population. In states where less than five places meet either of these criteria, we have included places with at least 10,000 total population with the highest percentage of Hispanic/Latino population. These places are identified with an asterisk (*); Please refer to the User's Guide for a full explanation of data.

Central American, ex. Mexican	175,000
Cuban	231,800
Dominican Republic	198,600
Mexican	151,000
Puerto Rican	193,800
South American	204,700
Colombian	214,100
Ecuadorian	313,500
Peruvian	186,300
Venezuelan	236,500

Median Gross Rent

Group	Dollars
Total Population	971
Hispanic or Latino (of any race)	934
Central American, ex. Mexican	975
Cuban	874
Dominican Republic	897
Mexican	1,003
Puerto Rican	919
South American	971
Colombian	924
Ecuadorian	986
Peruvian	982
Venezuelan	1,050

Median Household Income
(2010 Inflation-Adjusted Dollars)

Group	Dollars
Total Population	42,355
Hispanic or Latino (of any race)	34,541
Central American, ex. Mexican	30,833
Cuban	32,482
Dominican Republic	36,769
Mexican	37,208
Puerto Rican	31,916
South American	40,125
Colombian	39,722
Ecuadorian	47,054
Peruvian	52,179
Venezuelan	35,473

Per Capita Income
(2010 Inflation-Adjusted Dollars)

Group	Dollars
Total Population	25,854
Hispanic or Latino (of any race)	17,371
Central American, ex. Mexican	13,477
Cuban	24,139
Dominican Republic	17,489
Mexican	17,382
Puerto Rican	15,918
South American	18,911
Colombian	18,488
Ecuadorian	13,243
Peruvian	23,385
Venezuelan	23,937

Households with $100,000+ Income

Group	Number	%
Total Population	14,105	14.4
Hispanic or Latino (of any race)	1,832	9.5
Central American, ex. Mexican	11	1.3
Cuban	393	23.6
Dominican Republic	127	7.3
Mexican	165	10.6
Puerto Rican	701	7.5
South American	331	9.6
Colombian	133	8.8
Ecuadorian	20	4.5
Peruvian	80	16.2
Venezuelan	40	6.4

Households with Food Stamps/SNAP Benefits During Past 12 Months

Group	Number	%
Total Population	8,710	8.9
Hispanic or Latino (of any race)	2,308	11.9
Central American, ex. Mexican	66	7.6
Cuban	138	8.3
Dominican Republic	306	17.6
Mexican	167	10.8
Puerto Rican	1,478	15.7
South American	148	4.3
Colombian	37	2.5
Ecuadorian	41	9.1
Peruvian	46	9.3
Venezuelan	24	3.9

Poverty Rate
(Income in Past 12 Months Below Poverty Level)

Group	%
Total Population	16.6
Hispanic or Latino (of any race)	20.5
Central American, ex. Mexican	25.7
Cuban	19.0
Dominican Republic	24.6
Mexican	29.7
Puerto Rican	22.4
South American	11.7
Colombian	7.0
Ecuadorian	19.0
Peruvian	10.5
Venezuelan	4.5

Pembroke Pines

Population

Group	Number	%TP[1]	%HP[2]
Total Population	154,750	100.0	–
Hispanic or Latino (of any race)	64,061	41.4	100.0
Central American, ex. Mexican	4,614	3.0	7.2
Costa Rican	407	0.3	0.6
Guatemalan	529	0.3	0.8
Honduran	996	0.6	1.6
Nicaraguan	1,423	0.9	2.2
Panamanian	676	0.4	1.1
Salvadoran	575	0.4	0.9
Cuban	19,826	12.8	30.9
Dominican Republic	4,804	3.1	7.5
Mexican	1,658	1.1	2.6
Puerto Rican	10,490	6.8	16.4
South American	19,424	12.6	30.3
Argentinean	1,147	0.7	1.8
Bolivian	153	0.1	0.2
Chilean	558	0.4	0.9
Colombian	9,937	6.4	15.5
Ecuadorian	1,732	1.1	2.7
Peruvian	2,638	1.7	4.1
Uruguayan	243	0.2	0.4
Venezuelan	2,937	1.9	4.6
Spaniard	502	0.3	0.8

Population Growth: 2000–2010

Group	%
Total Population	12.6
Hispanic or Latino (of any race)	65.5
Central American, ex. Mexican	143.4
Costa Rican	79.3
Guatemalan	147.2
Honduran	264.8
Nicaraguan	167.0
Panamanian	84.2
Salvadoran	145.7
Cuban	66.6
Dominican Republic	193.5
Mexican	72.7
Puerto Rican	52.3
South American	134.2
Argentinean	147.7
Chilean	87.2
Colombian	141.0
Ecuadorian	136.0
Peruvian	143.8
Venezuelan	136.5
Spaniard	123.1

Males per 100 Females

Group	Number
Total Population	85.9
Hispanic or Latino (of any race)	85.6
Central American, ex. Mexican	76.5
Costa Rican	62.8
Guatemalan	86.9
Honduran	68.2
Nicaraguan	80.4
Panamanian	71.6
Salvadoran	92.3
Cuban	90.6
Dominican Republic	81.8
Mexican	91.7
Puerto Rican	87.8
South American	80.8
Argentinean	94.1
Bolivian	106.8
Chilean	89.8
Colombian	78.9
Ecuadorian	76.6
Peruvian	79.0
Uruguayan	88.4
Venezuelan	83.6
Spaniard	88.0

Average Household Size

Group	People
Total Population	2.70
Hispanic or Latino (of any race)	2.98
Central American, ex. Mexican	3.29
Costa Rican	2.80
Guatemalan	3.33
Honduran	3.32
Nicaraguan	3.46
Panamanian	3.05
Salvadoran	3.43
Cuban	2.84
Dominican Republic	3.23
Mexican	3.15
Puerto Rican	2.88
South American	3.10
Argentinean	2.99
Bolivian	3.22
Chilean	3.00
Colombian	3.14
Ecuadorian	3.11
Peruvian	3.18
Uruguayan	2.82
Venezuelan	3.00
Spaniard	2.57

Median Age

Group	Years
Total Population	39.5
Hispanic or Latino (of any race)	37.0
Central American, ex. Mexican	34.5
Costa Rican	38.1
Guatemalan	35.6
Honduran	33.2
Nicaraguan	32.7
Panamanian	39.1
Salvadoran	35.0
Cuban	40.0
Dominican Republic	33.4
Mexican	30.0
Puerto Rican	35.0
South American	38.2
Argentinean	38.4
Bolivian	36.8
Chilean	38.2
Colombian	38.2
Ecuadorian	39.2
Peruvian	39.9
Uruguayan	39.6
Venezuelan	36.7
Spaniard	45.0

High School Graduates
(Universe: Population 25 Years and Over)

Group	Number	%
Total Population	92,851	89.1
Hispanic or Latino (of any race)	33,694	86.4
Central American, ex. Mexican	2,314	84.4
Nicaraguan	771	81.8
Cuban	10,204	84.2
Dominican Republic	2,225	85.7
Mexican	1,085	88.2
Puerto Rican	4,247	86.9
South American	12,143	87.7
Argentinean	692	89.8
Colombian	6,146	86.3
Ecuadorian	1,448	84.3
Peruvian	1,774	97.4
Venezuelan	1,516	85.7

Notes: (1) Percent of total population; (2) Percent of Hispanic/Latino population; Profiles include places with an overall population of at least 125,000, OR an overall population of at least 25,000 where the Hispanic/Latino population is at least 20% of the overall population. In states where less than five places meet either of these criteria, we have included places with at least 10,000 total population with the highest percentage of Hispanic/Latino population. These places are identified with an asterisk (*); Please refer to the User's Guide for a full explanation of data.

Four-Year College Graduates
(Universe: Population 25 Years and Over)

Group	Number	%
Total Population	32,864	31.5
Hispanic or Latino (of any race)	11,392	29.2
Central American, ex. Mexican	664	24.2
Nicaraguan	266	28.2
Cuban	3,225	26.6
Dominican Republic	695	26.8
Mexican	296	24.1
Puerto Rican	1,331	27.2
South American	4,712	34.0
Argentinean	275	35.7
Colombian	2,352	33.0
Ecuadorian	332	19.3
Peruvian	768	42.2
Venezuelan	782	44.2

Population Age 3–17 Enrolled in Public School
(Universe: Population Age 3–17 Enrolled in School)

Group	Number	%
Total Population	24,087	82.6
Hispanic or Latino (of any race)	9,853	83.8
Central American, ex. Mexican	284	92.8
Nicaraguan	70	100.0
Cuban	2,889	81.0
Dominican Republic	634	94.5
Mexican	574	77.9
Puerto Rican	1,495	83.5
South American	2,829	83.6
Argentinean	131	69.3
Colombian	1,352	81.4
Ecuadorian	404	81.8
Peruvian	265	85.2
Venezuelan	363	93.3

Population Age 3–17 Enrolled in Private School
(Universe: Population Age 3–17 Enrolled in School)

Group	Number	%
Total Population	5,073	17.4
Hispanic or Latino (of any race)	1,904	16.2
Central American, ex. Mexican	22	7.2
Nicaraguan	0	0.0
Cuban	679	19.0
Dominican Republic	37	5.5
Mexican	163	22.1
Puerto Rican	295	16.5
South American	554	16.4
Argentinean	58	30.7
Colombian	308	18.6
Ecuadorian	90	18.2
Peruvian	46	14.8
Venezuelan	26	6.7

Foreign-Born Population

Group	Number	%
Total Population	56,539	37.1
Hispanic or Latino (of any race)	30,853	52.1
Central American, ex. Mexican	2,693	77.4
Nicaraguan	882	80.0
Cuban	8,727	48.2
Dominican Republic	2,196	54.8
Mexican	693	31.5
Puerto Rican	108	1.4
South American	15,151	75.0
Argentinean	698	61.8
Colombian	8,022	76.8
Ecuadorian	1,572	63.7
Peruvian	1,849	75.6
Venezuelan	2,309	90.4

Foreign-Born Naturalized U.S. Citizens

Group	Number	%
Total Population	35,050	62.0
Hispanic or Latino (of any race)	18,583	60.2
Central American, ex. Mexican	1,860	69.1
Nicaraguan	734	83.2
Cuban	7,147	81.9
Dominican Republic	1,611	73.4
Mexican	322	46.5
Puerto Rican	74	68.5
South American	6,961	45.9
Argentinean	475	68.1
Colombian	3,209	40.0
Ecuadorian	883	56.2
Peruvian	1,132	61.2
Venezuelan	733	31.7

Language Spoken at Home: English Only
(Universe: Population 5 Years and Over)

Group	Number	%
Total Population	74,967	52.0
Hispanic or Latino (of any race)	7,591	13.6
Central American, ex. Mexican	391	11.5
Nicaraguan	193	17.8
Cuban	2,699	15.8
Dominican Republic	252	6.9
Mexican	691	34.2
Puerto Rican	1,844	25.5
South American	979	5.1
Argentinean	110	10.5
Colombian	442	4.5
Ecuadorian	140	6.2
Peruvian	224	9.9
Venezuelan	23	0.9

Language Spoken at Home: Spanish
(Universe: Population 5 Years and Over)

Group	Number	%
Total Population	51,053	35.4
Hispanic or Latino (of any race)	47,886	86.0
Central American, ex. Mexican	3,001	88.5
Nicaraguan	891	82.2
Cuban	14,310	83.6
Dominican Republic	3,384	93.1
Mexican	1,320	65.3
Puerto Rican	5,356	74.0
South American	18,027	94.8
Argentinean	933	89.5
Colombian	9,417	95.5
Ecuadorian	2,111	93.8
Peruvian	2,022	89.3
Venezuelan	2,432	99.1

Unemployment Rate
(Universe: Population 16 Years and Over)

Group	%
Total Population	7.8
Hispanic or Latino (of any race)	7.7
Central American, ex. Mexican	5.8
Nicaraguan	9.0
Cuban	7.2
Dominican Republic	13.0
Mexican	4.1
Puerto Rican	5.4
South American	8.4
Argentinean	3.3
Colombian	9.6
Ecuadorian	4.6
Peruvian	7.6
Venezuelan	8.9

Class of Worker: Private Wage and Salary
(Universe: Civilian Employed Population 16 Years and Over)

Group	Number	%
Total Population	58,237	78.8
Hispanic or Latino (of any race)	24,847	82.2
Central American, ex. Mexican	1,852	85.4
Nicaraguan	617	86.8
Cuban	6,733	73.8
Dominican Republic	1,696	83.1
Mexican	785	83.7
Puerto Rican	3,160	81.6
South American	9,514	88.1
Argentinean	689	93.1
Colombian	4,665	87.5
Ecuadorian	1,029	83.2
Peruvian	1,259	88.2
Venezuelan	1,400	94.7

Class of Worker: Government
(Universe: Civilian Employed Population 16 Years and Over)

Group	Number	%
Total Population	12,352	16.7
Hispanic or Latino (of any race)	4,025	13.3
Central American, ex. Mexican	190	8.8
Nicaraguan	78	11.0
Cuban	1,910	20.9
Dominican Republic	303	14.9
Mexican	140	14.9
Puerto Rican	597	15.4
South American	767	7.1
Argentinean	51	6.9
Colombian	333	6.2
Ecuadorian	159	12.9
Peruvian	94	6.6
Venezuelan	57	3.9

Means of Transportation to Work: Car, Truck or Van
(Universe: Workers 16 Years and Over)

Group	Number	%
Total Population	67,751	94.3
Hispanic or Latino (of any race)	27,644	94.2
Central American, ex. Mexican	1,868	90.7
Nicaraguan	670	94.2
Cuban	8,336	95.2
Dominican Republic	1,893	96.8
Mexican	878	95.4
Puerto Rican	3,576	93.2
South American	9,878	93.6
Argentinean	633	87.6
Colombian	4,851	93.1
Ecuadorian	1,134	91.7
Peruvian	1,327	94.2
Venezuelan	1,381	98.2

Means of Transportation to Work: Public Transportation (ex. Taxicab)
(Universe: Workers 16 Years and Over)

Group	Number	%
Total Population	653	0.9
Hispanic or Latino (of any race)	247	0.8
Central American, ex. Mexican	59	2.9
Nicaraguan	0	0.0
Cuban	0	0.0
Dominican Republic	0	0.0
Mexican	14	1.5
Puerto Rican	51	1.3
South American	111	1.1
Argentinean	0	0.0
Colombian	50	1.0
Ecuadorian	21	1.7
Peruvian	40	2.8
Venezuelan	0	0.0

Homeownership Rate
(Universe: Occupied Housing Units)

Group	%
Total Population	75.8
Hispanic or Latino (of any race)	72.4
Central American, ex. Mexican	67.5
Costa Rican	67.2
Guatemalan	71.9
Honduran	65.7
Nicaraguan	65.1
Panamanian	67.1
Salvadoran	72.9
Cuban	81.2
Dominican Republic	61.8
Mexican	65.7
Puerto Rican	68.7
South American	69.0
Argentinean	78.1
Bolivian	69.0
Chilean	76.2
Colombian	68.7
Ecuadorian	70.3
Peruvian	67.8
Uruguayan	66.3
Venezuelan	64.7
Spaniard	80.8

Median Home Value

Group	Dollars
Total Population	277,600
Hispanic or Latino (of any race)	293,000
Central American, ex. Mexican	286,400
Nicaraguan	305,300
Cuban	314,000
Dominican Republic	281,500
Mexican	281,400
Puerto Rican	265,500
South American	271,800
Argentinean	351,200

Notes: (1) Percent of total population; (2) Percent of Hispanic/Latino population; Profiles include places with an overall population of at least 125,000, OR an overall population of at least 25,000 where the Hispanic/Latino population is at least 20% of the overall population. In states where less than five places meet either of these criteria, we have included places with at least 10,000 total population with the highest percentage of Hispanic/Latino population. These places are identified with an asterisk (*); Please refer to the User's Guide for a full explanation of data.

Colombian	259,600
Ecuadorian	276,400
Peruvian	319,600
Venezuelan	281,100

Median Gross Rent

Group	Dollars
Total Population	1,348
Hispanic or Latino (of any race)	1,315
Central American, ex. Mexican	1,384
Nicaraguan	1,314
Cuban	1,255
Dominican Republic	1,188
Mexican	1,494
Puerto Rican	1,386
South American	1,291
Argentinean	961
Colombian	1,288
Ecuadorian	1,201
Peruvian	1,282
Venezuelan	1,359

Median Household Income
(2010 Inflation-Adjusted Dollars)

Group	Dollars
Total Population	63,266
Hispanic or Latino (of any race)	66,453
Central American, ex. Mexican	65,943
Nicaraguan	68,867
Cuban	72,321
Dominican Republic	51,615
Mexican	93,717
Puerto Rican	66,000
South American	62,919
Argentinean	73,115
Colombian	55,875
Ecuadorian	43,977
Peruvian	70,994
Venezuelan	73,925

Per Capita Income
(2010 Inflation-Adjusted Dollars)

Group	Dollars
Total Population	28,615
Hispanic or Latino (of any race)	26,032
Central American, ex. Mexican	28,759
Nicaraguan	26,145
Cuban	29,111
Dominican Republic	24,807
Mexican	25,677
Puerto Rican	26,787
South American	23,100
Argentinean	32,140
Colombian	21,078
Ecuadorian	21,000
Peruvian	27,658
Venezuelan	24,646

Households with $100,000+ Income

Group	Number	%
Total Population	14,562	26.8
Hispanic or Latino (of any race)	5,013	26.9
Central American, ex. Mexican	248	22.8
Nicaraguan	93	27.8
Cuban	1,855	30.7
Dominican Republic	363	25.9
Mexican	210	39.7
Puerto Rican	755	28.6
South American	1,274	20.9
Argentinean	151	32.8
Colombian	563	19.6
Ecuadorian	93	15.4
Peruvian	211	24.1
Venezuelan	206	22.4

Households with Food Stamps/SNAP Benefits During Past 12 Months

Group	Number	%
Total Population	3,134	5.8
Hispanic or Latino (of any race)	1,595	8.5
Central American, ex. Mexican	83	7.6
Nicaraguan	0	0.0
Cuban	494	8.2
Dominican Republic	197	14.0
Mexican	14	2.6
Puerto Rican	229	8.7
South American	549	9.0
Argentinean	12	2.6
Colombian	340	11.8
Ecuadorian	75	12.5
Peruvian	63	7.2
Venezuelan	8	0.9

Poverty Rate
(Income in Past 12 Months Below Poverty Level)

Group	%
Total Population	6.4
Hispanic or Latino (of any race)	5.7
Central American, ex. Mexican	3.3
Nicaraguan	1.5
Cuban	3.2
Dominican Republic	6.8
Mexican	1.0
Puerto Rican	5.2
South American	8.6
Argentinean	1.1
Colombian	9.1
Ecuadorian	7.6
Peruvian	9.5
Venezuelan	10.6

Plant City

Population

Group	Number	%TP[1]	%HP[2]
Total Population	34,721	100.0	–
Hispanic or Latino (of any race)	9,984	28.8	100.0
Central American, ex. Mexican	403	1.2	4.0
Guatemalan	128	0.4	1.3
Cuban	419	1.2	4.2
Dominican Republic	113	0.3	1.1
Mexican	6,861	19.8	68.7
Puerto Rican	1,569	4.5	15.7
South American	258	0.7	2.6

Population Growth: 2000–2010

Group	%
Total Population	16.1
Hispanic or Latino (of any race)	91.6
Central American, ex. Mexican	172.3
Cuban	215.0
Mexican	86.4
Puerto Rican	147.1

Males per 100 Females

Group	Number
Total Population	93.8
Hispanic or Latino (of any race)	106.2
Central American, ex. Mexican	115.5
Guatemalan	184.4
Cuban	100.5
Dominican Republic	82.3
Mexican	113.0
Puerto Rican	87.5
South American	80.4

Average Household Size

Group	People
Total Population	2.82
Hispanic or Latino (of any race)	3.93
Central American, ex. Mexican	3.76
Guatemalan	3.74
Cuban	3.18
Dominican Republic	3.30
Mexican	4.42
Puerto Rican	3.03
South American	3.17

Median Age

Group	Years
Total Population	33.3
Hispanic or Latino (of any race)	24.1
Central American, ex. Mexican	29.1
Guatemalan	28.5
Cuban	26.2
Dominican Republic	32.5
Mexican	22.5
Puerto Rican	28.2
South American	37.8

High School Graduates
(Universe: Population 25 Years and Over)

Group	Number	%
Total Population	16,554	79.4
Hispanic or Latino (of any race)	2,665	55.7
Mexican	1,217	41.5
Puerto Rican	780	72.9

Four-Year College Graduates
(Universe: Population 25 Years and Over)

Group	Number	%
Total Population	3,675	17.6
Hispanic or Latino (of any race)	322	6.7
Mexican	84	2.9
Puerto Rican	55	5.1

Population Age 3–17 Enrolled in Public School
(Universe: Population Age 3–17 Enrolled in School)

Group	Number	%
Total Population	6,388	93.8
Hispanic or Latino (of any race)	1,985	98.6
Mexican	1,124	97.5
Puerto Rican	386	100.0

Population Age 3–17 Enrolled in Private School
(Universe: Population Age 3–17 Enrolled in School)

Group	Number	%
Total Population	421	6.2
Hispanic or Latino (of any race)	29	1.4
Mexican	29	2.5
Puerto Rican	0	0.0

Foreign-Born Population

Group	Number	%
Total Population	5,451	15.9
Hispanic or Latino (of any race)	4,502	47.3
Mexican	3,491	56.3
Puerto Rican	0	0.0

Foreign-Born Naturalized U.S. Citizens

Group	Number	%
Total Population	1,551	28.5
Hispanic or Latino (of any race)	1,057	23.5
Mexican	633	18.1
Puerto Rican	0	0.0

Language Spoken at Home: English Only
(Universe: Population 5 Years and Over)

Group	Number	%
Total Population	22,221	71.0
Hispanic or Latino (of any race)	709	8.7
Mexican	278	5.4
Puerto Rican	139	9.1

Language Spoken at Home: Spanish
(Universe: Population 5 Years and Over)

Group	Number	%
Total Population	7,897	25.2
Hispanic or Latino (of any race)	7,484	91.3
Mexican	4,891	94.6
Puerto Rican	1,382	90.9

Unemployment Rate
(Universe: Population 16 Years and Over)

Group	%
Total Population	7.4
Hispanic or Latino (of any race)	8.9
Mexican	7.1
Puerto Rican	17.6

Class of Worker: Private Wage and Salary
(Universe: Civilian Employed Population 16 Years and Over)

Group	Number	%
Total Population	13,006	83.3
Hispanic or Latino (of any race)	3,564	93.0
Mexican	2,362	93.1
Puerto Rican	541	86.7

Class of Worker: Government
(Universe: Civilian Employed Population 16 Years and Over)

Group	Number	%
Total Population	2,038	13.1
Hispanic or Latino (of any race)	107	2.8
Mexican	32	1.3
Puerto Rican	66	10.6

Notes: (1) Percent of total population; (2) Percent of Hispanic/Latino population; Profiles include places with an overall population of at least 125,000, OR an overall population of at least 25,000 where the Hispanic/Latino population is at least 20% of the overall population. In states where less than five places meet either of these criteria, we have included places with at least 10,000 total population with the highest percentage of Hispanic/Latino population. These places are identified with an asterisk (*); Please refer to the User's Guide for a full explanation of data.

Means of Transportation to Work: Car, Truck or Van
(Universe: Workers 16 Years and Over)

Group	Number	%
Total Population	14,002	92.0
Hispanic or Latino (of any race)	3,329	88.7
Mexican	2,159	85.7
Puerto Rican	563	90.2

Means of Transportation to Work: Public Transportation (ex. Taxicab)
(Universe: Workers 16 Years and Over)

Group	Number	%
Total Population	26	0.2
Hispanic or Latino (of any race)	26	0.7
Mexican	26	1.0
Puerto Rican	0	0.0

Homeownership Rate
(Universe: Occupied Housing Units)

Group	%
Total Population	61.0
Hispanic or Latino (of any race)	43.7
Central American, ex. Mexican	46.6
Guatemalan	53.8
Cuban	52.0
Dominican Republic	48.5
Mexican	40.8
Puerto Rican	43.1
South American	56.6

Median Home Value

Group	Dollars
Total Population	170,900
Hispanic or Latino (of any race)	147,100
Mexican	134,800
Puerto Rican	151,800

Median Gross Rent

Group	Dollars
Total Population	834
Hispanic or Latino (of any race)	831
Mexican	749
Puerto Rican	848

Median Household Income
(2010 Inflation-Adjusted Dollars)

Group	Dollars
Total Population	46,930
Hispanic or Latino (of any race)	35,273
Mexican	31,964
Puerto Rican	32,132

Per Capita Income
(2010 Inflation-Adjusted Dollars)

Group	Dollars
Total Population	21,962
Hispanic or Latino (of any race)	11,812
Mexican	9,882
Puerto Rican	13,853

Households with $100,000+ Income

Group	Number	%
Total Population	1,700	14.2
Hispanic or Latino (of any race)	43	1.7
Mexican	0	0.0
Puerto Rican	17	3.2

Households with Food Stamps/SNAP Benefits During Past 12 Months

Group	Number	%
Total Population	1,322	11.0
Hispanic or Latino (of any race)	708	28.8
Mexican	468	30.4
Puerto Rican	193	36.6

Poverty Rate
(Income in Past 12 Months Below Poverty Level)

Group	%
Total Population	15.1
Hispanic or Latino (of any race)	27.5
Mexican	33.4
Puerto Rican	27.2

Plantation

Population

Group	Number	%TP[1]	%HP[2]
Total Population	84,955	100.0	–
Hispanic or Latino (of any race)	17,372	20.4	100.0
Central American, ex. Mexican	1,325	1.6	7.6
Costa Rican	139	0.2	0.8
Guatemalan	197	0.2	1.1
Honduran	307	0.4	1.8
Nicaraguan	291	0.3	1.7
Panamanian	176	0.2	1.0
Salvadoran	213	0.3	1.2
Cuban	3,398	4.0	19.6
Dominican Republic	1,016	1.2	5.8
Mexican	817	1.0	4.7
Puerto Rican	3,221	3.8	18.5
South American	6,394	7.5	36.8
Argentinean	458	0.5	2.6
Chilean	212	0.2	1.2
Colombian	2,947	3.5	17.0
Ecuadorian	624	0.7	3.6
Peruvian	1,071	1.3	6.2
Uruguayan	115	0.1	0.7
Venezuelan	836	1.0	4.8
Spaniard	218	0.3	1.3

Population Growth: 2000–2010

Group	%
Total Population	2.4
Hispanic or Latino (of any race)	60.0
Central American, ex. Mexican	113.4
Honduran	127.4
Panamanian	76.0
Salvadoran	50.0
Cuban	66.3
Dominican Republic	162.5
Mexican	46.2
Puerto Rican	68.2
South American	103.8
Argentinean	158.8
Colombian	96.2
Ecuadorian	143.8
Peruvian	121.3
Venezuelan	78.6

Males per 100 Females

Group	Number
Total Population	90.3
Hispanic or Latino (of any race)	85.6
Central American, ex. Mexican	80.3
Costa Rican	78.2
Guatemalan	85.8
Honduran	70.6
Nicaraguan	85.4
Panamanian	76.0
Salvadoran	90.2
Cuban	95.6
Dominican Republic	75.5
Mexican	88.7
Puerto Rican	83.8
South American	82.3
Argentinean	83.2
Chilean	79.7
Colombian	80.9
Ecuadorian	85.2
Peruvian	78.2
Uruguayan	130.0
Venezuelan	88.7
Spaniard	118.0

Average Household Size

Group	People
Total Population	2.47
Hispanic or Latino (of any race)	2.76
Central American, ex. Mexican	3.01
Costa Rican	2.85
Guatemalan	3.13
Honduran	3.05
Nicaraguan	3.14
Panamanian	2.46
Salvadoran	3.42
Cuban	2.71
Dominican Republic	3.09
Mexican	2.86
Puerto Rican	2.63
South American	2.79
Argentinean	2.70
Chilean	2.66
Colombian	2.80
Ecuadorian	2.81
Peruvian	2.83
Uruguayan	2.78
Venezuelan	2.80
Spaniard	2.61

Median Age

Group	Years
Total Population	39.7
Hispanic or Latino (of any race)	34.0
Central American, ex. Mexican	33.5
Costa Rican	38.3
Guatemalan	31.9
Honduran	34.1
Nicaraguan	31.6
Panamanian	35.7
Salvadoran	31.9
Cuban	37.5
Dominican Republic	30.3
Mexican	29.9
Puerto Rican	31.7
South American	36.0
Argentinean	37.4
Chilean	36.8
Colombian	35.8
Ecuadorian	36.5
Peruvian	36.8
Uruguayan	37.3
Venezuelan	33.3
Spaniard	38.6

High School Graduates
(Universe: Population 25 Years and Over)

Group	Number	%
Total Population	56,211	94.0
Hispanic or Latino (of any race)	9,354	90.9
Central American, ex. Mexican	535	93.2
Cuban	2,081	90.5
Dominican Republic	650	76.6
Puerto Rican	1,522	94.0
South American	3,589	93.3
Colombian	1,523	91.9

Four-Year College Graduates
(Universe: Population 25 Years and Over)

Group	Number	%
Total Population	25,137	42.0
Hispanic or Latino (of any race)	4,178	40.6
Central American, ex. Mexican	189	32.9
Cuban	870	37.8
Dominican Republic	240	28.3
Puerto Rican	666	41.1
South American	1,763	45.8
Colombian	735	44.3

Population Age 3–17 Enrolled in Public School
(Universe: Population Age 3–17 Enrolled in School)

Group	Number	%
Total Population	9,877	68.7
Hispanic or Latino (of any race)	1,786	63.0
Central American, ex. Mexican	168	76.0
Cuban	258	58.8
Dominican Republic	214	71.3
Puerto Rican	266	69.5
South American	615	60.0
Colombian	326	72.1

Population Age 3–17 Enrolled in Private School
(Universe: Population Age 3–17 Enrolled in School)

Group	Number	%
Total Population	4,501	31.3
Hispanic or Latino (of any race)	1,049	37.0
Central American, ex. Mexican	53	24.0
Cuban	181	41.2
Dominican Republic	86	28.7
Puerto Rican	117	30.5
South American	410	40.0
Colombian	126	27.9

Notes: (1) Percent of total population; (2) Percent of Hispanic/Latino population; Profiles include places with an overall population of at least 125,000, OR an overall population of at least 25,000 where the Hispanic/Latino population is at least 20% of the overall population. In states where less than five places meet either of these criteria, we have included places with at least 10,000 total population with the highest percentage of Hispanic/Latino population. These places are identified with an asterisk (*); Please refer to the User's Guide for a full explanation of data.

Foreign-Born Population

Group	Number	%
Total Population	22,380	26.3
Hispanic or Latino (of any race)	7,992	51.8
Central American, ex. Mexican	588	61.4
Cuban	1,377	42.5
Dominican Republic	828	67.0
Puerto Rican	81	3.5
South American	4,369	73.6
Colombian	1,711	73.2

Foreign-Born Naturalized U.S. Citizens

Group	Number	%
Total Population	12,665	56.6
Hispanic or Latino (of any race)	4,250	53.2
Central American, ex. Mexican	180	30.6
Cuban	1,093	79.4
Dominican Republic	558	67.4
Puerto Rican	16	19.8
South American	1,978	45.3
Colombian	882	51.5

Language Spoken at Home: English Only
(Universe: Population 5 Years and Over)

Group	Number	%
Total Population	58,124	72.9
Hispanic or Latino (of any race)	3,077	21.4
Central American, ex. Mexican	193	22.0
Cuban	744	24.2
Dominican Republic	127	10.5
Puerto Rican	750	33.8
South American	580	10.7
Colombian	327	14.9

Language Spoken at Home: Spanish
(Universe: Population 5 Years and Over)

Group	Number	%
Total Population	12,529	15.7
Hispanic or Latino (of any race)	11,207	78.0
Central American, ex. Mexican	684	78.0
Cuban	2,309	75.1
Dominican Republic	1,086	89.5
Puerto Rican	1,468	66.2
South American	4,808	88.8
Colombian	1,866	85.1

Unemployment Rate
(Universe: Population 16 Years and Over)

Group	%
Total Population	6.5
Hispanic or Latino (of any race)	7.4
Central American, ex. Mexican	8.8
Cuban	5.0
Dominican Republic	7.6
Puerto Rican	8.8
South American	8.6
Colombian	8.2

Class of Worker: Private Wage and Salary
(Universe: Civilian Employed Population 16 Years and Over)

Group	Number	%
Total Population	37,116	80.6
Hispanic or Latino (of any race)	7,453	85.4
Central American, ex. Mexican	488	91.0
Cuban	1,518	85.4
Dominican Republic	571	87.2
Puerto Rican	1,194	80.5
South American	3,047	88.6
Colombian	1,181	87.3

Class of Worker: Government
(Universe: Civilian Employed Population 16 Years and Over)

Group	Number	%
Total Population	6,633	14.4
Hispanic or Latino (of any race)	833	9.5
Central American, ex. Mexican	13	2.4
Cuban	159	8.9
Dominican Republic	84	12.8
Puerto Rican	275	18.5
South American	187	5.4
Colombian	94	6.9

Means of Transportation to Work: Car, Truck or Van
(Universe: Workers 16 Years and Over)

Group	Number	%
Total Population	40,976	91.3
Hispanic or Latino (of any race)	7,885	92.2
Central American, ex. Mexican	505	97.5
Cuban	1,603	92.9
Dominican Republic	655	100.0
Puerto Rican	1,360	94.7
South American	2,947	87.1
Colombian	1,066	78.8

Means of Transportation to Work: Public Transportation (ex. Taxicab)
(Universe: Workers 16 Years and Over)

Group	Number	%
Total Population	747	1.7
Hispanic or Latino (of any race)	152	1.8
Central American, ex. Mexican	0	0.0
Cuban	0	0.0
Dominican Republic	0	0.0
Puerto Rican	49	3.4
South American	103	3.0
Colombian	90	6.7

Homeownership Rate
(Universe: Occupied Housing Units)

Group	%
Total Population	69.1
Hispanic or Latino (of any race)	57.9
Central American, ex. Mexican	56.5
Costa Rican	68.8
Guatemalan	57.1
Honduran	59.1
Nicaraguan	46.9
Panamanian	52.2
Salvadoran	58.3
Cuban	69.6
Dominican Republic	49.0
Mexican	49.4
Puerto Rican	49.9
South American	57.9
Argentinean	67.4
Chilean	62.4
Colombian	58.3
Ecuadorian	59.3
Peruvian	58.0
Uruguayan	49.0
Venezuelan	51.6
Spaniard	74.0

Median Home Value

Group	Dollars
Total Population	307,000
Hispanic or Latino (of any race)	265,900
Central American, ex. Mexican	274,200
Cuban	325,800
Dominican Republic	277,500
Puerto Rican	227,900
South American	230,900
Colombian	214,800

Median Gross Rent

Group	Dollars
Total Population	1,296
Hispanic or Latino (of any race)	1,295
Central American, ex. Mexican	1,233
Cuban	1,371
Dominican Republic	1,179
Puerto Rican	1,161
South American	1,300
Colombian	1,307

Median Household Income
(2010 Inflation-Adjusted Dollars)

Group	Dollars
Total Population	66,435
Hispanic or Latino (of any race)	60,770
Central American, ex. Mexican	72,232
Cuban	75,313
Dominican Republic	86,528
Puerto Rican	69,696
South American	50,412
Colombian	35,954

Per Capita Income
(2010 Inflation-Adjusted Dollars)

Group	Dollars
Total Population	35,994
Hispanic or Latino (of any race)	29,797
Central American, ex. Mexican	25,807
Cuban	33,816
Dominican Republic	21,653
Puerto Rican	33,314
South American	29,998
Colombian	24,687

Households with $100,000+ Income

Group	Number	%
Total Population	10,234	29.9
Hispanic or Latino (of any race)	1,483	26.4
Central American, ex. Mexican	74	29.1
Cuban	391	32.3
Dominican Republic	114	45.1
Puerto Rican	273	26.2
South American	467	21.9
Colombian	151	19.0

Households with Food Stamps/SNAP Benefits During Past 12 Months

Group	Number	%
Total Population	1,323	3.9
Hispanic or Latino (of any race)	266	4.7
Central American, ex. Mexican	0	0.0
Cuban	85	7.0
Dominican Republic	15	5.9
Puerto Rican	37	3.6
South American	105	4.9
Colombian	91	11.5

Poverty Rate
(Income in Past 12 Months Below Poverty Level)

Group	%
Total Population	7.3
Hispanic or Latino (of any race)	7.4
Central American, ex. Mexican	14.4
Cuban	6.9
Dominican Republic	1.2
Puerto Rican	6.5
South American	5.7
Colombian	5.4

Poinciana

Population

Group	Number	%TP[1]	%HP[2]
Total Population	53,193	100.0	–
Hispanic or Latino (of any race)	27,234	51.2	100.0
Central American, ex. Mexican	1,389	2.6	5.1
Guatemalan	176	0.3	0.6
Honduran	315	0.6	1.2
Nicaraguan	236	0.4	0.9
Panamanian	208	0.4	0.8
Salvadoran	349	0.7	1.3
Cuban	1,150	2.2	4.2
Dominican Republic	1,833	3.4	6.7
Mexican	927	1.7	3.4
Puerto Rican	19,055	35.8	70.0
South American	1,791	3.4	6.6
Argentinean	117	0.2	0.4
Colombian	828	1.6	3.0
Ecuadorian	285	0.5	1.0
Peruvian	280	0.5	1.0
Venezuelan	155	0.3	0.6

Population Growth: 2000–2010

Group	%
Total Population	289.8
Hispanic or Latino (of any race)	405.0
Central American, ex. Mexican	608.7
Cuban	751.9
Dominican Republic	744.7
Mexican	581.6
Puerto Rican	402.9
South American	495.0
Colombian	463.3

Notes: (1) Percent of total population; (2) Percent of Hispanic/Latino population; Profiles include places with an overall population of at least 125,000, OR an overall population of at least 25,000 where the Hispanic/Latino population is at least 20% of the overall population. In states where less than five places meet either of these criteria, we have included places with at least 10,000 total population with the highest percentage of Hispanic/Latino population. These places are identified with an asterisk (*); Please refer to the User's Guide for a full explanation of data.

Males per 100 Females

Group	Number
Total Population	92.5
Hispanic or Latino (of any race)	93.4
Central American, ex. Mexican	82.3
Guatemalan	87.2
Honduran	88.6
Nicaraguan	108.8
Panamanian	50.7
Salvadoran	84.7
Cuban	101.8
Dominican Republic	85.5
Mexican	109.3
Puerto Rican	94.7
South American	78.0
Argentinean	88.7
Colombian	72.9
Ecuadorian	74.8
Peruvian	73.9
Venezuelan	84.5

Average Household Size

Group	People
Total Population	3.14
Hispanic or Latino (of any race)	3.56
Central American, ex. Mexican	3.77
Guatemalan	4.15
Honduran	3.81
Nicaraguan	4.03
Panamanian	3.22
Salvadoran	3.84
Cuban	3.39
Dominican Republic	3.66
Mexican	4.13
Puerto Rican	3.55
South American	3.48
Argentinean	3.05
Colombian	3.58
Ecuadorian	3.30
Peruvian	3.65
Venezuelan	3.22

Median Age

Group	Years
Total Population	35.1
Hispanic or Latino (of any race)	31.1
Central American, ex. Mexican	35.5
Guatemalan	37.0
Honduran	35.2
Nicaraguan	34.0
Panamanian	37.3
Salvadoran	35.1
Cuban	35.9
Dominican Republic	32.3
Mexican	22.7
Puerto Rican	30.5
South American	39.1
Argentinean	40.8
Colombian	38.8
Ecuadorian	43.3
Peruvian	40.6
Venezuelan	33.5

High School Graduates
(Universe: Population 25 Years and Over)

Group	Number	%
Total Population	26,230	84.9
Hispanic or Latino (of any race)	12,031	82.9
Central American, ex. Mexican	666	71.1
Dominican Republic	707	82.3
Puerto Rican	8,769	86.2
South American	1,020	83.3

Four-Year College Graduates
(Universe: Population 25 Years and Over)

Group	Number	%
Total Population	4,907	15.9
Hispanic or Latino (of any race)	1,751	12.1
Central American, ex. Mexican	78	8.3
Dominican Republic	170	19.8
Puerto Rican	1,209	11.9
South American	172	14.0

Population Age 3–17 Enrolled in Public School
(Universe: Population Age 3–17 Enrolled in School)

Group	Number	%
Total Population	11,614	94.3
Hispanic or Latino (of any race)	6,883	94.8
Central American, ex. Mexican	415	82.8
Dominican Republic	390	95.8
Puerto Rican	5,324	95.9
South American	242	93.8

Population Age 3–17 Enrolled in Private School
(Universe: Population Age 3–17 Enrolled in School)

Group	Number	%
Total Population	696	5.7
Hispanic or Latino (of any race)	374	5.2
Central American, ex. Mexican	86	17.2
Dominican Republic	17	4.2
Puerto Rican	229	4.1
South American	16	6.2

Foreign-Born Population

Group	Number	%
Total Population	10,351	20.7
Hispanic or Latino (of any race)	4,144	16.0
Central American, ex. Mexican	1,040	61.4
Dominican Republic	733	51.3
Puerto Rican	50	0.3
South American	1,208	72.3

Foreign-Born Naturalized U.S. Citizens

Group	Number	%
Total Population	5,780	55.8
Hispanic or Latino (of any race)	2,023	48.8
Central American, ex. Mexican	453	43.6
Dominican Republic	599	81.7
Puerto Rican	50	100.0
South American	613	50.7

Language Spoken at Home: English Only
(Universe: Population 5 Years and Over)

Group	Number	%
Total Population	21,847	46.9
Hispanic or Latino (of any race)	3,064	12.9
Central American, ex. Mexican	380	25.1
Dominican Republic	122	9.2
Puerto Rican	2,181	12.5
South American	15	1.0

Language Spoken at Home: Spanish
(Universe: Population 5 Years and Over)

Group	Number	%
Total Population	21,189	45.5
Hispanic or Latino (of any race)	20,689	86.9
Central American, ex. Mexican	1,131	74.9
Dominican Republic	1,179	89.3
Puerto Rican	15,295	87.4
South American	1,471	98.4

Unemployment Rate
(Universe: Population 16 Years and Over)

Group	%
Total Population	13.7
Hispanic or Latino (of any race)	14.0
Central American, ex. Mexican	10.4
Dominican Republic	21.5
Puerto Rican	12.3
South American	23.8

Class of Worker: Private Wage and Salary
(Universe: Civilian Employed Population 16 Years and Over)

Group	Number	%
Total Population	17,366	87.3
Hispanic or Latino (of any race)	9,039	88.2
Central American, ex. Mexican	527	82.3
Dominican Republic	406	79.0
Puerto Rican	6,770	89.3
South American	668	96.8

Class of Worker: Government
(Universe: Civilian Employed Population 16 Years and Over)

Group	Number	%
Total Population	1,822	9.2
Hispanic or Latino (of any race)	977	9.5
Central American, ex. Mexican	96	15.0
Dominican Republic	108	21.0
Puerto Rican	659	8.7
South American	5	0.7

Means of Transportation to Work: Car, Truck or Van
(Universe: Workers 16 Years and Over)

Group	Number	%
Total Population	18,140	94.9
Hispanic or Latino (of any race)	9,510	96.1
Central American, ex. Mexican	640	100.0
Dominican Republic	501	97.5
Puerto Rican	6,969	95.4
South American	630	94.6

Means of Transportation to Work: Public Transportation (ex. Taxicab)
(Universe: Workers 16 Years and Over)

Group	Number	%
Total Population	256	1.3
Hispanic or Latino (of any race)	170	1.7
Central American, ex. Mexican	0	0.0
Dominican Republic	13	2.5
Puerto Rican	150	2.1
South American	0	0.0

Homeownership Rate
(Universe: Occupied Housing Units)

Group	%
Total Population	76.0
Hispanic or Latino (of any race)	71.4
Central American, ex. Mexican	80.4
Guatemalan	85.4
Honduran	79.7
Nicaraguan	81.2
Panamanian	84.1
Salvadoran	75.5
Cuban	72.0
Dominican Republic	72.6
Mexican	66.3
Puerto Rican	69.5
South American	83.0
Argentinean	79.5
Colombian	82.0
Ecuadorian	88.9
Peruvian	89.2
Venezuelan	67.6

Median Home Value

Group	Dollars
Total Population	189,500
Hispanic or Latino (of any race)	175,800
Central American, ex. Mexican	171,900
Dominican Republic	205,000
Puerto Rican	175,000
South American	230,600

Median Gross Rent

Group	Dollars
Total Population	1,126
Hispanic or Latino (of any race)	1,105
Central American, ex. Mexican	972
Dominican Republic	–
Puerto Rican	1,140
South American	1,082

Median Household Income
(2010 Inflation-Adjusted Dollars)

Group	Dollars
Total Population	45,210
Hispanic or Latino (of any race)	43,755
Central American, ex. Mexican	41,471
Dominican Republic	46,050
Puerto Rican	44,948
South American	35,882

Per Capita Income
(2010 Inflation-Adjusted Dollars)

Group	Dollars
Total Population	17,407
Hispanic or Latino (of any race)	14,519
Central American, ex. Mexican	17,543
Dominican Republic	13,667
Puerto Rican	14,312
South American	16,051

STATE & PLACE PROFILES

Notes: (1) Percent of total population; (2) Percent of Hispanic/Latino population; Profiles include places with an overall population of at least 125,000, OR an overall population of at least 25,000 where the Hispanic/Latino population is at least 20% of the overall population. In states where less than five places meet either of these criteria, we have included places with at least 10,000 total population with the highest percentage of Hispanic/Latino population. These places are identified with an asterisk (*); Please refer to the User's Guide for a full explanation of data.

Households with $100,000+ Income

Group	Number	%
Total Population	1,465	8.9
Hispanic or Latino (of any race)	407	5.5
Central American, ex. Mexican	30	5.9
Dominican Republic	67	15.3
Puerto Rican	260	5.0
South American	36	6.7

Households with Food Stamps/SNAP Benefits During Past 12 Months

Group	Number	%
Total Population	1,773	10.8
Hispanic or Latino (of any race)	960	12.9
Central American, ex. Mexican	0	0.0
Dominican Republic	42	9.6
Puerto Rican	724	13.8
South American	111	20.8

Poverty Rate
(Income in Past 12 Months Below Poverty Level)

Group	%
Total Population	16.1
Hispanic or Latino (of any race)	17.1
Central American, ex. Mexican	18.0
Dominican Republic	14.9
Puerto Rican	16.2
South American	14.3

Port Saint Lucie

Population

Group	Number	%TP[1]	%HP[2]
Total Population	164,603	100.0	–
Hispanic or Latino (of any race)	30,250	18.4	100.0
Central American, ex. Mexican	3,241	2.0	10.7
Costa Rican	170	0.1	0.6
Guatemalan	712	0.4	2.4
Honduran	967	0.6	3.2
Nicaraguan	537	0.3	1.8
Panamanian	263	0.2	0.9
Salvadoran	565	0.3	1.9
Cuban	4,120	2.5	13.6
Dominican Republic	1,686	1.0	5.6
Mexican	4,335	2.6	14.3
Puerto Rican	9,737	5.9	32.2
South American	5,157	3.1	17.0
Argentinean	369	0.2	1.2
Chilean	193	0.1	0.6
Colombian	2,518	1.5	8.3
Ecuadorian	718	0.4	2.4
Peruvian	701	0.4	2.3
Uruguayan	102	0.1	0.3
Venezuelan	441	0.3	1.5
Spaniard	337	0.2	1.1

Population Growth: 2000–2010

Group	%
Total Population	85.4
Hispanic or Latino (of any race)	353.0
Central American, ex. Mexican	757.4
Guatemalan	547.3
Cuban	424.2
Dominican Republic	773.6
Mexican	569.0
Puerto Rican	246.4
South American	713.4
Colombian	799.3
Ecuadorian	541.1

Males per 100 Females

Group	Number
Total Population	94.6
Hispanic or Latino (of any race)	95.6
Central American, ex. Mexican	104.4
Costa Rican	86.8
Guatemalan	138.9
Honduran	95.0
Nicaraguan	92.5
Panamanian	67.5
Salvadoran	121.6
Cuban	99.6
Dominican Republic	93.1
Mexican	103.5
Puerto Rican	96.4
South American	82.2
Argentinean	108.5
Chilean	94.9
Colombian	76.3
Ecuadorian	93.0
Peruvian	77.0
Uruguayan	85.5
Venezuelan	87.7
Spaniard	94.8

Average Household Size

Group	People
Total Population	2.69
Hispanic or Latino (of any race)	3.38
Central American, ex. Mexican	4.03
Costa Rican	3.33
Guatemalan	4.47
Honduran	4.17
Nicaraguan	3.90
Panamanian	2.79
Salvadoran	4.45
Cuban	3.12
Dominican Republic	3.67
Mexican	4.16
Puerto Rican	3.09
South American	3.35
Argentinean	3.39
Chilean	3.40
Colombian	3.38
Ecuadorian	3.22
Peruvian	3.30
Uruguayan	3.53
Venezuelan	3.40
Spaniard	2.81

Median Age

Group	Years
Total Population	39.8
Hispanic or Latino (of any race)	30.8
Central American, ex. Mexican	29.9
Costa Rican	36.5
Guatemalan	26.4
Honduran	29.5
Nicaraguan	31.1
Panamanian	38.1
Salvadoran	29.6
Cuban	35.7
Dominican Republic	31.2
Mexican	22.8
Puerto Rican	31.6
South American	36.0
Argentinean	36.3
Chilean	36.5
Colombian	36.1
Ecuadorian	36.2
Peruvian	36.3
Uruguayan	38.3
Venezuelan	33.1
Spaniard	39.1

High School Graduates
(Universe: Population 25 Years and Over)

Group	Number	%
Total Population	91,434	86.8
Hispanic or Latino (of any race)	11,490	76.8
Central American, ex. Mexican	1,336	74.1
Cuban	1,660	76.9
Dominican Republic	647	85.0
Mexican	1,340	63.1
Puerto Rican	3,671	75.7
South American	2,377	89.8
Colombian	1,485	91.0

Four-Year College Graduates
(Universe: Population 25 Years and Over)

Group	Number	%
Total Population	18,525	17.6
Hispanic or Latino (of any race)	2,074	13.9
Central American, ex. Mexican	309	17.1
Cuban	326	15.1
Dominican Republic	174	22.9
Mexican	155	7.3
Puerto Rican	414	8.5
South American	561	21.2
Colombian	356	21.8

Population Age 3–17 Enrolled in Public School
(Universe: Population Age 3–17 Enrolled in School)

Group	Number	%
Total Population	25,872	88.6
Hispanic or Latino (of any race)	6,227	91.2
Central American, ex. Mexican	473	81.6
Cuban	628	91.0
Dominican Republic	441	98.2
Mexican	1,360	95.8
Puerto Rican	2,138	92.2
South American	813	93.6
Colombian	539	95.4

Population Age 3–17 Enrolled in Private School
(Universe: Population Age 3–17 Enrolled in School)

Group	Number	%
Total Population	3,328	11.4
Hispanic or Latino (of any race)	601	8.8
Central American, ex. Mexican	107	18.4
Cuban	62	9.0
Dominican Republic	8	1.8
Mexican	60	4.2
Puerto Rican	182	7.8
South American	56	6.4
Colombian	26	4.6

Foreign-Born Population

Group	Number	%
Total Population	26,171	16.9
Hispanic or Latino (of any race)	8,960	34.3
Central American, ex. Mexican	2,147	71.9
Cuban	1,793	54.5
Dominican Republic	649	46.5
Mexican	1,267	28.8
Puerto Rican	91	1.1
South American	2,639	63.5
Colombian	1,630	62.5

Foreign-Born Naturalized U.S. Citizens

Group	Number	%
Total Population	14,244	54.4
Hispanic or Latino (of any race)	4,047	45.2
Central American, ex. Mexican	752	35.0
Cuban	1,186	66.1
Dominican Republic	420	64.7
Mexican	333	26.3
Puerto Rican	68	74.7
South American	1,121	42.5
Colombian	700	42.9

Language Spoken at Home: English Only
(Universe: Population 5 Years and Over)

Group	Number	%
Total Population	112,806	78.2
Hispanic or Latino (of any race)	5,499	23.3
Central American, ex. Mexican	211	7.8
Cuban	529	17.5
Dominican Republic	209	16.5
Mexican	1,085	28.4
Puerto Rican	2,624	34.0
South American	410	10.7
Colombian	187	7.6

Language Spoken at Home: Spanish
(Universe: Population 5 Years and Over)

Group	Number	%
Total Population	19,591	13.6
Hispanic or Latino (of any race)	17,969	76.3
Central American, ex. Mexican	2,502	92.2
Cuban	2,486	82.5
Dominican Republic	1,056	83.5
Mexican	2,739	71.6
Puerto Rican	5,088	65.9
South American	3,402	88.9
Colombian	2,264	92.4

Unemployment Rate
(Universe: Population 16 Years and Over)

Group	%
Total Population	11.5
Hispanic or Latino (of any race)	16.8
Central American, ex. Mexican	14.8

Notes: (1) Percent of total population; (2) Percent of Hispanic/Latino population; Profiles include places with an overall population of at least 125,000, OR an overall population of at least 25,000 where the Hispanic/Latino population is at least 20% of the overall population. In states where less than five places meet either of these criteria, we have included places with at least 10,000 total population with the highest percentage of Hispanic/Latino population. These places are identified with an asterisk (*); Please refer to the User's Guide for a full explanation of data.

Cuban		15.2
Dominican Republic		10.3
Mexican		24.5
Puerto Rican		15.8
South American		19.1
Colombian		23.0

Class of Worker: Private Wage and Salary
(Universe: Civilian Employed Population 16 Years and Over)

Group	Number	%
Total Population	55,829	81.6
Hispanic or Latino (of any race)	8,567	83.0
Central American, ex. Mexican	1,236	84.7
Cuban	1,069	75.1
Dominican Republic	517	86.2
Mexican	1,313	89.9
Puerto Rican	2,633	84.2
South American	1,446	83.6
Colombian	827	80.7

Class of Worker: Government
(Universe: Civilian Employed Population 16 Years and Over)

Group	Number	%
Total Population	8,695	12.7
Hispanic or Latino (of any race)	1,116	10.8
Central American, ex. Mexican	43	2.9
Cuban	284	20.0
Dominican Republic	55	9.2
Mexican	119	8.2
Puerto Rican	428	13.7
South American	105	6.1
Colombian	72	7.0

Means of Transportation to Work: Car, Truck or Van
(Universe: Workers 16 Years and Over)

Group	Number	%
Total Population	61,915	93.6
Hispanic or Latino (of any race)	9,168	92.4
Central American, ex. Mexican	1,125	84.6
Cuban	1,241	90.8
Dominican Republic	492	81.3
Mexican	1,380	97.5
Puerto Rican	3,011	97.4
South American	1,473	90.8
Colombian	885	96.4

Means of Transportation to Work: Public Transportation (ex. Taxicab)
(Universe: Workers 16 Years and Over)

Group	Number	%
Total Population	154	0.2
Hispanic or Latino (of any race)	22	0.2
Central American, ex. Mexican	0	0.0
Cuban	0	0.0
Dominican Republic	0	0.0
Mexican	0	0.0
Puerto Rican	10	0.3
South American	12	0.7
Colombian	0	0.0

Homeownership Rate
(Universe: Occupied Housing Units)

Group	%
Total Population	78.1
Hispanic or Latino (of any race)	70.4
Central American, ex. Mexican	69.4
Costa Rican	85.4
Guatemalan	69.8
Honduran	64.5
Nicaraguan	71.9
Panamanian	71.9
Salvadoran	66.4
Cuban	74.9
Dominican Republic	70.4
Mexican	63.7
Puerto Rican	69.4
South American	72.1
Argentinean	74.1
Chilean	84.2
Colombian	69.2
Ecuadorian	74.7
Peruvian	76.6
Uruguayan	70.6
Venezuelan	68.6
Spaniard	80.0

Median Home Value

Group	Dollars
Total Population	193,200
Hispanic or Latino (of any race)	194,100
Central American, ex. Mexican	164,400
Cuban	204,900
Dominican Republic	201,600
Mexican	217,700
Puerto Rican	192,300
South American	208,900
Colombian	212,300

Median Gross Rent

Group	Dollars
Total Population	1,176
Hispanic or Latino (of any race)	1,170
Central American, ex. Mexican	975
Cuban	1,153
Dominican Republic	984
Mexican	1,201
Puerto Rican	1,186
South American	1,308
Colombian	1,320

Median Household Income
(2010 Inflation-Adjusted Dollars)

Group	Dollars
Total Population	49,657
Hispanic or Latino (of any race)	48,922
Central American, ex. Mexican	49,227
Cuban	57,500
Dominican Republic	66,429
Mexican	44,750
Puerto Rican	48,196
South American	46,728
Colombian	45,037

Per Capita Income
(2010 Inflation-Adjusted Dollars)

Group	Dollars
Total Population	22,793
Hispanic or Latino (of any race)	16,302
Central American, ex. Mexican	15,830
Cuban	21,670
Dominican Republic	18,514
Mexican	12,407
Puerto Rican	15,080
South American	17,223
Colombian	17,609

Households with $100,000+ Income

Group	Number	%
Total Population	8,066	14.3
Hispanic or Latino (of any race)	623	8.5
Central American, ex. Mexican	118	14.8
Cuban	209	18.1
Dominican Republic	22	5.8
Mexican	66	8.6
Puerto Rican	119	4.6
South American	47	3.7
Colombian	27	3.8

Households with Food Stamps/SNAP Benefits During Past 12 Months

Group	Number	%
Total Population	3,886	6.9
Hispanic or Latino (of any race)	906	12.4
Central American, ex. Mexican	66	8.3
Cuban	125	10.9
Dominican Republic	55	14.4
Mexican	39	5.1
Puerto Rican	510	19.5
South American	111	8.7
Colombian	34	4.8

Poverty Rate
(Income in Past 12 Months Below Poverty Level)

Group	%
Total Population	11.0
Hispanic or Latino (of any race)	18.8
Central American, ex. Mexican	20.5
Cuban	12.9
Dominican Republic	1.1
Mexican	27.5
Puerto Rican	22.6
South American	12.4
Colombian	13.9

Richmond West

Population

Group	Number	%TP[1]	%HP[2]
Total Population	31,973	100.0	–
Hispanic or Latino (of any race)	25,110	78.5	100.0
Central American, ex. Mexican	3,300	10.3	13.1
Costa Rican	105	0.3	0.4
Guatemalan	172	0.5	0.7
Honduran	540	1.7	2.2
Nicaraguan	2,039	6.4	8.1
Panamanian	207	0.6	0.8
Salvadoran	235	0.7	0.9
Cuban	12,818	40.1	51.0
Dominican Republic	1,112	3.5	4.4
Mexican	363	1.1	1.4
Puerto Rican	1,924	6.0	7.7
South American	4,392	13.7	17.5
Argentinean	223	0.7	0.9
Chilean	165	0.5	0.7
Colombian	2,117	6.6	8.4
Ecuadorian	284	0.9	1.1
Peruvian	954	3.0	3.8
Venezuelan	537	1.7	2.1
Spaniard	140	0.4	0.6

Population Growth: 2000–2010

Group	%
Total Population	13.9
Hispanic or Latino (of any race)	27.7
Central American, ex. Mexican	68.1
Honduran	135.8
Nicaraguan	73.1
Panamanian	-1.4
Salvadoran	94.2
Cuban	55.8
Dominican Republic	59.8
Mexican	34.9
Puerto Rican	-5.9
South American	51.1
Argentinean	100.9
Chilean	27.9
Colombian	46.9
Ecuadorian	44.2
Peruvian	88.5
Venezuelan	40.9

Males per 100 Females

Group	Number
Total Population	94.6
Hispanic or Latino (of any race)	93.5
Central American, ex. Mexican	86.3
Costa Rican	56.7
Guatemalan	95.5
Honduran	75.3
Nicaraguan	91.3
Panamanian	78.4
Salvadoran	88.0
Cuban	101.2
Dominican Republic	87.2
Mexican	85.2
Puerto Rican	88.4
South American	80.9
Argentinean	110.4
Chilean	79.3
Colombian	75.1
Ecuadorian	100.0
Peruvian	80.0
Venezuelan	82.0
Spaniard	79.5

Average Household Size

Group	People
Total Population	3.57
Hispanic or Latino (of any race)	3.67
Central American, ex. Mexican	4.14
Costa Rican	3.74
Guatemalan	3.85

Notes: (1) Percent of total population; (2) Percent of Hispanic/Latino population; Profiles include places with an overall population of at least 125,000, OR an overall population of at least 25,000 where the Hispanic/Latino population is at least 20% of the overall population. In states where less than five places meet either of these criteria, we have included places with at least 10,000 total population with the highest percentage of Hispanic/Latino population. These places are identified with an asterisk (*); Please refer to the User's Guide for a full explanation of data.

Honduran	4.31
Nicaraguan	4.23
Panamanian	3.40
Salvadoran	4.08
Cuban	3.60
Dominican Republic	3.72
Mexican	3.86
Puerto Rican	3.39
South American	3.72
Argentinean	3.50
Chilean	3.64
Colombian	3.73
Ecuadorian	3.87
Peruvian	3.71
Venezuelan	3.78
Spaniard	2.95

Median Age

Group	Years
Total Population	36.6
Hispanic or Latino (of any race)	37.2
Central American, ex. Mexican	36.3
Costa Rican	37.5
Guatemalan	39.0
Honduran	35.2
Nicaraguan	35.4
Panamanian	42.4
Salvadoran	37.1
Cuban	38.3
Dominican Republic	35.8
Mexican	32.2
Puerto Rican	37.4
South American	38.9
Argentinean	36.6
Chilean	37.8
Colombian	38.9
Ecuadorian	41.1
Peruvian	40.9
Venezuelan	34.9
Spaniard	41.3

High School Graduates
(Universe: Population 25 Years and Over)

Group	Number	%
Total Population	17,322	85.9
Hispanic or Latino (of any race)	13,844	84.8
Central American, ex. Mexican	1,791	83.0
Nicaraguan	1,309	82.2
Cuban	6,824	81.9
Dominican Republic	794	90.5
Puerto Rican	967	91.6
South American	2,992	91.6
Colombian	1,569	89.2

Four-Year College Graduates
(Universe: Population 25 Years and Over)

Group	Number	%
Total Population	4,519	22.4
Hispanic or Latino (of any race)	3,496	21.4
Central American, ex. Mexican	621	28.8
Nicaraguan	495	31.1
Cuban	1,523	18.3
Dominican Republic	190	21.7
Puerto Rican	231	21.9
South American	803	24.6
Colombian	324	18.4

Population Age 3–17 Enrolled in Public School
(Universe: Population Age 3–17 Enrolled in School)

Group	Number	%
Total Population	5,642	82.7
Hispanic or Latino (of any race)	4,146	86.6
Central American, ex. Mexican	489	88.4
Nicaraguan	403	89.8
Cuban	2,193	85.5
Dominican Republic	87	77.0
Puerto Rican	314	85.3
South American	708	92.3
Colombian	388	91.9

Population Age 3–17 Enrolled in Private School
(Universe: Population Age 3–17 Enrolled in School)

Group	Number	%
Total Population	1,177	17.3
Hispanic or Latino (of any race)	644	13.4
Central American, ex. Mexican	64	11.6
Nicaraguan	46	10.2
Cuban	372	14.5
Dominican Republic	26	23.0
Puerto Rican	54	14.7
South American	59	7.7
Colombian	34	8.1

Foreign-Born Population

Group	Number	%
Total Population	16,623	51.2
Hispanic or Latino (of any race)	14,700	58.0
Central American, ex. Mexican	2,224	66.8
Nicaraguan	1,544	63.5
Cuban	7,625	60.3
Dominican Republic	694	62.5
Puerto Rican	0	0.0
South American	3,691	70.2
Colombian	1,895	66.6

Foreign-Born Naturalized U.S. Citizens

Group	Number	%
Total Population	10,323	62.1
Hispanic or Latino (of any race)	9,095	61.9
Central American, ex. Mexican	1,403	63.1
Nicaraguan	951	61.6
Cuban	4,922	64.6
Dominican Republic	617	88.9
Puerto Rican	0	0.0
South American	1,954	52.9
Colombian	1,047	55.3

Language Spoken at Home: English Only
(Universe: Population 5 Years and Over)

Group	Number	%
Total Population	5,353	17.5
Hispanic or Latino (of any race)	1,308	5.4
Central American, ex. Mexican	74	2.3
Nicaraguan	13	0.6
Cuban	750	6.3
Dominican Republic	58	5.4
Puerto Rican	254	16.3
South American	126	2.5
Colombian	0	0.0

Language Spoken at Home: Spanish
(Universe: Population 5 Years and Over)

Group	Number	%
Total Population	24,099	78.9
Hispanic or Latino (of any race)	22,608	94.0
Central American, ex. Mexican	3,122	97.7
Nicaraguan	2,312	99.4
Cuban	11,129	93.5
Dominican Republic	1,026	94.6
Puerto Rican	1,302	83.7
South American	4,919	97.0
Colombian	2,754	99.5

Unemployment Rate
(Universe: Population 16 Years and Over)

Group	%
Total Population	9.1
Hispanic or Latino (of any race)	8.8
Central American, ex. Mexican	10.3
Nicaraguan	9.9
Cuban	10.0
Dominican Republic	3.5
Puerto Rican	1.6
South American	7.5
Colombian	8.0

Class of Worker: Private Wage and Salary
(Universe: Civilian Employed Population 16 Years and Over)

Group	Number	%
Total Population	13,427	83.6
Hispanic or Latino (of any race)	10,892	84.4
Central American, ex. Mexican	1,809	94.5
Nicaraguan	1,360	98.3
Cuban	5,031	84.2
Dominican Republic	676	95.1
Puerto Rican	509	70.3
South American	2,487	82.5
Colombian	1,203	77.3

Class of Worker: Government
(Universe: Civilian Employed Population 16 Years and Over)

Group	Number	%
Total Population	1,753	10.9
Hispanic or Latino (of any race)	1,246	9.7
Central American, ex. Mexican	95	5.0
Nicaraguan	13	0.9
Cuban	692	11.6
Dominican Republic	35	4.9
Puerto Rican	161	22.2
South American	147	4.9
Colombian	93	6.0

Means of Transportation to Work: Car, Truck or Van
(Universe: Workers 16 Years and Over)

Group	Number	%
Total Population	14,346	90.8
Hispanic or Latino (of any race)	11,463	90.4
Central American, ex. Mexican	1,752	91.5
Nicaraguan	1,340	96.8
Cuban	5,331	91.3
Dominican Republic	649	91.3
Puerto Rican	678	93.6
South American	2,525	85.2
Colombian	1,257	83.0

Means of Transportation to Work: Public Transportation (ex. Taxicab)
(Universe: Workers 16 Years and Over)

Group	Number	%
Total Population	440	2.8
Hispanic or Latino (of any race)	390	3.1
Central American, ex. Mexican	108	5.6
Nicaraguan	21	1.5
Cuban	142	2.4
Dominican Republic	33	4.6
Puerto Rican	0	0.0
South American	107	3.6
Colombian	107	7.1

Homeownership Rate
(Universe: Occupied Housing Units)

Group	%
Total Population	86.5
Hispanic or Latino (of any race)	85.4
Central American, ex. Mexican	86.8
Costa Rican	85.2
Guatemalan	90.6
Honduran	81.1
Nicaraguan	88.2
Panamanian	86.5
Salvadoran	87.1
Cuban	86.0
Dominican Republic	82.8
Mexican	79.2
Puerto Rican	85.5
South American	84.0
Argentinean	75.7
Chilean	90.0
Colombian	84.5
Ecuadorian	88.1
Peruvian	83.0
Venezuelan	81.9
Spaniard	86.4

Median Home Value

Group	Dollars
Total Population	312,300
Hispanic or Latino (of any race)	310,400
Central American, ex. Mexican	255,000
Nicaraguan	271,500
Cuban	321,100
Dominican Republic	296,200
Puerto Rican	262,900
South American	311,300
Colombian	285,700

Median Gross Rent

Group	Dollars
Total Population	1,711
Hispanic or Latino (of any race)	1,728
Central American, ex. Mexican	1,701
Nicaraguan	–
Cuban	1,761

Notes: (1) Percent of total population; (2) Percent of Hispanic/Latino population; Profiles include places with an overall population of at least 125,000, OR an overall population of at least 25,000 where the Hispanic/Latino population is at least 20% of the overall population. In states where less than five places meet either of these criteria, we have included places with at least 10,000 total population with the highest percentage of Hispanic/Latino population. These places are identified with an asterisk (*); Please refer to the User's Guide for a full explanation of data.

Dominican Republic	-
Puerto Rican	-
South American	1,661
Colombian	1,447

Median Household Income
(2010 Inflation-Adjusted Dollars)

Group	Dollars
Total Population	70,033
Hispanic or Latino (of any race)	66,324
Central American, ex. Mexican	72,670
Nicaraguan	72,955
Cuban	68,472
Dominican Republic	77,917
Puerto Rican	59,408
South American	62,406
Colombian	60,533

Per Capita Income
(2010 Inflation-Adjusted Dollars)

Group	Dollars
Total Population	22,603
Hispanic or Latino (of any race)	22,775
Central American, ex. Mexican	20,964
Nicaraguan	20,552
Cuban	24,996
Dominican Republic	22,439
Puerto Rican	22,166
South American	20,921
Colombian	19,574

Households with $100,000+ Income

Group	Number	%
Total Population	2,225	24.8
Hispanic or Latino (of any race)	1,635	22.9
Central American, ex. Mexican	258	28.7
Nicaraguan	170	27.2
Cuban	1,005	26.4
Dominican Republic	44	16.1
Puerto Rican	41	8.9
South American	199	14.0
Colombian	63	7.9

Households with Food Stamps/SNAP Benefits During Past 12 Months

Group	Number	%
Total Population	1,268	14.1
Hispanic or Latino (of any race)	1,106	15.5
Central American, ex. Mexican	92	10.2
Nicaraguan	92	14.7
Cuban	721	18.9
Dominican Republic	61	22.3
Puerto Rican	33	7.2
South American	173	12.2
Colombian	119	14.9

Poverty Rate
(Income in Past 12 Months Below Poverty Level)

Group	%
Total Population	8.0
Hispanic or Latino (of any race)	8.1
Central American, ex. Mexican	3.6
Nicaraguan	2.3
Cuban	8.8
Dominican Republic	8.1
Puerto Rican	8.5
South American	7.9
Colombian	10.8

Riverview

Population

Group	Number	%TP[1]	%HP[2]
Total Population	71,050	100.0	-
Hispanic or Latino (of any race)	14,946	21.0	100.0
Central American, ex. Mexican	1,013	1.4	6.8
Guatemalan	143	0.2	1.0
Honduran	231	0.3	1.5
Nicaraguan	110	0.2	0.7
Panamanian	264	0.4	1.8
Salvadoran	178	0.3	1.2
Cuban	1,450	2.0	9.7
Dominican Republic	1,004	1.4	6.7
Mexican	2,904	4.1	19.4
Puerto Rican	5,992	8.4	40.1
South American	1,700	2.4	11.4
Colombian	899	1.3	6.0
Ecuadorian	193	0.3	1.3
Peruvian	224	0.3	1.5
Venezuelan	228	0.3	1.5
Spaniard	261	0.4	1.7

Population Growth: 2000–2010

Group	%
Total Population	490.4
Hispanic or Latino (of any race)	1,277.5
Cuban	1,015.4
Mexican	1,660.0
Puerto Rican	1,303.3

Males per 100 Females

Group	Number
Total Population	92.6
Hispanic or Latino (of any race)	89.9
Central American, ex. Mexican	83.2
Guatemalan	93.2
Honduran	90.9
Nicaraguan	66.7
Panamanian	66.0
Salvadoran	83.5
Cuban	94.9
Dominican Republic	88.7
Mexican	94.0
Puerto Rican	91.7
South American	79.9
Colombian	73.9
Ecuadorian	99.0
Peruvian	86.7
Venezuelan	83.9
Spaniard	97.7

Average Household Size

Group	People
Total Population	2.89
Hispanic or Latino (of any race)	3.49
Central American, ex. Mexican	3.66
Guatemalan	4.26
Honduran	3.67
Nicaraguan	3.72
Panamanian	3.24
Salvadoran	4.07
Cuban	3.22
Dominican Republic	3.82
Mexican	4.23
Puerto Rican	3.33
South American	3.35
Colombian	3.38
Ecuadorian	3.59
Peruvian	3.37
Venezuelan	3.25
Spaniard	2.44

Median Age

Group	Years
Total Population	34.1
Hispanic or Latino (of any race)	28.5
Central American, ex. Mexican	30.5
Guatemalan	31.4
Honduran	30.6
Nicaraguan	29.0
Panamanian	34.1
Salvadoran	28.3
Cuban	31.9
Dominican Republic	29.3
Mexican	21.8
Puerto Rican	28.7
South American	34.4
Colombian	34.3
Ecuadorian	32.7
Peruvian	36.2
Venezuelan	32.8
Spaniard	37.8

High School Graduates
(Universe: Population 25 Years and Over)

Group	Number	%
Total Population	37,265	89.2
Hispanic or Latino (of any race)	5,605	78.0
Central American, ex. Mexican	399	62.6
Cuban	653	80.1
Mexican	661	47.6
Puerto Rican	2,673	89.2
South American	609	89.8

Four-Year College Graduates
(Universe: Population 25 Years and Over)

Group	Number	%
Total Population	10,797	25.8
Hispanic or Latino (of any race)	1,208	16.8
Central American, ex. Mexican	85	13.3
Cuban	140	17.2
Mexican	95	6.8
Puerto Rican	460	15.4
South American	228	33.6

Population Age 3–17 Enrolled in Public School
(Universe: Population Age 3–17 Enrolled in School)

Group	Number	%
Total Population	12,514	89.1
Hispanic or Latino (of any race)	3,587	94.3
Central American, ex. Mexican	243	86.2
Cuban	157	68.6
Mexican	1,244	100.0
Puerto Rican	1,493	99.4
South American	48	73.8

Population Age 3–17 Enrolled in Private School
(Universe: Population Age 3–17 Enrolled in School)

Group	Number	%
Total Population	1,532	10.9
Hispanic or Latino (of any race)	215	5.7
Central American, ex. Mexican	39	13.8
Cuban	72	31.4
Mexican	0	0.0
Puerto Rican	9	0.6
South American	17	26.2

Foreign-Born Population

Group	Number	%
Total Population	6,781	10.4
Hispanic or Latino (of any race)	3,235	23.9
Central American, ex. Mexican	547	42.1
Cuban	655	53.2
Mexican	922	27.7
Puerto Rican	17	0.3
South American	680	74.6

Foreign-Born Naturalized U.S. Citizens

Group	Number	%
Total Population	3,576	52.7
Hispanic or Latino (of any race)	1,391	43.0
Central American, ex. Mexican	164	30.0
Cuban	293	44.7
Mexican	280	30.4
Puerto Rican	17	100.0
South American	328	48.2

Language Spoken at Home: English Only
(Universe: Population 5 Years and Over)

Group	Number	%
Total Population	46,342	76.8
Hispanic or Latino (of any race)	2,185	18.0
Central American, ex. Mexican	35	3.6
Cuban	276	24.9
Mexican	454	14.7
Puerto Rican	915	18.8
South American	44	5.6

Language Spoken at Home: Spanish
(Universe: Population 5 Years and Over)

Group	Number	%
Total Population	10,705	17.7
Hispanic or Latino (of any race)	9,954	81.9
Central American, ex. Mexican	925	96.4
Cuban	834	75.1
Mexican	2,643	85.3
Puerto Rican	3,948	81.2
South American	745	94.4

Unemployment Rate
(Universe: Population 16 Years and Over)

Group	%
Total Population	7.4
Hispanic or Latino (of any race)	8.9
Central American, ex. Mexican	4.2

Notes: (1) Percent of total population; (2) Percent of Hispanic/Latino population; Profiles include places with an overall population of at least 125,000, OR an overall population of at least 25,000 where the Hispanic/Latino population is at least 20% of the overall population. In states where less than five places meet either of these criteria, we have included places with at least 10,000 total population with the highest percentage of Hispanic/Latino population. These places are identified with an asterisk (*); Please refer to the User's Guide for a full explanation of data.

Cuban	6.6
Mexican	11.1
Puerto Rican	8.3
South American	8.7

Class of Worker: Private Wage and Salary
(Universe: Civilian Employed Population 16 Years and Over)

Group	Number	%
Total Population	25,351	80.6
Hispanic or Latino (of any race)	4,773	81.6
Central American, ex. Mexican	401	98.0
Cuban	454	75.2
Mexican	1,021	85.2
Puerto Rican	1,973	80.5
South American	477	82.7

Class of Worker: Government
(Universe: Civilian Employed Population 16 Years and Over)

Group	Number	%
Total Population	4,629	14.7
Hispanic or Latino (of any race)	855	14.6
Central American, ex. Mexican	8	2.0
Cuban	99	16.4
Mexican	148	12.3
Puerto Rican	407	16.6
South American	86	14.9

Means of Transportation to Work: Car, Truck or Van
(Universe: Workers 16 Years and Over)

Group	Number	%
Total Population	29,770	94.5
Hispanic or Latino (of any race)	5,484	93.9
Central American, ex. Mexican	317	77.5
Cuban	604	100.0
Mexican	1,097	92.4
Puerto Rican	2,405	97.2
South American	541	91.5

Means of Transportation to Work: Public Transportation (ex. Taxicab)
(Universe: Workers 16 Years and Over)

Group	Number	%
Total Population	291	0.9
Hispanic or Latino (of any race)	80	1.4
Central American, ex. Mexican	0	0.0
Cuban	0	0.0
Mexican	16	1.3
Puerto Rican	64	2.6
South American	0	0.0

Homeownership Rate
(Universe: Occupied Housing Units)

Group	%
Total Population	78.3
Hispanic or Latino (of any race)	73.1
Central American, ex. Mexican	77.2
Guatemalan	76.9
Honduran	78.6
Nicaraguan	69.0
Panamanian	82.7
Salvadoran	73.3
Cuban	79.9
Dominican Republic	72.6
Mexican	61.7
Puerto Rican	71.8
South American	81.5
Colombian	82.3
Ecuadorian	79.3
Peruvian	78.3
Venezuelan	79.4
Spaniard	84.2

Median Home Value

Group	Dollars
Total Population	206,200
Hispanic or Latino (of any race)	203,100
Central American, ex. Mexican	227,500
Cuban	254,700
Mexican	159,500
Puerto Rican	205,200
South American	195,400

Median Gross Rent

Group	Dollars
Total Population	1,162
Hispanic or Latino (of any race)	1,181
Central American, ex. Mexican	886
Cuban	–
Mexican	1,461
Puerto Rican	1,251
South American	1,313

Median Household Income
(2010 Inflation-Adjusted Dollars)

Group	Dollars
Total Population	65,020
Hispanic or Latino (of any race)	59,517
Central American, ex. Mexican	52,917
Cuban	79,412
Mexican	37,443
Puerto Rican	67,788
South American	51,193

Per Capita Income
(2010 Inflation-Adjusted Dollars)

Group	Dollars
Total Population	26,317
Hispanic or Latino (of any race)	19,595
Central American, ex. Mexican	15,744
Cuban	27,887
Mexican	11,979
Puerto Rican	22,087
South American	25,936

Households with $100,000+ Income

Group	Number	%
Total Population	5,082	22.1
Hispanic or Latino (of any race)	782	21.5
Central American, ex. Mexican	29	8.7
Cuban	159	41.6
Mexican	140	19.5
Puerto Rican	322	22.5
South American	49	15.3

Households with Food Stamps/SNAP Benefits During Past 12 Months

Group	Number	%
Total Population	1,278	5.6
Hispanic or Latino (of any race)	278	7.7
Central American, ex. Mexican	50	15.1
Cuban	50	13.1
Mexican	97	13.5
Puerto Rican	20	1.4
South American	15	4.7

Poverty Rate
(Income in Past 12 Months Below Poverty Level)

Group	%
Total Population	8.8
Hispanic or Latino (of any race)	12.8
Central American, ex. Mexican	8.2
Cuban	13.6
Mexican	37.5
Puerto Rican	1.8
South American	0.0

Royal Palm Beach

Population

Group	Number	%TP[1]	%HP[2]
Total Population	34,140	100.0	–
Hispanic or Latino (of any race)	6,950	20.4	100.0
Central American, ex. Mexican	522	1.5	7.5
Honduran	111	0.3	1.6
Nicaraguan	131	0.4	1.9
Cuban	1,521	4.5	21.9
Dominican Republic	471	1.4	6.8
Mexican	654	1.9	9.4
Puerto Rican	1,646	4.8	23.7
South American	1,764	5.2	25.4
Colombian	917	2.7	13.2
Ecuadorian	198	0.6	2.8
Peruvian	262	0.8	3.8
Venezuelan	195	0.6	2.8

Population Growth: 2000–2010

Group	%
Total Population	58.6
Hispanic or Latino (of any race)	173.0
Central American, ex. Mexican	252.7
Cuban	139.5
Mexican	144.9
Puerto Rican	140.6
South American	465.4
Colombian	445.8

Males per 100 Females

Group	Number
Total Population	91.6
Hispanic or Latino (of any race)	91.3
Central American, ex. Mexican	73.4
Honduran	79.0
Nicaraguan	65.8
Cuban	93.5
Dominican Republic	97.1
Mexican	107.0
Puerto Rican	94.6
South American	83.4
Colombian	78.8
Ecuadorian	92.2
Peruvian	73.5
Venezuelan	91.2

Average Household Size

Group	People
Total Population	2.93
Hispanic or Latino (of any race)	3.34
Central American, ex. Mexican	3.53
Honduran	3.34
Nicaraguan	4.36
Cuban	3.22
Dominican Republic	3.50
Mexican	3.74
Puerto Rican	3.16
South American	3.49
Colombian	3.50
Ecuadorian	3.62
Peruvian	3.58
Venezuelan	3.60

Median Age

Group	Years
Total Population	37.7
Hispanic or Latino (of any race)	33.6
Central American, ex. Mexican	33.3
Honduran	32.9
Nicaraguan	31.5
Cuban	37.5
Dominican Republic	30.8
Mexican	24.9
Puerto Rican	33.0
South American	36.4
Colombian	36.7
Ecuadorian	38.4
Peruvian	37.0
Venezuelan	34.3

High School Graduates
(Universe: Population 25 Years and Over)

Group	Number	%
Total Population	18,479	88.8
Hispanic or Latino (of any race)	3,083	82.3
Cuban	805	84.6
Mexican	385	82.3
Puerto Rican	672	86.7
South American	774	87.4
Colombian	368	81.2

Four-Year College Graduates
(Universe: Population 25 Years and Over)

Group	Number	%
Total Population	5,651	27.2
Hispanic or Latino (of any race)	781	20.9
Cuban	175	18.4
Mexican	17	3.6
Puerto Rican	155	20.0
South American	327	36.9
Colombian	113	24.9

Notes: (1) Percent of total population; (2) Percent of Hispanic/Latino population; Profiles include places with an overall population of at least 125,000, OR an overall population of at least 25,000 where the Hispanic/Latino population is at least 20% of the overall population. In states where less than five places meet either of these criteria, we have included places with at least 10,000 total population with the highest percentage of Hispanic/Latino population. These places are identified with an asterisk (*); Please refer to the User's Guide for a full explanation of data.

Population Age 3–17 Enrolled in Public School
(Universe: Population Age 3–17 Enrolled in School)

Group	Number	%
Total Population	5,946	82.4
Hispanic or Latino (of any race)	1,056	82.0
Cuban	123	45.1
Mexican	316	97.5
Puerto Rican	202	95.3
South American	268	83.2
Colombian	214	79.9

Population Age 3–17 Enrolled in Private School
(Universe: Population Age 3–17 Enrolled in School)

Group	Number	%
Total Population	1,274	17.6
Hispanic or Latino (of any race)	232	18.0
Cuban	150	54.9
Mexican	8	2.5
Puerto Rican	10	4.7
South American	54	16.8
Colombian	54	20.1

Foreign-Born Population

Group	Number	%
Total Population	6,729	20.9
Hispanic or Latino (of any race)	2,361	41.4
Cuban	856	64.2
Mexican	138	14.3
Puerto Rican	22	2.0
South American	858	63.8
Colombian	444	57.2

Foreign-Born Naturalized U.S. Citizens

Group	Number	%
Total Population	4,444	66.0
Hispanic or Latino (of any race)	1,290	54.6
Cuban	448	52.3
Mexican	75	54.3
Puerto Rican	22	100.0
South American	442	51.5
Colombian	183	41.2

Language Spoken at Home: English Only
(Universe: Population 5 Years and Over)

Group	Number	%
Total Population	23,372	76.7
Hispanic or Latino (of any race)	1,418	26.0
Cuban	281	21.8
Mexican	406	44.4
Puerto Rican	267	25.4
South American	275	21.3
Colombian	194	25.9

Language Spoken at Home: Spanish
(Universe: Population 5 Years and Over)

Group	Number	%
Total Population	4,390	14.4
Hispanic or Latino (of any race)	4,017	73.7
Cuban	1,010	78.2
Mexican	509	55.6
Puerto Rican	785	74.6
South American	1,018	78.7
Colombian	556	74.1

Unemployment Rate
(Universe: Population 16 Years and Over)

Group	%
Total Population	9.2
Hispanic or Latino (of any race)	5.6
Cuban	9.9
Mexican	5.0
Puerto Rican	4.8
South American	4.0
Colombian	5.1

Class of Worker: Private Wage and Salary
(Universe: Civilian Employed Population 16 Years and Over)

Group	Number	%
Total Population	12,386	76.9
Hispanic or Latino (of any race)	2,474	81.7
Cuban	601	86.8
Mexican	366	74.2
Puerto Rican	402	74.9
South American	573	81.3
Colombian	284	85.5

Class of Worker: Government
(Universe: Civilian Employed Population 16 Years and Over)

Group	Number	%
Total Population	3,147	19.5
Hispanic or Latino (of any race)	417	13.8
Cuban	69	10.0
Mexican	88	17.8
Puerto Rican	113	21.0
South American	91	12.9
Colombian	16	4.8

Means of Transportation to Work: Car, Truck or Van
(Universe: Workers 16 Years and Over)

Group	Number	%
Total Population	14,581	93.4
Hispanic or Latino (of any race)	2,862	95.6
Cuban	641	92.6
Mexican	454	92.1
Puerto Rican	518	100.0
South American	675	95.7
Colombian	302	91.0

Means of Transportation to Work: Public Transportation (ex. Taxicab)
(Universe: Workers 16 Years and Over)

Group	Number	%
Total Population	131	0.8
Hispanic or Latino (of any race)	0	0.0
Cuban	0	0.0
Mexican	0	0.0
Puerto Rican	0	0.0
South American	0	0.0
Colombian	0	0.0

Homeownership Rate
(Universe: Occupied Housing Units)

Group	%
Total Population	83.8
Hispanic or Latino (of any race)	79.3
Central American, ex. Mexican	82.5
Honduran	72.4
Nicaraguan	82.1
Cuban	83.9
Dominican Republic	74.0
Mexican	69.9
Puerto Rican	77.5
South American	81.3
Colombian	78.6
Ecuadorian	90.2
Peruvian	79.7
Venezuelan	80.8

Median Home Value

Group	Dollars
Total Population	256,400
Hispanic or Latino (of any race)	256,400
Cuban	256,100
Mexican	224,100
Puerto Rican	307,700
South American	236,500
Colombian	246,900

Median Gross Rent

Group	Dollars
Total Population	1,377
Hispanic or Latino (of any race)	1,384
Cuban	1,546
Mexican	1,509
Puerto Rican	1,296
South American	1,388
Colombian	1,385

Median Household Income
(2010 Inflation-Adjusted Dollars)

Group	Dollars
Total Population	65,459
Hispanic or Latino (of any race)	63,576
Cuban	61,477
Mexican	51,063
Puerto Rican	75,563
South American	72,778
Colombian	46,282

Per Capita Income
(2010 Inflation-Adjusted Dollars)

Group	Dollars
Total Population	27,169
Hispanic or Latino (of any race)	24,140
Cuban	19,582
Mexican	17,202
Puerto Rican	23,436
South American	27,118
Colombian	16,417

Households with $100,000+ Income

Group	Number	%
Total Population	2,891	26.6
Hispanic or Latino (of any race)	446	25.0
Cuban	78	22.2
Mexican	32	12.6
Puerto Rican	98	26.5
South American	140	28.3
Colombian	6	2.6

Households with Food Stamps/SNAP Benefits During Past 12 Months

Group	Number	%
Total Population	574	5.3
Hispanic or Latino (of any race)	139	7.8
Cuban	39	11.1
Mexican	41	16.1
Puerto Rican	11	3.0
South American	33	6.7
Colombian	27	11.6

Poverty Rate
(Income in Past 12 Months Below Poverty Level)

Group	%
Total Population	7.6
Hispanic or Latino (of any race)	8.2
Cuban	23.6
Mexican	9.1
Puerto Rican	3.7
South American	0.8
Colombian	1.4

Saint Cloud

Population

Group	Number	%TP[1]	%HP[2]
Total Population	35,183	100.0	–
Hispanic or Latino (of any race)	10,280	29.2	100.0
Central American, ex. Mexican	428	1.2	4.2
Cuban	536	1.5	5.2
Dominican Republic	693	2.0	6.7
Mexican	671	1.9	6.5
Puerto Rican	6,574	18.7	63.9
South American	1,056	3.0	10.3
Colombian	507	1.4	4.9
Ecuadorian	175	0.5	1.7
Venezuelan	161	0.5	1.6

Population Growth: 2000–2010

Group	%
Total Population	75.3
Hispanic or Latino (of any race)	283.4
Cuban	252.6
Mexican	171.7
Puerto Rican	297.7
South American	514.0

Males per 100 Females

Group	Number
Total Population	91.8
Hispanic or Latino (of any race)	91.9
Central American, ex. Mexican	92.8
Cuban	86.8
Dominican Republic	84.8
Mexican	112.3
Puerto Rican	92.4
South American	79.0
Colombian	77.9
Ecuadorian	68.3
Venezuelan	94.0

Notes: (1) Percent of total population; (2) Percent of Hispanic/Latino population; Profiles include places with an overall population of at least 125,000, OR an overall population of at least 25,000 where the Hispanic/Latino population is at least 20% of the overall population. In states where less than five places meet either of these criteria, we have included places with at least 10,000 total population with the highest percentage of Hispanic/Latino population. These places are identified with an asterisk (*); Please refer to the User's Guide for a full explanation of data.

Average Household Size	
Group	People
Total Population	2.76
Hispanic or Latino (of any race)	3.26
Central American, ex. Mexican	3.48
Cuban	3.07
Dominican Republic	3.64
Mexican	3.97
Puerto Rican	3.17
South American	3.34
Colombian	3.31
Ecuadorian	3.54
Venezuelan	3.93

Median Age	
Group	Years
Total Population	36.8
Hispanic or Latino (of any race)	30.4
Central American, ex. Mexican	31.8
Cuban	38.2
Dominican Republic	30.7
Mexican	24.1
Puerto Rican	30.4
South American	35.6
Colombian	36.3
Ecuadorian	37.8
Venezuelan	34.4

High School Graduates (Universe: Population 25 Years and Over)

Group	Number	%
Total Population	19,073	87.0
Hispanic or Latino (of any race)	4,099	79.4
Puerto Rican	2,634	82.0
South American	536	87.9

Four-Year College Graduates (Universe: Population 25 Years and Over)

Group	Number	%
Total Population	4,149	18.9
Hispanic or Latino (of any race)	961	18.6
Puerto Rican	555	17.3
South American	185	30.3

Population Age 3–17 Enrolled in Public School (Universe: Population Age 3–17 Enrolled in School)

Group	Number	%
Total Population	6,227	90.2
Hispanic or Latino (of any race)	2,333	94.0
Puerto Rican	1,566	95.4
South American	171	94.5

Population Age 3–17 Enrolled in Private School (Universe: Population Age 3–17 Enrolled in School)

Group	Number	%
Total Population	679	9.8
Hispanic or Latino (of any race)	148	6.0
Puerto Rican	76	4.6
South American	10	5.5

Foreign-Born Population

Group	Number	%
Total Population	3,276	9.7
Hispanic or Latino (of any race)	2,091	22.9
Puerto Rican	51	0.9
South American	565	64.4

Foreign-Born Naturalized U.S. Citizens

Group	Number	%
Total Population	1,558	47.6
Hispanic or Latino (of any race)	991	47.4
Puerto Rican	51	100.0
South American	280	49.6

Language Spoken at Home: English Only (Universe: Population 5 Years and Over)

Group	Number	%
Total Population	23,174	74.6
Hispanic or Latino (of any race)	1,420	16.9
Puerto Rican	1,015	18.8
South American	144	16.6

Language Spoken at Home: Spanish (Universe: Population 5 Years and Over)

Group	Number	%
Total Population	7,135	23.0
Hispanic or Latino (of any race)	7,002	83.1
Puerto Rican	4,396	81.2
South American	723	83.4

Unemployment Rate (Universe: Population 16 Years and Over)

Group	%
Total Population	9.8
Hispanic or Latino (of any race)	12.8
Puerto Rican	15.3
South American	4.2

Class of Worker: Private Wage and Salary (Universe: Civilian Employed Population 16 Years and Over)

Group	Number	%
Total Population	12,108	80.8
Hispanic or Latino (of any race)	3,282	88.4
Puerto Rican	1,855	86.0
South American	502	92.4

Class of Worker: Government (Universe: Civilian Employed Population 16 Years and Over)

Group	Number	%
Total Population	2,374	15.8
Hispanic or Latino (of any race)	337	9.1
Puerto Rican	266	12.3
South American	14	2.6

Means of Transportation to Work: Car, Truck or Van (Universe: Workers 16 Years and Over)

Group	Number	%
Total Population	13,759	93.5
Hispanic or Latino (of any race)	3,300	92.9
Puerto Rican	1,938	94.7
South American	531	100.0

Means of Transportation to Work: Public Transportation (ex. Taxicab) (Universe: Workers 16 Years and Over)

Group	Number	%
Total Population	54	0.4
Hispanic or Latino (of any race)	0	0.0
Puerto Rican	0	0.0
South American	0	0.0

Homeownership Rate (Universe: Occupied Housing Units)

Group	%
Total Population	70.8
Hispanic or Latino (of any race)	61.2
Central American, ex. Mexican	72.3
Cuban	59.7
Dominican Republic	70.2
Mexican	52.2
Puerto Rican	57.9
South American	77.3
Colombian	78.0
Ecuadorian	86.0
Venezuelan	75.0

Median Home Value

Group	Dollars
Total Population	182,000
Hispanic or Latino (of any race)	208,600
Puerto Rican	217,300
South American	191,500

Median Gross Rent

Group	Dollars
Total Population	955
Hispanic or Latino (of any race)	864
Puerto Rican	812
South American	–

Median Household Income (2010 Inflation-Adjusted Dollars)

Group	Dollars
Total Population	48,280
Hispanic or Latino (of any race)	35,969
Puerto Rican	37,184
South American	58,839

Per Capita Income (2010 Inflation-Adjusted Dollars)

Group	Dollars
Total Population	21,355
Hispanic or Latino (of any race)	14,680
Puerto Rican	14,628
South American	19,280

Households with $100,000+ Income

Group	Number	%
Total Population	1,243	9.7
Hispanic or Latino (of any race)	126	4.1
Puerto Rican	58	2.8
South American	22	8.4

Households with Food Stamps/SNAP Benefits During Past 12 Months

Group	Number	%
Total Population	1,419	11.1
Hispanic or Latino (of any race)	678	22.1
Puerto Rican	450	22.1
South American	32	12.3

Poverty Rate (Income in Past 12 Months Below Poverty Level)

Group	%
Total Population	12.0
Hispanic or Latino (of any race)	17.7
Puerto Rican	16.9
South American	4.2

Saint Petersburg

Population

Group	Number	%TP[1]	%HP[2]
Total Population	244,769	100.0	–
Hispanic or Latino (of any race)	16,214	6.6	100.0
Central American, ex. Mexican	921	0.4	5.7
Costa Rican	152	0.1	0.9
Guatemalan	142	0.1	0.9
Honduran	198	0.1	1.2
Nicaraguan	108	<0.1	0.7
Panamanian	221	0.1	1.4
Cuban	2,835	1.2	17.5
Dominican Republic	485	0.2	3.0
Mexican	2,855	1.2	17.6
Puerto Rican	5,272	2.2	32.5
South American	2,209	0.9	13.6
Argentinean	166	0.1	1.0
Colombian	844	0.3	5.2
Ecuadorian	229	0.1	1.4
Peruvian	321	0.1	2.0
Venezuelan	413	0.2	2.5
Spaniard	441	0.2	2.7

Population Growth: 2000–2010

Group	%
Total Population	-1.4
Hispanic or Latino (of any race)	54.4
Central American, ex. Mexican	99.4
Panamanian	92.2
Cuban	81.7
Dominican Republic	111.8
Mexican	93.7
Puerto Rican	47.5
South American	96.0
Colombian	123.9
Peruvian	134.3
Venezuelan	45.4
Spaniard	280.2

Males per 100 Females

Group	Number
Total Population	92.6
Hispanic or Latino (of any race)	98.8
Central American, ex. Mexican	90.7
Costa Rican	68.9
Guatemalan	115.2
Honduran	88.6
Nicaraguan	100.0
Panamanian	85.7
Cuban	110.0

Notes: (1) Percent of total population; (2) Percent of Hispanic/Latino population; Profiles include places with an overall population of at least 125,000, OR an overall population of at least 25,000 where the Hispanic/Latino population is at least 20% of the overall population. In states where less than five places meet either of these criteria, we have included places with at least 10,000 total population with the highest percentage of Hispanic/Latino population. These places are identified with an asterisk (*); Please refer to the User's Guide for a full explanation of data.

Dominican Republic	85.8
Mexican	118.1
Puerto Rican	96.0
South American	82.0
Argentinean	76.6
Colombian	75.1
Ecuadorian	97.4
Peruvian	81.4
Venezuelan	82.7
Spaniard	91.7

Average Household Size

Group	People
Total Population	2.19
Hispanic or Latino (of any race)	2.53
Central American, ex. Mexican	2.60
Costa Rican	2.45
Guatemalan	2.39
Honduran	2.88
Nicaraguan	2.76
Panamanian	2.49
Cuban	2.54
Dominican Republic	2.83
Mexican	2.75
Puerto Rican	2.52
South American	2.50
Argentinean	2.37
Colombian	2.50
Ecuadorian	2.98
Peruvian	2.48
Venezuelan	2.42
Spaniard	2.09

Median Age

Group	Years
Total Population	41.6
Hispanic or Latino (of any race)	31.0
Central American, ex. Mexican	32.4
Costa Rican	34.8
Guatemalan	27.5
Honduran	33.0
Nicaraguan	29.8
Panamanian	32.9
Cuban	37.2
Dominican Republic	28.2
Mexican	26.4
Puerto Rican	29.5
South American	36.0
Argentinean	38.6
Colombian	35.8
Ecuadorian	33.5
Peruvian	36.4
Venezuelan	35.6
Spaniard	41.9

High School Graduates
(Universe: Population 25 Years and Over)

Group	Number	%
Total Population	152,651	87.2
Hispanic or Latino (of any race)	7,443	79.4
Central American, ex. Mexican	707	84.4
Cuban	1,282	75.7
Mexican	942	61.9
Puerto Rican	2,576	81.7
South American	1,095	87.3

Four-Year College Graduates
(Universe: Population 25 Years and Over)

Group	Number	%
Total Population	48,665	27.8
Hispanic or Latino (of any race)	2,180	23.3
Central American, ex. Mexican	196	23.4
Cuban	417	24.6
Mexican	233	15.3
Puerto Rican	731	23.2
South American	372	29.7

Population Age 3–17 Enrolled in Public School
(Universe: Population Age 3–17 Enrolled in School)

Group	Number	%
Total Population	31,958	84.6
Hispanic or Latino (of any race)	2,578	86.2
Central American, ex. Mexican	232	94.7
Cuban	374	78.2
Mexican	540	89.4
Puerto Rican	1,139	88.0
South American	122	91.7

Population Age 3–17 Enrolled in Private School
(Universe: Population Age 3–17 Enrolled in School)

Group	Number	%
Total Population	5,812	15.4
Hispanic or Latino (of any race)	414	13.8
Central American, ex. Mexican	13	5.3
Cuban	104	21.8
Mexican	64	10.6
Puerto Rican	156	12.0
South American	11	8.3

Foreign-Born Population

Group	Number	%
Total Population	25,253	10.3
Hispanic or Latino (of any race)	4,667	30.7
Central American, ex. Mexican	748	55.7
Cuban	1,189	44.4
Mexican	1,107	36.9
Puerto Rican	13	0.3
South American	1,170	69.3

Foreign-Born Naturalized U.S. Citizens

Group	Number	%
Total Population	12,962	51.3
Hispanic or Latino (of any race)	2,212	47.4
Central American, ex. Mexican	350	46.8
Cuban	632	53.2
Mexican	295	26.6
Puerto Rican	13	100.0
South American	624	53.3

Language Spoken at Home: English Only
(Universe: Population 5 Years and Over)

Group	Number	%
Total Population	205,310	88.5
Hispanic or Latino (of any race)	5,393	39.2
Central American, ex. Mexican	182	16.2
Cuban	982	40.7
Mexican	1,003	38.6
Puerto Rican	2,034	42.4
South American	399	24.5

Language Spoken at Home: Spanish
(Universe: Population 5 Years and Over)

Group	Number	%
Total Population	9,974	4.3
Hispanic or Latino (of any race)	8,261	60.0
Central American, ex. Mexican	940	83.8
Cuban	1,394	57.8
Mexican	1,574	60.6
Puerto Rican	2,712	56.6
South American	1,231	75.5

Unemployment Rate
(Universe: Population 16 Years and Over)

Group	%
Total Population	8.1
Hispanic or Latino (of any race)	9.6
Central American, ex. Mexican	11.0
Cuban	7.6
Mexican	10.0
Puerto Rican	11.1
South American	5.3

Class of Worker: Private Wage and Salary
(Universe: Civilian Employed Population 16 Years and Over)

Group	Number	%
Total Population	99,287	81.8
Hispanic or Latino (of any race)	5,648	83.6
Central American, ex. Mexican	569	92.4
Cuban	994	81.9
Mexican	1,116	87.1
Puerto Rican	1,630	79.5
South American	797	84.9

Class of Worker: Government
(Universe: Civilian Employed Population 16 Years and Over)

Group	Number	%
Total Population	14,917	12.3
Hispanic or Latino (of any race)	657	9.7
Central American, ex. Mexican	31	5.0
Cuban	134	11.0
Mexican	68	5.3
Puerto Rican	263	12.8
South American	66	7.0

Means of Transportation to Work: Car, Truck or Van
(Universe: Workers 16 Years and Over)

Group	Number	%
Total Population	106,604	89.2
Hispanic or Latino (of any race)	6,107	90.4
Central American, ex. Mexican	513	84.9
Cuban	1,101	91.4
Mexican	1,139	87.0
Puerto Rican	1,957	93.7
South American	826	86.0

Means of Transportation to Work: Public Transportation (ex. Taxicab)
(Universe: Workers 16 Years and Over)

Group	Number	%
Total Population	2,551	2.1
Hispanic or Latino (of any race)	98	1.5
Central American, ex. Mexican	45	7.5
Cuban	0	0.0
Mexican	14	1.1
Puerto Rican	39	1.9
South American	0	0.0

Homeownership Rate
(Universe: Occupied Housing Units)

Group	%
Total Population	60.7
Hispanic or Latino (of any race)	48.4
Central American, ex. Mexican	54.0
Costa Rican	54.5
Guatemalan	61.1
Honduran	53.1
Nicaraguan	51.7
Panamanian	53.4
Cuban	61.6
Dominican Republic	50.3
Mexican	36.0
Puerto Rican	40.6
South American	54.6
Argentinean	70.8
Colombian	51.9
Ecuadorian	56.3
Peruvian	55.0
Venezuelan	51.7
Spaniard	67.5

Median Home Value

Group	Dollars
Total Population	177,800
Hispanic or Latino (of any race)	167,300
Central American, ex. Mexican	163,100
Cuban	147,800
Mexican	190,400
Puerto Rican	171,100
South American	158,500

Median Gross Rent

Group	Dollars
Total Population	874
Hispanic or Latino (of any race)	855
Central American, ex. Mexican	1,017
Cuban	827
Mexican	875
Puerto Rican	870
South American	912

Median Household Income
(2010 Inflation-Adjusted Dollars)

Group	Dollars
Total Population	44,041
Hispanic or Latino (of any race)	40,115
Central American, ex. Mexican	37,250
Cuban	50,179
Mexican	40,806
Puerto Rican	40,158
South American	29,241

Per Capita Income
(2010 Inflation-Adjusted Dollars)

Group	Dollars
Total Population	26,735

Notes: (1) Percent of total population; (2) Percent of Hispanic/Latino population; Profiles include places with an overall population of at least 125,000, OR an overall population of at least 25,000 where the Hispanic/Latino population is at least 20% of the overall population. In states where less than five places meet either of these criteria, we have included places with at least 10,000 total population with the highest percentage of Hispanic/Latino population. These places are identified with an asterisk (*); Please refer to the User's Guide for a full explanation of data.

Group	Number
Hispanic or Latino (of any race)	18,370
Central American, ex. Mexican	13,183
Cuban	21,060
Mexican	12,657
Puerto Rican	18,699
South American	22,836

Households with $100,000+ Income

Group	Number	%
Total Population	15,385	14.4
Hispanic or Latino (of any race)	681	13.0
Central American, ex. Mexican	18	4.8
Cuban	148	14.0
Mexican	82	10.1
Puerto Rican	236	13.1
South American	85	13.2

Households with Food Stamps/SNAP Benefits During Past 12 Months

Group	Number	%
Total Population	9,547	8.9
Hispanic or Latino (of any race)	725	13.8
Central American, ex. Mexican	10	2.7
Cuban	147	13.9
Mexican	84	10.3
Puerto Rican	345	19.2
South American	73	11.3

Poverty Rate
(Income in Past 12 Months Below Poverty Level)

Group	%
Total Population	14.3
Hispanic or Latino (of any race)	18.3
Central American, ex. Mexican	22.6
Cuban	11.3
Mexican	26.9
Puerto Rican	21.5
South American	8.2

Group	Number
Puerto Rican	90.8
South American	86.0
Argentinean	85.2
Colombian	88.9
Ecuadorian	72.3
Peruvian	81.7
Venezuelan	101.3

Average Household Size

Group	People
Total Population	2.59
Hispanic or Latino (of any race)	3.06
Central American, ex. Mexican	3.43
Guatemalan	4.25
Honduran	3.28
Panamanian	2.63
Salvadoran	3.56
Cuban	2.81
Dominican Republic	3.23
Mexican	3.66
Puerto Rican	2.94
South American	2.95
Argentinean	2.79
Colombian	2.88
Ecuadorian	3.13
Peruvian	3.16
Venezuelan	3.10

Foreign-Born Population

Group	Number	%
Total Population	5,250	10.2
Hispanic or Latino (of any race)	2,412	26.5
Mexican	944	51.3
Puerto Rican	20	0.5
South American	516	56.3

Foreign-Born Naturalized U.S. Citizens

Group	Number	%
Total Population	2,388	45.5
Hispanic or Latino (of any race)	738	30.6
Mexican	44	4.7
Puerto Rican	20	100.0
South American	264	51.2

Language Spoken at Home: English Only
(Universe: Population 5 Years and Over)

Group	Number	%
Total Population	39,315	82.8
Hispanic or Latino (of any race)	2,583	31.1
Mexican	448	28.8
Puerto Rican	1,477	37.1
South American	305	33.3

Language Spoken at Home: Spanish
(Universe: Population 5 Years and Over)

Group	Number	%
Total Population	6,161	13.0
Hispanic or Latino (of any race)	5,727	68.9
Mexican	1,107	71.2
Puerto Rican	2,502	62.9
South American	611	66.7

Unemployment Rate
(Universe: Population 16 Years and Over)

Group	%
Total Population	9.8
Hispanic or Latino (of any race)	14.9
Mexican	11.8
Puerto Rican	16.4
South American	10.7

Class of Worker: Private Wage and Salary
(Universe: Civilian Employed Population 16 Years and Over)

Group	Number	%
Total Population	19,876	82.5
Hispanic or Latino (of any race)	3,317	81.8
Mexican	821	96.7
Puerto Rican	1,454	80.1
South American	300	74.8

Class of Worker: Government
(Universe: Civilian Employed Population 16 Years and Over)

Group	Number	%
Total Population	3,241	13.4
Hispanic or Latino (of any race)	632	15.6
Mexican	14	1.6
Puerto Rican	334	18.4
South American	56	14.0

Means of Transportation to Work: Car, Truck or Van
(Universe: Workers 16 Years and Over)

Group	Number	%
Total Population	21,410	91.3
Hispanic or Latino (of any race)	3,533	91.2
Mexican	832	98.0
Puerto Rican	1,548	93.9
South American	303	77.7

Means of Transportation to Work: Public Transportation (ex. Taxicab)
(Universe: Workers 16 Years and Over)

Group	Number	%
Total Population	194	0.8
Hispanic or Latino (of any race)	69	1.8
Mexican	14	1.6
Puerto Rican	24	1.5
South American	19	4.9

Homeownership Rate
(Universe: Occupied Housing Units)

Group	%
Total Population	50.1

Sanford

Population

Group	Number	%TP[1]	%HP[2]
Total Population	53,570	100.0	–
Hispanic or Latino (of any race)	10,844	20.2	100.0
Central American, ex. Mexican	848	1.6	7.8
Guatemalan	274	0.5	2.5
Honduran	115	0.2	1.1
Panamanian	154	0.3	1.4
Salvadoran	171	0.3	1.6
Cuban	396	0.7	3.7
Dominican Republic	444	0.8	4.1
Mexican	1,776	3.3	16.4
Puerto Rican	5,538	10.3	51.1
South American	1,246	2.3	11.5
Argentinean	113	0.2	1.0
Colombian	563	1.1	5.2
Ecuadorian	205	0.4	1.9
Peruvian	129	0.2	1.2
Venezuelan	155	0.3	1.4

Population Growth: 2000–2010

Group	%
Total Population	39.9
Hispanic or Latino (of any race)	172.9
Central American, ex. Mexican	341.7
Cuban	214.3
Mexican	104.6
Puerto Rican	180.5
South American	368.4
Colombian	377.1

Males per 100 Females

Group	Number
Total Population	92.3
Hispanic or Latino (of any race)	97.9
Central American, ex. Mexican	121.4
Guatemalan	234.1
Honduran	117.0
Panamanian	73.0
Salvadoran	98.8
Cuban	104.1
Dominican Republic	87.3
Mexican	124.2

Median Age

Group	Years
Total Population	32.4
Hispanic or Latino (of any race)	27.1
Central American, ex. Mexican	28.5
Guatemalan	25.2
Honduran	29.6
Panamanian	33.0
Salvadoran	28.6
Cuban	33.3
Dominican Republic	29.1
Mexican	23.6
Puerto Rican	27.3
South American	32.8
Argentinean	31.3
Colombian	34.2
Ecuadorian	35.3
Peruvian	32.1
Venezuelan	31.3

High School Graduates
(Universe: Population 25 Years and Over)

Group	Number	%
Total Population	27,059	82.7
Hispanic or Latino (of any race)	3,892	76.3
Mexican	368	54.0
Puerto Rican	1,962	75.4
South American	551	97.9

Four-Year College Graduates
(Universe: Population 25 Years and Over)

Group	Number	%
Total Population	6,963	21.3
Hispanic or Latino (of any race)	831	16.3
Mexican	70	10.3
Puerto Rican	308	11.8
South American	156	27.7

Population Age 3–17 Enrolled in Public School
(Universe: Population Age 3–17 Enrolled in School)

Group	Number	%
Total Population	8,812	88.8
Hispanic or Latino (of any race)	1,790	90.5
Mexican	376	83.0
Puerto Rican	795	91.7
South American	253	86.9

Population Age 3–17 Enrolled in Private School
(Universe: Population Age 3–17 Enrolled in School)

Group	Number	%
Total Population	1,113	11.2
Hispanic or Latino (of any race)	187	9.5
Mexican	77	17.0
Puerto Rican	72	8.3
South American	38	13.1

Notes: (1) Percent of total population; (2) Percent of Hispanic/Latino population; Profiles include places with an overall population of at least 125,000, OR an overall population of at least 25,000 where the Hispanic/Latino population is at least 20% of the overall population. In states where less than five places meet either of these criteria, we have included places with at least 10,000 total population with the highest percentage of Hispanic/Latino population. These places are identified with an asterisk (*); Please refer to the User's Guide for a full explanation of data.

Hispanic or Latino (of any race)	39.2
Central American, ex. Mexican	32.9
Guatemalan	23.4
Honduran	27.8
Panamanian	38.1
Salvadoran	37.5
Cuban	48.2
Dominican Republic	40.4
Mexican	26.3
Puerto Rican	38.6
South American	57.1
Argentinean	59.5
Colombian	56.0
Ecuadorian	69.6
Peruvian	48.6
Venezuelan	58.8

Median Home Value

Group	Dollars
Total Population	165,400
Hispanic or Latino (of any race)	188,900
Mexican	122,200
Puerto Rican	162,200
South American	202,300

Median Gross Rent

Group	Dollars
Total Population	909
Hispanic or Latino (of any race)	906
Mexican	860
Puerto Rican	1,012
South American	1,349

Median Household Income
(2010 Inflation-Adjusted Dollars)

Group	Dollars
Total Population	43,470
Hispanic or Latino (of any race)	36,513
Mexican	39,018
Puerto Rican	35,566
South American	37,316

Per Capita Income
(2010 Inflation-Adjusted Dollars)

Group	Dollars
Total Population	20,588
Hispanic or Latino (of any race)	15,735
Mexican	12,606
Puerto Rican	14,958
South American	15,134

Households with $100,000+ Income

Group	Number	%
Total Population	2,006	10.6
Hispanic or Latino (of any race)	204	7.4
Mexican	24	5.5
Puerto Rican	72	5.2
South American	0	0.0

Households with Food Stamps/SNAP Benefits During Past 12 Months

Group	Number	%
Total Population	2,198	11.6
Hispanic or Latino (of any race)	422	15.4
Mexican	42	9.6
Puerto Rican	299	21.6
South American	21	8.5

Poverty Rate
(Income in Past 12 Months Below Poverty Level)

Group	%
Total Population	18.5
Hispanic or Latino (of any race)	16.1
Mexican	25.9
Puerto Rican	13.3
South American	7.3

South Miami Heights

Population

Group	Number	%TP[1]	%HP[2]
Total Population	35,696	100.0	–
Hispanic or Latino (of any race)	24,258	68.0	100.0
Central American, ex. Mexican	3,456	9.7	14.2
Costa Rican	106	0.3	0.4
Guatemalan	243	0.7	1.0
Honduran	839	2.4	3.5
Nicaraguan	1,585	4.4	6.5
Panamanian	158	0.4	0.7
Salvadoran	511	1.4	2.1
Cuban	13,466	37.7	55.5
Dominican Republic	988	2.8	4.1
Mexican	1,107	3.1	4.6
Puerto Rican	2,065	5.8	8.5
South American	2,066	5.8	8.5
Argentinean	115	0.3	0.5
Colombian	1,007	2.8	4.2
Ecuadorian	205	0.6	0.8
Peruvian	398	1.1	1.6
Venezuelan	170	0.5	0.7

Population Growth: 2000–2010

Group	%
Total Population	6.5
Hispanic or Latino (of any race)	28.8
Central American, ex. Mexican	85.0
Guatemalan	65.3
Honduran	129.2
Nicaraguan	69.3
Salvadoran	134.4
Cuban	56.3
Dominican Republic	16.1
Mexican	27.7
Puerto Rican	-9.6
South American	43.4
Colombian	26.2
Ecuadorian	61.4
Peruvian	63.8
Venezuelan	60.4

Males per 100 Females

Group	Number
Total Population	93.7
Hispanic or Latino (of any race)	95.1
Central American, ex. Mexican	91.8
Costa Rican	60.6
Guatemalan	105.9
Honduran	85.2
Nicaraguan	91.2
Panamanian	81.6
Salvadoran	112.0
Cuban	99.8
Dominican Republic	76.4
Mexican	117.1
Puerto Rican	94.8
South American	72.0
Argentinean	105.4
Colombian	67.8
Ecuadorian	76.7
Peruvian	67.2
Venezuelan	82.8

Average Household Size

Group	People
Total Population	3.30
Hispanic or Latino (of any race)	3.45
Central American, ex. Mexican	4.02
Costa Rican	2.97
Guatemalan	3.81
Honduran	4.09
Nicaraguan	3.97
Panamanian	3.65
Salvadoran	4.58
Cuban	3.33
Dominican Republic	3.39
Mexican	4.64
Puerto Rican	3.12
South American	3.45
Argentinean	3.15
Colombian	3.51
Ecuadorian	3.43
Peruvian	3.69
Venezuelan	3.42

Median Age

Group	Years
Total Population	37.0
Hispanic or Latino (of any race)	38.4
Central American, ex. Mexican	35.0
Costa Rican	42.5
Guatemalan	37.1
Honduran	34.8
Nicaraguan	35.1
Panamanian	41.0
Salvadoran	31.0
Cuban	41.7
Dominican Republic	38.3
Mexican	25.9
Puerto Rican	34.1
South American	39.6
Argentinean	32.5
Colombian	40.0
Ecuadorian	41.2
Peruvian	42.3
Venezuelan	36.0

High School Graduates
(Universe: Population 25 Years and Over)

Group	Number	%
Total Population	17,031	72.9
Hispanic or Latino (of any race)	10,856	67.0
Central American, ex. Mexican	1,322	58.6
Honduran	488	68.3
Nicaraguan	484	60.4
Cuban	6,580	66.8
Dominican Republic	530	73.9
Puerto Rican	946	75.3
South American	1,085	77.1
Colombian	574	75.3

Four-Year College Graduates
(Universe: Population 25 Years and Over)

Group	Number	%
Total Population	3,214	13.8
Hispanic or Latino (of any race)	2,232	13.8
Central American, ex. Mexican	378	16.8
Honduran	170	23.8
Nicaraguan	95	11.9
Cuban	1,325	13.4
Dominican Republic	16	2.2
Puerto Rican	131	10.4
South American	238	16.9
Colombian	128	16.8

Population Age 3–17 Enrolled in Public School
(Universe: Population Age 3–17 Enrolled in School)

Group	Number	%
Total Population	6,830	90.7
Hispanic or Latino (of any race)	3,526	88.7
Central American, ex. Mexican	511	99.8
Honduran	183	99.5
Nicaraguan	328	100.0
Cuban	2,062	89.6
Dominican Republic	173	87.4
Puerto Rican	349	66.5
South American	300	100.0
Colombian	162	100.0

Population Age 3–17 Enrolled in Private School
(Universe: Population Age 3–17 Enrolled in School)

Group	Number	%
Total Population	701	9.3
Hispanic or Latino (of any race)	448	11.3
Central American, ex. Mexican	1	0.2
Honduran	1	0.5
Nicaraguan	0	0.0
Cuban	240	10.4
Dominican Republic	25	12.6
Puerto Rican	176	33.5
South American	0	0.0
Colombian	0	0.0

Foreign-Born Population

Group	Number	%
Total Population	18,302	50.0
Hispanic or Latino (of any race)	14,809	63.0
Central American, ex. Mexican	2,466	75.3
Honduran	703	67.7
Nicaraguan	980	71.4
Cuban	9,783	71.5
Dominican Republic	634	59.8
Puerto Rican	14	0.6
South American	1,320	63.7
Colombian	688	61.6

Notes: (1) Percent of total population; (2) Percent of Hispanic/Latino population; Profiles include places with an overall population of at least 125,000, OR an overall population of at least 25,000 where the Hispanic/Latino population is at least 20% of the overall population. In states where less than five places meet either of these criteria, we have included places with at least 10,000 total population with the highest percentage of Hispanic/Latino population. These places are identified with an asterisk (*); Please refer to the User's Guide for a full explanation of data.

Foreign-Born Naturalized U.S. Citizens

Group	Number	%
Total Population	8,694	47.5
Hispanic or Latino (of any race)	6,466	43.7
Central American, ex. Mexican	976	39.6
Honduran	433	61.6
Nicaraguan	415	42.3
Cuban	4,333	44.3
Dominican Republic	354	55.8
Puerto Rican	0	0.0
South American	601	45.5
Colombian	347	50.4

Language Spoken at Home: English Only
(Universe: Population 5 Years and Over)

Group	Number	%
Total Population	10,987	32.1
Hispanic or Latino (of any race)	1,110	5.0
Central American, ex. Mexican	163	5.2
Honduran	24	2.5
Nicaraguan	139	10.4
Cuban	417	3.3
Dominican Republic	26	2.5
Puerto Rican	315	14.6
South American	155	7.9
Colombian	115	10.5

Language Spoken at Home: Spanish
(Universe: Population 5 Years and Over)

Group	Number	%
Total Population	21,851	63.9
Hispanic or Latino (of any race)	20,985	94.9
Central American, ex. Mexican	2,976	94.8
Honduran	943	97.5
Nicaraguan	1,193	89.6
Cuban	12,329	96.6
Dominican Republic	1,008	97.5
Puerto Rican	1,838	85.4
South American	1,799	92.1
Colombian	982	89.5

Unemployment Rate
(Universe: Population 16 Years and Over)

Group	%
Total Population	8.2
Hispanic or Latino (of any race)	7.0
Central American, ex. Mexican	4.6
Honduran	9.6
Nicaraguan	5.1
Cuban	8.9
Dominican Republic	3.5
Puerto Rican	8.1
South American	3.6
Colombian	6.0

Class of Worker: Private Wage and Salary
(Universe: Civilian Employed Population 16 Years and Over)

Group	Number	%
Total Population	12,785	78.7
Hispanic or Latino (of any race)	8,711	80.6
Central American, ex. Mexican	1,561	82.2
Honduran	360	79.6
Nicaraguan	719	88.7
Cuban	4,450	79.1
Dominican Republic	399	71.5
Puerto Rican	852	90.2
South American	960	80.4
Colombian	621	88.8

Class of Worker: Government
(Universe: Civilian Employed Population 16 Years and Over)

Group	Number	%
Total Population	1,983	12.2
Hispanic or Latino (of any race)	970	9.0
Central American, ex. Mexican	112	5.9
Honduran	46	10.2
Nicaraguan	43	5.3
Cuban	526	9.4
Dominican Republic	77	13.8
Puerto Rican	91	9.6
South American	131	11.0
Colombian	54	7.7

Means of Transportation to Work: Car, Truck or Van
(Universe: Workers 16 Years and Over)

Group	Number	%
Total Population	13,595	85.7
Hispanic or Latino (of any race)	8,918	85.0
Central American, ex. Mexican	1,619	89.0
Honduran	389	91.3
Nicaraguan	728	92.0
Cuban	4,668	84.8
Dominican Republic	470	87.0
Puerto Rican	789	84.3
South American	923	83.5
Colombian	627	93.9

Means of Transportation to Work: Public Transportation (ex. Taxicab)
(Universe: Workers 16 Years and Over)

Group	Number	%
Total Population	872	5.5
Hispanic or Latino (of any race)	493	4.7
Central American, ex. Mexican	145	8.0
Honduran	13	3.1
Nicaraguan	63	8.0
Cuban	114	2.1
Dominican Republic	17	3.1
Puerto Rican	116	12.4
South American	84	7.6
Colombian	41	6.1

Homeownership Rate
(Universe: Occupied Housing Units)

Group	%
Total Population	60.3
Hispanic or Latino (of any race)	62.4
Central American, ex. Mexican	70.7
Costa Rican	65.5
Guatemalan	62.5
Honduran	66.8
Nicaraguan	74.8
Panamanian	79.6
Salvadoran	65.9
Cuban	62.5
Dominican Republic	55.4
Mexican	60.0
Puerto Rican	54.1
South American	63.9
Argentinean	59.0
Colombian	62.9
Ecuadorian	62.3
Peruvian	70.9
Venezuelan	55.6

Median Home Value

Group	Dollars
Total Population	226,600
Hispanic or Latino (of any race)	238,100
Central American, ex. Mexican	239,500
Honduran	241,300
Nicaraguan	238,400
Cuban	243,900
Dominican Republic	147,200
Puerto Rican	206,600
South American	237,200
Colombian	245,100

Median Gross Rent

Group	Dollars
Total Population	880
Hispanic or Latino (of any race)	870
Central American, ex. Mexican	956
Honduran	1,098
Nicaraguan	956
Cuban	844
Dominican Republic	945
Puerto Rican	956
South American	833
Colombian	853

Median Household Income
(2010 Inflation-Adjusted Dollars)

Group	Dollars
Total Population	45,383
Hispanic or Latino (of any race)	43,125
Central American, ex. Mexican	47,288
Honduran	40,573
Nicaraguan	55,587
Cuban	42,239
Dominican Republic	26,759
Puerto Rican	41,339
South American	38,803
Colombian	39,241

Per Capita Income
(2010 Inflation-Adjusted Dollars)

Group	Dollars
Total Population	16,764
Hispanic or Latino (of any race)	16,099
Central American, ex. Mexican	13,782
Honduran	12,065
Nicaraguan	13,317
Cuban	15,765
Dominican Republic	14,498
Puerto Rican	17,850
South American	20,573
Colombian	25,900

Households with $100,000+ Income

Group	Number	%
Total Population	1,331	12.6
Hispanic or Latino (of any race)	840	12.0
Central American, ex. Mexican	73	9.0
Honduran	24	13.3
Nicaraguan	46	12.6
Cuban	413	10.0
Dominican Republic	9	2.5
Puerto Rican	189	26.7
South American	123	17.2
Colombian	72	18.5

Households with Food Stamps/SNAP Benefits During Past 12 Months

Group	Number	%
Total Population	2,942	27.9
Hispanic or Latino (of any race)	2,207	31.6
Central American, ex. Mexican	136	16.7
Honduran	63	34.8
Nicaraguan	57	15.6
Cuban	1,586	38.4
Dominican Republic	73	20.1
Puerto Rican	191	26.9
South American	157	22.0
Colombian	116	29.8

Poverty Rate
(Income in Past 12 Months Below Poverty Level)

Group	%
Total Population	16.8
Hispanic or Latino (of any race)	16.2
Central American, ex. Mexican	14.4
Honduran	19.3
Nicaraguan	9.2
Cuban	16.6
Dominican Republic	16.4
Puerto Rican	15.2
South American	19.8
Colombian	16.9

Sunrise

Population

Group	Number	%TP[1]	%HP[2]
Total Population	84,439	100.0	–
Hispanic or Latino (of any race)	21,621	25.6	100.0
Central American, ex. Mexican	1,785	2.1	8.3
Costa Rican	166	0.2	0.8
Guatemalan	280	0.3	1.3
Honduran	401	0.5	1.9
Nicaraguan	338	0.4	1.6
Panamanian	244	0.3	1.1
Salvadoran	346	0.4	1.6
Cuban	2,956	3.5	13.7
Dominican Republic	1,387	1.6	6.4
Mexican	722	0.9	3.3
Puerto Rican	4,210	5.0	19.5
South American	9,204	10.9	42.6
Argentinean	451	0.5	2.1
Chilean	171	0.2	0.8
Colombian	4,592	5.4	21.2

Notes: (1) Percent of total population; (2) Percent of Hispanic/Latino population; Profiles include places with an overall population of at least 125,000, OR an overall population of at least 25,000 where the Hispanic/Latino population is at least 20% of the overall population. In states where less than five places meet either of these criteria, we have included places with at least 10,000 total population with the highest percentage of Hispanic/Latino population. These places are identified with an asterisk (*); Please refer to the User's Guide for a full explanation of data.

Ecuadorian	995	1.2	4.6
Peruvian	1,503	1.8	7.0
Uruguayan	135	0.2	0.6
Venezuelan	1,241	1.5	5.7
Spaniard	173	0.2	0.8

Population Growth: 2000–2010

Group	%
Total Population	-1.6
Hispanic or Latino (of any race)	47.5
Central American, ex. Mexican	127.7
Honduran	182.4
Nicaraguan	156.1
Panamanian	80.7
Salvadoran	119.0
Cuban	50.4
Dominican Republic	142.1
Mexican	26.7
Puerto Rican	30.6
South American	113.1
Argentinean	93.6
Chilean	27.6
Colombian	119.7
Ecuadorian	153.8
Peruvian	118.5
Venezuelan	128.5

Males per 100 Females

Group	Number
Total Population	87.0
Hispanic or Latino (of any race)	86.9
Central American, ex. Mexican	87.7
Costa Rican	71.1
Guatemalan	110.5
Honduran	75.1
Nicaraguan	101.2
Panamanian	68.3
Salvadoran	100.0
Cuban	94.7
Dominican Republic	82.0
Mexican	107.5
Puerto Rican	89.0
South American	81.5
Argentinean	93.6
Chilean	87.9
Colombian	75.8
Ecuadorian	81.2
Peruvian	88.3
Uruguayan	104.5
Venezuelan	88.9
Spaniard	96.6

Average Household Size

Group	People
Total Population	2.58
Hispanic or Latino (of any race)	2.80
Central American, ex. Mexican	3.18
Costa Rican	3.25
Guatemalan	3.22
Honduran	3.32
Nicaraguan	3.18
Panamanian	2.70
Salvadoran	3.43
Cuban	2.53
Dominican Republic	3.10
Mexican	2.82
Puerto Rican	2.71
South American	2.86
Argentinean	2.54
Chilean	2.72
Colombian	2.81
Ecuadorian	3.08
Peruvian	2.95
Uruguayan	2.71
Venezuelan	2.97
Spaniard	2.63

Median Age

Group	Years
Total Population	39.1
Hispanic or Latino (of any race)	37.2
Central American, ex. Mexican	36.3
Costa Rican	36.0
Guatemalan	34.4
Honduran	32.9
Nicaraguan	34.5
Panamanian	43.2
Salvadoran	36.3
Cuban	41.3
Dominican Republic	34.2
Mexican	32.4
Puerto Rican	34.5
South American	38.8
Argentinean	38.8
Chilean	40.6
Colombian	39.4
Ecuadorian	39.5
Peruvian	40.1
Uruguayan	45.5
Venezuelan	34.0
Spaniard	44.5

High School Graduates
(Universe: Population 25 Years and Over)

Group	Number	%
Total Population	50,811	88.4
Hispanic or Latino (of any race)	12,203	85.3
Central American, ex. Mexican	752	67.1
Cuban	1,657	80.9
Dominican Republic	1,071	86.9
Puerto Rican	1,980	76.3
South American	5,870	94.0
Colombian	2,207	91.6
Ecuadorian	1,014	95.5
Peruvian	957	96.9
Venezuelan	1,148	94.6

Four-Year College Graduates
(Universe: Population 25 Years and Over)

Group	Number	%
Total Population	14,288	24.9
Hispanic or Latino (of any race)	3,809	26.6
Central American, ex. Mexican	212	18.9
Cuban	439	21.4
Dominican Republic	241	19.5
Puerto Rican	619	23.8
South American	2,051	32.8
Colombian	805	33.4
Ecuadorian	333	31.4
Peruvian	282	28.5
Venezuelan	394	32.5

Population Age 3–17 Enrolled in Public School
(Universe: Population Age 3–17 Enrolled in School)

Group	Number	%
Total Population	14,188	89.3
Hispanic or Latino (of any race)	3,338	90.8
Central American, ex. Mexican	285	96.6
Cuban	400	90.9
Dominican Republic	355	97.8
Puerto Rican	874	86.4
South American	1,084	91.1
Colombian	459	92.2
Ecuadorian	207	100.0
Peruvian	170	100.0
Venezuelan	248	83.8

Population Age 3–17 Enrolled in Private School
(Universe: Population Age 3–17 Enrolled in School)

Group	Number	%
Total Population	1,692	10.7
Hispanic or Latino (of any race)	338	9.2
Central American, ex. Mexican	10	3.4
Cuban	40	9.1
Dominican Republic	8	2.2
Puerto Rican	138	13.6
South American	106	8.9
Colombian	39	7.8
Ecuadorian	0	0.0
Peruvian	0	0.0
Venezuelan	48	16.2

Foreign-Born Population

Group	Number	%
Total Population	30,322	35.6
Hispanic or Latino (of any race)	11,322	53.0
Central American, ex. Mexican	1,163	70.0
Cuban	1,569	53.6
Dominican Republic	1,091	53.9
Puerto Rican	40	0.9
South American	6,785	77.3
Colombian	2,512	73.6
Ecuadorian	1,167	80.7
Peruvian	1,450	90.3
Venezuelan	1,167	71.3

Foreign-Born Naturalized U.S. Citizens

Group	Number	%
Total Population	16,445	54.2
Hispanic or Latino (of any race)	5,164	45.6
Central American, ex. Mexican	600	51.6
Cuban	916	58.4
Dominican Republic	770	70.6
Puerto Rican	24	60.0
South American	2,459	36.2
Colombian	1,052	41.9
Ecuadorian	630	54.0
Peruvian	302	20.8
Venezuelan	259	22.2

Language Spoken at Home: English Only
(Universe: Population 5 Years and Over)

Group	Number	%
Total Population	52,082	65.2
Hispanic or Latino (of any race)	3,513	17.6
Central American, ex. Mexican	153	9.5
Cuban	603	22.8
Dominican Republic	194	10.3
Puerto Rican	1,282	33.5
South American	568	6.7
Colombian	58	1.8
Ecuadorian	86	6.1
Peruvian	39	2.5
Venezuelan	349	22.6

Language Spoken at Home: Spanish
(Universe: Population 5 Years and Over)

Group	Number	%
Total Population	17,202	21.5
Hispanic or Latino (of any race)	16,461	82.3
Central American, ex. Mexican	1,452	90.5
Cuban	2,039	77.2
Dominican Republic	1,693	89.7
Puerto Rican	2,533	66.1
South American	7,866	93.3
Colombian	3,239	98.2
Ecuadorian	1,323	93.9
Peruvian	1,522	97.5
Venezuelan	1,192	77.4

Unemployment Rate
(Universe: Population 16 Years and Over)

Group	%
Total Population	9.1
Hispanic or Latino (of any race)	9.6
Central American, ex. Mexican	2.3
Cuban	3.4
Dominican Republic	13.6
Puerto Rican	8.0
South American	11.9
Colombian	12.3
Ecuadorian	2.9
Peruvian	22.5
Venezuelan	12.5

Class of Worker: Private Wage and Salary
(Universe: Civilian Employed Population 16 Years and Over)

Group	Number	%
Total Population	35,110	80.9
Hispanic or Latino (of any race)	9,684	84.2
Central American, ex. Mexican	800	77.5
Cuban	1,318	90.8
Dominican Republic	943	88.7
Puerto Rican	1,499	75.9
South American	4,453	86.6
Colombian	1,496	79.4
Ecuadorian	870	93.8
Peruvian	825	90.9
Venezuelan	828	84.6

Class of Worker: Government
(Universe: Civilian Employed Population 16 Years and Over)

Group	Number	%
Total Population	5,982	13.8
Hispanic or Latino (of any race)	1,029	8.9

Notes: (1) Percent of total population; (2) Percent of Hispanic/Latino population; Profiles include places with an overall population of at least 125,000, OR an overall population of at least 25,000 where the Hispanic/Latino population is at least 20% of the overall population. In states where less than five places meet either of these criteria, we have included places with at least 10,000 total population with the highest percentage of Hispanic/Latino population. These places are identified with an asterisk (*); Please refer to the User's Guide for a full explanation of data.

Group	Number	%
Central American, ex. Mexican	75	7.3
Cuban	107	7.4
Dominican Republic	88	8.3
Puerto Rican	356	18.0
South American	264	5.1
Colombian	197	10.5
Ecuadorian	0	0.0
Peruvian	0	0.0
Venezuelan	67	6.8

Means of Transportation to Work: Car, Truck or Van
(Universe: Workers 16 Years and Over)

Group	Number	%
Total Population	39,136	92.5
Hispanic or Latino (of any race)	10,238	92.4
Central American, ex. Mexican	939	91.9
Cuban	1,260	93.1
Dominican Republic	973	94.3
Puerto Rican	1,823	91.7
South American	4,460	92.1
Colombian	1,625	92.1
Ecuadorian	859	92.6
Peruvian	859	96.8
Venezuelan	673	82.0

Means of Transportation to Work: Public Transportation (ex. Taxicab)
(Universe: Workers 16 Years and Over)

Group	Number	%
Total Population	833	2.0
Hispanic or Latino (of any race)	194	1.8
Central American, ex. Mexican	0	0.0
Cuban	0	0.0
Dominican Republic	26	2.5
Puerto Rican	59	3.0
South American	53	1.1
Colombian	11	0.6
Ecuadorian	42	4.5
Peruvian	0	0.0
Venezuelan	0	0.0

Homeownership Rate
(Universe: Occupied Housing Units)

Group	%
Total Population	72.7
Hispanic or Latino (of any race)	68.5
Central American, ex. Mexican	69.1
Costa Rican	64.7
Guatemalan	71.0
Honduran	63.4
Nicaraguan	76.1
Panamanian	68.0
Salvadoran	69.5
Cuban	76.9
Dominican Republic	65.1
Mexican	56.7
Puerto Rican	68.0
South American	66.7
Argentinean	65.1
Chilean	60.3
Colombian	67.7
Ecuadorian	65.6
Peruvian	65.1
Uruguayan	76.3
Venezuelan	65.1
Spaniard	88.2

Median Home Value

Group	Dollars
Total Population	199,900
Hispanic or Latino (of any race)	206,200
Central American, ex. Mexican	254,300
Cuban	234,500
Dominican Republic	229,500
Puerto Rican	205,700
South American	192,100
Colombian	190,000
Ecuadorian	207,600
Peruvian	185,800
Venezuelan	168,800

Median Gross Rent

Group	Dollars
Total Population	1,265
Hispanic or Latino (of any race)	1,303
Central American, ex. Mexican	1,252
Cuban	1,375
Dominican Republic	1,313
Puerto Rican	1,347
South American	1,312
Colombian	1,313
Ecuadorian	1,399
Peruvian	1,142
Venezuelan	1,331

Median Household Income
(2010 Inflation-Adjusted Dollars)

Group	Dollars
Total Population	49,496
Hispanic or Latino (of any race)	50,837
Central American, ex. Mexican	47,589
Cuban	60,313
Dominican Republic	49,309
Puerto Rican	52,533
South American	50,820
Colombian	41,220
Ecuadorian	58,378
Peruvian	43,750
Venezuelan	53,264

Per Capita Income
(2010 Inflation-Adjusted Dollars)

Group	Dollars
Total Population	23,679
Hispanic or Latino (of any race)	22,255
Central American, ex. Mexican	21,115
Cuban	27,148
Dominican Republic	21,826
Puerto Rican	21,559
South American	22,017
Colombian	21,061
Ecuadorian	25,463
Peruvian	15,180
Venezuelan	23,285

Households with $100,000+ Income

Group	Number	%
Total Population	5,392	16.9
Hispanic or Latino (of any race)	1,136	15.7
Central American, ex. Mexican	123	24.2
Cuban	162	15.4
Dominican Republic	88	13.6
Puerto Rican	243	17.8
South American	460	14.7
Colombian	149	12.0
Ecuadorian	73	15.2
Peruvian	33	6.6
Venezuelan	133	23.1

Households with Food Stamps/SNAP Benefits During Past 12 Months

Group	Number	%
Total Population	1,921	6.0
Hispanic or Latino (of any race)	501	6.9
Central American, ex. Mexican	26	5.1
Cuban	103	9.8
Dominican Republic	37	5.7
Puerto Rican	99	7.3
South American	148	4.7
Colombian	43	3.5
Ecuadorian	36	7.5
Peruvian	14	2.8
Venezuelan	48	8.3

Poverty Rate
(Income in Past 12 Months Below Poverty Level)

Group	%
Total Population	10.3
Hispanic or Latino (of any race)	7.9
Central American, ex. Mexican	1.6
Cuban	6.8
Dominican Republic	5.3
Puerto Rican	10.8
South American	7.7
Colombian	11.7
Ecuadorian	1.5
Peruvian	1.7
Venezuelan	13.4

Tallahassee

Population

Group	Number	%TP[1]	%HP[2]
Total Population	181,376	100.0	–
Hispanic or Latino (of any race)	11,346	6.3	100.0
Central American, ex. Mexican	1,170	0.6	10.3
Guatemalan	160	0.1	1.4
Honduran	231	0.1	2.0
Nicaraguan	221	0.1	1.9
Panamanian	255	0.1	2.2
Salvadoran	218	0.1	1.9
Cuban	2,302	1.3	20.3
Dominican Republic	372	0.2	3.3
Mexican	2,354	1.3	20.7
Puerto Rican	2,275	1.3	20.1
South American	1,701	0.9	15.0
Argentinean	121	0.1	1.1
Colombian	800	0.4	7.1
Ecuadorian	106	0.1	0.9
Peruvian	244	0.1	2.2
Venezuelan	245	0.1	2.2
Spaniard	361	0.2	3.2

Population Growth: 2000–2010

Group	%
Total Population	20.4
Hispanic or Latino (of any race)	79.8
Central American, ex. Mexican	167.7
Panamanian	96.2
Cuban	72.0
Dominican Republic	184.0
Mexican	113.6
Puerto Rican	74.7
South American	129.6
Colombian	119.2

Males per 100 Females

Group	Number
Total Population	88.9
Hispanic or Latino (of any race)	93.4
Central American, ex. Mexican	99.0
Guatemalan	180.7
Honduran	102.6
Nicaraguan	87.3
Panamanian	86.1
Salvadoran	89.6
Cuban	90.4
Dominican Republic	74.6
Mexican	95.0
Puerto Rican	96.8
South American	91.6
Argentinean	152.1
Colombian	94.2
Ecuadorian	71.0
Peruvian	74.3
Venezuelan	80.1
Spaniard	74.4

Average Household Size

Group	People
Total Population	2.23
Hispanic or Latino (of any race)	2.45
Central American, ex. Mexican	2.55
Guatemalan	2.90
Honduran	2.56
Nicaraguan	2.38
Panamanian	2.38
Salvadoran	3.00
Cuban	2.25
Dominican Republic	2.55
Mexican	2.82
Puerto Rican	2.45
South American	2.39
Argentinean	2.70
Colombian	2.38
Ecuadorian	2.78
Peruvian	2.24
Venezuelan	2.32
Spaniard	2.27

Median Age

Group	Years
Total Population	26.1

Notes: (1) Percent of total population; (2) Percent of Hispanic/Latino population; Profiles include places with an overall population of at least 125,000, OR an overall population of at least 25,000 where the Hispanic/Latino population is at least 20% of the overall population. In states where less than five places meet either of these criteria, we have included places with at least 10,000 total population with the highest percentage of Hispanic/Latino population. These places are identified with an asterisk (*); Please refer to the User's Guide for a full explanation of data.

Group	%
Hispanic or Latino (of any race)	22.7
Central American, ex. Mexican	23.4
Guatemalan	23.6
Honduran	24.6
Nicaraguan	22.5
Panamanian	22.5
Salvadoran	26.8
Cuban	22.1
Dominican Republic	22.0
Mexican	23.6
Puerto Rican	22.8
South American	22.6
Argentinean	22.1
Colombian	22.7
Ecuadorian	22.4
Peruvian	22.8
Venezuelan	22.3
Spaniard	24.0

High School Graduates
(Universe: Population 25 Years and Over)

Group	Number	%
Total Population	83,891	90.9
Hispanic or Latino (of any race)	3,775	85.6
Cuban	640	86.8
Mexican	743	72.4
Puerto Rican	913	89.2
South American	900	94.9
Colombian	355	93.7

Four-Year College Graduates
(Universe: Population 25 Years and Over)

Group	Number	%
Total Population	41,501	44.9
Hispanic or Latino (of any race)	1,815	41.1
Cuban	479	65.0
Mexican	263	25.6
Puerto Rican	296	28.9
South American	442	46.6
Colombian	180	47.5

Population Age 3–17 Enrolled in Public School
(Universe: Population Age 3–17 Enrolled in School)

Group	Number	%
Total Population	16,958	75.9
Hispanic or Latino (of any race)	776	71.4
Cuban	117	51.3
Mexican	300	95.2
Puerto Rican	130	100.0
South American	43	23.1
Colombian	10	6.9

Population Age 3–17 Enrolled in Private School
(Universe: Population Age 3–17 Enrolled in School)

Group	Number	%
Total Population	5,391	24.1
Hispanic or Latino (of any race)	311	28.6
Cuban	111	48.7
Mexican	15	4.8
Puerto Rican	0	0.0
South American	143	76.9
Colombian	135	93.1

Foreign-Born Population

Group	Number	%
Total Population	13,649	7.7
Hispanic or Latino (of any race)	3,146	28.9
Cuban	356	17.2
Mexican	699	30.4
Puerto Rican	36	1.8
South American	1,225	57.1
Colombian	592	54.3

Foreign-Born Naturalized U.S. Citizens

Group	Number	%
Total Population	5,592	41.0
Hispanic or Latino (of any race)	926	29.4
Cuban	154	43.3
Mexican	81	11.6
Puerto Rican	36	100.0
South American	453	37.0
Colombian	167	28.2

Language Spoken at Home: English Only
(Universe: Population 5 Years and Over)

Group	Number	%
Total Population	150,314	90.0
Hispanic or Latino (of any race)	4,264	41.5
Cuban	876	44.9
Mexican	1,056	52.0
Puerto Rican	655	34.2
South American	512	25.1
Colombian	301	28.3

Language Spoken at Home: Spanish
(Universe: Population 5 Years and Over)

Group	Number	%
Total Population	7,693	4.6
Hispanic or Latino (of any race)	5,914	57.5
Cuban	1,042	53.4
Mexican	919	45.2
Puerto Rican	1,260	65.8
South American	1,524	74.9
Colombian	761	71.7

Unemployment Rate
(Universe: Population 16 Years and Over)

Group	%
Total Population	9.6
Hispanic or Latino (of any race)	11.5
Cuban	5.0
Mexican	17.5
Puerto Rican	13.5
South American	10.2
Colombian	19.6

Class of Worker: Private Wage and Salary
(Universe: Civilian Employed Population 16 Years and Over)

Group	Number	%
Total Population	56,196	63.4
Hispanic or Latino (of any race)	3,533	71.9
Cuban	707	69.9
Mexican	562	80.3
Puerto Rican	797	70.4
South American	707	74.8
Colombian	242	67.8

Class of Worker: Government
(Universe: Civilian Employed Population 16 Years and Over)

Group	Number	%
Total Population	28,861	32.5
Hispanic or Latino (of any race)	1,242	25.3
Cuban	304	30.1
Mexican	104	14.9
Puerto Rican	335	29.6
South American	168	17.8
Colombian	115	32.2

Means of Transportation to Work: Car, Truck or Van
(Universe: Workers 16 Years and Over)

Group	Number	%
Total Population	78,664	90.6
Hispanic or Latino (of any race)	4,416	89.2
Cuban	892	89.3
Mexican	699	94.1
Puerto Rican	945	84.7
South American	817	86.5
Colombian	268	75.1

Means of Transportation to Work: Public Transportation (ex. Taxicab)
(Universe: Workers 16 Years and Over)

Group	Number	%
Total Population	1,631	1.9
Hispanic or Latino (of any race)	50	1.0
Cuban	0	0.0
Mexican	35	4.7
Puerto Rican	0	0.0
South American	0	0.0
Colombian	0	0.0

Homeownership Rate
(Universe: Occupied Housing Units)

Group	%
Total Population	41.4
Hispanic or Latino (of any race)	27.0
Central American, ex. Mexican	22.9
Guatemalan	22.4
Honduran	24.7
Nicaraguan	18.5
Panamanian	19.6
Salvadoran	29.9
Cuban	27.6
Dominican Republic	20.5
Mexican	24.7
Puerto Rican	29.9
South American	25.9
Argentinean	38.6
Colombian	26.1
Ecuadorian	27.8
Peruvian	17.4
Venezuelan	18.9
Spaniard	44.8

Median Home Value

Group	Dollars
Total Population	194,500
Hispanic or Latino (of any race)	191,900
Cuban	197,800
Mexican	225,000
Puerto Rican	168,200
South American	177,200
Colombian	157,700

Median Gross Rent

Group	Dollars
Total Population	875
Hispanic or Latino (of any race)	992
Cuban	1,022
Mexican	926
Puerto Rican	879
South American	1,092
Colombian	1,215

Median Household Income
(2010 Inflation-Adjusted Dollars)

Group	Dollars
Total Population	37,451
Hispanic or Latino (of any race)	29,183
Cuban	28,784
Mexican	24,286
Puerto Rican	37,139
South American	20,467
Colombian	17,813

Per Capita Income
(2010 Inflation-Adjusted Dollars)

Group	Dollars
Total Population	23,598
Hispanic or Latino (of any race)	16,686
Cuban	19,793
Mexican	15,503
Puerto Rican	17,680
South American	14,712
Colombian	7,458

Households with $100,000+ Income

Group	Number	%
Total Population	10,462	14.3
Hispanic or Latino (of any race)	290	8.3
Cuban	71	10.7
Mexican	49	7.7
Puerto Rican	70	11.1
South American	18	2.4
Colombian	0	0.0

Households with Food Stamps/SNAP Benefits During Past 12 Months

Group	Number	%
Total Population	6,689	9.1
Hispanic or Latino (of any race)	195	5.6
Cuban	48	7.2
Mexican	51	8.0
Puerto Rican	58	9.2
South American	31	4.1
Colombian	17	5.2

Poverty Rate
(Income in Past 12 Months Below Poverty Level)

Group	%
Total Population	28.5
Hispanic or Latino (of any race)	34.3

STATE & PLACE PROFILES

Notes: (1) Percent of total population; (2) Percent of Hispanic/Latino population; Profiles include places with an overall population of at least 125,000, OR an overall population of at least 25,000 where the Hispanic/Latino population is at least 20% of the overall population. In states where less than five places meet either of these criteria, we have included places with at least 10,000 total population with the highest percentage of Hispanic/Latino population. These places are identified with an asterisk (*); Please refer to the User's Guide for a full explanation of data.

Cuban	34.4
Mexican	36.1
Puerto Rican	25.8
South American	37.7
Colombian	57.5

Tamarac

Population

Group	Number	%TP[1]	%HP[2]
Total Population	60,427	100.0	–
Hispanic or Latino (of any race)	14,713	24.3	100.0
Central American, ex. Mexican	1,205	2.0	8.2
Costa Rican	106	0.2	0.7
Guatemalan	151	0.2	1.0
Honduran	252	0.4	1.7
Nicaraguan	183	0.3	1.2
Panamanian	186	0.3	1.3
Salvadoran	326	0.5	2.2
Cuban	1,510	2.5	10.3
Dominican Republic	815	1.3	5.5
Mexican	617	1.0	4.2
Puerto Rican	3,029	5.0	20.6
South American	6,607	10.9	44.9
Argentinean	370	0.6	2.5
Chilean	129	0.2	0.9
Colombian	3,762	6.2	25.6
Ecuadorian	516	0.9	3.5
Peruvian	966	1.6	6.6
Uruguayan	125	0.2	0.8
Venezuelan	643	1.1	4.4
Spaniard	135	0.2	0.9

Population Growth: 2000–2010

Group	%
Total Population	8.7
Hispanic or Latino (of any race)	77.8
Central American, ex. Mexican	195.3
Honduran	93.8
Cuban	91.1
Dominican Republic	209.9
Mexican	21.7
Puerto Rican	54.9
South American	164.7
Argentinean	230.4
Colombian	147.0
Ecuadorian	232.9
Peruvian	182.5
Venezuelan	229.7

Males per 100 Females

Group	Number
Total Population	80.3
Hispanic or Latino (of any race)	88.8
Central American, ex. Mexican	95.3
Costa Rican	86.0
Guatemalan	91.1
Honduran	95.3
Nicaraguan	96.8
Panamanian	60.3
Salvadoran	128.0
Cuban	111.2
Dominican Republic	81.1
Mexican	101.0
Puerto Rican	90.5
South American	82.0
Argentinean	100.0
Chilean	92.5
Colombian	78.4
Ecuadorian	76.7
Peruvian	84.0
Uruguayan	127.3
Venezuelan	90.8
Spaniard	90.1

Average Household Size

Group	People
Total Population	2.12
Hispanic or Latino (of any race)	2.69
Central American, ex. Mexican	2.98
Costa Rican	2.75
Guatemalan	2.83
Honduran	3.01
Nicaraguan	3.02
Panamanian	2.61
Salvadoran	3.40
Cuban	2.38
Dominican Republic	2.77
Mexican	2.70
Puerto Rican	2.49
South American	2.84
Argentinean	2.47
Chilean	2.18
Colombian	2.92
Ecuadorian	2.79
Peruvian	2.86
Uruguayan	2.87
Venezuelan	2.82
Spaniard	2.25

Median Age

Group	Years
Total Population	47.1
Hispanic or Latino (of any race)	37.3
Central American, ex. Mexican	34.8
Costa Rican	37.7
Guatemalan	36.1
Honduran	36.3
Nicaraguan	34.3
Panamanian	43.0
Salvadoran	30.2
Cuban	41.7
Dominican Republic	35.5
Mexican	30.5
Puerto Rican	37.8
South American	39.0
Argentinean	42.9
Chilean	45.5
Colombian	39.7
Ecuadorian	39.2
Peruvian	39.1
Uruguayan	36.8
Venezuelan	34.5
Spaniard	45.7

High School Graduates
(Universe: Population 25 Years and Over)

Group	Number	%
Total Population	40,862	88.1
Hispanic or Latino (of any race)	9,188	87.2
Central American, ex. Mexican	680	68.3
Cuban	1,012	94.7
Puerto Rican	2,021	86.7
South American	4,468	91.8
Colombian	2,434	88.9

Four-Year College Graduates
(Universe: Population 25 Years and Over)

Group	Number	%
Total Population	11,041	23.8
Hispanic or Latino (of any race)	2,263	21.5
Central American, ex. Mexican	96	9.6
Cuban	145	13.6
Puerto Rican	512	22.0
South American	1,304	26.8
Colombian	600	21.9

Population Age 3–17 Enrolled in Public School
(Universe: Population Age 3–17 Enrolled in School)

Group	Number	%
Total Population	6,316	82.4
Hispanic or Latino (of any race)	2,238	86.6
Central American, ex. Mexican	133	81.6
Cuban	361	90.5
Puerto Rican	423	79.5
South American	926	88.5
Colombian	456	96.4

Population Age 3–17 Enrolled in Private School
(Universe: Population Age 3–17 Enrolled in School)

Group	Number	%
Total Population	1,347	17.6
Hispanic or Latino (of any race)	345	13.4
Central American, ex. Mexican	30	18.4
Cuban	38	9.5
Puerto Rican	109	20.5
South American	120	11.5
Colombian	17	3.6

Foreign-Born Population

Group	Number	%
Total Population	17,639	29.5
Hispanic or Latino (of any race)	7,896	51.0
Central American, ex. Mexican	1,005	69.1
Cuban	781	45.8
Puerto Rican	47	1.5
South American	5,147	73.1
Colombian	2,858	74.2

Foreign-Born Naturalized U.S. Citizens

Group	Number	%
Total Population	9,881	56.0
Hispanic or Latino (of any race)	3,672	46.5
Central American, ex. Mexican	441	43.9
Cuban	673	86.2
Puerto Rican	30	63.8
South American	2,087	40.5
Colombian	1,127	39.4

Language Spoken at Home: English Only
(Universe: Population 5 Years and Over)

Group	Number	%
Total Population	38,115	67.3
Hispanic or Latino (of any race)	2,183	15.4
Central American, ex. Mexican	106	8.4
Cuban	525	33.2
Puerto Rican	779	25.6
South American	296	4.6
Colombian	103	2.9

Language Spoken at Home: Spanish
(Universe: Population 5 Years and Over)

Group	Number	%
Total Population	12,903	22.8
Hispanic or Latino (of any race)	11,918	84.1
Central American, ex. Mexican	1,126	89.4
Cuban	1,056	66.8
Puerto Rican	2,262	74.4
South American	6,096	95.0
Colombian	3,457	97.1

Unemployment Rate
(Universe: Population 16 Years and Over)

Group	%
Total Population	9.4
Hispanic or Latino (of any race)	11.8
Central American, ex. Mexican	3.9
Cuban	2.3
Puerto Rican	10.1
South American	17.4
Colombian	16.4

Class of Worker: Private Wage and Salary
(Universe: Civilian Employed Population 16 Years and Over)

Group	Number	%
Total Population	22,170	81.7
Hispanic or Latino (of any race)	6,522	81.8
Central American, ex. Mexican	853	91.5
Cuban	678	72.4
Puerto Rican	1,284	78.1
South American	2,882	81.9
Colombian	1,738	82.1

Class of Worker: Government
(Universe: Civilian Employed Population 16 Years and Over)

Group	Number	%
Total Population	3,254	12.0
Hispanic or Latino (of any race)	823	10.3
Central American, ex. Mexican	79	8.5
Cuban	133	14.2
Puerto Rican	330	20.1
South American	230	6.5
Colombian	141	6.7

Means of Transportation to Work: Car, Truck or Van
(Universe: Workers 16 Years and Over)

Group	Number	%
Total Population	24,415	92.9
Hispanic or Latino (of any race)	7,278	92.9
Central American, ex. Mexican	852	91.4
Cuban	837	89.4
Puerto Rican	1,554	96.3
South American	3,161	92.3

Notes: (1) Percent of total population; (2) Percent of Hispanic/Latino population; Profiles include places with an overall population of at least 125,000, OR an overall population of at least 25,000 where the Hispanic/Latino population is at least 20% of the overall population. In states where less than five places meet either of these criteria, we have included places with at least 10,000 total population with the highest percentage of Hispanic/Latino population. These places are identified with an asterisk (*); Please refer to the User's Guide for a full explanation of data.

Colombian	1,909	92.0

Means of Transportation to Work: Public Transportation (ex. Taxicab)
(Universe: Workers 16 Years and Over)

Group	Number	%
Total Population	537	2.0
Hispanic or Latino (of any race)	256	3.3
Central American, ex. Mexican	49	5.3
Cuban	0	0.0
Puerto Rican	11	0.7
South American	196	5.7
Colombian	128	6.2

Homeownership Rate
(Universe: Occupied Housing Units)

Group	%
Total Population	78.0
Hispanic or Latino (of any race)	69.5
Central American, ex. Mexican	62.1
Costa Rican	66.7
Guatemalan	67.3
Honduran	57.4
Nicaraguan	72.9
Panamanian	66.3
Salvadoran	52.0
Cuban	79.3
Dominican Republic	66.1
Mexican	59.1
Puerto Rican	67.8
South American	70.3
Argentinean	75.2
Chilean	80.7
Colombian	71.0
Ecuadorian	75.0
Peruvian	61.2
Uruguayan	70.2
Venezuelan	69.1
Spaniard	85.5

Median Home Value

Group	Dollars
Total Population	175,200
Hispanic or Latino (of any race)	188,500
Central American, ex. Mexican	164,900
Cuban	217,200
Puerto Rican	214,800
South American	165,700
Colombian	166,400

Median Gross Rent

Group	Dollars
Total Population	1,170
Hispanic or Latino (of any race)	1,143
Central American, ex. Mexican	995
Cuban	1,644
Puerto Rican	1,261
South American	1,233
Colombian	1,396

Median Household Income
(2010 Inflation-Adjusted Dollars)

Group	Dollars
Total Population	40,934
Hispanic or Latino (of any race)	42,070
Central American, ex. Mexican	46,814
Cuban	56,944
Puerto Rican	48,142
South American	34,841
Colombian	39,593

Per Capita Income
(2010 Inflation-Adjusted Dollars)

Group	Dollars
Total Population	25,315
Hispanic or Latino (of any race)	17,990
Central American, ex. Mexican	18,752
Cuban	19,848
Puerto Rican	24,215
South American	15,201
Colombian	15,700

Households with $100,000+ Income

Group	Number	%
Total Population	3,066	11.0
Hispanic or Latino (of any race)	545	10.4
Central American, ex. Mexican	70	14.8
Cuban	91	16.4
Puerto Rican	152	12.4
South American	152	6.3
Colombian	95	7.7

Households with Food Stamps/SNAP Benefits During Past 12 Months

Group	Number	%
Total Population	1,382	5.0
Hispanic or Latino (of any race)	560	10.7
Central American, ex. Mexican	48	10.2
Cuban	30	5.4
Puerto Rican	81	6.6
South American	350	14.6
Colombian	155	12.5

Poverty Rate
(Income in Past 12 Months Below Poverty Level)

Group	%
Total Population	10.4
Hispanic or Latino (of any race)	10.0
Central American, ex. Mexican	11.1
Cuban	6.4
Puerto Rican	5.8
South American	12.8
Colombian	13.1

Tamiami

Population

Group	Number	%TP[1]	%HP[2]
Total Population	55,271	100.0	–
Hispanic or Latino (of any race)	51,217	92.7	100.0
Central American, ex. Mexican	4,850	8.8	9.5
Costa Rican	144	0.3	0.3
Guatemalan	228	0.4	0.4
Honduran	540	1.0	1.1
Nicaraguan	3,476	6.3	6.8
Panamanian	216	0.4	0.4
Salvadoran	239	0.4	0.5
Cuban	36,180	65.5	70.6
Dominican Republic	985	1.8	1.9
Mexican	464	0.8	0.9
Puerto Rican	1,307	2.4	2.6
South American	5,642	10.2	11.0
Argentinean	356	0.6	0.7
Chilean	301	0.5	0.6
Colombian	2,594	4.7	5.1
Ecuadorian	480	0.9	0.9
Peruvian	697	1.3	1.4
Venezuelan	1,018	1.8	2.0
Spaniard	254	0.5	0.5

Population Growth: 2000–2010

Group	%
Total Population	0.9
Hispanic or Latino (of any race)	7.5
Central American, ex. Mexican	40.5
Guatemalan	86.9
Honduran	50.8
Nicaraguan	36.3
Panamanian	52.1
Cuban	16.6
Dominican Republic	17.8
Mexican	23.1
Puerto Rican	-5.4
South American	30.5
Argentinean	41.8
Chilean	14.9
Colombian	20.0
Ecuadorian	49.1
Peruvian	32.5
Venezuelan	74.6
Spaniard	39.6

Males per 100 Females

Group	Number
Total Population	89.5
Hispanic or Latino (of any race)	88.1
Central American, ex. Mexican	80.1
Costa Rican	87.0
Guatemalan	82.4
Honduran	65.1
Nicaraguan	82.9
Panamanian	63.6
Salvadoran	86.7
Cuban	90.7
Dominican Republic	72.8
Mexican	95.8
Puerto Rican	90.8
South American	80.6
Argentinean	90.4
Chilean	88.1
Colombian	76.2
Ecuadorian	80.5
Peruvian	89.4
Venezuelan	77.7
Spaniard	88.1

Average Household Size

Group	People
Total Population	3.29
Hispanic or Latino (of any race)	3.32
Central American, ex. Mexican	3.97
Costa Rican	3.70
Guatemalan	3.52
Honduran	3.78
Nicaraguan	4.10
Panamanian	3.08
Salvadoran	4.02
Cuban	3.22
Dominican Republic	3.57
Mexican	3.65
Puerto Rican	3.14
South American	3.52
Argentinean	3.50
Chilean	3.49
Colombian	3.47
Ecuadorian	3.48
Peruvian	3.45
Venezuelan	3.79
Spaniard	2.77

Median Age

Group	Years
Total Population	42.0
Hispanic or Latino (of any race)	43.1
Central American, ex. Mexican	39.4
Costa Rican	39.6
Guatemalan	36.3
Honduran	38.8
Nicaraguan	39.5
Panamanian	42.5
Salvadoran	36.9
Cuban	45.0
Dominican Republic	40.6
Mexican	30.6
Puerto Rican	38.7
South American	39.9
Argentinean	38.0
Chilean	47.9
Colombian	40.5
Ecuadorian	41.3
Peruvian	42.3
Venezuelan	35.3
Spaniard	51.5

High School Graduates
(Universe: Population 25 Years and Over)

Group	Number	%
Total Population	29,360	76.4
Hispanic or Latino (of any race)	27,411	75.7
Central American, ex. Mexican	2,949	86.1
Nicaraguan	2,404	85.9
Cuban	19,234	74.3
Dominican Republic	339	60.9
Puerto Rican	919	80.8
South American	3,397	79.2
Colombian	1,135	76.8
Venezuelan	828	87.2

Four-Year College Graduates
(Universe: Population 25 Years and Over)

Group	Number	%
Total Population	9,863	25.7
Hispanic or Latino (of any race)	9,153	25.3
Central American, ex. Mexican	856	25.0

Notes: (1) Percent of total population; (2) Percent of Hispanic/Latino population; Profiles include places with an overall population of at least 125,000, OR an overall population of at least 25,000 where the Hispanic/Latino population is at least 20% of the overall population. In states where less than five places meet either of these criteria, we have included places with at least 10,000 total population with the highest percentage of Hispanic/Latino population. These places are identified with an asterisk (*); Please refer to the User's Guide for a full explanation of data.

Group	Number	%
Nicaraguan	694	24.8
Cuban	6,724	26.0
Dominican Republic	91	16.3
Puerto Rican	366	32.2
South American	948	22.1
Colombian	330	22.3
Venezuelan	282	29.7

Population Age 3–17 Enrolled in Public School
(Universe: Population Age 3–17 Enrolled in School)

Group	Number	%
Total Population	7,568	83.6
Hispanic or Latino (of any race)	6,800	85.3
Central American, ex. Mexican	919	96.4
Nicaraguan	637	94.9
Cuban	4,225	83.6
Dominican Republic	128	84.8
Puerto Rican	234	57.6
South American	952	96.5
Colombian	434	95.6
Venezuelan	113	94.2

Population Age 3–17 Enrolled in Private School
(Universe: Population Age 3–17 Enrolled in School)

Group	Number	%
Total Population	1,484	16.4
Hispanic or Latino (of any race)	1,172	14.7
Central American, ex. Mexican	34	3.6
Nicaraguan	34	5.1
Cuban	828	16.4
Dominican Republic	23	15.2
Puerto Rican	172	42.4
South American	35	3.5
Colombian	20	4.4
Venezuelan	7	5.8

Foreign-Born Population

Group	Number	%
Total Population	35,539	65.0
Hispanic or Latino (of any race)	34,528	68.3
Central American, ex. Mexican	3,340	65.6
Nicaraguan	2,709	67.4
Cuban	24,933	71.6
Dominican Republic	553	63.3
Puerto Rican	126	6.7
South American	4,936	77.0
Colombian	1,633	73.4
Venezuelan	1,075	78.1

Foreign-Born Naturalized U.S. Citizens

Group	Number	%
Total Population	21,543	60.6
Hispanic or Latino (of any race)	20,935	60.6
Central American, ex. Mexican	2,218	66.4
Nicaraguan	1,776	65.6
Cuban	15,632	62.7
Dominican Republic	366	66.2
Puerto Rican	56	44.4
South American	2,258	45.7
Colombian	990	60.6
Venezuelan	329	30.6

Language Spoken at Home: English Only
(Universe: Population 5 Years and Over)

Group	Number	%
Total Population	3,268	6.2
Hispanic or Latino (of any race)	1,489	3.1
Central American, ex. Mexican	340	6.8
Nicaraguan	297	7.5
Cuban	681	2.0
Dominican Republic	25	3.0
Puerto Rican	262	15.3
South American	80	1.3
Colombian	34	1.5
Venezuelan	11	0.8

Language Spoken at Home: Spanish
(Universe: Population 5 Years and Over)

Group	Number	%
Total Population	48,372	92.4
Hispanic or Latino (of any race)	46,941	96.8
Central American, ex. Mexican	4,625	93.2
Nicaraguan	3,674	92.5
Cuban	32,575	97.8
Dominican Republic	805	97.0
Puerto Rican	1,447	84.7
South American	6,179	98.3
Colombian	2,169	98.5
Venezuelan	1,354	99.2

Unemployment Rate
(Universe: Population 16 Years and Over)

Group	%
Total Population	6.7
Hispanic or Latino (of any race)	6.8
Central American, ex. Mexican	9.4
Nicaraguan	9.9
Cuban	6.5
Dominican Republic	9.4
Puerto Rican	10.6
South American	5.7
Colombian	4.5
Venezuelan	8.3

Class of Worker: Private Wage and Salary
(Universe: Civilian Employed Population 16 Years and Over)

Group	Number	%
Total Population	22,075	81.8
Hispanic or Latino (of any race)	20,565	81.7
Central American, ex. Mexican	2,413	89.0
Nicaraguan	2,081	93.4
Cuban	13,574	79.3
Dominican Republic	443	95.7
Puerto Rican	708	80.7
South American	2,810	86.7
Colombian	879	78.7
Venezuelan	644	88.2

Class of Worker: Government
(Universe: Civilian Employed Population 16 Years and Over)

Group	Number	%
Total Population	3,173	11.8
Hispanic or Latino (of any race)	2,895	11.5
Central American, ex. Mexican	178	6.6
Nicaraguan	59	2.6
Cuban	2,320	13.6
Dominican Republic	20	4.3
Puerto Rican	99	11.3
South American	184	5.7
Colombian	84	7.5
Venezuelan	45	6.2

Means of Transportation to Work: Car, Truck or Van
(Universe: Workers 16 Years and Over)

Group	Number	%
Total Population	24,711	93.2
Hispanic or Latino (of any race)	22,986	93.1
Central American, ex. Mexican	2,344	89.0
Nicaraguan	1,942	89.2
Cuban	15,892	94.6
Dominican Republic	410	93.4
Puerto Rican	769	88.9
South American	2,977	93.4
Colombian	1,043	96.0
Venezuelan	682	93.4

Means of Transportation to Work: Public Transportation (ex. Taxicab)
(Universe: Workers 16 Years and Over)

Group	Number	%
Total Population	565	2.1
Hispanic or Latino (of any race)	558	2.3
Central American, ex. Mexican	62	2.4
Nicaraguan	62	2.8
Cuban	189	1.1
Dominican Republic	0	0.0
Puerto Rican	58	6.7
South American	88	2.8
Colombian	27	2.5
Venezuelan	0	0.0

Homeownership Rate
(Universe: Occupied Housing Units)

Group	%
Total Population	79.3
Hispanic or Latino (of any race)	79.1
Central American, ex. Mexican	76.2
Costa Rican	78.3
Guatemalan	73.4
Honduran	72.2
Nicaraguan	75.8
Panamanian	85.2
Salvadoran	83.0
Cuban	80.6
Dominican Republic	77.9
Mexican	66.7
Puerto Rican	78.3
South American	71.1
Argentinean	72.0
Chilean	77.0
Colombian	73.5
Ecuadorian	78.4
Peruvian	71.5
Venezuelan	56.0
Spaniard	90.2

Median Home Value

Group	Dollars
Total Population	290,100
Hispanic or Latino (of any race)	289,400
Central American, ex. Mexican	243,000
Nicaraguan	235,900
Cuban	307,300
Dominican Republic	265,800
Puerto Rican	262,100
South American	255,500
Colombian	272,100
Venezuelan	215,100

Median Gross Rent

Group	Dollars
Total Population	1,258
Hispanic or Latino (of any race)	1,253
Central American, ex. Mexican	1,391
Nicaraguan	1,391
Cuban	1,192
Dominican Republic	1,240
Puerto Rican	1,347
South American	1,299
Colombian	1,260
Venezuelan	1,216

Median Household Income
(2010 Inflation-Adjusted Dollars)

Group	Dollars
Total Population	53,456
Hispanic or Latino (of any race)	52,778
Central American, ex. Mexican	51,250
Nicaraguan	51,776
Cuban	52,719
Dominican Republic	62,361
Puerto Rican	71,080
South American	50,793
Colombian	48,438
Venezuelan	32,179

Per Capita Income
(2010 Inflation-Adjusted Dollars)

Group	Dollars
Total Population	22,345
Hispanic or Latino (of any race)	22,108
Central American, ex. Mexican	18,797
Nicaraguan	19,372
Cuban	23,233
Dominican Republic	19,658
Puerto Rican	27,853
South American	16,910
Colombian	15,820
Venezuelan	16,469

Households with $100,000+ Income

Group	Number	%
Total Population	3,546	21.8
Hispanic or Latino (of any race)	3,236	21.0
Central American, ex. Mexican	294	21.9
Nicaraguan	269	24.7
Cuban	2,311	20.7
Dominican Republic	62	23.0
Puerto Rican	206	39.4
South American	260	15.0
Colombian	60	11.5
Venezuelan	44	9.8

Notes: (1) Percent of total population; (2) Percent of Hispanic/Latino population; Profiles include places with an overall population of at least 125,000, OR an overall population of at least 25,000 where the Hispanic/Latino population is at least 20% of the overall population. In states where less than five places meet either of these criteria, we have included places with at least 10,000 total population with the highest percentage of Hispanic/Latino population. These places are identified with an asterisk (*); Please refer to the User's Guide for a full explanation of data.

Households with Food Stamps/SNAP Benefits During Past 12 Months		
Group	Number	%
Total Population	2,732	16.8
Hispanic or Latino (of any race)	2,695	17.5
Central American, ex. Mexican	249	18.5
Nicaraguan	223	20.5
Cuban	2,056	18.4
Dominican Republic	60	22.3
Puerto Rican	72	13.8
South American	249	14.4
Colombian	95	18.3
Venezuelan	68	15.1

Poverty Rate (Income in Past 12 Months Below Poverty Level)	
Group	%
Total Population	9.5
Hispanic or Latino (of any race)	10.0
Central American, ex. Mexican	12.0
Nicaraguan	14.2
Cuban	9.9
Dominican Republic	12.2
Puerto Rican	0.0
South American	12.1
Colombian	15.0
Venezuelan	17.8

Tampa

Population			
Group	Number	%TP[1]	%HP[2]
Total Population	335,709	100.0	–
Hispanic or Latino (of any race)	77,472	23.1	100.0
Central American, ex. Mexican	5,234	1.6	6.8
Costa Rican	374	0.1	0.5
Guatemalan	842	0.3	1.1
Honduran	2,004	0.6	2.6
Nicaraguan	537	0.2	0.7
Panamanian	656	0.2	0.8
Salvadoran	787	0.2	1.0
Cuban	21,295	6.3	27.5
Dominican Republic	3,110	0.9	4.0
Mexican	9,583	2.9	12.4
Puerto Rican	24,057	7.2	31.1
South American	6,102	1.8	7.9
Argentinean	386	0.1	0.5
Bolivian	164	<0.1	0.2
Chilean	165	<0.1	0.2
Colombian	2,846	0.8	3.7
Ecuadorian	814	0.2	1.1
Peruvian	800	0.2	1.0
Venezuelan	785	0.2	1.0
Spaniard	3,018	0.9	3.9

Population Growth: 2000–2010	
Group	%
Total Population	10.6
Hispanic or Latino (of any race)	32.4
Central American, ex. Mexican	121.6
Costa Rican	60.5
Guatemalan	274.2
Honduran	157.6
Nicaraguan	101.1
Panamanian	61.2
Salvadoran	117.4
Cuban	45.1
Dominican Republic	122.6
Mexican	52.8
Puerto Rican	37.3
South American	118.6
Argentinean	229.9
Colombian	103.1
Ecuadorian	161.7
Peruvian	119.2
Venezuelan	122.4
Spaniard	343.2

Males per 100 Females	
Group	Number
Total Population	95.6
Hispanic or Latino (of any race)	97.9
Central American, ex. Mexican	95.5
Costa Rican	81.6
Guatemalan	128.8
Honduran	98.6
Nicaraguan	81.4
Panamanian	74.0
Salvadoran	95.8
Cuban	100.7
Dominican Republic	87.1
Mexican	125.5
Puerto Rican	92.8
South American	86.7
Argentinean	107.5
Bolivian	67.3
Chilean	94.1
Colombian	82.8
Ecuadorian	95.2
Peruvian	90.5
Venezuelan	80.9
Spaniard	84.9

Average Household Size	
Group	People
Total Population	2.38
Hispanic or Latino (of any race)	2.70
Central American, ex. Mexican	3.07
Costa Rican	2.74
Guatemalan	3.18
Honduran	3.21
Nicaraguan	3.13
Panamanian	2.46
Salvadoran	3.36
Cuban	2.59
Dominican Republic	3.00
Mexican	3.44
Puerto Rican	2.75
South American	2.58
Argentinean	2.63
Bolivian	2.68
Chilean	2.16
Colombian	2.57
Ecuadorian	2.93
Peruvian	2.39
Venezuelan	2.48
Spaniard	2.07

Median Age	
Group	Years
Total Population	34.6
Hispanic or Latino (of any race)	32.6
Central American, ex. Mexican	30.7
Costa Rican	34.0
Guatemalan	28.2
Honduran	30.4
Nicaraguan	33.8
Panamanian	33.7
Salvadoran	30.0
Cuban	41.2
Dominican Republic	30.7
Mexican	25.7
Puerto Rican	28.8
South American	34.3
Argentinean	34.2
Bolivian	35.4
Chilean	37.3
Colombian	34.6
Ecuadorian	32.6
Peruvian	35.0
Venezuelan	33.4
Spaniard	47.2

High School Graduates (Universe: Population 25 Years and Over)		
Group	Number	%
Total Population	179,023	83.6
Hispanic or Latino (of any race)	33,333	71.3
Central American, ex. Mexican	1,680	55.3
Honduran	621	47.1
Cuban	10,304	72.2
Dominican Republic	1,265	85.1
Mexican	2,773	49.6
Puerto Rican	9,367	72.2
South American	3,515	88.2
Colombian	1,701	82.7
Peruvian	489	94.4
Spaniard	1,949	86.0

Four-Year College Graduates (Universe: Population 25 Years and Over)		
Group	Number	%
Total Population	66,907	31.2
Hispanic or Latino (of any race)	8,230	17.6
Central American, ex. Mexican	457	15.1
Honduran	85	6.4
Cuban	2,338	16.4
Dominican Republic	260	17.5
Mexican	576	10.3
Puerto Rican	1,707	13.2
South American	1,428	35.8
Colombian	565	27.5
Peruvian	236	45.6
Spaniard	625	27.6

Population Age 3–17 Enrolled in Public School (Universe: Population Age 3–17 Enrolled in School)		
Group	Number	%
Total Population	51,403	86.2
Hispanic or Latino (of any race)	12,997	89.1
Central American, ex. Mexican	727	91.0
Honduran	289	96.0
Cuban	3,084	83.8
Dominican Republic	248	100.0
Mexican	1,873	95.0
Puerto Rican	5,250	92.9
South American	933	91.7
Colombian	555	96.2
Peruvian	88	70.4
Spaniard	345	71.9

Population Age 3–17 Enrolled in Private School (Universe: Population Age 3–17 Enrolled in School)		
Group	Number	%
Total Population	8,195	13.8
Hispanic or Latino (of any race)	1,595	10.9
Central American, ex. Mexican	72	9.0
Honduran	12	4.0
Cuban	598	16.2
Dominican Republic	0	0.0
Mexican	99	5.0
Puerto Rican	404	7.1
South American	85	8.3
Colombian	22	3.8
Peruvian	37	29.6
Spaniard	135	28.1

Foreign-Born Population		
Group	Number	%
Total Population	49,215	14.8
Hispanic or Latino (of any race)	27,352	35.5
Central American, ex. Mexican	3,275	62.4
Honduran	1,554	74.6
Cuban	11,873	56.2
Dominican Republic	1,675	68.2
Mexican	5,315	51.2
Puerto Rican	175	0.8
South American	4,229	67.9
Colombian	1,915	63.5
Peruvian	653	70.7
Spaniard	209	7.1

Foreign-Born Naturalized U.S. Citizens		
Group	Number	%
Total Population	20,791	42.2
Hispanic or Latino (of any race)	10,290	37.6
Central American, ex. Mexican	1,290	39.4
Honduran	549	35.3
Cuban	4,930	41.5
Dominican Republic	1,066	63.6
Mexican	635	11.9
Puerto Rican	52	29.7
South American	1,800	42.6
Colombian	942	49.2
Peruvian	309	47.3
Spaniard	174	83.3

Language Spoken at Home: English Only (Universe: Population 5 Years and Over)		
Group	Number	%
Total Population	233,001	74.9
Hispanic or Latino (of any race)	16,507	23.4
Central American, ex. Mexican	750	16.5
Honduran	185	10.0

Notes: (1) Percent of total population; (2) Percent of Hispanic/Latino population; Profiles include places with an overall population of at least 125,000, OR an overall population of at least 25,000 where the Hispanic/Latino population is at least 20% of the overall population. In states where less than five places meet either of these criteria, we have included places with at least 10,000 total population with the highest percentage of Hispanic/Latino population. These places are identified with an asterisk (*); Please refer to the User's Guide for a full explanation of data.

Cuban	3,974	19.8
Dominican Republic	274	11.8
Mexican	1,876	20.4
Puerto Rican	5,958	28.1
South American	620	10.5
Colombian	328	11.3
Peruvian	72	8.5
Spaniard	1,443	52.0

Language Spoken at Home: Spanish
(Universe: Population 5 Years and Over)

Group	Number	%
Total Population	59,165	19.0
Hispanic or Latino (of any race)	53,946	76.4
Central American, ex. Mexican	3,809	83.5
Honduran	1,659	90.0
Cuban	16,068	80.0
Dominican Republic	2,031	87.5
Mexican	7,308	79.5
Puerto Rican	15,247	71.8
South American	5,291	89.4
Colombian	2,575	88.7
Peruvian	771	90.6
Spaniard	1,309	47.2

Unemployment Rate
(Universe: Population 16 Years and Over)

Group	%
Total Population	9.9
Hispanic or Latino (of any race)	10.1
Central American, ex. Mexican	9.8
Honduran	9.4
Cuban	10.5
Dominican Republic	8.5
Mexican	9.1
Puerto Rican	11.8
South American	9.0
Colombian	7.3
Peruvian	20.4
Spaniard	8.5

Class of Worker: Private Wage and Salary
(Universe: Civilian Employed Population 16 Years and Over)

Group	Number	%
Total Population	128,593	82.6
Hispanic or Latino (of any race)	28,509	84.9
Central American, ex. Mexican	2,058	83.0
Honduran	943	88.0
Cuban	7,984	82.6
Dominican Republic	1,446	93.2
Mexican	4,378	89.7
Puerto Rican	7,225	85.7
South American	2,838	86.4
Colombian	1,382	80.5
Peruvian	404	97.6
Spaniard	1,016	79.3

Class of Worker: Government
(Universe: Civilian Employed Population 16 Years and Over)

Group	Number	%
Total Population	19,219	12.3
Hispanic or Latino (of any race)	3,533	10.5
Central American, ex. Mexican	209	8.4
Honduran	15	1.4
Cuban	1,137	11.8
Dominican Republic	43	2.8
Mexican	316	6.5
Puerto Rican	991	11.8
South American	211	6.4
Colombian	153	8.9
Peruvian	10	2.4
Spaniard	222	17.3

Means of Transportation to Work: Car, Truck or Van
(Universe: Workers 16 Years and Over)

Group	Number	%
Total Population	134,270	87.0
Hispanic or Latino (of any race)	29,605	89.1
Central American, ex. Mexican	2,163	86.2
Honduran	813	77.4
Cuban	8,647	90.9
Dominican Republic	1,412	92.7
Mexican	4,118	82.9
Puerto Rican	7,466	90.2
South American	2,891	89.1
Colombian	1,496	88.2
Peruvian	383	96.7
Spaniard	1,167	92.5

Means of Transportation to Work: Public Transportation (ex. Taxicab)
(Universe: Workers 16 Years and Over)

Group	Number	%
Total Population	4,350	2.8
Hispanic or Latino (of any race)	1,107	3.3
Central American, ex. Mexican	60	2.4
Honduran	33	3.1
Cuban	141	1.5
Dominican Republic	25	1.6
Mexican	367	7.4
Puerto Rican	272	3.3
South American	126	3.9
Colombian	87	5.1
Peruvian	13	3.3
Spaniard	0	0.0

Homeownership Rate
(Universe: Occupied Housing Units)

Group	%
Total Population	51.7
Hispanic or Latino (of any race)	46.5
Central American, ex. Mexican	40.6
Costa Rican	52.1
Guatemalan	35.8
Honduran	34.5
Nicaraguan	46.4
Panamanian	44.5
Salvadoran	46.9
Cuban	55.6
Dominican Republic	43.8
Mexican	34.8
Puerto Rican	34.5
South American	47.6
Argentinean	53.5
Bolivian	55.9
Chilean	53.2
Colombian	46.6
Ecuadorian	52.4
Peruvian	41.7
Venezuelan	48.5
Spaniard	76.8

Median Home Value

Group	Dollars
Total Population	199,300
Hispanic or Latino (of any race)	171,300
Central American, ex. Mexican	186,100
Honduran	215,900
Cuban	169,900
Dominican Republic	154,000
Mexican	161,600
Puerto Rican	164,100
South American	218,400
Colombian	227,600
Peruvian	214,600
Spaniard	200,400

Median Gross Rent

Group	Dollars
Total Population	874
Hispanic or Latino (of any race)	799
Central American, ex. Mexican	927
Honduran	1,070
Cuban	683
Dominican Republic	640
Mexican	849
Puerto Rican	804
South American	908
Colombian	964
Peruvian	813
Spaniard	699

Median Household Income
(2010 Inflation-Adjusted Dollars)

Group	Dollars
Total Population	43,117
Hispanic or Latino (of any race)	34,827
Central American, ex. Mexican	39,923
Honduran	41,200
Cuban	33,653
Dominican Republic	43,003
Mexican	35,824
Puerto Rican	28,144
South American	50,333
Colombian	53,601
Peruvian	42,500
Spaniard	36,667

Per Capita Income
(2010 Inflation-Adjusted Dollars)

Group	Dollars
Total Population	28,362
Hispanic or Latino (of any race)	17,709
Central American, ex. Mexican	15,058
Honduran	12,960
Cuban	18,655
Dominican Republic	21,078
Mexican	15,584
Puerto Rican	14,670
South American	24,306
Colombian	23,811
Peruvian	21,868
Spaniard	27,662

Households with $100,000+ Income

Group	Number	%
Total Population	24,444	18.3
Hispanic or Latino (of any race)	2,520	9.2
Central American, ex. Mexican	60	3.9
Honduran	15	2.4
Cuban	682	8.2
Dominican Republic	57	5.8
Mexican	260	8.6
Puerto Rican	543	7.0
South American	339	14.6
Colombian	195	16.6
Peruvian	12	3.6
Spaniard	282	17.0

Households with Food Stamps/SNAP Benefits During Past 12 Months

Group	Number	%
Total Population	15,894	11.9
Hispanic or Latino (of any race)	4,456	16.2
Central American, ex. Mexican	211	13.7
Honduran	89	14.5
Cuban	1,492	17.9
Dominican Republic	214	21.9
Mexican	368	12.2
Puerto Rican	1,911	24.6
South American	120	5.2
Colombian	77	6.6
Peruvian	43	12.7
Spaniard	56	3.4

Poverty Rate
(Income in Past 12 Months Below Poverty Level)

Group	%
Total Population	19.5
Hispanic or Latino (of any race)	23.0
Central American, ex. Mexican	24.7
Honduran	25.4
Cuban	20.8
Dominican Republic	6.2
Mexican	30.6
Puerto Rican	29.3
South American	11.7
Colombian	14.4
Peruvian	0.6
Spaniard	14.0

The Hammocks

Population

Group	Number	%TP[1]	%HP[2]
Total Population	51,003	100.0	–
Hispanic or Latino (of any race)	39,244	76.9	100.0
Central American, ex. Mexican	4,063	8.0	10.4
Costa Rican	190	0.4	0.5
Guatemalan	215	0.4	0.5
Honduran	588	1.2	1.5
Nicaraguan	2,391	4.7	6.1
Panamanian	310	0.6	0.8

Notes: (1) Percent of total population; (2) Percent of Hispanic/Latino population; Profiles include places with an overall population of at least 125,000, OR an overall population of at least 25,000 where the Hispanic/Latino population is at least 20% of the overall population. In states where less than five places meet either of these criteria, we have included places with at least 10,000 total population with the highest percentage of Hispanic/Latino population. These places are identified with an asterisk (*); Please refer to the User's Guide for a full explanation of data.

Salvadoran	357	0.7	0.9
Cuban	13,605	26.7	34.7
Dominican Republic	1,907	3.7	4.9
Mexican	579	1.1	1.5
Puerto Rican	2,934	5.8	7.5
South American	13,807	27.1	35.2
Argentinean	687	1.3	1.8
Bolivian	156	0.3	0.4
Chilean	564	1.1	1.4
Colombian	6,896	13.5	17.6
Ecuadorian	868	1.7	2.2
Peruvian	2,403	4.7	6.1
Uruguayan	130	0.3	0.3
Venezuelan	2,065	4.0	5.3
Spaniard	285	0.6	0.7

Population Growth: 2000–2010

Group	%
Total Population	7.6
Hispanic or Latino (of any race)	26.8
Central American, ex. Mexican	74.8
Costa Rican	50.8
Guatemalan	79.2
Honduran	152.4
Nicaraguan	75.3
Panamanian	37.2
Salvadoran	77.6
Cuban	63.2
Dominican Republic	63.4
Mexican	14.9
Puerto Rican	6.2
South American	45.4
Argentinean	71.3
Chilean	37.9
Colombian	45.2
Ecuadorian	66.3
Peruvian	51.0
Venezuelan	38.8
Spaniard	97.9

Males per 100 Females

Group	Number
Total Population	90.4
Hispanic or Latino (of any race)	88.3
Central American, ex. Mexican	84.5
Costa Rican	75.9
Guatemalan	102.8
Honduran	69.0
Nicaraguan	88.7
Panamanian	65.8
Salvadoran	100.6
Cuban	97.4
Dominican Republic	76.4
Mexican	88.0
Puerto Rican	85.5
South American	81.9
Argentinean	107.6
Bolivian	73.3
Chilean	90.5
Colombian	77.6
Ecuadorian	79.7
Peruvian	86.0
Uruguayan	88.4
Venezuelan	83.4
Spaniard	102.1

Average Household Size

Group	People
Total Population	3.09
Hispanic or Latino (of any race)	3.24
Central American, ex. Mexican	3.49
Costa Rican	3.65
Guatemalan	3.63
Honduran	3.73
Nicaraguan	3.50
Panamanian	2.94
Salvadoran	3.50
Cuban	3.09
Dominican Republic	3.47
Mexican	3.28
Puerto Rican	3.04
South American	3.38
Argentinean	3.23
Bolivian	3.16
Chilean	3.38
Colombian	3.37
Ecuadorian	3.65
Peruvian	3.44
Uruguayan	3.22
Venezuelan	3.31
Spaniard	2.78

Median Age

Group	Years
Total Population	36.3
Hispanic or Latino (of any race)	36.7
Central American, ex. Mexican	36.0
Costa Rican	37.3
Guatemalan	35.1
Honduran	31.9
Nicaraguan	36.4
Panamanian	41.2
Salvadoran	36.3
Cuban	38.3
Dominican Republic	33.4
Mexican	30.0
Puerto Rican	34.1
South American	38.3
Argentinean	38.5
Bolivian	35.0
Chilean	39.9
Colombian	38.4
Ecuadorian	38.9
Peruvian	40.7
Uruguayan	45.2
Venezuelan	34.1
Spaniard	40.2

High School Graduates
(Universe: Population 25 Years and Over)

Group	Number	%
Total Population	28,145	90.7
Hispanic or Latino (of any race)	21,314	89.6
Central American, ex. Mexican	2,806	87.6
Nicaraguan	1,795	90.5
Cuban	7,574	88.4
Dominican Republic	785	88.8
Puerto Rican	1,631	96.1
South American	7,512	91.9
Colombian	3,879	92.9
Peruvian	1,490	89.3
Venezuelan	1,024	96.5

Four-Year College Graduates
(Universe: Population 25 Years and Over)

Group	Number	%
Total Population	10,908	35.1
Hispanic or Latino (of any race)	8,052	33.8
Central American, ex. Mexican	1,066	33.3
Nicaraguan	736	37.1
Cuban	2,682	31.3
Dominican Republic	264	29.9
Puerto Rican	468	27.6
South American	3,151	38.5
Colombian	1,496	35.8
Peruvian	634	38.0
Venezuelan	636	59.9

Population Age 3–17 Enrolled in Public School
(Universe: Population Age 3–17 Enrolled in School)

Group	Number	%
Total Population	8,200	80.6
Hispanic or Latino (of any race)	6,084	84.0
Central American, ex. Mexican	620	67.0
Nicaraguan	391	62.5
Cuban	2,047	81.2
Dominican Republic	346	96.4
Puerto Rican	736	96.0
South American	1,719	88.3
Colombian	945	90.0
Peruvian	363	87.5
Venezuelan	224	75.9

Population Age 3–17 Enrolled in Private School
(Universe: Population Age 3–17 Enrolled in School)

Group	Number	%
Total Population	1,970	19.4
Hispanic or Latino (of any race)	1,160	16.0
Central American, ex. Mexican	306	33.0
Nicaraguan	235	37.5
Cuban	473	18.8
Dominican Republic	13	3.6
Puerto Rican	31	4.0
South American	228	11.7
Colombian	105	10.0
Peruvian	52	12.5
Venezuelan	71	24.1

Foreign-Born Population

Group	Number	%
Total Population	26,055	52.1
Hispanic or Latino (of any race)	22,077	58.9
Central American, ex. Mexican	3,313	65.8
Nicaraguan	2,085	72.0
Cuban	7,614	57.9
Dominican Republic	1,060	72.3
Puerto Rican	0	0.0
South American	8,762	72.0
Colombian	4,396	67.8
Peruvian	2,017	81.0
Venezuelan	1,106	74.8

Foreign-Born Naturalized U.S. Citizens

Group	Number	%
Total Population	14,939	57.3
Hispanic or Latino (of any race)	12,295	55.7
Central American, ex. Mexican	2,049	61.8
Nicaraguan	1,489	71.4
Cuban	4,829	63.4
Dominican Republic	729	68.8
Puerto Rican	0	0.0
South American	4,016	45.8
Colombian	2,050	46.6
Peruvian	924	45.8
Venezuelan	512	46.3

Language Spoken at Home: English Only
(Universe: Population 5 Years and Over)

Group	Number	%
Total Population	8,535	18.1
Hispanic or Latino (of any race)	1,861	5.2
Central American, ex. Mexican	28	0.6
Nicaraguan	0	0.0
Cuban	833	6.7
Dominican Republic	33	2.3
Puerto Rican	327	10.8
South American	454	3.9
Colombian	164	2.7
Peruvian	81	3.3
Venezuelan	139	9.5

Language Spoken at Home: Spanish
(Universe: Population 5 Years and Over)

Group	Number	%
Total Population	35,658	75.8
Hispanic or Latino (of any race)	33,594	94.5
Central American, ex. Mexican	4,625	99.2
Nicaraguan	2,687	100.0
Cuban	11,552	93.1
Dominican Republic	1,407	97.7
Puerto Rican	2,683	88.6
South American	11,243	95.9
Colombian	5,959	97.1
Peruvian	2,358	96.7
Venezuelan	1,314	89.9

Unemployment Rate
(Universe: Population 16 Years and Over)

Group	%
Total Population	8.4
Hispanic or Latino (of any race)	8.3
Central American, ex. Mexican	10.8
Nicaraguan	10.8
Cuban	8.0
Dominican Republic	6.3
Puerto Rican	4.8
South American	9.2
Colombian	11.4
Peruvian	6.2
Venezuelan	4.9

Class of Worker: Private Wage and Salary
(Universe: Civilian Employed Population 16 Years and Over)

Group	Number	%
Total Population	21,517	82.3

STATE & PLACE PROFILES

Notes: (1) Percent of total population; (2) Percent of Hispanic/Latino population; Profiles include places with an overall population of at least 125,000, OR an overall population of at least 25,000 where the Hispanic/Latino population is at least 20% of the overall population. In states where less than five places meet either of these criteria, we have included places with at least 10,000 total population with the highest percentage of Hispanic/Latino population. These places are identified with an asterisk (*); Please refer to the User's Guide for a full explanation of data.

Hispanic or Latino (of any race)	16,463	82.1
Central American, ex. Mexican	2,193	85.4
Nicaraguan	1,119	83.9
Cuban	5,444	78.1
Dominican Republic	807	99.1
Puerto Rican	1,224	72.2
South American	5,751	84.2
Colombian	3,041	86.0
Peruvian	1,173	82.8
Venezuelan	749	87.6

Class of Worker: Government
(Universe: Civilian Employed Population 16 Years and Over)

Group	Number	%
Total Population	3,141	12.0
Hispanic or Latino (of any race)	2,218	11.1
Central American, ex. Mexican	245	9.5
Nicaraguan	169	12.7
Cuban	888	12.7
Dominican Republic	7	0.9
Puerto Rican	368	21.7
South American	585	8.6
Colombian	265	7.5
Peruvian	150	10.6
Venezuelan	66	7.7

Means of Transportation to Work: Car, Truck or Van
(Universe: Workers 16 Years and Over)

Group	Number	%
Total Population	23,229	90.8
Hispanic or Latino (of any race)	17,789	90.9
Central American, ex. Mexican	2,287	89.1
Nicaraguan	1,259	94.4
Cuban	6,059	90.0
Dominican Republic	701	86.1
Puerto Rican	1,614	98.1
South American	6,125	92.0
Colombian	3,073	89.9
Peruvian	1,293	92.3
Venezuelan	802	96.3

Means of Transportation to Work: Public Transportation (ex. Taxicab)
(Universe: Workers 16 Years and Over)

Group	Number	%
Total Population	994	3.9
Hispanic or Latino (of any race)	789	4.0
Central American, ex. Mexican	163	6.3
Nicaraguan	43	3.2
Cuban	119	1.8
Dominican Republic	113	13.9
Puerto Rican	32	1.9
South American	323	4.8
Colombian	241	7.0
Peruvian	67	4.8
Venezuelan	10	1.2

Homeownership Rate
(Universe: Occupied Housing Units)

Group	%
Total Population	64.8
Hispanic or Latino (of any race)	63.9
Central American, ex. Mexican	63.0
Costa Rican	67.3
Guatemalan	64.4
Honduran	54.6
Nicaraguan	63.1
Panamanian	63.6
Salvadoran	70.3
Cuban	68.0
Dominican Republic	58.8
Mexican	56.2
Puerto Rican	60.1
South American	62.2
Argentinean	62.8
Bolivian	60.3
Chilean	62.5
Colombian	61.6
Ecuadorian	66.5
Peruvian	64.9
Uruguayan	64.4
Venezuelan	58.6
Spaniard	72.2

Median Home Value

Group	Dollars
Total Population	284,700
Hispanic or Latino (of any race)	288,700
Central American, ex. Mexican	291,400
Nicaraguan	291,300
Cuban	299,000
Dominican Republic	249,700
Puerto Rican	361,300
South American	266,300
Colombian	247,200
Peruvian	261,300
Venezuelan	277,400

Median Gross Rent

Group	Dollars
Total Population	1,245
Hispanic or Latino (of any race)	1,229
Central American, ex. Mexican	1,240
Nicaraguan	1,192
Cuban	1,202
Dominican Republic	1,259
Puerto Rican	1,412
South American	1,201
Colombian	1,188
Peruvian	1,156
Venezuelan	2,000+

Median Household Income
(2010 Inflation-Adjusted Dollars)

Group	Dollars
Total Population	59,843
Hispanic or Latino (of any race)	56,747
Central American, ex. Mexican	74,142
Nicaraguan	74,657
Cuban	57,083
Dominican Republic	42,308
Puerto Rican	60,167
South American	52,624
Colombian	53,464
Peruvian	52,614
Venezuelan	58,068

Per Capita Income
(2010 Inflation-Adjusted Dollars)

Group	Dollars
Total Population	23,656
Hispanic or Latino (of any race)	22,883
Central American, ex. Mexican	23,338
Nicaraguan	23,355
Cuban	23,931
Dominican Republic	15,476
Puerto Rican	24,455
South American	23,219
Colombian	19,768
Peruvian	26,061
Venezuelan	30,743

Households with $100,000+ Income

Group	Number	%
Total Population	3,615	22.6
Hispanic or Latino (of any race)	2,558	21.5
Central American, ex. Mexican	481	35.2
Nicaraguan	271	36.2
Cuban	1,080	25.1
Dominican Republic	45	9.6
Puerto Rican	159	15.7
South American	676	16.6
Colombian	211	11.2
Peruvian	206	24.6
Venezuelan	140	25.0

Households with Food Stamps/SNAP Benefits During Past 12 Months

Group	Number	%
Total Population	1,264	7.9
Hispanic or Latino (of any race)	1,111	9.3
Central American, ex. Mexican	101	7.4
Nicaraguan	45	6.0
Cuban	365	8.5
Dominican Republic	127	27.0
Puerto Rican	26	2.6
South American	344	8.4
Colombian	224	11.9
Peruvian	72	8.6
Venezuelan	27	4.8

Poverty Rate
(Income in Past 12 Months Below Poverty Level)

Group	%
Total Population	9.2
Hispanic or Latino (of any race)	9.8
Central American, ex. Mexican	5.3
Nicaraguan	2.2
Cuban	9.7
Dominican Republic	14.6
Puerto Rican	4.0
South American	11.4
Colombian	9.8
Peruvian	13.3
Venezuelan	17.6

Town 'n' Country

Population

Group	Number	%TP[1]	%HP[2]
Total Population	78,442	100.0	–
Hispanic or Latino (of any race)	34,380	43.8	100.0
Central American, ex. Mexican	1,444	1.8	4.2
Costa Rican	177	0.2	0.5
Guatemalan	191	0.2	0.6
Honduran	353	0.5	1.0
Nicaraguan	229	0.3	0.7
Panamanian	214	0.3	0.6
Salvadoran	273	0.3	0.8
Cuban	11,570	14.7	33.7
Dominican Republic	2,248	2.9	6.5
Mexican	1,505	1.9	4.4
Puerto Rican	10,742	13.7	31.2
South American	4,669	6.0	13.6
Argentinean	138	0.2	0.4
Colombian	2,631	3.4	7.7
Ecuadorian	454	0.6	1.3
Peruvian	800	1.0	2.3
Venezuelan	397	0.5	1.2
Spaniard	539	0.7	1.6

Population Growth: 2000–2010

Group	%
Total Population	8.2
Hispanic or Latino (of any race)	63.6
Central American, ex. Mexican	109.0
Honduran	161.5
Nicaraguan	86.2
Panamanian	62.1
Salvadoran	160.0
Cuban	124.8
Dominican Republic	156.6
Mexican	81.5
Puerto Rican	43.1
South American	132.5
Colombian	148.9
Ecuadorian	100.9
Peruvian	124.7
Venezuelan	148.1
Spaniard	213.4

Males per 100 Females

Group	Number
Total Population	95.1
Hispanic or Latino (of any race)	93.9
Central American, ex. Mexican	87.8
Costa Rican	113.3
Guatemalan	109.9
Honduran	78.3
Nicaraguan	77.5
Panamanian	64.6
Salvadoran	105.3
Cuban	101.6
Dominican Republic	84.0
Mexican	109.6
Puerto Rican	91.8
South American	83.8
Argentinean	137.9
Colombian	81.8
Ecuadorian	76.7
Peruvian	89.6
Venezuelan	82.9

Notes: (1) Percent of total population; (2) Percent of Hispanic/Latino population; Profiles include places with an overall population of at least 125,000, OR an overall population of at least 25,000 where the Hispanic/Latino population is at least 20% of the overall population. In states where less than five places meet either of these criteria, we have included places with at least 10,000 total population with the highest percentage of Hispanic/Latino population. These places are identified with an asterisk (*); Please refer to the User's Guide for a full explanation of data.

Spaniard		86.5

Average Household Size

Group	People
Total Population	2.57
Hispanic or Latino (of any race)	3.07
Central American, ex. Mexican	3.14
Costa Rican	2.90
Guatemalan	3.61
Honduran	3.43
Nicaraguan	3.23
Panamanian	2.28
Salvadoran	3.35
Cuban	3.12
Dominican Republic	3.39
Mexican	3.11
Puerto Rican	3.00
South American	3.14
Argentinean	2.88
Colombian	3.19
Ecuadorian	3.20
Peruvian	3.27
Venezuelan	2.86
Spaniard	2.37

Median Age

Group	Years
Total Population	37.2
Hispanic or Latino (of any race)	33.9
Central American, ex. Mexican	33.3
Costa Rican	35.5
Guatemalan	30.8
Honduran	32.5
Nicaraguan	31.3
Panamanian	39.0
Salvadoran	31.9
Cuban	37.6
Dominican Republic	31.1
Mexican	26.7
Puerto Rican	30.4
South American	36.5
Argentinean	37.3
Colombian	36.3
Ecuadorian	38.1
Peruvian	38.6
Venezuelan	32.9
Spaniard	47.9

High School Graduates
(Universe: Population 25 Years and Over)

Group	Number	%
Total Population	45,331	86.2
Hispanic or Latino (of any race)	15,184	81.2
Central American, ex. Mexican	836	74.5
Cuban	4,804	75.0
Dominican Republic	861	81.9
Mexican	641	84.5
Puerto Rican	4,670	83.6
South American	2,366	88.1
Colombian	1,399	82.9

Four-Year College Graduates
(Universe: Population 25 Years and Over)

Group	Number	%
Total Population	14,104	26.8
Hispanic or Latino (of any race)	3,215	17.2
Central American, ex. Mexican	258	23.0
Cuban	820	12.8
Dominican Republic	234	22.3
Mexican	198	26.1
Puerto Rican	779	14.0
South American	635	23.6
Colombian	441	26.1

Population Age 3–17 Enrolled in Public School
(Universe: Population Age 3–17 Enrolled in School)

Group	Number	%
Total Population	11,353	86.5
Hispanic or Latino (of any race)	5,980	91.0
Central American, ex. Mexican	457	96.2
Cuban	1,592	87.1
Dominican Republic	515	100.0
Mexican	371	89.6
Puerto Rican	1,696	89.6
South American	976	95.2
Colombian	709	93.5

Population Age 3–17 Enrolled in Private School
(Universe: Population Age 3–17 Enrolled in School)

Group	Number	%
Total Population	1,773	13.5
Hispanic or Latino (of any race)	594	9.0
Central American, ex. Mexican	18	3.8
Cuban	235	12.9
Dominican Republic	0	0.0
Mexican	43	10.4
Puerto Rican	196	10.4
South American	49	4.8
Colombian	49	6.5

Foreign-Born Population

Group	Number	%
Total Population	18,021	23.4
Hispanic or Latino (of any race)	12,074	39.7
Central American, ex. Mexican	1,135	62.7
Cuban	6,664	69.6
Dominican Republic	911	48.3
Mexican	311	21.6
Puerto Rican	30	0.3
South American	2,584	58.9
Colombian	1,723	57.1

Foreign-Born Naturalized U.S. Citizens

Group	Number	%
Total Population	8,211	45.6
Hispanic or Latino (of any race)	4,820	39.9
Central American, ex. Mexican	343	30.2
Cuban	2,505	37.6
Dominican Republic	598	65.6
Mexican	112	36.0
Puerto Rican	0	0.0
South American	1,104	42.7
Colombian	514	29.8

Language Spoken at Home: English Only
(Universe: Population 5 Years and Over)

Group	Number	%
Total Population	45,192	62.2
Hispanic or Latino (of any race)	6,247	21.9
Central American, ex. Mexican	225	12.9
Cuban	1,391	15.5
Dominican Republic	432	23.9
Mexican	444	33.5
Puerto Rican	2,740	31.1
South American	560	13.4
Colombian	300	10.5

Language Spoken at Home: Spanish
(Universe: Population 5 Years and Over)

Group	Number	%
Total Population	23,331	32.1
Hispanic or Latino (of any race)	22,151	77.8
Central American, ex. Mexican	1,518	87.1
Cuban	7,610	84.5
Dominican Republic	1,373	76.1
Mexican	853	64.3
Puerto Rican	6,038	68.5
South American	3,611	86.2
Colombian	2,546	88.8

Unemployment Rate
(Universe: Population 16 Years and Over)

Group	%
Total Population	8.1
Hispanic or Latino (of any race)	10.1
Central American, ex. Mexican	6.8
Cuban	11.1
Dominican Republic	20.8
Mexican	11.3
Puerto Rican	9.9
South American	7.6
Colombian	8.9

Class of Worker: Private Wage and Salary
(Universe: Civilian Employed Population 16 Years and Over)

Group	Number	%
Total Population	34,977	86.4
Hispanic or Latino (of any race)	12,424	84.4
Central American, ex. Mexican	865	86.8
Cuban	3,997	86.9
Dominican Republic	579	76.2
Mexican	585	88.6
Puerto Rican	3,841	83.8
South American	1,935	85.3
Colombian	1,277	91.0

Class of Worker: Government
(Universe: Civilian Employed Population 16 Years and Over)

Group	Number	%
Total Population	3,234	8.0
Hispanic or Latino (of any race)	1,297	8.8
Central American, ex. Mexican	86	8.6
Cuban	233	5.1
Dominican Republic	133	17.5
Mexican	59	8.9
Puerto Rican	474	10.3
South American	131	5.8
Colombian	75	5.3

Means of Transportation to Work: Car, Truck or Van
(Universe: Workers 16 Years and Over)

Group	Number	%
Total Population	36,322	90.9
Hispanic or Latino (of any race)	13,193	91.3
Central American, ex. Mexican	963	96.7
Cuban	4,091	90.5
Dominican Republic	728	95.8
Mexican	597	97.1
Puerto Rican	3,840	86.3
South American	2,219	97.8
Colombian	1,373	97.9

Means of Transportation to Work: Public Transportation (ex. Taxicab)
(Universe: Workers 16 Years and Over)

Group	Number	%
Total Population	429	1.1
Hispanic or Latino (of any race)	144	1.0
Central American, ex. Mexican	33	3.3
Cuban	58	1.3
Dominican Republic	0	0.0
Mexican	8	1.3
Puerto Rican	12	0.3
South American	0	0.0
Colombian	0	0.0

Homeownership Rate
(Universe: Occupied Housing Units)

Group	%
Total Population	60.8
Hispanic or Latino (of any race)	58.3
Central American, ex. Mexican	55.4
Costa Rican	48.3
Guatemalan	51.9
Honduran	55.3
Nicaraguan	50.0
Panamanian	54.3
Salvadoran	68.2
Cuban	69.0
Dominican Republic	53.0
Mexican	46.2
Puerto Rican	48.9
South American	57.7
Argentinean	65.5
Colombian	58.9
Ecuadorian	65.4
Peruvian	54.3
Venezuelan	43.5
Spaniard	82.0

Median Home Value

Group	Dollars
Total Population	182,100
Hispanic or Latino (of any race)	179,000
Central American, ex. Mexican	158,300
Cuban	171,500
Dominican Republic	174,600
Mexican	197,800
Puerto Rican	171,300
South American	219,300
Colombian	236,500

STATE & PLACE PROFILES

Notes: (1) Percent of total population; (2) Percent of Hispanic/Latino population; Profiles include places with an overall population of at least 125,000, OR an overall population of at least 25,000 where the Hispanic/Latino population is at least 20% of the overall population. In states where less than five places meet either of these criteria, we have included places with at least 10,000 total population with the highest percentage of Hispanic/Latino population. These places are identified with an asterisk (*); Please refer to the User's Guide for a full explanation of data.

Median Gross Rent

Group	Dollars
Total Population	979
Hispanic or Latino (of any race)	974
Central American, ex. Mexican	911
Cuban	962
Dominican Republic	799
Mexican	1,557
Puerto Rican	980
South American	963
Colombian	995

Median Household Income
(2010 Inflation-Adjusted Dollars)

Group	Dollars
Total Population	46,710
Hispanic or Latino (of any race)	41,927
Central American, ex. Mexican	35,795
Cuban	42,527
Dominican Republic	41,935
Mexican	52,500
Puerto Rican	40,827
South American	36,279
Colombian	29,428

Per Capita Income
(2010 Inflation-Adjusted Dollars)

Group	Dollars
Total Population	24,022
Hispanic or Latino (of any race)	17,547
Central American, ex. Mexican	13,972
Cuban	18,479
Dominican Republic	13,971
Mexican	20,953
Puerto Rican	17,263
South American	16,912
Colombian	15,013

Households with $100,000+ Income

Group	Number	%
Total Population	4,303	14.0
Hispanic or Latino (of any race)	923	9.2
Central American, ex. Mexican	19	3.6
Cuban	222	7.0
Dominican Republic	0	0.0
Mexican	134	27.8
Puerto Rican	344	10.5
South American	154	10.2
Colombian	89	9.9

Households with Food Stamps/SNAP Benefits During Past 12 Months

Group	Number	%
Total Population	2,136	6.9
Hispanic or Latino (of any race)	1,005	10.0
Central American, ex. Mexican	25	4.8
Cuban	445	14.1
Dominican Republic	47	8.8
Mexican	0	0.0
Puerto Rican	363	11.0
South American	116	7.7
Colombian	116	12.9

Poverty Rate
(Income in Past 12 Months Below Poverty Level)

Group	%
Total Population	12.5
Hispanic or Latino (of any race)	17.0
Central American, ex. Mexican	15.6
Cuban	13.2
Dominican Republic	21.3
Mexican	14.5
Puerto Rican	16.7
South American	30.0
Colombian	36.2

University (Hillsborough County)

Population

Group	Number	%TP[1]	%HP[2]
Total Population	41,163	100.0	–
Hispanic or Latino (of any race)	11,983	29.1	100.0
Central American, ex. Mexican	1,342	3.3	11.2
Guatemalan	100	0.2	0.8
Honduran	922	2.2	7.7
Salvadoran	111	0.3	0.9
Cuban	850	2.1	7.1
Dominican Republic	403	1.0	3.4
Mexican	3,058	7.4	25.5
Puerto Rican	4,854	11.8	40.5
South American	714	1.7	6.0
Colombian	321	0.8	2.7
Peruvian	154	0.4	1.3
Spaniard	105	0.3	0.9

Population Growth: 2000–2010

Group	%
Total Population	33.9
Hispanic or Latino (of any race)	101.9
Central American, ex. Mexican	247.7
Honduran	315.3
Cuban	110.9
Mexican	149.8
Puerto Rican	79.8
South American	157.8
Colombian	148.8

Males per 100 Females

Group	Number
Total Population	94.1
Hispanic or Latino (of any race)	110.3
Central American, ex. Mexican	138.4
Guatemalan	222.6
Honduran	142.0
Salvadoran	113.5
Cuban	84.0
Dominican Republic	90.1
Mexican	184.7
Puerto Rican	84.6
South American	91.4
Colombian	100.6
Peruvian	90.1
Spaniard	98.1

Average Household Size

Group	People
Total Population	2.19
Hispanic or Latino (of any race)	2.79
Central American, ex. Mexican	3.12
Guatemalan	2.74
Honduran	3.42
Salvadoran	3.25
Cuban	2.26
Dominican Republic	2.64
Mexican	3.55
Puerto Rican	2.62
South American	2.37
Colombian	2.37
Peruvian	2.30
Spaniard	1.87

Median Age

Group	Years
Total Population	26.7
Hispanic or Latino (of any race)	25.5
Central American, ex. Mexican	27.9
Guatemalan	27.3
Honduran	28.0
Salvadoran	26.2
Cuban	26.2
Dominican Republic	26.3
Mexican	24.1
Puerto Rican	25.7
South American	26.4
Colombian	24.7
Peruvian	27.8
Spaniard	27.5

High School Graduates
(Universe: Population 25 Years and Over)

Group	Number	%
Total Population	18,168	78.1
Hispanic or Latino (of any race)	3,974	66.8
Central American, ex. Mexican	466	62.2
Cuban	523	74.0
Mexican	562	38.5
Puerto Rican	1,763	77.5

Four-Year College Graduates
(Universe: Population 25 Years and Over)

Group	Number	%
Total Population	5,429	23.3
Hispanic or Latino (of any race)	874	14.7
Central American, ex. Mexican	86	11.5
Cuban	55	7.8
Mexican	54	3.7
Puerto Rican	338	14.9

Population Age 3–17 Enrolled in Public School
(Universe: Population Age 3–17 Enrolled in School)

Group	Number	%
Total Population	5,021	93.4
Hispanic or Latino (of any race)	2,014	95.6
Central American, ex. Mexican	250	100.0
Cuban	186	100.0
Mexican	356	97.0
Puerto Rican	1,115	93.2

Population Age 3–17 Enrolled in Private School
(Universe: Population Age 3–17 Enrolled in School)

Group	Number	%
Total Population	356	6.6
Hispanic or Latino (of any race)	92	4.4
Central American, ex. Mexican	0	0.0
Cuban	0	0.0
Mexican	11	3.0
Puerto Rican	81	6.8

Foreign-Born Population

Group	Number	%
Total Population	8,384	20.7
Hispanic or Latino (of any race)	4,191	36.4
Central American, ex. Mexican	991	68.3
Cuban	478	37.1
Mexican	1,895	72.0
Puerto Rican	70	1.4

Foreign-Born Naturalized U.S. Citizens

Group	Number	%
Total Population	2,309	27.5
Hispanic or Latino (of any race)	864	20.6
Central American, ex. Mexican	304	30.7
Cuban	232	48.5
Mexican	79	4.2
Puerto Rican	45	64.3

Language Spoken at Home: English Only
(Universe: Population 5 Years and Over)

Group	Number	%
Total Population	24,080	64.9
Hispanic or Latino (of any race)	1,369	13.4
Central American, ex. Mexican	96	8.0
Cuban	206	16.9
Mexican	92	3.7
Puerto Rican	839	20.2

Language Spoken at Home: Spanish
(Universe: Population 5 Years and Over)

Group	Number	%
Total Population	9,333	25.1
Hispanic or Latino (of any race)	8,823	86.1
Central American, ex. Mexican	1,107	92.0
Cuban	993	81.6
Mexican	2,410	96.3
Puerto Rican	3,324	79.8

Unemployment Rate
(Universe: Population 16 Years and Over)

Group	%
Total Population	15.8
Hispanic or Latino (of any race)	13.6
Central American, ex. Mexican	24.9
Cuban	8.4
Mexican	6.5
Puerto Rican	19.7

Class of Worker: Private Wage and Salary
(Universe: Civilian Employed Population 16 Years and Over)

Group	Number	%
Total Population	14,778	79.7
Hispanic or Latino (of any race)	4,336	86.8
Central American, ex. Mexican	500	87.4
Cuban	572	89.0

Notes: (1) Percent of total population; (2) Percent of Hispanic/Latino population; Profiles include places with an overall population of at least 125,000, OR an overall population of at least 25,000 where the Hispanic/Latino population is at least 20% of the overall population. In states where less than five places meet either of these criteria, we have included places with at least 10,000 total population with the highest percentage of Hispanic/Latino population. These places are identified with an asterisk (*); Please refer to the User's Guide for a full explanation of data.

Mexican	1,456	90.3
Puerto Rican	1,416	90.5

Class of Worker: Government
(Universe: Civilian Employed Population 16 Years and Over)

Group	Number	%
Total Population	3,012	16.2
Hispanic or Latino (of any race)	367	7.3
Central American, ex. Mexican	32	5.6
Cuban	46	7.2
Mexican	0	0.0
Puerto Rican	131	8.4

Means of Transportation to Work: Car, Truck or Van
(Universe: Workers 16 Years and Over)

Group	Number	%
Total Population	15,096	83.2
Hispanic or Latino (of any race)	4,024	81.6
Central American, ex. Mexican	421	73.6
Cuban	575	90.8
Mexican	1,333	82.6
Puerto Rican	1,298	84.9

Means of Transportation to Work: Public Transportation (ex. Taxicab)
(Universe: Workers 16 Years and Over)

Group	Number	%
Total Population	1,291	7.1
Hispanic or Latino (of any race)	319	6.5
Central American, ex. Mexican	0	0.0
Cuban	26	4.1
Mexican	225	13.9
Puerto Rican	20	1.3

Homeownership Rate
(Universe: Occupied Housing Units)

Group	%
Total Population	13.4
Hispanic or Latino (of any race)	12.0
Central American, ex. Mexican	9.0
Guatemalan	2.6
Honduran	7.9
Salvadoran	15.0
Cuban	20.9
Dominican Republic	16.1
Mexican	6.9
Puerto Rican	12.1
South American	17.3
Colombian	14.4
Peruvian	17.2
Spaniard	15.1

Median Home Value

Group	Dollars
Total Population	124,800
Hispanic or Latino (of any race)	120,400
Central American, ex. Mexican	144,400
Cuban	257,400
Mexican	102,700
Puerto Rican	109,900

Median Gross Rent

Group	Dollars
Total Population	759
Hispanic or Latino (of any race)	723
Central American, ex. Mexican	751
Cuban	668
Mexican	813
Puerto Rican	689

Median Household Income
(2010 Inflation-Adjusted Dollars)

Group	Dollars
Total Population	24,235
Hispanic or Latino (of any race)	21,836
Central American, ex. Mexican	23,750
Cuban	29,180
Mexican	30,486
Puerto Rican	18,750

Per Capita Income
(2010 Inflation-Adjusted Dollars)

Group	Dollars
Total Population	15,065
Hispanic or Latino (of any race)	12,277
Central American, ex. Mexican	10,838
Cuban	15,018
Mexican	12,748
Puerto Rican	11,402

Households with $100,000+ Income

Group	Number	%
Total Population	549	3.1
Hispanic or Latino (of any race)	136	3.3
Central American, ex. Mexican	0	0.0
Cuban	17	3.8
Mexican	13	1.5
Puerto Rican	96	5.4

Households with Food Stamps/SNAP Benefits During Past 12 Months

Group	Number	%
Total Population	3,432	19.6
Hispanic or Latino (of any race)	1,117	27.4
Central American, ex. Mexican	38	8.8
Cuban	109	24.4
Mexican	210	24.1
Puerto Rican	698	39.4

Poverty Rate
(Income in Past 12 Months Below Poverty Level)

Group	%
Total Population	36.7
Hispanic or Latino (of any race)	41.2
Central American, ex. Mexican	55.2
Cuban	21.3
Mexican	28.1
Puerto Rican	48.7

University (Orange County)

Population

Group	Number	%TP[1]	%HP[2]
Total Population	31,084	100.0	–
Hispanic or Latino (of any race)	6,527	21.0	100.0
Central American, ex. Mexican	272	0.9	4.2
Cuban	702	2.3	10.8
Dominican Republic	228	0.7	3.5
Mexican	496	1.6	7.6
Puerto Rican	2,980	9.6	45.7
South American	758	2.4	11.6
Colombian	355	1.1	5.4
Ecuadorian	114	0.4	1.7
Peruvian	100	0.3	1.5
Venezuelan	109	0.4	1.7

Population Growth: 2000–2010

Group	%
Total Population	n/a

Males per 100 Females

Group	Number
Total Population	102.1
Hispanic or Latino (of any race)	99.1
Central American, ex. Mexican	92.9
Cuban	102.9
Dominican Republic	94.9
Mexican	138.5
Puerto Rican	96.7
South American	96.4
Colombian	89.8
Ecuadorian	111.1
Peruvian	78.6
Venezuelan	105.7

Average Household Size

Group	People
Total Population	2.67
Hispanic or Latino (of any race)	2.96
Central American, ex. Mexican	2.91
Cuban	2.87
Dominican Republic	2.93
Mexican	3.13
Puerto Rican	3.01
South American	2.87
Colombian	2.66
Ecuadorian	3.69
Peruvian	2.88
Venezuelan	2.56

Median Age

Group	Years
Total Population	21.1
Hispanic or Latino (of any race)	21.6
Central American, ex. Mexican	25.4
Cuban	21.1
Dominican Republic	22.3
Mexican	22.1
Puerto Rican	24.3
South American	22.2
Colombian	22.3
Ecuadorian	26.3
Peruvian	21.5
Venezuelan	22.2

High School Graduates
(Universe: Population 25 Years and Over)

Group	Number	%
Total Population	7,861	86.6
Hispanic or Latino (of any race)	1,904	78.6
Puerto Rican	1,155	80.8

Four-Year College Graduates
(Universe: Population 25 Years and Over)

Group	Number	%
Total Population	3,282	36.2
Hispanic or Latino (of any race)	408	16.9
Puerto Rican	228	15.9

Population Age 3–17 Enrolled in Public School
(Universe: Population Age 3–17 Enrolled in School)

Group	Number	%
Total Population	2,128	90.5
Hispanic or Latino (of any race)	1,087	95.2
Puerto Rican	782	96.9

Population Age 3–17 Enrolled in Private School
(Universe: Population Age 3–17 Enrolled in School)

Group	Number	%
Total Population	224	9.5
Hispanic or Latino (of any race)	55	4.8
Puerto Rican	25	3.1

Foreign-Born Population

Group	Number	%
Total Population	2,977	14.1
Hispanic or Latino (of any race)	1,036	19.4
Puerto Rican	0	0.0

Foreign-Born Naturalized U.S. Citizens

Group	Number	%
Total Population	1,209	40.6
Hispanic or Latino (of any race)	332	32.0
Puerto Rican	0	0.0

Language Spoken at Home: English Only
(Universe: Population 5 Years and Over)

Group	Number	%
Total Population	15,080	73.9
Hispanic or Latino (of any race)	1,230	24.7
Puerto Rican	523	19.4

Language Spoken at Home: Spanish
(Universe: Population 5 Years and Over)

Group	Number	%
Total Population	3,806	18.6
Hispanic or Latino (of any race)	3,723	74.8
Puerto Rican	2,175	80.6

Unemployment Rate
(Universe: Population 16 Years and Over)

Group	%
Total Population	14.2
Hispanic or Latino (of any race)	13.3
Puerto Rican	19.4

Class of Worker: Private Wage and Salary
(Universe: Civilian Employed Population 16 Years and Over)

Group	Number	%
Total Population	8,320	82.2
Hispanic or Latino (of any race)	1,821	82.4
Puerto Rican	765	73.8

Notes: (1) Percent of total population; (2) Percent of Hispanic/Latino population; Profiles include places with an overall population of at least 125,000, OR an overall population of at least 25,000 where the Hispanic/Latino population is at least 20% of the overall population. In states where less than five places meet either of these criteria, we have included places with at least 10,000 total population with the highest percentage of Hispanic/Latino population. These places are identified with an asterisk (*); Please refer to the User's Guide for a full explanation of data.

Class of Worker: Government
(Universe: Civilian Employed Population 16 Years and Over)

Group	Number	%
Total Population	1,356	13.4
Hispanic or Latino (of any race)	239	10.8
Puerto Rican	153	14.8

Means of Transportation to Work: Car, Truck or Van
(Universe: Workers 16 Years and Over)

Group	Number	%
Total Population	8,594	88.4
Hispanic or Latino (of any race)	2,020	92.3
Puerto Rican	991	94.7

Means of Transportation to Work: Public Transportation (ex. Taxicab)
(Universe: Workers 16 Years and Over)

Group	Number	%
Total Population	194	2.0
Hispanic or Latino (of any race)	26	1.2
Puerto Rican	16	1.5

Homeownership Rate
(Universe: Occupied Housing Units)

Group	%
Total Population	41.6
Hispanic or Latino (of any race)	46.6
Central American, ex. Mexican	46.8
Cuban	29.6
Dominican Republic	38.4
Mexican	32.5
Puerto Rican	56.3
South American	36.2
Colombian	33.3
Ecuadorian	56.4
Peruvian	16.0
Venezuelan	40.7

Median Home Value

Group	Dollars
Total Population	197,200
Hispanic or Latino (of any race)	191,000
Puerto Rican	172,000

Median Gross Rent

Group	Dollars
Total Population	901
Hispanic or Latino (of any race)	883
Puerto Rican	863

Median Household Income
(2010 Inflation-Adjusted Dollars)

Group	Dollars
Total Population	36,038
Hispanic or Latino (of any race)	34,816
Puerto Rican	31,408

Per Capita Income
(2010 Inflation-Adjusted Dollars)

Group	Dollars
Total Population	17,196
Hispanic or Latino (of any race)	13,925
Puerto Rican	13,419

Households with $100,000+ Income

Group	Number	%
Total Population	747	11.1
Hispanic or Latino (of any race)	122	7.5
Puerto Rican	37	3.5

Households with Food Stamps/SNAP Benefits During Past 12 Months

Group	Number	%
Total Population	423	6.3
Hispanic or Latino (of any race)	236	14.6
Puerto Rican	153	14.5

Poverty Rate
(Income in Past 12 Months Below Poverty Level)

Group	%
Total Population	28.3
Hispanic or Latino (of any race)	21.5
Puerto Rican	21.3

University Park

Population

Group	Number	%TP[1]	%HP[2]
Total Population	26,995	100.0	–
Hispanic or Latino (of any race)	22,938	85.0	100.0
Central American, ex. Mexican	1,909	7.1	8.3
Guatemalan	174	0.6	0.8
Honduran	272	1.0	1.2
Nicaraguan	1,167	4.3	5.1
Salvadoran	156	0.6	0.7
Cuban	17,155	63.5	74.8
Dominican Republic	317	1.2	1.4
Mexican	251	0.9	1.1
Puerto Rican	572	2.1	2.5
South American	2,104	7.8	9.2
Argentinean	183	0.7	0.8
Chilean	104	0.4	0.5
Colombian	865	3.2	3.8
Ecuadorian	144	0.5	0.6
Peruvian	353	1.3	1.5
Venezuelan	306	1.1	1.3
Spaniard	145	0.5	0.6

Population Growth: 2000–2010

Group	%
Total Population	1.7
Hispanic or Latino (of any race)	4.5
Central American, ex. Mexican	54.0
Honduran	85.0
Nicaraguan	52.2
Salvadoran	36.8
Cuban	8.1
Dominican Republic	13.2
Mexican	49.4
Puerto Rican	-0.2
South American	34.9
Argentinean	45.2
Colombian	23.4
Peruvian	55.5
Venezuelan	15.9
Spaniard	22.9

Males per 100 Females

Group	Number
Total Population	88.0
Hispanic or Latino (of any race)	86.4
Central American, ex. Mexican	81.3
Guatemalan	107.1
Honduran	87.6
Nicaraguan	75.8
Salvadoran	95.0
Cuban	86.6
Dominican Republic	66.0
Mexican	109.2
Puerto Rican	82.2
South American	88.7
Argentinean	96.8
Chilean	79.3
Colombian	76.9
Ecuadorian	89.5
Peruvian	110.1
Venezuelan	91.3
Spaniard	98.6

Average Household Size

Group	People
Total Population	2.99
Hispanic or Latino (of any race)	3.05
Central American, ex. Mexican	3.86
Guatemalan	4.15
Honduran	3.82
Nicaraguan	3.88
Salvadoran	4.06
Cuban	2.97
Dominican Republic	3.08
Mexican	3.13
Puerto Rican	3.12
South American	3.34
Argentinean	3.17
Chilean	2.91
Colombian	3.33
Ecuadorian	3.62
Peruvian	3.52
Venezuelan	3.24
Spaniard	2.40

Median Age

Group	Years
Total Population	40.5
Hispanic or Latino (of any race)	44.5
Central American, ex. Mexican	36.8
Guatemalan	29.0
Honduran	35.0
Nicaraguan	39.1
Salvadoran	32.5
Cuban	47.3
Dominican Republic	32.9
Mexican	24.3
Puerto Rican	24.9
South American	36.0
Argentinean	35.6
Chilean	42.3
Colombian	39.5
Ecuadorian	33.0
Peruvian	35.1
Venezuelan	32.3
Spaniard	58.3

High School Graduates
(Universe: Population 25 Years and Over)

Group	Number	%
Total Population	13,523	77.7
Hispanic or Latino (of any race)	12,568	77.0
Central American, ex. Mexican	806	74.3
Nicaraguan	565	68.6
Cuban	9,800	75.4
South American	858	96.7

Four-Year College Graduates
(Universe: Population 25 Years and Over)

Group	Number	%
Total Population	4,798	27.6
Hispanic or Latino (of any race)	4,445	27.2
Central American, ex. Mexican	372	34.3
Nicaraguan	233	28.3
Cuban	3,377	26.0
South American	259	29.2

Population Age 3–17 Enrolled in Public School
(Universe: Population Age 3–17 Enrolled in School)

Group	Number	%
Total Population	2,417	80.7
Hispanic or Latino (of any race)	2,107	80.6
Central American, ex. Mexican	130	83.9
Nicaraguan	113	81.9
Cuban	1,449	79.2
South American	227	94.6

Population Age 3–17 Enrolled in Private School
(Universe: Population Age 3–17 Enrolled in School)

Group	Number	%
Total Population	577	19.3
Hispanic or Latino (of any race)	506	19.4
Central American, ex. Mexican	25	16.1
Nicaraguan	25	18.1
Cuban	380	20.8
South American	13	5.4

Foreign-Born Population

Group	Number	%
Total Population	16,209	66.7
Hispanic or Latino (of any race)	15,649	71.0
Central American, ex. Mexican	1,116	72.0
Nicaraguan	909	74.8
Cuban	12,545	73.7
South American	1,135	77.7

Foreign-Born Naturalized U.S. Citizens

Group	Number	%
Total Population	10,038	61.9
Hispanic or Latino (of any race)	9,881	63.1
Central American, ex. Mexican	742	66.5
Nicaraguan	569	62.6
Cuban	8,171	65.1
South American	505	44.5

Notes: (1) Percent of total population; (2) Percent of Hispanic/Latino population; Profiles include places with an overall population of at least 125,000, OR an overall population of at least 25,000 where the Hispanic/Latino population is at least 20% of the overall population. In states where less than five places meet either of these criteria, we have included places with at least 10,000 total population with the highest percentage of Hispanic/Latino population. These places are identified with an asterisk (*); Please refer to the User's Guide for a full explanation of data.

Language Spoken at Home: English Only
(Universe: Population 5 Years and Over)

Group	Number	%
Total Population	2,007	8.6
Hispanic or Latino (of any race)	757	3.6
Central American, ex. Mexican	39	2.8
Nicaraguan	8	0.8
Cuban	390	2.4
South American	86	6.2

Language Spoken at Home: Spanish
(Universe: Population 5 Years and Over)

Group	Number	%
Total Population	20,820	89.5
Hispanic or Latino (of any race)	20,310	96.3
Central American, ex. Mexican	1,308	95.1
Nicaraguan	1,012	96.5
Cuban	16,013	97.6
South American	1,300	93.8

Unemployment Rate
(Universe: Population 16 Years and Over)

Group	%
Total Population	4.8
Hispanic or Latino (of any race)	4.3
Central American, ex. Mexican	7.6
Nicaraguan	9.7
Cuban	3.2
South American	6.6

Class of Worker: Private Wage and Salary
(Universe: Civilian Employed Population 16 Years and Over)

Group	Number	%
Total Population	9,066	78.3
Hispanic or Latino (of any race)	8,700	80.2
Central American, ex. Mexican	650	80.6
Nicaraguan	531	86.8
Cuban	6,672	80.7
South American	585	82.0

Class of Worker: Government
(Universe: Civilian Employed Population 16 Years and Over)

Group	Number	%
Total Population	1,644	14.2
Hispanic or Latino (of any race)	1,357	12.5
Central American, ex. Mexican	72	8.9
Nicaraguan	48	7.8
Cuban	1,087	13.1
South American	63	8.8

Means of Transportation to Work: Car, Truck or Van
(Universe: Workers 16 Years and Over)

Group	Number	%
Total Population	10,314	90.9
Hispanic or Latino (of any race)	9,851	92.4
Central American, ex. Mexican	689	86.9
Nicaraguan	535	89.3
Cuban	7,657	94.3
South American	622	89.5

Means of Transportation to Work: Public Transportation (ex. Taxicab)
(Universe: Workers 16 Years and Over)

Group	Number	%
Total Population	207	1.8
Hispanic or Latino (of any race)	192	1.8
Central American, ex. Mexican	33	4.2
Nicaraguan	33	5.5
Cuban	58	0.7
South American	63	9.1

Homeownership Rate
(Universe: Occupied Housing Units)

Group	%
Total Population	65.1
Hispanic or Latino (of any race)	66.5
Central American, ex. Mexican	55.7
Guatemalan	61.0
Honduran	60.6
Nicaraguan	54.2
Salvadoran	54.8
Cuban	68.6
Dominican Republic	56.0
Mexican	50.0
Puerto Rican	55.8
South American	56.9
Argentinean	59.3
Chilean	44.1
Colombian	55.8
Ecuadorian	75.7
Peruvian	67.1
Venezuelan	47.6
Spaniard	82.4

Median Home Value

Group	Dollars
Total Population	332,500
Hispanic or Latino (of any race)	331,400
Central American, ex. Mexican	242,000
Nicaraguan	233,300
Cuban	341,300
South American	244,000

Median Gross Rent

Group	Dollars
Total Population	1,057
Hispanic or Latino (of any race)	1,060
Central American, ex. Mexican	1,079
Nicaraguan	1,059
Cuban	1,060
South American	985

Median Household Income
(2010 Inflation-Adjusted Dollars)

Group	Dollars
Total Population	46,008
Hispanic or Latino (of any race)	46,127
Central American, ex. Mexican	42,604
Nicaraguan	33,864
Cuban	44,722
South American	53,512

Per Capita Income
(2010 Inflation-Adjusted Dollars)

Group	Dollars
Total Population	21,556
Hispanic or Latino (of any race)	22,248
Central American, ex. Mexican	17,512
Nicaraguan	14,961
Cuban	23,172
South American	14,775

Households with $100,000+ Income

Group	Number	%
Total Population	1,416	18.0
Hispanic or Latino (of any race)	1,293	17.5
Central American, ex. Mexican	60	16.5
Nicaraguan	34	12.8
Cuban	1,078	17.6
South American	14	4.0

Households with Food Stamps/SNAP Benefits During Past 12 Months

Group	Number	%
Total Population	1,496	19.0
Hispanic or Latino (of any race)	1,473	20.0
Central American, ex. Mexican	54	14.9
Nicaraguan	43	16.2
Cuban	1,287	21.0
South American	60	17.2

Poverty Rate
(Income in Past 12 Months Below Poverty Level)

Group	%
Total Population	14.7
Hispanic or Latino (of any race)	15.0
Central American, ex. Mexican	4.6
Nicaraguan	5.9
Cuban	17.0
South American	12.2

Wesley Chapel

Population

Group	Number	%TP[1]	%HP[2]
Total Population	44,092	100.0	–
Hispanic or Latino (of any race)	8,871	20.1	100.0
Central American, ex. Mexican	523	1.2	5.9
Honduran	150	0.3	1.7
Panamanian	115	0.3	1.3
Cuban	956	2.2	10.8
Dominican Republic	499	1.1	5.6
Mexican	731	1.7	8.2
Puerto Rican	3,818	8.7	43.0
South American	1,739	3.9	19.6
Colombian	869	2.0	9.8
Ecuadorian	189	0.4	2.1
Peruvian	236	0.5	2.7
Venezuelan	313	0.7	3.5
Spaniard	222	0.5	2.5

Population Growth: 2000–2010

Group	%
Total Population	674.8
Hispanic or Latino (of any race)	1,214.2
Puerto Rican	1,221.1

Males per 100 Females

Group	Number
Total Population	94.0
Hispanic or Latino (of any race)	93.8
Central American, ex. Mexican	79.7
Honduran	56.3
Panamanian	76.9
Cuban	105.2
Dominican Republic	94.9
Mexican	104.2
Puerto Rican	97.0
South American	82.1
Colombian	74.1
Ecuadorian	65.8
Peruvian	98.3
Venezuelan	101.9
Spaniard	103.7

Average Household Size

Group	People
Total Population	2.80
Hispanic or Latino (of any race)	3.28
Central American, ex. Mexican	3.40
Honduran	3.63
Panamanian	3.05
Cuban	3.12
Dominican Republic	3.53
Mexican	3.37
Puerto Rican	3.29
South American	3.31
Colombian	3.31
Ecuadorian	3.47
Peruvian	3.26
Venezuelan	3.45
Spaniard	2.88

Median Age

Group	Years
Total Population	35.2
Hispanic or Latino (of any race)	30.9
Central American, ex. Mexican	32.8
Honduran	32.3
Panamanian	35.8
Cuban	30.6
Dominican Republic	28.6
Mexican	26.2
Puerto Rican	30.6
South American	35.0
Colombian	36.2
Ecuadorian	33.7
Peruvian	33.6
Venezuelan	32.7
Spaniard	31.0

High School Graduates
(Universe: Population 25 Years and Over)

Group	Number	%
Total Population	24,566	93.9
Hispanic or Latino (of any race)	3,772	87.1
Puerto Rican	1,139	87.3
South American	989	97.1

Four-Year College Graduates
(Universe: Population 25 Years and Over)

Group	Number	%
Total Population	9,177	35.1

Notes: (1) Percent of total population; (2) Percent of Hispanic/Latino population; Profiles include places with an overall population of at least 125,000, OR an overall population of at least 25,000 where the Hispanic/Latino population is at least 20% of the overall population. In states where less than five places meet either of these criteria, we have included places with at least 10,000 total population with the highest percentage of Hispanic/Latino population. These places are identified with an asterisk (*); Please refer to the User's Guide for a full explanation of data.

Hispanic or Latino (of any race)	1,220	28.2
Puerto Rican	433	33.2
South American	350	34.3

Population Age 3–17 Enrolled in Public School
(Universe: Population Age 3–17 Enrolled in School)

Group	Number	%
Total Population	6,584	85.6
Hispanic or Latino (of any race)	1,776	93.0
Puerto Rican	694	91.2
South American	367	100.0

Population Age 3–17 Enrolled in Private School
(Universe: Population Age 3–17 Enrolled in School)

Group	Number	%
Total Population	1,111	14.4
Hispanic or Latino (of any race)	133	7.0
Puerto Rican	67	8.8
South American	0	0.0

Foreign-Born Population

Group	Number	%
Total Population	5,545	14.1
Hispanic or Latino (of any race)	2,456	32.8
Puerto Rican	0	0.0
South American	1,142	76.9

Foreign-Born Naturalized U.S. Citizens

Group	Number	%
Total Population	3,481	62.8
Hispanic or Latino (of any race)	1,299	52.9
Puerto Rican	0	0.0
South American	717	62.8

Language Spoken at Home: English Only
(Universe: Population 5 Years and Over)

Group	Number	%
Total Population	28,112	77.6
Hispanic or Latino (of any race)	1,858	27.9
Puerto Rican	786	35.4
South American	60	4.5

Language Spoken at Home: Spanish
(Universe: Population 5 Years and Over)

Group	Number	%
Total Population	5,643	15.6
Hispanic or Latino (of any race)	4,810	72.1
Puerto Rican	1,432	64.6
South American	1,288	95.5

Unemployment Rate
(Universe: Population 16 Years and Over)

Group	%
Total Population	5.8
Hispanic or Latino (of any race)	7.9
Puerto Rican	3.2
South American	12.4

Class of Worker: Private Wage and Salary
(Universe: Civilian Employed Population 16 Years and Over)

Group	Number	%
Total Population	16,428	79.7
Hispanic or Latino (of any race)	2,860	79.9
Puerto Rican	828	69.8
South American	534	80.7

Class of Worker: Government
(Universe: Civilian Employed Population 16 Years and Over)

Group	Number	%
Total Population	3,261	15.8
Hispanic or Latino (of any race)	585	16.3
Puerto Rican	321	27.1
South American	114	17.2

Means of Transportation to Work: Car, Truck or Van
(Universe: Workers 16 Years and Over)

Group	Number	%
Total Population	18,960	92.7
Hispanic or Latino (of any race)	3,287	93.6
Puerto Rican	1,092	93.8
South American	640	98.2

Means of Transportation to Work: Public Transportation (ex. Taxicab)
(Universe: Workers 16 Years and Over)

Group	Number	%
Total Population	61	0.3
Hispanic or Latino (of any race)	50	1.4
Puerto Rican	0	0.0
South American	0	0.0

Homeownership Rate
(Universe: Occupied Housing Units)

Group	%
Total Population	77.3
Hispanic or Latino (of any race)	74.6
Central American, ex. Mexican	79.2
Honduran	72.5
Panamanian	75.7
Cuban	78.2
Dominican Republic	69.9
Mexican	62.4
Puerto Rican	72.8
South American	79.8
Colombian	79.3
Ecuadorian	84.5
Peruvian	85.1
Venezuelan	74.5
Spaniard	92.4

Median Home Value

Group	Dollars
Total Population	211,800
Hispanic or Latino (of any race)	222,100
Puerto Rican	222,100
South American	238,100

Median Gross Rent

Group	Dollars
Total Population	1,265
Hispanic or Latino (of any race)	1,276
Puerto Rican	1,384
South American	–

Median Household Income
(2010 Inflation-Adjusted Dollars)

Group	Dollars
Total Population	69,673
Hispanic or Latino (of any race)	68,056
Puerto Rican	75,187
South American	57,390

Per Capita Income
(2010 Inflation-Adjusted Dollars)

Group	Dollars
Total Population	29,355
Hispanic or Latino (of any race)	20,935
Puerto Rican	21,108
South American	22,377

Households with $100,000+ Income

Group	Number	%
Total Population	3,924	27.1
Hispanic or Latino (of any race)	441	20.5
Puerto Rican	105	14.8
South American	114	23.2

Households with Food Stamps/SNAP Benefits During Past 12 Months

Group	Number	%
Total Population	409	2.8
Hispanic or Latino (of any race)	62	2.9
Puerto Rican	0	0.0
South American	16	3.3

Poverty Rate
(Income in Past 12 Months Below Poverty Level)

Group	%
Total Population	6.0
Hispanic or Latino (of any race)	6.4
Puerto Rican	2.2
South American	0.0

West Little River

Population

Group	Number	%TP[1]	%HP[2]
Total Population	34,699	100.0	–
Hispanic or Latino (of any race)	17,550	50.6	100.0
Central American, ex. Mexican	5,083	14.6	29.0
Guatemalan	695	2.0	4.0
Honduran	1,902	5.5	10.8
Nicaraguan	2,112	6.1	12.0
Salvadoran	291	0.8	1.7
Cuban	8,014	23.1	45.7
Dominican Republic	1,179	3.4	6.7
Mexican	265	0.8	1.5
Puerto Rican	1,126	3.2	6.4
South American	686	2.0	3.9
Colombian	307	0.9	1.7
Peruvian	153	0.4	0.9

Population Growth: 2000–2010

Group	%
Total Population	6.8
Hispanic or Latino (of any race)	34.8
Central American, ex. Mexican	101.1
Guatemalan	77.7
Honduran	168.3
Nicaraguan	81.6
Salvadoran	129.1
Cuban	47.0
Dominican Republic	50.0
Mexican	41.7
Puerto Rican	0.8
South American	59.9
Colombian	65.1

Males per 100 Females

Group	Number
Total Population	99.7
Hispanic or Latino (of any race)	110.2
Central American, ex. Mexican	107.4
Guatemalan	143.0
Honduran	107.4
Nicaraguan	99.8
Salvadoran	107.9
Cuban	117.9
Dominican Republic	93.9
Mexican	112.0
Puerto Rican	106.2
South American	93.8
Colombian	79.5
Peruvian	125.0

Average Household Size

Group	People
Total Population	3.35
Hispanic or Latino (of any race)	3.78
Central American, ex. Mexican	4.28
Guatemalan	4.35
Honduran	4.24
Nicaraguan	4.42
Salvadoran	3.97
Cuban	3.56
Dominican Republic	3.96
Mexican	3.40
Puerto Rican	3.24
South American	3.96
Colombian	3.91
Peruvian	4.08

Median Age

Group	Years
Total Population	37.7
Hispanic or Latino (of any race)	38.5
Central American, ex. Mexican	34.2
Guatemalan	35.4
Honduran	32.8
Nicaraguan	35.1
Salvadoran	35.1
Cuban	44.0
Dominican Republic	38.9
Mexican	27.4
Puerto Rican	35.7
South American	41.8
Colombian	46.5

Notes: (1) Percent of total population; (2) Percent of Hispanic/Latino population; Profiles include places with an overall population of at least 125,000, OR an overall population of at least 25,000 where the Hispanic/Latino population is at least 20% of the overall population. In states where less than five places meet either of these criteria, we have included places with at least 10,000 total population with the highest percentage of Hispanic/Latino population. These places are identified with an asterisk (*); Please refer to the User's Guide for a full explanation of data.

Peruvian		32.8

High School Graduates
(Universe: Population 25 Years and Over)

Group	Number	%
Total Population	13,566	64.0
Hispanic or Latino (of any race)	5,681	53.4
Central American, ex. Mexican	1,831	47.6
Honduran	455	39.3
Nicaraguan	1,104	56.8
Cuban	2,546	54.6
Dominican Republic	356	60.5
Puerto Rican	414	50.6

Four-Year College Graduates
(Universe: Population 25 Years and Over)

Group	Number	%
Total Population	1,602	7.6
Hispanic or Latino (of any race)	729	6.9
Central American, ex. Mexican	261	6.8
Honduran	41	3.5
Nicaraguan	143	7.4
Cuban	189	4.0
Dominican Republic	24	4.1
Puerto Rican	58	7.1

Population Age 3–17 Enrolled in Public School
(Universe: Population Age 3–17 Enrolled in School)

Group	Number	%
Total Population	5,933	95.4
Hispanic or Latino (of any race)	1,920	94.8
Central American, ex. Mexican	864	100.0
Honduran	281	100.0
Nicaraguan	405	100.0
Cuban	530	91.2
Dominican Republic	65	89.0
Puerto Rican	246	90.4

Population Age 3–17 Enrolled in Private School
(Universe: Population Age 3–17 Enrolled in School)

Group	Number	%
Total Population	287	4.6
Hispanic or Latino (of any race)	105	5.2
Central American, ex. Mexican	0	0.0
Honduran	0	0.0
Nicaraguan	0	0.0
Cuban	51	8.8
Dominican Republic	8	11.0
Puerto Rican	26	9.6

Foreign-Born Population

Group	Number	%
Total Population	13,501	41.5
Hispanic or Latino (of any race)	10,639	69.6
Central American, ex. Mexican	4,453	75.4
Honduran	1,453	82.3
Nicaraguan	2,169	73.9
Cuban	4,756	77.1
Dominican Republic	638	74.0
Puerto Rican	58	4.7

Foreign-Born Naturalized U.S. Citizens

Group	Number	%
Total Population	5,016	37.2
Hispanic or Latino (of any race)	3,612	34.0
Central American, ex. Mexican	1,151	25.8
Honduran	139	9.6
Nicaraguan	776	35.8
Cuban	1,883	39.6
Dominican Republic	242	37.9
Puerto Rican	41	70.7

Language Spoken at Home: English Only
(Universe: Population 5 Years and Over)

Group	Number	%
Total Population	13,551	44.4
Hispanic or Latino (of any race)	447	3.1
Central American, ex. Mexican	191	3.5
Honduran	78	4.5
Nicaraguan	66	2.5
Cuban	135	2.4
Dominican Republic	11	1.3
Puerto Rican	49	4.3

Language Spoken at Home: Spanish
(Universe: Population 5 Years and Over)

Group	Number	%
Total Population	14,466	47.4
Hispanic or Latino (of any race)	13,725	96.6
Central American, ex. Mexican	5,339	96.5
Honduran	1,637	95.5
Nicaraguan	2,592	97.5
Cuban	5,546	97.6
Dominican Republic	805	97.5
Puerto Rican	1,081	95.7

Unemployment Rate
(Universe: Population 16 Years and Over)

Group	%
Total Population	13.2
Hispanic or Latino (of any race)	13.7
Central American, ex. Mexican	14.8
Honduran	18.8
Nicaraguan	11.6
Cuban	11.5
Dominican Republic	8.8
Puerto Rican	8.8

Class of Worker: Private Wage and Salary
(Universe: Civilian Employed Population 16 Years and Over)

Group	Number	%
Total Population	10,043	73.9
Hispanic or Latino (of any race)	5,661	80.4
Central American, ex. Mexican	2,352	79.0
Honduran	592	64.4
Nicaraguan	1,306	89.1
Cuban	2,184	84.2
Dominican Republic	409	77.0
Puerto Rican	388	87.2

Class of Worker: Government
(Universe: Civilian Employed Population 16 Years and Over)

Group	Number	%
Total Population	2,107	15.5
Hispanic or Latino (of any race)	238	3.4
Central American, ex. Mexican	54	1.8
Honduran	8	0.9
Nicaraguan	9	0.6
Cuban	90	3.5
Dominican Republic	49	9.2
Puerto Rican	45	10.1

Means of Transportation to Work: Car, Truck or Van
(Universe: Workers 16 Years and Over)

Group	Number	%
Total Population	11,015	82.1
Hispanic or Latino (of any race)	5,720	82.8
Central American, ex. Mexican	2,345	79.9
Honduran	595	65.9
Nicaraguan	1,300	90.3
Cuban	2,181	86.3
Dominican Republic	418	81.3
Puerto Rican	412	92.6

Means of Transportation to Work: Public Transportation (ex. Taxicab)
(Universe: Workers 16 Years and Over)

Group	Number	%
Total Population	1,657	12.4
Hispanic or Latino (of any race)	636	9.2
Central American, ex. Mexican	450	15.3
Honduran	275	30.5
Nicaraguan	85	5.9
Cuban	50	2.0
Dominican Republic	12	2.3
Puerto Rican	33	7.4

Homeownership Rate
(Universe: Occupied Housing Units)

Group	%
Total Population	59.7
Hispanic or Latino (of any race)	61.4
Central American, ex. Mexican	58.6
Guatemalan	45.3
Honduran	61.1
Nicaraguan	58.6
Salvadoran	70.9
Cuban	63.5
Dominican Republic	65.6
Mexican	52.6
Puerto Rican	57.5
South American	58.8
Colombian	69.6
Peruvian	46.2

Median Home Value

Group	Dollars
Total Population	168,700
Hispanic or Latino (of any race)	170,500
Central American, ex. Mexican	160,900
Honduran	150,800
Nicaraguan	163,000
Cuban	173,900
Dominican Republic	164,900
Puerto Rican	184,100

Median Gross Rent

Group	Dollars
Total Population	743
Hispanic or Latino (of any race)	713
Central American, ex. Mexican	904
Honduran	1,046
Nicaraguan	520
Cuban	649
Dominican Republic	544
Puerto Rican	476

Median Household Income
(2010 Inflation-Adjusted Dollars)

Group	Dollars
Total Population	32,974
Hispanic or Latino (of any race)	30,520
Central American, ex. Mexican	33,485
Honduran	30,671
Nicaraguan	53,641
Cuban	29,051
Dominican Republic	21,927
Puerto Rican	27,368

Per Capita Income
(2010 Inflation-Adjusted Dollars)

Group	Dollars
Total Population	13,126
Hispanic or Latino (of any race)	11,961
Central American, ex. Mexican	11,466
Honduran	10,271
Nicaraguan	12,456
Cuban	12,081
Dominican Republic	13,912
Puerto Rican	12,063

Households with $100,000+ Income

Group	Number	%
Total Population	434	4.5
Hispanic or Latino (of any race)	161	3.9
Central American, ex. Mexican	51	3.7
Honduran	13	2.9
Nicaraguan	31	5.7
Cuban	76	4.2
Dominican Republic	11	3.4
Puerto Rican	0	0.0

Households with Food Stamps/SNAP Benefits During Past 12 Months

Group	Number	%
Total Population	2,370	24.6
Hispanic or Latino (of any race)	1,315	31.6
Central American, ex. Mexican	315	23.1
Honduran	106	23.5
Nicaraguan	115	21.1
Cuban	704	38.7
Dominican Republic	61	18.7
Puerto Rican	144	40.9

Poverty Rate
(Income in Past 12 Months Below Poverty Level)

Group	%
Total Population	22.4
Hispanic or Latino (of any race)	22.8
Central American, ex. Mexican	21.0
Honduran	28.0
Nicaraguan	9.3
Cuban	26.0

STATE & PLACE PROFILES

Notes: (1) Percent of total population; (2) Percent of Hispanic/Latino population; Profiles include places with an overall population of at least 125,000, OR an overall population of at least 25,000 where the Hispanic/Latino population is at least 20% of the overall population. In states where less than five places meet either of these criteria, we have included places with at least 10,000 total population with the highest percentage of Hispanic/Latino population. These places are identified with an asterisk (*); Please refer to the User's Guide for a full explanation of data.

Dominican Republic	27.6
Puerto Rican	14.8

West Palm Beach

Population

Group	Number	%TP[1]	%HP[2]
Total Population	99,919	100.0	–
Hispanic or Latino (of any race)	22,601	22.6	100.0
Central American, ex. Mexican	5,454	5.5	24.1
Costa Rican	169	0.2	0.7
Guatemalan	3,897	3.9	17.2
Honduran	573	0.6	2.5
Nicaraguan	501	0.5	2.2
Panamanian	109	0.1	0.5
Salvadoran	179	0.2	0.8
Cuban	5,337	5.3	23.6
Dominican Republic	983	1.0	4.3
Mexican	2,805	2.8	12.4
Puerto Rican	3,291	3.3	14.6
South American	3,265	3.3	14.4
Argentinean	302	0.3	1.3
Chilean	115	0.1	0.5
Colombian	1,535	1.5	6.8
Ecuadorian	343	0.3	1.5
Peruvian	432	0.4	1.9
Uruguayan	128	0.1	0.6
Venezuelan	297	0.3	1.3
Spaniard	198	0.2	0.9

Population Growth: 2000–2010

Group	%
Total Population	21.7
Hispanic or Latino (of any race)	51.1
Central American, ex. Mexican	98.7
Costa Rican	45.7
Guatemalan	111.7
Honduran	86.0
Nicaraguan	89.1
Salvadoran	61.3
Cuban	22.9
Dominican Republic	135.2
Mexican	42.0
Puerto Rican	54.5
South American	178.8
Colombian	161.5
Ecuadorian	163.8
Peruvian	229.8

Males per 100 Females

Group	Number
Total Population	94.8
Hispanic or Latino (of any race)	109.9
Central American, ex. Mexican	152.4
Costa Rican	69.0
Guatemalan	190.4
Honduran	93.6
Nicaraguan	83.5
Panamanian	87.9
Salvadoran	110.6
Cuban	100.0
Dominican Republic	90.9
Mexican	128.4
Puerto Rican	93.7
South American	81.8
Argentinean	106.8
Chilean	105.4
Colombian	75.2
Ecuadorian	67.3
Peruvian	92.0
Uruguayan	88.2
Venezuelan	78.9
Spaniard	108.4

Average Household Size

Group	People
Total Population	2.26
Hispanic or Latino (of any race)	2.97
Central American, ex. Mexican	4.27
Costa Rican	2.79
Guatemalan	4.90
Honduran	3.39
Nicaraguan	3.48
Panamanian	2.26
Salvadoran	3.00
Cuban	2.54
Dominican Republic	2.99
Mexican	3.62
Puerto Rican	2.53
South American	2.47
Argentinean	2.34
Chilean	2.48
Colombian	2.48
Ecuadorian	2.51
Peruvian	2.64
Uruguayan	2.12
Venezuelan	2.51
Spaniard	2.27

Median Age

Group	Years
Total Population	38.1
Hispanic or Latino (of any race)	30.8
Central American, ex. Mexican	27.0
Costa Rican	37.5
Guatemalan	25.9
Honduran	30.5
Nicaraguan	31.9
Panamanian	39.8
Salvadoran	30.4
Cuban	43.1
Dominican Republic	31.1
Mexican	25.5
Puerto Rican	30.6
South American	36.7
Argentinean	37.6
Chilean	40.3
Colombian	37.3
Ecuadorian	34.3
Peruvian	37.6
Uruguayan	38.8
Venezuelan	33.6
Spaniard	40.0

High School Graduates
(Universe: Population 25 Years and Over)

Group	Number	%
Total Population	56,936	82.9
Hispanic or Latino (of any race)	8,662	65.6
Central American, ex. Mexican	1,134	32.8
Guatemalan	546	20.9
Cuban	2,670	79.3
Mexican	785	50.1
Puerto Rican	1,068	75.0
South American	2,420	91.1
Colombian	907	88.8

Four-Year College Graduates
(Universe: Population 25 Years and Over)

Group	Number	%
Total Population	20,210	29.4
Hispanic or Latino (of any race)	2,739	20.7
Central American, ex. Mexican	329	9.5
Guatemalan	122	4.7
Cuban	744	22.1
Mexican	254	16.2
Puerto Rican	341	23.9
South American	931	35.1
Colombian	322	31.5

Population Age 3–17 Enrolled in Public School
(Universe: Population Age 3–17 Enrolled in School)

Group	Number	%
Total Population	11,697	82.8
Hispanic or Latino (of any race)	3,164	87.6
Central American, ex. Mexican	811	97.6
Guatemalan	551	98.9
Cuban	470	83.9
Mexican	722	100.0
Puerto Rican	580	84.1
South American	370	63.1
Colombian	130	46.4

Population Age 3–17 Enrolled in Private School
(Universe: Population Age 3–17 Enrolled in School)

Group	Number	%
Total Population	2,427	17.2
Hispanic or Latino (of any race)	447	12.4
Central American, ex. Mexican	20	2.4
Guatemalan	6	1.1
Cuban	90	16.1
Mexican	0	0.0
Puerto Rican	110	15.9
South American	216	36.9
Colombian	150	53.6

Foreign-Born Population

Group	Number	%
Total Population	26,731	27.3
Hispanic or Latino (of any race)	12,727	59.8
Central American, ex. Mexican	4,619	77.0
Guatemalan	3,617	79.1
Cuban	2,900	65.9
Mexican	1,584	52.3
Puerto Rican	0	0.0
South American	2,948	75.0
Colombian	1,211	76.8

Foreign-Born Naturalized U.S. Citizens

Group	Number	%
Total Population	10,267	38.4
Hispanic or Latino (of any race)	3,103	24.4
Central American, ex. Mexican	340	7.4
Guatemalan	35	1.0
Cuban	1,410	48.6
Mexican	121	7.6
Puerto Rican	0	0.0
South American	945	32.1
Colombian	254	21.0

Language Spoken at Home: English Only
(Universe: Population 5 Years and Over)

Group	Number	%
Total Population	64,497	70.3
Hispanic or Latino (of any race)	2,765	14.2
Central American, ex. Mexican	93	1.8
Guatemalan	9	0.2
Cuban	692	17.0
Mexican	589	20.6
Puerto Rican	691	27.0
South American	429	11.9
Colombian	81	5.5

Language Spoken at Home: Spanish
(Universe: Population 5 Years and Over)

Group	Number	%
Total Population	18,364	20.0
Hispanic or Latino (of any race)	16,581	85.4
Central American, ex. Mexican	5,179	98.1
Guatemalan	3,943	99.8
Cuban	3,387	83.0
Mexican	2,267	79.1
Puerto Rican	1,872	73.0
South American	3,174	88.1
Colombian	1,398	94.5

Unemployment Rate
(Universe: Population 16 Years and Over)

Group	%
Total Population	10.1
Hispanic or Latino (of any race)	8.2
Central American, ex. Mexican	7.8
Guatemalan	8.1
Cuban	8.4
Mexican	8.4
Puerto Rican	9.5
South American	5.3
Colombian	7.3

Class of Worker: Private Wage and Salary
(Universe: Civilian Employed Population 16 Years and Over)

Group	Number	%
Total Population	38,747	82.4
Hispanic or Latino (of any race)	9,699	86.7
Central American, ex. Mexican	3,073	92.1
Guatemalan	2,439	97.5
Cuban	1,616	79.4
Mexican	1,512	92.3
Puerto Rican	1,118	86.3
South American	1,952	82.3
Colombian	816	91.1

Notes: (1) Percent of total population; (2) Percent of Hispanic/Latino population; Profiles include places with an overall population of at least 125,000, OR an overall population of at least 25,000 where the Hispanic/Latino population is at least 20% of the overall population. In states where less than five places meet either of these criteria, we have included places with at least 10,000 total population with the highest percentage of Hispanic/Latino population. These places are identified with an asterisk (*); Please refer to the User's Guide for a full explanation of data.

Class of Worker: Government
(Universe: Civilian Employed Population 16 Years and Over)

Group	Number	%
Total Population	5,483	11.7
Hispanic or Latino (of any race)	730	6.5
Central American, ex. Mexican	20	0.6
Guatemalan	0	0.0
Cuban	268	13.2
Mexican	34	2.1
Puerto Rican	178	13.7
South American	196	8.3
Colombian	34	3.8

Means of Transportation to Work: Car, Truck or Van
(Universe: Workers 16 Years and Over)

Group	Number	%
Total Population	39,952	86.8
Hispanic or Latino (of any race)	9,632	86.1
Central American, ex. Mexican	2,626	79.4
Guatemalan	2,045	82.5
Cuban	1,828	89.9
Mexican	1,314	80.0
Puerto Rican	1,182	89.3
South American	2,176	91.9
Colombian	847	94.5

Means of Transportation to Work: Public Transportation (ex. Taxicab)
(Universe: Workers 16 Years and Over)

Group	Number	%
Total Population	1,324	2.9
Hispanic or Latino (of any race)	292	2.6
Central American, ex. Mexican	163	4.9
Guatemalan	129	5.2
Cuban	28	1.4
Mexican	78	4.8
Puerto Rican	13	1.0
South American	10	0.4
Colombian	0	0.0

Homeownership Rate
(Universe: Occupied Housing Units)

Group	%
Total Population	50.6
Hispanic or Latino (of any race)	38.7
Central American, ex. Mexican	22.5
Costa Rican	42.4
Guatemalan	12.4
Honduran	36.9
Nicaraguan	47.7
Panamanian	34.8
Salvadoran	32.1
Cuban	51.4
Dominican Republic	38.2
Mexican	27.5
Puerto Rican	32.4
South American	46.0
Argentinean	48.4
Chilean	41.3
Colombian	50.4
Ecuadorian	39.8
Peruvian	42.8
Uruguayan	35.0
Venezuelan	38.6
Spaniard	57.6

Median Home Value

Group	Dollars
Total Population	239,700
Hispanic or Latino (of any race)	219,400
Central American, ex. Mexican	235,400
Guatemalan	212,100
Cuban	228,900
Mexican	277,500
Puerto Rican	188,900
South American	187,200
Colombian	176,600

Median Gross Rent

Group	Dollars
Total Population	1,010
Hispanic or Latino (of any race)	1,042
Central American, ex. Mexican	1,064
Guatemalan	1,085
Cuban	871
Mexican	990
Puerto Rican	1,154
South American	1,107
Colombian	1,105

Median Household Income
(2010 Inflation-Adjusted Dollars)

Group	Dollars
Total Population	44,905
Hispanic or Latino (of any race)	40,718
Central American, ex. Mexican	38,514
Guatemalan	37,127
Cuban	42,500
Mexican	31,344
Puerto Rican	44,574
South American	46,667
Colombian	49,453

Per Capita Income
(2010 Inflation-Adjusted Dollars)

Group	Dollars
Total Population	29,620
Hispanic or Latino (of any race)	17,421
Central American, ex. Mexican	11,024
Guatemalan	9,317
Cuban	20,785
Mexican	14,881
Puerto Rican	18,100
South American	24,563
Colombian	16,556

Households with $100,000+ Income

Group	Number	%
Total Population	6,977	17.1
Hispanic or Latino (of any race)	752	11.7
Central American, ex. Mexican	59	4.6
Guatemalan	6	0.8
Cuban	242	14.6
Mexican	71	8.9
Puerto Rican	67	6.4
South American	256	20.1
Colombian	21	5.5

Households with Food Stamps/SNAP Benefits During Past 12 Months

Group	Number	%
Total Population	4,024	9.9
Hispanic or Latino (of any race)	904	14.1
Central American, ex. Mexican	264	20.7
Guatemalan	144	18.8
Cuban	311	18.8
Mexican	70	8.7
Puerto Rican	116	11.0
South American	133	10.4
Colombian	48	12.5

Poverty Rate
(Income in Past 12 Months Below Poverty Level)

Group	%
Total Population	18.2
Hispanic or Latino (of any race)	27.0
Central American, ex. Mexican	43.8
Guatemalan	47.7
Cuban	19.6
Mexican	28.2
Puerto Rican	27.1
South American	12.6
Colombian	18.3

Westchester

Population

Group	Number	%TP[1]	%HP[2]
Total Population	29,862	100.0	–
Hispanic or Latino (of any race)	27,211	91.1	100.0
Central American, ex. Mexican	1,978	6.6	7.3
Costa Rican	103	0.3	0.4
Guatemalan	287	1.0	1.1
Honduran	344	1.2	1.3
Nicaraguan	1,013	3.4	3.7
Salvadoran	186	0.6	0.7
Cuban	21,391	71.6	78.6
Dominican Republic	382	1.3	1.4
Mexican	292	1.0	1.1
Puerto Rican	504	1.7	1.9
South American	1,805	6.0	6.6
Argentinean	174	0.6	0.6
Chilean	112	0.4	0.4
Colombian	665	2.2	2.4
Ecuadorian	178	0.6	0.7
Peruvian	317	1.1	1.2
Venezuelan	258	0.9	0.9
Spaniard	244	0.8	0.9

Population Growth: 2000–2010

Group	%
Total Population	-1.4
Hispanic or Latino (of any race)	5.4
Central American, ex. Mexican	60.8
Guatemalan	120.8
Honduran	116.4
Nicaraguan	48.5
Salvadoran	75.5
Cuban	7.6
Dominican Republic	20.5
Mexican	46.7
Puerto Rican	-1.0
South American	35.8
Colombian	24.1
Ecuadorian	49.6
Peruvian	34.3
Venezuelan	41.8
Spaniard	41.0

Males per 100 Females

Group	Number
Total Population	89.6
Hispanic or Latino (of any race)	88.0
Central American, ex. Mexican	85.9
Costa Rican	71.7
Guatemalan	149.6
Honduran	64.6
Nicaraguan	81.9
Salvadoran	100.0
Cuban	88.5
Dominican Republic	62.6
Mexican	139.3
Puerto Rican	88.8
South American	74.7
Argentinean	87.1
Chilean	83.6
Colombian	65.0
Ecuadorian	74.5
Peruvian	83.2
Venezuelan	80.4
Spaniard	125.9

Average Household Size

Group	People
Total Population	3.11
Hispanic or Latino (of any race)	3.18
Central American, ex. Mexican	4.19
Costa Rican	3.71
Guatemalan	4.86
Honduran	3.85
Nicaraguan	4.19
Salvadoran	4.19
Cuban	3.11
Dominican Republic	3.05
Mexican	4.14
Puerto Rican	3.07
South American	3.34
Argentinean	3.47
Chilean	3.45
Colombian	3.24
Ecuadorian	3.45
Peruvian	3.34
Venezuelan	3.28
Spaniard	2.57

Median Age

Group	Years
Total Population	45.2
Hispanic or Latino (of any race)	45.7
Central American, ex. Mexican	35.2
Costa Rican	40.8
Guatemalan	28.1
Honduran	34.6

Notes: (1) Percent of total population; (2) Percent of Hispanic/Latino population; Profiles include places with an overall population of at least 125,000, OR an overall population of at least 25,000 where the Hispanic/Latino population is at least 20% of the overall population. In states where less than five places meet either of these criteria, we have included places with at least 10,000 total population with the highest percentage of Hispanic/Latino population. These places are identified with an asterisk (*); Please refer to the User's Guide for a full explanation of data.

Nicaraguan		37.6
Salvadoran		35.5
Cuban		47.6
Dominican Republic		40.1
Mexican		27.3
Puerto Rican		42.6
South American		41.0
Argentinean		34.6
Chilean		41.5
Colombian		43.2
Ecuadorian		44.3
Peruvian		45.9
Venezuelan		35.2
Spaniard		60.9

High School Graduates
(Universe: Population 25 Years and Over)

Group	Number	%
Total Population	15,984	74.0
Hispanic or Latino (of any race)	14,438	72.9
Central American, ex. Mexican	630	60.2
Cuban	11,588	72.7
South American	1,072	77.0

Four-Year College Graduates
(Universe: Population 25 Years and Over)

Group	Number	%
Total Population	4,493	20.8
Hispanic or Latino (of any race)	4,114	20.8
Central American, ex. Mexican	167	16.0
Cuban	3,323	20.8
South American	375	26.9

Population Age 3–17 Enrolled in Public School
(Universe: Population Age 3–17 Enrolled in School)

Group	Number	%
Total Population	2,996	85.9
Hispanic or Latino (of any race)	2,600	87.7
Central American, ex. Mexican	194	100.0
Cuban	1,983	88.0
South American	146	77.7

Population Age 3–17 Enrolled in Private School
(Universe: Population Age 3–17 Enrolled in School)

Group	Number	%
Total Population	490	14.1
Hispanic or Latino (of any race)	363	12.3
Central American, ex. Mexican	0	0.0
Cuban	271	12.0
South American	42	22.3

Foreign-Born Population

Group	Number	%
Total Population	18,755	65.3
Hispanic or Latino (of any race)	18,159	70.5
Central American, ex. Mexican	1,065	79.5
Cuban	14,922	71.9
South American	1,396	80.4

Foreign-Born Naturalized U.S. Citizens

Group	Number	%
Total Population	10,837	57.8
Hispanic or Latino (of any race)	10,550	58.1
Central American, ex. Mexican	357	33.5
Cuban	9,000	60.3
South American	853	61.1

Language Spoken at Home: English Only
(Universe: Population 5 Years and Over)

Group	Number	%
Total Population	2,321	8.3
Hispanic or Latino (of any race)	879	3.5
Central American, ex. Mexican	26	2.0
Cuban	635	3.1
South American	25	1.5

Language Spoken at Home: Spanish
(Universe: Population 5 Years and Over)

Group	Number	%
Total Population	25,233	90.4
Hispanic or Latino (of any race)	24,157	96.4
Central American, ex. Mexican	1,250	98.0
Cuban	19,578	96.8
South American	1,647	98.5

Unemployment Rate
(Universe: Population 16 Years and Over)

Group	%
Total Population	6.8
Hispanic or Latino (of any race)	7.0
Central American, ex. Mexican	2.3
Cuban	7.9
South American	4.1

Class of Worker: Private Wage and Salary
(Universe: Civilian Employed Population 16 Years and Over)

Group	Number	%
Total Population	11,353	83.3
Hispanic or Latino (of any race)	10,305	84.2
Central American, ex. Mexican	426	72.3
Cuban	8,336	83.9
South American	607	83.3

Class of Worker: Government
(Universe: Civilian Employed Population 16 Years and Over)

Group	Number	%
Total Population	1,356	9.9
Hispanic or Latino (of any race)	1,104	9.0
Central American, ex. Mexican	30	5.1
Cuban	937	9.4
South American	106	14.5

Means of Transportation to Work: Car, Truck or Van
(Universe: Workers 16 Years and Over)

Group	Number	%
Total Population	12,244	91.1
Hispanic or Latino (of any race)	11,223	93.0
Central American, ex. Mexican	416	70.6
Cuban	9,158	93.9
South American	682	93.6

Means of Transportation to Work: Public Transportation (ex. Taxicab)
(Universe: Workers 16 Years and Over)

Group	Number	%
Total Population	314	2.3
Hispanic or Latino (of any race)	264	2.2
Central American, ex. Mexican	93	15.8
Cuban	153	1.6
South American	0	0.0

Homeownership Rate
(Universe: Occupied Housing Units)

Group	%
Total Population	68.0
Hispanic or Latino (of any race)	66.4
Central American, ex. Mexican	45.7
Costa Rican	61.9
Guatemalan	30.8
Honduran	44.0
Nicaraguan	47.7
Salvadoran	51.2
Cuban	68.1
Dominican Republic	64.9
Mexican	50.9
Puerto Rican	64.6
South American	57.8
Argentinean	49.1
Chilean	65.8
Colombian	61.8
Ecuadorian	62.5
Peruvian	59.1
Venezuelan	52.3
Spaniard	88.1

Median Home Value

Group	Dollars
Total Population	316,700
Hispanic or Latino (of any race)	321,600
Central American, ex. Mexican	286,700
Cuban	324,900
South American	369,700

Median Gross Rent

Group	Dollars
Total Population	1,126
Hispanic or Latino (of any race)	1,133
Central American, ex. Mexican	1,050
Cuban	1,146
South American	1,129

Median Household Income
(2010 Inflation-Adjusted Dollars)

Group	Dollars
Total Population	43,560
Hispanic or Latino (of any race)	42,071
Central American, ex. Mexican	38,482
Cuban	42,719
South American	38,333

Per Capita Income
(2010 Inflation-Adjusted Dollars)

Group	Dollars
Total Population	20,018
Hispanic or Latino (of any race)	19,750
Central American, ex. Mexican	13,200
Cuban	20,010
South American	16,718

Households with $100,000+ Income

Group	Number	%
Total Population	1,403	14.8
Hispanic or Latino (of any race)	1,321	15.2
Central American, ex. Mexican	32	9.9
Cuban	1,146	16.1
South American	0	0.0

Households with Food Stamps/SNAP Benefits During Past 12 Months

Group	Number	%
Total Population	1,623	17.1
Hispanic or Latino (of any race)	1,550	17.8
Central American, ex. Mexican	131	40.4
Cuban	1,333	18.8
South American	0	0.0

Poverty Rate
(Income in Past 12 Months Below Poverty Level)

Group	%
Total Population	11.7
Hispanic or Latino (of any race)	11.7
Central American, ex. Mexican	33.8
Cuban	10.7
South American	10.1

Weston

Population

Group	Number	%TP[1]	%HP[2]
Total Population	65,333	100.0	–
Hispanic or Latino (of any race)	29,353	44.9	100.0
Central American, ex. Mexican	1,215	1.9	4.1
Costa Rican	105	0.2	0.4
Guatemalan	282	0.4	1.0
Honduran	189	0.3	0.6
Nicaraguan	288	0.4	1.0
Panamanian	137	0.2	0.5
Salvadoran	213	0.3	0.7
Cuban	3,134	4.8	10.7
Dominican Republic	988	1.5	3.4
Mexican	1,293	2.0	4.4
Puerto Rican	2,695	4.1	9.2
South American	18,234	27.9	62.1
Argentinean	946	1.4	3.2
Bolivian	130	0.2	0.4
Chilean	306	0.5	1.0
Colombian	7,637	11.7	26.0
Ecuadorian	1,000	1.5	3.4
Peruvian	1,677	2.6	5.7
Uruguayan	133	0.2	0.5
Venezuelan	6,360	9.7	21.7
Spaniard	522	0.8	1.8

Population Growth: 2000–2010

Group	%
Total Population	32.6
Hispanic or Latino (of any race)	97.3
Central American, ex. Mexican	184.5
Nicaraguan	174.3
Cuban	57.1
Dominican Republic	171.4
Mexican	117.7
Puerto Rican	65.1

Notes: (1) Percent of total population; (2) Percent of Hispanic/Latino population; Profiles include places with an overall population of at least 125,000, OR an overall population of at least 25,000 where the Hispanic/Latino population is at least 20% of the overall population. In states where less than five places meet either of these criteria, we have included places with at least 10,000 total population with the highest percentage of Hispanic/Latino population. These places are identified with an asterisk (*); Please refer to the User's Guide for a full explanation of data.

Group	
South American	175.4
Argentinean	209.2
Chilean	163.8
Colombian	150.2
Ecuadorian	213.5
Peruvian	185.2
Venezuelan	214.9
Spaniard	262.5

Males per 100 Females

Group	Number
Total Population	94.4
Hispanic or Latino (of any race)	89.0
Central American, ex. Mexican	88.1
Costa Rican	105.9
Guatemalan	110.4
Honduran	96.9
Nicaraguan	73.5
Panamanian	65.1
Salvadoran	83.6
Cuban	96.4
Dominican Republic	87.1
Mexican	89.9
Puerto Rican	90.7
South American	86.8
Argentinean	99.6
Bolivian	83.1
Chilean	91.3
Colombian	81.4
Ecuadorian	89.8
Peruvian	80.5
Uruguayan	133.3
Venezuelan	92.3
Spaniard	98.5

Average Household Size

Group	People
Total Population	3.08
Hispanic or Latino (of any race)	3.36
Central American, ex. Mexican	3.45
Costa Rican	3.81
Guatemalan	3.78
Honduran	3.47
Nicaraguan	3.54
Panamanian	2.78
Salvadoran	3.29
Cuban	3.06
Dominican Republic	3.57
Mexican	3.58
Puerto Rican	3.19
South American	3.42
Argentinean	3.62
Bolivian	3.91
Chilean	3.46
Colombian	3.34
Ecuadorian	3.70
Peruvian	3.46
Uruguayan	3.59
Venezuelan	3.43
Spaniard	3.42

Median Age

Group	Years
Total Population	37.9
Hispanic or Latino (of any race)	36.0
Central American, ex. Mexican	35.8
Costa Rican	34.3
Guatemalan	34.9
Honduran	31.1
Nicaraguan	38.0
Panamanian	40.8
Salvadoran	35.6
Cuban	39.7
Dominican Republic	32.2
Mexican	28.9
Puerto Rican	34.4
South American	36.7
Argentinean	38.9
Bolivian	36.0
Chilean	38.5
Colombian	37.5
Ecuadorian	35.3
Peruvian	39.3
Uruguayan	40.7
Venezuelan	35.1
Spaniard	40.8

High School Graduates
(Universe: Population 25 Years and Over)

Group	Number	%
Total Population	36,187	95.9
Hispanic or Latino (of any race)	15,105	95.4
Central American, ex. Mexican	537	94.5
Cuban	1,820	90.9
Dominican Republic	531	88.1
Mexican	555	100.0
Puerto Rican	1,325	96.5
South American	9,388	96.8
Colombian	3,354	93.7
Peruvian	1,308	98.3
Venezuelan	3,689	98.8

Four-Year College Graduates
(Universe: Population 25 Years and Over)

Group	Number	%
Total Population	22,079	58.5
Hispanic or Latino (of any race)	9,106	57.5
Central American, ex. Mexican	267	47.0
Cuban	1,042	52.0
Dominican Republic	282	46.8
Mexican	375	67.6
Puerto Rican	822	59.9
South American	5,823	60.0
Colombian	2,047	57.2
Peruvian	727	54.7
Venezuelan	2,461	65.9

Population Age 3–17 Enrolled in Public School
(Universe: Population Age 3–17 Enrolled in School)

Group	Number	%
Total Population	13,141	79.5
Hispanic or Latino (of any race)	6,381	81.9
Central American, ex. Mexican	175	92.1
Cuban	580	75.8
Dominican Republic	332	100.0
Mexican	216	68.8
Puerto Rican	594	68.6
South American	3,891	84.6
Colombian	1,505	85.4
Peruvian	352	88.7
Venezuelan	1,774	85.7

Population Age 3–17 Enrolled in Private School
(Universe: Population Age 3–17 Enrolled in School)

Group	Number	%
Total Population	3,390	20.5
Hispanic or Latino (of any race)	1,406	18.1
Central American, ex. Mexican	15	7.9
Cuban	185	24.2
Dominican Republic	0	0.0
Mexican	98	31.2
Puerto Rican	272	31.4
South American	706	15.4
Colombian	258	14.6
Peruvian	45	11.3
Venezuelan	296	14.3

Foreign-Born Population

Group	Number	%
Total Population	25,095	40.0
Hispanic or Latino (of any race)	17,591	63.2
Central American, ex. Mexican	546	61.9
Cuban	1,416	46.4
Dominican Republic	514	49.0
Mexican	540	52.3
Puerto Rican	26	1.0
South American	13,350	79.3
Colombian	4,520	71.9
Peruvian	1,657	84.0
Venezuelan	5,959	86.2

Foreign-Born Naturalized U.S. Citizens

Group	Number	%
Total Population	9,118	36.3
Hispanic or Latino (of any race)	5,553	31.6
Central American, ex. Mexican	254	46.5
Cuban	1,063	75.1
Dominican Republic	231	44.9
Mexican	123	22.8
Puerto Rican	0	0.0
South American	3,465	26.0
Colombian	1,529	33.8
Peruvian	566	34.2
Venezuelan	819	13.7

Language Spoken at Home: English Only
(Universe: Population 5 Years and Over)

Group	Number	%
Total Population	28,514	48.5
Hispanic or Latino (of any race)	2,956	11.3
Central American, ex. Mexican	213	24.8
Cuban	517	18.2
Dominican Republic	38	3.9
Mexican	322	34.5
Puerto Rican	978	39.6
South American	540	3.4
Colombian	291	4.9
Peruvian	82	4.2
Venezuelan	50	0.8

Language Spoken at Home: Spanish
(Universe: Population 5 Years and Over)

Group	Number	%
Total Population	24,743	42.1
Hispanic or Latino (of any race)	22,876	87.8
Central American, ex. Mexican	645	75.2
Cuban	2,255	79.5
Dominican Republic	938	96.1
Mexican	611	65.5
Puerto Rican	1,491	60.4
South American	15,235	95.7
Colombian	5,607	95.1
Peruvian	1,850	95.8
Venezuelan	6,358	97.5

Unemployment Rate
(Universe: Population 16 Years and Over)

Group	%
Total Population	6.7
Hispanic or Latino (of any race)	8.5
Central American, ex. Mexican	15.2
Cuban	9.6
Dominican Republic	15.3
Mexican	2.3
Puerto Rican	13.1
South American	6.3
Colombian	10.6
Peruvian	2.3
Venezuelan	2.8

Class of Worker: Private Wage and Salary
(Universe: Civilian Employed Population 16 Years and Over)

Group	Number	%
Total Population	24,350	83.0
Hispanic or Latino (of any race)	10,537	84.9
Central American, ex. Mexican	444	91.7
Cuban	1,146	83.4
Dominican Republic	346	86.9
Mexican	432	92.9
Puerto Rican	779	75.0
South American	6,565	84.4
Colombian	2,670	88.6
Peruvian	861	81.6
Venezuelan	2,327	80.3

Class of Worker: Government
(Universe: Civilian Employed Population 16 Years and Over)

Group	Number	%
Total Population	3,044	10.4
Hispanic or Latino (of any race)	817	6.6
Central American, ex. Mexican	18	3.7
Cuban	168	12.2
Dominican Republic	0	0.0
Mexican	20	4.3
Puerto Rican	247	23.8
South American	351	4.5
Colombian	92	3.1
Peruvian	61	5.8
Venezuelan	176	6.1

Means of Transportation to Work: Car, Truck or Van
(Universe: Workers 16 Years and Over)

Group	Number	%
Total Population	25,775	89.4

STATE & PLACE PROFILES

Notes: (1) Percent of total population; (2) Percent of Hispanic/Latino population; Profiles include places with an overall population of at least 125,000, OR an overall population of at least 25,000 where the Hispanic/Latino population is at least 20% of the overall population. In states where less than five places meet either of these criteria, we have included places with at least 10,000 total population with the highest percentage of Hispanic/Latino population. These places are identified with an asterisk (*); Please refer to the User's Guide for a full explanation of data.

Group	Number	%
Hispanic or Latino (of any race)	10,739	89.4
Central American, ex. Mexican	428	88.4
Cuban	1,210	92.9
Dominican Republic	341	85.7
Mexican	426	91.6
Puerto Rican	875	87.5
South American	6,779	89.7
Colombian	2,467	87.5
Peruvian	935	89.9
Venezuelan	2,654	92.2

Means of Transportation to Work: Public Transportation (ex. Taxicab)
(Universe: Workers 16 Years and Over)

Group	Number	%
Total Population	62	0.2
Hispanic or Latino (of any race)	50	0.4
Central American, ex. Mexican	24	5.0
Cuban	0	0.0
Dominican Republic	0	0.0
Mexican	0	0.0
Puerto Rican	0	0.0
South American	13	0.2
Colombian	0	0.0
Peruvian	0	0.0
Venezuelan	13	0.5

Homeownership Rate
(Universe: Occupied Housing Units)

Group	%
Total Population	75.5
Hispanic or Latino (of any race)	69.3
Central American, ex. Mexican	69.5
Costa Rican	76.9
Guatemalan	68.9
Honduran	63.6
Nicaraguan	69.7
Panamanian	73.9
Salvadoran	68.3
Cuban	80.7
Dominican Republic	62.5
Mexican	72.3
Puerto Rican	69.7
South American	67.0
Argentinean	79.8
Bolivian	70.6
Chilean	63.3
Colombian	65.6
Ecuadorian	64.8
Peruvian	64.4
Uruguayan	64.7
Venezuelan	68.0
Spaniard	79.5

Median Home Value

Group	Dollars
Total Population	451,600
Hispanic or Latino (of any race)	418,900
Central American, ex. Mexican	548,000
Cuban	443,600
Dominican Republic	672,800
Mexican	520,000
Puerto Rican	399,100
South American	392,200
Colombian	372,800
Peruvian	432,600
Venezuelan	381,400

Median Gross Rent

Group	Dollars
Total Population	1,736
Hispanic or Latino (of any race)	1,655
Central American, ex. Mexican	–
Cuban	1,721
Dominican Republic	1,693
Mexican	1,844
Puerto Rican	1,625
South American	1,613
Colombian	1,550
Peruvian	1,353
Venezuelan	1,733

Median Household Income
(2010 Inflation-Adjusted Dollars)

Group	Dollars
Total Population	93,553
Hispanic or Latino (of any race)	79,375
Central American, ex. Mexican	114,107
Cuban	108,421
Dominican Republic	64,239
Mexican	144,750
Puerto Rican	87,390
South American	68,290
Colombian	68,750
Peruvian	65,147
Venezuelan	66,042

Per Capita Income
(2010 Inflation-Adjusted Dollars)

Group	Dollars
Total Population	40,432
Hispanic or Latino (of any race)	30,080
Central American, ex. Mexican	53,425
Cuban	33,743
Dominican Republic	26,325
Mexican	56,248
Puerto Rican	31,053
South American	26,903
Colombian	25,697
Peruvian	29,564
Venezuelan	21,513

Households with $100,000+ Income

Group	Number	%
Total Population	9,394	46.9
Hispanic or Latino (of any race)	2,905	37.4
Central American, ex. Mexican	170	55.9
Cuban	489	57.4
Dominican Republic	80	35.4
Mexican	202	67.3
Puerto Rican	349	46.3
South American	1,343	27.3
Colombian	536	29.3
Peruvian	195	31.3
Venezuelan	401	20.2

Households with Food Stamps/SNAP Benefits During Past 12 Months

Group	Number	%
Total Population	351	1.8
Hispanic or Latino (of any race)	194	2.5
Central American, ex. Mexican	12	3.9
Cuban	54	6.3
Dominican Republic	30	13.3
Mexican	0	0.0
Puerto Rican	17	2.3
South American	65	1.3
Colombian	28	1.5
Peruvian	0	0.0
Venezuelan	37	1.9

Poverty Rate
(Income in Past 12 Months Below Poverty Level)

Group	%
Total Population	4.9
Hispanic or Latino (of any race)	5.4
Central American, ex. Mexican	0.0
Cuban	4.7
Dominican Republic	18.4
Mexican	8.0
Puerto Rican	4.3
South American	5.5
Colombian	6.4
Peruvian	3.6
Venezuelan	5.6

Winter Garden

Population

Group	Number	%TP[1]	%HP[2]
Total Population	34,568	100.0	–
Hispanic or Latino (of any race)	7,606	22.0	100.0
Central American, ex. Mexican	504	1.5	6.6
Guatemalan	191	0.6	2.5
Honduran	110	0.3	1.4
Cuban	418	1.2	5.5
Dominican Republic	429	1.2	5.6
Mexican	2,242	6.5	29.5
Puerto Rican	2,640	7.6	34.7
South American	999	2.9	13.1
Colombian	461	1.3	6.1
Ecuadorian	139	0.4	1.8
Peruvian	100	0.3	1.3
Venezuelan	195	0.6	2.6

Population Growth: 2000–2010

Group	%
Total Population	140.9
Hispanic or Latino (of any race)	202.9
Cuban	266.7
Mexican	97.2
Puerto Rican	242.0
South American	784.1

Males per 100 Females

Group	Number
Total Population	93.7
Hispanic or Latino (of any race)	98.8
Central American, ex. Mexican	113.6
Guatemalan	180.9
Honduran	111.5
Cuban	90.9
Dominican Republic	89.8
Mexican	116.0
Puerto Rican	93.5
South American	81.0
Colombian	75.3
Ecuadorian	87.8
Peruvian	53.8
Venezuelan	101.0

Average Household Size

Group	People
Total Population	2.87
Hispanic or Latino (of any race)	3.50
Central American, ex. Mexican	3.72
Guatemalan	4.08
Honduran	4.34
Cuban	2.99
Dominican Republic	3.75
Mexican	4.09
Puerto Rican	3.22
South American	3.28
Colombian	3.37
Ecuadorian	3.83
Peruvian	3.52
Venezuelan	3.22

Median Age

Group	Years
Total Population	34.7
Hispanic or Latino (of any race)	27.9
Central American, ex. Mexican	29.2
Guatemalan	27.1
Honduran	30.0
Cuban	34.3
Dominican Republic	28.8
Mexican	24.5
Puerto Rican	29.0
South American	35.8
Colombian	35.2
Ecuadorian	37.5
Peruvian	39.3
Venezuelan	35.2

High School Graduates
(Universe: Population 25 Years and Over)

Group	Number	%
Total Population	17,722	88.6
Hispanic or Latino (of any race)	2,884	76.2
Mexican	806	60.7
Puerto Rican	1,043	78.4

Four-Year College Graduates
(Universe: Population 25 Years and Over)

Group	Number	%
Total Population	6,323	31.6
Hispanic or Latino (of any race)	763	20.2
Mexican	115	8.7
Puerto Rican	370	27.8

Notes: (1) Percent of total population; (2) Percent of Hispanic/Latino population; Profiles include places with an overall population of at least 125,000, OR an overall population of at least 25,000 where the Hispanic/Latino population is at least 20% of the overall population. In states where less than five places meet either of these criteria, we have included places with at least 10,000 total population with the highest percentage of Hispanic/Latino population. These places are identified with an asterisk (*); Please refer to the User's Guide for a full explanation of data.

Population Age 3–17 Enrolled in Public School
(Universe: Population Age 3–17 Enrolled in School)

Group	Number	%
Total Population	5,020	77.5
Hispanic or Latino (of any race)	1,411	93.8
Mexican	375	96.4
Puerto Rican	626	93.7

Population Age 3–17 Enrolled in Private School
(Universe: Population Age 3–17 Enrolled in School)

Group	Number	%
Total Population	1,456	22.5
Hispanic or Latino (of any race)	93	6.2
Mexican	14	3.6
Puerto Rican	42	6.3

Foreign-Born Population

Group	Number	%
Total Population	5,169	16.4
Hispanic or Latino (of any race)	2,738	41.2
Mexican	1,697	62.5
Puerto Rican	27	1.3

Foreign-Born Naturalized U.S. Citizens

Group	Number	%
Total Population	2,488	48.1
Hispanic or Latino (of any race)	1,051	38.4
Mexican	380	22.4
Puerto Rican	27	100.0

Language Spoken at Home: English Only
(Universe: Population 5 Years and Over)

Group	Number	%
Total Population	21,795	76.4
Hispanic or Latino (of any race)	1,036	17.2
Mexican	177	7.9
Puerto Rican	530	25.6

Language Spoken at Home: Spanish
(Universe: Population 5 Years and Over)

Group	Number	%
Total Population	5,266	18.5
Hispanic or Latino (of any race)	4,956	82.5
Mexican	2,055	92.1
Puerto Rican	1,537	74.4

Unemployment Rate
(Universe: Population 16 Years and Over)

Group	%
Total Population	7.8
Hispanic or Latino (of any race)	10.4
Mexican	12.7
Puerto Rican	4.3

Class of Worker: Private Wage and Salary
(Universe: Civilian Employed Population 16 Years and Over)

Group	Number	%
Total Population	13,115	84.5
Hispanic or Latino (of any race)	2,619	83.8
Mexican	1,232	95.1
Puerto Rican	651	72.9

Class of Worker: Government
(Universe: Civilian Employed Population 16 Years and Over)

Group	Number	%
Total Population	1,697	10.9
Hispanic or Latino (of any race)	354	11.3
Mexican	45	3.5
Puerto Rican	222	24.9

Means of Transportation to Work: Car, Truck or Van
(Universe: Workers 16 Years and Over)

Group	Number	%
Total Population	13,932	91.4
Hispanic or Latino (of any race)	2,661	87.5
Mexican	948	76.2
Puerto Rican	843	94.4

Means of Transportation to Work: Public Transportation (ex. Taxicab)
(Universe: Workers 16 Years and Over)

Group	Number	%
Total Population	40	0.3
Hispanic or Latino (of any race)	18	0.6
Mexican	0	0.0
Puerto Rican	18	2.0

Homeownership Rate
(Universe: Occupied Housing Units)

Group	%
Total Population	70.7
Hispanic or Latino (of any race)	55.1
Central American, ex. Mexican	45.3
Guatemalan	26.4
Honduran	48.3
Cuban	73.8
Dominican Republic	64.1
Mexican	40.1
Puerto Rican	54.1
South American	72.8
Colombian	72.2
Ecuadorian	80.5
Peruvian	69.0
Venezuelan	74.6

Median Home Value

Group	Dollars
Total Population	247,200
Hispanic or Latino (of any race)	258,000
Mexican	284,100
Puerto Rican	249,300

Median Gross Rent

Group	Dollars
Total Population	933
Hispanic or Latino (of any race)	904
Mexican	896
Puerto Rican	843

Median Household Income
(2010 Inflation-Adjusted Dollars)

Group	Dollars
Total Population	62,152
Hispanic or Latino (of any race)	50,456
Mexican	44,899
Puerto Rican	51,862

Per Capita Income
(2010 Inflation-Adjusted Dollars)

Group	Dollars
Total Population	25,803
Hispanic or Latino (of any race)	20,053
Mexican	15,100
Puerto Rican	26,138

Households with $100,000+ Income

Group	Number	%
Total Population	2,573	24.3
Hispanic or Latino (of any race)	356	18.5
Mexican	100	18.6
Puerto Rican	107	16.4

Households with Food Stamps/SNAP Benefits During Past 12 Months

Group	Number	%
Total Population	671	6.3
Hispanic or Latino (of any race)	250	13.0
Mexican	57	10.6
Puerto Rican	103	15.8

Poverty Rate
(Income in Past 12 Months Below Poverty Level)

Group	%
Total Population	7.7
Hispanic or Latino (of any race)	12.2
Mexican	20.9
Puerto Rican	7.2

Notes: (1) Percent of total population; (2) Percent of Hispanic/Latino population; Profiles include places with an overall population of at least 125,000, OR an overall population of at least 25,000 where the Hispanic/Latino population is at least 20% of the overall population. In states where less than five places meet either of these criteria, we have included places with at least 10,000 total population with the highest percentage of Hispanic/Latino population. These places are identified with an asterisk (*); Please refer to the User's Guide for a full explanation of data.

Georgia

EDITOR'S NOTE: For a place to be included in this edition, it must meet one of two criteria. Either its overall population is at least 125,000, OR its overall population is at least 25,000 and its Hispanic/Latino population is at least 20% of the overall population. For the state of Georgia, the following locations are included:

- Atlanta
- Augusta-Richmond County
- Columbus
- Dalton
- Gainesville
- Lawrenceville
- Marietta
- North Atlanta
- Savannah

Section Two: State & Place Profiles starts with the state profile, followed by place profiles that meet the criteria above. Places are listed alphabetically within each state. All states, all counties and places that meet the above criteria are ranked and compared in *Section Three: Rankings & Comparisons*, on page 1055.

For a more detailed look at the Hispanic/Latino population in Georgia, a companion web site is available at no additional charge with purchase of this print edition. Visit http://gold.greyhouse.com/page/info_hispanic for more information.

The web site includes data for all counties and places in Georgia with Hispanic/Latino population, plus ten additional topics: Self Employed Worker; Walked to Work; Worked from Home; Mean Travel Time to Work; Mean Household Income; Households with Cash Public Assistance; Mean Cash Pubic Assistance; Poverty Rates for 18 and Under, 18 to 64, and 65 and Over.

Population

Group	Number	%TP[1]	%HP[2]
Total Population	9,687,653	100.0	–
Hispanic or Latino (of any race)	853,689	8.8	100.0
Central American, ex. Mexican	106,987	1.1	12.5
Costa Rican	3,114	<0.1	0.4
Guatemalan	36,874	0.4	4.3
Honduran	20,577	0.2	2.4
Nicaraguan	4,787	<0.1	0.6
Panamanian	8,678	0.1	1.0
Salvadoran	32,107	0.3	3.8
Cuban	25,048	0.3	2.9
Dominican Republic	14,941	0.2	1.8
Mexican	519,502	5.4	60.9
Puerto Rican	71,987	0.7	8.4
South American	57,707	0.6	6.8
Argentinean	3,230	<0.1	0.4
Bolivian	872	<0.1	0.1
Chilean	2,249	<0.1	0.3
Colombian	26,013	0.3	3.0
Ecuadorian	4,886	0.1	0.6
Paraguayan	360	<0.1	<0.1
Peruvian	10,570	0.1	1.2
Uruguayan	2,708	<0.1	0.3
Venezuelan	6,289	0.1	0.7
Spaniard	7,466	0.1	0.9

Population Growth: 2000–2010

Group	%
Total Population	18.3
Hispanic or Latino (of any race)	96.1
Central American, ex. Mexican	236.3
Costa Rican	160.6
Guatemalan	244.0
Honduran	298.9
Nicaraguan	243.4
Panamanian	131.7
Salvadoran	277.9
Cuban	99.8
Dominican Republic	362.1
Mexican	88.7
Puerto Rican	102.6
South American	196.0
Argentinean	226.9
Bolivian	144.3
Chilean	157.9
Colombian	186.4
Ecuadorian	242.2
Paraguayan	120.9
Peruvian	234.4
Uruguayan	476.2
Venezuelan	180.3
Spaniard	567.2

Males per 100 Females

Group	Number
Total Population	95.4
Hispanic or Latino (of any race)	117.1
Central American, ex. Mexican	126.3
Costa Rican	96.6
Guatemalan	169.9
Honduran	124.4
Nicaraguan	94.2
Panamanian	65.9
Salvadoran	117.0
Cuban	104.4
Dominican Republic	85.7
Mexican	125.4
Puerto Rican	93.6
South American	89.4
Argentinean	101.2
Bolivian	87.1
Chilean	96.6
Colombian	85.4
Ecuadorian	94.5
Paraguayan	90.5
Peruvian	90.8
Uruguayan	107.4
Venezuelan	85.1
Spaniard	95.3

Average Household Size

Group	People
Total Population	2.63
Hispanic or Latino (of any race)	3.85
Central American, ex. Mexican	4.10
Costa Rican	2.95
Guatemalan	4.59
Honduran	4.08
Nicaraguan	3.47
Panamanian	2.76
Salvadoran	4.35
Cuban	2.80
Dominican Republic	3.29
Mexican	4.28
Puerto Rican	2.92
South American	3.08
Argentinean	2.89
Bolivian	3.00
Chilean	2.86
Colombian	3.03
Ecuadorian	3.35
Paraguayan	3.01
Peruvian	3.26
Uruguayan	3.33
Venezuelan	2.95
Spaniard	2.72

Median Age

Group	Years
Total Population	35.3
Hispanic or Latino (of any race)	25.3
Central American, ex. Mexican	27.9
Costa Rican	30.8
Guatemalan	26.2
Honduran	28.4
Nicaraguan	30.2
Panamanian	32.9
Salvadoran	28.8
Cuban	33.6
Dominican Republic	27.5
Mexican	23.6
Puerto Rican	26.1
South American	33.7
Argentinean	34.7
Bolivian	33.8
Chilean	33.7
Colombian	33.9
Ecuadorian	31.9
Paraguayan	27.7
Peruvian	34.5
Uruguayan	33.0
Venezuelan	33.2
Spaniard	33.2

High School Graduates

(Universe: Population 25 Years and Over)

Group	Number	%
Total Population	5,052,566	83.5
Hispanic or Latino (of any race)	223,237	56.1
Central American, ex. Mexican	26,215	44.1
Costa Rican	1,681	74.4
Guatemalan	6,233	32.9
Honduran	4,995	42.5
Nicaraguan	1,578	71.6
Panamanian	4,226	90.4
Salvadoran	7,168	37.6
Cuban	12,762	87.1
Dominican Republic	5,559	77.6
Mexican	106,010	45.6
Puerto Rican	30,123	87.4
South American	30,406	89.7
Argentinean	1,790	95.1
Chilean	1,437	94.0
Colombian	13,161	89.2
Ecuadorian	2,047	83.7
Peruvian	5,610	90.1
Uruguayan	1,593	81.3
Venezuelan	4,006	94.5
Spaniard	3,559	92.4

Four-Year College Graduates

(Universe: Population 25 Years and Over)

Group	Number	%
Total Population	1,647,046	27.2
Hispanic or Latino (of any race)	54,463	13.7
Central American, ex. Mexican	5,694	9.6
Costa Rican	562	24.9
Guatemalan	970	5.1
Honduran	1,090	9.3
Nicaraguan	452	20.5
Panamanian	1,346	28.8
Salvadoran	1,248	6.5
Cuban	5,150	35.1
Dominican Republic	1,884	26.3
Mexican	14,592	6.3
Puerto Rican	8,797	25.5
South American	13,915	41.1
Argentinean	1,020	54.2
Chilean	566	37.0
Colombian	6,057	41.0
Ecuadorian	841	34.4
Peruvian	2,519	40.5
Uruguayan	259	13.2
Venezuelan	2,325	54.8
Spaniard	1,723	44.8

Population Age 3–17 Enrolled in Public School

(Universe: Population Age 3–17 Enrolled in School)

Group	Number	%
Total Population	1,616,006	87.1
Hispanic or Latino (of any race)	173,272	93.9
Central American, ex. Mexican	18,077	94.0
Costa Rican	418	82.6
Guatemalan	5,646	91.1
Honduran	3,193	96.9
Nicaraguan	515	85.5
Panamanian	1,349	87.9

Notes: (1) Percent of total population; (2) Percent of Hispanic/Latino population; Profiles include places with an overall population of at least 125,000, OR an overall population of at least 25,000 where the Hispanic/Latino population is at least 20% of the overall population. In states where less than five places meet either of these criteria, we have included places with at least 10,000 total population with the highest percentage of Hispanic/Latino population. These places are identified with an asterisk (*); Please refer to the User's Guide for a full explanation of data.

Group	Number	%
Salvadoran	6,741	98.0
Cuban	4,236	80.9
Dominican Republic	3,710	93.6
Mexican	115,462	96.5
Puerto Rican	15,211	89.6
South American	9,603	82.7
Argentinean	404	59.4
Chilean	822	88.6
Colombian	4,098	83.0
Ecuadorian	975	89.5
Peruvian	1,459	88.7
Uruguayan	477	98.4
Venezuelan	1,110	78.3
Spaniard	1,266	82.5

Population Age 3–17 Enrolled in Private School
(Universe: Population Age 3–17 Enrolled in School)

Group	Number	%
Total Population	239,640	12.9
Hispanic or Latino (of any race)	11,270	6.1
Central American, ex. Mexican	1,162	6.0
Costa Rican	88	17.4
Guatemalan	552	8.9
Honduran	102	3.1
Nicaraguan	87	14.5
Panamanian	185	12.1
Salvadoran	136	2.0
Cuban	997	19.1
Dominican Republic	252	6.4
Mexican	4,223	3.5
Puerto Rican	1,761	10.4
South American	2,005	17.3
Argentinean	276	40.6
Chilean	106	11.4
Colombian	842	17.0
Ecuadorian	114	10.5
Peruvian	186	11.3
Uruguayan	8	1.6
Venezuelan	307	21.7
Spaniard	269	17.5

Foreign-Born Population

Group	Number	%
Total Population	909,022	9.6
Hispanic or Latino (of any race)	413,757	52.7
Central American, ex. Mexican	72,140	68.3
Costa Rican	1,975	56.9
Guatemalan	25,942	71.2
Honduran	14,948	75.1
Nicaraguan	2,104	62.0
Panamanian	3,674	49.0
Salvadoran	22,873	67.5
Cuban	9,584	40.9
Dominican Republic	6,820	48.0
Mexican	279,228	56.9
Puerto Rican	914	1.4
South American	36,298	66.3
Argentinean	1,844	60.9
Chilean	1,530	51.3
Colombian	15,746	66.5
Ecuadorian	2,692	62.3
Peruvian	6,662	69.6
Uruguayan	2,343	80.3
Venezuelan	4,621	68.7
Spaniard	1,391	22.2

Foreign-Born Naturalized U.S. Citizens

Group	Number	%
Total Population	307,045	33.8
Hispanic or Latino (of any race)	62,896	15.2
Central American, ex. Mexican	11,621	16.1
Costa Rican	648	32.8
Guatemalan	2,873	11.1
Honduran	1,804	12.1
Nicaraguan	632	30.0
Panamanian	2,177	59.3
Salvadoran	3,347	14.6
Cuban	6,125	63.9
Dominican Republic	2,818	41.3
Mexican	26,878	9.6
Puerto Rican	289	31.6
South American	12,596	34.7
Argentinean	625	33.9
Chilean	735	48.0
Colombian	5,969	37.9
Ecuadorian	1,116	41.5
Peruvian	2,410	36.2
Uruguayan	259	11.1
Venezuelan	1,152	24.9
Spaniard	776	55.8

Language Spoken at Home: English Only
(Universe: Population 5 Years and Over)

Group	Number	%
Total Population	7,666,663	87.3
Hispanic or Latino (of any race)	114,670	16.8
Central American, ex. Mexican	8,986	9.7
Costa Rican	888	27.8
Guatemalan	2,180	7.0
Honduran	1,256	7.1
Nicaraguan	693	22.0
Panamanian	2,380	34.9
Salvadoran	1,547	5.2
Cuban	7,919	36.8
Dominican Republic	2,826	22.3
Mexican	49,784	11.9
Puerto Rican	25,079	43.1
South American	8,580	17.0
Argentinean	768	28.0
Chilean	653	24.9
Colombian	3,236	14.8
Ecuadorian	774	19.1
Peruvian	1,400	15.7
Uruguayan	189	6.9
Venezuelan	1,250	20.0
Spaniard	3,658	64.9

Language Spoken at Home: Spanish
(Universe: Population 5 Years and Over)

Group	Number	%
Total Population	652,397	7.4
Hispanic or Latino (of any race)	562,423	82.6
Central American, ex. Mexican	83,233	89.7
Costa Rican	2,299	72.0
Guatemalan	28,609	91.9
Honduran	16,352	92.6
Nicaraguan	2,461	78.0
Panamanian	4,408	64.5
Salvadoran	28,352	94.5
Cuban	13,333	61.9
Dominican Republic	9,783	77.4
Mexican	367,995	87.9
Puerto Rican	32,792	56.3
South American	41,505	82.1
Argentinean	1,826	66.5
Chilean	1,927	73.4
Colombian	18,450	84.6
Ecuadorian	3,250	80.2
Peruvian	7,513	84.0
Uruguayan	2,559	93.1
Venezuelan	4,943	78.9
Spaniard	1,932	34.3

Unemployment Rate
(Universe: Population 16 Years and Over)

Group	%
Total Population	8.8
Hispanic or Latino (of any race)	8.7
Central American, ex. Mexican	9.8
Costa Rican	10.9
Guatemalan	8.3
Honduran	10.7
Nicaraguan	16.6
Panamanian	9.2
Salvadoran	10.0
Cuban	9.2
Dominican Republic	17.3
Mexican	7.8
Puerto Rican	11.4
South American	8.3
Argentinean	3.3
Chilean	7.0
Colombian	9.4
Ecuadorian	9.4
Peruvian	9.8
Uruguayan	2.4
Venezuelan	7.6
Spaniard	6.0

Class of Worker: Private Wage and Salary
(Universe: Civilian Employed Population 16 Years and Over)

Group	Number	%
Total Population	3,362,548	78.3
Hispanic or Latino (of any race)	301,842	88.2
Central American, ex. Mexican	47,142	89.0
Costa Rican	1,473	86.7
Guatemalan	16,395	89.5
Honduran	9,357	89.4
Nicaraguan	1,287	81.6
Panamanian	2,591	75.0
Salvadoran	15,669	91.8
Cuban	8,399	78.6
Dominican Republic	4,471	78.9
Mexican	190,012	91.2
Puerto Rican	20,204	78.6
South American	22,405	82.0
Argentinean	1,151	76.4
Chilean	993	87.1
Colombian	10,210	84.3
Ecuadorian	1,621	77.3
Peruvian	3,961	82.1
Uruguayan	1,335	80.1
Venezuelan	2,508	77.1
Spaniard	1,855	73.8

Class of Worker: Government
(Universe: Civilian Employed Population 16 Years and Over)

Group	Number	%
Total Population	675,962	15.7
Hispanic or Latino (of any race)	18,700	5.5
Central American, ex. Mexican	2,024	3.8
Costa Rican	97	5.7
Guatemalan	269	1.5
Honduran	504	4.8
Nicaraguan	126	8.0
Panamanian	670	19.4
Salvadoran	358	2.1
Cuban	1,420	13.3
Dominican Republic	711	12.6
Mexican	6,176	3.0
Puerto Rican	4,483	17.4
South American	2,522	9.2
Argentinean	204	13.5
Chilean	104	9.1
Colombian	872	7.2
Ecuadorian	191	9.1
Peruvian	525	10.9
Uruguayan	119	7.1
Venezuelan	449	13.8
Spaniard	452	18.0

Means of Transportation to Work: Car, Truck or Van
(Universe: Workers 16 Years and Over)

Group	Number	%
Total Population	3,811,245	89.9
Hispanic or Latino (of any race)	288,827	84.9
Central American, ex. Mexican	42,952	81.9
Costa Rican	1,479	87.7
Guatemalan	14,230	78.4
Honduran	8,600	83.5
Nicaraguan	1,420	88.4
Panamanian	3,048	88.0
Salvadoran	13,827	82.1
Cuban	9,358	89.0
Dominican Republic	4,689	86.1
Mexican	174,256	84.4
Puerto Rican	23,757	88.1
South American	23,677	88.3
Argentinean	1,260	83.8
Chilean	1,076	93.5
Colombian	10,521	88.6
Ecuadorian	1,576	78.4
Peruvian	4,276	89.5
Uruguayan	1,410	91.4
Venezuelan	2,967	91.7
Spaniard	2,135	82.6

Means of Transportation to Work: Public Transportation (ex. Taxicab)
(Universe: Workers 16 Years and Over)

Group	Number	%
Total Population	96,011	2.3
Hispanic or Latino (of any race)	12,512	3.7

Notes: (1) Percent of total population; (2) Percent of Hispanic/Latino population; Profiles include places with an overall population of at least 125,000, OR an overall population of at least 25,000 where the Hispanic/Latino population is at least 20% of the overall population. In states where less than five places meet either of these criteria, we have included places with at least 10,000 total population with the highest percentage of Hispanic/Latino population. These places are identified with an asterisk (*); Please refer to the User's Guide for a full explanation of data.

Group	Number	%
Central American, ex. Mexican	2,238	4.3
Costa Rican	30	1.8
Guatemalan	938	5.2
Honduran	447	4.3
Nicaraguan	27	1.7
Panamanian	116	3.3
Salvadoran	680	4.0
Cuban	257	2.4
Dominican Republic	200	3.7
Mexican	8,256	4.0
Puerto Rican	795	2.9
South American	582	2.2
Argentinean	33	2.2
Chilean	15	1.3
Colombian	264	2.2
Ecuadorian	0	0.0
Peruvian	157	3.3
Uruguayan	40	2.6
Venezuelan	18	0.6
Spaniard	34	1.3

Homeownership Rate
(Universe: Occupied Housing Units)

Group	%
Total Population	65.7
Hispanic or Latino (of any race)	44.4
Central American, ex. Mexican	41.4
Costa Rican	52.0
Guatemalan	26.7
Honduran	33.7
Nicaraguan	49.6
Panamanian	55.0
Salvadoran	53.6
Cuban	63.8
Dominican Republic	48.6
Mexican	38.7
Puerto Rican	53.7
South American	60.4
Argentinean	63.1
Bolivian	65.1
Chilean	57.0
Colombian	61.9
Ecuadorian	64.7
Paraguayan	64.8
Peruvian	57.8
Uruguayan	45.5
Venezuelan	60.8
Spaniard	66.4

Median Home Value

Group	Dollars
Total Population	161,400
Hispanic or Latino (of any race)	149,900
Central American, ex. Mexican	147,400
Costa Rican	196,900
Guatemalan	127,300
Honduran	143,000
Nicaraguan	162,000
Panamanian	155,200
Salvadoran	146,500
Cuban	204,000
Dominican Republic	177,300
Mexican	129,400
Puerto Rican	173,300
South American	185,800
Argentinean	260,200
Chilean	220,200
Colombian	182,400
Ecuadorian	176,100
Peruvian	180,700
Uruguayan	156,200
Venezuelan	199,300
Spaniard	221,300

Median Gross Rent

Group	Dollars
Total Population	808
Hispanic or Latino (of any race)	825
Central American, ex. Mexican	825
Costa Rican	849
Guatemalan	791
Honduran	832
Nicaraguan	988
Panamanian	961
Salvadoran	830
Cuban	869
Dominican Republic	933
Mexican	803
Puerto Rican	862
South American	935
Argentinean	840
Chilean	1,095
Colombian	931
Ecuadorian	893
Peruvian	954
Uruguayan	930
Venezuelan	935
Spaniard	866

Median Household Income
(2010 Inflation-Adjusted Dollars)

Group	Dollars
Total Population	49,347
Hispanic or Latino (of any race)	38,287
Central American, ex. Mexican	37,902
Costa Rican	44,440
Guatemalan	32,645
Honduran	39,538
Nicaraguan	46,615
Panamanian	43,962
Salvadoran	38,617
Cuban	57,055
Dominican Republic	40,260
Mexican	33,685
Puerto Rican	49,580
South American	50,712
Argentinean	65,729
Chilean	53,421
Colombian	50,109
Ecuadorian	48,750
Peruvian	50,265
Uruguayan	42,094
Venezuelan	52,056
Spaniard	61,737

Per Capita Income
(2010 Inflation-Adjusted Dollars)

Group	Dollars
Total Population	25,134
Hispanic or Latino (of any race)	13,580
Central American, ex. Mexican	13,273
Costa Rican	23,569
Guatemalan	11,125
Honduran	13,058
Nicaraguan	18,424
Panamanian	22,006
Salvadoran	12,248
Cuban	30,047
Dominican Republic	15,454
Mexican	10,753
Puerto Rican	19,894
South American	21,158
Argentinean	34,091
Chilean	18,956
Colombian	19,907
Ecuadorian	20,592
Peruvian	20,391
Uruguayan	18,823
Venezuelan	23,984
Spaniard	28,083

Households with $100,000+ Income

Group	Number	%
Total Population	655,603	18.9
Hispanic or Latino (of any race)	19,122	9.7
Central American, ex. Mexican	2,153	7.8
Costa Rican	203	19.2
Guatemalan	411	4.8
Honduran	440	8.4
Nicaraguan	93	8.9
Panamanian	507	20.0
Salvadoran	487	5.5
Cuban	2,100	25.7
Dominican Republic	589	14.5
Mexican	6,771	6.1
Puerto Rican	3,114	15.0
South American	2,876	17.2
Argentinean	395	38.6
Chilean	128	16.5
Colombian	1,011	14.1
Ecuadorian	250	18.8
Peruvian	498	17.3
Uruguayan	115	12.7
Venezuelan	413	19.6
Spaniard	713	29.9

Households with Food Stamps/SNAP Benefits During Past 12 Months

Group	Number	%
Total Population	344,023	9.9
Hispanic or Latino (of any race)	21,504	10.9
Central American, ex. Mexican	2,761	10.0
Costa Rican	113	10.7
Guatemalan	625	7.3
Honduran	848	16.1
Nicaraguan	40	3.8
Panamanian	417	16.4
Salvadoran	718	8.1
Cuban	691	8.5
Dominican Republic	639	15.7
Mexican	13,522	12.1
Puerto Rican	2,245	10.8
South American	1,054	6.3
Argentinean	11	1.1
Chilean	14	1.8
Colombian	466	6.5
Ecuadorian	166	12.5
Peruvian	181	6.3
Uruguayan	64	7.1
Venezuelan	152	7.2
Spaniard	106	4.4

Poverty Rate
(Income in Past 12 Months Below Poverty Level)

Group	%
Total Population	15.7
Hispanic or Latino (of any race)	28.1
Central American, ex. Mexican	28.1
Costa Rican	12.8
Guatemalan	38.9
Honduran	22.9
Nicaraguan	25.4
Panamanian	15.1
Salvadoran	24.4
Cuban	13.9
Dominican Republic	24.3
Mexican	32.5
Puerto Rican	16.7
South American	12.8
Argentinean	10.9
Chilean	2.4
Colombian	13.9
Ecuadorian	13.6
Peruvian	15.9
Uruguayan	11.6
Venezuelan	10.0
Spaniard	13.6

Atlanta

Population

Group	Number	%TP[1]	%HP[2]
Total Population	420,003	100.0	–
Hispanic or Latino (of any race)	21,815	5.2	100.0
Central American, ex. Mexican	1,840	0.4	8.4
Costa Rican	126	<0.1	0.6
Guatemalan	466	0.1	2.1
Honduran	518	0.1	2.4
Nicaraguan	113	<0.1	0.5
Panamanian	376	0.1	1.7
Salvadoran	217	0.1	1.0
Cuban	1,333	0.3	6.1
Dominican Republic	473	0.1	2.2
Mexican	11,827	2.8	54.2
Puerto Rican	2,258	0.5	10.4
South American	2,335	0.6	10.7
Argentinean	256	0.1	1.2
Chilean	134	<0.1	0.6
Colombian	989	0.2	4.5
Ecuadorian	137	<0.1	0.6
Peruvian	315	0.1	1.4
Venezuelan	350	0.1	1.6
Spaniard	438	0.1	2.0

Notes: (1) Percent of total population; (2) Percent of Hispanic/Latino population; Profiles include places with an overall population of at least 125,000, OR an overall population of at least 25,000 where the Hispanic/Latino population is at least 20% of the overall population. In states where less than five places meet either of these criteria, we have included places with at least 10,000 total population with the highest percentage of Hispanic/Latino population. These places are identified with an asterisk (*); Please refer to the User's Guide for a full explanation of data.

Population Growth: 2000–2010

Group	%
Total Population	0.8
Hispanic or Latino (of any race)	16.5
Central American, ex. Mexican	131.2
Guatemalan	288.3
Honduran	94.0
Panamanian	216.0
Salvadoran	33.1
Cuban	50.3
Dominican Republic	228.5
Mexican	-7.0
Puerto Rican	96.9
South American	173.7
Argentinean	156.0
Colombian	237.5
Peruvian	148.0
Venezuelan	171.3

Males per 100 Females

Group	Number
Total Population	99.0
Hispanic or Latino (of any race)	129.8
Central American, ex. Mexican	138.7
Costa Rican	96.9
Guatemalan	223.6
Honduran	127.2
Nicaraguan	105.5
Panamanian	97.9
Salvadoran	178.2
Cuban	121.8
Dominican Republic	94.7
Mexican	143.7
Puerto Rican	104.9
South American	107.7
Argentinean	108.1
Chilean	119.7
Colombian	104.8
Ecuadorian	104.5
Peruvian	98.1
Venezuelan	130.3
Spaniard	120.1

Average Household Size

Group	People
Total Population	2.11
Hispanic or Latino (of any race)	2.75
Central American, ex. Mexican	2.78
Costa Rican	1.81
Guatemalan	3.86
Honduran	3.37
Nicaraguan	2.17
Panamanian	1.98
Salvadoran	2.55
Cuban	2.03
Dominican Republic	1.96
Mexican	3.67
Puerto Rican	1.91
South American	1.92
Argentinean	1.97
Chilean	1.67
Colombian	1.94
Ecuadorian	2.12
Peruvian	1.89
Venezuelan	1.95
Spaniard	1.86

Median Age

Group	Years
Total Population	32.9
Hispanic or Latino (of any race)	28.0
Central American, ex. Mexican	28.1
Costa Rican	26.6
Guatemalan	26.9
Honduran	29.1
Nicaraguan	28.3
Panamanian	29.1
Salvadoran	27.3
Cuban	30.1
Dominican Republic	27.1
Mexican	27.0
Puerto Rican	27.7
South American	30.4
Argentinean	33.3
Chilean	33.8

Group	Years
Colombian	30.2
Ecuadorian	27.6
Peruvian	30.7
Venezuelan	29.9
Spaniard	32.4

High School Graduates
(Universe: Population 25 Years and Over)

Group	Number	%
Total Population	234,832	86.2
Hispanic or Latino (of any race)	7,729	64.1
Central American, ex. Mexican	659	56.9
Cuban	592	94.0
Mexican	3,893	52.3
Puerto Rican	815	92.1
South American	1,188	93.0

Four-Year College Graduates
(Universe: Population 25 Years and Over)

Group	Number	%
Total Population	122,488	45.0
Hispanic or Latino (of any race)	3,194	26.5
Central American, ex. Mexican	261	22.5
Cuban	410	65.1
Mexican	929	12.5
Puerto Rican	491	55.5
South American	831	65.1

Population Age 3–17 Enrolled in Public School
(Universe: Population Age 3–17 Enrolled in School)

Group	Number	%
Total Population	46,993	79.8
Hispanic or Latino (of any race)	2,300	84.7
Central American, ex. Mexican	0	0.0
Cuban	39	100.0
Mexican	1,871	90.6
Puerto Rican	137	74.5
South American	95	60.1

Population Age 3–17 Enrolled in Private School
(Universe: Population Age 3–17 Enrolled in School)

Group	Number	%
Total Population	11,920	20.2
Hispanic or Latino (of any race)	416	15.3
Central American, ex. Mexican	86	100.0
Cuban	0	0.0
Mexican	195	9.4
Puerto Rican	47	25.5
South American	63	39.9

Foreign-Born Population

Group	Number	%
Total Population	32,093	7.8
Hispanic or Latino (of any race)	10,830	54.4
Central American, ex. Mexican	1,126	67.5
Cuban	301	35.9
Mexican	7,995	61.8
Puerto Rican	17	1.1
South American	1,145	61.9

Foreign-Born Naturalized U.S. Citizens

Group	Number	%
Total Population	9,186	28.6
Hispanic or Latino (of any race)	1,441	13.3
Central American, ex. Mexican	317	28.2
Cuban	259	86.0
Mexican	424	5.3
Puerto Rican	0	0.0
South American	415	36.2

Language Spoken at Home: English Only
(Universe: Population 5 Years and Over)

Group	Number	%
Total Population	346,017	89.4
Hispanic or Latino (of any race)	3,474	19.3
Central American, ex. Mexican	223	15.7
Cuban	320	40.6
Mexican	1,456	12.6
Puerto Rican	728	51.3
South American	329	18.2

Language Spoken at Home: Spanish
(Universe: Population 5 Years and Over)

Group	Number	%
Total Population	20,047	5.2
Hispanic or Latino (of any race)	14,407	79.9
Central American, ex. Mexican	1,193	83.8
Cuban	443	56.1
Mexican	10,050	86.9
Puerto Rican	665	46.9
South American	1,454	80.6

Unemployment Rate
(Universe: Population 16 Years and Over)

Group	%
Total Population	9.9
Hispanic or Latino (of any race)	7.2
Central American, ex. Mexican	5.1
Cuban	7.1
Mexican	6.3
Puerto Rican	9.0
South American	9.3

Class of Worker: Private Wage and Salary
(Universe: Civilian Employed Population 16 Years and Over)

Group	Number	%
Total Population	161,618	80.9
Hispanic or Latino (of any race)	9,932	89.6
Central American, ex. Mexican	1,029	95.8
Cuban	369	78.3
Mexican	6,274	89.9
Puerto Rican	853	91.0
South American	939	85.6

Class of Worker: Government
(Universe: Civilian Employed Population 16 Years and Over)

Group	Number	%
Total Population	27,382	13.7
Hispanic or Latino (of any race)	424	3.8
Central American, ex. Mexican	10	0.9
Cuban	40	8.5
Mexican	150	2.1
Puerto Rican	84	9.0
South American	103	9.4

Means of Transportation to Work: Car, Truck or Van
(Universe: Workers 16 Years and Over)

Group	Number	%
Total Population	146,234	74.6
Hispanic or Latino (of any race)	7,084	65.2
Central American, ex. Mexican	660	64.0
Cuban	372	79.0
Mexican	4,343	63.3
Puerto Rican	604	65.3
South American	778	70.9

Means of Transportation to Work: Public Transportation (ex. Taxicab)
(Universe: Workers 16 Years and Over)

Group	Number	%
Total Population	24,808	12.7
Hispanic or Latino (of any race)	2,678	24.7
Central American, ex. Mexican	221	21.4
Cuban	59	12.5
Mexican	2,103	30.7
Puerto Rican	241	26.1
South American	29	2.6

Homeownership Rate
(Universe: Occupied Housing Units)

Group	%
Total Population	44.9
Hispanic or Latino (of any race)	30.0
Central American, ex. Mexican	27.8
Costa Rican	35.4
Guatemalan	14.4
Honduran	15.7
Nicaraguan	47.8
Panamanian	39.0
Salvadoran	34.8
Cuban	44.9
Dominican Republic	30.7
Mexican	20.3
Puerto Rican	33.6
South American	42.0
Argentinean	57.0
Chilean	31.1
Colombian	40.4
Ecuadorian	35.1
Peruvian	42.1

Notes: (1) Percent of total population; (2) Percent of Hispanic/Latino population; Profiles include places with an overall population of at least 125,000, OR an overall population of at least 25,000 where the Hispanic/Latino population is at least 20% of the overall population. In states where less than five places meet either of these criteria, we have included places with at least 10,000 total population with the highest percentage of Hispanic/Latino population. These places are identified with an asterisk (*); Please refer to the User's Guide for a full explanation of data.

Venezuelan	44.2
Spaniard	54.1

Median Home Value

Group	Dollars
Total Population	231,800
Hispanic or Latino (of any race)	208,000
Central American, ex. Mexican	277,200
Cuban	238,900
Mexican	161,400
Puerto Rican	240,000
South American	254,600

Median Gross Rent

Group	Dollars
Total Population	884
Hispanic or Latino (of any race)	885
Central American, ex. Mexican	740
Cuban	796
Mexican	898
Puerto Rican	829
South American	978

Median Household Income
(2010 Inflation-Adjusted Dollars)

Group	Dollars
Total Population	45,171
Hispanic or Latino (of any race)	43,301
Central American, ex. Mexican	44,950
Cuban	44,423
Mexican	40,742
Puerto Rican	48,971
South American	50,371

Per Capita Income
(2010 Inflation-Adjusted Dollars)

Group	Dollars
Total Population	35,453
Hispanic or Latino (of any race)	19,961
Central American, ex. Mexican	19,004
Cuban	43,315
Mexican	14,216
Puerto Rican	29,592
South American	39,726

Households with $100,000+ Income

Group	Number	%
Total Population	40,999	23.0
Hispanic or Latino (of any race)	919	14.8
Central American, ex. Mexican	72	16.0
Cuban	102	21.2
Mexican	306	8.8
Puerto Rican	109	19.0
South American	189	22.4

Households with Food Stamps/SNAP Benefits During Past 12 Months

Group	Number	%
Total Population	23,145	13.0
Hispanic or Latino (of any race)	736	11.8
Central American, ex. Mexican	68	15.1
Cuban	31	6.4
Mexican	499	14.4
Puerto Rican	79	13.8
South American	25	3.0

Poverty Rate
(Income in Past 12 Months Below Poverty Level)

Group	%
Total Population	22.6
Hispanic or Latino (of any race)	24.4
Central American, ex. Mexican	19.8
Cuban	8.3
Mexican	27.4
Puerto Rican	16.5
South American	18.9

Augusta-Richmond County

Population

Group	Number	%TP[1]	%HP[2]
Total Population	195,844	100.0	–
Hispanic or Latino (of any race)	8,053	4.1	100.0
Central American, ex. Mexican	746	0.4	9.3
Honduran	109	0.1	1.4
Panamanian	389	0.2	4.8
Cuban	278	0.1	3.5
Dominican Republic	217	0.1	2.7
Mexican	3,018	1.5	37.5
Puerto Rican	2,848	1.5	35.4
South American	278	0.1	3.5
Colombian	114	0.1	1.4
Spaniard	113	0.1	1.4

Population Growth: 2000–2010

Group	%
Total Population	0.3
Hispanic or Latino (of any race)	47.8
Central American, ex. Mexican	71.5
Panamanian	27.1
Cuban	102.9
Mexican	99.7
Puerto Rican	37.7
South American	66.5

Males per 100 Females

Group	Number
Total Population	93.8
Hispanic or Latino (of any race)	116.7
Central American, ex. Mexican	89.8
Honduran	109.6
Panamanian	66.2
Cuban	100.0
Dominican Republic	97.3
Mexican	132.0
Puerto Rican	116.4
South American	105.9
Colombian	86.9
Spaniard	117.3

Average Household Size

Group	People
Total Population	2.46
Hispanic or Latino (of any race)	2.84
Central American, ex. Mexican	2.63
Honduran	2.49
Panamanian	2.60
Cuban	2.61
Dominican Republic	3.04
Mexican	3.14
Puerto Rican	2.79
South American	2.29
Colombian	2.38
Spaniard	2.15

Median Age

Group	Years
Total Population	33.0
Hispanic or Latino (of any race)	24.5
Central American, ex. Mexican	29.7
Honduran	28.2
Panamanian	35.1
Cuban	25.6
Dominican Republic	23.8
Mexican	22.8
Puerto Rican	24.5
South American	28.5
Colombian	28.1
Spaniard	30.3

High School Graduates
(Universe: Population 25 Years and Over)

Group	Number	%
Total Population	99,536	82.4
Hispanic or Latino (of any race)	3,378	88.8
Mexican	779	76.8
Puerto Rican	1,379	93.0

Four-Year College Graduates
(Universe: Population 25 Years and Over)

Group	Number	%
Total Population	24,742	20.5
Hispanic or Latino (of any race)	675	17.7
Mexican	130	12.8
Puerto Rican	240	16.2

Population Age 3–17 Enrolled in Public School
(Universe: Population Age 3–17 Enrolled in School)

Group	Number	%
Total Population	30,785	89.0
Hispanic or Latino (of any race)	1,375	86.9
Mexican	572	96.0
Puerto Rican	530	88.5

Population Age 3–17 Enrolled in Private School
(Universe: Population Age 3–17 Enrolled in School)

Group	Number	%
Total Population	3,812	11.0
Hispanic or Latino (of any race)	208	13.1
Mexican	24	4.0
Puerto Rican	69	11.5

Foreign-Born Population

Group	Number	%
Total Population	7,364	3.8
Hispanic or Latino (of any race)	1,785	23.2
Mexican	763	31.3
Puerto Rican	18	0.6

Foreign-Born Naturalized U.S. Citizens

Group	Number	%
Total Population	3,665	49.8
Hispanic or Latino (of any race)	410	23.0
Mexican	50	6.6
Puerto Rican	0	0.0

Language Spoken at Home: English Only
(Universe: Population 5 Years and Over)

Group	Number	%
Total Population	167,624	93.6
Hispanic or Latino (of any race)	2,740	39.9
Mexican	819	38.2
Puerto Rican	1,089	39.7

Language Spoken at Home: Spanish
(Universe: Population 5 Years and Over)

Group	Number	%
Total Population	6,082	3.4
Hispanic or Latino (of any race)	4,088	59.5
Mexican	1,311	61.2
Puerto Rican	1,641	59.8

Unemployment Rate
(Universe: Population 16 Years and Over)

Group	%
Total Population	11.0
Hispanic or Latino (of any race)	17.5
Mexican	10.8
Puerto Rican	21.2

Class of Worker: Private Wage and Salary
(Universe: Civilian Employed Population 16 Years and Over)

Group	Number	%
Total Population	57,028	73.8
Hispanic or Latino (of any race)	2,089	76.4
Mexican	614	76.8
Puerto Rican	684	63.0

Class of Worker: Government
(Universe: Civilian Employed Population 16 Years and Over)

Group	Number	%
Total Population	16,964	22.0
Hispanic or Latino (of any race)	573	21.0
Mexican	131	16.4
Puerto Rican	384	35.4

Means of Transportation to Work: Car, Truck or Van
(Universe: Workers 16 Years and Over)

Group	Number	%
Total Population	74,298	90.4
Hispanic or Latino (of any race)	2,910	86.6
Mexican	792	78.9
Puerto Rican	1,266	87.7

Means of Transportation to Work: Public Transportation (ex. Taxicab)
(Universe: Workers 16 Years and Over)

Group	Number	%
Total Population	1,343	1.6
Hispanic or Latino (of any race)	84	2.5
Mexican	45	4.5

Notes: (1) Percent of total population; (2) Percent of Hispanic/Latino population; Profiles include places with an overall population of at least 125,000, OR an overall population of at least 25,000 where the Hispanic/Latino population is at least 20% of the overall population. In states where less than five places meet either of these criteria, we have included places with at least 10,000 total population with the highest percentage of Hispanic/Latino population. These places are identified with an asterisk (*); Please refer to the User's Guide for a full explanation of data.

Puerto Rican	24	1.7

Homeownership Rate
(Universe: Occupied Housing Units)

Group	%
Total Population	53.6
Hispanic or Latino (of any race)	41.2
Central American, ex. Mexican	44.4
Honduran	17.1
Panamanian	51.1
Cuban	52.4
Dominican Republic	36.8
Mexican	30.6
Puerto Rican	48.4
South American	46.7
Colombian	43.2
Spaniard	45.0

Median Home Value

Group	Dollars
Total Population	99,400
Hispanic or Latino (of any race)	104,400
Mexican	94,800
Puerto Rican	107,600

Median Gross Rent

Group	Dollars
Total Population	686
Hispanic or Latino (of any race)	726
Mexican	787
Puerto Rican	636

Median Household Income
(2010 Inflation-Adjusted Dollars)

Group	Dollars
Total Population	37,609
Hispanic or Latino (of any race)	37,845
Mexican	30,536
Puerto Rican	35,852

Per Capita Income
(2010 Inflation-Adjusted Dollars)

Group	Dollars
Total Population	20,629
Hispanic or Latino (of any race)	16,227
Mexican	11,219
Puerto Rican	19,464

Households with $100,000+ Income

Group	Number	%
Total Population	7,343	10.1
Hispanic or Latino (of any race)	116	5.4
Mexican	27	5.5
Puerto Rican	51	5.3

Households with Food Stamps/SNAP Benefits During Past 12 Months

Group	Number	%
Total Population	11,253	15.5
Hispanic or Latino (of any race)	301	13.9
Mexican	34	7.0
Puerto Rican	133	13.7

Poverty Rate
(Income in Past 12 Months Below Poverty Level)

Group	%
Total Population	23.7
Hispanic or Latino (of any race)	24.9
Mexican	31.8
Puerto Rican	23.5

Columbus

Population

Group	Number	%TP[1]	%HP[2]
Total Population	189,885	100.0	–
Hispanic or Latino (of any race)	12,110	6.4	100.0
Central American, ex. Mexican	1,585	0.8	13.1
Guatemalan	464	0.2	3.8
Honduran	186	0.1	1.5
Panamanian	696	0.4	5.7
Salvadoran	125	0.1	1.0
Cuban	328	0.2	2.7
Dominican Republic	275	0.1	2.3
Mexican	4,792	2.5	39.6
Puerto Rican	3,301	1.7	27.3
South American	652	0.3	5.4
Colombian	336	0.2	2.8
Peruvian	107	0.1	0.9
Spaniard	185	0.1	1.5

Population Growth: 2000–2010

Group	%
Total Population	2.2
Hispanic or Latino (of any race)	44.7
Central American, ex. Mexican	90.7
Guatemalan	163.6
Panamanian	45.0
Cuban	76.3
Dominican Republic	152.3
Mexican	74.3
Puerto Rican	23.1
South American	68.9
Colombian	121.1

Males per 100 Females

Group	Number
Total Population	91.8
Hispanic or Latino (of any race)	114.5
Central American, ex. Mexican	95.4
Guatemalan	179.5
Honduran	126.8
Panamanian	53.0
Salvadoran	150.0
Cuban	95.2
Dominican Republic	99.3
Mexican	140.7
Puerto Rican	102.9
South American	92.3
Colombian	96.5
Peruvian	101.9
Spaniard	88.8

Average Household Size

Group	People
Total Population	2.47
Hispanic or Latino (of any race)	3.06
Central American, ex. Mexican	3.21
Guatemalan	4.29
Honduran	3.54
Panamanian	2.76
Salvadoran	2.88
Cuban	2.67
Dominican Republic	3.04
Mexican	3.47
Puerto Rican	2.74
South American	2.76
Colombian	2.90
Peruvian	2.57
Spaniard	2.42

Median Age

Group	Years
Total Population	33.5
Hispanic or Latino (of any race)	25.3
Central American, ex. Mexican	28.3
Guatemalan	25.7
Honduran	29.0
Panamanian	34.1
Salvadoran	27.8
Cuban	25.8
Dominican Republic	25.6
Mexican	23.8
Puerto Rican	26.2
South American	30.6
Colombian	30.0
Peruvian	32.5
Spaniard	28.3

High School Graduates
(Universe: Population 25 Years and Over)

Group	Number	%
Total Population	97,291	83.8
Hispanic or Latino (of any race)	4,465	77.3
Central American, ex. Mexican	624	62.9
Mexican	1,526	68.5
Puerto Rican	1,726	88.9

Four-Year College Graduates
(Universe: Population 25 Years and Over)

Group	Number	%
Total Population	25,116	21.6
Hispanic or Latino (of any race)	949	16.4
Central American, ex. Mexican	138	13.9
Mexican	200	9.0
Puerto Rican	430	22.1

Population Age 3–17 Enrolled in Public School
(Universe: Population Age 3–17 Enrolled in School)

Group	Number	%
Total Population	33,163	90.1
Hispanic or Latino (of any race)	2,327	93.7
Central American, ex. Mexican	279	100.0
Mexican	880	88.5
Puerto Rican	857	95.2

Population Age 3–17 Enrolled in Private School
(Universe: Population Age 3–17 Enrolled in School)

Group	Number	%
Total Population	3,625	9.9
Hispanic or Latino (of any race)	157	6.3
Central American, ex. Mexican	0	0.0
Mexican	114	11.5
Puerto Rican	43	4.8

Foreign-Born Population

Group	Number	%
Total Population	9,116	4.9
Hispanic or Latino (of any race)	3,089	27.3
Central American, ex. Mexican	1,005	65.6
Mexican	1,619	33.0
Puerto Rican	41	1.2

Foreign-Born Naturalized U.S. Citizens

Group	Number	%
Total Population	4,644	50.9
Hispanic or Latino (of any race)	977	31.6
Central American, ex. Mexican	577	57.4
Mexican	188	11.6
Puerto Rican	19	46.3

Language Spoken at Home: English Only
(Universe: Population 5 Years and Over)

Group	Number	%
Total Population	157,996	90.9
Hispanic or Latino (of any race)	3,156	31.4
Central American, ex. Mexican	215	14.5
Mexican	1,329	32.1
Puerto Rican	1,021	32.3

Language Spoken at Home: Spanish
(Universe: Population 5 Years and Over)

Group	Number	%
Total Population	9,188	5.3
Hispanic or Latino (of any race)	6,738	67.1
Central American, ex. Mexican	1,212	81.6
Mexican	2,788	67.3
Puerto Rican	2,088	66.1

Unemployment Rate
(Universe: Population 16 Years and Over)

Group	%
Total Population	9.1
Hispanic or Latino (of any race)	11.0
Central American, ex. Mexican	12.0
Mexican	7.9
Puerto Rican	13.6

Class of Worker: Private Wage and Salary
(Universe: Civilian Employed Population 16 Years and Over)

Group	Number	%
Total Population	56,555	75.3
Hispanic or Latino (of any race)	3,189	78.5
Central American, ex. Mexican	555	86.0
Mexican	1,342	81.7
Puerto Rican	863	67.8

Class of Worker: Government
(Universe: Civilian Employed Population 16 Years and Over)

Group	Number	%
Total Population	14,598	19.4
Hispanic or Latino (of any race)	646	15.9
Central American, ex. Mexican	82	12.7

STATE & PLACE PROFILES

Notes: (1) Percent of total population; (2) Percent of Hispanic/Latino population; Profiles include places with an overall population of at least 125,000, OR an overall population of at least 25,000 where the Hispanic/Latino population is at least 20% of the overall population. In states where less than five places meet either of these criteria, we have included places with at least 10,000 total population with the highest percentage of Hispanic/Latino population. These places are identified with an asterisk (*); Please refer to the User's Guide for a full explanation of data.

Mexican	135	8.2
Puerto Rican	370	29.1

Means of Transportation to Work: Car, Truck or Van
(Universe: Workers 16 Years and Over)

Group	Number	%
Total Population	70,397	84.6
Hispanic or Latino (of any race)	3,858	74.0
Central American, ex. Mexican	643	84.5
Mexican	1,387	60.8
Puerto Rican	1,331	86.9

Means of Transportation to Work: Public Transportation (ex. Taxicab)
(Universe: Workers 16 Years and Over)

Group	Number	%
Total Population	738	0.9
Hispanic or Latino (of any race)	9	0.2
Central American, ex. Mexican	0	0.0
Mexican	0	0.0
Puerto Rican	9	0.6

Homeownership Rate
(Universe: Occupied Housing Units)

Group	%
Total Population	52.1
Hispanic or Latino (of any race)	38.6
Central American, ex. Mexican	40.5
Guatemalan	27.2
Honduran	29.8
Panamanian	51.0
Salvadoran	28.6
Cuban	39.6
Dominican Republic	29.0
Mexican	30.2
Puerto Rican	48.5
South American	36.6
Colombian	32.2
Peruvian	48.6
Spaniard	53.8

Median Home Value

Group	Dollars
Total Population	131,900
Hispanic or Latino (of any race)	143,000
Central American, ex. Mexican	122,100
Mexican	115,100
Puerto Rican	160,200

Median Gross Rent

Group	Dollars
Total Population	732
Hispanic or Latino (of any race)	793
Central American, ex. Mexican	752
Mexican	779
Puerto Rican	877

Median Household Income
(2010 Inflation-Adjusted Dollars)

Group	Dollars
Total Population	41,331
Hispanic or Latino (of any race)	43,314
Central American, ex. Mexican	46,250
Mexican	40,673
Puerto Rican	47,788

Per Capita Income
(2010 Inflation-Adjusted Dollars)

Group	Dollars
Total Population	22,514
Hispanic or Latino (of any race)	17,349
Central American, ex. Mexican	26,606
Mexican	14,023
Puerto Rican	16,911

Households with $100,000+ Income

Group	Number	%
Total Population	9,433	13.1
Hispanic or Latino (of any race)	344	10.6
Central American, ex. Mexican	103	20.3
Mexican	92	8.5
Puerto Rican	74	6.0

Households with Food Stamps/SNAP Benefits During Past 12 Months

Group	Number	%
Total Population	10,855	15.1
Hispanic or Latino (of any race)	286	8.8
Central American, ex. Mexican	13	2.6
Mexican	147	13.5
Puerto Rican	79	6.4

Poverty Rate
(Income in Past 12 Months Below Poverty Level)

Group	%
Total Population	18.2
Hispanic or Latino (of any race)	21.1
Central American, ex. Mexican	29.1
Mexican	19.0
Puerto Rican	20.6

Dalton

Population

Group	Number	%TP[1]	%HP[2]
Total Population	33,128	100.0	–
Hispanic or Latino (of any race)	15,891	48.0	100.0
Central American, ex. Mexican	1,538	4.6	9.7
Guatemalan	909	2.7	5.7
Honduran	101	0.3	0.6
Salvadoran	445	1.3	2.8
Cuban	139	0.4	0.9
Mexican	13,214	39.9	83.2
Puerto Rican	223	0.7	1.4
South American	103	0.3	0.6

Population Growth: 2000–2010

Group	%
Total Population	18.7
Hispanic or Latino (of any race)	41.6
Central American, ex. Mexican	171.3
Guatemalan	225.8
Salvadoran	134.2
Mexican	40.1
Puerto Rican	31.2

Males per 100 Females

Group	Number
Total Population	97.2
Hispanic or Latino (of any race)	111.1
Central American, ex. Mexican	130.9
Guatemalan	145.0
Honduran	119.6
Salvadoran	121.4
Cuban	104.4
Mexican	110.5
Puerto Rican	82.8
South American	90.7

Average Household Size

Group	People
Total Population	2.84
Hispanic or Latino (of any race)	4.23
Central American, ex. Mexican	4.38
Guatemalan	4.88
Honduran	4.29
Salvadoran	3.84
Cuban	3.06
Mexican	4.29
Puerto Rican	3.00
South American	2.66

Median Age

Group	Years
Total Population	31.3
Hispanic or Latino (of any race)	23.1
Central American, ex. Mexican	26.4
Guatemalan	24.1
Honduran	28.3
Salvadoran	30.5
Cuban	29.7
Mexican	22.5
Puerto Rican	26.1
South American	38.8

High School Graduates
(Universe: Population 25 Years and Over)

Group	Number	%
Total Population	12,281	63.0
Hispanic or Latino (of any race)	2,211	32.2
Mexican	1,561	29.7

Four-Year College Graduates
(Universe: Population 25 Years and Over)

Group	Number	%
Total Population	4,002	20.5
Hispanic or Latino (of any race)	368	5.4
Mexican	177	3.4

Population Age 3–17 Enrolled in Public School
(Universe: Population Age 3–17 Enrolled in School)

Group	Number	%
Total Population	5,929	91.1
Hispanic or Latino (of any race)	3,698	95.8
Mexican	3,157	99.1

Population Age 3–17 Enrolled in Private School
(Universe: Population Age 3–17 Enrolled in School)

Group	Number	%
Total Population	580	8.9
Hispanic or Latino (of any race)	163	4.2
Mexican	29	0.9

Foreign-Born Population

Group	Number	%
Total Population	9,598	29.6
Hispanic or Latino (of any race)	8,437	56.8
Mexican	6,986	58.5

Foreign-Born Naturalized U.S. Citizens

Group	Number	%
Total Population	1,351	14.1
Hispanic or Latino (of any race)	768	9.1
Mexican	535	7.7

Language Spoken at Home: English Only
(Universe: Population 5 Years and Over)

Group	Number	%
Total Population	15,603	53.4
Hispanic or Latino (of any race)	577	4.5
Mexican	366	3.6

Language Spoken at Home: Spanish
(Universe: Population 5 Years and Over)

Group	Number	%
Total Population	12,324	42.2
Hispanic or Latino (of any race)	12,132	95.2
Mexican	9,731	96.4

Unemployment Rate
(Universe: Population 16 Years and Over)

Group	%
Total Population	7.4
Hispanic or Latino (of any race)	7.5
Mexican	6.5

Class of Worker: Private Wage and Salary
(Universe: Civilian Employed Population 16 Years and Over)

Group	Number	%
Total Population	12,406	87.7
Hispanic or Latino (of any race)	6,017	94.6
Mexican	4,696	94.4

Class of Worker: Government
(Universe: Civilian Employed Population 16 Years and Over)

Group	Number	%
Total Population	1,049	7.4
Hispanic or Latino (of any race)	108	1.7
Mexican	85	1.7

Means of Transportation to Work: Car, Truck or Van
(Universe: Workers 16 Years and Over)

Group	Number	%
Total Population	12,630	90.6
Hispanic or Latino (of any race)	5,549	88.7
Mexican	4,374	89.5

Notes: (1) Percent of total population; (2) Percent of Hispanic/Latino population; Profiles include places with an overall population of at least 125,000, OR an overall population of at least 25,000 where the Hispanic/Latino population is at least 20% of the overall population. In states where less than five places meet either of these criteria, we have included places with at least 10,000 total population with the highest percentage of Hispanic/Latino population. These places are identified with an asterisk (*); Please refer to the User's Guide for a full explanation of data.

Means of Transportation to Work: Public Transportation (ex. Taxicab)
(Universe: Workers 16 Years and Over)

Group	Number	%
Total Population	33	0.2
Hispanic or Latino (of any race)	18	0.3
Mexican	0	0.0

Homeownership Rate
(Universe: Occupied Housing Units)

Group	%
Total Population	48.6
Hispanic or Latino (of any race)	43.4
Central American, ex. Mexican	28.9
Guatemalan	21.5
Honduran	32.1
Salvadoran	41.5
Cuban	31.4
Mexican	46.0
Puerto Rican	26.7
South American	52.6

Median Home Value

Group	Dollars
Total Population	145,200
Hispanic or Latino (of any race)	119,300
Mexican	116,800

Median Gross Rent

Group	Dollars
Total Population	633
Hispanic or Latino (of any race)	640
Mexican	619

Median Household Income
(2010 Inflation-Adjusted Dollars)

Group	Dollars
Total Population	38,798
Hispanic or Latino (of any race)	33,453
Mexican	29,700

Per Capita Income
(2010 Inflation-Adjusted Dollars)

Group	Dollars
Total Population	20,359
Hispanic or Latino (of any race)	11,004
Mexican	10,582

Households with $100,000+ Income

Group	Number	%
Total Population	1,601	14.2
Hispanic or Latino (of any race)	158	4.0
Mexican	99	3.2

Households with Food Stamps/SNAP Benefits During Past 12 Months

Group	Number	%
Total Population	1,442	12.7
Hispanic or Latino (of any race)	639	16.0
Mexican	471	15.3

Poverty Rate
(Income in Past 12 Months Below Poverty Level)

Group	%
Total Population	24.4
Hispanic or Latino (of any race)	36.4
Mexican	38.6

Gainesville

Population

Group	Number	%TP[1]	%HP[2]
Total Population	33,804	100.0	–
Hispanic or Latino (of any race)	14,058	41.6	100.0
Central American, ex. Mexican	1,844	5.5	13.1
Guatemalan	321	0.9	2.3
Honduran	400	1.2	2.8
Salvadoran	1,037	3.1	7.4
Mexican	10,940	32.4	77.8
Puerto Rican	350	1.0	2.5
South American	217	0.6	1.5
Colombian	150	0.4	1.1

Population Growth: 2000–2010

Group	%
Total Population	32.2
Hispanic or Latino (of any race)	65.7
Central American, ex. Mexican	310.7
Salvadoran	221.1
Mexican	54.5

Males per 100 Females

Group	Number
Total Population	91.6
Hispanic or Latino (of any race)	107.9
Central American, ex. Mexican	117.5
Guatemalan	156.8
Honduran	138.1
Salvadoran	102.5
Mexican	108.0
Puerto Rican	90.2
South American	82.4
Colombian	78.6

Average Household Size

Group	People
Total Population	2.85
Hispanic or Latino (of any race)	4.57
Central American, ex. Mexican	5.00
Guatemalan	5.39
Honduran	5.29
Salvadoran	4.88
Mexican	4.73
Puerto Rican	2.77
South American	2.75
Colombian	2.58

Median Age

Group	Years
Total Population	28.5
Hispanic or Latino (of any race)	22.5
Central American, ex. Mexican	27.2
Guatemalan	24.3
Honduran	28.7
Salvadoran	28.0
Mexican	20.9
Puerto Rican	26.8
South American	34.8
Colombian	33.7

High School Graduates
(Universe: Population 25 Years and Over)

Group	Number	%
Total Population	12,473	66.4
Hispanic or Latino (of any race)	2,618	36.5
Central American, ex. Mexican	158	11.8
Salvadoran	72	8.6
Mexican	2,174	40.3

Four-Year College Graduates
(Universe: Population 25 Years and Over)

Group	Number	%
Total Population	3,822	20.4
Hispanic or Latino (of any race)	302	4.2
Central American, ex. Mexican	0	0.0
Salvadoran	0	0.0
Mexican	238	4.4

Population Age 3–17 Enrolled in Public School
(Universe: Population Age 3–17 Enrolled in School)

Group	Number	%
Total Population	5,386	94.4
Hispanic or Latino (of any race)	3,401	98.2
Central American, ex. Mexican	395	100.0
Salvadoran	291	100.0
Mexican	2,892	98.3

Population Age 3–17 Enrolled in Private School
(Universe: Population Age 3–17 Enrolled in School)

Group	Number	%
Total Population	318	5.6
Hispanic or Latino (of any race)	61	1.8
Central American, ex. Mexican	0	0.0
Salvadoran	0	0.0
Mexican	51	1.7

Foreign-Born Population

Group	Number	%
Total Population	9,987	30.4
Hispanic or Latino (of any race)	9,031	57.8
Central American, ex. Mexican	1,840	69.2
Salvadoran	1,121	73.8
Mexican	6,828	56.7

Foreign-Born Naturalized U.S. Citizens

Group	Number	%
Total Population	908	9.1
Hispanic or Latino (of any race)	554	6.1
Central American, ex. Mexican	36	2.0
Salvadoran	14	1.2
Mexican	332	4.9

Language Spoken at Home: English Only
(Universe: Population 5 Years and Over)

Group	Number	%
Total Population	15,046	52.3
Hispanic or Latino (of any race)	803	6.1
Central American, ex. Mexican	0	0.0
Salvadoran	0	0.0
Mexican	715	7.1

Language Spoken at Home: Spanish
(Universe: Population 5 Years and Over)

Group	Number	%
Total Population	12,719	44.2
Hispanic or Latino (of any race)	12,368	93.9
Central American, ex. Mexican	2,336	100.0
Salvadoran	1,386	100.0
Mexican	9,373	92.9

Unemployment Rate
(Universe: Population 16 Years and Over)

Group	%
Total Population	6.2
Hispanic or Latino (of any race)	4.8
Central American, ex. Mexican	9.9
Salvadoran	14.4
Mexican	3.6

Class of Worker: Private Wage and Salary
(Universe: Civilian Employed Population 16 Years and Over)

Group	Number	%
Total Population	13,180	88.1
Hispanic or Latino (of any race)	6,684	95.4
Central American, ex. Mexican	1,427	94.4
Salvadoran	726	89.5
Mexican	4,896	96.4

Class of Worker: Government
(Universe: Civilian Employed Population 16 Years and Over)

Group	Number	%
Total Population	1,131	7.6
Hispanic or Latino (of any race)	218	3.1
Central American, ex. Mexican	56	3.7
Salvadoran	56	6.9
Mexican	125	2.5

Means of Transportation to Work: Car, Truck or Van
(Universe: Workers 16 Years and Over)

Group	Number	%
Total Population	13,310	90.7
Hispanic or Latino (of any race)	6,067	88.1
Central American, ex. Mexican	1,299	86.2
Salvadoran	631	77.8
Mexican	4,389	88.3

Means of Transportation to Work: Public Transportation (ex. Taxicab)
(Universe: Workers 16 Years and Over)

Group	Number	%
Total Population	44	0.3
Hispanic or Latino (of any race)	15	0.2
Central American, ex. Mexican	0	0.0
Salvadoran	0	0.0
Mexican	15	0.3

Homeownership Rate
(Universe: Occupied Housing Units)

Group	%
Total Population	38.0

Notes: (1) Percent of total population; (2) Percent of Hispanic/Latino population; Profiles include places with an overall population of at least 125,000, OR an overall population of at least 25,000 where the Hispanic/Latino population is at least 20% of the overall population. In states where less than five places meet either of these criteria, we have included places with at least 10,000 total population with the highest percentage of Hispanic/Latino population. These places are identified with an asterisk (*); Please refer to the User's Guide for a full explanation of data.

Group	%
Hispanic or Latino (of any race)	25.3
Central American, ex. Mexican	39.7
Guatemalan	11.9
Honduran	37.0
Salvadoran	48.4
Mexican	22.1
Puerto Rican	24.6
South American	35.5
Colombian	34.6

Median Home Value

Group	Dollars
Total Population	178,200
Hispanic or Latino (of any race)	139,700
Central American, ex. Mexican	132,800
Salvadoran	132,800
Mexican	136,900

Median Gross Rent

Group	Dollars
Total Population	779
Hispanic or Latino (of any race)	772
Central American, ex. Mexican	747
Salvadoran	739
Mexican	796

Median Household Income
(2010 Inflation-Adjusted Dollars)

Group	Dollars
Total Population	37,866
Hispanic or Latino (of any race)	37,379
Central American, ex. Mexican	39,196
Salvadoran	37,375
Mexican	36,946

Per Capita Income
(2010 Inflation-Adjusted Dollars)

Group	Dollars
Total Population	19,554
Hispanic or Latino (of any race)	11,114
Central American, ex. Mexican	11,949
Salvadoran	11,097
Mexican	10,646

Households with $100,000+ Income

Group	Number	%
Total Population	1,324	11.5
Hispanic or Latino (of any race)	257	7.0
Central American, ex. Mexican	34	4.9
Salvadoran	7	1.6
Mexican	212	8.0

Households with Food Stamps/SNAP Benefits During Past 12 Months

Group	Number	%
Total Population	1,659	14.4
Hispanic or Latino (of any race)	471	12.8
Central American, ex. Mexican	22	3.1
Salvadoran	0	0.0
Mexican	364	13.8

Poverty Rate
(Income in Past 12 Months Below Poverty Level)

Group	%
Total Population	22.8
Hispanic or Latino (of any race)	26.4
Central American, ex. Mexican	31.1
Salvadoran	36.4
Mexican	25.3

Lawrenceville

Population

Group	Number	%TP[1]	%HP[2]
Total Population	28,546	100.0	–
Hispanic or Latino (of any race)	6,378	22.3	100.0
Central American, ex. Mexican	922	3.2	14.5
Guatemalan	316	1.1	5.0
Honduran	156	0.5	2.4
Salvadoran	369	1.3	5.8
Cuban	178	0.6	2.8
Dominican Republic	177	0.6	2.8
Mexican	3,708	13.0	58.1
Puerto Rican	490	1.7	7.7
South American	473	1.7	7.4
Colombian	223	0.8	3.5

Population Growth: 2000–2010

Group	%
Total Population	27.5
Hispanic or Latino (of any race)	134.5
Central American, ex. Mexican	603.8
Mexican	104.1
Puerto Rican	210.1
South American	338.0

Males per 100 Females

Group	Number
Total Population	91.4
Hispanic or Latino (of any race)	111.1
Central American, ex. Mexican	123.8
Guatemalan	184.7
Honduran	92.6
Salvadoran	107.3
Cuban	117.1
Dominican Republic	67.0
Mexican	119.9
Puerto Rican	84.2
South American	92.3
Colombian	93.9

Average Household Size

Group	People
Total Population	2.84
Hispanic or Latino (of any race)	4.15
Central American, ex. Mexican	4.33
Guatemalan	4.77
Honduran	4.00
Salvadoran	4.64
Cuban	3.09
Dominican Republic	3.68
Mexican	4.55
Puerto Rican	3.43
South American	3.39
Colombian	3.20

Median Age

Group	Years
Total Population	32.4
Hispanic or Latino (of any race)	25.0
Central American, ex. Mexican	27.4
Guatemalan	25.9
Honduran	27.5
Salvadoran	28.4
Cuban	34.7
Dominican Republic	24.8
Mexican	23.4
Puerto Rican	23.9
South American	33.1
Colombian	32.6

High School Graduates
(Universe: Population 25 Years and Over)

Group	Number	%
Total Population	12,906	78.2
Hispanic or Latino (of any race)	1,380	47.3
Mexican	913	43.7

Four-Year College Graduates
(Universe: Population 25 Years and Over)

Group	Number	%
Total Population	3,136	19.0
Hispanic or Latino (of any race)	230	7.9
Mexican	70	3.4

Population Age 3–17 Enrolled in Public School
(Universe: Population Age 3–17 Enrolled in School)

Group	Number	%
Total Population	5,702	91.8
Hispanic or Latino (of any race)	1,630	95.1
Mexican	1,208	97.5

Population Age 3–17 Enrolled in Private School
(Universe: Population Age 3–17 Enrolled in School)

Group	Number	%
Total Population	511	8.2
Hispanic or Latino (of any race)	84	4.9
Mexican	31	2.5

Foreign-Born Population

Group	Number	%
Total Population	7,020	25.3
Hispanic or Latino (of any race)	3,789	57.8
Mexican	2,877	59.8

Foreign-Born Naturalized U.S. Citizens

Group	Number	%
Total Population	2,142	30.5
Hispanic or Latino (of any race)	469	12.4
Mexican	299	10.4

Language Spoken at Home: English Only
(Universe: Population 5 Years and Over)

Group	Number	%
Total Population	16,432	65.6
Hispanic or Latino (of any race)	329	6.0
Mexican	153	3.8

Language Spoken at Home: Spanish
(Universe: Population 5 Years and Over)

Group	Number	%
Total Population	5,395	21.6
Hispanic or Latino (of any race)	5,093	93.5
Mexican	3,848	96.2

Unemployment Rate
(Universe: Population 16 Years and Over)

Group	%
Total Population	10.4
Hispanic or Latino (of any race)	13.2
Mexican	12.9

Class of Worker: Private Wage and Salary
(Universe: Civilian Employed Population 16 Years and Over)

Group	Number	%
Total Population	10,526	83.4
Hispanic or Latino (of any race)	2,210	89.4
Mexican	1,513	87.7

Class of Worker: Government
(Universe: Civilian Employed Population 16 Years and Over)

Group	Number	%
Total Population	1,138	9.0
Hispanic or Latino (of any race)	25	1.0
Mexican	14	0.8

Means of Transportation to Work: Car, Truck or Van
(Universe: Workers 16 Years and Over)

Group	Number	%
Total Population	10,686	88.4
Hispanic or Latino (of any race)	1,964	82.2
Mexican	1,309	79.0

Means of Transportation to Work: Public Transportation (ex. Taxicab)
(Universe: Workers 16 Years and Over)

Group	Number	%
Total Population	328	2.7
Hispanic or Latino (of any race)	69	2.9
Mexican	37	2.2

Homeownership Rate
(Universe: Occupied Housing Units)

Group	%
Total Population	52.2
Hispanic or Latino (of any race)	39.3
Central American, ex. Mexican	43.2
Guatemalan	25.8
Honduran	32.4
Salvadoran	59.4
Cuban	41.4
Dominican Republic	41.5
Mexican	34.0
Puerto Rican	45.4
South American	52.7
Colombian	51.3

Median Home Value

Group	Dollars
Total Population	154,500
Hispanic or Latino (of any race)	158,200
Mexican	154,300

Notes: (1) Percent of total population; (2) Percent of Hispanic/Latino population; Profiles include places with an overall population of at least 125,000, OR an overall population of at least 25,000 where the Hispanic/Latino population is at least 20% of the overall population. In states where less than five places meet either of these criteria, we have included places with at least 10,000 total population with the highest percentage of Hispanic/Latino population. These places are identified with an asterisk (*); Please refer to the User's Guide for a full explanation of data.

Median Gross Rent

Group	Dollars
Total Population	860
Hispanic or Latino (of any race)	864
Mexican	857

Median Household Income
(2010 Inflation-Adjusted Dollars)

Group	Dollars
Total Population	47,689
Hispanic or Latino (of any race)	32,118
Mexican	31,302

Per Capita Income
(2010 Inflation-Adjusted Dollars)

Group	Dollars
Total Population	19,474
Hispanic or Latino (of any race)	9,704
Mexican	8,662

Households with $100,000+ Income

Group	Number	%
Total Population	1,252	13.7
Hispanic or Latino (of any race)	92	6.5
Mexican	51	5.1

Households with Food Stamps/SNAP Benefits During Past 12 Months

Group	Number	%
Total Population	1,220	13.4
Hispanic or Latino (of any race)	230	16.3
Mexican	180	17.9

Poverty Rate
(Income in Past 12 Months Below Poverty Level)

Group	%
Total Population	17.9
Hispanic or Latino (of any race)	38.1
Mexican	42.4

Marietta

Population

Group	Number	%TP[1]	%HP[2]
Total Population	56,579	100.0	–
Hispanic or Latino (of any race)	11,633	20.6	100.0
Central American, ex. Mexican	2,088	3.7	17.9
Guatemalan	1,152	2.0	9.9
Honduran	321	0.6	2.8
Salvadoran	460	0.8	4.0
Cuban	170	0.3	1.5
Dominican Republic	211	0.4	1.8
Mexican	7,330	13.0	63.0
Puerto Rican	609	1.1	5.2
South American	492	0.9	4.2
Colombian	192	0.3	1.7
Peruvian	103	0.2	0.9

Population Growth: 2000–2010

Group	%
Total Population	-3.7
Hispanic or Latino (of any race)	16.9
Central American, ex. Mexican	133.8
Guatemalan	143.6
Honduran	119.9
Salvadoran	202.6
Cuban	45.3
Mexican	2.2
Puerto Rican	14.7
South American	60.8
Colombian	43.3

Males per 100 Females

Group	Number
Total Population	95.9
Hispanic or Latino (of any race)	129.0
Central American, ex. Mexican	178.8
Guatemalan	233.9
Honduran	163.1
Salvadoran	128.9
Cuban	115.2
Dominican Republic	90.1
Mexican	128.3
Puerto Rican	87.4
South American	87.1
Colombian	77.8
Peruvian	110.2

Average Household Size

Group	People
Total Population	2.38
Hispanic or Latino (of any race)	3.79
Central American, ex. Mexican	4.03
Guatemalan	4.45
Honduran	3.80
Salvadoran	3.92
Cuban	2.41
Dominican Republic	2.83
Mexican	4.20
Puerto Rican	2.36
South American	2.88
Colombian	2.97
Peruvian	3.03

Median Age

Group	Years
Total Population	32.6
Hispanic or Latino (of any race)	25.8
Central American, ex. Mexican	27.0
Guatemalan	26.6
Honduran	27.2
Salvadoran	27.7
Cuban	32.5
Dominican Republic	26.1
Mexican	24.6
Puerto Rican	28.1
South American	34.0
Colombian	37.0
Peruvian	34.8

High School Graduates
(Universe: Population 25 Years and Over)

Group	Number	%
Total Population	30,320	83.0
Hispanic or Latino (of any race)	3,293	49.1
Central American, ex. Mexican	701	40.9
Guatemalan	382	39.4
Mexican	1,753	46.6

Four-Year College Graduates
(Universe: Population 25 Years and Over)

Group	Number	%
Total Population	13,273	36.4
Hispanic or Latino (of any race)	857	12.8
Central American, ex. Mexican	149	8.7
Guatemalan	118	12.2
Mexican	484	12.9

Population Age 3–17 Enrolled in Public School
(Universe: Population Age 3–17 Enrolled in School)

Group	Number	%
Total Population	7,073	81.4
Hispanic or Latino (of any race)	2,053	96.4
Central American, ex. Mexican	190	100.0
Guatemalan	84	100.0
Mexican	1,410	95.4

Population Age 3–17 Enrolled in Private School
(Universe: Population Age 3–17 Enrolled in School)

Group	Number	%
Total Population	1,612	18.6
Hispanic or Latino (of any race)	76	3.6
Central American, ex. Mexican	0	0.0
Guatemalan	0	0.0
Mexican	68	4.6

Foreign-Born Population

Group	Number	%
Total Population	13,482	23.6
Hispanic or Latino (of any race)	8,655	69.9
Central American, ex. Mexican	2,466	86.7
Guatemalan	1,419	88.7
Mexican	5,408	73.3

Foreign-Born Naturalized U.S. Citizens

Group	Number	%
Total Population	2,485	18.4
Hispanic or Latino (of any race)	615	7.1
Central American, ex. Mexican	80	3.2
Guatemalan	0	0.0
Mexican	368	6.8

Language Spoken at Home: English Only
(Universe: Population 5 Years and Over)

Group	Number	%
Total Population	37,289	71.4
Hispanic or Latino (of any race)	753	6.8
Central American, ex. Mexican	71	2.7
Guatemalan	23	1.5
Mexican	298	4.6

Language Spoken at Home: Spanish
(Universe: Population 5 Years and Over)

Group	Number	%
Total Population	10,702	20.5
Hispanic or Latino (of any race)	10,204	92.6
Central American, ex. Mexican	2,537	97.3
Guatemalan	1,480	98.5
Mexican	6,244	95.4

Unemployment Rate
(Universe: Population 16 Years and Over)

Group	%
Total Population	7.3
Hispanic or Latino (of any race)	8.3
Central American, ex. Mexican	8.1
Guatemalan	6.3
Mexican	5.6

Class of Worker: Private Wage and Salary
(Universe: Civilian Employed Population 16 Years and Over)

Group	Number	%
Total Population	25,017	81.5
Hispanic or Latino (of any race)	5,919	89.6
Central American, ex. Mexican	1,811	97.5
Guatemalan	1,049	96.8
Mexican	3,590	89.4

Class of Worker: Government
(Universe: Civilian Employed Population 16 Years and Over)

Group	Number	%
Total Population	3,753	12.2
Hispanic or Latino (of any race)	146	2.2
Central American, ex. Mexican	12	0.6
Guatemalan	0	0.0
Mexican	108	2.7

Means of Transportation to Work: Car, Truck or Van
(Universe: Workers 16 Years and Over)

Group	Number	%
Total Population	25,776	85.7
Hispanic or Latino (of any race)	4,967	77.4
Central American, ex. Mexican	1,201	65.8
Guatemalan	766	72.8
Mexican	3,246	82.2

Means of Transportation to Work: Public Transportation (ex. Taxicab)
(Universe: Workers 16 Years and Over)

Group	Number	%
Total Population	1,470	4.9
Hispanic or Latino (of any race)	657	10.2
Central American, ex. Mexican	303	16.6
Guatemalan	117	11.1
Mexican	315	8.0

Homeownership Rate
(Universe: Occupied Housing Units)

Group	%
Total Population	42.3
Hispanic or Latino (of any race)	17.4
Central American, ex. Mexican	10.1
Guatemalan	4.4
Honduran	8.9
Salvadoran	16.5
Cuban	38.0
Dominican Republic	15.6
Mexican	14.8
Puerto Rican	28.6
South American	41.0
Colombian	49.2
Peruvian	38.9

Notes: (1) Percent of total population; (2) Percent of Hispanic/Latino population; Profiles include places with an overall population of at least 125,000, OR an overall population of at least 25,000 where the Hispanic/Latino population is at least 20% of the overall population. In states where less than five places meet either of these criteria, we have included places with at least 10,000 total population with the highest percentage of Hispanic/Latino population. These places are identified with an asterisk (*); Please refer to the User's Guide for a full explanation of data.

Median Home Value

Group	Dollars
Total Population	220,600
Hispanic or Latino (of any race)	146,600
Central American, ex. Mexican	–
Guatemalan	–
Mexican	135,900

Median Gross Rent

Group	Dollars
Total Population	848
Hispanic or Latino (of any race)	832
Central American, ex. Mexican	835
Guatemalan	789
Mexican	821

Median Household Income
(2010 Inflation-Adjusted Dollars)

Group	Dollars
Total Population	45,233
Hispanic or Latino (of any race)	36,065
Central American, ex. Mexican	36,649
Guatemalan	36,188
Mexican	34,194

Per Capita Income
(2010 Inflation-Adjusted Dollars)

Group	Dollars
Total Population	26,710
Hispanic or Latino (of any race)	13,496
Central American, ex. Mexican	13,272
Guatemalan	12,374
Mexican	12,598

Households with $100,000+ Income

Group	Number	%
Total Population	3,939	16.9
Hispanic or Latino (of any race)	410	12.7
Central American, ex. Mexican	84	13.0
Guatemalan	51	15.8
Mexican	166	9.0

Households with Food Stamps/SNAP Benefits During Past 12 Months

Group	Number	%
Total Population	2,037	8.7
Hispanic or Latino (of any race)	394	12.2
Central American, ex. Mexican	0	0.0
Guatemalan	0	0.0
Mexican	310	16.7

Poverty Rate
(Income in Past 12 Months Below Poverty Level)

Group	%
Total Population	18.5
Hispanic or Latino (of any race)	32.8
Central American, ex. Mexican	36.7
Guatemalan	44.7
Mexican	30.7

North Atlanta

Population

Group	Number	%TP[1]	%HP[2]
Total Population	40,456	100.0	–
Hispanic or Latino (of any race)	14,426	35.7	100.0
Central American, ex. Mexican	1,366	3.4	9.5
Guatemalan	344	0.9	2.4
Honduran	471	1.2	3.3
Nicaraguan	183	0.5	1.3
Salvadoran	315	0.8	2.2
Cuban	145	0.4	1.0
Mexican	11,367	28.1	78.8
Puerto Rican	214	0.5	1.5
South American	551	1.4	3.8
Colombian	173	0.4	1.2
Peruvian	200	0.5	1.4
Spaniard	112	0.3	0.8

Population Growth: 2000–2010

Group	%
Total Population	4.9
Hispanic or Latino (of any race)	36.4
Central American, ex. Mexican	15.6
Guatemalan	132.4
Honduran	5.4
Nicaraguan	30.7
Salvadoran	-12.0
Cuban	-19.9
Mexican	54.2
Puerto Rican	-11.6
South American	38.8
Colombian	16.1

Males per 100 Females

Group	Number
Total Population	111.8
Hispanic or Latino (of any race)	140.0
Central American, ex. Mexican	161.2
Guatemalan	227.6
Honduran	182.0
Nicaraguan	125.9
Salvadoran	125.0
Cuban	119.7
Mexican	141.6
Puerto Rican	109.8
South American	110.3
Colombian	82.1
Peruvian	132.6
Spaniard	107.4

Average Household Size

Group	People
Total Population	2.44
Hispanic or Latino (of any race)	4.33
Central American, ex. Mexican	4.08
Guatemalan	3.83
Honduran	4.28
Nicaraguan	4.35
Salvadoran	4.13
Cuban	2.08
Mexican	4.72
Puerto Rican	2.13
South American	2.83
Colombian	2.32
Peruvian	3.78
Spaniard	2.91

Median Age

Group	Years
Total Population	31.0
Hispanic or Latino (of any race)	26.5
Central American, ex. Mexican	29.3
Guatemalan	27.4
Honduran	29.0
Nicaraguan	31.4
Salvadoran	32.1
Cuban	40.5
Mexican	25.6
Puerto Rican	30.9
South American	34.4
Colombian	36.3
Peruvian	35.4
Spaniard	32.3

High School Graduates
(Universe: Population 25 Years and Over)

Group	Number	%
Total Population	20,784	83.5
Hispanic or Latino (of any race)	3,029	46.8
Mexican	2,274	45.1

Four-Year College Graduates
(Universe: Population 25 Years and Over)

Group	Number	%
Total Population	12,798	51.4
Hispanic or Latino (of any race)	679	10.5
Mexican	263	5.2

Population Age 3–17 Enrolled in Public School
(Universe: Population Age 3–17 Enrolled in School)

Group	Number	%
Total Population	3,121	70.7
Hispanic or Latino (of any race)	2,224	98.2
Mexican	2,132	98.2

Population Age 3–17 Enrolled in Private School
(Universe: Population Age 3–17 Enrolled in School)

Group	Number	%
Total Population	1,293	29.3
Hispanic or Latino (of any race)	40	1.8
Mexican	40	1.8

Foreign-Born Population

Group	Number	%
Total Population	11,744	31.7
Hispanic or Latino (of any race)	8,210	68.2
Mexican	6,995	69.0

Foreign-Born Naturalized U.S. Citizens

Group	Number	%
Total Population	1,524	13.0
Hispanic or Latino (of any race)	226	2.8
Mexican	122	1.7

Language Spoken at Home: English Only
(Universe: Population 5 Years and Over)

Group	Number	%
Total Population	20,639	61.6
Hispanic or Latino (of any race)	624	6.1
Mexican	313	3.7

Language Spoken at Home: Spanish
(Universe: Population 5 Years and Over)

Group	Number	%
Total Population	9,842	29.4
Hispanic or Latino (of any race)	9,598	93.9
Mexican	8,196	96.3

Unemployment Rate
(Universe: Population 16 Years and Over)

Group	%
Total Population	6.4
Hispanic or Latino (of any race)	11.6
Mexican	9.3

Class of Worker: Private Wage and Salary
(Universe: Civilian Employed Population 16 Years and Over)

Group	Number	%
Total Population	17,363	84.2
Hispanic or Latino (of any race)	4,420	83.1
Mexican	3,505	81.0

Class of Worker: Government
(Universe: Civilian Employed Population 16 Years and Over)

Group	Number	%
Total Population	1,304	6.3
Hispanic or Latino (of any race)	58	1.1
Mexican	0	0.0

Means of Transportation to Work: Car, Truck or Van
(Universe: Workers 16 Years and Over)

Group	Number	%
Total Population	14,900	73.2
Hispanic or Latino (of any race)	2,672	51.2
Mexican	2,229	52.5

Means of Transportation to Work: Public Transportation (ex. Taxicab)
(Universe: Workers 16 Years and Over)

Group	Number	%
Total Population	2,362	11.6
Hispanic or Latino (of any race)	1,186	22.7
Mexican	1,092	25.7

Homeownership Rate
(Universe: Occupied Housing Units)

Group	%
Total Population	43.6
Hispanic or Latino (of any race)	7.7
Central American, ex. Mexican	4.5
Guatemalan	6.3
Honduran	1.7
Nicaraguan	2.1
Salvadoran	3.2
Cuban	57.6
Mexican	2.6
Puerto Rican	33.9
South American	30.0
Colombian	38.9
Peruvian	9.1

Notes: (1) Percent of total population; (2) Percent of Hispanic/Latino population; Profiles include places with an overall population of at least 125,000, OR an overall population of at least 25,000 where the Hispanic/Latino population is at least 20% of the overall population. In states where less than five places meet either of these criteria, we have included places with at least 10,000 total population with the highest percentage of Hispanic/Latino population. These places are identified with an asterisk (*); Please refer to the User's Guide for a full explanation of data.

Spaniard	44.4

Median Home Value

Group	Dollars
Total Population	402,900
Hispanic or Latino (of any race)	242,400
Mexican	328,600

Median Gross Rent

Group	Dollars
Total Population	994
Hispanic or Latino (of any race)	923
Mexican	925

Median Household Income
(2010 Inflation-Adjusted Dollars)

Group	Dollars
Total Population	58,112
Hispanic or Latino (of any race)	34,000
Mexican	27,392

Per Capita Income
(2010 Inflation-Adjusted Dollars)

Group	Dollars
Total Population	37,889
Hispanic or Latino (of any race)	10,350
Mexican	8,498

Households with $100,000+ Income

Group	Number	%
Total Population	4,462	29.9
Hispanic or Latino (of any race)	112	3.7
Mexican	42	1.8

Households with Food Stamps/SNAP Benefits During Past 12 Months

Group	Number	%
Total Population	533	3.6
Hispanic or Latino (of any race)	175	5.7
Mexican	152	6.7

Poverty Rate
(Income in Past 12 Months Below Poverty Level)

Group	%
Total Population	16.4
Hispanic or Latino (of any race)	33.6
Mexican	37.1

Savannah

Population

Group	Number	%TP[1]	%HP[2]
Total Population	136,286	100.0	–
Hispanic or Latino (of any race)	6,392	4.7	100.0
Central American, ex. Mexican	547	0.4	8.6
Honduran	126	0.1	2.0
Panamanian	166	0.1	2.6
Cuban	252	0.2	3.9
Dominican Republic	179	0.1	2.8
Mexican	2,876	2.1	45.0
Puerto Rican	1,401	1.0	21.9
South American	513	0.4	8.0
Colombian	197	0.1	3.1
Spaniard	126	0.1	2.0

Population Growth: 2000–2010

Group	%
Total Population	3.6
Hispanic or Latino (of any race)	117.6
Central American, ex. Mexican	202.2
Panamanian	33.9
Cuban	68.0
Mexican	160.5
Puerto Rican	74.5
South American	233.1

Males per 100 Females

Group	Number
Total Population	92.0
Hispanic or Latino (of any race)	118.2
Central American, ex. Mexican	104.1
Honduran	90.9
Panamanian	78.5
Cuban	80.0
Dominican Republic	88.4
Mexican	149.7
Puerto Rican	95.9
South American	72.7
Colombian	80.7
Spaniard	96.9

Average Household Size

Group	People
Total Population	2.40
Hispanic or Latino (of any race)	2.90
Central American, ex. Mexican	2.71
Honduran	2.85
Panamanian	2.37
Cuban	2.12
Dominican Republic	2.45
Mexican	3.53
Puerto Rican	2.57
South American	2.47
Colombian	2.62
Spaniard	2.44

Median Age

Group	Years
Total Population	31.3
Hispanic or Latino (of any race)	24.8
Central American, ex. Mexican	24.7
Honduran	24.0
Panamanian	23.9
Cuban	27.3
Dominican Republic	23.9
Mexican	24.9
Puerto Rican	23.7
South American	24.4
Colombian	25.3
Spaniard	32.0

High School Graduates
(Universe: Population 25 Years and Over)

Group	Number	%
Total Population	69,044	83.5
Hispanic or Latino (of any race)	2,139	64.7
Mexican	904	50.8
Puerto Rican	553	90.2

Four-Year College Graduates
(Universe: Population 25 Years and Over)

Group	Number	%
Total Population	19,250	23.3
Hispanic or Latino (of any race)	595	18.0
Mexican	120	6.7
Puerto Rican	145	23.7

Population Age 3–17 Enrolled in Public School
(Universe: Population Age 3–17 Enrolled in School)

Group	Number	%
Total Population	19,333	87.0
Hispanic or Latino (of any race)	573	91.7
Mexican	296	100.0
Puerto Rican	152	94.4

Population Age 3–17 Enrolled in Private School
(Universe: Population Age 3–17 Enrolled in School)

Group	Number	%
Total Population	2,877	13.0
Hispanic or Latino (of any race)	52	8.3
Mexican	0	0.0
Puerto Rican	9	5.6

Foreign-Born Population

Group	Number	%
Total Population	7,417	5.5
Hispanic or Latino (of any race)	3,138	52.0
Mexican	2,335	66.9
Puerto Rican	22	2.2

Foreign-Born Naturalized U.S. Citizens

Group	Number	%
Total Population	2,398	32.3
Hispanic or Latino (of any race)	403	12.8
Mexican	125	5.4
Puerto Rican	0	0.0

Language Spoken at Home: English Only
(Universe: Population 5 Years and Over)

Group	Number	%
Total Population	116,169	93.1
Hispanic or Latino (of any race)	1,410	25.6
Mexican	393	12.9
Puerto Rican	414	42.1

Language Spoken at Home: Spanish
(Universe: Population 5 Years and Over)

Group	Number	%
Total Population	4,931	4.0
Hispanic or Latino (of any race)	4,090	74.1
Mexican	2,655	87.1
Puerto Rican	569	57.9

Unemployment Rate
(Universe: Population 16 Years and Over)

Group	%
Total Population	8.0
Hispanic or Latino (of any race)	6.7
Mexican	6.3
Puerto Rican	11.9

Class of Worker: Private Wage and Salary
(Universe: Civilian Employed Population 16 Years and Over)

Group	Number	%
Total Population	45,134	79.4
Hispanic or Latino (of any race)	2,628	86.6
Mexican	1,758	93.7
Puerto Rican	283	73.3

Class of Worker: Government
(Universe: Civilian Employed Population 16 Years and Over)

Group	Number	%
Total Population	8,329	14.7
Hispanic or Latino (of any race)	295	9.7
Mexican	60	3.2
Puerto Rican	72	18.7

Means of Transportation to Work: Car, Truck or Van
(Universe: Workers 16 Years and Over)

Group	Number	%
Total Population	49,595	87.2
Hispanic or Latino (of any race)	2,665	83.7
Mexican	1,684	88.8
Puerto Rican	392	79.8

Means of Transportation to Work: Public Transportation (ex. Taxicab)
(Universe: Workers 16 Years and Over)

Group	Number	%
Total Population	2,690	4.7
Hispanic or Latino (of any race)	212	6.7
Mexican	165	8.7
Puerto Rican	0	0.0

Homeownership Rate
(Universe: Occupied Housing Units)

Group	%
Total Population	46.6
Hispanic or Latino (of any race)	28.5
Central American, ex. Mexican	28.0
Honduran	21.2
Panamanian	29.4
Cuban	40.5
Dominican Republic	24.5
Mexican	26.0
Puerto Rican	30.3
South American	30.3
Colombian	26.2
Spaniard	45.6

Median Home Value

Group	Dollars
Total Population	144,900
Hispanic or Latino (of any race)	191,400
Mexican	220,300
Puerto Rican	197,400

Median Gross Rent

Group	Dollars
Total Population	815
Hispanic or Latino (of any race)	822

Notes: (1) Percent of total population; (2) Percent of Hispanic/Latino population; Profiles include places with an overall population of at least 125,000, OR an overall population of at least 25,000 where the Hispanic/Latino population is at least 20% of the overall population. In states where less than five places meet either of these criteria, we have included places with at least 10,000 total population with the highest percentage of Hispanic/Latino population. These places are identified with an asterisk (*); Please refer to the User's Guide for a full explanation of data.

Mexican	784
Puerto Rican	800

Median Household Income
(2010 Inflation-Adjusted Dollars)

Group	Dollars
Total Population	33,316
Hispanic or Latino (of any race)	36,892
Mexican	35,805
Puerto Rican	49,219

Per Capita Income
(2010 Inflation-Adjusted Dollars)

Group	Dollars
Total Population	19,836
Hispanic or Latino (of any race)	15,891
Mexican	12,427
Puerto Rican	22,104

Households with $100,000+ Income

Group	Number	%
Total Population	5,026	9.6
Hispanic or Latino (of any race)	159	8.3
Mexican	63	7.2
Puerto Rican	38	9.0

Households with Food Stamps/SNAP Benefits During Past 12 Months

Group	Number	%
Total Population	4,999	9.5
Hispanic or Latino (of any race)	44	2.3
Mexican	11	1.3
Puerto Rican	0	0.0

Poverty Rate
(Income in Past 12 Months Below Poverty Level)

Group	%
Total Population	23.8
Hispanic or Latino (of any race)	30.2
Mexican	25.9
Puerto Rican	18.0

Notes: (1) Percent of total population; (2) Percent of Hispanic/Latino population; Profiles include places with an overall population of at least 125,000, OR an overall population of at least 25,000 where the Hispanic/Latino population is at least 20% of the overall population. In states where less than five places meet either of these criteria, we have included places with at least 10,000 total population with the highest percentage of Hispanic/Latino population. These places are identified with an asterisk (*); Please refer to the User's Guide for a full explanation of data.

Hawaii

EDITOR'S NOTE: For a place to be included in this edition, it must meet one of two criteria. Either its overall population is at least 125,000, OR its overall population is at least 25,000 and its Hispanic/Latino population is at least 20% of the overall population. In Hawaii, less than five places meet either of these criteria. In an effort to include at least five places for each state, we have included places with at least 10,000 total population with the highest percentage of Hispanic/Latino population. These places are identified with an asterisk (*). For the state of Hawaii, the following locations are included:

Hawaiian Paradise Park*
Makakilo*
Schofield Barracks*
Urban Honolulu
Waianae*

Section Two: State & Place Profiles starts with the state profile, followed by place profiles that meet the criteria above. Places are listed alphabetically within each state. All states, all counties and places that meet the above criteria are ranked and compared in *Section Three: Rankings & Comparisons*, on page 1055.

For a more detailed look at the Hispanic/Latino population in Hawaii, a companion web site is available at no additional charge with purchase of this print edition. Visit http://gold.greyhouse.com/page/info_hispanic for more information.

The web site includes data for all counties and places in Hawaii with Hispanic/Latino population, plus ten additional topics: Self Employed Worker; Walked to Work; Worked from Home; Mean Travel Time to Work; Mean Household Income; Households with Cash Public Assistance; Mean Cash Pubic Assistance; Poverty Rates for 18 and Under, 18 to 64, and 65 and Over.

Population

Group	Number	%TP[1]	%HP[2]
Total Population	1,360,301	100.0	–
Hispanic or Latino (of any race)	120,842	8.9	100.0
Central American, ex. Mexican	2,962	0.2	2.5
Costa Rican	289	<0.1	0.2
Guatemalan	565	<0.1	0.5
Honduran	390	<0.1	0.3
Nicaraguan	336	<0.1	0.3
Panamanian	527	<0.1	0.4
Salvadoran	801	0.1	0.7
Cuban	1,544	0.1	1.3
Dominican Republic	600	<0.1	0.5
Mexican	35,415	2.6	29.3
Puerto Rican	44,116	3.2	36.5
South American	3,549	0.3	2.9
Argentinean	588	<0.1	0.5
Bolivian	131	<0.1	0.1
Chilean	408	<0.1	0.3
Colombian	904	0.1	0.7
Ecuadorian	362	<0.1	0.3
Peruvian	721	0.1	0.6
Venezuelan	287	<0.1	0.2
Spaniard	10,265	0.8	8.5

Population Growth: 2000–2010

Group	%
Total Population	12.3
Hispanic or Latino (of any race)	37.8
Central American, ex. Mexican	133.4
Costa Rican	175.2
Guatemalan	112.4
Honduran	219.7
Nicaraguan	197.3
Panamanian	31.4
Salvadoran	256.0
Cuban	117.2
Dominican Republic	145.9
Mexican	78.7
Puerto Rican	47.0
South American	146.6
Argentinean	269.8
Chilean	209.1
Colombian	120.5
Ecuadorian	160.4
Peruvian	109.0
Venezuelan	145.3
Spaniard	978.3

Males per 100 Females

Group	Number
Total Population	100.3
Hispanic or Latino (of any race)	102.2
Central American, ex. Mexican	105.7
Costa Rican	82.9
Guatemalan	128.7
Honduran	105.3
Nicaraguan	108.7
Panamanian	86.2
Salvadoran	114.7
Cuban	106.7
Dominican Republic	123.9
Mexican	111.0
Puerto Rican	103.3
South American	96.8
Argentinean	126.2
Bolivian	79.5
Chilean	88.0
Colombian	84.9
Ecuadorian	116.8
Peruvian	90.7
Venezuelan	92.6
Spaniard	86.7

Average Household Size

Group	People
Total Population	2.89
Hispanic or Latino (of any race)	3.17
Central American, ex. Mexican	3.01
Costa Rican	2.63
Guatemalan	3.26
Honduran	3.24
Nicaraguan	2.94
Panamanian	2.82
Salvadoran	3.05
Cuban	2.66
Dominican Republic	2.84
Mexican	3.08
Puerto Rican	3.30
South American	2.69
Argentinean	2.68
Bolivian	2.66
Chilean	2.83
Colombian	2.52
Ecuadorian	2.72
Peruvian	2.89
Venezuelan	2.51
Spaniard	3.18

Median Age

Group	Years
Total Population	38.6
Hispanic or Latino (of any race)	24.9
Central American, ex. Mexican	26.1
Costa Rican	28.6
Guatemalan	26.0
Honduran	24.9
Nicaraguan	26.6
Panamanian	29.0
Salvadoran	24.4
Cuban	26.4
Dominican Republic	23.2
Mexican	23.9
Puerto Rican	23.4
South American	30.0
Argentinean	31.8
Bolivian	27.9
Chilean	32.0
Colombian	28.3
Ecuadorian	28.4
Peruvian	31.3
Venezuelan	30.9
Spaniard	29.0

High School Graduates
(Universe: Population 25 Years and Over)

Group	Number	%
Total Population	811,365	89.8
Hispanic or Latino (of any race)	49,736	86.8
Central American, ex. Mexican	1,140	80.3
Salvadoran	421	84.7
Cuban	721	96.3
Mexican	13,848	87.4
Puerto Rican	15,901	83.2
South American	2,097	95.8
Peruvian	646	96.4
Spaniard	4,484	92.9

Four-Year College Graduates
(Universe: Population 25 Years and Over)

Group	Number	%
Total Population	266,095	29.4
Hispanic or Latino (of any race)	9,995	17.5
Central American, ex. Mexican	408	28.8
Salvadoran	123	24.7
Cuban	269	35.9
Mexican	3,020	19.1
Puerto Rican	2,147	11.2
South American	847	38.7
Peruvian	250	37.3
Spaniard	1,042	21.6

Population Age 3–17 Enrolled in Public School
(Universe: Population Age 3–17 Enrolled in School)

Group	Number	%
Total Population	173,945	76.9
Hispanic or Latino (of any race)	25,600	84.0
Central American, ex. Mexican	549	71.4
Salvadoran	188	82.1
Cuban	237	85.6
Mexican	7,534	85.1
Puerto Rican	9,933	87.7
South American	409	67.9
Peruvian	135	74.2
Spaniard	2,022	82.2

Population Age 3–17 Enrolled in Private School
(Universe: Population Age 3–17 Enrolled in School)

Group	Number	%
Total Population	52,169	23.1
Hispanic or Latino (of any race)	4,864	16.0
Central American, ex. Mexican	220	28.6
Salvadoran	41	17.9
Cuban	40	14.4
Mexican	1,324	14.9
Puerto Rican	1,395	12.3
South American	193	32.1
Peruvian	47	25.8
Spaniard	438	17.8

Foreign-Born Population

Group	Number	%
Total Population	236,177	17.7
Hispanic or Latino (of any race)	12,312	10.7
Central American, ex. Mexican	1,185	39.4
Salvadoran	414	45.5
Cuban	296	20.0
Mexican	5,394	16.0
Puerto Rican	161	0.4
South American	1,871	53.6
Peruvian	611	54.3
Spaniard	929	10.3

Foreign-Born Naturalized U.S. Citizens

Group	Number	%
Total Population	133,315	56.4
Hispanic or Latino (of any race)	6,721	54.6

Notes: (1) Percent of total population; (2) Percent of Hispanic/Latino population; Profiles include places with an overall population of at least 125,000, OR an overall population of at least 25,000 where the Hispanic/Latino population is at least 20% of the overall population. In states where less than five places meet either of these criteria, we have included places with at least 10,000 total population with the highest percentage of Hispanic/Latino population. These places are identified with an asterisk (*); Please refer to the User's Guide for a full explanation of data.

Central American, ex. Mexican	531	44.8
Salvadoran	275	66.4
Cuban	266	89.9
Mexican	2,235	41.4
Puerto Rican	134	83.2
South American	1,293	69.1
Peruvian	531	86.9
Spaniard	646	69.5

Language Spoken at Home: English Only
(Universe: Population 5 Years and Over)

Group	Number	%
Total Population	929,303	74.5
Hispanic or Latino (of any race)	75,300	74.9
Central American, ex. Mexican	1,182	47.7
Salvadoran	366	44.6
Cuban	617	53.6
Mexican	17,891	61.6
Puerto Rican	29,854	87.3
South American	1,259	38.4
Peruvian	430	41.3
Spaniard	6,980	85.2

Language Spoken at Home: Spanish
(Universe: Population 5 Years and Over)

Group	Number	%
Total Population	25,285	2.0
Hispanic or Latino (of any race)	19,184	19.1
Central American, ex. Mexican	1,238	49.9
Salvadoran	446	54.3
Cuban	445	38.7
Mexican	10,149	34.9
Puerto Rican	3,186	9.3
South American	1,852	56.5
Peruvian	611	58.7
Spaniard	416	5.1

Unemployment Rate
(Universe: Population 16 Years and Over)

Group	%
Total Population	5.6
Hispanic or Latino (of any race)	9.6
Central American, ex. Mexican	5.6
Salvadoran	7.6
Cuban	13.7
Mexican	7.9
Puerto Rican	11.4
South American	6.5
Peruvian	2.9
Spaniard	11.0

Class of Worker: Private Wage and Salary
(Universe: Civilian Employed Population 16 Years and Over)

Group	Number	%
Total Population	455,520	71.6
Hispanic or Latino (of any race)	32,585	74.3
Central American, ex. Mexican	757	67.5
Salvadoran	350	92.8
Cuban	459	83.8
Mexican	9,879	74.9
Puerto Rican	10,088	74.0
South American	1,143	69.9
Peruvian	367	63.4
Spaniard	2,987	78.6

Class of Worker: Government
(Universe: Civilian Employed Population 16 Years and Over)

Group	Number	%
Total Population	128,536	20.2
Hispanic or Latino (of any race)	8,199	18.7
Central American, ex. Mexican	153	13.6
Salvadoran	0	0.0
Cuban	29	5.3
Mexican	2,337	17.7
Puerto Rican	2,807	20.6
South American	330	20.2
Peruvian	110	19.0
Spaniard	651	17.1

Means of Transportation to Work: Car, Truck or Van
(Universe: Workers 16 Years and Over)

Group	Number	%
Total Population	538,308	81.8
Hispanic or Latino (of any race)	39,266	81.9
Central American, ex. Mexican	1,067	74.8
Salvadoran	317	75.3
Cuban	547	77.4
Mexican	11,986	77.6
Puerto Rican	12,382	85.7
South American	1,425	79.9
Peruvian	529	86.6
Spaniard	3,118	82.6

Means of Transportation to Work: Public Transportation (ex. Taxicab)
(Universe: Workers 16 Years and Over)

Group	Number	%
Total Population	39,605	6.0
Hispanic or Latino (of any race)	2,511	5.2
Central American, ex. Mexican	65	4.6
Salvadoran	29	6.9
Cuban	0	0.0
Mexican	772	5.0
Puerto Rican	597	4.1
South American	110	6.2
Peruvian	45	7.4
Spaniard	241	6.4

Homeownership Rate
(Universe: Occupied Housing Units)

Group	%
Total Population	57.7
Hispanic or Latino (of any race)	39.5
Central American, ex. Mexican	29.2
Costa Rican	35.5
Guatemalan	26.2
Honduran	20.9
Nicaraguan	38.4
Panamanian	35.6
Salvadoran	24.1
Cuban	33.5
Dominican Republic	22.0
Mexican	30.7
Puerto Rican	41.8
South American	36.2
Argentinean	36.3
Bolivian	48.3
Chilean	38.0
Colombian	31.4
Ecuadorian	36.2
Peruvian	43.2
Venezuelan	28.0
Spaniard	54.1

Median Home Value

Group	Dollars
Total Population	537,400
Hispanic or Latino (of any race)	458,600
Central American, ex. Mexican	413,900
Salvadoran	354,300
Cuban	460,000
Mexican	429,400
Puerto Rican	419,700
South American	702,000
Peruvian	714,500
Spaniard	579,200

Median Gross Rent

Group	Dollars
Total Population	1,260
Hispanic or Latino (of any race)	1,294
Central American, ex. Mexican	1,405
Salvadoran	1,228
Cuban	1,266
Mexican	1,509
Puerto Rican	1,231
South American	1,424
Peruvian	1,325
Spaniard	1,156

Median Household Income
(2010 Inflation-Adjusted Dollars)

Group	Dollars
Total Population	66,420
Hispanic or Latino (of any race)	54,050
Central American, ex. Mexican	61,653
Salvadoran	75,222
Cuban	75,568
Mexican	52,885
Puerto Rican	50,776
South American	65,643
Peruvian	72,781
Spaniard	62,880

Per Capita Income
(2010 Inflation-Adjusted Dollars)

Group	Dollars
Total Population	28,882
Hispanic or Latino (of any race)	18,628
Central American, ex. Mexican	18,866
Salvadoran	21,168
Cuban	23,523
Mexican	19,523
Puerto Rican	16,578
South American	28,925
Peruvian	22,640
Spaniard	20,648

Households with $100,000+ Income

Group	Number	%
Total Population	127,936	28.9
Hispanic or Latino (of any race)	5,706	19.1
Central American, ex. Mexican	150	21.0
Salvadoran	22	8.7
Cuban	96	22.0
Mexican	1,592	17.9
Puerto Rican	1,607	17.0
South American	322	24.0
Peruvian	87	20.5
Spaniard	842	30.3

Households with Food Stamps/SNAP Benefits During Past 12 Months

Group	Number	%
Total Population	32,544	7.4
Hispanic or Latino (of any race)	3,966	13.3
Central American, ex. Mexican	0	0.0
Salvadoran	0	0.0
Cuban	0	0.0
Mexican	834	9.4
Puerto Rican	1,870	19.8
South American	54	4.0
Peruvian	0	0.0
Spaniard	224	8.1

Poverty Rate
(Income in Past 12 Months Below Poverty Level)

Group	%
Total Population	9.6
Hispanic or Latino (of any race)	13.7
Central American, ex. Mexican	13.3
Salvadoran	13.2
Cuban	4.7
Mexican	13.6
Puerto Rican	16.0
South American	14.1
Peruvian	11.1
Spaniard	11.4

Hawaiian Paradise Park*

Population

Group	Number	%TP[1]	%HP[2]
Total Population	11,404	100.0	–
Hispanic or Latino (of any race)	1,698	14.9	100.0
Mexican	338	3.0	19.9
Puerto Rican	898	7.9	52.9

Population Growth: 2000–2010

Group	%
Total Population	61.7
Hispanic or Latino (of any race)	70.5
Mexican	191.4
Puerto Rican	88.7

Males per 100 Females

Group	Number
Total Population	102.1
Hispanic or Latino (of any race)	99.8
Mexican	98.8
Puerto Rican	106.9

Notes: (1) Percent of total population; (2) Percent of Hispanic/Latino population; Profiles include places with an overall population of at least 125,000, OR an overall population of at least 25,000 where the Hispanic/Latino population is at least 20% of the overall population. In states where less than five places meet either of these criteria, we have included places with at least 10,000 total population with the highest percentage of Hispanic/Latino population. These places are identified with an asterisk (*); Please refer to the User's Guide for a full explanation of data.

Average Household Size

Group	People
Total Population	2.93
Hispanic or Latino (of any race)	3.35
Mexican	3.23
Puerto Rican	3.57

Median Age

Group	Years
Total Population	36.5
Hispanic or Latino (of any race)	22.8
Mexican	25.0
Puerto Rican	19.5

High School Graduates
(Universe: Population 25 Years and Over)

Group	Number	%
Total Population	4,678	91.2

Four-Year College Graduates
(Universe: Population 25 Years and Over)

Group	Number	%
Total Population	1,368	26.7

Population Age 3–17 Enrolled in Public School
(Universe: Population Age 3–17 Enrolled in School)

Group	Number	%
Total Population	1,445	88.9

Population Age 3–17 Enrolled in Private School
(Universe: Population Age 3–17 Enrolled in School)

Group	Number	%
Total Population	180	11.1

Foreign-Born Population

Group	Number	%
Total Population	656	8.4

Foreign-Born Naturalized U.S. Citizens

Group	Number	%
Total Population	314	47.9

Language Spoken at Home: English Only
(Universe: Population 5 Years and Over)

Group	Number	%
Total Population	5,661	78.0

Language Spoken at Home: Spanish
(Universe: Population 5 Years and Over)

Group	Number	%
Total Population	284	3.9

Unemployment Rate
(Universe: Population 16 Years and Over)

Group	%
Total Population	8.4

Class of Worker: Private Wage and Salary
(Universe: Civilian Employed Population 16 Years and Over)

Group	Number	%
Total Population	2,451	69.9

Class of Worker: Government
(Universe: Civilian Employed Population 16 Years and Over)

Group	Number	%
Total Population	584	16.7

Means of Transportation to Work: Car, Truck or Van
(Universe: Workers 16 Years and Over)

Group	Number	%
Total Population	3,148	92.7

Means of Transportation to Work: Public Transportation (ex. Taxicab)
(Universe: Workers 16 Years and Over)

Group	Number	%
Total Population	59	1.7

Homeownership Rate
(Universe: Occupied Housing Units)

Group	%
Total Population	73.0
Hispanic or Latino (of any race)	60.9
Mexican	59.3
Puerto Rican	56.0

Median Home Value

Group	Dollars
Total Population	283,400

Median Gross Rent

Group	Dollars
Total Population	1,157

Median Household Income
(2010 Inflation-Adjusted Dollars)

Group	Dollars
Total Population	36,051

Per Capita Income
(2010 Inflation-Adjusted Dollars)

Group	Dollars
Total Population	17,453

Households with $100,000+ Income

Group	Number	%
Total Population	315	10.8

Households with Food Stamps/SNAP Benefits During Past 12 Months

Group	Number	%
Total Population	455	15.6

Poverty Rate
(Income in Past 12 Months Below Poverty Level)

Group	%
Total Population	25.2

Makakilo*

Population

Group	Number	%TP[1]	%HP[2]
Total Population	18,248	100.0	–
Hispanic or Latino (of any race)	2,424	13.3	100.0
Mexican	505	2.8	20.8
Puerto Rican	990	5.4	40.8
Spaniard	315	1.7	13.0

Population Growth: 2000–2010

Group	%
Total Population	n/a

Males per 100 Females

Group	Number
Total Population	100.4
Hispanic or Latino (of any race)	99.7
Mexican	106.1
Puerto Rican	114.3
Spaniard	90.9

Average Household Size

Group	People
Total Population	3.35
Hispanic or Latino (of any race)	3.56
Mexican	3.29
Puerto Rican	3.77
Spaniard	3.59

Median Age

Group	Years
Total Population	33.4
Hispanic or Latino (of any race)	22.4
Mexican	22.6
Puerto Rican	21.1
Spaniard	24.2

High School Graduates
(Universe: Population 25 Years and Over)

Group	Number	%
Total Population	10,263	95.4
Hispanic or Latino (of any race)	1,118	97.0
Puerto Rican	414	92.2

Four-Year College Graduates
(Universe: Population 25 Years and Over)

Group	Number	%
Total Population	3,063	28.5
Hispanic or Latino (of any race)	222	19.3
Puerto Rican	59	13.1

Population Age 3–17 Enrolled in Public School
(Universe: Population Age 3–17 Enrolled in School)

Group	Number	%
Total Population	2,962	77.5
Hispanic or Latino (of any race)	522	84.5
Puerto Rican	324	85.0

Population Age 3–17 Enrolled in Private School
(Universe: Population Age 3–17 Enrolled in School)

Group	Number	%
Total Population	861	22.5
Hispanic or Latino (of any race)	96	15.5
Puerto Rican	57	15.0

Foreign-Born Population

Group	Number	%
Total Population	2,268	13.3
Hispanic or Latino (of any race)	231	9.7
Puerto Rican	0	0.0

Foreign-Born Naturalized U.S. Citizens

Group	Number	%
Total Population	1,505	66.4
Hispanic or Latino (of any race)	145	62.8
Puerto Rican	0	0.0

Language Spoken at Home: English Only
(Universe: Population 5 Years and Over)

Group	Number	%
Total Population	12,369	77.6
Hispanic or Latino (of any race)	1,754	82.4
Puerto Rican	904	97.1

Language Spoken at Home: Spanish
(Universe: Population 5 Years and Over)

Group	Number	%
Total Population	446	2.8
Hispanic or Latino (of any race)	374	17.6
Puerto Rican	27	2.9

Unemployment Rate
(Universe: Population 16 Years and Over)

Group	%
Total Population	5.4
Hispanic or Latino (of any race)	7.2
Puerto Rican	5.5

Class of Worker: Private Wage and Salary
(Universe: Civilian Employed Population 16 Years and Over)

Group	Number	%
Total Population	5,893	69.0
Hispanic or Latino (of any race)	856	76.5
Puerto Rican	319	68.3

Class of Worker: Government
(Universe: Civilian Employed Population 16 Years and Over)

Group	Number	%
Total Population	2,187	25.6
Hispanic or Latino (of any race)	227	20.3
Puerto Rican	148	31.7

Means of Transportation to Work: Car, Truck or Van
(Universe: Workers 16 Years and Over)

Group	Number	%
Total Population	8,103	90.5
Hispanic or Latino (of any race)	1,120	94.6
Puerto Rican	434	96.4

Means of Transportation to Work: Public Transportation (ex. Taxicab)
(Universe: Workers 16 Years and Over)

Group	Number	%
Total Population	450	5.0
Hispanic or Latino (of any race)	37	3.1
Puerto Rican	4	0.9

Homeownership Rate
(Universe: Occupied Housing Units)

Group	%
Total Population	70.2
Hispanic or Latino (of any race)	55.2
Mexican	62.6
Puerto Rican	49.3
Spaniard	62.3

Notes: (1) Percent of total population; (2) Percent of Hispanic/Latino population; Profiles include places with an overall population of at least 125,000, OR an overall population of at least 25,000 where the Hispanic/Latino population is at least 20% of the overall population. In states where less than five places meet either of these criteria, we have included places with at least 10,000 total population with the highest percentage of Hispanic/Latino population. These places are identified with an asterisk (*); Please refer to the User's Guide for a full explanation of data.

Median Home Value

Group	Dollars
Total Population	468,100
Hispanic or Latino (of any race)	442,000
Puerto Rican	620,700

Median Gross Rent

Group	Dollars
Total Population	1,551
Hispanic or Latino (of any race)	1,563
Puerto Rican	1,639

Median Household Income
(2010 Inflation-Adjusted Dollars)

Group	Dollars
Total Population	92,384
Hispanic or Latino (of any race)	68,056
Puerto Rican	63,083

Per Capita Income
(2010 Inflation-Adjusted Dollars)

Group	Dollars
Total Population	30,826
Hispanic or Latino (of any race)	21,587
Puerto Rican	21,665

Households with $100,000+ Income

Group	Number	%
Total Population	2,256	42.0
Hispanic or Latino (of any race)	74	14.7
Puerto Rican	33	23.1

Households with Food Stamps/SNAP Benefits During Past 12 Months

Group	Number	%
Total Population	211	3.9
Hispanic or Latino (of any race)	21	4.2
Puerto Rican	21	14.7

Poverty Rate
(Income in Past 12 Months Below Poverty Level)

Group	%
Total Population	3.4
Hispanic or Latino (of any race)	2.3
Puerto Rican	0.5

Schofield Barracks*

Population

Group	Number	%TP[1]	%HP[2]
Total Population	16,370	100.0	–
Hispanic or Latino (of any race)	2,835	17.3	100.0
Central American, ex. Mexican	161	1.0	5.7
Mexican	1,363	8.3	48.1
Puerto Rican	824	5.0	29.1

Population Growth: 2000–2010

Group	%
Total Population	13.5
Hispanic or Latino (of any race)	21.3
Central American, ex. Mexican	47.7
Mexican	19.2
Puerto Rican	27.0

Males per 100 Females

Group	Number
Total Population	137.5
Hispanic or Latino (of any race)	106.0
Central American, ex. Mexican	85.1
Mexican	105.6
Puerto Rican	112.4

Average Household Size

Group	People
Total Population	3.55
Hispanic or Latino (of any race)	3.51
Central American, ex. Mexican	3.63
Mexican	3.51
Puerto Rican	3.70

Median Age

Group	Years
Total Population	22.0
Hispanic or Latino (of any race)	19.8
Central American, ex. Mexican	14.8
Mexican	19.4
Puerto Rican	19.4

High School Graduates
(Universe: Population 25 Years and Over)

Group	Number	%
Total Population	4,645	97.0
Hispanic or Latino (of any race)	830	96.2
Mexican	354	96.7

Four-Year College Graduates
(Universe: Population 25 Years and Over)

Group	Number	%
Total Population	1,091	22.8
Hispanic or Latino (of any race)	115	13.3
Mexican	17	4.6

Population Age 3–17 Enrolled in Public School
(Universe: Population Age 3–17 Enrolled in School)

Group	Number	%
Total Population	2,263	90.2
Hispanic or Latino (of any race)	814	100.0
Mexican	334	100.0

Population Age 3–17 Enrolled in Private School
(Universe: Population Age 3–17 Enrolled in School)

Group	Number	%
Total Population	247	9.8
Hispanic or Latino (of any race)	0	0.0
Mexican	0	0.0

Foreign-Born Population

Group	Number	%
Total Population	605	5.0
Hispanic or Latino (of any race)	152	5.5
Mexican	17	1.2

Foreign-Born Naturalized U.S. Citizens

Group	Number	%
Total Population	324	53.6
Hispanic or Latino (of any race)	111	73.0
Mexican	17	100.0

Language Spoken at Home: English Only
(Universe: Population 5 Years and Over)

Group	Number	%
Total Population	8,786	83.7
Hispanic or Latino (of any race)	1,222	53.1
Mexican	716	65.9

Language Spoken at Home: Spanish
(Universe: Population 5 Years and Over)

Group	Number	%
Total Population	1,124	10.7
Hispanic or Latino (of any race)	1,049	45.6
Mexican	371	34.1

Unemployment Rate
(Universe: Population 16 Years and Over)

Group	%
Total Population	22.5
Hispanic or Latino (of any race)	36.2
Mexican	12.8

Class of Worker: Private Wage and Salary
(Universe: Civilian Employed Population 16 Years and Over)

Group	Number	%
Total Population	564	44.7
Hispanic or Latino (of any race)	68	28.6
Mexican	8	10.7

Class of Worker: Government
(Universe: Civilian Employed Population 16 Years and Over)

Group	Number	%
Total Population	572	45.4
Hispanic or Latino (of any race)	130	54.6
Mexican	27	36.0

Means of Transportation to Work: Car, Truck or Van
(Universe: Workers 16 Years and Over)

Group	Number	%
Total Population	3,732	61.3
Hispanic or Latino (of any race)	654	61.2
Mexican	236	42.4

Means of Transportation to Work: Public Transportation (ex. Taxicab)
(Universe: Workers 16 Years and Over)

Group	Number	%
Total Population	19	0.3
Hispanic or Latino (of any race)	0	0.0
Mexican	0	0.0

Homeownership Rate
(Universe: Occupied Housing Units)

Group	%
Total Population	0.5
Hispanic or Latino (of any race)	1.0
Central American, ex. Mexican	3.1
Mexican	0.7
Puerto Rican	1.1

Median Home Value

Group	Dollars
Total Population	–
Hispanic or Latino (of any race)	–
Mexican	–

Median Gross Rent

Group	Dollars
Total Population	2,000+
Hispanic or Latino (of any race)	2,000+
Mexican	2,000+

Median Household Income
(2010 Inflation-Adjusted Dollars)

Group	Dollars
Total Population	41,602
Hispanic or Latino (of any race)	44,755
Mexican	27,708

Per Capita Income
(2010 Inflation-Adjusted Dollars)

Group	Dollars
Total Population	18,665
Hispanic or Latino (of any race)	13,714
Mexican	14,302

Households with $100,000+ Income

Group	Number	%
Total Population	231	8.3
Hispanic or Latino (of any race)	9	1.5
Mexican	9	2.9

Households with Food Stamps/SNAP Benefits During Past 12 Months

Group	Number	%
Total Population	0	0.0
Hispanic or Latino (of any race)	0	0.0
Mexican	0	0.0

Poverty Rate
(Income in Past 12 Months Below Poverty Level)

Group	%
Total Population	18.2
Hispanic or Latino (of any race)	19.3
Mexican	35.6

Urban Honolulu

Population

Group	Number	%TP[1]	%HP[2]
Total Population	337,256	100.0	–
Hispanic or Latino (of any race)	18,301	5.4	100.0
Central American, ex. Mexican	619	0.2	3.4
Guatemalan	100	<0.1	0.5
Panamanian	133	<0.1	0.7
Salvadoran	163	<0.1	0.9
Cuban	307	0.1	1.7
Dominican Republic	133	<0.1	0.7
Mexican	5,601	1.7	30.6
Puerto Rican	5,397	1.6	29.5
South American	818	0.2	4.5
Argentinean	129	<0.1	0.7
Colombian	208	0.1	1.1
Peruvian	183	0.1	1.0
Spaniard	1,816	0.5	9.9

Notes: (1) Percent of total population; (2) Percent of Hispanic/Latino population; Profiles include places with an overall population of at least 125,000, OR an overall population of at least 25,000 where the Hispanic/Latino population is at least 20% of the overall population. In states where less than five places meet either of these criteria, we have included places with at least 10,000 total population with the highest percentage of Hispanic/Latino population. These places are identified with an asterisk (*); Please refer to the User's Guide for a full explanation of data.

Population Growth: 2000–2010

Group	%
Total Population	n/a

Males per 100 Females

Group	Number
Total Population	97.5
Hispanic or Latino (of any race)	105.9
Central American, ex. Mexican	120.3
Guatemalan	112.8
Panamanian	114.5
Salvadoran	123.3
Cuban	136.2
Dominican Republic	146.3
Mexican	116.2
Puerto Rican	106.5
South American	105.0
Argentinean	95.5
Colombian	84.1
Peruvian	117.9
Spaniard	85.1

Average Household Size

Group	People
Total Population	2.51
Hispanic or Latino (of any race)	2.55
Central American, ex. Mexican	2.34
Guatemalan	2.35
Panamanian	2.49
Salvadoran	2.25
Cuban	2.17
Dominican Republic	2.62
Mexican	2.49
Puerto Rican	2.56
South American	2.23
Argentinean	2.20
Colombian	2.09
Peruvian	2.44
Spaniard	2.66

Median Age

Group	Years
Total Population	41.3
Hispanic or Latino (of any race)	28.0
Central American, ex. Mexican	28.2
Guatemalan	29.0
Panamanian	30.5
Salvadoran	26.4
Cuban	31.9
Dominican Republic	24.4
Mexican	26.2
Puerto Rican	27.6
South American	29.9
Argentinean	31.1
Colombian	28.0
Peruvian	31.8
Spaniard	31.4

High School Graduates
(Universe: Population 25 Years and Over)

Group	Number	%
Total Population	210,841	87.6
Hispanic or Latino (of any race)	7,862	86.3
Mexican	2,219	89.6
Puerto Rican	1,832	79.8
Spaniard	787	91.1

Four-Year College Graduates
(Universe: Population 25 Years and Over)

Group	Number	%
Total Population	80,179	33.3
Hispanic or Latino (of any race)	2,379	26.1
Mexican	773	31.2
Puerto Rican	408	17.8
Spaniard	261	30.2

Population Age 3–17 Enrolled in Public School
(Universe: Population Age 3–17 Enrolled in School)

Group	Number	%
Total Population	32,300	73.2
Hispanic or Latino (of any race)	2,004	74.4
Mexican	465	72.1
Puerto Rican	556	87.3
Spaniard	188	83.6

Population Age 3–17 Enrolled in Private School
(Universe: Population Age 3–17 Enrolled in School)

Group	Number	%
Total Population	11,833	26.8
Hispanic or Latino (of any race)	690	25.6
Mexican	180	27.9
Puerto Rican	81	12.7
Spaniard	37	16.4

Foreign-Born Population

Group	Number	%
Total Population	93,847	28.4
Hispanic or Latino (of any race)	2,419	15.6
Mexican	860	19.8
Puerto Rican	9	0.2
Spaniard	97	6.9

Foreign-Born Naturalized U.S. Citizens

Group	Number	%
Total Population	49,613	52.9
Hispanic or Latino (of any race)	1,565	64.7
Mexican	478	55.6
Puerto Rican	9	100.0
Spaniard	74	76.3

Language Spoken at Home: English Only
(Universe: Population 5 Years and Over)

Group	Number	%
Total Population	195,391	62.2
Hispanic or Latino (of any race)	9,783	69.6
Mexican	2,210	57.1
Puerto Rican	3,024	87.9
Spaniard	1,082	83.9

Language Spoken at Home: Spanish
(Universe: Population 5 Years and Over)

Group	Number	%
Total Population	4,663	1.5
Hispanic or Latino (of any race)	3,158	22.5
Mexican	1,418	36.6
Puerto Rican	394	11.5
Spaniard	78	6.1

Unemployment Rate
(Universe: Population 16 Years and Over)

Group	%
Total Population	4.3
Hispanic or Latino (of any race)	10.0
Mexican	7.2
Puerto Rican	9.5
Spaniard	10.5

Class of Worker: Private Wage and Salary
(Universe: Civilian Employed Population 16 Years and Over)

Group	Number	%
Total Population	123,346	74.4
Hispanic or Latino (of any race)	5,110	72.8
Mexican	1,455	72.7
Puerto Rican	1,191	70.7
Spaniard	512	74.1

Class of Worker: Government
(Universe: Civilian Employed Population 16 Years and Over)

Group	Number	%
Total Population	30,920	18.6
Hispanic or Latino (of any race)	1,535	21.9
Mexican	507	25.3
Puerto Rican	406	24.1
Spaniard	167	24.2

Means of Transportation to Work: Car, Truck or Van
(Universe: Workers 16 Years and Over)

Group	Number	%
Total Population	119,401	70.9
Hispanic or Latino (of any race)	4,985	65.7
Mexican	1,244	54.8
Puerto Rican	1,318	71.3
Spaniard	541	77.0

Means of Transportation to Work: Public Transportation (ex. Taxicab)
(Universe: Workers 16 Years and Over)

Group	Number	%
Total Population	21,236	12.6
Hispanic or Latino (of any race)	1,129	14.9
Mexican	340	15.0
Puerto Rican	267	14.4
Spaniard	83	11.8

Homeownership Rate
(Universe: Occupied Housing Units)

Group	%
Total Population	43.8
Hispanic or Latino (of any race)	20.0
Central American, ex. Mexican	17.2
Guatemalan	5.9
Panamanian	27.7
Salvadoran	16.4
Cuban	18.3
Dominican Republic	14.9
Mexican	13.4
Puerto Rican	18.9
South American	24.3
Argentinean	27.5
Colombian	28.6
Peruvian	23.6
Spaniard	30.7

Median Home Value

Group	Dollars
Total Population	539,500
Hispanic or Latino (of any race)	406,400
Mexican	374,400
Puerto Rican	442,200
Spaniard	432,800

Median Gross Rent

Group	Dollars
Total Population	1,135
Hispanic or Latino (of any race)	1,171
Mexican	1,329
Puerto Rican	1,108
Spaniard	1,052

Median Household Income
(2010 Inflation-Adjusted Dollars)

Group	Dollars
Total Population	55,951
Hispanic or Latino (of any race)	44,936
Mexican	50,435
Puerto Rican	44,402
Spaniard	51,809

Per Capita Income
(2010 Inflation-Adjusted Dollars)

Group	Dollars
Total Population	30,002
Hispanic or Latino (of any race)	23,166
Mexican	23,329
Puerto Rican	24,215
Spaniard	22,008

Households with $100,000+ Income

Group	Number	%
Total Population	29,477	23.4
Hispanic or Latino (of any race)	765	13.4
Mexican	180	11.1
Puerto Rican	218	15.4
Spaniard	79	13.7

Households with Food Stamps/SNAP Benefits During Past 12 Months

Group	Number	%
Total Population	8,513	6.7
Hispanic or Latino (of any race)	514	9.0
Mexican	78	4.8
Puerto Rican	190	13.4
Spaniard	6	1.0

Poverty Rate
(Income in Past 12 Months Below Poverty Level)

Group	%
Total Population	11.3
Hispanic or Latino (of any race)	13.0
Mexican	11.1
Puerto Rican	13.5
Spaniard	6.8

Notes: (1) Percent of total population; (2) Percent of Hispanic/Latino population; Profiles include places with an overall population of at least 125,000, OR an overall population of at least 25,000 where the Hispanic/Latino population is at least 20% of the overall population. In states where less than five places meet either of these criteria, we have included places with at least 10,000 total population with the highest percentage of Hispanic/Latino population. These places are identified with an asterisk (*); Please refer to the User's Guide for a full explanation of data.

Waianae*

Population

Group	Number	%TP[1]	%HP[2]
Total Population	13,177	100.0	–
Hispanic or Latino (of any race)	2,099	15.9	100.0
Mexican	243	1.8	11.6
Puerto Rican	1,188	9.0	56.6
Spaniard	124	0.9	5.9

Population Growth: 2000–2010

Group	%
Total Population	25.4
Hispanic or Latino (of any race)	42.7
Mexican	66.4
Puerto Rican	98.0

Males per 100 Females

Group	Number
Total Population	97.6
Hispanic or Latino (of any race)	98.6
Mexican	115.0
Puerto Rican	107.7
Spaniard	67.6

Average Household Size

Group	People
Total Population	4.25
Hispanic or Latino (of any race)	4.23
Mexican	4.19
Puerto Rican	4.07
Spaniard	4.78

Median Age

Group	Years
Total Population	29.8
Hispanic or Latino (of any race)	19.5
Mexican	18.5
Puerto Rican	18.8
Spaniard	21.0

High School Graduates
(Universe: Population 25 Years and Over)

Group	Number	%
Total Population	6,309	87.3
Hispanic or Latino (of any race)	494	84.6
Puerto Rican	327	91.1

Four-Year College Graduates
(Universe: Population 25 Years and Over)

Group	Number	%
Total Population	654	9.0
Hispanic or Latino (of any race)	20	3.4
Puerto Rican	0	0.0

Population Age 3–17 Enrolled in Public School
(Universe: Population Age 3–17 Enrolled in School)

Group	Number	%
Total Population	2,857	89.8
Hispanic or Latino (of any race)	522	95.8
Puerto Rican	313	96.0

Population Age 3–17 Enrolled in Private School
(Universe: Population Age 3–17 Enrolled in School)

Group	Number	%
Total Population	326	10.2
Hispanic or Latino (of any race)	23	4.2
Puerto Rican	13	4.0

Foreign-Born Population

Group	Number	%
Total Population	927	7.3
Hispanic or Latino (of any race)	14	0.9
Puerto Rican	0	0.0

Foreign-Born Naturalized U.S. Citizens

Group	Number	%
Total Population	407	43.9
Hispanic or Latino (of any race)	14	100.0
Puerto Rican	0	0.0

Language Spoken at Home: English Only
(Universe: Population 5 Years and Over)

Group	Number	%
Total Population	9,449	82.8
Hispanic or Latino (of any race)	1,222	94.0
Puerto Rican	776	99.6

Language Spoken at Home: Spanish
(Universe: Population 5 Years and Over)

Group	Number	%
Total Population	11	0.1
Hispanic or Latino (of any race)	11	0.8
Puerto Rican	0	0.0

Unemployment Rate
(Universe: Population 16 Years and Over)

Group	%
Total Population	9.5
Hispanic or Latino (of any race)	15.3
Puerto Rican	18.0

Class of Worker: Private Wage and Salary
(Universe: Civilian Employed Population 16 Years and Over)

Group	Number	%
Total Population	3,565	70.0
Hispanic or Latino (of any race)	308	63.1
Puerto Rican	207	66.8

Class of Worker: Government
(Universe: Civilian Employed Population 16 Years and Over)

Group	Number	%
Total Population	1,210	23.8
Hispanic or Latino (of any race)	165	33.8
Puerto Rican	103	33.2

Means of Transportation to Work: Car, Truck or Van
(Universe: Workers 16 Years and Over)

Group	Number	%
Total Population	4,152	82.4
Hispanic or Latino (of any race)	390	83.2
Puerto Rican	252	86.6

Means of Transportation to Work: Public Transportation (ex. Taxicab)
(Universe: Workers 16 Years and Over)

Group	Number	%
Total Population	597	11.9
Hispanic or Latino (of any race)	34	7.2
Puerto Rican	9	3.1

Homeownership Rate
(Universe: Occupied Housing Units)

Group	%
Total Population	66.5
Hispanic or Latino (of any race)	51.1
Mexican	47.2
Puerto Rican	50.3
Spaniard	63.0

Median Home Value

Group	Dollars
Total Population	302,800
Hispanic or Latino (of any race)	361,200
Puerto Rican	760,600

Median Gross Rent

Group	Dollars
Total Population	1,120
Hispanic or Latino (of any race)	1,199
Puerto Rican	1,779

Median Household Income
(2010 Inflation-Adjusted Dollars)

Group	Dollars
Total Population	63,408
Hispanic or Latino (of any race)	62,833
Puerto Rican	63,167

Per Capita Income
(2010 Inflation-Adjusted Dollars)

Group	Dollars
Total Population	18,097
Hispanic or Latino (of any race)	15,016
Puerto Rican	17,537

Households with $100,000+ Income

Group	Number	%
Total Population	751	25.4
Hispanic or Latino (of any race)	74	29.6
Puerto Rican	47	32.6

Households with Food Stamps/SNAP Benefits During Past 12 Months

Group	Number	%
Total Population	678	22.9
Hispanic or Latino (of any race)	78	31.2
Puerto Rican	41	28.5

Poverty Rate
(Income in Past 12 Months Below Poverty Level)

Group	%
Total Population	15.6
Hispanic or Latino (of any race)	21.3
Puerto Rican	18.5

Notes: (1) Percent of total population; (2) Percent of Hispanic/Latino population; Profiles include places with an overall population of at least 125,000, OR an overall population of at least 25,000 where the Hispanic/Latino population is at least 20% of the overall population. In states where less than five places meet either of these criteria, we have included places with at least 10,000 total population with the highest percentage of Hispanic/Latino population. These places are identified with an asterisk (*); Please refer to the User's Guide for a full explanation of data.

Idaho

EDITOR'S NOTE: For a place to be included in this edition, it must meet one of two criteria. Either its overall population is at least 125,000, OR its overall population is at least 25,000 and its Hispanic/Latino population is at least 20% of the overall population. In Idaho, less than five places meet either of these criteria. In an effort to include at least five places for each state, we have included places with at least 10,000 total population with the highest percentage of Hispanic/Latino population. These places are identified with an asterisk (*). For the state of Idaho, the following locations are included:

Boise City
Burley*
Caldwell
Jerome*
Nampa

Section Two: State & Place Profiles starts with the state profile, followed by place profiles that meet the criteria above. Places are listed alphabetically within each state. All states, all counties and places that meet the above criteria are ranked and compared in *Section Three: Rankings & Comparisons*, on page 1055.

For a more detailed look at the Hispanic/Latino population in Idaho, a companion web site is available at no additional charge with purchase of this print edition. Visit http://gold.greyhouse.com/page/info_hispanic for more information.

The web site includes data for all counties and places in Idaho with Hispanic/Latino population, plus ten additional topics: Self Employed Worker; Walked to Work; Worked from Home; Mean Travel Time to Work; Mean Household Income; Households with Cash Public Assistance; Mean Cash Pubic Assistance; Poverty Rates for 18 and Under, 18 to 64, and 65 and Over.

Population

Group	Number	%TP[1]	%HP[2]
Total Population	1,567,582	100.0	–
Hispanic or Latino (of any race)	175,901	11.2	100.0
Central American, ex. Mexican	3,494	0.2	2.0
Costa Rican	230	<0.1	0.1
Guatemalan	1,168	0.1	0.7
Honduran	461	<0.1	0.3
Nicaraguan	222	<0.1	0.1
Panamanian	223	<0.1	0.1
Salvadoran	1,159	0.1	0.7
Cuban	825	0.1	0.5
Dominican Republic	185	<0.1	0.1
Mexican	148,923	9.5	84.7
Puerto Rican	2,910	0.2	1.7
South American	3,707	0.2	2.1
Argentinean	366	<0.1	0.2
Bolivian	122	<0.1	0.1
Chilean	336	<0.1	0.2
Colombian	734	<0.1	0.4
Ecuadorian	274	<0.1	0.2
Peruvian	1,560	0.1	0.9
Venezuelan	200	<0.1	0.1
Spaniard	3,425	0.2	1.9

Population Growth: 2000–2010

Group	%
Total Population	21.1
Hispanic or Latino (of any race)	73.0
Central American, ex. Mexican	232.4
Costa Rican	117.0
Guatemalan	263.9
Honduran	277.9
Panamanian	102.7
Salvadoran	340.7
Cuban	102.2
Mexican	87.7
Puerto Rican	92.8
South American	181.0
Argentinean	200.0
Chilean	111.3
Colombian	197.2
Peruvian	232.6
Venezuelan	90.5
Spaniard	733.3

Males per 100 Females

Group	Number
Total Population	100.4
Hispanic or Latino (of any race)	108.7
Central American, ex. Mexican	96.3
Costa Rican	85.5
Guatemalan	101.0
Honduran	96.2
Nicaraguan	91.4
Panamanian	90.6
Salvadoran	95.1
Cuban	98.3
Dominican Republic	85.0
Mexican	110.4
Puerto Rican	99.6
South American	103.7
Argentinean	96.8
Bolivian	71.8
Chilean	100.0
Colombian	76.4
Ecuadorian	97.1
Peruvian	134.6
Venezuelan	78.6
Spaniard	90.5

Average Household Size

Group	People
Total Population	2.66
Hispanic or Latino (of any race)	3.63
Central American, ex. Mexican	3.50
Costa Rican	3.04
Guatemalan	3.82
Honduran	3.87
Nicaraguan	3.31
Panamanian	2.72
Salvadoran	3.36
Cuban	2.79
Dominican Republic	3.17
Mexican	3.76
Puerto Rican	2.90
South American	3.09
Argentinean	2.91
Bolivian	2.75
Chilean	2.72
Colombian	2.99
Ecuadorian	3.14
Peruvian	3.28
Venezuelan	3.10
Spaniard	2.57

Median Age

Group	Years
Total Population	34.6
Hispanic or Latino (of any race)	22.5
Central American, ex. Mexican	27.1
Costa Rican	27.3
Guatemalan	25.8
Honduran	26.0
Nicaraguan	30.6
Panamanian	25.6
Salvadoran	28.3
Cuban	25.7
Dominican Republic	21.6
Mexican	21.9
Puerto Rican	23.7
South American	29.4
Argentinean	30.9
Bolivian	24.4
Chilean	25.6
Colombian	26.9
Ecuadorian	23.7
Peruvian	32.1
Venezuelan	26.3
Spaniard	33.6

High School Graduates
(Universe: Population 25 Years and Over)

Group	Number	%
Total Population	840,043	88.2
Hispanic or Latino (of any race)	38,779	53.1
Central American, ex. Mexican	1,099	59.0
Guatemalan	263	43.2
Salvadoran	300	50.8
Mexican	30,528	48.8
Puerto Rican	1,162	84.6
South American	1,513	88.4
Peruvian	733	87.0
Spaniard	1,583	90.2

Four-Year College Graduates
(Universe: Population 25 Years and Over)

Group	Number	%
Total Population	231,387	24.3
Hispanic or Latino (of any race)	5,724	7.8
Central American, ex. Mexican	145	7.8
Guatemalan	29	4.8
Salvadoran	46	7.8
Mexican	3,953	6.3
Puerto Rican	190	13.8
South American	511	29.8
Peruvian	193	22.9
Spaniard	338	19.3

Population Age 3–17 Enrolled in Public School
(Universe: Population Age 3–17 Enrolled in School)

Group	Number	%
Total Population	268,644	88.7
Hispanic or Latino (of any race)	42,603	94.1
Central American, ex. Mexican	455	88.2
Guatemalan	215	81.7
Salvadoran	56	100.0
Mexican	38,297	94.5
Puerto Rican	631	99.1
South American	895	84.4
Peruvian	441	90.0
Spaniard	683	93.6

Population Age 3–17 Enrolled in Private School
(Universe: Population Age 3–17 Enrolled in School)

Group	Number	%
Total Population	34,290	11.3
Hispanic or Latino (of any race)	2,648	5.9
Central American, ex. Mexican	61	11.8
Guatemalan	48	18.3
Salvadoran	0	0.0
Mexican	2,212	5.5
Puerto Rican	6	0.9
South American	165	15.6
Peruvian	49	10.0
Spaniard	47	6.4

Foreign-Born Population

Group	Number	%
Total Population	89,359	5.9
Hispanic or Latino (of any race)	53,413	33.1
Central American, ex. Mexican	2,021	59.1
Guatemalan	839	69.7
Salvadoran	569	65.5
Mexican	48,497	34.4
Puerto Rican	4	0.1
South American	1,909	54.2
Peruvian	947	61.9
Spaniard	213	7.1

Foreign-Born Naturalized U.S. Citizens

Group	Number	%
Total Population	29,286	32.8
Hispanic or Latino (of any race)	12,144	22.7
Central American, ex. Mexican	663	32.8
Guatemalan	252	30.0
Salvadoran	212	37.3

Notes: (1) Percent of total population; (2) Percent of Hispanic/Latino population; Profiles include places with an overall population of at least 125,000, OR an overall population of at least 25,000 where the Hispanic/Latino population is at least 20% of the overall population. In states where less than five places meet either of these criteria, we have included places with at least 10,000 total population with the highest percentage of Hispanic/Latino population. These places are identified with an asterisk (*); Please refer to the User's Guide for a full explanation of data.

Group	Number	%
Mexican	10,262	21.2
Puerto Rican	0	0.0
South American	782	41.0
Peruvian	338	35.7
Spaniard	122	57.3

Language Spoken at Home: English Only
(Universe: Population 5 Years and Over)

Group	Number	%
Total Population	1,263,694	89.8
Hispanic or Latino (of any race)	49,812	35.6
Central American, ex. Mexican	671	24.1
Guatemalan	128	13.0
Salvadoran	114	16.1
Mexican	39,793	32.6
Puerto Rican	1,776	67.7
South American	1,027	33.3
Peruvian	310	22.6
Spaniard	2,399	86.6

Language Spoken at Home: Spanish
(Universe: Population 5 Years and Over)

Group	Number	%
Total Population	106,792	7.6
Hispanic or Latino (of any race)	89,618	64.0
Central American, ex. Mexican	2,072	74.5
Guatemalan	823	83.3
Salvadoran	594	83.9
Mexican	82,106	67.2
Puerto Rican	831	31.7
South American	2,041	66.1
Peruvian	1,044	76.1
Spaniard	352	12.7

Unemployment Rate
(Universe: Population 16 Years and Over)

Group	%
Total Population	7.0
Hispanic or Latino (of any race)	10.1
Central American, ex. Mexican	6.0
Guatemalan	7.2
Salvadoran	8.2
Mexican	10.2
Puerto Rican	11.5
South American	5.7
Peruvian	2.2
Spaniard	14.9

Class of Worker: Private Wage and Salary
(Universe: Civilian Employed Population 16 Years and Over)

Group	Number	%
Total Population	530,315	75.9
Hispanic or Latino (of any race)	56,423	87.8
Central American, ex. Mexican	1,518	88.2
Guatemalan	545	91.3
Salvadoran	399	90.9
Mexican	49,196	88.6
Puerto Rican	1,057	79.6
South American	1,296	87.2
Peruvian	664	88.1
Spaniard	1,010	75.5

Class of Worker: Government
(Universe: Civilian Employed Population 16 Years and Over)

Group	Number	%
Total Population	108,582	15.5
Hispanic or Latino (of any race)	4,720	7.3
Central American, ex. Mexican	132	7.7
Guatemalan	11	1.8
Salvadoran	40	9.1
Mexican	3,647	6.6
Puerto Rican	212	16.0
South American	144	9.7
Peruvian	90	11.9
Spaniard	212	15.8

Means of Transportation to Work: Car, Truck or Van
(Universe: Workers 16 Years and Over)

Group	Number	%
Total Population	602,090	87.8
Hispanic or Latino (of any race)	55,824	88.6
Central American, ex. Mexican	1,515	86.8
Guatemalan	428	70.6
Salvadoran	462	100.0
Mexican	48,201	88.8
Puerto Rican	1,267	93.9
South American	1,270	85.5
Peruvian	609	80.8
Spaniard	1,089	84.1

Means of Transportation to Work: Public Transportation (ex. Taxicab)
(Universe: Workers 16 Years and Over)

Group	Number	%
Total Population	6,100	0.9
Hispanic or Latino (of any race)	541	0.9
Central American, ex. Mexican	0	0.0
Guatemalan	0	0.0
Salvadoran	0	0.0
Mexican	486	0.9
Puerto Rican	17	1.3
South American	38	2.6
Peruvian	38	5.0
Spaniard	0	0.0

Homeownership Rate
(Universe: Occupied Housing Units)

Group	%
Total Population	69.9
Hispanic or Latino (of any race)	53.1
Central American, ex. Mexican	54.0
Costa Rican	64.3
Guatemalan	46.7
Honduran	51.4
Nicaraguan	53.8
Panamanian	53.1
Salvadoran	59.8
Cuban	57.7
Dominican Republic	31.3
Mexican	53.2
Puerto Rican	46.7
South American	49.8
Argentinean	57.5
Bolivian	68.8
Chilean	50.6
Colombian	50.0
Ecuadorian	69.6
Peruvian	41.9
Venezuelan	64.0
Spaniard	64.7

Median Home Value

Group	Dollars
Total Population	172,700
Hispanic or Latino (of any race)	119,500
Central American, ex. Mexican	113,200
Guatemalan	150,000
Salvadoran	106,200
Mexican	113,400
Puerto Rican	173,000
South American	183,200
Peruvian	102,900
Spaniard	206,800

Median Gross Rent

Group	Dollars
Total Population	689
Hispanic or Latino (of any race)	636
Central American, ex. Mexican	610
Guatemalan	638
Salvadoran	632
Mexican	630
Puerto Rican	670
South American	711
Peruvian	891
Spaniard	642

Median Household Income
(2010 Inflation-Adjusted Dollars)

Group	Dollars
Total Population	46,423
Hispanic or Latino (of any race)	35,141
Central American, ex. Mexican	26,230
Guatemalan	37,829
Salvadoran	24,602
Mexican	34,787
Puerto Rican	38,042
South American	40,881
Peruvian	48,269
Spaniard	55,739

Per Capita Income
(2010 Inflation-Adjusted Dollars)

Group	Dollars
Total Population	22,518
Hispanic or Latino (of any race)	11,974
Central American, ex. Mexican	14,532
Guatemalan	8,037
Salvadoran	19,735
Mexican	11,435
Puerto Rican	13,740
South American	13,953
Peruvian	12,331
Spaniard	22,550

Households with $100,000+ Income

Group	Number	%
Total Population	77,992	13.7
Hispanic or Latino (of any race)	2,626	6.3
Central American, ex. Mexican	21	2.7
Guatemalan	0	0.0
Salvadoran	0	0.0
Mexican	1,853	5.3
Puerto Rican	160	14.7
South American	106	12.8
Peruvian	27	7.7
Spaniard	230	18.2

Households with Food Stamps/SNAP Benefits During Past 12 Months

Group	Number	%
Total Population	46,760	8.2
Hispanic or Latino (of any race)	7,261	17.5
Central American, ex. Mexican	106	13.4
Guatemalan	0	0.0
Salvadoran	42	16.5
Mexican	6,364	18.1
Puerto Rican	292	26.8
South American	43	5.2
Peruvian	2	0.6
Spaniard	198	15.7

Poverty Rate
(Income in Past 12 Months Below Poverty Level)

Group	%
Total Population	13.6
Hispanic or Latino (of any race)	26.2
Central American, ex. Mexican	27.7
Guatemalan	28.4
Salvadoran	17.2
Mexican	26.8
Puerto Rican	28.0
South American	22.5
Peruvian	26.4
Spaniard	12.3

Boise City

Population

Group	Number	%TP[1]	%HP[2]
Total Population	205,671	100.0	–
Hispanic or Latino (of any race)	14,606	7.1	100.0
Central American, ex. Mexican	483	0.2	3.3
Guatemalan	147	0.1	1.0
Salvadoran	131	0.1	0.9
Cuban	197	0.1	1.3
Mexican	11,065	5.4	75.8
Puerto Rican	488	0.2	3.3
South American	529	0.3	3.6
Colombian	204	0.1	1.4
Spaniard	577	0.3	4.0

Population Growth: 2000–2010

Group	%
Total Population	10.7
Hispanic or Latino (of any race)	73.7
Central American, ex. Mexican	222.0
Cuban	84.1
Mexican	92.2
Puerto Rican	64.3
South American	125.1

Notes: (1) Percent of total population; (2) Percent of Hispanic/Latino population; Profiles include places with an overall population of at least 125,000, OR an overall population of at least 25,000 where the Hispanic/Latino population is at least 20% of the overall population. In states where less than five places meet either of these criteria, we have included places with at least 10,000 total population with the highest percentage of Hispanic/Latino population. These places are identified with an asterisk (*); Please refer to the User's Guide for a full explanation of data.

Males per 100 Females	
Group	Number
Total Population	97.8
Hispanic or Latino (of any race)	100.9
Central American, ex. Mexican	87.2
Guatemalan	90.9
Salvadoran	87.1
Cuban	111.8
Mexican	104.1
Puerto Rican	98.4
South American	75.2
Colombian	70.0
Spaniard	83.2

Average Household Size	
Group	People
Total Population	2.36
Hispanic or Latino (of any race)	2.94
Central American, ex. Mexican	2.95
Guatemalan	3.41
Salvadoran	2.95
Cuban	2.50
Mexican	3.08
Puerto Rican	2.66
South American	2.69
Colombian	3.02
Spaniard	2.34

Median Age	
Group	Years
Total Population	35.3
Hispanic or Latino (of any race)	24.4
Central American, ex. Mexican	26.6
Guatemalan	23.8
Salvadoran	28.1
Cuban	28.3
Mexican	23.4
Puerto Rican	25.0
South American	30.6
Colombian	30.0
Spaniard	34.6

High School Graduates (Universe: Population 25 Years and Over)		
Group	Number	%
Total Population	125,669	93.2
Hispanic or Latino (of any race)	5,283	77.0
Mexican	3,732	73.2

Four-Year College Graduates (Universe: Population 25 Years and Over)		
Group	Number	%
Total Population	50,294	37.3
Hispanic or Latino (of any race)	1,560	22.7
Mexican	1,066	20.9

Population Age 3–17 Enrolled in Public School (Universe: Population Age 3–17 Enrolled in School)		
Group	Number	%
Total Population	30,173	86.6
Hispanic or Latino (of any race)	3,275	92.0
Mexican	2,743	94.8

Population Age 3–17 Enrolled in Private School (Universe: Population Age 3–17 Enrolled in School)		
Group	Number	%
Total Population	4,649	13.4
Hispanic or Latino (of any race)	284	8.0
Mexican	150	5.2

Foreign-Born Population		
Group	Number	%
Total Population	14,276	6.9
Hispanic or Latino (of any race)	3,454	24.6
Mexican	2,663	24.0

Foreign-Born Naturalized U.S. Citizens		
Group	Number	%
Total Population	5,767	40.4
Hispanic or Latino (of any race)	1,184	34.3
Mexican	757	28.4

Language Spoken at Home: English Only (Universe: Population 5 Years and Over)		
Group	Number	%
Total Population	172,859	89.8
Hispanic or Latino (of any race)	5,944	48.3
Mexican	4,416	45.8

Language Spoken at Home: Spanish (Universe: Population 5 Years and Over)		
Group	Number	%
Total Population	9,162	4.8
Hispanic or Latino (of any race)	6,201	50.4
Mexican	5,169	53.6

Unemployment Rate (Universe: Population 16 Years and Over)	
Group	%
Total Population	6.7
Hispanic or Latino (of any race)	8.6
Mexican	8.5

Class of Worker: Private Wage and Salary (Universe: Civilian Employed Population 16 Years and Over)		
Group	Number	%
Total Population	85,061	78.7
Hispanic or Latino (of any race)	5,494	84.8
Mexican	4,355	86.1

Class of Worker: Government (Universe: Civilian Employed Population 16 Years and Over)		
Group	Number	%
Total Population	15,651	14.5
Hispanic or Latino (of any race)	632	9.8
Mexican	417	8.2

Means of Transportation to Work: Car, Truck or Van (Universe: Workers 16 Years and Over)		
Group	Number	%
Total Population	92,403	86.9
Hispanic or Latino (of any race)	5,640	87.5
Mexican	4,460	88.8

Means of Transportation to Work: Public Transportation (ex. Taxicab) (Universe: Workers 16 Years and Over)		
Group	Number	%
Total Population	929	0.9
Hispanic or Latino (of any race)	20	0.3
Mexican	20	0.4

Homeownership Rate (Universe: Occupied Housing Units)	
Group	%
Total Population	61.1
Hispanic or Latino (of any race)	40.3
Central American, ex. Mexican	37.2
Guatemalan	26.1
Salvadoran	35.7
Cuban	45.5
Mexican	40.0
Puerto Rican	41.2
South American	45.7
Colombian	38.1
Spaniard	53.7

Median Home Value	
Group	Dollars
Total Population	205,000
Hispanic or Latino (of any race)	171,300
Mexican	160,800

Median Gross Rent	
Group	Dollars
Total Population	743
Hispanic or Latino (of any race)	723
Mexican	719

Median Household Income (2010 Inflation-Adjusted Dollars)	
Group	Dollars
Total Population	50,402
Hispanic or Latino (of any race)	42,831
Mexican	41,456

Per Capita Income (2010 Inflation-Adjusted Dollars)	
Group	Dollars
Total Population	28,162
Hispanic or Latino (of any race)	16,974
Mexican	15,758

Households with $100,000+ Income		
Group	Number	%
Total Population	16,006	18.6
Hispanic or Latino (of any race)	582	14.6
Mexican	303	10.4

Households with Food Stamps/SNAP Benefits During Past 12 Months		
Group	Number	%
Total Population	6,095	7.1
Hispanic or Latino (of any race)	447	11.2
Mexican	392	13.4

Poverty Rate (Income in Past 12 Months Below Poverty Level)	
Group	%
Total Population	12.3
Hispanic or Latino (of any race)	23.0
Mexican	24.2

Burley*

Population			
Group	Number	%TP[1]	%HP[2]
Total Population	10,345	100.0	–
Hispanic or Latino (of any race)	3,460	33.4	100.0
Mexican	3,183	30.8	92.0

Population Growth: 2000–2010	
Group	%
Total Population	11.0
Hispanic or Latino (of any race)	39.1
Mexican	71.4

Males per 100 Females	
Group	Number
Total Population	98.6
Hispanic or Latino (of any race)	109.1
Mexican	110.9

Average Household Size	
Group	People
Total Population	2.76
Hispanic or Latino (of any race)	3.52
Mexican	3.59

Median Age	
Group	Years
Total Population	30.8
Hispanic or Latino (of any race)	22.7
Mexican	22.3

High School Graduates (Universe: Population 25 Years and Over)		
Group	Number	%
Total Population	4,228	72.3
Hispanic or Latino (of any race)	594	37.4
Mexican	501	35.0

Four-Year College Graduates (Universe: Population 25 Years and Over)		
Group	Number	%
Total Population	862	14.7
Hispanic or Latino (of any race)	47	3.0
Mexican	38	2.7

Population Age 3–17 Enrolled in Public School (Universe: Population Age 3–17 Enrolled in School)		
Group	Number	%
Total Population	1,874	86.9
Hispanic or Latino (of any race)	997	99.3
Mexican	898	99.2

Population Age 3–17 Enrolled in Private School (Universe: Population Age 3–17 Enrolled in School)		
Group	Number	%
Total Population	283	13.1

Notes: (1) Percent of total population; (2) Percent of Hispanic/Latino population; Profiles include places with an overall population of at least 125,000, OR an overall population of at least 25,000 where the Hispanic/Latino population is at least 20% of the overall population. In states where less than five places meet either of these criteria, we have included places with at least 10,000 total population with the highest percentage of Hispanic/Latino population. These places are identified with an asterisk (*); Please refer to the User's Guide for a full explanation of data.

Hispanic or Latino (of any race)	7	0.7
Mexican	7	0.8

Foreign-Born Population

Group	Number	%
Total Population	993	10.0
Hispanic or Latino (of any race)	977	28.4
Mexican	928	29.4

Foreign-Born Naturalized U.S. Citizens

Group	Number	%
Total Population	349	35.1
Hispanic or Latino (of any race)	342	35.0
Mexican	333	35.9

Language Spoken at Home: English Only
(Universe: Population 5 Years and Over)

Group	Number	%
Total Population	6,931	78.0
Hispanic or Latino (of any race)	1,062	36.3
Mexican	931	35.1

Language Spoken at Home: Spanish
(Universe: Population 5 Years and Over)

Group	Number	%
Total Population	1,932	21.7
Hispanic or Latino (of any race)	1,867	63.7
Mexican	1,722	64.9

Unemployment Rate
(Universe: Population 16 Years and Over)

Group	%
Total Population	7.6
Hispanic or Latino (of any race)	5.1
Mexican	5.7

Class of Worker: Private Wage and Salary
(Universe: Civilian Employed Population 16 Years and Over)

Group	Number	%
Total Population	2,982	76.5
Hispanic or Latino (of any race)	1,019	84.1
Mexican	879	82.0

Class of Worker: Government
(Universe: Civilian Employed Population 16 Years and Over)

Group	Number	%
Total Population	530	13.6
Hispanic or Latino (of any race)	95	7.8
Mexican	95	8.9

Means of Transportation to Work: Car, Truck or Van
(Universe: Workers 16 Years and Over)

Group	Number	%
Total Population	3,437	93.2
Hispanic or Latino (of any race)	1,058	93.6
Mexican	943	92.9

Means of Transportation to Work: Public Transportation (ex. Taxicab)
(Universe: Workers 16 Years and Over)

Group	Number	%
Total Population	0	0.0
Hispanic or Latino (of any race)	0	0.0
Mexican	0	0.0

Homeownership Rate
(Universe: Occupied Housing Units)

Group	%
Total Population	59.9
Hispanic or Latino (of any race)	52.0
Mexican	51.8

Median Home Value

Group	Dollars
Total Population	95,600
Hispanic or Latino (of any race)	69,700
Mexican	69,500

Median Gross Rent

Group	Dollars
Total Population	539
Hispanic or Latino (of any race)	580
Mexican	567

Median Household Income
(2010 Inflation-Adjusted Dollars)

Group	Dollars
Total Population	34,257
Hispanic or Latino (of any race)	30,637
Mexican	28,924

Per Capita Income
(2010 Inflation-Adjusted Dollars)

Group	Dollars
Total Population	15,984
Hispanic or Latino (of any race)	10,330
Mexican	10,126

Households with $100,000+ Income

Group	Number	%
Total Population	196	5.5
Hispanic or Latino (of any race)	28	3.1
Mexican	19	2.4

Households with Food Stamps/SNAP Benefits During Past 12 Months

Group	Number	%
Total Population	653	18.2
Hispanic or Latino (of any race)	216	23.7
Mexican	201	25.0

Poverty Rate
(Income in Past 12 Months Below Poverty Level)

Group	%
Total Population	20.8
Hispanic or Latino (of any race)	33.4
Mexican	34.0

Caldwell

Population

Group	Number	%TP[1]	%HP[2]
Total Population	46,237	100.0	–
Hispanic or Latino (of any race)	16,347	35.4	100.0
Central American, ex. Mexican	235	0.5	1.4
Mexican	14,580	31.5	89.2
Puerto Rican	125	0.3	0.8
Spaniard	129	0.3	0.8

Population Growth: 2000–2010

Group	%
Total Population	78.1
Hispanic or Latino (of any race)	123.7
Mexican	155.7

Males per 100 Females

Group	Number
Total Population	97.5
Hispanic or Latino (of any race)	104.1
Central American, ex. Mexican	100.9
Mexican	105.1
Puerto Rican	92.3
Spaniard	81.7

Average Household Size

Group	People
Total Population	3.00
Hispanic or Latino (of any race)	4.01
Central American, ex. Mexican	4.19
Mexican	4.07
Puerto Rican	3.88
Spaniard	2.93

Median Age

Group	Years
Total Population	28.2
Hispanic or Latino (of any race)	21.0
Central American, ex. Mexican	28.5
Mexican	20.8
Puerto Rican	20.3
Spaniard	29.3

High School Graduates
(Universe: Population 25 Years and Over)

Group	Number	%
Total Population	19,062	76.0
Hispanic or Latino (of any race)	3,478	49.9
Mexican	3,090	49.5

Four-Year College Graduates
(Universe: Population 25 Years and Over)

Group	Number	%
Total Population	3,075	12.3
Hispanic or Latino (of any race)	228	3.3
Mexican	184	2.9

Population Age 3–17 Enrolled in Public School
(Universe: Population Age 3–17 Enrolled in School)

Group	Number	%
Total Population	8,354	91.9
Hispanic or Latino (of any race)	3,897	95.5
Mexican	3,616	95.4

Population Age 3–17 Enrolled in Private School
(Universe: Population Age 3–17 Enrolled in School)

Group	Number	%
Total Population	737	8.1
Hispanic or Latino (of any race)	183	4.5
Mexican	173	4.6

Foreign-Born Population

Group	Number	%
Total Population	5,672	13.0
Hispanic or Latino (of any race)	5,157	33.5
Mexican	4,644	33.3

Foreign-Born Naturalized U.S. Citizens

Group	Number	%
Total Population	1,203	21.2
Hispanic or Latino (of any race)	964	18.7
Mexican	933	20.1

Language Spoken at Home: English Only
(Universe: Population 5 Years and Over)

Group	Number	%
Total Population	28,337	72.8
Hispanic or Latino (of any race)	3,508	26.9
Mexican	2,928	24.8

Language Spoken at Home: Spanish
(Universe: Population 5 Years and Over)

Group	Number	%
Total Population	10,120	26.0
Hispanic or Latino (of any race)	9,509	73.1
Mexican	8,868	75.2

Unemployment Rate
(Universe: Population 16 Years and Over)

Group	%
Total Population	10.1
Hispanic or Latino (of any race)	13.5
Mexican	13.7

Class of Worker: Private Wage and Salary
(Universe: Civilian Employed Population 16 Years and Over)

Group	Number	%
Total Population	15,624	83.6
Hispanic or Latino (of any race)	5,402	87.7
Mexican	4,862	87.3

Class of Worker: Government
(Universe: Civilian Employed Population 16 Years and Over)

Group	Number	%
Total Population	2,023	10.8
Hispanic or Latino (of any race)	408	6.6
Mexican	384	6.9

Means of Transportation to Work: Car, Truck or Van
(Universe: Workers 16 Years and Over)

Group	Number	%
Total Population	16,420	90.2
Hispanic or Latino (of any race)	5,344	88.5
Mexican	4,840	88.9

Means of Transportation to Work: Public Transportation (ex. Taxicab)
(Universe: Workers 16 Years and Over)

Group	Number	%
Total Population	115	0.6
Hispanic or Latino (of any race)	38	0.6
Mexican	38	0.7

Notes: (1) Percent of total population; (2) Percent of Hispanic/Latino population; Profiles include places with an overall population of at least 125,000, OR an overall population of at least 25,000 where the Hispanic/Latino population is at least 20% of the overall population. In states where less than five places meet either of these criteria, we have included places with at least 10,000 total population with the highest percentage of Hispanic/Latino population. These places are identified with an asterisk (*); Please refer to the User's Guide for a full explanation of data.

Homeownership Rate
(Universe: Occupied Housing Units)

Group	%
Total Population	65.1
Hispanic or Latino (of any race)	60.7
Central American, ex. Mexican	68.5
Mexican	61.7
Puerto Rican	31.3
Spaniard	67.4

Median Home Value

Group	Dollars
Total Population	126,400
Hispanic or Latino (of any race)	111,800
Mexican	111,900

Median Gross Rent

Group	Dollars
Total Population	682
Hispanic or Latino (of any race)	663
Mexican	648

Median Household Income
(2010 Inflation-Adjusted Dollars)

Group	Dollars
Total Population	37,336
Hispanic or Latino (of any race)	33,969
Mexican	34,648

Per Capita Income
(2010 Inflation-Adjusted Dollars)

Group	Dollars
Total Population	15,731
Hispanic or Latino (of any race)	9,801
Mexican	9,888

Households with $100,000+ Income

Group	Number	%
Total Population	795	5.3
Hispanic or Latino (of any race)	119	3.1
Mexican	52	1.5

Households with Food Stamps/SNAP Benefits During Past 12 Months

Group	Number	%
Total Population	2,662	17.7
Hispanic or Latino (of any race)	1,104	28.9
Mexican	971	28.6

Poverty Rate
(Income in Past 12 Months Below Poverty Level)

Group	%
Total Population	20.2
Hispanic or Latino (of any race)	31.3
Mexican	32.3

Jerome*

Population

Group	Number	%TP[1]	%HP[2]
Total Population	10,890	100.0	–
Hispanic or Latino (of any race)	3,739	34.3	100.0
Mexican	3,342	30.7	89.4

Population Growth: 2000–2010

Group	%
Total Population	40.0
Hispanic or Latino (of any race)	184.1
Mexican	216.2

Males per 100 Females

Group	Number
Total Population	101.8
Hispanic or Latino (of any race)	115.6
Mexican	117.3

Average Household Size

Group	People
Total Population	2.92
Hispanic or Latino (of any race)	4.06
Mexican	4.11

Median Age

Group	Years
Total Population	28.9
Hispanic or Latino (of any race)	21.6
Mexican	21.4

High School Graduates
(Universe: Population 25 Years and Over)

Group	Number	%
Total Population	3,873	65.6
Hispanic or Latino (of any race)	366	25.3
Mexican	325	23.7

Four-Year College Graduates
(Universe: Population 25 Years and Over)

Group	Number	%
Total Population	429	7.3
Hispanic or Latino (of any race)	29	2.0
Mexican	29	2.1

Population Age 3–17 Enrolled in Public School
(Universe: Population Age 3–17 Enrolled in School)

Group	Number	%
Total Population	2,012	93.9
Hispanic or Latino (of any race)	924	98.0
Mexican	904	97.9

Population Age 3–17 Enrolled in Private School
(Universe: Population Age 3–17 Enrolled in School)

Group	Number	%
Total Population	130	6.1
Hispanic or Latino (of any race)	19	2.0
Mexican	19	2.1

Foreign-Born Population

Group	Number	%
Total Population	1,867	18.3
Hispanic or Latino (of any race)	1,736	50.5
Mexican	1,643	49.8

Foreign-Born Naturalized U.S. Citizens

Group	Number	%
Total Population	471	25.2
Hispanic or Latino (of any race)	423	24.4
Mexican	423	25.7

Language Spoken at Home: English Only
(Universe: Population 5 Years and Over)

Group	Number	%
Total Population	7,079	78.5
Hispanic or Latino (of any race)	991	34.7
Mexican	949	34.6

Language Spoken at Home: Spanish
(Universe: Population 5 Years and Over)

Group	Number	%
Total Population	1,882	20.9
Hispanic or Latino (of any race)	1,867	65.3
Mexican	1,796	65.4

Unemployment Rate
(Universe: Population 16 Years and Over)

Group	%
Total Population	4.1
Hispanic or Latino (of any race)	0.8
Mexican	0.8

Class of Worker: Private Wage and Salary
(Universe: Civilian Employed Population 16 Years and Over)

Group	Number	%
Total Population	3,814	86.0
Hispanic or Latino (of any race)	1,379	97.4
Mexican	1,326	97.3

Class of Worker: Government
(Universe: Civilian Employed Population 16 Years and Over)

Group	Number	%
Total Population	402	9.1
Hispanic or Latino (of any race)	24	1.7
Mexican	24	1.8

Means of Transportation to Work: Car, Truck or Van
(Universe: Workers 16 Years and Over)

Group	Number	%
Total Population	4,179	95.7
Hispanic or Latino (of any race)	1,387	98.0
Mexican	1,334	97.9

Means of Transportation to Work: Public Transportation (ex. Taxicab)
(Universe: Workers 16 Years and Over)

Group	Number	%
Total Population	0	0.0
Hispanic or Latino (of any race)	0	0.0
Mexican	0	0.0

Homeownership Rate
(Universe: Occupied Housing Units)

Group	%
Total Population	60.1
Hispanic or Latino (of any race)	45.3
Mexican	45.0

Median Home Value

Group	Dollars
Total Population	100,600
Hispanic or Latino (of any race)	106,500
Mexican	111,900

Median Gross Rent

Group	Dollars
Total Population	640
Hispanic or Latino (of any race)	622
Mexican	607

Median Household Income
(2010 Inflation-Adjusted Dollars)

Group	Dollars
Total Population	32,635
Hispanic or Latino (of any race)	29,343
Mexican	29,331

Per Capita Income
(2010 Inflation-Adjusted Dollars)

Group	Dollars
Total Population	14,681
Hispanic or Latino (of any race)	9,341
Mexican	9,325

Households with $100,000+ Income

Group	Number	%
Total Population	118	3.2
Hispanic or Latino (of any race)	12	1.4
Mexican	12	1.5

Households with Food Stamps/SNAP Benefits During Past 12 Months

Group	Number	%
Total Population	514	13.9
Hispanic or Latino (of any race)	154	18.5
Mexican	154	19.4

Poverty Rate
(Income in Past 12 Months Below Poverty Level)

Group	%
Total Population	20.9
Hispanic or Latino (of any race)	26.7
Mexican	27.9

Nampa

Population

Group	Number	%TP[1]	%HP[2]
Total Population	81,557	100.0	–
Hispanic or Latino (of any race)	18,653	22.9	100.0
Central American, ex. Mexican	534	0.7	2.9
Guatemalan	142	0.2	0.8
Salvadoran	241	0.3	1.3
Mexican	16,237	19.9	87.0
Puerto Rican	244	0.3	1.3
South American	204	0.3	1.1
Spaniard	213	0.3	1.1

Population Growth: 2000–2010

Group	%
Total Population	57.2
Hispanic or Latino (of any race)	101.0
Central American, ex. Mexican	418.4
Mexican	119.8

Notes: (1) Percent of total population; (2) Percent of Hispanic/Latino population; Profiles include places with an overall population of at least 125,000, OR an overall population of at least 25,000 where the Hispanic/Latino population is at least 20% of the overall population. In states where less than five places meet either of these criteria, we have included places with at least 10,000 total population with the highest percentage of Hispanic/Latino population. These places are identified with an asterisk (*); Please refer to the User's Guide for a full explanation of data.

Males per 100 Females

Group	Number
Total Population	96.0
Hispanic or Latino (of any race)	101.2
Central American, ex. Mexican	96.3
Guatemalan	79.7
Salvadoran	104.2
Mexican	102.3
Puerto Rican	100.0
South American	88.9
Spaniard	93.6

Average Household Size

Group	People
Total Population	2.88
Hispanic or Latino (of any race)	3.80
Central American, ex. Mexican	3.94
Guatemalan	4.52
Salvadoran	3.68
Mexican	3.87
Puerto Rican	3.17
South American	2.78
Spaniard	2.76

Median Age

Group	Years
Total Population	30.1
Hispanic or Latino (of any race)	21.3
Central American, ex. Mexican	29.3
Guatemalan	29.5
Salvadoran	29.3
Mexican	21.0
Puerto Rican	21.8
South American	28.1
Spaniard	31.6

High School Graduates
(Universe: Population 25 Years and Over)

Group	Number	%
Total Population	36,883	83.8
Hispanic or Latino (of any race)	3,655	51.6
Mexican	2,991	48.6

Four-Year College Graduates
(Universe: Population 25 Years and Over)

Group	Number	%
Total Population	7,379	16.8
Hispanic or Latino (of any race)	342	4.8
Mexican	259	4.2

Population Age 3–17 Enrolled in Public School
(Universe: Population Age 3–17 Enrolled in School)

Group	Number	%
Total Population	15,002	86.8
Hispanic or Latino (of any race)	5,054	95.2
Mexican	4,618	95.2

Population Age 3–17 Enrolled in Private School
(Universe: Population Age 3–17 Enrolled in School)

Group	Number	%
Total Population	2,279	13.2
Hispanic or Latino (of any race)	254	4.8
Mexican	234	4.8

Foreign-Born Population

Group	Number	%
Total Population	7,086	9.0
Hispanic or Latino (of any race)	5,489	31.4
Mexican	4,952	31.9

Foreign-Born Naturalized U.S. Citizens

Group	Number	%
Total Population	1,922	27.1
Hispanic or Latino (of any race)	1,142	20.8
Mexican	872	17.6

Language Spoken at Home: English Only
(Universe: Population 5 Years and Over)

Group	Number	%
Total Population	56,870	81.3
Hispanic or Latino (of any race)	4,201	28.2
Mexican	3,292	25.0

Language Spoken at Home: Spanish
(Universe: Population 5 Years and Over)

Group	Number	%
Total Population	11,556	16.5
Hispanic or Latino (of any race)	10,683	71.7
Mexican	9,850	74.9

Unemployment Rate
(Universe: Population 16 Years and Over)

Group	%
Total Population	10.6
Hispanic or Latino (of any race)	12.8
Mexican	14.3

Class of Worker: Private Wage and Salary
(Universe: Civilian Employed Population 16 Years and Over)

Group	Number	%
Total Population	25,758	80.5
Hispanic or Latino (of any race)	5,382	88.8
Mexican	4,553	90.7

Class of Worker: Government
(Universe: Civilian Employed Population 16 Years and Over)

Group	Number	%
Total Population	4,197	13.1
Hispanic or Latino (of any race)	467	7.7
Mexican	294	5.9

Means of Transportation to Work: Car, Truck or Van
(Universe: Workers 16 Years and Over)

Group	Number	%
Total Population	28,360	90.8
Hispanic or Latino (of any race)	5,191	89.4
Mexican	4,247	88.8

Means of Transportation to Work: Public Transportation (ex. Taxicab)
(Universe: Workers 16 Years and Over)

Group	Number	%
Total Population	89	0.3
Hispanic or Latino (of any race)	8	0.1
Mexican	8	0.2

Homeownership Rate
(Universe: Occupied Housing Units)

Group	%
Total Population	65.8
Hispanic or Latino (of any race)	55.8
Central American, ex. Mexican	60.5
Guatemalan	63.6
Salvadoran	58.8
Mexican	56.1
Puerto Rican	57.6
South American	71.2
Spaniard	63.4

Median Home Value

Group	Dollars
Total Population	143,700
Hispanic or Latino (of any race)	115,200
Mexican	116,300

Median Gross Rent

Group	Dollars
Total Population	741
Hispanic or Latino (of any race)	704
Mexican	696

Median Household Income
(2010 Inflation-Adjusted Dollars)

Group	Dollars
Total Population	42,697
Hispanic or Latino (of any race)	31,353
Mexican	30,333

Per Capita Income
(2010 Inflation-Adjusted Dollars)

Group	Dollars
Total Population	17,229
Hispanic or Latino (of any race)	9,235
Mexican	8,785

Households with $100,000+ Income

Group	Number	%
Total Population	1,748	6.7
Hispanic or Latino (of any race)	54	1.3
Mexican	54	1.5

Households with Food Stamps/SNAP Benefits During Past 12 Months

Group	Number	%
Total Population	3,534	13.5
Hispanic or Latino (of any race)	1,101	26.6
Mexican	986	27.4

Poverty Rate
(Income in Past 12 Months Below Poverty Level)

Group	%
Total Population	19.3
Hispanic or Latino (of any race)	35.7
Mexican	37.6

Notes: (1) Percent of total population; (2) Percent of Hispanic/Latino population; Profiles include places with an overall population of at least 125,000, OR an overall population of at least 25,000 where the Hispanic/Latino population is at least 20% of the overall population. In states where less than five places meet either of these criteria, we have included places with at least 10,000 total population with the highest percentage of Hispanic/Latino population. These places are identified with an asterisk (*); Please refer to the User's Guide for a full explanation of data.

Illinois

EDITOR'S NOTE: For a place to be included in this edition, it must meet one of two criteria. Either its overall population is at least 125,000, OR its overall population is at least 25,000 and its Hispanic/Latino population is at least 20% of the overall population. For the state of Illinois, the following locations are included:

- Addison
- Aurora
- Belvidere
- Berwyn
- Bolingbrook
- Burbank
- Carpentersville
- Chicago
- Chicago Heights
- Cicero
- Elgin
- Glendale Heights
- Hanover Park
- Joliet
- Melrose Park
- Mundelein
- Naperville
- North Chicago
- Rockford
- Romeoville
- Round Lake Beach
- Streamwood
- Waukegan
- West Chicago
- Wheeling

Section Two: State & Place Profiles starts with the state profile, followed by place profiles that meet the criteria above. Places are listed alphabetically within each state. All states, all counties and places that meet the above criteria are ranked and compared in *Section Three: Rankings & Comparisons*, on page 1055.

For a more detailed look at the Hispanic/Latino population in Illinois, a companion web site is available at no additional charge with purchase of this print edition. Visit http://gold.greyhouse.com/page/info_hispanic for more information.

The web site includes data for all counties and places in Illinois with Hispanic/Latino population, plus ten additional topics: Self Employed Worker; Walked to Work; Worked from Home; Mean Travel Time to Work; Mean Household Income; Households with Cash Public Assistance; Mean Cash Pubic Assistance; Poverty Rates for 18 and Under, 18 to 64, and 65 and Over.

Population

Group	Number	%TP[1]	%HP[2]
Total Population	12,830,632	100.0	–
Hispanic or Latino (of any race)	2,027,578	15.8	100.0
Central American, ex. Mexican	70,000	0.5	3.5
Costa Rican	1,874	<0.1	0.1
Guatemalan	35,321	0.3	1.7
Honduran	12,023	0.1	0.6
Nicaraguan	3,078	<0.1	0.2
Panamanian	2,843	<0.1	0.1
Salvadoran	14,217	0.1	0.7
Cuban	22,541	0.2	1.1
Dominican Republic	5,691	<0.1	0.3
Mexican	1,602,403	12.5	79.0
Puerto Rican	182,989	1.4	9.0
South American	67,862	0.5	3.3
Argentinean	5,294	<0.1	0.3
Bolivian	2,304	<0.1	0.1
Chilean	2,753	<0.1	0.1
Colombian	19,345	0.2	1.0
Ecuadorian	22,816	0.2	1.1
Paraguayan	423	<0.1	<0.1
Peruvian	10,213	0.1	0.5
Uruguayan	737	<0.1	<0.1
Venezuelan	3,283	<0.1	0.2
Spaniard	11,666	0.1	0.6

Population Growth: 2000–2010

Group	%
Total Population	3.3
Hispanic or Latino (of any race)	32.5
Central American, ex. Mexican	77.8
Costa Rican	49.0
Guatemalan	78.5
Honduran	100.7
Nicaraguan	105.2
Panamanian	70.6
Salvadoran	100.7
Cuban	22.3
Dominican Republic	94.0
Mexican	40.0
Puerto Rican	15.9
South American	75.5
Argentinean	110.7
Bolivian	89.3
Chilean	59.4
Colombian	63.2
Ecuadorian	89.2
Paraguayan	53.8
Peruvian	85.3
Uruguayan	129.6
Venezuelan	110.2
Spaniard	467.7

Males per 100 Females

Group	Number
Total Population	96.2
Hispanic or Latino (of any race)	106.7
Central American, ex. Mexican	101.2
Costa Rican	81.4
Guatemalan	108.0
Honduran	100.3
Nicaraguan	87.9
Panamanian	67.9
Salvadoran	100.4
Cuban	101.2
Dominican Republic	87.6
Mexican	108.8
Puerto Rican	95.1
South American	94.4
Argentinean	97.5
Bolivian	90.4
Chilean	90.5
Colombian	80.6
Ecuadorian	113.1
Paraguayan	88.0
Peruvian	89.1
Uruguayan	102.5
Venezuelan	83.4
Spaniard	93.4

Average Household Size

Group	People
Total Population	2.59
Hispanic or Latino (of any race)	3.78
Central American, ex. Mexican	3.59
Costa Rican	2.82
Guatemalan	3.66
Honduran	3.68
Nicaraguan	3.30
Panamanian	2.60
Salvadoran	3.79
Cuban	2.58
Dominican Republic	2.90
Mexican	4.02
Puerto Rican	2.95
South American	3.07
Argentinean	2.60
Bolivian	2.81
Chilean	2.60
Colombian	2.83
Ecuadorian	3.66
Paraguayan	2.51
Peruvian	2.93
Uruguayan	2.90
Venezuelan	2.76
Spaniard	2.55

Median Age

Group	Years
Total Population	36.6
Hispanic or Latino (of any race)	26.4
Central American, ex. Mexican	30.7
Costa Rican	31.2
Guatemalan	30.6
Honduran	30.4
Nicaraguan	30.9
Panamanian	31.7
Salvadoran	30.8
Cuban	33.5
Dominican Republic	28.7
Mexican	25.6
Puerto Rican	28.6
South American	33.3
Argentinean	35.6
Bolivian	34.5
Chilean	34.3
Colombian	33.5
Ecuadorian	32.1
Paraguayan	22.0
Peruvian	35.3
Uruguayan	35.8
Venezuelan	32.0
Spaniard	32.7

High School Graduates

(Universe: Population 25 Years and Over)

Group	Number	%
Total Population	7,194,979	86.2
Hispanic or Latino (of any race)	602,728	59.5
Central American, ex. Mexican	26,021	64.4
Costa Rican	1,182	83.2
Guatemalan	12,956	64.1
Honduran	4,266	61.9
Nicaraguan	1,216	77.7
Panamanian	1,402	93.9
Salvadoran	4,335	56.6
Cuban	10,644	81.0
Dominican Republic	2,637	78.8
Mexican	430,416	55.2
Puerto Rican	70,993	70.8
South American	38,751	82.9
Argentinean	3,751	90.5
Bolivian	1,171	95.6
Chilean	1,657	86.3
Colombian	11,181	87.4
Ecuadorian	11,067	70.4
Peruvian	6,260	89.9
Venezuelan	1,896	94.3
Spaniard	6,092	91.4

Four-Year College Graduates

(Universe: Population 25 Years and Over)

Group	Number	%
Total Population	2,526,884	30.3
Hispanic or Latino (of any race)	119,375	11.8
Central American, ex. Mexican	6,639	16.4
Costa Rican	619	43.6
Guatemalan	2,877	14.2
Honduran	924	13.4
Nicaraguan	276	17.6
Panamanian	774	51.8
Salvadoran	986	12.9
Cuban	4,742	36.1
Dominican Republic	999	29.8
Mexican	67,905	8.7
Puerto Rican	14,343	14.3
South American	16,393	35.1
Argentinean	2,093	50.5
Bolivian	627	51.2
Chilean	873	45.5

Notes: (1) Percent of total population; (2) Percent of Hispanic/Latino population; Profiles include places with an overall population of at least 125,000, OR an overall population of at least 25,000 where the Hispanic/Latino population is at least 20% of the overall population. In states where less than five places meet either of these criteria, we have included places with at least 10,000 total population with the highest percentage of Hispanic/Latino population. These places are identified with an asterisk (*); Please refer to the User's Guide for a full explanation of data.

Group	Number	%
Colombian	4,876	38.1
Ecuadorian	3,205	20.4
Peruvian	2,967	42.6
Venezuelan	1,076	53.5
Spaniard	2,841	42.6

Population Age 3–17 Enrolled in Public School
(Universe: Population Age 3–17 Enrolled in School)

Group	Number	%
Total Population	2,074,471	85.5
Hispanic or Latino (of any race)	458,353	91.5
Central American, ex. Mexican	11,550	85.7
Costa Rican	419	77.2
Guatemalan	6,050	84.4
Honduran	2,017	95.2
Nicaraguan	389	76.6
Panamanian	378	71.2
Salvadoran	2,090	89.0
Cuban	3,619	76.0
Dominican Republic	1,032	88.5
Mexican	378,866	92.8
Puerto Rican	35,277	88.0
South American	12,044	81.1
Argentinean	1,145	88.1
Bolivian	379	76.0
Chilean	536	81.8
Colombian	3,865	86.0
Ecuadorian	3,970	82.8
Peruvian	1,391	68.1
Venezuelan	484	77.4
Spaniard	1,773	88.4

Population Age 3–17 Enrolled in Private School
(Universe: Population Age 3–17 Enrolled in School)

Group	Number	%
Total Population	351,622	14.5
Hispanic or Latino (of any race)	42,799	8.5
Central American, ex. Mexican	1,925	14.3
Costa Rican	124	22.8
Guatemalan	1,122	15.6
Honduran	102	4.8
Nicaraguan	119	23.4
Panamanian	153	28.8
Salvadoran	258	11.0
Cuban	1,141	24.0
Dominican Republic	134	11.5
Mexican	29,575	7.2
Puerto Rican	4,796	12.0
South American	2,799	18.9
Argentinean	154	11.9
Bolivian	120	24.0
Chilean	119	18.2
Colombian	631	14.0
Ecuadorian	822	17.2
Peruvian	651	31.9
Venezuelan	141	22.6
Spaniard	232	11.6

Foreign-Born Population

Group	Number	%
Total Population	1,736,696	13.6
Hispanic or Latino (of any race)	802,182	41.4
Central American, ex. Mexican	40,977	62.4
Costa Rican	1,245	51.4
Guatemalan	20,779	62.6
Honduran	7,261	67.5
Nicaraguan	1,386	60.3
Panamanian	1,200	47.1
Salvadoran	7,986	61.9
Cuban	8,255	37.6
Dominican Republic	3,048	56.0
Mexican	690,885	45.0
Puerto Rican	1,981	1.1
South American	44,861	60.6
Argentinean	3,365	55.0
Bolivian	1,031	48.4
Chilean	1,680	53.4
Colombian	12,270	58.9
Ecuadorian	15,953	63.6
Peruvian	6,713	63.0
Venezuelan	2,008	63.9
Spaniard	2,275	21.6

Foreign-Born Naturalized U.S. Citizens

Group	Number	%
Total Population	769,086	44.3
Hispanic or Latino (of any race)	229,654	28.6
Central American, ex. Mexican	16,209	39.6
Costa Rican	470	37.8
Guatemalan	8,820	42.4
Honduran	2,360	32.5
Nicaraguan	807	58.2
Panamanian	483	40.3
Salvadoran	2,848	35.7
Cuban	5,793	70.2
Dominican Republic	1,839	60.3
Mexican	178,596	25.9
Puerto Rican	952	48.1
South American	20,365	45.4
Argentinean	1,717	51.0
Bolivian	588	57.0
Chilean	796	47.4
Colombian	6,397	52.1
Ecuadorian	6,228	39.0
Peruvian	2,751	41.0
Venezuelan	764	38.0
Spaniard	1,122	49.3

Language Spoken at Home: English Only
(Universe: Population 5 Years and Over)

Group	Number	%
Total Population	9,315,206	78.3
Hispanic or Latino (of any race)	316,369	18.3
Central American, ex. Mexican	8,193	13.6
Costa Rican	737	34.0
Guatemalan	3,665	12.1
Honduran	783	7.9
Nicaraguan	594	26.2
Panamanian	987	42.7
Salvadoran	1,258	10.7
Cuban	8,049	40.1
Dominican Republic	990	19.7
Mexican	210,250	15.4
Puerto Rican	52,026	32.5
South American	11,240	16.5
Argentinean	1,351	24.1
Bolivian	359	19.6
Chilean	1,077	36.9
Colombian	3,863	19.9
Ecuadorian	1,889	8.2
Peruvian	1,757	18.0
Venezuelan	637	21.9
Spaniard	6,228	62.8

Language Spoken at Home: Spanish
(Universe: Population 5 Years and Over)

Group	Number	%
Total Population	1,517,245	12.7
Hispanic or Latino (of any race)	1,407,288	81.4
Central American, ex. Mexican	51,651	85.9
Costa Rican	1,404	64.8
Guatemalan	26,500	87.8
Honduran	9,049	91.4
Nicaraguan	1,575	69.6
Panamanian	1,325	57.3
Salvadoran	10,530	89.2
Cuban	11,773	58.7
Dominican Republic	4,011	79.9
Mexican	1,148,007	84.3
Puerto Rican	107,333	67.1
South American	56,517	83.0
Argentinean	4,236	75.7
Bolivian	1,464	79.8
Chilean	1,819	62.4
Colombian	15,516	80.0
Ecuadorian	20,909	91.0
Peruvian	8,012	81.9
Venezuelan	2,221	76.2
Spaniard	3,312	33.4

Unemployment Rate
(Universe: Population 16 Years and Over)

Group	%
Total Population	8.6
Hispanic or Latino (of any race)	10.0
Central American, ex. Mexican	9.2
Costa Rican	16.6
Guatemalan	9.7
Honduran	12.8
Nicaraguan	10.7
Panamanian	6.0
Salvadoran	4.9
Cuban	10.9
Dominican Republic	13.4
Mexican	9.7
Puerto Rican	13.7
South American	6.9
Argentinean	5.9
Bolivian	12.0
Chilean	13.0
Colombian	6.1
Ecuadorian	7.0
Peruvian	5.4
Venezuelan	7.8
Spaniard	8.2

Class of Worker: Private Wage and Salary
(Universe: Civilian Employed Population 16 Years and Over)

Group	Number	%
Total Population	4,965,671	81.9
Hispanic or Latino (of any race)	756,887	89.4
Central American, ex. Mexican	29,163	88.1
Costa Rican	879	83.6
Guatemalan	14,177	86.8
Honduran	4,260	86.0
Nicaraguan	1,092	89.6
Panamanian	1,150	88.7
Salvadoran	6,775	92.3
Cuban	7,820	83.7
Dominican Republic	1,949	84.1
Mexican	607,733	91.0
Puerto Rican	57,118	80.5
South American	32,544	83.5
Argentinean	2,384	76.7
Bolivian	699	74.5
Chilean	1,192	80.2
Colombian	8,811	81.6
Ecuadorian	12,057	87.6
Peruvian	4,998	85.8
Venezuelan	1,214	77.9
Spaniard	4,460	83.4

Class of Worker: Government
(Universe: Civilian Employed Population 16 Years and Over)

Group	Number	%
Total Population	780,081	12.9
Hispanic or Latino (of any race)	61,733	7.3
Central American, ex. Mexican	2,299	6.9
Costa Rican	72	6.9
Guatemalan	1,217	7.5
Honduran	359	7.2
Nicaraguan	111	9.1
Panamanian	129	10.0
Salvadoran	369	5.0
Cuban	1,258	13.5
Dominican Republic	279	12.0
Mexican	39,356	5.9
Puerto Rican	11,952	16.8
South American	3,642	9.3
Argentinean	515	16.6
Bolivian	122	13.0
Chilean	191	12.9
Colombian	1,145	10.6
Ecuadorian	736	5.3
Peruvian	625	10.7
Venezuelan	182	11.7
Spaniard	661	12.4

Means of Transportation to Work: Car, Truck or Van
(Universe: Workers 16 Years and Over)

Group	Number	%
Total Population	4,906,968	82.7
Hispanic or Latino (of any race)	681,523	82.5
Central American, ex. Mexican	26,148	81.7
Costa Rican	831	83.1
Guatemalan	12,417	78.5
Honduran	4,016	84.0
Nicaraguan	967	80.1
Panamanian	1,123	86.9
Salvadoran	6,087	86.6
Cuban	7,298	80.4
Dominican Republic	1,784	77.8

Notes: (1) Percent of total population; (2) Percent of Hispanic/Latino population; Profiles include places with an overall population of at least 125,000, OR an overall population of at least 25,000 where the Hispanic/Latino population is at least 20% of the overall population. In states where less than five places meet either of these criteria, we have included places with at least 10,000 total population with the highest percentage of Hispanic/Latino population. These places are identified with an asterisk (*); Please refer to the User's Guide for a full explanation of data.

Mexican	546,009	83.9
Puerto Rican	53,224	76.7
South American	28,180	74.3
Argentinean	2,253	75.1
Bolivian	883	94.8
Chilean	1,061	74.1
Colombian	8,555	80.7
Ecuadorian	8,734	64.9
Peruvian	4,513	80.8
Venezuelan	1,046	68.8
Spaniard	4,221	78.0

Means of Transportation to Work: Public Transportation (ex. Taxicab)

(Universe: Workers 16 Years and Over)

Group	Number	%
Total Population	515,963	8.7
Hispanic or Latino (of any race)	82,573	10.0
Central American, ex. Mexican	3,541	11.1
Costa Rican	60	6.0
Guatemalan	2,270	14.3
Honduran	421	8.8
Nicaraguan	88	7.3
Panamanian	65	5.0
Salvadoran	540	7.7
Cuban	933	10.3
Dominican Republic	334	14.6
Mexican	58,514	9.0
Puerto Rican	10,531	15.2
South American	6,188	16.3
Argentinean	341	11.4
Bolivian	0	0.0
Chilean	147	10.3
Colombian	1,136	10.7
Ecuadorian	3,565	26.5
Peruvian	722	12.9
Venezuelan	185	12.2
Spaniard	455	8.4

Homeownership Rate

(Universe: Occupied Housing Units)

Group	%
Total Population	67.5
Hispanic or Latino (of any race)	52.6
Central American, ex. Mexican	48.5
Costa Rican	53.9
Guatemalan	48.6
Honduran	41.3
Nicaraguan	54.1
Panamanian	49.9
Salvadoran	52.7
Cuban	56.0
Dominican Republic	41.5
Mexican	54.3
Puerto Rican	43.3
South American	55.8
Argentinean	62.6
Bolivian	70.7
Chilean	56.1
Colombian	56.8
Ecuadorian	52.3
Paraguayan	54.0
Peruvian	54.4
Uruguayan	56.7
Venezuelan	53.3
Spaniard	60.5

Median Home Value

Group	Dollars
Total Population	202,500
Hispanic or Latino (of any race)	219,700
Central American, ex. Mexican	252,800
Costa Rican	242,400
Guatemalan	256,400
Honduran	246,700
Nicaraguan	260,200
Panamanian	260,200
Salvadoran	239,400
Cuban	317,500
Dominican Republic	241,600
Mexican	210,600
Puerto Rican	262,100
South American	276,200
Argentinean	284,800
Bolivian	273,900
Chilean	246,500
Colombian	269,000
Ecuadorian	303,800
Peruvian	246,700
Venezuelan	291,000
Spaniard	258,100

Median Gross Rent

Group	Dollars
Total Population	834
Hispanic or Latino (of any race)	860
Central American, ex. Mexican	885
Costa Rican	783
Guatemalan	912
Honduran	829
Nicaraguan	856
Panamanian	1,048
Salvadoran	907
Cuban	874
Dominican Republic	884
Mexican	851
Puerto Rican	874
South American	947
Argentinean	1,026
Bolivian	821
Chilean	917
Colombian	929
Ecuadorian	965
Peruvian	933
Venezuelan	1,043
Spaniard	1,047

Median Household Income

(2010 Inflation-Adjusted Dollars)

Group	Dollars
Total Population	55,735
Hispanic or Latino (of any race)	47,170
Central American, ex. Mexican	48,314
Costa Rican	50,250
Guatemalan	47,171
Honduran	46,833
Nicaraguan	51,600
Panamanian	67,871
Salvadoran	48,477
Cuban	54,667
Dominican Republic	53,873
Mexican	46,580
Puerto Rican	43,925
South American	57,836
Argentinean	65,514
Bolivian	64,297
Chilean	70,568
Colombian	55,376
Ecuadorian	56,284
Peruvian	57,383
Venezuelan	59,167
Spaniard	61,952

Per Capita Income

(2010 Inflation-Adjusted Dollars)

Group	Dollars
Total Population	28,782
Hispanic or Latino (of any race)	15,528
Central American, ex. Mexican	17,907
Costa Rican	26,508
Guatemalan	16,726
Honduran	15,609
Nicaraguan	22,961
Panamanian	28,726
Salvadoran	17,866
Cuban	29,871
Dominican Republic	19,887
Mexican	14,456
Puerto Rican	18,282
South American	22,548
Argentinean	28,486
Bolivian	28,751
Chilean	27,126
Colombian	22,455
Ecuadorian	18,986
Peruvian	24,484
Venezuelan	24,704
Spaniard	29,754

Households with $100,000+ Income

Group	Number	%
Total Population	1,094,563	22.9
Hispanic or Latino (of any race)	64,807	13.2
Central American, ex. Mexican	2,690	14.3
Costa Rican	189	25.0
Guatemalan	1,270	13.6
Honduran	337	12.5
Nicaraguan	177	21.4
Panamanian	172	19.4
Salvadoran	509	13.6
Cuban	1,831	24.7
Dominican Republic	255	16.5
Mexican	44,237	12.0
Puerto Rican	7,971	14.8
South American	4,752	21.5
Argentinean	565	28.9
Bolivian	175	25.0
Chilean	288	27.1
Colombian	1,259	20.2
Ecuadorian	1,298	18.6
Peruvian	647	20.9
Venezuelan	259	23.6
Spaniard	1,116	28.5

Households with Food Stamps/SNAP Benefits During Past 12 Months

Group	Number	%
Total Population	431,798	9.1
Hispanic or Latino (of any race)	68,796	14.0
Central American, ex. Mexican	2,518	13.4
Costa Rican	56	7.4
Guatemalan	1,407	15.0
Honduran	239	8.9
Nicaraguan	143	17.3
Panamanian	76	8.6
Salvadoran	434	11.6
Cuban	993	13.4
Dominican Republic	209	13.5
Mexican	49,341	13.3
Puerto Rican	12,311	22.8
South American	1,601	7.2
Argentinean	51	2.6
Bolivian	13	1.9
Chilean	53	5.0
Colombian	626	10.0
Ecuadorian	407	5.8
Peruvian	185	6.0
Venezuelan	192	17.5
Spaniard	221	5.6

Poverty Rate

(Income in Past 12 Months Below Poverty Level)

Group	%
Total Population	12.6
Hispanic or Latino (of any race)	18.2
Central American, ex. Mexican	13.6
Costa Rican	21.7
Guatemalan	14.1
Honduran	14.3
Nicaraguan	14.5
Panamanian	17.2
Salvadoran	9.2
Cuban	13.4
Dominican Republic	15.9
Mexican	18.4
Puerto Rican	21.6
South American	11.1
Argentinean	8.9
Bolivian	16.9
Chilean	8.8
Colombian	9.6
Ecuadorian	12.4
Peruvian	11.5
Venezuelan	16.5
Spaniard	12.3

Addison

Population

Group	Number	%TP[1]	%HP[2]
Total Population	36,942	100.0	–
Hispanic or Latino (of any race)	14,813	40.1	100.0

Notes: (1) Percent of total population; (2) Percent of Hispanic/Latino population; Profiles include places with an overall population of at least 125,000, OR an overall population of at least 25,000 where the Hispanic/Latino population is at least 20% of the overall population. In states where less than five places meet either of these criteria, we have included places with at least 10,000 total population with the highest percentage of Hispanic/Latino population. These places are identified with an asterisk (*); Please refer to the User's Guide for a full explanation of data.

Group	Number	%TP	%HP
Central American, ex. Mexican	561	1.5	3.8
Guatemalan	418	1.1	2.8
Cuban	150	0.4	1.0
Mexican	12,863	34.8	86.8
Puerto Rican	493	1.3	3.3
South American	265	0.7	1.8

Population Growth: 2000–2010

Group	%
Total Population	2.9
Hispanic or Latino (of any race)	45.3
Central American, ex. Mexican	119.1
Guatemalan	121.2
Mexican	47.2
Puerto Rican	40.5
South American	96.3

Males per 100 Females

Group	Number
Total Population	100.9
Hispanic or Latino (of any race)	108.6
Central American, ex. Mexican	134.7
Guatemalan	138.9
Cuban	108.3
Mexican	107.9
Puerto Rican	103.7
South American	105.4

Average Household Size

Group	People
Total Population	3.08
Hispanic or Latino (of any race)	4.24
Central American, ex. Mexican	4.17
Guatemalan	4.16
Cuban	3.00
Mexican	4.36
Puerto Rican	3.32
South American	3.57

Median Age

Group	Years
Total Population	33.7
Hispanic or Latino (of any race)	25.6
Central American, ex. Mexican	29.3
Guatemalan	28.6
Cuban	38.0
Mexican	25.0
Puerto Rican	29.3
South American	38.2

High School Graduates
(Universe: Population 25 Years and Over)

Group	Number	%
Total Population	18,812	79.2
Hispanic or Latino (of any race)	4,581	57.6
Mexican	3,787	54.1

Four-Year College Graduates
(Universe: Population 25 Years and Over)

Group	Number	%
Total Population	5,132	21.6
Hispanic or Latino (of any race)	817	10.3
Mexican	605	8.6

Population Age 3–17 Enrolled in Public School
(Universe: Population Age 3–17 Enrolled in School)

Group	Number	%
Total Population	5,763	88.8
Hispanic or Latino (of any race)	3,383	97.6
Mexican	2,906	97.2

Population Age 3–17 Enrolled in Private School
(Universe: Population Age 3–17 Enrolled in School)

Group	Number	%
Total Population	730	11.2
Hispanic or Latino (of any race)	84	2.4
Mexican	84	2.8

Foreign-Born Population

Group	Number	%
Total Population	13,026	35.5
Hispanic or Latino (of any race)	7,706	51.3
Mexican	7,263	54.7

Foreign-Born Naturalized U.S. Citizens

Group	Number	%
Total Population	5,033	38.6
Hispanic or Latino (of any race)	1,632	21.2
Mexican	1,437	19.8

Language Spoken at Home: English Only
(Universe: Population 5 Years and Over)

Group	Number	%
Total Population	14,976	44.8
Hispanic or Latino (of any race)	1,458	11.1
Mexican	782	6.8

Language Spoken at Home: Spanish
(Universe: Population 5 Years and Over)

Group	Number	%
Total Population	11,969	35.8
Hispanic or Latino (of any race)	11,652	88.9
Mexican	10,638	93.2

Unemployment Rate
(Universe: Population 16 Years and Over)

Group	%
Total Population	9.3
Hispanic or Latino (of any race)	10.5
Mexican	10.9

Class of Worker: Private Wage and Salary
(Universe: Civilian Employed Population 16 Years and Over)

Group	Number	%
Total Population	16,043	89.0
Hispanic or Latino (of any race)	6,807	94.5
Mexican	6,015	95.6

Class of Worker: Government
(Universe: Civilian Employed Population 16 Years and Over)

Group	Number	%
Total Population	1,269	7.0
Hispanic or Latino (of any race)	205	2.8
Mexican	128	2.0

Means of Transportation to Work: Car, Truck or Van
(Universe: Workers 16 Years and Over)

Group	Number	%
Total Population	15,983	92.3
Hispanic or Latino (of any race)	6,615	96.3
Mexican	5,822	97.0

Means of Transportation to Work: Public Transportation (ex. Taxicab)
(Universe: Workers 16 Years and Over)

Group	Number	%
Total Population	608	3.5
Hispanic or Latino (of any race)	128	1.9
Mexican	71	1.2

Homeownership Rate
(Universe: Occupied Housing Units)

Group	%
Total Population	68.4
Hispanic or Latino (of any race)	45.7
Central American, ex. Mexican	47.6
Guatemalan	45.6
Cuban	74.5
Mexican	44.0
Puerto Rican	58.1
South American	66.7

Median Home Value

Group	Dollars
Total Population	280,300
Hispanic or Latino (of any race)	260,600
Mexican	260,000

Median Gross Rent

Group	Dollars
Total Population	876
Hispanic or Latino (of any race)	912
Mexican	912

Median Household Income
(2010 Inflation-Adjusted Dollars)

Group	Dollars
Total Population	61,287
Hispanic or Latino (of any race)	51,139
Mexican	49,173

Per Capita Income
(2010 Inflation-Adjusted Dollars)

Group	Dollars
Total Population	24,605
Hispanic or Latino (of any race)	15,625
Mexican	14,872

Households with $100,000+ Income

Group	Number	%
Total Population	2,753	22.8
Hispanic or Latino (of any race)	414	11.0
Mexican	307	9.4

Households with Food Stamps/SNAP Benefits During Past 12 Months

Group	Number	%
Total Population	780	6.5
Hispanic or Latino (of any race)	379	10.1
Mexican	368	11.3

Poverty Rate
(Income in Past 12 Months Below Poverty Level)

Group	%
Total Population	10.6
Hispanic or Latino (of any race)	15.1
Mexican	17.1

Aurora

Population

Group	Number	%TP[1]	%HP[2]
Total Population	197,899	100.0	–
Hispanic or Latino (of any race)	81,809	41.3	100.0
Central American, ex. Mexican	1,086	0.5	1.3
Guatemalan	386	0.2	0.5
Honduran	211	0.1	0.3
Salvadoran	289	0.1	0.4
Cuban	318	0.2	0.4
Dominican Republic	110	0.1	0.1
Mexican	72,924	36.8	89.1
Puerto Rican	3,867	2.0	4.7
South American	1,010	0.5	1.2
Argentinean	133	0.1	0.2
Colombian	311	0.2	0.4
Ecuadorian	135	0.1	0.2
Peruvian	187	0.1	0.2
Spaniard	204	0.1	0.2

Population Growth: 2000–2010

Group	%
Total Population	38.4
Hispanic or Latino (of any race)	75.7
Central American, ex. Mexican	230.1
Guatemalan	257.4
Cuban	53.6
Mexican	85.3
Puerto Rican	48.1
South American	182.1
Colombian	161.3

Males per 100 Females

Group	Number
Total Population	98.4
Hispanic or Latino (of any race)	105.8
Central American, ex. Mexican	100.4
Guatemalan	96.9
Honduran	117.5
Salvadoran	99.3
Cuban	100.0
Dominican Republic	96.4
Mexican	107.2
Puerto Rican	97.8
South American	84.6
Argentinean	84.7
Colombian	96.8
Ecuadorian	73.1
Peruvian	70.0
Spaniard	71.4

Average Household Size

Group	People
Total Population	3.12

Notes: (1) Percent of total population; (2) Percent of Hispanic/Latino population; Profiles include places with an overall population of at least 125,000, OR an overall population of at least 25,000 where the Hispanic/Latino population is at least 20% of the overall population. In states where less than five places meet either of these criteria, we have included places with at least 10,000 total population with the highest percentage of Hispanic/Latino population. These places are identified with an asterisk (*); Please refer to the User's Guide for a full explanation of data.

Hispanic or Latino (of any race)	4.24
Central American, ex. Mexican	3.70
Guatemalan	3.64
Honduran	3.62
Salvadoran	4.14
Cuban	2.94
Dominican Republic	3.32
Mexican	4.37
Puerto Rican	3.18
South American	3.27
Argentinean	3.07
Colombian	3.13
Ecuadorian	3.34
Peruvian	3.32
Spaniard	3.00

Median Age

Group	Years
Total Population	30.7
Hispanic or Latino (of any race)	25.1
Central American, ex. Mexican	30.5
Guatemalan	29.8
Honduran	32.2
Salvadoran	30.1
Cuban	27.8
Dominican Republic	27.0
Mexican	24.8
Puerto Rican	28.7
South American	33.0
Argentinean	34.2
Colombian	34.4
Ecuadorian	29.8
Peruvian	34.5
Spaniard	28.3

High School Graduates
(Universe: Population 25 Years and Over)

Group	Number	%
Total Population	88,056	78.0
Hispanic or Latino (of any race)	19,292	49.7
Mexican	16,480	46.9
Puerto Rican	1,360	70.9
South American	475	93.3

Four-Year College Graduates
(Universe: Population 25 Years and Over)

Group	Number	%
Total Population	35,111	31.1
Hispanic or Latino (of any race)	2,890	7.4
Mexican	2,076	5.9
Puerto Rican	179	9.3
South American	262	51.5

Population Age 3–17 Enrolled in Public School
(Universe: Population Age 3–17 Enrolled in School)

Group	Number	%
Total Population	39,161	87.7
Hispanic or Latino (of any race)	19,678	93.1
Mexican	17,886	93.5
Puerto Rican	827	90.8
South American	294	91.6

Population Age 3–17 Enrolled in Private School
(Universe: Population Age 3–17 Enrolled in School)

Group	Number	%
Total Population	5,516	12.3
Hispanic or Latino (of any race)	1,464	6.9
Mexican	1,241	6.5
Puerto Rican	84	9.2
South American	27	8.4

Foreign-Born Population

Group	Number	%
Total Population	47,194	24.8
Hispanic or Latino (of any race)	34,540	44.5
Mexican	33,120	47.0
Puerto Rican	0	0.0
South American	549	53.5

Foreign-Born Naturalized U.S. Citizens

Group	Number	%
Total Population	14,085	29.8
Hispanic or Latino (of any race)	7,454	21.6
Mexican	6,711	20.3
Puerto Rican	0	0.0
South American	382	69.6

Language Spoken at Home: English Only
(Universe: Population 5 Years and Over)

Group	Number	%
Total Population	98,716	57.3
Hispanic or Latino (of any race)	9,522	14.0
Mexican	7,386	12.0
Puerto Rican	832	24.9
South American	294	30.7

Language Spoken at Home: Spanish
(Universe: Population 5 Years and Over)

Group	Number	%
Total Population	60,185	34.9
Hispanic or Latino (of any race)	58,596	85.9
Mexican	54,254	88.0
Puerto Rican	2,505	75.1
South American	651	68.0

Unemployment Rate
(Universe: Population 16 Years and Over)

Group	%
Total Population	8.4
Hispanic or Latino (of any race)	9.8
Mexican	9.7
Puerto Rican	15.3
South American	12.0

Class of Worker: Private Wage and Salary
(Universe: Civilian Employed Population 16 Years and Over)

Group	Number	%
Total Population	81,762	88.1
Hispanic or Latino (of any race)	31,973	92.4
Mexican	28,970	92.8
Puerto Rican	1,401	86.1
South American	388	80.0

Class of Worker: Government
(Universe: Civilian Employed Population 16 Years and Over)

Group	Number	%
Total Population	7,832	8.4
Hispanic or Latino (of any race)	1,673	4.8
Mexican	1,324	4.2
Puerto Rican	218	13.4
South American	64	13.2

Means of Transportation to Work: Car, Truck or Van
(Universe: Workers 16 Years and Over)

Group	Number	%
Total Population	79,388	88.1
Hispanic or Latino (of any race)	30,864	92.5
Mexican	27,757	92.3
Puerto Rican	1,517	95.8
South American	421	93.3

Means of Transportation to Work: Public Transportation (ex. Taxicab)
(Universe: Workers 16 Years and Over)

Group	Number	%
Total Population	4,344	4.8
Hispanic or Latino (of any race)	376	1.1
Mexican	318	1.1
Puerto Rican	23	1.5
South American	0	0.0

Homeownership Rate
(Universe: Occupied Housing Units)

Group	%
Total Population	69.6
Hispanic or Latino (of any race)	62.2
Central American, ex. Mexican	61.1
Guatemalan	56.1
Honduran	50.7
Salvadoran	68.4
Cuban	71.4
Dominican Republic	52.9
Mexican	62.6
Puerto Rican	59.3
South American	72.2
Argentinean	68.3
Colombian	68.7
Ecuadorian	76.3
Peruvian	72.0
Spaniard	57.6

Median Home Value

Group	Dollars
Total Population	205,600
Hispanic or Latino (of any race)	170,200
Mexican	168,000
Puerto Rican	191,800
South American	198,200

Median Gross Rent

Group	Dollars
Total Population	979
Hispanic or Latino (of any race)	924
Mexican	934
Puerto Rican	819
South American	1,194

Median Household Income
(2010 Inflation-Adjusted Dollars)

Group	Dollars
Total Population	60,689
Hispanic or Latino (of any race)	47,226
Mexican	46,655
Puerto Rican	50,685
South American	59,565

Per Capita Income
(2010 Inflation-Adjusted Dollars)

Group	Dollars
Total Population	25,491
Hispanic or Latino (of any race)	14,627
Mexican	14,009
Puerto Rican	21,306
South American	22,394

Households with $100,000+ Income

Group	Number	%
Total Population	15,556	24.9
Hispanic or Latino (of any race)	2,273	11.9
Mexican	1,833	10.9
Puerto Rican	250	22.9
South American	67	28.2

Households with Food Stamps/SNAP Benefits During Past 12 Months

Group	Number	%
Total Population	6,189	9.9
Hispanic or Latino (of any race)	3,244	17.0
Mexican	2,918	17.3
Puerto Rican	187	17.1
South American	17	7.1

Poverty Rate
(Income in Past 12 Months Below Poverty Level)

Group	%
Total Population	11.9
Hispanic or Latino (of any race)	16.9
Mexican	17.2
Puerto Rican	17.8
South American	6.2

Belvidere

Population

Group	Number	%TP[1]	%HP[2]
Total Population	25,585	100.0	–
Hispanic or Latino (of any race)	7,838	30.6	100.0
Mexican	7,169	28.0	91.5
Puerto Rican	291	1.1	3.7

Population Growth: 2000–2010

Group	%
Total Population	22.9
Hispanic or Latino (of any race)	87.6
Mexican	96.1
Puerto Rican	131.0

Males per 100 Females

Group	Number
Total Population	97.5
Hispanic or Latino (of any race)	110.9
Mexican	112.0
Puerto Rican	92.7

STATE & PLACE PROFILES

Notes: (1) Percent of total population; (2) Percent of Hispanic/Latino population; Profiles include places with an overall population of at least 125,000, OR an overall population of at least 25,000 where the Hispanic/Latino population is at least 20% of the overall population. In states where less than five places meet either of these criteria, we have included places with at least 10,000 total population with the highest percentage of Hispanic/Latino population. These places are identified with an asterisk (*); Please refer to the User's Guide for a full explanation of data.

Average Household Size

Group	People
Total Population	2.88
Hispanic or Latino (of any race)	4.28
Mexican	4.37
Puerto Rican	3.41

Median Age

Group	Years
Total Population	33.6
Hispanic or Latino (of any race)	23.0
Mexican	22.7
Puerto Rican	26.4

High School Graduates
(Universe: Population 25 Years and Over)

Group	Number	%
Total Population	11,705	77.1
Hispanic or Latino (of any race)	1,956	52.1
Mexican	1,793	51.2

Four-Year College Graduates
(Universe: Population 25 Years and Over)

Group	Number	%
Total Population	2,127	14.0
Hispanic or Latino (of any race)	336	9.0
Mexican	224	6.4

Population Age 3–17 Enrolled in Public School
(Universe: Population Age 3–17 Enrolled in School)

Group	Number	%
Total Population	5,392	94.1
Hispanic or Latino (of any race)	2,214	98.1
Mexican	2,148	98.5

Population Age 3–17 Enrolled in Private School
(Universe: Population Age 3–17 Enrolled in School)

Group	Number	%
Total Population	338	5.9
Hispanic or Latino (of any race)	43	1.9
Mexican	33	1.5

Foreign-Born Population

Group	Number	%
Total Population	3,933	15.5
Hispanic or Latino (of any race)	3,624	46.0
Mexican	3,557	47.5

Foreign-Born Naturalized U.S. Citizens

Group	Number	%
Total Population	993	25.2
Hispanic or Latino (of any race)	748	20.6
Mexican	681	19.1

Language Spoken at Home: English Only
(Universe: Population 5 Years and Over)

Group	Number	%
Total Population	16,623	72.3
Hispanic or Latino (of any race)	872	12.9
Mexican	697	10.9

Language Spoken at Home: Spanish
(Universe: Population 5 Years and Over)

Group	Number	%
Total Population	6,075	26.4
Hispanic or Latino (of any race)	5,876	87.1
Mexican	5,711	89.1

Unemployment Rate
(Universe: Population 16 Years and Over)

Group	%
Total Population	11.6
Hispanic or Latino (of any race)	14.7
Mexican	13.6

Class of Worker: Private Wage and Salary
(Universe: Civilian Employed Population 16 Years and Over)

Group	Number	%
Total Population	9,215	88.7
Hispanic or Latino (of any race)	2,733	96.8
Mexican	2,608	96.6

Class of Worker: Government
(Universe: Civilian Employed Population 16 Years and Over)

Group	Number	%
Total Population	893	8.6
Hispanic or Latino (of any race)	91	3.2
Mexican	91	3.4

Means of Transportation to Work: Car, Truck or Van
(Universe: Workers 16 Years and Over)

Group	Number	%
Total Population	9,354	92.6
Hispanic or Latino (of any race)	2,534	92.3
Mexican	2,409	92.0

Means of Transportation to Work: Public Transportation (ex. Taxicab)
(Universe: Workers 16 Years and Over)

Group	Number	%
Total Population	30	0.3
Hispanic or Latino (of any race)	0	0.0
Mexican	0	0.0

Homeownership Rate
(Universe: Occupied Housing Units)

Group	%
Total Population	70.3
Hispanic or Latino (of any race)	62.2
Mexican	62.2
Puerto Rican	66.7

Median Home Value

Group	Dollars
Total Population	138,000
Hispanic or Latino (of any race)	156,900
Mexican	158,800

Median Gross Rent

Group	Dollars
Total Population	678
Hispanic or Latino (of any race)	776
Mexican	758

Median Household Income
(2010 Inflation-Adjusted Dollars)

Group	Dollars
Total Population	46,580
Hispanic or Latino (of any race)	40,969
Mexican	40,232

Per Capita Income
(2010 Inflation-Adjusted Dollars)

Group	Dollars
Total Population	20,224
Hispanic or Latino (of any race)	12,110
Mexican	11,715

Households with $100,000+ Income

Group	Number	%
Total Population	1,067	12.3
Hispanic or Latino (of any race)	141	8.1
Mexican	130	8.1

Households with Food Stamps/SNAP Benefits During Past 12 Months

Group	Number	%
Total Population	1,050	12.1
Hispanic or Latino (of any race)	338	19.5
Mexican	327	20.5

Poverty Rate
(Income in Past 12 Months Below Poverty Level)

Group	%
Total Population	15.1
Hispanic or Latino (of any race)	27.7
Mexican	27.8

Berwyn

Population

Group	Number	%TP[1]	%HP[2]
Total Population	56,657	100.0	–
Hispanic or Latino (of any race)	33,676	59.4	100.0
Central American, ex. Mexican	825	1.5	2.4
Guatemalan	476	0.8	1.4
Salvadoran	182	0.3	0.5
Cuban	167	0.3	0.5
Mexican	28,185	49.7	83.7
Puerto Rican	2,918	5.2	8.7
South American	856	1.5	2.5
Colombian	276	0.5	0.8
Ecuadorian	257	0.5	0.8
Peruvian	128	0.2	0.4

Population Growth: 2000–2010

Group	%
Total Population	4.9
Hispanic or Latino (of any race)	63.9
Central American, ex. Mexican	135.7
Guatemalan	181.7
Cuban	31.5
Mexican	68.3
Puerto Rican	109.6
South American	92.4
Colombian	130.0
Ecuadorian	82.3

Males per 100 Females

Group	Number
Total Population	98.1
Hispanic or Latino (of any race)	101.5
Central American, ex. Mexican	97.4
Guatemalan	95.1
Salvadoran	109.2
Cuban	79.6
Mexican	103.1
Puerto Rican	93.1
South American	89.0
Colombian	80.4
Ecuadorian	86.2
Peruvian	116.9

Average Household Size

Group	People
Total Population	2.99
Hispanic or Latino (of any race)	3.88
Central American, ex. Mexican	3.65
Guatemalan	3.69
Salvadoran	3.98
Cuban	3.43
Mexican	3.98
Puerto Rican	3.35
South American	3.40
Colombian	3.59
Ecuadorian	3.57
Peruvian	3.07

Median Age

Group	Years
Total Population	32.9
Hispanic or Latino (of any race)	27.1
Central American, ex. Mexican	32.3
Guatemalan	33.0
Salvadoran	30.5
Cuban	38.2
Mexican	26.6
Puerto Rican	27.0
South American	36.4
Colombian	35.7
Ecuadorian	36.7
Peruvian	36.0

High School Graduates
(Universe: Population 25 Years and Over)

Group	Number	%
Total Population	26,289	76.0
Hispanic or Latino (of any race)	10,404	62.7
Mexican	8,628	60.6
Puerto Rican	853	74.6

Four-Year College Graduates
(Universe: Population 25 Years and Over)

Group	Number	%
Total Population	6,313	18.3
Hispanic or Latino (of any race)	1,534	9.2
Mexican	1,141	8.0
Puerto Rican	207	18.1

Population Age 3–17 Enrolled in Public School
(Universe: Population Age 3–17 Enrolled in School)

Group	Number	%
Total Population	10,211	86.2
Hispanic or Latino (of any race)	8,098	88.8

Notes: (1) Percent of total population; (2) Percent of Hispanic/Latino population; Profiles include places with an overall population of at least 125,000, OR an overall population of at least 25,000 where the Hispanic/Latino population is at least 20% of the overall population. In states where less than five places meet either of these criteria, we have included places with at least 10,000 total population with the highest percentage of Hispanic/Latino population. These places are identified with an asterisk (*); Please refer to the User's Guide for a full explanation of data.

Group	Number	%
Mexican	7,292	89.0
Puerto Rican	381	90.3

Population Age 3–17 Enrolled in Private School
(Universe: Population Age 3–17 Enrolled in School)

Group	Number	%
Total Population	1,638	13.8
Hispanic or Latino (of any race)	1,021	11.2
Mexican	899	11.0
Puerto Rican	41	9.7

Foreign-Born Population

Group	Number	%
Total Population	14,132	25.4
Hispanic or Latino (of any race)	11,926	36.9
Mexican	10,914	38.9
Puerto Rican	0	0.0

Foreign-Born Naturalized U.S. Citizens

Group	Number	%
Total Population	5,596	39.6
Hispanic or Latino (of any race)	4,041	33.9
Mexican	3,658	33.5
Puerto Rican	0	0.0

Language Spoken at Home: English Only
(Universe: Population 5 Years and Over)

Group	Number	%
Total Population	22,495	44.0
Hispanic or Latino (of any race)	3,603	12.4
Mexican	2,583	10.3
Puerto Rican	711	37.9

Language Spoken at Home: Spanish
(Universe: Population 5 Years and Over)

Group	Number	%
Total Population	26,039	50.9
Hispanic or Latino (of any race)	25,400	87.5
Mexican	22,592	89.7
Puerto Rican	1,167	62.1

Unemployment Rate
(Universe: Population 16 Years and Over)

Group	%
Total Population	10.3
Hispanic or Latino (of any race)	10.5
Mexican	10.1
Puerto Rican	14.0

Class of Worker: Private Wage and Salary
(Universe: Civilian Employed Population 16 Years and Over)

Group	Number	%
Total Population	22,158	86.1
Hispanic or Latino (of any race)	12,788	90.1
Mexican	11,191	90.9
Puerto Rican	723	87.5

Class of Worker: Government
(Universe: Civilian Employed Population 16 Years and Over)

Group	Number	%
Total Population	2,797	10.9
Hispanic or Latino (of any race)	1,015	7.1
Mexican	875	7.1
Puerto Rican	103	12.5

Means of Transportation to Work: Car, Truck or Van
(Universe: Workers 16 Years and Over)

Group	Number	%
Total Population	20,945	84.1
Hispanic or Latino (of any race)	11,927	87.1
Mexican	10,396	87.2
Puerto Rican	681	85.4

Means of Transportation to Work: Public Transportation (ex. Taxicab)
(Universe: Workers 16 Years and Over)

Group	Number	%
Total Population	2,469	9.9
Hispanic or Latino (of any race)	1,103	8.1
Mexican	921	7.7
Puerto Rican	101	12.7

Homeownership Rate
(Universe: Occupied Housing Units)

Group	%
Total Population	59.8
Hispanic or Latino (of any race)	58.8
Central American, ex. Mexican	62.6
Guatemalan	63.8
Salvadoran	72.7
Cuban	63.8
Mexican	59.6
Puerto Rican	51.3
South American	61.8
Colombian	61.6
Ecuadorian	72.0
Peruvian	62.8

Median Home Value

Group	Dollars
Total Population	244,100
Hispanic or Latino (of any race)	251,600
Mexican	252,600
Puerto Rican	234,700

Median Gross Rent

Group	Dollars
Total Population	843
Hispanic or Latino (of any race)	935
Mexican	939
Puerto Rican	781

Median Household Income
(2010 Inflation-Adjusted Dollars)

Group	Dollars
Total Population	48,710
Hispanic or Latino (of any race)	50,376
Mexican	50,696
Puerto Rican	47,168

Per Capita Income
(2010 Inflation-Adjusted Dollars)

Group	Dollars
Total Population	20,562
Hispanic or Latino (of any race)	14,764
Mexican	14,385
Puerto Rican	17,146

Households with $100,000+ Income

Group	Number	%
Total Population	2,859	15.4
Hispanic or Latino (of any race)	1,065	13.6
Mexican	935	14.2
Puerto Rican	67	8.7

Households with Food Stamps/SNAP Benefits During Past 12 Months

Group	Number	%
Total Population	2,036	10.9
Hispanic or Latino (of any race)	980	12.5
Mexican	811	12.3
Puerto Rican	113	14.7

Poverty Rate
(Income in Past 12 Months Below Poverty Level)

Group	%
Total Population	13.4
Hispanic or Latino (of any race)	14.7
Mexican	15.1
Puerto Rican	17.2

Bolingbrook

Population

Group	Number	%TP[1]	%HP[2]
Total Population	73,366	100.0	–
Hispanic or Latino (of any race)	17,957	24.5	100.0
Central American, ex. Mexican	460	0.6	2.6
Guatemalan	262	0.4	1.5
Cuban	117	0.2	0.7
Mexican	15,256	20.8	85.0
Puerto Rican	1,254	1.7	7.0
South American	405	0.6	2.3
Colombian	140	0.2	0.8
Spaniard	105	0.1	0.6

Population Growth: 2000–2010

Group	%
Total Population	30.3
Hispanic or Latino (of any race)	143.6
Central American, ex. Mexican	238.2
Cuban	15.8
Mexican	166.9
Puerto Rican	100.3
South American	151.6

Males per 100 Females

Group	Number
Total Population	98.3
Hispanic or Latino (of any race)	105.5
Central American, ex. Mexican	105.4
Guatemalan	122.0
Cuban	129.4
Mexican	106.4
Puerto Rican	99.0
South American	98.5
Colombian	100.0
Spaniard	59.1

Average Household Size

Group	People
Total Population	3.29
Hispanic or Latino (of any race)	4.41
Central American, ex. Mexican	3.96
Guatemalan	4.15
Cuban	3.13
Mexican	4.58
Puerto Rican	3.59
South American	3.42
Colombian	3.38
Spaniard	3.11

Median Age

Group	Years
Total Population	33.1
Hispanic or Latino (of any race)	24.9
Central American, ex. Mexican	31.7
Guatemalan	31.7
Cuban	38.3
Mexican	24.4
Puerto Rican	25.4
South American	34.5
Colombian	34.4
Spaniard	29.8

High School Graduates
(Universe: Population 25 Years and Over)

Group	Number	%
Total Population	38,630	88.8
Hispanic or Latino (of any race)	5,252	64.1
Mexican	4,076	61.1
Puerto Rican	552	88.9

Four-Year College Graduates
(Universe: Population 25 Years and Over)

Group	Number	%
Total Population	14,749	33.9
Hispanic or Latino (of any race)	840	10.3
Mexican	436	6.5
Puerto Rican	190	30.6

Population Age 3–17 Enrolled in Public School
(Universe: Population Age 3–17 Enrolled in School)

Group	Number	%
Total Population	15,331	89.7
Hispanic or Latino (of any race)	4,762	96.6
Mexican	3,940	98.9
Puerto Rican	583	94.0

Population Age 3–17 Enrolled in Private School
(Universe: Population Age 3–17 Enrolled in School)

Group	Number	%
Total Population	1,752	10.3
Hispanic or Latino (of any race)	168	3.4
Mexican	43	1.1
Puerto Rican	37	6.0

Foreign-Born Population

Group	Number	%
Total Population	16,543	22.8
Hispanic or Latino (of any race)	7,516	43.1

Notes: (1) Percent of total population; (2) Percent of Hispanic/Latino population; Profiles include places with an overall population of at least 125,000, OR an overall population of at least 25,000 where the Hispanic/Latino population is at least 20% of the overall population. In states where less than five places meet either of these criteria, we have included places with at least 10,000 total population with the highest percentage of Hispanic/Latino population. These places are identified with an asterisk (*); Please refer to the User's Guide for a full explanation of data.

STATE & PLACE PROFILES

Mexican	6,660	46.3
Puerto Rican	0	0.0

Foreign-Born Naturalized U.S. Citizens

Group	Number	%
Total Population	7,469	45.1
Hispanic or Latino (of any race)	2,229	29.7
Mexican	1,901	28.5
Puerto Rican	0	0.0

Language Spoken at Home: English Only
(Universe: Population 5 Years and Over)

Group	Number	%
Total Population	42,979	64.6
Hispanic or Latino (of any race)	2,202	14.3
Mexican	1,382	10.9
Puerto Rican	605	47.4

Language Spoken at Home: Spanish
(Universe: Population 5 Years and Over)

Group	Number	%
Total Population	13,761	20.7
Hispanic or Latino (of any race)	13,072	85.2
Mexican	11,266	88.9
Puerto Rican	671	52.6

Unemployment Rate
(Universe: Population 16 Years and Over)

Group	%
Total Population	8.7
Hispanic or Latino (of any race)	10.0
Mexican	9.0
Puerto Rican	12.1

Class of Worker: Private Wage and Salary
(Universe: Civilian Employed Population 16 Years and Over)

Group	Number	%
Total Population	32,677	87.3
Hispanic or Latino (of any race)	7,464	93.7
Mexican	6,382	94.6
Puerto Rican	391	88.1

Class of Worker: Government
(Universe: Civilian Employed Population 16 Years and Over)

Group	Number	%
Total Population	3,711	9.9
Hispanic or Latino (of any race)	327	4.1
Mexican	247	3.7
Puerto Rican	53	11.9

Means of Transportation to Work: Car, Truck or Van
(Universe: Workers 16 Years and Over)

Group	Number	%
Total Population	32,752	89.8
Hispanic or Latino (of any race)	7,161	93.2
Mexican	6,065	93.1
Puerto Rican	366	91.0

Means of Transportation to Work: Public Transportation (ex. Taxicab)
(Universe: Workers 16 Years and Over)

Group	Number	%
Total Population	1,149	3.2
Hispanic or Latino (of any race)	49	0.6
Mexican	37	0.6
Puerto Rican	12	3.0

Homeownership Rate
(Universe: Occupied Housing Units)

Group	%
Total Population	83.1
Hispanic or Latino (of any race)	76.8
Central American, ex. Mexican	75.9
Guatemalan	76.3
Cuban	86.8
Mexican	75.9
Puerto Rican	82.5
South American	86.6
Colombian	90.0
Spaniard	77.8

Median Home Value

Group	Dollars
Total Population	245,700
Hispanic or Latino (of any race)	224,800
Mexican	217,000
Puerto Rican	266,700

Median Gross Rent

Group	Dollars
Total Population	933
Hispanic or Latino (of any race)	1,019
Mexican	1,087
Puerto Rican	–

Median Household Income
(2010 Inflation-Adjusted Dollars)

Group	Dollars
Total Population	81,108
Hispanic or Latino (of any race)	62,852
Mexican	60,508
Puerto Rican	86,786

Per Capita Income
(2010 Inflation-Adjusted Dollars)

Group	Dollars
Total Population	27,593
Hispanic or Latino (of any race)	16,082
Mexican	15,312
Puerto Rican	23,190

Households with $100,000+ Income

Group	Number	%
Total Population	7,960	36.0
Hispanic or Latino (of any race)	880	22.9
Mexican	614	20.3
Puerto Rican	168	47.2

Households with Food Stamps/SNAP Benefits During Past 12 Months

Group	Number	%
Total Population	1,433	6.5
Hispanic or Latino (of any race)	535	13.9
Mexican	452	14.9
Puerto Rican	60	16.9

Poverty Rate
(Income in Past 12 Months Below Poverty Level)

Group	%
Total Population	6.1
Hispanic or Latino (of any race)	9.3
Mexican	8.4
Puerto Rican	0.0

Burbank

Population

Group	Number	%TP[1]	%HP[2]
Total Population	28,925	100.0	–
Hispanic or Latino (of any race)	7,680	26.6	100.0
Central American, ex. Mexican	142	0.5	1.8
Mexican	6,678	23.1	87.0
Puerto Rican	421	1.5	5.5
South American	151	0.5	2.0

Population Growth: 2000–2010

Group	%
Total Population	3.7
Hispanic or Latino (of any race)	148.1
Mexican	170.9
Puerto Rican	65.7

Males per 100 Females

Group	Number
Total Population	98.2
Hispanic or Latino (of any race)	100.8
Central American, ex. Mexican	105.8
Mexican	101.3
Puerto Rican	106.4
South American	69.7

Average Household Size

Group	People
Total Population	3.09
Hispanic or Latino (of any race)	4.05
Central American, ex. Mexican	4.10
Mexican	4.12
Puerto Rican	3.35
South American	4.25

Median Age

Group	Years
Total Population	36.8
Hispanic or Latino (of any race)	27.0
Central American, ex. Mexican	28.0
Mexican	26.7
Puerto Rican	31.8
South American	32.6

High School Graduates
(Universe: Population 25 Years and Over)

Group	Number	%
Total Population	13,531	74.1
Hispanic or Latino (of any race)	2,224	60.0
Mexican	1,673	56.2

Four-Year College Graduates
(Universe: Population 25 Years and Over)

Group	Number	%
Total Population	2,120	11.6
Hispanic or Latino (of any race)	384	10.4
Mexican	177	5.9

Population Age 3–17 Enrolled in Public School
(Universe: Population Age 3–17 Enrolled in School)

Group	Number	%
Total Population	4,639	86.7
Hispanic or Latino (of any race)	1,579	86.5
Mexican	1,398	89.6

Population Age 3–17 Enrolled in Private School
(Universe: Population Age 3–17 Enrolled in School)

Group	Number	%
Total Population	710	13.3
Hispanic or Latino (of any race)	246	13.5
Mexican	162	10.4

Foreign-Born Population

Group	Number	%
Total Population	9,196	32.3
Hispanic or Latino (of any race)	2,552	36.1
Mexican	2,029	34.4

Foreign-Born Naturalized U.S. Citizens

Group	Number	%
Total Population	4,742	51.6
Hispanic or Latino (of any race)	1,055	41.3
Mexican	878	43.3

Language Spoken at Home: English Only
(Universe: Population 5 Years and Over)

Group	Number	%
Total Population	12,854	48.3
Hispanic or Latino (of any race)	1,095	17.6
Mexican	904	17.6

Language Spoken at Home: Spanish
(Universe: Population 5 Years and Over)

Group	Number	%
Total Population	5,258	19.7
Hispanic or Latino (of any race)	5,104	82.1
Mexican	4,205	82.1

Unemployment Rate
(Universe: Population 16 Years and Over)

Group	%
Total Population	9.0
Hispanic or Latino (of any race)	5.5
Mexican	5.8

Class of Worker: Private Wage and Salary
(Universe: Civilian Employed Population 16 Years and Over)

Group	Number	%
Total Population	11,075	85.1
Hispanic or Latino (of any race)	2,448	80.6
Mexican	1,977	80.5

Class of Worker: Government
(Universe: Civilian Employed Population 16 Years and Over)

Group	Number	%
Total Population	1,319	10.1
Hispanic or Latino (of any race)	367	12.1
Mexican	295	12.0

Notes: (1) Percent of total population; (2) Percent of Hispanic/Latino population; Profiles include places with an overall population of at least 125,000, OR an overall population of at least 25,000 where the Hispanic/Latino population is at least 20% of the overall population. In states where less than five places meet either of these criteria, we have included places with at least 10,000 total population with the highest percentage of Hispanic/Latino population. These places are identified with an asterisk (*); Please refer to the User's Guide for a full explanation of data.

Means of Transportation to Work: Car, Truck or Van
(Universe: Workers 16 Years and Over)

Group	Number	%
Total Population	11,806	93.1
Hispanic or Latino (of any race)	2,775	91.3
Mexican	2,222	90.4

Means of Transportation to Work: Public Transportation (ex. Taxicab)
(Universe: Workers 16 Years and Over)

Group	Number	%
Total Population	467	3.7
Hispanic or Latino (of any race)	120	3.9
Mexican	120	4.9

Homeownership Rate
(Universe: Occupied Housing Units)

Group	%
Total Population	80.6
Hispanic or Latino (of any race)	78.5
Central American, ex. Mexican	80.0
Mexican	80.8
Puerto Rican	64.8
South American	66.7

Median Home Value

Group	Dollars
Total Population	235,900
Hispanic or Latino (of any race)	248,700
Mexican	239,000

Median Gross Rent

Group	Dollars
Total Population	890
Hispanic or Latino (of any race)	1,114
Mexican	1,189

Median Household Income
(2010 Inflation-Adjusted Dollars)

Group	Dollars
Total Population	56,386
Hispanic or Latino (of any race)	56,196
Mexican	59,219

Per Capita Income
(2010 Inflation-Adjusted Dollars)

Group	Dollars
Total Population	21,290
Hispanic or Latino (of any race)	16,168
Mexican	16,203

Households with $100,000+ Income

Group	Number	%
Total Population	1,542	17.6
Hispanic or Latino (of any race)	228	14.2
Mexican	206	15.3

Households with Food Stamps/SNAP Benefits During Past 12 Months

Group	Number	%
Total Population	553	6.3
Hispanic or Latino (of any race)	176	11.0
Mexican	107	8.0

Poverty Rate
(Income in Past 12 Months Below Poverty Level)

Group	%
Total Population	10.3
Hispanic or Latino (of any race)	16.9
Mexican	15.4

Carpentersville

Population

Group	Number	%TP[1]	%HP[2]
Total Population	37,691	100.0	–
Hispanic or Latino (of any race)	18,877	50.1	100.0
Central American, ex. Mexican	748	2.0	4.0
Guatemalan	173	0.5	0.9
Salvadoran	478	1.3	2.5
Mexican	16,794	44.6	89.0
Puerto Rican	601	1.6	3.2
South American	205	0.5	1.1

Population Growth: 2000–2010

Group	%
Total Population	23.2
Hispanic or Latino (of any race)	52.1
Central American, ex. Mexican	165.2
Salvadoran	204.5
Mexican	56.2
Puerto Rican	72.2

Males per 100 Females

Group	Number
Total Population	101.5
Hispanic or Latino (of any race)	108.2
Central American, ex. Mexican	111.3
Guatemalan	90.1
Salvadoran	119.3
Mexican	109.2
Puerto Rican	91.4
South American	86.4

Average Household Size

Group	People
Total Population	3.47
Hispanic or Latino (of any race)	4.69
Central American, ex. Mexican	4.69
Guatemalan	4.13
Salvadoran	4.87
Mexican	4.81
Puerto Rican	3.43
South American	3.19

Median Age

Group	Years
Total Population	29.4
Hispanic or Latino (of any race)	24.3
Central American, ex. Mexican	28.7
Guatemalan	27.9
Salvadoran	28.6
Mexican	24.0
Puerto Rican	21.7
South American	34.4

High School Graduates
(Universe: Population 25 Years and Over)

Group	Number	%
Total Population	15,124	70.8
Hispanic or Latino (of any race)	3,888	44.3
Mexican	3,333	42.2

Four-Year College Graduates
(Universe: Population 25 Years and Over)

Group	Number	%
Total Population	4,524	21.2
Hispanic or Latino (of any race)	467	5.3
Mexican	353	4.5

Population Age 3–17 Enrolled in Public School
(Universe: Population Age 3–17 Enrolled in School)

Group	Number	%
Total Population	8,346	91.1
Hispanic or Latino (of any race)	4,967	96.7
Mexican	4,602	96.5

Population Age 3–17 Enrolled in Private School
(Universe: Population Age 3–17 Enrolled in School)

Group	Number	%
Total Population	813	8.9
Hispanic or Latino (of any race)	168	3.3
Mexican	168	3.5

Foreign-Born Population

Group	Number	%
Total Population	11,656	31.4
Hispanic or Latino (of any race)	9,165	50.9
Mexican	8,486	51.5

Foreign-Born Naturalized U.S. Citizens

Group	Number	%
Total Population	3,725	32.0
Hispanic or Latino (of any race)	2,157	23.5
Mexican	1,848	21.8

Language Spoken at Home: English Only
(Universe: Population 5 Years and Over)

Group	Number	%
Total Population	15,746	46.8
Hispanic or Latino (of any race)	1,410	8.8
Mexican	1,136	7.8

Language Spoken at Home: Spanish
(Universe: Population 5 Years and Over)

Group	Number	%
Total Population	14,931	44.4
Hispanic or Latino (of any race)	14,562	91.2
Mexican	13,441	92.2

Unemployment Rate
(Universe: Population 16 Years and Over)

Group	%
Total Population	9.1
Hispanic or Latino (of any race)	9.1
Mexican	8.4

Class of Worker: Private Wage and Salary
(Universe: Civilian Employed Population 16 Years and Over)

Group	Number	%
Total Population	15,104	88.6
Hispanic or Latino (of any race)	6,835	90.2
Mexican	6,131	89.4

Class of Worker: Government
(Universe: Civilian Employed Population 16 Years and Over)

Group	Number	%
Total Population	1,176	6.9
Hispanic or Latino (of any race)	390	5.1
Mexican	374	5.5

Means of Transportation to Work: Car, Truck or Van
(Universe: Workers 16 Years and Over)

Group	Number	%
Total Population	15,709	93.6
Hispanic or Latino (of any race)	6,933	93.2
Mexican	6,280	92.9

Means of Transportation to Work: Public Transportation (ex. Taxicab)
(Universe: Workers 16 Years and Over)

Group	Number	%
Total Population	379	2.3
Hispanic or Latino (of any race)	77	1.0
Mexican	67	1.0

Homeownership Rate
(Universe: Occupied Housing Units)

Group	%
Total Population	75.9
Hispanic or Latino (of any race)	68.7
Central American, ex. Mexican	67.2
Guatemalan	70.0
Salvadoran	68.1
Mexican	68.9
Puerto Rican	58.8
South American	83.8

Median Home Value

Group	Dollars
Total Population	177,400
Hispanic or Latino (of any race)	165,800
Mexican	164,300

Median Gross Rent

Group	Dollars
Total Population	963
Hispanic or Latino (of any race)	927
Mexican	927

Median Household Income
(2010 Inflation-Adjusted Dollars)

Group	Dollars
Total Population	55,324
Hispanic or Latino (of any race)	46,847
Mexican	47,027

Per Capita Income
(2010 Inflation-Adjusted Dollars)

Group	Dollars
Total Population	20,882
Hispanic or Latino (of any race)	12,929
Mexican	12,389

Notes: (1) Percent of total population; (2) Percent of Hispanic/Latino population; Profiles include places with an overall population of at least 125,000, OR an overall population of at least 25,000 where the Hispanic/Latino population is at least 20% of the overall population. In states where less than five places meet either of these criteria, we have included places with at least 10,000 total population with the highest percentage of Hispanic/Latino population. These places are identified with an asterisk (*); Please refer to the User's Guide for a full explanation of data.

Households with $100,000+ Income

Group	Number	%
Total Population	2,266	20.2
Hispanic or Latino (of any race)	303	7.2
Mexican	286	7.7

Households with Food Stamps/SNAP Benefits During Past 12 Months

Group	Number	%
Total Population	785	7.0
Hispanic or Latino (of any race)	272	6.5
Mexican	262	7.1

Poverty Rate
(Income in Past 12 Months Below Poverty Level)

Group	%
Total Population	11.3
Hispanic or Latino (of any race)	14.1
Mexican	14.6

Chicago

Population

Group	Number	%TP[1]	%HP[2]
Total Population	2,695,598	100.0	–
Hispanic or Latino (of any race)	778,862	28.9	100.0
Central American, ex. Mexican	31,263	1.2	4.0
Costa Rican	681	<0.1	0.1
Guatemalan	17,973	0.7	2.3
Honduran	5,021	0.2	0.6
Nicaraguan	1,239	<0.1	0.2
Panamanian	883	<0.1	0.1
Salvadoran	5,204	0.2	0.7
Cuban	8,331	0.3	1.1
Dominican Republic	2,737	0.1	0.4
Mexican	578,100	21.4	74.2
Puerto Rican	102,703	3.8	13.2
South American	32,129	1.2	4.1
Argentinean	1,743	0.1	0.2
Bolivian	626	<0.1	0.1
Chilean	876	<0.1	0.1
Colombian	7,547	0.3	1.0
Ecuadorian	15,466	0.6	2.0
Paraguayan	101	<0.1	<0.1
Peruvian	4,075	0.2	0.5
Uruguayan	267	<0.1	<0.1
Venezuelan	1,121	<0.1	0.1
Spaniard	3,173	0.1	0.4

Population Growth: 2000–2010

Group	%
Total Population	-6.9
Hispanic or Latino (of any race)	3.3
Central American, ex. Mexican	34.0
Costa Rican	11.8
Guatemalan	32.1
Honduran	64.7
Nicaraguan	59.3
Panamanian	38.6
Salvadoran	50.1
Cuban	3.1
Dominican Republic	65.8
Mexican	9.0
Puerto Rican	-9.2
South American	54.3
Argentinean	92.0
Bolivian	51.2
Chilean	36.9
Colombian	34.2
Ecuadorian	73.0
Peruvian	48.9
Uruguayan	99.3
Venezuelan	86.8
Spaniard	293.2

Males per 100 Females

Group	Number
Total Population	94.3
Hispanic or Latino (of any race)	105.3
Central American, ex. Mexican	99.8
Costa Rican	83.1
Guatemalan	106.8
Honduran	89.8
Nicaraguan	88.9
Panamanian	74.9
Salvadoran	97.1
Cuban	101.7
Dominican Republic	83.3
Mexican	108.2
Puerto Rican	92.6
South American	101.7
Argentinean	96.7
Bolivian	103.9
Chilean	97.7
Colombian	78.0
Ecuadorian	122.4
Paraguayan	65.6
Peruvian	90.2
Uruguayan	105.4
Venezuelan	82.6
Spaniard	96.0

Average Household Size

Group	People
Total Population	2.52
Hispanic or Latino (of any race)	3.61
Central American, ex. Mexican	3.46
Costa Rican	2.39
Guatemalan	3.57
Honduran	3.50
Nicaraguan	3.20
Panamanian	2.31
Salvadoran	3.56
Cuban	2.28
Dominican Republic	2.75
Mexican	3.92
Puerto Rican	2.85
South American	3.05
Argentinean	2.18
Bolivian	2.44
Chilean	2.24
Colombian	2.59
Ecuadorian	3.76
Paraguayan	2.14
Peruvian	2.73
Uruguayan	2.66
Venezuelan	2.31
Spaniard	2.24

Median Age

Group	Years
Total Population	32.9
Hispanic or Latino (of any race)	28.0
Central American, ex. Mexican	32.3
Costa Rican	32.5
Guatemalan	32.6
Honduran	31.5
Nicaraguan	31.0
Panamanian	33.4
Salvadoran	32.1
Cuban	35.6
Dominican Republic	30.5
Mexican	26.8
Puerto Rican	30.7
South American	33.0
Argentinean	34.1
Bolivian	34.4
Chilean	33.9
Colombian	33.9
Ecuadorian	31.8
Paraguayan	27.4
Peruvian	36.4
Uruguayan	36.9
Venezuelan	31.3
Spaniard	32.6

High School Graduates
(Universe: Population 25 Years and Over)

Group	Number	%
Total Population	1,403,628	79.4
Hispanic or Latino (of any race)	235,015	56.6
Central American, ex. Mexican	11,674	60.5
Guatemalan	6,593	60.6
Honduran	1,764	55.9
Nicaraguan	565	75.9
Salvadoran	1,523	53.9
Cuban	4,067	75.2
Dominican Republic	1,297	72.3
Mexican	153,063	51.7
Puerto Rican	41,080	67.6
South American	17,075	73.9
Argentinean	1,095	86.2
Chilean	580	90.1
Colombian	4,467	82.6
Ecuadorian	6,873	62.5
Peruvian	2,760	84.0
Spaniard	1,478	90.6

Four-Year College Graduates
(Universe: Population 25 Years and Over)

Group	Number	%
Total Population	570,134	32.2
Hispanic or Latino (of any race)	46,857	11.3
Central American, ex. Mexican	2,774	14.4
Guatemalan	1,435	13.2
Honduran	351	11.1
Nicaraguan	80	10.8
Salvadoran	452	16.0
Cuban	1,824	33.7
Dominican Republic	342	19.1
Mexican	25,648	8.7
Puerto Rican	7,101	11.7
South American	6,498	28.1
Argentinean	656	51.6
Chilean	315	48.9
Colombian	1,986	36.7
Ecuadorian	1,769	16.1
Peruvian	1,145	34.9
Spaniard	814	49.9

Population Age 3–17 Enrolled in Public School
(Universe: Population Age 3–17 Enrolled in School)

Group	Number	%
Total Population	395,453	83.4
Hispanic or Latino (of any race)	161,362	90.0
Central American, ex. Mexican	4,512	87.4
Guatemalan	2,886	87.1
Honduran	857	90.5
Nicaraguan	102	79.1
Salvadoran	567	93.7
Cuban	938	81.1
Dominican Republic	541	97.5
Mexican	126,765	91.1
Puerto Rican	18,100	86.8
South American	4,767	85.2
Argentinean	174	74.0
Chilean	34	61.8
Colombian	1,069	93.3
Ecuadorian	2,729	87.6
Peruvian	528	72.2
Spaniard	301	79.4

Population Age 3–17 Enrolled in Private School
(Universe: Population Age 3–17 Enrolled in School)

Group	Number	%
Total Population	78,750	16.6
Hispanic or Latino (of any race)	17,855	10.0
Central American, ex. Mexican	652	12.6
Guatemalan	429	12.9
Honduran	90	9.5
Nicaraguan	27	20.9
Salvadoran	38	6.3
Cuban	219	18.9
Dominican Republic	14	2.5
Mexican	12,445	8.9
Puerto Rican	2,750	13.2
South American	830	14.8
Argentinean	61	26.0
Chilean	21	38.2
Colombian	77	6.7
Ecuadorian	388	12.4
Peruvian	203	27.8
Spaniard	78	20.6

Foreign-Born Population

Group	Number	%
Total Population	570,543	21.1
Hispanic or Latino (of any race)	314,643	41.8
Central American, ex. Mexican	18,869	65.1
Guatemalan	10,501	62.0
Honduran	3,320	69.8
Nicaraguan	777	79.1
Salvadoran	2,854	66.9

Notes: (1) Percent of total population; (2) Percent of Hispanic/Latino population; Profiles include places with an overall population of at least 125,000, OR an overall population of at least 25,000 where the Hispanic/Latino population is at least 20% of the overall population. In states where less than five places meet either of these criteria, we have included places with at least 10,000 total population with the highest percentage of Hispanic/Latino population. These places are identified with an asterisk (*); Please refer to the User's Guide for a full explanation of data.

Group	Number	%
Cuban	3,387	43.4
Dominican Republic	1,641	60.0
Mexican	262,573	47.1
Puerto Rican	1,389	1.4
South American	22,774	65.5
Argentinean	984	57.2
Chilean	515	58.9
Colombian	5,180	65.7
Ecuadorian	11,820	67.5
Peruvian	2,942	64.2
Spaniard	687	26.5

Foreign-Born Naturalized U.S. Citizens

Group	Number	%
Total Population	230,492	40.4
Hispanic or Latino (of any race)	93,768	29.8
Central American, ex. Mexican	7,644	40.5
Guatemalan	4,350	41.4
Honduran	1,038	31.3
Nicaraguan	395	50.8
Salvadoran	1,137	39.8
Cuban	2,407	71.1
Dominican Republic	949	57.8
Mexican	71,170	27.1
Puerto Rican	673	48.5
South American	9,169	40.3
Argentinean	442	44.9
Chilean	301	58.4
Colombian	2,408	46.5
Ecuadorian	3,987	33.7
Peruvian	1,451	49.3
Spaniard	352	51.2

Language Spoken at Home: English Only
(Universe: Population 5 Years and Over)

Group	Number	%
Total Population	1,627,190	64.7
Hispanic or Latino (of any race)	94,770	13.9
Central American, ex. Mexican	2,517	9.3
Guatemalan	1,468	9.3
Honduran	226	5.0
Nicaraguan	75	7.6
Salvadoran	337	8.6
Cuban	2,267	31.5
Dominican Republic	377	14.9
Mexican	56,338	11.3
Puerto Rican	23,986	25.7
South American	3,101	9.7
Argentinean	217	14.1
Chilean	159	20.1
Colombian	1,070	14.4
Ecuadorian	820	5.1
Peruvian	597	13.8
Spaniard	1,311	54.9

Language Spoken at Home: Spanish
(Universe: Population 5 Years and Over)

Group	Number	%
Total Population	608,618	24.2
Hispanic or Latino (of any race)	582,240	85.7
Central American, ex. Mexican	24,480	90.2
Guatemalan	14,303	90.6
Honduran	4,196	93.4
Nicaraguan	891	90.7
Salvadoran	3,603	91.4
Cuban	4,787	66.6
Dominican Republic	2,125	84.2
Mexican	441,756	88.5
Puerto Rican	68,943	73.9
South American	28,855	89.8
Argentinean	1,322	85.9
Chilean	631	79.9
Colombian	6,386	85.6
Ecuadorian	15,059	94.3
Peruvian	3,727	85.9
Spaniard	981	41.1

Unemployment Rate
(Universe: Population 16 Years and Over)

Group	%
Total Population	11.1
Hispanic or Latino (of any race)	10.6
Central American, ex. Mexican	8.6
Guatemalan	9.0
Honduran	11.3
Nicaraguan	9.5
Salvadoran	5.0
Cuban	9.3
Dominican Republic	13.7
Mexican	10.4
Puerto Rican	14.3
South American	6.3
Argentinean	0.8
Chilean	6.7
Colombian	6.4
Ecuadorian	6.7
Peruvian	5.5
Spaniard	7.8

Class of Worker: Private Wage and Salary
(Universe: Civilian Employed Population 16 Years and Over)

Group	Number	%
Total Population	1,024,780	81.8
Hispanic or Latino (of any race)	288,186	88.2
Central American, ex. Mexican	13,346	87.0
Guatemalan	7,754	87.0
Honduran	1,752	82.6
Nicaraguan	526	85.4
Salvadoran	2,205	89.3
Cuban	2,882	83.9
Dominican Republic	905	84.5
Mexican	216,191	90.3
Puerto Rican	31,946	79.2
South American	16,741	84.4
Argentinean	773	81.0
Chilean	375	70.9
Colombian	3,435	78.4
Ecuadorian	8,810	88.0
Peruvian	2,373	85.6
Spaniard	957	79.0

Class of Worker: Government
(Universe: Civilian Employed Population 16 Years and Over)

Group	Number	%
Total Population	167,678	13.4
Hispanic or Latino (of any race)	26,839	8.2
Central American, ex. Mexican	1,078	7.0
Guatemalan	630	7.1
Honduran	127	6.0
Nicaraguan	90	14.6
Salvadoran	135	5.5
Cuban	460	13.4
Dominican Republic	133	12.4
Mexican	15,358	6.4
Puerto Rican	7,339	18.2
South American	1,540	7.8
Argentinean	119	12.5
Chilean	79	14.9
Colombian	437	10.0
Ecuadorian	513	5.1
Peruvian	342	12.3
Spaniard	160	13.2

Means of Transportation to Work: Car, Truck or Van
(Universe: Workers 16 Years and Over)

Group	Number	%
Total Population	743,458	61.0
Hispanic or Latino (of any race)	227,492	71.7
Central American, ex. Mexican	10,746	72.6
Guatemalan	5,975	69.7
Honduran	1,626	79.5
Nicaraguan	481	78.1
Salvadoran	1,729	73.1
Cuban	2,138	64.9
Dominican Republic	771	72.9
Mexican	170,874	73.4
Puerto Rican	26,734	68.5
South American	11,873	62.0
Argentinean	500	56.7
Chilean	232	44.8
Colombian	2,954	69.3
Ecuadorian	5,522	57.2
Peruvian	1,832	68.1
Spaniard	596	47.7

Means of Transportation to Work: Public Transportation (ex. Taxicab)
(Universe: Workers 16 Years and Over)

Group	Number	%
Total Population	324,247	26.6
Hispanic or Latino (of any race)	63,634	20.1
Central American, ex. Mexican	2,887	19.5
Guatemalan	2,000	23.3
Honduran	205	10.0
Nicaraguan	58	9.4
Salvadoran	430	18.2
Cuban	706	21.4
Dominican Republic	254	24.0
Mexican	43,929	18.9
Puerto Rican	8,770	22.5
South American	5,319	27.8
Argentinean	224	25.4
Chilean	133	25.7
Colombian	835	19.6
Ecuadorian	3,361	34.8
Peruvian	614	22.8
Spaniard	356	28.5

Homeownership Rate
(Universe: Occupied Housing Units)

Group	%
Total Population	44.9
Hispanic or Latino (of any race)	42.2
Central American, ex. Mexican	40.0
Costa Rican	38.1
Guatemalan	41.2
Honduran	35.2
Nicaraguan	45.8
Panamanian	38.2
Salvadoran	40.4
Cuban	40.5
Dominican Republic	32.0
Mexican	44.6
Puerto Rican	34.8
South American	43.2
Argentinean	45.9
Bolivian	53.4
Chilean	39.6
Colombian	43.9
Ecuadorian	43.3
Paraguayan	40.5
Peruvian	40.2
Uruguayan	42.2
Venezuelan	40.7
Spaniard	41.6

Median Home Value

Group	Dollars
Total Population	269,200
Hispanic or Latino (of any race)	262,600
Central American, ex. Mexican	303,200
Guatemalan	308,500
Honduran	298,000
Nicaraguan	314,300
Salvadoran	308,500
Cuban	358,200
Dominican Republic	301,400
Mexican	247,400
Puerto Rican	304,100
South American	331,000
Argentinean	271,400
Chilean	268,800
Colombian	322,900
Ecuadorian	349,500
Peruvian	347,300
Spaniard	322,800

Median Gross Rent

Group	Dollars
Total Population	885
Hispanic or Latino (of any race)	839
Central American, ex. Mexican	871
Guatemalan	870
Honduran	840
Nicaraguan	869
Salvadoran	927
Cuban	886
Dominican Republic	839
Mexican	816
Puerto Rican	875

Notes: (1) Percent of total population; (2) Percent of Hispanic/Latino population; Profiles include places with an overall population of at least 125,000, OR an overall population of at least 25,000 where the Hispanic/Latino population is at least 20% of the overall population. In states where less than five places meet either of these criteria, we have included places with at least 10,000 total population with the highest percentage of Hispanic/Latino population. These places are identified with an asterisk (*); Please refer to the User's Guide for a full explanation of data.

Group	Dollars
South American	960
Argentinean	1,261
Chilean	796
Colombian	924
Ecuadorian	951
Peruvian	956
Spaniard	1,021

Median Household Income
(2010 Inflation-Adjusted Dollars)

Group	Dollars
Total Population	46,877
Hispanic or Latino (of any race)	41,979
Central American, ex. Mexican	44,605
Guatemalan	45,308
Honduran	48,140
Nicaraguan	41,979
Salvadoran	41,157
Cuban	46,295
Dominican Republic	36,354
Mexican	42,024
Puerto Rican	36,733
South American	50,762
Argentinean	48,208
Chilean	56,985
Colombian	46,667
Ecuadorian	50,435
Peruvian	52,443
Spaniard	53,125

Per Capita Income
(2010 Inflation-Adjusted Dollars)

Group	Dollars
Total Population	27,148
Hispanic or Latino (of any race)	14,986
Central American, ex. Mexican	17,654
Guatemalan	16,884
Honduran	15,358
Nicaraguan	22,691
Salvadoran	18,106
Cuban	28,552
Dominican Republic	14,149
Mexican	13,865
Puerto Rican	17,089
South American	21,315
Argentinean	22,774
Chilean	36,486
Colombian	23,487
Ecuadorian	17,569
Peruvian	27,064
Spaniard	32,738

Households with $100,000+ Income

Group	Number	%
Total Population	200,080	19.4
Hispanic or Latino (of any race)	22,452	11.1
Central American, ex. Mexican	1,035	11.8
Guatemalan	652	13.5
Honduran	124	10.2
Nicaraguan	45	10.0
Salvadoran	86	6.1
Cuban	599	18.7
Dominican Republic	28	3.7
Mexican	14,308	10.2
Puerto Rican	3,635	11.0
South American	2,041	18.8
Argentinean	182	25.3
Chilean	85	21.4
Colombian	503	18.7
Ecuadorian	767	16.7
Peruvian	298	19.7
Spaniard	207	19.3

Households with Food Stamps/SNAP Benefits During Past 12 Months

Group	Number	%
Total Population	152,490	14.8
Hispanic or Latino (of any race)	33,571	16.7
Central American, ex. Mexican	1,288	14.7
Guatemalan	737	15.2
Honduran	145	11.9
Nicaraguan	78	17.3
Salvadoran	114	8.1
Cuban	565	17.6
Dominican Republic	156	20.6
Mexican	21,144	15.1
Puerto Rican	8,896	26.8
South American	854	7.9
Argentinean	0	0.0
Chilean	0	0.0
Colombian	253	9.4
Ecuadorian	323	7.0
Peruvian	113	7.5
Spaniard	58	5.4

Poverty Rate
(Income in Past 12 Months Below Poverty Level)

Group	%
Total Population	20.9
Hispanic or Latino (of any race)	21.7
Central American, ex. Mexican	15.8
Guatemalan	15.4
Honduran	19.5
Nicaraguan	14.8
Salvadoran	13.3
Cuban	14.1
Dominican Republic	22.4
Mexican	22.0
Puerto Rican	25.4
South American	12.2
Argentinean	12.7
Chilean	19.7
Colombian	10.3
Ecuadorian	13.1
Peruvian	9.4
Spaniard	14.2

Chicago Heights

Population

Group	Number	%TP[1]	%HP[2]
Total Population	30,276	100.0	
Hispanic or Latino (of any race)	10,254	33.9	100.0
Mexican	9,438	31.2	92.0
Puerto Rican	281	0.9	2.7

Population Growth: 2000–2010

Group	%
Total Population	-7.6
Hispanic or Latino (of any race)	31.6
Mexican	37.8
Puerto Rican	46.4

Males per 100 Females

Group	Number
Total Population	95.9
Hispanic or Latino (of any race)	113.4
Mexican	113.9
Puerto Rican	116.2

Average Household Size

Group	People
Total Population	3.09
Hispanic or Latino (of any race)	4.20
Mexican	4.24
Puerto Rican	3.54

Median Age

Group	Years
Total Population	31.2
Hispanic or Latino (of any race)	24.6
Mexican	24.5
Puerto Rican	22.5

High School Graduates
(Universe: Population 25 Years and Over)

Group	Number	%
Total Population	13,931	79.8
Hispanic or Latino (of any race)	2,839	60.2
Mexican	2,551	57.8

Four-Year College Graduates
(Universe: Population 25 Years and Over)

Group	Number	%
Total Population	2,368	13.6
Hispanic or Latino (of any race)	214	4.5
Mexican	192	4.4

Population Age 3–17 Enrolled in Public School
(Universe: Population Age 3–17 Enrolled in School)

Group	Number	%
Total Population	6,597	88.6
Hispanic or Latino (of any race)	2,735	92.4
Mexican	2,283	91.0

Population Age 3–17 Enrolled in Private School
(Universe: Population Age 3–17 Enrolled in School)

Group	Number	%
Total Population	845	11.4
Hispanic or Latino (of any race)	225	7.6
Mexican	225	9.0

Foreign-Born Population

Group	Number	%
Total Population	4,213	13.9
Hispanic or Latino (of any race)	3,780	38.5
Mexican	3,690	41.6

Foreign-Born Naturalized U.S. Citizens

Group	Number	%
Total Population	1,043	24.8
Hispanic or Latino (of any race)	719	19.0
Mexican	709	19.2

Language Spoken at Home: English Only
(Universe: Population 5 Years and Over)

Group	Number	%
Total Population	20,455	73.1
Hispanic or Latino (of any race)	1,935	22.4
Mexican	1,326	17.1

Language Spoken at Home: Spanish
(Universe: Population 5 Years and Over)

Group	Number	%
Total Population	6,961	24.9
Hispanic or Latino (of any race)	6,687	77.6
Mexican	6,446	82.9

Unemployment Rate
(Universe: Population 16 Years and Over)

Group	%
Total Population	15.3
Hispanic or Latino (of any race)	10.9
Mexican	11.1

Class of Worker: Private Wage and Salary
(Universe: Civilian Employed Population 16 Years and Over)

Group	Number	%
Total Population	9,557	85.7
Hispanic or Latino (of any race)	3,375	92.7
Mexican	3,259	95.5

Class of Worker: Government
(Universe: Civilian Employed Population 16 Years and Over)

Group	Number	%
Total Population	1,369	12.3
Hispanic or Latino (of any race)	241	6.6
Mexican	129	3.8

Means of Transportation to Work: Car, Truck or Van
(Universe: Workers 16 Years and Over)

Group	Number	%
Total Population	9,812	90.2
Hispanic or Latino (of any race)	3,478	96.2
Mexican	3,260	96.2

Means of Transportation to Work: Public Transportation (ex. Taxicab)
(Universe: Workers 16 Years and Over)

Group	Number	%
Total Population	701	6.4
Hispanic or Latino (of any race)	38	1.1
Mexican	28	0.8

Homeownership Rate
(Universe: Occupied Housing Units)

Group	%
Total Population	61.4
Hispanic or Latino (of any race)	60.0
Mexican	60.2
Puerto Rican	59.7

Notes: (1) Percent of total population; (2) Percent of Hispanic/Latino population; Profiles include places with an overall population of at least 125,000, OR an overall population of at least 25,000 where the Hispanic/Latino population is at least 20% of the overall population. In states where less than five places meet either of these criteria, we have included places with at least 10,000 total population with the highest percentage of Hispanic/Latino population. These places are identified with an asterisk (*); Please refer to the User's Guide for a full explanation of data.

Median Home Value	
Group	Dollars
Total Population	135,400
Hispanic or Latino (of any race)	120,900
Mexican	121,600

Median Gross Rent	
Group	Dollars
Total Population	776
Hispanic or Latino (of any race)	739
Mexican	721

Median Household Income (2010 Inflation-Adjusted Dollars)	
Group	Dollars
Total Population	38,972
Hispanic or Latino (of any race)	34,598
Mexican	34,909

Per Capita Income (2010 Inflation-Adjusted Dollars)	
Group	Dollars
Total Population	16,646
Hispanic or Latino (of any race)	11,238
Mexican	11,496

Households with $100,000+ Income		
Group	Number	%
Total Population	989	10.0
Hispanic or Latino (of any race)	121	4.7
Mexican	121	5.0

Households with Food Stamps/SNAP Benefits During Past 12 Months		
Group	Number	%
Total Population	1,545	15.6
Hispanic or Latino (of any race)	336	13.0
Mexican	283	11.6

Poverty Rate (Income in Past 12 Months Below Poverty Level)	
Group	%
Total Population	24.4
Hispanic or Latino (of any race)	22.5
Mexican	21.2

Cicero

Population			
Group	Number	%TP[1]	%HP[2]
Total Population	83,891	100.0	–
Hispanic or Latino (of any race)	72,609	86.6	100.0
Central American, ex. Mexican	1,293	1.5	1.8
Guatemalan	650	0.8	0.9
Honduran	205	0.2	0.3
Nicaraguan	105	0.1	0.1
Salvadoran	278	0.3	0.4
Cuban	137	0.2	0.2
Dominican Republic	150	0.2	0.2
Mexican	65,694	78.3	90.5
Puerto Rican	2,782	3.3	3.8
South American	719	0.9	1.0
Colombian	145	0.2	0.2
Ecuadorian	365	0.4	0.5

Population Growth: 2000–2010	
Group	%
Total Population	-2.0
Hispanic or Latino (of any race)	9.5
Central American, ex. Mexican	47.1
Guatemalan	36.0
Honduran	53.0
Salvadoran	84.1
Cuban	11.4
Mexican	12.2
Puerto Rican	19.3
South American	32.2
Colombian	-15.2
Ecuadorian	75.5

Males per 100 Females	
Group	Number
Total Population	103.7
Hispanic or Latino (of any race)	105.5
Central American, ex. Mexican	98.6
Guatemalan	105.7
Honduran	83.0
Nicaraguan	75.0
Salvadoran	107.5
Cuban	136.2
Dominican Republic	89.9
Mexican	106.0
Puerto Rican	96.5
South American	105.4
Colombian	98.6
Ecuadorian	106.2

Average Household Size	
Group	People
Total Population	3.79
Hispanic or Latino (of any race)	4.24
Central American, ex. Mexican	3.98
Guatemalan	3.99
Honduran	3.96
Nicaraguan	4.09
Salvadoran	3.91
Cuban	3.35
Dominican Republic	3.53
Mexican	4.31
Puerto Rican	3.39
South American	3.65
Colombian	3.17
Ecuadorian	3.83

Median Age	
Group	Years
Total Population	27.8
Hispanic or Latino (of any race)	25.8
Central American, ex. Mexican	33.6
Guatemalan	34.2
Honduran	33.1
Nicaraguan	34.5
Salvadoran	33.3
Cuban	33.3
Dominican Republic	28.0
Mexican	25.6
Puerto Rican	27.3
South American	35.5
Colombian	38.6
Ecuadorian	35.8

High School Graduates (Universe: Population 25 Years and Over)		
Group	Number	%
Total Population	27,193	60.2
Hispanic or Latino (of any race)	20,151	55.6
Central American, ex. Mexican	706	67.9
Mexican	17,514	54.1
Puerto Rican	1,097	64.9

Four-Year College Graduates (Universe: Population 25 Years and Over)		
Group	Number	%
Total Population	3,732	8.3
Hispanic or Latino (of any race)	2,201	6.1
Central American, ex. Mexican	47	4.5
Mexican	1,747	5.4
Puerto Rican	212	12.6

Population Age 3–17 Enrolled in Public School (Universe: Population Age 3–17 Enrolled in School)		
Group	Number	%
Total Population	19,071	94.6
Hispanic or Latino (of any race)	17,868	95.0
Central American, ex. Mexican	285	100.0
Mexican	16,203	95.4
Puerto Rican	577	88.1

Population Age 3–17 Enrolled in Private School (Universe: Population Age 3–17 Enrolled in School)		
Group	Number	%
Total Population	1,098	5.4
Hispanic or Latino (of any race)	931	5.0
Central American, ex. Mexican	0	0.0
Mexican	776	4.6
Puerto Rican	78	11.9

Foreign-Born Population		
Group	Number	%
Total Population	35,945	43.1
Hispanic or Latino (of any race)	34,485	48.2
Central American, ex. Mexican	1,098	69.1
Mexican	32,639	50.9
Puerto Rican	35	1.1

Foreign-Born Naturalized U.S. Citizens		
Group	Number	%
Total Population	10,372	28.9
Hispanic or Latino (of any race)	9,536	27.7
Central American, ex. Mexican	484	44.1
Mexican	8,634	26.5
Puerto Rican	27	77.1

Language Spoken at Home: English Only (Universe: Population 5 Years and Over)		
Group	Number	%
Total Population	13,413	18.1
Hispanic or Latino (of any race)	4,225	6.7
Central American, ex. Mexican	96	6.6
Mexican	2,847	5.0
Puerto Rican	840	31.7

Language Spoken at Home: Spanish (Universe: Population 5 Years and Over)		
Group	Number	%
Total Population	59,164	79.8
Hispanic or Latino (of any race)	58,713	93.2
Central American, ex. Mexican	1,360	93.4
Mexican	53,941	95.0
Puerto Rican	1,780	67.2

Unemployment Rate (Universe: Population 16 Years and Over)	
Group	%
Total Population	11.1
Hispanic or Latino (of any race)	10.9
Central American, ex. Mexican	9.5
Mexican	10.3
Puerto Rican	19.9

Class of Worker: Private Wage and Salary (Universe: Civilian Employed Population 16 Years and Over)		
Group	Number	%
Total Population	31,378	90.0
Hispanic or Latino (of any race)	27,655	91.4
Central American, ex. Mexican	753	89.5
Mexican	25,364	92.2
Puerto Rican	915	82.5

Class of Worker: Government (Universe: Civilian Employed Population 16 Years and Over)		
Group	Number	%
Total Population	2,299	6.6
Hispanic or Latino (of any race)	1,669	5.5
Central American, ex. Mexican	42	5.0
Mexican	1,342	4.9
Puerto Rican	159	14.3

Means of Transportation to Work: Car, Truck or Van (Universe: Workers 16 Years and Over)		
Group	Number	%
Total Population	28,454	83.9
Hispanic or Latino (of any race)	25,002	84.9
Central American, ex. Mexican	675	86.1
Mexican	22,914	85.7
Puerto Rican	811	73.1

Means of Transportation to Work: Public Transportation (ex. Taxicab) (Universe: Workers 16 Years and Over)		
Group	Number	%
Total Population	3,295	9.7
Hispanic or Latino (of any race)	2,606	8.8
Central American, ex. Mexican	85	10.8
Mexican	2,046	7.7
Puerto Rican	287	25.9

Homeownership Rate (Universe: Occupied Housing Units)	
Group	%
Total Population	50.0

STATE & PLACE PROFILES

Notes: (1) Percent of total population; (2) Percent of Hispanic/Latino population; Profiles include places with an overall population of at least 125,000, OR an overall population of at least 25,000 where the Hispanic/Latino population is at least 20% of the overall population. In states where less than five places meet either of these criteria, we have included places with at least 10,000 total population with the highest percentage of Hispanic/Latino population. These places are identified with an asterisk (*); Please refer to the User's Guide for a full explanation of data.

Hispanic or Latino (of any race)	49.0
Central American, ex. Mexican	45.6
Guatemalan	46.8
Honduran	44.4
Nicaraguan	31.8
Salvadoran	47.4
Cuban	49.0
Dominican Republic	30.0
Mexican	49.9
Puerto Rican	37.9
South American	55.4
Colombian	54.8
Ecuadorian	60.9

Median Home Value

Group	Dollars
Total Population	219,800
Hispanic or Latino (of any race)	227,100
Central American, ex. Mexican	216,700
Mexican	228,600
Puerto Rican	197,600

Median Gross Rent

Group	Dollars
Total Population	778
Hispanic or Latino (of any race)	798
Central American, ex. Mexican	707
Mexican	812
Puerto Rican	742

Median Household Income
(2010 Inflation-Adjusted Dollars)

Group	Dollars
Total Population	43,799
Hispanic or Latino (of any race)	46,370
Central American, ex. Mexican	39,297
Mexican	46,946
Puerto Rican	27,010

Per Capita Income
(2010 Inflation-Adjusted Dollars)

Group	Dollars
Total Population	14,312
Hispanic or Latino (of any race)	13,096
Central American, ex. Mexican	14,459
Mexican	13,010
Puerto Rican	13,947

Households with $100,000+ Income

Group	Number	%
Total Population	2,076	9.6
Hispanic or Latino (of any race)	1,509	9.1
Central American, ex. Mexican	52	9.4
Mexican	1,363	9.4
Puerto Rican	66	6.6

Households with Food Stamps/SNAP Benefits During Past 12 Months

Group	Number	%
Total Population	4,137	19.1
Hispanic or Latino (of any race)	3,193	19.3
Central American, ex. Mexican	137	24.7
Mexican	2,616	18.1
Puerto Rican	363	36.2

Poverty Rate
(Income in Past 12 Months Below Poverty Level)

Group	%
Total Population	16.9
Hispanic or Latino (of any race)	15.9
Central American, ex. Mexican	24.4
Mexican	15.0
Puerto Rican	31.4

Elgin

Population

Group	Number	%TP[1]	%HP[2]
Total Population	108,188	100.0	–
Hispanic or Latino (of any race)	47,121	43.6	100.0
Central American, ex. Mexican	888	0.8	1.9
Guatemalan	356	0.3	0.8
Salvadoran	387	0.4	0.8
Cuban	204	0.2	0.4
Mexican	41,265	38.1	87.6
Puerto Rican	2,973	2.7	6.3
South American	637	0.6	1.4
Colombian	253	0.2	0.5
Ecuadorian	152	0.1	0.3
Peruvian	117	0.1	0.2
Spaniard	159	0.1	0.3

Population Growth: 2000–2010

Group	%
Total Population	14.5
Hispanic or Latino (of any race)	45.3
Central American, ex. Mexican	201.0
Guatemalan	206.9
Salvadoran	261.7
Cuban	82.1
Mexican	50.4
Puerto Rican	26.2
South American	250.0

Males per 100 Females

Group	Number
Total Population	99.2
Hispanic or Latino (of any race)	108.0
Central American, ex. Mexican	100.5
Guatemalan	111.9
Salvadoran	91.6
Cuban	90.7
Mexican	109.6
Puerto Rican	99.9
South American	82.5
Colombian	69.8
Ecuadorian	102.7
Peruvian	95.0
Spaniard	98.8

Average Household Size

Group	People
Total Population	3.03
Hispanic or Latino (of any race)	4.40
Central American, ex. Mexican	4.09
Guatemalan	4.25
Salvadoran	4.29
Cuban	2.79
Mexican	4.60
Puerto Rican	3.04
South American	3.42
Colombian	3.07
Ecuadorian	4.35
Peruvian	3.20
Spaniard	2.66

Median Age

Group	Years
Total Population	32.5
Hispanic or Latino (of any race)	24.9
Central American, ex. Mexican	30.0
Guatemalan	30.2
Salvadoran	28.5
Cuban	31.0
Mexican	24.4
Puerto Rican	28.6
South American	31.2
Colombian	31.9
Ecuadorian	28.0
Peruvian	31.5
Spaniard	32.7

High School Graduates
(Universe: Population 25 Years and Over)

Group	Number	%
Total Population	51,002	77.6
Hispanic or Latino (of any race)	10,894	51.4
Mexican	8,835	47.9
Puerto Rican	1,299	78.2

Four-Year College Graduates
(Universe: Population 25 Years and Over)

Group	Number	%
Total Population	15,417	23.5
Hispanic or Latino (of any race)	1,696	8.0
Mexican	1,005	5.4
Puerto Rican	415	25.0

Population Age 3–17 Enrolled in Public School
(Universe: Population Age 3–17 Enrolled in School)

Group	Number	%
Total Population	19,926	91.6
Hispanic or Latino (of any race)	11,684	97.9
Mexican	10,775	98.7
Puerto Rican	484	86.6

Population Age 3–17 Enrolled in Private School
(Universe: Population Age 3–17 Enrolled in School)

Group	Number	%
Total Population	1,830	8.4
Hispanic or Latino (of any race)	256	2.1
Mexican	144	1.3
Puerto Rican	75	13.4

Foreign-Born Population

Group	Number	%
Total Population	27,342	25.6
Hispanic or Latino (of any race)	20,822	47.8
Mexican	19,863	50.9
Puerto Rican	49	1.9

Foreign-Born Naturalized U.S. Citizens

Group	Number	%
Total Population	7,936	29.0
Hispanic or Latino (of any race)	3,631	17.4
Mexican	3,239	16.3
Puerto Rican	17	34.7

Language Spoken at Home: English Only
(Universe: Population 5 Years and Over)

Group	Number	%
Total Population	55,658	57.3
Hispanic or Latino (of any race)	4,339	11.5
Mexican	3,120	9.3
Puerto Rican	741	30.6

Language Spoken at Home: Spanish
(Universe: Population 5 Years and Over)

Group	Number	%
Total Population	34,177	35.2
Hispanic or Latino (of any race)	33,430	88.4
Mexican	30,601	90.7
Puerto Rican	1,661	68.7

Unemployment Rate
(Universe: Population 16 Years and Over)

Group	%
Total Population	8.1
Hispanic or Latino (of any race)	9.9
Mexican	9.8
Puerto Rican	16.0

Class of Worker: Private Wage and Salary
(Universe: Civilian Employed Population 16 Years and Over)

Group	Number	%
Total Population	45,283	86.4
Hispanic or Latino (of any race)	17,295	92.1
Mexican	15,521	93.8
Puerto Rican	994	75.5

Class of Worker: Government
(Universe: Civilian Employed Population 16 Years and Over)

Group	Number	%
Total Population	5,195	9.9
Hispanic or Latino (of any race)	1,039	5.5
Mexican	685	4.1
Puerto Rican	289	21.9

Means of Transportation to Work: Car, Truck or Van
(Universe: Workers 16 Years and Over)

Group	Number	%
Total Population	46,788	91.2
Hispanic or Latino (of any race)	17,046	93.1
Mexican	15,077	93.4
Puerto Rican	1,202	94.9

Means of Transportation to Work: Public Transportation (ex. Taxicab)
(Universe: Workers 16 Years and Over)

Group	Number	%
Total Population	1,205	2.3
Hispanic or Latino (of any race)	261	1.4
Mexican	174	1.1

Notes: (1) Percent of total population; (2) Percent of Hispanic/Latino population; Profiles include places with an overall population of at least 125,000, OR an overall population of at least 25,000 where the Hispanic/Latino population is at least 20% of the overall population. In states where less than five places meet either of these criteria, we have included places with at least 10,000 total population with the highest percentage of Hispanic/Latino population. These places are identified with an asterisk (*); Please refer to the User's Guide for a full explanation of data.

Puerto Rican	14	1.1

Homeownership Rate
(Universe: Occupied Housing Units)

Group	%
Total Population	70.0
Hispanic or Latino (of any race)	57.0
Central American, ex. Mexican	55.5
Guatemalan	63.3
Salvadoran	53.8
Cuban	74.6
Mexican	57.2
Puerto Rican	53.1
South American	67.6
Colombian	60.6
Ecuadorian	72.1
Peruvian	74.3
Spaniard	67.2

Median Home Value

Group	Dollars
Total Population	212,700
Hispanic or Latino (of any race)	196,800
Mexican	195,200
Puerto Rican	211,900

Median Gross Rent

Group	Dollars
Total Population	883
Hispanic or Latino (of any race)	913
Mexican	932
Puerto Rican	785

Median Household Income
(2010 Inflation-Adjusted Dollars)

Group	Dollars
Total Population	57,216
Hispanic or Latino (of any race)	46,713
Mexican	46,160
Puerto Rican	51,354

Per Capita Income
(2010 Inflation-Adjusted Dollars)

Group	Dollars
Total Population	23,407
Hispanic or Latino (of any race)	13,110
Mexican	12,006
Puerto Rican	23,097

Households with $100,000+ Income

Group	Number	%
Total Population	7,345	20.5
Hispanic or Latino (of any race)	1,051	10.4
Mexican	835	9.7
Puerto Rican	135	15.7

Households with Food Stamps/SNAP Benefits During Past 12 Months

Group	Number	%
Total Population	2,678	7.5
Hispanic or Latino (of any race)	1,107	11.0
Mexican	935	10.9
Puerto Rican	117	13.6

Poverty Rate
(Income in Past 12 Months Below Poverty Level)

Group	%
Total Population	11.9
Hispanic or Latino (of any race)	18.0
Mexican	18.5
Puerto Rican	15.5

Glendale Heights

Population

Group	Number	%TP[1]	%HP[2]
Total Population	34,208	100.0	–
Hispanic or Latino (of any race)	10,512	30.7	100.0
Central American, ex. Mexican	550	1.6	5.2
Guatemalan	357	1.0	3.4
Mexican	8,685	25.4	82.6
Puerto Rican	465	1.4	4.4
South American	323	0.9	3.1

Population Growth: 2000–2010

Group	%
Total Population	7.7
Hispanic or Latino (of any race)	79.9
Central American, ex. Mexican	89.7
Guatemalan	63.0
Mexican	87.9
Puerto Rican	98.7
South American	144.7

Males per 100 Females

Group	Number
Total Population	103.6
Hispanic or Latino (of any race)	109.2
Central American, ex. Mexican	109.1
Guatemalan	113.8
Mexican	109.7
Puerto Rican	109.5
South American	105.7

Average Household Size

Group	People
Total Population	3.04
Hispanic or Latino (of any race)	4.19
Central American, ex. Mexican	3.94
Guatemalan	4.05
Mexican	4.37
Puerto Rican	3.20
South American	3.22

Median Age

Group	Years
Total Population	32.0
Hispanic or Latino (of any race)	25.8
Central American, ex. Mexican	32.0
Guatemalan	32.5
Mexican	24.9
Puerto Rican	27.9
South American	35.7

High School Graduates
(Universe: Population 25 Years and Over)

Group	Number	%
Total Population	17,757	84.4
Hispanic or Latino (of any race)	2,932	64.5
Mexican	2,256	60.5

Four-Year College Graduates
(Universe: Population 25 Years and Over)

Group	Number	%
Total Population	6,043	28.7
Hispanic or Latino (of any race)	511	11.2
Mexican	217	5.8

Population Age 3–17 Enrolled in Public School
(Universe: Population Age 3–17 Enrolled in School)

Group	Number	%
Total Population	6,296	89.5
Hispanic or Latino (of any race)	2,805	92.2
Mexican	2,502	92.6

Population Age 3–17 Enrolled in Private School
(Universe: Population Age 3–17 Enrolled in School)

Group	Number	%
Total Population	741	10.5
Hispanic or Latino (of any race)	238	7.8
Mexican	200	7.4

Foreign-Born Population

Group	Number	%
Total Population	11,782	35.0
Hispanic or Latino (of any race)	4,427	45.2
Mexican	3,885	46.2

Foreign-Born Naturalized U.S. Citizens

Group	Number	%
Total Population	6,568	55.7
Hispanic or Latino (of any race)	1,575	35.6
Mexican	1,361	35.0

Language Spoken at Home: English Only
(Universe: Population 5 Years and Over)

Group	Number	%
Total Population	14,403	46.4
Hispanic or Latino (of any race)	699	8.2
Mexican	542	7.5

Language Spoken at Home: Spanish
(Universe: Population 5 Years and Over)

Group	Number	%
Total Population	8,011	25.8
Hispanic or Latino (of any race)	7,789	91.5
Mexican	6,713	92.3

Unemployment Rate
(Universe: Population 16 Years and Over)

Group	%
Total Population	9.5
Hispanic or Latino (of any race)	8.3
Mexican	8.9

Class of Worker: Private Wage and Salary
(Universe: Civilian Employed Population 16 Years and Over)

Group	Number	%
Total Population	15,899	89.7
Hispanic or Latino (of any race)	4,078	92.5
Mexican	3,401	93.3

Class of Worker: Government
(Universe: Civilian Employed Population 16 Years and Over)

Group	Number	%
Total Population	1,226	6.9
Hispanic or Latino (of any race)	112	2.5
Mexican	71	1.9

Means of Transportation to Work: Car, Truck or Van
(Universe: Workers 16 Years and Over)

Group	Number	%
Total Population	16,412	95.6
Hispanic or Latino (of any race)	4,124	98.4
Mexican	3,422	99.1

Means of Transportation to Work: Public Transportation (ex. Taxicab)
(Universe: Workers 16 Years and Over)

Group	Number	%
Total Population	271	1.6
Hispanic or Latino (of any race)	34	0.8
Mexican	0	0.0

Homeownership Rate
(Universe: Occupied Housing Units)

Group	%
Total Population	67.6
Hispanic or Latino (of any race)	60.0
Central American, ex. Mexican	53.8
Guatemalan	57.1
Mexican	60.5
Puerto Rican	64.1
South American	66.4

Median Home Value

Group	Dollars
Total Population	221,100
Hispanic or Latino (of any race)	220,500
Mexican	217,700

Median Gross Rent

Group	Dollars
Total Population	986
Hispanic or Latino (of any race)	995
Mexican	1,013

Median Household Income
(2010 Inflation-Adjusted Dollars)

Group	Dollars
Total Population	63,490
Hispanic or Latino (of any race)	60,761
Mexican	58,073

Per Capita Income
(2010 Inflation-Adjusted Dollars)

Group	Dollars
Total Population	25,620
Hispanic or Latino (of any race)	16,751
Mexican	14,919

Households with $100,000+ Income

Group	Number	%
Total Population	2,578	22.3
Hispanic or Latino (of any race)	480	18.6
Mexican	311	16.2

Notes: (1) Percent of total population; (2) Percent of Hispanic/Latino population; Profiles include places with an overall population of at least 125,000, OR an overall population of at least 25,000 where the Hispanic/Latino population is at least 20% of the overall population. In states where less than five places meet either of these criteria, we have included places with at least 10,000 total population with the highest percentage of Hispanic/Latino population. These places are identified with an asterisk (*); Please refer to the User's Guide for a full explanation of data.

Households with Food Stamps/SNAP Benefits During Past 12 Months

Group	Number	%
Total Population	893	7.7
Hispanic or Latino (of any race)	241	9.3
Mexican	153	8.0

Poverty Rate
(Income in Past 12 Months Below Poverty Level)

Group	%
Total Population	10.8
Hispanic or Latino (of any race)	12.9
Mexican	12.6

Hanover Park

Population

Group	Number	%TP[1]	%HP[2]
Total Population	37,973	100.0	–
Hispanic or Latino (of any race)	14,532	38.3	100.0
Central American, ex. Mexican	437	1.2	3.0
Guatemalan	223	0.6	1.5
Salvadoran	149	0.4	1.0
Mexican	12,691	33.4	87.3
Puerto Rican	572	1.5	3.9
South American	316	0.8	2.2
Colombian	139	0.4	1.0

Population Growth: 2000–2010

Group	%
Total Population	-0.8
Hispanic or Latino (of any race)	42.0
Central American, ex. Mexican	61.9
Guatemalan	81.3
Mexican	48.5
Puerto Rican	56.7
South American	60.4

Males per 100 Females

Group	Number
Total Population	102.2
Hispanic or Latino (of any race)	110.2
Central American, ex. Mexican	82.1
Guatemalan	79.8
Salvadoran	101.4
Mexican	113.0
Puerto Rican	90.7
South American	91.5
Colombian	87.8

Average Household Size

Group	People
Total Population	3.48
Hispanic or Latino (of any race)	4.68
Central American, ex. Mexican	4.20
Guatemalan	4.06
Salvadoran	4.33
Mexican	4.85
Puerto Rican	3.21
South American	3.69
Colombian	3.72

Median Age

Group	Years
Total Population	31.5
Hispanic or Latino (of any race)	24.9
Central American, ex. Mexican	28.9
Guatemalan	30.6
Salvadoran	28.2
Mexican	24.4
Puerto Rican	25.8
South American	32.5
Colombian	33.9

High School Graduates
(Universe: Population 25 Years and Over)

Group	Number	%
Total Population	18,132	80.5
Hispanic or Latino (of any race)	4,147	57.2
Mexican	3,414	53.9

Four-Year College Graduates
(Universe: Population 25 Years and Over)

Group	Number	%
Total Population	5,462	24.3
Hispanic or Latino (of any race)	532	7.3
Mexican	463	7.3

Population Age 3–17 Enrolled in Public School
(Universe: Population Age 3–17 Enrolled in School)

Group	Number	%
Total Population	7,693	93.6
Hispanic or Latino (of any race)	3,346	96.8
Mexican	3,025	96.5

Population Age 3–17 Enrolled in Private School
(Universe: Population Age 3–17 Enrolled in School)

Group	Number	%
Total Population	525	6.4
Hispanic or Latino (of any race)	111	3.2
Mexican	111	3.5

Foreign-Born Population

Group	Number	%
Total Population	14,393	38.1
Hispanic or Latino (of any race)	7,739	55.8
Mexican	7,309	59.1

Foreign-Born Naturalized U.S. Citizens

Group	Number	%
Total Population	5,682	39.5
Hispanic or Latino (of any race)	1,653	21.4
Mexican	1,459	20.0

Language Spoken at Home: English Only
(Universe: Population 5 Years and Over)

Group	Number	%
Total Population	15,622	45.4
Hispanic or Latino (of any race)	1,038	8.7
Mexican	727	6.8

Language Spoken at Home: Spanish
(Universe: Population 5 Years and Over)

Group	Number	%
Total Population	11,116	32.3
Hispanic or Latino (of any race)	10,955	91.3
Mexican	9,941	93.2

Unemployment Rate
(Universe: Population 16 Years and Over)

Group	%
Total Population	9.2
Hispanic or Latino (of any race)	7.8
Mexican	7.5

Class of Worker: Private Wage and Salary
(Universe: Civilian Employed Population 16 Years and Over)

Group	Number	%
Total Population	16,892	89.2
Hispanic or Latino (of any race)	6,303	92.5
Mexican	5,768	93.5

Class of Worker: Government
(Universe: Civilian Employed Population 16 Years and Over)

Group	Number	%
Total Population	1,460	7.7
Hispanic or Latino (of any race)	395	5.8
Mexican	283	4.6

Means of Transportation to Work: Car, Truck or Van
(Universe: Workers 16 Years and Over)

Group	Number	%
Total Population	16,693	90.1
Hispanic or Latino (of any race)	6,184	91.4
Mexican	5,608	91.3

Means of Transportation to Work: Public Transportation (ex. Taxicab)
(Universe: Workers 16 Years and Over)

Group	Number	%
Total Population	571	3.1
Hispanic or Latino (of any race)	114	1.7
Mexican	67	1.1

Homeownership Rate
(Universe: Occupied Housing Units)

Group	%
Total Population	79.1
Hispanic or Latino (of any race)	62.7
Central American, ex. Mexican	73.3
Guatemalan	86.3
Salvadoran	66.7
Mexican	60.8
Puerto Rican	71.1
South American	86.8
Colombian	86.1

Median Home Value

Group	Dollars
Total Population	219,400
Hispanic or Latino (of any race)	209,600
Mexican	204,400

Median Gross Rent

Group	Dollars
Total Population	958
Hispanic or Latino (of any race)	917
Mexican	915

Median Household Income
(2010 Inflation-Adjusted Dollars)

Group	Dollars
Total Population	63,649
Hispanic or Latino (of any race)	54,019
Mexican	53,872

Per Capita Income
(2010 Inflation-Adjusted Dollars)

Group	Dollars
Total Population	21,152
Hispanic or Latino (of any race)	15,183
Mexican	14,583

Households with $100,000+ Income

Group	Number	%
Total Population	2,139	19.4
Hispanic or Latino (of any race)	394	12.3
Mexican	332	12.3

Households with Food Stamps/SNAP Benefits During Past 12 Months

Group	Number	%
Total Population	950	8.6
Hispanic or Latino (of any race)	297	9.2
Mexican	196	7.2

Poverty Rate
(Income in Past 12 Months Below Poverty Level)

Group	%
Total Population	11.1
Hispanic or Latino (of any race)	12.1
Mexican	12.7

Joliet

Population

Group	Number	%TP[1]	%HP[2]
Total Population	147,433	100.0	–
Hispanic or Latino (of any race)	41,042	27.8	100.0
Central American, ex. Mexican	588	0.4	1.4
Guatemalan	323	0.2	0.8
Salvadoran	109	0.1	0.3
Cuban	151	0.1	0.4
Mexican	36,570	24.8	89.1
Puerto Rican	2,084	1.4	5.1
South American	485	0.3	1.2
Colombian	167	0.1	0.4
Peruvian	102	0.1	0.2
Spaniard	120	0.1	0.3

Population Growth: 2000–2010

Group	%
Total Population	38.8
Hispanic or Latino (of any race)	109.9
Mexican	115.9
Puerto Rican	255.6
South American	325.4

Notes: (1) Percent of total population; (2) Percent of Hispanic/Latino population; Profiles include places with an overall population of at least 125,000, OR an overall population of at least 25,000 where the Hispanic/Latino population is at least 20% of the overall population. In states where less than five places meet either of these criteria, we have included places with at least 10,000 total population with the highest percentage of Hispanic/Latino population. These places are identified with an asterisk (*); Please refer to the User's Guide for a full explanation of data.

Males per 100 Females

Group	Number
Total Population	97.8
Hispanic or Latino (of any race)	109.2
Central American, ex. Mexican	99.3
Guatemalan	97.0
Salvadoran	109.6
Cuban	73.6
Mexican	110.2
Puerto Rican	110.3
South American	90.9
Colombian	89.8
Peruvian	78.9
Spaniard	81.8

Average Household Size

Group	People
Total Population	3.01
Hispanic or Latino (of any race)	4.16
Central American, ex. Mexican	4.15
Guatemalan	3.95
Salvadoran	4.66
Cuban	3.43
Mexican	4.22
Puerto Rican	3.67
South American	3.46
Colombian	3.36
Peruvian	3.06
Spaniard	3.03

Median Age

Group	Years
Total Population	31.7
Hispanic or Latino (of any race)	24.6
Central American, ex. Mexican	29.4
Guatemalan	29.4
Salvadoran	29.8
Cuban	24.8
Mexican	24.5
Puerto Rican	23.3
South American	34.5
Colombian	34.9
Peruvian	40.0
Spaniard	27.5

High School Graduates
(Universe: Population 25 Years and Over)

Group	Number	%
Total Population	72,292	83.1
Hispanic or Latino (of any race)	11,011	57.2
Mexican	9,499	54.9
Puerto Rican	577	75.0

Four-Year College Graduates
(Universe: Population 25 Years and Over)

Group	Number	%
Total Population	18,612	21.4
Hispanic or Latino (of any race)	1,216	6.3
Mexican	917	5.3
Puerto Rican	77	10.0

Population Age 3–17 Enrolled in Public School
(Universe: Population Age 3–17 Enrolled in School)

Group	Number	%
Total Population	29,175	88.5
Hispanic or Latino (of any race)	9,625	92.8
Mexican	8,569	93.0
Puerto Rican	390	87.8

Population Age 3–17 Enrolled in Private School
(Universe: Population Age 3–17 Enrolled in School)

Group	Number	%
Total Population	3,800	11.5
Hispanic or Latino (of any race)	744	7.2
Mexican	642	7.0
Puerto Rican	54	12.2

Foreign-Born Population

Group	Number	%
Total Population	20,638	14.2
Hispanic or Latino (of any race)	15,788	40.6
Mexican	15,013	43.1
Puerto Rican	0	0.0

Foreign-Born Naturalized U.S. Citizens

Group	Number	%
Total Population	6,878	33.3
Hispanic or Latino (of any race)	3,885	24.6
Mexican	3,592	23.9
Puerto Rican	0	0.0

Language Spoken at Home: English Only
(Universe: Population 5 Years and Over)

Group	Number	%
Total Population	97,068	73.6
Hispanic or Latino (of any race)	6,270	18.4
Mexican	4,928	16.2
Puerto Rican	811	54.2

Language Spoken at Home: Spanish
(Universe: Population 5 Years and Over)

Group	Number	%
Total Population	29,121	22.1
Hispanic or Latino (of any race)	27,643	81.2
Mexican	25,316	83.4
Puerto Rican	685	45.8

Unemployment Rate
(Universe: Population 16 Years and Over)

Group	%
Total Population	9.8
Hispanic or Latino (of any race)	9.3
Mexican	9.2
Puerto Rican	10.2

Class of Worker: Private Wage and Salary
(Universe: Civilian Employed Population 16 Years and Over)

Group	Number	%
Total Population	56,613	85.7
Hispanic or Latino (of any race)	15,140	91.2
Mexican	13,638	91.4
Puerto Rican	614	89.9

Class of Worker: Government
(Universe: Civilian Employed Population 16 Years and Over)

Group	Number	%
Total Population	7,527	11.4
Hispanic or Latino (of any race)	933	5.6
Mexican	775	5.2
Puerto Rican	69	10.1

Means of Transportation to Work: Car, Truck or Van
(Universe: Workers 16 Years and Over)

Group	Number	%
Total Population	58,425	91.2
Hispanic or Latino (of any race)	14,701	92.1
Mexican	13,254	92.3
Puerto Rican	577	84.5

Means of Transportation to Work: Public Transportation (ex. Taxicab)
(Universe: Workers 16 Years and Over)

Group	Number	%
Total Population	1,747	2.7
Hispanic or Latino (of any race)	285	1.8
Mexican	242	1.7
Puerto Rican	27	4.0

Homeownership Rate
(Universe: Occupied Housing Units)

Group	%
Total Population	73.8
Hispanic or Latino (of any race)	69.9
Central American, ex. Mexican	74.3
Guatemalan	82.9
Salvadoran	75.9
Cuban	65.7
Mexican	69.8
Puerto Rican	73.3
South American	81.9
Colombian	79.5
Peruvian	78.1
Spaniard	75.8

Median Home Value

Group	Dollars
Total Population	195,300
Hispanic or Latino (of any race)	178,300
Mexican	171,400
Puerto Rican	236,800

Median Gross Rent

Group	Dollars
Total Population	819
Hispanic or Latino (of any race)	845
Mexican	850
Puerto Rican	725

Median Household Income
(2010 Inflation-Adjusted Dollars)

Group	Dollars
Total Population	60,714
Hispanic or Latino (of any race)	51,818
Mexican	49,692
Puerto Rican	56,810

Per Capita Income
(2010 Inflation-Adjusted Dollars)

Group	Dollars
Total Population	22,572
Hispanic or Latino (of any race)	14,414
Mexican	13,971
Puerto Rican	18,707

Households with $100,000+ Income

Group	Number	%
Total Population	10,127	21.7
Hispanic or Latino (of any race)	1,122	12.3
Mexican	973	12.3
Puerto Rican	60	11.4

Households with Food Stamps/SNAP Benefits During Past 12 Months

Group	Number	%
Total Population	5,524	11.8
Hispanic or Latino (of any race)	1,466	16.1
Mexican	1,283	16.3
Puerto Rican	92	17.5

Poverty Rate
(Income in Past 12 Months Below Poverty Level)

Group	%
Total Population	11.9
Hispanic or Latino (of any race)	17.4
Mexican	18.5
Puerto Rican	4.6

Melrose Park

Population

Group	Number	%TP[1]	%HP[2]
Total Population	25,411	100.0	–
Hispanic or Latino (of any race)	17,675	69.6	100.0
Central American, ex. Mexican	441	1.7	2.5
Guatemalan	297	1.2	1.7
Cuban	237	0.9	1.3
Mexican	15,141	59.6	85.7
Puerto Rican	1,095	4.3	6.2
South American	320	1.3	1.8
Colombian	111	0.4	0.6

Population Growth: 2000–2010

Group	%
Total Population	9.7
Hispanic or Latino (of any race)	41.6
Central American, ex. Mexican	81.5
Guatemalan	67.8
Cuban	-31.3
Mexican	44.2
Puerto Rican	144.4
South American	72.0

Males per 100 Females

Group	Number
Total Population	100.4
Hispanic or Latino (of any race)	107.8
Central American, ex. Mexican	111.0
Guatemalan	121.6
Cuban	107.9
Mexican	108.6
Puerto Rican	106.2
South American	87.1

Notes: (1) Percent of total population; (2) Percent of Hispanic/Latino population; Profiles include places with an overall population of at least 125,000, OR an overall population of at least 25,000 where the Hispanic/Latino population is at least 20% of the overall population. In states where less than five places meet either of these criteria, we have included places with at least 10,000 total population with the highest percentage of Hispanic/Latino population. These places are identified with an asterisk (*); Please refer to the User's Guide for a full explanation of data.

Group	People
Colombian	85.0

Average Household Size

Group	People
Total Population	3.19
Hispanic or Latino (of any race)	4.02
Central American, ex. Mexican	3.40
Guatemalan	3.33
Cuban	2.61
Mexican	4.22
Puerto Rican	2.97
South American	3.27
Colombian	2.96

Median Age

Group	Years
Total Population	30.9
Hispanic or Latino (of any race)	26.4
Central American, ex. Mexican	32.1
Guatemalan	32.0
Cuban	42.9
Mexican	25.6
Puerto Rican	28.6
South American	34.1
Colombian	36.3

High School Graduates
(Universe: Population 25 Years and Over)

Group	Number	%
Total Population	9,808	68.3
Hispanic or Latino (of any race)	4,897	56.8
Mexican	4,184	54.3

Four-Year College Graduates
(Universe: Population 25 Years and Over)

Group	Number	%
Total Population	1,517	10.6
Hispanic or Latino (of any race)	746	8.6
Mexican	568	7.4

Population Age 3–17 Enrolled in Public School
(Universe: Population Age 3–17 Enrolled in School)

Group	Number	%
Total Population	4,549	87.9
Hispanic or Latino (of any race)	3,886	90.4
Mexican	3,553	91.5

Population Age 3–17 Enrolled in Private School
(Universe: Population Age 3–17 Enrolled in School)

Group	Number	%
Total Population	627	12.1
Hispanic or Latino (of any race)	411	9.6
Mexican	331	8.5

Foreign-Born Population

Group	Number	%
Total Population	9,987	40.4
Hispanic or Latino (of any race)	8,762	50.8
Mexican	8,088	52.2

Foreign-Born Naturalized U.S. Citizens

Group	Number	%
Total Population	2,841	28.4
Hispanic or Latino (of any race)	2,213	25.3
Mexican	1,911	23.6

Language Spoken at Home: English Only
(Universe: Population 5 Years and Over)

Group	Number	%
Total Population	6,238	28.0
Hispanic or Latino (of any race)	738	4.9
Mexican	475	3.5

Language Spoken at Home: Spanish
(Universe: Population 5 Years and Over)

Group	Number	%
Total Population	14,423	64.8
Hispanic or Latino (of any race)	14,329	95.0
Mexican	13,121	96.4

Unemployment Rate
(Universe: Population 16 Years and Over)

Group	%
Total Population	11.1
Hispanic or Latino (of any race)	9.7
Mexican	9.8

Class of Worker: Private Wage and Salary
(Universe: Civilian Employed Population 16 Years and Over)

Group	Number	%
Total Population	9,221	86.0
Hispanic or Latino (of any race)	6,625	90.0
Mexican	6,016	91.8

Class of Worker: Government
(Universe: Civilian Employed Population 16 Years and Over)

Group	Number	%
Total Population	1,039	9.7
Hispanic or Latino (of any race)	470	6.4
Mexican	312	4.8

Means of Transportation to Work: Car, Truck or Van
(Universe: Workers 16 Years and Over)

Group	Number	%
Total Population	9,135	86.4
Hispanic or Latino (of any race)	6,348	87.1
Mexican	5,685	87.6

Means of Transportation to Work: Public Transportation (ex. Taxicab)
(Universe: Workers 16 Years and Over)

Group	Number	%
Total Population	804	7.6
Hispanic or Latino (of any race)	532	7.3
Mexican	426	6.6

Homeownership Rate
(Universe: Occupied Housing Units)

Group	%
Total Population	49.9
Hispanic or Latino (of any race)	43.3
Central American, ex. Mexican	40.1
Guatemalan	36.2
Cuban	54.7
Mexican	43.3
Puerto Rican	37.2
South American	64.5
Colombian	63.0

Median Home Value

Group	Dollars
Total Population	268,300
Hispanic or Latino (of any race)	265,500
Mexican	256,700

Median Gross Rent

Group	Dollars
Total Population	809
Hispanic or Latino (of any race)	841
Mexican	850

Median Household Income
(2010 Inflation-Adjusted Dollars)

Group	Dollars
Total Population	43,478
Hispanic or Latino (of any race)	44,486
Mexican	45,203

Per Capita Income
(2010 Inflation-Adjusted Dollars)

Group	Dollars
Total Population	16,847
Hispanic or Latino (of any race)	13,694
Mexican	13,248

Households with $100,000+ Income

Group	Number	%
Total Population	981	12.8
Hispanic or Latino (of any race)	505	11.7
Mexican	481	12.9

Households with Food Stamps/SNAP Benefits During Past 12 Months

Group	Number	%
Total Population	957	12.5
Hispanic or Latino (of any race)	596	13.8
Mexican	496	13.3

Poverty Rate
(Income in Past 12 Months Below Poverty Level)

Group	%
Total Population	14.5
Hispanic or Latino (of any race)	13.8
Mexican	14.0

Mundelein

Population

Group	Number	%TP[1]	%HP[2]
Total Population	31,064	100.0	–
Hispanic or Latino (of any race)	9,344	30.1	100.0
Central American, ex. Mexican	254	0.8	2.7
Salvadoran	115	0.4	1.2
Mexican	8,353	26.9	89.4
Puerto Rican	256	0.8	2.7
South American	223	0.7	2.4
Colombian	103	0.3	1.1

Population Growth: 2000–2010

Group	%
Total Population	0.4
Hispanic or Latino (of any race)	24.8
Central American, ex. Mexican	24.5
Salvadoran	7.5
Mexican	27.7
Puerto Rican	31.3
South American	95.6

Males per 100 Females

Group	Number
Total Population	102.8
Hispanic or Latino (of any race)	112.7
Central American, ex. Mexican	95.4
Salvadoran	101.8
Mexican	113.7
Puerto Rican	93.9
South American	108.4
Colombian	119.1

Average Household Size

Group	People
Total Population	2.94
Hispanic or Latino (of any race)	4.47
Central American, ex. Mexican	4.02
Salvadoran	3.83
Mexican	4.62
Puerto Rican	3.01
South American	3.20
Colombian	3.14

Median Age

Group	Years
Total Population	35.1
Hispanic or Latino (of any race)	25.4
Central American, ex. Mexican	32.8
Salvadoran	36.1
Mexican	24.8
Puerto Rican	26.5
South American	36.2
Colombian	33.8

High School Graduates
(Universe: Population 25 Years and Over)

Group	Number	%
Total Population	16,766	83.4
Hispanic or Latino (of any race)	2,276	46.3
Mexican	1,917	42.6

Four-Year College Graduates
(Universe: Population 25 Years and Over)

Group	Number	%
Total Population	8,177	40.7
Hispanic or Latino (of any race)	513	10.4
Mexican	405	9.0

Population Age 3–17 Enrolled in Public School
(Universe: Population Age 3–17 Enrolled in School)

Group	Number	%
Total Population	5,382	83.1
Hispanic or Latino (of any race)	2,268	96.0
Mexican	2,100	96.6

Population Age 3–17 Enrolled in Private School
(Universe: Population Age 3–17 Enrolled in School)

Group	Number	%
Total Population	1,097	16.9

Notes: (1) Percent of total population; (2) Percent of Hispanic/Latino population; Profiles include places with an overall population of at least 125,000, OR an overall population of at least 25,000 where the Hispanic/Latino population is at least 20% of the overall population. In states where less than five places meet either of these criteria, we have included places with at least 10,000 total population with the highest percentage of Hispanic/Latino population. These places are identified with an asterisk (*); Please refer to the User's Guide for a full explanation of data.

Hispanic or Latino (of any race)	95	4.0
Mexican	73	3.4

Foreign-Born Population

Group	Number	%
Total Population	9,083	29.2
Hispanic or Latino (of any race)	5,297	56.7
Mexican	4,971	57.7

Foreign-Born Naturalized U.S. Citizens

Group	Number	%
Total Population	3,494	38.5
Hispanic or Latino (of any race)	1,043	19.7
Mexican	927	18.6

Language Spoken at Home: English Only
(Universe: Population 5 Years and Over)

Group	Number	%
Total Population	16,608	57.7
Hispanic or Latino (of any race)	437	5.2
Mexican	281	3.6

Language Spoken at Home: Spanish
(Universe: Population 5 Years and Over)

Group	Number	%
Total Population	8,177	28.4
Hispanic or Latino (of any race)	8,043	94.8
Mexican	7,507	96.4

Unemployment Rate
(Universe: Population 16 Years and Over)

Group	%
Total Population	8.6
Hispanic or Latino (of any race)	15.2
Mexican	15.5

Class of Worker: Private Wage and Salary
(Universe: Civilian Employed Population 16 Years and Over)

Group	Number	%
Total Population	14,649	86.3
Hispanic or Latino (of any race)	4,151	91.0
Mexican	3,811	90.8

Class of Worker: Government
(Universe: Civilian Employed Population 16 Years and Over)

Group	Number	%
Total Population	1,555	9.2
Hispanic or Latino (of any race)	142	3.1
Mexican	117	2.8

Means of Transportation to Work: Car, Truck or Van
(Universe: Workers 16 Years and Over)

Group	Number	%
Total Population	14,810	89.2
Hispanic or Latino (of any race)	3,887	87.2
Mexican	3,542	86.6

Means of Transportation to Work: Public Transportation (ex. Taxicab)
(Universe: Workers 16 Years and Over)

Group	Number	%
Total Population	462	2.8
Hispanic or Latino (of any race)	91	2.0
Mexican	80	2.0

Homeownership Rate
(Universe: Occupied Housing Units)

Group	%
Total Population	78.0
Hispanic or Latino (of any race)	56.9
Central American, ex. Mexican	74.2
Salvadoran	74.3
Mexican	55.1
Puerto Rican	64.2
South American	71.2
Colombian	82.1

Median Home Value

Group	Dollars
Total Population	251,000
Hispanic or Latino (of any race)	217,600
Mexican	211,300

Median Gross Rent

Group	Dollars
Total Population	998
Hispanic or Latino (of any race)	1,008
Mexican	1,025

Median Household Income
(2010 Inflation-Adjusted Dollars)

Group	Dollars
Total Population	82,759
Hispanic or Latino (of any race)	56,956
Mexican	55,868

Per Capita Income
(2010 Inflation-Adjusted Dollars)

Group	Dollars
Total Population	33,804
Hispanic or Latino (of any race)	16,767
Mexican	16,109

Households with $100,000+ Income

Group	Number	%
Total Population	3,943	38.2
Hispanic or Latino (of any race)	426	21.0
Mexican	353	19.3

Households with Food Stamps/SNAP Benefits During Past 12 Months

Group	Number	%
Total Population	365	3.5
Hispanic or Latino (of any race)	47	2.3
Mexican	47	2.6

Poverty Rate
(Income in Past 12 Months Below Poverty Level)

Group	%
Total Population	4.8
Hispanic or Latino (of any race)	10.9
Mexican	11.7

Naperville

Population

Group	Number	%TP[1]	%HP[2]
Total Population	141,853	100.0	–
Hispanic or Latino (of any race)	7,574	5.3	100.0
Central American, ex. Mexican	320	0.2	4.2
Guatemalan	135	0.1	1.8
Cuban	286	0.2	3.8
Mexican	4,767	3.4	62.9
Puerto Rican	853	0.6	11.3
South American	798	0.6	10.5
Argentinean	111	0.1	1.5
Colombian	262	0.2	3.5
Peruvian	109	0.1	1.4
Venezuelan	108	0.1	1.4
Spaniard	177	0.1	2.3

Population Growth: 2000–2010

Group	%
Total Population	10.5
Hispanic or Latino (of any race)	82.1
Cuban	35.5
Mexican	91.4
Puerto Rican	73.7
South American	137.5
Colombian	162.0

Males per 100 Females

Group	Number
Total Population	94.7
Hispanic or Latino (of any race)	97.9
Central American, ex. Mexican	89.3
Guatemalan	104.5
Cuban	93.2
Mexican	102.5
Puerto Rican	104.1
South American	80.1
Argentinean	101.8
Colombian	74.7
Peruvian	70.3
Venezuelan	92.9
Spaniard	62.4

Average Household Size

Group	People
Total Population	2.79
Hispanic or Latino (of any race)	3.19
Central American, ex. Mexican	3.13
Guatemalan	3.44
Cuban	3.24
Mexican	3.29
Puerto Rican	3.07
South American	3.07
Argentinean	2.97
Colombian	2.97
Peruvian	2.91
Venezuelan	3.64
Spaniard	2.52

Median Age

Group	Years
Total Population	37.9
Hispanic or Latino (of any race)	25.9
Central American, ex. Mexican	27.0
Guatemalan	23.8
Cuban	28.3
Mexican	25.2
Puerto Rican	24.0
South American	32.7
Argentinean	39.3
Colombian	32.0
Peruvian	35.2
Venezuelan	32.3
Spaniard	32.4

High School Graduates
(Universe: Population 25 Years and Over)

Group	Number	%
Total Population	84,882	96.6
Hispanic or Latino (of any race)	2,857	81.6
Mexican	1,814	80.0

Four-Year College Graduates
(Universe: Population 25 Years and Over)

Group	Number	%
Total Population	57,226	65.1
Hispanic or Latino (of any race)	1,294	37.0
Mexican	643	28.4

Population Age 3–17 Enrolled in Public School
(Universe: Population Age 3–17 Enrolled in School)

Group	Number	%
Total Population	30,094	85.5
Hispanic or Latino (of any race)	2,141	88.8
Mexican	1,379	91.4

Population Age 3–17 Enrolled in Private School
(Universe: Population Age 3–17 Enrolled in School)

Group	Number	%
Total Population	5,119	14.5
Hispanic or Latino (of any race)	269	11.2
Mexican	130	8.6

Foreign-Born Population

Group	Number	%
Total Population	21,803	15.5
Hispanic or Latino (of any race)	2,710	34.2
Mexican	2,073	38.8

Foreign-Born Naturalized U.S. Citizens

Group	Number	%
Total Population	10,557	48.4
Hispanic or Latino (of any race)	742	27.4
Mexican	398	19.2

Language Spoken at Home: English Only
(Universe: Population 5 Years and Over)

Group	Number	%
Total Population	105,008	79.6
Hispanic or Latino (of any race)	2,691	37.1
Mexican	1,557	32.0

Language Spoken at Home: Spanish
(Universe: Population 5 Years and Over)

Group	Number	%
Total Population	5,894	4.5
Hispanic or Latino (of any race)	4,539	62.5
Mexican	3,293	67.7

Notes: (1) Percent of total population; (2) Percent of Hispanic/Latino population; Profiles include places with an overall population of at least 125,000, OR an overall population of at least 25,000 where the Hispanic/Latino population is at least 20% of the overall population. In states where less than five places meet either of these criteria, we have included places with at least 10,000 total population with the highest percentage of Hispanic/Latino population. These places are identified with an asterisk (*); Please refer to the User's Guide for a full explanation of data.

Unemployment Rate
(Universe: Population 16 Years and Over)

Group	%
Total Population	5.7
Hispanic or Latino (of any race)	6.3
Mexican	5.2

Class of Worker: Private Wage and Salary
(Universe: Civilian Employed Population 16 Years and Over)

Group	Number	%
Total Population	58,405	84.3
Hispanic or Latino (of any race)	3,350	90.6
Mexican	2,433	91.5

Class of Worker: Government
(Universe: Civilian Employed Population 16 Years and Over)

Group	Number	%
Total Population	7,739	11.2
Hispanic or Latino (of any race)	295	8.0
Mexican	187	7.0

Means of Transportation to Work: Car, Truck or Van
(Universe: Workers 16 Years and Over)

Group	Number	%
Total Population	54,879	80.6
Hispanic or Latino (of any race)	2,776	76.2
Mexican	1,982	75.3

Means of Transportation to Work: Public Transportation (ex. Taxicab)
(Universe: Workers 16 Years and Over)

Group	Number	%
Total Population	6,582	9.7
Hispanic or Latino (of any race)	161	4.4
Mexican	87	3.3

Homeownership Rate
(Universe: Occupied Housing Units)

Group	%
Total Population	75.9
Hispanic or Latino (of any race)	51.5
Central American, ex. Mexican	48.3
Guatemalan	50.0
Cuban	71.3
Mexican	48.1
Puerto Rican	49.4
South American	66.1
Argentinean	79.5
Colombian	66.7
Peruvian	42.9
Venezuelan	67.9
Spaniard	66.0

Median Home Value

Group	Dollars
Total Population	402,900
Hispanic or Latino (of any race)	316,600
Mexican	262,500

Median Gross Rent

Group	Dollars
Total Population	1,150
Hispanic or Latino (of any race)	1,094
Mexican	1,099

Median Household Income
(2010 Inflation-Adjusted Dollars)

Group	Dollars
Total Population	101,911
Hispanic or Latino (of any race)	57,963
Mexican	57,076

Per Capita Income
(2010 Inflation-Adjusted Dollars)

Group	Dollars
Total Population	45,488
Hispanic or Latino (of any race)	21,084
Mexican	18,170

Households with $100,000+ Income

Group	Number	%
Total Population	24,636	51.0
Hispanic or Latino (of any race)	554	25.7
Mexican	295	22.3

Households with Food Stamps/SNAP Benefits During Past 12 Months

Group	Number	%
Total Population	1,113	2.3
Hispanic or Latino (of any race)	253	11.8
Mexican	136	10.3

Poverty Rate
(Income in Past 12 Months Below Poverty Level)

Group	%
Total Population	3.4
Hispanic or Latino (of any race)	11.2
Mexican	14.2

North Chicago

Population

Group	Number	%TP[1]	%HP[2]
Total Population	32,574	100.0	–
Hispanic or Latino (of any race)	8,857	27.2	100.0
Central American, ex. Mexican	383	1.2	4.3
Honduran	157	0.5	1.8
Salvadoran	104	0.3	1.2
Mexican	6,915	21.2	78.1
Puerto Rican	731	2.2	8.3
South American	165	0.5	1.9

Population Growth: 2000–2010

Group	%
Total Population	-9.3
Hispanic or Latino (of any race)	35.2
Central American, ex. Mexican	64.4
Mexican	49.8
Puerto Rican	-5.7
South American	29.9

Males per 100 Females

Group	Number
Total Population	152.9
Hispanic or Latino (of any race)	125.7
Central American, ex. Mexican	105.9
Honduran	106.6
Salvadoran	121.3
Mexican	123.2
Puerto Rican	126.3
South American	179.7

Average Household Size

Group	People
Total Population	3.00
Hispanic or Latino (of any race)	4.60
Central American, ex. Mexican	4.00
Honduran	3.91
Salvadoran	4.48
Mexican	4.92
Puerto Rican	3.04
South American	3.00

Median Age

Group	Years
Total Population	22.8
Hispanic or Latino (of any race)	22.0
Central American, ex. Mexican	26.4
Honduran	28.2
Salvadoran	27.5
Mexican	21.9
Puerto Rican	21.7
South American	23.4

High School Graduates
(Universe: Population 25 Years and Over)

Group	Number	%
Total Population	11,578	78.1
Hispanic or Latino (of any race)	1,945	48.5
Mexican	1,362	41.9

Four-Year College Graduates
(Universe: Population 25 Years and Over)

Group	Number	%
Total Population	2,612	17.6
Hispanic or Latino (of any race)	330	8.2
Mexican	123	3.8

Population Age 3–17 Enrolled in Public School
(Universe: Population Age 3–17 Enrolled in School)

Group	Number	%
Total Population	4,452	87.4
Hispanic or Latino (of any race)	2,061	91.8
Mexican	1,776	95.4

Population Age 3–17 Enrolled in Private School
(Universe: Population Age 3–17 Enrolled in School)

Group	Number	%
Total Population	639	12.6
Hispanic or Latino (of any race)	183	8.2
Mexican	85	4.6

Foreign-Born Population

Group	Number	%
Total Population	6,333	19.2
Hispanic or Latino (of any race)	4,197	45.9
Mexican	3,730	53.9

Foreign-Born Naturalized U.S. Citizens

Group	Number	%
Total Population	1,849	29.2
Hispanic or Latino (of any race)	749	17.8
Mexican	552	14.8

Language Spoken at Home: English Only
(Universe: Population 5 Years and Over)

Group	Number	%
Total Population	21,336	69.0
Hispanic or Latino (of any race)	1,391	16.7
Mexican	551	8.9

Language Spoken at Home: Spanish
(Universe: Population 5 Years and Over)

Group	Number	%
Total Population	7,436	24.0
Hispanic or Latino (of any race)	6,934	83.3
Mexican	5,646	91.1

Unemployment Rate
(Universe: Population 16 Years and Over)

Group	%
Total Population	12.3
Hispanic or Latino (of any race)	12.5
Mexican	12.9

Class of Worker: Private Wage and Salary
(Universe: Civilian Employed Population 16 Years and Over)

Group	Number	%
Total Population	7,107	75.7
Hispanic or Latino (of any race)	2,825	88.6
Mexican	2,410	91.1

Class of Worker: Government
(Universe: Civilian Employed Population 16 Years and Over)

Group	Number	%
Total Population	1,815	19.3
Hispanic or Latino (of any race)	233	7.3
Mexican	127	4.8

Means of Transportation to Work: Car, Truck or Van
(Universe: Workers 16 Years and Over)

Group	Number	%
Total Population	9,026	48.8
Hispanic or Latino (of any race)	2,694	61.8
Mexican	2,218	72.2

Means of Transportation to Work: Public Transportation (ex. Taxicab)
(Universe: Workers 16 Years and Over)

Group	Number	%
Total Population	403	2.2
Hispanic or Latino (of any race)	253	5.8
Mexican	229	7.5

Homeownership Rate
(Universe: Occupied Housing Units)

Group	%
Total Population	37.1
Hispanic or Latino (of any race)	48.2
Central American, ex. Mexican	43.4
Honduran	36.4
Salvadoran	61.9
Mexican	53.5

Notes: (1) Percent of total population; (2) Percent of Hispanic/Latino population; Profiles include places with an overall population of at least 125,000, OR an overall population of at least 25,000 where the Hispanic/Latino population is at least 20% of the overall population. In states where less than five places meet either of these criteria, we have included places with at least 10,000 total population with the highest percentage of Hispanic/Latino population. These places are identified with an asterisk (*); Please refer to the User's Guide for a full explanation of data.

Puerto Rican	23.2
South American	23.1

Median Home Value

Group	Dollars
Total Population	146,300
Hispanic or Latino (of any race)	137,500
Mexican	135,100

Median Gross Rent

Group	Dollars
Total Population	1,005
Hispanic or Latino (of any race)	828
Mexican	865

Median Household Income
(2010 Inflation-Adjusted Dollars)

Group	Dollars
Total Population	44,904
Hispanic or Latino (of any race)	42,857
Mexican	41,895

Per Capita Income
(2010 Inflation-Adjusted Dollars)

Group	Dollars
Total Population	17,892
Hispanic or Latino (of any race)	13,106
Mexican	12,111

Households with $100,000+ Income

Group	Number	%
Total Population	663	8.9
Hispanic or Latino (of any race)	81	4.8
Mexican	71	5.0

Households with Food Stamps/SNAP Benefits During Past 12 Months

Group	Number	%
Total Population	1,154	15.5
Hispanic or Latino (of any race)	240	14.3
Mexican	221	15.6

Poverty Rate
(Income in Past 12 Months Below Poverty Level)

Group	%
Total Population	19.5
Hispanic or Latino (of any race)	20.2
Mexican	19.1

Rockford

Population

Group	Number	%TP[1]	%HP[2]
Total Population	152,871	100.0	–
Hispanic or Latino (of any race)	24,085	15.8	100.0
Central American, ex. Mexican	510	0.3	2.1
Guatemalan	240	0.2	1.0
Salvadoran	100	0.1	0.4
Cuban	418	0.3	1.7
Mexican	20,019	13.1	83.1
Puerto Rican	1,323	0.9	5.5
South American	494	0.3	2.1
Colombian	211	0.1	0.9
Spaniard	115	0.1	0.5

Population Growth: 2000–2010

Group	%
Total Population	1.8
Hispanic or Latino (of any race)	57.6
Central American, ex. Mexican	131.8
Cuban	34.8
Mexican	60.0
Puerto Rican	193.3
South American	63.0
Colombian	21.3

Males per 100 Females

Group	Number
Total Population	93.5
Hispanic or Latino (of any race)	106.8
Central American, ex. Mexican	91.0
Guatemalan	108.7
Salvadoran	100.0
Cuban	113.3
Mexican	107.3
Puerto Rican	101.1
South American	90.0
Colombian	77.3
Spaniard	113.0

Average Household Size

Group	People
Total Population	2.48
Hispanic or Latino (of any race)	3.77
Central American, ex. Mexican	3.56
Guatemalan	3.93
Salvadoran	3.54
Cuban	2.86
Mexican	3.93
Puerto Rican	3.13
South American	3.07
Colombian	3.26
Spaniard	2.47

Median Age

Group	Years
Total Population	35.8
Hispanic or Latino (of any race)	23.3
Central American, ex. Mexican	31.2
Guatemalan	28.0
Salvadoran	27.7
Cuban	30.2
Mexican	22.9
Puerto Rican	22.1
South American	32.8
Colombian	32.7
Spaniard	31.2

High School Graduates
(Universe: Population 25 Years and Over)

Group	Number	%
Total Population	80,504	80.3
Hispanic or Latino (of any race)	5,935	54.0
Mexican	4,451	50.6
Puerto Rican	389	55.5

Four-Year College Graduates
(Universe: Population 25 Years and Over)

Group	Number	%
Total Population	20,601	20.6
Hispanic or Latino (of any race)	882	8.0
Mexican	440	5.0
Puerto Rican	42	6.0

Population Age 3–17 Enrolled in Public School
(Universe: Population Age 3–17 Enrolled in School)

Group	Number	%
Total Population	24,184	82.4
Hispanic or Latino (of any race)	6,497	93.8
Mexican	5,540	95.2
Puerto Rican	445	92.7

Population Age 3–17 Enrolled in Private School
(Universe: Population Age 3–17 Enrolled in School)

Group	Number	%
Total Population	5,150	17.6
Hispanic or Latino (of any race)	428	6.2
Mexican	280	4.8
Puerto Rican	35	7.3

Foreign-Born Population

Group	Number	%
Total Population	16,139	10.4
Hispanic or Latino (of any race)	9,560	41.4
Mexican	8,399	44.1
Puerto Rican	17	1.1

Foreign-Born Naturalized U.S. Citizens

Group	Number	%
Total Population	6,186	38.3
Hispanic or Latino (of any race)	1,815	19.0
Mexican	1,333	15.9
Puerto Rican	0	0.0

Language Spoken at Home: English Only
(Universe: Population 5 Years and Over)

Group	Number	%
Total Population	119,519	83.7
Hispanic or Latino (of any race)	4,440	22.1
Mexican	3,079	18.7
Puerto Rican	609	41.9

Language Spoken at Home: Spanish
(Universe: Population 5 Years and Over)

Group	Number	%
Total Population	16,920	11.8
Hispanic or Latino (of any race)	15,556	77.6
Mexican	13,358	81.0
Puerto Rican	845	58.1

Unemployment Rate
(Universe: Population 16 Years and Over)

Group	%
Total Population	11.8
Hispanic or Latino (of any race)	14.3
Mexican	12.1
Puerto Rican	35.3

Class of Worker: Private Wage and Salary
(Universe: Civilian Employed Population 16 Years and Over)

Group	Number	%
Total Population	54,443	84.9
Hispanic or Latino (of any race)	7,691	93.6
Mexican	6,545	94.1
Puerto Rican	449	97.4

Class of Worker: Government
(Universe: Civilian Employed Population 16 Years and Over)

Group	Number	%
Total Population	6,556	10.2
Hispanic or Latino (of any race)	279	3.4
Mexican	228	3.3
Puerto Rican	0	0.0

Means of Transportation to Work: Car, Truck or Van
(Universe: Workers 16 Years and Over)

Group	Number	%
Total Population	57,631	92.0
Hispanic or Latino (of any race)	7,616	94.9
Mexican	6,438	95.2
Puerto Rican	398	86.3

Means of Transportation to Work: Public Transportation (ex. Taxicab)
(Universe: Workers 16 Years and Over)

Group	Number	%
Total Population	999	1.6
Hispanic or Latino (of any race)	151	1.9
Mexican	139	2.1
Puerto Rican	0	0.0

Homeownership Rate
(Universe: Occupied Housing Units)

Group	%
Total Population	58.4
Hispanic or Latino (of any race)	55.4
Central American, ex. Mexican	63.4
Guatemalan	55.9
Salvadoran	65.7
Cuban	51.0
Mexican	56.7
Puerto Rican	41.8
South American	68.6
Colombian	71.0
Spaniard	51.1

Median Home Value

Group	Dollars
Total Population	109,100
Hispanic or Latino (of any race)	98,500
Mexican	93,400
Puerto Rican	119,400

Median Gross Rent

Group	Dollars
Total Population	655
Hispanic or Latino (of any race)	664
Mexican	666
Puerto Rican	718

Median Household Income
(2010 Inflation-Adjusted Dollars)

Group	Dollars
Total Population	38,573
Hispanic or Latino (of any race)	32,791

Notes: (1) Percent of total population; (2) Percent of Hispanic/Latino population; Profiles include places with an overall population of at least 125,000, OR an overall population of at least 25,000 where the Hispanic/Latino population is at least 20% of the overall population. In states where less than five places meet either of these criteria, we have included places with at least 10,000 total population with the highest percentage of Hispanic/Latino population. These places are identified with an asterisk (*); Please refer to the User's Guide for a full explanation of data.

Group	Dollars
Mexican	33,180
Puerto Rican	26,119

Per Capita Income
(2010 Inflation-Adjusted Dollars)

Group	Dollars
Total Population	21,422
Hispanic or Latino (of any race)	11,130
Mexican	10,678
Puerto Rican	10,063

Households with $100,000+ Income

Group	Number	%
Total Population	7,153	12.0
Hispanic or Latino (of any race)	329	5.9
Mexican	248	5.6
Puerto Rican	10	2.3

Households with Food Stamps/SNAP Benefits During Past 12 Months

Group	Number	%
Total Population	9,690	16.2
Hispanic or Latino (of any race)	1,653	29.8
Mexican	1,160	26.1
Puerto Rican	229	53.0

Poverty Rate
(Income in Past 12 Months Below Poverty Level)

Group	%
Total Population	23.3
Hispanic or Latino (of any race)	38.6
Mexican	37.2
Puerto Rican	52.7

Romeoville

Population

Group	Number	%TP[1]	%HP[2]
Total Population	39,680	100.0	–
Hispanic or Latino (of any race)	11,883	29.9	100.0
Central American, ex. Mexican	275	0.7	2.3
Guatemalan	148	0.4	1.2
Mexican	9,992	25.2	84.1
Puerto Rican	931	2.3	7.8
South American	301	0.8	2.5

Population Growth: 2000–2010

Group	%
Total Population	87.6
Hispanic or Latino (of any race)	327.3
Mexican	380.6
Puerto Rican	183.8

Males per 100 Females

Group	Number
Total Population	97.7
Hispanic or Latino (of any race)	106.4
Central American, ex. Mexican	103.7
Guatemalan	111.4
Mexican	106.7
Puerto Rican	107.8
South American	87.0

Average Household Size

Group	People
Total Population	3.21
Hispanic or Latino (of any race)	4.26
Central American, ex. Mexican	3.88
Guatemalan	3.90
Mexican	4.40
Puerto Rican	3.54
South American	3.78

Median Age

Group	Years
Total Population	31.3
Hispanic or Latino (of any race)	24.0
Central American, ex. Mexican	30.4
Guatemalan	29.3
Mexican	23.5
Puerto Rican	22.1
South American	33.2

High School Graduates
(Universe: Population 25 Years and Over)

Group	Number	%
Total Population	19,102	84.3
Hispanic or Latino (of any race)	4,113	67.2
Mexican	2,977	62.2
Puerto Rican	538	85.3

Four-Year College Graduates
(Universe: Population 25 Years and Over)

Group	Number	%
Total Population	5,178	22.9
Hispanic or Latino (of any race)	731	11.9
Mexican	468	9.8
Puerto Rican	97	15.4

Population Age 3–17 Enrolled in Public School
(Universe: Population Age 3–17 Enrolled in School)

Group	Number	%
Total Population	8,192	91.6
Hispanic or Latino (of any race)	3,660	95.8
Mexican	3,070	95.6
Puerto Rican	262	95.6

Population Age 3–17 Enrolled in Private School
(Universe: Population Age 3–17 Enrolled in School)

Group	Number	%
Total Population	750	8.4
Hispanic or Latino (of any race)	160	4.2
Mexican	141	4.4
Puerto Rican	12	4.4

Foreign-Born Population

Group	Number	%
Total Population	7,474	19.9
Hispanic or Latino (of any race)	4,201	35.8
Mexican	3,663	38.3
Puerto Rican	6	0.6

Foreign-Born Naturalized U.S. Citizens

Group	Number	%
Total Population	3,450	46.2
Hispanic or Latino (of any race)	1,779	42.3
Mexican	1,418	38.7
Puerto Rican	0	0.0

Language Spoken at Home: English Only
(Universe: Population 5 Years and Over)

Group	Number	%
Total Population	21,588	62.7
Hispanic or Latino (of any race)	2,228	20.8
Mexican	1,631	18.8
Puerto Rican	406	41.4

Language Spoken at Home: Spanish
(Universe: Population 5 Years and Over)

Group	Number	%
Total Population	8,815	25.6
Hispanic or Latino (of any race)	8,488	79.1
Mexican	7,028	81.0
Puerto Rican	575	58.6

Unemployment Rate
(Universe: Population 16 Years and Over)

Group	%
Total Population	9.0
Hispanic or Latino (of any race)	7.1
Mexican	6.3
Puerto Rican	10.6

Class of Worker: Private Wage and Salary
(Universe: Civilian Employed Population 16 Years and Over)

Group	Number	%
Total Population	15,191	85.1
Hispanic or Latino (of any race)	4,234	87.6
Mexican	3,485	87.5
Puerto Rican	442	91.9

Class of Worker: Government
(Universe: Civilian Employed Population 16 Years and Over)

Group	Number	%
Total Population	1,823	10.2
Hispanic or Latino (of any race)	341	7.1
Mexican	243	6.1
Puerto Rican	39	8.1

Means of Transportation to Work: Car, Truck or Van
(Universe: Workers 16 Years and Over)

Group	Number	%
Total Population	15,671	91.3
Hispanic or Latino (of any race)	4,489	93.6
Mexican	3,713	93.6
Puerto Rican	425	88.4

Means of Transportation to Work: Public Transportation (ex. Taxicab)
(Universe: Workers 16 Years and Over)

Group	Number	%
Total Population	559	3.3
Hispanic or Latino (of any race)	56	1.2
Mexican	23	0.6
Puerto Rican	33	6.9

Homeownership Rate
(Universe: Occupied Housing Units)

Group	%
Total Population	85.0
Hispanic or Latino (of any race)	86.7
Central American, ex. Mexican	88.9
Guatemalan	87.5
Mexican	87.6
Puerto Rican	81.1
South American	83.3

Median Home Value

Group	Dollars
Total Population	206,400
Hispanic or Latino (of any race)	203,900
Mexican	203,900
Puerto Rican	157,400

Median Gross Rent

Group	Dollars
Total Population	1,321
Hispanic or Latino (of any race)	1,333
Mexican	1,351
Puerto Rican	–

Median Household Income
(2010 Inflation-Adjusted Dollars)

Group	Dollars
Total Population	67,165
Hispanic or Latino (of any race)	61,138
Mexican	61,207
Puerto Rican	66,321

Per Capita Income
(2010 Inflation-Adjusted Dollars)

Group	Dollars
Total Population	23,197
Hispanic or Latino (of any race)	16,333
Mexican	15,881
Puerto Rican	17,712

Households with $100,000+ Income

Group	Number	%
Total Population	2,612	22.9
Hispanic or Latino (of any race)	528	18.9
Mexican	447	20.7
Puerto Rican	18	8.0

Households with Food Stamps/SNAP Benefits During Past 12 Months

Group	Number	%
Total Population	457	4.0
Hispanic or Latino (of any race)	159	5.7
Mexican	159	7.4
Puerto Rican	0	0.0

Poverty Rate
(Income in Past 12 Months Below Poverty Level)

Group	%
Total Population	7.3
Hispanic or Latino (of any race)	9.7
Mexican	11.0
Puerto Rican	8.8

Notes: (1) Percent of total population; (2) Percent of Hispanic/Latino population; Profiles include places with an overall population of at least 125,000, OR an overall population of at least 25,000 where the Hispanic/Latino population is at least 20% of the overall population. In states where less than five places meet either of these criteria, we have included places with at least 10,000 total population with the highest percentage of Hispanic/Latino population. These places are identified with an asterisk (*); Please refer to the User's Guide for a full explanation of data.

Round Lake Beach

Population

Group	Number	%TP[1]	%HP[2]
Total Population	28,175	100.0	–
Hispanic or Latino (of any race)	13,530	48.0	100.0
Central American, ex. Mexican	357	1.3	2.6
Guatemalan	130	0.5	1.0
Salvadoran	151	0.5	1.1
Mexican	12,194	43.3	90.1
Puerto Rican	415	1.5	3.1
South American	225	0.8	1.7

Population Growth: 2000–2010

Group	%
Total Population	9.0
Hispanic or Latino (of any race)	67.4
Central American, ex. Mexican	96.2
Salvadoran	33.6
Mexican	77.2
Puerto Rican	30.5
South American	71.8

Males per 100 Females

Group	Number
Total Population	101.8
Hispanic or Latino (of any race)	109.8
Central American, ex. Mexican	112.5
Guatemalan	120.3
Salvadoran	106.8
Mexican	110.1
Puerto Rican	105.4
South American	87.5

Average Household Size

Group	People
Total Population	3.48
Hispanic or Latino (of any race)	4.80
Central American, ex. Mexican	3.79
Guatemalan	3.74
Salvadoran	3.94
Mexican	4.98
Puerto Rican	3.40
South American	3.37

Median Age

Group	Years
Total Population	30.2
Hispanic or Latino (of any race)	24.6
Central American, ex. Mexican	34.5
Guatemalan	34.8
Salvadoran	33.5
Mexican	24.1
Puerto Rican	25.4
South American	34.3

High School Graduates
(Universe: Population 25 Years and Over)

Group	Number	%
Total Population	11,698	75.7
Hispanic or Latino (of any race)	3,259	53.0
Mexican	2,839	51.5

Four-Year College Graduates
(Universe: Population 25 Years and Over)

Group	Number	%
Total Population	2,719	17.6
Hispanic or Latino (of any race)	392	6.4
Mexican	297	5.4

Population Age 3–17 Enrolled in Public School
(Universe: Population Age 3–17 Enrolled in School)

Group	Number	%
Total Population	6,187	91.2
Hispanic or Latino (of any race)	3,280	96.2
Mexican	2,953	95.8

Population Age 3–17 Enrolled in Private School
(Universe: Population Age 3–17 Enrolled in School)

Group	Number	%
Total Population	597	8.8
Hispanic or Latino (of any race)	131	3.8
Mexican	131	4.2

Foreign-Born Population

Group	Number	%
Total Population	7,525	26.9
Hispanic or Latino (of any race)	6,503	48.3
Mexican	6,148	50.3

Foreign-Born Naturalized U.S. Citizens

Group	Number	%
Total Population	1,944	25.8
Hispanic or Latino (of any race)	1,372	21.1
Mexican	1,157	18.8

Language Spoken at Home: English Only
(Universe: Population 5 Years and Over)

Group	Number	%
Total Population	13,313	53.7
Hispanic or Latino (of any race)	1,062	9.4
Mexican	888	8.7

Language Spoken at Home: Spanish
(Universe: Population 5 Years and Over)

Group	Number	%
Total Population	10,405	42.0
Hispanic or Latino (of any race)	10,222	90.5
Mexican	9,325	91.2

Unemployment Rate
(Universe: Population 16 Years and Over)

Group	%
Total Population	9.1
Hispanic or Latino (of any race)	11.6
Mexican	11.0

Class of Worker: Private Wage and Salary
(Universe: Civilian Employed Population 16 Years and Over)

Group	Number	%
Total Population	11,803	88.6
Hispanic or Latino (of any race)	4,995	91.1
Mexican	4,622	92.7

Class of Worker: Government
(Universe: Civilian Employed Population 16 Years and Over)

Group	Number	%
Total Population	1,127	8.5
Hispanic or Latino (of any race)	328	6.0
Mexican	241	4.8

Means of Transportation to Work: Car, Truck or Van
(Universe: Workers 16 Years and Over)

Group	Number	%
Total Population	12,161	93.5
Hispanic or Latino (of any race)	5,112	97.3
Mexican	4,674	97.5

Means of Transportation to Work: Public Transportation (ex. Taxicab)
(Universe: Workers 16 Years and Over)

Group	Number	%
Total Population	452	3.5
Hispanic or Latino (of any race)	59	1.1
Mexican	50	1.0

Homeownership Rate
(Universe: Occupied Housing Units)

Group	%
Total Population	81.2
Hispanic or Latino (of any race)	78.1
Central American, ex. Mexican	80.9
Guatemalan	93.0
Salvadoran	74.5
Mexican	78.1
Puerto Rican	73.9
South American	85.5

Median Home Value

Group	Dollars
Total Population	174,200
Hispanic or Latino (of any race)	177,600
Mexican	178,600

Median Gross Rent

Group	Dollars
Total Population	888
Hispanic or Latino (of any race)	1,068
Mexican	1,163

Median Household Income
(2010 Inflation-Adjusted Dollars)

Group	Dollars
Total Population	62,709
Hispanic or Latino (of any race)	52,511
Mexican	52,190

Per Capita Income
(2010 Inflation-Adjusted Dollars)

Group	Dollars
Total Population	20,513
Hispanic or Latino (of any race)	13,253
Mexican	12,732

Households with $100,000+ Income

Group	Number	%
Total Population	1,673	20.8
Hispanic or Latino (of any race)	414	15.0
Mexican	347	14.1

Households with Food Stamps/SNAP Benefits During Past 12 Months

Group	Number	%
Total Population	680	8.5
Hispanic or Latino (of any race)	306	11.1
Mexican	256	10.4

Poverty Rate
(Income in Past 12 Months Below Poverty Level)

Group	%
Total Population	14.7
Hispanic or Latino (of any race)	20.0
Mexican	20.1

Streamwood

Population

Group	Number	%TP[1]	%HP[2]
Total Population	39,858	100.0	–
Hispanic or Latino (of any race)	11,238	28.2	100.0
Central American, ex. Mexican	434	1.1	3.9
Guatemalan	134	0.3	1.2
Salvadoran	234	0.6	2.1
Mexican	9,416	23.6	83.8
Puerto Rican	555	1.4	4.9
South American	410	1.0	3.6
Colombian	131	0.3	1.2
Ecuadorian	126	0.3	1.1

Population Growth: 2000–2010

Group	%
Total Population	9.5
Hispanic or Latino (of any race)	84.0
Central American, ex. Mexican	142.5
Mexican	100.4
Puerto Rican	45.3
South American	73.7
Colombian	22.4

Males per 100 Females

Group	Number
Total Population	98.3
Hispanic or Latino (of any race)	108.7
Central American, ex. Mexican	104.7
Guatemalan	109.4
Salvadoran	114.7
Mexican	112.2
Puerto Rican	84.4
South American	89.8
Colombian	84.5
Ecuadorian	106.6

Average Household Size

Group	People
Total Population	3.04
Hispanic or Latino (of any race)	4.55
Central American, ex. Mexican	4.53
Guatemalan	3.72
Salvadoran	5.40
Mexican	4.76
Puerto Rican	3.12
South American	3.46
Colombian	3.28
Ecuadorian	3.89

STATE & PLACE PROFILES

Notes: (1) Percent of total population; (2) Percent of Hispanic/Latino population; Profiles include places with an overall population of at least 125,000, OR an overall population of at least 25,000 where the Hispanic/Latino population is at least 20% of the overall population. In states where less than five places meet either of these criteria, we have included places with at least 10,000 total population with the highest percentage of Hispanic/Latino population. These places are identified with an asterisk (*); Please refer to the User's Guide for a full explanation of data.

Median Age

Group	Years
Total Population	34.7
Hispanic or Latino (of any race)	26.4
Central American, ex. Mexican	31.0
Guatemalan	34.0
Salvadoran	29.1
Mexican	25.4
Puerto Rican	30.1
South American	33.8
Colombian	37.8
Ecuadorian	30.2

High School Graduates
(Universe: Population 25 Years and Over)

Group	Number	%
Total Population	21,451	84.2
Hispanic or Latino (of any race)	3,310	59.6
Mexican	2,469	54.3

Four-Year College Graduates
(Universe: Population 25 Years and Over)

Group	Number	%
Total Population	7,561	29.7
Hispanic or Latino (of any race)	710	12.8
Mexican	372	8.2

Population Age 3–17 Enrolled in Public School
(Universe: Population Age 3–17 Enrolled in School)

Group	Number	%
Total Population	6,690	89.9
Hispanic or Latino (of any race)	2,991	97.0
Mexican	2,685	98.7

Population Age 3–17 Enrolled in Private School
(Universe: Population Age 3–17 Enrolled in School)

Group	Number	%
Total Population	749	10.1
Hispanic or Latino (of any race)	91	3.0
Mexican	34	1.3

Foreign-Born Population

Group	Number	%
Total Population	12,125	30.9
Hispanic or Latino (of any race)	5,129	47.0
Mexican	4,437	47.5

Foreign-Born Naturalized U.S. Citizens

Group	Number	%
Total Population	5,907	48.7
Hispanic or Latino (of any race)	1,442	28.1
Mexican	1,076	24.3

Language Spoken at Home: English Only
(Universe: Population 5 Years and Over)

Group	Number	%
Total Population	19,339	53.8
Hispanic or Latino (of any race)	1,536	15.8
Mexican	1,159	13.9

Language Spoken at Home: Spanish
(Universe: Population 5 Years and Over)

Group	Number	%
Total Population	8,341	23.2
Hispanic or Latino (of any race)	8,041	82.6
Mexican	7,135	85.6

Unemployment Rate
(Universe: Population 16 Years and Over)

Group	%
Total Population	7.9
Hispanic or Latino (of any race)	9.3
Mexican	9.9

Class of Worker: Private Wage and Salary
(Universe: Civilian Employed Population 16 Years and Over)

Group	Number	%
Total Population	19,226	90.8
Hispanic or Latino (of any race)	5,067	94.2
Mexican	4,303	95.3

Class of Worker: Government
(Universe: Civilian Employed Population 16 Years and Over)

Group	Number	%
Total Population	1,356	6.4
Hispanic or Latino (of any race)	252	4.7
Mexican	164	3.6

Means of Transportation to Work: Car, Truck or Van
(Universe: Workers 16 Years and Over)

Group	Number	%
Total Population	19,359	92.4
Hispanic or Latino (of any race)	5,139	95.9
Mexican	4,337	96.5

Means of Transportation to Work: Public Transportation (ex. Taxicab)
(Universe: Workers 16 Years and Over)

Group	Number	%
Total Population	593	2.8
Hispanic or Latino (of any race)	63	1.2
Mexican	45	1.0

Homeownership Rate
(Universe: Occupied Housing Units)

Group	%
Total Population	88.4
Hispanic or Latino (of any race)	84.8
Central American, ex. Mexican	82.9
Guatemalan	93.0
Salvadoran	72.0
Mexican	85.4
Puerto Rican	80.1
South American	89.6
Colombian	91.7
Ecuadorian	88.6

Median Home Value

Group	Dollars
Total Population	230,700
Hispanic or Latino (of any race)	229,600
Mexican	230,500

Median Gross Rent

Group	Dollars
Total Population	1,410
Hispanic or Latino (of any race)	1,646
Mexican	1,607

Median Household Income
(2010 Inflation-Adjusted Dollars)

Group	Dollars
Total Population	69,710
Hispanic or Latino (of any race)	64,375
Mexican	60,035

Per Capita Income
(2010 Inflation-Adjusted Dollars)

Group	Dollars
Total Population	27,285
Hispanic or Latino (of any race)	16,938
Mexican	15,499

Households with $100,000+ Income

Group	Number	%
Total Population	3,536	27.1
Hispanic or Latino (of any race)	474	19.4
Mexican	350	18.3

Households with Food Stamps/SNAP Benefits During Past 12 Months

Group	Number	%
Total Population	438	3.4
Hispanic or Latino (of any race)	175	7.2
Mexican	114	6.0

Poverty Rate
(Income in Past 12 Months Below Poverty Level)

Group	%
Total Population	5.8
Hispanic or Latino (of any race)	8.7
Mexican	8.5

Waukegan

Population

Group	Number	%TP[1]	%HP[2]
Total Population	89,078	100.0	–
Hispanic or Latino (of any race)	47,612	53.4	100.0
Central American, ex. Mexican	3,653	4.1	7.7
Guatemalan	340	0.4	0.7
Honduran	2,311	2.6	4.9
Salvadoran	887	1.0	1.9
Cuban	136	0.2	0.3
Dominican Republic	103	0.1	0.2
Mexican	38,636	43.4	81.1
Puerto Rican	2,918	3.3	6.1
South American	546	0.6	1.1
Colombian	358	0.4	0.8
Spaniard	153	0.2	0.3

Population Growth: 2000–2010

Group	%
Total Population	1.3
Hispanic or Latino (of any race)	20.9
Central American, ex. Mexican	75.5
Guatemalan	79.9
Honduran	79.6
Salvadoran	107.2
Cuban	32.0
Mexican	25.8
Puerto Rican	-1.9
South American	44.4
Colombian	25.6

Males per 100 Females

Group	Number
Total Population	101.6
Hispanic or Latino (of any race)	107.7
Central American, ex. Mexican	107.9
Guatemalan	80.9
Honduran	116.0
Salvadoran	103.0
Cuban	126.7
Dominican Republic	83.9
Mexican	108.5
Puerto Rican	99.3
South American	75.0
Colombian	72.9
Spaniard	96.2

Average Household Size

Group	People
Total Population	3.10
Hispanic or Latino (of any race)	4.19
Central American, ex. Mexican	4.18
Guatemalan	3.97
Honduran	4.24
Salvadoran	4.17
Cuban	2.74
Dominican Republic	3.20
Mexican	4.39
Puerto Rican	2.94
South American	3.10
Colombian	3.20
Spaniard	3.49

Median Age

Group	Years
Total Population	30.5
Hispanic or Latino (of any race)	25.5
Central American, ex. Mexican	30.2
Guatemalan	33.6
Honduran	29.3
Salvadoran	31.8
Cuban	25.0
Dominican Republic	25.2
Mexican	24.7
Puerto Rican	27.8
South American	35.0
Colombian	31.6
Spaniard	30.3

High School Graduates
(Universe: Population 25 Years and Over)

Group	Number	%
Total Population	36,813	69.7
Hispanic or Latino (of any race)	11,579	48.8
Central American, ex. Mexican	1,026	49.0
Honduran	661	49.7
Mexican	8,709	46.2
Puerto Rican	1,204	58.5

Notes: (1) Percent of total population; (2) Percent of Hispanic/Latino population; Profiles include places with an overall population of at least 125,000, OR an overall population of at least 25,000 where the Hispanic/Latino population is at least 20% of the overall population. In states where less than five places meet either of these criteria, we have included places with at least 10,000 total population with the highest percentage of Hispanic/Latino population. These places are identified with an asterisk (*); Please refer to the User's Guide for a full explanation of data.

Four-Year College Graduates
(Universe: Population 25 Years and Over)

Group	Number	%
Total Population	8,371	15.9
Hispanic or Latino (of any race)	1,370	5.8
Central American, ex. Mexican	149	7.1
Honduran	33	2.5
Mexican	847	4.5
Puerto Rican	185	9.0

Population Age 3–17 Enrolled in Public School
(Universe: Population Age 3–17 Enrolled in School)

Group	Number	%
Total Population	18,501	92.7
Hispanic or Latino (of any race)	12,682	96.3
Central American, ex. Mexican	509	91.5
Honduran	385	100.0
Mexican	11,390	97.5
Puerto Rican	377	86.9

Population Age 3–17 Enrolled in Private School
(Universe: Population Age 3–17 Enrolled in School)

Group	Number	%
Total Population	1,463	7.3
Hispanic or Latino (of any race)	485	3.7
Central American, ex. Mexican	47	8.5
Honduran	0	0.0
Mexican	293	2.5
Puerto Rican	57	13.1

Foreign-Born Population

Group	Number	%
Total Population	29,184	32.7
Hispanic or Latino (of any race)	23,806	51.1
Central American, ex. Mexican	2,396	73.3
Honduran	1,537	72.9
Mexican	20,811	53.9
Puerto Rican	169	5.7

Foreign-Born Naturalized U.S. Citizens

Group	Number	%
Total Population	7,236	24.8
Hispanic or Latino (of any race)	4,436	18.6
Central American, ex. Mexican	358	14.9
Honduran	110	7.2
Mexican	3,764	18.1
Puerto Rican	59	34.9

Language Spoken at Home: English Only
(Universe: Population 5 Years and Over)

Group	Number	%
Total Population	36,791	44.9
Hispanic or Latino (of any race)	2,849	6.8
Central American, ex. Mexican	92	3.2
Honduran	17	0.9
Mexican	1,965	5.7
Puerto Rican	426	15.4

Language Spoken at Home: Spanish
(Universe: Population 5 Years and Over)

Group	Number	%
Total Population	40,394	49.3
Hispanic or Latino (of any race)	38,883	93.2
Central American, ex. Mexican	2,825	96.8
Honduran	1,812	99.1
Mexican	32,665	94.3
Puerto Rican	2,335	84.6

Unemployment Rate
(Universe: Population 16 Years and Over)

Group	%
Total Population	10.8
Hispanic or Latino (of any race)	10.9
Central American, ex. Mexican	12.8
Honduran	14.1
Mexican	10.8
Puerto Rican	9.5

Class of Worker: Private Wage and Salary
(Universe: Civilian Employed Population 16 Years and Over)

Group	Number	%
Total Population	34,682	85.7
Hispanic or Latino (of any race)	18,815	91.2
Central American, ex. Mexican	1,637	94.5
Honduran	1,014	96.0
Mexican	15,604	92.9
Puerto Rican	1,108	72.3

Class of Worker: Government
(Universe: Civilian Employed Population 16 Years and Over)

Group	Number	%
Total Population	4,225	10.4
Hispanic or Latino (of any race)	1,084	5.3
Central American, ex. Mexican	15	0.9
Honduran	0	0.0
Mexican	679	4.0
Puerto Rican	310	20.2

Means of Transportation to Work: Car, Truck or Van
(Universe: Workers 16 Years and Over)

Group	Number	%
Total Population	35,787	90.1
Hispanic or Latino (of any race)	18,287	91.4
Central American, ex. Mexican	1,463	85.8
Honduran	917	86.8
Mexican	14,958	92.2
Puerto Rican	1,315	88.4

Means of Transportation to Work: Public Transportation (ex. Taxicab)
(Universe: Workers 16 Years and Over)

Group	Number	%
Total Population	1,631	4.1
Hispanic or Latino (of any race)	725	3.6
Central American, ex. Mexican	103	6.0
Honduran	91	8.6
Mexican	598	3.7
Puerto Rican	24	1.6

Homeownership Rate
(Universe: Occupied Housing Units)

Group	%
Total Population	53.3
Hispanic or Latino (of any race)	52.9
Central American, ex. Mexican	43.2
Guatemalan	62.5
Honduran	32.9
Salvadoran	59.0
Cuban	47.8
Dominican Republic	48.6
Mexican	56.0
Puerto Rican	41.5
South American	48.3
Colombian	48.6
Spaniard	46.8

Median Home Value

Group	Dollars
Total Population	165,200
Hispanic or Latino (of any race)	153,400
Central American, ex. Mexican	185,000
Honduran	149,000
Mexican	150,300
Puerto Rican	160,500

Median Gross Rent

Group	Dollars
Total Population	821
Hispanic or Latino (of any race)	816
Central American, ex. Mexican	793
Honduran	823
Mexican	835
Puerto Rican	680

Median Household Income
(2010 Inflation-Adjusted Dollars)

Group	Dollars
Total Population	47,987
Hispanic or Latino (of any race)	45,292
Central American, ex. Mexican	40,773
Honduran	40,326
Mexican	47,276
Puerto Rican	43,875

Per Capita Income
(2010 Inflation-Adjusted Dollars)

Group	Dollars
Total Population	20,093
Hispanic or Latino (of any race)	13,666
Central American, ex. Mexican	13,330
Honduran	11,341
Mexican	13,281
Puerto Rican	19,797

Households with $100,000+ Income

Group	Number	%
Total Population	4,073	14.0
Hispanic or Latino (of any race)	845	7.5
Central American, ex. Mexican	77	8.9
Honduran	12	2.4
Mexican	582	6.5
Puerto Rican	126	11.2

Households with Food Stamps/SNAP Benefits During Past 12 Months

Group	Number	%
Total Population	3,185	10.9
Hispanic or Latino (of any race)	1,276	11.3
Central American, ex. Mexican	63	7.3
Honduran	22	4.3
Mexican	1,002	11.1
Puerto Rican	144	12.8

Poverty Rate
(Income in Past 12 Months Below Poverty Level)

Group	%
Total Population	13.9
Hispanic or Latino (of any race)	13.9
Central American, ex. Mexican	13.6
Honduran	9.9
Mexican	14.4
Puerto Rican	13.1

West Chicago

Population

Group	Number	%TP[1]	%HP[2]
Total Population	27,086	100.0	–
Hispanic or Latino (of any race)	13,837	51.1	100.0
Central American, ex. Mexican	103	0.4	0.7
Cuban	182	0.7	1.3
Mexican	12,797	47.2	92.5
Puerto Rican	186	0.7	1.3

Population Growth: 2000–2010

Group	%
Total Population	15.4
Hispanic or Latino (of any race)	21.3
Mexican	21.3
Puerto Rican	24.0

Males per 100 Females

Group	Number
Total Population	105.8
Hispanic or Latino (of any race)	113.0
Central American, ex. Mexican	119.1
Cuban	106.8
Mexican	113.3
Puerto Rican	126.8

Average Household Size

Group	People
Total Population	3.65
Hispanic or Latino (of any race)	4.76
Central American, ex. Mexican	4.38
Cuban	2.85
Mexican	4.86
Puerto Rican	3.31

Median Age

Group	Years
Total Population	30.1
Hispanic or Latino (of any race)	24.8
Central American, ex. Mexican	23.5
Cuban	37.4
Mexican	24.6
Puerto Rican	24.8

High School Graduates
(Universe: Population 25 Years and Over)

Group	Number	%
Total Population	11,004	74.3
Hispanic or Latino (of any race)	2,727	48.2
Mexican	2,522	48.1

Notes: (1) Percent of total population; (2) Percent of Hispanic/Latino population; Profiles include places with an overall population of at least 125,000, OR an overall population of at least 25,000 where the Hispanic/Latino population is at least 20% of the overall population. In states where less than five places meet either of these criteria, we have included places with at least 10,000 total population with the highest percentage of Hispanic/Latino population. These places are identified with an asterisk (*); Please refer to the User's Guide for a full explanation of data.

Four-Year College Graduates
(Universe: Population 25 Years and Over)

Group	Number	%
Total Population	4,144	28.0
Hispanic or Latino (of any race)	352	6.2
Mexican	342	6.5

Population Age 3–17 Enrolled in Public School
(Universe: Population Age 3–17 Enrolled in School)

Group	Number	%
Total Population	5,228	90.1
Hispanic or Latino (of any race)	2,978	98.8
Mexican	2,678	98.6

Population Age 3–17 Enrolled in Private School
(Universe: Population Age 3–17 Enrolled in School)

Group	Number	%
Total Population	575	9.9
Hispanic or Latino (of any race)	37	1.2
Mexican	37	1.4

Foreign-Born Population

Group	Number	%
Total Population	9,615	36.5
Hispanic or Latino (of any race)	7,016	55.3
Mexican	6,585	56.8

Foreign-Born Naturalized U.S. Citizens

Group	Number	%
Total Population	2,963	30.8
Hispanic or Latino (of any race)	1,237	17.6
Mexican	1,216	18.5

Language Spoken at Home: English Only
(Universe: Population 5 Years and Over)

Group	Number	%
Total Population	10,637	45.0
Hispanic or Latino (of any race)	740	6.8
Mexican	608	6.2

Language Spoken at Home: Spanish
(Universe: Population 5 Years and Over)

Group	Number	%
Total Population	10,365	43.9
Hispanic or Latino (of any race)	10,092	93.2
Mexican	9,252	93.8

Unemployment Rate
(Universe: Population 16 Years and Over)

Group	%
Total Population	7.8
Hispanic or Latino (of any race)	8.1
Mexican	8.4

Class of Worker: Private Wage and Salary
(Universe: Civilian Employed Population 16 Years and Over)

Group	Number	%
Total Population	11,781	90.0
Hispanic or Latino (of any race)	5,970	97.1
Mexican	5,368	96.7

Class of Worker: Government
(Universe: Civilian Employed Population 16 Years and Over)

Group	Number	%
Total Population	884	6.8
Hispanic or Latino (of any race)	177	2.9
Mexican	177	3.2

Means of Transportation to Work: Car, Truck or Van
(Universe: Workers 16 Years and Over)

Group	Number	%
Total Population	11,576	90.7
Hispanic or Latino (of any race)	5,461	91.3
Mexican	4,898	91.0

Means of Transportation to Work: Public Transportation (ex. Taxicab)
(Universe: Workers 16 Years and Over)

Group	Number	%
Total Population	275	2.2
Hispanic or Latino (of any race)	72	1.2
Mexican	72	1.3

Homeownership Rate
(Universe: Occupied Housing Units)

Group	%
Total Population	69.1
Hispanic or Latino (of any race)	48.9
Central American, ex. Mexican	38.1
Cuban	16.9
Mexican	49.4
Puerto Rican	75.6

Median Home Value

Group	Dollars
Total Population	260,500
Hispanic or Latino (of any race)	223,200
Mexican	223,200

Median Gross Rent

Group	Dollars
Total Population	854
Hispanic or Latino (of any race)	877
Mexican	880

Median Household Income
(2010 Inflation-Adjusted Dollars)

Group	Dollars
Total Population	64,795
Hispanic or Latino (of any race)	49,848
Mexican	50,843

Per Capita Income
(2010 Inflation-Adjusted Dollars)

Group	Dollars
Total Population	24,498
Hispanic or Latino (of any race)	13,163
Mexican	12,888

Households with $100,000+ Income

Group	Number	%
Total Population	2,318	30.5
Hispanic or Latino (of any race)	350	12.0
Mexican	258	9.6

Households with Food Stamps/SNAP Benefits During Past 12 Months

Group	Number	%
Total Population	585	7.7
Hispanic or Latino (of any race)	433	14.8
Mexican	284	10.6

Poverty Rate
(Income in Past 12 Months Below Poverty Level)

Group	%
Total Population	10.9
Hispanic or Latino (of any race)	16.7
Mexican	16.1

Wheeling

Population

Group	Number	%TP[1]	%HP[2]
Total Population	37,648	100.0	–
Hispanic or Latino (of any race)	11,758	31.2	100.0
Central American, ex. Mexican	329	0.9	2.8
Guatemalan	121	0.3	1.0
Salvadoran	167	0.4	1.4
Mexican	10,517	27.9	89.4
Puerto Rican	254	0.7	2.2
South American	283	0.8	2.4

Population Growth: 2000–2010

Group	%
Total Population	9.1
Hispanic or Latino (of any race)	64.8
Central American, ex. Mexican	72.3
Mexican	72.8
Puerto Rican	38.8
South American	59.9

Males per 100 Females

Group	Number
Total Population	96.9
Hispanic or Latino (of any race)	113.2
Central American, ex. Mexican	122.3
Guatemalan	116.1
Salvadoran	122.7
Mexican	113.8
Puerto Rican	122.8
South American	85.0

Average Household Size

Group	People
Total Population	2.57
Hispanic or Latino (of any race)	4.16
Central American, ex. Mexican	3.33
Guatemalan	2.80
Salvadoran	4.22
Mexican	4.32
Puerto Rican	2.96
South American	3.24

Median Age

Group	Years
Total Population	36.1
Hispanic or Latino (of any race)	26.3
Central American, ex. Mexican	33.2
Guatemalan	34.3
Salvadoran	31.2
Mexican	25.7
Puerto Rican	29.3
South American	37.1

High School Graduates
(Universe: Population 25 Years and Over)

Group	Number	%
Total Population	22,114	86.4
Hispanic or Latino (of any race)	3,836	64.1
Mexican	3,122	61.3

Four-Year College Graduates
(Universe: Population 25 Years and Over)

Group	Number	%
Total Population	9,633	37.6
Hispanic or Latino (of any race)	862	14.4
Mexican	647	12.7

Population Age 3–17 Enrolled in Public School
(Universe: Population Age 3–17 Enrolled in School)

Group	Number	%
Total Population	5,915	93.5
Hispanic or Latino (of any race)	2,779	98.7
Mexican	2,641	99.2

Population Age 3–17 Enrolled in Private School
(Universe: Population Age 3–17 Enrolled in School)

Group	Number	%
Total Population	408	6.5
Hispanic or Latino (of any race)	36	1.3
Mexican	20	0.8

Foreign-Born Population

Group	Number	%
Total Population	15,139	40.9
Hispanic or Latino (of any race)	5,914	53.6
Mexican	5,251	53.6

Foreign-Born Naturalized U.S. Citizens

Group	Number	%
Total Population	7,028	46.4
Hispanic or Latino (of any race)	1,794	30.3
Mexican	1,481	28.2

Language Spoken at Home: English Only
(Universe: Population 5 Years and Over)

Group	Number	%
Total Population	15,116	43.7
Hispanic or Latino (of any race)	614	6.2
Mexican	335	3.9

Language Spoken at Home: Spanish
(Universe: Population 5 Years and Over)

Group	Number	%
Total Population	9,576	27.7
Hispanic or Latino (of any race)	9,229	93.8
Mexican	8,335	96.1

Unemployment Rate
(Universe: Population 16 Years and Over)

Group	%
Total Population	6.5
Hispanic or Latino (of any race)	6.2

Notes: (1) Percent of total population; (2) Percent of Hispanic/Latino population; Profiles include places with an overall population of at least 125,000, OR an overall population of at least 25,000 where the Hispanic/Latino population is at least 20% of the overall population. In states where less than five places meet either of these criteria, we have included places with at least 10,000 total population with the highest percentage of Hispanic/Latino population. These places are identified with an asterisk (*); Please refer to the User's Guide for a full explanation of data.

Group		%
Mexican		5.6

Class of Worker: Private Wage and Salary
(Universe: Civilian Employed Population 16 Years and Over)

Group	Number	%
Total Population	17,881	88.2
Hispanic or Latino (of any race)	5,282	93.1
Mexican	4,627	93.4

Class of Worker: Government
(Universe: Civilian Employed Population 16 Years and Over)

Group	Number	%
Total Population	1,506	7.4
Hispanic or Latino (of any race)	327	5.8
Mexican	327	6.6

Means of Transportation to Work: Car, Truck or Van
(Universe: Workers 16 Years and Over)

Group	Number	%
Total Population	18,205	91.3
Hispanic or Latino (of any race)	5,431	96.9
Mexican	4,774	96.5

Means of Transportation to Work: Public Transportation (ex. Taxicab)
(Universe: Workers 16 Years and Over)

Group	Number	%
Total Population	459	2.3
Hispanic or Latino (of any race)	62	1.1
Mexican	62	1.3

Homeownership Rate
(Universe: Occupied Housing Units)

Group	%
Total Population	64.5
Hispanic or Latino (of any race)	53.7
Central American, ex. Mexican	59.6
Guatemalan	56.5
Salvadoran	63.3
Mexican	52.4
Puerto Rican	60.7
South American	69.9

Median Home Value

Group	Dollars
Total Population	238,300
Hispanic or Latino (of any race)	216,700
Mexican	217,100

Median Gross Rent

Group	Dollars
Total Population	980
Hispanic or Latino (of any race)	941
Mexican	935

Median Household Income
(2010 Inflation-Adjusted Dollars)

Group	Dollars
Total Population	55,869
Hispanic or Latino (of any race)	49,701
Mexican	46,813

Per Capita Income
(2010 Inflation-Adjusted Dollars)

Group	Dollars
Total Population	26,698
Hispanic or Latino (of any race)	15,122
Mexican	14,836

Households with $100,000+ Income

Group	Number	%
Total Population	2,714	18.6
Hispanic or Latino (of any race)	252	9.0
Mexican	209	8.5

Households with Food Stamps/SNAP Benefits During Past 12 Months

Group	Number	%
Total Population	922	6.3
Hispanic or Latino (of any race)	187	6.6
Mexican	187	7.6

Poverty Rate
(Income in Past 12 Months Below Poverty Level)

Group	%
Total Population	9.0
Hispanic or Latino (of any race)	15.5
Mexican	17.1

STATE & PLACE PROFILES

Notes: (1) Percent of total population; (2) Percent of Hispanic/Latino population; Profiles include places with an overall population of at least 125,000, OR an overall population of at least 25,000 where the Hispanic/Latino population is at least 20% of the overall population. In states where less than five places meet either of these criteria, we have included places with at least 10,000 total population with the highest percentage of Hispanic/Latino population. These places are identified with an asterisk (*); Please refer to the User's Guide for a full explanation of data.

Indiana

EDITOR'S NOTE: For a place to be included in this edition, it must meet one of two criteria. Either its overall population is at least 125,000, OR its overall population is at least 25,000 and its Hispanic/Latino population is at least 20% of the overall population. For the state of Indiana, the following locations are included:

- East Chicago
- Elkhart
- Fort Wayne
- Goshen
- Hammond
- Indianapolis

Section Two: State & Place Profiles starts with the state profile, followed by place profiles that meet the criteria above. Places are listed alphabetically within each state. All states, all counties and places that meet the above criteria are ranked and compared in *Section Three: Rankings & Comparisons*, on page 1055.

For a more detailed look at the Hispanic/Latino population in Indiana, a companion web site is available at no additional charge with purchase of this print edition. Visit http://gold.greyhouse.com/page/info_hispanic for more information.

The web site includes data for all counties and places in Indiana with Hispanic/Latino population, plus ten additional topics: Self Employed Worker; Walked to Work; Worked from Home; Mean Travel Time to Work; Mean Household Income; Households with Cash Public Assistance; Mean Cash Pubic Assistance; Poverty Rates for 18 and Under, 18 to 64, and 65 and Over.

Population

Group	Number	%TP[1]	%HP[2]
Total Population	6,483,802	100.0	–
Hispanic or Latino (of any race)	389,707	6.0	100.0
Central American, ex. Mexican	22,093	0.3	5.7
Costa Rican	592	<0.1	0.2
Guatemalan	5,933	0.1	1.5
Honduran	5,345	0.1	1.4
Nicaraguan	1,431	<0.1	0.4
Panamanian	1,218	<0.1	0.3
Salvadoran	7,401	0.1	1.9
Cuban	4,042	0.1	1.0
Dominican Republic	2,340	<0.1	0.6
Mexican	295,373	4.6	75.8
Puerto Rican	30,304	0.5	7.8
South American	10,032	0.2	2.6
Argentinean	1,027	<0.1	0.3
Bolivian	425	<0.1	0.1
Chilean	647	<0.1	0.2
Colombian	2,854	<0.1	0.7
Ecuadorian	1,092	<0.1	0.3
Peruvian	2,225	<0.1	0.6
Uruguayan	150	<0.1	<0.1
Venezuelan	1,440	<0.1	0.4
Spaniard	3,675	0.1	0.9

Population Growth: 2000–2010

Group	%
Total Population	6.6
Hispanic or Latino (of any race)	81.7
Central American, ex. Mexican	260.8
Costa Rican	116.8
Guatemalan	309.5
Honduran	286.2
Nicaraguan	186.8
Panamanian	113.7
Salvadoran	341.3
Cuban	46.8
Dominican Republic	262.8
Mexican	93.0
Puerto Rican	54.0
South American	154.7
Argentinean	137.7
Bolivian	148.5
Chilean	136.1
Colombian	149.7
Ecuadorian	163.8
Peruvian	238.7
Venezuelan	144.9
Spaniard	624.9

Males per 100 Females

Group	Number
Total Population	96.8
Hispanic or Latino (of any race)	110.9
Central American, ex. Mexican	115.0
Costa Rican	94.7
Guatemalan	126.6
Honduran	126.5
Nicaraguan	97.9
Panamanian	70.8
Salvadoran	112.2
Cuban	103.7
Dominican Republic	93.1
Mexican	113.6
Puerto Rican	98.8
South American	92.0
Argentinean	105.8
Bolivian	84.8
Chilean	93.1
Colombian	87.0
Ecuadorian	94.0
Peruvian	88.4
Uruguayan	87.5
Venezuelan	99.4
Spaniard	91.4

Average Household Size

Group	People
Total Population	2.52
Hispanic or Latino (of any race)	3.49
Central American, ex. Mexican	3.73
Costa Rican	2.70
Guatemalan	3.82
Honduran	3.81
Nicaraguan	3.42
Panamanian	2.60
Salvadoran	3.97
Cuban	2.72
Dominican Republic	3.19
Mexican	3.63
Puerto Rican	2.95
South American	2.87
Argentinean	2.96
Bolivian	2.88
Chilean	2.71
Colombian	2.65
Ecuadorian	3.05
Peruvian	3.02
Uruguayan	3.02
Venezuelan	2.93
Spaniard	2.65

Median Age

Group	Years
Total Population	37.0
Hispanic or Latino (of any race)	24.1
Central American, ex. Mexican	26.5
Costa Rican	28.9
Guatemalan	24.2
Honduran	27.1
Nicaraguan	29.3
Panamanian	28.7
Salvadoran	27.1
Cuban	27.3
Dominican Republic	26.3
Mexican	23.5
Puerto Rican	25.2
South American	31.3
Argentinean	34.4
Bolivian	28.2
Chilean	32.9
Colombian	30.5
Ecuadorian	29.6
Peruvian	32.5
Uruguayan	35.7
Venezuelan	31.6
Spaniard	31.1

High School Graduates
(Universe: Population 25 Years and Over)

Group	Number	%
Total Population	3,591,170	86.2
Hispanic or Latino (of any race)	107,651	61.1
Central American, ex. Mexican	5,238	47.3
Guatemalan	991	43.3
Honduran	1,460	44.3
Nicaraguan	547	71.2
Panamanian	533	87.8
Salvadoran	1,335	36.1
Cuban	2,044	81.4
Dominican Republic	992	78.0
Mexican	76,202	57.4
Puerto Rican	12,411	81.4
South American	5,102	89.8
Argentinean	650	91.0
Colombian	1,438	96.1
Ecuadorian	533	73.0
Peruvian	1,183	86.8
Venezuelan	678	98.5
Spaniard	1,288	84.3

Four-Year College Graduates
(Universe: Population 25 Years and Over)

Group	Number	%
Total Population	934,292	22.4
Hispanic or Latino (of any race)	20,316	11.5
Central American, ex. Mexican	1,536	13.9
Guatemalan	280	12.2
Honduran	347	10.5
Nicaraguan	238	31.0
Panamanian	203	33.4
Salvadoran	302	8.2
Cuban	725	28.9
Dominican Republic	358	28.1
Mexican	11,067	8.3
Puerto Rican	2,450	16.1
South American	2,578	45.4
Argentinean	343	48.0
Colombian	919	61.4
Ecuadorian	229	31.4
Peruvian	376	27.6
Venezuelan	366	53.2
Spaniard	527	34.5

Population Age 3–17 Enrolled in Public School
(Universe: Population Age 3–17 Enrolled in School)

Group	Number	%
Total Population	1,018,440	85.3
Hispanic or Latino (of any race)	83,722	89.4
Central American, ex. Mexican	3,865	83.9
Guatemalan	1,063	71.6
Honduran	966	89.7
Nicaraguan	163	74.4
Panamanian	112	90.3
Salvadoran	1,418	94.7
Cuban	679	71.3
Dominican Republic	455	80.4
Mexican	66,316	91.0
Puerto Rican	6,780	87.9
South American	1,801	76.7
Argentinean	231	89.9
Colombian	585	72.5
Ecuadorian	239	74.0
Peruvian	395	87.6
Venezuelan	150	64.4
Spaniard	642	89.0

Population Age 3–17 Enrolled in Private School
(Universe: Population Age 3–17 Enrolled in School)

Group	Number	%
Total Population	175,573	14.7

Notes: (1) Percent of total population; (2) Percent of Hispanic/Latino population; Profiles include places with an overall population of at least 125,000, OR an overall population of at least 25,000 where the Hispanic/Latino population is at least 20% of the overall population. In states where less than five places meet either of these criteria, we have included places with at least 10,000 total population with the highest percentage of Hispanic/Latino population. These places are identified with an asterisk (*); Please refer to the User's Guide for a full explanation of data.

Group	Number	%
Hispanic or Latino (of any race)	9,891	10.6
Central American, ex. Mexican	744	16.1
Guatemalan	421	28.4
Honduran	111	10.3
Nicaraguan	56	25.6
Panamanian	12	9.7
Salvadoran	79	5.3
Cuban	273	28.7
Dominican Republic	111	19.6
Mexican	6,592	9.0
Puerto Rican	933	12.1
South American	547	23.3
Argentinean	26	10.1
Colombian	222	27.5
Ecuadorian	84	26.0
Peruvian	56	12.4
Venezuelan	83	35.6
Spaniard	79	11.0

Foreign-Born Population

Group	Number	%
Total Population	285,300	4.4
Hispanic or Latino (of any race)	134,360	37.2
Central American, ex. Mexican	13,419	62.3
Guatemalan	3,606	67.1
Honduran	4,146	67.1
Nicaraguan	805	71.7
Panamanian	413	42.4
Salvadoran	4,122	58.0
Cuban	1,447	33.4
Dominican Republic	1,186	53.6
Mexican	109,123	39.2
Puerto Rican	186	0.6
South American	6,304	61.4
Argentinean	877	70.6
Colombian	1,560	49.5
Ecuadorian	839	60.8
Peruvian	1,554	68.6
Venezuelan	786	71.4
Spaniard	351	12.4

Foreign-Born Naturalized U.S. Citizens

Group	Number	%
Total Population	99,711	34.9
Hispanic or Latino (of any race)	28,005	20.8
Central American, ex. Mexican	3,294	24.5
Guatemalan	1,182	32.8
Honduran	508	12.3
Nicaraguan	240	29.8
Panamanian	248	60.0
Salvadoran	1,004	24.4
Cuban	920	63.6
Dominican Republic	575	48.5
Mexican	19,985	18.3
Puerto Rican	39	21.0
South American	2,060	32.7
Argentinean	291	33.2
Colombian	716	45.9
Ecuadorian	158	18.8
Peruvian	390	25.1
Venezuelan	202	25.7
Spaniard	184	52.4

Language Spoken at Home: English Only
(Universe: Population 5 Years and Over)

Group	Number	%
Total Population	5,514,295	92.2
Hispanic or Latino (of any race)	99,912	31.9
Central American, ex. Mexican	2,699	15.0
Guatemalan	912	20.7
Honduran	392	7.7
Nicaraguan	121	11.7
Panamanian	441	50.7
Salvadoran	461	7.9
Cuban	1,979	48.5
Dominican Republic	364	18.3
Mexican	72,518	30.3
Puerto Rican	12,302	47.6
South American	1,882	20.5
Argentinean	223	18.6
Colombian	743	27.7
Ecuadorian	186	15.7
Peruvian	323	15.6
Venezuelan	96	10.1
Spaniard	1,899	71.8

Language Spoken at Home: Spanish
(Universe: Population 5 Years and Over)

Group	Number	%
Total Population	264,317	4.4
Hispanic or Latino (of any race)	211,666	67.7
Central American, ex. Mexican	15,234	84.8
Guatemalan	3,477	78.8
Honduran	4,686	92.3
Nicaraguan	917	88.3
Panamanian	409	47.1
Salvadoran	5,391	92.1
Cuban	2,073	50.8
Dominican Republic	1,626	81.7
Mexican	166,507	69.5
Puerto Rican	13,454	52.0
South American	7,253	78.9
Argentinean	963	80.5
Colombian	1,900	70.8
Ecuadorian	987	83.4
Peruvian	1,743	84.4
Venezuelan	854	89.9
Spaniard	696	26.3

Unemployment Rate
(Universe: Population 16 Years and Over)

Group	%
Total Population	8.4
Hispanic or Latino (of any race)	11.0
Central American, ex. Mexican	15.9
Guatemalan	9.8
Honduran	19.8
Nicaraguan	19.1
Panamanian	2.7
Salvadoran	19.2
Cuban	16.3
Dominican Republic	4.4
Mexican	10.7
Puerto Rican	11.9
South American	5.5
Argentinean	9.1
Colombian	5.6
Ecuadorian	0.0
Peruvian	8.3
Venezuelan	2.4
Spaniard	9.5

Class of Worker: Private Wage and Salary
(Universe: Civilian Employed Population 16 Years and Over)

Group	Number	%
Total Population	2,492,633	83.1
Hispanic or Latino (of any race)	133,403	90.5
Central American, ex. Mexican	8,239	91.8
Guatemalan	1,960	88.8
Honduran	2,413	91.6
Nicaraguan	297	75.6
Panamanian	455	85.0
Salvadoran	2,798	98.0
Cuban	1,591	84.0
Dominican Republic	1,045	88.6
Mexican	103,817	91.9
Puerto Rican	9,700	84.4
South American	4,076	83.2
Argentinean	520	80.1
Colombian	1,171	81.0
Ecuadorian	567	79.0
Peruvian	865	88.8
Venezuelan	505	90.5
Spaniard	880	73.7

Class of Worker: Government
(Universe: Civilian Employed Population 16 Years and Over)

Group	Number	%
Total Population	350,347	11.7
Hispanic or Latino (of any race)	8,782	6.0
Central American, ex. Mexican	482	5.4
Guatemalan	167	7.6
Honduran	145	5.5
Nicaraguan	46	11.7
Panamanian	70	13.1
Salvadoran	17	0.6
Cuban	219	11.6
Dominican Republic	129	10.9
Mexican	5,163	4.6
Puerto Rican	1,493	13.0
South American	626	12.8

Group	Number	%
Argentinean	129	19.9
Colombian	194	13.4
Ecuadorian	151	21.0
Peruvian	48	4.9
Venezuelan	37	6.6
Spaniard	165	13.8

Means of Transportation to Work: Car, Truck or Van
(Universe: Workers 16 Years and Over)

Group	Number	%
Total Population	2,704,567	92.2
Hispanic or Latino (of any race)	131,930	91.7
Central American, ex. Mexican	8,279	95.1
Guatemalan	2,051	95.4
Honduran	2,432	94.1
Nicaraguan	357	100.0
Panamanian	498	92.9
Salvadoran	2,596	95.2
Cuban	1,643	91.0
Dominican Republic	1,139	97.9
Mexican	100,785	91.5
Puerto Rican	10,518	93.0
South American	4,308	89.0
Argentinean	564	88.3
Colombian	1,211	84.7
Ecuadorian	681	93.5
Peruvian	903	94.2
Venezuelan	567	98.4
Spaniard	891	75.8

Means of Transportation to Work: Public Transportation (ex. Taxicab)
(Universe: Workers 16 Years and Over)

Group	Number	%
Total Population	30,940	1.1
Hispanic or Latino (of any race)	2,932	2.0
Central American, ex. Mexican	76	0.9
Guatemalan	21	1.0
Honduran	31	1.2
Nicaraguan	0	0.0
Panamanian	0	0.0
Salvadoran	24	0.9
Cuban	42	2.3
Dominican Republic	0	0.0
Mexican	2,538	2.3
Puerto Rican	167	1.5
South American	0	0.0
Argentinean	0	0.0
Colombian	0	0.0
Ecuadorian	0	0.0
Peruvian	0	0.0
Venezuelan	0	0.0
Spaniard	35	3.0

Homeownership Rate
(Universe: Occupied Housing Units)

Group	%
Total Population	69.9
Hispanic or Latino (of any race)	52.2
Central American, ex. Mexican	48.0
Costa Rican	53.0
Guatemalan	44.4
Honduran	40.5
Nicaraguan	49.0
Panamanian	49.3
Salvadoran	54.7
Cuban	55.9
Dominican Republic	44.5
Mexican	52.2
Puerto Rican	53.9
South American	59.8
Argentinean	66.0
Bolivian	60.0
Chilean	61.8
Colombian	57.9
Ecuadorian	62.5
Peruvian	59.9
Uruguayan	63.2
Venezuelan	55.9
Spaniard	62.6

Median Home Value

Group	Dollars
Total Population	123,000

Notes: (1) Percent of total population; (2) Percent of Hispanic/Latino population; Profiles include places with an overall population of at least 125,000, OR an overall population of at least 25,000 where the Hispanic/Latino population is at least 20% of the overall population. In states where less than five places meet either of these criteria, we have included places with at least 10,000 total population with the highest percentage of Hispanic/Latino population. These places are identified with an asterisk (*); Please refer to the User's Guide for a full explanation of data.

Group	Dollars
Hispanic or Latino (of any race)	105,100
Central American, ex. Mexican	105,900
Guatemalan	88,000
Honduran	99,600
Nicaraguan	129,500
Panamanian	136,300
Salvadoran	99,800
Cuban	118,600
Dominican Republic	116,000
Mexican	98,900
Puerto Rican	124,600
South American	133,700
Argentinean	197,900
Colombian	122,800
Ecuadorian	123,000
Peruvian	121,000
Venezuelan	124,500
Spaniard	126,000

Median Gross Rent

Group	Dollars
Total Population	683
Hispanic or Latino (of any race)	679
Central American, ex. Mexican	685
Guatemalan	690
Honduran	643
Nicaraguan	0
Panamanian	694
Salvadoran	708
Cuban	855
Dominican Republic	591
Mexican	668
Puerto Rican	728
South American	731
Argentinean	855
Colombian	752
Ecuadorian	598
Peruvian	693
Venezuelan	610
Spaniard	838

Median Household Income
(2010 Inflation-Adjusted Dollars)

Group	Dollars
Total Population	47,697
Hispanic or Latino (of any race)	36,855
Central American, ex. Mexican	34,911
Guatemalan	32,147
Honduran	27,852
Nicaraguan	45,120
Panamanian	63,333
Salvadoran	36,979
Cuban	38,548
Dominican Republic	46,250
Mexican	36,166
Puerto Rican	42,715
South American	45,613
Argentinean	78,125
Colombian	43,984
Ecuadorian	34,796
Peruvian	41,212
Venezuelan	42,404
Spaniard	45,909

Per Capita Income
(2010 Inflation-Adjusted Dollars)

Group	Dollars
Total Population	24,058
Hispanic or Latino (of any race)	13,469
Central American, ex. Mexican	12,236
Guatemalan	9,832
Honduran	10,208
Nicaraguan	17,360
Panamanian	22,984
Salvadoran	11,962
Cuban	26,512
Dominican Republic	16,970
Mexican	12,421
Puerto Rican	17,890
South American	20,077
Argentinean	27,473
Colombian	17,866
Ecuadorian	13,651
Peruvian	18,017
Venezuelan	21,303
Spaniard	30,427

Households with $100,000+ Income

Group	Number	%
Total Population	378,026	15.3
Hispanic or Latino (of any race)	7,687	8.2
Central American, ex. Mexican	344	6.5
Guatemalan	36	3.4
Honduran	43	2.4
Nicaraguan	27	9.6
Panamanian	38	18.3
Salvadoran	109	6.3
Cuban	173	12.3
Dominican Republic	36	5.4
Mexican	4,996	7.2
Puerto Rican	1,183	13.2
South American	505	16.8
Argentinean	160	40.3
Colombian	137	15.3
Ecuadorian	28	6.6
Peruvian	57	9.9
Venezuelan	16	4.4
Spaniard	77	9.6

Households with Food Stamps/SNAP Benefits During Past 12 Months

Group	Number	%
Total Population	234,098	9.5
Hispanic or Latino (of any race)	14,322	15.4
Central American, ex. Mexican	953	18.1
Guatemalan	203	19.2
Honduran	394	22.4
Nicaraguan	30	10.7
Panamanian	0	0.0
Salvadoran	322	18.7
Cuban	179	12.8
Dominican Republic	89	13.3
Mexican	10,649	15.3
Puerto Rican	1,747	19.5
South American	129	4.3
Argentinean	0	0.0
Colombian	65	7.3
Ecuadorian	10	2.3
Peruvian	31	5.4
Venezuelan	11	3.0
Spaniard	47	5.8

Poverty Rate
(Income in Past 12 Months Below Poverty Level)

Group	%
Total Population	13.5
Hispanic or Latino (of any race)	25.4
Central American, ex. Mexican	26.6
Guatemalan	24.1
Honduran	34.6
Nicaraguan	28.6
Panamanian	15.8
Salvadoran	24.5
Cuban	14.8
Dominican Republic	11.5
Mexican	26.4
Puerto Rican	22.6
South American	16.3
Argentinean	20.2
Colombian	11.3
Ecuadorian	37.1
Peruvian	9.4
Venezuelan	13.6
Spaniard	8.4

East Chicago

Population

Group	Number	%TP[1]	%HP[2]
Total Population	29,698	100.0	–
Hispanic or Latino (of any race)	15,105	50.9	100.0
Central American, ex. Mexican	160	0.5	1.1
Mexican	11,819	39.8	78.2
Puerto Rican	2,528	8.5	16.7

Population Growth: 2000–2010

Group	%
Total Population	-8.4
Hispanic or Latino (of any race)	-9.7
Mexican	-3.5
Puerto Rican	-18.1

Males per 100 Females

Group	Number
Total Population	88.1
Hispanic or Latino (of any race)	100.2
Central American, ex. Mexican	107.8
Mexican	101.7
Puerto Rican	93.1

Average Household Size

Group	People
Total Population	2.75
Hispanic or Latino (of any race)	3.15
Central American, ex. Mexican	3.47
Mexican	3.25
Puerto Rican	2.77

Median Age

Group	Years
Total Population	30.9
Hispanic or Latino (of any race)	30.4
Central American, ex. Mexican	33.2
Mexican	30.1
Puerto Rican	32.5

High School Graduates
(Universe: Population 25 Years and Over)

Group	Number	%
Total Population	12,084	70.0
Hispanic or Latino (of any race)	5,393	62.1
Mexican	4,241	61.4
Puerto Rican	845	61.4

Four-Year College Graduates
(Universe: Population 25 Years and Over)

Group	Number	%
Total Population	1,488	8.6
Hispanic or Latino (of any race)	582	6.7
Mexican	470	6.8
Puerto Rican	44	3.2

Population Age 3–17 Enrolled in Public School
(Universe: Population Age 3–17 Enrolled in School)

Group	Number	%
Total Population	6,886	91.7
Hispanic or Latino (of any race)	3,023	88.5
Mexican	2,472	88.4
Puerto Rican	305	93.3

Population Age 3–17 Enrolled in Private School
(Universe: Population Age 3–17 Enrolled in School)

Group	Number	%
Total Population	626	8.3
Hispanic or Latino (of any race)	393	11.5
Mexican	324	11.6
Puerto Rican	22	6.7

Foreign-Born Population

Group	Number	%
Total Population	4,564	15.1
Hispanic or Latino (of any race)	4,257	28.5
Mexican	3,976	33.1
Puerto Rican	0	0.0

Foreign-Born Naturalized U.S. Citizens

Group	Number	%
Total Population	1,953	42.8
Hispanic or Latino (of any race)	1,763	41.4
Mexican	1,648	41.4
Puerto Rican	0	0.0

Language Spoken at Home: English Only
(Universe: Population 5 Years and Over)

Group	Number	%
Total Population	17,362	63.2
Hispanic or Latino (of any race)	3,977	29.3
Mexican	3,175	29.1
Puerto Rican	612	30.8

Language Spoken at Home: Spanish
(Universe: Population 5 Years and Over)

Group	Number	%
Total Population	9,849	35.8
Hispanic or Latino (of any race)	9,601	70.7

Notes: (1) Percent of total population; (2) Percent of Hispanic/Latino population; Profiles include places with an overall population of at least 125,000, OR an overall population of at least 25,000 where the Hispanic/Latino population is at least 20% of the overall population. In states where less than five places meet either of these criteria, we have included places with at least 10,000 total population with the highest percentage of Hispanic/Latino population. These places are identified with an asterisk (*); Please refer to the User's Guide for a full explanation of data.

Mexican	7,750	70.9
Puerto Rican	1,368	69.0

Unemployment Rate
(Universe: Population 16 Years and Over)

Group	%
Total Population	12.2
Hispanic or Latino (of any race)	11.9
Mexican	12.9
Puerto Rican	8.1

Class of Worker: Private Wage and Salary
(Universe: Civilian Employed Population 16 Years and Over)

Group	Number	%
Total Population	8,655	85.6
Hispanic or Latino (of any race)	4,489	87.7
Mexican	3,623	90.1
Puerto Rican	607	76.3

Class of Worker: Government
(Universe: Civilian Employed Population 16 Years and Over)

Group	Number	%
Total Population	1,273	12.6
Hispanic or Latino (of any race)	540	10.5
Mexican	342	8.5
Puerto Rican	189	23.7

Means of Transportation to Work: Car, Truck or Van
(Universe: Workers 16 Years and Over)

Group	Number	%
Total Population	8,857	89.4
Hispanic or Latino (of any race)	4,595	91.6
Mexican	3,506	89.6
Puerto Rican	785	98.6

Means of Transportation to Work: Public Transportation (ex. Taxicab)
(Universe: Workers 16 Years and Over)

Group	Number	%
Total Population	409	4.1
Hispanic or Latino (of any race)	152	3.0
Mexican	144	3.7
Puerto Rican	8	1.0

Homeownership Rate
(Universe: Occupied Housing Units)

Group	%
Total Population	41.5
Hispanic or Latino (of any race)	51.6
Central American, ex. Mexican	43.9
Mexican	54.7
Puerto Rican	42.3

Median Home Value

Group	Dollars
Total Population	89,100
Hispanic or Latino (of any race)	90,700
Mexican	89,000
Puerto Rican	94,500

Median Gross Rent

Group	Dollars
Total Population	655
Hispanic or Latino (of any race)	674
Mexican	668
Puerto Rican	685

Median Household Income
(2010 Inflation-Adjusted Dollars)

Group	Dollars
Total Population	28,999
Hispanic or Latino (of any race)	41,932
Mexican	42,522
Puerto Rican	37,625

Per Capita Income
(2010 Inflation-Adjusted Dollars)

Group	Dollars
Total Population	13,850
Hispanic or Latino (of any race)	14,255
Mexican	14,273
Puerto Rican	14,086

Households with $100,000+ Income

Group	Number	%
Total Population	668	6.9
Hispanic or Latino (of any race)	346	8.1
Mexican	278	8.2
Puerto Rican	68	10.1

Households with Food Stamps/SNAP Benefits During Past 12 Months

Group	Number	%
Total Population	3,083	31.7
Hispanic or Latino (of any race)	980	23.1
Mexican	796	23.3
Puerto Rican	184	27.3

Poverty Rate
(Income in Past 12 Months Below Poverty Level)

Group	%
Total Population	33.1
Hispanic or Latino (of any race)	21.5
Mexican	22.2
Puerto Rican	23.4

Elkhart

Population

Group	Number	%TP[1]	%HP[2]
Total Population	50,949	100.0	–
Hispanic or Latino (of any race)	11,451	22.5	100.0
Central American, ex. Mexican	912	1.8	8.0
Honduran	390	0.8	3.4
Salvadoran	400	0.8	3.5
Mexican	9,313	18.3	81.3
Puerto Rican	392	0.8	3.4
South American	121	0.2	1.1

Population Growth: 2000–2010

Group	%
Total Population	-1.8
Hispanic or Latino (of any race)	49.1
Central American, ex. Mexican	120.8
Honduran	133.5
Salvadoran	192.0
Mexican	50.8
Puerto Rican	17.7

Males per 100 Females

Group	Number
Total Population	93.0
Hispanic or Latino (of any race)	111.7
Central American, ex. Mexican	120.8
Honduran	143.8
Salvadoran	104.1
Mexican	112.7
Puerto Rican	105.2
South American	72.9

Average Household Size

Group	People
Total Population	2.60
Hispanic or Latino (of any race)	4.10
Central American, ex. Mexican	4.14
Honduran	4.31
Salvadoran	4.18
Mexican	4.25
Puerto Rican	2.89
South American	2.95

Median Age

Group	Years
Total Population	32.7
Hispanic or Latino (of any race)	22.5
Central American, ex. Mexican	27.3
Honduran	26.7
Salvadoran	27.6
Mexican	22.0
Puerto Rican	20.8
South American	35.3

High School Graduates
(Universe: Population 25 Years and Over)

Group	Number	%
Total Population	23,469	73.9
Hispanic or Latino (of any race)	2,420	41.5
Central American, ex. Mexican	282	26.1
Mexican	1,764	41.2

Four-Year College Graduates
(Universe: Population 25 Years and Over)

Group	Number	%
Total Population	4,444	14.0
Hispanic or Latino (of any race)	426	7.3
Central American, ex. Mexican	70	6.5
Mexican	218	5.1

Population Age 3–17 Enrolled in Public School
(Universe: Population Age 3–17 Enrolled in School)

Group	Number	%
Total Population	9,239	90.1
Hispanic or Latino (of any race)	3,031	93.9
Central American, ex. Mexican	370	95.1
Mexican	2,416	93.1

Population Age 3–17 Enrolled in Private School
(Universe: Population Age 3–17 Enrolled in School)

Group	Number	%
Total Population	1,016	9.9
Hispanic or Latino (of any race)	198	6.1
Central American, ex. Mexican	19	4.9
Mexican	179	6.9

Foreign-Born Population

Group	Number	%
Total Population	7,673	14.8
Hispanic or Latino (of any race)	6,782	55.1
Central American, ex. Mexican	1,233	56.8
Mexican	5,336	57.7

Foreign-Born Naturalized U.S. Citizens

Group	Number	%
Total Population	1,351	17.6
Hispanic or Latino (of any race)	847	12.5
Central American, ex. Mexican	124	10.1
Mexican	710	13.3

Language Spoken at Home: English Only
(Universe: Population 5 Years and Over)

Group	Number	%
Total Population	36,169	77.3
Hispanic or Latino (of any race)	1,065	10.3
Central American, ex. Mexican	41	2.6
Mexican	861	10.8

Language Spoken at Home: Spanish
(Universe: Population 5 Years and Over)

Group	Number	%
Total Population	9,750	20.8
Hispanic or Latino (of any race)	9,226	89.5
Central American, ex. Mexican	1,527	97.4
Mexican	7,110	89.1

Unemployment Rate
(Universe: Population 16 Years and Over)

Group	%
Total Population	14.1
Hispanic or Latino (of any race)	15.4
Central American, ex. Mexican	15.7
Mexican	14.6

Class of Worker: Private Wage and Salary
(Universe: Civilian Employed Population 16 Years and Over)

Group	Number	%
Total Population	19,844	89.4
Hispanic or Latino (of any race)	4,942	97.9
Central American, ex. Mexican	766	100.0
Mexican	3,855	97.3

Class of Worker: Government
(Universe: Civilian Employed Population 16 Years and Over)

Group	Number	%
Total Population	1,645	7.4
Hispanic or Latino (of any race)	89	1.8
Central American, ex. Mexican	0	0.0
Mexican	89	2.2

Means of Transportation to Work: Car, Truck or Van
(Universe: Workers 16 Years and Over)

Group	Number	%
Total Population	19,874	91.9

Notes: (1) Percent of total population; (2) Percent of Hispanic/Latino population; Profiles include places with an overall population of at least 125,000, OR an overall population of at least 25,000 where the Hispanic/Latino population is at least 20% of the overall population. In states where less than five places meet either of these criteria, we have included places with at least 10,000 total population with the highest percentage of Hispanic/Latino population. These places are identified with an asterisk (*); Please refer to the User's Guide for a full explanation of data.

Hispanic or Latino (of any race)	4,339	88.8
Central American, ex. Mexican	650	93.3
Mexican	3,417	87.9

Means of Transportation to Work: Public Transportation (ex. Taxicab)
(Universe: Workers 16 Years and Over)

Group	Number	%
Total Population	201	0.9
Hispanic or Latino (of any race)	80	1.6
Central American, ex. Mexican	31	4.4
Mexican	39	1.0

Homeownership Rate
(Universe: Occupied Housing Units)

Group	%
Total Population	50.8
Hispanic or Latino (of any race)	42.7
Central American, ex. Mexican	41.4
Honduran	41.0
Salvadoran	45.8
Mexican	44.3
Puerto Rican	29.5
South American	46.5

Median Home Value

Group	Dollars
Total Population	90,900
Hispanic or Latino (of any race)	88,700
Central American, ex. Mexican	82,600
Mexican	88,600

Median Gross Rent

Group	Dollars
Total Population	642
Hispanic or Latino (of any race)	598
Central American, ex. Mexican	589
Mexican	606

Median Household Income
(2010 Inflation-Adjusted Dollars)

Group	Dollars
Total Population	35,654
Hispanic or Latino (of any race)	32,258
Central American, ex. Mexican	27,391
Mexican	35,000

Per Capita Income
(2010 Inflation-Adjusted Dollars)

Group	Dollars
Total Population	17,879
Hispanic or Latino (of any race)	10,477
Central American, ex. Mexican	9,676
Mexican	10,557

Households with $100,000+ Income

Group	Number	%
Total Population	1,144	5.9
Hispanic or Latino (of any race)	96	3.2
Central American, ex. Mexican	22	4.2
Mexican	65	2.9

Households with Food Stamps/SNAP Benefits During Past 12 Months

Group	Number	%
Total Population	4,169	21.6
Hispanic or Latino (of any race)	776	25.7
Central American, ex. Mexican	196	37.5
Mexican	474	21.5

Poverty Rate
(Income in Past 12 Months Below Poverty Level)

Group	%
Total Population	22.7
Hispanic or Latino (of any race)	25.3
Central American, ex. Mexican	34.0
Mexican	23.7

Fort Wayne

Population

Group	Number	%TP[1]	%HP[2]
Total Population	253,691	100.0	–
Hispanic or Latino (of any race)	20,200	8.0	100.0
Central American, ex. Mexican	1,346	0.5	6.7
Guatemalan	729	0.3	3.6
Honduran	129	0.1	0.6
Salvadoran	369	0.1	1.8
Cuban	174	0.1	0.9
Mexican	15,545	6.1	77.0
Puerto Rican	939	0.4	4.6
South American	651	0.3	3.2
Colombian	235	0.1	1.2
Ecuadorian	159	0.1	0.8
Peruvian	128	0.1	0.6
Spaniard	176	0.1	0.9

Population Growth: 2000–2010

Group	%
Total Population	23.3
Hispanic or Latino (of any race)	70.0
Central American, ex. Mexican	185.8
Guatemalan	185.9
Salvadoran	220.9
Cuban	27.9
Mexican	80.4
Puerto Rican	76.2
South American	130.9
Colombian	102.6

Males per 100 Females

Group	Number
Total Population	93.8
Hispanic or Latino (of any race)	106.1
Central American, ex. Mexican	116.4
Guatemalan	147.1
Honduran	95.5
Salvadoran	87.3
Cuban	102.3
Mexican	107.5
Puerto Rican	98.1
South American	92.6
Colombian	89.5
Ecuadorian	96.3
Peruvian	116.9
Spaniard	89.2

Average Household Size

Group	People
Total Population	2.44
Hispanic or Latino (of any race)	3.43
Central American, ex. Mexican	3.71
Guatemalan	3.95
Honduran	3.43
Salvadoran	3.71
Cuban	2.34
Mexican	3.51
Puerto Rican	2.91
South American	3.10
Colombian	2.72
Ecuadorian	4.28
Peruvian	3.03
Spaniard	2.69

Median Age

Group	Years
Total Population	34.5
Hispanic or Latino (of any race)	22.9
Central American, ex. Mexican	28.0
Guatemalan	27.6
Honduran	27.2
Salvadoran	29.4
Cuban	35.5
Mexican	21.9
Puerto Rican	22.6
South American	32.1
Colombian	31.8
Ecuadorian	32.1
Peruvian	36.5
Spaniard	36.8

High School Graduates
(Universe: Population 25 Years and Over)

Group	Number	%
Total Population	141,212	87.7
Hispanic or Latino (of any race)	5,224	58.7
Central American, ex. Mexican	320	49.4
Mexican	3,682	54.3
Puerto Rican	491	87.5

Four-Year College Graduates
(Universe: Population 25 Years and Over)

Group	Number	%
Total Population	41,100	25.5
Hispanic or Latino (of any race)	904	10.2
Central American, ex. Mexican	94	14.5
Mexican	644	9.5
Puerto Rican	51	9.1

Population Age 3–17 Enrolled in Public School
(Universe: Population Age 3–17 Enrolled in School)

Group	Number	%
Total Population	40,035	81.3
Hispanic or Latino (of any race)	4,667	90.6
Central American, ex. Mexican	309	83.5
Mexican	3,673	93.0
Puerto Rican	317	85.2

Population Age 3–17 Enrolled in Private School
(Universe: Population Age 3–17 Enrolled in School)

Group	Number	%
Total Population	9,235	18.7
Hispanic or Latino (of any race)	484	9.4
Central American, ex. Mexican	61	16.5
Mexican	275	7.0
Puerto Rican	55	14.8

Foreign-Born Population

Group	Number	%
Total Population	16,471	6.5
Hispanic or Latino (of any race)	6,421	33.8
Central American, ex. Mexican	779	56.1
Mexican	5,157	35.7
Puerto Rican	0	0.0

Foreign-Born Naturalized U.S. Citizens

Group	Number	%
Total Population	6,039	36.7
Hispanic or Latino (of any race)	1,337	20.8
Central American, ex. Mexican	187	24.0
Mexican	1,008	19.5
Puerto Rican	0	0.0

Language Spoken at Home: English Only
(Universe: Population 5 Years and Over)

Group	Number	%
Total Population	211,517	90.4
Hispanic or Latino (of any race)	5,672	34.6
Central American, ex. Mexican	118	9.8
Mexican	4,246	33.9
Puerto Rican	596	50.9

Language Spoken at Home: Spanish
(Universe: Population 5 Years and Over)

Group	Number	%
Total Population	12,714	5.4
Hispanic or Latino (of any race)	10,644	64.9
Central American, ex. Mexican	1,090	90.2
Mexican	8,248	65.8
Puerto Rican	527	45.0

Unemployment Rate
(Universe: Population 16 Years and Over)

Group	%
Total Population	9.4
Hispanic or Latino (of any race)	13.0
Central American, ex. Mexican	11.6
Mexican	12.6
Puerto Rican	16.9

Class of Worker: Private Wage and Salary
(Universe: Civilian Employed Population 16 Years and Over)

Group	Number	%
Total Population	101,998	86.8
Hispanic or Latino (of any race)	6,976	93.6
Central American, ex. Mexican	423	88.3
Mexican	5,255	93.4
Puerto Rican	566	97.4

Class of Worker: Government
(Universe: Civilian Employed Population 16 Years and Over)

Group	Number	%
Total Population	10,550	9.0
Hispanic or Latino (of any race)	206	2.8
Central American, ex. Mexican	11	2.3

Notes: (1) Percent of total population; (2) Percent of Hispanic/Latino population; Profiles include places with an overall population of at least 125,000, OR an overall population of at least 25,000 where the Hispanic/Latino population is at least 20% of the overall population. In states where less than five places meet either of these criteria, we have included places with at least 10,000 total population with the highest percentage of Hispanic/Latino population. These places are identified with an asterisk (*); Please refer to the User's Guide for a full explanation of data.

Mexican	151	2.7
Puerto Rican	15	2.6

Means of Transportation to Work: Car, Truck or Van
(Universe: Workers 16 Years and Over)

Group	Number	%
Total Population	108,529	94.0
Hispanic or Latino (of any race)	6,781	93.5
Central American, ex. Mexican	448	100.0
Mexican	5,172	93.6
Puerto Rican	535	94.2

Means of Transportation to Work: Public Transportation (ex. Taxicab)
(Universe: Workers 16 Years and Over)

Group	Number	%
Total Population	941	0.8
Hispanic or Latino (of any race)	168	2.3
Central American, ex. Mexican	0	0.0
Mexican	136	2.5
Puerto Rican	0	0.0

Homeownership Rate
(Universe: Occupied Housing Units)

Group	%
Total Population	63.3
Hispanic or Latino (of any race)	53.6
Central American, ex. Mexican	57.4
Guatemalan	55.6
Honduran	48.6
Salvadoran	65.0
Cuban	57.4
Mexican	53.5
Puerto Rican	50.4
South American	58.6
Colombian	51.9
Ecuadorian	70.2
Peruvian	52.5
Spaniard	62.2

Median Home Value

Group	Dollars
Total Population	100,800
Hispanic or Latino (of any race)	75,300
Central American, ex. Mexican	85,200
Mexican	72,500
Puerto Rican	88,500

Median Gross Rent

Group	Dollars
Total Population	623
Hispanic or Latino (of any race)	594
Central American, ex. Mexican	615
Mexican	577
Puerto Rican	486

Median Household Income
(2010 Inflation-Adjusted Dollars)

Group	Dollars
Total Population	43,847
Hispanic or Latino (of any race)	30,989
Central American, ex. Mexican	31,442
Mexican	31,996
Puerto Rican	29,087

Per Capita Income
(2010 Inflation-Adjusted Dollars)

Group	Dollars
Total Population	23,145
Hispanic or Latino (of any race)	11,647
Central American, ex. Mexican	10,317
Mexican	11,435
Puerto Rican	13,672

Households with $100,000+ Income

Group	Number	%
Total Population	12,445	12.3
Hispanic or Latino (of any race)	144	2.7
Central American, ex. Mexican	37	11.4
Mexican	65	1.7
Puerto Rican	13	2.9

Households with Food Stamps/SNAP Benefits During Past 12 Months

Group	Number	%
Total Population	11,505	11.3
Hispanic or Latino (of any race)	885	16.8
Central American, ex. Mexican	32	9.9
Mexican	649	16.8
Puerto Rican	82	18.1

Poverty Rate
(Income in Past 12 Months Below Poverty Level)

Group	%
Total Population	15.0
Hispanic or Latino (of any race)	23.6
Central American, ex. Mexican	19.3
Mexican	22.8
Puerto Rican	34.8

Goshen

Population

Group	Number	%TP[1]	%HP[2]
Total Population	31,719	100.0	–
Hispanic or Latino (of any race)	8,903	28.1	100.0
Central American, ex. Mexican	310	1.0	3.5
Honduran	124	0.4	1.4
Mexican	7,781	24.5	87.4
Puerto Rican	347	1.1	3.9

Population Growth: 2000–2010

Group	%
Total Population	8.0
Hispanic or Latino (of any race)	56.8
Central American, ex. Mexican	206.9
Mexican	58.4
Puerto Rican	50.2

Males per 100 Females

Group	Number
Total Population	95.5
Hispanic or Latino (of any race)	115.2
Central American, ex. Mexican	113.8
Honduran	129.6
Mexican	116.7
Puerto Rican	90.7

Average Household Size

Group	People
Total Population	2.67
Hispanic or Latino (of any race)	4.24
Central American, ex. Mexican	4.14
Honduran	4.19
Mexican	4.35
Puerto Rican	3.25

Median Age

Group	Years
Total Population	32.4
Hispanic or Latino (of any race)	22.1
Central American, ex. Mexican	28.1
Honduran	26.7
Mexican	21.5
Puerto Rican	23.8

High School Graduates
(Universe: Population 25 Years and Over)

Group	Number	%
Total Population	15,125	78.4
Hispanic or Latino (of any race)	1,895	56.4
Mexican	1,583	57.3

Four-Year College Graduates
(Universe: Population 25 Years and Over)

Group	Number	%
Total Population	3,741	19.4
Hispanic or Latino (of any race)	140	4.2
Mexican	116	4.2

Population Age 3–17 Enrolled in Public School
(Universe: Population Age 3–17 Enrolled in School)

Group	Number	%
Total Population	5,572	93.5
Hispanic or Latino (of any race)	2,021	93.7
Mexican	1,795	93.9

Population Age 3–17 Enrolled in Private School
(Universe: Population Age 3–17 Enrolled in School)

Group	Number	%
Total Population	385	6.5
Hispanic or Latino (of any race)	136	6.3
Mexican	116	6.1

Foreign-Born Population

Group	Number	%
Total Population	4,539	14.5
Hispanic or Latino (of any race)	3,480	46.5
Mexican	3,129	48.0

Foreign-Born Naturalized U.S. Citizens

Group	Number	%
Total Population	952	21.0
Hispanic or Latino (of any race)	480	13.8
Mexican	360	11.5

Language Spoken at Home: English Only
(Universe: Population 5 Years and Over)

Group	Number	%
Total Population	21,630	76.0
Hispanic or Latino (of any race)	1,176	18.5
Mexican	944	17.5

Language Spoken at Home: Spanish
(Universe: Population 5 Years and Over)

Group	Number	%
Total Population	5,638	19.8
Hispanic or Latino (of any race)	5,167	81.5
Mexican	4,461	82.5

Unemployment Rate
(Universe: Population 16 Years and Over)

Group	%
Total Population	9.5
Hispanic or Latino (of any race)	15.0
Mexican	12.5

Class of Worker: Private Wage and Salary
(Universe: Civilian Employed Population 16 Years and Over)

Group	Number	%
Total Population	12,312	87.1
Hispanic or Latino (of any race)	2,516	88.9
Mexican	2,077	87.5

Class of Worker: Government
(Universe: Civilian Employed Population 16 Years and Over)

Group	Number	%
Total Population	1,241	8.8
Hispanic or Latino (of any race)	113	4.0
Mexican	97	4.1

Means of Transportation to Work: Car, Truck or Van
(Universe: Workers 16 Years and Over)

Group	Number	%
Total Population	12,522	90.4
Hispanic or Latino (of any race)	2,501	90.7
Mexican	2,124	92.3

Means of Transportation to Work: Public Transportation (ex. Taxicab)
(Universe: Workers 16 Years and Over)

Group	Number	%
Total Population	93	0.7
Hispanic or Latino (of any race)	39	1.4
Mexican	23	1.0

Homeownership Rate
(Universe: Occupied Housing Units)

Group	%
Total Population	58.6
Hispanic or Latino (of any race)	44.3
Central American, ex. Mexican	49.4
Honduran	46.9
Mexican	44.4
Puerto Rican	45.3

Median Home Value

Group	Dollars
Total Population	107,200
Hispanic or Latino (of any race)	88,100
Mexican	92,700

Notes: (1) Percent of total population; (2) Percent of Hispanic/Latino population; Profiles include places with an overall population of at least 125,000, OR an overall population of at least 25,000 where the Hispanic/Latino population is at least 20% of the overall population. In states where less than five places meet either of these criteria, we have included places with at least 10,000 total population with the highest percentage of Hispanic/Latino population. These places are identified with an asterisk (*); Please refer to the User's Guide for a full explanation of data.

Median Gross Rent

Group	Dollars
Total Population	717
Hispanic or Latino (of any race)	677
Mexican	676

Median Household Income
(2010 Inflation-Adjusted Dollars)

Group	Dollars
Total Population	39,384
Hispanic or Latino (of any race)	28,446
Mexican	27,343

Per Capita Income
(2010 Inflation-Adjusted Dollars)

Group	Dollars
Total Population	20,003
Hispanic or Latino (of any race)	10,455
Mexican	9,730

Households with $100,000+ Income

Group	Number	%
Total Population	943	8.0
Hispanic or Latino (of any race)	55	2.7
Mexican	48	3.0

Households with Food Stamps/SNAP Benefits During Past 12 Months

Group	Number	%
Total Population	1,489	12.7
Hispanic or Latino (of any race)	430	21.0
Mexican	340	21.1

Poverty Rate
(Income in Past 12 Months Below Poverty Level)

Group	%
Total Population	18.1
Hispanic or Latino (of any race)	31.2
Mexican	34.4

Hammond

Population

Group	Number	%TP[1]	%HP[2]
Total Population	80,830	100.0	–
Hispanic or Latino (of any race)	27,563	34.1	100.0
Central American, ex. Mexican	526	0.7	1.9
Guatemalan	172	0.2	0.6
Honduran	117	0.1	0.4
Salvadoran	174	0.2	0.6
Cuban	140	0.2	0.5
Mexican	22,684	28.1	82.3
Puerto Rican	3,081	3.8	11.2
South American	141	0.2	0.5
Spaniard	105	0.1	0.4

Population Growth: 2000–2010

Group	%
Total Population	-2.7
Hispanic or Latino (of any race)	57.7
Central American, ex. Mexican	152.9
Cuban	16.7
Mexican	67.0
Puerto Rican	53.1

Males per 100 Females

Group	Number
Total Population	96.2
Hispanic or Latino (of any race)	103.0
Central American, ex. Mexican	116.5
Guatemalan	104.8
Honduran	138.8
Salvadoran	114.8
Cuban	109.0
Mexican	104.1
Puerto Rican	94.3
South American	93.2
Spaniard	87.5

Average Household Size

Group	People
Total Population	2.67
Hispanic or Latino (of any race)	3.55
Central American, ex. Mexican	3.70
Guatemalan	4.02
Honduran	3.65
Salvadoran	3.69
Cuban	3.03
Mexican	3.64
Puerto Rican	3.02
South American	3.15
Spaniard	2.93

Median Age

Group	Years
Total Population	33.3
Hispanic or Latino (of any race)	25.9
Central American, ex. Mexican	29.5
Guatemalan	30.3
Honduran	30.5
Salvadoran	28.8
Cuban	25.5
Mexican	25.6
Puerto Rican	27.5
South American	30.1
Spaniard	25.3

High School Graduates
(Universe: Population 25 Years and Over)

Group	Number	%
Total Population	39,092	77.8
Hispanic or Latino (of any race)	8,880	63.8
Mexican	6,899	61.3
Puerto Rican	1,428	78.2

Four-Year College Graduates
(Universe: Population 25 Years and Over)

Group	Number	%
Total Population	6,060	12.1
Hispanic or Latino (of any race)	1,219	8.8
Mexican	1,021	9.1
Puerto Rican	116	6.4

Population Age 3–17 Enrolled in Public School
(Universe: Population Age 3–17 Enrolled in School)

Group	Number	%
Total Population	14,241	88.3
Hispanic or Latino (of any race)	6,507	87.6
Mexican	5,296	85.6
Puerto Rican	703	100.0

Population Age 3–17 Enrolled in Private School
(Universe: Population Age 3–17 Enrolled in School)

Group	Number	%
Total Population	1,896	11.7
Hispanic or Latino (of any race)	917	12.4
Mexican	889	14.4
Puerto Rican	0	0.0

Foreign-Born Population

Group	Number	%
Total Population	9,442	11.6
Hispanic or Latino (of any race)	7,874	28.3
Mexican	7,327	32.1
Puerto Rican	0	0.0

Foreign-Born Naturalized U.S. Citizens

Group	Number	%
Total Population	3,770	39.9
Hispanic or Latino (of any race)	2,865	36.4
Mexican	2,581	35.2
Puerto Rican	0	0.0

Language Spoken at Home: English Only
(Universe: Population 5 Years and Over)

Group	Number	%
Total Population	55,195	74.2
Hispanic or Latino (of any race)	8,023	32.6
Mexican	6,363	31.6
Puerto Rican	1,211	42.7

Language Spoken at Home: Spanish
(Universe: Population 5 Years and Over)

Group	Number	%
Total Population	17,248	23.2
Hispanic or Latino (of any race)	16,563	67.4
Mexican	13,791	68.4
Puerto Rican	1,622	57.3

Unemployment Rate
(Universe: Population 16 Years and Over)

Group	%
Total Population	11.3
Hispanic or Latino (of any race)	10.4
Mexican	10.6
Puerto Rican	8.2

Class of Worker: Private Wage and Salary
(Universe: Civilian Employed Population 16 Years and Over)

Group	Number	%
Total Population	29,942	87.8
Hispanic or Latino (of any race)	9,800	92.0
Mexican	8,206	94.1
Puerto Rican	1,123	82.0

Class of Worker: Government
(Universe: Civilian Employed Population 16 Years and Over)

Group	Number	%
Total Population	3,148	9.2
Hispanic or Latino (of any race)	589	5.5
Mexican	314	3.6
Puerto Rican	200	14.6

Means of Transportation to Work: Car, Truck or Van
(Universe: Workers 16 Years and Over)

Group	Number	%
Total Population	30,031	90.6
Hispanic or Latino (of any race)	9,249	89.7
Mexican	7,382	88.0
Puerto Rican	1,343	98.1

Means of Transportation to Work: Public Transportation (ex. Taxicab)
(Universe: Workers 16 Years and Over)

Group	Number	%
Total Population	1,590	4.8
Hispanic or Latino (of any race)	672	6.5
Mexican	621	7.4
Puerto Rican	26	1.9

Homeownership Rate
(Universe: Occupied Housing Units)

Group	%
Total Population	61.3
Hispanic or Latino (of any race)	66.0
Central American, ex. Mexican	69.7
Guatemalan	68.9
Honduran	64.5
Salvadoran	81.6
Cuban	55.0
Mexican	68.0
Puerto Rican	56.7
South American	69.6
Spaniard	63.3

Median Home Value

Group	Dollars
Total Population	97,800
Hispanic or Latino (of any race)	99,400
Mexican	98,700
Puerto Rican	102,300

Median Gross Rent

Group	Dollars
Total Population	736
Hispanic or Latino (of any race)	775
Mexican	771
Puerto Rican	812

Median Household Income
(2010 Inflation-Adjusted Dollars)

Group	Dollars
Total Population	38,539
Hispanic or Latino (of any race)	36,975
Mexican	36,924
Puerto Rican	40,395

Per Capita Income
(2010 Inflation-Adjusted Dollars)

Group	Dollars
Total Population	17,844
Hispanic or Latino (of any race)	12,648
Mexican	12,413

Notes: (1) Percent of total population; (2) Percent of Hispanic/Latino population; Profiles include places with an overall population of at least 125,000, OR an overall population of at least 25,000 where the Hispanic/Latino population is at least 20% of the overall population. In states where less than five places meet either of these criteria, we have included places with at least 10,000 total population with the highest percentage of Hispanic/Latino population. These places are identified with an asterisk (*); Please refer to the User's Guide for a full explanation of data.

Group	Number	%
Puerto Rican	15,435	

Households with $100,000+ Income

Group	Number	%
Total Population	2,188	7.4
Hispanic or Latino (of any race)	526	7.0
Mexican	398	6.5
Puerto Rican	111	11.7

Households with Food Stamps/SNAP Benefits During Past 12 Months

Group	Number	%
Total Population	4,897	16.5
Hispanic or Latino (of any race)	1,326	17.7
Mexican	976	15.8
Puerto Rican	303	32.0

Poverty Rate
(Income in Past 12 Months Below Poverty Level)

Group	%
Total Population	21.1
Hispanic or Latino (of any race)	24.7
Mexican	24.0
Puerto Rican	26.3

Indianapolis

Population

Group	Number	%TP[1]	%HP[2]
Total Population	820,445	100.0	–
Hispanic or Latino (of any race)	77,352	9.4	100.0
Central American, ex. Mexican	7,746	0.9	10.0
Costa Rican	125	<0.1	0.2
Guatemalan	1,616	0.2	2.1
Honduran	2,302	0.3	3.0
Nicaraguan	668	0.1	0.9
Panamanian	274	<0.1	0.4
Salvadoran	2,695	0.3	3.5
Cuban	739	0.1	1.0
Dominican Republic	1,124	0.1	1.5
Mexican	56,771	6.9	73.4
Puerto Rican	3,431	0.4	4.4
South American	2,068	0.3	2.7
Argentinean	207	<0.1	0.3
Colombian	587	0.1	0.8
Ecuadorian	160	<0.1	0.2
Peruvian	611	0.1	0.8
Venezuelan	314	<0.1	0.4
Spaniard	527	0.1	0.7

Population Growth: 2000–2010

Group	%
Total Population	4.9
Hispanic or Latino (of any race)	152.5
Central American, ex. Mexican	337.6
Guatemalan	546.4
Honduran	365.1
Nicaraguan	170.4
Panamanian	98.6
Salvadoran	429.5
Cuban	61.7
Dominican Republic	329.0
Mexican	169.7
Puerto Rican	80.2
South American	172.8
Colombian	164.4
Peruvian	245.2
Venezuelan	106.6

Males per 100 Females

Group	Number
Total Population	93.5
Hispanic or Latino (of any race)	118.0
Central American, ex. Mexican	119.9
Costa Rican	95.3
Guatemalan	139.8
Honduran	128.8
Nicaraguan	108.1
Panamanian	61.2
Salvadoran	112.5
Cuban	100.8
Dominican Republic	89.5
Mexican	121.8
Puerto Rican	95.3
South American	100.0
Argentinean	113.4
Colombian	100.3
Ecuadorian	116.2
Peruvian	88.6
Venezuelan	106.6
Spaniard	101.9

Average Household Size

Group	People
Total Population	2.42
Hispanic or Latino (of any race)	3.58
Central American, ex. Mexican	3.72
Costa Rican	2.74
Guatemalan	3.88
Honduran	3.66
Nicaraguan	3.56
Panamanian	2.53
Salvadoran	3.95
Cuban	2.59
Dominican Republic	3.22
Mexican	3.75
Puerto Rican	2.78
South American	2.68
Argentinean	2.73
Colombian	2.58
Ecuadorian	2.47
Peruvian	2.89
Venezuelan	2.64
Spaniard	2.47

Median Age

Group	Years
Total Population	33.7
Hispanic or Latino (of any race)	24.5
Central American, ex. Mexican	27.6
Costa Rican	28.2
Guatemalan	26.5
Honduran	27.7
Nicaraguan	30.4
Panamanian	31.7
Salvadoran	27.6
Cuban	29.8
Dominican Republic	27.5
Mexican	23.7
Puerto Rican	24.7
South American	33.5
Argentinean	36.5
Colombian	30.9
Ecuadorian	33.8
Peruvian	34.8
Venezuelan	31.8
Spaniard	31.1

High School Graduates
(Universe: Population 25 Years and Over)

Group	Number	%
Total Population	437,130	83.7
Hispanic or Latino (of any race)	16,553	49.1
Central American, ex. Mexican	1,488	40.0
Guatemalan	227	32.2
Honduran	512	32.9
Salvadoran	434	43.2
Mexican	11,500	45.0
Puerto Rican	1,142	75.2
South American	1,104	84.8
Colombian	373	97.4

Four-Year College Graduates
(Universe: Population 25 Years and Over)

Group	Number	%
Total Population	142,474	27.3
Hispanic or Latino (of any race)	3,074	9.1
Central American, ex. Mexican	292	7.9
Guatemalan	58	8.2
Honduran	61	3.9
Salvadoran	51	5.1
Mexican	1,467	5.7
Puerto Rican	346	22.8
South American	517	39.7
Colombian	214	55.9

Population Age 3–17 Enrolled in Public School
(Universe: Population Age 3–17 Enrolled in School)

Group	Number	%
Total Population	118,632	82.2
Hispanic or Latino (of any race)	14,277	90.8
Central American, ex. Mexican	979	83.9
Guatemalan	118	61.1
Honduran	403	82.8
Salvadoran	357	100.0
Mexican	11,578	93.4
Puerto Rican	803	85.7
South American	448	79.7
Colombian	174	84.1

Population Age 3–17 Enrolled in Private School
(Universe: Population Age 3–17 Enrolled in School)

Group	Number	%
Total Population	25,666	17.8
Hispanic or Latino (of any race)	1,443	9.2
Central American, ex. Mexican	188	16.1
Guatemalan	75	38.9
Honduran	84	17.2
Salvadoran	0	0.0
Mexican	814	6.6
Puerto Rican	134	14.3
South American	114	20.3
Colombian	33	15.9

Foreign-Born Population

Group	Number	%
Total Population	65,302	8.1
Hispanic or Latino (of any race)	37,296	54.6
Central American, ex. Mexican	4,750	72.6
Guatemalan	951	73.9
Honduran	2,157	77.8
Salvadoran	1,172	64.3
Mexican	29,911	56.0
Puerto Rican	45	1.4
South American	1,495	61.2
Colombian	458	52.1

Foreign-Born Naturalized U.S. Citizens

Group	Number	%
Total Population	16,371	25.1
Hispanic or Latino (of any race)	5,099	13.7
Central American, ex. Mexican	634	13.3
Guatemalan	112	11.8
Honduran	210	9.7
Salvadoran	134	11.4
Mexican	3,401	11.4
Puerto Rican	0	0.0
South American	482	32.2
Colombian	194	42.4

Language Spoken at Home: English Only
(Universe: Population 5 Years and Over)

Group	Number	%
Total Population	662,286	88.5
Hispanic or Latino (of any race)	9,386	16.3
Central American, ex. Mexican	487	8.6
Guatemalan	149	13.4
Honduran	150	6.2
Salvadoran	81	5.2
Mexican	6,224	14.0
Puerto Rican	1,312	49.9
South American	394	17.8
Colombian	114	16.0

Language Spoken at Home: Spanish
(Universe: Population 5 Years and Over)

Group	Number	%
Total Population	57,904	7.7
Hispanic or Latino (of any race)	48,058	83.4
Central American, ex. Mexican	5,206	91.4
Guatemalan	960	86.6
Honduran	2,259	93.8
Salvadoran	1,465	94.8
Mexican	38,316	85.9
Puerto Rican	1,315	50.1
South American	1,821	82.2
Colombian	600	84.0

Notes: (1) Percent of total population; (2) Percent of Hispanic/Latino population; Profiles include places with an overall population of at least 125,000, OR an overall population of at least 25,000 where the Hispanic/Latino population is at least 20% of the overall population. In states where less than five places meet either of these criteria, we have included places with at least 10,000 total population with the highest percentage of Hispanic/Latino population. These places are identified with an asterisk (*); Please refer to the User's Guide for a full explanation of data.

STATE & PLACE PROFILES

Unemployment Rate
(Universe: Population 16 Years and Over)

Group	%
Total Population	10.2
Hispanic or Latino (of any race)	11.5
Central American, ex. Mexican	21.0
Guatemalan	5.6
Honduran	24.2
Salvadoran	29.4
Mexican	10.4
Puerto Rican	18.1
South American	3.3
Colombian	8.0

Class of Worker: Private Wage and Salary
(Universe: Civilian Employed Population 16 Years and Over)

Group	Number	%
Total Population	328,760	84.4
Hispanic or Latino (of any race)	27,195	91.9
Central American, ex. Mexican	3,031	96.3
Guatemalan	797	97.7
Honduran	1,247	95.6
Salvadoran	808	98.3
Mexican	21,179	93.1
Puerto Rican	895	78.7
South American	979	82.1
Colombian	302	79.5

Class of Worker: Government
(Universe: Civilian Employed Population 16 Years and Over)

Group	Number	%
Total Population	43,418	11.1
Hispanic or Latino (of any race)	1,107	3.7
Central American, ex. Mexican	63	2.0
Guatemalan	19	2.3
Honduran	26	2.0
Salvadoran	6	0.7
Mexican	574	2.5
Puerto Rican	205	18.0
South American	95	8.0
Colombian	35	9.2

Means of Transportation to Work: Car, Truck or Van
(Universe: Workers 16 Years and Over)

Group	Number	%
Total Population	350,234	92.0
Hispanic or Latino (of any race)	26,687	92.9
Central American, ex. Mexican	2,834	92.3
Guatemalan	748	93.4
Honduran	1,166	93.0
Salvadoran	723	89.0
Mexican	20,539	93.3
Puerto Rican	1,028	89.9
South American	1,051	88.8
Colombian	312	84.3

Means of Transportation to Work: Public Transportation (ex. Taxicab)
(Universe: Workers 16 Years and Over)

Group	Number	%
Total Population	7,441	2.0
Hispanic or Latino (of any race)	517	1.8
Central American, ex. Mexican	12	0.4
Guatemalan	12	1.5
Honduran	0	0.0
Salvadoran	0	0.0
Mexican	461	2.1
Puerto Rican	12	1.0
South American	0	0.0
Colombian	0	0.0

Homeownership Rate
(Universe: Occupied Housing Units)

Group	%
Total Population	55.8
Hispanic or Latino (of any race)	33.0
Central American, ex. Mexican	37.0
Costa Rican	36.8
Guatemalan	27.9
Honduran	28.6
Nicaraguan	43.1
Panamanian	51.1
Salvadoran	45.2
Cuban	43.5
Dominican Republic	34.8
Mexican	31.0
Puerto Rican	37.8
South American	50.7
Argentinean	55.4
Colombian	51.5
Ecuadorian	52.9
Peruvian	49.8
Venezuelan	45.9
Spaniard	43.4

Median Home Value

Group	Dollars
Total Population	122,100
Hispanic or Latino (of any race)	104,700
Central American, ex. Mexican	113,600
Guatemalan	105,400
Honduran	133,200
Salvadoran	98,900
Mexican	96,600
Puerto Rican	128,300
South American	122,600
Colombian	113,700

Median Gross Rent

Group	Dollars
Total Population	716
Hispanic or Latino (of any race)	687
Central American, ex. Mexican	669
Guatemalan	676
Honduran	633
Salvadoran	734
Mexican	682
Puerto Rican	739
South American	739
Colombian	793

Median Household Income
(2010 Inflation-Adjusted Dollars)

Group	Dollars
Total Population	43,088
Hispanic or Latino (of any race)	30,295
Central American, ex. Mexican	29,446
Guatemalan	32,143
Honduran	26,071
Salvadoran	37,222
Mexican	29,227
Puerto Rican	30,436
South American	41,989
Colombian	34,049

Per Capita Income
(2010 Inflation-Adjusted Dollars)

Group	Dollars
Total Population	24,334
Hispanic or Latino (of any race)	11,713
Central American, ex. Mexican	10,549
Guatemalan	9,357
Honduran	8,999
Salvadoran	12,870
Mexican	10,215
Puerto Rican	14,480
South American	19,675
Colombian	13,401

Households with $100,000+ Income

Group	Number	%
Total Population	46,098	14.2
Hispanic or Latino (of any race)	880	5.0
Central American, ex. Mexican	76	4.7
Guatemalan	0	0.0
Honduran	22	3.0
Salvadoran	32	7.5
Mexican	524	3.9
Puerto Rican	71	7.4
South American	123	14.3
Colombian	8	2.5

Households with Food Stamps/SNAP Benefits During Past 12 Months

Group	Number	%
Total Population	39,293	12.1
Hispanic or Latino (of any race)	2,298	13.0
Central American, ex. Mexican	239	14.9
Guatemalan	25	8.8
Honduran	154	21.2
Salvadoran	44	10.3
Mexican	1,734	13.0
Puerto Rican	218	22.6
South American	23	2.7
Colombian	0	0.0

Poverty Rate
(Income in Past 12 Months Below Poverty Level)

Group	%
Total Population	17.9
Hispanic or Latino (of any race)	34.1
Central American, ex. Mexican	33.4
Guatemalan	36.3
Honduran	31.9
Salvadoran	35.6
Mexican	36.2
Puerto Rican	31.6
South American	10.4
Colombian	10.4

Notes: (1) Percent of total population; (2) Percent of Hispanic/Latino population; Profiles include places with an overall population of at least 125,000, OR an overall population of at least 25,000 where the Hispanic/Latino population is at least 20% of the overall population. In states where less than five places meet either of these criteria, we have included places with at least 10,000 total population with the highest percentage of Hispanic/Latino population. These places are identified with an asterisk (*); Please refer to the User's Guide for a full explanation of data.

Iowa

EDITOR'S NOTE: For a place to be included in this edition, it must meet one of two criteria. Either its overall population is at least 125,000, OR its overall population is at least 25,000 and its Hispanic/Latino population is at least 20% of the overall population. In Iowa, less than five places meet either of these criteria. In an effort to include at least five places for each state, we have included places with at least 10,000 total population with the highest percentage of Hispanic/Latino population. These places are identified with an asterisk (*). For the state of Iowa, the following locations are included:

- Cedar Rapids
- Des Moines
- Marshalltown
- Muscatine*
- Storm Lake*

Section Two: State & Place Profiles starts with the state profile, followed by place profiles that meet the criteria above. Places are listed alphabetically within each state. All states, all counties and places that meet the above criteria are ranked and compared in *Section Three: Rankings & Comparisons*, on page 1055.

For a more detailed look at the Hispanic/Latino population in Iowa, a companion web site is available at no additional charge with purchase of this print edition. Visit http://gold.greyhouse.com/page/info_hispanic for more information.

The web site includes data for all counties and places in Iowa with Hispanic/Latino population, plus ten additional topics: Self Employed Worker; Walked to Work; Worked from Home; Mean Travel Time to Work; Mean Household Income; Households with Cash Public Assistance; Mean Cash Pubic Assistance; Poverty Rates for 18 and Under, 18 to 64, and 65 and Over.

Population

Group	Number	%TP[1]	%HP[2]
Total Population	3,046,355	100.0	–
Hispanic or Latino (of any race)	151,544	5.0	100.0
Central American, ex. Mexican	13,289	0.4	8.8
Costa Rican	255	<0.1	0.2
Guatemalan	4,917	0.2	3.2
Honduran	1,539	0.1	1.0
Nicaraguan	472	<0.1	0.3
Panamanian	413	<0.1	0.3
Salvadoran	5,601	0.2	3.7
Cuban	1,226	<0.1	0.8
Dominican Republic	429	<0.1	0.3
Mexican	117,090	3.8	77.3
Puerto Rican	4,885	0.2	3.2
South American	3,754	0.1	2.5
Argentinean	344	<0.1	0.2
Bolivian	171	<0.1	0.1
Chilean	329	<0.1	0.2
Colombian	1,026	<0.1	0.7
Ecuadorian	795	<0.1	0.5
Peruvian	607	<0.1	0.4
Venezuelan	310	<0.1	0.2
Spaniard	1,552	0.1	1.0

Population Growth: 2000–2010

Group	%
Total Population	4.1
Hispanic or Latino (of any race)	83.7
Central American, ex. Mexican	233.6
Costa Rican	112.5
Guatemalan	278.8
Honduran	218.0
Nicaraguan	153.8
Panamanian	93.0
Salvadoran	281.0
Cuban	63.5
Dominican Republic	176.8
Mexican	91.5
Puerto Rican	81.6
South American	111.9
Argentinean	134.0
Chilean	74.1
Colombian	126.0
Ecuadorian	141.6
Peruvian	139.9
Venezuelan	49.0
Spaniard	888.5

Males per 100 Females

Group	Number
Total Population	98.1
Hispanic or Latino (of any race)	111.8
Central American, ex. Mexican	120.2
Costa Rican	112.5
Guatemalan	144.1
Honduran	115.2
Nicaraguan	101.7
Panamanian	72.1
Salvadoran	110.3
Cuban	108.9
Dominican Republic	102.4
Mexican	112.7
Puerto Rican	102.2
South American	98.4
Argentinean	106.0
Bolivian	111.1
Chilean	86.9
Colombian	91.1
Ecuadorian	116.6
Peruvian	82.8
Venezuelan	110.9
Spaniard	89.7

Average Household Size

Group	People
Total Population	2.41
Hispanic or Latino (of any race)	3.52
Central American, ex. Mexican	3.82
Costa Rican	2.84
Guatemalan	3.99
Honduran	3.49
Nicaraguan	3.37
Panamanian	2.60
Salvadoran	3.94
Cuban	2.63
Dominican Republic	2.91
Mexican	3.61
Puerto Rican	2.85
South American	2.78
Argentinean	2.43
Bolivian	2.74
Chilean	2.63
Colombian	2.59
Ecuadorian	3.36
Peruvian	2.80
Venezuelan	2.73
Spaniard	2.76

Median Age

Group	Years
Total Population	38.1
Hispanic or Latino (of any race)	22.2
Central American, ex. Mexican	26.4
Costa Rican	24.8
Guatemalan	24.6
Honduran	26.2
Nicaraguan	27.0
Panamanian	27.5
Salvadoran	28.3
Cuban	27.7
Dominican Republic	22.2
Mexican	21.4
Puerto Rican	21.9
South American	29.2
Argentinean	34.9
Bolivian	28.5
Chilean	26.7
Colombian	29.1
Ecuadorian	28.7
Peruvian	30.0
Venezuelan	28.2
Spaniard	27.2

High School Graduates
(Universe: Population 25 Years and Over)

Group	Number	%
Total Population	1,785,436	89.9
Hispanic or Latino (of any race)	34,534	55.5
Central American, ex. Mexican	2,784	40.3
Guatemalan	937	34.5
Honduran	364	60.3
Salvadoran	933	33.9
Cuban	526	88.6
Mexican	25,028	52.8
Puerto Rican	1,879	87.0
South American	1,793	86.2
Colombian	574	94.6
Ecuadorian	300	70.3
Spaniard	444	90.8

Four-Year College Graduates
(Universe: Population 25 Years and Over)

Group	Number	%
Total Population	486,646	24.5
Hispanic or Latino (of any race)	6,810	10.9
Central American, ex. Mexican	449	6.5
Guatemalan	217	8.0
Honduran	84	13.9
Salvadoran	96	3.5
Cuban	262	44.1
Mexican	3,775	8.0
Puerto Rican	620	28.7
South American	1,143	54.9
Colombian	313	51.6
Ecuadorian	146	34.2
Spaniard	197	40.3

Population Age 3–17 Enrolled in Public School
(Universe: Population Age 3–17 Enrolled in School)

Group	Number	%
Total Population	481,547	87.8
Hispanic or Latino (of any race)	36,349	94.4
Central American, ex. Mexican	2,903	98.9
Guatemalan	1,281	98.1
Honduran	342	98.3
Salvadoran	1,006	100.0
Cuban	246	73.9
Mexican	29,854	94.6
Puerto Rican	1,061	96.5
South American	699	90.2
Colombian	213	85.5
Ecuadorian	131	94.9
Spaniard	109	82.0

Population Age 3–17 Enrolled in Private School
(Universe: Population Age 3–17 Enrolled in School)

Group	Number	%
Total Population	66,769	12.2
Hispanic or Latino (of any race)	2,142	5.6
Central American, ex. Mexican	31	1.1
Guatemalan	25	1.9
Honduran	6	1.7
Salvadoran	0	0.0
Cuban	87	26.1
Mexican	1,712	5.4
Puerto Rican	39	3.5
South American	76	9.8
Colombian	36	14.5
Ecuadorian	7	5.1
Spaniard	24	18.0

Foreign-Born Population

Group	Number	%
Total Population	124,681	4.1
Hispanic or Latino (of any race)	51,938	37.9
Central American, ex. Mexican	8,415	65.2

Notes: (1) Percent of total population; (2) Percent of Hispanic/Latino population; Profiles include places with an overall population of at least 125,000, OR an overall population of at least 25,000 where the Hispanic/Latino population is at least 20% of the overall population. In states where less than five places meet either of these criteria, we have included places with at least 10,000 total population with the highest percentage of Hispanic/Latino population. These places are identified with an asterisk (*); Please refer to the User's Guide for a full explanation of data.

Group	Number	%
Guatemalan	3,566	68.1
Honduran	685	50.7
Salvadoran	3,390	67.9
Cuban	346	26.7
Mexican	39,135	36.2
Puerto Rican	87	1.9
South American	2,610	71.0
Colombian	752	64.9
Ecuadorian	495	66.5
Spaniard	144	17.1

Foreign-Born Naturalized U.S. Citizens

Group	Number	%
Total Population	44,755	35.9
Hispanic or Latino (of any race)	11,366	21.9
Central American, ex. Mexican	1,574	18.7
Guatemalan	484	13.6
Honduran	155	22.6
Salvadoran	603	17.8
Cuban	206	59.5
Mexican	8,031	20.5
Puerto Rican	8	9.2
South American	1,151	44.1
Colombian	381	50.7
Ecuadorian	175	35.4
Spaniard	32	22.2

Language Spoken at Home: English Only
(Universe: Population 5 Years and Over)

Group	Number	%
Total Population	2,625,703	93.2
Hispanic or Latino (of any race)	37,546	31.8
Central American, ex. Mexican	1,295	11.4
Guatemalan	511	11.0
Honduran	205	18.5
Salvadoran	253	5.8
Cuban	630	55.0
Mexican	29,296	31.7
Puerto Rican	2,197	54.4
South American	1,013	29.6
Colombian	372	35.6
Ecuadorian	166	24.7
Spaniard	590	72.8

Language Spoken at Home: Spanish
(Universe: Population 5 Years and Over)

Group	Number	%
Total Population	106,888	3.8
Hispanic or Latino (of any race)	79,967	67.8
Central American, ex. Mexican	10,076	88.5
Guatemalan	4,138	88.8
Honduran	906	81.5
Salvadoran	4,146	94.2
Cuban	493	43.0
Mexican	62,872	68.1
Puerto Rican	1,815	44.9
South American	2,370	69.3
Colombian	672	64.4
Ecuadorian	506	75.3
Spaniard	202	24.9

Unemployment Rate
(Universe: Population 16 Years and Over)

Group	%
Total Population	5.3
Hispanic or Latino (of any race)	9.8
Central American, ex. Mexican	8.8
Guatemalan	5.5
Honduran	7.5
Salvadoran	10.1
Cuban	17.0
Mexican	10.0
Puerto Rican	10.0
South American	6.9
Colombian	6.5
Ecuadorian	6.5
Spaniard	12.6

Class of Worker: Private Wage and Salary
(Universe: Civilian Employed Population 16 Years and Over)

Group	Number	%
Total Population	1,221,421	78.6
Hispanic or Latino (of any race)	49,972	88.5
Central American, ex. Mexican	5,880	92.2
Guatemalan	2,310	91.8
Honduran	491	94.4
Salvadoran	2,425	91.3
Cuban	410	80.1
Mexican	38,465	89.3
Puerto Rican	1,755	88.1
South American	1,356	71.9
Colombian	328	60.1
Ecuadorian	340	84.2
Spaniard	279	66.9

Class of Worker: Government
(Universe: Civilian Employed Population 16 Years and Over)

Group	Number	%
Total Population	215,073	13.8
Hispanic or Latino (of any race)	4,552	8.1
Central American, ex. Mexican	256	4.0
Guatemalan	82	3.3
Honduran	24	4.6
Salvadoran	122	4.6
Cuban	98	19.1
Mexican	3,137	7.3
Puerto Rican	236	11.9
South American	424	22.5
Colombian	204	37.4
Ecuadorian	37	9.2
Spaniard	116	27.8

Means of Transportation to Work: Car, Truck or Van
(Universe: Workers 16 Years and Over)

Group	Number	%
Total Population	1,352,588	89.0
Hispanic or Latino (of any race)	48,751	89.3
Central American, ex. Mexican	5,318	86.1
Guatemalan	1,917	76.2
Honduran	460	90.6
Salvadoran	2,311	93.5
Cuban	426	85.9
Mexican	37,437	90.1
Puerto Rican	1,758	88.4
South American	1,586	85.1
Colombian	388	74.0
Ecuadorian	404	100.0
Spaniard	341	84.6

Means of Transportation to Work: Public Transportation (ex. Taxicab)
(Universe: Workers 16 Years and Over)

Group	Number	%
Total Population	16,803	1.1
Hispanic or Latino (of any race)	754	1.4
Central American, ex. Mexican	127	2.1
Guatemalan	64	2.5
Honduran	30	5.9
Salvadoran	0	0.0
Cuban	13	2.6
Mexican	456	1.1
Puerto Rican	54	2.7
South American	65	3.5
Colombian	19	3.6
Ecuadorian	0	0.0
Spaniard	0	0.0

Homeownership Rate
(Universe: Occupied Housing Units)

Group	%
Total Population	72.1
Hispanic or Latino (of any race)	50.8
Central American, ex. Mexican	49.2
Costa Rican	49.0
Guatemalan	40.4
Honduran	41.1
Nicaraguan	47.2
Panamanian	55.7
Salvadoran	57.7
Cuban	51.0
Dominican Republic	47.0
Mexican	51.4
Puerto Rican	45.0
South American	54.1
Argentinean	61.1
Bolivian	69.0
Chilean	55.8
Colombian	51.0
Ecuadorian	53.6
Peruvian	51.2
Venezuelan	59.3
Spaniard	57.4

Median Home Value

Group	Dollars
Total Population	119,200
Hispanic or Latino (of any race)	85,700
Central American, ex. Mexican	91,700
Guatemalan	98,500
Honduran	130,800
Salvadoran	87,800
Cuban	123,700
Mexican	80,500
Puerto Rican	128,000
South American	167,700
Colombian	125,700
Ecuadorian	161,400
Spaniard	118,300

Median Gross Rent

Group	Dollars
Total Population	617
Hispanic or Latino (of any race)	619
Central American, ex. Mexican	550
Guatemalan	564
Honduran	482
Salvadoran	536
Cuban	808
Mexican	622
Puerto Rican	634
South American	635
Colombian	846
Ecuadorian	967
Spaniard	764

Median Household Income
(2010 Inflation-Adjusted Dollars)

Group	Dollars
Total Population	48,872
Hispanic or Latino (of any race)	38,388
Central American, ex. Mexican	36,326
Guatemalan	40,503
Honduran	45,833
Salvadoran	32,135
Cuban	41,520
Mexican	38,378
Puerto Rican	44,449
South American	56,122
Colombian	54,102
Ecuadorian	82,361
Spaniard	45,341

Per Capita Income
(2010 Inflation-Adjusted Dollars)

Group	Dollars
Total Population	25,335
Hispanic or Latino (of any race)	12,850
Central American, ex. Mexican	13,203
Guatemalan	12,094
Honduran	12,054
Salvadoran	14,163
Cuban	16,819
Mexican	12,064
Puerto Rican	15,433
South American	28,375
Colombian	24,977
Ecuadorian	21,870
Spaniard	21,931

Households with $100,000+ Income

Group	Number	%
Total Population	185,575	15.3
Hispanic or Latino (of any race)	2,372	6.8
Central American, ex. Mexican	240	7.4
Guatemalan	120	9.2
Honduran	46	14.7
Salvadoran	74	6.1
Cuban	37	10.9
Mexican	1,619	6.1
Puerto Rican	84	6.3
South American	191	19.3
Colombian	49	21.6
Ecuadorian	28	10.3
Spaniard	59	11.8

Notes: (1) Percent of total population; (2) Percent of Hispanic/Latino population; Profiles include places with an overall population of at least 125,000, OR an overall population of at least 25,000 where the Hispanic/Latino population is at least 20% of the overall population. In states where less than five places meet either of these criteria, we have included places with at least 10,000 total population with the highest percentage of Hispanic/Latino population. These places are identified with an asterisk (*); Please refer to the User's Guide for a full explanation of data.

Households with Food Stamps/SNAP Benefits During Past 12 Months

Group	Number	%
Total Population	109,037	9.0
Hispanic or Latino (of any race)	6,749	19.4
Central American, ex. Mexican	436	13.4
Guatemalan	171	13.2
Honduran	85	27.2
Salvadoran	120	9.9
Cuban	93	27.4
Mexican	5,472	20.5
Puerto Rican	373	27.8
South American	67	6.8
Colombian	0	0.0
Ecuadorian	9	3.3
Spaniard	36	7.2

Poverty Rate
(Income in Past 12 Months Below Poverty Level)

Group	%
Total Population	11.6
Hispanic or Latino (of any race)	24.4
Central American, ex. Mexican	19.1
Guatemalan	21.8
Honduran	27.4
Salvadoran	16.9
Cuban	23.3
Mexican	25.4
Puerto Rican	31.6
South American	11.1
Colombian	8.2
Ecuadorian	10.5
Spaniard	19.7

Cedar Rapids

Population

Group	Number	%TP[1]	%HP[2]
Total Population	126,326	100.0	–
Hispanic or Latino (of any race)	4,176	3.3	100.0
Central American, ex. Mexican	318	0.3	7.6
Guatemalan	108	0.1	2.6
Mexican	2,928	2.3	70.1
Puerto Rican	280	0.2	6.7
South American	185	0.1	4.4

Population Growth: 2000–2010

Group	%
Total Population	4.6
Hispanic or Latino (of any race)	102.2
Mexican	122.7
Puerto Rican	95.8

Males per 100 Females

Group	Number
Total Population	96.6
Hispanic or Latino (of any race)	114.4
Central American, ex. Mexican	122.4
Guatemalan	151.2
Mexican	116.4
Puerto Rican	112.1
South American	105.6

Average Household Size

Group	People
Total Population	2.31
Hispanic or Latino (of any race)	3.00
Central American, ex. Mexican	3.12
Guatemalan	3.50
Mexican	3.10
Puerto Rican	2.98
South American	2.96

Median Age

Group	Years
Total Population	35.3
Hispanic or Latino (of any race)	23.0
Central American, ex. Mexican	24.4
Guatemalan	21.9
Mexican	22.5
Puerto Rican	21.0
South American	26.5

High School Graduates
(Universe: Population 25 Years and Over)

Group	Number	%
Total Population	75,905	92.5
Hispanic or Latino (of any race)	1,578	84.6
Mexican	1,178	82.0

Four-Year College Graduates
(Universe: Population 25 Years and Over)

Group	Number	%
Total Population	24,013	29.3
Hispanic or Latino (of any race)	317	17.0
Mexican	155	10.8

Population Age 3–17 Enrolled in Public School
(Universe: Population Age 3–17 Enrolled in School)

Group	Number	%
Total Population	18,905	83.0
Hispanic or Latino (of any race)	928	89.6
Mexican	853	90.6

Population Age 3–17 Enrolled in Private School
(Universe: Population Age 3–17 Enrolled in School)

Group	Number	%
Total Population	3,863	17.0
Hispanic or Latino (of any race)	108	10.4
Mexican	88	9.4

Foreign-Born Population

Group	Number	%
Total Population	4,301	3.4
Hispanic or Latino (of any race)	786	19.9
Mexican	635	19.9

Foreign-Born Naturalized U.S. Citizens

Group	Number	%
Total Population	1,797	41.8
Hispanic or Latino (of any race)	128	16.3
Mexican	76	12.0

Language Spoken at Home: English Only
(Universe: Population 5 Years and Over)

Group	Number	%
Total Population	110,383	94.4
Hispanic or Latino (of any race)	2,143	61.8
Mexican	1,693	60.9

Language Spoken at Home: Spanish
(Universe: Population 5 Years and Over)

Group	Number	%
Total Population	2,571	2.2
Hispanic or Latino (of any race)	1,322	38.2
Mexican	1,085	39.1

Unemployment Rate
(Universe: Population 16 Years and Over)

Group	%
Total Population	5.2
Hispanic or Latino (of any race)	5.0
Mexican	3.2

Class of Worker: Private Wage and Salary
(Universe: Civilian Employed Population 16 Years and Over)

Group	Number	%
Total Population	56,317	84.9
Hispanic or Latino (of any race)	1,797	90.6
Mexican	1,392	92.2

Class of Worker: Government
(Universe: Civilian Employed Population 16 Years and Over)

Group	Number	%
Total Population	7,014	10.6
Hispanic or Latino (of any race)	158	8.0
Mexican	90	6.0

Means of Transportation to Work: Car, Truck or Van
(Universe: Workers 16 Years and Over)

Group	Number	%
Total Population	59,525	91.6
Hispanic or Latino (of any race)	1,664	84.8
Mexican	1,243	83.4

Means of Transportation to Work: Public Transportation (ex. Taxicab)
(Universe: Workers 16 Years and Over)

Group	Number	%
Total Population	833	1.3
Hispanic or Latino (of any race)	91	4.6
Mexican	91	6.1

Homeownership Rate
(Universe: Occupied Housing Units)

Group	%
Total Population	68.2
Hispanic or Latino (of any race)	45.6
Central American, ex. Mexican	39.0
Guatemalan	15.0
Mexican	45.2
Puerto Rican	48.4
South American	60.4

Median Home Value

Group	Dollars
Total Population	125,900
Hispanic or Latino (of any race)	122,500
Mexican	113,000

Median Gross Rent

Group	Dollars
Total Population	636
Hispanic or Latino (of any race)	679
Mexican	712

Median Household Income
(2010 Inflation-Adjusted Dollars)

Group	Dollars
Total Population	49,298
Hispanic or Latino (of any race)	50,171
Mexican	50,582

Per Capita Income
(2010 Inflation-Adjusted Dollars)

Group	Dollars
Total Population	27,167
Hispanic or Latino (of any race)	16,457
Mexican	15,842

Households with $100,000+ Income

Group	Number	%
Total Population	8,638	16.2
Hispanic or Latino (of any race)	89	8.2
Mexican	77	10.5

Households with Food Stamps/SNAP Benefits During Past 12 Months

Group	Number	%
Total Population	5,829	10.9
Hispanic or Latino (of any race)	190	17.6
Mexican	152	20.7

Poverty Rate
(Income in Past 12 Months Below Poverty Level)

Group	%
Total Population	12.0
Hispanic or Latino (of any race)	13.6
Mexican	15.2

Des Moines

Population

Group	Number	%TP[1]	%HP[2]
Total Population	203,433	100.0	–
Hispanic or Latino (of any race)	24,334	12.0	100.0
Central American, ex. Mexican	2,480	1.2	10.2
Guatemalan	544	0.3	2.2
Honduran	266	0.1	1.1
Salvadoran	1,515	0.7	6.2
Cuban	137	0.1	0.6
Mexican	19,167	9.4	78.8
Puerto Rican	531	0.3	2.2
South American	394	0.2	1.6
Ecuadorian	152	0.1	0.6
Spaniard	173	0.1	0.7

STATE & PLACE PROFILES

Notes: (1) Percent of total population; (2) Percent of Hispanic/Latino population; Profiles include places with an overall population of at least 125,000, OR an overall population of at least 25,000 where the Hispanic/Latino population is at least 20% of the overall population. In states where less than five places meet either of these criteria, we have included places with at least 10,000 total population with the highest percentage of Hispanic/Latino population. These places are identified with an asterisk (*); Please refer to the User's Guide for a full explanation of data.

Population Growth: 2000–2010

Group	%
Total Population	2.4
Hispanic or Latino (of any race)	85.2
Central American, ex. Mexican	227.2
Guatemalan	260.3
Honduran	166.0
Salvadoran	294.5
Mexican	93.2
Puerto Rican	72.4
South American	140.2

Males per 100 Females

Group	Number
Total Population	95.8
Hispanic or Latino (of any race)	110.4
Central American, ex. Mexican	115.1
Guatemalan	139.6
Honduran	129.3
Salvadoran	107.3
Cuban	90.3
Mexican	110.8
Puerto Rican	102.7
South American	114.1
Ecuadorian	137.5
Spaniard	103.5

Average Household Size

Group	People
Total Population	2.43
Hispanic or Latino (of any race)	3.72
Central American, ex. Mexican	4.00
Guatemalan	3.93
Honduran	3.77
Salvadoran	4.13
Cuban	2.45
Mexican	3.79
Puerto Rican	2.89
South American	3.13
Ecuadorian	3.85
Spaniard	2.61

Median Age

Group	Years
Total Population	33.5
Hispanic or Latino (of any race)	22.7
Central American, ex. Mexican	27.3
Guatemalan	26.5
Honduran	25.6
Salvadoran	28.5
Cuban	28.4
Mexican	21.9
Puerto Rican	25.5
South American	30.0
Ecuadorian	29.7
Spaniard	31.1

High School Graduates
(Universe: Population 25 Years and Over)

Group	Number	%
Total Population	112,015	85.8
Hispanic or Latino (of any race)	4,764	46.1
Central American, ex. Mexican	453	30.0
Salvadoran	190	22.7
Mexican	3,941	48.1

Four-Year College Graduates
(Universe: Population 25 Years and Over)

Group	Number	%
Total Population	30,590	23.4
Hispanic or Latino (of any race)	723	7.0
Central American, ex. Mexican	124	8.2
Salvadoran	40	4.8
Mexican	476	5.8

Population Age 3–17 Enrolled in Public School
(Universe: Population Age 3–17 Enrolled in School)

Group	Number	%
Total Population	32,005	88.7
Hispanic or Latino (of any race)	6,349	94.9
Central American, ex. Mexican	561	100.0
Salvadoran	234	100.0
Mexican	5,506	95.6

Population Age 3–17 Enrolled in Private School
(Universe: Population Age 3–17 Enrolled in School)

Group	Number	%
Total Population	4,066	11.3
Hispanic or Latino (of any race)	343	5.1
Central American, ex. Mexican	0	0.0
Salvadoran	0	0.0
Mexican	252	4.4

Foreign-Born Population

Group	Number	%
Total Population	20,985	10.4
Hispanic or Latino (of any race)	9,830	43.7
Central American, ex. Mexican	1,608	62.3
Salvadoran	915	69.6
Mexican	7,833	42.4

Foreign-Born Naturalized U.S. Citizens

Group	Number	%
Total Population	6,441	30.7
Hispanic or Latino (of any race)	1,273	13.0
Central American, ex. Mexican	130	8.1
Salvadoran	27	3.0
Mexican	1,031	13.2

Language Spoken at Home: English Only
(Universe: Population 5 Years and Over)

Group	Number	%
Total Population	156,392	84.0
Hispanic or Latino (of any race)	4,297	22.5
Central American, ex. Mexican	44	2.0
Salvadoran	11	0.9
Mexican	3,907	24.9

Language Spoken at Home: Spanish
(Universe: Population 5 Years and Over)

Group	Number	%
Total Population	17,340	9.3
Hispanic or Latino (of any race)	14,801	77.5
Central American, ex. Mexican	2,195	98.0
Salvadoran	1,172	99.1
Mexican	11,802	75.1

Unemployment Rate
(Universe: Population 16 Years and Over)

Group	%
Total Population	7.3
Hispanic or Latino (of any race)	9.7
Central American, ex. Mexican	8.1
Salvadoran	9.4
Mexican	9.9

Class of Worker: Private Wage and Salary
(Universe: Civilian Employed Population 16 Years and Over)

Group	Number	%
Total Population	87,007	84.0
Hispanic or Latino (of any race)	8,389	90.9
Central American, ex. Mexican	1,281	91.3
Salvadoran	668	84.6
Mexican	6,602	90.7

Class of Worker: Government
(Universe: Civilian Employed Population 16 Years and Over)

Group	Number	%
Total Population	11,721	11.3
Hispanic or Latino (of any race)	500	5.4
Central American, ex. Mexican	37	2.6
Salvadoran	37	4.7
Mexican	427	5.9

Means of Transportation to Work: Car, Truck or Van
(Universe: Workers 16 Years and Over)

Group	Number	%
Total Population	91,459	90.3
Hispanic or Latino (of any race)	8,052	90.5
Central American, ex. Mexican	1,343	94.0
Salvadoran	772	97.7
Mexican	6,292	90.7

Means of Transportation to Work: Public Transportation (ex. Taxicab)
(Universe: Workers 16 Years and Over)

Group	Number	%
Total Population	3,011	3.0
Hispanic or Latino (of any race)	248	2.8
Central American, ex. Mexican	43	3.0
Salvadoran	0	0.0
Mexican	152	2.2

Homeownership Rate
(Universe: Occupied Housing Units)

Group	%
Total Population	62.8
Hispanic or Latino (of any race)	51.5
Central American, ex. Mexican	56.1
Guatemalan	50.6
Honduran	33.8
Salvadoran	61.8
Cuban	52.6
Mexican	51.4
Puerto Rican	51.8
South American	57.9
Ecuadorian	69.6
Spaniard	46.3

Median Home Value

Group	Dollars
Total Population	117,600
Hispanic or Latino (of any race)	100,100
Central American, ex. Mexican	110,700
Salvadoran	106,500
Mexican	96,900

Median Gross Rent

Group	Dollars
Total Population	673
Hispanic or Latino (of any race)	640
Central American, ex. Mexican	626
Salvadoran	625
Mexican	638

Median Household Income
(2010 Inflation-Adjusted Dollars)

Group	Dollars
Total Population	44,178
Hispanic or Latino (of any race)	34,669
Central American, ex. Mexican	38,456
Salvadoran	32,589
Mexican	34,581

Per Capita Income
(2010 Inflation-Adjusted Dollars)

Group	Dollars
Total Population	24,096
Hispanic or Latino (of any race)	11,442
Central American, ex. Mexican	12,862
Salvadoran	14,059
Mexican	11,092

Households with $100,000+ Income

Group	Number	%
Total Population	10,013	12.0
Hispanic or Latino (of any race)	254	4.4
Central American, ex. Mexican	36	5.2
Salvadoran	28	7.4
Mexican	193	4.0

Households with Food Stamps/SNAP Benefits During Past 12 Months

Group	Number	%
Total Population	12,625	15.1
Hispanic or Latino (of any race)	1,248	21.5
Central American, ex. Mexican	73	10.5
Salvadoran	6	1.6
Mexican	1,090	22.8

Poverty Rate
(Income in Past 12 Months Below Poverty Level)

Group	%
Total Population	16.3
Hispanic or Latino (of any race)	28.9
Central American, ex. Mexican	13.5
Salvadoran	11.5
Mexican	32.0

Notes: (1) Percent of total population; (2) Percent of Hispanic/Latino population; Profiles include places with an overall population of at least 125,000, OR an overall population of at least 25,000 where the Hispanic/Latino population is at least 20% of the overall population. In states where less than five places meet either of these criteria, we have included places with at least 10,000 total population with the highest percentage of Hispanic/Latino population. These places are identified with an asterisk (*); Please refer to the User's Guide for a full explanation of data.

Marshalltown

Population

Group	Number	%TP[1]	%HP[2]
Total Population	27,552	100.0	–
Hispanic or Latino (of any race)	6,632	24.1	100.0
Central American, ex. Mexican	283	1.0	4.3
Guatemalan	111	0.4	1.7
Salvadoran	135	0.5	2.0
Mexican	6,003	21.8	90.5

Population Growth: 2000–2010

Group	%
Total Population	5.9
Hispanic or Latino (of any race)	103.1
Mexican	106.8

Males per 100 Females

Group	Number
Total Population	99.3
Hispanic or Latino (of any race)	110.1
Central American, ex. Mexican	114.4
Guatemalan	136.2
Salvadoran	98.5
Mexican	110.8

Average Household Size

Group	People
Total Population	2.55
Hispanic or Latino (of any race)	4.42
Central American, ex. Mexican	3.91
Guatemalan	4.24
Salvadoran	3.74
Mexican	4.51

Median Age

Group	Years
Total Population	37.3
Hispanic or Latino (of any race)	20.1
Central American, ex. Mexican	26.4
Guatemalan	24.2
Salvadoran	30.2
Mexican	19.8

High School Graduates
(Universe: Population 25 Years and Over)

Group	Number	%
Total Population	14,583	82.9
Hispanic or Latino (of any race)	1,007	42.0
Mexican	799	38.2

Four-Year College Graduates
(Universe: Population 25 Years and Over)

Group	Number	%
Total Population	3,370	19.2
Hispanic or Latino (of any race)	82	3.4
Mexican	75	3.6

Population Age 3–17 Enrolled in Public School
(Universe: Population Age 3–17 Enrolled in School)

Group	Number	%
Total Population	4,408	92.5
Hispanic or Latino (of any race)	1,748	100.0
Mexican	1,659	100.0

Population Age 3–17 Enrolled in Private School
(Universe: Population Age 3–17 Enrolled in School)

Group	Number	%
Total Population	359	7.5
Hispanic or Latino (of any race)	0	0.0
Mexican	0	0.0

Foreign-Born Population

Group	Number	%
Total Population	3,503	12.9
Hispanic or Latino (of any race)	2,926	50.2
Mexican	2,591	50.2

Foreign-Born Naturalized U.S. Citizens

Group	Number	%
Total Population	774	22.1
Hispanic or Latino (of any race)	522	17.8
Mexican	522	20.1

Language Spoken at Home: English Only
(Universe: Population 5 Years and Over)

Group	Number	%
Total Population	19,309	77.7
Hispanic or Latino (of any race)	312	6.4
Mexican	298	6.9

Language Spoken at Home: Spanish
(Universe: Population 5 Years and Over)

Group	Number	%
Total Population	5,004	20.1
Hispanic or Latino (of any race)	4,575	93.6
Mexican	4,016	93.1

Unemployment Rate
(Universe: Population 16 Years and Over)

Group	%
Total Population	7.7
Hispanic or Latino (of any race)	17.1
Mexican	17.3

Class of Worker: Private Wage and Salary
(Universe: Civilian Employed Population 16 Years and Over)

Group	Number	%
Total Population	9,589	79.6
Hispanic or Latino (of any race)	1,621	90.3
Mexican	1,346	89.7

Class of Worker: Government
(Universe: Civilian Employed Population 16 Years and Over)

Group	Number	%
Total Population	1,935	16.1
Hispanic or Latino (of any race)	128	7.1
Mexican	108	7.2

Means of Transportation to Work: Car, Truck or Van
(Universe: Workers 16 Years and Over)

Group	Number	%
Total Population	10,699	90.8
Hispanic or Latino (of any race)	1,623	93.8
Mexican	1,336	93.0

Means of Transportation to Work: Public Transportation (ex. Taxicab)
(Universe: Workers 16 Years and Over)

Group	Number	%
Total Population	55	0.5
Hispanic or Latino (of any race)	0	0.0
Mexican	0	0.0

Homeownership Rate
(Universe: Occupied Housing Units)

Group	%
Total Population	68.1
Hispanic or Latino (of any race)	59.7
Central American, ex. Mexican	43.5
Guatemalan	37.9
Salvadoran	48.9
Mexican	61.7

Median Home Value

Group	Dollars
Total Population	92,800
Hispanic or Latino (of any race)	74,700
Mexican	73,900

Median Gross Rent

Group	Dollars
Total Population	552
Hispanic or Latino (of any race)	586
Mexican	587

Median Household Income
(2010 Inflation-Adjusted Dollars)

Group	Dollars
Total Population	41,738
Hispanic or Latino (of any race)	36,581
Mexican	34,555

Per Capita Income
(2010 Inflation-Adjusted Dollars)

Group	Dollars
Total Population	21,430
Hispanic or Latino (of any race)	8,203
Mexican	8,093

Households with $100,000+ Income

Group	Number	%
Total Population	995	9.5
Hispanic or Latino (of any race)	15	1.2
Mexican	0	0.0

Households with Food Stamps/SNAP Benefits During Past 12 Months

Group	Number	%
Total Population	1,419	13.6
Hispanic or Latino (of any race)	328	27.3
Mexican	313	30.1

Poverty Rate
(Income in Past 12 Months Below Poverty Level)

Group	%
Total Population	14.5
Hispanic or Latino (of any race)	25.7
Mexican	25.1

Muscatine*

Population

Group	Number	%TP[1]	%HP[2]
Total Population	22,886	100.0	–
Hispanic or Latino (of any race)	3,794	16.6	100.0
Central American, ex. Mexican	236	1.0	6.2
Salvadoran	129	0.6	3.4
Mexican	3,190	13.9	84.1
Puerto Rican	105	0.5	2.8

Population Growth: 2000–2010

Group	%
Total Population	0.8
Hispanic or Latino (of any race)	35.9
Central American, ex. Mexican	120.6
Mexican	48.4

Males per 100 Females

Group	Number
Total Population	96.4
Hispanic or Latino (of any race)	102.2
Central American, ex. Mexican	107.0
Salvadoran	92.5
Mexican	101.1
Puerto Rican	162.5

Average Household Size

Group	People
Total Population	2.50
Hispanic or Latino (of any race)	3.63
Central American, ex. Mexican	4.09
Salvadoran	3.85
Mexican	3.72
Puerto Rican	2.63

Median Age

Group	Years
Total Population	36.1
Hispanic or Latino (of any race)	22.5
Central American, ex. Mexican	29.5
Salvadoran	32.2
Mexican	22.4
Puerto Rican	20.8

High School Graduates
(Universe: Population 25 Years and Over)

Group	Number	%
Total Population	12,397	82.1
Hispanic or Latino (of any race)	830	52.4
Mexican	582	46.3

Four-Year College Graduates
(Universe: Population 25 Years and Over)

Group	Number	%
Total Population	3,031	20.1
Hispanic or Latino (of any race)	36	2.3
Mexican	0	0.0

Population Age 3–17 Enrolled in Public School
(Universe: Population Age 3–17 Enrolled in School)

Group	Number	%
Total Population	4,216	97.5
Hispanic or Latino (of any race)	1,249	97.0

Notes: (1) Percent of total population; (2) Percent of Hispanic/Latino population; Profiles include places with an overall population of at least 125,000, OR an overall population of at least 25,000 where the Hispanic/Latino population is at least 20% of the overall population. In states where less than five places meet either of these criteria, we have included places with at least 10,000 total population with the highest percentage of Hispanic/Latino population. These places are identified with an asterisk (*); Please refer to the User's Guide for a full explanation of data.

Mexican	1,086	99.4

Population Age 3–17 Enrolled in Private School
(Universe: Population Age 3–17 Enrolled in School)

Group	Number	%
Total Population	108	2.5
Hispanic or Latino (of any race)	39	3.0
Mexican	7	0.6

Foreign-Born Population

Group	Number	%
Total Population	1,846	8.1
Hispanic or Latino (of any race)	1,446	40.3
Mexican	1,156	40.2

Foreign-Born Naturalized U.S. Citizens

Group	Number	%
Total Population	603	32.7
Hispanic or Latino (of any race)	360	24.9
Mexican	254	22.0

Language Spoken at Home: English Only
(Universe: Population 5 Years and Over)

Group	Number	%
Total Population	18,228	85.5
Hispanic or Latino (of any race)	753	23.5
Mexican	526	20.5

Language Spoken at Home: Spanish
(Universe: Population 5 Years and Over)

Group	Number	%
Total Population	2,633	12.4
Hispanic or Latino (of any race)	2,454	76.5
Mexican	2,039	79.5

Unemployment Rate
(Universe: Population 16 Years and Over)

Group	%
Total Population	8.3
Hispanic or Latino (of any race)	9.2
Mexican	10.8

Class of Worker: Private Wage and Salary
(Universe: Civilian Employed Population 16 Years and Over)

Group	Number	%
Total Population	9,053	81.3
Hispanic or Latino (of any race)	1,207	89.0
Mexican	892	86.5

Class of Worker: Government
(Universe: Civilian Employed Population 16 Years and Over)

Group	Number	%
Total Population	1,426	12.8
Hispanic or Latino (of any race)	53	3.9
Mexican	43	4.2

Means of Transportation to Work: Car, Truck or Van
(Universe: Workers 16 Years and Over)

Group	Number	%
Total Population	10,165	93.2
Hispanic or Latino (of any race)	1,314	98.4
Mexican	989	97.8

Means of Transportation to Work: Public Transportation (ex. Taxicab)
(Universe: Workers 16 Years and Over)

Group	Number	%
Total Population	79	0.7
Hispanic or Latino (of any race)	0	0.0
Mexican	0	0.0

Homeownership Rate
(Universe: Occupied Housing Units)

Group	%
Total Population	68.5
Hispanic or Latino (of any race)	60.7
Central American, ex. Mexican	76.6
Salvadoran	75.8
Mexican	60.5
Puerto Rican	66.7

Median Home Value

Group	Dollars
Total Population	98,000
Hispanic or Latino (of any race)	76,700
Mexican	73,500

Median Gross Rent

Group	Dollars
Total Population	595
Hispanic or Latino (of any race)	716
Mexican	713

Median Household Income
(2010 Inflation-Adjusted Dollars)

Group	Dollars
Total Population	46,178
Hispanic or Latino (of any race)	42,930
Mexican	44,406

Per Capita Income
(2010 Inflation-Adjusted Dollars)

Group	Dollars
Total Population	23,690
Hispanic or Latino (of any race)	12,163
Mexican	11,096

Households with $100,000+ Income

Group	Number	%
Total Population	1,160	12.3
Hispanic or Latino (of any race)	0	0.0
Mexican	0	0.0

Households with Food Stamps/SNAP Benefits During Past 12 Months

Group	Number	%
Total Population	1,331	14.2
Hispanic or Latino (of any race)	248	30.6
Mexican	212	29.5

Poverty Rate
(Income in Past 12 Months Below Poverty Level)

Group	%
Total Population	17.6
Hispanic or Latino (of any race)	28.4
Mexican	24.2

Storm Lake*

Population

Group	Number	%TP[1]	%HP[2]
Total Population	10,600	100.0	–
Hispanic or Latino (of any race)	3,822	36.1	100.0
Central American, ex. Mexican	461	4.3	12.1
Guatemalan	120	1.1	3.1
Salvadoran	272	2.6	7.1
Mexican	3,115	29.4	81.5

Population Growth: 2000–2010

Group	%
Total Population	5.2
Hispanic or Latino (of any race)	80.2
Central American, ex. Mexican	319.1
Mexican	82.4

Males per 100 Females

Group	Number
Total Population	100.3
Hispanic or Latino (of any race)	112.3
Central American, ex. Mexican	143.9
Guatemalan	144.9
Salvadoran	154.2
Mexican	110.8

Average Household Size

Group	People
Total Population	2.75
Hispanic or Latino (of any race)	4.17
Central American, ex. Mexican	3.89
Guatemalan	4.03
Salvadoran	3.90
Mexican	4.30

Median Age

Group	Years
Total Population	30.8
Hispanic or Latino (of any race)	23.6
Central American, ex. Mexican	28.8
Guatemalan	27.8
Salvadoran	30.7
Mexican	22.6

High School Graduates
(Universe: Population 25 Years and Over)

Group	Number	%
Total Population	3,982	70.6
Hispanic or Latino (of any race)	355	22.5
Mexican	238	18.3

Four-Year College Graduates
(Universe: Population 25 Years and Over)

Group	Number	%
Total Population	1,283	22.7
Hispanic or Latino (of any race)	127	8.1
Mexican	65	5.0

Population Age 3–17 Enrolled in Public School
(Universe: Population Age 3–17 Enrolled in School)

Group	Number	%
Total Population	2,007	95.8
Hispanic or Latino (of any race)	1,015	99.3
Mexican	740	99.1

Population Age 3–17 Enrolled in Private School
(Universe: Population Age 3–17 Enrolled in School)

Group	Number	%
Total Population	87	4.2
Hispanic or Latino (of any race)	7	0.7
Mexican	7	0.9

Foreign-Born Population

Group	Number	%
Total Population	2,497	24.1
Hispanic or Latino (of any race)	1,835	52.8
Mexican	1,531	54.4

Foreign-Born Naturalized U.S. Citizens

Group	Number	%
Total Population	470	18.8
Hispanic or Latino (of any race)	356	19.4
Mexican	306	20.0

Language Spoken at Home: English Only
(Universe: Population 5 Years and Over)

Group	Number	%
Total Population	5,692	59.3
Hispanic or Latino (of any race)	128	4.1
Mexican	102	4.1

Language Spoken at Home: Spanish
(Universe: Population 5 Years and Over)

Group	Number	%
Total Population	3,046	31.7
Hispanic or Latino (of any race)	2,965	95.9
Mexican	2,382	95.9

Unemployment Rate
(Universe: Population 16 Years and Over)

Group	%
Total Population	4.9
Hispanic or Latino (of any race)	11.7
Mexican	10.3

Class of Worker: Private Wage and Salary
(Universe: Civilian Employed Population 16 Years and Over)

Group	Number	%
Total Population	4,600	85.3
Hispanic or Latino (of any race)	1,570	97.6
Mexican	1,287	97.8

Class of Worker: Government
(Universe: Civilian Employed Population 16 Years and Over)

Group	Number	%
Total Population	541	10.0
Hispanic or Latino (of any race)	17	1.1
Mexican	7	0.5

Means of Transportation to Work: Car, Truck or Van
(Universe: Workers 16 Years and Over)

Group	Number	%
Total Population	4,239	80.5
Hispanic or Latino (of any race)	1,270	82.7
Mexican	1,041	83.8

Notes: (1) Percent of total population; (2) Percent of Hispanic/Latino population; Profiles include places with an overall population of at least 125,000, OR an overall population of at least 25,000 where the Hispanic/Latino population is at least 20% of the overall population. In states where less than five places meet either of these criteria, we have included places with at least 10,000 total population with the highest percentage of Hispanic/Latino population. These places are identified with an asterisk (*); Please refer to the User's Guide for a full explanation of data.

Means of Transportation to Work: Public Transportation (ex. Taxicab) *(Universe: Workers 16 Years and Over)*		
Group	Number	%
Total Population	17	0.3
Hispanic or Latino (of any race)	0	0.0
Mexican	0	0.0

Homeownership Rate *(Universe: Occupied Housing Units)*	
Group	%
Total Population	61.6
Hispanic or Latino (of any race)	55.7
Central American, ex. Mexican	62.9
Guatemalan	55.9
Salvadoran	67.5
Mexican	55.3

Median Home Value	
Group	Dollars
Total Population	89,100
Hispanic or Latino (of any race)	63,700
Mexican	63,000

Median Gross Rent	
Group	Dollars
Total Population	557
Hispanic or Latino (of any race)	602
Mexican	599

Median Household Income *(2010 Inflation-Adjusted Dollars)*	
Group	Dollars
Total Population	40,800
Hispanic or Latino (of any race)	39,433
Mexican	39,000

Per Capita Income *(2010 Inflation-Adjusted Dollars)*	
Group	Dollars
Total Population	17,449
Hispanic or Latino (of any race)	11,632
Mexican	11,678

Households with $100,000+ Income		
Group	Number	%
Total Population	236	6.6
Hispanic or Latino (of any race)	36	3.9
Mexican	36	5.2

Households with Food Stamps/SNAP Benefits During Past 12 Months		
Group	Number	%
Total Population	501	14.0
Hispanic or Latino (of any race)	153	16.7
Mexican	65	9.3

Poverty Rate *(Income in Past 12 Months Below Poverty Level)*	
Group	%
Total Population	15.1
Hispanic or Latino (of any race)	26.0
Mexican	18.6

STATE & PLACE PROFILES

Notes: (1) Percent of total population; (2) Percent of Hispanic/Latino population; Profiles include places with an overall population of at least 125,000, OR an overall population of at least 25,000 where the Hispanic/Latino population is at least 20% of the overall population. In states where less than five places meet either of these criteria, we have included places with at least 10,000 total population with the highest percentage of Hispanic/Latino population. These places are identified with an asterisk (*); Please refer to the User's Guide for a full explanation of data.

Kansas

EDITOR'S NOTE: For a place to be included in this edition, it must meet one of two criteria. Either its overall population is at least 125,000, OR its overall population is at least 25,000 and its Hispanic/Latino population is at least 20% of the overall population. For the state of Kansas, the following locations are included:

- Dodge City
- Garden City
- Kansas City
- Olathe
- Overland Park
- Topeka
- Wichita

Section Two: State & Place Profiles starts with the state profile, followed by place profiles that meet the criteria above. Places are listed alphabetically within each state. All states, all counties and places that meet the above criteria are ranked and compared in *Section Three: Rankings & Comparisons*, on page 1055.

For a more detailed look at the Hispanic/Latino population in Kansas, a companion web site is available at no additional charge with purchase of this print edition. Visit http://gold.greyhouse.com/page/info_hispanic for more information.

The web site includes data for all counties and places in Kansas with Hispanic/Latino population, plus ten additional topics: Self Employed Worker; Walked to Work; Worked from Home; Mean Travel Time to Work; Mean Household Income; Households with Cash Public Assistance; Mean Cash Pubic Assistance; Poverty Rates for 18 and Under, 18 to 64, and 65 and Over.

Population

Group	Number	%TP[1]	%HP[2]
Total Population	2,853,118	100.0	–
Hispanic or Latino (of any race)	300,042	10.5	100.0
Central American, ex. Mexican	15,293	0.5	5.1
Costa Rican	385	<0.1	0.1
Guatemalan	5,538	0.2	1.8
Honduran	2,689	0.1	0.9
Nicaraguan	537	<0.1	0.2
Panamanian	888	<0.1	0.3
Salvadoran	5,108	0.2	1.7
Cuban	2,723	0.1	0.9
Dominican Republic	764	<0.1	0.3
Mexican	247,297	8.7	82.4
Puerto Rican	9,247	0.3	3.1
South American	5,845	0.2	1.9
Argentinean	531	<0.1	0.2
Bolivian	332	<0.1	0.1
Chilean	346	<0.1	0.1
Colombian	1,769	0.1	0.6
Ecuadorian	701	<0.1	0.2
Paraguayan	212	<0.1	0.1
Peruvian	1,151	<0.1	0.4
Venezuelan	639	<0.1	0.2
Spaniard	3,034	0.1	1.0

Population Growth: 2000–2010

Group	%
Total Population	6.1
Hispanic or Latino (of any race)	59.4
Central American, ex. Mexican	241.1
Costa Rican	108.1
Guatemalan	412.8
Honduran	309.3
Nicaraguan	214.0
Panamanian	83.1
Salvadoran	209.8
Cuban	62.1
Dominican Republic	278.2
Mexican	66.8
Puerto Rican	76.6
South American	122.5
Argentinean	155.3
Bolivian	145.9
Chilean	113.6
Colombian	148.5
Ecuadorian	111.8
Paraguayan	81.2
Peruvian	167.7
Venezuelan	78.5
Spaniard	1,089.8

Males per 100 Females

Group	Number
Total Population	98.4
Hispanic or Latino (of any race)	109.0
Central American, ex. Mexican	123.5
Costa Rican	85.1
Guatemalan	157.1
Honduran	133.2
Nicaraguan	90.4
Panamanian	70.8
Salvadoran	107.9
Cuban	117.0
Dominican Republic	101.6
Mexican	109.5
Puerto Rican	103.4
South American	87.2
Argentinean	102.7
Bolivian	82.4
Chilean	101.2
Colombian	79.0
Ecuadorian	86.4
Paraguayan	98.1
Peruvian	85.3
Venezuelan	89.1
Spaniard	94.9

Average Household Size

Group	People
Total Population	2.49
Hispanic or Latino (of any race)	3.47
Central American, ex. Mexican	3.75
Costa Rican	2.70
Guatemalan	4.07
Honduran	3.68
Nicaraguan	3.43
Panamanian	2.84
Salvadoran	3.79
Cuban	2.70
Dominican Republic	3.11
Mexican	3.54
Puerto Rican	2.97
South American	2.81
Argentinean	2.86
Bolivian	2.77
Chilean	2.85
Colombian	2.73
Ecuadorian	3.02
Paraguayan	2.49
Peruvian	2.92
Venezuelan	2.73
Spaniard	2.74

Median Age

Group	Years
Total Population	36.0
Hispanic or Latino (of any race)	23.3
Central American, ex. Mexican	26.8
Costa Rican	29.1
Guatemalan	25.3
Honduran	27.4
Nicaraguan	27.9
Panamanian	27.9
Salvadoran	29.0
Cuban	27.0
Dominican Republic	23.8
Mexican	22.8
Puerto Rican	22.4
South American	29.9
Argentinean	34.4
Bolivian	30.6
Chilean	32.0
Colombian	29.1
Ecuadorian	30.3
Paraguayan	24.0
Peruvian	30.3
Venezuelan	29.8
Spaniard	28.5

High School Graduates
(Universe: Population 25 Years and Over)

Group	Number	%
Total Population	1,608,324	89.2
Hispanic or Latino (of any race)	76,335	58.8
Central American, ex. Mexican	3,442	44.3
Guatemalan	697	33.8
Honduran	983	49.4
Salvadoran	970	36.3
Cuban	1,091	88.3
Mexican	59,994	56.3
Puerto Rican	3,267	85.2
South American	3,340	93.3
Colombian	1,069	91.2
Ecuadorian	413	95.8
Peruvian	562	93.2
Spaniard	1,270	95.4

Four-Year College Graduates
(Universe: Population 25 Years and Over)

Group	Number	%
Total Population	529,091	29.3
Hispanic or Latino (of any race)	14,592	11.2
Central American, ex. Mexican	855	11.0
Guatemalan	178	8.6
Honduran	207	10.4
Salvadoran	108	4.0
Cuban	381	30.8
Mexican	9,398	8.8
Puerto Rican	871	22.7
South American	1,721	48.1
Colombian	442	37.7
Ecuadorian	252	58.5
Peruvian	390	64.7
Spaniard	476	35.8

Population Age 3–17 Enrolled in Public School
(Universe: Population Age 3–17 Enrolled in School)

Group	Number	%
Total Population	465,859	86.7
Hispanic or Latino (of any race)	72,404	92.3
Central American, ex. Mexican	2,884	88.2
Guatemalan	1,163	85.1
Honduran	359	92.1
Salvadoran	926	99.1
Cuban	346	85.9
Mexican	62,316	92.8
Puerto Rican	2,112	92.9
South American	755	70.7
Colombian	287	76.1
Ecuadorian	130	67.7
Peruvian	134	60.6
Spaniard	532	87.6

Population Age 3–17 Enrolled in Private School
(Universe: Population Age 3–17 Enrolled in School)

Group	Number	%
Total Population	71,316	13.3
Hispanic or Latino (of any race)	6,078	7.7
Central American, ex. Mexican	384	11.8
Guatemalan	203	14.9
Honduran	31	7.9
Salvadoran	8	0.9
Cuban	57	14.1
Mexican	4,837	7.2
Puerto Rican	162	7.1
South American	313	29.3
Colombian	90	23.9
Ecuadorian	62	32.3
Peruvian	87	39.4
Spaniard	75	12.4

Notes: (1) Percent of total population; (2) Percent of Hispanic/Latino population; Profiles include places with an overall population of at least 125,000, OR an overall population of at least 25,000 where the Hispanic/Latino population is at least 20% of the overall population. In states where less than five places meet either of these criteria, we have included places with at least 10,000 total population with the highest percentage of Hispanic/Latino population. These places are identified with an asterisk (*); Please refer to the User's Guide for a full explanation of data.

Foreign-Born Population

Group	Number	%
Total Population	177,139	6.3
Hispanic or Latino (of any race)	96,895	35.1
Central American, ex. Mexican	9,782	66.3
Guatemalan	3,289	71.3
Honduran	2,291	72.7
Salvadoran	3,047	63.0
Cuban	670	33.1
Mexican	80,364	34.9
Puerto Rican	149	1.7
South American	3,479	58.3
Colombian	1,157	62.1
Ecuadorian	409	41.2
Peruvian	611	67.8
Spaniard	250	9.8

Foreign-Born Naturalized U.S. Citizens

Group	Number	%
Total Population	57,708	32.6
Hispanic or Latino (of any race)	19,917	20.6
Central American, ex. Mexican	2,289	23.4
Guatemalan	665	20.2
Honduran	566	24.7
Salvadoran	598	19.6
Cuban	309	46.1
Mexican	15,327	19.1
Puerto Rican	64	43.0
South American	1,135	32.6
Colombian	416	36.0
Ecuadorian	82	20.0
Peruvian	216	35.4
Spaniard	52	20.8

Language Spoken at Home: English Only
(Universe: Population 5 Years and Over)

Group	Number	%
Total Population	2,335,053	89.5
Hispanic or Latino (of any race)	80,107	33.4
Central American, ex. Mexican	1,306	10.1
Guatemalan	423	10.2
Honduran	123	4.6
Salvadoran	205	4.9
Cuban	1,017	52.7
Mexican	65,575	32.9
Puerto Rican	4,137	55.2
South American	1,184	22.6
Colombian	312	18.6
Ecuadorian	240	31.6
Peruvian	158	18.0
Spaniard	1,695	73.8

Language Spoken at Home: Spanish
(Universe: Population 5 Years and Over)

Group	Number	%
Total Population	182,110	7.0
Hispanic or Latino (of any race)	158,888	66.2
Central American, ex. Mexican	11,564	89.4
Guatemalan	3,707	89.5
Honduran	2,570	95.4
Salvadoran	3,940	95.0
Cuban	913	47.3
Mexican	133,368	66.9
Puerto Rican	3,280	43.8
South American	4,004	76.5
Colombian	1,368	81.4
Ecuadorian	519	68.4
Peruvian	697	79.6
Spaniard	467	20.3

Unemployment Rate
(Universe: Population 16 Years and Over)

Group	%
Total Population	6.0
Hispanic or Latino (of any race)	8.4
Central American, ex. Mexican	8.5
Guatemalan	11.9
Honduran	8.3
Salvadoran	6.6
Cuban	10.3
Mexican	8.3
Puerto Rican	11.2
South American	5.5
Colombian	3.7
Ecuadorian	2.7
Peruvian	4.8
Spaniard	10.8

Class of Worker: Private Wage and Salary
(Universe: Civilian Employed Population 16 Years and Over)

Group	Number	%
Total Population	1,060,575	76.3
Hispanic or Latino (of any race)	100,122	86.3
Central American, ex. Mexican	6,581	89.7
Guatemalan	1,730	93.2
Honduran	1,667	93.8
Salvadoran	2,366	90.1
Cuban	970	92.4
Mexican	82,043	86.6
Puerto Rican	2,838	82.3
South American	2,523	78.0
Colombian	809	78.4
Ecuadorian	338	83.7
Peruvian	414	80.2
Spaniard	971	84.1

Class of Worker: Government
(Universe: Civilian Employed Population 16 Years and Over)

Group	Number	%
Total Population	228,678	16.4
Hispanic or Latino (of any race)	10,667	9.2
Central American, ex. Mexican	297	4.1
Guatemalan	13	0.7
Honduran	16	0.9
Salvadoran	126	4.8
Cuban	63	6.0
Mexican	8,548	9.0
Puerto Rican	474	13.7
South American	406	12.6
Colombian	102	9.9
Ecuadorian	31	7.7
Peruvian	79	15.3
Spaniard	163	14.1

Means of Transportation to Work: Car, Truck or Van
(Universe: Workers 16 Years and Over)

Group	Number	%
Total Population	1,252,229	91.1
Hispanic or Latino (of any race)	106,117	92.5
Central American, ex. Mexican	6,468	90.6
Guatemalan	1,635	88.1
Honduran	1,402	90.7
Salvadoran	2,401	92.6
Cuban	865	80.8
Mexican	86,705	93.0
Puerto Rican	3,375	90.7
South American	2,964	92.2
Colombian	896	89.2
Ecuadorian	381	92.5
Peruvian	516	100.0
Spaniard	1,148	95.9

Means of Transportation to Work: Public Transportation (ex. Taxicab)
(Universe: Workers 16 Years and Over)

Group	Number	%
Total Population	7,066	0.5
Hispanic or Latino (of any race)	694	0.6
Central American, ex. Mexican	23	0.3
Guatemalan	0	0.0
Honduran	0	0.0
Salvadoran	12	0.5
Cuban	17	1.6
Mexican	626	0.7
Puerto Rican	0	0.0
South American	12	0.4
Colombian	0	0.0
Ecuadorian	0	0.0
Peruvian	0	0.0
Spaniard	0	0.0

Homeownership Rate
(Universe: Occupied Housing Units)

Group	%
Total Population	67.8
Hispanic or Latino (of any race)	53.0
Central American, ex. Mexican	43.8
Costa Rican	50.4
Guatemalan	27.9
Honduran	36.1
Nicaraguan	50.6
Panamanian	50.0
Salvadoran	59.2
Cuban	51.3
Dominican Republic	36.6
Mexican	54.5
Puerto Rican	41.7
South American	55.5
Argentinean	64.8
Bolivian	66.7
Chilean	54.1
Colombian	53.6
Ecuadorian	62.4
Paraguayan	35.8
Peruvian	56.4
Venezuelan	50.2
Spaniard	59.4

Median Home Value

Group	Dollars
Total Population	122,600
Hispanic or Latino (of any race)	82,400
Central American, ex. Mexican	89,000
Guatemalan	85,600
Honduran	152,500
Salvadoran	75,500
Cuban	113,500
Mexican	78,900
Puerto Rican	130,800
South American	170,100
Colombian	143,800
Ecuadorian	144,600
Peruvian	185,600
Spaniard	163,300

Median Gross Rent

Group	Dollars
Total Population	671
Hispanic or Latino (of any race)	674
Central American, ex. Mexican	702
Guatemalan	704
Honduran	696
Salvadoran	706
Cuban	828
Mexican	669
Puerto Rican	637
South American	810
Colombian	1,010
Ecuadorian	1,025
Peruvian	756
Spaniard	687

Median Household Income
(2010 Inflation-Adjusted Dollars)

Group	Dollars
Total Population	49,424
Hispanic or Latino (of any race)	37,572
Central American, ex. Mexican	38,772
Guatemalan	30,114
Honduran	41,705
Salvadoran	39,862
Cuban	37,877
Mexican	37,289
Puerto Rican	36,955
South American	49,800
Colombian	78,415
Ecuadorian	52,298
Peruvian	42,143
Spaniard	44,135

Per Capita Income
(2010 Inflation-Adjusted Dollars)

Group	Dollars
Total Population	25,907
Hispanic or Latino (of any race)	13,264
Central American, ex. Mexican	13,645
Guatemalan	10,494
Honduran	13,947
Salvadoran	13,445
Cuban	24,710
Mexican	12,501
Puerto Rican	18,766
South American	25,103
Colombian	23,571

Notes: (1) Percent of total population; (2) Percent of Hispanic/Latino population; Profiles include places with an overall population of at least 125,000, OR an overall population of at least 25,000 where the Hispanic/Latino population is at least 20% of the overall population. In states where less than five places meet either of these criteria, we have included places with at least 10,000 total population with the highest percentage of Hispanic/Latino population. These places are identified with an asterisk (*); Please refer to the User's Guide for a full explanation of data.

Ecuadorian	21,807	
Peruvian	26,063	
Spaniard	21,939	

Households with $100,000+ Income

Group	Number	%
Total Population	191,354	17.4
Hispanic or Latino (of any race)	5,617	7.7
Central American, ex. Mexican	220	6.0
Guatemalan	61	6.0
Honduran	59	8.9
Salvadoran	66	4.7
Cuban	148	18.6
Mexican	4,141	7.0
Puerto Rican	229	9.2
South American	441	21.3
Colombian	187	35.3
Ecuadorian	55	16.7
Peruvian	56	15.8
Spaniard	205	24.7

Households with Food Stamps/SNAP Benefits During Past 12 Months

Group	Number	%
Total Population	79,862	7.2
Hispanic or Latino (of any race)	9,557	13.1
Central American, ex. Mexican	371	10.1
Guatemalan	45	4.4
Honduran	67	10.2
Salvadoran	233	16.6
Cuban	89	11.2
Mexican	7,802	13.1
Puerto Rican	524	21.1
South American	155	7.5
Colombian	0	0.0
Ecuadorian	24	7.3
Peruvian	49	13.8
Spaniard	27	3.3

Poverty Rate
(Income in Past 12 Months Below Poverty Level)

Group	%
Total Population	12.4
Hispanic or Latino (of any race)	24.1
Central American, ex. Mexican	28.3
Guatemalan	38.2
Honduran	35.4
Salvadoran	19.5
Cuban	15.9
Mexican	24.5
Puerto Rican	26.7
South American	13.3
Colombian	14.6
Ecuadorian	11.3
Peruvian	11.2
Spaniard	11.9

Dodge City

Population

Group	Number	%TP[1]	%HP[2]
Total Population	27,340	100.0	–
Hispanic or Latino (of any race)	15,730	57.5	100.0
Central American, ex. Mexican	1,446	5.3	9.2
Guatemalan	1,043	3.8	6.6
Salvadoran	316	1.2	2.0
Cuban	227	0.8	1.4
Mexican	13,105	47.9	83.3
Puerto Rican	140	0.5	0.9

Population Growth: 2000–2010

Group	%
Total Population	8.6
Hispanic or Latino (of any race)	45.7
Central American, ex. Mexican	443.6
Guatemalan	619.3
Mexican	42.7

Males per 100 Females

Group	Number
Total Population	105.7
Hispanic or Latino (of any race)	113.8
Central American, ex. Mexican	180.2
Guatemalan	207.7
Salvadoran	110.7
Cuban	152.2
Mexican	108.6
Puerto Rican	122.2

Average Household Size

Group	People
Total Population	3.05
Hispanic or Latino (of any race)	4.00
Central American, ex. Mexican	4.41
Guatemalan	4.54
Salvadoran	4.17
Cuban	2.67
Mexican	4.01
Puerto Rican	3.86

Median Age

Group	Years
Total Population	28.9
Hispanic or Latino (of any race)	23.0
Central American, ex. Mexican	25.8
Guatemalan	25.0
Salvadoran	28.0
Cuban	36.5
Mexican	22.1
Puerto Rican	19.7

High School Graduates
(Universe: Population 25 Years and Over)

Group	Number	%
Total Population	9,992	66.0
Hispanic or Latino (of any race)	2,791	41.1
Mexican	2,259	40.3

Four-Year College Graduates
(Universe: Population 25 Years and Over)

Group	Number	%
Total Population	2,570	17.0
Hispanic or Latino (of any race)	219	3.2
Mexican	127	2.3

Population Age 3–17 Enrolled in Public School
(Universe: Population Age 3–17 Enrolled in School)

Group	Number	%
Total Population	5,572	97.2
Hispanic or Latino (of any race)	3,903	98.5
Mexican	3,547	98.3

Population Age 3–17 Enrolled in Private School
(Universe: Population Age 3–17 Enrolled in School)

Group	Number	%
Total Population	159	2.8
Hispanic or Latino (of any race)	61	1.5
Mexican	61	1.7

Foreign-Born Population

Group	Number	%
Total Population	7,402	28.1
Hispanic or Latino (of any race)	6,772	46.8
Mexican	5,599	45.4

Foreign-Born Naturalized U.S. Citizens

Group	Number	%
Total Population	1,680	22.7
Hispanic or Latino (of any race)	1,460	21.6
Mexican	1,125	20.1

Language Spoken at Home: English Only
(Universe: Population 5 Years and Over)

Group	Number	%
Total Population	11,948	50.6
Hispanic or Latino (of any race)	1,686	13.6
Mexican	1,446	13.8

Language Spoken at Home: Spanish
(Universe: Population 5 Years and Over)

Group	Number	%
Total Population	10,919	46.2
Hispanic or Latino (of any race)	10,699	86.3
Mexican	9,028	86.2

Unemployment Rate
(Universe: Population 16 Years and Over)

Group	%
Total Population	4.0
Hispanic or Latino (of any race)	5.0
Mexican	3.4

Class of Worker: Private Wage and Salary
(Universe: Civilian Employed Population 16 Years and Over)

Group	Number	%
Total Population	10,611	82.3
Hispanic or Latino (of any race)	5,792	91.2
Mexican	4,818	91.5

Class of Worker: Government
(Universe: Civilian Employed Population 16 Years and Over)

Group	Number	%
Total Population	1,591	12.3
Hispanic or Latino (of any race)	389	6.1
Mexican	330	6.3

Means of Transportation to Work: Car, Truck or Van
(Universe: Workers 16 Years and Over)

Group	Number	%
Total Population	12,116	95.0
Hispanic or Latino (of any race)	6,036	96.4
Mexican	5,007	97.2

Means of Transportation to Work: Public Transportation (ex. Taxicab)
(Universe: Workers 16 Years and Over)

Group	Number	%
Total Population	0	0.0
Hispanic or Latino (of any race)	0	0.0
Mexican	0	0.0

Homeownership Rate
(Universe: Occupied Housing Units)

Group	%
Total Population	60.6
Hispanic or Latino (of any race)	55.0
Central American, ex. Mexican	28.1
Guatemalan	15.0
Salvadoran	57.3
Cuban	8.0
Mexican	59.9
Puerto Rican	32.1

Median Home Value

Group	Dollars
Total Population	84,000
Hispanic or Latino (of any race)	67,300
Mexican	62,400

Median Gross Rent

Group	Dollars
Total Population	595
Hispanic or Latino (of any race)	598
Mexican	609

Median Household Income
(2010 Inflation-Adjusted Dollars)

Group	Dollars
Total Population	43,994
Hispanic or Latino (of any race)	39,231
Mexican	40,066

Per Capita Income
(2010 Inflation-Adjusted Dollars)

Group	Dollars
Total Population	18,350
Hispanic or Latino (of any race)	11,367
Mexican	10,930

Households with $100,000+ Income

Group	Number	%
Total Population	899	10.3
Hispanic or Latino (of any race)	196	5.8
Mexican	130	4.7

Households with Food Stamps/SNAP Benefits During Past 12 Months

Group	Number	%
Total Population	1,262	14.4
Hispanic or Latino (of any race)	541	16.1
Mexican	387	14.1

Notes: (1) Percent of total population; (2) Percent of Hispanic/Latino population; Profiles include places with an overall population of at least 125,000, OR an overall population of at least 25,000 where the Hispanic/Latino population is at least 20% of the overall population. In states where less than five places meet either of these criteria, we have included places with at least 10,000 total population with the highest percentage of Hispanic/Latino population. These places are identified with an asterisk (*); Please refer to the User's Guide for a full explanation of data.

Poverty Rate
(Income in Past 12 Months Below Poverty Level)

Group	%
Total Population	19.0
Hispanic or Latino (of any race)	24.2
Mexican	25.1

Garden City

Population

Group	Number	%TP[1]	%HP[2]
Total Population	26,658	100.0	–
Hispanic or Latino (of any race)	12,946	48.6	100.0
Central American, ex. Mexican	868	3.3	6.7
Guatemalan	144	0.5	1.1
Salvadoran	648	2.4	5.0
Mexican	11,245	42.2	86.9

Population Growth: 2000–2010

Group	%
Total Population	-6.3
Hispanic or Latino (of any race)	3.6
Central American, ex. Mexican	55.6
Guatemalan	2.1
Salvadoran	87.8
Mexican	14.0

Males per 100 Females

Group	Number
Total Population	99.0
Hispanic or Latino (of any race)	104.7
Central American, ex. Mexican	120.3
Guatemalan	182.4
Salvadoran	112.5
Mexican	104.3

Average Household Size

Group	People
Total Population	2.88
Hispanic or Latino (of any race)	3.75
Central American, ex. Mexican	4.09
Guatemalan	4.26
Salvadoran	4.02
Mexican	3.75

Median Age

Group	Years
Total Population	29.9
Hispanic or Latino (of any race)	22.8
Central American, ex. Mexican	28.8
Guatemalan	27.8
Salvadoran	29.2
Mexican	22.4

High School Graduates
(Universe: Population 25 Years and Over)

Group	Number	%
Total Population	9,995	68.2
Hispanic or Latino (of any race)	2,399	40.8
Central American, ex. Mexican	82	14.3
Mexican	1,723	39.1

Four-Year College Graduates
(Universe: Population 25 Years and Over)

Group	Number	%
Total Population	2,405	16.4
Hispanic or Latino (of any race)	380	6.5
Central American, ex. Mexican	0	0.0
Mexican	256	5.8

Population Age 3–17 Enrolled in Public School
(Universe: Population Age 3–17 Enrolled in School)

Group	Number	%
Total Population	5,291	92.9
Hispanic or Latino (of any race)	3,459	96.2
Central American, ex. Mexican	374	100.0
Mexican	2,747	96.3

Population Age 3–17 Enrolled in Private School
(Universe: Population Age 3–17 Enrolled in School)

Group	Number	%
Total Population	406	7.1
Hispanic or Latino (of any race)	137	3.8
Central American, ex. Mexican	0	0.0
Mexican	105	3.7

Foreign-Born Population

Group	Number	%
Total Population	5,380	20.7
Hispanic or Latino (of any race)	4,508	35.9
Central American, ex. Mexican	743	57.8
Mexican	3,164	33.3

Foreign-Born Naturalized U.S. Citizens

Group	Number	%
Total Population	1,229	22.8
Hispanic or Latino (of any race)	966	21.4
Central American, ex. Mexican	88	11.8
Mexican	838	26.5

Language Spoken at Home: English Only
(Universe: Population 5 Years and Over)

Group	Number	%
Total Population	13,669	57.9
Hispanic or Latino (of any race)	2,317	21.1
Central American, ex. Mexican	0	0.0
Mexican	1,938	23.4

Language Spoken at Home: Spanish
(Universe: Population 5 Years and Over)

Group	Number	%
Total Population	8,862	37.5
Hispanic or Latino (of any race)	8,664	78.9
Central American, ex. Mexican	1,151	100.0
Mexican	6,327	76.6

Unemployment Rate
(Universe: Population 16 Years and Over)

Group	%
Total Population	3.8
Hispanic or Latino (of any race)	4.6
Central American, ex. Mexican	4.6
Mexican	3.8

Class of Worker: Private Wage and Salary
(Universe: Civilian Employed Population 16 Years and Over)

Group	Number	%
Total Population	10,603	80.3
Hispanic or Latino (of any race)	5,035	88.4
Central American, ex. Mexican	659	99.1
Mexican	3,519	85.4

Class of Worker: Government
(Universe: Civilian Employed Population 16 Years and Over)

Group	Number	%
Total Population	1,861	14.1
Hispanic or Latino (of any race)	542	9.5
Central American, ex. Mexican	0	0.0
Mexican	489	11.9

Means of Transportation to Work: Car, Truck or Van
(Universe: Workers 16 Years and Over)

Group	Number	%
Total Population	11,751	90.6
Hispanic or Latino (of any race)	5,133	91.1
Central American, ex. Mexican	612	92.0
Mexican	3,825	94.2

Means of Transportation to Work: Public Transportation (ex. Taxicab)
(Universe: Workers 16 Years and Over)

Group	Number	%
Total Population	55	0.4
Hispanic or Latino (of any race)	36	0.6
Central American, ex. Mexican	0	0.0
Mexican	36	0.9

Homeownership Rate
(Universe: Occupied Housing Units)

Group	%
Total Population	60.6
Hispanic or Latino (of any race)	60.3
Central American, ex. Mexican	61.0
Guatemalan	50.0
Salvadoran	64.8
Mexican	61.1

Median Home Value

Group	Dollars
Total Population	99,600
Hispanic or Latino (of any race)	87,700
Central American, ex. Mexican	103,900
Mexican	86,600

Median Gross Rent

Group	Dollars
Total Population	612
Hispanic or Latino (of any race)	728
Central American, ex. Mexican	784
Mexican	596

Median Household Income
(2010 Inflation-Adjusted Dollars)

Group	Dollars
Total Population	47,975
Hispanic or Latino (of any race)	48,815
Central American, ex. Mexican	58,458
Mexican	46,121

Per Capita Income
(2010 Inflation-Adjusted Dollars)

Group	Dollars
Total Population	20,066
Hispanic or Latino (of any race)	13,943
Central American, ex. Mexican	10,828
Mexican	13,468

Households with $100,000+ Income

Group	Number	%
Total Population	1,008	11.6
Hispanic or Latino (of any race)	212	6.5
Central American, ex. Mexican	21	8.7
Mexican	150	6.1

Households with Food Stamps/SNAP Benefits During Past 12 Months

Group	Number	%
Total Population	688	7.9
Hispanic or Latino (of any race)	282	8.6
Central American, ex. Mexican	26	10.8
Mexican	203	8.2

Poverty Rate
(Income in Past 12 Months Below Poverty Level)

Group	%
Total Population	12.5
Hispanic or Latino (of any race)	16.4
Central American, ex. Mexican	35.9
Mexican	15.2

Kansas City

Population

Group	Number	%TP[1]	%HP[2]
Total Population	145,786	100.0	–
Hispanic or Latino (of any race)	40,522	27.8	100.0
Central American, ex. Mexican	2,636	1.8	6.5
Guatemalan	917	0.6	2.3
Honduran	778	0.5	1.9
Salvadoran	800	0.5	2.0
Cuban	247	0.2	0.6
Mexican	34,764	23.8	85.8
Puerto Rican	397	0.3	1.0
South American	347	0.2	0.9
Colombian	110	0.1	0.3
Spaniard	143	0.1	0.4

Population Growth: 2000–2010

Group	%
Total Population	-0.7
Hispanic or Latino (of any race)	64.5
Central American, ex. Mexican	245.9
Guatemalan	238.4
Honduran	325.1
Salvadoran	257.1
Cuban	38.8
Mexican	68.8
Puerto Rican	56.9
South American	136.1

STATE & PLACE PROFILES

Notes: (1) Percent of total population; (2) Percent of Hispanic/Latino population; Profiles include places with an overall population of at least 125,000, OR an overall population of at least 25,000 where the Hispanic/Latino population is at least 20% of the overall population. In states where less than five places meet either of these criteria, we have included places with at least 10,000 total population with the highest percentage of Hispanic/Latino population. These places are identified with an asterisk (*); Please refer to the User's Guide for a full explanation of data.

Males per 100 Females

Group	Number
Total Population	97.7
Hispanic or Latino (of any race)	111.8
Central American, ex. Mexican	125.5
Guatemalan	149.9
Honduran	134.3
Salvadoran	102.0
Cuban	118.6
Mexican	111.7
Puerto Rican	106.8
South American	84.6
Colombian	86.4
Spaniard	104.3

Average Household Size

Group	People
Total Population	2.68
Hispanic or Latino (of any race)	3.78
Central American, ex. Mexican	4.13
Guatemalan	4.23
Honduran	4.24
Salvadoran	3.96
Cuban	2.52
Mexican	3.80
Puerto Rican	3.07
South American	3.29
Colombian	2.89
Spaniard	2.91

Median Age

Group	Years
Total Population	32.5
Hispanic or Latino (of any race)	24.4
Central American, ex. Mexican	28.5
Guatemalan	27.6
Honduran	28.0
Salvadoran	30.5
Cuban	33.3
Mexican	23.8
Puerto Rican	22.9
South American	32.1
Colombian	32.0
Spaniard	27.8

High School Graduates
(Universe: Population 25 Years and Over)

Group	Number	%
Total Population	69,240	77.9
Hispanic or Latino (of any race)	9,214	49.7
Central American, ex. Mexican	441	30.0
Mexican	8,130	49.9

Four-Year College Graduates
(Universe: Population 25 Years and Over)

Group	Number	%
Total Population	12,945	14.6
Hispanic or Latino (of any race)	756	4.1
Central American, ex. Mexican	58	3.9
Mexican	565	3.5

Population Age 3–17 Enrolled in Public School
(Universe: Population Age 3–17 Enrolled in School)

Group	Number	%
Total Population	26,605	90.5
Hispanic or Latino (of any race)	9,472	92.2
Central American, ex. Mexican	545	90.5
Mexican	8,554	92.0

Population Age 3–17 Enrolled in Private School
(Universe: Population Age 3–17 Enrolled in School)

Group	Number	%
Total Population	2,780	9.5
Hispanic or Latino (of any race)	803	7.8
Central American, ex. Mexican	57	9.5
Mexican	746	8.0

Foreign-Born Population

Group	Number	%
Total Population	21,646	15.0
Hispanic or Latino (of any race)	18,035	47.6
Central American, ex. Mexican	1,886	65.0
Mexican	15,720	46.9

Foreign-Born Naturalized U.S. Citizens

Group	Number	%
Total Population	3,899	18.0
Hispanic or Latino (of any race)	2,278	12.6
Central American, ex. Mexican	289	15.3
Mexican	1,882	12.0

Language Spoken at Home: English Only
(Universe: Population 5 Years and Over)

Group	Number	%
Total Population	99,002	75.1
Hispanic or Latino (of any race)	6,202	18.9
Central American, ex. Mexican	8	0.3
Mexican	5,625	19.3

Language Spoken at Home: Spanish
(Universe: Population 5 Years and Over)

Group	Number	%
Total Population	28,099	21.3
Hispanic or Latino (of any race)	26,555	80.9
Central American, ex. Mexican	2,391	99.7
Mexican	23,451	80.5

Unemployment Rate
(Universe: Population 16 Years and Over)

Group	%
Total Population	12.7
Hispanic or Latino (of any race)	10.5
Central American, ex. Mexican	13.3
Mexican	10.4

Class of Worker: Private Wage and Salary
(Universe: Civilian Employed Population 16 Years and Over)

Group	Number	%
Total Population	49,412	79.5
Hispanic or Latino (of any race)	14,085	88.7
Central American, ex. Mexican	1,171	88.6
Mexican	12,257	88.8

Class of Worker: Government
(Universe: Civilian Employed Population 16 Years and Over)

Group	Number	%
Total Population	9,588	15.4
Hispanic or Latino (of any race)	814	5.1
Central American, ex. Mexican	48	3.6
Mexican	729	5.3

Means of Transportation to Work: Car, Truck or Van
(Universe: Workers 16 Years and Over)

Group	Number	%
Total Population	55,276	91.8
Hispanic or Latino (of any race)	13,710	89.9
Central American, ex. Mexican	1,130	92.5
Mexican	11,853	89.3

Means of Transportation to Work: Public Transportation (ex. Taxicab)
(Universe: Workers 16 Years and Over)

Group	Number	%
Total Population	942	1.6
Hispanic or Latino (of any race)	117	0.8
Central American, ex. Mexican	0	0.0
Mexican	117	0.9

Homeownership Rate
(Universe: Occupied Housing Units)

Group	%
Total Population	59.5
Hispanic or Latino (of any race)	53.7
Central American, ex. Mexican	45.3
Guatemalan	35.2
Honduran	37.2
Salvadoran	60.9
Cuban	56.1
Mexican	55.0
Puerto Rican	45.8
South American	52.8
Colombian	44.7
Spaniard	63.8

Median Home Value

Group	Dollars
Total Population	94,500
Hispanic or Latino (of any race)	79,400
Central American, ex. Mexican	84,100
Mexican	78,600

Median Gross Rent

Group	Dollars
Total Population	701
Hispanic or Latino (of any race)	759
Central American, ex. Mexican	675
Mexican	773

Median Household Income
(2010 Inflation-Adjusted Dollars)

Group	Dollars
Total Population	37,295
Hispanic or Latino (of any race)	32,995
Central American, ex. Mexican	29,735
Mexican	33,033

Per Capita Income
(2010 Inflation-Adjusted Dollars)

Group	Dollars
Total Population	18,435
Hispanic or Latino (of any race)	11,064
Central American, ex. Mexican	10,640
Mexican	10,929

Households with $100,000+ Income

Group	Number	%
Total Population	5,207	9.8
Hispanic or Latino (of any race)	590	6.4
Central American, ex. Mexican	19	2.8
Mexican	543	6.7

Households with Food Stamps/SNAP Benefits During Past 12 Months

Group	Number	%
Total Population	6,635	12.5
Hispanic or Latino (of any race)	1,036	11.2
Central American, ex. Mexican	105	15.3
Mexican	895	11.1

Poverty Rate
(Income in Past 12 Months Below Poverty Level)

Group	%
Total Population	22.3
Hispanic or Latino (of any race)	30.1
Central American, ex. Mexican	38.8
Mexican	29.2

Olathe

Population

Group	Number	%TP[1]	%HP[2]
Total Population	125,872	100.0	–
Hispanic or Latino (of any race)	12,794	10.2	100.0
Central American, ex. Mexican	689	0.5	5.4
Guatemalan	161	0.1	1.3
Honduran	255	0.2	2.0
Salvadoran	162	0.1	1.3
Cuban	143	0.1	1.1
Mexican	9,995	7.9	78.1
Puerto Rican	441	0.4	3.4
South American	536	0.4	4.2
Colombian	166	0.1	1.3
Peruvian	115	0.1	0.9
Spaniard	155	0.1	1.2

Population Growth: 2000–2010

Group	%
Total Population	35.4
Hispanic or Latino (of any race)	152.8
Central American, ex. Mexican	422.0
Mexican	153.6
Puerto Rican	170.6
South American	224.8

Males per 100 Females

Group	Number
Total Population	98.2
Hispanic or Latino (of any race)	113.3
Central American, ex. Mexican	113.3
Guatemalan	101.3
Honduran	136.1
Salvadoran	121.9

Notes: (1) Percent of total population; (2) Percent of Hispanic/Latino population; Profiles include places with an overall population of at least 125,000, OR an overall population of at least 25,000 where the Hispanic/Latino population is at least 20% of the overall population. In states where less than five places meet either of these criteria, we have included places with at least 10,000 total population with the highest percentage of Hispanic/Latino population. These places are identified with an asterisk (*); Please refer to the User's Guide for a full explanation of data.

Group	People
Cuban	88.2
Mexican	115.9
Puerto Rican	112.0
South American	90.1
Colombian	76.6
Peruvian	85.5
Spaniard	118.3

Average Household Size

Group	People
Total Population	2.80
Hispanic or Latino (of any race)	3.74
Central American, ex. Mexican	3.48
Guatemalan	3.39
Honduran	3.65
Salvadoran	3.65
Cuban	3.26
Mexican	3.89
Puerto Rican	3.17
South American	3.18
Colombian	2.98
Peruvian	3.56
Spaniard	3.00

Median Age

Group	Years
Total Population	32.9
Hispanic or Latino (of any race)	24.3
Central American, ex. Mexican	27.1
Guatemalan	24.3
Honduran	26.1
Salvadoran	29.0
Cuban	27.3
Mexican	23.6
Puerto Rican	23.1
South American	33.3
Colombian	33.7
Peruvian	35.3
Spaniard	29.6

High School Graduates
(Universe: Population 25 Years and Over)

Group	Number	%
Total Population	70,226	94.0
Hispanic or Latino (of any race)	4,126	67.5
Mexican	2,787	60.8

Four-Year College Graduates
(Universe: Population 25 Years and Over)

Group	Number	%
Total Population	33,592	45.0
Hispanic or Latino (of any race)	1,252	20.5
Mexican	592	12.9

Population Age 3–17 Enrolled in Public School
(Universe: Population Age 3–17 Enrolled in School)

Group	Number	%
Total Population	23,071	85.6
Hispanic or Latino (of any race)	2,987	90.4
Mexican	2,428	93.6

Population Age 3–17 Enrolled in Private School
(Universe: Population Age 3–17 Enrolled in School)

Group	Number	%
Total Population	3,883	14.4
Hispanic or Latino (of any race)	319	9.6
Mexican	167	6.4

Foreign-Born Population

Group	Number	%
Total Population	11,450	9.5
Hispanic or Latino (of any race)	5,199	43.3
Mexican	4,139	44.0

Foreign-Born Naturalized U.S. Citizens

Group	Number	%
Total Population	3,549	31.0
Hispanic or Latino (of any race)	833	16.0
Mexican	521	12.6

Language Spoken at Home: English Only
(Universe: Population 5 Years and Over)

Group	Number	%
Total Population	94,944	86.5
Hispanic or Latino (of any race)	3,649	35.2
Mexican	2,728	34.1

Language Spoken at Home: Spanish
(Universe: Population 5 Years and Over)

Group	Number	%
Total Population	7,984	7.3
Hispanic or Latino (of any race)	6,708	64.6
Mexican	5,272	65.9

Unemployment Rate
(Universe: Population 16 Years and Over)

Group	%
Total Population	4.7
Hispanic or Latino (of any race)	7.8
Mexican	9.2

Class of Worker: Private Wage and Salary
(Universe: Civilian Employed Population 16 Years and Over)

Group	Number	%
Total Population	54,795	82.6
Hispanic or Latino (of any race)	5,322	91.1
Mexican	3,970	90.9

Class of Worker: Government
(Universe: Civilian Employed Population 16 Years and Over)

Group	Number	%
Total Population	8,126	12.3
Hispanic or Latino (of any race)	236	4.0
Mexican	202	4.6

Means of Transportation to Work: Car, Truck or Van
(Universe: Workers 16 Years and Over)

Group	Number	%
Total Population	59,072	91.7
Hispanic or Latino (of any race)	5,380	94.4
Mexican	4,001	93.5

Means of Transportation to Work: Public Transportation (ex. Taxicab)
(Universe: Workers 16 Years and Over)

Group	Number	%
Total Population	317	0.5
Hispanic or Latino (of any race)	21	0.4
Mexican	21	0.5

Homeownership Rate
(Universe: Occupied Housing Units)

Group	%
Total Population	72.7
Hispanic or Latino (of any race)	43.0
Central American, ex. Mexican	42.2
Guatemalan	52.3
Honduran	21.7
Salvadoran	37.5
Cuban	71.8
Mexican	39.5
Puerto Rican	55.9
South American	69.4
Colombian	67.4
Peruvian	59.4
Spaniard	77.4

Median Home Value

Group	Dollars
Total Population	193,300
Hispanic or Latino (of any race)	172,100
Mexican	164,500

Median Gross Rent

Group	Dollars
Total Population	801
Hispanic or Latino (of any race)	782
Mexican	765

Median Household Income
(2010 Inflation-Adjusted Dollars)

Group	Dollars
Total Population	75,228
Hispanic or Latino (of any race)	55,574
Mexican	54,681

Per Capita Income
(2010 Inflation-Adjusted Dollars)

Group	Dollars
Total Population	30,966
Hispanic or Latino (of any race)	15,455
Mexican	14,175

Households with $100,000+ Income

Group	Number	%
Total Population	13,605	31.8
Hispanic or Latino (of any race)	522	17.7
Mexican	383	16.9

Households with Food Stamps/SNAP Benefits During Past 12 Months

Group	Number	%
Total Population	1,592	3.7
Hispanic or Latino (of any race)	262	8.9
Mexican	205	9.1

Poverty Rate
(Income in Past 12 Months Below Poverty Level)

Group	%
Total Population	5.9
Hispanic or Latino (of any race)	15.4
Mexican	16.0

Overland Park

Population

Group	Number	%TP[1]	%HP[2]
Total Population	173,372	100.0	–
Hispanic or Latino (of any race)	10,911	6.3	100.0
Central American, ex. Mexican	749	0.4	6.9
Guatemalan	326	0.2	3.0
Honduran	156	0.1	1.4
Salvadoran	165	0.1	1.5
Cuban	244	0.1	2.2
Mexican	7,682	4.4	70.4
Puerto Rican	390	0.2	3.6
South American	960	0.6	8.8
Argentinean	120	0.1	1.1
Colombian	310	0.2	2.8
Peruvian	197	0.1	1.8
Spaniard	236	0.1	2.2

Population Growth: 2000–2010

Group	%
Total Population	16.3
Hispanic or Latino (of any race)	94.1
Central American, ex. Mexican	340.6
Cuban	51.6
Mexican	99.5
Puerto Rican	110.8
South American	143.7
Colombian	156.2

Males per 100 Females

Group	Number
Total Population	93.4
Hispanic or Latino (of any race)	103.6
Central American, ex. Mexican	108.1
Guatemalan	110.3
Honduran	140.0
Salvadoran	98.8
Cuban	117.9
Mexican	107.8
Puerto Rican	90.2
South American	74.2
Argentinean	100.0
Colombian	66.7
Peruvian	71.3
Spaniard	84.4

Average Household Size

Group	People
Total Population	2.41
Hispanic or Latino (of any race)	3.09
Central American, ex. Mexican	3.30
Guatemalan	3.16
Honduran	3.92
Salvadoran	3.59
Cuban	2.79
Mexican	3.19
Puerto Rican	2.45
South American	2.88
Argentinean	2.81
Colombian	2.87
Peruvian	3.18
Spaniard	2.51

STATE & PLACE PROFILES

Notes: (1) Percent of total population; (2) Percent of Hispanic/Latino population; Profiles include places with an overall population of at least 125,000, OR an overall population of at least 25,000 where the Hispanic/Latino population is at least 20% of the overall population. In states where less than five places meet either of these criteria, we have included places with at least 10,000 total population with the highest percentage of Hispanic/Latino population. These places are identified with an asterisk (*); Please refer to the User's Guide for a full explanation of data.

Median Age

Group	Years
Total Population	37.8
Hispanic or Latino (of any race)	26.1
Central American, ex. Mexican	26.5
Guatemalan	24.7
Honduran	26.8
Salvadoran	29.1
Cuban	32.0
Mexican	25.3
Puerto Rican	25.8
South American	32.7
Argentinean	35.5
Colombian	33.0
Peruvian	32.6
Spaniard	32.0

High School Graduates
(Universe: Population 25 Years and Over)

Group	Number	%
Total Population	111,843	96.5
Hispanic or Latino (of any race)	3,549	83.5
Mexican	2,278	80.5
South American	564	98.1

Four-Year College Graduates
(Universe: Population 25 Years and Over)

Group	Number	%
Total Population	65,354	56.4
Hispanic or Latino (of any race)	1,554	36.6
Mexican	878	31.0
South American	394	68.5

Population Age 3–17 Enrolled in Public School
(Universe: Population Age 3–17 Enrolled in School)

Group	Number	%
Total Population	26,033	78.0
Hispanic or Latino (of any race)	1,702	83.3
Mexican	1,361	88.5
South American	92	49.5

Population Age 3–17 Enrolled in Private School
(Universe: Population Age 3–17 Enrolled in School)

Group	Number	%
Total Population	7,333	22.0
Hispanic or Latino (of any race)	340	16.7
Mexican	177	11.5
South American	94	50.5

Foreign-Born Population

Group	Number	%
Total Population	14,893	8.7
Hispanic or Latino (of any race)	2,592	31.9
Mexican	1,527	26.0
South American	486	60.0

Foreign-Born Naturalized U.S. Citizens

Group	Number	%
Total Population	6,437	43.2
Hispanic or Latino (of any race)	789	30.4
Mexican	346	22.7
South American	273	56.2

Language Spoken at Home: English Only
(Universe: Population 5 Years and Over)

Group	Number	%
Total Population	140,727	88.1
Hispanic or Latino (of any race)	3,338	47.3
Mexican	2,387	47.9
South American	296	38.9

Language Spoken at Home: Spanish
(Universe: Population 5 Years and Over)

Group	Number	%
Total Population	5,503	3.4
Hispanic or Latino (of any race)	3,695	52.4
Mexican	2,600	52.1
South American	444	58.3

Unemployment Rate
(Universe: Population 16 Years and Over)

Group	%
Total Population	4.9
Hispanic or Latino (of any race)	3.8
Mexican	4.4
South American	2.2

Class of Worker: Private Wage and Salary
(Universe: Civilian Employed Population 16 Years and Over)

Group	Number	%
Total Population	77,794	83.9
Hispanic or Latino (of any race)	3,480	85.3
Mexican	2,334	84.8
South American	433	88.5

Class of Worker: Government
(Universe: Civilian Employed Population 16 Years and Over)

Group	Number	%
Total Population	9,495	10.2
Hispanic or Latino (of any race)	398	9.8
Mexican	296	10.8
South American	23	4.7

Means of Transportation to Work: Car, Truck or Van
(Universe: Workers 16 Years and Over)

Group	Number	%
Total Population	83,379	91.6
Hispanic or Latino (of any race)	3,815	94.9
Mexican	2,556	94.5
South American	462	97.3

Means of Transportation to Work: Public Transportation (ex. Taxicab)
(Universe: Workers 16 Years and Over)

Group	Number	%
Total Population	534	0.6
Hispanic or Latino (of any race)	0	0.0
Mexican	0	0.0
South American	0	0.0

Homeownership Rate
(Universe: Occupied Housing Units)

Group	%
Total Population	65.2
Hispanic or Latino (of any race)	37.2
Central American, ex. Mexican	31.1
Guatemalan	19.2
Honduran	25.0
Salvadoran	37.0
Cuban	75.3
Mexican	33.5
Puerto Rican	33.3
South American	53.0
Argentinean	64.3
Colombian	51.7
Peruvian	54.8
Spaniard	63.2

Median Home Value

Group	Dollars
Total Population	222,700
Hispanic or Latino (of any race)	191,700
Mexican	178,200
South American	218,900

Median Gross Rent

Group	Dollars
Total Population	893
Hispanic or Latino (of any race)	857
Mexican	873
South American	888

Median Household Income
(2010 Inflation-Adjusted Dollars)

Group	Dollars
Total Population	71,513
Hispanic or Latino (of any race)	52,446
Mexican	51,114
South American	46,131

Per Capita Income
(2010 Inflation-Adjusted Dollars)

Group	Dollars
Total Population	39,319
Hispanic or Latino (of any race)	20,882
Mexican	17,795
South American	31,995

Households with $100,000+ Income

Group	Number	%
Total Population	23,581	33.0
Hispanic or Latino (of any race)	505	18.2
Mexican	269	14.4
South American	93	26.6

Households with Food Stamps/SNAP Benefits During Past 12 Months

Group	Number	%
Total Population	1,865	2.6
Hispanic or Latino (of any race)	265	9.5
Mexican	196	10.5
South American	28	8.0

Poverty Rate
(Income in Past 12 Months Below Poverty Level)

Group	%
Total Population	4.9
Hispanic or Latino (of any race)	14.4
Mexican	16.9
South American	2.8

Topeka

Population

Group	Number	%TP[1]	%HP[2]
Total Population	127,473	100.0	–
Hispanic or Latino (of any race)	17,026	13.4	100.0
Central American, ex. Mexican	286	0.2	1.7
Guatemalan	106	0.1	0.6
Mexican	14,803	11.6	86.9
Puerto Rican	790	0.6	4.6
South American	213	0.2	1.3
Spaniard	114	0.1	0.7

Population Growth: 2000–2010

Group	%
Total Population	4.2
Hispanic or Latino (of any race)	57.0
Mexican	67.8
Puerto Rican	63.9

Males per 100 Females

Group	Number
Total Population	91.6
Hispanic or Latino (of any race)	101.8
Central American, ex. Mexican	127.0
Guatemalan	186.5
Mexican	101.4
Puerto Rican	110.1
South American	85.2
Spaniard	96.6

Average Household Size

Group	People
Total Population	2.29
Hispanic or Latino (of any race)	3.19
Central American, ex. Mexican	3.54
Guatemalan	4.25
Mexican	3.24
Puerto Rican	2.87
South American	2.66
Spaniard	2.73

Median Age

Group	Years
Total Population	36.0
Hispanic or Latino (of any race)	23.4
Central American, ex. Mexican	25.8
Guatemalan	23.3
Mexican	23.2
Puerto Rican	20.9
South American	29.9
Spaniard	33.5

High School Graduates
(Universe: Population 25 Years and Over)

Group	Number	%
Total Population	72,693	88.0
Hispanic or Latino (of any race)	4,659	60.9
Mexican	3,966	58.5

Notes: (1) Percent of total population; (2) Percent of Hispanic/Latino population; Profiles include places with an overall population of at least 125,000, OR an overall population of at least 25,000 where the Hispanic/Latino population is at least 20% of the overall population. In states where less than five places meet either of these criteria, we have included places with at least 10,000 total population with the highest percentage of Hispanic/Latino population. These places are identified with an asterisk (*); Please refer to the User's Guide for a full explanation of data.

Four-Year College Graduates
(Universe: Population 25 Years and Over)

Group	Number	%
Total Population	22,518	27.3
Hispanic or Latino (of any race)	807	10.6
Mexican	670	9.9

Population Age 3–17 Enrolled in Public School
(Universe: Population Age 3–17 Enrolled in School)

Group	Number	%
Total Population	19,358	87.6
Hispanic or Latino (of any race)	4,471	94.3
Mexican	3,940	94.0

Population Age 3–17 Enrolled in Private School
(Universe: Population Age 3–17 Enrolled in School)

Group	Number	%
Total Population	2,749	12.4
Hispanic or Latino (of any race)	271	5.7
Mexican	252	6.0

Foreign-Born Population

Group	Number	%
Total Population	6,781	5.4
Hispanic or Latino (of any race)	4,344	26.7
Mexican	3,914	27.2

Foreign-Born Naturalized U.S. Citizens

Group	Number	%
Total Population	1,813	26.7
Hispanic or Latino (of any race)	723	16.6
Mexican	604	15.4

Language Spoken at Home: English Only
(Universe: Population 5 Years and Over)

Group	Number	%
Total Population	104,649	89.6
Hispanic or Latino (of any race)	5,943	42.4
Mexican	5,231	42.1

Language Spoken at Home: Spanish
(Universe: Population 5 Years and Over)

Group	Number	%
Total Population	9,335	8.0
Hispanic or Latino (of any race)	8,066	57.5
Mexican	7,180	57.8

Unemployment Rate
(Universe: Population 16 Years and Over)

Group	%
Total Population	8.2
Hispanic or Latino (of any race)	9.4
Mexican	9.4

Class of Worker: Private Wage and Salary
(Universe: Civilian Employed Population 16 Years and Over)

Group	Number	%
Total Population	44,998	74.8
Hispanic or Latino (of any race)	5,563	83.2
Mexican	4,957	83.3

Class of Worker: Government
(Universe: Civilian Employed Population 16 Years and Over)

Group	Number	%
Total Population	12,231	20.3
Hispanic or Latino (of any race)	796	11.9
Mexican	686	11.5

Means of Transportation to Work: Car, Truck or Van
(Universe: Workers 16 Years and Over)

Group	Number	%
Total Population	54,993	92.8
Hispanic or Latino (of any race)	6,009	92.1
Mexican	5,289	92.0

Means of Transportation to Work: Public Transportation (ex. Taxicab)
(Universe: Workers 16 Years and Over)

Group	Number	%
Total Population	886	1.5
Hispanic or Latino (of any race)	131	2.0
Mexican	117	2.0

Homeownership Rate
(Universe: Occupied Housing Units)

Group	%
Total Population	58.3
Hispanic or Latino (of any race)	51.3
Central American, ex. Mexican	47.4
Guatemalan	46.4
Mexican	52.4
Puerto Rican	38.2
South American	54.3
Spaniard	64.4

Median Home Value

Group	Dollars
Total Population	94,200
Hispanic or Latino (of any race)	74,300
Mexican	72,400

Median Gross Rent

Group	Dollars
Total Population	628
Hispanic or Latino (of any race)	636
Mexican	616

Median Household Income
(2010 Inflation-Adjusted Dollars)

Group	Dollars
Total Population	40,342
Hispanic or Latino (of any race)	29,714
Mexican	28,738

Per Capita Income
(2010 Inflation-Adjusted Dollars)

Group	Dollars
Total Population	23,524
Hispanic or Latino (of any race)	12,176
Mexican	11,764

Households with $100,000+ Income

Group	Number	%
Total Population	6,639	12.2
Hispanic or Latino (of any race)	267	5.7
Mexican	211	5.1

Households with Food Stamps/SNAP Benefits During Past 12 Months

Group	Number	%
Total Population	6,485	11.9
Hispanic or Latino (of any race)	910	19.4
Mexican	819	19.8

Poverty Rate
(Income in Past 12 Months Below Poverty Level)

Group	%
Total Population	18.8
Hispanic or Latino (of any race)	36.6
Mexican	37.2

Wichita

Population

Group	Number	%TP[1]	%HP[2]
Total Population	382,368	100.0	–
Hispanic or Latino (of any race)	58,348	15.3	100.0
Central American, ex. Mexican	2,277	0.6	3.9
Guatemalan	435	0.1	0.7
Honduran	467	0.1	0.8
Nicaraguan	146	<0.1	0.3
Panamanian	128	<0.1	0.2
Salvadoran	1,021	0.3	1.7
Cuban	422	0.1	0.7
Mexican	49,700	13.0	85.2
Puerto Rican	1,553	0.4	2.7
South American	944	0.2	1.6
Colombian	252	0.1	0.4
Peruvian	219	0.1	0.4
Venezuelan	112	<0.1	0.2
Spaniard	498	0.1	0.9

Population Growth: 2000–2010

Group	%
Total Population	11.1
Hispanic or Latino (of any race)	76.2
Central American, ex. Mexican	282.7
Honduran	299.1
Salvadoran	338.2
Cuban	66.8
Mexican	84.4
Puerto Rican	89.2
South American	107.9
Colombian	103.2

Males per 100 Females

Group	Number
Total Population	97.3
Hispanic or Latino (of any race)	105.7
Central American, ex. Mexican	105.3
Guatemalan	118.6
Honduran	120.3
Nicaraguan	69.8
Panamanian	73.0
Salvadoran	104.6
Cuban	107.9
Mexican	106.5
Puerto Rican	100.1
South American	94.6
Colombian	88.1
Peruvian	99.1
Venezuelan	80.6
Spaniard	95.3

Average Household Size

Group	People
Total Population	2.48
Hispanic or Latino (of any race)	3.50
Central American, ex. Mexican	3.63
Guatemalan	3.99
Honduran	3.62
Nicaraguan	3.67
Panamanian	2.86
Salvadoran	3.68
Cuban	2.63
Mexican	3.57
Puerto Rican	3.00
South American	2.68
Colombian	2.63
Peruvian	2.58
Venezuelan	2.80
Spaniard	2.77

Median Age

Group	Years
Total Population	33.9
Hispanic or Latino (of any race)	22.6
Central American, ex. Mexican	28.3
Guatemalan	25.8
Honduran	28.0
Nicaraguan	29.5
Panamanian	28.2
Salvadoran	30.1
Cuban	27.5
Mexican	22.1
Puerto Rican	22.2
South American	31.6
Colombian	30.3
Peruvian	35.4
Venezuelan	33.7
Spaniard	27.7

High School Graduates
(Universe: Population 25 Years and Over)

Group	Number	%
Total Population	204,273	86.3
Hispanic or Latino (of any race)	13,663	56.7
Central American, ex. Mexican	657	57.6
Salvadoran	254	56.3
Mexican	11,201	53.9
Puerto Rican	397	78.3

Four-Year College Graduates
(Universe: Population 25 Years and Over)

Group	Number	%
Total Population	65,249	27.6
Hispanic or Latino (of any race)	2,444	10.1
Central American, ex. Mexican	101	8.9
Salvadoran	20	4.4
Mexican	1,755	8.4
Puerto Rican	65	12.8

Notes: (1) Percent of total population; (2) Percent of Hispanic/Latino population; Profiles include places with an overall population of at least 125,000, OR an overall population of at least 25,000 where the Hispanic/Latino population is at least 20% of the overall population. In states where less than five places meet either of these criteria, we have included places with at least 10,000 total population with the highest percentage of Hispanic/Latino population. These places are identified with an asterisk (*); Please refer to the User's Guide for a full explanation of data.

Population Age 3–17 Enrolled in Public School
(Universe: Population Age 3–17 Enrolled in School)

Group	Number	%
Total Population	60,363	83.9
Hispanic or Latino (of any race)	14,065	93.1
Central American, ex. Mexican	606	100.0
Salvadoran	161	100.0
Mexican	12,261	93.3
Puerto Rican	277	85.0

Population Age 3–17 Enrolled in Private School
(Universe: Population Age 3–17 Enrolled in School)

Group	Number	%
Total Population	11,585	16.1
Hispanic or Latino (of any race)	1,039	6.9
Central American, ex. Mexican	0	0.0
Salvadoran	0	0.0
Mexican	882	6.7
Puerto Rican	49	15.0

Foreign-Born Population

Group	Number	%
Total Population	34,405	9.2
Hispanic or Latino (of any race)	17,242	33.1
Central American, ex. Mexican	1,548	66.2
Salvadoran	632	63.3
Mexican	14,678	32.3
Puerto Rican	0	0.0

Foreign-Born Naturalized U.S. Citizens

Group	Number	%
Total Population	13,409	39.0
Hispanic or Latino (of any race)	4,010	23.3
Central American, ex. Mexican	355	22.9
Salvadoran	175	27.7
Mexican	3,232	22.0
Puerto Rican	0	0.0

Language Spoken at Home: English Only
(Universe: Population 5 Years and Over)

Group	Number	%
Total Population	291,910	84.8
Hispanic or Latino (of any race)	14,769	32.8
Central American, ex. Mexican	283	13.4
Salvadoran	55	6.2
Mexican	12,617	32.5
Puerto Rican	623	68.7

Language Spoken at Home: Spanish
(Universe: Population 5 Years and Over)

Group	Number	%
Total Population	33,338	9.7
Hispanic or Latino (of any race)	30,052	66.8
Central American, ex. Mexican	1,826	86.6
Salvadoran	828	93.8
Mexican	26,169	67.3
Puerto Rican	284	31.3

Unemployment Rate
(Universe: Population 16 Years and Over)

Group	%
Total Population	8.4
Hispanic or Latino (of any race)	9.7
Central American, ex. Mexican	8.5
Salvadoran	12.7
Mexican	9.1
Puerto Rican	28.4

Class of Worker: Private Wage and Salary
(Universe: Civilian Employed Population 16 Years and Over)

Group	Number	%
Total Population	148,538	82.2
Hispanic or Latino (of any race)	19,516	88.6
Central American, ex. Mexican	1,047	90.4
Salvadoran	436	81.0
Mexican	16,944	89.3
Puerto Rican	305	88.2

Class of Worker: Government
(Universe: Civilian Employed Population 16 Years and Over)

Group	Number	%
Total Population	22,229	12.3
Hispanic or Latino (of any race)	1,737	7.9
Central American, ex. Mexican	63	5.4
Salvadoran	54	10.0
Mexican	1,392	7.3
Puerto Rican	41	11.8

Means of Transportation to Work: Car, Truck or Van
(Universe: Workers 16 Years and Over)

Group	Number	%
Total Population	167,072	93.8
Hispanic or Latino (of any race)	20,526	95.3
Central American, ex. Mexican	1,045	96.9
Salvadoran	503	95.8
Mexican	17,671	95.0
Puerto Rican	335	96.8

Means of Transportation to Work: Public Transportation (ex. Taxicab)
(Universe: Workers 16 Years and Over)

Group	Number	%
Total Population	1,612	0.9
Hispanic or Latino (of any race)	217	1.0
Central American, ex. Mexican	23	2.1
Salvadoran	12	2.3
Mexican	194	1.0
Puerto Rican	0	0.0

Homeownership Rate
(Universe: Occupied Housing Units)

Group	%
Total Population	61.3
Hispanic or Latino (of any race)	49.8
Central American, ex. Mexican	53.4
Guatemalan	43.8
Honduran	43.9
Nicaraguan	51.1
Panamanian	58.1
Salvadoran	60.6
Cuban	56.0
Mexican	49.9
Puerto Rican	41.7
South American	61.3
Colombian	60.2
Peruvian	64.4
Venezuelan	57.5
Spaniard	58.8

Median Home Value

Group	Dollars
Total Population	111,300
Hispanic or Latino (of any race)	84,100
Central American, ex. Mexican	66,100
Salvadoran	76,900
Mexican	81,900
Puerto Rican	108,300

Median Gross Rent

Group	Dollars
Total Population	629
Hispanic or Latino (of any race)	609
Central American, ex. Mexican	697
Salvadoran	831
Mexican	606
Puerto Rican	555

Median Household Income
(2010 Inflation-Adjusted Dollars)

Group	Dollars
Total Population	44,360
Hispanic or Latino (of any race)	34,547
Central American, ex. Mexican	35,234
Salvadoran	36,510
Mexican	34,146
Puerto Rican	25,625

Per Capita Income
(2010 Inflation-Adjusted Dollars)

Group	Dollars
Total Population	24,715
Hispanic or Latino (of any race)	13,189
Central American, ex. Mexican	12,370
Salvadoran	12,579
Mexican	12,803
Puerto Rican	18,330

Households with $100,000+ Income

Group	Number	%
Total Population	23,342	15.5
Hispanic or Latino (of any race)	924	6.4
Central American, ex. Mexican	0	0.0
Salvadoran	0	0.0
Mexican	746	6.0
Puerto Rican	68	19.4

Households with Food Stamps/SNAP Benefits During Past 12 Months

Group	Number	%
Total Population	17,286	11.5
Hispanic or Latino (of any race)	2,479	17.1
Central American, ex. Mexican	84	13.1
Salvadoran	67	29.4
Mexican	2,130	17.1
Puerto Rican	96	27.4

Poverty Rate
(Income in Past 12 Months Below Poverty Level)

Group	%
Total Population	15.6
Hispanic or Latino (of any race)	26.9
Central American, ex. Mexican	22.4
Salvadoran	8.6
Mexican	27.5
Puerto Rican	21.3

Notes: (1) Percent of total population; (2) Percent of Hispanic/Latino population; Profiles include places with an overall population of at least 125,000, OR an overall population of at least 25,000 where the Hispanic/Latino population is at least 20% of the overall population. In states where less than five places meet either of these criteria, we have included places with at least 10,000 total population with the highest percentage of Hispanic/Latino population. These places are identified with an asterisk (*); Please refer to the User's Guide for a full explanation of data.

Kentucky

EDITOR'S NOTE: For a place to be included in this edition, it must meet one of two criteria. Either its overall population is at least 125,000, OR its overall population is at least 25,000 and its Hispanic/Latino population is at least 20% of the overall population. In Kentucky, less than five places meet either of these criteria. In an effort to include at least five places for each state, we have included places with at least 10,000 total population with the highest percentage of Hispanic/Latino population. These places are identified with an asterisk (*). For the state of Kentucky, the following locations are included:

Fort Campbell North*
Lexington-Fayette
Louisville-Jefferson County
Mayfield*
Shelbyville*

Section Two: State & Place Profiles starts with the state profile, followed by place profiles that meet the criteria above. Places are listed alphabetically within each state. All states, all counties and places that meet the above criteria are ranked and compared in *Section Three: Rankings & Comparisons*, on page 1055.

For a more detailed look at the Hispanic/Latino population in Kentucky, a companion web site is available at no additional charge with purchase of this print edition. Visit http://gold.greyhouse.com/page/info_hispanic for more information.

The web site includes data for all counties and places in Kentucky with Hispanic/Latino population, plus ten additional topics: Self Employed Worker; Walked to Work; Worked from Home; Mean Travel Time to Work; Mean Household Income; Households with Cash Public Assistance; Mean Cash Pubic Assistance; Poverty Rates for 18 and Under, 18 to 64, and 65 and Over.

Population

Group	Number	%TP[1]	%HP[2]
Total Population	4,339,367	100.0	–
Hispanic or Latino (of any race)	132,836	3.1	100.0
Central American, ex. Mexican	11,479	0.3	8.6
Costa Rican	253	<0.1	0.2
Guatemalan	5,231	0.1	3.9
Honduran	2,012	<0.1	1.5
Nicaraguan	526	<0.1	0.4
Panamanian	1,019	<0.1	0.8
Salvadoran	2,351	0.1	1.8
Cuban	9,323	0.2	7.0
Dominican Republic	1,065	<0.1	0.8
Mexican	82,110	1.9	61.8
Puerto Rican	11,454	0.3	8.6
South American	5,405	0.1	4.1
Argentinean	481	<0.1	0.4
Bolivian	227	<0.1	0.2
Chilean	332	<0.1	0.2
Colombian	1,729	<0.1	1.3
Ecuadorian	615	<0.1	0.5
Peruvian	1,174	<0.1	0.9
Venezuelan	637	<0.1	0.5
Spaniard	1,620	<0.1	1.2

Population Growth: 2000–2010

Group	%
Total Population	7.4
Hispanic or Latino (of any race)	121.6
Central American, ex. Mexican	268.4
Costa Rican	114.4
Guatemalan	379.9
Honduran	320.9
Nicaraguan	267.8
Panamanian	77.8
Salvadoran	263.9
Cuban	165.2
Dominican Republic	243.5
Mexican	161.6
Puerto Rican	77.1
South American	180.6
Argentinean	193.3
Bolivian	118.3
Chilean	179.0
Colombian	194.5
Ecuadorian	210.6
Peruvian	237.4
Venezuelan	141.3
Spaniard	694.1

Males per 100 Females

Group	Number
Total Population	96.8
Hispanic or Latino (of any race)	126.9
Central American, ex. Mexican	134.1
Costa Rican	102.4
Guatemalan	158.1
Honduran	148.1
Nicaraguan	93.4
Panamanian	74.8
Salvadoran	125.8
Cuban	111.9
Dominican Republic	101.7
Mexican	135.5
Puerto Rican	108.6
South American	89.4
Argentinean	103.0
Bolivian	97.4
Chilean	90.8
Colombian	83.5
Ecuadorian	85.2
Peruvian	93.1
Venezuelan	88.5
Spaniard	100.0

Average Household Size

Group	People
Total Population	2.45
Hispanic or Latino (of any race)	3.29
Central American, ex. Mexican	3.67
Costa Rican	2.50
Guatemalan	4.20
Honduran	3.51
Nicaraguan	2.94
Panamanian	2.62
Salvadoran	3.69
Cuban	2.90
Dominican Republic	3.27
Mexican	3.53
Puerto Rican	2.87
South American	2.76
Argentinean	2.70
Bolivian	2.72
Chilean	2.44
Colombian	2.73
Ecuadorian	2.99
Peruvian	2.90
Venezuelan	2.61
Spaniard	2.60

Median Age

Group	Years
Total Population	38.1
Hispanic or Latino (of any race)	24.6
Central American, ex. Mexican	25.2
Costa Rican	27.7
Guatemalan	23.3
Honduran	27.0
Nicaraguan	28.1
Panamanian	29.8
Salvadoran	27.1
Cuban	34.3
Dominican Republic	25.1
Mexican	23.2
Puerto Rican	23.7
South American	31.7
Argentinean	35.9
Bolivian	32.9
Chilean	31.1
Colombian	30.6
Ecuadorian	30.0
Peruvian	32.3
Venezuelan	32.2
Spaniard	31.8

High School Graduates
(Universe: Population 25 Years and Over)

Group	Number	%
Total Population	2,312,214	81.0
Hispanic or Latino (of any race)	36,237	63.4
Central American, ex. Mexican	2,464	51.3
Guatemalan	565	37.8
Honduran	391	44.4
Panamanian	727	94.3
Salvadoran	489	38.4
Cuban	4,233	82.7
Mexican	19,567	55.3
Puerto Rican	4,297	87.3
South American	2,523	91.1
Colombian	524	84.5
Peruvian	624	98.0
Spaniard	983	85.3

Four-Year College Graduates
(Universe: Population 25 Years and Over)

Group	Number	%
Total Population	580,971	20.3
Hispanic or Latino (of any race)	8,259	14.5
Central American, ex. Mexican	704	14.6
Guatemalan	226	15.1
Honduran	125	14.2
Panamanian	225	29.2
Salvadoran	54	4.2
Cuban	1,206	23.6
Mexican	3,036	8.6
Puerto Rican	1,099	22.3
South American	1,278	46.1
Colombian	312	50.3
Peruvian	173	27.2
Spaniard	440	38.2

Population Age 3–17 Enrolled in Public School
(Universe: Population Age 3–17 Enrolled in School)

Group	Number	%
Total Population	663,282	86.6
Hispanic or Latino (of any race)	26,697	92.3
Central American, ex. Mexican	2,932	88.8
Guatemalan	1,344	83.4
Honduran	408	96.2
Panamanian	98	57.6
Salvadoran	765	100.0
Cuban	1,594	93.6
Mexican	16,943	94.7
Puerto Rican	2,911	92.0
South American	818	72.6
Colombian	203	55.9
Peruvian	123	76.9
Spaniard	183	100.0

Population Age 3–17 Enrolled in Private School
(Universe: Population Age 3–17 Enrolled in School)

Group	Number	%
Total Population	102,236	13.4
Hispanic or Latino (of any race)	2,212	7.7
Central American, ex. Mexican	369	11.2
Guatemalan	268	16.6
Honduran	16	3.8
Panamanian	72	42.4
Salvadoran	0	0.0
Cuban	109	6.4
Mexican	944	5.3
Puerto Rican	252	8.0
South American	308	27.4
Colombian	160	44.1
Peruvian	37	23.1
Spaniard	0	0.0

Notes: (1) Percent of total population; (2) Percent of Hispanic/Latino population; Profiles include places with an overall population of at least 125,000, OR an overall population of at least 25,000 where the Hispanic/Latino population is at least 20% of the overall population. In states where less than five places meet either of these criteria, we have included places with at least 10,000 total population with the highest percentage of Hispanic/Latino population. These places are identified with an asterisk (*); Please refer to the User's Guide for a full explanation of data.

Foreign-Born Population

Group	Number	%
Total Population	130,794	3.1
Hispanic or Latino (of any race)	52,066	44.4
Central American, ex. Mexican	6,169	56.7
Guatemalan	3,063	64.9
Honduran	1,044	59.1
Panamanian	493	44.9
Salvadoran	1,266	52.0
Cuban	5,599	68.5
Mexican	35,735	47.5
Puerto Rican	57	0.6
South American	3,047	61.3
Colombian	594	45.4
Peruvian	692	60.8
Spaniard	472	29.2

Foreign-Born Naturalized U.S. Citizens

Group	Number	%
Total Population	43,223	33.0
Hispanic or Latino (of any race)	8,568	16.5
Central American, ex. Mexican	1,597	25.9
Guatemalan	767	25.0
Honduran	135	12.9
Panamanian	379	76.9
Salvadoran	207	16.4
Cuban	1,087	19.4
Mexican	4,273	12.0
Puerto Rican	22	38.6
South American	1,112	36.5
Colombian	259	43.6
Peruvian	330	47.7
Spaniard	76	16.1

Language Spoken at Home: English Only
(Universe: Population 5 Years and Over)

Group	Number	%
Total Population	3,822,840	95.4
Hispanic or Latino (of any race)	34,413	34.2
Central American, ex. Mexican	2,234	25.1
Guatemalan	772	22.7
Honduran	369	25.0
Panamanian	370	35.0
Salvadoran	339	15.7
Cuban	1,709	23.0
Mexican	19,136	30.1
Puerto Rican	5,137	56.6
South American	1,442	31.6
Colombian	422	36.6
Peruvian	226	23.7
Spaniard	923	59.2

Language Spoken at Home: Spanish
(Universe: Population 5 Years and Over)

Group	Number	%
Total Population	96,868	2.4
Hispanic or Latino (of any race)	65,770	65.5
Central American, ex. Mexican	6,597	74.2
Guatemalan	2,576	75.6
Honduran	1,109	75.0
Panamanian	688	65.0
Salvadoran	1,814	84.1
Cuban	5,732	77.0
Mexican	44,303	69.7
Puerto Rican	3,910	43.1
South American	3,098	68.0
Colombian	731	63.4
Peruvian	729	76.3
Spaniard	612	39.2

Unemployment Rate
(Universe: Population 16 Years and Over)

Group	%
Total Population	8.2
Hispanic or Latino (of any race)	9.7
Central American, ex. Mexican	9.9
Guatemalan	10.9
Honduran	8.4
Panamanian	9.0
Salvadoran	11.1
Cuban	19.4
Mexican	8.0
Puerto Rican	13.3
South American	7.3
Colombian	21.5
Peruvian	3.9
Spaniard	16.6

Class of Worker: Private Wage and Salary
(Universe: Civilian Employed Population 16 Years and Over)

Group	Number	%
Total Population	1,466,073	78.3
Hispanic or Latino (of any race)	43,300	88.9
Central American, ex. Mexican	3,712	90.5
Guatemalan	1,463	94.9
Honduran	756	95.1
Panamanian	478	85.8
Salvadoran	779	90.9
Cuban	3,019	88.2
Mexican	29,500	91.0
Puerto Rican	2,728	75.9
South American	1,887	82.2
Colombian	410	76.1
Peruvian	374	76.2
Spaniard	542	69.6

Class of Worker: Government
(Universe: Civilian Employed Population 16 Years and Over)

Group	Number	%
Total Population	286,254	15.3
Hispanic or Latino (of any race)	3,307	6.8
Central American, ex. Mexican	219	5.3
Guatemalan	68	4.4
Honduran	13	1.6
Panamanian	70	12.6
Salvadoran	16	1.9
Cuban	237	6.9
Mexican	1,531	4.7
Puerto Rican	720	20.0
South American	274	11.9
Colombian	114	21.2
Peruvian	57	11.6
Spaniard	184	23.6

Means of Transportation to Work: Car, Truck or Van
(Universe: Workers 16 Years and Over)

Group	Number	%
Total Population	1,701,262	92.5
Hispanic or Latino (of any race)	44,232	89.4
Central American, ex. Mexican	3,640	86.5
Guatemalan	1,254	82.7
Honduran	703	89.4
Panamanian	487	89.9
Salvadoran	858	87.6
Cuban	2,978	89.9
Mexican	29,501	90.1
Puerto Rican	3,482	88.6
South American	2,085	90.8
Colombian	486	82.8
Peruvian	474	98.5
Spaniard	608	77.9

Means of Transportation to Work: Public Transportation (ex. Taxicab)
(Universe: Workers 16 Years and Over)

Group	Number	%
Total Population	21,331	1.2
Hispanic or Latino (of any race)	1,071	2.2
Central American, ex. Mexican	241	5.7
Guatemalan	183	12.1
Honduran	25	3.2
Panamanian	25	4.6
Salvadoran	8	0.8
Cuban	82	2.5
Mexican	666	2.0
Puerto Rican	21	0.5
South American	34	1.5
Colombian	22	3.7
Peruvian	0	0.0
Spaniard	17	2.2

Homeownership Rate
(Universe: Occupied Housing Units)

Group	%
Total Population	68.7
Hispanic or Latino (of any race)	35.5
Central American, ex. Mexican	30.3
Costa Rican	42.6
Guatemalan	19.1
Honduran	28.5
Nicaraguan	40.4
Panamanian	43.0
Salvadoran	41.6
Cuban	44.8
Dominican Republic	35.1
Mexican	29.8
Puerto Rican	43.3
South American	54.3
Argentinean	58.9
Bolivian	67.1
Chilean	61.1
Colombian	50.5
Ecuadorian	53.6
Peruvian	52.2
Venezuelan	52.7
Spaniard	59.3

Median Home Value

Group	Dollars
Total Population	116,800
Hispanic or Latino (of any race)	126,000
Central American, ex. Mexican	135,500
Guatemalan	177,400
Honduran	93,200
Panamanian	174,300
Salvadoran	130,900
Cuban	124,400
Mexican	112,800
Puerto Rican	156,600
South American	168,800
Colombian	192,800
Peruvian	158,300
Spaniard	149,500

Median Gross Rent

Group	Dollars
Total Population	601
Hispanic or Latino (of any race)	609
Central American, ex. Mexican	609
Guatemalan	608
Honduran	615
Panamanian	662
Salvadoran	523
Cuban	545
Mexican	595
Puerto Rican	734
South American	674
Colombian	667
Peruvian	666
Spaniard	1,017

Median Household Income
(2010 Inflation-Adjusted Dollars)

Group	Dollars
Total Population	41,576
Hispanic or Latino (of any race)	34,639
Central American, ex. Mexican	31,262
Guatemalan	27,149
Honduran	33,168
Panamanian	29,750
Salvadoran	31,324
Cuban	38,229
Mexican	31,673
Puerto Rican	47,500
South American	51,042
Colombian	50,690
Peruvian	40,938
Spaniard	53,750

Per Capita Income
(2010 Inflation-Adjusted Dollars)

Group	Dollars
Total Population	22,515
Hispanic or Latino (of any race)	13,122
Central American, ex. Mexican	11,131
Guatemalan	7,896
Honduran	11,652
Panamanian	22,862
Salvadoran	10,673
Cuban	19,237
Mexican	11,383
Puerto Rican	17,699
South American	18,188
Colombian	18,985

Notes: (1) Percent of total population; (2) Percent of Hispanic/Latino population; Profiles include places with an overall population of at least 125,000, OR an overall population of at least 25,000 where the Hispanic/Latino population is at least 20% of the overall population. In states where less than five places meet either of these criteria, we have included places with at least 10,000 total population with the highest percentage of Hispanic/Latino population. These places are identified with an asterisk (*); Please refer to the User's Guide for a full explanation of data.

Peruvian	14,416	
Spaniard	23,323	

Households with $100,000+ Income

Group	Number	%
Total Population	223,774	13.3
Hispanic or Latino (of any race)	2,659	9.1
Central American, ex. Mexican	160	6.5
Guatemalan	62	6.8
Honduran	17	3.1
Panamanian	65	26.6
Salvadoran	0	0.0
Cuban	297	11.5
Mexican	1,277	7.3
Puerto Rican	276	9.3
South American	290	20.1
Colombian	62	19.9
Peruvian	34	9.5
Spaniard	73	15.5

Households with Food Stamps/SNAP Benefits During Past 12 Months

Group	Number	%
Total Population	234,426	14.0
Hispanic or Latino (of any race)	5,602	19.1
Central American, ex. Mexican	564	22.9
Guatemalan	264	28.9
Honduran	114	20.7
Panamanian	0	0.0
Salvadoran	111	20.1
Cuban	620	23.9
Mexican	3,262	18.7
Puerto Rican	748	25.2
South American	98	6.8
Colombian	13	4.2
Peruvian	55	15.4
Spaniard	115	24.5

Poverty Rate
(Income in Past 12 Months Below Poverty Level)

Group	%
Total Population	17.7
Hispanic or Latino (of any race)	31.0
Central American, ex. Mexican	34.1
Guatemalan	43.5
Honduran	30.3
Panamanian	14.0
Salvadoran	30.1
Cuban	22.7
Mexican	34.3
Puerto Rican	27.4
South American	15.2
Colombian	7.1
Peruvian	30.0
Spaniard	16.4

Fort Campbell North*

Population

Group	Number	%TP[1]	%HP[2]
Total Population	13,685	100.0	–
Hispanic or Latino (of any race)	2,057	15.0	100.0
Central American, ex. Mexican	103	0.8	5.0
Mexican	1,011	7.4	49.1
Puerto Rican	570	4.2	27.7

Population Growth: 2000–2010

Group	%
Total Population	-4.6
Hispanic or Latino (of any race)	3.6
Central American, ex. Mexican	-18.9
Mexican	31.5
Puerto Rican	-17.6

Males per 100 Females

Group	Number
Total Population	154.7
Hispanic or Latino (of any race)	135.1
Central American, ex. Mexican	98.1
Mexican	150.2
Puerto Rican	118.4

Average Household Size

Group	People
Total Population	3.93
Hispanic or Latino (of any race)	3.91
Central American, ex. Mexican	3.90
Mexican	3.91
Puerto Rican	4.08

Median Age

Group	Years
Total Population	21.3
Hispanic or Latino (of any race)	19.9
Central American, ex. Mexican	20.2
Mexican	19.8
Puerto Rican	18.3

High School Graduates
(Universe: Population 25 Years and Over)

Group	Number	%
Total Population	4,400	93.9
Hispanic or Latino (of any race)	536	94.5
Mexican	184	100.0

Four-Year College Graduates
(Universe: Population 25 Years and Over)

Group	Number	%
Total Population	262	5.6
Hispanic or Latino (of any race)	59	10.4
Mexican	0	0.0

Population Age 3–17 Enrolled in Public School
(Universe: Population Age 3–17 Enrolled in School)

Group	Number	%
Total Population	2,975	98.0
Hispanic or Latino (of any race)	422	100.0
Mexican	236	100.0

Population Age 3–17 Enrolled in Private School
(Universe: Population Age 3–17 Enrolled in School)

Group	Number	%
Total Population	61	2.0
Hispanic or Latino (of any race)	0	0.0
Mexican	0	0.0

Foreign-Born Population

Group	Number	%
Total Population	535	4.1
Hispanic or Latino (of any race)	90	5.0
Mexican	47	6.0

Foreign-Born Naturalized U.S. Citizens

Group	Number	%
Total Population	185	34.6
Hispanic or Latino (of any race)	27	30.0
Mexican	27	57.4

Language Spoken at Home: English Only
(Universe: Population 5 Years and Over)

Group	Number	%
Total Population	9,907	87.4
Hispanic or Latino (of any race)	803	52.2
Mexican	522	79.1

Language Spoken at Home: Spanish
(Universe: Population 5 Years and Over)

Group	Number	%
Total Population	790	7.0
Hispanic or Latino (of any race)	709	46.1
Mexican	112	17.0

Unemployment Rate
(Universe: Population 16 Years and Over)

Group	%
Total Population	20.2
Hispanic or Latino (of any race)	17.9
Mexican	44.3

Class of Worker: Private Wage and Salary
(Universe: Civilian Employed Population 16 Years and Over)

Group	Number	%
Total Population	811	62.6
Hispanic or Latino (of any race)	85	68.5
Mexican	34	100.0

Class of Worker: Government
(Universe: Civilian Employed Population 16 Years and Over)

Group	Number	%
Total Population	449	34.6
Hispanic or Latino (of any race)	39	31.5
Mexican	0	0.0

Means of Transportation to Work: Car, Truck or Van
(Universe: Workers 16 Years and Over)

Group	Number	%
Total Population	3,971	70.0
Hispanic or Latino (of any race)	470	61.0
Mexican	185	60.5

Means of Transportation to Work: Public Transportation (ex. Taxicab)
(Universe: Workers 16 Years and Over)

Group	Number	%
Total Population	0	0.0
Hispanic or Latino (of any race)	0	0.0
Mexican	0	0.0

Homeownership Rate
(Universe: Occupied Housing Units)

Group	%
Total Population	0.7
Hispanic or Latino (of any race)	0.8
Central American, ex. Mexican	0.0
Mexican	0.0
Puerto Rican	2.8

Median Home Value

Group	Dollars
Total Population	72,300
Hispanic or Latino (of any race)	–
Mexican	–

Median Gross Rent

Group	Dollars
Total Population	858
Hispanic or Latino (of any race)	884
Mexican	888

Median Household Income
(2010 Inflation-Adjusted Dollars)

Group	Dollars
Total Population	34,317
Hispanic or Latino (of any race)	39,167
Mexican	34,800

Per Capita Income
(2010 Inflation-Adjusted Dollars)

Group	Dollars
Total Population	13,941
Hispanic or Latino (of any race)	14,900
Mexican	12,761

Households with $100,000+ Income

Group	Number	%
Total Population	13	0.5
Hispanic or Latino (of any race)	0	0.0
Mexican	0	0.0

Households with Food Stamps/SNAP Benefits During Past 12 Months

Group	Number	%
Total Population	155	5.9
Hispanic or Latino (of any race)	25	9.5
Mexican	25	16.4

Poverty Rate
(Income in Past 12 Months Below Poverty Level)

Group	%
Total Population	24.1
Hispanic or Latino (of any race)	13.9
Mexican	21.3

Lexington-Fayette

Population

Group	Number	%TP[1]	%HP[2]
Total Population	295,803	100.0	–
Hispanic or Latino (of any race)	20,474	6.9	100.0

Notes: (1) Percent of total population; (2) Percent of Hispanic/Latino population; Profiles include places with an overall population of at least 125,000, OR an overall population of at least 25,000 where the Hispanic/Latino population is at least 20% of the overall population. In states where less than five places meet either of these criteria, we have included places with at least 10,000 total population with the highest percentage of Hispanic/Latino population. These places are identified with an asterisk (*); Please refer to the User's Guide for a full explanation of data.

STATE & PLACE PROFILES

Central American, ex. Mexican	1,305	0.4	6.4
Guatemalan	453	0.2	2.2
Honduran	387	0.1	1.9
Salvadoran	222	0.1	1.1
Cuban	488	0.2	2.4
Dominican Republic	171	0.1	0.8
Mexican	15,145	5.1	74.0
Puerto Rican	1,008	0.3	4.9
South American	1,027	0.3	5.0
Argentinean	112	<0.1	0.5
Colombian	296	0.1	1.4
Peruvian	246	0.1	1.2
Venezuelan	161	0.1	0.8
Spaniard	182	0.1	0.9

Population Growth: 2000–2010

Group	%
Total Population	13.5
Hispanic or Latino (of any race)	139.2
Central American, ex. Mexican	321.0
Guatemalan	353.0
Cuban	99.2
Mexican	151.8
Puerto Rican	103.6
South American	133.4
Colombian	144.6

Males per 100 Females

Group	Number
Total Population	96.9
Hispanic or Latino (of any race)	132.9
Central American, ex. Mexican	133.9
Guatemalan	186.7
Honduran	134.5
Salvadoran	136.2
Cuban	105.9
Dominican Republic	111.1
Mexican	140.3
Puerto Rican	106.6
South American	101.8
Argentinean	96.5
Colombian	98.7
Peruvian	110.3
Venezuelan	83.0
Spaniard	104.5

Average Household Size

Group	People
Total Population	2.30
Hispanic or Latino (of any race)	3.34
Central American, ex. Mexican	3.49
Guatemalan	3.79
Honduran	3.67
Salvadoran	3.74
Cuban	2.58
Dominican Republic	2.98
Mexican	3.57
Puerto Rican	2.49
South American	2.59
Argentinean	2.93
Colombian	2.33
Peruvian	2.90
Venezuelan	2.46
Spaniard	2.21

Median Age

Group	Years
Total Population	33.7
Hispanic or Latino (of any race)	25.5
Central American, ex. Mexican	25.8
Guatemalan	23.1
Honduran	26.9
Salvadoran	26.8
Cuban	33.1
Dominican Republic	26.8
Mexican	24.8
Puerto Rican	25.5
South American	33.8
Argentinean	32.6
Colombian	32.6
Peruvian	35.2
Venezuelan	35.8
Spaniard	35.3

High School Graduates
(Universe: Population 25 Years and Over)

Group	Number	%
Total Population	163,672	88.3
Hispanic or Latino (of any race)	5,232	56.7
Central American, ex. Mexican	362	52.5
Mexican	3,392	48.9
South American	509	97.1

Four-Year College Graduates
(Universe: Population 25 Years and Over)

Group	Number	%
Total Population	72,446	39.1
Hispanic or Latino (of any race)	1,471	15.9
Central American, ex. Mexican	73	10.6
Mexican	436	6.3
South American	432	82.4

Population Age 3–17 Enrolled in Public School
(Universe: Population Age 3–17 Enrolled in School)

Group	Number	%
Total Population	35,454	81.2
Hispanic or Latino (of any race)	3,294	93.5
Central American, ex. Mexican	328	86.1
Mexican	2,393	96.3
South American	174	79.5

Population Age 3–17 Enrolled in Private School
(Universe: Population Age 3–17 Enrolled in School)

Group	Number	%
Total Population	8,195	18.8
Hispanic or Latino (of any race)	229	6.5
Central American, ex. Mexican	53	13.9
Mexican	91	3.7
South American	45	20.5

Foreign-Born Population

Group	Number	%
Total Population	24,586	8.5
Hispanic or Latino (of any race)	10,823	60.6
Central American, ex. Mexican	924	54.8
Mexican	8,663	65.1
South American	750	80.2

Foreign-Born Naturalized U.S. Citizens

Group	Number	%
Total Population	6,392	26.0
Hispanic or Latino (of any race)	1,304	12.0
Central American, ex. Mexican	195	21.1
Mexican	835	9.6
South American	199	26.5

Language Spoken at Home: English Only
(Universe: Population 5 Years and Over)

Group	Number	%
Total Population	240,944	89.4
Hispanic or Latino (of any race)	2,927	19.1
Central American, ex. Mexican	182	15.4
Mexican	1,719	14.9
South American	134	14.9

Language Spoken at Home: Spanish
(Universe: Population 5 Years and Over)

Group	Number	%
Total Population	15,129	5.6
Hispanic or Latino (of any race)	12,326	80.4
Central American, ex. Mexican	1,002	84.6
Mexican	9,754	84.7
South American	763	85.1

Unemployment Rate
(Universe: Population 16 Years and Over)

Group	%
Total Population	6.3
Hispanic or Latino (of any race)	7.5
Central American, ex. Mexican	3.1
Mexican	8.5
South American	3.8

Class of Worker: Private Wage and Salary
(Universe: Civilian Employed Population 16 Years and Over)

Group	Number	%
Total Population	115,951	76.3
Hispanic or Latino (of any race)	7,650	88.5
Central American, ex. Mexican	603	92.2
Mexican	6,245	92.4
South American	251	65.7

Class of Worker: Government
(Universe: Civilian Employed Population 16 Years and Over)

Group	Number	%
Total Population	27,945	18.4
Hispanic or Latino (of any race)	604	7.0
Central American, ex. Mexican	36	5.5
Mexican	228	3.4
South American	118	30.9

Means of Transportation to Work: Car, Truck or Van
(Universe: Workers 16 Years and Over)

Group	Number	%
Total Population	134,526	90.7
Hispanic or Latino (of any race)	7,579	88.8
Central American, ex. Mexican	604	95.0
Mexican	6,002	89.8
South American	319	85.8

Means of Transportation to Work: Public Transportation (ex. Taxicab)
(Universe: Workers 16 Years and Over)

Group	Number	%
Total Population	2,091	1.4
Hispanic or Latino (of any race)	337	3.9
Central American, ex. Mexican	8	1.3
Mexican	307	4.6
South American	12	3.2

Homeownership Rate
(Universe: Occupied Housing Units)

Group	%
Total Population	55.9
Hispanic or Latino (of any race)	24.7
Central American, ex. Mexican	23.5
Guatemalan	16.0
Honduran	21.4
Salvadoran	29.2
Cuban	41.1
Dominican Republic	30.0
Mexican	19.9
Puerto Rican	36.1
South American	50.9
Argentinean	62.2
Colombian	45.7
Peruvian	51.3
Venezuelan	48.5
Spaniard	43.2

Median Home Value

Group	Dollars
Total Population	159,200
Hispanic or Latino (of any race)	144,000
Central American, ex. Mexican	131,300
Mexican	123,200
South American	200,300

Median Gross Rent

Group	Dollars
Total Population	693
Hispanic or Latino (of any race)	591
Central American, ex. Mexican	611
Mexican	579
South American	794

Median Household Income
(2010 Inflation-Adjusted Dollars)

Group	Dollars
Total Population	47,469
Hispanic or Latino (of any race)	31,376
Central American, ex. Mexican	21,927
Mexican	29,301
South American	46,866

Per Capita Income
(2010 Inflation-Adjusted Dollars)

Group	Dollars
Total Population	28,345
Hispanic or Latino (of any race)	11,977
Central American, ex. Mexican	8,585
Mexican	11,196
South American	18,174

Notes: (1) Percent of total population; (2) Percent of Hispanic/Latino population; Profiles include places with an overall population of at least 125,000, OR an overall population of at least 25,000 where the Hispanic/Latino population is at least 20% of the overall population. In states where less than five places meet either of these criteria, we have included places with at least 10,000 total population with the highest percentage of Hispanic/Latino population. These places are identified with an asterisk (*); Please refer to the User's Guide for a full explanation of data.

Households with $100,000+ Income		
Group	Number	%
Total Population	22,624	18.7
Hispanic or Latino (of any race)	318	7.0
Central American, ex. Mexican	11	2.6
Mexican	169	5.2
South American	38	13.5

Households with Food Stamps/SNAP Benefits During Past 12 Months		
Group	Number	%
Total Population	10,991	9.1
Hispanic or Latino (of any race)	688	15.1
Central American, ex. Mexican	96	22.5
Mexican	532	16.2
South American	0	0.0

Poverty Rate (Income in Past 12 Months Below Poverty Level)	
Group	%
Total Population	17.4
Hispanic or Latino (of any race)	34.9
Central American, ex. Mexican	44.5
Mexican	38.1
South American	6.8

Louisville-Jefferson County

Population			
Group	Number	%TP[1]	%HP[2]
Total Population	597,337	100.0	–
Hispanic or Latino (of any race)	26,790	4.5	100.0
Central American, ex. Mexican	2,149	0.4	8.0
Guatemalan	1,019	0.2	3.8
Honduran	313	0.1	1.2
Nicaraguan	112	<0.1	0.4
Panamanian	246	<0.1	0.9
Salvadoran	411	0.1	1.5
Cuban	6,575	1.1	24.5
Dominican Republic	198	<0.1	0.7
Mexican	12,537	2.1	46.8
Puerto Rican	2,112	0.4	7.9
South American	1,284	0.2	4.8
Argentinean	103	<0.1	0.4
Colombian	420	0.1	1.6
Ecuadorian	137	<0.1	0.5
Peruvian	289	<0.1	1.1
Venezuelan	132	<0.1	0.5
Spaniard	252	<0.1	0.9

Population Growth: 2000–2010	
Group	%
Total Population	n/a

Males per 100 Females	
Group	Number
Total Population	93.9
Hispanic or Latino (of any race)	119.2
Central American, ex. Mexican	149.0
Guatemalan	183.8
Honduran	172.2
Nicaraguan	93.1
Panamanian	89.2
Salvadoran	130.9
Cuban	112.5
Dominican Republic	81.7
Mexican	127.9
Puerto Rican	104.5
South American	86.4
Argentinean	83.9
Colombian	74.3
Ecuadorian	87.7
Peruvian	91.4
Venezuelan	100.0
Spaniard	115.4

Average Household Size	
Group	People
Total Population	2.37
Hispanic or Latino (of any race)	3.14
Central American, ex. Mexican	3.31
Guatemalan	3.83
Honduran	3.45
Nicaraguan	2.76
Panamanian	2.33
Salvadoran	3.18
Cuban	2.97
Dominican Republic	2.95
Mexican	3.52
Puerto Rican	2.63
South American	2.67
Argentinean	2.39
Colombian	2.63
Ecuadorian	2.69
Peruvian	2.98
Venezuelan	2.67
Spaniard	2.45

Median Age	
Group	Years
Total Population	37.1
Hispanic or Latino (of any race)	26.8
Central American, ex. Mexican	27.5
Guatemalan	25.4
Honduran	29.4
Nicaraguan	35.0
Panamanian	30.5
Salvadoran	29.9
Cuban	35.5
Dominican Republic	25.2
Mexican	23.6
Puerto Rican	24.2
South American	32.9
Argentinean	41.4
Colombian	31.7
Ecuadorian	32.5
Peruvian	34.1
Venezuelan	31.2
Spaniard	33.0

High School Graduates (Universe: Population 25 Years and Over)		
Group	Number	%
Total Population	336,101	85.5
Hispanic or Latino (of any race)	8,869	70.9
Central American, ex. Mexican	798	70.4
Cuban	3,010	80.5
Mexican	3,140	57.5
Puerto Rican	874	86.4
South American	588	92.2

Four-Year College Graduates (Universe: Population 25 Years and Over)		
Group	Number	%
Total Population	99,335	25.3
Hispanic or Latino (of any race)	2,341	18.7
Central American, ex. Mexican	250	22.0
Cuban	708	18.9
Mexican	563	10.3
Puerto Rican	319	31.6
South American	317	49.7

Population Age 3–17 Enrolled in Public School (Universe: Population Age 3–17 Enrolled in School)		
Group	Number	%
Total Population	81,993	78.1
Hispanic or Latino (of any race)	4,827	90.1
Central American, ex. Mexican	493	76.0
Cuban	1,124	98.7
Mexican	2,417	90.5
Puerto Rican	433	91.9
South American	112	76.2

Population Age 3–17 Enrolled in Private School (Universe: Population Age 3–17 Enrolled in School)		
Group	Number	%
Total Population	22,966	21.9
Hispanic or Latino (of any race)	528	9.9
Central American, ex. Mexican	156	24.0
Cuban	15	1.3
Mexican	253	9.5
Puerto Rican	38	8.1
South American	35	23.8

Foreign-Born Population		
Group	Number	%
Total Population	33,637	5.7
Hispanic or Latino (of any race)	12,319	52.3
Central American, ex. Mexican	1,120	51.7
Cuban	4,634	80.9
Mexican	5,714	48.4
Puerto Rican	27	1.5
South American	637	62.0

Foreign-Born Naturalized U.S. Citizens		
Group	Number	%
Total Population	11,128	33.1
Hispanic or Latino (of any race)	2,003	16.3
Central American, ex. Mexican	480	42.9
Cuban	791	17.1
Mexican	443	7.8
Puerto Rican	0	0.0
South American	245	38.5

Language Spoken at Home: English Only (Universe: Population 5 Years and Over)		
Group	Number	%
Total Population	506,438	92.5
Hispanic or Latino (of any race)	5,788	28.2
Central American, ex. Mexican	508	25.6
Cuban	571	10.9
Mexican	2,783	28.4
Puerto Rican	1,100	68.6
South American	279	29.7

Language Spoken at Home: Spanish (Universe: Population 5 Years and Over)		
Group	Number	%
Total Population	19,127	3.5
Hispanic or Latino (of any race)	14,667	71.6
Central American, ex. Mexican	1,477	74.4
Cuban	4,679	89.1
Mexican	7,000	71.4
Puerto Rican	504	31.4
South American	659	70.3

Unemployment Rate (Universe: Population 16 Years and Over)	
Group	%
Total Population	9.6
Hispanic or Latino (of any race)	11.8
Central American, ex. Mexican	12.8
Cuban	22.1
Mexican	8.9
Puerto Rican	7.1
South American	0.0

Class of Worker: Private Wage and Salary (Universe: Civilian Employed Population 16 Years and Over)		
Group	Number	%
Total Population	229,528	83.7
Hispanic or Latino (of any race)	9,379	89.0
Central American, ex. Mexican	868	87.0
Cuban	2,123	91.7
Mexican	4,839	92.3
Puerto Rican	505	65.8
South American	631	92.9

Class of Worker: Government (Universe: Civilian Employed Population 16 Years and Over)		
Group	Number	%
Total Population	31,743	11.6
Hispanic or Latino (of any race)	626	5.9
Central American, ex. Mexican	57	5.7
Cuban	83	3.6
Mexican	153	2.9
Puerto Rican	210	27.3
South American	48	7.1

Means of Transportation to Work: Car, Truck or Van (Universe: Workers 16 Years and Over)		
Group	Number	%
Total Population	242,622	90.3
Hispanic or Latino (of any race)	8,982	87.1
Central American, ex. Mexican	852	86.7
Cuban	1,957	89.6
Mexican	4,423	85.9
Puerto Rican	705	90.0
South American	573	84.4

Notes: (1) Percent of total population; (2) Percent of Hispanic/Latino population; Profiles include places with an overall population of at least 125,000, OR an overall population of at least 25,000 where the Hispanic/Latino population is at least 20% of the overall population. In states where less than five places meet either of these criteria, we have included places with at least 10,000 total population with the highest percentage of Hispanic/Latino population. These places are identified with an asterisk (*); Please refer to the User's Guide for a full explanation of data.

Means of Transportation to Work: Public Transportation (ex. Taxicab)
(Universe: Workers 16 Years and Over)

Group	Number	%
Total Population	10,317	3.8
Hispanic or Latino (of any race)	301	2.9
Central American, ex. Mexican	50	5.1
Cuban	64	2.9
Mexican	157	3.1
Puerto Rican	8	1.0
South American	22	3.2

Homeownership Rate
(Universe: Occupied Housing Units)

Group	%
Total Population	61.6
Hispanic or Latino (of any race)	37.3
Central American, ex. Mexican	27.4
Guatemalan	12.6
Honduran	27.4
Nicaraguan	44.1
Panamanian	44.8
Salvadoran	37.9
Cuban	43.6
Dominican Republic	26.3
Mexican	30.5
Puerto Rican	45.3
South American	55.9
Argentinean	54.5
Colombian	52.1
Ecuadorian	54.9
Peruvian	61.7
Venezuelan	48.9
Spaniard	57.0

Median Home Value

Group	Dollars
Total Population	137,400
Hispanic or Latino (of any race)	132,200
Central American, ex. Mexican	177,000
Cuban	119,700
Mexican	118,800
Puerto Rican	163,900
South American	176,000

Median Gross Rent

Group	Dollars
Total Population	647
Hispanic or Latino (of any race)	619
Central American, ex. Mexican	665
Cuban	533
Mexican	633
Puerto Rican	762
South American	1,031

Median Household Income
(2010 Inflation-Adjusted Dollars)

Group	Dollars
Total Population	43,009
Hispanic or Latino (of any race)	35,894
Central American, ex. Mexican	32,886
Cuban	35,373
Mexican	31,349
Puerto Rican	54,545
South American	70,234

Per Capita Income
(2010 Inflation-Adjusted Dollars)

Group	Dollars
Total Population	24,696
Hispanic or Latino (of any race)	15,289
Central American, ex. Mexican	14,772
Cuban	17,756
Mexican	10,951
Puerto Rican	24,957
South American	27,826

Households with $100,000+ Income

Group	Number	%
Total Population	36,303	15.2
Hispanic or Latino (of any race)	624	9.3
Central American, ex. Mexican	84	15.7
Cuban	183	10.4
Mexican	149	5.0
Puerto Rican	75	10.4
South American	97	27.7

Households with Food Stamps/SNAP Benefits During Past 12 Months

Group	Number	%
Total Population	31,643	13.2
Hispanic or Latino (of any race)	1,139	17.0
Central American, ex. Mexican	100	18.7
Cuban	473	26.9
Mexican	424	14.2
Puerto Rican	120	16.7
South American	11	3.1

Poverty Rate
(Income in Past 12 Months Below Poverty Level)

Group	%
Total Population	17.3
Hispanic or Latino (of any race)	28.5
Central American, ex. Mexican	34.0
Cuban	22.8
Mexican	34.6
Puerto Rican	22.3
South American	6.3

Mayfield*

Population

Group	Number	%TP[1]	%HP[2]
Total Population	10,024	100.0	–
Hispanic or Latino (of any race)	1,442	14.4	100.0
Central American, ex. Mexican	145	1.4	10.1
Guatemalan	135	1.3	9.4
Mexican	1,175	11.7	81.5

Population Growth: 2000–2010

Group	%
Total Population	-3.1
Hispanic or Latino (of any race)	138.0
Mexican	142.3

Males per 100 Females

Group	Number
Total Population	89.9
Hispanic or Latino (of any race)	124.3
Central American, ex. Mexican	202.1
Guatemalan	187.2
Mexican	117.6

Average Household Size

Group	People
Total Population	2.33
Hispanic or Latino (of any race)	3.91
Central American, ex. Mexican	4.19
Guatemalan	4.24
Mexican	4.02

Median Age

Group	Years
Total Population	37.3
Hispanic or Latino (of any race)	22.4
Central American, ex. Mexican	24.1
Guatemalan	23.9
Mexican	21.5

High School Graduates
(Universe: Population 25 Years and Over)

Group	Number	%
Total Population	4,768	73.1
Hispanic or Latino (of any race)	288	46.6
Mexican	230	49.1

Four-Year College Graduates
(Universe: Population 25 Years and Over)

Group	Number	%
Total Population	979	15.0
Hispanic or Latino (of any race)	23	3.7
Mexican	23	4.9

Population Age 3–17 Enrolled in Public School
(Universe: Population Age 3–17 Enrolled in School)

Group	Number	%
Total Population	2,029	97.2
Hispanic or Latino (of any race)	463	100.0
Mexican	309	100.0

Population Age 3–17 Enrolled in Private School
(Universe: Population Age 3–17 Enrolled in School)

Group	Number	%
Total Population	58	2.8
Hispanic or Latino (of any race)	0	0.0
Mexican	0	0.0

Foreign-Born Population

Group	Number	%
Total Population	858	8.6
Hispanic or Latino (of any race)	813	54.1
Mexican	601	60.3

Foreign-Born Naturalized U.S. Citizens

Group	Number	%
Total Population	79	9.2
Hispanic or Latino (of any race)	56	6.9
Mexican	39	6.5

Language Spoken at Home: English Only
(Universe: Population 5 Years and Over)

Group	Number	%
Total Population	8,014	85.9
Hispanic or Latino (of any race)	123	9.8
Mexican	85	9.9

Language Spoken at Home: Spanish
(Universe: Population 5 Years and Over)

Group	Number	%
Total Population	1,213	13.0
Hispanic or Latino (of any race)	1,109	88.5
Mexican	751	87.6

Unemployment Rate
(Universe: Population 16 Years and Over)

Group	%
Total Population	16.6
Hispanic or Latino (of any race)	37.7
Mexican	19.5

Class of Worker: Private Wage and Salary
(Universe: Civilian Employed Population 16 Years and Over)

Group	Number	%
Total Population	2,608	77.9
Hispanic or Latino (of any race)	325	84.9
Mexican	260	81.8

Class of Worker: Government
(Universe: Civilian Employed Population 16 Years and Over)

Group	Number	%
Total Population	390	11.7
Hispanic or Latino (of any race)	0	0.0
Mexican	0	0.0

Means of Transportation to Work: Car, Truck or Van
(Universe: Workers 16 Years and Over)

Group	Number	%
Total Population	3,171	96.4
Hispanic or Latino (of any race)	352	91.9
Mexican	287	90.3

Means of Transportation to Work: Public Transportation (ex. Taxicab)
(Universe: Workers 16 Years and Over)

Group	Number	%
Total Population	24	0.7
Hispanic or Latino (of any race)	0	0.0
Mexican	0	0.0

Homeownership Rate
(Universe: Occupied Housing Units)

Group	%
Total Population	53.6
Hispanic or Latino (of any race)	35.7
Central American, ex. Mexican	8.1
Guatemalan	2.9
Mexican	39.4

Median Home Value

Group	Dollars
Total Population	71,900
Hispanic or Latino (of any race)	45,200
Mexican	44,000

Notes: (1) Percent of total population; (2) Percent of Hispanic/Latino population; Profiles include places with an overall population of at least 125,000, OR an overall population of at least 25,000 where the Hispanic/Latino population is at least 20% of the overall population. In states where less than five places meet either of these criteria, we have included places with at least 10,000 total population with the highest percentage of Hispanic/Latino population. These places are identified with an asterisk (*); Please refer to the User's Guide for a full explanation of data.

Median Gross Rent	
Group	Dollars
Total Population	532
Hispanic or Latino (of any race)	660
Mexican	635

Median Household Income (2010 Inflation-Adjusted Dollars)	
Group	Dollars
Total Population	25,833
Hispanic or Latino (of any race)	22,006
Mexican	29,063

Per Capita Income (2010 Inflation-Adjusted Dollars)	
Group	Dollars
Total Population	15,876
Hispanic or Latino (of any race)	7,209
Mexican	8,388

Households with $100,000+ Income		
Group	Number	%
Total Population	265	6.5
Hispanic or Latino (of any race)	25	7.0
Mexican	25	10.9

Households with Food Stamps/SNAP Benefits During Past 12 Months		
Group	Number	%
Total Population	936	23.1
Hispanic or Latino (of any race)	65	18.2
Mexican	4	1.7

Poverty Rate (Income in Past 12 Months Below Poverty Level)	
Group	%
Total Population	33.7
Hispanic or Latino (of any race)	45.3
Mexican	26.0

Shelbyville*

Population			
Group	Number	%TP[1]	%HP[2]
Total Population	14,045	100.0	–
Hispanic or Latino (of any race)	2,494	17.8	100.0
Central American, ex. Mexican	568	4.0	22.8
Guatemalan	450	3.2	18.0
Mexican	1,665	11.9	66.8

Population Growth: 2000–2010	
Group	%
Total Population	39.3
Hispanic or Latino (of any race)	160.1
Central American, ex. Mexican	311.6
Guatemalan	271.9
Mexican	144.9

Males per 100 Females	
Group	Number
Total Population	94.7
Hispanic or Latino (of any race)	133.1
Central American, ex. Mexican	164.2
Guatemalan	171.1
Mexican	129.0

Average Household Size	
Group	People
Total Population	2.66
Hispanic or Latino (of any race)	4.22
Central American, ex. Mexican	4.47
Guatemalan	4.66
Mexican	4.27

Median Age	
Group	Years
Total Population	32.6
Hispanic or Latino (of any race)	24.3
Central American, ex. Mexican	26.9
Guatemalan	26.1
Mexican	23.0

High School Graduates (Universe: Population 25 Years and Over)		
Group	Number	%
Total Population	6,499	77.1
Hispanic or Latino (of any race)	354	37.4
Mexican	265	32.5

Four-Year College Graduates (Universe: Population 25 Years and Over)		
Group	Number	%
Total Population	1,963	23.3
Hispanic or Latino (of any race)	66	7.0
Mexican	48	5.9

Population Age 3–17 Enrolled in Public School (Universe: Population Age 3–17 Enrolled in School)		
Group	Number	%
Total Population	2,483	88.8
Hispanic or Latino (of any race)	463	96.1
Mexican	400	100.0

Population Age 3–17 Enrolled in Private School (Universe: Population Age 3–17 Enrolled in School)		
Group	Number	%
Total Population	314	11.2
Hispanic or Latino (of any race)	19	3.9
Mexican	0	0.0

Foreign-Born Population		
Group	Number	%
Total Population	1,334	10.0
Hispanic or Latino (of any race)	1,242	58.8
Mexican	1,119	59.1

Foreign-Born Naturalized U.S. Citizens		
Group	Number	%
Total Population	150	11.2
Hispanic or Latino (of any race)	126	10.1
Mexican	33	2.9

Language Spoken at Home: English Only (Universe: Population 5 Years and Over)		
Group	Number	%
Total Population	10,653	87.0
Hispanic or Latino (of any race)	425	23.5
Mexican	321	20.2

Language Spoken at Home: Spanish (Universe: Population 5 Years and Over)		
Group	Number	%
Total Population	1,518	12.4
Hispanic or Latino (of any race)	1,377	76.3
Mexican	1,269	79.8

Unemployment Rate (Universe: Population 16 Years and Over)	
Group	%
Total Population	5.2
Hispanic or Latino (of any race)	2.6
Mexican	2.9

Class of Worker: Private Wage and Salary (Universe: Civilian Employed Population 16 Years and Over)		
Group	Number	%
Total Population	5,969	85.0
Hispanic or Latino (of any race)	1,120	94.3
Mexican	1,043	97.7

Class of Worker: Government (Universe: Civilian Employed Population 16 Years and Over)		
Group	Number	%
Total Population	809	11.5
Hispanic or Latino (of any race)	43	3.6
Mexican	0	0.0

Means of Transportation to Work: Car, Truck or Van (Universe: Workers 16 Years and Over)		
Group	Number	%
Total Population	6,290	91.8
Hispanic or Latino (of any race)	1,092	91.9
Mexican	1,003	93.9

Means of Transportation to Work: Public Transportation (ex. Taxicab) (Universe: Workers 16 Years and Over)		
Group	Number	%
Total Population	16	0.2
Hispanic or Latino (of any race)	16	1.3
Mexican	16	1.5

Homeownership Rate (Universe: Occupied Housing Units)	
Group	%
Total Population	51.7
Hispanic or Latino (of any race)	17.2
Central American, ex. Mexican	12.0
Guatemalan	10.8
Mexican	16.2

Median Home Value	
Group	Dollars
Total Population	145,300
Hispanic or Latino (of any race)	123,000
Mexican	142,000

Median Gross Rent	
Group	Dollars
Total Population	654
Hispanic or Latino (of any race)	695
Mexican	715

Median Household Income (2010 Inflation-Adjusted Dollars)	
Group	Dollars
Total Population	46,186
Hispanic or Latino (of any race)	31,667
Mexican	31,722

Per Capita Income (2010 Inflation-Adjusted Dollars)	
Group	Dollars
Total Population	23,962
Hispanic or Latino (of any race)	15,591
Mexican	8,949

Households with $100,000+ Income		
Group	Number	%
Total Population	694	13.5
Hispanic or Latino (of any race)	0	0.0
Mexican	0	0.0

Households with Food Stamps/SNAP Benefits During Past 12 Months		
Group	Number	%
Total Population	740	14.4
Hispanic or Latino (of any race)	126	23.4
Mexican	108	24.0

Poverty Rate (Income in Past 12 Months Below Poverty Level)	
Group	%
Total Population	19.6
Hispanic or Latino (of any race)	49.0
Mexican	47.9

Notes: (1) Percent of total population; (2) Percent of Hispanic/Latino population; Profiles include places with an overall population of at least 125,000, OR an overall population of at least 25,000 where the Hispanic/Latino population is at least 20% of the overall population. In states where less than five places meet either of these criteria, we have included places with at least 10,000 total population with the highest percentage of Hispanic/Latino population. These places are identified with an asterisk (*); Please refer to the User's Guide for a full explanation of data.

Louisiana

EDITOR'S NOTE: For a place to be included in this edition, it must meet one of two criteria. Either its overall population is at least 125,000, OR its overall population is at least 25,000 and its Hispanic/Latino population is at least 20% of the overall population. For the state of Louisiana, the following locations are included:

- Baton Rouge
- Kenner
- Metairie
- New Orleans
- Shreveport

Section Two: State & Place Profiles starts with the state profile, followed by place profiles that meet the criteria above. Places are listed alphabetically within each state. All states, all counties and places that meet the above criteria are ranked and compared in *Section Three: Rankings & Comparisons*, on page 1055.

For a more detailed look at the Hispanic/Latino population in Louisiana, a companion web site is available at no additional charge with purchase of this print edition. Visit http://gold.greyhouse.com/page/info_hispanic for more information.

The web site includes data for all counties and places in Louisiana with Hispanic/Latino population, plus ten additional topics: Self Employed Worker; Walked to Work; Worked from Home; Mean Travel Time to Work; Mean Household Income; Households with Cash Public Assistance; Mean Cash Pubic Assistance; Poverty Rates for 18 and Under, 18 to 64, and 65 and Over.

Population

Group	Number	%TP[1]	%HP[2]
Total Population	4,533,372	100.0	–
Hispanic or Latino (of any race)	192,560	4.2	100.0
Central American, ex. Mexican	51,722	1.1	26.9
Costa Rican	1,212	<0.1	0.6
Guatemalan	6,660	0.1	3.5
Honduran	30,617	0.7	15.9
Nicaraguan	6,390	0.1	3.3
Panamanian	1,434	<0.1	0.7
Salvadoran	5,120	0.1	2.7
Cuban	10,330	0.2	5.4
Dominican Republic	3,238	0.1	1.7
Mexican	78,643	1.7	40.8
Puerto Rican	11,603	0.3	6.0
South American	8,871	0.2	4.6
Argentinean	707	<0.1	0.4
Bolivian	295	<0.1	0.2
Chilean	548	<0.1	0.3
Colombian	3,167	0.1	1.6
Ecuadorian	1,069	<0.1	0.6
Peruvian	1,229	<0.1	0.6
Uruguayan	109	<0.1	0.1
Venezuelan	1,591	<0.1	0.8
Spaniard	6,018	0.1	3.1

Population Growth: 2000–2010

Group	%
Total Population	1.4
Hispanic or Latino (of any race)	78.7
Central American, ex. Mexican	198.5
Costa Rican	79.8
Guatemalan	218.2
Honduran	248.2
Nicaraguan	127.9
Panamanian	67.7
Salvadoran	354.3
Cuban	22.3
Dominican Republic	244.5
Mexican	143.7
Puerto Rican	51.3
South American	117.5
Argentinean	135.7
Chilean	93.0
Colombian	106.6
Ecuadorian	123.6
Peruvian	154.5
Venezuelan	145.5
Spaniard	550.6

Males per 100 Females

Group	Number
Total Population	95.9
Hispanic or Latino (of any race)	123.5
Central American, ex. Mexican	123.4
Costa Rican	87.6
Guatemalan	132.1
Honduran	130.1
Nicaraguan	105.1
Panamanian	74.5
Salvadoran	126.4
Cuban	107.6
Dominican Republic	114.9
Mexican	139.1
Puerto Rican	107.1
South American	89.5
Argentinean	100.9
Bolivian	99.3
Chilean	89.0
Colombian	83.9
Ecuadorian	102.8
Peruvian	92.9
Uruguayan	87.9
Venezuelan	83.9
Spaniard	104.3

Average Household Size

Group	People
Total Population	2.55
Hispanic or Latino (of any race)	3.06
Central American, ex. Mexican	3.32
Costa Rican	2.74
Guatemalan	3.34
Honduran	3.41
Nicaraguan	3.10
Panamanian	2.69
Salvadoran	3.47
Cuban	2.60
Dominican Republic	3.16
Mexican	3.27
Puerto Rican	2.69
South American	2.63
Argentinean	2.42
Bolivian	2.79
Chilean	2.51
Colombian	2.56
Ecuadorian	2.69
Peruvian	2.73
Uruguayan	2.73
Venezuelan	2.77
Spaniard	2.41

Median Age

Group	Years
Total Population	35.8
Hispanic or Latino (of any race)	28.9
Central American, ex. Mexican	30.8
Costa Rican	35.5
Guatemalan	29.2
Honduran	30.5
Nicaraguan	34.5
Panamanian	35.3
Salvadoran	30.1
Cuban	37.7
Dominican Republic	30.3
Mexican	26.2
Puerto Rican	27.2
South American	34.0
Argentinean	37.0
Bolivian	34.3
Chilean	36.2
Colombian	35.0
Ecuadorian	33.2
Peruvian	34.3
Uruguayan	38.4
Venezuelan	30.7
Spaniard	41.0

High School Graduates

(Universe: Population 25 Years and Over)

Group	Number	%
Total Population	2,313,064	81.0
Hispanic or Latino (of any race)	69,239	69.3
Central American, ex. Mexican	20,628	66.5
Costa Rican	779	76.1
Guatemalan	2,334	65.8
Honduran	11,172	64.5
Nicaraguan	3,692	71.3
Panamanian	888	92.8
Salvadoran	1,487	56.9
Cuban	5,165	78.4
Dominican Republic	1,068	72.0
Mexican	22,811	60.8
Puerto Rican	4,533	86.2
South American	5,545	92.8
Argentinean	566	94.0
Colombian	1,714	87.2
Ecuadorian	554	97.4
Peruvian	1,014	96.3
Venezuelan	1,006	98.6
Spaniard	3,864	82.6

Four-Year College Graduates

(Universe: Population 25 Years and Over)

Group	Number	%
Total Population	597,856	20.9
Hispanic or Latino (of any race)	18,019	18.0
Central American, ex. Mexican	5,027	16.2
Costa Rican	226	22.1
Guatemalan	619	17.5
Honduran	2,178	12.6
Nicaraguan	1,265	24.4
Panamanian	372	38.9
Salvadoran	283	10.8
Cuban	1,664	25.2
Dominican Republic	297	20.0
Mexican	4,174	11.1
Puerto Rican	1,525	29.0
South American	2,823	47.3
Argentinean	333	55.3
Colombian	836	42.5
Ecuadorian	285	50.1
Peruvian	402	38.2
Venezuelan	551	54.0
Spaniard	1,238	26.5

Population Age 3–17 Enrolled in Public School

(Universe: Population Age 3–17 Enrolled in School)

Group	Number	%
Total Population	675,755	80.5
Hispanic or Latino (of any race)	27,162	80.2
Central American, ex. Mexican	5,399	74.5
Costa Rican	97	82.9
Guatemalan	683	61.3
Honduran	3,486	80.5
Nicaraguan	454	55.6
Panamanian	82	66.7
Salvadoran	476	79.6
Cuban	980	59.3
Dominican Republic	446	81.4
Mexican	14,826	89.4
Puerto Rican	1,623	72.2
South American	1,244	64.2
Argentinean	94	67.6
Colombian	434	65.1
Ecuadorian	27	22.3
Peruvian	204	97.6
Venezuelan	367	68.5
Spaniard	762	66.9

Notes: (1) Percent of total population; (2) Percent of Hispanic/Latino population; Profiles include places with an overall population of at least 125,000, OR an overall population of at least 25,000 where the Hispanic/Latino population is at least 20% of the overall population. In states where less than five places meet either of these criteria, we have included places with at least 10,000 total population with the highest percentage of Hispanic/Latino population. These places are identified with an asterisk (*); Please refer to the User's Guide for a full explanation of data.

Population Age 3–17 Enrolled in Private School
(Universe: Population Age 3–17 Enrolled in School)

Group	Number	%
Total Population	163,246	19.5
Hispanic or Latino (of any race)	6,699	19.8
Central American, ex. Mexican	1,851	25.5
Costa Rican	20	17.1
Guatemalan	432	38.7
Honduran	842	19.5
Nicaraguan	363	44.4
Panamanian	41	33.3
Salvadoran	122	20.4
Cuban	673	40.7
Dominican Republic	102	18.6
Mexican	1,766	10.6
Puerto Rican	625	27.8
South American	695	35.8
Argentinean	45	32.4
Colombian	233	34.9
Ecuadorian	94	77.7
Peruvian	5	2.4
Venezuelan	169	31.5
Spaniard	377	33.1

Foreign-Born Population

Group	Number	%
Total Population	157,697	3.6
Hispanic or Latino (of any race)	73,760	42.7
Central American, ex. Mexican	31,689	65.7
Costa Rican	848	59.0
Guatemalan	3,771	61.2
Honduran	18,614	66.8
Nicaraguan	4,807	69.5
Panamanian	565	44.0
Salvadoran	2,724	70.4
Cuban	4,624	45.2
Dominican Republic	1,628	64.9
Mexican	26,964	37.1
Puerto Rican	355	3.5
South American	5,493	56.7
Argentinean	411	46.4
Colombian	1,853	54.8
Ecuadorian	460	54.9
Peruvian	1,123	78.9
Venezuelan	911	46.2
Spaniard	589	8.8

Foreign-Born Naturalized U.S. Citizens

Group	Number	%
Total Population	65,998	41.9
Hispanic or Latino (of any race)	22,861	31.0
Central American, ex. Mexican	11,905	37.6
Costa Rican	441	52.0
Guatemalan	1,658	44.0
Honduran	5,857	31.5
Nicaraguan	2,562	53.3
Panamanian	382	67.6
Salvadoran	801	29.4
Cuban	2,649	57.3
Dominican Republic	646	39.7
Mexican	4,012	14.9
Puerto Rican	161	45.4
South American	1,970	35.9
Argentinean	183	44.5
Colombian	811	43.8
Ecuadorian	216	47.0
Peruvian	168	15.0
Venezuelan	312	34.2
Spaniard	258	43.8

Language Spoken at Home: English Only
(Universe: Population 5 Years and Over)

Group	Number	%
Total Population	3,764,360	91.3
Hispanic or Latino (of any race)	52,165	33.6
Central American, ex. Mexican	7,092	16.1
Costa Rican	303	22.6
Guatemalan	867	15.9
Honduran	3,924	15.5
Nicaraguan	846	13.2
Panamanian	550	44.6
Salvadoran	477	13.0
Cuban	3,308	35.2
Dominican Republic	283	12.0
Mexican	23,576	36.8
Puerto Rican	3,990	44.8
South American	2,108	23.9
Argentinean	289	38.4
Colombian	579	18.6
Ecuadorian	185	24.2
Peruvian	249	18.2
Venezuelan	607	35.2
Spaniard	4,923	77.3

Language Spoken at Home: Spanish
(Universe: Population 5 Years and Over)

Group	Number	%
Total Population	136,282	3.3
Hispanic or Latino (of any race)	101,555	65.4
Central American, ex. Mexican	36,785	83.7
Costa Rican	1,026	76.7
Guatemalan	4,529	83.3
Honduran	21,313	84.5
Nicaraguan	5,562	86.8
Panamanian	669	54.2
Salvadoran	3,196	87.0
Cuban	6,039	64.2
Dominican Republic	2,058	87.6
Mexican	39,980	62.3
Puerto Rican	4,889	54.9
South American	6,637	75.4
Argentinean	449	59.6
Colombian	2,529	81.4
Ecuadorian	565	74.0
Peruvian	1,089	79.7
Venezuelan	1,119	64.8
Spaniard	1,070	16.8

Unemployment Rate
(Universe: Population 16 Years and Over)

Group	%
Total Population	7.7
Hispanic or Latino (of any race)	7.4
Central American, ex. Mexican	8.2
Costa Rican	1.5
Guatemalan	8.0
Honduran	9.9
Nicaraguan	5.8
Panamanian	0.0
Salvadoran	6.7
Cuban	8.9
Dominican Republic	10.0
Mexican	5.9
Puerto Rican	8.0
South American	7.7
Argentinean	14.4
Colombian	7.8
Ecuadorian	8.8
Peruvian	1.0
Venezuelan	5.2
Spaniard	8.7

Class of Worker: Private Wage and Salary
(Universe: Civilian Employed Population 16 Years and Over)

Group	Number	%
Total Population	1,505,474	77.1
Hispanic or Latino (of any race)	67,863	83.6
Central American, ex. Mexican	21,737	84.1
Costa Rican	692	87.0
Guatemalan	2,502	80.4
Honduran	12,196	85.3
Nicaraguan	3,687	88.6
Panamanian	672	80.0
Salvadoran	1,837	75.0
Cuban	3,887	82.9
Dominican Republic	974	84.7
Mexican	27,338	85.4
Puerto Rican	3,223	80.2
South American	3,587	75.1
Argentinean	230	59.4
Colombian	1,242	77.9
Ecuadorian	291	68.3
Peruvian	626	72.0
Venezuelan	851	89.8
Spaniard	2,222	75.0

Class of Worker: Government
(Universe: Civilian Employed Population 16 Years and Over)

Group	Number	%
Total Population	323,145	16.5
Hispanic or Latino (of any race)	6,514	8.0
Central American, ex. Mexican	1,289	5.0
Costa Rican	45	5.7
Guatemalan	146	4.7
Honduran	616	4.3
Nicaraguan	246	5.9
Panamanian	150	17.9
Salvadoran	55	2.2
Cuban	504	10.8
Dominican Republic	56	4.9
Mexican	2,195	6.9
Puerto Rican	680	16.9
South American	787	16.5
Argentinean	138	35.7
Colombian	298	18.7
Ecuadorian	85	20.0
Peruvian	90	10.3
Venezuelan	44	4.6
Spaniard	481	16.2

Means of Transportation to Work: Car, Truck or Van
(Universe: Workers 16 Years and Over)

Group	Number	%
Total Population	1,770,677	92.5
Hispanic or Latino (of any race)	71,566	89.3
Central American, ex. Mexican	22,249	88.7
Costa Rican	723	92.9
Guatemalan	2,597	83.1
Honduran	12,155	87.8
Nicaraguan	3,840	94.8
Panamanian	771	93.7
Salvadoran	1,995	86.5
Cuban	3,953	87.2
Dominican Republic	913	82.0
Mexican	28,241	89.0
Puerto Rican	3,986	92.2
South American	4,231	90.3
Argentinean	379	97.2
Colombian	1,439	92.6
Ecuadorian	379	88.3
Peruvian	701	82.1
Venezuelan	894	95.0
Spaniard	2,691	89.0

Means of Transportation to Work: Public Transportation (ex. Taxicab)
(Universe: Workers 16 Years and Over)

Group	Number	%
Total Population	24,248	1.3
Hispanic or Latino (of any race)	2,247	2.8
Central American, ex. Mexican	1,091	4.3
Costa Rican	38	4.9
Guatemalan	154	4.9
Honduran	758	5.5
Nicaraguan	41	1.0
Panamanian	0	0.0
Salvadoran	100	4.3
Cuban	45	1.0
Dominican Republic	175	15.7
Mexican	532	1.7
Puerto Rican	94	2.2
South American	182	3.9
Argentinean	11	2.8
Colombian	44	2.8
Ecuadorian	0	0.0
Peruvian	127	14.9
Venezuelan	0	0.0
Spaniard	18	0.6

Homeownership Rate
(Universe: Occupied Housing Units)

Group	%
Total Population	67.2
Hispanic or Latino (of any race)	46.2
Central American, ex. Mexican	44.2
Costa Rican	60.9
Guatemalan	46.7
Honduran	40.4
Nicaraguan	54.1
Panamanian	56.3
Salvadoran	40.9
Cuban	59.7
Dominican Republic	39.6
Mexican	38.7

Notes: (1) Percent of total population; (2) Percent of Hispanic/Latino population; Profiles include places with an overall population of at least 125,000, OR an overall population of at least 25,000 where the Hispanic/Latino population is at least 20% of the overall population. In states where less than five places meet either of these criteria, we have included places with at least 10,000 total population with the highest percentage of Hispanic/Latino population. These places are identified with an asterisk (*); Please refer to the User's Guide for a full explanation of data.

Puerto Rican	44.1
South American	54.7
Argentinean	60.8
Bolivian	50.5
Chilean	60.7
Colombian	55.2
Ecuadorian	55.7
Peruvian	46.4
Uruguayan	46.2
Venezuelan	57.1
Spaniard	75.8

Median Home Value

Group	Dollars
Total Population	130,000
Hispanic or Latino (of any race)	156,200
Central American, ex. Mexican	166,200
Costa Rican	168,500
Guatemalan	146,100
Honduran	166,700
Nicaraguan	174,500
Panamanian	197,900
Salvadoran	160,800
Cuban	172,600
Dominican Republic	221,600
Mexican	121,100
Puerto Rican	165,700
South American	180,200
Argentinean	195,500
Colombian	153,000
Ecuadorian	186,900
Peruvian	160,800
Venezuelan	208,800
Spaniard	159,000

Median Gross Rent

Group	Dollars
Total Population	712
Hispanic or Latino (of any race)	775
Central American, ex. Mexican	852
Costa Rican	862
Guatemalan	825
Honduran	858
Nicaraguan	908
Panamanian	699
Salvadoran	745
Cuban	796
Dominican Republic	775
Mexican	726
Puerto Rican	799
South American	851
Argentinean	716
Colombian	777
Ecuadorian	659
Peruvian	839
Venezuelan	933
Spaniard	806

Median Household Income
(2010 Inflation-Adjusted Dollars)

Group	Dollars
Total Population	43,445
Hispanic or Latino (of any race)	42,007
Central American, ex. Mexican	42,755
Costa Rican	56,641
Guatemalan	41,998
Honduran	41,598
Nicaraguan	52,868
Panamanian	43,603
Salvadoran	34,747
Cuban	49,240
Dominican Republic	33,241
Mexican	39,447
Puerto Rican	46,868
South American	44,982
Argentinean	63,264
Colombian	42,777
Ecuadorian	56,750
Peruvian	35,313
Venezuelan	66,926
Spaniard	46,250

Per Capita Income
(2010 Inflation-Adjusted Dollars)

Group	Dollars
Total Population	23,094
Hispanic or Latino (of any race)	18,727
Central American, ex. Mexican	17,912
Costa Rican	26,916
Guatemalan	14,773
Honduran	16,394
Nicaraguan	23,068
Panamanian	26,865
Salvadoran	18,739
Cuban	25,495
Dominican Republic	23,472
Mexican	15,952
Puerto Rican	21,479
South American	26,871
Argentinean	30,301
Colombian	22,202
Ecuadorian	19,807
Peruvian	23,255
Venezuelan	27,121
Spaniard	23,486

Households with $100,000+ Income

Group	Number	%
Total Population	261,835	16.0
Hispanic or Latino (of any race)	6,792	13.3
Central American, ex. Mexican	1,794	12.3
Costa Rican	105	18.6
Guatemalan	155	9.2
Honduran	1,040	12.6
Nicaraguan	311	14.6
Panamanian	75	15.2
Salvadoran	102	8.6
Cuban	719	20.4
Dominican Republic	140	15.7
Mexican	2,223	12.0
Puerto Rican	411	13.4
South American	597	18.0
Argentinean	70	21.1
Colombian	202	15.9
Ecuadorian	3	1.5
Peruvian	62	14.7
Venezuelan	177	26.2
Spaniard	439	16.3

Households with Food Stamps/SNAP Benefits During Past 12 Months

Group	Number	%
Total Population	274,078	16.7
Hispanic or Latino (of any race)	7,088	13.9
Central American, ex. Mexican	2,029	13.9
Costa Rican	78	13.8
Guatemalan	273	16.3
Honduran	1,195	14.5
Nicaraguan	289	13.6
Panamanian	18	3.7
Salvadoran	71	6.0
Cuban	509	14.4
Dominican Republic	163	18.2
Mexican	2,375	12.8
Puerto Rican	583	19.0
South American	281	8.5
Argentinean	38	11.4
Colombian	148	11.7
Ecuadorian	7	3.5
Peruvian	35	8.3
Venezuelan	53	7.8
Spaniard	349	12.9

Poverty Rate
(Income in Past 12 Months Below Poverty Level)

Group	%
Total Population	18.1
Hispanic or Latino (of any race)	19.4
Central American, ex. Mexican	17.1
Costa Rican	10.1
Guatemalan	12.7
Honduran	19.9
Nicaraguan	12.3
Panamanian	8.6
Salvadoran	12.4
Cuban	14.4
Dominican Republic	20.9
Mexican	23.7
Puerto Rican	16.5
South American	15.0
Argentinean	5.9
Colombian	13.9
Ecuadorian	8.9
Peruvian	21.7
Venezuelan	18.5
Spaniard	10.6

Baton Rouge

Population

Group	Number	%TP[1]	%HP[2]
Total Population	229,493	100.0	–
Hispanic or Latino (of any race)	7,653	3.3	100.0
Central American, ex. Mexican	1,917	0.8	25.0
Guatemalan	271	0.1	3.5
Honduran	730	0.3	9.5
Nicaraguan	130	0.1	1.7
Salvadoran	647	0.3	8.5
Cuban	551	0.2	7.2
Mexican	3,070	1.3	40.1
Puerto Rican	489	0.2	6.4
South American	604	0.3	7.9
Colombian	245	0.1	3.2
Venezuelan	139	0.1	1.8
Spaniard	213	0.1	2.8

Population Growth: 2000–2010

Group	%
Total Population	0.7
Hispanic or Latino (of any race)	95.3
Central American, ex. Mexican	305.3
Honduran	444.8
Salvadoran	547.0
Cuban	29.6
Mexican	154.6
Puerto Rican	45.5
South American	79.8
Colombian	96.0

Males per 100 Females

Group	Number
Total Population	92.7
Hispanic or Latino (of any race)	131.8
Central American, ex. Mexican	144.2
Guatemalan	153.3
Honduran	159.8
Nicaraguan	94.0
Salvadoran	149.8
Cuban	98.9
Mexican	153.7
Puerto Rican	98.0
South American	98.0
Colombian	100.8
Venezuelan	69.5
Spaniard	124.2

Average Household Size

Group	People
Total Population	2.40
Hispanic or Latino (of any race)	2.90
Central American, ex. Mexican	3.30
Guatemalan	3.71
Honduran	3.06
Nicaraguan	2.46
Salvadoran	3.96
Cuban	2.27
Mexican	3.30
Puerto Rican	2.42
South American	2.43
Colombian	2.52
Venezuelan	2.59
Spaniard	1.88

Median Age

Group	Years
Total Population	30.7
Hispanic or Latino (of any race)	26.6
Central American, ex. Mexican	27.1
Guatemalan	27.6
Honduran	26.7
Nicaraguan	29.3

Notes: (1) Percent of total population; (2) Percent of Hispanic/Latino population; Profiles include places with an overall population of at least 125,000, OR an overall population of at least 25,000 where the Hispanic/Latino population is at least 20% of the overall population. In states where less than five places meet either of these criteria, we have included places with at least 10,000 total population with the highest percentage of Hispanic/Latino population. These places are identified with an asterisk (*); Please refer to the User's Guide for a full explanation of data.

Salvadoran		26.3
Cuban		33.0
Mexican		25.4
Puerto Rican		24.2
South American		29.6
Colombian		35.5
Venezuelan		26.6
Spaniard		36.4

High School Graduates
(Universe: Population 25 Years and Over)

Group	Number	%
Total Population	112,013	84.2
Hispanic or Latino (of any race)	2,429	74.1
Central American, ex. Mexican	684	88.6
Mexican	603	53.4

Four-Year College Graduates
(Universe: Population 25 Years and Over)

Group	Number	%
Total Population	42,584	32.0
Hispanic or Latino (of any race)	851	26.0
Central American, ex. Mexican	144	18.7
Mexican	112	9.9

Population Age 3–17 Enrolled in Public School
(Universe: Population Age 3–17 Enrolled in School)

Group	Number	%
Total Population	31,112	77.9
Hispanic or Latino (of any race)	759	82.8
Central American, ex. Mexican	52	61.9
Mexican	424	92.4

Population Age 3–17 Enrolled in Private School
(Universe: Population Age 3–17 Enrolled in School)

Group	Number	%
Total Population	8,847	22.1
Hispanic or Latino (of any race)	158	17.2
Central American, ex. Mexican	32	38.1
Mexican	35	7.6

Foreign-Born Population

Group	Number	%
Total Population	11,339	4.9
Hispanic or Latino (of any race)	2,911	41.6
Central American, ex. Mexican	666	46.3
Mexican	1,433	47.0

Foreign-Born Naturalized U.S. Citizens

Group	Number	%
Total Population	4,224	37.3
Hispanic or Latino (of any race)	844	29.0
Central American, ex. Mexican	397	59.6
Mexican	161	11.2

Language Spoken at Home: English Only
(Universe: Population 5 Years and Over)

Group	Number	%
Total Population	196,494	91.8
Hispanic or Latino (of any race)	2,069	33.5
Central American, ex. Mexican	269	21.1
Mexican	724	28.4

Language Spoken at Home: Spanish
(Universe: Population 5 Years and Over)

Group	Number	%
Total Population	6,365	3.0
Hispanic or Latino (of any race)	4,040	65.5
Central American, ex. Mexican	1,007	78.9
Mexican	1,825	71.6

Unemployment Rate
(Universe: Population 16 Years and Over)

Group	%
Total Population	8.8
Hispanic or Latino (of any race)	7.5
Central American, ex. Mexican	6.6
Mexican	4.7

Class of Worker: Private Wage and Salary
(Universe: Civilian Employed Population 16 Years and Over)

Group	Number	%
Total Population	77,856	72.8
Hispanic or Latino (of any race)	2,626	77.4
Central American, ex. Mexican	767	87.5
Mexican	985	76.4

Class of Worker: Government
(Universe: Civilian Employed Population 16 Years and Over)

Group	Number	%
Total Population	22,788	21.3
Hispanic or Latino (of any race)	478	14.1
Central American, ex. Mexican	40	4.6
Mexican	143	11.1

Means of Transportation to Work: Car, Truck or Van
(Universe: Workers 16 Years and Over)

Group	Number	%
Total Population	93,482	90.1
Hispanic or Latino (of any race)	2,724	84.3
Central American, ex. Mexican	729	91.0
Mexican	904	71.5

Means of Transportation to Work: Public Transportation (ex. Taxicab)
(Universe: Workers 16 Years and Over)

Group	Number	%
Total Population	2,510	2.4
Hispanic or Latino (of any race)	89	2.8
Central American, ex. Mexican	34	4.2
Mexican	55	4.4

Homeownership Rate
(Universe: Occupied Housing Units)

Group	%
Total Population	49.3
Hispanic or Latino (of any race)	29.5
Central American, ex. Mexican	25.9
Guatemalan	18.6
Honduran	18.1
Nicaraguan	36.5
Salvadoran	30.3
Cuban	49.4
Mexican	18.7
Puerto Rican	25.4
South American	41.4
Colombian	52.3
Venezuelan	23.5
Spaniard	58.2

Median Home Value

Group	Dollars
Total Population	144,900
Hispanic or Latino (of any race)	161,100
Central American, ex. Mexican	159,300
Mexican	150,400

Median Gross Rent

Group	Dollars
Total Population	733
Hispanic or Latino (of any race)	781
Central American, ex. Mexican	886
Mexican	764

Median Household Income
(2010 Inflation-Adjusted Dollars)

Group	Dollars
Total Population	36,964
Hispanic or Latino (of any race)	31,872
Central American, ex. Mexican	55,688
Mexican	25,769

Per Capita Income
(2010 Inflation-Adjusted Dollars)

Group	Dollars
Total Population	23,195
Hispanic or Latino (of any race)	18,150
Central American, ex. Mexican	24,854
Mexican	11,854

Households with $100,000+ Income

Group	Number	%
Total Population	12,842	14.5
Hispanic or Latino (of any race)	270	11.2
Central American, ex. Mexican	107	15.8
Mexican	26	3.1

Households with Food Stamps/SNAP Benefits During Past 12 Months

Group	Number	%
Total Population	15,051	17.0
Hispanic or Latino (of any race)	320	13.3
Central American, ex. Mexican	61	9.0
Mexican	80	9.7

Poverty Rate
(Income in Past 12 Months Below Poverty Level)

Group	%
Total Population	25.5
Hispanic or Latino (of any race)	35.2
Central American, ex. Mexican	27.8
Mexican	41.8

Kenner

Population

Group	Number	%TP[1]	%HP[2]
Total Population	66,702	100.0	–
Hispanic or Latino (of any race)	14,918	22.4	100.0
Central American, ex. Mexican	8,641	13.0	57.9
Costa Rican	158	0.2	1.1
Guatemalan	844	1.3	5.7
Honduran	5,556	8.3	37.2
Nicaraguan	1,306	2.0	8.8
Salvadoran	679	1.0	4.6
Cuban	1,101	1.7	7.4
Dominican Republic	287	0.4	1.9
Mexican	2,214	3.3	14.8
Puerto Rican	617	0.9	4.1
South American	538	0.8	3.6
Colombian	181	0.3	1.2
Ecuadorian	106	0.2	0.7
Venezuelan	101	0.2	0.7
Spaniard	136	0.2	0.9

Population Growth: 2000–2010

Group	%
Total Population	-5.4
Hispanic or Latino (of any race)	55.4
Central American, ex. Mexican	156.9
Costa Rican	18.8
Guatemalan	111.5
Honduran	213.2
Nicaraguan	104.7
Salvadoran	267.0
Cuban	11.8
Mexican	114.7
Puerto Rican	66.8
South American	101.5
Colombian	70.8

Males per 100 Females

Group	Number
Total Population	95.4
Hispanic or Latino (of any race)	111.7
Central American, ex. Mexican	107.2
Costa Rican	97.5
Guatemalan	113.1
Honduran	111.3
Nicaraguan	88.5
Salvadoran	113.5
Cuban	103.5
Dominican Republic	102.1
Mexican	149.0
Puerto Rican	117.3
South American	88.1
Colombian	70.8
Ecuadorian	100.0
Venezuelan	102.0
Spaniard	88.9

Average Household Size

Group	People
Total Population	2.67
Hispanic or Latino (of any race)	3.34
Central American, ex. Mexican	3.53
Costa Rican	3.21
Guatemalan	3.40
Honduran	3.57
Nicaraguan	3.48
Salvadoran	3.73
Cuban	2.65
Dominican Republic	3.32
Mexican	3.66
Puerto Rican	2.87

Notes: (1) Percent of total population; (2) Percent of Hispanic/Latino population; Profiles include places with an overall population of at least 125,000, OR an overall population of at least 25,000 where the Hispanic/Latino population is at least 20% of the overall population. In states where less than five places meet either of these criteria, we have included places with at least 10,000 total population with the highest percentage of Hispanic/Latino population. These places are identified with an asterisk (*); Please refer to the User's Guide for a full explanation of data.

Group	Years
South American	2.58
Colombian	2.26
Ecuadorian	2.80
Venezuelan	2.69
Spaniard	2.76

Median Age

Group	Years
Total Population	37.4
Hispanic or Latino (of any race)	31.6
Central American, ex. Mexican	32.6
Costa Rican	40.0
Guatemalan	35.0
Honduran	31.6
Nicaraguan	36.0
Salvadoran	33.1
Cuban	43.3
Dominican Republic	29.6
Mexican	27.6
Puerto Rican	30.8
South American	39.3
Colombian	45.3
Ecuadorian	38.5
Venezuelan	28.8
Spaniard	39.0

High School Graduates
(Universe: Population 25 Years and Over)

Group	Number	%
Total Population	37,607	82.8
Hispanic or Latino (of any race)	6,249	72.0
Central American, ex. Mexican	4,102	71.5
Honduran	2,405	69.9
Nicaraguan	1,044	79.2
Cuban	614	85.3
Mexican	508	50.4

Four-Year College Graduates
(Universe: Population 25 Years and Over)

Group	Number	%
Total Population	10,094	22.2
Hispanic or Latino (of any race)	1,336	15.4
Central American, ex. Mexican	722	12.6
Honduran	190	5.5
Nicaraguan	434	32.9
Cuban	132	18.3
Mexican	174	17.3

Population Age 3–17 Enrolled in Public School
(Universe: Population Age 3–17 Enrolled in School)

Group	Number	%
Total Population	7,398	65.3
Hispanic or Latino (of any race)	1,695	79.4
Central American, ex. Mexican	1,026	89.8
Honduran	711	92.9
Nicaraguan	200	87.3
Cuban	88	43.1
Mexican	170	66.9

Population Age 3–17 Enrolled in Private School
(Universe: Population Age 3–17 Enrolled in School)

Group	Number	%
Total Population	3,928	34.7
Hispanic or Latino (of any race)	441	20.6
Central American, ex. Mexican	116	10.2
Honduran	54	7.1
Nicaraguan	29	12.7
Cuban	116	56.9
Mexican	84	33.1

Foreign-Born Population

Group	Number	%
Total Population	11,231	16.9
Hispanic or Latino (of any race)	8,429	63.2
Central American, ex. Mexican	5,951	71.6
Honduran	3,632	66.5
Nicaraguan	1,313	81.5
Cuban	692	59.4
Mexican	1,013	56.6

Foreign-Born Naturalized U.S. Citizens

Group	Number	%
Total Population	5,121	45.6
Hispanic or Latino (of any race)	3,460	41.0
Central American, ex. Mexican	2,194	36.9
Honduran	1,040	28.6
Nicaraguan	593	45.2
Cuban	552	79.8
Mexican	302	29.8

Language Spoken at Home: English Only
(Universe: Population 5 Years and Over)

Group	Number	%
Total Population	48,414	77.7
Hispanic or Latino (of any race)	2,111	17.2
Central American, ex. Mexican	728	9.6
Honduran	575	11.9
Nicaraguan	67	4.4
Cuban	295	26.5
Mexican	352	20.3

Language Spoken at Home: Spanish
(Universe: Population 5 Years and Over)

Group	Number	%
Total Population	10,842	17.4
Hispanic or Latino (of any race)	10,118	82.5
Central American, ex. Mexican	6,816	90.2
Honduran	4,240	88.1
Nicaraguan	1,466	95.6
Cuban	819	73.5
Mexican	1,386	79.7

Unemployment Rate
(Universe: Population 16 Years and Over)

Group	%
Total Population	8.2
Hispanic or Latino (of any race)	8.9
Central American, ex. Mexican	9.6
Honduran	13.2
Nicaraguan	0.7
Cuban	7.2
Mexican	8.8

Class of Worker: Private Wage and Salary
(Universe: Civilian Employed Population 16 Years and Over)

Group	Number	%
Total Population	27,924	83.6
Hispanic or Latino (of any race)	6,127	87.5
Central American, ex. Mexican	3,859	89.8
Honduran	2,347	89.6
Nicaraguan	913	94.1
Cuban	489	88.7
Mexican	966	85.9

Class of Worker: Government
(Universe: Civilian Employed Population 16 Years and Over)

Group	Number	%
Total Population	3,499	10.5
Hispanic or Latino (of any race)	292	4.2
Central American, ex. Mexican	122	2.8
Honduran	65	2.5
Nicaraguan	8	0.8
Cuban	0	0.0
Mexican	17	1.5

Means of Transportation to Work: Car, Truck or Van
(Universe: Workers 16 Years and Over)

Group	Number	%
Total Population	29,985	92.9
Hispanic or Latino (of any race)	6,243	92.9
Central American, ex. Mexican	3,801	92.5
Honduran	2,300	92.3
Nicaraguan	851	92.1
Cuban	513	98.5
Mexican	966	89.9

Means of Transportation to Work: Public Transportation (ex. Taxicab)
(Universe: Workers 16 Years and Over)

Group	Number	%
Total Population	440	1.4
Hispanic or Latino (of any race)	182	2.7
Central American, ex. Mexican	130	3.2
Honduran	105	4.2
Nicaraguan	25	2.7
Cuban	0	0.0
Mexican	41	3.8

Homeownership Rate
(Universe: Occupied Housing Units)

Group	%
Total Population	60.5
Hispanic or Latino (of any race)	50.9
Central American, ex. Mexican	53.8
Costa Rican	66.1
Guatemalan	60.9
Honduran	50.2
Nicaraguan	63.0
Salvadoran	52.2
Cuban	62.6
Dominican Republic	37.6
Mexican	33.4
Puerto Rican	43.1
South American	58.5
Colombian	52.2
Ecuadorian	75.6
Venezuelan	40.6
Spaniard	75.9

Median Home Value

Group	Dollars
Total Population	184,900
Hispanic or Latino (of any race)	181,000
Central American, ex. Mexican	165,300
Honduran	161,100
Nicaraguan	201,300
Cuban	221,100
Mexican	180,400

Median Gross Rent

Group	Dollars
Total Population	882
Hispanic or Latino (of any race)	928
Central American, ex. Mexican	941
Honduran	959
Nicaraguan	717
Cuban	858
Mexican	946

Median Household Income
(2010 Inflation-Adjusted Dollars)

Group	Dollars
Total Population	48,567
Hispanic or Latino (of any race)	43,378
Central American, ex. Mexican	41,039
Honduran	36,397
Nicaraguan	58,482
Cuban	65,842
Mexican	37,417

Per Capita Income
(2010 Inflation-Adjusted Dollars)

Group	Dollars
Total Population	24,932
Hispanic or Latino (of any race)	17,401
Central American, ex. Mexican	14,945
Honduran	13,487
Nicaraguan	18,934
Cuban	23,346
Mexican	19,619

Households with $100,000+ Income

Group	Number	%
Total Population	4,601	18.9
Hispanic or Latino (of any race)	504	12.3
Central American, ex. Mexican	173	7.2
Honduran	72	4.8
Nicaraguan	70	13.8
Cuban	73	18.7
Mexican	127	23.7

Households with Food Stamps/SNAP Benefits During Past 12 Months

Group	Number	%
Total Population	3,537	14.6
Hispanic or Latino (of any race)	521	12.7
Central American, ex. Mexican	377	15.6
Honduran	289	19.4
Nicaraguan	33	6.5
Cuban	63	16.1
Mexican	17	3.2

Notes: (1) Percent of total population; (2) Percent of Hispanic/Latino population; Profiles include places with an overall population of at least 125,000, OR an overall population of at least 25,000 where the Hispanic/Latino population is at least 20% of the overall population. In states where less than five places meet either of these criteria, we have included places with at least 10,000 total population with the highest percentage of Hispanic/Latino population. These places are identified with an asterisk (*); Please refer to the User's Guide for a full explanation of data.

Poverty Rate
(Income in Past 12 Months Below Poverty Level)

Group	%
Total Population	14.2
Hispanic or Latino (of any race)	15.6
Central American, ex. Mexican	15.6
Honduran	21.0
Nicaraguan	0.0
Cuban	8.8
Mexican	17.6

Metairie

Population

Group	Number	%TP[1]	%HP[2]
Total Population	138,481	100.0	–
Hispanic or Latino (of any race)	17,447	12.6	100.0
Central American, ex. Mexican	9,085	6.6	52.1
Costa Rican	200	0.1	1.1
Guatemalan	1,096	0.8	6.3
Honduran	5,611	4.1	32.2
Nicaraguan	1,462	1.1	8.4
Salvadoran	579	0.4	3.3
Cuban	1,396	1.0	8.0
Dominican Republic	267	0.2	1.5
Mexican	2,779	2.0	15.9
Puerto Rican	650	0.5	3.7
South American	1,062	0.8	6.1
Argentinean	100	0.1	0.6
Colombian	331	0.2	1.9
Ecuadorian	179	0.1	1.0
Peruvian	186	0.1	1.1
Venezuelan	158	0.1	0.9
Spaniard	417	0.3	2.4

Population Growth: 2000–2010

Group	%
Total Population	-5.2
Hispanic or Latino (of any race)	64.7
Central American, ex. Mexican	165.8
Guatemalan	198.6
Honduran	222.3
Nicaraguan	81.4
Salvadoran	278.4
Cuban	20.0
Mexican	109.6
Puerto Rican	36.0
South American	77.6
Colombian	60.7

Males per 100 Females

Group	Number
Total Population	94.9
Hispanic or Latino (of any race)	117.2
Central American, ex. Mexican	120.0
Costa Rican	75.4
Guatemalan	132.7
Honduran	127.3
Nicaraguan	105.6
Salvadoran	103.2
Cuban	99.7
Dominican Republic	107.0
Mexican	128.3
Puerto Rican	102.5
South American	99.6
Argentinean	92.3
Colombian	93.6
Ecuadorian	94.6
Peruvian	121.4
Venezuelan	92.7
Spaniard	120.6

Average Household Size

Group	People
Total Population	2.30
Hispanic or Latino (of any race)	2.93
Central American, ex. Mexican	3.17
Costa Rican	2.73
Guatemalan	3.46
Honduran	3.25
Nicaraguan	2.91
Salvadoran	3.04
Cuban	2.50
Dominican Republic	2.88
Mexican	3.07
Puerto Rican	2.34
South American	2.67
Argentinean	2.62
Colombian	2.55
Ecuadorian	2.52
Peruvian	3.00
Venezuelan	2.82
Spaniard	2.25

Median Age

Group	Years
Total Population	41.0
Hispanic or Latino (of any race)	31.1
Central American, ex. Mexican	31.3
Costa Rican	35.3
Guatemalan	29.5
Honduran	30.5
Nicaraguan	36.4
Salvadoran	32.3
Cuban	43.2
Dominican Republic	28.1
Mexican	28.2
Puerto Rican	29.5
South American	39.0
Argentinean	35.5
Colombian	41.4
Ecuadorian	41.7
Peruvian	39.1
Venezuelan	34.2
Spaniard	46.4

High School Graduates
(Universe: Population 25 Years and Over)

Group	Number	%
Total Population	85,920	88.3
Hispanic or Latino (of any race)	6,883	69.5
Central American, ex. Mexican	3,067	58.7
Honduran	1,890	67.0
Nicaraguan	558	45.9
Cuban	535	68.9
Mexican	1,559	77.9
South American	617	94.1

Four-Year College Graduates
(Universe: Population 25 Years and Over)

Group	Number	%
Total Population	32,132	33.0
Hispanic or Latino (of any race)	1,879	19.0
Central American, ex. Mexican	848	16.2
Honduran	507	18.0
Nicaraguan	213	17.5
Cuban	88	11.3
Mexican	367	18.3
South American	304	46.3

Population Age 3–17 Enrolled in Public School
(Universe: Population Age 3–17 Enrolled in School)

Group	Number	%
Total Population	8,347	41.8
Hispanic or Latino (of any race)	1,307	57.0
Central American, ex. Mexican	648	59.1
Honduran	549	70.8
Nicaraguan	22	12.7
Cuban	0	0.0
Mexican	374	71.1
South American	147	61.0

Population Age 3–17 Enrolled in Private School
(Universe: Population Age 3–17 Enrolled in School)

Group	Number	%
Total Population	11,630	58.2
Hispanic or Latino (of any race)	986	43.0
Central American, ex. Mexican	448	40.9
Honduran	226	29.2
Nicaraguan	151	87.3
Cuban	124	100.0
Mexican	152	28.9
South American	94	39.0

Foreign-Born Population

Group	Number	%
Total Population	15,527	11.4
Hispanic or Latino (of any race)	8,663	56.6
Central American, ex. Mexican	5,435	70.6
Honduran	3,042	70.9
Nicaraguan	1,170	73.1
Cuban	549	53.5
Mexican	1,663	44.2
South American	710	69.3

Foreign-Born Naturalized U.S. Citizens

Group	Number	%
Total Population	6,101	39.3
Hispanic or Latino (of any race)	2,883	33.3
Central American, ex. Mexican	1,969	36.2
Honduran	1,163	38.2
Nicaraguan	552	47.2
Cuban	307	55.9
Mexican	184	11.1
South American	232	32.7

Language Spoken at Home: English Only
(Universe: Population 5 Years and Over)

Group	Number	%
Total Population	107,847	84.4
Hispanic or Latino (of any race)	3,105	22.0
Central American, ex. Mexican	841	11.7
Honduran	500	12.4
Nicaraguan	273	18.2
Cuban	236	25.3
Mexican	1,128	33.5
South American	133	14.4

Language Spoken at Home: Spanish
(Universe: Population 5 Years and Over)

Group	Number	%
Total Population	12,132	9.5
Hispanic or Latino (of any race)	10,955	77.7
Central American, ex. Mexican	6,331	88.0
Honduran	3,533	87.6
Nicaraguan	1,223	81.8
Cuban	696	74.7
Mexican	2,235	66.5
South American	792	85.6

Unemployment Rate
(Universe: Population 16 Years and Over)

Group	%
Total Population	5.5
Hispanic or Latino (of any race)	7.5
Central American, ex. Mexican	9.5
Honduran	8.6
Nicaraguan	9.7
Cuban	10.8
Mexican	4.7
South American	0.0

Class of Worker: Private Wage and Salary
(Universe: Civilian Employed Population 16 Years and Over)

Group	Number	%
Total Population	57,577	81.7
Hispanic or Latino (of any race)	7,101	84.2
Central American, ex. Mexican	3,631	83.7
Honduran	1,846	81.4
Nicaraguan	773	91.6
Cuban	394	81.9
Mexican	1,777	83.0
South American	456	87.5

Class of Worker: Government
(Universe: Civilian Employed Population 16 Years and Over)

Group	Number	%
Total Population	7,976	11.3
Hispanic or Latino (of any race)	387	4.6
Central American, ex. Mexican	167	3.8
Honduran	133	5.9
Nicaraguan	20	2.4
Cuban	61	12.7
Mexican	47	2.2
South American	20	3.8

Means of Transportation to Work: Car, Truck or Van
(Universe: Workers 16 Years and Over)

Group	Number	%
Total Population	63,991	92.3
Hispanic or Latino (of any race)	7,307	89.0
Central American, ex. Mexican	3,581	86.4

Notes: (1) Percent of total population; (2) Percent of Hispanic/Latino population; Profiles include places with an overall population of at least 125,000, OR an overall population of at least 25,000 where the Hispanic/Latino population is at least 20% of the overall population. In states where less than five places meet either of these criteria, we have included places with at least 10,000 total population with the highest percentage of Hispanic/Latino population. These places are identified with an asterisk (*); Please refer to the User's Guide for a full explanation of data.

Group	Number	%
Honduran	1,851	85.2
Nicaraguan	782	94.0
Cuban	414	89.0
Mexican	1,974	90.6
South American	461	90.9

Means of Transportation to Work: Public Transportation (ex. Taxicab)
(Universe: Workers 16 Years and Over)

Group	Number	%
Total Population	868	1.3
Hispanic or Latino (of any race)	277	3.4
Central American, ex. Mexican	140	3.4
Honduran	27	1.2
Nicaraguan	16	1.9
Cuban	27	5.8
Mexican	98	4.5
South American	0	0.0

Homeownership Rate
(Universe: Occupied Housing Units)

Group	%
Total Population	62.1
Hispanic or Latino (of any race)	36.1
Central American, ex. Mexican	31.4
Costa Rican	54.5
Guatemalan	32.5
Honduran	27.0
Nicaraguan	43.1
Salvadoran	27.8
Cuban	56.5
Dominican Republic	10.6
Mexican	25.3
Puerto Rican	35.4
South American	52.4
Argentinean	59.0
Colombian	57.8
Ecuadorian	63.0
Peruvian	29.0
Venezuelan	56.1
Spaniard	73.9

Median Home Value

Group	Dollars
Total Population	210,900
Hispanic or Latino (of any race)	188,100
Central American, ex. Mexican	185,800
Honduran	183,800
Nicaraguan	192,300
Cuban	192,000
Mexican	135,500
South American	189,900

Median Gross Rent

Group	Dollars
Total Population	863
Hispanic or Latino (of any race)	853
Central American, ex. Mexican	880
Honduran	873
Nicaraguan	1,027
Cuban	1,019
Mexican	808
South American	860

Median Household Income
(2010 Inflation-Adjusted Dollars)

Group	Dollars
Total Population	51,761
Hispanic or Latino (of any race)	39,536
Central American, ex. Mexican	40,273
Honduran	42,645
Nicaraguan	31,944
Cuban	44,375
Mexican	35,407
South American	36,591

Per Capita Income
(2010 Inflation-Adjusted Dollars)

Group	Dollars
Total Population	31,619
Hispanic or Latino (of any race)	18,806
Central American, ex. Mexican	16,946
Honduran	17,217
Nicaraguan	19,307
Cuban	26,833
Mexican	17,427
South American	20,435

Households with $100,000+ Income

Group	Number	%
Total Population	12,086	21.3
Hispanic or Latino (of any race)	683	13.3
Central American, ex. Mexican	312	13.4
Honduran	179	13.3
Nicaraguan	60	13.3
Cuban	114	27.5
Mexican	130	10.7
South American	50	17.9

Households with Food Stamps/SNAP Benefits During Past 12 Months

Group	Number	%
Total Population	6,068	10.7
Hispanic or Latino (of any race)	646	12.6
Central American, ex. Mexican	271	11.6
Honduran	169	12.5
Nicaraguan	23	5.1
Cuban	96	23.2
Mexican	115	9.5
South American	26	9.3

Poverty Rate
(Income in Past 12 Months Below Poverty Level)

Group	%
Total Population	9.5
Hispanic or Latino (of any race)	15.1
Central American, ex. Mexican	19.0
Honduran	16.4
Nicaraguan	20.7
Cuban	7.6
Mexican	9.2
South American	20.5

New Orleans

Population

Group	Number	%TP[1]	%HP[2]
Total Population	343,829	100.0	–
Hispanic or Latino (of any race)	18,051	5.2	100.0
Central American, ex. Mexican	7,325	2.1	40.6
Costa Rican	135	<0.1	0.7
Guatemalan	906	0.3	5.0
Honduran	4,572	1.3	25.3
Nicaraguan	976	0.3	5.4
Panamanian	165	<0.1	0.9
Salvadoran	505	0.1	2.8
Cuban	1,285	0.4	7.1
Dominican Republic	244	0.1	1.4
Mexican	4,298	1.3	23.8
Puerto Rican	948	0.3	5.3
South American	1,352	0.4	7.5
Argentinean	165	<0.1	0.9
Colombian	459	0.1	2.5
Ecuadorian	194	0.1	1.1
Peruvian	166	<0.1	0.9
Venezuelan	154	<0.1	0.9
Spaniard	523	0.2	2.9

Population Growth: 2000–2010

Group	%
Total Population	-29.1
Hispanic or Latino (of any race)	21.8
Central American, ex. Mexican	110.2
Costa Rican	20.5
Guatemalan	153.1
Honduran	133.5
Nicaraguan	100.0
Panamanian	13.0
Salvadoran	140.5
Cuban	-20.4
Dominican Republic	106.8
Mexican	66.7
Puerto Rican	-8.1
South American	69.4
Colombian	60.5
Ecuadorian	55.2
Spaniard	311.8

Males per 100 Females

Group	Number
Total Population	93.6
Hispanic or Latino (of any race)	133.2
Central American, ex. Mexican	140.3
Costa Rican	107.7
Guatemalan	142.9
Honduran	147.7
Nicaraguan	128.6
Panamanian	58.7
Salvadoran	145.1
Cuban	112.4
Dominican Republic	117.9
Mexican	165.3
Puerto Rican	114.5
South American	96.5
Argentinean	85.4
Colombian	82.1
Ecuadorian	86.5
Peruvian	144.1
Venezuelan	129.9
Spaniard	96.6

Average Household Size

Group	People
Total Population	2.33
Hispanic or Latino (of any race)	2.57
Central American, ex. Mexican	2.92
Costa Rican	2.07
Guatemalan	2.78
Honduran	3.02
Nicaraguan	2.92
Panamanian	2.21
Salvadoran	2.97
Cuban	2.18
Dominican Republic	2.57
Mexican	2.63
Puerto Rican	2.09
South American	2.17
Argentinean	2.17
Colombian	2.05
Ecuadorian	2.23
Peruvian	2.29
Venezuelan	2.19
Spaniard	1.98

Median Age

Group	Years
Total Population	34.6
Hispanic or Latino (of any race)	31.3
Central American, ex. Mexican	32.1
Costa Rican	37.5
Guatemalan	29.8
Honduran	32.0
Nicaraguan	32.4
Panamanian	32.9
Salvadoran	34.0
Cuban	34.2
Dominican Republic	29.1
Mexican	29.7
Puerto Rican	28.8
South American	33.0
Argentinean	35.5
Colombian	32.6
Ecuadorian	29.7
Peruvian	35.0
Venezuelan	32.0
Spaniard	39.8

High School Graduates
(Universe: Population 25 Years and Over)

Group	Number	%
Total Population	162,625	83.4
Hispanic or Latino (of any race)	7,159	71.5
Central American, ex. Mexican	2,221	58.2
Honduran	1,360	52.2
Cuban	512	96.4
Mexican	2,039	67.7
South American	1,149	92.5

Four-Year College Graduates
(Universe: Population 25 Years and Over)

Group	Number	%
Total Population	61,701	31.6
Hispanic or Latino (of any race)	2,963	29.6

Notes: (1) Percent of total population; (2) Percent of Hispanic/Latino population; Profiles include places with an overall population of at least 125,000, OR an overall population of at least 25,000 where the Hispanic/Latino population is at least 20% of the overall population. In states where less than five places meet either of these criteria, we have included places with at least 10,000 total population with the highest percentage of Hispanic/Latino population. These places are identified with an asterisk (*); Please refer to the User's Guide for a full explanation of data.

Central American, ex. Mexican	714	18.7
Honduran	287	11.0
Cuban	336	63.3
Mexican	654	21.7
South American	686	55.2

Population Age 3–17 Enrolled in Public School
(Universe: Population Age 3–17 Enrolled in School)

Group	Number	%
Total Population	33,901	72.1
Hispanic or Latino (of any race)	1,082	64.8
Central American, ex. Mexican	373	76.6
Honduran	346	90.1
Cuban	0	0.0
Mexican	486	75.2
South American	108	57.1

Population Age 3–17 Enrolled in Private School
(Universe: Population Age 3–17 Enrolled in School)

Group	Number	%
Total Population	13,110	27.9
Hispanic or Latino (of any race)	588	35.2
Central American, ex. Mexican	114	23.4
Honduran	38	9.9
Cuban	62	100.0
Mexican	160	24.8
South American	81	42.9

Foreign-Born Population

Group	Number	%
Total Population	17,773	6.0
Hispanic or Latino (of any race)	7,296	48.4
Central American, ex. Mexican	3,908	70.0
Honduran	2,709	71.8
Cuban	229	26.2
Mexican	1,533	32.5
South American	1,103	65.0

Foreign-Born Naturalized U.S. Citizens

Group	Number	%
Total Population	7,759	43.7
Hispanic or Latino (of any race)	2,024	27.7
Central American, ex. Mexican	1,152	29.5
Honduran	720	26.6
Cuban	192	83.8
Mexican	170	11.1
South American	323	29.3

Language Spoken at Home: English Only
(Universe: Population 5 Years and Over)

Group	Number	%
Total Population	250,255	90.3
Hispanic or Latino (of any race)	3,740	27.0
Central American, ex. Mexican	791	15.3
Honduran	538	15.6
Cuban	376	43.7
Mexican	1,250	29.1
South American	263	16.9

Language Spoken at Home: Spanish
(Universe: Population 5 Years and Over)

Group	Number	%
Total Population	13,410	4.8
Hispanic or Latino (of any race)	9,973	72.0
Central American, ex. Mexican	4,365	84.7
Honduran	2,918	84.4
Cuban	479	55.6
Mexican	2,996	69.8
South American	1,245	79.8

Unemployment Rate
(Universe: Population 16 Years and Over)

Group	%
Total Population	12.0
Hispanic or Latino (of any race)	10.1
Central American, ex. Mexican	13.0
Honduran	14.0
Cuban	11.2
Mexican	6.5
South American	9.6

Class of Worker: Private Wage and Salary
(Universe: Civilian Employed Population 16 Years and Over)

Group	Number	%
Total Population	101,110	76.6
Hispanic or Latino (of any race)	6,434	80.7
Central American, ex. Mexican	2,827	87.3
Honduran	1,822	87.3
Cuban	381	71.6
Mexican	1,734	76.2
South American	810	80.3

Class of Worker: Government
(Universe: Civilian Employed Population 16 Years and Over)

Group	Number	%
Total Population	20,821	15.8
Hispanic or Latino (of any race)	620	7.8
Central American, ex. Mexican	89	2.7
Honduran	58	2.8
Cuban	97	18.2
Mexican	185	8.1
South American	70	6.9

Means of Transportation to Work: Car, Truck or Van
(Universe: Workers 16 Years and Over)

Group	Number	%
Total Population	103,869	80.6
Hispanic or Latino (of any race)	5,876	75.5
Central American, ex. Mexican	2,295	71.9
Honduran	1,363	66.5
Cuban	369	72.2
Mexican	1,792	81.8
South American	719	74.6

Means of Transportation to Work: Public Transportation (ex. Taxicab)
(Universe: Workers 16 Years and Over)

Group	Number	%
Total Population	9,013	7.0
Hispanic or Latino (of any race)	1,035	13.3
Central American, ex. Mexican	613	19.2
Honduran	499	24.3
Cuban	18	3.5
Mexican	130	5.9
South American	173	17.9

Homeownership Rate
(Universe: Occupied Housing Units)

Group	%
Total Population	47.8
Hispanic or Latino (of any race)	34.4
Central American, ex. Mexican	34.7
Costa Rican	52.6
Guatemalan	34.3
Honduran	33.7
Nicaraguan	35.2
Panamanian	52.8
Salvadoran	30.3
Cuban	51.5
Dominican Republic	36.3
Mexican	23.6
Puerto Rican	29.7
South American	35.4
Argentinean	54.3
Colombian	32.2
Ecuadorian	40.3
Peruvian	27.8
Venezuelan	35.1
Spaniard	55.3

Median Home Value

Group	Dollars
Total Population	184,100
Hispanic or Latino (of any race)	208,200
Central American, ex. Mexican	192,300
Honduran	179,000
Cuban	265,500
Mexican	153,600
South American	268,900

Median Gross Rent

Group	Dollars
Total Population	899
Hispanic or Latino (of any race)	913
Central American, ex. Mexican	851
Honduran	847
Cuban	1,385
Mexican	957
South American	834

Median Household Income
(2010 Inflation-Adjusted Dollars)

Group	Dollars
Total Population	37,468
Hispanic or Latino (of any race)	37,337
Central American, ex. Mexican	34,151
Honduran	36,406
Cuban	61,274
Mexican	37,024
South American	37,663

Per Capita Income
(2010 Inflation-Adjusted Dollars)

Group	Dollars
Total Population	24,929
Hispanic or Latino (of any race)	20,870
Central American, ex. Mexican	17,694
Honduran	17,198
Cuban	35,149
Mexican	17,795
South American	26,714

Households with $100,000+ Income

Group	Number	%
Total Population	17,756	15.2
Hispanic or Latino (of any race)	669	13.1
Central American, ex. Mexican	162	8.8
Honduran	112	9.1
Cuban	110	27.8
Mexican	156	11.3
South American	93	15.5

Households with Food Stamps/SNAP Benefits During Past 12 Months

Group	Number	%
Total Population	22,309	19.1
Hispanic or Latino (of any race)	715	14.0
Central American, ex. Mexican	316	17.1
Honduran	200	16.3
Cuban	19	4.8
Mexican	180	13.0
South American	60	10.0

Poverty Rate
(Income in Past 12 Months Below Poverty Level)

Group	%
Total Population	24.4
Hispanic or Latino (of any race)	24.4
Central American, ex. Mexican	27.5
Honduran	27.1
Cuban	13.0
Mexican	31.2
South American	17.7

Shreveport

Population

Group	Number	%TP[1]	%HP[2]
Total Population	199,311	100.0	–
Hispanic or Latino (of any race)	5,018	2.5	100.0
Central American, ex. Mexican	382	0.2	7.6
Honduran	105	0.1	2.1
Cuban	121	0.1	2.4
Mexican	3,182	1.6	63.4
Puerto Rican	365	0.2	7.3
South American	246	0.1	4.9
Spaniard	123	0.1	2.5

Population Growth: 2000–2010

Group	%
Total Population	-0.4
Hispanic or Latino (of any race)	61.6
Central American, ex. Mexican	223.7
Mexican	104.2
Puerto Rican	30.4

Males per 100 Females

Group	Number
Total Population	88.1
Hispanic or Latino (of any race)	121.9
Central American, ex. Mexican	146.5
Honduran	133.3
Cuban	101.7
Mexican	132.1

Notes: (1) Percent of total population; (2) Percent of Hispanic/Latino population; Profiles include places with an overall population of at least 125,000, OR an overall population of at least 25,000 where the Hispanic/Latino population is at least 20% of the overall population. In states where less than five places meet either of these criteria, we have included places with at least 10,000 total population with the highest percentage of Hispanic/Latino population. These places are identified with an asterisk (*); Please refer to the User's Guide for a full explanation of data.

Group	
Puerto Rican	105.1
South American	82.2
Spaniard	86.4

Average Household Size

Group	People
Total Population	2.40
Hispanic or Latino (of any race)	2.75
Central American, ex. Mexican	2.73
Honduran	2.66
Cuban	2.25
Mexican	2.94
Puerto Rican	2.45
South American	2.49
Spaniard	1.90

Median Age

Group	Years
Total Population	34.6
Hispanic or Latino (of any race)	27.2
Central American, ex. Mexican	30.3
Honduran	30.5
Cuban	31.8
Mexican	25.3
Puerto Rican	26.3
South American	33.6
Spaniard	41.8

High School Graduates
(Universe: Population 25 Years and Over)

Group	Number	%
Total Population	107,080	84.9
Hispanic or Latino (of any race)	2,038	76.0
Mexican	965	73.2

Four-Year College Graduates
(Universe: Population 25 Years and Over)

Group	Number	%
Total Population	30,549	24.2
Hispanic or Latino (of any race)	601	22.4
Mexican	191	14.5

Population Age 3–17 Enrolled in Public School
(Universe: Population Age 3–17 Enrolled in School)

Group	Number	%
Total Population	34,634	89.5
Hispanic or Latino (of any race)	848	82.7
Mexican	510	93.9

Population Age 3–17 Enrolled in Private School
(Universe: Population Age 3–17 Enrolled in School)

Group	Number	%
Total Population	4,054	10.5
Hispanic or Latino (of any race)	177	17.3
Mexican	33	6.1

Foreign-Born Population

Group	Number	%
Total Population	5,282	2.7
Hispanic or Latino (of any race)	1,480	29.8
Mexican	734	28.0

Foreign-Born Naturalized U.S. Citizens

Group	Number	%
Total Population	2,452	46.4
Hispanic or Latino (of any race)	427	28.9
Mexican	97	13.2

Language Spoken at Home: English Only
(Universe: Population 5 Years and Over)

Group	Number	%
Total Population	175,922	95.6
Hispanic or Latino (of any race)	2,348	53.5
Mexican	1,377	60.5

Language Spoken at Home: Spanish
(Universe: Population 5 Years and Over)

Group	Number	%
Total Population	3,415	1.9
Hispanic or Latino (of any race)	2,025	46.1
Mexican	898	39.5

Unemployment Rate
(Universe: Population 16 Years and Over)

Group	%
Total Population	9.6
Hispanic or Latino (of any race)	8.2
Mexican	6.1

Class of Worker: Private Wage and Salary
(Universe: Civilian Employed Population 16 Years and Over)

Group	Number	%
Total Population	66,213	76.8
Hispanic or Latino (of any race)	2,258	88.9
Mexican	1,282	88.1

Class of Worker: Government
(Universe: Civilian Employed Population 16 Years and Over)

Group	Number	%
Total Population	15,421	17.9
Hispanic or Latino (of any race)	175	6.9
Mexican	116	8.0

Means of Transportation to Work: Car, Truck or Van
(Universe: Workers 16 Years and Over)

Group	Number	%
Total Population	77,157	91.1
Hispanic or Latino (of any race)	2,154	90.2
Mexican	1,240	92.6

Means of Transportation to Work: Public Transportation (ex. Taxicab)
(Universe: Workers 16 Years and Over)

Group	Number	%
Total Population	2,539	3.0
Hispanic or Latino (of any race)	127	5.3
Mexican	37	2.8

Homeownership Rate
(Universe: Occupied Housing Units)

Group	%
Total Population	55.5
Hispanic or Latino (of any race)	41.1
Central American, ex. Mexican	41.0
Honduran	40.6
Cuban	44.2
Mexican	36.9
Puerto Rican	40.0
South American	53.7
Spaniard	63.5

Median Home Value

Group	Dollars
Total Population	113,800
Hispanic or Latino (of any race)	159,100
Mexican	92,500

Median Gross Rent

Group	Dollars
Total Population	675
Hispanic or Latino (of any race)	639
Mexican	649

Median Household Income
(2010 Inflation-Adjusted Dollars)

Group	Dollars
Total Population	35,613
Hispanic or Latino (of any race)	31,159
Mexican	30,614

Per Capita Income
(2010 Inflation-Adjusted Dollars)

Group	Dollars
Total Population	22,047
Hispanic or Latino (of any race)	19,791
Mexican	19,791

Households with $100,000+ Income

Group	Number	%
Total Population	9,435	12.3
Hispanic or Latino (of any race)	142	9.4
Mexican	37	4.7

Households with Food Stamps/SNAP Benefits During Past 12 Months

Group	Number	%
Total Population	12,155	15.8
Hispanic or Latino (of any race)	122	8.1
Mexican	80	10.2

Poverty Rate
(Income in Past 12 Months Below Poverty Level)

Group	%
Total Population	22.1
Hispanic or Latino (of any race)	18.3
Mexican	25.1

Notes: (1) Percent of total population; (2) Percent of Hispanic/Latino population; Profiles include places with an overall population of at least 125,000, OR an overall population of at least 25,000 where the Hispanic/Latino population is at least 20% of the overall population. In states where less than five places meet either of these criteria, we have included places with at least 10,000 total population with the highest percentage of Hispanic/Latino population. These places are identified with an asterisk (*); Please refer to the User's Guide for a full explanation of data.

Maine

EDITOR'S NOTE: For a place to be included in this edition, it must meet one of two criteria. Either its overall population is at least 125,000, OR its overall population is at least 25,000 and its Hispanic/Latino population is at least 20% of the overall population. In Maine, less than five places meet either of these criteria. In an effort to include at least five places for each state, we have included places with at least 10,000 total population with the highest percentage of Hispanic/Latino population. These places are identified with an asterisk (*). For the state of Maine, the following locations are included:

- Brunswick*
- Lewiston*
- Portland*
- South Portland*
- Waterville*

Section Two: State & Place Profiles starts with the state profile, followed by place profiles that meet the criteria above. Places are listed alphabetically within each state. All states, all counties and places that meet the above criteria are ranked and compared in *Section Three: Rankings & Comparisons*, on page 1055.

For a more detailed look at the Hispanic/Latino population in Maine, a companion web site is available at no additional charge with purchase of this print edition. Visit http://gold.greyhouse.com/page/info_hispanic for more information.

The web site includes data for all counties and places in Maine with Hispanic/Latino population, plus ten additional topics: Self Employed Worker; Walked to Work; Worked from Home; Mean Travel Time to Work; Mean Household Income; Households with Cash Public Assistance; Mean Cash Pubic Assistance; Poverty Rates for 18 and Under, 18 to 64, and 65 and Over.

Population

Group	Number	%TP[1]	%HP[2]
Total Population	1,328,361	100.0	–
Hispanic or Latino (of any race)	16,935	1.3	100.0
Central American, ex. Mexican	1,708	0.1	10.1
Costa Rican	105	<0.1	0.6
Guatemalan	457	<0.1	2.7
Honduran	280	<0.1	1.7
Panamanian	141	<0.1	0.8
Salvadoran	618	<0.1	3.6
Cuban	783	0.1	4.6
Dominican Republic	610	<0.1	3.6
Mexican	5,134	0.4	30.3
Puerto Rican	4,377	0.3	25.8
South American	1,515	0.1	8.9
Argentinean	149	<0.1	0.9
Chilean	166	<0.1	1.0
Colombian	496	<0.1	2.9
Ecuadorian	178	<0.1	1.1
Peruvian	272	<0.1	1.6
Venezuelan	146	<0.1	0.9
Spaniard	672	0.1	4.0

Population Growth: 2000–2010

Group	%
Total Population	4.2
Hispanic or Latino (of any race)	80.9
Central American, ex. Mexican	220.5
Salvadoran	179.6
Cuban	63.8
Dominican Republic	185.0
Mexican	86.3
Puerto Rican	92.4
South American	133.8
Colombian	151.8
Peruvian	140.7
Spaniard	500.0

Males per 100 Females

Group	Number
Total Population	95.8
Hispanic or Latino (of any race)	101.2
Central American, ex. Mexican	114.6
Costa Rican	81.0
Guatemalan	129.6
Honduran	120.5
Panamanian	74.1
Salvadoran	128.0
Cuban	109.4
Dominican Republic	97.4
Mexican	99.0
Puerto Rican	108.7
South American	81.0
Argentinean	60.2
Chilean	107.5
Colombian	79.7
Ecuadorian	87.4
Peruvian	76.6
Venezuelan	78.0
Spaniard	77.8

Average Household Size

Group	People
Total Population	2.32
Hispanic or Latino (of any race)	2.74
Central American, ex. Mexican	3.37
Costa Rican	2.53
Guatemalan	3.55
Honduran	3.90
Panamanian	2.45
Salvadoran	3.66
Cuban	2.45
Dominican Republic	2.93
Mexican	2.76
Puerto Rican	2.81
South American	2.77
Argentinean	2.41
Chilean	2.75
Colombian	2.76
Ecuadorian	2.85
Peruvian	2.80
Venezuelan	3.18
Spaniard	2.35

Median Age

Group	Years
Total Population	42.7
Hispanic or Latino (of any race)	23.8
Central American, ex. Mexican	22.7
Costa Rican	26.8
Guatemalan	14.4
Honduran	20.7
Panamanian	25.5
Salvadoran	27.1
Cuban	28.2
Dominican Republic	21.8
Mexican	23.2
Puerto Rican	21.4
South American	27.8
Argentinean	36.3
Chilean	28.7
Colombian	27.7
Ecuadorian	22.8
Peruvian	29.6
Venezuelan	26.0
Spaniard	38.9

High School Graduates
(Universe: Population 25 Years and Over)

Group	Number	%
Total Population	834,106	89.8
Hispanic or Latino (of any race)	6,558	81.9
Central American, ex. Mexican	296	47.5
Cuban	470	94.6
Mexican	2,007	80.8
Puerto Rican	1,698	81.1
South American	563	95.9
Spaniard	631	95.2

Four-Year College Graduates
(Universe: Population 25 Years and Over)

Group	Number	%
Total Population	246,727	26.5
Hispanic or Latino (of any race)	1,631	20.4
Central American, ex. Mexican	38	6.1
Cuban	189	38.0
Mexican	427	17.2
Puerto Rican	292	13.9
South American	180	30.7
Spaniard	268	40.4

Population Age 3–17 Enrolled in Public School
(Universe: Population Age 3–17 Enrolled in School)

Group	Number	%
Total Population	189,743	87.8
Hispanic or Latino (of any race)	3,992	85.1
Central American, ex. Mexican	730	91.3
Cuban	127	68.6
Mexican	1,092	90.5
Puerto Rican	1,136	76.2
South American	431	89.4
Spaniard	102	100.0

Population Age 3–17 Enrolled in Private School
(Universe: Population Age 3–17 Enrolled in School)

Group	Number	%
Total Population	26,425	12.2
Hispanic or Latino (of any race)	700	14.9
Central American, ex. Mexican	70	8.8
Cuban	58	31.4
Mexican	115	9.5
Puerto Rican	354	23.8
South American	51	10.6
Spaniard	0	0.0

Foreign-Born Population

Group	Number	%
Total Population	43,911	3.3
Hispanic or Latino (of any race)	3,165	18.6
Central American, ex. Mexican	876	49.5
Cuban	231	28.9
Mexican	812	16.6
Puerto Rican	70	1.4
South American	700	50.1
Spaniard	220	24.7

Foreign-Born Naturalized U.S. Citizens

Group	Number	%
Total Population	24,092	54.9
Hispanic or Latino (of any race)	1,276	40.3
Central American, ex. Mexican	272	31.1
Cuban	133	57.6
Mexican	243	29.9
Puerto Rican	0	0.0
South American	452	64.6
Spaniard	110	50.0

Language Spoken at Home: English Only
(Universe: Population 5 Years and Over)

Group	Number	%
Total Population	1,167,970	92.9
Hispanic or Latino (of any race)	8,888	58.7
Central American, ex. Mexican	819	50.7
Cuban	544	68.5
Mexican	2,635	60.4
Puerto Rican	2,450	57.7
South American	582	44.1
Spaniard	493	58.9

Language Spoken at Home: Spanish
(Universe: Population 5 Years and Over)

Group	Number	%
Total Population	13,017	1.0
Hispanic or Latino (of any race)	5,936	39.2
Central American, ex. Mexican	796	49.3
Cuban	250	31.5
Mexican	1,673	38.3
Puerto Rican	1,796	42.3
South American	716	54.3

Notes: (1) Percent of total population; (2) Percent of Hispanic/Latino population; Profiles include places with an overall population of at least 125,000, OR an overall population of at least 25,000 where the Hispanic/Latino population is at least 20% of the overall population. In states where less than five places meet either of these criteria, we have included places with at least 10,000 total population with the highest percentage of Hispanic/Latino population. These places are identified with an asterisk (*); Please refer to the User's Guide for a full explanation of data.

STATE & PLACE PROFILES

Group	Number	%
Spaniard	259	30.9

Unemployment Rate
(Universe: Population 16 Years and Over)

Group	%
Total Population	6.5
Hispanic or Latino (of any race)	11.1
Central American, ex. Mexican	11.4
Cuban	12.4
Mexican	7.7
Puerto Rican	12.4
South American	2.1
Spaniard	31.2

Class of Worker: Private Wage and Salary
(Universe: Civilian Employed Population 16 Years and Over)

Group	Number	%
Total Population	499,172	75.9
Hispanic or Latino (of any race)	5,600	83.6
Central American, ex. Mexican	520	88.0
Cuban	236	72.8
Mexican	1,676	85.1
Puerto Rican	1,605	85.8
South American	579	88.8
Spaniard	222	73.5

Class of Worker: Government
(Universe: Civilian Employed Population 16 Years and Over)

Group	Number	%
Total Population	93,975	14.3
Hispanic or Latino (of any race)	706	10.5
Central American, ex. Mexican	29	4.9
Cuban	72	22.2
Mexican	185	9.4
Puerto Rican	194	10.4
South American	43	6.6
Spaniard	59	19.5

Means of Transportation to Work: Car, Truck or Van
(Universe: Workers 16 Years and Over)

Group	Number	%
Total Population	569,322	88.7
Hispanic or Latino (of any race)	5,367	81.6
Central American, ex. Mexican	439	77.3
Cuban	291	89.8
Mexican	1,643	81.6
Puerto Rican	1,545	84.0
South American	478	76.6
Spaniard	209	81.0

Means of Transportation to Work: Public Transportation (ex. Taxicab)
(Universe: Workers 16 Years and Over)

Group	Number	%
Total Population	4,107	0.6
Hispanic or Latino (of any race)	33	0.5
Central American, ex. Mexican	0	0.0
Cuban	0	0.0
Mexican	6	0.3
Puerto Rican	27	1.5
South American	0	0.0
Spaniard	0	0.0

Homeownership Rate
(Universe: Occupied Housing Units)

Group	%
Total Population	71.3
Hispanic or Latino (of any race)	47.0
Central American, ex. Mexican	40.7
Costa Rican	62.5
Guatemalan	41.1
Honduran	31.3
Panamanian	41.4
Salvadoran	37.2
Cuban	56.0
Dominican Republic	32.5
Mexican	45.6
Puerto Rican	40.3
South American	55.9
Argentinean	63.0
Chilean	51.0
Colombian	61.5
Ecuadorian	47.8
Peruvian	48.4
Venezuelan	62.5
Spaniard	69.1

Median Home Value

Group	Dollars
Total Population	176,200
Hispanic or Latino (of any race)	171,100
Central American, ex. Mexican	225,000
Cuban	187,500
Mexican	157,400
Puerto Rican	185,300
South American	182,500
Spaniard	148,700

Median Gross Rent

Group	Dollars
Total Population	707
Hispanic or Latino (of any race)	780
Central American, ex. Mexican	726
Cuban	767
Mexican	739
Puerto Rican	816
South American	1,258
Spaniard	644

Median Household Income
(2010 Inflation-Adjusted Dollars)

Group	Dollars
Total Population	46,933
Hispanic or Latino (of any race)	35,167
Central American, ex. Mexican	44,583
Cuban	34,453
Mexican	35,785
Puerto Rican	29,826
South American	58,333
Spaniard	27,214

Per Capita Income
(2010 Inflation-Adjusted Dollars)

Group	Dollars
Total Population	25,385
Hispanic or Latino (of any race)	13,594
Central American, ex. Mexican	8,976
Cuban	19,449
Mexican	15,183
Puerto Rican	10,343
South American	16,324
Spaniard	18,488

Households with $100,000+ Income

Group	Number	%
Total Population	80,334	14.6
Hispanic or Latino (of any race)	324	7.3
Central American, ex. Mexican	29	9.1
Cuban	27	8.7
Mexican	66	4.7
Puerto Rican	73	6.4
South American	44	15.8
Spaniard	29	8.9

Households with Food Stamps/SNAP Benefits During Past 12 Months

Group	Number	%
Total Population	74,929	13.6
Hispanic or Latino (of any race)	1,149	26.0
Central American, ex. Mexican	52	16.4
Cuban	22	7.1
Mexican	385	27.3
Puerto Rican	506	44.2
South American	41	14.7
Spaniard	85	26.2

Poverty Rate
(Income in Past 12 Months Below Poverty Level)

Group	%
Total Population	12.6
Hispanic or Latino (of any race)	25.5
Central American, ex. Mexican	25.7
Cuban	4.5
Mexican	27.8
Puerto Rican	33.5
South American	12.9
Spaniard	21.3

Brunswick*

Population

Group	Number	%TP[1]	%HP[2]
Total Population	20,278	100.0	–
Hispanic or Latino (of any race)	597	2.9	100.0
Mexican	215	1.1	36.0
Puerto Rican	128	0.6	21.4

Population Growth: 2000–2010

Group	%
Total Population	-4.2
Hispanic or Latino (of any race)	73.5
Mexican	77.7

Males per 100 Females

Group	Number
Total Population	89.1
Hispanic or Latino (of any race)	86.6
Mexican	108.7
Puerto Rican	75.3

Average Household Size

Group	People
Total Population	2.19
Hispanic or Latino (of any race)	2.78
Mexican	2.93
Puerto Rican	2.58

Median Age

Group	Years
Total Population	41.4
Hispanic or Latino (of any race)	20.6
Mexican	20.5
Puerto Rican	22.0

High School Graduates
(Universe: Population 25 Years and Over)

Group	Number	%
Total Population	12,045	91.7

Four-Year College Graduates
(Universe: Population 25 Years and Over)

Group	Number	%
Total Population	5,047	38.4

Population Age 3–17 Enrolled in Public School
(Universe: Population Age 3–17 Enrolled in School)

Group	Number	%
Total Population	2,475	84.2

Population Age 3–17 Enrolled in Private School
(Universe: Population Age 3–17 Enrolled in School)

Group	Number	%
Total Population	466	15.8

Foreign-Born Population

Group	Number	%
Total Population	647	3.1

Foreign-Born Naturalized U.S. Citizens

Group	Number	%
Total Population	349	53.9

Language Spoken at Home: English Only
(Universe: Population 5 Years and Over)

Group	Number	%
Total Population	17,855	92.0

Language Spoken at Home: Spanish
(Universe: Population 5 Years and Over)

Group	Number	%
Total Population	325	1.7

Unemployment Rate
(Universe: Population 16 Years and Over)

Group	%
Total Population	5.8

Class of Worker: Private Wage and Salary
(Universe: Civilian Employed Population 16 Years and Over)

Group	Number	%
Total Population	8,036	81.4

Notes: (1) Percent of total population; (2) Percent of Hispanic/Latino population; Profiles include places with an overall population of at least 125,000, OR an overall population of at least 25,000 where the Hispanic/Latino population is at least 20% of the overall population. In states where less than five places meet either of these criteria, we have included places with at least 10,000 total population with the highest percentage of Hispanic/Latino population. These places are identified with an asterisk (*); Please refer to the User's Guide for a full explanation of data.

Class of Worker: Government (Universe: Civilian Employed Population 16 Years and Over)		
Group	Number	%
Total Population	1,199	12.1

Means of Transportation to Work: Car, Truck or Van (Universe: Workers 16 Years and Over)		
Group	Number	%
Total Population	8,292	82.0

Means of Transportation to Work: Public Transportation (ex. Taxicab) (Universe: Workers 16 Years and Over)		
Group	Number	%
Total Population	25	0.2

Homeownership Rate (Universe: Occupied Housing Units)	
Group	%
Total Population	67.7
Hispanic or Latino (of any race)	50.4
Mexican	52.5
Puerto Rican	44.4

Median Home Value	
Group	Dollars
Total Population	213,800

Median Gross Rent	
Group	Dollars
Total Population	779

Median Household Income (2010 Inflation-Adjusted Dollars)	
Group	Dollars
Total Population	50,117

Per Capita Income (2010 Inflation-Adjusted Dollars)	
Group	Dollars
Total Population	27,453

Households with $100,000+ Income		
Group	Number	%
Total Population	1,565	18.5

Households with Food Stamps/SNAP Benefits During Past 12 Months		
Group	Number	%
Total Population	766	9.1

Poverty Rate (Income in Past 12 Months Below Poverty Level)	
Group	%
Total Population	11.0

Lewiston*

Population			
Group	Number	%TP[1]	%HP[2]
Total Population	36,592	100.0	–
Hispanic or Latino (of any race)	730	2.0	100.0
Mexican	273	0.7	37.4
Puerto Rican	232	0.6	31.8

Population Growth: 2000–2010	
Group	%
Total Population	2.5
Hispanic or Latino (of any race)	62.9
Mexican	48.4
Puerto Rican	85.6

Males per 100 Females	
Group	Number
Total Population	92.6
Hispanic or Latino (of any race)	102.8
Mexican	102.2
Puerto Rican	98.3

Average Household Size	
Group	People
Total Population	2.26
Hispanic or Latino (of any race)	2.82
Mexican	3.10
Puerto Rican	2.92

Median Age	
Group	Years
Total Population	37.4
Hispanic or Latino (of any race)	21.0
Mexican	20.8
Puerto Rican	20.7

High School Graduates (Universe: Population 25 Years and Over)		
Group	Number	%
Total Population	19,649	82.7

Four-Year College Graduates (Universe: Population 25 Years and Over)		
Group	Number	%
Total Population	3,566	15.0

Population Age 3–17 Enrolled in Public School (Universe: Population Age 3–17 Enrolled in School)		
Group	Number	%
Total Population	4,928	90.7

Population Age 3–17 Enrolled in Private School (Universe: Population Age 3–17 Enrolled in School)		
Group	Number	%
Total Population	503	9.3

Foreign-Born Population		
Group	Number	%
Total Population	1,763	4.8

Foreign-Born Naturalized U.S. Citizens		
Group	Number	%
Total Population	737	41.8

Language Spoken at Home: English Only (Universe: Population 5 Years and Over)		
Group	Number	%
Total Population	26,982	79.3

Language Spoken at Home: Spanish (Universe: Population 5 Years and Over)		
Group	Number	%
Total Population	694	2.0

Unemployment Rate (Universe: Population 16 Years and Over)	
Group	%
Total Population	9.7

Class of Worker: Private Wage and Salary (Universe: Civilian Employed Population 16 Years and Over)		
Group	Number	%
Total Population	14,112	85.1

Class of Worker: Government (Universe: Civilian Employed Population 16 Years and Over)		
Group	Number	%
Total Population	1,525	9.2

Means of Transportation to Work: Car, Truck or Van (Universe: Workers 16 Years and Over)		
Group	Number	%
Total Population	14,056	87.1

Means of Transportation to Work: Public Transportation (ex. Taxicab) (Universe: Workers 16 Years and Over)		
Group	Number	%
Total Population	108	0.7

Homeownership Rate (Universe: Occupied Housing Units)	
Group	%
Total Population	47.8
Hispanic or Latino (of any race)	31.6
Mexican	43.5
Puerto Rican	21.7

Median Home Value	
Group	Dollars
Total Population	150,500

Median Gross Rent	
Group	Dollars
Total Population	614

Median Household Income (2010 Inflation-Adjusted Dollars)	
Group	Dollars
Total Population	36,743

Per Capita Income (2010 Inflation-Adjusted Dollars)	
Group	Dollars
Total Population	20,014

Households with $100,000+ Income		
Group	Number	%
Total Population	1,217	8.1

Households with Food Stamps/SNAP Benefits During Past 12 Months		
Group	Number	%
Total Population	3,534	23.5

Poverty Rate (Income in Past 12 Months Below Poverty Level)	
Group	%
Total Population	21.7

Portland*

Population			
Group	Number	%TP[1]	%HP[2]
Total Population	66,194	100.0	–
Hispanic or Latino (of any race)	1,998	3.0	100.0
Central American, ex. Mexican	602	0.9	30.1
Guatemalan	123	0.2	6.2
Salvadoran	363	0.5	18.2
Cuban	117	0.2	5.9
Dominican Republic	123	0.2	6.2
Mexican	381	0.6	19.1
Puerto Rican	352	0.5	17.6
South American	179	0.3	9.0

Population Growth: 2000–2010	
Group	%
Total Population	3.0
Hispanic or Latino (of any race)	105.1
Central American, ex. Mexican	234.4
Salvadoran	166.9
Mexican	105.9
Puerto Rican	84.3

Males per 100 Females	
Group	Number
Total Population	95.3
Hispanic or Latino (of any race)	118.8
Central American, ex. Mexican	146.7
Guatemalan	167.4
Salvadoran	138.8
Cuban	116.7
Dominican Republic	92.2
Mexican	128.1
Puerto Rican	112.0
South American	75.5

Average Household Size	
Group	People
Total Population	2.07
Hispanic or Latino (of any race)	2.66
Central American, ex. Mexican	3.95
Guatemalan	4.07
Salvadoran	4.12
Cuban	2.30
Dominican Republic	2.50
Mexican	2.25
Puerto Rican	2.52
South American	2.18

Median Age	
Group	Years
Total Population	36.7
Hispanic or Latino (of any race)	27.3
Central American, ex. Mexican	26.6
Guatemalan	24.4

Notes: (1) Percent of total population; (2) Percent of Hispanic/Latino population; Profiles include places with an overall population of at least 125,000, OR an overall population of at least 25,000 where the Hispanic/Latino population is at least 20% of the overall population. In states where less than five places meet either of these criteria, we have included places with at least 10,000 total population with the highest percentage of Hispanic/Latino population. These places are identified with an asterisk (*); Please refer to the User's Guide for a full explanation of data.

Group	%
Salvadoran	26.8
Cuban	28.4
Dominican Republic	31.3
Mexican	27.2
Puerto Rican	25.5
South American	31.5

High School Graduates
(Universe: Population 25 Years and Over)

Group	Number	%
Total Population	43,118	91.3
Hispanic or Latino (of any race)	852	73.6

Four-Year College Graduates
(Universe: Population 25 Years and Over)

Group	Number	%
Total Population	20,400	43.2
Hispanic or Latino (of any race)	376	32.5

Population Age 3–17 Enrolled in Public School
(Universe: Population Age 3–17 Enrolled in School)

Group	Number	%
Total Population	7,168	85.1
Hispanic or Latino (of any race)	473	83.1

Population Age 3–17 Enrolled in Private School
(Universe: Population Age 3–17 Enrolled in School)

Group	Number	%
Total Population	1,255	14.9
Hispanic or Latino (of any race)	96	16.9

Foreign-Born Population

Group	Number	%
Total Population	7,261	11.0
Hispanic or Latino (of any race)	624	26.5

Foreign-Born Naturalized U.S. Citizens

Group	Number	%
Total Population	3,156	43.5
Hispanic or Latino (of any race)	124	19.9

Language Spoken at Home: English Only
(Universe: Population 5 Years and Over)

Group	Number	%
Total Population	53,878	85.9
Hispanic or Latino (of any race)	969	48.0

Language Spoken at Home: Spanish
(Universe: Population 5 Years and Over)

Group	Number	%
Total Population	1,701	2.7
Hispanic or Latino (of any race)	1,004	49.8

Unemployment Rate
(Universe: Population 16 Years and Over)

Group	%
Total Population	5.3
Hispanic or Latino (of any race)	14.1

Class of Worker: Private Wage and Salary
(Universe: Civilian Employed Population 16 Years and Over)

Group	Number	%
Total Population	29,988	81.4
Hispanic or Latino (of any race)	672	76.5

Class of Worker: Government
(Universe: Civilian Employed Population 16 Years and Over)

Group	Number	%
Total Population	3,846	10.4
Hispanic or Latino (of any race)	141	16.1

Means of Transportation to Work: Car, Truck or Van
(Universe: Workers 16 Years and Over)

Group	Number	%
Total Population	28,461	78.5
Hispanic or Latino (of any race)	606	69.3

Means of Transportation to Work: Public Transportation (ex. Taxicab)
(Universe: Workers 16 Years and Over)

Group	Number	%
Total Population	1,224	3.4
Hispanic or Latino (of any race)	19	2.2

Homeownership Rate
(Universe: Occupied Housing Units)

Group	%
Total Population	42.7
Hispanic or Latino (of any race)	22.1
Central American, ex. Mexican	29.9
Guatemalan	16.7
Salvadoran	33.3
Cuban	13.3
Dominican Republic	14.6
Mexican	16.8
Puerto Rican	11.9
South American	30.9

Median Home Value

Group	Dollars
Total Population	248,100
Hispanic or Latino (of any race)	197,100

Median Gross Rent

Group	Dollars
Total Population	840
Hispanic or Latino (of any race)	830

Median Household Income
(2010 Inflation-Adjusted Dollars)

Group	Dollars
Total Population	44,422
Hispanic or Latino (of any race)	25,466

Per Capita Income
(2010 Inflation-Adjusted Dollars)

Group	Dollars
Total Population	27,794
Hispanic or Latino (of any race)	12,707

Households with $100,000+ Income

Group	Number	%
Total Population	4,580	14.9
Hispanic or Latino (of any race)	6	0.8

Households with Food Stamps/SNAP Benefits During Past 12 Months

Group	Number	%
Total Population	5,040	16.4
Hispanic or Latino (of any race)	256	33.2

Poverty Rate
(Income in Past 12 Months Below Poverty Level)

Group	%
Total Population	17.5
Hispanic or Latino (of any race)	38.5

South Portland*

Population

Group	Number	%TP[1]	%HP[2]
Total Population	25,002	100.0	–
Hispanic or Latino (of any race)	554	2.2	100.0
Mexican	122	0.5	22.0
Puerto Rican	109	0.4	19.7
South American	103	0.4	18.6

Population Growth: 2000–2010

Group	%
Total Population	7.2
Hispanic or Latino (of any race)	110.6

Males per 100 Females

Group	Number
Total Population	91.1
Hispanic or Latino (of any race)	103.7
Mexican	121.8
Puerto Rican	127.1
South American	87.3

Average Household Size

Group	People
Total Population	2.24
Hispanic or Latino (of any race)	2.91
Mexican	3.00
Puerto Rican	2.74
South American	3.19

Median Age

Group	Years
Total Population	39.4
Hispanic or Latino (of any race)	25.3
Mexican	21.3
Puerto Rican	21.8
South American	29.5

High School Graduates
(Universe: Population 25 Years and Over)

Group	Number	%
Total Population	16,514	94.5

Four-Year College Graduates
(Universe: Population 25 Years and Over)

Group	Number	%
Total Population	6,664	38.1

Population Age 3–17 Enrolled in Public School
(Universe: Population Age 3–17 Enrolled in School)

Group	Number	%
Total Population	3,422	81.4

Population Age 3–17 Enrolled in Private School
(Universe: Population Age 3–17 Enrolled in School)

Group	Number	%
Total Population	782	18.6

Foreign-Born Population

Group	Number	%
Total Population	1,959	7.9

Foreign-Born Naturalized U.S. Citizens

Group	Number	%
Total Population	998	50.9

Language Spoken at Home: English Only
(Universe: Population 5 Years and Over)

Group	Number	%
Total Population	21,654	91.8

Language Spoken at Home: Spanish
(Universe: Population 5 Years and Over)

Group	Number	%
Total Population	171	0.7

Unemployment Rate
(Universe: Population 16 Years and Over)

Group	%
Total Population	4.8

Class of Worker: Private Wage and Salary
(Universe: Civilian Employed Population 16 Years and Over)

Group	Number	%
Total Population	11,408	81.1

Class of Worker: Government
(Universe: Civilian Employed Population 16 Years and Over)

Group	Number	%
Total Population	1,740	12.4

Means of Transportation to Work: Car, Truck or Van
(Universe: Workers 16 Years and Over)

Group	Number	%
Total Population	12,594	90.4

Means of Transportation to Work: Public Transportation (ex. Taxicab)
(Universe: Workers 16 Years and Over)

Group	Number	%
Total Population	157	1.1

Homeownership Rate
(Universe: Occupied Housing Units)

Group	%
Total Population	61.0
Hispanic or Latino (of any race)	33.6
Mexican	33.3
Puerto Rican	29.0
South American	25.9

Median Home Value

Group	Dollars
Total Population	226,000

Notes: (1) Percent of total population; (2) Percent of Hispanic/Latino population; Profiles include places with an overall population of at least 125,000, OR an overall population of at least 25,000 where the Hispanic/Latino population is at least 20% of the overall population. In states where less than five places meet either of these criteria, we have included places with at least 10,000 total population with the highest percentage of Hispanic/Latino population. These places are identified with an asterisk (*); Please refer to the User's Guide for a full explanation of data.

Median Gross Rent

Group	Dollars
Total Population	895

Median Household Income
(2010 Inflation-Adjusted Dollars)

Group	Dollars
Total Population	51,066

Per Capita Income
(2010 Inflation-Adjusted Dollars)

Group	Dollars
Total Population	28,597

Households with $100,000+ Income

Group	Number	%
Total Population	1,818	16.4

Households with Food Stamps/SNAP Benefits During Past 12 Months

Group	Number	%
Total Population	956	8.6

Poverty Rate
(Income in Past 12 Months Below Poverty Level)

Group	%
Total Population	10.4

Waterville*

Population

Group	Number	%TP[1]	%HP[2]
Total Population	15,722	100.0	–
Hispanic or Latino (of any race)	374	2.4	100.0
Mexican	101	0.6	27.0
Puerto Rican	137	0.9	36.6

Population Growth: 2000–2010

Group	%
Total Population	0.7
Hispanic or Latino (of any race)	118.7

Males per 100 Females

Group	Number
Total Population	87.8
Hispanic or Latino (of any race)	114.9
Mexican	129.5
Puerto Rican	124.6

Average Household Size

Group	People
Total Population	2.13
Hispanic or Latino (of any race)	2.69
Mexican	3.08
Puerto Rican	2.94

Median Age

Group	Years
Total Population	36.8
Hispanic or Latino (of any race)	20.9
Mexican	20.1
Puerto Rican	21.1

High School Graduates
(Universe: Population 25 Years and Over)

Group	Number	%
Total Population	8,421	86.9

Four-Year College Graduates
(Universe: Population 25 Years and Over)

Group	Number	%
Total Population	2,239	23.1

Population Age 3–17 Enrolled in Public School
(Universe: Population Age 3–17 Enrolled in School)

Group	Number	%
Total Population	1,658	88.3

Population Age 3–17 Enrolled in Private School
(Universe: Population Age 3–17 Enrolled in School)

Group	Number	%
Total Population	220	11.7

Foreign-Born Population

Group	Number	%
Total Population	647	4.1

Foreign-Born Naturalized U.S. Citizens

Group	Number	%
Total Population	130	20.1

Language Spoken at Home: English Only
(Universe: Population 5 Years and Over)

Group	Number	%
Total Population	13,652	91.0

Language Spoken at Home: Spanish
(Universe: Population 5 Years and Over)

Group	Number	%
Total Population	354	2.4

Unemployment Rate
(Universe: Population 16 Years and Over)

Group	%
Total Population	10.0

Class of Worker: Private Wage and Salary
(Universe: Civilian Employed Population 16 Years and Over)

Group	Number	%
Total Population	5,613	80.5

Class of Worker: Government
(Universe: Civilian Employed Population 16 Years and Over)

Group	Number	%
Total Population	898	12.9

Means of Transportation to Work: Car, Truck or Van
(Universe: Workers 16 Years and Over)

Group	Number	%
Total Population	5,483	80.8

Means of Transportation to Work: Public Transportation (ex. Taxicab)
(Universe: Workers 16 Years and Over)

Group	Number	%
Total Population	9	0.1

Homeownership Rate
(Universe: Occupied Housing Units)

Group	%
Total Population	47.8
Hispanic or Latino (of any race)	25.6
Mexican	37.5
Puerto Rican	14.7

Median Home Value

Group	Dollars
Total Population	109,000

Median Gross Rent

Group	Dollars
Total Population	614

Median Household Income
(2010 Inflation-Adjusted Dollars)

Group	Dollars
Total Population	33,461

Per Capita Income
(2010 Inflation-Adjusted Dollars)

Group	Dollars
Total Population	19,411

Households with $100,000+ Income

Group	Number	%
Total Population	504	8.0

Households with Food Stamps/SNAP Benefits During Past 12 Months

Group	Number	%
Total Population	1,562	24.8

Poverty Rate
(Income in Past 12 Months Below Poverty Level)

Group	%
Total Population	23.5

Notes: (1) Percent of total population; (2) Percent of Hispanic/Latino population; Profiles include places with an overall population of at least 125,000, OR an overall population of at least 25,000 where the Hispanic/Latino population is at least 20% of the overall population. In states where less than five places meet either of these criteria, we have included places with at least 10,000 total population with the highest percentage of Hispanic/Latino population. These places are identified with an asterisk (*); Please refer to the User's Guide for a full explanation of data.

Maryland

EDITOR'S NOTE: For a place to be included in this edition, it must meet one of two criteria. Either its overall population is at least 125,000, OR its overall population is at least 25,000 and its Hispanic/Latino population is at least 20% of the overall population. For the state of Maryland, the following locations are included:

- Aspen Hill
- Baltimore
- Chillum
- Gaithersburg
- Montgomery Village
- Silver Spring
- Wheaton

Section Two: State & Place Profiles starts with the state profile, followed by place profiles that meet the criteria above. Places are listed alphabetically within each state. All states, all counties and places that meet the above criteria are ranked and compared in *Section Three: Rankings & Comparisons*, on page 1055.

For a more detailed look at the Hispanic/Latino population in Maryland, a companion web site is available at no additional charge with purchase of this print edition. Visit http://gold.greyhouse.com/page/info_hispanic for more information.

The web site includes data for all counties and places in Maryland with Hispanic/Latino population, plus ten additional topics: Self Employed Worker; Walked to Work; Worked from Home; Mean Travel Time to Work; Mean Household Income; Households with Cash Public Assistance; Mean Cash Pubic Assistance; Poverty Rates for 18 and Under, 18 to 64, and 65 and Over.

Population

Group	Number	%TP[1]	%HP[2]
Total Population	5,773,552	100.0	–
Hispanic or Latino (of any race)	470,632	8.2	100.0
Central American, ex. Mexican	195,692	3.4	41.6
Costa Rican	2,304	<0.1	0.5
Guatemalan	34,491	0.6	7.3
Honduran	20,576	0.4	4.4
Nicaraguan	8,196	0.1	1.7
Panamanian	5,341	0.1	1.1
Salvadoran	123,789	2.1	26.3
Cuban	10,366	0.2	2.2
Dominican Republic	14,873	0.3	3.2
Mexican	88,004	1.5	18.7
Puerto Rican	42,572	0.7	9.0
South American	61,400	1.1	13.0
Argentinean	5,138	0.1	1.1
Bolivian	7,496	0.1	1.6
Chilean	4,146	0.1	0.9
Colombian	12,990	0.2	2.8
Ecuadorian	7,076	0.1	1.5
Paraguayan	1,161	<0.1	0.2
Peruvian	18,229	0.3	3.9
Uruguayan	1,282	<0.1	0.3
Venezuelan	3,328	0.1	0.7
Spaniard	7,530	0.1	1.6

Population Growth: 2000–2010

Group	%
Total Population	9.0
Hispanic or Latino (of any race)	106.5
Central American, ex. Mexican	248.6
Costa Rican	133.7
Guatemalan	315.4
Honduran	405.9
Nicaraguan	138.3
Panamanian	115.0
Salvadoran	259.5
Cuban	53.5
Dominican Republic	165.8
Mexican	120.6
Puerto Rican	66.5
South American	138.8
Argentinean	125.3
Bolivian	150.0
Chilean	79.0
Colombian	146.7
Ecuadorian	170.3
Paraguayan	157.4
Peruvian	186.4
Uruguayan	199.5
Venezuelan	128.9
Spaniard	362.2

Males per 100 Females

Group	Number
Total Population	93.6
Hispanic or Latino (of any race)	110.0
Central American, ex. Mexican	119.6
Costa Rican	93.3
Guatemalan	157.6
Honduran	134.3
Nicaraguan	87.6
Panamanian	66.8
Salvadoran	114.4
Cuban	95.7
Dominican Republic	89.0
Mexican	122.9
Puerto Rican	92.5
South American	86.0
Argentinean	92.1
Bolivian	90.9
Chilean	86.5
Colombian	79.8
Ecuadorian	90.0
Paraguayan	81.4
Peruvian	86.1
Uruguayan	92.8
Venezuelan	79.2
Spaniard	92.9

Average Household Size

Group	People
Total Population	2.61
Hispanic or Latino (of any race)	3.87
Central American, ex. Mexican	4.65
Costa Rican	3.11
Guatemalan	4.59
Honduran	4.62
Nicaraguan	3.88
Panamanian	2.81
Salvadoran	4.90
Cuban	2.64
Dominican Republic	3.55
Mexican	3.98
Puerto Rican	2.85
South American	3.28
Argentinean	2.89
Bolivian	3.67
Chilean	2.98
Colombian	3.01
Ecuadorian	3.47
Paraguayan	3.29
Peruvian	3.57
Uruguayan	2.85
Venezuelan	2.98
Spaniard	2.69

Median Age

Group	Years
Total Population	38.0
Hispanic or Latino (of any race)	27.8
Central American, ex. Mexican	28.6
Costa Rican	31.5
Guatemalan	28.2
Honduran	28.6
Nicaraguan	31.7
Panamanian	33.5
Salvadoran	28.4
Cuban	31.6
Dominican Republic	27.3
Mexican	25.7
Puerto Rican	26.8
South American	34.7
Argentinean	36.1
Bolivian	34.6
Chilean	36.1
Colombian	34.3
Ecuadorian	33.2
Paraguayan	32.4
Peruvian	35.3
Uruguayan	35.5
Venezuelan	33.4
Spaniard	34.4

High School Graduates
(Universe: Population 25 Years and Over)

Group	Number	%
Total Population	3,325,937	87.8
Hispanic or Latino (of any race)	148,545	62.2
Central American, ex. Mexican	48,867	45.4
Costa Rican	1,381	86.3
Guatemalan	7,824	38.6
Honduran	4,935	46.5
Nicaraguan	3,092	69.8
Panamanian	2,875	93.3
Salvadoran	27,841	42.1
Cuban	5,183	89.9
Dominican Republic	4,870	74.7
Mexican	23,766	57.6
Puerto Rican	19,643	88.6
South American	32,896	87.0
Argentinean	3,546	90.2
Bolivian	4,035	90.5
Chilean	2,293	84.4
Colombian	6,627	89.6
Ecuadorian	3,501	75.7
Paraguayan	621	90.5
Peruvian	9,352	87.2
Uruguayan	816	80.6
Venezuelan	1,433	94.6
Spaniard	3,833	93.5

Four-Year College Graduates
(Universe: Population 25 Years and Over)

Group	Number	%
Total Population	1,353,079	35.7
Hispanic or Latino (of any race)	47,730	20.0
Central American, ex. Mexican	9,206	8.5
Costa Rican	648	40.5
Guatemalan	1,355	6.7
Honduran	1,262	11.9
Nicaraguan	732	16.5
Panamanian	1,340	43.5
Salvadoran	3,520	5.3
Cuban	2,405	41.7
Dominican Republic	1,231	18.9
Mexican	7,364	17.9
Puerto Rican	8,165	36.8
South American	14,018	37.1
Argentinean	2,127	54.1
Bolivian	1,525	34.2
Chilean	1,027	37.8
Colombian	2,745	37.1
Ecuadorian	1,264	27.3
Paraguayan	203	29.6
Peruvian	3,593	33.5
Uruguayan	372	36.7
Venezuelan	802	52.9
Spaniard	1,913	46.7

Population Age 3–17 Enrolled in Public School
(Universe: Population Age 3–17 Enrolled in School)

Group	Number	%
Total Population	842,228	80.8
Hispanic or Latino (of any race)	80,772	88.3
Central American, ex. Mexican	32,896	93.6
Costa Rican	361	59.7
Guatemalan	4,661	93.9
Honduran	2,244	95.7
Nicaraguan	770	78.4

Notes: (1) Percent of total population; (2) Percent of Hispanic/Latino population; Profiles include places with an overall population of at least 125,000, OR an overall population of at least 25,000 where the Hispanic/Latino population is at least 20% of the overall population. In states where less than five places meet either of these criteria, we have included places with at least 10,000 total population with the highest percentage of Hispanic/Latino population. These places are identified with an asterisk (*); Please refer to the User's Guide for a full explanation of data.

Group	Number	%
Panamanian	526	67.3
Salvadoran	23,815	95.6
Cuban	1,181	66.3
Dominican Republic	2,840	91.6
Mexican	16,677	88.6
Puerto Rican	8,962	83.6
South American	9,628	81.4
Argentinean	853	69.6
Bolivian	1,056	88.1
Chilean	835	89.0
Colombian	2,020	83.9
Ecuadorian	1,542	88.8
Paraguayan	223	93.7
Peruvian	2,300	77.4
Uruguayan	246	95.0
Venezuelan	202	51.5
Spaniard	952	68.2

Population Age 3–17 Enrolled in Private School
(Universe: Population Age 3–17 Enrolled in School)

Group	Number	%
Total Population	200,106	19.2
Hispanic or Latino (of any race)	10,722	11.7
Central American, ex. Mexican	2,260	6.4
Costa Rican	244	40.3
Guatemalan	301	6.1
Honduran	102	4.3
Nicaraguan	212	21.6
Panamanian	256	32.7
Salvadoran	1,105	4.4
Cuban	600	33.7
Dominican Republic	261	8.4
Mexican	2,140	11.4
Puerto Rican	1,761	16.4
South American	2,196	18.6
Argentinean	373	30.4
Bolivian	142	11.9
Chilean	103	11.0
Colombian	389	16.1
Ecuadorian	194	11.2
Paraguayan	15	6.3
Peruvian	672	22.6
Uruguayan	13	5.0
Venezuelan	190	48.5
Spaniard	443	31.8

Foreign-Born Population

Group	Number	%
Total Population	750,533	13.2
Hispanic or Latino (of any race)	231,068	53.7
Central American, ex. Mexican	127,841	67.6
Costa Rican	1,596	56.9
Guatemalan	26,430	76.1
Honduran	12,263	71.7
Nicaraguan	4,262	64.0
Panamanian	2,216	48.6
Salvadoran	79,178	65.8
Cuban	3,180	34.1
Dominican Republic	6,482	53.2
Mexican	39,484	48.2
Puerto Rican	533	1.3
South American	40,434	67.1
Argentinean	3,845	62.4
Bolivian	5,193	73.3
Chilean	3,053	69.2
Colombian	7,649	65.3
Ecuadorian	5,024	65.1
Paraguayan	876	73.9
Peruvian	11,551	70.5
Uruguayan	1,049	72.5
Venezuelan	1,519	59.6
Spaniard	1,886	28.8

Foreign-Born Naturalized U.S. Citizens

Group	Number	%
Total Population	335,717	44.7
Hispanic or Latino (of any race)	59,393	25.7
Central American, ex. Mexican	25,923	20.3
Costa Rican	638	40.0
Guatemalan	4,450	16.8
Honduran	1,599	13.0
Nicaraguan	1,841	43.2
Panamanian	1,428	64.4
Salvadoran	15,589	19.7
Cuban	2,373	74.6
Dominican Republic	3,051	47.1
Mexican	5,743	14.5
Puerto Rican	335	62.9
South American	16,161	40.0
Argentinean	1,449	37.7
Bolivian	2,436	46.9
Chilean	1,325	43.4
Colombian	3,588	46.9
Ecuadorian	1,982	39.5
Paraguayan	357	40.8
Peruvian	3,782	32.7
Uruguayan	239	22.8
Venezuelan	498	32.8
Spaniard	1,048	55.6

Language Spoken at Home: English Only
(Universe: Population 5 Years and Over)

Group	Number	%
Total Population	4,483,607	84.1
Hispanic or Latino (of any race)	93,075	24.4
Central American, ex. Mexican	25,449	15.2
Costa Rican	700	28.0
Guatemalan	5,086	16.3
Honduran	2,221	14.5
Nicaraguan	946	15.0
Panamanian	1,783	42.1
Salvadoran	14,531	13.7
Cuban	3,646	43.3
Dominican Republic	1,928	17.8
Mexican	26,458	37.4
Puerto Rican	16,570	44.4
South American	9,713	17.5
Argentinean	1,183	21.0
Bolivian	828	12.7
Chilean	861	21.1
Colombian	2,367	21.5
Ecuadorian	996	14.1
Paraguayan	138	13.0
Peruvian	2,198	14.5
Uruguayan	64	4.8
Venezuelan	638	28.2
Spaniard	3,268	53.2

Language Spoken at Home: Spanish
(Universe: Population 5 Years and Over)

Group	Number	%
Total Population	344,255	6.5
Hispanic or Latino (of any race)	285,451	74.7
Central American, ex. Mexican	142,172	84.7
Costa Rican	1,782	71.4
Guatemalan	25,911	83.3
Honduran	13,124	85.5
Nicaraguan	5,367	85.0
Panamanian	2,437	57.5
Salvadoran	91,150	86.2
Cuban	4,627	55.0
Dominican Republic	8,793	81.1
Mexican	43,557	61.6
Puerto Rican	20,423	54.8
South American	44,836	80.9
Argentinean	4,266	75.9
Bolivian	5,508	84.6
Chilean	3,175	77.8
Colombian	8,611	78.2
Ecuadorian	6,005	84.9
Paraguayan	916	86.3
Peruvian	12,826	84.9
Uruguayan	1,051	79.4
Venezuelan	1,579	69.8
Spaniard	2,553	41.6

Unemployment Rate
(Universe: Population 16 Years and Over)

Group	%
Total Population	6.6
Hispanic or Latino (of any race)	7.7
Central American, ex. Mexican	9.0
Costa Rican	9.0
Guatemalan	8.6
Honduran	9.4
Nicaraguan	7.4
Panamanian	7.8
Salvadoran	9.3
Cuban	4.9
Dominican Republic	9.3
Mexican	6.3
Puerto Rican	8.0
South American	5.8
Argentinean	5.6
Bolivian	4.2
Chilean	5.3
Colombian	7.3
Ecuadorian	5.4
Paraguayan	2.4
Peruvian	6.0
Uruguayan	3.5
Venezuelan	8.3
Spaniard	4.4

Class of Worker: Private Wage and Salary
(Universe: Civilian Employed Population 16 Years and Over)

Group	Number	%
Total Population	2,107,477	72.6
Hispanic or Latino (of any race)	184,245	83.3
Central American, ex. Mexican	92,265	88.7
Costa Rican	1,095	83.5
Guatemalan	19,100	91.3
Honduran	8,832	87.3
Nicaraguan	3,404	76.6
Panamanian	1,639	67.7
Salvadoran	57,041	89.8
Cuban	3,155	69.8
Dominican Republic	4,418	77.4
Mexican	34,782	87.7
Puerto Rican	12,620	67.9
South American	24,981	75.3
Argentinean	2,057	64.1
Bolivian	3,333	80.5
Chilean	1,718	75.7
Colombian	4,556	74.6
Ecuadorian	3,423	81.8
Paraguayan	449	60.2
Peruvian	7,281	76.4
Uruguayan	530	62.0
Venezuelan	1,106	76.9
Spaniard	2,308	68.8

Class of Worker: Government
(Universe: Civilian Employed Population 16 Years and Over)

Group	Number	%
Total Population	643,957	22.2
Hispanic or Latino (of any race)	23,459	10.6
Central American, ex. Mexican	5,322	5.1
Costa Rican	173	13.2
Guatemalan	718	3.4
Honduran	483	4.8
Nicaraguan	594	13.4
Panamanian	608	25.1
Salvadoran	2,642	4.2
Cuban	1,031	22.8
Dominican Republic	952	16.7
Mexican	3,547	8.9
Puerto Rican	5,409	29.1
South American	4,884	14.7
Argentinean	805	25.1
Bolivian	471	11.4
Chilean	380	16.7
Colombian	1,105	18.1
Ecuadorian	437	10.4
Paraguayan	130	17.4
Peruvian	1,105	11.6
Uruguayan	153	17.9
Venezuelan	238	16.6
Spaniard	770	23.0

Means of Transportation to Work: Car, Truck or Van
(Universe: Workers 16 Years and Over)

Group	Number	%
Total Population	2,392,766	83.8
Hispanic or Latino (of any race)	172,461	79.1
Central American, ex. Mexican	78,535	77.3
Costa Rican	1,175	93.8
Guatemalan	15,570	76.7
Honduran	6,504	66.1
Nicaraguan	2,867	66.3
Panamanian	1,961	80.2
Salvadoran	49,399	79.5
Cuban	3,465	78.8
Dominican Republic	4,544	79.5

Notes: (1) Percent of total population; (2) Percent of Hispanic/Latino population; Profiles include places with an overall population of at least 125,000, OR an overall population of at least 25,000 where the Hispanic/Latino population is at least 20% of the overall population. In states where less than five places meet either of these criteria, we have included places with at least 10,000 total population with the highest percentage of Hispanic/Latino population. These places are identified with an asterisk (*); Please refer to the User's Guide for a full explanation of data.

Mexican	30,707	77.8
Puerto Rican	16,233	85.5
South American	26,660	81.9
Argentinean	2,493	79.2
Bolivian	3,490	85.8
Chilean	1,916	83.6
Colombian	5,127	85.0
Ecuadorian	3,218	76.3
Paraguayan	628	87.8
Peruvian	7,487	80.9
Uruguayan	632	80.7
Venezuelan	1,097	79.8
Spaniard	2,728	81.8

Means of Transportation to Work: Public Transportation (ex. Taxicab)

(Universe: Workers 16 Years and Over)

Group	Number	%
Total Population	248,485	8.7
Hispanic or Latino (of any race)	29,662	13.6
Central American, ex. Mexican	17,181	16.9
Costa Rican	58	4.6
Guatemalan	3,421	16.9
Honduran	2,440	24.8
Nicaraguan	1,010	23.3
Panamanian	207	8.5
Salvadoran	9,883	15.9
Cuban	478	10.9
Dominican Republic	807	14.1
Mexican	4,333	11.0
Puerto Rican	1,782	9.4
South American	3,271	10.1
Argentinean	381	12.1
Bolivian	418	10.3
Chilean	159	6.9
Colombian	485	8.0
Ecuadorian	651	15.4
Paraguayan	35	4.9
Peruvian	968	10.5
Uruguayan	45	5.7
Venezuelan	120	8.7
Spaniard	256	7.7

Homeownership Rate

(Universe: Occupied Housing Units)

Group	%
Total Population	67.5
Hispanic or Latino (of any race)	50.8
Central American, ex. Mexican	49.6
Costa Rican	54.4
Guatemalan	34.6
Honduran	36.2
Nicaraguan	54.3
Panamanian	53.3
Salvadoran	55.1
Cuban	62.0
Dominican Republic	47.0
Mexican	40.7
Puerto Rican	52.2
South American	62.8
Argentinean	65.8
Bolivian	67.3
Chilean	63.5
Colombian	62.6
Ecuadorian	63.5
Paraguayan	58.7
Peruvian	60.6
Uruguayan	58.9
Venezuelan	62.3
Spaniard	68.9

Median Home Value

Group	Dollars
Total Population	329,400
Hispanic or Latino (of any race)	338,500
Central American, ex. Mexican	330,600
Costa Rican	381,600
Guatemalan	303,100
Honduran	312,200
Nicaraguan	358,300
Panamanian	304,500
Salvadoran	333,300
Cuban	364,500
Dominican Republic	290,900
Mexican	328,500
Puerto Rican	333,700
South American	361,400
Argentinean	428,700
Bolivian	397,900
Chilean	325,800
Colombian	350,100
Ecuadorian	367,500
Paraguayan	312,800
Peruvian	346,200
Uruguayan	346,900
Venezuelan	361,900
Spaniard	375,900

Median Gross Rent

Group	Dollars
Total Population	1,091
Hispanic or Latino (of any race)	1,199
Central American, ex. Mexican	1,201
Costa Rican	1,439
Guatemalan	1,134
Honduran	1,255
Nicaraguan	1,215
Panamanian	1,057
Salvadoran	1,234
Cuban	1,096
Dominican Republic	1,273
Mexican	1,164
Puerto Rican	1,176
South American	1,261
Argentinean	1,221
Bolivian	1,204
Chilean	1,579
Colombian	1,273
Ecuadorian	998
Paraguayan	1,461
Peruvian	1,281
Uruguayan	1,314
Venezuelan	1,398
Spaniard	1,386

Median Household Income

(2010 Inflation-Adjusted Dollars)

Group	Dollars
Total Population	70,647
Hispanic or Latino (of any race)	61,818
Central American, ex. Mexican	57,874
Costa Rican	73,203
Guatemalan	57,952
Honduran	56,914
Nicaraguan	66,300
Panamanian	58,415
Salvadoran	57,283
Cuban	71,167
Dominican Republic	55,000
Mexican	59,381
Puerto Rican	70,795
South American	66,489
Argentinean	78,800
Bolivian	69,742
Chilean	69,718
Colombian	60,030
Ecuadorian	66,543
Paraguayan	72,318
Peruvian	62,066
Uruguayan	69,676
Venezuelan	74,417
Spaniard	73,155

Per Capita Income

(2010 Inflation-Adjusted Dollars)

Group	Dollars
Total Population	34,849
Hispanic or Latino (of any race)	20,490
Central American, ex. Mexican	16,651
Costa Rican	21,496
Guatemalan	16,964
Honduran	16,460
Nicaraguan	23,036
Panamanian	29,615
Salvadoran	15,498
Cuban	35,791
Dominican Republic	17,444
Mexican	19,353
Puerto Rican	25,984
South American	26,527
Argentinean	33,220
Bolivian	24,989
Chilean	26,458
Colombian	25,443
Ecuadorian	23,065
Paraguayan	23,514
Peruvian	25,412
Uruguayan	32,692
Venezuelan	35,750
Spaniard	43,673

Households with $100,000+ Income

Group	Number	%
Total Population	699,260	33.0
Hispanic or Latino (of any race)	25,977	23.9
Central American, ex. Mexican	8,022	18.7
Costa Rican	197	34.1
Guatemalan	1,192	15.0
Honduran	763	21.1
Nicaraguan	610	32.9
Panamanian	320	20.4
Salvadoran	4,739	17.7
Cuban	1,295	36.4
Dominican Republic	647	20.4
Mexican	3,947	21.8
Puerto Rican	3,928	29.4
South American	5,270	29.2
Argentinean	675	36.3
Bolivian	692	32.2
Chilean	434	34.0
Colombian	903	25.5
Ecuadorian	599	27.4
Paraguayan	50	14.8
Peruvian	1,352	27.7
Uruguayan	141	27.4
Venezuelan	284	32.6
Spaniard	998	39.7

Households with Food Stamps/SNAP Benefits During Past 12 Months

Group	Number	%
Total Population	127,819	6.0
Hispanic or Latino (of any race)	7,759	7.2
Central American, ex. Mexican	3,168	7.4
Costa Rican	0	0.0
Guatemalan	445	5.6
Honduran	239	6.6
Nicaraguan	166	8.9
Panamanian	118	7.5
Salvadoran	2,182	8.2
Cuban	309	8.7
Dominican Republic	500	15.8
Mexican	1,214	6.7
Puerto Rican	1,229	9.2
South American	843	4.7
Argentinean	32	1.7
Bolivian	40	1.9
Chilean	47	3.7
Colombian	221	6.2
Ecuadorian	141	6.5
Paraguayan	0	0.0
Peruvian	224	4.6
Uruguayan	19	3.7
Venezuelan	14	1.6
Spaniard	76	3.0

Poverty Rate

(Income in Past 12 Months Below Poverty Level)

Group	%
Total Population	8.6
Hispanic or Latino (of any race)	12.2
Central American, ex. Mexican	13.7
Costa Rican	5.2
Guatemalan	14.9
Honduran	18.2
Nicaraguan	6.2
Panamanian	10.8
Salvadoran	13.7
Cuban	12.2
Dominican Republic	18.6
Mexican	13.3
Puerto Rican	11.6
South American	5.9
Argentinean	4.3
Bolivian	8.6

Notes: (1) Percent of total population; (2) Percent of Hispanic/Latino population; Profiles include places with an overall population of at least 125,000, OR an overall population of at least 25,000 where the Hispanic/Latino population is at least 20% of the overall population. In states where less than five places meet either of these criteria, we have included places with at least 10,000 total population with the highest percentage of Hispanic/Latino population. These places are identified with an asterisk (*); Please refer to the User's Guide for a full explanation of data.

Chilean	6.3
Colombian	6.7
Ecuadorian	4.5
Paraguayan	4.3
Peruvian	6.0
Uruguayan	4.6
Venezuelan	5.2
Spaniard	7.9

Aspen Hill

Population

Group	Number	%TP[1]	%HP[2]
Total Population	48,759	100.0	–
Hispanic or Latino (of any race)	13,593	27.9	100.0
Central American, ex. Mexican	7,037	14.4	51.8
Guatemalan	712	1.5	5.2
Honduran	755	1.5	5.6
Nicaraguan	384	0.8	2.8
Panamanian	100	0.2	0.7
Salvadoran	5,023	10.3	37.0
Cuban	179	0.4	1.3
Dominican Republic	348	0.7	2.6
Mexican	1,084	2.2	8.0
Puerto Rican	379	0.8	2.8
South American	3,025	6.2	22.3
Argentinean	127	0.3	0.9
Bolivian	521	1.1	3.8
Chilean	212	0.4	1.6
Colombian	546	1.1	4.0
Ecuadorian	258	0.5	1.9
Peruvian	1,144	2.3	8.4

Population Growth: 2000–2010

Group	%
Total Population	-2.9
Hispanic or Latino (of any race)	75.2
Central American, ex. Mexican	218.6
Guatemalan	165.7
Honduran	494.5
Nicaraguan	108.7
Salvadoran	262.9
Cuban	7.8
Dominican Republic	150.4
Mexican	67.8
Puerto Rican	35.4
South American	103.2
Bolivian	79.7
Chilean	64.3
Colombian	109.2
Ecuadorian	70.9
Peruvian	181.8

Males per 100 Females

Group	Number
Total Population	92.3
Hispanic or Latino (of any race)	103.3
Central American, ex. Mexican	108.5
Guatemalan	128.2
Honduran	125.4
Nicaraguan	91.0
Panamanian	61.3
Salvadoran	106.5
Cuban	96.7
Dominican Republic	89.1
Mexican	124.9
Puerto Rican	85.8
South American	89.1
Argentinean	92.4
Bolivian	95.1
Chilean	87.6
Colombian	79.6
Ecuadorian	104.8
Peruvian	92.3

Average Household Size

Group	People
Total Population	2.90
Hispanic or Latino (of any race)	4.28
Central American, ex. Mexican	4.90
Guatemalan	4.50
Honduran	5.50
Nicaraguan	4.29
Panamanian	3.41
Salvadoran	5.02
Cuban	2.79
Dominican Republic	3.88
Mexican	4.22
Puerto Rican	2.70
South American	3.82
Argentinean	3.13
Bolivian	4.11
Chilean	3.34
Colombian	3.38
Ecuadorian	3.95
Peruvian	4.18

Median Age

Group	Years
Total Population	37.2
Hispanic or Latino (of any race)	29.5
Central American, ex. Mexican	29.2
Guatemalan	29.9
Honduran	29.5
Nicaraguan	29.4
Panamanian	33.0
Salvadoran	28.8
Cuban	37.1
Dominican Republic	29.0
Mexican	27.2
Puerto Rican	29.3
South American	36.7
Argentinean	36.5
Bolivian	36.1
Chilean	43.5
Colombian	39.7
Ecuadorian	37.2
Peruvian	34.9

High School Graduates
(Universe: Population 25 Years and Over)

Group	Number	%
Total Population	26,605	84.1
Hispanic or Latino (of any race)	3,350	57.0
Central American, ex. Mexican	1,466	43.7
Salvadoran	1,196	44.1
Mexican	316	61.2
South American	1,063	80.2

Four-Year College Graduates
(Universe: Population 25 Years and Over)

Group	Number	%
Total Population	13,191	41.7
Hispanic or Latino (of any race)	816	13.9
Central American, ex. Mexican	261	7.8
Salvadoran	162	6.0
Mexican	80	15.5
South American	263	19.8

Population Age 3–17 Enrolled in Public School
(Universe: Population Age 3–17 Enrolled in School)

Group	Number	%
Total Population	7,489	84.1
Hispanic or Latino (of any race)	2,022	95.7
Central American, ex. Mexican	1,439	97.4
Salvadoran	1,327	98.8
Mexican	249	100.0
South American	191	100.0

Population Age 3–17 Enrolled in Private School
(Universe: Population Age 3–17 Enrolled in School)

Group	Number	%
Total Population	1,415	15.9
Hispanic or Latino (of any race)	91	4.3
Central American, ex. Mexican	39	2.6
Salvadoran	16	1.2
Mexican	0	0.0
South American	0	0.0

Foreign-Born Population

Group	Number	%
Total Population	16,978	36.1
Hispanic or Latino (of any race)	6,771	65.9
Central American, ex. Mexican	4,467	69.9
Salvadoran	3,743	68.7
Mexican	370	34.2
South American	1,473	84.0

Foreign-Born Naturalized U.S. Citizens

Group	Number	%
Total Population	7,133	42.0
Hispanic or Latino (of any race)	1,757	25.9
Central American, ex. Mexican	708	15.8
Salvadoran	468	12.5
Mexican	85	23.0
South American	722	49.0

Language Spoken at Home: English Only
(Universe: Population 5 Years and Over)

Group	Number	%
Total Population	24,560	55.7
Hispanic or Latino (of any race)	703	7.6
Central American, ex. Mexican	225	3.9
Salvadoran	158	3.2
Mexican	175	20.9
South American	45	2.7

Language Spoken at Home: Spanish
(Universe: Population 5 Years and Over)

Group	Number	%
Total Population	9,150	20.8
Hispanic or Latino (of any race)	8,455	91.4
Central American, ex. Mexican	5,512	95.3
Salvadoran	4,684	95.8
Mexican	661	79.1
South American	1,601	97.3

Unemployment Rate
(Universe: Population 16 Years and Over)

Group	%
Total Population	8.2
Hispanic or Latino (of any race)	9.5
Central American, ex. Mexican	11.0
Salvadoran	10.9
Mexican	12.7
South American	2.4

Class of Worker: Private Wage and Salary
(Universe: Civilian Employed Population 16 Years and Over)

Group	Number	%
Total Population	17,798	72.3
Hispanic or Latino (of any race)	4,342	79.4
Central American, ex. Mexican	2,775	80.2
Salvadoran	2,283	80.6
Mexican	391	84.8
South American	853	81.8

Class of Worker: Government
(Universe: Civilian Employed Population 16 Years and Over)

Group	Number	%
Total Population	4,324	17.6
Hispanic or Latino (of any race)	352	6.4
Central American, ex. Mexican	154	4.5
Salvadoran	127	4.5
Mexican	58	12.6
South American	79	7.6

Means of Transportation to Work: Car, Truck or Van
(Universe: Workers 16 Years and Over)

Group	Number	%
Total Population	18,777	77.3
Hispanic or Latino (of any race)	4,000	73.0
Central American, ex. Mexican	2,459	71.7
Salvadoran	1,965	70.1
Mexican	348	68.4
South American	801	77.5

Means of Transportation to Work: Public Transportation (ex. Taxicab)
(Universe: Workers 16 Years and Over)

Group	Number	%
Total Population	4,086	16.8
Hispanic or Latino (of any race)	1,326	24.2
Central American, ex. Mexican	917	26.7
Salvadoran	785	28.0
Mexican	161	31.6
South American	192	18.6

Homeownership Rate
(Universe: Occupied Housing Units)

Group	%
Total Population	65.8

Notes: (1) Percent of total population; (2) Percent of Hispanic/Latino population; Profiles include places with an overall population of at least 125,000, OR an overall population of at least 25,000 where the Hispanic/Latino population is at least 20% of the overall population. In states where less than five places meet either of these criteria, we have included places with at least 10,000 total population with the highest percentage of Hispanic/Latino population. These places are identified with an asterisk (*); Please refer to the User's Guide for a full explanation of data.

Hispanic or Latino (of any race)	56.9
Central American, ex. Mexican	57.2
Guatemalan	52.7
Honduran	43.7
Nicaraguan	42.4
Panamanian	59.4
Salvadoran	60.5
Cuban	58.6
Dominican Republic	36.7
Mexican	47.0
Puerto Rican	51.5
South American	64.1
Argentinean	60.5
Bolivian	70.7
Chilean	64.2
Colombian	64.2
Ecuadorian	59.0
Peruvian	62.0

Median Home Value

Group	Dollars
Total Population	422,900
Hispanic or Latino (of any race)	355,000
Central American, ex. Mexican	365,000
Salvadoran	364,300
Mexican	365,300
South American	315,400

Median Gross Rent

Group	Dollars
Total Population	1,367
Hispanic or Latino (of any race)	1,274
Central American, ex. Mexican	1,236
Salvadoran	1,204
Mexican	1,621
South American	1,143

Median Household Income
(2010 Inflation-Adjusted Dollars)

Group	Dollars
Total Population	73,513
Hispanic or Latino (of any race)	57,059
Central American, ex. Mexican	56,166
Salvadoran	46,806
Mexican	50,565
South American	58,576

Per Capita Income
(2010 Inflation-Adjusted Dollars)

Group	Dollars
Total Population	33,509
Hispanic or Latino (of any race)	20,949
Central American, ex. Mexican	15,333
Salvadoran	13,996
Mexican	17,315
South American	21,880

Households with $100,000+ Income

Group	Number	%
Total Population	5,948	35.5
Hispanic or Latino (of any race)	498	18.5
Central American, ex. Mexican	224	15.6
Salvadoran	163	13.2
Mexican	28	11.7
South American	92	13.7

Households with Food Stamps/SNAP Benefits During Past 12 Months

Group	Number	%
Total Population	1,113	6.6
Hispanic or Latino (of any race)	124	4.6
Central American, ex. Mexican	82	5.7
Salvadoran	82	6.6
Mexican	0	0.0
South American	42	6.2

Poverty Rate
(Income in Past 12 Months Below Poverty Level)

Group	%
Total Population	9.6
Hispanic or Latino (of any race)	11.8
Central American, ex. Mexican	12.8
Salvadoran	14.3
Mexican	16.3
South American	10.2

Baltimore

Population

Group	Number	%TP[1]	%HP[2]
Total Population	620,961	100.0	–
Hispanic or Latino (of any race)	25,960	4.2	100.0
Central American, ex. Mexican	6,921	1.1	26.7
Guatemalan	1,246	0.2	4.8
Honduran	2,386	0.4	9.2
Nicaraguan	101	<0.1	0.4
Panamanian	269	<0.1	1.0
Salvadoran	2,796	0.5	10.8
Cuban	824	0.1	3.2
Dominican Republic	1,111	0.2	4.3
Mexican	7,855	1.3	30.3
Puerto Rican	3,137	0.5	12.1
South American	2,554	0.4	9.8
Argentinean	276	<0.1	1.1
Chilean	111	<0.1	0.4
Colombian	492	0.1	1.9
Ecuadorian	755	0.1	2.9
Peruvian	537	0.1	2.1
Venezuelan	195	<0.1	0.8
Spaniard	413	0.1	1.6

Population Growth: 2000–2010

Group	%
Total Population	-4.6
Hispanic or Latino (of any race)	134.7
Central American, ex. Mexican	474.4
Guatemalan	559.3
Honduran	758.3
Panamanian	156.2
Salvadoran	455.9
Cuban	62.2
Dominican Republic	223.0
Mexican	161.9
Puerto Rican	42.1
South American	227.9
Colombian	174.9
Ecuadorian	467.7
Peruvian	198.3

Males per 100 Females

Group	Number
Total Population	88.9
Hispanic or Latino (of any race)	124.3
Central American, ex. Mexican	147.5
Guatemalan	178.7
Honduran	170.8
Nicaraguan	102.0
Panamanian	71.3
Salvadoran	133.2
Cuban	94.8
Dominican Republic	95.9
Mexican	137.9
Puerto Rican	91.2
South American	110.9
Argentinean	122.6
Chilean	136.2
Colombian	110.3
Ecuadorian	113.3
Peruvian	116.5
Venezuelan	87.5
Spaniard	93.9

Average Household Size

Group	People
Total Population	2.38
Hispanic or Latino (of any race)	3.23
Central American, ex. Mexican	4.10
Guatemalan	3.84
Honduran	4.53
Nicaraguan	2.67
Panamanian	2.28
Salvadoran	4.40
Cuban	2.14
Dominican Republic	3.13
Mexican	3.59
Puerto Rican	2.43
South American	2.68
Argentinean	2.19
Chilean	2.17
Colombian	2.19
Ecuadorian	3.90
Peruvian	2.53
Venezuelan	2.46
Spaniard	1.92

Median Age

Group	Years
Total Population	34.4
Hispanic or Latino (of any race)	27.5
Central American, ex. Mexican	28.1
Guatemalan	27.4
Honduran	28.0
Nicaraguan	29.8
Panamanian	30.9
Salvadoran	28.3
Cuban	29.0
Dominican Republic	27.3
Mexican	26.2
Puerto Rican	27.1
South American	30.6
Argentinean	32.8
Chilean	30.6
Colombian	29.9
Ecuadorian	28.7
Peruvian	32.4
Venezuelan	31.9
Spaniard	30.7

High School Graduates
(Universe: Population 25 Years and Over)

Group	Number	%
Total Population	313,747	77.4
Hispanic or Latino (of any race)	7,541	58.1
Central American, ex. Mexican	1,582	48.5
Honduran	585	51.4
Salvadoran	511	39.3
Cuban	567	91.9
Mexican	2,055	46.4
Puerto Rican	1,095	72.8
South American	1,376	67.9

Four-Year College Graduates
(Universe: Population 25 Years and Over)

Group	Number	%
Total Population	102,068	25.2
Hispanic or Latino (of any race)	2,311	17.8
Central American, ex. Mexican	317	9.7
Honduran	49	4.3
Salvadoran	83	6.4
Cuban	193	31.3
Mexican	435	9.8
Puerto Rican	328	21.8
South American	658	32.4

Population Age 3–17 Enrolled in Public School
(Universe: Population Age 3–17 Enrolled in School)

Group	Number	%
Total Population	85,309	84.5
Hispanic or Latino (of any race)	3,181	84.5
Central American, ex. Mexican	537	80.9
Honduran	82	98.8
Salvadoran	376	75.0
Cuban	111	51.2
Mexican	1,234	89.9
Puerto Rican	547	90.7
South American	298	77.8

Population Age 3–17 Enrolled in Private School
(Universe: Population Age 3–17 Enrolled in School)

Group	Number	%
Total Population	15,660	15.5
Hispanic or Latino (of any race)	585	15.5
Central American, ex. Mexican	127	19.1
Honduran	1	1.2
Salvadoran	125	25.0
Cuban	106	48.8
Mexican	139	10.1
Puerto Rican	56	9.3
South American	85	22.2

Foreign-Born Population

Group	Number	%
Total Population	43,571	7.0
Hispanic or Latino (of any race)	11,339	49.7
Central American, ex. Mexican	3,669	69.4

Notes: (1) Percent of total population; (2) Percent of Hispanic/Latino population; Profiles include places with an overall population of at least 125,000, OR an overall population of at least 25,000 where the Hispanic/Latino population is at least 20% of the overall population. In states where less than five places meet either of these criteria, we have included places with at least 10,000 total population with the highest percentage of Hispanic/Latino population. These places are identified with an asterisk (*); Please refer to the User's Guide for a full explanation of data.

Group	Number	%
Honduran	1,190	76.1
Salvadoran	1,503	65.6
Cuban	292	29.0
Mexican	4,754	56.1
Puerto Rican	83	3.0
South American	1,911	60.6

Foreign-Born Naturalized U.S. Citizens

Group	Number	%
Total Population	16,928	38.9
Hispanic or Latino (of any race)	2,853	25.2
Central American, ex. Mexican	775	21.1
Honduran	136	11.4
Salvadoran	405	26.9
Cuban	168	57.5
Mexican	843	17.7
Puerto Rican	63	75.9
South American	723	37.8

Language Spoken at Home: English Only
(Universe: Population 5 Years and Over)

Group	Number	%
Total Population	526,705	90.9
Hispanic or Latino (of any race)	5,569	27.8
Central American, ex. Mexican	788	17.3
Honduran	223	16.1
Salvadoran	239	12.1
Cuban	319	33.8
Mexican	1,891	25.5
Puerto Rican	1,360	56.6
South American	547	19.6

Language Spoken at Home: Spanish
(Universe: Population 5 Years and Over)

Group	Number	%
Total Population	21,661	3.7
Hispanic or Latino (of any race)	14,283	71.3
Central American, ex. Mexican	3,742	82.3
Honduran	1,164	83.9
Salvadoran	1,719	87.0
Cuban	611	64.7
Mexican	5,441	73.3
Puerto Rican	1,036	43.1
South American	2,241	80.1

Unemployment Rate
(Universe: Population 16 Years and Over)

Group	%
Total Population	11.5
Hispanic or Latino (of any race)	8.3
Central American, ex. Mexican	7.5
Honduran	14.7
Salvadoran	4.6
Cuban	4.0
Mexican	6.5
Puerto Rican	14.7
South American	7.9

Class of Worker: Private Wage and Salary
(Universe: Civilian Employed Population 16 Years and Over)

Group	Number	%
Total Population	203,381	74.2
Hispanic or Latino (of any race)	10,566	88.4
Central American, ex. Mexican	2,740	89.5
Honduran	813	89.5
Salvadoran	1,084	89.3
Cuban	323	74.4
Mexican	4,480	94.4
Puerto Rican	985	85.1
South American	1,376	84.8

Class of Worker: Government
(Universe: Civilian Employed Population 16 Years and Over)

Group	Number	%
Total Population	59,446	21.7
Hispanic or Latino (of any race)	885	7.4
Central American, ex. Mexican	207	6.8
Honduran	59	6.5
Salvadoran	90	7.4
Cuban	99	22.8
Mexican	169	3.6
Puerto Rican	173	14.9
South American	49	3.0

Means of Transportation to Work: Car, Truck or Van
(Universe: Workers 16 Years and Over)

Group	Number	%
Total Population	187,044	70.2
Hispanic or Latino (of any race)	7,595	64.2
Central American, ex. Mexican	2,038	67.6
Honduran	527	61.2
Salvadoran	849	69.9
Cuban	301	70.2
Mexican	2,719	57.5
Puerto Rican	923	80.4
South American	1,027	63.3

Means of Transportation to Work: Public Transportation (ex. Taxicab)
(Universe: Workers 16 Years and Over)

Group	Number	%
Total Population	49,262	18.5
Hispanic or Latino (of any race)	2,516	21.3
Central American, ex. Mexican	643	21.3
Honduran	219	25.4
Salvadoran	319	26.3
Cuban	10	2.3
Mexican	1,261	26.6
Puerto Rican	107	9.3
South American	379	23.4

Homeownership Rate
(Universe: Occupied Housing Units)

Group	%
Total Population	47.7
Hispanic or Latino (of any race)	31.1
Central American, ex. Mexican	27.6
Guatemalan	18.8
Honduran	17.0
Nicaraguan	46.7
Panamanian	43.5
Salvadoran	36.1
Cuban	42.5
Dominican Republic	45.7
Mexican	20.9
Puerto Rican	37.9
South American	40.1
Argentinean	44.2
Chilean	38.9
Colombian	42.1
Ecuadorian	34.8
Peruvian	42.3
Venezuelan	41.8
Spaniard	48.1

Median Home Value

Group	Dollars
Total Population	160,400
Hispanic or Latino (of any race)	193,600
Central American, ex. Mexican	163,000
Honduran	97,800
Salvadoran	164,400
Cuban	254,400
Mexican	181,200
Puerto Rican	194,200
South American	249,100

Median Gross Rent

Group	Dollars
Total Population	859
Hispanic or Latino (of any race)	1,064
Central American, ex. Mexican	1,110
Honduran	1,253
Salvadoran	1,074
Cuban	853
Mexican	1,118
Puerto Rican	970
South American	1,085

Median Household Income
(2010 Inflation-Adjusted Dollars)

Group	Dollars
Total Population	39,386
Hispanic or Latino (of any race)	40,104
Central American, ex. Mexican	57,069
Honduran	35,417
Salvadoran	58,409
Cuban	47,860
Mexican	38,690
Puerto Rican	25,063
South American	48,194

Per Capita Income
(2010 Inflation-Adjusted Dollars)

Group	Dollars
Total Population	23,333
Hispanic or Latino (of any race)	18,485
Central American, ex. Mexican	16,427
Honduran	13,732
Salvadoran	17,268
Cuban	24,391
Mexican	15,087
Puerto Rican	15,549
South American	29,724

Households with $100,000+ Income

Group	Number	%
Total Population	31,968	13.4
Hispanic or Latino (of any race)	782	12.6
Central American, ex. Mexican	184	15.4
Honduran	38	9.3
Salvadoran	54	11.6
Cuban	35	8.6
Mexican	93	5.0
Puerto Rican	64	6.9
South American	286	27.4

Households with Food Stamps/SNAP Benefits During Past 12 Months

Group	Number	%
Total Population	35,296	14.8
Hispanic or Latino (of any race)	863	13.9
Central American, ex. Mexican	120	10.1
Honduran	40	9.8
Salvadoran	75	16.1
Cuban	152	37.3
Mexican	164	8.8
Puerto Rican	218	23.6
South American	59	5.7

Poverty Rate
(Income in Past 12 Months Below Poverty Level)

Group	%
Total Population	21.3
Hispanic or Latino (of any race)	24.1
Central American, ex. Mexican	19.8
Honduran	32.9
Salvadoran	19.5
Cuban	40.5
Mexican	26.6
Puerto Rican	23.4
South American	16.8

Chillum

Population

Group	Number	%TP[1]	%HP[2]
Total Population	33,513	100.0	–
Hispanic or Latino (of any race)	14,099	42.1	100.0
Central American, ex. Mexican	9,869	29.4	70.0
Guatemalan	1,569	4.7	11.1
Honduran	620	1.9	4.4
Nicaraguan	261	0.8	1.9
Salvadoran	7,315	21.8	51.9
Dominican Republic	723	2.2	5.1
Mexican	993	3.0	7.0
Puerto Rican	179	0.5	1.3
South American	350	1.0	2.5
Peruvian	111	0.3	0.8

Population Growth: 2000–2010

Group	%
Total Population	-2.2
Hispanic or Latino (of any race)	73.9
Central American, ex. Mexican	171.5
Guatemalan	399.7
Honduran	289.9
Nicaraguan	78.8
Salvadoran	163.3
Dominican Republic	41.8
Mexican	32.2
Puerto Rican	-20.8

Notes: (1) Percent of total population; (2) Percent of Hispanic/Latino population; Profiles include places with an overall population of at least 125,000, OR an overall population of at least 25,000 where the Hispanic/Latino population is at least 20% of the overall population. In states where less than five places meet either of these criteria, we have included places with at least 10,000 total population with the highest percentage of Hispanic/Latino population. These places are identified with an asterisk (*); Please refer to the User's Guide for a full explanation of data.

South American	65.1

Males per 100 Females

Group	Number
Total Population	100.1
Hispanic or Latino (of any race)	119.9
Central American, ex. Mexican	124.1
Guatemalan	176.2
Honduran	122.2
Nicaraguan	96.2
Salvadoran	117.3
Dominican Republic	102.5
Mexican	119.2
Puerto Rican	90.4
South American	95.5
Peruvian	98.2

Average Household Size

Group	People
Total Population	3.07
Hispanic or Latino (of any race)	4.73
Central American, ex. Mexican	5.03
Guatemalan	5.01
Honduran	4.93
Nicaraguan	4.17
Salvadoran	5.12
Dominican Republic	4.07
Mexican	4.18
Puerto Rican	3.26
South American	3.55
Peruvian	3.39

Median Age

Group	Years
Total Population	32.2
Hispanic or Latino (of any race)	28.1
Central American, ex. Mexican	29.3
Guatemalan	28.9
Honduran	29.7
Nicaraguan	30.9
Salvadoran	29.2
Dominican Republic	30.9
Mexican	27.0
Puerto Rican	30.8
South American	36.7
Peruvian	40.4

High School Graduates
(Universe: Population 25 Years and Over)

Group	Number	%
Total Population	15,358	67.8
Hispanic or Latino (of any race)	2,953	37.0
Central American, ex. Mexican	1,709	28.5
Guatemalan	300	29.1
Salvadoran	1,208	26.9

Four-Year College Graduates
(Universe: Population 25 Years and Over)

Group	Number	%
Total Population	3,676	16.2
Hispanic or Latino (of any race)	372	4.7
Central American, ex. Mexican	151	2.5
Guatemalan	6	0.6
Salvadoran	49	1.1

Population Age 3–17 Enrolled in Public School
(Universe: Population Age 3–17 Enrolled in School)

Group	Number	%
Total Population	4,513	93.1
Hispanic or Latino (of any race)	2,359	99.1
Central American, ex. Mexican	1,760	100.0
Guatemalan	306	100.0
Salvadoran	1,257	100.0

Population Age 3–17 Enrolled in Private School
(Universe: Population Age 3–17 Enrolled in School)

Group	Number	%
Total Population	336	6.9
Hispanic or Latino (of any race)	21	0.9
Central American, ex. Mexican	0	0.0
Guatemalan	0	0.0
Salvadoran	0	0.0

Foreign-Born Population

Group	Number	%
Total Population	15,247	43.5
Hispanic or Latino (of any race)	9,509	67.5
Central American, ex. Mexican	7,541	71.4
Guatemalan	1,088	68.6
Salvadoran	5,712	71.7

Foreign-Born Naturalized U.S. Citizens

Group	Number	%
Total Population	3,214	21.1
Hispanic or Latino (of any race)	1,452	15.3
Central American, ex. Mexican	905	12.0
Guatemalan	140	12.9
Salvadoran	664	11.6

Language Spoken at Home: English Only
(Universe: Population 5 Years and Over)

Group	Number	%
Total Population	16,413	51.4
Hispanic or Latino (of any race)	1,255	10.2
Central American, ex. Mexican	800	8.7
Guatemalan	169	12.7
Salvadoran	608	8.7

Language Spoken at Home: Spanish
(Universe: Population 5 Years and Over)

Group	Number	%
Total Population	11,601	36.4
Hispanic or Latino (of any race)	11,035	89.5
Central American, ex. Mexican	8,398	91.3
Guatemalan	1,160	87.3
Salvadoran	6,341	91.3

Unemployment Rate
(Universe: Population 16 Years and Over)

Group	%
Total Population	11.3
Hispanic or Latino (of any race)	14.2
Central American, ex. Mexican	17.7
Guatemalan	25.0
Salvadoran	17.2

Class of Worker: Private Wage and Salary
(Universe: Civilian Employed Population 16 Years and Over)

Group	Number	%
Total Population	14,510	79.9
Hispanic or Latino (of any race)	6,557	89.5
Central American, ex. Mexican	4,868	92.9
Guatemalan	632	94.8
Salvadoran	3,722	93.2

Class of Worker: Government
(Universe: Civilian Employed Population 16 Years and Over)

Group	Number	%
Total Population	2,624	14.4
Hispanic or Latino (of any race)	399	5.4
Central American, ex. Mexican	143	2.7
Guatemalan	12	1.8
Salvadoran	120	3.0

Means of Transportation to Work: Car, Truck or Van
(Universe: Workers 16 Years and Over)

Group	Number	%
Total Population	12,206	69.3
Hispanic or Latino (of any race)	5,197	72.9
Central American, ex. Mexican	3,825	75.6
Guatemalan	597	94.8
Salvadoran	2,978	76.1

Means of Transportation to Work: Public Transportation (ex. Taxicab)
(Universe: Workers 16 Years and Over)

Group	Number	%
Total Population	4,689	26.6
Hispanic or Latino (of any race)	1,704	23.9
Central American, ex. Mexican	1,143	22.6
Guatemalan	33	5.2
Salvadoran	880	22.5

Homeownership Rate
(Universe: Occupied Housing Units)

Group	%
Total Population	40.7
Hispanic or Latino (of any race)	46.1
Central American, ex. Mexican	48.1
Guatemalan	30.7
Honduran	34.4
Nicaraguan	63.3
Salvadoran	52.2
Dominican Republic	46.6
Mexican	28.9
Puerto Rican	30.3
South American	54.8
Peruvian	61.3

Median Home Value

Group	Dollars
Total Population	312,700
Hispanic or Latino (of any race)	265,300
Central American, ex. Mexican	301,300
Guatemalan	303,300
Salvadoran	299,300

Median Gross Rent

Group	Dollars
Total Population	1,110
Hispanic or Latino (of any race)	1,119
Central American, ex. Mexican	1,110
Guatemalan	989
Salvadoran	1,138

Median Household Income
(2010 Inflation-Adjusted Dollars)

Group	Dollars
Total Population	52,457
Hispanic or Latino (of any race)	54,696
Central American, ex. Mexican	57,016
Guatemalan	36,511
Salvadoran	68,042

Per Capita Income
(2010 Inflation-Adjusted Dollars)

Group	Dollars
Total Population	21,464
Hispanic or Latino (of any race)	15,827
Central American, ex. Mexican	14,696
Guatemalan	14,694
Salvadoran	14,292

Households with $100,000+ Income

Group	Number	%
Total Population	2,082	19.3
Hispanic or Latino (of any race)	555	18.6
Central American, ex. Mexican	361	17.7
Guatemalan	22	5.9
Salvadoran	291	19.2

Households with Food Stamps/SNAP Benefits During Past 12 Months

Group	Number	%
Total Population	986	9.1
Hispanic or Latino (of any race)	285	9.6
Central American, ex. Mexican	159	7.8
Guatemalan	0	0.0
Salvadoran	135	8.9

Poverty Rate
(Income in Past 12 Months Below Poverty Level)

Group	%
Total Population	16.4
Hispanic or Latino (of any race)	17.0
Central American, ex. Mexican	18.2
Guatemalan	8.1
Salvadoran	19.6

Gaithersburg

Population

Group	Number	%TP[1]	%HP[2]
Total Population	59,933	100.0	–
Hispanic or Latino (of any race)	14,499	24.2	100.0
Central American, ex. Mexican	7,812	13.0	53.9
Guatemalan	1,009	1.7	7.0
Honduran	1,211	2.0	8.4
Nicaraguan	415	0.7	2.9
Panamanian	100	0.2	0.7
Salvadoran	4,994	8.3	34.4
Cuban	154	0.3	1.1
Dominican Republic	328	0.5	2.3
Mexican	1,161	1.9	8.0
Puerto Rican	471	0.8	3.2

Notes: (1) Percent of total population; (2) Percent of Hispanic/Latino population; Profiles include places with an overall population of at least 125,000, OR an overall population of at least 25,000 where the Hispanic/Latino population is at least 20% of the overall population. In states where less than five places meet either of these criteria, we have included places with at least 10,000 total population with the highest percentage of Hispanic/Latino population. These places are identified with an asterisk (*); Please refer to the User's Guide for a full explanation of data.

South American	2,870	4.8	19.8
Argentinean	112	0.2	0.8
Bolivian	443	0.7	3.1
Chilean	143	0.2	1.0
Colombian	456	0.8	3.1
Ecuadorian	280	0.5	1.9
Peruvian	1,150	1.9	7.9
Venezuelan	114	0.2	0.8
Spaniard	121	0.2	0.8

Population Growth: 2000–2010

Group	%
Total Population	13.9
Hispanic or Latino (of any race)	39.4
Central American, ex. Mexican	103.5
Guatemalan	195.0
Honduran	260.4
Nicaraguan	73.6
Salvadoran	87.6
Cuban	5.5
Dominican Republic	144.8
Mexican	9.5
Puerto Rican	19.2
South American	108.3
Bolivian	135.6
Colombian	92.4
Ecuadorian	135.3
Peruvian	112.2

Males per 100 Females

Group	Number
Total Population	94.7
Hispanic or Latino (of any race)	110.6
Central American, ex. Mexican	122.9
Guatemalan	132.0
Honduran	141.7
Nicaraguan	93.0
Panamanian	63.9
Salvadoran	122.1
Cuban	108.1
Dominican Republic	84.3
Mexican	123.7
Puerto Rican	83.3
South American	87.0
Argentinean	103.6
Bolivian	80.8
Chilean	78.8
Colombian	80.2
Ecuadorian	85.4
Peruvian	87.6
Venezuelan	81.0
Spaniard	108.6

Average Household Size

Group	People
Total Population	2.70
Hispanic or Latino (of any race)	4.05
Central American, ex. Mexican	4.68
Guatemalan	4.29
Honduran	5.16
Nicaraguan	4.09
Panamanian	3.05
Salvadoran	4.82
Cuban	2.64
Dominican Republic	3.37
Mexican	3.76
Puerto Rican	2.60
South American	3.39
Argentinean	2.69
Bolivian	3.62
Chilean	3.20
Colombian	2.93
Ecuadorian	3.40
Peruvian	3.72
Venezuelan	3.03
Spaniard	2.67

Median Age

Group	Years
Total Population	35.1
Hispanic or Latino (of any race)	28.9
Central American, ex. Mexican	29.1
Guatemalan	29.3
Honduran	29.3
Nicaraguan	31.9
Panamanian	39.5
Salvadoran	28.7
Cuban	37.4
Dominican Republic	27.2
Mexican	28.2
Puerto Rican	27.3
South American	35.5
Argentinean	35.6
Bolivian	34.9
Chilean	35.9
Colombian	36.0
Ecuadorian	33.9
Peruvian	36.2
Venezuelan	36.5
Spaniard	35.9

High School Graduates
(Universe: Population 25 Years and Over)

Group	Number	%
Total Population	35,657	89.9
Hispanic or Latino (of any race)	5,205	67.4
Central American, ex. Mexican	2,074	54.2
Salvadoran	1,052	49.9
South American	1,497	93.9

Four-Year College Graduates
(Universe: Population 25 Years and Over)

Group	Number	%
Total Population	20,942	52.8
Hispanic or Latino (of any race)	1,260	16.3
Central American, ex. Mexican	246	6.4
Salvadoran	35	1.7
South American	434	27.2

Population Age 3–17 Enrolled in Public School
(Universe: Population Age 3–17 Enrolled in School)

Group	Number	%
Total Population	7,845	83.6
Hispanic or Latino (of any race)	2,328	89.1
Central American, ex. Mexican	1,147	90.7
Salvadoran	846	92.1
South American	267	96.4

Population Age 3–17 Enrolled in Private School
(Universe: Population Age 3–17 Enrolled in School)

Group	Number	%
Total Population	1,534	16.4
Hispanic or Latino (of any race)	286	10.9
Central American, ex. Mexican	118	9.3
Salvadoran	73	7.9
South American	10	3.6

Foreign-Born Population

Group	Number	%
Total Population	23,390	40.2
Hispanic or Latino (of any race)	8,707	63.2
Central American, ex. Mexican	4,928	67.6
Salvadoran	2,904	65.2
South American	2,132	88.2

Foreign-Born Naturalized U.S. Citizens

Group	Number	%
Total Population	10,008	42.8
Hispanic or Latino (of any race)	2,585	29.7
Central American, ex. Mexican	1,365	27.7
Salvadoran	822	28.3
South American	753	35.3

Language Spoken at Home: English Only
(Universe: Population 5 Years and Over)

Group	Number	%
Total Population	27,771	51.5
Hispanic or Latino (of any race)	1,545	12.3
Central American, ex. Mexican	569	8.8
Salvadoran	426	10.8
South American	190	8.0

Language Spoken at Home: Spanish
(Universe: Population 5 Years and Over)

Group	Number	%
Total Population	11,635	21.6
Hispanic or Latino (of any race)	10,983	87.2
Central American, ex. Mexican	5,889	91.2
Salvadoran	3,515	89.2
South American	2,161	91.4

Unemployment Rate
(Universe: Population 16 Years and Over)

Group	%
Total Population	5.2
Hispanic or Latino (of any race)	7.7
Central American, ex. Mexican	8.3
Salvadoran	8.1
South American	5.5

Class of Worker: Private Wage and Salary
(Universe: Civilian Employed Population 16 Years and Over)

Group	Number	%
Total Population	25,560	75.9
Hispanic or Latino (of any race)	6,616	83.5
Central American, ex. Mexican	3,656	89.1
Salvadoran	2,188	90.5
South American	1,253	79.2

Class of Worker: Government
(Universe: Civilian Employed Population 16 Years and Over)

Group	Number	%
Total Population	6,216	18.4
Hispanic or Latino (of any race)	722	9.1
Central American, ex. Mexican	228	5.6
Salvadoran	157	6.5
South American	77	4.9

Means of Transportation to Work: Car, Truck or Van
(Universe: Workers 16 Years and Over)

Group	Number	%
Total Population	27,072	82.2
Hispanic or Latino (of any race)	6,375	81.4
Central American, ex. Mexican	3,303	82.4
Salvadoran	2,107	87.1
South American	1,278	81.5

Means of Transportation to Work: Public Transportation (ex. Taxicab)
(Universe: Workers 16 Years and Over)

Group	Number	%
Total Population	3,580	10.9
Hispanic or Latino (of any race)	1,040	13.3
Central American, ex. Mexican	485	12.1
Salvadoran	300	12.4
South American	154	9.8

Homeownership Rate
(Universe: Occupied Housing Units)

Group	%
Total Population	56.3
Hispanic or Latino (of any race)	42.7
Central American, ex. Mexican	37.2
Guatemalan	33.3
Honduran	33.5
Nicaraguan	49.1
Panamanian	47.5
Salvadoran	37.1
Cuban	69.8
Dominican Republic	39.1
Mexican	40.5
Puerto Rican	35.4
South American	53.0
Argentinean	44.4
Bolivian	51.2
Chilean	53.6
Colombian	58.4
Ecuadorian	56.1
Peruvian	52.2
Venezuelan	63.9
Spaniard	68.9

Median Home Value

Group	Dollars
Total Population	390,100
Hispanic or Latino (of any race)	342,600
Central American, ex. Mexican	329,900
Salvadoran	350,000
South American	322,100

Median Gross Rent

Group	Dollars
Total Population	1,355
Hispanic or Latino (of any race)	1,334
Central American, ex. Mexican	1,294

STATE & PLACE PROFILES

Notes: (1) Percent of total population; (2) Percent of Hispanic/Latino population; Profiles include places with an overall population of at least 125,000, OR an overall population of at least 25,000 where the Hispanic/Latino population is at least 20% of the overall population. In states where less than five places meet either of these criteria, we have included places with at least 10,000 total population with the highest percentage of Hispanic/Latino population. These places are identified with an asterisk (*); Please refer to the User's Guide for a full explanation of data.

Group	Number
Salvadoran	1,193
South American	1,283

Median Household Income
(2010 Inflation-Adjusted Dollars)

Group	Dollars
Total Population	78,736
Hispanic or Latino (of any race)	61,127
Central American, ex. Mexican	59,991
Salvadoran	58,116
South American	50,542

Per Capita Income
(2010 Inflation-Adjusted Dollars)

Group	Dollars
Total Population	37,955
Hispanic or Latino (of any race)	20,701
Central American, ex. Mexican	17,714
Salvadoran	16,527
South American	26,097

Households with $100,000+ Income

Group	Number	%
Total Population	8,835	38.7
Hispanic or Latino (of any race)	886	22.7
Central American, ex. Mexican	402	23.6
Salvadoran	190	16.8
South American	137	15.8

Households with Food Stamps/SNAP Benefits During Past 12 Months

Group	Number	%
Total Population	1,056	4.6
Hispanic or Latino (of any race)	306	7.8
Central American, ex. Mexican	114	6.7
Salvadoran	89	7.9
South American	36	4.2

Poverty Rate
(Income in Past 12 Months Below Poverty Level)

Group	%
Total Population	7.5
Hispanic or Latino (of any race)	12.1
Central American, ex. Mexican	10.2
Salvadoran	11.9
South American	7.8

Montgomery Village

Population

Group	Number	%TP[1]	%HP[2]
Total Population	32,032	100.0	–
Hispanic or Latino (of any race)	7,812	24.4	100.0
Central American, ex. Mexican	3,662	11.4	46.9
Guatemalan	461	1.4	5.9
Honduran	329	1.0	4.2
Nicaraguan	263	0.8	3.4
Salvadoran	2,522	7.9	32.3
Cuban	132	0.4	1.7
Dominican Republic	188	0.6	2.4
Mexican	597	1.9	7.6
Puerto Rican	377	1.2	4.8
South American	2,083	6.5	26.7
Bolivian	216	0.7	2.8
Chilean	108	0.3	1.4
Colombian	436	1.4	5.6
Ecuadorian	252	0.8	3.2
Peruvian	842	2.6	10.8

Population Growth: 2000–2010

Group	%
Total Population	-15.8
Hispanic or Latino (of any race)	75.2
Central American, ex. Mexican	260.4
Guatemalan	205.3
Nicaraguan	134.8
Salvadoran	326.0
Mexican	51.9
Puerto Rican	11.5
South American	101.5
Bolivian	77.0
Colombian	90.4
Ecuadorian	125.0
Peruvian	173.4

Males per 100 Females

Group	Number
Total Population	93.2
Hispanic or Latino (of any race)	101.4
Central American, ex. Mexican	109.4
Guatemalan	111.5
Honduran	140.1
Nicaraguan	96.3
Salvadoran	107.7
Cuban	85.9
Dominican Republic	79.0
Mexican	105.2
Puerto Rican	106.0
South American	87.2
Bolivian	87.8
Chilean	89.5
Colombian	78.7
Ecuadorian	83.9
Peruvian	91.4

Average Household Size

Group	People
Total Population	2.70
Hispanic or Latino (of any race)	3.74
Central American, ex. Mexican	4.34
Guatemalan	4.00
Honduran	4.25
Nicaraguan	4.12
Salvadoran	4.50
Cuban	2.82
Dominican Republic	3.68
Mexican	3.42
Puerto Rican	2.57
South American	3.39
Bolivian	3.30
Chilean	2.74
Colombian	3.09
Ecuadorian	3.51
Peruvian	3.74

Median Age

Group	Years
Total Population	35.7
Hispanic or Latino (of any race)	29.6
Central American, ex. Mexican	28.8
Guatemalan	29.1
Honduran	31.3
Nicaraguan	32.4
Salvadoran	28.1
Cuban	32.5
Dominican Republic	27.4
Mexican	30.0
Puerto Rican	29.1
South American	35.8
Bolivian	35.8
Chilean	38.5
Colombian	37.1
Ecuadorian	32.3
Peruvian	35.9

High School Graduates
(Universe: Population 25 Years and Over)

Group	Number	%
Total Population	19,289	91.0
Hispanic or Latino (of any race)	2,540	68.4
Central American, ex. Mexican	1,152	59.1
Salvadoran	756	55.0
South American	800	92.5

Four-Year College Graduates
(Universe: Population 25 Years and Over)

Group	Number	%
Total Population	10,608	50.0
Hispanic or Latino (of any race)	613	16.5
Central American, ex. Mexican	137	7.0
Salvadoran	53	3.9
South American	252	29.1

Population Age 3–17 Enrolled in Public School
(Universe: Population Age 3–17 Enrolled in School)

Group	Number	%
Total Population	5,055	86.1
Hispanic or Latino (of any race)	1,522	92.0
Central American, ex. Mexican	757	100.0
Salvadoran	467	100.0
South American	251	82.8

Population Age 3–17 Enrolled in Private School
(Universe: Population Age 3–17 Enrolled in School)

Group	Number	%
Total Population	813	13.9
Hispanic or Latino (of any race)	132	8.0
Central American, ex. Mexican	0	0.0
Salvadoran	0	0.0
South American	52	17.2

Foreign-Born Population

Group	Number	%
Total Population	10,282	32.4
Hispanic or Latino (of any race)	4,066	60.3
Central American, ex. Mexican	2,517	71.4
Salvadoran	1,766	73.0
South American	909	68.2

Foreign-Born Naturalized U.S. Citizens

Group	Number	%
Total Population	3,829	37.2
Hispanic or Latino (of any race)	1,014	24.9
Central American, ex. Mexican	511	20.3
Salvadoran	251	14.2
South American	347	38.2

Language Spoken at Home: English Only
(Universe: Population 5 Years and Over)

Group	Number	%
Total Population	17,720	60.9
Hispanic or Latino (of any race)	575	9.5
Central American, ex. Mexican	41	1.3
Salvadoran	0	0.0
South American	109	8.5

Language Spoken at Home: Spanish
(Universe: Population 5 Years and Over)

Group	Number	%
Total Population	5,816	20.0
Hispanic or Latino (of any race)	5,423	89.8
Central American, ex. Mexican	3,039	98.2
Salvadoran	2,075	100.0
South American	1,169	91.5

Unemployment Rate
(Universe: Population 16 Years and Over)

Group	%
Total Population	4.6
Hispanic or Latino (of any race)	4.7
Central American, ex. Mexican	6.6
Salvadoran	7.5
South American	1.7

Class of Worker: Private Wage and Salary
(Universe: Civilian Employed Population 16 Years and Over)

Group	Number	%
Total Population	13,408	75.0
Hispanic or Latino (of any race)	2,905	86.1
Central American, ex. Mexican	1,591	87.7
Salvadoran	1,127	91.7
South American	623	84.9

Class of Worker: Government
(Universe: Civilian Employed Population 16 Years and Over)

Group	Number	%
Total Population	3,500	19.6
Hispanic or Latino (of any race)	199	5.9
Central American, ex. Mexican	62	3.4
Salvadoran	45	3.7
South American	18	2.5

Means of Transportation to Work: Car, Truck or Van
(Universe: Workers 16 Years and Over)

Group	Number	%
Total Population	13,953	80.7
Hispanic or Latino (of any race)	2,519	77.7
Central American, ex. Mexican	1,317	76.9
Salvadoran	802	70.4
South American	603	83.6

Notes: (1) Percent of total population; (2) Percent of Hispanic/Latino population; Profiles include places with an overall population of at least 125,000, OR an overall population of at least 25,000 where the Hispanic/Latino population is at least 20% of the overall population. In states where less than five places meet either of these criteria, we have included places with at least 10,000 total population with the highest percentage of Hispanic/Latino population. These places are identified with an asterisk (*); Please refer to the User's Guide for a full explanation of data.

Means of Transportation to Work: Public Transportation (ex. Taxicab)
(Universe: Workers 16 Years and Over)

Group	Number	%
Total Population	2,383	13.8
Hispanic or Latino (of any race)	553	17.1
Central American, ex. Mexican	269	15.7
Salvadoran	257	22.6
South American	83	11.5

Homeownership Rate
(Universe: Occupied Housing Units)

Group	%
Total Population	70.3
Hispanic or Latino (of any race)	59.7
Central American, ex. Mexican	55.1
Guatemalan	63.9
Honduran	43.8
Nicaraguan	58.8
Salvadoran	54.0
Cuban	74.5
Dominican Republic	68.1
Mexican	51.3
Puerto Rican	54.0
South American	69.5
Bolivian	79.7
Chilean	68.6
Colombian	70.4
Ecuadorian	72.2
Peruvian	63.6

Median Home Value

Group	Dollars
Total Population	334,500
Hispanic or Latino (of any race)	303,400
Central American, ex. Mexican	258,700
Salvadoran	239,300
South American	363,100

Median Gross Rent

Group	Dollars
Total Population	1,340
Hispanic or Latino (of any race)	1,396
Central American, ex. Mexican	1,408
Salvadoran	1,421
South American	1,222

Median Household Income
(2010 Inflation-Adjusted Dollars)

Group	Dollars
Total Population	81,912
Hispanic or Latino (of any race)	55,279
Central American, ex. Mexican	55,219
Salvadoran	49,004
South American	76,375

Per Capita Income
(2010 Inflation-Adjusted Dollars)

Group	Dollars
Total Population	36,383
Hispanic or Latino (of any race)	17,909
Central American, ex. Mexican	15,212
Salvadoran	13,961
South American	22,502

Households with $100,000+ Income

Group	Number	%
Total Population	4,649	39.3
Hispanic or Latino (of any race)	339	20.2
Central American, ex. Mexican	127	14.8
Salvadoran	99	14.9
South American	106	28.3

Households with Food Stamps/SNAP Benefits During Past 12 Months

Group	Number	%
Total Population	494	4.2
Hispanic or Latino (of any race)	136	8.1
Central American, ex. Mexican	83	9.7
Salvadoran	37	5.6
South American	19	5.1

Poverty Rate
(Income in Past 12 Months Below Poverty Level)

Group	%
Total Population	6.3
Hispanic or Latino (of any race)	10.1
Central American, ex. Mexican	10.3
Salvadoran	14.3
South American	13.1

Silver Spring

Population

Group	Number	%TP[1]	%HP[2]
Total Population	71,452	100.0	–
Hispanic or Latino (of any race)	18,759	26.3	100.0
Central American, ex. Mexican	11,474	16.1	61.2
Guatemalan	2,360	3.3	12.6
Honduran	1,166	1.6	6.2
Nicaraguan	610	0.9	3.3
Panamanian	151	0.2	0.8
Salvadoran	7,103	9.9	37.9
Cuban	280	0.4	1.5
Dominican Republic	829	1.2	4.4
Mexican	1,887	2.6	10.1
Puerto Rican	564	0.8	3.0
South American	1,695	2.4	9.0
Argentinean	118	0.2	0.6
Bolivian	348	0.5	1.9
Colombian	372	0.5	2.0
Ecuadorian	185	0.3	1.0
Peruvian	446	0.6	2.4
Spaniard	192	0.3	1.0

Population Growth: 2000–2010

Group	%
Total Population	-6.6
Hispanic or Latino (of any race)	10.3
Central American, ex. Mexican	64.5
Guatemalan	177.0
Honduran	193.7
Nicaraguan	22.0
Panamanian	22.8
Salvadoran	49.1
Cuban	-11.1
Dominican Republic	23.9
Mexican	38.3
Puerto Rican	-4.9
South American	36.5
Bolivian	21.3
Colombian	60.3
Ecuadorian	26.7
Peruvian	55.9

Males per 100 Females

Group	Number
Total Population	94.9
Hispanic or Latino (of any race)	113.3
Central American, ex. Mexican	125.4
Guatemalan	168.2
Honduran	168.0
Nicaraguan	83.2
Panamanian	71.6
Salvadoran	114.3
Cuban	98.6
Dominican Republic	77.1
Mexican	111.1
Puerto Rican	81.9
South American	83.4
Argentinean	87.3
Bolivian	101.2
Colombian	79.7
Ecuadorian	69.7
Peruvian	89.0
Spaniard	106.5

Average Household Size

Group	People
Total Population	2.49
Hispanic or Latino (of any race)	3.85
Central American, ex. Mexican	4.50
Guatemalan	4.50
Honduran	4.60
Nicaraguan	3.69
Panamanian	2.48
Salvadoran	4.66
Cuban	2.22
Dominican Republic	3.25
Mexican	3.74
Puerto Rican	1.96
South American	2.84
Argentinean	2.27
Bolivian	3.79
Colombian	2.37
Ecuadorian	2.72
Peruvian	3.10
Spaniard	2.40

Median Age

Group	Years
Total Population	33.8
Hispanic or Latino (of any race)	28.6
Central American, ex. Mexican	28.9
Guatemalan	27.9
Honduran	29.0
Nicaraguan	33.9
Panamanian	32.4
Salvadoran	29.1
Cuban	37.5
Dominican Republic	29.8
Mexican	26.8
Puerto Rican	31.3
South American	36.5
Argentinean	35.5
Bolivian	35.6
Colombian	35.7
Ecuadorian	39.2
Peruvian	38.1
Spaniard	34.7

High School Graduates
(Universe: Population 25 Years and Over)

Group	Number	%
Total Population	39,717	82.9
Hispanic or Latino (of any race)	5,247	46.8
Central American, ex. Mexican	2,494	33.3
Guatemalan	441	28.6
Salvadoran	1,726	36.4
Mexican	668	67.4
South American	1,029	91.8

Four-Year College Graduates
(Universe: Population 25 Years and Over)

Group	Number	%
Total Population	24,186	50.5
Hispanic or Latino (of any race)	1,417	12.6
Central American, ex. Mexican	336	4.5
Guatemalan	52	3.4
Salvadoran	184	3.9
Mexican	189	19.1
South American	454	40.5

Population Age 3–17 Enrolled in Public School
(Universe: Population Age 3–17 Enrolled in School)

Group	Number	%
Total Population	8,415	80.0
Hispanic or Latino (of any race)	3,248	89.4
Central American, ex. Mexican	2,071	93.8
Guatemalan	283	100.0
Salvadoran	1,615	94.3
Mexican	407	80.9
South American	191	82.3

Population Age 3–17 Enrolled in Private School
(Universe: Population Age 3–17 Enrolled in School)

Group	Number	%
Total Population	2,102	20.0
Hispanic or Latino (of any race)	384	10.6
Central American, ex. Mexican	137	6.2
Guatemalan	0	0.0
Salvadoran	97	5.7
Mexican	96	19.1
South American	41	17.7

Foreign-Born Population

Group	Number	%
Total Population	25,599	36.5
Hispanic or Latino (of any race)	12,612	64.9
Central American, ex. Mexican	9,521	70.9

Notes: (1) Percent of total population; (2) Percent of Hispanic/Latino population; Profiles include places with an overall population of at least 125,000, OR an overall population of at least 25,000 where the Hispanic/Latino population is at least 20% of the overall population. In states where less than five places meet either of these criteria, we have included places with at least 10,000 total population with the highest percentage of Hispanic/Latino population. These places are identified with an asterisk (*); Please refer to the User's Guide for a full explanation of data.

Guatemalan	2,372	82.3
Salvadoran	5,751	65.9
Mexican	846	47.0
South American	1,148	70.9

Foreign-Born Naturalized U.S. Citizens

Group	Number	%
Total Population	8,036	31.4
Hispanic or Latino (of any race)	2,265	18.0
Central American, ex. Mexican	1,067	11.2
Guatemalan	135	5.7
Salvadoran	825	14.3
Mexican	326	38.5
South American	363	31.6

Language Spoken at Home: English Only
(Universe: Population 5 Years and Over)

Group	Number	%
Total Population	36,556	56.4
Hispanic or Latino (of any race)	1,514	8.7
Central American, ex. Mexican	323	2.7
Guatemalan	25	1.0
Salvadoran	104	1.3
Mexican	296	19.5
South American	188	12.6

Language Spoken at Home: Spanish
(Universe: Population 5 Years and Over)

Group	Number	%
Total Population	16,474	25.4
Hispanic or Latino (of any race)	15,862	90.8
Central American, ex. Mexican	11,670	97.3
Guatemalan	2,575	99.0
Salvadoran	7,705	98.7
Mexican	1,156	76.0
South American	1,306	87.4

Unemployment Rate
(Universe: Population 16 Years and Over)

Group	%
Total Population	6.4
Hispanic or Latino (of any race)	8.9
Central American, ex. Mexican	11.0
Guatemalan	11.9
Salvadoran	10.7
Mexican	0.0
South American	4.9

Class of Worker: Private Wage and Salary
(Universe: Civilian Employed Population 16 Years and Over)

Group	Number	%
Total Population	30,818	73.7
Hispanic or Latino (of any race)	9,064	84.3
Central American, ex. Mexican	6,899	89.2
Guatemalan	1,711	91.3
Salvadoran	4,210	88.1
Mexican	650	76.4
South American	580	63.8

Class of Worker: Government
(Universe: Civilian Employed Population 16 Years and Over)

Group	Number	%
Total Population	8,273	19.8
Hispanic or Latino (of any race)	861	8.0
Central American, ex. Mexican	360	4.7
Guatemalan	32	1.7
Salvadoran	265	5.5
Mexican	122	14.3
South American	171	18.8

Means of Transportation to Work: Car, Truck or Van
(Universe: Workers 16 Years and Over)

Group	Number	%
Total Population	25,710	62.5
Hispanic or Latino (of any race)	7,001	65.9
Central American, ex. Mexican	5,117	67.8
Guatemalan	943	52.5
Salvadoran	3,658	77.9
Mexican	544	56.6
South American	605	67.4

Means of Transportation to Work: Public Transportation (ex. Taxicab)
(Universe: Workers 16 Years and Over)

Group	Number	%
Total Population	11,822	28.7
Hispanic or Latino (of any race)	3,169	29.8
Central American, ex. Mexican	2,230	29.5
Guatemalan	852	47.5
Salvadoran	847	18.0
Mexican	417	43.4
South American	178	19.8

Homeownership Rate
(Universe: Occupied Housing Units)

Group	%
Total Population	39.4
Hispanic or Latino (of any race)	25.3
Central American, ex. Mexican	22.2
Guatemalan	12.3
Honduran	9.4
Nicaraguan	23.6
Panamanian	24.2
Salvadoran	27.0
Cuban	48.8
Dominican Republic	23.2
Mexican	23.5
Puerto Rican	24.7
South American	37.4
Argentinean	35.3
Bolivian	42.0
Colombian	31.9
Ecuadorian	43.4
Peruvian	36.4
Spaniard	42.4

Median Home Value

Group	Dollars
Total Population	462,400
Hispanic or Latino (of any race)	416,900
Central American, ex. Mexican	416,300
Guatemalan	247,200
Salvadoran	412,700
Mexican	361,100
South American	449,500

Median Gross Rent

Group	Dollars
Total Population	1,281
Hispanic or Latino (of any race)	1,250
Central American, ex. Mexican	1,219
Guatemalan	1,130
Salvadoran	1,296
Mexican	1,375
South American	1,277

Median Household Income
(2010 Inflation-Adjusted Dollars)

Group	Dollars
Total Population	67,918
Hispanic or Latino (of any race)	58,199
Central American, ex. Mexican	52,781
Guatemalan	58,125
Salvadoran	52,939
Mexican	71,047
South American	44,349

Per Capita Income
(2010 Inflation-Adjusted Dollars)

Group	Dollars
Total Population	36,381
Hispanic or Latino (of any race)	17,087
Central American, ex. Mexican	14,958
Guatemalan	16,026
Salvadoran	14,405
Mexican	17,349
South American	23,616

Households with $100,000+ Income

Group	Number	%
Total Population	8,445	30.0
Hispanic or Latino (of any race)	870	17.2
Central American, ex. Mexican	445	15.0
Guatemalan	118	18.0
Salvadoran	272	14.2
Mexican	81	19.2
South American	106	14.5

Households with Food Stamps/SNAP Benefits During Past 12 Months

Group	Number	%
Total Population	994	3.5
Hispanic or Latino (of any race)	185	3.7
Central American, ex. Mexican	173	5.8
Guatemalan	89	13.6
Salvadoran	71	3.7
Mexican	0	0.0
South American	0	0.0

Poverty Rate
(Income in Past 12 Months Below Poverty Level)

Group	%
Total Population	10.0
Hispanic or Latino (of any race)	15.2
Central American, ex. Mexican	17.3
Guatemalan	14.7
Salvadoran	18.3
Mexican	9.7
South American	8.9

Wheaton

Population

Group	Number	%TP[1]	%HP[2]
Total Population	48,284	100.0	–
Hispanic or Latino (of any race)	20,155	41.7	100.0
Central American, ex. Mexican	12,072	25.0	59.9
Guatemalan	1,354	2.8	6.7
Honduran	1,101	2.3	5.5
Nicaraguan	561	1.2	2.8
Salvadoran	8,912	18.5	44.2
Cuban	168	0.3	0.8
Dominican Republic	626	1.3	3.1
Mexican	1,530	3.2	7.6
Puerto Rican	368	0.8	1.8
South American	2,789	5.8	13.8
Argentinean	122	0.3	0.6
Bolivian	476	1.0	2.4
Chilean	151	0.3	0.7
Colombian	411	0.9	2.0
Ecuadorian	319	0.7	1.6
Peruvian	1,130	2.3	5.6
Spaniard	123	0.3	0.6

Population Growth: 2000–2010

Group	%
Total Population	n/a

Males per 100 Females

Group	Number
Total Population	98.5
Hispanic or Latino (of any race)	110.7
Central American, ex. Mexican	117.6
Guatemalan	132.2
Honduran	150.2
Nicaraguan	90.8
Salvadoran	114.8
Cuban	130.1
Dominican Republic	81.4
Mexican	109.9
Puerto Rican	93.7
South American	93.4
Argentinean	93.7
Bolivian	122.4
Chilean	84.1
Colombian	84.3
Ecuadorian	87.6
Peruvian	92.2
Spaniard	112.1

Average Household Size

Group	People
Total Population	3.27
Hispanic or Latino (of any race)	4.84
Central American, ex. Mexican	5.35
Guatemalan	5.01
Honduran	5.38
Nicaraguan	4.49
Salvadoran	5.49
Cuban	3.45

Notes: (1) Percent of total population; (2) Percent of Hispanic/Latino population; Profiles include places with an overall population of at least 125,000, OR an overall population of at least 25,000 where the Hispanic/Latino population is at least 20% of the overall population. In states where less than five places meet either of these criteria, we have included places with at least 10,000 total population with the highest percentage of Hispanic/Latino population. These places are identified with an asterisk (*); Please refer to the User's Guide for a full explanation of data.

Dominican Republic	4.11
Mexican	4.59
Puerto Rican	2.94
South American	4.09
Argentinean	3.38
Bolivian	4.19
Chilean	3.84
Colombian	3.93
Ecuadorian	4.10
Peruvian	4.39
Spaniard	2.92

Median Age

Group	Years
Total Population	34.5
Hispanic or Latino (of any race)	29.2
Central American, ex. Mexican	29.7
Guatemalan	30.2
Honduran	28.9
Nicaraguan	34.1
Salvadoran	29.4
Cuban	37.1
Dominican Republic	29.3
Mexican	26.8
Puerto Rican	28.3
South American	37.8
Argentinean	35.2
Bolivian	38.0
Chilean	40.6
Colombian	40.3
Ecuadorian	40.9
Peruvian	35.3
Spaniard	32.8

High School Graduates
(Universe: Population 25 Years and Over)

Group	Number	%
Total Population	21,905	73.9
Hispanic or Latino (of any race)	5,493	50.0
Central American, ex. Mexican	2,817	38.7
Guatemalan	269	36.8
Honduran	428	41.6
Salvadoran	1,899	36.8
Mexican	564	66.8
South American	1,268	78.8

Four-Year College Graduates
(Universe: Population 25 Years and Over)

Group	Number	%
Total Population	9,287	31.3
Hispanic or Latino (of any race)	1,261	11.5
Central American, ex. Mexican	554	7.6
Guatemalan	91	12.4
Honduran	74	7.2
Salvadoran	319	6.2
Mexican	80	9.5
South American	365	22.7

Population Age 3–17 Enrolled in Public School
(Universe: Population Age 3–17 Enrolled in School)

Group	Number	%
Total Population	6,995	90.0
Hispanic or Latino (of any race)	3,672	95.9
Central American, ex. Mexican	2,237	97.3
Guatemalan	144	100.0
Honduran	128	100.0
Salvadoran	1,894	96.8
Mexican	388	95.8
South American	329	81.0

Population Age 3–17 Enrolled in Private School
(Universe: Population Age 3–17 Enrolled in School)

Group	Number	%
Total Population	774	10.0
Hispanic or Latino (of any race)	156	4.1
Central American, ex. Mexican	62	2.7
Guatemalan	0	0.0
Honduran	0	0.0
Salvadoran	62	3.2
Mexican	17	4.2
South American	77	19.0

Foreign-Born Population

Group	Number	%
Total Population	20,274	45.0
Hispanic or Latino (of any race)	11,865	62.4
Central American, ex. Mexican	7,974	65.1
Guatemalan	779	68.2
Honduran	1,152	77.3
Salvadoran	5,712	62.4
Mexican	1,017	58.4
South American	1,715	63.8

Foreign-Born Naturalized U.S. Citizens

Group	Number	%
Total Population	6,593	32.5
Hispanic or Latino (of any race)	2,459	20.7
Central American, ex. Mexican	1,191	14.9
Guatemalan	176	22.6
Honduran	78	6.8
Salvadoran	856	15.0
Mexican	73	7.2
South American	867	50.6

Language Spoken at Home: English Only
(Universe: Population 5 Years and Over)

Group	Number	%
Total Population	16,770	40.9
Hispanic or Latino (of any race)	600	3.6
Central American, ex. Mexican	106	1.0
Guatemalan	4	0.4
Honduran	0	0.0
Salvadoran	94	1.2
Mexican	187	12.0
South American	90	3.9

Language Spoken at Home: Spanish
(Universe: Population 5 Years and Over)

Group	Number	%
Total Population	16,148	39.4
Hispanic or Latino (of any race)	15,820	95.4
Central American, ex. Mexican	10,477	99.0
Guatemalan	1,065	99.6
Honduran	1,391	100.0
Salvadoran	7,570	98.8
Mexican	1,354	86.7
South American	2,202	95.7

Unemployment Rate
(Universe: Population 16 Years and Over)

Group	%
Total Population	6.4
Hispanic or Latino (of any race)	7.5
Central American, ex. Mexican	7.1
Guatemalan	2.6
Honduran	9.8
Salvadoran	7.5
Mexican	6.6
South American	11.3

Class of Worker: Private Wage and Salary
(Universe: Civilian Employed Population 16 Years and Over)

Group	Number	%
Total Population	19,131	78.6
Hispanic or Latino (of any race)	8,936	87.6
Central American, ex. Mexican	6,241	91.9
Guatemalan	544	86.2
Honduran	1,057	98.4
Salvadoran	4,344	91.6
Mexican	788	83.7
South American	972	69.5

Class of Worker: Government
(Universe: Civilian Employed Population 16 Years and Over)

Group	Number	%
Total Population	3,498	14.4
Hispanic or Latino (of any race)	525	5.1
Central American, ex. Mexican	200	2.9
Guatemalan	0	0.0
Honduran	17	1.6
Salvadoran	159	3.4
Mexican	25	2.7
South American	192	13.7

Means of Transportation to Work: Car, Truck or Van
(Universe: Workers 16 Years and Over)

Group	Number	%
Total Population	17,633	73.5
Hispanic or Latino (of any race)	7,172	71.0
Central American, ex. Mexican	4,491	67.0
Guatemalan	443	70.2
Honduran	443	41.2
Salvadoran	3,355	72.1
Mexican	650	69.1
South American	1,241	89.7

Means of Transportation to Work: Public Transportation (ex. Taxicab)
(Universe: Workers 16 Years and Over)

Group	Number	%
Total Population	5,080	21.2
Hispanic or Latino (of any race)	2,502	24.8
Central American, ex. Mexican	2,032	30.3
Guatemalan	123	19.5
Honduran	631	58.8
Salvadoran	1,184	25.4
Mexican	162	17.2
South American	79	5.7

Homeownership Rate
(Universe: Occupied Housing Units)

Group	%
Total Population	67.8
Hispanic or Latino (of any race)	62.5
Central American, ex. Mexican	64.7
Guatemalan	57.2
Honduran	47.8
Nicaraguan	60.0
Salvadoran	68.1
Cuban	72.5
Dominican Republic	49.7
Mexican	55.4
Puerto Rican	52.9
South American	63.9
Argentinean	66.0
Bolivian	66.9
Chilean	65.9
Colombian	60.0
Ecuadorian	73.3
Peruvian	58.9
Spaniard	79.5

Median Home Value

Group	Dollars
Total Population	379,300
Hispanic or Latino (of any race)	365,300
Central American, ex. Mexican	360,300
Guatemalan	380,100
Honduran	334,500
Salvadoran	361,300
Mexican	412,800
South American	369,400

Median Gross Rent

Group	Dollars
Total Population	1,408
Hispanic or Latino (of any race)	1,453
Central American, ex. Mexican	1,494
Guatemalan	2,000+
Honduran	1,804
Salvadoran	1,434
Mexican	1,800
South American	1,463

Median Household Income
(2010 Inflation-Adjusted Dollars)

Group	Dollars
Total Population	69,008
Hispanic or Latino (of any race)	65,231
Central American, ex. Mexican	60,423
Guatemalan	74,516
Honduran	64,589
Salvadoran	56,238
Mexican	73,000
South American	69,821

Per Capita Income
(2010 Inflation-Adjusted Dollars)

Group	Dollars
Total Population	26,770
Hispanic or Latino (of any race)	16,502
Central American, ex. Mexican	14,822
Guatemalan	16,244
Honduran	16,694

Notes: (1) Percent of total population; (2) Percent of Hispanic/Latino population; Profiles include places with an overall population of at least 125,000, OR an overall population of at least 25,000 where the Hispanic/Latino population is at least 20% of the overall population. In states where less than five places meet either of these criteria, we have included places with at least 10,000 total population with the highest percentage of Hispanic/Latino population. These places are identified with an asterisk (*); Please refer to the User's Guide for a full explanation of data.

Salvadoran	13,861	
Mexican	16,683	
South American	22,096	

Households with $100,000+ Income

Group	Number	%
Total Population	4,415	31.1
Hispanic or Latino (of any race)	902	22.3
Central American, ex. Mexican	481	18.6
Guatemalan	25	11.1
Honduran	124	39.7
Salvadoran	253	13.5
Mexican	61	17.5
South American	210	38.3

Households with Food Stamps/SNAP Benefits During Past 12 Months

Group	Number	%
Total Population	1,142	8.0
Hispanic or Latino (of any race)	456	11.3
Central American, ex. Mexican	382	14.8
Guatemalan	40	17.7
Honduran	46	14.7
Salvadoran	296	15.8
Mexican	11	3.2
South American	22	4.0

Poverty Rate
(Income in Past 12 Months Below Poverty Level)

Group	%
Total Population	11.5
Hispanic or Latino (of any race)	17.3
Central American, ex. Mexican	19.3
Guatemalan	32.9
Honduran	24.4
Salvadoran	17.4
Mexican	11.1
South American	8.2

Notes: (1) Percent of total population; (2) Percent of Hispanic/Latino population; Profiles include places with an overall population of at least 125,000, OR an overall population of at least 25,000 where the Hispanic/Latino population is at least 20% of the overall population. In states where less than five places meet either of these criteria, we have included places with at least 10,000 total population with the highest percentage of Hispanic/Latino population. These places are identified with an asterisk (*); Please refer to the User's Guide for a full explanation of data.

Massachusetts

EDITOR'S NOTE: For a place to be included in this edition, it must meet one of two criteria. Either its overall population is at least 125,000, OR its overall population is at least 25,000 and its Hispanic/Latino population is at least 20% of the overall population. For the state of Massachusetts, the following locations are included:

- Boston
- Chelsea
- Everett
- Fitchburg
- Holyoke
- Lawrence
- Lynn
- Revere
- Springfield
- Worcester

Section Two: State & Place Profiles starts with the state profile, followed by place profiles that meet the criteria above. Places are listed alphabetically within each state. All states, all counties and places that meet the above criteria are ranked and compared in *Section Three: Rankings & Comparisons*, on page 1055.

For a more detailed look at the Hispanic/Latino population in Massachusetts, a companion web site is available at no additional charge with purchase of this print edition. Visit http://gold.greyhouse.com/page/info_hispanic for more information.

The web site includes data for all counties and places in Massachusetts with Hispanic/Latino population, plus ten additional topics: Self Employed Worker; Walked to Work; Worked from Home; Mean Travel Time to Work; Mean Household Income; Households with Cash Public Assistance; Mean Cash Pubic Assistance; Poverty Rates for 18 and Under, 18 to 64, and 65 and Over.

Population

Group	Number	%TP[1]	%HP[2]
Total Population	6,547,629	100.0	–
Hispanic or Latino (of any race)	627,654	9.6	100.0
Central American, ex. Mexican	96,958	1.5	15.4
Costa Rican	2,951	<0.1	0.5
Guatemalan	32,812	0.5	5.2
Honduran	12,533	0.2	2.0
Nicaraguan	1,722	<0.1	0.3
Panamanian	2,436	<0.1	0.4
Salvadoran	43,400	0.7	6.9
Cuban	11,306	0.2	1.8
Dominican Republic	103,292	1.6	16.5
Mexican	38,379	0.6	6.1
Puerto Rican	266,125	4.1	42.4
South American	54,398	0.8	8.7
Argentinean	4,022	0.1	0.6
Bolivian	1,401	<0.1	0.2
Chilean	3,045	<0.1	0.5
Colombian	23,843	0.4	3.8
Ecuadorian	7,592	0.1	1.2
Paraguayan	380	<0.1	0.1
Peruvian	7,360	0.1	1.2
Uruguayan	2,317	<0.1	0.4
Venezuelan	3,982	0.1	0.6
Spaniard	6,829	0.1	1.1

Population Growth: 2000–2010

Group	%
Total Population	3.1
Hispanic or Latino (of any race)	46.4
Central American, ex. Mexican	153.0
Costa Rican	68.0
Guatemalan	186.9
Honduran	144.5
Nicaraguan	147.1
Panamanian	70.8
Salvadoran	173.0
Cuban	27.5
Dominican Republic	106.9
Mexican	72.2
Puerto Rican	33.6
South American	94.0
Argentinean	78.9
Bolivian	122.0
Chilean	74.0
Colombian	86.4
Ecuadorian	161.0
Paraguayan	106.5
Peruvian	122.4
Uruguayan	234.8
Venezuelan	83.8
Spaniard	319.7

Males per 100 Females

Group	Number
Total Population	93.7
Hispanic or Latino (of any race)	96.4
Central American, ex. Mexican	118.8
Costa Rican	83.2
Guatemalan	136.8
Honduran	99.2
Nicaraguan	89.9
Panamanian	74.7
Salvadoran	119.5
Cuban	95.2
Dominican Republic	83.5
Mexican	109.0
Puerto Rican	91.0
South American	91.4
Argentinean	93.8
Bolivian	88.3
Chilean	95.9
Colombian	88.3
Ecuadorian	105.0
Paraguayan	77.6
Peruvian	88.0
Uruguayan	101.0
Venezuelan	82.6
Spaniard	95.6

Average Household Size

Group	People
Total Population	2.48
Hispanic or Latino (of any race)	3.11
Central American, ex. Mexican	3.98
Costa Rican	2.86
Guatemalan	4.23
Honduran	3.55
Nicaraguan	3.12
Panamanian	2.64
Salvadoran	4.20
Cuban	2.47
Dominican Republic	3.30
Mexican	2.99
Puerto Rican	2.91
South American	2.91
Argentinean	2.55
Bolivian	3.05
Chilean	2.71
Colombian	2.91
Ecuadorian	3.32
Paraguayan	2.70
Peruvian	3.04
Uruguayan	3.00
Venezuelan	2.51
Spaniard	2.47

Median Age

Group	Years
Total Population	39.1
Hispanic or Latino (of any race)	26.3
Central American, ex. Mexican	28.4
Costa Rican	31.7
Guatemalan	27.5
Honduran	28.9
Nicaraguan	29.8
Panamanian	32.1
Salvadoran	28.7
Cuban	30.5
Dominican Republic	27.4
Mexican	25.7
Puerto Rican	24.1
South American	32.1
Argentinean	34.7
Bolivian	31.7
Chilean	34.2
Colombian	32.1
Ecuadorian	29.3
Paraguayan	21.1
Peruvian	34.5
Uruguayan	32.6
Venezuelan	29.9
Spaniard	31.2

High School Graduates
(Universe: Population 25 Years and Over)

Group	Number	%
Total Population	3,886,556	88.7
Hispanic or Latino (of any race)	199,138	65.4
Central American, ex. Mexican	29,733	55.9
Costa Rican	2,193	88.6
Guatemalan	9,635	52.4
Honduran	4,659	68.3
Nicaraguan	938	82.4
Panamanian	1,565	80.3
Salvadoran	9,844	46.6
Cuban	5,428	85.1
Dominican Republic	31,681	61.0
Mexican	15,152	74.6
Puerto Rican	76,444	62.5
South American	28,909	82.0
Argentinean	2,501	91.8
Bolivian	962	91.4
Chilean	2,053	95.4
Colombian	12,220	76.7
Ecuadorian	3,190	82.6
Peruvian	4,401	87.1
Uruguayan	999	60.8
Venezuelan	1,974	91.4
Spaniard	3,274	92.5

Four-Year College Graduates
(Universe: Population 25 Years and Over)

Group	Number	%
Total Population	1,678,209	38.3
Hispanic or Latino (of any race)	48,828	16.0
Central American, ex. Mexican	6,214	11.7
Costa Rican	631	25.5
Guatemalan	2,052	11.2
Honduran	1,284	18.8
Nicaraguan	189	16.6
Panamanian	647	33.2
Salvadoran	1,151	5.4
Cuban	2,688	42.1
Dominican Republic	5,306	10.2
Mexican	5,865	28.9
Puerto Rican	12,570	10.3
South American	11,844	33.6
Argentinean	1,475	54.2
Bolivian	358	34.0
Chilean	947	44.0
Colombian	4,317	27.1
Ecuadorian	946	24.5
Peruvian	1,769	35.0
Uruguayan	271	16.5
Venezuelan	1,523	70.5
Spaniard	1,678	47.4

Population Age 3–17 Enrolled in Public School
(Universe: Population Age 3–17 Enrolled in School)

Group	Number	%
Total Population	944,445	84.0
Hispanic or Latino (of any race)	135,698	92.5
Central American, ex. Mexican	17,793	92.3
Costa Rican	501	66.7
Guatemalan	6,450	92.3

Notes: (1) Percent of total population; (2) Percent of Hispanic/Latino population; Profiles include places with an overall population of at least 125,000, OR an overall population of at least 25,000 where the Hispanic/Latino population is at least 20% of the overall population. In states where less than five places meet either of these criteria, we have included places with at least 10,000 total population with the highest percentage of Hispanic/Latino population. These places are identified with an asterisk (*); Please refer to the User's Guide for a full explanation of data.

STATE & PLACE PROFILES

Group	Number	%
Honduran	2,947	91.3
Nicaraguan	412	93.0
Panamanian	535	88.4
Salvadoran	6,609	96.6
Cuban	1,537	85.1
Dominican Republic	24,312	92.7
Mexican	7,653	89.7
Puerto Rican	69,229	94.8
South American	8,942	84.8
Argentinean	418	64.7
Bolivian	318	71.8
Chilean	515	90.5
Colombian	4,106	85.0
Ecuadorian	1,226	92.9
Peruvian	1,175	90.4
Uruguayan	342	80.5
Venezuelan	505	82.1
Spaniard	647	81.1

Population Age 3–17 Enrolled in Private School
(Universe: Population Age 3–17 Enrolled in School)

Group	Number	%
Total Population	179,840	16.0
Hispanic or Latino (of any race)	11,027	7.5
Central American, ex. Mexican	1,480	7.7
Costa Rican	250	33.3
Guatemalan	537	7.7
Honduran	281	8.7
Nicaraguan	31	7.0
Panamanian	70	11.6
Salvadoran	232	3.4
Cuban	270	14.9
Dominican Republic	1,924	7.3
Mexican	883	10.3
Puerto Rican	3,784	5.2
South American	1,602	15.2
Argentinean	228	35.3
Bolivian	125	28.2
Chilean	54	9.5
Colombian	722	15.0
Ecuadorian	94	7.1
Peruvian	125	9.6
Uruguayan	83	19.5
Venezuelan	110	17.9
Spaniard	151	18.9

Foreign-Born Population

Group	Number	%
Total Population	942,255	14.5
Hispanic or Latino (of any race)	190,946	32.6
Central American, ex. Mexican	62,302	65.6
Costa Rican	2,122	54.7
Guatemalan	22,715	67.8
Honduran	7,869	60.8
Nicaraguan	1,182	57.4
Panamanian	1,693	50.4
Salvadoran	25,363	68.2
Cuban	3,650	35.6
Dominican Republic	59,684	58.6
Mexican	14,929	38.0
Puerto Rican	2,235	0.9
South American	38,895	69.7
Argentinean	2,592	67.8
Bolivian	1,157	60.3
Chilean	2,053	63.3
Colombian	17,987	70.8
Ecuadorian	4,048	63.5
Peruvian	5,530	72.8
Uruguayan	1,905	78.9
Venezuelan	2,658	72.3
Spaniard	1,467	29.1

Foreign-Born Naturalized U.S. Citizens

Group	Number	%
Total Population	455,803	48.4
Hispanic or Latino (of any race)	68,055	35.6
Central American, ex. Mexican	15,807	25.4
Costa Rican	987	46.5
Guatemalan	5,542	24.4
Honduran	2,460	31.3
Nicaraguan	579	49.0
Panamanian	934	55.2
Salvadoran	4,858	19.2
Cuban	2,588	70.9
Dominican Republic	27,150	45.5
Mexican	3,153	21.1
Puerto Rican	1,069	47.8
South American	14,203	36.5
Argentinean	1,325	51.1
Bolivian	429	37.1
Chilean	798	38.9
Colombian	6,225	34.6
Ecuadorian	1,753	43.3
Peruvian	1,835	33.2
Uruguayan	380	19.9
Venezuelan	990	37.2
Spaniard	596	40.6

Language Spoken at Home: English Only
(Universe: Population 5 Years and Over)

Group	Number	%
Total Population	4,823,127	79.0
Hispanic or Latino (of any race)	111,125	21.1
Central American, ex. Mexican	9,127	10.7
Costa Rican	722	20.8
Guatemalan	2,403	8.1
Honduran	1,851	15.4
Nicaraguan	564	29.2
Panamanian	1,204	39.5
Salvadoran	2,150	6.5
Cuban	4,376	45.0
Dominican Republic	6,068	6.6
Mexican	14,612	41.5
Puerto Rican	59,673	26.4
South American	8,168	15.7
Argentinean	594	16.7
Bolivian	251	14.1
Chilean	763	25.6
Colombian	3,197	13.6
Ecuadorian	1,225	20.3
Peruvian	1,062	14.7
Uruguayan	216	10.0
Venezuelan	509	14.9
Spaniard	2,695	57.1

Language Spoken at Home: Spanish
(Universe: Population 5 Years and Over)

Group	Number	%
Total Population	457,990	7.5
Hispanic or Latino (of any race)	408,535	77.6
Central American, ex. Mexican	75,443	88.6
Costa Rican	2,739	78.9
Guatemalan	26,881	90.9
Honduran	9,993	83.4
Nicaraguan	1,352	69.9
Panamanian	1,820	59.7
Salvadoran	30,923	93.2
Cuban	5,230	53.7
Dominican Republic	85,406	92.7
Mexican	19,767	56.1
Puerto Rican	165,348	73.2
South American	42,946	82.6
Argentinean	2,802	78.6
Bolivian	1,524	85.7
Chilean	2,083	70.0
Colombian	20,302	86.1
Ecuadorian	4,767	79.1
Peruvian	6,087	84.5
Uruguayan	1,904	88.0
Venezuelan	2,812	82.1
Spaniard	1,588	33.6

Unemployment Rate
(Universe: Population 16 Years and Over)

Group	%
Total Population	7.4
Hispanic or Latino (of any race)	12.4
Central American, ex. Mexican	9.1
Costa Rican	5.0
Guatemalan	8.8
Honduran	11.2
Nicaraguan	15.5
Panamanian	9.7
Salvadoran	9.3
Cuban	11.6
Dominican Republic	11.5
Mexican	11.6
Puerto Rican	16.2
South American	9.8
Argentinean	10.1
Bolivian	4.2
Chilean	5.3
Colombian	9.2
Ecuadorian	14.4
Peruvian	8.1
Uruguayan	18.3
Venezuelan	11.2
Spaniard	4.6

Class of Worker: Private Wage and Salary
(Universe: Civilian Employed Population 16 Years and Over)

Group	Number	%
Total Population	2,629,874	80.4
Hispanic or Latino (of any race)	207,439	87.3
Central American, ex. Mexican	46,404	92.4
Costa Rican	1,673	80.2
Guatemalan	15,798	92.3
Honduran	5,934	90.8
Nicaraguan	836	94.9
Panamanian	1,479	84.8
Salvadoran	19,698	95.6
Cuban	3,780	81.6
Dominican Republic	37,941	89.1
Mexican	16,061	87.7
Puerto Rican	66,457	83.9
South American	26,943	88.1
Argentinean	1,821	84.9
Bolivian	995	92.6
Chilean	1,509	83.4
Colombian	12,818	90.2
Ecuadorian	2,786	84.4
Peruvian	3,885	87.7
Uruguayan	1,178	92.0
Venezuelan	1,434	83.9
Spaniard	1,933	75.1

Class of Worker: Government
(Universe: Civilian Employed Population 16 Years and Over)

Group	Number	%
Total Population	426,584	13.0
Hispanic or Latino (of any race)	21,011	8.8
Central American, ex. Mexican	2,019	4.0
Costa Rican	268	12.8
Guatemalan	486	2.8
Honduran	478	7.3
Nicaraguan	17	1.9
Panamanian	205	11.7
Salvadoran	378	1.8
Cuban	677	14.6
Dominican Republic	2,802	6.6
Mexican	1,381	7.5
Puerto Rican	10,624	13.4
South American	2,250	7.4
Argentinean	141	6.6
Bolivian	72	6.7
Chilean	169	9.3
Colombian	970	6.8
Ecuadorian	390	11.8
Peruvian	323	7.3
Uruguayan	44	3.4
Venezuelan	114	6.7
Spaniard	423	16.4

Means of Transportation to Work: Car, Truck or Van
(Universe: Workers 16 Years and Over)

Group	Number	%
Total Population	2,576,773	80.8
Hispanic or Latino (of any race)	167,245	72.3
Central American, ex. Mexican	33,012	67.0
Costa Rican	1,557	77.5
Guatemalan	11,983	71.1
Honduran	4,585	71.1
Nicaraguan	544	61.7
Panamanian	1,106	64.8
Salvadoran	12,513	62.2
Cuban	3,255	70.9
Dominican Republic	30,795	74.6
Mexican	11,408	63.5
Puerto Rican	61,733	80.1
South American	18,732	63.2
Argentinean	1,491	70.9
Bolivian	757	77.2
Chilean	1,322	73.9
Colombian	7,603	55.1

Notes: (1) Percent of total population; (2) Percent of Hispanic/Latino population; Profiles include places with an overall population of at least 125,000, OR an overall population of at least 25,000 where the Hispanic/Latino population is at least 20% of the overall population. In states where less than five places meet either of these criteria, we have included places with at least 10,000 total population with the highest percentage of Hispanic/Latino population. These places are identified with an asterisk (*); Please refer to the User's Guide for a full explanation of data.

Group	Number	%
Ecuadorian	2,251	69.7
Peruvian	2,719	62.3
Uruguayan	883	73.1
Venezuelan	1,208	75.7
Spaniard	1,659	67.5

Means of Transportation to Work: Public Transportation (ex. Taxicab)
(Universe: Workers 16 Years and Over)

Group	Number	%
Total Population	289,058	9.1
Hispanic or Latino (of any race)	37,272	16.1
Central American, ex. Mexican	10,687	21.7
Costa Rican	280	13.9
Guatemalan	2,607	15.5
Honduran	1,261	19.5
Nicaraguan	212	24.1
Panamanian	362	21.2
Salvadoran	5,581	27.7
Cuban	664	14.5
Dominican Republic	5,563	13.5
Mexican	3,623	20.2
Puerto Rican	7,951	10.3
South American	7,243	24.4
Argentinean	288	13.7
Bolivian	84	8.6
Chilean	288	16.1
Colombian	4,662	33.8
Ecuadorian	467	14.5
Peruvian	1,053	24.1
Uruguayan	230	19.0
Venezuelan	113	7.1
Spaniard	254	10.3

Homeownership Rate
(Universe: Occupied Housing Units)

Group	%
Total Population	62.3
Hispanic or Latino (of any race)	24.8
Central American, ex. Mexican	28.4
Costa Rican	41.6
Guatemalan	24.4
Honduran	23.9
Nicaraguan	31.8
Panamanian	40.4
Salvadoran	30.7
Cuban	44.6
Dominican Republic	19.7
Mexican	33.3
Puerto Rican	19.8
South American	39.7
Argentinean	54.1
Bolivian	41.0
Chilean	48.5
Colombian	35.7
Ecuadorian	36.1
Paraguayan	38.3
Peruvian	43.6
Uruguayan	31.5
Venezuelan	42.5
Spaniard	52.8

Median Home Value

Group	Dollars
Total Population	352,300
Hispanic or Latino (of any race)	294,500
Central American, ex. Mexican	327,700
Costa Rican	292,000
Guatemalan	330,800
Honduran	298,400
Nicaraguan	403,300
Panamanian	279,000
Salvadoran	340,200
Cuban	366,700
Dominican Republic	281,200
Mexican	356,000
Puerto Rican	233,300
South American	336,000
Argentinean	390,600
Bolivian	382,200
Chilean	380,800
Colombian	313,600
Ecuadorian	318,500
Peruvian	272,800
Uruguayan	375,600
Venezuelan	443,200
Spaniard	386,100

Median Gross Rent

Group	Dollars
Total Population	1,006
Hispanic or Latino (of any race)	882
Central American, ex. Mexican	1,121
Costa Rican	844
Guatemalan	1,174
Honduran	1,077
Nicaraguan	1,077
Panamanian	1,160
Salvadoran	1,121
Cuban	1,203
Dominican Republic	862
Mexican	1,139
Puerto Rican	722
South American	1,159
Argentinean	1,377
Bolivian	996
Chilean	1,482
Colombian	1,210
Ecuadorian	874
Peruvian	1,125
Uruguayan	852
Venezuelan	976
Spaniard	1,081

Median Household Income
(2010 Inflation-Adjusted Dollars)

Group	Dollars
Total Population	64,509
Hispanic or Latino (of any race)	32,206
Central American, ex. Mexican	48,278
Costa Rican	59,653
Guatemalan	46,583
Honduran	46,225
Nicaraguan	41,545
Panamanian	41,458
Salvadoran	50,493
Cuban	46,552
Dominican Republic	26,650
Mexican	53,743
Puerto Rican	22,816
South American	54,035
Argentinean	81,364
Bolivian	39,946
Chilean	59,153
Colombian	52,144
Ecuadorian	45,250
Peruvian	47,389
Uruguayan	44,487
Venezuelan	54,375
Spaniard	56,497

Per Capita Income
(2010 Inflation-Adjusted Dollars)

Group	Dollars
Total Population	33,966
Hispanic or Latino (of any race)	15,688
Central American, ex. Mexican	16,685
Costa Rican	22,112
Guatemalan	16,125
Honduran	15,995
Nicaraguan	16,395
Panamanian	23,418
Salvadoran	16,081
Cuban	27,737
Dominican Republic	13,170
Mexican	20,867
Puerto Rican	12,608
South American	23,634
Argentinean	38,745
Bolivian	20,557
Chilean	29,118
Colombian	22,071
Ecuadorian	19,068
Peruvian	21,946
Uruguayan	20,481
Venezuelan	29,610
Spaniard	35,869

Households with $100,000+ Income

Group	Number	%
Total Population	749,692	29.8
Hispanic or Latino (of any race)	18,900	10.6
Central American, ex. Mexican	3,315	13.0
Costa Rican	183	14.1
Guatemalan	1,162	12.9
Honduran	344	9.6
Nicaraguan	74	13.8
Panamanian	222	19.8
Salvadoran	1,156	12.5
Cuban	907	23.7
Dominican Republic	2,137	6.6
Mexican	2,135	20.6
Puerto Rican	5,584	6.9
South American	3,315	19.5
Argentinean	616	45.8
Bolivian	149	33.0
Chilean	249	22.3
Colombian	1,305	16.9
Ecuadorian	207	11.9
Peruvian	317	14.5
Uruguayan	64	8.3
Venezuelan	317	24.6
Spaniard	489	22.3

Households with Food Stamps/SNAP Benefits During Past 12 Months

Group	Number	%
Total Population	211,519	8.4
Hispanic or Latino (of any race)	56,728	31.8
Central American, ex. Mexican	3,621	14.2
Costa Rican	159	12.2
Guatemalan	1,051	11.7
Honduran	567	15.8
Nicaraguan	115	21.5
Panamanian	144	12.9
Salvadoran	1,416	15.3
Cuban	534	14.0
Dominican Republic	12,078	37.1
Mexican	1,141	11.0
Puerto Rican	36,895	45.7
South American	1,283	7.6
Argentinean	105	7.8
Bolivian	0	0.0
Chilean	31	2.8
Colombian	680	8.8
Ecuadorian	279	16.0
Peruvian	100	4.6
Uruguayan	35	4.5
Venezuelan	53	4.1
Spaniard	92	4.2

Poverty Rate
(Income in Past 12 Months Below Poverty Level)

Group	%
Total Population	10.5
Hispanic or Latino (of any race)	29.6
Central American, ex. Mexican	19.1
Costa Rican	10.8
Guatemalan	21.1
Honduran	22.7
Nicaraguan	24.4
Panamanian	20.4
Salvadoran	16.7
Cuban	16.3
Dominican Republic	32.5
Mexican	18.1
Puerto Rican	40.0
South American	11.5
Argentinean	7.8
Bolivian	4.7
Chilean	9.7
Colombian	12.1
Ecuadorian	19.4
Peruvian	8.2
Uruguayan	11.3
Venezuelan	9.9
Spaniard	11.0

Notes: (1) Percent of total population; (2) Percent of Hispanic/Latino population; Profiles include places with an overall population of at least 125,000, OR an overall population of at least 25,000 where the Hispanic/Latino population is at least 20% of the overall population. In states where less than five places meet either of these criteria, we have included places with at least 10,000 total population with the highest percentage of Hispanic/Latino population. These places are identified with an asterisk (*); Please refer to the User's Guide for a full explanation of data.

Boston

Population

Group	Number	%TP[1]	%HP[2]
Total Population	617,594	100.0	–
Hispanic or Latino (of any race)	107,917	17.5	100.0
Central American, ex. Mexican	21,286	3.4	19.7
Costa Rican	652	0.1	0.6
Guatemalan	4,451	0.7	4.1
Honduran	4,017	0.7	3.7
Nicaraguan	397	0.1	0.4
Panamanian	737	0.1	0.7
Salvadoran	10,850	1.8	10.1
Cuban	2,319	0.4	2.1
Dominican Republic	25,648	4.2	23.8
Mexican	5,961	1.0	5.5
Puerto Rican	30,506	4.9	28.3
South American	11,184	1.8	10.4
Argentinean	631	0.1	0.6
Bolivian	263	<0.1	0.2
Chilean	405	0.1	0.4
Colombian	6,649	1.1	6.2
Ecuadorian	732	0.1	0.7
Peruvian	1,286	0.2	1.2
Venezuelan	1,019	0.2	0.9
Spaniard	1,066	0.2	1.0

Population Growth: 2000–2010

Group	%
Total Population	4.8
Hispanic or Latino (of any race)	26.8
Central American, ex. Mexican	84.6
Costa Rican	49.2
Guatemalan	74.3
Honduran	120.5
Nicaraguan	60.7
Panamanian	39.8
Salvadoran	103.5
Cuban	4.4
Dominican Republic	97.6
Mexican	44.5
Puerto Rican	11.2
South American	59.7
Argentinean	49.9
Bolivian	128.7
Chilean	28.6
Colombian	63.6
Ecuadorian	90.1
Peruvian	69.4
Venezuelan	59.7
Spaniard	195.3

Males per 100 Females

Group	Number
Total Population	92.0
Hispanic or Latino (of any race)	94.4
Central American, ex. Mexican	115.5
Costa Rican	74.8
Guatemalan	133.2
Honduran	93.5
Nicaraguan	82.1
Panamanian	77.6
Salvadoran	125.9
Cuban	93.9
Dominican Republic	78.0
Mexican	127.8
Puerto Rican	86.4
South American	99.9
Argentinean	92.4
Bolivian	92.0
Chilean	94.7
Colombian	105.9
Ecuadorian	100.0
Peruvian	93.1
Venezuelan	82.3
Spaniard	95.2

Average Household Size

Group	People
Total Population	2.26
Hispanic or Latino (of any race)	2.93
Central American, ex. Mexican	3.68
Costa Rican	2.44
Guatemalan	3.66
Honduran	3.17
Nicaraguan	2.71
Panamanian	2.57
Salvadoran	4.24
Cuban	2.14
Dominican Republic	3.10
Mexican	2.43
Puerto Rican	2.71
South American	2.66
Argentinean	2.24
Bolivian	2.80
Chilean	2.26
Colombian	2.83
Ecuadorian	2.59
Peruvian	2.75
Venezuelan	2.14
Spaniard	2.11

Median Age

Group	Years
Total Population	30.8
Hispanic or Latino (of any race)	27.5
Central American, ex. Mexican	29.4
Costa Rican	33.5
Guatemalan	30.2
Honduran	29.9
Nicaraguan	30.9
Panamanian	34.0
Salvadoran	28.7
Cuban	30.6
Dominican Republic	27.6
Mexican	26.5
Puerto Rican	25.7
South American	31.4
Argentinean	31.3
Bolivian	30.7
Chilean	32.4
Colombian	32.3
Ecuadorian	28.3
Peruvian	32.8
Venezuelan	27.5
Spaniard	27.1

High School Graduates

(Universe: Population 25 Years and Over)

Group	Number	%
Total Population	324,570	84.3
Hispanic or Latino (of any race)	35,590	63.8
Central American, ex. Mexican	6,711	54.6
Guatemalan	1,733	57.0
Honduran	1,472	69.1
Salvadoran	2,500	42.6
Cuban	1,317	83.9
Dominican Republic	7,516	59.8
Mexican	2,365	65.7
Puerto Rican	9,775	64.9
South American	5,833	71.7
Colombian	3,652	67.1
Peruvian	606	94.7

Four-Year College Graduates

(Universe: Population 25 Years and Over)

Group	Number	%
Total Population	163,609	42.5
Hispanic or Latino (of any race)	8,945	16.0
Central American, ex. Mexican	1,604	13.1
Guatemalan	452	14.9
Honduran	439	20.6
Salvadoran	416	7.1
Cuban	826	52.6
Dominican Republic	1,099	8.7
Mexican	934	26.0
Puerto Rican	1,752	11.6
South American	2,042	25.1
Colombian	985	18.1
Peruvian	276	43.1

Population Age 3–17 Enrolled in Public School

(Universe: Population Age 3–17 Enrolled in School)

Group	Number	%
Total Population	61,771	79.9
Hispanic or Latino (of any race)	19,604	88.9
Central American, ex. Mexican	2,953	87.7
Guatemalan	629	91.3
Honduran	737	81.7
Salvadoran	1,394	99.4
Cuban	108	100.0
Dominican Republic	5,269	89.6
Mexican	802	93.3
Puerto Rican	7,593	89.9
South American	1,620	84.9
Colombian	1,149	92.3
Peruvian	143	73.3

Population Age 3–17 Enrolled in Private School

(Universe: Population Age 3–17 Enrolled in School)

Group	Number	%
Total Population	15,585	20.1
Hispanic or Latino (of any race)	2,456	11.1
Central American, ex. Mexican	414	12.3
Guatemalan	60	8.7
Honduran	165	18.3
Salvadoran	9	0.6
Cuban	0	0.0
Dominican Republic	611	10.4
Mexican	58	6.7
Puerto Rican	857	10.1
South American	288	15.1
Colombian	96	7.7
Peruvian	52	26.7

Foreign-Born Population

Group	Number	%
Total Population	163,625	27.2
Hispanic or Latino (of any race)	44,428	44.1
Central American, ex. Mexican	14,023	70.0
Guatemalan	3,313	69.5
Honduran	2,442	61.8
Salvadoran	7,055	76.6
Cuban	831	36.5
Dominican Republic	15,035	62.1
Mexican	2,929	47.8
Puerto Rican	316	1.1
South American	9,405	74.0
Colombian	6,382	77.2
Peruvian	753	72.1

Foreign-Born Naturalized U.S. Citizens

Group	Number	%
Total Population	72,447	44.3
Hispanic or Latino (of any race)	14,819	33.4
Central American, ex. Mexican	3,895	27.8
Guatemalan	1,254	37.9
Honduran	848	34.7
Salvadoran	1,075	15.2
Cuban	654	78.7
Dominican Republic	6,204	41.3
Mexican	619	21.1
Puerto Rican	150	47.5
South American	2,301	24.5
Colombian	1,315	20.6
Peruvian	265	35.2

Language Spoken at Home: English Only

(Universe: Population 5 Years and Over)

Group	Number	%
Total Population	368,845	64.5
Hispanic or Latino (of any race)	12,969	14.0
Central American, ex. Mexican	1,663	9.1
Guatemalan	415	9.6
Honduran	511	13.9
Salvadoran	309	3.6
Cuban	743	33.7
Dominican Republic	839	3.8
Mexican	1,479	26.5
Puerto Rican	5,846	21.3
South American	1,362	11.4
Colombian	644	8.2
Peruvian	185	19.1

Language Spoken at Home: Spanish

(Universe: Population 5 Years and Over)

Group	Number	%
Total Population	85,588	15.0
Hispanic or Latino (of any race)	78,546	84.9
Central American, ex. Mexican	16,514	90.0
Guatemalan	3,795	87.8
Honduran	3,113	84.7
Salvadoran	8,181	96.4
Cuban	1,378	62.4

Notes: (1) Percent of total population; (2) Percent of Hispanic/Latino population; Profiles include places with an overall population of at least 125,000, OR an overall population of at least 25,000 where the Hispanic/Latino population is at least 20% of the overall population. In states where less than five places meet either of these criteria, we have included places with at least 10,000 total population with the highest percentage of Hispanic/Latino population. These places are identified with an asterisk (*); Please refer to the User's Guide for a full explanation of data.

Group	Number	%
Dominican Republic	21,095	95.2
Mexican	4,039	72.3
Puerto Rican	21,450	78.1
South American	10,452	87.4
Colombian	7,178	91.8
Peruvian	752	77.8

Unemployment Rate
(Universe: Population 16 Years and Over)

Group	%
Total Population	9.3
Hispanic or Latino (of any race)	12.9
Central American, ex. Mexican	10.7
Guatemalan	14.0
Honduran	19.9
Salvadoran	7.0
Cuban	12.9
Dominican Republic	12.3
Mexican	11.7
Puerto Rican	19.1
South American	7.0
Colombian	8.8
Peruvian	6.2

Class of Worker: Private Wage and Salary
(Universe: Civilian Employed Population 16 Years and Over)

Group	Number	%
Total Population	265,867	83.6
Hispanic or Latino (of any race)	40,323	87.9
Central American, ex. Mexican	10,094	90.8
Guatemalan	2,280	89.4
Honduran	1,643	87.2
Salvadoran	5,403	96.4
Cuban	1,031	79.2
Dominican Republic	9,474	88.2
Mexican	3,062	90.9
Puerto Rican	8,085	82.4
South American	6,931	91.2
Colombian	4,722	92.6
Peruvian	487	92.6

Class of Worker: Government
(Universe: Civilian Employed Population 16 Years and Over)

Group	Number	%
Total Population	38,185	12.0
Hispanic or Latino (of any race)	3,937	8.6
Central American, ex. Mexican	679	6.1
Guatemalan	121	4.7
Honduran	232	12.3
Salvadoran	84	1.5
Cuban	234	18.0
Dominican Republic	774	7.2
Mexican	213	6.3
Puerto Rican	1,529	15.6
South American	346	4.6
Colombian	232	4.5
Peruvian	12	2.3

Means of Transportation to Work: Car, Truck or Van
(Universe: Workers 16 Years and Over)

Group	Number	%
Total Population	142,973	46.3
Hispanic or Latino (of any race)	20,895	46.7
Central American, ex. Mexican	5,406	49.3
Guatemalan	1,451	57.6
Honduran	1,039	56.4
Salvadoran	2,425	44.1
Cuban	600	46.1
Dominican Republic	5,537	53.4
Mexican	1,186	36.7
Puerto Rican	5,063	52.4
South American	2,140	29.4
Colombian	1,216	24.6
Peruvian	116	23.0

Means of Transportation to Work: Public Transportation (ex. Taxicab)
(Universe: Workers 16 Years and Over)

Group	Number	%
Total Population	101,584	32.9
Hispanic or Latino (of any race)	17,493	39.1
Central American, ex. Mexican	4,199	38.3
Guatemalan	753	29.9
Honduran	640	34.7
Salvadoran	2,386	43.4
Cuban	401	30.8
Dominican Republic	3,650	35.2
Mexican	1,309	40.5
Puerto Rican	3,428	35.5
South American	3,931	54.0
Colombian	2,980	60.2
Peruvian	289	57.3

Homeownership Rate
(Universe: Occupied Housing Units)

Group	%
Total Population	33.9
Hispanic or Latino (of any race)	16.6
Central American, ex. Mexican	22.1
Costa Rican	28.8
Guatemalan	22.9
Honduran	20.3
Nicaraguan	22.8
Panamanian	36.1
Salvadoran	20.3
Cuban	32.0
Dominican Republic	10.7
Mexican	19.1
Puerto Rican	13.2
South American	24.1
Argentinean	29.2
Bolivian	33.0
Chilean	32.7
Colombian	19.8
Ecuadorian	27.3
Peruvian	30.5
Venezuelan	27.7
Spaniard	29.8

Median Home Value

Group	Dollars
Total Population	395,200
Hispanic or Latino (of any race)	366,300
Central American, ex. Mexican	347,000
Guatemalan	363,600
Honduran	316,300
Salvadoran	348,800
Cuban	367,000
Dominican Republic	365,000
Mexican	381,400
Puerto Rican	361,900
South American	386,100
Colombian	360,900
Peruvian	365,700

Median Gross Rent

Group	Dollars
Total Population	1,199
Hispanic or Latino (of any race)	936
Central American, ex. Mexican	1,145
Guatemalan	1,173
Honduran	1,095
Salvadoran	1,198
Cuban	1,406
Dominican Republic	594
Mexican	1,187
Puerto Rican	625
South American	1,353
Colombian	1,348
Peruvian	1,311

Median Household Income
(2010 Inflation-Adjusted Dollars)

Group	Dollars
Total Population	50,684
Hispanic or Latino (of any race)	29,886
Central American, ex. Mexican	50,322
Guatemalan	45,000
Honduran	47,475
Salvadoran	54,076
Cuban	42,782
Dominican Republic	21,949
Mexican	48,051
Puerto Rican	18,499
South American	47,399
Colombian	56,446
Peruvian	36,033

Per Capita Income
(2010 Inflation-Adjusted Dollars)

Group	Dollars
Total Population	31,856
Hispanic or Latino (of any race)	16,723
Central American, ex. Mexican	19,239
Guatemalan	22,313
Honduran	17,288
Salvadoran	17,045
Cuban	30,521
Dominican Republic	12,443
Mexican	23,815
Puerto Rican	12,945
South American	22,604
Colombian	22,581
Peruvian	18,355

Households with $100,000+ Income

Group	Number	%
Total Population	58,190	23.7
Hispanic or Latino (of any race)	3,356	9.9
Central American, ex. Mexican	809	14.3
Guatemalan	240	19.0
Honduran	198	16.4
Salvadoran	271	11.5
Cuban	245	24.6
Dominican Republic	403	4.7
Mexican	336	16.5
Puerto Rican	591	5.4
South American	716	18.0
Colombian	533	21.7
Peruvian	11	3.1

Households with Food Stamps/SNAP Benefits During Past 12 Months

Group	Number	%
Total Population	33,984	13.8
Hispanic or Latino (of any race)	10,531	31.2
Central American, ex. Mexican	920	16.3
Guatemalan	117	9.3
Honduran	313	25.9
Salvadoran	250	10.6
Cuban	20	2.0
Dominican Republic	3,767	44.0
Mexican	205	10.0
Puerto Rican	4,931	44.9
South American	285	7.2
Colombian	204	8.3
Peruvian	31	8.9

Poverty Rate
(Income in Past 12 Months Below Poverty Level)

Group	%
Total Population	21.2
Hispanic or Latino (of any race)	29.8
Central American, ex. Mexican	18.4
Guatemalan	19.1
Honduran	22.8
Salvadoran	15.0
Cuban	27.8
Dominican Republic	35.6
Mexican	16.0
Puerto Rican	42.9
South American	13.4
Colombian	11.5
Peruvian	17.7

Chelsea

Population

Group	Number	%TP[1]	%HP[2]
Total Population	35,177	100.0	–
Hispanic or Latino (of any race)	21,855	62.1	100.0
Central American, ex. Mexican	12,682	36.1	58.0
Costa Rican	163	0.5	0.7
Guatemalan	2,553	7.3	11.7
Honduran	2,938	8.4	13.4
Nicaraguan	136	0.4	0.6
Salvadoran	6,391	18.2	29.2
Cuban	182	0.5	0.8
Dominican Republic	774	2.2	3.5
Mexican	997	2.8	4.6
Puerto Rican	4,458	12.7	20.4

STATE & PLACE PROFILES

Notes: (1) Percent of total population; (2) Percent of Hispanic/Latino population; Profiles include places with an overall population of at least 125,000, OR an overall population of at least 25,000 where the Hispanic/Latino population is at least 20% of the overall population. In states where less than five places meet either of these criteria, we have included places with at least 10,000 total population with the highest percentage of Hispanic/Latino population. These places are identified with an asterisk (*); Please refer to the User's Guide for a full explanation of data.

Group	Number	% (1)	% (2)
South American	884	2.5	4.0
Colombian	554	1.6	2.5
Peruvian	170	0.5	0.8
Spaniard	121	0.3	0.6

Population Growth: 2000–2010

Group	%
Total Population	0.3
Hispanic or Latino (of any race)	28.7
Central American, ex. Mexican	111.0
Costa Rican	4.5
Guatemalan	116.9
Honduran	85.7
Salvadoran	135.7
Cuban	-19.8
Dominican Republic	45.2
Mexican	51.1
Puerto Rican	-16.9
South American	-2.3
Colombian	-15.8
Peruvian	51.8

Males per 100 Females

Group	Number
Total Population	103.6
Hispanic or Latino (of any race)	108.0
Central American, ex. Mexican	118.4
Costa Rican	69.8
Guatemalan	130.2
Honduran	112.9
Nicaraguan	74.4
Salvadoran	119.6
Cuban	149.3
Dominican Republic	79.2
Mexican	107.3
Puerto Rican	91.6
South American	79.7
Colombian	73.7
Peruvian	88.9
Spaniard	157.4

Average Household Size

Group	People
Total Population	2.92
Hispanic or Latino (of any race)	3.72
Central American, ex. Mexican	4.39
Costa Rican	3.45
Guatemalan	4.50
Honduran	4.38
Nicaraguan	3.97
Salvadoran	4.41
Cuban	2.47
Dominican Republic	3.05
Mexican	4.26
Puerto Rican	2.75
South American	2.96
Colombian	2.98
Peruvian	3.07
Spaniard	3.21

Median Age

Group	Years
Total Population	31.8
Hispanic or Latino (of any race)	28.0
Central American, ex. Mexican	29.0
Costa Rican	31.5
Guatemalan	29.9
Honduran	28.8
Nicaraguan	34.4
Salvadoran	28.9
Cuban	42.3
Dominican Republic	29.2
Mexican	24.3
Puerto Rican	27.2
South American	37.4
Colombian	37.5
Peruvian	36.0
Spaniard	20.5

High School Graduates

(Universe: Population 25 Years and Over)

Group	Number	%
Total Population	14,186	65.6
Hispanic or Latino (of any race)	5,516	51.6
Central American, ex. Mexican	2,706	43.3
Guatemalan	441	50.1
Honduran	712	52.7
Salvadoran	1,432	36.7
Dominican Republic	277	56.3
Mexican	545	60.4
Puerto Rican	1,287	61.2

Four-Year College Graduates

(Universe: Population 25 Years and Over)

Group	Number	%
Total Population	2,936	13.6
Hispanic or Latino (of any race)	636	6.0
Central American, ex. Mexican	249	4.0
Guatemalan	0	0.0
Honduran	94	7.0
Salvadoran	139	3.6
Dominican Republic	0	0.0
Mexican	78	8.6
Puerto Rican	208	9.9

Population Age 3–17 Enrolled in Public School

(Universe: Population Age 3–17 Enrolled in School)

Group	Number	%
Total Population	5,945	93.7
Hispanic or Latino (of any race)	4,415	95.6
Central American, ex. Mexican	2,533	96.9
Guatemalan	397	92.3
Honduran	457	100.0
Salvadoran	1,522	96.9
Dominican Republic	295	83.6
Mexican	354	100.0
Puerto Rican	883	94.6

Population Age 3–17 Enrolled in Private School

(Universe: Population Age 3–17 Enrolled in School)

Group	Number	%
Total Population	398	6.3
Hispanic or Latino (of any race)	205	4.4
Central American, ex. Mexican	82	3.1
Guatemalan	33	7.7
Honduran	0	0.0
Salvadoran	49	3.1
Dominican Republic	58	16.4
Mexican	0	0.0
Puerto Rican	50	5.4

Foreign-Born Population

Group	Number	%
Total Population	14,510	42.0
Hispanic or Latino (of any race)	10,492	51.2
Central American, ex. Mexican	7,750	64.9
Guatemalan	1,090	59.2
Honduran	1,639	72.6
Salvadoran	4,972	65.7
Dominican Republic	509	44.4
Mexican	1,047	64.4
Puerto Rican	97	2.3

Foreign-Born Naturalized U.S. Citizens

Group	Number	%
Total Population	3,815	26.3
Hispanic or Latino (of any race)	1,748	16.7
Central American, ex. Mexican	928	12.0
Guatemalan	132	12.1
Honduran	271	16.5
Salvadoran	492	9.9
Dominican Republic	302	59.3
Mexican	88	8.4
Puerto Rican	72	74.2

Language Spoken at Home: English Only

(Universe: Population 5 Years and Over)

Group	Number	%
Total Population	10,580	34.1
Hispanic or Latino (of any race)	1,117	6.3
Central American, ex. Mexican	355	3.4
Guatemalan	87	5.6
Honduran	53	2.6
Salvadoran	59	0.9
Dominican Republic	182	17.6
Mexican	135	10.4
Puerto Rican	410	11.3

Language Spoken at Home: Spanish

(Universe: Population 5 Years and Over)

Group	Number	%
Total Population	16,800	54.2
Hispanic or Latino (of any race)	16,560	93.6
Central American, ex. Mexican	9,952	96.6
Guatemalan	1,473	94.4
Honduran	2,024	97.4
Salvadoran	6,325	99.1
Dominican Republic	854	82.4
Mexican	1,169	89.6
Puerto Rican	3,199	88.4

Unemployment Rate

(Universe: Population 16 Years and Over)

Group	%
Total Population	11.5
Hispanic or Latino (of any race)	12.9
Central American, ex. Mexican	14.5
Guatemalan	12.7
Honduran	10.7
Salvadoran	16.6
Dominican Republic	18.5
Mexican	10.2
Puerto Rican	10.5

Class of Worker: Private Wage and Salary

(Universe: Civilian Employed Population 16 Years and Over)

Group	Number	%
Total Population	13,543	87.6
Hispanic or Latino (of any race)	8,508	91.9
Central American, ex. Mexican	5,570	96.3
Guatemalan	772	90.0
Honduran	1,267	98.0
Salvadoran	3,429	97.6
Dominican Republic	370	87.5
Mexican	723	96.9
Puerto Rican	1,116	73.8

Class of Worker: Government

(Universe: Civilian Employed Population 16 Years and Over)

Group	Number	%
Total Population	1,312	8.5
Hispanic or Latino (of any race)	497	5.4
Central American, ex. Mexican	69	1.2
Guatemalan	14	1.6
Honduran	0	0.0
Salvadoran	39	1.1
Dominican Republic	29	6.9
Mexican	0	0.0
Puerto Rican	334	22.1

Means of Transportation to Work: Car, Truck or Van

(Universe: Workers 16 Years and Over)

Group	Number	%
Total Population	9,543	64.6
Hispanic or Latino (of any race)	5,077	57.9
Central American, ex. Mexican	3,043	55.3
Guatemalan	558	66.8
Honduran	675	53.1
Salvadoran	1,756	53.7
Dominican Republic	246	60.7
Mexican	456	62.5
Puerto Rican	940	70.3

Means of Transportation to Work: Public Transportation (ex. Taxicab)

(Universe: Workers 16 Years and Over)

Group	Number	%
Total Population	3,398	23.0
Hispanic or Latino (of any race)	2,465	28.1
Central American, ex. Mexican	1,696	30.8
Guatemalan	159	19.0
Honduran	321	25.2
Salvadoran	1,152	35.2
Dominican Republic	128	31.6
Mexican	197	27.0
Puerto Rican	121	9.0

Homeownership Rate

(Universe: Occupied Housing Units)

Group	%
Total Population	28.7
Hispanic or Latino (of any race)	19.0

Notes: (1) Percent of total population; (2) Percent of Hispanic/Latino population; Profiles include places with an overall population of at least 125,000, OR an overall population of at least 25,000 where the Hispanic/Latino population is at least 20% of the overall population. In states where less than five places meet either of these criteria, we have included places with at least 10,000 total population with the highest percentage of Hispanic/Latino population. These places are identified with an asterisk (*); Please refer to the User's Guide for a full explanation of data.

Central American, ex. Mexican	20.0
Costa Rican	24.1
Guatemalan	16.8
Honduran	15.8
Nicaraguan	29.7
Salvadoran	23.5
Cuban	23.3
Dominican Republic	16.4
Mexican	17.4
Puerto Rican	15.4
South American	28.3
Colombian	26.6
Peruvian	20.0
Spaniard	33.3

Median Home Value

Group	Dollars
Total Population	318,000
Hispanic or Latino (of any race)	346,300
Central American, ex. Mexican	365,200
Guatemalan	356,300
Honduran	246,900
Salvadoran	373,100
Dominican Republic	272,500
Mexican	406,700
Puerto Rican	333,400

Median Gross Rent

Group	Dollars
Total Population	1,006
Hispanic or Latino (of any race)	1,081
Central American, ex. Mexican	1,240
Guatemalan	1,191
Honduran	1,181
Salvadoran	1,300
Dominican Republic	210
Mexican	1,089
Puerto Rican	763

Median Household Income
(2010 Inflation-Adjusted Dollars)

Group	Dollars
Total Population	40,487
Hispanic or Latino (of any race)	41,201
Central American, ex. Mexican	50,575
Guatemalan	40,856
Honduran	51,250
Salvadoran	51,404
Dominican Republic	16,987
Mexican	44,853
Puerto Rican	23,750

Per Capita Income
(2010 Inflation-Adjusted Dollars)

Group	Dollars
Total Population	18,630
Hispanic or Latino (of any race)	14,330
Central American, ex. Mexican	14,220
Guatemalan	13,232
Honduran	17,303
Salvadoran	13,382
Dominican Republic	9,993
Mexican	16,585
Puerto Rican	13,611

Households with $100,000+ Income

Group	Number	%
Total Population	1,227	10.3
Hispanic or Latino (of any race)	459	8.1
Central American, ex. Mexican	306	11.3
Guatemalan	48	8.6
Honduran	7	1.3
Salvadoran	235	15.6
Dominican Republic	0	0.0
Mexican	45	8.2
Puerto Rican	108	6.5

Households with Food Stamps/SNAP Benefits During Past 12 Months

Group	Number	%
Total Population	2,386	20.1
Hispanic or Latino (of any race)	1,411	24.9
Central American, ex. Mexican	620	23.0
Guatemalan	134	24.1
Honduran	76	13.7
Salvadoran	402	26.7
Dominican Republic	161	54.6
Mexican	73	13.4
Puerto Rican	499	30.1

Poverty Rate
(Income in Past 12 Months Below Poverty Level)

Group	%
Total Population	24.2
Hispanic or Latino (of any race)	26.9
Central American, ex. Mexican	20.9
Guatemalan	23.1
Honduran	25.4
Salvadoran	19.7
Dominican Republic	44.2
Mexican	26.9
Puerto Rican	42.1

Everett

Population

Group	Number	%TP[1]	%HP[2]
Total Population	41,667	100.0	–
Hispanic or Latino (of any race)	8,792	21.1	100.0
Central American, ex. Mexican	4,673	11.2	53.2
Guatemalan	422	1.0	4.8
Honduran	241	0.6	2.7
Salvadoran	3,895	9.3	44.3
Dominican Republic	462	1.1	5.3
Mexican	353	0.8	4.0
Puerto Rican	1,242	3.0	14.1
South American	833	2.0	9.5
Colombian	478	1.1	5.4
Peruvian	181	0.4	2.1

Population Growth: 2000–2010

Group	%
Total Population	9.5
Hispanic or Latino (of any race)	143.1
Central American, ex. Mexican	289.1
Guatemalan	232.3
Salvadoran	338.6
Mexican	89.8
Puerto Rican	129.2
South American	79.9
Colombian	64.8

Males per 100 Females

Group	Number
Total Population	96.3
Hispanic or Latino (of any race)	108.4
Central American, ex. Mexican	118.1
Guatemalan	108.9
Honduran	109.6
Salvadoran	120.1
Dominican Republic	79.1
Mexican	126.3
Puerto Rican	91.4
South American	88.5
Colombian	79.7
Peruvian	88.5

Average Household Size

Group	People
Total Population	2.67
Hispanic or Latino (of any race)	3.70
Central American, ex. Mexican	4.27
Guatemalan	4.04
Honduran	3.73
Salvadoran	4.36
Dominican Republic	3.25
Mexican	3.04
Puerto Rican	2.94
South American	3.18
Colombian	3.27
Peruvian	3.33

Median Age

Group	Years
Total Population	35.3
Hispanic or Latino (of any race)	28.0
Central American, ex. Mexican	29.2
Guatemalan	31.9
Honduran	29.1
Salvadoran	28.7
Dominican Republic	29.0
Mexican	28.4
Puerto Rican	24.0
South American	33.6
Colombian	32.3
Peruvian	35.9

High School Graduates
(Universe: Population 25 Years and Over)

Group	Number	%
Total Population	22,122	78.9
Hispanic or Latino (of any race)	2,488	60.6
Central American, ex. Mexican	1,139	49.8
Salvadoran	907	53.6

Four-Year College Graduates
(Universe: Population 25 Years and Over)

Group	Number	%
Total Population	4,425	15.8
Hispanic or Latino (of any race)	340	8.3
Central American, ex. Mexican	56	2.4
Salvadoran	26	1.5

Population Age 3–17 Enrolled in Public School
(Universe: Population Age 3–17 Enrolled in School)

Group	Number	%
Total Population	5,564	89.5
Hispanic or Latino (of any race)	1,395	97.3
Central American, ex. Mexican	688	100.0
Salvadoran	431	100.0

Population Age 3–17 Enrolled in Private School
(Universe: Population Age 3–17 Enrolled in School)

Group	Number	%
Total Population	655	10.5
Hispanic or Latino (of any race)	39	2.7
Central American, ex. Mexican	0	0.0
Salvadoran	0	0.0

Foreign-Born Population

Group	Number	%
Total Population	14,186	35.0
Hispanic or Latino (of any race)	4,243	59.2
Central American, ex. Mexican	2,709	66.0
Salvadoran	1,955	67.4

Foreign-Born Naturalized U.S. Citizens

Group	Number	%
Total Population	5,203	36.7
Hispanic or Latino (of any race)	1,177	27.7
Central American, ex. Mexican	716	26.4
Salvadoran	584	29.9

Language Spoken at Home: English Only
(Universe: Population 5 Years and Over)

Group	Number	%
Total Population	21,352	56.2
Hispanic or Latino (of any race)	883	13.9
Central American, ex. Mexican	317	9.1
Salvadoran	283	11.5

Language Spoken at Home: Spanish
(Universe: Population 5 Years and Over)

Group	Number	%
Total Population	5,703	15.0
Hispanic or Latino (of any race)	5,279	83.2
Central American, ex. Mexican	3,161	90.9
Salvadoran	2,177	88.5

Unemployment Rate
(Universe: Population 16 Years and Over)

Group	%
Total Population	9.0
Hispanic or Latino (of any race)	10.1
Central American, ex. Mexican	8.1
Salvadoran	10.4

Class of Worker: Private Wage and Salary
(Universe: Civilian Employed Population 16 Years and Over)

Group	Number	%
Total Population	18,198	84.0
Hispanic or Latino (of any race)	3,523	91.8
Central American, ex. Mexican	2,039	94.0
Salvadoran	1,554	99.2

Notes: (1) Percent of total population; (2) Percent of Hispanic/Latino population; Profiles include places with an overall population of at least 125,000, OR an overall population of at least 25,000 where the Hispanic/Latino population is at least 20% of the overall population. In states where less than five places meet either of these criteria, we have included places with at least 10,000 total population with the highest percentage of Hispanic/Latino population. These places are identified with an asterisk (*); Please refer to the User's Guide for a full explanation of data.

Class of Worker: Government
(Universe: Civilian Employed Population 16 Years and Over)

Group	Number	%
Total Population	2,035	9.4
Hispanic or Latino (of any race)	93	2.4
Central American, ex. Mexican	37	1.7
Salvadoran	13	0.8

Means of Transportation to Work: Car, Truck or Van
(Universe: Workers 16 Years and Over)

Group	Number	%
Total Population	14,941	70.5
Hispanic or Latino (of any race)	2,200	57.9
Central American, ex. Mexican	1,339	62.8
Salvadoran	1,041	68.1

Means of Transportation to Work: Public Transportation (ex. Taxicab)
(Universe: Workers 16 Years and Over)

Group	Number	%
Total Population	4,629	21.8
Hispanic or Latino (of any race)	1,326	34.9
Central American, ex. Mexican	662	31.1
Salvadoran	377	24.7

Homeownership Rate
(Universe: Occupied Housing Units)

Group	%
Total Population	39.9
Hispanic or Latino (of any race)	28.3
Central American, ex. Mexican	35.0
Guatemalan	43.8
Honduran	18.3
Salvadoran	35.4
Dominican Republic	19.5
Mexican	14.7
Puerto Rican	13.4
South American	33.6
Colombian	30.0
Peruvian	38.3

Median Home Value

Group	Dollars
Total Population	355,900
Hispanic or Latino (of any race)	349,000
Central American, ex. Mexican	355,400
Salvadoran	380,200

Median Gross Rent

Group	Dollars
Total Population	1,111
Hispanic or Latino (of any race)	1,242
Central American, ex. Mexican	1,172
Salvadoran	1,339

Median Household Income
(2010 Inflation-Adjusted Dollars)

Group	Dollars
Total Population	49,737
Hispanic or Latino (of any race)	42,832
Central American, ex. Mexican	39,982
Salvadoran	44,205

Per Capita Income
(2010 Inflation-Adjusted Dollars)

Group	Dollars
Total Population	23,876
Hispanic or Latino (of any race)	15,546
Central American, ex. Mexican	14,915
Salvadoran	15,344

Households with $100,000+ Income

Group	Number	%
Total Population	2,402	15.7
Hispanic or Latino (of any race)	170	10.4
Central American, ex. Mexican	95	9.4
Salvadoran	83	11.9

Households with Food Stamps/SNAP Benefits During Past 12 Months

Group	Number	%
Total Population	1,853	12.1
Hispanic or Latino (of any race)	222	13.6
Central American, ex. Mexican	124	12.3
Salvadoran	66	9.5

Poverty Rate
(Income in Past 12 Months Below Poverty Level)

Group	%
Total Population	11.9
Hispanic or Latino (of any race)	15.3
Central American, ex. Mexican	12.8
Salvadoran	9.4

Fitchburg

Population

Group	Number	%TP[1]	%HP[2]
Total Population	40,318	100.0	–
Hispanic or Latino (of any race)	8,727	21.6	100.0
Central American, ex. Mexican	236	0.6	2.7
Dominican Republic	706	1.8	8.1
Mexican	551	1.4	6.3
Puerto Rican	5,871	14.6	67.3
South American	951	2.4	10.9
Ecuadorian	106	0.3	1.2
Uruguayan	650	1.6	7.4

Population Growth: 2000–2010

Group	%
Total Population	3.1
Hispanic or Latino (of any race)	49.1
Dominican Republic	145.1
Mexican	40.9
Puerto Rican	39.8
South American	242.1
Uruguayan	357.7

Males per 100 Females

Group	Number
Total Population	94.5
Hispanic or Latino (of any race)	96.9
Central American, ex. Mexican	95.0
Dominican Republic	82.4
Mexican	100.4
Puerto Rican	98.0
South American	98.1
Ecuadorian	79.7
Uruguayan	97.0

Average Household Size

Group	People
Total Population	2.49
Hispanic or Latino (of any race)	3.19
Central American, ex. Mexican	3.74
Dominican Republic	3.46
Mexican	3.73
Puerto Rican	3.12
South American	3.21
Ecuadorian	3.16
Uruguayan	3.33

Median Age

Group	Years
Total Population	34.7
Hispanic or Latino (of any race)	24.3
Central American, ex. Mexican	24.6
Dominican Republic	24.8
Mexican	22.0
Puerto Rican	23.3
South American	31.3
Ecuadorian	31.0
Uruguayan	31.3

High School Graduates
(Universe: Population 25 Years and Over)

Group	Number	%
Total Population	20,803	84.4
Hispanic or Latino (of any race)	2,766	72.4
Puerto Rican	1,725	68.8

Four-Year College Graduates
(Universe: Population 25 Years and Over)

Group	Number	%
Total Population	5,107	20.7
Hispanic or Latino (of any race)	241	6.3
Puerto Rican	96	3.8

Population Age 3–17 Enrolled in Public School
(Universe: Population Age 3–17 Enrolled in School)

Group	Number	%
Total Population	6,046	89.2
Hispanic or Latino (of any race)	1,856	100.0
Puerto Rican	1,199	100.0

Population Age 3–17 Enrolled in Private School
(Universe: Population Age 3–17 Enrolled in School)

Group	Number	%
Total Population	730	10.8
Hispanic or Latino (of any race)	0	0.0
Puerto Rican	0	0.0

Foreign-Born Population

Group	Number	%
Total Population	3,951	9.8
Hispanic or Latino (of any race)	1,348	17.8
Puerto Rican	15	0.3

Foreign-Born Naturalized U.S. Citizens

Group	Number	%
Total Population	1,921	48.6
Hispanic or Latino (of any race)	503	37.3
Puerto Rican	15	100.0

Language Spoken at Home: English Only
(Universe: Population 5 Years and Over)

Group	Number	%
Total Population	29,423	77.8
Hispanic or Latino (of any race)	1,554	22.8
Puerto Rican	1,136	25.6

Language Spoken at Home: Spanish
(Universe: Population 5 Years and Over)

Group	Number	%
Total Population	5,529	14.6
Hispanic or Latino (of any race)	5,211	76.5
Puerto Rican	3,294	74.4

Unemployment Rate
(Universe: Population 16 Years and Over)

Group	%
Total Population	10.4
Hispanic or Latino (of any race)	16.3
Puerto Rican	21.9

Class of Worker: Private Wage and Salary
(Universe: Civilian Employed Population 16 Years and Over)

Group	Number	%
Total Population	15,439	82.5
Hispanic or Latino (of any race)	2,273	85.6
Puerto Rican	1,253	85.9

Class of Worker: Government
(Universe: Civilian Employed Population 16 Years and Over)

Group	Number	%
Total Population	2,607	13.9
Hispanic or Latino (of any race)	245	9.2
Puerto Rican	156	10.7

Means of Transportation to Work: Car, Truck or Van
(Universe: Workers 16 Years and Over)

Group	Number	%
Total Population	16,204	89.1
Hispanic or Latino (of any race)	2,290	89.3
Puerto Rican	1,304	92.4

Means of Transportation to Work: Public Transportation (ex. Taxicab)
(Universe: Workers 16 Years and Over)

Group	Number	%
Total Population	366	2.0
Hispanic or Latino (of any race)	122	4.8
Puerto Rican	0	0.0

Homeownership Rate
(Universe: Occupied Housing Units)

Group	%
Total Population	54.0
Hispanic or Latino (of any race)	26.9
Central American, ex. Mexican	38.6
Dominican Republic	28.3
Mexican	44.5
Puerto Rican	23.0

Notes: (1) Percent of total population; (2) Percent of Hispanic/Latino population; Profiles include places with an overall population of at least 125,000, OR an overall population of at least 25,000 where the Hispanic/Latino population is at least 20% of the overall population. In states where less than five places meet either of these criteria, we have included places with at least 10,000 total population with the highest percentage of Hispanic/Latino population. These places are identified with an asterisk (*); Please refer to the User's Guide for a full explanation of data.

South American	38.9
Ecuadorian	39.5
Uruguayan	34.4

Median Home Value

Group	Dollars
Total Population	223,400
Hispanic or Latino (of any race)	226,400
Puerto Rican	225,900

Median Gross Rent

Group	Dollars
Total Population	820
Hispanic or Latino (of any race)	855
Puerto Rican	817

Median Household Income
(2010 Inflation-Adjusted Dollars)

Group	Dollars
Total Population	47,019
Hispanic or Latino (of any race)	24,259
Puerto Rican	21,901

Per Capita Income
(2010 Inflation-Adjusted Dollars)

Group	Dollars
Total Population	22,972
Hispanic or Latino (of any race)	11,911
Puerto Rican	11,473

Households with $100,000+ Income

Group	Number	%
Total Population	2,396	16.4
Hispanic or Latino (of any race)	130	5.6
Puerto Rican	63	4.1

Households with Food Stamps/SNAP Benefits During Past 12 Months

Group	Number	%
Total Population	2,169	14.8
Hispanic or Latino (of any race)	953	41.3
Puerto Rican	709	45.7

Poverty Rate
(Income in Past 12 Months Below Poverty Level)

Group	%
Total Population	19.4
Hispanic or Latino (of any race)	36.0
Puerto Rican	40.7

Holyoke

Population

Group	Number	%TP[1]	%HP[2]
Total Population	39,880	100.0	–
Hispanic or Latino (of any race)	19,313	48.4	100.0
Central American, ex. Mexican	135	0.3	0.7
Dominican Republic	349	0.9	1.8
Mexican	167	0.4	0.9
Puerto Rican	17,825	44.7	92.3
South American	297	0.7	1.5
Colombian	202	0.5	1.0

Population Growth: 2000–2010

Group	%
Total Population	0.1
Hispanic or Latino (of any race)	17.2
Dominican Republic	107.7
Puerto Rican	22.6
South American	26.9
Colombian	6.3

Males per 100 Females

Group	Number
Total Population	88.3
Hispanic or Latino (of any race)	88.6
Central American, ex. Mexican	84.9
Dominican Republic	83.7
Mexican	89.8
Puerto Rican	88.7
South American	89.2
Colombian	68.3

Average Household Size

Group	People
Total Population	2.51
Hispanic or Latino (of any race)	3.00
Central American, ex. Mexican	3.32
Dominican Republic	3.19
Mexican	2.67
Puerto Rican	3.00
South American	2.85
Colombian	2.97

Median Age

Group	Years
Total Population	35.0
Hispanic or Latino (of any race)	23.9
Central American, ex. Mexican	25.5
Dominican Republic	29.7
Mexican	24.4
Puerto Rican	23.8
South American	35.3
Colombian	34.8

High School Graduates
(Universe: Population 25 Years and Over)

Group	Number	%
Total Population	19,157	74.0
Hispanic or Latino (of any race)	4,887	51.0
Puerto Rican	4,365	51.0

Four-Year College Graduates
(Universe: Population 25 Years and Over)

Group	Number	%
Total Population	5,128	19.8
Hispanic or Latino (of any race)	584	6.1
Puerto Rican	404	4.7

Population Age 3–17 Enrolled in Public School
(Universe: Population Age 3–17 Enrolled in School)

Group	Number	%
Total Population	7,228	88.5
Hispanic or Latino (of any race)	5,602	97.0
Puerto Rican	5,205	99.3

Population Age 3–17 Enrolled in Private School
(Universe: Population Age 3–17 Enrolled in School)

Group	Number	%
Total Population	936	11.5
Hispanic or Latino (of any race)	175	3.0
Puerto Rican	37	0.7

Foreign-Born Population

Group	Number	%
Total Population	2,232	5.6
Hispanic or Latino (of any race)	644	3.3
Puerto Rican	40	0.2

Foreign-Born Naturalized U.S. Citizens

Group	Number	%
Total Population	1,338	59.9
Hispanic or Latino (of any race)	368	57.1
Puerto Rican	33	82.5

Language Spoken at Home: English Only
(Universe: Population 5 Years and Over)

Group	Number	%
Total Population	20,165	54.2
Hispanic or Latino (of any race)	2,441	14.1
Puerto Rican	2,070	13.3

Language Spoken at Home: Spanish
(Universe: Population 5 Years and Over)

Group	Number	%
Total Population	15,113	40.6
Hispanic or Latino (of any race)	14,854	85.7
Puerto Rican	13,517	86.5

Unemployment Rate
(Universe: Population 16 Years and Over)

Group	%
Total Population	13.1
Hispanic or Latino (of any race)	24.0
Puerto Rican	24.8

Class of Worker: Private Wage and Salary
(Universe: Civilian Employed Population 16 Years and Over)

Group	Number	%
Total Population	11,592	79.6
Hispanic or Latino (of any race)	3,801	82.6
Puerto Rican	3,286	83.0

Class of Worker: Government
(Universe: Civilian Employed Population 16 Years and Over)

Group	Number	%
Total Population	2,459	16.9
Hispanic or Latino (of any race)	700	15.2
Puerto Rican	586	14.8

Means of Transportation to Work: Car, Truck or Van
(Universe: Workers 16 Years and Over)

Group	Number	%
Total Population	12,725	89.7
Hispanic or Latino (of any race)	3,717	82.9
Puerto Rican	3,226	83.3

Means of Transportation to Work: Public Transportation (ex. Taxicab)
(Universe: Workers 16 Years and Over)

Group	Number	%
Total Population	357	2.5
Hispanic or Latino (of any race)	242	5.4
Puerto Rican	212	5.5

Homeownership Rate
(Universe: Occupied Housing Units)

Group	%
Total Population	41.6
Hispanic or Latino (of any race)	15.5
Central American, ex. Mexican	43.9
Dominican Republic	25.2
Mexican	39.1
Puerto Rican	14.4
South American	47.4
Colombian	54.0

Median Home Value

Group	Dollars
Total Population	189,100
Hispanic or Latino (of any race)	144,700
Puerto Rican	145,000

Median Gross Rent

Group	Dollars
Total Population	678
Hispanic or Latino (of any race)	628
Puerto Rican	590

Median Household Income
(2010 Inflation-Adjusted Dollars)

Group	Dollars
Total Population	31,948
Hispanic or Latino (of any race)	15,531
Puerto Rican	14,664

Per Capita Income
(2010 Inflation-Adjusted Dollars)

Group	Dollars
Total Population	18,766
Hispanic or Latino (of any race)	9,747
Puerto Rican	9,341

Households with $100,000+ Income

Group	Number	%
Total Population	1,582	9.8
Hispanic or Latino (of any race)	215	3.2
Puerto Rican	133	2.2

Households with Food Stamps/SNAP Benefits During Past 12 Months

Group	Number	%
Total Population	5,494	34.1
Hispanic or Latino (of any race)	4,493	67.0
Puerto Rican	4,228	68.7

Poverty Rate
(Income in Past 12 Months Below Poverty Level)

Group	%
Total Population	31.7
Hispanic or Latino (of any race)	51.8

Notes: (1) Percent of total population; (2) Percent of Hispanic/Latino population; Profiles include places with an overall population of at least 125,000, OR an overall population of at least 25,000 where the Hispanic/Latino population is at least 20% of the overall population. In states where less than five places meet either of these criteria, we have included places with at least 10,000 total population with the highest percentage of Hispanic/Latino population. These places are identified with an asterisk (*); Please refer to the User's Guide for a full explanation of data.

Puerto Rican	55.5

Lawrence

Population

Group	Number	%TP[1]	%HP[2]
Total Population	76,377	100.0	–
Hispanic or Latino (of any race)	56,363	73.8	100.0
Central American, ex. Mexican	3,052	4.0	5.4
Guatemalan	2,262	3.0	4.0
Honduran	155	0.2	0.3
Salvadoran	495	0.6	0.9
Cuban	369	0.5	0.7
Dominican Republic	30,243	39.6	53.7
Mexican	551	0.7	1.0
Puerto Rican	16,953	22.2	30.1
South American	1,185	1.6	2.1
Colombian	335	0.4	0.6
Ecuadorian	597	0.8	1.1
Peruvian	100	0.1	0.2

Population Growth: 2000–2010

Group	%
Total Population	6.0
Hispanic or Latino (of any race)	31.0
Central American, ex. Mexican	204.9
Guatemalan	184.9
Cuban	-9.6
Dominican Republic	86.8
Mexican	74.4
Puerto Rican	7.2
South American	63.4
Colombian	69.2
Ecuadorian	60.5

Males per 100 Females

Group	Number
Total Population	92.9
Hispanic or Latino (of any race)	91.7
Central American, ex. Mexican	150.8
Guatemalan	170.9
Honduran	96.2
Salvadoran	117.1
Cuban	112.1
Dominican Republic	87.0
Mexican	136.5
Puerto Rican	86.8
South American	101.2
Colombian	97.1
Ecuadorian	105.9
Peruvian	100.0

Average Household Size

Group	People
Total Population	3.00
Hispanic or Latino (of any race)	3.41
Central American, ex. Mexican	4.38
Guatemalan	4.55
Honduran	3.76
Salvadoran	4.26
Cuban	2.44
Dominican Republic	3.53
Mexican	3.42
Puerto Rican	3.13
South American	3.34
Colombian	2.70
Ecuadorian	3.74
Peruvian	3.33

Median Age

Group	Years
Total Population	30.5
Hispanic or Latino (of any race)	27.1
Central American, ex. Mexican	28.1
Guatemalan	27.8
Honduran	32.2
Salvadoran	28.2
Cuban	39.8
Dominican Republic	29.3
Mexican	23.9
Puerto Rican	24.6
South American	32.5
Colombian	36.8
Ecuadorian	31.8
Peruvian	37.0

High School Graduates
(Universe: Population 25 Years and Over)

Group	Number	%
Total Population	28,206	64.3
Hispanic or Latino (of any race)	15,903	55.8
Central American, ex. Mexican	1,435	58.5
Guatemalan	704	47.3
Dominican Republic	8,188	53.6
Puerto Rican	4,769	56.5
South American	765	76.3

Four-Year College Graduates
(Universe: Population 25 Years and Over)

Group	Number	%
Total Population	5,080	11.6
Hispanic or Latino (of any race)	1,974	6.9
Central American, ex. Mexican	318	13.0
Guatemalan	154	10.3
Dominican Republic	983	6.4
Puerto Rican	405	4.8
South American	172	17.1

Population Age 3–17 Enrolled in Public School
(Universe: Population Age 3–17 Enrolled in School)

Group	Number	%
Total Population	14,575	90.8
Hispanic or Latino (of any race)	12,797	92.4
Central American, ex. Mexican	751	96.2
Guatemalan	433	99.1
Dominican Republic	6,507	90.4
Puerto Rican	4,735	96.5
South American	182	94.8

Population Age 3–17 Enrolled in Private School
(Universe: Population Age 3–17 Enrolled in School)

Group	Number	%
Total Population	1,475	9.2
Hispanic or Latino (of any race)	1,059	7.6
Central American, ex. Mexican	30	3.8
Guatemalan	4	0.9
Dominican Republic	689	9.6
Puerto Rican	172	3.5
South American	10	5.2

Foreign-Born Population

Group	Number	%
Total Population	27,086	36.0
Hispanic or Latino (of any race)	23,447	43.0
Central American, ex. Mexican	2,693	73.0
Guatemalan	1,584	69.7
Dominican Republic	18,145	62.6
Puerto Rican	329	1.9
South American	1,112	77.4

Foreign-Born Naturalized U.S. Citizens

Group	Number	%
Total Population	10,845	40.0
Hispanic or Latino (of any race)	8,821	37.6
Central American, ex. Mexican	324	12.0
Guatemalan	193	12.2
Dominican Republic	7,371	40.6
Puerto Rican	223	67.8
South American	423	38.0

Language Spoken at Home: English Only
(Universe: Population 5 Years and Over)

Group	Number	%
Total Population	17,324	25.1
Hispanic or Latino (of any race)	2,924	5.9
Central American, ex. Mexican	129	3.7
Guatemalan	13	0.6
Dominican Republic	374	1.4
Puerto Rican	1,807	11.3
South American	116	8.8

Language Spoken at Home: Spanish
(Universe: Population 5 Years and Over)

Group	Number	%
Total Population	46,962	68.2
Hispanic or Latino (of any race)	46,150	93.6
Central American, ex. Mexican	3,316	96.3
Guatemalan	2,056	99.4
Dominican Republic	25,695	98.5
Puerto Rican	14,146	88.4
South American	1,205	91.2

Unemployment Rate
(Universe: Population 16 Years and Over)

Group	%
Total Population	8.0
Hispanic or Latino (of any race)	8.7
Central American, ex. Mexican	6.9
Guatemalan	3.1
Dominican Republic	8.2
Puerto Rican	10.9
South American	5.6

Class of Worker: Private Wage and Salary
(Universe: Civilian Employed Population 16 Years and Over)

Group	Number	%
Total Population	26,724	86.0
Hispanic or Latino (of any race)	18,660	88.7
Central American, ex. Mexican	1,974	93.3
Guatemalan	1,258	92.2
Dominican Republic	10,671	89.5
Puerto Rican	4,459	84.6
South American	756	96.1

Class of Worker: Government
(Universe: Civilian Employed Population 16 Years and Over)

Group	Number	%
Total Population	3,021	9.7
Hispanic or Latino (of any race)	1,793	8.5
Central American, ex. Mexican	99	4.7
Guatemalan	65	4.8
Dominican Republic	831	7.0
Puerto Rican	731	13.9
South American	16	2.0

Means of Transportation to Work: Car, Truck or Van
(Universe: Workers 16 Years and Over)

Group	Number	%
Total Population	26,453	88.0
Hispanic or Latino (of any race)	17,579	86.1
Central American, ex. Mexican	1,837	86.9
Guatemalan	1,151	84.3
Dominican Republic	9,762	84.8
Puerto Rican	4,452	86.2
South American	751	97.3

Means of Transportation to Work: Public Transportation (ex. Taxicab)
(Universe: Workers 16 Years and Over)

Group	Number	%
Total Population	1,032	3.4
Hispanic or Latino (of any race)	709	3.5
Central American, ex. Mexican	135	6.4
Guatemalan	135	9.9
Dominican Republic	340	3.0
Puerto Rican	200	3.9
South American	0	0.0

Homeownership Rate
(Universe: Occupied Housing Units)

Group	%
Total Population	31.2
Hispanic or Latino (of any race)	21.1
Central American, ex. Mexican	22.0
Guatemalan	13.6
Honduran	37.8
Salvadoran	41.6
Cuban	27.5
Dominican Republic	23.4
Mexican	29.9
Puerto Rican	15.7
South American	32.1
Colombian	33.6
Ecuadorian	31.9
Peruvian	40.0

Median Home Value

Group	Dollars
Total Population	258,100
Hispanic or Latino (of any race)	283,100
Central American, ex. Mexican	326,400
Guatemalan	303,800
Dominican Republic	287,900
Puerto Rican	261,800

Notes: (1) Percent of total population; (2) Percent of Hispanic/Latino population; Profiles include places with an overall population of at least 125,000, OR an overall population of at least 25,000 where the Hispanic/Latino population is at least 20% of the overall population. In states where less than five places meet either of these criteria, we have included places with at least 10,000 total population with the highest percentage of Hispanic/Latino population. These places are identified with an asterisk (*); Please refer to the User's Guide for a full explanation of data.

South American	314,200

Median Gross Rent

Group	Dollars
Total Population	922
Hispanic or Latino (of any race)	934
Central American, ex. Mexican	1,048
Guatemalan	1,044
Dominican Republic	961
Puerto Rican	876
South American	820

Median Household Income
(2010 Inflation-Adjusted Dollars)

Group	Dollars
Total Population	31,631
Hispanic or Latino (of any race)	27,363
Central American, ex. Mexican	42,009
Guatemalan	29,816
Dominican Republic	28,075
Puerto Rican	22,584
South American	36,619

Per Capita Income
(2010 Inflation-Adjusted Dollars)

Group	Dollars
Total Population	16,557
Hispanic or Latino (of any race)	12,673
Central American, ex. Mexican	17,113
Guatemalan	15,163
Dominican Republic	12,874
Puerto Rican	11,059
South American	19,502

Households with $100,000+ Income

Group	Number	%
Total Population	2,500	9.5
Hispanic or Latino (of any race)	1,017	5.8
Central American, ex. Mexican	89	7.3
Guatemalan	0	0.0
Dominican Republic	533	5.7
Puerto Rican	343	6.0
South American	33	7.8

Households with Food Stamps/SNAP Benefits During Past 12 Months

Group	Number	%
Total Population	6,688	25.3
Hispanic or Latino (of any race)	5,657	32.5
Central American, ex. Mexican	70	5.7
Guatemalan	36	4.9
Dominican Republic	3,054	32.7
Puerto Rican	2,257	39.7
South American	34	8.1

Poverty Rate
(Income in Past 12 Months Below Poverty Level)

Group	%
Total Population	26.5
Hispanic or Latino (of any race)	31.9
Central American, ex. Mexican	18.8
Guatemalan	21.5
Dominican Republic	32.6
Puerto Rican	36.6
South American	10.8

Lynn

Population

Group	Number	%TP[1]	%HP[2]
Total Population	90,329	100.0	–
Hispanic or Latino (of any race)	29,013	32.1	100.0
Central American, ex. Mexican	9,049	10.0	31.2
Costa Rican	115	0.1	0.4
Guatemalan	5,715	6.3	19.7
Honduran	523	0.6	1.8
Salvadoran	2,509	2.8	8.6
Cuban	179	0.2	0.6
Dominican Republic	9,528	10.5	32.8
Mexican	1,519	1.7	5.2
Puerto Rican	4,894	5.4	16.9
South American	878	1.0	3.0
Colombian	387	0.4	1.3
Peruvian	204	0.2	0.7
Spaniard	103	0.1	0.4

Population Growth: 2000–2010

Group	%
Total Population	1.4
Hispanic or Latino (of any race)	77.1
Central American, ex. Mexican	361.0
Guatemalan	296.3
Honduran	402.9
Salvadoran	832.7
Cuban	20.9
Dominican Republic	72.7
Mexican	78.1
Puerto Rican	29.8
South American	177.8
Colombian	168.8

Males per 100 Females

Group	Number
Total Population	95.9
Hispanic or Latino (of any race)	104.1
Central American, ex. Mexican	131.5
Costa Rican	74.2
Guatemalan	145.7
Honduran	98.1
Salvadoran	114.3
Cuban	105.7
Dominican Republic	84.4
Mexican	126.4
Puerto Rican	94.8
South American	91.7
Colombian	95.5
Peruvian	96.2
Spaniard	106.0

Average Household Size

Group	People
Total Population	2.69
Hispanic or Latino (of any race)	3.66
Central American, ex. Mexican	4.82
Costa Rican	3.17
Guatemalan	5.16
Honduran	3.82
Salvadoran	4.56
Cuban	2.56
Dominican Republic	3.30
Mexican	3.88
Puerto Rican	2.99
South American	3.29
Colombian	3.31
Peruvian	3.72
Spaniard	1.96

Median Age

Group	Years
Total Population	34.7
Hispanic or Latino (of any race)	25.2
Central American, ex. Mexican	26.1
Costa Rican	31.5
Guatemalan	25.3
Honduran	29.9
Salvadoran	27.7
Cuban	30.8
Dominican Republic	27.2
Mexican	24.9
Puerto Rican	23.3
South American	31.9
Colombian	31.9
Peruvian	34.0
Spaniard	29.5

High School Graduates
(Universe: Population 25 Years and Over)

Group	Number	%
Total Population	45,253	77.9
Hispanic or Latino (of any race)	6,619	52.1
Central American, ex. Mexican	1,402	31.1
Guatemalan	400	15.7
Salvadoran	555	49.2
Dominican Republic	2,887	61.7
Mexican	474	69.5
Puerto Rican	1,282	65.2
South American	350	78.1

Four-Year College Graduates
(Universe: Population 25 Years and Over)

Group	Number	%
Total Population	10,452	18.0
Hispanic or Latino (of any race)	750	5.9
Central American, ex. Mexican	186	4.1
Guatemalan	17	0.7
Salvadoran	90	8.0
Dominican Republic	297	6.3
Mexican	83	12.2
Puerto Rican	86	4.4
South American	70	15.6

Population Age 3–17 Enrolled in Public School
(Universe: Population Age 3–17 Enrolled in School)

Group	Number	%
Total Population	13,692	86.3
Hispanic or Latino (of any race)	5,673	95.8
Central American, ex. Mexican	1,851	98.3
Guatemalan	1,119	100.0
Salvadoran	493	98.2
Dominican Republic	2,053	97.7
Mexican	203	79.9
Puerto Rican	1,273	92.0
South American	157	95.7

Population Age 3–17 Enrolled in Private School
(Universe: Population Age 3–17 Enrolled in School)

Group	Number	%
Total Population	2,172	13.7
Hispanic or Latino (of any race)	250	4.2
Central American, ex. Mexican	32	1.7
Guatemalan	0	0.0
Salvadoran	9	1.8
Dominican Republic	49	2.3
Mexican	51	20.1
Puerto Rican	111	8.0
South American	7	4.3

Foreign-Born Population

Group	Number	%
Total Population	25,794	28.8
Hispanic or Latino (of any race)	13,444	53.3
Central American, ex. Mexican	6,479	68.9
Guatemalan	3,849	68.6
Salvadoran	1,617	68.6
Dominican Republic	5,313	59.8
Mexican	647	58.3
Puerto Rican	127	3.1
South American	553	68.4

Foreign-Born Naturalized U.S. Citizens

Group	Number	%
Total Population	10,727	41.6
Hispanic or Latino (of any race)	3,935	29.3
Central American, ex. Mexican	510	7.9
Guatemalan	259	6.7
Salvadoran	132	8.2
Dominican Republic	2,740	51.6
Mexican	117	18.1
Puerto Rican	78	61.4
South American	340	61.5

Language Spoken at Home: English Only
(Universe: Population 5 Years and Over)

Group	Number	%
Total Population	50,083	60.0
Hispanic or Latino (of any race)	2,397	10.6
Central American, ex. Mexican	365	4.4
Guatemalan	88	1.8
Salvadoran	131	6.3
Dominican Republic	650	8.1
Mexican	179	18.2
Puerto Rican	1,089	29.8
South American	29	3.8

Language Spoken at Home: Spanish
(Universe: Population 5 Years and Over)

Group	Number	%
Total Population	20,812	25.0
Hispanic or Latino (of any race)	19,984	88.6
Central American, ex. Mexican	7,966	95.1
Guatemalan	4,788	97.3
Salvadoran	1,958	93.7
Dominican Republic	7,385	91.9

Notes: (1) Percent of total population; (2) Percent of Hispanic/Latino population; Profiles include places with an overall population of at least 125,000, OR an overall population of at least 25,000 where the Hispanic/Latino population is at least 20% of the overall population. In states where less than five places meet either of these criteria, we have included places with at least 10,000 total population with the highest percentage of Hispanic/Latino population. These places are identified with an asterisk (*); Please refer to the User's Guide for a full explanation of data.

Mexican	666	67.6
Puerto Rican	2,569	70.2
South American	744	96.2

Unemployment Rate
(Universe: Population 16 Years and Over)

Group	%
Total Population	9.7
Hispanic or Latino (of any race)	11.8
Central American, ex. Mexican	10.7
Guatemalan	9.1
Salvadoran	12.6
Dominican Republic	13.7
Mexican	3.4
Puerto Rican	14.6
South American	14.0

Class of Worker: Private Wage and Salary
(Universe: Civilian Employed Population 16 Years and Over)

Group	Number	%
Total Population	34,855	82.2
Hispanic or Latino (of any race)	10,167	87.5
Central American, ex. Mexican	4,490	90.4
Guatemalan	2,771	94.4
Salvadoran	952	80.5
Dominican Republic	3,432	89.5
Mexican	468	86.7
Puerto Rican	1,054	74.0
South American	363	80.0

Class of Worker: Government
(Universe: Civilian Employed Population 16 Years and Over)

Group	Number	%
Total Population	5,723	13.5
Hispanic or Latino (of any race)	817	7.0
Central American, ex. Mexican	178	3.6
Guatemalan	8	0.3
Salvadoran	89	7.5
Dominican Republic	156	4.1
Mexican	72	13.3
Puerto Rican	305	21.4
South American	91	20.0

Means of Transportation to Work: Car, Truck or Van
(Universe: Workers 16 Years and Over)

Group	Number	%
Total Population	34,348	83.0
Hispanic or Latino (of any race)	8,860	78.1
Central American, ex. Mexican	3,708	76.0
Guatemalan	2,046	70.9
Salvadoran	979	85.4
Dominican Republic	2,953	79.7
Mexican	405	75.0
Puerto Rican	1,138	83.2
South American	334	73.6

Means of Transportation to Work: Public Transportation (ex. Taxicab)
(Universe: Workers 16 Years and Over)

Group	Number	%
Total Population	3,478	8.4
Hispanic or Latino (of any race)	1,037	9.1
Central American, ex. Mexican	490	10.0
Guatemalan	287	9.9
Salvadoran	145	12.7
Dominican Republic	260	7.0
Mexican	61	11.3
Puerto Rican	119	8.7
South American	86	18.9

Homeownership Rate
(Universe: Occupied Housing Units)

Group	%
Total Population	47.4
Hispanic or Latino (of any race)	24.9
Central American, ex. Mexican	32.2
Costa Rican	37.1
Guatemalan	18.7
Honduran	39.9
Salvadoran	57.5
Cuban	27.1
Dominican Republic	20.1
Mexican	26.3
Puerto Rican	19.7
South American	51.1
Colombian	53.4
Peruvian	54.1
Spaniard	47.8

Median Home Value

Group	Dollars
Total Population	283,600
Hispanic or Latino (of any race)	289,800
Central American, ex. Mexican	298,300
Guatemalan	259,000
Salvadoran	331,500
Dominican Republic	300,500
Mexican	56,100
Puerto Rican	280,400
South American	262,000

Median Gross Rent

Group	Dollars
Total Population	907
Hispanic or Latino (of any race)	981
Central American, ex. Mexican	1,146
Guatemalan	1,201
Salvadoran	1,043
Dominican Republic	880
Mexican	1,034
Puerto Rican	840
South American	825

Median Household Income
(2010 Inflation-Adjusted Dollars)

Group	Dollars
Total Population	43,200
Hispanic or Latino (of any race)	32,079
Central American, ex. Mexican	43,188
Guatemalan	41,025
Salvadoran	48,917
Dominican Republic	20,206
Mexican	40,476
Puerto Rican	34,063
South American	36,500

Per Capita Income
(2010 Inflation-Adjusted Dollars)

Group	Dollars
Total Population	21,616
Hispanic or Latino (of any race)	13,568
Central American, ex. Mexican	13,432
Guatemalan	12,797
Salvadoran	14,710
Dominican Republic	11,970
Mexican	19,424
Puerto Rican	14,039
South American	19,099

Households with $100,000+ Income

Group	Number	%
Total Population	5,094	14.9
Hispanic or Latino (of any race)	503	6.5
Central American, ex. Mexican	175	7.4
Guatemalan	125	9.4
Salvadoran	35	5.6
Dominican Republic	169	5.2
Mexican	39	15.5
Puerto Rican	75	5.5
South American	27	11.2

Households with Food Stamps/SNAP Benefits During Past 12 Months

Group	Number	%
Total Population	6,739	19.8
Hispanic or Latino (of any race)	2,295	29.8
Central American, ex. Mexican	321	13.6
Guatemalan	241	18.1
Salvadoran	49	7.8
Dominican Republic	1,293	39.7
Mexican	19	7.5
Puerto Rican	574	42.3
South American	33	13.6

Poverty Rate
(Income in Past 12 Months Below Poverty Level)

Group	%
Total Population	19.3
Hispanic or Latino (of any race)	30.3
Central American, ex. Mexican	19.3
Guatemalan	24.1
Salvadoran	5.2
Dominican Republic	41.9
Mexican	32.9
Puerto Rican	37.9
South American	4.8

Revere

Population

Group	Number	%TP[1]	%HP[2]
Total Population	51,755	100.0	–
Hispanic or Latino (of any race)	12,617	24.4	100.0
Central American, ex. Mexican	4,457	8.6	35.3
Guatemalan	769	1.5	6.1
Honduran	505	1.0	4.0
Salvadoran	3,024	5.8	24.0
Cuban	138	0.3	1.1
Dominican Republic	661	1.3	5.2
Mexican	966	1.9	7.7
Puerto Rican	1,897	3.7	15.0
South American	3,184	6.2	25.2
Colombian	2,520	4.9	20.0
Peruvian	325	0.6	2.6
Spaniard	104	0.2	0.8

Population Growth: 2000–2010

Group	%
Total Population	9.5
Hispanic or Latino (of any race)	182.6
Central American, ex. Mexican	491.9
Guatemalan	487.0
Salvadoran	587.3
Dominican Republic	420.5
Mexican	104.2
Puerto Rican	136.5
South American	271.5
Colombian	305.1

Males per 100 Females

Group	Number
Total Population	96.2
Hispanic or Latino (of any race)	100.6
Central American, ex. Mexican	113.7
Guatemalan	119.7
Honduran	96.5
Salvadoran	115.8
Cuban	89.0
Dominican Republic	89.4
Mexican	104.7
Puerto Rican	96.4
South American	89.6
Colombian	91.1
Peruvian	92.3
Spaniard	112.2

Average Household Size

Group	People
Total Population	2.52
Hispanic or Latino (of any race)	3.59
Central American, ex. Mexican	4.21
Guatemalan	4.18
Honduran	3.76
Salvadoran	4.36
Cuban	2.56
Dominican Republic	3.32
Mexican	3.91
Puerto Rican	2.83
South American	3.45
Colombian	3.55
Peruvian	3.56
Spaniard	2.94

Median Age

Group	Years
Total Population	37.9
Hispanic or Latino (of any race)	28.3
Central American, ex. Mexican	28.8
Guatemalan	30.5
Honduran	28.3
Salvadoran	28.1
Cuban	34.4
Dominican Republic	25.9

Notes: (1) Percent of total population; (2) Percent of Hispanic/Latino population; Profiles include places with an overall population of at least 125,000, OR an overall population of at least 25,000 where the Hispanic/Latino population is at least 20% of the overall population. In states where less than five places meet either of these criteria, we have included places with at least 10,000 total population with the highest percentage of Hispanic/Latino population. These places are identified with an asterisk (*); Please refer to the User's Guide for a full explanation of data.

Mexican	26.3
Puerto Rican	25.9
South American	32.3
Colombian	30.8
Peruvian	36.4
Spaniard	32.5

High School Graduates
(Universe: Population 25 Years and Over)

Group	Number	%
Total Population	27,697	77.8
Hispanic or Latino (of any race)	3,610	54.3
Central American, ex. Mexican	975	38.7
Salvadoran	326	23.7
Puerto Rican	742	66.1
South American	1,419	63.6
Colombian	963	57.3

Four-Year College Graduates
(Universe: Population 25 Years and Over)

Group	Number	%
Total Population	6,459	18.1
Hispanic or Latino (of any race)	668	10.0
Central American, ex. Mexican	174	6.9
Salvadoran	0	0.0
Puerto Rican	85	7.6
South American	335	15.0
Colombian	297	17.7

Population Age 3–17 Enrolled in Public School
(Universe: Population Age 3–17 Enrolled in School)

Group	Number	%
Total Population	6,443	84.8
Hispanic or Latino (of any race)	2,552	89.3
Central American, ex. Mexican	806	91.7
Salvadoran	458	88.9
Puerto Rican	322	70.6
South American	979	90.9
Colombian	744	88.4

Population Age 3–17 Enrolled in Private School
(Universe: Population Age 3–17 Enrolled in School)

Group	Number	%
Total Population	1,156	15.2
Hispanic or Latino (of any race)	305	10.7
Central American, ex. Mexican	73	8.3
Salvadoran	57	11.1
Puerto Rican	134	29.4
South American	98	9.1
Colombian	98	11.6

Foreign-Born Population

Group	Number	%
Total Population	14,789	29.6
Hispanic or Latino (of any race)	6,429	54.2
Central American, ex. Mexican	2,900	66.1
Salvadoran	1,737	66.8
Puerto Rican	31	1.7
South American	2,818	69.3
Colombian	2,152	72.7

Foreign-Born Naturalized U.S. Citizens

Group	Number	%
Total Population	5,364	36.3
Hispanic or Latino (of any race)	1,399	21.8
Central American, ex. Mexican	587	20.2
Salvadoran	206	11.9
Puerto Rican	0	0.0
South American	588	20.9
Colombian	437	20.3

Language Spoken at Home: English Only
(Universe: Population 5 Years and Over)

Group	Number	%
Total Population	27,313	58.3
Hispanic or Latino (of any race)	1,292	11.9
Central American, ex. Mexican	252	6.3
Salvadoran	124	5.3
Puerto Rican	531	31.5
South American	303	8.3
Colombian	150	5.5

Language Spoken at Home: Spanish
(Universe: Population 5 Years and Over)

Group	Number	%
Total Population	9,989	21.3
Hispanic or Latino (of any race)	9,558	87.8
Central American, ex. Mexican	3,776	93.7
Salvadoran	2,200	94.7
Puerto Rican	1,157	68.5
South American	3,348	91.7
Colombian	2,578	94.5

Unemployment Rate
(Universe: Population 16 Years and Over)

Group	%
Total Population	8.2
Hispanic or Latino (of any race)	8.2
Central American, ex. Mexican	4.5
Salvadoran	3.6
Puerto Rican	14.0
South American	7.2
Colombian	2.0

Class of Worker: Private Wage and Salary
(Universe: Civilian Employed Population 16 Years and Over)

Group	Number	%
Total Population	20,375	83.7
Hispanic or Latino (of any race)	5,780	93.5
Central American, ex. Mexican	2,390	97.2
Salvadoran	1,448	100.0
Puerto Rican	777	86.6
South American	2,062	93.8
Colombian	1,535	94.3

Class of Worker: Government
(Universe: Civilian Employed Population 16 Years and Over)

Group	Number	%
Total Population	2,527	10.4
Hispanic or Latino (of any race)	269	4.3
Central American, ex. Mexican	0	0.0
Salvadoran	0	0.0
Puerto Rican	120	13.4
South American	93	4.2
Colombian	93	5.7

Means of Transportation to Work: Car, Truck or Van
(Universe: Workers 16 Years and Over)

Group	Number	%
Total Population	16,272	68.9
Hispanic or Latino (of any race)	3,192	52.5
Central American, ex. Mexican	1,299	53.5
Salvadoran	882	60.9
Puerto Rican	605	73.3
South American	1,019	46.4
Colombian	672	41.3

Means of Transportation to Work: Public Transportation (ex. Taxicab)
(Universe: Workers 16 Years and Over)

Group	Number	%
Total Population	6,191	26.2
Hispanic or Latino (of any race)	2,643	43.4
Central American, ex. Mexican	1,071	44.1
Salvadoran	506	34.9
Puerto Rican	169	20.5
South American	1,053	47.9
Colombian	830	51.0

Homeownership Rate
(Universe: Occupied Housing Units)

Group	%
Total Population	47.6
Hispanic or Latino (of any race)	35.0
Central American, ex. Mexican	42.5
Guatemalan	46.0
Honduran	38.0
Salvadoran	42.2
Cuban	47.9
Dominican Republic	18.5
Mexican	35.1
Puerto Rican	21.6
South American	37.0
Colombian	36.0
Peruvian	41.7
Spaniard	51.5

Median Home Value

Group	Dollars
Total Population	337,400
Hispanic or Latino (of any race)	339,000
Central American, ex. Mexican	337,900
Salvadoran	331,100
Puerto Rican	330,500
South American	343,100
Colombian	362,300

Median Gross Rent

Group	Dollars
Total Population	1,122
Hispanic or Latino (of any race)	1,174
Central American, ex. Mexican	1,237
Salvadoran	1,309
Puerto Rican	1,155
South American	1,182
Colombian	1,203

Median Household Income
(2010 Inflation-Adjusted Dollars)

Group	Dollars
Total Population	49,759
Hispanic or Latino (of any race)	45,956
Central American, ex. Mexican	61,587
Salvadoran	60,433
Puerto Rican	33,565
South American	44,850
Colombian	38,563

Per Capita Income
(2010 Inflation-Adjusted Dollars)

Group	Dollars
Total Population	23,928
Hispanic or Latino (of any race)	16,736
Central American, ex. Mexican	16,762
Salvadoran	14,403
Puerto Rican	19,719
South American	16,234
Colombian	16,652

Households with $100,000+ Income

Group	Number	%
Total Population	3,511	18.5
Hispanic or Latino (of any race)	527	16.3
Central American, ex. Mexican	263	25.1
Salvadoran	90	16.6
Puerto Rican	133	20.1
South American	80	6.9
Colombian	49	5.4

Households with Food Stamps/SNAP Benefits During Past 12 Months

Group	Number	%
Total Population	2,810	14.8
Hispanic or Latino (of any race)	542	16.7
Central American, ex. Mexican	172	16.4
Salvadoran	121	22.3
Puerto Rican	185	27.9
South American	113	9.7
Colombian	100	11.0

Poverty Rate
(Income in Past 12 Months Below Poverty Level)

Group	%
Total Population	14.7
Hispanic or Latino (of any race)	15.6
Central American, ex. Mexican	14.6
Salvadoran	18.0
Puerto Rican	30.9
South American	10.5
Colombian	12.3

Springfield

Population

Group	Number	%TP[1]	%HP[2]
Total Population	153,060	100.0	–
Hispanic or Latino (of any race)	59,451	38.8	100.0
Central American, ex. Mexican	1,399	0.9	2.4
Costa Rican	122	0.1	0.2
Guatemalan	727	0.5	1.2
Honduran	121	0.1	0.2
Panamanian	157	0.1	0.3
Salvadoran	234	0.2	0.4
Cuban	384	0.3	0.6

Notes: (1) Percent of total population; (2) Percent of Hispanic/Latino population; Profiles include places with an overall population of at least 125,000, OR an overall population of at least 25,000 where the Hispanic/Latino population is at least 20% of the overall population. In states where less than five places meet either of these criteria, we have included places with at least 10,000 total population with the highest percentage of Hispanic/Latino population. These places are identified with an asterisk (*); Please refer to the User's Guide for a full explanation of data.

Dominican Republic	2,649	1.7	4.5
Mexican	1,514	1.0	2.5
Puerto Rican	50,798	33.2	85.4
South American	893	0.6	1.5
Colombian	375	0.2	0.6
Ecuadorian	193	0.1	0.3
Peruvian	196	0.1	0.3
Spaniard	175	0.1	0.3

Population Growth: 2000–2010

Group	%
Total Population	0.6
Hispanic or Latino (of any race)	43.8
Central American, ex. Mexican	267.2
Panamanian	42.7
Cuban	65.5
Dominican Republic	331.4
Mexican	140.3
Puerto Rican	44.1
South American	113.6
Colombian	116.8

Males per 100 Females

Group	Number
Total Population	90.2
Hispanic or Latino (of any race)	87.7
Central American, ex. Mexican	116.2
Costa Rican	90.6
Guatemalan	137.6
Honduran	124.1
Panamanian	68.8
Salvadoran	100.0
Cuban	106.5
Dominican Republic	83.2
Mexican	146.2
Puerto Rican	85.4
South American	92.5
Colombian	84.7
Ecuadorian	89.2
Peruvian	98.0
Spaniard	80.4

Average Household Size

Group	People
Total Population	2.60
Hispanic or Latino (of any race)	3.07
Central American, ex. Mexican	4.32
Costa Rican	2.88
Guatemalan	5.65
Honduran	4.64
Panamanian	2.40
Salvadoran	4.18
Cuban	2.62
Dominican Republic	3.41
Mexican	3.95
Puerto Rican	3.02
South American	2.90
Colombian	2.85
Ecuadorian	3.07
Peruvian	2.93
Spaniard	2.65

Median Age

Group	Years
Total Population	32.2
Hispanic or Latino (of any race)	24.4
Central American, ex. Mexican	25.9
Costa Rican	34.0
Guatemalan	24.1
Honduran	27.6
Panamanian	31.8
Salvadoran	28.0
Cuban	26.7
Dominican Republic	26.4
Mexican	24.4
Puerto Rican	24.1
South American	36.2
Colombian	34.8
Ecuadorian	36.5
Peruvian	39.0
Spaniard	26.9

High School Graduates
(Universe: Population 25 Years and Over)

Group	Number	%
Total Population	69,176	75.9
Hispanic or Latino (of any race)	15,520	59.6
Central American, ex. Mexican	331	52.0
Dominican Republic	737	60.8
Mexican	287	36.9
Puerto Rican	13,156	59.5
South American	510	85.6

Four-Year College Graduates
(Universe: Population 25 Years and Over)

Group	Number	%
Total Population	15,437	16.9
Hispanic or Latino (of any race)	2,059	7.9
Central American, ex. Mexican	34	5.3
Dominican Republic	151	12.5
Mexican	9	1.2
Puerto Rican	1,624	7.3
South American	125	21.0

Population Age 3–17 Enrolled in Public School
(Universe: Population Age 3–17 Enrolled in School)

Group	Number	%
Total Population	27,841	90.7
Hispanic or Latino (of any race)	15,113	96.0
Central American, ex. Mexican	238	88.5
Dominican Republic	515	84.3
Mexican	259	100.0
Puerto Rican	13,616	97.9
South American	77	60.6

Population Age 3–17 Enrolled in Private School
(Universe: Population Age 3–17 Enrolled in School)

Group	Number	%
Total Population	2,858	9.3
Hispanic or Latino (of any race)	622	4.0
Central American, ex. Mexican	31	11.5
Dominican Republic	96	15.7
Mexican	0	0.0
Puerto Rican	295	2.1
South American	50	39.4

Foreign-Born Population

Group	Number	%
Total Population	15,776	10.3
Hispanic or Latino (of any race)	4,252	7.7
Central American, ex. Mexican	650	50.6
Dominican Republic	1,435	57.6
Mexican	949	49.1
Puerto Rican	361	0.8
South American	576	70.8

Foreign-Born Naturalized U.S. Citizens

Group	Number	%
Total Population	7,817	49.5
Hispanic or Latino (of any race)	1,416	33.3
Central American, ex. Mexican	142	21.8
Dominican Republic	681	47.5
Mexican	57	6.0
Puerto Rican	69	19.1
South American	304	52.8

Language Spoken at Home: English Only
(Universe: Population 5 Years and Over)

Group	Number	%
Total Population	93,611	66.3
Hispanic or Latino (of any race)	12,202	25.0
Central American, ex. Mexican	176	16.2
Dominican Republic	59	2.8
Mexican	143	8.8
Puerto Rican	11,034	26.4
South American	121	16.1

Language Spoken at Home: Spanish
(Universe: Population 5 Years and Over)

Group	Number	%
Total Population	37,465	26.5
Hispanic or Latino (of any race)	36,482	74.8
Central American, ex. Mexican	911	83.8
Dominican Republic	2,066	97.2
Mexican	1,483	91.2
Puerto Rican	30,711	73.5
South American	617	82.3

Unemployment Rate
(Universe: Population 16 Years and Over)

Group	%
Total Population	14.2
Hispanic or Latino (of any race)	20.4
Central American, ex. Mexican	19.7
Dominican Republic	9.0
Mexican	36.2
Puerto Rican	20.3
South American	10.7

Class of Worker: Private Wage and Salary
(Universe: Civilian Employed Population 16 Years and Over)

Group	Number	%
Total Population	46,914	80.4
Hispanic or Latino (of any race)	13,561	84.1
Central American, ex. Mexican	352	88.9
Dominican Republic	917	89.3
Mexican	586	100.0
Puerto Rican	11,029	82.7
South American	364	88.8

Class of Worker: Government
(Universe: Civilian Employed Population 16 Years and Over)

Group	Number	%
Total Population	8,581	14.7
Hispanic or Latino (of any race)	2,028	12.6
Central American, ex. Mexican	44	11.1
Dominican Republic	47	4.6
Mexican	0	0.0
Puerto Rican	1,859	13.9
South American	46	11.2

Means of Transportation to Work: Car, Truck or Van
(Universe: Workers 16 Years and Over)

Group	Number	%
Total Population	50,326	88.4
Hispanic or Latino (of any race)	13,578	85.4
Central American, ex. Mexican	367	92.7
Dominican Republic	858	84.4
Mexican	453	77.3
Puerto Rican	11,191	85.3
South American	390	95.1

Means of Transportation to Work: Public Transportation (ex. Taxicab)
(Universe: Workers 16 Years and Over)

Group	Number	%
Total Population	2,860	5.0
Hispanic or Latino (of any race)	1,163	7.3
Central American, ex. Mexican	0	0.0
Dominican Republic	86	8.5
Mexican	103	17.6
Puerto Rican	968	7.4
South American	0	0.0

Homeownership Rate
(Universe: Occupied Housing Units)

Group	%
Total Population	49.8
Hispanic or Latino (of any race)	24.6
Central American, ex. Mexican	34.3
Costa Rican	51.2
Guatemalan	9.2
Honduran	46.4
Panamanian	44.6
Salvadoran	60.0
Cuban	29.3
Dominican Republic	33.0
Mexican	27.1
Puerto Rican	23.2
South American	56.2
Colombian	56.3
Ecuadorian	53.7
Peruvian	54.2
Spaniard	49.1

Median Home Value

Group	Dollars
Total Population	155,500
Hispanic or Latino (of any race)	156,900
Central American, ex. Mexican	143,800
Dominican Republic	188,900
Mexican	206,000

Notes: (1) Percent of total population; (2) Percent of Hispanic/Latino population; Profiles include places with an overall population of at least 125,000, OR an overall population of at least 25,000 where the Hispanic/Latino population is at least 20% of the overall population. In states where less than five places meet either of these criteria, we have included places with at least 10,000 total population with the highest percentage of Hispanic/Latino population. These places are identified with an asterisk (*); Please refer to the User's Guide for a full explanation of data.

Puerto Rican	156,300
South American	155,500

Median Gross Rent

Group	Dollars
Total Population	737
Hispanic or Latino (of any race)	692
Central American, ex. Mexican	1,058
Dominican Republic	837
Mexican	938
Puerto Rican	659
South American	238

Median Household Income
(2010 Inflation-Adjusted Dollars)

Group	Dollars
Total Population	34,628
Hispanic or Latino (of any race)	21,364
Central American, ex. Mexican	21,639
Dominican Republic	21,635
Mexican	20,781
Puerto Rican	20,729
South American	47,083

Per Capita Income
(2010 Inflation-Adjusted Dollars)

Group	Dollars
Total Population	17,962
Hispanic or Latino (of any race)	10,992
Central American, ex. Mexican	8,898
Dominican Republic	12,052
Mexican	8,465
Puerto Rican	10,921
South American	20,046

Households with $100,000+ Income

Group	Number	%
Total Population	5,156	9.2
Hispanic or Latino (of any race)	617	3.6
Central American, ex. Mexican	0	0.0
Dominican Republic	43	5.3
Mexican	0	0.0
Puerto Rican	542	3.6
South American	7	2.4

Households with Food Stamps/SNAP Benefits During Past 12 Months

Group	Number	%
Total Population	15,826	28.1
Hispanic or Latino (of any race)	8,986	52.1
Central American, ex. Mexican	205	50.5
Dominican Republic	385	47.6
Mexican	164	41.0
Puerto Rican	8,002	53.9
South American	74	25.3

Poverty Rate
(Income in Past 12 Months Below Poverty Level)

Group	%
Total Population	27.6
Hispanic or Latino (of any race)	43.0
Central American, ex. Mexican	57.1
Dominican Republic	30.1
Mexican	54.5
Puerto Rican	44.1
South American	10.4

Worcester

Population

Group	Number	%TP[1]	%HP[2]
Total Population	181,045	100.0	–
Hispanic or Latino (of any race)	37,818	20.9	100.0
Central American, ex. Mexican	3,792	2.1	10.0
Costa Rican	116	0.1	0.3
Guatemalan	474	0.3	1.3
Honduran	206	0.1	0.5
Panamanian	129	0.1	0.3
Salvadoran	2,776	1.5	7.3
Cuban	490	0.3	1.3
Dominican Republic	4,221	2.3	11.2
Mexican	1,356	0.7	3.6
Puerto Rican	23,074	12.7	61.0
South American	2,351	1.3	6.2
Chilean	102	0.1	0.3
Colombian	769	0.4	2.0
Ecuadorian	953	0.5	2.5
Peruvian	252	0.1	0.7
Venezuelan	109	0.1	0.3
Spaniard	177	0.1	0.5

Population Growth: 2000–2010

Group	%
Total Population	4.9
Hispanic or Latino (of any race)	44.6
Central American, ex. Mexican	169.5
Guatemalan	259.1
Salvadoran	177.6
Cuban	22.8
Dominican Republic	162.0
Mexican	92.1
Puerto Rican	35.0
South American	107.0
Colombian	100.8
Ecuadorian	130.8

Males per 100 Females

Group	Number
Total Population	94.9
Hispanic or Latino (of any race)	95.4
Central American, ex. Mexican	117.3
Costa Rican	103.5
Guatemalan	135.8
Honduran	136.8
Panamanian	89.7
Salvadoran	116.4
Cuban	101.6
Dominican Republic	81.2
Mexican	118.7
Puerto Rican	91.7
South American	100.3
Chilean	82.1
Colombian	96.2
Ecuadorian	105.4
Peruvian	108.3
Venezuelan	75.8
Spaniard	98.9

Average Household Size

Group	People
Total Population	2.46
Hispanic or Latino (of any race)	3.05
Central American, ex. Mexican	3.82
Costa Rican	3.30
Guatemalan	3.83
Honduran	3.53
Panamanian	2.87
Salvadoran	3.94
Cuban	2.42
Dominican Republic	3.26
Mexican	3.44
Puerto Rican	2.92
South American	3.04
Chilean	2.88
Colombian	2.77
Ecuadorian	3.45
Peruvian	3.21
Venezuelan	2.54
Spaniard	2.48

Median Age

Group	Years
Total Population	33.4
Hispanic or Latino (of any race)	25.0
Central American, ex. Mexican	28.9
Costa Rican	28.6
Guatemalan	26.6
Honduran	24.8
Panamanian	28.5
Salvadoran	29.6
Cuban	27.4
Dominican Republic	27.6
Mexican	23.3
Puerto Rican	23.7
South American	32.6
Chilean	35.3
Colombian	34.6
Ecuadorian	31.5
Peruvian	34.0
Venezuelan	31.4
Spaniard	29.3

High School Graduates
(Universe: Population 25 Years and Over)

Group	Number	%
Total Population	95,795	84.0
Hispanic or Latino (of any race)	11,579	65.4
Central American, ex. Mexican	1,431	66.9
Salvadoran	809	63.5
Dominican Republic	1,680	67.9
Mexican	420	78.8
Puerto Rican	6,301	60.1
South American	1,261	90.7
Colombian	471	82.5

Four-Year College Graduates
(Universe: Population 25 Years and Over)

Group	Number	%
Total Population	33,758	29.6
Hispanic or Latino (of any race)	1,987	11.2
Central American, ex. Mexican	246	11.5
Salvadoran	19	1.5
Dominican Republic	300	12.1
Mexican	32	6.0
Puerto Rican	813	7.8
South American	400	28.8
Colombian	182	31.9

Population Age 3–17 Enrolled in Public School
(Universe: Population Age 3–17 Enrolled in School)

Group	Number	%
Total Population	25,941	85.7
Hispanic or Latino (of any race)	9,050	96.1
Central American, ex. Mexican	546	96.3
Salvadoran	336	94.1
Dominican Republic	1,422	95.4
Mexican	366	94.8
Puerto Rican	5,958	96.9
South American	419	88.4
Colombian	200	86.6

Population Age 3–17 Enrolled in Private School
(Universe: Population Age 3–17 Enrolled in School)

Group	Number	%
Total Population	4,335	14.3
Hispanic or Latino (of any race)	363	3.9
Central American, ex. Mexican	21	3.7
Salvadoran	21	5.9
Dominican Republic	69	4.6
Mexican	20	5.2
Puerto Rican	188	3.1
South American	55	11.6
Colombian	31	13.4

Foreign-Born Population

Group	Number	%
Total Population	35,304	19.6
Hispanic or Latino (of any race)	7,942	22.6
Central American, ex. Mexican	2,342	71.4
Salvadoran	1,359	68.9
Dominican Republic	3,114	66.0
Mexican	523	35.4
Puerto Rican	108	0.5
South American	1,405	59.6
Colombian	595	56.7

Foreign-Born Naturalized U.S. Citizens

Group	Number	%
Total Population	15,153	42.9
Hispanic or Latino (of any race)	3,163	39.8
Central American, ex. Mexican	869	37.1
Salvadoran	484	35.6
Dominican Republic	1,497	48.1
Mexican	128	24.5
Puerto Rican	28	25.9
South American	534	38.0
Colombian	357	60.0

Language Spoken at Home: English Only
(Universe: Population 5 Years and Over)

Group	Number	%
Total Population	114,142	67.6
Hispanic or Latino (of any race)	5,562	17.7
Central American, ex. Mexican	169	5.8

Notes: (1) Percent of total population; (2) Percent of Hispanic/Latino population; Profiles include places with an overall population of at least 125,000, OR an overall population of at least 25,000 where the Hispanic/Latino population is at least 20% of the overall population. In states where less than five places meet either of these criteria, we have included places with at least 10,000 total population with the highest percentage of Hispanic/Latino population. These places are identified with an asterisk (*); Please refer to the User's Guide for a full explanation of data.

Group	Number	%
Salvadoran	62	3.6
Dominican Republic	412	9.4
Mexican	643	48.4
Puerto Rican	3,759	19.4
South American	306	14.0
Colombian	170	17.3

Language Spoken at Home: Spanish
(Universe: Population 5 Years and Over)

Group	Number	%
Total Population	27,011	16.0
Hispanic or Latino (of any race)	25,791	82.0
Central American, ex. Mexican	2,727	94.2
Salvadoran	1,667	96.4
Dominican Republic	3,960	90.0
Mexican	686	51.6
Puerto Rican	15,600	80.6
South American	1,876	86.0
Colombian	815	82.7

Unemployment Rate
(Universe: Population 16 Years and Over)

Group	%
Total Population	8.9
Hispanic or Latino (of any race)	15.8
Central American, ex. Mexican	10.5
Salvadoran	9.0
Dominican Republic	10.8
Mexican	24.2
Puerto Rican	18.2
South American	11.6
Colombian	23.2

Class of Worker: Private Wage and Salary
(Universe: Civilian Employed Population 16 Years and Over)

Group	Number	%
Total Population	68,753	82.1
Hispanic or Latino (of any race)	10,504	88.4
Central American, ex. Mexican	1,635	95.6
Salvadoran	1,098	98.4
Dominican Republic	1,791	91.8
Mexican	429	95.5
Puerto Rican	5,167	84.4
South American	1,070	91.1
Colombian	311	78.9

Class of Worker: Government
(Universe: Civilian Employed Population 16 Years and Over)

Group	Number	%
Total Population	11,378	13.6
Hispanic or Latino (of any race)	1,150	9.7
Central American, ex. Mexican	23	1.3
Salvadoran	0	0.0
Dominican Republic	78	4.0
Mexican	10	2.2
Puerto Rican	907	14.8
South American	91	7.7
Colombian	69	17.5

Means of Transportation to Work: Car, Truck or Van
(Universe: Workers 16 Years and Over)

Group	Number	%
Total Population	70,073	85.9
Hispanic or Latino (of any race)	9,459	81.2
Central American, ex. Mexican	1,523	89.4
Salvadoran	1,016	91.0
Dominican Republic	1,570	82.2
Mexican	351	80.0
Puerto Rican	4,816	80.7
South American	876	75.7
Colombian	351	89.1

Means of Transportation to Work: Public Transportation (ex. Taxicab)
(Universe: Workers 16 Years and Over)

Group	Number	%
Total Population	2,613	3.2
Hispanic or Latino (of any race)	793	6.8
Central American, ex. Mexican	95	5.6
Salvadoran	83	7.4
Dominican Republic	54	2.8
Mexican	32	7.3
Puerto Rican	402	6.7
South American	198	17.1
Colombian	13	3.3

Homeownership Rate
(Universe: Occupied Housing Units)

Group	%
Total Population	44.5
Hispanic or Latino (of any race)	17.9
Central American, ex. Mexican	30.3
Costa Rican	40.0
Guatemalan	23.9
Honduran	9.8
Panamanian	21.7
Salvadoran	33.1
Cuban	23.8
Dominican Republic	17.6
Mexican	25.3
Puerto Rican	13.3
South American	41.1
Chilean	68.8
Colombian	41.3
Ecuadorian	35.4
Peruvian	43.8
Venezuelan	51.4
Spaniard	29.0

Median Home Value

Group	Dollars
Total Population	242,800
Hispanic or Latino (of any race)	238,300
Central American, ex. Mexican	221,400
Salvadoran	233,200
Dominican Republic	234,100
Mexican	277,100
Puerto Rican	240,900
South American	233,900
Colombian	217,500

Median Gross Rent

Group	Dollars
Total Population	861
Hispanic or Latino (of any race)	767
Central American, ex. Mexican	930
Salvadoran	935
Dominican Republic	825
Mexican	930
Puerto Rican	695
South American	847
Colombian	999

Median Household Income
(2010 Inflation-Adjusted Dollars)

Group	Dollars
Total Population	45,036
Hispanic or Latino (of any race)	22,213
Central American, ex. Mexican	49,203
Salvadoran	48,388
Dominican Republic	28,181
Mexican	31,354
Puerto Rican	18,007
South American	44,459
Colombian	65,653

Per Capita Income
(2010 Inflation-Adjusted Dollars)

Group	Dollars
Total Population	24,326
Hispanic or Latino (of any race)	12,329
Central American, ex. Mexican	16,171
Salvadoran	17,228
Dominican Republic	12,845
Mexican	11,245
Puerto Rican	10,694
South American	18,921
Colombian	18,498

Households with $100,000+ Income

Group	Number	%
Total Population	11,694	16.6
Hispanic or Latino (of any race)	693	6.2
Central American, ex. Mexican	130	12.9
Salvadoran	84	13.6
Dominican Republic	69	4.6
Mexican	87	26.8
Puerto Rican	226	3.2
South American	108	14.6
Colombian	46	14.5

Households with Food Stamps/SNAP Benefits During Past 12 Months

Group	Number	%
Total Population	11,489	16.3
Hispanic or Latino (of any race)	5,023	45.1
Central American, ex. Mexican	119	11.8
Salvadoran	80	12.9
Dominican Republic	739	49.7
Mexican	65	20.0
Puerto Rican	3,859	54.4
South American	55	7.4
Colombian	28	8.8

Poverty Rate
(Income in Past 12 Months Below Poverty Level)

Group	%
Total Population	18.3
Hispanic or Latino (of any race)	40.5
Central American, ex. Mexican	20.7
Salvadoran	20.6
Dominican Republic	31.6
Mexican	19.4
Puerto Rican	49.8
South American	17.1
Colombian	9.0

Notes: (1) Percent of total population; (2) Percent of Hispanic/Latino population; Profiles include places with an overall population of at least 125,000, OR an overall population of at least 25,000 where the Hispanic/Latino population is at least 20% of the overall population. In states where less than five places meet either of these criteria, we have included places with at least 10,000 total population with the highest percentage of Hispanic/Latino population. These places are identified with an asterisk (*); Please refer to the User's Guide for a full explanation of data.

Michigan

EDITOR'S NOTE: For a place to be included in this edition, it must meet one of two criteria. Either its overall population is at least 125,000, OR its overall population is at least 25,000 and its Hispanic/Latino population is at least 20% of the overall population. For the state of Michigan, the following locations are included:

- Detroit
- Grand Rapids
- Holland (charter township)
- Holland (city)
- Sterling Heights
- Warren

Section Two: State & Place Profiles starts with the state profile, followed by place profiles that meet the criteria above. Places are listed alphabetically within each state. All states, all counties and places that meet the above criteria are ranked and compared in *Section Three: Rankings & Comparisons*, on page 1055.

For a more detailed look at the Hispanic/Latino population in Michigan, a companion web site is available at no additional charge with purchase of this print edition. Visit http://gold.greyhouse.com/page/info_hispanic for more information.

The web site includes data for all counties and places in Michigan with Hispanic/Latino population, plus ten additional topics: Self Employed Worker; Walked to Work; Worked from Home; Mean Travel Time to Work; Mean Household Income; Households with Cash Public Assistance; Mean Cash Pubic Assistance; Poverty Rates for 18 and Under, 18 to 64, and 65 and Over.

Population

Group	Number	%TP[1]	%HP[2]
Total Population	9,883,640	100.0	–
Hispanic or Latino (of any race)	436,358	4.4	100.0
Central American, ex. Mexican	17,785	0.2	4.1
Costa Rican	903	<0.1	0.2
Guatemalan	8,428	0.1	1.9
Honduran	2,694	<0.1	0.6
Nicaraguan	870	<0.1	0.2
Panamanian	1,359	<0.1	0.3
Salvadoran	3,401	<0.1	0.8
Cuban	9,922	0.1	2.3
Dominican Republic	5,012	0.1	1.1
Mexican	317,903	3.2	72.9
Puerto Rican	37,267	0.4	8.5
South American	13,243	0.1	3.0
Argentinean	2,113	<0.1	0.5
Bolivian	512	<0.1	0.1
Chilean	1,160	<0.1	0.3
Colombian	3,991	<0.1	0.9
Ecuadorian	1,312	<0.1	0.3
Paraguayan	225	<0.1	0.1
Peruvian	2,040	<0.1	0.5
Uruguayan	224	<0.1	0.1
Venezuelan	1,496	<0.1	0.3
Spaniard	7,009	0.1	1.6

Population Growth: 2000–2010

Group	%
Total Population	-0.6
Hispanic or Latino (of any race)	34.7
Central American, ex. Mexican	147.4
Costa Rican	66.0
Guatemalan	175.5
Honduran	159.8
Nicaraguan	112.7
Panamanian	78.3
Salvadoran	199.4
Cuban	37.4
Dominican Republic	124.2
Mexican	44.0
Puerto Rican	38.3
South American	92.8
Argentinean	96.6
Bolivian	146.2
Chilean	75.8
Colombian	90.7
Ecuadorian	151.3
Paraguayan	97.4
Peruvian	121.0
Venezuelan	72.5
Spaniard	686.6

Males per 100 Females

Group	Number
Total Population	96.3
Hispanic or Latino (of any race)	103.5
Central American, ex. Mexican	108.6
Costa Rican	80.2
Guatemalan	120.9
Honduran	102.4
Nicaraguan	96.8
Panamanian	69.7
Salvadoran	116.2
Cuban	105.5
Dominican Republic	92.9
Mexican	105.1
Puerto Rican	98.2
South American	88.2
Argentinean	96.6
Bolivian	97.7
Chilean	93.0
Colombian	80.3
Ecuadorian	101.2
Paraguayan	87.5
Peruvian	84.8
Uruguayan	88.2
Venezuelan	86.1
Spaniard	93.8

Average Household Size

Group	People
Total Population	2.49
Hispanic or Latino (of any race)	3.23
Central American, ex. Mexican	3.68
Costa Rican	2.72
Guatemalan	4.35
Honduran	3.55
Nicaraguan	2.83
Panamanian	2.60
Salvadoran	3.64
Cuban	2.67
Dominican Republic	3.19
Mexican	3.35
Puerto Rican	2.96
South American	2.63
Argentinean	2.66
Bolivian	2.82
Chilean	2.69
Colombian	2.55
Ecuadorian	2.63
Paraguayan	2.37
Peruvian	2.62
Uruguayan	2.60
Venezuelan	2.71
Spaniard	2.57

Median Age

Group	Years
Total Population	38.9
Hispanic or Latino (of any race)	24.0
Central American, ex. Mexican	24.6
Costa Rican	29.2
Guatemalan	20.6
Honduran	26.6
Nicaraguan	29.0
Panamanian	30.9
Salvadoran	28.6
Cuban	29.8
Dominican Republic	25.1
Mexican	23.3
Puerto Rican	23.2
South American	31.2
Argentinean	36.9
Bolivian	24.6
Chilean	30.4
Colombian	29.7
Ecuadorian	27.3
Paraguayan	21.7
Peruvian	32.1
Uruguayan	35.0
Venezuelan	32.2
Spaniard	32.9

High School Graduates
(Universe: Population 25 Years and Over)

Group	Number	%
Total Population	5,776,855	88.0
Hispanic or Latino (of any race)	138,029	67.1
Central American, ex. Mexican	4,338	54.2
Costa Rican	328	84.8
Guatemalan	1,338	37.0
Honduran	688	66.4
Nicaraguan	452	95.0
Panamanian	669	92.1
Salvadoran	735	46.1
Cuban	4,769	86.2
Dominican Republic	1,131	81.5
Mexican	94,533	63.4
Puerto Rican	13,353	74.9
South American	6,892	92.9
Argentinean	1,468	93.9
Chilean	591	98.0
Colombian	1,663	89.3
Ecuadorian	646	98.8
Peruvian	1,353	96.6
Venezuelan	559	81.5
Spaniard	3,896	91.2

Four-Year College Graduates
(Universe: Population 25 Years and Over)

Group	Number	%
Total Population	1,641,383	25.0
Hispanic or Latino (of any race)	30,547	14.9
Central American, ex. Mexican	1,227	15.3
Costa Rican	112	28.9
Guatemalan	293	8.1
Honduran	151	14.6
Nicaraguan	271	56.9
Panamanian	205	28.2
Salvadoran	113	7.1
Cuban	1,794	32.4
Dominican Republic	327	23.6
Mexican	15,931	10.7
Puerto Rican	3,342	18.7
South American	3,886	52.4
Argentinean	958	61.3
Chilean	254	42.1
Colombian	1,051	56.4
Ecuadorian	281	43.0
Peruvian	526	37.5
Venezuelan	428	62.4
Spaniard	1,670	39.1

Population Age 3–17 Enrolled in Public School
(Universe: Population Age 3–17 Enrolled in School)

Group	Number	%
Total Population	1,645,770	88.1
Hispanic or Latino (of any race)	109,820	91.3
Central American, ex. Mexican	3,890	83.1
Costa Rican	208	93.7
Guatemalan	2,130	79.1
Honduran	490	95.5
Nicaraguan	210	91.7
Panamanian	368	96.3
Salvadoran	411	77.5
Cuban	1,888	89.4
Dominican Republic	677	76.5
Mexican	83,999	92.6
Puerto Rican	8,906	89.9
South American	2,116	80.2
Argentinean	206	73.0

Notes: (1) Percent of total population; (2) Percent of Hispanic/Latino population; Profiles include places with an overall population of at least 125,000, OR an overall population of at least 25,000 where the Hispanic/Latino population is at least 20% of the overall population. In states where less than five places meet either of these criteria, we have included places with at least 10,000 total population with the highest percentage of Hispanic/Latino population. These places are identified with an asterisk (*); Please refer to the User's Guide for a full explanation of data.

Chilean	260	82.8
Colombian	602	74.0
Ecuadorian	285	96.6
Peruvian	251	83.4
Venezuelan	216	74.7
Spaniard	1,599	86.2

Population Age 3–17 Enrolled in Private School
(Universe: Population Age 3–17 Enrolled in School)

Group	Number	%
Total Population	222,360	11.9
Hispanic or Latino (of any race)	10,490	8.7
Central American, ex. Mexican	790	16.9
Costa Rican	14	6.3
Guatemalan	563	20.9
Honduran	23	4.5
Nicaraguan	19	8.3
Panamanian	14	3.7
Salvadoran	119	22.5
Cuban	223	10.6
Dominican Republic	208	23.5
Mexican	6,677	7.4
Puerto Rican	999	10.1
South American	524	19.8
Argentinean	76	27.0
Chilean	54	17.2
Colombian	211	26.0
Ecuadorian	10	3.4
Peruvian	50	16.6
Venezuelan	73	25.3
Spaniard	256	13.8

Foreign-Born Population

Group	Number	%
Total Population	591,534	5.9
Hispanic or Latino (of any race)	107,312	25.3
Central American, ex. Mexican	10,145	59.8
Costa Rican	474	56.0
Guatemalan	5,672	64.9
Honduran	1,191	59.9
Nicaraguan	353	44.6
Panamanian	476	33.5
Salvadoran	1,803	63.1
Cuban	3,830	40.0
Dominican Republic	1,386	45.3
Mexican	79,403	25.3
Puerto Rican	291	0.8
South American	7,129	57.5
Argentinean	1,499	65.5
Chilean	625	52.3
Colombian	1,814	55.2
Ecuadorian	577	51.7
Peruvian	1,320	65.6
Venezuelan	667	51.9
Spaniard	1,214	15.9

Foreign-Born Naturalized U.S. Citizens

Group	Number	%
Total Population	286,257	48.4
Hispanic or Latino (of any race)	24,548	22.9
Central American, ex. Mexican	2,728	26.9
Costa Rican	191	40.3
Guatemalan	1,488	26.2
Honduran	288	24.2
Nicaraguan	132	37.4
Panamanian	250	52.5
Salvadoran	306	17.0
Cuban	1,603	41.9
Dominican Republic	673	48.6
Mexican	14,102	17.8
Puerto Rican	131	45.0
South American	3,504	49.2
Argentinean	532	35.5
Chilean	287	45.9
Colombian	844	46.5
Ecuadorian	265	45.9
Peruvian	846	64.1
Venezuelan	287	43.0
Spaniard	450	37.1

Language Spoken at Home: English Only
(Universe: Population 5 Years and Over)

Group	Number	%
Total Population	8,507,947	91.1
Hispanic or Latino (of any race)	169,378	45.5
Central American, ex. Mexican	3,613	25.0
Costa Rican	182	24.8
Guatemalan	1,565	22.4
Honduran	330	18.1
Nicaraguan	308	41.0
Panamanian	758	57.6
Salvadoran	324	12.8
Cuban	3,807	43.0
Dominican Republic	698	25.8
Mexican	123,917	45.2
Puerto Rican	15,259	48.1
South American	3,604	32.3
Argentinean	437	22.4
Chilean	357	35.8
Colombian	1,151	38.1
Ecuadorian	250	24.7
Peruvian	489	26.0
Venezuelan	412	37.1
Spaniard	5,038	71.4

Language Spoken at Home: Spanish
(Universe: Population 5 Years and Over)

Group	Number	%
Total Population	274,586	2.9
Hispanic or Latino (of any race)	200,269	53.8
Central American, ex. Mexican	10,708	74.1
Costa Rican	553	75.2
Guatemalan	5,303	76.0
Honduran	1,491	81.9
Nicaraguan	430	57.3
Panamanian	559	42.4
Salvadoran	2,217	87.2
Cuban	4,924	55.7
Dominican Republic	1,982	73.2
Mexican	148,991	54.4
Puerto Rican	16,400	51.7
South American	7,349	65.9
Argentinean	1,439	73.9
Chilean	623	62.6
Colombian	1,816	60.1
Ecuadorian	762	75.3
Peruvian	1,391	73.9
Venezuelan	675	60.8
Spaniard	1,816	25.7

Unemployment Rate
(Universe: Population 16 Years and Over)

Group	%
Total Population	11.5
Hispanic or Latino (of any race)	15.1
Central American, ex. Mexican	12.7
Costa Rican	15.8
Guatemalan	14.0
Honduran	9.7
Nicaraguan	16.3
Panamanian	8.2
Salvadoran	11.9
Cuban	14.6
Dominican Republic	14.8
Mexican	15.3
Puerto Rican	18.7
South American	8.3
Argentinean	7.2
Chilean	3.1
Colombian	9.5
Ecuadorian	14.3
Peruvian	6.4
Venezuelan	6.5
Spaniard	13.1

Class of Worker: Private Wage and Salary
(Universe: Civilian Employed Population 16 Years and Over)

Group	Number	%
Total Population	3,593,359	82.2
Hispanic or Latino (of any race)	139,044	87.6
Central American, ex. Mexican	6,443	89.1
Costa Rican	246	68.7
Guatemalan	2,896	93.9
Honduran	879	95.4
Nicaraguan	261	76.8
Panamanian	511	80.1
Salvadoran	1,534	88.4
Cuban	3,309	81.6
Dominican Republic	1,015	87.4
Mexican	103,403	88.9
Puerto Rican	10,151	84.5
South American	4,722	82.6
Argentinean	918	81.8
Chilean	379	85.9
Colombian	1,197	86.6
Ecuadorian	471	91.1
Peruvian	868	72.7
Venezuelan	511	90.6
Spaniard	2,475	78.4

Class of Worker: Government
(Universe: Civilian Employed Population 16 Years and Over)

Group	Number	%
Total Population	530,927	12.1
Hispanic or Latino (of any race)	13,397	8.4
Central American, ex. Mexican	394	5.4
Costa Rican	37	10.3
Guatemalan	58	1.9
Honduran	20	2.2
Nicaraguan	77	22.6
Panamanian	123	19.3
Salvadoran	58	3.3
Cuban	551	13.6
Dominican Republic	84	7.2
Mexican	8,763	7.5
Puerto Rican	1,391	11.6
South American	729	12.8
Argentinean	107	9.5
Chilean	62	14.1
Colombian	126	9.1
Ecuadorian	33	6.4
Peruvian	245	20.5
Venezuelan	46	8.2
Spaniard	524	16.6

Means of Transportation to Work: Car, Truck or Van
(Universe: Workers 16 Years and Over)

Group	Number	%
Total Population	3,907,914	91.8
Hispanic or Latino (of any race)	138,658	89.8
Central American, ex. Mexican	6,450	92.0
Costa Rican	246	75.5
Guatemalan	2,715	91.2
Honduran	866	99.5
Nicaraguan	307	99.0
Panamanian	587	92.0
Salvadoran	1,585	91.6
Cuban	3,635	90.9
Dominican Republic	1,041	91.6
Mexican	101,153	89.5
Puerto Rican	10,661	90.4
South American	4,995	89.0
Argentinean	974	90.4
Chilean	398	90.2
Colombian	1,248	89.2
Ecuadorian	379	76.0
Peruvian	1,047	89.3
Venezuelan	530	94.3
Spaniard	2,798	90.8

Means of Transportation to Work: Public Transportation (ex. Taxicab)
(Universe: Workers 16 Years and Over)

Group	Number	%
Total Population	53,244	1.3
Hispanic or Latino (of any race)	2,284	1.5
Central American, ex. Mexican	111	1.6
Costa Rican	0	0.0
Guatemalan	66	2.2
Honduran	0	0.0
Nicaraguan	0	0.0
Panamanian	23	3.6
Salvadoran	22	1.3
Cuban	0	0.0
Dominican Republic	0	0.0
Mexican	1,625	1.4
Puerto Rican	139	1.2
South American	167	3.0
Argentinean	31	2.9
Chilean	0	0.0
Colombian	0	0.0
Ecuadorian	59	11.8
Peruvian	67	5.7
Venezuelan	10	1.8

Notes: (1) Percent of total population; (2) Percent of Hispanic/Latino population; Profiles include places with an overall population of at least 125,000, OR an overall population of at least 25,000 where the Hispanic/Latino population is at least 20% of the overall population. In states where less than five places meet either of these criteria, we have included places with at least 10,000 total population with the highest percentage of Hispanic/Latino population. These places are identified with an asterisk (*); Please refer to the User's Guide for a full explanation of data.

Spaniard	104	3.4

Homeownership Rate
(Universe: Occupied Housing Units)

Group	%
Total Population	72.1
Hispanic or Latino (of any race)	56.2
Central American, ex. Mexican	44.6
Costa Rican	61.7
Guatemalan	35.7
Honduran	41.9
Nicaraguan	52.4
Panamanian	56.9
Salvadoran	49.6
Cuban	54.8
Dominican Republic	47.2
Mexican	57.6
Puerto Rican	48.7
South American	62.8
Argentinean	72.8
Bolivian	77.4
Chilean	62.0
Colombian	58.7
Ecuadorian	56.2
Paraguayan	47.6
Peruvian	59.4
Uruguayan	65.1
Venezuelan	64.1
Spaniard	70.0

Median Home Value

Group	Dollars
Total Population	144,200
Hispanic or Latino (of any race)	109,600
Central American, ex. Mexican	104,500
Costa Rican	190,200
Guatemalan	104,400
Honduran	49,300
Nicaraguan	120,000
Panamanian	107,000
Salvadoran	98,800
Cuban	148,000
Dominican Republic	98,800
Mexican	101,900
Puerto Rican	114,100
South American	186,200
Argentinean	221,200
Chilean	187,900
Colombian	174,700
Ecuadorian	114,400
Peruvian	185,200
Venezuelan	192,900
Spaniard	164,400

Median Gross Rent

Group	Dollars
Total Population	723
Hispanic or Latino (of any race)	715
Central American, ex. Mexican	727
Costa Rican	835
Guatemalan	699
Honduran	713
Nicaraguan	750
Panamanian	747
Salvadoran	700
Cuban	620
Dominican Republic	618
Mexican	713
Puerto Rican	744
South American	804
Argentinean	803
Chilean	651
Colombian	641
Ecuadorian	876
Peruvian	908
Venezuelan	825
Spaniard	710

Median Household Income
(2010 Inflation-Adjusted Dollars)

Group	Dollars
Total Population	48,432
Hispanic or Latino (of any race)	38,175
Central American, ex. Mexican	36,308
Costa Rican	36,211
Guatemalan	30,299
Honduran	36,453
Nicaraguan	71,413
Panamanian	61,458
Salvadoran	38,681
Cuban	43,369
Dominican Republic	28,125
Mexican	37,014
Puerto Rican	38,385
South American	52,554
Argentinean	52,309
Chilean	67,957
Colombian	52,788
Ecuadorian	39,500
Peruvian	54,792
Venezuelan	65,139
Spaniard	54,395

Per Capita Income
(2010 Inflation-Adjusted Dollars)

Group	Dollars
Total Population	25,135
Hispanic or Latino (of any race)	14,564
Central American, ex. Mexican	13,207
Costa Rican	12,533
Guatemalan	9,591
Honduran	12,360
Nicaraguan	23,538
Panamanian	22,517
Salvadoran	16,930
Cuban	20,165
Dominican Republic	11,903
Mexican	13,493
Puerto Rican	15,814
South American	31,427
Argentinean	46,541
Chilean	28,373
Colombian	27,832
Ecuadorian	21,475
Peruvian	32,978
Venezuelan	23,858
Spaniard	21,571

Households with $100,000+ Income

Group	Number	%
Total Population	673,242	17.5
Hispanic or Latino (of any race)	12,568	11.3
Central American, ex. Mexican	466	10.8
Costa Rican	27	14.6
Guatemalan	184	9.5
Honduran	83	15.9
Nicaraguan	29	12.1
Panamanian	92	23.9
Salvadoran	43	4.8
Cuban	498	16.3
Dominican Republic	30	3.8
Mexican	8,014	10.1
Puerto Rican	1,244	12.7
South American	986	25.8
Argentinean	302	32.8
Chilean	50	23.0
Colombian	248	28.9
Ecuadorian	47	11.5
Peruvian	165	21.4
Venezuelan	66	18.3
Spaniard	556	20.0

Households with Food Stamps/SNAP Benefits During Past 12 Months

Group	Number	%
Total Population	484,952	12.6
Hispanic or Latino (of any race)	25,218	22.7
Central American, ex. Mexican	588	13.7
Costa Rican	17	9.2
Guatemalan	426	22.0
Honduran	31	5.9
Nicaraguan	6	2.5
Panamanian	40	10.4
Salvadoran	68	7.6
Cuban	583	19.1
Dominican Republic	302	37.8
Mexican	18,776	23.7
Puerto Rican	2,835	28.9
South American	347	9.1
Argentinean	30	3.3
Chilean	19	8.8
Colombian	49	5.7
Ecuadorian	110	27.0
Peruvian	84	10.9
Venezuelan	55	15.3
Spaniard	414	14.9

Poverty Rate
(Income in Past 12 Months Below Poverty Level)

Group	%
Total Population	14.8
Hispanic or Latino (of any race)	26.5
Central American, ex. Mexican	24.5
Costa Rican	19.1
Guatemalan	34.2
Honduran	21.8
Nicaraguan	13.8
Panamanian	10.0
Salvadoran	10.5
Cuban	22.2
Dominican Republic	29.3
Mexican	27.2
Puerto Rican	29.4
South American	12.3
Argentinean	19.8
Chilean	7.4
Colombian	11.3
Ecuadorian	7.9
Peruvian	8.4
Venezuelan	13.2
Spaniard	18.3

Detroit

Population

Group	Number	%TP[1]	%HP[2]
Total Population	713,777	100.0	–
Hispanic or Latino (of any race)	48,679	6.8	100.0
Central American, ex. Mexican	1,813	0.3	3.7
Guatemalan	542	0.1	1.1
Honduran	566	0.1	1.2
Panamanian	124	<0.1	0.3
Salvadoran	451	0.1	0.9
Cuban	773	0.1	1.6
Dominican Republic	688	0.1	1.4
Mexican	36,452	5.1	74.9
Puerto Rican	5,783	0.8	11.9
South American	337	<0.1	0.7
Colombian	101	<0.1	0.2
Spaniard	174	<0.1	0.4

Population Growth: 2000–2010

Group	%
Total Population	-25.0
Hispanic or Latino (of any race)	3.2
Central American, ex. Mexican	108.6
Guatemalan	194.6
Honduran	173.4
Salvadoran	95.2
Cuban	-11.3
Dominican Republic	78.2
Mexican	10.0
Puerto Rican	-12.6
South American	17.0
Colombian	-22.9

Males per 100 Females

Group	Number
Total Population	89.8
Hispanic or Latino (of any race)	108.3
Central American, ex. Mexican	126.9
Guatemalan	144.1
Honduran	134.9
Panamanian	55.0
Salvadoran	134.9
Cuban	126.7
Dominican Republic	96.0
Mexican	109.6
Puerto Rican	95.8
South American	111.9
Colombian	94.2
Spaniard	81.3

Notes: (1) Percent of total population; (2) Percent of Hispanic/Latino population; Profiles include places with an overall population of at least 125,000, OR an overall population of at least 25,000 where the Hispanic/Latino population is at least 20% of the overall population. In states where less than five places meet either of these criteria, we have included places with at least 10,000 total population with the highest percentage of Hispanic/Latino population. These places are identified with an asterisk (*); Please refer to the User's Guide for a full explanation of data.

Average Household Size

Group	People
Total Population	2.59
Hispanic or Latino (of any race)	3.66
Central American, ex. Mexican	4.03
Guatemalan	5.08
Honduran	4.23
Panamanian	2.44
Salvadoran	3.98
Cuban	2.21
Dominican Republic	3.40
Mexican	3.88
Puerto Rican	3.10
South American	2.19
Colombian	2.17
Spaniard	2.29

Median Age

Group	Years
Total Population	34.8
Hispanic or Latino (of any race)	25.1
Central American, ex. Mexican	28.2
Guatemalan	25.0
Honduran	26.8
Panamanian	42.0
Salvadoran	31.3
Cuban	33.6
Dominican Republic	30.1
Mexican	24.4
Puerto Rican	24.7
South American	33.3
Colombian	37.3
Spaniard	33.5

High School Graduates
(Universe: Population 25 Years and Over)

Group	Number	%
Total Population	356,831	76.8
Hispanic or Latino (of any race)	10,395	43.9
Central American, ex. Mexican	397	42.6
Mexican	6,970	39.2
Puerto Rican	1,656	61.7

Four-Year College Graduates
(Universe: Population 25 Years and Over)

Group	Number	%
Total Population	54,808	11.8
Hispanic or Latino (of any race)	1,202	5.1
Central American, ex. Mexican	58	6.2
Mexican	685	3.9
Puerto Rican	182	6.8

Population Age 3–17 Enrolled in Public School
(Universe: Population Age 3–17 Enrolled in School)

Group	Number	%
Total Population	154,323	92.9
Hispanic or Latino (of any race)	13,533	95.2
Central American, ex. Mexican	259	100.0
Mexican	10,502	96.5
Puerto Rican	1,500	86.8

Population Age 3–17 Enrolled in Private School
(Universe: Population Age 3–17 Enrolled in School)

Group	Number	%
Total Population	11,752	7.1
Hispanic or Latino (of any race)	675	4.8
Central American, ex. Mexican	0	0.0
Mexican	385	3.5
Puerto Rican	228	13.2

Foreign-Born Population

Group	Number	%
Total Population	38,435	5.1
Hispanic or Latino (of any race)	19,076	39.0
Central American, ex. Mexican	1,268	79.2
Mexican	16,189	43.9
Puerto Rican	34	0.6

Foreign-Born Naturalized U.S. Citizens

Group	Number	%
Total Population	11,617	30.2
Hispanic or Latino (of any race)	2,935	15.4
Central American, ex. Mexican	68	5.4
Mexican	2,465	15.2
Puerto Rican	34	100.0

Language Spoken at Home: English Only
(Universe: Population 5 Years and Over)

Group	Number	%
Total Population	641,155	90.8
Hispanic or Latino (of any race)	9,208	21.6
Central American, ex. Mexican	142	9.5
Mexican	5,934	18.6
Puerto Rican	1,514	30.8

Language Spoken at Home: Spanish
(Universe: Population 5 Years and Over)

Group	Number	%
Total Population	41,094	5.8
Hispanic or Latino (of any race)	33,160	78.0
Central American, ex. Mexican	1,351	90.5
Mexican	25,817	81.0
Puerto Rican	3,396	69.1

Unemployment Rate
(Universe: Population 16 Years and Over)

Group	%
Total Population	24.8
Hispanic or Latino (of any race)	19.0
Central American, ex. Mexican	8.9
Mexican	17.9
Puerto Rican	24.9

Class of Worker: Private Wage and Salary
(Universe: Civilian Employed Population 16 Years and Over)

Group	Number	%
Total Population	190,232	80.7
Hispanic or Latino (of any race)	14,310	90.5
Central American, ex. Mexican	847	94.3
Mexican	11,191	92.1
Puerto Rican	1,145	80.9

Class of Worker: Government
(Universe: Civilian Employed Population 16 Years and Over)

Group	Number	%
Total Population	34,854	14.8
Hispanic or Latino (of any race)	724	4.6
Central American, ex. Mexican	8	0.9
Mexican	497	4.1
Puerto Rican	80	5.7

Means of Transportation to Work: Car, Truck or Van
(Universe: Workers 16 Years and Over)

Group	Number	%
Total Population	192,353	84.4
Hispanic or Latino (of any race)	13,986	90.2
Central American, ex. Mexican	848	96.1
Mexican	10,791	90.8
Puerto Rican	1,219	86.6

Means of Transportation to Work: Public Transportation (ex. Taxicab)
(Universe: Workers 16 Years and Over)

Group	Number	%
Total Population	18,122	7.9
Hispanic or Latino (of any race)	379	2.4
Central American, ex. Mexican	8	0.9
Mexican	307	2.6
Puerto Rican	20	1.4

Homeownership Rate
(Universe: Occupied Housing Units)

Group	%
Total Population	51.1
Hispanic or Latino (of any race)	48.5
Central American, ex. Mexican	37.8
Guatemalan	31.3
Honduran	28.0
Panamanian	48.0
Salvadoran	45.8
Cuban	37.6
Dominican Republic	56.7
Mexican	51.3
Puerto Rican	41.6
South American	43.5
Colombian	54.3
Spaniard	55.4

Median Home Value

Group	Dollars
Total Population	80,400
Hispanic or Latino (of any race)	73,900
Central American, ex. Mexican	75,800
Mexican	73,000
Puerto Rican	74,300

Median Gross Rent

Group	Dollars
Total Population	747
Hispanic or Latino (of any race)	705
Central American, ex. Mexican	685
Mexican	689
Puerto Rican	687

Median Household Income
(2010 Inflation-Adjusted Dollars)

Group	Dollars
Total Population	28,357
Hispanic or Latino (of any race)	29,109
Central American, ex. Mexican	40,288
Mexican	29,688
Puerto Rican	22,250

Per Capita Income
(2010 Inflation-Adjusted Dollars)

Group	Dollars
Total Population	15,062
Hispanic or Latino (of any race)	10,378
Central American, ex. Mexican	17,095
Mexican	10,237
Puerto Rican	9,833

Households with $100,000+ Income

Group	Number	%
Total Population	17,691	6.5
Hispanic or Latino (of any race)	678	5.4
Central American, ex. Mexican	40	9.1
Mexican	567	6.2
Puerto Rican	47	2.9

Households with Food Stamps/SNAP Benefits During Past 12 Months

Group	Number	%
Total Population	85,433	31.5
Hispanic or Latino (of any race)	3,739	29.9
Central American, ex. Mexican	77	17.5
Mexican	2,515	27.6
Puerto Rican	710	44.4

Poverty Rate
(Income in Past 12 Months Below Poverty Level)

Group	%
Total Population	34.5
Hispanic or Latino (of any race)	36.7
Central American, ex. Mexican	19.2
Mexican	35.2
Puerto Rican	49.4

Grand Rapids

Population

Group	Number	%TP[1]	%HP[2]
Total Population	188,040	100.0	–
Hispanic or Latino (of any race)	29,261	15.6	100.0
Central American, ex. Mexican	4,051	2.2	13.8
Guatemalan	3,372	1.8	11.5
Honduran	197	0.1	0.7
Salvadoran	348	0.2	1.2
Cuban	417	0.2	1.4
Dominican Republic	1,342	0.7	4.6
Mexican	18,698	9.9	63.9
Puerto Rican	2,712	1.4	9.3
South American	337	0.2	1.2
Spaniard	166	0.1	0.6

Population Growth: 2000–2010

Group	%
Total Population	-4.9
Hispanic or Latino (of any race)	13.3
Central American, ex. Mexican	84.9
Guatemalan	91.4
Honduran	60.2

Notes: (1) Percent of total population; (2) Percent of Hispanic/Latino population; Profiles include places with an overall population of at least 125,000, OR an overall population of at least 25,000 where the Hispanic/Latino population is at least 20% of the overall population. In states where less than five places meet either of these criteria, we have included places with at least 10,000 total population with the highest percentage of Hispanic/Latino population. These places are identified with an asterisk (*); Please refer to the User's Guide for a full explanation of data.

Salvadoran	75.8
Cuban	-1.9
Dominican Republic	55.5
Mexican	12.6
Puerto Rican	16.3
South American	92.6

Males per 100 Females

Group	Number
Total Population	94.9
Hispanic or Latino (of any race)	106.9
Central American, ex. Mexican	123.8
Guatemalan	134.3
Honduran	82.4
Salvadoran	85.1
Cuban	124.2
Dominican Republic	83.8
Mexican	107.0
Puerto Rican	101.0
South American	71.9
Spaniard	84.4

Average Household Size

Group	People
Total Population	2.49
Hispanic or Latino (of any race)	3.92
Central American, ex. Mexican	4.84
Guatemalan	5.16
Honduran	3.72
Salvadoran	3.89
Cuban	2.51
Dominican Republic	3.46
Mexican	4.03
Puerto Rican	3.16
South American	2.58
Spaniard	2.69

Median Age

Group	Years
Total Population	30.8
Hispanic or Latino (of any race)	22.4
Central American, ex. Mexican	24.8
Guatemalan	24.4
Honduran	24.3
Salvadoran	30.0
Cuban	26.5
Dominican Republic	27.0
Mexican	21.5
Puerto Rican	22.1
South American	28.6
Spaniard	28.2

High School Graduates
(Universe: Population 25 Years and Over)

Group	Number	%
Total Population	95,212	82.6
Hispanic or Latino (of any race)	6,146	44.2
Central American, ex. Mexican	351	18.3
Guatemalan	213	13.3
Dominican Republic	383	78.6
Mexican	4,062	43.3
Puerto Rican	665	56.4

Four-Year College Graduates
(Universe: Population 25 Years and Over)

Group	Number	%
Total Population	31,971	27.7
Hispanic or Latino (of any race)	951	6.8
Central American, ex. Mexican	62	3.2
Guatemalan	62	3.9
Dominican Republic	118	24.2
Mexican	356	3.8
Puerto Rican	83	7.0

Population Age 3–17 Enrolled in Public School
(Universe: Population Age 3–17 Enrolled in School)

Group	Number	%
Total Population	26,899	77.1
Hispanic or Latino (of any race)	8,062	89.3
Central American, ex. Mexican	848	92.9
Guatemalan	756	95.6
Dominican Republic	260	70.3
Mexican	5,770	88.8
Puerto Rican	790	96.0

Population Age 3–17 Enrolled in Private School
(Universe: Population Age 3–17 Enrolled in School)

Group	Number	%
Total Population	7,994	22.9
Hispanic or Latino (of any race)	967	10.7
Central American, ex. Mexican	65	7.1
Guatemalan	35	4.4
Dominican Republic	110	29.7
Mexican	726	11.2
Puerto Rican	33	4.0

Foreign-Born Population

Group	Number	%
Total Population	20,443	10.7
Hispanic or Latino (of any race)	12,703	41.7
Central American, ex. Mexican	2,362	63.1
Guatemalan	2,012	63.1
Dominican Republic	515	52.2
Mexican	9,217	43.1
Puerto Rican	83	3.3

Foreign-Born Naturalized U.S. Citizens

Group	Number	%
Total Population	5,949	29.1
Hispanic or Latino (of any race)	2,217	17.5
Central American, ex. Mexican	298	12.6
Guatemalan	144	7.2
Dominican Republic	238	46.2
Mexican	1,297	14.1
Puerto Rican	12	14.5

Language Spoken at Home: English Only
(Universe: Population 5 Years and Over)

Group	Number	%
Total Population	145,916	83.1
Hispanic or Latino (of any race)	6,018	22.8
Central American, ex. Mexican	117	3.7
Guatemalan	61	2.3
Dominican Republic	95	10.1
Mexican	4,322	23.4
Puerto Rican	802	33.9

Language Spoken at Home: Spanish
(Universe: Population 5 Years and Over)

Group	Number	%
Total Population	22,198	12.6
Hispanic or Latino (of any race)	20,345	76.9
Central American, ex. Mexican	3,032	96.1
Guatemalan	2,605	97.5
Dominican Republic	842	89.9
Mexican	14,093	76.4
Puerto Rican	1,531	64.8

Unemployment Rate
(Universe: Population 16 Years and Over)

Group	%
Total Population	11.7
Hispanic or Latino (of any race)	16.2
Central American, ex. Mexican	18.1
Guatemalan	16.1
Dominican Republic	16.2
Mexican	15.3
Puerto Rican	26.2

Class of Worker: Private Wage and Salary
(Universe: Civilian Employed Population 16 Years and Over)

Group	Number	%
Total Population	75,749	86.5
Hispanic or Latino (of any race)	10,589	92.5
Central American, ex. Mexican	1,410	93.8
Guatemalan	1,213	97.1
Dominican Republic	329	92.2
Mexican	7,389	93.7
Puerto Rican	815	92.5

Class of Worker: Government
(Universe: Civilian Employed Population 16 Years and Over)

Group	Number	%
Total Population	7,155	8.2
Hispanic or Latino (of any race)	369	3.2
Central American, ex. Mexican	23	1.5
Guatemalan	0	0.0
Dominican Republic	16	4.5
Mexican	219	2.8
Puerto Rican	27	3.1

Means of Transportation to Work: Car, Truck or Van
(Universe: Workers 16 Years and Over)

Group	Number	%
Total Population	74,065	87.1
Hispanic or Latino (of any race)	9,907	89.6
Central American, ex. Mexican	1,341	91.1
Guatemalan	1,086	89.2
Dominican Republic	327	91.6
Mexican	6,949	91.4
Puerto Rican	688	81.3

Means of Transportation to Work: Public Transportation (ex. Taxicab)
(Universe: Workers 16 Years and Over)

Group	Number	%
Total Population	2,777	3.3
Hispanic or Latino (of any race)	327	3.0
Central American, ex. Mexican	0	0.0
Guatemalan	0	0.0
Dominican Republic	0	0.0
Mexican	202	2.7
Puerto Rican	41	4.8

Homeownership Rate
(Universe: Occupied Housing Units)

Group	%
Total Population	56.0
Hispanic or Latino (of any race)	45.1
Central American, ex. Mexican	33.4
Guatemalan	27.3
Honduran	43.1
Salvadoran	62.4
Cuban	40.7
Dominican Republic	50.0
Mexican	49.4
Puerto Rican	37.0
South American	46.7
Spaniard	38.2

Median Home Value

Group	Dollars
Total Population	122,000
Hispanic or Latino (of any race)	91,400
Central American, ex. Mexican	94,100
Guatemalan	95,000
Dominican Republic	99,900
Mexican	89,100
Puerto Rican	91,100

Median Gross Rent

Group	Dollars
Total Population	716
Hispanic or Latino (of any race)	717
Central American, ex. Mexican	729
Guatemalan	740
Dominican Republic	636
Mexican	725
Puerto Rican	708

Median Household Income
(2010 Inflation-Adjusted Dollars)

Group	Dollars
Total Population	38,344
Hispanic or Latino (of any race)	29,532
Central American, ex. Mexican	28,797
Guatemalan	27,610
Dominican Republic	27,083
Mexican	30,144
Puerto Rican	30,114

Per Capita Income
(2010 Inflation-Adjusted Dollars)

Group	Dollars
Total Population	19,868
Hispanic or Latino (of any race)	9,725
Central American, ex. Mexican	8,450
Guatemalan	7,830
Dominican Republic	10,010
Mexican	8,893
Puerto Rican	15,334

Households with $100,000+ Income

Group	Number	%
Total Population	7,247	9.9

Notes: (1) Percent of total population; (2) Percent of Hispanic/Latino population; Profiles include places with an overall population of at least 125,000, OR an overall population of at least 25,000 where the Hispanic/Latino population is at least 20% of the overall population. In states where less than five places meet either of these criteria, we have included places with at least 10,000 total population with the highest percentage of Hispanic/Latino population. These places are identified with an asterisk (*); Please refer to the User's Guide for a full explanation of data.

Hispanic or Latino (of any race)	252	3.4
Central American, ex. Mexican	51	5.5
Guatemalan	42	5.4
Dominican Republic	0	0.0
Mexican	144	2.9
Puerto Rican	23	3.0

Households with Food Stamps/SNAP Benefits During Past 12 Months

Group	Number	%
Total Population	14,543	19.9
Hispanic or Latino (of any race)	2,583	34.6
Central American, ex. Mexican	194	20.7
Guatemalan	194	24.8
Dominican Republic	151	45.6
Mexican	1,864	37.8
Puerto Rican	281	37.0

Poverty Rate
(Income in Past 12 Months Below Poverty Level)

Group	%
Total Population	24.3
Hispanic or Latino (of any race)	39.5
Central American, ex. Mexican	47.0
Guatemalan	51.4
Dominican Republic	25.5
Mexican	39.0
Puerto Rican	41.2

Holland (charter township)

Population

Group	Number	%TP[1]	%HP[2]
Total Population	35,636	100.0	–
Hispanic or Latino (of any race)	8,347	23.4	100.0
Central American, ex. Mexican	171	0.5	2.0
Cuban	123	0.3	1.5
Mexican	6,950	19.5	83.3
Puerto Rican	340	1.0	4.1
South American	134	0.4	1.6

Population Growth: 2000–2010

Group	%
Total Population	23.3
Hispanic or Latino (of any race)	82.5
Mexican	89.5
Puerto Rican	172.0

Males per 100 Females

Group	Number
Total Population	99.7
Hispanic or Latino (of any race)	107.7
Central American, ex. Mexican	119.2
Cuban	112.1
Mexican	108.5
Puerto Rican	107.3
South American	83.6

Average Household Size

Group	People
Total Population	2.85
Hispanic or Latino (of any race)	3.73
Central American, ex. Mexican	3.91
Cuban	3.23
Mexican	3.80
Puerto Rican	3.23
South American	3.51

Median Age

Group	Years
Total Population	32.0
Hispanic or Latino (of any race)	22.8
Central American, ex. Mexican	26.3
Cuban	35.2
Mexican	22.5
Puerto Rican	24.8
South American	31.0

High School Graduates
(Universe: Population 25 Years and Over)

Group	Number	%
Total Population	16,944	82.6
Hispanic or Latino (of any race)	2,053	59.0
Mexican	1,672	55.9

Four-Year College Graduates
(Universe: Population 25 Years and Over)

Group	Number	%
Total Population	4,660	22.7
Hispanic or Latino (of any race)	322	9.3
Mexican	264	8.8

Population Age 3–17 Enrolled in Public School
(Universe: Population Age 3–17 Enrolled in School)

Group	Number	%
Total Population	6,265	85.7
Hispanic or Latino (of any race)	1,769	92.4
Mexican	1,426	92.4

Population Age 3–17 Enrolled in Private School
(Universe: Population Age 3–17 Enrolled in School)

Group	Number	%
Total Population	1,043	14.3
Hispanic or Latino (of any race)	146	7.6
Mexican	117	7.6

Foreign-Born Population

Group	Number	%
Total Population	5,367	15.5
Hispanic or Latino (of any race)	2,400	33.0
Mexican	2,171	35.1

Foreign-Born Naturalized U.S. Citizens

Group	Number	%
Total Population	2,451	45.7
Hispanic or Latino (of any race)	664	27.7
Mexican	557	25.7

Language Spoken at Home: English Only
(Universe: Population 5 Years and Over)

Group	Number	%
Total Population	23,541	74.0
Hispanic or Latino (of any race)	1,673	26.9
Mexican	1,217	23.3

Language Spoken at Home: Spanish
(Universe: Population 5 Years and Over)

Group	Number	%
Total Population	4,899	15.4
Hispanic or Latino (of any race)	4,536	72.9
Mexican	4,005	76.5

Unemployment Rate
(Universe: Population 16 Years and Over)

Group	%
Total Population	9.9
Hispanic or Latino (of any race)	13.8
Mexican	12.6

Class of Worker: Private Wage and Salary
(Universe: Civilian Employed Population 16 Years and Over)

Group	Number	%
Total Population	15,634	90.4
Hispanic or Latino (of any race)	2,862	95.8
Mexican	2,485	96.2

Class of Worker: Government
(Universe: Civilian Employed Population 16 Years and Over)

Group	Number	%
Total Population	1,017	5.9
Hispanic or Latino (of any race)	82	2.7
Mexican	57	2.2

Means of Transportation to Work: Car, Truck or Van
(Universe: Workers 16 Years and Over)

Group	Number	%
Total Population	16,352	96.0
Hispanic or Latino (of any race)	2,840	97.8
Mexican	2,452	98.0

Means of Transportation to Work: Public Transportation (ex. Taxicab)
(Universe: Workers 16 Years and Over)

Group	Number	%
Total Population	62	0.4
Hispanic or Latino (of any race)	0	0.0
Mexican	0	0.0

Homeownership Rate
(Universe: Occupied Housing Units)

Group	%
Total Population	70.1
Hispanic or Latino (of any race)	56.4
Central American, ex. Mexican	57.8
Cuban	60.5
Mexican	57.8
Puerto Rican	44.4
South American	68.9

Median Home Value

Group	Dollars
Total Population	142,100
Hispanic or Latino (of any race)	111,300
Mexican	113,700

Median Gross Rent

Group	Dollars
Total Population	725
Hispanic or Latino (of any race)	731
Mexican	728

Median Household Income
(2010 Inflation-Adjusted Dollars)

Group	Dollars
Total Population	50,547
Hispanic or Latino (of any race)	37,119
Mexican	37,073

Per Capita Income
(2010 Inflation-Adjusted Dollars)

Group	Dollars
Total Population	20,894
Hispanic or Latino (of any race)	12,517
Mexican	12,564

Households with $100,000+ Income

Group	Number	%
Total Population	1,486	12.2
Hispanic or Latino (of any race)	100	5.7
Mexican	86	5.6

Households with Food Stamps/SNAP Benefits During Past 12 Months

Group	Number	%
Total Population	1,610	13.2
Hispanic or Latino (of any race)	582	33.2
Mexican	520	34.1

Poverty Rate
(Income in Past 12 Months Below Poverty Level)

Group	%
Total Population	10.3
Hispanic or Latino (of any race)	18.4
Mexican	19.6

Holland (city)

Population

Group	Number	%TP[1]	%HP[2]
Total Population	33,051	100.0	–
Hispanic or Latino (of any race)	7,512	22.7	100.0
Central American, ex. Mexican	125	0.4	1.7
Mexican	6,241	18.9	83.1
Puerto Rican	450	1.4	6.0

Population Growth: 2000–2010

Group	%
Total Population	-5.7
Hispanic or Latino (of any race)	-3.5
Mexican	6.5
Puerto Rican	38.0

Males per 100 Females

Group	Number
Total Population	90.6
Hispanic or Latino (of any race)	103.5
Central American, ex. Mexican	101.6
Mexican	104.1
Puerto Rican	112.3

Notes: (1) Percent of total population; (2) Percent of Hispanic/Latino population; Profiles include places with an overall population of at least 125,000, OR an overall population of at least 25,000 where the Hispanic/Latino population is at least 20% of the overall population. In states where less than five places meet either of these criteria, we have included places with at least 10,000 total population with the highest percentage of Hispanic/Latino population. These places are identified with an asterisk (*); Please refer to the User's Guide for a full explanation of data.

Average Household Size

Group	People
Total Population	2.52
Hispanic or Latino (of any race)	3.49
Central American, ex. Mexican	3.15
Mexican	3.57
Puerto Rican	3.11

Median Age

Group	Years
Total Population	31.7
Hispanic or Latino (of any race)	23.9
Central American, ex. Mexican	23.3
Mexican	23.9
Puerto Rican	24.4

High School Graduates
(Universe: Population 25 Years and Over)

Group	Number	%
Total Population	16,872	83.9
Hispanic or Latino (of any race)	2,402	59.1
Mexican	2,085	61.5

Four-Year College Graduates
(Universe: Population 25 Years and Over)

Group	Number	%
Total Population	6,352	31.6
Hispanic or Latino (of any race)	335	8.2
Mexican	254	7.5

Population Age 3–17 Enrolled in Public School
(Universe: Population Age 3–17 Enrolled in School)

Group	Number	%
Total Population	4,898	82.3
Hispanic or Latino (of any race)	2,013	88.6
Mexican	1,588	88.4

Population Age 3–17 Enrolled in Private School
(Universe: Population Age 3–17 Enrolled in School)

Group	Number	%
Total Population	1,054	17.7
Hispanic or Latino (of any race)	259	11.4
Mexican	208	11.6

Foreign-Born Population

Group	Number	%
Total Population	3,662	10.9
Hispanic or Latino (of any race)	2,316	28.1
Mexican	1,893	27.9

Foreign-Born Naturalized U.S. Citizens

Group	Number	%
Total Population	1,508	41.2
Hispanic or Latino (of any race)	827	35.7
Mexican	645	34.1

Language Spoken at Home: English Only
(Universe: Population 5 Years and Over)

Group	Number	%
Total Population	24,025	77.4
Hispanic or Latino (of any race)	1,960	27.2
Mexican	1,572	26.8

Language Spoken at Home: Spanish
(Universe: Population 5 Years and Over)

Group	Number	%
Total Population	5,496	17.7
Hispanic or Latino (of any race)	5,235	72.6
Mexican	4,292	73.1

Unemployment Rate
(Universe: Population 16 Years and Over)

Group	%
Total Population	8.2
Hispanic or Latino (of any race)	14.9
Mexican	13.1

Class of Worker: Private Wage and Salary
(Universe: Civilian Employed Population 16 Years and Over)

Group	Number	%
Total Population	13,489	86.0
Hispanic or Latino (of any race)	2,829	88.3
Mexican	2,450	89.4

Class of Worker: Government
(Universe: Civilian Employed Population 16 Years and Over)

Group	Number	%
Total Population	1,347	8.6
Hispanic or Latino (of any race)	193	6.0
Mexican	120	4.4

Means of Transportation to Work: Car, Truck or Van
(Universe: Workers 16 Years and Over)

Group	Number	%
Total Population	12,949	84.9
Hispanic or Latino (of any race)	2,885	91.8
Mexican	2,440	91.5

Means of Transportation to Work: Public Transportation (ex. Taxicab)
(Universe: Workers 16 Years and Over)

Group	Number	%
Total Population	171	1.1
Hispanic or Latino (of any race)	9	0.3
Mexican	9	0.3

Homeownership Rate
(Universe: Occupied Housing Units)

Group	%
Total Population	63.7
Hispanic or Latino (of any race)	52.5
Central American, ex. Mexican	53.8
Mexican	54.1
Puerto Rican	33.3

Median Home Value

Group	Dollars
Total Population	132,600
Hispanic or Latino (of any race)	104,800
Mexican	105,100

Median Gross Rent

Group	Dollars
Total Population	667
Hispanic or Latino (of any race)	648
Mexican	697

Median Household Income
(2010 Inflation-Adjusted Dollars)

Group	Dollars
Total Population	42,987
Hispanic or Latino (of any race)	37,207
Mexican	40,590

Per Capita Income
(2010 Inflation-Adjusted Dollars)

Group	Dollars
Total Population	20,668
Hispanic or Latino (of any race)	12,464
Mexican	13,059

Households with $100,000+ Income

Group	Number	%
Total Population	1,492	12.1
Hispanic or Latino (of any race)	127	5.5
Mexican	107	5.7

Households with Food Stamps/SNAP Benefits During Past 12 Months

Group	Number	%
Total Population	1,522	12.3
Hispanic or Latino (of any race)	608	26.5
Mexican	492	26.2

Poverty Rate
(Income in Past 12 Months Below Poverty Level)

Group	%
Total Population	15.4
Hispanic or Latino (of any race)	25.2
Mexican	23.6

Sterling Heights

Population

Group	Number	%TP[1]	%HP[2]
Total Population	129,699	100.0	–
Hispanic or Latino (of any race)	2,523	1.9	100.0
Mexican	1,537	1.2	60.9
Puerto Rican	301	0.2	11.9
South American	192	0.1	7.6

Population Growth: 2000–2010

Group	%
Total Population	4.2
Hispanic or Latino (of any race)	51.5
Mexican	72.7
Puerto Rican	98.0
South American	40.1

Males per 100 Females

Group	Number
Total Population	94.1
Hispanic or Latino (of any race)	106.8
Mexican	107.1
Puerto Rican	103.4
South American	88.2

Average Household Size

Group	People
Total Population	2.61
Hispanic or Latino (of any race)	2.96
Mexican	3.05
Puerto Rican	2.81
South American	2.87

Median Age

Group	Years
Total Population	40.4
Hispanic or Latino (of any race)	27.0
Mexican	25.6
Puerto Rican	22.1
South American	35.0

High School Graduates
(Universe: Population 25 Years and Over)

Group	Number	%
Total Population	76,829	85.9
Hispanic or Latino (of any race)	1,356	83.9
Mexican	644	74.0

Four-Year College Graduates
(Universe: Population 25 Years and Over)

Group	Number	%
Total Population	23,838	26.7
Hispanic or Latino (of any race)	523	32.3
Mexican	285	32.8

Population Age 3–17 Enrolled in Public School
(Universe: Population Age 3–17 Enrolled in School)

Group	Number	%
Total Population	20,471	90.3
Hispanic or Latino (of any race)	481	88.7
Mexican	341	91.7

Population Age 3–17 Enrolled in Private School
(Universe: Population Age 3–17 Enrolled in School)

Group	Number	%
Total Population	2,187	9.7
Hispanic or Latino (of any race)	61	11.3
Mexican	31	8.3

Foreign-Born Population

Group	Number	%
Total Population	28,837	22.2
Hispanic or Latino (of any race)	948	33.8
Mexican	542	31.4

Foreign-Born Naturalized U.S. Citizens

Group	Number	%
Total Population	16,557	57.4
Hispanic or Latino (of any race)	190	20.0
Mexican	46	8.5

Language Spoken at Home: English Only
(Universe: Population 5 Years and Over)

Group	Number	%
Total Population	88,399	72.2
Hispanic or Latino (of any race)	1,027	42.6
Mexican	702	49.3

Notes: (1) Percent of total population; (2) Percent of Hispanic/Latino population; Profiles include places with an overall population of at least 125,000, OR an overall population of at least 25,000 where the Hispanic/Latino population is at least 20% of the overall population. In states where less than five places meet either of these criteria, we have included places with at least 10,000 total population with the highest percentage of Hispanic/Latino population. These places are identified with an asterisk (*); Please refer to the User's Guide for a full explanation of data.

Language Spoken at Home: Spanish
(Universe: Population 5 Years and Over)

Group	Number	%
Total Population	1,676	1.4
Hispanic or Latino (of any race)	1,294	53.7
Mexican	711	49.9

Unemployment Rate
(Universe: Population 16 Years and Over)

Group	%
Total Population	10.6
Hispanic or Latino (of any race)	9.8
Mexican	6.0

Class of Worker: Private Wage and Salary
(Universe: Civilian Employed Population 16 Years and Over)

Group	Number	%
Total Population	53,378	87.6
Hispanic or Latino (of any race)	1,058	83.2
Mexican	564	77.0

Class of Worker: Government
(Universe: Civilian Employed Population 16 Years and Over)

Group	Number	%
Total Population	5,347	8.8
Hispanic or Latino (of any race)	134	10.5
Mexican	103	14.1

Means of Transportation to Work: Car, Truck or Van
(Universe: Workers 16 Years and Over)

Group	Number	%
Total Population	56,831	96.3
Hispanic or Latino (of any race)	1,157	96.7
Mexican	639	97.3

Means of Transportation to Work: Public Transportation (ex. Taxicab)
(Universe: Workers 16 Years and Over)

Group	Number	%
Total Population	240	0.4
Hispanic or Latino (of any race)	5	0.4
Mexican	5	0.8

Homeownership Rate
(Universe: Occupied Housing Units)

Group	%
Total Population	76.2
Hispanic or Latino (of any race)	66.3
Mexican	64.4
Puerto Rican	62.9
South American	63.9

Median Home Value

Group	Dollars
Total Population	173,700
Hispanic or Latino (of any race)	137,700
Mexican	111,600

Median Gross Rent

Group	Dollars
Total Population	794
Hispanic or Latino (of any race)	736
Mexican	1,043

Median Household Income
(2010 Inflation-Adjusted Dollars)

Group	Dollars
Total Population	58,073
Hispanic or Latino (of any race)	60,292
Mexican	74,444

Per Capita Income
(2010 Inflation-Adjusted Dollars)

Group	Dollars
Total Population	26,475
Hispanic or Latino (of any race)	19,687
Mexican	17,386

Households with $100,000+ Income

Group	Number	%
Total Population	10,624	21.7
Hispanic or Latino (of any race)	174	20.3
Mexican	99	20.4

Households with Food Stamps/SNAP Benefits During Past 12 Months

Group	Number	%
Total Population	3,977	8.1
Hispanic or Latino (of any race)	100	11.7
Mexican	92	18.9

Poverty Rate
(Income in Past 12 Months Below Poverty Level)

Group	%
Total Population	8.8
Hispanic or Latino (of any race)	11.8
Mexican	15.4

Warren

Population

Group	Number	%TP[1]	%HP[2]
Total Population	134,056	100.0	–
Hispanic or Latino (of any race)	2,758	2.1	100.0
Mexican	1,650	1.2	59.8
Puerto Rican	405	0.3	14.7
South American	135	0.1	4.9
Spaniard	113	0.1	4.1

Population Growth: 2000–2010

Group	%
Total Population	-3.0
Hispanic or Latino (of any race)	47.6
Mexican	50.8
Puerto Rican	131.4

Males per 100 Females

Group	Number
Total Population	93.8
Hispanic or Latino (of any race)	104.8
Mexican	108.3
Puerto Rican	93.8
South American	107.7
Spaniard	68.7

Average Household Size

Group	People
Total Population	2.49
Hispanic or Latino (of any race)	3.00
Mexican	3.10
Puerto Rican	3.08
South American	2.41
Spaniard	2.59

Median Age

Group	Years
Total Population	39.4
Hispanic or Latino (of any race)	25.3
Mexican	24.1
Puerto Rican	22.1
South American	34.5
Spaniard	40.5

High School Graduates
(Universe: Population 25 Years and Over)

Group	Number	%
Total Population	77,240	83.2
Hispanic or Latino (of any race)	1,032	76.3
Mexican	649	79.0

Four-Year College Graduates
(Universe: Population 25 Years and Over)

Group	Number	%
Total Population	14,562	15.7
Hispanic or Latino (of any race)	207	15.3
Mexican	76	9.3

Population Age 3–17 Enrolled in Public School
(Universe: Population Age 3–17 Enrolled in School)

Group	Number	%
Total Population	21,769	92.9
Hispanic or Latino (of any race)	820	94.1
Mexican	512	93.4

Population Age 3–17 Enrolled in Private School
(Universe: Population Age 3–17 Enrolled in School)

Group	Number	%
Total Population	1,655	7.1
Hispanic or Latino (of any race)	51	5.9
Mexican	36	6.6

Foreign-Born Population

Group	Number	%
Total Population	13,915	10.2
Hispanic or Latino (of any race)	319	10.8
Mexican	121	6.6

Foreign-Born Naturalized U.S. Citizens

Group	Number	%
Total Population	8,739	62.8
Hispanic or Latino (of any race)	120	37.6
Mexican	8	6.6

Language Spoken at Home: English Only
(Universe: Population 5 Years and Over)

Group	Number	%
Total Population	109,649	86.0
Hispanic or Latino (of any race)	1,673	64.3
Mexican	1,159	72.9

Language Spoken at Home: Spanish
(Universe: Population 5 Years and Over)

Group	Number	%
Total Population	1,307	1.0
Hispanic or Latino (of any race)	824	31.7
Mexican	431	27.1

Unemployment Rate
(Universe: Population 16 Years and Over)

Group	%
Total Population	13.1
Hispanic or Latino (of any race)	3.9
Mexican	2.2

Class of Worker: Private Wage and Salary
(Universe: Civilian Employed Population 16 Years and Over)

Group	Number	%
Total Population	50,235	86.0
Hispanic or Latino (of any race)	991	92.2
Mexican	691	92.3

Class of Worker: Government
(Universe: Civilian Employed Population 16 Years and Over)

Group	Number	%
Total Population	5,691	9.7
Hispanic or Latino (of any race)	84	7.8
Mexican	58	7.7

Means of Transportation to Work: Car, Truck or Van
(Universe: Workers 16 Years and Over)

Group	Number	%
Total Population	53,495	94.4
Hispanic or Latino (of any race)	919	86.9
Mexican	590	83.7

Means of Transportation to Work: Public Transportation (ex. Taxicab)
(Universe: Workers 16 Years and Over)

Group	Number	%
Total Population	630	1.1
Hispanic or Latino (of any race)	9	0.9
Mexican	9	1.3

Homeownership Rate
(Universe: Occupied Housing Units)

Group	%
Total Population	74.3
Hispanic or Latino (of any race)	66.5
Mexican	65.0
Puerto Rican	64.1
South American	65.9
Spaniard	73.2

Median Home Value

Group	Dollars
Total Population	127,400
Hispanic or Latino (of any race)	128,400
Mexican	95,400

Median Gross Rent

Group	Dollars
Total Population	755
Hispanic or Latino (of any race)	821

Notes: (1) Percent of total population; (2) Percent of Hispanic/Latino population; Profiles include places with an overall population of at least 125,000, OR an overall population of at least 25,000 where the Hispanic/Latino population is at least 20% of the overall population. In states where less than five places meet either of these criteria, we have included places with at least 10,000 total population with the highest percentage of Hispanic/Latino population. These places are identified with an asterisk (*); Please refer to the User's Guide for a full explanation of data.

Mexican	738

Median Household Income
(2010 Inflation-Adjusted Dollars)

Group	Dollars
Total Population	45,337
Hispanic or Latino (of any race)	46,434
Mexican	32,028

Per Capita Income
(2010 Inflation-Adjusted Dollars)

Group	Dollars
Total Population	22,110
Hispanic or Latino (of any race)	15,205
Mexican	14,073

Households with $100,000+ Income

Group	Number	%
Total Population	6,341	11.6
Hispanic or Latino (of any race)	160	20.0
Mexican	71	14.8

Households with Food Stamps/SNAP Benefits During Past 12 Months

Group	Number	%
Total Population	6,829	12.5
Hispanic or Latino (of any race)	178	22.3
Mexican	92	19.2

Poverty Rate
(Income in Past 12 Months Below Poverty Level)

Group	%
Total Population	14.2
Hispanic or Latino (of any race)	28.6
Mexican	25.8

STATE & PLACE PROFILES

Notes: (1) Percent of total population; (2) Percent of Hispanic/Latino population; Profiles include places with an overall population of at least 125,000, OR an overall population of at least 25,000 where the Hispanic/Latino population is at least 20% of the overall population. In states where less than five places meet either of these criteria, we have included places with at least 10,000 total population with the highest percentage of Hispanic/Latino population. These places are identified with an asterisk (*); Please refer to the User's Guide for a full explanation of data.

Minnesota

EDITOR'S NOTE: For a place to be included in this edition, it must meet one of two criteria. Either its overall population is at least 125,000, OR its overall population is at least 25,000 and its Hispanic/Latino population is at least 20% of the overall population. In Minnesota, less than five places meet either of these criteria. In an effort to include at least five places for each state, we have included places with at least 10,000 total population with the highest percentage of Hispanic/Latino population. These places are identified with an asterisk (*). For the state of Minnesota, the following locations are included:

Minneapolis
Saint Paul
West Saint Paul*
Willmar*
Worthington*

Section Two: State & Place Profiles starts with the state profile, followed by place profiles that meet the criteria above. Places are listed alphabetically within each state. All states, all counties and places that meet the above criteria are ranked and compared in *Section Three: Rankings & Comparisons*, on page 1055.

For a more detailed look at the Hispanic/Latino population in Minnesota, a companion web site is available at no additional charge with purchase of this print edition. Visit http://gold.greyhouse.com/page/info_hispanic for more information.

The web site includes data for all counties and places in Minnesota with Hispanic/Latino population, plus ten additional topics: Self Employed Worker; Walked to Work; Worked from Home; Mean Travel Time to Work; Mean Household Income; Households with Cash Public Assistance; Mean Cash Pubic Assistance; Poverty Rates for 18 and Under, 18 to 64, and 65 and Over.

Population

Group	Number	%TP[1]	%HP[2]
Total Population	5,303,925	100.0	–
Hispanic or Latino (of any race)	250,258	4.7	100.0
Central American, ex. Mexican	19,908	0.4	8.0
Costa Rican	785	<0.1	0.3
Guatemalan	6,754	0.1	2.7
Honduran	3,186	0.1	1.3
Nicaraguan	970	<0.1	0.4
Panamanian	906	<0.1	0.4
Salvadoran	7,175	0.1	2.9
Cuban	3,661	0.1	1.5
Dominican Republic	1,294	<0.1	0.5
Mexican	176,007	3.3	70.3
Puerto Rican	10,807	0.2	4.3
South American	18,075	0.3	7.2
Argentinean	1,008	<0.1	0.4
Bolivian	430	<0.1	0.2
Chilean	1,057	<0.1	0.4
Colombian	4,484	0.1	1.8
Ecuadorian	7,290	0.1	2.9
Paraguayan	287	<0.1	0.1
Peruvian	2,028	<0.1	0.8
Uruguayan	223	<0.1	0.1
Venezuelan	1,017	<0.1	0.4
Spaniard	3,255	0.1	1.3

Population Growth: 2000–2010

Group	%
Total Population	7.8
Hispanic or Latino (of any race)	74.5
Central American, ex. Mexican	222.1
Costa Rican	126.2
Guatemalan	301.1
Honduran	244.4
Nicaraguan	158.0
Panamanian	84.5
Salvadoran	257.9
Cuban	44.9
Dominican Republic	171.3
Mexican	84.1
Puerto Rican	63.3
South American	149.7
Argentinean	148.3
Bolivian	173.9
Chilean	111.8
Colombian	114.8
Ecuadorian	228.2
Paraguayan	45.7
Peruvian	149.8
Venezuelan	116.4
Spaniard	591.1

Males per 100 Females

Group	Number
Total Population	98.5
Hispanic or Latino (of any race)	111.4
Central American, ex. Mexican	115.4
Costa Rican	102.8
Guatemalan	123.7
Honduran	122.5
Nicaraguan	101.7
Panamanian	76.6
Salvadoran	114.4
Cuban	115.7
Dominican Republic	96.1
Mexican	113.0
Puerto Rican	101.5
South American	103.6
Argentinean	86.7
Bolivian	99.1
Chilean	92.2
Colombian	87.6
Ecuadorian	131.9
Paraguayan	91.3
Peruvian	83.2
Uruguayan	85.8
Venezuelan	93.3
Spaniard	90.6

Average Household Size

Group	People
Total Population	2.48
Hispanic or Latino (of any race)	3.60
Central American, ex. Mexican	3.85
Costa Rican	2.82
Guatemalan	4.06
Honduran	3.75
Nicaraguan	3.46
Panamanian	2.84
Salvadoran	4.06
Cuban	2.53
Dominican Republic	3.14
Mexican	3.78
Puerto Rican	2.78
South American	3.37
Argentinean	2.72
Bolivian	2.65
Chilean	2.75
Colombian	2.64
Ecuadorian	4.44
Paraguayan	2.88
Peruvian	2.85
Uruguayan	2.91
Venezuelan	2.79
Spaniard	2.64

Median Age

Group	Years
Total Population	37.4
Hispanic or Latino (of any race)	23.5
Central American, ex. Mexican	25.5
Costa Rican	27.6
Guatemalan	21.4
Honduran	25.3
Nicaraguan	28.6
Panamanian	30.1
Salvadoran	28.2
Cuban	26.6
Dominican Republic	25.7
Mexican	22.6
Puerto Rican	23.3
South American	27.8
Argentinean	34.7
Bolivian	28.3
Chilean	28.7
Colombian	22.3
Ecuadorian	28.2
Paraguayan	18.2
Peruvian	30.9
Uruguayan	32.6
Venezuelan	32.2
Spaniard	29.7

High School Graduates
(Universe: Population 25 Years and Over)

Group	Number	%
Total Population	3,151,753	91.3
Hispanic or Latino (of any race)	67,955	61.3
Central American, ex. Mexican	4,887	51.9
Costa Rican	489	94.2
Guatemalan	1,024	46.2
Honduran	798	47.2
Nicaraguan	329	56.5
Panamanian	343	100.0
Salvadoran	1,858	46.9
Cuban	1,442	79.7
Dominican Republic	310	74.0
Mexican	44,930	57.8
Puerto Rican	4,689	87.4
South American	6,516	69.4
Argentinean	564	98.8
Chilean	364	90.8
Colombian	1,910	99.1
Ecuadorian	1,828	40.4
Peruvian	957	95.3
Venezuelan	599	94.5
Spaniard	1,369	90.8

Four-Year College Graduates
(Universe: Population 25 Years and Over)

Group	Number	%
Total Population	1,084,157	31.4
Hispanic or Latino (of any race)	16,821	15.2
Central American, ex. Mexican	1,350	14.3
Costa Rican	269	51.8
Guatemalan	276	12.4
Honduran	234	13.8
Nicaraguan	173	29.7
Panamanian	105	30.6
Salvadoran	256	6.5
Cuban	500	27.6
Dominican Republic	105	25.1
Mexican	8,223	10.6
Puerto Rican	1,827	34.1
South American	3,086	32.9
Argentinean	298	52.2
Chilean	237	59.1
Colombian	832	43.2
Ecuadorian	559	12.4
Peruvian	493	49.1
Venezuelan	482	76.0
Spaniard	643	42.6

Population Age 3–17 Enrolled in Public School
(Universe: Population Age 3–17 Enrolled in School)

Group	Number	%
Total Population	827,714	86.1
Hispanic or Latino (of any race)	58,571	92.0
Central American, ex. Mexican	4,362	89.3
Costa Rican	205	69.3
Guatemalan	1,557	80.8
Honduran	485	94.0
Nicaraguan	262	94.6
Panamanian	137	100.0
Salvadoran	1,699	99.2
Cuban	408	81.9

Notes: (1) Percent of total population; (2) Percent of Hispanic/Latino population; Profiles include places with an overall population of at least 125,000, OR an overall population of at least 25,000 where the Hispanic/Latino population is at least 20% of the overall population. In states where less than five places meet either of these criteria, we have included places with at least 10,000 total population with the highest percentage of Hispanic/Latino population. These places are identified with an asterisk (*); Please refer to the User's Guide for a full explanation of data.

Dominican Republic	69	76.7
Mexican	44,218	94.2
Puerto Rican	2,624	89.0
South American	3,435	80.2
Argentinean	125	63.5
Chilean	165	89.7
Colombian	1,290	79.1
Ecuadorian	1,243	89.9
Peruvian	266	81.1
Venezuelan	159	79.5
Spaniard	612	77.4

Population Age 3–17 Enrolled in Private School
(Universe: Population Age 3–17 Enrolled in School)

Group	Number	%
Total Population	133,706	13.9
Hispanic or Latino (of any race)	5,086	8.0
Central American, ex. Mexican	521	10.7
Costa Rican	91	30.7
Guatemalan	370	19.2
Honduran	31	6.0
Nicaraguan	15	5.4
Panamanian	0	0.0
Salvadoran	14	0.8
Cuban	90	18.1
Dominican Republic	21	23.3
Mexican	2,702	5.8
Puerto Rican	324	11.0
South American	850	19.8
Argentinean	72	36.5
Chilean	19	10.3
Colombian	340	20.9
Ecuadorian	139	10.1
Peruvian	62	18.9
Venezuelan	41	20.5
Spaniard	179	22.6

Foreign-Born Population

Group	Number	%
Total Population	366,951	7.0
Hispanic or Latino (of any race)	93,736	40.1
Central American, ex. Mexican	12,527	64.1
Costa Rican	479	46.8
Guatemalan	4,054	67.8
Honduran	2,054	70.1
Nicaraguan	658	58.8
Panamanian	126	17.1
Salvadoran	5,038	66.0
Cuban	992	34.9
Dominican Republic	368	46.6
Mexican	64,953	38.7
Puerto Rican	128	1.2
South American	12,093	67.1
Argentinean	580	62.9
Chilean	511	64.8
Colombian	2,964	66.0
Ecuadorian	5,701	69.5
Peruvian	1,089	66.3
Venezuelan	682	61.9
Spaniard	601	22.3

Foreign-Born Naturalized U.S. Citizens

Group	Number	%
Total Population	159,386	43.4
Hispanic or Latino (of any race)	19,995	21.3
Central American, ex. Mexican	3,277	26.2
Costa Rican	142	29.6
Guatemalan	1,569	38.7
Honduran	411	20.0
Nicaraguan	142	21.6
Panamanian	26	20.6
Salvadoran	952	18.9
Cuban	538	54.2
Dominican Republic	221	60.1
Mexican	10,354	15.9
Puerto Rican	48	37.5
South American	4,516	37.3
Argentinean	259	44.7
Chilean	230	45.0
Colombian	1,963	66.2
Ecuadorian	825	14.5
Peruvian	574	52.7
Venezuelan	197	28.9
Spaniard	349	58.1

Language Spoken at Home: English Only
(Universe: Population 5 Years and Over)

Group	Number	%
Total Population	4,386,970	89.7
Hispanic or Latino (of any race)	63,142	31.4
Central American, ex. Mexican	3,163	18.9
Costa Rican	294	30.6
Guatemalan	1,211	25.2
Honduran	421	16.8
Nicaraguan	194	19.1
Panamanian	280	42.6
Salvadoran	729	10.9
Cuban	1,407	53.2
Dominican Republic	148	22.9
Mexican	41,739	29.1
Puerto Rican	5,236	55.1
South American	4,701	29.4
Argentinean	180	22.4
Chilean	288	41.6
Colombian	2,428	60.3
Ecuadorian	497	7.1
Peruvian	344	22.3
Venezuelan	438	42.8
Spaniard	1,700	65.1

Language Spoken at Home: Spanish
(Universe: Population 5 Years and Over)

Group	Number	%
Total Population	183,397	3.8
Hispanic or Latino (of any race)	136,421	67.8
Central American, ex. Mexican	13,060	78.0
Costa Rican	667	69.4
Guatemalan	3,059	63.8
Honduran	2,081	83.2
Nicaraguan	820	80.9
Panamanian	377	57.4
Salvadoran	5,962	89.1
Cuban	1,227	46.4
Dominican Republic	497	77.1
Mexican	101,152	70.5
Puerto Rican	4,165	43.9
South American	11,238	70.3
Argentinean	625	77.6
Chilean	384	55.5
Colombian	1,594	39.6
Ecuadorian	6,527	92.9
Peruvian	1,202	77.7
Venezuelan	586	57.2
Spaniard	824	31.6

Unemployment Rate
(Universe: Population 16 Years and Over)

Group	%
Total Population	6.4
Hispanic or Latino (of any race)	8.9
Central American, ex. Mexican	10.9
Costa Rican	14.7
Guatemalan	9.3
Honduran	5.3
Nicaraguan	14.6
Panamanian	12.2
Salvadoran	12.6
Cuban	9.8
Dominican Republic	7.7
Mexican	8.9
Puerto Rican	10.0
South American	5.5
Argentinean	0.0
Chilean	4.4
Colombian	6.6
Ecuadorian	5.1
Peruvian	1.4
Venezuelan	15.4
Spaniard	6.3

Class of Worker: Private Wage and Salary
(Universe: Civilian Employed Population 16 Years and Over)

Group	Number	%
Total Population	2,216,606	81.2
Hispanic or Latino (of any race)	91,155	90.1
Central American, ex. Mexican	8,362	91.0
Costa Rican	361	81.7
Guatemalan	1,991	85.7
Honduran	1,299	90.0
Nicaraguan	500	89.0
Panamanian	381	89.6
Salvadoran	3,739	95.7
Cuban	1,219	90.5
Dominican Republic	345	82.7
Mexican	64,333	91.4
Puerto Rican	4,062	84.8
South American	8,217	88.4
Argentinean	537	91.2
Chilean	146	60.8
Colombian	1,604	82.0
Ecuadorian	4,542	95.5
Peruvian	680	88.2
Venezuelan	403	71.2
Spaniard	1,186	81.0

Class of Worker: Government
(Universe: Civilian Employed Population 16 Years and Over)

Group	Number	%
Total Population	334,700	12.3
Hispanic or Latino (of any race)	6,033	6.0
Central American, ex. Mexican	360	3.9
Costa Rican	12	2.7
Guatemalan	104	4.5
Honduran	31	2.1
Nicaraguan	9	1.6
Panamanian	40	9.4
Salvadoran	164	4.2
Cuban	84	6.2
Dominican Republic	15	3.6
Mexican	3,601	5.1
Puerto Rican	508	10.6
South American	724	7.8
Argentinean	31	5.3
Chilean	46	19.2
Colombian	294	15.0
Ecuadorian	90	1.9
Peruvian	59	7.7
Venezuelan	149	26.3
Spaniard	207	14.1

Means of Transportation to Work: Car, Truck or Van
(Universe: Workers 16 Years and Over)

Group	Number	%
Total Population	2,327,571	87.0
Hispanic or Latino (of any race)	83,929	84.9
Central American, ex. Mexican	7,599	84.2
Costa Rican	342	79.0
Guatemalan	1,965	85.1
Honduran	1,189	85.2
Nicaraguan	356	64.6
Panamanian	400	94.1
Salvadoran	3,278	85.8
Cuban	1,067	79.6
Dominican Republic	277	75.7
Mexican	59,601	86.5
Puerto Rican	4,022	86.3
South American	6,791	75.0
Argentinean	543	98.9
Chilean	213	88.8
Colombian	1,592	84.9
Ecuadorian	3,138	66.9
Peruvian	649	86.2
Venezuelan	424	79.8
Spaniard	1,089	79.2

Means of Transportation to Work: Public Transportation (ex. Taxicab)
(Universe: Workers 16 Years and Over)

Group	Number	%
Total Population	90,712	3.4
Hispanic or Latino (of any race)	6,963	7.0
Central American, ex. Mexican	578	6.4
Costa Rican	6	1.4
Guatemalan	110	4.8
Honduran	71	5.1
Nicaraguan	136	24.7
Panamanian	15	3.5
Salvadoran	222	5.8
Cuban	110	8.2
Dominican Republic	45	12.3
Mexican	4,012	5.8
Puerto Rican	333	7.1
South American	1,565	17.3
Argentinean	0	0.0

Notes: (1) Percent of total population; (2) Percent of Hispanic/Latino population; Profiles include places with an overall population of at least 125,000, OR an overall population of at least 25,000 where the Hispanic/Latino population is at least 20% of the overall population. In states where less than five places meet either of these criteria, we have included places with at least 10,000 total population with the highest percentage of Hispanic/Latino population. These places are identified with an asterisk (*); Please refer to the User's Guide for a full explanation of data.

Group	Number	%
Chilean	2	0.8
Colombian	102	5.4
Ecuadorian	1,299	27.7
Peruvian	44	5.8
Venezuelan	10	1.9
Spaniard	103	7.5

Homeownership Rate
(Universe: Occupied Housing Units)

Group	%
Total Population	73.0
Hispanic or Latino (of any race)	44.3
Central American, ex. Mexican	42.8
Costa Rican	60.7
Guatemalan	36.2
Honduran	34.7
Nicaraguan	51.7
Panamanian	61.2
Salvadoran	44.9
Cuban	48.1
Dominican Republic	39.0
Mexican	43.2
Puerto Rican	44.4
South American	52.0
Argentinean	64.2
Bolivian	61.4
Chilean	58.9
Colombian	55.1
Ecuadorian	41.7
Paraguayan	43.8
Peruvian	58.9
Uruguayan	50.0
Venezuelan	61.1
Spaniard	62.6

Median Home Value

Group	Dollars
Total Population	206,200
Hispanic or Latino (of any race)	176,700
Central American, ex. Mexican	182,600
Costa Rican	196,100
Guatemalan	166,000
Honduran	156,800
Nicaraguan	231,500
Panamanian	345,300
Salvadoran	168,800
Cuban	205,600
Dominican Republic	193,800
Mexican	164,700
Puerto Rican	216,300
South American	218,600
Argentinean	219,600
Chilean	377,900
Colombian	199,500
Ecuadorian	212,600
Peruvian	223,000
Venezuelan	233,300
Spaniard	193,600

Median Gross Rent

Group	Dollars
Total Population	759
Hispanic or Latino (of any race)	761
Central American, ex. Mexican	752
Costa Rican	1,125
Guatemalan	774
Honduran	708
Nicaraguan	616
Panamanian	897
Salvadoran	763
Cuban	763
Dominican Republic	737
Mexican	757
Puerto Rican	809
South American	834
Argentinean	899
Chilean	544
Colombian	854
Ecuadorian	837
Peruvian	685
Venezuelan	842
Spaniard	677

Median Household Income
(2010 Inflation-Adjusted Dollars)

Group	Dollars
Total Population	57,243
Hispanic or Latino (of any race)	40,163
Central American, ex. Mexican	41,286
Costa Rican	57,125
Guatemalan	41,027
Honduran	28,173
Nicaraguan	67,333
Panamanian	126,250
Salvadoran	38,359
Cuban	41,618
Dominican Republic	40,000
Mexican	38,148
Puerto Rican	46,566
South American	51,954
Argentinean	69,698
Chilean	66,354
Colombian	59,279
Ecuadorian	43,375
Peruvian	59,450
Venezuelan	43,264
Spaniard	51,800

Per Capita Income
(2010 Inflation-Adjusted Dollars)

Group	Dollars
Total Population	29,582
Hispanic or Latino (of any race)	14,202
Central American, ex. Mexican	14,386
Costa Rican	16,856
Guatemalan	11,387
Honduran	13,485
Nicaraguan	17,367
Panamanian	35,867
Salvadoran	13,852
Cuban	25,579
Dominican Republic	19,579
Mexican	12,741
Puerto Rican	20,194
South American	19,391
Argentinean	34,539
Chilean	26,968
Colombian	22,886
Ecuadorian	13,914
Peruvian	20,836
Venezuelan	23,956
Spaniard	28,268

Households with $100,000+ Income

Group	Number	%
Total Population	461,271	22.1
Hispanic or Latino (of any race)	6,483	11.0
Central American, ex. Mexican	725	14.3
Costa Rican	64	23.4
Guatemalan	127	9.9
Honduran	78	10.2
Nicaraguan	64	22.2
Panamanian	136	60.7
Salvadoran	242	11.1
Cuban	160	18.4
Dominican Republic	58	20.3
Mexican	3,582	8.7
Puerto Rican	582	18.4
South American	792	17.2
Argentinean	121	38.2
Chilean	78	35.6
Colombian	181	17.9
Ecuadorian	196	9.7
Peruvian	111	28.8
Venezuelan	71	15.4
Spaniard	224	22.6

Households with Food Stamps/SNAP Benefits During Past 12 Months

Group	Number	%
Total Population	123,923	5.9
Hispanic or Latino (of any race)	7,434	12.6
Central American, ex. Mexican	367	7.2
Costa Rican	31	11.4
Guatemalan	72	5.6
Honduran	87	11.4
Nicaraguan	0	0.0
Panamanian	18	8.0
Salvadoran	159	7.3
Cuban	178	20.5
Dominican Republic	57	19.9
Mexican	5,866	14.3
Puerto Rican	348	11.0
South American	149	3.2
Argentinean	0	0.0
Chilean	0	0.0
Colombian	22	2.2
Ecuadorian	99	4.9
Peruvian	0	0.0
Venezuelan	28	6.1
Spaniard	88	8.9

Poverty Rate
(Income in Past 12 Months Below Poverty Level)

Group	%
Total Population	10.6
Hispanic or Latino (of any race)	23.9
Central American, ex. Mexican	22.3
Costa Rican	10.5
Guatemalan	23.6
Honduran	34.8
Nicaraguan	17.4
Panamanian	4.6
Salvadoran	20.8
Cuban	19.8
Dominican Republic	21.2
Mexican	25.4
Puerto Rican	15.1
South American	18.9
Argentinean	1.9
Chilean	29.6
Colombian	7.1
Ecuadorian	28.5
Peruvian	11.5
Venezuelan	25.6
Spaniard	11.7

Minneapolis

Population

Group	Number	%TP[1]	%HP[2]
Total Population	382,578	100.0	–
Hispanic or Latino (of any race)	40,073	10.5	100.0
Central American, ex. Mexican	2,258	0.6	5.6
Costa Rican	113	<0.1	0.3
Guatemalan	980	0.3	2.4
Honduran	286	0.1	0.7
Nicaraguan	152	<0.1	0.4
Panamanian	126	<0.1	0.3
Salvadoran	586	0.2	1.5
Cuban	553	0.1	1.4
Dominican Republic	177	<0.1	0.4
Mexican	26,643	7.0	66.5
Puerto Rican	1,364	0.4	3.4
South American	6,270	1.6	15.6
Argentinean	174	<0.1	0.4
Chilean	155	<0.1	0.4
Colombian	568	0.1	1.4
Ecuadorian	4,792	1.3	12.0
Peruvian	263	0.1	0.7
Venezuelan	142	<0.1	0.4
Spaniard	468	0.1	1.2

Population Growth: 2000–2010

Group	%
Total Population	0.0
Hispanic or Latino (of any race)	37.4
Central American, ex. Mexican	104.0
Guatemalan	155.2
Honduran	128.8
Salvadoran	73.4
Cuban	12.9
Dominican Republic	40.5
Mexican	34.3
Puerto Rican	13.5
South American	155.2
Chilean	38.4
Colombian	96.5
Ecuadorian	192.4
Peruvian	115.6
Spaniard	368.0

Notes: (1) Percent of total population; (2) Percent of Hispanic/Latino population; Profiles include places with an overall population of at least 125,000, OR an overall population of at least 25,000 where the Hispanic/Latino population is at least 20% of the overall population. In states where less than five places meet either of these criteria, we have included places with at least 10,000 total population with the highest percentage of Hispanic/Latino population. These places are identified with an asterisk (*); Please refer to the User's Guide for a full explanation of data.

Males per 100 Females

Group	Number
Total Population	101.2
Hispanic or Latino (of any race)	121.0
Central American, ex. Mexican	125.3
Costa Rican	101.8
Guatemalan	140.8
Honduran	134.4
Nicaraguan	145.2
Panamanian	80.0
Salvadoran	113.1
Cuban	145.8
Dominican Republic	71.8
Mexican	119.9
Puerto Rican	103.6
South American	131.1
Argentinean	91.2
Chilean	91.4
Colombian	97.2
Ecuadorian	144.0
Peruvian	87.9
Venezuelan	121.9
Spaniard	105.3

Average Household Size

Group	People
Total Population	2.23
Hispanic or Latino (of any race)	3.75
Central American, ex. Mexican	3.49
Costa Rican	2.33
Guatemalan	3.90
Honduran	3.09
Nicaraguan	3.07
Panamanian	2.61
Salvadoran	3.75
Cuban	2.03
Dominican Republic	2.59
Mexican	4.06
Puerto Rican	2.27
South American	3.88
Argentinean	2.05
Chilean	2.15
Colombian	2.18
Ecuadorian	4.67
Peruvian	2.22
Venezuelan	2.25
Spaniard	2.33

Median Age

Group	Years
Total Population	31.4
Hispanic or Latino (of any race)	25.6
Central American, ex. Mexican	26.9
Costa Rican	29.4
Guatemalan	25.6
Honduran	25.9
Nicaraguan	28.3
Panamanian	30.6
Salvadoran	29.5
Cuban	30.6
Dominican Republic	25.9
Mexican	24.6
Puerto Rican	25.7
South American	28.4
Argentinean	32.5
Chilean	27.9
Colombian	25.7
Ecuadorian	28.3
Peruvian	30.5
Venezuelan	30.4
Spaniard	28.2

High School Graduates
(Universe: Population 25 Years and Over)

Group	Number	%
Total Population	217,017	87.9
Hispanic or Latino (of any race)	9,459	52.9
Central American, ex. Mexican	767	64.6
Guatemalan	238	73.9
Mexican	5,383	49.5
Puerto Rican	560	84.1
South American	1,743	45.6
Ecuadorian	999	33.3

Four-Year College Graduates
(Universe: Population 25 Years and Over)

Group	Number	%
Total Population	107,585	43.6
Hispanic or Latino (of any race)	2,930	16.4
Central American, ex. Mexican	314	26.5
Guatemalan	103	32.0
Mexican	1,280	11.8
Puerto Rican	249	37.4
South American	613	16.0
Ecuadorian	230	7.7

Population Age 3–17 Enrolled in Public School
(Universe: Population Age 3–17 Enrolled in School)

Group	Number	%
Total Population	45,089	84.1
Hispanic or Latino (of any race)	6,904	91.2
Central American, ex. Mexican	454	93.8
Guatemalan	235	88.7
Mexican	4,705	93.4
Puerto Rican	193	79.8
South American	1,194	86.9
Ecuadorian	952	95.3

Population Age 3–17 Enrolled in Private School
(Universe: Population Age 3–17 Enrolled in School)

Group	Number	%
Total Population	8,528	15.9
Hispanic or Latino (of any race)	669	8.8
Central American, ex. Mexican	30	6.2
Guatemalan	30	11.3
Mexican	334	6.6
Puerto Rican	49	20.2
South American	180	13.1
Ecuadorian	47	4.7

Foreign-Born Population

Group	Number	%
Total Population	57,202	15.1
Hispanic or Latino (of any race)	19,124	54.9
Central American, ex. Mexican	1,466	70.0
Guatemalan	641	76.9
Mexican	11,990	54.0
Puerto Rican	0	0.0
South American	4,906	68.8
Ecuadorian	3,934	71.6

Foreign-Born Naturalized U.S. Citizens

Group	Number	%
Total Population	20,665	36.1
Hispanic or Latino (of any race)	3,039	15.9
Central American, ex. Mexican	283	19.3
Guatemalan	168	26.2
Mexican	1,439	12.0
Puerto Rican	0	0.0
South American	1,013	20.6
Ecuadorian	432	11.0

Language Spoken at Home: English Only
(Universe: Population 5 Years and Over)

Group	Number	%
Total Population	284,308	80.4
Hispanic or Latino (of any race)	5,802	19.7
Central American, ex. Mexican	438	23.6
Guatemalan	229	31.5
Mexican	3,104	16.8
Puerto Rican	427	40.2
South American	950	15.5
Ecuadorian	147	3.2

Language Spoken at Home: Spanish
(Universe: Population 5 Years and Over)

Group	Number	%
Total Population	28,494	8.1
Hispanic or Latino (of any race)	23,549	80.0
Central American, ex. Mexican	1,418	76.4
Guatemalan	499	68.5
Mexican	15,292	83.0
Puerto Rican	636	59.8
South American	5,193	84.5
Ecuadorian	4,482	96.8

Unemployment Rate
(Universe: Population 16 Years and Over)

Group	%
Total Population	9.0
Hispanic or Latino (of any race)	8.0
Central American, ex. Mexican	11.1
Guatemalan	14.3
Mexican	8.0
Puerto Rican	7.4
South American	6.2
Ecuadorian	5.2

Class of Worker: Private Wage and Salary
(Universe: Civilian Employed Population 16 Years and Over)

Group	Number	%
Total Population	166,985	80.7
Hispanic or Latino (of any race)	15,087	91.5
Central American, ex. Mexican	1,084	95.1
Guatemalan	354	96.7
Mexican	9,035	92.1
Puerto Rican	517	83.8
South American	3,740	94.2
Ecuadorian	3,031	96.4

Class of Worker: Government
(Universe: Civilian Employed Population 16 Years and Over)

Group	Number	%
Total Population	27,737	13.4
Hispanic or Latino (of any race)	798	4.8
Central American, ex. Mexican	0	0.0
Guatemalan	0	0.0
Mexican	532	5.4
Puerto Rican	65	10.5
South American	85	2.1
Ecuadorian	48	1.5

Means of Transportation to Work: Car, Truck or Van
(Universe: Workers 16 Years and Over)

Group	Number	%
Total Population	141,569	70.0
Hispanic or Latino (of any race)	11,093	68.6
Central American, ex. Mexican	828	72.6
Guatemalan	303	82.8
Mexican	6,832	71.0
Puerto Rican	388	67.8
South American	2,333	59.8
Ecuadorian	1,772	57.2

Means of Transportation to Work: Public Transportation (ex. Taxicab)
(Universe: Workers 16 Years and Over)

Group	Number	%
Total Population	28,137	13.9
Hispanic or Latino (of any race)	3,743	23.2
Central American, ex. Mexican	146	12.8
Guatemalan	26	7.1
Mexican	1,964	20.4
Puerto Rican	128	22.4
South American	1,374	35.2
Ecuadorian	1,211	39.1

Homeownership Rate
(Universe: Occupied Housing Units)

Group	%
Total Population	49.2
Hispanic or Latino (of any race)	28.2
Central American, ex. Mexican	31.1
Costa Rican	51.5
Guatemalan	22.6
Honduran	20.0
Nicaraguan	40.9
Panamanian	53.1
Salvadoran	36.5
Cuban	30.5
Dominican Republic	20.3
Mexican	25.5
Puerto Rican	30.6
South American	35.3
Argentinean	48.0
Chilean	43.6
Colombian	40.7
Ecuadorian	32.8
Peruvian	38.4
Venezuelan	45.1

Notes: (1) Percent of total population; (2) Percent of Hispanic/Latino population; Profiles include places with an overall population of at least 125,000, OR an overall population of at least 25,000 where the Hispanic/Latino population is at least 20% of the overall population. In states where less than five places meet either of these criteria, we have included places with at least 10,000 total population with the highest percentage of Hispanic/Latino population. These places are identified with an asterisk (*); Please refer to the User's Guide for a full explanation of data.

Spaniard	43.0

Median Home Value

Group	Dollars
Total Population	228,700
Hispanic or Latino (of any race)	201,300
Central American, ex. Mexican	211,600
Guatemalan	229,000
Mexican	207,300
Puerto Rican	148,600
South American	199,600
Ecuadorian	201,100

Median Gross Rent

Group	Dollars
Total Population	774
Hispanic or Latino (of any race)	732
Central American, ex. Mexican	691
Guatemalan	912
Mexican	724
Puerto Rican	891
South American	836
Ecuadorian	836

Median Household Income
(2010 Inflation-Adjusted Dollars)

Group	Dollars
Total Population	46,075
Hispanic or Latino (of any race)	34,901
Central American, ex. Mexican	48,324
Guatemalan	53,650
Mexican	31,268
Puerto Rican	30,000
South American	40,915
Ecuadorian	40,148

Per Capita Income
(2010 Inflation-Adjusted Dollars)

Group	Dollars
Total Population	29,551
Hispanic or Latino (of any race)	13,622
Central American, ex. Mexican	16,345
Guatemalan	14,665
Mexican	11,682
Puerto Rican	22,960
South American	14,885
Ecuadorian	12,119

Households with $100,000+ Income

Group	Number	%
Total Population	31,050	18.6
Hispanic or Latino (of any race)	717	7.5
Central American, ex. Mexican	42	6.1
Guatemalan	16	8.5
Mexican	378	6.7
Puerto Rican	38	8.0
South American	166	9.0
Ecuadorian	56	4.1

Households with Food Stamps/SNAP Benefits During Past 12 Months

Group	Number	%
Total Population	20,055	12.0
Hispanic or Latino (of any race)	1,421	14.8
Central American, ex. Mexican	28	4.1
Guatemalan	0	0.0
Mexican	1,080	19.0
Puerto Rican	117	24.6
South American	63	3.4
Ecuadorian	43	3.2

Poverty Rate
(Income in Past 12 Months Below Poverty Level)

Group	%
Total Population	22.7
Hispanic or Latino (of any race)	30.4
Central American, ex. Mexican	11.5
Guatemalan	13.5
Mexican	33.1
Puerto Rican	19.1
South American	30.4
Ecuadorian	31.1

Saint Paul

Population

Group	Number	%TP[1]	%HP[2]
Total Population	285,068	100.0	–
Hispanic or Latino (of any race)	27,311	9.6	100.0
Central American, ex. Mexican	2,933	1.0	10.7
Guatemalan	583	0.2	2.1
Honduran	377	0.1	1.4
Salvadoran	1,731	0.6	6.3
Cuban	445	0.2	1.6
Dominican Republic	209	0.1	0.8
Mexican	19,490	6.8	71.4
Puerto Rican	1,310	0.5	4.8
South American	1,032	0.4	3.8
Colombian	351	0.1	1.3
Ecuadorian	148	0.1	0.5
Peruvian	154	0.1	0.6
Spaniard	293	0.1	1.1

Population Growth: 2000–2010

Group	%
Total Population	-0.7
Hispanic or Latino (of any race)	20.2
Central American, ex. Mexican	158.0
Guatemalan	185.8
Honduran	137.1
Salvadoran	191.9
Cuban	25.0
Dominican Republic	109.0
Mexican	17.7
Puerto Rican	26.3
South American	76.4
Colombian	97.2

Males per 100 Females

Group	Number
Total Population	95.6
Hispanic or Latino (of any race)	110.1
Central American, ex. Mexican	120.7
Guatemalan	115.9
Honduran	138.6
Salvadoran	122.2
Cuban	115.0
Dominican Republic	90.0
Mexican	112.0
Puerto Rican	96.7
South American	85.9
Colombian	80.0
Ecuadorian	117.6
Peruvian	75.0
Spaniard	73.4

Average Household Size

Group	People
Total Population	2.47
Hispanic or Latino (of any race)	3.47
Central American, ex. Mexican	3.88
Guatemalan	3.74
Honduran	3.56
Salvadoran	4.19
Cuban	2.34
Dominican Republic	3.19
Mexican	3.62
Puerto Rican	2.85
South American	2.49
Colombian	2.38
Ecuadorian	3.38
Peruvian	2.42
Spaniard	2.25

Median Age

Group	Years
Total Population	30.9
Hispanic or Latino (of any race)	24.2
Central American, ex. Mexican	27.5
Guatemalan	23.3
Honduran	26.6
Salvadoran	28.3
Cuban	26.7
Dominican Republic	25.6
Mexican	23.6
Puerto Rican	21.1
South American	25.5

Colombian	22.6
Ecuadorian	24.0
Peruvian	31.3
Spaniard	29.7

High School Graduates
(Universe: Population 25 Years and Over)

Group	Number	%
Total Population	149,275	86.6
Hispanic or Latino (of any race)	8,069	59.6
Central American, ex. Mexican	736	42.6
Salvadoran	416	36.0
Mexican	5,452	56.6
Puerto Rican	569	95.2
South American	656	94.3

Four-Year College Graduates
(Universe: Population 25 Years and Over)

Group	Number	%
Total Population	64,267	37.3
Hispanic or Latino (of any race)	2,027	15.0
Central American, ex. Mexican	92	5.3
Salvadoran	0	0.0
Mexican	1,002	10.4
Puerto Rican	181	30.3
South American	497	71.4

Population Age 3–17 Enrolled in Public School
(Universe: Population Age 3–17 Enrolled in School)

Group	Number	%
Total Population	41,877	82.8
Hispanic or Latino (of any race)	6,122	92.3
Central American, ex. Mexican	723	90.6
Salvadoran	497	100.0
Mexican	4,426	93.7
Puerto Rican	409	96.2
South American	200	78.4

Population Age 3–17 Enrolled in Private School
(Universe: Population Age 3–17 Enrolled in School)

Group	Number	%
Total Population	8,706	17.2
Hispanic or Latino (of any race)	513	7.7
Central American, ex. Mexican	75	9.4
Salvadoran	0	0.0
Mexican	297	6.3
Puerto Rican	16	3.8
South American	55	21.6

Foreign-Born Population

Group	Number	%
Total Population	47,543	16.9
Hispanic or Latino (of any race)	10,933	40.5
Central American, ex. Mexican	2,022	62.1
Salvadoran	1,372	65.1
Mexican	7,730	40.0
Puerto Rican	9	0.6
South American	772	67.1

Foreign-Born Naturalized U.S. Citizens

Group	Number	%
Total Population	19,461	40.9
Hispanic or Latino (of any race)	2,180	19.9
Central American, ex. Mexican	527	26.1
Salvadoran	369	26.9
Mexican	1,076	13.9
Puerto Rican	0	0.0
South American	361	46.8

Language Spoken at Home: English Only
(Universe: Population 5 Years and Over)

Group	Number	%
Total Population	193,267	74.3
Hispanic or Latino (of any race)	6,868	29.3
Central American, ex. Mexican	240	8.8
Salvadoran	75	4.1
Mexican	4,752	28.3
Puerto Rican	791	61.9
South American	410	37.6

Language Spoken at Home: Spanish
(Universe: Population 5 Years and Over)

Group	Number	%
Total Population	19,187	7.4
Hispanic or Latino (of any race)	16,463	70.1
Central American, ex. Mexican	2,484	91.2

Notes: (1) Percent of total population; (2) Percent of Hispanic/Latino population; Profiles include places with an overall population of at least 125,000, OR an overall population of at least 25,000 where the Hispanic/Latino population is at least 20% of the overall population. In states where less than five places meet either of these criteria, we have included places with at least 10,000 total population with the highest percentage of Hispanic/Latino population. These places are identified with an asterisk (*); Please refer to the User's Guide for a full explanation of data.

Salvadoran	1,746	95.9
Mexican	11,947	71.1
Puerto Rican	479	37.5
South American	679	62.4

Unemployment Rate
(Universe: Population 16 Years and Over)

Group	%
Total Population	9.0
Hispanic or Latino (of any race)	10.8
Central American, ex. Mexican	11.2
Salvadoran	13.8
Mexican	10.7
Puerto Rican	16.8
South American	0.0

Class of Worker: Private Wage and Salary
(Universe: Civilian Employed Population 16 Years and Over)

Group	Number	%
Total Population	114,779	81.7
Hispanic or Latino (of any race)	10,381	89.9
Central American, ex. Mexican	1,361	95.6
Salvadoran	934	98.6
Mexican	7,540	91.2
Puerto Rican	474	82.7
South American	398	69.1

Class of Worker: Government
(Universe: Civilian Employed Population 16 Years and Over)

Group	Number	%
Total Population	19,124	13.6
Hispanic or Latino (of any race)	682	5.9
Central American, ex. Mexican	54	3.8
Salvadoran	13	1.4
Mexican	407	4.9
Puerto Rican	46	8.0
South American	114	19.8

Means of Transportation to Work: Car, Truck or Van
(Universe: Workers 16 Years and Over)

Group	Number	%
Total Population	109,881	79.8
Hispanic or Latino (of any race)	9,150	80.7
Central American, ex. Mexican	1,091	80.0
Salvadoran	740	83.4
Mexican	6,705	82.1
Puerto Rican	468	81.7
South American	453	80.7

Means of Transportation to Work: Public Transportation (ex. Taxicab)
(Universe: Workers 16 Years and Over)

Group	Number	%
Total Population	12,617	9.2
Hispanic or Latino (of any race)	1,434	12.6
Central American, ex. Mexican	184	13.5
Salvadoran	100	11.3
Mexican	963	11.8
Puerto Rican	59	10.3
South American	21	3.7

Homeownership Rate
(Universe: Occupied Housing Units)

Group	%
Total Population	51.3
Hispanic or Latino (of any race)	36.9
Central American, ex. Mexican	31.9
Guatemalan	34.5
Honduran	13.1
Salvadoran	33.3
Cuban	35.7
Dominican Republic	46.6
Mexican	37.5
Puerto Rican	30.7
South American	48.9
Colombian	35.6
Ecuadorian	56.3
Peruvian	53.3
Spaniard	55.5

Median Home Value

Group	Dollars
Total Population	205,400
Hispanic or Latino (of any race)	182,000
Central American, ex. Mexican	170,600
Salvadoran	158,300
Mexican	178,100
Puerto Rican	196,900
South American	194,800

Median Gross Rent

Group	Dollars
Total Population	756
Hispanic or Latino (of any race)	764
Central American, ex. Mexican	769
Salvadoran	782
Mexican	762
Puerto Rican	617
South American	783

Median Household Income
(2010 Inflation-Adjusted Dollars)

Group	Dollars
Total Population	45,439
Hispanic or Latino (of any race)	33,210
Central American, ex. Mexican	34,306
Salvadoran	38,309
Mexican	32,229
Puerto Rican	37,756
South American	60,397

Per Capita Income
(2010 Inflation-Adjusted Dollars)

Group	Dollars
Total Population	25,066
Hispanic or Latino (of any race)	13,579
Central American, ex. Mexican	11,919
Salvadoran	11,654
Mexican	12,911
Puerto Rican	15,826
South American	25,321

Households with $100,000+ Income

Group	Number	%
Total Population	18,377	16.5
Hispanic or Latino (of any race)	591	7.9
Central American, ex. Mexican	59	7.2
Salvadoran	37	6.9
Mexican	297	5.6
Puerto Rican	67	14.0
South American	87	22.4

Households with Food Stamps/SNAP Benefits During Past 12 Months

Group	Number	%
Total Population	14,522	13.0
Hispanic or Latino (of any race)	1,085	14.4
Central American, ex. Mexican	29	3.5
Salvadoran	29	5.4
Mexican	769	14.6
Puerto Rican	124	25.8
South American	29	7.5

Poverty Rate
(Income in Past 12 Months Below Poverty Level)

Group	%
Total Population	22.0
Hispanic or Latino (of any race)	30.6
Central American, ex. Mexican	29.6
Salvadoran	28.1
Mexican	31.4
Puerto Rican	29.0
South American	10.6

West Saint Paul*

Population

Group	Number	%TP[1]	%HP[2]
Total Population	19,540	100.0	–
Hispanic or Latino (of any race)	3,803	19.5	100.0
Central American, ex. Mexican	294	1.5	7.7
Salvadoran	150	0.8	3.9
Mexican	3,023	15.5	79.5
Puerto Rican	158	0.8	4.2

Population Growth: 2000–2010

Group	%
Total Population	0.7
Hispanic or Latino (of any race)	96.3
Central American, ex. Mexican	182.7
Mexican	109.9
Puerto Rican	19.7

Males per 100 Females

Group	Number
Total Population	90.7
Hispanic or Latino (of any race)	111.0
Central American, ex. Mexican	122.7
Salvadoran	134.4
Mexican	111.4
Puerto Rican	122.5

Average Household Size

Group	People
Total Population	2.25
Hispanic or Latino (of any race)	3.17
Central American, ex. Mexican	3.52
Salvadoran	3.47
Mexican	3.22
Puerto Rican	2.61

Median Age

Group	Years
Total Population	39.7
Hispanic or Latino (of any race)	25.5
Central American, ex. Mexican	29.0
Salvadoran	28.6
Mexican	24.8
Puerto Rican	28.0

High School Graduates
(Universe: Population 25 Years and Over)

Group	Number	%
Total Population	12,069	87.6
Hispanic or Latino (of any race)	1,062	60.0
Mexican	787	60.5

Four-Year College Graduates
(Universe: Population 25 Years and Over)

Group	Number	%
Total Population	3,910	28.4
Hispanic or Latino (of any race)	190	10.7
Mexican	96	7.4

Population Age 3–17 Enrolled in Public School
(Universe: Population Age 3–17 Enrolled in School)

Group	Number	%
Total Population	2,335	79.8
Hispanic or Latino (of any race)	702	88.5
Mexican	526	88.9

Population Age 3–17 Enrolled in Private School
(Universe: Population Age 3–17 Enrolled in School)

Group	Number	%
Total Population	592	20.2
Hispanic or Latino (of any race)	91	11.5
Mexican	66	11.1

Foreign-Born Population

Group	Number	%
Total Population	2,011	10.2
Hispanic or Latino (of any race)	1,379	37.9
Mexican	810	31.4

Foreign-Born Naturalized U.S. Citizens

Group	Number	%
Total Population	638	31.7
Hispanic or Latino (of any race)	270	19.6
Mexican	103	12.7

Language Spoken at Home: English Only
(Universe: Population 5 Years and Over)

Group	Number	%
Total Population	15,238	83.3
Hispanic or Latino (of any race)	936	30.7
Mexican	797	36.2

Language Spoken at Home: Spanish
(Universe: Population 5 Years and Over)

Group	Number	%
Total Population	2,229	12.2
Hispanic or Latino (of any race)	2,090	68.5
Mexican	1,395	63.3

Notes: (1) Percent of total population; (2) Percent of Hispanic/Latino population; Profiles include places with an overall population of at least 125,000, OR an overall population of at least 25,000 where the Hispanic/Latino population is at least 20% of the overall population. In states where less than five places meet either of these criteria, we have included places with at least 10,000 total population with the highest percentage of Hispanic/Latino population. These places are identified with an asterisk (*); Please refer to the User's Guide for a full explanation of data.

Unemployment Rate
(Universe: Population 16 Years and Over)

Group	%
Total Population	6.8
Hispanic or Latino (of any race)	7.8
Mexican	7.4

Class of Worker: Private Wage and Salary
(Universe: Civilian Employed Population 16 Years and Over)

Group	Number	%
Total Population	8,008	79.5
Hispanic or Latino (of any race)	1,484	85.3
Mexican	1,021	83.0

Class of Worker: Government
(Universe: Civilian Employed Population 16 Years and Over)

Group	Number	%
Total Population	1,750	17.4
Hispanic or Latino (of any race)	203	11.7
Mexican	157	12.8

Means of Transportation to Work: Car, Truck or Van
(Universe: Workers 16 Years and Over)

Group	Number	%
Total Population	8,816	88.6
Hispanic or Latino (of any race)	1,599	92.8
Mexican	1,122	92.4

Means of Transportation to Work: Public Transportation (ex. Taxicab)
(Universe: Workers 16 Years and Over)

Group	Number	%
Total Population	505	5.1
Hispanic or Latino (of any race)	23	1.3
Mexican	23	1.9

Homeownership Rate
(Universe: Occupied Housing Units)

Group	%
Total Population	58.1
Hispanic or Latino (of any race)	33.1
Central American, ex. Mexican	31.5
Salvadoran	28.6
Mexican	33.9
Puerto Rican	27.8

Median Home Value

Group	Dollars
Total Population	215,800
Hispanic or Latino (of any race)	219,300
Mexican	216,800

Median Gross Rent

Group	Dollars
Total Population	805
Hispanic or Latino (of any race)	741
Mexican	732

Median Household Income
(2010 Inflation-Adjusted Dollars)

Group	Dollars
Total Population	48,440
Hispanic or Latino (of any race)	37,112
Mexican	44,028

Per Capita Income
(2010 Inflation-Adjusted Dollars)

Group	Dollars
Total Population	29,327
Hispanic or Latino (of any race)	15,824
Mexican	16,493

Households with $100,000+ Income

Group	Number	%
Total Population	1,541	17.5
Hispanic or Latino (of any race)	56	5.2
Mexican	56	6.9

Households with Food Stamps/SNAP Benefits During Past 12 Months

Group	Number	%
Total Population	711	8.1
Hispanic or Latino (of any race)	98	9.0
Mexican	64	7.9

Poverty Rate
(Income in Past 12 Months Below Poverty Level)

Group	%
Total Population	8.4
Hispanic or Latino (of any race)	13.9
Mexican	10.5

Willmar*

Population

Group	Number	%TP[1]	%HP[2]
Total Population	19,610	100.0	–
Hispanic or Latino (of any race)	4,099	20.9	100.0
Central American, ex. Mexican	566	2.9	13.8
Guatemalan	135	0.7	3.3
Honduran	337	1.7	8.2
Mexican	2,934	15.0	71.6

Population Growth: 2000–2010

Group	%
Total Population	6.9
Hispanic or Latino (of any race)	40.8
Mexican	62.5

Males per 100 Females

Group	Number
Total Population	95.3
Hispanic or Latino (of any race)	110.2
Central American, ex. Mexican	140.9
Guatemalan	125.0
Honduran	165.4
Mexican	107.9

Average Household Size

Group	People
Total Population	2.43
Hispanic or Latino (of any race)	3.87
Central American, ex. Mexican	4.53
Guatemalan	4.43
Honduran	4.78
Mexican	3.81

Median Age

Group	Years
Total Population	33.8
Hispanic or Latino (of any race)	21.1
Central American, ex. Mexican	27.1
Guatemalan	27.9
Honduran	24.4
Mexican	20.3

High School Graduates
(Universe: Population 25 Years and Over)

Group	Number	%
Total Population	9,806	82.2
Hispanic or Latino (of any race)	713	43.8
Mexican	682	45.8

Four-Year College Graduates
(Universe: Population 25 Years and Over)

Group	Number	%
Total Population	2,254	18.9
Hispanic or Latino (of any race)	32	2.0
Mexican	16	1.1

Population Age 3–17 Enrolled in Public School
(Universe: Population Age 3–17 Enrolled in School)

Group	Number	%
Total Population	3,427	93.8
Hispanic or Latino (of any race)	1,273	97.8
Mexican	1,224	98.9

Population Age 3–17 Enrolled in Private School
(Universe: Population Age 3–17 Enrolled in School)

Group	Number	%
Total Population	225	6.2
Hispanic or Latino (of any race)	28	2.2
Mexican	14	1.1

Foreign-Born Population

Group	Number	%
Total Population	1,720	8.9
Hispanic or Latino (of any race)	1,030	25.6
Mexican	936	25.3

Foreign-Born Naturalized U.S. Citizens

Group	Number	%
Total Population	454	26.4
Hispanic or Latino (of any race)	275	26.7
Mexican	246	26.3

Language Spoken at Home: English Only
(Universe: Population 5 Years and Over)

Group	Number	%
Total Population	14,287	79.7
Hispanic or Latino (of any race)	835	24.5
Mexican	817	25.5

Language Spoken at Home: Spanish
(Universe: Population 5 Years and Over)

Group	Number	%
Total Population	2,946	16.4
Hispanic or Latino (of any race)	2,571	75.5
Mexican	2,389	74.5

Unemployment Rate
(Universe: Population 16 Years and Over)

Group	%
Total Population	7.5
Hispanic or Latino (of any race)	12.8
Mexican	13.7

Class of Worker: Private Wage and Salary
(Universe: Civilian Employed Population 16 Years and Over)

Group	Number	%
Total Population	7,558	81.1
Hispanic or Latino (of any race)	1,337	98.3
Mexican	1,235	98.2

Class of Worker: Government
(Universe: Civilian Employed Population 16 Years and Over)

Group	Number	%
Total Population	1,186	12.7
Hispanic or Latino (of any race)	23	1.7
Mexican	23	1.8

Means of Transportation to Work: Car, Truck or Van
(Universe: Workers 16 Years and Over)

Group	Number	%
Total Population	8,340	90.8
Hispanic or Latino (of any race)	1,336	98.2
Mexican	1,234	98.1

Means of Transportation to Work: Public Transportation (ex. Taxicab)
(Universe: Workers 16 Years and Over)

Group	Number	%
Total Population	249	2.7
Hispanic or Latino (of any race)	0	0.0
Mexican	0	0.0

Homeownership Rate
(Universe: Occupied Housing Units)

Group	%
Total Population	58.8
Hispanic or Latino (of any race)	32.6
Central American, ex. Mexican	36.6
Guatemalan	28.6
Honduran	39.7
Mexican	33.0

Median Home Value

Group	Dollars
Total Population	128,500
Hispanic or Latino (of any race)	134,200
Mexican	133,600

Median Gross Rent

Group	Dollars
Total Population	550
Hispanic or Latino (of any race)	457
Mexican	458

Median Household Income
(2010 Inflation-Adjusted Dollars)

Group	Dollars
Total Population	38,529
Hispanic or Latino (of any race)	31,577
Mexican	31,990

Notes: (1) Percent of total population; (2) Percent of Hispanic/Latino population; Profiles include places with an overall population of at least 125,000, OR an overall population of at least 25,000 where the Hispanic/Latino population is at least 20% of the overall population. In states where less than five places meet either of these criteria, we have included places with at least 10,000 total population with the highest percentage of Hispanic/Latino population. These places are identified with an asterisk (*); Please refer to the User's Guide for a full explanation of data.

Per Capita Income (2010 Inflation-Adjusted Dollars)	
Group	Dollars
Total Population	20,118
Hispanic or Latino (of any race)	10,175
Mexican	10,213

Households with $100,000+ Income		
Group	Number	%
Total Population	770	9.7
Hispanic or Latino (of any race)	143	14.1
Mexican	143	15.4

Households with Food Stamps/SNAP Benefits During Past 12 Months		
Group	Number	%
Total Population	1,015	12.8
Hispanic or Latino (of any race)	309	30.4
Mexican	253	27.2

Poverty Rate (Income in Past 12 Months Below Poverty Level)	
Group	%
Total Population	20.7
Hispanic or Latino (of any race)	41.3
Mexican	41.7

Worthington*

Population			
Group	Number	%TP[1]	%HP[2]
Total Population	12,764	100.0	–
Hispanic or Latino (of any race)	4,521	35.4	100.0
Central American, ex. Mexican	1,619	12.7	35.8
Guatemalan	906	7.1	20.0
Honduran	139	1.1	3.1
Salvadoran	500	3.9	11.1
Mexican	2,367	18.5	52.4

Population Growth: 2000–2010	
Group	%
Total Population	13.1
Hispanic or Latino (of any race)	107.9
Central American, ex. Mexican	497.4
Guatemalan	630.6
Mexican	52.3

Males per 100 Females	
Group	Number
Total Population	104.6
Hispanic or Latino (of any race)	118.4
Central American, ex. Mexican	137.4
Guatemalan	143.5
Honduran	127.9
Salvadoran	140.4
Mexican	106.7

Average Household Size	
Group	People
Total Population	2.79
Hispanic or Latino (of any race)	4.59
Central American, ex. Mexican	5.15
Guatemalan	5.09
Honduran	4.75
Salvadoran	5.43
Mexican	4.30

Median Age	
Group	Years
Total Population	33.5
Hispanic or Latino (of any race)	23.4
Central American, ex. Mexican	25.4
Guatemalan	24.8
Honduran	21.8
Salvadoran	26.9
Mexican	22.3

High School Graduates (Universe: Population 25 Years and Over)		
Group	Number	%
Total Population	5,615	72.4
Hispanic or Latino (of any race)	512	28.9
Central American, ex. Mexican	79	13.9
Mexican	433	38.7

Four-Year College Graduates (Universe: Population 25 Years and Over)		
Group	Number	%
Total Population	1,347	17.4
Hispanic or Latino (of any race)	58	3.3
Central American, ex. Mexican	0	0.0
Mexican	58	5.2

Population Age 3–17 Enrolled in Public School (Universe: Population Age 3–17 Enrolled in School)		
Group	Number	%
Total Population	1,948	90.2
Hispanic or Latino (of any race)	764	95.6
Central American, ex. Mexican	131	100.0
Mexican	602	94.5

Population Age 3–17 Enrolled in Private School (Universe: Population Age 3–17 Enrolled in School)		
Group	Number	%
Total Population	211	9.8
Hispanic or Latino (of any race)	35	4.4
Central American, ex. Mexican	0	0.0
Mexican	35	5.5

Foreign-Born Population		
Group	Number	%
Total Population	2,955	23.9
Hispanic or Latino (of any race)	2,099	54.5
Central American, ex. Mexican	850	66.8
Mexican	1,249	51.2

Foreign-Born Naturalized U.S. Citizens		
Group	Number	%
Total Population	842	28.5
Hispanic or Latino (of any race)	430	20.5
Central American, ex. Mexican	49	5.8
Mexican	381	30.5

Language Spoken at Home: English Only (Universe: Population 5 Years and Over)		
Group	Number	%
Total Population	7,305	64.3
Hispanic or Latino (of any race)	228	7.1
Central American, ex. Mexican	55	5.4
Mexican	167	8.1

Language Spoken at Home: Spanish (Universe: Population 5 Years and Over)		
Group	Number	%
Total Population	2,548	22.4
Hispanic or Latino (of any race)	2,490	77.5
Central American, ex. Mexican	459	45.4
Mexican	1,896	91.9

Unemployment Rate (Universe: Population 16 Years and Over)	
Group	%
Total Population	5.9
Hispanic or Latino (of any race)	12.9
Central American, ex. Mexican	16.8
Mexican	9.1

Class of Worker: Private Wage and Salary (Universe: Civilian Employed Population 16 Years and Over)		
Group	Number	%
Total Population	4,886	83.2
Hispanic or Latino (of any race)	1,447	92.8
Central American, ex. Mexican	481	100.0
Mexican	889	88.8

Class of Worker: Government (Universe: Civilian Employed Population 16 Years and Over)		
Group	Number	%
Total Population	669	11.4
Hispanic or Latino (of any race)	78	5.0
Central American, ex. Mexican	0	0.0
Mexican	78	7.8

Means of Transportation to Work: Car, Truck or Van (Universe: Workers 16 Years and Over)		
Group	Number	%
Total Population	4,927	86.5
Hispanic or Latino (of any race)	1,209	80.1
Central American, ex. Mexican	460	95.6
Mexican	693	72.8

Means of Transportation to Work: Public Transportation (ex. Taxicab) (Universe: Workers 16 Years and Over)		
Group	Number	%
Total Population	64	1.1
Hispanic or Latino (of any race)	45	3.0
Central American, ex. Mexican	10	2.1
Mexican	35	3.7

Homeownership Rate (Universe: Occupied Housing Units)	
Group	%
Total Population	63.0
Hispanic or Latino (of any race)	44.7
Central American, ex. Mexican	34.3
Guatemalan	23.4
Honduran	46.9
Salvadoran	46.4
Mexican	53.9

Median Home Value	
Group	Dollars
Total Population	101,100
Hispanic or Latino (of any race)	51,100
Central American, ex. Mexican	<10,000
Mexican	52,100

Median Gross Rent	
Group	Dollars
Total Population	570
Hispanic or Latino (of any race)	698
Central American, ex. Mexican	765
Mexican	604

Median Household Income (2010 Inflation-Adjusted Dollars)	
Group	Dollars
Total Population	40,703
Hispanic or Latino (of any race)	31,806
Central American, ex. Mexican	30,781
Mexican	32,012

Per Capita Income (2010 Inflation-Adjusted Dollars)	
Group	Dollars
Total Population	18,743
Hispanic or Latino (of any race)	8,941
Central American, ex. Mexican	9,553
Mexican	8,737

Households with $100,000+ Income		
Group	Number	%
Total Population	407	8.9
Hispanic or Latino (of any race)	14	1.5
Central American, ex. Mexican	8	2.7
Mexican	0	0.0

Households with Food Stamps/SNAP Benefits During Past 12 Months		
Group	Number	%
Total Population	423	9.3
Hispanic or Latino (of any race)	92	9.8
Central American, ex. Mexican	25	8.4
Mexican	67	11.1

Poverty Rate (Income in Past 12 Months Below Poverty Level)	
Group	%
Total Population	25.6
Hispanic or Latino (of any race)	45.4
Central American, ex. Mexican	38.2
Mexican	48.2

Notes: (1) Percent of total population; (2) Percent of Hispanic/Latino population; Profiles include places with an overall population of at least 125,000, OR an overall population of at least 25,000 where the Hispanic/Latino population is at least 20% of the overall population. In states where less than five places meet either of these criteria, we have included places with at least 10,000 total population with the highest percentage of Hispanic/Latino population. These places are identified with an asterisk (*); Please refer to the User's Guide for a full explanation of data.

Mississippi

EDITOR'S NOTE: For a place to be included in this edition, it must meet one of two criteria. Either its overall population is at least 125,000, OR its overall population is at least 25,000 and its Hispanic/Latino population is at least 20% of the overall population. In Mississippi, less than five places meet either of these criteria. In an effort to include at least five places for each state, we have included places with at least 10,000 total population with the highest percentage of Hispanic/Latino population. These places are identified with an asterisk (*). For the state of Mississippi, the following locations are included:

Biloxi*
Horn Lake*
Jackson
Laurel*
Pascagoula*

Section Two: State & Place Profiles starts with the state profile, followed by place profiles that meet the criteria above. Places are listed alphabetically within each state. All states, all counties and places that meet the above criteria are ranked and compared in *Section Three: Rankings & Comparisons*, on page 1055.

For a more detailed look at the Hispanic/Latino population in Mississippi, a companion web site is available at no additional charge with purchase of this print edition. Visit http://gold.greyhouse.com/page/info_hispanic for more information.

The web site includes data for all counties and places in Mississippi with Hispanic/Latino population, plus ten additional topics: Self Employed Worker; Walked to Work; Worked from Home; Mean Travel Time to Work; Mean Household Income; Households with Cash Public Assistance; Mean Cash Pubic Assistance; Poverty Rates for 18 and Under, 18 to 64, and 65 and Over.

Population

Group	Number	%TP[1]	%HP[2]
Total Population	2,967,297	100.0	–
Hispanic or Latino (of any race)	81,481	2.7	100.0
Central American, ex. Mexican	8,343	0.3	10.2
Costa Rican	317	<0.1	0.4
Guatemalan	2,978	0.1	3.7
Honduran	2,448	0.1	3.0
Nicaraguan	700	<0.1	0.9
Panamanian	670	<0.1	0.8
Salvadoran	1,174	<0.1	1.4
Cuban	2,063	0.1	2.5
Dominican Republic	733	<0.1	0.9
Mexican	52,459	1.8	64.4
Puerto Rican	5,888	0.2	7.2
South American	2,833	0.1	3.5
Argentinean	276	<0.1	0.3
Chilean	146	<0.1	0.2
Colombian	1,025	<0.1	1.3
Ecuadorian	298	<0.1	0.4
Peruvian	473	<0.1	0.6
Venezuelan	412	<0.1	0.5
Spaniard	1,353	<0.1	1.7

Population Growth: 2000–2010

Group	%
Total Population	4.3
Hispanic or Latino (of any race)	105.9
Central American, ex. Mexican	390.5
Costa Rican	124.8
Guatemalan	778.5
Honduran	429.9
Nicaraguan	295.5
Panamanian	104.9
Salvadoran	484.1
Cuban	36.8
Dominican Republic	285.8
Mexican	142.7
Puerto Rican	104.4
South American	139.9
Colombian	119.0
Peruvian	261.1
Venezuelan	62.2
Spaniard	720.0

Males per 100 Females

Group	Number
Total Population	94.4
Hispanic or Latino (of any race)	141.1
Central American, ex. Mexican	147.8
Costa Rican	80.1
Guatemalan	178.8
Honduran	164.6
Nicaraguan	100.6
Panamanian	82.6
Salvadoran	151.9
Cuban	127.7
Dominican Republic	134.2
Mexican	153.1
Puerto Rican	111.8
South American	100.2
Argentinean	117.3
Chilean	97.3
Colombian	113.5
Ecuadorian	106.9
Peruvian	77.8
Venezuelan	89.9
Spaniard	99.0

Average Household Size

Group	People
Total Population	2.58
Hispanic or Latino (of any race)	3.47
Central American, ex. Mexican	3.75
Costa Rican	2.81
Guatemalan	4.55
Honduran	3.62
Nicaraguan	3.19
Panamanian	2.72
Salvadoran	3.67
Cuban	2.74
Dominican Republic	3.09
Mexican	3.76
Puerto Rican	2.89
South American	2.85
Argentinean	2.95
Chilean	2.63
Colombian	2.74
Ecuadorian	2.78
Peruvian	3.11
Venezuelan	2.87
Spaniard	2.67

Median Age

Group	Years
Total Population	36.0
Hispanic or Latino (of any race)	26.3
Central American, ex. Mexican	27.8
Costa Rican	34.6
Guatemalan	26.0
Honduran	28.2
Nicaraguan	31.7
Panamanian	32.0
Salvadoran	29.1
Cuban	34.5
Dominican Republic	29.7
Mexican	25.2
Puerto Rican	26.3
South American	33.5
Argentinean	34.7
Chilean	35.0
Colombian	34.6
Ecuadorian	30.4
Peruvian	33.8
Venezuelan	32.4
Spaniard	35.6

High School Graduates
(Universe: Population 25 Years and Over)

Group	Number	%
Total Population	1,494,328	79.6
Hispanic or Latino (of any race)	20,323	57.2
Central American, ex. Mexican	2,109	53.1
Guatemalan	327	33.6
Honduran	628	47.6
Panamanian	382	93.9
Cuban	731	63.7
Mexican	10,574	48.0
Puerto Rican	2,007	88.6
South American	2,073	94.0
Spaniard	671	74.4

Four-Year College Graduates
(Universe: Population 25 Years and Over)

Group	Number	%
Total Population	365,159	19.5
Hispanic or Latino (of any race)	4,110	11.6
Central American, ex. Mexican	549	13.8
Guatemalan	64	6.6
Honduran	162	12.3
Panamanian	131	32.2
Cuban	293	25.5
Mexican	1,378	6.2
Puerto Rican	357	15.8
South American	1,045	47.4
Spaniard	157	17.4

Population Age 3–17 Enrolled in Public School
(Universe: Population Age 3–17 Enrolled in School)

Group	Number	%
Total Population	496,586	87.3
Hispanic or Latino (of any race)	12,872	89.7
Central American, ex. Mexican	959	80.0
Guatemalan	229	70.9
Honduran	248	70.7
Panamanian	92	100.0
Cuban	521	88.2
Mexican	9,031	93.4
Puerto Rican	1,074	83.4
South American	363	80.8
Spaniard	103	52.6

Population Age 3–17 Enrolled in Private School
(Universe: Population Age 3–17 Enrolled in School)

Group	Number	%
Total Population	72,272	12.7
Hispanic or Latino (of any race)	1,472	10.3
Central American, ex. Mexican	240	20.0
Guatemalan	94	29.1
Honduran	103	29.3
Panamanian	0	0.0
Cuban	70	11.8
Mexican	636	6.6
Puerto Rican	213	16.6
South American	86	19.2
Spaniard	93	47.4

Foreign-Born Population

Group	Number	%
Total Population	63,518	2.2
Hispanic or Latino (of any race)	31,654	45.3
Central American, ex. Mexican	4,743	66.3
Guatemalan	1,676	83.5
Honduran	1,527	68.7
Panamanian	293	33.1
Cuban	892	44.4
Mexican	22,185	48.5
Puerto Rican	100	1.9
South American	2,273	69.4
Spaniard	204	16.3

Foreign-Born Naturalized U.S. Citizens

Group	Number	%
Total Population	20,476	32.2
Hispanic or Latino (of any race)	4,915	15.5
Central American, ex. Mexican	767	16.2
Guatemalan	132	7.9

Notes: (1) Percent of total population; (2) Percent of Hispanic/Latino population; Profiles include places with an overall population of at least 125,000, OR an overall population of at least 25,000 where the Hispanic/Latino population is at least 20% of the overall population. In states where less than five places meet either of these criteria, we have included places with at least 10,000 total population with the highest percentage of Hispanic/Latino population. These places are identified with an asterisk (*); Please refer to the User's Guide for a full explanation of data.

Honduran	189	12.4
Panamanian	160	54.6
Cuban	339	38.0
Mexican	2,426	10.9
Puerto Rican	44	44.0
South American	743	32.7
Spaniard	157	77.0

Language Spoken at Home: English Only
(Universe: Population 5 Years and Over)

Group	Number	%
Total Population	2,629,581	96.2
Hispanic or Latino (of any race)	18,852	30.7
Central American, ex. Mexican	1,255	19.5
Guatemalan	160	8.9
Honduran	432	21.5
Panamanian	188	28.5
Cuban	796	41.5
Mexican	10,563	26.6
Puerto Rican	2,059	46.9
South American	566	19.2
Spaniard	963	78.2

Language Spoken at Home: Spanish
(Universe: Population 5 Years and Over)

Group	Number	%
Total Population	62,571	2.3
Hispanic or Latino (of any race)	42,097	68.6
Central American, ex. Mexican	5,137	80.0
Guatemalan	1,613	90.1
Honduran	1,569	78.0
Panamanian	472	71.5
Cuban	1,042	54.4
Mexican	28,978	73.0
Puerto Rican	2,321	52.8
South American	2,339	79.4
Spaniard	269	21.8

Unemployment Rate
(Universe: Population 16 Years and Over)

Group	%
Total Population	9.6
Hispanic or Latino (of any race)	8.5
Central American, ex. Mexican	10.6
Guatemalan	4.7
Honduran	6.6
Panamanian	40.3
Cuban	13.2
Mexican	7.7
Puerto Rican	7.1
South American	6.5
Spaniard	0.7

Class of Worker: Private Wage and Salary
(Universe: Civilian Employed Population 16 Years and Over)

Group	Number	%
Total Population	906,153	74.5
Hispanic or Latino (of any race)	24,815	84.2
Central American, ex. Mexican	3,053	88.4
Guatemalan	1,120	94.6
Honduran	944	88.7
Panamanian	98	55.7
Cuban	493	77.5
Mexican	17,221	88.5
Puerto Rican	1,428	78.1
South American	908	55.1
Spaniard	348	58.6

Class of Worker: Government
(Universe: Civilian Employed Population 16 Years and Over)

Group	Number	%
Total Population	229,171	18.8
Hispanic or Latino (of any race)	2,561	8.7
Central American, ex. Mexican	160	4.6
Guatemalan	34	2.9
Honduran	6	0.6
Panamanian	76	43.2
Cuban	40	6.3
Mexican	935	4.8
Puerto Rican	358	19.6
South American	539	32.7
Spaniard	171	28.8

Means of Transportation to Work: Car, Truck or Van
(Universe: Workers 16 Years and Over)

Group	Number	%
Total Population	1,126,454	94.1
Hispanic or Latino (of any race)	27,159	91.2
Central American, ex. Mexican	3,135	91.9
Guatemalan	1,073	94.8
Honduran	1,009	94.2
Panamanian	176	84.2
Cuban	559	93.8
Mexican	18,302	93.8
Puerto Rican	1,707	82.8
South American	1,373	82.2
Spaniard	453	85.6

Means of Transportation to Work: Public Transportation (ex. Taxicab)
(Universe: Workers 16 Years and Over)

Group	Number	%
Total Population	4,913	0.4
Hispanic or Latino (of any race)	135	0.5
Central American, ex. Mexican	13	0.4
Guatemalan	0	0.0
Honduran	13	1.2
Panamanian	0	0.0
Cuban	0	0.0
Mexican	119	0.6
Puerto Rican	3	0.1
South American	0	0.0
Spaniard	0	0.0

Homeownership Rate
(Universe: Occupied Housing Units)

Group	%
Total Population	69.6
Hispanic or Latino (of any race)	41.4
Central American, ex. Mexican	37.7
Costa Rican	68.2
Guatemalan	19.7
Honduran	34.7
Nicaraguan	49.8
Panamanian	58.2
Salvadoran	50.3
Cuban	52.5
Dominican Republic	38.6
Mexican	37.3
Puerto Rican	42.4
South American	54.1
Argentinean	61.0
Chilean	55.1
Colombian	53.7
Ecuadorian	48.9
Peruvian	47.9
Venezuelan	59.7
Spaniard	68.6

Median Home Value

Group	Dollars
Total Population	96,500
Hispanic or Latino (of any race)	114,200
Central American, ex. Mexican	122,200
Guatemalan	59,400
Honduran	117,800
Panamanian	99,000
Cuban	159,700
Mexican	89,600
Puerto Rican	142,400
South American	139,300
Spaniard	136,300

Median Gross Rent

Group	Dollars
Total Population	648
Hispanic or Latino (of any race)	729
Central American, ex. Mexican	759
Guatemalan	732
Honduran	780
Panamanian	0
Cuban	772
Mexican	727
Puerto Rican	691
South American	795
Spaniard	743

Median Household Income
(2010 Inflation-Adjusted Dollars)

Group	Dollars
Total Population	37,881
Hispanic or Latino (of any race)	40,051
Central American, ex. Mexican	42,303
Guatemalan	38,621
Honduran	37,445
Panamanian	42,292
Cuban	41,033
Mexican	37,503
Puerto Rican	47,096
South American	43,260
Spaniard	42,500

Per Capita Income
(2010 Inflation-Adjusted Dollars)

Group	Dollars
Total Population	19,977
Hispanic or Latino (of any race)	14,458
Central American, ex. Mexican	15,633
Guatemalan	10,756
Honduran	15,747
Panamanian	10,394
Cuban	22,236
Mexican	12,139
Puerto Rican	18,089
South American	25,293
Spaniard	17,106

Households with $100,000+ Income

Group	Number	%
Total Population	129,412	12.0
Hispanic or Latino (of any race)	1,674	10.0
Central American, ex. Mexican	184	10.1
Guatemalan	13	2.6
Honduran	64	9.7
Panamanian	51	30.0
Cuban	123	24.8
Mexican	866	8.9
Puerto Rican	124	8.5
South American	161	15.6
Spaniard	30	5.5

Households with Food Stamps/SNAP Benefits During Past 12 Months

Group	Number	%
Total Population	159,806	14.8
Hispanic or Latino (of any race)	1,619	9.7
Central American, ex. Mexican	241	13.3
Guatemalan	75	15.1
Honduran	166	25.1
Panamanian	0	0.0
Cuban	40	8.1
Mexican	878	9.1
Puerto Rican	183	12.6
South American	0	0.0
Spaniard	76	13.9

Poverty Rate
(Income in Past 12 Months Below Poverty Level)

Group	%
Total Population	21.2
Hispanic or Latino (of any race)	25.5
Central American, ex. Mexican	21.8
Guatemalan	39.6
Honduran	20.9
Panamanian	14.7
Cuban	19.3
Mexican	28.9
Puerto Rican	17.7
South American	5.1
Spaniard	13.1

Biloxi*

Population

Group	Number	%TP[1]	%HP[2]
Total Population	44,054	100.0	–
Hispanic or Latino (of any race)	3,847	8.7	100.0
Central American, ex. Mexican	655	1.5	17.0
Guatemalan	244	0.6	6.3
Honduran	195	0.4	5.1

Notes: (1) Percent of total population; (2) Percent of Hispanic/Latino population; Profiles include places with an overall population of at least 125,000, OR an overall population of at least 25,000 where the Hispanic/Latino population is at least 20% of the overall population. In states where less than five places meet either of these criteria, we have included places with at least 10,000 total population with the highest percentage of Hispanic/Latino population. These places are identified with an asterisk (*); Please refer to the User's Guide for a full explanation of data.

Mexican	2,107	4.8	54.8
Puerto Rican	382	0.9	9.9
South American	256	0.6	6.7

Population Growth: 2000–2010

Group	%
Total Population	-13.0
Hispanic or Latino (of any race)	108.2
Central American, ex. Mexican	469.6
Mexican	181.3
Puerto Rican	5.5

Males per 100 Females

Group	Number
Total Population	105.9
Hispanic or Latino (of any race)	145.5
Central American, ex. Mexican	151.0
Guatemalan	212.8
Honduran	167.1
Mexican	153.9
Puerto Rican	126.0
South American	118.8

Average Household Size

Group	People
Total Population	2.40
Hispanic or Latino (of any race)	3.27
Central American, ex. Mexican	3.95
Guatemalan	5.02
Honduran	3.72
Mexican	3.55
Puerto Rican	2.35
South American	2.98

Median Age

Group	Years
Total Population	33.5
Hispanic or Latino (of any race)	25.7
Central American, ex. Mexican	27.2
Guatemalan	25.5
Honduran	28.6
Mexican	24.7
Puerto Rican	27.1
South American	30.6

High School Graduates
(Universe: Population 25 Years and Over)

Group	Number	%
Total Population	24,443	85.3
Hispanic or Latino (of any race)	885	52.5
Mexican	338	37.6

Four-Year College Graduates
(Universe: Population 25 Years and Over)

Group	Number	%
Total Population	6,559	22.9
Hispanic or Latino (of any race)	287	17.0
Mexican	79	8.8

Population Age 3–17 Enrolled in Public School
(Universe: Population Age 3–17 Enrolled in School)

Group	Number	%
Total Population	5,447	83.6
Hispanic or Latino (of any race)	208	80.3
Mexican	152	100.0

Population Age 3–17 Enrolled in Private School
(Universe: Population Age 3–17 Enrolled in School)

Group	Number	%
Total Population	1,065	16.4
Hispanic or Latino (of any race)	51	19.7
Mexican	0	0.0

Foreign-Born Population

Group	Number	%
Total Population	3,667	8.3
Hispanic or Latino (of any race)	1,615	53.3
Mexican	1,172	62.9

Foreign-Born Naturalized U.S. Citizens

Group	Number	%
Total Population	1,230	33.5
Hispanic or Latino (of any race)	102	6.3
Mexican	13	1.1

Language Spoken at Home: English Only
(Universe: Population 5 Years and Over)

Group	Number	%
Total Population	36,886	89.7
Hispanic or Latino (of any race)	725	26.6
Mexican	264	16.2

Language Spoken at Home: Spanish
(Universe: Population 5 Years and Over)

Group	Number	%
Total Population	2,270	5.5
Hispanic or Latino (of any race)	1,958	72.0
Mexican	1,363	83.8

Unemployment Rate
(Universe: Population 16 Years and Over)

Group	%
Total Population	5.8
Hispanic or Latino (of any race)	4.6
Mexican	5.7

Class of Worker: Private Wage and Salary
(Universe: Civilian Employed Population 16 Years and Over)

Group	Number	%
Total Population	15,980	75.8
Hispanic or Latino (of any race)	1,443	85.5
Mexican	958	98.3

Class of Worker: Government
(Universe: Civilian Employed Population 16 Years and Over)

Group	Number	%
Total Population	4,004	19.0
Hispanic or Latino (of any race)	228	13.5
Mexican	0	0.0

Means of Transportation to Work: Car, Truck or Van
(Universe: Workers 16 Years and Over)

Group	Number	%
Total Population	20,697	91.5
Hispanic or Latino (of any race)	1,521	89.2
Mexican	914	94.2

Means of Transportation to Work: Public Transportation (ex. Taxicab)
(Universe: Workers 16 Years and Over)

Group	Number	%
Total Population	78	0.3
Hispanic or Latino (of any race)	0	0.0
Mexican	0	0.0

Homeownership Rate
(Universe: Occupied Housing Units)

Group	%
Total Population	49.2
Hispanic or Latino (of any race)	19.9
Central American, ex. Mexican	12.7
Guatemalan	0.0
Honduran	6.5
Mexican	15.7
Puerto Rican	33.1
South American	20.0

Median Home Value

Group	Dollars
Total Population	157,300
Hispanic or Latino (of any race)	132,100
Mexican	58,000

Median Gross Rent

Group	Dollars
Total Population	835
Hispanic or Latino (of any race)	860
Mexican	933

Median Household Income
(2010 Inflation-Adjusted Dollars)

Group	Dollars
Total Population	47,772
Hispanic or Latino (of any race)	65,978
Mexican	47,045

Per Capita Income
(2010 Inflation-Adjusted Dollars)

Group	Dollars
Total Population	26,714
Hispanic or Latino (of any race)	19,297
Mexican	16,692

Households with $100,000+ Income

Group	Number	%
Total Population	2,800	16.3
Hispanic or Latino (of any race)	198	22.4
Mexican	122	32.1

Households with Food Stamps/SNAP Benefits During Past 12 Months

Group	Number	%
Total Population	2,222	12.9
Hispanic or Latino (of any race)	76	8.6
Mexican	30	7.9

Poverty Rate
(Income in Past 12 Months Below Poverty Level)

Group	%
Total Population	12.9
Hispanic or Latino (of any race)	18.6
Mexican	16.8

Horn Lake*

Population

Group	Number	%TP[1]	%HP[2]
Total Population	26,066	100.0	–
Hispanic or Latino (of any race)	2,093	8.0	100.0
Central American, ex. Mexican	103	0.4	4.9
Mexican	1,701	6.5	81.3

Population Growth: 2000–2010

Group	%
Total Population	84.9
Hispanic or Latino (of any race)	247.1
Mexican	276.3

Males per 100 Females

Group	Number
Total Population	94.2
Hispanic or Latino (of any race)	125.8
Central American, ex. Mexican	90.7
Mexican	134.3

Average Household Size

Group	People
Total Population	2.87
Hispanic or Latino (of any race)	4.12
Central American, ex. Mexican	3.14
Mexican	4.40

Median Age

Group	Years
Total Population	30.7
Hispanic or Latino (of any race)	24.5
Central American, ex. Mexican	32.4
Mexican	24.1

High School Graduates
(Universe: Population 25 Years and Over)

Group	Number	%
Total Population	12,644	82.7
Hispanic or Latino (of any race)	466	44.6
Mexican	269	37.1

Four-Year College Graduates
(Universe: Population 25 Years and Over)

Group	Number	%
Total Population	1,783	11.7
Hispanic or Latino (of any race)	63	6.0
Mexican	63	8.7

Population Age 3–17 Enrolled in Public School
(Universe: Population Age 3–17 Enrolled in School)

Group	Number	%
Total Population	5,158	92.3
Hispanic or Latino (of any race)	513	86.5
Mexican	497	86.1

Population Age 3–17 Enrolled in Private School
(Universe: Population Age 3–17 Enrolled in School)

Group	Number	%
Total Population	428	7.7

Notes: (1) Percent of total population; (2) Percent of Hispanic/Latino population; Profiles include places with an overall population of at least 125,000, OR an overall population of at least 25,000 where the Hispanic/Latino population is at least 20% of the overall population. In states where less than five places meet either of these criteria, we have included places with at least 10,000 total population with the highest percentage of Hispanic/Latino population. These places are identified with an asterisk (*); Please refer to the User's Guide for a full explanation of data.

Hispanic or Latino (of any race)	80	13.5
Mexican	80	13.9

Foreign-Born Population

Group	Number	%
Total Population	1,245	4.9
Hispanic or Latino (of any race)	1,002	42.8
Mexican	729	39.5

Foreign-Born Naturalized U.S. Citizens

Group	Number	%
Total Population	300	24.1
Hispanic or Latino (of any race)	115	11.5
Mexican	30	4.1

Language Spoken at Home: English Only
(Universe: Population 5 Years and Over)

Group	Number	%
Total Population	21,378	91.4
Hispanic or Latino (of any race)	530	27.2
Mexican	357	23.8

Language Spoken at Home: Spanish
(Universe: Population 5 Years and Over)

Group	Number	%
Total Population	1,618	6.9
Hispanic or Latino (of any race)	1,418	72.8
Mexican	1,146	76.2

Unemployment Rate
(Universe: Population 16 Years and Over)

Group	%
Total Population	7.1
Hispanic or Latino (of any race)	19.6
Mexican	10.8

Class of Worker: Private Wage and Salary
(Universe: Civilian Employed Population 16 Years and Over)

Group	Number	%
Total Population	11,028	86.3
Hispanic or Latino (of any race)	730	92.4
Mexican	530	98.3

Class of Worker: Government
(Universe: Civilian Employed Population 16 Years and Over)

Group	Number	%
Total Population	1,185	9.3
Hispanic or Latino (of any race)	46	5.8
Mexican	9	1.7

Means of Transportation to Work: Car, Truck or Van
(Universe: Workers 16 Years and Over)

Group	Number	%
Total Population	12,146	96.2
Hispanic or Latino (of any race)	703	91.8
Mexican	452	87.8

Means of Transportation to Work: Public Transportation (ex. Taxicab)
(Universe: Workers 16 Years and Over)

Group	Number	%
Total Population	63	0.5
Hispanic or Latino (of any race)	63	8.2
Mexican	63	12.2

Homeownership Rate
(Universe: Occupied Housing Units)

Group	%
Total Population	65.5
Hispanic or Latino (of any race)	54.3
Central American, ex. Mexican	69.0
Mexican	54.0

Median Home Value

Group	Dollars
Total Population	99,300
Hispanic or Latino (of any race)	83,500
Mexican	78,600

Median Gross Rent

Group	Dollars
Total Population	877
Hispanic or Latino (of any race)	798
Mexican	782

Median Household Income
(2010 Inflation-Adjusted Dollars)

Group	Dollars
Total Population	46,357
Hispanic or Latino (of any race)	47,727
Mexican	48,532

Per Capita Income
(2010 Inflation-Adjusted Dollars)

Group	Dollars
Total Population	18,799
Hispanic or Latino (of any race)	12,657
Mexican	9,864

Households with $100,000+ Income

Group	Number	%
Total Population	844	9.3
Hispanic or Latino (of any race)	10	1.8
Mexican	10	2.7

Households with Food Stamps/SNAP Benefits During Past 12 Months

Group	Number	%
Total Population	1,134	12.5
Hispanic or Latino (of any race)	77	13.9
Mexican	34	9.3

Poverty Rate
(Income in Past 12 Months Below Poverty Level)

Group	%
Total Population	14.6
Hispanic or Latino (of any race)	17.7
Mexican	18.1

Jackson

Population

Group	Number	%TP[1]	%HP[2]
Total Population	173,514	100.0	–
Hispanic or Latino (of any race)	2,723	1.6	100.0
Central American, ex. Mexican	296	0.2	10.9
Honduran	155	0.1	5.7
Mexican	1,694	1.0	62.2
Puerto Rican	169	0.1	6.2

Population Growth: 2000–2010

Group	%
Total Population	-5.8
Hispanic or Latino (of any race)	87.7
Mexican	152.8
Puerto Rican	22.5

Males per 100 Females

Group	Number
Total Population	86.8
Hispanic or Latino (of any race)	144.7
Central American, ex. Mexican	169.1
Honduran	252.3
Mexican	158.2
Puerto Rican	94.3

Average Household Size

Group	People
Total Population	2.60
Hispanic or Latino (of any race)	3.44
Central American, ex. Mexican	3.93
Honduran	4.47
Mexican	3.78
Puerto Rican	2.92

Median Age

Group	Years
Total Population	31.2
Hispanic or Latino (of any race)	25.8
Central American, ex. Mexican	27.5
Honduran	27.3
Mexican	24.6
Puerto Rican	22.9

High School Graduates
(Universe: Population 25 Years and Over)

Group	Number	%
Total Population	85,643	81.8
Hispanic or Latino (of any race)	793	54.6

Four-Year College Graduates
(Universe: Population 25 Years and Over)

Group	Number	%
Total Population	27,696	26.5
Hispanic or Latino (of any race)	281	19.4

Population Age 3–17 Enrolled in Public School
(Universe: Population Age 3–17 Enrolled in School)

Group	Number	%
Total Population	34,043	87.3
Hispanic or Latino (of any race)	180	65.2

Population Age 3–17 Enrolled in Private School
(Universe: Population Age 3–17 Enrolled in School)

Group	Number	%
Total Population	4,967	12.7
Hispanic or Latino (of any race)	96	34.8

Foreign-Born Population

Group	Number	%
Total Population	3,229	1.8
Hispanic or Latino (of any race)	1,803	60.1

Foreign-Born Naturalized U.S. Citizens

Group	Number	%
Total Population	1,005	31.1
Hispanic or Latino (of any race)	385	21.4

Language Spoken at Home: English Only
(Universe: Population 5 Years and Over)

Group	Number	%
Total Population	156,474	96.7
Hispanic or Latino (of any race)	657	24.8

Language Spoken at Home: Spanish
(Universe: Population 5 Years and Over)

Group	Number	%
Total Population	3,227	2.0
Hispanic or Latino (of any race)	1,962	74.1

Unemployment Rate
(Universe: Population 16 Years and Over)

Group	%
Total Population	10.3
Hispanic or Latino (of any race)	7.1

Class of Worker: Private Wage and Salary
(Universe: Civilian Employed Population 16 Years and Over)

Group	Number	%
Total Population	52,800	70.7
Hispanic or Latino (of any race)	1,369	78.8

Class of Worker: Government
(Universe: Civilian Employed Population 16 Years and Over)

Group	Number	%
Total Population	17,802	23.8
Hispanic or Latino (of any race)	146	8.4

Means of Transportation to Work: Car, Truck or Van
(Universe: Workers 16 Years and Over)

Group	Number	%
Total Population	68,464	93.5
Hispanic or Latino (of any race)	1,532	91.1

Means of Transportation to Work: Public Transportation (ex. Taxicab)
(Universe: Workers 16 Years and Over)

Group	Number	%
Total Population	630	0.9
Hispanic or Latino (of any race)	0	0.0

Homeownership Rate
(Universe: Occupied Housing Units)

Group	%
Total Population	53.1
Hispanic or Latino (of any race)	26.6
Central American, ex. Mexican	20.9
Honduran	23.5
Mexican	23.4
Puerto Rican	29.2

Median Home Value

Group	Dollars
Total Population	89,100
Hispanic or Latino (of any race)	134,100

Notes: (1) Percent of total population; (2) Percent of Hispanic/Latino population; Profiles include places with an overall population of at least 125,000, OR an overall population of at least 25,000 where the Hispanic/Latino population is at least 20% of the overall population. In states where less than five places meet either of these criteria, we have included places with at least 10,000 total population with the highest percentage of Hispanic/Latino population. These places are identified with an asterisk (*); Please refer to the User's Guide for a full explanation of data.

Median Gross Rent

Group	Dollars
Total Population	752
Hispanic or Latino (of any race)	728

Median Household Income
(2010 Inflation-Adjusted Dollars)

Group	Dollars
Total Population	34,555
Hispanic or Latino (of any race)	26,573

Per Capita Income
(2010 Inflation-Adjusted Dollars)

Group	Dollars
Total Population	19,095
Hispanic or Latino (of any race)	14,326

Households with $100,000+ Income

Group	Number	%
Total Population	6,509	10.4
Hispanic or Latino (of any race)	84	9.3

Households with Food Stamps/SNAP Benefits During Past 12 Months

Group	Number	%
Total Population	11,546	18.5
Hispanic or Latino (of any race)	89	9.8

Poverty Rate
(Income in Past 12 Months Below Poverty Level)

Group	%
Total Population	26.6
Hispanic or Latino (of any race)	34.9

Laurel*

Population

Group	Number	%TP[1]	%HP[2]
Total Population	18,540	100.0	–
Hispanic or Latino (of any race)	1,424	7.7	100.0
Central American, ex. Mexican	118	0.6	8.3
Mexican	1,148	6.2	80.6

Population Growth: 2000–2010

Group	%
Total Population	0.8
Hispanic or Latino (of any race)	100.0
Mexican	102.1

Males per 100 Females

Group	Number
Total Population	88.8
Hispanic or Latino (of any race)	173.3
Central American, ex. Mexican	136.0
Mexican	180.7

Average Household Size

Group	People
Total Population	2.69
Hispanic or Latino (of any race)	4.20
Central American, ex. Mexican	4.00
Mexican	4.49

Median Age

Group	Years
Total Population	33.2
Hispanic or Latino (of any race)	25.9
Central American, ex. Mexican	29.7
Mexican	25.4

High School Graduates
(Universe: Population 25 Years and Over)

Group	Number	%
Total Population	8,287	71.6
Hispanic or Latino (of any race)	431	55.5
Mexican	184	37.2

Four-Year College Graduates
(Universe: Population 25 Years and Over)

Group	Number	%
Total Population	1,858	16.0
Hispanic or Latino (of any race)	48	6.2
Mexican	48	9.7

Population Age 3–17 Enrolled in Public School
(Universe: Population Age 3–17 Enrolled in School)

Group	Number	%
Total Population	2,695	87.0
Hispanic or Latino (of any race)	165	90.2
Mexican	105	85.4

Population Age 3–17 Enrolled in Private School
(Universe: Population Age 3–17 Enrolled in School)

Group	Number	%
Total Population	401	13.0
Hispanic or Latino (of any race)	18	9.8
Mexican	18	14.6

Foreign-Born Population

Group	Number	%
Total Population	1,099	5.9
Hispanic or Latino (of any race)	978	55.7
Mexican	679	76.0

Foreign-Born Naturalized U.S. Citizens

Group	Number	%
Total Population	85	7.7
Hispanic or Latino (of any race)	61	6.2
Mexican	28	4.1

Language Spoken at Home: English Only
(Universe: Population 5 Years and Over)

Group	Number	%
Total Population	15,295	91.4
Hispanic or Latino (of any race)	301	20.8
Mexican	115	14.3

Language Spoken at Home: Spanish
(Universe: Population 5 Years and Over)

Group	Number	%
Total Population	1,256	7.5
Hispanic or Latino (of any race)	1,071	74.1
Mexican	614	76.6

Unemployment Rate
(Universe: Population 16 Years and Over)

Group	%
Total Population	9.6
Hispanic or Latino (of any race)	14.6
Mexican	15.8

Class of Worker: Private Wage and Salary
(Universe: Civilian Employed Population 16 Years and Over)

Group	Number	%
Total Population	5,539	81.9
Hispanic or Latino (of any race)	684	97.0
Mexican	425	95.3

Class of Worker: Government
(Universe: Civilian Employed Population 16 Years and Over)

Group	Number	%
Total Population	875	12.9
Hispanic or Latino (of any race)	21	3.0
Mexican	21	4.7

Means of Transportation to Work: Car, Truck or Van
(Universe: Workers 16 Years and Over)

Group	Number	%
Total Population	6,400	95.8
Hispanic or Latino (of any race)	620	87.9
Mexican	432	96.9

Means of Transportation to Work: Public Transportation (ex. Taxicab)
(Universe: Workers 16 Years and Over)

Group	Number	%
Total Population	26	0.4
Hispanic or Latino (of any race)	14	2.0
Mexican	14	3.1

Homeownership Rate
(Universe: Occupied Housing Units)

Group	%
Total Population	56.2
Hispanic or Latino (of any race)	21.0
Central American, ex. Mexican	41.4
Mexican	16.9

Median Home Value

Group	Dollars
Total Population	76,900
Hispanic or Latino (of any race)	–
Mexican	–

Median Gross Rent

Group	Dollars
Total Population	536
Hispanic or Latino (of any race)	724
Mexican	854

Median Household Income
(2010 Inflation-Adjusted Dollars)

Group	Dollars
Total Population	27,056
Hispanic or Latino (of any race)	53,954
Mexican	72,045

Per Capita Income
(2010 Inflation-Adjusted Dollars)

Group	Dollars
Total Population	18,273
Hispanic or Latino (of any race)	10,633
Mexican	10,802

Households with $100,000+ Income

Group	Number	%
Total Population	602	8.4
Hispanic or Latino (of any race)	34	13.7
Mexican	34	27.9

Households with Food Stamps/SNAP Benefits During Past 12 Months

Group	Number	%
Total Population	1,283	17.9
Hispanic or Latino (of any race)	8	3.2
Mexican	0	0.0

Poverty Rate
(Income in Past 12 Months Below Poverty Level)

Group	%
Total Population	32.5
Hispanic or Latino (of any race)	44.3
Mexican	31.5

Pascagoula*

Population

Group	Number	%TP[1]	%HP[2]
Total Population	22,392	100.0	–
Hispanic or Latino (of any race)	2,472	11.0	100.0
Central American, ex. Mexican	121	0.5	4.9
Dominican Republic	177	0.8	7.2
Mexican	909	4.1	36.8
Puerto Rican	1,014	4.5	41.0

Population Growth: 2000–2010

Group	%
Total Population	-14.5
Hispanic or Latino (of any race)	142.6
Mexican	33.9
Puerto Rican	580.5

Males per 100 Females

Group	Number
Total Population	99.8
Hispanic or Latino (of any race)	139.5
Central American, ex. Mexican	188.1
Dominican Republic	129.9
Mexican	148.4
Puerto Rican	126.3

Average Household Size

Group	People
Total Population	2.54
Hispanic or Latino (of any race)	3.16
Central American, ex. Mexican	3.00
Dominican Republic	3.12
Mexican	3.41
Puerto Rican	3.05

Notes: (1) Percent of total population; (2) Percent of Hispanic/Latino population; Profiles include places with an overall population of at least 125,000, OR an overall population of at least 25,000 where the Hispanic/Latino population is at least 20% of the overall population. In states where less than five places meet either of these criteria, we have included places with at least 10,000 total population with the highest percentage of Hispanic/Latino population. These places are identified with an asterisk (*); Please refer to the User's Guide for a full explanation of data.

Median Age

Group	Years
Total Population	34.9
Hispanic or Latino (of any race)	26.9
Central American, ex. Mexican	30.3
Dominican Republic	27.1
Mexican	25.9
Puerto Rican	26.4

High School Graduates
(Universe: Population 25 Years and Over)

Group	Number	%
Total Population	12,236	84.0
Hispanic or Latino (of any race)	843	67.3
Mexican	470	58.2

Four-Year College Graduates
(Universe: Population 25 Years and Over)

Group	Number	%
Total Population	2,592	17.8
Hispanic or Latino (of any race)	61	4.9
Mexican	0	0.0

Population Age 3–17 Enrolled in Public School
(Universe: Population Age 3–17 Enrolled in School)

Group	Number	%
Total Population	4,274	90.9
Hispanic or Latino (of any race)	616	100.0
Mexican	352	100.0

Population Age 3–17 Enrolled in Private School
(Universe: Population Age 3–17 Enrolled in School)

Group	Number	%
Total Population	430	9.1
Hispanic or Latino (of any race)	0	0.0
Mexican	0	0.0

Foreign-Born Population

Group	Number	%
Total Population	1,369	6.0
Hispanic or Latino (of any race)	1,125	43.8
Mexican	1,066	69.5

Foreign-Born Naturalized U.S. Citizens

Group	Number	%
Total Population	135	9.9
Hispanic or Latino (of any race)	90	8.0
Mexican	68	6.4

Language Spoken at Home: English Only
(Universe: Population 5 Years and Over)

Group	Number	%
Total Population	18,826	88.7
Hispanic or Latino (of any race)	417	17.9
Mexican	285	19.5

Language Spoken at Home: Spanish
(Universe: Population 5 Years and Over)

Group	Number	%
Total Population	2,038	9.6
Hispanic or Latino (of any race)	1,907	82.1
Mexican	1,180	80.5

Unemployment Rate
(Universe: Population 16 Years and Over)

Group	%
Total Population	9.2
Hispanic or Latino (of any race)	3.0
Mexican	4.7

Class of Worker: Private Wage and Salary
(Universe: Civilian Employed Population 16 Years and Over)

Group	Number	%
Total Population	7,500	78.4
Hispanic or Latino (of any race)	1,230	93.5
Mexican	825	98.9

Class of Worker: Government
(Universe: Civilian Employed Population 16 Years and Over)

Group	Number	%
Total Population	1,482	15.5
Hispanic or Latino (of any race)	76	5.8
Mexican	0	0.0

Means of Transportation to Work: Car, Truck or Van
(Universe: Workers 16 Years and Over)

Group	Number	%
Total Population	9,021	96.1
Hispanic or Latino (of any race)	1,286	100.0
Mexican	834	100.0

Means of Transportation to Work: Public Transportation (ex. Taxicab)
(Universe: Workers 16 Years and Over)

Group	Number	%
Total Population	0	0.0
Hispanic or Latino (of any race)	0	0.0
Mexican	0	0.0

Homeownership Rate
(Universe: Occupied Housing Units)

Group	%
Total Population	56.8
Hispanic or Latino (of any race)	20.2
Central American, ex. Mexican	15.4
Dominican Republic	24.1
Mexican	20.2
Puerto Rican	18.0

Median Home Value

Group	Dollars
Total Population	114,900
Hispanic or Latino (of any race)	95,300
Mexican	95,000

Median Gross Rent

Group	Dollars
Total Population	718
Hispanic or Latino (of any race)	782
Mexican	825

Median Household Income
(2010 Inflation-Adjusted Dollars)

Group	Dollars
Total Population	38,245
Hispanic or Latino (of any race)	46,086
Mexican	41,729

Per Capita Income
(2010 Inflation-Adjusted Dollars)

Group	Dollars
Total Population	21,288
Hispanic or Latino (of any race)	20,579
Mexican	13,779

Households with $100,000+ Income

Group	Number	%
Total Population	995	11.6
Hispanic or Latino (of any race)	49	7.6
Mexican	27	8.4

Households with Food Stamps/SNAP Benefits During Past 12 Months

Group	Number	%
Total Population	1,868	21.7
Hispanic or Latino (of any race)	74	11.5
Mexican	11	3.4

Poverty Rate
(Income in Past 12 Months Below Poverty Level)

Group	%
Total Population	22.1
Hispanic or Latino (of any race)	20.0
Mexican	23.7

STATE & PLACE PROFILES

Notes: (1) Percent of total population; (2) Percent of Hispanic/Latino population; Profiles include places with an overall population of at least 125,000, OR an overall population of at least 25,000 where the Hispanic/Latino population is at least 20% of the overall population. In states where less than five places meet either of these criteria, we have included places with at least 10,000 total population with the highest percentage of Hispanic/Latino population. These places are identified with an asterisk (*); Please refer to the User's Guide for a full explanation of data.

Missouri

EDITOR'S NOTE: For a place to be included in this edition, it must meet one of two criteria. Either its overall population is at least 125,000, OR its overall population is at least 25,000 and its Hispanic/Latino population is at least 20% of the overall population. In Missouri, less than five places meet either of these criteria. In an effort to include at least five places for each state, we have included places with at least 10,000 total population with the highest percentage of Hispanic/Latino population. These places are identified with an asterisk (*). For the state of Missouri, the following locations are included:

Carthage*
Fort Leonard Wood*
Kansas City
Saint Louis
Springfield

Section Two: State & Place Profiles starts with the state profile, followed by place profiles that meet the criteria above. Places are listed alphabetically within each state. All states, all counties and places that meet the above criteria are ranked and compared in *Section Three: Rankings & Comparisons*, on page 1055.

For a more detailed look at the Hispanic/Latino population in Missouri, a companion web site is available at no additional charge with purchase of this print edition. Visit http://gold.greyhouse.com/page/info_hispanic for more information.

The web site includes data for all counties and places in Missouri with Hispanic/Latino population, plus ten additional topics: Self Employed Worker; Walked to Work; Worked from Home; Mean Travel Time to Work; Mean Household Income; Households with Cash Public Assistance; Mean Cash Pubic Assistance; Poverty Rates for 18 and Under, 18 to 64, and 65 and Over.

Population

Group	Number	%TP[1]	%HP[2]
Total Population	5,988,927	100.0	–
Hispanic or Latino (of any race)	212,470	3.5	100.0
Central American, ex. Mexican	17,763	0.3	8.4
Costa Rican	587	<0.1	0.3
Guatemalan	6,610	0.1	3.1
Honduran	3,657	0.1	1.7
Nicaraguan	843	<0.1	0.4
Panamanian	1,349	<0.1	0.6
Salvadoran	4,628	0.1	2.2
Cuban	4,979	0.1	2.3
Dominican Republic	1,503	<0.1	0.7
Mexican	147,254	2.5	69.3
Puerto Rican	12,236	0.2	5.8
South American	8,731	0.1	4.1
Argentinean	991	<0.1	0.5
Bolivian	471	<0.1	0.2
Chilean	665	<0.1	0.3
Colombian	2,659	<0.1	1.3
Ecuadorian	937	<0.1	0.4
Paraguayan	128	<0.1	0.1
Peruvian	1,687	<0.1	0.8
Uruguayan	179	<0.1	0.1
Venezuelan	901	<0.1	0.4
Spaniard	4,413	0.1	2.1

Population Growth: 2000–2010

Group	%
Total Population	7.0
Hispanic or Latino (of any race)	79.2
Central American, ex. Mexican	249.3
Costa Rican	142.6
Guatemalan	319.9
Honduran	278.6
Nicaraguan	201.1
Panamanian	83.3
Salvadoran	324.2
Cuban	64.8
Dominican Republic	177.3
Mexican	89.1
Puerto Rican	83.3
South American	144.6
Argentinean	158.1
Bolivian	124.3
Chilean	119.5
Colombian	163.0
Ecuadorian	178.9
Peruvian	148.8
Venezuelan	130.4
Spaniard	808.0

Males per 100 Females

Group	Number
Total Population	96.0
Hispanic or Latino (of any race)	108.9
Central American, ex. Mexican	112.5
Costa Rican	91.2
Guatemalan	118.5
Honduran	125.5
Nicaraguan	104.1
Panamanian	74.5
Salvadoran	112.9
Cuban	112.2
Dominican Republic	99.3
Mexican	110.9
Puerto Rican	106.4
South American	88.3
Argentinean	88.0
Bolivian	97.1
Chilean	90.5
Colombian	87.0
Ecuadorian	94.0
Paraguayan	82.9
Peruvian	79.9
Uruguayan	121.0
Venezuelan	92.9
Spaniard	90.0

Average Household Size

Group	People
Total Population	2.45
Hispanic or Latino (of any race)	3.19
Central American, ex. Mexican	3.63
Costa Rican	2.75
Guatemalan	4.16
Honduran	3.55
Nicaraguan	3.10
Panamanian	2.61
Salvadoran	3.72
Cuban	2.61
Dominican Republic	2.95
Mexican	3.34
Puerto Rican	2.77
South American	2.68
Argentinean	2.59
Bolivian	2.70
Chilean	2.64
Colombian	2.59
Ecuadorian	2.76
Paraguayan	2.85
Peruvian	2.73
Uruguayan	3.41
Venezuelan	2.82
Spaniard	2.50

Median Age

Group	Years
Total Population	37.9
Hispanic or Latino (of any race)	24.4
Central American, ex. Mexican	25.1
Costa Rican	28.8
Guatemalan	21.4
Honduran	26.9
Nicaraguan	27.1
Panamanian	27.7
Salvadoran	27.5
Cuban	31.2
Dominican Republic	24.2
Mexican	23.4
Puerto Rican	24.4
South American	30.1
Argentinean	35.0
Bolivian	31.3
Chilean	31.4
Colombian	28.5
Ecuadorian	27.3
Paraguayan	25.5
Peruvian	30.1
Uruguayan	29.8
Venezuelan	31.3
Spaniard	32.5

High School Graduates
(Universe: Population 25 Years and Over)

Group	Number	%
Total Population	3,366,197	86.2
Hispanic or Latino (of any race)	64,289	66.3
Central American, ex. Mexican	3,796	49.3
Guatemalan	611	27.6
Honduran	813	53.2
Nicaraguan	443	83.0
Panamanian	676	89.5
Salvadoran	875	39.0
Cuban	2,229	79.6
Dominican Republic	605	81.6
Mexican	40,637	61.4
Puerto Rican	5,458	89.6
South American	4,851	95.7
Argentinean	546	93.2
Chilean	540	100.0
Colombian	1,498	96.1
Ecuadorian	361	89.8
Peruvian	786	93.9
Venezuelan	430	96.4
Spaniard	2,345	86.4

Four-Year College Graduates
(Universe: Population 25 Years and Over)

Group	Number	%
Total Population	978,650	25.0
Hispanic or Latino (of any race)	16,359	16.9
Central American, ex. Mexican	1,281	16.6
Guatemalan	119	5.4
Honduran	196	12.8
Nicaraguan	191	35.8
Panamanian	320	42.4
Salvadoran	312	13.9
Cuban	989	35.3
Dominican Republic	140	18.9
Mexican	7,245	10.9
Puerto Rican	1,773	29.1
South American	2,995	59.1
Argentinean	434	74.1
Chilean	335	62.0
Colombian	861	55.2
Ecuadorian	197	49.0
Peruvian	455	54.4
Venezuelan	288	64.6
Spaniard	680	25.0

Population Age 3–17 Enrolled in Public School
(Universe: Population Age 3–17 Enrolled in School)

Group	Number	%
Total Population	897,312	83.9
Hispanic or Latino (of any race)	44,502	87.9
Central American, ex. Mexican	3,263	84.9
Guatemalan	1,205	82.5
Honduran	595	88.8
Nicaraguan	232	93.5
Panamanian	256	80.8
Salvadoran	755	84.6
Cuban	671	94.0
Dominican Republic	324	95.6
Mexican	32,944	89.9
Puerto Rican	2,296	83.6
South American	1,515	70.5

Notes: (1) Percent of total population; (2) Percent of Hispanic/Latino population; Profiles include places with an overall population of at least 125,000, OR an overall population of at least 25,000 where the Hispanic/Latino population is at least 20% of the overall population. In states where less than five places meet either of these criteria, we have included places with at least 10,000 total population with the highest percentage of Hispanic/Latino population. These places are identified with an asterisk (*); Please refer to the User's Guide for a full explanation of data.

Group	Number	%
Argentinean	93	100.0
Chilean	198	83.9
Colombian	601	71.5
Ecuadorian	130	100.0
Peruvian	167	43.4
Venezuelan	233	80.3
Spaniard	839	78.2

Population Age 3–17 Enrolled in Private School
(Universe: Population Age 3–17 Enrolled in School)

Group	Number	%
Total Population	172,486	16.1
Hispanic or Latino (of any race)	6,120	12.1
Central American, ex. Mexican	581	15.1
Guatemalan	255	17.5
Honduran	75	11.2
Nicaraguan	16	6.5
Panamanian	61	19.2
Salvadoran	137	15.4
Cuban	43	6.0
Dominican Republic	15	4.4
Mexican	3,688	10.1
Puerto Rican	452	16.4
South American	633	29.5
Argentinean	0	0.0
Chilean	38	16.1
Colombian	239	28.5
Ecuadorian	0	0.0
Peruvian	218	56.6
Venezuelan	57	19.7
Spaniard	234	21.8

Foreign-Born Population

Group	Number	%
Total Population	216,698	3.7
Hispanic or Latino (of any race)	64,111	32.3
Central American, ex. Mexican	9,638	59.8
Guatemalan	3,768	63.9
Honduran	1,984	66.2
Nicaraguan	437	46.1
Panamanian	470	34.4
Salvadoran	2,603	63.4
Cuban	2,324	50.7
Dominican Republic	683	50.5
Mexican	44,453	31.6
Puerto Rican	212	1.8
South American	4,913	57.3
Argentinean	618	83.9
Chilean	479	53.0
Colombian	1,514	56.3
Ecuadorian	312	36.2
Peruvian	817	52.3
Venezuelan	521	67.2
Spaniard	580	12.0

Foreign-Born Naturalized U.S. Citizens

Group	Number	%
Total Population	90,473	41.8
Hispanic or Latino (of any race)	15,039	23.5
Central American, ex. Mexican	2,936	30.5
Guatemalan	750	19.9
Honduran	650	32.8
Nicaraguan	234	53.5
Panamanian	326	69.4
Salvadoran	764	29.4
Cuban	961	41.4
Dominican Republic	372	54.5
Mexican	7,864	17.7
Puerto Rican	33	15.6
South American	2,055	41.8
Argentinean	204	33.0
Chilean	192	40.1
Colombian	667	44.1
Ecuadorian	175	56.1
Peruvian	407	49.8
Venezuelan	146	28.0
Spaniard	195	33.6

Language Spoken at Home: English Only
(Universe: Population 5 Years and Over)

Group	Number	%
Total Population	5,209,395	94.1
Hispanic or Latino (of any race)	74,932	43.3
Central American, ex. Mexican	3,001	22.3
Guatemalan	866	19.5
Honduran	313	11.7
Nicaraguan	283	34.9
Panamanian	654	53.5
Salvadoran	635	17.4
Cuban	1,442	34.1
Dominican Republic	277	23.0
Mexican	51,437	42.4
Puerto Rican	6,411	59.9
South American	2,494	32.2
Argentinean	168	23.3
Chilean	233	29.3
Colombian	882	35.1
Ecuadorian	400	60.7
Peruvian	355	26.5
Venezuelan	170	22.4
Spaniard	3,279	72.7

Language Spoken at Home: Spanish
(Universe: Population 5 Years and Over)

Group	Number	%
Total Population	147,188	2.7
Hispanic or Latino (of any race)	97,083	56.2
Central American, ex. Mexican	10,377	77.0
Guatemalan	3,511	79.1
Honduran	2,357	88.3
Nicaraguan	528	65.1
Panamanian	534	43.7
Salvadoran	3,004	82.6
Cuban	2,765	65.4
Dominican Republic	886	73.6
Mexican	69,565	57.4
Puerto Rican	4,258	39.8
South American	5,162	66.7
Argentinean	552	76.7
Chilean	562	70.7
Colombian	1,607	63.9
Ecuadorian	259	39.3
Peruvian	968	72.1
Venezuelan	553	73.0
Spaniard	1,173	26.0

Unemployment Rate
(Universe: Population 16 Years and Over)

Group	%
Total Population	7.4
Hispanic or Latino (of any race)	8.9
Central American, ex. Mexican	7.0
Guatemalan	4.4
Honduran	7.5
Nicaraguan	12.8
Panamanian	6.8
Salvadoran	9.3
Cuban	11.6
Dominican Republic	6.1
Mexican	8.7
Puerto Rican	12.5
South American	3.8
Argentinean	5.0
Chilean	2.6
Colombian	4.0
Ecuadorian	3.2
Peruvian	3.8
Venezuelan	4.9
Spaniard	14.8

Class of Worker: Private Wage and Salary
(Universe: Civilian Employed Population 16 Years and Over)

Group	Number	%
Total Population	2,238,929	80.1
Hispanic or Latino (of any race)	73,825	87.6
Central American, ex. Mexican	6,278	87.5
Guatemalan	2,143	90.9
Honduran	1,299	94.0
Nicaraguan	227	69.4
Panamanian	580	78.3
Salvadoran	1,778	86.1
Cuban	1,863	89.7
Dominican Republic	621	94.4
Mexican	52,895	89.3
Puerto Rican	3,824	76.6
South American	3,600	83.4
Argentinean	416	83.5
Chilean	401	90.7
Colombian	1,161	85.6
Ecuadorian	195	72.5
Peruvian	720	84.2
Venezuelan	280	79.8
Spaniard	1,644	88.9

Class of Worker: Government
(Universe: Civilian Employed Population 16 Years and Over)

Group	Number	%
Total Population	371,076	13.3
Hispanic or Latino (of any race)	6,527	7.7
Central American, ex. Mexican	461	6.4
Guatemalan	58	2.5
Honduran	61	4.4
Nicaraguan	33	10.1
Panamanian	111	15.0
Salvadoran	145	7.0
Cuban	152	7.3
Dominican Republic	37	5.6
Mexican	3,681	6.2
Puerto Rican	1,001	20.0
South American	515	11.9
Argentinean	59	11.8
Chilean	35	7.9
Colombian	137	10.1
Ecuadorian	74	27.5
Peruvian	84	9.8
Venezuelan	36	10.3
Spaniard	135	7.3

Means of Transportation to Work: Car, Truck or Van
(Universe: Workers 16 Years and Over)

Group	Number	%
Total Population	2,505,332	91.0
Hispanic or Latino (of any race)	75,336	89.0
Central American, ex. Mexican	6,009	83.9
Guatemalan	1,641	70.4
Honduran	1,223	88.9
Nicaraguan	337	93.4
Panamanian	661	91.0
Salvadoran	1,884	90.3
Cuban	1,899	89.9
Dominican Republic	620	89.9
Mexican	53,156	89.7
Puerto Rican	4,743	85.8
South American	3,808	90.2
Argentinean	393	78.9
Chilean	348	87.4
Colombian	1,277	94.2
Ecuadorian	217	81.9
Peruvian	789	97.6
Venezuelan	312	89.4
Spaniard	1,725	93.4

Means of Transportation to Work: Public Transportation (ex. Taxicab)
(Universe: Workers 16 Years and Over)

Group	Number	%
Total Population	41,045	1.5
Hispanic or Latino (of any race)	1,464	1.7
Central American, ex. Mexican	96	1.3
Guatemalan	25	1.1
Honduran	63	4.6
Nicaraguan	0	0.0
Panamanian	8	1.1
Salvadoran	0	0.0
Cuban	61	2.9
Dominican Republic	0	0.0
Mexican	1,086	1.8
Puerto Rican	81	1.5
South American	83	2.0
Argentinean	17	3.4
Chilean	6	1.5
Colombian	23	1.7
Ecuadorian	0	0.0
Peruvian	0	0.0
Venezuelan	0	0.0
Spaniard	18	1.0

Homeownership Rate
(Universe: Occupied Housing Units)

Group	%
Total Population	68.8
Hispanic or Latino (of any race)	49.4
Central American, ex. Mexican	43.5
Costa Rican	55.0

STATE & PLACE PROFILES

Notes: (1) Percent of total population; (2) Percent of Hispanic/Latino population; Profiles include places with an overall population of at least 125,000, OR an overall population of at least 25,000 where the Hispanic/Latino population is at least 20% of the overall population. In states where less than five places meet either of these criteria, we have included places with at least 10,000 total population with the highest percentage of Hispanic/Latino population. These places are identified with an asterisk (*); Please refer to the User's Guide for a full explanation of data.

Group	%
Guatemalan	30.9
Honduran	38.4
Nicaraguan	48.6
Panamanian	53.3
Salvadoran	54.7
Cuban	50.4
Dominican Republic	45.6
Mexican	49.3
Puerto Rican	47.1
South American	58.9
Argentinean	62.5
Bolivian	62.7
Chilean	59.6
Colombian	57.8
Ecuadorian	62.4
Paraguayan	42.4
Peruvian	58.6
Uruguayan	40.7
Venezuelan	58.1
Spaniard	61.3

Median Home Value

Group	Dollars
Total Population	137,700
Hispanic or Latino (of any race)	118,400
Central American, ex. Mexican	97,600
Guatemalan	70,600
Honduran	79,400
Nicaraguan	156,400
Panamanian	224,000
Salvadoran	97,600
Cuban	145,400
Dominican Republic	154,600
Mexican	108,300
Puerto Rican	156,200
South American	182,600
Argentinean	331,900
Chilean	189,700
Colombian	177,600
Ecuadorian	95,000
Peruvian	168,300
Venezuelan	176,100
Spaniard	173,800

Median Gross Rent

Group	Dollars
Total Population	667
Hispanic or Latino (of any race)	685
Central American, ex. Mexican	672
Guatemalan	608
Honduran	756
Nicaraguan	818
Panamanian	623
Salvadoran	655
Cuban	738
Dominican Republic	954
Mexican	676
Puerto Rican	706
South American	763
Argentinean	835
Chilean	813
Colombian	760
Ecuadorian	821
Peruvian	625
Venezuelan	646
Spaniard	718

Median Household Income
(2010 Inflation-Adjusted Dollars)

Group	Dollars
Total Population	46,262
Hispanic or Latino (of any race)	38,811
Central American, ex. Mexican	37,620
Guatemalan	27,712
Honduran	33,173
Nicaraguan	50,000
Panamanian	58,750
Salvadoran	41,649
Cuban	34,252
Dominican Republic	53,707
Mexican	37,231
Puerto Rican	42,778
South American	56,217
Argentinean	75,096
Chilean	57,093
Colombian	56,250
Ecuadorian	25,313
Peruvian	71,595
Venezuelan	50,395
Spaniard	39,084

Per Capita Income
(2010 Inflation-Adjusted Dollars)

Group	Dollars
Total Population	24,724
Hispanic or Latino (of any race)	14,961
Central American, ex. Mexican	12,125
Guatemalan	8,372
Honduran	10,895
Nicaraguan	15,200
Panamanian	21,987
Salvadoran	14,191
Cuban	22,562
Dominican Republic	16,149
Mexican	13,638
Puerto Rican	20,603
South American	26,522
Argentinean	38,972
Chilean	22,335
Colombian	26,604
Ecuadorian	17,629
Peruvian	25,585
Venezuelan	22,619
Spaniard	19,602

Households with $100,000+ Income

Group	Number	%
Total Population	366,970	15.6
Hispanic or Latino (of any race)	5,799	10.8
Central American, ex. Mexican	311	7.8
Guatemalan	54	4.8
Honduran	9	1.3
Nicaraguan	25	7.3
Panamanian	114	32.5
Salvadoran	83	6.9
Cuban	240	14.0
Dominican Republic	20	5.0
Mexican	3,348	9.3
Puerto Rican	592	15.4
South American	699	26.5
Argentinean	79	32.5
Chilean	81	29.1
Colombian	198	24.8
Ecuadorian	11	4.2
Peruvian	145	34.8
Venezuelan	60	27.0
Spaniard	228	13.2

Households with Food Stamps/SNAP Benefits During Past 12 Months

Group	Number	%
Total Population	267,850	11.4
Hispanic or Latino (of any race)	8,264	15.4
Central American, ex. Mexican	616	15.4
Guatemalan	193	17.3
Honduran	186	26.0
Nicaraguan	41	12.0
Panamanian	35	10.0
Salvadoran	132	11.0
Cuban	284	16.6
Dominican Republic	52	13.0
Mexican	5,768	16.0
Puerto Rican	443	11.5
South American	161	6.1
Argentinean	5	2.1
Chilean	14	5.0
Colombian	42	5.3
Ecuadorian	84	31.8
Peruvian	0	0.0
Venezuelan	8	3.6
Spaniard	320	18.5

Poverty Rate
(Income in Past 12 Months Below Poverty Level)

Group	%
Total Population	14.0
Hispanic or Latino (of any race)	24.3
Central American, ex. Mexican	28.6
Guatemalan	35.9
Honduran	42.6
Nicaraguan	23.4
Panamanian	4.3
Salvadoran	16.7
Cuban	20.4
Dominican Republic	6.7
Mexican	26.3
Puerto Rican	17.2
South American	9.0
Argentinean	3.9
Chilean	4.1
Colombian	5.3
Ecuadorian	54.8
Peruvian	5.2
Venezuelan	0.8
Spaniard	15.5

Carthage*

Population

Group	Number	%TP[1]	%HP[2]
Total Population	14,378	100.0	–
Hispanic or Latino (of any race)	3,685	25.6	100.0
Central American, ex. Mexican	2,060	14.3	55.9
Guatemalan	1,840	12.8	49.9
Salvadoran	175	1.2	4.7
Mexican	1,286	8.9	34.9

Population Growth: 2000–2010

Group	%
Total Population	13.5
Hispanic or Latino (of any race)	131.9
Central American, ex. Mexican	250.3
Guatemalan	258.0
Mexican	69.2

Males per 100 Females

Group	Number
Total Population	95.8
Hispanic or Latino (of any race)	109.7
Central American, ex. Mexican	114.4
Guatemalan	113.2
Salvadoran	130.3
Mexican	98.5

Average Household Size

Group	People
Total Population	2.69
Hispanic or Latino (of any race)	4.51
Central American, ex. Mexican	4.81
Guatemalan	4.92
Salvadoran	4.08
Mexican	4.13

Median Age

Group	Years
Total Population	32.0
Hispanic or Latino (of any race)	21.9
Central American, ex. Mexican	24.2
Guatemalan	23.8
Salvadoran	29.3
Mexican	18.3

High School Graduates
(Universe: Population 25 Years and Over)

Group	Number	%
Total Population	5,732	66.9
Hispanic or Latino (of any race)	406	21.8
Central American, ex. Mexican	118	13.2
Guatemalan	87	11.3
Mexican	176	20.5

Four-Year College Graduates
(Universe: Population 25 Years and Over)

Group	Number	%
Total Population	1,181	13.8
Hispanic or Latino (of any race)	95	5.1
Central American, ex. Mexican	32	3.6
Guatemalan	18	2.3
Mexican	21	2.4

Population Age 3–17 Enrolled in Public School
(Universe: Population Age 3–17 Enrolled in School)

Group	Number	%
Total Population	2,766	95.2

Notes: (1) Percent of total population; (2) Percent of Hispanic/Latino population; Profiles include places with an overall population of at least 125,000, OR an overall population of at least 25,000 where the Hispanic/Latino population is at least 20% of the overall population. In states where less than five places meet either of these criteria, we have included places with at least 10,000 total population with the highest percentage of Hispanic/Latino population. These places are identified with an asterisk (*); Please refer to the User's Guide for a full explanation of data.

Group	Number	%
Hispanic or Latino (of any race)	1,136	98.2
Central American, ex. Mexican	461	95.6
Guatemalan	446	95.5
Mexican	657	100.0

Population Age 3–17 Enrolled in Private School
(Universe: Population Age 3–17 Enrolled in School)

Group	Number	%
Total Population	138	4.8
Hispanic or Latino (of any race)	21	1.8
Central American, ex. Mexican	21	4.4
Guatemalan	21	4.5
Mexican	0	0.0

Foreign-Born Population

Group	Number	%
Total Population	2,419	17.1
Hispanic or Latino (of any race)	2,278	54.0
Central American, ex. Mexican	1,244	58.4
Guatemalan	1,135	60.3
Mexican	992	51.6

Foreign-Born Naturalized U.S. Citizens

Group	Number	%
Total Population	205	8.5
Hispanic or Latino (of any race)	88	3.9
Central American, ex. Mexican	70	5.6
Guatemalan	46	4.1
Mexican	18	1.8

Language Spoken at Home: English Only
(Universe: Population 5 Years and Over)

Group	Number	%
Total Population	9,084	72.1
Hispanic or Latino (of any race)	214	6.2
Central American, ex. Mexican	103	6.5
Guatemalan	69	4.8
Mexican	70	4.2

Language Spoken at Home: Spanish
(Universe: Population 5 Years and Over)

Group	Number	%
Total Population	3,399	27.0
Hispanic or Latino (of any race)	3,216	93.8
Central American, ex. Mexican	1,493	93.5
Guatemalan	1,369	95.2
Mexican	1,616	95.8

Unemployment Rate
(Universe: Population 16 Years and Over)

Group	%
Total Population	14.3
Hispanic or Latino (of any race)	21.4
Central American, ex. Mexican	11.2
Guatemalan	9.8
Mexican	31.5

Class of Worker: Private Wage and Salary
(Universe: Civilian Employed Population 16 Years and Over)

Group	Number	%
Total Population	4,644	86.0
Hispanic or Latino (of any race)	1,236	94.1
Central American, ex. Mexican	841	98.7
Guatemalan	736	100.0
Mexican	374	84.8

Class of Worker: Government
(Universe: Civilian Employed Population 16 Years and Over)

Group	Number	%
Total Population	439	8.1
Hispanic or Latino (of any race)	0	0.0
Central American, ex. Mexican	0	0.0
Guatemalan	0	0.0
Mexican	0	0.0

Means of Transportation to Work: Car, Truck or Van
(Universe: Workers 16 Years and Over)

Group	Number	%
Total Population	4,572	85.6
Hispanic or Latino (of any race)	895	69.6
Central American, ex. Mexican	481	57.6
Guatemalan	393	54.7
Mexican	393	91.6

Means of Transportation to Work: Public Transportation (ex. Taxicab)
(Universe: Workers 16 Years and Over)

Group	Number	%
Total Population	11	0.2
Hispanic or Latino (of any race)	11	0.9
Central American, ex. Mexican	11	1.3
Guatemalan	11	1.5
Mexican	0	0.0

Homeownership Rate
(Universe: Occupied Housing Units)

Group	%
Total Population	56.7
Hispanic or Latino (of any race)	34.9
Central American, ex. Mexican	29.2
Guatemalan	26.7
Salvadoran	52.1
Mexican	44.7

Median Home Value

Group	Dollars
Total Population	81,300
Hispanic or Latino (of any race)	69,300
Central American, ex. Mexican	39,000
Guatemalan	32,300
Mexican	71,300

Median Gross Rent

Group	Dollars
Total Population	545
Hispanic or Latino (of any race)	574
Central American, ex. Mexican	589
Guatemalan	586
Mexican	548

Median Household Income
(2010 Inflation-Adjusted Dollars)

Group	Dollars
Total Population	29,024
Hispanic or Latino (of any race)	27,647
Central American, ex. Mexican	28,538
Guatemalan	27,807
Mexican	26,328

Per Capita Income
(2010 Inflation-Adjusted Dollars)

Group	Dollars
Total Population	15,189
Hispanic or Latino (of any race)	8,056
Central American, ex. Mexican	9,309
Guatemalan	8,504
Mexican	6,415

Households with $100,000+ Income

Group	Number	%
Total Population	361	7.2
Hispanic or Latino (of any race)	59	6.3
Central American, ex. Mexican	41	8.3
Guatemalan	41	9.3
Mexican	18	5.2

Households with Food Stamps/SNAP Benefits During Past 12 Months

Group	Number	%
Total Population	1,102	22.0
Hispanic or Latino (of any race)	233	24.8
Central American, ex. Mexican	96	19.5
Guatemalan	80	18.1
Mexican	126	36.5

Poverty Rate
(Income in Past 12 Months Below Poverty Level)

Group	%
Total Population	30.9
Hispanic or Latino (of any race)	48.7
Central American, ex. Mexican	43.0
Guatemalan	41.2
Mexican	55.6

Fort Leonard Wood*

Population

Group	Number	%TP[1]	%HP[2]
Total Population	15,061	100.0	–
Hispanic or Latino (of any race)	2,200	14.6	100.0
Central American, ex. Mexican	122	0.8	5.5
Mexican	1,068	7.1	48.5
Puerto Rican	600	4.0	27.3
South American	123	0.8	5.6

Population Growth: 2000–2010

Group	%
Total Population	10.2
Hispanic or Latino (of any race)	40.8
Central American, ex. Mexican	16.2
Mexican	53.7
Puerto Rican	44.9

Males per 100 Females

Group	Number
Total Population	255.9
Hispanic or Latino (of any race)	248.1
Central American, ex. Mexican	248.6
Mexican	240.1
Puerto Rican	240.9
South American	284.4

Average Household Size

Group	People
Total Population	3.27
Hispanic or Latino (of any race)	3.21
Central American, ex. Mexican	2.89
Mexican	3.16
Puerto Rican	3.43
South American	3.33

Median Age

Group	Years
Total Population	21.2
Hispanic or Latino (of any race)	20.9
Central American, ex. Mexican	21.2
Mexican	20.5
Puerto Rican	21.2
South American	21.5

High School Graduates
(Universe: Population 25 Years and Over)

Group	Number	%
Total Population	4,362	96.0
Hispanic or Latino (of any race)	485	100.0
Mexican	115	100.0

Four-Year College Graduates
(Universe: Population 25 Years and Over)

Group	Number	%
Total Population	887	19.5
Hispanic or Latino (of any race)	127	26.2
Mexican	11	9.6

Population Age 3–17 Enrolled in Public School
(Universe: Population Age 3–17 Enrolled in School)

Group	Number	%
Total Population	1,743	92.8
Hispanic or Latino (of any race)	245	100.0
Mexican	82	100.0

Population Age 3–17 Enrolled in Private School
(Universe: Population Age 3–17 Enrolled in School)

Group	Number	%
Total Population	136	7.2
Hispanic or Latino (of any race)	0	0.0
Mexican	0	0.0

Foreign-Born Population

Group	Number	%
Total Population	783	5.1
Hispanic or Latino (of any race)	278	12.9
Mexican	137	12.2

Foreign-Born Naturalized U.S. Citizens

Group	Number	%
Total Population	299	38.2
Hispanic or Latino (of any race)	86	30.9
Mexican	32	23.4

Notes: (1) Percent of total population; (2) Percent of Hispanic/Latino population; Profiles include places with an overall population of at least 125,000, OR an overall population of at least 25,000 where the Hispanic/Latino population is at least 20% of the overall population. In states where less than five places meet either of these criteria, we have included places with at least 10,000 total population with the highest percentage of Hispanic/Latino population. These places are identified with an asterisk (*); Please refer to the User's Guide for a full explanation of data.

Language Spoken at Home: English Only
(Universe: Population 5 Years and Over)

Group	Number	%
Total Population	11,766	81.3
Hispanic or Latino (of any race)	704	35.5
Mexican	405	38.4

Language Spoken at Home: Spanish
(Universe: Population 5 Years and Over)

Group	Number	%
Total Population	1,605	11.1
Hispanic or Latino (of any race)	1,248	62.9
Mexican	635	60.1

Unemployment Rate
(Universe: Population 16 Years and Over)

Group	%
Total Population	15.1
Hispanic or Latino (of any race)	23.1
Mexican	46.4

Class of Worker: Private Wage and Salary
(Universe: Civilian Employed Population 16 Years and Over)

Group	Number	%
Total Population	769	46.5
Hispanic or Latino (of any race)	79	51.6
Mexican	11	36.7

Class of Worker: Government
(Universe: Civilian Employed Population 16 Years and Over)

Group	Number	%
Total Population	821	49.6
Hispanic or Latino (of any race)	71	46.4
Mexican	19	63.3

Means of Transportation to Work: Car, Truck or Van
(Universe: Workers 16 Years and Over)

Group	Number	%
Total Population	2,487	22.2
Hispanic or Latino (of any race)	287	17.8
Mexican	124	13.7

Means of Transportation to Work: Public Transportation (ex. Taxicab)
(Universe: Workers 16 Years and Over)

Group	Number	%
Total Population	90	0.8
Hispanic or Latino (of any race)	0	0.0
Mexican	0	0.0

Homeownership Rate
(Universe: Occupied Housing Units)

Group	%
Total Population	0.6
Hispanic or Latino (of any race)	0.0
Central American, ex. Mexican	0.0
Mexican	0.0
Puerto Rican	0.0
South American	0.0

Median Home Value

Group	Dollars
Total Population	–
Hispanic or Latino (of any race)	–
Mexican	–

Median Gross Rent

Group	Dollars
Total Population	1,014
Hispanic or Latino (of any race)	972
Mexican	1,020

Median Household Income
(2010 Inflation-Adjusted Dollars)

Group	Dollars
Total Population	40,784
Hispanic or Latino (of any race)	44,000
Mexican	37,102

Per Capita Income
(2010 Inflation-Adjusted Dollars)

Group	Dollars
Total Population	17,691
Hispanic or Latino (of any race)	15,961
Mexican	14,228

Households with $100,000+ Income

Group	Number	%
Total Population	138	6.3
Hispanic or Latino (of any race)	25	10.2
Mexican	25	24.3

Households with Food Stamps/SNAP Benefits During Past 12 Months

Group	Number	%
Total Population	85	3.9
Hispanic or Latino (of any race)	0	0.0
Mexican	0	0.0

Poverty Rate
(Income in Past 12 Months Below Poverty Level)

Group	%
Total Population	12.8
Hispanic or Latino (of any race)	1.4
Mexican	3.7

Kansas City

Population

Group	Number	%TP[1]	%HP[2]
Total Population	459,787	100.0	–
Hispanic or Latino (of any race)	45,953	10.0	100.0
Central American, ex. Mexican	2,758	0.6	6.0
Guatemalan	671	0.1	1.5
Honduran	884	0.2	1.9
Panamanian	127	<0.1	0.3
Salvadoran	893	0.2	1.9
Cuban	1,327	0.3	2.9
Dominican Republic	301	0.1	0.7
Mexican	35,930	7.8	78.2
Puerto Rican	1,474	0.3	3.2
South American	1,108	0.2	2.4
Argentinean	103	<0.1	0.2
Colombian	364	0.1	0.8
Ecuadorian	132	<0.1	0.3
Peruvian	176	<0.1	0.4
Venezuelan	111	<0.1	0.2
Spaniard	454	0.1	1.0

Population Growth: 2000–2010

Group	%
Total Population	4.1
Hispanic or Latino (of any race)	50.2
Central American, ex. Mexican	196.9
Guatemalan	258.8
Honduran	199.7
Salvadoran	227.1
Cuban	68.6
Mexican	49.4
Puerto Rican	99.2
South American	110.2
Colombian	120.6

Males per 100 Females

Group	Number
Total Population	94.3
Hispanic or Latino (of any race)	109.0
Central American, ex. Mexican	118.9
Guatemalan	109.0
Honduran	141.5
Panamanian	78.9
Salvadoran	115.7
Cuban	123.4
Dominican Republic	109.0
Mexican	109.1
Puerto Rican	101.4
South American	89.7
Argentinean	68.9
Colombian	84.8
Ecuadorian	100.0
Peruvian	81.4
Venezuelan	101.8
Spaniard	88.4

Average Household Size

Group	People
Total Population	2.34
Hispanic or Latino (of any race)	3.22
Central American, ex. Mexican	3.55
Guatemalan	3.86
Honduran	3.61
Panamanian	2.33
Salvadoran	3.74
Cuban	2.60
Dominican Republic	3.05
Mexican	3.34
Puerto Rican	2.51
South American	2.61
Argentinean	2.48
Colombian	2.90
Ecuadorian	2.44
Peruvian	2.59
Venezuelan	2.47
Spaniard	2.31

Median Age

Group	Years
Total Population	34.6
Hispanic or Latino (of any race)	26.2
Central American, ex. Mexican	28.1
Guatemalan	25.9
Honduran	28.9
Panamanian	27.2
Salvadoran	28.1
Cuban	36.7
Dominican Republic	27.4
Mexican	25.5
Puerto Rican	27.1
South American	32.4
Argentinean	38.2
Colombian	29.8
Ecuadorian	33.3
Peruvian	30.0
Venezuelan	34.8
Spaniard	34.6

High School Graduates
(Universe: Population 25 Years and Over)

Group	Number	%
Total Population	259,309	86.4
Hispanic or Latino (of any race)	13,716	58.9
Central American, ex. Mexican	787	44.6
Cuban	638	66.7
Mexican	10,196	56.5
Puerto Rican	565	96.1
South American	551	87.0

Four-Year College Graduates
(Universe: Population 25 Years and Over)

Group	Number	%
Total Population	88,692	29.6
Hispanic or Latino (of any race)	2,795	12.0
Central American, ex. Mexican	114	6.5
Cuban	303	31.7
Mexican	1,687	9.3
Puerto Rican	213	36.2
South American	277	43.8

Population Age 3–17 Enrolled in Public School
(Universe: Population Age 3–17 Enrolled in School)

Group	Number	%
Total Population	66,637	82.6
Hispanic or Latino (of any race)	9,334	88.2
Central American, ex. Mexican	481	95.4
Cuban	202	96.2
Mexican	7,589	88.5
Puerto Rican	172	68.0
South American	187	70.8

Population Age 3–17 Enrolled in Private School
(Universe: Population Age 3–17 Enrolled in School)

Group	Number	%
Total Population	14,020	17.4
Hispanic or Latino (of any race)	1,245	11.8
Central American, ex. Mexican	23	4.6
Cuban	8	3.8
Mexican	989	11.5
Puerto Rican	81	32.0
South American	77	29.2

Foreign-Born Population

Group	Number	%
Total Population	34,031	7.5
Hispanic or Latino (of any race)	16,645	37.6

Notes: (1) Percent of total population; (2) Percent of Hispanic/Latino population; Profiles include places with an overall population of at least 125,000, OR an overall population of at least 25,000 where the Hispanic/Latino population is at least 20% of the overall population. In states where less than five places meet either of these criteria, we have included places with at least 10,000 total population with the highest percentage of Hispanic/Latino population. These places are identified with an asterisk (*); Please refer to the User's Guide for a full explanation of data.

Central American, ex. Mexican	1,895	65.5
Cuban	1,108	70.9
Mexican	12,499	35.5
Puerto Rican	0	0.0
South American	640	63.7

Foreign-Born Naturalized U.S. Citizens

Group	Number	%
Total Population	12,613	37.1
Hispanic or Latino (of any race)	3,594	21.6
Central American, ex. Mexican	416	22.0
Cuban	358	32.3
Mexican	2,255	18.0
Puerto Rican	0	0.0
South American	322	50.3

Language Spoken at Home: English Only
(Universe: Population 5 Years and Over)

Group	Number	%
Total Population	371,885	88.4
Hispanic or Latino (of any race)	12,528	32.6
Central American, ex. Mexican	120	4.8
Cuban	186	12.9
Mexican	10,162	33.5
Puerto Rican	681	70.0
South American	141	16.0

Language Spoken at Home: Spanish
(Universe: Population 5 Years and Over)

Group	Number	%
Total Population	30,011	7.1
Hispanic or Latino (of any race)	25,825	67.2
Central American, ex. Mexican	2,335	93.2
Cuban	1,256	87.1
Mexican	20,128	66.4
Puerto Rican	282	29.0
South American	739	84.0

Unemployment Rate
(Universe: Population 16 Years and Over)

Group	%
Total Population	9.2
Hispanic or Latino (of any race)	9.4
Central American, ex. Mexican	3.6
Cuban	13.8
Mexican	10.2
Puerto Rican	1.8
South American	7.9

Class of Worker: Private Wage and Salary
(Universe: Civilian Employed Population 16 Years and Over)

Group	Number	%
Total Population	181,366	81.4
Hispanic or Latino (of any race)	16,777	87.2
Central American, ex. Mexican	1,308	87.8
Cuban	756	95.7
Mexican	12,958	87.0
Puerto Rican	505	86.5
South American	407	81.1

Class of Worker: Government
(Universe: Civilian Employed Population 16 Years and Over)

Group	Number	%
Total Population	30,023	13.5
Hispanic or Latino (of any race)	1,578	8.2
Central American, ex. Mexican	83	5.6
Cuban	34	4.3
Mexican	1,272	8.5
Puerto Rican	47	8.0
South American	46	9.2

Means of Transportation to Work: Car, Truck or Van
(Universe: Workers 16 Years and Over)

Group	Number	%
Total Population	196,199	89.8
Hispanic or Latino (of any race)	17,067	91.0
Central American, ex. Mexican	1,319	92.0
Cuban	684	88.8
Mexican	13,128	90.6
Puerto Rican	553	94.7
South American	502	100.0

Means of Transportation to Work: Public Transportation (ex. Taxicab)
(Universe: Workers 16 Years and Over)

Group	Number	%
Total Population	8,121	3.7
Hispanic or Latino (of any race)	525	2.8
Central American, ex. Mexican	12	0.8
Cuban	40	5.2
Mexican	461	3.2
Puerto Rican	0	0.0
South American	0	0.0

Homeownership Rate
(Universe: Occupied Housing Units)

Group	%
Total Population	56.2
Hispanic or Latino (of any race)	49.1
Central American, ex. Mexican	43.5
Guatemalan	40.3
Honduran	42.1
Panamanian	32.6
Salvadoran	48.0
Cuban	45.3
Dominican Republic	43.0
Mexican	50.5
Puerto Rican	41.9
South American	54.3
Argentinean	50.0
Colombian	58.3
Ecuadorian	54.2
Peruvian	44.6
Venezuelan	52.6
Spaniard	54.8

Median Home Value

Group	Dollars
Total Population	135,000
Hispanic or Latino (of any race)	98,900
Central American, ex. Mexican	74,000
Cuban	131,900
Mexican	94,700
Puerto Rican	165,600
South American	118,300

Median Gross Rent

Group	Dollars
Total Population	721
Hispanic or Latino (of any race)	705
Central American, ex. Mexican	823
Cuban	792
Mexican	684
Puerto Rican	572
South American	749

Median Household Income
(2010 Inflation-Adjusted Dollars)

Group	Dollars
Total Population	44,113
Hispanic or Latino (of any race)	36,956
Central American, ex. Mexican	32,628
Cuban	40,259
Mexican	35,216
Puerto Rican	53,182
South American	56,417

Per Capita Income
(2010 Inflation-Adjusted Dollars)

Group	Dollars
Total Population	25,683
Hispanic or Latino (of any race)	14,156
Central American, ex. Mexican	12,646
Cuban	18,247
Mexican	13,673
Puerto Rican	21,220
South American	21,614

Households with $100,000+ Income

Group	Number	%
Total Population	30,805	16.0
Hispanic or Latino (of any race)	1,055	8.0
Central American, ex. Mexican	43	5.1
Cuban	48	8.5
Mexican	777	7.6
Puerto Rican	75	17.0
South American	39	13.6

Households with Food Stamps/SNAP Benefits During Past 12 Months

Group	Number	%
Total Population	24,784	12.9
Hispanic or Latino (of any race)	2,354	17.9
Central American, ex. Mexican	278	33.2
Cuban	93	16.5
Mexican	1,746	17.0
Puerto Rican	60	13.6
South American	33	11.5

Poverty Rate
(Income in Past 12 Months Below Poverty Level)

Group	%
Total Population	18.1
Hispanic or Latino (of any race)	29.4
Central American, ex. Mexican	39.3
Cuban	10.7
Mexican	30.2
Puerto Rican	24.1
South American	3.9

Saint Louis

Population

Group	Number	%TP[1]	%HP[2]
Total Population	319,294	100.0	–
Hispanic or Latino (of any race)	11,130	3.5	100.0
Central American, ex. Mexican	954	0.3	8.6
Guatemalan	139	<0.1	1.2
Honduran	449	0.1	4.0
Nicaraguan	106	<0.1	1.0
Salvadoran	138	<0.1	1.2
Cuban	474	0.1	4.3
Mexican	7,163	2.2	64.4
Puerto Rican	700	0.2	6.3
South American	590	0.2	5.3
Colombian	178	0.1	1.6
Peruvian	115	<0.1	1.0
Spaniard	310	0.1	2.8

Population Growth: 2000–2010

Group	%
Total Population	-8.3
Hispanic or Latino (of any race)	58.5
Central American, ex. Mexican	219.1
Cuban	27.1
Mexican	74.2
Puerto Rican	40.0
South American	130.5

Males per 100 Females

Group	Number
Total Population	93.4
Hispanic or Latino (of any race)	119.5
Central American, ex. Mexican	138.5
Guatemalan	139.7
Honduran	167.3
Nicaraguan	135.6
Salvadoran	115.6
Cuban	112.6
Mexican	122.9
Puerto Rican	107.1
South American	100.7
Colombian	95.6
Peruvian	88.5
Spaniard	103.9

Average Household Size

Group	People
Total Population	2.16
Hispanic or Latino (of any race)	2.71
Central American, ex. Mexican	2.90
Guatemalan	2.53
Honduran	3.44
Nicaraguan	2.78
Salvadoran	3.04
Cuban	2.24
Mexican	3.03
Puerto Rican	2.15
South American	2.02
Colombian	2.11
Peruvian	1.92

Notes: (1) Percent of total population; (2) Percent of Hispanic/Latino population; Profiles include places with an overall population of at least 125,000, OR an overall population of at least 25,000 where the Hispanic/Latino population is at least 20% of the overall population. In states where less than five places meet either of these criteria, we have included places with at least 10,000 total population with the highest percentage of Hispanic/Latino population. These places are identified with an asterisk (*); Please refer to the User's Guide for a full explanation of data.

Group	Years
Spaniard	2.04

Median Age

Group	Years
Total Population	33.9
Hispanic or Latino (of any race)	27.2
Central American, ex. Mexican	28.1
Guatemalan	19.5
Honduran	28.1
Nicaraguan	30.5
Salvadoran	26.6
Cuban	33.0
Mexican	26.0
Puerto Rican	26.7
South American	31.4
Colombian	30.4
Peruvian	32.3
Spaniard	34.7

High School Graduates
(Universe: Population 25 Years and Over)

Group	Number	%
Total Population	169,115	80.6
Hispanic or Latino (of any race)	3,847	66.8
Mexican	2,341	58.5

Four-Year College Graduates
(Universe: Population 25 Years and Over)

Group	Number	%
Total Population	56,448	26.9
Hispanic or Latino (of any race)	1,222	21.2
Mexican	513	12.8

Population Age 3–17 Enrolled in Public School
(Universe: Population Age 3–17 Enrolled in School)

Group	Number	%
Total Population	39,787	77.7
Hispanic or Latino (of any race)	1,405	71.8
Mexican	1,161	78.0

Population Age 3–17 Enrolled in Private School
(Universe: Population Age 3–17 Enrolled in School)

Group	Number	%
Total Population	11,449	22.3
Hispanic or Latino (of any race)	552	28.2
Mexican	328	22.0

Foreign-Born Population

Group	Number	%
Total Population	21,256	6.7
Hispanic or Latino (of any race)	4,245	41.0
Mexican	3,307	44.2

Foreign-Born Naturalized U.S. Citizens

Group	Number	%
Total Population	7,418	34.9
Hispanic or Latino (of any race)	915	21.6
Mexican	467	14.1

Language Spoken at Home: English Only
(Universe: Population 5 Years and Over)

Group	Number	%
Total Population	270,934	91.1
Hispanic or Latino (of any race)	3,297	36.0
Mexican	1,985	30.3

Language Spoken at Home: Spanish
(Universe: Population 5 Years and Over)

Group	Number	%
Total Population	8,516	2.9
Hispanic or Latino (of any race)	5,829	63.7
Mexican	4,542	69.4

Unemployment Rate
(Universe: Population 16 Years and Over)

Group	%
Total Population	12.7
Hispanic or Latino (of any race)	7.0
Mexican	6.3

Class of Worker: Private Wage and Salary
(Universe: Civilian Employed Population 16 Years and Over)

Group	Number	%
Total Population	121,167	82.3
Hispanic or Latino (of any race)	4,680	88.7
Mexican	3,582	90.9

Class of Worker: Government
(Universe: Civilian Employed Population 16 Years and Over)

Group	Number	%
Total Population	19,549	13.3
Hispanic or Latino (of any race)	426	8.1
Mexican	249	6.3

Means of Transportation to Work: Car, Truck or Van
(Universe: Workers 16 Years and Over)

Group	Number	%
Total Population	116,533	81.0
Hispanic or Latino (of any race)	4,565	87.2
Mexican	3,503	89.2

Means of Transportation to Work: Public Transportation (ex. Taxicab)
(Universe: Workers 16 Years and Over)

Group	Number	%
Total Population	15,230	10.6
Hispanic or Latino (of any race)	414	7.9
Mexican	293	7.5

Homeownership Rate
(Universe: Occupied Housing Units)

Group	%
Total Population	45.4
Hispanic or Latino (of any race)	36.7
Central American, ex. Mexican	26.3
Guatemalan	23.3
Honduran	16.4
Nicaraguan	40.0
Salvadoran	37.0
Cuban	42.0
Mexican	35.4
Puerto Rican	30.8
South American	49.1
Colombian	44.9
Peruvian	52.0
Spaniard	54.2

Median Home Value

Group	Dollars
Total Population	122,200
Hispanic or Latino (of any race)	124,000
Mexican	110,900

Median Gross Rent

Group	Dollars
Total Population	658
Hispanic or Latino (of any race)	669
Mexican	654

Median Household Income
(2010 Inflation-Adjusted Dollars)

Group	Dollars
Total Population	33,652
Hispanic or Latino (of any race)	36,979
Mexican	36,538

Per Capita Income
(2010 Inflation-Adjusted Dollars)

Group	Dollars
Total Population	21,406
Hispanic or Latino (of any race)	17,082
Mexican	14,593

Households with $100,000+ Income

Group	Number	%
Total Population	14,232	10.1
Hispanic or Latino (of any race)	312	9.8
Mexican	183	8.8

Households with Food Stamps/SNAP Benefits During Past 12 Months

Group	Number	%
Total Population	30,501	21.7
Hispanic or Latino (of any race)	422	13.3
Mexican	312	15.0

Poverty Rate
(Income in Past 12 Months Below Poverty Level)

Group	%
Total Population	26.0
Hispanic or Latino (of any race)	29.1
Mexican	32.5

Springfield

Population

Group	Number	%TP[1]	%HP[2]
Total Population	159,498	100.0	–
Hispanic or Latino (of any race)	5,851	3.7	100.0
Central American, ex. Mexican	427	0.3	7.3
Honduran	120	0.1	2.1
Salvadoran	154	0.1	2.6
Cuban	107	0.1	1.8
Mexican	3,879	2.4	66.3
Puerto Rican	470	0.3	8.0
South American	256	0.2	4.4
Spaniard	212	0.1	3.6

Population Growth: 2000–2010

Group	%
Total Population	5.2
Hispanic or Latino (of any race)	67.1
Central American, ex. Mexican	223.5
Cuban	-0.9
Mexican	88.8
Puerto Rican	55.1
South American	85.5

Males per 100 Females

Group	Number
Total Population	94.1
Hispanic or Latino (of any race)	116.5
Central American, ex. Mexican	128.3
Honduran	126.4
Salvadoran	133.3
Cuban	148.8
Mexican	117.9
Puerto Rican	102.6
South American	100.0
Spaniard	105.8

Average Household Size

Group	People
Total Population	2.13
Hispanic or Latino (of any race)	2.79
Central American, ex. Mexican	3.07
Honduran	4.00
Salvadoran	3.21
Cuban	2.53
Mexican	2.98
Puerto Rican	2.55
South American	2.32
Spaniard	2.34

Median Age

Group	Years
Total Population	33.2
Hispanic or Latino (of any race)	23.9
Central American, ex. Mexican	24.8
Honduran	22.6
Salvadoran	26.0
Cuban	25.5
Mexican	23.0
Puerto Rican	22.9
South American	28.8
Spaniard	26.0

High School Graduates
(Universe: Population 25 Years and Over)

Group	Number	%
Total Population	86,371	86.6
Hispanic or Latino (of any race)	1,639	66.8
Mexican	952	62.6

Four-Year College Graduates
(Universe: Population 25 Years and Over)

Group	Number	%
Total Population	25,566	25.6
Hispanic or Latino (of any race)	566	23.1
Mexican	325	21.4

Population Age 3–17 Enrolled in Public School
(Universe: Population Age 3–17 Enrolled in School)

Group	Number	%
Total Population	17,436	87.2
Hispanic or Latino (of any race)	898	88.7
Mexican	642	90.4

Notes: (1) Percent of total population; (2) Percent of Hispanic/Latino population; Profiles include places with an overall population of at least 125,000, OR an overall population of at least 25,000 where the Hispanic/Latino population is at least 20% of the overall population. In states where less than five places meet either of these criteria, we have included places with at least 10,000 total population with the highest percentage of Hispanic/Latino population. These places are identified with an asterisk (*); Please refer to the User's Guide for a full explanation of data.

Population Age 3–17 Enrolled in Private School
(Universe: Population Age 3–17 Enrolled in School)

Group	Number	%
Total Population	2,565	12.8
Hispanic or Latino (of any race)	114	11.3
Mexican	68	9.6

Foreign-Born Population

Group	Number	%
Total Population	4,971	3.1
Hispanic or Latino (of any race)	1,406	27.0
Mexican	992	28.8

Foreign-Born Naturalized U.S. Citizens

Group	Number	%
Total Population	1,950	39.2
Hispanic or Latino (of any race)	330	23.5
Mexican	150	15.1

Language Spoken at Home: English Only
(Universe: Population 5 Years and Over)

Group	Number	%
Total Population	141,261	94.1
Hispanic or Latino (of any race)	2,123	46.8
Mexican	1,369	45.1

Language Spoken at Home: Spanish
(Universe: Population 5 Years and Over)

Group	Number	%
Total Population	4,500	3.0
Hispanic or Latino (of any race)	2,394	52.8
Mexican	1,666	54.9

Unemployment Rate
(Universe: Population 16 Years and Over)

Group	%
Total Population	8.1
Hispanic or Latino (of any race)	6.5
Mexican	5.7

Class of Worker: Private Wage and Salary
(Universe: Civilian Employed Population 16 Years and Over)

Group	Number	%
Total Population	65,569	84.4
Hispanic or Latino (of any race)	2,121	87.9
Mexican	1,549	93.1

Class of Worker: Government
(Universe: Civilian Employed Population 16 Years and Over)

Group	Number	%
Total Population	7,630	9.8
Hispanic or Latino (of any race)	205	8.5
Mexican	27	1.6

Means of Transportation to Work: Car, Truck or Van
(Universe: Workers 16 Years and Over)

Group	Number	%
Total Population	68,265	89.1
Hispanic or Latino (of any race)	2,027	85.7
Mexican	1,431	86.0

Means of Transportation to Work: Public Transportation (ex. Taxicab)
(Universe: Workers 16 Years and Over)

Group	Number	%
Total Population	781	1.0
Hispanic or Latino (of any race)	93	3.9
Mexican	60	3.6

Homeownership Rate
(Universe: Occupied Housing Units)

Group	%
Total Population	49.2
Hispanic or Latino (of any race)	33.0
Central American, ex. Mexican	35.8
Honduran	23.1
Salvadoran	40.4
Cuban	28.1
Mexican	32.5
Puerto Rican	24.4
South American	42.3
Spaniard	39.1

Median Home Value

Group	Dollars
Total Population	103,800
Hispanic or Latino (of any race)	96,000
Mexican	61,600

Median Gross Rent

Group	Dollars
Total Population	612
Hispanic or Latino (of any race)	560
Mexican	594

Median Household Income
(2010 Inflation-Adjusted Dollars)

Group	Dollars
Total Population	33,082
Hispanic or Latino (of any race)	30,374
Mexican	34,728

Per Capita Income
(2010 Inflation-Adjusted Dollars)

Group	Dollars
Total Population	20,793
Hispanic or Latino (of any race)	11,954
Mexican	11,352

Households with $100,000+ Income

Group	Number	%
Total Population	5,220	7.4
Hispanic or Latino (of any race)	39	2.2
Mexican	16	1.6

Households with Food Stamps/SNAP Benefits During Past 12 Months

Group	Number	%
Total Population	9,323	13.3
Hispanic or Latino (of any race)	218	12.3
Mexican	163	16.0

Poverty Rate
(Income in Past 12 Months Below Poverty Level)

Group	%
Total Population	21.7
Hispanic or Latino (of any race)	25.5
Mexican	21.7

STATE & PLACE PROFILES

Notes: (1) Percent of total population; (2) Percent of Hispanic/Latino population; Profiles include places with an overall population of at least 125,000, OR an overall population of at least 25,000 where the Hispanic/Latino population is at least 20% of the overall population. In states where less than five places meet either of these criteria, we have included places with at least 10,000 total population with the highest percentage of Hispanic/Latino population. These places are identified with an asterisk (*); Please refer to the User's Guide for a full explanation of data.

Montana

EDITOR'S NOTE: For a place to be included in this edition, it must meet one of two criteria. Either its overall population is at least 125,000, OR its overall population is at least 25,000 and its Hispanic/Latino population is at least 20% of the overall population. In Montana, less than five places meet either of these criteria. In an effort to include at least five places for each state, we have included places with at least 10,000 total population with the highest percentage of Hispanic/Latino population. These places are identified with an asterisk (*). For the state of Montana, the following locations are included:

Billings*
Bozeman*
Butte-Silver Bow*
Great Falls*
Missoula*

Section Two: State & Place Profiles starts with the state profile, followed by place profiles that meet the criteria above. Places are listed alphabetically within each state. All states, all counties and places that meet the above criteria are ranked and compared in *Section Three: Rankings & Comparisons*, on page 1055.

For a more detailed look at the Hispanic/Latino population in Montana, a companion web site is available at no additional charge with purchase of this print edition. Visit http://gold.greyhouse.com/page/info_hispanic for more information.

The web site includes data for all counties and places in Montana with Hispanic/Latino population, plus ten additional topics: Self Employed Worker; Walked to Work; Worked from Home; Mean Travel Time to Work; Mean Household Income; Households with Cash Public Assistance; Mean Cash Pubic Assistance; Poverty Rates for 18 and Under, 18 to 64, and 65 and Over.

Population

Group	Number	%TP[1]	%HP[2]
Total Population	989,415	100.0	–
Hispanic or Latino (of any race)	28,565	2.9	100.0
Central American, ex. Mexican	735	0.1	2.6
Guatemalan	200	<0.1	0.7
Panamanian	131	<0.1	0.5
Salvadoran	140	<0.1	0.5
Cuban	421	<0.1	1.5
Mexican	20,048	2.0	70.2
Puerto Rican	1,491	0.2	5.2
South American	997	0.1	3.5
Argentinean	115	<0.1	0.4
Chilean	105	<0.1	0.4
Colombian	288	<0.1	1.0
Peruvian	237	<0.1	0.8
Spaniard	1,360	0.1	4.8

Population Growth: 2000–2010

Group	%
Total Population	9.7
Hispanic or Latino (of any race)	58.0
Central American, ex. Mexican	212.8
Cuban	47.7
Mexican	70.8
Puerto Rican	60.2
South American	223.7
Spaniard	900.0

Males per 100 Females

Group	Number
Total Population	100.8
Hispanic or Latino (of any race)	102.9
Central American, ex. Mexican	80.1
Guatemalan	83.5
Panamanian	74.7
Salvadoran	97.2
Cuban	94.9
Mexican	106.0
Puerto Rican	101.2
South American	82.3
Argentinean	88.5
Chilean	94.4
Colombian	67.4
Peruvian	89.6
Spaniard	91.5

Average Household Size

Group	People
Total Population	2.35
Hispanic or Latino (of any race)	2.70
Central American, ex. Mexican	2.65
Guatemalan	2.58
Panamanian	2.65
Salvadoran	2.97
Cuban	2.28
Mexican	2.83
Puerto Rican	2.65
South American	2.53
Argentinean	2.42
Chilean	2.25
Colombian	2.29
Peruvian	2.80
Spaniard	2.39

Median Age

Group	Years
Total Population	39.8
Hispanic or Latino (of any race)	23.6
Central American, ex. Mexican	21.9
Guatemalan	12.0
Panamanian	26.5
Salvadoran	22.8
Cuban	28.7
Mexican	22.4
Puerto Rican	23.4
South American	26.5
Argentinean	32.5
Chilean	27.8
Colombian	24.6
Peruvian	27.1
Spaniard	31.8

High School Graduates
(Universe: Population 25 Years and Over)

Group	Number	%
Total Population	594,992	91.0
Hispanic or Latino (of any race)	10,670	83.3
Mexican	7,316	81.4
Puerto Rican	617	87.5
South American	461	90.9
Spaniard	748	92.3

Four-Year College Graduates
(Universe: Population 25 Years and Over)

Group	Number	%
Total Population	182,330	27.9
Hispanic or Latino (of any race)	2,412	18.8
Mexican	1,523	16.9
Puerto Rican	137	19.4
South American	160	31.6
Spaniard	150	18.5

Population Age 3–17 Enrolled in Public School
(Universe: Population Age 3–17 Enrolled in School)

Group	Number	%
Total Population	144,534	88.2
Hispanic or Latino (of any race)	6,595	90.0
Mexican	4,917	88.9
Puerto Rican	367	100.0
South American	152	92.1
Spaniard	139	93.3

Population Age 3–17 Enrolled in Private School
(Universe: Population Age 3–17 Enrolled in School)

Group	Number	%
Total Population	19,268	11.8
Hispanic or Latino (of any race)	730	10.0
Mexican	611	11.1
Puerto Rican	0	0.0
South American	13	7.9
Spaniard	10	6.7

Foreign-Born Population

Group	Number	%
Total Population	19,119	2.0
Hispanic or Latino (of any race)	2,335	8.6
Mexican	1,347	6.9
Puerto Rican	0	0.0
South American	522	50.3
Spaniard	126	11.5

Foreign-Born Naturalized U.S. Citizens

Group	Number	%
Total Population	10,366	54.2
Hispanic or Latino (of any race)	1,287	55.1
Mexican	628	46.6
Puerto Rican	0	0.0
South American	328	62.8
Spaniard	58	46.0

Language Spoken at Home: English Only
(Universe: Population 5 Years and Over)

Group	Number	%
Total Population	871,548	95.4
Hispanic or Latino (of any race)	18,615	77.8
Mexican	13,388	79.4
Puerto Rican	1,062	70.7
South American	467	47.8
Spaniard	839	82.3

Language Spoken at Home: Spanish
(Universe: Population 5 Years and Over)

Group	Number	%
Total Population	12,822	1.4
Hispanic or Latino (of any race)	5,102	21.3
Mexican	3,359	19.9
Puerto Rican	440	29.3
South American	494	50.5
Spaniard	132	12.9

Unemployment Rate
(Universe: Population 16 Years and Over)

Group	%
Total Population	5.7
Hispanic or Latino (of any race)	8.1
Mexican	8.2
Puerto Rican	4.2
South American	11.9
Spaniard	3.0

Class of Worker: Private Wage and Salary
(Universe: Civilian Employed Population 16 Years and Over)

Group	Number	%
Total Population	336,831	70.7
Hispanic or Latino (of any race)	8,352	78.9
Mexican	5,962	80.9
Puerto Rican	406	70.9
South American	396	77.8
Spaniard	405	69.7

Class of Worker: Government
(Universe: Civilian Employed Population 16 Years and Over)

Group	Number	%
Total Population	88,177	18.5
Hispanic or Latino (of any race)	1,622	15.3
Mexican	1,103	15.0
Puerto Rican	141	24.6
South American	48	9.4
Spaniard	79	13.6

Means of Transportation to Work: Car, Truck or Van
(Universe: Workers 16 Years and Over)

Group	Number	%
Total Population	396,379	84.6
Hispanic or Latino (of any race)	9,260	86.7
Mexican	6,533	88.0

Notes: (1) Percent of total population; (2) Percent of Hispanic/Latino population; Profiles include places with an overall population of at least 125,000, OR an overall population of at least 25,000 where the Hispanic/Latino population is at least 20% of the overall population. In states where less than five places meet either of these criteria, we have included places with at least 10,000 total population with the highest percentage of Hispanic/Latino population. These places are identified with an asterisk (*); Please refer to the User's Guide for a full explanation of data.

Group	Number	%
Puerto Rican	522	87.9
South American	450	80.5
Spaniard	477	83.7

Means of Transportation to Work: Public Transportation (ex. Taxicab)
(Universe: Workers 16 Years and Over)

Group	Number	%
Total Population	4,722	1.0
Hispanic or Latino (of any race)	160	1.5
Mexican	152	2.0
Puerto Rican	0	0.0
South American	0	0.0
Spaniard	0	0.0

Homeownership Rate
(Universe: Occupied Housing Units)

Group	%
Total Population	68.0
Hispanic or Latino (of any race)	48.0
Central American, ex. Mexican	48.1
Guatemalan	42.3
Panamanian	54.8
Salvadoran	47.4
Cuban	53.7
Mexican	47.4
Puerto Rican	43.8
South American	43.7
Argentinean	55.3
Chilean	50.0
Colombian	37.9
Peruvian	33.9
Spaniard	57.7

Median Home Value

Group	Dollars
Total Population	173,300
Hispanic or Latino (of any race)	163,800
Mexican	161,300
Puerto Rican	160,500
South American	207,400
Spaniard	196,900

Median Gross Rent

Group	Dollars
Total Population	629
Hispanic or Latino (of any race)	649
Mexican	666
Puerto Rican	513
South American	879
Spaniard	643

Median Household Income
(2010 Inflation-Adjusted Dollars)

Group	Dollars
Total Population	43,872
Hispanic or Latino (of any race)	32,182
Mexican	31,872
Puerto Rican	25,917
South American	40,568
Spaniard	43,427

Per Capita Income
(2010 Inflation-Adjusted Dollars)

Group	Dollars
Total Population	23,836
Hispanic or Latino (of any race)	14,009
Mexican	13,241
Puerto Rican	13,665
South American	16,302
Spaniard	26,946

Households with $100,000+ Income

Group	Number	%
Total Population	52,469	13.1
Hispanic or Latino (of any race)	413	5.5
Mexican	217	4.4
Puerto Rican	16	3.0
South American	29	11.6
Spaniard	35	6.0

Households with Food Stamps/SNAP Benefits During Past 12 Months

Group	Number	%
Total Population	32,783	8.2
Hispanic or Latino (of any race)	1,211	16.1
Mexican	884	18.0
Puerto Rican	46	8.7
South American	15	6.0
Spaniard	27	4.6

Poverty Rate
(Income in Past 12 Months Below Poverty Level)

Group	%
Total Population	14.5
Hispanic or Latino (of any race)	26.5
Mexican	27.1
Puerto Rican	30.1
South American	10.0
Spaniard	16.8

Billings*

Population

Group	Number	%TP[1]	%HP[2]
Total Population	104,170	100.0	–
Hispanic or Latino (of any race)	5,456	5.2	100.0
Central American, ex. Mexican	103	0.1	1.9
Mexican	4,214	4.0	77.2
Puerto Rican	227	0.2	4.2
Spaniard	172	0.2	3.2

Population Growth: 2000–2010

Group	%
Total Population	15.9
Hispanic or Latino (of any race)	45.2
Mexican	55.7
Puerto Rican	89.2

Males per 100 Females

Group	Number
Total Population	93.3
Hispanic or Latino (of any race)	103.5
Central American, ex. Mexican	66.1
Mexican	104.4
Puerto Rican	122.5
Spaniard	93.3

Average Household Size

Group	People
Total Population	2.29
Hispanic or Latino (of any race)	2.71
Central American, ex. Mexican	2.53
Mexican	2.81
Puerto Rican	2.56
Spaniard	2.30

Median Age

Group	Years
Total Population	37.5
Hispanic or Latino (of any race)	23.6
Central American, ex. Mexican	14.9
Mexican	22.8
Puerto Rican	23.4
Spaniard	35.7

High School Graduates
(Universe: Population 25 Years and Over)

Group	Number	%
Total Population	62,860	92.0
Hispanic or Latino (of any race)	1,716	74.5
Mexican	1,389	72.1

Four-Year College Graduates
(Universe: Population 25 Years and Over)

Group	Number	%
Total Population	21,179	31.0
Hispanic or Latino (of any race)	357	15.5
Mexican	286	14.8

Population Age 3–17 Enrolled in Public School
(Universe: Population Age 3–17 Enrolled in School)

Group	Number	%
Total Population	14,276	88.1
Hispanic or Latino (of any race)	1,132	93.9
Mexican	923	92.6

Population Age 3–17 Enrolled in Private School
(Universe: Population Age 3–17 Enrolled in School)

Group	Number	%
Total Population	1,926	11.9
Hispanic or Latino (of any race)	74	6.1
Mexican	74	7.4

Foreign-Born Population

Group	Number	%
Total Population	1,851	1.8
Hispanic or Latino (of any race)	199	4.0
Mexican	68	1.7

Foreign-Born Naturalized U.S. Citizens

Group	Number	%
Total Population	1,122	60.6
Hispanic or Latino (of any race)	163	81.9
Mexican	46	67.6

Language Spoken at Home: English Only
(Universe: Population 5 Years and Over)

Group	Number	%
Total Population	89,765	95.3
Hispanic or Latino (of any race)	3,373	81.8
Mexican	2,775	83.8

Language Spoken at Home: Spanish
(Universe: Population 5 Years and Over)

Group	Number	%
Total Population	1,566	1.7
Hispanic or Latino (of any race)	737	17.9
Mexican	535	16.2

Unemployment Rate
(Universe: Population 16 Years and Over)

Group	%
Total Population	4.4
Hispanic or Latino (of any race)	3.8
Mexican	3.1

Class of Worker: Private Wage and Salary
(Universe: Civilian Employed Population 16 Years and Over)

Group	Number	%
Total Population	43,351	82.3
Hispanic or Latino (of any race)	1,906	91.3
Mexican	1,544	94.3

Class of Worker: Government
(Universe: Civilian Employed Population 16 Years and Over)

Group	Number	%
Total Population	5,845	11.1
Hispanic or Latino (of any race)	136	6.5
Mexican	94	5.7

Means of Transportation to Work: Car, Truck or Van
(Universe: Workers 16 Years and Over)

Group	Number	%
Total Population	46,903	90.5
Hispanic or Latino (of any race)	1,929	92.3
Mexican	1,508	92.0

Means of Transportation to Work: Public Transportation (ex. Taxicab)
(Universe: Workers 16 Years and Over)

Group	Number	%
Total Population	821	1.6
Hispanic or Latino (of any race)	60	2.9
Mexican	60	3.7

Homeownership Rate
(Universe: Occupied Housing Units)

Group	%
Total Population	63.6
Hispanic or Latino (of any race)	44.4
Central American, ex. Mexican	82.4
Mexican	42.9
Puerto Rican	44.3
Spaniard	49.3

Median Home Value

Group	Dollars
Total Population	169,000
Hispanic or Latino (of any race)	150,000
Mexican	152,200

Notes: (1) Percent of total population; (2) Percent of Hispanic/Latino population; Profiles include places with an overall population of at least 125,000, OR an overall population of at least 25,000 where the Hispanic/Latino population is at least 20% of the overall population. In states where less than five places meet either of these criteria, we have included places with at least 10,000 total population with the highest percentage of Hispanic/Latino population. These places are identified with an asterisk (*); Please refer to the User's Guide for a full explanation of data.

Median Gross Rent

Group	Dollars
Total Population	656
Hispanic or Latino (of any race)	659
Mexican	669

Median Household Income
(2010 Inflation-Adjusted Dollars)

Group	Dollars
Total Population	46,433
Hispanic or Latino (of any race)	32,766
Mexican	33,032

Per Capita Income
(2010 Inflation-Adjusted Dollars)

Group	Dollars
Total Population	26,449
Hispanic or Latino (of any race)	13,621
Mexican	13,718

Households with $100,000+ Income

Group	Number	%
Total Population	6,628	15.4
Hispanic or Latino (of any race)	51	3.6
Mexican	36	3.1

Households with Food Stamps/SNAP Benefits During Past 12 Months

Group	Number	%
Total Population	3,501	8.1
Hispanic or Latino (of any race)	361	25.2
Mexican	250	21.5

Poverty Rate
(Income in Past 12 Months Below Poverty Level)

Group	%
Total Population	12.1
Hispanic or Latino (of any race)	26.6
Mexican	25.0

Bozeman*

Population

Group	Number	%TP[1]	%HP[2]
Total Population	37,280	100.0	–
Hispanic or Latino (of any race)	1,096	2.9	100.0
Mexican	665	1.8	60.7
South American	104	0.3	9.5

Population Growth: 2000–2010

Group	%
Total Population	35.5
Hispanic or Latino (of any race)	150.2
Mexican	215.2

Males per 100 Females

Group	Number
Total Population	111.1
Hispanic or Latino (of any race)	111.6
Mexican	126.2
South American	67.7

Average Household Size

Group	People
Total Population	2.17
Hispanic or Latino (of any race)	2.44
Mexican	2.63
South American	2.24

Median Age

Group	Years
Total Population	27.2
Hispanic or Latino (of any race)	23.9
Mexican	23.1
South American	26.6

High School Graduates
(Universe: Population 25 Years and Over)

Group	Number	%
Total Population	19,690	97.2
Hispanic or Latino (of any race)	495	96.9

Four-Year College Graduates
(Universe: Population 25 Years and Over)

Group	Number	%
Total Population	10,344	51.1
Hispanic or Latino (of any race)	197	38.6

Population Age 3–17 Enrolled in Public School
(Universe: Population Age 3–17 Enrolled in School)

Group	Number	%
Total Population	3,146	88.4
Hispanic or Latino (of any race)	99	100.0

Population Age 3–17 Enrolled in Private School
(Universe: Population Age 3–17 Enrolled in School)

Group	Number	%
Total Population	412	11.6
Hispanic or Latino (of any race)	0	0.0

Foreign-Born Population

Group	Number	%
Total Population	1,405	3.9
Hispanic or Latino (of any race)	40	4.1

Foreign-Born Naturalized U.S. Citizens

Group	Number	%
Total Population	583	41.5
Hispanic or Latino (of any race)	33	82.5

Language Spoken at Home: English Only
(Universe: Population 5 Years and Over)

Group	Number	%
Total Population	32,540	94.1
Hispanic or Latino (of any race)	744	87.4

Language Spoken at Home: Spanish
(Universe: Population 5 Years and Over)

Group	Number	%
Total Population	497	1.4
Hispanic or Latino (of any race)	107	12.6

Unemployment Rate
(Universe: Population 16 Years and Over)

Group	%
Total Population	5.7
Hispanic or Latino (of any race)	5.3

Class of Worker: Private Wage and Salary
(Universe: Civilian Employed Population 16 Years and Over)

Group	Number	%
Total Population	16,202	75.5
Hispanic or Latino (of any race)	518	87.9

Class of Worker: Government
(Universe: Civilian Employed Population 16 Years and Over)

Group	Number	%
Total Population	3,699	17.2
Hispanic or Latino (of any race)	59	10.0

Means of Transportation to Work: Car, Truck or Van
(Universe: Workers 16 Years and Over)

Group	Number	%
Total Population	16,146	77.3
Hispanic or Latino (of any race)	428	75.8

Means of Transportation to Work: Public Transportation (ex. Taxicab)
(Universe: Workers 16 Years and Over)

Group	Number	%
Total Population	249	1.2
Hispanic or Latino (of any race)	0	0.0

Homeownership Rate
(Universe: Occupied Housing Units)

Group	%
Total Population	43.5
Hispanic or Latino (of any race)	23.9
Mexican	20.1
South American	32.4

Median Home Value

Group	Dollars
Total Population	268,100
Hispanic or Latino (of any race)	203,600

Median Gross Rent

Group	Dollars
Total Population	787
Hispanic or Latino (of any race)	889

Median Household Income
(2010 Inflation-Adjusted Dollars)

Group	Dollars
Total Population	42,218
Hispanic or Latino (of any race)	43,409

Per Capita Income
(2010 Inflation-Adjusted Dollars)

Group	Dollars
Total Population	26,038
Hispanic or Latino (of any race)	17,767

Households with $100,000+ Income

Group	Number	%
Total Population	2,053	13.3
Hispanic or Latino (of any race)	26	11.1

Households with Food Stamps/SNAP Benefits During Past 12 Months

Group	Number	%
Total Population	729	4.7
Hispanic or Latino (of any race)	8	3.4

Poverty Rate
(Income in Past 12 Months Below Poverty Level)

Group	%
Total Population	20.9
Hispanic or Latino (of any race)	15.0

Butte-Silver Bow*

Population

Group	Number	%TP[1]	%HP[2]
Total Population	33,525	100.0	–
Hispanic or Latino (of any race)	1,227	3.7	100.0
Mexican	923	2.8	75.2

Population Growth: 2000–2010

Group	%
Total Population	-1.1
Hispanic or Latino (of any race)	32.4
Mexican	48.4

Males per 100 Females

Group	Number
Total Population	102.2
Hispanic or Latino (of any race)	102.5
Mexican	106.5

Average Household Size

Group	People
Total Population	2.22
Hispanic or Latino (of any race)	2.52
Mexican	2.58

Median Age

Group	Years
Total Population	41.3
Hispanic or Latino (of any race)	26.8
Mexican	25.8

High School Graduates
(Universe: Population 25 Years and Over)

Group	Number	%
Total Population	20,578	91.5
Hispanic or Latino (of any race)	581	87.4

Four-Year College Graduates
(Universe: Population 25 Years and Over)

Group	Number	%
Total Population	5,181	23.0
Hispanic or Latino (of any race)	150	22.6

Population Age 3–17 Enrolled in Public School
(Universe: Population Age 3–17 Enrolled in School)

Group	Number	%
Total Population	4,803	88.6
Hispanic or Latino (of any race)	330	100.0

Notes: (1) Percent of total population; (2) Percent of Hispanic/Latino population; Profiles include places with an overall population of at least 125,000, OR an overall population of at least 25,000 where the Hispanic/Latino population is at least 20% of the overall population. In states where less than five places meet either of these criteria, we have included places with at least 10,000 total population with the highest percentage of Hispanic/Latino population. These places are identified with an asterisk (*); Please refer to the User's Guide for a full explanation of data.

Population Age 3–17 Enrolled in Private School
(Universe: Population Age 3–17 Enrolled in School)

Group	Number	%
Total Population	619	11.4
Hispanic or Latino (of any race)	0	0.0

Foreign-Born Population

Group	Number	%
Total Population	712	2.2
Hispanic or Latino (of any race)	63	5.2

Foreign-Born Naturalized U.S. Citizens

Group	Number	%
Total Population	447	62.8
Hispanic or Latino (of any race)	63	100.0

Language Spoken at Home: English Only
(Universe: Population 5 Years and Over)

Group	Number	%
Total Population	29,388	94.6
Hispanic or Latino (of any race)	866	76.2

Language Spoken at Home: Spanish
(Universe: Population 5 Years and Over)

Group	Number	%
Total Population	628	2.0
Hispanic or Latino (of any race)	228	20.1

Unemployment Rate
(Universe: Population 16 Years and Over)

Group	%
Total Population	5.2
Hispanic or Latino (of any race)	11.4

Class of Worker: Private Wage and Salary
(Universe: Civilian Employed Population 16 Years and Over)

Group	Number	%
Total Population	12,052	76.8
Hispanic or Latino (of any race)	460	86.1

Class of Worker: Government
(Universe: Civilian Employed Population 16 Years and Over)

Group	Number	%
Total Population	2,417	15.4
Hispanic or Latino (of any race)	74	13.9

Means of Transportation to Work: Car, Truck or Van
(Universe: Workers 16 Years and Over)

Group	Number	%
Total Population	13,634	89.5
Hispanic or Latino (of any race)	505	94.6

Means of Transportation to Work: Public Transportation (ex. Taxicab)
(Universe: Workers 16 Years and Over)

Group	Number	%
Total Population	139	0.9
Hispanic or Latino (of any race)	0	0.0

Homeownership Rate
(Universe: Occupied Housing Units)

Group	%
Total Population	67.3
Hispanic or Latino (of any race)	55.6
Mexican	54.4

Median Home Value

Group	Dollars
Total Population	118,700
Hispanic or Latino (of any race)	96,400

Median Gross Rent

Group	Dollars
Total Population	516
Hispanic or Latino (of any race)	507

Median Household Income
(2010 Inflation-Adjusted Dollars)

Group	Dollars
Total Population	38,178
Hispanic or Latino (of any race)	30,267

Per Capita Income
(2010 Inflation-Adjusted Dollars)

Group	Dollars
Total Population	21,479
Hispanic or Latino (of any race)	10,530

Households with $100,000+ Income

Group	Number	%
Total Population	1,418	9.8
Hispanic or Latino (of any race)	26	6.7

Households with Food Stamps/SNAP Benefits During Past 12 Months

Group	Number	%
Total Population	1,680	11.6
Hispanic or Latino (of any race)	63	16.3

Poverty Rate
(Income in Past 12 Months Below Poverty Level)

Group	%
Total Population	17.5
Hispanic or Latino (of any race)	45.3

Great Falls*

Population

Group	Number	%TP[1]	%HP[2]
Total Population	58,505	100.0	–
Hispanic or Latino (of any race)	1,978	3.4	100.0
Mexican	1,319	2.3	66.7
Puerto Rican	176	0.3	8.9
Spaniard	112	0.2	5.7

Population Growth: 2000–2010

Group	%
Total Population	3.2
Hispanic or Latino (of any race)	46.1
Mexican	68.2
Puerto Rican	61.5

Males per 100 Females

Group	Number
Total Population	95.5
Hispanic or Latino (of any race)	103.7
Mexican	110.0
Puerto Rican	120.0
Spaniard	86.7

Average Household Size

Group	People
Total Population	2.26
Hispanic or Latino (of any race)	2.57
Mexican	2.65
Puerto Rican	2.65
Spaniard	2.25

Median Age

Group	Years
Total Population	39.0
Hispanic or Latino (of any race)	22.5
Mexican	21.7
Puerto Rican	22.5
Spaniard	32.0

High School Graduates
(Universe: Population 25 Years and Over)

Group	Number	%
Total Population	35,181	90.6
Hispanic or Latino (of any race)	557	72.0
Mexican	342	71.1

Four-Year College Graduates
(Universe: Population 25 Years and Over)

Group	Number	%
Total Population	9,422	24.3
Hispanic or Latino (of any race)	67	8.7
Mexican	23	4.8

Population Age 3–17 Enrolled in Public School
(Universe: Population Age 3–17 Enrolled in School)

Group	Number	%
Total Population	8,418	86.6
Hispanic or Latino (of any race)	342	78.3
Mexican	215	71.7

Population Age 3–17 Enrolled in Private School
(Universe: Population Age 3–17 Enrolled in School)

Group	Number	%
Total Population	1,305	13.4
Hispanic or Latino (of any race)	95	21.7
Mexican	85	28.3

Foreign-Born Population

Group	Number	%
Total Population	1,389	2.4
Hispanic or Latino (of any race)	75	4.7
Mexican	68	7.0

Foreign-Born Naturalized U.S. Citizens

Group	Number	%
Total Population	923	66.5
Hispanic or Latino (of any race)	7	9.3
Mexican	0	0.0

Language Spoken at Home: English Only
(Universe: Population 5 Years and Over)

Group	Number	%
Total Population	51,431	95.1
Hispanic or Latino (of any race)	1,000	70.8
Mexican	641	73.8

Language Spoken at Home: Spanish
(Universe: Population 5 Years and Over)

Group	Number	%
Total Population	911	1.7
Hispanic or Latino (of any race)	377	26.7
Mexican	193	22.2

Unemployment Rate
(Universe: Population 16 Years and Over)

Group	%
Total Population	5.6
Hispanic or Latino (of any race)	13.8
Mexican	18.3

Class of Worker: Private Wage and Salary
(Universe: Civilian Employed Population 16 Years and Over)

Group	Number	%
Total Population	20,750	77.9
Hispanic or Latino (of any race)	425	72.4
Mexican	238	72.8

Class of Worker: Government
(Universe: Civilian Employed Population 16 Years and Over)

Group	Number	%
Total Population	4,299	16.1
Hispanic or Latino (of any race)	138	23.5
Mexican	76	23.2

Means of Transportation to Work: Car, Truck or Van
(Universe: Workers 16 Years and Over)

Group	Number	%
Total Population	25,058	91.4
Hispanic or Latino (of any race)	545	84.8
Mexican	340	90.4

Means of Transportation to Work: Public Transportation (ex. Taxicab)
(Universe: Workers 16 Years and Over)

Group	Number	%
Total Population	459	1.7
Hispanic or Latino (of any race)	29	4.5
Mexican	29	7.7

Homeownership Rate
(Universe: Occupied Housing Units)

Group	%
Total Population	63.2
Hispanic or Latino (of any race)	41.0
Mexican	43.4
Puerto Rican	40.3
Spaniard	43.8

Median Home Value

Group	Dollars
Total Population	144,200
Hispanic or Latino (of any race)	154,300
Mexican	162,100

STATE & PLACE PROFILES

Notes: (1) Percent of total population; (2) Percent of Hispanic/Latino population; Profiles include places with an overall population of at least 125,000, OR an overall population of at least 25,000 where the Hispanic/Latino population is at least 20% of the overall population. In states where less than five places meet either of these criteria, we have included places with at least 10,000 total population with the highest percentage of Hispanic/Latino population. These places are identified with an asterisk (*); Please refer to the User's Guide for a full explanation of data.

Median Gross Rent

Group	Dollars
Total Population	547
Hispanic or Latino (of any race)	602
Mexican	574

Median Household Income
(2010 Inflation-Adjusted Dollars)

Group	Dollars
Total Population	40,935
Hispanic or Latino (of any race)	41,683
Mexican	40,096

Per Capita Income
(2010 Inflation-Adjusted Dollars)

Group	Dollars
Total Population	22,450
Hispanic or Latino (of any race)	21,263
Mexican	24,544

Households with $100,000+ Income

Group	Number	%
Total Population	2,504	10.2
Hispanic or Latino (of any race)	68	14.3
Mexican	42	19.1

Households with Food Stamps/SNAP Benefits During Past 12 Months

Group	Number	%
Total Population	2,471	10.1
Hispanic or Latino (of any race)	53	11.2
Mexican	28	12.7

Poverty Rate
(Income in Past 12 Months Below Poverty Level)

Group	%
Total Population	15.0
Hispanic or Latino (of any race)	30.7
Mexican	24.2

Missoula*

Population

Group	Number	%TP[1]	%HP[2]
Total Population	66,788	100.0	–
Hispanic or Latino (of any race)	1,943	2.9	100.0
Mexican	1,173	1.8	60.4
Puerto Rican	139	0.2	7.2
South American	147	0.2	7.6
Spaniard	117	0.2	6.0

Population Growth: 2000–2010

Group	%
Total Population	17.1
Hispanic or Latino (of any race)	93.5
Mexican	103.3

Males per 100 Females

Group	Number
Total Population	99.6
Hispanic or Latino (of any race)	97.3
Mexican	94.5
Puerto Rican	117.2
South American	90.9
Spaniard	82.8

Average Household Size

Group	People
Total Population	2.18
Hispanic or Latino (of any race)	2.43
Mexican	2.56
Puerto Rican	2.56
South American	2.28
Spaniard	2.33

Median Age

Group	Years
Total Population	30.9
Hispanic or Latino (of any race)	23.7
Mexican	23.3
Puerto Rican	24.5
South American	23.4
Spaniard	25.1

High School Graduates
(Universe: Population 25 Years and Over)

Group	Number	%
Total Population	36,909	92.0
Hispanic or Latino (of any race)	776	94.3

Four-Year College Graduates
(Universe: Population 25 Years and Over)

Group	Number	%
Total Population	16,729	41.7
Hispanic or Latino (of any race)	250	30.4

Population Age 3–17 Enrolled in Public School
(Universe: Population Age 3–17 Enrolled in School)

Group	Number	%
Total Population	7,228	88.1
Hispanic or Latino (of any race)	305	69.6

Population Age 3–17 Enrolled in Private School
(Universe: Population Age 3–17 Enrolled in School)

Group	Number	%
Total Population	980	11.9
Hispanic or Latino (of any race)	133	30.4

Foreign-Born Population

Group	Number	%
Total Population	1,791	2.7
Hispanic or Latino (of any race)	231	12.2

Foreign-Born Naturalized U.S. Citizens

Group	Number	%
Total Population	819	45.7
Hispanic or Latino (of any race)	148	64.1

Language Spoken at Home: English Only
(Universe: Population 5 Years and Over)

Group	Number	%
Total Population	59,074	95.0
Hispanic or Latino (of any race)	1,372	78.2

Language Spoken at Home: Spanish
(Universe: Population 5 Years and Over)

Group	Number	%
Total Population	988	1.6
Hispanic or Latino (of any race)	349	19.9

Unemployment Rate
(Universe: Population 16 Years and Over)

Group	%
Total Population	6.1
Hispanic or Latino (of any race)	11.7

Class of Worker: Private Wage and Salary
(Universe: Civilian Employed Population 16 Years and Over)

Group	Number	%
Total Population	26,098	74.7
Hispanic or Latino (of any race)	513	75.0

Class of Worker: Government
(Universe: Civilian Employed Population 16 Years and Over)

Group	Number	%
Total Population	6,593	18.9
Hispanic or Latino (of any race)	127	18.6

Means of Transportation to Work: Car, Truck or Van
(Universe: Workers 16 Years and Over)

Group	Number	%
Total Population	26,318	77.1
Hispanic or Latino (of any race)	564	81.7

Means of Transportation to Work: Public Transportation (ex. Taxicab)
(Universe: Workers 16 Years and Over)

Group	Number	%
Total Population	920	2.7
Hispanic or Latino (of any race)	0	0.0

Homeownership Rate
(Universe: Occupied Housing Units)

Group	%
Total Population	48.2
Hispanic or Latino (of any race)	26.4
Mexican	26.3
Puerto Rican	20.0
South American	28.2
Spaniard	28.9

Median Home Value

Group	Dollars
Total Population	232,700
Hispanic or Latino (of any race)	195,100

Median Gross Rent

Group	Dollars
Total Population	691
Hispanic or Latino (of any race)	715

Median Household Income
(2010 Inflation-Adjusted Dollars)

Group	Dollars
Total Population	36,547
Hispanic or Latino (of any race)	30,793

Per Capita Income
(2010 Inflation-Adjusted Dollars)

Group	Dollars
Total Population	22,543
Hispanic or Latino (of any race)	16,066

Households with $100,000+ Income

Group	Number	%
Total Population	3,335	11.8
Hispanic or Latino (of any race)	41	6.0

Households with Food Stamps/SNAP Benefits During Past 12 Months

Group	Number	%
Total Population	3,204	11.3
Hispanic or Latino (of any race)	162	23.9

Poverty Rate
(Income in Past 12 Months Below Poverty Level)

Group	%
Total Population	22.1
Hispanic or Latino (of any race)	22.5

Notes: (1) Percent of total population; (2) Percent of Hispanic/Latino population; Profiles include places with an overall population of at least 125,000, OR an overall population of at least 25,000 where the Hispanic/Latino population is at least 20% of the overall population. In states where less than five places meet either of these criteria, we have included places with at least 10,000 total population with the highest percentage of Hispanic/Latino population. These places are identified with an asterisk (*); Please refer to the User's Guide for a full explanation of data.

Nebraska

EDITOR'S NOTE: For a place to be included in this edition, it must meet one of two criteria. Either its overall population is at least 125,000, OR its overall population is at least 25,000 and its Hispanic/Latino population is at least 20% of the overall population. In Nebraska, less than five places meet either of these criteria. In an effort to include at least five places for each state, we have included places with at least 10,000 total population with the highest percentage of Hispanic/Latino population. These places are identified with an asterisk (*). For the state of Nebraska, the following locations are included:

Grand Island
Lexington*
Lincoln
Omaha
South Sioux City*

Section Two: State & Place Profiles starts with the state profile, followed by place profiles that meet the criteria above. Places are listed alphabetically within each state. All states, all counties and places that meet the above criteria are ranked and compared in *Section Three: Rankings & Comparisons*, on page 1055.

For a more detailed look at the Hispanic/Latino population in Nebraska, a companion web site is available at no additional charge with purchase of this print edition. Visit http://gold.greyhouse.com/page/info_hispanic for more information.

The web site includes data for all counties and places in Nebraska with Hispanic/Latino population, plus ten additional topics: Self Employed Worker; Walked to Work; Worked from Home; Mean Travel Time to Work; Mean Household Income; Households with Cash Public Assistance; Mean Cash Pubic Assistance; Poverty Rates for 18 and Under, 18 to 64, and 65 and Over.

Population

Group	Number	%TP[1]	%HP[2]
Total Population	1,826,341	100.0	–
Hispanic or Latino (of any race)	167,405	9.2	100.0
Central American, ex. Mexican	17,242	0.9	10.3
Costa Rican	166	<0.1	0.1
Guatemalan	8,616	0.5	5.1
Honduran	1,547	0.1	0.9
Nicaraguan	347	<0.1	0.2
Panamanian	398	<0.1	0.2
Salvadoran	6,016	0.3	3.6
Cuban	2,152	0.1	1.3
Dominican Republic	358	<0.1	0.2
Mexican	128,060	7.0	76.5
Puerto Rican	3,242	0.2	1.9
South American	2,824	0.2	1.7
Argentinean	243	<0.1	0.1
Chilean	228	<0.1	0.1
Colombian	974	0.1	0.6
Ecuadorian	233	<0.1	0.1
Peruvian	628	<0.1	0.4
Venezuelan	319	<0.1	0.2
Spaniard	1,644	0.1	1.0

Population Growth: 2000–2010

Group	%
Total Population	6.7
Hispanic or Latino (of any race)	77.3
Central American, ex. Mexican	227.2
Guatemalan	243.5
Honduran	225.0
Nicaraguan	199.1
Panamanian	71.6
Salvadoran	270.0
Cuban	150.5
Dominican Republic	177.5
Mexican	80.3
Puerto Rican	62.7
South American	135.9
Chilean	75.4
Colombian	145.3
Peruvian	160.6
Venezuelan	103.2
Spaniard	813.3

Males per 100 Females

Group	Number
Total Population	98.5
Hispanic or Latino (of any race)	111.2
Central American, ex. Mexican	120.3
Costa Rican	86.5
Guatemalan	135.1
Honduran	111.1
Nicaraguan	99.4
Panamanian	77.7
Salvadoran	109.3
Cuban	141.5
Dominican Republic	91.4
Mexican	110.6
Puerto Rican	107.3
South American	86.2
Argentinean	133.7
Chilean	82.4
Colombian	74.2
Ecuadorian	100.9
Peruvian	88.6
Venezuelan	80.2
Spaniard	92.3

Average Household Size

Group	People
Total Population	2.46
Hispanic or Latino (of any race)	3.65
Central American, ex. Mexican	4.15
Costa Rican	2.63
Guatemalan	4.45
Honduran	3.78
Nicaraguan	3.39
Panamanian	2.53
Salvadoran	4.11
Cuban	2.68
Dominican Republic	3.20
Mexican	3.70
Puerto Rican	2.91
South American	2.84
Argentinean	2.82
Chilean	2.94
Colombian	2.60
Ecuadorian	3.17
Peruvian	2.98
Venezuelan	2.98
Spaniard	2.79

Median Age

Group	Years
Total Population	36.2
Hispanic or Latino (of any race)	22.8
Central American, ex. Mexican	26.9
Costa Rican	28.0
Guatemalan	25.9
Honduran	26.7
Nicaraguan	28.1
Panamanian	29.9
Salvadoran	28.7
Cuban	32.2
Dominican Republic	26.2
Mexican	21.9
Puerto Rican	22.4
South American	30.1
Argentinean	33.9
Chilean	32.5
Colombian	28.7
Ecuadorian	28.8
Peruvian	31.2
Venezuelan	30.4
Spaniard	27.9

High School Graduates

(Universe: Population 25 Years and Over)

Group	Number	%
Total Population	1,044,835	90.0
Hispanic or Latino (of any race)	36,296	51.8
Central American, ex. Mexican	3,050	35.6
Guatemalan	1,020	26.4
Honduran	354	40.2
Salvadoran	1,074	34.5
Cuban	527	57.8
Mexican	27,761	50.9
Puerto Rican	1,098	84.6
South American	1,465	91.4
Colombian	472	83.7
Spaniard	777	81.0

Four-Year College Graduates

(Universe: Population 25 Years and Over)

Group	Number	%
Total Population	321,224	27.7
Hispanic or Latino (of any race)	6,948	9.9
Central American, ex. Mexican	493	5.8
Guatemalan	185	4.8
Honduran	69	7.8
Salvadoran	55	1.8
Cuban	201	22.0
Mexican	4,309	7.9
Puerto Rican	377	29.0
South American	855	53.3
Colombian	259	45.9
Spaniard	342	35.7

Population Age 3–17 Enrolled in Public School

(Universe: Population Age 3–17 Enrolled in School)

Group	Number	%
Total Population	283,314	84.0
Hispanic or Latino (of any race)	39,217	92.1
Central American, ex. Mexican	3,589	96.1
Guatemalan	1,635	96.3
Honduran	346	91.3
Salvadoran	1,236	97.9
Cuban	283	90.4
Mexican	32,064	92.4
Puerto Rican	716	81.4
South American	334	76.6
Colombian	121	64.0
Spaniard	457	89.8

Population Age 3–17 Enrolled in Private School

(Universe: Population Age 3–17 Enrolled in School)

Group	Number	%
Total Population	53,904	16.0
Hispanic or Latino (of any race)	3,357	7.9
Central American, ex. Mexican	146	3.9
Guatemalan	62	3.7
Honduran	33	8.7
Salvadoran	26	2.1
Cuban	30	9.6
Mexican	2,626	7.6
Puerto Rican	164	18.6
South American	102	23.4
Colombian	68	36.0
Spaniard	52	10.2

Foreign-Born Population

Group	Number	%
Total Population	106,298	5.9
Hispanic or Latino (of any race)	59,444	39.1
Central American, ex. Mexican	10,480	61.5
Guatemalan	4,844	60.9
Honduran	1,221	69.9
Salvadoran	3,804	64.3
Cuban	607	40.0
Mexican	45,350	37.6
Puerto Rican	21	0.8
South American	1,851	70.0
Colombian	841	81.4
Spaniard	323	17.9

Notes: (1) Percent of total population; (2) Percent of Hispanic/Latino population; Profiles include places with an overall population of at least 125,000, OR an overall population of at least 25,000 where the Hispanic/Latino population is at least 20% of the overall population. In states where less than five places meet either of these criteria, we have included places with at least 10,000 total population with the highest percentage of Hispanic/Latino population. These places are identified with an asterisk (*); Please refer to the User's Guide for a full explanation of data.

Foreign-Born Naturalized U.S. Citizens

Group	Number	%
Total Population	35,603	33.5
Hispanic or Latino (of any race)	13,825	23.3
Central American, ex. Mexican	2,189	20.9
Guatemalan	786	16.2
Honduran	441	36.1
Salvadoran	735	19.3
Cuban	311	51.2
Mexican	10,284	22.7
Puerto Rican	0	0.0
South American	585	31.6
Colombian	168	20.0
Spaniard	136	42.1

Language Spoken at Home: English Only
(Universe: Population 5 Years and Over)

Group	Number	%
Total Population	1,507,705	90.3
Hispanic or Latino (of any race)	38,642	29.6
Central American, ex. Mexican	1,442	9.8
Guatemalan	486	7.4
Honduran	212	13.3
Salvadoran	350	6.7
Cuban	542	38.3
Mexican	30,740	29.8
Puerto Rican	1,549	63.2
South American	524	21.7
Colombian	81	8.7
Spaniard	1,229	75.1

Language Spoken at Home: Spanish
(Universe: Population 5 Years and Over)

Group	Number	%
Total Population	107,428	6.4
Hispanic or Latino (of any race)	91,688	70.2
Central American, ex. Mexican	13,200	90.0
Guatemalan	6,050	92.5
Honduran	1,376	86.0
Salvadoran	4,877	93.3
Cuban	872	61.7
Mexican	72,155	70.0
Puerto Rican	891	36.4
South American	1,889	78.3
Colombian	850	91.3
Spaniard	389	23.8

Unemployment Rate
(Universe: Population 16 Years and Over)

Group	%
Total Population	5.1
Hispanic or Latino (of any race)	7.9
Central American, ex. Mexican	6.3
Guatemalan	5.4
Honduran	6.6
Salvadoran	8.6
Cuban	8.8
Mexican	8.2
Puerto Rican	8.6
South American	5.0
Colombian	8.3
Spaniard	8.7

Class of Worker: Private Wage and Salary
(Universe: Civilian Employed Population 16 Years and Over)

Group	Number	%
Total Population	729,846	77.8
Hispanic or Latino (of any race)	58,083	89.5
Central American, ex. Mexican	7,476	92.8
Guatemalan	3,322	94.2
Honduran	590	82.4
Salvadoran	2,974	95.0
Cuban	733	94.1
Mexican	45,090	89.3
Puerto Rican	1,048	83.8
South American	1,187	78.8
Colombian	522	82.6
Spaniard	664	86.2

Class of Worker: Government
(Universe: Civilian Employed Population 16 Years and Over)

Group	Number	%
Total Population	132,571	14.1
Hispanic or Latino (of any race)	4,195	6.5
Central American, ex. Mexican	317	3.9
Guatemalan	81	2.3
Honduran	95	13.3
Salvadoran	87	2.8
Cuban	11	1.4
Mexican	3,246	6.4
Puerto Rican	131	10.5
South American	252	16.7
Colombian	97	15.3
Spaniard	91	11.8

Means of Transportation to Work: Car, Truck or Van
(Universe: Workers 16 Years and Over)

Group	Number	%
Total Population	830,972	90.0
Hispanic or Latino (of any race)	58,469	92.1
Central American, ex. Mexican	7,527	94.8
Guatemalan	3,377	96.8
Honduran	548	88.4
Salvadoran	2,921	94.1
Cuban	761	95.4
Mexican	45,254	92.0
Puerto Rican	1,117	90.0
South American	1,250	85.7
Colombian	484	80.5
Spaniard	742	97.5

Means of Transportation to Work: Public Transportation (ex. Taxicab)
(Universe: Workers 16 Years and Over)

Group	Number	%
Total Population	6,086	0.7
Hispanic or Latino (of any race)	645	1.0
Central American, ex. Mexican	153	1.9
Guatemalan	37	1.1
Honduran	25	4.0
Salvadoran	68	2.2
Cuban	8	1.0
Mexican	436	0.9
Puerto Rican	0	0.0
South American	35	2.4
Colombian	35	5.8
Spaniard	0	0.0

Homeownership Rate
(Universe: Occupied Housing Units)

Group	%
Total Population	67.2
Hispanic or Latino (of any race)	49.3
Central American, ex. Mexican	47.7
Costa Rican	59.2
Guatemalan	40.1
Honduran	42.8
Nicaraguan	47.2
Panamanian	54.6
Salvadoran	57.8
Cuban	31.9
Dominican Republic	40.4
Mexican	50.6
Puerto Rican	41.0
South American	52.7
Argentinean	55.7
Chilean	50.0
Colombian	50.5
Ecuadorian	51.5
Peruvian	49.2
Venezuelan	62.7
Spaniard	61.4

Median Home Value

Group	Dollars
Total Population	123,900
Hispanic or Latino (of any race)	91,200
Central American, ex. Mexican	93,500
Guatemalan	86,700
Honduran	68,400
Salvadoran	97,200
Cuban	126,000
Mexican	87,400
Puerto Rican	150,900
South American	139,200
Colombian	141,700
Spaniard	128,800

Median Gross Rent

Group	Dollars
Total Population	648
Hispanic or Latino (of any race)	642
Central American, ex. Mexican	635
Guatemalan	614
Honduran	699
Salvadoran	693
Cuban	604
Mexican	640
Puerto Rican	716
South American	642
Colombian	643
Spaniard	929

Median Household Income
(2010 Inflation-Adjusted Dollars)

Group	Dollars
Total Population	49,342
Hispanic or Latino (of any race)	37,714
Central American, ex. Mexican	41,169
Guatemalan	38,919
Honduran	44,293
Salvadoran	45,179
Cuban	55,713
Mexican	36,875
Puerto Rican	61,429
South American	38,917
Colombian	63,438
Spaniard	34,450

Per Capita Income
(2010 Inflation-Adjusted Dollars)

Group	Dollars
Total Population	25,229
Hispanic or Latino (of any race)	12,519
Central American, ex. Mexican	12,237
Guatemalan	10,936
Honduran	11,593
Salvadoran	13,094
Cuban	23,107
Mexican	11,843
Puerto Rican	17,530
South American	21,561
Colombian	23,008
Spaniard	19,350

Households with $100,000+ Income

Group	Number	%
Total Population	113,842	16.0
Hispanic or Latino (of any race)	2,124	5.5
Central American, ex. Mexican	88	2.0
Guatemalan	17	0.9
Honduran	15	4.9
Salvadoran	7	0.4
Cuban	107	17.3
Mexican	1,459	4.9
Puerto Rican	105	11.9
South American	115	13.5
Colombian	59	18.8
Spaniard	92	18.7

Households with Food Stamps/SNAP Benefits During Past 12 Months

Group	Number	%
Total Population	53,473	7.5
Hispanic or Latino (of any race)	5,455	14.2
Central American, ex. Mexican	511	11.9
Guatemalan	197	10.8
Honduran	78	25.4
Salvadoran	182	10.1
Cuban	109	17.7
Mexican	4,383	14.6
Puerto Rican	176	19.9
South American	52	6.1
Colombian	22	7.0
Spaniard	39	7.9

Poverty Rate
(Income in Past 12 Months Below Poverty Level)

Group	%
Total Population	11.8
Hispanic or Latino (of any race)	23.0
Central American, ex. Mexican	20.7
Guatemalan	29.5

Notes: (1) Percent of total population; (2) Percent of Hispanic/Latino population; Profiles include places with an overall population of at least 125,000, OR an overall population of at least 25,000 where the Hispanic/Latino population is at least 20% of the overall population. In states where less than five places meet either of these criteria, we have included places with at least 10,000 total population with the highest percentage of Hispanic/Latino population. These places are identified with an asterisk (*); Please refer to the User's Guide for a full explanation of data.

Honduran	5.2
Salvadoran	16.6
Cuban	11.7
Mexican	23.8
Puerto Rican	23.6
South American	12.8
Colombian	8.5
Spaniard	25.1

Grand Island

Population

Group	Number	%TP[1]	%HP[2]
Total Population	48,520	100.0	–
Hispanic or Latino (of any race)	12,933	26.7	100.0
Central American, ex. Mexican	2,689	5.5	20.8
Guatemalan	1,665	3.4	12.9
Honduran	225	0.5	1.7
Salvadoran	757	1.6	5.9
Cuban	528	1.1	4.1
Mexican	8,126	16.7	62.8
South American	109	0.2	0.8

Population Growth: 2000–2010

Group	%
Total Population	13.0
Hispanic or Latino (of any race)	88.9
Central American, ex. Mexican	181.9
Guatemalan	191.6
Salvadoran	209.0
Mexican	67.7

Males per 100 Females

Group	Number
Total Population	99.2
Hispanic or Latino (of any race)	116.5
Central American, ex. Mexican	128.1
Guatemalan	137.5
Honduran	139.4
Salvadoran	106.3
Cuban	210.6
Mexican	108.1
South American	81.7

Average Household Size

Group	People
Total Population	2.59
Hispanic or Latino (of any race)	3.88
Central American, ex. Mexican	4.45
Guatemalan	4.62
Honduran	4.33
Salvadoran	4.28
Cuban	2.82
Mexican	3.81
South American	3.26

Median Age

Group	Years
Total Population	34.7
Hispanic or Latino (of any race)	23.1
Central American, ex. Mexican	27.3
Guatemalan	26.6
Honduran	27.3
Salvadoran	30.0
Cuban	35.1
Mexican	20.2
South American	34.6

High School Graduates

(Universe: Population 25 Years and Over)

Group	Number	%
Total Population	23,869	80.8
Hispanic or Latino (of any race)	1,995	38.1
Central American, ex. Mexican	584	31.8
Guatemalan	253	26.5
Salvadoran	273	42.0
Mexican	1,371	43.7

Four-Year College Graduates

(Universe: Population 25 Years and Over)

Group	Number	%
Total Population	4,610	15.6
Hispanic or Latino (of any race)	267	5.1
Central American, ex. Mexican	50	2.7
Guatemalan	22	2.3
Salvadoran	0	0.0
Mexican	207	6.6

Population Age 3–17 Enrolled in Public School

(Universe: Population Age 3–17 Enrolled in School)

Group	Number	%
Total Population	8,589	91.3
Hispanic or Latino (of any race)	3,352	97.8
Central American, ex. Mexican	1,075	98.9
Guatemalan	537	98.2
Salvadoran	398	99.5
Mexican	2,160	97.2

Population Age 3–17 Enrolled in Private School

(Universe: Population Age 3–17 Enrolled in School)

Group	Number	%
Total Population	822	8.7
Hispanic or Latino (of any race)	75	2.2
Central American, ex. Mexican	12	1.1
Guatemalan	10	1.8
Salvadoran	2	0.5
Mexican	63	2.8

Foreign-Born Population

Group	Number	%
Total Population	6,446	13.7
Hispanic or Latino (of any race)	5,577	49.2
Central American, ex. Mexican	2,337	60.2
Guatemalan	1,233	62.0
Salvadoran	873	58.4
Mexican	2,998	42.9

Foreign-Born Naturalized U.S. Citizens

Group	Number	%
Total Population	1,424	22.1
Hispanic or Latino (of any race)	990	17.8
Central American, ex. Mexican	369	15.8
Guatemalan	163	13.2
Salvadoran	129	14.8
Mexican	578	19.3

Language Spoken at Home: English Only

(Universe: Population 5 Years and Over)

Group	Number	%
Total Population	33,823	78.8
Hispanic or Latino (of any race)	1,870	19.1
Central American, ex. Mexican	216	6.2
Guatemalan	168	9.5
Salvadoran	48	3.6
Mexican	1,564	26.4

Language Spoken at Home: Spanish

(Universe: Population 5 Years and Over)

Group	Number	%
Total Population	8,175	19.0
Hispanic or Latino (of any race)	7,936	80.9
Central American, ex. Mexican	3,242	93.5
Guatemalan	1,585	90.0
Salvadoran	1,286	96.4
Mexican	4,355	73.6

Unemployment Rate

(Universe: Population 16 Years and Over)

Group	%
Total Population	4.9
Hispanic or Latino (of any race)	8.1
Central American, ex. Mexican	10.1
Guatemalan	7.8
Salvadoran	15.3
Mexican	7.7

Class of Worker: Private Wage and Salary

(Universe: Civilian Employed Population 16 Years and Over)

Group	Number	%
Total Population	20,282	82.4
Hispanic or Latino (of any race)	4,774	92.2
Central American, ex. Mexican	1,732	94.8
Guatemalan	840	90.0
Salvadoran	696	99.7
Mexican	2,725	90.1

Class of Worker: Government

(Universe: Civilian Employed Population 16 Years and Over)

Group	Number	%
Total Population	2,699	11.0
Hispanic or Latino (of any race)	222	4.3
Central American, ex. Mexican	23	1.3
Guatemalan	23	2.5
Salvadoran	0	0.0
Mexican	199	6.6

Means of Transportation to Work: Car, Truck or Van

(Universe: Workers 16 Years and Over)

Group	Number	%
Total Population	22,688	93.9
Hispanic or Latino (of any race)	4,775	94.0
Central American, ex. Mexican	1,719	94.6
Guatemalan	869	94.0
Salvadoran	654	93.7
Mexican	2,740	93.3

Means of Transportation to Work: Public Transportation (ex. Taxicab)

(Universe: Workers 16 Years and Over)

Group	Number	%
Total Population	109	0.5
Hispanic or Latino (of any race)	87	1.7
Central American, ex. Mexican	79	4.3
Guatemalan	37	4.0
Salvadoran	42	6.0
Mexican	8	0.3

Homeownership Rate

(Universe: Occupied Housing Units)

Group	%
Total Population	61.0
Hispanic or Latino (of any race)	47.6
Central American, ex. Mexican	47.0
Guatemalan	38.8
Honduran	51.7
Salvadoran	61.5
Cuban	7.9
Mexican	53.0
South American	38.7

Median Home Value

Group	Dollars
Total Population	102,800
Hispanic or Latino (of any race)	83,100
Central American, ex. Mexican	78,400
Guatemalan	72,100
Salvadoran	95,200
Mexican	83,000

Median Gross Rent

Group	Dollars
Total Population	593
Hispanic or Latino (of any race)	609
Central American, ex. Mexican	584
Guatemalan	556
Salvadoran	707
Mexican	608

Median Household Income

(2010 Inflation-Adjusted Dollars)

Group	Dollars
Total Population	43,495
Hispanic or Latino (of any race)	38,451
Central American, ex. Mexican	48,750
Guatemalan	36,141
Salvadoran	49,579
Mexican	36,223

Per Capita Income

(2010 Inflation-Adjusted Dollars)

Group	Dollars
Total Population	21,220
Hispanic or Latino (of any race)	11,512
Central American, ex. Mexican	11,960
Guatemalan	10,968
Salvadoran	11,829
Mexican	10,828

Households with $100,000+ Income

Group	Number	%
Total Population	1,881	10.4
Hispanic or Latino (of any race)	99	3.5
Central American, ex. Mexican	0	0.0
Guatemalan	0	0.0
Salvadoran	0	0.0

Notes: (1) Percent of total population; (2) Percent of Hispanic/Latino population; Profiles include places with an overall population of at least 125,000, OR an overall population of at least 25,000 where the Hispanic/Latino population is at least 20% of the overall population. In states where less than five places meet either of these criteria, we have included places with at least 10,000 total population with the highest percentage of Hispanic/Latino population. These places are identified with an asterisk (*); Please refer to the User's Guide for a full explanation of data.

Mexican	56	3.1

Households with Food Stamps/SNAP Benefits During Past 12 Months

Group	Number	%
Total Population	1,918	10.6
Hispanic or Latino (of any race)	615	21.7
Central American, ex. Mexican	186	20.4
Guatemalan	67	15.5
Salvadoran	84	21.6
Mexican	411	22.6

Poverty Rate
(Income in Past 12 Months Below Poverty Level)

Group	%
Total Population	12.1
Hispanic or Latino (of any race)	20.5
Central American, ex. Mexican	17.2
Guatemalan	22.8
Salvadoran	12.6
Mexican	22.4

Lexington*

Population

Group	Number	%TP[1]	%HP[2]
Total Population	10,230	100.0	–
Hispanic or Latino (of any race)	6,183	60.4	100.0
Central American, ex. Mexican	1,243	12.2	20.1
Guatemalan	891	8.7	14.4
Salvadoran	281	2.7	4.5
Mexican	4,524	44.2	73.2

Population Growth: 2000–2010

Group	%
Total Population	2.2
Hispanic or Latino (of any race)	20.7
Central American, ex. Mexican	78.1
Guatemalan	81.8
Salvadoran	79.0
Mexican	20.5

Males per 100 Females

Group	Number
Total Population	106.8
Hispanic or Latino (of any race)	113.3
Central American, ex. Mexican	122.8
Guatemalan	132.0
Salvadoran	100.7
Mexican	111.3

Average Household Size

Group	People
Total Population	3.17
Hispanic or Latino (of any race)	4.20
Central American, ex. Mexican	4.21
Guatemalan	4.41
Salvadoran	3.83
Mexican	4.26

Median Age

Group	Years
Total Population	29.4
Hispanic or Latino (of any race)	23.2
Central American, ex. Mexican	29.1
Guatemalan	27.5
Salvadoran	34.1
Mexican	21.8

High School Graduates
(Universe: Population 25 Years and Over)

Group	Number	%
Total Population	3,149	53.8
Hispanic or Latino (of any race)	841	29.5
Central American, ex. Mexican	86	15.3
Guatemalan	41	11.1
Mexican	682	31.7

Four-Year College Graduates
(Universe: Population 25 Years and Over)

Group	Number	%
Total Population	536	9.2
Hispanic or Latino (of any race)	64	2.2
Central American, ex. Mexican	0	0.0
Guatemalan	0	0.0
Mexican	41	1.9

Population Age 3–17 Enrolled in Public School
(Universe: Population Age 3–17 Enrolled in School)

Group	Number	%
Total Population	2,336	98.1
Hispanic or Latino (of any race)	1,897	98.8
Central American, ex. Mexican	329	96.5
Guatemalan	159	93.0
Mexican	1,560	99.2

Population Age 3–17 Enrolled in Private School
(Universe: Population Age 3–17 Enrolled in School)

Group	Number	%
Total Population	46	1.9
Hispanic or Latino (of any race)	24	1.2
Central American, ex. Mexican	12	3.5
Guatemalan	12	7.0
Mexican	12	0.8

Foreign-Born Population

Group	Number	%
Total Population	3,800	37.6
Hispanic or Latino (of any race)	3,224	52.4
Central American, ex. Mexican	713	59.2
Guatemalan	480	60.8
Mexican	2,414	50.4

Foreign-Born Naturalized U.S. Citizens

Group	Number	%
Total Population	1,050	27.6
Hispanic or Latino (of any race)	935	29.0
Central American, ex. Mexican	103	14.4
Guatemalan	46	9.6
Mexican	780	32.3

Language Spoken at Home: English Only
(Universe: Population 5 Years and Over)

Group	Number	%
Total Population	3,282	36.3
Hispanic or Latino (of any race)	236	4.4
Central American, ex. Mexican	16	1.5
Guatemalan	0	0.0
Mexican	180	4.3

Language Spoken at Home: Spanish
(Universe: Population 5 Years and Over)

Group	Number	%
Total Population	5,174	57.2
Hispanic or Latino (of any race)	5,109	95.6
Central American, ex. Mexican	1,020	98.5
Guatemalan	646	100.0
Mexican	3,981	95.7

Unemployment Rate
(Universe: Population 16 Years and Over)

Group	%
Total Population	5.5
Hispanic or Latino (of any race)	7.8
Central American, ex. Mexican	10.7
Guatemalan	7.9
Mexican	7.5

Class of Worker: Private Wage and Salary
(Universe: Civilian Employed Population 16 Years and Over)

Group	Number	%
Total Population	4,352	90.0
Hispanic or Latino (of any race)	2,372	91.9
Central American, ex. Mexican	395	89.0
Guatemalan	269	92.8
Mexican	1,873	92.2

Class of Worker: Government
(Universe: Civilian Employed Population 16 Years and Over)

Group	Number	%
Total Population	214	4.4
Hispanic or Latino (of any race)	50	1.9
Central American, ex. Mexican	0	0.0
Guatemalan	0	0.0
Mexican	50	2.5

Means of Transportation to Work: Car, Truck or Van
(Universe: Workers 16 Years and Over)

Group	Number	%
Total Population	4,114	86.7
Hispanic or Latino (of any race)	2,257	90.4
Central American, ex. Mexican	395	89.0
Guatemalan	269	92.8
Mexican	1,799	92.3

Means of Transportation to Work: Public Transportation (ex. Taxicab)
(Universe: Workers 16 Years and Over)

Group	Number	%
Total Population	0	0.0
Hispanic or Latino (of any race)	0	0.0
Central American, ex. Mexican	0	0.0
Guatemalan	0	0.0
Mexican	0	0.0

Homeownership Rate
(Universe: Occupied Housing Units)

Group	%
Total Population	62.6
Hispanic or Latino (of any race)	63.1
Central American, ex. Mexican	60.0
Guatemalan	59.7
Salvadoran	65.2
Mexican	64.9

Median Home Value

Group	Dollars
Total Population	82,700
Hispanic or Latino (of any race)	74,000
Central American, ex. Mexican	70,300
Guatemalan	93,100
Mexican	74,600

Median Gross Rent

Group	Dollars
Total Population	585
Hispanic or Latino (of any race)	659
Central American, ex. Mexican	672
Guatemalan	672
Mexican	653

Median Household Income
(2010 Inflation-Adjusted Dollars)

Group	Dollars
Total Population	40,216
Hispanic or Latino (of any race)	42,248
Central American, ex. Mexican	40,572
Guatemalan	39,219
Mexican	43,511

Per Capita Income
(2010 Inflation-Adjusted Dollars)

Group	Dollars
Total Population	14,769
Hispanic or Latino (of any race)	10,086
Central American, ex. Mexican	9,150
Guatemalan	9,343
Mexican	9,937

Households with $100,000+ Income

Group	Number	%
Total Population	203	6.7
Hispanic or Latino (of any race)	23	1.8
Central American, ex. Mexican	0	0.0
Guatemalan	0	0.0
Mexican	14	1.4

Households with Food Stamps/SNAP Benefits During Past 12 Months

Group	Number	%
Total Population	304	10.0
Hispanic or Latino (of any race)	112	8.5
Central American, ex. Mexican	0	0.0
Guatemalan	0	0.0
Mexican	112	11.2

Poverty Rate
(Income in Past 12 Months Below Poverty Level)

Group	%
Total Population	16.5

Notes: (1) Percent of total population; (2) Percent of Hispanic/Latino population; Profiles include places with an overall population of at least 125,000, OR an overall population of at least 25,000 where the Hispanic/Latino population is at least 20% of the overall population. In states where less than five places meet either of these criteria, we have included places with at least 10,000 total population with the highest percentage of Hispanic/Latino population. These places are identified with an asterisk (*); Please refer to the User's Guide for a full explanation of data.

Hispanic or Latino (of any race)	19.5
Central American, ex. Mexican	20.4
Guatemalan	17.8
Mexican	19.7

Lincoln

Population

Group	Number	%TP[1]	%HP[2]
Total Population	258,379	100.0	–
Hispanic or Latino (of any race)	16,182	6.3	100.0
Central American, ex. Mexican	1,430	0.6	8.8
Guatemalan	682	0.3	4.2
Honduran	149	0.1	0.9
Salvadoran	459	0.2	2.8
Cuban	212	0.1	1.3
Mexican	12,073	4.7	74.6
Puerto Rican	475	0.2	2.9
South American	702	0.3	4.3
Colombian	196	0.1	1.2
Peruvian	211	0.1	1.3
Spaniard	229	0.1	1.4

Population Growth: 2000–2010

Group	%
Total Population	14.5
Hispanic or Latino (of any race)	98.5
Central American, ex. Mexican	254.0
Guatemalan	405.2
Salvadoran	267.2
Cuban	51.4
Mexican	127.4
Puerto Rican	50.8
South American	132.5

Males per 100 Females

Group	Number
Total Population	100.1
Hispanic or Latino (of any race)	112.6
Central American, ex. Mexican	122.0
Guatemalan	142.7
Honduran	104.1
Salvadoran	118.6
Cuban	109.9
Mexican	112.7
Puerto Rican	114.9
South American	90.8
Colombian	64.7
Peruvian	108.9
Spaniard	81.7

Average Household Size

Group	People
Total Population	2.36
Hispanic or Latino (of any race)	3.11
Central American, ex. Mexican	3.29
Guatemalan	3.44
Honduran	3.14
Salvadoran	3.33
Cuban	2.31
Mexican	3.23
Puerto Rican	2.47
South American	2.57
Colombian	2.23
Peruvian	2.83
Spaniard	2.38

Median Age

Group	Years
Total Population	31.8
Hispanic or Latino (of any race)	23.2
Central American, ex. Mexican	26.6
Guatemalan	25.9
Honduran	25.6
Salvadoran	28.0
Cuban	26.5
Mexican	22.3
Puerto Rican	22.2
South American	30.3
Colombian	28.0
Peruvian	31.7
Spaniard	23.3

High School Graduates
(Universe: Population 25 Years and Over)

Group	Number	%
Total Population	142,792	92.7
Hispanic or Latino (of any race)	4,527	66.6
Central American, ex. Mexican	378	57.7
Mexican	3,121	62.9

Four-Year College Graduates
(Universe: Population 25 Years and Over)

Group	Number	%
Total Population	54,155	35.1
Hispanic or Latino (of any race)	1,327	19.5
Central American, ex. Mexican	103	15.7
Mexican	647	13.0

Population Age 3–17 Enrolled in Public School
(Universe: Population Age 3–17 Enrolled in School)

Group	Number	%
Total Population	32,431	79.5
Hispanic or Latino (of any race)	2,844	87.4
Central American, ex. Mexican	148	85.1
Mexican	2,257	91.3

Population Age 3–17 Enrolled in Private School
(Universe: Population Age 3–17 Enrolled in School)

Group	Number	%
Total Population	8,363	20.5
Hispanic or Latino (of any race)	411	12.6
Central American, ex. Mexican	26	14.9
Mexican	216	8.7

Foreign-Born Population

Group	Number	%
Total Population	18,766	7.4
Hispanic or Latino (of any race)	4,913	33.6
Central American, ex. Mexican	746	48.7
Mexican	3,428	31.7

Foreign-Born Naturalized U.S. Citizens

Group	Number	%
Total Population	7,708	41.1
Hispanic or Latino (of any race)	1,067	21.7
Central American, ex. Mexican	208	27.9
Mexican	669	19.5

Language Spoken at Home: English Only
(Universe: Population 5 Years and Over)

Group	Number	%
Total Population	208,508	88.9
Hispanic or Latino (of any race)	4,995	39.7
Central American, ex. Mexican	140	13.2
Mexican	3,774	40.3

Language Spoken at Home: Spanish
(Universe: Population 5 Years and Over)

Group	Number	%
Total Population	10,175	4.3
Hispanic or Latino (of any race)	7,506	59.6
Central American, ex. Mexican	912	85.7
Mexican	5,557	59.4

Unemployment Rate
(Universe: Population 16 Years and Over)

Group	%
Total Population	5.6
Hispanic or Latino (of any race)	9.4
Central American, ex. Mexican	3.6
Mexican	10.0

Class of Worker: Private Wage and Salary
(Universe: Civilian Employed Population 16 Years and Over)

Group	Number	%
Total Population	106,030	76.3
Hispanic or Latino (of any race)	5,519	82.9
Central American, ex. Mexican	523	80.8
Mexican	4,078	84.0

Class of Worker: Government
(Universe: Civilian Employed Population 16 Years and Over)

Group	Number	%
Total Population	25,826	18.6
Hispanic or Latino (of any race)	821	12.3
Central American, ex. Mexican	124	19.2
Mexican	496	10.2

Means of Transportation to Work: Car, Truck or Van
(Universe: Workers 16 Years and Over)

Group	Number	%
Total Population	122,832	90.2
Hispanic or Latino (of any race)	5,546	86.1
Central American, ex. Mexican	624	99.2
Mexican	3,969	85.3

Means of Transportation to Work: Public Transportation (ex. Taxicab)
(Universe: Workers 16 Years and Over)

Group	Number	%
Total Population	1,830	1.3
Hispanic or Latino (of any race)	174	2.7
Central American, ex. Mexican	0	0.0
Mexican	139	3.0

Homeownership Rate
(Universe: Occupied Housing Units)

Group	%
Total Population	58.6
Hispanic or Latino (of any race)	37.7
Central American, ex. Mexican	30.6
Guatemalan	19.2
Honduran	47.7
Salvadoran	36.7
Cuban	40.3
Mexican	39.3
Puerto Rican	33.5
South American	37.1
Colombian	31.9
Peruvian	36.2
Spaniard	42.3

Median Home Value

Group	Dollars
Total Population	140,600
Hispanic or Latino (of any race)	117,100
Central American, ex. Mexican	134,100
Mexican	114,400

Median Gross Rent

Group	Dollars
Total Population	667
Hispanic or Latino (of any race)	586
Central American, ex. Mexican	479
Mexican	596

Median Household Income
(2010 Inflation-Adjusted Dollars)

Group	Dollars
Total Population	48,846
Hispanic or Latino (of any race)	34,800
Central American, ex. Mexican	35,977
Mexican	33,718

Per Capita Income
(2010 Inflation-Adjusted Dollars)

Group	Dollars
Total Population	25,146
Hispanic or Latino (of any race)	13,281
Central American, ex. Mexican	11,517
Mexican	13,054

Households with $100,000+ Income

Group	Number	%
Total Population	15,999	15.7
Hispanic or Latino (of any race)	199	4.5
Central American, ex. Mexican	12	3.0
Mexican	171	5.2

Households with Food Stamps/SNAP Benefits During Past 12 Months

Group	Number	%
Total Population	8,004	7.8
Hispanic or Latino (of any race)	576	12.9
Central American, ex. Mexican	45	11.1
Mexican	437	13.2

Poverty Rate
(Income in Past 12 Months Below Poverty Level)

Group	%
Total Population	14.9
Hispanic or Latino (of any race)	25.5

STATE & PLACE PROFILES

Notes: (1) Percent of total population; (2) Percent of Hispanic/Latino population; Profiles include places with an overall population of at least 125,000, OR an overall population of at least 25,000 where the Hispanic/Latino population is at least 20% of the overall population. In states where less than five places meet either of these criteria, we have included places with at least 10,000 total population with the highest percentage of Hispanic/Latino population. These places are identified with an asterisk (*); Please refer to the User's Guide for a full explanation of data.

Central American, ex. Mexican	26.8
Mexican	25.4

Omaha

Population

Group	Number	%TP[1]	%HP[2]
Total Population	408,958	100.0	–
Hispanic or Latino (of any race)	53,553	13.1	100.0
Central American, ex. Mexican	4,943	1.2	9.2
Guatemalan	1,853	0.5	3.5
Honduran	518	0.1	1.0
Panamanian	124	<0.1	0.2
Salvadoran	2,276	0.6	4.2
Cuban	365	0.1	0.7
Dominican Republic	152	<0.1	0.3
Mexican	42,701	10.4	79.7
Puerto Rican	930	0.2	1.7
South American	749	0.2	1.4
Colombian	270	0.1	0.5
Peruvian	123	<0.1	0.2
Spaniard	420	0.1	0.8

Population Growth: 2000–2010

Group	%
Total Population	4.9
Hispanic or Latino (of any race)	82.2
Central American, ex. Mexican	261.1
Guatemalan	383.8
Honduran	307.9
Salvadoran	242.8
Cuban	34.2
Mexican	83.3
Puerto Rican	57.4
South American	73.8
Colombian	57.9

Males per 100 Females

Group	Number
Total Population	96.7
Hispanic or Latino (of any race)	113.4
Central American, ex. Mexican	119.5
Guatemalan	139.1
Honduran	118.6
Panamanian	69.9
Salvadoran	110.0
Cuban	128.1
Dominican Republic	83.1
Mexican	113.7
Puerto Rican	109.9
South American	84.9
Colombian	82.4
Peruvian	89.2
Spaniard	95.3

Average Household Size

Group	People
Total Population	2.45
Hispanic or Latino (of any race)	3.84
Central American, ex. Mexican	4.36
Guatemalan	4.92
Honduran	3.78
Panamanian	2.79
Salvadoran	4.35
Cuban	2.26
Dominican Republic	3.52
Mexican	3.90
Puerto Rican	2.92
South American	2.71
Colombian	2.40
Peruvian	2.83
Spaniard	2.73

Median Age

Group	Years
Total Population	33.5
Hispanic or Latino (of any race)	23.3
Central American, ex. Mexican	26.5
Guatemalan	25.2
Honduran	25.5
Panamanian	29.0
Salvadoran	28.0
Cuban	30.3
Dominican Republic	26.5
Mexican	22.7
Puerto Rican	23.7
South American	29.3
Colombian	28.3
Peruvian	28.8
Spaniard	28.9

High School Graduates
(Universe: Population 25 Years and Over)

Group	Number	%
Total Population	228,350	88.3
Hispanic or Latino (of any race)	10,687	46.5
Central American, ex. Mexican	679	27.4
Guatemalan	128	17.0
Salvadoran	309	23.8
Mexican	8,512	45.7
Puerto Rican	292	82.5

Four-Year College Graduates
(Universe: Population 25 Years and Over)

Group	Number	%
Total Population	83,770	32.4
Hispanic or Latino (of any race)	2,048	8.9
Central American, ex. Mexican	76	3.1
Guatemalan	25	3.3
Salvadoran	5	0.4
Mexican	1,304	7.0
Puerto Rican	75	21.2

Population Age 3–17 Enrolled in Public School
(Universe: Population Age 3–17 Enrolled in School)

Group	Number	%
Total Population	61,935	81.9
Hispanic or Latino (of any race)	12,023	92.4
Central American, ex. Mexican	938	98.9
Guatemalan	314	100.0
Salvadoran	402	100.0
Mexican	10,045	92.6
Puerto Rican	189	73.5

Population Age 3–17 Enrolled in Private School
(Universe: Population Age 3–17 Enrolled in School)

Group	Number	%
Total Population	13,688	18.1
Hispanic or Latino (of any race)	992	7.6
Central American, ex. Mexican	10	1.1
Guatemalan	0	0.0
Salvadoran	0	0.0
Mexican	806	7.4
Puerto Rican	68	26.5

Foreign-Born Population

Group	Number	%
Total Population	36,950	9.1
Hispanic or Latino (of any race)	21,840	44.5
Central American, ex. Mexican	2,932	64.1
Guatemalan	949	64.8
Salvadoran	1,565	67.7
Mexican	18,057	44.5
Puerto Rican	0	0.0

Foreign-Born Naturalized U.S. Citizens

Group	Number	%
Total Population	10,815	29.3
Hispanic or Latino (of any race)	4,381	20.1
Central American, ex. Mexican	617	21.0
Guatemalan	195	20.5
Salvadoran	294	18.8
Mexican	3,352	18.6
Puerto Rican	0	0.0

Language Spoken at Home: English Only
(Universe: Population 5 Years and Over)

Group	Number	%
Total Population	326,486	86.6
Hispanic or Latino (of any race)	10,397	24.8
Central American, ex. Mexican	457	11.4
Guatemalan	182	14.5
Salvadoran	67	3.3
Mexican	8,127	23.6
Puerto Rican	373	55.5

Language Spoken at Home: Spanish
(Universe: Population 5 Years and Over)

Group	Number	%
Total Population	35,176	9.3
Hispanic or Latino (of any race)	31,450	75.1
Central American, ex. Mexican	3,557	88.6
Guatemalan	1,074	85.5
Salvadoran	1,974	96.7
Mexican	26,280	76.3
Puerto Rican	299	44.5

Unemployment Rate
(Universe: Population 16 Years and Over)

Group	%
Total Population	6.9
Hispanic or Latino (of any race)	8.5
Central American, ex. Mexican	6.2
Guatemalan	0.0
Salvadoran	7.6
Mexican	8.7
Puerto Rican	15.6

Class of Worker: Private Wage and Salary
(Universe: Civilian Employed Population 16 Years and Over)

Group	Number	%
Total Population	176,381	84.6
Hispanic or Latino (of any race)	19,874	92.5
Central American, ex. Mexican	2,269	95.7
Guatemalan	644	97.1
Salvadoran	1,251	96.5
Mexican	16,142	92.3
Puerto Rican	258	88.4

Class of Worker: Government
(Universe: Civilian Employed Population 16 Years and Over)

Group	Number	%
Total Population	21,865	10.5
Hispanic or Latino (of any race)	853	4.0
Central American, ex. Mexican	45	1.9
Guatemalan	19	2.9
Salvadoran	0	0.0
Mexican	723	4.1
Puerto Rican	0	0.0

Means of Transportation to Work: Car, Truck or Van
(Universe: Workers 16 Years and Over)

Group	Number	%
Total Population	186,941	91.5
Hispanic or Latino (of any race)	19,303	92.7
Central American, ex. Mexican	2,132	91.0
Guatemalan	615	95.3
Salvadoran	1,175	91.4
Mexican	15,758	92.9
Puerto Rican	292	100.0

Means of Transportation to Work: Public Transportation (ex. Taxicab)
(Universe: Workers 16 Years and Over)

Group	Number	%
Total Population	2,820	1.4
Hispanic or Latino (of any race)	189	0.9
Central American, ex. Mexican	74	3.2
Guatemalan	0	0.0
Salvadoran	26	2.0
Mexican	107	0.6
Puerto Rican	0	0.0

Homeownership Rate
(Universe: Occupied Housing Units)

Group	%
Total Population	58.3
Hispanic or Latino (of any race)	43.5
Central American, ex. Mexican	46.7
Guatemalan	37.1
Honduran	33.1
Panamanian	52.6
Salvadoran	56.7
Cuban	49.3
Dominican Republic	35.7
Mexican	43.6
Puerto Rican	33.2
South American	50.0
Colombian	46.0
Peruvian	33.3
Spaniard	57.6

Notes: (1) Percent of total population; (2) Percent of Hispanic/Latino population; Profiles include places with an overall population of at least 125,000, OR an overall population of at least 25,000 where the Hispanic/Latino population is at least 20% of the overall population. In states where less than five places meet either of these criteria, we have included places with at least 10,000 total population with the highest percentage of Hispanic/Latino population. These places are identified with an asterisk (*); Please refer to the User's Guide for a full explanation of data.

Median Home Value	
Group	Dollars
Total Population	131,900
Hispanic or Latino (of any race)	97,800
Central American, ex. Mexican	107,300
Guatemalan	108,300
Salvadoran	106,800
Mexican	93,400
Puerto Rican	142,500

Median Gross Rent	
Group	Dollars
Total Population	712
Hispanic or Latino (of any race)	707
Central American, ex. Mexican	732
Guatemalan	743
Salvadoran	727
Mexican	694
Puerto Rican	751

Median Household Income (2010 Inflation-Adjusted Dollars)	
Group	Dollars
Total Population	46,230
Hispanic or Latino (of any race)	36,741
Central American, ex. Mexican	38,520
Guatemalan	36,118
Salvadoran	39,507
Mexican	36,465
Puerto Rican	24,821

Per Capita Income (2010 Inflation-Adjusted Dollars)	
Group	Dollars
Total Population	26,123
Hispanic or Latino (of any race)	12,280
Central American, ex. Mexican	13,455
Guatemalan	11,897
Salvadoran	13,754
Mexican	11,485
Puerto Rican	19,150

Households with $100,000+ Income		
Group	Number	%
Total Population	26,605	16.3
Hispanic or Latino (of any race)	578	4.7
Central American, ex. Mexican	35	2.6
Guatemalan	4	1.2
Salvadoran	6	0.8
Mexican	379	3.9
Puerto Rican	21	12.9

Households with Food Stamps/SNAP Benefits During Past 12 Months		
Group	Number	%
Total Population	17,851	11.0
Hispanic or Latino (of any race)	1,624	13.3
Central American, ex. Mexican	168	12.4
Guatemalan	63	18.2
Salvadoran	58	7.6
Mexican	1,364	14.0
Puerto Rican	29	17.8

Poverty Rate (Income in Past 12 Months Below Poverty Level)	
Group	%
Total Population	15.3
Hispanic or Latino (of any race)	25.3
Central American, ex. Mexican	20.9
Guatemalan	32.1
Salvadoran	16.9
Mexican	26.5
Puerto Rican	19.4

South Sioux City*

Population			
Group	Number	%TP[1]	%HP[2]
Total Population	13,353	100.0	–
Hispanic or Latino (of any race)	6,047	45.3	100.0
Central American, ex. Mexican	499	3.7	8.3
Guatemalan	306	2.3	5.1
Salvadoran	156	1.2	2.6
Mexican	5,246	39.3	86.8

Population Growth: 2000–2010	
Group	%
Total Population	12.0
Hispanic or Latino (of any race)	104.4
Central American, ex. Mexican	389.2
Mexican	108.9

Males per 100 Females	
Group	Number
Total Population	98.4
Hispanic or Latino (of any race)	109.1
Central American, ex. Mexican	126.8
Guatemalan	159.3
Salvadoran	75.3
Mexican	107.9

Average Household Size	
Group	People
Total Population	2.93
Hispanic or Latino (of any race)	4.31
Central American, ex. Mexican	4.56
Guatemalan	4.77
Salvadoran	4.48
Mexican	4.31

Median Age	
Group	Years
Total Population	30.5
Hispanic or Latino (of any race)	21.5
Central American, ex. Mexican	28.7
Guatemalan	27.6
Salvadoran	29.5
Mexican	21.0

High School Graduates (Universe: Population 25 Years and Over)		
Group	Number	%
Total Population	5,698	72.5
Hispanic or Latino (of any race)	938	40.9
Mexican	878	40.7

Four-Year College Graduates (Universe: Population 25 Years and Over)		
Group	Number	%
Total Population	773	9.8
Hispanic or Latino (of any race)	103	4.5
Mexican	103	4.8

Population Age 3–17 Enrolled in Public School (Universe: Population Age 3–17 Enrolled in School)		
Group	Number	%
Total Population	2,338	86.6
Hispanic or Latino (of any race)	1,389	88.8
Mexican	1,353	89.2

Population Age 3–17 Enrolled in Private School (Universe: Population Age 3–17 Enrolled in School)		
Group	Number	%
Total Population	362	13.4
Hispanic or Latino (of any race)	176	11.2
Mexican	164	10.8

Foreign-Born Population		
Group	Number	%
Total Population	3,357	25.9
Hispanic or Latino (of any race)	2,451	47.2
Mexican	2,307	46.3

Foreign-Born Naturalized U.S. Citizens		
Group	Number	%
Total Population	829	24.7
Hispanic or Latino (of any race)	580	23.7
Mexican	580	25.1

Language Spoken at Home: English Only (Universe: Population 5 Years and Over)		
Group	Number	%
Total Population	7,034	59.7
Hispanic or Latino (of any race)	621	13.9
Mexican	587	13.8

Language Spoken at Home: Spanish (Universe: Population 5 Years and Over)		
Group	Number	%
Total Population	3,899	33.1
Hispanic or Latino (of any race)	3,832	86.1
Mexican	3,665	86.2

Unemployment Rate (Universe: Population 16 Years and Over)	
Group	%
Total Population	5.6
Hispanic or Latino (of any race)	4.7
Mexican	5.0

Class of Worker: Private Wage and Salary (Universe: Civilian Employed Population 16 Years and Over)		
Group	Number	%
Total Population	5,536	83.9
Hispanic or Latino (of any race)	2,103	91.0
Mexican	1,977	90.5

Class of Worker: Government (Universe: Civilian Employed Population 16 Years and Over)		
Group	Number	%
Total Population	675	10.2
Hispanic or Latino (of any race)	117	5.1
Mexican	117	5.4

Means of Transportation to Work: Car, Truck or Van (Universe: Workers 16 Years and Over)		
Group	Number	%
Total Population	5,815	90.4
Hispanic or Latino (of any race)	2,080	93.9
Mexican	1,954	93.6

Means of Transportation to Work: Public Transportation (ex. Taxicab) (Universe: Workers 16 Years and Over)		
Group	Number	%
Total Population	45	0.7
Hispanic or Latino (of any race)	29	1.3
Mexican	29	1.4

Homeownership Rate (Universe: Occupied Housing Units)	
Group	%
Total Population	56.5
Hispanic or Latino (of any race)	56.4
Central American, ex. Mexican	44.3
Guatemalan	41.1
Salvadoran	40.9
Mexican	58.4

Median Home Value	
Group	Dollars
Total Population	94,900
Hispanic or Latino (of any race)	90,200
Mexican	89,300

Median Gross Rent	
Group	Dollars
Total Population	634
Hispanic or Latino (of any race)	637
Mexican	626

Median Household Income (2010 Inflation-Adjusted Dollars)	
Group	Dollars
Total Population	40,457
Hispanic or Latino (of any race)	42,303
Mexican	41,162

Per Capita Income (2010 Inflation-Adjusted Dollars)	
Group	Dollars
Total Population	17,490
Hispanic or Latino (of any race)	11,102
Mexican	11,024

Households with $100,000+ Income		
Group	Number	%
Total Population	410	9.0
Hispanic or Latino (of any race)	34	2.9
Mexican	34	3.0

Households with Food Stamps/SNAP Benefits During Past 12 Months		
Group	Number	%
Total Population	712	15.7
Hispanic or Latino (of any race)	187	16.0

Notes: (1) Percent of total population; (2) Percent of Hispanic/Latino population; Profiles include places with an overall population of at least 125,000, OR an overall population of at least 25,000 where the Hispanic/Latino population is at least 20% of the overall population. In states where less than five places meet either of these criteria, we have included places with at least 10,000 total population with the highest percentage of Hispanic/Latino population. These places are identified with an asterisk (*); Please refer to the User's Guide for a full explanation of data.

Mexican	187	16.7

Poverty Rate
(Income in Past 12 Months Below Poverty Level)

Group	%
Total Population	17.8
Hispanic or Latino (of any race)	21.7
Mexican	21.9

Notes: (1) Percent of total population; (2) Percent of Hispanic/Latino population; Profiles include places with an overall population of at least 125,000, OR an overall population of at least 25,000 where the Hispanic/Latino population is at least 20% of the overall population. In states where less than five places meet either of these criteria, we have included places with at least 10,000 total population with the highest percentage of Hispanic/Latino population. These places are identified with an asterisk (*); Please refer to the User's Guide for a full explanation of data.

Nevada

EDITOR'S NOTE: For a place to be included in this edition, it must meet one of two criteria. Either its overall population is at least 125,000, OR its overall population is at least 25,000 and its Hispanic/Latino population is at least 20% of the overall population. For the state of Nevada, the following locations are included:

- Carson City
- Henderson
- Las Vegas
- North Las Vegas
- Paradise
- Reno
- Sparks
- Spring Valley
- Sunrise Manor
- Whitney
- Winchester

Section Two: State & Place Profiles starts with the state profile, followed by place profiles that meet the criteria above. Places are listed alphabetically within each state. All states, all counties and places that meet the above criteria are ranked and compared in *Section Three: Rankings & Comparisons*, on page 1055.

For a more detailed look at the Hispanic/Latino population in Nevada, a companion web site is available at no additional charge with purchase of this print edition. Visit http://gold.greyhouse.com/page/info_hispanic for more information.

The web site includes data for all counties and places in Nevada with Hispanic/Latino population, plus ten additional topics: Self Employed Worker; Walked to Work; Worked from Home; Mean Travel Time to Work; Mean Household Income; Households with Cash Public Assistance; Mean Cash Pubic Assistance; Poverty Rates for 18 and Under, 18 to 64, and 65 and Over.

Population

Group	Number	%TP[1]	%HP[2]
Total Population	2,700,551	100.0	–
Hispanic or Latino (of any race)	716,501	26.5	100.0
Central American, ex. Mexican	55,937	2.1	7.8
Costa Rican	1,433	0.1	0.2
Guatemalan	13,407	0.5	1.9
Honduran	4,481	0.2	0.6
Nicaraguan	4,475	0.2	0.6
Panamanian	1,615	0.1	0.2
Salvadoran	30,043	1.1	4.2
Cuban	21,459	0.8	3.0
Dominican Republic	2,446	0.1	0.3
Mexican	540,978	20.0	75.5
Puerto Rican	20,664	0.8	2.9
South American	19,056	0.7	2.7
Argentinean	3,419	0.1	0.5
Bolivian	481	<0.1	0.1
Chilean	1,683	0.1	0.2
Colombian	5,230	0.2	0.7
Ecuadorian	2,045	0.1	0.3
Paraguayan	116	<0.1	<0.1
Peruvian	4,581	0.2	0.6
Uruguayan	407	<0.1	0.1
Venezuelan	878	<0.1	0.1
Spaniard	10,980	0.4	1.5

Population Growth: 2000–2010

Group	%
Total Population	35.1
Hispanic or Latino (of any race)	81.9
Central American, ex. Mexican	198.4
Costa Rican	114.8
Guatemalan	226.5
Honduran	240.5
Nicaraguan	182.7
Panamanian	141.4
Salvadoran	220.1
Cuban	86.6
Dominican Republic	181.5
Mexican	89.3
Puerto Rican	98.3
South American	180.1
Argentinean	153.3
Bolivian	291.1
Chilean	141.5
Colombian	187.2
Ecuadorian	226.7
Peruvian	223.7
Venezuelan	259.8
Spaniard	608.4

Males per 100 Females

Group	Number
Total Population	102.0
Hispanic or Latino (of any race)	105.0
Central American, ex. Mexican	101.7
Costa Rican	85.9
Guatemalan	112.2
Honduran	94.4
Nicaraguan	94.1
Panamanian	74.4
Salvadoran	102.2
Cuban	110.2
Dominican Republic	86.6
Mexican	105.9
Puerto Rican	98.0
South American	87.1
Argentinean	98.0
Bolivian	89.4
Chilean	89.1
Colombian	76.3
Ecuadorian	85.2
Paraguayan	70.6
Peruvian	93.9
Uruguayan	91.1
Venezuelan	81.8
Spaniard	92.0

Average Household Size

Group	People
Total Population	2.65
Hispanic or Latino (of any race)	3.66
Central American, ex. Mexican	3.82
Costa Rican	3.06
Guatemalan	3.95
Honduran	3.70
Nicaraguan	3.56
Panamanian	2.82
Salvadoran	3.92
Cuban	2.90
Dominican Republic	3.08
Mexican	3.85
Puerto Rican	2.76
South American	2.87
Argentinean	2.68
Bolivian	2.84
Chilean	2.72
Colombian	2.86
Ecuadorian	3.18
Paraguayan	2.73
Peruvian	3.06
Uruguayan	2.73
Venezuelan	2.71
Spaniard	2.64

Median Age

Group	Years
Total Population	36.3
Hispanic or Latino (of any race)	26.0
Central American, ex. Mexican	30.8
Costa Rican	33.0
Guatemalan	30.3
Honduran	30.5
Nicaraguan	32.8
Panamanian	32.8
Salvadoran	30.6
Cuban	37.1
Dominican Republic	28.9
Mexican	24.5
Puerto Rican	28.1
South American	36.3
Argentinean	38.2
Bolivian	35.5
Chilean	37.8
Colombian	34.8
Ecuadorian	34.2
Paraguayan	43.0
Peruvian	36.8
Uruguayan	37.1
Venezuelan	35.1
Spaniard	36.2

High School Graduates
(Universe: Population 25 Years and Over)

Group	Number	%
Total Population	1,461,183	84.3
Hispanic or Latino (of any race)	200,100	58.0
Central American, ex. Mexican	17,153	54.8
Costa Rican	806	74.8
Guatemalan	5,000	57.3
Honduran	1,355	56.9
Nicaraguan	1,765	73.9
Panamanian	712	93.1
Salvadoran	7,038	45.9
Cuban	9,258	74.0
Dominican Republic	1,283	73.6
Mexican	135,593	53.0
Puerto Rican	10,200	85.0
South American	9,555	88.3
Argentinean	1,493	82.2
Chilean	820	90.4
Colombian	2,537	87.2
Ecuadorian	923	92.1
Peruvian	2,667	91.0
Spaniard	5,477	87.2

Four-Year College Graduates
(Universe: Population 25 Years and Over)

Group	Number	%
Total Population	378,792	21.8
Hispanic or Latino (of any race)	28,966	8.4
Central American, ex. Mexican	2,199	7.0
Costa Rican	167	15.5
Guatemalan	406	4.7
Honduran	182	7.6
Nicaraguan	241	10.1
Panamanian	163	21.3
Salvadoran	976	6.4
Cuban	1,955	15.6
Dominican Republic	399	22.9
Mexican	16,078	6.3
Puerto Rican	2,214	18.5
South American	2,559	23.6
Argentinean	253	13.9
Chilean	330	36.4
Colombian	714	24.5
Ecuadorian	178	17.8
Peruvian	836	28.5
Spaniard	1,441	22.9

Population Age 3–17 Enrolled in Public School
(Universe: Population Age 3–17 Enrolled in School)

Group	Number	%
Total Population	432,725	92.5
Hispanic or Latino (of any race)	163,445	96.5
Central American, ex. Mexican	10,591	96.0
Costa Rican	266	92.0
Guatemalan	2,638	93.2
Honduran	545	91.3
Nicaraguan	732	94.3
Panamanian	240	90.2
Salvadoran	6,000	98.3
Cuban	3,266	90.6
Dominican Republic	386	79.1
Mexican	134,216	97.2

Notes: (1) Percent of total population; (2) Percent of Hispanic/Latino population; Profiles include places with an overall population of at least 125,000, OR an overall population of at least 25,000 where the Hispanic/Latino population is at least 20% of the overall population. In states where less than five places meet either of these criteria, we have included places with at least 10,000 total population with the highest percentage of Hispanic/Latino population. These places are identified with an asterisk (*); Please refer to the User's Guide for a full explanation of data.

Group	Number	%
Puerto Rican	4,361	94.3
South American	3,278	88.2
Argentinean	399	92.6
Chilean	250	82.2
Colombian	1,096	88.6
Ecuadorian	262	83.7
Peruvian	784	93.0
Spaniard	1,448	88.8

Population Age 3–17 Enrolled in Private School

(Universe: Population Age 3–17 Enrolled in School)

Group	Number	%
Total Population	35,214	7.5
Hispanic or Latino (of any race)	5,932	3.5
Central American, ex. Mexican	440	4.0
Costa Rican	23	8.0
Guatemalan	192	6.8
Honduran	52	8.7
Nicaraguan	44	5.7
Panamanian	26	9.8
Salvadoran	103	1.7
Cuban	339	9.4
Dominican Republic	102	20.9
Mexican	3,817	2.8
Puerto Rican	262	5.7
South American	439	11.8
Argentinean	32	7.4
Chilean	54	17.8
Colombian	141	11.4
Ecuadorian	51	16.3
Peruvian	59	7.0
Spaniard	182	11.2

Foreign-Born Population

Group	Number	%
Total Population	508,882	19.3
Hispanic or Latino (of any race)	290,989	43.2
Central American, ex. Mexican	34,112	63.5
Costa Rican	1,138	65.9
Guatemalan	9,520	65.2
Honduran	2,555	67.0
Nicaraguan	2,684	65.3
Panamanian	541	39.8
Salvadoran	17,154	62.8
Cuban	11,998	62.4
Dominican Republic	1,476	56.7
Mexican	226,405	43.1
Puerto Rican	639	3.1
South American	10,992	65.0
Argentinean	1,743	70.5
Chilean	906	64.3
Colombian	2,972	61.2
Ecuadorian	806	50.3
Peruvian	3,191	69.9
Spaniard	1,007	10.5

Foreign-Born Naturalized U.S. Citizens

Group	Number	%
Total Population	199,952	39.3
Hispanic or Latino (of any race)	73,584	25.3
Central American, ex. Mexican	10,511	30.8
Costa Rican	488	42.9
Guatemalan	2,429	25.5
Honduran	661	25.9
Nicaraguan	916	34.1
Panamanian	429	79.3
Salvadoran	5,324	31.0
Cuban	4,931	41.1
Dominican Republic	891	60.4
Mexican	49,065	21.7
Puerto Rican	329	51.5
South American	5,001	45.5
Argentinean	807	46.3
Chilean	434	47.9
Colombian	1,575	53.0
Ecuadorian	423	52.5
Peruvian	1,377	43.2
Spaniard	586	58.2

Language Spoken at Home: English Only

(Universe: Population 5 Years and Over)

Group	Number	%
Total Population	1,755,755	71.8
Hispanic or Latino (of any race)	143,157	24.0
Central American, ex. Mexican	6,129	12.5
Costa Rican	373	23.5
Guatemalan	1,582	12.1
Honduran	483	13.6
Nicaraguan	595	15.3
Panamanian	563	45.1
Salvadoran	2,285	9.2
Cuban	3,097	17.3
Dominican Republic	484	19.9
Mexican	99,741	21.7
Puerto Rican	10,793	57.1
South American	2,976	18.5
Argentinean	452	19.0
Chilean	394	30.1
Colombian	874	18.9
Ecuadorian	453	30.8
Peruvian	612	13.8
Spaniard	6,368	72.7

Language Spoken at Home: Spanish

(Universe: Population 5 Years and Over)

Group	Number	%
Total Population	480,267	19.6
Hispanic or Latino (of any race)	452,093	75.7
Central American, ex. Mexican	42,862	87.5
Costa Rican	1,213	76.5
Guatemalan	11,526	87.9
Honduran	3,062	86.4
Nicaraguan	3,298	84.7
Panamanian	686	54.9
Salvadoran	22,524	90.8
Cuban	14,664	82.1
Dominican Republic	1,931	79.5
Mexican	359,796	78.2
Puerto Rican	7,952	42.1
South American	12,920	80.3
Argentinean	1,871	78.4
Chilean	915	69.9
Colombian	3,736	80.7
Ecuadorian	1,007	68.5
Peruvian	3,812	86.0
Spaniard	2,147	24.5

Unemployment Rate

(Universe: Population 16 Years and Over)

Group	%
Total Population	9.0
Hispanic or Latino (of any race)	9.8
Central American, ex. Mexican	8.4
Costa Rican	13.8
Guatemalan	8.7
Honduran	8.3
Nicaraguan	10.7
Panamanian	10.4
Salvadoran	7.3
Cuban	9.1
Dominican Republic	9.6
Mexican	10.2
Puerto Rican	6.8
South American	9.5
Argentinean	6.1
Chilean	6.1
Colombian	13.8
Ecuadorian	9.6
Peruvian	8.6
Spaniard	12.9

Class of Worker: Private Wage and Salary

(Universe: Civilian Employed Population 16 Years and Over)

Group	Number	%
Total Population	1,035,934	82.6
Hispanic or Latino (of any race)	266,555	90.4
Central American, ex. Mexican	26,231	92.0
Costa Rican	672	82.8
Guatemalan	7,261	93.4
Honduran	2,091	91.9
Nicaraguan	1,879	87.6
Panamanian	532	80.5
Salvadoran	13,445	93.2
Cuban	8,472	88.5
Dominican Republic	1,227	78.5
Mexican	201,580	91.4
Puerto Rican	8,411	83.0
South American	7,689	88.1
Argentinean	1,165	87.6
Chilean	645	83.9
Colombian	1,750	85.0
Ecuadorian	754	95.2
Peruvian	2,517	89.0
Spaniard	3,532	78.6

Class of Worker: Government

(Universe: Civilian Employed Population 16 Years and Over)

Group	Number	%
Total Population	155,498	12.4
Hispanic or Latino (of any race)	17,312	5.9
Central American, ex. Mexican	1,289	4.5
Costa Rican	81	10.0
Guatemalan	265	3.4
Honduran	78	3.4
Nicaraguan	203	9.5
Panamanian	108	16.3
Salvadoran	517	3.6
Cuban	651	6.8
Dominican Republic	172	11.0
Mexican	11,377	5.2
Puerto Rican	1,384	13.7
South American	620	7.1
Argentinean	100	7.5
Chilean	76	9.9
Colombian	211	10.2
Ecuadorian	38	4.8
Peruvian	161	5.7
Spaniard	690	15.4

Means of Transportation to Work: Car, Truck or Van

(Universe: Workers 16 Years and Over)

Group	Number	%
Total Population	1,103,495	89.3
Hispanic or Latino (of any race)	256,866	88.8
Central American, ex. Mexican	24,051	86.9
Costa Rican	720	88.7
Guatemalan	6,757	88.7
Honduran	1,833	85.8
Nicaraguan	1,882	88.7
Panamanian	635	96.1
Salvadoran	11,858	85.4
Cuban	8,223	87.7
Dominican Republic	1,477	95.6
Mexican	192,464	88.9
Puerto Rican	9,067	90.6
South American	7,763	90.7
Argentinean	1,188	93.2
Chilean	645	83.9
Colombian	1,934	96.1
Ecuadorian	621	81.2
Peruvian	2,554	91.0
Spaniard	3,835	87.9

Means of Transportation to Work: Public Transportation (ex. Taxicab)

(Universe: Workers 16 Years and Over)

Group	Number	%
Total Population	41,976	3.4
Hispanic or Latino (of any race)	14,668	5.1
Central American, ex. Mexican	2,020	7.3
Costa Rican	0	0.0
Guatemalan	544	7.1
Honduran	124	5.8
Nicaraguan	129	6.1
Panamanian	26	3.9
Salvadoran	1,175	8.5
Cuban	370	3.9
Dominican Republic	23	1.5
Mexican	11,057	5.1
Puerto Rican	385	3.8
South American	320	3.7
Argentinean	9	0.7
Chilean	90	11.7
Colombian	9	0.4
Ecuadorian	88	11.5
Peruvian	80	2.9
Spaniard	141	3.2

Homeownership Rate

(Universe: Occupied Housing Units)

Group	%
Total Population	58.8
Hispanic or Latino (of any race)	46.6
Central American, ex. Mexican	48.0

Notes: (1) Percent of total population; (2) Percent of Hispanic/Latino population; Profiles include places with an overall population of at least 125,000, OR an overall population of at least 25,000 where the Hispanic/Latino population is at least 20% of the overall population. In states where less than five places meet either of these criteria, we have included places with at least 10,000 total population with the highest percentage of Hispanic/Latino population. These places are identified with an asterisk (*); Please refer to the User's Guide for a full explanation of data.

Costa Rican	48.9
Guatemalan	43.7
Honduran	40.2
Nicaraguan	50.9
Panamanian	46.1
Salvadoran	50.8
Cuban	49.4
Dominican Republic	47.7
Mexican	45.8
Puerto Rican	43.0
South American	55.4
Argentinean	59.1
Bolivian	60.0
Chilean	59.9
Colombian	54.9
Ecuadorian	56.4
Paraguayan	63.6
Peruvian	52.2
Uruguayan	46.3
Venezuelan	49.1
Spaniard	60.3

Median Home Value

Group	Dollars
Total Population	254,200
Hispanic or Latino (of any race)	219,500
Central American, ex. Mexican	221,300
Costa Rican	225,400
Guatemalan	235,900
Honduran	166,500
Nicaraguan	226,200
Panamanian	268,500
Salvadoran	216,500
Cuban	239,800
Dominican Republic	226,500
Mexican	210,800
Puerto Rican	255,600
South American	257,500
Argentinean	232,700
Chilean	259,100
Colombian	273,200
Ecuadorian	349,000
Peruvian	233,300
Spaniard	230,300

Median Gross Rent

Group	Dollars
Total Population	998
Hispanic or Latino (of any race)	918
Central American, ex. Mexican	880
Costa Rican	1,101
Guatemalan	854
Honduran	966
Nicaraguan	1,095
Panamanian	983
Salvadoran	866
Cuban	914
Dominican Republic	1,159
Mexican	907
Puerto Rican	1,034
South American	1,008
Argentinean	995
Chilean	1,031
Colombian	1,066
Ecuadorian	1,088
Peruvian	913
Spaniard	1,015

Median Household Income
(2010 Inflation-Adjusted Dollars)

Group	Dollars
Total Population	55,726
Hispanic or Latino (of any race)	46,605
Central American, ex. Mexican	46,093
Costa Rican	50,958
Guatemalan	43,276
Honduran	45,023
Nicaraguan	51,803
Panamanian	21,172
Salvadoran	48,387
Cuban	43,789
Dominican Republic	71,607
Mexican	45,757
Puerto Rican	57,229
South American	45,847
Argentinean	48,534
Chilean	46,000
Colombian	53,015
Ecuadorian	33,205
Peruvian	47,740
Spaniard	52,439

Per Capita Income
(2010 Inflation-Adjusted Dollars)

Group	Dollars
Total Population	27,589
Hispanic or Latino (of any race)	15,724
Central American, ex. Mexican	17,466
Costa Rican	22,882
Guatemalan	16,359
Honduran	18,072
Nicaraguan	20,667
Panamanian	17,676
Salvadoran	17,039
Cuban	19,679
Dominican Republic	35,248
Mexican	14,427
Puerto Rican	22,782
South American	19,991
Argentinean	23,395
Chilean	21,739
Colombian	16,740
Ecuadorian	16,485
Peruvian	19,381
Spaniard	25,789

Households with $100,000+ Income

Group	Number	%
Total Population	204,752	20.9
Hispanic or Latino (of any race)	20,329	11.5
Central American, ex. Mexican	1,623	10.6
Costa Rican	45	10.0
Guatemalan	477	10.9
Honduran	144	12.7
Nicaraguan	176	14.3
Panamanian	61	15.8
Salvadoran	685	9.2
Cuban	769	11.1
Dominican Republic	203	25.6
Mexican	13,859	10.7
Puerto Rican	1,240	17.9
South American	790	13.9
Argentinean	166	16.8
Chilean	72	11.2
Colombian	227	15.9
Ecuadorian	64	11.0
Peruvian	182	13.3
Spaniard	640	17.6

Households with Food Stamps/SNAP Benefits During Past 12 Months

Group	Number	%
Total Population	58,099	5.9
Hispanic or Latino (of any race)	14,987	8.5
Central American, ex. Mexican	839	5.5
Costa Rican	55	12.2
Guatemalan	261	6.0
Honduran	100	8.8
Nicaraguan	59	4.8
Panamanian	38	9.8
Salvadoran	313	4.2
Cuban	1,006	14.5
Dominican Republic	5	0.6
Mexican	11,614	8.9
Puerto Rican	656	9.5
South American	259	4.6
Argentinean	35	3.5
Chilean	14	2.2
Colombian	115	8.1
Ecuadorian	0	0.0
Peruvian	40	2.9
Spaniard	266	7.3

Poverty Rate
(Income in Past 12 Months Below Poverty Level)

Group	%
Total Population	11.9
Hispanic or Latino (of any race)	18.2
Central American, ex. Mexican	14.8
Costa Rican	14.2
Guatemalan	15.4
Honduran	21.9
Nicaraguan	7.8
Panamanian	10.3
Salvadoran	15.1
Cuban	18.1
Dominican Republic	6.4
Mexican	19.5
Puerto Rican	11.4
South American	14.4
Argentinean	8.8
Chilean	14.3
Colombian	18.4
Ecuadorian	18.4
Peruvian	10.4
Spaniard	11.9

Carson City

Population

Group	Number	%TP[1]	%HP[2]
Total Population	55,274	100.0	–
Hispanic or Latino (of any race)	11,777	21.3	100.0
Central American, ex. Mexican	838	1.5	7.1
Nicaraguan	320	0.6	2.7
Salvadoran	330	0.6	2.8
Mexican	9,215	16.7	78.2
Puerto Rican	167	0.3	1.4
South American	138	0.2	1.2
Spaniard	197	0.4	1.7

Population Growth: 2000–2010

Group	%
Total Population	5.4
Hispanic or Latino (of any race)	57.7
Central American, ex. Mexican	81.8
Nicaraguan	48.1
Salvadoran	148.1
Mexican	66.9

Males per 100 Females

Group	Number
Total Population	107.9
Hispanic or Latino (of any race)	113.0
Central American, ex. Mexican	116.5
Nicaraguan	92.8
Salvadoran	144.4
Mexican	102.8
Puerto Rican	138.6
South American	76.9
Spaniard	107.4

Average Household Size

Group	People
Total Population	2.41
Hispanic or Latino (of any race)	3.64
Central American, ex. Mexican	3.60
Nicaraguan	3.51
Salvadoran	3.69
Mexican	3.81
Puerto Rican	2.57
South American	2.59
Spaniard	2.21

Median Age

Group	Years
Total Population	41.7
Hispanic or Latino (of any race)	25.4
Central American, ex. Mexican	30.9
Nicaraguan	30.9
Salvadoran	31.2
Mexican	23.3
Puerto Rican	31.5
South American	42.0
Spaniard	45.9

High School Graduates
(Universe: Population 25 Years and Over)

Group	Number	%
Total Population	33,448	88.0
Hispanic or Latino (of any race)	3,780	67.6
Mexican	2,555	62.9

STATE & PLACE PROFILES

Notes: (1) Percent of total population; (2) Percent of Hispanic/Latino population; Profiles include places with an overall population of at least 125,000, OR an overall population of at least 25,000 where the Hispanic/Latino population is at least 20% of the overall population. In states where less than five places meet either of these criteria, we have included places with at least 10,000 total population with the highest percentage of Hispanic/Latino population. These places are identified with an asterisk (*); Please refer to the User's Guide for a full explanation of data.

Four-Year College Graduates
(Universe: Population 25 Years and Over)

Group	Number	%
Total Population	8,211	21.6
Hispanic or Latino (of any race)	588	10.5
Mexican	220	5.4

Population Age 3–17 Enrolled in Public School
(Universe: Population Age 3–17 Enrolled in School)

Group	Number	%
Total Population	8,586	94.3
Hispanic or Latino (of any race)	2,921	97.4
Mexican	2,456	98.8

Population Age 3–17 Enrolled in Private School
(Universe: Population Age 3–17 Enrolled in School)

Group	Number	%
Total Population	518	5.7
Hispanic or Latino (of any race)	78	2.6
Mexican	31	1.2

Foreign-Born Population

Group	Number	%
Total Population	6,426	11.6
Hispanic or Latino (of any race)	4,727	42.4
Mexican	3,686	43.6

Foreign-Born Naturalized U.S. Citizens

Group	Number	%
Total Population	2,185	34.0
Hispanic or Latino (of any race)	991	21.0
Mexican	646	17.5

Language Spoken at Home: English Only
(Universe: Population 5 Years and Over)

Group	Number	%
Total Population	42,697	82.3
Hispanic or Latino (of any race)	2,875	29.4
Mexican	1,848	25.0

Language Spoken at Home: Spanish
(Universe: Population 5 Years and Over)

Group	Number	%
Total Population	7,325	14.1
Hispanic or Latino (of any race)	6,883	70.5
Mexican	5,537	74.9

Unemployment Rate
(Universe: Population 16 Years and Over)

Group	%
Total Population	12.9
Hispanic or Latino (of any race)	14.5
Mexican	14.5

Class of Worker: Private Wage and Salary
(Universe: Civilian Employed Population 16 Years and Over)

Group	Number	%
Total Population	16,792	67.1
Hispanic or Latino (of any race)	3,960	86.3
Mexican	2,942	88.5

Class of Worker: Government
(Universe: Civilian Employed Population 16 Years and Over)

Group	Number	%
Total Population	6,406	25.6
Hispanic or Latino (of any race)	473	10.3
Mexican	248	7.5

Means of Transportation to Work: Car, Truck or Van
(Universe: Workers 16 Years and Over)

Group	Number	%
Total Population	22,260	91.3
Hispanic or Latino (of any race)	4,173	94.0
Mexican	3,083	94.4

Means of Transportation to Work: Public Transportation (ex. Taxicab)
(Universe: Workers 16 Years and Over)

Group	Number	%
Total Population	99	0.4
Hispanic or Latino (of any race)	46	1.0
Mexican	0	0.0

Homeownership Rate
(Universe: Occupied Housing Units)

Group	%
Total Population	59.4
Hispanic or Latino (of any race)	45.1
Central American, ex. Mexican	42.6
Nicaraguan	50.6
Salvadoran	36.4
Mexican	44.9
Puerto Rican	41.3
South American	60.9
Spaniard	66.7

Median Home Value

Group	Dollars
Total Population	270,500
Hispanic or Latino (of any race)	217,600
Mexican	202,100

Median Gross Rent

Group	Dollars
Total Population	885
Hispanic or Latino (of any race)	834
Mexican	777

Median Household Income
(2010 Inflation-Adjusted Dollars)

Group	Dollars
Total Population	52,067
Hispanic or Latino (of any race)	40,804
Mexican	39,073

Per Capita Income
(2010 Inflation-Adjusted Dollars)

Group	Dollars
Total Population	27,568
Hispanic or Latino (of any race)	15,810
Mexican	14,895

Households with $100,000+ Income

Group	Number	%
Total Population	4,079	19.0
Hispanic or Latino (of any race)	229	8.2
Mexican	164	8.2

Households with Food Stamps/SNAP Benefits During Past 12 Months

Group	Number	%
Total Population	1,419	6.6
Hispanic or Latino (of any race)	293	10.5
Mexican	217	10.9

Poverty Rate
(Income in Past 12 Months Below Poverty Level)

Group	%
Total Population	14.0
Hispanic or Latino (of any race)	22.8
Mexican	19.0

Henderson

Population

Group	Number	%TP[1]	%HP[2]
Total Population	257,729	100.0	–
Hispanic or Latino (of any race)	38,377	14.9	100.0
Central American, ex. Mexican	2,333	0.9	6.1
Costa Rican	119	<0.1	0.3
Guatemalan	545	0.2	1.4
Honduran	173	0.1	0.5
Nicaraguan	315	0.1	0.8
Panamanian	171	0.1	0.4
Salvadoran	992	0.4	2.6
Cuban	1,550	0.6	4.0
Dominican Republic	201	0.1	0.5
Mexican	25,405	9.9	66.2
Puerto Rican	2,325	0.9	6.1
South American	2,157	0.8	5.6
Argentinean	437	0.2	1.1
Chilean	173	0.1	0.5
Colombian	592	0.2	1.5
Ecuadorian	199	0.1	0.5
Peruvian	493	0.2	1.3
Venezuelan	122	<0.1	0.3
Spaniard	1,277	0.5	3.3

Population Growth: 2000–2010

Group	%
Total Population	47.0
Hispanic or Latino (of any race)	104.3
Central American, ex. Mexican	318.1
Guatemalan	325.8
Salvadoran	372.4
Cuban	97.0
Mexican	131.0
Puerto Rican	111.4
South American	200.0
Argentinean	136.2
Colombian	169.1
Peruvian	297.6
Spaniard	853.0

Males per 100 Females

Group	Number
Total Population	96.8
Hispanic or Latino (of any race)	96.3
Central American, ex. Mexican	91.7
Costa Rican	65.3
Guatemalan	94.6
Honduran	90.1
Nicaraguan	94.4
Panamanian	67.6
Salvadoran	97.6
Cuban	107.5
Dominican Republic	82.7
Mexican	97.5
Puerto Rican	98.5
South American	85.8
Argentinean	95.1
Chilean	82.1
Colombian	71.6
Ecuadorian	101.0
Peruvian	93.3
Venezuelan	74.3
Spaniard	89.2

Average Household Size

Group	People
Total Population	2.53
Hispanic or Latino (of any race)	3.15
Central American, ex. Mexican	3.44
Costa Rican	3.35
Guatemalan	3.54
Honduran	3.32
Nicaraguan	3.38
Panamanian	2.86
Salvadoran	3.55
Cuban	2.78
Dominican Republic	2.52
Mexican	3.30
Puerto Rican	2.74
South American	2.80
Argentinean	2.54
Chilean	2.90
Colombian	2.94
Ecuadorian	2.90
Peruvian	2.90
Venezuelan	2.80
Spaniard	2.71

Median Age

Group	Years
Total Population	39.6
Hispanic or Latino (of any race)	28.2
Central American, ex. Mexican	30.8
Costa Rican	32.8
Guatemalan	30.4
Honduran	29.5
Nicaraguan	30.2
Panamanian	33.6
Salvadoran	30.9
Cuban	35.2
Dominican Republic	29.4
Mexican	26.8
Puerto Rican	28.7
South American	36.7
Argentinean	41.8
Chilean	38.4
Colombian	33.8
Ecuadorian	34.2
Peruvian	35.4

Notes: (1) Percent of total population; (2) Percent of Hispanic/Latino population; Profiles include places with an overall population of at least 125,000, OR an overall population of at least 25,000 where the Hispanic/Latino population is at least 20% of the overall population. In states where less than five places meet either of these criteria, we have included places with at least 10,000 total population with the highest percentage of Hispanic/Latino population. These places are identified with an asterisk (*); Please refer to the User's Guide for a full explanation of data.

Group	Number	%
Venezuelan		34.5
Spaniard		35.9

High School Graduates
(Universe: Population 25 Years and Over)

Group	Number	%
Total Population	161,013	92.0
Hispanic or Latino (of any race)	15,208	79.0
Central American, ex. Mexican	699	76.6
Cuban	979	75.5
Mexican	8,668	76.6
Puerto Rican	1,167	91.5
South American	986	88.1
Spaniard	545	82.2

Four-Year College Graduates
(Universe: Population 25 Years and Over)

Group	Number	%
Total Population	51,145	29.2
Hispanic or Latino (of any race)	3,298	17.1
Central American, ex. Mexican	223	24.4
Cuban	85	6.6
Mexican	1,656	14.6
Puerto Rican	374	29.3
South American	382	34.1
Spaniard	200	30.2

Population Age 3–17 Enrolled in Public School
(Universe: Population Age 3–17 Enrolled in School)

Group	Number	%
Total Population	37,161	90.5
Hispanic or Latino (of any race)	8,307	95.2
Central American, ex. Mexican	273	81.0
Cuban	366	96.3
Mexican	5,588	94.8
Puerto Rican	546	100.0
South American	228	93.4
Spaniard	214	100.0

Population Age 3–17 Enrolled in Private School
(Universe: Population Age 3–17 Enrolled in School)

Group	Number	%
Total Population	3,918	9.5
Hispanic or Latino (of any race)	417	4.8
Central American, ex. Mexican	64	19.0
Cuban	14	3.7
Mexican	306	5.2
Puerto Rican	0	0.0
South American	16	6.6
Spaniard	0	0.0

Foreign-Born Population

Group	Number	%
Total Population	29,302	11.8
Hispanic or Latino (of any race)	8,106	23.5
Central American, ex. Mexican	814	52.5
Cuban	924	42.9
Mexican	4,397	20.4
Puerto Rican	49	2.2
South American	1,054	67.5
Spaniard	152	15.8

Foreign-Born Naturalized U.S. Citizens

Group	Number	%
Total Population	17,840	60.9
Hispanic or Latino (of any race)	4,140	51.1
Central American, ex. Mexican	341	41.9
Cuban	661	71.5
Mexican	2,064	46.9
Puerto Rican	0	0.0
South American	556	52.8
Spaniard	78	51.3

Language Spoken at Home: English Only
(Universe: Population 5 Years and Over)

Group	Number	%
Total Population	195,744	83.8
Hispanic or Latino (of any race)	15,087	48.8
Central American, ex. Mexican	454	32.8
Cuban	760	40.6
Mexican	9,289	49.0
Puerto Rican	1,181	57.1
South American	247	16.4
Spaniard	461	49.8

Language Spoken at Home: Spanish
(Universe: Population 5 Years and Over)

Group	Number	%
Total Population	18,246	7.8
Hispanic or Latino (of any race)	15,658	50.6
Central American, ex. Mexican	929	67.2
Cuban	1,112	59.4
Mexican	9,573	50.5
Puerto Rican	856	41.4
South American	1,259	83.6
Spaniard	407	44.0

Unemployment Rate
(Universe: Population 16 Years and Over)

Group	%
Total Population	7.5
Hispanic or Latino (of any race)	9.9
Central American, ex. Mexican	4.3
Cuban	10.5
Mexican	11.7
Puerto Rican	2.9
South American	16.3
Spaniard	17.7

Class of Worker: Private Wage and Salary
(Universe: Civilian Employed Population 16 Years and Over)

Group	Number	%
Total Population	100,477	80.6
Hispanic or Latino (of any race)	12,912	84.9
Central American, ex. Mexican	744	88.6
Cuban	800	90.3
Mexican	7,654	84.5
Puerto Rican	873	78.9
South American	656	87.1
Spaniard	282	76.0

Class of Worker: Government
(Universe: Civilian Employed Population 16 Years and Over)

Group	Number	%
Total Population	17,984	14.4
Hispanic or Latino (of any race)	1,546	10.2
Central American, ex. Mexican	44	5.2
Cuban	43	4.9
Mexican	1,050	11.6
Puerto Rican	122	11.0
South American	57	7.6
Spaniard	89	24.0

Means of Transportation to Work: Car, Truck or Van
(Universe: Workers 16 Years and Over)

Group	Number	%
Total Population	112,319	91.5
Hispanic or Latino (of any race)	13,880	93.0
Central American, ex. Mexican	749	93.7
Cuban	776	88.7
Mexican	8,306	93.7
Puerto Rican	1,105	100.0
South American	753	100.0
Spaniard	308	85.1

Means of Transportation to Work: Public Transportation (ex. Taxicab)
(Universe: Workers 16 Years and Over)

Group	Number	%
Total Population	1,434	1.2
Hispanic or Latino (of any race)	368	2.5
Central American, ex. Mexican	30	3.8
Cuban	35	4.0
Mexican	162	1.8
Puerto Rican	0	0.0
South American	0	0.0
Spaniard	39	10.8

Homeownership Rate
(Universe: Occupied Housing Units)

Group	%
Total Population	65.8
Hispanic or Latino (of any race)	53.5
Central American, ex. Mexican	51.8
Costa Rican	64.9
Guatemalan	43.8
Honduran	48.9
Nicaraguan	49.0
Panamanian	57.9
Salvadoran	54.5
Cuban	62.7
Dominican Republic	49.2
Mexican	52.4
Puerto Rican	51.0
South American	61.3
Argentinean	70.5
Chilean	60.4
Colombian	61.2
Ecuadorian	56.5
Peruvian	55.4
Venezuelan	67.5
Spaniard	60.2

Median Home Value

Group	Dollars
Total Population	311,600
Hispanic or Latino (of any race)	286,400
Central American, ex. Mexican	325,000
Cuban	473,500
Mexican	284,000
Puerto Rican	295,000
South American	337,500
Spaniard	225,000

Median Gross Rent

Group	Dollars
Total Population	1,188
Hispanic or Latino (of any race)	1,184
Central American, ex. Mexican	1,532
Cuban	1,448
Mexican	1,149
Puerto Rican	1,194
South American	1,280
Spaniard	1,739

Median Household Income
(2010 Inflation-Adjusted Dollars)

Group	Dollars
Total Population	68,039
Hispanic or Latino (of any race)	60,189
Central American, ex. Mexican	55,486
Cuban	61,555
Mexican	60,244
Puerto Rican	76,727
South American	47,315
Spaniard	50,288

Per Capita Income
(2010 Inflation-Adjusted Dollars)

Group	Dollars
Total Population	35,050
Hispanic or Latino (of any race)	22,718
Central American, ex. Mexican	25,698
Cuban	27,069
Mexican	19,918
Puerto Rican	32,324
South American	23,274
Spaniard	23,217

Households with $100,000+ Income

Group	Number	%
Total Population	29,165	29.7
Hispanic or Latino (of any race)	2,306	22.9
Central American, ex. Mexican	39	8.9
Cuban	156	21.5
Mexican	1,340	22.4
Puerto Rican	233	31.9
South American	128	29.0
Spaniard	75	21.4

Households with Food Stamps/SNAP Benefits During Past 12 Months

Group	Number	%
Total Population	2,861	2.9
Hispanic or Latino (of any race)	582	5.8
Central American, ex. Mexican	0	0.0
Cuban	92	12.7
Mexican	357	6.0
Puerto Rican	45	6.2
South American	0	0.0
Spaniard	18	5.1

STATE & PLACE PROFILES

Notes: (1) Percent of total population; (2) Percent of Hispanic/Latino population; Profiles include places with an overall population of at least 125,000, OR an overall population of at least 25,000 where the Hispanic/Latino population is at least 20% of the overall population. In states where less than five places meet either of these criteria, we have included places with at least 10,000 total population with the highest percentage of Hispanic/Latino population. These places are identified with an asterisk (*); Please refer to the User's Guide for a full explanation of data.

Poverty Rate
(Income in Past 12 Months Below Poverty Level)

Group	%
Total Population	7.3
Hispanic or Latino (of any race)	11.3
Central American, ex. Mexican	18.7
Cuban	21.6
Mexican	11.5
Puerto Rican	7.8
South American	5.0
Spaniard	5.5

Las Vegas

Population

Group	Number	%TP[1]	%HP[2]
Total Population	583,756	100.0	–
Hispanic or Latino (of any race)	183,859	31.5	100.0
Central American, ex. Mexican	15,318	2.6	8.3
Costa Rican	292	0.1	0.2
Guatemalan	3,592	0.6	2.0
Honduran	1,360	0.2	0.7
Nicaraguan	1,217	0.2	0.7
Panamanian	367	0.1	0.2
Salvadoran	8,392	1.4	4.6
Cuban	5,471	0.9	3.0
Dominican Republic	700	0.1	0.4
Mexican	140,104	24.0	76.2
Puerto Rican	5,209	0.9	2.8
South American	4,838	0.8	2.6
Argentinean	935	0.2	0.5
Chilean	467	0.1	0.3
Colombian	1,297	0.2	0.7
Ecuadorian	537	0.1	0.3
Peruvian	1,068	0.2	0.6
Uruguayan	117	<0.1	0.1
Venezuelan	230	<0.1	0.1
Spaniard	2,268	0.4	1.2

Population Growth: 2000–2010

Group	%
Total Population	22.0
Hispanic or Latino (of any race)	62.8
Central American, ex. Mexican	170.2
Costa Rican	84.8
Guatemalan	184.4
Honduran	220.8
Nicaraguan	146.9
Panamanian	89.2
Salvadoran	196.3
Cuban	61.2
Dominican Republic	138.9
Mexican	67.8
Puerto Rican	81.8
South American	161.5
Argentinean	147.4
Chilean	142.0
Colombian	165.2
Ecuadorian	174.0
Peruvian	219.8
Spaniard	779.1

Males per 100 Females

Group	Number
Total Population	101.5
Hispanic or Latino (of any race)	106.7
Central American, ex. Mexican	105.8
Costa Rican	89.6
Guatemalan	118.1
Honduran	103.6
Nicaraguan	95.0
Panamanian	73.1
Salvadoran	105.5
Cuban	113.6
Dominican Republic	81.8
Mexican	108.3
Puerto Rican	96.1
South American	89.0
Argentinean	96.0
Chilean	100.4
Colombian	81.7
Ecuadorian	74.4
Peruvian	95.6
Uruguayan	88.7
Venezuelan	82.5
Spaniard	91.1

Average Household Size

Group	People
Total Population	2.71
Hispanic or Latino (of any race)	3.80
Central American, ex. Mexican	3.92
Costa Rican	2.75
Guatemalan	4.15
Honduran	3.66
Nicaraguan	3.83
Panamanian	2.60
Salvadoran	4.00
Cuban	2.86
Dominican Republic	3.10
Mexican	4.02
Puerto Rican	2.79
South American	2.88
Argentinean	2.65
Chilean	2.92
Colombian	2.71
Ecuadorian	3.30
Peruvian	3.08
Uruguayan	3.11
Venezuelan	2.86
Spaniard	2.78

Median Age

Group	Years
Total Population	35.9
Hispanic or Latino (of any race)	26.1
Central American, ex. Mexican	31.1
Costa Rican	34.0
Guatemalan	30.3
Honduran	31.0
Nicaraguan	31.9
Panamanian	37.5
Salvadoran	31.1
Cuban	38.1
Dominican Republic	30.3
Mexican	24.7
Puerto Rican	28.0
South American	37.1
Argentinean	38.9
Chilean	37.7
Colombian	36.5
Ecuadorian	34.8
Peruvian	37.1
Uruguayan	37.4
Venezuelan	37.0
Spaniard	35.3

High School Graduates
(Universe: Population 25 Years and Over)

Group	Number	%
Total Population	308,986	81.6
Hispanic or Latino (of any race)	49,320	53.9
Central American, ex. Mexican	4,454	47.4
Guatemalan	1,056	53.5
Honduran	559	60.7
Nicaraguan	432	68.5
Salvadoran	1,919	36.6
Cuban	2,067	72.7
Mexican	34,274	49.6
Puerto Rican	2,386	89.2
South American	2,524	86.9
Colombian	597	86.1
Peruvian	721	97.7
Spaniard	850	86.1

Four-Year College Graduates
(Universe: Population 25 Years and Over)

Group	Number	%
Total Population	79,787	21.1
Hispanic or Latino (of any race)	6,869	7.5
Central American, ex. Mexican	668	7.1
Guatemalan	100	5.1
Honduran	140	15.2
Nicaraguan	49	7.8
Salvadoran	328	6.3
Cuban	417	14.7
Mexican	4,035	5.8
Puerto Rican	413	15.4
South American	588	20.3
Colombian	175	25.3
Peruvian	145	19.6
Spaniard	182	18.4

Population Age 3–17 Enrolled in Public School
(Universe: Population Age 3–17 Enrolled in School)

Group	Number	%
Total Population	96,590	91.5
Hispanic or Latino (of any race)	42,660	96.2
Central American, ex. Mexican	3,254	95.0
Guatemalan	607	85.0
Honduran	104	100.0
Nicaraguan	140	83.3
Salvadoran	2,208	98.4
Cuban	749	94.1
Mexican	35,447	97.2
Puerto Rican	761	89.2
South American	975	81.5
Colombian	181	63.5
Peruvian	448	89.8
Spaniard	175	82.9

Population Age 3–17 Enrolled in Private School
(Universe: Population Age 3–17 Enrolled in School)

Group	Number	%
Total Population	8,996	8.5
Hispanic or Latino (of any race)	1,674	3.8
Central American, ex. Mexican	171	5.0
Guatemalan	107	15.0
Honduran	0	0.0
Nicaraguan	28	16.7
Salvadoran	36	1.6
Cuban	47	5.9
Mexican	1,007	2.8
Puerto Rican	92	10.8
South American	221	18.5
Colombian	104	36.5
Peruvian	51	10.2
Spaniard	36	17.1

Foreign-Born Population

Group	Number	%
Total Population	129,367	22.3
Hispanic or Latino (of any race)	83,541	46.6
Central American, ex. Mexican	10,303	62.5
Guatemalan	2,031	58.7
Honduran	860	66.6
Nicaraguan	661	64.4
Salvadoran	6,192	63.4
Cuban	2,728	64.9
Mexican	66,255	46.7
Puerto Rican	137	3.1
South American	2,741	58.5
Colombian	617	54.9
Peruvian	790	62.4
Spaniard	36	2.3

Foreign-Born Naturalized U.S. Citizens

Group	Number	%
Total Population	43,532	33.7
Hispanic or Latino (of any race)	17,605	21.1
Central American, ex. Mexican	2,983	29.0
Guatemalan	560	27.6
Honduran	285	33.1
Nicaraguan	287	43.4
Salvadoran	1,568	25.3
Cuban	934	34.2
Mexican	11,900	18.0
Puerto Rican	40	29.2
South American	1,091	39.8
Colombian	333	54.0
Peruvian	211	26.7
Spaniard	26	72.2

Language Spoken at Home: English Only
(Universe: Population 5 Years and Over)

Group	Number	%
Total Population	359,119	66.9
Hispanic or Latino (of any race)	32,873	20.7
Central American, ex. Mexican	1,740	11.5
Guatemalan	411	12.9
Honduran	269	21.5
Nicaraguan	97	9.7
Salvadoran	793	9.0

Notes: (1) Percent of total population; (2) Percent of Hispanic/Latino population; Profiles include places with an overall population of at least 125,000, OR an overall population of at least 25,000 where the Hispanic/Latino population is at least 20% of the overall population. In states where less than five places meet either of these criteria, we have included places with at least 10,000 total population with the highest percentage of Hispanic/Latino population. These places are identified with an asterisk (*); Please refer to the User's Guide for a full explanation of data.

Cuban	687	17.1
Mexican	23,636	19.0
Puerto Rican	2,255	56.4
South American	744	17.0
Colombian	107	9.6
Peruvian	128	10.6
Spaniard	969	70.8

Language Spoken at Home: Spanish
(Universe: Population 5 Years and Over)

Group	Number	%
Total Population	133,021	24.8
Hispanic or Latino (of any race)	125,333	78.9
Central American, ex. Mexican	13,373	88.5
Guatemalan	2,764	87.1
Honduran	981	78.5
Nicaraguan	907	90.3
Salvadoran	8,050	91.0
Cuban	3,283	81.7
Mexican	100,330	80.8
Puerto Rican	1,714	42.9
South American	3,588	81.8
Colombian	1,007	90.4
Peruvian	1,073	88.8
Spaniard	348	25.4

Unemployment Rate
(Universe: Population 16 Years and Over)

Group	%
Total Population	9.8
Hispanic or Latino (of any race)	10.5
Central American, ex. Mexican	9.4
Guatemalan	12.7
Honduran	5.9
Nicaraguan	17.0
Salvadoran	7.7
Cuban	11.8
Mexican	11.0
Puerto Rican	2.4
South American	10.5
Colombian	28.2
Peruvian	0.0
Spaniard	10.2

Class of Worker: Private Wage and Salary
(Universe: Civilian Employed Population 16 Years and Over)

Group	Number	%
Total Population	224,421	84.0
Hispanic or Latino (of any race)	69,962	91.0
Central American, ex. Mexican	7,751	93.4
Guatemalan	1,534	89.1
Honduran	728	85.8
Nicaraguan	460	88.0
Salvadoran	4,650	96.9
Cuban	1,759	87.7
Mexican	53,655	92.0
Puerto Rican	2,043	82.9
South American	1,863	84.3
Colombian	383	78.0
Peruvian	525	76.6
Spaniard	510	75.9

Class of Worker: Government
(Universe: Civilian Employed Population 16 Years and Over)

Group	Number	%
Total Population	29,551	11.1
Hispanic or Latino (of any race)	3,639	4.7
Central American, ex. Mexican	259	3.1
Guatemalan	137	8.0
Honduran	68	8.0
Nicaraguan	10	1.9
Salvadoran	35	0.7
Cuban	61	3.0
Mexican	2,376	4.1
Puerto Rican	351	14.2
South American	149	6.7
Colombian	84	17.1
Peruvian	35	5.1
Spaniard	130	19.3

Means of Transportation to Work: Car, Truck or Van
(Universe: Workers 16 Years and Over)

Group	Number	%
Total Population	233,509	88.8
Hispanic or Latino (of any race)	66,203	87.7
Central American, ex. Mexican	7,015	86.7
Guatemalan	1,411	84.5
Honduran	776	92.4
Nicaraguan	462	86.0
Salvadoran	4,010	86.7
Cuban	1,607	81.3
Mexican	50,224	87.6
Puerto Rican	2,149	90.5
South American	2,036	92.6
Colombian	463	94.3
Peruvian	588	86.7
Spaniard	599	89.1

Means of Transportation to Work: Public Transportation (ex. Taxicab)
(Universe: Workers 16 Years and Over)

Group	Number	%
Total Population	11,554	4.4
Hispanic or Latino (of any race)	4,338	5.7
Central American, ex. Mexican	590	7.3
Guatemalan	149	8.9
Honduran	24	2.9
Nicaraguan	39	7.3
Salvadoran	356	7.7
Cuban	37	1.9
Mexican	3,465	6.0
Puerto Rican	98	4.1
South American	12	0.5
Colombian	0	0.0
Peruvian	5	0.7
Spaniard	12	1.8

Homeownership Rate
(Universe: Occupied Housing Units)

Group	%
Total Population	56.5
Hispanic or Latino (of any race)	44.1
Central American, ex. Mexican	48.2
Costa Rican	53.1
Guatemalan	43.4
Honduran	37.9
Nicaraguan	50.3
Panamanian	39.4
Salvadoran	51.9
Cuban	46.2
Dominican Republic	49.1
Mexican	42.9
Puerto Rican	39.5
South American	58.1
Argentinean	60.2
Chilean	66.7
Colombian	56.6
Ecuadorian	64.3
Peruvian	52.0
Uruguayan	42.2
Venezuelan	53.5
Spaniard	57.6

Median Home Value

Group	Dollars
Total Population	251,300
Hispanic or Latino (of any race)	215,400
Central American, ex. Mexican	205,700
Guatemalan	226,300
Honduran	159,200
Nicaraguan	276,900
Salvadoran	172,900
Cuban	224,000
Mexican	212,500
Puerto Rican	308,100
South American	250,400
Colombian	268,200
Peruvian	112,500
Spaniard	203,200

Median Gross Rent

Group	Dollars
Total Population	999
Hispanic or Latino (of any race)	913
Central American, ex. Mexican	857
Guatemalan	797
Honduran	869
Nicaraguan	1,071
Salvadoran	886
Cuban	793
Mexican	918
Puerto Rican	1,016
South American	914
Colombian	996
Peruvian	821
Spaniard	832

Median Household Income
(2010 Inflation-Adjusted Dollars)

Group	Dollars
Total Population	54,334
Hispanic or Latino (of any race)	45,778
Central American, ex. Mexican	44,862
Guatemalan	39,250
Honduran	61,566
Nicaraguan	51,857
Salvadoran	47,235
Cuban	40,266
Mexican	45,861
Puerto Rican	53,026
South American	44,781
Colombian	53,409
Peruvian	44,924
Spaniard	57,500

Per Capita Income
(2010 Inflation-Adjusted Dollars)

Group	Dollars
Total Population	26,993
Hispanic or Latino (of any race)	14,935
Central American, ex. Mexican	15,846
Guatemalan	16,094
Honduran	24,930
Nicaraguan	23,053
Salvadoran	13,975
Cuban	20,647
Mexican	13,876
Puerto Rican	24,112
South American	18,429
Colombian	22,982
Peruvian	15,800
Spaniard	23,136

Households with $100,000+ Income

Group	Number	%
Total Population	44,001	20.8
Hispanic or Latino (of any race)	4,921	10.8
Central American, ex. Mexican	503	11.1
Guatemalan	137	12.0
Honduran	119	23.2
Nicaraguan	45	14.4
Salvadoran	202	9.1
Cuban	170	11.0
Mexican	3,277	9.6
Puerto Rican	289	18.9
South American	225	15.1
Colombian	98	22.2
Peruvian	38	10.8
Spaniard	119	21.0

Households with Food Stamps/SNAP Benefits During Past 12 Months

Group	Number	%
Total Population	14,825	7.0
Hispanic or Latino (of any race)	3,948	8.7
Central American, ex. Mexican	276	6.1
Guatemalan	63	5.5
Honduran	62	12.1
Nicaraguan	22	7.1
Salvadoran	98	4.4
Cuban	266	17.2
Mexican	2,964	8.7
Puerto Rican	119	7.8
South American	121	8.1
Colombian	66	14.9
Peruvian	0	0.0
Spaniard	50	8.8

Poverty Rate
(Income in Past 12 Months Below Poverty Level)

Group	%
Total Population	13.1
Hispanic or Latino (of any race)	19.4
Central American, ex. Mexican	14.9

Notes: (1) Percent of total population; (2) Percent of Hispanic/Latino population; Profiles include places with an overall population of at least 125,000, OR an overall population of at least 25,000 where the Hispanic/Latino population is at least 20% of the overall population. In states where less than five places meet either of these criteria, we have included places with at least 10,000 total population with the highest percentage of Hispanic/Latino population. These places are identified with an asterisk (*); Please refer to the User's Guide for a full explanation of data.

Guatemalan	19.4
Honduran	17.9
Nicaraguan	8.3
Salvadoran	14.2
Cuban	14.8
Mexican	20.9
Puerto Rican	13.5
South American	11.9
Colombian	23.1
Peruvian	0.4
Spaniard	12.3

North Las Vegas

Population

Group	Number	%TP[1]	%HP[2]
Total Population	216,961	100.0	–
Hispanic or Latino (of any race)	84,134	38.8	100.0
Central American, ex. Mexican	5,734	2.6	6.8
Costa Rican	102	<0.1	0.1
Guatemalan	1,137	0.5	1.4
Honduran	507	0.2	0.6
Nicaraguan	375	0.2	0.4
Panamanian	244	0.1	0.3
Salvadoran	3,293	1.5	3.9
Cuban	1,151	0.5	1.4
Dominican Republic	236	0.1	0.3
Mexican	68,610	31.6	81.5
Puerto Rican	2,141	1.0	2.5
South American	1,220	0.6	1.5
Argentinean	221	0.1	0.3
Colombian	316	0.1	0.4
Ecuadorian	187	0.1	0.2
Peruvian	273	0.1	0.3
Spaniard	751	0.3	0.9

Population Growth: 2000–2010

Group	%
Total Population	87.9
Hispanic or Latino (of any race)	93.7
Central American, ex. Mexican	252.0
Guatemalan	241.4
Honduran	352.7
Nicaraguan	244.0
Salvadoran	275.9
Cuban	141.8
Mexican	96.9
Puerto Rican	187.4
South American	300.0
Colombian	184.7

Males per 100 Females

Group	Number
Total Population	99.3
Hispanic or Latino (of any race)	104.3
Central American, ex. Mexican	97.8
Costa Rican	104.0
Guatemalan	107.1
Honduran	81.7
Nicaraguan	102.7
Panamanian	78.1
Salvadoran	97.8
Cuban	113.5
Dominican Republic	77.4
Mexican	105.5
Puerto Rican	106.1
South American	99.7
Argentinean	104.6
Colombian	89.2
Ecuadorian	90.8
Peruvian	110.0
Spaniard	99.2

Average Household Size

Group	People
Total Population	3.23
Hispanic or Latino (of any race)	4.18
Central American, ex. Mexican	4.13
Costa Rican	3.53
Guatemalan	4.19
Honduran	4.21
Nicaraguan	3.85
Panamanian	2.93
Salvadoran	4.25
Cuban	3.38
Dominican Republic	3.53
Mexican	4.32
Puerto Rican	3.07
South American	3.31
Argentinean	3.13
Colombian	3.13
Ecuadorian	3.80
Peruvian	3.80
Spaniard	3.36

Median Age

Group	Years
Total Population	30.6
Hispanic or Latino (of any race)	24.2
Central American, ex. Mexican	30.5
Costa Rican	31.5
Guatemalan	30.4
Honduran	30.8
Nicaraguan	35.1
Panamanian	27.3
Salvadoran	30.0
Cuban	29.9
Dominican Republic	25.0
Mexican	23.2
Puerto Rican	26.5
South American	33.8
Argentinean	32.8
Colombian	33.4
Ecuadorian	33.1
Peruvian	35.1
Spaniard	31.6

High School Graduates
(Universe: Population 25 Years and Over)

Group	Number	%
Total Population	90,566	76.6
Hispanic or Latino (of any race)	17,515	47.6
Central American, ex. Mexican	1,439	48.0
Guatemalan	364	50.8
Salvadoran	721	41.0
Mexican	12,730	42.7
Puerto Rican	974	83.3
South American	677	95.9
Spaniard	593	87.1

Four-Year College Graduates
(Universe: Population 25 Years and Over)

Group	Number	%
Total Population	18,225	15.4
Hispanic or Latino (of any race)	1,709	4.6
Central American, ex. Mexican	117	3.9
Guatemalan	0	0.0
Salvadoran	5	0.3
Mexican	1,115	3.7
Puerto Rican	71	6.1
South American	143	20.3
Spaniard	133	19.5

Population Age 3–17 Enrolled in Public School
(Universe: Population Age 3–17 Enrolled in School)

Group	Number	%
Total Population	44,185	95.1
Hispanic or Latino (of any race)	19,937	96.8
Central American, ex. Mexican	1,070	95.2
Guatemalan	154	100.0
Salvadoran	761	93.4
Mexican	17,146	97.4
Puerto Rican	748	100.0
South American	79	77.5
Spaniard	101	100.0

Population Age 3–17 Enrolled in Private School
(Universe: Population Age 3–17 Enrolled in School)

Group	Number	%
Total Population	2,267	4.9
Hispanic or Latino (of any race)	658	3.2
Central American, ex. Mexican	54	4.8
Guatemalan	0	0.0
Salvadoran	54	6.6
Mexican	466	2.6
Puerto Rican	0	0.0
South American	23	22.5
Spaniard	0	0.0

Foreign-Born Population

Group	Number	%
Total Population	47,603	23.3
Hispanic or Latino (of any race)	35,263	46.5
Central American, ex. Mexican	3,316	61.3
Guatemalan	799	73.2
Salvadoran	1,928	55.9
Mexican	30,305	47.9
Puerto Rican	23	1.0
South American	639	70.9
Spaniard	62	7.2

Foreign-Born Naturalized U.S. Citizens

Group	Number	%
Total Population	14,675	30.8
Hispanic or Latino (of any race)	7,383	20.9
Central American, ex. Mexican	807	24.3
Guatemalan	103	12.9
Salvadoran	522	27.1
Mexican	5,688	18.8
Puerto Rican	0	0.0
South American	377	59.0
Spaniard	22	35.5

Language Spoken at Home: English Only
(Universe: Population 5 Years and Over)

Group	Number	%
Total Population	114,998	62.2
Hispanic or Latino (of any race)	11,134	16.7
Central American, ex. Mexican	509	11.0
Guatemalan	201	21.1
Salvadoran	221	7.7
Mexican	8,078	14.5
Puerto Rican	928	44.5
South American	101	11.3
Spaniard	622	72.8

Language Spoken at Home: Spanish
(Universe: Population 5 Years and Over)

Group	Number	%
Total Population	57,349	31.0
Hispanic or Latino (of any race)	55,537	83.2
Central American, ex. Mexican	4,115	89.0
Guatemalan	751	78.9
Salvadoran	2,631	92.3
Mexican	47,480	85.4
Puerto Rican	1,159	55.5
South American	789	88.7
Spaniard	218	25.5

Unemployment Rate
(Universe: Population 16 Years and Over)

Group	%
Total Population	8.7
Hispanic or Latino (of any race)	9.2
Central American, ex. Mexican	7.8
Guatemalan	8.3
Salvadoran	5.8
Mexican	9.4
Puerto Rican	9.1
South American	13.2
Spaniard	13.8

Class of Worker: Private Wage and Salary
(Universe: Civilian Employed Population 16 Years and Over)

Group	Number	%
Total Population	75,157	83.4
Hispanic or Latino (of any race)	29,045	92.2
Central American, ex. Mexican	2,712	92.8
Guatemalan	576	93.5
Salvadoran	1,633	92.0
Mexican	23,531	92.9
Puerto Rican	841	87.7
South American	490	89.7
Spaniard	316	71.0

Class of Worker: Government
(Universe: Civilian Employed Population 16 Years and Over)

Group	Number	%
Total Population	11,959	13.3
Hispanic or Latino (of any race)	1,545	4.9
Central American, ex. Mexican	109	3.7
Guatemalan	11	1.8
Salvadoran	80	4.5
Mexican	1,058	4.2

Notes: (1) Percent of total population; (2) Percent of Hispanic/Latino population; Profiles include places with an overall population of at least 125,000, OR an overall population of at least 25,000 where the Hispanic/Latino population is at least 20% of the overall population. In states where less than five places meet either of these criteria, we have included places with at least 10,000 total population with the highest percentage of Hispanic/Latino population. These places are identified with an asterisk (*); Please refer to the User's Guide for a full explanation of data.

Puerto Rican	118	12.3
South American	56	10.3
Spaniard	111	24.9

Means of Transportation to Work: Car, Truck or Van
(Universe: Workers 16 Years and Over)

Group	Number	%
Total Population	84,634	93.3
Hispanic or Latino (of any race)	28,934	93.3
Central American, ex. Mexican	2,666	94.3
Guatemalan	616	100.0
Salvadoran	1,566	93.2
Mexican	23,165	92.9
Puerto Rican	938	95.5
South American	528	98.5
Spaniard	384	95.5

Means of Transportation to Work: Public Transportation (ex. Taxicab)
(Universe: Workers 16 Years and Over)

Group	Number	%
Total Population	2,175	2.4
Hispanic or Latino (of any race)	853	2.8
Central American, ex. Mexican	36	1.3
Guatemalan	0	0.0
Salvadoran	24	1.4
Mexican	755	3.0
Puerto Rican	35	3.6
South American	0	0.0
Spaniard	0	0.0

Homeownership Rate
(Universe: Occupied Housing Units)

Group	%
Total Population	62.4
Hispanic or Latino (of any race)	56.4
Central American, ex. Mexican	62.0
Costa Rican	52.8
Guatemalan	57.9
Honduran	55.9
Nicaraguan	65.9
Panamanian	61.1
Salvadoran	64.5
Cuban	61.6
Dominican Republic	58.1
Mexican	55.7
Puerto Rican	55.4
South American	67.6
Argentinean	68.4
Colombian	66.0
Ecuadorian	60.7
Peruvian	72.5
Spaniard	66.4

Median Home Value

Group	Dollars
Total Population	236,400
Hispanic or Latino (of any race)	215,700
Central American, ex. Mexican	255,000
Guatemalan	276,500
Salvadoran	241,900
Mexican	205,000
Puerto Rican	282,400
South American	239,100
Spaniard	254,700

Median Gross Rent

Group	Dollars
Total Population	1,140
Hispanic or Latino (of any race)	941
Central American, ex. Mexican	924
Guatemalan	816
Salvadoran	1,070
Mexican	930
Puerto Rican	1,175
South American	1,025
Spaniard	780

Median Household Income
(2010 Inflation-Adjusted Dollars)

Group	Dollars
Total Population	59,256
Hispanic or Latino (of any race)	49,682
Central American, ex. Mexican	49,298
Guatemalan	39,688
Salvadoran	55,789
Mexican	48,855
Puerto Rican	56,615
South American	64,434
Spaniard	62,059

Per Capita Income
(2010 Inflation-Adjusted Dollars)

Group	Dollars
Total Population	21,657
Hispanic or Latino (of any race)	14,190
Central American, ex. Mexican	16,866
Guatemalan	18,582
Salvadoran	13,443
Mexican	13,169
Puerto Rican	21,071
South American	25,877
Spaniard	36,666

Households with $100,000+ Income

Group	Number	%
Total Population	12,627	20.4
Hispanic or Latino (of any race)	2,068	11.9
Central American, ex. Mexican	184	11.6
Guatemalan	29	8.0
Salvadoran	107	11.3
Mexican	1,541	11.2
Puerto Rican	135	20.4
South American	66	19.9
Spaniard	92	27.4

Households with Food Stamps/SNAP Benefits During Past 12 Months

Group	Number	%
Total Population	4,427	7.1
Hispanic or Latino (of any race)	1,617	9.3
Central American, ex. Mexican	81	5.1
Guatemalan	0	0.0
Salvadoran	70	7.4
Mexican	1,369	9.9
Puerto Rican	70	10.6
South American	31	9.3
Spaniard	0	0.0

Poverty Rate
(Income in Past 12 Months Below Poverty Level)

Group	%
Total Population	12.2
Hispanic or Latino (of any race)	18.3
Central American, ex. Mexican	18.1
Guatemalan	14.1
Salvadoran	20.3
Mexican	19.4
Puerto Rican	13.3
South American	7.2
Spaniard	4.0

Paradise

Population

Group	Number	%TP[1]	%HP[2]
Total Population	223,167	100.0	–
Hispanic or Latino (of any race)	69,599	31.2	100.0
Central American, ex. Mexican	6,648	3.0	9.6
Costa Rican	153	0.1	0.2
Guatemalan	1,669	0.7	2.4
Honduran	508	0.2	0.7
Nicaraguan	520	0.2	0.7
Panamanian	147	0.1	0.2
Salvadoran	3,578	1.6	5.1
Cuban	4,405	2.0	6.3
Dominican Republic	300	0.1	0.4
Mexican	48,022	21.5	69.0
Puerto Rican	2,213	1.0	3.2
South American	2,619	1.2	3.8
Argentinean	442	0.2	0.6
Chilean	202	0.1	0.3
Colombian	681	0.3	1.0
Ecuadorian	304	0.1	0.4
Peruvian	719	0.3	1.0
Venezuelan	111	<0.1	0.2
Spaniard	957	0.4	1.4

Population Growth: 2000–2010

Group	%
Total Population	19.9
Hispanic or Latino (of any race)	59.4
Central American, ex. Mexican	150.2
Guatemalan	174.1
Honduran	137.4
Nicaraguan	173.7
Salvadoran	172.1
Cuban	64.1
Dominican Republic	105.5
Mexican	66.0
Puerto Rican	57.4
South American	110.4
Argentinean	63.7
Chilean	66.9
Colombian	126.2
Peruvian	147.9
Spaniard	521.4

Males per 100 Females

Group	Number
Total Population	107.3
Hispanic or Latino (of any race)	109.6
Central American, ex. Mexican	112.2
Costa Rican	121.7
Guatemalan	134.4
Honduran	104.8
Nicaraguan	88.4
Panamanian	70.9
Salvadoran	109.7
Cuban	110.6
Dominican Republic	104.1
Mexican	111.2
Puerto Rican	101.9
South American	92.4
Argentinean	98.2
Chilean	90.6
Colombian	94.6
Ecuadorian	101.3
Peruvian	89.7
Venezuelan	113.5
Spaniard	90.3

Average Household Size

Group	People
Total Population	2.46
Hispanic or Latino (of any race)	3.27
Central American, ex. Mexican	3.55
Costa Rican	2.82
Guatemalan	3.75
Honduran	3.36
Nicaraguan	3.21
Panamanian	2.72
Salvadoran	3.61
Cuban	2.73
Dominican Republic	2.84
Mexican	3.46
Puerto Rican	2.44
South American	2.74
Argentinean	2.67
Chilean	2.33
Colombian	2.82
Ecuadorian	2.94
Peruvian	2.95
Venezuelan	2.48
Spaniard	2.45

Median Age

Group	Years
Total Population	36.0
Hispanic or Latino (of any race)	27.8
Central American, ex. Mexican	30.8
Costa Rican	36.3
Guatemalan	30.2
Honduran	29.8
Nicaraguan	36.1
Panamanian	33.2
Salvadoran	30.4
Cuban	39.2
Dominican Republic	30.1
Mexican	26.1
Puerto Rican	29.5
South American	37.4
Argentinean	38.3

Notes: (1) Percent of total population; (2) Percent of Hispanic/Latino population; Profiles include places with an overall population of at least 125,000, OR an overall population of at least 25,000 where the Hispanic/Latino population is at least 20% of the overall population. In states where less than five places meet either of these criteria, we have included places with at least 10,000 total population with the highest percentage of Hispanic/Latino population. These places are identified with an asterisk (*); Please refer to the User's Guide for a full explanation of data.

Group	Number	%
Chilean		43.7
Colombian		36.6
Ecuadorian		35.4
Peruvian		37.3
Venezuelan		35.3
Spaniard		35.5

High School Graduates
(Universe: Population 25 Years and Over)

Group	Number	%
Total Population	123,519	83.7
Hispanic or Latino (of any race)	23,114	63.1
Central American, ex. Mexican	2,186	55.3
Guatemalan	811	56.6
Salvadoran	861	48.8
Cuban	2,126	79.8
Mexican	14,124	57.9
Puerto Rican	1,343	83.5
South American	1,494	86.7
Spaniard	592	86.8

Four-Year College Graduates
(Universe: Population 25 Years and Over)

Group	Number	%
Total Population	30,573	20.7
Hispanic or Latino (of any race)	3,307	9.0
Central American, ex. Mexican	134	3.4
Guatemalan	32	2.2
Salvadoran	102	5.8
Cuban	516	19.4
Mexican	1,798	7.4
Puerto Rican	261	16.2
South American	237	13.7
Spaniard	132	19.4

Population Age 3–17 Enrolled in Public School
(Universe: Population Age 3–17 Enrolled in School)

Group	Number	%
Total Population	31,781	94.7
Hispanic or Latino (of any race)	14,306	97.3
Central American, ex. Mexican	1,019	100.0
Guatemalan	179	100.0
Salvadoran	633	100.0
Cuban	730	95.4
Mexican	10,620	96.9
Puerto Rican	415	100.0
South American	917	100.0
Spaniard	207	100.0

Population Age 3–17 Enrolled in Private School
(Universe: Population Age 3–17 Enrolled in School)

Group	Number	%
Total Population	1,774	5.3
Hispanic or Latino (of any race)	396	2.7
Central American, ex. Mexican	0	0.0
Guatemalan	0	0.0
Salvadoran	0	0.0
Cuban	35	4.6
Mexican	343	3.1
Puerto Rican	0	0.0
South American	0	0.0
Spaniard	0	0.0

Foreign-Born Population

Group	Number	%
Total Population	55,789	25.6
Hispanic or Latino (of any race)	31,314	47.9
Central American, ex. Mexican	4,219	70.3
Guatemalan	1,490	78.3
Salvadoran	1,883	65.0
Cuban	2,667	69.3
Mexican	21,365	45.9
Puerto Rican	123	4.8
South American	2,028	70.6
Spaniard	255	22.4

Foreign-Born Naturalized U.S. Citizens

Group	Number	%
Total Population	20,869	37.4
Hispanic or Latino (of any race)	7,158	22.9
Central American, ex. Mexican	1,207	28.6
Guatemalan	280	18.8
Salvadoran	591	31.4
Cuban	1,002	37.6
Mexican	3,684	17.2
Puerto Rican	114	92.7
South American	792	39.1
Spaniard	45	17.6

Language Spoken at Home: English Only
(Universe: Population 5 Years and Over)

Group	Number	%
Total Population	132,591	64.7
Hispanic or Latino (of any race)	13,499	22.7
Central American, ex. Mexican	651	11.2
Guatemalan	103	5.8
Salvadoran	253	8.9
Cuban	397	10.8
Mexican	8,561	20.6
Puerto Rican	1,575	66.8
South American	427	15.2
Spaniard	730	71.8

Language Spoken at Home: Spanish
(Universe: Population 5 Years and Over)

Group	Number	%
Total Population	48,262	23.6
Hispanic or Latino (of any race)	45,522	76.6
Central American, ex. Mexican	5,144	88.8
Guatemalan	1,668	94.2
Salvadoran	2,599	91.1
Cuban	3,246	88.4
Mexican	32,822	79.1
Puerto Rican	765	32.5
South American	2,267	80.5
Spaniard	227	22.3

Unemployment Rate
(Universe: Population 16 Years and Over)

Group	%
Total Population	8.8
Hispanic or Latino (of any race)	7.5
Central American, ex. Mexican	7.0
Guatemalan	9.7
Salvadoran	4.3
Cuban	9.7
Mexican	7.9
Puerto Rican	7.8
South American	6.2
Spaniard	3.6

Class of Worker: Private Wage and Salary
(Universe: Civilian Employed Population 16 Years and Over)

Group	Number	%
Total Population	100,431	88.0
Hispanic or Latino (of any race)	30,890	92.3
Central American, ex. Mexican	3,595	95.2
Guatemalan	1,278	96.9
Salvadoran	1,687	95.6
Cuban	1,893	90.8
Mexican	21,009	93.0
Puerto Rican	1,203	84.7
South American	1,357	92.6
Spaniard	558	85.8

Class of Worker: Government
(Universe: Civilian Employed Population 16 Years and Over)

Group	Number	%
Total Population	9,579	8.4
Hispanic or Latino (of any race)	1,532	4.6
Central American, ex. Mexican	60	1.6
Guatemalan	32	2.4
Salvadoran	0	0.0
Cuban	164	7.9
Mexican	907	4.0
Puerto Rican	158	11.1
South American	85	5.8
Spaniard	21	3.2

Means of Transportation to Work: Car, Truck or Van
(Universe: Workers 16 Years and Over)

Group	Number	%
Total Population	95,348	85.3
Hispanic or Latino (of any race)	26,986	82.2
Central American, ex. Mexican	3,053	81.8
Guatemalan	1,096	83.9
Salvadoran	1,450	82.2
Cuban	1,733	85.2
Mexican	18,162	81.9
Puerto Rican	1,105	80.8
South American	1,256	87.4
Spaniard	469	73.2

Means of Transportation to Work: Public Transportation (ex. Taxicab)
(Universe: Workers 16 Years and Over)

Group	Number	%
Total Population	7,351	6.6
Hispanic or Latino (of any race)	2,959	9.0
Central American, ex. Mexican	451	12.1
Guatemalan	123	9.4
Salvadoran	217	12.3
Cuban	177	8.7
Mexican	1,976	8.9
Puerto Rican	155	11.3
South American	47	3.3
Spaniard	90	14.0

Homeownership Rate
(Universe: Occupied Housing Units)

Group	%
Total Population	43.2
Hispanic or Latino (of any race)	31.2
Central American, ex. Mexican	29.8
Costa Rican	41.7
Guatemalan	25.3
Honduran	30.3
Nicaraguan	34.9
Panamanian	32.6
Salvadoran	30.4
Cuban	37.8
Dominican Republic	31.7
Mexican	29.8
Puerto Rican	32.2
South American	42.9
Argentinean	46.5
Chilean	45.5
Colombian	44.0
Ecuadorian	45.1
Peruvian	39.4
Venezuelan	40.9
Spaniard	48.5

Median Home Value

Group	Dollars
Total Population	241,600
Hispanic or Latino (of any race)	222,500
Central American, ex. Mexican	258,200
Guatemalan	231,700
Salvadoran	280,800
Cuban	231,600
Mexican	202,100
Puerto Rican	188,000
South American	304,000
Spaniard	263,300

Median Gross Rent

Group	Dollars
Total Population	925
Hispanic or Latino (of any race)	890
Central American, ex. Mexican	831
Guatemalan	851
Salvadoran	806
Cuban	893
Mexican	882
Puerto Rican	941
South American	1,042
Spaniard	1,167

Median Household Income
(2010 Inflation-Adjusted Dollars)

Group	Dollars
Total Population	49,408
Hispanic or Latino (of any race)	43,795
Central American, ex. Mexican	44,921
Guatemalan	56,023
Salvadoran	42,341
Cuban	47,826
Mexican	42,797
Puerto Rican	45,735
South American	46,603
Spaniard	38,438

Notes: (1) Percent of total population; (2) Percent of Hispanic/Latino population; Profiles include places with an overall population of at least 125,000, OR an overall population of at least 25,000 where the Hispanic/Latino population is at least 20% of the overall population. In states where less than five places meet either of these criteria, we have included places with at least 10,000 total population with the highest percentage of Hispanic/Latino population. These places are identified with an asterisk (*); Please refer to the User's Guide for a full explanation of data.

Per Capita Income
(2010 Inflation-Adjusted Dollars)

Group	Dollars
Total Population	25,761
Hispanic or Latino (of any race)	16,681
Central American, ex. Mexican	17,450
Guatemalan	17,402
Salvadoran	17,850
Cuban	19,870
Mexican	15,460
Puerto Rican	20,142
South American	19,714
Spaniard	19,682

Households with $100,000+ Income

Group	Number	%
Total Population	13,436	15.3
Hispanic or Latino (of any race)	1,671	8.4
Central American, ex. Mexican	124	6.5
Guatemalan	53	9.1
Salvadoran	46	4.7
Cuban	120	8.1
Mexican	1,076	7.9
Puerto Rican	87	11.4
South American	114	12.5
Spaniard	68	18.2

Households with Food Stamps/SNAP Benefits During Past 12 Months

Group	Number	%
Total Population	5,626	6.4
Hispanic or Latino (of any race)	1,706	8.6
Central American, ex. Mexican	155	8.1
Guatemalan	32	5.5
Salvadoran	50	5.1
Cuban	238	16.1
Mexican	1,105	8.1
Puerto Rican	94	12.3
South American	21	2.3
Spaniard	52	13.9

Poverty Rate
(Income in Past 12 Months Below Poverty Level)

Group	%
Total Population	13.0
Hispanic or Latino (of any race)	17.6
Central American, ex. Mexican	15.3
Guatemalan	11.1
Salvadoran	20.0
Cuban	10.6
Mexican	19.9
Puerto Rican	15.7
South American	10.0
Spaniard	4.6

Reno

Population

Group	Number	%TP[1]	%HP[2]
Total Population	225,221	100.0	–
Hispanic or Latino (of any race)	54,640	24.3	100.0
Central American, ex. Mexican	5,366	2.4	9.8
Costa Rican	168	0.1	0.3
Guatemalan	1,825	0.8	3.3
Honduran	222	0.1	0.4
Nicaraguan	246	0.1	0.5
Salvadoran	2,783	1.2	5.1
Cuban	318	0.1	0.6
Mexican	42,271	18.8	77.4
Puerto Rican	1,015	0.5	1.9
South American	1,118	0.5	2.0
Argentinean	150	0.1	0.3
Chilean	162	0.1	0.3
Colombian	316	0.1	0.6
Peruvian	304	0.1	0.6
Spaniard	940	0.4	1.7

Population Growth: 2000–2010

Group	%
Total Population	24.8
Hispanic or Latino (of any race)	57.8
Central American, ex. Mexican	113.9
Costa Rican	68.0
Guatemalan	145.3
Salvadoran	106.0
Cuban	56.7
Mexican	65.1
Puerto Rican	57.9
South American	178.1
Colombian	195.3
Peruvian	178.9
Spaniard	586.1

Males per 100 Females

Group	Number
Total Population	103.4
Hispanic or Latino (of any race)	106.6
Central American, ex. Mexican	99.0
Costa Rican	73.2
Guatemalan	109.0
Honduran	103.7
Nicaraguan	86.4
Salvadoran	95.0
Cuban	112.0
Mexican	108.0
Puerto Rican	105.9
South American	76.9
Argentinean	111.3
Chilean	74.2
Colombian	59.6
Peruvian	82.0
Spaniard	93.0

Average Household Size

Group	People
Total Population	2.43
Hispanic or Latino (of any race)	3.55
Central American, ex. Mexican	3.54
Costa Rican	2.81
Guatemalan	3.73
Honduran	3.36
Nicaraguan	2.91
Salvadoran	3.58
Cuban	2.23
Mexican	3.73
Puerto Rican	2.45
South American	2.75
Argentinean	2.62
Chilean	2.64
Colombian	2.61
Peruvian	2.95
Spaniard	2.25

Median Age

Group	Years
Total Population	34.6
Hispanic or Latino (of any race)	24.8
Central American, ex. Mexican	30.1
Costa Rican	33.6
Guatemalan	29.4
Honduran	30.9
Nicaraguan	33.7
Salvadoran	30.4
Cuban	30.0
Mexican	23.6
Puerto Rican	27.4
South American	33.1
Argentinean	33.7
Chilean	32.0
Colombian	31.5
Peruvian	34.8
Spaniard	35.2

High School Graduates
(Universe: Population 25 Years and Over)

Group	Number	%
Total Population	119,591	85.2
Hispanic or Latino (of any race)	12,614	51.8
Central American, ex. Mexican	1,595	53.0
Guatemalan	442	44.7
Salvadoran	849	55.0
Mexican	8,457	46.1
South American	532	87.4
Spaniard	561	89.3

Four-Year College Graduates
(Universe: Population 25 Years and Over)

Group	Number	%
Total Population	40,013	28.5
Hispanic or Latino (of any race)	2,424	10.0
Central American, ex. Mexican	222	7.4
Guatemalan	53	5.4
Salvadoran	143	9.3
Mexican	1,212	6.6
South American	238	39.1
Spaniard	228	36.3

Population Age 3–17 Enrolled in Public School
(Universe: Population Age 3–17 Enrolled in School)

Group	Number	%
Total Population	33,370	90.7
Hispanic or Latino (of any race)	12,381	96.2
Central American, ex. Mexican	773	97.1
Guatemalan	287	100.0
Salvadoran	397	100.0
Mexican	10,607	97.2
South American	255	87.3
Spaniard	144	65.2

Population Age 3–17 Enrolled in Private School
(Universe: Population Age 3–17 Enrolled in School)

Group	Number	%
Total Population	3,402	9.3
Hispanic or Latino (of any race)	484	3.8
Central American, ex. Mexican	23	2.9
Guatemalan	0	0.0
Salvadoran	0	0.0
Mexican	311	2.8
South American	37	12.7
Spaniard	77	34.8

Foreign-Born Population

Group	Number	%
Total Population	38,609	17.5
Hispanic or Latino (of any race)	22,012	43.6
Central American, ex. Mexican	3,412	70.9
Guatemalan	1,279	67.0
Salvadoran	1,576	75.6
Mexican	17,255	42.6
South American	711	69.8
Spaniard	131	12.0

Foreign-Born Naturalized U.S. Citizens

Group	Number	%
Total Population	14,486	37.5
Hispanic or Latino (of any race)	5,664	25.7
Central American, ex. Mexican	927	27.2
Guatemalan	355	27.8
Salvadoran	442	28.0
Mexican	3,999	23.2
South American	381	53.6
Spaniard	113	86.3

Language Spoken at Home: English Only
(Universe: Population 5 Years and Over)

Group	Number	%
Total Population	155,080	75.6
Hispanic or Latino (of any race)	10,820	24.5
Central American, ex. Mexican	629	14.5
Guatemalan	237	14.9
Salvadoran	236	11.8
Mexican	7,446	21.2
South American	235	24.1
Spaniard	853	85.2

Language Spoken at Home: Spanish
(Universe: Population 5 Years and Over)

Group	Number	%
Total Population	35,597	17.4
Hispanic or Latino (of any race)	33,338	75.4
Central American, ex. Mexican	3,710	85.5
Guatemalan	1,352	85.1
Salvadoran	1,763	88.2
Mexican	27,633	78.7
South American	741	75.9
Spaniard	148	14.8

Notes: (1) Percent of total population; (2) Percent of Hispanic/Latino population; Profiles include places with an overall population of at least 125,000, OR an overall population of at least 25,000 where the Hispanic/Latino population is at least 20% of the overall population. In states where less than five places meet either of these criteria, we have included places with at least 10,000 total population with the highest percentage of Hispanic/Latino population. These places are identified with an asterisk (*); Please refer to the User's Guide for a full explanation of data.

Unemployment Rate
(Universe: Population 16 Years and Over)

Group	%
Total Population	8.7
Hispanic or Latino (of any race)	10.3
Central American, ex. Mexican	7.8
Guatemalan	2.5
Salvadoran	9.9
Mexican	10.8
South American	6.5
Spaniard	3.8

Class of Worker: Private Wage and Salary
(Universe: Civilian Employed Population 16 Years and Over)

Group	Number	%
Total Population	90,933	82.4
Hispanic or Latino (of any race)	19,794	91.8
Central American, ex. Mexican	2,484	92.4
Guatemalan	960	100.0
Salvadoran	1,226	96.0
Mexican	15,494	93.1
South American	520	92.5
Spaniard	424	79.3

Class of Worker: Government
(Universe: Civilian Employed Population 16 Years and Over)

Group	Number	%
Total Population	13,732	12.4
Hispanic or Latino (of any race)	1,270	5.9
Central American, ex. Mexican	158	5.9
Guatemalan	0	0.0
Salvadoran	37	2.9
Mexican	812	4.9
South American	29	5.2
Spaniard	95	17.8

Means of Transportation to Work: Car, Truck or Van
(Universe: Workers 16 Years and Over)

Group	Number	%
Total Population	93,559	86.1
Hispanic or Latino (of any race)	18,052	85.1
Central American, ex. Mexican	1,975	78.3
Guatemalan	818	85.2
Salvadoran	793	68.4
Mexican	14,258	86.5
South American	471	83.8
Spaniard	444	87.1

Means of Transportation to Work: Public Transportation (ex. Taxicab)
(Universe: Workers 16 Years and Over)

Group	Number	%
Total Population	4,581	4.2
Hispanic or Latino (of any race)	1,578	7.4
Central American, ex. Mexican	418	16.6
Guatemalan	132	13.8
Salvadoran	265	22.9
Mexican	1,076	6.5
South American	41	7.3
Spaniard	0	0.0

Homeownership Rate
(Universe: Occupied Housing Units)

Group	%
Total Population	48.0
Hispanic or Latino (of any race)	35.6
Central American, ex. Mexican	37.6
Costa Rican	35.1
Guatemalan	35.9
Honduran	22.7
Nicaraguan	45.9
Salvadoran	39.8
Cuban	31.6
Mexican	35.1
Puerto Rican	27.6
South American	45.1
Argentinean	45.0
Chilean	44.4
Colombian	41.1
Peruvian	50.0
Spaniard	49.8

Median Home Value

Group	Dollars
Total Population	290,100
Hispanic or Latino (of any race)	219,800
Central American, ex. Mexican	244,900
Guatemalan	328,100
Salvadoran	266,200
Mexican	198,200
South American	248,600
Spaniard	253,100

Median Gross Rent

Group	Dollars
Total Population	872
Hispanic or Latino (of any race)	810
Central American, ex. Mexican	826
Guatemalan	817
Salvadoran	810
Mexican	799
South American	775
Spaniard	976

Median Household Income
(2010 Inflation-Adjusted Dollars)

Group	Dollars
Total Population	48,895
Hispanic or Latino (of any race)	37,044
Central American, ex. Mexican	38,467
Guatemalan	37,258
Salvadoran	38,750
Mexican	35,944
South American	46,203
Spaniard	65,284

Per Capita Income
(2010 Inflation-Adjusted Dollars)

Group	Dollars
Total Population	27,714
Hispanic or Latino (of any race)	13,581
Central American, ex. Mexican	16,432
Guatemalan	14,383
Salvadoran	18,952
Mexican	12,186
South American	23,137
Spaniard	24,426

Households with $100,000+ Income

Group	Number	%
Total Population	16,662	18.7
Hispanic or Latino (of any race)	1,230	9.0
Central American, ex. Mexican	100	6.6
Guatemalan	0	0.0
Salvadoran	100	13.5
Mexican	837	8.1
South American	46	12.5
Spaniard	90	22.1

Households with Food Stamps/SNAP Benefits During Past 12 Months

Group	Number	%
Total Population	5,845	6.6
Hispanic or Latino (of any race)	1,351	9.8
Central American, ex. Mexican	34	2.3
Guatemalan	0	0.0
Salvadoran	34	4.6
Mexican	1,079	10.4
South American	26	7.0
Spaniard	67	16.4

Poverty Rate
(Income in Past 12 Months Below Poverty Level)

Group	%
Total Population	16.3
Hispanic or Latino (of any race)	27.5
Central American, ex. Mexican	20.5
Guatemalan	23.1
Salvadoran	18.4
Mexican	29.3
South American	11.1
Spaniard	34.0

Sparks

Population

Group	Number	%TP[1]	%HP[2]
Total Population	90,264	100.0	–
Hispanic or Latino (of any race)	23,698	26.3	100.0
Central American, ex. Mexican	2,087	2.3	8.8
Guatemalan	512	0.6	2.2
Nicaraguan	104	0.1	0.4
Salvadoran	1,285	1.4	5.4
Cuban	116	0.1	0.5
Mexican	19,135	21.2	80.7
Puerto Rican	422	0.5	1.8
South American	383	0.4	1.6
Peruvian	144	0.2	0.6
Spaniard	393	0.4	1.7

Population Growth: 2000–2010

Group	%
Total Population	36.1
Hispanic or Latino (of any race)	81.3
Central American, ex. Mexican	177.9
Guatemalan	255.6
Salvadoran	175.8
Mexican	91.0
Puerto Rican	124.5
South American	171.6

Males per 100 Females

Group	Number
Total Population	97.8
Hispanic or Latino (of any race)	104.0
Central American, ex. Mexican	94.0
Guatemalan	91.0
Nicaraguan	67.7
Salvadoran	98.0
Cuban	110.9
Mexican	105.8
Puerto Rican	103.9
South American	85.0
Peruvian	92.0
Spaniard	88.9

Average Household Size

Group	People
Total Population	2.68
Hispanic or Latino (of any race)	3.77
Central American, ex. Mexican	3.88
Guatemalan	4.10
Nicaraguan	3.92
Salvadoran	3.85
Cuban	2.82
Mexican	3.90
Puerto Rican	2.84
South American	3.02
Peruvian	3.38
Spaniard	2.54

Median Age

Group	Years
Total Population	35.5
Hispanic or Latino (of any race)	24.9
Central American, ex. Mexican	28.9
Guatemalan	29.2
Nicaraguan	24.7
Salvadoran	29.0
Cuban	32.0
Mexican	24.0
Puerto Rican	25.1
South American	35.3
Peruvian	35.5
Spaniard	39.1

High School Graduates
(Universe: Population 25 Years and Over)

Group	Number	%
Total Population	49,346	86.1
Hispanic or Latino (of any race)	7,178	59.9
Central American, ex. Mexican	627	70.7
Mexican	5,475	56.3

Notes: (1) Percent of total population; (2) Percent of Hispanic/Latino population; Profiles include places with an overall population of at least 125,000, OR an overall population of at least 25,000 where the Hispanic/Latino population is at least 20% of the overall population. In states where less than five places meet either of these criteria, we have included places with at least 10,000 total population with the highest percentage of Hispanic/Latino population. These places are identified with an asterisk (*); Please refer to the User's Guide for a full explanation of data.

Four-Year College Graduates
(Universe: Population 25 Years and Over)

Group	Number	%
Total Population	11,656	20.3
Hispanic or Latino (of any race)	862	7.2
Central American, ex. Mexican	46	5.2
Mexican	648	6.7

Population Age 3–17 Enrolled in Public School
(Universe: Population Age 3–17 Enrolled in School)

Group	Number	%
Total Population	15,192	93.0
Hispanic or Latino (of any race)	5,960	96.5
Central American, ex. Mexican	261	100.0
Mexican	5,251	96.1

Population Age 3–17 Enrolled in Private School
(Universe: Population Age 3–17 Enrolled in School)

Group	Number	%
Total Population	1,139	7.0
Hispanic or Latino (of any race)	215	3.5
Central American, ex. Mexican	0	0.0
Mexican	211	3.9

Foreign-Born Population

Group	Number	%
Total Population	14,512	16.6
Hispanic or Latino (of any race)	9,501	40.9
Central American, ex. Mexican	867	54.9
Mexican	8,091	41.6

Foreign-Born Naturalized U.S. Citizens

Group	Number	%
Total Population	6,281	43.3
Hispanic or Latino (of any race)	2,828	29.8
Central American, ex. Mexican	335	38.6
Mexican	2,129	26.3

Language Spoken at Home: English Only
(Universe: Population 5 Years and Over)

Group	Number	%
Total Population	59,960	74.3
Hispanic or Latino (of any race)	5,464	26.7
Central American, ex. Mexican	291	21.2
Mexican	4,181	24.4

Language Spoken at Home: Spanish
(Universe: Population 5 Years and Over)

Group	Number	%
Total Population	15,737	19.5
Hispanic or Latino (of any race)	14,902	72.7
Central American, ex. Mexican	1,081	78.8
Mexican	12,934	75.3

Unemployment Rate
(Universe: Population 16 Years and Over)

Group	%
Total Population	7.9
Hispanic or Latino (of any race)	8.9
Central American, ex. Mexican	11.9
Mexican	8.8

Class of Worker: Private Wage and Salary
(Universe: Civilian Employed Population 16 Years and Over)

Group	Number	%
Total Population	35,499	81.3
Hispanic or Latino (of any race)	9,206	88.9
Central American, ex. Mexican	645	83.9
Mexican	7,654	89.3

Class of Worker: Government
(Universe: Civilian Employed Population 16 Years and Over)

Group	Number	%
Total Population	5,999	13.7
Hispanic or Latino (of any race)	698	6.7
Central American, ex. Mexican	37	4.8
Mexican	604	7.1

Means of Transportation to Work: Car, Truck or Van
(Universe: Workers 16 Years and Over)

Group	Number	%
Total Population	38,204	89.7
Hispanic or Latino (of any race)	9,231	91.2
Central American, ex. Mexican	668	93.8
Mexican	7,591	90.2

Means of Transportation to Work: Public Transportation (ex. Taxicab)
(Universe: Workers 16 Years and Over)

Group	Number	%
Total Population	933	2.2
Hispanic or Latino (of any race)	389	3.8
Central American, ex. Mexican	22	3.1
Mexican	367	4.4

Homeownership Rate
(Universe: Occupied Housing Units)

Group	%
Total Population	58.5
Hispanic or Latino (of any race)	44.5
Central American, ex. Mexican	45.0
Guatemalan	43.7
Nicaraguan	26.9
Salvadoran	47.0
Cuban	52.6
Mexican	43.9
Puerto Rican	37.0
South American	61.5
Peruvian	68.9
Spaniard	62.7

Median Home Value

Group	Dollars
Total Population	263,900
Hispanic or Latino (of any race)	229,500
Central American, ex. Mexican	226,100
Mexican	227,100

Median Gross Rent

Group	Dollars
Total Population	960
Hispanic or Latino (of any race)	871
Central American, ex. Mexican	823
Mexican	866

Median Household Income
(2010 Inflation-Adjusted Dollars)

Group	Dollars
Total Population	56,775
Hispanic or Latino (of any race)	45,237
Central American, ex. Mexican	39,888
Mexican	44,577

Per Capita Income
(2010 Inflation-Adjusted Dollars)

Group	Dollars
Total Population	25,717
Hispanic or Latino (of any race)	16,003
Central American, ex. Mexican	20,998
Mexican	14,865

Households with $100,000+ Income

Group	Number	%
Total Population	6,634	20.1
Hispanic or Latino (of any race)	796	12.6
Central American, ex. Mexican	66	15.5
Mexican	617	12.0

Households with Food Stamps/SNAP Benefits During Past 12 Months

Group	Number	%
Total Population	1,722	5.2
Hispanic or Latino (of any race)	431	6.8
Central American, ex. Mexican	51	11.9
Mexican	380	7.4

Poverty Rate
(Income in Past 12 Months Below Poverty Level)

Group	%
Total Population	11.0
Hispanic or Latino (of any race)	17.6
Central American, ex. Mexican	20.3
Mexican	18.7

Spring Valley

Population

Group	Number	%TP[1]	%HP[2]
Total Population	178,395	100.0	–
Hispanic or Latino (of any race)	36,691	20.6	100.0
Central American, ex. Mexican	3,447	1.9	9.4
Costa Rican	150	0.1	0.4
Guatemalan	810	0.5	2.2
Honduran	272	0.2	0.7
Nicaraguan	277	0.2	0.8
Panamanian	126	0.1	0.3
Salvadoran	1,776	1.0	4.8
Cuban	2,010	1.1	5.5
Dominican Republic	291	0.2	0.8
Mexican	23,871	13.4	65.1
Puerto Rican	1,589	0.9	4.3
South American	2,163	1.2	5.9
Argentinean	442	0.2	1.2
Chilean	200	0.1	0.5
Colombian	693	0.4	1.9
Ecuadorian	174	0.1	0.5
Peruvian	475	0.3	1.3
Spaniard	706	0.4	1.9

Population Growth: 2000–2010

Group	%
Total Population	52.0
Hispanic or Latino (of any race)	127.0
Central American, ex. Mexican	308.9
Guatemalan	373.7
Salvadoran	364.9
Cuban	125.3
Dominican Republic	144.5
Mexican	146.0
Puerto Rican	105.8
South American	191.5
Argentinean	138.9
Colombian	259.1
Peruvian	306.0
Spaniard	503.4

Males per 100 Females

Group	Number
Total Population	99.2
Hispanic or Latino (of any race)	97.1
Central American, ex. Mexican	91.0
Costa Rican	85.2
Guatemalan	99.0
Honduran	70.0
Nicaraguan	97.9
Panamanian	57.5
Salvadoran	95.2
Cuban	97.6
Dominican Republic	80.7
Mexican	100.4
Puerto Rican	97.1
South American	79.2
Argentinean	85.7
Chilean	86.9
Colombian	68.6
Ecuadorian	79.4
Peruvian	84.1
Spaniard	83.9

Average Household Size

Group	People
Total Population	2.48
Hispanic or Latino (of any race)	3.22
Central American, ex. Mexican	3.65
Costa Rican	2.87
Guatemalan	3.92
Honduran	3.36
Nicaraguan	3.43
Panamanian	2.73
Salvadoran	3.78
Cuban	2.88
Dominican Republic	2.91
Mexican	3.38
Puerto Rican	2.58
South American	2.81
Argentinean	2.75
Chilean	2.67
Colombian	2.85
Ecuadorian	2.92
Peruvian	3.12
Spaniard	2.52

Median Age

Group	Years
Total Population	37.2

Notes: (1) Percent of total population; (2) Percent of Hispanic/Latino population; Profiles include places with an overall population of at least 125,000, OR an overall population of at least 25,000 where the Hispanic/Latino population is at least 20% of the overall population. In states where less than five places meet either of these criteria, we have included places with at least 10,000 total population with the highest percentage of Hispanic/Latino population. These places are identified with an asterisk (*); Please refer to the User's Guide for a full explanation of data.

STATE & PLACE PROFILES

Hispanic or Latino (of any race)		28.8
Central American, ex. Mexican		31.4
Costa Rican		34.3
Guatemalan		31.1
Honduran		30.5
Nicaraguan		33.1
Panamanian		36.7
Salvadoran		30.9
Cuban		36.4
Dominican Republic		29.1
Mexican		27.1
Puerto Rican		29.9
South American		36.4
Argentinean		38.0
Chilean		37.0
Colombian		35.4
Ecuadorian		33.0
Peruvian		37.4
Spaniard		34.8

High School Graduates
(Universe: Population 25 Years and Over)

Group	Number	%
Total Population	107,149	88.8
Hispanic or Latino (of any race)	13,311	73.6
Central American, ex. Mexican	1,307	72.2
Guatemalan	494	65.3
Salvadoran	330	58.7
Cuban	1,010	90.8
Mexican	7,895	68.6
Puerto Rican	995	92.9
South American	1,154	87.2

Four-Year College Graduates
(Universe: Population 25 Years and Over)

Group	Number	%
Total Population	29,667	24.6
Hispanic or Latino (of any race)	2,298	12.7
Central American, ex. Mexican	190	10.5
Guatemalan	32	4.2
Salvadoran	56	10.0
Cuban	200	18.0
Mexican	1,026	8.9
Puerto Rican	181	16.9
South American	429	32.4

Population Age 3–17 Enrolled in Public School
(Universe: Population Age 3–17 Enrolled in School)

Group	Number	%
Total Population	22,072	90.9
Hispanic or Latino (of any race)	6,421	93.3
Central American, ex. Mexican	653	96.2
Guatemalan	374	100.0
Salvadoran	100	100.0
Cuban	203	69.3
Mexican	4,719	95.9
Puerto Rican	284	96.9
South American	291	72.9

Population Age 3–17 Enrolled in Private School
(Universe: Population Age 3–17 Enrolled in School)

Group	Number	%
Total Population	2,214	9.1
Hispanic or Latino (of any race)	460	6.7
Central American, ex. Mexican	26	3.8
Guatemalan	0	0.0
Salvadoran	0	0.0
Cuban	90	30.7
Mexican	203	4.1
Puerto Rican	9	3.1
South American	108	27.1

Foreign-Born Population

Group	Number	%
Total Population	46,806	27.4
Hispanic or Latino (of any race)	13,123	41.4
Central American, ex. Mexican	1,729	56.6
Guatemalan	768	58.0
Salvadoran	536	57.1
Cuban	1,168	63.0
Mexican	8,105	38.4
Puerto Rican	0	0.0
South American	1,303	60.9

Foreign-Born Naturalized U.S. Citizens

Group	Number	%
Total Population	23,579	50.4
Hispanic or Latino (of any race)	5,013	38.2
Central American, ex. Mexican	661	38.2
Guatemalan	141	18.4
Salvadoran	275	51.3
Cuban	484	41.4
Mexican	2,479	30.6
Puerto Rican	0	0.0
South American	773	59.3

Language Spoken at Home: English Only
(Universe: Population 5 Years and Over)

Group	Number	%
Total Population	105,050	65.5
Hispanic or Latino (of any race)	7,466	25.9
Central American, ex. Mexican	502	18.3
Guatemalan	52	4.2
Salvadoran	106	13.2
Cuban	181	10.1
Mexican	4,839	25.5
Puerto Rican	644	43.7
South American	561	27.7

Language Spoken at Home: Spanish
(Universe: Population 5 Years and Over)

Group	Number	%
Total Population	22,789	14.2
Hispanic or Latino (of any race)	21,255	73.7
Central American, ex. Mexican	2,234	81.4
Guatemalan	1,183	95.8
Salvadoran	688	85.6
Cuban	1,612	89.9
Mexican	14,040	74.1
Puerto Rican	831	56.3
South American	1,454	71.8

Unemployment Rate
(Universe: Population 16 Years and Over)

Group	%
Total Population	8.8
Hispanic or Latino (of any race)	7.8
Central American, ex. Mexican	3.9
Guatemalan	2.6
Salvadoran	6.8
Cuban	7.0
Mexican	8.2
Puerto Rican	3.2
South American	6.3

Class of Worker: Private Wage and Salary
(Universe: Civilian Employed Population 16 Years and Over)

Group	Number	%
Total Population	80,654	87.4
Hispanic or Latino (of any race)	14,893	88.9
Central American, ex. Mexican	1,637	91.9
Guatemalan	718	97.7
Salvadoran	539	93.9
Cuban	1,195	95.1
Mexican	9,214	87.9
Puerto Rican	959	97.6
South American	1,074	84.6

Class of Worker: Government
(Universe: Civilian Employed Population 16 Years and Over)

Group	Number	%
Total Population	6,999	7.6
Hispanic or Latino (of any race)	1,090	6.5
Central American, ex. Mexican	106	6.0
Guatemalan	0	0.0
Salvadoran	27	4.7
Cuban	15	1.2
Mexican	736	7.0
Puerto Rican	10	1.0
South American	114	9.0

Means of Transportation to Work: Car, Truck or Van
(Universe: Workers 16 Years and Over)

Group	Number	%
Total Population	82,326	91.0
Hispanic or Latino (of any race)	15,090	91.9
Central American, ex. Mexican	1,537	89.5
Guatemalan	735	100.0
Salvadoran	391	76.5
Cuban	1,243	100.0
Mexican	9,300	90.7
Puerto Rican	912	93.8
South American	1,166	92.9

Means of Transportation to Work: Public Transportation (ex. Taxicab)
(Universe: Workers 16 Years and Over)

Group	Number	%
Total Population	2,924	3.2
Hispanic or Latino (of any race)	622	3.8
Central American, ex. Mexican	99	5.8
Guatemalan	0	0.0
Salvadoran	94	18.4
Cuban	0	0.0
Mexican	429	4.2
Puerto Rican	44	4.5
South American	50	4.0

Homeownership Rate
(Universe: Occupied Housing Units)

Group	%
Total Population	51.3
Hispanic or Latino (of any race)	42.8
Central American, ex. Mexican	45.9
Costa Rican	26.7
Guatemalan	45.6
Honduran	29.9
Nicaraguan	46.5
Panamanian	50.0
Salvadoran	49.2
Cuban	50.4
Dominican Republic	40.6
Mexican	41.7
Puerto Rican	31.9
South American	49.4
Argentinean	54.9
Chilean	50.0
Colombian	47.4
Ecuadorian	46.0
Peruvian	53.0
Spaniard	48.7

Median Home Value

Group	Dollars
Total Population	273,200
Hispanic or Latino (of any race)	264,100
Central American, ex. Mexican	239,600
Guatemalan	220,400
Salvadoran	229,800
Cuban	198,200
Mexican	273,200
Puerto Rican	258,800
South American	279,400

Median Gross Rent

Group	Dollars
Total Population	1,134
Hispanic or Latino (of any race)	1,114
Central American, ex. Mexican	1,259
Guatemalan	1,414
Salvadoran	979
Cuban	1,000
Mexican	1,109
Puerto Rican	1,120
South American	1,131

Median Household Income
(2010 Inflation-Adjusted Dollars)

Group	Dollars
Total Population	56,135
Hispanic or Latino (of any race)	54,200
Central American, ex. Mexican	61,116
Guatemalan	51,655
Salvadoran	33,844
Cuban	46,227
Mexican	52,929
Puerto Rican	72,903
South American	46,486

Per Capita Income
(2010 Inflation-Adjusted Dollars)

Group	Dollars
Total Population	31,242

Notes: (1) Percent of total population; (2) Percent of Hispanic/Latino population; Profiles include places with an overall population of at least 125,000, OR an overall population of at least 25,000 where the Hispanic/Latino population is at least 20% of the overall population. In states where less than five places meet either of these criteria, we have included places with at least 10,000 total population with the highest percentage of Hispanic/Latino population. These places are identified with an asterisk (*); Please refer to the User's Guide for a full explanation of data.

Hispanic or Latino (of any race)	20,699
Central American, ex. Mexican	21,245
Guatemalan	15,320
Salvadoran	19,498
Cuban	21,201
Mexican	19,171
Puerto Rican	27,131
South American	18,531

Households with $100,000+ Income

Group	Number	%
Total Population	13,589	19.4
Hispanic or Latino (of any race)	1,387	13.8
Central American, ex. Mexican	235	24.0
Guatemalan	44	12.9
Salvadoran	53	18.3
Cuban	98	13.2
Mexican	847	13.9
Puerto Rican	52	8.3
South American	47	5.9

Households with Food Stamps/SNAP Benefits During Past 12 Months

Group	Number	%
Total Population	2,461	3.5
Hispanic or Latino (of any race)	588	5.9
Central American, ex. Mexican	8	0.8
Guatemalan	0	0.0
Salvadoran	8	2.8
Cuban	14	1.9
Mexican	481	7.9
Puerto Rican	85	13.5
South American	0	0.0

Poverty Rate
(Income in Past 12 Months Below Poverty Level)

Group	%
Total Population	9.1
Hispanic or Latino (of any race)	13.6
Central American, ex. Mexican	4.2
Guatemalan	5.0
Salvadoran	0.0
Cuban	25.6
Mexican	13.8
Puerto Rican	2.6
South American	25.0

Sunrise Manor

Population

Group	Number	%TP[1]	%HP[2]
Total Population	189,372	100.0	–
Hispanic or Latino (of any race)	91,764	48.5	100.0
Central American, ex. Mexican	6,672	3.5	7.3
Guatemalan	1,532	0.8	1.7
Honduran	741	0.4	0.8
Nicaraguan	458	0.2	0.5
Panamanian	142	0.1	0.2
Salvadoran	3,655	1.9	4.0
Cuban	2,604	1.4	2.8
Dominican Republic	199	0.1	0.2
Mexican	74,476	39.3	81.2
Puerto Rican	1,685	0.9	1.8
South American	1,001	0.5	1.1
Argentinean	219	0.1	0.2
Colombian	216	0.1	0.2
Ecuadorian	169	0.1	0.2
Peruvian	192	0.1	0.2
Spaniard	629	0.3	0.7

Population Growth: 2000–2010

Group	%
Total Population	21.3
Hispanic or Latino (of any race)	125.9
Central American, ex. Mexican	285.7
Guatemalan	367.1
Honduran	311.7
Nicaraguan	239.3
Salvadoran	297.7
Cuban	94.0
Mexican	149.2
Puerto Rican	42.6
South American	86.8
Argentinean	112.6
Colombian	53.2
Spaniard	424.2

Males per 100 Females

Group	Number
Total Population	99.4
Hispanic or Latino (of any race)	103.7
Central American, ex. Mexican	104.9
Guatemalan	119.2
Honduran	89.0
Nicaraguan	98.3
Panamanian	69.0
Salvadoran	105.9
Cuban	109.3
Dominican Republic	86.0
Mexican	104.4
Puerto Rican	93.0
South American	87.5
Argentinean	85.6
Colombian	86.2
Ecuadorian	74.2
Peruvian	95.9
Spaniard	87.8

Average Household Size

Group	People
Total Population	3.11
Hispanic or Latino (of any race)	4.08
Central American, ex. Mexican	4.11
Guatemalan	4.14
Honduran	4.15
Nicaraguan	3.66
Panamanian	2.77
Salvadoran	4.22
Cuban	3.18
Dominican Republic	3.44
Mexican	4.22
Puerto Rican	3.04
South American	3.16
Argentinean	2.74
Colombian	3.17
Ecuadorian	3.55
Peruvian	3.45
Spaniard	2.87

Median Age

Group	Years
Total Population	31.6
Hispanic or Latino (of any race)	24.3
Central American, ex. Mexican	30.9
Guatemalan	30.8
Honduran	29.4
Nicaraguan	32.4
Panamanian	28.8
Salvadoran	31.0
Cuban	36.5
Dominican Republic	26.2
Mexican	23.1
Puerto Rican	27.2
South American	37.5
Argentinean	38.5
Colombian	34.0
Ecuadorian	38.6
Peruvian	41.3
Spaniard	32.9

High School Graduates
(Universe: Population 25 Years and Over)

Group	Number	%
Total Population	82,523	72.1
Hispanic or Latino (of any race)	20,857	49.6
Central American, ex. Mexican	2,016	53.2
Guatemalan	761	63.4
Salvadoran	925	45.2
Cuban	1,005	59.2
Mexican	15,512	46.4
Puerto Rican	787	80.8

Four-Year College Graduates
(Universe: Population 25 Years and Over)

Group	Number	%
Total Population	12,851	11.2
Hispanic or Latino (of any race)	2,032	4.8
Central American, ex. Mexican	212	5.6
Guatemalan	66	5.5
Salvadoran	129	6.3
Cuban	262	15.4
Mexican	1,170	3.5
Puerto Rican	207	21.3

Population Age 3–17 Enrolled in Public School
(Universe: Population Age 3–17 Enrolled in School)

Group	Number	%
Total Population	39,512	96.7
Hispanic or Latino (of any race)	22,770	98.0
Central American, ex. Mexican	1,495	100.0
Guatemalan	431	100.0
Salvadoran	865	100.0
Cuban	351	94.9
Mexican	19,693	98.1
Puerto Rican	387	91.7

Population Age 3–17 Enrolled in Private School
(Universe: Population Age 3–17 Enrolled in School)

Group	Number	%
Total Population	1,367	3.3
Hispanic or Latino (of any race)	453	2.0
Central American, ex. Mexican	0	0.0
Guatemalan	0	0.0
Salvadoran	0	0.0
Cuban	19	5.1
Mexican	380	1.9
Puerto Rican	35	8.3

Foreign-Born Population

Group	Number	%
Total Population	52,166	26.9
Hispanic or Latino (of any race)	39,891	45.7
Central American, ex. Mexican	4,396	66.6
Guatemalan	1,371	67.7
Salvadoran	2,445	66.9
Cuban	1,744	73.2
Mexican	32,596	45.0
Puerto Rican	39	1.9

Foreign-Born Naturalized U.S. Citizens

Group	Number	%
Total Population	17,594	33.7
Hispanic or Latino (of any race)	9,904	24.8
Central American, ex. Mexican	1,527	34.7
Guatemalan	317	23.1
Salvadoran	1,031	42.2
Cuban	842	48.3
Mexican	7,096	21.8
Puerto Rican	17	43.6

Language Spoken at Home: English Only
(Universe: Population 5 Years and Over)

Group	Number	%
Total Population	97,440	55.0
Hispanic or Latino (of any race)	10,716	14.0
Central American, ex. Mexican	265	4.4
Guatemalan	66	3.7
Salvadoran	192	5.7
Cuban	239	10.3
Mexican	8,187	13.1
Puerto Rican	947	51.8

Language Spoken at Home: Spanish
(Universe: Population 5 Years and Over)

Group	Number	%
Total Population	67,807	38.3
Hispanic or Latino (of any race)	65,606	85.9
Central American, ex. Mexican	5,817	95.6
Guatemalan	1,718	96.3
Salvadoran	3,198	94.3
Cuban	2,088	89.7
Mexican	54,425	86.9
Puerto Rican	871	47.7

Unemployment Rate
(Universe: Population 16 Years and Over)

Group	%
Total Population	11.2
Hispanic or Latino (of any race)	11.3
Central American, ex. Mexican	7.3
Guatemalan	6.1
Salvadoran	8.4
Cuban	11.9
Mexican	11.4

Notes: (1) Percent of total population; (2) Percent of Hispanic/Latino population; Profiles include places with an overall population of at least 125,000, OR an overall population of at least 25,000 where the Hispanic/Latino population is at least 20% of the overall population. In states where less than five places meet either of these criteria, we have included places with at least 10,000 total population with the highest percentage of Hispanic/Latino population. These places are identified with an asterisk (*); Please refer to the User's Guide for a full explanation of data.

Group	Number	%
Puerto Rican		18.5

Class of Worker: Private Wage and Salary
(Universe: Civilian Employed Population 16 Years and Over)

Group	Number	%
Total Population	73,148	86.4
Hispanic or Latino (of any race)	32,827	91.7
Central American, ex. Mexican	3,241	91.8
Guatemalan	999	93.8
Salvadoran	1,769	90.3
Cuban	873	80.7
Mexican	26,608	92.5
Puerto Rican	608	76.9

Class of Worker: Government
(Universe: Civilian Employed Population 16 Years and Over)

Group	Number	%
Total Population	8,698	10.3
Hispanic or Latino (of any race)	1,745	4.9
Central American, ex. Mexican	144	4.1
Guatemalan	25	2.3
Salvadoran	119	6.1
Cuban	149	13.8
Mexican	1,165	4.0
Puerto Rican	183	23.1

Means of Transportation to Work: Car, Truck or Van
(Universe: Workers 16 Years and Over)

Group	Number	%
Total Population	74,185	89.4
Hispanic or Latino (of any race)	31,693	90.6
Central American, ex. Mexican	2,964	84.9
Guatemalan	911	85.5
Salvadoran	1,692	87.8
Cuban	973	93.6
Mexican	25,712	91.5
Puerto Rican	650	83.8

Means of Transportation to Work: Public Transportation (ex. Taxicab)
(Universe: Workers 16 Years and Over)

Group	Number	%
Total Population	4,390	5.3
Hispanic or Latino (of any race)	1,884	5.4
Central American, ex. Mexican	254	7.3
Guatemalan	100	9.4
Salvadoran	132	6.8
Cuban	0	0.0
Mexican	1,459	5.2
Puerto Rican	53	6.8

Homeownership Rate
(Universe: Occupied Housing Units)

Group	%
Total Population	55.9
Hispanic or Latino (of any race)	50.1
Central American, ex. Mexican	53.9
Guatemalan	49.6
Honduran	42.4
Nicaraguan	52.0
Panamanian	35.5
Salvadoran	58.7
Cuban	59.8
Dominican Republic	65.4
Mexican	49.2
Puerto Rican	43.3
South American	60.9
Argentinean	62.5
Colombian	59.7
Ecuadorian	72.7
Peruvian	58.3
Spaniard	67.0

Median Home Value

Group	Dollars
Total Population	181,500
Hispanic or Latino (of any race)	183,500
Central American, ex. Mexican	181,600
Guatemalan	159,000
Salvadoran	209,900
Cuban	117,200
Mexican	185,000
Puerto Rican	154,500

Median Gross Rent

Group	Dollars
Total Population	915
Hispanic or Latino (of any race)	896
Central American, ex. Mexican	820
Guatemalan	740
Salvadoran	902
Cuban	753
Mexican	896
Puerto Rican	1,070

Median Household Income
(2010 Inflation-Adjusted Dollars)

Group	Dollars
Total Population	46,478
Hispanic or Latino (of any race)	42,228
Central American, ex. Mexican	45,189
Guatemalan	36,793
Salvadoran	51,449
Cuban	26,443
Mexican	42,123
Puerto Rican	49,702

Per Capita Income
(2010 Inflation-Adjusted Dollars)

Group	Dollars
Total Population	18,998
Hispanic or Latino (of any race)	13,035
Central American, ex. Mexican	15,235
Guatemalan	16,975
Salvadoran	14,679
Cuban	15,987
Mexican	12,505
Puerto Rican	17,170

Households with $100,000+ Income

Group	Number	%
Total Population	8,088	12.8
Hispanic or Latino (of any race)	1,654	7.7
Central American, ex. Mexican	158	9.0
Guatemalan	85	13.1
Salvadoran	65	7.5
Cuban	75	7.7
Mexican	1,302	7.6
Puerto Rican	51	7.9

Households with Food Stamps/SNAP Benefits During Past 12 Months

Group	Number	%
Total Population	7,155	11.3
Hispanic or Latino (of any race)	2,461	11.4
Central American, ex. Mexican	103	5.9
Guatemalan	73	11.2
Salvadoran	23	2.7
Cuban	211	21.6
Mexican	1,996	11.7
Puerto Rican	101	15.7

Poverty Rate
(Income in Past 12 Months Below Poverty Level)

Group	%
Total Population	17.2
Hispanic or Latino (of any race)	20.9
Central American, ex. Mexican	16.5
Guatemalan	14.0
Salvadoran	16.3
Cuban	33.5
Mexican	21.4
Puerto Rican	11.7

Whitney

Population

Group	Number	%TP[1]	%HP[2]
Total Population	38,585	100.0	–
Hispanic or Latino (of any race)	13,960	36.2	100.0
Central American, ex. Mexican	1,427	3.7	10.2
Guatemalan	288	0.7	2.1
Honduran	101	0.3	0.7
Nicaraguan	119	0.3	0.9
Salvadoran	834	2.2	6.0
Cuban	965	2.5	6.9
Mexican	9,597	24.9	68.7
Puerto Rican	386	1.0	2.8
South American	425	1.1	3.0
Peruvian	130	0.3	0.9
Spaniard	146	0.4	1.0

Population Growth: 2000–2010

Group	%
Total Population	111.2
Hispanic or Latino (of any race)	202.0
Central American, ex. Mexican	494.6
Salvadoran	595.0
Cuban	278.4
Mexican	208.3
Puerto Rican	177.7

Males per 100 Females

Group	Number
Total Population	98.6
Hispanic or Latino (of any race)	98.9
Central American, ex. Mexican	95.5
Guatemalan	85.8
Honduran	87.0
Nicaraguan	95.1
Salvadoran	101.9
Cuban	102.3
Mexican	101.0
Puerto Rican	82.1
South American	77.1
Peruvian	75.7
Spaniard	117.9

Average Household Size

Group	People
Total Population	2.73
Hispanic or Latino (of any race)	3.65
Central American, ex. Mexican	4.09
Guatemalan	4.05
Honduran	3.83
Nicaraguan	4.09
Salvadoran	4.17
Cuban	3.16
Mexican	3.79
Puerto Rican	2.76
South American	3.13
Peruvian	3.43
Spaniard	2.64

Median Age

Group	Years
Total Population	33.3
Hispanic or Latino (of any race)	26.2
Central American, ex. Mexican	30.3
Guatemalan	33.0
Honduran	32.9
Nicaraguan	34.5
Salvadoran	29.5
Cuban	36.0
Mexican	24.4
Puerto Rican	28.5
South American	34.6
Peruvian	34.0
Spaniard	37.8

High School Graduates
(Universe: Population 25 Years and Over)

Group	Number	%
Total Population	17,982	80.5
Hispanic or Latino (of any race)	4,470	61.9
Mexican	3,005	56.6

Four-Year College Graduates
(Universe: Population 25 Years and Over)

Group	Number	%
Total Population	3,338	14.9
Hispanic or Latino (of any race)	544	7.5
Mexican	189	3.6

Population Age 3–17 Enrolled in Public School
(Universe: Population Age 3–17 Enrolled in School)

Group	Number	%
Total Population	5,865	98.0
Hispanic or Latino (of any race)	3,289	97.9
Mexican	2,717	97.5

Notes: (1) Percent of total population; (2) Percent of Hispanic/Latino population; Profiles include places with an overall population of at least 125,000, OR an overall population of at least 25,000 where the Hispanic/Latino population is at least 20% of the overall population. In states where less than five places meet either of these criteria, we have included places with at least 10,000 total population with the highest percentage of Hispanic/Latino population. These places are identified with an asterisk (*); Please refer to the User's Guide for a full explanation of data.

Population Age 3–17 Enrolled in Private School
(Universe: Population Age 3–17 Enrolled in School)

Group	Number	%
Total Population	119	2.0
Hispanic or Latino (of any race)	71	2.1
Mexican	71	2.5

Foreign-Born Population

Group	Number	%
Total Population	9,946	27.8
Hispanic or Latino (of any race)	6,653	47.5
Mexican	4,816	45.7

Foreign-Born Naturalized U.S. Citizens

Group	Number	%
Total Population	3,660	36.8
Hispanic or Latino (of any race)	1,707	25.7
Mexican	1,106	23.0

Language Spoken at Home: English Only
(Universe: Population 5 Years and Over)

Group	Number	%
Total Population	18,759	57.8
Hispanic or Latino (of any race)	2,383	19.2
Mexican	1,533	16.4

Language Spoken at Home: Spanish
(Universe: Population 5 Years and Over)

Group	Number	%
Total Population	10,383	32.0
Hispanic or Latino (of any race)	9,971	80.5
Mexican	7,787	83.3

Unemployment Rate
(Universe: Population 16 Years and Over)

Group	%
Total Population	11.3
Hispanic or Latino (of any race)	9.9
Mexican	10.8

Class of Worker: Private Wage and Salary
(Universe: Civilian Employed Population 16 Years and Over)

Group	Number	%
Total Population	15,437	87.5
Hispanic or Latino (of any race)	6,067	91.7
Mexican	4,324	90.8

Class of Worker: Government
(Universe: Civilian Employed Population 16 Years and Over)

Group	Number	%
Total Population	1,729	9.8
Hispanic or Latino (of any race)	368	5.6
Mexican	294	6.2

Means of Transportation to Work: Car, Truck or Van
(Universe: Workers 16 Years and Over)

Group	Number	%
Total Population	15,611	90.3
Hispanic or Latino (of any race)	5,727	89.6
Mexican	4,118	89.4

Means of Transportation to Work: Public Transportation (ex. Taxicab)
(Universe: Workers 16 Years and Over)

Group	Number	%
Total Population	1,057	6.1
Hispanic or Latino (of any race)	497	7.8
Mexican	379	8.2

Homeownership Rate
(Universe: Occupied Housing Units)

Group	%
Total Population	55.3
Hispanic or Latino (of any race)	53.2
Central American, ex. Mexican	60.6
Guatemalan	65.0
Honduran	65.5
Nicaraguan	64.7
Salvadoran	60.2
Cuban	61.9
Mexican	51.6
Puerto Rican	43.1
South American	59.9
Peruvian	77.1
Spaniard	60.7

Median Home Value

Group	Dollars
Total Population	180,600
Hispanic or Latino (of any race)	210,000
Mexican	216,000

Median Gross Rent

Group	Dollars
Total Population	1,002
Hispanic or Latino (of any race)	942
Mexican	946

Median Household Income
(2010 Inflation-Adjusted Dollars)

Group	Dollars
Total Population	49,355
Hispanic or Latino (of any race)	45,634
Mexican	46,725

Per Capita Income
(2010 Inflation-Adjusted Dollars)

Group	Dollars
Total Population	20,997
Hispanic or Latino (of any race)	13,953
Mexican	13,693

Households with $100,000+ Income

Group	Number	%
Total Population	1,430	11.1
Hispanic or Latino (of any race)	241	6.6
Mexican	181	7.2

Households with Food Stamps/SNAP Benefits During Past 12 Months

Group	Number	%
Total Population	1,108	8.6
Hispanic or Latino (of any race)	446	12.3
Mexican	432	17.1

Poverty Rate
(Income in Past 12 Months Below Poverty Level)

Group	%
Total Population	12.6
Hispanic or Latino (of any race)	16.1
Mexican	18.4

Winchester

Population

Group	Number	%TP[1]	%HP[2]
Total Population	27,978	100.0	–
Hispanic or Latino (of any race)	12,491	44.6	100.0
Central American, ex. Mexican	1,437	5.1	11.5
Guatemalan	333	1.2	2.7
Honduran	135	0.5	1.1
Salvadoran	845	3.0	6.8
Cuban	985	3.5	7.9
Mexican	8,620	30.8	69.0
Puerto Rican	252	0.9	2.0
South American	326	1.2	2.6

Population Growth: 2000–2010

Group	%
Total Population	3.8
Hispanic or Latino (of any race)	59.7
Central American, ex. Mexican	205.1
Salvadoran	199.6
Cuban	33.6
Mexican	65.6
Puerto Rican	21.2
South American	148.9

Males per 100 Females

Group	Number
Total Population	110.0
Hispanic or Latino (of any race)	106.5
Central American, ex. Mexican	112.3
Guatemalan	117.6
Honduran	150.0
Salvadoran	105.1
Cuban	120.9
Mexican	106.5
Puerto Rican	83.9
South American	84.2

Average Household Size

Group	People
Total Population	2.38
Hispanic or Latino (of any race)	3.38
Central American, ex. Mexican	3.83
Guatemalan	4.14
Honduran	3.78
Salvadoran	3.84
Cuban	2.74
Mexican	3.59
Puerto Rican	2.38
South American	2.52

Median Age

Group	Years
Total Population	38.2
Hispanic or Latino (of any race)	28.2
Central American, ex. Mexican	31.1
Guatemalan	30.4
Honduran	31.3
Salvadoran	31.3
Cuban	41.4
Mexican	25.8
Puerto Rican	32.4
South American	46.4

High School Graduates
(Universe: Population 25 Years and Over)

Group	Number	%
Total Population	14,206	74.3
Hispanic or Latino (of any race)	3,398	51.2
Central American, ex. Mexican	439	65.4
Mexican	2,175	45.0

Four-Year College Graduates
(Universe: Population 25 Years and Over)

Group	Number	%
Total Population	3,153	16.5
Hispanic or Latino (of any race)	470	7.1
Central American, ex. Mexican	28	4.2
Mexican	271	5.6

Population Age 3–17 Enrolled in Public School
(Universe: Population Age 3–17 Enrolled in School)

Group	Number	%
Total Population	3,500	96.4
Hispanic or Latino (of any race)	2,415	98.1
Central American, ex. Mexican	240	100.0
Mexican	1,916	98.7

Population Age 3–17 Enrolled in Private School
(Universe: Population Age 3–17 Enrolled in School)

Group	Number	%
Total Population	131	3.6
Hispanic or Latino (of any race)	46	1.9
Central American, ex. Mexican	0	0.0
Mexican	26	1.3

Foreign-Born Population

Group	Number	%
Total Population	8,631	31.7
Hispanic or Latino (of any race)	6,096	52.7
Central American, ex. Mexican	679	65.4
Mexican	4,439	49.7

Foreign-Born Naturalized U.S. Citizens

Group	Number	%
Total Population	2,840	32.9
Hispanic or Latino (of any race)	1,307	21.4
Central American, ex. Mexican	156	23.0
Mexican	757	17.1

Language Spoken at Home: English Only
(Universe: Population 5 Years and Over)

Group	Number	%
Total Population	13,759	54.3
Hispanic or Latino (of any race)	1,297	12.5
Central American, ex. Mexican	55	5.5
Mexican	1,002	12.7

Language Spoken at Home: Spanish
(Universe: Population 5 Years and Over)

Group	Number	%
Total Population	9,173	36.2
Hispanic or Latino (of any race)	9,062	87.4

Notes: (1) Percent of total population; (2) Percent of Hispanic/Latino population; Profiles include places with an overall population of at least 125,000, OR an overall population of at least 25,000 where the Hispanic/Latino population is at least 20% of the overall population. In states where less than five places meet either of these criteria, we have included places with at least 10,000 total population with the highest percentage of Hispanic/Latino population. These places are identified with an asterisk (*); Please refer to the User's Guide for a full explanation of data.

Central American, ex. Mexican	940	94.5
Mexican	6,858	87.3

Unemployment Rate
(Universe: Population 16 Years and Over)

Group	%
Total Population	11.7
Hispanic or Latino (of any race)	9.1
Central American, ex. Mexican	16.1
Mexican	8.6

Class of Worker: Private Wage and Salary
(Universe: Civilian Employed Population 16 Years and Over)

Group	Number	%
Total Population	10,788	88.0
Hispanic or Latino (of any race)	4,617	91.0
Central American, ex. Mexican	348	77.7
Mexican	3,559	94.2

Class of Worker: Government
(Universe: Civilian Employed Population 16 Years and Over)

Group	Number	%
Total Population	775	6.3
Hispanic or Latino (of any race)	91	1.8
Central American, ex. Mexican	31	6.9
Mexican	23	0.6

Means of Transportation to Work: Car, Truck or Van
(Universe: Workers 16 Years and Over)

Group	Number	%
Total Population	9,777	81.7
Hispanic or Latino (of any race)	4,154	83.3
Central American, ex. Mexican	352	78.6
Mexican	3,088	83.2

Means of Transportation to Work: Public Transportation (ex. Taxicab)
(Universe: Workers 16 Years and Over)

Group	Number	%
Total Population	826	6.9
Hispanic or Latino (of any race)	452	9.1
Central American, ex. Mexican	16	3.6
Mexican	383	10.3

Homeownership Rate
(Universe: Occupied Housing Units)

Group	%
Total Population	41.5
Hispanic or Latino (of any race)	32.6
Central American, ex. Mexican	34.4
Guatemalan	32.6
Honduran	28.9
Salvadoran	37.1
Cuban	37.9
Mexican	30.3
Puerto Rican	25.8
South American	41.7

Median Home Value

Group	Dollars
Total Population	179,200
Hispanic or Latino (of any race)	178,800
Central American, ex. Mexican	212,500
Mexican	133,900

Median Gross Rent

Group	Dollars
Total Population	881
Hispanic or Latino (of any race)	913
Central American, ex. Mexican	1,510
Mexican	913

Median Household Income
(2010 Inflation-Adjusted Dollars)

Group	Dollars
Total Population	37,367
Hispanic or Latino (of any race)	38,288
Central American, ex. Mexican	33,657
Mexican	38,505

Per Capita Income
(2010 Inflation-Adjusted Dollars)

Group	Dollars
Total Population	24,280
Hispanic or Latino (of any race)	14,703
Central American, ex. Mexican	15,530
Mexican	13,348

Households with $100,000+ Income

Group	Number	%
Total Population	1,337	11.6
Hispanic or Latino (of any race)	319	9.9
Central American, ex. Mexican	26	12.8
Mexican	191	7.9

Households with Food Stamps/SNAP Benefits During Past 12 Months

Group	Number	%
Total Population	1,281	11.1
Hispanic or Latino (of any race)	366	11.3
Central American, ex. Mexican	42	20.7
Mexican	254	10.5

Poverty Rate
(Income in Past 12 Months Below Poverty Level)

Group	%
Total Population	19.5
Hispanic or Latino (of any race)	18.9
Central American, ex. Mexican	2.7
Mexican	20.9

Notes: (1) Percent of total population; (2) Percent of Hispanic/Latino population; Profiles include places with an overall population of at least 125,000, OR an overall population of at least 25,000 where the Hispanic/Latino population is at least 20% of the overall population. In states where less than five places meet either of these criteria, we have included places with at least 10,000 total population with the highest percentage of Hispanic/Latino population. These places are identified with an asterisk (*); Please refer to the User's Guide for a full explanation of data.

New Hampshire

EDITOR'S NOTE: For a place to be included in this edition, it must meet one of two criteria. Either its overall population is at least 125,000, OR its overall population is at least 25,000 and its Hispanic/Latino population is at least 20% of the overall population. In New Hampshire, less than five places meet either of these criteria. In an effort to include at least five places for each state, we have included places with at least 10,000 total population with the highest percentage of Hispanic/Latino population. These places are identified with an asterisk (*). For the state of New Hampshire, the following locations are included:

Derry*
Hanover*
Manchester*
Nashua*
Salem*

Section Two: State & Place Profiles starts with the state profile, followed by place profiles that meet the criteria above. Places are listed alphabetically within each state. All states, all counties and places that meet the above criteria are ranked and compared in *Section Three: Rankings & Comparisons*, on page 1055.

For a more detailed look at the Hispanic/Latino population in New Hampshire, a companion web site is available at no additional charge with purchase of this print edition. Visit http://gold.greyhouse.com/page/info_hispanic for more information.

The web site includes data for all counties and places in New Hampshire with Hispanic/Latino population, plus ten additional topics: Self Employed Worker; Walked to Work; Worked from Home; Mean Travel Time to Work; Mean Household Income; Households with Cash Public Assistance; Mean Cash Pubic Assistance; Poverty Rates for 18 and Under, 18 to 64, and 65 and Over.

Population

Group	Number	%TP[1]	%HP[2]
Total Population	1,316,470	100.0	–
Hispanic or Latino (of any race)	36,704	2.8	100.0
Central American, ex. Mexican	2,731	0.2	7.4
Costa Rican	233	<0.1	0.6
Guatemalan	743	0.1	2.0
Honduran	506	<0.1	1.4
Nicaraguan	174	<0.1	0.5
Panamanian	214	<0.1	0.6
Salvadoran	823	0.1	2.2
Cuban	1,349	0.1	3.7
Dominican Republic	4,460	0.3	12.2
Mexican	7,822	0.6	21.3
Puerto Rican	11,729	0.9	32.0
South American	4,266	0.3	11.6
Argentinean	322	<0.1	0.9
Chilean	224	<0.1	0.6
Colombian	1,899	0.1	5.2
Ecuadorian	595	<0.1	1.6
Peruvian	471	<0.1	1.3
Uruguayan	351	<0.1	1.0
Venezuelan	243	<0.1	0.7
Spaniard	1,032	0.1	2.8

Population Growth: 2000–2010

Group	%
Total Population	6.5
Hispanic or Latino (of any race)	79.1
Central American, ex. Mexican	202.4
Guatemalan	301.6
Honduran	232.9
Panamanian	62.1
Salvadoran	245.8
Cuban	71.8
Dominican Republic	201.4
Mexican	70.4
Puerto Rican	88.7
South American	119.1
Colombian	102.0
Ecuadorian	179.3
Peruvian	178.7
Uruguayan	96.1
Venezuelan	88.4
Spaniard	448.9

Males per 100 Females

Group	Number
Total Population	97.3
Hispanic or Latino (of any race)	100.4
Central American, ex. Mexican	106.7
Costa Rican	84.9
Guatemalan	115.4
Honduran	115.3
Nicaraguan	77.6
Panamanian	71.2
Salvadoran	120.1
Cuban	93.8
Dominican Republic	93.2
Mexican	107.9
Puerto Rican	102.1
South American	82.8
Argentinean	85.1
Chilean	86.7
Colombian	80.9
Ecuadorian	90.7
Peruvian	79.1
Uruguayan	84.7
Venezuelan	65.3
Spaniard	93.6

Average Household Size

Group	People
Total Population	2.46
Hispanic or Latino (of any race)	3.07
Central American, ex. Mexican	3.49
Costa Rican	3.24
Guatemalan	3.44
Honduran	3.57
Nicaraguan	3.44
Panamanian	2.52
Salvadoran	3.84
Cuban	2.66
Dominican Republic	3.31
Mexican	3.27
Puerto Rican	2.99
South American	3.02
Argentinean	2.82
Chilean	2.83
Colombian	3.09
Ecuadorian	3.20
Peruvian	2.95
Uruguayan	2.79
Venezuelan	2.76
Spaniard	2.58

Median Age

Group	Years
Total Population	41.1
Hispanic or Latino (of any race)	24.6
Central American, ex. Mexican	25.8
Costa Rican	26.1
Guatemalan	20.0
Honduran	26.4
Nicaraguan	28.5
Panamanian	34.5
Salvadoran	27.3
Cuban	29.2
Dominican Republic	25.1
Mexican	22.8
Puerto Rican	21.9
South American	32.0
Argentinean	32.8
Chilean	27.9
Colombian	32.1
Ecuadorian	32.0
Peruvian	28.4
Uruguayan	38.6
Venezuelan	35.1
Spaniard	33.1

High School Graduates

(Universe: Population 25 Years and Over)

Group	Number	%
Total Population	814,346	90.9
Hispanic or Latino (of any race)	13,823	79.8
Central American, ex. Mexican	994	65.5
Guatemalan	205	52.3
Cuban	718	87.9
Dominican Republic	1,374	82.3
Mexican	2,429	68.0
Puerto Rican	3,911	79.1
South American	2,514	91.2
Colombian	1,113	89.0
Spaniard	657	96.9

Four-Year College Graduates

(Universe: Population 25 Years and Over)

Group	Number	%
Total Population	294,200	32.9
Hispanic or Latino (of any race)	4,419	25.5
Central American, ex. Mexican	112	7.4
Guatemalan	17	4.3
Cuban	251	30.7
Dominican Republic	343	20.6
Mexican	841	23.5
Puerto Rican	1,003	20.3
South American	1,186	43.0
Colombian	427	34.2
Spaniard	252	37.2

Population Age 3–17 Enrolled in Public School

(Universe: Population Age 3–17 Enrolled in School)

Group	Number	%
Total Population	196,698	84.5
Hispanic or Latino (of any race)	8,597	88.6
Central American, ex. Mexican	659	91.0
Guatemalan	236	92.9
Cuban	190	80.5
Dominican Republic	680	82.3
Mexican	1,901	91.9
Puerto Rican	3,144	90.2
South American	1,176	82.4
Colombian	749	93.3
Spaniard	206	91.2

Population Age 3–17 Enrolled in Private School

(Universe: Population Age 3–17 Enrolled in School)

Group	Number	%
Total Population	35,995	15.5
Hispanic or Latino (of any race)	1,102	11.4
Central American, ex. Mexican	65	9.0
Guatemalan	18	7.1
Cuban	46	19.5
Dominican Republic	146	17.7
Mexican	167	8.1
Puerto Rican	340	9.8
South American	251	17.6
Colombian	54	6.7
Spaniard	20	8.8

Foreign-Born Population

Group	Number	%
Total Population	68,999	5.3
Hispanic or Latino (of any race)	10,019	28.4
Central American, ex. Mexican	1,739	60.2
Guatemalan	603	70.9
Cuban	414	29.7
Dominican Republic	1,689	50.4
Mexican	2,375	31.9
Puerto Rican	58	0.5
South American	2,795	55.3
Colombian	1,384	55.2
Spaniard	174	16.6

Notes: (1) Percent of total population; (2) Percent of Hispanic/Latino population; Profiles include places with an overall population of at least 125,000, OR an overall population of at least 25,000 where the Hispanic/Latino population is at least 20% of the overall population. In states where less than five places meet either of these criteria, we have included places with at least 10,000 total population with the highest percentage of Hispanic/Latino population. These places are identified with an asterisk (*); Please refer to the User's Guide for a full explanation of data.

Foreign-Born Naturalized U.S. Citizens

Group	Number	%
Total Population	35,302	51.2
Hispanic or Latino (of any race)	4,314	43.1
Central American, ex. Mexican	824	47.4
Guatemalan	279	46.3
Cuban	302	72.9
Dominican Republic	763	45.2
Mexican	509	21.4
Puerto Rican	30	51.7
South American	1,553	55.6
Colombian	742	53.6
Spaniard	79	45.4

Language Spoken at Home: English Only
(Universe: Population 5 Years and Over)

Group	Number	%
Total Population	1,141,853	92.0
Hispanic or Latino (of any race)	12,770	40.8
Central American, ex. Mexican	609	24.6
Guatemalan	212	30.3
Cuban	759	58.7
Dominican Republic	353	11.9
Mexican	3,051	46.7
Puerto Rican	4,931	49.3
South American	1,180	26.0
Colombian	489	21.8
Spaniard	661	66.0

Language Spoken at Home: Spanish
(Universe: Population 5 Years and Over)

Group	Number	%
Total Population	26,623	2.1
Hispanic or Latino (of any race)	18,342	58.5
Central American, ex. Mexican	1,864	75.4
Guatemalan	488	69.7
Cuban	535	41.3
Dominican Republic	2,604	88.1
Mexican	3,463	53.0
Puerto Rican	5,036	50.4
South American	3,358	73.9
Colombian	1,754	78.0
Spaniard	302	30.1

Unemployment Rate
(Universe: Population 16 Years and Over)

Group	%
Total Population	5.9
Hispanic or Latino (of any race)	11.1
Central American, ex. Mexican	18.4
Guatemalan	2.3
Cuban	4.0
Dominican Republic	11.6
Mexican	10.9
Puerto Rican	12.9
South American	8.7
Colombian	9.2
Spaniard	17.3

Class of Worker: Private Wage and Salary
(Universe: Civilian Employed Population 16 Years and Over)

Group	Number	%
Total Population	545,954	78.5
Hispanic or Latino (of any race)	12,835	88.8
Central American, ex. Mexican	1,016	91.1
Guatemalan	302	100.0
Cuban	562	82.8
Dominican Republic	1,438	87.9
Mexican	2,815	94.4
Puerto Rican	3,407	87.8
South American	2,163	88.5
Colombian	976	85.2
Spaniard	352	85.6

Class of Worker: Government
(Universe: Civilian Employed Population 16 Years and Over)

Group	Number	%
Total Population	92,838	13.4
Hispanic or Latino (of any race)	1,179	8.2
Central American, ex. Mexican	60	5.4
Guatemalan	0	0.0
Cuban	96	14.1
Dominican Republic	198	12.1
Mexican	115	3.9
Puerto Rican	327	8.4
South American	193	7.9
Colombian	116	10.1
Spaniard	49	11.9

Means of Transportation to Work: Car, Truck or Van
(Universe: Workers 16 Years and Over)

Group	Number	%
Total Population	608,212	89.8
Hispanic or Latino (of any race)	12,403	88.2
Central American, ex. Mexican	859	80.7
Guatemalan	173	65.3
Cuban	651	95.9
Dominican Republic	1,489	92.9
Mexican	2,336	82.3
Puerto Rican	3,444	88.6
South American	2,105	89.5
Colombian	1,018	92.9
Spaniard	358	87.1

Means of Transportation to Work: Public Transportation (ex. Taxicab)
(Universe: Workers 16 Years and Over)

Group	Number	%
Total Population	5,050	0.7
Hispanic or Latino (of any race)	188	1.3
Central American, ex. Mexican	12	1.1
Guatemalan	12	4.5
Cuban	18	2.7
Dominican Republic	0	0.0
Mexican	104	3.7
Puerto Rican	35	0.9
South American	19	0.8
Colombian	7	0.6
Spaniard	0	0.0

Homeownership Rate
(Universe: Occupied Housing Units)

Group	%
Total Population	71.0
Hispanic or Latino (of any race)	39.7
Central American, ex. Mexican	41.4
Costa Rican	59.2
Guatemalan	42.5
Honduran	25.2
Nicaraguan	46.2
Panamanian	55.8
Salvadoran	40.5
Cuban	61.8
Dominican Republic	29.4
Mexican	41.4
Puerto Rican	32.1
South American	50.2
Argentinean	62.1
Chilean	51.6
Colombian	45.8
Ecuadorian	45.0
Peruvian	48.2
Uruguayan	57.6
Venezuelan	64.5
Spaniard	67.7

Median Home Value

Group	Dollars
Total Population	253,200
Hispanic or Latino (of any race)	242,100
Central American, ex. Mexican	269,100
Guatemalan	182,200
Cuban	303,300
Dominican Republic	216,200
Mexican	236,700
Puerto Rican	235,600
South American	294,000
Colombian	295,700
Spaniard	219,300

Median Gross Rent

Group	Dollars
Total Population	933
Hispanic or Latino (of any race)	1,011
Central American, ex. Mexican	1,140
Guatemalan	939
Cuban	1,335
Dominican Republic	800
Mexican	943
Puerto Rican	995
South American	1,103
Colombian	1,113
Spaniard	1,186

Median Household Income
(2010 Inflation-Adjusted Dollars)

Group	Dollars
Total Population	63,277
Hispanic or Latino (of any race)	51,336
Central American, ex. Mexican	47,262
Guatemalan	49,630
Cuban	72,986
Dominican Republic	38,984
Mexican	41,007
Puerto Rican	49,145
South American	73,375
Colombian	70,087
Spaniard	65,323

Per Capita Income
(2010 Inflation-Adjusted Dollars)

Group	Dollars
Total Population	31,422
Hispanic or Latino (of any race)	17,813
Central American, ex. Mexican	13,922
Guatemalan	9,903
Cuban	30,224
Dominican Republic	16,864
Mexican	14,485
Puerto Rican	16,278
South American	23,202
Colombian	19,139
Spaniard	28,660

Households with $100,000+ Income

Group	Number	%
Total Population	136,096	26.5
Hispanic or Latino (of any race)	1,761	18.6
Central American, ex. Mexican	74	10.2
Guatemalan	9	5.6
Cuban	143	31.8
Dominican Republic	143	13.4
Mexican	263	14.5
Puerto Rican	466	15.7
South American	397	30.4
Colombian	179	27.5
Spaniard	77	24.5

Households with Food Stamps/SNAP Benefits During Past 12 Months

Group	Number	%
Total Population	29,881	5.8
Hispanic or Latino (of any race)	1,497	15.8
Central American, ex. Mexican	129	17.8
Guatemalan	6	3.7
Cuban	26	5.8
Dominican Republic	224	21.0
Mexican	230	12.7
Puerto Rican	705	23.7
South American	97	7.4
Colombian	78	12.0
Spaniard	0	0.0

Poverty Rate
(Income in Past 12 Months Below Poverty Level)

Group	%
Total Population	7.8
Hispanic or Latino (of any race)	15.8
Central American, ex. Mexican	16.1
Guatemalan	9.8
Cuban	11.1
Dominican Republic	10.4
Mexican	16.9
Puerto Rican	22.6
South American	5.4
Colombian	5.2
Spaniard	10.0

Derry*

Population

Group	Number	%TP[1]	%HP[2]
Total Population	22,015	100.0	-

Notes: (1) Percent of total population; (2) Percent of Hispanic/Latino population; Profiles include places with an overall population of at least 125,000, OR an overall population of at least 25,000 where the Hispanic/Latino population is at least 20% of the overall population. In states where less than five places meet either of these criteria, we have included places with at least 10,000 total population with the highest percentage of Hispanic/Latino population. These places are identified with an asterisk (*); Please refer to the User's Guide for a full explanation of data.

Hispanic or Latino (of any race)	793	3.6	100.0
Mexican	124	0.6	15.6
Puerto Rican	291	1.3	36.7

Population Growth: 2000–2010

Group	%
Total Population	-2.9
Hispanic or Latino (of any race)	58.3
Puerto Rican	72.2

Males per 100 Females

Group	Number
Total Population	98.6
Hispanic or Latino (of any race)	102.3
Mexican	96.8
Puerto Rican	102.1

Average Household Size

Group	People
Total Population	2.48
Hispanic or Latino (of any race)	2.84
Mexican	2.94
Puerto Rican	2.85

Median Age

Group	Years
Total Population	37.5
Hispanic or Latino (of any race)	25.8
Mexican	26.0
Puerto Rican	22.9

High School Graduates
(Universe: Population 25 Years and Over)

Group	Number	%
Total Population	13,411	90.3

Four-Year College Graduates
(Universe: Population 25 Years and Over)

Group	Number	%
Total Population	4,219	28.4

Population Age 3–17 Enrolled in Public School
(Universe: Population Age 3–17 Enrolled in School)

Group	Number	%
Total Population	3,468	85.8

Population Age 3–17 Enrolled in Private School
(Universe: Population Age 3–17 Enrolled in School)

Group	Number	%
Total Population	573	14.2

Foreign-Born Population

Group	Number	%
Total Population	1,545	6.8

Foreign-Born Naturalized U.S. Citizens

Group	Number	%
Total Population	810	52.4

Language Spoken at Home: English Only
(Universe: Population 5 Years and Over)

Group	Number	%
Total Population	19,287	89.9

Language Spoken at Home: Spanish
(Universe: Population 5 Years and Over)

Group	Number	%
Total Population	456	2.1

Unemployment Rate
(Universe: Population 16 Years and Over)

Group	%
Total Population	8.3

Class of Worker: Private Wage and Salary
(Universe: Civilian Employed Population 16 Years and Over)

Group	Number	%
Total Population	10,619	85.1

Class of Worker: Government
(Universe: Civilian Employed Population 16 Years and Over)

Group	Number	%
Total Population	1,169	9.4

Means of Transportation to Work: Car, Truck or Van
(Universe: Workers 16 Years and Over)

Group	Number	%
Total Population	11,371	94.5

Means of Transportation to Work: Public Transportation (ex. Taxicab)
(Universe: Workers 16 Years and Over)

Group	Number	%
Total Population	31	0.3

Homeownership Rate
(Universe: Occupied Housing Units)

Group	%
Total Population	57.3
Hispanic or Latino (of any race)	37.9
Mexican	33.3
Puerto Rican	28.8

Median Home Value

Group	Dollars
Total Population	225,600

Median Gross Rent

Group	Dollars
Total Population	972

Median Household Income
(2010 Inflation-Adjusted Dollars)

Group	Dollars
Total Population	63,526

Per Capita Income
(2010 Inflation-Adjusted Dollars)

Group	Dollars
Total Population	28,048

Households with $100,000+ Income

Group	Number	%
Total Population	2,307	26.4

Households with Food Stamps/SNAP Benefits During Past 12 Months

Group	Number	%
Total Population	538	6.1

Poverty Rate
(Income in Past 12 Months Below Poverty Level)

Group	%
Total Population	10.0

Hanover*

Population

Group	Number	%TP[1]	%HP[2]
Total Population	11,260	100.0	–
Hispanic or Latino (of any race)	438	3.9	100.0
Mexican	111	1.0	25.3
South American	112	1.0	25.6

Population Growth: 2000–2010

Group	%
Total Population	3.8
Hispanic or Latino (of any race)	58.7

Males per 100 Females

Group	Number
Total Population	96.2
Hispanic or Latino (of any race)	102.8
Mexican	109.4
South American	119.6

Average Household Size

Group	People
Total Population	2.37
Hispanic or Latino (of any race)	2.92
Mexican	3.27
South American	2.64

Median Age

Group	Years
Total Population	23.0
Hispanic or Latino (of any race)	20.7
Mexican	19.9
South American	21.2

High School Graduates
(Universe: Population 25 Years and Over)

Group	Number	%
Total Population	4,704	97.1

Four-Year College Graduates
(Universe: Population 25 Years and Over)

Group	Number	%
Total Population	3,993	82.4

Population Age 3–17 Enrolled in Public School
(Universe: Population Age 3–17 Enrolled in School)

Group	Number	%
Total Population	1,407	92.2

Population Age 3–17 Enrolled in Private School
(Universe: Population Age 3–17 Enrolled in School)

Group	Number	%
Total Population	119	7.8

Foreign-Born Population

Group	Number	%
Total Population	1,526	13.5

Foreign-Born Naturalized U.S. Citizens

Group	Number	%
Total Population	446	29.2

Language Spoken at Home: English Only
(Universe: Population 5 Years and Over)

Group	Number	%
Total Population	8,739	79.8

Language Spoken at Home: Spanish
(Universe: Population 5 Years and Over)

Group	Number	%
Total Population	341	3.1

Unemployment Rate
(Universe: Population 16 Years and Over)

Group	%
Total Population	1.8

Class of Worker: Private Wage and Salary
(Universe: Civilian Employed Population 16 Years and Over)

Group	Number	%
Total Population	3,971	82.4

Class of Worker: Government
(Universe: Civilian Employed Population 16 Years and Over)

Group	Number	%
Total Population	458	9.5

Means of Transportation to Work: Car, Truck or Van
(Universe: Workers 16 Years and Over)

Group	Number	%
Total Population	2,319	49.2

Means of Transportation to Work: Public Transportation (ex. Taxicab)
(Universe: Workers 16 Years and Over)

Group	Number	%
Total Population	79	1.7

Homeownership Rate
(Universe: Occupied Housing Units)

Group	%
Total Population	62.5
Hispanic or Latino (of any race)	40.8
Mexican	27.3
South American	63.6

Median Home Value

Group	Dollars
Total Population	494,800

Median Gross Rent

Group	Dollars
Total Population	1,230

Notes: (1) Percent of total population; (2) Percent of Hispanic/Latino population; Profiles include places with an overall population of at least 125,000, OR an overall population of at least 25,000 where the Hispanic/Latino population is at least 20% of the overall population. In states where less than five places meet either of these criteria, we have included places with at least 10,000 total population with the highest percentage of Hispanic/Latino population. These places are identified with an asterisk (*); Please refer to the User's Guide for a full explanation of data.

Median Household Income
(2010 Inflation-Adjusted Dollars)

Group	Dollars
Total Population	88,485

Per Capita Income
(2010 Inflation-Adjusted Dollars)

Group	Dollars
Total Population	34,915

Households with $100,000+ Income

Group	Number	%
Total Population	1,356	45.7

Households with Food Stamps/SNAP Benefits During Past 12 Months

Group	Number	%
Total Population	0	0.0

Poverty Rate
(Income in Past 12 Months Below Poverty Level)

Group	%
Total Population	11.0

Manchester*

Population

Group	Number	%TP[1]	%HP[2]
Total Population	109,565	100.0	–
Hispanic or Latino (of any race)	8,883	8.1	100.0
Central American, ex. Mexican	862	0.8	9.7
Guatemalan	134	0.1	1.5
Honduran	242	0.2	2.7
Salvadoran	386	0.4	4.3
Cuban	109	0.1	1.2
Dominican Republic	1,215	1.1	13.7
Mexican	1,914	1.7	21.5
Puerto Rican	3,315	3.0	37.3
South American	762	0.7	8.6
Colombian	334	0.3	3.8
Uruguayan	211	0.2	2.4

Population Growth: 2000–2010

Group	%
Total Population	2.4
Hispanic or Latino (of any race)	79.7
Central American, ex. Mexican	342.1
Dominican Republic	231.1
Mexican	56.9
Puerto Rican	83.0
South American	94.4
Colombian	94.2
Uruguayan	74.4

Males per 100 Females

Group	Number
Total Population	98.5
Hispanic or Latino (of any race)	108.2
Central American, ex. Mexican	134.2
Guatemalan	162.7
Honduran	137.3
Salvadoran	132.5
Cuban	94.6
Dominican Republic	98.9
Mexican	118.2
Puerto Rican	106.7
South American	83.6
Colombian	86.6
Uruguayan	85.1

Average Household Size

Group	People
Total Population	2.34
Hispanic or Latino (of any race)	3.25
Central American, ex. Mexican	3.87
Guatemalan	3.71
Honduran	3.96
Salvadoran	4.16
Cuban	2.92
Dominican Republic	3.32
Mexican	3.71
Puerto Rican	3.08
South American	2.86
Colombian	2.97
Uruguayan	2.61

Median Age

Group	Years
Total Population	36.0
Hispanic or Latino (of any race)	24.3
Central American, ex. Mexican	27.5
Guatemalan	26.5
Honduran	26.2
Salvadoran	28.7
Cuban	26.5
Dominican Republic	25.1
Mexican	23.6
Puerto Rican	21.4
South American	34.2
Colombian	31.6
Uruguayan	40.7

High School Graduates
(Universe: Population 25 Years and Over)

Group	Number	%
Total Population	63,778	86.1
Hispanic or Latino (of any race)	2,887	72.4
Mexican	562	56.1
Puerto Rican	721	66.6
South American	570	93.3

Four-Year College Graduates
(Universe: Population 25 Years and Over)

Group	Number	%
Total Population	18,734	25.3
Hispanic or Latino (of any race)	612	15.4
Mexican	161	16.1
Puerto Rican	107	9.9
South American	259	42.4

Population Age 3–17 Enrolled in Public School
(Universe: Population Age 3–17 Enrolled in School)

Group	Number	%
Total Population	15,078	84.6
Hispanic or Latino (of any race)	2,116	95.1
Mexican	615	91.8
Puerto Rican	625	98.9
South American	273	97.5

Population Age 3–17 Enrolled in Private School
(Universe: Population Age 3–17 Enrolled in School)

Group	Number	%
Total Population	2,742	15.4
Hispanic or Latino (of any race)	108	4.9
Mexican	55	8.2
Puerto Rican	7	1.1
South American	7	2.5

Foreign-Born Population

Group	Number	%
Total Population	12,676	11.5
Hispanic or Latino (of any race)	2,658	33.1
Mexican	833	39.7
Puerto Rican	7	0.3
South American	634	57.2

Foreign-Born Naturalized U.S. Citizens

Group	Number	%
Total Population	5,692	44.9
Hispanic or Latino (of any race)	861	32.4
Mexican	143	17.2
Puerto Rican	0	0.0
South American	420	66.2

Language Spoken at Home: English Only
(Universe: Population 5 Years and Over)

Group	Number	%
Total Population	82,978	81.2
Hispanic or Latino (of any race)	1,591	22.9
Mexican	471	25.8
Puerto Rican	664	31.5
South American	36	3.7

Language Spoken at Home: Spanish
(Universe: Population 5 Years and Over)

Group	Number	%
Total Population	6,230	6.1
Hispanic or Latino (of any race)	5,370	77.1
Mexican	1,358	74.2
Puerto Rican	1,442	68.5
South American	933	96.3

Unemployment Rate
(Universe: Population 16 Years and Over)

Group	%
Total Population	7.1
Hispanic or Latino (of any race)	10.7
Mexican	14.0
Puerto Rican	10.3
South American	12.0

Class of Worker: Private Wage and Salary
(Universe: Civilian Employed Population 16 Years and Over)

Group	Number	%
Total Population	48,283	84.0
Hispanic or Latino (of any race)	2,993	90.7
Mexican	774	96.4
Puerto Rican	683	90.0
South American	432	81.8

Class of Worker: Government
(Universe: Civilian Employed Population 16 Years and Over)

Group	Number	%
Total Population	6,370	11.1
Hispanic or Latino (of any race)	219	6.6
Mexican	11	1.4
Puerto Rican	76	10.0
South American	74	14.0

Means of Transportation to Work: Car, Truck or Van
(Universe: Workers 16 Years and Over)

Group	Number	%
Total Population	52,089	92.8
Hispanic or Latino (of any race)	2,779	87.7
Mexican	635	84.3
Puerto Rican	610	81.4
South American	484	91.7

Means of Transportation to Work: Public Transportation (ex. Taxicab)
(Universe: Workers 16 Years and Over)

Group	Number	%
Total Population	500	0.9
Hispanic or Latino (of any race)	49	1.5
Mexican	14	1.9
Puerto Rican	28	3.7
South American	7	1.3

Homeownership Rate
(Universe: Occupied Housing Units)

Group	%
Total Population	47.3
Hispanic or Latino (of any race)	20.8
Central American, ex. Mexican	28.3
Guatemalan	14.7
Honduran	17.5
Salvadoran	34.4
Cuban	29.7
Dominican Republic	20.1
Mexican	20.9
Puerto Rican	14.1
South American	38.7
Colombian	38.6
Uruguayan	46.8

Median Home Value

Group	Dollars
Total Population	235,700
Hispanic or Latino (of any race)	230,300
Mexican	217,800
Puerto Rican	215,300
South American	237,100

Median Gross Rent

Group	Dollars
Total Population	949
Hispanic or Latino (of any race)	947
Mexican	981
Puerto Rican	845
South American	757

Median Household Income
(2010 Inflation-Adjusted Dollars)

Group	Dollars
Total Population	53,377

Notes: (1) Percent of total population; (2) Percent of Hispanic/Latino population; Profiles include places with an overall population of at least 125,000, OR an overall population of at least 25,000 where the Hispanic/Latino population is at least 20% of the overall population. In states where less than five places meet either of these criteria, we have included places with at least 10,000 total population with the highest percentage of Hispanic/Latino population. These places are identified with an asterisk (*); Please refer to the User's Guide for a full explanation of data.

Hispanic or Latino (of any race)	37,479
Mexican	36,905
Puerto Rican	26,297
South American	54,188

Per Capita Income
(2010 Inflation-Adjusted Dollars)

Group	Dollars
Total Population	27,002
Hispanic or Latino (of any race)	14,204
Mexican	11,457
Puerto Rican	9,925
South American	19,139

Households with $100,000+ Income

Group	Number	%
Total Population	7,853	17.3
Hispanic or Latino (of any race)	129	5.8
Mexican	0	0.0
Puerto Rican	0	0.0
South American	43	13.6

Households with Food Stamps/SNAP Benefits During Past 12 Months

Group	Number	%
Total Population	5,159	11.4
Hispanic or Latino (of any race)	532	23.9
Mexican	59	10.5
Puerto Rican	356	46.5
South American	0	0.0

Poverty Rate
(Income in Past 12 Months Below Poverty Level)

Group	%
Total Population	13.2
Hispanic or Latino (of any race)	21.1
Mexican	20.5
Puerto Rican	37.7
South American	0.0

Nashua*

Population

Group	Number	%TP[1]	%HP[2]
Total Population	86,494	100.0	–
Hispanic or Latino (of any race)	8,510	9.8	100.0
Central American, ex. Mexican	400	0.5	4.7
Honduran	110	0.1	1.3
Salvadoran	150	0.2	1.8
Cuban	179	0.2	2.1
Dominican Republic	1,639	1.9	19.3
Mexican	1,825	2.1	21.4
Puerto Rican	2,577	3.0	30.3
South American	1,047	1.2	12.3
Colombian	671	0.8	7.9
Ecuadorian	195	0.2	2.3

Population Growth: 2000–2010

Group	%
Total Population	-0.1
Hispanic or Latino (of any race)	57.9
Central American, ex. Mexican	135.3
Dominican Republic	162.7
Mexican	39.7
Puerto Rican	75.5
South American	77.2
Colombian	69.4

Males per 100 Females

Group	Number
Total Population	97.3
Hispanic or Latino (of any race)	99.5
Central American, ex. Mexican	98.0
Honduran	107.5
Salvadoran	108.3
Cuban	105.7
Dominican Republic	90.8
Mexican	118.0
Puerto Rican	95.5
South American	93.2
Colombian	82.3
Ecuadorian	124.1

Average Household Size

Group	People
Total Population	2.42
Hispanic or Latino (of any race)	3.24
Central American, ex. Mexican	3.54
Honduran	3.69
Salvadoran	3.59
Cuban	2.59
Dominican Republic	3.51
Mexican	3.75
Puerto Rican	2.91
South American	3.17
Colombian	3.22
Ecuadorian	3.42

Median Age

Group	Years
Total Population	38.5
Hispanic or Latino (of any race)	25.1
Central American, ex. Mexican	29.1
Honduran	31.0
Salvadoran	28.5
Cuban	32.5
Dominican Republic	26.2
Mexican	22.9
Puerto Rican	22.5
South American	34.0
Colombian	34.4
Ecuadorian	34.2

High School Graduates
(Universe: Population 25 Years and Over)

Group	Number	%
Total Population	53,055	89.8
Hispanic or Latino (of any race)	2,524	70.9
Dominican Republic	498	64.5
Mexican	305	52.3
Puerto Rican	919	83.3

Four-Year College Graduates
(Universe: Population 25 Years and Over)

Group	Number	%
Total Population	20,855	35.3
Hispanic or Latino (of any race)	636	17.9
Dominican Republic	147	19.0
Mexican	40	6.9
Puerto Rican	177	16.0

Population Age 3–17 Enrolled in Public School
(Universe: Population Age 3–17 Enrolled in School)

Group	Number	%
Total Population	12,326	82.8
Hispanic or Latino (of any race)	1,790	92.0
Dominican Republic	315	97.2
Mexican	299	100.0
Puerto Rican	731	86.5

Population Age 3–17 Enrolled in Private School
(Universe: Population Age 3–17 Enrolled in School)

Group	Number	%
Total Population	2,555	17.2
Hispanic or Latino (of any race)	156	8.0
Dominican Republic	9	2.8
Mexican	0	0.0
Puerto Rican	114	13.5

Foreign-Born Population

Group	Number	%
Total Population	10,692	12.3
Hispanic or Latino (of any race)	2,657	36.6
Dominican Republic	899	63.0
Mexican	556	46.8
Puerto Rican	0	0.0

Foreign-Born Naturalized U.S. Citizens

Group	Number	%
Total Population	4,608	43.1
Hispanic or Latino (of any race)	806	30.3
Dominican Republic	470	52.3
Mexican	44	7.9
Puerto Rican	0	0.0

Language Spoken at Home: English Only
(Universe: Population 5 Years and Over)

Group	Number	%
Total Population	65,321	80.1
Hispanic or Latino (of any race)	1,579	24.4
Dominican Republic	69	5.3
Mexican	239	22.8
Puerto Rican	849	37.7

Language Spoken at Home: Spanish
(Universe: Population 5 Years and Over)

Group	Number	%
Total Population	5,708	7.0
Hispanic or Latino (of any race)	4,867	75.2
Dominican Republic	1,243	94.7
Mexican	809	77.2
Puerto Rican	1,402	62.3

Unemployment Rate
(Universe: Population 16 Years and Over)

Group	%
Total Population	7.2
Hispanic or Latino (of any race)	11.9
Dominican Republic	17.0
Mexican	5.5
Puerto Rican	14.3

Class of Worker: Private Wage and Salary
(Universe: Civilian Employed Population 16 Years and Over)

Group	Number	%
Total Population	39,889	85.7
Hispanic or Latino (of any race)	2,925	91.0
Dominican Republic	736	98.0
Mexican	584	96.2
Puerto Rican	718	86.7

Class of Worker: Government
(Universe: Civilian Employed Population 16 Years and Over)

Group	Number	%
Total Population	4,163	8.9
Hispanic or Latino (of any race)	145	4.5
Dominican Republic	15	2.0
Mexican	13	2.1
Puerto Rican	55	6.6

Means of Transportation to Work: Car, Truck or Van
(Universe: Workers 16 Years and Over)

Group	Number	%
Total Population	40,788	89.7
Hispanic or Latino (of any race)	2,886	93.1
Dominican Republic	626	87.3
Mexican	474	83.7
Puerto Rican	814	98.3

Means of Transportation to Work: Public Transportation (ex. Taxicab)
(Universe: Workers 16 Years and Over)

Group	Number	%
Total Population	967	2.1
Hispanic or Latino (of any race)	36	1.2
Dominican Republic	0	0.0
Mexican	11	1.9
Puerto Rican	7	0.8

Homeownership Rate
(Universe: Occupied Housing Units)

Group	%
Total Population	59.0
Hispanic or Latino (of any race)	25.3
Central American, ex. Mexican	30.4
Honduran	18.8
Salvadoran	31.7
Cuban	54.5
Dominican Republic	24.5
Mexican	28.4
Puerto Rican	19.2
South American	30.1
Colombian	25.9
Ecuadorian	23.7

Median Home Value

Group	Dollars
Total Population	262,100
Hispanic or Latino (of any race)	224,300

Notes: (1) Percent of total population; (2) Percent of Hispanic/Latino population; Profiles include places with an overall population of at least 125,000, OR an overall population of at least 25,000 where the Hispanic/Latino population is at least 20% of the overall population. In states where less than five places meet either of these criteria, we have included places with at least 10,000 total population with the highest percentage of Hispanic/Latino population. These places are identified with an asterisk (*); Please refer to the User's Guide for a full explanation of data.

Dominican Republic	223,800
Mexican	163,500
Puerto Rican	218,700

Median Gross Rent

Group	Dollars
Total Population	1,063
Hispanic or Latino (of any race)	1,038
Dominican Republic	756
Mexican	826
Puerto Rican	1,302

Median Household Income
(2010 Inflation-Adjusted Dollars)

Group	Dollars
Total Population	65,476
Hispanic or Latino (of any race)	38,792
Dominican Republic	27,323
Mexican	27,065
Puerto Rican	37,955

Per Capita Income
(2010 Inflation-Adjusted Dollars)

Group	Dollars
Total Population	33,200
Hispanic or Latino (of any race)	15,156
Dominican Republic	15,635
Mexican	13,859
Puerto Rican	14,792

Households with $100,000+ Income

Group	Number	%
Total Population	9,707	27.6
Hispanic or Latino (of any race)	223	10.0
Dominican Republic	28	4.7
Mexican	29	9.0
Puerto Rican	46	6.5

Households with Food Stamps/SNAP Benefits During Past 12 Months

Group	Number	%
Total Population	2,694	7.7
Hispanic or Latino (of any race)	630	28.3
Dominican Republic	134	22.7
Mexican	97	30.1
Puerto Rican	229	32.5

Poverty Rate
(Income in Past 12 Months Below Poverty Level)

Group	%
Total Population	7.3
Hispanic or Latino (of any race)	22.3
Dominican Republic	12.6
Mexican	36.8
Puerto Rican	31.8

Salem*

Population

Group	Number	%TP[1]	%HP[2]
Total Population	28,776	100.0	–
Hispanic or Latino (of any race)	1,270	4.4	100.0
Central American, ex. Mexican	124	0.4	9.8
Dominican Republic	371	1.3	29.2
Puerto Rican	410	1.4	32.3
South American	113	0.4	8.9

Population Growth: 2000–2010

Group	%
Total Population	2.4
Hispanic or Latino (of any race)	130.1
Puerto Rican	166.2

Males per 100 Females

Group	Number
Total Population	98.1
Hispanic or Latino (of any race)	93.3
Central American, ex. Mexican	121.4
Dominican Republic	83.7
Puerto Rican	106.0
South American	73.8

Average Household Size

Group	People
Total Population	2.57
Hispanic or Latino (of any race)	2.98
Central American, ex. Mexican	3.72
Dominican Republic	2.95
Puerto Rican	2.98
South American	3.53

Median Age

Group	Years
Total Population	43.2
Hispanic or Latino (of any race)	27.4
Central American, ex. Mexican	30.7
Dominican Republic	28.6
Puerto Rican	23.6
South American	34.8

High School Graduates
(Universe: Population 25 Years and Over)

Group	Number	%
Total Population	18,191	90.4
Hispanic or Latino (of any race)	824	86.1

Four-Year College Graduates
(Universe: Population 25 Years and Over)

Group	Number	%
Total Population	5,877	29.2
Hispanic or Latino (of any race)	169	17.7

Population Age 3–17 Enrolled in Public School
(Universe: Population Age 3–17 Enrolled in School)

Group	Number	%
Total Population	4,399	82.7
Hispanic or Latino (of any race)	268	65.5

Population Age 3–17 Enrolled in Private School
(Universe: Population Age 3–17 Enrolled in School)

Group	Number	%
Total Population	918	17.3
Hispanic or Latino (of any race)	141	34.5

Foreign-Born Population

Group	Number	%
Total Population	2,692	9.3
Hispanic or Latino (of any race)	782	43.4

Foreign-Born Naturalized U.S. Citizens

Group	Number	%
Total Population	1,450	53.9
Hispanic or Latino (of any race)	451	57.7

Language Spoken at Home: English Only
(Universe: Population 5 Years and Over)

Group	Number	%
Total Population	23,488	85.6
Hispanic or Latino (of any race)	294	18.6

Language Spoken at Home: Spanish
(Universe: Population 5 Years and Over)

Group	Number	%
Total Population	1,605	5.9
Hispanic or Latino (of any race)	1,285	81.4

Unemployment Rate
(Universe: Population 16 Years and Over)

Group	%
Total Population	6.4
Hispanic or Latino (of any race)	7.7

Class of Worker: Private Wage and Salary
(Universe: Civilian Employed Population 16 Years and Over)

Group	Number	%
Total Population	12,761	82.4
Hispanic or Latino (of any race)	792	92.2

Class of Worker: Government
(Universe: Civilian Employed Population 16 Years and Over)

Group	Number	%
Total Population	1,891	12.2
Hispanic or Latino (of any race)	47	5.5

Means of Transportation to Work: Car, Truck or Van
(Universe: Workers 16 Years and Over)

Group	Number	%
Total Population	14,366	95.8
Hispanic or Latino (of any race)	822	100.0

Means of Transportation to Work: Public Transportation (ex. Taxicab)
(Universe: Workers 16 Years and Over)

Group	Number	%
Total Population	76	0.5
Hispanic or Latino (of any race)	0	0.0

Homeownership Rate
(Universe: Occupied Housing Units)

Group	%
Total Population	77.5
Hispanic or Latino (of any race)	41.6
Central American, ex. Mexican	37.5
Dominican Republic	44.2
Puerto Rican	37.4
South American	56.7

Median Home Value

Group	Dollars
Total Population	312,900
Hispanic or Latino (of any race)	257,900

Median Gross Rent

Group	Dollars
Total Population	988
Hispanic or Latino (of any race)	1,032

Median Household Income
(2010 Inflation-Adjusted Dollars)

Group	Dollars
Total Population	70,502
Hispanic or Latino (of any race)	50,170

Per Capita Income
(2010 Inflation-Adjusted Dollars)

Group	Dollars
Total Population	33,751
Hispanic or Latino (of any race)	21,206

Households with $100,000+ Income

Group	Number	%
Total Population	3,514	31.4
Hispanic or Latino (of any race)	143	30.2

Households with Food Stamps/SNAP Benefits During Past 12 Months

Group	Number	%
Total Population	367	3.3
Hispanic or Latino (of any race)	0	0.0

Poverty Rate
(Income in Past 12 Months Below Poverty Level)

Group	%
Total Population	3.5
Hispanic or Latino (of any race)	5.8

Notes: (1) Percent of total population; (2) Percent of Hispanic/Latino population; Profiles include places with an overall population of at least 125,000, OR an overall population of at least 25,000 where the Hispanic/Latino population is at least 20% of the overall population. In states where less than five places meet either of these criteria, we have included places with at least 10,000 total population with the highest percentage of Hispanic/Latino population. These places are identified with an asterisk (*); Please refer to the User's Guide for a full explanation of data.

New Jersey

EDITOR'S NOTE: For a place to be included in this edition, it must meet one of two criteria. Either its overall population is at least 125,000, OR its overall population is at least 25,000 and its Hispanic/Latino population is at least 20% of the overall population. For the state of New Jersey, the following locations are included:

- Atlantic City
- Bayonne
- Belleville
- Bergenfield
- Bloomfield
- Bridgeton
- Camden
- City of Orange
- Clifton
- Elizabeth
- Englewood
- Garfield
- Hackensack
- Jersey City
- Kearny
- Linden
- Long Branch
- New Brunswick
- Newark
- North Bergen
- Passaic
- Paterson
- Pennsauken
- Perth Amboy
- Plainfield
- Rahway
- Trenton
- Union City
- Vineland
- West New York

Section Two: State & Place Profiles starts with the state profile, followed by place profiles that meet the criteria above. Places are listed alphabetically within each state. All states, all counties and places that meet the above criteria are ranked and compared in *Section Three: Rankings & Comparisons*, on page 1055.

For a more detailed look at the Hispanic/Latino population in New Jersey, a companion web site is available at no additional charge with purchase of this print edition. Visit http://gold.greyhouse.com/page/info_hispanic for more information.

The web site includes data for all counties and places in New Jersey with Hispanic/Latino population, plus ten additional topics: Self Employed Worker; Walked to Work; Worked from Home; Mean Travel Time to Work; Mean Household Income; Households with Cash Public Assistance; Mean Cash Pubic Assistance; Poverty Rates for 18 and Under, 18 to 64, and 65 and Over.

Population

Group	Number	%TP[1]	%HP[2]
Total Population	8,791,894	100.0	–
Hispanic or Latino (of any race)	1,555,144	17.7	100.0
Central American, ex. Mexican	176,611	2.0	11.4
Costa Rican	19,933	0.2	1.3
Guatemalan	48,869	0.6	3.1
Honduran	36,556	0.4	2.4
Nicaraguan	8,222	0.1	0.5
Panamanian	5,431	0.1	0.3
Salvadoran	56,532	0.6	3.6
Cuban	83,362	0.9	5.4
Dominican Republic	197,922	2.3	12.7
Mexican	217,715	2.5	14.0
Puerto Rican	434,092	4.9	27.9
South American	325,179	3.7	20.9
Argentinean	14,272	0.2	0.9
Bolivian	3,361	<0.1	0.2
Chilean	8,100	0.1	0.5
Colombian	101,593	1.2	6.5
Ecuadorian	100,480	1.1	6.5
Paraguayan	1,964	<0.1	0.1
Peruvian	75,869	0.9	4.9
Uruguayan	10,902	0.1	0.7
Venezuelan	6,950	0.1	0.4
Spaniard	21,791	0.2	1.4

Population Growth: 2000–2010

Group	%
Total Population	4.5
Hispanic or Latino (of any race)	39.2
Central American, ex. Mexican	119.4
Costa Rican	78.4
Guatemalan	187.6
Honduran	136.9
Nicaraguan	87.5
Panamanian	79.8
Salvadoran	124.1
Cuban	7.8
Dominican Republic	92.9
Mexican	111.5
Puerto Rican	18.3
South American	83.7
Argentinean	83.1
Bolivian	91.5
Chilean	57.9
Colombian	56.1
Ecuadorian	121.4
Paraguayan	144.6
Peruvian	101.4
Uruguayan	167.3
Venezuelan	75.4
Spaniard	137.3

Males per 100 Females

Group	Number
Total Population	94.8
Hispanic or Latino (of any race)	101.5
Central American, ex. Mexican	124.4
Costa Rican	133.9
Guatemalan	165.5
Honduran	111.6
Nicaraguan	93.6
Panamanian	75.9
Salvadoran	112.1
Cuban	94.4
Dominican Republic	87.3
Mexican	127.0
Puerto Rican	93.9
South American	94.8
Argentinean	102.7
Bolivian	94.2
Chilean	96.4
Colombian	82.7
Ecuadorian	108.2
Paraguayan	98.6
Peruvian	94.7
Uruguayan	100.6
Venezuelan	79.6
Spaniard	100.0

Average Household Size

Group	People
Total Population	2.68
Hispanic or Latino (of any race)	3.39
Central American, ex. Mexican	4.00
Costa Rican	3.63
Guatemalan	4.29
Honduran	4.01
Nicaraguan	3.59
Panamanian	2.73
Salvadoran	4.14
Cuban	2.57
Dominican Republic	3.66
Mexican	4.64
Puerto Rican	2.94
South American	3.41
Argentinean	2.89
Bolivian	3.34
Chilean	2.97
Colombian	3.19
Ecuadorian	3.75
Paraguayan	3.58
Peruvian	3.57
Uruguayan	3.05
Venezuelan	2.95
Spaniard	2.67

Median Age

Group	Years
Total Population	39.0
Hispanic or Latino (of any race)	30.0
Central American, ex. Mexican	30.0
Costa Rican	31.5
Guatemalan	28.5
Honduran	30.0
Nicaraguan	33.1
Panamanian	37.3
Salvadoran	30.2
Cuban	42.3
Dominican Republic	29.9
Mexican	25.1
Puerto Rican	29.2
South American	35.2
Argentinean	37.3
Bolivian	37.0
Chilean	38.5
Colombian	36.4
Ecuadorian	32.9
Paraguayan	33.0
Peruvian	36.5
Uruguayan	35.6
Venezuelan	32.6
Spaniard	39.6

High School Graduates

(Universe: Population 25 Years and Over)

Group	Number	%
Total Population	5,139,449	87.3
Hispanic or Latino (of any race)	597,803	69.6
Central American, ex. Mexican	54,395	54.6
Costa Rican	7,825	64.6
Guatemalan	12,135	45.6
Honduran	11,067	56.1
Nicaraguan	3,754	72.9
Panamanian	3,515	93.3
Salvadoran	15,483	49.3
Cuban	45,025	75.4
Dominican Republic	67,302	66.8
Mexican	53,976	52.7
Puerto Rican	170,525	71.7
South American	171,877	79.9
Argentinean	7,976	82.0
Bolivian	2,360	83.8
Chilean	4,908	85.6
Colombian	53,579	82.3
Ecuadorian	47,037	71.2
Paraguayan	859	70.4
Peruvian	44,452	87.3
Uruguayan	5,695	70.7
Venezuelan	3,566	91.7
Spaniard	11,999	82.6

Four-Year College Graduates

(Universe: Population 25 Years and Over)

Group	Number	%
Total Population	2,037,395	34.6
Hispanic or Latino (of any race)	134,127	15.6
Central American, ex. Mexican	9,872	9.9
Costa Rican	1,380	11.4
Guatemalan	2,046	7.7
Honduran	1,949	9.9
Nicaraguan	867	16.8
Panamanian	1,340	35.6
Salvadoran	2,119	6.8
Cuban	16,445	27.5

Notes: (1) Percent of total population; (2) Percent of Hispanic/Latino population; Profiles include places with an overall population of at least 125,000, OR an overall population of at least 25,000 where the Hispanic/Latino population is at least 20% of the overall population. In states where less than five places meet either of these criteria, we have included places with at least 10,000 total population with the highest percentage of Hispanic/Latino population. These places are identified with an asterisk (*); Please refer to the User's Guide for a full explanation of data.

Dominican Republic	14,486	14.4
Mexican	8,539	8.3
Puerto Rican	30,343	12.8
South American	42,235	19.6
Argentinean	2,501	25.7
Bolivian	765	27.2
Chilean	1,477	25.8
Colombian	14,548	22.4
Ecuadorian	10,105	15.3
Paraguayan	133	10.9
Peruvian	9,924	19.5
Uruguayan	916	11.4
Venezuelan	1,460	37.6
Spaniard	5,457	37.6

Population Age 3–17 Enrolled in Public School

(Universe: Population Age 3–17 Enrolled in School)

Group	Number	%
Total Population	1,361,928	83.3
Hispanic or Latino (of any race)	293,234	91.0
Central American, ex. Mexican	27,936	92.6
Costa Rican	2,919	89.3
Guatemalan	6,866	89.4
Honduran	5,411	95.6
Nicaraguan	1,340	96.1
Panamanian	954	80.6
Salvadoran	10,056	95.1
Cuban	11,440	83.2
Dominican Republic	39,691	93.3
Mexican	43,509	95.1
Puerto Rican	97,767	90.2
South American	54,000	89.8
Argentinean	1,785	75.3
Bolivian	502	96.9
Chilean	1,066	74.1
Colombian	17,076	91.1
Ecuadorian	18,098	91.8
Paraguayan	323	74.3
Peruvian	11,885	89.6
Uruguayan	1,982	93.8
Venezuelan	866	84.9
Spaniard	2,825	77.8

Population Age 3–17 Enrolled in Private School

(Universe: Population Age 3–17 Enrolled in School)

Group	Number	%
Total Population	272,484	16.7
Hispanic or Latino (of any race)	29,098	9.0
Central American, ex. Mexican	2,228	7.4
Costa Rican	349	10.7
Guatemalan	813	10.6
Honduran	248	4.4
Nicaraguan	54	3.9
Panamanian	229	19.4
Salvadoran	522	4.9
Cuban	2,310	16.8
Dominican Republic	2,829	6.7
Mexican	2,236	4.9
Puerto Rican	10,630	9.8
South American	6,109	10.2
Argentinean	586	24.7
Bolivian	16	3.1
Chilean	373	25.9
Colombian	1,669	8.9
Ecuadorian	1,617	8.2
Paraguayan	112	25.7
Peruvian	1,382	10.4
Uruguayan	132	6.2
Venezuelan	154	15.1
Spaniard	807	22.2

Foreign-Born Population

Group	Number	%
Total Population	1,773,859	20.3
Hispanic or Latino (of any race)	652,005	44.4
Central American, ex. Mexican	117,023	70.9
Costa Rican	14,658	77.9
Guatemalan	33,789	74.1
Honduran	24,143	74.7
Nicaraguan	4,697	59.8
Panamanian	3,043	52.4
Salvadoran	35,700	67.3
Cuban	48,138	56.9
Dominican Republic	105,062	58.7
Mexican	123,050	60.6
Puerto Rican	5,642	1.3
South American	228,358	69.3
Argentinean	9,279	66.1
Bolivian	3,251	75.2
Chilean	5,732	67.2
Colombian	68,227	68.5
Ecuadorian	71,934	69.4
Paraguayan	1,293	66.9
Peruvian	53,643	70.1
Uruguayan	9,222	76.0
Venezuelan	4,189	68.8
Spaniard	7,008	32.8

Foreign-Born Naturalized U.S. Citizens

Group	Number	%
Total Population	882,018	49.7
Hispanic or Latino (of any race)	234,840	36.0
Central American, ex. Mexican	28,632	24.5
Costa Rican	2,462	16.8
Guatemalan	6,211	18.4
Honduran	5,872	24.3
Nicaraguan	2,064	43.9
Panamanian	1,725	56.7
Salvadoran	9,992	28.0
Cuban	35,071	72.9
Dominican Republic	48,516	46.2
Mexican	11,832	9.6
Puerto Rican	2,951	52.3
South American	95,248	41.7
Argentinean	4,338	46.8
Bolivian	1,069	32.9
Chilean	2,872	50.1
Colombian	32,432	47.5
Ecuadorian	26,848	37.3
Paraguayan	426	32.9
Peruvian	21,772	40.6
Uruguayan	2,640	28.6
Venezuelan	1,830	43.7
Spaniard	3,744	53.4

Language Spoken at Home: English Only

(Universe: Population 5 Years and Over)

Group	Number	%
Total Population	5,830,812	71.3
Hispanic or Latino (of any race)	228,792	17.1
Central American, ex. Mexican	12,862	8.5
Costa Rican	1,260	7.3
Guatemalan	3,459	8.4
Honduran	1,718	5.7
Nicaraguan	1,374	18.8
Panamanian	2,055	36.9
Salvadoran	2,694	5.6
Cuban	17,008	21.2
Dominican Republic	11,120	6.8
Mexican	19,597	11.1
Puerto Rican	116,903	30.3
South American	26,263	8.6
Argentinean	2,173	16.9
Bolivian	352	9.0
Chilean	1,406	17.7
Colombian	8,437	9.0
Ecuadorian	6,583	6.9
Paraguayan	208	12.1
Peruvian	4,857	6.9
Uruguayan	669	6.0
Venezuelan	1,120	19.6
Spaniard	9,229	46.2

Language Spoken at Home: Spanish

(Universe: Population 5 Years and Over)

Group	Number	%
Total Population	1,191,818	14.6
Hispanic or Latino (of any race)	1,097,492	82.3
Central American, ex. Mexican	138,128	91.2
Costa Rican	15,798	91.9
Guatemalan	37,719	91.2
Honduran	28,360	94.1
Nicaraguan	5,863	80.4
Panamanian	3,439	61.8
Salvadoran	45,720	94.4
Cuban	62,508	78.1
Dominican Republic	151,709	93.0
Mexican	155,683	88.3
Puerto Rican	268,351	69.4
South American	276,900	90.8
Argentinean	10,330	80.4
Bolivian	3,533	90.4
Chilean	6,463	81.4
Colombian	84,740	90.8
Ecuadorian	88,079	92.5
Paraguayan	1,504	87.4
Peruvian	65,644	92.7
Uruguayan	10,371	93.3
Venezuelan	4,335	75.9
Spaniard	10,188	51.0

Unemployment Rate

(Universe: Population 16 Years and Over)

Group	%
Total Population	7.8
Hispanic or Latino (of any race)	9.1
Central American, ex. Mexican	8.2
Costa Rican	8.0
Guatemalan	7.3
Honduran	9.0
Nicaraguan	11.3
Panamanian	7.9
Salvadoran	8.3
Cuban	8.1
Dominican Republic	9.1
Mexican	7.1
Puerto Rican	11.6
South American	8.1
Argentinean	4.9
Bolivian	1.4
Chilean	6.0
Colombian	7.9
Ecuadorian	9.0
Paraguayan	18.7
Peruvian	8.3
Uruguayan	7.1
Venezuelan	8.3
Spaniard	7.7

Class of Worker: Private Wage and Salary

(Universe: Civilian Employed Population 16 Years and Over)

Group	Number	%
Total Population	3,400,308	80.4
Hispanic or Latino (of any race)	604,565	87.0
Central American, ex. Mexican	84,382	91.6
Costa Rican	9,174	87.7
Guatemalan	24,995	93.9
Honduran	17,071	91.9
Nicaraguan	3,854	89.9
Panamanian	2,203	75.7
Salvadoran	26,413	92.9
Cuban	30,328	78.3
Dominican Republic	74,139	89.0
Mexican	91,352	94.1
Puerto Rican	140,728	81.4
South American	156,639	87.9
Argentinean	6,235	85.5
Bolivian	2,265	89.8
Chilean	4,092	87.4
Colombian	46,212	85.3
Ecuadorian	50,224	90.1
Paraguayan	732	80.4
Peruvian	37,447	89.4
Uruguayan	5,539	86.1
Venezuelan	2,699	84.9
Spaniard	8,325	80.2

Class of Worker: Government

(Universe: Civilian Employed Population 16 Years and Over)

Group	Number	%
Total Population	615,807	14.6
Hispanic or Latino (of any race)	62,732	9.0
Central American, ex. Mexican	3,721	4.0
Costa Rican	301	2.9
Guatemalan	547	2.1
Honduran	690	3.7
Nicaraguan	282	6.6
Panamanian	579	19.9
Salvadoran	1,176	4.1
Cuban	6,855	17.7
Dominican Republic	5,873	7.1
Mexican	2,247	2.3
Puerto Rican	27,853	16.1
South American	11,995	6.7
Argentinean	586	8.0

Notes: (1) Percent of total population; (2) Percent of Hispanic/Latino population; Profiles include places with an overall population of at least 125,000, OR an overall population of at least 25,000 where the Hispanic/Latino population is at least 20% of the overall population. In states where less than five places meet either of these criteria, we have included places with at least 10,000 total population with the highest percentage of Hispanic/Latino population. These places are identified with an asterisk (*); Please refer to the User's Guide for a full explanation of data.

Group	Number	%
Bolivian	147	5.8
Chilean	249	5.3
Colombian	4,723	8.7
Ecuadorian	3,019	5.4
Paraguayan	7	0.8
Peruvian	2,504	6.0
Uruguayan	321	5.0
Venezuelan	323	10.2
Spaniard	1,576	15.2

Means of Transportation to Work: Car, Truck or Van
(Universe: Workers 16 Years and Over)

Group	Number	%
Total Population	3,323,938	80.6
Hispanic or Latino (of any race)	474,013	69.8
Central American, ex. Mexican	56,541	62.7
Costa Rican	6,917	68.2
Guatemalan	14,941	57.0
Honduran	11,555	63.3
Nicaraguan	3,153	75.3
Panamanian	2,060	72.9
Salvadoran	17,318	62.4
Cuban	28,411	74.8
Dominican Republic	58,159	71.3
Mexican	53,645	56.0
Puerto Rican	131,504	78.2
South American	122,128	70.3
Argentinean	5,225	73.9
Bolivian	1,543	62.2
Chilean	3,567	78.0
Colombian	39,550	75.0
Ecuadorian	35,696	65.7
Paraguayan	664	73.5
Peruvian	28,370	69.6
Uruguayan	4,221	67.0
Venezuelan	2,129	68.9
Spaniard	7,670	77.2

Means of Transportation to Work: Public Transportation (ex. Taxicab)
(Universe: Workers 16 Years and Over)

Group	Number	%
Total Population	438,293	10.6
Hispanic or Latino (of any race)	106,979	15.8
Central American, ex. Mexican	15,478	17.2
Costa Rican	895	8.8
Guatemalan	5,209	19.9
Honduran	3,373	18.5
Nicaraguan	652	15.6
Panamanian	589	20.8
Salvadoran	4,578	16.5
Cuban	4,865	12.8
Dominican Republic	13,367	16.4
Mexican	17,055	17.8
Puerto Rican	21,714	12.9
South American	29,800	17.2
Argentinean	1,031	14.6
Bolivian	595	24.0
Chilean	515	11.3
Colombian	7,168	13.6
Ecuadorian	11,572	21.3
Paraguayan	101	11.2
Peruvian	7,133	17.5
Uruguayan	991	15.7
Venezuelan	527	17.0
Spaniard	1,251	12.6

Homeownership Rate
(Universe: Occupied Housing Units)

Group	%
Total Population	65.4
Hispanic or Latino (of any race)	36.3
Central American, ex. Mexican	29.4
Costa Rican	27.6
Guatemalan	24.3
Honduran	27.3
Nicaraguan	41.1
Panamanian	51.0
Salvadoran	30.4
Cuban	46.7
Dominican Republic	32.9
Mexican	20.8
Puerto Rican	38.5
South American	39.2

Group	
Argentinean	54.0
Bolivian	47.1
Chilean	44.8
Colombian	40.1
Ecuadorian	36.2
Paraguayan	37.0
Peruvian	37.7
Uruguayan	32.6
Venezuelan	45.8
Spaniard	71.3

Median Home Value

Group	Dollars
Total Population	357,000
Hispanic or Latino (of any race)	344,000
Central American, ex. Mexican	330,900
Costa Rican	349,600
Guatemalan	281,700
Honduran	331,500
Nicaraguan	267,500
Panamanian	322,200
Salvadoran	362,500
Cuban	395,200
Dominican Republic	359,300
Mexican	317,700
Puerto Rican	302,100
South American	367,300
Argentinean	367,400
Bolivian	378,900
Chilean	325,200
Colombian	367,400
Ecuadorian	376,100
Paraguayan	351,900
Peruvian	358,500
Uruguayan	351,000
Venezuelan	442,000
Spaniard	383,300

Median Gross Rent

Group	Dollars
Total Population	1,092
Hispanic or Latino (of any race)	1,080
Central American, ex. Mexican	1,152
Costa Rican	1,287
Guatemalan	1,199
Honduran	1,106
Nicaraguan	1,124
Panamanian	1,007
Salvadoran	1,113
Cuban	924
Dominican Republic	1,070
Mexican	1,209
Puerto Rican	983
South American	1,120
Argentinean	1,219
Bolivian	1,234
Chilean	1,161
Colombian	1,115
Ecuadorian	1,127
Paraguayan	1,361
Peruvian	1,092
Uruguayan	1,095
Venezuelan	1,204
Spaniard	1,063

Median Household Income
(2010 Inflation-Adjusted Dollars)

Group	Dollars
Total Population	69,811
Hispanic or Latino (of any race)	48,578
Central American, ex. Mexican	49,461
Costa Rican	47,178
Guatemalan	49,361
Honduran	46,205
Nicaraguan	59,940
Panamanian	62,721
Salvadoran	49,035
Cuban	52,177
Dominican Republic	44,492
Mexican	43,419
Puerto Rican	45,207
South American	53,778
Argentinean	66,111
Bolivian	55,923
Chilean	61,975
Colombian	56,837
Ecuadorian	51,542
Paraguayan	55,815
Peruvian	50,283
Uruguayan	49,252
Venezuelan	54,948
Spaniard	74,461

Per Capita Income
(2010 Inflation-Adjusted Dollars)

Group	Dollars
Total Population	34,858
Hispanic or Latino (of any race)	19,221
Central American, ex. Mexican	17,154
Costa Rican	17,640
Guatemalan	15,229
Honduran	17,537
Nicaraguan	21,926
Panamanian	28,305
Salvadoran	16,306
Cuban	29,994
Dominican Republic	16,205
Mexican	13,618
Puerto Rican	19,503
South American	21,069
Argentinean	32,542
Bolivian	24,939
Chilean	25,769
Colombian	21,694
Ecuadorian	18,755
Paraguayan	23,059
Peruvian	19,788
Uruguayan	21,575
Venezuelan	26,469
Spaniard	36,544

Households with $100,000+ Income

Group	Number	%
Total Population	1,059,839	33.4
Hispanic or Latino (of any race)	74,933	17.8
Central American, ex. Mexican	6,340	14.8
Costa Rican	707	14.1
Guatemalan	1,282	12.0
Honduran	1,227	14.3
Nicaraguan	532	23.4
Panamanian	612	28.1
Salvadoran	1,882	13.7
Cuban	8,245	26.0
Dominican Republic	6,325	12.6
Mexican	5,710	13.0
Puerto Rican	23,461	17.7
South American	19,153	19.6
Argentinean	1,655	31.9
Bolivian	316	25.4
Chilean	590	20.6
Colombian	6,370	21.6
Ecuadorian	4,756	15.9
Paraguayan	93	16.7
Peruvian	4,008	18.4
Uruguayan	576	14.0
Venezuelan	540	30.2
Spaniard	2,818	35.4

Households with Food Stamps/SNAP Benefits During Past 12 Months

Group	Number	%
Total Population	159,394	5.0
Hispanic or Latino (of any race)	52,232	12.4
Central American, ex. Mexican	3,671	8.5
Costa Rican	403	8.0
Guatemalan	856	8.0
Honduran	812	9.5
Nicaraguan	226	10.0
Panamanian	103	4.7
Salvadoran	1,266	9.2
Cuban	3,475	10.9
Dominican Republic	8,609	17.2
Mexican	5,905	13.4
Puerto Rican	21,972	16.6
South American	7,292	7.5
Argentinean	275	5.3
Bolivian	56	4.5
Chilean	155	5.4
Colombian	1,775	6.0
Ecuadorian	2,318	7.8

Notes: (1) Percent of total population; (2) Percent of Hispanic/Latino population; Profiles include places with an overall population of at least 125,000, OR an overall population of at least 25,000 where the Hispanic/Latino population is at least 20% of the overall population. In states where less than five places meet either of these criteria, we have included places with at least 10,000 total population with the highest percentage of Hispanic/Latino population. These places are identified with an asterisk (*); Please refer to the User's Guide for a full explanation of data.

Paraguayan	0	0.0
Peruvian	2,317	10.6
Uruguayan	224	5.4
Venezuelan	105	5.9
Spaniard	375	4.7

Poverty Rate
(Income in Past 12 Months Below Poverty Level)

Group	%
Total Population	9.1
Hispanic or Latino (of any race)	17.6
Central American, ex. Mexican	17.0
Costa Rican	20.8
Guatemalan	18.2
Honduran	18.4
Nicaraguan	12.4
Panamanian	10.2
Salvadoran	15.5
Cuban	11.0
Dominican Republic	18.8
Mexican	25.1
Puerto Rican	20.6
South American	11.7
Argentinean	11.2
Bolivian	11.4
Chilean	8.2
Colombian	9.3
Ecuadorian	13.0
Paraguayan	5.7
Peruvian	12.9
Uruguayan	18.3
Venezuelan	10.2
Spaniard	6.8

Atlantic City

Population

Group	Number	%TP[1]	%HP[2]
Total Population	39,558	100.0	–
Hispanic or Latino (of any race)	12,044	30.4	100.0
Central American, ex. Mexican	1,396	3.5	11.6
Honduran	857	2.2	7.1
Salvadoran	377	1.0	3.1
Cuban	234	0.6	1.9
Dominican Republic	1,419	3.6	11.8
Mexican	3,861	9.8	32.1
Puerto Rican	3,506	8.9	29.1
South American	910	2.3	7.6
Colombian	495	1.3	4.1
Ecuadorian	110	0.3	0.9
Peruvian	240	0.6	2.0

Population Growth: 2000–2010

Group	%
Total Population	-2.4
Hispanic or Latino (of any race)	19.2
Central American, ex. Mexican	70.7
Honduran	90.4
Salvadoran	70.6
Cuban	-1.7
Dominican Republic	68.9
Mexican	75.6
Puerto Rican	-3.5
South American	35.4
Colombian	11.5
Peruvian	122.2

Males per 100 Females

Group	Number
Total Population	96.2
Hispanic or Latino (of any race)	104.1
Central American, ex. Mexican	114.1
Honduran	124.9
Salvadoran	97.4
Cuban	118.7
Dominican Republic	93.3
Mexican	123.1
Puerto Rican	93.3
South American	87.6
Colombian	80.0
Ecuadorian	86.4
Peruvian	100.0

Average Household Size

Group	People
Total Population	2.50
Hispanic or Latino (of any race)	3.40
Central American, ex. Mexican	3.99
Honduran	4.13
Salvadoran	4.20
Cuban	2.09
Dominican Republic	3.38
Mexican	4.64
Puerto Rican	2.75
South American	2.82
Colombian	2.73
Ecuadorian	3.42
Peruvian	2.85

Median Age

Group	Years
Total Population	36.3
Hispanic or Latino (of any race)	27.5
Central American, ex. Mexican	29.4
Honduran	28.7
Salvadoran	31.1
Cuban	45.5
Dominican Republic	30.6
Mexican	25.1
Puerto Rican	27.8
South American	40.5
Colombian	43.8
Ecuadorian	32.3
Peruvian	39.7

High School Graduates
(Universe: Population 25 Years and Over)

Group	Number	%
Total Population	19,702	74.3
Hispanic or Latino (of any race)	3,358	62.6
Dominican Republic	452	60.8
Mexican	824	61.0
Puerto Rican	1,057	64.9

Four-Year College Graduates
(Universe: Population 25 Years and Over)

Group	Number	%
Total Population	4,391	16.6
Hispanic or Latino (of any race)	392	7.3
Dominican Republic	11	1.5
Mexican	159	11.8
Puerto Rican	44	2.7

Population Age 3–17 Enrolled in Public School
(Universe: Population Age 3–17 Enrolled in School)

Group	Number	%
Total Population	6,330	90.2
Hispanic or Latino (of any race)	2,005	96.3
Dominican Republic	178	100.0
Mexican	711	96.3
Puerto Rican	768	96.5

Population Age 3–17 Enrolled in Private School
(Universe: Population Age 3–17 Enrolled in School)

Group	Number	%
Total Population	690	9.8
Hispanic or Latino (of any race)	76	3.7
Dominican Republic	0	0.0
Mexican	27	3.7
Puerto Rican	28	3.5

Foreign-Born Population

Group	Number	%
Total Population	11,194	27.9
Hispanic or Latino (of any race)	3,982	42.0
Dominican Republic	882	71.1
Mexican	1,486	52.5
Puerto Rican	80	2.6

Foreign-Born Naturalized U.S. Citizens

Group	Number	%
Total Population	4,946	44.2
Hispanic or Latino (of any race)	1,155	29.0
Dominican Republic	190	21.5
Mexican	366	24.6
Puerto Rican	15	18.8

Language Spoken at Home: English Only
(Universe: Population 5 Years and Over)

Group	Number	%
Total Population	21,730	59.4
Hispanic or Latino (of any race)	1,190	14.3
Dominican Republic	4	0.4
Mexican	257	10.7
Puerto Rican	708	26.0

Language Spoken at Home: Spanish
(Universe: Population 5 Years and Over)

Group	Number	%
Total Population	7,578	20.7
Hispanic or Latino (of any race)	7,126	85.7
Dominican Republic	1,063	99.6
Mexican	2,145	89.3
Puerto Rican	2,012	74.0

Unemployment Rate
(Universe: Population 16 Years and Over)

Group	%
Total Population	13.9
Hispanic or Latino (of any race)	10.1
Dominican Republic	11.6
Mexican	8.6
Puerto Rican	12.6

Class of Worker: Private Wage and Salary
(Universe: Civilian Employed Population 16 Years and Over)

Group	Number	%
Total Population	13,937	84.8
Hispanic or Latino (of any race)	4,063	95.8
Dominican Republic	576	94.6
Mexican	1,140	98.8
Puerto Rican	1,149	95.0

Class of Worker: Government
(Universe: Civilian Employed Population 16 Years and Over)

Group	Number	%
Total Population	1,857	11.3
Hispanic or Latino (of any race)	71	1.7
Dominican Republic	0	0.0
Mexican	0	0.0
Puerto Rican	61	5.0

Means of Transportation to Work: Car, Truck or Van
(Universe: Workers 16 Years and Over)

Group	Number	%
Total Population	8,058	51.0
Hispanic or Latino (of any race)	1,854	45.6
Dominican Republic	244	43.5
Mexican	566	52.3
Puerto Rican	529	45.4

Means of Transportation to Work: Public Transportation (ex. Taxicab)
(Universe: Workers 16 Years and Over)

Group	Number	%
Total Population	4,456	28.2
Hispanic or Latino (of any race)	1,496	36.8
Dominican Republic	145	25.8
Mexican	366	33.8
Puerto Rican	523	44.9

Homeownership Rate
(Universe: Occupied Housing Units)

Group	%
Total Population	28.6
Hispanic or Latino (of any race)	15.1
Central American, ex. Mexican	22.3
Honduran	17.7
Salvadoran	29.7
Cuban	19.8
Dominican Republic	17.7
Mexican	13.4
Puerto Rican	9.7
South American	28.1
Colombian	28.0
Ecuadorian	22.6
Peruvian	31.8

Median Home Value

Group	Dollars
Total Population	238,200

Notes: (1) Percent of total population; (2) Percent of Hispanic/Latino population; Profiles include places with an overall population of at least 125,000, OR an overall population of at least 25,000 where the Hispanic/Latino population is at least 20% of the overall population. In states where less than five places meet either of these criteria, we have included places with at least 10,000 total population with the highest percentage of Hispanic/Latino population. These places are identified with an asterisk (*); Please refer to the User's Guide for a full explanation of data.

Hispanic or Latino (of any race)	216,200
Dominican Republic	458,700
Mexican	218,500
Puerto Rican	190,700

Median Gross Rent

Group	Dollars
Total Population	780
Hispanic or Latino (of any race)	934
Dominican Republic	893
Mexican	1,082
Puerto Rican	883

Median Household Income
(2010 Inflation-Adjusted Dollars)

Group	Dollars
Total Population	30,237
Hispanic or Latino (of any race)	27,341
Dominican Republic	33,076
Mexican	31,987
Puerto Rican	22,721

Per Capita Income
(2010 Inflation-Adjusted Dollars)

Group	Dollars
Total Population	20,069
Hispanic or Latino (of any race)	12,486
Dominican Republic	13,851
Mexican	11,349
Puerto Rican	10,218

Households with $100,000+ Income

Group	Number	%
Total Population	1,422	8.4
Hispanic or Latino (of any race)	173	5.6
Dominican Republic	23	5.7
Mexican	71	9.7
Puerto Rican	15	1.4

Households with Food Stamps/SNAP Benefits During Past 12 Months

Group	Number	%
Total Population	2,950	17.5
Hispanic or Latino (of any race)	658	21.3
Dominican Republic	88	21.9
Mexican	70	9.6
Puerto Rican	407	37.6

Poverty Rate
(Income in Past 12 Months Below Poverty Level)

Group	%
Total Population	25.3
Hispanic or Latino (of any race)	29.7
Dominican Republic	15.0
Mexican	27.6
Puerto Rican	41.5

Bayonne

Population

Group	Number	%TP[1]	%HP[2]
Total Population	63,024	100.0	–
Hispanic or Latino (of any race)	16,251	25.8	100.0
Central American, ex. Mexican	1,729	2.7	10.6
Guatemalan	502	0.8	3.1
Honduran	489	0.8	3.0
Nicaraguan	103	0.2	0.6
Panamanian	107	0.2	0.7
Salvadoran	476	0.8	2.9
Cuban	553	0.9	3.4
Dominican Republic	2,464	3.9	15.2
Mexican	1,317	2.1	8.1
Puerto Rican	6,209	9.9	38.2
South American	2,116	3.4	13.0
Argentinean	124	0.2	0.8
Chilean	167	0.3	1.0
Colombian	618	1.0	3.8
Ecuadorian	709	1.1	4.4
Peruvian	284	0.5	1.7
Spaniard	720	1.1	4.4

Population Growth: 2000–2010

Group	%
Total Population	1.9
Hispanic or Latino (of any race)	47.5
Central American, ex. Mexican	73.2
Guatemalan	69.0
Honduran	136.2
Salvadoran	95.9
Cuban	21.8
Dominican Republic	129.9
Mexican	108.7
Puerto Rican	46.3
South American	86.3
Chilean	30.5
Colombian	72.1
Ecuadorian	141.2
Peruvian	80.9
Spaniard	69.8

Males per 100 Females

Group	Number
Total Population	91.7
Hispanic or Latino (of any race)	90.0
Central American, ex. Mexican	90.4
Guatemalan	95.3
Honduran	88.1
Nicaraguan	90.7
Panamanian	84.5
Salvadoran	89.6
Cuban	101.8
Dominican Republic	80.5
Mexican	123.2
Puerto Rican	85.2
South American	88.3
Argentinean	100.0
Chilean	101.2
Colombian	72.6
Ecuadorian	94.2
Peruvian	101.4
Spaniard	91.0

Average Household Size

Group	People
Total Population	2.49
Hispanic or Latino (of any race)	3.01
Central American, ex. Mexican	3.33
Guatemalan	3.36
Honduran	3.45
Nicaraguan	2.78
Panamanian	2.67
Salvadoran	3.62
Cuban	2.56
Dominican Republic	3.36
Mexican	3.77
Puerto Rican	2.82
South American	3.06
Argentinean	2.70
Chilean	2.80
Colombian	2.86
Ecuadorian	3.33
Peruvian	3.07
Spaniard	2.52

Median Age

Group	Years
Total Population	38.4
Hispanic or Latino (of any race)	29.5
Central American, ex. Mexican	33.2
Guatemalan	35.6
Honduran	30.7
Nicaraguan	36.4
Panamanian	49.1
Salvadoran	31.3
Cuban	36.6
Dominican Republic	29.0
Mexican	26.1
Puerto Rican	27.2
South American	34.0
Argentinean	34.6
Chilean	37.8
Colombian	32.3
Ecuadorian	32.7
Peruvian	36.9
Spaniard	42.0

High School Graduates
(Universe: Population 25 Years and Over)

Group	Number	%
Total Population	38,057	86.5
Hispanic or Latino (of any race)	6,058	73.4
Central American, ex. Mexican	850	63.2
Dominican Republic	1,222	74.1
Mexican	640	59.6
Puerto Rican	1,454	78.9
South American	1,161	86.0

Four-Year College Graduates
(Universe: Population 25 Years and Over)

Group	Number	%
Total Population	12,389	28.1
Hispanic or Latino (of any race)	1,395	16.9
Central American, ex. Mexican	236	17.5
Dominican Republic	297	18.0
Mexican	99	9.2
Puerto Rican	229	12.4
South American	328	24.3

Population Age 3–17 Enrolled in Public School
(Universe: Population Age 3–17 Enrolled in School)

Group	Number	%
Total Population	8,417	88.6
Hispanic or Latino (of any race)	2,126	88.4
Central American, ex. Mexican	299	87.4
Dominican Republic	460	100.0
Mexican	124	100.0
Puerto Rican	873	92.7
South American	168	68.3

Population Age 3–17 Enrolled in Private School
(Universe: Population Age 3–17 Enrolled in School)

Group	Number	%
Total Population	1,086	11.4
Hispanic or Latino (of any race)	280	11.6
Central American, ex. Mexican	43	12.6
Dominican Republic	0	0.0
Mexican	0	0.0
Puerto Rican	69	7.3
South American	78	31.7

Foreign-Born Population

Group	Number	%
Total Population	16,376	26.4
Hispanic or Latino (of any race)	6,590	50.7
Central American, ex. Mexican	1,433	71.5
Dominican Republic	1,658	67.7
Mexican	1,333	68.9
Puerto Rican	3	0.1
South American	1,454	82.3

Foreign-Born Naturalized U.S. Citizens

Group	Number	%
Total Population	8,421	51.4
Hispanic or Latino (of any race)	2,823	42.8
Central American, ex. Mexican	395	27.6
Dominican Republic	866	52.2
Mexican	319	23.9
Puerto Rican	3	100.0
South American	746	51.3

Language Spoken at Home: English Only
(Universe: Population 5 Years and Over)

Group	Number	%
Total Population	36,556	62.4
Hispanic or Latino (of any race)	2,300	19.0
Central American, ex. Mexican	86	4.7
Dominican Republic	196	8.5
Mexican	144	8.5
Puerto Rican	1,433	44.4
South American	175	10.0

Language Spoken at Home: Spanish
(Universe: Population 5 Years and Over)

Group	Number	%
Total Population	12,092	20.7
Hispanic or Latino (of any race)	9,794	80.9
Central American, ex. Mexican	1,754	95.3
Dominican Republic	2,098	91.5
Mexican	1,547	91.2
Puerto Rican	1,798	55.6
South American	1,571	90.0

Notes: (1) Percent of total population; (2) Percent of Hispanic/Latino population; Profiles include places with an overall population of at least 125,000, OR an overall population of at least 25,000 where the Hispanic/Latino population is at least 20% of the overall population. In states where less than five places meet either of these criteria, we have included places with at least 10,000 total population with the highest percentage of Hispanic/Latino population. These places are identified with an asterisk (*); Please refer to the User's Guide for a full explanation of data.

Unemployment Rate
(Universe: Population 16 Years and Over)

Group	%
Total Population	8.8
Hispanic or Latino (of any race)	9.3
Central American, ex. Mexican	7.5
Dominican Republic	11.4
Mexican	10.8
Puerto Rican	11.6
South American	2.9

Class of Worker: Private Wage and Salary
(Universe: Civilian Employed Population 16 Years and Over)

Group	Number	%
Total Population	23,447	77.6
Hispanic or Latino (of any race)	5,351	84.8
Central American, ex. Mexican	909	92.0
Dominican Republic	1,095	92.3
Mexican	880	96.2
Puerto Rican	1,161	73.5
South American	797	77.3

Class of Worker: Government
(Universe: Civilian Employed Population 16 Years and Over)

Group	Number	%
Total Population	5,644	18.7
Hispanic or Latino (of any race)	671	10.6
Central American, ex. Mexican	23	2.3
Dominican Republic	78	6.6
Mexican	7	0.8
Puerto Rican	385	24.4
South American	85	8.2

Means of Transportation to Work: Car, Truck or Van
(Universe: Workers 16 Years and Over)

Group	Number	%
Total Population	19,749	66.9
Hispanic or Latino (of any race)	3,995	64.2
Central American, ex. Mexican	714	72.3
Dominican Republic	745	64.6
Mexican	505	55.2
Puerto Rican	1,081	70.4
South American	511	49.6

Means of Transportation to Work: Public Transportation (ex. Taxicab)
(Universe: Workers 16 Years and Over)

Group	Number	%
Total Population	6,328	21.4
Hispanic or Latino (of any race)	1,624	26.1
Central American, ex. Mexican	220	22.3
Dominican Republic	386	33.4
Mexican	102	11.1
Puerto Rican	368	24.0
South American	429	41.6

Homeownership Rate
(Universe: Occupied Housing Units)

Group	%
Total Population	38.8
Hispanic or Latino (of any race)	24.2
Central American, ex. Mexican	21.8
Guatemalan	18.7
Honduran	21.6
Nicaraguan	37.8
Panamanian	15.6
Salvadoran	24.3
Cuban	28.5
Dominican Republic	24.7
Mexican	10.3
Puerto Rican	18.3
South American	32.7
Argentinean	48.8
Chilean	38.2
Colombian	26.5
Ecuadorian	34.7
Peruvian	28.9
Spaniard	66.1

Median Home Value

Group	Dollars
Total Population	363,600
Hispanic or Latino (of any race)	376,000
Central American, ex. Mexican	370,500
Dominican Republic	461,500
Mexican	206,800
Puerto Rican	374,100
South American	363,300

Median Gross Rent

Group	Dollars
Total Population	967
Hispanic or Latino (of any race)	981
Central American, ex. Mexican	952
Dominican Republic	1,024
Mexican	1,089
Puerto Rican	924
South American	1,137

Median Household Income
(2010 Inflation-Adjusted Dollars)

Group	Dollars
Total Population	53,587
Hispanic or Latino (of any race)	45,298
Central American, ex. Mexican	53,216
Dominican Republic	27,917
Mexican	50,156
Puerto Rican	41,009
South American	54,938

Per Capita Income
(2010 Inflation-Adjusted Dollars)

Group	Dollars
Total Population	28,698
Hispanic or Latino (of any race)	19,723
Central American, ex. Mexican	20,391
Dominican Republic	15,024
Mexican	14,281
Puerto Rican	19,493
South American	23,525

Households with $100,000+ Income

Group	Number	%
Total Population	5,662	22.5
Hispanic or Latino (of any race)	659	15.0
Central American, ex. Mexican	124	17.6
Dominican Republic	44	5.8
Mexican	7	1.4
Puerto Rican	195	15.4
South American	153	22.6

Households with Food Stamps/SNAP Benefits During Past 12 Months

Group	Number	%
Total Population	1,620	6.4
Hispanic or Latino (of any race)	513	11.6
Central American, ex. Mexican	39	5.5
Dominican Republic	261	34.5
Mexican	0	0.0
Puerto Rican	126	10.0
South American	71	10.5

Poverty Rate
(Income in Past 12 Months Below Poverty Level)

Group	%
Total Population	12.3
Hispanic or Latino (of any race)	17.7
Central American, ex. Mexican	5.9
Dominican Republic	24.2
Mexican	38.0
Puerto Rican	17.0
South American	8.7

Belleville

Population

Group	Number	%TP[1]	%HP[2]
Total Population	35,926	100.0	–
Hispanic or Latino (of any race)	14,133	39.3	100.0
Central American, ex. Mexican	814	2.3	5.8
Guatemalan	196	0.5	1.4
Honduran	192	0.5	1.4
Salvadoran	249	0.7	1.8
Cuban	500	1.4	3.5
Dominican Republic	1,352	3.8	9.6
Mexican	323	0.9	2.3
Puerto Rican	5,001	13.9	35.4
South American	5,012	14.0	35.5
Argentinean	121	0.3	0.9
Colombian	561	1.6	4.0
Ecuadorian	2,824	7.9	20.0
Peruvian	1,239	3.4	8.8
Uruguayan	119	0.3	0.8
Spaniard	188	0.5	1.3

Population Growth: 2000–2010

Group	%
Total Population	0.0
Hispanic or Latino (of any race)	66.1
Central American, ex. Mexican	132.6
Guatemalan	56.8
Cuban	10.1
Dominican Republic	230.6
Mexican	104.4
Puerto Rican	45.8
South American	158.5
Colombian	141.8
Ecuadorian	157.2
Peruvian	224.3

Males per 100 Females

Group	Number
Total Population	93.1
Hispanic or Latino (of any race)	97.4
Central American, ex. Mexican	114.8
Guatemalan	104.2
Honduran	104.3
Salvadoran	105.8
Cuban	86.6
Dominican Republic	92.6
Mexican	98.2
Puerto Rican	91.3
South American	100.2
Argentinean	132.7
Colombian	77.5
Ecuadorian	108.0
Peruvian	94.8
Uruguayan	112.5
Spaniard	118.6

Average Household Size

Group	People
Total Population	2.68
Hispanic or Latino (of any race)	3.31
Central American, ex. Mexican	3.62
Guatemalan	3.92
Honduran	3.48
Salvadoran	3.65
Cuban	2.74
Dominican Republic	3.42
Mexican	3.30
Puerto Rican	2.99
South American	3.68
Argentinean	2.81
Colombian	3.12
Ecuadorian	3.95
Peruvian	3.73
Uruguayan	2.71
Spaniard	2.80

Median Age

Group	Years
Total Population	37.2
Hispanic or Latino (of any race)	31.3
Central American, ex. Mexican	33.0
Guatemalan	35.3
Honduran	32.6
Salvadoran	34.1
Cuban	35.6
Dominican Republic	30.4
Mexican	29.2
Puerto Rican	29.3
South American	34.1
Argentinean	37.4
Colombian	35.5
Ecuadorian	33.3
Peruvian	35.6
Uruguayan	34.2
Spaniard	42.3

Notes: (1) Percent of total population; (2) Percent of Hispanic/Latino population; Profiles include places with an overall population of at least 125,000, OR an overall population of at least 25,000 where the Hispanic/Latino population is at least 20% of the overall population. In states where less than five places meet either of these criteria, we have included places with at least 10,000 total population with the highest percentage of Hispanic/Latino population. These places are identified with an asterisk (*); Please refer to the User's Guide for a full explanation of data.

High School Graduates
(Universe: Population 25 Years and Over)

Group	Number	%
Total Population	20,957	84.7
Hispanic or Latino (of any race)	6,220	76.3
Central American, ex. Mexican	237	48.2
Dominican Republic	493	63.9
Puerto Rican	2,417	80.6
South American	2,439	79.2
Ecuadorian	1,310	83.9
Peruvian	431	70.2

Four-Year College Graduates
(Universe: Population 25 Years and Over)

Group	Number	%
Total Population	6,719	27.2
Hispanic or Latino (of any race)	1,304	16.0
Central American, ex. Mexican	52	10.6
Dominican Republic	180	23.3
Puerto Rican	475	15.8
South American	427	13.9
Ecuadorian	181	11.6
Peruvian	82	13.4

Population Age 3–17 Enrolled in Public School
(Universe: Population Age 3–17 Enrolled in School)

Group	Number	%
Total Population	4,810	84.8
Hispanic or Latino (of any race)	2,569	90.3
Central American, ex. Mexican	147	100.0
Dominican Republic	244	83.6
Puerto Rican	1,049	92.5
South American	966	93.6
Ecuadorian	571	94.2
Peruvian	120	79.5

Population Age 3–17 Enrolled in Private School
(Universe: Population Age 3–17 Enrolled in School)

Group	Number	%
Total Population	864	15.2
Hispanic or Latino (of any race)	275	9.7
Central American, ex. Mexican	0	0.0
Dominican Republic	48	16.4
Puerto Rican	85	7.5
South American	66	6.4
Ecuadorian	35	5.8
Peruvian	31	20.5

Foreign-Born Population

Group	Number	%
Total Population	12,038	33.7
Hispanic or Latino (of any race)	5,659	42.0
Central American, ex. Mexican	665	65.8
Dominican Republic	796	69.7
Puerto Rican	0	0.0
South American	3,572	73.4
Ecuadorian	1,884	74.0
Peruvian	674	75.2

Foreign-Born Naturalized U.S. Citizens

Group	Number	%
Total Population	6,003	49.9
Hispanic or Latino (of any race)	2,548	45.0
Central American, ex. Mexican	203	30.5
Dominican Republic	527	66.2
Puerto Rican	0	0.0
South American	1,323	37.0
Ecuadorian	712	37.8
Peruvian	211	31.3

Language Spoken at Home: English Only
(Universe: Population 5 Years and Over)

Group	Number	%
Total Population	16,295	48.4
Hispanic or Latino (of any race)	1,693	13.6
Central American, ex. Mexican	37	3.9
Dominican Republic	55	5.2
Puerto Rican	1,127	24.8
South American	163	3.5
Ecuadorian	69	2.8
Peruvian	35	4.0

Language Spoken at Home: Spanish
(Universe: Population 5 Years and Over)

Group	Number	%
Total Population	11,242	33.4
Hispanic or Latino (of any race)	10,681	86.0
Central American, ex. Mexican	900	96.1
Dominican Republic	978	93.1
Puerto Rican	3,418	75.2
South American	4,475	96.5
Ecuadorian	2,363	97.2
Peruvian	842	96.0

Unemployment Rate
(Universe: Population 16 Years and Over)

Group	%
Total Population	8.5
Hispanic or Latino (of any race)	8.9
Central American, ex. Mexican	7.9
Dominican Republic	2.3
Puerto Rican	5.5
South American	15.6
Ecuadorian	12.2
Peruvian	29.0

Class of Worker: Private Wage and Salary
(Universe: Civilian Employed Population 16 Years and Over)

Group	Number	%
Total Population	14,869	81.6
Hispanic or Latino (of any race)	5,746	84.3
Central American, ex. Mexican	437	80.0
Dominican Republic	625	93.1
Puerto Rican	2,032	81.8
South American	2,023	86.2
Ecuadorian	1,078	87.4
Peruvian	252	76.4

Class of Worker: Government
(Universe: Civilian Employed Population 16 Years and Over)

Group	Number	%
Total Population	2,728	15.0
Hispanic or Latino (of any race)	840	12.3
Central American, ex. Mexican	49	9.0
Dominican Republic	28	4.2
Puerto Rican	423	17.0
South American	215	9.2
Ecuadorian	148	12.0
Peruvian	34	10.3

Means of Transportation to Work: Car, Truck or Van
(Universe: Workers 16 Years and Over)

Group	Number	%
Total Population	14,691	82.5
Hispanic or Latino (of any race)	5,397	80.6
Central American, ex. Mexican	360	65.9
Dominican Republic	569	89.3
Puerto Rican	2,071	84.4
South American	1,802	77.8
Ecuadorian	889	73.0
Peruvian	263	83.5

Means of Transportation to Work: Public Transportation (ex. Taxicab)
(Universe: Workers 16 Years and Over)

Group	Number	%
Total Population	1,547	8.7
Hispanic or Latino (of any race)	552	8.2
Central American, ex. Mexican	145	26.6
Dominican Republic	34	5.3
Puerto Rican	183	7.5
South American	121	5.2
Ecuadorian	48	3.9
Peruvian	34	10.8

Homeownership Rate
(Universe: Occupied Housing Units)

Group	%
Total Population	53.3
Hispanic or Latino (of any race)	47.5
Central American, ex. Mexican	48.3
Guatemalan	54.7
Honduran	54.0
Salvadoran	47.3
Cuban	57.0
Dominican Republic	49.5
Mexican	39.5
Puerto Rican	39.9
South American	53.2
Argentinean	50.0
Colombian	49.1
Ecuadorian	54.7
Peruvian	56.0
Uruguayan	33.3
Spaniard	77.5

Median Home Value

Group	Dollars
Total Population	325,400
Hispanic or Latino (of any race)	339,200
Central American, ex. Mexican	308,100
Dominican Republic	389,000
Puerto Rican	330,300
South American	346,600
Ecuadorian	343,100
Peruvian	365,200

Median Gross Rent

Group	Dollars
Total Population	1,123
Hispanic or Latino (of any race)	1,182
Central American, ex. Mexican	1,355
Dominican Republic	970
Puerto Rican	1,113
South American	1,328
Ecuadorian	1,304
Peruvian	1,099

Median Household Income
(2010 Inflation-Adjusted Dollars)

Group	Dollars
Total Population	60,127
Hispanic or Latino (of any race)	59,195
Central American, ex. Mexican	48,385
Dominican Republic	85,972
Puerto Rican	60,268
South American	52,911
Ecuadorian	38,986
Peruvian	78,333

Per Capita Income
(2010 Inflation-Adjusted Dollars)

Group	Dollars
Total Population	27,668
Hispanic or Latino (of any race)	22,407
Central American, ex. Mexican	15,771
Dominican Republic	27,251
Puerto Rican	23,979
South American	19,442
Ecuadorian	14,706
Peruvian	23,659

Households with $100,000+ Income

Group	Number	%
Total Population	2,910	22.1
Hispanic or Latino (of any race)	789	19.1
Central American, ex. Mexican	35	15.3
Dominican Republic	115	32.5
Puerto Rican	327	17.8
South American	257	19.3
Ecuadorian	53	7.2
Peruvian	70	36.8

Households with Food Stamps/SNAP Benefits During Past 12 Months

Group	Number	%
Total Population	716	5.4
Hispanic or Latino (of any race)	280	6.8
Central American, ex. Mexican	0	0.0
Dominican Republic	18	5.1
Puerto Rican	158	8.6
South American	104	7.8
Ecuadorian	76	10.3
Peruvian	0	0.0

Poverty Rate
(Income in Past 12 Months Below Poverty Level)

Group	%
Total Population	6.0
Hispanic or Latino (of any race)	8.7
Central American, ex. Mexican	0.0

Notes: (1) Percent of total population; (2) Percent of Hispanic/Latino population; Profiles include places with an overall population of at least 125,000, OR an overall population of at least 25,000 where the Hispanic/Latino population is at least 20% of the overall population. In states where less than five places meet either of these criteria, we have included places with at least 10,000 total population with the highest percentage of Hispanic/Latino population. These places are identified with an asterisk (*); Please refer to the User's Guide for a full explanation of data.

Group	%
Dominican Republic	1.6
Puerto Rican	14.1
South American	6.9
Ecuadorian	11.7
Peruvian	4.1

Bergenfield

Population

Group	Number	%TP[1]	%HP[2]
Total Population	26,764	100.0	–
Hispanic or Latino (of any race)	7,097	26.5	100.0
Central American, ex. Mexican	631	2.4	8.9
Guatemalan	105	0.4	1.5
Salvadoran	313	1.2	4.4
Cuban	323	1.2	4.6
Dominican Republic	1,818	6.8	25.6
Mexican	534	2.0	7.5
Puerto Rican	1,197	4.5	16.9
South American	2,143	8.0	30.2
Colombian	1,566	5.9	22.1
Ecuadorian	280	1.0	3.9
Peruvian	133	0.5	1.9

Population Growth: 2000–2010

Group	%
Total Population	2.0
Hispanic or Latino (of any race)	58.6
Central American, ex. Mexican	132.0
Salvadoran	187.2
Cuban	30.8
Dominican Republic	185.0
Mexican	142.7
Puerto Rican	29.3
South American	91.2
Colombian	84.2
Ecuadorian	133.3

Males per 100 Females

Group	Number
Total Population	91.7
Hispanic or Latino (of any race)	92.4
Central American, ex. Mexican	96.6
Guatemalan	90.9
Salvadoran	87.4
Cuban	78.5
Dominican Republic	92.4
Mexican	184.0
Puerto Rican	90.0
South American	80.5
Colombian	80.6
Ecuadorian	81.8
Peruvian	79.7

Average Household Size

Group	People
Total Population	3.02
Hispanic or Latino (of any race)	3.61
Central American, ex. Mexican	3.96
Guatemalan	3.55
Salvadoran	4.38
Cuban	3.16
Dominican Republic	4.07
Mexican	4.03
Puerto Rican	3.08
South American	3.51
Colombian	3.52
Ecuadorian	3.62
Peruvian	3.86

Median Age

Group	Years
Total Population	39.0
Hispanic or Latino (of any race)	32.3
Central American, ex. Mexican	32.2
Guatemalan	30.6
Salvadoran	31.9
Cuban	37.7
Dominican Republic	29.7
Mexican	28.3
Puerto Rican	34.1
South American	37.2
Colombian	38.2
Ecuadorian	34.0
Peruvian	36.8

High School Graduates
(Universe: Population 25 Years and Over)

Group	Number	%
Total Population	16,286	89.1
Hispanic or Latino (of any race)	2,840	80.3
Puerto Rican	609	87.6
South American	857	74.3
Colombian	553	65.8

Four-Year College Graduates
(Universe: Population 25 Years and Over)

Group	Number	%
Total Population	7,048	38.6
Hispanic or Latino (of any race)	912	25.8
Puerto Rican	164	23.6
South American	362	31.4
Colombian	240	28.5

Population Age 3–17 Enrolled in Public School
(Universe: Population Age 3–17 Enrolled in School)

Group	Number	%
Total Population	3,643	74.7
Hispanic or Latino (of any race)	1,049	89.8
Puerto Rican	110	84.6
South American	403	90.8
Colombian	290	100.0

Population Age 3–17 Enrolled in Private School
(Universe: Population Age 3–17 Enrolled in School)

Group	Number	%
Total Population	1,232	25.3
Hispanic or Latino (of any race)	119	10.2
Puerto Rican	20	15.4
South American	41	9.2
Colombian	0	0.0

Foreign-Born Population

Group	Number	%
Total Population	10,057	37.9
Hispanic or Latino (of any race)	2,866	52.3
Puerto Rican	15	1.5
South American	1,256	69.0
Colombian	916	70.4

Foreign-Born Naturalized U.S. Citizens

Group	Number	%
Total Population	6,343	63.1
Hispanic or Latino (of any race)	1,588	55.4
Puerto Rican	15	100.0
South American	571	45.5
Colombian	336	36.7

Language Spoken at Home: English Only
(Universe: Population 5 Years and Over)

Group	Number	%
Total Population	13,536	54.1
Hispanic or Latino (of any race)	949	18.9
Puerto Rican	401	45.9
South American	142	8.2
Colombian	44	3.5

Language Spoken at Home: Spanish
(Universe: Population 5 Years and Over)

Group	Number	%
Total Population	4,706	18.8
Hispanic or Latino (of any race)	4,045	80.7
Puerto Rican	472	54.1
South American	1,563	90.7
Colombian	1,212	96.5

Unemployment Rate
(Universe: Population 16 Years and Over)

Group	%
Total Population	5.4
Hispanic or Latino (of any race)	5.1
Puerto Rican	5.5
South American	9.1
Colombian	5.3

Class of Worker: Private Wage and Salary
(Universe: Civilian Employed Population 16 Years and Over)

Group	Number	%
Total Population	11,149	79.3
Hispanic or Latino (of any race)	2,429	83.4
Puerto Rican	401	65.1
South American	765	81.8
Colombian	629	85.1

Class of Worker: Government
(Universe: Civilian Employed Population 16 Years and Over)

Group	Number	%
Total Population	2,279	16.2
Hispanic or Latino (of any race)	335	11.5
Puerto Rican	195	31.7
South American	77	8.2
Colombian	33	4.5

Means of Transportation to Work: Car, Truck or Van
(Universe: Workers 16 Years and Over)

Group	Number	%
Total Population	11,161	81.4
Hispanic or Latino (of any race)	2,115	74.5
Puerto Rican	493	83.4
South American	694	77.6
Colombian	535	76.0

Means of Transportation to Work: Public Transportation (ex. Taxicab)
(Universe: Workers 16 Years and Over)

Group	Number	%
Total Population	1,782	13.0
Hispanic or Latino (of any race)	404	14.2
Puerto Rican	88	14.9
South American	92	10.3
Colombian	83	11.8

Homeownership Rate
(Universe: Occupied Housing Units)

Group	%
Total Population	70.3
Hispanic or Latino (of any race)	57.1
Central American, ex. Mexican	42.2
Guatemalan	45.2
Salvadoran	41.8
Cuban	73.7
Dominican Republic	73.4
Mexican	16.8
Puerto Rican	72.4
South American	45.3
Colombian	37.9
Ecuadorian	74.1
Peruvian	59.5

Median Home Value

Group	Dollars
Total Population	381,400
Hispanic or Latino (of any race)	375,000
Puerto Rican	355,500
South American	399,300
Colombian	338,800

Median Gross Rent

Group	Dollars
Total Population	1,148
Hispanic or Latino (of any race)	1,148
Puerto Rican	1,172
South American	1,166
Colombian	1,152

Median Household Income
(2010 Inflation-Adjusted Dollars)

Group	Dollars
Total Population	82,546
Hispanic or Latino (of any race)	69,226
Puerto Rican	125,168
South American	54,063
Colombian	49,957

Per Capita Income
(2010 Inflation-Adjusted Dollars)

Group	Dollars
Total Population	35,034
Hispanic or Latino (of any race)	27,325
Puerto Rican	38,085
South American	20,280
Colombian	19,853

Notes: (1) Percent of total population; (2) Percent of Hispanic/Latino population; Profiles include places with an overall population of at least 125,000, OR an overall population of at least 25,000 where the Hispanic/Latino population is at least 20% of the overall population. In states where less than five places meet either of these criteria, we have included places with at least 10,000 total population with the highest percentage of Hispanic/Latino population. These places are identified with an asterisk (*); Please refer to the User's Guide for a full explanation of data.

Households with $100,000+ Income

Group	Number	%
Total Population	3,677	39.8
Hispanic or Latino (of any race)	641	35.5
Puerto Rican	204	60.9
South American	146	25.2
Colombian	77	17.5

Households with Food Stamps/SNAP Benefits During Past 12 Months

Group	Number	%
Total Population	312	3.4
Hispanic or Latino (of any race)	82	4.5
Puerto Rican	17	5.1
South American	58	10.0
Colombian	58	13.2

Poverty Rate
(Income in Past 12 Months Below Poverty Level)

Group	%
Total Population	5.7
Hispanic or Latino (of any race)	11.0
Puerto Rican	12.8
South American	13.6
Colombian	15.6

Bloomfield

Population

Group	Number	%TP[1]	%HP[2]
Total Population	47,315	100.0	–
Hispanic or Latino (of any race)	11,606	24.5	100.0
Central American, ex. Mexican	1,031	2.2	8.9
Costa Rican	319	0.7	2.7
Guatemalan	243	0.5	2.1
Honduran	115	0.2	1.0
Salvadoran	251	0.5	2.2
Cuban	427	0.9	3.7
Dominican Republic	1,340	2.8	11.5
Mexican	420	0.9	3.6
Puerto Rican	4,156	8.8	35.8
South American	3,347	7.1	28.8
Argentinean	134	0.3	1.2
Colombian	521	1.1	4.5
Ecuadorian	1,635	3.5	14.1
Peruvian	820	1.7	7.1
Uruguayan	108	0.2	0.9
Spaniard	112	0.2	1.0

Population Growth: 2000–2010

Group	%
Total Population	-0.8
Hispanic or Latino (of any race)	68.2
Central American, ex. Mexican	89.5
Costa Rican	61.9
Guatemalan	77.4
Cuban	13.3
Dominican Republic	235.8
Mexican	162.5
Puerto Rican	52.6
South American	159.3
Colombian	122.6
Ecuadorian	218.1
Peruvian	176.1

Males per 100 Females

Group	Number
Total Population	89.6
Hispanic or Latino (of any race)	95.0
Central American, ex. Mexican	107.4
Costa Rican	168.1
Guatemalan	100.8
Honduran	64.3
Salvadoran	100.8
Cuban	88.1
Dominican Republic	85.3
Mexican	107.9
Puerto Rican	92.8
South American	96.5
Argentinean	127.1
Colombian	88.8
Ecuadorian	101.6
Peruvian	88.9
Uruguayan	116.0
Spaniard	69.7

Average Household Size

Group	People
Total Population	2.54
Hispanic or Latino (of any race)	3.29
Central American, ex. Mexican	3.43
Costa Rican	3.14
Guatemalan	3.28
Honduran	3.38
Salvadoran	3.96
Cuban	2.90
Dominican Republic	3.74
Mexican	3.32
Puerto Rican	2.93
South American	3.68
Argentinean	3.14
Colombian	3.23
Ecuadorian	3.96
Peruvian	3.72
Uruguayan	3.34
Spaniard	2.63

Median Age

Group	Years
Total Population	37.7
Hispanic or Latino (of any race)	30.4
Central American, ex. Mexican	30.6
Costa Rican	29.2
Guatemalan	34.6
Honduran	32.1
Salvadoran	31.1
Cuban	36.6
Dominican Republic	29.5
Mexican	26.7
Puerto Rican	29.8
South American	33.7
Argentinean	34.6
Colombian	33.5
Ecuadorian	32.2
Peruvian	37.7
Uruguayan	33.6
Spaniard	36.0

High School Graduates
(Universe: Population 25 Years and Over)

Group	Number	%
Total Population	29,878	90.1
Hispanic or Latino (of any race)	5,255	85.0
Puerto Rican	2,357	86.8
South American	1,722	86.6
Ecuadorian	712	80.0
Peruvian	580	94.3

Four-Year College Graduates
(Universe: Population 25 Years and Over)

Group	Number	%
Total Population	11,633	35.1
Hispanic or Latino (of any race)	1,116	18.0
Puerto Rican	410	15.1
South American	407	20.5
Ecuadorian	130	14.6
Peruvian	107	17.4

Population Age 3–17 Enrolled in Public School
(Universe: Population Age 3–17 Enrolled in School)

Group	Number	%
Total Population	5,890	81.5
Hispanic or Latino (of any race)	1,801	83.7
Puerto Rican	779	76.4
South American	493	92.5
Ecuadorian	239	93.4
Peruvian	180	95.7

Population Age 3–17 Enrolled in Private School
(Universe: Population Age 3–17 Enrolled in School)

Group	Number	%
Total Population	1,336	18.5
Hispanic or Latino (of any race)	350	16.3
Puerto Rican	240	23.6
South American	40	7.5
Ecuadorian	17	6.6
Peruvian	8	4.3

Foreign-Born Population

Group	Number	%
Total Population	12,171	25.8
Hispanic or Latino (of any race)	3,789	37.5
Puerto Rican	51	1.2
South American	2,193	67.4
Ecuadorian	1,040	73.3
Peruvian	743	62.7

Foreign-Born Naturalized U.S. Citizens

Group	Number	%
Total Population	6,851	56.3
Hispanic or Latino (of any race)	1,870	49.4
Puerto Rican	51	100.0
South American	1,014	46.2
Ecuadorian	445	42.8
Peruvian	297	40.0

Language Spoken at Home: English Only
(Universe: Population 5 Years and Over)

Group	Number	%
Total Population	28,554	64.4
Hispanic or Latino (of any race)	1,506	16.0
Puerto Rican	982	24.5
South American	210	7.2
Ecuadorian	22	1.7
Peruvian	33	3.4

Language Spoken at Home: Spanish
(Universe: Population 5 Years and Over)

Group	Number	%
Total Population	8,202	18.5
Hispanic or Latino (of any race)	7,742	82.5
Puerto Rican	2,978	74.3
South American	2,678	91.3
Ecuadorian	1,296	98.3
Peruvian	912	93.4

Unemployment Rate
(Universe: Population 16 Years and Over)

Group	%
Total Population	5.6
Hispanic or Latino (of any race)	5.1
Puerto Rican	5.0
South American	5.4
Ecuadorian	9.0
Peruvian	2.0

Class of Worker: Private Wage and Salary
(Universe: Civilian Employed Population 16 Years and Over)

Group	Number	%
Total Population	19,698	79.7
Hispanic or Latino (of any race)	4,369	83.5
Puerto Rican	1,908	80.5
South American	1,398	86.4
Ecuadorian	663	88.9
Peruvian	421	84.9

Class of Worker: Government
(Universe: Civilian Employed Population 16 Years and Over)

Group	Number	%
Total Population	3,815	15.4
Hispanic or Latino (of any race)	579	11.1
Puerto Rican	436	18.4
South American	70	4.3
Ecuadorian	24	3.2
Peruvian	27	5.4

Means of Transportation to Work: Car, Truck or Van
(Universe: Workers 16 Years and Over)

Group	Number	%
Total Population	18,464	77.3
Hispanic or Latino (of any race)	3,698	72.4
Puerto Rican	1,739	74.2
South American	1,110	71.3
Ecuadorian	499	70.9
Peruvian	388	78.2

Means of Transportation to Work: Public Transportation (ex. Taxicab)
(Universe: Workers 16 Years and Over)

Group	Number	%
Total Population	3,393	14.2
Hispanic or Latino (of any race)	757	14.8

Notes: (1) Percent of total population; (2) Percent of Hispanic/Latino population; Profiles include places with an overall population of at least 125,000, OR an overall population of at least 25,000 where the Hispanic/Latino population is at least 20% of the overall population. In states where less than five places meet either of these criteria, we have included places with at least 10,000 total population with the highest percentage of Hispanic/Latino population. These places are identified with an asterisk (*); Please refer to the User's Guide for a full explanation of data.

Puerto Rican	434	18.5
South American	218	14.0
Ecuadorian	71	10.1
Peruvian	54	10.9

Homeownership Rate
(Universe: Occupied Housing Units)

Group	%
Total Population	54.0
Hispanic or Latino (of any race)	48.3
Central American, ex. Mexican	36.9
Costa Rican	15.1
Guatemalan	44.9
Honduran	42.3
Salvadoran	56.9
Cuban	66.4
Dominican Republic	49.2
Mexican	38.5
Puerto Rican	46.2
South American	53.3
Argentinean	46.9
Colombian	54.3
Ecuadorian	56.0
Peruvian	52.6
Uruguayan	31.6
Spaniard	70.6

Median Home Value

Group	Dollars
Total Population	364,400
Hispanic or Latino (of any race)	385,400
Puerto Rican	388,600
South American	388,500
Ecuadorian	398,100
Peruvian	429,200

Median Gross Rent

Group	Dollars
Total Population	1,111
Hispanic or Latino (of any race)	1,136
Puerto Rican	1,158
South American	1,207
Ecuadorian	1,201
Peruvian	995

Median Household Income
(2010 Inflation-Adjusted Dollars)

Group	Dollars
Total Population	62,831
Hispanic or Latino (of any race)	52,479
Puerto Rican	66,833
South American	41,027
Ecuadorian	36,500
Peruvian	35,787

Per Capita Income
(2010 Inflation-Adjusted Dollars)

Group	Dollars
Total Population	30,421
Hispanic or Latino (of any race)	22,296
Puerto Rican	26,694
South American	18,126
Ecuadorian	18,480
Peruvian	13,672

Households with $100,000+ Income

Group	Number	%
Total Population	5,019	27.8
Hispanic or Latino (of any race)	757	21.9
Puerto Rican	387	25.3
South American	192	19.7
Ecuadorian	55	13.6
Peruvian	41	13.9

Households with Food Stamps/SNAP Benefits During Past 12 Months

Group	Number	%
Total Population	544	3.0
Hispanic or Latino (of any race)	234	6.8
Puerto Rican	61	4.0
South American	58	5.9
Ecuadorian	9	2.2
Peruvian	49	16.6

Poverty Rate
(Income in Past 12 Months Below Poverty Level)

Group	%
Total Population	7.4
Hispanic or Latino (of any race)	12.0
Puerto Rican	7.6
South American	19.1
Ecuadorian	20.2
Peruvian	22.7

Bridgeton

Population

Group	Number	%TP[1]	%HP[2]
Total Population	25,349	100.0	–
Hispanic or Latino (of any race)	11,046	43.6	100.0
Central American, ex. Mexican	348	1.4	3.2
Guatemalan	255	1.0	2.3
Mexican	8,063	31.8	73.0
Puerto Rican	1,439	5.7	13.0

Population Growth: 2000–2010

Group	%
Total Population	11.3
Hispanic or Latino (of any race)	98.1
Mexican	147.0
Puerto Rican	-7.6

Males per 100 Females

Group	Number
Total Population	135.3
Hispanic or Latino (of any race)	132.4
Central American, ex. Mexican	140.0
Guatemalan	168.4
Mexican	121.7
Puerto Rican	94.7

Average Household Size

Group	People
Total Population	3.36
Hispanic or Latino (of any race)	5.30
Central American, ex. Mexican	5.89
Guatemalan	6.67
Mexican	6.12
Puerto Rican	3.12

Median Age

Group	Years
Total Population	29.7
Hispanic or Latino (of any race)	24.2
Central American, ex. Mexican	25.7
Guatemalan	25.3
Mexican	22.4
Puerto Rican	24.7

High School Graduates
(Universe: Population 25 Years and Over)

Group	Number	%
Total Population	9,427	61.4
Hispanic or Latino (of any race)	1,823	34.8
Mexican	881	26.4
Puerto Rican	469	41.5

Four-Year College Graduates
(Universe: Population 25 Years and Over)

Group	Number	%
Total Population	1,097	7.1
Hispanic or Latino (of any race)	150	2.9
Mexican	76	2.3
Puerto Rican	11	1.0

Population Age 3–17 Enrolled in Public School
(Universe: Population Age 3–17 Enrolled in School)

Group	Number	%
Total Population	4,252	91.0
Hispanic or Latino (of any race)	2,090	90.7
Mexican	1,640	97.3
Puerto Rican	289	68.3

Population Age 3–17 Enrolled in Private School
(Universe: Population Age 3–17 Enrolled in School)

Group	Number	%
Total Population	418	9.0
Hispanic or Latino (of any race)	215	9.3
Mexican	45	2.7
Puerto Rican	134	31.7

Foreign-Born Population

Group	Number	%
Total Population	5,954	23.8
Hispanic or Latino (of any race)	5,368	51.6
Mexican	4,812	66.3
Puerto Rican	0	0.0

Foreign-Born Naturalized U.S. Citizens

Group	Number	%
Total Population	889	14.9
Hispanic or Latino (of any race)	630	11.7
Mexican	413	8.6
Puerto Rican	0	0.0

Language Spoken at Home: English Only
(Universe: Population 5 Years and Over)

Group	Number	%
Total Population	13,532	59.9
Hispanic or Latino (of any race)	766	8.6
Mexican	190	3.1
Puerto Rican	402	22.6

Language Spoken at Home: Spanish
(Universe: Population 5 Years and Over)

Group	Number	%
Total Population	8,555	37.9
Hispanic or Latino (of any race)	8,087	90.9
Mexican	5,900	96.8
Puerto Rican	1,368	77.0

Unemployment Rate
(Universe: Population 16 Years and Over)

Group	%
Total Population	20.4
Hispanic or Latino (of any race)	19.9
Mexican	19.5
Puerto Rican	42.8

Class of Worker: Private Wage and Salary
(Universe: Civilian Employed Population 16 Years and Over)

Group	Number	%
Total Population	5,724	82.1
Hispanic or Latino (of any race)	3,137	94.9
Mexican	2,527	95.5
Puerto Rican	214	94.3

Class of Worker: Government
(Universe: Civilian Employed Population 16 Years and Over)

Group	Number	%
Total Population	971	13.9
Hispanic or Latino (of any race)	71	2.1
Mexican	30	1.1
Puerto Rican	13	5.7

Means of Transportation to Work: Car, Truck or Van
(Universe: Workers 16 Years and Over)

Group	Number	%
Total Population	5,961	87.7
Hispanic or Latino (of any race)	2,867	88.0
Mexican	2,316	89.2
Puerto Rican	179	78.9

Means of Transportation to Work: Public Transportation (ex. Taxicab)
(Universe: Workers 16 Years and Over)

Group	Number	%
Total Population	385	5.7
Hispanic or Latino (of any race)	98	3.0
Mexican	69	2.7
Puerto Rican	16	7.0

Homeownership Rate
(Universe: Occupied Housing Units)

Group	%
Total Population	39.7
Hispanic or Latino (of any race)	23.0
Central American, ex. Mexican	13.1
Guatemalan	9.5
Mexican	21.6
Puerto Rican	26.6

Notes: (1) Percent of total population; (2) Percent of Hispanic/Latino population; Profiles include places with an overall population of at least 125,000, OR an overall population of at least 25,000 where the Hispanic/Latino population is at least 20% of the overall population. In states where less than five places meet either of these criteria, we have included places with at least 10,000 total population with the highest percentage of Hispanic/Latino population. These places are identified with an asterisk (*); Please refer to the User's Guide for a full explanation of data.

Median Home Value

Group	Dollars
Total Population	123,600
Hispanic or Latino (of any race)	141,900
Mexican	131,700
Puerto Rican	350,000

Median Gross Rent

Group	Dollars
Total Population	873
Hispanic or Latino (of any race)	1,049
Mexican	1,167
Puerto Rican	651

Median Household Income
(2010 Inflation-Adjusted Dollars)

Group	Dollars
Total Population	31,044
Hispanic or Latino (of any race)	32,383
Mexican	42,165
Puerto Rican	9,519

Per Capita Income
(2010 Inflation-Adjusted Dollars)

Group	Dollars
Total Population	12,418
Hispanic or Latino (of any race)	11,092
Mexican	11,560
Puerto Rican	6,537

Households with $100,000+ Income

Group	Number	%
Total Population	532	8.5
Hispanic or Latino (of any race)	263	15.0
Mexican	198	17.0
Puerto Rican	6	1.6

Households with Food Stamps/SNAP Benefits During Past 12 Months

Group	Number	%
Total Population	1,510	24.2
Hispanic or Latino (of any race)	574	32.7
Mexican	394	33.9
Puerto Rican	137	35.4

Poverty Rate
(Income in Past 12 Months Below Poverty Level)

Group	%
Total Population	27.7
Hispanic or Latino (of any race)	30.9
Mexican	28.9
Puerto Rican	51.4

Camden

Population

Group	Number	%TP[1]	%HP[2]
Total Population	77,344	100.0	–
Hispanic or Latino (of any race)	36,379	47.0	100.0
Central American, ex. Mexican	1,737	2.2	4.8
Guatemalan	439	0.6	1.2
Honduran	110	0.1	0.3
Nicaraguan	880	1.1	2.4
Salvadoran	188	0.2	0.5
Cuban	218	0.3	0.6
Dominican Republic	4,006	5.2	11.0
Mexican	5,035	6.5	13.8
Puerto Rican	23,759	30.7	65.3
South American	279	0.4	0.8
Ecuadorian	118	0.2	0.3

Population Growth: 2000–2010

Group	%
Total Population	-3.2
Hispanic or Latino (of any race)	17.3
Central American, ex. Mexican	88.8
Guatemalan	295.5
Nicaraguan	45.0
Cuban	5.8
Dominican Republic	113.8
Mexican	163.9
Puerto Rican	3.1
South American	61.3

Males per 100 Females

Group	Number
Total Population	94.7
Hispanic or Latino (of any race)	100.8
Central American, ex. Mexican	119.3
Guatemalan	179.6
Honduran	115.7
Nicaraguan	94.7
Salvadoran	144.2
Cuban	113.7
Dominican Republic	93.9
Mexican	144.8
Puerto Rican	92.7
South American	121.4
Ecuadorian	118.5

Average Household Size

Group	People
Total Population	3.02
Hispanic or Latino (of any race)	3.50
Central American, ex. Mexican	4.20
Guatemalan	4.86
Honduran	4.44
Nicaraguan	3.97
Salvadoran	4.27
Cuban	3.19
Dominican Republic	4.05
Mexican	5.18
Puerto Rican	3.18
South American	3.33
Ecuadorian	3.97

Median Age

Group	Years
Total Population	28.5
Hispanic or Latino (of any race)	26.2
Central American, ex. Mexican	30.0
Guatemalan	27.2
Honduran	33.0
Nicaraguan	32.7
Salvadoran	28.9
Cuban	28.7
Dominican Republic	28.0
Mexican	24.5
Puerto Rican	26.5
South American	34.4
Ecuadorian	35.0

High School Graduates
(Universe: Population 25 Years and Over)

Group	Number	%
Total Population	26,774	62.0
Hispanic or Latino (of any race)	9,021	49.1
Central American, ex. Mexican	601	45.0
Dominican Republic	1,147	54.4
Mexican	792	34.7
Puerto Rican	5,643	50.1

Four-Year College Graduates
(Universe: Population 25 Years and Over)

Group	Number	%
Total Population	2,936	6.8
Hispanic or Latino (of any race)	885	4.8
Central American, ex. Mexican	27	2.0
Dominican Republic	249	11.8
Mexican	63	2.8
Puerto Rican	304	2.7

Population Age 3–17 Enrolled in Public School
(Universe: Population Age 3–17 Enrolled in School)

Group	Number	%
Total Population	17,174	92.1
Hispanic or Latino (of any race)	7,912	91.9
Central American, ex. Mexican	464	88.2
Dominican Republic	701	92.5
Mexican	842	97.6
Puerto Rican	5,501	91.1

Population Age 3–17 Enrolled in Private School
(Universe: Population Age 3–17 Enrolled in School)

Group	Number	%
Total Population	1,473	7.9
Hispanic or Latino (of any race)	693	8.1
Central American, ex. Mexican	62	11.8
Dominican Republic	57	7.5
Mexican	21	2.4
Puerto Rican	539	8.9

Foreign-Born Population

Group	Number	%
Total Population	11,043	14.1
Hispanic or Latino (of any race)	8,390	24.1
Central American, ex. Mexican	1,655	76.6
Dominican Republic	2,594	69.9
Mexican	3,004	67.6
Puerto Rican	170	0.8

Foreign-Born Naturalized U.S. Citizens

Group	Number	%
Total Population	2,842	25.7
Hispanic or Latino (of any race)	1,574	18.8
Central American, ex. Mexican	164	9.9
Dominican Republic	739	28.5
Mexican	188	6.3
Puerto Rican	86	50.6

Language Spoken at Home: English Only
(Universe: Population 5 Years and Over)

Group	Number	%
Total Population	42,558	60.1
Hispanic or Latino (of any race)	6,093	19.6
Central American, ex. Mexican	144	7.2
Dominican Republic	111	3.2
Mexican	151	3.9
Puerto Rican	5,306	26.9

Language Spoken at Home: Spanish
(Universe: Population 5 Years and Over)

Group	Number	%
Total Population	25,787	36.4
Hispanic or Latino (of any race)	24,988	80.4
Central American, ex. Mexican	1,867	92.8
Dominican Republic	3,306	96.8
Mexican	3,720	96.1
Puerto Rican	14,394	73.1

Unemployment Rate
(Universe: Population 16 Years and Over)

Group	%
Total Population	19.3
Hispanic or Latino (of any race)	18.3
Central American, ex. Mexican	16.0
Dominican Republic	6.7
Mexican	6.7
Puerto Rican	25.5

Class of Worker: Private Wage and Salary
(Universe: Civilian Employed Population 16 Years and Over)

Group	Number	%
Total Population	21,331	82.5
Hispanic or Latino (of any race)	10,653	87.2
Central American, ex. Mexican	979	92.6
Dominican Republic	1,525	82.9
Mexican	2,241	97.6
Puerto Rican	5,251	84.4

Class of Worker: Government
(Universe: Civilian Employed Population 16 Years and Over)

Group	Number	%
Total Population	3,664	14.2
Hispanic or Latino (of any race)	1,106	9.1
Central American, ex. Mexican	66	6.2
Dominican Republic	124	6.7
Mexican	9	0.4
Puerto Rican	829	13.3

Means of Transportation to Work: Car, Truck or Van
(Universe: Workers 16 Years and Over)

Group	Number	%
Total Population	18,164	73.4
Hispanic or Latino (of any race)	8,936	76.5
Central American, ex. Mexican	674	65.8
Dominican Republic	1,417	81.8
Mexican	1,685	75.7
Puerto Rican	4,608	77.7

Notes: (1) Percent of total population; (2) Percent of Hispanic/Latino population; Profiles include places with an overall population of at least 125,000, OR an overall population of at least 25,000 where the Hispanic/Latino population is at least 20% of the overall population. In states where less than five places meet either of these criteria, we have included places with at least 10,000 total population with the highest percentage of Hispanic/Latino population. These places are identified with an asterisk (*); Please refer to the User's Guide for a full explanation of data.

Means of Transportation to Work: Public Transportation (ex. Taxicab)
(Universe: Workers 16 Years and Over)

Group	Number	%
Total Population	4,062	16.4
Hispanic or Latino (of any race)	1,354	11.6
Central American, ex. Mexican	149	14.6
Dominican Republic	133	7.7
Mexican	236	10.6
Puerto Rican	719	12.1

Homeownership Rate
(Universe: Occupied Housing Units)

Group	%
Total Population	39.2
Hispanic or Latino (of any race)	37.1
Central American, ex. Mexican	51.3
Guatemalan	29.0
Honduran	64.0
Nicaraguan	60.7
Salvadoran	44.4
Cuban	40.3
Dominican Republic	55.4
Mexican	18.2
Puerto Rican	36.2
South American	44.0
Ecuadorian	50.0

Median Home Value

Group	Dollars
Total Population	88,300
Hispanic or Latino (of any race)	98,400
Central American, ex. Mexican	80,500
Dominican Republic	106,600
Mexican	68,600
Puerto Rican	97,300

Median Gross Rent

Group	Dollars
Total Population	783
Hispanic or Latino (of any race)	853
Central American, ex. Mexican	880
Dominican Republic	972
Mexican	1,088
Puerto Rican	766

Median Household Income
(2010 Inflation-Adjusted Dollars)

Group	Dollars
Total Population	27,027
Hispanic or Latino (of any race)	27,828
Central American, ex. Mexican	42,989
Dominican Republic	37,500
Mexican	42,311
Puerto Rican	25,842

Per Capita Income
(2010 Inflation-Adjusted Dollars)

Group	Dollars
Total Population	12,807
Hispanic or Latino (of any race)	10,941
Central American, ex. Mexican	12,645
Dominican Republic	13,359
Mexican	10,324
Puerto Rican	10,341

Households with $100,000+ Income

Group	Number	%
Total Population	1,405	5.6
Hispanic or Latino (of any race)	471	4.7
Central American, ex. Mexican	66	13.4
Dominican Republic	57	5.9
Mexican	108	11.0
Puerto Rican	218	3.2

Households with Food Stamps/SNAP Benefits During Past 12 Months

Group	Number	%
Total Population	6,860	27.1
Hispanic or Latino (of any race)	3,094	30.6
Central American, ex. Mexican	49	10.0
Dominican Republic	275	28.6
Mexican	139	14.2
Puerto Rican	2,398	35.2

Poverty Rate
(Income in Past 12 Months Below Poverty Level)

Group	%
Total Population	36.1
Hispanic or Latino (of any race)	34.7
Central American, ex. Mexican	28.1
Dominican Republic	22.3
Mexican	40.6
Puerto Rican	36.8

City of Orange

Population

Group	Number	%TP[1]	%HP[2]
Total Population	30,134	100.0	–
Hispanic or Latino (of any race)	6,531	21.7	100.0
Central American, ex. Mexican	1,514	5.0	23.2
Guatemalan	434	1.4	6.6
Honduran	144	0.5	2.2
Salvadoran	809	2.7	12.4
Dominican Republic	509	1.7	7.8
Mexican	856	2.8	13.1
Puerto Rican	523	1.7	8.0
South American	2,375	7.9	36.4
Ecuadorian	1,210	4.0	18.5
Peruvian	491	1.6	7.5
Uruguayan	445	1.5	6.8

Population Growth: 2000–2010

Group	%
Total Population	-8.3
Hispanic or Latino (of any race)	59.4
Central American, ex. Mexican	160.6
Guatemalan	325.5
Salvadoran	131.1
Dominican Republic	56.1
Mexican	121.2
Puerto Rican	-2.8
South American	109.4
Ecuadorian	317.2
Peruvian	25.6
Uruguayan	134.2

Males per 100 Females

Group	Number
Total Population	89.0
Hispanic or Latino (of any race)	133.0
Central American, ex. Mexican	176.8
Guatemalan	317.3
Honduran	242.9
Salvadoran	133.1
Dominican Republic	93.5
Mexican	143.2
Puerto Rican	95.1
South American	132.4
Ecuadorian	154.2
Peruvian	115.4
Uruguayan	118.1

Average Household Size

Group	People
Total Population	2.66
Hispanic or Latino (of any race)	3.58
Central American, ex. Mexican	3.97
Guatemalan	4.18
Honduran	3.29
Salvadoran	4.16
Dominican Republic	3.40
Mexican	4.14
Puerto Rican	2.63
South American	3.63
Ecuadorian	4.53
Peruvian	2.95
Uruguayan	3.01

Median Age

Group	Years
Total Population	34.4
Hispanic or Latino (of any race)	29.0
Central American, ex. Mexican	29.2
Guatemalan	28.5
Honduran	30.1
Salvadoran	29.0
Dominican Republic	29.3
Mexican	26.2
Puerto Rican	25.4
South American	31.1
Ecuadorian	28.4
Peruvian	34.9
Uruguayan	34.4

High School Graduates
(Universe: Population 25 Years and Over)

Group	Number	%
Total Population	14,955	77.5
Hispanic or Latino (of any race)	2,113	60.3
Central American, ex. Mexican	254	36.3
South American	938	62.7
Ecuadorian	232	43.7

Four-Year College Graduates
(Universe: Population 25 Years and Over)

Group	Number	%
Total Population	3,463	18.0
Hispanic or Latino (of any race)	143	4.1
Central American, ex. Mexican	9	1.3
South American	45	3.0
Ecuadorian	5	0.9

Population Age 3–17 Enrolled in Public School
(Universe: Population Age 3–17 Enrolled in School)

Group	Number	%
Total Population	4,639	80.2
Hispanic or Latino (of any race)	902	89.7
Central American, ex. Mexican	225	72.6
South American	226	95.4
Ecuadorian	72	100.0

Population Age 3–17 Enrolled in Private School
(Universe: Population Age 3–17 Enrolled in School)

Group	Number	%
Total Population	1,148	19.8
Hispanic or Latino (of any race)	104	10.3
Central American, ex. Mexican	85	27.4
South American	11	4.6
Ecuadorian	0	0.0

Foreign-Born Population

Group	Number	%
Total Population	10,947	36.0
Hispanic or Latino (of any race)	3,709	62.9
Central American, ex. Mexican	924	78.6
South American	1,827	77.5
Ecuadorian	813	84.1

Foreign-Born Naturalized U.S. Citizens

Group	Number	%
Total Population	3,850	35.2
Hispanic or Latino (of any race)	476	12.8
Central American, ex. Mexican	83	9.0
South American	192	10.5
Ecuadorian	92	11.3

Language Spoken at Home: English Only
(Universe: Population 5 Years and Over)

Group	Number	%
Total Population	17,796	64.6
Hispanic or Latino (of any race)	433	8.4
Central American, ex. Mexican	28	2.5
South American	162	7.7
Ecuadorian	63	7.3

Language Spoken at Home: Spanish
(Universe: Population 5 Years and Over)

Group	Number	%
Total Population	4,884	17.7
Hispanic or Latino (of any race)	4,680	91.1
Central American, ex. Mexican	1,085	97.5
South American	1,931	92.3
Ecuadorian	798	92.7

Unemployment Rate
(Universe: Population 16 Years and Over)

Group	%
Total Population	10.2
Hispanic or Latino (of any race)	6.3
Central American, ex. Mexican	8.0
South American	2.6
Ecuadorian	0.8

Notes: (1) Percent of total population; (2) Percent of Hispanic/Latino population; Profiles include places with an overall population of at least 125,000, OR an overall population of at least 25,000 where the Hispanic/Latino population is at least 20% of the overall population. In states where less than five places meet either of these criteria, we have included places with at least 10,000 total population with the highest percentage of Hispanic/Latino population. These places are identified with an asterisk (*); Please refer to the User's Guide for a full explanation of data.

Class of Worker: Private Wage and Salary
(Universe: Civilian Employed Population 16 Years and Over)

Group	Number	%
Total Population	11,812	80.9
Hispanic or Latino (of any race)	2,871	89.1
Central American, ex. Mexican	642	91.7
South American	1,401	94.9
Ecuadorian	573	93.9

Class of Worker: Government
(Universe: Civilian Employed Population 16 Years and Over)

Group	Number	%
Total Population	2,360	16.2
Hispanic or Latino (of any race)	191	5.9
Central American, ex. Mexican	28	4.0
South American	9	0.6
Ecuadorian	0	0.0

Means of Transportation to Work: Car, Truck or Van
(Universe: Workers 16 Years and Over)

Group	Number	%
Total Population	9,780	68.7
Hispanic or Latino (of any race)	2,029	64.4
Central American, ex. Mexican	392	56.1
South American	996	69.7
Ecuadorian	380	62.3

Means of Transportation to Work: Public Transportation (ex. Taxicab)
(Universe: Workers 16 Years and Over)

Group	Number	%
Total Population	3,146	22.1
Hispanic or Latino (of any race)	546	17.3
Central American, ex. Mexican	59	8.4
South American	236	16.5
Ecuadorian	128	21.0

Homeownership Rate
(Universe: Occupied Housing Units)

Group	%
Total Population	25.1
Hispanic or Latino (of any race)	16.6
Central American, ex. Mexican	14.6
Guatemalan	6.6
Honduran	14.7
Salvadoran	18.2
Dominican Republic	22.0
Mexican	11.0
Puerto Rican	20.0
South American	16.5
Ecuadorian	10.6
Peruvian	13.6
Uruguayan	20.6

Median Home Value

Group	Dollars
Total Population	292,800
Hispanic or Latino (of any race)	289,500
Central American, ex. Mexican	336,500
South American	287,500
Ecuadorian	291,300

Median Gross Rent

Group	Dollars
Total Population	964
Hispanic or Latino (of any race)	1,055
Central American, ex. Mexican	1,123
South American	1,099
Ecuadorian	1,129

Median Household Income
(2010 Inflation-Adjusted Dollars)

Group	Dollars
Total Population	40,818
Hispanic or Latino (of any race)	38,638
Central American, ex. Mexican	53,182
South American	36,042
Ecuadorian	38,043

Per Capita Income
(2010 Inflation-Adjusted Dollars)

Group	Dollars
Total Population	19,816
Hispanic or Latino (of any race)	14,034
Central American, ex. Mexican	15,268
South American	14,776
Ecuadorian	14,263

Households with $100,000+ Income

Group	Number	%
Total Population	1,139	10.2
Hispanic or Latino (of any race)	148	8.6
Central American, ex. Mexican	70	24.3
South American	9	1.2
Ecuadorian	0	0.0

Households with Food Stamps/SNAP Benefits During Past 12 Months

Group	Number	%
Total Population	1,226	11.0
Hispanic or Latino (of any race)	329	19.2
Central American, ex. Mexican	65	22.6
South American	104	14.0
Ecuadorian	43	16.7

Poverty Rate
(Income in Past 12 Months Below Poverty Level)

Group	%
Total Population	18.1
Hispanic or Latino (of any race)	23.2
Central American, ex. Mexican	21.1
South American	25.3
Ecuadorian	29.0

Clifton

Population

Group	Number	%TP[1]	%HP[2]
Total Population	84,136	100.0	–
Hispanic or Latino (of any race)	26,854	31.9	100.0
Central American, ex. Mexican	1,036	1.2	3.9
Costa Rican	163	0.2	0.6
Guatemalan	227	0.3	0.8
Honduran	215	0.3	0.8
Salvadoran	345	0.4	1.3
Cuban	754	0.9	2.8
Dominican Republic	4,561	5.4	17.0
Mexican	3,538	4.2	13.2
Puerto Rican	5,969	7.1	22.2
South American	9,347	11.1	34.8
Argentinean	243	0.3	0.9
Bolivian	255	0.3	0.9
Chilean	149	0.2	0.6
Colombian	2,973	3.5	11.1
Ecuadorian	993	1.2	3.7
Peruvian	4,473	5.3	16.7
Venezuelan	153	0.2	0.6
Spaniard	127	0.2	0.5

Population Growth: 2000–2010

Group	%
Total Population	6.9
Hispanic or Latino (of any race)	72.1
Central American, ex. Mexican	125.7
Honduran	64.1
Cuban	47.8
Dominican Republic	146.1
Mexican	122.4
Puerto Rican	52.2
South American	117.1
Argentinean	51.9
Bolivian	116.1
Colombian	88.0
Ecuadorian	144.6
Peruvian	150.2

Males per 100 Females

Group	Number
Total Population	93.2
Hispanic or Latino (of any race)	92.1
Central American, ex. Mexican	101.9
Costa Rican	98.8
Guatemalan	138.9
Honduran	87.0
Salvadoran	94.9
Cuban	106.0
Dominican Republic	80.5
Mexican	114.3
Puerto Rican	93.5
South American	87.5
Argentinean	122.9
Bolivian	88.9
Chilean	91.0
Colombian	81.9
Ecuadorian	88.8
Peruvian	89.9
Venezuelan	68.1
Spaniard	122.8

Average Household Size

Group	People
Total Population	2.74
Hispanic or Latino (of any race)	3.52
Central American, ex. Mexican	3.69
Costa Rican	3.04
Guatemalan	4.15
Honduran	3.91
Salvadoran	3.83
Cuban	3.00
Dominican Republic	3.66
Mexican	4.63
Puerto Rican	3.00
South American	3.60
Argentinean	3.08
Bolivian	3.96
Chilean	3.21
Colombian	3.44
Ecuadorian	3.66
Peruvian	3.74
Venezuelan	3.42
Spaniard	2.34

Median Age

Group	Years
Total Population	38.4
Hispanic or Latino (of any race)	31.2
Central American, ex. Mexican	32.3
Costa Rican	33.2
Guatemalan	34.8
Honduran	30.3
Salvadoran	31.0
Cuban	36.6
Dominican Republic	30.2
Mexican	26.5
Puerto Rican	30.8
South American	35.6
Argentinean	37.4
Bolivian	34.1
Chilean	36.5
Colombian	35.6
Ecuadorian	35.1
Peruvian	35.9
Venezuelan	27.5
Spaniard	40.3

High School Graduates
(Universe: Population 25 Years and Over)

Group	Number	%
Total Population	50,632	86.8
Hispanic or Latino (of any race)	12,969	81.9
Dominican Republic	1,791	78.4
Mexican	1,221	60.4
Puerto Rican	2,802	82.5
South American	6,046	89.1
Colombian	1,687	92.4
Ecuadorian	660	84.9
Peruvian	3,263	92.1

Four-Year College Graduates
(Universe: Population 25 Years and Over)

Group	Number	%
Total Population	18,082	31.0
Hispanic or Latino (of any race)	3,295	20.8
Dominican Republic	403	17.6
Mexican	199	9.8
Puerto Rican	608	17.9
South American	1,863	27.5
Colombian	507	27.8
Ecuadorian	98	12.6
Peruvian	1,126	31.8

STATE & PLACE PROFILES

Notes: (1) Percent of total population; (2) Percent of Hispanic/Latino population; Profiles include places with an overall population of at least 125,000, OR an overall population of at least 25,000 where the Hispanic/Latino population is at least 20% of the overall population. In states where less than five places meet either of these criteria, we have included places with at least 10,000 total population with the highest percentage of Hispanic/Latino population. These places are identified with an asterisk (*); Please refer to the User's Guide for a full explanation of data.

Population Age 3–17 Enrolled in Public School
(Universe: Population Age 3–17 Enrolled in School)

Group	Number	%
Total Population	10,118	81.8
Hispanic or Latino (of any race)	4,521	91.6
Dominican Republic	772	96.7
Mexican	949	94.6
Puerto Rican	995	90.4
South American	1,237	86.9
Colombian	384	91.6
Ecuadorian	243	100.0
Peruvian	518	79.7

Population Age 3–17 Enrolled in Private School
(Universe: Population Age 3–17 Enrolled in School)

Group	Number	%
Total Population	2,256	18.2
Hispanic or Latino (of any race)	413	8.4
Dominican Republic	26	3.3
Mexican	54	5.4
Puerto Rican	106	9.6
South American	187	13.1
Colombian	35	8.4
Ecuadorian	0	0.0
Peruvian	132	20.3

Foreign-Born Population

Group	Number	%
Total Population	28,552	34.5
Hispanic or Latino (of any race)	12,280	49.3
Dominican Republic	2,408	64.2
Mexican	1,745	48.2
Puerto Rican	91	1.6
South American	6,894	71.8
Colombian	1,619	62.3
Ecuadorian	748	63.6
Peruvian	3,728	77.8

Foreign-Born Naturalized U.S. Citizens

Group	Number	%
Total Population	16,213	56.8
Hispanic or Latino (of any race)	5,572	45.4
Dominican Republic	1,363	56.6
Mexican	387	22.2
Puerto Rican	36	39.6
South American	3,087	44.8
Colombian	1,010	62.4
Ecuadorian	335	44.8
Peruvian	1,518	40.7

Language Spoken at Home: English Only
(Universe: Population 5 Years and Over)

Group	Number	%
Total Population	36,758	47.2
Hispanic or Latino (of any race)	2,248	9.7
Dominican Republic	140	4.1
Mexican	156	4.8
Puerto Rican	933	18.3
South American	576	6.3
Colombian	233	9.4
Ecuadorian	34	2.9
Peruvian	220	4.9

Language Spoken at Home: Spanish
(Universe: Population 5 Years and Over)

Group	Number	%
Total Population	21,997	28.2
Hispanic or Latino (of any race)	20,697	89.4
Dominican Republic	3,282	95.4
Mexican	3,094	95.2
Puerto Rican	4,121	80.8
South American	8,476	92.6
Colombian	2,256	90.6
Ecuadorian	1,053	90.5
Peruvian	4,275	95.1

Unemployment Rate
(Universe: Population 16 Years and Over)

Group	%
Total Population	6.7
Hispanic or Latino (of any race)	8.3
Dominican Republic	4.8
Mexican	4.0
Puerto Rican	14.8
South American	7.3
Colombian	4.1
Ecuadorian	0.0
Peruvian	11.4

Class of Worker: Private Wage and Salary
(Universe: Civilian Employed Population 16 Years and Over)

Group	Number	%
Total Population	35,799	85.0
Hispanic or Latino (of any race)	11,469	89.3
Dominican Republic	1,802	87.4
Mexican	1,687	97.2
Puerto Rican	2,348	86.2
South American	4,690	89.8
Colombian	1,246	80.9
Ecuadorian	422	79.0
Peruvian	2,421	96.1

Class of Worker: Government
(Universe: Civilian Employed Population 16 Years and Over)

Group	Number	%
Total Population	4,889	11.6
Hispanic or Latino (of any race)	1,148	8.9
Dominican Republic	260	12.6
Mexican	0	0.0
Puerto Rican	367	13.5
South American	381	7.3
Colombian	189	12.3
Ecuadorian	112	21.0
Peruvian	71	2.8

Means of Transportation to Work: Car, Truck or Van
(Universe: Workers 16 Years and Over)

Group	Number	%
Total Population	34,294	83.8
Hispanic or Latino (of any race)	9,765	78.5
Dominican Republic	1,660	83.8
Mexican	1,116	64.3
Puerto Rican	2,347	86.5
South American	3,776	76.3
Colombian	1,308	87.7
Ecuadorian	401	84.1
Peruvian	1,669	70.5

Means of Transportation to Work: Public Transportation (ex. Taxicab)
(Universe: Workers 16 Years and Over)

Group	Number	%
Total Population	3,768	9.2
Hispanic or Latino (of any race)	1,413	11.4
Dominican Republic	217	11.0
Mexican	255	14.7
Puerto Rican	180	6.6
South American	659	13.3
Colombian	104	7.0
Ecuadorian	12	2.5
Peruvian	409	17.3

Homeownership Rate
(Universe: Occupied Housing Units)

Group	%
Total Population	59.9
Hispanic or Latino (of any race)	44.8
Central American, ex. Mexican	50.0
Costa Rican	36.7
Guatemalan	51.6
Honduran	58.5
Salvadoran	54.0
Cuban	65.5
Dominican Republic	46.5
Mexican	31.1
Puerto Rican	42.9
South American	45.9
Argentinean	45.3
Bolivian	33.3
Chilean	58.3
Colombian	49.4
Ecuadorian	52.4
Peruvian	42.5
Venezuelan	26.3
Spaniard	64.0

Median Home Value

Group	Dollars
Total Population	369,800
Hispanic or Latino (of any race)	371,500
Dominican Republic	434,300
Mexican	361,200
Puerto Rican	342,900
South American	384,800
Colombian	395,600
Ecuadorian	390,500
Peruvian	377,100

Median Gross Rent

Group	Dollars
Total Population	1,139
Hispanic or Latino (of any race)	1,235
Dominican Republic	1,334
Mexican	1,213
Puerto Rican	1,314
South American	1,166
Colombian	1,172
Ecuadorian	931
Peruvian	1,192

Median Household Income
(2010 Inflation-Adjusted Dollars)

Group	Dollars
Total Population	62,271
Hispanic or Latino (of any race)	54,479
Dominican Republic	55,888
Mexican	40,536
Puerto Rican	65,613
South American	54,794
Colombian	59,549
Ecuadorian	70,192
Peruvian	40,758

Per Capita Income
(2010 Inflation-Adjusted Dollars)

Group	Dollars
Total Population	29,812
Hispanic or Latino (of any race)	20,405
Dominican Republic	20,645
Mexican	13,534
Puerto Rican	26,144
South American	19,606
Colombian	23,523
Ecuadorian	23,241
Peruvian	16,416

Households with $100,000+ Income

Group	Number	%
Total Population	8,187	27.7
Hispanic or Latino (of any race)	1,274	18.8
Dominican Republic	179	17.2
Mexican	56	6.4
Puerto Rican	356	19.4
South American	566	23.4
Colombian	187	24.0
Ecuadorian	133	42.4
Peruvian	224	20.3

Households with Food Stamps/SNAP Benefits During Past 12 Months

Group	Number	%
Total Population	1,032	3.5
Hispanic or Latino (of any race)	476	7.0
Dominican Republic	91	8.7
Mexican	82	9.3
Puerto Rican	101	5.5
South American	202	8.3
Colombian	17	2.2
Ecuadorian	0	0.0
Peruvian	185	16.7

Poverty Rate
(Income in Past 12 Months Below Poverty Level)

Group	%
Total Population	9.3
Hispanic or Latino (of any race)	13.4
Dominican Republic	19.9
Mexican	16.0
Puerto Rican	9.5
South American	12.5
Colombian	7.1
Ecuadorian	15.4
Peruvian	16.8

Notes: (1) Percent of total population; (2) Percent of Hispanic/Latino population; Profiles include places with an overall population of at least 125,000, OR an overall population of at least 25,000 where the Hispanic/Latino population is at least 20% of the overall population. In states where less than five places meet either of these criteria, we have included places with at least 10,000 total population with the highest percentage of Hispanic/Latino population. These places are identified with an asterisk (*); Please refer to the User's Guide for a full explanation of data.

Elizabeth

Population

Group	Number	%TP[1]	%HP[2]
Total Population	124,969	100.0	–
Hispanic or Latino (of any race)	74,353	59.5	100.0
Central American, ex. Mexican	12,097	9.7	16.3
Costa Rican	660	0.5	0.9
Guatemalan	1,131	0.9	1.5
Honduran	2,338	1.9	3.1
Nicaraguan	407	0.3	0.5
Panamanian	127	0.1	0.2
Salvadoran	7,364	5.9	9.9
Cuban	6,570	5.3	8.8
Dominican Republic	7,073	5.7	9.5
Mexican	4,126	3.3	5.5
Puerto Rican	13,488	10.8	18.1
South American	25,649	20.5	34.5
Argentinean	557	0.4	0.7
Bolivian	164	0.1	0.2
Chilean	212	0.2	0.3
Colombian	10,692	8.6	14.4
Ecuadorian	5,591	4.5	7.5
Peruvian	5,419	4.3	7.3
Uruguayan	2,553	2.0	3.4
Venezuelan	389	0.3	0.5
Spaniard	417	0.3	0.6

Population Growth: 2000–2010

Group	%
Total Population	3.7
Hispanic or Latino (of any race)	24.7
Central American, ex. Mexican	97.5
Costa Rican	104.3
Guatemalan	110.6
Honduran	113.7
Nicaraguan	46.9
Salvadoran	109.3
Cuban	-7.1
Dominican Republic	94.9
Mexican	156.0
Puerto Rican	3.8
South American	72.9
Argentinean	78.5
Bolivian	35.5
Chilean	1.4
Colombian	37.2
Ecuadorian	161.9
Peruvian	91.5
Uruguayan	230.7
Venezuelan	31.4
Spaniard	44.3

Males per 100 Females

Group	Number
Total Population	98.6
Hispanic or Latino (of any race)	100.5
Central American, ex. Mexican	118.2
Costa Rican	154.8
Guatemalan	133.7
Honduran	113.7
Nicaraguan	101.5
Panamanian	64.9
Salvadoran	116.8
Cuban	98.5
Dominican Republic	85.6
Mexican	138.2
Puerto Rican	93.3
South American	95.3
Argentinean	109.4
Bolivian	97.6
Chilean	112.0
Colombian	83.1
Ecuadorian	118.1
Peruvian	96.6
Uruguayan	98.8
Venezuelan	89.8
Spaniard	112.8

Average Household Size

Group	People
Total Population	2.94
Hispanic or Latino (of any race)	3.29
Central American, ex. Mexican	4.05
Costa Rican	3.26
Guatemalan	4.04
Honduran	3.77
Nicaraguan	3.57
Panamanian	2.92
Salvadoran	4.30
Cuban	2.53
Dominican Republic	3.55
Mexican	4.37
Puerto Rican	2.90
South American	3.35
Argentinean	2.94
Bolivian	3.09
Chilean	2.56
Colombian	3.15
Ecuadorian	3.77
Peruvian	3.66
Uruguayan	3.10
Venezuelan	2.95
Spaniard	2.57

Median Age

Group	Years
Total Population	33.2
Hispanic or Latino (of any race)	31.7
Central American, ex. Mexican	30.5
Costa Rican	33.7
Guatemalan	30.5
Honduran	31.5
Nicaraguan	36.3
Panamanian	31.5
Salvadoran	29.6
Cuban	45.4
Dominican Republic	30.1
Mexican	25.5
Puerto Rican	29.4
South American	35.1
Argentinean	34.0
Bolivian	39.6
Chilean	45.6
Colombian	37.0
Ecuadorian	32.4
Peruvian	36.4
Uruguayan	33.4
Venezuelan	32.1
Spaniard	43.3

High School Graduates

(Universe: Population 25 Years and Over)

Group	Number	%
Total Population	55,117	70.9
Hispanic or Latino (of any race)	28,915	67.0
Central American, ex. Mexican	3,609	48.3
Guatemalan	500	58.6
Honduran	660	56.1
Salvadoran	1,963	41.9
Cuban	2,470	67.4
Dominican Republic	2,417	71.6
Mexican	1,036	45.8
Puerto Rican	5,343	70.3
South American	13,370	74.9
Colombian	5,660	79.7
Ecuadorian	2,865	66.7
Peruvian	3,236	84.6
Uruguayan	1,090	63.6

Four-Year College Graduates

(Universe: Population 25 Years and Over)

Group	Number	%
Total Population	9,126	11.7
Hispanic or Latino (of any race)	3,296	7.6
Central American, ex. Mexican	185	2.5
Guatemalan	45	5.3
Honduran	14	1.2
Salvadoran	115	2.5
Cuban	411	11.2
Dominican Republic	240	7.1
Mexican	127	5.6
Puerto Rican	476	6.3
South American	1,739	9.7
Colombian	812	11.4
Ecuadorian	312	7.3
Peruvian	441	11.5
Uruguayan	108	6.3

Population Age 3–17 Enrolled in Public School

(Universe: Population Age 3–17 Enrolled in School)

Group	Number	%
Total Population	21,980	92.0
Hispanic or Latino (of any race)	13,526	95.4
Central American, ex. Mexican	2,235	92.3
Guatemalan	166	100.0
Honduran	377	94.5
Salvadoran	1,443	100.0
Cuban	399	93.0
Dominican Republic	1,788	96.3
Mexican	574	97.6
Puerto Rican	3,148	97.0
South American	5,028	95.6
Colombian	1,706	95.1
Ecuadorian	1,205	91.3
Peruvian	1,061	98.4
Uruguayan	752	100.0

Population Age 3–17 Enrolled in Private School

(Universe: Population Age 3–17 Enrolled in School)

Group	Number	%
Total Population	1,924	8.0
Hispanic or Latino (of any race)	651	4.6
Central American, ex. Mexican	186	7.7
Guatemalan	0	0.0
Honduran	22	5.5
Salvadoran	0	0.0
Cuban	30	7.0
Dominican Republic	69	3.7
Mexican	14	2.4
Puerto Rican	97	3.0
South American	234	4.4
Colombian	88	4.9
Ecuadorian	115	8.7
Peruvian	17	1.6
Uruguayan	0	0.0

Foreign-Born Population

Group	Number	%
Total Population	57,475	46.7
Hispanic or Latino (of any race)	40,878	57.7
Central American, ex. Mexican	9,115	71.5
Guatemalan	997	75.5
Honduran	1,563	77.9
Salvadoran	5,777	72.1
Cuban	3,399	74.5
Dominican Republic	3,845	60.5
Mexican	3,086	70.3
Puerto Rican	259	2.0
South American	20,447	73.4
Colombian	7,765	73.7
Ecuadorian	4,770	72.0
Peruvian	4,244	70.2
Uruguayan	2,494	77.6

Foreign-Born Naturalized U.S. Citizens

Group	Number	%
Total Population	19,149	33.3
Hispanic or Latino (of any race)	12,140	29.7
Central American, ex. Mexican	1,364	15.0
Guatemalan	124	12.4
Honduran	338	21.6
Salvadoran	751	13.0
Cuban	2,127	62.6
Dominican Republic	1,552	40.4
Mexican	266	8.6
Puerto Rican	164	63.3
South American	6,329	31.0
Colombian	3,205	41.3
Ecuadorian	1,314	27.5
Peruvian	1,343	31.6
Uruguayan	248	9.9

Language Spoken at Home: English Only

(Universe: Population 5 Years and Over)

Group	Number	%
Total Population	33,221	29.4
Hispanic or Latino (of any race)	4,233	6.6
Central American, ex. Mexican	519	4.5
Guatemalan	40	3.4
Honduran	23	1.3
Salvadoran	253	3.5
Cuban	240	5.6
Dominican Republic	245	4.2

Notes: (1) Percent of total population; (2) Percent of Hispanic/Latino population; Profiles include places with an overall population of at least 125,000, OR an overall population of at least 25,000 where the Hispanic/Latino population is at least 20% of the overall population. In states where less than five places meet either of these criteria, we have included places with at least 10,000 total population with the highest percentage of Hispanic/Latino population. These places are identified with an asterisk (*); Please refer to the User's Guide for a full explanation of data.

Group	Number	%
Mexican	105	2.7
Puerto Rican	2,233	18.8
South American	713	2.8
Colombian	279	2.8
Ecuadorian	220	3.6
Peruvian	119	2.2
Uruguayan	69	2.5

Language Spoken at Home: Spanish
(Universe: Population 5 Years and Over)

Group	Number	%
Total Population	61,977	54.9
Hispanic or Latino (of any race)	59,841	93.1
Central American, ex. Mexican	10,925	95.5
Guatemalan	1,123	96.6
Honduran	1,763	98.7
Salvadoran	7,059	96.5
Cuban	4,022	94.1
Dominican Republic	5,530	95.8
Mexican	3,725	96.6
Puerto Rican	9,664	81.2
South American	24,765	96.8
Colombian	9,567	97.2
Ecuadorian	5,836	95.3
Peruvian	5,291	97.8
Uruguayan	2,734	97.2

Unemployment Rate
(Universe: Population 16 Years and Over)

Group	%
Total Population	9.7
Hispanic or Latino (of any race)	10.1
Central American, ex. Mexican	8.1
Guatemalan	4.2
Honduran	4.3
Salvadoran	9.7
Cuban	7.4
Dominican Republic	11.0
Mexican	14.3
Puerto Rican	12.2
South American	9.9
Colombian	10.6
Ecuadorian	12.6
Peruvian	6.5
Uruguayan	8.6

Class of Worker: Private Wage and Salary
(Universe: Civilian Employed Population 16 Years and Over)

Group	Number	%
Total Population	49,517	85.4
Hispanic or Latino (of any race)	31,089	88.9
Central American, ex. Mexican	6,561	95.3
Guatemalan	669	97.5
Honduran	1,082	93.6
Salvadoran	4,239	95.4
Cuban	1,378	80.9
Dominican Republic	2,612	89.2
Mexican	2,220	94.6
Puerto Rican	4,200	81.2
South American	13,595	89.4
Colombian	4,993	86.4
Ecuadorian	3,195	90.4
Peruvian	3,327	93.3
Uruguayan	1,393	87.5

Class of Worker: Government
(Universe: Civilian Employed Population 16 Years and Over)

Group	Number	%
Total Population	5,665	9.8
Hispanic or Latino (of any race)	2,023	5.8
Central American, ex. Mexican	157	2.3
Guatemalan	0	0.0
Honduran	54	4.7
Salvadoran	77	1.7
Cuban	267	15.7
Dominican Republic	124	4.2
Mexican	57	2.4
Puerto Rican	717	13.9
South American	651	4.3
Colombian	472	8.2
Ecuadorian	53	1.5
Peruvian	79	2.2
Uruguayan	36	2.3

Means of Transportation to Work: Car, Truck or Van
(Universe: Workers 16 Years and Over)

Group	Number	%
Total Population	37,126	66.0
Hispanic or Latino (of any race)	21,185	62.4
Central American, ex. Mexican	3,548	52.1
Guatemalan	282	42.5
Honduran	484	42.1
Salvadoran	2,406	54.5
Cuban	1,298	77.6
Dominican Republic	1,948	67.0
Mexican	737	34.8
Puerto Rican	3,551	72.1
South American	9,535	64.3
Colombian	4,106	72.7
Ecuadorian	2,212	63.7
Peruvian	2,190	64.0
Uruguayan	706	44.3

Means of Transportation to Work: Public Transportation (ex. Taxicab)
(Universe: Workers 16 Years and Over)

Group	Number	%
Total Population	5,891	10.5
Hispanic or Latino (of any race)	3,290	9.7
Central American, ex. Mexican	384	5.6
Guatemalan	56	8.4
Honduran	150	13.0
Salvadoran	154	3.5
Cuban	81	4.8
Dominican Republic	310	10.7
Mexican	519	24.5
Puerto Rican	402	8.2
South American	1,548	10.4
Colombian	435	7.7
Ecuadorian	561	16.2
Peruvian	161	4.7
Uruguayan	302	19.0

Homeownership Rate
(Universe: Occupied Housing Units)

Group	%
Total Population	26.7
Hispanic or Latino (of any race)	23.4
Central American, ex. Mexican	23.7
Costa Rican	14.0
Guatemalan	25.8
Honduran	21.1
Nicaraguan	28.8
Panamanian	17.9
Salvadoran	25.1
Cuban	33.0
Dominican Republic	21.3
Mexican	12.9
Puerto Rican	18.1
South American	24.4
Argentinean	20.5
Bolivian	26.2
Chilean	29.2
Colombian	23.9
Ecuadorian	29.2
Peruvian	25.8
Uruguayan	15.1
Venezuelan	23.4
Spaniard	59.5

Median Home Value

Group	Dollars
Total Population	356,600
Hispanic or Latino (of any race)	361,600
Central American, ex. Mexican	420,800
Guatemalan	494,200
Honduran	356,300
Salvadoran	432,600
Cuban	299,100
Dominican Republic	375,200
Mexican	273,400
Puerto Rican	339,500
South American	355,300
Colombian	344,900
Ecuadorian	358,900
Peruvian	390,900
Uruguayan	359,100

Median Gross Rent

Group	Dollars
Total Population	970
Hispanic or Latino (of any race)	1,000
Central American, ex. Mexican	1,097
Guatemalan	1,086
Honduran	1,088
Salvadoran	1,114
Cuban	832
Dominican Republic	1,071
Mexican	1,169
Puerto Rican	969
South American	986
Colombian	942
Ecuadorian	1,022
Peruvian	1,025
Uruguayan	1,084

Median Household Income
(2010 Inflation-Adjusted Dollars)

Group	Dollars
Total Population	43,770
Hispanic or Latino (of any race)	44,120
Central American, ex. Mexican	49,520
Guatemalan	51,585
Honduran	54,000
Salvadoran	50,847
Cuban	32,028
Dominican Republic	54,161
Mexican	57,608
Puerto Rican	38,179
South American	45,835
Colombian	46,596
Ecuadorian	45,625
Peruvian	59,104
Uruguayan	43,948

Per Capita Income
(2010 Inflation-Adjusted Dollars)

Group	Dollars
Total Population	19,196
Hispanic or Latino (of any race)	16,667
Central American, ex. Mexican	14,872
Guatemalan	14,641
Honduran	15,899
Salvadoran	15,314
Cuban	20,213
Dominican Republic	16,870
Mexican	14,342
Puerto Rican	16,375
South American	17,076
Colombian	17,934
Ecuadorian	16,383
Peruvian	18,442
Uruguayan	13,682

Households with $100,000+ Income

Group	Number	%
Total Population	4,908	12.3
Hispanic or Latino (of any race)	2,107	10.0
Central American, ex. Mexican	318	9.8
Guatemalan	20	5.9
Honduran	43	7.5
Salvadoran	232	12.2
Cuban	221	10.2
Dominican Republic	203	11.0
Mexican	145	18.4
Puerto Rican	391	8.8
South American	787	9.8
Colombian	239	7.3
Ecuadorian	246	13.6
Peruvian	271	17.8
Uruguayan	8	0.9

Households with Food Stamps/SNAP Benefits During Past 12 Months

Group	Number	%
Total Population	3,688	9.2
Hispanic or Latino (of any race)	1,829	8.7
Central American, ex. Mexican	242	7.5
Guatemalan	0	0.0
Honduran	44	7.7
Salvadoran	138	7.2
Cuban	444	20.4
Dominican Republic	165	8.9

Notes: (1) Percent of total population; (2) Percent of Hispanic/Latino population; Profiles include places with an overall population of at least 125,000, OR an overall population of at least 25,000 where the Hispanic/Latino population is at least 20% of the overall population. In states where less than five places meet either of these criteria, we have included places with at least 10,000 total population with the highest percentage of Hispanic/Latino population. These places are identified with an asterisk (*); Please refer to the User's Guide for a full explanation of data.

Group	Number	%
Mexican	45	5.7
Puerto Rican	607	13.7
South American	302	3.8
Colombian	138	4.2
Ecuadorian	70	3.9
Peruvian	49	3.2
Uruguayan	28	3.2

Poverty Rate
(Income in Past 12 Months Below Poverty Level)

Group	%
Total Population	16.7
Hispanic or Latino (of any race)	17.8
Central American, ex. Mexican	20.6
Guatemalan	5.0
Honduran	22.8
Salvadoran	20.2
Cuban	18.9
Dominican Republic	10.6
Mexican	18.0
Puerto Rican	29.2
South American	12.9
Colombian	8.5
Ecuadorian	19.0
Peruvian	6.9
Uruguayan	24.1

Englewood

Population

Group	Number	%TP[1]	%HP[2]
Total Population	27,147	100.0	–
Hispanic or Latino (of any race)	7,460	27.5	100.0
Central American, ex. Mexican	1,042	3.8	14.0
Guatemalan	282	1.0	3.8
Honduran	148	0.5	2.0
Salvadoran	488	1.8	6.5
Cuban	259	1.0	3.5
Dominican Republic	1,180	4.3	15.8
Mexican	728	2.7	9.8
Puerto Rican	854	3.1	11.4
South American	2,767	10.2	37.1
Colombian	2,306	8.5	30.9
Ecuadorian	204	0.8	2.7
Peruvian	111	0.4	1.5

Population Growth: 2000–2010

Group	%
Total Population	3.6
Hispanic or Latino (of any race)	30.8
Central American, ex. Mexican	149.3
Salvadoran	158.2
Cuban	0.8
Dominican Republic	91.2
Mexican	190.0
Puerto Rican	28.2
South American	29.9
Colombian	22.8

Males per 100 Females

Group	Number
Total Population	90.0
Hispanic or Latino (of any race)	98.8
Central American, ex. Mexican	128.0
Guatemalan	166.0
Honduran	100.0
Salvadoran	128.0
Cuban	114.0
Dominican Republic	87.3
Mexican	157.2
Puerto Rican	73.2
South American	89.5
Colombian	90.1
Ecuadorian	90.7
Peruvian	98.2

Average Household Size

Group	People
Total Population	2.68
Hispanic or Latino (of any race)	3.53
Central American, ex. Mexican	4.16
Guatemalan	4.39
Honduran	3.44
Salvadoran	4.62
Cuban	2.69
Dominican Republic	3.77
Mexican	4.63
Puerto Rican	2.72
South American	3.47
Colombian	3.56
Ecuadorian	3.62
Peruvian	3.10

Median Age

Group	Years
Total Population	38.9
Hispanic or Latino (of any race)	33.4
Central American, ex. Mexican	31.9
Guatemalan	30.2
Honduran	34.0
Salvadoran	31.3
Cuban	45.1
Dominican Republic	32.1
Mexican	27.2
Puerto Rican	32.5
South American	39.9
Colombian	40.3
Ecuadorian	35.8
Peruvian	38.9

High School Graduates
(Universe: Population 25 Years and Over)

Group	Number	%
Total Population	16,537	89.3
Hispanic or Latino (of any race)	3,162	77.9
Dominican Republic	487	84.3
South American	1,695	83.9
Colombian	1,478	82.0

Four-Year College Graduates
(Universe: Population 25 Years and Over)

Group	Number	%
Total Population	7,903	42.7
Hispanic or Latino (of any race)	1,075	26.5
Dominican Republic	63	10.9
South American	632	31.3
Colombian	539	29.9

Population Age 3–17 Enrolled in Public School
(Universe: Population Age 3–17 Enrolled in School)

Group	Number	%
Total Population	3,230	64.7
Hispanic or Latino (of any race)	1,222	88.0
Dominican Republic	252	93.3
South American	473	96.5
Colombian	300	94.6

Population Age 3–17 Enrolled in Private School
(Universe: Population Age 3–17 Enrolled in School)

Group	Number	%
Total Population	1,760	35.3
Hispanic or Latino (of any race)	166	12.0
Dominican Republic	18	6.7
South American	17	3.5
Colombian	17	5.4

Foreign-Born Population

Group	Number	%
Total Population	7,815	29.1
Hispanic or Latino (of any race)	3,656	57.9
Dominican Republic	484	52.8
South American	2,221	79.4
Colombian	1,976	83.3

Foreign-Born Naturalized U.S. Citizens

Group	Number	%
Total Population	4,546	58.2
Hispanic or Latino (of any race)	2,014	55.1
Dominican Republic	338	69.8
South American	1,314	59.2
Colombian	1,252	63.4

Language Spoken at Home: English Only
(Universe: Population 5 Years and Over)

Group	Number	%
Total Population	16,853	67.3
Hispanic or Latino (of any race)	750	12.7
Dominican Republic	20	2.3
South American	180	6.8
Colombian	139	6.1

Language Spoken at Home: Spanish
(Universe: Population 5 Years and Over)

Group	Number	%
Total Population	5,637	22.5
Hispanic or Latino (of any race)	5,147	87.3
Dominican Republic	868	97.7
South American	2,481	93.2
Colombian	2,143	93.9

Unemployment Rate
(Universe: Population 16 Years and Over)

Group	%
Total Population	6.2
Hispanic or Latino (of any race)	5.4
Dominican Republic	3.9
South American	5.8
Colombian	5.3

Class of Worker: Private Wage and Salary
(Universe: Civilian Employed Population 16 Years and Over)

Group	Number	%
Total Population	11,176	81.8
Hispanic or Latino (of any race)	2,794	88.0
Dominican Republic	340	80.6
South American	1,527	91.5
Colombian	1,351	90.5

Class of Worker: Government
(Universe: Civilian Employed Population 16 Years and Over)

Group	Number	%
Total Population	1,430	10.5
Hispanic or Latino (of any race)	126	4.0
Dominican Republic	0	0.0
South American	89	5.3
Colombian	89	6.0

Means of Transportation to Work: Car, Truck or Van
(Universe: Workers 16 Years and Over)

Group	Number	%
Total Population	9,966	74.4
Hispanic or Latino (of any race)	2,055	66.8
Dominican Republic	312	84.8
South American	1,198	72.3
Colombian	1,080	72.9

Means of Transportation to Work: Public Transportation (ex. Taxicab)
(Universe: Workers 16 Years and Over)

Group	Number	%
Total Population	1,969	14.7
Hispanic or Latino (of any race)	409	13.3
Dominican Republic	37	10.1
South American	203	12.2
Colombian	145	9.8

Homeownership Rate
(Universe: Occupied Housing Units)

Group	%
Total Population	54.2
Hispanic or Latino (of any race)	39.3
Central American, ex. Mexican	30.0
Guatemalan	13.4
Honduran	39.5
Salvadoran	27.0
Cuban	55.3
Dominican Republic	56.5
Mexican	20.9
Puerto Rican	49.4
South American	32.3
Colombian	29.3
Ecuadorian	45.3
Peruvian	39.0

Median Home Value

Group	Dollars
Total Population	435,200
Hispanic or Latino (of any race)	461,100
Dominican Republic	484,600
South American	452,100
Colombian	486,100

Median Gross Rent

Group	Dollars
Total Population	1,179

Notes: (1) Percent of total population; (2) Percent of Hispanic/Latino population; Profiles include places with an overall population of at least 125,000, OR an overall population of at least 25,000 where the Hispanic/Latino population is at least 20% of the overall population. In states where less than five places meet either of these criteria, we have included places with at least 10,000 total population with the highest percentage of Hispanic/Latino population. These places are identified with an asterisk (*); Please refer to the User's Guide for a full explanation of data.

Hispanic or Latino (of any race)	1,176
Dominican Republic	343
South American	1,243
Colombian	1,233

Median Household Income
(2010 Inflation-Adjusted Dollars)

Group	Dollars
Total Population	69,915
Hispanic or Latino (of any race)	58,446
Dominican Republic	30,139
South American	73,147
Colombian	68,292

Per Capita Income
(2010 Inflation-Adjusted Dollars)

Group	Dollars
Total Population	41,533
Hispanic or Latino (of any race)	26,016
Dominican Republic	15,990
South American	28,101
Colombian	29,076

Households with $100,000+ Income

Group	Number	%
Total Population	3,731	36.0
Hispanic or Latino (of any race)	519	25.9
Dominican Republic	38	13.1
South American	354	34.6
Colombian	296	33.1

Households with Food Stamps/SNAP Benefits During Past 12 Months

Group	Number	%
Total Population	630	6.1
Hispanic or Latino (of any race)	112	5.6
Dominican Republic	0	0.0
South American	36	3.5
Colombian	36	4.0

Poverty Rate
(Income in Past 12 Months Below Poverty Level)

Group	%
Total Population	10.0
Hispanic or Latino (of any race)	9.7
Dominican Republic	4.8
South American	10.6
Colombian	6.5

Garfield

Population

Group	Number	%TP[1]	%HP[2]
Total Population	30,487	100.0	–
Hispanic or Latino (of any race)	9,830	32.2	100.0
Central American, ex. Mexican	498	1.6	5.1
Honduran	109	0.4	1.1
Salvadoran	186	0.6	1.9
Cuban	216	0.7	2.2
Dominican Republic	2,057	6.7	20.9
Mexican	852	2.8	8.7
Puerto Rican	2,210	7.2	22.5
South American	3,338	10.9	34.0
Argentinean	151	0.5	1.5
Bolivian	102	0.3	1.0
Colombian	880	2.9	9.0
Ecuadorian	619	2.0	6.3
Peruvian	1,462	4.8	14.9

Population Growth: 2000–2010

Group	%
Total Population	2.4
Hispanic or Latino (of any race)	64.1
Central American, ex. Mexican	217.2
Cuban	66.2
Dominican Republic	230.2
Mexican	81.7
Puerto Rican	63.9
South American	78.7
Argentinean	18.0
Colombian	62.4
Ecuadorian	138.1
Peruvian	92.1

Males per 100 Females

Group	Number
Total Population	91.3
Hispanic or Latino (of any race)	89.0
Central American, ex. Mexican	104.9
Honduran	91.2
Salvadoran	100.0
Cuban	118.2
Dominican Republic	79.5
Mexican	105.3
Puerto Rican	91.8
South American	82.2
Argentinean	81.9
Bolivian	88.9
Colombian	75.0
Ecuadorian	94.0
Peruvian	81.4

Average Household Size

Group	People
Total Population	2.75
Hispanic or Latino (of any race)	3.57
Central American, ex. Mexican	3.91
Honduran	4.00
Salvadoran	3.89
Cuban	2.85
Dominican Republic	3.87
Mexican	4.27
Puerto Rican	3.16
South American	3.66
Argentinean	2.84
Bolivian	3.50
Colombian	3.49
Ecuadorian	3.82
Peruvian	3.89

Median Age

Group	Years
Total Population	35.5
Hispanic or Latino (of any race)	28.8
Central American, ex. Mexican	30.6
Honduran	31.3
Salvadoran	32.0
Cuban	32.7
Dominican Republic	26.9
Mexican	25.5
Puerto Rican	26.4
South American	34.0
Argentinean	36.9
Bolivian	35.0
Colombian	32.7
Ecuadorian	32.7
Peruvian	35.0

High School Graduates
(Universe: Population 25 Years and Over)

Group	Number	%
Total Population	16,511	81.5
Hispanic or Latino (of any race)	4,176	77.5
Dominican Republic	877	85.0
Mexican	331	55.2
Puerto Rican	1,175	78.5
South American	1,427	79.9
Colombian	404	60.1

Four-Year College Graduates
(Universe: Population 25 Years and Over)

Group	Number	%
Total Population	3,613	17.8
Hispanic or Latino (of any race)	635	11.8
Dominican Republic	249	24.1
Mexican	25	4.2
Puerto Rican	60	4.0
South American	235	13.2
Colombian	44	6.5

Population Age 3–17 Enrolled in Public School
(Universe: Population Age 3–17 Enrolled in School)

Group	Number	%
Total Population	4,859	91.1
Hispanic or Latino (of any race)	2,520	91.5
Dominican Republic	528	79.8
Mexican	278	100.0
Puerto Rican	951	90.4
South American	560	100.0
Colombian	174	100.0

Population Age 3–17 Enrolled in Private School
(Universe: Population Age 3–17 Enrolled in School)

Group	Number	%
Total Population	476	8.9
Hispanic or Latino (of any race)	235	8.5
Dominican Republic	134	20.2
Mexican	0	0.0
Puerto Rican	101	9.6
South American	0	0.0
Colombian	0	0.0

Foreign-Born Population

Group	Number	%
Total Population	11,977	39.7
Hispanic or Latino (of any race)	4,240	42.2
Dominican Republic	1,174	54.5
Mexican	610	52.0
Puerto Rican	0	0.0
South American	1,969	67.2
Colombian	751	67.2

Foreign-Born Naturalized U.S. Citizens

Group	Number	%
Total Population	5,667	47.3
Hispanic or Latino (of any race)	2,193	51.7
Dominican Republic	658	56.0
Mexican	229	37.5
Puerto Rican	0	0.0
South American	1,095	55.6
Colombian	452	60.2

Language Spoken at Home: English Only
(Universe: Population 5 Years and Over)

Group	Number	%
Total Population	11,841	41.8
Hispanic or Latino (of any race)	1,552	16.8
Dominican Republic	101	5.5
Mexican	56	5.3
Puerto Rican	1,146	41.7
South American	184	6.5
Colombian	68	6.3

Language Spoken at Home: Spanish
(Universe: Population 5 Years and Over)

Group	Number	%
Total Population	8,139	28.7
Hispanic or Latino (of any race)	7,688	83.2
Dominican Republic	1,735	94.5
Mexican	1,007	94.7
Puerto Rican	1,602	58.3
South American	2,650	93.5
Colombian	1,009	93.7

Unemployment Rate
(Universe: Population 16 Years and Over)

Group	%
Total Population	7.6
Hispanic or Latino (of any race)	9.8
Dominican Republic	7.5
Mexican	11.3
Puerto Rican	16.5
South American	7.5
Colombian	11.7

Class of Worker: Private Wage and Salary
(Universe: Civilian Employed Population 16 Years and Over)

Group	Number	%
Total Population	13,515	86.0
Hispanic or Latino (of any race)	4,346	89.1
Dominican Republic	897	90.3
Mexican	479	93.9
Puerto Rican	1,041	87.1
South American	1,542	87.4
Colombian	640	97.1

Class of Worker: Government
(Universe: Civilian Employed Population 16 Years and Over)

Group	Number	%
Total Population	1,600	10.2
Hispanic or Latino (of any race)	384	7.9
Dominican Republic	60	6.0
Mexican	15	2.9
Puerto Rican	132	11.0
South American	170	9.6

Notes: (1) Percent of total population; (2) Percent of Hispanic/Latino population; Profiles include places with an overall population of at least 125,000, OR an overall population of at least 25,000 where the Hispanic/Latino population is at least 20% of the overall population. In states where less than five places meet either of these criteria, we have included places with at least 10,000 total population with the highest percentage of Hispanic/Latino population. These places are identified with an asterisk (*); Please refer to the User's Guide for a full explanation of data.

Group	Number	%
Colombian	19	2.9

Means of Transportation to Work: Car, Truck or Van
(Universe: Workers 16 Years and Over)

Group	Number	%
Total Population	13,048	85.2
Hispanic or Latino (of any race)	3,950	83.1
Dominican Republic	819	82.5
Mexican	348	70.0
Puerto Rican	922	82.9
South American	1,559	89.2
Colombian	546	82.9

Means of Transportation to Work: Public Transportation (ex. Taxicab)
(Universe: Workers 16 Years and Over)

Group	Number	%
Total Population	1,049	6.8
Hispanic or Latino (of any race)	406	8.5
Dominican Republic	125	12.6
Mexican	75	15.1
Puerto Rican	51	4.6
South American	96	5.5
Colombian	51	7.7

Homeownership Rate
(Universe: Occupied Housing Units)

Group	%
Total Population	38.4
Hispanic or Latino (of any race)	28.3
Central American, ex. Mexican	34.8
Honduran	25.8
Salvadoran	47.2
Cuban	31.1
Dominican Republic	33.7
Mexican	28.9
Puerto Rican	19.6
South American	30.5
Argentinean	26.8
Bolivian	17.6
Colombian	32.5
Ecuadorian	39.0
Peruvian	27.7

Median Home Value

Group	Dollars
Total Population	371,900
Hispanic or Latino (of any race)	394,600
Dominican Republic	443,500
Mexican	391,700
Puerto Rican	338,100
South American	408,900
Colombian	364,200

Median Gross Rent

Group	Dollars
Total Population	1,130
Hispanic or Latino (of any race)	1,215
Dominican Republic	1,195
Mexican	1,490
Puerto Rican	1,191
South American	1,144
Colombian	1,071

Median Household Income
(2010 Inflation-Adjusted Dollars)

Group	Dollars
Total Population	51,407
Hispanic or Latino (of any race)	52,981
Dominican Republic	55,075
Mexican	63,438
Puerto Rican	41,944
South American	73,008
Colombian	85,556

Per Capita Income
(2010 Inflation-Adjusted Dollars)

Group	Dollars
Total Population	24,022
Hispanic or Latino (of any race)	18,161
Dominican Republic	14,764
Mexican	16,043
Puerto Rican	18,491
South American	21,726
Colombian	23,033

Households with $100,000+ Income

Group	Number	%
Total Population	2,122	18.9
Hispanic or Latino (of any race)	429	15.5
Dominican Republic	103	19.6
Mexican	54	21.6
Puerto Rican	122	11.9
South American	141	17.6
Colombian	56	21.5

Households with Food Stamps/SNAP Benefits During Past 12 Months

Group	Number	%
Total Population	667	6.0
Hispanic or Latino (of any race)	289	10.5
Dominican Republic	77	14.7
Mexican	0	0.0
Puerto Rican	166	16.2
South American	27	3.4
Colombian	10	3.8

Poverty Rate
(Income in Past 12 Months Below Poverty Level)

Group	%
Total Population	13.0
Hispanic or Latino (of any race)	15.1
Dominican Republic	12.8
Mexican	0.0
Puerto Rican	25.7
South American	9.0
Colombian	2.2

Hackensack

Population

Group	Number	%TP[1]	%HP[2]
Total Population	43,010	100.0	–
Hispanic or Latino (of any race)	15,186	35.3	100.0
Central American, ex. Mexican	884	2.1	5.8
Guatemalan	158	0.4	1.0
Honduran	103	0.2	0.7
Salvadoran	417	1.0	2.7
Cuban	339	0.8	2.2
Dominican Republic	3,021	7.0	19.9
Mexican	827	1.9	5.4
Puerto Rican	1,658	3.9	10.9
South American	6,917	16.1	45.5
Colombian	1,835	4.3	12.1
Ecuadorian	4,291	10.0	28.3
Peruvian	483	1.1	3.2

Population Growth: 2000–2010

Group	%
Total Population	0.8
Hispanic or Latino (of any race)	37.3
Central American, ex. Mexican	59.6
Salvadoran	64.2
Cuban	13.8
Dominican Republic	92.1
Mexican	143.2
Puerto Rican	20.9
South American	62.1
Colombian	12.3
Ecuadorian	110.3
Peruvian	63.2

Males per 100 Females

Group	Number
Total Population	98.0
Hispanic or Latino (of any race)	106.8
Central American, ex. Mexican	126.7
Guatemalan	222.4
Honduran	110.2
Salvadoran	138.3
Cuban	105.5
Dominican Republic	86.3
Mexican	126.6
Puerto Rican	99.0
South American	110.9
Colombian	83.5
Ecuadorian	129.1
Peruvian	84.4

Average Household Size

Group	People
Total Population	2.30
Hispanic or Latino (of any race)	3.27
Central American, ex. Mexican	3.21
Guatemalan	3.24
Honduran	3.26
Salvadoran	3.66
Cuban	2.06
Dominican Republic	3.28
Mexican	4.04
Puerto Rican	2.31
South American	3.61
Colombian	2.76
Ecuadorian	4.34
Peruvian	2.90

Median Age

Group	Years
Total Population	37.5
Hispanic or Latino (of any race)	31.4
Central American, ex. Mexican	32.9
Guatemalan	29.9
Honduran	33.4
Salvadoran	31.6
Cuban	40.7
Dominican Republic	30.0
Mexican	27.6
Puerto Rican	34.6
South American	33.0
Colombian	40.9
Ecuadorian	30.4
Peruvian	36.9

High School Graduates
(Universe: Population 25 Years and Over)

Group	Number	%
Total Population	26,838	85.5
Hispanic or Latino (of any race)	6,790	75.7
Central American, ex. Mexican	454	60.9
Dominican Republic	917	64.4
Puerto Rican	1,139	87.5
South American	3,839	80.0
Colombian	1,459	85.4
Ecuadorian	1,659	75.9

Four-Year College Graduates
(Universe: Population 25 Years and Over)

Group	Number	%
Total Population	10,689	34.0
Hispanic or Latino (of any race)	1,711	19.1
Central American, ex. Mexican	57	7.6
Dominican Republic	212	14.9
Puerto Rican	317	24.4
South American	956	19.9
Colombian	451	26.4
Ecuadorian	251	11.5

Population Age 3–17 Enrolled in Public School
(Universe: Population Age 3–17 Enrolled in School)

Group	Number	%
Total Population	4,598	86.1
Hispanic or Latino (of any race)	1,993	89.4
Central American, ex. Mexican	107	69.9
Dominican Republic	405	94.4
Puerto Rican	259	69.3
South American	1,084	95.5
Colombian	283	100.0
Ecuadorian	654	97.9

Population Age 3–17 Enrolled in Private School
(Universe: Population Age 3–17 Enrolled in School)

Group	Number	%
Total Population	744	13.9
Hispanic or Latino (of any race)	236	10.6
Central American, ex. Mexican	46	30.1
Dominican Republic	24	5.6
Puerto Rican	115	30.7
South American	51	4.5
Colombian	0	0.0
Ecuadorian	14	2.1

Foreign-Born Population

Group	Number	%
Total Population	15,875	37.2

Notes: (1) Percent of total population; (2) Percent of Hispanic/Latino population; Profiles include places with an overall population of at least 125,000, OR an overall population of at least 25,000 where the Hispanic/Latino population is at least 20% of the overall population. In states where less than five places meet either of these criteria, we have included places with at least 10,000 total population with the highest percentage of Hispanic/Latino population. These places are identified with an asterisk (*); Please refer to the User's Guide for a full explanation of data.

Group	Number	%
Hispanic or Latino (of any race)	8,258	58.9
Central American, ex. Mexican	965	83.3
Dominican Republic	1,546	65.0
Puerto Rican	0	0.0
South American	5,242	73.0
Colombian	1,741	78.2
Ecuadorian	2,685	72.3

Foreign-Born Naturalized U.S. Citizens

Group	Number	%
Total Population	6,707	42.2
Hispanic or Latino (of any race)	3,095	37.5
Central American, ex. Mexican	359	37.2
Dominican Republic	642	41.5
Puerto Rican	0	0.0
South American	1,987	37.9
Colombian	858	49.3
Ecuadorian	815	30.4

Language Spoken at Home: English Only
(Universe: Population 5 Years and Over)

Group	Number	%
Total Population	21,966	54.7
Hispanic or Latino (of any race)	1,237	9.6
Central American, ex. Mexican	165	15.1
Dominican Republic	193	8.5
Puerto Rican	440	22.1
South American	341	5.1
Colombian	112	5.4
Ecuadorian	45	1.3

Language Spoken at Home: Spanish
(Universe: Population 5 Years and Over)

Group	Number	%
Total Population	12,275	30.5
Hispanic or Latino (of any race)	11,606	89.6
Central American, ex. Mexican	926	84.9
Dominican Republic	2,070	91.5
Puerto Rican	1,471	73.8
South American	6,294	94.7
Colombian	1,964	94.6
Ecuadorian	3,291	98.3

Unemployment Rate
(Universe: Population 16 Years and Over)

Group	%
Total Population	4.8
Hispanic or Latino (of any race)	5.3
Central American, ex. Mexican	1.1
Dominican Republic	5.8
Puerto Rican	2.5
South American	5.8
Colombian	6.7
Ecuadorian	5.2

Class of Worker: Private Wage and Salary
(Universe: Civilian Employed Population 16 Years and Over)

Group	Number	%
Total Population	20,210	84.3
Hispanic or Latino (of any race)	7,439	92.8
Central American, ex. Mexican	788	98.5
Dominican Republic	1,252	95.5
Puerto Rican	1,274	98.5
South American	3,651	89.1
Colombian	1,095	84.2
Ecuadorian	1,950	96.0

Class of Worker: Government
(Universe: Civilian Employed Population 16 Years and Over)

Group	Number	%
Total Population	2,878	12.0
Hispanic or Latino (of any race)	330	4.1
Central American, ex. Mexican	12	1.5
Dominican Republic	17	1.3
Puerto Rican	19	1.5
South American	271	6.6
Colombian	140	10.8
Ecuadorian	65	3.2

Means of Transportation to Work: Car, Truck or Van
(Universe: Workers 16 Years and Over)

Group	Number	%
Total Population	16,063	68.7
Hispanic or Latino (of any race)	4,239	54.2
Central American, ex. Mexican	353	44.1
Dominican Republic	663	50.9
Puerto Rican	676	52.3
South American	2,238	56.8
Colombian	958	73.6
Ecuadorian	796	42.2

Means of Transportation to Work: Public Transportation (ex. Taxicab)
(Universe: Workers 16 Years and Over)

Group	Number	%
Total Population	4,910	21.0
Hispanic or Latino (of any race)	2,358	30.2
Central American, ex. Mexican	197	24.6
Dominican Republic	362	27.8
Puerto Rican	537	41.5
South American	1,216	30.9
Colombian	295	22.7
Ecuadorian	723	38.3

Homeownership Rate
(Universe: Occupied Housing Units)

Group	%
Total Population	35.2
Hispanic or Latino (of any race)	26.4
Central American, ex. Mexican	30.2
Guatemalan	21.4
Honduran	34.3
Salvadoran	29.4
Cuban	43.4
Dominican Republic	26.1
Mexican	20.8
Puerto Rican	31.3
South American	24.2
Colombian	29.9
Ecuadorian	19.2
Peruvian	27.4

Median Home Value

Group	Dollars
Total Population	362,400
Hispanic or Latino (of any race)	397,300
Central American, ex. Mexican	351,600
Dominican Republic	440,400
Puerto Rican	368,200
South American	422,700
Colombian	335,900
Ecuadorian	467,600

Median Gross Rent

Group	Dollars
Total Population	1,203
Hispanic or Latino (of any race)	1,222
Central American, ex. Mexican	1,086
Dominican Republic	1,047
Puerto Rican	1,381
South American	1,215
Colombian	1,354
Ecuadorian	1,199

Median Household Income
(2010 Inflation-Adjusted Dollars)

Group	Dollars
Total Population	57,676
Hispanic or Latino (of any race)	55,873
Central American, ex. Mexican	53,486
Dominican Republic	62,014
Puerto Rican	76,741
South American	49,081
Colombian	51,335
Ecuadorian	41,129

Per Capita Income
(2010 Inflation-Adjusted Dollars)

Group	Dollars
Total Population	32,036
Hispanic or Latino (of any race)	20,708
Central American, ex. Mexican	18,034
Dominican Republic	19,374
Puerto Rican	27,585
South American	19,661
Colombian	22,636
Ecuadorian	16,013

Households with $100,000+ Income

Group	Number	%
Total Population	4,326	23.4
Hispanic or Latino (of any race)	946	21.4
Central American, ex. Mexican	60	15.5
Dominican Republic	130	16.2
Puerto Rican	321	39.1
South American	346	15.7
Colombian	103	14.9
Ecuadorian	125	11.5

Households with Food Stamps/SNAP Benefits During Past 12 Months

Group	Number	%
Total Population	1,166	6.3
Hispanic or Latino (of any race)	499	11.3
Central American, ex. Mexican	0	0.0
Dominican Republic	157	19.6
Puerto Rican	151	18.4
South American	191	8.7
Colombian	89	12.9
Ecuadorian	102	9.4

Poverty Rate
(Income in Past 12 Months Below Poverty Level)

Group	%
Total Population	10.7
Hispanic or Latino (of any race)	13.7
Central American, ex. Mexican	20.2
Dominican Republic	9.6
Puerto Rican	15.8
South American	12.6
Colombian	6.5
Ecuadorian	12.9

Jersey City

Population

Group	Number	%TP[1]	%HP[2]
Total Population	247,597	100.0	–
Hispanic or Latino (of any race)	68,256	27.6	100.0
Central American, ex. Mexican	6,838	2.8	10.0
Costa Rican	229	0.1	0.3
Guatemalan	1,148	0.5	1.7
Honduran	3,041	1.2	4.5
Nicaraguan	528	0.2	0.8
Panamanian	384	0.2	0.6
Salvadoran	1,427	0.6	2.1
Cuban	1,641	0.7	2.4
Dominican Republic	13,512	5.5	19.8
Mexican	4,535	1.8	6.6
Puerto Rican	25,677	10.4	37.6
South American	11,034	4.5	16.2
Argentinean	558	0.2	0.8
Bolivian	337	0.1	0.5
Chilean	316	0.1	0.5
Colombian	2,246	0.9	3.3
Ecuadorian	5,754	2.3	8.4
Peruvian	1,221	0.5	1.8
Uruguayan	149	0.1	0.2
Venezuelan	303	0.1	0.4
Spaniard	463	0.2	0.7

Population Growth: 2000–2010

Group	%
Total Population	3.1
Hispanic or Latino (of any race)	0.4
Central American, ex. Mexican	43.9
Costa Rican	21.8
Guatemalan	120.8
Honduran	38.7
Nicaraguan	50.4
Panamanian	62.7
Salvadoran	53.1
Cuban	-11.8
Dominican Republic	47.1
Mexican	81.8
Puerto Rican	-13.8
South American	41.3
Argentinean	86.0
Bolivian	38.1
Chilean	17.5
Colombian	33.5

Notes: (1) Percent of total population; (2) Percent of Hispanic/Latino population; Profiles include places with an overall population of at least 125,000, OR an overall population of at least 25,000 where the Hispanic/Latino population is at least 20% of the overall population. In states where less than five places meet either of these criteria, we have included places with at least 10,000 total population with the highest percentage of Hispanic/Latino population. These places are identified with an asterisk (*); Please refer to the User's Guide for a full explanation of data.

Group	
Ecuadorian	46.8
Peruvian	55.3
Venezuelan	83.6
Spaniard	102.2

Males per 100 Females

Group	Number
Total Population	97.6
Hispanic or Latino (of any race)	95.4
Central American, ex. Mexican	107.8
Costa Rican	120.2
Guatemalan	133.3
Honduran	106.4
Nicaraguan	97.8
Panamanian	83.7
Salvadoran	101.3
Cuban	109.3
Dominican Republic	87.3
Mexican	128.8
Puerto Rican	90.5
South American	96.5
Argentinean	108.2
Bolivian	97.1
Chilean	109.3
Colombian	97.0
Ecuadorian	94.0
Peruvian	98.2
Uruguayan	109.9
Venezuelan	104.7
Spaniard	101.3

Average Household Size

Group	People
Total Population	2.53
Hispanic or Latino (of any race)	2.91
Central American, ex. Mexican	3.43
Costa Rican	2.78
Guatemalan	3.88
Honduran	3.47
Nicaraguan	3.31
Panamanian	2.56
Salvadoran	3.56
Cuban	2.22
Dominican Republic	3.30
Mexican	3.50
Puerto Rican	2.62
South American	2.98
Argentinean	2.45
Bolivian	3.13
Chilean	2.45
Colombian	2.63
Ecuadorian	3.27
Peruvian	3.06
Uruguayan	2.72
Venezuelan	2.32
Spaniard	2.28

Median Age

Group	Years
Total Population	33.2
Hispanic or Latino (of any race)	31.4
Central American, ex. Mexican	32.4
Costa Rican	34.1
Guatemalan	29.9
Honduran	32.7
Nicaraguan	34.0
Panamanian	35.5
Salvadoran	32.6
Cuban	37.6
Dominican Republic	30.7
Mexican	27.5
Puerto Rican	31.0
South American	36.6
Argentinean	36.5
Bolivian	38.3
Chilean	40.0
Colombian	37.1
Ecuadorian	36.3
Peruvian	36.8
Uruguayan	35.3
Venezuelan	35.0
Spaniard	36.6

High School Graduates
(Universe: Population 25 Years and Over)

Group	Number	%
Total Population	137,348	83.1
Hispanic or Latino (of any race)	28,670	70.4
Central American, ex. Mexican	2,858	60.0
Guatemalan	391	57.4
Honduran	1,376	56.9
Salvadoran	374	56.7
Cuban	1,064	87.0
Dominican Republic	4,213	67.3
Mexican	1,662	69.9
Puerto Rican	10,743	71.9
South American	6,724	70.3
Colombian	1,380	71.5
Ecuadorian	3,531	64.8
Peruvian	785	89.7

Four-Year College Graduates
(Universe: Population 25 Years and Over)

Group	Number	%
Total Population	65,360	39.6
Hispanic or Latino (of any race)	7,121	17.5
Central American, ex. Mexican	803	16.9
Guatemalan	83	12.2
Honduran	398	16.5
Salvadoran	45	6.8
Cuban	416	34.0
Dominican Republic	964	15.4
Mexican	528	22.2
Puerto Rican	1,991	13.3
South American	1,923	20.1
Colombian	388	20.1
Ecuadorian	875	16.0
Peruvian	197	22.5

Population Age 3–17 Enrolled in Public School
(Universe: Population Age 3–17 Enrolled in School)

Group	Number	%
Total Population	33,817	85.8
Hispanic or Latino (of any race)	13,765	89.2
Central American, ex. Mexican	1,405	92.3
Guatemalan	295	93.7
Honduran	713	92.6
Salvadoran	93	88.6
Cuban	366	92.7
Dominican Republic	2,511	92.3
Mexican	861	94.6
Puerto Rican	6,144	89.5
South American	1,643	81.5
Colombian	421	88.6
Ecuadorian	1,005	85.8
Peruvian	131	87.3

Population Age 3–17 Enrolled in Private School
(Universe: Population Age 3–17 Enrolled in School)

Group	Number	%
Total Population	5,579	14.2
Hispanic or Latino (of any race)	1,670	10.8
Central American, ex. Mexican	118	7.7
Guatemalan	20	6.3
Honduran	57	7.4
Salvadoran	12	11.4
Cuban	29	7.3
Dominican Republic	210	7.7
Mexican	49	5.4
Puerto Rican	721	10.5
South American	374	18.5
Colombian	54	11.4
Ecuadorian	167	14.2
Peruvian	19	12.7

Foreign-Born Population

Group	Number	%
Total Population	93,023	38.2
Hispanic or Latino (of any race)	26,011	38.0
Central American, ex. Mexican	4,873	66.3
Guatemalan	797	59.1
Honduran	2,383	69.6
Salvadoran	720	73.7
Cuban	753	41.8
Dominican Republic	7,372	65.1
Mexican	2,519	55.8
Puerto Rican	248	0.9
South American	9,576	71.5
Colombian	1,742	65.3
Ecuadorian	5,748	74.0
Peruvian	891	76.6

Foreign-Born Naturalized U.S. Citizens

Group	Number	%
Total Population	41,578	44.7
Hispanic or Latino (of any race)	10,909	41.9
Central American, ex. Mexican	2,024	41.5
Guatemalan	212	26.6
Honduran	1,215	51.0
Salvadoran	333	46.3
Cuban	305	40.5
Dominican Republic	3,289	44.6
Mexican	182	7.2
Puerto Rican	76	30.6
South American	4,673	48.8
Colombian	926	53.2
Ecuadorian	2,706	47.1
Peruvian	437	49.0

Language Spoken at Home: English Only
(Universe: Population 5 Years and Over)

Group	Number	%
Total Population	108,731	48.0
Hispanic or Latino (of any race)	10,895	17.4
Central American, ex. Mexican	547	7.9
Guatemalan	68	5.2
Honduran	113	3.5
Salvadoran	175	19.0
Cuban	382	22.6
Dominican Republic	535	5.1
Mexican	678	17.2
Puerto Rican	6,570	27.0
South American	949	7.7
Colombian	402	16.0
Ecuadorian	438	6.0
Peruvian	37	3.7

Language Spoken at Home: Spanish
(Universe: Population 5 Years and Over)

Group	Number	%
Total Population	55,192	24.4
Hispanic or Latino (of any race)	51,527	82.1
Central American, ex. Mexican	6,339	91.6
Guatemalan	1,230	94.8
Honduran	3,094	95.6
Salvadoran	748	81.0
Cuban	1,292	76.5
Dominican Republic	9,999	94.9
Mexican	3,209	81.4
Puerto Rican	17,665	72.6
South American	11,393	92.0
Colombian	2,103	84.0
Ecuadorian	6,804	94.0
Peruvian	946	94.1

Unemployment Rate
(Universe: Population 16 Years and Over)

Group	%
Total Population	9.7
Hispanic or Latino (of any race)	11.4
Central American, ex. Mexican	10.2
Guatemalan	7.6
Honduran	13.1
Salvadoran	17.1
Cuban	11.3
Dominican Republic	9.6
Mexican	15.2
Puerto Rican	13.7
South American	9.4
Colombian	8.1
Ecuadorian	11.0
Peruvian	2.8

Class of Worker: Private Wage and Salary
(Universe: Civilian Employed Population 16 Years and Over)

Group	Number	%
Total Population	102,472	83.4
Hispanic or Latino (of any race)	26,932	85.1
Central American, ex. Mexican	3,587	88.1
Guatemalan	775	97.0
Honduran	1,526	85.3
Salvadoran	464	84.2
Cuban	619	73.9

STATE & PLACE PROFILES

Notes: (1) Percent of total population; (2) Percent of Hispanic/Latino population; Profiles include places with an overall population of at least 125,000, OR an overall population of at least 25,000 where the Hispanic/Latino population is at least 20% of the overall population. In states where less than five places meet either of these criteria, we have included places with at least 10,000 total population with the highest percentage of Hispanic/Latino population. These places are identified with an asterisk (*); Please refer to the User's Guide for a full explanation of data.

Dominican Republic	4,860	89.4
Mexican	2,124	95.9
Puerto Rican	8,119	77.7
South American	6,289	88.5
Colombian	1,001	85.9
Ecuadorian	3,778	88.8
Peruvian	601	85.2

Class of Worker: Government
(Universe: Civilian Employed Population 16 Years and Over)

Group	Number	%
Total Population	15,342	12.5
Hispanic or Latino (of any race)	3,631	11.5
Central American, ex. Mexican	250	6.1
Guatemalan	8	1.0
Honduran	111	6.2
Salvadoran	74	13.4
Cuban	188	22.4
Dominican Republic	352	6.5
Mexican	0	0.0
Puerto Rican	2,098	20.1
South American	571	8.0
Colombian	109	9.4
Ecuadorian	361	8.5
Peruvian	68	9.6

Means of Transportation to Work: Car, Truck or Van
(Universe: Workers 16 Years and Over)

Group	Number	%
Total Population	50,123	41.6
Hispanic or Latino (of any race)	14,650	47.0
Central American, ex. Mexican	2,037	50.7
Guatemalan	369	46.2
Honduran	798	45.5
Salvadoran	247	44.8
Cuban	399	47.6
Dominican Republic	2,519	47.0
Mexican	725	32.4
Puerto Rican	5,193	50.3
South American	3,160	45.7
Colombian	467	42.5
Ecuadorian	1,960	47.3
Peruvian	291	41.3

Means of Transportation to Work: Public Transportation (ex. Taxicab)
(Universe: Workers 16 Years and Over)

Group	Number	%
Total Population	55,256	45.9
Hispanic or Latino (of any race)	12,288	39.5
Central American, ex. Mexican	1,389	34.6
Guatemalan	174	21.8
Honduran	678	38.7
Salvadoran	257	46.6
Cuban	332	39.6
Dominican Republic	1,916	35.7
Mexican	1,097	49.0
Puerto Rican	3,770	36.5
South American	3,087	44.7
Colombian	466	42.4
Ecuadorian	1,760	42.5
Peruvian	406	57.6

Homeownership Rate
(Universe: Occupied Housing Units)

Group	%
Total Population	29.5
Hispanic or Latino (of any race)	21.2
Central American, ex. Mexican	23.4
Costa Rican	24.7
Guatemalan	20.1
Honduran	20.3
Nicaraguan	27.3
Panamanian	30.3
Salvadoran	28.4
Cuban	29.5
Dominican Republic	19.9
Mexican	12.5
Puerto Rican	18.8
South American	28.4
Argentinean	26.6
Bolivian	28.8
Chilean	23.1
Colombian	30.6
Ecuadorian	27.6
Peruvian	30.0
Uruguayan	24.5
Venezuelan	25.4
Spaniard	41.9

Median Home Value

Group	Dollars
Total Population	360,400
Hispanic or Latino (of any race)	362,100
Central American, ex. Mexican	353,900
Guatemalan	278,600
Honduran	342,600
Salvadoran	393,400
Cuban	341,700
Dominican Republic	423,500
Mexican	336,700
Puerto Rican	363,900
South American	358,600
Colombian	365,400
Ecuadorian	351,600
Peruvian	361,700

Median Gross Rent

Group	Dollars
Total Population	1,082
Hispanic or Latino (of any race)	982
Central American, ex. Mexican	1,071
Guatemalan	1,132
Honduran	1,052
Salvadoran	839
Cuban	1,104
Dominican Republic	978
Mexican	1,063
Puerto Rican	928
South American	1,036
Colombian	881
Ecuadorian	1,062
Peruvian	1,026

Median Household Income
(2010 Inflation-Adjusted Dollars)

Group	Dollars
Total Population	54,280
Hispanic or Latino (of any race)	40,909
Central American, ex. Mexican	40,182
Guatemalan	35,912
Honduran	40,729
Salvadoran	26,058
Cuban	52,292
Dominican Republic	34,939
Mexican	48,574
Puerto Rican	38,662
South American	44,497
Colombian	39,136
Ecuadorian	41,141
Peruvian	54,333

Per Capita Income
(2010 Inflation-Adjusted Dollars)

Group	Dollars
Total Population	30,490
Hispanic or Latino (of any race)	19,594
Central American, ex. Mexican	18,386
Guatemalan	11,497
Honduran	17,755
Salvadoran	20,769
Cuban	23,702
Dominican Republic	16,392
Mexican	18,523
Puerto Rican	19,637
South American	22,057
Colombian	23,782
Ecuadorian	17,764
Peruvian	20,738

Households with $100,000+ Income

Group	Number	%
Total Population	23,622	25.4
Hispanic or Latino (of any race)	3,230	14.4
Central American, ex. Mexican	170	7.3
Guatemalan	0	0.0
Honduran	53	4.7
Salvadoran	37	9.3
Cuban	118	16.3
Dominican Republic	388	11.4
Mexican	198	15.7
Puerto Rican	1,345	14.8
South American	792	17.2
Colombian	170	17.8
Ecuadorian	261	10.2
Peruvian	66	17.1

Households with Food Stamps/SNAP Benefits During Past 12 Months

Group	Number	%
Total Population	9,522	10.2
Hispanic or Latino (of any race)	3,481	15.5
Central American, ex. Mexican	348	14.9
Guatemalan	64	18.9
Honduran	182	16.2
Salvadoran	42	10.6
Cuban	112	15.4
Dominican Republic	633	18.6
Mexican	153	12.1
Puerto Rican	1,617	17.8
South American	595	12.9
Colombian	110	11.5
Ecuadorian	283	11.0
Peruvian	98	25.4

Poverty Rate
(Income in Past 12 Months Below Poverty Level)

Group	%
Total Population	17.5
Hispanic or Latino (of any race)	22.1
Central American, ex. Mexican	14.6
Guatemalan	16.8
Honduran	13.8
Salvadoran	20.2
Cuban	23.8
Dominican Republic	24.8
Mexican	20.4
Puerto Rican	26.4
South American	16.9
Colombian	19.1
Ecuadorian	18.2
Peruvian	11.6

Kearny

Population

Group	Number	%TP[1]	%HP[2]
Total Population	40,684	100.0	–
Hispanic or Latino (of any race)	16,253	39.9	100.0
Central American, ex. Mexican	1,041	2.6	6.4
Guatemalan	264	0.6	1.6
Honduran	183	0.4	1.1
Salvadoran	432	1.1	2.7
Cuban	719	1.8	4.4
Dominican Republic	1,009	2.5	6.2
Mexican	913	2.2	5.6
Puerto Rican	2,730	6.7	16.8
South American	7,015	17.2	43.2
Argentinean	177	0.4	1.1
Colombian	623	1.5	3.8
Ecuadorian	2,230	5.5	13.7
Peruvian	3,315	8.1	20.4
Uruguayan	418	1.0	2.6
Venezuelan	104	0.3	0.6
Spaniard	898	2.2	5.5

Population Growth: 2000–2010

Group	%
Total Population	0.4
Hispanic or Latino (of any race)	46.8
Central American, ex. Mexican	104.1
Guatemalan	61.0
Salvadoran	111.8
Cuban	-15.1
Dominican Republic	115.1
Mexican	143.5
Puerto Rican	22.0
South American	116.8
Argentinean	68.6
Colombian	63.1
Ecuadorian	160.5
Peruvian	114.0

Notes: (1) Percent of total population; (2) Percent of Hispanic/Latino population; Profiles include places with an overall population of at least 125,000, OR an overall population of at least 25,000 where the Hispanic/Latino population is at least 20% of the overall population. In states where less than five places meet either of these criteria, we have included places with at least 10,000 total population with the highest percentage of Hispanic/Latino population. These places are identified with an asterisk (*); Please refer to the User's Guide for a full explanation of data.

Group	
Spaniard	36.1

Males per 100 Females

Group	Number
Total Population	106.0
Hispanic or Latino (of any race)	107.4
Central American, ex. Mexican	101.7
Guatemalan	104.7
Honduran	94.7
Salvadoran	95.5
Cuban	83.0
Dominican Republic	96.3
Mexican	123.2
Puerto Rican	99.3
South American	97.3
Argentinean	115.9
Colombian	82.7
Ecuadorian	106.1
Peruvian	93.7
Uruguayan	101.0
Venezuelan	100.0
Spaniard	108.8

Average Household Size

Group	People
Total Population	2.83
Hispanic or Latino (of any race)	3.37
Central American, ex. Mexican	3.66
Guatemalan	3.62
Honduran	3.81
Salvadoran	3.90
Cuban	2.67
Dominican Republic	3.40
Mexican	4.21
Puerto Rican	3.07
South American	3.59
Argentinean	3.06
Colombian	3.20
Ecuadorian	3.77
Peruvian	3.68
Uruguayan	3.19
Venezuelan	3.17
Spaniard	2.85

Median Age

Group	Years
Total Population	36.4
Hispanic or Latino (of any race)	32.3
Central American, ex. Mexican	32.6
Guatemalan	34.7
Honduran	32.4
Salvadoran	30.0
Cuban	42.4
Dominican Republic	28.1
Mexican	26.1
Puerto Rican	28.5
South American	35.2
Argentinean	38.3
Colombian	35.9
Ecuadorian	33.4
Peruvian	36.8
Uruguayan	32.8
Venezuelan	29.5
Spaniard	45.5

High School Graduates
(Universe: Population 25 Years and Over)

Group	Number	%
Total Population	21,383	78.3
Hispanic or Latino (of any race)	7,913	77.1
Central American, ex. Mexican	488	60.2
Cuban	434	70.5
Dominican Republic	343	62.0
Puerto Rican	1,345	74.6
South American	4,096	86.1
Ecuadorian	1,376	85.6
Peruvian	1,767	84.8
Spaniard	473	58.7

Four-Year College Graduates
(Universe: Population 25 Years and Over)

Group	Number	%
Total Population	5,003	18.3
Hispanic or Latino (of any race)	1,216	11.9
Central American, ex. Mexican	125	15.4
Cuban	118	19.2
Dominican Republic	38	6.9
Puerto Rican	104	5.8
South American	640	13.4
Ecuadorian	242	15.1
Peruvian	303	14.5
Spaniard	101	12.5

Population Age 3–17 Enrolled in Public School
(Universe: Population Age 3–17 Enrolled in School)

Group	Number	%
Total Population	6,155	91.5
Hispanic or Latino (of any race)	3,339	94.0
Central American, ex. Mexican	290	100.0
Cuban	154	100.0
Dominican Republic	273	84.8
Puerto Rican	586	100.0
South American	1,508	99.0
Ecuadorian	589	100.0
Peruvian	553	98.9
Spaniard	197	83.1

Population Age 3–17 Enrolled in Private School
(Universe: Population Age 3–17 Enrolled in School)

Group	Number	%
Total Population	572	8.5
Hispanic or Latino (of any race)	215	6.0
Central American, ex. Mexican	0	0.0
Cuban	0	0.0
Dominican Republic	49	15.2
Puerto Rican	0	0.0
South American	16	1.0
Ecuadorian	0	0.0
Peruvian	6	1.1
Spaniard	40	16.9

Foreign-Born Population

Group	Number	%
Total Population	16,242	40.4
Hispanic or Latino (of any race)	9,156	54.7
Central American, ex. Mexican	786	61.1
Cuban	448	46.5
Dominican Republic	642	63.2
Puerto Rican	40	1.3
South American	5,602	76.1
Ecuadorian	1,938	74.6
Peruvian	2,488	79.8
Spaniard	739	58.5

Foreign-Born Naturalized U.S. Citizens

Group	Number	%
Total Population	6,916	42.6
Hispanic or Latino (of any race)	3,208	35.0
Central American, ex. Mexican	167	21.2
Cuban	344	76.8
Dominican Republic	358	55.8
Puerto Rican	40	100.0
South American	1,822	32.5
Ecuadorian	618	31.9
Peruvian	858	34.5
Spaniard	248	33.6

Language Spoken at Home: English Only
(Universe: Population 5 Years and Over)

Group	Number	%
Total Population	13,838	36.8
Hispanic or Latino (of any race)	1,445	9.4
Central American, ex. Mexican	0	0.0
Cuban	241	26.3
Dominican Republic	50	5.2
Puerto Rican	594	22.2
South American	195	2.9
Ecuadorian	82	3.6
Peruvian	89	3.0
Spaniard	240	19.6

Language Spoken at Home: Spanish
(Universe: Population 5 Years and Over)

Group	Number	%
Total Population	14,779	39.3
Hispanic or Latino (of any race)	13,600	88.3
Central American, ex. Mexican	1,267	100.0
Cuban	676	73.7
Dominican Republic	906	94.8
Puerto Rican	2,058	76.9
South American	6,352	93.1
Ecuadorian	2,030	88.3
Peruvian	2,916	97.0
Spaniard	985	80.4

Unemployment Rate
(Universe: Population 16 Years and Over)

Group	%
Total Population	10.3
Hispanic or Latino (of any race)	13.4
Central American, ex. Mexican	17.5
Cuban	9.9
Dominican Republic	12.5
Puerto Rican	17.1
South American	11.6
Ecuadorian	12.6
Peruvian	10.5
Spaniard	16.6

Class of Worker: Private Wage and Salary
(Universe: Civilian Employed Population 16 Years and Over)

Group	Number	%
Total Population	16,099	82.4
Hispanic or Latino (of any race)	7,028	91.7
Central American, ex. Mexican	591	100.0
Cuban	288	80.9
Dominican Republic	427	89.5
Puerto Rican	1,065	85.5
South American	3,518	92.9
Ecuadorian	1,115	92.8
Peruvian	1,709	97.8
Spaniard	474	89.8

Class of Worker: Government
(Universe: Civilian Employed Population 16 Years and Over)

Group	Number	%
Total Population	2,524	12.9
Hispanic or Latino (of any race)	422	5.5
Central American, ex. Mexican	0	0.0
Cuban	68	19.1
Dominican Republic	32	6.7
Puerto Rican	146	11.7
South American	137	3.6
Ecuadorian	47	3.9
Peruvian	29	1.7
Spaniard	22	4.2

Means of Transportation to Work: Car, Truck or Van
(Universe: Workers 16 Years and Over)

Group	Number	%
Total Population	14,620	75.9
Hispanic or Latino (of any race)	5,422	71.5
Central American, ex. Mexican	440	74.5
Cuban	335	97.7
Dominican Republic	277	63.0
Puerto Rican	917	73.7
South American	2,485	65.9
Ecuadorian	893	74.4
Peruvian	1,173	67.8
Spaniard	446	84.5

Means of Transportation to Work: Public Transportation (ex. Taxicab)
(Universe: Workers 16 Years and Over)

Group	Number	%
Total Population	2,720	14.1
Hispanic or Latino (of any race)	1,302	17.2
Central American, ex. Mexican	77	13.0
Cuban	8	2.3
Dominican Republic	81	18.4
Puerto Rican	179	14.4
South American	813	21.6
Ecuadorian	177	14.7
Peruvian	334	19.3
Spaniard	70	13.3

Homeownership Rate
(Universe: Occupied Housing Units)

Group	%
Total Population	45.8
Hispanic or Latino (of any race)	32.3
Central American, ex. Mexican	26.1
Guatemalan	19.5
Honduran	34.6

Notes: (1) Percent of total population; (2) Percent of Hispanic/Latino population; Profiles include places with an overall population of at least 125,000, OR an overall population of at least 25,000 where the Hispanic/Latino population is at least 20% of the overall population. In states where less than five places meet either of these criteria, we have included places with at least 10,000 total population with the highest percentage of Hispanic/Latino population. These places are identified with an asterisk (*); Please refer to the User's Guide for a full explanation of data.

Salvadoran	31.9
Cuban	52.6
Dominican Republic	26.1
Mexican	19.3
Puerto Rican	23.3
South American	29.5
Argentinean	37.9
Colombian	25.8
Ecuadorian	34.1
Peruvian	27.9
Uruguayan	17.3
Venezuelan	29.2
Spaniard	74.2

Median Home Value

Group	Dollars
Total Population	369,700
Hispanic or Latino (of any race)	382,100
Central American, ex. Mexican	417,600
Cuban	441,100
Dominican Republic	446,200
Puerto Rican	298,200
South American	350,000
Ecuadorian	283,000
Peruvian	382,700
Spaniard	481,800

Median Gross Rent

Group	Dollars
Total Population	1,097
Hispanic or Latino (of any race)	1,133
Central American, ex. Mexican	1,189
Cuban	787
Dominican Republic	1,349
Puerto Rican	1,073
South American	1,127
Ecuadorian	1,260
Peruvian	1,033
Spaniard	978

Median Household Income
(2010 Inflation-Adjusted Dollars)

Group	Dollars
Total Population	58,698
Hispanic or Latino (of any race)	57,539
Central American, ex. Mexican	39,758
Cuban	111,473
Dominican Republic	42,083
Puerto Rican	61,034
South American	57,860
Ecuadorian	55,030
Peruvian	74,125
Spaniard	77,823

Per Capita Income
(2010 Inflation-Adjusted Dollars)

Group	Dollars
Total Population	24,977
Hispanic or Latino (of any race)	19,964
Central American, ex. Mexican	15,774
Cuban	31,553
Dominican Republic	20,681
Puerto Rican	19,264
South American	19,401
Ecuadorian	15,641
Peruvian	20,005
Spaniard	26,438

Households with $100,000+ Income

Group	Number	%
Total Population	3,248	24.0
Hispanic or Latino (of any race)	994	20.4
Central American, ex. Mexican	86	21.3
Cuban	133	57.1
Dominican Republic	55	18.2
Puerto Rican	99	12.0
South American	384	18.0
Ecuadorian	59	8.9
Peruvian	229	25.0
Spaniard	157	33.0

Households with Food Stamps/SNAP Benefits During Past 12 Months

Group	Number	%
Total Population	605	4.5
Hispanic or Latino (of any race)	382	7.9
Central American, ex. Mexican	18	4.5
Cuban	8	3.4
Dominican Republic	18	5.9
Puerto Rican	61	7.4
South American	187	8.8
Ecuadorian	88	13.3
Peruvian	80	8.7
Spaniard	0	0.0

Poverty Rate
(Income in Past 12 Months Below Poverty Level)

Group	%
Total Population	10.3
Hispanic or Latino (of any race)	11.3
Central American, ex. Mexican	25.5
Cuban	1.3
Dominican Republic	13.3
Puerto Rican	11.8
South American	11.4
Ecuadorian	10.9
Peruvian	12.4
Spaniard	6.1

Linden

Population

Group	Number	%TP[1]	%HP[2]
Total Population	40,499	100.0	–
Hispanic or Latino (of any race)	10,095	24.9	100.0
Central American, ex. Mexican	1,019	2.5	10.1
Costa Rican	109	0.3	1.1
Guatemalan	137	0.3	1.4
Honduran	199	0.5	2.0
Salvadoran	457	1.1	4.5
Cuban	780	1.9	7.7
Dominican Republic	957	2.4	9.5
Mexican	295	0.7	2.9
Puerto Rican	2,484	6.1	24.6
South American	3,608	8.9	35.7
Argentinean	149	0.4	1.5
Colombian	1,652	4.1	16.4
Ecuadorian	563	1.4	5.6
Peruvian	906	2.2	9.0
Uruguayan	209	0.5	2.1
Spaniard	222	0.5	2.2

Population Growth: 2000–2010

Group	%
Total Population	2.8
Hispanic or Latino (of any race)	77.9
Central American, ex. Mexican	204.2
Salvadoran	287.3
Cuban	31.5
Dominican Republic	248.0
Mexican	92.8
Puerto Rican	64.3
South American	143.9
Colombian	93.9
Ecuadorian	407.2
Peruvian	244.5
Spaniard	115.5

Males per 100 Females

Group	Number
Total Population	91.1
Hispanic or Latino (of any race)	92.6
Central American, ex. Mexican	103.0
Costa Rican	142.2
Guatemalan	132.2
Honduran	80.9
Salvadoran	101.3
Cuban	95.0
Dominican Republic	88.4
Mexican	100.7
Puerto Rican	95.4
South American	87.4
Argentinean	81.7
Colombian	80.5
Ecuadorian	98.9
Peruvian	99.1
Uruguayan	80.2
Spaniard	88.1

Average Household Size

Group	People
Total Population	2.70
Hispanic or Latino (of any race)	3.42
Central American, ex. Mexican	3.91
Costa Rican	3.47
Guatemalan	4.02
Honduran	3.72
Salvadoran	4.15
Cuban	2.90
Dominican Republic	3.66
Mexican	3.68
Puerto Rican	3.13
South American	3.63
Argentinean	3.00
Colombian	3.66
Ecuadorian	3.95
Peruvian	3.67
Uruguayan	3.32
Spaniard	2.71

Median Age

Group	Years
Total Population	38.8
Hispanic or Latino (of any race)	32.5
Central American, ex. Mexican	32.3
Costa Rican	31.5
Guatemalan	31.8
Honduran	34.5
Salvadoran	30.9
Cuban	42.4
Dominican Republic	30.8
Mexican	28.1
Puerto Rican	30.1
South American	35.4
Argentinean	37.3
Colombian	34.7
Ecuadorian	33.6
Peruvian	37.5
Uruguayan	35.4
Spaniard	39.5

High School Graduates
(Universe: Population 25 Years and Over)

Group	Number	%
Total Population	23,704	83.9
Hispanic or Latino (of any race)	4,680	80.8
Central American, ex. Mexican	497	80.0
Cuban	326	80.9
Dominican Republic	501	83.4
Puerto Rican	719	65.1
South American	2,120	85.6
Colombian	680	95.2
Peruvian	660	91.3

Four-Year College Graduates
(Universe: Population 25 Years and Over)

Group	Number	%
Total Population	5,206	18.4
Hispanic or Latino (of any race)	762	13.2
Central American, ex. Mexican	38	6.1
Cuban	55	13.6
Dominican Republic	129	21.5
Puerto Rican	103	9.3
South American	319	12.9
Colombian	121	16.9
Peruvian	112	15.5

Population Age 3–17 Enrolled in Public School
(Universe: Population Age 3–17 Enrolled in School)

Group	Number	%
Total Population	5,423	87.8
Hispanic or Latino (of any race)	1,772	94.0
Central American, ex. Mexican	210	95.0
Cuban	106	96.4
Dominican Republic	137	100.0
Puerto Rican	378	95.5
South American	678	96.0
Colombian	152	96.2
Peruvian	162	89.0

Population Age 3–17 Enrolled in Private School
(Universe: Population Age 3–17 Enrolled in School)

Group	Number	%
Total Population	753	12.2

Notes: (1) Percent of total population; (2) Percent of Hispanic/Latino population; Profiles include places with an overall population of at least 125,000, OR an overall population of at least 25,000 where the Hispanic/Latino population is at least 20% of the overall population. In states where less than five places meet either of these criteria, we have included places with at least 10,000 total population with the highest percentage of Hispanic/Latino population. These places are identified with an asterisk (*); Please refer to the User's Guide for a full explanation of data.

Hispanic or Latino (of any race)	113	6.0
Central American, ex. Mexican	11	5.0
Cuban	4	3.6
Dominican Republic	0	0.0
Puerto Rican	18	4.5
South American	28	4.0
Colombian	6	3.8
Peruvian	20	11.0

Foreign-Born Population

Group	Number	%
Total Population	12,796	32.0
Hispanic or Latino (of any race)	4,414	46.7
Central American, ex. Mexican	480	48.4
Cuban	394	65.6
Dominican Republic	650	69.8
Puerto Rican	12	0.6
South American	2,595	68.2
Colombian	695	66.3
Peruvian	923	78.4

Foreign-Born Naturalized U.S. Citizens

Group	Number	%
Total Population	6,385	49.9
Hispanic or Latino (of any race)	2,179	49.4
Central American, ex. Mexican	324	67.5
Cuban	293	74.4
Dominican Republic	294	45.2
Puerto Rican	12	100.0
South American	1,163	44.8
Colombian	539	77.6
Peruvian	296	32.1

Language Spoken at Home: English Only
(Universe: Population 5 Years and Over)

Group	Number	%
Total Population	20,714	54.5
Hispanic or Latino (of any race)	1,242	14.2
Central American, ex. Mexican	62	7.2
Cuban	73	12.2
Dominican Republic	49	5.6
Puerto Rican	592	30.8
South American	252	7.2
Colombian	82	8.6
Peruvian	8	0.7

Language Spoken at Home: Spanish
(Universe: Population 5 Years and Over)

Group	Number	%
Total Population	7,761	20.4
Hispanic or Latino (of any race)	7,439	85.2
Central American, ex. Mexican	799	92.8
Cuban	480	80.5
Dominican Republic	831	94.4
Puerto Rican	1,333	69.2
South American	3,261	92.5
Colombian	874	91.4
Peruvian	1,114	99.3

Unemployment Rate
(Universe: Population 16 Years and Over)

Group	%
Total Population	8.8
Hispanic or Latino (of any race)	7.6
Central American, ex. Mexican	17.0
Cuban	5.4
Dominican Republic	10.8
Puerto Rican	8.7
South American	4.3
Colombian	2.4
Peruvian	3.6

Class of Worker: Private Wage and Salary
(Universe: Civilian Employed Population 16 Years and Over)

Group	Number	%
Total Population	16,577	80.9
Hispanic or Latino (of any race)	4,497	87.8
Central American, ex. Mexican	384	90.6
Cuban	323	88.0
Dominican Republic	449	82.5
Puerto Rican	1,044	88.4
South American	1,921	90.9
Colombian	522	80.8
Peruvian	661	90.5

Class of Worker: Government
(Universe: Civilian Employed Population 16 Years and Over)

Group	Number	%
Total Population	2,931	14.3
Hispanic or Latino (of any race)	507	9.9
Central American, ex. Mexican	29	6.8
Cuban	44	12.0
Dominican Republic	86	15.8
Puerto Rican	127	10.8
South American	104	4.9
Colombian	81	12.5
Peruvian	23	3.2

Means of Transportation to Work: Car, Truck or Van
(Universe: Workers 16 Years and Over)

Group	Number	%
Total Population	15,963	80.6
Hispanic or Latino (of any race)	3,530	70.9
Central American, ex. Mexican	291	70.5
Cuban	230	67.6
Dominican Republic	358	65.8
Puerto Rican	868	74.9
South American	1,374	66.9
Colombian	468	74.9
Peruvian	475	68.8

Means of Transportation to Work: Public Transportation (ex. Taxicab)
(Universe: Workers 16 Years and Over)

Group	Number	%
Total Population	1,551	7.8
Hispanic or Latino (of any race)	525	10.5
Central American, ex. Mexican	64	15.5
Cuban	15	4.4
Dominican Republic	104	19.1
Puerto Rican	181	15.6
South American	150	7.3
Colombian	104	16.6
Peruvian	0	0.0

Homeownership Rate
(Universe: Occupied Housing Units)

Group	%
Total Population	57.0
Hispanic or Latino (of any race)	55.1
Central American, ex. Mexican	60.0
Costa Rican	50.0
Guatemalan	58.1
Honduran	62.1
Salvadoran	57.9
Cuban	61.8
Dominican Republic	54.6
Mexican	35.4
Puerto Rican	48.8
South American	56.7
Argentinean	58.0
Colombian	58.9
Ecuadorian	64.7
Peruvian	51.9
Uruguayan	47.8
Spaniard	79.8

Median Home Value

Group	Dollars
Total Population	335,900
Hispanic or Latino (of any race)	363,100
Central American, ex. Mexican	375,600
Cuban	360,500
Dominican Republic	338,100
Puerto Rican	369,700
South American	369,100
Colombian	370,400
Peruvian	388,400

Median Gross Rent

Group	Dollars
Total Population	1,075
Hispanic or Latino (of any race)	1,121
Central American, ex. Mexican	1,354
Cuban	1,026
Dominican Republic	–
Puerto Rican	1,040
South American	1,191
Colombian	1,114
Peruvian	987

Median Household Income
(2010 Inflation-Adjusted Dollars)

Group	Dollars
Total Population	55,859
Hispanic or Latino (of any race)	58,578
Central American, ex. Mexican	47,154
Cuban	52,188
Dominican Republic	68,590
Puerto Rican	55,349
South American	60,945
Colombian	70,000
Peruvian	61,389

Per Capita Income
(2010 Inflation-Adjusted Dollars)

Group	Dollars
Total Population	27,011
Hispanic or Latino (of any race)	21,140
Central American, ex. Mexican	18,432
Cuban	27,058
Dominican Republic	20,416
Puerto Rican	21,169
South American	21,185
Colombian	31,097
Peruvian	19,838

Households with $100,000+ Income

Group	Number	%
Total Population	3,066	20.7
Hispanic or Latino (of any race)	503	17.4
Central American, ex. Mexican	8	2.5
Cuban	59	24.9
Dominican Republic	53	21.2
Puerto Rican	110	16.5
South American	227	20.6
Colombian	101	27.2
Peruvian	102	30.7

Households with Food Stamps/SNAP Benefits During Past 12 Months

Group	Number	%
Total Population	608	4.1
Hispanic or Latino (of any race)	151	5.2
Central American, ex. Mexican	0	0.0
Cuban	17	7.2
Dominican Republic	0	0.0
Puerto Rican	83	12.5
South American	51	4.6
Colombian	0	0.0
Peruvian	4	1.2

Poverty Rate
(Income in Past 12 Months Below Poverty Level)

Group	%
Total Population	7.5
Hispanic or Latino (of any race)	10.2
Central American, ex. Mexican	11.2
Cuban	8.9
Dominican Republic	11.4
Puerto Rican	14.0
South American	5.3
Colombian	5.6
Peruvian	5.9

Long Branch

Population

Group	Number	%TP[1]	%HP[2]
Total Population	30,719	100.0	–
Hispanic or Latino (of any race)	8,624	28.1	100.0
Central American, ex. Mexican	1,499	4.9	17.4
Guatemalan	479	1.6	5.6
Honduran	147	0.5	1.7
Salvadoran	733	2.4	8.5
Cuban	103	0.3	1.2
Dominican Republic	215	0.7	2.5
Mexican	3,496	11.4	40.5
Puerto Rican	2,187	7.1	25.4
South American	655	2.1	7.6
Colombian	231	0.8	2.7
Ecuadorian	166	0.5	1.9

Notes: (1) Percent of total population; (2) Percent of Hispanic/Latino population; Profiles include places with an overall population of at least 125,000, OR an overall population of at least 25,000 where the Hispanic/Latino population is at least 20% of the overall population. In states where less than five places meet either of these criteria, we have included places with at least 10,000 total population with the highest percentage of Hispanic/Latino population. These places are identified with an asterisk (*); Please refer to the User's Guide for a full explanation of data.

Population Growth: 2000–2010

Group	%
Total Population	-2.0
Hispanic or Latino (of any race)	33.1
Central American, ex. Mexican	173.5
Guatemalan	188.6
Salvadoran	214.6
Dominican Republic	97.2
Mexican	141.4
Puerto Rican	-21.3
South American	59.4
Colombian	22.9

Males per 100 Females

Group	Number
Total Population	100.3
Hispanic or Latino (of any race)	114.2
Central American, ex. Mexican	117.6
Guatemalan	130.3
Honduran	75.0
Salvadoran	118.2
Cuban	114.6
Dominican Republic	100.9
Mexican	128.9
Puerto Rican	96.3
South American	98.5
Colombian	92.5
Ecuadorian	88.6

Average Household Size

Group	People
Total Population	2.60
Hispanic or Latino (of any race)	3.96
Central American, ex. Mexican	4.52
Guatemalan	4.50
Honduran	4.66
Salvadoran	4.71
Cuban	2.45
Dominican Republic	3.76
Mexican	5.07
Puerto Rican	3.05
South American	3.33
Colombian	3.59
Ecuadorian	3.53

Median Age

Group	Years
Total Population	33.8
Hispanic or Latino (of any race)	27.1
Central American, ex. Mexican	29.2
Guatemalan	29.0
Honduran	28.4
Salvadoran	29.2
Cuban	31.5
Dominican Republic	31.5
Mexican	25.4
Puerto Rican	27.9
South American	35.9
Colombian	33.9
Ecuadorian	35.0

High School Graduates
(Universe: Population 25 Years and Over)

Group	Number	%
Total Population	16,262	78.4
Hispanic or Latino (of any race)	3,149	59.6
Central American, ex. Mexican	319	51.9
Mexican	1,274	56.1
Puerto Rican	927	58.6

Four-Year College Graduates
(Universe: Population 25 Years and Over)

Group	Number	%
Total Population	4,890	23.6
Hispanic or Latino (of any race)	496	9.4
Central American, ex. Mexican	42	6.8
Mexican	102	4.5
Puerto Rican	128	8.1

Population Age 3–17 Enrolled in Public School
(Universe: Population Age 3–17 Enrolled in School)

Group	Number	%
Total Population	4,090	87.5
Hispanic or Latino (of any race)	2,134	97.8
Central American, ex. Mexican	150	100.0
Mexican	721	98.4
Puerto Rican	988	99.6

Population Age 3–17 Enrolled in Private School
(Universe: Population Age 3–17 Enrolled in School)

Group	Number	%
Total Population	584	12.5
Hispanic or Latino (of any race)	47	2.2
Central American, ex. Mexican	0	0.0
Mexican	12	1.6
Puerto Rican	4	0.4

Foreign-Born Population

Group	Number	%
Total Population	9,450	30.6
Hispanic or Latino (of any race)	4,302	47.0
Central American, ex. Mexican	651	72.9
Mexican	2,810	71.4
Puerto Rican	12	0.4

Foreign-Born Naturalized U.S. Citizens

Group	Number	%
Total Population	1,804	19.1
Hispanic or Latino (of any race)	433	10.1
Central American, ex. Mexican	129	19.8
Mexican	75	2.7
Puerto Rican	0	0.0

Language Spoken at Home: English Only
(Universe: Population 5 Years and Over)

Group	Number	%
Total Population	16,622	57.6
Hispanic or Latino (of any race)	1,436	17.6
Central American, ex. Mexican	0	0.0
Mexican	140	4.2
Puerto Rican	1,084	39.7

Language Spoken at Home: Spanish
(Universe: Population 5 Years and Over)

Group	Number	%
Total Population	7,168	24.8
Hispanic or Latino (of any race)	6,677	81.9
Central American, ex. Mexican	816	100.0
Mexican	3,188	95.2
Puerto Rican	1,649	60.3

Unemployment Rate
(Universe: Population 16 Years and Over)

Group	%
Total Population	7.8
Hispanic or Latino (of any race)	11.9
Central American, ex. Mexican	10.9
Mexican	8.3
Puerto Rican	20.1

Class of Worker: Private Wage and Salary
(Universe: Civilian Employed Population 16 Years and Over)

Group	Number	%
Total Population	13,737	81.0
Hispanic or Latino (of any race)	3,800	88.7
Central American, ex. Mexican	437	84.7
Mexican	1,992	94.3
Puerto Rican	854	84.6

Class of Worker: Government
(Universe: Civilian Employed Population 16 Years and Over)

Group	Number	%
Total Population	1,559	9.2
Hispanic or Latino (of any race)	211	4.9
Central American, ex. Mexican	20	3.9
Mexican	8	0.4
Puerto Rican	118	11.7

Means of Transportation to Work: Car, Truck or Van
(Universe: Workers 16 Years and Over)

Group	Number	%
Total Population	13,084	79.3
Hispanic or Latino (of any race)	2,594	62.4
Central American, ex. Mexican	323	65.8
Mexican	1,075	51.9
Puerto Rican	806	83.0

Means of Transportation to Work: Public Transportation (ex. Taxicab)
(Universe: Workers 16 Years and Over)

Group	Number	%
Total Population	1,382	8.4
Hispanic or Latino (of any race)	606	14.6
Central American, ex. Mexican	117	23.8
Mexican	368	17.8
Puerto Rican	9	0.9

Homeownership Rate
(Universe: Occupied Housing Units)

Group	%
Total Population	42.0
Hispanic or Latino (of any race)	23.8
Central American, ex. Mexican	32.3
Guatemalan	30.6
Honduran	45.7
Salvadoran	29.3
Cuban	23.7
Dominican Republic	31.4
Mexican	10.9
Puerto Rican	25.7
South American	43.4
Colombian	52.4
Ecuadorian	43.6

Median Home Value

Group	Dollars
Total Population	383,500
Hispanic or Latino (of any race)	322,800
Central American, ex. Mexican	345,800
Mexican	417,400
Puerto Rican	228,800

Median Gross Rent

Group	Dollars
Total Population	1,166
Hispanic or Latino (of any race)	1,148
Central American, ex. Mexican	1,072
Mexican	1,369
Puerto Rican	1,082

Median Household Income
(2010 Inflation-Adjusted Dollars)

Group	Dollars
Total Population	52,792
Hispanic or Latino (of any race)	44,223
Central American, ex. Mexican	43,542
Mexican	49,316
Puerto Rican	27,885

Per Capita Income
(2010 Inflation-Adjusted Dollars)

Group	Dollars
Total Population	30,381
Hispanic or Latino (of any race)	13,584
Central American, ex. Mexican	18,148
Mexican	11,900
Puerto Rican	13,308

Households with $100,000+ Income

Group	Number	%
Total Population	2,627	22.2
Hispanic or Latino (of any race)	169	7.2
Central American, ex. Mexican	15	5.4
Mexican	63	7.6
Puerto Rican	47	5.0

Households with Food Stamps/SNAP Benefits During Past 12 Months

Group	Number	%
Total Population	766	6.5
Hispanic or Latino (of any race)	342	14.7
Central American, ex. Mexican	26	9.4
Mexican	116	14.1
Puerto Rican	162	17.3

Poverty Rate
(Income in Past 12 Months Below Poverty Level)

Group	%
Total Population	14.5
Hispanic or Latino (of any race)	23.9
Central American, ex. Mexican	14.7
Mexican	28.5

Notes: (1) Percent of total population; (2) Percent of Hispanic/Latino population; Profiles include places with an overall population of at least 125,000, OR an overall population of at least 25,000 where the Hispanic/Latino population is at least 20% of the overall population. In states where less than five places meet either of these criteria, we have included places with at least 10,000 total population with the highest percentage of Hispanic/Latino population. These places are identified with an asterisk (*); Please refer to the User's Guide for a full explanation of data.

Puerto Rican	24.7

New Brunswick

Population

Group	Number	%TP[1]	%HP[2]
Total Population	55,181	100.0	–
Hispanic or Latino (of any race)	27,553	49.9	100.0
Central American, ex. Mexican	3,761	6.8	13.7
Guatemalan	353	0.6	1.3
Honduran	2,772	5.0	10.1
Nicaraguan	244	0.4	0.9
Salvadoran	313	0.6	1.1
Cuban	273	0.5	1.0
Dominican Republic	4,139	7.5	15.0
Mexican	14,104	25.6	51.2
Puerto Rican	2,832	5.1	10.3
South American	1,103	2.0	4.0
Colombian	274	0.5	1.0
Ecuadorian	334	0.6	1.2
Peruvian	335	0.6	1.2
Spaniard	115	0.2	0.4

Population Growth: 2000–2010

Group	%
Total Population	13.6
Hispanic or Latino (of any race)	45.4
Central American, ex. Mexican	71.1
Guatemalan	116.6
Honduran	91.0
Nicaraguan	-5.4
Salvadoran	213.0
Cuban	7.5
Dominican Republic	45.0
Mexican	91.5
Puerto Rican	-10.9
South American	55.6
Colombian	30.5
Ecuadorian	74.0
Peruvian	129.5

Males per 100 Females

Group	Number
Total Population	105.0
Hispanic or Latino (of any race)	114.0
Central American, ex. Mexican	121.1
Guatemalan	132.2
Honduran	124.5
Nicaraguan	86.3
Salvadoran	117.4
Cuban	97.8
Dominican Republic	91.2
Mexican	127.6
Puerto Rican	92.9
South American	97.7
Colombian	85.1
Ecuadorian	106.2
Peruvian	97.1
Spaniard	117.0

Average Household Size

Group	People
Total Population	3.36
Hispanic or Latino (of any race)	4.81
Central American, ex. Mexican	5.02
Guatemalan	4.72
Honduran	5.28
Nicaraguan	4.92
Salvadoran	4.37
Cuban	2.54
Dominican Republic	4.26
Mexican	6.08
Puerto Rican	2.99
South American	3.24
Colombian	2.96
Ecuadorian	3.51
Peruvian	3.58
Spaniard	2.46

Median Age

Group	Years
Total Population	23.3
Hispanic or Latino (of any race)	25.3
Central American, ex. Mexican	28.6
Guatemalan	30.4
Honduran	28.5
Nicaraguan	29.4
Salvadoran	26.9
Cuban	22.8
Dominican Republic	28.0
Mexican	24.2
Puerto Rican	27.1
South American	30.1
Colombian	24.8
Ecuadorian	30.0
Peruvian	35.3
Spaniard	21.1

High School Graduates
(Universe: Population 25 Years and Over)

Group	Number	%
Total Population	16,580	66.1
Hispanic or Latino (of any race)	6,746	48.5
Central American, ex. Mexican	858	45.3
Honduran	510	41.4
Dominican Republic	1,325	57.5
Mexican	2,423	37.2
Puerto Rican	1,512	64.8
South American	426	72.8

Four-Year College Graduates
(Universe: Population 25 Years and Over)

Group	Number	%
Total Population	5,512	22.0
Hispanic or Latino (of any race)	1,180	8.5
Central American, ex. Mexican	177	9.3
Honduran	35	2.8
Dominican Republic	297	12.9
Mexican	197	3.0
Puerto Rican	257	11.0
South American	155	26.5

Population Age 3–17 Enrolled in Public School
(Universe: Population Age 3–17 Enrolled in School)

Group	Number	%
Total Population	8,097	92.6
Hispanic or Latino (of any race)	6,389	98.0
Central American, ex. Mexican	788	100.0
Honduran	616	100.0
Dominican Republic	1,030	98.0
Mexican	3,575	100.0
Puerto Rican	684	86.3
South American	200	100.0

Population Age 3–17 Enrolled in Private School
(Universe: Population Age 3–17 Enrolled in School)

Group	Number	%
Total Population	643	7.4
Hispanic or Latino (of any race)	130	2.0
Central American, ex. Mexican	0	0.0
Honduran	0	0.0
Dominican Republic	21	2.0
Mexican	0	0.0
Puerto Rican	109	13.7
South American	0	0.0

Foreign-Born Population

Group	Number	%
Total Population	19,538	36.2
Hispanic or Latino (of any race)	15,563	58.3
Central American, ex. Mexican	2,357	72.3
Honduran	1,644	73.8
Dominican Republic	2,978	68.8
Mexican	9,081	68.2
Puerto Rican	222	5.4
South American	718	65.5

Foreign-Born Naturalized U.S. Citizens

Group	Number	%
Total Population	3,507	17.9
Hispanic or Latino (of any race)	1,675	10.8
Central American, ex. Mexican	256	10.9
Honduran	182	11.1
Dominican Republic	693	23.3
Mexican	387	4.3
Puerto Rican	0	0.0
South American	254	35.4

Language Spoken at Home: English Only
(Universe: Population 5 Years and Over)

Group	Number	%
Total Population	23,696	47.5
Hispanic or Latino (of any race)	1,355	5.7
Central American, ex. Mexican	54	1.8
Honduran	19	0.9
Dominican Republic	70	1.8
Mexican	184	1.6
Puerto Rican	788	21.3
South American	109	11.3

Language Spoken at Home: Spanish
(Universe: Population 5 Years and Over)

Group	Number	%
Total Population	22,723	45.5
Hispanic or Latino (of any race)	22,233	94.2
Central American, ex. Mexican	2,974	98.2
Honduran	2,093	99.1
Dominican Republic	3,870	98.2
Mexican	11,249	98.4
Puerto Rican	2,911	78.7
South American	856	88.7

Unemployment Rate
(Universe: Population 16 Years and Over)

Group	%
Total Population	10.0
Hispanic or Latino (of any race)	10.5
Central American, ex. Mexican	14.3
Honduran	18.2
Dominican Republic	11.1
Mexican	6.9
Puerto Rican	17.5
South American	10.8

Class of Worker: Private Wage and Salary
(Universe: Civilian Employed Population 16 Years and Over)

Group	Number	%
Total Population	21,543	87.4
Hispanic or Latino (of any race)	11,849	94.3
Central American, ex. Mexican	1,529	90.8
Honduran	1,033	94.8
Dominican Republic	1,817	93.4
Mexican	6,471	99.8
Puerto Rican	1,356	78.2
South American	500	96.3

Class of Worker: Government
(Universe: Civilian Employed Population 16 Years and Over)

Group	Number	%
Total Population	2,676	10.9
Hispanic or Latino (of any race)	538	4.3
Central American, ex. Mexican	45	2.7
Honduran	39	3.6
Dominican Republic	71	3.6
Mexican	0	0.0
Puerto Rican	378	21.8
South American	19	3.7

Means of Transportation to Work: Car, Truck or Van
(Universe: Workers 16 Years and Over)

Group	Number	%
Total Population	16,254	67.0
Hispanic or Latino (of any race)	8,230	66.9
Central American, ex. Mexican	1,107	67.0
Honduran	732	69.1
Dominican Republic	1,680	90.2
Mexican	3,643	56.7
Puerto Rican	1,295	77.9
South American	380	77.1

Means of Transportation to Work: Public Transportation (ex. Taxicab)
(Universe: Workers 16 Years and Over)

Group	Number	%
Total Population	2,556	10.5
Hispanic or Latino (of any race)	1,390	11.3
Central American, ex. Mexican	174	10.5
Honduran	47	4.4
Dominican Republic	54	2.9
Mexican	915	14.2
Puerto Rican	143	8.6
South American	55	11.2

Notes: (1) Percent of total population; (2) Percent of Hispanic/Latino population; Profiles include places with an overall population of at least 125,000, OR an overall population of at least 25,000 where the Hispanic/Latino population is at least 20% of the overall population. In states where less than five places meet either of these criteria, we have included places with at least 10,000 total population with the highest percentage of Hispanic/Latino population. These places are identified with an asterisk (*); Please refer to the User's Guide for a full explanation of data.

Homeownership Rate (Universe: Occupied Housing Units)	
Group	%
Total Population	23.9
Hispanic or Latino (of any race)	19.9
Central American, ex. Mexican	20.1
Guatemalan	17.9
Honduran	20.6
Nicaraguan	27.5
Salvadoran	14.7
Cuban	21.4
Dominican Republic	33.8
Mexican	9.6
Puerto Rican	25.3
South American	31.9
Colombian	39.4
Ecuadorian	27.5
Peruvian	38.2
Spaniard	20.8

Median Home Value	
Group	Dollars
Total Population	285,900
Hispanic or Latino (of any race)	292,800
Central American, ex. Mexican	365,900
Honduran	357,200
Dominican Republic	309,600
Mexican	298,900
Puerto Rican	236,900
South American	299,100

Median Gross Rent	
Group	Dollars
Total Population	1,273
Hispanic or Latino (of any race)	1,299
Central American, ex. Mexican	1,193
Honduran	1,172
Dominican Republic	1,151
Mexican	1,542
Puerto Rican	1,036
South American	1,250

Median Household Income (2010 Inflation-Adjusted Dollars)	
Group	Dollars
Total Population	44,543
Hispanic or Latino (of any race)	44,975
Central American, ex. Mexican	41,383
Honduran	40,798
Dominican Republic	41,942
Mexican	52,140
Puerto Rican	30,799
South American	36,031

Per Capita Income (2010 Inflation-Adjusted Dollars)	
Group	Dollars
Total Population	16,395
Hispanic or Latino (of any race)	12,948
Central American, ex. Mexican	13,430
Honduran	12,815
Dominican Republic	13,929
Mexican	11,816
Puerto Rican	14,930
South American	13,642

Households with $100,000+ Income		
Group	Number	%
Total Population	2,204	15.2
Hispanic or Latino (of any race)	508	8.3
Central American, ex. Mexican	23	3.3
Honduran	23	4.8
Dominican Republic	51	4.4
Mexican	297	13.1
Puerto Rican	69	4.8
South American	50	13.5

Households with Food Stamps/SNAP Benefits During Past 12 Months		
Group	Number	%
Total Population	1,343	9.2
Hispanic or Latino (of any race)	810	13.2
Central American, ex. Mexican	61	8.6
Honduran	43	8.9
Dominican Republic	220	18.9
Mexican	339	15.0
Puerto Rican	160	11.2
South American	8	2.2

Poverty Rate (Income in Past 12 Months Below Poverty Level)	
Group	%
Total Population	25.8
Hispanic or Latino (of any race)	20.8
Central American, ex. Mexican	21.2
Honduran	23.0
Dominican Republic	18.3
Mexican	21.7
Puerto Rican	19.1
South American	29.2

Newark

Population			
Group	Number	%TP[1]	%HP[2]
Total Population	277,140	100.0	–
Hispanic or Latino (of any race)	93,746	33.8	100.0
Central American, ex. Mexican	7,497	2.7	8.0
Costa Rican	444	0.2	0.5
Guatemalan	1,375	0.5	1.5
Honduran	2,126	0.8	2.3
Nicaraguan	285	0.1	0.3
Panamanian	220	0.1	0.2
Salvadoran	3,000	1.1	3.2
Cuban	2,241	0.8	2.4
Dominican Republic	12,527	4.5	13.4
Mexican	4,336	1.6	4.6
Puerto Rican	35,993	13.0	38.4
South American	22,413	8.1	23.9
Argentinean	351	0.1	0.4
Bolivian	105	<0.1	0.1
Chilean	125	<0.1	0.1
Colombian	1,393	0.5	1.5
Ecuadorian	16,847	6.1	18.0
Peruvian	2,448	0.9	2.6
Uruguayan	634	0.2	0.7
Venezuelan	299	0.1	0.3
Spaniard	1,293	0.5	1.4

Population Growth: 2000–2010	
Group	%
Total Population	1.3
Hispanic or Latino (of any race)	16.3
Central American, ex. Mexican	98.1
Costa Rican	57.4
Guatemalan	77.2
Honduran	223.6
Nicaraguan	63.8
Panamanian	44.7
Salvadoran	91.7
Cuban	-24.3
Dominican Republic	99.9
Mexican	88.9
Puerto Rican	-9.2
South American	101.3
Argentinean	64.8
Colombian	30.1
Ecuadorian	121.4
Peruvian	74.2
Uruguayan	165.3
Venezuelan	21.5
Spaniard	3.9

Males per 100 Females	
Group	Number
Total Population	97.9
Hispanic or Latino (of any race)	106.8
Central American, ex. Mexican	124.1
Costa Rican	115.5
Guatemalan	138.3
Honduran	128.1
Nicaraguan	100.7
Panamanian	78.9
Salvadoran	123.2
Cuban	109.2
Dominican Republic	88.2
Mexican	130.8
Puerto Rican	90.2
South American	127.7
Argentinean	112.7
Bolivian	110.0
Chilean	86.6
Colombian	80.9
Ecuadorian	140.1
Peruvian	102.8
Uruguayan	107.9
Venezuelan	79.0
Spaniard	109.2

Average Household Size	
Group	People
Total Population	2.76
Hispanic or Latino (of any race)	3.19
Central American, ex. Mexican	3.72
Costa Rican	3.26
Guatemalan	3.71
Honduran	3.82
Nicaraguan	3.19
Panamanian	2.49
Salvadoran	3.96
Cuban	2.22
Dominican Republic	3.56
Mexican	3.73
Puerto Rican	2.84
South American	3.62
Argentinean	2.61
Bolivian	3.47
Chilean	2.65
Colombian	3.04
Ecuadorian	3.85
Peruvian	3.21
Uruguayan	2.86
Venezuelan	2.69
Spaniard	2.52

Median Age	
Group	Years
Total Population	32.3
Hispanic or Latino (of any race)	30.2
Central American, ex. Mexican	29.7
Costa Rican	33.7
Guatemalan	30.2
Honduran	28.4
Nicaraguan	32.9
Panamanian	31.5
Salvadoran	29.8
Cuban	46.0
Dominican Republic	29.4
Mexican	25.6
Puerto Rican	29.8
South American	32.2
Argentinean	36.6
Bolivian	32.1
Chilean	36.4
Colombian	34.1
Ecuadorian	31.3
Peruvian	38.1
Uruguayan	35.1
Venezuelan	31.9
Spaniard	43.9

High School Graduates (Universe: Population 25 Years and Over)		
Group	Number	%
Total Population	117,172	68.1
Hispanic or Latino (of any race)	29,889	56.2
Central American, ex. Mexican	1,850	44.2
Guatemalan	369	43.2
Honduran	350	40.6
Salvadoran	558	33.0
Cuban	942	61.6
Dominican Republic	3,507	59.6
Mexican	1,162	42.5
Puerto Rican	12,738	55.5
South American	8,393	61.2
Colombian	738	70.9
Ecuadorian	5,290	55.3
Peruvian	1,701	77.1
Spaniard	676	58.0

Notes: (1) Percent of total population; (2) Percent of Hispanic/Latino population; Profiles include places with an overall population of at least 125,000, OR an overall population of at least 25,000 where the Hispanic/Latino population is at least 20% of the overall population. In states where less than five places meet either of these criteria, we have included places with at least 10,000 total population with the highest percentage of Hispanic/Latino population. These places are identified with an asterisk (*); Please refer to the User's Guide for a full explanation of data.

Four-Year College Graduates
(Universe: Population 25 Years and Over)

Group	Number	%
Total Population	21,186	12.3
Hispanic or Latino (of any race)	4,375	8.2
Central American, ex. Mexican	286	6.8
Guatemalan	89	10.4
Honduran	21	2.4
Salvadoran	87	5.2
Cuban	119	7.8
Dominican Republic	795	13.5
Mexican	108	3.9
Puerto Rican	1,352	5.9
South American	1,502	11.0
Colombian	110	10.6
Ecuadorian	971	10.1
Peruvian	316	14.3
Spaniard	111	9.5

Population Age 3–17 Enrolled in Public School
(Universe: Population Age 3–17 Enrolled in School)

Group	Number	%
Total Population	48,524	90.0
Hispanic or Latino (of any race)	17,511	91.8
Central American, ex. Mexican	1,006	96.4
Guatemalan	42	100.0
Honduran	191	100.0
Salvadoran	672	96.4
Cuban	43	100.0
Dominican Republic	2,072	89.6
Mexican	682	100.0
Puerto Rican	9,535	93.2
South American	3,543	87.8
Colombian	395	95.2
Ecuadorian	2,546	85.8
Peruvian	392	88.5
Spaniard	112	80.0

Population Age 3–17 Enrolled in Private School
(Universe: Population Age 3–17 Enrolled in School)

Group	Number	%
Total Population	5,419	10.0
Hispanic or Latino (of any race)	1,570	8.2
Central American, ex. Mexican	38	3.6
Guatemalan	0	0.0
Honduran	0	0.0
Salvadoran	25	3.6
Cuban	0	0.0
Dominican Republic	240	10.4
Mexican	0	0.0
Puerto Rican	699	6.8
South American	492	12.2
Colombian	20	4.8
Ecuadorian	421	14.2
Peruvian	51	11.5
Spaniard	28	20.0

Foreign-Born Population

Group	Number	%
Total Population	71,461	26.0
Hispanic or Latino (of any race)	32,806	36.6
Central American, ex. Mexican	4,814	70.7
Guatemalan	914	82.2
Honduran	1,081	81.6
Salvadoran	2,122	62.9
Cuban	1,125	56.7
Dominican Republic	6,762	64.9
Mexican	2,890	61.3
Puerto Rican	459	1.1
South American	15,376	70.2
Colombian	1,013	56.9
Ecuadorian	11,029	70.8
Peruvian	2,284	72.9
Spaniard	843	55.0

Foreign-Born Naturalized U.S. Citizens

Group	Number	%
Total Population	24,088	33.7
Hispanic or Latino (of any race)	8,941	27.3
Central American, ex. Mexican	1,059	22.0
Guatemalan	201	22.0
Honduran	152	14.1
Salvadoran	410	19.3
Cuban	672	59.7
Dominican Republic	2,050	30.3
Mexican	315	10.9
Puerto Rican	215	46.8
South American	3,938	25.6
Colombian	440	43.4
Ecuadorian	2,392	21.7
Peruvian	761	33.3
Spaniard	391	46.4

Language Spoken at Home: English Only
(Universe: Population 5 Years and Over)

Group	Number	%
Total Population	141,580	55.6
Hispanic or Latino (of any race)	7,798	9.6
Central American, ex. Mexican	394	6.4
Guatemalan	0	0.0
Honduran	53	4.3
Salvadoran	158	5.3
Cuban	187	10.3
Dominican Republic	398	4.2
Mexican	216	5.1
Puerto Rican	5,235	14.2
South American	810	4.1
Colombian	39	2.4
Ecuadorian	445	3.2
Peruvian	199	6.9
Spaniard	289	20.8

Language Spoken at Home: Spanish
(Universe: Population 5 Years and Over)

Group	Number	%
Total Population	77,031	30.3
Hispanic or Latino (of any race)	73,289	89.8
Central American, ex. Mexican	5,744	92.7
Guatemalan	979	100.0
Honduran	1,174	95.7
Salvadoran	2,827	94.7
Cuban	1,620	88.9
Dominican Republic	9,103	95.4
Mexican	3,981	94.9
Puerto Rican	31,455	85.5
South American	18,902	95.3
Colombian	1,557	96.9
Ecuadorian	13,623	96.7
Peruvian	2,654	92.3
Spaniard	1,072	77.0

Unemployment Rate
(Universe: Population 16 Years and Over)

Group	%
Total Population	14.3
Hispanic or Latino (of any race)	11.5
Central American, ex. Mexican	8.3
Guatemalan	10.1
Honduran	11.6
Salvadoran	3.2
Cuban	6.7
Dominican Republic	11.0
Mexican	8.2
Puerto Rican	15.1
South American	9.7
Colombian	9.1
Ecuadorian	10.6
Peruvian	5.2
Spaniard	2.9

Class of Worker: Private Wage and Salary
(Universe: Civilian Employed Population 16 Years and Over)

Group	Number	%
Total Population	89,901	80.4
Hispanic or Latino (of any race)	33,147	87.6
Central American, ex. Mexican	3,398	90.8
Guatemalan	650	92.5
Honduran	715	86.8
Salvadoran	1,559	95.3
Cuban	580	81.3
Dominican Republic	4,038	90.4
Mexican	2,256	98.3
Puerto Rican	10,981	82.4
South American	10,666	90.1
Colombian	592	73.9
Ecuadorian	7,931	92.5
Peruvian	1,577	86.6
Spaniard	562	77.4

Class of Worker: Government
(Universe: Civilian Employed Population 16 Years and Over)

Group	Number	%
Total Population	18,461	16.5
Hispanic or Latino (of any race)	3,410	9.0
Central American, ex. Mexican	269	7.2
Guatemalan	38	5.4
Honduran	81	9.8
Salvadoran	59	3.6
Cuban	97	13.6
Dominican Republic	234	5.2
Mexican	8	0.3
Puerto Rican	2,114	15.9
South American	518	4.4
Colombian	126	15.7
Ecuadorian	161	1.9
Peruvian	192	10.5
Spaniard	141	19.4

Means of Transportation to Work: Car, Truck or Van
(Universe: Workers 16 Years and Over)

Group	Number	%
Total Population	68,561	63.5
Hispanic or Latino (of any race)	22,906	62.2
Central American, ex. Mexican	2,165	58.9
Guatemalan	382	55.8
Honduran	421	51.1
Salvadoran	1,115	69.7
Cuban	548	76.9
Dominican Republic	2,643	59.4
Mexican	702	30.6
Puerto Rican	9,015	70.0
South American	6,908	60.2
Colombian	536	72.8
Ecuadorian	4,883	58.6
Peruvian	1,046	58.0
Spaniard	416	59.9

Means of Transportation to Work: Public Transportation (ex. Taxicab)
(Universe: Workers 16 Years and Over)

Group	Number	%
Total Population	26,739	24.8
Hispanic or Latino (of any race)	8,753	23.8
Central American, ex. Mexican	1,008	27.4
Guatemalan	179	26.1
Honduran	288	35.0
Salvadoran	281	17.6
Cuban	62	8.7
Dominican Republic	1,304	29.3
Mexican	765	33.3
Puerto Rican	2,740	21.3
South American	2,586	22.5
Colombian	143	19.4
Ecuadorian	1,833	22.0
Peruvian	481	26.6
Spaniard	194	28.0

Homeownership Rate
(Universe: Occupied Housing Units)

Group	%
Total Population	22.1
Hispanic or Latino (of any race)	19.0
Central American, ex. Mexican	19.7
Costa Rican	23.7
Guatemalan	21.5
Honduran	12.0
Nicaraguan	14.9
Panamanian	30.0
Salvadoran	23.2
Cuban	25.2
Dominican Republic	20.6
Mexican	8.3
Puerto Rican	16.9
South American	20.8
Argentinean	17.8
Bolivian	13.3
Chilean	26.5
Colombian	24.6
Ecuadorian	20.0
Peruvian	25.6
Uruguayan	13.6
Venezuelan	23.2
Spaniard	41.7

Notes: (1) Percent of total population; (2) Percent of Hispanic/Latino population; Profiles include places with an overall population of at least 125,000, OR an overall population of at least 25,000 where the Hispanic/Latino population is at least 20% of the overall population. In states where less than five places meet either of these criteria, we have included places with at least 10,000 total population with the highest percentage of Hispanic/Latino population. These places are identified with an asterisk (*); Please refer to the User's Guide for a full explanation of data.

Median Home Value

Group	Dollars
Total Population	287,800
Hispanic or Latino (of any race)	316,100
Central American, ex. Mexican	286,900
Guatemalan	412,500
Honduran	–
Salvadoran	307,900
Cuban	300,800
Dominican Republic	313,900
Mexican	376,900
Puerto Rican	288,600
South American	368,000
Colombian	410,000
Ecuadorian	376,700
Peruvian	354,400
Spaniard	359,200

Median Gross Rent

Group	Dollars
Total Population	902
Hispanic or Latino (of any race)	947
Central American, ex. Mexican	983
Guatemalan	1,018
Honduran	1,066
Salvadoran	985
Cuban	897
Dominican Republic	936
Mexican	1,080
Puerto Rican	880
South American	1,045
Colombian	1,262
Ecuadorian	1,077
Peruvian	888
Spaniard	880

Median Household Income
(2010 Inflation-Adjusted Dollars)

Group	Dollars
Total Population	35,659
Hispanic or Latino (of any race)	35,350
Central American, ex. Mexican	45,238
Guatemalan	60,139
Honduran	45,952
Salvadoran	47,618
Cuban	36,713
Dominican Republic	35,043
Mexican	37,317
Puerto Rican	30,300
South American	41,255
Colombian	55,125
Ecuadorian	43,741
Peruvian	37,040
Spaniard	56,915

Per Capita Income
(2010 Inflation-Adjusted Dollars)

Group	Dollars
Total Population	17,367
Hispanic or Latino (of any race)	14,602
Central American, ex. Mexican	17,516
Guatemalan	20,570
Honduran	19,863
Salvadoran	15,055
Cuban	22,477
Dominican Republic	13,300
Mexican	12,317
Puerto Rican	13,500
South American	15,402
Colombian	15,415
Ecuadorian	15,089
Peruvian	17,222
Spaniard	24,630

Households with $100,000+ Income

Group	Number	%
Total Population	9,881	10.7
Hispanic or Latino (of any race)	2,304	8.6
Central American, ex. Mexican	244	14.0
Guatemalan	48	16.6
Honduran	25	11.1
Salvadoran	116	14.6
Cuban	118	15.0
Dominican Republic	136	4.3
Mexican	85	7.1
Puerto Rican	997	7.8
South American	531	8.8
Colombian	88	20.0
Ecuadorian	347	8.4
Peruvian	68	8.1
Spaniard	122	17.3

Households with Food Stamps/SNAP Benefits During Past 12 Months

Group	Number	%
Total Population	16,479	17.8
Hispanic or Latino (of any race)	5,617	20.9
Central American, ex. Mexican	258	14.8
Guatemalan	48	16.6
Honduran	37	16.4
Salvadoran	88	11.1
Cuban	117	14.9
Dominican Republic	749	23.7
Mexican	150	12.6
Puerto Rican	3,696	28.9
South American	511	8.4
Colombian	0	0.0
Ecuadorian	373	9.0
Peruvian	90	10.7
Spaniard	82	11.6

Poverty Rate
(Income in Past 12 Months Below Poverty Level)

Group	%
Total Population	25.0
Hispanic or Latino (of any race)	25.9
Central American, ex. Mexican	19.2
Guatemalan	8.5
Honduran	22.4
Salvadoran	21.6
Cuban	13.1
Dominican Republic	28.6
Mexican	24.3
Puerto Rican	31.1
South American	20.7
Colombian	21.2
Ecuadorian	19.3
Peruvian	22.2
Spaniard	15.3

North Bergen

Population

Group	Number	%TP[1]	%HP[2]
Total Population	60,773	100.0	–
Hispanic or Latino (of any race)	41,569	68.4	100.0
Central American, ex. Mexican	5,991	9.9	14.4
Costa Rican	167	0.3	0.4
Guatemalan	1,596	2.6	3.8
Honduran	1,081	1.8	2.6
Nicaraguan	240	0.4	0.6
Salvadoran	2,825	4.6	6.8
Cuban	7,248	11.9	17.4
Dominican Republic	5,999	9.9	14.4
Mexican	1,440	2.4	3.5
Puerto Rican	5,090	8.4	12.2
South American	13,026	21.4	31.3
Argentinean	494	0.8	1.2
Chilean	472	0.8	1.1
Colombian	4,784	7.9	11.5
Ecuadorian	5,064	8.3	12.2
Peruvian	1,590	2.6	3.8
Uruguayan	201	0.3	0.5
Venezuelan	267	0.4	0.6
Spaniard	336	0.6	0.8

Population Growth: 2000–2010

Group	%
Total Population	4.6
Hispanic or Latino (of any race)	25.0
Central American, ex. Mexican	118.7
Costa Rican	44.0
Guatemalan	241.8
Honduran	112.4
Nicaraguan	60.0
Salvadoran	121.9
Cuban	-5.1
Dominican Republic	85.8
Mexican	160.4
Puerto Rican	12.2
South American	67.4
Argentinean	19.3
Chilean	49.8
Colombian	42.8
Ecuadorian	117.0
Peruvian	87.5
Uruguayan	93.3
Venezuelan	78.0
Spaniard	56.3

Males per 100 Females

Group	Number
Total Population	94.4
Hispanic or Latino (of any race)	95.4
Central American, ex. Mexican	121.9
Costa Rican	101.2
Guatemalan	236.0
Honduran	81.4
Nicaraguan	100.0
Salvadoran	104.7
Cuban	93.0
Dominican Republic	82.6
Mexican	113.0
Puerto Rican	92.7
South American	90.6
Argentinean	117.6
Chilean	108.8
Colombian	79.6
Ecuadorian	94.5
Peruvian	100.8
Uruguayan	142.2
Venezuelan	71.2
Spaniard	115.4

Average Household Size

Group	People
Total Population	2.73
Hispanic or Latino (of any race)	3.06
Central American, ex. Mexican	3.87
Costa Rican	2.97
Guatemalan	4.38
Honduran	3.61
Nicaraguan	3.35
Salvadoran	3.90
Cuban	2.44
Dominican Republic	3.38
Mexican	3.90
Puerto Rican	2.63
South American	3.22
Argentinean	2.83
Chilean	2.99
Colombian	2.97
Ecuadorian	3.54
Peruvian	3.34
Uruguayan	3.08
Venezuelan	3.10
Spaniard	2.54

Median Age

Group	Years
Total Population	37.1
Hispanic or Latino (of any race)	34.9
Central American, ex. Mexican	31.2
Costa Rican	39.2
Guatemalan	27.9
Honduran	33.1
Nicaraguan	39.8
Salvadoran	32.7
Cuban	47.6
Dominican Republic	31.5
Mexican	27.5
Puerto Rican	31.6
South American	37.3
Argentinean	38.8
Chilean	41.0
Colombian	38.8
Ecuadorian	35.4
Peruvian	39.1
Uruguayan	37.1
Venezuelan	34.1
Spaniard	42.0

Notes: (1) Percent of total population; (2) Percent of Hispanic/Latino population; Profiles include places with an overall population of at least 125,000, OR an overall population of at least 25,000 where the Hispanic/Latino population is at least 20% of the overall population. In states where less than five places meet either of these criteria, we have included places with at least 10,000 total population with the highest percentage of Hispanic/Latino population. These places are identified with an asterisk (*); Please refer to the User's Guide for a full explanation of data.

High School Graduates
(Universe: Population 25 Years and Over)

Group	Number	%
Total Population	30,794	76.9
Hispanic or Latino (of any race)	18,910	73.8
Central American, ex. Mexican	2,302	65.3
Guatemalan	234	37.9
Salvadoran	1,108	66.2
Cuban	4,317	69.3
Dominican Republic	2,546	77.6
Puerto Rican	2,634	76.9
South American	6,408	78.6
Colombian	2,235	81.3
Ecuadorian	2,278	75.1
Peruvian	1,066	88.0

Four-Year College Graduates
(Universe: Population 25 Years and Over)

Group	Number	%
Total Population	10,165	25.4
Hispanic or Latino (of any race)	4,937	19.3
Central American, ex. Mexican	362	10.3
Guatemalan	14	2.3
Salvadoran	272	16.3
Cuban	1,253	20.1
Dominican Republic	565	17.2
Puerto Rican	671	19.6
South American	1,801	22.1
Colombian	614	22.3
Ecuadorian	574	18.9
Peruvian	338	27.9

Population Age 3–17 Enrolled in Public School
(Universe: Population Age 3–17 Enrolled in School)

Group	Number	%
Total Population	9,081	88.3
Hispanic or Latino (of any race)	7,326	88.8
Central American, ex. Mexican	1,411	96.1
Guatemalan	296	100.0
Salvadoran	835	97.4
Cuban	326	75.8
Dominican Republic	1,285	92.0
Puerto Rican	1,352	86.9
South American	2,610	89.4
Colombian	968	89.3
Ecuadorian	1,145	96.5
Peruvian	177	83.9

Population Age 3–17 Enrolled in Private School
(Universe: Population Age 3–17 Enrolled in School)

Group	Number	%
Total Population	1,208	11.7
Hispanic or Latino (of any race)	924	11.2
Central American, ex. Mexican	58	3.9
Guatemalan	0	0.0
Salvadoran	22	2.6
Cuban	104	24.2
Dominican Republic	111	8.0
Puerto Rican	204	13.1
South American	308	10.6
Colombian	116	10.7
Ecuadorian	41	3.5
Peruvian	34	16.1

Foreign-Born Population

Group	Number	%
Total Population	29,127	48.9
Hispanic or Latino (of any race)	22,621	55.2
Central American, ex. Mexican	3,822	62.4
Guatemalan	794	60.5
Salvadoran	1,811	59.0
Cuban	5,751	75.5
Dominican Republic	3,044	52.3
Puerto Rican	131	2.1
South American	8,838	66.5
Colombian	3,102	67.6
Ecuadorian	3,259	62.2
Peruvian	1,276	81.0

Foreign-Born Naturalized U.S. Citizens

Group	Number	%
Total Population	16,766	57.6
Hispanic or Latino (of any race)	12,604	55.7
Central American, ex. Mexican	1,613	42.2
Guatemalan	116	14.6
Salvadoran	927	51.2
Cuban	4,427	77.0
Dominican Republic	2,043	67.1
Puerto Rican	80	61.1
South American	4,071	46.1
Colombian	1,382	44.6
Ecuadorian	1,449	44.5
Peruvian	702	55.0

Language Spoken at Home: English Only
(Universe: Population 5 Years and Over)

Group	Number	%
Total Population	13,894	24.9
Hispanic or Latino (of any race)	4,126	10.9
Central American, ex. Mexican	429	7.7
Guatemalan	94	8.1
Salvadoran	273	9.7
Cuban	633	8.5
Dominican Republic	609	11.4
Puerto Rican	1,388	24.6
South American	649	5.3
Colombian	166	3.8
Ecuadorian	324	6.9
Peruvian	15	1.0

Language Spoken at Home: Spanish
(Universe: Population 5 Years and Over)

Group	Number	%
Total Population	34,803	62.5
Hispanic or Latino (of any race)	33,807	89.0
Central American, ex. Mexican	5,178	92.3
Guatemalan	1,060	91.9
Salvadoran	2,528	90.3
Cuban	6,833	91.5
Dominican Republic	4,722	88.6
Puerto Rican	4,249	75.2
South American	11,563	94.7
Colombian	4,149	96.2
Ecuadorian	4,372	93.1
Peruvian	1,542	99.0

Unemployment Rate
(Universe: Population 16 Years and Over)

Group	%
Total Population	10.7
Hispanic or Latino (of any race)	11.8
Central American, ex. Mexican	9.4
Guatemalan	9.6
Salvadoran	10.0
Cuban	15.5
Dominican Republic	14.3
Puerto Rican	13.2
South American	9.4
Colombian	6.6
Ecuadorian	9.2
Peruvian	15.4

Class of Worker: Private Wage and Salary
(Universe: Civilian Employed Population 16 Years and Over)

Group	Number	%
Total Population	24,114	82.1
Hispanic or Latino (of any race)	16,914	84.1
Central American, ex. Mexican	2,701	84.3
Guatemalan	596	80.4
Salvadoran	1,274	84.0
Cuban	2,564	77.5
Dominican Republic	2,210	83.9
Puerto Rican	2,371	81.0
South American	6,270	87.7
Colombian	2,154	84.8
Ecuadorian	2,472	93.3
Peruvian	873	84.5

Class of Worker: Government
(Universe: Civilian Employed Population 16 Years and Over)

Group	Number	%
Total Population	3,754	12.8
Hispanic or Latino (of any race)	2,172	10.8
Central American, ex. Mexican	227	7.1
Guatemalan	22	3.0
Salvadoran	150	9.9
Cuban	611	18.5
Dominican Republic	309	11.7
Puerto Rican	501	17.1
South American	467	6.5
Colombian	193	7.6
Ecuadorian	74	2.8
Peruvian	155	15.0

Means of Transportation to Work: Car, Truck or Van
(Universe: Workers 16 Years and Over)

Group	Number	%
Total Population	17,778	62.1
Hispanic or Latino (of any race)	12,302	62.7
Central American, ex. Mexican	2,089	66.0
Guatemalan	293	39.5
Salvadoran	1,075	70.9
Cuban	2,379	73.2
Dominican Republic	1,667	65.2
Puerto Rican	1,730	61.2
South American	4,012	57.5
Colombian	1,330	53.1
Ecuadorian	1,480	58.3
Peruvian	741	73.5

Means of Transportation to Work: Public Transportation (ex. Taxicab)
(Universe: Workers 16 Years and Over)

Group	Number	%
Total Population	7,993	27.9
Hispanic or Latino (of any race)	5,401	27.5
Central American, ex. Mexican	725	22.9
Guatemalan	247	33.3
Salvadoran	330	21.8
Cuban	481	14.8
Dominican Republic	613	24.0
Puerto Rican	884	31.3
South American	2,326	33.3
Colombian	856	34.2
Ecuadorian	913	36.0
Peruvian	262	26.0

Homeownership Rate
(Universe: Occupied Housing Units)

Group	%
Total Population	39.5
Hispanic or Latino (of any race)	34.3
Central American, ex. Mexican	29.0
Costa Rican	25.4
Guatemalan	15.2
Honduran	30.3
Nicaraguan	31.3
Salvadoran	34.8
Cuban	40.4
Dominican Republic	32.6
Mexican	26.3
Puerto Rican	28.0
South American	35.4
Argentinean	43.4
Chilean	32.9
Colombian	32.0
Ecuadorian	39.1
Peruvian	31.8
Uruguayan	37.3
Venezuelan	31.8
Spaniard	64.9

Median Home Value

Group	Dollars
Total Population	374,600
Hispanic or Latino (of any race)	388,700
Central American, ex. Mexican	354,200
Guatemalan	–
Salvadoran	366,200
Cuban	382,500
Dominican Republic	419,300
Puerto Rican	338,100
South American	417,500
Colombian	435,700
Ecuadorian	399,700
Peruvian	448,100

Median Gross Rent

Group	Dollars
Total Population	1,043
Hispanic or Latino (of any race)	1,065
Central American, ex. Mexican	1,114
Guatemalan	1,257
Salvadoran	1,110

Notes: (1) Percent of total population; (2) Percent of Hispanic/Latino population; Profiles include places with an overall population of at least 125,000, OR an overall population of at least 25,000 where the Hispanic/Latino population is at least 20% of the overall population. In states where less than five places meet either of these criteria, we have included places with at least 10,000 total population with the highest percentage of Hispanic/Latino population. These places are identified with an asterisk (*); Please refer to the User's Guide for a full explanation of data.

Cuban	784
Dominican Republic	1,127
Puerto Rican	1,051
South American	1,115
Colombian	1,168
Ecuadorian	1,103
Peruvian	966

Median Household Income
(2010 Inflation-Adjusted Dollars)

Group	Dollars
Total Population	52,726
Hispanic or Latino (of any race)	50,631
Central American, ex. Mexican	52,027
Guatemalan	36,713
Salvadoran	51,622
Cuban	32,667
Dominican Republic	55,960
Puerto Rican	41,875
South American	57,734
Colombian	61,733
Ecuadorian	59,093
Peruvian	62,564

Per Capita Income
(2010 Inflation-Adjusted Dollars)

Group	Dollars
Total Population	25,674
Hispanic or Latino (of any race)	21,405
Central American, ex. Mexican	18,193
Guatemalan	12,633
Salvadoran	17,868
Cuban	24,101
Dominican Republic	18,191
Puerto Rican	22,873
South American	22,431
Colombian	23,721
Ecuadorian	20,055
Peruvian	31,454

Households with $100,000+ Income

Group	Number	%
Total Population	4,954	23.2
Hispanic or Latino (of any race)	2,649	19.6
Central American, ex. Mexican	329	18.3
Guatemalan	14	4.5
Salvadoran	145	16.0
Cuban	475	14.1
Dominican Republic	354	22.3
Puerto Rican	476	21.7
South American	872	21.7
Colombian	271	19.6
Ecuadorian	313	21.0
Peruvian	179	31.5

Households with Food Stamps/SNAP Benefits During Past 12 Months

Group	Number	%
Total Population	1,712	8.0
Hispanic or Latino (of any race)	1,443	10.7
Central American, ex. Mexican	123	6.8
Guatemalan	13	4.2
Salvadoran	67	7.4
Cuban	255	7.5
Dominican Republic	328	20.6
Puerto Rican	337	15.4
South American	355	8.8
Colombian	132	9.6
Ecuadorian	149	10.0
Peruvian	55	9.7

Poverty Rate
(Income in Past 12 Months Below Poverty Level)

Group	%
Total Population	9.9
Hispanic or Latino (of any race)	10.5
Central American, ex. Mexican	10.8
Guatemalan	19.3
Salvadoran	6.8
Cuban	10.6
Dominican Republic	16.2
Puerto Rican	15.5
South American	5.3
Colombian	6.1
Ecuadorian	4.7
Peruvian	1.3

Passaic

Population

Group	Number	%TP[1]	%HP[2]
Total Population	69,781	100.0	–
Hispanic or Latino (of any race)	49,557	71.0	100.0
Central American, ex. Mexican	1,372	2.0	2.8
Guatemalan	409	0.6	0.8
Honduran	499	0.7	1.0
Salvadoran	318	0.5	0.6
Cuban	481	0.7	1.0
Dominican Republic	12,340	17.7	24.9
Mexican	21,123	30.3	42.6
Puerto Rican	7,368	10.6	14.9
South American	4,723	6.8	9.5
Argentinean	133	0.2	0.3
Bolivian	139	0.2	0.3
Colombian	1,251	1.8	2.5
Ecuadorian	761	1.1	1.5
Peruvian	2,228	3.2	4.5

Population Growth: 2000–2010

Group	%
Total Population	2.8
Hispanic or Latino (of any race)	16.9
Central American, ex. Mexican	69.6
Guatemalan	150.9
Honduran	65.8
Salvadoran	45.9
Cuban	-26.5
Dominican Republic	39.2
Mexican	58.3
Puerto Rican	-19.2
South American	24.4
Bolivian	35.0
Colombian	-0.7
Ecuadorian	48.6
Peruvian	35.6

Males per 100 Females

Group	Number
Total Population	100.9
Hispanic or Latino (of any race)	104.2
Central American, ex. Mexican	132.9
Guatemalan	240.8
Honduran	104.5
Salvadoran	100.0
Cuban	104.7
Dominican Republic	87.8
Mexican	122.1
Puerto Rican	91.4
South American	95.3
Argentinean	104.6
Bolivian	87.8
Colombian	83.2
Ecuadorian	99.2
Peruvian	101.1

Average Household Size

Group	People
Total Population	3.57
Hispanic or Latino (of any race)	3.99
Central American, ex. Mexican	3.89
Guatemalan	3.94
Honduran	4.21
Salvadoran	3.73
Cuban	2.61
Dominican Republic	3.74
Mexican	5.35
Puerto Rican	2.87
South American	3.34
Argentinean	3.23
Bolivian	4.02
Colombian	3.05
Ecuadorian	3.25
Peruvian	3.54

Median Age

Group	Years
Total Population	29.2
Hispanic or Latino (of any race)	27.8
Central American, ex. Mexican	31.5
Guatemalan	29.9
Honduran	31.9
Salvadoran	32.7
Cuban	47.7
Dominican Republic	30.7
Mexican	24.1
Puerto Rican	31.4
South American	39.8
Argentinean	35.2
Bolivian	39.1
Colombian	39.7
Ecuadorian	38.2
Peruvian	41.3

High School Graduates
(Universe: Population 25 Years and Over)

Group	Number	%
Total Population	25,202	65.4
Hispanic or Latino (of any race)	14,059	55.7
Central American, ex. Mexican	537	62.1
Dominican Republic	3,208	53.5
Mexican	3,630	40.7
Puerto Rican	3,046	60.5
South American	3,010	83.5
Colombian	813	80.3
Peruvian	1,344	88.8

Four-Year College Graduates
(Universe: Population 25 Years and Over)

Group	Number	%
Total Population	6,503	16.9
Hispanic or Latino (of any race)	1,845	7.3
Central American, ex. Mexican	163	18.8
Dominican Republic	540	9.0
Mexican	49	0.6
Puerto Rican	446	8.9
South American	444	12.3
Colombian	109	10.8
Peruvian	132	8.7

Population Age 3–17 Enrolled in Public School
(Universe: Population Age 3–17 Enrolled in School)

Group	Number	%
Total Population	13,603	78.3
Hispanic or Latino (of any race)	11,320	94.4
Central American, ex. Mexican	392	93.3
Dominican Republic	3,101	98.5
Mexican	5,076	98.0
Puerto Rican	1,358	81.2
South American	1,040	91.3
Colombian	181	100.0
Peruvian	382	79.4

Population Age 3–17 Enrolled in Private School
(Universe: Population Age 3–17 Enrolled in School)

Group	Number	%
Total Population	3,772	21.7
Hispanic or Latino (of any race)	674	5.6
Central American, ex. Mexican	28	6.7
Dominican Republic	46	1.5
Mexican	105	2.0
Puerto Rican	314	18.8
South American	99	8.7
Colombian	0	0.0
Peruvian	99	20.6

Foreign-Born Population

Group	Number	%
Total Population	31,107	45.1
Hispanic or Latino (of any race)	25,508	54.3
Central American, ex. Mexican	1,015	67.7
Dominican Republic	7,380	66.2
Mexican	11,878	62.7
Puerto Rican	185	2.3
South American	4,148	70.5
Colombian	1,076	74.2
Peruvian	1,623	68.4

Foreign-Born Naturalized U.S. Citizens

Group	Number	%
Total Population	7,433	23.9
Hispanic or Latino (of any race)	4,733	18.6
Central American, ex. Mexican	276	27.2
Dominican Republic	2,214	30.0
Mexican	629	5.3

Notes: (1) Percent of total population; (2) Percent of Hispanic/Latino population; Profiles include places with an overall population of at least 125,000, OR an overall population of at least 25,000 where the Hispanic/Latino population is at least 20% of the overall population. In states where less than five places meet either of these criteria, we have included places with at least 10,000 total population with the highest percentage of Hispanic/Latino population. These places are identified with an asterisk (*); Please refer to the User's Guide for a full explanation of data.

Group	Number	%
Puerto Rican	130	70.3
South American	1,246	30.0
Colombian	464	43.1
Peruvian	544	33.5

Language Spoken at Home: English Only
(Universe: Population 5 Years and Over)

Group	Number	%
Total Population	16,267	26.3
Hispanic or Latino (of any race)	1,850	4.5
Central American, ex. Mexican	32	2.4
Dominican Republic	365	3.7
Mexican	536	3.3
Puerto Rican	720	9.9
South American	123	2.3
Colombian	19	1.4
Peruvian	87	4.2

Language Spoken at Home: Spanish
(Universe: Population 5 Years and Over)

Group	Number	%
Total Population	40,288	65.1
Hispanic or Latino (of any race)	39,701	95.5
Central American, ex. Mexican	1,304	97.6
Dominican Republic	9,590	96.3
Mexican	15,731	96.7
Puerto Rican	6,574	90.1
South American	5,202	97.7
Colombian	1,385	98.6
Peruvian	1,973	95.8

Unemployment Rate
(Universe: Population 16 Years and Over)

Group	%
Total Population	7.1
Hispanic or Latino (of any race)	6.4
Central American, ex. Mexican	7.3
Dominican Republic	7.0
Mexican	2.7
Puerto Rican	8.0
South American	13.0
Colombian	18.6
Peruvian	12.4

Class of Worker: Private Wage and Salary
(Universe: Civilian Employed Population 16 Years and Over)

Group	Number	%
Total Population	25,076	90.3
Hispanic or Latino (of any race)	17,679	92.6
Central American, ex. Mexican	664	100.0
Dominican Republic	4,191	95.3
Mexican	7,163	93.1
Puerto Rican	2,808	90.8
South American	2,247	86.8
Colombian	536	85.9
Peruvian	979	89.7

Class of Worker: Government
(Universe: Civilian Employed Population 16 Years and Over)

Group	Number	%
Total Population	1,840	6.6
Hispanic or Latino (of any race)	852	4.5
Central American, ex. Mexican	0	0.0
Dominican Republic	167	3.8
Mexican	189	2.5
Puerto Rican	269	8.7
South American	185	7.1
Colombian	56	9.0
Peruvian	57	5.2

Means of Transportation to Work: Car, Truck or Van
(Universe: Workers 16 Years and Over)

Group	Number	%
Total Population	14,156	52.0
Hispanic or Latino (of any race)	8,743	46.5
Central American, ex. Mexican	346	52.1
Dominican Republic	2,581	61.1
Mexican	1,709	22.3
Puerto Rican	2,151	71.2
South American	1,567	60.5
Colombian	504	80.8
Peruvian	684	62.7

Means of Transportation to Work: Public Transportation (ex. Taxicab)
(Universe: Workers 16 Years and Over)

Group	Number	%
Total Population	4,991	18.3
Hispanic or Latino (of any race)	3,224	17.1
Central American, ex. Mexican	62	9.3
Dominican Republic	602	14.2
Mexican	1,726	22.5
Puerto Rican	324	10.7
South American	386	14.9
Colombian	35	5.6
Peruvian	59	5.4

Homeownership Rate
(Universe: Occupied Housing Units)

Group	%
Total Population	25.4
Hispanic or Latino (of any race)	16.7
Central American, ex. Mexican	20.7
Guatemalan	22.9
Honduran	17.3
Salvadoran	18.8
Cuban	33.7
Dominican Republic	18.8
Mexican	9.5
Puerto Rican	16.7
South American	25.6
Argentinean	38.6
Bolivian	41.5
Colombian	26.0
Ecuadorian	26.3
Peruvian	23.6

Median Home Value

Group	Dollars
Total Population	361,700
Hispanic or Latino (of any race)	369,400
Central American, ex. Mexican	357,400
Dominican Republic	403,300
Mexican	375,100
Puerto Rican	357,400
South American	284,700
Colombian	331,600
Peruvian	261,900

Median Gross Rent

Group	Dollars
Total Population	979
Hispanic or Latino (of any race)	1,007
Central American, ex. Mexican	1,122
Dominican Republic	980
Mexican	1,078
Puerto Rican	959
South American	913
Colombian	893
Peruvian	928

Median Household Income
(2010 Inflation-Adjusted Dollars)

Group	Dollars
Total Population	31,135
Hispanic or Latino (of any race)	26,776
Central American, ex. Mexican	35,810
Dominican Republic	25,597
Mexican	22,161
Puerto Rican	26,659
South American	39,796
Colombian	30,250
Peruvian	37,452

Per Capita Income
(2010 Inflation-Adjusted Dollars)

Group	Dollars
Total Population	14,424
Hispanic or Latino (of any race)	11,029
Central American, ex. Mexican	13,621
Dominican Republic	10,652
Mexican	7,293
Puerto Rican	15,675
South American	15,175
Colombian	14,934
Peruvian	17,303

Households with $100,000+ Income

Group	Number	%
Total Population	2,089	10.4
Hispanic or Latino (of any race)	633	4.9
Central American, ex. Mexican	29	5.2
Dominican Republic	107	3.4
Mexican	31	0.7
Puerto Rican	278	9.8
South American	105	7.2
Colombian	30	7.1
Peruvian	49	7.8

Households with Food Stamps/SNAP Benefits During Past 12 Months

Group	Number	%
Total Population	3,978	19.7
Hispanic or Latino (of any race)	3,181	24.6
Central American, ex. Mexican	157	27.9
Dominican Republic	731	23.2
Mexican	1,105	25.1
Puerto Rican	778	27.4
South American	321	22.0
Colombian	152	35.8
Peruvian	129	20.5

Poverty Rate
(Income in Past 12 Months Below Poverty Level)

Group	%
Total Population	27.5
Hispanic or Latino (of any race)	33.2
Central American, ex. Mexican	22.1
Dominican Republic	26.7
Mexican	45.6
Puerto Rican	26.9
South American	17.0
Colombian	22.0
Peruvian	11.8

Paterson

Population

Group	Number	%TP[1]	%HP[2]
Total Population	146,199	100.0	–
Hispanic or Latino (of any race)	84,254	57.6	100.0
Central American, ex. Mexican	4,281	2.9	5.1
Costa Rican	1,241	0.8	1.5
Guatemalan	879	0.6	1.0
Honduran	453	0.3	0.5
Nicaraguan	339	0.2	0.4
Salvadoran	1,292	0.9	1.5
Cuban	783	0.5	0.9
Dominican Republic	27,426	18.8	32.6
Mexican	8,136	5.6	9.7
Puerto Rican	21,015	14.4	24.9
South American	17,383	11.9	20.6
Argentinean	327	0.2	0.4
Chilean	101	0.1	0.1
Colombian	5,204	3.6	6.2
Ecuadorian	1,243	0.9	1.5
Peruvian	9,943	6.8	11.8
Uruguayan	204	0.1	0.2
Venezuelan	273	0.2	0.3
Spaniard	147	0.1	0.2

Population Growth: 2000–2010

Group	%
Total Population	-2.0
Hispanic or Latino (of any race)	12.7
Central American, ex. Mexican	87.4
Costa Rican	57.3
Guatemalan	89.4
Honduran	155.9
Nicaraguan	91.5
Salvadoran	151.4
Cuban	-8.7
Dominican Republic	78.9
Mexican	62.6
Puerto Rican	-12.5
South American	25.5
Argentinean	53.5
Colombian	1.8
Ecuadorian	59.8
Peruvian	41.3

Notes: (1) Percent of total population; (2) Percent of Hispanic/Latino population; Profiles include places with an overall population of at least 125,000, OR an overall population of at least 25,000 where the Hispanic/Latino population is at least 20% of the overall population. In states where less than five places meet either of these criteria, we have included places with at least 10,000 total population with the highest percentage of Hispanic/Latino population. These places are identified with an asterisk (*); Please refer to the User's Guide for a full explanation of data.

Venezuelan	10.1

Males per 100 Females

Group	Number
Total Population	93.6
Hispanic or Latino (of any race)	98.6
Central American, ex. Mexican	132.2
Costa Rican	165.2
Guatemalan	151.9
Honduran	108.8
Nicaraguan	117.3
Salvadoran	109.4
Cuban	100.3
Dominican Republic	90.6
Mexican	126.3
Puerto Rican	94.1
South American	99.8
Argentinean	113.7
Chilean	98.0
Colombian	88.8
Ecuadorian	117.7
Peruvian	103.3
Uruguayan	108.2
Venezuelan	88.3
Spaniard	107.0

Average Household Size

Group	People
Total Population	3.24
Hispanic or Latino (of any race)	3.67
Central American, ex. Mexican	3.93
Costa Rican	3.53
Guatemalan	4.27
Honduran	3.97
Nicaraguan	4.15
Salvadoran	4.12
Cuban	2.50
Dominican Republic	4.11
Mexican	4.86
Puerto Rican	3.07
South American	3.54
Argentinean	3.08
Chilean	3.24
Colombian	3.40
Ecuadorian	3.74
Peruvian	3.64
Uruguayan	3.42
Venezuelan	3.44
Spaniard	2.85

Median Age

Group	Years
Total Population	32.1
Hispanic or Latino (of any race)	30.4
Central American, ex. Mexican	31.8
Costa Rican	31.7
Guatemalan	31.5
Honduran	32.0
Nicaraguan	33.2
Salvadoran	31.3
Cuban	44.8
Dominican Republic	29.4
Mexican	25.0
Puerto Rican	30.3
South American	38.1
Argentinean	34.8
Chilean	48.8
Colombian	41.3
Ecuadorian	33.9
Peruvian	37.8
Uruguayan	36.0
Venezuelan	28.3
Spaniard	41.8

High School Graduates
(Universe: Population 25 Years and Over)

Group	Number	%
Total Population	63,798	71.7
Hispanic or Latino (of any race)	30,945	66.3
Central American, ex. Mexican	2,003	62.8
Guatemalan	568	53.2
Salvadoran	618	60.2
Dominican Republic	8,123	59.4
Mexican	2,297	54.5
Puerto Rican	6,960	60.1
South American	10,209	85.0
Colombian	2,904	82.9
Ecuadorian	996	91.0
Peruvian	5,774	84.3

Four-Year College Graduates
(Universe: Population 25 Years and Over)

Group	Number	%
Total Population	8,729	9.8
Hispanic or Latino (of any race)	3,563	7.6
Central American, ex. Mexican	232	7.3
Guatemalan	70	6.6
Salvadoran	37	3.6
Dominican Republic	1,245	9.1
Mexican	101	2.4
Puerto Rican	329	2.8
South American	1,419	11.8
Colombian	430	12.3
Ecuadorian	110	10.1
Peruvian	879	12.8

Population Age 3–17 Enrolled in Public School
(Universe: Population Age 3–17 Enrolled in School)

Group	Number	%
Total Population	27,784	92.5
Hispanic or Latino (of any race)	16,170	93.5
Central American, ex. Mexican	689	82.3
Guatemalan	212	90.2
Salvadoran	177	65.8
Dominican Republic	5,852	96.2
Mexican	2,241	98.2
Puerto Rican	4,466	92.4
South American	2,222	89.4
Colombian	470	84.7
Ecuadorian	113	100.0
Peruvian	1,540	89.6

Population Age 3–17 Enrolled in Private School
(Universe: Population Age 3–17 Enrolled in School)

Group	Number	%
Total Population	2,243	7.5
Hispanic or Latino (of any race)	1,119	6.5
Central American, ex. Mexican	148	17.7
Guatemalan	23	9.8
Salvadoran	92	34.2
Dominican Republic	233	3.8
Mexican	42	1.8
Puerto Rican	365	7.6
South American	264	10.6
Colombian	85	15.3
Ecuadorian	0	0.0
Peruvian	179	10.4

Foreign-Born Population

Group	Number	%
Total Population	42,405	29.1
Hispanic or Latino (of any race)	31,513	39.3
Central American, ex. Mexican	3,002	60.9
Guatemalan	967	55.1
Salvadoran	897	60.4
Dominican Republic	12,075	48.0
Mexican	4,056	44.9
Puerto Rican	366	1.8
South American	10,544	60.6
Colombian	3,003	57.9
Ecuadorian	942	72.5
Peruvian	6,028	59.6

Foreign-Born Naturalized U.S. Citizens

Group	Number	%
Total Population	19,388	45.7
Hispanic or Latino (of any race)	12,474	39.6
Central American, ex. Mexican	839	27.9
Guatemalan	200	20.7
Salvadoran	280	31.2
Dominican Republic	5,238	43.4
Mexican	757	18.7
Puerto Rican	200	54.6
South American	4,527	42.9
Colombian	1,534	51.1
Ecuadorian	552	58.6
Peruvian	2,242	37.2

Language Spoken at Home: English Only
(Universe: Population 5 Years and Over)

Group	Number	%
Total Population	53,268	39.7
Hispanic or Latino (of any race)	4,323	5.9
Central American, ex. Mexican	179	4.0
Guatemalan	71	4.5
Salvadoran	70	5.3
Dominican Republic	782	3.5
Mexican	360	4.6
Puerto Rican	2,105	11.4
South American	732	4.4
Colombian	157	3.2
Ecuadorian	138	10.9
Peruvian	430	4.5

Language Spoken at Home: Spanish
(Universe: Population 5 Years and Over)

Group	Number	%
Total Population	70,199	52.4
Hispanic or Latino (of any race)	68,432	93.8
Central American, ex. Mexican	4,254	94.6
Guatemalan	1,501	95.5
Salvadoran	1,243	94.7
Dominican Republic	21,779	96.5
Mexican	7,319	94.4
Puerto Rican	16,368	88.5
South American	15,684	95.3
Colombian	4,810	96.8
Ecuadorian	1,132	89.1
Peruvian	9,025	95.5

Unemployment Rate
(Universe: Population 16 Years and Over)

Group	%
Total Population	8.6
Hispanic or Latino (of any race)	6.6
Central American, ex. Mexican	3.3
Guatemalan	0.0
Salvadoran	3.5
Dominican Republic	6.0
Mexican	4.5
Puerto Rican	9.0
South American	5.8
Colombian	7.3
Ecuadorian	10.2
Peruvian	4.7

Class of Worker: Private Wage and Salary
(Universe: Civilian Employed Population 16 Years and Over)

Group	Number	%
Total Population	50,444	85.5
Hispanic or Latino (of any race)	30,538	91.0
Central American, ex. Mexican	2,438	98.5
Guatemalan	882	99.2
Salvadoran	651	98.0
Dominican Republic	9,620	92.5
Mexican	3,468	95.1
Puerto Rican	5,612	84.8
South American	8,415	91.0
Colombian	2,778	91.7
Ecuadorian	642	91.6
Peruvian	4,626	90.2

Class of Worker: Government
(Universe: Civilian Employed Population 16 Years and Over)

Group	Number	%
Total Population	6,802	11.5
Hispanic or Latino (of any race)	2,024	6.0
Central American, ex. Mexican	9	0.4
Guatemalan	0	0.0
Salvadoran	0	0.0
Dominican Republic	514	4.9
Mexican	95	2.6
Puerto Rican	811	12.3
South American	409	4.4
Colombian	164	5.4
Ecuadorian	39	5.6
Peruvian	206	4.0

Means of Transportation to Work: Car, Truck or Van
(Universe: Workers 16 Years and Over)

Group	Number	%
Total Population	43,284	74.7

Notes: (1) Percent of total population; (2) Percent of Hispanic/Latino population; Profiles include places with an overall population of at least 125,000, OR an overall population of at least 25,000 where the Hispanic/Latino population is at least 20% of the overall population. In states where less than five places meet either of these criteria, we have included places with at least 10,000 total population with the highest percentage of Hispanic/Latino population. These places are identified with an asterisk (*); Please refer to the User's Guide for a full explanation of data.

Hispanic or Latino (of any race)	23,681	71.3
Central American, ex. Mexican	1,480	59.8
Guatemalan	476	53.5
Salvadoran	451	67.9
Dominican Republic	8,124	78.8
Mexican	2,011	55.1
Puerto Rican	5,058	77.5
South American	5,963	65.8
Colombian	2,198	72.9
Ecuadorian	535	77.4
Peruvian	2,989	60.2

Means of Transportation to Work: Public Transportation (ex. Taxicab)
(Universe: Workers 16 Years and Over)

Group	Number	%
Total Population	7,031	12.1
Hispanic or Latino (of any race)	4,222	12.7
Central American, ex. Mexican	468	18.9
Guatemalan	274	30.8
Salvadoran	99	14.9
Dominican Republic	717	7.0
Mexican	922	25.3
Puerto Rican	605	9.3
South American	1,437	15.9
Colombian	316	10.5
Ecuadorian	0	0.0
Peruvian	1,043	21.0

Homeownership Rate
(Universe: Occupied Housing Units)

Group	%
Total Population	29.6
Hispanic or Latino (of any race)	26.4
Central American, ex. Mexican	24.6
Costa Rican	15.0
Guatemalan	27.9
Honduran	30.0
Nicaraguan	22.5
Salvadoran	30.5
Cuban	35.2
Dominican Republic	27.8
Mexican	15.0
Puerto Rican	23.8
South American	30.9
Argentinean	39.8
Chilean	36.4
Colombian	30.9
Ecuadorian	33.3
Peruvian	30.1
Uruguayan	28.1
Venezuelan	26.4
Spaniard	52.1

Median Home Value

Group	Dollars
Total Population	331,200
Hispanic or Latino (of any race)	345,800
Central American, ex. Mexican	331,200
Guatemalan	381,500
Salvadoran	316,000
Dominican Republic	350,800
Mexican	299,100
Puerto Rican	343,600
South American	357,000
Colombian	377,700
Ecuadorian	361,000
Peruvian	345,400

Median Gross Rent

Group	Dollars
Total Population	1,030
Hispanic or Latino (of any race)	1,077
Central American, ex. Mexican	1,232
Guatemalan	1,405
Salvadoran	1,127
Dominican Republic	1,143
Mexican	1,112
Puerto Rican	1,000
South American	1,077
Colombian	1,033
Ecuadorian	1,092
Peruvian	1,088

Median Household Income
(2010 Inflation-Adjusted Dollars)

Group	Dollars
Total Population	34,086
Hispanic or Latino (of any race)	33,345
Central American, ex. Mexican	41,958
Guatemalan	47,404
Salvadoran	36,250
Dominican Republic	35,052
Mexican	27,026
Puerto Rican	26,355
South American	39,666
Colombian	48,712
Ecuadorian	37,806
Peruvian	39,464

Per Capita Income
(2010 Inflation-Adjusted Dollars)

Group	Dollars
Total Population	15,543
Hispanic or Latino (of any race)	13,032
Central American, ex. Mexican	14,236
Guatemalan	13,565
Salvadoran	15,053
Dominican Republic	11,757
Mexican	9,859
Puerto Rican	13,069
South American	16,024
Colombian	15,988
Ecuadorian	23,297
Peruvian	15,263

Households with $100,000+ Income

Group	Number	%
Total Population	4,041	9.0
Hispanic or Latino (of any race)	1,364	6.1
Central American, ex. Mexican	77	5.7
Guatemalan	17	5.1
Salvadoran	21	4.7
Dominican Republic	371	5.9
Mexican	107	5.3
Puerto Rican	377	5.6
South American	325	6.7
Colombian	83	6.8
Ecuadorian	87	18.9
Peruvian	155	5.5

Households with Food Stamps/SNAP Benefits During Past 12 Months

Group	Number	%
Total Population	8,035	17.9
Hispanic or Latino (of any race)	4,540	20.4
Central American, ex. Mexican	80	5.9
Guatemalan	32	9.6
Salvadoran	10	2.2
Dominican Republic	1,391	22.1
Mexican	411	20.2
Puerto Rican	1,922	28.7
South American	577	11.9
Colombian	80	6.6
Ecuadorian	44	9.5
Peruvian	414	14.8

Poverty Rate
(Income in Past 12 Months Below Poverty Level)

Group	%
Total Population	26.6
Hispanic or Latino (of any race)	27.0
Central American, ex. Mexican	21.6
Guatemalan	29.9
Salvadoran	9.0
Dominican Republic	25.1
Mexican	31.8
Puerto Rican	36.6
South American	18.2
Colombian	13.4
Ecuadorian	10.6
Peruvian	21.2

Pennsauken

Population

Group	Number	%TP[1]	%HP[2]
Total Population	35,885	100.0	–
Hispanic or Latino (of any race)	9,657	26.9	100.0
Central American, ex. Mexican	650	1.8	6.7
Guatemalan	123	0.3	1.3
Nicaraguan	336	0.9	3.5
Cuban	101	0.3	1.0
Dominican Republic	1,347	3.8	13.9
Mexican	822	2.3	8.5
Puerto Rican	6,038	16.8	62.5
South American	312	0.9	3.2
Colombian	107	0.3	1.1

Population Growth: 2000–2010

Group	%
Total Population	0.4
Hispanic or Latino (of any race)	88.4
Central American, ex. Mexican	138.1
Nicaraguan	89.8
Dominican Republic	434.5
Mexican	277.1
Puerto Rican	66.4

Males per 100 Females

Group	Number
Total Population	91.8
Hispanic or Latino (of any race)	95.0
Central American, ex. Mexican	101.9
Guatemalan	123.6
Nicaraguan	103.6
Cuban	102.0
Dominican Republic	93.0
Mexican	111.3
Puerto Rican	91.6
South American	109.4
Colombian	81.4

Average Household Size

Group	People
Total Population	2.83
Hispanic or Latino (of any race)	3.61
Central American, ex. Mexican	4.15
Guatemalan	4.56
Nicaraguan	4.11
Cuban	2.87
Dominican Republic	4.16
Mexican	5.07
Puerto Rican	3.36
South American	3.58
Colombian	3.13

Median Age

Group	Years
Total Population	38.0
Hispanic or Latino (of any race)	27.6
Central American, ex. Mexican	30.8
Guatemalan	29.1
Nicaraguan	32.8
Cuban	37.5
Dominican Republic	28.3
Mexican	24.6
Puerto Rican	27.9
South American	33.3
Colombian	35.5

High School Graduates
(Universe: Population 25 Years and Over)

Group	Number	%
Total Population	19,180	80.8
Hispanic or Latino (of any race)	2,920	64.4
Dominican Republic	362	45.4
Puerto Rican	1,900	69.9

Four-Year College Graduates
(Universe: Population 25 Years and Over)

Group	Number	%
Total Population	4,692	19.8
Hispanic or Latino (of any race)	478	10.5
Dominican Republic	55	6.9
Puerto Rican	295	10.8

STATE & PLACE PROFILES

Notes: (1) Percent of total population; (2) Percent of Hispanic/Latino population; Profiles include places with an overall population of at least 125,000, OR an overall population of at least 25,000 where the Hispanic/Latino population is at least 20% of the overall population. In states where less than five places meet either of these criteria, we have included places with at least 10,000 total population with the highest percentage of Hispanic/Latino population. These places are identified with an asterisk (*); Please refer to the User's Guide for a full explanation of data.

Population Age 3–17 Enrolled in Public School
(Universe: Population Age 3–17 Enrolled in School)

Group	Number	%
Total Population	5,814	82.5
Hispanic or Latino (of any race)	2,153	90.7
Dominican Republic	349	79.3
Puerto Rican	1,235	92.4

Population Age 3–17 Enrolled in Private School
(Universe: Population Age 3–17 Enrolled in School)

Group	Number	%
Total Population	1,230	17.5
Hispanic or Latino (of any race)	220	9.3
Dominican Republic	91	20.7
Puerto Rican	102	7.6

Foreign-Born Population

Group	Number	%
Total Population	4,715	13.1
Hispanic or Latino (of any race)	1,879	21.9
Dominican Republic	858	54.4
Puerto Rican	27	0.5

Foreign-Born Naturalized U.S. Citizens

Group	Number	%
Total Population	2,282	48.4
Hispanic or Latino (of any race)	790	42.0
Dominican Republic	399	46.5
Puerto Rican	10	37.0

Language Spoken at Home: English Only
(Universe: Population 5 Years and Over)

Group	Number	%
Total Population	23,795	70.4
Hispanic or Latino (of any race)	1,349	17.3
Dominican Republic	103	7.2
Puerto Rican	862	18.9

Language Spoken at Home: Spanish
(Universe: Population 5 Years and Over)

Group	Number	%
Total Population	6,788	20.1
Hispanic or Latino (of any race)	6,378	81.7
Dominican Republic	1,321	92.8
Puerto Rican	3,698	81.1

Unemployment Rate
(Universe: Population 16 Years and Over)

Group	%
Total Population	10.0
Hispanic or Latino (of any race)	9.5
Dominican Republic	2.3
Puerto Rican	12.8

Class of Worker: Private Wage and Salary
(Universe: Civilian Employed Population 16 Years and Over)

Group	Number	%
Total Population	14,564	81.0
Hispanic or Latino (of any race)	3,057	79.8
Dominican Republic	514	74.2
Puerto Rican	1,795	78.3

Class of Worker: Government
(Universe: Civilian Employed Population 16 Years and Over)

Group	Number	%
Total Population	2,691	15.0
Hispanic or Latino (of any race)	533	13.9
Dominican Republic	93	13.4
Puerto Rican	395	17.2

Means of Transportation to Work: Car, Truck or Van
(Universe: Workers 16 Years and Over)

Group	Number	%
Total Population	15,682	89.6
Hispanic or Latino (of any race)	3,426	91.0
Dominican Republic	611	91.6
Puerto Rican	2,125	94.3

Means of Transportation to Work: Public Transportation (ex. Taxicab)
(Universe: Workers 16 Years and Over)

Group	Number	%
Total Population	1,087	6.2
Hispanic or Latino (of any race)	250	6.6
Dominican Republic	12	1.8
Puerto Rican	106	4.7

Homeownership Rate
(Universe: Occupied Housing Units)

Group	%
Total Population	77.3
Hispanic or Latino (of any race)	69.9
Central American, ex. Mexican	80.2
Guatemalan	77.8
Nicaraguan	80.2
Cuban	58.1
Dominican Republic	78.4
Mexican	48.4
Puerto Rican	69.0
South American	81.6
Colombian	89.5

Median Home Value

Group	Dollars
Total Population	187,800
Hispanic or Latino (of any race)	199,100
Dominican Republic	205,700
Puerto Rican	195,600

Median Gross Rent

Group	Dollars
Total Population	899
Hispanic or Latino (of any race)	1,076
Dominican Republic	641
Puerto Rican	1,060

Median Household Income
(2010 Inflation-Adjusted Dollars)

Group	Dollars
Total Population	57,241
Hispanic or Latino (of any race)	58,575
Dominican Republic	45,565
Puerto Rican	66,936

Per Capita Income
(2010 Inflation-Adjusted Dollars)

Group	Dollars
Total Population	26,048
Hispanic or Latino (of any race)	17,298
Dominican Republic	11,888
Puerto Rican	19,316

Households with $100,000+ Income

Group	Number	%
Total Population	2,634	20.3
Hispanic or Latino (of any race)	364	16.8
Dominican Republic	0	0.0
Puerto Rican	286	22.6

Households with Food Stamps/SNAP Benefits During Past 12 Months

Group	Number	%
Total Population	668	5.2
Hispanic or Latino (of any race)	203	9.4
Dominican Republic	21	5.2
Puerto Rican	163	12.9

Poverty Rate
(Income in Past 12 Months Below Poverty Level)

Group	%
Total Population	8.9
Hispanic or Latino (of any race)	9.7
Dominican Republic	11.2
Puerto Rican	9.3

Perth Amboy

Population

Group	Number	%TP[1]	%HP[2]
Total Population	50,814	100.0	–
Hispanic or Latino (of any race)	39,685	78.1	100.0
Central American, ex. Mexican	1,441	2.8	3.6
Guatemalan	181	0.4	0.5
Honduran	404	0.8	1.0
Salvadoran	670	1.3	1.7
Cuban	824	1.6	2.1
Dominican Republic	14,773	29.1	37.2
Mexican	5,183	10.2	13.1
Puerto Rican	12,090	23.8	30.5
South American	3,538	7.0	8.9
Argentinean	427	0.8	1.1
Colombian	530	1.0	1.3
Ecuadorian	366	0.7	0.9
Peruvian	1,979	3.9	5.0

Population Growth: 2000–2010

Group	%
Total Population	7.4
Hispanic or Latino (of any race)	20.1
Central American, ex. Mexican	87.6
Honduran	78.0
Salvadoran	111.4
Cuban	-10.2
Dominican Republic	66.0
Mexican	69.6
Puerto Rican	-8.0
South American	81.0
Argentinean	157.2
Colombian	38.7
Ecuadorian	120.5
Peruvian	90.1

Males per 100 Females

Group	Number
Total Population	97.3
Hispanic or Latino (of any race)	99.1
Central American, ex. Mexican	114.8
Guatemalan	178.5
Honduran	104.0
Salvadoran	114.7
Cuban	112.4
Dominican Republic	91.5
Mexican	131.0
Puerto Rican	94.1
South American	101.7
Argentinean	128.3
Colombian	74.9
Ecuadorian	102.2
Peruvian	104.9

Average Household Size

Group	People
Total Population	3.25
Hispanic or Latino (of any race)	3.67
Central American, ex. Mexican	4.06
Guatemalan	4.41
Honduran	4.13
Salvadoran	4.15
Cuban	2.72
Dominican Republic	4.14
Mexican	4.83
Puerto Rican	3.02
South American	3.54
Argentinean	3.44
Colombian	3.15
Ecuadorian	3.34
Peruvian	3.81

Median Age

Group	Years
Total Population	32.4
Hispanic or Latino (of any race)	29.8
Central American, ex. Mexican	30.9
Guatemalan	29.2
Honduran	29.5
Salvadoran	31.9
Cuban	43.7
Dominican Republic	30.0
Mexican	24.8
Puerto Rican	31.7
South American	35.1
Argentinean	31.7
Colombian	35.6
Ecuadorian	32.8
Peruvian	36.5

High School Graduates
(Universe: Population 25 Years and Over)

Group	Number	%
Total Population	20,821	67.0
Hispanic or Latino (of any race)	13,580	61.5
Central American, ex. Mexican	496	52.5
Cuban	625	75.4
Dominican Republic	3,727	52.8

Notes: (1) Percent of total population; (2) Percent of Hispanic/Latino population; Profiles include places with an overall population of at least 125,000, OR an overall population of at least 25,000 where the Hispanic/Latino population is at least 20% of the overall population. In states where less than five places meet either of these criteria, we have included places with at least 10,000 total population with the highest percentage of Hispanic/Latino population. These places are identified with an asterisk (*); Please refer to the User's Guide for a full explanation of data.

Mexican	1,232	56.7
Puerto Rican	5,014	62.2
South American	2,096	87.2
Peruvian	995	90.5

Four-Year College Graduates
(Universe: Population 25 Years and Over)

Group	Number	%
Total Population	4,326	13.9
Hispanic or Latino (of any race)	2,233	10.1
Central American, ex. Mexican	105	11.1
Cuban	356	42.9
Dominican Republic	501	7.1
Mexican	107	4.9
Puerto Rican	640	7.9
South American	462	19.2
Peruvian	284	25.8

Population Age 3–17 Enrolled in Public School
(Universe: Population Age 3–17 Enrolled in School)

Group	Number	%
Total Population	9,294	94.1
Hispanic or Latino (of any race)	7,884	96.0
Central American, ex. Mexican	456	100.0
Cuban	270	89.4
Dominican Republic	2,640	98.7
Mexican	929	99.1
Puerto Rican	2,746	94.3
South American	620	90.8
Peruvian	401	94.8

Population Age 3–17 Enrolled in Private School
(Universe: Population Age 3–17 Enrolled in School)

Group	Number	%
Total Population	586	5.9
Hispanic or Latino (of any race)	325	4.0
Central American, ex. Mexican	0	0.0
Cuban	32	10.6
Dominican Republic	35	1.3
Mexican	8	0.9
Puerto Rican	165	5.7
South American	63	9.2
Peruvian	22	5.2

Foreign-Born Population

Group	Number	%
Total Population	18,588	37.0
Hispanic or Latino (of any race)	15,863	41.4
Central American, ex. Mexican	1,125	67.6
Cuban	712	54.2
Dominican Republic	7,715	62.5
Mexican	2,608	61.9
Puerto Rican	279	2.0
South American	3,016	76.6
Peruvian	1,488	70.5

Foreign-Born Naturalized U.S. Citizens

Group	Number	%
Total Population	6,685	36.0
Hispanic or Latino (of any race)	5,213	32.9
Central American, ex. Mexican	265	23.6
Cuban	475	66.7
Dominican Republic	2,813	36.5
Mexican	195	7.5
Puerto Rican	105	37.6
South American	1,261	41.8
Peruvian	794	53.4

Language Spoken at Home: English Only
(Universe: Population 5 Years and Over)

Group	Number	%
Total Population	11,852	25.5
Hispanic or Latino (of any race)	3,788	10.8
Central American, ex. Mexican	190	12.2
Cuban	198	15.9
Dominican Republic	480	4.2
Mexican	184	4.8
Puerto Rican	2,396	19.2
South American	184	4.9
Peruvian	95	4.9

Language Spoken at Home: Spanish
(Universe: Population 5 Years and Over)

Group	Number	%
Total Population	32,335	69.5
Hispanic or Latino (of any race)	31,328	89.1
Central American, ex. Mexican	1,357	87.2
Cuban	1,047	84.1
Dominican Republic	10,968	95.8
Mexican	3,613	95.2
Puerto Rican	10,097	80.7
South American	3,538	95.1
Peruvian	1,841	95.1

Unemployment Rate
(Universe: Population 16 Years and Over)

Group	%
Total Population	7.3
Hispanic or Latino (of any race)	6.3
Central American, ex. Mexican	3.9
Cuban	5.7
Dominican Republic	7.4
Mexican	4.2
Puerto Rican	7.5
South American	2.6
Peruvian	2.8

Class of Worker: Private Wage and Salary
(Universe: Civilian Employed Population 16 Years and Over)

Group	Number	%
Total Population	19,743	86.6
Hispanic or Latino (of any race)	15,437	88.4
Central American, ex. Mexican	741	90.1
Cuban	479	82.7
Dominican Republic	5,585	93.5
Mexican	1,606	89.2
Puerto Rican	4,714	82.3
South American	1,947	89.5
Peruvian	873	85.3

Class of Worker: Government
(Universe: Civilian Employed Population 16 Years and Over)

Group	Number	%
Total Population	2,376	10.4
Hispanic or Latino (of any race)	1,723	9.9
Central American, ex. Mexican	81	9.9
Cuban	100	17.3
Dominican Republic	344	5.8
Mexican	122	6.8
Puerto Rican	943	16.5
South American	104	4.8
Peruvian	60	5.9

Means of Transportation to Work: Car, Truck or Van
(Universe: Workers 16 Years and Over)

Group	Number	%
Total Population	19,144	85.1
Hispanic or Latino (of any race)	14,936	86.5
Central American, ex. Mexican	767	93.3
Cuban	539	93.1
Dominican Republic	4,934	83.9
Mexican	1,467	81.6
Puerto Rican	5,008	88.8
South American	1,904	88.2
Peruvian	893	89.0

Means of Transportation to Work: Public Transportation (ex. Taxicab)
(Universe: Workers 16 Years and Over)

Group	Number	%
Total Population	1,562	6.9
Hispanic or Latino (of any race)	1,090	6.3
Central American, ex. Mexican	21	2.6
Cuban	0	0.0
Dominican Republic	427	7.3
Mexican	195	10.8
Puerto Rican	326	5.8
South American	101	4.7
Peruvian	36	3.6

Homeownership Rate
(Universe: Occupied Housing Units)

Group	%
Total Population	35.5
Hispanic or Latino (of any race)	29.8
Central American, ex. Mexican	26.0
Guatemalan	28.3
Honduran	27.6
Salvadoran	27.3
Cuban	42.7
Dominican Republic	29.3
Mexican	17.0
Puerto Rican	33.2
South American	30.4
Argentinean	22.3
Colombian	25.6
Ecuadorian	31.3
Peruvian	33.1

Median Home Value

Group	Dollars
Total Population	310,500
Hispanic or Latino (of any race)	320,000
Central American, ex. Mexican	342,100
Cuban	323,300
Dominican Republic	358,500
Mexican	224,000
Puerto Rican	307,800
South American	271,200
Peruvian	242,100

Median Gross Rent

Group	Dollars
Total Population	1,070
Hispanic or Latino (of any race)	1,089
Central American, ex. Mexican	1,253
Cuban	1,077
Dominican Republic	1,124
Mexican	1,183
Puerto Rican	1,042
South American	1,070
Peruvian	1,130

Median Household Income
(2010 Inflation-Adjusted Dollars)

Group	Dollars
Total Population	47,696
Hispanic or Latino (of any race)	41,745
Central American, ex. Mexican	52,938
Cuban	41,442
Dominican Republic	39,935
Mexican	34,145
Puerto Rican	41,875
South American	47,944
Peruvian	35,469

Per Capita Income
(2010 Inflation-Adjusted Dollars)

Group	Dollars
Total Population	20,162
Hispanic or Latino (of any race)	17,341
Central American, ex. Mexican	19,944
Cuban	20,578
Dominican Republic	14,268
Mexican	14,952
Puerto Rican	19,558
South American	18,789
Peruvian	15,263

Households with $100,000+ Income

Group	Number	%
Total Population	2,729	16.7
Hispanic or Latino (of any race)	1,679	14.4
Central American, ex. Mexican	113	26.5
Cuban	133	28.9
Dominican Republic	284	7.9
Mexican	171	17.0
Puerto Rican	631	13.7
South American	254	18.8
Peruvian	92	11.9

Households with Food Stamps/SNAP Benefits During Past 12 Months

Group	Number	%
Total Population	1,712	10.5
Hispanic or Latino (of any race)	1,425	12.2
Central American, ex. Mexican	15	3.5
Cuban	69	15.0
Dominican Republic	455	12.7
Mexican	162	16.1
Puerto Rican	647	14.0
South American	77	5.7
Peruvian	38	4.9

Notes: (1) Percent of total population; (2) Percent of Hispanic/Latino population; Profiles include places with an overall population of at least 125,000, OR an overall population of at least 25,000 where the Hispanic/Latino population is at least 20% of the overall population. In states where less than five places meet either of these criteria, we have included places with at least 10,000 total population with the highest percentage of Hispanic/Latino population. These places are identified with an asterisk (*); Please refer to the User's Guide for a full explanation of data.

Poverty Rate
(Income in Past 12 Months Below Poverty Level)

Group	%
Total Population	19.4
Hispanic or Latino (of any race)	21.8
Central American, ex. Mexican	8.6
Cuban	26.8
Dominican Republic	19.9
Mexican	30.1
Puerto Rican	22.6
South American	17.9
Peruvian	27.0

Plainfield

Population

Group	Number	%TP[1]	%HP[2]
Total Population	49,808	100.0	–
Hispanic or Latino (of any race)	20,105	40.4	100.0
Central American, ex. Mexican	9,822	19.7	48.9
Costa Rican	128	0.3	0.6
Guatemalan	4,302	8.6	21.4
Honduran	1,493	3.0	7.4
Salvadoran	3,684	7.4	18.3
Cuban	168	0.3	0.8
Dominican Republic	1,601	3.2	8.0
Mexican	1,568	3.1	7.8
Puerto Rican	1,822	3.7	9.1
South American	3,400	6.8	16.9
Colombian	748	1.5	3.7
Ecuadorian	2,061	4.1	10.3
Peruvian	450	0.9	2.2
Spaniard	113	0.2	0.6

Population Growth: 2000–2010

Group	%
Total Population	4.1
Hispanic or Latino (of any race)	67.1
Central American, ex. Mexican	155.4
Guatemalan	198.1
Honduran	91.7
Salvadoran	192.4
Cuban	15.9
Dominican Republic	128.1
Mexican	94.3
Puerto Rican	2.2
South American	86.2
Colombian	21.4
Ecuadorian	138.8
Peruvian	93.1

Males per 100 Females

Group	Number
Total Population	101.3
Hispanic or Latino (of any race)	129.7
Central American, ex. Mexican	158.1
Costa Rican	103.2
Guatemalan	201.0
Honduran	117.0
Salvadoran	144.3
Cuban	107.4
Dominican Republic	92.0
Mexican	119.6
Puerto Rican	98.5
South American	112.6
Colombian	89.4
Ecuadorian	122.8
Peruvian	108.3
Spaniard	182.5

Average Household Size

Group	People
Total Population	3.23
Hispanic or Latino (of any race)	4.53
Central American, ex. Mexican	5.10
Costa Rican	3.79
Guatemalan	5.14
Honduran	4.80
Salvadoran	5.30
Cuban	2.80
Dominican Republic	4.45
Mexican	4.31
Puerto Rican	3.38
South American	4.30
Colombian	3.61
Ecuadorian	4.75
Peruvian	4.01
Spaniard	3.00

Median Age

Group	Years
Total Population	33.3
Hispanic or Latino (of any race)	28.1
Central American, ex. Mexican	28.2
Costa Rican	32.0
Guatemalan	27.8
Honduran	29.3
Salvadoran	28.2
Cuban	41.3
Dominican Republic	28.6
Mexican	25.2
Puerto Rican	28.9
South American	32.9
Colombian	36.2
Ecuadorian	31.0
Peruvian	36.9
Spaniard	27.5

High School Graduates
(Universe: Population 25 Years and Over)

Group	Number	%
Total Population	23,862	74.5
Hispanic or Latino (of any race)	5,400	50.2
Central American, ex. Mexican	2,000	35.2
Guatemalan	421	21.9
Honduran	639	39.0
Salvadoran	697	39.1
Dominican Republic	289	48.2
Mexican	815	61.5
Puerto Rican	749	75.7
South American	1,004	68.6
Ecuadorian	478	55.4

Four-Year College Graduates
(Universe: Population 25 Years and Over)

Group	Number	%
Total Population	6,270	19.6
Hispanic or Latino (of any race)	628	5.8
Central American, ex. Mexican	247	4.3
Guatemalan	43	2.2
Honduran	142	8.7
Salvadoran	22	1.2
Dominican Republic	0	0.0
Mexican	80	6.0
Puerto Rican	61	6.2
South American	162	11.1
Ecuadorian	62	7.2

Population Age 3–17 Enrolled in Public School
(Universe: Population Age 3–17 Enrolled in School)

Group	Number	%
Total Population	7,691	86.4
Hispanic or Latino (of any race)	2,618	94.2
Central American, ex. Mexican	1,023	100.0
Guatemalan	319	100.0
Honduran	209	100.0
Salvadoran	471	100.0
Dominican Republic	359	95.0
Mexican	394	91.2
Puerto Rican	208	71.0
South American	356	95.2
Ecuadorian	252	100.0

Population Age 3–17 Enrolled in Private School
(Universe: Population Age 3–17 Enrolled in School)

Group	Number	%
Total Population	1,210	13.6
Hispanic or Latino (of any race)	160	5.8
Central American, ex. Mexican	0	0.0
Guatemalan	0	0.0
Honduran	0	0.0
Salvadoran	0	0.0
Dominican Republic	19	5.0
Mexican	38	8.8
Puerto Rican	85	29.0
South American	18	4.8
Ecuadorian	0	0.0

Foreign-Born Population

Group	Number	%
Total Population	16,124	32.9
Hispanic or Latino (of any race)	11,966	67.9
Central American, ex. Mexican	7,515	83.3
Guatemalan	2,883	85.7
Honduran	2,118	87.1
Salvadoran	2,165	76.8
Dominican Republic	586	56.2
Mexican	1,470	59.6
Puerto Rican	80	4.9
South American	1,769	74.7
Ecuadorian	1,063	75.8

Foreign-Born Naturalized U.S. Citizens

Group	Number	%
Total Population	4,350	27.0
Hispanic or Latino (of any race)	1,914	16.0
Central American, ex. Mexican	647	8.6
Guatemalan	99	3.4
Honduran	292	13.8
Salvadoran	237	10.9
Dominican Republic	127	21.7
Mexican	233	15.9
Puerto Rican	10	12.5
South American	631	35.7
Ecuadorian	317	29.8

Language Spoken at Home: English Only
(Universe: Population 5 Years and Over)

Group	Number	%
Total Population	26,775	59.3
Hispanic or Latino (of any race)	661	4.1
Central American, ex. Mexican	85	1.0
Guatemalan	41	1.3
Honduran	13	0.6
Salvadoran	15	0.6
Dominican Republic	0	0.0
Mexican	55	2.6
Puerto Rican	235	17.2
South American	92	4.3
Ecuadorian	48	3.8

Language Spoken at Home: Spanish
(Universe: Population 5 Years and Over)

Group	Number	%
Total Population	16,649	36.9
Hispanic or Latino (of any race)	15,211	95.3
Central American, ex. Mexican	8,199	98.0
Guatemalan	2,974	96.0
Honduran	2,286	99.4
Salvadoran	2,566	99.4
Dominican Republic	990	100.0
Mexican	2,052	97.4
Puerto Rican	1,132	82.8
South American	2,069	95.7
Ecuadorian	1,222	96.2

Unemployment Rate
(Universe: Population 16 Years and Over)

Group	%
Total Population	11.6
Hispanic or Latino (of any race)	10.4
Central American, ex. Mexican	8.2
Guatemalan	5.0
Honduran	11.4
Salvadoran	10.4
Dominican Republic	11.8
Mexican	12.8
Puerto Rican	14.8
South American	18.2
Ecuadorian	18.6

Class of Worker: Private Wage and Salary
(Universe: Civilian Employed Population 16 Years and Over)

Group	Number	%
Total Population	20,735	84.1
Hispanic or Latino (of any race)	9,646	94.2
Central American, ex. Mexican	5,867	96.3
Guatemalan	2,372	95.6
Honduran	1,584	99.3
Salvadoran	1,659	97.3
Dominican Republic	461	93.7
Mexican	1,176	98.3
Puerto Rican	565	80.6

Notes: (1) Percent of total population; (2) Percent of Hispanic/Latino population; Profiles include places with an overall population of at least 125,000, OR an overall population of at least 25,000 where the Hispanic/Latino population is at least 20% of the overall population. In states where less than five places meet either of these criteria, we have included places with at least 10,000 total population with the highest percentage of Hispanic/Latino population. These places are identified with an asterisk (*); Please refer to the User's Guide for a full explanation of data.

South American	1,164	93.6
Ecuadorian	726	100.0

Class of Worker: Government
(Universe: Civilian Employed Population 16 Years and Over)

Group	Number	%
Total Population	3,030	12.3
Hispanic or Latino (of any race)	296	2.9
Central American, ex. Mexican	52	0.9
Guatemalan	36	1.5
Honduran	0	0.0
Salvadoran	0	0.0
Dominican Republic	31	6.3
Mexican	9	0.8
Puerto Rican	99	14.1
South American	58	4.7
Ecuadorian	0	0.0

Means of Transportation to Work: Car, Truck or Van
(Universe: Workers 16 Years and Over)

Group	Number	%
Total Population	16,689	69.3
Hispanic or Latino (of any race)	5,496	54.6
Central American, ex. Mexican	2,855	47.4
Guatemalan	1,027	41.4
Honduran	626	39.6
Salvadoran	989	59.8
Dominican Republic	445	90.4
Mexican	562	47.0
Puerto Rican	585	84.8
South American	833	71.4
Ecuadorian	444	68.3

Means of Transportation to Work: Public Transportation (ex. Taxicab)
(Universe: Workers 16 Years and Over)

Group	Number	%
Total Population	2,178	9.0
Hispanic or Latino (of any race)	697	6.9
Central American, ex. Mexican	323	5.4
Guatemalan	179	7.2
Honduran	57	3.6
Salvadoran	63	3.8
Dominican Republic	7	1.4
Mexican	135	11.3
Puerto Rican	27	3.9
South American	154	13.2
Ecuadorian	53	8.2

Homeownership Rate
(Universe: Occupied Housing Units)

Group	%
Total Population	50.0
Hispanic or Latino (of any race)	29.5
Central American, ex. Mexican	21.3
Costa Rican	17.9
Guatemalan	14.5
Honduran	21.8
Salvadoran	27.2
Cuban	53.8
Dominican Republic	32.8
Mexican	21.7
Puerto Rican	38.3
South American	41.1
Colombian	42.4
Ecuadorian	40.2
Peruvian	40.6
Spaniard	71.4

Median Home Value

Group	Dollars
Total Population	305,700
Hispanic or Latino (of any race)	293,600
Central American, ex. Mexican	248,800
Guatemalan	302,500
Honduran	120,000
Salvadoran	255,000
Dominican Republic	269,400
Mexican	286,800
Puerto Rican	280,400
South American	346,700
Ecuadorian	366,700

Median Gross Rent

Group	Dollars
Total Population	1,061
Hispanic or Latino (of any race)	1,139
Central American, ex. Mexican	1,260
Guatemalan	1,288
Honduran	1,280
Salvadoran	1,247
Dominican Republic	1,126
Mexican	1,234
Puerto Rican	858
South American	1,081
Ecuadorian	1,082

Median Household Income
(2010 Inflation-Adjusted Dollars)

Group	Dollars
Total Population	52,056
Hispanic or Latino (of any race)	51,898
Central American, ex. Mexican	58,700
Guatemalan	65,625
Honduran	51,118
Salvadoran	56,793
Dominican Republic	39,182
Mexican	68,469
Puerto Rican	32,396
South American	51,364
Ecuadorian	61,490

Per Capita Income
(2010 Inflation-Adjusted Dollars)

Group	Dollars
Total Population	23,767
Hispanic or Latino (of any race)	16,213
Central American, ex. Mexican	14,606
Guatemalan	13,940
Honduran	14,983
Salvadoran	14,255
Dominican Republic	14,268
Mexican	14,066
Puerto Rican	17,947
South American	23,157
Ecuadorian	15,176

Households with $100,000+ Income

Group	Number	%
Total Population	3,559	22.1
Hispanic or Latino (of any race)	660	15.6
Central American, ex. Mexican	271	14.8
Guatemalan	50	8.4
Honduran	163	35.5
Salvadoran	58	8.7
Dominican Republic	21	6.8
Mexican	124	29.2
Puerto Rican	92	15.7
South American	117	17.3
Ecuadorian	57	14.9

Households with Food Stamps/SNAP Benefits During Past 12 Months

Group	Number	%
Total Population	1,549	9.6
Hispanic or Latino (of any race)	535	12.6
Central American, ex. Mexican	126	6.9
Guatemalan	60	10.1
Honduran	17	3.7
Salvadoran	49	7.4
Dominican Republic	22	7.2
Mexican	55	12.9
Puerto Rican	173	29.5
South American	128	18.9
Ecuadorian	108	28.3

Poverty Rate
(Income in Past 12 Months Below Poverty Level)

Group	%
Total Population	16.8
Hispanic or Latino (of any race)	18.8
Central American, ex. Mexican	20.1
Guatemalan	21.3
Honduran	25.6
Salvadoran	14.5
Dominican Republic	23.8
Mexican	18.1
Puerto Rican	19.7

South American	14.0
Ecuadorian	16.3

Rahway

Population

Group	Number	%TP[1]	%HP[2]
Total Population	27,346	100.0	–
Hispanic or Latino (of any race)	6,433	23.5	100.0
Central American, ex. Mexican	1,081	4.0	16.8
Guatemalan	121	0.4	1.9
Honduran	149	0.5	2.3
Salvadoran	681	2.5	10.6
Cuban	345	1.3	5.4
Dominican Republic	567	2.1	8.8
Mexican	745	2.7	11.6
Puerto Rican	1,653	6.0	25.7
South American	1,572	5.7	24.4
Colombian	525	1.9	8.2
Ecuadorian	227	0.8	3.5
Peruvian	644	2.4	10.0

Population Growth: 2000–2010

Group	%
Total Population	3.2
Hispanic or Latino (of any race)	75.0
Central American, ex. Mexican	158.0
Salvadoran	171.3
Cuban	59.7
Dominican Republic	265.8
Mexican	75.7
Puerto Rican	86.4
South American	101.5
Colombian	97.4
Peruvian	122.1

Males per 100 Females

Group	Number
Total Population	91.1
Hispanic or Latino (of any race)	97.3
Central American, ex. Mexican	113.6
Guatemalan	142.0
Honduran	112.9
Salvadoran	125.5
Cuban	84.5
Dominican Republic	84.7
Mexican	123.1
Puerto Rican	94.9
South American	87.1
Colombian	72.1
Ecuadorian	116.2
Peruvian	91.1

Average Household Size

Group	People
Total Population	2.58
Hispanic or Latino (of any race)	3.52
Central American, ex. Mexican	4.25
Guatemalan	4.14
Honduran	4.24
Salvadoran	4.59
Cuban	2.65
Dominican Republic	3.91
Mexican	4.81
Puerto Rican	3.04
South American	3.41
Colombian	3.23
Ecuadorian	3.54
Peruvian	3.49

Median Age

Group	Years
Total Population	38.8
Hispanic or Latino (of any race)	30.4
Central American, ex. Mexican	30.5
Guatemalan	33.6
Honduran	30.6
Salvadoran	29.6
Cuban	35.5
Dominican Republic	30.0
Mexican	24.8
Puerto Rican	28.7
South American	37.1
Colombian	36.8

Notes: (1) Percent of total population; (2) Percent of Hispanic/Latino population; Profiles include places with an overall population of at least 125,000, OR an overall population of at least 25,000 where the Hispanic/Latino population is at least 20% of the overall population. In states where less than five places meet either of these criteria, we have included places with at least 10,000 total population with the highest percentage of Hispanic/Latino population. These places are identified with an asterisk (*); Please refer to the User's Guide for a full explanation of data.

Ecuadorian		34.9
Peruvian		38.1

High School Graduates
(Universe: Population 25 Years and Over)

Group	Number	%
Total Population	16,056	87.1
Hispanic or Latino (of any race)	2,595	76.5
Puerto Rican	681	81.8
South American	658	88.7

Four-Year College Graduates
(Universe: Population 25 Years and Over)

Group	Number	%
Total Population	3,927	21.3
Hispanic or Latino (of any race)	601	17.7
Puerto Rican	113	13.6
South American	191	25.7

Population Age 3–17 Enrolled in Public School
(Universe: Population Age 3–17 Enrolled in School)

Group	Number	%
Total Population	4,231	87.3
Hispanic or Latino (of any race)	1,172	82.8
Puerto Rican	242	85.8
South American	121	55.5

Population Age 3–17 Enrolled in Private School
(Universe: Population Age 3–17 Enrolled in School)

Group	Number	%
Total Population	615	12.7
Hispanic or Latino (of any race)	244	17.2
Puerto Rican	40	14.2
South American	97	44.5

Foreign-Born Population

Group	Number	%
Total Population	6,003	22.3
Hispanic or Latino (of any race)	2,572	43.1
Puerto Rican	20	1.4
South American	949	75.9

Foreign-Born Naturalized U.S. Citizens

Group	Number	%
Total Population	2,999	50.0
Hispanic or Latino (of any race)	805	31.3
Puerto Rican	20	100.0
South American	374	39.4

Language Spoken at Home: English Only
(Universe: Population 5 Years and Over)

Group	Number	%
Total Population	17,180	67.2
Hispanic or Latino (of any race)	739	13.4
Puerto Rican	376	28.2
South American	33	3.0

Language Spoken at Home: Spanish
(Universe: Population 5 Years and Over)

Group	Number	%
Total Population	5,313	20.8
Hispanic or Latino (of any race)	4,745	86.0
Puerto Rican	956	71.8
South American	1,055	97.0

Unemployment Rate
(Universe: Population 16 Years and Over)

Group	%
Total Population	8.5
Hispanic or Latino (of any race)	11.3
Puerto Rican	4.2
South American	20.6

Class of Worker: Private Wage and Salary
(Universe: Civilian Employed Population 16 Years and Over)

Group	Number	%
Total Population	10,516	81.0
Hispanic or Latino (of any race)	2,316	83.9
Puerto Rican	626	81.0
South American	389	63.1

Class of Worker: Government
(Universe: Civilian Employed Population 16 Years and Over)

Group	Number	%
Total Population	2,127	16.4
Hispanic or Latino (of any race)	362	13.1
Puerto Rican	139	18.0
South American	151	24.5

Means of Transportation to Work: Car, Truck or Van
(Universe: Workers 16 Years and Over)

Group	Number	%
Total Population	10,451	82.9
Hispanic or Latino (of any race)	1,977	74.4
Puerto Rican	592	81.3
South American	454	79.5

Means of Transportation to Work: Public Transportation (ex. Taxicab)
(Universe: Workers 16 Years and Over)

Group	Number	%
Total Population	1,284	10.2
Hispanic or Latino (of any race)	291	10.9
Puerto Rican	84	11.5
South American	106	18.6

Homeownership Rate
(Universe: Occupied Housing Units)

Group	%
Total Population	59.5
Hispanic or Latino (of any race)	52.9
Central American, ex. Mexican	44.2
Guatemalan	42.9
Honduran	66.7
Salvadoran	40.6
Cuban	68.9
Dominican Republic	56.4
Mexican	22.2
Puerto Rican	56.3
South American	58.6
Colombian	67.1
Ecuadorian	65.9
Peruvian	49.0

Median Home Value

Group	Dollars
Total Population	331,500
Hispanic or Latino (of any race)	344,700
Puerto Rican	333,700
South American	335,100

Median Gross Rent

Group	Dollars
Total Population	1,098
Hispanic or Latino (of any race)	1,170
Puerto Rican	998
South American	1,160

Median Household Income
(2010 Inflation-Adjusted Dollars)

Group	Dollars
Total Population	58,551
Hispanic or Latino (of any race)	57,064
Puerto Rican	98,000
South American	63,750

Per Capita Income
(2010 Inflation-Adjusted Dollars)

Group	Dollars
Total Population	28,855
Hispanic or Latino (of any race)	21,281
Puerto Rican	27,498
South American	21,049

Households with $100,000+ Income

Group	Number	%
Total Population	2,710	26.9
Hispanic or Latino (of any race)	447	26.0
Puerto Rican	211	47.3
South American	122	39.6

Households with Food Stamps/SNAP Benefits During Past 12 Months

Group	Number	%
Total Population	569	5.6
Hispanic or Latino (of any race)	33	1.9
Puerto Rican	0	0.0
South American	4	1.3

Poverty Rate
(Income in Past 12 Months Below Poverty Level)

Group	%
Total Population	8.7
Hispanic or Latino (of any race)	8.0
Puerto Rican	4.4
South American	0.6

Trenton

Population

Group	Number	%TP[1]	%HP[2]
Total Population	84,913	100.0	–
Hispanic or Latino (of any race)	28,621	33.7	100.0
Central American, ex. Mexican	11,346	13.4	39.6
Costa Rican	1,279	1.5	4.5
Guatemalan	8,691	10.2	30.4
Honduran	820	1.0	2.9
Salvadoran	414	0.5	1.4
Cuban	250	0.3	0.9
Dominican Republic	1,707	2.0	6.0
Mexican	2,337	2.8	8.2
Puerto Rican	9,746	11.5	34.1
South American	1,238	1.5	4.3
Colombian	250	0.3	0.9
Ecuadorian	802	0.9	2.8
Spaniard	110	0.1	0.4

Population Growth: 2000–2010

Group	%
Total Population	-0.6
Hispanic or Latino (of any race)	55.6
Central American, ex. Mexican	190.8
Costa Rican	60.9
Guatemalan	228.7
Honduran	443.0
Cuban	25.0
Dominican Republic	272.7
Mexican	152.6
Puerto Rican	8.9
South American	104.3
Colombian	53.4
Ecuadorian	159.5

Males per 100 Females

Group	Number
Total Population	106.5
Hispanic or Latino (of any race)	132.1
Central American, ex. Mexican	171.4
Costa Rican	165.9
Guatemalan	177.1
Honduran	155.5
Salvadoran	131.3
Cuban	121.2
Dominican Republic	101.5
Mexican	141.9
Puerto Rican	102.4
South American	120.7
Colombian	96.9
Ecuadorian	129.8
Spaniard	107.5

Average Household Size

Group	People
Total Population	2.79
Hispanic or Latino (of any race)	3.84
Central American, ex. Mexican	4.67
Costa Rican	3.92
Guatemalan	4.79
Honduran	4.94
Salvadoran	4.78
Cuban	2.84
Dominican Republic	4.00
Mexican	4.37
Puerto Rican	3.06
South American	4.20
Colombian	3.45
Ecuadorian	4.91
Spaniard	3.45

Median Age

Group	Years
Total Population	32.6

Notes: (1) Percent of total population; (2) Percent of Hispanic/Latino population; Profiles include places with an overall population of at least 125,000, OR an overall population of at least 25,000 where the Hispanic/Latino population is at least 20% of the overall population. In states where less than five places meet either of these criteria, we have included places with at least 10,000 total population with the highest percentage of Hispanic/Latino population. These places are identified with an asterisk (*); Please refer to the User's Guide for a full explanation of data.

Hispanic or Latino (of any race)		28.2
Central American, ex. Mexican		28.8
Costa Rican		31.2
Guatemalan		28.5
Honduran		27.7
Salvadoran		28.6
Cuban		35.0
Dominican Republic		28.3
Mexican		26.8
Puerto Rican		28.6
South American		31.0
Colombian		34.3
Ecuadorian		29.4
Spaniard		19.8

High School Graduates
(Universe: Population 25 Years and Over)

Group	Number	%
Total Population	37,635	69.5
Hispanic or Latino (of any race)	8,307	51.5
Central American, ex. Mexican	2,269	35.3
Guatemalan	1,768	35.6
Dominican Republic	468	59.8
Mexican	898	59.0
Puerto Rican	3,064	62.3
South American	912	70.2

Four-Year College Graduates
(Universe: Population 25 Years and Over)

Group	Number	%
Total Population	5,961	11.0
Hispanic or Latino (of any race)	958	5.9
Central American, ex. Mexican	151	2.3
Guatemalan	123	2.5
Dominican Republic	125	16.0
Mexican	87	5.7
Puerto Rican	292	5.9
South American	147	11.3

Population Age 3–17 Enrolled in Public School
(Universe: Population Age 3–17 Enrolled in School)

Group	Number	%
Total Population	14,310	88.5
Hispanic or Latino (of any race)	4,827	90.8
Central American, ex. Mexican	1,294	94.3
Guatemalan	1,119	94.2
Dominican Republic	334	100.0
Mexican	412	77.9
Puerto Rican	2,398	91.7
South American	219	90.5

Population Age 3–17 Enrolled in Private School
(Universe: Population Age 3–17 Enrolled in School)

Group	Number	%
Total Population	1,863	11.5
Hispanic or Latino (of any race)	487	9.2
Central American, ex. Mexican	78	5.7
Guatemalan	69	5.8
Dominican Republic	0	0.0
Mexican	117	22.1
Puerto Rican	216	8.3
South American	23	9.5

Foreign-Born Population

Group	Number	%
Total Population	19,887	23.3
Hispanic or Latino (of any race)	14,077	51.1
Central American, ex. Mexican	8,376	79.1
Guatemalan	6,456	76.1
Dominican Republic	911	61.6
Mexican	2,166	75.7
Puerto Rican	216	2.4
South American	1,418	73.7

Foreign-Born Naturalized U.S. Citizens

Group	Number	%
Total Population	4,449	22.4
Hispanic or Latino (of any race)	2,213	15.7
Central American, ex. Mexican	666	8.0
Guatemalan	470	7.3
Dominican Republic	371	40.7
Mexican	356	16.4
Puerto Rican	30	13.9
South American	472	33.3

Language Spoken at Home: English Only
(Universe: Population 5 Years and Over)

Group	Number	%
Total Population	50,739	64.6
Hispanic or Latino (of any race)	2,698	10.8
Central American, ex. Mexican	784	8.0
Guatemalan	593	7.7
Dominican Republic	58	4.6
Mexican	183	7.3
Puerto Rican	1,451	17.9
South American	76	4.4

Language Spoken at Home: Spanish
(Universe: Population 5 Years and Over)

Group	Number	%
Total Population	22,866	29.1
Hispanic or Latino (of any race)	21,852	87.7
Central American, ex. Mexican	9,028	92.0
Guatemalan	7,148	92.3
Dominican Republic	1,208	95.4
Mexican	2,330	92.7
Puerto Rican	6,635	81.7
South American	1,653	95.2

Unemployment Rate
(Universe: Population 16 Years and Over)

Group	%
Total Population	14.5
Hispanic or Latino (of any race)	9.4
Central American, ex. Mexican	7.7
Guatemalan	6.1
Dominican Republic	13.3
Mexican	6.3
Puerto Rican	17.0
South American	0.0

Class of Worker: Private Wage and Salary
(Universe: Civilian Employed Population 16 Years and Over)

Group	Number	%
Total Population	27,724	77.7
Hispanic or Latino (of any race)	12,266	89.3
Central American, ex. Mexican	6,233	94.3
Guatemalan	5,044	95.3
Dominican Republic	645	87.6
Mexican	1,564	95.8
Puerto Rican	2,161	74.4
South American	1,091	91.3

Class of Worker: Government
(Universe: Civilian Employed Population 16 Years and Over)

Group	Number	%
Total Population	6,842	19.2
Hispanic or Latino (of any race)	936	6.8
Central American, ex. Mexican	168	2.5
Guatemalan	108	2.0
Dominican Republic	62	8.4
Mexican	19	1.2
Puerto Rican	561	19.3
South American	50	4.2

Means of Transportation to Work: Car, Truck or Van
(Universe: Workers 16 Years and Over)

Group	Number	%
Total Population	26,128	76.6
Hispanic or Latino (of any race)	9,718	73.5
Central American, ex. Mexican	4,507	70.6
Guatemalan	3,561	68.5
Dominican Republic	486	66.9
Mexican	1,160	72.2
Puerto Rican	2,029	76.0
South American	1,063	89.7

Means of Transportation to Work: Public Transportation (ex. Taxicab)
(Universe: Workers 16 Years and Over)

Group	Number	%
Total Population	4,003	11.7
Hispanic or Latino (of any race)	1,684	12.7
Central American, ex. Mexican	894	14.0
Guatemalan	715	13.8
Dominican Republic	122	16.8
Mexican	277	17.2
Puerto Rican	142	5.3
South American	80	6.8

Homeownership Rate
(Universe: Occupied Housing Units)

Group	%
Total Population	38.3
Hispanic or Latino (of any race)	31.0
Central American, ex. Mexican	22.6
Costa Rican	22.3
Guatemalan	22.4
Honduran	19.3
Salvadoran	28.1
Cuban	34.1
Dominican Republic	46.7
Mexican	14.8
Puerto Rican	37.1
South American	46.2
Colombian	54.9
Ecuadorian	46.7
Spaniard	18.2

Median Home Value

Group	Dollars
Total Population	131,000
Hispanic or Latino (of any race)	147,100
Central American, ex. Mexican	124,900
Guatemalan	120,900
Dominican Republic	208,700
Mexican	207,400
Puerto Rican	133,100
South American	171,100

Median Gross Rent

Group	Dollars
Total Population	916
Hispanic or Latino (of any race)	1,125
Central American, ex. Mexican	1,193
Guatemalan	1,147
Dominican Republic	889
Mexican	1,304
Puerto Rican	880
South American	1,548

Median Household Income
(2010 Inflation-Adjusted Dollars)

Group	Dollars
Total Population	36,601
Hispanic or Latino (of any race)	47,099
Central American, ex. Mexican	54,382
Guatemalan	55,230
Dominican Republic	21,111
Mexican	62,684
Puerto Rican	34,583
South American	60,457

Per Capita Income
(2010 Inflation-Adjusted Dollars)

Group	Dollars
Total Population	17,400
Hispanic or Latino (of any race)	14,286
Central American, ex. Mexican	14,478
Guatemalan	14,707
Dominican Republic	14,175
Mexican	12,935
Puerto Rican	11,911
South American	16,914

Households with $100,000+ Income

Group	Number	%
Total Population	2,965	10.6
Hispanic or Latino (of any race)	717	11.7
Central American, ex. Mexican	266	12.6
Guatemalan	225	13.9
Dominican Republic	29	6.4
Mexican	71	12.8
Puerto Rican	213	9.0
South American	85	20.6

Households with Food Stamps/SNAP Benefits During Past 12 Months

Group	Number	%
Total Population	4,235	15.2
Hispanic or Latino (of any race)	1,021	16.6
Central American, ex. Mexican	147	7.0
Guatemalan	121	7.5
Dominican Republic	182	40.1
Mexican	96	17.4

Notes: (1) Percent of total population; (2) Percent of Hispanic/Latino population; Profiles include places with an overall population of at least 125,000, OR an overall population of at least 25,000 where the Hispanic/Latino population is at least 20% of the overall population. In states where less than five places meet either of these criteria, we have included places with at least 10,000 total population with the highest percentage of Hispanic/Latino population. These places are identified with an asterisk (*); Please refer to the User's Guide for a full explanation of data.

Puerto Rican	582	24.7
South American	4	1.0

Poverty Rate
(Income in Past 12 Months Below Poverty Level)

Group	%
Total Population	24.5
Hispanic or Latino (of any race)	23.8
Central American, ex. Mexican	23.6
Guatemalan	21.1
Dominican Republic	37.7
Mexican	21.4
Puerto Rican	28.9
South American	6.2

Union City

Population

Group	Number	%TP[1]	%HP[2]
Total Population	66,455	100.0	–
Hispanic or Latino (of any race)	56,291	84.7	100.0
Central American, ex. Mexican	9,159	13.8	16.3
Guatemalan	1,097	1.7	1.9
Honduran	2,533	3.8	4.5
Nicaraguan	294	0.4	0.5
Salvadoran	5,060	7.6	9.0
Cuban	7,510	11.3	13.3
Dominican Republic	10,020	15.1	17.8
Mexican	5,189	7.8	9.2
Puerto Rican	6,643	10.0	11.8
South American	13,923	21.0	24.7
Argentinean	448	0.7	0.8
Bolivian	145	0.2	0.3
Chilean	372	0.6	0.7
Colombian	3,224	4.9	5.7
Ecuadorian	6,135	9.2	10.9
Peruvian	3,111	4.7	5.5
Uruguayan	181	0.3	0.3
Venezuelan	266	0.4	0.5
Spaniard	264	0.4	0.5

Population Growth: 2000–2010

Group	%
Total Population	-0.9
Hispanic or Latino (of any race)	1.9
Central American, ex. Mexican	59.3
Guatemalan	109.0
Honduran	64.4
Nicaraguan	50.0
Salvadoran	63.3
Cuban	-27.1
Dominican Republic	30.3
Mexican	88.6
Puerto Rican	-10.1
South American	38.1
Argentinean	10.9
Chilean	5.7
Colombian	6.1
Ecuadorian	54.0
Peruvian	83.6
Uruguayan	81.0
Venezuelan	22.0
Spaniard	20.0

Males per 100 Females

Group	Number
Total Population	100.4
Hispanic or Latino (of any race)	99.5
Central American, ex. Mexican	114.3
Guatemalan	155.1
Honduran	96.5
Nicaraguan	124.4
Salvadoran	116.1
Cuban	96.9
Dominican Republic	82.6
Mexican	127.9
Puerto Rican	95.2
South American	98.5
Argentinean	111.3
Bolivian	104.2
Chilean	128.2
Colombian	84.8
Ecuadorian	98.2
Peruvian	112.2
Uruguayan	94.6
Venezuelan	78.5
Spaniard	142.2

Average Household Size

Group	People
Total Population	2.88
Hispanic or Latino (of any race)	3.09
Central American, ex. Mexican	3.79
Guatemalan	3.87
Honduran	3.55
Nicaraguan	3.12
Salvadoran	4.03
Cuban	2.22
Dominican Republic	3.30
Mexican	4.18
Puerto Rican	2.65
South American	3.16
Argentinean	2.76
Bolivian	3.59
Chilean	2.70
Colombian	2.81
Ecuadorian	3.32
Peruvian	3.45
Uruguayan	2.61
Venezuelan	3.05
Spaniard	2.35

Median Age

Group	Years
Total Population	33.9
Hispanic or Latino (of any race)	33.8
Central American, ex. Mexican	31.1
Guatemalan	30.7
Honduran	32.4
Nicaraguan	40.2
Salvadoran	30.0
Cuban	50.9
Dominican Republic	32.2
Mexican	26.4
Puerto Rican	32.5
South American	37.5
Argentinean	35.7
Bolivian	38.5
Chilean	41.0
Colombian	41.8
Ecuadorian	37.0
Peruvian	36.0
Uruguayan	37.8
Venezuelan	32.4
Spaniard	39.5

High School Graduates
(Universe: Population 25 Years and Over)

Group	Number	%
Total Population	28,441	65.9
Hispanic or Latino (of any race)	22,025	62.2
Central American, ex. Mexican	2,180	41.7
Guatemalan	320	31.8
Honduran	616	47.3
Salvadoran	1,185	42.2
Cuban	4,124	62.2
Dominican Republic	3,419	65.3
Mexican	1,741	54.8
Puerto Rican	2,810	63.3
South American	7,151	73.1
Colombian	2,079	77.3
Ecuadorian	2,705	65.1
Peruvian	1,937	83.4

Four-Year College Graduates
(Universe: Population 25 Years and Over)

Group	Number	%
Total Population	7,227	16.7
Hispanic or Latino (of any race)	4,290	12.1
Central American, ex. Mexican	331	6.3
Guatemalan	65	6.5
Honduran	62	4.8
Salvadoran	179	6.4
Cuban	1,168	17.6
Dominican Republic	656	12.5
Mexican	242	7.6
Puerto Rican	183	4.1
South American	1,561	16.0
Colombian	506	18.8
Ecuadorian	539	13.0
Peruvian	397	17.1

Population Age 3–17 Enrolled in Public School
(Universe: Population Age 3–17 Enrolled in School)

Group	Number	%
Total Population	11,487	92.8
Hispanic or Latino (of any race)	8,534	94.0
Central American, ex. Mexican	1,143	92.3
Guatemalan	123	92.5
Honduran	162	84.8
Salvadoran	858	95.4
Cuban	775	89.4
Dominican Republic	1,790	97.2
Mexican	1,146	98.3
Puerto Rican	1,259	90.5
South American	1,895	93.4
Colombian	486	91.0
Ecuadorian	840	96.9
Peruvian	434	88.0

Population Age 3–17 Enrolled in Private School
(Universe: Population Age 3–17 Enrolled in School)

Group	Number	%
Total Population	885	7.2
Hispanic or Latino (of any race)	541	6.0
Central American, ex. Mexican	96	7.7
Guatemalan	10	7.5
Honduran	29	15.2
Salvadoran	41	4.6
Cuban	92	10.6
Dominican Republic	51	2.8
Mexican	20	1.7
Puerto Rican	132	9.5
South American	134	6.6
Colombian	48	9.0
Ecuadorian	27	3.1
Peruvian	59	12.0

Foreign-Born Population

Group	Number	%
Total Population	37,519	57.0
Hispanic or Latino (of any race)	34,620	66.3
Central American, ex. Mexican	5,887	75.2
Guatemalan	1,173	90.4
Honduran	1,458	80.2
Salvadoran	3,151	69.4
Cuban	6,583	81.2
Dominican Republic	5,811	69.8
Mexican	4,288	73.8
Puerto Rican	228	3.4
South American	11,033	81.6
Colombian	2,965	80.3
Ecuadorian	4,658	81.4
Peruvian	2,690	81.3

Foreign-Born Naturalized U.S. Citizens

Group	Number	%
Total Population	14,273	38.0
Hispanic or Latino (of any race)	13,011	37.6
Central American, ex. Mexican	1,349	22.9
Guatemalan	128	10.9
Honduran	469	32.2
Salvadoran	734	23.3
Cuban	4,427	67.2
Dominican Republic	2,609	44.9
Mexican	304	7.1
Puerto Rican	136	59.6
South American	3,768	34.2
Colombian	1,097	37.0
Ecuadorian	1,744	37.4
Peruvian	643	23.9

Language Spoken at Home: English Only
(Universe: Population 5 Years and Over)

Group	Number	%
Total Population	7,795	12.8
Hispanic or Latino (of any race)	2,826	5.8
Central American, ex. Mexican	408	5.6
Guatemalan	151	11.8
Honduran	26	1.5
Salvadoran	194	4.7
Cuban	206	2.6
Dominican Republic	366	4.7

Notes: (1) Percent of total population; (2) Percent of Hispanic/Latino population; Profiles include places with an overall population of at least 125,000, OR an overall population of at least 25,000 where the Hispanic/Latino population is at least 20% of the overall population. In states where less than five places meet either of these criteria, we have included places with at least 10,000 total population with the highest percentage of Hispanic/Latino population. These places are identified with an asterisk (*); Please refer to the User's Guide for a full explanation of data.

Group	Number	%
Mexican	336	6.6
Puerto Rican	784	12.7
South American	557	4.3
Colombian	247	6.9
Ecuadorian	136	2.5
Peruvian	165	5.3

Language Spoken at Home: Spanish
(Universe: Population 5 Years and Over)

Group	Number	%
Total Population	50,055	82.1
Hispanic or Latino (of any race)	45,821	93.8
Central American, ex. Mexican	6,850	94.4
Guatemalan	1,132	88.2
Honduran	1,684	98.5
Salvadoran	3,901	95.3
Cuban	7,688	97.0
Dominican Republic	7,471	95.3
Mexican	4,715	93.1
Puerto Rican	5,334	86.3
South American	12,326	95.3
Colombian	3,299	92.7
Ecuadorian	5,321	97.5
Peruvian	2,950	94.7

Unemployment Rate
(Universe: Population 16 Years and Over)

Group	%
Total Population	10.4
Hispanic or Latino (of any race)	10.6
Central American, ex. Mexican	11.2
Guatemalan	9.5
Honduran	8.8
Salvadoran	13.3
Cuban	6.2
Dominican Republic	9.4
Mexican	10.1
Puerto Rican	16.7
South American	10.3
Colombian	12.4
Ecuadorian	12.0
Peruvian	7.5

Class of Worker: Private Wage and Salary
(Universe: Civilian Employed Population 16 Years and Over)

Group	Number	%
Total Population	28,076	87.3
Hispanic or Latino (of any race)	23,505	88.7
Central American, ex. Mexican	4,310	93.7
Guatemalan	935	97.8
Honduran	1,021	90.0
Salvadoran	2,264	93.9
Cuban	2,869	78.6
Dominican Republic	3,659	87.1
Mexican	2,700	94.8
Puerto Rican	2,322	85.6
South American	7,056	90.9
Colombian	1,854	94.4
Ecuadorian	2,708	89.3
Peruvian	2,081	93.0

Class of Worker: Government
(Universe: Civilian Employed Population 16 Years and Over)

Group	Number	%
Total Population	2,801	8.7
Hispanic or Latino (of any race)	2,015	7.6
Central American, ex. Mexican	149	3.2
Guatemalan	0	0.0
Honduran	53	4.7
Salvadoran	96	4.0
Cuban	681	18.7
Dominican Republic	306	7.3
Mexican	9	0.3
Puerto Rican	337	12.4
South American	446	5.7
Colombian	65	3.3
Ecuadorian	217	7.2
Peruvian	89	4.0

Means of Transportation to Work: Car, Truck or Van
(Universe: Workers 16 Years and Over)

Group	Number	%
Total Population	13,747	43.7
Hispanic or Latino (of any race)	11,515	44.4
Central American, ex. Mexican	2,128	46.9
Guatemalan	360	37.7
Honduran	564	49.7
Salvadoran	1,148	48.8
Cuban	1,770	50.2
Dominican Republic	2,019	48.7
Mexican	734	25.9
Puerto Rican	1,263	48.3
South American	3,261	43.1
Colombian	848	44.7
Ecuadorian	1,198	40.1
Peruvian	925	42.9

Means of Transportation to Work: Public Transportation (ex. Taxicab)
(Universe: Workers 16 Years and Over)

Group	Number	%
Total Population	12,241	38.9
Hispanic or Latino (of any race)	9,802	37.8
Central American, ex. Mexican	1,702	37.5
Guatemalan	507	53.0
Honduran	367	32.3
Salvadoran	787	33.4
Cuban	844	23.9
Dominican Republic	1,435	34.6
Mexican	1,286	45.5
Puerto Rican	984	37.6
South American	3,302	43.7
Colombian	735	38.8
Ecuadorian	1,450	48.6
Peruvian	967	44.9

Homeownership Rate
(Universe: Occupied Housing Units)

Group	%
Total Population	20.1
Hispanic or Latino (of any race)	15.0
Central American, ex. Mexican	10.4
Guatemalan	7.1
Honduran	9.2
Nicaraguan	12.9
Salvadoran	11.3
Cuban	22.7
Dominican Republic	11.8
Mexican	7.1
Puerto Rican	11.6
South American	17.4
Argentinean	22.1
Bolivian	37.0
Chilean	19.9
Colombian	17.4
Ecuadorian	19.1
Peruvian	11.9
Uruguayan	14.5
Venezuelan	15.3
Spaniard	28.4

Median Home Value

Group	Dollars
Total Population	380,700
Hispanic or Latino (of any race)	400,900
Central American, ex. Mexican	431,600
Guatemalan	0
Honduran	428,800
Salvadoran	445,300
Cuban	398,800
Dominican Republic	395,700
Mexican	459,100
Puerto Rican	250,000
South American	425,200
Colombian	415,100
Ecuadorian	479,000
Peruvian	352,700

Median Gross Rent

Group	Dollars
Total Population	973
Hispanic or Latino (of any race)	970
Central American, ex. Mexican	1,037
Guatemalan	1,219
Honduran	920
Salvadoran	1,071
Cuban	875
Dominican Republic	947
Mexican	1,227
Puerto Rican	939
South American	984
Colombian	912
Ecuadorian	972
Peruvian	1,073

Median Household Income
(2010 Inflation-Adjusted Dollars)

Group	Dollars
Total Population	40,173
Hispanic or Latino (of any race)	36,737
Central American, ex. Mexican	40,290
Guatemalan	68,929
Honduran	30,717
Salvadoran	41,703
Cuban	30,804
Dominican Republic	32,540
Mexican	43,448
Puerto Rican	30,880
South American	41,529
Colombian	35,978
Ecuadorian	38,719
Peruvian	44,306

Per Capita Income
(2010 Inflation-Adjusted Dollars)

Group	Dollars
Total Population	18,506
Hispanic or Latino (of any race)	17,098
Central American, ex. Mexican	16,240
Guatemalan	23,474
Honduran	14,320
Salvadoran	14,537
Cuban	20,325
Dominican Republic	15,896
Mexican	13,414
Puerto Rican	14,865
South American	19,222
Colombian	18,629
Ecuadorian	17,834
Peruvian	19,994

Households with $100,000+ Income

Group	Number	%
Total Population	2,501	11.3
Hispanic or Latino (of any race)	1,604	9.2
Central American, ex. Mexican	217	9.5
Guatemalan	86	28.1
Honduran	29	3.7
Salvadoran	90	8.0
Cuban	225	6.4
Dominican Republic	262	9.8
Mexican	145	11.4
Puerto Rican	102	4.2
South American	603	12.7
Colombian	163	13.6
Ecuadorian	161	7.7
Peruvian	179	16.3

Households with Food Stamps/SNAP Benefits During Past 12 Months

Group	Number	%
Total Population	3,160	14.3
Hispanic or Latino (of any race)	2,945	17.0
Central American, ex. Mexican	315	13.8
Guatemalan	0	0.0
Honduran	101	13.0
Salvadoran	188	16.7
Cuban	611	17.5
Dominican Republic	728	27.2
Mexican	198	15.6
Puerto Rican	498	20.5
South American	582	12.2
Colombian	163	13.6
Ecuadorian	303	14.5
Peruvian	116	10.6

Poverty Rate
(Income in Past 12 Months Below Poverty Level)

Group	%
Total Population	20.0
Hispanic or Latino (of any race)	20.3
Central American, ex. Mexican	20.7
Guatemalan	14.0
Honduran	24.6

Notes: (1) Percent of total population; (2) Percent of Hispanic/Latino population; Profiles include places with an overall population of at least 125,000, OR an overall population of at least 25,000 where the Hispanic/Latino population is at least 20% of the overall population. In states where less than five places meet either of these criteria, we have included places with at least 10,000 total population with the highest percentage of Hispanic/Latino population. These places are identified with an asterisk (*); Please refer to the User's Guide for a full explanation of data.

Salvadoran	21.7
Cuban	14.4
Dominican Republic	27.5
Mexican	28.4
Puerto Rican	25.0
South American	15.2
Colombian	18.5
Ecuadorian	17.5
Peruvian	9.5

Vineland

Population

Group	Number	%TP[1]	%HP[2]
Total Population	60,724	100.0	–
Hispanic or Latino (of any race)	23,093	38.0	100.0
Central American, ex. Mexican	407	0.7	1.8
Guatemalan	126	0.2	0.5
Salvadoran	124	0.2	0.5
Cuban	200	0.3	0.9
Dominican Republic	819	1.3	3.5
Mexican	4,383	7.2	19.0
Puerto Rican	16,236	26.7	70.3
South American	402	0.7	1.7
Colombian	170	0.3	0.7

Population Growth: 2000–2010

Group	%
Total Population	7.9
Hispanic or Latino (of any race)	36.8
Central American, ex. Mexican	169.5
Cuban	-13.8
Dominican Republic	189.4
Mexican	221.1
Puerto Rican	22.2
South American	120.9
Colombian	57.4

Males per 100 Females

Group	Number
Total Population	92.4
Hispanic or Latino (of any race)	100.5
Central American, ex. Mexican	107.7
Guatemalan	147.1
Salvadoran	106.7
Cuban	98.0
Dominican Republic	86.1
Mexican	126.7
Puerto Rican	95.7
South American	74.8
Colombian	75.3

Average Household Size

Group	People
Total Population	2.76
Hispanic or Latino (of any race)	3.35
Central American, ex. Mexican	3.96
Guatemalan	4.69
Salvadoran	4.29
Cuban	2.59
Dominican Republic	3.74
Mexican	5.14
Puerto Rican	3.07
South American	3.14
Colombian	3.20

Median Age

Group	Years
Total Population	37.7
Hispanic or Latino (of any race)	28.3
Central American, ex. Mexican	28.6
Guatemalan	28.0
Salvadoran	28.2
Cuban	38.5
Dominican Republic	28.8
Mexican	24.0
Puerto Rican	30.2
South American	35.9
Colombian	39.0

High School Graduates
(Universe: Population 25 Years and Over)

Group	Number	%
Total Population	30,337	77.9
Hispanic or Latino (of any race)	6,713	59.4
Mexican	644	40.4
Puerto Rican	4,660	60.7
South American	611	75.9

Four-Year College Graduates
(Universe: Population 25 Years and Over)

Group	Number	%
Total Population	6,086	15.6
Hispanic or Latino (of any race)	731	6.5
Mexican	28	1.8
Puerto Rican	355	4.6
South American	126	15.7

Population Age 3–17 Enrolled in Public School
(Universe: Population Age 3–17 Enrolled in School)

Group	Number	%
Total Population	10,318	88.4
Hispanic or Latino (of any race)	5,017	98.1
Mexican	918	100.0
Puerto Rican	3,572	98.1
South American	80	100.0

Population Age 3–17 Enrolled in Private School
(Universe: Population Age 3–17 Enrolled in School)

Group	Number	%
Total Population	1,352	11.6
Hispanic or Latino (of any race)	99	1.9
Mexican	0	0.0
Puerto Rican	71	1.9
South American	0	0.0

Foreign-Born Population

Group	Number	%
Total Population	7,240	12.1
Hispanic or Latino (of any race)	4,202	19.9
Mexican	2,317	67.4
Puerto Rican	17	0.1
South American	850	75.6

Foreign-Born Naturalized U.S. Citizens

Group	Number	%
Total Population	2,886	39.9
Hispanic or Latino (of any race)	975	23.2
Mexican	111	4.8
Puerto Rican	11	64.7
South American	335	39.4

Language Spoken at Home: English Only
(Universe: Population 5 Years and Over)

Group	Number	%
Total Population	37,364	67.3
Hispanic or Latino (of any race)	3,954	20.9
Mexican	154	5.2
Puerto Rican	3,271	25.4
South American	102	10.3

Language Spoken at Home: Spanish
(Universe: Population 5 Years and Over)

Group	Number	%
Total Population	15,446	27.8
Hispanic or Latino (of any race)	14,925	78.9
Mexican	2,827	94.8
Puerto Rican	9,617	74.6
South American	892	89.7

Unemployment Rate
(Universe: Population 16 Years and Over)

Group	%
Total Population	9.7
Hispanic or Latino (of any race)	11.1
Mexican	14.7
Puerto Rican	11.5
South American	7.3

Class of Worker: Private Wage and Salary
(Universe: Civilian Employed Population 16 Years and Over)

Group	Number	%
Total Population	20,748	74.1
Hispanic or Latino (of any race)	7,253	80.5
Mexican	1,436	95.9
Puerto Rican	4,450	75.4
South American	585	92.7

Class of Worker: Government
(Universe: Civilian Employed Population 16 Years and Over)

Group	Number	%
Total Population	6,393	22.8
Hispanic or Latino (of any race)	1,603	17.8
Mexican	32	2.1
Puerto Rican	1,374	23.3
South American	33	5.2

Means of Transportation to Work: Car, Truck or Van
(Universe: Workers 16 Years and Over)

Group	Number	%
Total Population	25,163	93.4
Hispanic or Latino (of any race)	7,968	91.3
Mexican	1,348	91.3
Puerto Rican	5,142	91.1
South American	563	89.2

Means of Transportation to Work: Public Transportation (ex. Taxicab)
(Universe: Workers 16 Years and Over)

Group	Number	%
Total Population	404	1.5
Hispanic or Latino (of any race)	236	2.7
Mexican	66	4.5
Puerto Rican	113	2.0
South American	23	3.6

Homeownership Rate
(Universe: Occupied Housing Units)

Group	%
Total Population	68.0
Hispanic or Latino (of any race)	47.4
Central American, ex. Mexican	52.9
Guatemalan	46.2
Salvadoran	48.4
Cuban	63.0
Dominican Republic	51.5
Mexican	25.1
Puerto Rican	49.5
South American	71.1
Colombian	72.0

Median Home Value

Group	Dollars
Total Population	184,400
Hispanic or Latino (of any race)	168,400
Mexican	168,800
Puerto Rican	162,200
South American	204,400

Median Gross Rent

Group	Dollars
Total Population	901
Hispanic or Latino (of any race)	876
Mexican	1,056
Puerto Rican	820
South American	944

Median Household Income
(2010 Inflation-Adjusted Dollars)

Group	Dollars
Total Population	54,024
Hispanic or Latino (of any race)	48,713
Mexican	51,596
Puerto Rican	47,696
South American	50,638

Per Capita Income
(2010 Inflation-Adjusted Dollars)

Group	Dollars
Total Population	24,512
Hispanic or Latino (of any race)	16,848
Mexican	11,257
Puerto Rican	17,174
South American	16,023

Households with $100,000+ Income

Group	Number	%
Total Population	4,381	21.1
Hispanic or Latino (of any race)	813	14.4
Mexican	64	9.8
Puerto Rican	548	13.8
South American	25	6.8

Notes: (1) Percent of total population; (2) Percent of Hispanic/Latino population; Profiles include places with an overall population of at least 125,000, OR an overall population of at least 25,000 where the Hispanic/Latino population is at least 20% of the overall population. In states where less than five places meet either of these criteria, we have included places with at least 10,000 total population with the highest percentage of Hispanic/Latino population. These places are identified with an asterisk (*); Please refer to the User's Guide for a full explanation of data.

Households with Food Stamps/SNAP Benefits During Past 12 Months

Group	Number	%
Total Population	2,114	10.2
Hispanic or Latino (of any race)	1,082	19.2
Mexican	143	21.8
Puerto Rican	855	21.5
South American	34	9.3

Poverty Rate
(Income in Past 12 Months Below Poverty Level)

Group	%
Total Population	12.8
Hispanic or Latino (of any race)	19.0
Mexican	29.6
Puerto Rican	17.0
South American	19.9

West New York

Population

Group	Number	%TP[1]	%HP[2]
Total Population	49,708	100.0	–
Hispanic or Latino (of any race)	38,812	78.1	100.0
Central American, ex. Mexican	7,421	14.9	19.1
Costa Rican	114	0.2	0.3
Guatemalan	1,594	3.2	4.1
Honduran	970	2.0	2.5
Nicaraguan	182	0.4	0.5
Salvadoran	4,504	9.1	11.6
Cuban	7,514	15.1	19.4
Dominican Republic	4,935	9.9	12.7
Mexican	4,944	9.9	12.7
Puerto Rican	2,849	5.7	7.3
South American	8,700	17.5	22.4
Argentinean	312	0.6	0.8
Chilean	279	0.6	0.7
Colombian	3,077	6.2	7.9
Ecuadorian	3,348	6.7	8.6
Peruvian	1,205	2.4	3.1
Uruguayan	127	0.3	0.3
Venezuelan	243	0.5	0.6
Spaniard	216	0.4	0.6

Population Growth: 2000–2010

Group	%
Total Population	8.6
Hispanic or Latino (of any race)	7.7
Central American, ex. Mexican	86.6
Guatemalan	337.9
Honduran	79.0
Nicaraguan	61.1
Salvadoran	80.8
Cuban	-16.4
Dominican Republic	28.3
Mexican	65.8
Puerto Rican	2.1
South American	39.5
Argentinean	74.3
Chilean	42.3
Colombian	15.5
Ecuadorian	64.5
Peruvian	56.3
Venezuelan	64.2
Spaniard	57.7

Males per 100 Females

Group	Number
Total Population	98.4
Hispanic or Latino (of any race)	98.1
Central American, ex. Mexican	124.0
Costa Rican	93.2
Guatemalan	224.0
Honduran	102.1
Nicaraguan	93.6
Salvadoran	109.0
Cuban	85.7
Dominican Republic	82.0
Mexican	122.2
Puerto Rican	88.2
South American	89.3
Argentinean	106.6
Chilean	103.6
Colombian	82.6
Ecuadorian	91.0
Peruvian	102.9
Uruguayan	71.6
Venezuelan	64.2
Spaniard	96.4

Average Household Size

Group	People
Total Population	2.64
Hispanic or Latino (of any race)	2.94
Central American, ex. Mexican	3.85
Costa Rican	2.95
Guatemalan	4.19
Honduran	3.54
Nicaraguan	3.05
Salvadoran	3.92
Cuban	2.12
Dominican Republic	3.14
Mexican	4.28
Puerto Rican	2.38
South American	2.93
Argentinean	2.23
Chilean	2.77
Colombian	2.71
Ecuadorian	3.23
Peruvian	3.13
Uruguayan	2.27
Venezuelan	2.73
Spaniard	2.26

Median Age

Group	Years
Total Population	34.8
Hispanic or Latino (of any race)	34.6
Central American, ex. Mexican	30.6
Costa Rican	40.5
Guatemalan	28.3
Honduran	31.4
Nicaraguan	39.3
Salvadoran	31.0
Cuban	53.8
Dominican Republic	33.8
Mexican	26.2
Puerto Rican	35.0
South American	38.9
Argentinean	36.6
Chilean	40.9
Colombian	42.1
Ecuadorian	37.0
Peruvian	38.8
Uruguayan	40.5
Venezuelan	32.7
Spaniard	43.5

High School Graduates
(Universe: Population 25 Years and Over)

Group	Number	%
Total Population	22,360	68.3
Hispanic or Latino (of any race)	15,402	61.1
Central American, ex. Mexican	1,929	43.5
Guatemalan	382	37.1
Salvadoran	1,009	43.1
Cuban	4,036	62.3
Dominican Republic	2,127	62.3
Mexican	1,237	49.7
Puerto Rican	1,422	70.0
South American	4,316	73.6
Colombian	1,465	71.5
Ecuadorian	1,754	74.5
Peruvian	530	75.1

Four-Year College Graduates
(Universe: Population 25 Years and Over)

Group	Number	%
Total Population	8,138	24.8
Hispanic or Latino (of any race)	3,859	15.3
Central American, ex. Mexican	296	6.7
Guatemalan	61	5.9
Salvadoran	76	3.2
Cuban	1,410	21.8
Dominican Republic	463	13.6
Mexican	197	7.9
Puerto Rican	180	8.9
South American	1,265	21.6
Colombian	312	15.2
Ecuadorian	483	20.5
Peruvian	245	34.7

Population Age 3–17 Enrolled in Public School
(Universe: Population Age 3–17 Enrolled in School)

Group	Number	%
Total Population	6,981	90.8
Hispanic or Latino (of any race)	5,928	92.0
Central American, ex. Mexican	1,170	98.9
Guatemalan	59	100.0
Salvadoran	853	98.5
Cuban	795	90.0
Dominican Republic	814	77.7
Mexican	942	100.0
Puerto Rican	607	95.9
South American	1,303	90.2
Colombian	266	84.2
Ecuadorian	707	91.0
Peruvian	153	100.0

Population Age 3–17 Enrolled in Private School
(Universe: Population Age 3–17 Enrolled in School)

Group	Number	%
Total Population	709	9.2
Hispanic or Latino (of any race)	517	8.0
Central American, ex. Mexican	13	1.1
Guatemalan	0	0.0
Salvadoran	13	1.5
Cuban	88	10.0
Dominican Republic	234	22.3
Mexican	0	0.0
Puerto Rican	26	4.1
South American	141	9.8
Colombian	50	15.8
Ecuadorian	70	9.0
Peruvian	0	0.0

Foreign-Born Population

Group	Number	%
Total Population	29,396	60.7
Hispanic or Latino (of any race)	25,474	66.2
Central American, ex. Mexican	5,226	72.7
Guatemalan	1,393	89.3
Salvadoran	2,614	63.8
Cuban	6,556	81.0
Dominican Republic	3,726	66.2
Mexican	3,138	68.6
Puerto Rican	91	2.8
South American	6,358	72.4
Colombian	2,132	70.2
Ecuadorian	2,620	69.8
Peruvian	756	80.0

Foreign-Born Naturalized U.S. Citizens

Group	Number	%
Total Population	11,374	38.7
Hispanic or Latino (of any race)	9,993	39.2
Central American, ex. Mexican	979	18.7
Guatemalan	45	3.2
Salvadoran	654	25.0
Cuban	4,477	68.3
Dominican Republic	1,781	47.8
Mexican	232	7.4
Puerto Rican	62	68.1
South American	2,229	35.1
Colombian	764	35.8
Ecuadorian	906	34.6
Peruvian	305	40.3

Language Spoken at Home: English Only
(Universe: Population 5 Years and Over)

Group	Number	%
Total Population	7,449	16.7
Hispanic or Latino (of any race)	3,013	8.5
Central American, ex. Mexican	766	11.5
Guatemalan	256	16.6
Salvadoran	146	4.0
Cuban	400	5.1
Dominican Republic	463	9.1
Mexican	201	5.2
Puerto Rican	508	17.3
South American	624	7.6
Colombian	129	4.6
Ecuadorian	431	12.4

Notes: (1) Percent of total population; (2) Percent of Hispanic/Latino population; Profiles include places with an overall population of at least 125,000, OR an overall population of at least 25,000 where the Hispanic/Latino population is at least 20% of the overall population. In states where less than five places meet either of these criteria, we have included places with at least 10,000 total population with the highest percentage of Hispanic/Latino population. These places are identified with an asterisk (*); Please refer to the User's Guide for a full explanation of data.

Group	Number	%
Peruvian	21	2.4

Language Spoken at Home: Spanish
(Universe: Population 5 Years and Over)

Group	Number	%
Total Population	33,362	74.7
Hispanic or Latino (of any race)	32,315	91.3
Central American, ex. Mexican	5,895	88.5
Guatemalan	1,282	83.4
Salvadoran	3,472	96.0
Cuban	7,381	94.9
Dominican Republic	4,652	90.9
Mexican	3,680	94.8
Puerto Rican	2,402	81.9
South American	7,542	92.0
Colombian	2,672	94.3
Ecuadorian	3,039	87.6
Peruvian	865	97.6

Unemployment Rate
(Universe: Population 16 Years and Over)

Group	%
Total Population	10.3
Hispanic or Latino (of any race)	11.1
Central American, ex. Mexican	11.7
Guatemalan	5.5
Salvadoran	12.5
Cuban	14.5
Dominican Republic	11.2
Mexican	6.6
Puerto Rican	13.4
South American	9.2
Colombian	12.4
Ecuadorian	6.7
Peruvian	9.8

Class of Worker: Private Wage and Salary
(Universe: Civilian Employed Population 16 Years and Over)

Group	Number	%
Total Population	21,210	86.3
Hispanic or Latino (of any race)	16,272	86.0
Central American, ex. Mexican	4,018	93.7
Guatemalan	1,283	99.1
Salvadoran	1,952	90.6
Cuban	2,292	74.4
Dominican Republic	2,422	84.8
Mexican	2,139	91.1
Puerto Rican	1,119	78.4
South American	4,074	87.4
Colombian	1,175	78.6
Ecuadorian	1,970	93.3
Peruvian	498	98.4

Class of Worker: Government
(Universe: Civilian Employed Population 16 Years and Over)

Group	Number	%
Total Population	2,209	9.0
Hispanic or Latino (of any race)	1,803	9.5
Central American, ex. Mexican	108	2.5
Guatemalan	8	0.6
Salvadoran	97	4.5
Cuban	624	20.2
Dominican Republic	313	11.0
Mexican	80	3.4
Puerto Rican	255	17.9
South American	405	8.7
Colombian	244	16.3
Ecuadorian	93	4.4
Peruvian	8	1.6

Means of Transportation to Work: Car, Truck or Van
(Universe: Workers 16 Years and Over)

Group	Number	%
Total Population	10,810	44.9
Hispanic or Latino (of any race)	8,531	46.1
Central American, ex. Mexican	1,862	44.8
Guatemalan	629	48.6
Salvadoran	895	44.0
Cuban	1,810	60.1
Dominican Republic	1,642	58.1
Mexican	441	19.1
Puerto Rican	575	42.4
South American	2,101	45.7
Colombian	697	46.7
Ecuadorian	993	48.5
Peruvian	248	49.0

Means of Transportation to Work: Public Transportation (ex. Taxicab)
(Universe: Workers 16 Years and Over)

Group	Number	%
Total Population	9,513	39.5
Hispanic or Latino (of any race)	6,717	36.3
Central American, ex. Mexican	1,683	40.5
Guatemalan	612	47.3
Salvadoran	720	35.4
Cuban	513	17.0
Dominican Republic	802	28.4
Mexican	1,403	60.9
Puerto Rican	585	43.1
South American	1,610	35.0
Colombian	442	29.6
Ecuadorian	767	37.5
Peruvian	188	37.2

Homeownership Rate
(Universe: Occupied Housing Units)

Group	%
Total Population	21.3
Hispanic or Latino (of any race)	14.1
Central American, ex. Mexican	9.6
Costa Rican	9.3
Guatemalan	6.2
Honduran	5.4
Nicaraguan	16.4
Salvadoran	11.3
Cuban	17.8
Dominican Republic	10.6
Mexican	6.8
Puerto Rican	15.2
South American	15.9
Argentinean	17.2
Chilean	13.5
Colombian	13.4
Ecuadorian	18.4
Peruvian	16.8
Uruguayan	13.3
Venezuelan	12.1
Spaniard	39.6

Median Home Value

Group	Dollars
Total Population	391,200
Hispanic or Latino (of any race)	398,100
Central American, ex. Mexican	470,700
Guatemalan	–
Salvadoran	464,100
Cuban	376,100
Dominican Republic	357,700
Mexican	337,500
Puerto Rican	259,600
South American	468,000
Colombian	246,800
Ecuadorian	484,000
Peruvian	448,400

Median Gross Rent

Group	Dollars
Total Population	1,015
Hispanic or Latino (of any race)	963
Central American, ex. Mexican	1,051
Guatemalan	1,209
Salvadoran	1,038
Cuban	806
Dominican Republic	998
Mexican	1,180
Puerto Rican	1,036
South American	937
Colombian	952
Ecuadorian	951
Peruvian	740

Median Household Income
(2010 Inflation-Adjusted Dollars)

Group	Dollars
Total Population	44,657
Hispanic or Latino (of any race)	36,494
Central American, ex. Mexican	43,390
Guatemalan	56,490
Salvadoran	43,533
Cuban	32,302
Dominican Republic	37,872
Mexican	32,170
Puerto Rican	35,840
South American	41,353
Colombian	35,762
Ecuadorian	48,376
Peruvian	34,118

Per Capita Income
(2010 Inflation-Adjusted Dollars)

Group	Dollars
Total Population	24,419
Hispanic or Latino (of any race)	17,551
Central American, ex. Mexican	16,179
Guatemalan	19,278
Salvadoran	14,765
Cuban	21,842
Dominican Republic	15,149
Mexican	13,173
Puerto Rican	20,609
South American	17,931
Colombian	16,263
Ecuadorian	19,093
Peruvian	13,995

Households with $100,000+ Income

Group	Number	%
Total Population	2,910	16.5
Hispanic or Latino (of any race)	1,136	8.8
Central American, ex. Mexican	171	8.4
Guatemalan	112	27.8
Salvadoran	59	5.7
Cuban	228	6.2
Dominican Republic	89	5.2
Mexican	88	8.6
Puerto Rican	272	21.1
South American	256	8.8
Colombian	21	2.1
Ecuadorian	130	11.4
Peruvian	10	2.6

Households with Food Stamps/SNAP Benefits During Past 12 Months

Group	Number	%
Total Population	2,394	13.5
Hispanic or Latino (of any race)	2,285	17.7
Central American, ex. Mexican	241	11.9
Guatemalan	53	13.2
Salvadoran	153	14.9
Cuban	873	23.6
Dominican Republic	391	22.7
Mexican	172	16.8
Puerto Rican	160	12.4
South American	416	14.3
Colombian	95	9.6
Ecuadorian	121	10.6
Peruvian	116	29.7

Poverty Rate
(Income in Past 12 Months Below Poverty Level)

Group	%
Total Population	18.1
Hispanic or Latino (of any race)	19.6
Central American, ex. Mexican	18.8
Guatemalan	13.8
Salvadoran	19.1
Cuban	18.3
Dominican Republic	14.7
Mexican	29.2
Puerto Rican	22.0
South American	16.6
Colombian	19.3
Ecuadorian	8.9
Peruvian	28.0

Notes: (1) Percent of total population; (2) Percent of Hispanic/Latino population; Profiles include places with an overall population of at least 125,000, OR an overall population of at least 25,000 where the Hispanic/Latino population is at least 20% of the overall population. In states where less than five places meet either of these criteria, we have included places with at least 10,000 total population with the highest percentage of Hispanic/Latino population. These places are identified with an asterisk (*); Please refer to the User's Guide for a full explanation of data.

New Mexico

EDITOR'S NOTE: For a place to be included in this edition, it must meet one of two criteria. Either its overall population is at least 125,000, OR its overall population is at least 25,000 and its Hispanic/Latino population is at least 20% of the overall population. For the state of New Mexico, the following locations are included:

- Alamogordo
- Albuquerque
- Carlsbad
- Clovis
- Farmington
- Hobbs
- Las Cruces
- Rio Rancho
- Roswell
- Santa Fe
- South Valley

Section Two: State & Place Profiles starts with the state profile, followed by place profiles that meet the criteria above. Places are listed alphabetically within each state. All states, all counties and places that meet the above criteria are ranked and compared in *Section Three: Rankings & Comparisons*, on page 1055.

For a more detailed look at the Hispanic/Latino population in New Mexico, a companion web site is available at no additional charge with purchase of this print edition. Visit http://gold.greyhouse.com/page/info_hispanic for more information.

The web site includes data for all counties and places in New Mexico with Hispanic/Latino population, plus ten additional topics: Self Employed Worker; Walked to Work; Worked from Home; Mean Travel Time to Work; Mean Household Income; Households with Cash Public Assistance; Mean Cash Pubic Assistance; Poverty Rates for 18 and Under, 18 to 64, and 65 and Over.

Population

Group	Number	%TP[1]	%HP[2]
Total Population	2,059,179	100.0	–
Hispanic or Latino (of any race)	953,403	46.3	100.0
Central American, ex. Mexican	6,621	0.3	0.7
Costa Rican	342	<0.1	<0.1
Guatemalan	2,386	0.1	0.3
Honduran	657	<0.1	0.1
Nicaraguan	493	<0.1	0.1
Panamanian	625	<0.1	0.1
Salvadoran	2,051	0.1	0.2
Cuban	4,298	0.2	0.5
Dominican Republic	492	<0.1	0.1
Mexican	590,890	28.7	62.0
Puerto Rican	7,964	0.4	0.8
South American	4,841	0.2	0.5
Argentinean	653	<0.1	0.1
Bolivian	229	<0.1	<0.1
Chilean	569	<0.1	0.1
Colombian	1,347	0.1	0.1
Ecuadorian	548	<0.1	0.1
Peruvian	913	<0.1	0.1
Venezuelan	394	<0.1	<0.1
Spaniard	65,045	3.2	6.8

Population Growth: 2000–2010

Group	%
Total Population	13.2
Hispanic or Latino (of any race)	24.6
Central American, ex. Mexican	185.6
Costa Rican	140.8
Guatemalan	239.4
Honduran	185.7
Nicaraguan	132.5
Panamanian	66.7
Salvadoran	299.0
Cuban	66.1
Dominican Republic	234.7
Mexican	79.0
Puerto Rican	77.5
South American	151.9
Argentinean	281.9
Bolivian	129.0
Chilean	125.8
Colombian	144.9
Ecuadorian	179.6
Peruvian	176.7
Venezuelan	171.7
Spaniard	3,178.5

Males per 100 Females

Group	Number
Total Population	97.7
Hispanic or Latino (of any race)	98.4
Central American, ex. Mexican	104.4
Costa Rican	80.0
Guatemalan	123.0
Honduran	99.1
Nicaraguan	94.9
Panamanian	56.6
Salvadoran	112.1
Cuban	111.3
Dominican Republic	100.0
Mexican	100.7
Puerto Rican	106.1
South American	83.0
Argentinean	96.7
Bolivian	72.2
Chilean	86.6
Colombian	71.4
Ecuadorian	88.3
Peruvian	85.6
Venezuelan	91.3
Spaniard	89.9

Average Household Size

Group	People
Total Population	2.55
Hispanic or Latino (of any race)	2.87
Central American, ex. Mexican	3.32
Costa Rican	2.60
Guatemalan	3.75
Honduran	3.16
Nicaraguan	2.80
Panamanian	2.44
Salvadoran	3.41
Cuban	2.57
Dominican Republic	2.83
Mexican	3.08
Puerto Rican	2.65
South American	2.51
Argentinean	2.52
Bolivian	2.24
Chilean	2.37
Colombian	2.51
Ecuadorian	2.59
Peruvian	2.62
Venezuelan	2.61
Spaniard	2.59

Median Age

Group	Years
Total Population	36.7
Hispanic or Latino (of any race)	29.8
Central American, ex. Mexican	31.4
Costa Rican	34.8
Guatemalan	30.6
Honduran	30.9
Nicaraguan	32.6
Panamanian	36.3
Salvadoran	31.0
Cuban	35.2
Dominican Republic	28.6
Mexican	28.1
Puerto Rican	28.8
South American	34.9
Argentinean	37.8
Bolivian	38.6
Chilean	36.1
Colombian	34.4
Ecuadorian	34.5
Peruvian	33.3
Venezuelan	34.0
Spaniard	35.8

High School Graduates

(Universe: Population 25 Years and Over)

Group	Number	%
Total Population	1,072,474	82.7
Hispanic or Latino (of any race)	364,439	70.4
Central American, ex. Mexican	2,696	66.7
Guatemalan	1,128	64.6
Panamanian	344	81.9
Salvadoran	595	53.5
Cuban	1,632	75.1
Mexican	176,406	62.4
Puerto Rican	3,696	85.5
South American	2,841	95.0
Colombian	671	87.6
Peruvian	705	100.0
Spaniard	26,977	85.4

Four-Year College Graduates

(Universe: Population 25 Years and Over)

Group	Number	%
Total Population	330,033	25.5
Hispanic or Latino (of any race)	66,753	12.9
Central American, ex. Mexican	776	19.2
Guatemalan	272	15.6
Panamanian	104	24.8
Salvadoran	142	12.8
Cuban	576	26.5
Mexican	32,193	11.4
Puerto Rican	1,215	28.1
South American	1,368	45.8
Colombian	325	42.4
Peruvian	239	33.9
Spaniard	5,922	18.8

Population Age 3–17 Enrolled in Public School

(Universe: Population Age 3–17 Enrolled in School)

Group	Number	%
Total Population	337,289	89.8
Hispanic or Latino (of any race)	194,883	92.6
Central American, ex. Mexican	1,132	85.6
Guatemalan	409	78.4
Panamanian	275	96.8
Salvadoran	240	96.4
Cuban	592	80.0
Mexican	122,200	94.2
Puerto Rican	1,167	79.5
South American	869	90.1
Colombian	123	87.2
Peruvian	394	94.9
Spaniard	7,834	88.8

Population Age 3–17 Enrolled in Private School

(Universe: Population Age 3–17 Enrolled in School)

Group	Number	%
Total Population	38,401	10.2
Hispanic or Latino (of any race)	15,603	7.4
Central American, ex. Mexican	190	14.4
Guatemalan	113	21.6
Panamanian	9	3.2
Salvadoran	9	3.6
Cuban	148	20.0
Mexican	7,519	5.8
Puerto Rican	301	20.5
South American	95	9.9
Colombian	18	12.8
Peruvian	21	5.1
Spaniard	987	11.2

Foreign-Born Population

Group	Number	%
Total Population	195,770	9.7

Notes: (1) Percent of total population; (2) Percent of Hispanic/Latino population; Profiles include places with an overall population of at least 125,000, OR an overall population of at least 25,000 where the Hispanic/Latino population is at least 20% of the overall population. In states where less than five places meet either of these criteria, we have included places with at least 10,000 total population with the highest percentage of Hispanic/Latino population. These places are identified with an asterisk (*); Please refer to the User's Guide for a full explanation of data.

Group	Number	%
Hispanic or Latino (of any race)	152,658	16.7
Central American, ex. Mexican	3,894	60.6
Guatemalan	1,900	67.1
Panamanian	248	30.2
Salvadoran	1,123	69.5
Cuban	1,874	52.9
Mexican	132,954	25.3
Puerto Rican	78	1.0
South American	2,687	57.3
Colombian	598	53.2
Peruvian	667	50.6
Spaniard	821	1.7

Foreign-Born Naturalized U.S. Citizens

Group	Number	%
Total Population	62,168	31.8
Hispanic or Latino (of any race)	38,629	25.3
Central American, ex. Mexican	1,292	33.2
Guatemalan	535	28.2
Panamanian	148	59.7
Salvadoran	346	30.8
Cuban	448	23.9
Mexican	31,737	23.9
Puerto Rican	0	0.0
South American	1,265	47.1
Colombian	248	41.5
Peruvian	335	50.2
Spaniard	378	46.0

Language Spoken at Home: English Only
(Universe: Population 5 Years and Over)

Group	Number	%
Total Population	1,197,144	64.0
Hispanic or Latino (of any race)	327,541	39.4
Central American, ex. Mexican	1,329	22.4
Guatemalan	403	15.7
Panamanian	473	62.6
Salvadoran	133	8.8
Cuban	808	24.8
Mexican	148,120	31.2
Puerto Rican	3,420	51.1
South American	1,062	25.2
Colombian	207	20.9
Peruvian	413	36.5
Spaniard	25,405	56.8

Language Spoken at Home: Spanish
(Universe: Population 5 Years and Over)

Group	Number	%
Total Population	532,568	28.5
Hispanic or Latino (of any race)	500,159	60.2
Central American, ex. Mexican	4,556	76.9
Guatemalan	2,159	84.0
Panamanian	283	37.4
Salvadoran	1,360	89.8
Cuban	2,440	75.0
Mexican	324,632	68.5
Puerto Rican	3,175	47.5
South American	3,105	73.8
Colombian	783	79.1
Peruvian	717	63.5
Spaniard	19,240	43.0

Unemployment Rate
(Universe: Population 16 Years and Over)

Group	%
Total Population	7.2
Hispanic or Latino (of any race)	8.3
Central American, ex. Mexican	2.8
Guatemalan	2.2
Panamanian	5.5
Salvadoran	3.2
Cuban	5.9
Mexican	8.9
Puerto Rican	3.5
South American	3.7
Colombian	0.0
Peruvian	0.0
Spaniard	7.8

Class of Worker: Private Wage and Salary
(Universe: Civilian Employed Population 16 Years and Over)

Group	Number	%
Total Population	621,318	69.9
Hispanic or Latino (of any race)	273,168	71.8
Central American, ex. Mexican	2,692	80.0
Guatemalan	1,227	82.3
Panamanian	215	78.2
Salvadoran	814	78.0
Cuban	1,382	83.0
Mexican	159,047	74.4
Puerto Rican	2,524	72.3
South American	1,296	55.6
Colombian	378	69.7
Peruvian	307	44.2
Spaniard	13,943	65.6

Class of Worker: Government
(Universe: Civilian Employed Population 16 Years and Over)

Group	Number	%
Total Population	198,160	22.3
Hispanic or Latino (of any race)	82,406	21.7
Central American, ex. Mexican	303	9.0
Guatemalan	64	4.3
Panamanian	60	21.8
Salvadoran	81	7.8
Cuban	147	8.8
Mexican	40,434	18.9
Puerto Rican	732	21.0
South American	696	29.9
Colombian	128	23.6
Peruvian	187	26.9
Spaniard	5,722	26.9

Means of Transportation to Work: Car, Truck or Van
(Universe: Workers 16 Years and Over)

Group	Number	%
Total Population	784,854	89.7
Hispanic or Latino (of any race)	343,729	92.2
Central American, ex. Mexican	3,117	91.2
Guatemalan	1,318	88.1
Panamanian	293	100.0
Salvadoran	1,029	94.8
Cuban	1,462	87.8
Mexican	193,570	92.3
Puerto Rican	3,190	92.1
South American	2,078	90.7
Colombian	502	96.7
Peruvian	570	87.7
Spaniard	19,132	92.5

Means of Transportation to Work: Public Transportation (ex. Taxicab)
(Universe: Workers 16 Years and Over)

Group	Number	%
Total Population	9,167	1.0
Hispanic or Latino (of any race)	3,793	1.0
Central American, ex. Mexican	29	0.8
Guatemalan	29	1.9
Panamanian	0	0.0
Salvadoran	0	0.0
Cuban	14	0.8
Mexican	1,943	0.9
Puerto Rican	74	2.1
South American	11	0.5
Colombian	0	0.0
Peruvian	11	1.7
Spaniard	145	0.7

Homeownership Rate
(Universe: Occupied Housing Units)

Group	%
Total Population	68.5
Hispanic or Latino (of any race)	66.2
Central American, ex. Mexican	55.3
Costa Rican	52.9
Guatemalan	56.2
Honduran	50.0
Nicaraguan	59.4
Panamanian	62.3
Salvadoran	53.3
Cuban	45.9
Dominican Republic	46.8
Mexican	64.7
Puerto Rican	55.2
South American	63.0
Argentinean	60.9
Bolivian	74.7
Chilean	75.4
Colombian	61.0
Ecuadorian	58.0
Peruvian	63.7
Venezuelan	61.3
Spaniard	76.1

Median Home Value

Group	Dollars
Total Population	158,400
Hispanic or Latino (of any race)	129,200
Central American, ex. Mexican	163,200
Guatemalan	186,900
Panamanian	154,200
Salvadoran	119,100
Cuban	171,600
Mexican	110,200
Puerto Rican	180,100
South American	234,500
Colombian	172,300
Peruvian	211,100
Spaniard	161,800

Median Gross Rent

Group	Dollars
Total Population	683
Hispanic or Latino (of any race)	651
Central American, ex. Mexican	725
Guatemalan	818
Panamanian	806
Salvadoran	694
Cuban	548
Mexican	625
Puerto Rican	753
South American	703
Colombian	761
Peruvian	667
Spaniard	630

Median Household Income
(2010 Inflation-Adjusted Dollars)

Group	Dollars
Total Population	43,820
Hispanic or Latino (of any race)	36,392
Central American, ex. Mexican	45,448
Guatemalan	46,132
Panamanian	26,509
Salvadoran	50,236
Cuban	37,581
Mexican	34,238
Puerto Rican	44,941
South American	43,310
Colombian	35,625
Peruvian	42,853
Spaniard	41,417

Per Capita Income
(2010 Inflation-Adjusted Dollars)

Group	Dollars
Total Population	22,966
Hispanic or Latino (of any race)	16,209
Central American, ex. Mexican	16,748
Guatemalan	15,884
Panamanian	12,955
Salvadoran	18,385
Cuban	16,310
Mexican	14,267
Puerto Rican	24,715
South American	21,016
Colombian	17,539
Peruvian	17,881
Spaniard	21,332

Households with $100,000+ Income

Group	Number	%
Total Population	117,443	15.5
Hispanic or Latino (of any race)	27,912	9.4
Central American, ex. Mexican	260	14.6
Guatemalan	119	15.8
Panamanian	6	2.8
Salvadoran	80	16.0
Cuban	97	8.2
Mexican	12,554	8.0
Puerto Rican	380	14.4
South American	256	17.5
Colombian	29	8.5

Notes: (1) Percent of total population; (2) Percent of Hispanic/Latino population; Profiles include places with an overall population of at least 125,000, OR an overall population of at least 25,000 where the Hispanic/Latino population is at least 20% of the overall population. In states where less than five places meet either of these criteria, we have included places with at least 10,000 total population with the highest percentage of Hispanic/Latino population. These places are identified with an asterisk (*); Please refer to the User's Guide for a full explanation of data.

Group	Number	%
Peruvian	56	16.3
Spaniard	2,607	13.5

Households with Food Stamps/SNAP Benefits During Past 12 Months

Group	Number	%
Total Population	75,872	10.0
Hispanic or Latino (of any race)	45,184	15.3
Central American, ex. Mexican	219	12.3
Guatemalan	119	15.8
Panamanian	24	11.1
Salvadoran	27	5.4
Cuban	222	18.9
Mexican	27,069	17.3
Puerto Rican	348	13.2
South American	133	9.1
Colombian	51	14.9
Peruvian	44	12.8
Spaniard	2,135	11.1

Poverty Rate
(Income in Past 12 Months Below Poverty Level)

Group	%
Total Population	18.4
Hispanic or Latino (of any race)	23.1
Central American, ex. Mexican	17.9
Guatemalan	11.8
Panamanian	34.9
Salvadoran	25.5
Cuban	23.8
Mexican	26.2
Puerto Rican	19.9
South American	10.5
Colombian	13.3
Peruvian	12.7
Spaniard	15.1

Alamogordo

Population

Group	Number	%TP[1]	%HP[2]
Total Population	30,403	100.0	–
Hispanic or Latino (of any race)	9,271	30.5	100.0
Mexican	7,061	23.2	76.2
Puerto Rican	243	0.8	2.6
Spaniard	339	1.1	3.7

Population Growth: 2000–2010

Group	%
Total Population	-14.6
Hispanic or Latino (of any race)	-18.6
Mexican	-10.7
Puerto Rican	-6.9

Males per 100 Females

Group	Number
Total Population	96.6
Hispanic or Latino (of any race)	92.1
Mexican	94.5
Puerto Rican	143.0
Spaniard	84.2

Average Household Size

Group	People
Total Population	2.33
Hispanic or Latino (of any race)	2.63
Mexican	2.68
Puerto Rican	2.46
Spaniard	2.36

Median Age

Group	Years
Total Population	37.4
Hispanic or Latino (of any race)	29.5
Mexican	29.0
Puerto Rican	25.8
Spaniard	38.5

High School Graduates
(Universe: Population 25 Years and Over)

Group	Number	%
Total Population	17,871	89.1
Hispanic or Latino (of any race)	3,936	78.0
Mexican	2,900	76.2

Four-Year College Graduates
(Universe: Population 25 Years and Over)

Group	Number	%
Total Population	3,545	17.7
Hispanic or Latino (of any race)	443	8.8
Mexican	257	6.8

Population Age 3–17 Enrolled in Public School
(Universe: Population Age 3–17 Enrolled in School)

Group	Number	%
Total Population	4,283	90.7
Hispanic or Latino (of any race)	1,822	92.2
Mexican	1,361	90.9

Population Age 3–17 Enrolled in Private School
(Universe: Population Age 3–17 Enrolled in School)

Group	Number	%
Total Population	441	9.3
Hispanic or Latino (of any race)	155	7.8
Mexican	136	9.1

Foreign-Born Population

Group	Number	%
Total Population	2,699	9.1
Hispanic or Latino (of any race)	824	9.2
Mexican	746	10.7

Foreign-Born Naturalized U.S. Citizens

Group	Number	%
Total Population	938	34.8
Hispanic or Latino (of any race)	477	57.9
Mexican	429	57.5

Language Spoken at Home: English Only
(Universe: Population 5 Years and Over)

Group	Number	%
Total Population	20,533	74.2
Hispanic or Latino (of any race)	3,330	41.5
Mexican	2,507	40.7

Language Spoken at Home: Spanish
(Universe: Population 5 Years and Over)

Group	Number	%
Total Population	5,253	19.0
Hispanic or Latino (of any race)	4,623	57.6
Mexican	3,577	58.1

Unemployment Rate
(Universe: Population 16 Years and Over)

Group	%
Total Population	8.1
Hispanic or Latino (of any race)	8.1
Mexican	8.4

Class of Worker: Private Wage and Salary
(Universe: Civilian Employed Population 16 Years and Over)

Group	Number	%
Total Population	8,319	66.4
Hispanic or Latino (of any race)	2,678	70.6
Mexican	2,137	72.5

Class of Worker: Government
(Universe: Civilian Employed Population 16 Years and Over)

Group	Number	%
Total Population	3,437	27.4
Hispanic or Latino (of any race)	825	21.8
Mexican	563	19.1

Means of Transportation to Work: Car, Truck or Van
(Universe: Workers 16 Years and Over)

Group	Number	%
Total Population	12,600	95.4
Hispanic or Latino (of any race)	3,643	94.4
Mexican	2,867	95.9

Means of Transportation to Work: Public Transportation (ex. Taxicab)
(Universe: Workers 16 Years and Over)

Group	Number	%
Total Population	13	0.1
Hispanic or Latino (of any race)	0	0.0
Mexican	0	0.0

Homeownership Rate
(Universe: Occupied Housing Units)

Group	%
Total Population	62.1
Hispanic or Latino (of any race)	61.0
Mexican	61.7
Puerto Rican	54.9
Spaniard	65.5

Median Home Value

Group	Dollars
Total Population	103,900
Hispanic or Latino (of any race)	88,300
Mexican	85,100

Median Gross Rent

Group	Dollars
Total Population	581
Hispanic or Latino (of any race)	509
Mexican	508

Median Household Income
(2010 Inflation-Adjusted Dollars)

Group	Dollars
Total Population	41,640
Hispanic or Latino (of any race)	36,205
Mexican	38,561

Per Capita Income
(2010 Inflation-Adjusted Dollars)

Group	Dollars
Total Population	21,093
Hispanic or Latino (of any race)	15,214
Mexican	15,115

Households with $100,000+ Income

Group	Number	%
Total Population	1,201	9.7
Hispanic or Latino (of any race)	202	7.3
Mexican	160	7.6

Households with Food Stamps/SNAP Benefits During Past 12 Months

Group	Number	%
Total Population	1,194	9.7
Hispanic or Latino (of any race)	578	20.9
Mexican	466	22.1

Poverty Rate
(Income in Past 12 Months Below Poverty Level)

Group	%
Total Population	14.1
Hispanic or Latino (of any race)	17.0
Mexican	16.1

Albuquerque

Population

Group	Number	%TP[1]	%HP[2]
Total Population	545,852	100.0	–
Hispanic or Latino (of any race)	255,055	46.7	100.0
Central American, ex. Mexican	2,310	0.4	0.9
Costa Rican	136	<0.1	0.1
Guatemalan	724	0.1	0.3
Honduran	202	<0.1	0.1
Nicaraguan	205	<0.1	0.1
Panamanian	306	0.1	0.1
Salvadoran	723	0.1	0.3
Cuban	2,915	0.5	1.1
Dominican Republic	183	<0.1	0.1
Mexican	146,035	26.8	57.3
Puerto Rican	2,802	0.5	1.1
South American	2,220	0.4	0.9
Argentinean	250	<0.1	0.1
Chilean	282	0.1	0.1
Colombian	627	0.1	0.2
Ecuadorian	309	0.1	0.1
Peruvian	426	0.1	0.2
Venezuelan	171	<0.1	0.1
Spaniard	23,386	4.3	9.2

Population Growth: 2000–2010

Group	%
Total Population	21.7

Notes: (1) Percent of total population; (2) Percent of Hispanic/Latino population; Profiles include places with an overall population of at least 125,000, OR an overall population of at least 25,000 where the Hispanic/Latino population is at least 20% of the overall population. In states where less than five places meet either of these criteria, we have included places with at least 10,000 total population with the highest percentage of Hispanic/Latino population. These places are identified with an asterisk (*); Please refer to the User's Guide for a full explanation of data.

Group	
Hispanic or Latino (of any race)	42.4
Central American, ex. Mexican	179.7
Guatemalan	267.5
Panamanian	117.0
Salvadoran	224.2
Cuban	72.1
Mexican	113.1
Puerto Rican	63.3
South American	154.9
Chilean	112.0
Colombian	162.3
Ecuadorian	200.0
Peruvian	202.1
Spaniard	3,193.8

Males per 100 Females

Group	Number
Total Population	94.4
Hispanic or Latino (of any race)	94.4
Central American, ex. Mexican	93.5
Costa Rican	74.4
Guatemalan	109.2
Honduran	85.3
Nicaraguan	84.7
Panamanian	56.9
Salvadoran	108.4
Cuban	110.5
Dominican Republic	112.8
Mexican	98.8
Puerto Rican	101.4
South American	81.7
Argentinean	93.8
Chilean	93.2
Colombian	68.1
Ecuadorian	93.1
Peruvian	80.5
Venezuelan	96.6
Spaniard	84.9

Average Household Size

Group	People
Total Population	2.40
Hispanic or Latino (of any race)	2.76
Central American, ex. Mexican	2.99
Costa Rican	2.52
Guatemalan	3.31
Honduran	2.72
Nicaraguan	2.72
Panamanian	2.46
Salvadoran	3.11
Cuban	2.64
Dominican Republic	2.39
Mexican	2.97
Puerto Rican	2.53
South American	2.44
Argentinean	2.53
Chilean	2.32
Colombian	2.42
Ecuadorian	2.62
Peruvian	2.48
Venezuelan	2.69
Spaniard	2.52

Median Age

Group	Years
Total Population	35.1
Hispanic or Latino (of any race)	28.8
Central American, ex. Mexican	32.3
Costa Rican	33.0
Guatemalan	30.9
Honduran	32.7
Nicaraguan	32.3
Panamanian	36.5
Salvadoran	32.1
Cuban	34.6
Dominican Republic	28.9
Mexican	27.6
Puerto Rican	28.3
South American	34.4
Argentinean	36.8
Chilean	33.5
Colombian	34.4
Ecuadorian	33.6
Peruvian	34.0
Venezuelan	34.3

Group		
Spaniard		33.0

High School Graduates
(Universe: Population 25 Years and Over)

Group	Number	%
Total Population	302,186	87.1
Hispanic or Latino (of any race)	103,512	75.7
Central American, ex. Mexican	765	71.7
Cuban	1,048	82.7
Mexican	42,269	66.7
Puerto Rican	1,211	83.0
South American	1,401	94.3
Spaniard	7,891	89.0

Four-Year College Graduates
(Universe: Population 25 Years and Over)

Group	Number	%
Total Population	111,829	32.2
Hispanic or Latino (of any race)	22,900	16.7
Central American, ex. Mexican	176	16.5
Cuban	342	27.0
Mexican	10,146	16.0
Puerto Rican	383	26.3
South American	727	49.0
Spaniard	2,256	25.5

Population Age 3–17 Enrolled in Public School
(Universe: Population Age 3–17 Enrolled in School)

Group	Number	%
Total Population	77,042	84.6
Hispanic or Latino (of any race)	46,852	88.5
Central American, ex. Mexican	178	70.6
Cuban	387	88.0
Mexican	24,402	90.4
Puerto Rican	468	70.8
South American	352	96.7
Spaniard	2,269	82.9

Population Age 3–17 Enrolled in Private School
(Universe: Population Age 3–17 Enrolled in School)

Group	Number	%
Total Population	14,072	15.4
Hispanic or Latino (of any race)	6,084	11.5
Central American, ex. Mexican	74	29.4
Cuban	53	12.0
Mexican	2,587	9.6
Puerto Rican	193	29.2
South American	12	3.3
Spaniard	467	17.1

Foreign-Born Population

Group	Number	%
Total Population	57,851	10.9
Hispanic or Latino (of any race)	39,522	16.4
Central American, ex. Mexican	883	55.0
Cuban	1,360	66.8
Mexican	30,152	26.3
Puerto Rican	50	1.8
South American	1,192	50.9
Spaniard	351	2.5

Foreign-Born Naturalized U.S. Citizens

Group	Number	%
Total Population	19,149	33.1
Hispanic or Latino (of any race)	8,699	22.0
Central American, ex. Mexican	445	50.4
Cuban	305	22.4
Mexican	5,741	19.0
Puerto Rican	0	0.0
South American	517	43.4
Spaniard	177	50.4

Language Spoken at Home: English Only
(Universe: Population 5 Years and Over)

Group	Number	%
Total Population	345,818	70.1
Hispanic or Latino (of any race)	105,387	48.3
Central American, ex. Mexican	338	23.7
Cuban	258	13.8
Mexican	38,684	37.4
Puerto Rican	1,468	59.4
South American	538	26.5
Spaniard	9,506	71.8

Language Spoken at Home: Spanish
(Universe: Population 5 Years and Over)

Group	Number	%
Total Population	120,629	24.4
Hispanic or Latino (of any race)	112,097	51.4
Central American, ex. Mexican	1,080	75.7
Cuban	1,605	86.2
Mexican	64,546	62.4
Puerto Rican	971	39.3
South American	1,479	72.7
Spaniard	3,726	28.1

Unemployment Rate
(Universe: Population 16 Years and Over)

Group	%
Total Population	6.3
Hispanic or Latino (of any race)	7.4
Central American, ex. Mexican	2.9
Cuban	8.7
Mexican	7.8
Puerto Rican	4.4
South American	5.1
Spaniard	6.9

Class of Worker: Private Wage and Salary
(Universe: Civilian Employed Population 16 Years and Over)

Group	Number	%
Total Population	195,658	74.7
Hispanic or Latino (of any race)	84,781	77.0
Central American, ex. Mexican	640	78.6
Cuban	852	91.3
Mexican	40,054	78.6
Puerto Rican	1,155	81.3
South American	610	51.0
Spaniard	4,985	71.9

Class of Worker: Government
(Universe: Civilian Employed Population 16 Years and Over)

Group	Number	%
Total Population	51,698	19.7
Hispanic or Latino (of any race)	20,088	18.2
Central American, ex. Mexican	109	13.4
Cuban	81	8.7
Mexican	8,352	16.4
Puerto Rican	170	12.0
South American	493	41.3
Spaniard	1,558	22.5

Means of Transportation to Work: Car, Truck or Van
(Universe: Workers 16 Years and Over)

Group	Number	%
Total Population	230,797	89.5
Hispanic or Latino (of any race)	99,783	92.2
Central American, ex. Mexican	744	94.7
Cuban	902	96.7
Mexican	46,093	91.7
Puerto Rican	1,204	90.9
South American	1,128	95.6
Spaniard	6,277	92.3

Means of Transportation to Work: Public Transportation (ex. Taxicab)
(Universe: Workers 16 Years and Over)

Group	Number	%
Total Population	5,389	2.1
Hispanic or Latino (of any race)	2,174	2.0
Central American, ex. Mexican	0	0.0
Cuban	14	1.5
Mexican	1,176	2.3
Puerto Rican	0	0.0
South American	0	0.0
Spaniard	70	1.0

Homeownership Rate
(Universe: Occupied Housing Units)

Group	%
Total Population	60.3
Hispanic or Latino (of any race)	58.0
Central American, ex. Mexican	56.1
Costa Rican	45.2
Guatemalan	60.6
Honduran	49.3
Nicaraguan	53.7
Panamanian	59.4

Notes: (1) Percent of total population; (2) Percent of Hispanic/Latino population; Profiles include places with an overall population of at least 125,000, OR an overall population of at least 25,000 where the Hispanic/Latino population is at least 20% of the overall population. In states where less than five places meet either of these criteria, we have included places with at least 10,000 total population with the highest percentage of Hispanic/Latino population. These places are identified with an asterisk (*); Please refer to the User's Guide for a full explanation of data.

Salvadoran	54.8
Cuban	38.8
Dominican Republic	33.3
Mexican	56.9
Puerto Rican	47.1
South American	62.3
Argentinean	54.0
Chilean	76.7
Colombian	62.4
Ecuadorian	55.7
Peruvian	62.9
Venezuelan	50.0
Spaniard	71.0

Median Home Value

Group	Dollars
Total Population	188,600
Hispanic or Latino (of any race)	163,300
Central American, ex. Mexican	169,000
Cuban	172,200
Mexican	156,500
Puerto Rican	205,800
South American	262,800
Spaniard	194,500

Median Gross Rent

Group	Dollars
Total Population	712
Hispanic or Latino (of any race)	695
Central American, ex. Mexican	807
Cuban	496
Mexican	679
Puerto Rican	715
South American	763
Spaniard	713

Median Household Income
(2010 Inflation-Adjusted Dollars)

Group	Dollars
Total Population	46,662
Hispanic or Latino (of any race)	39,628
Central American, ex. Mexican	44,038
Cuban	31,082
Mexican	37,666
Puerto Rican	59,643
South American	45,954
Spaniard	49,102

Per Capita Income
(2010 Inflation-Adjusted Dollars)

Group	Dollars
Total Population	25,819
Hispanic or Latino (of any race)	18,186
Central American, ex. Mexican	21,036
Cuban	15,932
Mexican	16,376
Puerto Rican	26,389
South American	21,826
Spaniard	25,079

Households with $100,000+ Income

Group	Number	%
Total Population	36,909	17.0
Hispanic or Latino (of any race)	8,618	10.4
Central American, ex. Mexican	86	18.9
Cuban	79	11.6
Mexican	3,123	8.7
Puerto Rican	178	17.3
South American	134	16.6
Spaniard	1,070	18.8

Households with Food Stamps/SNAP Benefits During Past 12 Months

Group	Number	%
Total Population	18,902	8.7
Hispanic or Latino (of any race)	11,098	13.4
Central American, ex. Mexican	67	14.8
Cuban	148	21.7
Mexican	5,298	14.8
Puerto Rican	84	8.2
South American	82	10.2
Spaniard	504	8.8

Poverty Rate
(Income in Past 12 Months Below Poverty Level)

Group	%
Total Population	15.7
Hispanic or Latino (of any race)	20.1
Central American, ex. Mexican	15.9
Cuban	18.9
Mexican	22.2
Puerto Rican	26.4
South American	10.9
Spaniard	12.0

Carlsbad

Population

Group	Number	%TP[1]	%HP[2]
Total Population	26,138	100.0	–
Hispanic or Latino (of any race)	11,105	42.5	100.0
Mexican	8,803	33.7	79.3
Spaniard	172	0.7	1.5

Population Growth: 2000–2010

Group	%
Total Population	2.0
Hispanic or Latino (of any race)	17.9
Mexican	74.1

Males per 100 Females

Group	Number
Total Population	96.5
Hispanic or Latino (of any race)	96.8
Mexican	99.5
Spaniard	77.3

Average Household Size

Group	People
Total Population	2.50
Hispanic or Latino (of any race)	2.86
Mexican	2.89
Spaniard	2.54

Median Age

Group	Years
Total Population	37.6
Hispanic or Latino (of any race)	29.3
Mexican	29.3
Spaniard	40.0

High School Graduates
(Universe: Population 25 Years and Over)

Group	Number	%
Total Population	13,974	82.6
Hispanic or Latino (of any race)	4,019	69.4
Mexican	3,197	68.9

Four-Year College Graduates
(Universe: Population 25 Years and Over)

Group	Number	%
Total Population	2,701	16.0
Hispanic or Latino (of any race)	682	11.8
Mexican	558	12.0

Population Age 3–17 Enrolled in Public School
(Universe: Population Age 3–17 Enrolled in School)

Group	Number	%
Total Population	4,208	90.4
Hispanic or Latino (of any race)	2,372	94.4
Mexican	1,873	93.0

Population Age 3–17 Enrolled in Private School
(Universe: Population Age 3–17 Enrolled in School)

Group	Number	%
Total Population	447	9.6
Hispanic or Latino (of any race)	140	5.6
Mexican	140	7.0

Foreign-Born Population

Group	Number	%
Total Population	694	2.7
Hispanic or Latino (of any race)	494	4.7
Mexican	494	5.9

Foreign-Born Naturalized U.S. Citizens

Group	Number	%
Total Population	277	39.9
Hispanic or Latino (of any race)	129	26.1
Mexican	129	26.1

Language Spoken at Home: English Only
(Universe: Population 5 Years and Over)

Group	Number	%
Total Population	17,263	73.1
Hispanic or Latino (of any race)	3,669	39.8
Mexican	3,070	41.6

Language Spoken at Home: Spanish
(Universe: Population 5 Years and Over)

Group	Number	%
Total Population	6,099	25.8
Hispanic or Latino (of any race)	5,498	59.7
Mexican	4,269	57.8

Unemployment Rate
(Universe: Population 16 Years and Over)

Group	%
Total Population	7.0
Hispanic or Latino (of any race)	6.5
Mexican	6.7

Class of Worker: Private Wage and Salary
(Universe: Civilian Employed Population 16 Years and Over)

Group	Number	%
Total Population	8,300	72.9
Hispanic or Latino (of any race)	3,212	72.3
Mexican	2,596	71.6

Class of Worker: Government
(Universe: Civilian Employed Population 16 Years and Over)

Group	Number	%
Total Population	2,435	21.4
Hispanic or Latino (of any race)	1,039	23.4
Mexican	868	23.9

Means of Transportation to Work: Car, Truck or Van
(Universe: Workers 16 Years and Over)

Group	Number	%
Total Population	9,795	90.5
Hispanic or Latino (of any race)	3,898	93.1
Mexican	3,202	92.9

Means of Transportation to Work: Public Transportation (ex. Taxicab)
(Universe: Workers 16 Years and Over)

Group	Number	%
Total Population	60	0.6
Hispanic or Latino (of any race)	26	0.6
Mexican	26	0.8

Homeownership Rate
(Universe: Occupied Housing Units)

Group	%
Total Population	70.1
Hispanic or Latino (of any race)	66.5
Mexican	68.3
Spaniard	69.2

Median Home Value

Group	Dollars
Total Population	87,300
Hispanic or Latino (of any race)	75,700
Mexican	79,900

Median Gross Rent

Group	Dollars
Total Population	618
Hispanic or Latino (of any race)	635
Mexican	634

Median Household Income
(2010 Inflation-Adjusted Dollars)

Group	Dollars
Total Population	43,955
Hispanic or Latino (of any race)	43,091
Mexican	44,929

Notes: (1) Percent of total population; (2) Percent of Hispanic/Latino population; Profiles include places with an overall population of at least 125,000, OR an overall population of at least 25,000 where the Hispanic/Latino population is at least 20% of the overall population. In states where less than five places meet either of these criteria, we have included places with at least 10,000 total population with the highest percentage of Hispanic/Latino population. These places are identified with an asterisk (*); Please refer to the User's Guide for a full explanation of data.

Per Capita Income
(2010 Inflation-Adjusted Dollars)

Group	Dollars
Total Population	22,619
Hispanic or Latino (of any race)	16,626
Mexican	17,058

Households with $100,000+ Income

Group	Number	%
Total Population	1,465	15.2
Hispanic or Latino (of any race)	380	11.7
Mexican	314	11.8

Households with Food Stamps/SNAP Benefits During Past 12 Months

Group	Number	%
Total Population	1,328	13.8
Hispanic or Latino (of any race)	791	24.3
Mexican	674	25.4

Poverty Rate
(Income in Past 12 Months Below Poverty Level)

Group	%
Total Population	12.1
Hispanic or Latino (of any race)	14.2
Mexican	15.8

Clovis

Population

Group	Number	%TP[1]	%HP[2]
Total Population	37,775	100.0	–
Hispanic or Latino (of any race)	15,804	41.8	100.0
Central American, ex. Mexican	142	0.4	0.9
Mexican	10,901	28.9	69.0
Puerto Rican	265	0.7	1.7
Spaniard	611	1.6	3.9

Population Growth: 2000–2010

Group	%
Total Population	15.6
Hispanic or Latino (of any race)	44.7
Mexican	112.5
Puerto Rican	134.5

Males per 100 Females

Group	Number
Total Population	98.5
Hispanic or Latino (of any race)	98.8
Central American, ex. Mexican	91.9
Mexican	103.4
Puerto Rican	103.8
Spaniard	87.4

Average Household Size

Group	People
Total Population	2.60
Hispanic or Latino (of any race)	3.08
Central American, ex. Mexican	3.22
Mexican	3.22
Puerto Rican	3.04
Spaniard	2.95

Median Age

Group	Years
Total Population	31.8
Hispanic or Latino (of any race)	25.3
Central American, ex. Mexican	27.2
Mexican	24.4
Puerto Rican	21.8
Spaniard	29.9

High School Graduates
(Universe: Population 25 Years and Over)

Group	Number	%
Total Population	17,855	81.2
Hispanic or Latino (of any race)	4,435	63.1
Mexican	2,927	60.3

Four-Year College Graduates
(Universe: Population 25 Years and Over)

Group	Number	%
Total Population	4,044	18.4
Hispanic or Latino (of any race)	526	7.5
Mexican	394	8.1

Population Age 3–17 Enrolled in Public School
(Universe: Population Age 3–17 Enrolled in School)

Group	Number	%
Total Population	7,406	95.0
Hispanic or Latino (of any race)	4,020	98.6
Mexican	3,304	98.3

Population Age 3–17 Enrolled in Private School
(Universe: Population Age 3–17 Enrolled in School)

Group	Number	%
Total Population	390	5.0
Hispanic or Latino (of any race)	56	1.4
Mexican	56	1.7

Foreign-Born Population

Group	Number	%
Total Population	2,842	7.8
Hispanic or Latino (of any race)	2,165	14.9
Mexican	2,100	19.1

Foreign-Born Naturalized U.S. Citizens

Group	Number	%
Total Population	987	34.7
Hispanic or Latino (of any race)	628	29.0
Mexican	609	29.0

Language Spoken at Home: English Only
(Universe: Population 5 Years and Over)

Group	Number	%
Total Population	25,449	76.6
Hispanic or Latino (of any race)	5,841	45.5
Mexican	4,030	42.1

Language Spoken at Home: Spanish
(Universe: Population 5 Years and Over)

Group	Number	%
Total Population	7,261	21.9
Hispanic or Latino (of any race)	6,991	54.5
Mexican	5,537	57.9

Unemployment Rate
(Universe: Population 16 Years and Over)

Group	%
Total Population	5.6
Hispanic or Latino (of any race)	8.2
Mexican	8.7

Class of Worker: Private Wage and Salary
(Universe: Civilian Employed Population 16 Years and Over)

Group	Number	%
Total Population	11,929	73.9
Hispanic or Latino (of any race)	4,601	79.7
Mexican	3,589	85.2

Class of Worker: Government
(Universe: Civilian Employed Population 16 Years and Over)

Group	Number	%
Total Population	3,319	20.6
Hispanic or Latino (of any race)	1,037	18.0
Mexican	515	12.2

Means of Transportation to Work: Car, Truck or Van
(Universe: Workers 16 Years and Over)

Group	Number	%
Total Population	15,302	93.6
Hispanic or Latino (of any race)	5,273	92.5
Mexican	3,813	91.0

Means of Transportation to Work: Public Transportation (ex. Taxicab)
(Universe: Workers 16 Years and Over)

Group	Number	%
Total Population	65	0.4
Hispanic or Latino (of any race)	0	0.0
Mexican	0	0.0

Homeownership Rate
(Universe: Occupied Housing Units)

Group	%
Total Population	61.0
Hispanic or Latino (of any race)	53.4
Central American, ex. Mexican	48.9
Mexican	53.1
Puerto Rican	46.3
Spaniard	62.8

Median Home Value

Group	Dollars
Total Population	99,500
Hispanic or Latino (of any race)	73,200
Mexican	74,300

Median Gross Rent

Group	Dollars
Total Population	547
Hispanic or Latino (of any race)	541
Mexican	552

Median Household Income
(2010 Inflation-Adjusted Dollars)

Group	Dollars
Total Population	36,638
Hispanic or Latino (of any race)	27,836
Mexican	30,149

Per Capita Income
(2010 Inflation-Adjusted Dollars)

Group	Dollars
Total Population	19,946
Hispanic or Latino (of any race)	11,492
Mexican	10,748

Households with $100,000+ Income

Group	Number	%
Total Population	1,551	11.3
Hispanic or Latino (of any race)	210	4.8
Mexican	166	5.7

Households with Food Stamps/SNAP Benefits During Past 12 Months

Group	Number	%
Total Population	2,423	17.6
Hispanic or Latino (of any race)	1,428	32.8
Mexican	1,071	36.8

Poverty Rate
(Income in Past 12 Months Below Poverty Level)

Group	%
Total Population	21.7
Hispanic or Latino (of any race)	35.0
Mexican	37.0

Farmington

Population

Group	Number	%TP[1]	%HP[2]
Total Population	45,877	100.0	–
Hispanic or Latino (of any race)	10,298	22.4	100.0
Mexican	6,054	13.2	58.8
Spaniard	1,086	2.4	10.5

Population Growth: 2000–2010

Group	%
Total Population	21.2
Hispanic or Latino (of any race)	54.1
Mexican	125.9

Males per 100 Females

Group	Number
Total Population	97.3
Hispanic or Latino (of any race)	100.8
Mexican	106.1
Spaniard	95.3

Average Household Size

Group	People
Total Population	2.70
Hispanic or Latino (of any race)	3.06
Mexican	3.32
Spaniard	2.89

Median Age

Group	Years
Total Population	32.7
Hispanic or Latino (of any race)	25.5
Mexican	23.8
Spaniard	28.1

Notes: (1) Percent of total population; (2) Percent of Hispanic/Latino population; Profiles include places with an overall population of at least 125,000, OR an overall population of at least 25,000 where the Hispanic/Latino population is at least 20% of the overall population. In states where less than five places meet either of these criteria, we have included places with at least 10,000 total population with the highest percentage of Hispanic/Latino population. These places are identified with an asterisk (*); Please refer to the User's Guide for a full explanation of data.

High School Graduates
(Universe: Population 25 Years and Over)

Group	Number	%
Total Population	22,945	84.5
Hispanic or Latino (of any race)	3,301	63.5
Mexican	1,203	51.0

Four-Year College Graduates
(Universe: Population 25 Years and Over)

Group	Number	%
Total Population	5,356	19.7
Hispanic or Latino (of any race)	457	8.8
Mexican	186	7.9

Population Age 3–17 Enrolled in Public School
(Universe: Population Age 3–17 Enrolled in School)

Group	Number	%
Total Population	7,883	91.7
Hispanic or Latino (of any race)	2,516	90.1
Mexican	1,287	95.1

Population Age 3–17 Enrolled in Private School
(Universe: Population Age 3–17 Enrolled in School)

Group	Number	%
Total Population	712	8.3
Hispanic or Latino (of any race)	276	9.9
Mexican	66	4.9

Foreign-Born Population

Group	Number	%
Total Population	2,366	5.3
Hispanic or Latino (of any race)	1,866	18.2
Mexican	1,568	32.7

Foreign-Born Naturalized U.S. Citizens

Group	Number	%
Total Population	673	28.4
Hispanic or Latino (of any race)	492	26.4
Mexican	340	21.7

Language Spoken at Home: English Only
(Universe: Population 5 Years and Over)

Group	Number	%
Total Population	29,978	74.5
Hispanic or Latino (of any race)	3,876	43.0
Mexican	1,166	27.7

Language Spoken at Home: Spanish
(Universe: Population 5 Years and Over)

Group	Number	%
Total Population	5,563	13.8
Hispanic or Latino (of any race)	5,092	56.5
Mexican	3,044	72.3

Unemployment Rate
(Universe: Population 16 Years and Over)

Group	%
Total Population	4.0
Hispanic or Latino (of any race)	5.3
Mexican	5.8

Class of Worker: Private Wage and Salary
(Universe: Civilian Employed Population 16 Years and Over)

Group	Number	%
Total Population	16,195	79.7
Hispanic or Latino (of any race)	3,302	83.2
Mexican	1,572	87.1

Class of Worker: Government
(Universe: Civilian Employed Population 16 Years and Over)

Group	Number	%
Total Population	2,901	14.3
Hispanic or Latino (of any race)	451	11.4
Mexican	182	10.1

Means of Transportation to Work: Car, Truck or Van
(Universe: Workers 16 Years and Over)

Group	Number	%
Total Population	18,793	94.2
Hispanic or Latino (of any race)	3,790	97.5
Mexican	1,716	97.7

Means of Transportation to Work: Public Transportation (ex. Taxicab)
(Universe: Workers 16 Years and Over)

Group	Number	%
Total Population	18	0.1
Hispanic or Latino (of any race)	0	0.0
Mexican	0	0.0

Homeownership Rate
(Universe: Occupied Housing Units)

Group	%
Total Population	65.9
Hispanic or Latino (of any race)	63.5
Mexican	63.6
Spaniard	71.7

Median Home Value

Group	Dollars
Total Population	171,700
Hispanic or Latino (of any race)	152,400
Mexican	152,800

Median Gross Rent

Group	Dollars
Total Population	718
Hispanic or Latino (of any race)	707
Mexican	781

Median Household Income
(2010 Inflation-Adjusted Dollars)

Group	Dollars
Total Population	49,705
Hispanic or Latino (of any race)	37,585
Mexican	38,936

Per Capita Income
(2010 Inflation-Adjusted Dollars)

Group	Dollars
Total Population	24,883
Hispanic or Latino (of any race)	15,213
Mexican	14,952

Households with $100,000+ Income

Group	Number	%
Total Population	3,120	20.0
Hispanic or Latino (of any race)	270	9.0
Mexican	139	10.0

Households with Food Stamps/SNAP Benefits During Past 12 Months

Group	Number	%
Total Population	941	6.0
Hispanic or Latino (of any race)	367	12.3
Mexican	187	13.5

Poverty Rate
(Income in Past 12 Months Below Poverty Level)

Group	%
Total Population	16.9
Hispanic or Latino (of any race)	22.0
Mexican	19.7

Hobbs

Population

Group	Number	%TP[1]	%HP[2]
Total Population	34,122	100.0	–
Hispanic or Latino (of any race)	18,317	53.7	100.0
Mexican	16,023	47.0	87.5
Spaniard	151	0.4	0.8

Population Growth: 2000–2010

Group	%
Total Population	19.1
Hispanic or Latino (of any race)	51.5
Mexican	100.4

Males per 100 Females

Group	Number
Total Population	105.9
Hispanic or Latino (of any race)	109.0
Mexican	107.8
Spaniard	135.9

Average Household Size

Group	People
Total Population	2.81
Hispanic or Latino (of any race)	3.40
Mexican	3.45
Spaniard	2.89

Median Age

Group	Years
Total Population	30.8
Hispanic or Latino (of any race)	25.1
Mexican	24.8
Spaniard	35.2

High School Graduates
(Universe: Population 25 Years and Over)

Group	Number	%
Total Population	14,802	74.6
Hispanic or Latino (of any race)	4,686	55.6
Mexican	3,991	53.1

Four-Year College Graduates
(Universe: Population 25 Years and Over)

Group	Number	%
Total Population	2,782	14.0
Hispanic or Latino (of any race)	437	5.2
Mexican	250	3.3

Population Age 3–17 Enrolled in Public School
(Universe: Population Age 3–17 Enrolled in School)

Group	Number	%
Total Population	6,207	94.8
Hispanic or Latino (of any race)	4,339	97.5
Mexican	4,129	98.1

Population Age 3–17 Enrolled in Private School
(Universe: Population Age 3–17 Enrolled in School)

Group	Number	%
Total Population	338	5.2
Hispanic or Latino (of any race)	110	2.5
Mexican	78	1.9

Foreign-Born Population

Group	Number	%
Total Population	3,477	10.6
Hispanic or Latino (of any race)	3,289	19.5
Mexican	3,240	20.9

Foreign-Born Naturalized U.S. Citizens

Group	Number	%
Total Population	1,020	29.3
Hispanic or Latino (of any race)	916	27.9
Mexican	895	27.6

Language Spoken at Home: English Only
(Universe: Population 5 Years and Over)

Group	Number	%
Total Population	19,656	65.4
Hispanic or Latino (of any race)	4,932	33.1
Mexican	4,243	31.1

Language Spoken at Home: Spanish
(Universe: Population 5 Years and Over)

Group	Number	%
Total Population	10,144	33.7
Hispanic or Latino (of any race)	9,968	66.9
Mexican	9,400	68.9

Unemployment Rate
(Universe: Population 16 Years and Over)

Group	%
Total Population	8.8
Hispanic or Latino (of any race)	10.2
Mexican	11.2

Class of Worker: Private Wage and Salary
(Universe: Civilian Employed Population 16 Years and Over)

Group	Number	%
Total Population	9,502	75.5
Hispanic or Latino (of any race)	4,504	79.8
Mexican	4,126	81.4

Class of Worker: Government
(Universe: Civilian Employed Population 16 Years and Over)

Group	Number	%
Total Population	2,062	16.4

STATE & PLACE PROFILES

Notes: (1) Percent of total population; (2) Percent of Hispanic/Latino population; Profiles include places with an overall population of at least 125,000, OR an overall population of at least 25,000 where the Hispanic/Latino population is at least 20% of the overall population. In states where less than five places meet either of these criteria, we have included places with at least 10,000 total population with the highest percentage of Hispanic/Latino population. These places are identified with an asterisk (*); Please refer to the User's Guide for a full explanation of data.

Group	Number	%
Hispanic or Latino (of any race)	795	14.1
Mexican	639	12.6

Means of Transportation to Work: Car, Truck or Van
(Universe: Workers 16 Years and Over)

Group	Number	%
Total Population	11,690	95.3
Hispanic or Latino (of any race)	5,117	94.4
Mexican	4,657	95.9

Means of Transportation to Work: Public Transportation (ex. Taxicab)
(Universe: Workers 16 Years and Over)

Group	Number	%
Total Population	0	0.0
Hispanic or Latino (of any race)	0	0.0
Mexican	0	0.0

Homeownership Rate
(Universe: Occupied Housing Units)

Group	%
Total Population	62.8
Hispanic or Latino (of any race)	60.3
Mexican	61.0
Spaniard	60.4

Median Home Value

Group	Dollars
Total Population	93,000
Hispanic or Latino (of any race)	77,600
Mexican	75,900

Median Gross Rent

Group	Dollars
Total Population	645
Hispanic or Latino (of any race)	607
Mexican	607

Median Household Income
(2010 Inflation-Adjusted Dollars)

Group	Dollars
Total Population	43,194
Hispanic or Latino (of any race)	34,703
Mexican	34,481

Per Capita Income
(2010 Inflation-Adjusted Dollars)

Group	Dollars
Total Population	19,509
Hispanic or Latino (of any race)	13,485
Mexican	12,643

Households with $100,000+ Income

Group	Number	%
Total Population	1,565	14.1
Hispanic or Latino (of any race)	431	9.6
Mexican	343	8.6

Households with Food Stamps/SNAP Benefits During Past 12 Months

Group	Number	%
Total Population	1,270	11.5
Hispanic or Latino (of any race)	601	13.4
Mexican	509	12.7

Poverty Rate
(Income in Past 12 Months Below Poverty Level)

Group	%
Total Population	20.3
Hispanic or Latino (of any race)	27.2
Mexican	28.1

Las Cruces

Population

Group	Number	%TP[1]	%HP[2]
Total Population	97,618	100.0	–
Hispanic or Latino (of any race)	55,443	56.8	100.0
Central American, ex. Mexican	232	0.2	0.4
Cuban	115	0.1	0.2
Mexican	45,747	46.9	82.5
Puerto Rican	594	0.6	1.1
South American	262	0.3	0.5
Spaniard	1,522	1.6	2.7

Population Growth: 2000–2010

Group	%
Total Population	31.4
Hispanic or Latino (of any race)	44.3
Mexican	89.4
Puerto Rican	108.4
South American	142.6

Males per 100 Females

Group	Number
Total Population	94.9
Hispanic or Latino (of any race)	92.0
Central American, ex. Mexican	90.2
Cuban	125.5
Mexican	93.2
Puerto Rican	111.4
South American	73.5
Spaniard	80.3

Average Household Size

Group	People
Total Population	2.43
Hispanic or Latino (of any race)	2.79
Central American, ex. Mexican	2.49
Cuban	2.04
Mexican	2.84
Puerto Rican	2.57
South American	2.61
Spaniard	2.51

Median Age

Group	Years
Total Population	32.4
Hispanic or Latino (of any race)	27.3
Central American, ex. Mexican	33.8
Cuban	44.8
Mexican	27.1
Puerto Rican	28.7
South American	34.0
Spaniard	30.2

High School Graduates
(Universe: Population 25 Years and Over)

Group	Number	%
Total Population	47,386	83.3
Hispanic or Latino (of any race)	20,423	72.3
Mexican	17,707	70.8
Spaniard	386	83.4

Four-Year College Graduates
(Universe: Population 25 Years and Over)

Group	Number	%
Total Population	17,696	31.1
Hispanic or Latino (of any race)	4,790	17.0
Mexican	3,965	15.9
Spaniard	100	21.6

Population Age 3–17 Enrolled in Public School
(Universe: Population Age 3–17 Enrolled in School)

Group	Number	%
Total Population	15,850	95.1
Hispanic or Latino (of any race)	11,802	96.8
Mexican	10,653	96.9
Spaniard	251	100.0

Population Age 3–17 Enrolled in Private School
(Universe: Population Age 3–17 Enrolled in School)

Group	Number	%
Total Population	809	4.9
Hispanic or Latino (of any race)	389	3.2
Mexican	342	3.1
Spaniard	0	0.0

Foreign-Born Population

Group	Number	%
Total Population	12,224	13.2
Hispanic or Latino (of any race)	9,444	17.8
Mexican	9,173	19.3
Spaniard	0	0.0

Foreign-Born Naturalized U.S. Citizens

Group	Number	%
Total Population	4,295	35.1
Hispanic or Latino (of any race)	2,858	30.3
Mexican	2,643	28.8
Spaniard	0	0.0

Language Spoken at Home: English Only
(Universe: Population 5 Years and Over)

Group	Number	%
Total Population	51,771	59.9
Hispanic or Latino (of any race)	17,304	35.9
Mexican	14,999	34.8
Spaniard	466	56.3

Language Spoken at Home: Spanish
(Universe: Population 5 Years and Over)

Group	Number	%
Total Population	32,304	37.4
Hispanic or Latino (of any race)	30,843	64.0
Mexican	28,121	65.2
Spaniard	362	43.7

Unemployment Rate
(Universe: Population 16 Years and Over)

Group	%
Total Population	8.5
Hispanic or Latino (of any race)	8.9
Mexican	9.3
Spaniard	0.0

Class of Worker: Private Wage and Salary
(Universe: Civilian Employed Population 16 Years and Over)

Group	Number	%
Total Population	27,014	66.4
Hispanic or Latino (of any race)	15,203	68.3
Mexican	13,749	68.7
Spaniard	301	88.0

Class of Worker: Government
(Universe: Civilian Employed Population 16 Years and Over)

Group	Number	%
Total Population	10,773	26.5
Hispanic or Latino (of any race)	5,513	24.8
Mexican	4,805	24.0
Spaniard	34	9.9

Means of Transportation to Work: Car, Truck or Van
(Universe: Workers 16 Years and Over)

Group	Number	%
Total Population	36,449	90.8
Hispanic or Latino (of any race)	20,424	93.1
Mexican	18,451	93.1
Spaniard	279	94.9

Means of Transportation to Work: Public Transportation (ex. Taxicab)
(Universe: Workers 16 Years and Over)

Group	Number	%
Total Population	197	0.5
Hispanic or Latino (of any race)	103	0.5
Mexican	91	0.5
Spaniard	0	0.0

Homeownership Rate
(Universe: Occupied Housing Units)

Group	%
Total Population	56.3
Hispanic or Latino (of any race)	52.4
Central American, ex. Mexican	47.3
Cuban	49.1
Mexican	53.0
Puerto Rican	52.0
South American	50.6
Spaniard	58.1

Median Home Value

Group	Dollars
Total Population	152,400
Hispanic or Latino (of any race)	128,700
Mexican	127,600
Spaniard	110,600

Median Gross Rent

Group	Dollars
Total Population	674
Hispanic or Latino (of any race)	652
Mexican	656
Spaniard	489

Notes: (1) Percent of total population; (2) Percent of Hispanic/Latino population; Profiles include places with an overall population of at least 125,000, OR an overall population of at least 25,000 where the Hispanic/Latino population is at least 20% of the overall population. In states where less than five places meet either of these criteria, we have included places with at least 10,000 total population with the highest percentage of Hispanic/Latino population. These places are identified with an asterisk (*); Please refer to the User's Guide for a full explanation of data.

Median Household Income
(2010 Inflation-Adjusted Dollars)

Group	Dollars
Total Population	38,391
Hispanic or Latino (of any race)	32,786
Mexican	32,543
Spaniard	22,782

Per Capita Income
(2010 Inflation-Adjusted Dollars)

Group	Dollars
Total Population	19,943
Hispanic or Latino (of any race)	14,185
Mexican	13,821
Spaniard	16,774

Households with $100,000+ Income

Group	Number	%
Total Population	4,005	11.0
Hispanic or Latino (of any race)	966	5.5
Mexican	840	5.5
Spaniard	40	12.5

Households with Food Stamps/SNAP Benefits During Past 12 Months

Group	Number	%
Total Population	4,279	11.7
Hispanic or Latino (of any race)	3,115	17.8
Mexican	2,902	19.0
Spaniard	56	17.4

Poverty Rate
(Income in Past 12 Months Below Poverty Level)

Group	%
Total Population	20.4
Hispanic or Latino (of any race)	24.9
Mexican	25.8
Spaniard	23.6

Rio Rancho

Population

Group	Number	%TP[1]	%HP[2]
Total Population	87,521	100.0	–
Hispanic or Latino (of any race)	32,153	36.7	100.0
Central American, ex. Mexican	451	0.5	1.4
Guatemalan	108	0.1	0.3
Salvadoran	180	0.2	0.6
Cuban	160	0.2	0.5
Mexican	16,070	18.4	50.0
Puerto Rican	783	0.9	2.4
South American	389	0.4	1.2
Colombian	111	0.1	0.3
Spaniard	3,882	4.4	12.1

Population Growth: 2000–2010

Group	%
Total Population	69.1
Hispanic or Latino (of any race)	124.4
Central American, ex. Mexican	313.8
Mexican	276.7
Puerto Rican	147.0

Males per 100 Females

Group	Number
Total Population	94.9
Hispanic or Latino (of any race)	93.3
Central American, ex. Mexican	92.7
Guatemalan	96.4
Salvadoran	91.5
Cuban	95.1
Mexican	96.3
Puerto Rican	107.1
South American	89.8
Colombian	79.0
Spaniard	93.9

Average Household Size

Group	People
Total Population	2.74
Hispanic or Latino (of any race)	3.08
Central American, ex. Mexican	3.40
Guatemalan	3.94
Salvadoran	3.42
Cuban	2.94
Mexican	3.24
Puerto Rican	2.94
South American	3.14
Colombian	3.26
Spaniard	2.93

Median Age

Group	Years
Total Population	35.9
Hispanic or Latino (of any race)	28.0
Central American, ex. Mexican	33.5
Guatemalan	34.5
Salvadoran	33.5
Cuban	29.0
Mexican	27.0
Puerto Rican	31.6
South American	37.1
Colombian	38.5
Spaniard	30.4

High School Graduates
(Universe: Population 25 Years and Over)

Group	Number	%
Total Population	48,288	93.4
Hispanic or Latino (of any race)	14,042	89.5
Mexican	5,784	89.0
Puerto Rican	495	93.8
Spaniard	1,087	95.7

Four-Year College Graduates
(Universe: Population 25 Years and Over)

Group	Number	%
Total Population	14,602	28.2
Hispanic or Latino (of any race)	3,021	19.3
Mexican	1,238	19.0
Puerto Rican	111	21.0
Spaniard	312	27.5

Population Age 3–17 Enrolled in Public School
(Universe: Population Age 3–17 Enrolled in School)

Group	Number	%
Total Population	15,593	88.8
Hispanic or Latino (of any race)	7,212	89.5
Mexican	3,297	90.6
Puerto Rican	106	95.5
Spaniard	654	83.7

Population Age 3–17 Enrolled in Private School
(Universe: Population Age 3–17 Enrolled in School)

Group	Number	%
Total Population	1,957	11.2
Hispanic or Latino (of any race)	844	10.5
Mexican	341	9.4
Puerto Rican	5	4.5
Spaniard	127	16.3

Foreign-Born Population

Group	Number	%
Total Population	4,573	5.6
Hispanic or Latino (of any race)	2,460	8.4
Mexican	1,611	12.8
Puerto Rican	0	0.0
Spaniard	30	1.3

Foreign-Born Naturalized U.S. Citizens

Group	Number	%
Total Population	2,306	50.4
Hispanic or Latino (of any race)	1,025	41.7
Mexican	691	42.9
Puerto Rican	0	0.0
Spaniard	16	53.3

Language Spoken at Home: English Only
(Universe: Population 5 Years and Over)

Group	Number	%
Total Population	60,718	81.0
Hispanic or Latino (of any race)	15,746	60.2
Mexican	5,882	52.3
Puerto Rican	271	31.5
Spaniard	1,617	83.4

Language Spoken at Home: Spanish
(Universe: Population 5 Years and Over)

Group	Number	%
Total Population	11,396	15.2
Hispanic or Latino (of any race)	10,369	39.7
Mexican	5,348	47.6
Puerto Rican	589	68.5
Spaniard	323	16.6

Unemployment Rate
(Universe: Population 16 Years and Over)

Group	%
Total Population	6.0
Hispanic or Latino (of any race)	5.7
Mexican	6.1
Puerto Rican	0.0
Spaniard	8.8

Class of Worker: Private Wage and Salary
(Universe: Civilian Employed Population 16 Years and Over)

Group	Number	%
Total Population	30,126	77.8
Hispanic or Latino (of any race)	10,322	78.1
Mexican	4,296	77.5
Puerto Rican	482	81.4
Spaniard	628	75.9

Class of Worker: Government
(Universe: Civilian Employed Population 16 Years and Over)

Group	Number	%
Total Population	6,674	17.2
Hispanic or Latino (of any race)	2,242	17.0
Mexican	1,051	19.0
Puerto Rican	69	11.7
Spaniard	131	15.8

Means of Transportation to Work: Car, Truck or Van
(Universe: Workers 16 Years and Over)

Group	Number	%
Total Population	34,640	91.9
Hispanic or Latino (of any race)	12,026	94.0
Mexican	5,192	96.8
Puerto Rican	583	98.5
Spaniard	658	83.7

Means of Transportation to Work: Public Transportation (ex. Taxicab)
(Universe: Workers 16 Years and Over)

Group	Number	%
Total Population	346	0.9
Hispanic or Latino (of any race)	107	0.8
Mexican	50	0.9
Puerto Rican	0	0.0
Spaniard	10	1.3

Homeownership Rate
(Universe: Occupied Housing Units)

Group	%
Total Population	78.9
Hispanic or Latino (of any race)	77.3
Central American, ex. Mexican	81.3
Guatemalan	90.3
Salvadoran	77.2
Cuban	85.1
Mexican	76.3
Puerto Rican	79.2
South American	81.9
Colombian	73.5
Spaniard	83.1

Median Home Value

Group	Dollars
Total Population	179,700
Hispanic or Latino (of any race)	173,000
Mexican	166,700
Puerto Rican	175,000
Spaniard	190,300

Median Gross Rent

Group	Dollars
Total Population	973
Hispanic or Latino (of any race)	945
Mexican	894
Puerto Rican	877
Spaniard	938

Notes: (1) Percent of total population; (2) Percent of Hispanic/Latino population; Profiles include places with an overall population of at least 125,000, OR an overall population of at least 25,000 where the Hispanic/Latino population is at least 20% of the overall population. In states where less than five places meet either of these criteria, we have included places with at least 10,000 total population with the highest percentage of Hispanic/Latino population. These places are identified with an asterisk (*); Please refer to the User's Guide for a full explanation of data.

Median Household Income
(2010 Inflation-Adjusted Dollars)

Group	Dollars
Total Population	59,063
Hispanic or Latino (of any race)	54,310
Mexican	50,759
Puerto Rican	54,615
Spaniard	60,817

Per Capita Income
(2010 Inflation-Adjusted Dollars)

Group	Dollars
Total Population	26,372
Hispanic or Latino (of any race)	20,244
Mexican	19,423
Puerto Rican	23,258
Spaniard	17,583

Households with $100,000+ Income

Group	Number	%
Total Population	6,065	20.4
Hispanic or Latino (of any race)	1,576	18.2
Mexican	659	19.3
Puerto Rican	62	18.9
Spaniard	139	20.7

Households with Food Stamps/SNAP Benefits During Past 12 Months

Group	Number	%
Total Population	1,860	6.3
Hispanic or Latino (of any race)	837	9.6
Mexican	320	9.4
Puerto Rican	53	16.2
Spaniard	124	18.5

Poverty Rate
(Income in Past 12 Months Below Poverty Level)

Group	%
Total Population	7.9
Hispanic or Latino (of any race)	10.3
Mexican	12.5
Puerto Rican	1.6
Spaniard	5.4

Roswell

Population

Group	Number	%TP[1]	%HP[2]
Total Population	48,366	100.0	–
Hispanic or Latino (of any race)	25,832	53.4	100.0
Central American, ex. Mexican	161	0.3	0.6
Mexican	20,586	42.6	79.7
Puerto Rican	155	0.3	0.6
Spaniard	633	1.3	2.5

Population Growth: 2000–2010

Group	%
Total Population	6.8
Hispanic or Latino (of any race)	28.6
Mexican	67.6

Males per 100 Females

Group	Number
Total Population	94.9
Hispanic or Latino (of any race)	96.4
Central American, ex. Mexican	91.7
Mexican	98.4
Puerto Rican	121.4
Spaniard	79.8

Average Household Size

Group	People
Total Population	2.66
Hispanic or Latino (of any race)	3.19
Central American, ex. Mexican	3.71
Mexican	3.28
Puerto Rican	3.33
Spaniard	2.77

Median Age

Group	Years
Total Population	33.5
Hispanic or Latino (of any race)	25.8
Central American, ex. Mexican	34.4
Mexican	25.6
Puerto Rican	21.9
Spaniard	30.2

High School Graduates
(Universe: Population 25 Years and Over)

Group	Number	%
Total Population	22,602	78.2
Hispanic or Latino (of any race)	7,766	63.8
Mexican	5,798	60.0

Four-Year College Graduates
(Universe: Population 25 Years and Over)

Group	Number	%
Total Population	4,768	16.5
Hispanic or Latino (of any race)	1,037	8.5
Mexican	743	7.7

Population Age 3–17 Enrolled in Public School
(Universe: Population Age 3–17 Enrolled in School)

Group	Number	%
Total Population	8,757	89.0
Hispanic or Latino (of any race)	6,246	91.8
Mexican	5,094	91.4

Population Age 3–17 Enrolled in Private School
(Universe: Population Age 3–17 Enrolled in School)

Group	Number	%
Total Population	1,082	11.0
Hispanic or Latino (of any race)	558	8.2
Mexican	480	8.6

Foreign-Born Population

Group	Number	%
Total Population	5,446	11.5
Hispanic or Latino (of any race)	4,920	20.0
Mexican	4,564	22.8

Foreign-Born Naturalized U.S. Citizens

Group	Number	%
Total Population	1,685	30.9
Hispanic or Latino (of any race)	1,317	26.8
Mexican	1,167	25.6

Language Spoken at Home: English Only
(Universe: Population 5 Years and Over)

Group	Number	%
Total Population	27,885	64.3
Hispanic or Latino (of any race)	7,913	36.4
Mexican	5,863	33.3

Language Spoken at Home: Spanish
(Universe: Population 5 Years and Over)

Group	Number	%
Total Population	14,737	34.0
Hispanic or Latino (of any race)	13,799	63.5
Mexican	11,733	66.7

Unemployment Rate
(Universe: Population 16 Years and Over)

Group	%
Total Population	7.2
Hispanic or Latino (of any race)	8.7
Mexican	8.1

Class of Worker: Private Wage and Salary
(Universe: Civilian Employed Population 16 Years and Over)

Group	Number	%
Total Population	15,319	76.6
Hispanic or Latino (of any race)	7,371	76.6
Mexican	6,090	78.0

Class of Worker: Government
(Universe: Civilian Employed Population 16 Years and Over)

Group	Number	%
Total Population	3,338	16.7
Hispanic or Latino (of any race)	1,643	17.1
Mexican	1,191	15.3

Means of Transportation to Work: Car, Truck or Van
(Universe: Workers 16 Years and Over)

Group	Number	%
Total Population	18,186	94.5
Hispanic or Latino (of any race)	8,505	93.7
Mexican	6,855	94.3

Means of Transportation to Work: Public Transportation (ex. Taxicab)
(Universe: Workers 16 Years and Over)

Group	Number	%
Total Population	68	0.4
Hispanic or Latino (of any race)	48	0.5
Mexican	30	0.4

Homeownership Rate
(Universe: Occupied Housing Units)

Group	%
Total Population	66.6
Hispanic or Latino (of any race)	64.2
Central American, ex. Mexican	73.3
Mexican	64.9
Puerto Rican	57.5
Spaniard	66.7

Median Home Value

Group	Dollars
Total Population	83,700
Hispanic or Latino (of any race)	64,600
Mexican	65,200

Median Gross Rent

Group	Dollars
Total Population	568
Hispanic or Latino (of any race)	539
Mexican	550

Median Household Income
(2010 Inflation-Adjusted Dollars)

Group	Dollars
Total Population	36,237
Hispanic or Latino (of any race)	31,340
Mexican	31,620

Per Capita Income
(2010 Inflation-Adjusted Dollars)

Group	Dollars
Total Population	18,448
Hispanic or Latino (of any race)	12,405
Mexican	11,959

Households with $100,000+ Income

Group	Number	%
Total Population	1,514	8.6
Hispanic or Latino (of any race)	344	4.7
Mexican	242	4.3

Households with Food Stamps/SNAP Benefits During Past 12 Months

Group	Number	%
Total Population	2,790	15.8
Hispanic or Latino (of any race)	1,827	25.2
Mexican	1,377	24.2

Poverty Rate
(Income in Past 12 Months Below Poverty Level)

Group	%
Total Population	21.8
Hispanic or Latino (of any race)	27.9
Mexican	28.3

Santa Fe

Population

Group	Number	%TP[1]	%HP[2]
Total Population	67,947	100.0	–
Hispanic or Latino (of any race)	33,089	48.7	100.0
Central American, ex. Mexican	1,190	1.8	3.6
Guatemalan	648	1.0	2.0
Salvadoran	369	0.5	1.1
Cuban	107	0.2	0.3
Mexican	14,084	20.7	42.6
Puerto Rican	205	0.3	0.6
South American	384	0.6	1.2
Spaniard	4,015	5.9	12.1

Population Growth: 2000–2010

Group	%
Total Population	9.2
Hispanic or Latino (of any race)	11.2
Central American, ex. Mexican	257.4

Notes: (1) Percent of total population; (2) Percent of Hispanic/Latino population; Profiles include places with an overall population of at least 125,000, OR an overall population of at least 25,000 where the Hispanic/Latino population is at least 20% of the overall population. In states where less than five places meet either of these criteria, we have included places with at least 10,000 total population with the highest percentage of Hispanic/Latino population. These places are identified with an asterisk (*); Please refer to the User's Guide for a full explanation of data.

Group	Number
Guatemalan	274.6
Mexican	69.2
Puerto Rican	60.2
South American	146.2
Spaniard	2,612.8

Males per 100 Females

Group	Number
Total Population	90.0
Hispanic or Latino (of any race)	96.6
Central American, ex. Mexican	148.4
Guatemalan	165.6
Salvadoran	135.0
Cuban	87.7
Mexican	103.2
Puerto Rican	95.2
South American	96.9
Spaniard	88.4

Average Household Size

Group	People
Total Population	2.10
Hispanic or Latino (of any race)	2.55
Central American, ex. Mexican	3.83
Guatemalan	4.20
Salvadoran	3.57
Cuban	2.06
Mexican	2.93
Puerto Rican	1.93
South American	2.09
Spaniard	2.33

Median Age

Group	Years
Total Population	44.0
Hispanic or Latino (of any race)	34.8
Central American, ex. Mexican	30.2
Guatemalan	29.7
Salvadoran	30.1
Cuban	39.8
Mexican	29.7
Puerto Rican	39.1
South American	35.0
Spaniard	43.3

High School Graduates
(Universe: Population 25 Years and Over)

Group	Number	%
Total Population	43,416	88.1
Hispanic or Latino (of any race)	15,397	75.4
Central American, ex. Mexican	304	38.3
Mexican	4,348	62.0
Spaniard	1,585	91.7

Four-Year College Graduates
(Universe: Population 25 Years and Over)

Group	Number	%
Total Population	21,822	44.3
Hispanic or Latino (of any race)	4,118	20.2
Central American, ex. Mexican	104	13.1
Mexican	1,316	18.8
Spaniard	494	28.6

Population Age 3–17 Enrolled in Public School
(Universe: Population Age 3–17 Enrolled in School)

Group	Number	%
Total Population	7,209	78.1
Hispanic or Latino (of any race)	5,121	85.7
Central American, ex. Mexican	163	76.2
Mexican	2,082	84.2
Spaniard	282	94.3

Population Age 3–17 Enrolled in Private School
(Universe: Population Age 3–17 Enrolled in School)

Group	Number	%
Total Population	2,027	21.9
Hispanic or Latino (of any race)	855	14.3
Central American, ex. Mexican	51	23.8
Mexican	391	15.8
Spaniard	17	5.7

Foreign-Born Population

Group	Number	%
Total Population	8,399	12.4
Hispanic or Latino (of any race)	6,255	19.5
Central American, ex. Mexican	977	75.7
Mexican	4,446	36.9
Spaniard	61	2.4

Foreign-Born Naturalized U.S. Citizens

Group	Number	%
Total Population	2,037	24.3
Hispanic or Latino (of any race)	980	15.7
Central American, ex. Mexican	212	21.7
Mexican	438	9.9
Spaniard	20	32.8

Language Spoken at Home: English Only
(Universe: Population 5 Years and Over)

Group	Number	%
Total Population	43,822	68.4
Hispanic or Latino (of any race)	13,071	44.2
Central American, ex. Mexican	45	3.8
Mexican	3,254	30.2
Spaniard	1,340	58.5

Language Spoken at Home: Spanish
(Universe: Population 5 Years and Over)

Group	Number	%
Total Population	17,844	27.9
Hispanic or Latino (of any race)	16,380	55.4
Central American, ex. Mexican	1,150	96.2
Mexican	7,520	69.8
Spaniard	936	40.9

Unemployment Rate
(Universe: Population 16 Years and Over)

Group	%
Total Population	6.1
Hispanic or Latino (of any race)	7.5
Central American, ex. Mexican	5.2
Mexican	6.9
Spaniard	9.8

Class of Worker: Private Wage and Salary
(Universe: Civilian Employed Population 16 Years and Over)

Group	Number	%
Total Population	22,947	65.2
Hispanic or Latino (of any race)	9,958	64.9
Central American, ex. Mexican	708	83.3
Mexican	4,170	71.1
Spaniard	630	54.5

Class of Worker: Government
(Universe: Civilian Employed Population 16 Years and Over)

Group	Number	%
Total Population	7,552	21.4
Hispanic or Latino (of any race)	3,972	25.9
Central American, ex. Mexican	50	5.9
Mexican	1,098	18.7
Spaniard	408	35.3

Means of Transportation to Work: Car, Truck or Van
(Universe: Workers 16 Years and Over)

Group	Number	%
Total Population	28,714	83.2
Hispanic or Latino (of any race)	13,871	91.6
Central American, ex. Mexican	756	88.9
Mexican	5,160	89.6
Spaniard	1,077	95.2

Means of Transportation to Work: Public Transportation (ex. Taxicab)
(Universe: Workers 16 Years and Over)

Group	Number	%
Total Population	516	1.5
Hispanic or Latino (of any race)	250	1.7
Central American, ex. Mexican	29	3.4
Mexican	98	1.7
Spaniard	0	0.0

Homeownership Rate
(Universe: Occupied Housing Units)

Group	%
Total Population	60.5
Hispanic or Latino (of any race)	59.5
Central American, ex. Mexican	31.5
Guatemalan	31.3
Salvadoran	30.5
Cuban	46.3
Mexican	53.1
Puerto Rican	40.0
South American	54.0
Spaniard	74.6

Median Home Value

Group	Dollars
Total Population	311,300
Hispanic or Latino (of any race)	258,300
Central American, ex. Mexican	235,400
Mexican	244,400
Spaniard	285,300

Median Gross Rent

Group	Dollars
Total Population	879
Hispanic or Latino (of any race)	791
Central American, ex. Mexican	842
Mexican	779
Spaniard	454

Median Household Income
(2010 Inflation-Adjusted Dollars)

Group	Dollars
Total Population	49,947
Hispanic or Latino (of any race)	43,428
Central American, ex. Mexican	45,495
Mexican	36,611
Spaniard	58,750

Per Capita Income
(2010 Inflation-Adjusted Dollars)

Group	Dollars
Total Population	34,428
Hispanic or Latino (of any race)	21,174
Central American, ex. Mexican	16,261
Mexican	17,664
Spaniard	26,732

Households with $100,000+ Income

Group	Number	%
Total Population	6,269	19.8
Hispanic or Latino (of any race)	1,536	12.7
Central American, ex. Mexican	31	8.8
Mexican	406	9.9
Spaniard	200	17.5

Households with Food Stamps/SNAP Benefits During Past 12 Months

Group	Number	%
Total Population	2,202	7.0
Hispanic or Latino (of any race)	1,262	10.4
Central American, ex. Mexican	45	12.8
Mexican	543	13.2
Spaniard	160	14.0

Poverty Rate
(Income in Past 12 Months Below Poverty Level)

Group	%
Total Population	14.8
Hispanic or Latino (of any race)	19.3
Central American, ex. Mexican	17.7
Mexican	28.3
Spaniard	15.1

South Valley

Population

Group	Number	%TP[1]	%HP[2]
Total Population	40,976	100.0	–
Hispanic or Latino (of any race)	32,860	80.2	100.0
Mexican	21,189	51.7	64.5
Puerto Rican	119	0.3	0.4
Spaniard	1,891	4.6	5.8

Population Growth: 2000–2010

Group	%
Total Population	4.9
Hispanic or Latino (of any race)	8.4
Mexican	72.5

Males per 100 Females

Group	Number
Total Population	98.8
Hispanic or Latino (of any race)	99.8

STATE & PLACE PROFILES

Notes: (1) Percent of total population; (2) Percent of Hispanic/Latino population; Profiles include places with an overall population of at least 125,000, OR an overall population of at least 25,000 where the Hispanic/Latino population is at least 20% of the overall population. In states where less than five places meet either of these criteria, we have included places with at least 10,000 total population with the highest percentage of Hispanic/Latino population. These places are identified with an asterisk (*); Please refer to the User's Guide for a full explanation of data.

Mexican	103.9
Puerto Rican	138.0
Spaniard	86.3

Average Household Size

Group	People
Total Population	2.93
Hispanic or Latino (of any race)	3.12
Mexican	3.38
Puerto Rican	2.71
Spaniard	2.70

Median Age

Group	Years
Total Population	35.5
Hispanic or Latino (of any race)	32.1
Mexican	29.8
Puerto Rican	30.5
Spaniard	45.2

High School Graduates
(Universe: Population 25 Years and Over)

Group	Number	%
Total Population	18,647	70.2
Hispanic or Latino (of any race)	12,854	64.2
Mexican	6,323	59.0
Spaniard	544	70.3

Four-Year College Graduates
(Universe: Population 25 Years and Over)

Group	Number	%
Total Population	3,373	12.7
Hispanic or Latino (of any race)	1,600	8.0
Mexican	883	8.2
Spaniard	81	10.5

Population Age 3–17 Enrolled in Public School
(Universe: Population Age 3–17 Enrolled in School)

Group	Number	%
Total Population	7,560	90.8
Hispanic or Latino (of any race)	6,701	90.7
Mexican	3,888	92.3
Spaniard	76	77.6

Population Age 3–17 Enrolled in Private School
(Universe: Population Age 3–17 Enrolled in School)

Group	Number	%
Total Population	770	9.2
Hispanic or Latino (of any race)	691	9.3
Mexican	323	7.7
Spaniard	22	22.4

Foreign-Born Population

Group	Number	%
Total Population	6,910	16.5
Hispanic or Latino (of any race)	6,564	19.5
Mexican	6,045	31.8
Spaniard	0	0.0

Foreign-Born Naturalized U.S. Citizens

Group	Number	%
Total Population	1,060	15.3
Hispanic or Latino (of any race)	832	12.7
Mexican	742	12.3
Spaniard	0	0.0

Language Spoken at Home: English Only
(Universe: Population 5 Years and Over)

Group	Number	%
Total Population	18,764	47.8
Hispanic or Latino (of any race)	11,933	38.1
Mexican	4,706	27.1
Spaniard	444	48.2

Language Spoken at Home: Spanish
(Universe: Population 5 Years and Over)

Group	Number	%
Total Population	20,043	51.0
Hispanic or Latino (of any race)	19,358	61.8
Mexican	12,621	72.8
Spaniard	478	51.8

Unemployment Rate
(Universe: Population 16 Years and Over)

Group	%
Total Population	7.2
Hispanic or Latino (of any race)	7.3
Mexican	7.8
Spaniard	4.6

Class of Worker: Private Wage and Salary
(Universe: Civilian Employed Population 16 Years and Over)

Group	Number	%
Total Population	12,240	71.0
Hispanic or Latino (of any race)	9,649	73.0
Mexican	5,564	73.4
Spaniard	265	79.1

Class of Worker: Government
(Universe: Civilian Employed Population 16 Years and Over)

Group	Number	%
Total Population	3,386	19.6
Hispanic or Latino (of any race)	2,411	18.2
Mexican	1,221	16.1
Spaniard	29	8.7

Means of Transportation to Work: Car, Truck or Van
(Universe: Workers 16 Years and Over)

Group	Number	%
Total Population	15,773	93.6
Hispanic or Latino (of any race)	12,176	94.2
Mexican	7,044	94.2
Spaniard	317	94.6

Means of Transportation to Work: Public Transportation (ex. Taxicab)
(Universe: Workers 16 Years and Over)

Group	Number	%
Total Population	84	0.5
Hispanic or Latino (of any race)	35	0.3
Mexican	13	0.2
Spaniard	0	0.0

Homeownership Rate
(Universe: Occupied Housing Units)

Group	%
Total Population	72.1
Hispanic or Latino (of any race)	70.0
Mexican	66.8
Puerto Rican	69.0
Spaniard	83.2

Median Home Value

Group	Dollars
Total Population	133,000
Hispanic or Latino (of any race)	131,200
Mexican	126,500
Spaniard	153,400

Median Gross Rent

Group	Dollars
Total Population	689
Hispanic or Latino (of any race)	663
Mexican	676
Spaniard	–

Median Household Income
(2010 Inflation-Adjusted Dollars)

Group	Dollars
Total Population	37,203
Hispanic or Latino (of any race)	34,066
Mexican	34,615
Spaniard	33,529

Per Capita Income
(2010 Inflation-Adjusted Dollars)

Group	Dollars
Total Population	17,300
Hispanic or Latino (of any race)	14,521
Mexican	13,658
Spaniard	18,475

Households with $100,000+ Income

Group	Number	%
Total Population	1,459	10.1
Hispanic or Latino (of any race)	805	7.5
Mexican	469	8.5
Spaniard	38	9.0

Households with Food Stamps/SNAP Benefits During Past 12 Months

Group	Number	%
Total Population	1,820	12.6
Hispanic or Latino (of any race)	1,440	13.4
Mexican	667	12.1
Spaniard	68	16.0

Poverty Rate
(Income in Past 12 Months Below Poverty Level)

Group	%
Total Population	21.7
Hispanic or Latino (of any race)	23.4
Mexican	24.2
Spaniard	8.8

Notes: (1) Percent of total population; (2) Percent of Hispanic/Latino population; Profiles include places with an overall population of at least 125,000, OR an overall population of at least 25,000 where the Hispanic/Latino population is at least 20% of the overall population. In states where less than five places meet either of these criteria, we have included places with at least 10,000 total population with the highest percentage of Hispanic/Latino population. These places are identified with an asterisk (*); Please refer to the User's Guide for a full explanation of data.

New York

EDITOR'S NOTE: For a place to be included in this edition, it must meet one of two criteria. Either its overall population is at least 125,000, OR its overall population is at least 25,000 and its Hispanic/Latino population is at least 20% of the overall population. For the state of New York, the following locations are included:

- Babylon
- Bay Shore
- Brentwood
- Bronx
- Brookhaven
- Brooklyn
- Buffalo
- Central Islip
- Elmont
- Freeport
- Glen Cove
- Haverstraw
- Hempstead (town)
- Hempstead (village)
- Huntington
- Huntington Station
- Islip
- Manhattan
- Middletown
- New Rochelle
- New York City
- Newburgh
- North Hempstead
- Ossining (town)
- Ossining (village)
- Oyster Bay
- Port Chester
- Queens
- Ramapo
- Rochester
- Rye
- Spring Valley
- Staten Island
- Syracuse
- Valley Stream
- Wallkill
- White Plains
- Yonkers

Section Two: State & Place Profiles starts with the state profile, followed by place profiles that meet the criteria above. Places are listed alphabetically within each state. All states, all counties and places that meet the above criteria are ranked and compared in *Section Three: Rankings & Comparisons*, on page 1055.

For a more detailed look at the Hispanic/Latino population in New York, a companion web site is available at no additional charge with purchase of this print edition. Visit http://gold.greyhouse.com/page/info_hispanic for more information.

The web site includes data for all counties and places in New York with Hispanic/Latino population, plus ten additional topics: Self Employed Worker; Walked to Work; Worked from Home; Mean Travel Time to Work; Mean Household Income; Households with Cash Public Assistance; Mean Cash Pubic Assistance; Poverty Rates for 18 and Under, 18 to 64, and 65 and Over.

Population

Group	Number	%TP[1]	%HP[2]
Total Population	19,378,102	100.0	–
Hispanic or Latino (of any race)	3,416,922	17.6	100.0
Central American, ex. Mexican	353,589	1.8	10.3
Costa Rican	11,576	0.1	0.3
Guatemalan	73,806	0.4	2.2
Honduran	71,919	0.4	2.1
Nicaraguan	13,006	0.1	0.4
Panamanian	28,200	0.1	0.8
Salvadoran	152,130	0.8	4.5
Cuban	70,803	0.4	2.1
Dominican Republic	674,787	3.5	19.7
Mexican	457,288	2.4	13.4
Puerto Rican	1,070,558	5.5	31.3
South American	513,417	2.6	15.0
Argentinean	24,969	0.1	0.7
Bolivian	7,122	<0.1	0.2
Chilean	15,050	0.1	0.4
Colombian	141,879	0.7	4.2
Ecuadorian	228,216	1.2	6.7
Paraguayan	5,940	<0.1	0.2
Peruvian	66,318	0.3	1.9
Uruguayan	6,021	<0.1	0.2
Venezuelan	13,910	0.1	0.4
Spaniard	35,571	0.2	1.0

Population Growth: 2000–2010

Group	%
Total Population	2.1
Hispanic or Latino (of any race)	19.2
Central American, ex. Mexican	94.4
Costa Rican	47.6
Guatemalan	153.9
Honduran	104.7
Nicaraguan	61.9
Panamanian	40.6
Salvadoran	109.2
Cuban	13.1
Dominican Republic	48.3
Mexican	75.3
Puerto Rican	1.9
South American	61.3
Argentinean	73.3
Bolivian	68.7
Chilean	51.5
Colombian	36.2
Ecuadorian	84.8
Paraguayan	122.6
Peruvian	77.6
Uruguayan	78.9
Venezuelan	57.6
Spaniard	173.3

Males per 100 Females

Group	Number
Total Population	93.8
Hispanic or Latino (of any race)	97.2
Central American, ex. Mexican	110.6
Costa Rican	80.0
Guatemalan	150.3
Honduran	102.8
Nicaraguan	87.9
Panamanian	73.4
Salvadoran	111.8
Cuban	98.1
Dominican Republic	83.0
Mexican	128.1
Puerto Rican	89.6
South American	98.0
Argentinean	100.0
Bolivian	86.9
Chilean	101.5
Colombian	80.7
Ecuadorian	113.3
Paraguayan	92.1
Peruvian	92.8
Uruguayan	105.5
Venezuelan	84.3
Spaniard	96.3

Average Household Size

Group	People
Total Population	2.57
Hispanic or Latino (of any race)	3.22
Central American, ex. Mexican	4.06
Costa Rican	2.78
Guatemalan	4.21
Honduran	3.85
Nicaraguan	3.26
Panamanian	2.63
Salvadoran	4.87
Cuban	2.35
Dominican Republic	3.42
Mexican	4.34
Puerto Rican	2.68
South American	3.38
Argentinean	2.59
Bolivian	3.14
Chilean	2.76
Colombian	2.99
Ecuadorian	3.96
Paraguayan	3.31
Peruvian	3.35
Uruguayan	2.79
Venezuelan	2.63
Spaniard	2.44

Median Age

Group	Years
Total Population	38.0
Hispanic or Latino (of any race)	30.3
Central American, ex. Mexican	30.4
Costa Rican	36.9
Guatemalan	28.9
Honduran	30.4
Nicaraguan	34.7
Panamanian	40.4
Salvadoran	29.7
Cuban	39.3
Dominican Republic	31.4
Mexican	25.6
Puerto Rican	31.1
South American	35.0
Argentinean	37.9
Bolivian	36.7
Chilean	37.9
Colombian	37.4
Ecuadorian	32.7
Paraguayan	33.6
Peruvian	37.7
Uruguayan	39.4
Venezuelan	32.5
Spaniard	37.3

High School Graduates

(Universe: Population 25 Years and Over)

Group	Number	%
Total Population	10,905,648	84.4
Hispanic or Latino (of any race)	1,250,438	64.6
Central American, ex. Mexican	114,288	56.1
Costa Rican	6,045	78.4
Guatemalan	20,327	51.5
Honduran	22,455	54.6
Nicaraguan	6,397	71.9
Panamanian	17,562	89.6
Salvadoran	39,207	46.9
Cuban	39,584	79.1
Dominican Republic	228,846	59.3
Mexican	110,889	51.0
Puerto Rican	432,536	67.3
South American	258,050	73.6
Argentinean	14,984	85.9
Bolivian	4,655	87.8
Chilean	8,932	83.5
Colombian	79,976	80.4
Ecuadorian	90,710	61.3
Paraguayan	3,487	78.5
Peruvian	40,332	86.0
Uruguayan	3,008	73.3
Venezuelan	8,255	86.5
Spaniard	21,247	88.2

Four-Year College Graduates

(Universe: Population 25 Years and Over)

Group	Number	%
Total Population	4,149,168	32.1

Notes: (1) Percent of total population; (2) Percent of Hispanic/Latino population; Profiles include places with an overall population of at least 125,000, OR an overall population of at least 25,000 where the Hispanic/Latino population is at least 20% of the overall population. In states where less than five places meet either of these criteria, we have included places with at least 10,000 total population with the highest percentage of Hispanic/Latino population. These places are identified with an asterisk (*); Please refer to the User's Guide for a full explanation of data.

Hispanic or Latino (of any race)	304,711	15.7
Central American, ex. Mexican	23,946	11.8
Costa Rican	1,683	21.8
Guatemalan	3,731	9.5
Honduran	4,937	12.0
Nicaraguan	2,054	23.1
Panamanian	4,790	24.4
Salvadoran	6,214	7.4
Cuban	15,508	31.0
Dominican Republic	53,405	13.8
Mexican	23,114	10.6
Puerto Rican	90,126	14.0
South American	74,214	21.2
Argentinean	6,987	40.1
Bolivian	1,599	30.2
Chilean	3,361	31.4
Colombian	24,135	24.3
Ecuadorian	18,419	12.5
Paraguayan	841	18.9
Peruvian	12,593	26.9
Uruguayan	976	23.8
Venezuelan	3,883	40.7
Spaniard	10,157	42.2

Population Age 3–17 Enrolled in Public School

(Universe: Population Age 3–17 Enrolled in School)

Group	Number	%
Total Population	2,813,896	82.7
Hispanic or Latino (of any race)	633,498	89.5
Central American, ex. Mexican	58,166	93.1
Costa Rican	1,691	90.8
Guatemalan	10,696	91.4
Honduran	11,871	92.0
Nicaraguan	1,702	90.4
Panamanian	4,466	91.0
Salvadoran	26,608	94.8
Cuban	7,604	75.3
Dominican Republic	136,948	90.9
Mexican	95,307	94.7
Puerto Rican	227,352	88.6
South American	76,902	85.7
Argentinean	2,515	78.0
Bolivian	881	61.4
Chilean	2,161	85.6
Colombian	21,434	85.6
Ecuadorian	35,430	88.1
Paraguayan	1,199	93.3
Peruvian	9,662	84.4
Uruguayan	711	74.3
Venezuelan	1,902	83.6
Spaniard	3,620	73.4

Population Age 3–17 Enrolled in Private School

(Universe: Population Age 3–17 Enrolled in School)

Group	Number	%
Total Population	589,586	17.3
Hispanic or Latino (of any race)	73,986	10.5
Central American, ex. Mexican	4,313	6.9
Costa Rican	171	9.2
Guatemalan	1,008	8.6
Honduran	1,029	8.0
Nicaraguan	181	9.6
Panamanian	442	9.0
Salvadoran	1,445	5.2
Cuban	2,500	24.7
Dominican Republic	13,728	9.1
Mexican	5,340	5.3
Puerto Rican	29,255	11.4
South American	12,804	14.3
Argentinean	709	22.0
Bolivian	554	38.6
Chilean	363	14.4
Colombian	3,619	14.4
Ecuadorian	4,778	11.9
Paraguayan	86	6.7
Peruvian	1,783	15.6
Uruguayan	246	25.7
Venezuelan	372	16.4
Spaniard	1,312	26.6

Foreign-Born Population

Group	Number	%
Total Population	4,180,075	21.7
Hispanic or Latino (of any race)	1,310,773	39.9
Central American, ex. Mexican	219,846	65.5
Costa Rican	6,617	58.4
Guatemalan	47,347	71.9
Honduran	45,894	66.4
Nicaraguan	7,978	61.8
Panamanian	15,743	53.1
Salvadoran	93,381	66.1
Cuban	30,152	43.2
Dominican Republic	400,918	59.7
Mexican	239,451	56.7
Puerto Rican	11,935	1.1
South American	361,188	67.8
Argentinean	15,765	66.1
Bolivian	5,137	65.6
Chilean	10,100	64.9
Colombian	96,977	65.7
Ecuadorian	161,322	68.8
Paraguayan	4,864	73.3
Peruvian	48,639	70.7
Uruguayan	4,174	68.7
Venezuelan	9,586	66.1
Spaniard	9,837	29.2

Foreign-Born Naturalized U.S. Citizens

Group	Number	%
Total Population	2,170,747	51.9
Hispanic or Latino (of any race)	488,365	37.3
Central American, ex. Mexican	70,817	32.2
Costa Rican	4,238	64.0
Guatemalan	12,186	25.7
Honduran	13,337	29.1
Nicaraguan	3,837	48.1
Panamanian	10,494	66.7
Salvadoran	25,137	26.9
Cuban	21,842	72.4
Dominican Republic	183,124	45.7
Mexican	27,058	11.3
Puerto Rican	6,428	53.9
South American	154,121	42.7
Argentinean	7,503	47.6
Bolivian	2,747	53.5
Chilean	4,981	49.3
Colombian	53,144	54.8
Ecuadorian	54,428	33.7
Paraguayan	1,167	24.0
Peruvian	22,582	46.4
Uruguayan	1,694	40.6
Venezuelan	3,145	32.8
Spaniard	4,500	45.7

Language Spoken at Home: English Only

(Universe: Population 5 Years and Over)

Group	Number	%
Total Population	12,788,323	70.8
Hispanic or Latino (of any race)	559,145	18.6
Central American, ex. Mexican	31,856	10.4
Costa Rican	2,674	25.1
Guatemalan	5,045	8.3
Honduran	5,282	8.4
Nicaraguan	1,687	13.8
Panamanian	10,034	35.9
Salvadoran	6,337	5.0
Cuban	23,509	35.5
Dominican Republic	34,632	5.6
Mexican	46,803	12.5
Puerto Rican	324,593	32.0
South American	48,893	9.9
Argentinean	3,910	17.5
Bolivian	855	11.8
Chilean	2,814	19.0
Colombian	15,856	11.5
Ecuadorian	12,114	5.7
Paraguayan	591	9.5
Peruvian	6,852	10.6
Uruguayan	654	11.6
Venezuelan	3,258	24.0
Spaniard	15,949	50.3

Language Spoken at Home: Spanish

(Universe: Population 5 Years and Over)

Group	Number	%
Total Population	2,613,816	14.5
Hispanic or Latino (of any race)	2,435,438	80.9
Central American, ex. Mexican	272,361	89.0
Costa Rican	7,977	74.8
Guatemalan	55,259	91.4
Honduran	56,980	90.6
Nicaraguan	10,433	85.5
Panamanian	17,740	63.5
Salvadoran	120,051	94.6
Cuban	42,031	63.4
Dominican Republic	584,085	94.2
Mexican	323,954	86.8
Puerto Rican	685,246	67.6
South American	441,267	89.5
Argentinean	17,818	79.6
Bolivian	6,410	88.1
Chilean	11,859	80.2
Colombian	121,384	88.1
Ecuadorian	201,260	94.1
Paraguayan	5,456	87.5
Peruvian	57,434	88.9
Uruguayan	4,809	85.4
Venezuelan	10,031	73.8
Spaniard	14,658	46.3

Unemployment Rate

(Universe: Population 16 Years and Over)

Group	%
Total Population	7.5
Hispanic or Latino (of any race)	10.0
Central American, ex. Mexican	8.6
Costa Rican	9.4
Guatemalan	7.4
Honduran	8.7
Nicaraguan	10.3
Panamanian	9.4
Salvadoran	8.7
Cuban	9.1
Dominican Republic	11.8
Mexican	6.7
Puerto Rican	12.4
South American	7.6
Argentinean	5.9
Bolivian	7.3
Chilean	7.4
Colombian	7.9
Ecuadorian	7.7
Paraguayan	6.4
Peruvian	7.1
Uruguayan	6.3
Venezuelan	10.7
Spaniard	7.5

Class of Worker: Private Wage and Salary

(Universe: Civilian Employed Population 16 Years and Over)

Group	Number	%
Total Population	6,951,209	76.8
Hispanic or Latino (of any race)	1,155,761	81.6
Central American, ex. Mexican	147,505	85.1
Costa Rican	3,944	76.0
Guatemalan	31,052	85.6
Honduran	30,343	85.9
Nicaraguan	5,709	82.1
Panamanian	10,076	69.7
Salvadoran	64,284	88.6
Cuban	23,863	77.4
Dominican Republic	232,067	82.4
Mexican	174,453	90.0
Puerto Rican	298,358	75.2
South American	232,734	82.8
Argentinean	10,907	82.2
Bolivian	3,463	85.5
Chilean	6,546	75.2
Colombian	62,595	81.1
Ecuadorian	103,600	85.1
Paraguayan	3,054	76.8
Peruvian	30,771	82.0
Uruguayan	2,602	81.4
Venezuelan	6,411	80.6
Spaniard	12,762	73.9

Class of Worker: Government

(Universe: Civilian Employed Population 16 Years and Over)

Group	Number	%
Total Population	1,520,566	16.8
Hispanic or Latino (of any race)	175,155	12.4
Central American, ex. Mexican	13,564	7.8
Costa Rican	862	16.6
Guatemalan	1,885	5.2
Honduran	2,745	7.8

Notes: (1) Percent of total population; (2) Percent of Hispanic/Latino population; Profiles include places with an overall population of at least 125,000, OR an overall population of at least 25,000 where the Hispanic/Latino population is at least 20% of the overall population. In states where less than five places meet either of these criteria, we have included places with at least 10,000 total population with the highest percentage of Hispanic/Latino population. These places are identified with an asterisk (*); Please refer to the User's Guide for a full explanation of data.

Group	Number	%
Nicaraguan	707	10.2
Panamanian	3,641	25.2
Salvadoran	3,432	4.7
Cuban	5,457	17.7
Dominican Republic	30,265	10.8
Mexican	7,491	3.9
Puerto Rican	85,316	21.5
South American	23,561	8.4
Argentinean	1,197	9.0
Bolivian	190	4.7
Chilean	1,074	12.3
Colombian	7,343	9.5
Ecuadorian	8,157	6.7
Paraguayan	117	2.9
Peruvian	3,629	9.7
Uruguayan	311	9.7
Venezuelan	959	12.1
Spaniard	3,703	21.4

Means of Transportation to Work: Car, Truck or Van

(Universe: Workers 16 Years and Over)

Group	Number	%
Total Population	5,422,644	61.5
Hispanic or Latino (of any race)	565,551	41.0
Central American, ex. Mexican	86,484	50.9
Costa Rican	2,583	51.8
Guatemalan	15,739	44.0
Honduran	13,063	37.9
Nicaraguan	2,145	31.7
Panamanian	4,807	33.6
Salvadoran	46,970	66.0
Cuban	15,877	52.6
Dominican Republic	87,909	32.5
Mexican	50,516	26.3
Puerto Rican	180,027	46.7
South American	116,193	42.5
Argentinean	5,771	45.3
Bolivian	1,937	49.6
Chilean	4,474	52.5
Colombian	34,299	45.8
Ecuadorian	44,494	37.4
Paraguayan	2,195	56.0
Peruvian	17,174	47.2
Uruguayan	1,498	47.1
Venezuelan	2,735	35.8
Spaniard	9,626	56.5

Means of Transportation to Work: Public Transportation (ex. Taxicab)

(Universe: Workers 16 Years and Over)

Group	Number	%
Total Population	2,338,345	26.5
Hispanic or Latino (of any race)	619,743	44.9
Central American, ex. Mexican	61,068	35.9
Costa Rican	2,102	42.2
Guatemalan	13,455	37.6
Honduran	16,408	47.6
Nicaraguan	3,628	53.6
Panamanian	8,036	56.2
Salvadoran	16,274	22.9
Cuban	10,189	33.8
Dominican Republic	138,155	51.1
Mexican	105,149	54.8
Puerto Rican	157,980	41.0
South American	125,110	45.7
Argentinean	4,785	37.6
Bolivian	1,552	39.8
Chilean	2,763	32.4
Colombian	32,425	43.3
Ecuadorian	60,827	51.2
Paraguayan	1,371	35.0
Peruvian	14,980	41.2
Uruguayan	1,168	36.7
Venezuelan	3,661	47.9
Spaniard	5,362	31.5

Homeownership Rate

(Universe: Occupied Housing Units)

Group	%
Total Population	53.3
Hispanic or Latino (of any race)	23.2
Central American, ex. Mexican	28.8
Costa Rican	35.7
Guatemalan	19.5
Honduran	19.1
Nicaraguan	23.1
Panamanian	30.9
Salvadoran	38.5
Cuban	36.2
Dominican Republic	14.1
Mexican	13.9
Puerto Rican	23.4
South American	31.0
Argentinean	42.9
Bolivian	44.4
Chilean	35.7
Colombian	31.9
Ecuadorian	26.0
Paraguayan	23.5
Peruvian	34.5
Uruguayan	38.8
Venezuelan	30.7
Spaniard	53.6

Median Home Value

Group	Dollars
Total Population	303,900
Hispanic or Latino (of any race)	405,800
Central American, ex. Mexican	385,900
Costa Rican	371,600
Guatemalan	386,300
Honduran	392,300
Nicaraguan	455,600
Panamanian	438,000
Salvadoran	373,100
Cuban	417,600
Dominican Republic	439,000
Mexican	380,100
Puerto Rican	371,800
South American	454,700
Argentinean	496,500
Bolivian	527,500
Chilean	459,800
Colombian	432,200
Ecuadorian	470,600
Paraguayan	426,800
Peruvian	455,500
Uruguayan	469,800
Venezuelan	378,300
Spaniard	449,800

Median Gross Rent

Group	Dollars
Total Population	977
Hispanic or Latino (of any race)	986
Central American, ex. Mexican	1,110
Costa Rican	1,095
Guatemalan	1,215
Honduran	997
Nicaraguan	1,077
Panamanian	1,000
Salvadoran	1,212
Cuban	877
Dominican Republic	937
Mexican	1,194
Puerto Rican	826
South American	1,170
Argentinean	1,243
Bolivian	1,365
Chilean	1,167
Colombian	1,163
Ecuadorian	1,156
Paraguayan	1,287
Peruvian	1,175
Uruguayan	1,291
Venezuelan	1,216
Spaniard	1,206

Median Household Income

(2010 Inflation-Adjusted Dollars)

Group	Dollars
Total Population	55,603
Hispanic or Latino (of any race)	39,541
Central American, ex. Mexican	47,388
Costa Rican	50,805
Guatemalan	46,127
Honduran	40,571
Nicaraguan	52,500
Panamanian	49,707
Salvadoran	51,329
Cuban	49,639
Dominican Republic	31,880
Mexican	40,788
Puerto Rican	33,436
South American	51,599
Argentinean	64,446
Bolivian	58,411
Chilean	64,706
Colombian	52,149
Ecuadorian	48,040
Paraguayan	49,915
Peruvian	51,978
Uruguayan	59,125
Venezuelan	53,305
Spaniard	66,478

Per Capita Income

(2010 Inflation-Adjusted Dollars)

Group	Dollars
Total Population	30,948
Hispanic or Latino (of any race)	17,528
Central American, ex. Mexican	17,209
Costa Rican	21,182
Guatemalan	15,915
Honduran	16,289
Nicaraguan	22,202
Panamanian	23,531
Salvadoran	15,975
Cuban	29,901
Dominican Republic	14,091
Mexican	13,913
Puerto Rican	17,867
South American	21,411
Argentinean	38,302
Bolivian	25,868
Chilean	28,508
Colombian	22,258
Ecuadorian	17,129
Paraguayan	21,045
Peruvian	23,113
Uruguayan	26,543
Venezuelan	32,560
Spaniard	35,721

Households with $100,000+ Income

Group	Number	%
Total Population	1,806,762	25.1
Hispanic or Latino (of any race)	136,343	13.7
Central American, ex. Mexican	13,503	15.1
Costa Rican	550	14.7
Guatemalan	2,299	13.4
Honduran	2,187	11.4
Nicaraguan	846	22.0
Panamanian	1,551	13.4
Salvadoran	5,679	17.5
Cuban	6,382	22.5
Dominican Republic	16,900	8.4
Mexican	11,561	12.1
Puerto Rican	48,256	13.0
South American	30,220	18.4
Argentinean	2,892	31.4
Bolivian	606	23.5
Chilean	1,392	25.4
Colombian	8,815	18.0
Ecuadorian	9,537	14.7
Paraguayan	333	18.5
Peruvian	4,343	19.9
Uruguayan	514	24.3
Venezuelan	1,191	22.8
Spaniard	4,370	30.6

Households with Food Stamps/SNAP Benefits During Past 12 Months

Group	Number	%
Total Population	806,295	11.2
Hispanic or Latino (of any race)	255,528	25.7
Central American, ex. Mexican	12,864	14.4
Costa Rican	492	13.2
Guatemalan	1,988	11.6
Honduran	4,190	21.8
Nicaraguan	737	19.1
Panamanian	1,901	16.4
Salvadoran	3,399	10.5
Cuban	5,525	19.5

Notes: (1) Percent of total population; (2) Percent of Hispanic/Latino population; Profiles include places with an overall population of at least 125,000, OR an overall population of at least 25,000 where the Hispanic/Latino population is at least 20% of the overall population. In states where less than five places meet either of these criteria, we have included places with at least 10,000 total population with the highest percentage of Hispanic/Latino population. These places are identified with an asterisk (*); Please refer to the User's Guide for a full explanation of data.

Group	Number	%
Dominican Republic	75,289	37.6
Mexican	21,792	22.8
Puerto Rican	110,948	29.9
South American	23,210	14.1
Argentinean	923	10.0
Bolivian	248	9.6
Chilean	330	6.0
Colombian	6,155	12.5
Ecuadorian	11,854	18.3
Paraguayan	132	7.3
Peruvian	2,475	11.3
Uruguayan	111	5.3
Venezuelan	771	14.8
Spaniard	670	4.7

Poverty Rate
(Income in Past 12 Months Below Poverty Level)

Group	%
Total Population	14.2
Hispanic or Latino (of any race)	24.5
Central American, ex. Mexican	17.5
Costa Rican	14.1
Guatemalan	18.1
Honduran	22.5
Nicaraguan	14.6
Panamanian	16.2
Salvadoran	15.7
Cuban	16.1
Dominican Republic	28.3
Mexican	28.9
Puerto Rican	29.0
South American	14.4
Argentinean	9.6
Bolivian	9.3
Chilean	6.8
Colombian	12.6
Ecuadorian	17.5
Paraguayan	13.7
Peruvian	12.8
Uruguayan	7.5
Venezuelan	16.0
Spaniard	7.1

Babylon

Population

Group	Number	%TP[1]	%HP[2]
Total Population	213,603	100.0	–
Hispanic or Latino (of any race)	35,793	16.8	100.0
Central American, ex. Mexican	11,096	5.2	31.0
Costa Rican	146	0.1	0.4
Guatemalan	884	0.4	2.5
Honduran	1,756	0.8	4.9
Nicaraguan	112	0.1	0.3
Panamanian	305	0.1	0.9
Salvadoran	7,805	3.7	21.8
Cuban	550	0.3	1.5
Dominican Republic	6,543	3.1	18.3
Mexican	1,145	0.5	3.2
Puerto Rican	7,562	3.5	21.1
South American	5,576	2.6	15.6
Argentinean	336	0.2	0.9
Chilean	226	0.1	0.6
Colombian	2,036	1.0	5.7
Ecuadorian	1,348	0.6	3.8
Peruvian	1,313	0.6	3.7
Venezuelan	104	<0.1	0.3
Spaniard	506	0.2	1.4

Population Growth: 2000–2010

Group	%
Total Population	0.9
Hispanic or Latino (of any race)	68.2
Central American, ex. Mexican	212.4
Guatemalan	277.8
Honduran	365.8
Panamanian	76.3
Salvadoran	206.2
Cuban	12.9
Dominican Republic	105.2
Mexican	51.5
Puerto Rican	22.6
South American	121.8
Argentinean	125.5
Chilean	115.2
Colombian	90.1
Ecuadorian	149.6
Peruvian	226.6
Spaniard	283.3

Males per 100 Females

Group	Number
Total Population	93.7
Hispanic or Latino (of any race)	101.6
Central American, ex. Mexican	119.2
Costa Rican	53.7
Guatemalan	132.6
Honduran	134.8
Nicaraguan	133.3
Panamanian	62.2
Salvadoran	118.8
Cuban	87.7
Dominican Republic	95.3
Mexican	117.7
Puerto Rican	93.6
South American	89.4
Argentinean	108.7
Chilean	76.6
Colombian	77.8
Ecuadorian	92.3
Peruvian	103.3
Venezuelan	82.5
Spaniard	96.9

Average Household Size

Group	People
Total Population	2.98
Hispanic or Latino (of any race)	4.39
Central American, ex. Mexican	5.64
Costa Rican	3.85
Guatemalan	5.02
Honduran	5.54
Nicaraguan	4.52
Panamanian	3.09
Salvadoran	5.99
Cuban	2.89
Dominican Republic	5.05
Mexican	3.79
Puerto Rican	3.23
South American	4.05
Argentinean	3.43
Chilean	3.30
Colombian	3.80
Ecuadorian	4.40
Peruvian	4.67
Venezuelan	2.84
Spaniard	3.18

Median Age

Group	Years
Total Population	39.2
Hispanic or Latino (of any race)	29.4
Central American, ex. Mexican	28.5
Costa Rican	35.3
Guatemalan	28.6
Honduran	28.5
Nicaraguan	32.2
Panamanian	36.8
Salvadoran	28.1
Cuban	35.7
Dominican Republic	29.5
Mexican	26.6
Puerto Rican	29.9
South American	35.3
Argentinean	39.1
Chilean	36.3
Colombian	35.7
Ecuadorian	33.7
Peruvian	34.9
Venezuelan	31.5
Spaniard	33.9

High School Graduates
(Universe: Population 25 Years and Over)

Group	Number	%
Total Population	122,951	86.8
Hispanic or Latino (of any race)	11,975	66.3
Central American, ex. Mexican	2,503	44.0
Salvadoran	1,700	44.4
Dominican Republic	1,878	61.5
Mexican	314	78.5
Puerto Rican	3,523	84.0
South American	2,596	80.9
Colombian	953	78.2
Ecuadorian	865	84.1

Four-Year College Graduates
(Universe: Population 25 Years and Over)

Group	Number	%
Total Population	31,689	22.4
Hispanic or Latino (of any race)	2,169	12.0
Central American, ex. Mexican	448	7.9
Salvadoran	258	6.7
Dominican Republic	226	7.4
Mexican	29	7.3
Puerto Rican	612	14.6
South American	591	18.4
Colombian	260	21.3
Ecuadorian	116	11.3

Population Age 3–17 Enrolled in Public School
(Universe: Population Age 3–17 Enrolled in School)

Group	Number	%
Total Population	36,291	88.7
Hispanic or Latino (of any race)	7,446	96.3
Central American, ex. Mexican	2,194	99.5
Salvadoran	1,556	99.3
Dominican Republic	1,337	96.3
Mexican	222	87.1
Puerto Rican	2,024	92.4
South American	1,067	99.3
Colombian	422	98.1
Ecuadorian	386	100.0

Population Age 3–17 Enrolled in Private School
(Universe: Population Age 3–17 Enrolled in School)

Group	Number	%
Total Population	4,609	11.3
Hispanic or Latino (of any race)	287	3.7
Central American, ex. Mexican	11	0.5
Salvadoran	11	0.7
Dominican Republic	52	3.7
Mexican	33	12.9
Puerto Rican	167	7.6
South American	8	0.7
Colombian	8	1.9
Ecuadorian	0	0.0

Foreign-Born Population

Group	Number	%
Total Population	36,312	17.0
Hispanic or Latino (of any race)	13,650	41.8
Central American, ex. Mexican	6,619	65.4
Salvadoran	4,401	63.7
Dominican Republic	3,121	55.2
Mexican	258	28.0
Puerto Rican	79	1.0
South American	2,911	54.4
Colombian	916	45.4
Ecuadorian	926	50.4

Foreign-Born Naturalized U.S. Citizens

Group	Number	%
Total Population	19,230	53.0
Hispanic or Latino (of any race)	5,006	36.7
Central American, ex. Mexican	1,506	22.8
Salvadoran	1,057	24.0
Dominican Republic	1,305	41.8
Mexican	117	45.3
Puerto Rican	53	67.1
South American	1,662	57.1
Colombian	569	62.1
Ecuadorian	465	50.2

Language Spoken at Home: English Only
(Universe: Population 5 Years and Over)

Group	Number	%
Total Population	158,352	78.8
Hispanic or Latino (of any race)	7,893	26.6
Central American, ex. Mexican	468	5.2
Salvadoran	242	3.9
Dominican Republic	587	11.3
Mexican	519	60.0

Notes: (1) Percent of total population; (2) Percent of Hispanic/Latino population; Profiles include places with an overall population of at least 125,000, OR an overall population of at least 25,000 where the Hispanic/Latino population is at least 20% of the overall population. In states where less than five places meet either of these criteria, we have included places with at least 10,000 total population with the highest percentage of Hispanic/Latino population. These places are identified with an asterisk (*); Please refer to the User's Guide for a full explanation of data.

Group	Number	%
Puerto Rican	3,965	54.2
South American	1,259	25.4
Colombian	491	26.9
Ecuadorian	274	16.4

Language Spoken at Home: Spanish
(Universe: Population 5 Years and Over)

Group	Number	%
Total Population	23,069	11.5
Hispanic or Latino (of any race)	21,689	73.1
Central American, ex. Mexican	8,571	94.8
Salvadoran	5,947	96.1
Dominican Republic	4,611	88.4
Mexican	346	40.0
Puerto Rican	3,347	45.8
South American	3,659	73.8
Colombian	1,331	73.1
Ecuadorian	1,392	83.6

Unemployment Rate
(Universe: Population 16 Years and Over)

Group	%
Total Population	5.8
Hispanic or Latino (of any race)	5.6
Central American, ex. Mexican	6.0
Salvadoran	4.6
Dominican Republic	5.0
Mexican	0.0
Puerto Rican	5.7
South American	4.9
Colombian	7.5
Ecuadorian	6.2

Class of Worker: Private Wage and Salary
(Universe: Civilian Employed Population 16 Years and Over)

Group	Number	%
Total Population	83,449	79.6
Hispanic or Latino (of any race)	13,066	85.9
Central American, ex. Mexican	4,407	88.8
Salvadoran	3,125	88.4
Dominican Republic	2,168	80.2
Mexican	362	90.0
Puerto Rican	2,799	85.1
South American	2,364	86.0
Colombian	815	83.8
Ecuadorian	846	89.1

Class of Worker: Government
(Universe: Civilian Employed Population 16 Years and Over)

Group	Number	%
Total Population	16,855	16.1
Hispanic or Latino (of any race)	1,346	8.9
Central American, ex. Mexican	246	5.0
Salvadoran	125	3.5
Dominican Republic	297	11.0
Mexican	40	10.0
Puerto Rican	433	13.2
South American	269	9.8
Colombian	66	6.8
Ecuadorian	104	10.9

Means of Transportation to Work: Car, Truck or Van
(Universe: Workers 16 Years and Over)

Group	Number	%
Total Population	87,432	85.2
Hispanic or Latino (of any race)	12,762	85.5
Central American, ex. Mexican	4,211	85.7
Salvadoran	2,985	85.2
Dominican Republic	2,289	87.1
Mexican	251	62.1
Puerto Rican	2,843	89.4
South American	2,305	85.1
Colombian	743	78.5
Ecuadorian	813	85.2

Means of Transportation to Work: Public Transportation (ex. Taxicab)
(Universe: Workers 16 Years and Over)

Group	Number	%
Total Population	9,205	9.0
Hispanic or Latino (of any race)	1,131	7.6
Central American, ex. Mexican	303	6.2
Salvadoran	288	8.2
Dominican Republic	174	6.6
Mexican	96	23.8
Puerto Rican	205	6.4
South American	178	6.6
Colombian	123	13.0
Ecuadorian	55	5.8

Homeownership Rate
(Universe: Occupied Housing Units)

Group	%
Total Population	74.2
Hispanic or Latino (of any race)	63.4
Central American, ex. Mexican	59.3
Costa Rican	61.0
Guatemalan	49.4
Honduran	42.0
Nicaraguan	60.9
Panamanian	68.8
Salvadoran	63.8
Cuban	74.5
Dominican Republic	60.6
Mexican	47.5
Puerto Rican	65.6
South American	68.4
Argentinean	76.8
Chilean	66.7
Colombian	67.7
Ecuadorian	67.4
Peruvian	66.6
Venezuelan	64.0
Spaniard	81.0

Median Home Value

Group	Dollars
Total Population	387,800
Hispanic or Latino (of any race)	379,900
Central American, ex. Mexican	381,300
Salvadoran	364,400
Dominican Republic	377,000
Mexican	334,200
Puerto Rican	384,700
South American	406,700
Colombian	411,300
Ecuadorian	394,200

Median Gross Rent

Group	Dollars
Total Population	1,410
Hispanic or Latino (of any race)	1,475
Central American, ex. Mexican	1,619
Salvadoran	1,585
Dominican Republic	1,330
Mexican	865
Puerto Rican	1,566
South American	1,311
Colombian	1,137
Ecuadorian	1,288

Median Household Income
(2010 Inflation-Adjusted Dollars)

Group	Dollars
Total Population	77,407
Hispanic or Latino (of any race)	64,499
Central American, ex. Mexican	70,196
Salvadoran	64,786
Dominican Republic	53,856
Mexican	62,941
Puerto Rican	62,132
South American	69,190
Colombian	67,589
Ecuadorian	67,161

Per Capita Income
(2010 Inflation-Adjusted Dollars)

Group	Dollars
Total Population	30,107
Hispanic or Latino (of any race)	18,991
Central American, ex. Mexican	16,733
Salvadoran	15,711
Dominican Republic	16,861
Mexican	15,056
Puerto Rican	20,473
South American	20,555
Colombian	20,012
Ecuadorian	18,691

Households with $100,000+ Income

Group	Number	%
Total Population	24,909	35.8
Hispanic or Latino (of any race)	1,965	27.9
Central American, ex. Mexican	550	26.4
Salvadoran	374	25.8
Dominican Republic	236	16.7
Mexican	0	0.0
Puerto Rican	662	39.0
South American	307	26.9
Colombian	107	30.3
Ecuadorian	91	23.3

Households with Food Stamps/SNAP Benefits During Past 12 Months

Group	Number	%
Total Population	2,847	4.1
Hispanic or Latino (of any race)	427	6.1
Central American, ex. Mexican	127	6.1
Salvadoran	100	6.9
Dominican Republic	132	9.4
Mexican	0	0.0
Puerto Rican	98	5.8
South American	62	5.4
Colombian	27	7.6
Ecuadorian	14	3.6

Poverty Rate
(Income in Past 12 Months Below Poverty Level)

Group	%
Total Population	6.1
Hispanic or Latino (of any race)	9.5
Central American, ex. Mexican	10.6
Salvadoran	12.2
Dominican Republic	8.7
Mexican	25.1
Puerto Rican	9.5
South American	9.1
Colombian	15.8
Ecuadorian	5.8

Bay Shore

Population

Group	Number	%TP[1]	%HP[2]
Total Population	26,337	100.0	–
Hispanic or Latino (of any race)	8,101	30.8	100.0
Central American, ex. Mexican	1,992	7.6	24.6
Guatemalan	159	0.6	2.0
Honduran	239	0.9	3.0
Salvadoran	1,477	5.6	18.2
Dominican Republic	806	3.1	9.9
Mexican	336	1.3	4.1
Puerto Rican	2,245	8.5	27.7
South American	1,997	7.6	24.7
Colombian	500	1.9	6.2
Ecuadorian	1,038	3.9	12.8
Peruvian	305	1.2	3.8

Population Growth: 2000–2010

Group	%
Total Population	10.4
Hispanic or Latino (of any race)	71.0
Central American, ex. Mexican	222.3
Salvadoran	251.7
Dominican Republic	167.8
Mexican	202.7
Puerto Rican	21.0
South American	151.2
Colombian	77.3
Ecuadorian	181.3

Males per 100 Females

Group	Number
Total Population	94.1
Hispanic or Latino (of any race)	97.7
Central American, ex. Mexican	109.0
Guatemalan	101.3
Honduran	111.5
Salvadoran	109.2
Dominican Republic	74.8
Mexican	124.0
Puerto Rican	91.9

Notes: (1) Percent of total population; (2) Percent of Hispanic/Latino population; Profiles include places with an overall population of at least 125,000, OR an overall population of at least 25,000 where the Hispanic/Latino population is at least 20% of the overall population. In states where less than five places meet either of these criteria, we have included places with at least 10,000 total population with the highest percentage of Hispanic/Latino population. These places are identified with an asterisk (*); Please refer to the User's Guide for a full explanation of data.

Group	
South American	102.7
Colombian	87.3
Ecuadorian	119.9
Peruvian	88.3

Average Household Size

Group	People
Total Population	2.88
Hispanic or Latino (of any race)	3.94
Central American, ex. Mexican	5.02
Guatemalan	4.50
Honduran	4.81
Salvadoran	5.35
Dominican Republic	4.25
Mexican	4.28
Puerto Rican	2.98
South American	4.35
Colombian	3.97
Ecuadorian	4.76
Peruvian	4.06

Median Age

Group	Years
Total Population	37.4
Hispanic or Latino (of any race)	29.3
Central American, ex. Mexican	29.1
Guatemalan	28.2
Honduran	31.3
Salvadoran	28.6
Dominican Republic	27.2
Mexican	25.7
Puerto Rican	30.4
South American	32.4
Colombian	31.6
Ecuadorian	31.1
Peruvian	34.5

High School Graduates
(Universe: Population 25 Years and Over)

Group	Number	%
Total Population	15,558	84.3
Hispanic or Latino (of any race)	3,131	71.5
Puerto Rican	1,188	79.9
South American	803	70.4

Four-Year College Graduates
(Universe: Population 25 Years and Over)

Group	Number	%
Total Population	4,278	23.2
Hispanic or Latino (of any race)	641	14.6
Puerto Rican	128	8.6
South American	236	20.7

Population Age 3–17 Enrolled in Public School
(Universe: Population Age 3–17 Enrolled in School)

Group	Number	%
Total Population	4,844	88.6
Hispanic or Latino (of any race)	1,563	91.9
Puerto Rican	436	86.2
South American	449	100.0

Population Age 3–17 Enrolled in Private School
(Universe: Population Age 3–17 Enrolled in School)

Group	Number	%
Total Population	624	11.4
Hispanic or Latino (of any race)	137	8.1
Puerto Rican	70	13.8
South American	0	0.0

Foreign-Born Population

Group	Number	%
Total Population	5,285	18.9
Hispanic or Latino (of any race)	2,650	36.0
Puerto Rican	27	1.2
South American	1,293	62.9

Foreign-Born Naturalized U.S. Citizens

Group	Number	%
Total Population	2,295	43.4
Hispanic or Latino (of any race)	734	27.7
Puerto Rican	0	0.0
South American	415	32.1

Language Spoken at Home: English Only
(Universe: Population 5 Years and Over)

Group	Number	%
Total Population	18,571	71.8
Hispanic or Latino (of any race)	1,429	21.6
Puerto Rican	852	39.4
South American	66	3.7

Language Spoken at Home: Spanish
(Universe: Population 5 Years and Over)

Group	Number	%
Total Population	5,320	20.6
Hispanic or Latino (of any race)	5,189	78.4
Puerto Rican	1,313	60.6
South American	1,734	96.3

Unemployment Rate
(Universe: Population 16 Years and Over)

Group	%
Total Population	7.6
Hispanic or Latino (of any race)	5.9
Puerto Rican	8.4
South American	1.4

Class of Worker: Private Wage and Salary
(Universe: Civilian Employed Population 16 Years and Over)

Group	Number	%
Total Population	10,106	77.2
Hispanic or Latino (of any race)	3,104	86.6
Puerto Rican	773	82.9
South American	1,031	89.0

Class of Worker: Government
(Universe: Civilian Employed Population 16 Years and Over)

Group	Number	%
Total Population	2,343	17.9
Hispanic or Latino (of any race)	270	7.5
Puerto Rican	155	16.6
South American	22	1.9

Means of Transportation to Work: Car, Truck or Van
(Universe: Workers 16 Years and Over)

Group	Number	%
Total Population	10,405	84.1
Hispanic or Latino (of any race)	3,013	87.1
Puerto Rican	741	91.5
South American	905	78.1

Means of Transportation to Work: Public Transportation (ex. Taxicab)
(Universe: Workers 16 Years and Over)

Group	Number	%
Total Population	943	7.6
Hispanic or Latino (of any race)	261	7.5
Puerto Rican	36	4.4
South American	130	11.2

Homeownership Rate
(Universe: Occupied Housing Units)

Group	%
Total Population	59.0
Hispanic or Latino (of any race)	49.2
Central American, ex. Mexican	61.1
Guatemalan	60.5
Honduran	47.4
Salvadoran	67.0
Dominican Republic	44.6
Mexican	46.9
Puerto Rican	42.5
South American	50.7
Colombian	53.5
Ecuadorian	45.0
Peruvian	56.6

Median Home Value

Group	Dollars
Total Population	359,900
Hispanic or Latino (of any race)	368,600
Puerto Rican	378,700
South American	336,800

Median Gross Rent

Group	Dollars
Total Population	1,299
Hispanic or Latino (of any race)	1,317
Puerto Rican	1,259
South American	1,215

Median Household Income
(2010 Inflation-Adjusted Dollars)

Group	Dollars
Total Population	66,382
Hispanic or Latino (of any race)	69,148
Puerto Rican	47,813
South American	71,181

Per Capita Income
(2010 Inflation-Adjusted Dollars)

Group	Dollars
Total Population	27,648
Hispanic or Latino (of any race)	22,199
Puerto Rican	25,216
South American	18,443

Households with $100,000+ Income

Group	Number	%
Total Population	2,534	28.2
Hispanic or Latino (of any race)	505	29.1
Puerto Rican	188	24.5
South American	103	23.9

Households with Food Stamps/SNAP Benefits During Past 12 Months

Group	Number	%
Total Population	700	7.8
Hispanic or Latino (of any race)	127	7.3
Puerto Rican	115	15.0
South American	5	1.2

Poverty Rate
(Income in Past 12 Months Below Poverty Level)

Group	%
Total Population	9.1
Hispanic or Latino (of any race)	9.6
Puerto Rican	13.3
South American	14.7

Brentwood

Population

Group	Number	%TP[1]	%HP[2]
Total Population	60,664	100.0	–
Hispanic or Latino (of any race)	41,529	68.5	100.0
Central American, ex. Mexican	19,957	32.9	48.1
Guatemalan	1,553	2.6	3.7
Honduran	2,062	3.4	5.0
Panamanian	148	0.2	0.4
Salvadoran	15,946	26.3	38.4
Cuban	223	0.4	0.5
Dominican Republic	4,205	6.9	10.1
Mexican	1,193	2.0	2.9
Puerto Rican	6,125	10.1	14.7
South American	6,350	10.5	15.3
Argentinean	203	0.3	0.5
Chilean	153	0.3	0.4
Colombian	2,083	3.4	5.0
Ecuadorian	1,985	3.3	4.8
Peruvian	1,610	2.7	3.9
Venezuelan	113	0.2	0.3
Spaniard	158	0.3	0.4

Population Growth: 2000–2010

Group	%
Total Population	12.5
Hispanic or Latino (of any race)	42.0
Central American, ex. Mexican	142.8
Guatemalan	118.7
Honduran	277.7
Panamanian	8.0
Salvadoran	149.7
Cuban	8.8
Dominican Republic	53.2
Mexican	154.4
Puerto Rican	-25.8
South American	102.3
Colombian	53.5
Ecuadorian	148.7
Peruvian	196.0

Notes: (1) Percent of total population; (2) Percent of Hispanic/Latino population; Profiles include places with an overall population of at least 125,000, OR an overall population of at least 25,000 where the Hispanic/Latino population is at least 20% of the overall population. In states where less than five places meet either of these criteria, we have included places with at least 10,000 total population with the highest percentage of Hispanic/Latino population. These places are identified with an asterisk (*); Please refer to the User's Guide for a full explanation of data.

Males per 100 Females

Group	Number
Total Population	103.6
Hispanic or Latino (of any race)	108.3
Central American, ex. Mexican	114.5
Guatemalan	134.6
Honduran	113.2
Panamanian	92.2
Salvadoran	113.4
Cuban	102.7
Dominican Republic	94.0
Mexican	122.2
Puerto Rican	101.1
South American	102.0
Argentinean	116.0
Chilean	139.1
Colombian	93.6
Ecuadorian	105.3
Peruvian	104.8
Venezuelan	94.8
Spaniard	105.2

Average Household Size

Group	People
Total Population	4.35
Hispanic or Latino (of any race)	5.13
Central American, ex. Mexican	5.95
Guatemalan	5.50
Honduran	5.72
Panamanian	4.51
Salvadoran	6.08
Cuban	3.28
Dominican Republic	4.97
Mexican	5.30
Puerto Rican	3.70
South American	4.98
Argentinean	4.37
Chilean	4.15
Colombian	4.67
Ecuadorian	5.25
Peruvian	5.30
Venezuelan	4.61
Spaniard	3.79

Median Age

Group	Years
Total Population	32.0
Hispanic or Latino (of any race)	29.6
Central American, ex. Mexican	28.8
Guatemalan	30.0
Honduran	28.9
Panamanian	35.0
Salvadoran	28.5
Cuban	37.5
Dominican Republic	32.0
Mexican	25.2
Puerto Rican	33.6
South American	35.2
Argentinean	35.3
Chilean	40.8
Colombian	37.7
Ecuadorian	33.7
Peruvian	35.4
Venezuelan	28.1
Spaniard	27.0

High School Graduates
(Universe: Population 25 Years and Over)

Group	Number	%
Total Population	23,801	69.0
Hispanic or Latino (of any race)	12,280	59.2
Central American, ex. Mexican	3,574	41.7
Guatemalan	523	51.5
Honduran	351	29.1
Salvadoran	2,575	42.0
Dominican Republic	1,389	64.1
Puerto Rican	3,109	68.4
South American	3,330	85.4
Colombian	851	83.8
Ecuadorian	836	74.1
Peruvian	1,153	96.1

Four-Year College Graduates
(Universe: Population 25 Years and Over)

Group	Number	%
Total Population	4,956	14.4
Hispanic or Latino (of any race)	1,980	9.5
Central American, ex. Mexican	343	4.0
Guatemalan	77	7.6
Honduran	41	3.4
Salvadoran	187	3.0
Dominican Republic	288	13.3
Puerto Rican	468	10.3
South American	674	17.3
Colombian	168	16.6
Ecuadorian	225	19.9
Peruvian	143	11.9

Population Age 3–17 Enrolled in Public School
(Universe: Population Age 3–17 Enrolled in School)

Group	Number	%
Total Population	9,996	94.4
Hispanic or Latino (of any race)	7,187	95.8
Central American, ex. Mexican	3,160	97.3
Guatemalan	344	93.7
Honduran	125	91.9
Salvadoran	2,547	98.2
Dominican Republic	505	90.7
Puerto Rican	1,429	97.2
South American	1,133	90.3
Colombian	169	95.5
Ecuadorian	553	82.9
Peruvian	250	100.0

Population Age 3–17 Enrolled in Private School
(Universe: Population Age 3–17 Enrolled in School)

Group	Number	%
Total Population	588	5.6
Hispanic or Latino (of any race)	313	4.2
Central American, ex. Mexican	88	2.7
Guatemalan	23	6.3
Honduran	11	8.1
Salvadoran	46	1.8
Dominican Republic	52	9.3
Puerto Rican	41	2.8
South American	122	9.7
Colombian	8	4.5
Ecuadorian	114	17.1
Peruvian	0	0.0

Foreign-Born Population

Group	Number	%
Total Population	23,162	42.3
Hispanic or Latino (of any race)	17,936	50.9
Central American, ex. Mexican	9,586	65.0
Guatemalan	1,053	71.2
Honduran	1,409	80.8
Salvadoran	6,901	62.0
Dominican Republic	2,252	62.8
Puerto Rican	196	2.7
South American	4,208	64.8
Colombian	1,078	68.7
Ecuadorian	1,285	54.3
Peruvian	1,303	76.4

Foreign-Born Naturalized U.S. Citizens

Group	Number	%
Total Population	8,109	35.0
Hispanic or Latino (of any race)	5,277	29.4
Central American, ex. Mexican	2,331	24.3
Guatemalan	241	22.9
Honduran	259	18.4
Salvadoran	1,689	24.5
Dominican Republic	1,007	44.7
Puerto Rican	98	50.0
South American	1,407	33.4
Colombian	330	30.6
Ecuadorian	459	35.7
Peruvian	384	29.5

Language Spoken at Home: English Only
(Universe: Population 5 Years and Over)

Group	Number	%
Total Population	17,755	34.9
Hispanic or Latino (of any race)	3,564	11.1
Central American, ex. Mexican	275	2.1
Guatemalan	33	2.5
Honduran	0	0.0
Salvadoran	143	1.4
Dominican Republic	157	4.8
Puerto Rican	2,571	36.6
South American	232	4.0
Colombian	64	4.8
Ecuadorian	21	1.0
Peruvian	47	3.0

Language Spoken at Home: Spanish
(Universe: Population 5 Years and Over)

Group	Number	%
Total Population	28,968	57.0
Hispanic or Latino (of any race)	28,439	88.6
Central American, ex. Mexican	12,938	97.9
Guatemalan	1,288	97.5
Honduran	1,567	100.0
Salvadoran	9,797	98.6
Dominican Republic	3,072	94.8
Puerto Rican	4,422	63.0
South American	5,638	96.0
Colombian	1,274	95.2
Ecuadorian	2,081	99.0
Peruvian	1,544	97.0

Unemployment Rate
(Universe: Population 16 Years and Over)

Group	%
Total Population	8.5
Hispanic or Latino (of any race)	8.8
Central American, ex. Mexican	9.8
Guatemalan	5.7
Honduran	0.0
Salvadoran	12.3
Dominican Republic	8.8
Puerto Rican	12.1
South American	6.0
Colombian	7.5
Ecuadorian	9.2
Peruvian	4.5

Class of Worker: Private Wage and Salary
(Universe: Civilian Employed Population 16 Years and Over)

Group	Number	%
Total Population	23,711	85.8
Hispanic or Latino (of any race)	16,270	90.2
Central American, ex. Mexican	7,189	93.7
Guatemalan	736	91.0
Honduran	1,031	92.0
Salvadoran	5,344	95.5
Dominican Republic	1,715	84.7
Puerto Rican	2,702	83.9
South American	3,229	87.9
Colombian	834	83.3
Ecuadorian	936	92.4
Peruvian	965	90.3

Class of Worker: Government
(Universe: Civilian Employed Population 16 Years and Over)

Group	Number	%
Total Population	3,022	10.9
Hispanic or Latino (of any race)	1,185	6.6
Central American, ex. Mexican	253	3.3
Guatemalan	45	5.6
Honduran	39	3.5
Salvadoran	96	1.7
Dominican Republic	247	12.2
Puerto Rican	465	14.4
South American	210	5.7
Colombian	85	8.5
Ecuadorian	21	2.1
Peruvian	45	4.2

Means of Transportation to Work: Car, Truck or Van
(Universe: Workers 16 Years and Over)

Group	Number	%
Total Population	23,226	86.7
Hispanic or Latino (of any race)	15,541	87.8
Central American, ex. Mexican	6,544	87.3
Guatemalan	705	88.0
Honduran	981	89.5
Salvadoran	4,718	86.6
Dominican Republic	1,787	89.8
Puerto Rican	2,737	87.5

STATE & PLACE PROFILES

Notes: (1) Percent of total population; (2) Percent of Hispanic/Latino population; Profiles include places with an overall population of at least 125,000, OR an overall population of at least 25,000 where the Hispanic/Latino population is at least 20% of the overall population. In states where less than five places meet either of these criteria, we have included places with at least 10,000 total population with the highest percentage of Hispanic/Latino population. These places are identified with an asterisk (*); Please refer to the User's Guide for a full explanation of data.

South American	3,121	85.4
Colombian	795	80.0
Ecuadorian	922	92.1
Peruvian	865	80.9

Means of Transportation to Work: Public Transportation (ex. Taxicab)
(Universe: Workers 16 Years and Over)

Group	Number	%
Total Population	1,733	6.5
Hispanic or Latino (of any race)	766	4.3
Central American, ex. Mexican	260	3.5
Guatemalan	45	5.6
Honduran	33	3.0
Salvadoran	171	3.1
Dominican Republic	82	4.1
Puerto Rican	143	4.6
South American	239	6.5
Colombian	76	7.6
Ecuadorian	39	3.9
Peruvian	114	10.7

Homeownership Rate
(Universe: Occupied Housing Units)

Group	%
Total Population	69.6
Hispanic or Latino (of any race)	65.0
Central American, ex. Mexican	63.7
Guatemalan	59.8
Honduran	55.5
Panamanian	82.2
Salvadoran	64.7
Cuban	68.1
Dominican Republic	65.3
Mexican	52.0
Puerto Rican	66.9
South American	67.2
Argentinean	55.8
Chilean	74.4
Colombian	64.8
Ecuadorian	67.7
Peruvian	69.5
Venezuelan	69.6
Spaniard	76.3

Median Home Value

Group	Dollars
Total Population	343,300
Hispanic or Latino (of any race)	346,700
Central American, ex. Mexican	349,900
Guatemalan	341,700
Honduran	430,700
Salvadoran	343,800
Dominican Republic	328,200
Puerto Rican	338,000
South American	359,700
Colombian	367,500
Ecuadorian	333,300
Peruvian	349,000

Median Gross Rent

Group	Dollars
Total Population	1,266
Hispanic or Latino (of any race)	1,208
Central American, ex. Mexican	1,175
Guatemalan	1,442
Honduran	606
Salvadoran	1,315
Dominican Republic	791
Puerto Rican	1,112
South American	1,352
Colombian	1,457
Ecuadorian	1,321
Peruvian	853

Median Household Income
(2010 Inflation-Adjusted Dollars)

Group	Dollars
Total Population	68,750
Hispanic or Latino (of any race)	66,373
Central American, ex. Mexican	67,077
Guatemalan	76,555
Honduran	80,662
Salvadoran	64,622
Dominican Republic	65,684
Puerto Rican	62,109
South American	64,638
Colombian	67,596
Ecuadorian	53,833
Peruvian	60,563

Per Capita Income
(2010 Inflation-Adjusted Dollars)

Group	Dollars
Total Population	20,705
Hispanic or Latino (of any race)	17,994
Central American, ex. Mexican	16,189
Guatemalan	23,065
Honduran	19,636
Salvadoran	14,485
Dominican Republic	17,809
Puerto Rican	21,299
South American	20,160
Colombian	21,403
Ecuadorian	16,219
Peruvian	23,361

Households with $100,000+ Income

Group	Number	%
Total Population	4,043	29.9
Hispanic or Latino (of any race)	2,294	29.2
Central American, ex. Mexican	785	26.9
Guatemalan	132	27.1
Honduran	118	32.3
Salvadoran	526	26.7
Dominican Republic	197	25.8
Puerto Rican	677	33.0
South American	514	32.2
Colombian	114	27.2
Ecuadorian	115	25.3
Peruvian	135	32.1

Households with Food Stamps/SNAP Benefits During Past 12 Months

Group	Number	%
Total Population	1,482	10.9
Hispanic or Latino (of any race)	976	12.4
Central American, ex. Mexican	297	10.2
Guatemalan	0	0.0
Honduran	45	12.3
Salvadoran	252	12.8
Dominican Republic	118	15.4
Puerto Rican	389	19.0
South American	120	7.5
Colombian	10	2.4
Ecuadorian	67	14.8
Peruvian	31	7.4

Poverty Rate
(Income in Past 12 Months Below Poverty Level)

Group	%
Total Population	8.2
Hispanic or Latino (of any race)	8.0
Central American, ex. Mexican	9.1
Guatemalan	1.6
Honduran	9.9
Salvadoran	10.1
Dominican Republic	6.3
Puerto Rican	8.0
South American	6.8
Colombian	9.2
Ecuadorian	4.0
Peruvian	11.0

Bronx

Population

Group	Number	%TP[1]	%HP[2]
Total Population	1,385,108	100.0	–
Hispanic or Latino (of any race)	741,413	53.5	100.0
Central American, ex. Mexican	34,492	2.5	4.7
Costa Rican	1,095	0.1	0.1
Guatemalan	4,645	0.3	0.6
Honduran	17,990	1.3	2.4
Nicaraguan	2,342	0.2	0.3
Panamanian	2,372	0.2	0.3
Salvadoran	5,469	0.4	0.7
Cuban	8,785	0.6	1.2
Dominican Republic	240,987	17.4	32.5
Mexican	71,194	5.1	9.6
Puerto Rican	298,921	21.6	40.3
South American	35,463	2.6	4.8
Argentinean	1,117	0.1	0.2
Bolivian	227	<0.1	<0.1
Chilean	646	<0.1	0.1
Colombian	4,635	0.3	0.6
Ecuadorian	23,206	1.7	3.1
Paraguayan	223	<0.1	<0.1
Peruvian	3,596	0.3	0.5
Uruguayan	148	<0.1	<0.1
Venezuelan	1,296	0.1	0.2
Spaniard	2,097	0.2	0.3

Population Growth: 2000–2010

Group	%
Total Population	3.9
Hispanic or Latino (of any race)	15.0
Central American, ex. Mexican	61.1
Costa Rican	29.4
Guatemalan	93.3
Honduran	76.3
Nicaraguan	41.4
Panamanian	49.7
Salvadoran	67.0
Cuban	6.7
Dominican Republic	81.1
Mexican	107.1
Puerto Rican	-6.4
South American	70.6
Argentinean	74.3
Chilean	30.8
Colombian	52.0
Ecuadorian	80.1
Paraguayan	100.9
Peruvian	96.4
Venezuelan	49.8
Spaniard	96.0

Males per 100 Females

Group	Number
Total Population	88.3
Hispanic or Latino (of any race)	88.7
Central American, ex. Mexican	88.5
Costa Rican	78.9
Guatemalan	105.3
Honduran	84.6
Nicaraguan	84.7
Panamanian	76.0
Salvadoran	99.3
Cuban	103.1
Dominican Republic	80.5
Mexican	131.3
Puerto Rican	83.7
South American	94.9
Argentinean	112.8
Bolivian	87.6
Chilean	84.0
Colombian	76.8
Ecuadorian	98.2
Paraguayan	82.8
Peruvian	101.1
Uruguayan	111.4
Venezuelan	82.8
Spaniard	96.5

Average Household Size

Group	People
Total Population	2.77
Hispanic or Latino (of any race)	3.06
Central American, ex. Mexican	3.35
Costa Rican	2.61
Guatemalan	3.59
Honduran	3.47
Nicaraguan	3.31
Panamanian	2.45
Salvadoran	3.53
Cuban	2.26
Dominican Republic	3.37
Mexican	4.69
Puerto Rican	2.62
South American	3.22
Argentinean	2.55
Bolivian	2.97
Chilean	2.56

Notes: (1) Percent of total population; (2) Percent of Hispanic/Latino population; Profiles include places with an overall population of at least 125,000, OR an overall population of at least 25,000 where the Hispanic/Latino population is at least 20% of the overall population. In states where less than five places meet either of these criteria, we have included places with at least 10,000 total population with the highest percentage of Hispanic/Latino population. These places are identified with an asterisk (*); Please refer to the User's Guide for a full explanation of data.

Colombian	2.63
Ecuadorian	3.47
Paraguayan	3.12
Peruvian	3.10
Uruguayan	2.11
Venezuelan	2.98
Spaniard	2.67

Median Age

Group	Years
Total Population	32.8
Hispanic or Latino (of any race)	29.7
Central American, ex. Mexican	31.7
Costa Rican	39.1
Guatemalan	30.7
Honduran	30.5
Nicaraguan	35.6
Panamanian	38.1
Salvadoran	32.0
Cuban	39.8
Dominican Republic	29.9
Mexican	24.5
Puerto Rican	32.2
South American	35.1
Argentinean	37.8
Bolivian	35.1
Chilean	41.7
Colombian	37.4
Ecuadorian	34.3
Paraguayan	32.3
Peruvian	38.1
Uruguayan	41.0
Venezuelan	28.9
Spaniard	33.4

High School Graduates
(Universe: Population 25 Years and Over)

Group	Number	%
Total Population	578,214	68.8
Hispanic or Latino (of any race)	241,009	58.7
Central American, ex. Mexican	12,583	56.4
Costa Rican	423	65.8
Guatemalan	1,520	45.5
Honduran	5,968	52.1
Nicaraguan	1,375	70.3
Panamanian	1,298	81.6
Salvadoran	1,749	58.8
Cuban	4,033	68.4
Dominican Republic	73,799	58.7
Mexican	14,437	41.2
Puerto Rican	110,615	60.3
South American	18,567	66.5
Argentinean	735	78.4
Colombian	2,901	72.9
Ecuadorian	10,841	61.2
Peruvian	2,184	81.6
Venezuelan	704	83.7
Spaniard	1,572	85.9

Four-Year College Graduates
(Universe: Population 25 Years and Over)

Group	Number	%
Total Population	148,227	17.6
Hispanic or Latino (of any race)	46,757	11.4
Central American, ex. Mexican	2,558	11.5
Costa Rican	82	12.8
Guatemalan	233	7.0
Honduran	1,147	10.0
Nicaraguan	264	13.5
Panamanian	408	25.7
Salvadoran	364	12.2
Cuban	1,084	18.4
Dominican Republic	14,961	11.9
Mexican	1,580	4.5
Puerto Rican	20,122	11.0
South American	4,169	14.9
Argentinean	274	29.2
Colombian	980	24.6
Ecuadorian	1,939	10.9
Peruvian	444	16.6
Venezuelan	208	24.7
Spaniard	852	46.6

Population Age 3–17 Enrolled in Public School
(Universe: Population Age 3–17 Enrolled in School)

Group	Number	%
Total Population	241,152	85.3
Hispanic or Latino (of any race)	146,210	88.2
Central American, ex. Mexican	6,418	90.1
Costa Rican	25	100.0
Guatemalan	634	90.3
Honduran	3,593	89.7
Nicaraguan	327	77.7
Panamanian	515	92.5
Salvadoran	1,120	93.4
Cuban	974	82.4
Dominican Republic	49,492	89.5
Mexican	16,763	95.5
Puerto Rican	62,973	86.6
South American	4,955	82.9
Argentinean	82	85.4
Colombian	578	83.5
Ecuadorian	3,513	81.5
Peruvian	413	84.3
Venezuelan	198	95.2
Spaniard	198	68.0

Population Age 3–17 Enrolled in Private School
(Universe: Population Age 3–17 Enrolled in School)

Group	Number	%
Total Population	41,583	14.7
Hispanic or Latino (of any race)	19,548	11.8
Central American, ex. Mexican	708	9.9
Costa Rican	0	0.0
Guatemalan	68	9.7
Honduran	411	10.3
Nicaraguan	94	22.3
Panamanian	42	7.5
Salvadoran	79	6.6
Cuban	208	17.6
Dominican Republic	5,824	10.5
Mexican	791	4.5
Puerto Rican	9,726	13.4
South American	1,019	17.1
Argentinean	14	14.6
Colombian	114	16.5
Ecuadorian	796	18.5
Peruvian	77	15.7
Venezuelan	10	4.8
Spaniard	93	32.0

Foreign-Born Population

Group	Number	%
Total Population	443,968	32.5
Hispanic or Latino (of any race)	247,987	34.5
Central American, ex. Mexican	23,521	64.3
Costa Rican	425	53.9
Guatemalan	3,703	72.4
Honduran	12,830	65.9
Nicaraguan	1,720	62.4
Panamanian	1,259	47.9
Salvadoran	3,292	63.8
Cuban	3,870	46.5
Dominican Republic	140,358	61.2
Mexican	42,611	60.4
Puerto Rican	2,988	1.0
South American	28,607	70.3
Argentinean	818	72.8
Colombian	3,663	67.8
Ecuadorian	18,700	69.6
Peruvian	2,734	74.4
Venezuelan	917	66.9
Spaniard	1,010	41.2

Foreign-Born Naturalized U.S. Citizens

Group	Number	%
Total Population	193,010	43.5
Hispanic or Latino (of any race)	87,550	35.3
Central American, ex. Mexican	8,996	38.2
Costa Rican	320	75.3
Guatemalan	1,433	38.7
Honduran	4,562	35.6
Nicaraguan	963	56.0
Panamanian	596	47.3
Salvadoran	1,015	30.8
Cuban	2,553	66.0
Dominican Republic	56,919	40.6
Mexican	2,926	6.9
Puerto Rican	1,595	53.4
South American	11,426	39.9
Argentinean	354	43.3
Colombian	1,915	52.3
Ecuadorian	6,849	36.6
Peruvian	1,044	38.2
Venezuelan	284	31.0
Spaniard	406	40.2

Language Spoken at Home: English Only
(Universe: Population 5 Years and Over)

Group	Number	%
Total Population	555,767	44.0
Hispanic or Latino (of any race)	85,678	13.0
Central American, ex. Mexican	3,091	9.1
Costa Rican	170	22.3
Guatemalan	286	6.0
Honduran	1,208	6.8
Nicaraguan	113	4.4
Panamanian	947	37.5
Salvadoran	295	6.0
Cuban	2,279	28.7
Dominican Republic	6,989	3.3
Mexican	2,865	4.6
Puerto Rican	64,033	22.3
South American	2,343	6.2
Argentinean	118	11.2
Colombian	621	11.9
Ecuadorian	926	3.7
Peruvian	149	4.3
Venezuelan	228	17.5
Spaniard	692	29.2

Language Spoken at Home: Spanish
(Universe: Population 5 Years and Over)

Group	Number	%
Total Population	584,463	46.3
Hispanic or Latino (of any race)	569,607	86.7
Central American, ex. Mexican	30,248	89.1
Costa Rican	593	77.7
Guatemalan	4,427	92.4
Honduran	16,117	90.6
Nicaraguan	2,439	95.3
Panamanian	1,544	61.1
Salvadoran	4,618	94.0
Cuban	5,547	69.8
Dominican Republic	202,708	96.6
Mexican	58,620	95.1
Puerto Rican	222,629	77.6
South American	35,612	93.5
Argentinean	928	88.0
Colombian	4,585	88.1
Ecuadorian	23,929	96.1
Peruvian	3,300	94.7
Venezuelan	1,077	82.5
Spaniard	1,662	70.2

Unemployment Rate
(Universe: Population 16 Years and Over)

Group	%
Total Population	12.1
Hispanic or Latino (of any race)	12.6
Central American, ex. Mexican	10.0
Costa Rican	0.0
Guatemalan	7.7
Honduran	11.5
Nicaraguan	4.9
Panamanian	14.6
Salvadoran	9.3
Cuban	21.0
Dominican Republic	12.3
Mexican	6.8
Puerto Rican	14.7
South American	11.5
Argentinean	7.9
Colombian	12.1
Ecuadorian	11.3
Peruvian	13.8
Venezuelan	19.9
Spaniard	10.0

Class of Worker: Private Wage and Salary
(Universe: Civilian Employed Population 16 Years and Over)

Group	Number	%
Total Population	411,009	76.5

STATE & PLACE PROFILES

Notes: (1) Percent of total population; (2) Percent of Hispanic/Latino population; Profiles include places with an overall population of at least 125,000, OR an overall population of at least 25,000 where the Hispanic/Latino population is at least 20% of the overall population. In states where less than five places meet either of these criteria, we have included places with at least 10,000 total population with the highest percentage of Hispanic/Latino population. These places are identified with an asterisk (*); Please refer to the User's Guide for a full explanation of data.

Group	Number	%
Hispanic or Latino (of any race)	214,697	79.2
Central American, ex. Mexican	13,923	81.3
Costa Rican	330	84.4
Guatemalan	2,240	81.2
Honduran	7,086	82.4
Nicaraguan	1,167	79.0
Panamanian	762	69.3
Salvadoran	2,178	84.8
Cuban	1,707	67.2
Dominican Republic	76,765	81.3
Mexican	27,927	91.2
Puerto Rican	73,471	73.5
South American	15,828	79.1
Argentinean	508	82.5
Colombian	2,057	77.5
Ecuadorian	10,232	79.0
Peruvian	1,490	81.5
Venezuelan	548	82.0
Spaniard	914	71.2

Class of Worker: Government
(Universe: Civilian Employed Population 16 Years and Over)

Group	Number	%
Total Population	95,095	17.7
Hispanic or Latino (of any race)	38,665	14.3
Central American, ex. Mexican	1,718	10.0
Costa Rican	40	10.2
Guatemalan	171	6.2
Honduran	829	9.6
Nicaraguan	211	14.3
Panamanian	286	26.0
Salvadoran	139	5.4
Cuban	717	28.2
Dominican Republic	9,388	9.9
Mexican	637	2.1
Puerto Rican	22,716	22.7
South American	2,436	12.2
Argentinean	23	3.7
Colombian	422	15.9
Ecuadorian	1,577	12.2
Peruvian	212	11.6
Venezuelan	112	16.8
Spaniard	278	21.7

Means of Transportation to Work: Car, Truck or Van
(Universe: Workers 16 Years and Over)

Group	Number	%
Total Population	158,403	30.5
Hispanic or Latino (of any race)	69,137	26.4
Central American, ex. Mexican	3,269	19.5
Costa Rican	87	22.3
Guatemalan	412	15.1
Honduran	1,339	16.1
Nicaraguan	463	31.3
Panamanian	322	29.3
Salvadoran	591	23.2
Cuban	986	39.7
Dominican Republic	24,125	26.6
Mexican	3,048	10.1
Puerto Rican	30,775	31.9
South American	5,255	27.0
Argentinean	289	48.0
Colombian	1,058	40.6
Ecuadorian	2,775	22.2
Peruvian	528	30.2
Venezuelan	385	58.4
Spaniard	464	37.2

Means of Transportation to Work: Public Transportation (ex. Taxicab)
(Universe: Workers 16 Years and Over)

Group	Number	%
Total Population	297,629	57.4
Hispanic or Latino (of any race)	156,329	59.7
Central American, ex. Mexican	11,298	67.3
Costa Rican	278	71.1
Guatemalan	2,042	74.7
Honduran	5,725	68.9
Nicaraguan	745	50.4
Panamanian	690	62.8
Salvadoran	1,676	65.7
Cuban	1,097	44.2
Dominican Republic	52,459	57.9
Mexican	22,432	74.4
Puerto Rican	53,480	55.4
South American	11,941	61.4
Argentinean	156	25.9
Colombian	1,297	49.7
Ecuadorian	8,385	67.0
Peruvian	1,069	61.1
Venezuelan	214	32.5
Spaniard	628	50.4

Homeownership Rate
(Universe: Occupied Housing Units)

Group	%
Total Population	19.3
Hispanic or Latino (of any race)	11.1
Central American, ex. Mexican	10.7
Costa Rican	24.9
Guatemalan	9.1
Honduran	7.8
Nicaraguan	13.0
Panamanian	19.5
Salvadoran	11.4
Cuban	17.4
Dominican Republic	7.9
Mexican	4.8
Puerto Rican	13.2
South American	16.9
Argentinean	25.3
Bolivian	27.6
Chilean	20.6
Colombian	17.0
Ecuadorian	15.5
Paraguayan	11.8
Peruvian	18.0
Uruguayan	24.6
Venezuelan	17.1
Spaniard	27.1

Median Home Value

Group	Dollars
Total Population	386,200
Hispanic or Latino (of any race)	368,100
Central American, ex. Mexican	387,400
Costa Rican	345,500
Guatemalan	429,000
Honduran	310,400
Nicaraguan	460,200
Panamanian	378,400
Salvadoran	406,900
Cuban	366,300
Dominican Republic	405,400
Mexican	411,800
Puerto Rican	353,800
South American	400,700
Argentinean	430,400
Colombian	404,800
Ecuadorian	414,200
Peruvian	358,300
Venezuelan	366,700
Spaniard	377,100

Median Gross Rent

Group	Dollars
Total Population	923
Hispanic or Latino (of any race)	911
Central American, ex. Mexican	896
Costa Rican	768
Guatemalan	906
Honduran	885
Nicaraguan	892
Panamanian	994
Salvadoran	936
Cuban	744
Dominican Republic	937
Mexican	1,076
Puerto Rican	840
South American	971
Argentinean	829
Colombian	972
Ecuadorian	980
Peruvian	952
Venezuelan	1,128
Spaniard	998

Median Household Income
(2010 Inflation-Adjusted Dollars)

Group	Dollars
Total Population	34,264
Hispanic or Latino (of any race)	27,800
Central American, ex. Mexican	33,293
Costa Rican	42,891
Guatemalan	37,038
Honduran	30,600
Nicaraguan	35,536
Panamanian	39,127
Salvadoran	27,591
Cuban	22,123
Dominican Republic	27,076
Mexican	32,505
Puerto Rican	25,425
South American	39,853
Argentinean	42,500
Colombian	43,013
Ecuadorian	38,565
Peruvian	36,500
Venezuelan	37,533
Spaniard	51,455

Per Capita Income
(2010 Inflation-Adjusted Dollars)

Group	Dollars
Total Population	17,575
Hispanic or Latino (of any race)	13,842
Central American, ex. Mexican	15,311
Costa Rican	21,674
Guatemalan	16,100
Honduran	14,545
Nicaraguan	18,559
Panamanian	20,431
Salvadoran	11,780
Cuban	17,596
Dominican Republic	12,099
Mexican	10,123
Puerto Rican	15,227
South American	17,316
Argentinean	26,308
Colombian	18,082
Ecuadorian	16,353
Peruvian	17,997
Venezuelan	17,695
Spaniard	33,963

Households with $100,000+ Income

Group	Number	%
Total Population	49,901	10.6
Hispanic or Latino (of any race)	16,109	6.9
Central American, ex. Mexican	793	6.8
Costa Rican	13	3.3
Guatemalan	78	4.8
Honduran	352	5.8
Nicaraguan	93	11.9
Panamanian	134	12.0
Salvadoran	89	6.4
Cuban	344	10.9
Dominican Republic	3,074	4.3
Mexican	922	6.4
Puerto Rican	9,074	8.0
South American	1,354	10.1
Argentinean	90	18.4
Colombian	253	12.9
Ecuadorian	859	10.5
Peruvian	76	5.3
Venezuelan	21	4.8
Spaniard	289	26.2

Households with Food Stamps/SNAP Benefits During Past 12 Months

Group	Number	%
Total Population	133,714	28.3
Hispanic or Latino (of any race)	89,119	38.3
Central American, ex. Mexican	3,439	29.7
Costa Rican	101	25.3
Guatemalan	418	25.6
Honduran	1,967	32.4
Nicaraguan	160	20.4
Panamanian	329	29.4
Salvadoran	418	30.2
Cuban	1,363	43.3
Dominican Republic	31,014	43.2

Notes: (1) Percent of total population; (2) Percent of Hispanic/Latino population; Profiles include places with an overall population of at least 125,000, OR an overall population of at least 25,000 where the Hispanic/Latino population is at least 20% of the overall population. In states where less than five places meet either of these criteria, we have included places with at least 10,000 total population with the highest percentage of Hispanic/Latino population. These places are identified with an asterisk (*); Please refer to the User's Guide for a full explanation of data.

Group	Number	%
Mexican	5,227	36.2
Puerto Rican	42,918	38.0
South American	3,442	25.7
Argentinean	139	28.4
Colombian	445	22.6
Ecuadorian	2,345	28.7
Peruvian	367	25.6
Venezuelan	77	17.7
Spaniard	144	13.1

Poverty Rate
(Income in Past 12 Months Below Poverty Level)

Group	%
Total Population	28.4
Hispanic or Latino (of any race)	34.8
Central American, ex. Mexican	27.9
Costa Rican	18.2
Guatemalan	20.9
Honduran	29.4
Nicaraguan	19.1
Panamanian	27.1
Salvadoran	33.0
Cuban	26.3
Dominican Republic	34.3
Mexican	39.9
Puerto Rican	37.3
South American	19.4
Argentinean	16.6
Colombian	14.9
Ecuadorian	19.7
Peruvian	28.5
Venezuelan	22.1
Spaniard	10.4

Brookhaven

Population

Group	Number	%TP[1]	%HP[2]
Total Population	486,040	100.0	–
Hispanic or Latino (of any race)	60,270	12.4	100.0
Central American, ex. Mexican	9,259	1.9	15.4
Costa Rican	198	<0.1	0.3
Guatemalan	1,411	0.3	2.3
Honduran	1,195	0.2	2.0
Nicaraguan	159	<0.1	0.3
Panamanian	291	0.1	0.5
Salvadoran	5,899	1.2	9.8
Cuban	1,500	0.3	2.5
Dominican Republic	4,781	1.0	7.9
Mexican	4,926	1.0	8.2
Puerto Rican	21,429	4.4	35.6
South American	12,182	2.5	20.2
Argentinean	653	0.1	1.1
Bolivian	148	<0.1	0.2
Chilean	363	0.1	0.6
Colombian	2,970	0.6	4.9
Ecuadorian	6,437	1.3	10.7
Peruvian	1,074	0.2	1.8
Venezuelan	302	0.1	0.5
Spaniard	1,440	0.3	2.4

Population Growth: 2000–2010

Group	%
Total Population	8.4
Hispanic or Latino (of any race)	67.2
Central American, ex. Mexican	255.6
Guatemalan	208.8
Honduran	628.7
Panamanian	117.2
Salvadoran	273.1
Cuban	45.3
Dominican Republic	124.2
Mexican	144.1
Puerto Rican	30.4
South American	156.7
Argentinean	146.4
Chilean	116.1
Colombian	112.1
Ecuadorian	213.2
Peruvian	158.8
Venezuelan	193.2
Spaniard	263.6

Males per 100 Females

Group	Number
Total Population	97.2
Hispanic or Latino (of any race)	103.7
Central American, ex. Mexican	121.7
Costa Rican	106.3
Guatemalan	137.9
Honduran	132.0
Nicaraguan	76.7
Panamanian	92.7
Salvadoran	119.8
Cuban	97.4
Dominican Republic	84.5
Mexican	141.1
Puerto Rican	95.4
South American	100.7
Argentinean	96.1
Bolivian	72.1
Chilean	89.1
Colombian	81.0
Ecuadorian	120.7
Peruvian	75.5
Venezuelan	77.6
Spaniard	92.8

Average Household Size

Group	People
Total Population	2.89
Hispanic or Latino (of any race)	3.93
Central American, ex. Mexican	5.21
Costa Rican	3.52
Guatemalan	4.58
Honduran	5.12
Nicaraguan	4.34
Panamanian	2.90
Salvadoran	5.72
Cuban	3.00
Dominican Republic	4.58
Mexican	4.42
Puerto Rican	3.31
South American	4.34
Argentinean	3.40
Bolivian	3.95
Chilean	3.50
Colombian	3.75
Ecuadorian	5.06
Peruvian	3.78
Venezuelan	3.48
Spaniard	2.98

Median Age

Group	Years
Total Population	38.5
Hispanic or Latino (of any race)	28.2
Central American, ex. Mexican	27.9
Costa Rican	33.0
Guatemalan	27.6
Honduran	28.2
Nicaraguan	31.1
Panamanian	35.9
Salvadoran	27.5
Cuban	32.3
Dominican Republic	26.3
Mexican	26.4
Puerto Rican	27.8
South American	31.5
Argentinean	35.6
Bolivian	31.0
Chilean	34.6
Colombian	33.3
Ecuadorian	30.2
Peruvian	35.3
Venezuelan	33.6
Spaniard	38.9

High School Graduates
(Universe: Population 25 Years and Over)

Group	Number	%
Total Population	286,218	90.4
Hispanic or Latino (of any race)	24,218	77.3
Central American, ex. Mexican	2,687	55.7
Guatemalan	506	75.3
Salvadoran	1,589	47.4
Cuban	899	93.5
Dominican Republic	1,643	65.5
Mexican	2,035	67.7
Puerto Rican	9,745	84.3
South American	5,136	83.9
Colombian	1,477	92.2
Ecuadorian	2,134	76.9
Spaniard	924	93.9

Four-Year College Graduates
(Universe: Population 25 Years and Over)

Group	Number	%
Total Population	93,115	29.4
Hispanic or Latino (of any race)	5,982	19.1
Central American, ex. Mexican	413	8.6
Guatemalan	23	3.4
Salvadoran	288	8.6
Cuban	351	36.5
Dominican Republic	342	13.6
Mexican	332	11.0
Puerto Rican	2,349	20.3
South American	1,498	24.5
Colombian	443	27.7
Ecuadorian	462	16.6
Spaniard	354	36.0

Population Age 3–17 Enrolled in Public School
(Universe: Population Age 3–17 Enrolled in School)

Group	Number	%
Total Population	83,128	90.3
Hispanic or Latino (of any race)	11,907	90.5
Central American, ex. Mexican	1,574	91.0
Guatemalan	227	88.7
Salvadoran	1,046	89.2
Cuban	167	78.4
Dominican Republic	1,223	92.9
Mexican	722	80.7
Puerto Rican	4,868	92.8
South American	2,000	89.4
Colombian	611	93.0
Ecuadorian	728	84.7
Spaniard	266	74.7

Population Age 3–17 Enrolled in Private School
(Universe: Population Age 3–17 Enrolled in School)

Group	Number	%
Total Population	8,970	9.7
Hispanic or Latino (of any race)	1,246	9.5
Central American, ex. Mexican	155	9.0
Guatemalan	29	11.3
Salvadoran	126	10.8
Cuban	46	21.6
Dominican Republic	93	7.1
Mexican	173	19.3
Puerto Rican	375	7.2
South American	236	10.6
Colombian	46	7.0
Ecuadorian	132	15.3
Spaniard	90	25.3

Foreign-Born Population

Group	Number	%
Total Population	50,933	10.6
Hispanic or Latino (of any race)	17,378	30.9
Central American, ex. Mexican	5,665	65.8
Guatemalan	888	76.9
Salvadoran	4,033	67.9
Cuban	323	21.6
Dominican Republic	2,264	48.0
Mexican	2,379	43.8
Puerto Rican	131	0.6
South American	5,637	52.9
Colombian	1,461	51.5
Ecuadorian	2,682	55.4
Spaniard	319	19.4

Foreign-Born Naturalized U.S. Citizens

Group	Number	%
Total Population	25,326	49.7
Hispanic or Latino (of any race)	5,986	34.4
Central American, ex. Mexican	1,477	26.1
Guatemalan	298	33.6
Salvadoran	969	24.0
Cuban	281	87.0
Dominican Republic	901	39.8
Mexican	144	6.1
Puerto Rican	80	61.1

Notes: (1) Percent of total population; (2) Percent of Hispanic/Latino population; Profiles include places with an overall population of at least 125,000, OR an overall population of at least 25,000 where the Hispanic/Latino population is at least 20% of the overall population. In states where less than five places meet either of these criteria, we have included places with at least 10,000 total population with the highest percentage of Hispanic/Latino population. These places are identified with an asterisk (*); Please refer to the User's Guide for a full explanation of data.

STATE & PLACE PROFILES

Group	Number	%
South American	2,576	45.7
Colombian	882	60.4
Ecuadorian	1,022	38.1
Spaniard	154	48.3

Language Spoken at Home: English Only
(Universe: Population 5 Years and Over)

Group	Number	%
Total Population	379,978	84.4
Hispanic or Latino (of any race)	19,743	39.1
Central American, ex. Mexican	763	9.9
Guatemalan	91	8.2
Salvadoran	352	6.8
Cuban	870	65.1
Dominican Republic	677	15.9
Mexican	1,207	25.9
Puerto Rican	11,488	61.5
South American	1,997	21.0
Colombian	532	20.1
Ecuadorian	724	17.5
Spaniard	1,159	77.2

Language Spoken at Home: Spanish
(Universe: Population 5 Years and Over)

Group	Number	%
Total Population	33,824	7.5
Hispanic or Latino (of any race)	30,396	60.2
Central American, ex. Mexican	6,873	89.1
Guatemalan	1,025	91.8
Salvadoran	4,775	91.7
Cuban	435	32.6
Dominican Republic	3,573	84.1
Mexican	3,427	73.7
Puerto Rican	7,138	38.2
South American	7,442	78.3
Colombian	2,099	79.4
Ecuadorian	3,411	82.5
Spaniard	331	22.0

Unemployment Rate
(Universe: Population 16 Years and Over)

Group	%
Total Population	5.3
Hispanic or Latino (of any race)	6.4
Central American, ex. Mexican	6.2
Guatemalan	0.0
Salvadoran	7.6
Cuban	0.5
Dominican Republic	6.8
Mexican	16.4
Puerto Rican	6.4
South American	2.9
Colombian	4.7
Ecuadorian	1.3
Spaniard	3.2

Class of Worker: Private Wage and Salary
(Universe: Civilian Employed Population 16 Years and Over)

Group	Number	%
Total Population	175,834	73.7
Hispanic or Latino (of any race)	21,578	79.8
Central American, ex. Mexican	3,973	90.6
Guatemalan	593	97.9
Salvadoran	2,694	89.1
Cuban	631	80.2
Dominican Republic	1,659	75.0
Mexican	1,993	85.6
Puerto Rican	6,974	72.2
South American	4,679	84.5
Colombian	1,228	84.5
Ecuadorian	2,439	90.0
Spaniard	619	75.0

Class of Worker: Government
(Universe: Civilian Employed Population 16 Years and Over)

Group	Number	%
Total Population	52,433	22.0
Hispanic or Latino (of any race)	4,538	16.8
Central American, ex. Mexican	283	6.5
Guatemalan	0	0.0
Salvadoran	214	7.1
Cuban	156	19.8
Dominican Republic	519	23.5
Mexican	48	2.1
Puerto Rican	2,377	24.6
South American	705	12.7
Colombian	195	13.4
Ecuadorian	216	8.0
Spaniard	195	23.6

Means of Transportation to Work: Car, Truck or Van
(Universe: Workers 16 Years and Over)

Group	Number	%
Total Population	212,279	91.3
Hispanic or Latino (of any race)	24,044	90.5
Central American, ex. Mexican	3,955	91.7
Guatemalan	560	92.4
Salvadoran	2,708	91.5
Cuban	695	92.8
Dominican Republic	2,141	96.1
Mexican	1,913	84.0
Puerto Rican	8,480	88.7
South American	5,004	93.6
Colombian	1,256	93.9
Ecuadorian	2,495	93.0
Spaniard	712	89.2

Means of Transportation to Work: Public Transportation (ex. Taxicab)
(Universe: Workers 16 Years and Over)

Group	Number	%
Total Population	8,992	3.9
Hispanic or Latino (of any race)	1,308	4.9
Central American, ex. Mexican	172	4.0
Guatemalan	46	7.6
Salvadoran	90	3.0
Cuban	41	5.5
Dominican Republic	9	0.4
Mexican	24	1.1
Puerto Rican	788	8.2
South American	145	2.7
Colombian	27	2.0
Ecuadorian	87	3.2
Spaniard	59	7.4

Homeownership Rate
(Universe: Occupied Housing Units)

Group	%
Total Population	78.8
Hispanic or Latino (of any race)	64.1
Central American, ex. Mexican	59.5
Costa Rican	79.6
Guatemalan	53.0
Honduran	45.9
Nicaraguan	77.3
Panamanian	61.7
Salvadoran	62.3
Cuban	77.5
Dominican Republic	60.8
Mexican	42.8
Puerto Rican	67.7
South American	63.6
Argentinean	79.5
Bolivian	70.0
Chilean	76.2
Colombian	67.3
Ecuadorian	55.0
Peruvian	77.0
Venezuelan	67.6
Spaniard	80.9

Median Home Value

Group	Dollars
Total Population	371,300
Hispanic or Latino (of any race)	357,900
Central American, ex. Mexican	325,200
Guatemalan	405,700
Salvadoran	326,800
Cuban	394,600
Dominican Republic	360,300
Mexican	374,300
Puerto Rican	353,200
South American	378,800
Colombian	360,900
Ecuadorian	388,000
Spaniard	325,000

Median Gross Rent

Group	Dollars
Total Population	1,456
Hispanic or Latino (of any race)	1,444
Central American, ex. Mexican	1,235
Guatemalan	800
Salvadoran	1,233
Cuban	1,839
Dominican Republic	861
Mexican	1,654
Puerto Rican	1,513
South American	1,450
Colombian	1,099
Ecuadorian	1,532
Spaniard	–

Median Household Income
(2010 Inflation-Adjusted Dollars)

Group	Dollars
Total Population	81,937
Hispanic or Latino (of any race)	69,408
Central American, ex. Mexican	62,548
Guatemalan	52,690
Salvadoran	62,188
Cuban	97,432
Dominican Republic	49,694
Mexican	45,147
Puerto Rican	76,835
South American	79,361
Colombian	74,511
Ecuadorian	82,056
Spaniard	82,721

Per Capita Income
(2010 Inflation-Adjusted Dollars)

Group	Dollars
Total Population	33,324
Hispanic or Latino (of any race)	21,590
Central American, ex. Mexican	15,912
Guatemalan	13,583
Salvadoran	15,266
Cuban	39,937
Dominican Republic	17,544
Mexican	16,038
Puerto Rican	24,074
South American	22,355
Colombian	23,508
Ecuadorian	20,004
Spaniard	31,467

Households with $100,000+ Income

Group	Number	%
Total Population	62,935	39.0
Hispanic or Latino (of any race)	3,681	27.5
Central American, ex. Mexican	333	17.6
Guatemalan	78	30.4
Salvadoran	179	13.9
Cuban	249	46.8
Dominican Republic	240	21.0
Mexican	93	8.5
Puerto Rican	1,573	30.4
South American	792	32.4
Colombian	190	23.5
Ecuadorian	334	34.3
Spaniard	167	30.9

Households with Food Stamps/SNAP Benefits During Past 12 Months

Group	Number	%
Total Population	5,573	3.5
Hispanic or Latino (of any race)	1,176	8.8
Central American, ex. Mexican	5	0.3
Guatemalan	5	1.9
Salvadoran	0	0.0
Cuban	47	8.8
Dominican Republic	85	7.4
Mexican	198	18.2
Puerto Rican	747	14.4
South American	94	3.8
Colombian	29	3.6
Ecuadorian	35	3.6
Spaniard	0	0.0

Notes: (1) Percent of total population; (2) Percent of Hispanic/Latino population; Profiles include places with an overall population of at least 125,000, OR an overall population of at least 25,000 where the Hispanic/Latino population is at least 20% of the overall population. In states where less than five places meet either of these criteria, we have included places with at least 10,000 total population with the highest percentage of Hispanic/Latino population. These places are identified with an asterisk (*); Please refer to the User's Guide for a full explanation of data.

Poverty Rate (Income in Past 12 Months Below Poverty Level)	
Group	%
Total Population	6.5
Hispanic or Latino (of any race)	10.0
Central American, ex. Mexican	11.0
Guatemalan	19.4
Salvadoran	11.6
Cuban	2.1
Dominican Republic	12.6
Mexican	25.5
Puerto Rican	11.3
South American	2.0
Colombian	1.3
Ecuadorian	3.1
Spaniard	0.5

Brooklyn

Population			
Group	Number	%TP[1]	%HP[2]
Total Population	2,504,700	100.0	–
Hispanic or Latino (of any race)	496,285	19.8	100.0
Central American, ex. Mexican	46,119	1.8	9.3
Costa Rican	2,576	0.1	0.5
Guatemalan	9,160	0.4	1.8
Honduran	10,071	0.4	2.0
Nicaraguan	2,407	0.1	0.5
Panamanian	13,681	0.5	2.8
Salvadoran	7,737	0.3	1.6
Cuban	7,581	0.3	1.5
Dominican Republic	86,764	3.5	17.5
Mexican	94,585	3.8	19.1
Puerto Rican	176,528	7.0	35.6
South American	49,003	2.0	9.9
Argentinean	2,760	0.1	0.6
Bolivian	310	<0.1	0.1
Chilean	1,026	<0.1	0.2
Colombian	8,861	0.4	1.8
Ecuadorian	28,684	1.1	5.8
Paraguayan	230	<0.1	<0.1
Peruvian	4,222	0.2	0.9
Uruguayan	488	<0.1	0.1
Venezuelan	1,916	0.1	0.4
Spaniard	3,249	0.1	0.7

Population Growth: 2000–2010	
Group	%
Total Population	1.6
Hispanic or Latino (of any race)	1.7
Central American, ex. Mexican	43.6
Costa Rican	39.5
Guatemalan	126.9
Honduran	47.3
Nicaraguan	19.0
Panamanian	28.9
Salvadoran	52.2
Cuban	12.2
Dominican Republic	32.1
Mexican	60.8
Puerto Rican	-17.1
South American	46.5
Argentinean	86.7
Bolivian	69.4
Chilean	70.4
Colombian	27.1
Ecuadorian	51.4
Paraguayan	119.0
Peruvian	56.6
Uruguayan	99.2
Venezuelan	61.7
Spaniard	139.4

Males per 100 Females	
Group	Number
Total Population	89.3
Hispanic or Latino (of any race)	95.9
Central American, ex. Mexican	94.6
Costa Rican	64.7
Guatemalan	176.7
Honduran	92.6
Nicaraguan	85.9
Panamanian	67.8
Salvadoran	98.9
Cuban	91.6
Dominican Republic	85.1
Mexican	124.9
Puerto Rican	86.3
South American	103.2
Argentinean	98.3
Bolivian	83.4
Chilean	115.5
Colombian	82.6
Ecuadorian	114.9
Paraguayan	84.0
Peruvian	92.4
Uruguayan	96.0
Venezuelan	81.8
Spaniard	92.6

Average Household Size	
Group	People
Total Population	2.69
Hispanic or Latino (of any race)	3.11
Central American, ex. Mexican	3.15
Costa Rican	2.52
Guatemalan	4.05
Honduran	3.50
Nicaraguan	3.21
Panamanian	2.60
Salvadoran	3.61
Cuban	2.19
Dominican Republic	3.48
Mexican	4.55
Puerto Rican	2.57
South American	3.24
Argentinean	2.55
Bolivian	2.36
Chilean	2.42
Colombian	2.69
Ecuadorian	3.77
Paraguayan	2.89
Peruvian	2.85
Uruguayan	2.59
Venezuelan	2.53
Spaniard	2.26

Median Age	
Group	Years
Total Population	34.1
Hispanic or Latino (of any race)	30.6
Central American, ex. Mexican	34.4
Costa Rican	43.1
Guatemalan	28.9
Honduran	32.8
Nicaraguan	36.7
Panamanian	43.1
Salvadoran	32.2
Cuban	37.2
Dominican Republic	31.1
Mexican	25.5
Puerto Rican	33.5
South American	34.2
Argentinean	36.1
Bolivian	36.0
Chilean	35.3
Colombian	35.4
Ecuadorian	32.8
Paraguayan	35.3
Peruvian	37.7
Uruguayan	39.1
Venezuelan	33.1
Spaniard	34.7

High School Graduates (Universe: Population 25 Years and Over)		
Group	Number	%
Total Population	1,254,863	77.8
Hispanic or Latino (of any race)	171,983	59.0
Central American, ex. Mexican	19,854	65.8
Costa Rican	1,249	74.6
Guatemalan	2,459	52.8
Honduran	3,550	56.8
Nicaraguan	923	65.3
Panamanian	8,385	88.8
Salvadoran	2,846	46.6
Cuban	4,384	81.0
Dominican Republic	26,567	55.5
Mexican	19,807	42.9
Puerto Rican	70,656	61.1
South American	23,400	64.9
Argentinean	1,540	84.1
Chilean	799	76.4
Colombian	5,586	75.7
Ecuadorian	10,288	54.3
Peruvian	2,682	77.1
Venezuelan	1,260	78.5
Spaniard	2,313	87.4

Four-Year College Graduates (Universe: Population 25 Years and Over)		
Group	Number	%
Total Population	463,908	28.8
Hispanic or Latino (of any race)	37,095	12.7
Central American, ex. Mexican	3,974	13.2
Costa Rican	380	22.7
Guatemalan	471	10.1
Honduran	879	14.1
Nicaraguan	252	17.8
Panamanian	1,384	14.7
Salvadoran	437	7.2
Cuban	1,746	32.3
Dominican Republic	5,338	11.2
Mexican	4,369	9.5
Puerto Rican	12,006	10.4
South American	7,039	19.5
Argentinean	733	40.0
Chilean	441	42.2
Colombian	2,039	27.6
Ecuadorian	1,953	10.3
Peruvian	819	23.6
Venezuelan	548	34.1
Spaniard	1,073	40.6

Population Age 3–17 Enrolled in Public School (Universe: Population Age 3–17 Enrolled in School)		
Group	Number	%
Total Population	338,020	75.0
Hispanic or Latino (of any race)	94,256	93.0
Central American, ex. Mexican	7,062	92.0
Costa Rican	417	91.4
Guatemalan	654	95.2
Honduran	2,080	94.0
Nicaraguan	245	100.0
Panamanian	2,204	93.0
Salvadoran	1,317	84.9
Cuban	583	85.1
Dominican Republic	18,633	95.5
Mexican	21,099	96.1
Puerto Rican	34,910	92.0
South American	8,420	89.6
Argentinean	383	73.1
Chilean	239	90.5
Colombian	1,745	87.3
Ecuadorian	4,900	94.3
Peruvian	622	78.4
Venezuelan	244	84.4
Spaniard	218	66.7

Population Age 3–17 Enrolled in Private School (Universe: Population Age 3–17 Enrolled in School)		
Group	Number	%
Total Population	112,797	25.0
Hispanic or Latino (of any race)	7,046	7.0
Central American, ex. Mexican	615	8.0
Costa Rican	39	8.6
Guatemalan	33	4.8
Honduran	133	6.0
Nicaraguan	0	0.0
Panamanian	166	7.0
Salvadoran	235	15.1
Cuban	102	14.9
Dominican Republic	875	4.5
Mexican	858	3.9
Puerto Rican	3,038	8.0
South American	979	10.4
Argentinean	141	26.9
Chilean	25	9.5
Colombian	255	12.8
Ecuadorian	297	5.7
Peruvian	171	21.6
Venezuelan	45	15.6
Spaniard	109	33.3

Notes: (1) Percent of total population; (2) Percent of Hispanic/Latino population; Profiles include places with an overall population of at least 125,000, OR an overall population of at least 25,000 where the Hispanic/Latino population is at least 20% of the overall population. In states where less than five places meet either of these criteria, we have included places with at least 10,000 total population with the highest percentage of Hispanic/Latino population. These places are identified with an asterisk (*); Please refer to the User's Guide for a full explanation of data.

Foreign-Born Population

Group	Number	%
Total Population	921,519	37.4
Hispanic or Latino (of any race)	180,828	37.1
Central American, ex. Mexican	30,208	65.0
Costa Rican	1,444	57.5
Guatemalan	5,111	74.0
Honduran	6,710	63.9
Nicaraguan	1,311	64.7
Panamanian	8,428	59.5
Salvadoran	6,692	70.8
Cuban	2,818	39.9
Dominican Republic	51,531	60.9
Mexican	51,285	58.2
Puerto Rican	2,444	1.3
South American	37,242	67.3
Argentinean	1,764	63.5
Chilean	901	59.5
Colombian	7,193	63.1
Ecuadorian	20,919	69.2
Peruvian	3,631	74.8
Venezuelan	1,367	61.9
Spaniard	865	26.7

Foreign-Born Naturalized U.S. Citizens

Group	Number	%
Total Population	509,392	55.3
Hispanic or Latino (of any race)	65,078	36.0
Central American, ex. Mexican	13,606	45.0
Costa Rican	990	68.6
Guatemalan	1,309	25.6
Honduran	2,620	39.0
Nicaraguan	563	42.9
Panamanian	5,613	66.6
Salvadoran	2,224	33.2
Cuban	2,074	73.6
Dominican Republic	23,845	46.3
Mexican	6,592	12.9
Puerto Rican	1,318	53.9
South American	14,910	40.0
Argentinean	732	41.5
Chilean	470	52.2
Colombian	3,624	50.4
Ecuadorian	6,795	32.5
Peruvian	1,893	52.1
Venezuelan	499	36.5
Spaniard	437	50.5

Language Spoken at Home: English Only

(Universe: Population 5 Years and Over)

Group	Number	%
Total Population	1,240,416	54.1
Hispanic or Latino (of any race)	75,575	16.9
Central American, ex. Mexican	6,641	15.4
Costa Rican	663	28.8
Guatemalan	407	6.4
Honduran	682	7.1
Nicaraguan	321	16.3
Panamanian	4,028	30.1
Salvadoran	275	3.2
Cuban	2,528	36.8
Dominican Republic	4,981	6.4
Mexican	6,071	7.8
Puerto Rican	44,763	25.8
South American	5,365	10.5
Argentinean	423	17.1
Chilean	361	26.6
Colombian	1,482	14.2
Ecuadorian	1,570	5.7
Peruvian	362	7.7
Venezuelan	798	39.1
Spaniard	1,340	42.3

Language Spoken at Home: Spanish

(Universe: Population 5 Years and Over)

Group	Number	%
Total Population	393,340	17.2
Hispanic or Latino (of any race)	368,824	82.5
Central American, ex. Mexican	36,285	84.2
Costa Rican	1,628	70.8
Guatemalan	5,946	92.8
Honduran	8,908	92.4
Nicaraguan	1,642	83.3
Panamanian	9,334	69.7
Salvadoran	8,271	96.8
Cuban	4,197	61.1
Dominican Republic	72,792	93.2
Mexican	71,705	91.6
Puerto Rican	128,440	73.9
South American	45,190	88.8
Argentinean	1,970	79.7
Chilean	965	71.2
Colombian	8,926	85.8
Ecuadorian	25,982	93.9
Peruvian	4,285	91.3
Venezuelan	1,195	58.6
Spaniard	1,692	53.5

Unemployment Rate

(Universe: Population 16 Years and Over)

Group	%
Total Population	8.4
Hispanic or Latino (of any race)	9.0
Central American, ex. Mexican	7.2
Costa Rican	6.9
Guatemalan	4.5
Honduran	7.7
Nicaraguan	7.6
Panamanian	7.3
Salvadoran	7.9
Cuban	8.0
Dominican Republic	9.4
Mexican	5.7
Puerto Rican	12.0
South American	6.7
Argentinean	9.3
Chilean	7.8
Colombian	6.0
Ecuadorian	6.9
Peruvian	8.6
Venezuelan	5.9
Spaniard	7.1

Class of Worker: Private Wage and Salary

(Universe: Civilian Employed Population 16 Years and Over)

Group	Number	%
Total Population	835,561	76.9
Hispanic or Latino (of any race)	160,451	80.5
Central American, ex. Mexican	18,842	79.5
Costa Rican	779	70.7
Guatemalan	3,588	86.0
Honduran	4,328	82.8
Nicaraguan	851	78.2
Panamanian	4,834	70.5
Salvadoran	4,095	84.9
Cuban	2,744	77.5
Dominican Republic	28,398	83.9
Mexican	35,439	89.0
Puerto Rican	46,956	72.9
South American	22,841	84.7
Argentinean	1,207	88.2
Chilean	511	70.8
Colombian	4,237	82.4
Ecuadorian	12,753	88.2
Peruvian	2,051	82.8
Venezuelan	1,093	75.6
Spaniard	1,198	70.6

Class of Worker: Government

(Universe: Civilian Employed Population 16 Years and Over)

Group	Number	%
Total Population	181,256	16.7
Hispanic or Latino (of any race)	26,534	13.3
Central American, ex. Mexican	3,094	13.0
Costa Rican	232	21.1
Guatemalan	311	7.5
Honduran	563	10.8
Nicaraguan	129	11.9
Panamanian	1,586	23.1
Salvadoran	205	4.2
Cuban	509	14.4
Dominican Republic	3,330	9.8
Mexican	1,420	3.6
Puerto Rican	15,111	23.5
South American	1,814	6.7
Argentinean	41	3.0
Chilean	93	12.9
Colombian	496	9.6
Ecuadorian	583	4.0
Peruvian	295	11.9
Venezuelan	180	12.5
Spaniard	388	22.9

Means of Transportation to Work: Car, Truck or Van

(Universe: Workers 16 Years and Over)

Group	Number	%
Total Population	264,770	25.0
Hispanic or Latino (of any race)	39,989	20.4
Central American, ex. Mexican	4,301	18.5
Costa Rican	203	18.7
Guatemalan	661	16.1
Honduran	751	14.7
Nicaraguan	128	11.8
Panamanian	1,295	19.2
Salvadoran	1,173	24.7
Cuban	861	24.8
Dominican Republic	6,890	20.7
Mexican	4,894	12.4
Puerto Rican	15,894	25.2
South American	5,854	22.1
Argentinean	161	12.1
Chilean	33	4.8
Colombian	1,217	24.1
Ecuadorian	3,167	22.3
Peruvian	472	19.4
Venezuelan	297	21.0
Spaniard	328	19.8

Means of Transportation to Work: Public Transportation (ex. Taxicab)

(Universe: Workers 16 Years and Over)

Group	Number	%
Total Population	641,106	60.5
Hispanic or Latino (of any race)	122,814	62.7
Central American, ex. Mexican	15,612	67.0
Costa Rican	840	77.6
Guatemalan	2,680	65.2
Honduran	3,253	63.7
Nicaraguan	797	73.3
Panamanian	4,890	72.3
Salvadoran	2,851	60.1
Cuban	2,078	59.9
Dominican Republic	20,156	60.7
Mexican	26,499	67.2
Puerto Rican	37,387	59.2
South American	16,540	62.5
Argentinean	1,003	75.5
Chilean	515	74.6
Colombian	3,263	64.5
Ecuadorian	8,549	60.1
Peruvian	1,603	65.9
Venezuelan	986	69.8
Spaniard	1,153	69.5

Homeownership Rate

(Universe: Occupied Housing Units)

Group	%
Total Population	27.7
Hispanic or Latino (of any race)	14.1
Central American, ex. Mexican	17.4
Costa Rican	29.5
Guatemalan	8.8
Honduran	13.0
Nicaraguan	16.4
Panamanian	22.6
Salvadoran	11.6
Cuban	25.8
Dominican Republic	13.4
Mexican	6.9
Puerto Rican	13.7
South American	18.1
Argentinean	29.2
Bolivian	32.6
Chilean	17.5
Colombian	17.2
Ecuadorian	16.0
Paraguayan	12.7
Peruvian	19.2
Uruguayan	24.4
Venezuelan	21.2
Spaniard	34.6

Notes: (1) Percent of total population; (2) Percent of Hispanic/Latino population; Profiles include places with an overall population of at least 125,000, OR an overall population of at least 25,000 where the Hispanic/Latino population is at least 20% of the overall population. In states where less than five places meet either of these criteria, we have included places with at least 10,000 total population with the highest percentage of Hispanic/Latino population. These places are identified with an asterisk (*); Please refer to the User's Guide for a full explanation of data.

Median Home Value

Group	Dollars
Total Population	562,400
Hispanic or Latino (of any race)	540,300
Central American, ex. Mexican	499,800
Costa Rican	437,800
Guatemalan	384,300
Honduran	528,200
Nicaraguan	546,900
Panamanian	551,600
Salvadoran	353,300
Cuban	483,300
Dominican Republic	549,900
Mexican	590,400
Puerto Rican	539,400
South American	540,400
Argentinean	720,400
Chilean	470,000
Colombian	522,800
Ecuadorian	525,800
Peruvian	569,400
Venezuelan	450,000
Spaniard	615,000

Median Gross Rent

Group	Dollars
Total Population	1,021
Hispanic or Latino (of any race)	955
Central American, ex. Mexican	977
Costa Rican	1,037
Guatemalan	983
Honduran	997
Nicaraguan	1,027
Panamanian	916
Salvadoran	1,003
Cuban	1,063
Dominican Republic	912
Mexican	1,152
Puerto Rican	803
South American	1,070
Argentinean	1,129
Chilean	1,315
Colombian	1,074
Ecuadorian	1,053
Peruvian	1,029
Venezuelan	1,109
Spaniard	1,195

Median Household Income
(2010 Inflation-Adjusted Dollars)

Group	Dollars
Total Population	43,567
Hispanic or Latino (of any race)	33,906
Central American, ex. Mexican	41,388
Costa Rican	39,063
Guatemalan	36,402
Honduran	42,407
Nicaraguan	39,688
Panamanian	44,407
Salvadoran	37,526
Cuban	43,861
Dominican Republic	30,054
Mexican	37,650
Puerto Rican	27,602
South American	41,180
Argentinean	39,208
Chilean	65,526
Colombian	44,822
Ecuadorian	37,720
Peruvian	41,971
Venezuelan	36,920
Spaniard	57,321

Per Capita Income
(2010 Inflation-Adjusted Dollars)

Group	Dollars
Total Population	23,605
Hispanic or Latino (of any race)	15,832
Central American, ex. Mexican	17,941
Costa Rican	19,924
Guatemalan	17,062
Honduran	16,091
Nicaraguan	18,831
Panamanian	20,287
Salvadoran	15,839
Cuban	29,702
Dominican Republic	13,455
Mexican	12,302
Puerto Rican	16,301
South American	18,458
Argentinean	30,468
Chilean	20,862
Colombian	20,965
Ecuadorian	14,917
Peruvian	19,090
Venezuelan	26,713
Spaniard	34,729

Households with $100,000+ Income

Group	Number	%
Total Population	162,415	18.0
Hispanic or Latino (of any race)	15,288	9.5
Central American, ex. Mexican	1,524	9.6
Costa Rican	93	9.4
Guatemalan	301	14.3
Honduran	238	6.6
Nicaraguan	122	17.0
Panamanian	411	7.2
Salvadoran	289	11.7
Cuban	467	14.9
Dominican Republic	2,050	7.8
Mexican	2,173	9.8
Puerto Rican	6,341	9.1
South American	2,041	11.4
Argentinean	217	20.1
Chilean	114	19.4
Colombian	436	11.7
Ecuadorian	786	8.6
Peruvian	224	13.1
Venezuelan	128	16.1
Spaniard	290	19.3

Households with Food Stamps/SNAP Benefits During Past 12 Months

Group	Number	%
Total Population	169,644	18.8
Hispanic or Latino (of any race)	48,933	30.5
Central American, ex. Mexican	3,091	19.4
Costa Rican	164	16.6
Guatemalan	387	18.4
Honduran	898	25.0
Nicaraguan	99	13.8
Panamanian	878	15.4
Salvadoran	643	26.1
Cuban	518	16.5
Dominican Republic	10,370	39.4
Mexican	6,510	29.3
Puerto Rican	23,618	33.9
South American	3,875	21.6
Argentinean	126	11.7
Chilean	70	11.9
Colombian	728	19.5
Ecuadorian	2,345	25.7
Peruvian	303	17.7
Venezuelan	231	29.1
Spaniard	39	2.6

Poverty Rate
(Income in Past 12 Months Below Poverty Level)

Group	%
Total Population	22.0
Hispanic or Latino (of any race)	29.5
Central American, ex. Mexican	19.4
Costa Rican	17.0
Guatemalan	20.6
Honduran	24.2
Nicaraguan	19.1
Panamanian	17.6
Salvadoran	16.3
Cuban	17.0
Dominican Republic	29.8
Mexican	32.9
Puerto Rican	34.0
South American	20.3
Argentinean	18.5
Chilean	12.6
Colombian	16.4
Ecuadorian	24.0
Peruvian	15.5
Venezuelan	17.9
Spaniard	11.2

Buffalo

Population

Group	Number	%TP[1]	%HP[2]
Total Population	261,310	100.0	–
Hispanic or Latino (of any race)	27,519	10.5	100.0
Central American, ex. Mexican	386	0.1	1.4
Cuban	795	0.3	2.9
Dominican Republic	707	0.3	2.6
Mexican	1,382	0.5	5.0
Puerto Rican	22,076	8.4	80.2
South American	679	0.3	2.5
Argentinean	117	<0.1	0.4
Colombian	215	0.1	0.8
Ecuadorian	106	<0.1	0.4
Peruvian	105	<0.1	0.4
Spaniard	217	0.1	0.8

Population Growth: 2000–2010

Group	%
Total Population	-10.7
Hispanic or Latino (of any race)	24.7
Central American, ex. Mexican	65.7
Cuban	125.2
Dominican Republic	58.9
Mexican	34.2
Puerto Rican	28.0
South American	103.9
Colombian	100.9

Males per 100 Females

Group	Number
Total Population	92.0
Hispanic or Latino (of any race)	93.7
Central American, ex. Mexican	87.4
Cuban	110.3
Dominican Republic	101.4
Mexican	96.0
Puerto Rican	92.7
South American	102.7
Argentinean	101.7
Colombian	92.0
Ecuadorian	140.9
Peruvian	98.1
Spaniard	88.7

Average Household Size

Group	People
Total Population	2.24
Hispanic or Latino (of any race)	2.75
Central American, ex. Mexican	2.60
Cuban	2.69
Dominican Republic	2.88
Mexican	2.53
Puerto Rican	2.79
South American	2.59
Argentinean	2.63
Colombian	2.42
Ecuadorian	3.13
Peruvian	2.47
Spaniard	2.04

Median Age

Group	Years
Total Population	33.2
Hispanic or Latino (of any race)	23.9
Central American, ex. Mexican	25.4
Cuban	30.6
Dominican Republic	22.4
Mexican	25.0
Puerto Rican	23.5
South American	27.3
Argentinean	29.5
Colombian	24.4
Ecuadorian	26.7
Peruvian	34.3
Spaniard	36.4

High School Graduates
(Universe: Population 25 Years and Over)

Group	Number	%
Total Population	134,730	80.6

Notes: (1) Percent of total population; (2) Percent of Hispanic/Latino population; Profiles include places with an overall population of at least 125,000, OR an overall population of at least 25,000 where the Hispanic/Latino population is at least 20% of the overall population. In states where less than five places meet either of these criteria, we have included places with at least 10,000 total population with the highest percentage of Hispanic/Latino population. These places are identified with an asterisk (*); Please refer to the User's Guide for a full explanation of data.

Group	Number	%
Hispanic or Latino (of any race)	6,795	60.9
Mexican	508	65.5
Puerto Rican	4,894	58.2

Four-Year College Graduates
(Universe: Population 25 Years and Over)

Group	Number	%
Total Population	36,329	21.7
Hispanic or Latino (of any race)	1,288	11.6
Mexican	195	25.2
Puerto Rican	671	8.0

Population Age 3–17 Enrolled in Public School
(Universe: Population Age 3–17 Enrolled in School)

Group	Number	%
Total Population	42,229	84.1
Hispanic or Latino (of any race)	6,281	88.0
Mexican	191	95.5
Puerto Rican	5,512	90.7

Population Age 3–17 Enrolled in Private School
(Universe: Population Age 3–17 Enrolled in School)

Group	Number	%
Total Population	7,961	15.9
Hispanic or Latino (of any race)	858	12.0
Mexican	9	4.5
Puerto Rican	566	9.3

Foreign-Born Population

Group	Number	%
Total Population	18,599	7.0
Hispanic or Latino (of any race)	1,696	7.0
Mexican	344	23.8
Puerto Rican	17	0.1

Foreign-Born Naturalized U.S. Citizens

Group	Number	%
Total Population	8,383	45.1
Hispanic or Latino (of any race)	665	39.2
Mexican	169	49.1
Puerto Rican	8	47.1

Language Spoken at Home: English Only
(Universe: Population 5 Years and Over)

Group	Number	%
Total Population	214,749	86.3
Hispanic or Latino (of any race)	6,838	32.0
Mexican	639	51.7
Puerto Rican	4,692	28.5

Language Spoken at Home: Spanish
(Universe: Population 5 Years and Over)

Group	Number	%
Total Population	16,814	6.8
Hispanic or Latino (of any race)	14,358	67.2
Mexican	506	40.9
Puerto Rican	11,702	71.1

Unemployment Rate
(Universe: Population 16 Years and Over)

Group	%
Total Population	12.4
Hispanic or Latino (of any race)	18.4
Mexican	9.8
Puerto Rican	18.6

Class of Worker: Private Wage and Salary
(Universe: Civilian Employed Population 16 Years and Over)

Group	Number	%
Total Population	85,536	78.6
Hispanic or Latino (of any race)	5,755	83.1
Mexican	442	90.9
Puerto Rican	4,019	83.7

Class of Worker: Government
(Universe: Civilian Employed Population 16 Years and Over)

Group	Number	%
Total Population	19,096	17.6
Hispanic or Latino (of any race)	943	13.6
Mexican	44	9.1
Puerto Rican	672	14.0

Means of Transportation to Work: Car, Truck or Van
(Universe: Workers 16 Years and Over)

Group	Number	%
Total Population	80,152	76.3
Hispanic or Latino (of any race)	5,036	74.8
Mexican	463	98.1
Puerto Rican	3,435	73.8

Means of Transportation to Work: Public Transportation (ex. Taxicab)
(Universe: Workers 16 Years and Over)

Group	Number	%
Total Population	13,912	13.2
Hispanic or Latino (of any race)	972	14.4
Mexican	9	1.9
Puerto Rican	683	14.7

Homeownership Rate
(Universe: Occupied Housing Units)

Group	%
Total Population	40.7
Hispanic or Latino (of any race)	22.8
Central American, ex. Mexican	28.3
Cuban	20.6
Dominican Republic	28.4
Mexican	30.8
Puerto Rican	21.9
South American	35.2
Argentinean	31.4
Colombian	32.8
Ecuadorian	47.8
Peruvian	44.7
Spaniard	42.6

Median Home Value

Group	Dollars
Total Population	65,700
Hispanic or Latino (of any race)	59,000
Mexican	78,400
Puerto Rican	55,400

Median Gross Rent

Group	Dollars
Total Population	646
Hispanic or Latino (of any race)	606
Mexican	726
Puerto Rican	593

Median Household Income
(2010 Inflation-Adjusted Dollars)

Group	Dollars
Total Population	30,043
Hispanic or Latino (of any race)	15,899
Mexican	24,444
Puerto Rican	15,132

Per Capita Income
(2010 Inflation-Adjusted Dollars)

Group	Dollars
Total Population	19,409
Hispanic or Latino (of any race)	10,096
Mexican	16,064
Puerto Rican	8,829

Households with $100,000+ Income

Group	Number	%
Total Population	9,604	8.5
Hispanic or Latino (of any race)	266	3.3
Mexican	41	9.2
Puerto Rican	177	2.7

Households with Food Stamps/SNAP Benefits During Past 12 Months

Group	Number	%
Total Population	29,934	26.5
Hispanic or Latino (of any race)	4,316	53.1
Mexican	145	32.4
Puerto Rican	3,693	57.4

Poverty Rate
(Income in Past 12 Months Below Poverty Level)

Group	%
Total Population	29.6
Hispanic or Latino (of any race)	51.7
Mexican	40.4
Puerto Rican	56.3

Central Islip

Population

Group	Number	%TP[1]	%HP[2]
Total Population	34,450	100.0	–
Hispanic or Latino (of any race)	17,938	52.1	100.0
Central American, ex. Mexican	8,487	24.6	47.3
Guatemalan	677	2.0	3.8
Honduran	1,118	3.2	6.2
Panamanian	134	0.4	0.7
Salvadoran	6,381	18.5	35.6
Cuban	146	0.4	0.8
Dominican Republic	1,261	3.7	7.0
Mexican	598	1.7	3.3
Puerto Rican	3,452	10.0	19.2
South American	2,327	6.8	13.0
Argentinean	116	0.3	0.6
Colombian	711	2.1	4.0
Ecuadorian	676	2.0	3.8
Peruvian	558	1.6	3.1
Spaniard	104	0.3	0.6

Population Growth: 2000–2010

Group	%
Total Population	7.8
Hispanic or Latino (of any race)	56.6
Central American, ex. Mexican	200.9
Guatemalan	186.9
Honduran	272.7
Salvadoran	224.4
Cuban	13.2
Dominican Republic	77.4
Mexican	110.6
Puerto Rican	-14.8
South American	101.3
Colombian	75.1
Ecuadorian	108.6
Peruvian	134.5

Males per 100 Females

Group	Number
Total Population	98.5
Hispanic or Latino (of any race)	105.4
Central American, ex. Mexican	113.4
Guatemalan	110.2
Honduran	123.6
Panamanian	81.1
Salvadoran	113.0
Cuban	111.6
Dominican Republic	84.4
Mexican	129.1
Puerto Rican	90.1
South American	100.1
Argentinean	114.8
Colombian	91.6
Ecuadorian	100.6
Peruvian	111.4
Spaniard	126.1

Average Household Size

Group	People
Total Population	3.66
Hispanic or Latino (of any race)	4.99
Central American, ex. Mexican	6.24
Guatemalan	5.27
Honduran	6.14
Panamanian	3.40
Salvadoran	6.54
Cuban	3.30
Dominican Republic	4.66
Mexican	5.40
Puerto Rican	3.50
South American	4.53
Argentinean	3.43
Colombian	4.32
Ecuadorian	4.92
Peruvian	4.85
Spaniard	3.12

Notes: (1) Percent of total population; (2) Percent of Hispanic/Latino population; Profiles include places with an overall population of at least 125,000, OR an overall population of at least 25,000 where the Hispanic/Latino population is at least 20% of the overall population. In states where less than five places meet either of these criteria, we have included places with at least 10,000 total population with the highest percentage of Hispanic/Latino population. These places are identified with an asterisk (*); Please refer to the User's Guide for a full explanation of data.

Median Age	
Group	Years
Total Population	32.6
Hispanic or Latino (of any race)	28.5
Central American, ex. Mexican	28.2
Guatemalan	29.7
Honduran	29.4
Panamanian	47.0
Salvadoran	27.6
Cuban	38.0
Dominican Republic	29.7
Mexican	25.3
Puerto Rican	30.9
South American	35.0
Argentinean	33.5
Colombian	36.9
Ecuadorian	33.4
Peruvian	34.9
Spaniard	26.0

High School Graduates (Universe: Population 25 Years and Over)		
Group	Number	%
Total Population	16,489	72.9
Hispanic or Latino (of any race)	6,302	58.1
Central American, ex. Mexican	2,744	47.7
Guatemalan	726	71.4
Salvadoran	1,566	39.3
Puerto Rican	1,515	69.4
South American	1,277	68.5
Ecuadorian	333	49.7

Four-Year College Graduates (Universe: Population 25 Years and Over)		
Group	Number	%
Total Population	3,720	16.5
Hispanic or Latino (of any race)	1,201	11.1
Central American, ex. Mexican	423	7.4
Guatemalan	109	10.7
Salvadoran	192	4.8
Puerto Rican	361	16.5
South American	288	15.4
Ecuadorian	95	14.2

Population Age 3–17 Enrolled in Public School (Universe: Population Age 3–17 Enrolled in School)		
Group	Number	%
Total Population	6,202	87.5
Hispanic or Latino (of any race)	3,715	89.3
Central American, ex. Mexican	2,074	94.4
Guatemalan	195	70.4
Salvadoran	1,464	97.3
Puerto Rican	759	87.9
South American	536	86.3
Ecuadorian	356	82.6

Population Age 3–17 Enrolled in Private School (Universe: Population Age 3–17 Enrolled in School)		
Group	Number	%
Total Population	889	12.5
Hispanic or Latino (of any race)	443	10.7
Central American, ex. Mexican	122	5.6
Guatemalan	82	29.6
Salvadoran	40	2.7
Puerto Rican	104	12.1
South American	85	13.7
Ecuadorian	75	17.4

Foreign-Born Population		
Group	Number	%
Total Population	13,178	36.7
Hispanic or Latino (of any race)	9,296	50.0
Central American, ex. Mexican	6,411	66.8
Guatemalan	1,117	71.0
Salvadoran	4,483	66.7
Puerto Rican	68	1.8
South American	2,048	65.4
Ecuadorian	791	60.2

Foreign-Born Naturalized U.S. Citizens		
Group	Number	%
Total Population	5,130	38.9
Hispanic or Latino (of any race)	2,803	30.2
Central American, ex. Mexican	1,933	30.2
Guatemalan	708	63.4
Salvadoran	1,115	24.9
Puerto Rican	42	61.8
South American	511	25.0
Ecuadorian	207	26.2

Language Spoken at Home: English Only (Universe: Population 5 Years and Over)		
Group	Number	%
Total Population	15,500	47.2
Hispanic or Latino (of any race)	2,310	14.0
Central American, ex. Mexican	417	4.9
Guatemalan	88	6.0
Salvadoran	126	2.2
Puerto Rican	1,366	41.4
South American	93	3.2
Ecuadorian	10	0.8

Language Spoken at Home: Spanish (Universe: Population 5 Years and Over)		
Group	Number	%
Total Population	14,440	44.0
Hispanic or Latino (of any race)	14,228	86.0
Central American, ex. Mexican	8,068	95.1
Guatemalan	1,368	94.0
Salvadoran	5,697	97.8
Puerto Rican	1,936	58.6
South American	2,808	96.8
Ecuadorian	1,167	99.2

Unemployment Rate (Universe: Population 16 Years and Over)	
Group	%
Total Population	11.6
Hispanic or Latino (of any race)	11.0
Central American, ex. Mexican	12.0
Guatemalan	5.3
Salvadoran	11.9
Puerto Rican	9.8
South American	10.4
Ecuadorian	5.6

Class of Worker: Private Wage and Salary (Universe: Civilian Employed Population 16 Years and Over)		
Group	Number	%
Total Population	13,940	81.3
Hispanic or Latino (of any race)	7,834	88.7
Central American, ex. Mexican	4,357	93.1
Guatemalan	908	91.1
Salvadoran	2,942	93.2
Puerto Rican	1,218	74.6
South American	1,374	86.8
Ecuadorian	545	85.7

Class of Worker: Government (Universe: Civilian Employed Population 16 Years and Over)		
Group	Number	%
Total Population	2,791	16.3
Hispanic or Latino (of any race)	800	9.1
Central American, ex. Mexican	215	4.6
Guatemalan	60	6.0
Salvadoran	136	4.3
Puerto Rican	408	25.0
South American	148	9.3
Ecuadorian	91	14.3

Means of Transportation to Work: Car, Truck or Van (Universe: Workers 16 Years and Over)		
Group	Number	%
Total Population	14,557	89.9
Hispanic or Latino (of any race)	7,860	94.2
Central American, ex. Mexican	4,323	93.6
Guatemalan	983	98.6
Salvadoran	2,852	92.1
Puerto Rican	1,254	93.9
South American	1,399	93.8
Ecuadorian	564	97.1

Means of Transportation to Work: Public Transportation (ex. Taxicab) (Universe: Workers 16 Years and Over)		
Group	Number	%
Total Population	716	4.4
Hispanic or Latino (of any race)	245	2.9
Central American, ex. Mexican	134	2.9
Guatemalan	14	1.4
Salvadoran	101	3.3
Puerto Rican	0	0.0
South American	92	6.2
Ecuadorian	17	2.9

Homeownership Rate (Universe: Occupied Housing Units)	
Group	%
Total Population	68.9
Hispanic or Latino (of any race)	64.5
Central American, ex. Mexican	66.5
Guatemalan	65.2
Honduran	51.4
Panamanian	82.2
Salvadoran	68.6
Cuban	66.0
Dominican Republic	61.1
Mexican	49.4
Puerto Rican	61.5
South American	68.6
Argentinean	65.7
Colombian	68.7
Ecuadorian	73.3
Peruvian	65.0
Spaniard	56.0

Median Home Value	
Group	Dollars
Total Population	327,000
Hispanic or Latino (of any race)	310,300
Central American, ex. Mexican	306,600
Guatemalan	281,500
Salvadoran	316,400
Puerto Rican	290,900
South American	317,800
Ecuadorian	269,300

Median Gross Rent	
Group	Dollars
Total Population	1,415
Hispanic or Latino (of any race)	1,391
Central American, ex. Mexican	1,660
Guatemalan	–
Salvadoran	1,688
Puerto Rican	1,269
South American	1,519
Ecuadorian	853

Median Household Income (2010 Inflation-Adjusted Dollars)	
Group	Dollars
Total Population	68,876
Hispanic or Latino (of any race)	68,611
Central American, ex. Mexican	61,196
Guatemalan	73,309
Salvadoran	58,851
Puerto Rican	71,486
South American	90,729
Ecuadorian	71,611

Per Capita Income (2010 Inflation-Adjusted Dollars)	
Group	Dollars
Total Population	21,925
Hispanic or Latino (of any race)	17,198
Central American, ex. Mexican	15,807
Guatemalan	21,856
Salvadoran	14,806
Puerto Rican	18,608
South American	20,040
Ecuadorian	16,467

Households with $100,000+ Income		
Group	Number	%
Total Population	2,411	24.8
Hispanic or Latino (of any race)	875	22.6
Central American, ex. Mexican	418	25.2
Guatemalan	111	38.1
Salvadoran	236	20.1
Puerto Rican	127	12.8
South American	242	36.7
Ecuadorian	72	25.4

Notes: (1) Percent of total population; (2) Percent of Hispanic/Latino population; Profiles include places with an overall population of at least 125,000, OR an overall population of at least 25,000 where the Hispanic/Latino population is at least 20% of the overall population. In states where less than five places meet either of these criteria, we have included places with at least 10,000 total population with the highest percentage of Hispanic/Latino population. These places are identified with an asterisk (*); Please refer to the User's Guide for a full explanation of data.

Households with Food Stamps/SNAP Benefits During Past 12 Months

Group	Number	%
Total Population	1,127	11.6
Hispanic or Latino (of any race)	411	10.6
Central American, ex. Mexican	126	7.6
Guatemalan	12	4.1
Salvadoran	114	9.7
Puerto Rican	136	13.7
South American	42	6.4
Ecuadorian	26	9.2

Poverty Rate
(Income in Past 12 Months Below Poverty Level)

Group	%
Total Population	9.4
Hispanic or Latino (of any race)	11.4
Central American, ex. Mexican	13.1
Guatemalan	5.6
Salvadoran	15.0
Puerto Rican	8.1
South American	4.1
Ecuadorian	6.6

Elmont

Population

Group	Number	%TP[1]	%HP[2]
Total Population	33,198	100.0	–
Hispanic or Latino (of any race)	7,236	21.8	100.0
Central American, ex. Mexican	1,681	5.1	23.2
Guatemalan	340	1.0	4.7
Honduran	289	0.9	4.0
Panamanian	143	0.4	2.0
Salvadoran	862	2.6	11.9
Cuban	143	0.4	2.0
Dominican Republic	772	2.3	10.7
Mexican	811	2.4	11.2
Puerto Rican	1,250	3.8	17.3
South American	1,941	5.8	26.8
Argentinean	122	0.4	1.7
Chilean	119	0.4	1.6
Colombian	698	2.1	9.6
Ecuadorian	426	1.3	5.9
Peruvian	465	1.4	6.4

Population Growth: 2000–2010

Group	%
Total Population	1.7
Hispanic or Latino (of any race)	54.9
Central American, ex. Mexican	133.8
Salvadoran	132.3
Cuban	21.2
Dominican Republic	92.0
Mexican	81.8
Puerto Rican	28.7
South American	100.9
Chilean	11.2
Colombian	63.5
Ecuadorian	238.1
Peruvian	194.3

Males per 100 Females

Group	Number
Total Population	92.9
Hispanic or Latino (of any race)	107.0
Central American, ex. Mexican	110.1
Guatemalan	142.9
Honduran	112.5
Panamanian	83.3
Salvadoran	106.7
Cuban	101.4
Dominican Republic	84.7
Mexican	145.8
Puerto Rican	92.9
South American	105.8
Argentinean	87.7
Chilean	230.6
Colombian	97.2
Ecuadorian	106.8
Peruvian	106.7

Average Household Size

Group	People
Total Population	3.37
Hispanic or Latino (of any race)	3.71
Central American, ex. Mexican	4.19
Guatemalan	3.72
Honduran	4.22
Panamanian	3.98
Salvadoran	4.61
Cuban	3.00
Dominican Republic	3.95
Mexican	3.29
Puerto Rican	3.37
South American	3.81
Argentinean	2.98
Chilean	2.70
Colombian	4.04
Ecuadorian	4.59
Peruvian	3.67

Median Age

Group	Years
Total Population	37.1
Hispanic or Latino (of any race)	31.8
Central American, ex. Mexican	31.5
Guatemalan	32.9
Honduran	30.7
Panamanian	31.9
Salvadoran	30.6
Cuban	37.8
Dominican Republic	30.4
Mexican	30.4
Puerto Rican	30.3
South American	37.7
Argentinean	40.5
Chilean	40.5
Colombian	39.8
Ecuadorian	35.3
Peruvian	36.9

High School Graduates
(Universe: Population 25 Years and Over)

Group	Number	%
Total Population	18,818	85.1
Hispanic or Latino (of any race)	3,040	73.3
Central American, ex. Mexican	499	60.4
Dominican Republic	353	45.6
Puerto Rican	670	97.5
South American	1,216	90.2
Colombian	460	87.3

Four-Year College Graduates
(Universe: Population 25 Years and Over)

Group	Number	%
Total Population	6,412	29.0
Hispanic or Latino (of any race)	717	17.3
Central American, ex. Mexican	56	6.8
Dominican Republic	115	14.9
Puerto Rican	72	10.5
South American	416	30.9
Colombian	34	6.5

Population Age 3–17 Enrolled in Public School
(Universe: Population Age 3–17 Enrolled in School)

Group	Number	%
Total Population	6,522	90.8
Hispanic or Latino (of any race)	1,710	94.1
Central American, ex. Mexican	439	87.3
Dominican Republic	406	100.0
Puerto Rican	209	100.0
South American	254	85.2
Colombian	105	78.4

Population Age 3–17 Enrolled in Private School
(Universe: Population Age 3–17 Enrolled in School)

Group	Number	%
Total Population	663	9.2
Hispanic or Latino (of any race)	108	5.9
Central American, ex. Mexican	64	12.7
Dominican Republic	0	0.0
Puerto Rican	0	0.0
South American	44	14.8
Colombian	29	21.6

Foreign-Born Population

Group	Number	%
Total Population	14,520	42.1
Hispanic or Latino (of any race)	3,581	47.9
Central American, ex. Mexican	853	54.0
Dominican Republic	836	60.0
Puerto Rican	0	0.0
South American	1,390	65.5
Colombian	686	72.8

Foreign-Born Naturalized U.S. Citizens

Group	Number	%
Total Population	9,294	64.0
Hispanic or Latino (of any race)	1,628	45.5
Central American, ex. Mexican	251	29.4
Dominican Republic	418	50.0
Puerto Rican	0	0.0
South American	787	56.6
Colombian	307	44.8

Language Spoken at Home: English Only
(Universe: Population 5 Years and Over)

Group	Number	%
Total Population	16,073	49.6
Hispanic or Latino (of any race)	657	9.7
Central American, ex. Mexican	92	7.0
Dominican Republic	17	1.3
Puerto Rican	267	22.9
South American	90	4.5
Colombian	21	2.5

Language Spoken at Home: Spanish
(Universe: Population 5 Years and Over)

Group	Number	%
Total Population	6,278	19.4
Hispanic or Latino (of any race)	6,040	89.2
Central American, ex. Mexican	1,147	87.2
Dominican Republic	1,255	98.7
Puerto Rican	899	77.1
South American	1,923	95.5
Colombian	835	97.5

Unemployment Rate
(Universe: Population 16 Years and Over)

Group	%
Total Population	6.5
Hispanic or Latino (of any race)	8.3
Central American, ex. Mexican	5.4
Dominican Republic	6.2
Puerto Rican	24.2
South American	3.9
Colombian	2.7

Class of Worker: Private Wage and Salary
(Universe: Civilian Employed Population 16 Years and Over)

Group	Number	%
Total Population	13,886	79.5
Hispanic or Latino (of any race)	2,963	79.2
Central American, ex. Mexican	654	90.6
Dominican Republic	463	78.7
Puerto Rican	420	76.4
South American	971	72.0
Colombian	500	87.3

Class of Worker: Government
(Universe: Civilian Employed Population 16 Years and Over)

Group	Number	%
Total Population	2,549	14.6
Hispanic or Latino (of any race)	448	12.0
Central American, ex. Mexican	27	3.7
Dominican Republic	52	8.8
Puerto Rican	117	21.3
South American	204	15.1
Colombian	12	2.1

Means of Transportation to Work: Car, Truck or Van
(Universe: Workers 16 Years and Over)

Group	Number	%
Total Population	12,656	75.2
Hispanic or Latino (of any race)	2,618	73.3
Central American, ex. Mexican	454	65.0
Dominican Republic	275	52.8
Puerto Rican	497	92.2
South American	902	69.7

Notes: (1) Percent of total population; (2) Percent of Hispanic/Latino population; Profiles include places with an overall population of at least 125,000, OR an overall population of at least 25,000 where the Hispanic/Latino population is at least 20% of the overall population. In states where less than five places meet either of these criteria, we have included places with at least 10,000 total population with the highest percentage of Hispanic/Latino population. These places are identified with an asterisk (*); Please refer to the User's Guide for a full explanation of data.

Colombian	436	76.1

Means of Transportation to Work: Public Transportation (ex. Taxicab)
(Universe: Workers 16 Years and Over)

Group	Number	%
Total Population	3,050	18.1
Hispanic or Latino (of any race)	565	15.8
Central American, ex. Mexican	143	20.5
Dominican Republic	142	27.3
Puerto Rican	20	3.7
South American	233	18.0
Colombian	58	10.1

Homeownership Rate
(Universe: Occupied Housing Units)

Group	%
Total Population	72.4
Hispanic or Latino (of any race)	53.7
Central American, ex. Mexican	47.8
Guatemalan	36.1
Honduran	28.1
Panamanian	70.0
Salvadoran	54.9
Cuban	59.2
Dominican Republic	64.1
Mexican	19.3
Puerto Rican	63.7
South American	60.0
Argentinean	53.3
Chilean	29.5
Colombian	67.0
Ecuadorian	79.4
Peruvian	47.1

Median Home Value

Group	Dollars
Total Population	420,000
Hispanic or Latino (of any race)	446,600
Central American, ex. Mexican	435,000
Dominican Republic	464,800
Puerto Rican	452,100
South American	436,200
Colombian	411,300

Median Gross Rent

Group	Dollars
Total Population	1,332
Hispanic or Latino (of any race)	1,657
Central American, ex. Mexican	1,246
Dominican Republic	448
Puerto Rican	–
South American	1,929
Colombian	2,000+

Median Household Income
(2010 Inflation-Adjusted Dollars)

Group	Dollars
Total Population	80,356
Hispanic or Latino (of any race)	82,827
Central American, ex. Mexican	57,069
Dominican Republic	84,521
Puerto Rican	110,893
South American	96,208
Colombian	103,068

Per Capita Income
(2010 Inflation-Adjusted Dollars)

Group	Dollars
Total Population	25,961
Hispanic or Latino (of any race)	18,424
Central American, ex. Mexican	15,703
Dominican Republic	12,034
Puerto Rican	23,987
South American	22,776
Colombian	20,634

Households with $100,000+ Income

Group	Number	%
Total Population	3,655	38.4
Hispanic or Latino (of any race)	505	36.1
Central American, ex. Mexican	27	12.6
Dominican Republic	93	44.5
Puerto Rican	124	56.9
South American	249	47.1

Colombian	100	51.3

Households with Food Stamps/SNAP Benefits During Past 12 Months

Group	Number	%
Total Population	559	5.9
Hispanic or Latino (of any race)	98	7.0
Central American, ex. Mexican	24	11.2
Dominican Republic	33	15.8
Puerto Rican	0	0.0
South American	41	7.8
Colombian	0	0.0

Poverty Rate
(Income in Past 12 Months Below Poverty Level)

Group	%
Total Population	5.4
Hispanic or Latino (of any race)	7.5
Central American, ex. Mexican	13.9
Dominican Republic	2.4
Puerto Rican	8.4
South American	5.7
Colombian	1.7

Freeport

Population

Group	Number	%TP[1]	%HP[2]
Total Population	42,860	100.0	–
Hispanic or Latino (of any race)	17,858	41.7	100.0
Central American, ex. Mexican	6,668	15.6	37.3
Costa Rican	108	0.3	0.6
Guatemalan	1,070	2.5	6.0
Honduran	785	1.8	4.4
Panamanian	149	0.3	0.8
Salvadoran	4,439	10.4	24.9
Cuban	379	0.9	2.1
Dominican Republic	5,539	12.9	31.0
Mexican	408	1.0	2.3
Puerto Rican	1,626	3.8	9.1
South American	1,604	3.7	9.0
Colombian	692	1.6	3.9
Ecuadorian	432	1.0	2.4
Peruvian	275	0.6	1.5
Spaniard	127	0.3	0.7

Population Growth: 2000–2010

Group	%
Total Population	-2.1
Hispanic or Latino (of any race)	21.9
Central American, ex. Mexican	56.9
Guatemalan	100.0
Honduran	209.1
Salvadoran	43.5
Cuban	-11.7
Dominican Republic	71.7
Mexican	35.5
Puerto Rican	4.6
South American	49.3
Colombian	23.1
Ecuadorian	87.8
Peruvian	92.3

Males per 100 Females

Group	Number
Total Population	94.9
Hispanic or Latino (of any race)	105.6
Central American, ex. Mexican	117.6
Costa Rican	86.2
Guatemalan	134.1
Honduran	160.8
Panamanian	84.0
Salvadoran	110.1
Cuban	89.5
Dominican Republic	97.0
Mexican	104.0
Puerto Rican	96.6
South American	93.3
Colombian	77.4
Ecuadorian	103.8
Peruvian	118.3
Spaniard	135.2

Average Household Size

Group	People
Total Population	3.18
Hispanic or Latino (of any race)	4.40
Central American, ex. Mexican	5.11
Costa Rican	3.69
Guatemalan	4.64
Honduran	5.36
Panamanian	3.47
Salvadoran	5.34
Cuban	2.96
Dominican Republic	4.61
Mexican	4.38
Puerto Rican	3.26
South American	3.66
Colombian	3.27
Ecuadorian	4.31
Peruvian	4.25
Spaniard	3.05

Median Age

Group	Years
Total Population	37.2
Hispanic or Latino (of any race)	30.4
Central American, ex. Mexican	30.5
Costa Rican	44.0
Guatemalan	30.7
Honduran	29.2
Panamanian	37.8
Salvadoran	30.4
Cuban	44.3
Dominican Republic	30.0
Mexican	27.1
Puerto Rican	32.5
South American	37.1
Colombian	39.8
Ecuadorian	33.1
Peruvian	35.9
Spaniard	28.5

High School Graduates
(Universe: Population 25 Years and Over)

Group	Number	%
Total Population	22,552	78.2
Hispanic or Latino (of any race)	6,186	58.9
Central American, ex. Mexican	1,311	49.7
Salvadoran	802	44.7
Dominican Republic	1,728	44.3
Puerto Rican	904	74.5
South American	1,549	84.5

Four-Year College Graduates
(Universe: Population 25 Years and Over)

Group	Number	%
Total Population	7,236	25.1
Hispanic or Latino (of any race)	1,432	13.6
Central American, ex. Mexican	329	12.5
Salvadoran	236	13.1
Dominican Republic	428	11.0
Puerto Rican	263	21.7
South American	174	9.5

Population Age 3–17 Enrolled in Public School
(Universe: Population Age 3–17 Enrolled in School)

Group	Number	%
Total Population	6,308	85.3
Hispanic or Latino (of any race)	2,898	89.9
Central American, ex. Mexican	890	90.7
Salvadoran	603	87.9
Dominican Republic	1,502	91.3
Puerto Rican	112	91.1
South American	246	91.8

Population Age 3–17 Enrolled in Private School
(Universe: Population Age 3–17 Enrolled in School)

Group	Number	%
Total Population	1,084	14.7
Hispanic or Latino (of any race)	327	10.1
Central American, ex. Mexican	91	9.3
Salvadoran	83	12.1
Dominican Republic	144	8.7
Puerto Rican	11	8.9
South American	22	8.2

Notes: (1) Percent of total population; (2) Percent of Hispanic/Latino population; Profiles include places with an overall population of at least 125,000, OR an overall population of at least 25,000 where the Hispanic/Latino population is at least 20% of the overall population. In states where less than five places meet either of these criteria, we have included places with at least 10,000 total population with the highest percentage of Hispanic/Latino population. These places are identified with an asterisk (*); Please refer to the User's Guide for a full explanation of data.

Foreign-Born Population

Group	Number	%
Total Population	14,633	34.3
Hispanic or Latino (of any race)	9,939	58.8
Central American, ex. Mexican	3,104	66.4
Salvadoran	2,162	64.6
Dominican Republic	4,260	63.0
Puerto Rican	23	1.4
South American	1,870	78.5

Foreign-Born Naturalized U.S. Citizens

Group	Number	%
Total Population	7,779	53.2
Hispanic or Latino (of any race)	4,610	46.4
Central American, ex. Mexican	1,008	32.5
Salvadoran	598	27.7
Dominican Republic	1,992	46.8
Puerto Rican	23	100.0
South American	1,231	65.8

Language Spoken at Home: English Only
(Universe: Population 5 Years and Over)

Group	Number	%
Total Population	22,879	57.6
Hispanic or Latino (of any race)	1,559	10.2
Central American, ex. Mexican	182	4.3
Salvadoran	141	4.8
Dominican Republic	285	4.8
Puerto Rican	747	46.5
South American	149	6.6

Language Spoken at Home: Spanish
(Universe: Population 5 Years and Over)

Group	Number	%
Total Population	14,545	36.6
Hispanic or Latino (of any race)	13,766	89.8
Central American, ex. Mexican	4,006	95.7
Salvadoran	2,820	95.2
Dominican Republic	5,664	95.1
Puerto Rican	859	53.5
South American	2,107	93.4

Unemployment Rate
(Universe: Population 16 Years and Over)

Group	%
Total Population	8.3
Hispanic or Latino (of any race)	9.3
Central American, ex. Mexican	8.2
Salvadoran	8.1
Dominican Republic	10.4
Puerto Rican	7.8
South American	11.0

Class of Worker: Private Wage and Salary
(Universe: Civilian Employed Population 16 Years and Over)

Group	Number	%
Total Population	17,342	78.6
Hispanic or Latino (of any race)	7,705	85.0
Central American, ex. Mexican	2,413	87.0
Salvadoran	1,787	90.4
Dominican Republic	2,633	88.7
Puerto Rican	732	68.4
South American	1,221	84.1

Class of Worker: Government
(Universe: Civilian Employed Population 16 Years and Over)

Group	Number	%
Total Population	3,578	16.2
Hispanic or Latino (of any race)	845	9.3
Central American, ex. Mexican	228	8.2
Salvadoran	154	7.8
Dominican Republic	189	6.4
Puerto Rican	266	24.9
South American	89	6.1

Means of Transportation to Work: Car, Truck or Van
(Universe: Workers 16 Years and Over)

Group	Number	%
Total Population	16,109	75.2
Hispanic or Latino (of any race)	6,593	74.9
Central American, ex. Mexican	1,931	72.5
Salvadoran	1,392	72.8
Dominican Republic	2,079	73.3
Puerto Rican	934	88.2
South American	1,136	79.4

Means of Transportation to Work: Public Transportation (ex. Taxicab)
(Universe: Workers 16 Years and Over)

Group	Number	%
Total Population	3,639	17.0
Hispanic or Latino (of any race)	1,282	14.6
Central American, ex. Mexican	420	15.8
Salvadoran	303	15.8
Dominican Republic	406	14.3
Puerto Rican	82	7.7
South American	177	12.4

Homeownership Rate
(Universe: Occupied Housing Units)

Group	%
Total Population	66.9
Hispanic or Latino (of any race)	44.3
Central American, ex. Mexican	43.6
Costa Rican	68.6
Guatemalan	29.0
Honduran	26.6
Panamanian	74.5
Salvadoran	47.3
Cuban	59.0
Dominican Republic	33.6
Mexican	43.7
Puerto Rican	61.3
South American	54.4
Colombian	45.2
Ecuadorian	64.2
Peruvian	55.4
Spaniard	67.5

Median Home Value

Group	Dollars
Total Population	382,100
Hispanic or Latino (of any race)	393,200
Central American, ex. Mexican	379,300
Salvadoran	359,000
Dominican Republic	395,100
Puerto Rican	408,900
South American	381,500

Median Gross Rent

Group	Dollars
Total Population	1,202
Hispanic or Latino (of any race)	1,199
Central American, ex. Mexican	1,300
Salvadoran	1,348
Dominican Republic	1,115
Puerto Rican	1,227
South American	1,356

Median Household Income
(2010 Inflation-Adjusted Dollars)

Group	Dollars
Total Population	69,081
Hispanic or Latino (of any race)	56,848
Central American, ex. Mexican	57,907
Salvadoran	62,604
Dominican Republic	43,587
Puerto Rican	57,453
South American	69,568

Per Capita Income
(2010 Inflation-Adjusted Dollars)

Group	Dollars
Total Population	29,930
Hispanic or Latino (of any race)	21,169
Central American, ex. Mexican	20,814
Salvadoran	21,663
Dominican Republic	15,025
Puerto Rican	32,241
South American	23,357

Households with $100,000+ Income

Group	Number	%
Total Population	4,630	32.6
Hispanic or Latino (of any race)	999	22.9
Central American, ex. Mexican	195	17.4
Salvadoran	155	21.4
Dominican Republic	293	18.6
Puerto Rican	171	29.8
South American	197	28.9

Households with Food Stamps/SNAP Benefits During Past 12 Months

Group	Number	%
Total Population	1,240	8.7
Hispanic or Latino (of any race)	629	14.4
Central American, ex. Mexican	76	6.8
Salvadoran	65	9.0
Dominican Republic	316	20.1
Puerto Rican	74	12.9
South American	122	17.9

Poverty Rate
(Income in Past 12 Months Below Poverty Level)

Group	%
Total Population	11.3
Hispanic or Latino (of any race)	17.2
Central American, ex. Mexican	11.7
Salvadoran	8.6
Dominican Republic	27.5
Puerto Rican	5.7
South American	9.0

Glen Cove

Population

Group	Number	%TP[1]	%HP[2]
Total Population	26,964	100.0	–
Hispanic or Latino (of any race)	7,513	27.9	100.0
Central American, ex. Mexican	3,158	11.7	42.0
Guatemalan	142	0.5	1.9
Honduran	364	1.3	4.8
Salvadoran	2,544	9.4	33.9
Cuban	114	0.4	1.5
Dominican Republic	194	0.7	2.6
Mexican	318	1.2	4.2
Puerto Rican	924	3.4	12.3
South American	1,715	6.4	22.8
Chilean	217	0.8	2.9
Colombian	351	1.3	4.7
Ecuadorian	108	0.4	1.4
Peruvian	883	3.3	11.8

Population Growth: 2000–2010

Group	%
Total Population	1.3
Hispanic or Latino (of any race)	40.8
Central American, ex. Mexican	120.2
Honduran	160.0
Salvadoran	124.9
Dominican Republic	31.1
Mexican	42.0
Puerto Rican	-5.2
South American	42.0
Chilean	64.4
Colombian	58.8
Peruvian	34.0

Males per 100 Females

Group	Number
Total Population	94.9
Hispanic or Latino (of any race)	108.1
Central American, ex. Mexican	129.0
Guatemalan	111.9
Honduran	124.7
Salvadoran	134.5
Cuban	100.0
Dominican Republic	76.4
Mexican	96.3
Puerto Rican	100.0
South American	83.2
Chilean	85.5
Colombian	65.6
Ecuadorian	61.2
Peruvian	89.5

Average Household Size

Group	People
Total Population	2.69
Hispanic or Latino (of any race)	3.86
Central American, ex. Mexican	4.63
Guatemalan	3.51
Honduran	4.53

Notes: (1) Percent of total population; (2) Percent of Hispanic/Latino population; Profiles include places with an overall population of at least 125,000, OR an overall population of at least 25,000 where the Hispanic/Latino population is at least 20% of the overall population. In states where less than five places meet either of these criteria, we have included places with at least 10,000 total population with the highest percentage of Hispanic/Latino population. These places are identified with an asterisk (*); Please refer to the User's Guide for a full explanation of data.

Salvadoran	4.80
Cuban	2.55
Dominican Republic	3.43
Mexican	3.39
Puerto Rican	2.90
South American	3.62
Chilean	3.46
Colombian	3.32
Ecuadorian	3.48
Peruvian	3.95

Median Age

Group	Years
Total Population	40.6
Hispanic or Latino (of any race)	30.6
Central American, ex. Mexican	29.2
Guatemalan	32.0
Honduran	29.3
Salvadoran	29.0
Cuban	42.0
Dominican Republic	27.8
Mexican	28.7
Puerto Rican	32.9
South American	38.3
Chilean	43.8
Colombian	37.6
Ecuadorian	39.0
Peruvian	37.9

High School Graduates
(Universe: Population 25 Years and Over)

Group	Number	%
Total Population	15,523	84.7
Hispanic or Latino (of any race)	2,297	62.9
Central American, ex. Mexican	699	42.8
Salvadoran	463	35.5

Four-Year College Graduates
(Universe: Population 25 Years and Over)

Group	Number	%
Total Population	7,005	38.2
Hispanic or Latino (of any race)	668	18.3
Central American, ex. Mexican	124	7.6
Salvadoran	47	3.6

Population Age 3–17 Enrolled in Public School
(Universe: Population Age 3–17 Enrolled in School)

Group	Number	%
Total Population	3,699	80.2
Hispanic or Latino (of any race)	1,439	97.9
Central American, ex. Mexican	761	98.8
Salvadoran	653	98.6

Population Age 3–17 Enrolled in Private School
(Universe: Population Age 3–17 Enrolled in School)

Group	Number	%
Total Population	916	19.8
Hispanic or Latino (of any race)	31	2.1
Central American, ex. Mexican	9	1.2
Salvadoran	9	1.4

Foreign-Born Population

Group	Number	%
Total Population	7,197	26.9
Hispanic or Latino (of any race)	3,829	56.4
Central American, ex. Mexican	2,371	70.5
Salvadoran	2,043	70.7

Foreign-Born Naturalized U.S. Citizens

Group	Number	%
Total Population	2,954	41.0
Hispanic or Latino (of any race)	727	19.0
Central American, ex. Mexican	226	9.5
Salvadoran	138	6.8

Language Spoken at Home: English Only
(Universe: Population 5 Years and Over)

Group	Number	%
Total Population	15,560	62.1
Hispanic or Latino (of any race)	571	9.7
Central American, ex. Mexican	97	3.4
Salvadoran	73	3.0

Language Spoken at Home: Spanish
(Universe: Population 5 Years and Over)

Group	Number	%
Total Population	5,847	23.3
Hispanic or Latino (of any race)	5,239	89.4
Central American, ex. Mexican	2,779	96.6
Salvadoran	2,364	97.0

Unemployment Rate
(Universe: Population 16 Years and Over)

Group	%
Total Population	4.9
Hispanic or Latino (of any race)	5.4
Central American, ex. Mexican	1.9
Salvadoran	2.2

Class of Worker: Private Wage and Salary
(Universe: Civilian Employed Population 16 Years and Over)

Group	Number	%
Total Population	10,751	81.8
Hispanic or Latino (of any race)	2,658	87.5
Central American, ex. Mexican	1,406	85.9
Salvadoran	1,193	85.2

Class of Worker: Government
(Universe: Civilian Employed Population 16 Years and Over)

Group	Number	%
Total Population	1,566	11.9
Hispanic or Latino (of any race)	160	5.3
Central American, ex. Mexican	12	0.7
Salvadoran	12	0.9

Means of Transportation to Work: Car, Truck or Van
(Universe: Workers 16 Years and Over)

Group	Number	%
Total Population	10,121	79.2
Hispanic or Latino (of any race)	2,196	74.1
Central American, ex. Mexican	1,045	63.8
Salvadoran	902	64.4

Means of Transportation to Work: Public Transportation (ex. Taxicab)
(Universe: Workers 16 Years and Over)

Group	Number	%
Total Population	914	7.2
Hispanic or Latino (of any race)	272	9.2
Central American, ex. Mexican	157	9.6
Salvadoran	124	8.9

Homeownership Rate
(Universe: Occupied Housing Units)

Group	%
Total Population	56.1
Hispanic or Latino (of any race)	25.0
Central American, ex. Mexican	15.1
Guatemalan	17.9
Honduran	11.5
Salvadoran	14.8
Cuban	34.1
Dominican Republic	25.5
Mexican	32.1
Puerto Rican	27.3
South American	32.5
Chilean	28.4
Colombian	34.7
Ecuadorian	45.5
Peruvian	27.7

Median Home Value

Group	Dollars
Total Population	560,900
Hispanic or Latino (of any race)	493,800
Central American, ex. Mexican	479,400
Salvadoran	454,200

Median Gross Rent

Group	Dollars
Total Population	1,514
Hispanic or Latino (of any race)	1,561
Central American, ex. Mexican	1,650
Salvadoran	1,721

Median Household Income
(2010 Inflation-Adjusted Dollars)

Group	Dollars
Total Population	73,624
Hispanic or Latino (of any race)	40,757
Central American, ex. Mexican	31,301
Salvadoran	29,097

Per Capita Income
(2010 Inflation-Adjusted Dollars)

Group	Dollars
Total Population	36,233
Hispanic or Latino (of any race)	15,493
Central American, ex. Mexican	9,960
Salvadoran	8,663

Households with $100,000+ Income

Group	Number	%
Total Population	3,475	36.6
Hispanic or Latino (of any race)	247	15.3
Central American, ex. Mexican	106	14.8
Salvadoran	48	9.0

Households with Food Stamps/SNAP Benefits During Past 12 Months

Group	Number	%
Total Population	440	4.6
Hispanic or Latino (of any race)	181	11.2
Central American, ex. Mexican	0	0.0
Salvadoran	0	0.0

Poverty Rate
(Income in Past 12 Months Below Poverty Level)

Group	%
Total Population	13.1
Hispanic or Latino (of any race)	33.4
Central American, ex. Mexican	42.4
Salvadoran	49.4

Haverstraw

Population

Group	Number	%TP[1]	%HP[2]
Total Population	36,634	100.0	–
Hispanic or Latino (of any race)	15,012	41.0	100.0
Central American, ex. Mexican	1,009	2.8	6.7
Guatemalan	325	0.9	2.2
Salvadoran	532	1.5	3.5
Cuban	152	0.4	1.0
Dominican Republic	6,277	17.1	41.8
Mexican	1,425	3.9	9.5
Puerto Rican	4,061	11.1	27.1
South American	1,067	2.9	7.1
Colombian	174	0.5	1.2
Ecuadorian	669	1.8	4.5
Peruvian	134	0.4	0.9

Population Growth: 2000–2010

Group	%
Total Population	8.3
Hispanic or Latino (of any race)	39.9
Central American, ex. Mexican	260.4
Cuban	32.2
Dominican Republic	66.8
Mexican	142.8
Puerto Rican	6.5
South American	154.0
Ecuadorian	248.4

Males per 100 Females

Group	Number
Total Population	94.0
Hispanic or Latino (of any race)	96.3
Central American, ex. Mexican	112.4
Guatemalan	133.8
Salvadoran	108.6
Cuban	85.4
Dominican Republic	85.9
Mexican	126.6
Puerto Rican	96.7
South American	118.6
Colombian	74.0
Ecuadorian	155.3
Peruvian	83.6

Notes: (1) Percent of total population; (2) Percent of Hispanic/Latino population; Profiles include places with an overall population of at least 125,000, OR an overall population of at least 25,000 where the Hispanic/Latino population is at least 20% of the overall population. In states where less than five places meet either of these criteria, we have included places with at least 10,000 total population with the highest percentage of Hispanic/Latino population. These places are identified with an asterisk (*); Please refer to the User's Guide for a full explanation of data.

Average Household Size

Group	People
Total Population	2.96
Hispanic or Latino (of any race)	3.89
Central American, ex. Mexican	4.24
Guatemalan	4.13
Salvadoran	4.54
Cuban	2.65
Dominican Republic	4.20
Mexican	5.26
Puerto Rican	3.21
South American	4.05
Colombian	3.30
Ecuadorian	4.60
Peruvian	3.76

Median Age

Group	Years
Total Population	37.1
Hispanic or Latino (of any race)	28.9
Central American, ex. Mexican	28.0
Guatemalan	28.4
Salvadoran	26.5
Cuban	36.0
Dominican Republic	29.7
Mexican	25.7
Puerto Rican	31.5
South American	31.1
Colombian	34.3
Ecuadorian	29.8
Peruvian	34.2

High School Graduates
(Universe: Population 25 Years and Over)

Group	Number	%
Total Population	18,628	79.7
Hispanic or Latino (of any race)	4,409	58.9
Dominican Republic	1,690	55.4
Mexican	354	44.0
Puerto Rican	1,690	73.8

Four-Year College Graduates
(Universe: Population 25 Years and Over)

Group	Number	%
Total Population	6,650	28.4
Hispanic or Latino (of any race)	967	12.9
Dominican Republic	289	9.5
Mexican	76	9.5
Puerto Rican	400	17.5

Population Age 3–17 Enrolled in Public School
(Universe: Population Age 3–17 Enrolled in School)

Group	Number	%
Total Population	6,202	87.4
Hispanic or Latino (of any race)	3,141	93.9
Dominican Republic	1,625	96.6
Mexican	237	100.0
Puerto Rican	715	86.9

Population Age 3–17 Enrolled in Private School
(Universe: Population Age 3–17 Enrolled in School)

Group	Number	%
Total Population	891	12.6
Hispanic or Latino (of any race)	203	6.1
Dominican Republic	58	3.4
Mexican	0	0.0
Puerto Rican	108	13.1

Foreign-Born Population

Group	Number	%
Total Population	9,734	27.1
Hispanic or Latino (of any race)	6,271	46.7
Dominican Republic	3,575	61.4
Mexican	939	69.1
Puerto Rican	0	0.0

Foreign-Born Naturalized U.S. Citizens

Group	Number	%
Total Population	4,486	46.1
Hispanic or Latino (of any race)	2,425	38.7
Dominican Republic	1,880	52.6
Mexican	126	13.4
Puerto Rican	0	0.0

Language Spoken at Home: English Only
(Universe: Population 5 Years and Over)

Group	Number	%
Total Population	18,260	55.0
Hispanic or Latino (of any race)	1,696	13.9
Dominican Republic	236	4.5
Mexican	135	11.4
Puerto Rican	1,065	31.2

Language Spoken at Home: Spanish
(Universe: Population 5 Years and Over)

Group	Number	%
Total Population	11,099	33.4
Hispanic or Latino (of any race)	10,460	85.9
Dominican Republic	5,030	95.5
Mexican	1,033	87.0
Puerto Rican	2,353	68.8

Unemployment Rate
(Universe: Population 16 Years and Over)

Group	%
Total Population	6.1
Hispanic or Latino (of any race)	6.9
Dominican Republic	6.2
Mexican	3.0
Puerto Rican	10.6

Class of Worker: Private Wage and Salary
(Universe: Civilian Employed Population 16 Years and Over)

Group	Number	%
Total Population	13,301	76.6
Hispanic or Latino (of any race)	4,981	82.2
Dominican Republic	2,013	82.8
Mexican	704	89.7
Puerto Rican	1,165	71.6

Class of Worker: Government
(Universe: Civilian Employed Population 16 Years and Over)

Group	Number	%
Total Population	3,546	20.4
Hispanic or Latino (of any race)	844	13.9
Dominican Republic	307	12.6
Mexican	37	4.7
Puerto Rican	420	25.8

Means of Transportation to Work: Car, Truck or Van
(Universe: Workers 16 Years and Over)

Group	Number	%
Total Population	14,502	85.1
Hispanic or Latino (of any race)	4,660	77.6
Dominican Republic	1,961	81.5
Mexican	421	54.8
Puerto Rican	1,366	84.5

Means of Transportation to Work: Public Transportation (ex. Taxicab)
(Universe: Workers 16 Years and Over)

Group	Number	%
Total Population	1,565	9.2
Hispanic or Latino (of any race)	828	13.8
Dominican Republic	190	7.9
Mexican	256	33.3
Puerto Rican	158	9.8

Homeownership Rate
(Universe: Occupied Housing Units)

Group	%
Total Population	62.4
Hispanic or Latino (of any race)	41.9
Central American, ex. Mexican	47.2
Guatemalan	43.8
Salvadoran	49.6
Cuban	59.6
Dominican Republic	38.7
Mexican	18.1
Puerto Rican	51.0
South American	35.8
Colombian	48.1
Ecuadorian	24.1
Peruvian	57.6

Median Home Value

Group	Dollars
Total Population	372,600
Hispanic or Latino (of any race)	353,600
Dominican Republic	345,600
Mexican	364,300
Puerto Rican	366,800

Median Gross Rent

Group	Dollars
Total Population	1,223
Hispanic or Latino (of any race)	1,190
Dominican Republic	1,264
Mexican	1,184
Puerto Rican	1,196

Median Household Income
(2010 Inflation-Adjusted Dollars)

Group	Dollars
Total Population	66,633
Hispanic or Latino (of any race)	49,798
Dominican Republic	47,935
Mexican	56,488
Puerto Rican	74,727

Per Capita Income
(2010 Inflation-Adjusted Dollars)

Group	Dollars
Total Population	30,080
Hispanic or Latino (of any race)	18,829
Dominican Republic	15,739
Mexican	19,221
Puerto Rican	24,072

Households with $100,000+ Income

Group	Number	%
Total Population	3,946	32.4
Hispanic or Latino (of any race)	841	22.5
Dominican Republic	263	16.2
Mexican	121	37.0
Puerto Rican	360	35.5

Households with Food Stamps/SNAP Benefits During Past 12 Months

Group	Number	%
Total Population	769	6.3
Hispanic or Latino (of any race)	504	13.5
Dominican Republic	224	13.8
Mexican	36	11.0
Puerto Rican	187	18.5

Poverty Rate
(Income in Past 12 Months Below Poverty Level)

Group	%
Total Population	10.9
Hispanic or Latino (of any race)	16.2
Dominican Republic	11.7
Mexican	26.2
Puerto Rican	12.4

Hempstead (town)

Population

Group	Number	%TP[1]	%HP[2]
Total Population	759,757	100.0	–
Hispanic or Latino (of any race)	132,154	17.4	100.0
Central American, ex. Mexican	49,236	6.5	37.3
Costa Rican	664	0.1	0.5
Guatemalan	5,948	0.8	4.5
Honduran	7,842	1.0	5.9
Nicaraguan	656	0.1	0.5
Panamanian	1,163	0.2	0.9
Salvadoran	32,681	4.3	24.7
Cuban	3,597	0.5	2.7
Dominican Republic	16,914	2.2	12.8
Mexican	5,000	0.7	3.8
Puerto Rican	20,508	2.7	15.5
South American	23,626	3.1	17.9
Argentinean	1,500	0.2	1.1
Bolivian	494	0.1	0.4
Chilean	1,415	0.2	1.1
Colombian	8,522	1.1	6.4
Ecuadorian	5,881	0.8	4.5
Paraguayan	185	<0.1	0.1
Peruvian	4,510	0.6	3.4
Uruguayan	359	<0.1	0.3
Venezuelan	517	0.1	0.4

Notes: (1) Percent of total population; (2) Percent of Hispanic/Latino population; Profiles include places with an overall population of at least 125,000, OR an overall population of at least 25,000 where the Hispanic/Latino population is at least 20% of the overall population. In states where less than five places meet either of these criteria, we have included places with at least 10,000 total population with the highest percentage of Hispanic/Latino population. These places are identified with an asterisk (*); Please refer to the User's Guide for a full explanation of data.

Spaniard	1,955	0.3	1.5

Population Growth: 2000–2010

Group	%
Total Population	0.5
Hispanic or Latino (of any race)	52.5
Central American, ex. Mexican	119.3
Costa Rican	49.2
Guatemalan	184.0
Honduran	219.8
Nicaraguan	250.8
Panamanian	94.8
Salvadoran	108.7
Cuban	22.6
Dominican Republic	100.6
Mexican	68.3
Puerto Rican	30.0
South American	106.7
Argentinean	74.6
Bolivian	116.7
Chilean	58.5
Colombian	93.5
Ecuadorian	151.0
Peruvian	161.6
Uruguayan	94.1
Venezuelan	120.0
Spaniard	202.6

Males per 100 Females

Group	Number
Total Population	93.3
Hispanic or Latino (of any race)	102.4
Central American, ex. Mexican	116.6
Costa Rican	88.6
Guatemalan	128.9
Honduran	138.6
Nicaraguan	115.1
Panamanian	85.2
Salvadoran	112.0
Cuban	95.9
Dominican Republic	89.2
Mexican	110.4
Puerto Rican	93.2
South American	91.1
Argentinean	100.0
Bolivian	96.8
Chilean	113.4
Colombian	85.2
Ecuadorian	90.6
Paraguayan	90.7
Peruvian	94.6
Uruguayan	93.0
Venezuelan	79.5
Spaniard	95.7

Average Household Size

Group	People
Total Population	3.03
Hispanic or Latino (of any race)	4.25
Central American, ex. Mexican	5.27
Costa Rican	3.57
Guatemalan	4.76
Honduran	5.41
Nicaraguan	4.50
Panamanian	3.52
Salvadoran	5.50
Cuban	3.14
Dominican Republic	4.32
Mexican	3.99
Puerto Rican	3.30
South American	3.87
Argentinean	3.21
Bolivian	3.64
Chilean	3.47
Colombian	3.76
Ecuadorian	4.37
Paraguayan	4.14
Peruvian	4.04
Uruguayan	3.32
Venezuelan	3.51
Spaniard	2.98

Median Age

Group	Years
Total Population	40.0
Hispanic or Latino (of any race)	30.3
Central American, ex. Mexican	29.9
Costa Rican	39.1
Guatemalan	30.0
Honduran	29.1
Nicaraguan	30.6
Panamanian	37.5
Salvadoran	29.8
Cuban	38.4
Dominican Republic	29.8
Mexican	26.9
Puerto Rican	30.8
South American	36.3
Argentinean	41.5
Bolivian	35.5
Chilean	37.1
Colombian	36.7
Ecuadorian	35.0
Paraguayan	28.8
Peruvian	36.0
Uruguayan	41.9
Venezuelan	32.0
Spaniard	38.7

High School Graduates
(Universe: Population 25 Years and Over)

Group	Number	%
Total Population	445,288	88.3
Hispanic or Latino (of any race)	48,841	66.7
Central American, ex. Mexican	11,974	46.7
Guatemalan	1,220	53.9
Honduran	1,873	41.8
Panamanian	911	96.5
Salvadoran	7,216	42.4
Cuban	1,919	84.6
Dominican Republic	6,251	57.1
Mexican	1,794	68.2
Puerto Rican	9,631	85.7
South American	13,467	84.2
Argentinean	680	75.8
Chilean	635	73.0
Colombian	5,166	86.3
Ecuadorian	2,923	82.4
Peruvian	2,605	87.0
Spaniard	1,131	82.8

Four-Year College Graduates
(Universe: Population 25 Years and Over)

Group	Number	%
Total Population	183,313	36.3
Hispanic or Latino (of any race)	12,439	17.0
Central American, ex. Mexican	1,950	7.6
Guatemalan	232	10.3
Honduran	282	6.3
Panamanian	377	39.9
Salvadoran	917	5.4
Cuban	783	34.5
Dominican Republic	1,540	14.1
Mexican	338	12.8
Puerto Rican	2,710	24.1
South American	3,852	24.1
Argentinean	320	35.7
Chilean	63	7.2
Colombian	1,302	21.8
Ecuadorian	816	23.0
Peruvian	941	31.4
Spaniard	471	34.5

Population Age 3–17 Enrolled in Public School
(Universe: Population Age 3–17 Enrolled in School)

Group	Number	%
Total Population	118,505	80.3
Hispanic or Latino (of any race)	24,007	90.2
Central American, ex. Mexican	8,198	94.3
Guatemalan	1,012	95.3
Honduran	994	93.3
Panamanian	257	74.9
Salvadoran	5,655	95.6
Cuban	513	73.5
Dominican Republic	4,120	92.0
Mexican	1,114	84.5
Puerto Rican	4,216	89.5
South American	3,644	87.7
Argentinean	114	79.2
Chilean	180	92.8
Colombian	1,262	86.4
Ecuadorian	1,105	86.0
Peruvian	671	90.8
Spaniard	264	55.2

Population Age 3–17 Enrolled in Private School
(Universe: Population Age 3–17 Enrolled in School)

Group	Number	%
Total Population	28,985	19.7
Hispanic or Latino (of any race)	2,610	9.8
Central American, ex. Mexican	491	5.7
Guatemalan	50	4.7
Honduran	71	6.7
Panamanian	86	25.1
Salvadoran	263	4.4
Cuban	185	26.5
Dominican Republic	358	8.0
Mexican	204	15.5
Puerto Rican	497	10.5
South American	510	12.3
Argentinean	30	20.8
Chilean	14	7.2
Colombian	198	13.6
Ecuadorian	180	14.0
Peruvian	68	9.2
Spaniard	214	44.8

Foreign-Born Population

Group	Number	%
Total Population	160,052	21.2
Hispanic or Latino (of any race)	62,073	50.3
Central American, ex. Mexican	28,711	65.9
Guatemalan	2,608	62.3
Honduran	5,069	70.1
Panamanian	675	47.0
Salvadoran	19,577	67.1
Cuban	1,515	44.7
Dominican Republic	11,343	59.4
Mexican	2,173	44.9
Puerto Rican	277	1.4
South American	15,831	66.3
Argentinean	887	69.0
Chilean	920	70.9
Colombian	5,853	67.7
Ecuadorian	3,596	62.6
Peruvian	2,872	65.1
Spaniard	471	20.7

Foreign-Born Naturalized U.S. Citizens

Group	Number	%
Total Population	97,007	60.6
Hispanic or Latino (of any race)	26,141	42.1
Central American, ex. Mexican	7,522	26.2
Guatemalan	908	34.8
Honduran	403	8.0
Panamanian	620	91.9
Salvadoran	5,126	26.2
Cuban	1,327	87.6
Dominican Republic	5,875	51.8
Mexican	708	32.6
Puerto Rican	218	78.7
South American	9,205	58.1
Argentinean	612	69.0
Chilean	357	38.8
Colombian	3,804	65.0
Ecuadorian	1,997	55.5
Peruvian	1,679	58.5
Spaniard	335	71.1

Language Spoken at Home: English Only
(Universe: Population 5 Years and Over)

Group	Number	%
Total Population	516,972	72.9
Hispanic or Latino (of any race)	21,287	18.9
Central American, ex. Mexican	2,835	7.3
Guatemalan	403	10.9
Honduran	441	7.0
Panamanian	568	41.6
Salvadoran	1,124	4.3
Cuban	1,234	37.7
Dominican Republic	1,605	9.3
Mexican	1,182	27.9
Puerto Rican	8,651	47.4
South American	2,965	13.3
Argentinean	236	19.6

Notes: (1) Percent of total population; (2) Percent of Hispanic/Latino population; Profiles include places with an overall population of at least 125,000, OR an overall population of at least 25,000 where the Hispanic/Latino population is at least 20% of the overall population. In states where less than five places meet either of these criteria, we have included places with at least 10,000 total population with the highest percentage of Hispanic/Latino population. These places are identified with an asterisk (*); Please refer to the User's Guide for a full explanation of data.

Group	Number	%
Chilean	111	8.7
Colombian	1,279	16.0
Ecuadorian	634	11.8
Peruvian	267	6.4
Spaniard	992	48.0

Language Spoken at Home: Spanish
(Universe: Population 5 Years and Over)

Group	Number	%
Total Population	98,366	13.9
Hispanic or Latino (of any race)	90,687	80.5
Central American, ex. Mexican	36,069	92.4
Guatemalan	3,306	89.1
Honduran	5,830	93.0
Panamanian	797	58.4
Salvadoran	25,024	95.2
Cuban	2,034	62.1
Dominican Republic	15,625	90.6
Mexican	3,009	71.2
Puerto Rican	9,471	51.9
South American	19,238	86.1
Argentinean	908	75.2
Chilean	1,172	91.3
Colombian	6,679	83.6
Ecuadorian	4,726	88.2
Peruvian	3,928	93.6
Spaniard	953	46.1

Unemployment Rate
(Universe: Population 16 Years and Over)

Group	%
Total Population	6.3
Hispanic or Latino (of any race)	7.9
Central American, ex. Mexican	6.6
Guatemalan	10.7
Honduran	5.4
Panamanian	8.0
Salvadoran	6.3
Cuban	10.3
Dominican Republic	11.9
Mexican	5.6
Puerto Rican	9.7
South American	6.6
Argentinean	1.0
Chilean	10.4
Colombian	11.5
Ecuadorian	3.6
Peruvian	3.0
Spaniard	5.2

Class of Worker: Private Wage and Salary
(Universe: Civilian Employed Population 16 Years and Over)

Group	Number	%
Total Population	285,329	76.7
Hispanic or Latino (of any race)	52,576	82.9
Central American, ex. Mexican	20,767	87.2
Guatemalan	1,517	80.2
Honduran	4,253	95.8
Panamanian	549	70.0
Salvadoran	13,774	87.0
Cuban	1,198	72.7
Dominican Republic	7,649	84.0
Mexican	1,932	86.9
Puerto Rican	7,090	75.5
South American	10,572	79.2
Argentinean	560	77.6
Chilean	747	83.9
Colombian	3,555	82.6
Ecuadorian	2,509	77.8
Peruvian	2,001	71.6
Spaniard	1,068	87.3

Class of Worker: Government
(Universe: Civilian Employed Population 16 Years and Over)

Group	Number	%
Total Population	67,455	18.1
Hispanic or Latino (of any race)	6,428	10.1
Central American, ex. Mexican	1,296	5.4
Guatemalan	53	2.8
Honduran	25	0.6
Panamanian	223	28.4
Salvadoran	854	5.4
Cuban	381	23.1
Dominican Republic	747	8.2
Mexican	186	8.4
Puerto Rican	1,973	21.0
South American	1,424	10.7
Argentinean	105	14.5
Chilean	48	5.4
Colombian	439	10.2
Ecuadorian	449	13.9
Peruvian	287	10.3
Spaniard	144	11.8

Means of Transportation to Work: Car, Truck or Van
(Universe: Workers 16 Years and Over)

Group	Number	%
Total Population	278,914	77.0
Hispanic or Latino (of any race)	46,074	74.6
Central American, ex. Mexican	16,935	72.7
Guatemalan	1,234	65.5
Honduran	2,446	56.8
Panamanian	564	74.1
Salvadoran	11,948	76.9
Cuban	1,204	77.9
Dominican Republic	6,276	72.2
Mexican	1,661	76.3
Puerto Rican	7,232	78.9
South American	9,877	75.9
Argentinean	540	76.6
Chilean	591	67.2
Colombian	3,211	77.7
Ecuadorian	2,413	76.1
Peruvian	2,037	74.2
Spaniard	889	74.6

Means of Transportation to Work: Public Transportation (ex. Taxicab)
(Universe: Workers 16 Years and Over)

Group	Number	%
Total Population	59,115	16.3
Hispanic or Latino (of any race)	10,445	16.9
Central American, ex. Mexican	4,353	18.7
Guatemalan	435	23.1
Honduran	1,425	33.1
Panamanian	153	20.1
Salvadoran	2,275	14.6
Cuban	236	15.3
Dominican Republic	1,317	15.2
Mexican	398	18.3
Puerto Rican	1,398	15.2
South American	2,129	16.4
Argentinean	83	11.8
Chilean	122	13.9
Colombian	669	16.2
Ecuadorian	560	17.7
Peruvian	427	15.5
Spaniard	230	19.3

Homeownership Rate
(Universe: Occupied Housing Units)

Group	%
Total Population	80.0
Hispanic or Latino (of any race)	58.0
Central American, ex. Mexican	47.3
Costa Rican	62.1
Guatemalan	37.7
Honduran	32.5
Nicaraguan	40.0
Panamanian	74.0
Salvadoran	50.7
Cuban	74.7
Dominican Republic	49.0
Mexican	44.3
Puerto Rican	70.9
South American	67.3
Argentinean	76.2
Bolivian	55.5
Chilean	50.5
Colombian	68.5
Ecuadorian	74.2
Paraguayan	68.6
Peruvian	58.3
Uruguayan	75.4
Venezuelan	66.4
Spaniard	83.9

Median Home Value

Group	Dollars
Total Population	456,700
Hispanic or Latino (of any race)	431,000
Central American, ex. Mexican	405,600
Guatemalan	438,800
Honduran	383,800
Panamanian	475,400
Salvadoran	397,400
Cuban	439,900
Dominican Republic	425,600
Mexican	418,200
Puerto Rican	434,500
South American	448,100
Argentinean	425,400
Chilean	431,100
Colombian	446,800
Ecuadorian	450,700
Peruvian	461,900
Spaniard	456,900

Median Gross Rent

Group	Dollars
Total Population	1,340
Hispanic or Latino (of any race)	1,332
Central American, ex. Mexican	1,371
Guatemalan	1,343
Honduran	1,363
Panamanian	1,231
Salvadoran	1,382
Cuban	1,511
Dominican Republic	1,161
Mexican	1,495
Puerto Rican	1,256
South American	1,448
Argentinean	–
Chilean	1,225
Colombian	1,455
Ecuadorian	1,382
Peruvian	1,750
Spaniard	1,622

Median Household Income
(2010 Inflation-Adjusted Dollars)

Group	Dollars
Total Population	89,722
Hispanic or Latino (of any race)	69,322
Central American, ex. Mexican	61,515
Guatemalan	53,900
Honduran	53,719
Panamanian	88,884
Salvadoran	61,534
Cuban	96,094
Dominican Republic	56,412
Mexican	55,956
Puerto Rican	79,234
South American	76,223
Argentinean	86,208
Chilean	70,843
Colombian	81,338
Ecuadorian	71,339
Peruvian	73,750
Spaniard	81,842

Per Capita Income
(2010 Inflation-Adjusted Dollars)

Group	Dollars
Total Population	36,416
Hispanic or Latino (of any race)	21,368
Central American, ex. Mexican	17,449
Guatemalan	16,250
Honduran	13,439
Panamanian	32,411
Salvadoran	17,130
Cuban	34,071
Dominican Republic	17,201
Mexican	22,420
Puerto Rican	26,491
South American	25,069
Argentinean	29,318
Chilean	25,840
Colombian	26,966
Ecuadorian	21,338
Peruvian	23,075
Spaniard	28,410

Notes: (1) Percent of total population; (2) Percent of Hispanic/Latino population; Profiles include places with an overall population of at least 125,000, OR an overall population of at least 25,000 where the Hispanic/Latino population is at least 20% of the overall population. In states where less than five places meet either of these criteria, we have included places with at least 10,000 total population with the highest percentage of Hispanic/Latino population. These places are identified with an asterisk (*); Please refer to the User's Guide for a full explanation of data.

Households with $100,000+ Income		
Group	Number	%
Total Population	109,027	44.7
Hispanic or Latino (of any race)	9,079	30.7
Central American, ex. Mexican	2,263	23.5
Guatemalan	205	21.3
Honduran	270	17.5
Panamanian	237	47.5
Salvadoran	1,388	22.2
Cuban	504	46.7
Dominican Republic	1,134	25.0
Mexican	210	20.3
Puerto Rican	1,808	36.6
South American	2,241	35.7
Argentinean	170	42.4
Chilean	115	30.2
Colombian	988	42.3
Ecuadorian	404	26.6
Peruvian	296	30.5
Spaniard	317	45.9

Households with Food Stamps/SNAP Benefits During Past 12 Months		
Group	Number	%
Total Population	9,706	4.0
Hispanic or Latino (of any race)	2,350	7.9
Central American, ex. Mexican	578	6.0
Guatemalan	66	6.8
Honduran	94	6.1
Panamanian	30	6.0
Salvadoran	388	6.2
Cuban	50	4.6
Dominican Republic	803	17.7
Mexican	51	4.9
Puerto Rican	388	7.8
South American	428	6.8
Argentinean	47	11.7
Chilean	0	0.0
Colombian	207	8.9
Ecuadorian	132	8.7
Peruvian	28	2.9
Spaniard	10	1.4

Poverty Rate (Income in Past 12 Months Below Poverty Level)	
Group	%
Total Population	5.3
Hispanic or Latino (of any race)	9.8
Central American, ex. Mexican	10.1
Guatemalan	16.9
Honduran	12.5
Panamanian	8.4
Salvadoran	9.2
Cuban	1.6
Dominican Republic	18.4
Mexican	13.5
Puerto Rican	9.3
South American	4.2
Argentinean	9.8
Chilean	6.6
Colombian	2.6
Ecuadorian	4.9
Peruvian	3.9
Spaniard	4.3

Hempstead (village)

Population			
Group	Number	%TP[1]	%HP[2]
Total Population	53,891	100.0	–
Hispanic or Latino (of any race)	23,823	44.2	100.0
Central American, ex. Mexican	16,171	30.0	67.9
Guatemalan	1,402	2.6	5.9
Honduran	3,758	7.0	15.8
Panamanian	138	0.3	0.6
Salvadoran	10,707	19.9	44.9
Cuban	174	0.3	0.7
Dominican Republic	1,398	2.6	5.9
Mexican	752	1.4	3.2
Puerto Rican	1,144	2.1	4.8
South American	1,575	2.9	6.6
Colombian	506	0.9	2.1
Ecuadorian	641	1.2	2.7
Peruvian	279	0.5	1.2
Spaniard	133	0.2	0.6

Population Growth: 2000–2010	
Group	%
Total Population	-4.7
Hispanic or Latino (of any race)	32.4
Central American, ex. Mexican	92.9
Guatemalan	190.9
Honduran	159.2
Panamanian	16.0
Salvadoran	80.0
Cuban	-19.4
Dominican Republic	57.6
Mexican	48.9
Puerto Rican	-17.2
South American	47.2
Colombian	30.4
Ecuadorian	62.3
Peruvian	61.3

Males per 100 Females	
Group	Number
Total Population	97.1
Hispanic or Latino (of any race)	120.3
Central American, ex. Mexican	129.2
Guatemalan	178.7
Honduran	151.0
Panamanian	79.2
Salvadoran	118.6
Cuban	112.2
Dominican Republic	81.1
Mexican	125.8
Puerto Rican	93.9
South American	111.7
Colombian	93.1
Ecuadorian	124.9
Peruvian	128.7
Spaniard	107.8

Average Household Size	
Group	People
Total Population	3.45
Hispanic or Latino (of any race)	5.00
Central American, ex. Mexican	5.53
Guatemalan	5.36
Honduran	5.43
Panamanian	3.40
Salvadoran	5.63
Cuban	3.10
Dominican Republic	4.02
Mexican	5.05
Puerto Rican	3.17
South American	4.16
Colombian	3.68
Ecuadorian	4.68
Peruvian	4.68
Spaniard	3.60

Median Age	
Group	Years
Total Population	32.5
Hispanic or Latino (of any race)	28.7
Central American, ex. Mexican	29.3
Guatemalan	29.0
Honduran	28.9
Panamanian	40.3
Salvadoran	29.4
Cuban	36.7
Dominican Republic	29.4
Mexican	25.0
Puerto Rican	29.2
South American	35.8
Colombian	39.5
Ecuadorian	33.7
Peruvian	35.5
Spaniard	18.5

High School Graduates (Universe: Population 25 Years and Over)		
Group	Number	%
Total Population	23,131	68.4
Hispanic or Latino (of any race)	5,811	44.2
Central American, ex. Mexican	3,251	35.6
Honduran	1,002	40.6
Salvadoran	1,865	32.0
Dominican Republic	939	55.5
Puerto Rican	480	76.6
South American	641	75.1

Four-Year College Graduates (Universe: Population 25 Years and Over)		
Group	Number	%
Total Population	5,650	16.7
Hispanic or Latino (of any race)	1,015	7.7
Central American, ex. Mexican	365	4.0
Honduran	134	5.4
Salvadoran	166	2.8
Dominican Republic	244	14.4
Puerto Rican	62	9.9
South American	272	31.9

Population Age 3–17 Enrolled in Public School (Universe: Population Age 3–17 Enrolled in School)		
Group	Number	%
Total Population	8,409	86.7
Hispanic or Latino (of any race)	3,532	91.0
Central American, ex. Mexican	2,259	95.5
Honduran	340	100.0
Salvadoran	1,720	97.4
Dominican Republic	554	92.6
Puerto Rican	272	66.7
South American	122	71.8

Population Age 3–17 Enrolled in Private School (Universe: Population Age 3–17 Enrolled in School)		
Group	Number	%
Total Population	1,293	13.3
Hispanic or Latino (of any race)	350	9.0
Central American, ex. Mexican	107	4.5
Honduran	0	0.0
Salvadoran	46	2.6
Dominican Republic	44	7.4
Puerto Rican	136	33.3
South American	48	28.2

Foreign-Born Population		
Group	Number	%
Total Population	20,895	39.2
Hispanic or Latino (of any race)	13,813	63.2
Central American, ex. Mexican	10,411	71.0
Honduran	2,889	76.8
Salvadoran	6,620	70.2
Dominican Republic	1,577	56.5
Puerto Rican	0	0.0
South American	1,058	75.8

Foreign-Born Naturalized U.S. Citizens		
Group	Number	%
Total Population	7,060	33.8
Hispanic or Latino (of any race)	2,783	20.1
Central American, ex. Mexican	1,344	12.9
Honduran	27	0.9
Salvadoran	1,091	16.5
Dominican Republic	860	54.5
Puerto Rican	0	0.0
South American	391	37.0

Language Spoken at Home: English Only (Universe: Population 5 Years and Over)		
Group	Number	%
Total Population	26,626	54.6
Hispanic or Latino (of any race)	1,473	7.7
Central American, ex. Mexican	530	4.1
Honduran	196	5.9
Salvadoran	204	2.5
Dominican Republic	129	5.2
Puerto Rican	491	39.5
South American	36	2.9

Language Spoken at Home: Spanish (Universe: Population 5 Years and Over)		
Group	Number	%
Total Population	18,145	37.2
Hispanic or Latino (of any race)	17,619	91.9
Central American, ex. Mexican	12,290	95.5
Honduran	3,133	94.1
Salvadoran	8,049	97.0
Dominican Republic	2,358	94.8
Puerto Rican	726	58.4

Notes: (1) Percent of total population; (2) Percent of Hispanic/Latino population; Profiles include places with an overall population of at least 125,000, OR an overall population of at least 25,000 where the Hispanic/Latino population is at least 20% of the overall population. In states where less than five places meet either of these criteria, we have included places with at least 10,000 total population with the highest percentage of Hispanic/Latino population. These places are identified with an asterisk (*); Please refer to the User's Guide for a full explanation of data.

South American	1,198	97.1

Unemployment Rate
(Universe: Population 16 Years and Over)

Group	%
Total Population	11.3
Hispanic or Latino (of any race)	9.3
Central American, ex. Mexican	8.0
Honduran	4.3
Salvadoran	8.3
Dominican Republic	21.5
Puerto Rican	9.6
South American	5.3

Class of Worker: Private Wage and Salary
(Universe: Civilian Employed Population 16 Years and Over)

Group	Number	%
Total Population	21,399	83.3
Hispanic or Latino (of any race)	10,313	89.9
Central American, ex. Mexican	7,613	93.4
Honduran	2,450	98.1
Salvadoran	4,676	93.1
Dominican Republic	930	79.3
Puerto Rican	305	61.1
South American	731	83.8

Class of Worker: Government
(Universe: Civilian Employed Population 16 Years and Over)

Group	Number	%
Total Population	3,003	11.7
Hispanic or Latino (of any race)	337	2.9
Central American, ex. Mexican	64	0.8
Honduran	0	0.0
Salvadoran	18	0.4
Dominican Republic	110	9.4
Puerto Rican	128	25.7
South American	18	2.1

Means of Transportation to Work: Car, Truck or Van
(Universe: Workers 16 Years and Over)

Group	Number	%
Total Population	16,734	66.2
Hispanic or Latino (of any race)	6,933	61.9
Central American, ex. Mexican	4,868	61.3
Honduran	1,196	50.3
Salvadoran	3,298	66.6
Dominican Republic	720	63.7
Puerto Rican	269	53.9
South American	612	71.8

Means of Transportation to Work: Public Transportation (ex. Taxicab)
(Universe: Workers 16 Years and Over)

Group	Number	%
Total Population	5,917	23.4
Hispanic or Latino (of any race)	2,644	23.6
Central American, ex. Mexican	2,035	25.6
Honduran	873	36.7
Salvadoran	984	19.9
Dominican Republic	144	12.7
Puerto Rican	123	24.6
South American	140	16.4

Homeownership Rate
(Universe: Occupied Housing Units)

Group	%
Total Population	42.1
Hispanic or Latino (of any race)	32.1
Central American, ex. Mexican	31.9
Guatemalan	22.9
Honduran	17.6
Panamanian	57.4
Salvadoran	36.5
Cuban	38.3
Dominican Republic	23.0
Mexican	20.7
Puerto Rican	41.8
South American	35.5
Colombian	29.7
Ecuadorian	41.9
Peruvian	38.5
Spaniard	48.0

Median Home Value

Group	Dollars
Total Population	365,000
Hispanic or Latino (of any race)	373,700
Central American, ex. Mexican	374,500
Honduran	359,800
Salvadoran	376,200
Dominican Republic	430,100
Puerto Rican	283,300
South American	416,400

Median Gross Rent

Group	Dollars
Total Population	1,207
Hispanic or Latino (of any race)	1,285
Central American, ex. Mexican	1,345
Honduran	1,386
Salvadoran	1,349
Dominican Republic	1,148
Puerto Rican	740
South American	995

Median Household Income
(2010 Inflation-Adjusted Dollars)

Group	Dollars
Total Population	53,333
Hispanic or Latino (of any race)	52,289
Central American, ex. Mexican	53,170
Honduran	53,802
Salvadoran	53,122
Dominican Republic	50,646
Puerto Rican	28,968
South American	34,926

Per Capita Income
(2010 Inflation-Adjusted Dollars)

Group	Dollars
Total Population	20,713
Hispanic or Latino (of any race)	14,934
Central American, ex. Mexican	14,509
Honduran	12,966
Salvadoran	14,855
Dominican Republic	15,312
Puerto Rican	17,554
South American	19,480

Households with $100,000+ Income

Group	Number	%
Total Population	3,315	20.3
Hispanic or Latino (of any race)	679	13.0
Central American, ex. Mexican	426	12.8
Honduran	113	13.1
Salvadoran	268	12.4
Dominican Republic	128	17.2
Puerto Rican	83	19.9
South American	30	8.2

Households with Food Stamps/SNAP Benefits During Past 12 Months

Group	Number	%
Total Population	2,769	16.9
Hispanic or Latino (of any race)	772	14.8
Central American, ex. Mexican	328	9.8
Honduran	94	10.9
Salvadoran	190	8.8
Dominican Republic	268	36.0
Puerto Rican	110	26.3
South American	37	10.1

Poverty Rate
(Income in Past 12 Months Below Poverty Level)

Group	%
Total Population	14.8
Hispanic or Latino (of any race)	15.0
Central American, ex. Mexican	12.5
Honduran	7.7
Salvadoran	13.7
Dominican Republic	25.3
Puerto Rican	27.4
South American	8.9

Huntington

Population

Group	Number	%TP[1]	%HP[2]
Total Population	203,264	100.0	–
Hispanic or Latino (of any race)	22,362	11.0	100.0
Central American, ex. Mexican	9,599	4.7	42.9
Costa Rican	118	0.1	0.5
Guatemalan	1,080	0.5	4.8
Honduran	1,651	0.8	7.4
Salvadoran	6,563	3.2	29.3
Cuban	603	0.3	2.7
Dominican Republic	1,011	0.5	4.5
Mexican	1,440	0.7	6.4
Puerto Rican	4,187	2.1	18.7
South American	3,043	1.5	13.6
Argentinean	329	0.2	1.5
Chilean	252	0.1	1.1
Colombian	957	0.5	4.3
Ecuadorian	637	0.3	2.8
Peruvian	538	0.3	2.4
Spaniard	542	0.3	2.4

Population Growth: 2000–2010

Group	%
Total Population	4.1
Hispanic or Latino (of any race)	74.1
Central American, ex. Mexican	164.9
Guatemalan	262.4
Honduran	366.4
Salvadoran	138.9
Cuban	64.8
Dominican Republic	106.7
Mexican	99.7
Puerto Rican	20.8
South American	98.2
Argentinean	105.6
Chilean	119.1
Colombian	95.7
Ecuadorian	90.7
Peruvian	125.1
Spaniard	313.7

Males per 100 Females

Group	Number
Total Population	96.9
Hispanic or Latino (of any race)	108.3
Central American, ex. Mexican	128.5
Costa Rican	66.2
Guatemalan	162.1
Honduran	145.0
Salvadoran	123.1
Cuban	101.0
Dominican Republic	92.9
Mexican	118.5
Puerto Rican	90.5
South American	82.2
Argentinean	109.6
Chilean	85.3
Colombian	70.3
Ecuadorian	85.7
Peruvian	88.1
Spaniard	96.4

Average Household Size

Group	People
Total Population	2.89
Hispanic or Latino (of any race)	4.38
Central American, ex. Mexican	5.66
Costa Rican	3.71
Guatemalan	5.46
Honduran	5.69
Salvadoran	5.79
Cuban	2.96
Dominican Republic	4.52
Mexican	4.13
Puerto Rican	3.37
South American	3.63
Argentinean	3.04
Chilean	3.86
Colombian	3.55
Ecuadorian	3.83
Peruvian	3.79
Spaniard	2.98

Notes: (1) Percent of total population; (2) Percent of Hispanic/Latino population; Profiles include places with an overall population of at least 125,000, OR an overall population of at least 25,000 where the Hispanic/Latino population is at least 20% of the overall population. In states where less than five places meet either of these criteria, we have included places with at least 10,000 total population with the highest percentage of Hispanic/Latino population. These places are identified with an asterisk (*); Please refer to the User's Guide for a full explanation of data.

Median Age	
Group	Years
Total Population	42.5
Hispanic or Latino (of any race)	28.9
Central American, ex. Mexican	28.1
Costa Rican	33.5
Guatemalan	28.4
Honduran	28.2
Salvadoran	27.9
Cuban	35.5
Dominican Republic	29.2
Mexican	26.8
Puerto Rican	29.9
South American	36.6
Argentinean	39.1
Chilean	35.8
Colombian	36.5
Ecuadorian	36.7
Peruvian	36.1
Spaniard	35.8

High School Graduates (Universe: Population 25 Years and Over)		
Group	Number	%
Total Population	128,254	93.0
Hispanic or Latino (of any race)	7,984	70.2
Central American, ex. Mexican	2,668	52.0
Honduran	789	68.2
Salvadoran	1,658	45.1
Dominican Republic	535	69.4
Mexican	245	60.0
Puerto Rican	1,775	88.1
South American	1,708	95.7
Colombian	643	96.0

Four-Year College Graduates (Universe: Population 25 Years and Over)		
Group	Number	%
Total Population	65,454	47.5
Hispanic or Latino (of any race)	2,176	19.1
Central American, ex. Mexican	373	7.3
Honduran	139	12.0
Salvadoran	194	5.3
Dominican Republic	130	16.9
Mexican	75	18.4
Puerto Rican	506	25.1
South American	650	36.4
Colombian	254	37.9

Population Age 3–17 Enrolled in Public School (Universe: Population Age 3–17 Enrolled in School)		
Group	Number	%
Total Population	36,151	85.5
Hispanic or Latino (of any race)	4,055	90.1
Central American, ex. Mexican	1,325	99.0
Honduran	255	100.0
Salvadoran	1,047	100.0
Dominican Republic	362	82.1
Mexican	425	88.9
Puerto Rican	1,109	91.5
South American	462	80.6
Colombian	289	86.3

Population Age 3–17 Enrolled in Private School (Universe: Population Age 3–17 Enrolled in School)		
Group	Number	%
Total Population	6,144	14.5
Hispanic or Latino (of any race)	447	9.9
Central American, ex. Mexican	14	1.0
Honduran	0	0.0
Salvadoran	0	0.0
Dominican Republic	79	17.9
Mexican	53	11.1
Puerto Rican	103	8.5
South American	111	19.4
Colombian	46	13.7

Foreign-Born Population		
Group	Number	%
Total Population	27,333	13.5
Hispanic or Latino (of any race)	9,120	46.2
Central American, ex. Mexican	5,880	69.0
Honduran	1,317	68.3
Salvadoran	4,202	68.7
Dominican Republic	709	48.0
Mexican	359	30.9
Puerto Rican	0	0.0
South American	1,638	61.3
Colombian	621	57.7

Foreign-Born Naturalized U.S. Citizens		
Group	Number	%
Total Population	15,233	55.7
Hispanic or Latino (of any race)	2,452	26.9
Central American, ex. Mexican	948	16.1
Honduran	176	13.4
Salvadoran	666	15.8
Dominican Republic	237	33.4
Mexican	52	14.5
Puerto Rican	0	0.0
South American	920	56.2
Colombian	364	58.6

Language Spoken at Home: English Only (Universe: Population 5 Years and Over)		
Group	Number	%
Total Population	155,062	81.4
Hispanic or Latino (of any race)	4,193	23.5
Central American, ex. Mexican	191	2.5
Honduran	20	1.2
Salvadoran	58	1.1
Dominican Republic	211	15.2
Mexican	361	35.9
Puerto Rican	2,035	55.6
South American	380	16.3
Colombian	229	23.9

Language Spoken at Home: Spanish (Universe: Population 5 Years and Over)		
Group	Number	%
Total Population	15,093	7.9
Hispanic or Latino (of any race)	13,265	74.4
Central American, ex. Mexican	7,230	95.1
Honduran	1,699	98.8
Salvadoran	5,213	95.6
Dominican Republic	1,123	81.0
Mexican	644	64.1
Puerto Rican	1,598	43.7
South American	1,891	81.0
Colombian	728	76.1

Unemployment Rate (Universe: Population 16 Years and Over)	
Group	%
Total Population	5.1
Hispanic or Latino (of any race)	6.5
Central American, ex. Mexican	8.4
Honduran	10.7
Salvadoran	8.5
Dominican Republic	4.4
Mexican	0.0
Puerto Rican	5.8
South American	5.7
Colombian	3.1

Class of Worker: Private Wage and Salary (Universe: Civilian Employed Population 16 Years and Over)		
Group	Number	%
Total Population	77,395	79.0
Hispanic or Latino (of any race)	8,708	85.3
Central American, ex. Mexican	4,455	93.2
Honduran	999	98.7
Salvadoran	3,173	93.0
Dominican Republic	593	83.2
Mexican	327	81.3
Puerto Rican	1,395	76.7
South American	1,169	81.4
Colombian	470	77.9

Class of Worker: Government (Universe: Civilian Employed Population 16 Years and Over)		
Group	Number	%
Total Population	13,887	14.2
Hispanic or Latino (of any race)	1,024	10.0
Central American, ex. Mexican	140	2.9
Honduran	13	1.3
Salvadoran	114	3.3
Dominican Republic	77	10.8
Mexican	63	15.7
Puerto Rican	371	20.4
South American	136	9.5
Colombian	14	2.3

Means of Transportation to Work: Car, Truck or Van (Universe: Workers 16 Years and Over)		
Group	Number	%
Total Population	78,729	82.2
Hispanic or Latino (of any race)	8,444	83.8
Central American, ex. Mexican	3,991	83.6
Honduran	775	76.6
Salvadoran	3,038	89.2
Dominican Republic	619	88.2
Mexican	274	65.7
Puerto Rican	1,472	83.1
South American	1,217	88.2
Colombian	517	85.7

Means of Transportation to Work: Public Transportation (ex. Taxicab) (Universe: Workers 16 Years and Over)		
Group	Number	%
Total Population	9,371	9.8
Hispanic or Latino (of any race)	789	7.8
Central American, ex. Mexican	413	8.7
Honduran	144	14.2
Salvadoran	123	3.6
Dominican Republic	24	3.4
Mexican	75	18.0
Puerto Rican	125	7.1
South American	90	6.5
Colombian	46	7.6

Homeownership Rate (Universe: Occupied Housing Units)	
Group	%
Total Population	83.9
Hispanic or Latino (of any race)	56.3
Central American, ex. Mexican	42.2
Costa Rican	58.1
Guatemalan	33.5
Honduran	23.0
Salvadoran	47.1
Cuban	78.5
Dominican Republic	67.5
Mexican	44.9
Puerto Rican	61.0
South American	70.8
Argentinean	68.7
Chilean	73.4
Colombian	75.7
Ecuadorian	73.2
Peruvian	61.5
Spaniard	84.0

Median Home Value	
Group	Dollars
Total Population	573,300
Hispanic or Latino (of any race)	471,900
Central American, ex. Mexican	375,800
Honduran	338,800
Salvadoran	389,000
Dominican Republic	495,200
Mexican	591,300
Puerto Rican	561,100
South American	497,000
Colombian	581,200

Median Gross Rent	
Group	Dollars
Total Population	1,381
Hispanic or Latino (of any race)	1,428
Central American, ex. Mexican	1,369
Honduran	1,354
Salvadoran	1,428
Dominican Republic	1,392
Mexican	1,536
Puerto Rican	1,574
South American	1,563
Colombian	1,628

Median Household Income (2010 Inflation-Adjusted Dollars)	
Group	Dollars
Total Population	102,782

STATE & PLACE PROFILES

Notes: (1) Percent of total population; (2) Percent of Hispanic/Latino population; Profiles include places with an overall population of at least 125,000, OR an overall population of at least 25,000 where the Hispanic/Latino population is at least 20% of the overall population. In states where less than five places meet either of these criteria, we have included places with at least 10,000 total population with the highest percentage of Hispanic/Latino population. These places are identified with an asterisk (*); Please refer to the User's Guide for a full explanation of data.

Group	Dollars
Hispanic or Latino (of any race)	75,858
Central American, ex. Mexican	58,811
Honduran	43,016
Salvadoran	70,268
Dominican Republic	80,625
Mexican	87,778
Puerto Rican	81,250
South American	90,500
Colombian	98,438

Per Capita Income
(2010 Inflation-Adjusted Dollars)

Group	Dollars
Total Population	46,862
Hispanic or Latino (of any race)	22,310
Central American, ex. Mexican	15,347
Honduran	14,103
Salvadoran	15,174
Dominican Republic	17,261
Mexican	15,822
Puerto Rican	29,218
South American	33,014
Colombian	33,048

Households with $100,000+ Income

Group	Number	%
Total Population	35,687	52.3
Hispanic or Latino (of any race)	1,477	33.5
Central American, ex. Mexican	322	19.1
Honduran	28	8.9
Salvadoran	267	20.5
Dominican Republic	86	30.1
Mexican	81	30.2
Puerto Rican	402	46.7
South American	297	42.9
Colombian	114	46.0

Households with Food Stamps/SNAP Benefits During Past 12 Months

Group	Number	%
Total Population	1,247	1.8
Hispanic or Latino (of any race)	181	4.1
Central American, ex. Mexican	65	3.9
Honduran	38	12.1
Salvadoran	27	2.1
Dominican Republic	0	0.0
Mexican	14	5.2
Puerto Rican	72	8.4
South American	30	4.3
Colombian	0	0.0

Poverty Rate
(Income in Past 12 Months Below Poverty Level)

Group	%
Total Population	4.4
Hispanic or Latino (of any race)	12.6
Central American, ex. Mexican	22.4
Honduran	48.2
Salvadoran	13.4
Dominican Republic	7.8
Mexican	8.8
Puerto Rican	4.2
South American	1.6
Colombian	2.5

Huntington Station

Population

Group	Number	%TP[1]	%HP[2]
Total Population	33,029	100.0	–
Hispanic or Latino (of any race)	12,109	36.7	100.0
Central American, ex. Mexican	7,370	22.3	60.9
Guatemalan	739	2.2	6.1
Honduran	1,260	3.8	10.4
Salvadoran	5,233	15.8	43.2
Dominican Republic	451	1.4	3.7
Mexican	710	2.1	5.9
Puerto Rican	1,455	4.4	12.0
South American	863	2.6	7.1
Colombian	230	0.7	1.9
Ecuadorian	199	0.6	1.6
Peruvian	213	0.6	1.8

Population Growth: 2000–2010

Group	%
Total Population	10.4
Hispanic or Latino (of any race)	78.0
Central American, ex. Mexican	158.5
Guatemalan	337.3
Honduran	400.0
Salvadoran	127.1
Dominican Republic	71.5
Mexican	98.9
Puerto Rican	2.0
South American	64.7
Colombian	39.4
Ecuadorian	41.1
Peruvian	82.1

Males per 100 Females

Group	Number
Total Population	104.4
Hispanic or Latino (of any race)	123.9
Central American, ex. Mexican	135.3
Guatemalan	204.1
Honduran	155.6
Salvadoran	125.2
Dominican Republic	116.8
Mexican	136.7
Puerto Rican	89.5
South American	98.8
Colombian	82.5
Ecuadorian	93.2
Peruvian	117.3

Average Household Size

Group	People
Total Population	3.26
Hispanic or Latino (of any race)	5.10
Central American, ex. Mexican	5.88
Guatemalan	5.50
Honduran	6.04
Salvadoran	5.95
Dominican Republic	5.11
Mexican	4.61
Puerto Rican	3.56
South American	3.91
Colombian	3.57
Ecuadorian	4.25
Peruvian	4.17

Median Age

Group	Years
Total Population	35.4
Hispanic or Latino (of any race)	28.2
Central American, ex. Mexican	28.1
Guatemalan	28.8
Honduran	28.3
Salvadoran	27.9
Dominican Republic	32.2
Mexican	27.8
Puerto Rican	29.3
South American	35.9
Colombian	37.0
Ecuadorian	35.8
Peruvian	35.1

High School Graduates
(Universe: Population 25 Years and Over)

Group	Number	%
Total Population	17,269	81.0
Hispanic or Latino (of any race)	3,515	57.7
Central American, ex. Mexican	2,133	51.4
Honduran	715	69.6
Salvadoran	1,324	44.6
Puerto Rican	528	91.5

Four-Year College Graduates
(Universe: Population 25 Years and Over)

Group	Number	%
Total Population	6,292	29.5
Hispanic or Latino (of any race)	561	9.2
Central American, ex. Mexican	278	6.7
Honduran	108	10.5
Salvadoran	170	5.7
Puerto Rican	136	23.6

Population Age 3–17 Enrolled in Public School
(Universe: Population Age 3–17 Enrolled in School)

Group	Number	%
Total Population	5,175	91.3
Hispanic or Latino (of any race)	1,935	94.7
Central American, ex. Mexican	1,134	100.0
Honduran	255	100.0
Salvadoran	879	100.0
Puerto Rican	271	100.0

Population Age 3–17 Enrolled in Private School
(Universe: Population Age 3–17 Enrolled in School)

Group	Number	%
Total Population	495	8.7
Hispanic or Latino (of any race)	109	5.3
Central American, ex. Mexican	0	0.0
Honduran	0	0.0
Salvadoran	0	0.0
Puerto Rican	0	0.0

Foreign-Born Population

Group	Number	%
Total Population	8,642	27.3
Hispanic or Latino (of any race)	6,225	60.0
Central American, ex. Mexican	4,763	70.2
Honduran	1,188	66.5
Salvadoran	3,337	70.2
Puerto Rican	0	0.0

Foreign-Born Naturalized U.S. Citizens

Group	Number	%
Total Population	2,727	31.6
Hispanic or Latino (of any race)	1,118	18.0
Central American, ex. Mexican	692	14.5
Honduran	131	11.0
Salvadoran	549	16.5
Puerto Rican	0	0.0

Language Spoken at Home: English Only
(Universe: Population 5 Years and Over)

Group	Number	%
Total Population	18,094	61.4
Hispanic or Latino (of any race)	888	9.5
Central American, ex. Mexican	61	1.0
Honduran	20	1.3
Salvadoran	29	0.7
Puerto Rican	600	61.0

Language Spoken at Home: Spanish
(Universe: Population 5 Years and Over)

Group	Number	%
Total Population	8,479	28.8
Hispanic or Latino (of any race)	8,178	87.3
Central American, ex. Mexican	5,906	96.0
Honduran	1,570	98.7
Salvadoran	4,121	95.1
Puerto Rican	383	39.0

Unemployment Rate
(Universe: Population 16 Years and Over)

Group	%
Total Population	6.7
Hispanic or Latino (of any race)	6.8
Central American, ex. Mexican	7.7
Honduran	10.6
Salvadoran	7.2
Puerto Rican	7.5

Class of Worker: Private Wage and Salary
(Universe: Civilian Employed Population 16 Years and Over)

Group	Number	%
Total Population	14,122	85.6
Hispanic or Latino (of any race)	4,899	92.2
Central American, ex. Mexican	3,527	94.8
Honduran	907	100.0
Salvadoran	2,405	92.6
Puerto Rican	376	84.3

Class of Worker: Government
(Universe: Civilian Employed Population 16 Years and Over)

Group	Number	%
Total Population	1,639	9.9
Hispanic or Latino (of any race)	215	4.0
Central American, ex. Mexican	106	2.9
Honduran	0	0.0

Notes: (1) Percent of total population; (2) Percent of Hispanic/Latino population; Profiles include places with an overall population of at least 125,000, OR an overall population of at least 25,000 where the Hispanic/Latino population is at least 20% of the overall population. In states where less than five places meet either of these criteria, we have included places with at least 10,000 total population with the highest percentage of Hispanic/Latino population. These places are identified with an asterisk (*); Please refer to the User's Guide for a full explanation of data.

Salvadoran	106	4.1
Puerto Rican	46	10.3

Means of Transportation to Work: Car, Truck or Van
(Universe: Workers 16 Years and Over)

Group	Number	%
Total Population	13,443	82.9
Hispanic or Latino (of any race)	4,353	82.6
Central American, ex. Mexican	3,068	82.6
Honduran	698	77.0
Salvadoran	2,292	88.5
Puerto Rican	390	94.4

Means of Transportation to Work: Public Transportation (ex. Taxicab)
(Universe: Workers 16 Years and Over)

Group	Number	%
Total Population	1,458	9.0
Hispanic or Latino (of any race)	438	8.3
Central American, ex. Mexican	351	9.5
Honduran	131	14.4
Salvadoran	104	4.0
Puerto Rican	12	2.9

Homeownership Rate
(Universe: Occupied Housing Units)

Group	%
Total Population	69.5
Hispanic or Latino (of any race)	43.3
Central American, ex. Mexican	39.2
Guatemalan	20.0
Honduran	21.5
Salvadoran	45.8
Dominican Republic	55.9
Mexican	30.6
Puerto Rican	42.9
South American	62.1
Colombian	66.7
Ecuadorian	60.8
Peruvian	54.7

Median Home Value

Group	Dollars
Total Population	419,100
Hispanic or Latino (of any race)	389,700
Central American, ex. Mexican	368,900
Honduran	–
Salvadoran	379,100
Puerto Rican	388,000

Median Gross Rent

Group	Dollars
Total Population	1,354
Hispanic or Latino (of any race)	1,441
Central American, ex. Mexican	1,430
Honduran	1,383
Salvadoran	1,471
Puerto Rican	1,354

Median Household Income
(2010 Inflation-Adjusted Dollars)

Group	Dollars
Total Population	74,667
Hispanic or Latino (of any race)	48,858
Central American, ex. Mexican	56,120
Honduran	43,671
Salvadoran	60,068
Puerto Rican	26,056

Per Capita Income
(2010 Inflation-Adjusted Dollars)

Group	Dollars
Total Population	30,052
Hispanic or Latino (of any race)	13,910
Central American, ex. Mexican	14,025
Honduran	14,006
Salvadoran	14,118
Puerto Rican	14,809

Households with $100,000+ Income

Group	Number	%
Total Population	3,570	34.6
Hispanic or Latino (of any race)	293	13.7
Central American, ex. Mexican	160	12.2
Honduran	28	10.0
Salvadoran	132	13.0
Puerto Rican	13	6.1

Households with Food Stamps/SNAP Benefits During Past 12 Months

Group	Number	%
Total Population	562	5.5
Hispanic or Latino (of any race)	145	6.8
Central American, ex. Mexican	65	5.0
Honduran	38	13.5
Salvadoran	27	2.7
Puerto Rican	72	34.0

Poverty Rate
(Income in Past 12 Months Below Poverty Level)

Group	%
Total Population	11.3
Hispanic or Latino (of any race)	21.0
Central American, ex. Mexican	26.4
Honduran	49.7
Salvadoran	16.3
Puerto Rican	10.6

Islip

Population

Group	Number	%TP[1]	%HP[2]
Total Population	335,543	100.0	–
Hispanic or Latino (of any race)	97,371	29.0	100.0
Central American, ex. Mexican	38,530	11.5	39.6
Costa Rican	297	0.1	0.3
Guatemalan	3,256	1.0	3.3
Honduran	4,232	1.3	4.3
Nicaraguan	253	0.1	0.3
Panamanian	466	0.1	0.5
Salvadoran	29,849	8.9	30.7
Cuban	1,113	0.3	1.1
Dominican Republic	8,547	2.5	8.8
Mexican	3,139	0.9	3.2
Puerto Rican	21,506	6.4	22.1
South American	16,012	4.8	16.4
Argentinean	616	0.2	0.6
Bolivian	220	0.1	0.2
Chilean	448	0.1	0.5
Colombian	5,156	1.5	5.3
Ecuadorian	5,323	1.6	5.5
Peruvian	3,599	1.1	3.7
Uruguayan	216	0.1	0.2
Venezuelan	322	0.1	0.3
Spaniard	835	0.2	0.9

Population Growth: 2000–2010

Group	%
Total Population	4.0
Hispanic or Latino (of any race)	49.7
Central American, ex. Mexican	159.4
Costa Rican	58.8
Guatemalan	141.7
Honduran	249.5
Nicaraguan	141.0
Panamanian	56.4
Salvadoran	170.2
Cuban	19.8
Dominican Republic	78.4
Mexican	122.6
Puerto Rican	-3.6
South American	116.4
Argentinean	105.3
Bolivian	105.6
Chilean	79.9
Colombian	74.7
Ecuadorian	159.4
Peruvian	189.3
Venezuelan	131.7
Spaniard	181.1

Males per 100 Females

Group	Number
Total Population	97.2
Hispanic or Latino (of any race)	103.8
Central American, ex. Mexican	113.6
Costa Rican	102.0
Guatemalan	124.6
Honduran	116.9
Nicaraguan	100.8
Panamanian	86.4
Salvadoran	112.8
Cuban	92.9
Dominican Republic	89.2
Mexican	113.4
Puerto Rican	95.2
South American	98.6
Argentinean	108.1
Bolivian	100.0
Chilean	113.3
Colombian	88.4
Ecuadorian	106.0
Peruvian	102.1
Uruguayan	101.9
Venezuelan	77.9
Spaniard	113.6

Average Household Size

Group	People
Total Population	3.20
Hispanic or Latino (of any race)	4.66
Central American, ex. Mexican	5.85
Costa Rican	4.10
Guatemalan	5.27
Honduran	5.64
Nicaraguan	4.59
Panamanian	3.69
Salvadoran	6.05
Cuban	3.12
Dominican Republic	4.74
Mexican	4.56
Puerto Rican	3.45
South American	4.55
Argentinean	3.64
Bolivian	4.63
Chilean	3.91
Colombian	4.19
Ecuadorian	4.94
Peruvian	4.93
Uruguayan	4.20
Venezuelan	4.17
Spaniard	3.21

Median Age

Group	Years
Total Population	37.6
Hispanic or Latino (of any race)	29.5
Central American, ex. Mexican	28.8
Costa Rican	32.8
Guatemalan	30.2
Honduran	29.2
Nicaraguan	30.5
Panamanian	41.8
Salvadoran	28.4
Cuban	34.2
Dominican Republic	30.3
Mexican	25.4
Puerto Rican	31.5
South American	34.6
Argentinean	37.1
Bolivian	33.3
Chilean	36.8
Colombian	36.4
Ecuadorian	32.9
Peruvian	35.1
Uruguayan	35.6
Venezuelan	29.5
Spaniard	35.2

High School Graduates
(Universe: Population 25 Years and Over)

Group	Number	%
Total Population	186,884	85.2
Hispanic or Latino (of any race)	34,855	64.9
Central American, ex. Mexican	9,265	46.0
Guatemalan	1,558	62.0
Honduran	987	44.8
Salvadoran	6,173	42.2
Cuban	556	93.0
Dominican Republic	3,468	71.7
Mexican	864	56.3
Puerto Rican	11,445	76.4
South American	7,538	80.1
Colombian	1,904	86.3

STATE & PLACE PROFILES

Notes: (1) Percent of total population; (2) Percent of Hispanic/Latino population; Profiles include places with an overall population of at least 125,000, OR an overall population of at least 25,000 where the Hispanic/Latino population is at least 20% of the overall population. In states where less than five places meet either of these criteria, we have included places with at least 10,000 total population with the highest percentage of Hispanic/Latino population. These places are identified with an asterisk (*); Please refer to the User's Guide for a full explanation of data.

Group	Number	%
Ecuadorian	1,852	64.6
Peruvian	2,454	88.0

Four-Year College Graduates
(Universe: Population 25 Years and Over)

Group	Number	%
Total Population	55,854	25.5
Hispanic or Latino (of any race)	6,565	12.2
Central American, ex. Mexican	1,080	5.4
Guatemalan	193	7.7
Honduran	180	8.2
Salvadoran	568	3.9
Cuban	152	25.4
Dominican Republic	800	16.5
Mexican	202	13.2
Puerto Rican	1,917	12.8
South American	1,923	20.4
Colombian	395	17.9
Ecuadorian	525	18.3
Peruvian	511	18.3

Population Age 3–17 Enrolled in Public School
(Universe: Population Age 3–17 Enrolled in School)

Group	Number	%
Total Population	61,320	90.7
Hispanic or Latino (of any race)	19,191	93.3
Central American, ex. Mexican	6,852	95.3
Guatemalan	750	84.1
Honduran	522	97.9
Salvadoran	5,188	97.3
Cuban	265	81.8
Dominican Republic	1,525	94.1
Mexican	909	92.7
Puerto Rican	5,688	93.1
South American	2,810	91.9
Colombian	645	97.3
Ecuadorian	1,229	86.7
Peruvian	624	94.0

Population Age 3–17 Enrolled in Private School
(Universe: Population Age 3–17 Enrolled in School)

Group	Number	%
Total Population	6,309	9.3
Hispanic or Latino (of any race)	1,376	6.7
Central American, ex. Mexican	335	4.7
Guatemalan	142	15.9
Honduran	11	2.1
Salvadoran	143	2.7
Cuban	59	18.2
Dominican Republic	96	5.9
Mexican	72	7.3
Puerto Rican	424	6.9
South American	248	8.1
Colombian	18	2.7
Ecuadorian	189	13.3
Peruvian	40	6.0

Foreign-Born Population

Group	Number	%
Total Population	64,409	19.3
Hispanic or Latino (of any race)	40,348	43.9
Central American, ex. Mexican	22,031	65.2
Guatemalan	2,648	68.4
Honduran	2,539	73.1
Salvadoran	16,070	64.1
Cuban	199	18.6
Dominican Republic	4,537	52.8
Mexican	1,375	46.2
Puerto Rican	433	1.7
South American	10,213	65.7
Colombian	2,249	65.8
Ecuadorian	3,166	57.3
Peruvian	3,165	71.0

Foreign-Born Naturalized U.S. Citizens

Group	Number	%
Total Population	27,720	43.0
Hispanic or Latino (of any race)	12,509	31.0
Central American, ex. Mexican	5,511	25.0
Guatemalan	1,101	41.6
Honduran	458	18.0
Salvadoran	3,523	21.9
Cuban	199	100.0
Dominican Republic	2,174	47.9
Mexican	209	15.2
Puerto Rican	160	37.0
South American	3,610	35.3
Colombian	755	33.6
Ecuadorian	1,106	34.9
Peruvian	1,143	36.1

Language Spoken at Home: English Only
(Universe: Population 5 Years and Over)

Group	Number	%
Total Population	222,229	71.1
Hispanic or Latino (of any race)	16,853	20.2
Central American, ex. Mexican	1,339	4.4
Guatemalan	218	6.2
Honduran	259	8.2
Salvadoran	530	2.4
Cuban	580	56.5
Dominican Republic	865	11.3
Mexican	871	32.6
Puerto Rican	11,119	47.1
South American	984	6.9
Colombian	269	8.5
Ecuadorian	263	5.3
Peruvian	232	5.7

Language Spoken at Home: Spanish
(Universe: Population 5 Years and Over)

Group	Number	%
Total Population	68,731	22.0
Hispanic or Latino (of any race)	66,218	79.5
Central American, ex. Mexican	28,770	95.4
Guatemalan	3,288	93.8
Honduran	2,890	91.8
Salvadoran	21,682	97.5
Cuban	446	43.5
Dominican Republic	6,731	88.1
Mexican	1,787	67.0
Puerto Rican	12,470	52.8
South American	13,360	93.1
Colombian	2,900	91.5
Ecuadorian	4,680	94.7
Peruvian	3,874	94.3

Unemployment Rate
(Universe: Population 16 Years and Over)

Group	%
Total Population	7.1
Hispanic or Latino (of any race)	8.8
Central American, ex. Mexican	10.2
Guatemalan	6.9
Honduran	6.9
Salvadoran	11.5
Cuban	2.5
Dominican Republic	6.4
Mexican	6.1
Puerto Rican	10.1
South American	6.6
Colombian	7.7
Ecuadorian	7.8
Peruvian	7.5

Class of Worker: Private Wage and Salary
(Universe: Civilian Employed Population 16 Years and Over)

Group	Number	%
Total Population	130,018	78.0
Hispanic or Latino (of any race)	39,901	87.0
Central American, ex. Mexican	16,411	93.5
Guatemalan	2,045	92.4
Honduran	1,882	93.7
Salvadoran	11,965	94.1
Cuban	445	94.7
Dominican Republic	3,789	86.1
Mexican	1,255	85.1
Puerto Rican	9,040	78.4
South American	7,495	86.2
Colombian	1,673	82.6
Ecuadorian	2,394	89.4
Peruvian	2,194	89.8

Class of Worker: Government
(Universe: Civilian Employed Population 16 Years and Over)

Group	Number	%
Total Population	29,936	17.9
Hispanic or Latino (of any race)	4,150	9.0
Central American, ex. Mexican	595	3.4
Guatemalan	112	5.1
Honduran	76	3.8
Salvadoran	315	2.5
Cuban	25	5.3
Dominican Republic	411	9.3
Mexican	157	10.6
Puerto Rican	2,197	19.1
South American	586	6.7
Colombian	213	10.5
Ecuadorian	112	4.2
Peruvian	118	4.8

Means of Transportation to Work: Car, Truck or Van
(Universe: Workers 16 Years and Over)

Group	Number	%
Total Population	142,993	88.7
Hispanic or Latino (of any race)	39,317	88.6
Central American, ex. Mexican	15,252	89.0
Guatemalan	2,070	93.8
Honduran	1,770	89.2
Salvadoran	10,945	88.5
Cuban	445	94.7
Dominican Republic	3,856	89.7
Mexican	1,374	93.2
Puerto Rican	9,580	88.9
South American	7,301	85.3
Colombian	1,658	83.7
Ecuadorian	2,170	83.8
Peruvian	2,130	87.2

Means of Transportation to Work: Public Transportation (ex. Taxicab)
(Universe: Workers 16 Years and Over)

Group	Number	%
Total Population	9,324	5.8
Hispanic or Latino (of any race)	1,996	4.5
Central American, ex. Mexican	583	3.4
Guatemalan	85	3.9
Honduran	33	1.7
Salvadoran	364	2.9
Cuban	25	5.3
Dominican Republic	222	5.2
Mexican	64	4.3
Puerto Rican	504	4.7
South American	545	6.4
Colombian	160	8.1
Ecuadorian	149	5.8
Peruvian	189	7.7

Homeownership Rate
(Universe: Occupied Housing Units)

Group	%
Total Population	76.4
Hispanic or Latino (of any race)	64.2
Central American, ex. Mexican	63.9
Costa Rican	67.6
Guatemalan	61.9
Honduran	52.5
Nicaraguan	63.2
Panamanian	77.1
Salvadoran	65.3
Cuban	73.9
Dominican Republic	62.2
Mexican	55.3
Puerto Rican	63.8
South American	66.2
Argentinean	67.0
Bolivian	86.3
Chilean	72.8
Colombian	66.5
Ecuadorian	64.7
Peruvian	66.4
Uruguayan	54.3
Venezuelan	61.4
Spaniard	78.1

Median Home Value

Group	Dollars
Total Population	395,500
Hispanic or Latino (of any race)	351,500
Central American, ex. Mexican	344,000
Guatemalan	315,000
Honduran	374,600
Salvadoran	345,100
Cuban	369,100

Notes: (1) Percent of total population; (2) Percent of Hispanic/Latino population; Profiles include places with an overall population of at least 125,000, OR an overall population of at least 25,000 where the Hispanic/Latino population is at least 20% of the overall population. In states where less than five places meet either of these criteria, we have included places with at least 10,000 total population with the highest percentage of Hispanic/Latino population. These places are identified with an asterisk (*); Please refer to the User's Guide for a full explanation of data.

Dominican Republic	352,500
Mexican	349,600
Puerto Rican	355,000
South American	351,500
Colombian	354,200
Ecuadorian	324,600
Peruvian	352,800

Median Gross Rent

Group	Dollars
Total Population	1,425
Hispanic or Latino (of any race)	1,366
Central American, ex. Mexican	1,543
Guatemalan	1,487
Honduran	619
Salvadoran	1,774
Cuban	–
Dominican Republic	1,454
Mexican	1,670
Puerto Rican	1,270
South American	1,330
Colombian	1,636
Ecuadorian	1,245
Peruvian	734

Median Household Income
(2010 Inflation-Adjusted Dollars)

Group	Dollars
Total Population	82,160
Hispanic or Latino (of any race)	70,507
Central American, ex. Mexican	70,735
Guatemalan	75,213
Honduran	80,882
Salvadoran	67,469
Cuban	87,069
Dominican Republic	66,370
Mexican	80,196
Puerto Rican	69,272
South American	71,933
Colombian	75,337
Ecuadorian	69,274
Peruvian	62,390

Per Capita Income
(2010 Inflation-Adjusted Dollars)

Group	Dollars
Total Population	30,893
Hispanic or Latino (of any race)	19,506
Central American, ex. Mexican	17,105
Guatemalan	21,513
Honduran	18,421
Salvadoran	15,921
Cuban	25,887
Dominican Republic	18,650
Mexican	19,156
Puerto Rican	22,355
South American	20,412
Colombian	21,258
Ecuadorian	17,587
Peruvian	20,286

Households with $100,000+ Income

Group	Number	%
Total Population	39,967	38.7
Hispanic or Latino (of any race)	6,218	30.4
Central American, ex. Mexican	1,912	30.5
Guatemalan	288	30.7
Honduran	265	40.4
Salvadoran	1,248	28.5
Cuban	137	48.2
Dominican Republic	509	25.3
Mexican	125	28.1
Puerto Rican	2,085	30.2
South American	1,228	33.0
Colombian	216	26.2
Ecuadorian	348	30.2
Peruvian	340	32.9

Households with Food Stamps/SNAP Benefits During Past 12 Months

Group	Number	%
Total Population	5,141	5.0
Hispanic or Latino (of any race)	1,956	9.5
Central American, ex. Mexican	495	7.9
Guatemalan	12	1.3
Honduran	45	6.9
Salvadoran	438	10.0
Cuban	17	6.0
Dominican Republic	276	13.7
Mexican	43	9.7
Puerto Rican	863	12.5
South American	236	6.3
Colombian	26	3.2
Ecuadorian	104	9.0
Peruvian	94	9.1

Poverty Rate
(Income in Past 12 Months Below Poverty Level)

Group	%
Total Population	5.5
Hispanic or Latino (of any race)	8.5
Central American, ex. Mexican	9.8
Guatemalan	3.6
Honduran	12.0
Salvadoran	10.9
Cuban	6.5
Dominican Republic	7.9
Mexican	7.8
Puerto Rican	7.6
South American	7.8
Colombian	13.4
Ecuadorian	4.2
Peruvian	11.2

Manhattan

Population

Group	Number	%TP[1]	%HP[2]
Total Population	1,585,873	100.0	–
Hispanic or Latino (of any race)	403,577	25.4	100.0
Central American, ex. Mexican	13,948	0.9	3.5
Costa Rican	987	0.1	0.2
Guatemalan	2,051	0.1	0.5
Honduran	4,058	0.3	1.0
Nicaraguan	1,556	0.1	0.4
Panamanian	1,716	0.1	0.4
Salvadoran	3,419	0.2	0.8
Cuban	11,623	0.7	2.9
Dominican Republic	155,971	9.8	38.6
Mexican	41,965	2.6	10.4
Puerto Rican	107,774	6.8	26.7
South American	36,748	2.3	9.1
Argentinean	4,339	0.3	1.1
Bolivian	522	<0.1	0.1
Chilean	1,824	0.1	0.5
Colombian	8,411	0.5	2.1
Ecuadorian	14,132	0.9	3.5
Paraguayan	268	<0.1	0.1
Peruvian	3,852	0.2	1.0
Uruguayan	549	<0.1	0.1
Venezuelan	2,573	0.2	0.6
Spaniard	5,629	0.4	1.4

Population Growth: 2000–2010

Group	%
Total Population	3.2
Hispanic or Latino (of any race)	-3.4
Central American, ex. Mexican	47.9
Costa Rican	48.9
Guatemalan	79.0
Honduran	48.9
Nicaraguan	49.9
Panamanian	53.2
Salvadoran	57.3
Cuban	-2.7
Dominican Republic	14.4
Mexican	38.1
Puerto Rican	-10.0
South American	45.9
Argentinean	67.9
Bolivian	108.8
Chilean	58.1
Colombian	56.7
Ecuadorian	37.3
Paraguayan	117.9
Peruvian	54.9
Uruguayan	98.9
Venezuelan	56.0
Spaniard	184.0

Males per 100 Females

Group	Number
Total Population	88.5
Hispanic or Latino (of any race)	89.1
Central American, ex. Mexican	82.7
Costa Rican	74.4
Guatemalan	99.5
Honduran	80.2
Nicaraguan	75.6
Panamanian	77.5
Salvadoran	85.4
Cuban	98.1
Dominican Republic	80.8
Mexican	131.1
Puerto Rican	84.1
South American	93.9
Argentinean	95.1
Bolivian	75.2
Chilean	93.2
Colombian	83.7
Ecuadorian	102.7
Paraguayan	81.1
Peruvian	90.3
Uruguayan	92.6
Venezuelan	94.2
Spaniard	94.9

Average Household Size

Group	People
Total Population	1.99
Hispanic or Latino (of any race)	2.68
Central American, ex. Mexican	2.55
Costa Rican	2.03
Guatemalan	2.56
Honduran	2.84
Nicaraguan	2.47
Panamanian	1.97
Salvadoran	2.86
Cuban	1.82
Dominican Republic	3.21
Mexican	3.43
Puerto Rican	2.23
South American	2.36
Argentinean	1.91
Bolivian	2.06
Chilean	1.93
Colombian	2.02
Ecuadorian	3.16
Paraguayan	1.89
Peruvian	2.12
Uruguayan	1.95
Venezuelan	1.90
Spaniard	1.79

Median Age

Group	Years
Total Population	36.4
Hispanic or Latino (of any race)	34.5
Central American, ex. Mexican	35.2
Costa Rican	36.6
Guatemalan	31.8
Honduran	34.7
Nicaraguan	38.5
Panamanian	39.0
Salvadoran	34.0
Cuban	45.5
Dominican Republic	36.0
Mexican	27.3
Puerto Rican	38.8
South American	36.4
Argentinean	37.3
Bolivian	33.8
Chilean	36.3
Colombian	35.9
Ecuadorian	37.0
Paraguayan	29.8
Peruvian	38.5
Uruguayan	36.9
Venezuelan	33.4
Spaniard	34.9

Notes: (1) Percent of total population; (2) Percent of Hispanic/Latino population; Profiles include places with an overall population of at least 125,000, OR an overall population of at least 25,000 where the Hispanic/Latino population is at least 20% of the overall population. In states where less than five places meet either of these criteria, we have included places with at least 10,000 total population with the highest percentage of Hispanic/Latino population. These places are identified with an asterisk (*); Please refer to the User's Guide for a full explanation of data.

High School Graduates
(Universe: Population 25 Years and Over)

Group	Number	%
Total Population	987,572	84.6
Hispanic or Latino (of any race)	162,831	61.7
Central American, ex. Mexican	7,142	68.1
Guatemalan	962	59.9
Honduran	1,471	53.0
Nicaraguan	1,031	73.3
Panamanian	1,440	93.4
Salvadoran	1,333	66.4
Cuban	6,893	71.8
Dominican Republic	56,697	54.8
Mexican	13,767	59.0
Puerto Rican	47,722	61.8
South American	21,239	76.3
Argentinean	3,029	95.2
Chilean	961	92.2
Colombian	5,093	82.4
Ecuadorian	6,643	59.7
Peruvian	2,794	86.4
Venezuelan	1,627	89.1
Spaniard	3,017	89.9

Four-Year College Graduates
(Universe: Population 25 Years and Over)

Group	Number	%
Total Population	665,064	57.0
Hispanic or Latino (of any race)	55,322	21.0
Central American, ex. Mexican	2,882	27.5
Guatemalan	418	26.0
Honduran	412	14.8
Nicaraguan	428	30.4
Panamanian	758	49.2
Salvadoran	465	23.1
Cuban	3,254	33.9
Dominican Republic	15,202	14.7
Mexican	6,253	26.8
Puerto Rican	11,948	15.5
South American	10,701	38.4
Argentinean	2,173	68.3
Chilean	680	65.3
Colombian	2,622	42.4
Ecuadorian	1,762	15.8
Peruvian	1,672	51.7
Venezuelan	1,076	58.9
Spaniard	2,248	67.0

Population Age 3–17 Enrolled in Public School
(Universe: Population Age 3–17 Enrolled in School)

Group	Number	%
Total Population	123,604	69.6
Hispanic or Latino (of any race)	63,463	87.9
Central American, ex. Mexican	2,139	87.8
Guatemalan	279	79.3
Honduran	846	86.0
Nicaraguan	251	95.1
Panamanian	251	100.0
Salvadoran	426	85.5
Cuban	559	74.5
Dominican Republic	28,643	90.9
Mexican	8,071	92.5
Puerto Rican	17,989	87.1
South American	3,239	72.2
Argentinean	180	49.6
Chilean	90	67.2
Colombian	394	49.9
Ecuadorian	2,135	85.2
Peruvian	176	66.2
Venezuelan	149	77.2
Spaniard	90	55.9

Population Age 3–17 Enrolled in Private School
(Universe: Population Age 3–17 Enrolled in School)

Group	Number	%
Total Population	53,919	30.4
Hispanic or Latino (of any race)	8,751	12.1
Central American, ex. Mexican	296	12.2
Guatemalan	73	20.7
Honduran	138	14.0
Nicaraguan	13	4.9
Panamanian	0	0.0
Salvadoran	72	14.5
Cuban	191	25.5
Dominican Republic	2,865	9.1
Mexican	656	7.5
Puerto Rican	2,670	12.9
South American	1,245	27.8
Argentinean	183	50.4
Chilean	44	32.8
Colombian	395	50.1
Ecuadorian	371	14.8
Peruvian	90	33.8
Venezuelan	44	22.8
Spaniard	71	44.1

Foreign-Born Population

Group	Number	%
Total Population	452,102	28.6
Hispanic or Latino (of any race)	176,684	43.4
Central American, ex. Mexican	9,733	61.3
Guatemalan	1,679	63.8
Honduran	2,928	65.4
Nicaraguan	1,324	67.9
Panamanian	891	38.3
Salvadoran	1,950	63.2
Cuban	5,815	49.0
Dominican Republic	103,506	62.9
Mexican	23,497	55.9
Puerto Rican	1,165	1.0
South American	25,484	66.8
Argentinean	2,465	63.6
Chilean	897	58.2
Colombian	5,231	65.9
Ecuadorian	11,301	68.3
Peruvian	2,876	70.7
Venezuelan	1,732	69.5
Spaniard	2,024	52.8

Foreign-Born Naturalized U.S. Citizens

Group	Number	%
Total Population	204,851	45.3
Hispanic or Latino (of any race)	75,859	42.9
Central American, ex. Mexican	4,669	48.0
Guatemalan	744	44.3
Honduran	893	30.5
Nicaraguan	780	58.9
Panamanian	609	68.4
Salvadoran	979	50.2
Cuban	4,248	73.1
Dominican Republic	48,373	46.7
Mexican	2,880	12.3
Puerto Rican	656	56.3
South American	11,255	44.2
Argentinean	745	30.2
Chilean	468	52.2
Colombian	2,736	52.3
Ecuadorian	4,855	43.0
Peruvian	1,463	50.9
Venezuelan	569	32.9
Spaniard	559	27.6

Language Spoken at Home: English Only
(Universe: Population 5 Years and Over)

Group	Number	%
Total Population	902,267	60.0
Hispanic or Latino (of any race)	53,226	13.9
Central American, ex. Mexican	2,946	19.4
Guatemalan	438	17.7
Honduran	457	10.8
Nicaraguan	284	14.7
Panamanian	1,305	58.0
Salvadoran	394	13.7
Cuban	2,892	25.5
Dominican Republic	5,414	3.5
Mexican	6,018	15.7
Puerto Rican	27,248	25.0
South American	4,004	11.2
Argentinean	645	17.7
Chilean	387	27.1
Colombian	1,005	13.3
Ecuadorian	685	4.5
Peruvian	664	17.2
Venezuelan	367	16.0
Spaniard	1,192	32.0

Language Spoken at Home: Spanish
(Universe: Population 5 Years and Over)

Group	Number	%
Total Population	347,033	23.1
Hispanic or Latino (of any race)	326,345	85.5
Central American, ex. Mexican	12,054	79.5
Guatemalan	2,034	82.3
Honduran	3,731	87.8
Nicaraguan	1,589	82.4
Panamanian	897	39.9
Salvadoran	2,492	86.3
Cuban	8,333	73.5
Dominican Republic	149,472	96.3
Mexican	31,991	83.7
Puerto Rican	81,318	74.7
South American	31,303	87.8
Argentinean	2,943	80.8
Chilean	1,027	71.9
Colombian	6,474	85.4
Ecuadorian	14,578	95.4
Peruvian	3,158	81.8
Venezuelan	1,841	80.5
Spaniard	2,267	60.8

Unemployment Rate
(Universe: Population 16 Years and Over)

Group	%
Total Population	7.9
Hispanic or Latino (of any race)	13.1
Central American, ex. Mexican	11.4
Guatemalan	6.9
Honduran	9.0
Nicaraguan	21.2
Panamanian	16.4
Salvadoran	11.0
Cuban	9.8
Dominican Republic	14.5
Mexican	8.1
Puerto Rican	16.4
South American	7.6
Argentinean	6.7
Chilean	5.0
Colombian	3.2
Ecuadorian	11.0
Peruvian	4.5
Venezuelan	11.2
Spaniard	6.1

Class of Worker: Private Wage and Salary
(Universe: Civilian Employed Population 16 Years and Over)

Group	Number	%
Total Population	696,866	82.2
Hispanic or Latino (of any race)	137,767	82.8
Central American, ex. Mexican	6,799	84.4
Guatemalan	1,395	91.8
Honduran	1,596	81.4
Nicaraguan	908	89.3
Panamanian	920	77.8
Salvadoran	1,296	84.3
Cuban	4,270	83.0
Dominican Republic	55,100	82.8
Mexican	19,432	91.8
Puerto Rican	28,459	76.1
South American	17,747	85.9
Argentinean	2,151	88.8
Chilean	568	80.6
Colombian	4,058	86.0
Ecuadorian	7,119	86.3
Peruvian	2,055	86.5
Venezuelan	1,135	86.8
Spaniard	1,787	79.7

Class of Worker: Government
(Universe: Civilian Employed Population 16 Years and Over)

Group	Number	%
Total Population	79,799	9.4
Hispanic or Latino (of any race)	19,360	11.6
Central American, ex. Mexican	640	7.9
Guatemalan	48	3.2
Honduran	195	9.9
Nicaraguan	0	0.0
Panamanian	220	18.6
Salvadoran	141	9.2
Cuban	499	9.7
Dominican Republic	7,222	10.9
Mexican	836	3.9
Puerto Rican	7,640	20.4
South American	1,622	7.9
Argentinean	208	8.6

Notes: (1) Percent of total population; (2) Percent of Hispanic/Latino population; Profiles include places with an overall population of at least 125,000, OR an overall population of at least 25,000 where the Hispanic/Latino population is at least 20% of the overall population. In states where less than five places meet either of these criteria, we have included places with at least 10,000 total population with the highest percentage of Hispanic/Latino population. These places are identified with an asterisk (*); Please refer to the User's Guide for a full explanation of data.

Chilean	85	12.1
Colombian	361	7.6
Ecuadorian	630	7.6
Peruvian	140	5.9
Venezuelan	72	5.5
Spaniard	382	17.0

Means of Transportation to Work: Car, Truck or Van
(Universe: Workers 16 Years and Over)

Group	Number	%
Total Population	75,058	9.1
Hispanic or Latino (of any race)	17,968	11.2
Central American, ex. Mexican	554	7.1
Guatemalan	62	4.2
Honduran	79	4.2
Nicaraguan	69	7.0
Panamanian	127	10.9
Salvadoran	144	9.7
Cuban	595	12.0
Dominican Republic	10,292	16.3
Mexican	712	3.4
Puerto Rican	3,443	9.6
South American	1,744	8.7
Argentinean	126	5.3
Chilean	76	11.2
Colombian	360	7.9
Ecuadorian	942	11.8
Peruvian	144	6.3
Venezuelan	36	2.8
Spaniard	74	3.4

Means of Transportation to Work: Public Transportation (ex. Taxicab)
(Universe: Workers 16 Years and Over)

Group	Number	%
Total Population	480,415	58.1
Hispanic or Latino (of any race)	102,770	64.3
Central American, ex. Mexican	5,635	72.2
Guatemalan	996	66.8
Honduran	1,524	80.6
Nicaraguan	786	79.7
Panamanian	793	67.9
Salvadoran	964	64.7
Cuban	2,814	56.7
Dominican Republic	39,192	62.1
Mexican	14,321	68.8
Puerto Rican	23,306	64.9
South American	12,895	64.4
Argentinean	1,462	61.5
Chilean	382	56.5
Colombian	2,794	61.5
Ecuadorian	5,430	67.8
Peruvian	1,457	64.0
Venezuelan	865	66.8
Spaniard	1,390	63.3

Homeownership Rate
(Universe: Occupied Housing Units)

Group	%
Total Population	22.8
Hispanic or Latino (of any race)	7.3
Central American, ex. Mexican	8.2
Costa Rican	9.5
Guatemalan	7.2
Honduran	5.5
Nicaraguan	8.2
Panamanian	14.4
Salvadoran	7.1
Cuban	15.7
Dominican Republic	3.4
Mexican	7.5
Puerto Rican	7.0
South American	14.2
Argentinean	25.2
Bolivian	18.8
Chilean	15.6
Colombian	14.5
Ecuadorian	6.3
Paraguayan	10.9
Peruvian	13.0
Uruguayan	21.8
Venezuelan	22.0
Spaniard	23.4

Median Home Value

Group	Dollars
Total Population	825,200
Hispanic or Latino (of any race)	617,100
Central American, ex. Mexican	496,100
Guatemalan	–
Honduran	414,700
Nicaraguan	–
Panamanian	463,200
Salvadoran	676,500
Cuban	778,700
Dominican Republic	347,000
Mexican	667,200
Puerto Rican	591,700
South American	671,500
Argentinean	684,800
Chilean	1,000,000+
Colombian	606,100
Ecuadorian	496,400
Peruvian	619,100
Venezuelan	902,000
Spaniard	868,400

Median Gross Rent

Group	Dollars
Total Population	1,234
Hispanic or Latino (of any race)	795
Central American, ex. Mexican	875
Guatemalan	687
Honduran	650
Nicaraguan	940
Panamanian	881
Salvadoran	1,044
Cuban	785
Dominican Republic	827
Mexican	1,297
Puerto Rican	579
South American	1,090
Argentinean	1,631
Chilean	1,140
Colombian	1,187
Ecuadorian	859
Peruvian	1,248
Venezuelan	1,192
Spaniard	1,624

Median Household Income
(2010 Inflation-Adjusted Dollars)

Group	Dollars
Total Population	64,971
Hispanic or Latino (of any race)	30,269
Central American, ex. Mexican	35,729
Guatemalan	37,568
Honduran	22,153
Nicaraguan	33,417
Panamanian	39,293
Salvadoran	50,685
Cuban	36,844
Dominican Republic	26,712
Mexican	45,004
Puerto Rican	23,794
South American	51,724
Argentinean	100,600
Chilean	50,739
Colombian	54,422
Ecuadorian	39,134
Peruvian	58,281
Venezuelan	60,754
Spaniard	65,432

Per Capita Income
(2010 Inflation-Adjusted Dollars)

Group	Dollars
Total Population	59,149
Hispanic or Latino (of any race)	20,008
Central American, ex. Mexican	22,558
Guatemalan	20,228
Honduran	15,247
Nicaraguan	26,114
Panamanian	27,849
Salvadoran	26,760
Cuban	38,532
Dominican Republic	13,516
Mexican	22,558
Puerto Rican	19,424
South American	35,893
Argentinean	68,661
Chilean	35,808
Colombian	39,494
Ecuadorian	18,228
Peruvian	49,219
Venezuelan	62,922
Spaniard	53,800

Households with $100,000+ Income

Group	Number	%
Total Population	257,814	35.2
Hispanic or Latino (of any race)	16,194	11.6
Central American, ex. Mexican	745	13.4
Guatemalan	107	14.7
Honduran	60	4.3
Nicaraguan	133	19.6
Panamanian	95	9.1
Salvadoran	193	16.3
Cuban	1,230	19.3
Dominican Republic	3,012	6.0
Mexican	2,141	20.4
Puerto Rican	4,059	8.8
South American	3,826	25.8
Argentinean	923	50.3
Chilean	165	24.5
Colombian	804	22.5
Ecuadorian	605	12.0
Peruvian	604	35.6
Venezuelan	456	37.0
Spaniard	601	26.9

Households with Food Stamps/SNAP Benefits During Past 12 Months

Group	Number	%
Total Population	82,243	11.2
Hispanic or Latino (of any race)	43,964	31.5
Central American, ex. Mexican	1,335	24.0
Guatemalan	39	5.3
Honduran	433	31.4
Nicaraguan	226	33.4
Panamanian	387	37.2
Salvadoran	197	16.7
Cuban	1,541	24.2
Dominican Republic	21,877	43.7
Mexican	2,148	20.5
Puerto Rican	13,843	30.1
South American	2,146	14.5
Argentinean	116	6.3
Chilean	46	6.8
Colombian	512	14.3
Ecuadorian	1,120	22.3
Peruvian	228	13.4
Venezuelan	88	7.1
Spaniard	86	3.9

Poverty Rate
(Income in Past 12 Months Below Poverty Level)

Group	%
Total Population	17.8
Hispanic or Latino (of any race)	29.8
Central American, ex. Mexican	23.6
Guatemalan	10.7
Honduran	40.4
Nicaraguan	12.9
Panamanian	20.4
Salvadoran	25.5
Cuban	27.6
Dominican Republic	32.2
Mexican	29.9
Puerto Rican	32.4
South American	17.2
Argentinean	13.3
Chilean	9.4
Colombian	15.6
Ecuadorian	20.1
Peruvian	16.9
Venezuelan	19.4
Spaniard	9.7

STATE & PLACE PROFILES

Notes: (1) Percent of total population; (2) Percent of Hispanic/Latino population; Profiles include places with an overall population of at least 125,000, OR an overall population of at least 25,000 where the Hispanic/Latino population is at least 20% of the overall population. In states where less than five places meet either of these criteria, we have included places with at least 10,000 total population with the highest percentage of Hispanic/Latino population. These places are identified with an asterisk (*); Please refer to the User's Guide for a full explanation of data.

Middletown

Population

Group	Number	%TP[1]	%HP[2]
Total Population	28,086	100.0	–
Hispanic or Latino (of any race)	11,158	39.7	100.0
Central American, ex. Mexican	547	1.9	4.9
Honduran	272	1.0	2.4
Salvadoran	104	0.4	0.9
Cuban	105	0.4	0.9
Dominican Republic	628	2.2	5.6
Mexican	4,208	15.0	37.7
Puerto Rican	4,533	16.1	40.6
South American	724	2.6	6.5
Colombian	266	0.9	2.4
Ecuadorian	281	1.0	2.5

Population Growth: 2000–2010

Group	%
Total Population	10.6
Hispanic or Latino (of any race)	75.0
Central American, ex. Mexican	110.4
Honduran	119.4
Dominican Republic	406.5
Mexican	106.5
Puerto Rican	47.8
South American	251.5
Colombian	144.0

Males per 100 Females

Group	Number
Total Population	95.6
Hispanic or Latino (of any race)	105.1
Central American, ex. Mexican	122.4
Honduran	124.8
Salvadoran	131.1
Cuban	90.9
Dominican Republic	84.7
Mexican	125.0
Puerto Rican	91.5
South American	106.3
Colombian	77.3
Ecuadorian	165.1

Average Household Size

Group	People
Total Population	2.77
Hispanic or Latino (of any race)	3.79
Central American, ex. Mexican	3.92
Honduran	3.94
Salvadoran	4.63
Cuban	2.77
Dominican Republic	3.82
Mexican	4.92
Puerto Rican	3.15
South American	3.92
Colombian	3.72
Ecuadorian	4.77

Median Age

Group	Years
Total Population	33.7
Hispanic or Latino (of any race)	25.3
Central American, ex. Mexican	30.2
Honduran	28.9
Salvadoran	29.3
Cuban	36.8
Dominican Republic	28.3
Mexican	23.5
Puerto Rican	25.4
South American	31.2
Colombian	37.0
Ecuadorian	27.6

High School Graduates
(Universe: Population 25 Years and Over)

Group	Number	%
Total Population	12,863	75.3
Hispanic or Latino (of any race)	2,718	52.1
Mexican	585	32.7
Puerto Rican	1,234	64.5

Four-Year College Graduates
(Universe: Population 25 Years and Over)

Group	Number	%
Total Population	2,917	17.1
Hispanic or Latino (of any race)	490	9.4
Mexican	19	1.1
Puerto Rican	224	11.7

Population Age 3–17 Enrolled in Public School
(Universe: Population Age 3–17 Enrolled in School)

Group	Number	%
Total Population	5,381	91.0
Hispanic or Latino (of any race)	2,869	95.6
Mexican	1,100	96.5
Puerto Rican	1,085	92.3

Population Age 3–17 Enrolled in Private School
(Universe: Population Age 3–17 Enrolled in School)

Group	Number	%
Total Population	532	9.0
Hispanic or Latino (of any race)	131	4.4
Mexican	40	3.5
Puerto Rican	91	7.7

Foreign-Born Population

Group	Number	%
Total Population	5,530	19.9
Hispanic or Latino (of any race)	4,085	38.7
Mexican	2,447	61.2
Puerto Rican	17	0.5

Foreign-Born Naturalized U.S. Citizens

Group	Number	%
Total Population	1,995	36.1
Hispanic or Latino (of any race)	971	23.8
Mexican	308	12.6
Puerto Rican	7	41.2

Language Spoken at Home: English Only
(Universe: Population 5 Years and Over)

Group	Number	%
Total Population	16,321	63.6
Hispanic or Latino (of any race)	1,522	16.2
Mexican	146	4.2
Puerto Rican	1,070	31.9

Language Spoken at Home: Spanish
(Universe: Population 5 Years and Over)

Group	Number	%
Total Population	8,180	31.9
Hispanic or Latino (of any race)	7,829	83.5
Mexican	3,333	95.8
Puerto Rican	2,274	67.8

Unemployment Rate
(Universe: Population 16 Years and Over)

Group	%
Total Population	9.2
Hispanic or Latino (of any race)	13.3
Mexican	13.1
Puerto Rican	15.8

Class of Worker: Private Wage and Salary
(Universe: Civilian Employed Population 16 Years and Over)

Group	Number	%
Total Population	9,726	76.0
Hispanic or Latino (of any race)	3,637	83.8
Mexican	1,502	91.0
Puerto Rican	1,124	79.9

Class of Worker: Government
(Universe: Civilian Employed Population 16 Years and Over)

Group	Number	%
Total Population	2,461	19.2
Hispanic or Latino (of any race)	455	10.5
Mexican	102	6.2
Puerto Rican	211	15.0

Means of Transportation to Work: Car, Truck or Van
(Universe: Workers 16 Years and Over)

Group	Number	%
Total Population	10,076	81.2
Hispanic or Latino (of any race)	3,205	75.1
Mexican	1,041	65.1
Puerto Rican	1,115	80.3

Means of Transportation to Work: Public Transportation (ex. Taxicab)
(Universe: Workers 16 Years and Over)

Group	Number	%
Total Population	709	5.7
Hispanic or Latino (of any race)	190	4.4
Mexican	31	1.9
Puerto Rican	109	7.8

Homeownership Rate
(Universe: Occupied Housing Units)

Group	%
Total Population	49.0
Hispanic or Latino (of any race)	35.2
Central American, ex. Mexican	43.8
Honduran	22.9
Salvadoran	54.2
Cuban	61.4
Dominican Republic	65.3
Mexican	15.0
Puerto Rican	39.9
South American	47.7
Colombian	51.9
Ecuadorian	32.3

Median Home Value

Group	Dollars
Total Population	228,300
Hispanic or Latino (of any race)	252,600
Mexican	204,700
Puerto Rican	259,800

Median Gross Rent

Group	Dollars
Total Population	998
Hispanic or Latino (of any race)	1,099
Mexican	1,126
Puerto Rican	992

Median Household Income
(2010 Inflation-Adjusted Dollars)

Group	Dollars
Total Population	54,354
Hispanic or Latino (of any race)	39,838
Mexican	34,020
Puerto Rican	35,246

Per Capita Income
(2010 Inflation-Adjusted Dollars)

Group	Dollars
Total Population	22,614
Hispanic or Latino (of any race)	13,174
Mexican	9,684
Puerto Rican	14,992

Households with $100,000+ Income

Group	Number	%
Total Population	1,620	17.0
Hispanic or Latino (of any race)	369	14.5
Mexican	89	11.8
Puerto Rican	177	15.1

Households with Food Stamps/SNAP Benefits During Past 12 Months

Group	Number	%
Total Population	1,178	12.4
Hispanic or Latino (of any race)	487	19.2
Mexican	70	9.3
Puerto Rican	319	27.2

Poverty Rate
(Income in Past 12 Months Below Poverty Level)

Group	%
Total Population	17.8
Hispanic or Latino (of any race)	29.1
Mexican	40.0
Puerto Rican	29.5

New Rochelle

Population

Group	Number	%TP[1]	%HP[2]
Total Population	77,062	100.0	–
Hispanic or Latino (of any race)	21,452	27.8	100.0

Notes: (1) Percent of total population; (2) Percent of Hispanic/Latino population; Profiles include places with an overall population of at least 125,000, OR an overall population of at least 25,000 where the Hispanic/Latino population is at least 20% of the overall population. In states where less than five places meet either of these criteria, we have included places with at least 10,000 total population with the highest percentage of Hispanic/Latino population. These places are identified with an asterisk (*); Please refer to the User's Guide for a full explanation of data.

Central American, ex. Mexican	2,017	2.6	9.4
Guatemalan	1,232	1.6	5.7
Honduran	242	0.3	1.1
Salvadoran	330	0.4	1.5
Cuban	371	0.5	1.7
Dominican Republic	960	1.2	4.5
Mexican	10,363	13.4	48.3
Puerto Rican	2,779	3.6	13.0
South American	3,697	4.8	17.2
Argentinean	170	0.2	0.8
Colombian	1,451	1.9	6.8
Ecuadorian	378	0.5	1.8
Peruvian	1,297	1.7	6.0
Venezuelan	131	0.2	0.6
Spaniard	191	0.2	0.9

Population Growth: 2000–2010

Group	%
Total Population	6.8
Hispanic or Latino (of any race)	48.0
Central American, ex. Mexican	172.2
Guatemalan	273.3
Salvadoran	127.6
Cuban	56.5
Dominican Republic	152.0
Mexican	50.2
Puerto Rican	44.9
South American	51.8
Colombian	35.5
Ecuadorian	129.1
Peruvian	64.0

Males per 100 Females

Group	Number
Total Population	92.3
Hispanic or Latino (of any race)	102.7
Central American, ex. Mexican	132.9
Guatemalan	153.0
Honduran	105.1
Salvadoran	126.0
Cuban	90.3
Dominican Republic	73.3
Mexican	116.2
Puerto Rican	82.9
South American	86.3
Argentinean	88.9
Colombian	81.6
Ecuadorian	90.9
Peruvian	91.6
Venezuelan	65.8
Spaniard	94.9

Average Household Size

Group	People
Total Population	2.64
Hispanic or Latino (of any race)	3.60
Central American, ex. Mexican	4.19
Guatemalan	4.83
Honduran	3.63
Salvadoran	3.83
Cuban	2.64
Dominican Republic	3.07
Mexican	4.36
Puerto Rican	2.55
South American	3.11
Argentinean	2.54
Colombian	2.97
Ecuadorian	3.00
Peruvian	3.43
Venezuelan	3.33
Spaniard	2.67

Median Age

Group	Years
Total Population	38.4
Hispanic or Latino (of any race)	28.6
Central American, ex. Mexican	28.7
Guatemalan	27.4
Honduran	31.8
Salvadoran	29.0
Cuban	38.5
Dominican Republic	26.8
Mexican	25.9
Puerto Rican	30.3
South American	37.2
Argentinean	39.5
Colombian	37.1
Ecuadorian	35.1
Peruvian	38.4
Venezuelan	33.1
Spaniard	37.5

High School Graduates
(Universe: Population 25 Years and Over)

Group	Number	%
Total Population	41,239	83.4
Hispanic or Latino (of any race)	5,720	57.8
Central American, ex. Mexican	638	48.8
Mexican	1,997	42.4
Puerto Rican	1,102	86.2
South American	1,477	78.7
Colombian	637	77.5

Four-Year College Graduates
(Universe: Population 25 Years and Over)

Group	Number	%
Total Population	19,621	39.7
Hispanic or Latino (of any race)	1,139	11.5
Central American, ex. Mexican	84	6.4
Mexican	263	5.6
Puerto Rican	270	21.1
South American	331	17.6
Colombian	80	9.7

Population Age 3–17 Enrolled in Public School
(Universe: Population Age 3–17 Enrolled in School)

Group	Number	%
Total Population	11,246	77.9
Hispanic or Latino (of any race)	4,164	94.3
Central American, ex. Mexican	401	96.9
Mexican	2,525	96.8
Puerto Rican	391	85.2
South American	387	86.4
Colombian	167	77.7

Population Age 3–17 Enrolled in Private School
(Universe: Population Age 3–17 Enrolled in School)

Group	Number	%
Total Population	3,199	22.1
Hispanic or Latino (of any race)	254	5.7
Central American, ex. Mexican	13	3.1
Mexican	84	3.2
Puerto Rican	68	14.8
South American	61	13.6
Colombian	48	22.3

Foreign-Born Population

Group	Number	%
Total Population	20,595	27.2
Hispanic or Latino (of any race)	9,961	54.4
Central American, ex. Mexican	1,425	71.1
Mexican	5,590	59.8
Puerto Rican	20	0.8
South American	2,226	75.9
Colombian	977	71.0

Foreign-Born Naturalized U.S. Citizens

Group	Number	%
Total Population	8,547	41.5
Hispanic or Latino (of any race)	2,522	25.3
Central American, ex. Mexican	542	38.0
Mexican	798	14.3
Puerto Rican	0	0.0
South American	938	42.1
Colombian	483	49.4

Language Spoken at Home: English Only
(Universe: Population 5 Years and Over)

Group	Number	%
Total Population	48,355	67.6
Hispanic or Latino (of any race)	2,727	16.7
Central American, ex. Mexican	163	8.8
Mexican	613	7.6
Puerto Rican	1,025	46.8
South American	389	14.2
Colombian	191	14.9

Language Spoken at Home: Spanish
(Universe: Population 5 Years and Over)

Group	Number	%
Total Population	14,303	20.0
Hispanic or Latino (of any race)	13,571	82.9
Central American, ex. Mexican	1,699	91.2
Mexican	7,471	92.4
Puerto Rican	1,129	51.6
South American	2,319	84.4
Colombian	1,077	84.2

Unemployment Rate
(Universe: Population 16 Years and Over)

Group	%
Total Population	7.0
Hispanic or Latino (of any race)	8.2
Central American, ex. Mexican	4.9
Mexican	8.4
Puerto Rican	12.1
South American	6.8
Colombian	7.4

Class of Worker: Private Wage and Salary
(Universe: Civilian Employed Population 16 Years and Over)

Group	Number	%
Total Population	26,823	76.6
Hispanic or Latino (of any race)	6,327	76.7
Central American, ex. Mexican	740	69.2
Mexican	3,170	81.4
Puerto Rican	795	72.9
South American	1,298	80.0
Colombian	617	81.6

Class of Worker: Government
(Universe: Civilian Employed Population 16 Years and Over)

Group	Number	%
Total Population	4,978	14.2
Hispanic or Latino (of any race)	777	9.4
Central American, ex. Mexican	79	7.4
Mexican	130	3.3
Puerto Rican	285	26.1
South American	95	5.9
Colombian	16	2.1

Means of Transportation to Work: Car, Truck or Van
(Universe: Workers 16 Years and Over)

Group	Number	%
Total Population	21,339	62.7
Hispanic or Latino (of any race)	4,386	54.8
Central American, ex. Mexican	432	44.0
Mexican	1,867	49.2
Puerto Rican	780	71.5
South American	1,001	64.4
Colombian	380	54.0

Means of Transportation to Work: Public Transportation (ex. Taxicab)
(Universe: Workers 16 Years and Over)

Group	Number	%
Total Population	6,586	19.3
Hispanic or Latino (of any race)	1,251	15.6
Central American, ex. Mexican	211	21.5
Mexican	455	12.0
Puerto Rican	178	16.3
South American	273	17.6
Colombian	224	31.8

Homeownership Rate
(Universe: Occupied Housing Units)

Group	%
Total Population	51.2
Hispanic or Latino (of any race)	26.2
Central American, ex. Mexican	18.0
Guatemalan	15.6
Honduran	18.6
Salvadoran	16.0
Cuban	47.1
Dominican Republic	32.7
Mexican	21.5
Puerto Rican	31.0
South American	29.2
Argentinean	47.4
Colombian	28.8
Ecuadorian	32.3
Peruvian	25.6
Venezuelan	22.5
Spaniard	64.4

Notes: (1) Percent of total population; (2) Percent of Hispanic/Latino population; Profiles include places with an overall population of at least 125,000, OR an overall population of at least 25,000 where the Hispanic/Latino population is at least 20% of the overall population. In states where less than five places meet either of these criteria, we have included places with at least 10,000 total population with the highest percentage of Hispanic/Latino population. These places are identified with an asterisk (*); Please refer to the User's Guide for a full explanation of data.

Median Home Value

Group	Dollars
Total Population	605,500
Hispanic or Latino (of any race)	531,200
Central American, ex. Mexican	453,500
Mexican	565,300
Puerto Rican	487,900
South American	500,000
Colombian	367,300

Median Gross Rent

Group	Dollars
Total Population	1,183
Hispanic or Latino (of any race)	1,196
Central American, ex. Mexican	1,292
Mexican	1,177
Puerto Rican	1,248
South American	1,137
Colombian	1,292

Median Household Income
(2010 Inflation-Adjusted Dollars)

Group	Dollars
Total Population	65,317
Hispanic or Latino (of any race)	46,525
Central American, ex. Mexican	51,719
Mexican	44,489
Puerto Rican	59,300
South American	50,563
Colombian	40,170

Per Capita Income
(2010 Inflation-Adjusted Dollars)

Group	Dollars
Total Population	40,787
Hispanic or Latino (of any race)	16,465
Central American, ex. Mexican	15,536
Mexican	12,275
Puerto Rican	24,266
South American	23,487
Colombian	17,835

Households with $100,000+ Income

Group	Number	%
Total Population	9,388	33.5
Hispanic or Latino (of any race)	607	11.9
Central American, ex. Mexican	0	0.0
Mexican	140	6.4
Puerto Rican	174	25.0
South American	262	23.0
Colombian	79	15.9

Households with Food Stamps/SNAP Benefits During Past 12 Months

Group	Number	%
Total Population	1,345	4.8
Hispanic or Latino (of any race)	301	5.9
Central American, ex. Mexican	22	4.3
Mexican	131	6.0
Puerto Rican	40	5.7
South American	59	5.2
Colombian	33	6.7

Poverty Rate
(Income in Past 12 Months Below Poverty Level)

Group	%
Total Population	10.7
Hispanic or Latino (of any race)	16.1
Central American, ex. Mexican	21.4
Mexican	17.4
Puerto Rican	12.9
South American	13.9
Colombian	4.8

New York City

Population

Group	Number	%TP[1]	%HP[2]
Total Population	8,175,133	100.0	–
Hispanic or Latino (of any race)	2,336,076	28.6	100.0
Central American, ex. Mexican	151,378	1.9	6.5
Costa Rican	6,673	0.1	0.3
Guatemalan	30,420	0.4	1.3
Honduran	42,400	0.5	1.8
Nicaraguan	9,346	0.1	0.4
Panamanian	22,353	0.3	1.0
Salvadoran	38,559	0.5	1.7
Cuban	40,840	0.5	1.7
Dominican Republic	576,701	7.1	24.7
Mexican	319,263	3.9	13.7
Puerto Rican	723,621	8.9	31.0
South American	343,468	4.2	14.7
Argentinean	15,169	0.2	0.6
Bolivian	4,488	0.1	0.2
Chilean	7,026	0.1	0.3
Colombian	94,723	1.2	4.1
Ecuadorian	167,209	2.0	7.2
Paraguayan	3,534	<0.1	0.2
Peruvian	36,018	0.4	1.5
Uruguayan	3,004	<0.1	0.1
Venezuelan	9,619	0.1	0.4
Spaniard	17,793	0.2	0.8

Population Growth: 2000–2010

Group	%
Total Population	2.1
Hispanic or Latino (of any race)	8.1
Central American, ex. Mexican	52.8
Costa Rican	35.1
Guatemalan	100.0
Honduran	65.6
Nicaraguan	44.9
Panamanian	32.7
Salvadoran	57.3
Cuban	-0.7
Dominican Republic	41.8
Mexican	70.8
Puerto Rican	-8.3
South American	45.3
Argentinean	58.4
Bolivian	52.5
Chilean	40.1
Colombian	22.8
Ecuadorian	65.5
Paraguayan	113.1
Peruvian	52.8
Uruguayan	57.5
Venezuelan	43.3
Spaniard	116.1

Males per 100 Females

Group	Number
Total Population	90.4
Hispanic or Latino (of any race)	93.8
Central American, ex. Mexican	96.7
Costa Rican	71.5
Guatemalan	141.2
Honduran	89.5
Nicaraguan	85.8
Panamanian	70.9
Salvadoran	101.8
Cuban	95.7
Dominican Republic	81.9
Mexican	130.7
Puerto Rican	86.0
South American	98.0
Argentinean	101.0
Bolivian	85.7
Chilean	104.0
Colombian	79.3
Ecuadorian	112.0
Paraguayan	92.5
Peruvian	94.4
Uruguayan	108.2
Venezuelan	85.7
Spaniard	95.2

Average Household Size

Group	People
Total Population	2.57
Hispanic or Latino (of any race)	3.08
Central American, ex. Mexican	3.31
Costa Rican	2.53
Guatemalan	3.79
Honduran	3.43
Nicaraguan	3.17
Panamanian	2.56
Salvadoran	3.73
Cuban	2.12
Dominican Republic	3.36
Mexican	4.48
Puerto Rican	2.57
South American	3.24
Argentinean	2.36
Bolivian	2.93
Chilean	2.41
Colombian	2.83
Ecuadorian	3.82
Paraguayan	3.15
Peruvian	3.06
Uruguayan	2.55
Venezuelan	2.48
Spaniard	2.19

Median Age

Group	Years
Total Population	35.5
Hispanic or Latino (of any race)	31.2
Central American, ex. Mexican	33.2
Costa Rican	40.3
Guatemalan	30.2
Honduran	32.0
Nicaraguan	35.8
Panamanian	42.2
Salvadoran	32.1
Cuban	42.6
Dominican Republic	31.9
Mexican	25.8
Puerto Rican	33.2
South American	35.6
Argentinean	37.9
Bolivian	39.0
Chilean	39.4
Colombian	38.9
Ecuadorian	33.3
Paraguayan	34.6
Peruvian	39.5
Uruguayan	39.9
Venezuelan	32.7
Spaniard	36.8

High School Graduates
(Universe: Population 25 Years and Over)

Group	Number	%
Total Population	4,314,755	79.0
Hispanic or Latino (of any race)	867,402	62.8
Central American, ex. Mexican	61,977	62.4
Costa Rican	3,473	76.6
Guatemalan	9,562	53.4
Honduran	15,213	56.5
Nicaraguan	4,910	70.9
Panamanian	14,030	89.3
Salvadoran	13,447	52.9
Cuban	23,866	75.6
Dominican Republic	193,362	58.2
Mexican	73,096	47.9
Puerto Rican	299,268	64.3
South American	176,213	71.4
Argentinean	9,198	85.1
Bolivian	2,995	83.8
Chilean	4,535	82.5
Colombian	54,227	78.4
Ecuadorian	69,184	60.5
Paraguayan	1,859	77.0
Peruvian	24,192	85.1
Uruguayan	1,651	76.3
Venezuelan	6,148	83.7
Spaniard	11,402	87.6

Four-Year College Graduates
(Universe: Population 25 Years and Over)

Group	Number	%
Total Population	1,816,233	33.3
Hispanic or Latino (of any race)	206,669	15.0
Central American, ex. Mexican	14,636	14.7
Costa Rican	1,096	24.2
Guatemalan	2,061	11.5
Honduran	3,421	12.7
Nicaraguan	1,442	20.8
Panamanian	3,453	22.0
Salvadoran	2,734	10.7
Cuban	9,192	29.1
Dominican Republic	43,952	13.2
Mexican	15,604	10.2

Notes: (1) Percent of total population; (2) Percent of Hispanic/Latino population; Profiles include places with an overall population of at least 125,000, OR an overall population of at least 25,000 where the Hispanic/Latino population is at least 20% of the overall population. In states where less than five places meet either of these criteria, we have included places with at least 10,000 total population with the highest percentage of Hispanic/Latino population. These places are identified with an asterisk (*); Please refer to the User's Guide for a full explanation of data.

Group	Number	%
Puerto Rican	59,035	12.7
South American	49,250	19.9
Argentinean	4,274	39.6
Bolivian	976	27.3
Chilean	2,006	36.5
Colombian	16,235	23.5
Ecuadorian	13,070	11.4
Paraguayan	578	24.0
Peruvian	7,990	28.1
Uruguayan	572	26.4
Venezuelan	2,740	37.3
Spaniard	6,057	46.5

Population Age 3–17 Enrolled in Public School
(Universe: Population Age 3–17 Enrolled in School)

Group	Number	%
Total Population	1,047,997	77.9
Hispanic or Latino (of any race)	416,151	88.7
Central American, ex. Mexican	24,068	90.8
Costa Rican	782	93.0
Guatemalan	3,485	89.5
Honduran	8,119	90.8
Nicaraguan	1,281	89.6
Panamanian	3,406	93.0
Salvadoran	6,450	90.1
Cuban	3,386	71.4
Dominican Republic	114,782	90.7
Mexican	64,969	95.4
Puerto Rican	144,445	87.2
South American	47,573	84.3
Argentinean	1,312	76.0
Bolivian	437	48.9
Chilean	651	71.9
Colombian	12,612	83.0
Ecuadorian	25,362	88.3
Paraguayan	473	87.9
Peruvian	4,961	80.1
Uruguayan	200	58.7
Venezuelan	1,100	83.7
Spaniard	1,129	63.7

Population Age 3–17 Enrolled in Private School
(Universe: Population Age 3–17 Enrolled in School)

Group	Number	%
Total Population	298,131	22.1
Hispanic or Latino (of any race)	52,952	11.3
Central American, ex. Mexican	2,430	9.2
Costa Rican	59	7.0
Guatemalan	411	10.5
Honduran	822	9.2
Nicaraguan	149	10.4
Panamanian	257	7.0
Salvadoran	709	9.9
Cuban	1,357	28.6
Dominican Republic	11,724	9.3
Mexican	3,150	4.6
Puerto Rican	21,204	12.8
South American	8,828	15.7
Argentinean	415	24.0
Bolivian	457	51.1
Chilean	254	28.1
Colombian	2,591	17.0
Ecuadorian	3,347	11.7
Paraguayan	65	12.1
Peruvian	1,233	19.9
Uruguayan	141	41.3
Venezuelan	215	16.3
Spaniard	642	36.3

Foreign-Born Population

Group	Number	%
Total Population	2,971,143	36.8
Hispanic or Latino (of any race)	939,329	41.2
Central American, ex. Mexican	101,164	65.0
Costa Rican	3,891	61.6
Guatemalan	19,805	70.6
Honduran	29,387	65.8
Nicaraguan	6,398	64.2
Panamanian	12,919	55.1
Salvadoran	27,115	67.1
Cuban	19,341	46.4
Dominican Republic	347,933	60.8
Mexican	175,988	60.3
Puerto Rican	8,982	1.2
South American	252,750	69.5
Argentinean	9,405	66.6
Bolivian	3,316	67.6
Chilean	4,981	65.1
Colombian	67,316	68.0
Ecuadorian	124,046	70.2
Paraguayan	2,465	70.7
Peruvian	28,844	72.3
Uruguayan	2,131	72.3
Venezuelan	7,323	69.1
Spaniard	6,388	38.9

Foreign-Born Naturalized U.S. Citizens

Group	Number	%
Total Population	1,528,135	51.4
Hispanic or Latino (of any race)	361,223	38.5
Central American, ex. Mexican	41,687	41.2
Costa Rican	2,832	72.8
Guatemalan	6,347	32.0
Honduran	10,554	35.9
Nicaraguan	3,161	49.4
Panamanian	8,531	66.0
Salvadoran	9,290	34.3
Cuban	14,271	73.8
Dominican Republic	156,979	45.1
Mexican	18,218	10.4
Puerto Rican	5,061	56.3
South American	106,999	42.3
Argentinean	4,053	43.1
Bolivian	2,014	60.7
Chilean	2,679	53.8
Colombian	35,981	53.5
Ecuadorian	42,633	34.4
Paraguayan	623	25.3
Peruvian	13,991	48.5
Uruguayan	841	39.5
Venezuelan	2,273	31.0
Spaniard	2,876	45.0

Language Spoken at Home: English Only
(Universe: Population 5 Years and Over)

Group	Number	%
Total Population	3,910,650	51.7
Hispanic or Latino (of any race)	310,498	14.8
Central American, ex. Mexican	17,920	12.4
Costa Rican	1,378	22.9
Guatemalan	2,087	8.0
Honduran	3,248	7.9
Nicaraguan	1,175	12.4
Panamanian	7,412	33.4
Salvadoran	2,191	5.9
Cuban	11,879	29.7
Dominican Republic	23,599	4.5
Mexican	19,839	7.7
Puerto Rican	189,308	26.8
South American	25,561	7.6
Argentinean	2,051	15.6
Bolivian	529	11.3
Chilean	1,150	15.8
Colombian	7,299	7.9
Ecuadorian	7,260	4.5
Paraguayan	254	7.8
Peruvian	3,494	9.3
Uruguayan	227	8.3
Venezuelan	2,082	20.9
Spaniard	6,036	38.4

Language Spoken at Home: Spanish
(Universe: Population 5 Years and Over)

Group	Number	%
Total Population	1,861,885	24.6
Hispanic or Latino (of any race)	1,780,137	84.7
Central American, ex. Mexican	125,825	86.9
Costa Rican	4,637	77.0
Guatemalan	23,942	91.4
Honduran	37,303	90.7
Nicaraguan	8,209	86.8
Panamanian	14,650	66.0
Salvadoran	34,872	94.0
Cuban	27,567	69.0
Dominican Republic	504,900	95.3
Mexican	237,363	91.7
Puerto Rican	515,835	72.9
South American	310,678	91.9
Argentinean	10,797	82.1
Bolivian	4,154	88.7
Chilean	6,045	83.2
Colombian	85,166	91.7
Ecuadorian	154,541	95.3
Paraguayan	2,844	86.9
Peruvian	34,062	90.2
Uruguayan	2,427	88.5
Venezuelan	7,701	77.3
Spaniard	9,061	57.6

Unemployment Rate
(Universe: Population 16 Years and Over)

Group	%
Total Population	8.8
Hispanic or Latino (of any race)	10.6
Central American, ex. Mexican	9.3
Costa Rican	8.0
Guatemalan	6.8
Honduran	9.7
Nicaraguan	11.3
Panamanian	9.7
Salvadoran	10.4
Cuban	10.5
Dominican Republic	12.1
Mexican	6.3
Puerto Rican	13.2
South American	8.2
Argentinean	6.2
Bolivian	9.9
Chilean	8.8
Colombian	8.3
Ecuadorian	8.1
Paraguayan	7.8
Peruvian	8.2
Uruguayan	5.1
Venezuelan	11.5
Spaniard	7.1

Class of Worker: Private Wage and Salary
(Universe: Civilian Employed Population 16 Years and Over)

Group	Number	%
Total Population	2,940,465	78.5
Hispanic or Latino (of any race)	783,992	81.4
Central American, ex. Mexican	64,881	81.8
Costa Rican	2,167	73.9
Guatemalan	13,502	85.0
Honduran	17,820	82.8
Nicaraguan	4,319	81.5
Panamanian	7,998	70.3
Salvadoran	17,926	86.0
Cuban	13,846	79.2
Dominican Republic	196,541	82.6
Mexican	123,977	90.8
Puerto Rican	197,991	74.5
South American	159,054	83.4
Argentinean	6,786	85.7
Bolivian	2,154	84.5
Chilean	2,986	72.3
Colombian	42,355	81.4
Ecuadorian	77,920	85.9
Paraguayan	1,682	77.1
Peruvian	17,421	81.7
Uruguayan	1,198	80.7
Venezuelan	4,886	81.4
Spaniard	6,510	74.4

Class of Worker: Government
(Universe: Civilian Employed Population 16 Years and Over)

Group	Number	%
Total Population	557,478	14.9
Hispanic or Latino (of any race)	119,303	12.4
Central American, ex. Mexican	8,273	10.4
Costa Rican	559	19.1
Guatemalan	1,013	6.4
Honduran	2,078	9.7
Nicaraguan	542	10.2
Panamanian	2,699	23.7
Salvadoran	1,205	5.8
Cuban	2,666	15.2
Dominican Republic	24,833	10.4
Mexican	4,060	3.0
Puerto Rican	58,826	22.1
South American	15,171	8.0
Argentinean	476	6.0
Bolivian	148	5.8
Chilean	524	12.7

Notes: (1) Percent of total population; (2) Percent of Hispanic/Latino population; Profiles include places with an overall population of at least 125,000, OR an overall population of at least 25,000 where the Hispanic/Latino population is at least 20% of the overall population. In states where less than five places meet either of these criteria, we have included places with at least 10,000 total population with the highest percentage of Hispanic/Latino population. These places are identified with an asterisk (*); Please refer to the User's Guide for a full explanation of data.

Colombian	4,745	9.1
Ecuadorian	5,822	6.4
Paraguayan	61	2.8
Peruvian	2,212	10.4
Uruguayan	99	6.7
Venezuelan	680	11.3
Spaniard	1,887	21.6

Means of Transportation to Work: Car, Truck or Van
(Universe: Workers 16 Years and Over)

Group	Number	%
Total Population	1,033,954	28.4
Hispanic or Latino (of any race)	229,103	24.5
Central American, ex. Mexican	17,723	22.8
Costa Rican	647	23.0
Guatemalan	3,285	21.0
Honduran	3,672	17.5
Nicaraguan	959	18.6
Panamanian	2,604	23.2
Salvadoran	6,281	30.9
Cuban	5,044	29.6
Dominican Republic	56,389	24.7
Mexican	14,538	10.8
Puerto Rican	76,655	29.7
South American	49,482	26.6
Argentinean	1,699	22.2
Bolivian	853	34.3
Chilean	1,033	25.5
Colombian	15,327	30.2
Ecuadorian	22,012	24.9
Paraguayan	800	36.8
Peruvian	5,616	27.1
Uruguayan	219	14.9
Venezuelan	1,356	23.2
Spaniard	2,742	32.1

Means of Transportation to Work: Public Transportation (ex. Taxicab)
(Universe: Workers 16 Years and Over)

Group	Number	%
Total Population	2,008,737	55.2
Hispanic or Latino (of any race)	566,320	60.6
Central American, ex. Mexican	49,267	63.5
Costa Rican	2,008	71.4
Guatemalan	10,068	64.3
Honduran	14,078	67.0
Nicaraguan	3,296	64.0
Panamanian	7,511	66.9
Salvadoran	11,265	55.5
Cuban	8,988	52.7
Dominican Republic	132,556	58.1
Mexican	96,792	71.8
Puerto Rican	144,786	56.2
South American	114,075	61.4
Argentinean	4,395	57.4
Bolivian	1,299	52.2
Chilean	2,336	57.7
Colombian	29,650	58.5
Ecuadorian	56,594	63.9
Paraguayan	1,189	54.7
Peruvian	12,774	61.7
Uruguayan	970	66.1
Venezuelan	3,422	58.5
Spaniard	4,526	53.1

Homeownership Rate
(Universe: Occupied Housing Units)

Group	%
Total Population	31.0
Hispanic or Latino (of any race)	15.3
Central American, ex. Mexican	17.3
Costa Rican	27.9
Guatemalan	13.2
Honduran	12.4
Nicaraguan	16.3
Panamanian	26.2
Salvadoran	15.5
Cuban	24.7
Dominican Republic	10.1
Mexican	7.7
Puerto Rican	15.6
South American	23.0
Argentinean	30.6
Bolivian	37.7
Chilean	23.6
Colombian	23.4
Ecuadorian	20.5
Paraguayan	16.3
Peruvian	24.9
Uruguayan	28.3
Venezuelan	22.4
Spaniard	36.9

Median Home Value

Group	Dollars
Total Population	513,900
Hispanic or Latino (of any race)	459,300
Central American, ex. Mexican	447,500
Costa Rican	410,300
Guatemalan	430,800
Honduran	453,700
Nicaraguan	476,900
Panamanian	470,500
Salvadoran	438,200
Cuban	458,400
Dominican Republic	467,900
Mexican	516,400
Puerto Rican	429,900
South American	496,300
Argentinean	607,700
Bolivian	591,900
Chilean	498,900
Colombian	474,600
Ecuadorian	499,000
Paraguayan	485,600
Peruvian	493,900
Uruguayan	465,300
Venezuelan	451,300
Spaniard	580,100

Median Gross Rent

Group	Dollars
Total Population	1,071
Hispanic or Latino (of any race)	968
Central American, ex. Mexican	1,014
Costa Rican	1,066
Guatemalan	1,047
Honduran	953
Nicaraguan	1,048
Panamanian	958
Salvadoran	1,091
Cuban	871
Dominican Republic	924
Mexican	1,208
Puerto Rican	823
South American	1,152
Argentinean	1,245
Bolivian	1,278
Chilean	1,183
Colombian	1,155
Ecuadorian	1,132
Paraguayan	1,129
Peruvian	1,145
Uruguayan	1,336
Venezuelan	1,220
Spaniard	1,221

Median Household Income
(2010 Inflation-Adjusted Dollars)

Group	Dollars
Total Population	50,285
Hispanic or Latino (of any race)	35,603
Central American, ex. Mexican	41,482
Costa Rican	48,487
Guatemalan	43,245
Honduran	36,336
Nicaraguan	43,839
Panamanian	46,146
Salvadoran	41,171
Cuban	41,587
Dominican Republic	29,994
Mexican	39,597
Puerto Rican	30,572
South American	47,863
Argentinean	58,718
Bolivian	53,214
Chilean	57,133
Colombian	48,441
Ecuadorian	45,414
Paraguayan	50,427
Peruvian	48,219
Uruguayan	59,333
Venezuelan	49,229
Spaniard	65,538

Per Capita Income
(2010 Inflation-Adjusted Dollars)

Group	Dollars
Total Population	30,498
Hispanic or Latino (of any race)	16,972
Central American, ex. Mexican	18,019
Costa Rican	22,497
Guatemalan	16,933
Honduran	16,036
Nicaraguan	20,939
Panamanian	22,613
Salvadoran	16,511
Cuban	29,101
Dominican Republic	13,570
Mexican	13,644
Puerto Rican	17,464
South American	21,041
Argentinean	39,871
Bolivian	23,984
Chilean	27,395
Colombian	21,982
Ecuadorian	16,977
Paraguayan	22,909
Peruvian	23,879
Uruguayan	29,413
Venezuelan	33,107
Spaniard	39,604

Households with $100,000+ Income

Group	Number	%
Total Population	696,100	22.8
Hispanic or Latino (of any race)	81,398	11.1
Central American, ex. Mexican	5,394	10.8
Costa Rican	359	14.7
Guatemalan	971	11.4
Honduran	1,120	8.0
Nicaraguan	551	18.1
Panamanian	994	10.3
Salvadoran	1,193	10.7
Cuban	3,412	18.1
Dominican Republic	12,136	6.9
Mexican	8,154	12.2
Puerto Rican	29,140	10.5
South American	18,410	15.5
Argentinean	1,718	29.4
Bolivian	390	20.4
Chilean	612	19.5
Colombian	4,935	14.0
Ecuadorian	6,699	13.2
Paraguayan	262	24.3
Peruvian	2,336	17.0
Uruguayan	251	22.7
Venezuelan	811	20.0
Spaniard	2,239	28.3

Households with Food Stamps/SNAP Benefits During Past 12 Months

Group	Number	%
Total Population	480,945	15.8
Hispanic or Latino (of any race)	216,371	29.5
Central American, ex. Mexican	9,913	19.9
Costa Rican	422	17.3
Guatemalan	1,271	14.9
Honduran	3,675	26.3
Nicaraguan	651	21.4
Panamanian	1,819	18.8
Salvadoran	1,955	17.5
Cuban	4,416	23.4
Dominican Republic	70,528	40.3
Mexican	18,411	27.6
Puerto Rican	88,354	31.9
South American	19,948	16.8
Argentinean	710	12.1
Bolivian	132	6.9
Chilean	305	9.7
Colombian	5,333	15.1
Ecuadorian	10,423	20.6
Paraguayan	118	10.9
Peruvian	1,997	14.5

Notes: (1) Percent of total population; (2) Percent of Hispanic/Latino population; Profiles include places with an overall population of at least 125,000, OR an overall population of at least 25,000 where the Hispanic/Latino population is at least 20% of the overall population. In states where less than five places meet either of these criteria, we have included places with at least 10,000 total population with the highest percentage of Hispanic/Latino population. These places are identified with an asterisk (*); Please refer to the User's Guide for a full explanation of data.

Uruguayan	92	8.3
Venezuelan	719	17.8
Spaniard	390	4.9

Poverty Rate
(Income in Past 12 Months Below Poverty Level)

Group	%
Total Population	19.1
Hispanic or Latino (of any race)	27.4
Central American, ex. Mexican	19.7
Costa Rican	12.0
Guatemalan	18.5
Honduran	25.1
Nicaraguan	14.5
Panamanian	17.5
Salvadoran	18.2
Cuban	20.0
Dominican Republic	30.1
Mexican	31.9
Puerto Rican	31.5
South American	16.5
Argentinean	12.3
Bolivian	13.2
Chilean	7.9
Colombian	14.6
Ecuadorian	18.6
Paraguayan	24.1
Peruvian	15.7
Uruguayan	6.5
Venezuelan	18.8
Spaniard	7.6

Newburgh

Population

Group	Number	%TP[1]	%HP[2]
Total Population	28,866	100.0	–
Hispanic or Latino (of any race)	13,814	47.9	100.0
Central American, ex. Mexican	2,381	8.2	17.2
Guatemalan	380	1.3	2.8
Honduran	1,545	5.4	11.2
Salvadoran	381	1.3	2.8
Dominican Republic	234	0.8	1.7
Mexican	6,181	21.4	44.7
Puerto Rican	2,962	10.3	21.4
South American	1,252	4.3	9.1
Colombian	195	0.7	1.4
Ecuadorian	229	0.8	1.7
Peruvian	691	2.4	5.0

Population Growth: 2000–2010

Group	%
Total Population	2.1
Hispanic or Latino (of any race)	34.7
Central American, ex. Mexican	119.4
Honduran	106.0
Salvadoran	99.5
Dominican Republic	114.7
Mexican	50.4
Puerto Rican	-3.5
South American	114.4
Peruvian	109.4

Males per 100 Females

Group	Number
Total Population	94.6
Hispanic or Latino (of any race)	106.6
Central American, ex. Mexican	121.9
Guatemalan	206.5
Honduran	112.8
Salvadoran	103.7
Dominican Republic	78.6
Mexican	110.7
Puerto Rican	92.1
South American	108.0
Colombian	103.1
Ecuadorian	124.5
Peruvian	100.3

Average Household Size

Group	People
Total Population	3.09
Hispanic or Latino (of any race)	4.07
Central American, ex. Mexican	4.33
Guatemalan	4.70
Honduran	4.30
Salvadoran	4.31
Dominican Republic	3.25
Mexican	5.07
Puerto Rican	3.00
South American	3.83
Colombian	3.57
Ecuadorian	4.03
Peruvian	3.93

Median Age

Group	Years
Total Population	28.2
Hispanic or Latino (of any race)	25.1
Central American, ex. Mexican	28.2
Guatemalan	26.1
Honduran	29.0
Salvadoran	27.9
Dominican Republic	22.6
Mexican	22.2
Puerto Rican	26.3
South American	32.8
Colombian	37.3
Ecuadorian	30.1
Peruvian	33.0

High School Graduates
(Universe: Population 25 Years and Over)

Group	Number	%
Total Population	10,889	67.2
Hispanic or Latino (of any race)	3,381	50.6
Central American, ex. Mexican	600	47.5
Honduran	358	47.5
Mexican	1,258	39.4
Puerto Rican	861	61.9
South American	579	82.1

Four-Year College Graduates
(Universe: Population 25 Years and Over)

Group	Number	%
Total Population	2,001	12.3
Hispanic or Latino (of any race)	463	6.9
Central American, ex. Mexican	57	4.5
Honduran	39	5.2
Mexican	105	3.3
Puerto Rican	99	7.1
South American	194	27.5

Population Age 3–17 Enrolled in Public School
(Universe: Population Age 3–17 Enrolled in School)

Group	Number	%
Total Population	6,253	95.5
Hispanic or Latino (of any race)	3,507	97.7
Central American, ex. Mexican	247	100.0
Honduran	152	100.0
Mexican	2,151	98.0
Puerto Rican	810	100.0
South American	278	87.7

Population Age 3–17 Enrolled in Private School
(Universe: Population Age 3–17 Enrolled in School)

Group	Number	%
Total Population	292	4.5
Hispanic or Latino (of any race)	84	2.3
Central American, ex. Mexican	0	0.0
Honduran	0	0.0
Mexican	45	2.0
Puerto Rican	0	0.0
South American	39	12.3

Foreign-Born Population

Group	Number	%
Total Population	7,239	25.0
Hispanic or Latino (of any race)	6,341	46.6
Central American, ex. Mexican	1,471	74.7
Honduran	893	74.7
Mexican	3,809	53.3
Puerto Rican	0	0.0
South American	911	65.1

Foreign-Born Naturalized U.S. Citizens

Group	Number	%
Total Population	1,409	19.5
Hispanic or Latino (of any race)	975	15.4
Central American, ex. Mexican	210	14.3
Honduran	89	10.0
Mexican	317	8.3
Puerto Rican	0	0.0
South American	343	37.7

Language Spoken at Home: English Only
(Universe: Population 5 Years and Over)

Group	Number	%
Total Population	14,551	56.0
Hispanic or Latino (of any race)	1,251	10.6
Central American, ex. Mexican	154	8.4
Honduran	104	9.4
Mexican	212	3.5
Puerto Rican	704	28.5
South American	131	11.1

Language Spoken at Home: Spanish
(Universe: Population 5 Years and Over)

Group	Number	%
Total Population	10,713	41.3
Hispanic or Latino (of any race)	10,516	89.3
Central American, ex. Mexican	1,681	91.6
Honduran	1,008	90.6
Mexican	5,772	96.5
Puerto Rican	1,765	71.5
South American	1,038	87.9

Unemployment Rate
(Universe: Population 16 Years and Over)

Group	%
Total Population	7.5
Hispanic or Latino (of any race)	3.8
Central American, ex. Mexican	1.8
Honduran	2.7
Mexican	3.2
Puerto Rican	11.4
South American	0.0

Class of Worker: Private Wage and Salary
(Universe: Civilian Employed Population 16 Years and Over)

Group	Number	%
Total Population	9,559	78.1
Hispanic or Latino (of any race)	5,257	87.8
Central American, ex. Mexican	1,157	86.9
Honduran	800	91.7
Mexican	2,735	93.6
Puerto Rican	639	71.6
South American	519	86.8

Class of Worker: Government
(Universe: Civilian Employed Population 16 Years and Over)

Group	Number	%
Total Population	2,178	17.8
Hispanic or Latino (of any race)	524	8.8
Central American, ex. Mexican	128	9.6
Honduran	59	6.8
Mexican	147	5.0
Puerto Rican	232	26.0
South American	0	0.0

Means of Transportation to Work: Car, Truck or Van
(Universe: Workers 16 Years and Over)

Group	Number	%
Total Population	8,643	74.4
Hispanic or Latino (of any race)	4,081	70.1
Central American, ex. Mexican	887	70.3
Honduran	586	73.1
Mexican	1,854	64.6
Puerto Rican	680	78.7
South American	493	84.6

Means of Transportation to Work: Public Transportation (ex. Taxicab)
(Universe: Workers 16 Years and Over)

Group	Number	%
Total Population	486	4.2
Hispanic or Latino (of any race)	271	4.7
Central American, ex. Mexican	33	2.6
Honduran	0	0.0
Mexican	238	8.3
Puerto Rican	0	0.0
South American	0	0.0

Notes: (1) Percent of total population; (2) Percent of Hispanic/Latino population; Profiles include places with an overall population of at least 125,000, OR an overall population of at least 25,000 where the Hispanic/Latino population is at least 20% of the overall population. In states where less than five places meet either of these criteria, we have included places with at least 10,000 total population with the highest percentage of Hispanic/Latino population. These places are identified with an asterisk (*); Please refer to the User's Guide for a full explanation of data.

Homeownership Rate
(Universe: Occupied Housing Units)

Group	%
Total Population	31.7
Hispanic or Latino (of any race)	23.6
Central American, ex. Mexican	24.9
Guatemalan	6.5
Honduran	27.3
Salvadoran	31.0
Dominican Republic	32.8
Mexican	19.6
Puerto Rican	24.1
South American	31.3
Colombian	28.6
Ecuadorian	40.9
Peruvian	28.1

Median Home Value

Group	Dollars
Total Population	219,100
Hispanic or Latino (of any race)	217,300
Central American, ex. Mexican	228,400
Honduran	324,600
Mexican	195,900
Puerto Rican	211,600
South American	242,500

Median Gross Rent

Group	Dollars
Total Population	960
Hispanic or Latino (of any race)	1,052
Central American, ex. Mexican	1,088
Honduran	1,087
Mexican	1,116
Puerto Rican	1,002
South American	884

Median Household Income
(2010 Inflation-Adjusted Dollars)

Group	Dollars
Total Population	36,153
Hispanic or Latino (of any race)	36,717
Central American, ex. Mexican	61,419
Honduran	60,405
Mexican	34,591
Puerto Rican	28,894
South American	39,955

Per Capita Income
(2010 Inflation-Adjusted Dollars)

Group	Dollars
Total Population	15,897
Hispanic or Latino (of any race)	12,577
Central American, ex. Mexican	18,108
Honduran	17,530
Mexican	10,138
Puerto Rican	13,259
South American	15,157

Households with $100,000+ Income

Group	Number	%
Total Population	958	10.5
Hispanic or Latino (of any race)	332	10.3
Central American, ex. Mexican	153	29.3
Honduran	84	26.1
Mexican	66	5.0
Puerto Rican	59	6.6
South American	42	10.6

Households with Food Stamps/SNAP Benefits During Past 12 Months

Group	Number	%
Total Population	1,782	19.5
Hispanic or Latino (of any race)	550	17.1
Central American, ex. Mexican	17	3.3
Honduran	17	5.3
Mexican	136	10.3
Puerto Rican	323	36.3
South American	56	14.1

Poverty Rate
(Income in Past 12 Months Below Poverty Level)

Group	%
Total Population	25.8
Hispanic or Latino (of any race)	25.5
Central American, ex. Mexican	2.4
Honduran	3.8
Mexican	29.7
Puerto Rican	35.0
South American	19.2

North Hempstead

Population

Group	Number	%TP[1]	%HP[2]
Total Population	226,322	100.0	–
Hispanic or Latino (of any race)	29,074	12.8	100.0
Central American, ex. Mexican	11,455	5.1	39.4
Costa Rican	124	0.1	0.4
Guatemalan	1,193	0.5	4.1
Honduran	1,572	0.7	5.4
Nicaraguan	110	<0.1	0.4
Salvadoran	8,262	3.7	28.4
Cuban	660	0.3	2.3
Dominican Republic	1,362	0.6	4.7
Mexican	3,488	1.5	12.0
Puerto Rican	2,705	1.2	9.3
South American	6,333	2.8	21.8
Argentinean	435	0.2	1.5
Chilean	664	0.3	2.3
Colombian	1,914	0.8	6.6
Ecuadorian	1,966	0.9	6.8
Paraguayan	140	0.1	0.5
Peruvian	925	0.4	3.2
Spaniard	519	0.2	1.8

Population Growth: 2000–2010

Group	%
Total Population	1.7
Hispanic or Latino (of any race)	32.9
Central American, ex. Mexican	74.3
Guatemalan	116.9
Honduran	164.6
Salvadoran	65.5
Cuban	25.5
Dominican Republic	57.6
Mexican	45.2
Puerto Rican	22.5
South American	70.8
Argentinean	46.5
Chilean	27.4
Colombian	57.0
Ecuadorian	141.2
Peruvian	102.4
Spaniard	129.6

Males per 100 Females

Group	Number
Total Population	94.5
Hispanic or Latino (of any race)	106.1
Central American, ex. Mexican	116.6
Costa Rican	77.1
Guatemalan	108.6
Honduran	134.3
Nicaraguan	74.6
Salvadoran	116.9
Cuban	88.6
Dominican Republic	90.8
Mexican	123.2
Puerto Rican	91.6
South American	92.1
Argentinean	101.4
Chilean	109.5
Colombian	72.4
Ecuadorian	113.9
Paraguayan	77.2
Peruvian	85.7
Spaniard	112.7

Average Household Size

Group	People
Total Population	2.87
Hispanic or Latino (of any race)	4.29
Central American, ex. Mexican	5.32
Costa Rican	3.44
Guatemalan	4.28
Honduran	5.64
Nicaraguan	4.67
Salvadoran	5.53
Cuban	2.94
Dominican Republic	3.94
Mexican	5.55
Puerto Rican	2.99
South American	3.64
Argentinean	2.98
Chilean	3.36
Colombian	3.23
Ecuadorian	4.32
Paraguayan	4.34
Peruvian	3.85
Spaniard	2.92

Median Age

Group	Years
Total Population	42.4
Hispanic or Latino (of any race)	30.4
Central American, ex. Mexican	29.8
Costa Rican	42.0
Guatemalan	30.9
Honduran	29.1
Nicaraguan	34.3
Salvadoran	29.6
Cuban	38.9
Dominican Republic	32.2
Mexican	25.5
Puerto Rican	34.8
South American	36.4
Argentinean	42.9
Chilean	37.8
Colombian	39.0
Ecuadorian	31.8
Paraguayan	36.5
Peruvian	39.4
Spaniard	38.3

High School Graduates
(Universe: Population 25 Years and Over)

Group	Number	%
Total Population	138,858	90.2
Hispanic or Latino (of any race)	10,472	67.0
Central American, ex. Mexican	2,964	48.7
Guatemalan	374	54.6
Salvadoran	2,155	45.1
Cuban	618	86.4
Dominican Republic	437	75.0
Mexican	613	45.0
Puerto Rican	1,625	87.3
South American	3,508	84.5
Colombian	1,461	86.7
Ecuadorian	707	73.6

Four-Year College Graduates
(Universe: Population 25 Years and Over)

Group	Number	%
Total Population	79,244	51.5
Hispanic or Latino (of any race)	3,537	22.6
Central American, ex. Mexican	536	8.8
Guatemalan	117	17.1
Salvadoran	343	7.2
Cuban	447	62.5
Dominican Republic	188	32.2
Mexican	197	14.5
Puerto Rican	549	29.5
South American	1,284	30.9
Colombian	556	33.0
Ecuadorian	186	19.4

Population Age 3–17 Enrolled in Public School
(Universe: Population Age 3–17 Enrolled in School)

Group	Number	%
Total Population	36,324	81.1
Hispanic or Latino (of any race)	5,846	90.5
Central American, ex. Mexican	2,590	98.8
Guatemalan	419	100.0
Salvadoran	1,884	100.0
Cuban	95	54.3
Dominican Republic	279	62.7
Mexican	625	94.0
Puerto Rican	712	89.3
South American	1,212	90.2
Colombian	461	84.3
Ecuadorian	251	91.3

Notes: (1) Percent of total population; (2) Percent of Hispanic/Latino population; Profiles include places with an overall population of at least 125,000, OR an overall population of at least 25,000 where the Hispanic/Latino population is at least 20% of the overall population. In states where less than five places meet either of these criteria, we have included places with at least 10,000 total population with the highest percentage of Hispanic/Latino population. These places are identified with an asterisk (*); Please refer to the User's Guide for a full explanation of data.

Population Age 3–17 Enrolled in Private School
(Universe: Population Age 3–17 Enrolled in School)

Group	Number	%
Total Population	8,439	18.9
Hispanic or Latino (of any race)	615	9.5
Central American, ex. Mexican	32	1.2
Guatemalan	0	0.0
Salvadoran	0	0.0
Cuban	80	45.7
Dominican Republic	166	37.3
Mexican	40	6.0
Puerto Rican	85	10.7
South American	131	9.8
Colombian	86	15.7
Ecuadorian	24	8.7

Foreign-Born Population

Group	Number	%
Total Population	61,137	27.3
Hispanic or Latino (of any race)	14,275	53.0
Central American, ex. Mexican	6,910	65.1
Guatemalan	755	55.3
Salvadoran	5,329	67.5
Cuban	268	26.4
Dominican Republic	547	44.4
Mexican	1,457	59.7
Puerto Rican	23	0.7
South American	4,411	66.2
Colombian	1,438	55.6
Ecuadorian	1,206	73.1

Foreign-Born Naturalized U.S. Citizens

Group	Number	%
Total Population	38,683	63.3
Hispanic or Latino (of any race)	5,593	39.2
Central American, ex. Mexican	2,149	31.1
Guatemalan	402	53.2
Salvadoran	1,550	29.1
Cuban	268	100.0
Dominican Republic	447	81.7
Mexican	189	13.0
Puerto Rican	23	100.0
South American	2,277	51.6
Colombian	883	61.4
Ecuadorian	398	33.0

Language Spoken at Home: English Only
(Universe: Population 5 Years and Over)

Group	Number	%
Total Population	132,054	62.4
Hispanic or Latino (of any race)	4,064	16.4
Central American, ex. Mexican	390	4.0
Guatemalan	29	2.2
Salvadoran	306	4.2
Cuban	444	49.0
Dominican Republic	63	5.5
Mexican	354	15.6
Puerto Rican	1,467	47.4
South American	868	13.9
Colombian	475	20.2
Ecuadorian	98	6.2

Language Spoken at Home: Spanish
(Universe: Population 5 Years and Over)

Group	Number	%
Total Population	22,740	10.7
Hispanic or Latino (of any race)	20,571	83.1
Central American, ex. Mexican	9,276	96.0
Guatemalan	1,275	97.8
Salvadoran	6,932	95.8
Cuban	436	48.1
Dominican Republic	1,082	94.5
Mexican	1,912	84.3
Puerto Rican	1,606	51.9
South American	5,322	85.4
Colombian	1,839	78.1
Ecuadorian	1,473	93.8

Unemployment Rate
(Universe: Population 16 Years and Over)

Group	%
Total Population	6.1
Hispanic or Latino (of any race)	7.1
Central American, ex. Mexican	8.4
Guatemalan	14.3
Salvadoran	6.9
Cuban	8.8
Dominican Republic	9.5
Mexican	0.3
Puerto Rican	11.1
South American	4.7
Colombian	5.4
Ecuadorian	8.4

Class of Worker: Private Wage and Salary
(Universe: Civilian Employed Population 16 Years and Over)

Group	Number	%
Total Population	82,058	77.3
Hispanic or Latino (of any race)	11,559	81.9
Central American, ex. Mexican	4,651	85.4
Guatemalan	438	67.1
Salvadoran	3,738	89.7
Cuban	488	84.6
Dominican Republic	337	80.0
Mexican	1,095	85.7
Puerto Rican	1,079	65.0
South American	3,283	81.9
Colombian	1,183	79.1
Ecuadorian	923	85.7

Class of Worker: Government
(Universe: Civilian Employed Population 16 Years and Over)

Group	Number	%
Total Population	15,527	14.6
Hispanic or Latino (of any race)	1,301	9.2
Central American, ex. Mexican	354	6.5
Guatemalan	96	14.7
Salvadoran	167	4.0
Cuban	57	9.9
Dominican Republic	64	15.2
Mexican	29	2.3
Puerto Rican	477	28.8
South American	242	6.0
Colombian	100	6.7
Ecuadorian	42	3.9

Means of Transportation to Work: Car, Truck or Van
(Universe: Workers 16 Years and Over)

Group	Number	%
Total Population	74,534	72.2
Hispanic or Latino (of any race)	8,989	65.8
Central American, ex. Mexican	3,511	66.4
Guatemalan	364	62.8
Salvadoran	2,764	67.3
Cuban	458	79.4
Dominican Republic	299	73.3
Mexican	676	52.9
Puerto Rican	1,066	65.0
South American	2,431	64.1
Colombian	955	63.9
Ecuadorian	582	56.2

Means of Transportation to Work: Public Transportation (ex. Taxicab)
(Universe: Workers 16 Years and Over)

Group	Number	%
Total Population	20,112	19.5
Hispanic or Latino (of any race)	2,706	19.8
Central American, ex. Mexican	1,080	20.4
Guatemalan	106	18.3
Salvadoran	787	19.1
Cuban	93	16.1
Dominican Republic	109	26.7
Mexican	210	16.4
Puerto Rican	341	20.8
South American	844	22.2
Colombian	395	26.4
Ecuadorian	217	21.0

Homeownership Rate
(Universe: Occupied Housing Units)

Group	%
Total Population	78.1
Hispanic or Latino (of any race)	46.0
Central American, ex. Mexican	34.2
Costa Rican	44.4
Guatemalan	18.9
Honduran	30.7
Nicaraguan	38.1
Salvadoran	36.8
Cuban	71.4
Dominican Republic	62.1
Mexican	28.4
Puerto Rican	61.1
South American	51.2
Argentinean	70.6
Chilean	36.9
Colombian	56.0
Ecuadorian	42.2
Paraguayan	44.8
Peruvian	52.7
Spaniard	84.0

Median Home Value

Group	Dollars
Total Population	659,200
Hispanic or Latino (of any race)	480,300
Central American, ex. Mexican	413,600
Guatemalan	–
Salvadoran	398,500
Cuban	545,000
Dominican Republic	563,800
Mexican	717,700
Puerto Rican	473,700
South American	538,900
Colombian	508,300
Ecuadorian	529,800

Median Gross Rent

Group	Dollars
Total Population	1,484
Hispanic or Latino (of any race)	1,453
Central American, ex. Mexican	1,541
Guatemalan	1,585
Salvadoran	1,678
Cuban	1,318
Dominican Republic	–
Mexican	1,372
Puerto Rican	1,407
South American	1,456
Colombian	1,508
Ecuadorian	1,551

Median Household Income
(2010 Inflation-Adjusted Dollars)

Group	Dollars
Total Population	100,760
Hispanic or Latino (of any race)	68,484
Central American, ex. Mexican	57,462
Guatemalan	37,083
Salvadoran	61,563
Cuban	129,375
Dominican Republic	107,583
Mexican	39,762
Puerto Rican	90,230
South American	75,587
Colombian	81,932
Ecuadorian	63,375

Per Capita Income
(2010 Inflation-Adjusted Dollars)

Group	Dollars
Total Population	51,663
Hispanic or Latino (of any race)	23,051
Central American, ex. Mexican	15,353
Guatemalan	16,381
Salvadoran	15,142
Cuban	52,895
Dominican Republic	26,686
Mexican	17,220
Puerto Rican	29,949
South American	27,315
Colombian	23,205
Ecuadorian	22,901

Households with $100,000+ Income

Group	Number	%
Total Population	38,966	50.5
Hispanic or Latino (of any race)	1,982	31.1
Central American, ex. Mexican	435	19.7
Guatemalan	51	13.7
Salvadoran	336	20.7
Cuban	157	58.1
Dominican Republic	134	50.2

Notes: (1) Percent of total population; (2) Percent of Hispanic/Latino population; Profiles include places with an overall population of at least 125,000, OR an overall population of at least 25,000 where the Hispanic/Latino population is at least 20% of the overall population. In states where less than five places meet either of these criteria, we have included places with at least 10,000 total population with the highest percentage of Hispanic/Latino population. These places are identified with an asterisk (*); Please refer to the User's Guide for a full explanation of data.

Mexican	109	22.0
Puerto Rican	327	38.9
South American	684	35.8
Colombian	298	39.7
Ecuadorian	98	23.7

Households with Food Stamps/SNAP Benefits During Past 12 Months

Group	Number	%
Total Population	1,745	2.3
Hispanic or Latino (of any race)	416	6.5
Central American, ex. Mexican	135	6.1
Guatemalan	0	0.0
Salvadoran	100	6.2
Cuban	0	0.0
Dominican Republic	37	13.9
Mexican	116	23.4
Puerto Rican	50	5.9
South American	78	4.1
Colombian	49	6.5
Ecuadorian	29	7.0

Poverty Rate
(Income in Past 12 Months Below Poverty Level)

Group	%
Total Population	4.7
Hispanic or Latino (of any race)	13.1
Central American, ex. Mexican	21.0
Guatemalan	12.9
Salvadoran	21.6
Cuban	0.0
Dominican Republic	1.7
Mexican	14.9
Puerto Rican	12.4
South American	6.5
Colombian	4.6
Ecuadorian	6.1

Ossining (town)

Population

Group	Number	%TP[1]	%HP[2]
Total Population	37,674	100.0	–
Hispanic or Latino (of any race)	11,403	30.3	100.0
Central American, ex. Mexican	694	1.8	6.1
Guatemalan	422	1.1	3.7
Honduran	104	0.3	0.9
Cuban	234	0.6	2.1
Dominican Republic	664	1.8	5.8
Mexican	482	1.3	4.2
Puerto Rican	1,452	3.9	12.7
South American	6,825	18.1	59.9
Chilean	190	0.5	1.7
Colombian	805	2.1	7.1
Ecuadorian	4,988	13.2	43.7
Peruvian	411	1.1	3.6
Uruguayan	273	0.7	2.4
Spaniard	110	0.3	1.0

Population Growth: 2000–2010

Group	%
Total Population	3.1
Hispanic or Latino (of any race)	56.6
Central American, ex. Mexican	123.9
Guatemalan	237.6
Cuban	27.2
Dominican Republic	47.2
Mexican	129.5
Puerto Rican	4.2
South American	132.0
Chilean	19.5
Colombian	65.6
Ecuadorian	174.4
Peruvian	263.7
Uruguayan	33.2

Males per 100 Females

Group	Number
Total Population	104.3
Hispanic or Latino (of any race)	121.9
Central American, ex. Mexican	121.7
Guatemalan	135.8
Honduran	121.3
Cuban	93.4
Dominican Republic	93.0
Mexican	100.8
Puerto Rican	131.6
South American	126.4
Chilean	134.6
Colombian	77.7
Ecuadorian	143.3
Peruvian	99.5
Uruguayan	93.6
Spaniard	93.0

Average Household Size

Group	People
Total Population	2.72
Hispanic or Latino (of any race)	3.89
Central American, ex. Mexican	3.91
Guatemalan	4.13
Honduran	3.76
Cuban	2.76
Dominican Republic	3.35
Mexican	3.62
Puerto Rican	3.01
South American	4.25
Chilean	3.36
Colombian	3.21
Ecuadorian	4.68
Peruvian	3.92
Uruguayan	3.04
Spaniard	2.66

Median Age

Group	Years
Total Population	39.3
Hispanic or Latino (of any race)	30.4
Central American, ex. Mexican	29.8
Guatemalan	27.9
Honduran	31.3
Cuban	35.3
Dominican Republic	29.3
Mexican	28.2
Puerto Rican	33.1
South American	31.1
Chilean	41.4
Colombian	34.8
Ecuadorian	30.1
Peruvian	35.6
Uruguayan	40.1
Spaniard	43.3

High School Graduates
(Universe: Population 25 Years and Over)

Group	Number	%
Total Population	21,505	82.3
Hispanic or Latino (of any race)	3,675	54.8
Puerto Rican	667	63.7
South American	2,127	49.8
Ecuadorian	1,095	37.6

Four-Year College Graduates
(Universe: Population 25 Years and Over)

Group	Number	%
Total Population	12,011	46.0
Hispanic or Latino (of any race)	1,367	20.4
Puerto Rican	221	21.1
South American	845	19.8
Ecuadorian	458	15.7

Population Age 3–17 Enrolled in Public School
(Universe: Population Age 3–17 Enrolled in School)

Group	Number	%
Total Population	5,251	82.5
Hispanic or Latino (of any race)	1,902	93.0
Puerto Rican	348	93.3
South American	1,293	95.2
Ecuadorian	846	95.5

Population Age 3–17 Enrolled in Private School
(Universe: Population Age 3–17 Enrolled in School)

Group	Number	%
Total Population	1,114	17.5
Hispanic or Latino (of any race)	143	7.0
Puerto Rican	25	6.7
South American	65	4.8
Ecuadorian	40	4.5

Foreign-Born Population

Group	Number	%
Total Population	10,556	28.3
Hispanic or Latino (of any race)	6,315	59.2
Puerto Rican	82	4.0
South American	4,889	73.6
Ecuadorian	3,378	75.7

Foreign-Born Naturalized U.S. Citizens

Group	Number	%
Total Population	4,123	39.1
Hispanic or Latino (of any race)	1,409	22.3
Puerto Rican	0	0.0
South American	892	18.2
Ecuadorian	470	13.9

Language Spoken at Home: English Only
(Universe: Population 5 Years and Over)

Group	Number	%
Total Population	21,485	61.2
Hispanic or Latino (of any race)	1,117	11.7
Puerto Rican	484	28.8
South American	274	4.5
Ecuadorian	150	3.7

Language Spoken at Home: Spanish
(Universe: Population 5 Years and Over)

Group	Number	%
Total Population	9,176	26.1
Hispanic or Latino (of any race)	8,412	87.9
Puerto Rican	1,195	71.2
South American	5,742	94.8
Ecuadorian	3,890	96.3

Unemployment Rate
(Universe: Population 16 Years and Over)

Group	%
Total Population	7.0
Hispanic or Latino (of any race)	8.2
Puerto Rican	5.3
South American	7.6
Ecuadorian	9.3

Class of Worker: Private Wage and Salary
(Universe: Civilian Employed Population 16 Years and Over)

Group	Number	%
Total Population	14,773	80.3
Hispanic or Latino (of any race)	4,829	82.8
Puerto Rican	601	82.7
South American	3,307	81.8
Ecuadorian	2,078	77.6

Class of Worker: Government
(Universe: Civilian Employed Population 16 Years and Over)

Group	Number	%
Total Population	2,263	12.3
Hispanic or Latino (of any race)	443	7.6
Puerto Rican	105	14.4
South American	221	5.5
Ecuadorian	108	4.0

Means of Transportation to Work: Car, Truck or Van
(Universe: Workers 16 Years and Over)

Group	Number	%
Total Population	13,133	73.2
Hispanic or Latino (of any race)	4,120	73.3
Puerto Rican	558	80.6
South American	2,860	74.0
Ecuadorian	1,762	69.0

Means of Transportation to Work: Public Transportation (ex. Taxicab)
(Universe: Workers 16 Years and Over)

Group	Number	%
Total Population	3,052	17.0
Hispanic or Latino (of any race)	790	14.1
Puerto Rican	104	15.0
South American	510	13.2
Ecuadorian	393	15.4

Homeownership Rate
(Universe: Occupied Housing Units)

Group	%
Total Population	64.2

Notes: (1) Percent of total population; (2) Percent of Hispanic/Latino population; Profiles include places with an overall population of at least 125,000, OR an overall population of at least 25,000 where the Hispanic/Latino population is at least 20% of the overall population. In states where less than five places meet either of these criteria, we have included places with at least 10,000 total population with the highest percentage of Hispanic/Latino population. These places are identified with an asterisk (*); Please refer to the User's Guide for a full explanation of data.

Group	%
Hispanic or Latino (of any race)	31.9
Central American, ex. Mexican	21.2
Guatemalan	11.3
Honduran	16.0
Cuban	56.3
Dominican Republic	38.0
Mexican	35.8
Puerto Rican	46.5
South American	26.7
Chilean	26.6
Colombian	27.4
Ecuadorian	24.9
Peruvian	35.4
Uruguayan	30.3
Spaniard	61.4

Median Home Value

Group	Dollars
Total Population	483,500
Hispanic or Latino (of any race)	511,700
Puerto Rican	360,700
South American	592,600
Ecuadorian	596,400

Median Gross Rent

Group	Dollars
Total Population	1,278
Hispanic or Latino (of any race)	1,213
Puerto Rican	1,256
South American	1,229
Ecuadorian	1,338

Median Household Income
(2010 Inflation-Adjusted Dollars)

Group	Dollars
Total Population	85,749
Hispanic or Latino (of any race)	54,093
Puerto Rican	55,179
South American	50,738
Ecuadorian	48,402

Per Capita Income
(2010 Inflation-Adjusted Dollars)

Group	Dollars
Total Population	43,721
Hispanic or Latino (of any race)	17,843
Puerto Rican	20,861
South American	15,004
Ecuadorian	12,859

Households with $100,000+ Income

Group	Number	%
Total Population	5,644	44.2
Hispanic or Latino (of any race)	574	20.2
Puerto Rican	128	31.7
South American	232	12.7
Ecuadorian	75	7.2

Households with Food Stamps/SNAP Benefits During Past 12 Months

Group	Number	%
Total Population	272	2.1
Hispanic or Latino (of any race)	134	4.7
Puerto Rican	29	7.2
South American	105	5.7
Ecuadorian	105	10.1

Poverty Rate
(Income in Past 12 Months Below Poverty Level)

Group	%
Total Population	12.3
Hispanic or Latino (of any race)	30.4
Puerto Rican	31.1
South American	32.6
Ecuadorian	40.9

Ossining (village)

Population

Group	Number	%TP[1]	%HP[2]
Total Population	25,060	100.0	–
Hispanic or Latino (of any race)	10,375	41.4	100.0
Central American, ex. Mexican	640	2.6	6.2
Guatemalan	395	1.6	3.8
Honduran	102	0.4	1.0
Cuban	170	0.7	1.6
Dominican Republic	575	2.3	5.5
Mexican	421	1.7	4.1
Puerto Rican	1,183	4.7	11.4
South American	6,440	25.7	62.1
Chilean	169	0.7	1.6
Colombian	703	2.8	6.8
Ecuadorian	4,840	19.3	46.7
Peruvian	381	1.5	3.7
Uruguayan	230	0.9	2.2

Population Growth: 2000–2010

Group	%
Total Population	4.4
Hispanic or Latino (of any race)	55.9
Central American, ex. Mexican	128.6
Guatemalan	255.9
Cuban	28.8
Dominican Republic	35.9
Mexican	150.6
Puerto Rican	-0.9
South American	128.4
Chilean	11.2
Colombian	54.2
Ecuadorian	169.5
Uruguayan	28.5

Males per 100 Females

Group	Number
Total Population	113.0
Hispanic or Latino (of any race)	127.2
Central American, ex. Mexican	128.6
Guatemalan	143.8
Honduran	117.0
Cuban	107.3
Dominican Republic	101.0
Mexican	110.5
Puerto Rican	144.4
South American	128.6
Chilean	141.4
Colombian	81.2
Ecuadorian	144.0
Peruvian	98.4
Uruguayan	91.7

Average Household Size

Group	People
Total Population	2.78
Hispanic or Latino (of any race)	3.96
Central American, ex. Mexican	3.92
Guatemalan	4.12
Honduran	3.88
Cuban	2.70
Dominican Republic	3.28
Mexican	3.89
Puerto Rican	3.03
South American	4.30
Chilean	3.28
Colombian	3.24
Ecuadorian	4.70
Peruvian	3.92
Uruguayan	3.07

Median Age

Group	Years
Total Population	36.6
Hispanic or Latino (of any race)	30.4
Central American, ex. Mexican	29.9
Guatemalan	28.0
Honduran	31.3
Cuban	35.0
Dominican Republic	30.0
Mexican	28.4
Puerto Rican	34.3
South American	31.1
Chilean	42.3
Colombian	36.4
Ecuadorian	30.1
Peruvian	35.4
Uruguayan	40.3

High School Graduates
(Universe: Population 25 Years and Over)

Group	Number	%
Total Population	13,383	76.5
Hispanic or Latino (of any race)	3,166	53.1
Puerto Rican	636	64.0
South American	1,810	47.7
Ecuadorian	956	36.0

Four-Year College Graduates
(Universe: Population 25 Years and Over)

Group	Number	%
Total Population	6,247	35.7
Hispanic or Latino (of any race)	1,070	18.0
Puerto Rican	200	20.1
South American	681	18.0
Ecuadorian	400	15.1

Population Age 3–17 Enrolled in Public School
(Universe: Population Age 3–17 Enrolled in School)

Group	Number	%
Total Population	3,349	87.0
Hispanic or Latino (of any race)	1,753	93.8
Puerto Rican	348	93.3
South American	1,178	94.8
Ecuadorian	791	95.2

Population Age 3–17 Enrolled in Private School
(Universe: Population Age 3–17 Enrolled in School)

Group	Number	%
Total Population	502	13.0
Hispanic or Latino (of any race)	115	6.2
Puerto Rican	25	6.7
South American	65	5.2
Ecuadorian	40	4.8

Foreign-Born Population

Group	Number	%
Total Population	8,609	34.7
Hispanic or Latino (of any race)	5,714	59.4
Puerto Rican	82	4.1
South American	4,458	74.8
Ecuadorian	3,133	76.5

Foreign-Born Naturalized U.S. Citizens

Group	Number	%
Total Population	2,816	32.7
Hispanic or Latino (of any race)	1,112	19.5
Puerto Rican	0	0.0
South American	700	15.7
Ecuadorian	425	13.6

Language Spoken at Home: English Only
(Universe: Population 5 Years and Over)

Group	Number	%
Total Population	12,020	52.0
Hispanic or Latino (of any race)	961	11.2
Puerto Rican	472	29.3
South American	229	4.2
Ecuadorian	105	2.8

Language Spoken at Home: Spanish
(Universe: Population 5 Years and Over)

Group	Number	%
Total Population	8,081	35.0
Hispanic or Latino (of any race)	7,600	88.3
Puerto Rican	1,141	70.7
South American	5,177	95.1
Ecuadorian	3,622	97.2

Unemployment Rate
(Universe: Population 16 Years and Over)

Group	%
Total Population	8.1
Hispanic or Latino (of any race)	8.4
Puerto Rican	5.5
South American	7.8
Ecuadorian	9.7

Class of Worker: Private Wage and Salary
(Universe: Civilian Employed Population 16 Years and Over)

Group	Number	%
Total Population	10,297	80.7
Hispanic or Latino (of any race)	4,313	82.3
Puerto Rican	601	85.1

Notes: (1) Percent of total population; (2) Percent of Hispanic/Latino population; Profiles include places with an overall population of at least 125,000, OR an overall population of at least 25,000 where the Hispanic/Latino population is at least 20% of the overall population. In states where less than five places meet either of these criteria, we have included places with at least 10,000 total population with the highest percentage of Hispanic/Latino population. These places are identified with an asterisk (*); Please refer to the User's Guide for a full explanation of data.

South American	2,919	79.8
Ecuadorian	1,893	76.0

Class of Worker: Government
(Universe: Civilian Employed Population 16 Years and Over)

Group	Number	%
Total Population	1,504	11.8
Hispanic or Latino (of any race)	408	7.8
Puerto Rican	105	14.9
South American	221	6.0
Ecuadorian	108	4.3

Means of Transportation to Work: Car, Truck or Van
(Universe: Workers 16 Years and Over)

Group	Number	%
Total Population	9,381	75.9
Hispanic or Latino (of any race)	3,661	72.9
Puerto Rican	558	83.2
South American	2,555	73.4
Ecuadorian	1,577	66.6

Means of Transportation to Work: Public Transportation (ex. Taxicab)
(Universe: Workers 16 Years and Over)

Group	Number	%
Total Population	1,764	14.3
Hispanic or Latino (of any race)	656	13.1
Puerto Rican	83	12.4
South American	427	12.3
Ecuadorian	393	16.6

Homeownership Rate
(Universe: Occupied Housing Units)

Group	%
Total Population	53.1
Hispanic or Latino (of any race)	28.5
Central American, ex. Mexican	19.0
Guatemalan	10.9
Honduran	12.5
Cuban	48.2
Dominican Republic	34.2
Mexican	28.4
Puerto Rican	39.2
South American	25.4
Chilean	26.7
Colombian	25.5
Ecuadorian	24.0
Peruvian	34.0
Uruguayan	30.2

Median Home Value

Group	Dollars
Total Population	426,700
Hispanic or Latino (of any race)	407,300
Puerto Rican	343,400
South American	578,200
Ecuadorian	575,800

Median Gross Rent

Group	Dollars
Total Population	1,288
Hispanic or Latino (of any race)	1,230
Puerto Rican	1,256
South American	1,250
Ecuadorian	1,338

Median Household Income
(2010 Inflation-Adjusted Dollars)

Group	Dollars
Total Population	70,864
Hispanic or Latino (of any race)	53,022
Puerto Rican	39,050
South American	49,684
Ecuadorian	47,176

Per Capita Income
(2010 Inflation-Adjusted Dollars)

Group	Dollars
Total Population	31,192
Hispanic or Latino (of any race)	15,557
Puerto Rican	15,442
South American	14,366
Ecuadorian	12,480

Households with $100,000+ Income

Group	Number	%
Total Population	2,905	33.9
Hispanic or Latino (of any race)	422	16.6
Puerto Rican	107	27.9
South American	193	11.5
Ecuadorian	69	7.1

Households with Food Stamps/SNAP Benefits During Past 12 Months

Group	Number	%
Total Population	244	2.9
Hispanic or Latino (of any race)	134	5.3
Puerto Rican	29	7.6
South American	105	6.3
Ecuadorian	105	10.8

Poverty Rate
(Income in Past 12 Months Below Poverty Level)

Group	%
Total Population	16.0
Hispanic or Latino (of any race)	33.7
Puerto Rican	32.0
South American	36.3
Ecuadorian	44.7

Oyster Bay

Population

Group	Number	%TP[1]	%HP[2]
Total Population	293,214	100.0	–
Hispanic or Latino (of any race)	21,923	7.5	100.0
Central American, ex. Mexican	4,958	1.7	22.6
Costa Rican	101	<0.1	0.5
Guatemalan	397	0.1	1.8
Honduran	952	0.3	4.3
Salvadoran	3,297	1.1	15.0
Cuban	906	0.3	4.1
Dominican Republic	1,429	0.5	6.5
Mexican	1,550	0.5	7.1
Puerto Rican	4,810	1.6	21.9
South American	5,752	2.0	26.2
Argentinean	441	0.2	2.0
Bolivian	110	<0.1	0.5
Chilean	569	0.2	2.6
Colombian	2,035	0.7	9.3
Ecuadorian	1,082	0.4	4.9
Peruvian	1,156	0.4	5.3
Uruguayan	134	<0.1	0.6
Venezuelan	129	<0.1	0.6
Spaniard	693	0.2	3.2

Population Growth: 2000–2010

Group	%
Total Population	-0.2
Hispanic or Latino (of any race)	47.4
Central American, ex. Mexican	90.1
Guatemalan	200.8
Honduran	199.4
Salvadoran	73.7
Cuban	21.3
Dominican Republic	190.4
Mexican	83.9
Puerto Rican	37.2
South American	88.5
Argentinean	82.2
Chilean	39.1
Colombian	90.9
Ecuadorian	145.4
Peruvian	114.9
Spaniard	264.7

Males per 100 Females

Group	Number
Total Population	94.0
Hispanic or Latino (of any race)	94.8
Central American, ex. Mexican	117.9
Costa Rican	110.4
Guatemalan	100.5
Honduran	157.3
Salvadoran	113.5
Cuban	94.0
Dominican Republic	80.0
Mexican	110.0
Puerto Rican	89.1
South American	82.0
Argentinean	109.0
Bolivian	74.6
Chilean	100.4
Colombian	76.0
Ecuadorian	83.4
Peruvian	75.2
Uruguayan	100.0
Venezuelan	69.7
Spaniard	92.5

Average Household Size

Group	People
Total Population	2.89
Hispanic or Latino (of any race)	3.81
Central American, ex. Mexican	4.99
Costa Rican	3.32
Guatemalan	4.17
Honduran	5.08
Salvadoran	5.27
Cuban	2.99
Dominican Republic	4.26
Mexican	4.31
Puerto Rican	3.21
South American	3.67
Argentinean	3.36
Bolivian	3.97
Chilean	3.73
Colombian	3.56
Ecuadorian	3.78
Peruvian	3.90
Uruguayan	3.80
Venezuelan	3.38
Spaniard	2.97

Median Age

Group	Years
Total Population	43.1
Hispanic or Latino (of any race)	31.0
Central American, ex. Mexican	29.2
Costa Rican	36.3
Guatemalan	29.1
Honduran	27.3
Salvadoran	29.5
Cuban	40.7
Dominican Republic	28.4
Mexican	26.9
Puerto Rican	31.9
South American	37.3
Argentinean	42.1
Bolivian	34.3
Chilean	37.4
Colombian	36.1
Ecuadorian	36.8
Peruvian	37.2
Uruguayan	46.0
Venezuelan	40.1
Spaniard	35.9

High School Graduates
(Universe: Population 25 Years and Over)

Group	Number	%
Total Population	188,344	93.2
Hispanic or Latino (of any race)	10,345	84.0
Central American, ex. Mexican	1,318	63.0
Salvadoran	741	56.0
Cuban	791	97.4
Dominican Republic	494	68.1
Mexican	518	57.6
Puerto Rican	2,657	94.0
South American	3,531	91.5
Colombian	1,008	87.4
Ecuadorian	670	89.9
Peruvian	819	98.7
Spaniard	514	91.3

Four-Year College Graduates
(Universe: Population 25 Years and Over)

Group	Number	%
Total Population	89,073	44.1
Hispanic or Latino (of any race)	3,109	25.2
Central American, ex. Mexican	436	20.8
Salvadoran	241	18.2

Notes: (1) Percent of total population; (2) Percent of Hispanic/Latino population; Profiles include places with an overall population of at least 125,000, OR an overall population of at least 25,000 where the Hispanic/Latino population is at least 20% of the overall population. In states where less than five places meet either of these criteria, we have included places with at least 10,000 total population with the highest percentage of Hispanic/Latino population. These places are identified with an asterisk (*); Please refer to the User's Guide for a full explanation of data.

Cuban	352	43.3
Dominican Republic	163	22.5
Mexican	73	8.1
Puerto Rican	732	25.9
South American	978	25.3
Colombian	197	17.1
Ecuadorian	253	34.0
Peruvian	202	24.3
Spaniard	231	41.0

Population Age 3–17 Enrolled in Public School
(Universe: Population Age 3–17 Enrolled in School)

Group	Number	%
Total Population	46,067	82.6
Hispanic or Latino (of any race)	4,039	85.3
Central American, ex. Mexican	625	92.6
Salvadoran	454	95.2
Cuban	177	75.6
Dominican Republic	136	85.0
Mexican	441	91.1
Puerto Rican	974	81.2
South American	1,159	82.4
Colombian	398	92.3
Ecuadorian	156	66.1
Peruvian	314	91.5
Spaniard	141	94.0

Population Age 3–17 Enrolled in Private School
(Universe: Population Age 3–17 Enrolled in School)

Group	Number	%
Total Population	9,705	17.4
Hispanic or Latino (of any race)	696	14.7
Central American, ex. Mexican	50	7.4
Salvadoran	23	4.8
Cuban	57	24.4
Dominican Republic	24	15.0
Mexican	43	8.9
Puerto Rican	226	18.8
South American	248	17.6
Colombian	33	7.7
Ecuadorian	80	33.9
Peruvian	29	8.5
Spaniard	9	6.0

Foreign-Born Population

Group	Number	%
Total Population	41,716	14.3
Hispanic or Latino (of any race)	7,764	38.4
Central American, ex. Mexican	2,051	61.2
Salvadoran	1,302	57.1
Cuban	441	35.3
Dominican Republic	774	61.1
Mexican	776	41.8
Puerto Rican	39	0.8
South American	3,358	58.6
Colombian	1,144	64.7
Ecuadorian	549	50.8
Peruvian	709	59.4
Spaniard	105	13.3

Foreign-Born Naturalized U.S. Citizens

Group	Number	%
Total Population	29,523	70.8
Hispanic or Latino (of any race)	4,473	57.6
Central American, ex. Mexican	919	44.8
Salvadoran	565	43.4
Cuban	407	92.3
Dominican Republic	475	61.4
Mexican	143	18.4
Puerto Rican	14	35.9
South American	2,305	68.6
Colombian	826	72.2
Ecuadorian	355	64.7
Peruvian	443	62.5
Spaniard	25	23.8

Language Spoken at Home: English Only
(Universe: Population 5 Years and Over)

Group	Number	%
Total Population	221,749	80.2
Hispanic or Latino (of any race)	6,678	36.2
Central American, ex. Mexican	638	21.0
Salvadoran	309	15.6
Cuban	585	53.2
Dominican Republic	172	14.3
Mexican	394	25.1
Puerto Rican	2,562	60.0
South American	1,320	24.9
Colombian	301	18.6
Ecuadorian	235	24.8
Peruvian	483	40.8
Spaniard	525	71.3

Language Spoken at Home: Spanish
(Universe: Population 5 Years and Over)

Group	Number	%
Total Population	14,229	5.1
Hispanic or Latino (of any race)	11,489	62.3
Central American, ex. Mexican	2,394	79.0
Salvadoran	1,677	84.4
Cuban	514	46.8
Dominican Republic	1,033	85.7
Mexican	1,066	67.8
Puerto Rican	1,706	40.0
South American	3,886	73.3
Colombian	1,316	81.4
Ecuadorian	712	75.2
Peruvian	616	52.1
Spaniard	211	28.7

Unemployment Rate
(Universe: Population 16 Years and Over)

Group	%
Total Population	4.9
Hispanic or Latino (of any race)	4.6
Central American, ex. Mexican	4.5
Salvadoran	5.6
Cuban	6.2
Dominican Republic	1.5
Mexican	1.2
Puerto Rican	6.0
South American	4.5
Colombian	5.1
Ecuadorian	3.4
Peruvian	6.6
Spaniard	0.0

Class of Worker: Private Wage and Salary
(Universe: Civilian Employed Population 16 Years and Over)

Group	Number	%
Total Population	107,879	76.8
Hispanic or Latino (of any race)	8,041	80.5
Central American, ex. Mexican	1,480	77.4
Salvadoran	1,023	84.3
Cuban	313	52.6
Dominican Republic	671	83.3
Mexican	554	93.1
Puerto Rican	1,835	81.7
South American	2,432	84.6
Colombian	802	89.8
Ecuadorian	380	82.6
Peruvian	417	74.2
Spaniard	322	69.0

Class of Worker: Government
(Universe: Civilian Employed Population 16 Years and Over)

Group	Number	%
Total Population	24,643	17.5
Hispanic or Latino (of any race)	1,351	13.5
Central American, ex. Mexican	266	13.9
Salvadoran	94	7.7
Cuban	257	43.2
Dominican Republic	96	11.9
Mexican	41	6.9
Puerto Rican	329	14.7
South American	183	6.4
Colombian	24	2.7
Ecuadorian	49	10.7
Peruvian	57	10.1
Spaniard	119	25.5

Means of Transportation to Work: Car, Truck or Van
(Universe: Workers 16 Years and Over)

Group	Number	%
Total Population	110,508	80.3
Hispanic or Latino (of any race)	7,383	75.3
Central American, ex. Mexican	1,315	69.2
Salvadoran	852	70.2
Cuban	515	90.7
Dominican Republic	541	68.9
Mexican	303	51.4
Puerto Rican	1,701	78.1
South American	2,159	76.0
Colombian	747	85.7
Ecuadorian	360	78.3
Peruvian	394	71.9
Spaniard	408	87.4

Means of Transportation to Work: Public Transportation (ex. Taxicab)
(Universe: Workers 16 Years and Over)

Group	Number	%
Total Population	17,981	13.1
Hispanic or Latino (of any race)	1,325	13.5
Central American, ex. Mexican	249	13.1
Salvadoran	125	10.3
Cuban	39	6.9
Dominican Republic	170	21.7
Mexican	157	26.6
Puerto Rican	295	13.5
South American	347	12.2
Colombian	42	4.8
Ecuadorian	43	9.3
Peruvian	108	19.7
Spaniard	59	12.6

Homeownership Rate
(Universe: Occupied Housing Units)

Group	%
Total Population	86.9
Hispanic or Latino (of any race)	67.9
Central American, ex. Mexican	48.8
Costa Rican	80.6
Guatemalan	69.5
Honduran	29.5
Salvadoran	48.2
Cuban	85.6
Dominican Republic	74.5
Mexican	52.0
Puerto Rican	79.9
South American	68.6
Argentinean	82.3
Bolivian	60.0
Chilean	47.1
Colombian	68.5
Ecuadorian	78.4
Peruvian	63.4
Uruguayan	85.4
Venezuelan	74.4
Spaniard	88.5

Median Home Value

Group	Dollars
Total Population	517,100
Hispanic or Latino (of any race)	474,200
Central American, ex. Mexican	438,900
Salvadoran	431,800
Cuban	470,000
Dominican Republic	624,100
Mexican	422,900
Puerto Rican	478,600
South American	487,000
Colombian	451,900
Ecuadorian	467,900
Peruvian	496,600
Spaniard	500,000

Median Gross Rent

Group	Dollars
Total Population	1,531
Hispanic or Latino (of any race)	1,572
Central American, ex. Mexican	1,774
Salvadoran	1,794
Cuban	1,634
Dominican Republic	–
Mexican	–
Puerto Rican	1,295
South American	1,614
Colombian	1,295
Ecuadorian	–
Peruvian	1,762
Spaniard	–

Notes: (1) Percent of total population; (2) Percent of Hispanic/Latino population; Profiles include places with an overall population of at least 125,000, OR an overall population of at least 25,000 where the Hispanic/Latino population is at least 20% of the overall population. In states where less than five places meet either of these criteria, we have included places with at least 10,000 total population with the highest percentage of Hispanic/Latino population. These places are identified with an asterisk (*); Please refer to the User's Guide for a full explanation of data.

Median Household Income
(2010 Inflation-Adjusted Dollars)

Group	Dollars
Total Population	104,453
Hispanic or Latino (of any race)	98,982
Central American, ex. Mexican	71,439
Salvadoran	72,212
Cuban	116,184
Dominican Republic	97,981
Mexican	58,788
Puerto Rican	107,143
South American	110,417
Colombian	79,200
Ecuadorian	119,583
Peruvian	112,361
Spaniard	146,400

Per Capita Income
(2010 Inflation-Adjusted Dollars)

Group	Dollars
Total Population	46,598
Hispanic or Latino (of any race)	30,139
Central American, ex. Mexican	29,118
Salvadoran	24,292
Cuban	38,197
Dominican Republic	27,243
Mexican	10,280
Puerto Rican	35,955
South American	31,124
Colombian	26,569
Ecuadorian	30,007
Peruvian	34,225
Spaniard	45,473

Households with $100,000+ Income

Group	Number	%
Total Population	50,794	52.0
Hispanic or Latino (of any race)	2,353	48.9
Central American, ex. Mexican	333	42.5
Salvadoran	221	46.5
Cuban	181	55.5
Dominican Republic	73	34.9
Mexican	118	34.5
Puerto Rican	615	54.1
South American	794	52.5
Colombian	207	42.2
Ecuadorian	199	71.6
Peruvian	220	68.5
Spaniard	164	54.7

Households with Food Stamps/SNAP Benefits During Past 12 Months

Group	Number	%
Total Population	1,446	1.5
Hispanic or Latino (of any race)	224	4.7
Central American, ex. Mexican	10	1.3
Salvadoran	10	2.1
Cuban	0	0.0
Dominican Republic	37	17.7
Mexican	33	9.6
Puerto Rican	12	1.1
South American	118	7.8
Colombian	0	0.0
Ecuadorian	14	5.0
Peruvian	18	5.6
Spaniard	14	4.7

Poverty Rate
(Income in Past 12 Months Below Poverty Level)

Group	%
Total Population	3.2
Hispanic or Latino (of any race)	7.0
Central American, ex. Mexican	8.1
Salvadoran	8.7
Cuban	0.0
Dominican Republic	0.8
Mexican	38.6
Puerto Rican	6.5
South American	1.2
Colombian	1.2
Ecuadorian	3.0
Peruvian	0.0
Spaniard	0.0

Port Chester

Population

Group	Number	%TP[1]	%HP[2]
Total Population	28,967	100.0	–
Hispanic or Latino (of any race)	17,193	59.4	100.0
Central American, ex. Mexican	3,577	12.3	20.8
Guatemalan	2,433	8.4	14.2
Honduran	169	0.6	1.0
Salvadoran	915	3.2	5.3
Cuban	359	1.2	2.1
Dominican Republic	556	1.9	3.2
Mexican	4,864	16.8	28.3
Puerto Rican	855	3.0	5.0
South American	5,769	19.9	33.6
Bolivian	350	1.2	2.0
Chilean	123	0.4	0.7
Colombian	724	2.5	4.2
Ecuadorian	2,774	9.6	16.1
Peruvian	1,485	5.1	8.6
Uruguayan	159	0.5	0.9

Population Growth: 2000–2010

Group	%
Total Population	3.9
Hispanic or Latino (of any race)	33.4
Central American, ex. Mexican	96.6
Guatemalan	134.6
Salvadoran	64.0
Cuban	-22.8
Dominican Republic	103.7
Mexican	56.5
Puerto Rican	1.5
South American	64.1
Bolivian	114.7
Chilean	10.8
Colombian	4.0
Ecuadorian	103.1
Peruvian	61.6

Males per 100 Females

Group	Number
Total Population	110.3
Hispanic or Latino (of any race)	128.1
Central American, ex. Mexican	150.5
Guatemalan	173.1
Honduran	106.1
Salvadoran	117.3
Cuban	100.6
Dominican Republic	90.4
Mexican	136.0
Puerto Rican	95.2
South American	122.2
Bolivian	117.4
Chilean	136.5
Colombian	90.5
Ecuadorian	147.7
Peruvian	104.3
Uruguayan	117.8

Average Household Size

Group	People
Total Population	3.08
Hispanic or Latino (of any race)	4.08
Central American, ex. Mexican	4.51
Guatemalan	4.45
Honduran	4.17
Salvadoran	4.84
Cuban	2.32
Dominican Republic	3.69
Mexican	4.96
Puerto Rican	2.97
South American	3.81
Bolivian	4.08
Chilean	3.08
Colombian	2.95
Ecuadorian	4.35
Peruvian	3.67
Uruguayan	3.11

Median Age

Group	Years
Total Population	34.4
Hispanic or Latino (of any race)	30.2
Central American, ex. Mexican	30.4
Guatemalan	30.3
Honduran	29.6
Salvadoran	30.9
Cuban	50.3
Dominican Republic	26.8
Mexican	26.7
Puerto Rican	31.3
South American	34.0
Bolivian	34.1
Chilean	46.2
Colombian	39.3
Ecuadorian	31.3
Peruvian	37.7
Uruguayan	36.8

High School Graduates
(Universe: Population 25 Years and Over)

Group	Number	%
Total Population	14,083	72.1
Hispanic or Latino (of any race)	4,810	54.0
Central American, ex. Mexican	693	35.7
Guatemalan	562	35.9
Mexican	720	39.1
Puerto Rican	610	81.0
South American	2,321	66.2
Ecuadorian	517	41.1
Peruvian	995	83.8

Four-Year College Graduates
(Universe: Population 25 Years and Over)

Group	Number	%
Total Population	4,526	23.2
Hispanic or Latino (of any race)	931	10.5
Central American, ex. Mexican	80	4.1
Guatemalan	59	3.8
Mexican	138	7.5
Puerto Rican	231	30.7
South American	384	11.0
Ecuadorian	58	4.6
Peruvian	121	10.2

Population Age 3–17 Enrolled in Public School
(Universe: Population Age 3–17 Enrolled in School)

Group	Number	%
Total Population	3,788	85.7
Hispanic or Latino (of any race)	2,271	89.5
Central American, ex. Mexican	295	86.0
Guatemalan	131	82.9
Mexican	880	97.9
Puerto Rican	285	87.4
South American	536	77.2
Ecuadorian	217	86.5
Peruvian	128	54.2

Population Age 3–17 Enrolled in Private School
(Universe: Population Age 3–17 Enrolled in School)

Group	Number	%
Total Population	631	14.3
Hispanic or Latino (of any race)	266	10.5
Central American, ex. Mexican	48	14.0
Guatemalan	27	17.1
Mexican	19	2.1
Puerto Rican	41	12.6
South American	158	22.8
Ecuadorian	34	13.5
Peruvian	108	45.8

Foreign-Born Population

Group	Number	%
Total Population	12,897	45.1
Hispanic or Latino (of any race)	9,882	68.1
Central American, ex. Mexican	2,532	85.7
Guatemalan	2,108	93.4
Mexican	2,374	66.9
Puerto Rican	0	0.0
South American	4,269	83.2
Ecuadorian	1,578	84.7
Peruvian	1,485	88.2

Foreign-Born Naturalized U.S. Citizens

Group	Number	%
Total Population	3,321	25.8
Hispanic or Latino (of any race)	2,027	20.5
Central American, ex. Mexican	284	11.2

Notes: (1) Percent of total population; (2) Percent of Hispanic/Latino population; Profiles include places with an overall population of at least 125,000, OR an overall population of at least 25,000 where the Hispanic/Latino population is at least 20% of the overall population. In states where less than five places meet either of these criteria, we have included places with at least 10,000 total population with the highest percentage of Hispanic/Latino population. These places are identified with an asterisk (*); Please refer to the User's Guide for a full explanation of data.

Guatemalan	222	10.5
Mexican	182	7.7
Puerto Rican	0	0.0
South American	1,170	27.4
Ecuadorian	507	32.1
Peruvian	375	25.3

Language Spoken at Home: English Only
(Universe: Population 5 Years and Over)

Group	Number	%
Total Population	11,233	42.0
Hispanic or Latino (of any race)	1,083	8.1
Central American, ex. Mexican	70	2.5
Guatemalan	70	3.2
Mexican	131	4.2
Puerto Rican	561	44.3
South American	197	4.1
Ecuadorian	59	3.3
Peruvian	73	4.5

Language Spoken at Home: Spanish
(Universe: Population 5 Years and Over)

Group	Number	%
Total Population	12,652	47.3
Hispanic or Latino (of any race)	12,187	91.6
Central American, ex. Mexican	2,683	97.5
Guatemalan	2,102	96.8
Mexican	2,966	95.8
Puerto Rican	664	52.4
South American	4,625	95.9
Ecuadorian	1,729	96.7
Peruvian	1,533	95.5

Unemployment Rate
(Universe: Population 16 Years and Over)

Group	%
Total Population	8.3
Hispanic or Latino (of any race)	7.6
Central American, ex. Mexican	3.8
Guatemalan	4.5
Mexican	4.8
Puerto Rican	17.1
South American	7.3
Ecuadorian	9.8
Peruvian	6.7

Class of Worker: Private Wage and Salary
(Universe: Civilian Employed Population 16 Years and Over)

Group	Number	%
Total Population	13,249	84.7
Hispanic or Latino (of any race)	7,593	90.3
Central American, ex. Mexican	1,827	96.1
Guatemalan	1,536	95.4
Mexican	1,758	93.2
Puerto Rican	472	75.0
South American	2,819	89.2
Ecuadorian	942	85.6
Peruvian	1,111	96.9

Class of Worker: Government
(Universe: Civilian Employed Population 16 Years and Over)

Group	Number	%
Total Population	1,615	10.3
Hispanic or Latino (of any race)	374	4.4
Central American, ex. Mexican	43	2.3
Guatemalan	43	2.7
Mexican	90	4.8
Puerto Rican	55	8.7
South American	87	2.8
Ecuadorian	48	4.4
Peruvian	10	0.9

Means of Transportation to Work: Car, Truck or Van
(Universe: Workers 16 Years and Over)

Group	Number	%
Total Population	9,475	62.3
Hispanic or Latino (of any race)	4,198	51.4
Central American, ex. Mexican	672	35.8
Guatemalan	541	34.1
Mexican	843	45.4
Puerto Rican	430	73.1
South American	1,624	53.8
Ecuadorian	612	56.2
Peruvian	455	42.3

Means of Transportation to Work: Public Transportation (ex. Taxicab)
(Universe: Workers 16 Years and Over)

Group	Number	%
Total Population	2,590	17.0
Hispanic or Latino (of any race)	1,560	19.1
Central American, ex. Mexican	452	24.1
Guatemalan	388	24.5
Mexican	182	9.8
Puerto Rican	58	9.9
South American	824	27.3
Ecuadorian	206	18.9
Peruvian	417	38.8

Homeownership Rate
(Universe: Occupied Housing Units)

Group	%
Total Population	43.2
Hispanic or Latino (of any race)	21.8
Central American, ex. Mexican	15.0
Guatemalan	13.5
Honduran	12.2
Salvadoran	17.8
Cuban	44.9
Dominican Republic	12.6
Mexican	15.9
Puerto Rican	27.3
South American	25.8
Bolivian	38.8
Chilean	30.0
Colombian	28.1
Ecuadorian	20.6
Peruvian	28.9
Uruguayan	30.6

Median Home Value

Group	Dollars
Total Population	472,900
Hispanic or Latino (of any race)	437,600
Central American, ex. Mexican	419,200
Guatemalan	240,700
Mexican	–
Puerto Rican	160,300
South American	540,900
Ecuadorian	489,700
Peruvian	596,700

Median Gross Rent

Group	Dollars
Total Population	1,313
Hispanic or Latino (of any race)	1,416
Central American, ex. Mexican	1,485
Guatemalan	1,503
Mexican	1,517
Puerto Rican	906
South American	1,450
Ecuadorian	1,208
Peruvian	1,426

Median Household Income
(2010 Inflation-Adjusted Dollars)

Group	Dollars
Total Population	52,758
Hispanic or Latino (of any race)	44,144
Central American, ex. Mexican	43,466
Guatemalan	47,083
Mexican	37,788
Puerto Rican	48,571
South American	52,903
Ecuadorian	68,182
Peruvian	54,758

Per Capita Income
(2010 Inflation-Adjusted Dollars)

Group	Dollars
Total Population	26,744
Hispanic or Latino (of any race)	15,492
Central American, ex. Mexican	13,990
Guatemalan	15,067
Mexican	11,759
Puerto Rican	19,683
South American	16,915
Ecuadorian	17,976
Peruvian	18,895

Households with $100,000+ Income

Group	Number	%
Total Population	2,035	20.1
Hispanic or Latino (of any race)	331	7.8
Central American, ex. Mexican	63	8.4
Guatemalan	63	10.9
Mexican	31	3.7
Puerto Rican	58	13.0
South American	93	5.5
Ecuadorian	55	9.7
Peruvian	38	6.2

Households with Food Stamps/SNAP Benefits During Past 12 Months

Group	Number	%
Total Population	705	6.9
Hispanic or Latino (of any race)	375	8.9
Central American, ex. Mexican	112	15.0
Guatemalan	112	19.4
Mexican	136	16.1
Puerto Rican	24	5.4
South American	78	4.6
Ecuadorian	25	4.4
Peruvian	0	0.0

Poverty Rate
(Income in Past 12 Months Below Poverty Level)

Group	%
Total Population	16.0
Hispanic or Latino (of any race)	22.7
Central American, ex. Mexican	30.3
Guatemalan	28.3
Mexican	35.7
Puerto Rican	15.6
South American	8.6
Ecuadorian	5.9
Peruvian	3.2

Queens

Population

Group	Number	%TP[1]	%HP[2]
Total Population	2,230,722	100.0	–
Hispanic or Latino (of any race)	613,750	27.5	100.0
Central American, ex. Mexican	52,509	2.4	8.6
Costa Rican	1,749	0.1	0.3
Guatemalan	13,700	0.6	2.2
Honduran	8,546	0.4	1.4
Nicaraguan	2,842	0.1	0.5
Panamanian	3,977	0.2	0.6
Salvadoran	21,342	1.0	3.5
Cuban	11,020	0.5	1.8
Dominican Republic	88,061	3.9	14.3
Mexican	92,835	4.2	15.1
Puerto Rican	102,881	4.6	16.8
South American	214,022	9.6	34.9
Argentinean	6,345	0.3	1.0
Bolivian	3,268	0.1	0.5
Chilean	3,184	0.1	0.5
Colombian	70,290	3.2	11.5
Ecuadorian	98,512	4.4	16.1
Paraguayan	2,775	0.1	0.5
Peruvian	22,886	1.0	3.7
Uruguayan	1,743	0.1	0.3
Venezuelan	3,580	0.2	0.6
Spaniard	5,485	0.2	0.9

Population Growth: 2000–2010

Group	%
Total Population	0.1
Hispanic or Latino (of any race)	10.3
Central American, ex. Mexican	53.6
Costa Rican	28.0
Guatemalan	85.7
Honduran	70.2
Nicaraguan	71.6
Panamanian	24.2
Salvadoran	54.7
Cuban	-13.9
Dominican Republic	26.0
Mexican	67.3
Puerto Rican	-5.3
South American	40.2

Notes: (1) Percent of total population; (2) Percent of Hispanic/Latino population; Profiles include places with an overall population of at least 125,000, OR an overall population of at least 25,000 where the Hispanic/Latino population is at least 20% of the overall population. In states where less than five places meet either of these criteria, we have included places with at least 10,000 total population with the highest percentage of Hispanic/Latino population. These places are identified with an asterisk (*); Please refer to the User's Guide for a full explanation of data.

Group	
Argentinean	40.0
Bolivian	41.0
Chilean	24.8
Colombian	16.6
Ecuadorian	70.7
Paraguayan	112.2
Peruvian	43.4
Uruguayan	38.9
Venezuelan	22.4
Spaniard	63.5

Males per 100 Females

Group	Number
Total Population	93.8
Hispanic or Latino (of any race)	101.2
Central American, ex. Mexican	109.1
Costa Rican	74.9
Guatemalan	142.0
Honduran	101.7
Nicaraguan	92.3
Panamanian	75.0
Salvadoran	107.2
Cuban	91.5
Dominican Republic	85.0
Mexican	136.0
Puerto Rican	92.3
South American	98.6
Argentinean	106.1
Bolivian	87.9
Chilean	112.7
Colombian	78.8
Ecuadorian	116.8
Paraguayan	96.0
Peruvian	94.2
Uruguayan	116.0
Venezuelan	83.9
Spaniard	97.3

Average Household Size

Group	People
Total Population	2.82
Hispanic or Latino (of any race)	3.39
Central American, ex. Mexican	3.70
Costa Rican	2.79
Guatemalan	3.93
Honduran	3.61
Nicaraguan	3.49
Panamanian	2.77
Salvadoran	4.00
Cuban	2.27
Dominican Republic	3.53
Mexican	4.76
Puerto Rican	2.69
South American	3.43
Argentinean	2.57
Bolivian	3.17
Chilean	2.68
Colombian	2.98
Ecuadorian	4.06
Paraguayan	3.32
Peruvian	3.28
Uruguayan	2.79
Venezuelan	2.84
Spaniard	2.39

Median Age

Group	Years
Total Population	37.2
Hispanic or Latino (of any race)	32.0
Central American, ex. Mexican	32.7
Costa Rican	39.7
Guatemalan	30.9
Honduran	32.8
Nicaraguan	34.7
Panamanian	43.7
Salvadoran	31.9
Cuban	46.6
Dominican Republic	32.3
Mexican	26.5
Puerto Rican	32.6
South American	35.9
Argentinean	39.1
Bolivian	40.5
Chilean	42.9
Colombian	40.0
Ecuadorian	32.8
Paraguayan	35.2
Peruvian	40.3
Uruguayan	41.5
Venezuelan	33.4
Spaniard	42.6

High School Graduates

(Universe: Population 25 Years and Over)

Group	Number	%
Total Population	1,221,800	80.0
Hispanic or Latino (of any race)	258,592	69.3
Central American, ex. Mexican	20,671	60.6
Costa Rican	1,051	74.6
Guatemalan	4,273	54.2
Honduran	3,700	65.5
Nicaraguan	1,487	72.3
Panamanian	2,665	93.4
Salvadoran	7,232	52.2
Cuban	7,389	78.3
Dominican Republic	34,443	65.3
Mexican	21,935	51.9
Puerto Rican	53,155	77.4
South American	107,662	72.3
Argentinean	3,476	79.4
Bolivian	1,855	82.8
Chilean	2,344	83.8
Colombian	39,054	78.3
Ecuadorian	39,905	61.8
Paraguayan	1,367	78.7
Peruvian	15,519	86.7
Uruguayan	802	71.5
Venezuelan	2,419	82.7
Spaniard	3,341	84.2

Four-Year College Graduates

(Universe: Population 25 Years and Over)

Group	Number	%
Total Population	450,252	29.5
Hispanic or Latino (of any race)	59,895	16.0
Central American, ex. Mexican	4,720	13.8
Costa Rican	373	26.5
Guatemalan	872	11.1
Honduran	816	14.4
Nicaraguan	445	21.6
Panamanian	785	27.5
Salvadoran	1,397	10.1
Cuban	2,937	31.1
Dominican Republic	7,876	14.9
Mexican	2,998	7.1
Puerto Rican	11,554	16.8
South American	25,844	17.4
Argentinean	937	21.4
Bolivian	566	25.3
Chilean	690	24.7
Colombian	10,132	20.3
Ecuadorian	7,132	11.0
Paraguayan	420	24.2
Peruvian	4,652	26.0
Uruguayan	157	14.0
Venezuelan	861	29.4
Spaniard	1,262	31.8

Population Age 3–17 Enrolled in Public School

(Universe: Population Age 3–17 Enrolled in School)

Group	Number	%
Total Population	281,512	80.7
Hispanic or Latino (of any race)	96,682	87.0
Central American, ex. Mexican	7,897	91.8
Costa Rican	213	91.4
Guatemalan	1,863	89.1
Honduran	1,511	92.5
Nicaraguan	411	93.8
Panamanian	334	87.2
Salvadoran	3,483	93.2
Cuban	965	54.7
Dominican Republic	17,002	89.7
Mexican	15,959	95.8
Puerto Rican	20,208	83.9
South American	29,543	85.5
Argentinean	595	90.2
Bolivian	311	42.7
Chilean	244	59.4
Colombian	9,549	86.3
Ecuadorian	14,377	89.2
Paraguayan	323	85.7
Peruvian	3,417	80.0
Uruguayan	77	65.8
Venezuelan	507	83.3
Spaniard	286	46.7

Population Age 3–17 Enrolled in Private School

(Universe: Population Age 3–17 Enrolled in School)

Group	Number	%
Total Population	67,374	19.3
Hispanic or Latino (of any race)	14,385	13.0
Central American, ex. Mexican	702	8.2
Costa Rican	20	8.6
Guatemalan	228	10.9
Honduran	123	7.5
Nicaraguan	27	6.2
Panamanian	49	12.8
Salvadoran	255	6.8
Cuban	798	45.3
Dominican Republic	1,945	10.3
Mexican	699	4.2
Puerto Rican	3,876	16.1
South American	5,027	14.5
Argentinean	65	9.8
Bolivian	417	57.3
Chilean	167	40.6
Colombian	1,513	13.7
Ecuadorian	1,740	10.8
Paraguayan	54	14.3
Peruvian	855	20.0
Uruguayan	40	34.2
Venezuelan	102	16.7
Spaniard	327	53.3

Foreign-Born Population

Group	Number	%
Total Population	1,057,296	48.1
Hispanic or Latino (of any race)	314,615	53.0
Central American, ex. Mexican	35,711	67.1
Costa Rican	1,260	65.9
Guatemalan	8,898	69.8
Honduran	6,137	68.1
Nicaraguan	1,990	64.5
Panamanian	2,235	57.8
Salvadoran	14,762	67.0
Cuban	6,209	49.6
Dominican Republic	50,658	56.9
Mexican	50,794	65.1
Puerto Rican	2,151	1.9
South American	155,649	70.9
Argentinean	4,044	70.8
Bolivian	2,116	63.8
Chilean	2,617	69.4
Colombian	49,800	69.8
Ecuadorian	71,111	71.1
Paraguayan	1,916	76.3
Peruvian	18,474	72.6
Uruguayan	1,059	75.0
Venezuelan	3,219	74.6
Spaniard	2,266	45.5

Foreign-Born Naturalized U.S. Citizens

Group	Number	%
Total Population	560,466	53.0
Hispanic or Latino (of any race)	125,497	39.9
Central American, ex. Mexican	13,289	37.2
Costa Rican	1,033	82.0
Guatemalan	2,673	30.0
Honduran	2,055	33.5
Nicaraguan	822	41.3
Panamanian	1,629	72.9
Salvadoran	4,862	32.9
Cuban	4,919	79.2
Dominican Republic	26,741	52.8
Mexican	5,187	10.2
Puerto Rican	1,427	66.3
South American	66,201	42.5
Argentinean	1,981	49.0
Bolivian	1,221	57.7
Chilean	1,390	53.1
Colombian	26,543	53.3
Ecuadorian	23,288	32.7
Paraguayan	335	17.5
Peruvian	9,140	49.5
Uruguayan	508	48.0

Notes: (1) Percent of total population; (2) Percent of Hispanic/Latino population; Profiles include places with an overall population of at least 125,000, OR an overall population of at least 25,000 where the Hispanic/Latino population is at least 20% of the overall population. In states where less than five places meet either of these criteria, we have included places with at least 10,000 total population with the highest percentage of Hispanic/Latino population. These places are identified with an asterisk (*); Please refer to the User's Guide for a full explanation of data.

Venezuelan	908	28.2
Spaniard	1,339	59.1

Language Spoken at Home: English Only
(Universe: Population 5 Years and Over)

Group	Number	%
Total Population	905,890	43.8
Hispanic or Latino (of any race)	68,541	12.5
Central American, ex. Mexican	4,508	9.2
Costa Rican	380	20.1
Guatemalan	916	7.6
Honduran	695	8.3
Nicaraguan	395	13.9
Panamanian	951	26.4
Salvadoran	1,135	5.7
Cuban	3,180	26.4
Dominican Republic	5,405	6.5
Mexican	3,715	5.4
Puerto Rican	34,012	33.2
South American	12,113	5.9
Argentinean	704	13.0
Bolivian	270	8.6
Chilean	250	6.8
Colombian	3,482	5.2
Ecuadorian	3,901	4.3
Paraguayan	75	3.2
Peruvian	2,046	8.5
Uruguayan	80	6.2
Venezuelan	640	15.4
Spaniard	1,491	31.3

Language Spoken at Home: Spanish
(Universe: Population 5 Years and Over)

Group	Number	%
Total Population	493,462	23.9
Hispanic or Latino (of any race)	474,977	86.8
Central American, ex. Mexican	44,604	90.6
Costa Rican	1,508	79.9
Guatemalan	11,060	92.3
Honduran	7,607	91.2
Nicaraguan	2,445	85.9
Panamanian	2,625	73.0
Salvadoran	18,878	94.1
Cuban	8,744	72.5
Dominican Republic	76,867	93.0
Mexican	65,077	93.8
Puerto Rican	67,873	66.2
South American	191,527	93.6
Argentinean	4,572	84.6
Bolivian	2,869	91.4
Chilean	3,428	93.0
Colombian	63,166	94.3
Ecuadorian	87,572	95.5
Paraguayan	2,166	91.6
Peruvian	22,007	91.2
Uruguayan	1,171	90.4
Venezuelan	3,473	83.4
Spaniard	3,116	65.4

Unemployment Rate
(Universe: Population 16 Years and Over)

Group	%
Total Population	8.5
Hispanic or Latino (of any race)	8.7
Central American, ex. Mexican	10.3
Costa Rican	10.3
Guatemalan	7.9
Honduran	9.6
Nicaraguan	11.5
Panamanian	11.3
Salvadoran	11.9
Cuban	7.7
Dominican Republic	9.9
Mexican	5.7
Puerto Rican	10.1
South American	8.2
Argentinean	4.7
Bolivian	14.3
Chilean	8.8
Colombian	9.0
Ecuadorian	7.3
Paraguayan	10.5
Peruvian	8.2
Uruguayan	6.7
Venezuelan	12.2

Spaniard	6.9

Class of Worker: Private Wage and Salary
(Universe: Civilian Employed Population 16 Years and Over)

Group	Number	%
Total Population	844,822	79.3
Hispanic or Latino (of any race)	247,108	84.0
Central American, ex. Mexican	23,638	83.3
Costa Rican	648	70.3
Guatemalan	6,003	84.7
Honduran	4,048	82.8
Nicaraguan	1,333	80.4
Panamanian	1,294	65.1
Salvadoran	10,086	87.5
Cuban	4,478	82.0
Dominican Republic	35,131	84.5
Mexican	36,880	92.5
Puerto Rican	37,791	78.2
South American	99,210	83.8
Argentinean	2,688	84.0
Bolivian	1,461	88.8
Chilean	1,599	69.0
Colombian	30,951	81.1
Ecuadorian	46,799	87.2
Paraguayan	1,238	78.4
Peruvian	11,206	81.1
Uruguayan	606	92.0
Venezuelan	2,043	82.2
Spaniard	2,056	79.6

Class of Worker: Government
(Universe: Civilian Employed Population 16 Years and Over)

Group	Number	%
Total Population	154,944	14.5
Hispanic or Latino (of any race)	28,618	9.7
Central American, ex. Mexican	2,515	8.9
Costa Rican	230	24.9
Guatemalan	426	6.0
Honduran	444	9.1
Nicaraguan	202	12.2
Panamanian	549	27.6
Salvadoran	642	5.6
Cuban	812	14.9
Dominican Republic	4,626	11.1
Mexican	895	2.2
Puerto Rican	9,473	19.6
South American	8,654	7.3
Argentinean	180	5.6
Bolivian	96	5.8
Chilean	285	12.3
Colombian	3,304	8.7
Ecuadorian	2,747	5.1
Paraguayan	42	2.7
Peruvian	1,472	10.7
Uruguayan	13	2.0
Venezuelan	287	11.6
Spaniard	478	18.5

Means of Transportation to Work: Car, Truck or Van
(Universe: Workers 16 Years and Over)

Group	Number	%
Total Population	407,032	39.5
Hispanic or Latino (of any race)	85,820	30.0
Central American, ex. Mexican	8,809	31.8
Costa Rican	249	28.9
Guatemalan	2,039	29.2
Honduran	1,156	23.7
Nicaraguan	299	19.4
Panamanian	775	39.6
Salvadoran	4,220	37.8
Cuban	2,172	41.0
Dominican Republic	14,424	36.2
Mexican	4,444	11.3
Puerto Rican	17,513	37.3
South American	34,211	29.6
Argentinean	963	31.5
Bolivian	507	31.1
Chilean	757	33.0
Colombian	11,948	32.2
Ecuadorian	14,276	27.2
Paraguayan	497	31.6
Peruvian	4,171	31.1
Uruguayan	166	25.2
Venezuelan	573	24.0

Spaniard	1,198	48.3

Means of Transportation to Work: Public Transportation (ex. Taxicab)
(Universe: Workers 16 Years and Over)

Group	Number	%
Total Population	526,040	51.0
Hispanic or Latino (of any race)	171,290	59.8
Central American, ex. Mexican	15,582	56.3
Costa Rican	600	69.7
Guatemalan	4,160	59.5
Honduran	3,132	64.3
Nicaraguan	932	60.6
Panamanian	977	49.9
Salvadoran	5,571	49.9
Cuban	2,687	50.7
Dominican Republic	20,289	50.9
Mexican	30,390	77.2
Puerto Rican	25,067	53.4
South American	70,847	61.4
Argentinean	1,659	54.3
Bolivian	950	58.3
Chilean	1,328	57.8
Colombian	21,739	58.6
Ecuadorian	33,747	64.4
Paraguayan	978	62.2
Peruvian	8,182	61.0
Uruguayan	446	67.7
Venezuelan	1,339	56.1
Spaniard	1,155	46.5

Homeownership Rate
(Universe: Occupied Housing Units)

Group	%
Total Population	43.0
Hispanic or Latino (of any race)	25.1
Central American, ex. Mexican	22.9
Costa Rican	35.7
Guatemalan	17.3
Honduran	21.4
Nicaraguan	23.6
Panamanian	45.9
Salvadoran	18.9
Cuban	37.0
Dominican Republic	25.3
Mexican	9.5
Puerto Rican	28.2
South American	26.1
Argentinean	34.1
Bolivian	42.4
Chilean	29.2
Colombian	24.9
Ecuadorian	24.7
Paraguayan	17.4
Peruvian	29.0
Uruguayan	31.1
Venezuelan	23.6
Spaniard	50.7

Median Home Value

Group	Dollars
Total Population	479,300
Hispanic or Latino (of any race)	484,500
Central American, ex. Mexican	448,200
Costa Rican	432,900
Guatemalan	441,100
Honduran	507,800
Nicaraguan	479,800
Panamanian	427,800
Salvadoran	459,800
Cuban	450,400
Dominican Republic	530,400
Mexican	505,600
Puerto Rican	440,000
South American	509,500
Argentinean	583,700
Bolivian	607,300
Chilean	463,600
Colombian	474,100
Ecuadorian	532,200
Paraguayan	483,300
Peruvian	511,300
Uruguayan	530,800
Venezuelan	281,000
Spaniard	604,600

STATE & PLACE PROFILES

Notes: (1) Percent of total population; (2) Percent of Hispanic/Latino population; Profiles include places with an overall population of at least 125,000, OR an overall population of at least 25,000 where the Hispanic/Latino population is at least 20% of the overall population. In states where less than five places meet either of these criteria, we have included places with at least 10,000 total population with the highest percentage of Hispanic/Latino population. These places are identified with an asterisk (*); Please refer to the User's Guide for a full explanation of data.

Median Gross Rent

Group	Dollars
Total Population	1,181
Hispanic or Latino (of any race)	1,201
Central American, ex. Mexican	1,187
Costa Rican	1,253
Guatemalan	1,191
Honduran	1,157
Nicaraguan	1,359
Panamanian	1,172
Salvadoran	1,176
Cuban	1,016
Dominican Republic	1,150
Mexican	1,395
Puerto Rican	1,132
South American	1,218
Argentinean	1,223
Bolivian	1,221
Chilean	1,180
Colombian	1,178
Ecuadorian	1,273
Paraguayan	1,148
Peruvian	1,198
Uruguayan	1,205
Venezuelan	1,309
Spaniard	1,127

Median Household Income
(2010 Inflation-Adjusted Dollars)

Group	Dollars
Total Population	55,291
Hispanic or Latino (of any race)	50,331
Central American, ex. Mexican	48,679
Costa Rican	73,534
Guatemalan	47,889
Honduran	51,706
Nicaraguan	77,042
Panamanian	69,306
Salvadoran	42,925
Cuban	50,602
Dominican Republic	48,593
Mexican	48,059
Puerto Rican	52,841
South American	50,451
Argentinean	52,696
Bolivian	55,238
Chilean	59,234
Colombian	48,450
Ecuadorian	51,207
Paraguayan	52,391
Peruvian	49,979
Uruguayan	52,303
Venezuelan	50,615
Spaniard	67,120

Per Capita Income
(2010 Inflation-Adjusted Dollars)

Group	Dollars
Total Population	25,553
Hispanic or Latino (of any race)	19,056
Central American, ex. Mexican	18,242
Costa Rican	26,058
Guatemalan	16,221
Honduran	18,188
Nicaraguan	21,149
Panamanian	29,494
Salvadoran	16,305
Cuban	27,990
Dominican Republic	17,395
Mexican	13,801
Puerto Rican	21,999
South American	19,622
Argentinean	26,172
Bolivian	21,012
Chilean	26,199
Colombian	20,440
Ecuadorian	17,393
Paraguayan	21,223
Peruvian	21,648
Uruguayan	26,517
Venezuelan	24,319
Spaniard	35,299

Households with $100,000+ Income

Group	Number	%
Total Population	171,703	22.2
Hispanic or Latino (of any race)	28,292	15.8
Central American, ex. Mexican	2,078	13.4
Costa Rican	162	25.6
Guatemalan	443	11.5
Honduran	363	14.6
Nicaraguan	203	25.0
Panamanian	320	19.8
Salvadoran	575	9.7
Cuban	1,223	22.2
Dominican Republic	3,718	14.6
Mexican	2,528	15.2
Puerto Rican	6,557	17.4
South American	10,501	15.1
Argentinean	394	17.3
Bolivian	194	17.3
Chilean	277	18.5
Colombian	3,172	12.6
Ecuadorian	4,302	15.7
Paraguayan	242	30.4
Peruvian	1,368	16.5
Uruguayan	126	23.6
Venezuelan	199	12.8
Spaniard	723	29.7

Households with Food Stamps/SNAP Benefits During Past 12 Months

Group	Number	%
Total Population	81,582	10.5
Hispanic or Latino (of any race)	30,581	17.1
Central American, ex. Mexican	1,911	12.3
Costa Rican	104	16.4
Guatemalan	425	11.0
Honduran	341	13.7
Nicaraguan	150	18.5
Panamanian	208	12.9
Salvadoran	659	11.1
Cuban	949	17.2
Dominican Republic	6,914	27.1
Mexican	3,641	21.9
Puerto Rican	6,047	16.0
South American	10,146	14.6
Argentinean	324	14.2
Bolivian	82	7.3
Chilean	169	11.3
Colombian	3,600	14.3
Ecuadorian	4,503	16.4
Paraguayan	62	7.8
Peruvian	923	11.1
Uruguayan	92	17.3
Venezuelan	323	20.8
Spaniard	121	5.0

Poverty Rate
(Income in Past 12 Months Below Poverty Level)

Group	%
Total Population	13.0
Hispanic or Latino (of any race)	16.3
Central American, ex. Mexican	14.4
Costa Rican	3.0
Guatemalan	18.8
Honduran	11.8
Nicaraguan	9.1
Panamanian	10.7
Salvadoran	15.2
Cuban	11.7
Dominican Republic	15.9
Mexican	23.4
Puerto Rican	16.4
South American	14.9
Argentinean	9.0
Bolivian	16.6
Chilean	5.8
Colombian	14.1
Ecuadorian	16.6
Paraguayan	26.3
Peruvian	12.3
Uruguayan	5.6
Venezuelan	18.8
Spaniard	4.0

Ramapo

Population

Group	Number	%TP[1]	%HP[2]
Total Population	126,595	100.0	–
Hispanic or Latino (of any race)	17,223	13.6	100.0
Central American, ex. Mexican	5,319	4.2	30.9
Costa Rican	103	0.1	0.6
Guatemalan	4,050	3.2	23.5
Honduran	182	0.1	1.1
Salvadoran	872	0.7	5.1
Cuban	279	0.2	1.6
Dominican Republic	1,021	0.8	5.9
Mexican	2,433	1.9	14.1
Puerto Rican	2,904	2.3	16.9
South American	3,759	3.0	21.8
Argentinean	166	0.1	1.0
Colombian	308	0.2	1.8
Ecuadorian	2,915	2.3	16.9
Peruvian	204	0.2	1.2
Spaniard	136	0.1	0.8

Population Growth: 2000–2010

Group	%
Total Population	16.2
Hispanic or Latino (of any race)	93.0
Central American, ex. Mexican	244.0
Guatemalan	262.9
Salvadoran	379.1
Cuban	34.8
Dominican Republic	165.2
Mexican	91.9
Puerto Rican	10.2
South American	209.4
Colombian	18.0
Ecuadorian	362.0
Peruvian	72.9

Males per 100 Females

Group	Number
Total Population	100.0
Hispanic or Latino (of any race)	126.4
Central American, ex. Mexican	154.3
Costa Rican	77.6
Guatemalan	170.2
Honduran	119.3
Salvadoran	122.4
Cuban	80.0
Dominican Republic	83.3
Mexican	148.8
Puerto Rican	94.6
South American	124.0
Argentinean	93.0
Colombian	78.0
Ecuadorian	139.9
Peruvian	68.6
Spaniard	100.0

Average Household Size

Group	People
Total Population	3.58
Hispanic or Latino (of any race)	4.35
Central American, ex. Mexican	5.12
Costa Rican	3.62
Guatemalan	5.38
Honduran	4.08
Salvadoran	4.75
Cuban	3.25
Dominican Republic	3.97
Mexican	4.36
Puerto Rican	2.99
South American	4.98
Argentinean	3.52
Colombian	3.02
Ecuadorian	5.76
Peruvian	3.53
Spaniard	2.96

Median Age

Group	Years
Total Population	28.9
Hispanic or Latino (of any race)	28.5
Central American, ex. Mexican	27.9
Costa Rican	34.5

Notes: (1) Percent of total population; (2) Percent of Hispanic/Latino population; Profiles include places with an overall population of at least 125,000, OR an overall population of at least 25,000 where the Hispanic/Latino population is at least 20% of the overall population. In states where less than five places meet either of these criteria, we have included places with at least 10,000 total population with the highest percentage of Hispanic/Latino population. These places are identified with an asterisk (*); Please refer to the User's Guide for a full explanation of data.

Group	Number	%
Guatemalan		27.7
Honduran		29.3
Salvadoran		28.3
Cuban		39.2
Dominican Republic		28.7
Mexican		28.0
Puerto Rican		34.3
South American		29.8
Argentinean		36.5
Colombian		38.7
Ecuadorian		28.5
Peruvian		37.5
Spaniard		38.5

High School Graduates
(Universe: Population 25 Years and Over)

Group	Number	%
Total Population	59,635	85.3
Hispanic or Latino (of any race)	5,697	61.8
Central American, ex. Mexican	1,211	42.0
Guatemalan	854	39.3
Dominican Republic	550	84.4
Mexican	766	67.5
Puerto Rican	1,532	82.4
South American	1,288	60.6
Ecuadorian	703	50.0

Four-Year College Graduates
(Universe: Population 25 Years and Over)

Group	Number	%
Total Population	25,214	36.1
Hispanic or Latino (of any race)	1,784	19.4
Central American, ex. Mexican	227	7.9
Guatemalan	171	7.9
Dominican Republic	289	44.3
Mexican	119	10.5
Puerto Rican	625	33.6
South American	285	13.4
Ecuadorian	158	11.2

Population Age 3–17 Enrolled in Public School
(Universe: Population Age 3–17 Enrolled in School)

Group	Number	%
Total Population	12,707	38.8
Hispanic or Latino (of any race)	2,846	88.0
Central American, ex. Mexican	912	100.0
Guatemalan	696	100.0
Dominican Republic	184	80.0
Mexican	230	71.2
Puerto Rican	931	86.1
South American	530	90.4
Ecuadorian	356	89.9

Population Age 3–17 Enrolled in Private School
(Universe: Population Age 3–17 Enrolled in School)

Group	Number	%
Total Population	20,057	61.2
Hispanic or Latino (of any race)	389	12.0
Central American, ex. Mexican	0	0.0
Guatemalan	0	0.0
Dominican Republic	46	20.0
Mexican	93	28.8
Puerto Rican	150	13.9
South American	56	9.6
Ecuadorian	40	10.1

Foreign-Born Population

Group	Number	%
Total Population	31,448	25.6
Hispanic or Latino (of any race)	9,038	56.1
Central American, ex. Mexican	3,871	77.5
Guatemalan	3,070	80.1
Dominican Republic	431	43.5
Mexican	1,490	76.1
Puerto Rican	47	1.3
South American	2,741	72.6
Ecuadorian	2,038	72.9

Foreign-Born Naturalized U.S. Citizens

Group	Number	%
Total Population	15,193	48.3
Hispanic or Latino (of any race)	1,848	20.4
Central American, ex. Mexican	475	12.3
Guatemalan	225	7.3
Dominican Republic	346	80.3
Mexican	198	13.3
Puerto Rican	0	0.0
South American	597	21.8
Ecuadorian	135	6.6

Language Spoken at Home: English Only
(Universe: Population 5 Years and Over)

Group	Number	%
Total Population	58,291	52.8
Hispanic or Latino (of any race)	2,370	16.4
Central American, ex. Mexican	224	4.9
Guatemalan	65	1.8
Dominican Republic	182	20.3
Mexican	112	6.3
Puerto Rican	1,493	46.1
South American	195	6.0
Ecuadorian	23	1.0

Language Spoken at Home: Spanish
(Universe: Population 5 Years and Over)

Group	Number	%
Total Population	12,791	11.6
Hispanic or Latino (of any race)	11,831	82.0
Central American, ex. Mexican	4,350	95.1
Guatemalan	3,464	98.2
Dominican Republic	697	77.8
Mexican	1,589	89.0
Puerto Rican	1,712	52.9
South American	2,995	92.5
Ecuadorian	2,290	99.0

Unemployment Rate
(Universe: Population 16 Years and Over)

Group	%
Total Population	5.2
Hispanic or Latino (of any race)	6.5
Central American, ex. Mexican	6.3
Guatemalan	4.1
Dominican Republic	3.3
Mexican	7.6
Puerto Rican	10.8
South American	4.4
Ecuadorian	4.9

Class of Worker: Private Wage and Salary
(Universe: Civilian Employed Population 16 Years and Over)

Group	Number	%
Total Population	41,625	79.3
Hispanic or Latino (of any race)	7,318	82.7
Central American, ex. Mexican	2,683	85.8
Guatemalan	2,127	85.9
Dominican Republic	335	86.8
Mexican	1,070	93.2
Puerto Rican	1,275	78.0
South American	1,572	75.9
Ecuadorian	1,110	74.6

Class of Worker: Government
(Universe: Civilian Employed Population 16 Years and Over)

Group	Number	%
Total Population	7,360	14.0
Hispanic or Latino (of any race)	703	7.9
Central American, ex. Mexican	98	3.1
Guatemalan	57	2.3
Dominican Republic	51	13.2
Mexican	10	0.9
Puerto Rican	344	21.1
South American	129	6.2
Ecuadorian	51	3.4

Means of Transportation to Work: Car, Truck or Van
(Universe: Workers 16 Years and Over)

Group	Number	%
Total Population	39,006	76.4
Hispanic or Latino (of any race)	5,687	65.5
Central American, ex. Mexican	1,749	56.5
Guatemalan	1,331	54.4
Dominican Republic	290	76.7
Mexican	648	56.4
Puerto Rican	1,400	86.9
South American	1,226	61.6
Ecuadorian	758	53.3

Means of Transportation to Work: Public Transportation (ex. Taxicab)
(Universe: Workers 16 Years and Over)

Group	Number	%
Total Population	5,652	11.1
Hispanic or Latino (of any race)	1,848	21.3
Central American, ex. Mexican	761	24.6
Guatemalan	563	23.0
Dominican Republic	88	23.3
Mexican	381	33.2
Puerto Rican	100	6.2
South American	469	23.6
Ecuadorian	442	31.1

Homeownership Rate
(Universe: Occupied Housing Units)

Group	%
Total Population	59.8
Hispanic or Latino (of any race)	33.8
Central American, ex. Mexican	12.6
Costa Rican	34.5
Guatemalan	8.3
Honduran	31.6
Salvadoran	19.0
Cuban	71.4
Dominican Republic	57.9
Mexican	11.8
Puerto Rican	66.4
South American	30.1
Argentinean	65.4
Colombian	50.5
Ecuadorian	19.2
Peruvian	40.4
Spaniard	68.1

Median Home Value

Group	Dollars
Total Population	468,500
Hispanic or Latino (of any race)	467,700
Central American, ex. Mexican	343,800
Guatemalan	112,500
Dominican Republic	599,200
Mexican	33,000
Puerto Rican	553,600
South American	360,400
Ecuadorian	333,300

Median Gross Rent

Group	Dollars
Total Population	1,157
Hispanic or Latino (of any race)	1,337
Central American, ex. Mexican	1,408
Guatemalan	1,346
Dominican Republic	–
Mexican	1,218
Puerto Rican	1,346
South American	1,123
Ecuadorian	1,226

Median Household Income
(2010 Inflation-Adjusted Dollars)

Group	Dollars
Total Population	68,819
Hispanic or Latino (of any race)	67,802
Central American, ex. Mexican	53,611
Guatemalan	58,071
Dominican Republic	125,938
Mexican	54,609
Puerto Rican	81,953
South American	68,393
Ecuadorian	66,908

Per Capita Income
(2010 Inflation-Adjusted Dollars)

Group	Dollars
Total Population	27,345
Hispanic or Latino (of any race)	19,181
Central American, ex. Mexican	13,998
Guatemalan	12,816
Dominican Republic	27,998
Mexican	15,315
Puerto Rican	25,988
South American	16,877
Ecuadorian	12,584

Notes: (1) Percent of total population; (2) Percent of Hispanic/Latino population; Profiles include places with an overall population of at least 125,000, OR an overall population of at least 25,000 where the Hispanic/Latino population is at least 20% of the overall population. In states where less than five places meet either of these criteria, we have included places with at least 10,000 total population with the highest percentage of Hispanic/Latino population. These places are identified with an asterisk (*); Please refer to the User's Guide for a full explanation of data.

Households with $100,000+ Income

Group	Number	%
Total Population	12,095	34.7
Hispanic or Latino (of any race)	1,116	29.8
Central American, ex. Mexican	132	13.6
Guatemalan	116	17.4
Dominican Republic	135	51.7
Mexican	20	5.1
Puerto Rican	412	42.7
South American	307	33.5
Ecuadorian	140	28.2

Households with Food Stamps/SNAP Benefits During Past 12 Months

Group	Number	%
Total Population	4,076	11.7
Hispanic or Latino (of any race)	289	7.7
Central American, ex. Mexican	96	9.9
Guatemalan	79	11.8
Dominican Republic	0	0.0
Mexican	16	4.1
Puerto Rican	89	9.2
South American	88	9.6
Ecuadorian	84	16.9

Poverty Rate
(Income in Past 12 Months Below Poverty Level)

Group	%
Total Population	18.6
Hispanic or Latino (of any race)	13.9
Central American, ex. Mexican	22.4
Guatemalan	22.4
Dominican Republic	2.7
Mexican	8.3
Puerto Rican	12.6
South American	12.7
Ecuadorian	16.0

Rochester

Population

Group	Number	%TP[1]	%HP[2]
Total Population	210,565	100.0	–
Hispanic or Latino (of any race)	34,456	16.4	100.0
Central American, ex. Mexican	569	0.3	1.7
Honduran	129	0.1	0.4
Panamanian	123	0.1	0.4
Cuban	1,616	0.8	4.7
Dominican Republic	1,373	0.7	4.0
Mexican	1,168	0.6	3.4
Puerto Rican	27,734	13.2	80.5
South American	517	0.2	1.5
Colombian	182	0.1	0.5
Spaniard	153	0.1	0.4

Population Growth: 2000–2010

Group	%
Total Population	-4.2
Hispanic or Latino (of any race)	22.9
Central American, ex. Mexican	105.4
Cuban	37.3
Dominican Republic	69.9
Mexican	37.3
Puerto Rican	26.7
South American	42.8
Colombian	54.2

Males per 100 Females

Group	Number
Total Population	93.4
Hispanic or Latino (of any race)	92.4
Central American, ex. Mexican	94.9
Honduran	69.7
Panamanian	64.0
Cuban	121.1
Dominican Republic	88.1
Mexican	95.0
Puerto Rican	91.0
South American	99.6
Colombian	111.6
Spaniard	88.9

Average Household Size

Group	People
Total Population	2.30
Hispanic or Latino (of any race)	2.82
Central American, ex. Mexican	2.79
Honduran	3.05
Panamanian	2.64
Cuban	2.40
Dominican Republic	3.11
Mexican	2.51
Puerto Rican	2.89
South American	2.21
Colombian	2.14
Spaniard	2.03

Median Age

Group	Years
Total Population	30.8
Hispanic or Latino (of any race)	24.6
Central American, ex. Mexican	28.3
Honduran	28.4
Panamanian	25.5
Cuban	35.8
Dominican Republic	27.3
Mexican	24.0
Puerto Rican	23.8
South American	29.0
Colombian	26.7
Spaniard	30.8

High School Graduates
(Universe: Population 25 Years and Over)

Group	Number	%
Total Population	101,361	78.2
Hispanic or Latino (of any race)	9,614	59.5
Central American, ex. Mexican	387	69.7
Cuban	470	74.6
Dominican Republic	503	62.9
Mexican	478	61.4
Puerto Rican	7,078	56.8

Four-Year College Graduates
(Universe: Population 25 Years and Over)

Group	Number	%
Total Population	31,250	24.1
Hispanic or Latino (of any race)	1,417	8.8
Central American, ex. Mexican	85	15.3
Cuban	96	15.2
Dominican Republic	33	4.1
Mexican	67	8.6
Puerto Rican	877	7.0

Population Age 3–17 Enrolled in Public School
(Universe: Population Age 3–17 Enrolled in School)

Group	Number	%
Total Population	35,461	88.8
Hispanic or Latino (of any race)	8,262	93.2
Central American, ex. Mexican	203	100.0
Cuban	237	95.6
Dominican Republic	443	88.2
Mexican	317	95.2
Puerto Rican	6,506	94.2

Population Age 3–17 Enrolled in Private School
(Universe: Population Age 3–17 Enrolled in School)

Group	Number	%
Total Population	4,462	11.2
Hispanic or Latino (of any race)	606	6.8
Central American, ex. Mexican	0	0.0
Cuban	11	4.4
Dominican Republic	59	11.8
Mexican	16	4.8
Puerto Rican	398	5.8

Foreign-Born Population

Group	Number	%
Total Population	17,281	8.2
Hispanic or Latino (of any race)	3,015	9.3
Central American, ex. Mexican	456	48.4
Cuban	529	55.1
Dominican Republic	821	50.2
Mexican	457	36.0
Puerto Rican	146	0.6

Foreign-Born Naturalized U.S. Citizens

Group	Number	%
Total Population	8,322	48.2
Hispanic or Latino (of any race)	1,418	47.0
Central American, ex. Mexican	129	28.3
Cuban	158	29.9
Dominican Republic	471	57.4
Mexican	174	38.1
Puerto Rican	78	53.4

Language Spoken at Home: English Only
(Universe: Population 5 Years and Over)

Group	Number	%
Total Population	163,276	82.9
Hispanic or Latino (of any race)	9,388	32.8
Central American, ex. Mexican	365	45.4
Cuban	146	16.5
Dominican Republic	228	15.6
Mexican	569	47.3
Puerto Rican	7,366	32.8

Language Spoken at Home: Spanish
(Universe: Population 5 Years and Over)

Group	Number	%
Total Population	21,423	10.9
Hispanic or Latino (of any race)	19,175	66.9
Central American, ex. Mexican	439	54.6
Cuban	737	83.5
Dominican Republic	1,236	84.4
Mexican	620	51.6
Puerto Rican	15,036	66.9

Unemployment Rate
(Universe: Population 16 Years and Over)

Group	%
Total Population	11.7
Hispanic or Latino (of any race)	16.4
Central American, ex. Mexican	19.3
Cuban	2.4
Dominican Republic	18.0
Mexican	10.6
Puerto Rican	17.4

Class of Worker: Private Wage and Salary
(Universe: Civilian Employed Population 16 Years and Over)

Group	Number	%
Total Population	72,255	82.6
Hispanic or Latino (of any race)	9,040	83.9
Central American, ex. Mexican	303	82.6
Cuban	326	74.3
Dominican Republic	470	83.3
Mexican	522	92.4
Puerto Rican	6,831	84.1

Class of Worker: Government
(Universe: Civilian Employed Population 16 Years and Over)

Group	Number	%
Total Population	10,959	12.5
Hispanic or Latino (of any race)	1,086	10.1
Central American, ex. Mexican	30	8.2
Cuban	54	12.3
Dominican Republic	47	8.3
Mexican	5	0.9
Puerto Rican	890	11.0

Means of Transportation to Work: Car, Truck or Van
(Universe: Workers 16 Years and Over)

Group	Number	%
Total Population	68,063	80.2
Hispanic or Latino (of any race)	8,116	79.8
Central American, ex. Mexican	147	41.2
Cuban	376	86.4
Dominican Republic	351	67.1
Mexican	385	68.1
Puerto Rican	6,328	82.2

Means of Transportation to Work: Public Transportation (ex. Taxicab)
(Universe: Workers 16 Years and Over)

Group	Number	%
Total Population	7,167	8.4
Hispanic or Latino (of any race)	915	9.0
Central American, ex. Mexican	64	17.9
Cuban	12	2.8

Notes: (1) Percent of total population; (2) Percent of Hispanic/Latino population; Profiles include places with an overall population of at least 125,000, OR an overall population of at least 25,000 where the Hispanic/Latino population is at least 20% of the overall population. In states where less than five places meet either of these criteria, we have included places with at least 10,000 total population with the highest percentage of Hispanic/Latino population. These places are identified with an asterisk (*); Please refer to the User's Guide for a full explanation of data.

Group	Number	%
Dominican Republic	115	22.0
Mexican	31	5.5
Puerto Rican	693	9.0

Homeownership Rate
(Universe: Occupied Housing Units)

Group	%
Total Population	37.7
Hispanic or Latino (of any race)	25.6
Central American, ex. Mexican	41.6
Honduran	30.2
Panamanian	44.4
Cuban	30.6
Dominican Republic	33.6
Mexican	28.8
Puerto Rican	24.5
South American	36.3
Colombian	33.3
Spaniard	43.3

Median Home Value

Group	Dollars
Total Population	73,600
Hispanic or Latino (of any race)	62,100
Central American, ex. Mexican	56,400
Cuban	34,600
Dominican Republic	78,300
Mexican	80,900
Puerto Rican	61,200

Median Gross Rent

Group	Dollars
Total Population	714
Hispanic or Latino (of any race)	691
Central American, ex. Mexican	890
Cuban	495
Dominican Republic	805
Mexican	983
Puerto Rican	675

Median Household Income
(2010 Inflation-Adjusted Dollars)

Group	Dollars
Total Population	30,138
Hispanic or Latino (of any race)	23,347
Central American, ex. Mexican	30,895
Cuban	21,081
Dominican Republic	26,500
Mexican	38,088
Puerto Rican	22,009

Per Capita Income
(2010 Inflation-Adjusted Dollars)

Group	Dollars
Total Population	17,865
Hispanic or Latino (of any race)	10,723
Central American, ex. Mexican	12,042
Cuban	12,824
Dominican Republic	9,663
Mexican	13,706
Puerto Rican	10,264

Households with $100,000+ Income

Group	Number	%
Total Population	6,344	7.4
Hispanic or Latino (of any race)	404	3.9
Central American, ex. Mexican	0	0.0
Cuban	9	2.1
Dominican Republic	33	8.0
Mexican	50	13.4
Puerto Rican	254	3.0

Households with Food Stamps/SNAP Benefits During Past 12 Months

Group	Number	%
Total Population	22,522	26.3
Hispanic or Latino (of any race)	4,370	41.7
Central American, ex. Mexican	73	21.0
Cuban	133	30.9
Dominican Republic	217	52.9
Mexican	113	30.4
Puerto Rican	3,672	44.0

Poverty Rate
(Income in Past 12 Months Below Poverty Level)

Group	%
Total Population	30.4
Hispanic or Latino (of any race)	42.0
Central American, ex. Mexican	44.4
Cuban	33.0
Dominican Republic	37.7
Mexican	25.4
Puerto Rican	44.7

Rye

Population

Group	Number	%TP[1]	%HP[2]
Total Population	45,928	100.0	–
Hispanic or Latino (of any race)	19,477	42.4	100.0
Central American, ex. Mexican	3,923	8.5	20.1
Guatemalan	2,654	5.8	13.6
Honduran	191	0.4	1.0
Salvadoran	1,004	2.2	5.2
Cuban	463	1.0	2.4
Dominican Republic	655	1.4	3.4
Mexican	5,313	11.6	27.3
Puerto Rican	1,093	2.4	5.6
South American	6,585	14.3	33.8
Argentinean	128	0.3	0.7
Bolivian	375	0.8	1.9
Chilean	192	0.4	1.0
Colombian	891	1.9	4.6
Ecuadorian	2,901	6.3	14.9
Paraguayan	102	0.2	0.5
Peruvian	1,734	3.8	8.9
Uruguayan	211	0.5	1.1
Spaniard	173	0.4	0.9

Population Growth: 2000–2010

Group	%
Total Population	4.7
Hispanic or Latino (of any race)	36.5
Central American, ex. Mexican	94.6
Guatemalan	132.2
Honduran	85.4
Salvadoran	61.4
Cuban	-14.3
Dominican Republic	119.1
Mexican	63.3
Puerto Rican	6.8
South American	71.4
Bolivian	108.3
Chilean	38.1
Colombian	20.6
Ecuadorian	108.1
Peruvian	69.8
Uruguayan	73.0

Males per 100 Females

Group	Number
Total Population	102.9
Hispanic or Latino (of any race)	124.6
Central American, ex. Mexican	148.1
Guatemalan	173.0
Honduran	103.2
Salvadoran	111.8
Cuban	98.7
Dominican Republic	92.1
Mexican	135.1
Puerto Rican	96.9
South American	116.8
Argentinean	85.5
Bolivian	114.3
Chilean	111.0
Colombian	91.2
Ecuadorian	143.6
Paraguayan	100.0
Peruvian	99.3
Uruguayan	117.5
Spaniard	98.9

Average Household Size

Group	People
Total Population	2.93
Hispanic or Latino (of any race)	4.01

Group	People
Central American, ex. Mexican	4.51
Guatemalan	4.47
Honduran	4.09
Salvadoran	4.79
Cuban	2.44
Dominican Republic	3.64
Mexican	4.89
Puerto Rican	2.89
South American	3.76
Argentinean	2.80
Bolivian	4.06
Chilean	3.15
Colombian	2.99
Ecuadorian	4.34
Paraguayan	3.06
Peruvian	3.64
Uruguayan	3.09
Spaniard	3.02

Median Age

Group	Years
Total Population	37.2
Hispanic or Latino (of any race)	30.3
Central American, ex. Mexican	30.4
Guatemalan	30.3
Honduran	29.6
Salvadoran	30.8
Cuban	48.0
Dominican Republic	27.9
Mexican	26.7
Puerto Rican	32.0
South American	34.3
Argentinean	39.2
Bolivian	34.2
Chilean	43.2
Colombian	38.4
Ecuadorian	31.3
Paraguayan	40.0
Peruvian	37.3
Uruguayan	39.3
Spaniard	39.2

High School Graduates
(Universe: Population 25 Years and Over)

Group	Number	%
Total Population	24,719	79.9
Hispanic or Latino (of any race)	5,900	57.8
Central American, ex. Mexican	732	36.4
Guatemalan	575	35.6
Mexican	860	42.1
Puerto Rican	829	82.8
South American	2,981	70.5
Ecuadorian	566	43.3
Peruvian	1,281	86.9

Four-Year College Graduates
(Universe: Population 25 Years and Over)

Group	Number	%
Total Population	10,556	34.1
Hispanic or Latino (of any race)	1,315	12.9
Central American, ex. Mexican	92	4.6
Guatemalan	59	3.7
Mexican	154	7.5
Puerto Rican	394	39.4
South American	553	13.1
Ecuadorian	71	5.4
Peruvian	171	11.6

Population Age 3–17 Enrolled in Public School
(Universe: Population Age 3–17 Enrolled in School)

Group	Number	%
Total Population	6,698	85.7
Hispanic or Latino (of any race)	2,690	89.6
Central American, ex. Mexican	307	86.5
Guatemalan	143	84.1
Mexican	976	98.1
Puerto Rican	370	90.0
South American	714	80.0
Ecuadorian	320	90.4
Peruvian	153	58.6

Population Age 3–17 Enrolled in Private School
(Universe: Population Age 3–17 Enrolled in School)

Group	Number	%
Total Population	1,119	14.3

Notes: (1) Percent of total population; (2) Percent of Hispanic/Latino population; Profiles include places with an overall population of at least 125,000, OR an overall population of at least 25,000 where the Hispanic/Latino population is at least 20% of the overall population. In states where less than five places meet either of these criteria, we have included places with at least 10,000 total population with the highest percentage of Hispanic/Latino population. These places are identified with an asterisk (*); Please refer to the User's Guide for a full explanation of data.

Group	Number	%
Hispanic or Latino (of any race)	311	10.4
Central American, ex. Mexican	48	13.5
Guatemalan	27	15.9
Mexican	19	1.9
Puerto Rican	41	10.0
South American	178	20.0
Ecuadorian	34	9.6
Peruvian	108	41.4

Foreign-Born Population

Group	Number	%
Total Population	16,368	36.1
Hispanic or Latino (of any race)	10,915	65.1
Central American, ex. Mexican	2,662	85.3
Guatemalan	2,212	92.4
Mexican	2,544	64.6
Puerto Rican	0	0.0
South American	4,953	78.5
Ecuadorian	1,627	77.5
Peruvian	1,846	87.8

Foreign-Born Naturalized U.S. Citizens

Group	Number	%
Total Population	5,022	30.7
Hispanic or Latino (of any race)	2,393	21.9
Central American, ex. Mexican	322	12.1
Guatemalan	234	10.6
Mexican	196	7.7
Puerto Rican	0	0.0
South American	1,471	29.7
Ecuadorian	543	33.4
Peruvian	470	25.5

Language Spoken at Home: English Only

(Universe: Population 5 Years and Over)

Group	Number	%
Total Population	22,317	52.8
Hispanic or Latino (of any race)	1,451	9.5
Central American, ex. Mexican	82	2.8
Guatemalan	82	3.6
Mexican	243	7.1
Puerto Rican	679	41.6
South American	287	4.9
Ecuadorian	71	3.7
Peruvian	73	3.7

Language Spoken at Home: Spanish

(Universe: Population 5 Years and Over)

Group	Number	%
Total Population	14,451	34.2
Hispanic or Latino (of any race)	13,745	90.0
Central American, ex. Mexican	2,801	97.2
Guatemalan	2,194	96.4
Mexican	3,185	92.9
Puerto Rican	911	55.9
South American	5,489	94.5
Ecuadorian	1,835	96.3
Peruvian	1,919	96.3

Unemployment Rate

(Universe: Population 16 Years and Over)

Group	%
Total Population	7.4
Hispanic or Latino (of any race)	7.1
Central American, ex. Mexican	3.7
Guatemalan	4.3
Mexican	4.5
Puerto Rican	13.6
South American	7.1
Ecuadorian	9.4
Peruvian	8.3

Class of Worker: Private Wage and Salary

(Universe: Civilian Employed Population 16 Years and Over)

Group	Number	%
Total Population	19,725	83.2
Hispanic or Latino (of any race)	8,611	89.6
Central American, ex. Mexican	1,899	96.2
Guatemalan	1,582	95.5
Mexican	1,916	93.7
Puerto Rican	585	70.8
South American	3,455	88.7
Ecuadorian	991	86.2
Peruvian	1,359	94.0

Class of Worker: Government

(Universe: Civilian Employed Population 16 Years and Over)

Group	Number	%
Total Population	2,700	11.4
Hispanic or Latino (of any race)	559	5.8
Central American, ex. Mexican	43	2.2
Guatemalan	43	2.6
Mexican	90	4.4
Puerto Rican	139	16.8
South American	188	4.8
Ecuadorian	48	4.2
Peruvian	60	4.2

Means of Transportation to Work: Car, Truck or Van

(Universe: Workers 16 Years and Over)

Group	Number	%
Total Population	14,841	64.8
Hispanic or Latino (of any race)	4,972	53.7
Central American, ex. Mexican	719	37.1
Guatemalan	574	35.2
Mexican	952	47.3
Puerto Rican	562	71.6
South American	2,097	57.4
Ecuadorian	661	58.1
Peruvian	624	46.7

Means of Transportation to Work: Public Transportation (ex. Taxicab)

(Universe: Workers 16 Years and Over)

Group	Number	%
Total Population	4,115	18.0
Hispanic or Latino (of any race)	1,760	19.0
Central American, ex. Mexican	465	24.0
Guatemalan	401	24.6
Mexican	231	11.5
Puerto Rican	123	15.7
South American	897	24.6
Ecuadorian	206	18.1
Peruvian	417	31.2

Homeownership Rate

(Universe: Occupied Housing Units)

Group	%
Total Population	55.5
Hispanic or Latino (of any race)	24.2
Central American, ex. Mexican	15.9
Guatemalan	14.4
Honduran	13.0
Salvadoran	18.6
Cuban	48.2
Dominican Republic	18.4
Mexican	16.7
Puerto Rican	32.9
South American	27.7
Argentinean	38.8
Bolivian	41.8
Chilean	36.1
Colombian	29.3
Ecuadorian	21.5
Paraguayan	17.6
Peruvian	31.1
Uruguayan	27.5
Spaniard	63.0

Median Home Value

Group	Dollars
Total Population	572,300
Hispanic or Latino (of any race)	475,800
Central American, ex. Mexican	427,400
Guatemalan	240,700
Mexican	534,100
Puerto Rican	174,800
South American	565,100
Ecuadorian	489,700
Peruvian	598,800

Median Gross Rent

Group	Dollars
Total Population	1,353
Hispanic or Latino (of any race)	1,411
Central American, ex. Mexican	1,499
Guatemalan	1,544
Mexican	1,535
Puerto Rican	740
South American	1,407
Ecuadorian	1,208
Peruvian	1,399

Median Household Income

(2010 Inflation-Adjusted Dollars)

Group	Dollars
Total Population	67,083
Hispanic or Latino (of any race)	47,348
Central American, ex. Mexican	39,853
Guatemalan	44,830
Mexican	39,263
Puerto Rican	49,881
South American	55,108
Ecuadorian	68,182
Peruvian	54,424

Per Capita Income

(2010 Inflation-Adjusted Dollars)

Group	Dollars
Total Population	39,563
Hispanic or Latino (of any race)	18,246
Central American, ex. Mexican	14,213
Guatemalan	14,805
Mexican	13,702
Puerto Rican	26,515
South American	20,955
Ecuadorian	17,261
Peruvian	18,899

Households with $100,000+ Income

Group	Number	%
Total Population	5,145	32.0
Hispanic or Latino (of any race)	458	9.6
Central American, ex. Mexican	63	7.9
Guatemalan	63	10.3
Mexican	47	4.9
Puerto Rican	93	17.7
South American	169	8.5
Ecuadorian	55	9.7
Peruvian	38	4.9

Households with Food Stamps/SNAP Benefits During Past 12 Months

Group	Number	%
Total Population	881	5.5
Hispanic or Latino (of any race)	499	10.4
Central American, ex. Mexican	145	18.2
Guatemalan	145	23.8
Mexican	136	14.3
Puerto Rican	37	7.1
South American	143	7.2
Ecuadorian	25	4.4
Peruvian	33	4.3

Poverty Rate

(Income in Past 12 Months Below Poverty Level)

Group	%
Total Population	11.6
Hispanic or Latino (of any race)	20.5
Central American, ex. Mexican	28.7
Guatemalan	26.7
Mexican	32.7
Puerto Rican	14.0
South American	8.7
Ecuadorian	5.2
Peruvian	7.6

Spring Valley

Population

Group	Number	%TP[1]	%HP[2]
Total Population	31,347	100.0	–
Hispanic or Latino (of any race)	9,588	30.6	100.0
Central American, ex. Mexican	4,034	12.9	42.1
Guatemalan	3,265	10.4	34.1
Honduran	123	0.4	1.3
Salvadoran	529	1.7	5.5
Dominican Republic	324	1.0	3.4
Mexican	885	2.8	9.2
Puerto Rican	611	1.9	6.4
South American	2,841	9.1	29.6
Ecuadorian	2,681	8.6	28.0

Notes: (1) Percent of total population; (2) Percent of Hispanic/Latino population; Profiles include places with an overall population of at least 125,000, OR an overall population of at least 25,000 where the Hispanic/Latino population is at least 20% of the overall population. In states where less than five places meet either of these criteria, we have included places with at least 10,000 total population with the highest percentage of Hispanic/Latino population. These places are identified with an asterisk (*); Please refer to the User's Guide for a full explanation of data.

Population Growth: 2000–2010

Group	%
Total Population	23.1
Hispanic or Latino (of any race)	144.5
Central American, ex. Mexican	238.1
Guatemalan	240.1
Salvadoran	323.2
Mexican	90.7
Puerto Rican	-11.7
South American	345.3
Ecuadorian	436.2

Males per 100 Females

Group	Number
Total Population	103.1
Hispanic or Latino (of any race)	143.5
Central American, ex. Mexican	159.8
Guatemalan	176.5
Honduran	115.8
Salvadoran	111.6
Dominican Republic	68.8
Mexican	165.8
Puerto Rican	107.1
South American	138.1
Ecuadorian	144.4

Average Household Size

Group	People
Total Population	3.56
Hispanic or Latino (of any race)	4.84
Central American, ex. Mexican	5.08
Guatemalan	5.25
Honduran	3.88
Salvadoran	4.71
Dominican Republic	3.80
Mexican	4.66
Puerto Rican	2.87
South American	5.51
Ecuadorian	5.76

Median Age

Group	Years
Total Population	28.8
Hispanic or Latino (of any race)	27.5
Central American, ex. Mexican	28.0
Guatemalan	28.0
Honduran	29.1
Salvadoran	27.6
Dominican Republic	26.6
Mexican	27.3
Puerto Rican	28.2
South American	28.3
Ecuadorian	28.0

High School Graduates
(Universe: Population 25 Years and Over)

Group	Number	%
Total Population	13,226	74.8
Hispanic or Latino (of any race)	2,554	53.2
Central American, ex. Mexican	856	41.7
Guatemalan	666	39.4
South American	674	51.4
Ecuadorian	505	45.3

Four-Year College Graduates
(Universe: Population 25 Years and Over)

Group	Number	%
Total Population	3,933	22.3
Hispanic or Latino (of any race)	675	14.1
Central American, ex. Mexican	169	8.2
Guatemalan	112	6.6
South American	153	11.7
Ecuadorian	145	13.0

Population Age 3–17 Enrolled in Public School
(Universe: Population Age 3–17 Enrolled in School)

Group	Number	%
Total Population	4,367	62.6
Hispanic or Latino (of any race)	1,388	93.4
Central American, ex. Mexican	684	100.0
Guatemalan	607	100.0
South American	309	94.2
Ecuadorian	309	94.2

Population Age 3–17 Enrolled in Private School
(Universe: Population Age 3–17 Enrolled in School)

Group	Number	%
Total Population	2,608	37.4
Hispanic or Latino (of any race)	98	6.6
Central American, ex. Mexican	0	0.0
Guatemalan	0	0.0
South American	19	5.8
Ecuadorian	19	5.8

Foreign-Born Population

Group	Number	%
Total Population	14,453	47.7
Hispanic or Latino (of any race)	5,792	66.0
Central American, ex. Mexican	2,863	73.8
Guatemalan	2,444	75.5
South American	1,834	73.8
Ecuadorian	1,646	71.9

Foreign-Born Naturalized U.S. Citizens

Group	Number	%
Total Population	4,141	28.7
Hispanic or Latino (of any race)	568	9.8
Central American, ex. Mexican	179	6.3
Guatemalan	81	3.3
South American	107	5.8
Ecuadorian	33	2.0

Language Spoken at Home: English Only
(Universe: Population 5 Years and Over)

Group	Number	%
Total Population	8,874	32.8
Hispanic or Latino (of any race)	411	5.5
Central American, ex. Mexican	56	1.6
Guatemalan	37	1.3
South American	8	0.4
Ecuadorian	0	0.0

Language Spoken at Home: Spanish
(Universe: Population 5 Years and Over)

Group	Number	%
Total Population	7,219	26.7
Hispanic or Latino (of any race)	7,032	93.5
Central American, ex. Mexican	3,407	98.4
Guatemalan	2,892	98.7
South American	2,014	99.6
Ecuadorian	1,826	100.0

Unemployment Rate
(Universe: Population 16 Years and Over)

Group	%
Total Population	9.1
Hispanic or Latino (of any race)	10.1
Central American, ex. Mexican	10.3
Guatemalan	9.5
South American	7.8
Ecuadorian	8.7

Class of Worker: Private Wage and Salary
(Universe: Civilian Employed Population 16 Years and Over)

Group	Number	%
Total Population	11,214	79.8
Hispanic or Latino (of any race)	3,600	80.1
Central American, ex. Mexican	1,919	85.1
Guatemalan	1,672	85.9
South American	869	69.1
Ecuadorian	742	66.5

Class of Worker: Government
(Universe: Civilian Employed Population 16 Years and Over)

Group	Number	%
Total Population	1,709	12.2
Hispanic or Latino (of any race)	291	6.5
Central American, ex. Mexican	91	4.0
Guatemalan	47	2.4
South American	39	3.1
Ecuadorian	31	2.8

Means of Transportation to Work: Car, Truck or Van
(Universe: Workers 16 Years and Over)

Group	Number	%
Total Population	9,743	70.6
Hispanic or Latino (of any race)	2,348	53.3
Central American, ex. Mexican	1,257	56.5
Guatemalan	1,018	53.1
South American	550	45.4
Ecuadorian	436	40.7

Means of Transportation to Work: Public Transportation (ex. Taxicab)
(Universe: Workers 16 Years and Over)

Group	Number	%
Total Population	2,537	18.4
Hispanic or Latino (of any race)	1,339	30.4
Central American, ex. Mexican	476	21.4
Guatemalan	442	23.0
South American	507	41.8
Ecuadorian	480	44.8

Homeownership Rate
(Universe: Occupied Housing Units)

Group	%
Total Population	28.7
Hispanic or Latino (of any race)	12.8
Central American, ex. Mexican	6.1
Guatemalan	4.0
Honduran	15.4
Salvadoran	9.9
Dominican Republic	30.4
Mexican	6.1
Puerto Rican	41.2
South American	11.1
Ecuadorian	9.1

Median Home Value

Group	Dollars
Total Population	301,500
Hispanic or Latino (of any race)	172,600
Central American, ex. Mexican	118,000
Guatemalan	112,500
South American	158,700
Ecuadorian	0

Median Gross Rent

Group	Dollars
Total Population	1,108
Hispanic or Latino (of any race)	1,278
Central American, ex. Mexican	1,287
Guatemalan	1,249
South American	1,214
Ecuadorian	1,253

Median Household Income
(2010 Inflation-Adjusted Dollars)

Group	Dollars
Total Population	48,125
Hispanic or Latino (of any race)	55,134
Central American, ex. Mexican	51,055
Guatemalan	57,375
South American	59,844
Ecuadorian	68,929

Per Capita Income
(2010 Inflation-Adjusted Dollars)

Group	Dollars
Total Population	18,033
Hispanic or Latino (of any race)	13,362
Central American, ex. Mexican	12,072
Guatemalan	11,704
South American	11,596
Ecuadorian	10,934

Households with $100,000+ Income

Group	Number	%
Total Population	1,334	15.1
Hispanic or Latino (of any race)	254	13.5
Central American, ex. Mexican	65	9.1
Guatemalan	46	8.9
South American	84	17.4
Ecuadorian	84	22.1

Households with Food Stamps/SNAP Benefits During Past 12 Months

Group	Number	%
Total Population	1,252	14.2
Hispanic or Latino (of any race)	264	14.1
Central American, ex. Mexican	118	16.5
Guatemalan	101	19.6
South American	103	21.3
Ecuadorian	103	27.1

Notes: (1) Percent of total population; (2) Percent of Hispanic/Latino population; Profiles include places with an overall population of at least 125,000, OR an overall population of at least 25,000 where the Hispanic/Latino population is at least 20% of the overall population. In states where less than five places meet either of these criteria, we have included places with at least 10,000 total population with the highest percentage of Hispanic/Latino population. These places are identified with an asterisk (*); Please refer to the User's Guide for a full explanation of data.

Poverty Rate
(Income in Past 12 Months Below Poverty Level)

Group	%
Total Population	21.0
Hispanic or Latino (of any race)	21.9
Central American, ex. Mexican	27.3
Guatemalan	28.7
South American	19.6
Ecuadorian	21.2

Staten Island

Population

Group	Number	%TP[1]	%HP[2]
Total Population	468,730	100.0	–
Hispanic or Latino (of any race)	81,051	17.3	100.0
Central American, ex. Mexican	4,310	0.9	5.3
Costa Rican	266	0.1	0.3
Guatemalan	864	0.2	1.1
Honduran	1,735	0.4	2.1
Nicaraguan	199	<0.1	0.2
Panamanian	607	0.1	0.7
Salvadoran	592	0.1	0.7
Cuban	1,831	0.4	2.3
Dominican Republic	4,918	1.0	6.1
Mexican	18,684	4.0	23.1
Puerto Rican	37,517	8.0	46.3
South American	8,232	1.8	10.2
Argentinean	608	0.1	0.8
Bolivian	161	<0.1	0.2
Chilean	346	0.1	0.4
Colombian	2,526	0.5	3.1
Ecuadorian	2,675	0.6	3.3
Peruvian	1,462	0.3	1.8
Venezuelan	254	0.1	0.3
Spaniard	1,333	0.3	1.6

Population Growth: 2000–2010

Group	%
Total Population	5.6
Hispanic or Latino (of any race)	51.4
Central American, ex. Mexican	119.5
Costa Rican	22.6
Guatemalan	249.8
Honduran	113.9
Panamanian	86.8
Salvadoran	213.2
Cuban	31.5
Dominican Republic	163.4
Mexican	139.6
Puerto Rican	31.5
South American	93.6
Argentinean	77.3
Bolivian	49.1
Chilean	62.4
Colombian	72.0
Ecuadorian	130.8
Peruvian	144.9
Spaniard	184.2

Males per 100 Females

Group	Number
Total Population	94.1
Hispanic or Latino (of any race)	99.0
Central American, ex. Mexican	95.2
Costa Rican	79.7
Guatemalan	146.9
Honduran	90.0
Nicaraguan	91.3
Panamanian	77.5
Salvadoran	80.5
Cuban	89.5
Dominican Republic	82.5
Mexican	131.6
Puerto Rican	91.8
South American	86.2
Argentinean	86.5
Bolivian	78.9
Chilean	96.6
Colombian	74.7
Ecuadorian	92.2
Peruvian	98.1
Venezuelan	74.0

Spaniard	92.4

Average Household Size

Group	People
Total Population	2.78
Hispanic or Latino (of any race)	3.39
Central American, ex. Mexican	3.40
Costa Rican	2.93
Guatemalan	3.73
Honduran	3.52
Nicaraguan	3.45
Panamanian	2.87
Salvadoran	3.66
Cuban	2.73
Dominican Republic	3.51
Mexican	4.93
Puerto Rican	3.00
South American	3.31
Argentinean	2.94
Bolivian	3.26
Chilean	2.75
Colombian	3.09
Ecuadorian	3.68
Peruvian	3.50
Venezuelan	2.89
Spaniard	2.51

Median Age

Group	Years
Total Population	38.4
Hispanic or Latino (of any race)	28.1
Central American, ex. Mexican	32.1
Costa Rican	40.5
Guatemalan	28.4
Honduran	32.0
Nicaraguan	30.9
Panamanian	37.2
Salvadoran	31.8
Cuban	33.4
Dominican Republic	28.5
Mexican	24.6
Puerto Rican	28.5
South American	35.6
Argentinean	39.9
Bolivian	39.5
Chilean	38.8
Colombian	34.4
Ecuadorian	33.4
Peruvian	38.1
Venezuelan	33.0
Spaniard	39.7

High School Graduates
(Universe: Population 25 Years and Over)

Group	Number	%
Total Population	272,306	87.5
Hispanic or Latino (of any race)	32,987	79.2
Central American, ex. Mexican	1,727	74.2
Honduran	524	65.3
Cuban	1,167	94.0
Dominican Republic	1,856	76.3
Mexican	3,150	54.0
Puerto Rican	17,120	83.2
South American	5,345	84.1
Colombian	1,593	90.3
Ecuadorian	1,507	74.4
Peruvian	1,013	89.0
Spaniard	1,159	94.7

Four-Year College Graduates
(Universe: Population 25 Years and Over)

Group	Number	%
Total Population	88,782	28.5
Hispanic or Latino (of any race)	7,600	18.2
Central American, ex. Mexican	502	21.6
Honduran	167	20.8
Cuban	171	13.8
Dominican Republic	575	23.6
Mexican	404	6.9
Puerto Rican	3,405	16.6
South American	1,497	23.6
Colombian	462	26.2
Ecuadorian	284	14.0
Peruvian	403	35.4
Spaniard	622	50.8

Population Age 3–17 Enrolled in Public School
(Universe: Population Age 3–17 Enrolled in School)

Group	Number	%
Total Population	63,709	73.9
Hispanic or Latino (of any race)	15,540	82.8
Central American, ex. Mexican	552	83.5
Honduran	89	84.0
Cuban	305	84.0
Dominican Republic	1,012	82.5
Mexican	3,077	95.5
Puerto Rican	8,365	81.5
South American	1,416	71.7
Colombian	346	52.4
Ecuadorian	437	75.3
Peruvian	333	89.3
Spaniard	337	88.9

Population Age 3–17 Enrolled in Private School
(Universe: Population Age 3–17 Enrolled in School)

Group	Number	%
Total Population	22,458	26.1
Hispanic or Latino (of any race)	3,222	17.2
Central American, ex. Mexican	109	16.5
Honduran	17	16.0
Cuban	58	16.0
Dominican Republic	215	17.5
Mexican	146	4.5
Puerto Rican	1,894	18.5
South American	558	28.3
Colombian	314	47.6
Ecuadorian	143	24.7
Peruvian	40	10.7
Spaniard	42	11.1

Foreign-Born Population

Group	Number	%
Total Population	96,258	20.8
Hispanic or Latino (of any race)	19,215	25.4
Central American, ex. Mexican	1,991	55.0
Honduran	782	65.6
Cuban	629	33.6
Dominican Republic	1,880	42.1
Mexican	7,801	59.0
Puerto Rican	234	0.6
South American	5,768	58.8
Colombian	1,429	49.0
Ecuadorian	2,015	67.4
Peruvian	1,129	60.4
Spaniard	223	11.7

Foreign-Born Naturalized U.S. Citizens

Group	Number	%
Total Population	60,416	62.8
Hispanic or Latino (of any race)	7,239	37.7
Central American, ex. Mexican	1,127	56.6
Honduran	424	54.2
Cuban	477	75.8
Dominican Republic	1,101	58.6
Mexican	633	8.1
Puerto Rican	65	27.8
South American	3,207	55.6
Colombian	1,163	81.4
Ecuadorian	846	42.0
Peruvian	451	39.9
Spaniard	135	60.5

Language Spoken at Home: English Only
(Universe: Population 5 Years and Over)

Group	Number	%
Total Population	306,310	70.4
Hispanic or Latino (of any race)	27,478	40.2
Central American, ex. Mexican	734	21.7
Honduran	206	18.0
Cuban	1,000	56.9
Dominican Republic	810	20.8
Mexican	1,170	10.4
Puerto Rican	19,252	55.1
South American	1,736	19.6
Colombian	709	26.0
Ecuadorian	178	6.6
Peruvian	273	17.2
Spaniard	1,321	76.9

Notes: (1) Percent of total population; (2) Percent of Hispanic/Latino population; Profiles include places with an overall population of at least 125,000, OR an overall population of at least 25,000 where the Hispanic/Latino population is at least 20% of the overall population. In states where less than five places meet either of these criteria, we have included places with at least 10,000 total population with the highest percentage of Hispanic/Latino population. These places are identified with an asterisk (*); Please refer to the User's Guide for a full explanation of data.

Language Spoken at Home: Spanish
(Universe: Population 5 Years and Over)

Group	Number	%
Total Population	43,587	10.0
Hispanic or Latino (of any race)	40,384	59.0
Central American, ex. Mexican	2,634	77.9
Honduran	940	82.0
Cuban	746	42.4
Dominican Republic	3,061	78.7
Mexican	9,970	88.4
Puerto Rican	15,575	44.6
South American	7,046	79.4
Colombian	2,015	74.0
Ecuadorian	2,480	91.3
Peruvian	1,312	82.8
Spaniard	324	18.9

Unemployment Rate
(Universe: Population 16 Years and Over)

Group	%
Total Population	6.2
Hispanic or Latino (of any race)	7.3
Central American, ex. Mexican	5.4
Honduran	5.0
Cuban	6.9
Dominican Republic	13.1
Mexican	6.1
Puerto Rican	8.8
South American	3.2
Colombian	3.9
Ecuadorian	1.8
Peruvian	2.2
Spaniard	6.1

Class of Worker: Private Wage and Salary
(Universe: Civilian Employed Population 16 Years and Over)

Group	Number	%
Total Population	152,207	73.2
Hispanic or Latino (of any race)	23,969	75.6
Central American, ex. Mexican	1,679	81.7
Honduran	762	91.3
Cuban	647	81.4
Dominican Republic	1,147	79.9
Mexican	4,299	83.8
Puerto Rican	11,314	73.1
South American	3,428	74.9
Colombian	1,052	76.5
Ecuadorian	1,017	71.3
Peruvian	619	74.2
Spaniard	555	58.7

Class of Worker: Government
(Universe: Civilian Employed Population 16 Years and Over)

Group	Number	%
Total Population	46,384	22.3
Hispanic or Latino (of any race)	6,126	19.3
Central American, ex. Mexican	306	14.9
Honduran	47	5.6
Cuban	129	16.2
Dominican Republic	267	18.6
Mexican	272	5.3
Puerto Rican	3,886	25.1
South American	645	14.1
Colombian	162	11.8
Ecuadorian	285	20.0
Peruvian	93	11.2
Spaniard	361	38.2

Means of Transportation to Work: Car, Truck or Van
(Universe: Workers 16 Years and Over)

Group	Number	%
Total Population	128,691	63.1
Hispanic or Latino (of any race)	16,189	51.9
Central American, ex. Mexican	790	39.2
Honduran	347	41.6
Cuban	430	51.3
Dominican Republic	658	51.9
Mexican	1,440	28.2
Puerto Rican	9,030	59.2
South American	2,418	53.6
Colombian	744	54.1
Ecuadorian	852	60.9
Peruvian	301	37.0
Spaniard	678	71.7

Means of Transportation to Work: Public Transportation (ex. Taxicab)
(Universe: Workers 16 Years and Over)

Group	Number	%
Total Population	63,547	31.1
Hispanic or Latino (of any race)	13,117	42.1
Central American, ex. Mexican	1,140	56.5
Honduran	444	53.2
Cuban	312	37.2
Dominican Republic	460	36.3
Mexican	3,150	61.7
Puerto Rican	5,546	36.4
South American	1,852	41.1
Colombian	557	40.5
Ecuadorian	483	34.5
Peruvian	463	56.9
Spaniard	200	21.2

Homeownership Rate
(Universe: Occupied Housing Units)

Group	%
Total Population	64.1
Hispanic or Latino (of any race)	41.4
Central American, ex. Mexican	43.1
Costa Rican	56.1
Guatemalan	38.1
Honduran	36.4
Nicaraguan	41.8
Panamanian	51.3
Salvadoran	50.0
Cuban	56.4
Dominican Republic	42.4
Mexican	15.2
Puerto Rican	44.7
South American	53.6
Argentinean	61.9
Bolivian	54.3
Chilean	51.7
Colombian	56.8
Ecuadorian	57.0
Peruvian	39.0
Venezuelan	50.7
Spaniard	67.7

Median Home Value

Group	Dollars
Total Population	461,700
Hispanic or Latino (of any race)	416,900
Central American, ex. Mexican	422,600
Honduran	464,400
Cuban	377,100
Dominican Republic	392,000
Mexican	482,400
Puerto Rican	408,900
South American	439,200
Colombian	431,800
Ecuadorian	463,100
Peruvian	362,400
Spaniard	496,200

Median Gross Rent

Group	Dollars
Total Population	1,107
Hispanic or Latino (of any race)	1,181
Central American, ex. Mexican	1,105
Honduran	978
Cuban	1,059
Dominican Republic	1,265
Mexican	1,413
Puerto Rican	1,115
South American	1,100
Colombian	1,076
Ecuadorian	1,089
Peruvian	1,074
Spaniard	1,106

Median Household Income
(2010 Inflation-Adjusted Dollars)

Group	Dollars
Total Population	71,084
Hispanic or Latino (of any race)	57,890
Central American, ex. Mexican	58,074
Honduran	46,333
Cuban	51,509
Dominican Republic	57,143
Mexican	31,220
Puerto Rican	65,520
South American	57,000
Colombian	53,816
Ecuadorian	59,450
Peruvian	46,440
Spaniard	100,732

Per Capita Income
(2010 Inflation-Adjusted Dollars)

Group	Dollars
Total Population	30,843
Hispanic or Latino (of any race)	21,379
Central American, ex. Mexican	23,188
Honduran	26,602
Cuban	25,675
Dominican Republic	17,044
Mexican	12,117
Puerto Rican	22,308
South American	25,076
Colombian	23,232
Ecuadorian	22,597
Peruvian	23,131
Spaniard	37,848

Households with $100,000+ Income

Group	Number	%
Total Population	54,267	33.0
Hispanic or Latino (of any race)	5,515	25.3
Central American, ex. Mexican	254	21.3
Honduran	107	22.7
Cuban	148	20.4
Dominican Republic	282	24.4
Mexican	390	12.7
Puerto Rican	3,109	28.3
South American	688	22.8
Colombian	270	31.4
Ecuadorian	147	16.5
Peruvian	64	10.2
Spaniard	336	51.9

Households with Food Stamps/SNAP Benefits During Past 12 Months

Group	Number	%
Total Population	13,762	8.4
Hispanic or Latino (of any race)	3,774	17.3
Central American, ex. Mexican	137	11.5
Honduran	36	7.6
Cuban	45	6.2
Dominican Republic	353	30.6
Mexican	885	28.8
Puerto Rican	1,928	17.6
South American	339	11.2
Colombian	48	5.6
Ecuadorian	110	12.4
Peruvian	176	28.1
Spaniard	0	0.0

Poverty Rate
(Income in Past 12 Months Below Poverty Level)

Group	%
Total Population	10.3
Hispanic or Latino (of any race)	18.2
Central American, ex. Mexican	3.5
Honduran	6.1
Cuban	11.8
Dominican Republic	27.9
Mexican	37.9
Puerto Rican	14.5
South American	14.9
Colombian	16.2
Ecuadorian	10.3
Peruvian	34.8
Spaniard	2.9

Syracuse

Population

Group	Number	%TP[1]	%HP[2]
Total Population	145,170	100.0	–
Hispanic or Latino (of any race)	12,036	8.3	100.0
Central American, ex. Mexican	348	0.2	2.9
Guatemalan	133	0.1	1.1
Cuban	1,192	0.8	9.9

Notes: (1) Percent of total population; (2) Percent of Hispanic/Latino population; Profiles include places with an overall population of at least 125,000, OR an overall population of at least 25,000 where the Hispanic/Latino population is at least 20% of the overall population. In states where less than five places meet either of these criteria, we have included places with at least 10,000 total population with the highest percentage of Hispanic/Latino population. These places are identified with an asterisk (*); Please refer to the User's Guide for a full explanation of data.

Dominican Republic	689	0.5	5.7
Mexican	958	0.7	8.0
Puerto Rican	7,594	5.2	63.1
South American	530	0.4	4.4
Colombian	173	0.1	1.4
Ecuadorian	101	0.1	0.8
Spaniard	140	0.1	1.2

Population Growth: 2000–2010

Group	%
Total Population	-1.5
Hispanic or Latino (of any race)	54.9
Central American, ex. Mexican	128.9
Cuban	115.9
Dominican Republic	160.0
Mexican	57.0
Puerto Rican	55.5
South American	83.4

Males per 100 Females

Group	Number
Total Population	91.0
Hispanic or Latino (of any race)	92.4
Central American, ex. Mexican	85.1
Guatemalan	111.1
Cuban	108.4
Dominican Republic	86.2
Mexican	81.8
Puerto Rican	92.8
South American	89.3
Colombian	73.0
Ecuadorian	124.4
Spaniard	86.7

Average Household Size

Group	People
Total Population	2.31
Hispanic or Latino (of any race)	2.88
Central American, ex. Mexican	3.00
Guatemalan	4.00
Cuban	2.75
Dominican Republic	2.91
Mexican	2.45
Puerto Rican	3.02
South American	2.66
Colombian	2.46
Ecuadorian	3.45
Spaniard	2.22

Median Age

Group	Years
Total Population	29.6
Hispanic or Latino (of any race)	21.3
Central American, ex. Mexican	20.9
Guatemalan	20.5
Cuban	31.6
Dominican Republic	20.8
Mexican	22.7
Puerto Rican	20.5
South American	22.1
Colombian	21.8
Ecuadorian	21.1
Spaniard	24.7

High School Graduates
(Universe: Population 25 Years and Over)

Group	Number	%
Total Population	67,455	80.6
Hispanic or Latino (of any race)	3,201	68.1
Cuban	555	83.3
Dominican Republic	273	78.0
Puerto Rican	1,400	56.8

Four-Year College Graduates
(Universe: Population 25 Years and Over)

Group	Number	%
Total Population	21,438	25.6
Hispanic or Latino (of any race)	658	14.0
Cuban	86	12.9
Dominican Republic	79	22.6
Puerto Rican	109	4.4

Population Age 3–17 Enrolled in Public School
(Universe: Population Age 3–17 Enrolled in School)

Group	Number	%
Total Population	22,456	89.1
Hispanic or Latino (of any race)	2,849	96.5
Cuban	137	100.0
Dominican Republic	304	88.9
Puerto Rican	1,985	97.4

Population Age 3–17 Enrolled in Private School
(Universe: Population Age 3–17 Enrolled in School)

Group	Number	%
Total Population	2,760	10.9
Hispanic or Latino (of any race)	104	3.5
Cuban	0	0.0
Dominican Republic	38	11.1
Puerto Rican	53	2.6

Foreign-Born Population

Group	Number	%
Total Population	14,855	10.3
Hispanic or Latino (of any race)	2,225	20.9
Cuban	947	88.8
Dominican Republic	384	34.3
Puerto Rican	59	1.0

Foreign-Born Naturalized U.S. Citizens

Group	Number	%
Total Population	5,234	35.2
Hispanic or Latino (of any race)	671	30.2
Cuban	148	15.6
Dominican Republic	182	47.4
Puerto Rican	0	0.0

Language Spoken at Home: English Only
(Universe: Population 5 Years and Over)

Group	Number	%
Total Population	113,775	84.4
Hispanic or Latino (of any race)	2,740	28.8
Cuban	46	4.4
Dominican Republic	139	14.4
Puerto Rican	1,644	31.5

Language Spoken at Home: Spanish
(Universe: Population 5 Years and Over)

Group	Number	%
Total Population	7,710	5.7
Hispanic or Latino (of any race)	6,674	70.3
Cuban	1,003	95.6
Dominican Republic	813	84.5
Puerto Rican	3,541	67.8

Unemployment Rate
(Universe: Population 16 Years and Over)

Group	%
Total Population	10.2
Hispanic or Latino (of any race)	16.5
Cuban	13.6
Dominican Republic	26.0
Puerto Rican	20.0

Class of Worker: Private Wage and Salary
(Universe: Civilian Employed Population 16 Years and Over)

Group	Number	%
Total Population	47,602	80.1
Hispanic or Latino (of any race)	3,144	87.0
Cuban	557	95.4
Dominican Republic	260	70.8
Puerto Rican	1,437	89.0

Class of Worker: Government
(Universe: Civilian Employed Population 16 Years and Over)

Group	Number	%
Total Population	9,115	15.3
Hispanic or Latino (of any race)	308	8.5
Cuban	27	4.6
Dominican Republic	46	12.5
Puerto Rican	162	10.0

Means of Transportation to Work: Car, Truck or Van
(Universe: Workers 16 Years and Over)

Group	Number	%
Total Population	43,944	76.4
Hispanic or Latino (of any race)	2,519	71.5
Cuban	514	88.0
Dominican Republic	168	45.8
Puerto Rican	1,213	77.8

Means of Transportation to Work: Public Transportation (ex. Taxicab)
(Universe: Workers 16 Years and Over)

Group	Number	%
Total Population	4,363	7.6
Hispanic or Latino (of any race)	492	14.0
Cuban	24	4.1
Dominican Republic	69	18.8
Puerto Rican	206	13.2

Homeownership Rate
(Universe: Occupied Housing Units)

Group	%
Total Population	38.5
Hispanic or Latino (of any race)	20.1
Central American, ex. Mexican	30.0
Guatemalan	25.9
Cuban	25.7
Dominican Republic	19.7
Mexican	23.9
Puerto Rican	17.3
South American	32.1
Colombian	22.0
Ecuadorian	40.0
Spaniard	35.2

Median Home Value

Group	Dollars
Total Population	83,400
Hispanic or Latino (of any race)	82,300
Cuban	74,000
Dominican Republic	80,700
Puerto Rican	83,000

Median Gross Rent

Group	Dollars
Total Population	673
Hispanic or Latino (of any race)	656
Cuban	676
Dominican Republic	928
Puerto Rican	627

Median Household Income
(2010 Inflation-Adjusted Dollars)

Group	Dollars
Total Population	30,891
Hispanic or Latino (of any race)	20,526
Cuban	38,202
Dominican Republic	16,961
Puerto Rican	18,233

Per Capita Income
(2010 Inflation-Adjusted Dollars)

Group	Dollars
Total Population	17,866
Hispanic or Latino (of any race)	11,024
Cuban	16,384
Dominican Republic	9,166
Puerto Rican	8,672

Households with $100,000+ Income

Group	Number	%
Total Population	4,780	8.5
Hispanic or Latino (of any race)	189	5.5
Cuban	22	5.0
Dominican Republic	18	8.0
Puerto Rican	32	1.7

Households with Food Stamps/SNAP Benefits During Past 12 Months

Group	Number	%
Total Population	12,277	21.8
Hispanic or Latino (of any race)	1,304	38.2
Cuban	170	38.5
Dominican Republic	82	36.6
Puerto Rican	913	47.3

Poverty Rate
(Income in Past 12 Months Below Poverty Level)

Group	%
Total Population	31.1
Hispanic or Latino (of any race)	41.7

Notes: (1) Percent of total population; (2) Percent of Hispanic/Latino population; Profiles include places with an overall population of at least 125,000, OR an overall population of at least 25,000 where the Hispanic/Latino population is at least 20% of the overall population. In states where less than five places meet either of these criteria, we have included places with at least 10,000 total population with the highest percentage of Hispanic/Latino population. These places are identified with an asterisk (*); Please refer to the User's Guide for a full explanation of data.

Cuban	15.0
Dominican Republic	43.9
Puerto Rican	49.7

Valley Stream

Population

Group	Number	%TP[1]	%HP[2]
Total Population	37,511	100.0	–
Hispanic or Latino (of any race)	8,344	22.2	100.0
Central American, ex. Mexican	1,565	4.2	18.8
Guatemalan	302	0.8	3.6
Honduran	155	0.4	1.9
Panamanian	110	0.3	1.3
Salvadoran	873	2.3	10.5
Cuban	207	0.6	2.5
Dominican Republic	1,281	3.4	15.4
Mexican	253	0.7	3.0
Puerto Rican	1,706	4.5	20.4
South American	2,609	7.0	31.3
Chilean	211	0.6	2.5
Colombian	944	2.5	11.3
Ecuadorian	650	1.7	7.8
Peruvian	513	1.4	6.1

Population Growth: 2000–2010

Group	%
Total Population	3.1
Hispanic or Latino (of any race)	87.0
Central American, ex. Mexican	170.3
Salvadoran	126.2
Cuban	59.2
Dominican Republic	207.9
Puerto Rican	47.2
South American	155.0
Chilean	78.8
Colombian	173.6
Ecuadorian	220.2
Peruvian	165.8

Males per 100 Females

Group	Number
Total Population	92.6
Hispanic or Latino (of any race)	96.2
Central American, ex. Mexican	109.5
Guatemalan	102.7
Honduran	112.3
Panamanian	83.3
Salvadoran	116.6
Cuban	113.4
Dominican Republic	79.4
Mexican	96.1
Puerto Rican	101.7
South American	90.9
Chilean	108.9
Colombian	88.0
Ecuadorian	85.2
Peruvian	93.6

Average Household Size

Group	People
Total Population	3.07
Hispanic or Latino (of any race)	3.96
Central American, ex. Mexican	4.65
Guatemalan	4.69
Honduran	5.04
Panamanian	3.35
Salvadoran	4.88
Cuban	2.95
Dominican Republic	4.09
Mexican	4.22
Puerto Rican	3.39
South American	4.08
Chilean	3.57
Colombian	3.95
Ecuadorian	4.49
Peruvian	4.24

Median Age

Group	Years
Total Population	39.7
Hispanic or Latino (of any race)	31.5
Central American, ex. Mexican	31.0
Guatemalan	31.1
Honduran	29.9
Panamanian	34.3
Salvadoran	30.5
Cuban	38.6
Dominican Republic	29.7
Mexican	25.8
Puerto Rican	32.5
South American	36.1
Chilean	36.5
Colombian	35.5
Ecuadorian	35.5
Peruvian	37.2

High School Graduates
(Universe: Population 25 Years and Over)

Group	Number	%
Total Population	22,257	89.2
Hispanic or Latino (of any race)	3,469	77.5
Central American, ex. Mexican	460	57.1
Dominican Republic	405	78.9
Puerto Rican	801	85.4
South American	1,248	78.9

Four-Year College Graduates
(Universe: Population 25 Years and Over)

Group	Number	%
Total Population	8,239	33.0
Hispanic or Latino (of any race)	1,085	24.2
Central American, ex. Mexican	120	14.9
Dominican Republic	103	20.1
Puerto Rican	354	37.7
South American	307	19.4

Population Age 3–17 Enrolled in Public School
(Universe: Population Age 3–17 Enrolled in School)

Group	Number	%
Total Population	5,755	85.4
Hispanic or Latino (of any race)	1,518	91.8
Central American, ex. Mexican	225	86.5
Dominican Republic	242	88.0
Puerto Rican	317	93.8
South American	351	100.0

Population Age 3–17 Enrolled in Private School
(Universe: Population Age 3–17 Enrolled in School)

Group	Number	%
Total Population	985	14.6
Hispanic or Latino (of any race)	136	8.2
Central American, ex. Mexican	35	13.5
Dominican Republic	33	12.0
Puerto Rican	21	6.2
South American	0	0.0

Foreign-Born Population

Group	Number	%
Total Population	12,202	33.0
Hispanic or Latino (of any race)	3,693	49.4
Central American, ex. Mexican	872	59.6
Dominican Republic	510	54.3
Puerto Rican	0	0.0
South American	1,740	74.5

Foreign-Born Naturalized U.S. Citizens

Group	Number	%
Total Population	7,861	64.4
Hispanic or Latino (of any race)	1,999	54.1
Central American, ex. Mexican	435	49.9
Dominican Republic	311	61.0
Puerto Rican	0	0.0
South American	940	54.0

Language Spoken at Home: English Only
(Universe: Population 5 Years and Over)

Group	Number	%
Total Population	20,692	59.0
Hispanic or Latino (of any race)	1,176	16.7
Central American, ex. Mexican	215	16.4
Dominican Republic	91	10.5
Puerto Rican	628	45.4
South American	71	3.1

Language Spoken at Home: Spanish
(Universe: Population 5 Years and Over)

Group	Number	%
Total Population	6,281	17.9
Hispanic or Latino (of any race)	5,839	82.9
Central American, ex. Mexican	1,093	83.6
Dominican Republic	774	89.5
Puerto Rican	754	54.6
South American	2,196	96.2

Unemployment Rate
(Universe: Population 16 Years and Over)

Group	%
Total Population	8.4
Hispanic or Latino (of any race)	6.7
Central American, ex. Mexican	1.1
Dominican Republic	0.0
Puerto Rican	16.8
South American	5.8

Class of Worker: Private Wage and Salary
(Universe: Civilian Employed Population 16 Years and Over)

Group	Number	%
Total Population	14,274	75.8
Hispanic or Latino (of any race)	3,108	81.6
Central American, ex. Mexican	759	95.6
Dominican Republic	376	79.7
Puerto Rican	497	70.8
South American	1,116	84.2

Class of Worker: Government
(Universe: Civilian Employed Population 16 Years and Over)

Group	Number	%
Total Population	3,697	19.6
Hispanic or Latino (of any race)	431	11.3
Central American, ex. Mexican	0	0.0
Dominican Republic	68	14.4
Puerto Rican	181	25.8
South American	98	7.4

Means of Transportation to Work: Car, Truck or Van
(Universe: Workers 16 Years and Over)

Group	Number	%
Total Population	13,641	75.1
Hispanic or Latino (of any race)	2,710	73.7
Central American, ex. Mexican	669	84.3
Dominican Republic	350	79.5
Puerto Rican	509	78.2
South American	816	63.5

Means of Transportation to Work: Public Transportation (ex. Taxicab)
(Universe: Workers 16 Years and Over)

Group	Number	%
Total Population	3,314	18.2
Hispanic or Latino (of any race)	648	17.6
Central American, ex. Mexican	78	9.8
Dominican Republic	76	17.3
Puerto Rican	102	15.7
South American	296	23.0

Homeownership Rate
(Universe: Occupied Housing Units)

Group	%
Total Population	79.1
Hispanic or Latino (of any race)	71.6
Central American, ex. Mexican	60.6
Guatemalan	62.7
Honduran	57.1
Panamanian	70.6
Salvadoran	59.8
Cuban	69.0
Dominican Republic	70.6
Mexican	63.6
Puerto Rican	77.1
South American	74.5
Chilean	52.8
Colombian	80.2
Ecuadorian	85.5
Peruvian	56.9

Median Home Value

Group	Dollars
Total Population	429,900
Hispanic or Latino (of any race)	450,000
Central American, ex. Mexican	442,700
Dominican Republic	409,600
Puerto Rican	447,800
South American	484,700

Notes: (1) Percent of total population; (2) Percent of Hispanic/Latino population; Profiles include places with an overall population of at least 125,000, OR an overall population of at least 25,000 where the Hispanic/Latino population is at least 20% of the overall population. In states where less than five places meet either of these criteria, we have included places with at least 10,000 total population with the highest percentage of Hispanic/Latino population. These places are identified with an asterisk (*); Please refer to the User's Guide for a full explanation of data.

Median Gross Rent

Group	Dollars
Total Population	1,306
Hispanic or Latino (of any race)	1,113
Central American, ex. Mexican	1,349
Dominican Republic	380
Puerto Rican	884
South American	1,165

Median Household Income
(2010 Inflation-Adjusted Dollars)

Group	Dollars
Total Population	82,279
Hispanic or Latino (of any race)	69,000
Central American, ex. Mexican	66,716
Dominican Republic	82,813
Puerto Rican	94,643
South American	64,886

Per Capita Income
(2010 Inflation-Adjusted Dollars)

Group	Dollars
Total Population	30,608
Hispanic or Latino (of any race)	22,446
Central American, ex. Mexican	19,136
Dominican Republic	26,748
Puerto Rican	27,507
South American	21,919

Households with $100,000+ Income

Group	Number	%
Total Population	4,597	39.5
Hispanic or Latino (of any race)	613	31.5
Central American, ex. Mexican	118	30.4
Dominican Republic	74	29.0
Puerto Rican	160	44.9
South American	180	29.3

Households with Food Stamps/SNAP Benefits During Past 12 Months

Group	Number	%
Total Population	331	2.8
Hispanic or Latino (of any race)	80	4.1
Central American, ex. Mexican	0	0.0
Dominican Republic	6	2.4
Puerto Rican	34	9.6
South American	30	4.9

Poverty Rate
(Income in Past 12 Months Below Poverty Level)

Group	%
Total Population	4.5
Hispanic or Latino (of any race)	5.1
Central American, ex. Mexican	9.5
Dominican Republic	4.3
Puerto Rican	9.2
South American	2.2

Wallkill

Population

Group	Number	%TP[1]	%HP[2]
Total Population	27,426	100.0	–
Hispanic or Latino (of any race)	6,162	22.5	100.0
Central American, ex. Mexican	321	1.2	5.2
Honduran	114	0.4	1.9
Cuban	125	0.5	2.0
Dominican Republic	463	1.7	7.5
Mexican	879	3.2	14.3
Puerto Rican	3,386	12.3	54.9
South American	608	2.2	9.9
Colombian	301	1.1	4.9
Ecuadorian	115	0.4	1.9
Peruvian	114	0.4	1.9

Population Growth: 2000–2010

Group	%
Total Population	11.2
Hispanic or Latino (of any race)	86.5
Mexican	161.6
Puerto Rican	69.0
South American	136.6
Colombian	77.1

Males per 100 Females

Group	Number
Total Population	92.5
Hispanic or Latino (of any race)	92.6
Central American, ex. Mexican	112.6
Honduran	86.9
Cuban	62.3
Dominican Republic	89.0
Mexican	104.4
Puerto Rican	92.1
South American	82.6
Colombian	77.1
Ecuadorian	79.7
Peruvian	111.1

Average Household Size

Group	People
Total Population	2.67
Hispanic or Latino (of any race)	3.28
Central American, ex. Mexican	3.55
Honduran	3.68
Cuban	2.77
Dominican Republic	3.76
Mexican	4.22
Puerto Rican	3.05
South American	3.32
Colombian	3.06
Ecuadorian	4.09
Peruvian	3.48

Median Age

Group	Years
Total Population	39.1
Hispanic or Latino (of any race)	29.2
Central American, ex. Mexican	30.1
Honduran	28.6
Cuban	37.5
Dominican Republic	27.1
Mexican	24.4
Puerto Rican	30.6
South American	35.5
Colombian	37.8
Ecuadorian	32.5
Peruvian	32.6

High School Graduates
(Universe: Population 25 Years and Over)

Group	Number	%
Total Population	16,500	88.8
Hispanic or Latino (of any race)	2,515	81.3
Puerto Rican	1,182	78.6

Four-Year College Graduates
(Universe: Population 25 Years and Over)

Group	Number	%
Total Population	4,623	24.9
Hispanic or Latino (of any race)	523	16.9
Puerto Rican	271	18.0

Population Age 3–17 Enrolled in Public School
(Universe: Population Age 3–17 Enrolled in School)

Group	Number	%
Total Population	4,590	88.4
Hispanic or Latino (of any race)	1,332	84.4
Puerto Rican	807	82.0

Population Age 3–17 Enrolled in Private School
(Universe: Population Age 3–17 Enrolled in School)

Group	Number	%
Total Population	603	11.6
Hispanic or Latino (of any race)	247	15.6
Puerto Rican	177	18.0

Foreign-Born Population

Group	Number	%
Total Population	3,522	13.0
Hispanic or Latino (of any race)	1,527	27.2
Puerto Rican	17	0.6

Foreign-Born Naturalized U.S. Citizens

Group	Number	%
Total Population	1,428	40.5
Hispanic or Latino (of any race)	472	30.9
Puerto Rican	17	100.0

Language Spoken at Home: English Only
(Universe: Population 5 Years and Over)

Group	Number	%
Total Population	20,795	80.9
Hispanic or Latino (of any race)	2,040	40.0
Puerto Rican	1,481	55.4

Language Spoken at Home: Spanish
(Universe: Population 5 Years and Over)

Group	Number	%
Total Population	3,404	13.2
Hispanic or Latino (of any race)	3,066	60.0
Puerto Rican	1,194	44.6

Unemployment Rate
(Universe: Population 16 Years and Over)

Group	%
Total Population	7.5
Hispanic or Latino (of any race)	14.8
Puerto Rican	13.9

Class of Worker: Private Wage and Salary
(Universe: Civilian Employed Population 16 Years and Over)

Group	Number	%
Total Population	9,952	72.2
Hispanic or Latino (of any race)	1,926	78.0
Puerto Rican	804	66.1

Class of Worker: Government
(Universe: Civilian Employed Population 16 Years and Over)

Group	Number	%
Total Population	3,304	24.0
Hispanic or Latino (of any race)	503	20.4
Puerto Rican	394	32.4

Means of Transportation to Work: Car, Truck or Van
(Universe: Workers 16 Years and Over)

Group	Number	%
Total Population	12,081	91.6
Hispanic or Latino (of any race)	2,144	90.1
Puerto Rican	1,034	87.5

Means of Transportation to Work: Public Transportation (ex. Taxicab)
(Universe: Workers 16 Years and Over)

Group	Number	%
Total Population	494	3.7
Hispanic or Latino (of any race)	90	3.8
Puerto Rican	51	4.3

Homeownership Rate
(Universe: Occupied Housing Units)

Group	%
Total Population	63.5
Hispanic or Latino (of any race)	52.9
Central American, ex. Mexican	56.1
Honduran	38.7
Cuban	58.3
Dominican Republic	64.4
Mexican	24.7
Puerto Rican	57.7
South American	43.0
Colombian	35.1
Ecuadorian	73.5
Peruvian	27.5

Median Home Value

Group	Dollars
Total Population	287,100
Hispanic or Latino (of any race)	261,100
Puerto Rican	239,700

Median Gross Rent

Group	Dollars
Total Population	1,012
Hispanic or Latino (of any race)	1,067
Puerto Rican	993

Median Household Income
(2010 Inflation-Adjusted Dollars)

Group	Dollars
Total Population	65,949
Hispanic or Latino (of any race)	68,598
Puerto Rican	66,645

Notes: (1) Percent of total population; (2) Percent of Hispanic/Latino population; Profiles include places with an overall population of at least 125,000, OR an overall population of at least 25,000 where the Hispanic/Latino population is at least 20% of the overall population. In states where less than five places meet either of these criteria, we have included places with at least 10,000 total population with the highest percentage of Hispanic/Latino population. These places are identified with an asterisk (*); Please refer to the User's Guide for a full explanation of data.

Per Capita Income (2010 Inflation-Adjusted Dollars)	
Group	Dollars
Total Population	28,625
Hispanic or Latino (of any race)	20,567
Puerto Rican	20,425

Households with $100,000+ Income		
Group	Number	%
Total Population	2,759	27.4
Hispanic or Latino (of any race)	489	29.4
Puerto Rican	234	29.3

Households with Food Stamps/SNAP Benefits During Past 12 Months		
Group	Number	%
Total Population	573	5.7
Hispanic or Latino (of any race)	139	8.4
Puerto Rican	47	5.9

Poverty Rate (Income in Past 12 Months Below Poverty Level)	
Group	%
Total Population	8.1
Hispanic or Latino (of any race)	8.8
Puerto Rican	11.9

White Plains

Population			
Group	Number	%TP[1]	%HP[2]
Total Population	56,853	100.0	–
Hispanic or Latino (of any race)	16,839	29.6	100.0
Central American, ex. Mexican	968	1.7	5.7
Guatemalan	551	1.0	3.3
Salvadoran	204	0.4	1.2
Cuban	321	0.6	1.9
Dominican Republic	1,177	2.1	7.0
Mexican	5,773	10.2	34.3
Puerto Rican	1,541	2.7	9.2
South American	5,850	10.3	34.7
Argentinean	189	0.3	1.1
Colombian	1,838	3.2	10.9
Ecuadorian	1,001	1.8	5.9
Paraguayan	260	0.5	1.5
Peruvian	2,260	4.0	13.4
Spaniard	279	0.5	1.7

Population Growth: 2000–2010	
Group	%
Total Population	7.1
Hispanic or Latino (of any race)	35.0
Central American, ex. Mexican	113.7
Guatemalan	178.3
Salvadoran	78.9
Cuban	7.4
Dominican Republic	76.5
Mexican	69.3
Puerto Rican	32.6
South American	60.7
Colombian	26.1
Ecuadorian	121.5
Paraguayan	52.0
Peruvian	78.5
Spaniard	92.4

Males per 100 Females	
Group	Number
Total Population	92.7
Hispanic or Latino (of any race)	102.0
Central American, ex. Mexican	102.1
Guatemalan	120.4
Salvadoran	83.8
Cuban	82.4
Dominican Republic	82.5
Mexican	121.1
Puerto Rican	81.9
South American	96.1
Argentinean	101.1
Colombian	82.2
Ecuadorian	138.3
Paraguayan	104.7
Peruvian	93.5
Spaniard	102.2

Average Household Size	
Group	People
Total Population	2.40
Hispanic or Latino (of any race)	3.58
Central American, ex. Mexican	3.56
Guatemalan	4.29
Salvadoran	3.12
Cuban	2.22
Dominican Republic	3.63
Mexican	4.74
Puerto Rican	2.33
South American	3.42
Argentinean	2.70
Colombian	3.05
Ecuadorian	3.93
Paraguayan	3.88
Peruvian	3.72
Spaniard	2.56

Median Age	
Group	Years
Total Population	39.2
Hispanic or Latino (of any race)	30.9
Central American, ex. Mexican	32.2
Guatemalan	29.6
Salvadoran	36.5
Cuban	42.3
Dominican Republic	29.7
Mexican	26.2
Puerto Rican	33.5
South American	36.7
Argentinean	36.4
Colombian	39.1
Ecuadorian	32.2
Paraguayan	37.5
Peruvian	37.4
Spaniard	43.3

High School Graduates (Universe: Population 25 Years and Over)		
Group	Number	%
Total Population	35,296	87.2
Hispanic or Latino (of any race)	7,032	70.6
Mexican	1,217	51.7
Puerto Rican	1,139	85.3
South American	3,616	77.3
Colombian	1,198	82.5
Ecuadorian	231	34.0
Peruvian	1,638	87.4

Four-Year College Graduates (Universe: Population 25 Years and Over)		
Group	Number	%
Total Population	18,883	46.7
Hispanic or Latino (of any race)	1,842	18.5
Mexican	126	5.4
Puerto Rican	599	44.9
South American	726	15.5
Colombian	266	18.3
Ecuadorian	0	0.0
Peruvian	215	11.5

Population Age 3–17 Enrolled in Public School (Universe: Population Age 3–17 Enrolled in School)		
Group	Number	%
Total Population	7,753	85.1
Hispanic or Latino (of any race)	3,447	94.3
Mexican	1,287	96.0
Puerto Rican	310	78.3
South American	1,344	95.9
Colombian	376	100.0
Ecuadorian	264	100.0
Peruvian	484	94.7

Population Age 3–17 Enrolled in Private School (Universe: Population Age 3–17 Enrolled in School)		
Group	Number	%
Total Population	1,355	14.9
Hispanic or Latino (of any race)	208	5.7
Mexican	53	4.0
Puerto Rican	86	21.7
South American	58	4.1
Colombian	0	0.0
Ecuadorian	0	0.0
Peruvian	27	5.3

Foreign-Born Population		
Group	Number	%
Total Population	16,700	29.9
Hispanic or Latino (of any race)	9,803	59.0
Mexican	2,794	59.6
Puerto Rican	0	0.0
South American	5,268	77.2
Colombian	1,565	75.4
Ecuadorian	906	78.4
Peruvian	2,041	79.7

Foreign-Born Naturalized U.S. Citizens		
Group	Number	%
Total Population	6,817	40.8
Hispanic or Latino (of any race)	3,035	31.0
Mexican	432	15.5
Puerto Rican	0	0.0
South American	1,694	32.2
Colombian	615	39.3
Ecuadorian	52	5.7
Peruvian	702	34.4

Language Spoken at Home: English Only (Universe: Population 5 Years and Over)		
Group	Number	%
Total Population	33,029	62.6
Hispanic or Latino (of any race)	1,868	12.2
Mexican	99	2.5
Puerto Rican	997	45.3
South American	385	5.9
Colombian	169	8.7
Ecuadorian	0	0.0
Peruvian	134	5.3

Language Spoken at Home: Spanish (Universe: Population 5 Years and Over)		
Group	Number	%
Total Population	13,904	26.4
Hispanic or Latino (of any race)	13,316	87.3
Mexican	3,821	97.0
Puerto Rican	1,203	54.7
South American	6,133	93.4
Colombian	1,776	91.3
Ecuadorian	1,110	98.7
Peruvian	2,373	94.2

Unemployment Rate (Universe: Population 16 Years and Over)	
Group	%
Total Population	5.9
Hispanic or Latino (of any race)	5.3
Mexican	6.3
Puerto Rican	9.5
South American	1.8
Colombian	1.0
Ecuadorian	0.0
Peruvian	3.0

Class of Worker: Private Wage and Salary (Universe: Civilian Employed Population 16 Years and Over)		
Group	Number	%
Total Population	22,555	76.0
Hispanic or Latino (of any race)	6,697	75.1
Mexican	1,657	76.0
Puerto Rican	942	76.9
South American	3,154	76.4
Colombian	1,006	79.3
Ecuadorian	546	72.3
Peruvian	1,108	76.9

Class of Worker: Government (Universe: Civilian Employed Population 16 Years and Over)		
Group	Number	%
Total Population	3,926	13.2
Hispanic or Latino (of any race)	636	7.1
Mexican	43	2.0
Puerto Rican	198	16.2
South American	222	5.4
Colombian	70	5.5
Ecuadorian	40	5.3
Peruvian	65	4.5

Notes: (1) Percent of total population; (2) Percent of Hispanic/Latino population; Profiles include places with an overall population of at least 125,000, OR an overall population of at least 25,000 where the Hispanic/Latino population is at least 20% of the overall population. In states where less than five places meet either of these criteria, we have included places with at least 10,000 total population with the highest percentage of Hispanic/Latino population. These places are identified with an asterisk (*); Please refer to the User's Guide for a full explanation of data.

Means of Transportation to Work: Car, Truck or Van
(Universe: Workers 16 Years and Over)

Group	Number	%
Total Population	17,669	60.9
Hispanic or Latino (of any race)	4,349	49.1
Mexican	740	33.9
Puerto Rican	889	72.3
South American	2,059	50.4
Colombian	635	50.0
Ecuadorian	172	22.8
Peruvian	771	54.1

Means of Transportation to Work: Public Transportation (ex. Taxicab)
(Universe: Workers 16 Years and Over)

Group	Number	%
Total Population	5,964	20.5
Hispanic or Latino (of any race)	2,043	23.1
Mexican	649	29.8
Puerto Rican	165	13.4
South American	868	21.3
Colombian	288	22.7
Ecuadorian	345	45.7
Peruvian	196	13.7

Homeownership Rate
(Universe: Occupied Housing Units)

Group	%
Total Population	53.8
Hispanic or Latino (of any race)	26.2
Central American, ex. Mexican	26.5
Guatemalan	22.2
Salvadoran	20.3
Cuban	40.7
Dominican Republic	24.3
Mexican	12.4
Puerto Rican	35.2
South American	27.9
Argentinean	43.8
Colombian	26.9
Ecuadorian	24.2
Paraguayan	32.4
Peruvian	26.5
Spaniard	72.2

Median Home Value

Group	Dollars
Total Population	510,400
Hispanic or Latino (of any race)	435,000
Mexican	375,400
Puerto Rican	442,900
South American	409,400
Colombian	260,900
Ecuadorian	1,000,000+
Peruvian	461,100

Median Gross Rent

Group	Dollars
Total Population	1,281
Hispanic or Latino (of any race)	1,323
Mexican	1,412
Puerto Rican	1,417
South American	1,323
Colombian	1,283
Ecuadorian	1,609
Peruvian	1,277

Median Household Income
(2010 Inflation-Adjusted Dollars)

Group	Dollars
Total Population	73,522
Hispanic or Latino (of any race)	45,101
Mexican	34,898
Puerto Rican	94,470
South American	47,591
Colombian	41,761
Ecuadorian	48,884
Peruvian	44,074

Per Capita Income
(2010 Inflation-Adjusted Dollars)

Group	Dollars
Total Population	43,938
Hispanic or Latino (of any race)	19,464
Mexican	10,975
Puerto Rican	27,752
South American	19,572
Colombian	20,142
Ecuadorian	13,852
Peruvian	17,449

Households with $100,000+ Income

Group	Number	%
Total Population	8,383	36.4
Hispanic or Latino (of any race)	850	17.0
Mexican	94	8.6
Puerto Rican	300	44.5
South American	297	13.3
Colombian	51	6.7
Ecuadorian	47	19.2
Peruvian	117	15.2

Households with Food Stamps/SNAP Benefits During Past 12 Months

Group	Number	%
Total Population	889	3.9
Hispanic or Latino (of any race)	395	7.9
Mexican	36	3.3
Puerto Rican	97	14.4
South American	146	6.6
Colombian	64	8.4
Ecuadorian	0	0.0
Peruvian	61	7.9

Poverty Rate
(Income in Past 12 Months Below Poverty Level)

Group	%
Total Population	8.9
Hispanic or Latino (of any race)	14.2
Mexican	21.6
Puerto Rican	12.1
South American	12.1
Colombian	11.9
Ecuadorian	17.6
Peruvian	13.8

Yonkers

Population

Group	Number	%TP[1]	%HP[2]
Total Population	195,976	100.0	–
Hispanic or Latino (of any race)	67,927	34.7	100.0
Central American, ex. Mexican	5,822	3.0	8.6
Costa Rican	156	0.1	0.2
Guatemalan	765	0.4	1.1
Honduran	1,451	0.7	2.1
Nicaraguan	534	0.3	0.8
Panamanian	185	0.1	0.3
Salvadoran	2,691	1.4	4.0
Cuban	1,501	0.8	2.2
Dominican Republic	15,903	8.1	23.4
Mexican	13,761	7.0	20.3
Puerto Rican	19,875	10.1	29.3
South American	6,622	3.4	9.7
Argentinean	273	0.1	0.4
Chilean	215	0.1	0.3
Colombian	1,493	0.8	2.2
Ecuadorian	3,271	1.7	4.8
Peruvian	946	0.5	1.4
Venezuelan	207	0.1	0.3
Spaniard	436	0.2	0.6

Population Growth: 2000–2010

Group	%
Total Population	-0.1
Hispanic or Latino (of any race)	33.6
Central American, ex. Mexican	72.6
Costa Rican	15.6
Guatemalan	123.0
Honduran	97.1
Nicaraguan	36.6
Panamanian	60.9
Salvadoran	77.3
Cuban	3.5
Dominican Republic	102.9
Mexican	88.7
Puerto Rican	9.8
South American	67.9
Argentinean	43.7
Chilean	62.9
Colombian	50.7
Ecuadorian	77.9
Peruvian	103.9
Venezuelan	64.3
Spaniard	128.3

Males per 100 Females

Group	Number
Total Population	90.0
Hispanic or Latino (of any race)	94.3
Central American, ex. Mexican	99.5
Costa Rican	52.9
Guatemalan	129.7
Honduran	93.2
Nicaraguan	84.8
Panamanian	72.9
Salvadoran	106.4
Cuban	88.3
Dominican Republic	80.8
Mexican	127.6
Puerto Rican	87.4
South American	89.0
Argentinean	100.7
Chilean	85.3
Colombian	80.3
Ecuadorian	93.2
Peruvian	86.2
Venezuelan	99.0
Spaniard	83.2

Average Household Size

Group	People
Total Population	2.58
Hispanic or Latino (of any race)	3.23
Central American, ex. Mexican	3.49
Costa Rican	2.68
Guatemalan	3.91
Honduran	3.52
Nicaraguan	3.04
Panamanian	2.30
Salvadoran	3.67
Cuban	2.43
Dominican Republic	3.25
Mexican	4.70
Puerto Rican	2.73
South American	3.07
Argentinean	2.53
Chilean	2.90
Colombian	2.85
Ecuadorian	3.24
Peruvian	3.20
Venezuelan	2.83
Spaniard	2.36

Median Age

Group	Years
Total Population	37.6
Hispanic or Latino (of any race)	29.2
Central American, ex. Mexican	32.6
Costa Rican	42.2
Guatemalan	29.4
Honduran	31.5
Nicaraguan	38.3
Panamanian	36.5
Salvadoran	32.6
Cuban	41.6
Dominican Republic	29.9
Mexican	25.0
Puerto Rican	30.2
South American	36.0
Argentinean	36.8
Chilean	39.5
Colombian	37.4
Ecuadorian	35.7
Peruvian	36.2
Venezuelan	32.6
Spaniard	43.2

High School Graduates
(Universe: Population 25 Years and Over)

Group	Number	%
Total Population	106,713	80.9
Hispanic or Latino (of any race)	24,590	66.2

Notes: (1) Percent of total population; (2) Percent of Hispanic/Latino population; Profiles include places with an overall population of at least 125,000, OR an overall population of at least 25,000 where the Hispanic/Latino population is at least 20% of the overall population. In states where less than five places meet either of these criteria, we have included places with at least 10,000 total population with the highest percentage of Hispanic/Latino population. These places are identified with an asterisk (*); Please refer to the User's Guide for a full explanation of data.

Group	Number	%
Central American, ex. Mexican	1,861	56.0
Guatemalan	248	37.3
Honduran	513	67.9
Salvadoran	551	44.5
Cuban	798	73.6
Dominican Republic	5,323	65.8
Mexican	3,096	46.8
Puerto Rican	8,965	75.4
South American	3,581	71.8
Colombian	1,071	75.5
Ecuadorian	1,411	64.5

Four-Year College Graduates
(Universe: Population 25 Years and Over)

Group	Number	%
Total Population	38,403	29.1
Hispanic or Latino (of any race)	6,064	16.3
Central American, ex. Mexican	386	11.6
Guatemalan	0	0.0
Honduran	127	16.8
Salvadoran	119	9.6
Cuban	176	16.2
Dominican Republic	1,385	17.1
Mexican	357	5.4
Puerto Rican	2,358	19.8
South American	996	20.0
Colombian	333	23.5
Ecuadorian	298	13.6

Population Age 3–17 Enrolled in Public School
(Universe: Population Age 3–17 Enrolled in School)

Group	Number	%
Total Population	26,383	78.6
Hispanic or Latino (of any race)	12,438	90.4
Central American, ex. Mexican	708	91.9
Guatemalan	184	95.8
Honduran	142	91.0
Salvadoran	294	88.0
Cuban	146	68.5
Dominican Republic	2,849	92.1
Mexican	2,809	97.3
Puerto Rican	4,329	90.9
South American	990	71.5
Colombian	298	100.0
Ecuadorian	440	62.5

Population Age 3–17 Enrolled in Private School
(Universe: Population Age 3–17 Enrolled in School)

Group	Number	%
Total Population	7,200	21.4
Hispanic or Latino (of any race)	1,325	9.6
Central American, ex. Mexican	62	8.1
Guatemalan	8	4.2
Honduran	14	9.0
Salvadoran	40	12.0
Cuban	67	31.5
Dominican Republic	243	7.9
Mexican	79	2.7
Puerto Rican	435	9.1
South American	395	28.5
Colombian	0	0.0
Ecuadorian	264	37.5

Foreign-Born Population

Group	Number	%
Total Population	58,821	30.2
Hispanic or Latino (of any race)	26,646	41.7
Central American, ex. Mexican	3,476	70.3
Guatemalan	760	73.8
Honduran	874	71.1
Salvadoran	1,276	67.4
Cuban	821	53.7
Dominican Republic	8,392	61.1
Mexican	7,840	61.3
Puerto Rican	459	2.2
South American	4,948	63.8
Colombian	1,280	61.0
Ecuadorian	2,282	64.0

Foreign-Born Naturalized U.S. Citizens

Group	Number	%
Total Population	28,970	49.3
Hispanic or Latino (of any race)	9,305	34.9
Central American, ex. Mexican	1,033	29.7
Guatemalan	49	6.4
Honduran	218	24.9
Salvadoran	400	31.3
Cuban	605	73.7
Dominican Republic	3,689	44.0
Mexican	869	11.1
Puerto Rican	230	50.1
South American	2,488	50.3
Colombian	766	59.8
Ecuadorian	1,071	46.9

Language Spoken at Home: English Only
(Universe: Population 5 Years and Over)

Group	Number	%
Total Population	99,843	55.1
Hispanic or Latino (of any race)	7,624	13.2
Central American, ex. Mexican	270	5.8
Guatemalan	46	4.8
Honduran	82	7.0
Salvadoran	84	4.8
Cuban	298	21.4
Dominican Republic	613	4.9
Mexican	606	5.5
Puerto Rican	4,543	23.9
South American	820	11.3
Colombian	148	7.5
Ecuadorian	353	10.6

Language Spoken at Home: Spanish
(Universe: Population 5 Years and Over)

Group	Number	%
Total Population	52,489	29.0
Hispanic or Latino (of any race)	49,932	86.2
Central American, ex. Mexican	4,389	94.1
Guatemalan	920	95.2
Honduran	1,089	93.0
Salvadoran	1,661	95.2
Cuban	1,096	78.6
Dominican Republic	11,859	94.8
Mexican	10,424	94.0
Puerto Rican	14,335	75.4
South American	6,360	87.7
Colombian	1,821	92.5
Ecuadorian	2,989	89.4

Unemployment Rate
(Universe: Population 16 Years and Over)

Group	%
Total Population	7.0
Hispanic or Latino (of any race)	7.7
Central American, ex. Mexican	7.3
Guatemalan	1.7
Honduran	8.2
Salvadoran	14.6
Cuban	6.0
Dominican Republic	8.0
Mexican	5.3
Puerto Rican	9.3
South American	7.2
Colombian	6.5
Ecuadorian	6.5

Class of Worker: Private Wage and Salary
(Universe: Civilian Employed Population 16 Years and Over)

Group	Number	%
Total Population	70,197	77.4
Hispanic or Latino (of any race)	23,541	80.6
Central American, ex. Mexican	2,104	81.0
Guatemalan	548	87.8
Honduran	498	74.4
Salvadoran	655	83.8
Cuban	582	80.2
Dominican Republic	5,274	83.7
Mexican	5,376	90.6
Puerto Rican	6,549	74.5
South American	3,049	74.0
Colombian	723	67.5
Ecuadorian	1,474	75.6

Class of Worker: Government
(Universe: Civilian Employed Population 16 Years and Over)

Group	Number	%
Total Population	16,083	17.7
Hispanic or Latino (of any race)	4,004	13.7
Central American, ex. Mexican	323	12.4
Guatemalan	40	6.4
Honduran	135	20.2
Salvadoran	45	5.8
Cuban	144	19.8
Dominican Republic	728	11.5
Mexican	131	2.2
Puerto Rican	1,983	22.6
South American	569	13.8
Colombian	249	23.2
Ecuadorian	163	8.4

Means of Transportation to Work: Car, Truck or Van
(Universe: Workers 16 Years and Over)

Group	Number	%
Total Population	58,217	65.6
Hispanic or Latino (of any race)	15,735	54.8
Central American, ex. Mexican	1,336	52.3
Guatemalan	149	24.3
Honduran	359	54.9
Salvadoran	614	80.7
Cuban	456	66.1
Dominican Republic	3,843	62.6
Mexican	2,140	36.5
Puerto Rican	5,147	59.4
South American	2,361	58.3
Colombian	621	60.3
Ecuadorian	1,106	57.4

Means of Transportation to Work: Public Transportation (ex. Taxicab)
(Universe: Workers 16 Years and Over)

Group	Number	%
Total Population	22,906	25.8
Hispanic or Latino (of any race)	9,595	33.4
Central American, ex. Mexican	814	31.9
Guatemalan	432	70.4
Honduran	53	8.1
Salvadoran	124	16.3
Cuban	178	25.8
Dominican Republic	1,770	28.8
Mexican	2,924	49.8
Puerto Rican	2,433	28.1
South American	1,212	29.9
Colombian	237	23.0
Ecuadorian	543	28.2

Homeownership Rate
(Universe: Occupied Housing Units)

Group	%
Total Population	46.1
Hispanic or Latino (of any race)	25.9
Central American, ex. Mexican	19.3
Costa Rican	26.3
Guatemalan	12.9
Honduran	20.9
Nicaraguan	24.4
Panamanian	28.0
Salvadoran	17.5
Cuban	34.6
Dominican Republic	26.8
Mexican	10.0
Puerto Rican	29.3
South American	32.9
Argentinean	53.5
Chilean	38.1
Colombian	32.4
Ecuadorian	27.8
Peruvian	35.4
Venezuelan	41.4
Spaniard	59.3

Median Home Value

Group	Dollars
Total Population	428,900
Hispanic or Latino (of any race)	407,300
Central American, ex. Mexican	347,100
Guatemalan	431,800
Honduran	875,000
Salvadoran	458,300
Cuban	375,200
Dominican Republic	497,600
Mexican	424,100
Puerto Rican	369,400
South American	377,100
Colombian	396,300

STATE & PLACE PROFILES

Notes: (1) Percent of total population; (2) Percent of Hispanic/Latino population; Profiles include places with an overall population of at least 125,000, OR an overall population of at least 25,000 where the Hispanic/Latino population is at least 20% of the overall population. In states where less than five places meet either of these criteria, we have included places with at least 10,000 total population with the highest percentage of Hispanic/Latino population. These places are identified with an asterisk (*); Please refer to the User's Guide for a full explanation of data.

Ecuadorian	448,200

Median Gross Rent

Group	Dollars
Total Population	1,082
Hispanic or Latino (of any race)	1,092
Central American, ex. Mexican	1,117
Guatemalan	1,348
Honduran	1,149
Salvadoran	1,043
Cuban	972
Dominican Republic	971
Mexican	1,134
Puerto Rican	1,128
South American	1,132
Colombian	1,291
Ecuadorian	1,001

Median Household Income
(2010 Inflation-Adjusted Dollars)

Group	Dollars
Total Population	55,715
Hispanic or Latino (of any race)	42,252
Central American, ex. Mexican	34,315
Guatemalan	26,442
Honduran	37,292
Salvadoran	29,861
Cuban	55,625
Dominican Republic	37,960
Mexican	40,659
Puerto Rican	46,741
South American	47,500
Colombian	78,380
Ecuadorian	30,434

Per Capita Income
(2010 Inflation-Adjusted Dollars)

Group	Dollars
Total Population	29,191
Hispanic or Latino (of any race)	17,745
Central American, ex. Mexican	16,533
Guatemalan	12,687
Honduran	17,743
Salvadoran	13,678
Cuban	24,528
Dominican Republic	16,858
Mexican	11,250
Puerto Rican	20,846
South American	20,459
Colombian	21,107
Ecuadorian	17,383

Households with $100,000+ Income

Group	Number	%
Total Population	18,308	24.5
Hispanic or Latino (of any race)	2,753	13.6
Central American, ex. Mexican	165	10.6
Guatemalan	37	14.0
Honduran	13	4.0
Salvadoran	52	8.6
Cuban	70	11.3
Dominican Republic	419	8.6
Mexican	214	7.6
Puerto Rican	1,264	17.3
South American	510	20.4
Colombian	150	27.3
Ecuadorian	108	9.4

Households with Food Stamps/SNAP Benefits During Past 12 Months

Group	Number	%
Total Population	9,294	12.4
Hispanic or Latino (of any race)	4,980	24.6
Central American, ex. Mexican	310	19.8
Guatemalan	90	34.0
Honduran	54	16.4
Salvadoran	127	21.0
Cuban	87	14.1
Dominican Republic	1,526	31.2
Mexican	654	23.2
Puerto Rican	1,854	25.4
South American	479	19.2
Colombian	84	15.3
Ecuadorian	301	26.3

Poverty Rate
(Income in Past 12 Months Below Poverty Level)

Group	%
Total Population	13.8
Hispanic or Latino (of any race)	22.4
Central American, ex. Mexican	27.2
Guatemalan	22.8
Honduran	15.7
Salvadoran	38.5
Cuban	21.8
Dominican Republic	23.2
Mexican	24.2
Puerto Rican	23.4
South American	15.2
Colombian	10.7
Ecuadorian	21.2

Notes: (1) Percent of total population; (2) Percent of Hispanic/Latino population; Profiles include places with an overall population of at least 125,000, OR an overall population of at least 25,000 where the Hispanic/Latino population is at least 20% of the overall population. In states where less than five places meet either of these criteria, we have included places with at least 10,000 total population with the highest percentage of Hispanic/Latino population. These places are identified with an asterisk (*); Please refer to the User's Guide for a full explanation of data.

North Carolina

EDITOR'S NOTE: For a place to be included in this edition, it must meet one of two criteria. Either its overall population is at least 125,000, OR its overall population is at least 25,000 and its Hispanic/Latino population is at least 20% of the overall population. For the state of North Carolina, the following locations are included:

- Asheboro
- Cary
- Charlotte
- Durham
- Fayetteville
- Greensboro
- Monroe
- Raleigh
- Sanford
- Winston-Salem

Section Two: State & Place Profiles starts with the state profile, followed by place profiles that meet the criteria above. Places are listed alphabetically within each state. All states, all counties and places that meet the above criteria are ranked and compared in *Section Three: Rankings & Comparisons*, on page 1055.

For a more detailed look at the Hispanic/Latino population in North Carolina, a companion web site is available at no additional charge with purchase of this print edition. Visit http://gold.greyhouse.com/page/info_hispanic for more information.

The web site includes data for all counties and places in North Carolina with Hispanic/Latino population, plus ten additional topics: Self Employed Worker; Walked to Work; Worked from Home; Mean Travel Time to Work; Mean Household Income; Households with Cash Public Assistance; Mean Cash Pubic Assistance; Poverty Rates for 18 and Under, 18 to 64, and 65 and Over.

Population

Group	Number	%TP[1]	%HP[2]
Total Population	9,535,483	100.0	–
Hispanic or Latino (of any race)	800,120	8.4	100.0
Central American, ex. Mexican	105,066	1.1	13.1
Costa Rican	4,658	<0.1	0.6
Guatemalan	20,206	0.2	2.5
Honduran	30,900	0.3	3.9
Nicaraguan	4,964	0.1	0.6
Panamanian	5,708	0.1	0.7
Salvadoran	37,778	0.4	4.7
Cuban	18,079	0.2	2.3
Dominican Republic	15,225	0.2	1.9
Mexican	486,960	5.1	60.9
Puerto Rican	71,800	0.8	9.0
South American	46,307	0.5	5.8
Argentinean	3,210	<0.1	0.4
Bolivian	878	<0.1	0.1
Chilean	2,525	<0.1	0.3
Colombian	17,648	0.2	2.2
Ecuadorian	8,110	0.1	1.0
Paraguayan	245	<0.1	<0.1
Peruvian	8,247	0.1	1.0
Uruguayan	980	<0.1	0.1
Venezuelan	4,070	<0.1	0.5
Spaniard	6,945	0.1	0.9

Population Growth: 2000–2010

Group	%
Total Population	18.5
Hispanic or Latino (of any race)	111.1
Central American, ex. Mexican	241.3
Costa Rican	77.5
Guatemalan	238.7
Honduran	271.3
Nicaraguan	242.6
Panamanian	105.8
Salvadoran	335.3
Cuban	144.7
Dominican Republic	431.4
Mexican	97.5
Puerto Rican	130.7
South American	257.4
Argentinean	255.1
Bolivian	164.5
Chilean	173.3
Colombian	254.0
Ecuadorian	332.8
Peruvian	315.9
Uruguayan	636.8
Venezuelan	232.8
Spaniard	713.2

Males per 100 Females

Group	Number
Total Population	95.0
Hispanic or Latino (of any race)	114.9
Central American, ex. Mexican	116.0
Costa Rican	97.1
Guatemalan	143.8
Honduran	123.2
Nicaraguan	95.5
Panamanian	64.1
Salvadoran	113.3
Cuban	98.7
Dominican Republic	87.6
Mexican	123.6
Puerto Rican	95.5
South American	85.8
Argentinean	92.3
Bolivian	93.4
Chilean	91.4
Colombian	80.8
Ecuadorian	89.2
Paraguayan	82.8
Peruvian	87.3
Uruguayan	109.0
Venezuelan	83.7
Spaniard	92.1

Average Household Size

Group	People
Total Population	2.48
Hispanic or Latino (of any race)	3.70
Central American, ex. Mexican	3.86
Costa Rican	3.13
Guatemalan	4.11
Honduran	3.97
Nicaraguan	3.40
Panamanian	2.72
Salvadoran	4.03
Cuban	2.73
Dominican Republic	3.32
Mexican	4.03
Puerto Rican	2.92
South American	3.02
Argentinean	2.85
Bolivian	2.82
Chilean	2.89
Colombian	2.94
Ecuadorian	3.34
Paraguayan	2.88
Peruvian	3.14
Uruguayan	3.09
Venezuelan	2.83
Spaniard	2.64

Median Age

Group	Years
Total Population	37.4
Hispanic or Latino (of any race)	24.5
Central American, ex. Mexican	27.6
Costa Rican	30.5
Guatemalan	26.0
Honduran	27.5
Nicaraguan	29.6
Panamanian	31.0
Salvadoran	27.8
Cuban	31.1
Dominican Republic	26.1
Mexican	23.1
Puerto Rican	24.3
South American	32.6
Argentinean	35.1
Bolivian	29.8
Chilean	33.5
Colombian	32.2
Ecuadorian	31.4
Paraguayan	25.8
Peruvian	34.0
Uruguayan	32.4
Venezuelan	32.7
Spaniard	31.2

High School Graduates
(Universe: Population 25 Years and Over)

Group	Number	%
Total Population	5,115,556	83.6
Hispanic or Latino (of any race)	188,745	53.2
Central American, ex. Mexican	24,092	45.5
Costa Rican	2,123	74.6
Guatemalan	3,145	34.6
Honduran	6,318	39.2
Nicaraguan	2,271	81.8
Panamanian	2,995	95.2
Salvadoran	6,963	37.6
Cuban	8,437	86.7
Dominican Republic	4,820	76.4
Mexican	89,182	41.9
Puerto Rican	27,268	85.5
South American	24,355	87.9
Argentinean	1,967	92.6
Bolivian	391	98.2
Chilean	1,253	95.2
Colombian	8,792	84.8
Ecuadorian	4,749	86.4
Peruvian	3,996	90.2
Venezuelan	2,324	93.4
Spaniard	3,667	91.4

Four-Year College Graduates
(Universe: Population 25 Years and Over)

Group	Number	%
Total Population	1,597,840	26.1
Hispanic or Latino (of any race)	42,042	11.8
Central American, ex. Mexican	5,029	9.5
Costa Rican	720	25.3
Guatemalan	622	6.8
Honduran	1,124	7.0
Nicaraguan	712	25.6
Panamanian	680	21.6
Salvadoran	1,110	6.0
Cuban	3,524	36.2
Dominican Republic	1,283	20.3
Mexican	12,066	5.7
Puerto Rican	6,527	20.5
South American	9,529	34.4
Argentinean	1,129	53.2
Bolivian	176	44.2
Chilean	524	39.8
Colombian	3,523	34.0
Ecuadorian	1,136	20.7
Peruvian	1,500	33.9
Venezuelan	1,248	50.2
Spaniard	1,620	40.4

Population Age 3–17 Enrolled in Public School
(Universe: Population Age 3–17 Enrolled in School)

Group	Number	%
Total Population	1,465,699	87.6
Hispanic or Latino (of any race)	166,982	95.1
Central American, ex. Mexican	19,863	94.3
Costa Rican	1,154	92.3
Guatemalan	2,847	85.7
Honduran	5,589	96.0
Nicaraguan	608	82.8
Panamanian	1,090	91.8

STATE & PLACE PROFILES

Notes: (1) Percent of total population; (2) Percent of Hispanic/Latino population; Profiles include places with an overall population of at least 125,000, OR an overall population of at least 25,000 where the Hispanic/Latino population is at least 20% of the overall population. In states where less than five places meet either of these criteria, we have included places with at least 10,000 total population with the highest percentage of Hispanic/Latino population. These places are identified with an asterisk (*); Please refer to the User's Guide for a full explanation of data.

Group	Number	%
Salvadoran	8,436	98.2
Cuban	2,790	88.8
Dominican Republic	3,041	94.6
Mexican	109,972	97.0
Puerto Rican	16,422	91.4
South American	7,314	87.6
Argentinean	646	92.6
Bolivian	75	57.7
Chilean	376	78.7
Colombian	2,195	81.5
Ecuadorian	1,814	97.3
Peruvian	1,281	90.9
Venezuelan	616	84.3
Spaniard	1,023	77.6

Population Age 3–17 Enrolled in Private School
(Universe: Population Age 3–17 Enrolled in School)

Group	Number	%
Total Population	208,274	12.4
Hispanic or Latino (of any race)	8,623	4.9
Central American, ex. Mexican	1,190	5.7
Costa Rican	96	7.7
Guatemalan	475	14.3
Honduran	233	4.0
Nicaraguan	126	17.2
Panamanian	98	8.2
Salvadoran	156	1.8
Cuban	353	11.2
Dominican Republic	173	5.4
Mexican	3,361	3.0
Puerto Rican	1,546	8.6
South American	1,037	12.4
Argentinean	52	7.4
Bolivian	55	42.3
Chilean	102	21.3
Colombian	498	18.5
Ecuadorian	50	2.7
Peruvian	129	9.1
Venezuelan	115	15.7
Spaniard	296	22.4

Foreign-Born Population

Group	Number	%
Total Population	682,955	7.4
Hispanic or Latino (of any race)	378,127	52.3
Central American, ex. Mexican	67,743	67.5
Costa Rican	3,467	66.2
Guatemalan	13,689	71.1
Honduran	21,477	71.5
Nicaraguan	3,131	68.8
Panamanian	2,494	46.5
Salvadoran	22,911	65.3
Cuban	5,892	38.0
Dominican Republic	5,778	47.7
Mexican	262,895	57.3
Puerto Rican	877	1.4
South American	27,720	63.5
Argentinean	1,923	59.6
Bolivian	401	58.9
Chilean	1,303	56.6
Colombian	10,142	65.0
Ecuadorian	5,608	61.9
Peruvian	4,421	61.2
Venezuelan	2,637	68.7
Spaniard	1,478	22.5

Foreign-Born Naturalized U.S. Citizens

Group	Number	%
Total Population	195,984	28.7
Hispanic or Latino (of any race)	49,592	13.1
Central American, ex. Mexican	11,571	17.1
Costa Rican	881	25.4
Guatemalan	2,590	18.9
Honduran	1,404	6.5
Nicaraguan	1,475	47.1
Panamanian	1,573	63.1
Salvadoran	3,580	15.6
Cuban	3,484	59.1
Dominican Republic	2,470	42.7
Mexican	18,899	7.2
Puerto Rican	287	32.7
South American	10,581	38.2
Argentinean	912	47.4
Bolivian	156	38.9
Chilean	488	37.5
Colombian	3,914	38.6
Ecuadorian	2,161	38.5
Peruvian	1,614	36.5
Venezuelan	937	35.5
Spaniard	600	40.6

Language Spoken at Home: English Only
(Universe: Population 5 Years and Over)

Group	Number	%
Total Population	7,750,904	89.6
Hispanic or Latino (of any race)	104,681	16.8
Central American, ex. Mexican	8,069	9.2
Costa Rican	723	15.6
Guatemalan	1,442	9.1
Honduran	1,061	4.1
Nicaraguan	776	18.8
Panamanian	1,735	34.3
Salvadoran	2,282	7.3
Cuban	5,329	36.9
Dominican Republic	1,814	16.7
Mexican	45,873	11.8
Puerto Rican	25,293	44.2
South American	7,404	18.6
Argentinean	618	21.1
Bolivian	196	33.4
Chilean	419	20.4
Colombian	2,629	18.0
Ecuadorian	1,104	13.4
Peruvian	1,196	19.0
Venezuelan	922	26.0
Spaniard	3,631	61.2

Language Spoken at Home: Spanish
(Universe: Population 5 Years and Over)

Group	Number	%
Total Population	601,101	6.9
Hispanic or Latino (of any race)	515,742	82.8
Central American, ex. Mexican	79,119	90.5
Costa Rican	3,915	84.4
Guatemalan	14,331	90.1
Honduran	24,760	95.7
Nicaraguan	3,311	80.3
Panamanian	3,325	65.7
Salvadoran	28,854	92.5
Cuban	8,974	62.2
Dominican Republic	9,043	83.0
Mexican	341,134	88.0
Puerto Rican	31,728	55.5
South American	32,255	80.8
Argentinean	2,280	77.8
Bolivian	379	64.7
Chilean	1,634	79.6
Colombian	11,933	81.7
Ecuadorian	7,122	86.3
Peruvian	5,020	79.7
Venezuelan	2,599	73.3
Spaniard	2,185	36.8

Unemployment Rate
(Universe: Population 16 Years and Over)

Group	%
Total Population	8.8
Hispanic or Latino (of any race)	10.3
Central American, ex. Mexican	11.3
Costa Rican	12.5
Guatemalan	10.9
Honduran	14.0
Nicaraguan	8.1
Panamanian	13.9
Salvadoran	9.0
Cuban	7.9
Dominican Republic	16.4
Mexican	9.9
Puerto Rican	11.6
South American	9.6
Argentinean	8.5
Bolivian	11.7
Chilean	8.7
Colombian	9.6
Ecuadorian	10.9
Peruvian	9.6
Venezuelan	7.6
Spaniard	10.4

Class of Worker: Private Wage and Salary
(Universe: Civilian Employed Population 16 Years and Over)

Group	Number	%
Total Population	3,319,505	78.4
Hispanic or Latino (of any race)	276,119	90.3
Central American, ex. Mexican	43,297	90.5
Costa Rican	2,114	86.0
Guatemalan	8,342	93.9
Honduran	13,156	92.9
Nicaraguan	1,813	79.8
Panamanian	1,694	69.1
Salvadoran	15,759	92.0
Cuban	5,900	77.3
Dominican Republic	3,922	88.1
Mexican	177,908	93.7
Puerto Rican	18,819	80.2
South American	17,769	81.2
Argentinean	1,242	77.7
Bolivian	194	77.6
Chilean	784	74.4
Colombian	6,626	81.5
Ecuadorian	3,985	86.3
Peruvian	2,730	82.2
Venezuelan	1,537	74.7
Spaniard	2,096	73.3

Class of Worker: Government
(Universe: Civilian Employed Population 16 Years and Over)

Group	Number	%
Total Population	641,586	15.2
Hispanic or Latino (of any race)	16,044	5.2
Central American, ex. Mexican	2,230	4.7
Costa Rican	130	5.3
Guatemalan	268	3.0
Honduran	372	2.6
Nicaraguan	250	11.0
Panamanian	619	25.3
Salvadoran	554	3.2
Cuban	1,129	14.8
Dominican Republic	381	8.6
Mexican	4,890	2.6
Puerto Rican	3,867	16.5
South American	2,339	10.7
Argentinean	145	9.1
Bolivian	56	22.4
Chilean	210	19.9
Colombian	941	11.6
Ecuadorian	294	6.4
Peruvian	271	8.2
Venezuelan	347	16.9
Spaniard	456	15.9

Means of Transportation to Work: Car, Truck or Van
(Universe: Workers 16 Years and Over)

Group	Number	%
Total Population	3,866,995	91.9
Hispanic or Latino (of any race)	283,433	92.0
Central American, ex. Mexican	43,164	91.3
Costa Rican	2,371	95.3
Guatemalan	7,964	89.6
Honduran	12,461	90.1
Nicaraguan	2,223	94.6
Panamanian	2,213	92.2
Salvadoran	15,482	91.7
Cuban	6,828	89.6
Dominican Republic	4,505	90.9
Mexican	176,134	92.7
Puerto Rican	23,075	89.8
South American	20,094	91.7
Argentinean	1,543	96.2
Bolivian	232	89.9
Chilean	939	89.6
Colombian	7,276	90.6
Ecuadorian	4,310	91.5
Peruvian	3,093	91.9
Venezuelan	1,900	93.0
Spaniard	2,695	89.7

Means of Transportation to Work: Public Transportation (ex. Taxicab)
(Universe: Workers 16 Years and Over)

Group	Number	%
Total Population	42,731	1.0
Hispanic or Latino (of any race)	3,932	1.3

Notes: (1) Percent of total population; (2) Percent of Hispanic/Latino population; Profiles include places with an overall population of at least 125,000, OR an overall population of at least 25,000 where the Hispanic/Latino population is at least 20% of the overall population. In states where less than five places meet either of these criteria, we have included places with at least 10,000 total population with the highest percentage of Hispanic/Latino population. These places are identified with an asterisk (*); Please refer to the User's Guide for a full explanation of data.

Central American, ex. Mexican	809	1.7
Costa Rican	11	0.4
Guatemalan	112	1.3
Honduran	317	2.3
Nicaraguan	11	0.5
Panamanian	0	0.0
Salvadoran	358	2.1
Cuban	103	1.4
Dominican Republic	74	1.5
Mexican	2,271	1.2
Puerto Rican	347	1.4
South American	211	1.0
Argentinean	0	0.0
Bolivian	0	0.0
Chilean	0	0.0
Colombian	108	1.3
Ecuadorian	75	1.6
Peruvian	11	0.3
Venezuelan	9	0.4
Spaniard	11	0.4

Homeownership Rate
(Universe: Occupied Housing Units)

Group	%
Total Population	66.7
Hispanic or Latino (of any race)	42.9
Central American, ex. Mexican	42.6
Costa Rican	50.0
Guatemalan	33.0
Honduran	31.8
Nicaraguan	51.5
Panamanian	51.5
Salvadoran	52.0
Cuban	58.9
Dominican Republic	46.0
Mexican	38.5
Puerto Rican	49.2
South American	58.6
Argentinean	64.8
Bolivian	59.7
Chilean	57.4
Colombian	59.8
Ecuadorian	60.3
Paraguayan	57.9
Peruvian	55.2
Uruguayan	47.0
Venezuelan	57.2
Spaniard	62.9

Median Home Value

Group	Dollars
Total Population	149,100
Hispanic or Latino (of any race)	120,500
Central American, ex. Mexican	126,800
Costa Rican	149,300
Guatemalan	100,500
Honduran	117,200
Nicaraguan	117,500
Panamanian	148,300
Salvadoran	133,600
Cuban	188,900
Dominican Republic	156,200
Mexican	83,200
Puerto Rican	154,000
South American	169,600
Argentinean	191,700
Bolivian	206,000
Chilean	179,200
Colombian	162,900
Ecuadorian	164,300
Peruvian	174,600
Venezuelan	180,500
Spaniard	177,900

Median Gross Rent

Group	Dollars
Total Population	718
Hispanic or Latino (of any race)	697
Central American, ex. Mexican	701
Costa Rican	639
Guatemalan	682
Honduran	715
Nicaraguan	904
Panamanian	649
Salvadoran	704
Cuban	801
Dominican Republic	798
Mexican	671
Puerto Rican	821
South American	796
Argentinean	912
Bolivian	685
Chilean	946
Colombian	772
Ecuadorian	755
Peruvian	894
Venezuelan	972
Spaniard	761

Median Household Income
(2010 Inflation-Adjusted Dollars)

Group	Dollars
Total Population	45,570
Hispanic or Latino (of any race)	34,523
Central American, ex. Mexican	35,965
Costa Rican	35,568
Guatemalan	32,931
Honduran	32,298
Nicaraguan	49,276
Panamanian	52,019
Salvadoran	38,915
Cuban	42,845
Dominican Republic	36,779
Mexican	31,065
Puerto Rican	44,633
South American	49,178
Argentinean	51,795
Bolivian	63,917
Chilean	57,938
Colombian	49,324
Ecuadorian	42,438
Peruvian	52,842
Venezuelan	49,523
Spaniard	50,347

Per Capita Income
(2010 Inflation-Adjusted Dollars)

Group	Dollars
Total Population	24,745
Hispanic or Latino (of any race)	12,287
Central American, ex. Mexican	12,358
Costa Rican	13,871
Guatemalan	11,172
Honduran	11,136
Nicaraguan	16,550
Panamanian	20,551
Salvadoran	12,014
Cuban	28,324
Dominican Republic	14,977
Mexican	10,021
Puerto Rican	16,829
South American	20,116
Argentinean	27,433
Bolivian	20,401
Chilean	22,442
Colombian	20,582
Ecuadorian	16,921
Peruvian	18,442
Venezuelan	20,324
Spaniard	24,972

Households with $100,000+ Income

Group	Number	%
Total Population	577,912	15.9
Hispanic or Latino (of any race)	12,533	6.8
Central American, ex. Mexican	1,522	5.7
Costa Rican	131	8.7
Guatemalan	181	3.8
Honduran	360	4.8
Nicaraguan	193	13.2
Panamanian	147	8.2
Salvadoran	504	5.4
Cuban	1,127	20.0
Dominican Republic	149	4.3
Mexican	4,545	4.2
Puerto Rican	2,156	11.2
South American	1,888	13.9
Argentinean	153	13.2
Bolivian	52	34.4
Chilean	184	25.3
Colombian	677	13.9
Ecuadorian	376	13.8
Peruvian	245	11.7
Venezuelan	130	10.0
Spaniard	436	21.2

Households with Food Stamps/SNAP Benefits During Past 12 Months

Group	Number	%
Total Population	372,066	10.3
Hispanic or Latino (of any race)	25,600	13.9
Central American, ex. Mexican	3,380	12.8
Costa Rican	148	9.8
Guatemalan	914	19.4
Honduran	1,193	15.9
Nicaraguan	200	13.7
Panamanian	94	5.2
Salvadoran	816	8.8
Cuban	495	8.8
Dominican Republic	665	19.4
Mexican	16,554	15.3
Puerto Rican	2,878	14.9
South American	1,056	7.8
Argentinean	0	0.0
Bolivian	18	11.9
Chilean	14	1.9
Colombian	569	11.7
Ecuadorian	210	7.7
Peruvian	133	6.3
Venezuelan	68	5.3
Spaniard	117	5.7

Poverty Rate
(Income in Past 12 Months Below Poverty Level)

Group	%
Total Population	15.5
Hispanic or Latino (of any race)	29.8
Central American, ex. Mexican	28.4
Costa Rican	20.5
Guatemalan	31.7
Honduran	30.8
Nicaraguan	16.0
Panamanian	14.2
Salvadoran	29.3
Cuban	15.2
Dominican Republic	29.1
Mexican	34.9
Puerto Rican	17.9
South American	10.4
Argentinean	1.9
Bolivian	13.4
Chilean	11.5
Colombian	10.1
Ecuadorian	12.0
Peruvian	14.7
Venezuelan	6.9
Spaniard	13.9

Asheboro

Population

Group	Number	%TP[1]	%HP[2]
Total Population	25,012	100.0	–
Hispanic or Latino (of any race)	6,719	26.9	100.0
Central American, ex. Mexican	607	2.4	9.0
Guatemalan	180	0.7	2.7
Salvadoran	183	0.7	2.7
Mexican	5,469	21.9	81.4
Puerto Rican	137	0.5	2.0

Population Growth: 2000–2010

Group	%
Total Population	15.4
Hispanic or Latino (of any race)	55.6
Central American, ex. Mexican	155.0
Mexican	51.6

Males per 100 Females

Group	Number
Total Population	90.8
Hispanic or Latino (of any race)	111.9
Central American, ex. Mexican	116.0
Guatemalan	150.0
Salvadoran	96.8

Notes: (1) Percent of total population; (2) Percent of Hispanic/Latino population; Profiles include places with an overall population of at least 125,000, OR an overall population of at least 25,000 where the Hispanic/Latino population is at least 20% of the overall population. In states where less than five places meet either of these criteria, we have included places with at least 10,000 total population with the highest percentage of Hispanic/Latino population. These places are identified with an asterisk (*); Please refer to the User's Guide for a full explanation of data.

Mexican	112.9
Puerto Rican	77.9

Average Household Size

Group	People
Total Population	2.46
Hispanic or Latino (of any race)	3.76
Central American, ex. Mexican	3.71
Guatemalan	4.13
Salvadoran	3.83
Mexican	3.86
Puerto Rican	2.75

Median Age

Group	Years
Total Population	34.0
Hispanic or Latino (of any race)	23.7
Central American, ex. Mexican	30.4
Guatemalan	28.0
Salvadoran	30.4
Mexican	22.6
Puerto Rican	27.8

High School Graduates
(Universe: Population 25 Years and Over)

Group	Number	%
Total Population	11,720	72.5
Hispanic or Latino (of any race)	1,580	50.3
Mexican	1,339	48.9

Four-Year College Graduates
(Universe: Population 25 Years and Over)

Group	Number	%
Total Population	2,832	17.5
Hispanic or Latino (of any race)	138	4.4
Mexican	57	2.1

Population Age 3–17 Enrolled in Public School
(Universe: Population Age 3–17 Enrolled in School)

Group	Number	%
Total Population	4,120	94.0
Hispanic or Latino (of any race)	1,591	100.0
Mexican	1,265	100.0

Population Age 3–17 Enrolled in Private School
(Universe: Population Age 3–17 Enrolled in School)

Group	Number	%
Total Population	264	6.0
Hispanic or Latino (of any race)	0	0.0
Mexican	0	0.0

Foreign-Born Population

Group	Number	%
Total Population	4,507	18.4
Hispanic or Latino (of any race)	4,178	65.6
Mexican	3,810	71.2

Foreign-Born Naturalized U.S. Citizens

Group	Number	%
Total Population	583	12.9
Hispanic or Latino (of any race)	386	9.2
Mexican	272	7.1

Language Spoken at Home: English Only
(Universe: Population 5 Years and Over)

Group	Number	%
Total Population	16,831	74.2
Hispanic or Latino (of any race)	395	7.0
Mexican	185	3.8

Language Spoken at Home: Spanish
(Universe: Population 5 Years and Over)

Group	Number	%
Total Population	5,509	24.3
Hispanic or Latino (of any race)	5,257	93.0
Mexican	4,624	96.2

Unemployment Rate
(Universe: Population 16 Years and Over)

Group	%
Total Population	10.1
Hispanic or Latino (of any race)	11.3
Mexican	10.6

Class of Worker: Private Wage and Salary
(Universe: Civilian Employed Population 16 Years and Over)

Group	Number	%
Total Population	8,516	81.4
Hispanic or Latino (of any race)	2,613	97.4
Mexican	2,287	99.0

Class of Worker: Government
(Universe: Civilian Employed Population 16 Years and Over)

Group	Number	%
Total Population	1,457	13.9
Hispanic or Latino (of any race)	38	1.4
Mexican	0	0.0

Means of Transportation to Work: Car, Truck or Van
(Universe: Workers 16 Years and Over)

Group	Number	%
Total Population	9,870	96.1
Hispanic or Latino (of any race)	2,556	97.0
Mexican	2,203	96.5

Means of Transportation to Work: Public Transportation (ex. Taxicab)
(Universe: Workers 16 Years and Over)

Group	Number	%
Total Population	35	0.3
Hispanic or Latino (of any race)	20	0.8
Mexican	20	0.9

Homeownership Rate
(Universe: Occupied Housing Units)

Group	%
Total Population	48.5
Hispanic or Latino (of any race)	30.6
Central American, ex. Mexican	28.8
Guatemalan	20.4
Salvadoran	48.1
Mexican	31.4
Puerto Rican	24.5

Median Home Value

Group	Dollars
Total Population	112,900
Hispanic or Latino (of any race)	72,300
Mexican	69,000

Median Gross Rent

Group	Dollars
Total Population	585
Hispanic or Latino (of any race)	581
Mexican	578

Median Household Income
(2010 Inflation-Adjusted Dollars)

Group	Dollars
Total Population	30,198
Hispanic or Latino (of any race)	21,676
Mexican	22,064

Per Capita Income
(2010 Inflation-Adjusted Dollars)

Group	Dollars
Total Population	18,126
Hispanic or Latino (of any race)	8,518
Mexican	8,516

Households with $100,000+ Income

Group	Number	%
Total Population	738	7.2
Hispanic or Latino (of any race)	33	1.9
Mexican	33	2.3

Households with Food Stamps/SNAP Benefits During Past 12 Months

Group	Number	%
Total Population	1,551	15.1
Hispanic or Latino (of any race)	352	20.1
Mexican	287	19.7

Poverty Rate
(Income in Past 12 Months Below Poverty Level)

Group	%
Total Population	27.6
Hispanic or Latino (of any race)	45.3
Mexican	48.4

Cary

Population

Group	Number	%TP[1]	%HP[2]
Total Population	135,234	100.0	–
Hispanic or Latino (of any race)	10,364	7.7	100.0
Central American, ex. Mexican	1,351	1.0	13.0
Guatemalan	391	0.3	3.8
Honduran	244	0.2	2.4
Salvadoran	450	0.3	4.3
Cuban	529	0.4	5.1
Dominican Republic	248	0.2	2.4
Mexican	5,012	3.7	48.4
Puerto Rican	1,169	0.9	11.3
South American	1,259	0.9	12.1
Argentinean	115	0.1	1.1
Colombian	423	0.3	4.1
Ecuadorian	140	0.1	1.4
Peruvian	258	0.2	2.5
Venezuelan	156	0.1	1.5
Spaniard	259	0.2	2.5

Population Growth: 2000–2010

Group	%
Total Population	43.1
Hispanic or Latino (of any race)	156.1
Central American, ex. Mexican	275.3
Salvadoran	287.9
Cuban	165.8
Mexican	132.4
Puerto Rican	199.7
South American	248.8
Colombian	264.7

Males per 100 Females

Group	Number
Total Population	94.8
Hispanic or Latino (of any race)	105.6
Central American, ex. Mexican	109.1
Guatemalan	138.4
Honduran	103.3
Salvadoran	114.3
Cuban	88.3
Dominican Republic	85.1
Mexican	119.9
Puerto Rican	94.5
South American	82.5
Argentinean	79.7
Colombian	75.5
Ecuadorian	64.7
Peruvian	95.5
Venezuelan	90.2
Spaniard	96.2

Average Household Size

Group	People
Total Population	2.61
Hispanic or Latino (of any race)	3.45
Central American, ex. Mexican	3.73
Guatemalan	4.39
Honduran	3.72
Salvadoran	3.74
Cuban	2.95
Dominican Republic	3.68
Mexican	3.96
Puerto Rican	2.73
South American	2.96
Argentinean	2.95
Colombian	2.96
Ecuadorian	3.51
Peruvian	3.06
Venezuelan	2.67
Spaniard	2.65

Median Age

Group	Years
Total Population	36.6
Hispanic or Latino (of any race)	26.9
Central American, ex. Mexican	26.9
Guatemalan	23.4
Honduran	27.4
Salvadoran	28.5
Cuban	35.0
Dominican Republic	28.0

Notes: (1) Percent of total population; (2) Percent of Hispanic/Latino population; Profiles include places with an overall population of at least 125,000, OR an overall population of at least 25,000 where the Hispanic/Latino population is at least 20% of the overall population. In states where less than five places meet either of these criteria, we have included places with at least 10,000 total population with the highest percentage of Hispanic/Latino population. These places are identified with an asterisk (*); Please refer to the User's Guide for a full explanation of data.

Mexican	25.0
Puerto Rican	28.3
South American	34.3
Argentinean	40.3
Colombian	35.4
Ecuadorian	32.3
Peruvian	34.6
Venezuelan	32.0
Spaniard	34.9

High School Graduates
(Universe: Population 25 Years and Over)

Group	Number	%
Total Population	79,591	95.4
Hispanic or Latino (of any race)	3,697	65.9
Central American, ex. Mexican	514	63.1
Mexican	1,364	48.7

Four-Year College Graduates
(Universe: Population 25 Years and Over)

Group	Number	%
Total Population	51,920	62.3
Hispanic or Latino (of any race)	1,258	22.4
Central American, ex. Mexican	157	19.3
Mexican	274	9.8

Population Age 3–17 Enrolled in Public School
(Universe: Population Age 3–17 Enrolled in School)

Group	Number	%
Total Population	23,263	81.5
Hispanic or Latino (of any race)	2,596	92.2
Central American, ex. Mexican	408	85.7
Mexican	1,405	97.6

Population Age 3–17 Enrolled in Private School
(Universe: Population Age 3–17 Enrolled in School)

Group	Number	%
Total Population	5,267	18.5
Hispanic or Latino (of any race)	219	7.8
Central American, ex. Mexican	68	14.3
Mexican	35	2.4

Foreign-Born Population

Group	Number	%
Total Population	22,648	17.8
Hispanic or Latino (of any race)	5,697	53.9
Central American, ex. Mexican	1,468	83.0
Mexican	3,153	56.8

Foreign-Born Naturalized U.S. Citizens

Group	Number	%
Total Population	9,795	43.2
Hispanic or Latino (of any race)	1,179	20.7
Central American, ex. Mexican	300	20.4
Mexican	340	10.8

Language Spoken at Home: English Only
(Universe: Population 5 Years and Over)

Group	Number	%
Total Population	92,660	78.3
Hispanic or Latino (of any race)	2,207	24.1
Central American, ex. Mexican	273	16.8
Mexican	712	15.3

Language Spoken at Home: Spanish
(Universe: Population 5 Years and Over)

Group	Number	%
Total Population	8,352	7.1
Hispanic or Latino (of any race)	6,887	75.3
Central American, ex. Mexican	1,349	83.2
Mexican	3,918	84.1

Unemployment Rate
(Universe: Population 16 Years and Over)

Group	%
Total Population	4.5
Hispanic or Latino (of any race)	8.5
Central American, ex. Mexican	12.9
Mexican	7.9

Class of Worker: Private Wage and Salary
(Universe: Civilian Employed Population 16 Years and Over)

Group	Number	%
Total Population	55,685	82.5
Hispanic or Latino (of any race)	4,580	88.5
Central American, ex. Mexican	890	88.8
Mexican	2,503	96.7

Class of Worker: Government
(Universe: Civilian Employed Population 16 Years and Over)

Group	Number	%
Total Population	8,670	12.8
Hispanic or Latino (of any race)	311	6.0
Central American, ex. Mexican	0	0.0
Mexican	38	1.5

Means of Transportation to Work: Car, Truck or Van
(Universe: Workers 16 Years and Over)

Group	Number	%
Total Population	58,870	88.7
Hispanic or Latino (of any race)	4,555	88.0
Central American, ex. Mexican	888	88.6
Mexican	2,194	84.7

Means of Transportation to Work: Public Transportation (ex. Taxicab)
(Universe: Workers 16 Years and Over)

Group	Number	%
Total Population	467	0.7
Hispanic or Latino (of any race)	61	1.2
Central American, ex. Mexican	0	0.0
Mexican	61	2.4

Homeownership Rate
(Universe: Occupied Housing Units)

Group	%
Total Population	68.8
Hispanic or Latino (of any race)	41.5
Central American, ex. Mexican	31.0
Guatemalan	24.1
Honduran	25.0
Salvadoran	33.9
Cuban	68.6
Dominican Republic	39.7
Mexican	31.4
Puerto Rican	49.3
South American	58.2
Argentinean	94.9
Colombian	60.7
Ecuadorian	59.5
Peruvian	47.7
Venezuelan	39.7
Spaniard	70.8

Median Home Value

Group	Dollars
Total Population	289,000
Hispanic or Latino (of any race)	213,900
Central American, ex. Mexican	227,300
Mexican	158,000

Median Gross Rent

Group	Dollars
Total Population	888
Hispanic or Latino (of any race)	796
Central American, ex. Mexican	803
Mexican	779

Median Household Income
(2010 Inflation-Adjusted Dollars)

Group	Dollars
Total Population	89,542
Hispanic or Latino (of any race)	38,971
Central American, ex. Mexican	55,079
Mexican	30,680

Per Capita Income
(2010 Inflation-Adjusted Dollars)

Group	Dollars
Total Population	41,700
Hispanic or Latino (of any race)	17,088
Central American, ex. Mexican	14,275
Mexican	12,339

Households with $100,000+ Income

Group	Number	%
Total Population	21,271	44.7
Hispanic or Latino (of any race)	499	16.5
Central American, ex. Mexican	30	6.3
Mexican	89	6.6

Households with Food Stamps/SNAP Benefits During Past 12 Months

Group	Number	%
Total Population	1,111	2.3
Hispanic or Latino (of any race)	291	9.6
Central American, ex. Mexican	42	8.8
Mexican	106	7.9

Poverty Rate
(Income in Past 12 Months Below Poverty Level)

Group	%
Total Population	5.0
Hispanic or Latino (of any race)	23.2
Central American, ex. Mexican	38.0
Mexican	25.1

Charlotte

Population

Group	Number	%TP[1]	%HP[2]
Total Population	731,424	100.0	–
Hispanic or Latino (of any race)	95,688	13.1	100.0
Central American, ex. Mexican	22,359	3.1	23.4
Costa Rican	673	0.1	0.7
Guatemalan	2,421	0.3	2.5
Honduran	7,557	1.0	7.9
Nicaraguan	1,320	0.2	1.4
Panamanian	608	0.1	0.6
Salvadoran	9,516	1.3	9.9
Cuban	2,902	0.4	3.0
Dominican Republic	3,280	0.4	3.4
Mexican	40,601	5.6	42.4
Puerto Rican	7,521	1.0	7.9
South American	10,729	1.5	11.2
Argentinean	514	0.1	0.5
Bolivian	138	<0.1	0.1
Chilean	368	0.1	0.4
Colombian	3,338	0.5	3.5
Ecuadorian	3,008	0.4	3.1
Peruvian	2,177	0.3	2.3
Uruguayan	262	<0.1	0.3
Venezuelan	818	0.1	0.9
Spaniard	660	0.1	0.7

Population Growth: 2000–2010

Group	%
Total Population	35.2
Hispanic or Latino (of any race)	140.4
Central American, ex. Mexican	347.1
Costa Rican	137.0
Guatemalan	439.2
Honduran	379.2
Nicaraguan	187.6
Panamanian	357.1
Salvadoran	403.2
Cuban	164.3
Dominican Republic	594.9
Mexican	83.2
Puerto Rican	211.4
South American	292.7
Argentinean	317.9
Chilean	162.9
Colombian	299.8
Ecuadorian	276.0
Peruvian	422.1
Venezuelan	255.7

Males per 100 Females

Group	Number
Total Population	93.5
Hispanic or Latino (of any race)	112.7
Central American, ex. Mexican	120.5
Costa Rican	90.1
Guatemalan	157.0
Honduran	132.1
Nicaraguan	95.0
Panamanian	82.6
Salvadoran	113.5
Cuban	94.1
Dominican Republic	86.0
Mexican	126.5
Puerto Rican	89.7
South American	86.6

Notes: (1) Percent of total population; (2) Percent of Hispanic/Latino population; Profiles include places with an overall population of at least 125,000, OR an overall population of at least 25,000 where the Hispanic/Latino population is at least 20% of the overall population. In states where less than five places meet either of these criteria, we have included places with at least 10,000 total population with the highest percentage of Hispanic/Latino population. These places are identified with an asterisk (*); Please refer to the User's Guide for a full explanation of data.

Group	
Argentinean	91.1
Bolivian	119.0
Chilean	84.0
Colombian	80.0
Ecuadorian	90.9
Peruvian	86.7
Uruguayan	114.8
Venezuelan	85.5
Spaniard	95.3

Average Household Size

Group	People
Total Population	2.48
Hispanic or Latino (of any race)	3.62
Central American, ex. Mexican	3.99
Costa Rican	3.16
Guatemalan	3.96
Honduran	4.11
Nicaraguan	3.50
Panamanian	2.68
Salvadoran	4.16
Cuban	2.82
Dominican Republic	3.42
Mexican	3.98
Puerto Rican	2.79
South American	3.10
Argentinean	2.96
Bolivian	2.95
Chilean	3.03
Colombian	2.84
Ecuadorian	3.47
Peruvian	3.26
Uruguayan	3.16
Venezuelan	2.88
Spaniard	2.54

Median Age

Group	Years
Total Population	33.2
Hispanic or Latino (of any race)	26.4
Central American, ex. Mexican	27.8
Costa Rican	30.1
Guatemalan	27.6
Honduran	27.4
Nicaraguan	29.8
Panamanian	31.3
Salvadoran	27.8
Cuban	32.3
Dominican Republic	28.4
Mexican	24.6
Puerto Rican	26.0
South American	33.4
Argentinean	34.3
Bolivian	35.0
Chilean	35.9
Colombian	33.5
Ecuadorian	31.7
Peruvian	35.6
Uruguayan	30.5
Venezuelan	33.1
Spaniard	31.8

High School Graduates
(Universe: Population 25 Years and Over)

Group	Number	%
Total Population	398,403	87.4
Hispanic or Latino (of any race)	26,435	57.2
Central American, ex. Mexican	4,873	42.9
Guatemalan	301	36.1
Honduran	1,187	33.1
Nicaraguan	693	81.6
Salvadoran	1,748	34.7
Cuban	1,282	90.0
Dominican Republic	792	65.2
Mexican	9,228	45.5
Puerto Rican	2,833	85.0
South American	5,807	84.4
Colombian	2,183	80.1
Ecuadorian	1,746	81.3
Peruvian	942	93.8

Four-Year College Graduates
(Universe: Population 25 Years and Over)

Group	Number	%
Total Population	178,392	39.1
Hispanic or Latino (of any race)	7,009	15.2
Central American, ex. Mexican	1,241	10.9
Guatemalan	178	21.3
Honduran	206	5.8
Nicaraguan	200	23.6
Salvadoran	329	6.5
Cuban	463	32.5
Dominican Republic	170	14.0
Mexican	1,546	7.6
Puerto Rican	738	22.1
South American	2,055	29.9
Colombian	972	35.6
Ecuadorian	380	17.7
Peruvian	390	38.8

Population Age 3–17 Enrolled in Public School
(Universe: Population Age 3–17 Enrolled in School)

Group	Number	%
Total Population	110,724	82.8
Hispanic or Latino (of any race)	18,909	94.4
Central American, ex. Mexican	4,671	95.4
Guatemalan	158	72.5
Honduran	1,538	92.3
Nicaraguan	182	100.0
Salvadoran	2,390	98.5
Cuban	549	92.4
Dominican Republic	557	92.8
Mexican	9,296	96.6
Puerto Rican	1,489	88.3
South American	1,388	91.5
Colombian	274	93.5
Ecuadorian	740	100.0
Peruvian	196	100.0

Population Age 3–17 Enrolled in Private School
(Universe: Population Age 3–17 Enrolled in School)

Group	Number	%
Total Population	23,065	17.2
Hispanic or Latino (of any race)	1,118	5.6
Central American, ex. Mexican	225	4.6
Guatemalan	60	27.5
Honduran	128	7.7
Nicaraguan	0	0.0
Salvadoran	37	1.5
Cuban	45	7.6
Dominican Republic	43	7.2
Mexican	323	3.4
Puerto Rican	198	11.7
South American	129	8.5
Colombian	19	6.5
Ecuadorian	0	0.0
Peruvian	0	0.0

Foreign-Born Population

Group	Number	%
Total Population	103,196	14.6
Hispanic or Latino (of any race)	51,069	58.7
Central American, ex. Mexican	15,691	70.1
Guatemalan	1,460	74.0
Honduran	5,615	73.7
Nicaraguan	959	74.5
Salvadoran	6,702	68.1
Cuban	990	41.6
Dominican Republic	1,236	52.2
Mexican	24,852	62.1
Puerto Rican	145	2.3
South American	6,930	68.5
Colombian	2,496	71.5
Ecuadorian	2,415	65.1
Peruvian	993	69.9

Foreign-Born Naturalized U.S. Citizens

Group	Number	%
Total Population	28,404	27.5
Hispanic or Latino (of any race)	6,389	12.5
Central American, ex. Mexican	1,672	10.7
Guatemalan	100	6.8
Honduran	130	2.3
Nicaraguan	244	25.4
Salvadoran	894	13.3
Cuban	455	46.0
Dominican Republic	356	28.8
Mexican	1,484	6.0
Puerto Rican	47	32.4
South American	1,966	28.4
Colombian	758	30.4
Ecuadorian	644	26.7
Peruvian	281	28.3

Language Spoken at Home: English Only
(Universe: Population 5 Years and Over)

Group	Number	%
Total Population	529,450	81.2
Hispanic or Latino (of any race)	10,074	13.3
Central American, ex. Mexican	1,210	6.2
Guatemalan	74	4.5
Honduran	178	2.7
Nicaraguan	135	12.1
Salvadoran	485	5.6
Cuban	517	23.1
Dominican Republic	174	8.3
Mexican	2,618	7.7
Puerto Rican	3,047	54.6
South American	1,271	13.9
Colombian	499	15.0
Ecuadorian	474	14.6
Peruvian	109	8.7

Language Spoken at Home: Spanish
(Universe: Population 5 Years and Over)

Group	Number	%
Total Population	71,628	11.0
Hispanic or Latino (of any race)	65,216	86.2
Central American, ex. Mexican	18,213	93.5
Guatemalan	1,535	92.9
Honduran	6,336	97.3
Nicaraguan	978	87.9
Salvadoran	8,128	94.2
Cuban	1,704	76.1
Dominican Republic	1,918	91.7
Mexican	31,420	92.2
Puerto Rican	2,494	44.7
South American	7,778	85.0
Colombian	2,819	85.0
Ecuadorian	2,762	85.4
Peruvian	1,054	84.5

Unemployment Rate
(Universe: Population 16 Years and Over)

Group	%
Total Population	9.2
Hispanic or Latino (of any race)	10.5
Central American, ex. Mexican	10.1
Guatemalan	16.4
Honduran	11.3
Nicaraguan	8.7
Salvadoran	6.3
Cuban	3.0
Dominican Republic	9.1
Mexican	10.9
Puerto Rican	7.8
South American	12.6
Colombian	13.7
Ecuadorian	12.3
Peruvian	9.9

Class of Worker: Private Wage and Salary
(Universe: Civilian Employed Population 16 Years and Over)

Group	Number	%
Total Population	307,526	84.9
Hispanic or Latino (of any race)	37,313	91.4
Central American, ex. Mexican	10,277	92.1
Guatemalan	1,004	98.8
Honduran	3,408	96.1
Nicaraguan	537	77.3
Salvadoran	4,561	90.4
Cuban	923	78.6
Dominican Republic	896	94.1
Mexican	16,456	92.4
Puerto Rican	2,431	87.3
South American	5,248	92.9
Colombian	1,917	94.4
Ecuadorian	1,837	92.7
Peruvian	640	86.4

Class of Worker: Government
(Universe: Civilian Employed Population 16 Years and Over)

Group	Number	%
Total Population	35,787	9.9
Hispanic or Latino (of any race)	1,446	3.5

Notes: (1) Percent of total population; (2) Percent of Hispanic/Latino population; Profiles include places with an overall population of at least 125,000, OR an overall population of at least 25,000 where the Hispanic/Latino population is at least 20% of the overall population. In states where less than five places meet either of these criteria, we have included places with at least 10,000 total population with the highest percentage of Hispanic/Latino population. These places are identified with an asterisk (*); Please refer to the User's Guide for a full explanation of data.

Group	Number	%
Central American, ex. Mexican	303	2.7
Guatemalan	12	1.2
Honduran	77	2.2
Nicaraguan	118	17.0
Salvadoran	55	1.1
Cuban	179	15.2
Dominican Republic	56	5.9
Mexican	280	1.6
Puerto Rican	314	11.3
South American	231	4.1
Colombian	91	4.5
Ecuadorian	93	4.7
Peruvian	25	3.4

Means of Transportation to Work: Car, Truck or Van
(Universe: Workers 16 Years and Over)

Group	Number	%
Total Population	314,323	88.7
Hispanic or Latino (of any race)	36,068	90.2
Central American, ex. Mexican	9,714	89.5
Guatemalan	747	75.8
Honduran	3,020	87.9
Nicaraguan	695	100.0
Salvadoran	4,469	90.5
Cuban	996	86.1
Dominican Republic	825	89.6
Mexican	15,767	90.0
Puerto Rican	2,511	89.6
South American	5,117	93.3
Colombian	1,763	93.3
Ecuadorian	1,780	89.8
Peruvian	707	95.4

Means of Transportation to Work: Public Transportation (ex. Taxicab)
(Universe: Workers 16 Years and Over)

Group	Number	%
Total Population	13,147	3.7
Hispanic or Latino (of any race)	1,644	4.1
Central American, ex. Mexican	556	5.1
Guatemalan	100	10.2
Honduran	214	6.2
Nicaraguan	0	0.0
Salvadoran	242	4.9
Cuban	43	3.7
Dominican Republic	44	4.8
Mexican	828	4.7
Puerto Rican	113	4.0
South American	49	0.9
Colombian	0	0.0
Ecuadorian	41	2.1
Peruvian	0	0.0

Homeownership Rate
(Universe: Occupied Housing Units)

Group	%
Total Population	57.4
Hispanic or Latino (of any race)	37.8
Central American, ex. Mexican	38.1
Costa Rican	43.1
Guatemalan	24.6
Honduran	22.3
Nicaraguan	49.4
Panamanian	49.6
Salvadoran	50.8
Cuban	55.1
Dominican Republic	49.1
Mexican	27.0
Puerto Rican	44.4
South American	54.6
Argentinean	61.8
Bolivian	54.5
Chilean	56.6
Colombian	57.6
Ecuadorian	53.3
Peruvian	50.7
Uruguayan	46.0
Venezuelan	57.5
Spaniard	59.3

Median Home Value

Group	Dollars
Total Population	173,300
Hispanic or Latino (of any race)	147,000
Central American, ex. Mexican	145,800
Guatemalan	147,700
Honduran	144,400
Nicaraguan	120,300
Salvadoran	148,900
Cuban	154,800
Dominican Republic	148,800
Mexican	131,000
Puerto Rican	145,500
South American	170,300
Colombian	179,700
Ecuadorian	159,400
Peruvian	161,700

Median Gross Rent

Group	Dollars
Total Population	823
Hispanic or Latino (of any race)	766
Central American, ex. Mexican	733
Guatemalan	677
Honduran	764
Nicaraguan	952
Salvadoran	711
Cuban	858
Dominican Republic	855
Mexican	747
Puerto Rican	940
South American	828
Colombian	843
Ecuadorian	739
Peruvian	930

Median Household Income
(2010 Inflation-Adjusted Dollars)

Group	Dollars
Total Population	52,446
Hispanic or Latino (of any race)	37,416
Central American, ex. Mexican	39,264
Guatemalan	50,526
Honduran	34,654
Nicaraguan	51,472
Salvadoran	40,500
Cuban	37,632
Dominican Republic	35,017
Mexican	33,142
Puerto Rican	53,125
South American	48,889
Colombian	52,173
Ecuadorian	37,401
Peruvian	41,339

Per Capita Income
(2010 Inflation-Adjusted Dollars)

Group	Dollars
Total Population	30,984
Hispanic or Latino (of any race)	13,848
Central American, ex. Mexican	11,835
Guatemalan	13,144
Honduran	10,160
Nicaraguan	14,084
Salvadoran	11,664
Cuban	24,788
Dominican Republic	14,073
Mexican	11,685
Puerto Rican	18,914
South American	18,562
Colombian	22,397
Ecuadorian	14,386
Peruvian	18,539

Households with $100,000+ Income

Group	Number	%
Total Population	60,780	21.5
Hispanic or Latino (of any race)	1,892	7.9
Central American, ex. Mexican	284	4.9
Guatemalan	39	7.4
Honduran	38	2.2
Nicaraguan	28	7.8
Salvadoran	164	6.3
Cuban	99	10.7
Dominican Republic	43	6.5
Mexican	604	5.8
Puerto Rican	167	8.6
South American	505	15.2
Colombian	262	21.6
Ecuadorian	169	14.7
Peruvian	28	5.1

Households with Food Stamps/SNAP Benefits During Past 12 Months

Group	Number	%
Total Population	26,144	9.3
Hispanic or Latino (of any race)	3,227	13.5
Central American, ex. Mexican	737	12.8
Guatemalan	71	13.5
Honduran	331	19.2
Nicaraguan	20	5.5
Salvadoran	277	10.7
Cuban	114	12.3
Dominican Republic	220	33.4
Mexican	1,436	13.8
Puerto Rican	236	12.2
South American	416	12.5
Colombian	178	14.7
Ecuadorian	122	10.6
Peruvian	47	8.6

Poverty Rate
(Income in Past 12 Months Below Poverty Level)

Group	%
Total Population	13.9
Hispanic or Latino (of any race)	25.1
Central American, ex. Mexican	25.3
Guatemalan	29.9
Honduran	26.0
Nicaraguan	11.4
Salvadoran	29.2
Cuban	25.4
Dominican Republic	41.2
Mexican	29.8
Puerto Rican	14.8
South American	11.8
Colombian	5.2
Ecuadorian	15.0
Peruvian	14.6

Durham

Population

Group	Number	%TP[1]	%HP[2]
Total Population	228,330	100.0	–
Hispanic or Latino (of any race)	32,459	14.2	100.0
Central American, ex. Mexican	8,052	3.5	24.8
Guatemalan	1,323	0.6	4.1
Honduran	3,451	1.5	10.6
Panamanian	159	0.1	0.5
Salvadoran	2,929	1.3	9.0
Cuban	445	0.2	1.4
Dominican Republic	428	0.2	1.3
Mexican	17,626	7.7	54.3
Puerto Rican	1,641	0.7	5.1
South American	1,448	0.6	4.5
Argentinean	210	0.1	0.6
Chilean	140	0.1	0.4
Colombian	478	0.2	1.5
Ecuadorian	169	0.1	0.5
Peruvian	193	0.1	0.6
Venezuelan	143	0.1	0.4
Spaniard	241	0.1	0.7

Population Growth: 2000–2010

Group	%
Total Population	22.1
Hispanic or Latino (of any race)	102.7
Central American, ex. Mexican	249.3
Guatemalan	326.8
Honduran	217.8
Salvadoran	308.5
Cuban	88.6
Mexican	70.4
Puerto Rican	135.8
South American	176.9
Colombian	282.4

Males per 100 Females

Group	Number
Total Population	90.6
Hispanic or Latino (of any race)	123.4
Central American, ex. Mexican	130.4

Notes: (1) Percent of total population; (2) Percent of Hispanic/Latino population; Profiles include places with an overall population of at least 125,000, OR an overall population of at least 25,000 where the Hispanic/Latino population is at least 20% of the overall population. In states where less than five places meet either of these criteria, we have included places with at least 10,000 total population with the highest percentage of Hispanic/Latino population. These places are identified with an asterisk (*); Please refer to the User's Guide for a full explanation of data.

Guatemalan	148.7
Honduran	139.5
Panamanian	89.3
Salvadoran	119.1
Cuban	79.4
Dominican Republic	84.5
Mexican	132.2
Puerto Rican	96.1
South American	90.5
Argentinean	114.3
Chilean	86.7
Colombian	85.3
Ecuadorian	98.8
Peruvian	87.4
Venezuelan	93.2
Spaniard	111.4

Average Household Size

Group	People
Total Population	2.34
Hispanic or Latino (of any race)	3.67
Central American, ex. Mexican	3.95
Guatemalan	4.22
Honduran	3.94
Panamanian	2.65
Salvadoran	4.10
Cuban	2.09
Dominican Republic	3.01
Mexican	3.96
Puerto Rican	2.62
South American	2.58
Argentinean	2.57
Chilean	2.43
Colombian	2.55
Ecuadorian	2.76
Peruvian	2.77
Venezuelan	2.28
Spaniard	2.26

Median Age

Group	Years
Total Population	32.1
Hispanic or Latino (of any race)	25.9
Central American, ex. Mexican	27.8
Guatemalan	26.1
Honduran	27.9
Panamanian	29.4
Salvadoran	28.7
Cuban	28.7
Dominican Republic	29.3
Mexican	25.1
Puerto Rican	26.2
South American	31.6
Argentinean	32.8
Chilean	31.5
Colombian	30.9
Ecuadorian	30.5
Peruvian	33.1
Venezuelan	31.4
Spaniard	30.9

High School Graduates
(Universe: Population 25 Years and Over)

Group	Number	%
Total Population	121,548	85.9
Hispanic or Latino (of any race)	7,172	47.0
Central American, ex. Mexican	1,507	35.0
Guatemalan	89	14.4
Honduran	742	33.5
Salvadoran	537	41.7
Mexican	3,431	40.5
Puerto Rican	721	82.7
South American	846	100.0

Four-Year College Graduates
(Universe: Population 25 Years and Over)

Group	Number	%
Total Population	64,519	45.6
Hispanic or Latino (of any race)	2,345	15.4
Central American, ex. Mexican	220	5.1
Guatemalan	27	4.4
Honduran	38	1.7
Salvadoran	78	6.1
Mexican	768	9.1
Puerto Rican	354	40.6
South American	571	67.5

Population Age 3–17 Enrolled in Public School
(Universe: Population Age 3–17 Enrolled in School)

Group	Number	%
Total Population	29,609	84.0
Hispanic or Latino (of any race)	5,292	96.4
Central American, ex. Mexican	1,312	98.5
Guatemalan	178	89.9
Honduran	652	100.0
Salvadoran	482	100.0
Mexican	3,355	96.0
Puerto Rican	163	92.6
South American	160	87.0

Population Age 3–17 Enrolled in Private School
(Universe: Population Age 3–17 Enrolled in School)

Group	Number	%
Total Population	5,628	16.0
Hispanic or Latino (of any race)	197	3.6
Central American, ex. Mexican	20	1.5
Guatemalan	20	10.1
Honduran	0	0.0
Salvadoran	0	0.0
Mexican	140	4.0
Puerto Rican	13	7.4
South American	24	13.0

Foreign-Born Population

Group	Number	%
Total Population	32,442	14.7
Hispanic or Latino (of any race)	17,036	58.7
Central American, ex. Mexican	5,110	69.4
Guatemalan	752	63.8
Honduran	2,680	73.9
Salvadoran	1,555	67.2
Mexican	10,685	62.6
Puerto Rican	11	0.7
South American	904	63.1

Foreign-Born Naturalized U.S. Citizens

Group	Number	%
Total Population	7,211	22.2
Hispanic or Latino (of any race)	1,459	8.6
Central American, ex. Mexican	350	6.8
Guatemalan	116	15.4
Honduran	32	1.2
Salvadoran	181	11.6
Mexican	543	5.1
Puerto Rican	0	0.0
South American	389	43.0

Language Spoken at Home: English Only
(Universe: Population 5 Years and Over)

Group	Number	%
Total Population	162,895	80.0
Hispanic or Latino (of any race)	2,528	10.2
Central American, ex. Mexican	145	2.3
Guatemalan	68	7.3
Honduran	17	0.5
Salvadoran	26	1.3
Mexican	1,031	7.2
Puerto Rican	610	40.6
South American	399	30.0

Language Spoken at Home: Spanish
(Universe: Population 5 Years and Over)

Group	Number	%
Total Population	25,410	12.5
Hispanic or Latino (of any race)	22,166	89.1
Central American, ex. Mexican	6,168	96.8
Guatemalan	832	89.0
Honduran	3,219	99.5
Salvadoran	1,951	97.5
Mexican	13,338	92.5
Puerto Rican	891	59.4
South American	890	66.9

Unemployment Rate
(Universe: Population 16 Years and Over)

Group	%
Total Population	8.4
Hispanic or Latino (of any race)	10.1
Central American, ex. Mexican	11.2
Guatemalan	2.7
Honduran	15.5
Salvadoran	7.2
Mexican	10.8
Puerto Rican	6.1
South American	3.1

Class of Worker: Private Wage and Salary
(Universe: Civilian Employed Population 16 Years and Over)

Group	Number	%
Total Population	86,665	77.9
Hispanic or Latino (of any race)	12,608	88.6
Central American, ex. Mexican	3,460	91.5
Guatemalan	477	84.3
Honduran	1,873	96.6
Salvadoran	1,033	92.6
Mexican	7,454	93.2
Puerto Rican	626	69.1
South American	686	79.7

Class of Worker: Government
(Universe: Civilian Employed Population 16 Years and Over)

Group	Number	%
Total Population	19,897	17.9
Hispanic or Latino (of any race)	1,000	7.0
Central American, ex. Mexican	273	7.2
Guatemalan	52	9.2
Honduran	56	2.9
Salvadoran	82	7.4
Mexican	184	2.3
Puerto Rican	269	29.7
South American	112	13.0

Means of Transportation to Work: Car, Truck or Van
(Universe: Workers 16 Years and Over)

Group	Number	%
Total Population	95,563	88.0
Hispanic or Latino (of any race)	12,749	91.7
Central American, ex. Mexican	3,493	96.4
Guatemalan	566	100.0
Honduran	1,739	94.4
Salvadoran	1,028	97.5
Mexican	7,312	93.0
Puerto Rican	635	69.9
South American	727	90.4

Means of Transportation to Work: Public Transportation (ex. Taxicab)
(Universe: Workers 16 Years and Over)

Group	Number	%
Total Population	3,883	3.6
Hispanic or Latino (of any race)	389	2.8
Central American, ex. Mexican	64	1.8
Guatemalan	0	0.0
Honduran	38	2.1
Salvadoran	26	2.5
Mexican	230	2.9
Puerto Rican	33	3.6
South American	34	4.2

Homeownership Rate
(Universe: Occupied Housing Units)

Group	%
Total Population	49.8
Hispanic or Latino (of any race)	24.6
Central American, ex. Mexican	25.8
Guatemalan	13.0
Honduran	16.7
Panamanian	38.0
Salvadoran	38.8
Cuban	42.0
Dominican Republic	30.4
Mexican	17.9
Puerto Rican	37.4
South American	48.6
Argentinean	55.8
Chilean	45.6
Colombian	48.2
Ecuadorian	47.0
Peruvian	48.0
Venezuelan	45.0
Spaniard	49.0

Notes: (1) Percent of total population; (2) Percent of Hispanic/Latino population; Profiles include places with an overall population of at least 125,000, OR an overall population of at least 25,000 where the Hispanic/Latino population is at least 20% of the overall population. In states where less than five places meet either of these criteria, we have included places with at least 10,000 total population with the highest percentage of Hispanic/Latino population. These places are identified with an asterisk (*); Please refer to the User's Guide for a full explanation of data.

Median Home Value

Group	Dollars
Total Population	176,600
Hispanic or Latino (of any race)	173,800
Central American, ex. Mexican	135,000
Guatemalan	223,500
Honduran	123,200
Salvadoran	136,300
Mexican	148,500
Puerto Rican	189,400
South American	219,800

Median Gross Rent

Group	Dollars
Total Population	786
Hispanic or Latino (of any race)	740
Central American, ex. Mexican	740
Guatemalan	750
Honduran	711
Salvadoran	802
Mexican	721
Puerto Rican	805
South American	948

Median Household Income
(2010 Inflation-Adjusted Dollars)

Group	Dollars
Total Population	46,972
Hispanic or Latino (of any race)	38,179
Central American, ex. Mexican	36,457
Guatemalan	29,096
Honduran	38,637
Salvadoran	38,882
Mexican	34,848
Puerto Rican	49,750
South American	53,365

Per Capita Income
(2010 Inflation-Adjusted Dollars)

Group	Dollars
Total Population	26,725
Hispanic or Latino (of any race)	12,185
Central American, ex. Mexican	10,308
Guatemalan	10,749
Honduran	9,241
Salvadoran	9,706
Mexican	10,207
Puerto Rican	22,586
South American	27,303

Households with $100,000+ Income

Group	Number	%
Total Population	16,901	18.6
Hispanic or Latino (of any race)	593	7.6
Central American, ex. Mexican	64	3.4
Guatemalan	6	2.1
Honduran	0	0.0
Salvadoran	49	7.6
Mexican	166	4.0
Puerto Rican	129	18.6
South American	155	25.1

Households with Food Stamps/SNAP Benefits During Past 12 Months

Group	Number	%
Total Population	9,411	10.4
Hispanic or Latino (of any race)	760	9.7
Central American, ex. Mexican	219	11.7
Guatemalan	36	12.5
Honduran	152	19.5
Salvadoran	31	4.8
Mexican	371	8.9
Puerto Rican	149	21.5
South American	11	1.8

Poverty Rate
(Income in Past 12 Months Below Poverty Level)

Group	%
Total Population	17.9
Hispanic or Latino (of any race)	29.1
Central American, ex. Mexican	32.1
Guatemalan	28.0
Honduran	32.6
Salvadoran	35.7
Mexican	29.3
Puerto Rican	29.0
South American	11.3

Fayetteville

Population

Group	Number	%TP[1]	%HP[2]
Total Population	200,564	100.0	–
Hispanic or Latino (of any race)	20,256	10.1	100.0
Central American, ex. Mexican	2,238	1.1	11.0
Guatemalan	176	0.1	0.9
Honduran	282	0.1	1.4
Nicaraguan	157	0.1	0.8
Panamanian	1,154	0.6	5.7
Salvadoran	379	0.2	1.9
Cuban	534	0.3	2.6
Dominican Republic	730	0.4	3.6
Mexican	6,448	3.2	31.8
Puerto Rican	7,526	3.8	37.2
South American	1,227	0.6	6.1
Colombian	492	0.2	2.4
Ecuadorian	195	0.1	1.0
Peruvian	244	0.1	1.2
Spaniard	363	0.2	1.8

Population Growth: 2000–2010

Group	%
Total Population	65.7
Hispanic or Latino (of any race)	195.2
Central American, ex. Mexican	218.3
Panamanian	138.9
Cuban	301.5
Dominican Republic	470.3
Mexican	213.9
Puerto Rican	202.5
South American	292.0
Colombian	339.3

Males per 100 Females

Group	Number
Total Population	93.6
Hispanic or Latino (of any race)	99.5
Central American, ex. Mexican	78.0
Guatemalan	112.0
Honduran	95.8
Nicaraguan	109.3
Panamanian	54.3
Salvadoran	144.5
Cuban	124.4
Dominican Republic	97.3
Mexican	112.9
Puerto Rican	100.4
South American	68.5
Colombian	62.9
Ecuadorian	74.1
Peruvian	69.4
Spaniard	98.4

Average Household Size

Group	People
Total Population	2.45
Hispanic or Latino (of any race)	2.86
Central American, ex. Mexican	2.93
Guatemalan	3.16
Honduran	2.96
Nicaraguan	2.92
Panamanian	2.75
Salvadoran	3.38
Cuban	2.62
Dominican Republic	3.03
Mexican	2.89
Puerto Rican	2.89
South American	2.69
Colombian	2.53
Ecuadorian	2.85
Peruvian	2.65
Spaniard	2.64

Median Age

Group	Years
Total Population	29.9
Hispanic or Latino (of any race)	24.0
Central American, ex. Mexican	27.7
Guatemalan	26.2
Honduran	25.4
Nicaraguan	27.3
Panamanian	31.8
Salvadoran	25.1
Cuban	24.9
Dominican Republic	23.6
Mexican	22.3
Puerto Rican	24.5
South American	27.3
Colombian	25.7
Ecuadorian	28.3
Peruvian	28.6
Spaniard	25.2

High School Graduates
(Universe: Population 25 Years and Over)

Group	Number	%
Total Population	105,053	89.7
Hispanic or Latino (of any race)	7,674	89.7
Central American, ex. Mexican	994	95.3
Panamanian	706	98.9
Mexican	2,058	82.6
Puerto Rican	3,188	93.9
South American	788	92.9

Four-Year College Graduates
(Universe: Population 25 Years and Over)

Group	Number	%
Total Population	27,984	23.9
Hispanic or Latino (of any race)	1,638	19.2
Central American, ex. Mexican	99	9.5
Panamanian	99	13.9
Mexican	468	18.8
Puerto Rican	624	18.4
South American	219	25.8

Population Age 3–17 Enrolled in Public School
(Universe: Population Age 3–17 Enrolled in School)

Group	Number	%
Total Population	32,688	90.1
Hispanic or Latino (of any race)	3,606	87.8
Central American, ex. Mexican	312	86.7
Panamanian	215	85.7
Mexican	1,183	85.4
Puerto Rican	1,369	89.5
South American	328	90.9

Population Age 3–17 Enrolled in Private School
(Universe: Population Age 3–17 Enrolled in School)

Group	Number	%
Total Population	3,582	9.9
Hispanic or Latino (of any race)	503	12.2
Central American, ex. Mexican	48	13.3
Panamanian	36	14.3
Mexican	202	14.6
Puerto Rican	161	10.5
South American	33	9.1

Foreign-Born Population

Group	Number	%
Total Population	11,931	6.0
Hispanic or Latino (of any race)	3,036	16.7
Central American, ex. Mexican	937	50.7
Panamanian	529	47.0
Mexican	928	14.9
Puerto Rican	45	0.7
South American	784	50.8

Foreign-Born Naturalized U.S. Citizens

Group	Number	%
Total Population	6,692	56.1
Hispanic or Latino (of any race)	1,423	46.9
Central American, ex. Mexican	547	58.4
Panamanian	366	69.2
Mexican	343	37.0
Puerto Rican	28	62.2
South American	326	41.6

Language Spoken at Home: English Only
(Universe: Population 5 Years and Over)

Group	Number	%
Total Population	161,678	88.6
Hispanic or Latino (of any race)	6,543	40.9
Central American, ex. Mexican	457	26.4
Panamanian	346	32.4

Notes: (1) Percent of total population; (2) Percent of Hispanic/Latino population; Profiles include places with an overall population of at least 125,000, OR an overall population of at least 25,000 where the Hispanic/Latino population is at least 20% of the overall population. In states where less than five places meet either of these criteria, we have included places with at least 10,000 total population with the highest percentage of Hispanic/Latino population. These places are identified with an asterisk (*); Please refer to the User's Guide for a full explanation of data.

STATE & PLACE PROFILES

Group	Number	%
Mexican	2,887	53.5
Puerto Rican	1,950	33.2
South American	343	24.6

Language Spoken at Home: Spanish
(Universe: Population 5 Years and Over)

Group	Number	%
Total Population	11,881	6.5
Hispanic or Latino (of any race)	9,296	58.1
Central American, ex. Mexican	1,251	72.2
Panamanian	721	67.6
Mexican	2,459	45.6
Puerto Rican	3,854	65.7
South American	1,049	75.4

Unemployment Rate
(Universe: Population 16 Years and Over)

Group	%
Total Population	11.7
Hispanic or Latino (of any race)	12.7
Central American, ex. Mexican	4.4
Panamanian	7.0
Mexican	14.1
Puerto Rican	15.8
South American	12.6

Class of Worker: Private Wage and Salary
(Universe: Civilian Employed Population 16 Years and Over)

Group	Number	%
Total Population	48,204	67.7
Hispanic or Latino (of any race)	3,851	71.3
Central American, ex. Mexican	570	64.4
Panamanian	339	62.5
Mexican	937	61.7
Puerto Rican	1,620	80.3
South American	418	74.4

Class of Worker: Government
(Universe: Civilian Employed Population 16 Years and Over)

Group	Number	%
Total Population	19,526	27.4
Hispanic or Latino (of any race)	1,286	23.8
Central American, ex. Mexican	258	29.2
Panamanian	175	32.3
Mexican	546	36.0
Puerto Rican	318	15.8
South American	62	11.0

Means of Transportation to Work: Car, Truck or Van
(Universe: Workers 16 Years and Over)

Group	Number	%
Total Population	79,965	87.9
Hispanic or Latino (of any race)	7,323	87.7
Central American, ex. Mexican	947	89.8
Panamanian	514	97.0
Mexican	2,490	85.4
Puerto Rican	2,497	87.8
South American	719	96.4

Means of Transportation to Work: Public Transportation (ex. Taxicab)
(Universe: Workers 16 Years and Over)

Group	Number	%
Total Population	513	0.6
Hispanic or Latino (of any race)	13	0.2
Central American, ex. Mexican	0	0.0
Panamanian	0	0.0
Mexican	0	0.0
Puerto Rican	0	0.0
South American	13	1.7

Homeownership Rate
(Universe: Occupied Housing Units)

Group	%
Total Population	50.3
Hispanic or Latino (of any race)	42.1
Central American, ex. Mexican	45.3
Guatemalan	35.7
Honduran	32.1
Nicaraguan	39.2
Panamanian	53.0
Salvadoran	32.4
Cuban	39.2
Dominican Republic	39.4

Group	%
Mexican	35.5
Puerto Rican	45.7
South American	48.5
Colombian	44.6
Ecuadorian	60.0
Peruvian	41.6
Spaniard	44.5

Median Home Value

Group	Dollars
Total Population	116,000
Hispanic or Latino (of any race)	120,800
Central American, ex. Mexican	98,100
Panamanian	97,500
Mexican	126,300
Puerto Rican	114,900
South American	130,400

Median Gross Rent

Group	Dollars
Total Population	800
Hispanic or Latino (of any race)	815
Central American, ex. Mexican	639
Panamanian	620
Mexican	818
Puerto Rican	855
South American	792

Median Household Income
(2010 Inflation-Adjusted Dollars)

Group	Dollars
Total Population	43,284
Hispanic or Latino (of any race)	41,281
Central American, ex. Mexican	50,087
Panamanian	60,096
Mexican	37,690
Puerto Rican	41,354
South American	60,909

Per Capita Income
(2010 Inflation-Adjusted Dollars)

Group	Dollars
Total Population	22,572
Hispanic or Latino (of any race)	17,514
Central American, ex. Mexican	20,651
Panamanian	21,511
Mexican	17,125
Puerto Rican	17,759
South American	17,801

Households with $100,000+ Income

Group	Number	%
Total Population	9,633	12.9
Hispanic or Latino (of any race)	356	6.3
Central American, ex. Mexican	31	4.6
Panamanian	31	8.4
Mexican	78	4.0
Puerto Rican	158	7.1
South American	57	15.5

Households with Food Stamps/SNAP Benefits During Past 12 Months

Group	Number	%
Total Population	9,439	12.6
Hispanic or Latino (of any race)	507	9.0
Central American, ex. Mexican	14	2.1
Panamanian	14	3.8
Mexican	132	6.7
Puerto Rican	309	13.9
South American	45	12.2

Poverty Rate
(Income in Past 12 Months Below Poverty Level)

Group	%
Total Population	16.1
Hispanic or Latino (of any race)	15.3
Central American, ex. Mexican	19.1
Panamanian	20.2
Mexican	18.2
Puerto Rican	13.7
South American	7.5

Greensboro

Population

Group	Number	%TP[1]	%HP[2]
Total Population	269,666	100.0	–
Hispanic or Latino (of any race)	20,336	7.5	100.0
Central American, ex. Mexican	2,246	0.8	11.0
Costa Rican	132	<0.1	0.6
Guatemalan	518	0.2	2.5
Honduran	352	0.1	1.7
Nicaraguan	159	0.1	0.8
Panamanian	191	0.1	0.9
Salvadoran	887	0.3	4.4
Cuban	520	0.2	2.6
Dominican Republic	568	0.2	2.8
Mexican	12,293	4.6	60.4
Puerto Rican	1,872	0.7	9.2
South American	1,456	0.5	7.2
Chilean	102	<0.1	0.5
Colombian	562	0.2	2.8
Ecuadorian	128	<0.1	0.6
Peruvian	285	0.1	1.4
Venezuelan	203	0.1	1.0
Spaniard	201	0.1	1.0

Population Growth: 2000–2010

Group	%
Total Population	20.4
Hispanic or Latino (of any race)	108.7
Central American, ex. Mexican	274.3
Guatemalan	384.1
Honduran	206.1
Salvadoran	336.9
Cuban	45.7
Dominican Republic	462.4
Mexican	98.1
Puerto Rican	138.5
South American	213.1
Colombian	202.2

Males per 100 Females

Group	Number
Total Population	88.7
Hispanic or Latino (of any race)	113.3
Central American, ex. Mexican	111.5
Costa Rican	103.1
Guatemalan	153.9
Honduran	113.3
Nicaraguan	63.9
Panamanian	76.9
Salvadoran	111.7
Cuban	84.4
Dominican Republic	80.3
Mexican	128.6
Puerto Rican	78.1
South American	88.1
Chilean	85.5
Colombian	79.6
Ecuadorian	109.8
Peruvian	96.6
Venezuelan	84.5
Spaniard	84.4

Average Household Size

Group	People
Total Population	2.31
Hispanic or Latino (of any race)	3.53
Central American, ex. Mexican	3.47
Costa Rican	3.07
Guatemalan	3.93
Honduran	3.35
Nicaraguan	3.14
Panamanian	2.32
Salvadoran	3.72
Cuban	2.49
Dominican Republic	3.33
Mexican	3.97
Puerto Rican	2.71
South American	2.82
Chilean	2.68
Colombian	2.90
Ecuadorian	2.95
Peruvian	3.01
Venezuelan	2.64

Notes: (1) Percent of total population; (2) Percent of Hispanic/Latino population; Profiles include places with an overall population of at least 125,000, OR an overall population of at least 25,000 where the Hispanic/Latino population is at least 20% of the overall population. In states where less than five places meet either of these criteria, we have included places with at least 10,000 total population with the highest percentage of Hispanic/Latino population. These places are identified with an asterisk (*); Please refer to the User's Guide for a full explanation of data.

Spaniard		2.37

Median Age

Group		Years
Total Population		33.4
Hispanic or Latino (of any race)		24.5
Central American, ex. Mexican		27.2
Costa Rican		32.6
Guatemalan		26.3
Honduran		29.9
Nicaraguan		28.1
Panamanian		26.2
Salvadoran		26.8
Cuban		31.3
Dominican Republic		22.9
Mexican		23.9
Puerto Rican		22.3
South American		32.5
Chilean		33.5
Colombian		31.4
Ecuadorian		30.0
Peruvian		32.8
Venezuelan		33.6
Spaniard		30.9

High School Graduates
(Universe: Population 25 Years and Over)

Group	Number	%
Total Population	144,796	87.1
Hispanic or Latino (of any race)	4,810	51.5
Central American, ex. Mexican	439	30.7
Salvadoran	129	16.8
Mexican	2,455	43.3
Puerto Rican	463	93.0
South American	803	78.7

Four-Year College Graduates
(Universe: Population 25 Years and Over)

Group	Number	%
Total Population	58,798	35.4
Hispanic or Latino (of any race)	1,155	12.4
Central American, ex. Mexican	106	7.4
Salvadoran	0	0.0
Mexican	235	4.1
Puerto Rican	170	34.1
South American	334	32.7

Population Age 3–17 Enrolled in Public School
(Universe: Population Age 3–17 Enrolled in School)

Group	Number	%
Total Population	37,842	87.8
Hispanic or Latino (of any race)	3,891	93.6
Central American, ex. Mexican	481	93.8
Salvadoran	186	98.4
Mexican	2,680	97.6
Puerto Rican	343	86.4
South American	204	88.7

Population Age 3–17 Enrolled in Private School
(Universe: Population Age 3–17 Enrolled in School)

Group	Number	%
Total Population	5,236	12.2
Hispanic or Latino (of any race)	264	6.4
Central American, ex. Mexican	32	6.2
Salvadoran	3	1.6
Mexican	65	2.4
Puerto Rican	54	13.6
South American	26	11.3

Foreign-Born Population

Group	Number	%
Total Population	26,807	10.2
Hispanic or Latino (of any race)	10,422	56.4
Central American, ex. Mexican	1,909	74.6
Salvadoran	870	78.5
Mexican	6,949	59.1
Puerto Rican	0	0.0
South American	1,085	78.7

Foreign-Born Naturalized U.S. Citizens

Group	Number	%
Total Population	8,306	31.0
Hispanic or Latino (of any race)	1,357	13.0
Central American, ex. Mexican	186	9.7
Salvadoran	48	5.5
Mexican	575	8.3
Puerto Rican	0	0.0
South American	337	31.1

Language Spoken at Home: English Only
(Universe: Population 5 Years and Over)

Group	Number	%
Total Population	213,165	86.7
Hispanic or Latino (of any race)	2,285	14.3
Central American, ex. Mexican	156	6.9
Salvadoran	53	5.0
Mexican	909	9.2
Puerto Rican	583	43.8
South American	202	15.0

Language Spoken at Home: Spanish
(Universe: Population 5 Years and Over)

Group	Number	%
Total Population	16,560	6.7
Hispanic or Latino (of any race)	13,649	85.2
Central American, ex. Mexican	2,103	93.1
Salvadoran	1,015	95.0
Mexican	8,905	90.0
Puerto Rican	748	56.2
South American	1,149	85.0

Unemployment Rate
(Universe: Population 16 Years and Over)

Group		%
Total Population		9.1
Hispanic or Latino (of any race)		8.7
Central American, ex. Mexican		13.9
Salvadoran		16.2
Mexican		6.9
Puerto Rican		14.9
South American		6.0

Class of Worker: Private Wage and Salary
(Universe: Civilian Employed Population 16 Years and Over)

Group	Number	%
Total Population	105,060	82.0
Hispanic or Latino (of any race)	7,510	92.5
Central American, ex. Mexican	1,125	93.6
Salvadoran	664	99.0
Mexican	4,731	96.2
Puerto Rican	622	82.7
South American	613	83.5

Class of Worker: Government
(Universe: Civilian Employed Population 16 Years and Over)

Group	Number	%
Total Population	16,442	12.8
Hispanic or Latino (of any race)	382	4.7
Central American, ex. Mexican	38	3.2
Salvadoran	7	1.0
Mexican	53	1.1
Puerto Rican	112	14.9
South American	101	13.8

Means of Transportation to Work: Car, Truck or Van
(Universe: Workers 16 Years and Over)

Group	Number	%
Total Population	113,983	91.4
Hispanic or Latino (of any race)	7,201	91.7
Central American, ex. Mexican	1,134	99.4
Salvadoran	603	98.9
Mexican	4,255	89.3
Puerto Rican	641	90.2
South American	707	98.6

Means of Transportation to Work: Public Transportation (ex. Taxicab)
(Universe: Workers 16 Years and Over)

Group	Number	%
Total Population	2,507	2.0
Hispanic or Latino (of any race)	256	3.3
Central American, ex. Mexican	0	0.0
Salvadoran	0	0.0
Mexican	226	4.7
Puerto Rican	30	4.2
South American	0	0.0

Homeownership Rate
(Universe: Occupied Housing Units)

Group		%
Total Population		52.5
Hispanic or Latino (of any race)		34.4
Central American, ex. Mexican		36.7
Costa Rican		56.1
Guatemalan		32.6
Honduran		30.7
Nicaraguan		35.3
Panamanian		35.1
Salvadoran		38.9
Cuban		51.0
Dominican Republic		40.2
Mexican		30.7
Puerto Rican		30.8
South American		50.5
Chilean		55.3
Colombian		50.3
Ecuadorian		50.0
Peruvian		48.9
Venezuelan		51.4
Spaniard		56.1

Median Home Value

Group		Dollars
Total Population		146,500
Hispanic or Latino (of any race)		120,700
Central American, ex. Mexican		93,200
Salvadoran		97,900
Mexican		110,000
Puerto Rican		125,000
South American		204,400

Median Gross Rent

Group		Dollars
Total Population		717
Hispanic or Latino (of any race)		710
Central American, ex. Mexican		684
Salvadoran		665
Mexican		697
Puerto Rican		765
South American		784

Median Household Income
(2010 Inflation-Adjusted Dollars)

Group		Dollars
Total Population		41,530
Hispanic or Latino (of any race)		33,388
Central American, ex. Mexican		32,813
Salvadoran		30,272
Mexican		31,261
Puerto Rican		43,221
South American		59,500

Per Capita Income
(2010 Inflation-Adjusted Dollars)

Group		Dollars
Total Population		25,707
Hispanic or Latino (of any race)		13,329
Central American, ex. Mexican		13,066
Salvadoran		12,458
Mexican		10,637
Puerto Rican		20,068
South American		21,438

Households with $100,000+ Income

Group	Number	%
Total Population	16,099	14.9
Hispanic or Latino (of any race)	355	6.8
Central American, ex. Mexican	0	0.0
Salvadoran	0	0.0
Mexican	105	3.3
Puerto Rican	82	17.8
South American	62	14.2

Households with Food Stamps/SNAP Benefits During Past 12 Months

Group	Number	%
Total Population	11,508	10.7
Hispanic or Latino (of any race)	600	11.5
Central American, ex. Mexican	112	16.0
Salvadoran	34	11.7
Mexican	329	10.4
Puerto Rican	82	17.8

Notes: (1) Percent of total population; (2) Percent of Hispanic/Latino population; Profiles include places with an overall population of at least 125,000, OR an overall population of at least 25,000 where the Hispanic/Latino population is at least 20% of the overall population. In states where less than five places meet either of these criteria, we have included places with at least 10,000 total population with the highest percentage of Hispanic/Latino population. These places are identified with an asterisk (*); Please refer to the User's Guide for a full explanation of data.

Group		
South American	0	0.0

Poverty Rate
(Income in Past 12 Months Below Poverty Level)

Group	%
Total Population	18.1
Hispanic or Latino (of any race)	27.9
Central American, ex. Mexican	44.6
Salvadoran	35.1
Mexican	28.9
Puerto Rican	18.1
South American	8.3

Monroe

Population

Group	Number	%TP[1]	%HP[2]
Total Population	32,797	100.0	–
Hispanic or Latino (of any race)	9,651	29.4	100.0
Central American, ex. Mexican	778	2.4	8.1
Guatemalan	342	1.0	3.5
Honduran	156	0.5	1.6
Salvadoran	212	0.6	2.2
Dominican Republic	112	0.3	1.2
Mexican	7,773	23.7	80.5
Puerto Rican	359	1.1	3.7
South American	244	0.7	2.5
Colombian	114	0.3	1.2

Population Growth: 2000–2010

Group	%
Total Population	25.0
Hispanic or Latino (of any race)	72.0
Central American, ex. Mexican	342.0
Mexican	64.0
Puerto Rican	194.3

Males per 100 Females

Group	Number
Total Population	96.8
Hispanic or Latino (of any race)	124.0
Central American, ex. Mexican	139.4
Guatemalan	173.6
Honduran	136.4
Salvadoran	109.9
Dominican Republic	93.1
Mexican	126.2
Puerto Rican	92.0
South American	92.1
Colombian	78.1

Average Household Size

Group	People
Total Population	2.92
Hispanic or Latino (of any race)	4.66
Central American, ex. Mexican	4.53
Guatemalan	4.88
Honduran	4.24
Salvadoran	4.55
Dominican Republic	3.68
Mexican	4.91
Puerto Rican	2.93
South American	3.60
Colombian	3.69

Median Age

Group	Years
Total Population	32.5
Hispanic or Latino (of any race)	23.6
Central American, ex. Mexican	26.6
Guatemalan	25.5
Honduran	29.0
Salvadoran	26.3
Dominican Republic	26.5
Mexican	22.9
Puerto Rican	25.5
South American	36.4
Colombian	33.3

High School Graduates
(Universe: Population 25 Years and Over)

Group	Number	%
Total Population	14,980	75.7
Hispanic or Latino (of any race)	1,810	42.1
Mexican	1,262	36.8

Four-Year College Graduates
(Universe: Population 25 Years and Over)

Group	Number	%
Total Population	3,162	16.0
Hispanic or Latino (of any race)	452	10.5
Mexican	264	7.7

Population Age 3–17 Enrolled in Public School
(Universe: Population Age 3–17 Enrolled in School)

Group	Number	%
Total Population	5,897	93.5
Hispanic or Latino (of any race)	1,794	97.5
Mexican	1,496	99.1

Population Age 3–17 Enrolled in Private School
(Universe: Population Age 3–17 Enrolled in School)

Group	Number	%
Total Population	410	6.5
Hispanic or Latino (of any race)	46	2.5
Mexican	14	0.9

Foreign-Born Population

Group	Number	%
Total Population	5,787	17.9
Hispanic or Latino (of any race)	5,460	62.2
Mexican	4,705	66.1

Foreign-Born Naturalized U.S. Citizens

Group	Number	%
Total Population	434	7.5
Hispanic or Latino (of any race)	292	5.3
Mexican	109	2.3

Language Spoken at Home: English Only
(Universe: Population 5 Years and Over)

Group	Number	%
Total Population	21,519	73.4
Hispanic or Latino (of any race)	244	3.3
Mexican	137	2.3

Language Spoken at Home: Spanish
(Universe: Population 5 Years and Over)

Group	Number	%
Total Population	7,327	25.0
Hispanic or Latino (of any race)	7,100	96.1
Mexican	5,834	97.0

Unemployment Rate
(Universe: Population 16 Years and Over)

Group	%
Total Population	9.6
Hispanic or Latino (of any race)	7.9
Mexican	8.2

Class of Worker: Private Wage and Salary
(Universe: Civilian Employed Population 16 Years and Over)

Group	Number	%
Total Population	12,606	85.5
Hispanic or Latino (of any race)	3,766	93.9
Mexican	3,217	98.8

Class of Worker: Government
(Universe: Civilian Employed Population 16 Years and Over)

Group	Number	%
Total Population	1,538	10.4
Hispanic or Latino (of any race)	203	5.1
Mexican	16	0.5

Means of Transportation to Work: Car, Truck or Van
(Universe: Workers 16 Years and Over)

Group	Number	%
Total Population	13,532	94.2
Hispanic or Latino (of any race)	3,663	94.5
Mexican	2,970	94.1

Means of Transportation to Work: Public Transportation (ex. Taxicab)
(Universe: Workers 16 Years and Over)

Group	Number	%
Total Population	149	1.0
Hispanic or Latino (of any race)	83	2.1
Mexican	83	2.6

Homeownership Rate
(Universe: Occupied Housing Units)

Group	%
Total Population	56.5
Hispanic or Latino (of any race)	34.4
Central American, ex. Mexican	40.8
Guatemalan	24.3
Honduran	35.7
Salvadoran	60.3
Dominican Republic	57.1
Mexican	30.5
Puerto Rican	45.0
South American	69.2
Colombian	77.1

Median Home Value

Group	Dollars
Total Population	149,900
Hispanic or Latino (of any race)	115,200
Mexican	105,900

Median Gross Rent

Group	Dollars
Total Population	744
Hispanic or Latino (of any race)	767
Mexican	809

Median Household Income
(2010 Inflation-Adjusted Dollars)

Group	Dollars
Total Population	43,457
Hispanic or Latino (of any race)	35,293
Mexican	33,431

Per Capita Income
(2010 Inflation-Adjusted Dollars)

Group	Dollars
Total Population	18,994
Hispanic or Latino (of any race)	10,096
Mexican	9,237

Households with $100,000+ Income

Group	Number	%
Total Population	1,263	11.1
Hispanic or Latino (of any race)	77	3.6
Mexican	77	4.5

Households with Food Stamps/SNAP Benefits During Past 12 Months

Group	Number	%
Total Population	1,846	16.2
Hispanic or Latino (of any race)	420	19.8
Mexican	386	22.5

Poverty Rate
(Income in Past 12 Months Below Poverty Level)

Group	%
Total Population	19.7
Hispanic or Latino (of any race)	23.4
Mexican	25.6

Raleigh

Population

Group	Number	%TP[1]	%HP[2]
Total Population	403,892	100.0	–
Hispanic or Latino (of any race)	45,868	11.4	100.0
Central American, ex. Mexican	7,519	1.9	16.4
Costa Rican	164	<0.1	0.4
Guatemalan	978	0.2	2.1
Honduran	2,345	0.6	5.1
Nicaraguan	184	<0.1	0.4
Panamanian	313	0.1	0.7
Salvadoran	3,476	0.9	7.6
Cuban	1,082	0.3	2.4
Dominican Republic	2,378	0.6	5.2
Mexican	23,867	5.9	52.0
Puerto Rican	4,340	1.1	9.5
South American	3,574	0.9	7.8
Argentinean	313	0.1	0.7
Chilean	196	<0.1	0.4
Colombian	1,261	0.3	2.7
Ecuadorian	352	0.1	0.8
Peruvian	729	0.2	1.6

Notes: (1) Percent of total population; (2) Percent of Hispanic/Latino population; Profiles include places with an overall population of at least 125,000, OR an overall population of at least 25,000 where the Hispanic/Latino population is at least 20% of the overall population. In states where less than five places meet either of these criteria, we have included places with at least 10,000 total population with the highest percentage of Hispanic/Latino population. These places are identified with an asterisk (*); Please refer to the User's Guide for a full explanation of data.

Uruguayan	146	<0.1	0.3
Venezuelan	457	0.1	1.0
Spaniard	433	0.1	0.9

Population Growth: 2000–2010

Group	%
Total Population	46.3
Hispanic or Latino (of any race)	137.6
Central American, ex. Mexican	290.4
Guatemalan	246.8
Honduran	392.6
Panamanian	174.6
Salvadoran	315.3
Cuban	171.2
Dominican Republic	647.8
Mexican	95.2
Puerto Rican	232.3
South American	304.8
Colombian	291.6
Peruvian	305.0
Venezuelan	311.7

Males per 100 Females

Group	Number
Total Population	93.5
Hispanic or Latino (of any race)	111.8
Central American, ex. Mexican	118.6
Costa Rican	78.3
Guatemalan	140.9
Honduran	125.7
Nicaraguan	78.6
Panamanian	71.0
Salvadoran	119.3
Cuban	101.5
Dominican Republic	75.5
Mexican	125.9
Puerto Rican	88.4
South American	89.9
Argentinean	90.9
Chilean	98.0
Colombian	83.6
Ecuadorian	87.2
Peruvian	85.5
Uruguayan	139.3
Venezuelan	96.1
Spaniard	74.6

Average Household Size

Group	People
Total Population	2.36
Hispanic or Latino (of any race)	3.61
Central American, ex. Mexican	3.84
Costa Rican	2.65
Guatemalan	3.88
Honduran	3.86
Nicaraguan	2.94
Panamanian	2.59
Salvadoran	4.14
Cuban	2.53
Dominican Republic	3.29
Mexican	4.13
Puerto Rican	2.72
South American	2.80
Argentinean	2.71
Chilean	2.88
Colombian	2.69
Ecuadorian	2.71
Peruvian	3.02
Uruguayan	3.20
Venezuelan	2.69
Spaniard	2.28

Median Age

Group	Years
Total Population	31.9
Hispanic or Latino (of any race)	25.5
Central American, ex. Mexican	27.3
Costa Rican	32.0
Guatemalan	26.3
Honduran	27.9
Nicaraguan	28.8
Panamanian	27.2
Salvadoran	27.0
Cuban	29.8
Dominican Republic	27.0
Mexican	24.4
Puerto Rican	24.7
South American	32.1
Argentinean	32.1
Chilean	33.8
Colombian	31.9
Ecuadorian	29.5
Peruvian	34.8
Uruguayan	31.5
Venezuelan	31.5
Spaniard	29.5

High School Graduates
(Universe: Population 25 Years and Over)

Group	Number	%
Total Population	217,952	90.4
Hispanic or Latino (of any race)	12,296	57.4
Central American, ex. Mexican	1,838	51.3
Honduran	595	53.1
Salvadoran	714	39.5
Dominican Republic	532	74.3
Mexican	5,714	47.1
Puerto Rican	1,555	84.4
South American	1,270	88.9
Colombian	457	98.1

Four-Year College Graduates
(Universe: Population 25 Years and Over)

Group	Number	%
Total Population	112,405	46.6
Hispanic or Latino (of any race)	3,211	15.0
Central American, ex. Mexican	616	17.2
Honduran	241	21.5
Salvadoran	148	8.2
Dominican Republic	176	24.6
Mexican	1,078	8.9
Puerto Rican	485	26.3
South American	494	34.6
Colombian	176	37.8

Population Age 3–17 Enrolled in Public School
(Universe: Population Age 3–17 Enrolled in School)

Group	Number	%
Total Population	53,286	83.4
Hispanic or Latino (of any race)	7,492	93.1
Central American, ex. Mexican	1,149	91.9
Honduran	100	100.0
Salvadoran	756	95.7
Dominican Republic	288	100.0
Mexican	4,007	95.8
Puerto Rican	990	92.9
South American	454	82.2
Colombian	118	73.3

Population Age 3–17 Enrolled in Private School
(Universe: Population Age 3–17 Enrolled in School)

Group	Number	%
Total Population	10,588	16.6
Hispanic or Latino (of any race)	556	6.9
Central American, ex. Mexican	101	8.1
Honduran	0	0.0
Salvadoran	34	4.3
Dominican Republic	0	0.0
Mexican	174	4.2
Puerto Rican	76	7.1
South American	98	17.8
Colombian	43	26.7

Foreign-Born Population

Group	Number	%
Total Population	55,518	14.5
Hispanic or Latino (of any race)	24,442	59.5
Central American, ex. Mexican	4,136	66.0
Honduran	1,225	75.0
Salvadoran	2,039	62.9
Dominican Republic	670	51.9
Mexican	16,209	66.7
Puerto Rican	61	1.7
South American	1,466	62.9
Colombian	459	61.9

Foreign-Born Naturalized U.S. Citizens

Group	Number	%
Total Population	15,600	28.1
Hispanic or Latino (of any race)	2,303	9.4
Central American, ex. Mexican	912	22.1
Honduran	47	3.8
Salvadoran	431	21.1
Dominican Republic	86	12.8
Mexican	431	2.7
Puerto Rican	12	19.7
South American	370	25.2
Colombian	200	43.6

Language Spoken at Home: English Only
(Universe: Population 5 Years and Over)

Group	Number	%
Total Population	291,817	82.3
Hispanic or Latino (of any race)	4,474	12.7
Central American, ex. Mexican	555	10.0
Honduran	82	5.5
Salvadoran	139	4.8
Dominican Republic	203	16.3
Mexican	1,153	5.7
Puerto Rican	1,226	38.3
South American	494	23.3
Colombian	126	18.9

Language Spoken at Home: Spanish
(Universe: Population 5 Years and Over)

Group	Number	%
Total Population	34,842	9.8
Hispanic or Latino (of any race)	30,753	87.1
Central American, ex. Mexican	4,987	90.0
Honduran	1,404	94.5
Salvadoran	2,751	95.2
Dominican Republic	1,043	83.7
Mexican	19,094	94.2
Puerto Rican	1,979	61.7
South American	1,624	76.7
Colombian	542	81.1

Unemployment Rate
(Universe: Population 16 Years and Over)

Group	%
Total Population	7.1
Hispanic or Latino (of any race)	8.9
Central American, ex. Mexican	11.0
Honduran	15.9
Salvadoran	7.4
Dominican Republic	27.9
Mexican	6.7
Puerto Rican	9.7
South American	11.0
Colombian	13.5

Class of Worker: Private Wage and Salary
(Universe: Civilian Employed Population 16 Years and Over)

Group	Number	%
Total Population	160,305	79.8
Hispanic or Latino (of any race)	17,788	92.3
Central American, ex. Mexican	2,832	91.2
Honduran	889	93.7
Salvadoran	1,434	91.7
Dominican Republic	424	92.4
Mexican	10,969	96.2
Puerto Rican	1,341	83.3
South American	836	79.1
Colombian	284	86.9

Class of Worker: Government
(Universe: Civilian Employed Population 16 Years and Over)

Group	Number	%
Total Population	31,750	15.8
Hispanic or Latino (of any race)	896	4.6
Central American, ex. Mexican	215	6.9
Honduran	60	6.3
Salvadoran	100	6.4
Dominican Republic	23	5.0
Mexican	135	1.2
Puerto Rican	223	13.9
South American	139	13.2
Colombian	31	9.5

Means of Transportation to Work: Car, Truck or Van
(Universe: Workers 16 Years and Over)

Group	Number	%
Total Population	176,377	89.4
Hispanic or Latino (of any race)	17,289	90.3

Notes: (1) Percent of total population; (2) Percent of Hispanic/Latino population; Profiles include places with an overall population of at least 125,000, OR an overall population of at least 25,000 where the Hispanic/Latino population is at least 20% of the overall population. In states where less than five places meet either of these criteria, we have included places with at least 10,000 total population with the highest percentage of Hispanic/Latino population. These places are identified with an asterisk (*); Please refer to the User's Guide for a full explanation of data.

Central American, ex. Mexican	2,757	89.3
Honduran	850	89.6
Salvadoran	1,366	88.4
Dominican Republic	413	90.0
Mexican	10,515	93.1
Puerto Rican	1,359	84.9
South American	878	82.6
Colombian	274	76.3

Means of Transportation to Work: Public Transportation (ex. Taxicab)
(Universe: Workers 16 Years and Over)

Group	Number	%
Total Population	3,661	1.9
Hispanic or Latino (of any race)	471	2.5
Central American, ex. Mexican	99	3.2
Honduran	31	3.3
Salvadoran	68	4.4
Dominican Republic	15	3.3
Mexican	183	1.6
Puerto Rican	94	5.9
South American	0	0.0
Colombian	0	0.0

Homeownership Rate
(Universe: Occupied Housing Units)

Group	%
Total Population	53.5
Hispanic or Latino (of any race)	30.3
Central American, ex. Mexican	31.3
Costa Rican	40.3
Guatemalan	27.4
Honduran	18.7
Nicaraguan	40.0
Panamanian	36.2
Salvadoran	39.5
Cuban	46.0
Dominican Republic	33.9
Mexican	21.4
Puerto Rican	37.0
South American	50.8
Argentinean	66.7
Chilean	53.1
Colombian	52.4
Ecuadorian	46.1
Peruvian	49.2
Uruguayan	24.5
Venezuelan	45.3
Spaniard	55.7

Median Home Value

Group	Dollars
Total Population	203,300
Hispanic or Latino (of any race)	155,100
Central American, ex. Mexican	161,300
Honduran	139,400
Salvadoran	161,400
Dominican Republic	131,500
Mexican	129,300
Puerto Rican	161,800
South American	169,800
Colombian	179,900

Median Gross Rent

Group	Dollars
Total Population	828
Hispanic or Latino (of any race)	804
Central American, ex. Mexican	853
Honduran	864
Salvadoran	828
Dominican Republic	895
Mexican	759
Puerto Rican	876
South American	970
Colombian	1,142

Median Household Income
(2010 Inflation-Adjusted Dollars)

Group	Dollars
Total Population	52,219
Hispanic or Latino (of any race)	32,980
Central American, ex. Mexican	35,897
Honduran	35,156
Salvadoran	35,543
Dominican Republic	21,111
Mexican	31,776
Puerto Rican	38,393
South American	56,685
Colombian	31,125

Per Capita Income
(2010 Inflation-Adjusted Dollars)

Group	Dollars
Total Population	30,079
Hispanic or Latino (of any race)	12,870
Central American, ex. Mexican	14,012
Honduran	15,548
Salvadoran	11,810
Dominican Republic	11,994
Mexican	11,078
Puerto Rican	16,844
South American	18,296
Colombian	18,939

Households with $100,000+ Income

Group	Number	%
Total Population	33,823	21.9
Hispanic or Latino (of any race)	778	6.9
Central American, ex. Mexican	144	7.5
Honduran	71	13.1
Salvadoran	0	0.0
Dominican Republic	0	0.0
Mexican	258	4.2
Puerto Rican	157	14.3
South American	96	14.3
Colombian	39	24.8

Households with Food Stamps/SNAP Benefits During Past 12 Months

Group	Number	%
Total Population	10,114	6.5
Hispanic or Latino (of any race)	1,007	9.0
Central American, ex. Mexican	153	8.0
Honduran	36	6.6
Salvadoran	35	4.0
Dominican Republic	59	16.6
Mexican	506	8.3
Puerto Rican	178	16.2
South American	17	2.5
Colombian	0	0.0

Poverty Rate
(Income in Past 12 Months Below Poverty Level)

Group	%
Total Population	14.6
Hispanic or Latino (of any race)	30.6
Central American, ex. Mexican	28.3
Honduran	32.7
Salvadoran	33.1
Dominican Republic	32.0
Mexican	33.7
Puerto Rican	20.7
South American	21.9
Colombian	24.2

Sanford

Population

Group	Number	%TP[1]	%HP[2]
Total Population	28,094	100.0	–
Hispanic or Latino (of any race)	7,190	25.6	100.0
Central American, ex. Mexican	1,749	6.2	24.3
Guatemalan	429	1.5	6.0
Honduran	351	1.2	4.9
Salvadoran	880	3.1	12.2
Mexican	4,409	15.7	61.3
Puerto Rican	379	1.3	5.3
South American	161	0.6	2.2

Population Growth: 2000–2010

Group	%
Total Population	21.0
Hispanic or Latino (of any race)	62.7
Central American, ex. Mexican	146.7
Guatemalan	171.5
Honduran	143.8
Salvadoran	167.5
Mexican	48.7
Puerto Rican	117.8

Males per 100 Females

Group	Number
Total Population	94.2
Hispanic or Latino (of any race)	113.1
Central American, ex. Mexican	118.6
Guatemalan	137.0
Honduran	114.0
Salvadoran	118.9
Mexican	117.8
Puerto Rican	78.8
South American	87.2

Average Household Size

Group	People
Total Population	2.60
Hispanic or Latino (of any race)	3.99
Central American, ex. Mexican	4.02
Guatemalan	4.33
Honduran	3.91
Salvadoran	4.01
Mexican	4.20
Puerto Rican	3.07
South American	3.02

Median Age

Group	Years
Total Population	33.3
Hispanic or Latino (of any race)	24.2
Central American, ex. Mexican	28.7
Guatemalan	27.6
Honduran	27.7
Salvadoran	29.2
Mexican	22.1
Puerto Rican	25.6
South American	35.5

High School Graduates
(Universe: Population 25 Years and Over)

Group	Number	%
Total Population	12,608	75.8
Hispanic or Latino (of any race)	1,094	34.4
Central American, ex. Mexican	384	42.4
Mexican	459	23.8

Four-Year College Graduates
(Universe: Population 25 Years and Over)

Group	Number	%
Total Population	3,418	20.5
Hispanic or Latino (of any race)	124	3.9
Central American, ex. Mexican	0	0.0
Mexican	48	2.5

Population Age 3–17 Enrolled in Public School
(Universe: Population Age 3–17 Enrolled in School)

Group	Number	%
Total Population	5,184	92.4
Hispanic or Latino (of any race)	1,893	100.0
Central American, ex. Mexican	461	100.0
Mexican	1,182	100.0

Population Age 3–17 Enrolled in Private School
(Universe: Population Age 3–17 Enrolled in School)

Group	Number	%
Total Population	429	7.6
Hispanic or Latino (of any race)	0	0.0
Central American, ex. Mexican	0	0.0
Mexican	0	0.0

Foreign-Born Population

Group	Number	%
Total Population	4,655	17.3
Hispanic or Latino (of any race)	4,190	61.4
Central American, ex. Mexican	1,234	67.0
Mexican	2,800	67.7

Foreign-Born Naturalized U.S. Citizens

Group	Number	%
Total Population	501	10.8
Hispanic or Latino (of any race)	298	7.1
Central American, ex. Mexican	104	8.4
Mexican	194	6.9

Notes: (1) Percent of total population; (2) Percent of Hispanic/Latino population; Profiles include places with an overall population of at least 125,000, OR an overall population of at least 25,000 where the Hispanic/Latino population is at least 20% of the overall population. In states where less than five places meet either of these criteria, we have included places with at least 10,000 total population with the highest percentage of Hispanic/Latino population. These places are identified with an asterisk (*); Please refer to the User's Guide for a full explanation of data.

Language Spoken at Home: English Only (Universe: Population 5 Years and Over)		
Group	Number	%
Total Population	18,282	73.7
Hispanic or Latino (of any race)	371	6.2
Central American, ex. Mexican	187	11.2
Mexican	130	3.6

Language Spoken at Home: Spanish (Universe: Population 5 Years and Over)		
Group	Number	%
Total Population	5,978	24.1
Hispanic or Latino (of any race)	5,658	93.8
Central American, ex. Mexican	1,489	88.8
Mexican	3,491	96.4

Unemployment Rate (Universe: Population 16 Years and Over)	
Group	%
Total Population	10.9
Hispanic or Latino (of any race)	11.5
Central American, ex. Mexican	2.5
Mexican	12.3

Class of Worker: Private Wage and Salary (Universe: Civilian Employed Population 16 Years and Over)		
Group	Number	%
Total Population	9,962	84.3
Hispanic or Latino (of any race)	2,884	94.8
Central American, ex. Mexican	1,012	94.1
Mexican	1,653	100.0

Class of Worker: Government (Universe: Civilian Employed Population 16 Years and Over)		
Group	Number	%
Total Population	1,466	12.4
Hispanic or Latino (of any race)	91	3.0
Central American, ex. Mexican	63	5.9
Mexican	0	0.0

Means of Transportation to Work: Car, Truck or Van (Universe: Workers 16 Years and Over)		
Group	Number	%
Total Population	11,026	94.1
Hispanic or Latino (of any race)	2,785	91.7
Central American, ex. Mexican	1,040	96.7
Mexican	1,533	91.6

Means of Transportation to Work: Public Transportation (ex. Taxicab) (Universe: Workers 16 Years and Over)		
Group	Number	%
Total Population	0	0.0
Hispanic or Latino (of any race)	0	0.0
Central American, ex. Mexican	0	0.0
Mexican	0	0.0

Homeownership Rate (Universe: Occupied Housing Units)	
Group	%
Total Population	52.6
Hispanic or Latino (of any race)	42.2
Central American, ex. Mexican	47.5
Guatemalan	36.7
Honduran	38.9
Salvadoran	56.1
Mexican	40.1
Puerto Rican	33.9
South American	40.8

Median Home Value	
Group	Dollars
Total Population	131,800
Hispanic or Latino (of any race)	93,300
Central American, ex. Mexican	111,600
Mexican	77,900

Median Gross Rent	
Group	Dollars
Total Population	627
Hispanic or Latino (of any race)	613
Central American, ex. Mexican	602
Mexican	620

Median Household Income (2010 Inflation-Adjusted Dollars)	
Group	Dollars
Total Population	39,231
Hispanic or Latino (of any race)	33,049
Central American, ex. Mexican	46,364
Mexican	30,429

Per Capita Income (2010 Inflation-Adjusted Dollars)	
Group	Dollars
Total Population	19,870
Hispanic or Latino (of any race)	11,039
Central American, ex. Mexican	15,752
Mexican	8,498

Households with $100,000+ Income		
Group	Number	%
Total Population	1,343	13.5
Hispanic or Latino (of any race)	136	8.3
Central American, ex. Mexican	119	26.2
Mexican	0	0.0

Households with Food Stamps/SNAP Benefits During Past 12 Months		
Group	Number	%
Total Population	1,436	14.5
Hispanic or Latino (of any race)	222	13.5
Central American, ex. Mexican	12	2.6
Mexican	123	13.4

Poverty Rate (Income in Past 12 Months Below Poverty Level)	
Group	%
Total Population	21.3
Hispanic or Latino (of any race)	25.9
Central American, ex. Mexican	12.7
Mexican	33.6

Winston-Salem

Population			
Group	Number	%TP[1]	%HP[2]
Total Population	229,617	100.0	–
Hispanic or Latino (of any race)	33,753	14.7	100.0
Central American, ex. Mexican	3,757	1.6	11.1
Guatemalan	882	0.4	2.6
Honduran	497	0.2	1.5
Nicaraguan	199	0.1	0.6
Panamanian	115	0.1	0.3
Salvadoran	1,954	0.9	5.8
Cuban	503	0.2	1.5
Dominican Republic	472	0.2	1.4
Mexican	23,427	10.2	69.4
Puerto Rican	1,965	0.9	5.8
South American	1,344	0.6	4.0
Argentinean	121	0.1	0.4
Colombian	463	0.2	1.4
Ecuadorian	243	0.1	0.7
Peruvian	236	0.1	0.7
Venezuelan	137	0.1	0.4
Spaniard	207	0.1	0.6

Population Growth: 2000–2010	
Group	%
Total Population	23.6
Hispanic or Latino (of any race)	110.4
Central American, ex. Mexican	241.2
Guatemalan	151.3
Honduran	387.3
Salvadoran	270.8
Cuban	113.1
Dominican Republic	349.5
Mexican	96.7
Puerto Rican	210.9
South American	269.2
Colombian	295.7

Males per 100 Females	
Group	Number
Total Population	88.6
Hispanic or Latino (of any race)	108.5
Central American, ex. Mexican	109.7
Guatemalan	128.5
Honduran	102.9
Nicaraguan	103.1
Panamanian	76.9
Salvadoran	107.4
Cuban	101.2
Dominican Republic	82.2
Mexican	113.2
Puerto Rican	87.9
South American	79.9
Argentinean	98.4
Colombian	72.8
Ecuadorian	86.9
Peruvian	84.4
Venezuelan	63.1
Spaniard	91.7

Average Household Size	
Group	People
Total Population	2.38
Hispanic or Latino (of any race)	3.97
Central American, ex. Mexican	3.90
Guatemalan	4.08
Honduran	3.72
Nicaraguan	3.46
Panamanian	2.55
Salvadoran	4.09
Cuban	2.52
Dominican Republic	3.31
Mexican	4.31
Puerto Rican	2.94
South American	2.90
Argentinean	2.54
Colombian	2.77
Ecuadorian	3.49
Peruvian	3.35
Venezuelan	2.57
Spaniard	2.60

Median Age	
Group	Years
Total Population	34.6
Hispanic or Latino (of any race)	23.1
Central American, ex. Mexican	27.5
Guatemalan	27.1
Honduran	27.7
Nicaraguan	29.8
Panamanian	29.9
Salvadoran	27.0
Cuban	31.9
Dominican Republic	26.8
Mexican	21.6
Puerto Rican	23.9
South American	32.9
Argentinean	35.5
Colombian	34.4
Ecuadorian	29.4
Peruvian	32.0
Venezuelan	32.2
Spaniard	35.4

High School Graduates (Universe: Population 25 Years and Over)		
Group	Number	%
Total Population	121,972	85.5
Hispanic or Latino (of any race)	7,340	51.4
Central American, ex. Mexican	1,207	50.0
Guatemalan	390	58.6
Salvadoran	446	39.3
Mexican	3,626	41.0
Puerto Rican	733	66.9
South American	1,129	96.6

Four-Year College Graduates (Universe: Population 25 Years and Over)		
Group	Number	%
Total Population	45,363	31.8
Hispanic or Latino (of any race)	1,380	9.7
Central American, ex. Mexican	252	10.4
Guatemalan	130	19.5
Salvadoran	0	0.0
Mexican	347	3.9
Puerto Rican	85	7.8
South American	456	39.0

Notes: (1) Percent of total population; (2) Percent of Hispanic/Latino population; Profiles include places with an overall population of at least 125,000, OR an overall population of at least 25,000 where the Hispanic/Latino population is at least 20% of the overall population. In states where less than five places meet either of these criteria, we have included places with at least 10,000 total population with the highest percentage of Hispanic/Latino population. These places are identified with an asterisk (*); Please refer to the User's Guide for a full explanation of data.

Population Age 3–17 Enrolled in Public School
(Universe: Population Age 3–17 Enrolled in School)

Group	Number	%
Total Population	35,303	88.2
Hispanic or Latino (of any race)	7,386	97.3
Central American, ex. Mexican	958	97.2
Guatemalan	391	93.3
Salvadoran	467	100.0
Mexican	5,145	98.8
Puerto Rican	554	89.2
South American	384	98.0

Population Age 3–17 Enrolled in Private School
(Universe: Population Age 3–17 Enrolled in School)

Group	Number	%
Total Population	4,703	11.8
Hispanic or Latino (of any race)	202	2.7
Central American, ex. Mexican	28	2.8
Guatemalan	28	6.7
Salvadoran	0	0.0
Mexican	63	1.2
Puerto Rican	67	10.8
South American	8	2.0

Foreign-Born Population

Group	Number	%
Total Population	24,322	10.8
Hispanic or Latino (of any race)	16,983	56.1
Central American, ex. Mexican	3,045	63.8
Guatemalan	855	57.9
Salvadoran	1,373	63.0
Mexican	12,151	60.1
Puerto Rican	50	2.5
South American	1,131	64.0

Foreign-Born Naturalized U.S. Citizens

Group	Number	%
Total Population	5,303	21.8
Hispanic or Latino (of any race)	1,852	10.9
Central American, ex. Mexican	507	16.7
Guatemalan	96	11.2
Salvadoran	220	16.0
Mexican	383	3.2
Puerto Rican	50	100.0
South American	588	52.0

Language Spoken at Home: English Only
(Universe: Population 5 Years and Over)

Group	Number	%
Total Population	174,067	83.6
Hispanic or Latino (of any race)	2,483	9.7
Central American, ex. Mexican	182	4.6
Guatemalan	101	8.0
Salvadoran	50	2.8
Mexican	950	5.7
Puerto Rican	691	37.7
South American	274	16.0

Language Spoken at Home: Spanish
(Universe: Population 5 Years and Over)

Group	Number	%
Total Population	26,223	12.6
Hispanic or Latino (of any race)	23,098	90.2
Central American, ex. Mexican	3,780	95.1
Guatemalan	1,159	92.0
Salvadoran	1,750	97.2
Mexican	15,754	94.3
Puerto Rican	1,144	62.3
South American	1,438	84.0

Unemployment Rate
(Universe: Population 16 Years and Over)

Group	%
Total Population	8.5
Hispanic or Latino (of any race)	8.0
Central American, ex. Mexican	6.4
Guatemalan	0.0
Salvadoran	9.4
Mexican	8.2
Puerto Rican	9.4
South American	4.6

Class of Worker: Private Wage and Salary
(Universe: Civilian Employed Population 16 Years and Over)

Group	Number	%
Total Population	84,775	83.4
Hispanic or Latino (of any race)	12,266	93.5
Central American, ex. Mexican	2,162	95.6
Guatemalan	510	85.7
Salvadoran	1,143	100.0
Mexican	7,939	96.3
Puerto Rican	695	83.5
South American	884	81.1

Class of Worker: Government
(Universe: Civilian Employed Population 16 Years and Over)

Group	Number	%
Total Population	11,693	11.5
Hispanic or Latino (of any race)	535	4.1
Central American, ex. Mexican	30	1.3
Guatemalan	30	5.0
Salvadoran	0	0.0
Mexican	149	1.8
Puerto Rican	137	16.5
South American	137	12.6

Means of Transportation to Work: Car, Truck or Van
(Universe: Workers 16 Years and Over)

Group	Number	%
Total Population	90,408	91.2
Hispanic or Latino (of any race)	11,878	92.1
Central American, ex. Mexican	2,026	90.9
Guatemalan	488	86.7
Salvadoran	1,015	88.8
Mexican	7,498	92.5
Puerto Rican	692	83.2
South American	1,016	95.8

Means of Transportation to Work: Public Transportation (ex. Taxicab)
(Universe: Workers 16 Years and Over)

Group	Number	%
Total Population	1,864	1.9
Hispanic or Latino (of any race)	93	0.7
Central American, ex. Mexican	0	0.0
Guatemalan	0	0.0
Salvadoran	0	0.0
Mexican	93	1.1
Puerto Rican	0	0.0
South American	0	0.0

Homeownership Rate
(Universe: Occupied Housing Units)

Group	%
Total Population	56.3
Hispanic or Latino (of any race)	32.8
Central American, ex. Mexican	42.3
Guatemalan	37.6
Honduran	23.1
Nicaraguan	44.1
Panamanian	47.5
Salvadoran	48.3
Cuban	51.6
Dominican Republic	42.3
Mexican	26.7
Puerto Rican	39.8
South American	57.6
Argentinean	56.8
Colombian	57.3
Ecuadorian	63.5
Peruvian	60.6
Venezuelan	51.8
Spaniard	54.2

Median Home Value

Group	Dollars
Total Population	141,200
Hispanic or Latino (of any race)	125,100
Central American, ex. Mexican	106,600
Guatemalan	121,300
Salvadoran	106,600
Mexican	88,300
Puerto Rican	139,400
South American	153,900

Median Gross Rent

Group	Dollars
Total Population	662
Hispanic or Latino (of any race)	591
Central American, ex. Mexican	623
Guatemalan	716
Salvadoran	529
Mexican	576
Puerto Rican	742
South American	848

Median Household Income
(2010 Inflation-Adjusted Dollars)

Group	Dollars
Total Population	41,483
Hispanic or Latino (of any race)	29,859
Central American, ex. Mexican	44,228
Guatemalan	65,049
Salvadoran	21,731
Mexican	26,032
Puerto Rican	30,993
South American	60,833

Per Capita Income
(2010 Inflation-Adjusted Dollars)

Group	Dollars
Total Population	24,472
Hispanic or Latino (of any race)	10,420
Central American, ex. Mexican	11,047
Guatemalan	11,160
Salvadoran	10,620
Mexican	8,115
Puerto Rican	13,475
South American	22,703

Households with $100,000+ Income

Group	Number	%
Total Population	13,482	15.1
Hispanic or Latino (of any race)	251	3.5
Central American, ex. Mexican	19	1.8
Guatemalan	10	3.4
Salvadoran	0	0.0
Mexican	64	1.4
Puerto Rican	0	0.0
South American	61	11.2

Households with Food Stamps/SNAP Benefits During Past 12 Months

Group	Number	%
Total Population	9,503	10.6
Hispanic or Latino (of any race)	903	12.5
Central American, ex. Mexican	246	23.4
Guatemalan	98	33.8
Salvadoran	103	19.6
Mexican	467	10.6
Puerto Rican	113	15.7
South American	16	2.9

Poverty Rate
(Income in Past 12 Months Below Poverty Level)

Group	%
Total Population	19.3
Hispanic or Latino (of any race)	38.8
Central American, ex. Mexican	32.8
Guatemalan	14.7
Salvadoran	46.5
Mexican	46.8
Puerto Rican	19.3
South American	0.5

Notes: (1) Percent of total population; (2) Percent of Hispanic/Latino population; Profiles include places with an overall population of at least 125,000, OR an overall population of at least 25,000 where the Hispanic/Latino population is at least 20% of the overall population. In states where less than five places meet either of these criteria, we have included places with at least 10,000 total population with the highest percentage of Hispanic/Latino population. These places are identified with an asterisk (*); Please refer to the User's Guide for a full explanation of data.

North Dakota

EDITOR'S NOTE: For a place to be included in this edition, it must meet one of two criteria. Either its overall population is at least 125,000, OR its overall population is at least 25,000 and its Hispanic/Latino population is at least 20% of the overall population. In North Dakota, less than five places meet either of these criteria. In an effort to include at least five places for each state, we have included places with at least 10,000 total population with the highest percentage of Hispanic/Latino population. These places are identified with an asterisk (*). For the state of North Dakota, the following locations are included:

- Dickinson*
- Fargo*
- Grand Forks*
- Minot*
- Williston*

Section Two: State & Place Profiles starts with the state profile, followed by place profiles that meet the criteria above. Places are listed alphabetically within each state. All states, all counties and places that meet the above criteria are ranked and compared in *Section Three: Rankings & Comparisons*, on page 1055.

For a more detailed look at the Hispanic/Latino population in North Dakota, a companion web site is available at no additional charge with purchase of this print edition. Visit http://gold.greyhouse.com/page/info_hispanic for more information.

The web site includes data for all counties and places in North Dakota with Hispanic/Latino population, plus ten additional topics: Self Employed Worker; Walked to Work; Worked from Home; Mean Travel Time to Work; Mean Household Income; Households with Cash Public Assistance; Mean Cash Pubic Assistance; Poverty Rates for 18 and Under, 18 to 64, and 65 and Over.

Population

Group	Number	%TP[1]	%HP[2]
Total Population	672,591	100.0	–
Hispanic or Latino (of any race)	13,467	2.0	100.0
Central American, ex. Mexican	452	0.1	3.4
Guatemalan	134	<0.1	1.0
Panamanian	100	<0.1	0.7
Cuban	260	<0.1	1.9
Mexican	9,223	1.4	68.5
Puerto Rican	987	0.1	7.3
South American	539	0.1	4.0
Colombian	244	<0.1	1.8
Spaniard	381	0.1	2.8

Population Growth: 2000–2010

Group	%
Total Population	4.7
Hispanic or Latino (of any race)	73.0
Central American, ex. Mexican	137.9
Cuban	4.0
Mexican	114.7
Puerto Rican	94.7
South American	124.6
Colombian	117.9

Males per 100 Females

Group	Number
Total Population	102.1
Hispanic or Latino (of any race)	114.4
Central American, ex. Mexican	94.0
Guatemalan	116.1
Panamanian	63.9
Cuban	124.1
Mexican	119.3
Puerto Rican	116.9
South American	88.5
Colombian	93.7
Spaniard	98.4

Average Household Size

Group	People
Total Population	2.30
Hispanic or Latino (of any race)	2.82
Central American, ex. Mexican	2.55
Guatemalan	2.81
Panamanian	2.32
Cuban	2.32
Mexican	2.97
Puerto Rican	2.57
South American	2.49
Colombian	2.40
Spaniard	2.56

Median Age

Group	Years
Total Population	37.0
Hispanic or Latino (of any race)	21.9
Central American, ex. Mexican	22.3
Guatemalan	15.4
Panamanian	22.8
Cuban	25.0
Mexican	21.0
Puerto Rican	22.4
South American	25.7
Colombian	24.2
Spaniard	24.9

High School Graduates
(Universe: Population 25 Years and Over)

Group	Number	%
Total Population	383,914	89.4
Hispanic or Latino (of any race)	4,411	77.4
Mexican	3,000	74.7
Puerto Rican	315	100.0
South American	352	93.9

Four-Year College Graduates
(Universe: Population 25 Years and Over)

Group	Number	%
Total Population	112,977	26.3
Hispanic or Latino (of any race)	915	16.0
Mexican	432	10.8
Puerto Rican	93	29.5
South American	139	37.1

Population Age 3–17 Enrolled in Public School
(Universe: Population Age 3–17 Enrolled in School)

Group	Number	%
Total Population	95,224	89.8
Hispanic or Latino (of any race)	3,102	90.9
Mexican	2,396	94.2
Puerto Rican	268	72.2
South American	127	88.8

Population Age 3–17 Enrolled in Private School
(Universe: Population Age 3–17 Enrolled in School)

Group	Number	%
Total Population	10,789	10.2
Hispanic or Latino (of any race)	309	9.1
Mexican	148	5.8
Puerto Rican	103	27.8
South American	16	11.2

Foreign-Born Population

Group	Number	%
Total Population	15,807	2.4
Hispanic or Latino (of any race)	1,441	11.2
Mexican	801	8.6
Puerto Rican	0	0.0
South American	417	54.4

Foreign-Born Naturalized U.S. Citizens

Group	Number	%
Total Population	6,157	39.0
Hispanic or Latino (of any race)	632	43.9
Mexican	289	36.1
Puerto Rican	0	0.0
South American	224	53.7

Language Spoken at Home: English Only
(Universe: Population 5 Years and Over)

Group	Number	%
Total Population	584,946	94.6
Hispanic or Latino (of any race)	6,965	61.9
Mexican	4,893	60.4
Puerto Rican	634	71.5
South American	266	44.7

Language Spoken at Home: Spanish
(Universe: Population 5 Years and Over)

Group	Number	%
Total Population	8,183	1.3
Hispanic or Latino (of any race)	4,202	37.3
Mexican	3,147	38.8
Puerto Rican	253	28.5
South American	329	55.3

Unemployment Rate
(Universe: Population 16 Years and Over)

Group	%
Total Population	3.6
Hispanic or Latino (of any race)	7.6
Mexican	7.3
Puerto Rican	2.6
South American	15.8

Class of Worker: Private Wage and Salary
(Universe: Civilian Employed Population 16 Years and Over)

Group	Number	%
Total Population	258,494	73.4
Hispanic or Latino (of any race)	4,216	79.4
Mexican	3,069	80.3
Puerto Rican	226	67.5
South American	242	72.0

Class of Worker: Government
(Universe: Civilian Employed Population 16 Years and Over)

Group	Number	%
Total Population	60,231	17.1
Hispanic or Latino (of any race)	831	15.7
Mexican	621	16.3
Puerto Rican	66	19.7
South American	40	11.9

Means of Transportation to Work: Car, Truck or Van
(Universe: Workers 16 Years and Over)

Group	Number	%
Total Population	309,234	88.3
Hispanic or Latino (of any race)	5,110	90.4
Mexican	3,651	91.5
Puerto Rican	396	95.2
South American	271	83.1

Means of Transportation to Work: Public Transportation (ex. Taxicab)
(Universe: Workers 16 Years and Over)

Group	Number	%
Total Population	2,003	0.6
Hispanic or Latino (of any race)	60	1.1
Mexican	42	1.1
Puerto Rican	0	0.0
South American	0	0.0

Homeownership Rate
(Universe: Occupied Housing Units)

Group	%
Total Population	65.4
Hispanic or Latino (of any race)	35.4
Central American, ex. Mexican	29.8
Guatemalan	33.3
Panamanian	36.0
Cuban	40.5
Mexican	34.0
Puerto Rican	31.6
South American	36.3
Colombian	28.4
Spaniard	46.7

Notes: (1) Percent of total population; (2) Percent of Hispanic/Latino population; Profiles include places with an overall population of at least 125,000, OR an overall population of at least 25,000 where the Hispanic/Latino population is at least 20% of the overall population. In states where less than five places meet either of these criteria, we have included places with at least 10,000 total population with the highest percentage of Hispanic/Latino population. These places are identified with an asterisk (*); Please refer to the User's Guide for a full explanation of data.

Median Home Value

Group	Dollars
Total Population	111,300
Hispanic or Latino (of any race)	84,900
Mexican	92,300
Puerto Rican	69,200
South American	88,400

Median Gross Rent

Group	Dollars
Total Population	555
Hispanic or Latino (of any race)	543
Mexican	526
Puerto Rican	579
South American	470

Median Household Income
(2010 Inflation-Adjusted Dollars)

Group	Dollars
Total Population	46,781
Hispanic or Latino (of any race)	38,156
Mexican	38,148
Puerto Rican	33,472
South American	38,316

Per Capita Income
(2010 Inflation-Adjusted Dollars)

Group	Dollars
Total Population	25,803
Hispanic or Latino (of any race)	14,216
Mexican	13,418
Puerto Rican	12,426
South American	13,116

Households with $100,000+ Income

Group	Number	%
Total Population	40,309	14.6
Hispanic or Latino (of any race)	341	9.5
Mexican	265	10.7
Puerto Rican	0	0.0
South American	18	8.3

Households with Food Stamps/SNAP Benefits During Past 12 Months

Group	Number	%
Total Population	19,803	7.2
Hispanic or Latino (of any race)	739	20.7
Mexican	580	23.4
Puerto Rican	23	10.9
South American	72	33.3

Poverty Rate
(Income in Past 12 Months Below Poverty Level)

Group	%
Total Population	12.3
Hispanic or Latino (of any race)	22.0
Mexican	24.5
Puerto Rican	16.4
South American	8.4

Dickinson*

Population

Group	Number	%TP[1]	%HP[2]
Total Population	17,787	100.0	–
Hispanic or Latino (of any race)	382	2.1	100.0
Mexican	270	1.5	70.7

Population Growth: 2000–2010

Group	%
Total Population	11.1
Hispanic or Latino (of any race)	127.4

Males per 100 Females

Group	Number
Total Population	97.3
Hispanic or Latino (of any race)	119.5
Mexican	141.1

Average Household Size

Group	People
Total Population	2.25
Hispanic or Latino (of any race)	2.66
Mexican	2.80

Median Age

Group	Years
Total Population	35.6
Hispanic or Latino (of any race)	22.2
Mexican	21.4

High School Graduates
(Universe: Population 25 Years and Over)

Group	Number	%
Total Population	9,712	87.7

Four-Year College Graduates
(Universe: Population 25 Years and Over)

Group	Number	%
Total Population	2,677	24.2

Population Age 3–17 Enrolled in Public School
(Universe: Population Age 3–17 Enrolled in School)

Group	Number	%
Total Population	2,207	83.8

Population Age 3–17 Enrolled in Private School
(Universe: Population Age 3–17 Enrolled in School)

Group	Number	%
Total Population	426	16.2

Foreign-Born Population

Group	Number	%
Total Population	381	2.2

Foreign-Born Naturalized U.S. Citizens

Group	Number	%
Total Population	59	15.5

Language Spoken at Home: English Only
(Universe: Population 5 Years and Over)

Group	Number	%
Total Population	15,301	94.4

Language Spoken at Home: Spanish
(Universe: Population 5 Years and Over)

Group	Number	%
Total Population	179	1.1

Unemployment Rate
(Universe: Population 16 Years and Over)

Group	%
Total Population	3.0

Class of Worker: Private Wage and Salary
(Universe: Civilian Employed Population 16 Years and Over)

Group	Number	%
Total Population	7,519	78.2

Class of Worker: Government
(Universe: Civilian Employed Population 16 Years and Over)

Group	Number	%
Total Population	1,372	14.3

Means of Transportation to Work: Car, Truck or Van
(Universe: Workers 16 Years and Over)

Group	Number	%
Total Population	8,798	92.5

Means of Transportation to Work: Public Transportation (ex. Taxicab)
(Universe: Workers 16 Years and Over)

Group	Number	%
Total Population	3	<0.1

Homeownership Rate
(Universe: Occupied Housing Units)

Group	%
Total Population	61.5
Hispanic or Latino (of any race)	26.9
Mexican	24.1

Median Home Value

Group	Dollars
Total Population	118,000

Median Gross Rent

Group	Dollars
Total Population	584

Median Household Income
(2010 Inflation-Adjusted Dollars)

Group	Dollars
Total Population	50,022

Per Capita Income
(2010 Inflation-Adjusted Dollars)

Group	Dollars
Total Population	25,463

Households with $100,000+ Income

Group	Number	%
Total Population	1,099	15.3

Households with Food Stamps/SNAP Benefits During Past 12 Months

Group	Number	%
Total Population	641	8.9

Poverty Rate
(Income in Past 12 Months Below Poverty Level)

Group	%
Total Population	9.7

Fargo*

Population

Group	Number	%TP[1]	%HP[2]
Total Population	105,549	100.0	–
Hispanic or Latino (of any race)	2,308	2.2	100.0
Mexican	1,546	1.5	67.0
Puerto Rican	131	0.1	5.7
South American	147	0.1	6.4

Population Growth: 2000–2010

Group	%
Total Population	16.5
Hispanic or Latino (of any race)	97.8
Mexican	131.4

Males per 100 Females

Group	Number
Total Population	101.8
Hispanic or Latino (of any race)	115.3
Mexican	119.6
Puerto Rican	125.9
South American	107.0

Average Household Size

Group	People
Total Population	2.15
Hispanic or Latino (of any race)	2.58
Mexican	2.67
Puerto Rican	2.17
South American	2.45

Median Age

Group	Years
Total Population	30.2
Hispanic or Latino (of any race)	22.7
Mexican	21.9
Puerto Rican	22.8
South American	27.5

High School Graduates
(Universe: Population 25 Years and Over)

Group	Number	%
Total Population	57,760	93.9
Hispanic or Latino (of any race)	804	85.3
Mexican	509	78.5

Four-Year College Graduates
(Universe: Population 25 Years and Over)

Group	Number	%
Total Population	23,856	38.8
Hispanic or Latino (of any race)	201	21.3
Mexican	21	3.2

Population Age 3–17 Enrolled in Public School
(Universe: Population Age 3–17 Enrolled in School)

Group	Number	%
Total Population	11,985	85.1
Hispanic or Latino (of any race)	518	96.5
Mexican	489	98.2

Notes: (1) Percent of total population; (2) Percent of Hispanic/Latino population; Profiles include places with an overall population of at least 125,000, OR an overall population of at least 25,000 where the Hispanic/Latino population is at least 20% of the overall population. In states where less than five places meet either of these criteria, we have included places with at least 10,000 total population with the highest percentage of Hispanic/Latino population. These places are identified with an asterisk (*); Please refer to the User's Guide for a full explanation of data.

Population Age 3–17 Enrolled in Private School
(Universe: Population Age 3–17 Enrolled in School)

Group	Number	%
Total Population	2,100	14.9
Hispanic or Latino (of any race)	19	3.5
Mexican	9	1.8

Foreign-Born Population

Group	Number	%
Total Population	5,551	5.4
Hispanic or Latino (of any race)	278	12.8
Mexican	172	9.9

Foreign-Born Naturalized U.S. Citizens

Group	Number	%
Total Population	1,738	31.3
Hispanic or Latino (of any race)	120	43.2
Mexican	62	36.0

Language Spoken at Home: English Only
(Universe: Population 5 Years and Over)

Group	Number	%
Total Population	89,457	93.0
Hispanic or Latino (of any race)	1,007	53.2
Mexican	723	49.6

Language Spoken at Home: Spanish
(Universe: Population 5 Years and Over)

Group	Number	%
Total Population	1,509	1.6
Hispanic or Latino (of any race)	874	46.1
Mexican	723	49.6

Unemployment Rate
(Universe: Population 16 Years and Over)

Group	%
Total Population	4.7
Hispanic or Latino (of any race)	7.7
Mexican	11.4

Class of Worker: Private Wage and Salary
(Universe: Civilian Employed Population 16 Years and Over)

Group	Number	%
Total Population	50,102	82.4
Hispanic or Latino (of any race)	929	89.2
Mexican	626	92.7

Class of Worker: Government
(Universe: Civilian Employed Population 16 Years and Over)

Group	Number	%
Total Population	8,374	13.8
Hispanic or Latino (of any race)	107	10.3
Mexican	43	6.4

Means of Transportation to Work: Car, Truck or Van
(Universe: Workers 16 Years and Over)

Group	Number	%
Total Population	53,992	90.3
Hispanic or Latino (of any race)	949	92.0
Mexican	605	91.0

Means of Transportation to Work: Public Transportation (ex. Taxicab)
(Universe: Workers 16 Years and Over)

Group	Number	%
Total Population	749	1.3
Hispanic or Latino (of any race)	42	4.1
Mexican	42	6.3

Homeownership Rate
(Universe: Occupied Housing Units)

Group	%
Total Population	45.8
Hispanic or Latino (of any race)	22.2
Mexican	20.2
Puerto Rican	14.3
South American	29.4

Median Home Value

Group	Dollars
Total Population	146,600
Hispanic or Latino (of any race)	164,000
Mexican	196,300

Median Gross Rent

Group	Dollars
Total Population	606
Hispanic or Latino (of any race)	526
Mexican	498

Median Household Income
(2010 Inflation-Adjusted Dollars)

Group	Dollars
Total Population	41,558
Hispanic or Latino (of any race)	29,792
Mexican	17,326

Per Capita Income
(2010 Inflation-Adjusted Dollars)

Group	Dollars
Total Population	26,997
Hispanic or Latino (of any race)	14,836
Mexican	13,050

Households with $100,000+ Income

Group	Number	%
Total Population	6,905	14.8
Hispanic or Latino (of any race)	78	11.2
Mexican	78	15.1

Households with Food Stamps/SNAP Benefits During Past 12 Months

Group	Number	%
Total Population	3,082	6.6
Hispanic or Latino (of any race)	187	26.8
Mexican	173	33.5

Poverty Rate
(Income in Past 12 Months Below Poverty Level)

Group	%
Total Population	15.5
Hispanic or Latino (of any race)	39.7
Mexican	44.9

Grand Forks*

Population

Group	Number	%TP[1]	%HP[2]
Total Population	52,838	100.0	–
Hispanic or Latino (of any race)	1,473	2.8	100.0
Mexican	995	1.9	67.5

Population Growth: 2000–2010

Group	%
Total Population	7.1
Hispanic or Latino (of any race)	59.9
Mexican	82.6

Males per 100 Females

Group	Number
Total Population	104.9
Hispanic or Latino (of any race)	116.6
Mexican	118.2

Average Household Size

Group	People
Total Population	2.21
Hispanic or Latino (of any race)	2.50
Mexican	2.58

Median Age

Group	Years
Total Population	28.4
Hispanic or Latino (of any race)	22.3
Mexican	21.8

High School Graduates
(Universe: Population 25 Years and Over)

Group	Number	%
Total Population	26,624	92.8
Hispanic or Latino (of any race)	426	71.5
Mexican	316	81.0

Four-Year College Graduates
(Universe: Population 25 Years and Over)

Group	Number	%
Total Population	10,228	35.7
Hispanic or Latino (of any race)	42	7.0
Mexican	15	3.8

Population Age 3–17 Enrolled in Public School
(Universe: Population Age 3–17 Enrolled in School)

Group	Number	%
Total Population	6,161	91.6
Hispanic or Latino (of any race)	143	65.9
Mexican	84	66.7

Population Age 3–17 Enrolled in Private School
(Universe: Population Age 3–17 Enrolled in School)

Group	Number	%
Total Population	564	8.4
Hispanic or Latino (of any race)	74	34.1
Mexican	42	33.3

Foreign-Born Population

Group	Number	%
Total Population	1,939	3.7
Hispanic or Latino (of any race)	149	10.5
Mexican	56	6.1

Foreign-Born Naturalized U.S. Citizens

Group	Number	%
Total Population	624	32.2
Hispanic or Latino (of any race)	57	38.3
Mexican	0	0.0

Language Spoken at Home: English Only
(Universe: Population 5 Years and Over)

Group	Number	%
Total Population	46,390	94.0
Hispanic or Latino (of any race)	777	63.8
Mexican	451	56.3

Language Spoken at Home: Spanish
(Universe: Population 5 Years and Over)

Group	Number	%
Total Population	846	1.7
Hispanic or Latino (of any race)	440	36.2
Mexican	350	43.7

Unemployment Rate
(Universe: Population 16 Years and Over)

Group	%
Total Population	4.9
Hispanic or Latino (of any race)	2.4
Mexican	1.8

Class of Worker: Private Wage and Salary
(Universe: Civilian Employed Population 16 Years and Over)

Group	Number	%
Total Population	22,807	75.9
Hispanic or Latino (of any race)	589	84.5
Mexican	428	86.1

Class of Worker: Government
(Universe: Civilian Employed Population 16 Years and Over)

Group	Number	%
Total Population	6,166	20.5
Hispanic or Latino (of any race)	96	13.8
Mexican	69	13.9

Means of Transportation to Work: Car, Truck or Van
(Universe: Workers 16 Years and Over)

Group	Number	%
Total Population	26,516	89.5
Hispanic or Latino (of any race)	638	85.3
Mexican	442	86.0

Means of Transportation to Work: Public Transportation (ex. Taxicab)
(Universe: Workers 16 Years and Over)

Group	Number	%
Total Population	545	1.8
Hispanic or Latino (of any race)	0	0.0
Mexican	0	0.0

Homeownership Rate
(Universe: Occupied Housing Units)

Group	%
Total Population	47.3
Hispanic or Latino (of any race)	24.6
Mexican	23.0

Notes: (1) Percent of total population; (2) Percent of Hispanic/Latino population; Profiles include places with an overall population of at least 125,000, OR an overall population of at least 25,000 where the Hispanic/Latino population is at least 20% of the overall population. In states where less than five places meet either of these criteria, we have included places with at least 10,000 total population with the highest percentage of Hispanic/Latino population. These places are identified with an asterisk (*); Please refer to the User's Guide for a full explanation of data.

STATE & PLACE PROFILES

Median Home Value

Group	Dollars
Total Population	144,300
Hispanic or Latino (of any race)	94,500
Mexican	99,500

Median Gross Rent

Group	Dollars
Total Population	628
Hispanic or Latino (of any race)	734
Mexican	675

Median Household Income
(2010 Inflation-Adjusted Dollars)

Group	Dollars
Total Population	40,352
Hispanic or Latino (of any race)	42,668
Mexican	53,917

Per Capita Income
(2010 Inflation-Adjusted Dollars)

Group	Dollars
Total Population	24,098
Hispanic or Latino (of any race)	13,912
Mexican	16,470

Households with $100,000+ Income

Group	Number	%
Total Population	2,885	13.3
Hispanic or Latino (of any race)	59	16.2
Mexican	47	22.4

Households with Food Stamps/SNAP Benefits During Past 12 Months

Group	Number	%
Total Population	1,723	8.0
Hispanic or Latino (of any race)	60	16.4
Mexican	37	17.6

Poverty Rate
(Income in Past 12 Months Below Poverty Level)

Group	%
Total Population	20.6
Hispanic or Latino (of any race)	13.0
Mexican	10.3

Minot*

Population

Group	Number	%TP[1]	%HP[2]
Total Population	40,888	100.0	–
Hispanic or Latino (of any race)	1,117	2.7	100.0
Mexican	708	1.7	63.4
Puerto Rican	159	0.4	14.2

Population Growth: 2000–2010

Group	%
Total Population	11.8
Hispanic or Latino (of any race)	107.2
Mexican	175.5
Puerto Rican	55.9

Males per 100 Females

Group	Number
Total Population	97.3
Hispanic or Latino (of any race)	114.4
Mexican	113.3
Puerto Rican	140.9

Average Household Size

Group	People
Total Population	2.20
Hispanic or Latino (of any race)	2.35
Mexican	2.52
Puerto Rican	2.17

Median Age

Group	Years
Total Population	33.8
Hispanic or Latino (of any race)	23.3
Mexican	22.3
Puerto Rican	23.6

High School Graduates
(Universe: Population 25 Years and Over)

Group	Number	%
Total Population	22,691	91.9
Hispanic or Latino (of any race)	417	78.5

Four-Year College Graduates
(Universe: Population 25 Years and Over)

Group	Number	%
Total Population	6,785	27.5
Hispanic or Latino (of any race)	119	22.4

Population Age 3–17 Enrolled in Public School
(Universe: Population Age 3–17 Enrolled in School)

Group	Number	%
Total Population	5,172	88.4
Hispanic or Latino (of any race)	269	96.1

Population Age 3–17 Enrolled in Private School
(Universe: Population Age 3–17 Enrolled in School)

Group	Number	%
Total Population	678	11.6
Hispanic or Latino (of any race)	11	3.9

Foreign-Born Population

Group	Number	%
Total Population	1,571	4.0
Hispanic or Latino (of any race)	219	18.4

Foreign-Born Naturalized U.S. Citizens

Group	Number	%
Total Population	592	37.7
Hispanic or Latino (of any race)	94	42.9

Language Spoken at Home: English Only
(Universe: Population 5 Years and Over)

Group	Number	%
Total Population	33,852	93.0
Hispanic or Latino (of any race)	485	48.7

Language Spoken at Home: Spanish
(Universe: Population 5 Years and Over)

Group	Number	%
Total Population	989	2.7
Hispanic or Latino (of any race)	511	51.3

Unemployment Rate
(Universe: Population 16 Years and Over)

Group	%
Total Population	3.1
Hispanic or Latino (of any race)	9.3

Class of Worker: Private Wage and Salary
(Universe: Civilian Employed Population 16 Years and Over)

Group	Number	%
Total Population	16,171	79.3
Hispanic or Latino (of any race)	454	84.5

Class of Worker: Government
(Universe: Civilian Employed Population 16 Years and Over)

Group	Number	%
Total Population	3,121	15.3
Hispanic or Latino (of any race)	33	6.1

Means of Transportation to Work: Car, Truck or Van
(Universe: Workers 16 Years and Over)

Group	Number	%
Total Population	19,845	93.0
Hispanic or Latino (of any race)	520	86.4

Means of Transportation to Work: Public Transportation (ex. Taxicab)
(Universe: Workers 16 Years and Over)

Group	Number	%
Total Population	89	0.4
Hispanic or Latino (of any race)	0	0.0

Homeownership Rate
(Universe: Occupied Housing Units)

Group	%
Total Population	60.7
Hispanic or Latino (of any race)	33.8
Mexican	33.6
Puerto Rican	27.8

Median Home Value

Group	Dollars
Total Population	118,600
Hispanic or Latino (of any race)	88,900

Median Gross Rent

Group	Dollars
Total Population	569
Hispanic or Latino (of any race)	476

Median Household Income
(2010 Inflation-Adjusted Dollars)

Group	Dollars
Total Population	44,452
Hispanic or Latino (of any race)	30,483

Per Capita Income
(2010 Inflation-Adjusted Dollars)

Group	Dollars
Total Population	25,507
Hispanic or Latino (of any race)	14,773

Households with $100,000+ Income

Group	Number	%
Total Population	1,827	10.7
Hispanic or Latino (of any race)	7	1.8

Households with Food Stamps/SNAP Benefits During Past 12 Months

Group	Number	%
Total Population	1,524	8.9
Hispanic or Latino (of any race)	102	26.2

Poverty Rate
(Income in Past 12 Months Below Poverty Level)

Group	%
Total Population	11.3
Hispanic or Latino (of any race)	18.0

Williston*

Population

Group	Number	%TP[1]	%HP[2]
Total Population	14,716	100.0	–
Hispanic or Latino (of any race)	328	2.2	100.0
Mexican	213	1.4	64.9

Population Growth: 2000–2010

Group	%
Total Population	17.6
Hispanic or Latino (of any race)	113.0

Males per 100 Females

Group	Number
Total Population	104.1
Hispanic or Latino (of any race)	97.6
Mexican	97.2

Average Household Size

Group	People
Total Population	2.31
Hispanic or Latino (of any race)	2.94
Mexican	3.13

Median Age

Group	Years
Total Population	35.5
Hispanic or Latino (of any race)	24.3
Mexican	22.4

High School Graduates
(Universe: Population 25 Years and Over)

Group	Number	%
Total Population	7,948	87.7

Four-Year College Graduates
(Universe: Population 25 Years and Over)

Group	Number	%
Total Population	1,884	20.8

Population Age 3–17 Enrolled in Public School
(Universe: Population Age 3–17 Enrolled in School)

Group	Number	%
Total Population	1,912	85.5

Notes: (1) Percent of total population; (2) Percent of Hispanic/Latino population; Profiles include places with an overall population of at least 125,000, OR an overall population of at least 25,000 where the Hispanic/Latino population is at least 20% of the overall population. In states where less than five places meet either of these criteria, we have included places with at least 10,000 total population with the highest percentage of Hispanic/Latino population. These places are identified with an asterisk (*); Please refer to the User's Guide for a full explanation of data.

Population Age 3–17 Enrolled in Private School
(Universe: Population Age 3–17 Enrolled in School)

Group	Number	%
Total Population	323	14.5

Foreign-Born Population

Group	Number	%
Total Population	302	2.2

Foreign-Born Naturalized U.S. Citizens

Group	Number	%
Total Population	155	51.3

Language Spoken at Home: English Only
(Universe: Population 5 Years and Over)

Group	Number	%
Total Population	12,384	96.7

Language Spoken at Home: Spanish
(Universe: Population 5 Years and Over)

Group	Number	%
Total Population	108	0.8

Unemployment Rate
(Universe: Population 16 Years and Over)

Group	%
Total Population	1.4

Class of Worker: Private Wage and Salary
(Universe: Civilian Employed Population 16 Years and Over)

Group	Number	%
Total Population	6,158	79.9

Class of Worker: Government
(Universe: Civilian Employed Population 16 Years and Over)

Group	Number	%
Total Population	1,105	14.3

Means of Transportation to Work: Car, Truck or Van
(Universe: Workers 16 Years and Over)

Group	Number	%
Total Population	6,928	91.8

Means of Transportation to Work: Public Transportation (ex. Taxicab)
(Universe: Workers 16 Years and Over)

Group	Number	%
Total Population	23	0.3

Homeownership Rate
(Universe: Occupied Housing Units)

Group	%
Total Population	62.4
Hispanic or Latino (of any race)	29.9
Mexican	26.1

Median Home Value

Group	Dollars
Total Population	95,200

Median Gross Rent

Group	Dollars
Total Population	527

Median Household Income
(2010 Inflation-Adjusted Dollars)

Group	Dollars
Total Population	52,926

Per Capita Income
(2010 Inflation-Adjusted Dollars)

Group	Dollars
Total Population	28,707

Households with $100,000+ Income

Group	Number	%
Total Population	1,068	17.8

Households with Food Stamps/SNAP Benefits During Past 12 Months

Group	Number	%
Total Population	275	4.6

Poverty Rate
(Income in Past 12 Months Below Poverty Level)

Group	%
Total Population	10.0

Notes: (1) Percent of total population; (2) Percent of Hispanic/Latino population; Profiles include places with an overall population of at least 125,000, OR an overall population of at least 25,000 where the Hispanic/Latino population is at least 20% of the overall population. In states where less than five places meet either of these criteria, we have included places with at least 10,000 total population with the highest percentage of Hispanic/Latino population. These places are identified with an asterisk (*); Please refer to the User's Guide for a full explanation of data.

Ohio

EDITOR'S NOTE: For a place to be included in this edition, it must meet one of two criteria. Either its overall population is at least 125,000, OR its overall population is at least 25,000 and its Hispanic/Latino population is at least 20% of the overall population. For the state of Ohio, the following locations are included:

- Akron
- Cincinnati
- Cleveland
- Columbus
- Dayton
- Lorain
- Toledo

Section Two: State & Place Profiles starts with the state profile, followed by place profiles that meet the criteria above. Places are listed alphabetically within each state. All states, all counties and places that meet the above criteria are ranked and compared in *Section Three: Rankings & Comparisons*, on page 1055.

For a more detailed look at the Hispanic/Latino population in Ohio, a companion web site is available at no additional charge with purchase of this print edition. Visit http://gold.greyhouse.com/page/info_hispanic for more information.

The web site includes data for all counties and places in Ohio with Hispanic/Latino population, plus ten additional topics: Self Employed Worker; Walked to Work; Worked from Home; Mean Travel Time to Work; Mean Household Income; Households with Cash Public Assistance; Mean Cash Pubic Assistance; Poverty Rates for 18 and Under, 18 to 64, and 65 and Over.

Population

Group	Number	%TP[1]	%HP[2]
Total Population	11,536,504	100.0	–
Hispanic or Latino (of any race)	354,674	3.1	100.0
Central American, ex. Mexican	22,756	0.2	6.4
Costa Rican	1,093	<0.1	0.3
Guatemalan	8,680	0.1	2.4
Honduran	3,699	<0.1	1.0
Nicaraguan	1,383	<0.1	0.4
Panamanian	2,055	<0.1	0.6
Salvadoran	5,627	<0.1	1.6
Cuban	7,523	0.1	2.1
Dominican Republic	6,453	0.1	1.8
Mexican	172,029	1.5	48.5
Puerto Rican	94,965	0.8	26.8
South American	17,571	0.2	5.0
Argentinean	1,921	<0.1	0.5
Bolivian	649	<0.1	0.2
Chilean	1,065	<0.1	0.3
Colombian	5,247	<0.1	1.5
Ecuadorian	2,090	<0.1	0.6
Paraguayan	205	<0.1	0.1
Peruvian	3,741	<0.1	1.1
Uruguayan	291	<0.1	0.1
Venezuelan	2,190	<0.1	0.6
Spaniard	6,426	0.1	1.8

Population Growth: 2000–2010

Group	%
Total Population	1.6
Hispanic or Latino (of any race)	63.4
Central American, ex. Mexican	246.0
Costa Rican	109.8
Guatemalan	426.7
Honduran	270.6
Nicaraguan	133.2
Panamanian	102.3
Salvadoran	271.7
Cuban	46.0
Dominican Republic	227.9
Mexican	89.7
Puerto Rican	43.3
South American	133.1
Argentinean	145.7
Bolivian	117.1
Chilean	72.9
Colombian	133.3
Ecuadorian	196.9
Paraguayan	86.4
Peruvian	184.3
Venezuelan	108.8
Spaniard	566.6

Males per 100 Females

Group	Number
Total Population	95.4
Hispanic or Latino (of any race)	106.4
Central American, ex. Mexican	113.7
Costa Rican	88.8
Guatemalan	131.9
Honduran	109.3
Nicaraguan	88.9
Panamanian	69.3
Salvadoran	122.9
Cuban	101.6
Dominican Republic	94.8
Mexican	113.8
Puerto Rican	97.5
South American	89.6
Argentinean	93.8
Bolivian	83.3
Chilean	83.9
Colombian	86.6
Ecuadorian	107.1
Paraguayan	83.0
Peruvian	82.7
Uruguayan	95.3
Venezuelan	92.1
Spaniard	86.6

Average Household Size

Group	People
Total Population	2.44
Hispanic or Latino (of any race)	3.03
Central American, ex. Mexican	3.49
Costa Rican	2.84
Guatemalan	4.05
Honduran	3.37
Nicaraguan	3.10
Panamanian	2.69
Salvadoran	3.53
Cuban	2.56
Dominican Republic	3.21
Mexican	3.23
Puerto Rican	2.87
South American	2.75
Argentinean	2.61
Bolivian	2.87
Chilean	2.54
Colombian	2.67
Ecuadorian	2.98
Paraguayan	3.00
Peruvian	2.84
Uruguayan	2.66
Venezuelan	2.82
Spaniard	2.45

Median Age

Group	Years
Total Population	38.8
Hispanic or Latino (of any race)	24.5
Central American, ex. Mexican	24.8
Costa Rican	30.7
Guatemalan	21.7
Honduran	25.8
Nicaraguan	28.7
Panamanian	30.2
Salvadoran	26.6
Cuban	27.8
Dominican Republic	26.3
Mexican	23.2
Puerto Rican	24.4
South American	31.3
Argentinean	34.9
Bolivian	30.3
Chilean	33.2
Colombian	30.1
Ecuadorian	29.2
Paraguayan	20.4
Peruvian	32.6
Uruguayan	36.9
Venezuelan	31.2
Spaniard	34.5

High School Graduates
(Universe: Population 25 Years and Over)

Group	Number	%
Total Population	6,693,408	87.4
Hispanic or Latino (of any race)	115,760	70.5
Central American, ex. Mexican	6,087	56.0
Guatemalan	1,850	44.2
Honduran	766	57.0
Nicaraguan	721	89.8
Panamanian	1,020	86.7
Salvadoran	1,130	43.1
Cuban	3,198	87.0
Dominican Republic	2,229	78.1
Mexican	52,820	66.1
Puerto Rican	31,143	71.9
South American	9,116	91.1
Argentinean	1,081	88.1
Chilean	529	94.6
Colombian	2,749	98.6
Ecuadorian	989	74.6
Peruvian	2,115	94.4
Venezuelan	990	94.4
Spaniard	3,621	90.1

Four-Year College Graduates
(Universe: Population 25 Years and Over)

Group	Number	%
Total Population	1,848,454	24.1
Hispanic or Latino (of any race)	27,600	16.8
Central American, ex. Mexican	1,814	16.7
Guatemalan	526	12.6
Honduran	238	17.7
Nicaraguan	278	34.6
Panamanian	434	36.9
Salvadoran	218	8.3
Cuban	1,286	35.0
Dominican Republic	500	17.5
Mexican	9,700	12.1
Puerto Rican	6,129	14.2
South American	4,825	48.2
Argentinean	593	48.3
Chilean	371	66.4
Colombian	1,569	56.3
Ecuadorian	327	24.7
Peruvian	983	43.9
Venezuelan	677	64.5
Spaniard	1,421	35.4

Population Age 3–17 Enrolled in Public School
(Universe: Population Age 3–17 Enrolled in School)

Group	Number	%
Total Population	1,766,122	84.1
Hispanic or Latino (of any race)	75,215	85.2
Central American, ex. Mexican	3,670	77.4
Guatemalan	1,535	72.7
Honduran	535	83.1
Nicaraguan	187	53.9
Panamanian	392	75.0
Salvadoran	1,011	91.7
Cuban	1,466	79.9
Dominican Republic	1,326	91.6
Mexican	40,285	87.5
Puerto Rican	20,453	84.5
South American	2,682	71.2
Argentinean	107	79.3
Chilean	122	63.2
Colombian	995	64.0

Notes: (1) Percent of total population; (2) Percent of Hispanic/Latino population; Profiles include places with an overall population of at least 125,000, OR an overall population of at least 25,000 where the Hispanic/Latino population is at least 20% of the overall population. In states where less than five places meet either of these criteria, we have included places with at least 10,000 total population with the highest percentage of Hispanic/Latino population. These places are identified with an asterisk (*); Please refer to the User's Guide for a full explanation of data.

Group	Number	%
Ecuadorian	440	95.0
Peruvian	733	79.9
Venezuelan	103	36.1
Spaniard	983	77.3

Population Age 3–17 Enrolled in Private School
(Universe: Population Age 3–17 Enrolled in School)

Group	Number	%
Total Population	335,092	15.9
Hispanic or Latino (of any race)	13,027	14.8
Central American, ex. Mexican	1,074	22.6
Guatemalan	577	27.3
Honduran	109	16.9
Nicaraguan	160	46.1
Panamanian	131	25.0
Salvadoran	91	8.3
Cuban	369	20.1
Dominican Republic	121	8.4
Mexican	5,738	12.5
Puerto Rican	3,740	15.5
South American	1,086	28.8
Argentinean	28	20.7
Chilean	71	36.8
Colombian	559	36.0
Ecuadorian	23	5.0
Peruvian	184	20.1
Venezuelan	182	63.9
Spaniard	288	22.7

Foreign-Born Population

Group	Number	%
Total Population	440,761	3.8
Hispanic or Latino (of any race)	80,346	24.1
Central American, ex. Mexican	13,398	60.5
Guatemalan	6,529	67.9
Honduran	1,702	61.0
Nicaraguan	538	36.0
Panamanian	773	38.1
Salvadoran	3,378	63.7
Cuban	1,808	25.1
Dominican Republic	2,363	45.9
Mexican	48,772	28.9
Puerto Rican	532	0.6
South American	9,698	58.0
Argentinean	994	65.4
Chilean	539	60.0
Colombian	2,757	52.6
Ecuadorian	1,180	55.9
Peruvian	2,377	66.4
Venezuelan	1,182	60.8
Spaniard	943	14.3

Foreign-Born Naturalized U.S. Citizens

Group	Number	%
Total Population	212,015	48.1
Hispanic or Latino (of any race)	20,628	25.7
Central American, ex. Mexican	3,912	29.2
Guatemalan	1,743	26.7
Honduran	564	33.1
Nicaraguan	326	60.6
Panamanian	371	48.0
Salvadoran	676	20.0
Cuban	1,239	68.5
Dominican Republic	1,283	54.3
Mexican	8,193	16.8
Puerto Rican	212	39.8
South American	4,212	43.4
Argentinean	460	46.3
Chilean	237	44.0
Colombian	1,421	51.5
Ecuadorian	405	34.3
Peruvian	877	36.9
Venezuelan	423	35.8
Spaniard	395	41.9

Language Spoken at Home: English Only
(Universe: Population 5 Years and Over)

Group	Number	%
Total Population	10,104,160	93.7
Hispanic or Latino (of any race)	130,287	44.8
Central American, ex. Mexican	4,673	24.7
Guatemalan	1,379	17.5
Honduran	593	23.7
Nicaraguan	582	44.5
Panamanian	1,019	54.1
Salvadoran	714	15.7
Cuban	3,710	57.5
Dominican Republic	844	18.2
Mexican	70,198	48.2
Puerto Rican	30,942	40.2
South American	4,341	28.3
Argentinean	415	28.4
Chilean	364	42.8
Colombian	1,495	31.2
Ecuadorian	485	24.8
Peruvian	650	19.5
Venezuelan	452	26.9
Spaniard	4,710	78.5

Language Spoken at Home: Spanish
(Universe: Population 5 Years and Over)

Group	Number	%
Total Population	236,444	2.2
Hispanic or Latino (of any race)	158,453	54.5
Central American, ex. Mexican	14,187	75.0
Guatemalan	6,427	81.8
Honduran	1,908	76.3
Nicaraguan	727	55.5
Panamanian	862	45.7
Salvadoran	3,821	84.0
Cuban	2,702	41.9
Dominican Republic	3,789	81.7
Mexican	74,428	51.1
Puerto Rican	45,619	59.3
South American	10,790	70.3
Argentinean	1,013	69.2
Chilean	482	56.7
Colombian	3,287	68.7
Ecuadorian	1,467	75.2
Peruvian	2,661	79.9
Venezuelan	1,131	67.2
Spaniard	1,248	20.8

Unemployment Rate
(Universe: Population 16 Years and Over)

Group	%
Total Population	8.6
Hispanic or Latino (of any race)	11.7
Central American, ex. Mexican	8.2
Guatemalan	8.7
Honduran	15.9
Nicaraguan	10.6
Panamanian	3.2
Salvadoran	5.0
Cuban	11.4
Dominican Republic	10.4
Mexican	11.3
Puerto Rican	15.0
South American	6.6
Argentinean	12.8
Chilean	4.7
Colombian	5.1
Ecuadorian	10.9
Peruvian	5.2
Venezuelan	3.5
Spaniard	9.9

Class of Worker: Private Wage and Salary
(Universe: Civilian Employed Population 16 Years and Over)

Group	Number	%
Total Population	4,377,198	81.5
Hispanic or Latino (of any race)	115,154	87.4
Central American, ex. Mexican	8,669	89.0
Guatemalan	3,449	91.2
Honduran	1,117	96.1
Nicaraguan	497	75.6
Panamanian	909	89.4
Salvadoran	2,364	89.9
Cuban	2,453	79.4
Dominican Republic	2,048	90.2
Mexican	59,518	90.1
Puerto Rican	27,062	84.4
South American	6,498	78.2
Argentinean	618	78.1
Chilean	369	79.7
Colombian	1,828	77.2
Ecuadorian	794	72.7
Peruvian	1,621	87.8
Venezuelan	743	71.9
Spaniard	2,393	82.5

Class of Worker: Government
(Universe: Civilian Employed Population 16 Years and Over)

Group	Number	%
Total Population	693,114	12.9
Hispanic or Latino (of any race)	12,029	9.1
Central American, ex. Mexican	482	4.9
Guatemalan	93	2.5
Honduran	45	3.9
Nicaraguan	146	22.2
Panamanian	78	7.7
Salvadoran	55	2.1
Cuban	453	14.7
Dominican Republic	122	5.4
Mexican	4,441	6.7
Puerto Rican	3,954	12.3
South American	1,502	18.1
Argentinean	162	20.5
Chilean	68	14.7
Colombian	466	19.7
Ecuadorian	227	20.8
Peruvian	181	9.8
Venezuelan	277	26.8
Spaniard	460	15.9

Means of Transportation to Work: Car, Truck or Van
(Universe: Workers 16 Years and Over)

Group	Number	%
Total Population	4,795,529	91.4
Hispanic or Latino (of any race)	114,942	89.3
Central American, ex. Mexican	8,411	88.4
Guatemalan	3,239	87.7
Honduran	1,021	87.9
Nicaraguan	547	84.2
Panamanian	866	85.5
Salvadoran	2,332	89.8
Cuban	2,716	89.5
Dominican Republic	1,960	88.2
Mexican	57,993	89.9
Puerto Rican	28,180	89.8
South American	6,969	87.1
Argentinean	730	94.9
Chilean	386	83.4
Colombian	2,046	87.6
Ecuadorian	808	83.7
Peruvian	1,535	87.5
Venezuelan	872	87.4
Spaniard	2,573	90.5

Means of Transportation to Work: Public Transportation (ex. Taxicab)
(Universe: Workers 16 Years and Over)

Group	Number	%
Total Population	96,351	1.8
Hispanic or Latino (of any race)	3,666	2.8
Central American, ex. Mexican	371	3.9
Guatemalan	125	3.4
Honduran	67	5.8
Nicaraguan	63	9.7
Panamanian	9	0.9
Salvadoran	107	4.1
Cuban	39	1.3
Dominican Republic	114	5.1
Mexican	1,400	2.2
Puerto Rican	1,076	3.4
South American	294	3.7
Argentinean	10	1.3
Chilean	12	2.6
Colombian	75	3.2
Ecuadorian	71	7.4
Peruvian	69	3.9
Venezuelan	23	2.3
Spaniard	88	3.1

Homeownership Rate
(Universe: Occupied Housing Units)

Group	%
Total Population	67.6
Hispanic or Latino (of any race)	44.4
Central American, ex. Mexican	36.4
Costa Rican	50.6
Guatemalan	25.7
Honduran	34.0
Nicaraguan	46.7
Panamanian	53.9

Notes: (1) Percent of total population; (2) Percent of Hispanic/Latino population; Profiles include places with an overall population of at least 125,000, OR an overall population of at least 25,000 where the Hispanic/Latino population is at least 20% of the overall population. In states where less than five places meet either of these criteria, we have included places with at least 10,000 total population with the highest percentage of Hispanic/Latino population. These places are identified with an asterisk (*); Please refer to the User's Guide for a full explanation of data.

Salvadoran	37.5
Cuban	53.2
Dominican Republic	38.4
Mexican	43.1
Puerto Rican	43.3
South American	57.1
Argentinean	65.3
Bolivian	64.4
Chilean	62.1
Colombian	54.0
Ecuadorian	51.8
Paraguayan	54.8
Peruvian	56.5
Uruguayan	54.6
Venezuelan	57.1
Spaniard	66.7

Median Home Value

Group	Dollars
Total Population	136,400
Hispanic or Latino (of any race)	117,000
Central American, ex. Mexican	123,800
Guatemalan	115,200
Honduran	106,300
Nicaraguan	131,500
Panamanian	159,100
Salvadoran	114,300
Cuban	161,600
Dominican Republic	114,900
Mexican	110,600
Puerto Rican	102,000
South American	177,700
Argentinean	175,800
Chilean	212,700
Colombian	181,500
Ecuadorian	215,200
Peruvian	146,600
Venezuelan	207,800
Spaniard	159,200

Median Gross Rent

Group	Dollars
Total Population	678
Hispanic or Latino (of any race)	679
Central American, ex. Mexican	671
Guatemalan	663
Honduran	696
Nicaraguan	527
Panamanian	787
Salvadoran	658
Cuban	745
Dominican Republic	773
Mexican	687
Puerto Rican	649
South American	707
Argentinean	806
Chilean	714
Colombian	734
Ecuadorian	657
Peruvian	692
Venezuelan	838
Spaniard	752

Median Household Income
(2010 Inflation-Adjusted Dollars)

Group	Dollars
Total Population	47,358
Hispanic or Latino (of any race)	36,350
Central American, ex. Mexican	37,177
Guatemalan	36,350
Honduran	36,708
Nicaraguan	36,635
Panamanian	44,543
Salvadoran	35,818
Cuban	43,313
Dominican Republic	29,755
Mexican	37,722
Puerto Rican	30,691
South American	53,384
Argentinean	58,333
Chilean	83,125
Colombian	53,413
Ecuadorian	37,396
Peruvian	47,204
Venezuelan	84,952
Spaniard	61,439

Per Capita Income
(2010 Inflation-Adjusted Dollars)

Group	Dollars
Total Population	25,113
Hispanic or Latino (of any race)	15,126
Central American, ex. Mexican	13,968
Guatemalan	10,783
Honduran	11,553
Nicaraguan	18,636
Panamanian	27,517
Salvadoran	13,305
Cuban	25,184
Dominican Republic	15,718
Mexican	14,018
Puerto Rican	13,745
South American	24,712
Argentinean	31,701
Chilean	29,290
Colombian	23,806
Ecuadorian	22,618
Peruvian	21,738
Venezuelan	30,199
Spaniard	26,411

Households with $100,000+ Income

Group	Number	%
Total Population	743,956	16.3
Hispanic or Latino (of any race)	10,453	11.4
Central American, ex. Mexican	614	11.4
Guatemalan	197	11.0
Honduran	45	6.3
Nicaraguan	59	14.2
Panamanian	138	19.8
Salvadoran	119	8.0
Cuban	496	21.9
Dominican Republic	131	8.1
Mexican	4,010	9.5
Puerto Rican	2,337	8.7
South American	1,421	27.1
Argentinean	161	25.9
Chilean	167	42.0
Colombian	419	30.1
Ecuadorian	86	13.1
Peruvian	200	19.2
Venezuelan	265	46.1
Spaniard	603	22.2

Households with Food Stamps/SNAP Benefits During Past 12 Months

Group	Number	%
Total Population	498,685	11.0
Hispanic or Latino (of any race)	19,383	21.1
Central American, ex. Mexican	663	12.3
Guatemalan	99	5.5
Honduran	127	17.8
Nicaraguan	71	17.1
Panamanian	169	24.2
Salvadoran	140	9.4
Cuban	423	18.7
Dominican Republic	453	27.9
Mexican	7,908	18.8
Puerto Rican	8,108	30.2
South American	500	9.5
Argentinean	0	0.0
Chilean	15	3.8
Colombian	143	10.3
Ecuadorian	110	16.8
Peruvian	137	13.2
Venezuelan	19	3.3
Spaniard	257	9.5

Poverty Rate
(Income in Past 12 Months Below Poverty Level)

Group	%
Total Population	14.2
Hispanic or Latino (of any race)	26.8
Central American, ex. Mexican	27.8
Guatemalan	35.9
Honduran	27.6
Nicaraguan	20.8
Panamanian	17.0
Salvadoran	21.0
Cuban	17.6
Dominican Republic	29.2
Mexican	27.3
Puerto Rican	30.1
South American	15.1
Argentinean	15.7
Chilean	7.4
Colombian	12.6
Ecuadorian	25.0
Peruvian	14.0
Venezuelan	10.6
Spaniard	13.3

Akron

Population

Group	Number	%TP[1]	%HP[2]
Total Population	199,110	100.0	–
Hispanic or Latino (of any race)	4,255	2.1	100.0
Central American, ex. Mexican	341	0.2	8.0
Cuban	148	0.1	3.5
Mexican	1,784	0.9	41.9
Puerto Rican	1,091	0.5	25.6
South American	251	0.1	5.9
Colombian	101	0.1	2.4
Spaniard	128	0.1	3.0

Population Growth: 2000–2010

Group	%
Total Population	-8.3
Hispanic or Latino (of any race)	69.3
Central American, ex. Mexican	154.5
Mexican	89.8
Puerto Rican	66.8
South American	118.3

Males per 100 Females

Group	Number
Total Population	93.6
Hispanic or Latino (of any race)	105.7
Central American, ex. Mexican	105.4
Cuban	70.1
Mexican	118.1
Puerto Rican	94.8
South American	85.9
Colombian	80.4
Spaniard	70.7

Average Household Size

Group	People
Total Population	2.31
Hispanic or Latino (of any race)	2.83
Central American, ex. Mexican	2.99
Cuban	2.41
Mexican	3.11
Puerto Rican	2.77
South American	2.41
Colombian	2.27
Spaniard	2.47

Median Age

Group	Years
Total Population	35.7
Hispanic or Latino (of any race)	24.8
Central American, ex. Mexican	26.5
Cuban	26.5
Mexican	24.6
Puerto Rican	21.9
South American	28.3
Colombian	28.5
Spaniard	31.3

High School Graduates
(Universe: Population 25 Years and Over)

Group	Number	%
Total Population	110,673	84.5
Hispanic or Latino (of any race)	1,124	54.3
Mexican	575	43.6
Puerto Rican	240	65.6

Four-Year College Graduates
(Universe: Population 25 Years and Over)

Group	Number	%
Total Population	26,295	20.1
Hispanic or Latino (of any race)	339	16.4

Notes: (1) Percent of total population; (2) Percent of Hispanic/Latino population; Profiles include places with an overall population of at least 125,000, OR an overall population of at least 25,000 where the Hispanic/Latino population is at least 20% of the overall population. In states where less than five places meet either of these criteria, we have included places with at least 10,000 total population with the highest percentage of Hispanic/Latino population. These places are identified with an asterisk (*); Please refer to the User's Guide for a full explanation of data.

Group	Number	%
Mexican	135	10.2
Puerto Rican	21	5.7

Population Age 3–17 Enrolled in Public School
(Universe: Population Age 3–17 Enrolled in School)

Group	Number	%
Total Population	29,800	83.2
Hispanic or Latino (of any race)	730	84.6
Mexican	401	77.9
Puerto Rican	198	100.0

Population Age 3–17 Enrolled in Private School
(Universe: Population Age 3–17 Enrolled in School)

Group	Number	%
Total Population	5,998	16.8
Hispanic or Latino (of any race)	133	15.4
Mexican	114	22.1
Puerto Rican	0	0.0

Foreign-Born Population

Group	Number	%
Total Population	8,882	4.4
Hispanic or Latino (of any race)	1,511	35.7
Mexican	1,190	45.6
Puerto Rican	0	0.0

Foreign-Born Naturalized U.S. Citizens

Group	Number	%
Total Population	3,924	44.2
Hispanic or Latino (of any race)	601	39.8
Mexican	388	32.6
Puerto Rican	0	0.0

Language Spoken at Home: English Only
(Universe: Population 5 Years and Over)

Group	Number	%
Total Population	177,208	93.8
Hispanic or Latino (of any race)	1,131	31.1
Mexican	786	34.4
Puerto Rican	195	28.6

Language Spoken at Home: Spanish
(Universe: Population 5 Years and Over)

Group	Number	%
Total Population	3,855	2.0
Hispanic or Latino (of any race)	2,504	68.9
Mexican	1,497	65.6
Puerto Rican	488	71.4

Unemployment Rate
(Universe: Population 16 Years and Over)

Group	%
Total Population	12.9
Hispanic or Latino (of any race)	11.1
Mexican	6.3
Puerto Rican	11.3

Class of Worker: Private Wage and Salary
(Universe: Civilian Employed Population 16 Years and Over)

Group	Number	%
Total Population	75,380	83.3
Hispanic or Latino (of any race)	1,741	90.9
Mexican	1,278	98.3
Puerto Rican	245	80.1

Class of Worker: Government
(Universe: Civilian Employed Population 16 Years and Over)

Group	Number	%
Total Population	11,081	12.2
Hispanic or Latino (of any race)	175	9.1
Mexican	22	1.7
Puerto Rican	61	19.9

Means of Transportation to Work: Car, Truck or Van
(Universe: Workers 16 Years and Over)

Group	Number	%
Total Population	80,289	90.7
Hispanic or Latino (of any race)	1,501	78.8
Mexican	1,087	84.4
Puerto Rican	200	65.4

Means of Transportation to Work: Public Transportation (ex. Taxicab)
(Universe: Workers 16 Years and Over)

Group	Number	%
Total Population	3,067	3.5
Hispanic or Latino (of any race)	158	8.3
Mexican	92	7.1
Puerto Rican	40	13.1

Homeownership Rate
(Universe: Occupied Housing Units)

Group	%
Total Population	54.5
Hispanic or Latino (of any race)	34.7
Central American, ex. Mexican	25.8
Cuban	42.9
Mexican	31.3
Puerto Rican	33.6
South American	49.4
Colombian	43.2
Spaniard	66.0

Median Home Value

Group	Dollars
Total Population	91,800
Hispanic or Latino (of any race)	78,600
Mexican	83,300
Puerto Rican	57,600

Median Gross Rent

Group	Dollars
Total Population	657
Hispanic or Latino (of any race)	569
Mexican	581
Puerto Rican	543

Median Household Income
(2010 Inflation-Adjusted Dollars)

Group	Dollars
Total Population	34,359
Hispanic or Latino (of any race)	29,917
Mexican	32,614
Puerto Rican	23,047

Per Capita Income
(2010 Inflation-Adjusted Dollars)

Group	Dollars
Total Population	19,664
Hispanic or Latino (of any race)	13,843
Mexican	13,396
Puerto Rican	15,118

Households with $100,000+ Income

Group	Number	%
Total Population	6,467	7.5
Hispanic or Latino (of any race)	65	4.9
Mexican	49	6.5
Puerto Rican	0	0.0

Households with Food Stamps/SNAP Benefits During Past 12 Months

Group	Number	%
Total Population	16,768	19.5
Hispanic or Latino (of any race)	198	15.0
Mexican	123	16.2
Puerto Rican	60	17.6

Poverty Rate
(Income in Past 12 Months Below Poverty Level)

Group	%
Total Population	23.9
Hispanic or Latino (of any race)	32.6
Mexican	31.2
Puerto Rican	49.3

Cincinnati

Population

Group	Number	%TP[1]	%HP[2]
Total Population	296,943	100.0	–
Hispanic or Latino (of any race)	8,308	2.8	100.0
Central American, ex. Mexican	1,860	0.6	22.4
Guatemalan	1,257	0.4	15.1
Honduran	230	0.1	2.8
Salvadoran	132	<0.1	1.6
Cuban	320	0.1	3.9
Dominican Republic	119	<0.1	1.4
Mexican	3,244	1.1	39.0
Puerto Rican	973	0.3	11.7
South American	668	0.2	8.0
Colombian	215	0.1	2.6
Peruvian	138	<0.1	1.7
Venezuelan	107	<0.1	1.3
Spaniard	192	0.1	2.3

Population Growth: 2000–2010

Group	%
Total Population	-10.4
Hispanic or Latino (of any race)	96.4
Central American, ex. Mexican	368.5
Guatemalan	495.7
Cuban	45.5
Mexican	110.4
Puerto Rican	50.2
South American	108.8

Males per 100 Females

Group	Number
Total Population	92.5
Hispanic or Latino (of any race)	118.3
Central American, ex. Mexican	138.2
Guatemalan	153.9
Honduran	117.0
Salvadoran	127.6
Cuban	98.8
Dominican Republic	95.1
Mexican	128.0
Puerto Rican	99.8
South American	94.8
Colombian	88.6
Peruvian	68.3
Venezuelan	122.9
Spaniard	79.4

Average Household Size

Group	People
Total Population	2.12
Hispanic or Latino (of any race)	2.68
Central American, ex. Mexican	3.77
Guatemalan	4.31
Honduran	3.39
Salvadoran	3.24
Cuban	2.03
Dominican Republic	2.64
Mexican	2.74
Puerto Rican	2.27
South American	1.95
Colombian	1.88
Peruvian	2.02
Venezuelan	1.81
Spaniard	2.10

Median Age

Group	Years
Total Population	32.5
Hispanic or Latino (of any race)	25.4
Central American, ex. Mexican	24.5
Guatemalan	23.8
Honduran	25.5
Salvadoran	24.8
Cuban	28.0
Dominican Republic	26.1
Mexican	24.8
Puerto Rican	24.3
South American	31.2
Colombian	28.9
Peruvian	34.5
Venezuelan	30.1
Spaniard	31.1

High School Graduates
(Universe: Population 25 Years and Over)

Group	Number	%
Total Population	159,490	83.6
Hispanic or Latino (of any race)	2,517	64.3
Central American, ex. Mexican	125	14.5
Guatemalan	61	9.0
Mexican	1,270	83.4
Puerto Rican	435	66.5

STATE & PLACE PROFILES

Notes: (1) Percent of total population; (2) Percent of Hispanic/Latino population; Profiles include places with an overall population of at least 125,000, OR an overall population of at least 25,000 where the Hispanic/Latino population is at least 20% of the overall population. In states where less than five places meet either of these criteria, we have included places with at least 10,000 total population with the highest percentage of Hispanic/Latino population. These places are identified with an asterisk (*); Please refer to the User's Guide for a full explanation of data.

Four-Year College Graduates
(Universe: Population 25 Years and Over)

Group	Number	%
Total Population	58,729	30.8
Hispanic or Latino (of any race)	946	24.2
Central American, ex. Mexican	0	0.0
Guatemalan	0	0.0
Mexican	422	27.7
Puerto Rican	297	45.4

Population Age 3–17 Enrolled in Public School
(Universe: Population Age 3–17 Enrolled in School)

Group	Number	%
Total Population	37,116	78.4
Hispanic or Latino (of any race)	1,169	77.4
Central American, ex. Mexican	194	85.8
Guatemalan	139	81.3
Mexican	367	85.7
Puerto Rican	206	72.3

Population Age 3–17 Enrolled in Private School
(Universe: Population Age 3–17 Enrolled in School)

Group	Number	%
Total Population	10,237	21.6
Hispanic or Latino (of any race)	342	22.6
Central American, ex. Mexican	32	14.2
Guatemalan	32	18.7
Mexican	61	14.3
Puerto Rican	79	27.7

Foreign-Born Population

Group	Number	%
Total Population	13,449	4.5
Hispanic or Latino (of any race)	3,121	38.5
Central American, ex. Mexican	1,263	66.0
Guatemalan	996	65.6
Mexican	1,098	37.8
Puerto Rican	53	4.1

Foreign-Born Naturalized U.S. Citizens

Group	Number	%
Total Population	4,756	35.4
Hispanic or Latino (of any race)	559	17.9
Central American, ex. Mexican	128	10.1
Guatemalan	43	4.3
Mexican	113	10.3
Puerto Rican	0	0.0

Language Spoken at Home: English Only
(Universe: Population 5 Years and Over)

Group	Number	%
Total Population	259,753	93.2
Hispanic or Latino (of any race)	2,039	29.8
Central American, ex. Mexican	62	4.3
Guatemalan	16	1.4
Mexican	1,102	43.9
Puerto Rican	377	32.8

Language Spoken at Home: Spanish
(Universe: Population 5 Years and Over)

Group	Number	%
Total Population	7,970	2.9
Hispanic or Latino (of any race)	4,787	69.9
Central American, ex. Mexican	1,374	95.0
Guatemalan	1,099	97.6
Mexican	1,410	56.1
Puerto Rican	772	67.2

Unemployment Rate
(Universe: Population 16 Years and Over)

Group	%
Total Population	10.7
Hispanic or Latino (of any race)	15.2
Central American, ex. Mexican	17.4
Guatemalan	20.9
Mexican	7.0
Puerto Rican	21.9

Class of Worker: Private Wage and Salary
(Universe: Civilian Employed Population 16 Years and Over)

Group	Number	%
Total Population	111,658	82.2
Hispanic or Latino (of any race)	2,587	81.6
Central American, ex. Mexican	512	71.8
Guatemalan	354	65.9
Mexican	1,165	88.7
Puerto Rican	400	89.5

Class of Worker: Government
(Universe: Civilian Employed Population 16 Years and Over)

Group	Number	%
Total Population	16,330	12.0
Hispanic or Latino (of any race)	287	9.0
Central American, ex. Mexican	36	5.0
Guatemalan	36	6.7
Mexican	84	6.4
Puerto Rican	31	6.9

Means of Transportation to Work: Car, Truck or Van
(Universe: Workers 16 Years and Over)

Group	Number	%
Total Population	106,875	80.6
Hispanic or Latino (of any race)	2,493	81.4
Central American, ex. Mexican	582	83.6
Guatemalan	424	81.5
Mexican	1,016	80.2
Puerto Rican	320	77.5

Means of Transportation to Work: Public Transportation (ex. Taxicab)
(Universe: Workers 16 Years and Over)

Group	Number	%
Total Population	12,822	9.7
Hispanic or Latino (of any race)	371	12.1
Central American, ex. Mexican	91	13.1
Guatemalan	73	14.0
Mexican	207	16.3
Puerto Rican	34	8.2

Homeownership Rate
(Universe: Occupied Housing Units)

Group	%
Total Population	38.9
Hispanic or Latino (of any race)	23.9
Central American, ex. Mexican	12.6
Guatemalan	5.4
Honduran	11.9
Salvadoran	32.4
Cuban	33.3
Dominican Republic	31.0
Mexican	20.9
Puerto Rican	27.0
South American	42.1
Colombian	33.7
Peruvian	44.1
Venezuelan	45.3
Spaniard	41.1

Median Home Value

Group	Dollars
Total Population	129,700
Hispanic or Latino (of any race)	152,400
Central American, ex. Mexican	105,000
Guatemalan	–
Mexican	163,300
Puerto Rican	143,200

Median Gross Rent

Group	Dollars
Total Population	593
Hispanic or Latino (of any race)	716
Central American, ex. Mexican	714
Guatemalan	731
Mexican	706
Puerto Rican	746

Median Household Income
(2010 Inflation-Adjusted Dollars)

Group	Dollars
Total Population	33,681
Hispanic or Latino (of any race)	27,334
Central American, ex. Mexican	34,737
Guatemalan	34,276
Mexican	27,106
Puerto Rican	20,809

Per Capita Income
(2010 Inflation-Adjusted Dollars)

Group	Dollars
Total Population	23,982
Hispanic or Latino (of any race)	14,021
Central American, ex. Mexican	8,043
Guatemalan	7,551
Mexican	16,204
Puerto Rican	11,533

Households with $100,000+ Income

Group	Number	%
Total Population	16,061	12.1
Hispanic or Latino (of any race)	183	8.4
Central American, ex. Mexican	0	0.0
Guatemalan	0	0.0
Mexican	82	9.2
Puerto Rican	6	1.5

Households with Food Stamps/SNAP Benefits During Past 12 Months

Group	Number	%
Total Population	22,700	17.1
Hispanic or Latino (of any race)	327	15.0
Central American, ex. Mexican	35	10.5
Guatemalan	27	10.3
Mexican	110	12.4
Puerto Rican	110	28.0

Poverty Rate
(Income in Past 12 Months Below Poverty Level)

Group	%
Total Population	27.2
Hispanic or Latino (of any race)	40.4
Central American, ex. Mexican	58.2
Guatemalan	62.0
Mexican	33.8
Puerto Rican	45.1

Cleveland

Population

Group	Number	%TP[1]	%HP[2]
Total Population	396,815	100.0	–
Hispanic or Latino (of any race)	39,534	10.0	100.0
Central American, ex. Mexican	2,085	0.5	5.3
Guatemalan	786	0.2	2.0
Honduran	324	0.1	0.8
Salvadoran	738	0.2	1.9
Cuban	463	0.1	1.2
Dominican Republic	1,140	0.3	2.9
Mexican	3,593	0.9	9.1
Puerto Rican	29,286	7.4	74.1
South American	959	0.2	2.4
Colombian	320	0.1	0.8
Ecuadorian	113	<0.1	0.3
Peruvian	276	0.1	0.7
Spaniard	177	<0.1	0.4

Population Growth: 2000–2010

Group	%
Total Population	-17.1
Hispanic or Latino (of any race)	13.8
Central American, ex. Mexican	78.8
Guatemalan	82.4
Honduran	90.6
Salvadoran	127.8
Cuban	-9.6
Dominican Republic	110.3
Mexican	20.9
Puerto Rican	15.4
South American	72.2
Colombian	97.5
Peruvian	94.4

Males per 100 Females

Group	Number
Total Population	92.1
Hispanic or Latino (of any race)	97.8
Central American, ex. Mexican	106.4
Guatemalan	113.0
Honduran	95.2
Salvadoran	110.9
Cuban	117.4
Dominican Republic	85.7
Mexican	107.6
Puerto Rican	95.8
South American	97.7

Notes: (1) Percent of total population; (2) Percent of Hispanic/Latino population; Profiles include places with an overall population of at least 125,000, OR an overall population of at least 25,000 where the Hispanic/Latino population is at least 20% of the overall population. In states where less than five places meet either of these criteria, we have included places with at least 10,000 total population with the highest percentage of Hispanic/Latino population. These places are identified with an asterisk (*); Please refer to the User's Guide for a full explanation of data.

Colombian	93.9
Ecuadorian	130.6
Peruvian	81.6
Spaniard	71.8

Average Household Size

Group	People
Total Population	2.29
Hispanic or Latino (of any race)	2.92
Central American, ex. Mexican	3.35
Guatemalan	3.56
Honduran	3.27
Salvadoran	3.35
Cuban	2.17
Dominican Republic	3.15
Mexican	2.87
Puerto Rican	2.95
South American	2.63
Colombian	2.90
Ecuadorian	2.80
Peruvian	2.65
Spaniard	2.53

Median Age

Group	Years
Total Population	35.7
Hispanic or Latino (of any race)	26.3
Central American, ex. Mexican	29.2
Guatemalan	30.2
Honduran	28.5
Salvadoran	29.5
Cuban	31.8
Dominican Republic	27.4
Mexican	25.1
Puerto Rican	25.9
South American	32.4
Colombian	28.3
Ecuadorian	36.5
Peruvian	36.3
Spaniard	30.2

High School Graduates
(Universe: Population 25 Years and Over)

Group	Number	%
Total Population	200,837	75.7
Hispanic or Latino (of any race)	12,008	62.3
Central American, ex. Mexican	540	45.5
Dominican Republic	441	75.4
Mexican	1,400	65.2
Puerto Rican	8,299	60.6
South American	508	70.2

Four-Year College Graduates
(Universe: Population 25 Years and Over)

Group	Number	%
Total Population	34,655	13.1
Hispanic or Latino (of any race)	1,289	6.7
Central American, ex. Mexican	133	11.2
Dominican Republic	14	2.4
Mexican	129	6.0
Puerto Rican	685	5.0
South American	123	17.0

Population Age 3–17 Enrolled in Public School
(Universe: Population Age 3–17 Enrolled in School)

Group	Number	%
Total Population	61,033	78.2
Hispanic or Latino (of any race)	8,192	80.2
Central American, ex. Mexican	283	64.6
Dominican Republic	222	82.2
Mexican	663	60.2
Puerto Rican	6,225	82.7
South American	179	81.0

Population Age 3–17 Enrolled in Private School
(Universe: Population Age 3–17 Enrolled in School)

Group	Number	%
Total Population	17,060	21.8
Hispanic or Latino (of any race)	2,023	19.8
Central American, ex. Mexican	155	35.4
Dominican Republic	48	17.8
Mexican	438	39.8
Puerto Rican	1,306	17.3
South American	42	19.0

Foreign-Born Population

Group	Number	%
Total Population	18,932	4.6
Hispanic or Latino (of any race)	3,566	9.5
Central American, ex. Mexican	1,238	66.5
Dominican Republic	434	38.5
Mexican	914	20.9
Puerto Rican	94	0.3
South American	569	51.5

Foreign-Born Naturalized U.S. Citizens

Group	Number	%
Total Population	9,055	47.8
Hispanic or Latino (of any race)	1,427	40.0
Central American, ex. Mexican	406	32.8
Dominican Republic	296	68.2
Mexican	178	19.5
Puerto Rican	34	36.2
South American	315	55.4

Language Spoken at Home: English Only
(Universe: Population 5 Years and Over)

Group	Number	%
Total Population	337,658	88.4
Hispanic or Latino (of any race)	9,487	28.3
Central American, ex. Mexican	186	11.0
Dominican Republic	138	14.7
Mexican	2,215	56.7
Puerto Rican	5,814	24.1
South American	147	14.2

Language Spoken at Home: Spanish
(Universe: Population 5 Years and Over)

Group	Number	%
Total Population	27,262	7.1
Hispanic or Latino (of any race)	23,938	71.3
Central American, ex. Mexican	1,510	89.0
Dominican Republic	799	85.3
Mexican	1,690	43.3
Puerto Rican	18,269	75.7
South American	863	83.6

Unemployment Rate
(Universe: Population 16 Years and Over)

Group	%
Total Population	17.8
Hispanic or Latino (of any race)	17.4
Central American, ex. Mexican	2.2
Dominican Republic	21.0
Mexican	16.7
Puerto Rican	18.4
South American	12.4

Class of Worker: Private Wage and Salary
(Universe: Civilian Employed Population 16 Years and Over)

Group	Number	%
Total Population	126,822	80.4
Hispanic or Latino (of any race)	11,227	84.4
Central American, ex. Mexican	721	87.0
Dominican Republic	396	92.3
Mexican	1,544	84.6
Puerto Rican	7,566	83.8
South American	483	80.4

Class of Worker: Government
(Universe: Civilian Employed Population 16 Years and Over)

Group	Number	%
Total Population	24,589	15.6
Hispanic or Latino (of any race)	1,594	12.0
Central American, ex. Mexican	36	4.3
Dominican Republic	7	1.6
Mexican	174	9.5
Puerto Rican	1,212	13.4
South American	89	14.8

Means of Transportation to Work: Car, Truck or Van
(Universe: Workers 16 Years and Over)

Group	Number	%
Total Population	121,737	79.5
Hispanic or Latino (of any race)	10,597	82.5
Central American, ex. Mexican	647	86.7
Dominican Republic	375	87.4
Mexican	1,395	78.6
Puerto Rican	7,464	85.5
South American	404	67.2

Means of Transportation to Work: Public Transportation (ex. Taxicab)
(Universe: Workers 16 Years and Over)

Group	Number	%
Total Population	18,366	12.0
Hispanic or Latino (of any race)	1,178	9.2
Central American, ex. Mexican	38	5.1
Dominican Republic	20	4.7
Mexican	148	8.3
Puerto Rican	652	7.5
South American	195	32.4

Homeownership Rate
(Universe: Occupied Housing Units)

Group	%
Total Population	44.1
Hispanic or Latino (of any race)	38.5
Central American, ex. Mexican	45.3
Guatemalan	47.6
Honduran	36.3
Salvadoran	47.8
Cuban	33.3
Dominican Republic	38.3
Mexican	36.8
Puerto Rican	38.1
South American	47.9
Colombian	48.6
Ecuadorian	52.3
Peruvian	50.0
Spaniard	50.0

Median Home Value

Group	Dollars
Total Population	86,700
Hispanic or Latino (of any race)	87,900
Central American, ex. Mexican	105,800
Dominican Republic	92,800
Mexican	102,900
Puerto Rican	86,200
South American	67,100

Median Gross Rent

Group	Dollars
Total Population	628
Hispanic or Latino (of any race)	657
Central American, ex. Mexican	657
Dominican Republic	664
Mexican	702
Puerto Rican	659
South American	641

Median Household Income
(2010 Inflation-Adjusted Dollars)

Group	Dollars
Total Population	27,349
Hispanic or Latino (of any race)	26,103
Central American, ex. Mexican	34,825
Dominican Republic	21,755
Mexican	40,737
Puerto Rican	25,629
South American	26,563

Per Capita Income
(2010 Inflation-Adjusted Dollars)

Group	Dollars
Total Population	16,302
Hispanic or Latino (of any race)	11,648
Central American, ex. Mexican	13,379
Dominican Republic	9,901
Mexican	13,739
Puerto Rican	11,147
South American	16,690

Households with $100,000+ Income

Group	Number	%
Total Population	9,017	5.3
Hispanic or Latino (of any race)	423	3.5
Central American, ex. Mexican	0	0.0
Dominican Republic	0	0.0
Mexican	84	6.5
Puerto Rican	306	3.5
South American	21	4.6

Notes: (1) Percent of total population; (2) Percent of Hispanic/Latino population; Profiles include places with an overall population of at least 125,000, OR an overall population of at least 25,000 where the Hispanic/Latino population is at least 20% of the overall population. In states where less than five places meet either of these criteria, we have included places with at least 10,000 total population with the highest percentage of Hispanic/Latino population. These places are identified with an asterisk (*); Please refer to the User's Guide for a full explanation of data.

Households with Food Stamps/SNAP Benefits During Past 12 Months

Group	Number	%
Total Population	44,627	26.2
Hispanic or Latino (of any race)	4,434	36.8
Central American, ex. Mexican	163	26.1
Dominican Republic	167	48.5
Mexican	208	16.2
Puerto Rican	3,659	42.2
South American	104	22.6

Poverty Rate
(Income in Past 12 Months Below Poverty Level)

Group	%
Total Population	31.2
Hispanic or Latino (of any race)	37.0
Central American, ex. Mexican	28.2
Dominican Republic	30.3
Mexican	32.7
Puerto Rican	38.6
South American	22.5

Columbus

Population

Group	Number	%TP[1]	%HP[2]
Total Population	787,033	100.0	–
Hispanic or Latino (of any race)	44,359	5.6	100.0
Central American, ex. Mexican	4,017	0.5	9.1
Costa Rican	129	<0.1	0.3
Guatemalan	645	0.1	1.5
Honduran	784	0.1	1.8
Nicaraguan	157	<0.1	0.4
Panamanian	294	<0.1	0.7
Salvadoran	1,954	0.2	4.4
Cuban	922	0.1	2.1
Dominican Republic	1,553	0.2	3.5
Mexican	25,973	3.3	58.6
Puerto Rican	5,034	0.6	11.3
South American	2,730	0.3	6.2
Argentinean	273	<0.1	0.6
Chilean	112	<0.1	0.3
Colombian	797	0.1	1.8
Ecuadorian	491	0.1	1.1
Peruvian	543	0.1	1.2
Venezuelan	355	<0.1	0.8
Spaniard	561	0.1	1.3

Population Growth: 2000–2010

Group	%
Total Population	10.6
Hispanic or Latino (of any race)	153.9
Central American, ex. Mexican	286.3
Guatemalan	460.9
Honduran	625.9
Panamanian	69.9
Salvadoran	329.5
Cuban	47.0
Dominican Republic	421.1
Mexican	199.0
Puerto Rican	80.4
South American	189.2
Colombian	175.8
Peruvian	203.4
Venezuelan	97.2

Males per 100 Females

Group	Number
Total Population	95.4
Hispanic or Latino (of any race)	117.1
Central American, ex. Mexican	121.4
Costa Rican	115.0
Guatemalan	152.9
Honduran	107.4
Nicaraguan	82.6
Panamanian	81.5
Salvadoran	128.8
Cuban	101.3
Dominican Republic	92.7
Mexican	128.4
Puerto Rican	91.0
South American	99.1
Argentinean	105.3
Chilean	69.7
Colombian	93.4
Ecuadorian	116.3
Peruvian	97.5
Venezuelan	88.8
Spaniard	80.4

Average Household Size

Group	People
Total Population	2.31
Hispanic or Latino (of any race)	3.20
Central American, ex. Mexican	3.49
Costa Rican	3.21
Guatemalan	3.64
Honduran	3.40
Nicaraguan	2.79
Panamanian	2.62
Salvadoran	3.75
Cuban	2.41
Dominican Republic	3.15
Mexican	3.49
Puerto Rican	2.60
South American	2.63
Argentinean	2.35
Chilean	2.18
Colombian	2.46
Ecuadorian	3.23
Peruvian	2.59
Venezuelan	2.69
Spaniard	2.19

Median Age

Group	Years
Total Population	31.2
Hispanic or Latino (of any race)	24.6
Central American, ex. Mexican	26.9
Costa Rican	29.5
Guatemalan	24.7
Honduran	26.0
Nicaraguan	28.3
Panamanian	30.8
Salvadoran	27.4
Cuban	26.6
Dominican Republic	25.4
Mexican	24.0
Puerto Rican	23.7
South American	29.8
Argentinean	29.3
Chilean	32.3
Colombian	29.2
Ecuadorian	28.2
Peruvian	31.3
Venezuelan	30.5
Spaniard	30.3

High School Graduates
(Universe: Population 25 Years and Over)

Group	Number	%
Total Population	424,643	87.3
Hispanic or Latino (of any race)	12,846	66.6
Central American, ex. Mexican	1,283	51.0
Guatemalan	318	55.3
Salvadoran	317	29.0
Cuban	331	82.5
Dominican Republic	751	87.9
Mexican	6,986	60.6
Puerto Rican	1,402	85.8
South American	1,270	94.8

Four-Year College Graduates
(Universe: Population 25 Years and Over)

Group	Number	%
Total Population	155,161	31.9
Hispanic or Latino (of any race)	3,032	15.7
Central American, ex. Mexican	276	11.0
Guatemalan	92	16.0
Salvadoran	21	1.9
Cuban	165	41.1
Dominican Republic	85	10.0
Mexican	1,311	11.4
Puerto Rican	389	23.8
South American	543	40.5

Population Age 3–17 Enrolled in Public School
(Universe: Population Age 3–17 Enrolled in School)

Group	Number	%
Total Population	109,490	86.7
Hispanic or Latino (of any race)	7,489	90.0
Central American, ex. Mexican	617	80.0
Guatemalan	121	59.6
Salvadoran	342	91.7
Cuban	141	100.0
Dominican Republic	229	100.0
Mexican	5,104	93.3
Puerto Rican	895	82.5
South American	176	66.2

Population Age 3–17 Enrolled in Private School
(Universe: Population Age 3–17 Enrolled in School)

Group	Number	%
Total Population	16,744	13.3
Hispanic or Latino (of any race)	830	10.0
Central American, ex. Mexican	154	20.0
Guatemalan	82	40.4
Salvadoran	31	8.3
Cuban	0	0.0
Dominican Republic	0	0.0
Mexican	367	6.7
Puerto Rican	190	17.5
South American	90	33.8

Foreign-Born Population

Group	Number	%
Total Population	78,121	10.1
Hispanic or Latino (of any race)	19,291	49.3
Central American, ex. Mexican	3,019	64.3
Guatemalan	825	64.8
Salvadoran	1,491	73.0
Cuban	307	36.5
Dominican Republic	773	60.9
Mexican	13,315	53.9
Puerto Rican	46	1.3
South American	1,229	60.0

Foreign-Born Naturalized U.S. Citizens

Group	Number	%
Total Population	25,180	32.2
Hispanic or Latino (of any race)	2,983	15.5
Central American, ex. Mexican	607	20.1
Guatemalan	150	18.2
Salvadoran	152	10.2
Cuban	178	58.0
Dominican Republic	377	48.8
Mexican	1,384	10.4
Puerto Rican	11	23.9
South American	358	29.1

Language Spoken at Home: English Only
(Universe: Population 5 Years and Over)

Group	Number	%
Total Population	622,574	87.4
Hispanic or Latino (of any race)	8,790	26.2
Central American, ex. Mexican	852	20.6
Guatemalan	86	8.8
Salvadoran	139	7.5
Cuban	331	47.0
Dominican Republic	53	4.3
Mexican	4,235	20.3
Puerto Rican	1,618	53.7
South American	706	37.0

Language Spoken at Home: Spanish
(Universe: Population 5 Years and Over)

Group	Number	%
Total Population	30,861	4.3
Hispanic or Latino (of any race)	24,651	73.5
Central American, ex. Mexican	3,288	79.4
Guatemalan	893	91.2
Salvadoran	1,711	92.5
Cuban	373	53.0
Dominican Republic	1,170	95.7
Mexican	16,581	79.6
Puerto Rican	1,381	45.8
South American	1,193	62.5

Notes: (1) Percent of total population; (2) Percent of Hispanic/Latino population; Profiles include places with an overall population of at least 125,000, OR an overall population of at least 25,000 where the Hispanic/Latino population is at least 20% of the overall population. In states where less than five places meet either of these criteria, we have included places with at least 10,000 total population with the highest percentage of Hispanic/Latino population. These places are identified with an asterisk (*); Please refer to the User's Guide for a full explanation of data.

Unemployment Rate
(Universe: Population 16 Years and Over)

Group	%
Total Population	8.9
Hispanic or Latino (of any race)	7.4
Central American, ex. Mexican	5.6
Guatemalan	4.9
Salvadoran	9.6
Cuban	8.2
Dominican Republic	3.0
Mexican	7.1
Puerto Rican	13.0
South American	8.4

Class of Worker: Private Wage and Salary
(Universe: Civilian Employed Population 16 Years and Over)

Group	Number	%
Total Population	312,773	80.3
Hispanic or Latino (of any race)	16,766	91.7
Central American, ex. Mexican	2,290	90.5
Guatemalan	585	98.2
Salvadoran	988	97.9
Cuban	278	70.7
Dominican Republic	730	86.6
Mexican	10,723	96.5
Puerto Rican	1,098	80.0
South American	934	82.9

Class of Worker: Government
(Universe: Civilian Employed Population 16 Years and Over)

Group	Number	%
Total Population	61,372	15.8
Hispanic or Latino (of any race)	1,067	5.8
Central American, ex. Mexican	96	3.8
Guatemalan	0	0.0
Salvadoran	0	0.0
Cuban	104	26.5
Dominican Republic	65	7.7
Mexican	290	2.6
Puerto Rican	139	10.1
South American	180	16.0

Means of Transportation to Work: Car, Truck or Van
(Universe: Workers 16 Years and Over)

Group	Number	%
Total Population	339,232	89.3
Hispanic or Latino (of any race)	16,412	92.5
Central American, ex. Mexican	2,224	93.6
Guatemalan	596	100.0
Salvadoran	894	91.7
Cuban	369	96.6
Dominican Republic	746	93.8
Mexican	10,130	93.3
Puerto Rican	1,217	92.0
South American	963	86.4

Means of Transportation to Work: Public Transportation (ex. Taxicab)
(Universe: Workers 16 Years and Over)

Group	Number	%
Total Population	11,625	3.1
Hispanic or Latino (of any race)	360	2.0
Central American, ex. Mexican	95	4.0
Guatemalan	0	0.0
Salvadoran	24	2.5
Cuban	0	0.0
Dominican Republic	12	1.5
Mexican	196	1.8
Puerto Rican	11	0.8
South American	35	3.1

Homeownership Rate
(Universe: Occupied Housing Units)

Group	%
Total Population	47.0
Hispanic or Latino (of any race)	26.5
Central American, ex. Mexican	29.1
Costa Rican	23.8
Guatemalan	21.7
Honduran	26.9
Nicaraguan	25.0
Panamanian	45.9
Salvadoran	29.3
Cuban	35.7
Dominican Republic	31.3
Mexican	22.4
Puerto Rican	29.4
South American	40.9
Argentinean	42.6
Chilean	48.9
Colombian	38.2
Ecuadorian	37.8
Peruvian	45.2
Venezuelan	40.4
Spaniard	37.4

Median Home Value

Group	Dollars
Total Population	138,700
Hispanic or Latino (of any race)	135,800
Central American, ex. Mexican	124,100
Guatemalan	130,700
Salvadoran	102,500
Cuban	148,500
Dominican Republic	138,000
Mexican	122,100
Puerto Rican	165,600
South American	173,400

Median Gross Rent

Group	Dollars
Total Population	753
Hispanic or Latino (of any race)	721
Central American, ex. Mexican	655
Guatemalan	585
Salvadoran	684
Cuban	769
Dominican Republic	752
Mexican	722
Puerto Rican	784
South American	694

Median Household Income
(2010 Inflation-Adjusted Dollars)

Group	Dollars
Total Population	43,122
Hispanic or Latino (of any race)	32,579
Central American, ex. Mexican	35,035
Guatemalan	35,563
Salvadoran	28,385
Cuban	41,563
Dominican Republic	29,968
Mexican	31,084
Puerto Rican	39,583
South American	47,965

Per Capita Income
(2010 Inflation-Adjusted Dollars)

Group	Dollars
Total Population	23,144
Hispanic or Latino (of any race)	13,395
Central American, ex. Mexican	12,505
Guatemalan	10,601
Salvadoran	12,519
Cuban	20,525
Dominican Republic	15,040
Mexican	12,391
Puerto Rican	13,984
South American	21,296

Households with $100,000+ Income

Group	Number	%
Total Population	40,183	12.6
Hispanic or Latino (of any race)	916	8.1
Central American, ex. Mexican	114	9.7
Guatemalan	43	19.6
Salvadoran	37	6.9
Cuban	42	11.2
Dominican Republic	46	9.9
Mexican	374	5.5
Puerto Rican	123	10.0
South American	187	23.7

Households with Food Stamps/SNAP Benefits During Past 12 Months

Group	Number	%
Total Population	43,257	13.6
Hispanic or Latino (of any race)	2,120	18.8
Central American, ex. Mexican	150	12.7
Guatemalan	0	0.0
Salvadoran	85	15.8
Cuban	48	12.8
Dominican Republic	52	11.1
Mexican	1,442	21.4
Puerto Rican	236	19.1
South American	97	12.3

Poverty Rate
(Income in Past 12 Months Below Poverty Level)

Group	%
Total Population	21.4
Hispanic or Latino (of any race)	29.9
Central American, ex. Mexican	24.0
Guatemalan	17.0
Salvadoran	33.5
Cuban	23.3
Dominican Republic	17.4
Mexican	34.1
Puerto Rican	22.1
South American	21.8

Dayton

Population

Group	Number	%TP[1]	%HP[2]
Total Population	141,527	100.0	–
Hispanic or Latino (of any race)	4,180	3.0	100.0
Central American, ex. Mexican	269	0.2	6.4
Cuban	147	0.1	3.5
Mexican	2,541	1.8	60.8
Puerto Rican	515	0.4	12.3
South American	217	0.2	5.2
Ecuadorian	115	0.1	2.8

Population Growth: 2000–2010

Group	%
Total Population	-14.8
Hispanic or Latino (of any race)	59.2
Cuban	25.6
Mexican	86.8
Puerto Rican	12.9

Males per 100 Females

Group	Number
Total Population	95.0
Hispanic or Latino (of any race)	124.2
Central American, ex. Mexican	138.1
Cuban	126.2
Mexican	126.3
Puerto Rican	105.2
South American	126.0
Ecuadorian	180.5

Average Household Size

Group	People
Total Population	2.26
Hispanic or Latino (of any race)	3.04
Central American, ex. Mexican	2.81
Cuban	2.25
Mexican	3.40
Puerto Rican	2.68
South American	2.97
Ecuadorian	3.25

Median Age

Group	Years
Total Population	34.4
Hispanic or Latino (of any race)	24.5
Central American, ex. Mexican	28.1
Cuban	28.1
Mexican	23.7
Puerto Rican	22.4
South American	26.4
Ecuadorian	25.3

High School Graduates
(Universe: Population 25 Years and Over)

Group	Number	%
Total Population	73,389	81.1
Hispanic or Latino (of any race)	819	56.3
Mexican	455	47.1

Notes: (1) Percent of total population; (2) Percent of Hispanic/Latino population; Profiles include places with an overall population of at least 125,000, OR an overall population of at least 25,000 where the Hispanic/Latino population is at least 20% of the overall population. In states where less than five places meet either of these criteria, we have included places with at least 10,000 total population with the highest percentage of Hispanic/Latino population. These places are identified with an asterisk (*); Please refer to the User's Guide for a full explanation of data.

Four-Year College Graduates
(Universe: Population 25 Years and Over)

Group	Number	%
Total Population	13,871	15.3
Hispanic or Latino (of any race)	124	8.5
Mexican	60	6.2

Population Age 3–17 Enrolled in Public School
(Universe: Population Age 3–17 Enrolled in School)

Group	Number	%
Total Population	20,118	79.2
Hispanic or Latino (of any race)	823	80.9
Mexican	640	81.5

Population Age 3–17 Enrolled in Private School
(Universe: Population Age 3–17 Enrolled in School)

Group	Number	%
Total Population	5,294	20.8
Hispanic or Latino (of any race)	194	19.1
Mexican	145	18.5

Foreign-Born Population

Group	Number	%
Total Population	3,648	2.5
Hispanic or Latino (of any race)	1,276	38.0
Mexican	983	44.1

Foreign-Born Naturalized U.S. Citizens

Group	Number	%
Total Population	1,055	28.9
Hispanic or Latino (of any race)	101	7.9
Mexican	57	5.8

Language Spoken at Home: English Only
(Universe: Population 5 Years and Over)

Group	Number	%
Total Population	129,970	96.1
Hispanic or Latino (of any race)	885	31.2
Mexican	480	26.2

Language Spoken at Home: Spanish
(Universe: Population 5 Years and Over)

Group	Number	%
Total Population	2,691	2.0
Hispanic or Latino (of any race)	1,956	68.8
Mexican	1,355	73.8

Unemployment Rate
(Universe: Population 16 Years and Over)

Group	%
Total Population	16.1
Hispanic or Latino (of any race)	17.5
Mexican	16.0

Class of Worker: Private Wage and Salary
(Universe: Civilian Employed Population 16 Years and Over)

Group	Number	%
Total Population	46,288	79.9
Hispanic or Latino (of any race)	880	76.7
Mexican	613	79.9

Class of Worker: Government
(Universe: Civilian Employed Population 16 Years and Over)

Group	Number	%
Total Population	9,394	16.2
Hispanic or Latino (of any race)	124	10.8
Mexican	81	10.6

Means of Transportation to Work: Car, Truck or Van
(Universe: Workers 16 Years and Over)

Group	Number	%
Total Population	47,429	83.9
Hispanic or Latino (of any race)	836	73.8
Mexican	601	79.8

Means of Transportation to Work: Public Transportation (ex. Taxicab)
(Universe: Workers 16 Years and Over)

Group	Number	%
Total Population	3,665	6.5
Hispanic or Latino (of any race)	60	5.3
Mexican	20	2.7

Homeownership Rate
(Universe: Occupied Housing Units)

Group	%
Total Population	49.9
Hispanic or Latino (of any race)	34.8
Central American, ex. Mexican	21.5
Cuban	50.0
Mexican	31.8
Puerto Rican	41.6
South American	35.3
Ecuadorian	28.1

Median Home Value

Group	Dollars
Total Population	79,100
Hispanic or Latino (of any race)	91,000
Mexican	92,500

Median Gross Rent

Group	Dollars
Total Population	609
Hispanic or Latino (of any race)	621
Mexican	686

Median Household Income
(2010 Inflation-Adjusted Dollars)

Group	Dollars
Total Population	29,368
Hispanic or Latino (of any race)	30,058
Mexican	31,299

Per Capita Income
(2010 Inflation-Adjusted Dollars)

Group	Dollars
Total Population	16,702
Hispanic or Latino (of any race)	9,630
Mexican	9,022

Households with $100,000+ Income

Group	Number	%
Total Population	3,328	5.6
Hispanic or Latino (of any race)	32	4.2
Mexican	21	4.1

Households with Food Stamps/SNAP Benefits During Past 12 Months

Group	Number	%
Total Population	14,063	23.5
Hispanic or Latino (of any race)	197	26.0
Mexican	63	12.4

Poverty Rate
(Income in Past 12 Months Below Poverty Level)

Group	%
Total Population	31.0
Hispanic or Latino (of any race)	40.2
Mexican	39.0

Lorain

Population

Group	Number	%TP[1]	%HP[2]
Total Population	64,097	100.0	–
Hispanic or Latino (of any race)	16,177	25.2	100.0
Central American, ex. Mexican	118	0.2	0.7
Dominican Republic	115	0.2	0.7
Mexican	2,934	4.6	18.1
Puerto Rican	12,413	19.4	76.7

Population Growth: 2000–2010

Group	%
Total Population	-6.6
Hispanic or Latino (of any race)	12.0
Mexican	20.4
Puerto Rican	17.8

Males per 100 Females

Group	Number
Total Population	90.5
Hispanic or Latino (of any race)	97.7
Central American, ex. Mexican	76.1
Dominican Republic	94.9
Mexican	102.2
Puerto Rican	97.5

Average Household Size

Group	People
Total Population	2.48
Hispanic or Latino (of any race)	2.89
Central American, ex. Mexican	3.03
Dominican Republic	2.85
Mexican	3.03
Puerto Rican	2.88

Median Age

Group	Years
Total Population	36.8
Hispanic or Latino (of any race)	26.6
Central American, ex. Mexican	25.7
Dominican Republic	27.5
Mexican	25.6
Puerto Rican	26.6

High School Graduates
(Universe: Population 25 Years and Over)

Group	Number	%
Total Population	33,875	81.3
Hispanic or Latino (of any race)	5,627	68.1
Mexican	1,140	70.9
Puerto Rican	4,188	67.9

Four-Year College Graduates
(Universe: Population 25 Years and Over)

Group	Number	%
Total Population	4,984	12.0
Hispanic or Latino (of any race)	648	7.8
Mexican	145	9.0
Puerto Rican	433	7.0

Population Age 3–17 Enrolled in Public School
(Universe: Population Age 3–17 Enrolled in School)

Group	Number	%
Total Population	11,598	86.6
Hispanic or Latino (of any race)	3,967	85.1
Mexican	752	72.4
Puerto Rican	2,717	87.0

Population Age 3–17 Enrolled in Private School
(Universe: Population Age 3–17 Enrolled in School)

Group	Number	%
Total Population	1,789	13.4
Hispanic or Latino (of any race)	693	14.9
Mexican	286	27.6
Puerto Rican	407	13.0

Foreign-Born Population

Group	Number	%
Total Population	2,302	3.5
Hispanic or Latino (of any race)	931	5.7
Mexican	609	17.7
Puerto Rican	0	0.0

Foreign-Born Naturalized U.S. Citizens

Group	Number	%
Total Population	1,301	56.5
Hispanic or Latino (of any race)	231	24.8
Mexican	80	13.1
Puerto Rican	0	0.0

Language Spoken at Home: English Only
(Universe: Population 5 Years and Over)

Group	Number	%
Total Population	49,540	82.4
Hispanic or Latino (of any race)	6,236	43.0
Mexican	1,870	61.4
Puerto Rican	3,671	36.2

Language Spoken at Home: Spanish
(Universe: Population 5 Years and Over)

Group	Number	%
Total Population	8,710	14.5
Hispanic or Latino (of any race)	8,208	56.7
Mexican	1,174	38.6
Puerto Rican	6,466	63.7

Unemployment Rate
(Universe: Population 16 Years and Over)

Group	%
Total Population	15.0
Hispanic or Latino (of any race)	19.2
Mexican	12.5

Notes: (1) Percent of total population; (2) Percent of Hispanic/Latino population; Profiles include places with an overall population of at least 125,000, OR an overall population of at least 25,000 where the Hispanic/Latino population is at least 20% of the overall population. In states where less than five places meet either of these criteria, we have included places with at least 10,000 total population with the highest percentage of Hispanic/Latino population. These places are identified with an asterisk (*); Please refer to the User's Guide for a full explanation of data.

Puerto Rican		19.7

Class of Worker: Private Wage and Salary
(Universe: Civilian Employed Population 16 Years and Over)

Group	Number	%
Total Population	21,052	82.9
Hispanic or Latino (of any race)	4,373	81.3
Mexican	1,136	87.9
Puerto Rican	2,960	78.4

Class of Worker: Government
(Universe: Civilian Employed Population 16 Years and Over)

Group	Number	%
Total Population	3,254	12.8
Hispanic or Latino (of any race)	700	13.0
Mexican	88	6.8
Puerto Rican	578	15.3

Means of Transportation to Work: Car, Truck or Van
(Universe: Workers 16 Years and Over)

Group	Number	%
Total Population	23,746	95.8
Hispanic or Latino (of any race)	5,104	96.3
Mexican	1,219	94.3
Puerto Rican	3,616	97.2

Means of Transportation to Work: Public Transportation (ex. Taxicab)
(Universe: Workers 16 Years and Over)

Group	Number	%
Total Population	219	0.9
Hispanic or Latino (of any race)	20	0.4
Mexican	0	0.0
Puerto Rican	11	0.3

Homeownership Rate
(Universe: Occupied Housing Units)

Group	%
Total Population	57.8
Hispanic or Latino (of any race)	47.4
Central American, ex. Mexican	24.2
Dominican Republic	41.0
Mexican	55.4
Puerto Rican	46.1

Median Home Value

Group	Dollars
Total Population	104,700
Hispanic or Latino (of any race)	96,700
Mexican	108,500
Puerto Rican	94,100

Median Gross Rent

Group	Dollars
Total Population	608
Hispanic or Latino (of any race)	568
Mexican	671
Puerto Rican	532

Median Household Income
(2010 Inflation-Adjusted Dollars)

Group	Dollars
Total Population	35,353
Hispanic or Latino (of any race)	28,495
Mexican	34,975
Puerto Rican	26,412

Per Capita Income
(2010 Inflation-Adjusted Dollars)

Group	Dollars
Total Population	18,212
Hispanic or Latino (of any race)	12,685
Mexican	15,487
Puerto Rican	12,359

Households with $100,000+ Income

Group	Number	%
Total Population	2,271	8.8
Hispanic or Latino (of any race)	289	5.4
Mexican	99	10.0
Puerto Rican	168	4.3

Households with Food Stamps/SNAP Benefits During Past 12 Months

Group	Number	%
Total Population	5,775	22.3
Hispanic or Latino (of any race)	1,825	34.3
Mexican	276	27.8
Puerto Rican	1,440	36.5

Poverty Rate
(Income in Past 12 Months Below Poverty Level)

Group	%
Total Population	27.9
Hispanic or Latino (of any race)	35.5
Mexican	30.1
Puerto Rican	36.5

Toledo

Population

Group	Number	%TP[1]	%HP[2]
Total Population	287,208	100.0	–
Hispanic or Latino (of any race)	21,231	7.4	100.0
Central American, ex. Mexican	240	0.1	1.1
Cuban	299	0.1	1.4
Mexican	17,576	6.1	82.8
Puerto Rican	1,143	0.4	5.4
South American	219	0.1	1.0
Spaniard	166	0.1	0.8

Population Growth: 2000–2010

Group	%
Total Population	-8.4
Hispanic or Latino (of any race)	23.9
Central American, ex. Mexican	58.9
Cuban	65.2
Mexican	32.0
Puerto Rican	54.0
South American	37.7

Males per 100 Females

Group	Number
Total Population	93.8
Hispanic or Latino (of any race)	98.1
Central American, ex. Mexican	72.7
Cuban	96.7
Mexican	98.9
Puerto Rican	99.5
South American	87.2
Spaniard	80.4

Average Household Size

Group	People
Total Population	2.33
Hispanic or Latino (of any race)	2.98
Central American, ex. Mexican	3.43
Cuban	2.68
Mexican	3.03
Puerto Rican	2.80
South American	2.46
Spaniard	2.11

Median Age

Group	Years
Total Population	34.2
Hispanic or Latino (of any race)	22.4
Central American, ex. Mexican	28.0
Cuban	25.4
Mexican	22.2
Puerto Rican	21.2
South American	25.9
Spaniard	27.6

High School Graduates
(Universe: Population 25 Years and Over)

Group	Number	%
Total Population	155,877	84.5
Hispanic or Latino (of any race)	5,910	67.8
Mexican	4,216	65.3
Puerto Rican	442	65.1

Four-Year College Graduates
(Universe: Population 25 Years and Over)

Group	Number	%
Total Population	32,469	17.6
Hispanic or Latino (of any race)	819	9.4
Mexican	471	7.3
Puerto Rican	66	9.7

Population Age 3–17 Enrolled in Public School
(Universe: Population Age 3–17 Enrolled in School)

Group	Number	%
Total Population	41,867	80.7
Hispanic or Latino (of any race)	5,029	85.0
Mexican	3,960	83.2
Puerto Rican	373	100.0

Population Age 3–17 Enrolled in Private School
(Universe: Population Age 3–17 Enrolled in School)

Group	Number	%
Total Population	10,043	19.3
Hispanic or Latino (of any race)	886	15.0
Mexican	799	16.8
Puerto Rican	0	0.0

Foreign-Born Population

Group	Number	%
Total Population	10,299	3.5
Hispanic or Latino (of any race)	2,375	11.9
Mexican	1,661	10.9
Puerto Rican	0	0.0

Foreign-Born Naturalized U.S. Citizens

Group	Number	%
Total Population	4,691	45.5
Hispanic or Latino (of any race)	770	32.4
Mexican	388	23.4
Puerto Rican	0	0.0

Language Spoken at Home: English Only
(Universe: Population 5 Years and Over)

Group	Number	%
Total Population	253,227	93.5
Hispanic or Latino (of any race)	10,892	63.8
Mexican	8,626	66.0
Puerto Rican	848	63.6

Language Spoken at Home: Spanish
(Universe: Population 5 Years and Over)

Group	Number	%
Total Population	8,314	3.1
Hispanic or Latino (of any race)	6,135	36.0
Mexican	4,425	33.9
Puerto Rican	485	36.4

Unemployment Rate
(Universe: Population 16 Years and Over)

Group	%
Total Population	15.0
Hispanic or Latino (of any race)	20.6
Mexican	18.9
Puerto Rican	36.0

Class of Worker: Private Wage and Salary
(Universe: Civilian Employed Population 16 Years and Over)

Group	Number	%
Total Population	103,662	82.7
Hispanic or Latino (of any race)	5,838	89.1
Mexican	4,363	89.5
Puerto Rican	474	87.0

Class of Worker: Government
(Universe: Civilian Employed Population 16 Years and Over)

Group	Number	%
Total Population	16,290	13.0
Hispanic or Latino (of any race)	547	8.3
Mexican	398	8.2
Puerto Rican	71	13.0

Means of Transportation to Work: Car, Truck or Van
(Universe: Workers 16 Years and Over)

Group	Number	%
Total Population	111,970	91.7
Hispanic or Latino (of any race)	6,113	96.0
Mexican	4,544	95.7
Puerto Rican	454	92.5

Notes: (1) Percent of total population; (2) Percent of Hispanic/Latino population; Profiles include places with an overall population of at least 125,000, OR an overall population of at least 25,000 where the Hispanic/Latino population is at least 20% of the overall population. In states where less than five places meet either of these criteria, we have included places with at least 10,000 total population with the highest percentage of Hispanic/Latino population. These places are identified with an asterisk (*); Please refer to the User's Guide for a full explanation of data.

Means of Transportation to Work: Public Transportation (ex. Taxicab) (Universe: Workers 16 Years and Over)		
Group	Number	%
Total Population	3,000	2.5
Hispanic or Latino (of any race)	108	1.7
Mexican	98	2.1
Puerto Rican	0	0.0

Homeownership Rate (Universe: Occupied Housing Units)	
Group	%
Total Population	55.5
Hispanic or Latino (of any race)	46.4
Central American, ex. Mexican	54.0
Cuban	51.5
Mexican	47.2
Puerto Rican	41.6
South American	47.7
Spaniard	53.8

Median Home Value	
Group	Dollars
Total Population	96,500
Hispanic or Latino (of any race)	83,600
Mexican	81,200
Puerto Rican	82,400

Median Gross Rent	
Group	Dollars
Total Population	617
Hispanic or Latino (of any race)	632
Mexican	614
Puerto Rican	642

Median Household Income (2010 Inflation-Adjusted Dollars)	
Group	Dollars
Total Population	34,260
Hispanic or Latino (of any race)	33,433
Mexican	33,962
Puerto Rican	25,833

Per Capita Income (2010 Inflation-Adjusted Dollars)	
Group	Dollars
Total Population	18,758
Hispanic or Latino (of any race)	11,735
Mexican	11,445
Puerto Rican	13,206

Households with $100,000+ Income		
Group	Number	%
Total Population	9,293	7.7
Hispanic or Latino (of any race)	334	6.4
Mexican	204	5.4
Puerto Rican	64	14.7

Households with Food Stamps/SNAP Benefits During Past 12 Months		
Group	Number	%
Total Population	23,865	19.8
Hispanic or Latino (of any race)	1,548	29.6
Mexican	957	25.6
Puerto Rican	149	34.3

Poverty Rate (Income in Past 12 Months Below Poverty Level)	
Group	%
Total Population	23.8
Hispanic or Latino (of any race)	30.9
Mexican	28.9
Puerto Rican	35.9

Notes: (1) Percent of total population; (2) Percent of Hispanic/Latino population; Profiles include places with an overall population of at least 125,000, OR an overall population of at least 25,000 where the Hispanic/Latino population is at least 20% of the overall population. In states where less than five places meet either of these criteria, we have included places with at least 10,000 total population with the highest percentage of Hispanic/Latino population. These places are identified with an asterisk (*); Please refer to the User's Guide for a full explanation of data.

Oklahoma

EDITOR'S NOTE: For a place to be included in this edition, it must meet one of two criteria. Either its overall population is at least 125,000, OR its overall population is at least 25,000 and its Hispanic/Latino population is at least 20% of the overall population. In Oklahoma, less than five places meet either of these criteria. In an effort to include at least five places for each state, we have included places with at least 10,000 total population with the highest percentage of Hispanic/Latino population. These places are identified with an asterisk (*). For the state of Oklahoma, the following locations are included:

- Altus*
- Guymon*
- Oklahoma City
- Tulsa
- Warr Acres*

Section Two: State & Place Profiles starts with the state profile, followed by place profiles that meet the criteria above. Places are listed alphabetically within each state. All states, all counties and places that meet the above criteria are ranked and compared in *Section Three: Rankings & Comparisons*, on page 1055.

For a more detailed look at the Hispanic/Latino population in Oklahoma, a companion web site is available at no additional charge with purchase of this print edition. Visit http://gold.greyhouse.com/page/info_hispanic for more information.

The web site includes data for all counties and places in Oklahoma with Hispanic/Latino population, plus ten additional topics: Self Employed Worker; Walked to Work; Worked from Home; Mean Travel Time to Work; Mean Household Income; Households with Cash Public Assistance; Mean Cash Pubic Assistance; Poverty Rates for 18 and Under, 18 to 64, and 65 and Over.

Population

Group	Number	%TP[1]	%HP[2]
Total Population	3,751,351	100.0	–
Hispanic or Latino (of any race)	332,007	8.9	100.0
Central American, ex. Mexican	15,641	0.4	4.7
Costa Rican	413	<0.1	0.1
Guatemalan	7,960	0.2	2.4
Honduran	2,711	0.1	0.8
Nicaraguan	470	<0.1	0.1
Panamanian	1,122	<0.1	0.3
Salvadoran	2,788	0.1	0.8
Cuban	2,755	0.1	0.8
Dominican Republic	727	<0.1	0.2
Mexican	267,016	7.1	80.4
Puerto Rican	12,223	0.3	3.7
South American	7,134	0.2	2.1
Argentinean	590	<0.1	0.2
Bolivian	300	<0.1	0.1
Chilean	289	<0.1	0.1
Colombian	2,122	0.1	0.6
Ecuadorian	474	<0.1	0.1
Peruvian	1,805	<0.1	0.5
Venezuelan	1,352	<0.1	0.4
Spaniard	5,047	0.1	1.5

Population Growth: 2000–2010

Group	%
Total Population	8.7
Hispanic or Latino (of any race)	85.2
Central American, ex. Mexican	259.7
Costa Rican	60.1
Guatemalan	332.8
Honduran	296.9
Nicaraguan	178.1
Panamanian	52.7
Salvadoran	421.1
Cuban	56.6
Dominican Republic	170.3
Mexican	101.0
Puerto Rican	49.9
South American	122.1
Argentinean	130.5
Bolivian	120.6
Colombian	146.5
Ecuadorian	87.4
Peruvian	140.3
Venezuelan	92.6
Spaniard	913.5

Males per 100 Females

Group	Number
Total Population	98.0
Hispanic or Latino (of any race)	114.1
Central American, ex. Mexican	131.3
Costa Rican	95.7
Guatemalan	146.3
Honduran	136.4
Nicaraguan	97.5
Panamanian	77.3
Salvadoran	125.2
Cuban	115.1
Dominican Republic	106.5
Mexican	115.7
Puerto Rican	105.8
South American	83.5
Argentinean	113.8
Bolivian	96.1
Chilean	80.6
Colombian	77.1
Ecuadorian	74.3
Peruvian	78.7
Venezuelan	92.0
Spaniard	88.1

Average Household Size

Group	People
Total Population	2.49
Hispanic or Latino (of any race)	3.43
Central American, ex. Mexican	3.64
Costa Rican	2.70
Guatemalan	4.02
Honduran	3.62
Nicaraguan	3.03
Panamanian	2.55
Salvadoran	3.45
Cuban	2.65
Dominican Republic	2.98
Mexican	3.54
Puerto Rican	2.84
South American	2.73
Argentinean	2.75
Bolivian	2.62
Chilean	2.74
Colombian	2.69
Ecuadorian	2.65
Peruvian	2.89
Venezuelan	2.69
Spaniard	2.72

Median Age

Group	Years
Total Population	36.2
Hispanic or Latino (of any race)	23.4
Central American, ex. Mexican	26.7
Costa Rican	30.9
Guatemalan	25.7
Honduran	28.1
Nicaraguan	29.8
Panamanian	29.8
Salvadoran	27.4
Cuban	28.1
Dominican Republic	22.8
Mexican	22.7
Puerto Rican	23.9
South American	31.0
Argentinean	31.5
Bolivian	29.4
Chilean	28.0
Colombian	29.3
Ecuadorian	30.1
Peruvian	34.0
Venezuelan	30.9
Spaniard	28.3

High School Graduates
(Universe: Population 25 Years and Over)

Group	Number	%
Total Population	2,032,584	85.4
Hispanic or Latino (of any race)	78,993	56.1
Central American, ex. Mexican	3,808	48.1
Guatemalan	1,136	29.8
Honduran	820	54.3
Panamanian	592	96.3
Salvadoran	741	54.4
Cuban	852	77.0
Mexican	59,278	52.3
Puerto Rican	4,207	85.2
South American	3,705	92.0
Colombian	886	90.5
Ecuadorian	488	100.0
Peruvian	1,016	90.3
Venezuelan	755	93.0
Spaniard	2,255	84.1

Four-Year College Graduates
(Universe: Population 25 Years and Over)

Group	Number	%
Total Population	538,182	22.6
Hispanic or Latino (of any race)	13,311	9.5
Central American, ex. Mexican	917	11.6
Guatemalan	285	7.5
Honduran	128	8.5
Panamanian	211	34.3
Salvadoran	220	16.1
Cuban	294	26.6
Mexican	7,951	7.0
Puerto Rican	1,069	21.7
South American	1,516	37.7
Colombian	338	34.5
Ecuadorian	153	31.4
Peruvian	330	29.3
Venezuelan	364	44.8
Spaniard	546	20.4

Population Age 3–17 Enrolled in Public School
(Universe: Population Age 3–17 Enrolled in School)

Group	Number	%
Total Population	617,714	91.1
Hispanic or Latino (of any race)	77,477	95.2
Central American, ex. Mexican	2,686	95.4
Guatemalan	1,153	96.2
Honduran	465	96.5
Panamanian	91	64.1
Salvadoran	560	97.2
Cuban	208	65.4
Mexican	65,771	95.8
Puerto Rican	2,672	91.8
South American	1,513	90.0
Colombian	145	96.7
Ecuadorian	295	84.5
Peruvian	524	88.8
Venezuelan	352	95.9
Spaniard	1,208	95.2

Population Age 3–17 Enrolled in Private School
(Universe: Population Age 3–17 Enrolled in School)

Group	Number	%
Total Population	60,097	8.9
Hispanic or Latino (of any race)	3,898	4.8
Central American, ex. Mexican	129	4.6
Guatemalan	45	3.8
Honduran	17	3.5
Panamanian	51	35.9
Salvadoran	16	2.8
Cuban	110	34.6
Mexican	2,912	4.2
Puerto Rican	240	8.2

STATE & PLACE PROFILES

Notes: (1) Percent of total population; (2) Percent of Hispanic/Latino population; Profiles include places with an overall population of at least 125,000, OR an overall population of at least 25,000 where the Hispanic/Latino population is at least 20% of the overall population. In states where less than five places meet either of these criteria, we have included places with at least 10,000 total population with the highest percentage of Hispanic/Latino population. These places are identified with an asterisk (*); Please refer to the User's Guide for a full explanation of data.

Group	Number	%
South American	169	10.0
Colombian	5	3.3
Ecuadorian	54	15.5
Peruvian	66	11.2
Venezuelan	15	4.1
Spaniard	61	4.8

Foreign-Born Population

Group	Number	%
Total Population	192,788	5.2
Hispanic or Latino (of any race)	111,054	36.8
Central American, ex. Mexican	9,608	63.7
Guatemalan	5,252	70.1
Honduran	2,040	69.2
Panamanian	397	38.1
Salvadoran	1,351	56.8
Cuban	624	31.8
Mexican	93,461	37.6
Puerto Rican	183	1.8
South American	4,324	59.2
Colombian	983	63.5
Ecuadorian	623	64.7
Peruvian	1,233	56.8
Venezuelan	882	59.0
Spaniard	723	13.9

Foreign-Born Naturalized U.S. Citizens

Group	Number	%
Total Population	62,165	32.2
Hispanic or Latino (of any race)	20,977	18.9
Central American, ex. Mexican	1,864	19.4
Guatemalan	517	9.8
Honduran	480	23.5
Panamanian	199	50.1
Salvadoran	363	26.9
Cuban	299	47.9
Mexican	16,047	17.2
Puerto Rican	90	49.2
South American	1,624	37.6
Colombian	377	38.4
Ecuadorian	212	34.0
Peruvian	544	44.1
Venezuelan	139	15.8
Spaniard	268	37.1

Language Spoken at Home: English Only
(Universe: Population 5 Years and Over)

Group	Number	%
Total Population	3,117,161	91.2
Hispanic or Latino (of any race)	84,954	32.6
Central American, ex. Mexican	2,031	15.4
Guatemalan	554	8.8
Honduran	164	6.5
Panamanian	509	54.3
Salvadoran	307	13.7
Cuban	818	46.9
Mexican	64,750	30.4
Puerto Rican	5,234	56.2
South American	1,907	28.0
Colombian	413	28.5
Ecuadorian	380	43.2
Peruvian	637	31.2
Venezuelan	147	10.3
Spaniard	3,128	68.9

Language Spoken at Home: Spanish
(Universe: Population 5 Years and Over)

Group	Number	%
Total Population	200,871	5.9
Hispanic or Latino (of any race)	174,875	67.1
Central American, ex. Mexican	11,133	84.6
Guatemalan	5,739	91.2
Honduran	2,351	93.5
Panamanian	428	45.7
Salvadoran	1,933	86.3
Cuban	911	52.2
Mexican	147,995	69.4
Puerto Rican	4,024	43.2
South American	4,885	71.8
Colombian	1,036	71.5
Ecuadorian	499	56.8
Peruvian	1,403	68.8
Venezuelan	1,275	89.7
Spaniard	1,311	28.9

Unemployment Rate
(Universe: Population 16 Years and Over)

Group	%
Total Population	6.2
Hispanic or Latino (of any race)	6.5
Central American, ex. Mexican	5.2
Guatemalan	3.8
Honduran	5.0
Panamanian	7.0
Salvadoran	9.3
Cuban	16.0
Mexican	6.1
Puerto Rican	11.1
South American	5.4
Colombian	7.9
Ecuadorian	1.7
Peruvian	0.9
Venezuelan	11.1
Spaniard	12.0

Class of Worker: Private Wage and Salary
(Universe: Civilian Employed Population 16 Years and Over)

Group	Number	%
Total Population	1,260,965	75.3
Hispanic or Latino (of any race)	107,466	86.0
Central American, ex. Mexican	7,171	90.4
Guatemalan	3,765	91.9
Honduran	1,477	96.4
Panamanian	446	76.6
Salvadoran	1,035	84.8
Cuban	806	85.7
Mexican	87,680	86.7
Puerto Rican	3,056	75.3
South American	2,958	80.9
Colombian	652	74.6
Ecuadorian	327	82.0
Peruvian	1,036	92.5
Venezuelan	501	69.7
Spaniard	1,586	79.4

Class of Worker: Government
(Universe: Civilian Employed Population 16 Years and Over)

Group	Number	%
Total Population	285,562	17.1
Hispanic or Latino (of any race)	10,715	8.6
Central American, ex. Mexican	362	4.6
Guatemalan	75	1.8
Honduran	22	1.4
Panamanian	130	22.3
Salvadoran	107	8.8
Cuban	86	9.1
Mexican	7,952	7.9
Puerto Rican	905	22.3
South American	347	9.5
Colombian	148	16.9
Ecuadorian	54	13.5
Peruvian	21	1.9
Venezuelan	38	5.3
Spaniard	346	17.3

Means of Transportation to Work: Car, Truck or Van
(Universe: Workers 16 Years and Over)

Group	Number	%
Total Population	1,529,604	92.4
Hispanic or Latino (of any race)	115,417	93.2
Central American, ex. Mexican	7,408	93.6
Guatemalan	3,874	95.5
Honduran	1,350	88.0
Panamanian	598	98.0
Salvadoran	1,102	91.8
Cuban	762	81.6
Mexican	93,226	93.8
Puerto Rican	3,985	89.8
South American	3,301	89.4
Colombian	926	97.2
Ecuadorian	411	97.6
Peruvian	894	80.6
Venezuelan	643	91.5
Spaniard	1,932	96.2

Means of Transportation to Work: Public Transportation (ex. Taxicab)
(Universe: Workers 16 Years and Over)

Group	Number	%
Total Population	7,672	0.5
Hispanic or Latino (of any race)	817	0.7
Central American, ex. Mexican	39	0.5
Guatemalan	25	0.6
Honduran	0	0.0
Panamanian	0	0.0
Salvadoran	0	0.0
Cuban	0	0.0
Mexican	617	0.6
Puerto Rican	17	0.4
South American	83	2.2
Colombian	0	0.0
Ecuadorian	0	0.0
Peruvian	46	4.1
Venezuelan	0	0.0
Spaniard	0	0.0

Homeownership Rate
(Universe: Occupied Housing Units)

Group	%
Total Population	67.2
Hispanic or Latino (of any race)	48.8
Central American, ex. Mexican	41.2
Costa Rican	50.7
Guatemalan	33.1
Honduran	38.4
Nicaraguan	57.2
Panamanian	59.2
Salvadoran	53.0
Cuban	53.8
Dominican Republic	43.0
Mexican	48.9
Puerto Rican	49.3
South American	57.2
Argentinean	62.7
Bolivian	57.7
Chilean	51.5
Colombian	56.1
Ecuadorian	58.3
Peruvian	58.9
Venezuelan	54.8
Spaniard	59.4

Median Home Value

Group	Dollars
Total Population	104,300
Hispanic or Latino (of any race)	79,100
Central American, ex. Mexican	94,100
Guatemalan	87,300
Honduran	91,600
Panamanian	119,200
Salvadoran	89,700
Cuban	156,100
Mexican	72,200
Puerto Rican	129,800
South American	123,600
Colombian	115,100
Ecuadorian	88,700
Peruvian	99,300
Venezuelan	147,800
Spaniard	107,100

Median Gross Rent

Group	Dollars
Total Population	633
Hispanic or Latino (of any race)	613
Central American, ex. Mexican	618
Guatemalan	608
Honduran	599
Panamanian	709
Salvadoran	677
Cuban	630
Mexican	604
Puerto Rican	650
South American	670
Colombian	664
Ecuadorian	580
Peruvian	636
Venezuelan	779
Spaniard	627

Notes: (1) Percent of total population; (2) Percent of Hispanic/Latino population; Profiles include places with an overall population of at least 125,000, OR an overall population of at least 25,000 where the Hispanic/Latino population is at least 20% of the overall population. In states where less than five places meet either of these criteria, we have included places with at least 10,000 total population with the highest percentage of Hispanic/Latino population. These places are identified with an asterisk (*); Please refer to the User's Guide for a full explanation of data.

Median Household Income (2010 Inflation-Adjusted Dollars)	
Group	Dollars
Total Population	42,979
Hispanic or Latino (of any race)	34,193
Central American, ex. Mexican	32,799
Guatemalan	32,897
Honduran	28,446
Panamanian	44,844
Salvadoran	35,125
Cuban	47,679
Mexican	33,683
Puerto Rican	54,541
South American	33,642
Colombian	35,579
Ecuadorian	33,750
Peruvian	30,115
Venezuelan	45,375
Spaniard	39,494

Per Capita Income (2010 Inflation-Adjusted Dollars)	
Group	Dollars
Total Population	23,094
Hispanic or Latino (of any race)	12,191
Central American, ex. Mexican	12,959
Guatemalan	11,194
Honduran	14,083
Panamanian	20,137
Salvadoran	13,555
Cuban	18,686
Mexican	11,524
Puerto Rican	18,445
South American	17,280
Colombian	16,976
Ecuadorian	12,331
Peruvian	14,747
Venezuelan	19,811
Spaniard	16,167

Households with $100,000+ Income		
Group	Number	%
Total Population	195,581	13.8
Hispanic or Latino (of any race)	4,696	6.0
Central American, ex. Mexican	185	4.3
Guatemalan	87	4.2
Honduran	40	5.1
Panamanian	13	3.9
Salvadoran	18	2.6
Cuban	112	15.6
Mexican	3,285	5.3
Puerto Rican	503	16.0
South American	277	12.3
Colombian	29	4.7
Ecuadorian	21	9.5
Peruvian	48	7.8
Venezuelan	104	24.9
Spaniard	106	7.0

Households with Food Stamps/SNAP Benefits During Past 12 Months		
Group	Number	%
Total Population	161,699	11.4
Hispanic or Latino (of any race)	12,744	16.2
Central American, ex. Mexican	567	13.3
Guatemalan	305	14.7
Honduran	120	15.2
Panamanian	17	5.1
Salvadoran	56	8.2
Cuban	190	26.5
Mexican	10,204	16.3
Puerto Rican	491	15.7
South American	132	5.8
Colombian	54	8.8
Ecuadorian	22	10.0
Peruvian	35	5.7
Venezuelan	4	1.0
Spaniard	301	19.8

Poverty Rate (Income in Past 12 Months Below Poverty Level)	
Group	%
Total Population	16.2
Hispanic or Latino (of any race)	28.2
Central American, ex. Mexican	26.6
Guatemalan	35.1
Honduran	24.3
Panamanian	8.5
Salvadoran	14.1
Cuban	23.5
Mexican	29.2
Puerto Rican	20.6
South American	13.9
Colombian	17.6
Ecuadorian	0.0
Peruvian	19.4
Venezuelan	8.0
Spaniard	25.7

Altus*

Population			
Group	Number	%TP[1]	%HP[2]
Total Population	19,813	100.0	–
Hispanic or Latino (of any race)	4,699	23.7	100.0
Mexican	4,089	20.6	87.0
Puerto Rican	107	0.5	2.3

Population Growth: 2000–2010	
Group	%
Total Population	-7.6
Hispanic or Latino (of any race)	27.0
Mexican	51.1
Puerto Rican	4.9

Males per 100 Females	
Group	Number
Total Population	98.5
Hispanic or Latino (of any race)	103.9
Mexican	102.9
Puerto Rican	143.2

Average Household Size	
Group	People
Total Population	2.51
Hispanic or Latino (of any race)	3.14
Mexican	3.18
Puerto Rican	3.00

Median Age	
Group	Years
Total Population	32.9
Hispanic or Latino (of any race)	24.5
Mexican	24.7
Puerto Rican	24.3

High School Graduates (Universe: Population 25 Years and Over)		
Group	Number	%
Total Population	9,627	80.0
Hispanic or Latino (of any race)	1,074	48.6
Mexican	835	45.2

Four-Year College Graduates (Universe: Population 25 Years and Over)		
Group	Number	%
Total Population	2,562	21.3
Hispanic or Latino (of any race)	191	8.7
Mexican	70	3.8

Population Age 3–17 Enrolled in Public School (Universe: Population Age 3–17 Enrolled in School)		
Group	Number	%
Total Population	3,650	94.9
Hispanic or Latino (of any race)	1,354	98.8
Mexican	1,241	100.0

Population Age 3–17 Enrolled in Private School (Universe: Population Age 3–17 Enrolled in School)		
Group	Number	%
Total Population	195	5.1
Hispanic or Latino (of any race)	17	1.2
Mexican	0	0.0

Foreign-Born Population		
Group	Number	%
Total Population	1,337	6.8
Hispanic or Latino (of any race)	818	17.7
Mexican	701	17.5

Foreign-Born Naturalized U.S. Citizens		
Group	Number	%
Total Population	531	39.7
Hispanic or Latino (of any race)	255	31.2
Mexican	226	32.2

Language Spoken at Home: English Only (Universe: Population 5 Years and Over)		
Group	Number	%
Total Population	14,898	82.2
Hispanic or Latino (of any race)	1,526	37.6
Mexican	1,380	39.4

Language Spoken at Home: Spanish (Universe: Population 5 Years and Over)		
Group	Number	%
Total Population	2,724	15.0
Hispanic or Latino (of any race)	2,532	62.4
Mexican	2,120	60.6

Unemployment Rate (Universe: Population 16 Years and Over)	
Group	%
Total Population	8.7
Hispanic or Latino (of any race)	10.8
Mexican	11.0

Class of Worker: Private Wage and Salary (Universe: Civilian Employed Population 16 Years and Over)		
Group	Number	%
Total Population	5,560	67.0
Hispanic or Latino (of any race)	1,536	86.9
Mexican	1,304	86.6

Class of Worker: Government (Universe: Civilian Employed Population 16 Years and Over)		
Group	Number	%
Total Population	2,213	26.7
Hispanic or Latino (of any race)	158	8.9
Mexican	138	9.2

Means of Transportation to Work: Car, Truck or Van (Universe: Workers 16 Years and Over)		
Group	Number	%
Total Population	8,032	88.4
Hispanic or Latino (of any race)	1,534	86.1
Mexican	1,345	90.0

Means of Transportation to Work: Public Transportation (ex. Taxicab) (Universe: Workers 16 Years and Over)		
Group	Number	%
Total Population	0	0.0
Hispanic or Latino (of any race)	0	0.0
Mexican	0	0.0

Homeownership Rate (Universe: Occupied Housing Units)	
Group	%
Total Population	55.3
Hispanic or Latino (of any race)	50.2
Mexican	51.5
Puerto Rican	36.4

Median Home Value	
Group	Dollars
Total Population	86,500
Hispanic or Latino (of any race)	34,000
Mexican	31,900

Median Gross Rent	
Group	Dollars
Total Population	609
Hispanic or Latino (of any race)	517
Mexican	517

Median Household Income (2010 Inflation-Adjusted Dollars)	
Group	Dollars
Total Population	40,607
Hispanic or Latino (of any race)	25,385
Mexican	22,222

Notes: (1) Percent of total population; (2) Percent of Hispanic/Latino population; Profiles include places with an overall population of at least 125,000, OR an overall population of at least 25,000 where the Hispanic/Latino population is at least 20% of the overall population. In states where less than five places meet either of these criteria, we have included places with at least 10,000 total population with the highest percentage of Hispanic/Latino population. These places are identified with an asterisk (*); Please refer to the User's Guide for a full explanation of data.

Per Capita Income
(2010 Inflation-Adjusted Dollars)

Group	Dollars
Total Population	20,214
Hispanic or Latino (of any race)	10,340
Mexican	9,706

Households with $100,000+ Income

Group	Number	%
Total Population	928	12.1
Hispanic or Latino (of any race)	48	3.5
Mexican	36	3.2

Households with Food Stamps/SNAP Benefits During Past 12 Months

Group	Number	%
Total Population	1,280	16.7
Hispanic or Latino (of any race)	397	29.0
Mexican	344	30.5

Poverty Rate
(Income in Past 12 Months Below Poverty Level)

Group	%
Total Population	19.5
Hispanic or Latino (of any race)	38.9
Mexican	39.9

Guymon*

Population

Group	Number	%TP[1]	%HP[2]
Total Population	11,442	100.0	–
Hispanic or Latino (of any race)	5,896	51.5	100.0
Central American, ex. Mexican	803	7.0	13.6
Guatemalan	704	6.2	11.9
Cuban	122	1.1	2.1
Mexican	4,578	40.0	77.6

Population Growth: 2000–2010

Group	%
Total Population	9.3
Hispanic or Latino (of any race)	46.7
Central American, ex. Mexican	303.5
Guatemalan	297.7
Mexican	55.6

Males per 100 Females

Group	Number
Total Population	107.5
Hispanic or Latino (of any race)	116.4
Central American, ex. Mexican	195.2
Guatemalan	193.3
Cuban	110.3
Mexican	110.0

Average Household Size

Group	People
Total Population	2.86
Hispanic or Latino (of any race)	3.61
Central American, ex. Mexican	4.06
Guatemalan	4.00
Cuban	3.15
Mexican	3.61

Median Age

Group	Years
Total Population	30.4
Hispanic or Latino (of any race)	24.6
Central American, ex. Mexican	26.1
Guatemalan	26.0
Cuban	35.0
Mexican	23.5

High School Graduates
(Universe: Population 25 Years and Over)

Group	Number	%
Total Population	4,550	69.8
Hispanic or Latino (of any race)	967	38.6
Mexican	849	41.9

Four-Year College Graduates
(Universe: Population 25 Years and Over)

Group	Number	%
Total Population	1,246	19.1
Hispanic or Latino (of any race)	148	5.9
Mexican	137	6.8

Population Age 3–17 Enrolled in Public School
(Universe: Population Age 3–17 Enrolled in School)

Group	Number	%
Total Population	2,134	94.7
Hispanic or Latino (of any race)	1,352	98.4
Mexican	1,179	98.2

Population Age 3–17 Enrolled in Private School
(Universe: Population Age 3–17 Enrolled in School)

Group	Number	%
Total Population	120	5.3
Hispanic or Latino (of any race)	22	1.6
Mexican	22	1.8

Foreign-Born Population

Group	Number	%
Total Population	2,861	26.2
Hispanic or Latino (of any race)	2,749	52.6
Mexican	2,223	52.5

Foreign-Born Naturalized U.S. Citizens

Group	Number	%
Total Population	466	16.3
Hispanic or Latino (of any race)	405	14.7
Mexican	318	14.3

Language Spoken at Home: English Only
(Universe: Population 5 Years and Over)

Group	Number	%
Total Population	5,835	59.5
Hispanic or Latino (of any race)	770	17.1
Mexican	581	15.6

Language Spoken at Home: Spanish
(Universe: Population 5 Years and Over)

Group	Number	%
Total Population	3,870	39.4
Hispanic or Latino (of any race)	3,730	82.9
Mexican	3,132	84.4

Unemployment Rate
(Universe: Population 16 Years and Over)

Group	%
Total Population	9.1
Hispanic or Latino (of any race)	13.6
Mexican	10.3

Class of Worker: Private Wage and Salary
(Universe: Civilian Employed Population 16 Years and Over)

Group	Number	%
Total Population	4,418	82.3
Hispanic or Latino (of any race)	2,169	94.5
Mexican	1,763	93.3

Class of Worker: Government
(Universe: Civilian Employed Population 16 Years and Over)

Group	Number	%
Total Population	572	10.7
Hispanic or Latino (of any race)	102	4.4
Mexican	102	5.4

Means of Transportation to Work: Car, Truck or Van
(Universe: Workers 16 Years and Over)

Group	Number	%
Total Population	4,924	93.6
Hispanic or Latino (of any race)	2,221	96.8
Mexican	1,815	96.1

Means of Transportation to Work: Public Transportation (ex. Taxicab)
(Universe: Workers 16 Years and Over)

Group	Number	%
Total Population	67	1.3
Hispanic or Latino (of any race)	11	0.5
Mexican	11	0.6

Homeownership Rate
(Universe: Occupied Housing Units)

Group	%
Total Population	57.5
Hispanic or Latino (of any race)	45.1
Central American, ex. Mexican	10.1
Guatemalan	8.9
Cuban	17.1
Mexican	52.7

Median Home Value

Group	Dollars
Total Population	87,600
Hispanic or Latino (of any race)	58,300
Mexican	56,800

Median Gross Rent

Group	Dollars
Total Population	606
Hispanic or Latino (of any race)	619
Mexican	580

Median Household Income
(2010 Inflation-Adjusted Dollars)

Group	Dollars
Total Population	44,487
Hispanic or Latino (of any race)	39,744
Mexican	44,005

Per Capita Income
(2010 Inflation-Adjusted Dollars)

Group	Dollars
Total Population	21,893
Hispanic or Latino (of any race)	12,203
Mexican	12,344

Households with $100,000+ Income

Group	Number	%
Total Population	507	13.3
Hispanic or Latino (of any race)	111	8.3
Mexican	111	10.0

Households with Food Stamps/SNAP Benefits During Past 12 Months

Group	Number	%
Total Population	330	8.7
Hispanic or Latino (of any race)	189	14.2
Mexican	152	13.7

Poverty Rate
(Income in Past 12 Months Below Poverty Level)

Group	%
Total Population	14.6
Hispanic or Latino (of any race)	23.8
Mexican	21.1

Oklahoma City

Population

Group	Number	%TP[1]	%HP[2]
Total Population	579,999	100.0	–
Hispanic or Latino (of any race)	100,038	17.2	100.0
Central American, ex. Mexican	6,506	1.1	6.5
Guatemalan	4,256	0.7	4.3
Honduran	944	0.2	0.9
Nicaraguan	140	<0.1	0.1
Panamanian	228	<0.1	0.2
Salvadoran	799	0.1	0.8
Cuban	594	0.1	0.6
Dominican Republic	106	<0.1	0.1
Mexican	82,318	14.2	82.3
Puerto Rican	2,211	0.4	2.2
South American	1,762	0.3	1.8
Argentinean	125	<0.1	0.1
Colombian	552	0.1	0.6
Ecuadorian	137	<0.1	0.1
Peruvian	540	0.1	0.5
Venezuelan	257	<0.1	0.3
Spaniard	844	0.1	0.8

Population Growth: 2000–2010

Group	%
Total Population	14.6
Hispanic or Latino (of any race)	94.7
Central American, ex. Mexican	268.2
Guatemalan	298.5
Honduran	216.8
Panamanian	70.1
Salvadoran	519.4
Cuban	62.7

Notes: (1) Percent of total population; (2) Percent of Hispanic/Latino population; Profiles include places with an overall population of at least 125,000, OR an overall population of at least 25,000 where the Hispanic/Latino population is at least 20% of the overall population. In states where less than five places meet either of these criteria, we have included places with at least 10,000 total population with the highest percentage of Hispanic/Latino population. These places are identified with an asterisk (*); Please refer to the User's Guide for a full explanation of data.

Group	Number
Mexican	100.8
Puerto Rican	83.5
South American	146.1
Colombian	166.7
Peruvian	170.0
Spaniard	703.8

Males per 100 Females

Group	Number
Total Population	97.0
Hispanic or Latino (of any race)	112.3
Central American, ex. Mexican	135.5
Guatemalan	147.3
Honduran	130.8
Nicaraguan	89.2
Panamanian	81.0
Salvadoran	118.3
Cuban	120.0
Dominican Republic	79.7
Mexican	112.1
Puerto Rican	102.1
South American	87.8
Argentinean	111.9
Colombian	73.0
Ecuadorian	71.3
Peruvian	93.5
Venezuelan	104.0
Spaniard	88.4

Average Household Size

Group	People
Total Population	2.47
Hispanic or Latino (of any race)	3.59
Central American, ex. Mexican	3.85
Guatemalan	4.15
Honduran	3.66
Nicaraguan	3.37
Panamanian	2.54
Salvadoran	3.49
Cuban	2.38
Dominican Republic	3.30
Mexican	3.67
Puerto Rican	2.79
South American	2.73
Argentinean	2.83
Colombian	2.59
Ecuadorian	2.91
Peruvian	2.83
Venezuelan	2.61
Spaniard	2.67

Median Age

Group	Years
Total Population	34.0
Hispanic or Latino (of any race)	23.4
Central American, ex. Mexican	26.8
Guatemalan	25.8
Honduran	29.5
Nicaraguan	31.5
Panamanian	31.0
Salvadoran	29.8
Cuban	30.8
Dominican Republic	22.8
Mexican	22.8
Puerto Rican	24.4
South American	32.2
Argentinean	31.5
Colombian	30.4
Ecuadorian	27.9
Peruvian	36.7
Venezuelan	31.3
Spaniard	32.5

High School Graduates
(Universe: Population 25 Years and Over)

Group	Number	%
Total Population	306,196	84.4
Hispanic or Latino (of any race)	20,554	48.8
Central American, ex. Mexican	1,375	38.2
Guatemalan	619	27.8
Honduran	304	44.9
Mexican	15,983	45.9
Puerto Rican	542	80.7
South American	1,169	95.7
Spaniard	609	90.5

Four-Year College Graduates
(Universe: Population 25 Years and Over)

Group	Number	%
Total Population	97,803	27.0
Hispanic or Latino (of any race)	3,313	7.9
Central American, ex. Mexican	434	12.0
Guatemalan	203	9.1
Honduran	73	10.8
Mexican	1,795	5.2
Puerto Rican	143	21.3
South American	525	43.0
Spaniard	194	28.8

Population Age 3–17 Enrolled in Public School
(Universe: Population Age 3–17 Enrolled in School)

Group	Number	%
Total Population	89,419	88.3
Hispanic or Latino (of any race)	22,290	94.1
Central American, ex. Mexican	1,022	96.4
Guatemalan	535	98.2
Honduran	170	93.4
Mexican	19,615	94.6
Puerto Rican	270	81.1
South American	357	85.8
Spaniard	281	100.0

Population Age 3–17 Enrolled in Private School
(Universe: Population Age 3–17 Enrolled in School)

Group	Number	%
Total Population	11,870	11.7
Hispanic or Latino (of any race)	1,391	5.9
Central American, ex. Mexican	38	3.6
Guatemalan	10	1.8
Honduran	12	6.6
Mexican	1,109	5.4
Puerto Rican	63	18.9
South American	59	14.2
Spaniard	0	0.0

Foreign-Born Population

Group	Number	%
Total Population	64,793	11.5
Hispanic or Latino (of any race)	41,567	45.6
Central American, ex. Mexican	4,476	69.6
Guatemalan	3,024	72.6
Honduran	739	70.8
Mexican	35,058	45.3
Puerto Rican	4	0.3
South American	1,389	70.7
Spaniard	321	24.4

Foreign-Born Naturalized U.S. Citizens

Group	Number	%
Total Population	18,903	29.2
Hispanic or Latino (of any race)	6,152	14.8
Central American, ex. Mexican	536	12.0
Guatemalan	227	7.5
Honduran	154	20.8
Mexican	4,994	14.2
Puerto Rican	4	100.0
South American	359	25.8
Spaniard	93	29.0

Language Spoken at Home: English Only
(Universe: Population 5 Years and Over)

Group	Number	%
Total Population	426,350	82.2
Hispanic or Latino (of any race)	16,386	21.0
Central American, ex. Mexican	322	5.8
Guatemalan	71	2.1
Honduran	25	2.8
Mexican	12,691	19.3
Puerto Rican	712	65.6
South American	539	28.0
Spaniard	564	52.4

Language Spoken at Home: Spanish
(Universe: Population 5 Years and Over)

Group	Number	%
Total Population	65,825	12.7
Hispanic or Latino (of any race)	61,496	78.9
Central American, ex. Mexican	5,193	94.2
Guatemalan	3,374	97.9
Honduran	884	97.2
Mexican	53,107	80.7
Puerto Rican	373	34.4
South American	1,387	72.0
Spaniard	502	46.7

Unemployment Rate
(Universe: Population 16 Years and Over)

Group	%
Total Population	6.4
Hispanic or Latino (of any race)	6.2
Central American, ex. Mexican	2.0
Guatemalan	0.4
Honduran	6.4
Mexican	6.8
Puerto Rican	2.6
South American	1.6
Spaniard	9.1

Class of Worker: Private Wage and Salary
(Universe: Civilian Employed Population 16 Years and Over)

Group	Number	%
Total Population	213,894	78.3
Hispanic or Latino (of any race)	33,898	86.8
Central American, ex. Mexican	3,353	91.4
Guatemalan	2,239	90.9
Honduran	531	93.3
Mexican	28,121	87.3
Puerto Rican	471	83.5
South American	881	76.4
Spaniard	355	77.7

Class of Worker: Government
(Universe: Civilian Employed Population 16 Years and Over)

Group	Number	%
Total Population	41,143	15.1
Hispanic or Latino (of any race)	2,692	6.9
Central American, ex. Mexican	119	3.2
Guatemalan	57	2.3
Honduran	21	3.7
Mexican	2,153	6.7
Puerto Rican	82	14.5
South American	118	10.2
Spaniard	87	19.0

Means of Transportation to Work: Car, Truck or Van
(Universe: Workers 16 Years and Over)

Group	Number	%
Total Population	251,992	93.5
Hispanic or Latino (of any race)	35,998	95.0
Central American, ex. Mexican	3,518	96.1
Guatemalan	2,395	98.0
Honduran	509	90.7
Mexican	29,574	95.2
Puerto Rican	526	94.8
South American	1,065	93.0
Spaniard	455	100.0

Means of Transportation to Work: Public Transportation (ex. Taxicab)
(Universe: Workers 16 Years and Over)

Group	Number	%
Total Population	1,933	0.7
Hispanic or Latino (of any race)	218	0.6
Central American, ex. Mexican	25	0.7
Guatemalan	25	1.0
Honduran	0	0.0
Mexican	141	0.5
Puerto Rican	11	2.0
South American	23	2.0
Spaniard	0	0.0

Homeownership Rate
(Universe: Occupied Housing Units)

Group	%
Total Population	59.7
Hispanic or Latino (of any race)	46.1
Central American, ex. Mexican	37.8
Guatemalan	32.0
Honduran	40.6
Nicaraguan	58.8
Panamanian	56.6
Salvadoran	50.2
Cuban	55.3
Dominican Republic	56.7
Mexican	46.6

Notes: (1) Percent of total population; (2) Percent of Hispanic/Latino population; Profiles include places with an overall population of at least 125,000, OR an overall population of at least 25,000 where the Hispanic/Latino population is at least 20% of the overall population. In states where less than five places meet either of these criteria, we have included places with at least 10,000 total population with the highest percentage of Hispanic/Latino population. These places are identified with an asterisk (*); Please refer to the User's Guide for a full explanation of data.

Group	
Puerto Rican	46.3
South American	58.2
Argentinean	60.4
Colombian	59.6
Ecuadorian	60.0
Peruvian	57.5
Venezuelan	51.6
Spaniard	53.8

Median Home Value

Group	Dollars
Total Population	124,600
Hispanic or Latino (of any race)	75,200
Central American, ex. Mexican	92,000
Guatemalan	89,000
Honduran	85,500
Mexican	71,000
Puerto Rican	171,800
South American	130,600
Spaniard	95,000

Median Gross Rent

Group	Dollars
Total Population	669
Hispanic or Latino (of any race)	625
Central American, ex. Mexican	634
Guatemalan	636
Honduran	609
Mexican	621
Puerto Rican	565
South American	672
Spaniard	575

Median Household Income
(2010 Inflation-Adjusted Dollars)

Group	Dollars
Total Population	43,798
Hispanic or Latino (of any race)	32,508
Central American, ex. Mexican	32,229
Guatemalan	31,066
Honduran	29,286
Mexican	32,307
Puerto Rican	49,432
South American	33,418
Spaniard	37,432

Per Capita Income
(2010 Inflation-Adjusted Dollars)

Group	Dollars
Total Population	25,042
Hispanic or Latino (of any race)	11,599
Central American, ex. Mexican	12,167
Guatemalan	11,473
Honduran	10,715
Mexican	10,873
Puerto Rican	17,427
South American	23,201
Spaniard	20,000

Households with $100,000+ Income

Group	Number	%
Total Population	35,721	16.0
Hispanic or Latino (of any race)	1,184	5.0
Central American, ex. Mexican	63	3.5
Guatemalan	57	4.8
Honduran	0	0.0
Mexican	790	4.1
Puerto Rican	81	18.7
South American	117	18.0
Spaniard	40	9.6

Households with Food Stamps/SNAP Benefits During Past 12 Months

Group	Number	%
Total Population	27,900	12.5
Hispanic or Latino (of any race)	3,934	16.7
Central American, ex. Mexican	229	12.6
Guatemalan	106	9.0
Honduran	50	22.1
Mexican	3,414	17.6
Puerto Rican	46	10.6
South American	0	0.0
Spaniard	79	18.9

Poverty Rate
(Income in Past 12 Months Below Poverty Level)

Group	%
Total Population	16.6
Hispanic or Latino (of any race)	30.1
Central American, ex. Mexican	32.4
Guatemalan	40.2
Honduran	36.4
Mexican	30.9
Puerto Rican	28.4
South American	11.2
Spaniard	17.8

Tulsa

Population

Group	Number	%TP[1]	%HP[2]
Total Population	391,906	100.0	–
Hispanic or Latino (of any race)	55,266	14.1	100.0
Central American, ex. Mexican	3,059	0.8	5.5
Costa Rican	101	<0.1	0.2
Guatemalan	1,352	0.3	2.4
Honduran	803	0.2	1.5
Panamanian	122	<0.1	0.2
Salvadoran	594	0.2	1.1
Cuban	458	0.1	0.8
Dominican Republic	168	<0.1	0.3
Mexican	45,013	11.5	81.4
Puerto Rican	1,574	0.4	2.8
South American	1,615	0.4	2.9
Argentinean	119	<0.1	0.2
Colombian	382	0.1	0.7
Peruvian	457	0.1	0.8
Venezuelan	388	0.1	0.7
Spaniard	580	0.1	1.0

Population Growth: 2000–2010

Group	%
Total Population	-0.3
Hispanic or Latino (of any race)	96.6
Central American, ex. Mexican	323.1
Guatemalan	461.0
Honduran	428.3
Salvadoran	324.3
Cuban	41.4
Mexican	113.2
Puerto Rican	37.1
South American	80.2
Colombian	81.0
Peruvian	119.7
Venezuelan	48.7

Males per 100 Females

Group	Number
Total Population	95.0
Hispanic or Latino (of any race)	117.4
Central American, ex. Mexican	144.5
Costa Rican	80.4
Guatemalan	152.2
Honduran	169.5
Panamanian	93.7
Salvadoran	131.1
Cuban	105.4
Dominican Republic	95.3
Mexican	119.3
Puerto Rican	104.7
South American	80.6
Argentinean	142.9
Colombian	63.9
Peruvian	66.2
Venezuelan	93.0
Spaniard	91.4

Average Household Size

Group	People
Total Population	2.34
Hispanic or Latino (of any race)	3.53
Central American, ex. Mexican	3.68
Costa Rican	2.75
Guatemalan	4.07
Honduran	3.83
Panamanian	2.23
Salvadoran	3.38
Cuban	2.34
Dominican Republic	2.80
Mexican	3.67
Puerto Rican	2.75
South American	2.58
Argentinean	2.55
Colombian	2.45
Peruvian	2.83
Venezuelan	2.62
Spaniard	2.56

Median Age

Group	Years
Total Population	34.7
Hispanic or Latino (of any race)	23.6
Central American, ex. Mexican	26.8
Costa Rican	34.3
Guatemalan	25.4
Honduran	27.7
Panamanian	30.0
Salvadoran	27.7
Cuban	28.6
Dominican Republic	23.3
Mexican	22.9
Puerto Rican	24.3
South American	33.9
Argentinean	36.3
Colombian	34.6
Peruvian	36.4
Venezuelan	32.3
Spaniard	30.0

High School Graduates
(Universe: Population 25 Years and Over)

Group	Number	%
Total Population	217,076	86.4
Hispanic or Latino (of any race)	12,830	54.2
Central American, ex. Mexican	615	46.1
Mexican	9,910	50.7
Puerto Rican	482	80.5
South American	817	90.0

Four-Year College Graduates
(Universe: Population 25 Years and Over)

Group	Number	%
Total Population	73,848	29.4
Hispanic or Latino (of any race)	2,012	8.5
Central American, ex. Mexican	28	2.1
Mexican	1,278	6.5
Puerto Rican	144	24.0
South American	209	23.0

Population Age 3–17 Enrolled in Public School
(Universe: Population Age 3–17 Enrolled in School)

Group	Number	%
Total Population	58,141	85.2
Hispanic or Latino (of any race)	11,640	95.7
Central American, ex. Mexican	319	94.9
Mexican	10,346	96.8
Puerto Rican	278	87.7
South American	232	82.9

Population Age 3–17 Enrolled in Private School
(Universe: Population Age 3–17 Enrolled in School)

Group	Number	%
Total Population	10,079	14.8
Hispanic or Latino (of any race)	517	4.3
Central American, ex. Mexican	17	5.1
Mexican	339	3.2
Puerto Rican	39	12.3
South American	48	17.1

Foreign-Born Population

Group	Number	%
Total Population	36,235	9.3
Hispanic or Latino (of any race)	22,558	45.1
Central American, ex. Mexican	1,961	72.3
Mexican	19,097	45.1
Puerto Rican	49	4.4
South American	989	66.5

Foreign-Born Naturalized U.S. Citizens

Group	Number	%
Total Population	9,664	26.7
Hispanic or Latino (of any race)	3,407	15.1

Notes: (1) Percent of total population; (2) Percent of Hispanic/Latino population; Profiles include places with an overall population of at least 125,000, OR an overall population of at least 25,000 where the Hispanic/Latino population is at least 20% of the overall population. In states where less than five places meet either of these criteria, we have included places with at least 10,000 total population with the highest percentage of Hispanic/Latino population. These places are identified with an asterisk (*); Please refer to the User's Guide for a full explanation of data.

Central American, ex. Mexican	315	16.1
Mexican	2,543	13.3
Puerto Rican	38	77.6
South American	370	37.4

Language Spoken at Home: English Only
(Universe: Population 5 Years and Over)

Group	Number	%
Total Population	309,933	86.3
Hispanic or Latino (of any race)	10,638	25.1
Central American, ex. Mexican	221	9.1
Mexican	8,542	24.0
Puerto Rican	572	55.1
South American	237	16.7

Language Spoken at Home: Spanish
(Universe: Population 5 Years and Over)

Group	Number	%
Total Population	35,720	9.9
Hispanic or Latino (of any race)	31,766	74.8
Central American, ex. Mexican	2,219	90.9
Mexican	26,960	75.9
Puerto Rican	467	44.9
South American	1,183	83.3

Unemployment Rate
(Universe: Population 16 Years and Over)

Group	%
Total Population	7.0
Hispanic or Latino (of any race)	5.9
Central American, ex. Mexican	4.7
Mexican	6.0
Puerto Rican	8.8
South American	2.7

Class of Worker: Private Wage and Salary
(Universe: Civilian Employed Population 16 Years and Over)

Group	Number	%
Total Population	156,580	83.8
Hispanic or Latino (of any race)	19,865	89.4
Central American, ex. Mexican	1,558	96.5
Mexican	16,237	89.1
Puerto Rican	420	81.1
South American	873	91.4

Class of Worker: Government
(Universe: Civilian Employed Population 16 Years and Over)

Group	Number	%
Total Population	18,063	9.7
Hispanic or Latino (of any race)	1,093	4.9
Central American, ex. Mexican	27	1.7
Mexican	813	4.5
Puerto Rican	85	16.4
South American	73	7.6

Means of Transportation to Work: Car, Truck or Van
(Universe: Workers 16 Years and Over)

Group	Number	%
Total Population	167,745	91.6
Hispanic or Latino (of any race)	20,527	94.2
Central American, ex. Mexican	1,423	92.2
Mexican	17,169	95.6
Puerto Rican	447	89.6
South American	780	85.3

Means of Transportation to Work: Public Transportation (ex. Taxicab)
(Universe: Workers 16 Years and Over)

Group	Number	%
Total Population	1,896	1.0
Hispanic or Latino (of any race)	168	0.8
Central American, ex. Mexican	0	0.0
Mexican	138	0.8
Puerto Rican	0	0.0
South American	0	0.0

Homeownership Rate
(Universe: Occupied Housing Units)

Group	%
Total Population	53.5
Hispanic or Latino (of any race)	36.3
Central American, ex. Mexican	31.4
Costa Rican	52.8
Guatemalan	22.9
Honduran	22.9
Panamanian	48.9
Salvadoran	44.8
Cuban	43.5
Dominican Republic	29.6
Mexican	36.1
Puerto Rican	34.5
South American	48.7
Argentinean	54.9
Colombian	46.9
Peruvian	50.8
Venezuelan	47.9
Spaniard	47.0

Median Home Value

Group	Dollars
Total Population	117,000
Hispanic or Latino (of any race)	90,200
Central American, ex. Mexican	98,100
Mexican	85,200
Puerto Rican	98,000
South American	109,100

Median Gross Rent

Group	Dollars
Total Population	676
Hispanic or Latino (of any race)	622
Central American, ex. Mexican	561
Mexican	624
Puerto Rican	690
South American	822

Median Household Income
(2010 Inflation-Adjusted Dollars)

Group	Dollars
Total Population	39,289
Hispanic or Latino (of any race)	32,112
Central American, ex. Mexican	31,010
Mexican	32,343
Puerto Rican	35,444
South American	29,598

Per Capita Income
(2010 Inflation-Adjusted Dollars)

Group	Dollars
Total Population	26,069
Hispanic or Latino (of any race)	11,626
Central American, ex. Mexican	14,091
Mexican	10,971
Puerto Rican	17,232
South American	15,922

Households with $100,000+ Income

Group	Number	%
Total Population	23,415	14.2
Hispanic or Latino (of any race)	488	3.5
Central American, ex. Mexican	16	1.8
Mexican	336	3.0
Puerto Rican	18	4.6
South American	11	1.8

Households with Food Stamps/SNAP Benefits During Past 12 Months

Group	Number	%
Total Population	20,817	12.6
Hispanic or Latino (of any race)	2,056	14.6
Central American, ex. Mexican	156	17.1
Mexican	1,573	13.9
Puerto Rican	48	12.2
South American	11	1.8

Poverty Rate
(Income in Past 12 Months Below Poverty Level)

Group	%
Total Population	19.3
Hispanic or Latino (of any race)	31.8
Central American, ex. Mexican	15.9
Mexican	32.8
Puerto Rican	30.2
South American	16.1

Warr Acres*

Population

Group	Number	%TP[1]	%HP[2]
Total Population	10,043	100.0	–
Hispanic or Latino (of any race)	2,030	20.2	100.0
Central American, ex. Mexican	166	1.7	8.2
Mexican	1,622	16.2	79.9

Population Growth: 2000–2010

Group	%
Total Population	3.2
Hispanic or Latino (of any race)	171.4
Mexican	176.8

Males per 100 Females

Group	Number
Total Population	93.1
Hispanic or Latino (of any race)	118.8
Central American, ex. Mexican	147.8
Mexican	118.0

Average Household Size

Group	People
Total Population	2.52
Hispanic or Latino (of any race)	3.78
Central American, ex. Mexican	3.93
Mexican	3.91

Median Age

Group	Years
Total Population	35.3
Hispanic or Latino (of any race)	23.5
Central American, ex. Mexican	28.3
Mexican	22.6

High School Graduates
(Universe: Population 25 Years and Over)

Group	Number	%
Total Population	5,782	87.1
Hispanic or Latino (of any race)	388	61.2

Four-Year College Graduates
(Universe: Population 25 Years and Over)

Group	Number	%
Total Population	1,342	20.2
Hispanic or Latino (of any race)	17	2.7

Population Age 3–17 Enrolled in Public School
(Universe: Population Age 3–17 Enrolled in School)

Group	Number	%
Total Population	1,539	85.5
Hispanic or Latino (of any race)	338	91.8

Population Age 3–17 Enrolled in Private School
(Universe: Population Age 3–17 Enrolled in School)

Group	Number	%
Total Population	260	14.5
Hispanic or Latino (of any race)	30	8.2

Foreign-Born Population

Group	Number	%
Total Population	1,117	11.2
Hispanic or Latino (of any race)	487	42.4

Foreign-Born Naturalized U.S. Citizens

Group	Number	%
Total Population	420	37.6
Hispanic or Latino (of any race)	133	27.3

Language Spoken at Home: English Only
(Universe: Population 5 Years and Over)

Group	Number	%
Total Population	8,139	85.6
Hispanic or Latino (of any race)	189	16.9

Language Spoken at Home: Spanish
(Universe: Population 5 Years and Over)

Group	Number	%
Total Population	1,028	10.8
Hispanic or Latino (of any race)	898	80.3

STATE & PLACE PROFILES

Notes: (1) Percent of total population; (2) Percent of Hispanic/Latino population; Profiles include places with an overall population of at least 125,000, OR an overall population of at least 25,000 where the Hispanic/Latino population is at least 20% of the overall population. In states where less than five places meet either of these criteria, we have included places with at least 10,000 total population with the highest percentage of Hispanic/Latino population. These places are identified with an asterisk (*); Please refer to the User's Guide for a full explanation of data.

Unemployment Rate
(Universe: Population 16 Years and Over)

Group	%
Total Population	3.0
Hispanic or Latino (of any race)	1.9

Class of Worker: Private Wage and Salary
(Universe: Civilian Employed Population 16 Years and Over)

Group	Number	%
Total Population	4,318	81.6
Hispanic or Latino (of any race)	406	78.4

Class of Worker: Government
(Universe: Civilian Employed Population 16 Years and Over)

Group	Number	%
Total Population	535	10.1
Hispanic or Latino (of any race)	0	0.0

Means of Transportation to Work: Car, Truck or Van
(Universe: Workers 16 Years and Over)

Group	Number	%
Total Population	4,843	93.0
Hispanic or Latino (of any race)	505	97.5

Means of Transportation to Work: Public Transportation (ex. Taxicab)
(Universe: Workers 16 Years and Over)

Group	Number	%
Total Population	13	0.2
Hispanic or Latino (of any race)	13	2.5

Homeownership Rate
(Universe: Occupied Housing Units)

Group	%
Total Population	62.3
Hispanic or Latino (of any race)	37.3
Central American, ex. Mexican	25.0
Mexican	38.1

Median Home Value

Group	Dollars
Total Population	96,700
Hispanic or Latino (of any race)	105,400

Median Gross Rent

Group	Dollars
Total Population	679
Hispanic or Latino (of any race)	621

Median Household Income
(2010 Inflation-Adjusted Dollars)

Group	Dollars
Total Population	37,510
Hispanic or Latino (of any race)	32,200

Per Capita Income
(2010 Inflation-Adjusted Dollars)

Group	Dollars
Total Population	21,134
Hispanic or Latino (of any race)	12,193

Households with $100,000+ Income

Group	Number	%
Total Population	271	6.6
Hispanic or Latino (of any race)	0	0.0

Households with Food Stamps/SNAP Benefits During Past 12 Months

Group	Number	%
Total Population	420	10.3
Hispanic or Latino (of any race)	93	25.5

Poverty Rate
(Income in Past 12 Months Below Poverty Level)

Group	%
Total Population	15.3
Hispanic or Latino (of any race)	13.8

Notes: (1) Percent of total population; (2) Percent of Hispanic/Latino population; Profiles include places with an overall population of at least 125,000, OR an overall population of at least 25,000 where the Hispanic/Latino population is at least 20% of the overall population. In states where less than five places meet either of these criteria, we have included places with at least 10,000 total population with the highest percentage of Hispanic/Latino population. These places are identified with an asterisk (*); Please refer to the User's Guide for a full explanation of data.

Oregon

EDITOR'S NOTE: For a place to be included in this edition, it must meet one of two criteria. Either its overall population is at least 125,000, OR its overall population is at least 25,000 and its Hispanic/Latino population is at least 20% of the overall population. For the state of Oregon, the following locations are included:

- Aloha
- Eugene
- Hillsboro
- McMinnville
- Portland
- Salem

Section Two: State & Place Profiles starts with the state profile, followed by place profiles that meet the criteria above. Places are listed alphabetically within each state. All states, all counties and places that meet the above criteria are ranked and compared in *Section Three: Rankings & Comparisons*, on page 1055.

For a more detailed look at the Hispanic/Latino population in Oregon, a companion web site is available at no additional charge with purchase of this print edition. Visit http://gold.greyhouse.com/page/info_hispanic for more information.

The web site includes data for all counties and places in Oregon with Hispanic/Latino population, plus ten additional topics: Self Employed Worker; Walked to Work; Worked from Home; Mean Travel Time to Work; Mean Household Income; Households with Cash Public Assistance; Mean Cash Pubic Assistance; Poverty Rates for 18 and Under, 18 to 64, and 65 and Over.

Population

Group	Number	%TP[1]	%HP[2]
Total Population	3,831,074	100.0	–
Hispanic or Latino (of any race)	450,062	11.7	100.0
Central American, ex. Mexican	18,190	0.5	4.0
Costa Rican	911	<0.1	0.2
Guatemalan	7,703	0.2	1.7
Honduran	1,644	<0.1	0.4
Nicaraguan	1,104	<0.1	0.2
Panamanian	725	<0.1	0.2
Salvadoran	5,906	0.2	1.3
Cuban	4,923	0.1	1.1
Dominican Republic	574	<0.1	0.1
Mexican	369,817	9.7	82.2
Puerto Rican	8,845	0.2	2.0
South American	9,648	0.3	2.1
Argentinean	1,381	<0.1	0.3
Bolivian	345	<0.1	0.1
Chilean	1,274	<0.1	0.3
Colombian	2,067	0.1	0.5
Ecuadorian	851	<0.1	0.2
Paraguayan	112	<0.1	<0.1
Peruvian	2,650	0.1	0.6
Uruguayan	132	<0.1	<0.1
Venezuelan	712	<0.1	0.2
Spaniard	7,995	0.2	1.8

Population Growth: 2000–2010

Group	%
Total Population	12.0
Hispanic or Latino (of any race)	63.5
Central American, ex. Mexican	128.7
Costa Rican	86.7
Guatemalan	119.3
Honduran	151.4
Nicaraguan	180.9
Panamanian	98.6
Salvadoran	171.2
Cuban	59.3
Dominican Republic	222.5
Mexican	72.3
Puerto Rican	73.7
South American	142.7
Argentinean	200.9
Bolivian	143.0
Chilean	109.9
Colombian	134.6
Ecuadorian	166.8
Peruvian	184.0
Venezuelan	140.5
Spaniard	790.3

Males per 100 Females

Group	Number
Total Population	98.0
Hispanic or Latino (of any race)	110.2
Central American, ex. Mexican	106.8
Costa Rican	79.0
Guatemalan	130.3
Honduran	96.7
Nicaraguan	85.5
Panamanian	78.6
Salvadoran	96.5
Cuban	113.6
Dominican Republic	99.3
Mexican	112.4
Puerto Rican	94.5
South American	86.2
Argentinean	96.4
Bolivian	94.9
Chilean	88.2
Colombian	77.6
Ecuadorian	94.7
Paraguayan	69.7
Peruvian	83.8
Uruguayan	103.1
Venezuelan	84.0
Spaniard	91.1

Average Household Size

Group	People
Total Population	2.47
Hispanic or Latino (of any race)	3.68
Central American, ex. Mexican	3.62
Costa Rican	2.73
Guatemalan	4.01
Honduran	3.49
Nicaraguan	3.07
Panamanian	2.57
Salvadoran	3.63
Cuban	2.68
Dominican Republic	2.72
Mexican	3.86
Puerto Rican	2.58
South American	2.68
Argentinean	2.66
Bolivian	2.71
Chilean	2.73
Colombian	2.60
Ecuadorian	2.69
Paraguayan	2.55
Peruvian	2.76
Uruguayan	2.51
Venezuelan	2.64
Spaniard	2.56

Median Age

Group	Years
Total Population	38.4
Hispanic or Latino (of any race)	23.6
Central American, ex. Mexican	28.2
Costa Rican	30.3
Guatemalan	27.1
Honduran	27.2
Nicaraguan	30.2
Panamanian	33.3
Salvadoran	29.3
Cuban	31.6
Dominican Republic	27.2
Mexican	22.7
Puerto Rican	26.9
South American	32.4
Argentinean	33.4
Bolivian	33.6
Chilean	33.2
Colombian	30.4
Ecuadorian	29.2
Paraguayan	28.5
Peruvian	34.1
Uruguayan	37.0
Venezuelan	31.4
Spaniard	33.9

High School Graduates

(Universe: Population 25 Years and Over)

Group	Number	%
Total Population	2,252,046	88.6
Hispanic or Latino (of any race)	110,191	55.1
Central American, ex. Mexican	6,202	54.9
Costa Rican	436	82.9
Guatemalan	2,142	41.7
Honduran	647	59.6
Nicaraguan	376	79.8
Salvadoran	2,181	60.6
Cuban	1,788	80.9
Mexican	82,047	50.3
Puerto Rican	3,518	85.4
South American	5,152	90.3
Argentinean	821	97.7
Chilean	655	91.6
Colombian	871	91.5
Ecuadorian	363	59.9
Peruvian	1,522	92.0
Spaniard	4,233	92.2

Four-Year College Graduates

(Universe: Population 25 Years and Over)

Group	Number	%
Total Population	728,241	28.6
Hispanic or Latino (of any race)	21,741	10.9
Central American, ex. Mexican	1,205	10.7
Costa Rican	161	30.6
Guatemalan	297	5.8
Honduran	146	13.5
Nicaraguan	123	26.1
Salvadoran	348	9.7
Cuban	541	24.5
Mexican	13,316	8.2
Puerto Rican	1,160	28.1
South American	2,464	43.2
Argentinean	443	52.7
Chilean	282	39.4
Colombian	413	43.4
Ecuadorian	187	30.9
Peruvian	662	40.0
Spaniard	1,206	26.3

Population Age 3–17 Enrolled in Public School

(Universe: Population Age 3–17 Enrolled in School)

Group	Number	%
Total Population	555,511	86.8
Hispanic or Latino (of any race)	108,638	94.6
Central American, ex. Mexican	4,468	96.1
Costa Rican	103	87.3
Guatemalan	2,182	96.9
Honduran	372	100.0
Nicaraguan	115	77.2
Salvadoran	1,418	95.7
Cuban	636	82.2
Mexican	95,689	95.6
Puerto Rican	1,558	82.9
South American	1,165	76.2
Argentinean	161	74.5
Chilean	147	100.0
Colombian	309	78.6
Ecuadorian	31	29.5
Peruvian	369	79.7
Spaniard	1,156	84.7

Notes: (1) Percent of total population; (2) Percent of Hispanic/Latino population; Profiles include places with an overall population of at least 125,000, OR an overall population of at least 25,000 where the Hispanic/Latino population is at least 20% of the overall population. In states where less than five places meet either of these criteria, we have included places with at least 10,000 total population with the highest percentage of Hispanic/Latino population. These places are identified with an asterisk (*); Please refer to the User's Guide for a full explanation of data.

Population Age 3–17 Enrolled in Private School
(Universe: Population Age 3–17 Enrolled in School)

Group	Number	%
Total Population	84,397	13.2
Hispanic or Latino (of any race)	6,148	5.4
Central American, ex. Mexican	183	3.9
Costa Rican	15	12.7
Guatemalan	70	3.1
Honduran	0	0.0
Nicaraguan	34	22.8
Salvadoran	64	4.3
Cuban	138	17.8
Mexican	4,400	4.4
Puerto Rican	321	17.1
South American	363	23.8
Argentinean	55	25.5
Chilean	0	0.0
Colombian	84	21.4
Ecuadorian	74	70.5
Peruvian	94	20.3
Spaniard	209	15.3

Foreign-Born Population

Group	Number	%
Total Population	364,898	9.7
Hispanic or Latino (of any race)	171,391	40.8
Central American, ex. Mexican	12,332	58.2
Costa Rican	358	47.0
Guatemalan	6,455	63.3
Honduran	1,016	57.3
Nicaraguan	427	43.0
Salvadoran	3,742	57.3
Cuban	1,553	38.9
Mexican	148,772	42.1
Puerto Rican	161	2.0
South American	5,349	60.5
Argentinean	681	55.1
Chilean	758	69.1
Colombian	845	51.7
Ecuadorian	536	63.4
Peruvian	1,689	66.6
Spaniard	470	6.4

Foreign-Born Naturalized U.S. Citizens

Group	Number	%
Total Population	131,305	36.0
Hispanic or Latino (of any race)	27,928	16.3
Central American, ex. Mexican	3,138	25.4
Costa Rican	171	47.8
Guatemalan	1,322	20.5
Honduran	247	24.3
Nicaraguan	188	44.0
Salvadoran	1,056	28.2
Cuban	668	43.0
Mexican	20,659	13.9
Puerto Rican	27	16.8
South American	2,390	44.7
Argentinean	364	53.5
Chilean	278	36.7
Colombian	463	54.8
Ecuadorian	260	48.5
Peruvian	788	46.7
Spaniard	256	54.5

Language Spoken at Home: English Only
(Universe: Population 5 Years and Over)

Group	Number	%
Total Population	3,021,536	85.7
Hispanic or Latino (of any race)	103,392	28.2
Central American, ex. Mexican	3,638	19.4
Costa Rican	331	46.0
Guatemalan	1,016	11.4
Honduran	459	29.1
Nicaraguan	349	39.0
Salvadoran	1,019	17.4
Cuban	1,586	43.1
Mexican	76,261	24.8
Puerto Rican	4,651	68.4
South American	2,171	27.4
Argentinean	438	38.5
Chilean	187	19.3
Colombian	486	34.3
Ecuadorian	209	27.7
Peruvian	355	15.7
Spaniard	5,779	83.4

Language Spoken at Home: Spanish
(Universe: Population 5 Years and Over)

Group	Number	%
Total Population	302,701	8.6
Hispanic or Latino (of any race)	260,879	71.2
Central American, ex. Mexican	14,978	79.8
Costa Rican	388	54.0
Guatemalan	7,772	87.3
Honduran	1,121	70.9
Nicaraguan	526	58.7
Salvadoran	4,822	82.6
Cuban	2,096	56.9
Mexican	229,415	74.7
Puerto Rican	2,042	30.0
South American	5,594	70.7
Argentinean	632	55.5
Chilean	771	79.4
Colombian	896	63.3
Ecuadorian	532	70.5
Peruvian	1,905	84.3
Spaniard	1,092	15.8

Unemployment Rate
(Universe: Population 16 Years and Over)

Group	%
Total Population	8.7
Hispanic or Latino (of any race)	10.1
Central American, ex. Mexican	10.3
Costa Rican	15.2
Guatemalan	8.4
Honduran	22.8
Nicaraguan	5.2
Salvadoran	10.0
Cuban	10.1
Mexican	10.1
Puerto Rican	11.9
South American	6.2
Argentinean	5.3
Chilean	6.8
Colombian	7.1
Ecuadorian	6.8
Peruvian	6.7
Spaniard	14.6

Class of Worker: Private Wage and Salary
(Universe: Civilian Employed Population 16 Years and Over)

Group	Number	%
Total Population	1,361,846	77.2
Hispanic or Latino (of any race)	152,495	86.6
Central American, ex. Mexican	8,752	86.7
Costa Rican	341	80.6
Guatemalan	4,290	88.7
Honduran	739	91.9
Nicaraguan	396	83.9
Salvadoran	2,683	83.9
Cuban	1,419	79.5
Mexican	128,157	87.6
Puerto Rican	2,517	78.6
South American	3,510	75.0
Argentinean	456	62.4
Chilean	379	72.6
Colombian	615	76.9
Ecuadorian	290	75.3
Peruvian	1,093	82.6
Spaniard	2,509	75.3

Class of Worker: Government
(Universe: Civilian Employed Population 16 Years and Over)

Group	Number	%
Total Population	247,860	14.1
Hispanic or Latino (of any race)	13,946	7.9
Central American, ex. Mexican	692	6.9
Costa Rican	82	19.4
Guatemalan	208	4.3
Honduran	65	8.1
Nicaraguan	36	7.6
Salvadoran	264	8.3
Cuban	283	15.8
Mexican	10,490	7.2
Puerto Rican	473	14.8
South American	740	15.8
Argentinean	123	16.8
Chilean	92	17.6
Colombian	149	18.6
Ecuadorian	95	24.7
Peruvian	143	10.8
Spaniard	556	16.7

Means of Transportation to Work: Car, Truck or Van
(Universe: Workers 16 Years and Over)

Group	Number	%
Total Population	1,422,920	82.7
Hispanic or Latino (of any race)	144,098	83.9
Central American, ex. Mexican	8,320	84.1
Costa Rican	334	82.7
Guatemalan	4,062	85.1
Honduran	668	88.6
Nicaraguan	334	72.6
Salvadoran	2,628	83.3
Cuban	1,368	78.0
Mexican	120,581	84.4
Puerto Rican	2,276	75.9
South American	3,689	81.4
Argentinean	602	82.4
Chilean	500	95.8
Colombian	625	81.4
Ecuadorian	336	87.3
Peruvian	1,006	78.7
Spaniard	2,660	81.4

Means of Transportation to Work: Public Transportation (ex. Taxicab)
(Universe: Workers 16 Years and Over)

Group	Number	%
Total Population	72,614	4.2
Hispanic or Latino (of any race)	9,790	5.7
Central American, ex. Mexican	974	9.8
Costa Rican	0	0.0
Guatemalan	470	9.9
Honduran	67	8.9
Nicaraguan	83	18.0
Salvadoran	325	10.3
Cuban	96	5.5
Mexican	7,440	5.2
Puerto Rican	292	9.7
South American	275	6.1
Argentinean	27	3.7
Chilean	8	1.5
Colombian	54	7.0
Ecuadorian	24	6.2
Peruvian	116	9.1
Spaniard	188	5.8

Homeownership Rate
(Universe: Occupied Housing Units)

Group	%
Total Population	62.2
Hispanic or Latino (of any race)	40.2
Central American, ex. Mexican	41.9
Costa Rican	51.1
Guatemalan	35.3
Honduran	39.1
Nicaraguan	51.1
Panamanian	53.5
Salvadoran	45.0
Cuban	42.4
Dominican Republic	37.9
Mexican	39.0
Puerto Rican	44.7
South American	52.3
Argentinean	55.5
Bolivian	51.7
Chilean	57.3
Colombian	51.0
Ecuadorian	45.7
Paraguayan	48.3
Peruvian	52.4
Uruguayan	47.4
Venezuelan	49.5
Spaniard	57.0

Median Home Value

Group	Dollars
Total Population	252,600
Hispanic or Latino (of any race)	203,900
Central American, ex. Mexican	218,600
Costa Rican	397,100
Guatemalan	211,700
Honduran	213,100

Notes: (1) Percent of total population; (2) Percent of Hispanic/Latino population; Profiles include places with an overall population of at least 125,000, OR an overall population of at least 25,000 where the Hispanic/Latino population is at least 20% of the overall population. In states where less than five places meet either of these criteria, we have included places with at least 10,000 total population with the highest percentage of Hispanic/Latino population. These places are identified with an asterisk (*); Please refer to the User's Guide for a full explanation of data.

Group	Dollars
Nicaraguan	292,800
Salvadoran	194,700
Cuban	247,900
Mexican	194,600
Puerto Rican	260,000
South American	275,000
Argentinean	370,100
Chilean	240,600
Colombian	272,300
Ecuadorian	260,700
Peruvian	261,900
Spaniard	246,400

Median Gross Rent

Group	Dollars
Total Population	795
Hispanic or Latino (of any race)	755
Central American, ex. Mexican	782
Costa Rican	539
Guatemalan	766
Honduran	777
Nicaraguan	845
Salvadoran	832
Cuban	812
Mexican	747
Puerto Rican	769
South American	865
Argentinean	782
Chilean	950
Colombian	1,125
Ecuadorian	935
Peruvian	741
Spaniard	761

Median Household Income
(2010 Inflation-Adjusted Dollars)

Group	Dollars
Total Population	49,260
Hispanic or Latino (of any race)	37,397
Central American, ex. Mexican	37,913
Costa Rican	62,868
Guatemalan	34,659
Honduran	28,581
Nicaraguan	43,514
Salvadoran	39,396
Cuban	39,291
Mexican	36,527
Puerto Rican	42,893
South American	50,634
Argentinean	50,921
Chilean	71,442
Colombian	59,375
Ecuadorian	35,893
Peruvian	50,743
Spaniard	43,045

Per Capita Income
(2010 Inflation-Adjusted Dollars)

Group	Dollars
Total Population	26,171
Hispanic or Latino (of any race)	12,751
Central American, ex. Mexican	13,839
Costa Rican	25,348
Guatemalan	11,253
Honduran	15,665
Nicaraguan	15,214
Salvadoran	15,760
Cuban	19,969
Mexican	11,860
Puerto Rican	17,551
South American	23,669
Argentinean	29,313
Chilean	25,258
Colombian	23,082
Ecuadorian	17,261
Peruvian	21,726
Spaniard	22,456

Households with $100,000+ Income

Group	Number	%
Total Population	263,152	17.6
Hispanic or Latino (of any race)	8,682	8.3
Central American, ex. Mexican	417	7.6
Costa Rican	69	23.4
Guatemalan	106	4.2
Honduran	13	2.7
Nicaraguan	7	2.2
Salvadoran	177	10.7
Cuban	199	14.3
Mexican	6,030	7.2
Puerto Rican	250	11.0
South American	714	23.9
Argentinean	208	40.9
Chilean	78	26.7
Colombian	202	33.0
Ecuadorian	14	7.5
Peruvian	99	13.6
Spaniard	436	12.9

Households with Food Stamps/SNAP Benefits During Past 12 Months

Group	Number	%
Total Population	194,544	13.0
Hispanic or Latino (of any race)	24,040	22.9
Central American, ex. Mexican	894	16.3
Costa Rican	30	10.2
Guatemalan	417	16.4
Honduran	139	29.2
Nicaraguan	107	33.6
Salvadoran	187	11.3
Cuban	350	25.2
Mexican	20,574	24.4
Puerto Rican	539	23.7
South American	318	10.7
Argentinean	80	15.7
Chilean	52	17.8
Colombian	10	1.6
Ecuadorian	49	26.3
Peruvian	72	9.9
Spaniard	429	12.7

Poverty Rate
(Income in Past 12 Months Below Poverty Level)

Group	%
Total Population	14.0
Hispanic or Latino (of any race)	25.6
Central American, ex. Mexican	21.8
Costa Rican	14.1
Guatemalan	25.4
Honduran	28.2
Nicaraguan	10.3
Salvadoran	17.8
Cuban	27.0
Mexican	26.7
Puerto Rican	24.0
South American	11.6
Argentinean	15.4
Chilean	13.2
Colombian	11.1
Ecuadorian	4.5
Peruvian	11.1
Spaniard	14.3

Aloha

Population

Group	Number	%TP[1]	%HP[2]
Total Population	49,425	100.0	–
Hispanic or Latino (of any race)	10,443	21.1	100.0
Central American, ex. Mexican	751	1.5	7.2
Guatemalan	430	0.9	4.1
Salvadoran	184	0.4	1.8
Mexican	8,417	17.0	80.6
Puerto Rican	186	0.4	1.8
South American	237	0.5	2.3
Spaniard	125	0.3	1.2

Population Growth: 2000–2010

Group	%
Total Population	18.4
Hispanic or Latino (of any race)	93.5
Central American, ex. Mexican	191.1
Guatemalan	211.6
Mexican	108.0
Puerto Rican	72.2

Males per 100 Females

Group	Number
Total Population	100.0
Hispanic or Latino (of any race)	105.3
Central American, ex. Mexican	100.8
Guatemalan	110.8
Salvadoran	82.2
Mexican	106.5
Puerto Rican	73.8
South American	74.3
Spaniard	115.5

Average Household Size

Group	People
Total Population	2.91
Hispanic or Latino (of any race)	4.24
Central American, ex. Mexican	4.18
Guatemalan	4.34
Salvadoran	3.98
Mexican	4.38
Puerto Rican	2.51
South American	3.39
Spaniard	3.15

Median Age

Group	Years
Total Population	32.8
Hispanic or Latino (of any race)	23.0
Central American, ex. Mexican	30.2
Guatemalan	30.0
Salvadoran	30.4
Mexican	21.9
Puerto Rican	30.0
South American	32.5
Spaniard	30.9

High School Graduates
(Universe: Population 25 Years and Over)

Group	Number	%
Total Population	26,490	87.6
Hispanic or Latino (of any race)	2,234	56.8
Mexican	1,666	53.0

Four-Year College Graduates
(Universe: Population 25 Years and Over)

Group	Number	%
Total Population	8,061	26.7
Hispanic or Latino (of any race)	314	8.0
Mexican	156	5.0

Population Age 3–17 Enrolled in Public School
(Universe: Population Age 3–17 Enrolled in School)

Group	Number	%
Total Population	8,391	86.6
Hispanic or Latino (of any race)	2,257	91.6
Mexican	1,986	96.6

Population Age 3–17 Enrolled in Private School
(Universe: Population Age 3–17 Enrolled in School)

Group	Number	%
Total Population	1,293	13.4
Hispanic or Latino (of any race)	208	8.4
Mexican	70	3.4

Foreign-Born Population

Group	Number	%
Total Population	9,016	19.0
Hispanic or Latino (of any race)	3,724	41.8
Mexican	3,184	43.4

Foreign-Born Naturalized U.S. Citizens

Group	Number	%
Total Population	3,632	40.3
Hispanic or Latino (of any race)	603	16.2
Mexican	380	11.9

Language Spoken at Home: English Only
(Universe: Population 5 Years and Over)

Group	Number	%
Total Population	32,299	74.1
Hispanic or Latino (of any race)	1,671	22.2
Mexican	1,294	20.9

Language Spoken at Home: Spanish
(Universe: Population 5 Years and Over)

Group	Number	%
Total Population	6,160	14.1
Hispanic or Latino (of any race)	5,831	77.5
Mexican	4,889	79.1

Notes: (1) Percent of total population; (2) Percent of Hispanic/Latino population; Profiles include places with an overall population of at least 125,000, OR an overall population of at least 25,000 where the Hispanic/Latino population is at least 20% of the overall population. In states where less than five places meet either of these criteria, we have included places with at least 10,000 total population with the highest percentage of Hispanic/Latino population. These places are identified with an asterisk (*); Please refer to the User's Guide for a full explanation of data.

STATE & PLACE PROFILES

Unemployment Rate
(Universe: Population 16 Years and Over)

Group	%
Total Population	9.4
Hispanic or Latino (of any race)	10.7
Mexican	10.7

Class of Worker: Private Wage and Salary
(Universe: Civilian Employed Population 16 Years and Over)

Group	Number	%
Total Population	19,597	84.2
Hispanic or Latino (of any race)	3,386	89.3
Mexican	2,751	91.7

Class of Worker: Government
(Universe: Civilian Employed Population 16 Years and Over)

Group	Number	%
Total Population	2,328	10.0
Hispanic or Latino (of any race)	261	6.9
Mexican	134	4.5

Means of Transportation to Work: Car, Truck or Van
(Universe: Workers 16 Years and Over)

Group	Number	%
Total Population	19,685	86.0
Hispanic or Latino (of any race)	3,188	87.6
Mexican	2,541	88.7

Means of Transportation to Work: Public Transportation (ex. Taxicab)
(Universe: Workers 16 Years and Over)

Group	Number	%
Total Population	1,537	6.7
Hispanic or Latino (of any race)	209	5.7
Mexican	134	4.7

Homeownership Rate
(Universe: Occupied Housing Units)

Group	%
Total Population	67.3
Hispanic or Latino (of any race)	45.8
Central American, ex. Mexican	58.1
Guatemalan	57.6
Salvadoran	52.1
Mexican	43.4
Puerto Rican	60.5
South American	67.2
Spaniard	70.7

Median Home Value

Group	Dollars
Total Population	244,500
Hispanic or Latino (of any race)	234,900
Mexican	231,300

Median Gross Rent

Group	Dollars
Total Population	974
Hispanic or Latino (of any race)	797
Mexican	800

Median Household Income
(2010 Inflation-Adjusted Dollars)

Group	Dollars
Total Population	58,450
Hispanic or Latino (of any race)	43,132
Mexican	42,377

Per Capita Income
(2010 Inflation-Adjusted Dollars)

Group	Dollars
Total Population	22,799
Hispanic or Latino (of any race)	13,099
Mexican	11,872

Households with $100,000+ Income

Group	Number	%
Total Population	2,814	17.1
Hispanic or Latino (of any race)	262	13.8
Mexican	195	11.6

Households with Food Stamps/SNAP Benefits During Past 12 Months

Group	Number	%
Total Population	1,944	11.8
Hispanic or Latino (of any race)	306	16.1
Mexican	276	16.4

Poverty Rate
(Income in Past 12 Months Below Poverty Level)

Group	%
Total Population	14.0
Hispanic or Latino (of any race)	22.0
Mexican	24.9

Eugene

Population

Group	Number	%TP[1]	%HP[2]
Total Population	156,185	100.0	–
Hispanic or Latino (of any race)	12,200	7.8	100.0
Central American, ex. Mexican	789	0.5	6.5
Guatemalan	229	0.1	1.9
Salvadoran	302	0.2	2.5
Cuban	155	0.1	1.3
Mexican	8,830	5.7	72.4
Puerto Rican	374	0.2	3.1
South American	625	0.4	5.1
Colombian	117	0.1	1.0
Peruvian	217	0.1	1.8
Spaniard	375	0.2	3.1

Population Growth: 2000–2010

Group	%
Total Population	13.3
Hispanic or Latino (of any race)	78.3
Central American, ex. Mexican	224.7
Mexican	87.4
Puerto Rican	52.7
South American	148.0

Males per 100 Females

Group	Number
Total Population	95.6
Hispanic or Latino (of any race)	103.8
Central American, ex. Mexican	100.8
Guatemalan	100.9
Salvadoran	98.7
Cuban	93.8
Mexican	108.6
Puerto Rican	92.8
South American	84.4
Colombian	77.3
Peruvian	70.9
Spaniard	82.0

Average Household Size

Group	People
Total Population	2.24
Hispanic or Latino (of any race)	3.00
Central American, ex. Mexican	3.05
Guatemalan	3.44
Salvadoran	3.19
Cuban	2.34
Mexican	3.15
Puerto Rican	2.32
South American	2.79
Colombian	2.72
Peruvian	2.88
Spaniard	2.34

Median Age

Group	Years
Total Population	33.8
Hispanic or Latino (of any race)	23.8
Central American, ex. Mexican	25.8
Guatemalan	23.4
Salvadoran	27.1
Cuban	24.4
Mexican	23.2
Puerto Rican	24.2
South American	28.2
Colombian	23.3
Peruvian	31.1
Spaniard	30.3

High School Graduates
(Universe: Population 25 Years and Over)

Group	Number	%
Total Population	89,776	92.6
Hispanic or Latino (of any race)	3,870	70.6
Mexican	2,604	66.9

Four-Year College Graduates
(Universe: Population 25 Years and Over)

Group	Number	%
Total Population	39,027	40.2
Hispanic or Latino (of any race)	1,406	25.6
Mexican	861	22.1

Population Age 3–17 Enrolled in Public School
(Universe: Population Age 3–17 Enrolled in School)

Group	Number	%
Total Population	19,026	88.6
Hispanic or Latino (of any race)	2,793	95.5
Mexican	2,315	95.2

Population Age 3–17 Enrolled in Private School
(Universe: Population Age 3–17 Enrolled in School)

Group	Number	%
Total Population	2,458	11.4
Hispanic or Latino (of any race)	133	4.5
Mexican	116	4.8

Foreign-Born Population

Group	Number	%
Total Population	11,703	7.6
Hispanic or Latino (of any race)	3,267	28.9
Mexican	2,517	29.3

Foreign-Born Naturalized U.S. Citizens

Group	Number	%
Total Population	3,849	32.9
Hispanic or Latino (of any race)	483	14.8
Mexican	274	10.9

Language Spoken at Home: English Only
(Universe: Population 5 Years and Over)

Group	Number	%
Total Population	127,252	87.2
Hispanic or Latino (of any race)	4,604	46.2
Mexican	3,275	43.7

Language Spoken at Home: Spanish
(Universe: Population 5 Years and Over)

Group	Number	%
Total Population	8,717	6.0
Hispanic or Latino (of any race)	5,304	53.3
Mexican	4,164	55.6

Unemployment Rate
(Universe: Population 16 Years and Over)

Group	%
Total Population	8.2
Hispanic or Latino (of any race)	8.6
Mexican	7.4

Class of Worker: Private Wage and Salary
(Universe: Civilian Employed Population 16 Years and Over)

Group	Number	%
Total Population	54,066	73.6
Hispanic or Latino (of any race)	3,822	83.4
Mexican	2,939	83.6

Class of Worker: Government
(Universe: Civilian Employed Population 16 Years and Over)

Group	Number	%
Total Population	13,614	18.5
Hispanic or Latino (of any race)	631	13.8
Mexican	458	13.0

Means of Transportation to Work: Car, Truck or Van
(Universe: Workers 16 Years and Over)

Group	Number	%
Total Population	52,479	74.2
Hispanic or Latino (of any race)	3,193	73.1
Mexican	2,437	73.1

Notes: (1) Percent of total population; (2) Percent of Hispanic/Latino population; Profiles include places with an overall population of at least 125,000, OR an overall population of at least 25,000 where the Hispanic/Latino population is at least 20% of the overall population. In states where less than five places meet either of these criteria, we have included places with at least 10,000 total population with the highest percentage of Hispanic/Latino population. These places are identified with an asterisk (*); Please refer to the User's Guide for a full explanation of data.

Means of Transportation to Work: Public Transportation (ex. Taxicab)
(Universe: Workers 16 Years and Over)

Group	Number	%
Total Population	4,131	5.8
Hispanic or Latino (of any race)	315	7.2
Mexican	249	7.5

Homeownership Rate
(Universe: Occupied Housing Units)

Group	%
Total Population	50.1
Hispanic or Latino (of any race)	33.5
Central American, ex. Mexican	37.2
Guatemalan	26.9
Salvadoran	37.2
Cuban	36.2
Mexican	31.9
Puerto Rican	30.9
South American	43.5
Colombian	40.6
Peruvian	42.6
Spaniard	50.7

Median Home Value

Group	Dollars
Total Population	245,500
Hispanic or Latino (of any race)	208,100
Mexican	181,600

Median Gross Rent

Group	Dollars
Total Population	781
Hispanic or Latino (of any race)	735
Mexican	714

Median Household Income
(2010 Inflation-Adjusted Dollars)

Group	Dollars
Total Population	41,701
Hispanic or Latino (of any race)	31,738
Mexican	31,190

Per Capita Income
(2010 Inflation-Adjusted Dollars)

Group	Dollars
Total Population	24,917
Hispanic or Latino (of any race)	13,329
Mexican	12,539

Households with $100,000+ Income

Group	Number	%
Total Population	9,662	14.9
Hispanic or Latino (of any race)	296	8.3
Mexican	209	8.3

Households with Food Stamps/SNAP Benefits During Past 12 Months

Group	Number	%
Total Population	9,418	14.5
Hispanic or Latino (of any race)	918	25.6
Mexican	651	25.9

Poverty Rate
(Income in Past 12 Months Below Poverty Level)

Group	%
Total Population	20.7
Hispanic or Latino (of any race)	26.8
Mexican	27.1

Hillsboro

Population

Group	Number	%TP[1]	%HP[2]
Total Population	91,611	100.0	–
Hispanic or Latino (of any race)	20,726	22.6	100.0
Central American, ex. Mexican	1,005	1.1	4.8
Guatemalan	604	0.7	2.9
Salvadoran	188	0.2	0.9
Cuban	123	0.1	0.6
Mexican	17,490	19.1	84.4
Puerto Rican	400	0.4	1.9
South American	376	0.4	1.8
Peruvian	109	0.1	0.5
Spaniard	240	0.3	1.2

Population Growth: 2000–2010

Group	%
Total Population	30.5
Hispanic or Latino (of any race)	56.3
Central American, ex. Mexican	71.8
Guatemalan	46.6
Mexican	60.1
Puerto Rican	109.4

Males per 100 Females

Group	Number
Total Population	100.6
Hispanic or Latino (of any race)	110.7
Central American, ex. Mexican	134.8
Guatemalan	177.1
Salvadoran	97.9
Cuban	78.3
Mexican	111.6
Puerto Rican	109.4
South American	85.2
Peruvian	75.8
Spaniard	72.7

Average Household Size

Group	People
Total Population	2.71
Hispanic or Latino (of any race)	3.97
Central American, ex. Mexican	3.90
Guatemalan	4.17
Salvadoran	3.90
Cuban	2.72
Mexican	4.14
Puerto Rican	2.78
South American	2.59
Peruvian	2.49
Spaniard	2.51

Median Age

Group	Years
Total Population	32.0
Hispanic or Latino (of any race)	23.8
Central American, ex. Mexican	28.5
Guatemalan	27.4
Salvadoran	28.9
Cuban	30.3
Mexican	22.9
Puerto Rican	28.0
South American	32.8
Peruvian	31.5
Spaniard	31.3

High School Graduates
(Universe: Population 25 Years and Over)

Group	Number	%
Total Population	47,668	86.4
Hispanic or Latino (of any race)	4,709	47.9
Central American, ex. Mexican	543	54.2
Mexican	3,404	42.8

Four-Year College Graduates
(Universe: Population 25 Years and Over)

Group	Number	%
Total Population	18,323	33.2
Hispanic or Latino (of any race)	772	7.9
Central American, ex. Mexican	59	5.9
Mexican	484	6.1

Population Age 3–17 Enrolled in Public School
(Universe: Population Age 3–17 Enrolled in School)

Group	Number	%
Total Population	14,516	85.5
Hispanic or Latino (of any race)	5,208	95.9
Central American, ex. Mexican	313	100.0
Mexican	4,637	96.0

Population Age 3–17 Enrolled in Private School
(Universe: Population Age 3–17 Enrolled in School)

Group	Number	%
Total Population	2,453	14.5
Hispanic or Latino (of any race)	222	4.1
Central American, ex. Mexican	0	0.0
Mexican	192	4.0

Foreign-Born Population

Group	Number	%
Total Population	16,927	19.2
Hispanic or Latino (of any race)	9,569	46.7
Central American, ex. Mexican	1,245	71.0
Mexican	7,931	45.9

Foreign-Born Naturalized U.S. Citizens

Group	Number	%
Total Population	4,365	25.8
Hispanic or Latino (of any race)	1,254	13.1
Central American, ex. Mexican	159	12.8
Mexican	909	11.5

Language Spoken at Home: English Only
(Universe: Population 5 Years and Over)

Group	Number	%
Total Population	58,014	72.1
Hispanic or Latino (of any race)	3,319	18.7
Central American, ex. Mexican	81	5.2
Mexican	2,514	16.8

Language Spoken at Home: Spanish
(Universe: Population 5 Years and Over)

Group	Number	%
Total Population	15,105	18.8
Hispanic or Latino (of any race)	14,414	81.0
Central American, ex. Mexican	1,465	94.8
Mexican	12,451	83.2

Unemployment Rate
(Universe: Population 16 Years and Over)

Group	%
Total Population	8.1
Hispanic or Latino (of any race)	10.8
Central American, ex. Mexican	14.1
Mexican	10.4

Class of Worker: Private Wage and Salary
(Universe: Civilian Employed Population 16 Years and Over)

Group	Number	%
Total Population	37,900	85.5
Hispanic or Latino (of any race)	8,343	88.8
Central American, ex. Mexican	891	86.5
Mexican	6,847	89.2

Class of Worker: Government
(Universe: Civilian Employed Population 16 Years and Over)

Group	Number	%
Total Population	4,468	10.1
Hispanic or Latino (of any race)	656	7.0
Central American, ex. Mexican	60	5.8
Mexican	521	6.8

Means of Transportation to Work: Car, Truck or Van
(Universe: Workers 16 Years and Over)

Group	Number	%
Total Population	36,317	84.3
Hispanic or Latino (of any race)	7,522	83.0
Central American, ex. Mexican	849	83.6
Mexican	6,096	82.6

Means of Transportation to Work: Public Transportation (ex. Taxicab)
(Universe: Workers 16 Years and Over)

Group	Number	%
Total Population	3,091	7.2
Hispanic or Latino (of any race)	927	10.2
Central American, ex. Mexican	122	12.0
Mexican	759	10.3

Homeownership Rate
(Universe: Occupied Housing Units)

Group	%
Total Population	54.5
Hispanic or Latino (of any race)	34.8
Central American, ex. Mexican	35.4
Guatemalan	28.3
Salvadoran	52.5
Cuban	51.1
Mexican	33.9
Puerto Rican	47.3
South American	50.4
Peruvian	38.5

Notes: (1) Percent of total population; (2) Percent of Hispanic/Latino population; Profiles include places with an overall population of at least 125,000, OR an overall population of at least 25,000 where the Hispanic/Latino population is at least 20% of the overall population. In states where less than five places meet either of these criteria, we have included places with at least 10,000 total population with the highest percentage of Hispanic/Latino population. These places are identified with an asterisk (*); Please refer to the User's Guide for a full explanation of data.

Spaniard	42.2

Median Home Value

Group	Dollars
Total Population	264,600
Hispanic or Latino (of any race)	230,700
Central American, ex. Mexican	260,500
Mexican	224,100

Median Gross Rent

Group	Dollars
Total Population	947
Hispanic or Latino (of any race)	834
Central American, ex. Mexican	874
Mexican	799

Median Household Income
(2010 Inflation-Adjusted Dollars)

Group	Dollars
Total Population	60,695
Hispanic or Latino (of any race)	42,529
Central American, ex. Mexican	52,109
Mexican	40,752

Per Capita Income
(2010 Inflation-Adjusted Dollars)

Group	Dollars
Total Population	25,697
Hispanic or Latino (of any race)	12,285
Central American, ex. Mexican	15,394
Mexican	11,342

Households with $100,000+ Income

Group	Number	%
Total Population	6,702	21.2
Hispanic or Latino (of any race)	364	8.4
Central American, ex. Mexican	42	11.1
Mexican	264	7.4

Households with Food Stamps/SNAP Benefits During Past 12 Months

Group	Number	%
Total Population	2,990	9.5
Hispanic or Latino (of any race)	1,138	26.2
Central American, ex. Mexican	85	22.4
Mexican	953	26.6

Poverty Rate
(Income in Past 12 Months Below Poverty Level)

Group	%
Total Population	10.9
Hispanic or Latino (of any race)	23.8
Central American, ex. Mexican	22.3
Mexican	24.6

McMinnville

Population

Group	Number	%TP[1]	%HP[2]
Total Population	32,187	100.0	–
Hispanic or Latino (of any race)	6,630	20.6	100.0
Central American, ex. Mexican	151	0.5	2.3
Mexican	5,890	18.3	88.8

Population Growth: 2000–2010

Group	%
Total Population	21.5
Hispanic or Latino (of any race)	70.9
Mexican	86.6

Males per 100 Females

Group	Number
Total Population	93.0
Hispanic or Latino (of any race)	113.0
Central American, ex. Mexican	109.7
Mexican	114.9

Average Household Size

Group	People
Total Population	2.61
Hispanic or Latino (of any race)	4.11
Central American, ex. Mexican	4.34
Mexican	4.23

Median Age

Group	Years
Total Population	34.0
Hispanic or Latino (of any race)	22.4
Central American, ex. Mexican	28.3
Mexican	22.0

High School Graduates
(Universe: Population 25 Years and Over)

Group	Number	%
Total Population	15,809	82.4
Hispanic or Latino (of any race)	1,280	42.5
Mexican	1,045	39.8

Four-Year College Graduates
(Universe: Population 25 Years and Over)

Group	Number	%
Total Population	4,121	21.5
Hispanic or Latino (of any race)	102	3.4
Mexican	70	2.7

Population Age 3–17 Enrolled in Public School
(Universe: Population Age 3–17 Enrolled in School)

Group	Number	%
Total Population	4,950	88.6
Hispanic or Latino (of any race)	1,632	96.9
Mexican	1,423	97.7

Population Age 3–17 Enrolled in Private School
(Universe: Population Age 3–17 Enrolled in School)

Group	Number	%
Total Population	639	11.4
Hispanic or Latino (of any race)	52	3.1
Mexican	34	2.3

Foreign-Born Population

Group	Number	%
Total Population	3,475	11.1
Hispanic or Latino (of any race)	2,586	40.3
Mexican	2,397	42.9

Foreign-Born Naturalized U.S. Citizens

Group	Number	%
Total Population	1,104	31.8
Hispanic or Latino (of any race)	452	17.5
Mexican	376	15.7

Language Spoken at Home: English Only
(Universe: Population 5 Years and Over)

Group	Number	%
Total Population	23,200	80.3
Hispanic or Latino (of any race)	950	17.8
Mexican	588	12.6

Language Spoken at Home: Spanish
(Universe: Population 5 Years and Over)

Group	Number	%
Total Population	4,691	16.2
Hispanic or Latino (of any race)	4,340	81.3
Mexican	4,092	87.4

Unemployment Rate
(Universe: Population 16 Years and Over)

Group	%
Total Population	10.3
Hispanic or Latino (of any race)	12.4
Mexican	6.8

Class of Worker: Private Wage and Salary
(Universe: Civilian Employed Population 16 Years and Over)

Group	Number	%
Total Population	10,695	80.2
Hispanic or Latino (of any race)	2,223	92.2
Mexican	2,054	92.8

Class of Worker: Government
(Universe: Civilian Employed Population 16 Years and Over)

Group	Number	%
Total Population	1,850	13.9
Hispanic or Latino (of any race)	122	5.1
Mexican	93	4.2

Means of Transportation to Work: Car, Truck or Van
(Universe: Workers 16 Years and Over)

Group	Number	%
Total Population	11,465	87.5
Hispanic or Latino (of any race)	2,332	96.3
Mexican	2,141	96.3

Means of Transportation to Work: Public Transportation (ex. Taxicab)
(Universe: Workers 16 Years and Over)

Group	Number	%
Total Population	60	0.5
Hispanic or Latino (of any race)	9	0.4
Mexican	9	0.4

Homeownership Rate
(Universe: Occupied Housing Units)

Group	%
Total Population	58.0
Hispanic or Latino (of any race)	43.1
Central American, ex. Mexican	68.6
Mexican	43.5

Median Home Value

Group	Dollars
Total Population	213,900
Hispanic or Latino (of any race)	195,800
Mexican	187,100

Median Gross Rent

Group	Dollars
Total Population	729
Hispanic or Latino (of any race)	682
Mexican	677

Median Household Income
(2010 Inflation-Adjusted Dollars)

Group	Dollars
Total Population	41,457
Hispanic or Latino (of any race)	35,577
Mexican	32,610

Per Capita Income
(2010 Inflation-Adjusted Dollars)

Group	Dollars
Total Population	21,341
Hispanic or Latino (of any race)	10,103
Mexican	9,425

Households with $100,000+ Income

Group	Number	%
Total Population	1,600	14.1
Hispanic or Latino (of any race)	30	1.9
Mexican	30	2.4

Households with Food Stamps/SNAP Benefits During Past 12 Months

Group	Number	%
Total Population	1,920	16.9
Hispanic or Latino (of any race)	479	30.9
Mexican	331	26.2

Poverty Rate
(Income in Past 12 Months Below Poverty Level)

Group	%
Total Population	19.0
Hispanic or Latino (of any race)	31.9
Mexican	34.1

Portland

Population

Group	Number	%TP[1]	%HP[2]
Total Population	583,776	100.0	–
Hispanic or Latino (of any race)	54,840	9.4	100.0
Central American, ex. Mexican	3,941	0.7	7.2
Costa Rican	144	<0.1	0.3
Guatemalan	1,894	0.3	3.5
Honduran	423	0.1	0.8
Nicaraguan	284	<0.1	0.5
Panamanian	137	<0.1	0.2
Salvadoran	1,027	0.2	1.9
Cuban	2,172	0.4	4.0

Notes: (1) Percent of total population; (2) Percent of Hispanic/Latino population; Profiles include places with an overall population of at least 125,000, OR an overall population of at least 25,000 where the Hispanic/Latino population is at least 20% of the overall population. In states where less than five places meet either of these criteria, we have included places with at least 10,000 total population with the highest percentage of Hispanic/Latino population. These places are identified with an asterisk (*); Please refer to the User's Guide for a full explanation of data.

Dominican Republic	138	<0.1	0.3
Mexican	39,181	6.7	71.4
Puerto Rican	1,729	0.3	3.2
South American	2,215	0.4	4.0
Argentinean	381	0.1	0.7
Chilean	307	0.1	0.6
Colombian	446	0.1	0.8
Ecuadorian	215	<0.1	0.4
Peruvian	537	0.1	1.0
Venezuelan	161	<0.1	0.3
Spaniard	1,215	0.2	2.2

Population Growth: 2000–2010

Group	%
Total Population	10.3
Hispanic or Latino (of any race)	52.1
Central American, ex. Mexican	92.2
Guatemalan	86.8
Honduran	108.4
Nicaraguan	140.7
Salvadoran	119.0
Cuban	63.4
Mexican	55.9
Puerto Rican	70.3
South American	136.9
Chilean	147.6
Colombian	93.9
Peruvian	138.7
Spaniard	699.3

Males per 100 Females

Group	Number
Total Population	98.2
Hispanic or Latino (of any race)	111.2
Central American, ex. Mexican	108.5
Costa Rican	63.6
Guatemalan	126.3
Honduran	92.3
Nicaraguan	91.9
Panamanian	85.1
Salvadoran	101.0
Cuban	122.8
Dominican Republic	130.0
Mexican	112.6
Puerto Rican	103.2
South American	90.6
Argentinean	90.5
Chilean	94.3
Colombian	83.5
Ecuadorian	106.7
Peruvian	93.9
Venezuelan	75.0
Spaniard	86.3

Average Household Size

Group	People
Total Population	2.28
Hispanic or Latino (of any race)	3.26
Central American, ex. Mexican	3.60
Costa Rican	2.00
Guatemalan	4.15
Honduran	3.75
Nicaraguan	3.10
Panamanian	2.43
Salvadoran	3.42
Cuban	2.65
Dominican Republic	2.48
Mexican	3.51
Puerto Rican	2.28
South American	2.38
Argentinean	2.43
Chilean	2.45
Colombian	2.34
Ecuadorian	2.52
Peruvian	2.43
Venezuelan	2.08
Spaniard	2.25

Median Age

Group	Years
Total Population	35.8
Hispanic or Latino (of any race)	26.1
Central American, ex. Mexican	27.4
Costa Rican	32.0
Guatemalan	25.5
Honduran	26.6
Nicaraguan	28.9
Panamanian	32.3
Salvadoran	29.7
Cuban	34.0
Dominican Republic	28.5
Mexican	24.9
Puerto Rican	28.4
South American	31.5
Argentinean	32.0
Chilean	31.5
Colombian	30.7
Ecuadorian	28.6
Peruvian	32.9
Venezuelan	31.4
Spaniard	33.7

High School Graduates
(Universe: Population 25 Years and Over)

Group	Number	%
Total Population	359,185	89.5
Hispanic or Latino (of any race)	15,408	60.1
Central American, ex. Mexican	911	35.1
Guatemalan	189	15.2
Salvadoran	411	54.9
Cuban	649	77.7
Mexican	10,351	56.9
Puerto Rican	886	90.9
South American	1,051	96.0
Spaniard	680	97.3

Four-Year College Graduates
(Universe: Population 25 Years and Over)

Group	Number	%
Total Population	165,053	41.1
Hispanic or Latino (of any race)	4,973	19.4
Central American, ex. Mexican	275	10.6
Guatemalan	50	4.0
Salvadoran	150	20.0
Cuban	221	26.5
Mexican	2,858	15.7
Puerto Rican	357	36.6
South American	574	52.4
Spaniard	342	48.9

Population Age 3–17 Enrolled in Public School
(Universe: Population Age 3–17 Enrolled in School)

Group	Number	%
Total Population	64,966	81.6
Hispanic or Latino (of any race)	11,161	92.5
Central American, ex. Mexican	827	91.3
Guatemalan	613	96.7
Salvadoran	129	84.3
Cuban	260	93.9
Mexican	9,093	93.2
Puerto Rican	181	90.5
South American	211	70.8
Spaniard	174	82.5

Population Age 3–17 Enrolled in Private School
(Universe: Population Age 3–17 Enrolled in School)

Group	Number	%
Total Population	14,671	18.4
Hispanic or Latino (of any race)	910	7.5
Central American, ex. Mexican	79	8.7
Guatemalan	21	3.3
Salvadoran	24	15.7
Cuban	17	6.1
Mexican	660	6.8
Puerto Rican	19	9.5
South American	87	29.2
Spaniard	37	17.5

Foreign-Born Population

Group	Number	%
Total Population	76,132	13.4
Hispanic or Latino (of any race)	20,241	40.6
Central American, ex. Mexican	3,128	66.5
Guatemalan	1,831	66.4
Salvadoran	828	78.0
Cuban	689	45.2
Mexican	14,986	40.5
Puerto Rican	111	7.3
South American	783	47.7
Spaniard	65	5.4

Foreign-Born Naturalized U.S. Citizens

Group	Number	%
Total Population	30,647	40.3
Hispanic or Latino (of any race)	2,739	13.5
Central American, ex. Mexican	724	23.1
Guatemalan	292	15.9
Salvadoran	298	36.0
Cuban	216	31.3
Mexican	1,313	8.8
Puerto Rican	9	8.1
South American	348	44.4
Spaniard	27	41.5

Language Spoken at Home: English Only
(Universe: Population 5 Years and Over)

Group	Number	%
Total Population	432,927	81.4
Hispanic or Latino (of any race)	13,011	29.9
Central American, ex. Mexican	496	11.7
Guatemalan	144	5.9
Salvadoran	50	4.9
Cuban	388	27.9
Mexican	8,855	27.6
Puerto Rican	855	61.0
South American	519	35.7
Spaniard	973	86.5

Language Spoken at Home: Spanish
(Universe: Population 5 Years and Over)

Group	Number	%
Total Population	37,266	7.0
Hispanic or Latino (of any race)	30,035	69.0
Central American, ex. Mexican	3,632	85.6
Guatemalan	2,167	89.3
Salvadoran	980	95.1
Cuban	1,004	72.1
Mexican	22,895	71.5
Puerto Rican	521	37.2
South American	917	63.0
Spaniard	130	11.6

Unemployment Rate
(Universe: Population 16 Years and Over)

Group	%
Total Population	8.8
Hispanic or Latino (of any race)	10.8
Central American, ex. Mexican	12.0
Guatemalan	14.2
Salvadoran	1.4
Cuban	13.1
Mexican	10.6
Puerto Rican	22.4
South American	4.8
Spaniard	5.0

Class of Worker: Private Wage and Salary
(Universe: Civilian Employed Population 16 Years and Over)

Group	Number	%
Total Population	236,065	79.1
Hispanic or Latino (of any race)	18,788	85.3
Central American, ex. Mexican	1,898	84.3
Guatemalan	1,000	87.2
Salvadoran	527	72.8
Cuban	601	83.9
Mexican	13,476	86.5
Puerto Rican	591	75.3
South American	818	76.5
Spaniard	470	72.9

Class of Worker: Government
(Universe: Civilian Employed Population 16 Years and Over)

Group	Number	%
Total Population	36,323	12.2
Hispanic or Latino (of any race)	1,678	7.6
Central American, ex. Mexican	173	7.7
Guatemalan	24	2.1
Salvadoran	139	19.2
Cuban	72	10.1
Mexican	1,026	6.6
Puerto Rican	141	18.0
South American	126	11.8
Spaniard	112	17.4

Notes: (1) Percent of total population; (2) Percent of Hispanic/Latino population; Profiles include places with an overall population of at least 125,000, OR an overall population of at least 25,000 where the Hispanic/Latino population is at least 20% of the overall population. In states where less than five places meet either of these criteria, we have included places with at least 10,000 total population with the highest percentage of Hispanic/Latino population. These places are identified with an asterisk (*); Please refer to the User's Guide for a full explanation of data.

Means of Transportation to Work: Car, Truck or Van
(Universe: Workers 16 Years and Over)

Group	Number	%
Total Population	203,734	69.8
Hispanic or Latino (of any race)	15,127	70.7
Central American, ex. Mexican	1,739	79.0
Guatemalan	947	84.6
Salvadoran	529	73.1
Cuban	446	64.3
Mexican	10,776	71.2
Puerto Rican	549	75.9
South American	684	66.5
Spaniard	421	66.3

Means of Transportation to Work: Public Transportation (ex. Taxicab)
(Universe: Workers 16 Years and Over)

Group	Number	%
Total Population	35,140	12.0
Hispanic or Latino (of any race)	3,965	18.5
Central American, ex. Mexican	330	15.0
Guatemalan	83	7.4
Salvadoran	188	26.0
Cuban	80	11.5
Mexican	2,858	18.9
Puerto Rican	96	13.3
South American	145	14.1
Spaniard	125	19.7

Homeownership Rate
(Universe: Occupied Housing Units)

Group	%
Total Population	53.7
Hispanic or Latino (of any race)	34.3
Central American, ex. Mexican	37.6
Costa Rican	39.1
Guatemalan	32.4
Honduran	29.2
Nicaraguan	39.7
Panamanian	47.5
Salvadoran	45.4
Cuban	32.2
Dominican Republic	30.2
Mexican	33.0
Puerto Rican	36.1
South American	45.0
Argentinean	43.3
Chilean	50.5
Colombian	42.2
Ecuadorian	39.4
Peruvian	46.0
Venezuelan	50.8
Spaniard	48.0

Median Home Value

Group	Dollars
Total Population	292,000
Hispanic or Latino (of any race)	237,000
Central American, ex. Mexican	247,000
Guatemalan	199,000
Salvadoran	233,900
Cuban	305,600
Mexican	226,800
Puerto Rican	329,200
South American	322,600
Spaniard	270,500

Median Gross Rent

Group	Dollars
Total Population	813
Hispanic or Latino (of any race)	778
Central American, ex. Mexican	768
Guatemalan	762
Salvadoran	839
Cuban	756
Mexican	786
Puerto Rican	798
South American	748
Spaniard	749

Median Household Income
(2010 Inflation-Adjusted Dollars)

Group	Dollars
Total Population	48,831
Hispanic or Latino (of any race)	36,963
Central American, ex. Mexican	30,676
Guatemalan	31,875
Salvadoran	34,706
Cuban	31,250
Mexican	36,198
Puerto Rican	42,647
South American	50,895
Spaniard	48,750

Per Capita Income
(2010 Inflation-Adjusted Dollars)

Group	Dollars
Total Population	29,797
Hispanic or Latino (of any race)	15,172
Central American, ex. Mexican	12,339
Guatemalan	9,872
Salvadoran	13,566
Cuban	16,686
Mexican	13,950
Puerto Rican	22,887
South American	33,685
Spaniard	26,321

Households with $100,000+ Income

Group	Number	%
Total Population	46,456	19.0
Hispanic or Latino (of any race)	1,402	10.2
Central American, ex. Mexican	56	4.2
Guatemalan	34	5.1
Salvadoran	0	0.0
Cuban	43	7.4
Mexican	955	10.2
Puerto Rican	78	13.5
South American	145	20.7
Spaniard	66	11.1

Households with Food Stamps/SNAP Benefits During Past 12 Months

Group	Number	%
Total Population	33,822	13.8
Hispanic or Latino (of any race)	2,896	21.0
Central American, ex. Mexican	313	23.2
Guatemalan	152	22.7
Salvadoran	52	17.6
Cuban	164	28.2
Mexican	2,069	22.1
Puerto Rican	172	29.8
South American	1	0.1
Spaniard	64	10.8

Poverty Rate
(Income in Past 12 Months Below Poverty Level)

Group	%
Total Population	16.3
Hispanic or Latino (of any race)	27.7
Central American, ex. Mexican	26.3
Guatemalan	24.7
Salvadoran	31.6
Cuban	27.6
Mexican	29.1
Puerto Rican	26.2
South American	11.5
Spaniard	16.5

Salem

Population

Group	Number	%TP[1]	%HP[2]
Total Population	154,637	100.0	–
Hispanic or Latino (of any race)	31,359	20.3	100.0
Central American, ex. Mexican	759	0.5	2.4
Guatemalan	271	0.2	0.9
Salvadoran	320	0.2	1.0
Cuban	121	0.1	0.4
Mexican	27,534	17.8	87.8
Puerto Rican	357	0.2	1.1
South American	343	0.2	1.1
Peruvian	108	0.1	0.3
Spaniard	352	0.2	1.1

Population Growth: 2000–2010

Group	%
Total Population	12.9
Hispanic or Latino (of any race)	57.0
Central American, ex. Mexican	144.8
Salvadoran	162.3
Cuban	18.6
Mexican	65.5
Puerto Rican	42.2
South American	174.4

Males per 100 Females

Group	Number
Total Population	99.5
Hispanic or Latino (of any race)	112.7
Central American, ex. Mexican	112.6
Guatemalan	148.6
Salvadoran	101.3
Cuban	95.2
Mexican	114.8
Puerto Rican	76.7
South American	86.4
Peruvian	80.0
Spaniard	88.2

Average Household Size

Group	People
Total Population	2.55
Hispanic or Latino (of any race)	3.89
Central American, ex. Mexican	3.79
Guatemalan	3.92
Salvadoran	3.73
Cuban	2.52
Mexican	3.99
Puerto Rican	2.73
South American	2.61
Peruvian	2.63
Spaniard	2.54

Median Age

Group	Years
Total Population	34.5
Hispanic or Latino (of any race)	22.0
Central American, ex. Mexican	28.7
Guatemalan	28.2
Salvadoran	29.4
Cuban	32.6
Mexican	21.7
Puerto Rican	23.4
South American	30.9
Peruvian	27.0
Spaniard	28.8

High School Graduates
(Universe: Population 25 Years and Over)

Group	Number	%
Total Population	82,215	84.5
Hispanic or Latino (of any race)	6,309	48.5
Mexican	4,856	43.2

Four-Year College Graduates
(Universe: Population 25 Years and Over)

Group	Number	%
Total Population	24,476	25.2
Hispanic or Latino (of any race)	1,021	7.9
Mexican	674	6.0

Population Age 3–17 Enrolled in Public School
(Universe: Population Age 3–17 Enrolled in School)

Group	Number	%
Total Population	24,432	89.9
Hispanic or Latino (of any race)	8,209	95.3
Mexican	7,809	97.4

Population Age 3–17 Enrolled in Private School
(Universe: Population Age 3–17 Enrolled in School)

Group	Number	%
Total Population	2,753	10.1
Hispanic or Latino (of any race)	402	4.7
Mexican	210	2.6

Foreign-Born Population

Group	Number	%
Total Population	19,340	12.7
Hispanic or Latino (of any race)	12,772	43.5
Mexican	11,828	44.9

Notes: (1) Percent of total population; (2) Percent of Hispanic/Latino population; Profiles include places with an overall population of at least 125,000, OR an overall population of at least 25,000 where the Hispanic/Latino population is at least 20% of the overall population. In states where less than five places meet either of these criteria, we have included places with at least 10,000 total population with the highest percentage of Hispanic/Latino population. These places are identified with an asterisk (*); Please refer to the User's Guide for a full explanation of data.

Foreign-Born Naturalized U.S. Citizens

Group	Number	%
Total Population	5,239	27.1
Hispanic or Latino (of any race)	2,035	15.9
Mexican	1,777	15.0

Language Spoken at Home: English Only
(Universe: Population 5 Years and Over)

Group	Number	%
Total Population	110,844	78.7
Hispanic or Latino (of any race)	5,530	21.9
Mexican	4,441	19.6

Language Spoken at Home: Spanish
(Universe: Population 5 Years and Over)

Group	Number	%
Total Population	22,041	15.6
Hispanic or Latino (of any race)	19,488	77.3
Mexican	18,113	80.0

Unemployment Rate
(Universe: Population 16 Years and Over)

Group	%
Total Population	9.7
Hispanic or Latino (of any race)	9.6
Mexican	10.1

Class of Worker: Private Wage and Salary
(Universe: Civilian Employed Population 16 Years and Over)

Group	Number	%
Total Population	47,353	71.5
Hispanic or Latino (of any race)	9,306	83.9
Mexican	8,408	84.5

Class of Worker: Government
(Universe: Civilian Employed Population 16 Years and Over)

Group	Number	%
Total Population	14,289	21.6
Hispanic or Latino (of any race)	1,138	10.3
Mexican	904	9.1

Means of Transportation to Work: Car, Truck or Van
(Universe: Workers 16 Years and Over)

Group	Number	%
Total Population	56,332	86.6
Hispanic or Latino (of any race)	9,511	87.9
Mexican	8,594	88.3

Means of Transportation to Work: Public Transportation (ex. Taxicab)
(Universe: Workers 16 Years and Over)

Group	Number	%
Total Population	1,740	2.7
Hispanic or Latino (of any race)	195	1.8
Mexican	183	1.9

Homeownership Rate
(Universe: Occupied Housing Units)

Group	%
Total Population	55.7
Hispanic or Latino (of any race)	37.3
Central American, ex. Mexican	46.3
Guatemalan	48.1
Salvadoran	47.0
Cuban	66.7
Mexican	36.6
Puerto Rican	32.6
South American	45.0
Peruvian	36.7
Spaniard	52.8

Median Home Value

Group	Dollars
Total Population	197,500
Hispanic or Latino (of any race)	170,200
Mexican	167,400

Median Gross Rent

Group	Dollars
Total Population	702
Hispanic or Latino (of any race)	680
Mexican	671

Median Household Income
(2010 Inflation-Adjusted Dollars)

Group	Dollars
Total Population	43,770
Hispanic or Latino (of any race)	34,072
Mexican	33,256

Per Capita Income
(2010 Inflation-Adjusted Dollars)

Group	Dollars
Total Population	22,196
Hispanic or Latino (of any race)	10,681
Mexican	10,179

Households with $100,000+ Income

Group	Number	%
Total Population	8,177	14.5
Hispanic or Latino (of any race)	278	4.0
Mexican	211	3.4

Households with Food Stamps/SNAP Benefits During Past 12 Months

Group	Number	%
Total Population	9,374	16.6
Hispanic or Latino (of any race)	1,794	25.9
Mexican	1,670	26.9

Poverty Rate
(Income in Past 12 Months Below Poverty Level)

Group	%
Total Population	16.7
Hispanic or Latino (of any race)	30.5
Mexican	31.8

Notes: (1) Percent of total population; (2) Percent of Hispanic/Latino population; Profiles include places with an overall population of at least 125,000, OR an overall population of at least 25,000 where the Hispanic/Latino population is at least 20% of the overall population. In states where less than five places meet either of these criteria, we have included places with at least 10,000 total population with the highest percentage of Hispanic/Latino population. These places are identified with an asterisk (*); Please refer to the User's Guide for a full explanation of data.

STATE & PLACE PROFILES

Pennsylvania

EDITOR'S NOTE: For a place to be included in this edition, it must meet one of two criteria. Either its overall population is at least 125,000, OR its overall population is at least 25,000 and its Hispanic/Latino population is at least 20% of the overall population. For the state of Pennsylvania, the following locations are included:

- Allentown
- Bethlehem
- Hazleton
- Lancaster
- Lebanon
- Norristown
- Philadelphia
- Pittsburgh
- Reading
- York

Section Two: State & Place Profiles starts with the state profile, followed by place profiles that meet the criteria above. Places are listed alphabetically within each state. All states, all counties and places that meet the above criteria are ranked and compared in *Section Three: Rankings & Comparisons*, on page 1055.

For a more detailed look at the Hispanic/Latino population in Pennsylvania, a companion web site is available at no additional charge with purchase of this print edition. Visit http://gold.greyhouse.com/page/info_hispanic for more information.

The web site includes data for all counties and places in Pennsylvania with Hispanic/Latino population, plus ten additional topics: Self Employed Worker; Walked to Work; Worked from Home; Mean Travel Time to Work; Mean Household Income; Households with Cash Public Assistance; Mean Cash Pubic Assistance; Poverty Rates for 18 and Under, 18 to 64, and 65 and Over.

Population

Group	Number	%TP[1]	%HP[2]
Total Population	12,702,379	100.0	–
Hispanic or Latino (of any race)	719,660	5.7	100.0
Central American, ex. Mexican	35,453	0.3	4.9
Costa Rican	3,048	<0.1	0.4
Guatemalan	11,462	0.1	1.6
Honduran	7,055	0.1	1.0
Nicaraguan	2,400	<0.1	0.3
Panamanian	3,234	<0.1	0.4
Salvadoran	7,952	0.1	1.1
Cuban	17,930	0.1	2.5
Dominican Republic	62,348	0.5	8.7
Mexican	129,568	1.0	18.0
Puerto Rican	366,082	2.9	50.9
South American	48,126	0.4	6.7
Argentinean	4,269	<0.1	0.6
Bolivian	895	<0.1	0.1
Chilean	2,521	<0.1	0.4
Colombian	16,525	0.1	2.3
Ecuadorian	10,680	0.1	1.5
Paraguayan	500	<0.1	0.1
Peruvian	7,783	0.1	1.1
Uruguayan	1,181	<0.1	0.2
Venezuelan	3,243	<0.1	0.5
Spaniard	8,554	0.1	1.2

Population Growth: 2000–2010

Group	%
Total Population	3.4
Hispanic or Latino (of any race)	82.6
Central American, ex. Mexican	260.1
Costa Rican	173.1
Guatemalan	393.6
Honduran	306.4
Nicaraguan	146.9
Panamanian	131.5
Salvadoran	324.8
Cuban	73.0
Dominican Republic	411.6
Mexican	134.8
Puerto Rican	60.2
South American	163.4
Argentinean	126.5
Bolivian	173.7
Chilean	118.8
Colombian	130.6
Ecuadorian	334.3
Paraguayan	141.5
Peruvian	200.2
Uruguayan	359.5
Venezuelan	130.0
Spaniard	502.4

Males per 100 Females

Group	Number
Total Population	95.1
Hispanic or Latino (of any race)	104.5
Central American, ex. Mexican	120.1
Costa Rican	114.6
Guatemalan	147.9
Honduran	123.5
Nicaraguan	93.5
Panamanian	78.1
Salvadoran	113.6
Cuban	103.5
Dominican Republic	94.3
Mexican	130.4
Puerto Rican	95.3
South American	94.4
Argentinean	94.6
Bolivian	89.2
Chilean	106.8
Colombian	85.4
Ecuadorian	112.6
Paraguayan	93.1
Peruvian	89.3
Uruguayan	94.2
Venezuelan	92.6
Spaniard	94.4

Average Household Size

Group	People
Total Population	2.45
Hispanic or Latino (of any race)	3.24
Central American, ex. Mexican	3.56
Costa Rican	3.21
Guatemalan	3.88
Honduran	3.71
Nicaraguan	3.32
Panamanian	2.72
Salvadoran	3.73
Cuban	2.65
Dominican Republic	3.65
Mexican	3.74
Puerto Rican	3.14
South American	3.03
Argentinean	2.62
Bolivian	2.78
Chilean	2.70
Colombian	2.95
Ecuadorian	3.62
Paraguayan	2.93
Peruvian	3.02
Uruguayan	2.97
Venezuelan	2.80
Spaniard	2.44

Median Age

Group	Years
Total Population	40.1
Hispanic or Latino (of any race)	25.2
Central American, ex. Mexican	26.8
Costa Rican	29.1
Guatemalan	24.3
Honduran	27.7
Nicaraguan	29.8
Panamanian	30.3
Salvadoran	27.4
Cuban	29.4
Dominican Republic	26.4
Mexican	24.7
Puerto Rican	23.8
South American	31.7
Argentinean	35.9
Bolivian	29.4
Chilean	31.7
Colombian	32.1
Ecuadorian	29.9
Paraguayan	21.9
Peruvian	32.6
Uruguayan	33.3
Venezuelan	31.2
Spaniard	34.8

High School Graduates

(Universe: Population 25 Years and Over)

Group	Number	%
Total Population	7,481,469	87.4
Hispanic or Latino (of any race)	215,325	65.6
Central American, ex. Mexican	10,159	59.6
Costa Rican	1,751	77.0
Guatemalan	2,123	45.6
Honduran	1,603	54.2
Nicaraguan	1,128	81.3
Panamanian	1,525	93.7
Salvadoran	1,880	48.0
Cuban	7,480	82.6
Dominican Republic	16,131	61.6
Mexican	33,174	57.5
Puerto Rican	109,792	64.5
South American	23,008	82.9
Argentinean	2,280	92.0
Bolivian	425	99.3
Chilean	1,264	96.3
Colombian	8,175	84.8
Ecuadorian	4,431	68.1
Peruvian	4,004	90.4
Uruguayan	502	68.9
Venezuelan	1,581	88.5
Spaniard	4,658	92.6

Four-Year College Graduates

(Universe: Population 25 Years and Over)

Group	Number	%
Total Population	2,258,056	26.4
Hispanic or Latino (of any race)	44,803	13.6
Central American, ex. Mexican	2,665	15.6
Costa Rican	375	16.5
Guatemalan	622	13.4
Honduran	350	11.8
Nicaraguan	362	26.1
Panamanian	602	37.0
Salvadoran	297	7.6
Cuban	3,124	34.5
Dominican Republic	2,898	11.1
Mexican	7,220	12.5
Puerto Rican	14,317	8.4
South American	9,351	33.7
Argentinean	1,278	51.6
Bolivian	178	41.6
Chilean	646	49.2
Colombian	3,423	35.5
Ecuadorian	1,168	17.9
Peruvian	1,414	31.9
Uruguayan	179	24.6
Venezuelan	843	47.2
Spaniard	2,119	42.1

Population Age 3–17 Enrolled in Public School

(Universe: Population Age 3–17 Enrolled in School)

Group	Number	%
Total Population	1,767,108	81.9
Hispanic or Latino (of any race)	149,856	89.0
Central American, ex. Mexican	5,866	81.7
Costa Rican	749	76.1
Guatemalan	1,721	70.7

Notes: (1) Percent of total population; (2) Percent of Hispanic/Latino population; Profiles include places with an overall population of at least 125,000, OR an overall population of at least 25,000 where the Hispanic/Latino population is at least 20% of the overall population. In states where less than five places meet either of these criteria, we have included places with at least 10,000 total population with the highest percentage of Hispanic/Latino population. These places are identified with an asterisk (*); Please refer to the User's Guide for a full explanation of data.

Honduran	911	92.1
Nicaraguan	300	76.5
Panamanian	747	92.5
Salvadoran	1,378	96.6
Cuban	3,370	90.4
Dominican Republic	13,333	94.3
Mexican	25,101	89.8
Puerto Rican	85,190	89.8
South American	7,599	81.4
Argentinean	328	78.8
Bolivian	73	76.0
Chilean	422	82.3
Colombian	2,785	74.7
Ecuadorian	2,257	90.5
Peruvian	952	82.8
Uruguayan	199	100.0
Venezuelan	532	86.4
Spaniard	1,467	77.2

Population Age 3–17 Enrolled in Private School

(Universe: Population Age 3–17 Enrolled in School)

Group	Number	%
Total Population	391,562	18.1
Hispanic or Latino (of any race)	18,544	11.0
Central American, ex. Mexican	1,317	18.3
Costa Rican	235	23.9
Guatemalan	712	29.3
Honduran	78	7.9
Nicaraguan	92	23.5
Panamanian	61	7.5
Salvadoran	48	3.4
Cuban	359	9.6
Dominican Republic	808	5.7
Mexican	2,839	10.2
Puerto Rican	9,707	10.2
South American	1,742	18.6
Argentinean	88	21.2
Bolivian	23	24.0
Chilean	91	17.7
Colombian	943	25.3
Ecuadorian	238	9.5
Peruvian	198	17.2
Uruguayan	0	0.0
Venezuelan	84	13.6
Spaniard	433	22.8

Foreign-Born Population

Group	Number	%
Total Population	704,332	5.6
Hispanic or Latino (of any race)	147,115	22.4
Central American, ex. Mexican	19,591	61.0
Costa Rican	2,324	54.6
Guatemalan	6,702	68.8
Honduran	3,376	68.9
Nicaraguan	1,354	57.0
Panamanian	1,209	37.9
Salvadoran	4,325	60.8
Cuban	5,305	31.7
Dominican Republic	30,579	58.2
Mexican	51,762	44.9
Puerto Rican	2,634	0.8
South American	29,156	61.8
Argentinean	2,291	62.4
Bolivian	404	60.7
Chilean	1,166	52.2
Colombian	10,098	60.0
Ecuadorian	7,478	63.9
Peruvian	4,454	63.6
Uruguayan	838	64.2
Venezuelan	1,854	62.3
Spaniard	1,626	19.2

Foreign-Born Naturalized U.S. Citizens

Group	Number	%
Total Population	346,978	49.3
Hispanic or Latino (of any race)	47,332	32.2
Central American, ex. Mexican	6,533	33.3
Costa Rican	617	26.5
Guatemalan	2,214	33.0
Honduran	964	28.6
Nicaraguan	621	45.9
Panamanian	521	43.1
Salvadoran	1,487	34.4
Cuban	3,250	61.3
Dominican Republic	12,125	39.7
Mexican	8,653	16.7
Puerto Rican	1,306	49.6
South American	11,942	41.0
Argentinean	910	39.7
Bolivian	236	58.4
Chilean	383	32.8
Colombian	4,581	45.4
Ecuadorian	2,420	32.4
Peruvian	2,217	49.8
Uruguayan	149	17.8
Venezuelan	702	37.9
Spaniard	728	44.8

Language Spoken at Home: English Only

(Universe: Population 5 Years and Over)

Group	Number	%
Total Population	10,710,239	90.1
Hispanic or Latino (of any race)	174,167	30.0
Central American, ex. Mexican	6,792	23.9
Costa Rican	806	20.8
Guatemalan	1,921	23.2
Honduran	864	18.9
Nicaraguan	510	24.1
Panamanian	1,316	44.7
Salvadoran	1,313	21.0
Cuban	7,095	46.6
Dominican Republic	4,814	10.2
Mexican	32,808	32.4
Puerto Rican	95,744	31.0
South American	8,590	19.8
Argentinean	890	25.3
Bolivian	268	42.9
Chilean	779	38.3
Colombian	2,939	18.9
Ecuadorian	1,430	13.4
Peruvian	994	15.5
Uruguayan	242	20.6
Venezuelan	872	32.2
Spaniard	5,142	66.2

Language Spoken at Home: Spanish

(Universe: Population 5 Years and Over)

Group	Number	%
Total Population	490,488	4.1
Hispanic or Latino (of any race)	403,318	69.4
Central American, ex. Mexican	21,551	75.7
Costa Rican	3,054	78.7
Guatemalan	6,319	76.4
Honduran	3,696	80.9
Nicaraguan	1,574	74.5
Panamanian	1,613	54.8
Salvadoran	4,938	78.8
Cuban	7,847	51.5
Dominican Republic	42,254	89.6
Mexican	67,530	66.8
Puerto Rican	212,573	68.8
South American	34,173	78.9
Argentinean	2,396	68.2
Bolivian	357	57.1
Chilean	1,226	60.2
Colombian	12,524	80.6
Ecuadorian	9,084	85.4
Peruvian	5,427	84.5
Uruguayan	875	74.5
Venezuelan	1,762	65.2
Spaniard	2,340	30.1

Unemployment Rate

(Universe: Population 16 Years and Over)

Group	%
Total Population	7.3
Hispanic or Latino (of any race)	12.8
Central American, ex. Mexican	9.0
Costa Rican	14.1
Guatemalan	7.9
Honduran	9.5
Nicaraguan	7.2
Panamanian	13.4
Salvadoran	5.1
Cuban	9.8
Dominican Republic	17.1
Mexican	7.2
Puerto Rican	16.4
South American	7.5
Argentinean	2.6
Bolivian	10.1
Chilean	4.1
Colombian	7.9
Ecuadorian	8.5
Peruvian	9.7
Uruguayan	7.3
Venezuelan	6.4
Spaniard	7.2

Class of Worker: Private Wage and Salary

(Universe: Civilian Employed Population 16 Years and Over)

Group	Number	%
Total Population	4,896,263	82.4
Hispanic or Latino (of any race)	213,841	88.0
Central American, ex. Mexican	13,293	90.4
Costa Rican	1,478	79.8
Guatemalan	3,852	93.4
Honduran	2,115	93.8
Nicaraguan	1,111	84.2
Panamanian	1,182	82.9
Salvadoran	3,422	95.3
Cuban	5,894	85.4
Dominican Republic	17,769	89.8
Mexican	48,653	92.2
Puerto Rican	95,154	86.2
South American	20,054	86.0
Argentinean	2,004	81.1
Bolivian	258	85.4
Chilean	818	77.0
Colombian	7,041	87.5
Ecuadorian	4,862	86.5
Peruvian	3,122	89.3
Uruguayan	380	76.9
Venezuelan	1,319	87.7
Spaniard	3,198	84.7

Class of Worker: Government

(Universe: Civilian Employed Population 16 Years and Over)

Group	Number	%
Total Population	694,589	11.7
Hispanic or Latino (of any race)	19,393	8.0
Central American, ex. Mexican	575	3.9
Costa Rican	81	4.4
Guatemalan	76	1.8
Honduran	69	3.1
Nicaraguan	92	7.0
Panamanian	149	10.4
Salvadoran	104	2.9
Cuban	494	7.2
Dominican Republic	1,020	5.2
Mexican	2,081	3.9
Puerto Rican	12,301	11.1
South American	1,703	7.3
Argentinean	200	8.1
Bolivian	39	12.9
Chilean	142	13.4
Colombian	602	7.5
Ecuadorian	340	6.0
Peruvian	212	6.1
Uruguayan	37	7.5
Venezuelan	100	6.6
Spaniard	352	9.3

Means of Transportation to Work: Car, Truck or Van

(Universe: Workers 16 Years and Over)

Group	Number	%
Total Population	4,979,288	85.9
Hispanic or Latino (of any race)	185,288	78.4
Central American, ex. Mexican	11,041	75.9
Costa Rican	1,482	84.4
Guatemalan	3,099	75.5
Honduran	1,632	72.9
Nicaraguan	1,189	91.0
Panamanian	979	68.6
Salvadoran	2,542	71.4
Cuban	5,465	80.9
Dominican Republic	15,846	82.7
Mexican	39,330	76.1
Puerto Rican	83,703	78.2
South American	18,032	79.9
Argentinean	1,556	64.7
Bolivian	254	90.1
Chilean	685	68.9
Colombian	6,358	81.3

Notes: (1) Percent of total population; (2) Percent of Hispanic/Latino population; Profiles include places with an overall population of at least 125,000, OR an overall population of at least 25,000 where the Hispanic/Latino population is at least 20% of the overall population. In states where less than five places meet either of these criteria, we have included places with at least 10,000 total population with the highest percentage of Hispanic/Latino population. These places are identified with an asterisk (*); Please refer to the User's Guide for a full explanation of data.

Group	Number	%
Ecuadorian	4,619	84.9
Peruvian	2,818	84.1
Uruguayan	400	81.0
Venezuelan	1,085	72.2
Spaniard	2,945	80.2

Means of Transportation to Work: Public Transportation (ex. Taxicab)

(Universe: Workers 16 Years and Over)

Group	Number	%
Total Population	312,308	5.4
Hispanic or Latino (of any race)	24,353	10.3
Central American, ex. Mexican	1,337	9.2
Costa Rican	114	6.5
Guatemalan	454	11.1
Honduran	117	5.2
Nicaraguan	40	3.1
Panamanian	209	14.6
Salvadoran	378	10.6
Cuban	498	7.4
Dominican Republic	1,671	8.7
Mexican	4,468	8.6
Puerto Rican	12,925	12.1
South American	2,143	9.5
Argentinean	341	14.2
Bolivian	15	5.3
Chilean	175	17.6
Colombian	792	10.1
Ecuadorian	442	8.1
Peruvian	186	5.6
Uruguayan	32	6.5
Venezuelan	160	10.7
Spaniard	245	6.7

Homeownership Rate

(Universe: Occupied Housing Units)

Group	%
Total Population	69.6
Hispanic or Latino (of any race)	42.4
Central American, ex. Mexican	43.2
Costa Rican	46.4
Guatemalan	31.2
Honduran	40.7
Nicaraguan	55.3
Panamanian	54.1
Salvadoran	49.0
Cuban	54.0
Dominican Republic	46.4
Mexican	35.8
Puerto Rican	40.3
South American	56.7
Argentinean	61.3
Bolivian	62.0
Chilean	49.8
Colombian	59.1
Ecuadorian	55.2
Paraguayan	54.5
Peruvian	54.7
Uruguayan	46.2
Venezuelan	55.4
Spaniard	64.6

Median Home Value

Group	Dollars
Total Population	159,300
Hispanic or Latino (of any race)	132,400
Central American, ex. Mexican	174,200
Costa Rican	191,100
Guatemalan	178,200
Honduran	177,400
Nicaraguan	127,300
Panamanian	210,200
Salvadoran	151,500
Cuban	213,900
Dominican Republic	108,400
Mexican	148,900
Puerto Rican	110,300
South American	187,100
Argentinean	278,800
Bolivian	171,000
Chilean	268,400
Colombian	173,000
Ecuadorian	165,400
Peruvian	198,400
Uruguayan	147,700
Venezuelan	264,800
Spaniard	205,500

Median Gross Rent

Group	Dollars
Total Population	739
Hispanic or Latino (of any race)	764
Central American, ex. Mexican	873
Costa Rican	928
Guatemalan	782
Honduran	916
Nicaraguan	952
Panamanian	1,066
Salvadoran	739
Cuban	824
Dominican Republic	777
Mexican	834
Puerto Rican	721
South American	823
Argentinean	744
Bolivian	780
Chilean	762
Colombian	913
Ecuadorian	862
Peruvian	730
Uruguayan	929
Venezuelan	764
Spaniard	898

Median Household Income

(2010 Inflation-Adjusted Dollars)

Group	Dollars
Total Population	50,398
Hispanic or Latino (of any race)	32,876
Central American, ex. Mexican	41,375
Costa Rican	28,359
Guatemalan	38,737
Honduran	48,482
Nicaraguan	44,268
Panamanian	41,168
Salvadoran	42,759
Cuban	51,750
Dominican Republic	29,852
Mexican	40,448
Puerto Rican	26,966
South American	46,157
Argentinean	60,000
Bolivian	47,670
Chilean	48,603
Colombian	46,425
Ecuadorian	42,466
Peruvian	47,063
Uruguayan	27,008
Venezuelan	47,119
Spaniard	61,758

Per Capita Income

(2010 Inflation-Adjusted Dollars)

Group	Dollars
Total Population	27,049
Hispanic or Latino (of any race)	14,164
Central American, ex. Mexican	15,544
Costa Rican	17,291
Guatemalan	13,445
Honduran	16,534
Nicaraguan	22,002
Panamanian	18,568
Salvadoran	13,412
Cuban	26,533
Dominican Republic	11,829
Mexican	14,804
Puerto Rican	12,134
South American	21,063
Argentinean	39,018
Bolivian	23,676
Chilean	24,103
Colombian	20,441
Ecuadorian	15,479
Peruvian	20,755
Uruguayan	18,203
Venezuelan	23,626
Spaniard	32,732

Households with $100,000+ Income

Group	Number	%
Total Population	938,986	19.0
Hispanic or Latino (of any race)	17,910	9.7
Central American, ex. Mexican	1,139	13.3
Costa Rican	210	17.0
Guatemalan	257	10.7
Honduran	154	13.7
Nicaraguan	202	27.0
Panamanian	155	16.1
Salvadoran	142	7.3
Cuban	1,305	23.9
Dominican Republic	832	5.9
Mexican	3,304	11.7
Puerto Rican	6,974	6.9
South American	2,247	15.3
Argentinean	331	22.9
Bolivian	18	7.6
Chilean	164	23.6
Colombian	696	13.4
Ecuadorian	396	12.3
Peruvian	296	14.0
Uruguayan	41	10.0
Venezuelan	255	23.3
Spaniard	841	28.7

Households with Food Stamps/SNAP Benefits During Past 12 Months

Group	Number	%
Total Population	445,506	9.0
Hispanic or Latino (of any race)	55,522	30.1
Central American, ex. Mexican	1,311	15.3
Costa Rican	150	12.1
Guatemalan	383	15.9
Honduran	213	19.0
Nicaraguan	160	21.4
Panamanian	176	18.3
Salvadoran	229	11.7
Cuban	1,037	19.0
Dominican Republic	5,088	36.4
Mexican	3,837	13.6
Puerto Rican	39,896	39.4
South American	1,694	11.6
Argentinean	174	12.0
Bolivian	32	13.4
Chilean	49	7.1
Colombian	548	10.5
Ecuadorian	519	16.1
Peruvian	245	11.6
Uruguayan	36	8.8
Venezuelan	82	7.5
Spaniard	205	7.0

Poverty Rate

(Income in Past 12 Months Below Poverty Level)

Group	%
Total Population	12.4
Hispanic or Latino (of any race)	31.0
Central American, ex. Mexican	19.3
Costa Rican	27.9
Guatemalan	18.5
Honduran	19.7
Nicaraguan	11.3
Panamanian	15.3
Salvadoran	19.7
Cuban	18.8
Dominican Republic	34.1
Mexican	21.6
Puerto Rican	37.6
South American	16.6
Argentinean	11.6
Bolivian	14.5
Chilean	23.5
Colombian	17.9
Ecuadorian	19.8
Peruvian	10.6
Uruguayan	19.7
Venezuelan	11.3
Spaniard	11.0

Notes: (1) Percent of total population; (2) Percent of Hispanic/Latino population; Profiles include places with an overall population of at least 125,000, OR an overall population of at least 25,000 where the Hispanic/Latino population is at least 20% of the overall population. In states where less than five places meet either of these criteria, we have included places with at least 10,000 total population with the highest percentage of Hispanic/Latino population. These places are identified with an asterisk (*); Please refer to the User's Guide for a full explanation of data.

Allentown

Population

Group	Number	%TP[1]	%HP[2]
Total Population	118,032	100.0	–
Hispanic or Latino (of any race)	50,461	42.8	100.0
Central American, ex. Mexican	1,911	1.6	3.8
Guatemalan	420	0.4	0.8
Honduran	749	0.6	1.5
Panamanian	143	0.1	0.3
Salvadoran	440	0.4	0.9
Cuban	458	0.4	0.9
Dominican Republic	9,340	7.9	18.5
Mexican	2,448	2.1	4.9
Puerto Rican	29,640	25.1	58.7
South American	3,048	2.6	6.0
Chilean	259	0.2	0.5
Colombian	755	0.6	1.5
Ecuadorian	1,241	1.1	2.5
Peruvian	565	0.5	1.1
Spaniard	143	0.1	0.3

Population Growth: 2000–2010

Group	%
Total Population	10.7
Hispanic or Latino (of any race)	93.6
Central American, ex. Mexican	283.7
Honduran	231.4
Cuban	93.2
Dominican Republic	440.2
Mexican	137.0
Puerto Rican	67.6
South American	157.2
Chilean	53.3
Colombian	136.7
Ecuadorian	255.6
Peruvian	141.5

Males per 100 Females

Group	Number
Total Population	93.0
Hispanic or Latino (of any race)	97.0
Central American, ex. Mexican	109.5
Guatemalan	144.2
Honduran	106.9
Panamanian	93.2
Salvadoran	102.8
Cuban	98.3
Dominican Republic	93.5
Mexican	133.6
Puerto Rican	93.9
South American	96.3
Chilean	119.5
Colombian	81.1
Ecuadorian	101.5
Peruvian	97.6
Spaniard	83.3

Average Household Size

Group	People
Total Population	2.64
Hispanic or Latino (of any race)	3.45
Central American, ex. Mexican	3.79
Guatemalan	3.86
Honduran	3.89
Panamanian	3.32
Salvadoran	3.81
Cuban	2.61
Dominican Republic	3.78
Mexican	4.11
Puerto Rican	3.31
South American	3.49
Chilean	3.49
Colombian	3.20
Ecuadorian	3.87
Peruvian	3.12
Spaniard	3.37

Median Age

Group	Years
Total Population	32.7
Hispanic or Latino (of any race)	24.4
Central American, ex. Mexican	30.0
Guatemalan	28.6
Honduran	30.4
Panamanian	27.1
Salvadoran	31.2
Cuban	25.5
Dominican Republic	26.8
Mexican	25.2
Puerto Rican	23.1
South American	33.0
Chilean	36.4
Colombian	33.0
Ecuadorian	31.5
Peruvian	35.9
Spaniard	31.4

High School Graduates
(Universe: Population 25 Years and Over)

Group	Number	%
Total Population	54,776	76.2
Hispanic or Latino (of any race)	12,801	59.4
Central American, ex. Mexican	562	64.2
Dominican Republic	2,314	66.0
Mexican	553	61.2
Puerto Rican	6,956	55.7
South American	1,553	75.3
Ecuadorian	760	76.8

Four-Year College Graduates
(Universe: Population 25 Years and Over)

Group	Number	%
Total Population	11,939	16.6
Hispanic or Latino (of any race)	1,133	5.3
Central American, ex. Mexican	58	6.6
Dominican Republic	235	6.7
Mexican	55	6.1
Puerto Rican	422	3.4
South American	277	13.4
Ecuadorian	89	9.0

Population Age 3–17 Enrolled in Public School
(Universe: Population Age 3–17 Enrolled in School)

Group	Number	%
Total Population	18,552	87.2
Hispanic or Latino (of any race)	11,535	95.0
Central American, ex. Mexican	207	85.5
Dominican Republic	1,729	99.3
Mexican	510	100.0
Puerto Rican	6,992	93.6
South American	585	98.3
Ecuadorian	405	100.0

Population Age 3–17 Enrolled in Private School
(Universe: Population Age 3–17 Enrolled in School)

Group	Number	%
Total Population	2,723	12.8
Hispanic or Latino (of any race)	602	5.0
Central American, ex. Mexican	35	14.5
Dominican Republic	13	0.7
Mexican	0	0.0
Puerto Rican	482	6.4
South American	10	1.7
Ecuadorian	0	0.0

Foreign-Born Population

Group	Number	%
Total Population	16,292	14.0
Hispanic or Latino (of any race)	9,701	21.6
Central American, ex. Mexican	839	58.1
Dominican Republic	4,259	60.8
Mexican	821	40.9
Puerto Rican	136	0.5
South American	2,272	69.8
Ecuadorian	1,111	64.0

Foreign-Born Naturalized U.S. Citizens

Group	Number	%
Total Population	7,041	43.2
Hispanic or Latino (of any race)	3,423	35.3
Central American, ex. Mexican	421	50.2
Dominican Republic	1,626	38.2
Mexican	104	12.7
Puerto Rican	13	9.6
South American	720	31.7
Ecuadorian	310	27.9

Language Spoken at Home: English Only
(Universe: Population 5 Years and Over)

Group	Number	%
Total Population	66,788	62.6
Hispanic or Latino (of any race)	7,607	19.4
Central American, ex. Mexican	128	9.9
Dominican Republic	208	3.5
Mexican	437	25.6
Puerto Rican	5,845	25.0
South American	210	6.8
Ecuadorian	141	8.4

Language Spoken at Home: Spanish
(Universe: Population 5 Years and Over)

Group	Number	%
Total Population	32,738	30.7
Hispanic or Latino (of any race)	31,429	80.1
Central American, ex. Mexican	1,167	90.1
Dominican Republic	5,811	96.4
Mexican	1,258	73.7
Puerto Rican	17,550	75.0
South American	2,815	90.8
Ecuadorian	1,464	87.1

Unemployment Rate
(Universe: Population 16 Years and Over)

Group	%
Total Population	11.4
Hispanic or Latino (of any race)	17.6
Central American, ex. Mexican	7.1
Dominican Republic	18.9
Mexican	15.2
Puerto Rican	18.5
South American	10.2
Ecuadorian	14.5

Class of Worker: Private Wage and Salary
(Universe: Civilian Employed Population 16 Years and Over)

Group	Number	%
Total Population	43,221	88.4
Hispanic or Latino (of any race)	13,994	93.4
Central American, ex. Mexican	664	97.5
Dominican Republic	2,729	95.4
Mexican	737	98.7
Puerto Rican	7,395	92.5
South American	1,368	88.3
Ecuadorian	559	79.3

Class of Worker: Government
(Universe: Civilian Employed Population 16 Years and Over)

Group	Number	%
Total Population	3,770	7.7
Hispanic or Latino (of any race)	633	4.2
Central American, ex. Mexican	17	2.5
Dominican Republic	37	1.3
Mexican	10	1.3
Puerto Rican	512	6.4
South American	38	2.5
Ecuadorian	22	3.1

Means of Transportation to Work: Car, Truck or Van
(Universe: Workers 16 Years and Over)

Group	Number	%
Total Population	40,949	86.3
Hispanic or Latino (of any race)	12,352	85.1
Central American, ex. Mexican	610	89.6
Dominican Republic	2,422	85.8
Mexican	661	89.4
Puerto Rican	6,324	82.8
South American	1,340	88.9
Ecuadorian	598	86.3

Means of Transportation to Work: Public Transportation (ex. Taxicab)
(Universe: Workers 16 Years and Over)

Group	Number	%
Total Population	2,303	4.9
Hispanic or Latino (of any race)	1,000	6.9
Central American, ex. Mexican	0	0.0
Dominican Republic	177	6.3
Mexican	15	2.0
Puerto Rican	642	8.4
South American	50	3.3
Ecuadorian	8	1.2

Notes: (1) Percent of total population; (2) Percent of Hispanic/Latino population; Profiles include places with an overall population of at least 125,000, OR an overall population of at least 25,000 where the Hispanic/Latino population is at least 20% of the overall population. In states where less than five places meet either of these criteria, we have included places with at least 10,000 total population with the highest percentage of Hispanic/Latino population. These places are identified with an asterisk (*); Please refer to the User's Guide for a full explanation of data.

Homeownership Rate (Universe: Occupied Housing Units)	
Group	%
Total Population	48.4
Hispanic or Latino (of any race)	33.1
Central American, ex. Mexican	49.0
Guatemalan	45.7
Honduran	48.0
Panamanian	34.0
Salvadoran	58.7
Cuban	34.5
Dominican Republic	45.6
Mexican	31.3
Puerto Rican	26.0
South American	54.4
Chilean	45.5
Colombian	54.7
Ecuadorian	57.2
Peruvian	55.9
Spaniard	62.8

Median Home Value	
Group	Dollars
Total Population	143,500
Hispanic or Latino (of any race)	126,000
Central American, ex. Mexican	135,900
Dominican Republic	130,600
Mexican	96,600
Puerto Rican	123,100
South American	137,500
Ecuadorian	138,600

Median Gross Rent	
Group	Dollars
Total Population	786
Hispanic or Latino (of any race)	779
Central American, ex. Mexican	895
Dominican Republic	916
Mexican	753
Puerto Rican	761
South American	848
Ecuadorian	865

Median Household Income (2010 Inflation-Adjusted Dollars)	
Group	Dollars
Total Population	36,202
Hispanic or Latino (of any race)	26,173
Central American, ex. Mexican	43,409
Dominican Republic	30,591
Mexican	26,113
Puerto Rican	22,028
South American	54,512
Ecuadorian	28,661

Per Capita Income (2010 Inflation-Adjusted Dollars)	
Group	Dollars
Total Population	18,139
Hispanic or Latino (of any race)	10,456
Central American, ex. Mexican	17,087
Dominican Republic	11,617
Mexican	9,865
Puerto Rican	9,513
South American	15,107
Ecuadorian	11,869

Households with $100,000+ Income		
Group	Number	%
Total Population	3,806	8.7
Hispanic or Latino (of any race)	475	3.6
Central American, ex. Mexican	18	3.7
Dominican Republic	82	4.6
Mexican	0	0.0
Puerto Rican	237	2.8
South American	70	7.2
Ecuadorian	32	6.9

Households with Food Stamps/SNAP Benefits During Past 12 Months		
Group	Number	%
Total Population	8,758	20.0
Hispanic or Latino (of any race)	5,303	39.7
Central American, ex. Mexican	73	14.9
Dominican Republic	611	34.5
Mexican	139	20.3
Puerto Rican	3,841	45.5
South American	113	11.6
Ecuadorian	70	15.1

Poverty Rate (Income in Past 12 Months Below Poverty Level)	
Group	%
Total Population	24.6
Hispanic or Latino (of any race)	37.3
Central American, ex. Mexican	20.4
Dominican Republic	31.0
Mexican	23.3
Puerto Rican	43.5
South American	20.5
Ecuadorian	31.8

Bethlehem

Population			
Group	Number	%TP[1]	%HP[2]
Total Population	74,982	100.0	–
Hispanic or Latino (of any race)	18,268	24.4	100.0
Central American, ex. Mexican	643	0.9	3.5
Guatemalan	275	0.4	1.5
Salvadoran	116	0.2	0.6
Cuban	196	0.3	1.1
Dominican Republic	1,010	1.3	5.5
Mexican	1,085	1.4	5.9
Puerto Rican	13,722	18.3	75.1
South American	804	1.1	4.4
Colombian	240	0.3	1.3
Ecuadorian	200	0.3	1.1
Peruvian	155	0.2	0.8
Spaniard	115	0.2	0.6

Population Growth: 2000–2010	
Group	%
Total Population	5.1
Hispanic or Latino (of any race)	40.5
Central American, ex. Mexican	257.2
Cuban	66.1
Dominican Republic	337.2
Mexican	49.0
Puerto Rican	35.9
South American	136.5
Colombian	65.5

Males per 100 Females	
Group	Number
Total Population	92.5
Hispanic or Latino (of any race)	93.0
Central American, ex. Mexican	115.1
Guatemalan	143.4
Salvadoran	152.2
Cuban	98.0
Dominican Republic	85.3
Mexican	115.3
Puerto Rican	91.0
South American	84.8
Colombian	75.2
Ecuadorian	100.0
Peruvian	72.2
Spaniard	82.5

Average Household Size	
Group	People
Total Population	2.34
Hispanic or Latino (of any race)	3.04
Central American, ex. Mexican	3.74
Guatemalan	3.77
Salvadoran	3.86
Cuban	2.69
Dominican Republic	3.52
Mexican	3.27
Puerto Rican	2.98
South American	3.01
Colombian	2.72
Ecuadorian	3.28
Peruvian	3.15
Spaniard	2.21

Median Age	
Group	Years
Total Population	35.7
Hispanic or Latino (of any race)	25.6
Central American, ex. Mexican	29.0
Guatemalan	28.4
Salvadoran	30.0
Cuban	22.3
Dominican Republic	25.9
Mexican	25.1
Puerto Rican	25.6
South American	29.5
Colombian	27.8
Ecuadorian	28.5
Peruvian	32.3
Spaniard	32.8

High School Graduates (Universe: Population 25 Years and Over)		
Group	Number	%
Total Population	39,600	84.1
Hispanic or Latino (of any race)	5,686	64.5
Dominican Republic	337	64.6
Mexican	429	55.0
Puerto Rican	4,322	66.1

Four-Year College Graduates (Universe: Population 25 Years and Over)		
Group	Number	%
Total Population	12,517	26.6
Hispanic or Latino (of any race)	670	7.6
Dominican Republic	48	9.2
Mexican	33	4.2
Puerto Rican	419	6.4

Population Age 3–17 Enrolled in Public School (Universe: Population Age 3–17 Enrolled in School)		
Group	Number	%
Total Population	10,020	87.2
Hispanic or Latino (of any race)	4,486	95.7
Dominican Republic	231	100.0
Mexican	262	93.9
Puerto Rican	3,702	97.4

Population Age 3–17 Enrolled in Private School (Universe: Population Age 3–17 Enrolled in School)		
Group	Number	%
Total Population	1,475	12.8
Hispanic or Latino (of any race)	201	4.3
Dominican Republic	0	0.0
Mexican	17	6.1
Puerto Rican	97	2.6

Foreign-Born Population		
Group	Number	%
Total Population	5,129	6.9
Hispanic or Latino (of any race)	1,448	8.2
Dominican Republic	513	53.0
Mexican	285	21.6
Puerto Rican	22	0.2

Foreign-Born Naturalized U.S. Citizens		
Group	Number	%
Total Population	2,054	40.0
Hispanic or Latino (of any race)	381	26.3
Dominican Republic	162	31.6
Mexican	0	0.0
Puerto Rican	22	100.0

Language Spoken at Home: English Only (Universe: Population 5 Years and Over)		
Group	Number	%
Total Population	55,170	77.9
Hispanic or Latino (of any race)	4,763	29.9
Dominican Republic	46	5.2
Mexican	443	36.9
Puerto Rican	3,505	29.0

Language Spoken at Home: Spanish (Universe: Population 5 Years and Over)		
Group	Number	%
Total Population	11,665	16.5
Hispanic or Latino (of any race)	11,175	70.1
Dominican Republic	831	94.8
Mexican	756	63.1

Notes: (1) Percent of total population; (2) Percent of Hispanic/Latino population; Profiles include places with an overall population of at least 125,000, OR an overall population of at least 25,000 where the Hispanic/Latino population is at least 20% of the overall population. In states where less than five places meet either of these criteria, we have included places with at least 10,000 total population with the highest percentage of Hispanic/Latino population. These places are identified with an asterisk (*); Please refer to the User's Guide for a full explanation of data.

Puerto Rican	8,587	71.0

Unemployment Rate
(Universe: Population 16 Years and Over)

Group	%
Total Population	7.6
Hispanic or Latino (of any race)	12.5
Dominican Republic	16.7
Mexican	1.8
Puerto Rican	12.9

Class of Worker: Private Wage and Salary
(Universe: Civilian Employed Population 16 Years and Over)

Group	Number	%
Total Population	29,028	86.6
Hispanic or Latino (of any race)	5,657	88.9
Dominican Republic	322	93.3
Mexican	481	87.3
Puerto Rican	4,232	88.6

Class of Worker: Government
(Universe: Civilian Employed Population 16 Years and Over)

Group	Number	%
Total Population	3,137	9.4
Hispanic or Latino (of any race)	521	8.2
Dominican Republic	0	0.0
Mexican	27	4.9
Puerto Rican	453	9.5

Means of Transportation to Work: Car, Truck or Van
(Universe: Workers 16 Years and Over)

Group	Number	%
Total Population	28,792	88.4
Hispanic or Latino (of any race)	5,178	85.3
Dominican Republic	291	85.3
Mexican	509	92.4
Puerto Rican	3,865	86.1

Means of Transportation to Work: Public Transportation (ex. Taxicab)
(Universe: Workers 16 Years and Over)

Group	Number	%
Total Population	908	2.8
Hispanic or Latino (of any race)	404	6.7
Dominican Republic	24	7.0
Mexican	42	7.6
Puerto Rican	208	4.6

Homeownership Rate
(Universe: Occupied Housing Units)

Group	%
Total Population	53.6
Hispanic or Latino (of any race)	32.2
Central American, ex. Mexican	45.2
Guatemalan	41.1
Salvadoran	41.7
Cuban	42.2
Dominican Republic	40.3
Mexican	47.8
Puerto Rican	28.8
South American	50.8
Colombian	44.0
Ecuadorian	55.2
Peruvian	60.4
Spaniard	54.2

Median Home Value

Group	Dollars
Total Population	175,900
Hispanic or Latino (of any race)	144,900
Dominican Republic	119,200
Mexican	165,000
Puerto Rican	143,400

Median Gross Rent

Group	Dollars
Total Population	821
Hispanic or Latino (of any race)	753
Dominican Republic	389
Mexican	957
Puerto Rican	717

Median Household Income
(2010 Inflation-Adjusted Dollars)

Group	Dollars
Total Population	44,310
Hispanic or Latino (of any race)	26,538
Dominican Republic	23,043
Mexican	33,067
Puerto Rican	26,066

Per Capita Income
(2010 Inflation-Adjusted Dollars)

Group	Dollars
Total Population	23,042
Hispanic or Latino (of any race)	11,436
Dominican Republic	8,927
Mexican	13,371
Puerto Rican	11,410

Households with $100,000+ Income

Group	Number	%
Total Population	3,870	13.1
Hispanic or Latino (of any race)	254	4.6
Dominican Republic	12	4.1
Mexican	26	6.3
Puerto Rican	148	3.6

Households with Food Stamps/SNAP Benefits During Past 12 Months

Group	Number	%
Total Population	3,533	11.9
Hispanic or Latino (of any race)	2,430	44.1
Dominican Republic	196	66.7
Mexican	60	14.6
Puerto Rican	1,881	45.7

Poverty Rate
(Income in Past 12 Months Below Poverty Level)

Group	%
Total Population	16.8
Hispanic or Latino (of any race)	34.9
Dominican Republic	42.1
Mexican	29.0
Puerto Rican	34.9

Hazleton

Population

Group	Number	%TP[1]	%HP[2]
Total Population	25,340	100.0	–
Hispanic or Latino (of any race)	9,454	37.3	100.0
Central American, ex. Mexican	225	0.9	2.4
Dominican Republic	5,327	21.0	56.3
Mexican	886	3.5	9.4
Puerto Rican	1,699	6.7	18.0
South American	338	1.3	3.6
Ecuadorian	141	0.6	1.5

Population Growth: 2000–2010

Group	%
Total Population	8.6
Hispanic or Latino (of any race)	735.2
Dominican Republic	1,519.1
Mexican	457.2
Puerto Rican	526.9

Males per 100 Females

Group	Number
Total Population	93.6
Hispanic or Latino (of any race)	98.6
Central American, ex. Mexican	134.4
Dominican Republic	94.1
Mexican	136.9
Puerto Rican	94.4
South American	93.1
Ecuadorian	95.8

Average Household Size

Group	People
Total Population	2.54
Hispanic or Latino (of any race)	3.80
Central American, ex. Mexican	3.48
Dominican Republic	3.89
Mexican	4.13
Puerto Rican	3.62
South American	3.49
Ecuadorian	4.47

Median Age

Group	Years
Total Population	37.6
Hispanic or Latino (of any race)	22.8
Central American, ex. Mexican	28.3
Dominican Republic	25.4
Mexican	21.0
Puerto Rican	19.4
South American	29.3
Ecuadorian	27.9

High School Graduates
(Universe: Population 25 Years and Over)

Group	Number	%
Total Population	12,967	77.7
Hispanic or Latino (of any race)	1,810	47.0
Dominican Republic	1,007	46.6
Mexican	128	26.9
Puerto Rican	246	59.6

Four-Year College Graduates
(Universe: Population 25 Years and Over)

Group	Number	%
Total Population	1,962	11.8
Hispanic or Latino (of any race)	201	5.2
Dominican Republic	57	2.6
Mexican	0	0.0
Puerto Rican	38	9.2

Population Age 3–17 Enrolled in Public School
(Universe: Population Age 3–17 Enrolled in School)

Group	Number	%
Total Population	3,705	86.1
Hispanic or Latino (of any race)	2,137	98.3
Dominican Republic	1,117	96.9
Mexican	377	100.0
Puerto Rican	237	100.0

Population Age 3–17 Enrolled in Private School
(Universe: Population Age 3–17 Enrolled in School)

Group	Number	%
Total Population	597	13.9
Hispanic or Latino (of any race)	36	1.7
Dominican Republic	36	3.1
Mexican	0	0.0
Puerto Rican	0	0.0

Foreign-Born Population

Group	Number	%
Total Population	4,943	19.9
Hispanic or Latino (of any race)	4,449	56.7
Dominican Republic	3,044	70.4
Mexican	505	48.6
Puerto Rican	10	1.1

Foreign-Born Naturalized U.S. Citizens

Group	Number	%
Total Population	1,467	29.7
Hispanic or Latino (of any race)	1,135	25.5
Dominican Republic	965	31.7
Mexican	13	2.6
Puerto Rican	10	100.0

Language Spoken at Home: English Only
(Universe: Population 5 Years and Over)

Group	Number	%
Total Population	16,608	71.2
Hispanic or Latino (of any race)	1,019	14.7
Dominican Republic	267	6.8
Mexican	230	26.0
Puerto Rican	259	33.0

Language Spoken at Home: Spanish
(Universe: Population 5 Years and Over)

Group	Number	%
Total Population	6,084	26.1
Hispanic or Latino (of any race)	5,905	85.3
Dominican Republic	3,637	93.2
Mexican	654	74.0
Puerto Rican	525	67.0

Notes: (1) Percent of total population; (2) Percent of Hispanic/Latino population; Profiles include places with an overall population of at least 125,000, OR an overall population of at least 25,000 where the Hispanic/Latino population is at least 20% of the overall population. In states where less than five places meet either of these criteria, we have included places with at least 10,000 total population with the highest percentage of Hispanic/Latino population. These places are identified with an asterisk (*); Please refer to the User's Guide for a full explanation of data.

Unemployment Rate
(Universe: Population 16 Years and Over)

Group	%
Total Population	8.4
Hispanic or Latino (of any race)	15.9
Dominican Republic	14.6
Mexican	16.0
Puerto Rican	8.6

Class of Worker: Private Wage and Salary
(Universe: Civilian Employed Population 16 Years and Over)

Group	Number	%
Total Population	9,319	88.4
Hispanic or Latino (of any race)	2,546	95.3
Dominican Republic	1,615	98.2
Mexican	326	100.0
Puerto Rican	222	72.3

Class of Worker: Government
(Universe: Civilian Employed Population 16 Years and Over)

Group	Number	%
Total Population	875	8.3
Hispanic or Latino (of any race)	90	3.4
Dominican Republic	17	1.0
Mexican	0	0.0
Puerto Rican	61	19.9

Means of Transportation to Work: Car, Truck or Van
(Universe: Workers 16 Years and Over)

Group	Number	%
Total Population	9,333	90.3
Hispanic or Latino (of any race)	2,414	93.0
Dominican Republic	1,405	89.5
Mexican	326	100.0
Puerto Rican	307	100.0

Means of Transportation to Work: Public Transportation (ex. Taxicab)
(Universe: Workers 16 Years and Over)

Group	Number	%
Total Population	141	1.4
Hispanic or Latino (of any race)	93	3.6
Dominican Republic	85	5.4
Mexican	0	0.0
Puerto Rican	0	0.0

Homeownership Rate
(Universe: Occupied Housing Units)

Group	%
Total Population	53.3
Hispanic or Latino (of any race)	35.3
Central American, ex. Mexican	42.6
Dominican Republic	40.8
Mexican	29.1
Puerto Rican	17.2
South American	48.1
Ecuadorian	61.8

Median Home Value

Group	Dollars
Total Population	93,300
Hispanic or Latino (of any race)	103,200
Dominican Republic	101,200
Mexican	62,400
Puerto Rican	89,800

Median Gross Rent

Group	Dollars
Total Population	599
Hispanic or Latino (of any race)	666
Dominican Republic	675
Mexican	676
Puerto Rican	609

Median Household Income
(2010 Inflation-Adjusted Dollars)

Group	Dollars
Total Population	32,169
Hispanic or Latino (of any race)	29,025
Dominican Republic	28,305
Mexican	38,555
Puerto Rican	17,684

Per Capita Income
(2010 Inflation-Adjusted Dollars)

Group	Dollars
Total Population	18,215
Hispanic or Latino (of any race)	10,271
Dominican Republic	11,178
Mexican	10,172
Puerto Rican	7,981

Households with $100,000+ Income

Group	Number	%
Total Population	611	6.1
Hispanic or Latino (of any race)	61	2.8
Dominican Republic	60	4.9
Mexican	1	0.5
Puerto Rican	0	0.0

Households with Food Stamps/SNAP Benefits During Past 12 Months

Group	Number	%
Total Population	1,902	18.9
Hispanic or Latino (of any race)	964	44.4
Dominican Republic	543	44.1
Mexican	99	50.8
Puerto Rican	161	51.8

Poverty Rate
(Income in Past 12 Months Below Poverty Level)

Group	%
Total Population	20.1
Hispanic or Latino (of any race)	38.5
Dominican Republic	39.3
Mexican	19.8
Puerto Rican	49.4

Lancaster

Population

Group	Number	%TP[1]	%HP[2]
Total Population	59,322	100.0	–
Hispanic or Latino (of any race)	23,329	39.3	100.0
Central American, ex. Mexican	405	0.7	1.7
Guatemalan	103	0.2	0.4
Salvadoran	143	0.2	0.6
Cuban	994	1.7	4.3
Dominican Republic	1,905	3.2	8.2
Mexican	1,046	1.8	4.5
Puerto Rican	17,341	29.2	74.3
South American	571	1.0	2.4
Colombian	208	0.4	0.9
Ecuadorian	157	0.3	0.7
Peruvian	108	0.2	0.5

Population Growth: 2000–2010

Group	%
Total Population	5.3
Hispanic or Latino (of any race)	34.6
Central American, ex. Mexican	132.8
Cuban	232.4
Dominican Republic	258.8
Mexican	118.4
Puerto Rican	26.4
South American	108.4
Colombian	82.5

Males per 100 Females

Group	Number
Total Population	98.7
Hispanic or Latino (of any race)	99.4
Central American, ex. Mexican	101.5
Guatemalan	134.1
Salvadoran	101.4
Cuban	130.6
Dominican Republic	92.2
Mexican	144.4
Puerto Rican	97.0
South American	97.6
Colombian	82.5
Ecuadorian	89.2
Peruvian	151.2

Average Household Size

Group	People
Total Population	2.58
Hispanic or Latino (of any race)	3.18
Central American, ex. Mexican	3.57
Guatemalan	3.74
Salvadoran	3.64
Cuban	2.76
Dominican Republic	3.69
Mexican	3.59
Puerto Rican	3.14
South American	3.16
Colombian	2.90
Ecuadorian	3.89
Peruvian	2.95

Median Age

Group	Years
Total Population	30.5
Hispanic or Latino (of any race)	25.1
Central American, ex. Mexican	27.4
Guatemalan	26.3
Salvadoran	27.5
Cuban	35.6
Dominican Republic	27.8
Mexican	24.3
Puerto Rican	24.4
South American	30.2
Colombian	32.2
Ecuadorian	26.6
Peruvian	36.5

High School Graduates
(Universe: Population 25 Years and Over)

Group	Number	%
Total Population	25,368	73.7
Hispanic or Latino (of any race)	5,982	57.4
Dominican Republic	438	58.9
Mexican	259	50.7
Puerto Rican	4,412	56.0

Four-Year College Graduates
(Universe: Population 25 Years and Over)

Group	Number	%
Total Population	5,649	16.4
Hispanic or Latino (of any race)	639	6.1
Dominican Republic	11	1.5
Mexican	31	6.1
Puerto Rican	309	3.9

Population Age 3–17 Enrolled in Public School
(Universe: Population Age 3–17 Enrolled in School)

Group	Number	%
Total Population	9,578	88.8
Hispanic or Latino (of any race)	5,295	95.8
Dominican Republic	206	86.9
Mexican	114	93.4
Puerto Rican	4,438	96.4

Population Age 3–17 Enrolled in Private School
(Universe: Population Age 3–17 Enrolled in School)

Group	Number	%
Total Population	1,213	11.2
Hispanic or Latino (of any race)	234	4.2
Dominican Republic	31	13.1
Mexican	8	6.6
Puerto Rican	168	3.6

Foreign-Born Population

Group	Number	%
Total Population	5,759	9.8
Hispanic or Latino (of any race)	2,541	11.9
Dominican Republic	832	60.5
Mexican	300	35.7
Puerto Rican	68	0.4

Foreign-Born Naturalized U.S. Citizens

Group	Number	%
Total Population	2,231	38.7
Hispanic or Latino (of any race)	885	34.8
Dominican Republic	439	52.8
Mexican	37	12.3
Puerto Rican	40	58.8

Language Spoken at Home: English Only
(Universe: Population 5 Years and Over)

Group	Number	%
Total Population	34,587	64.4
Hispanic or Latino (of any race)	3,427	18.5

Notes: (1) Percent of total population; (2) Percent of Hispanic/Latino population; Profiles include places with an overall population of at least 125,000, OR an overall population of at least 25,000 where the Hispanic/Latino population is at least 20% of the overall population. In states where less than five places meet either of these criteria, we have included places with at least 10,000 total population with the highest percentage of Hispanic/Latino population. These places are identified with an asterisk (*); Please refer to the User's Guide for a full explanation of data.

Dominican Republic	25	2.0
Mexican	188	25.0
Puerto Rican	2,801	19.4

Language Spoken at Home: Spanish
(Universe: Population 5 Years and Over)

Group	Number	%
Total Population	15,986	29.8
Hispanic or Latino (of any race)	14,999	80.8
Dominican Republic	1,214	98.0
Mexican	563	75.0
Puerto Rican	11,529	79.8

Unemployment Rate
(Universe: Population 16 Years and Over)

Group	%
Total Population	12.3
Hispanic or Latino (of any race)	15.7
Dominican Republic	22.4
Mexican	5.7
Puerto Rican	16.7

Class of Worker: Private Wage and Salary
(Universe: Civilian Employed Population 16 Years and Over)

Group	Number	%
Total Population	21,498	87.1
Hispanic or Latino (of any race)	6,607	92.0
Dominican Republic	506	83.2
Mexican	306	92.2
Puerto Rican	4,908	92.2

Class of Worker: Government
(Universe: Civilian Employed Population 16 Years and Over)

Group	Number	%
Total Population	2,143	8.7
Hispanic or Latino (of any race)	437	6.1
Dominican Republic	70	11.5
Mexican	26	7.8
Puerto Rican	325	6.1

Means of Transportation to Work: Car, Truck or Van
(Universe: Workers 16 Years and Over)

Group	Number	%
Total Population	18,403	76.8
Hispanic or Latino (of any race)	5,492	77.8
Dominican Republic	486	79.9
Mexican	234	70.5
Puerto Rican	3,976	76.4

Means of Transportation to Work: Public Transportation (ex. Taxicab)
(Universe: Workers 16 Years and Over)

Group	Number	%
Total Population	1,477	6.2
Hispanic or Latino (of any race)	637	9.0
Dominican Republic	80	13.2
Mexican	55	16.6
Puerto Rican	484	9.3

Homeownership Rate
(Universe: Occupied Housing Units)

Group	%
Total Population	43.9
Hispanic or Latino (of any race)	29.1
Central American, ex. Mexican	33.3
Guatemalan	39.1
Salvadoran	38.5
Cuban	32.1
Dominican Republic	37.8
Mexican	24.2
Puerto Rican	27.4
South American	54.6
Colombian	53.4
Ecuadorian	58.7
Peruvian	51.2

Median Home Value

Group	Dollars
Total Population	94,900
Hispanic or Latino (of any race)	84,900
Dominican Republic	89,000
Mexican	90,200
Puerto Rican	82,800

Median Gross Rent

Group	Dollars
Total Population	671
Hispanic or Latino (of any race)	674
Dominican Republic	743
Mexican	825
Puerto Rican	658

Median Household Income
(2010 Inflation-Adjusted Dollars)

Group	Dollars
Total Population	32,737
Hispanic or Latino (of any race)	25,177
Dominican Republic	45,776
Mexican	30,742
Puerto Rican	24,207

Per Capita Income
(2010 Inflation-Adjusted Dollars)

Group	Dollars
Total Population	15,768
Hispanic or Latino (of any race)	10,122
Dominican Republic	13,243
Mexican	10,878
Puerto Rican	9,719

Households with $100,000+ Income

Group	Number	%
Total Population	1,263	5.8
Hispanic or Latino (of any race)	255	3.8
Dominican Republic	46	10.0
Mexican	0	0.0
Puerto Rican	198	3.8

Households with Food Stamps/SNAP Benefits During Past 12 Months

Group	Number	%
Total Population	5,008	22.8
Hispanic or Latino (of any race)	2,861	43.0
Dominican Republic	78	17.0
Mexican	62	30.2
Puerto Rican	2,495	47.7

Poverty Rate
(Income in Past 12 Months Below Poverty Level)

Group	%
Total Population	27.6
Hispanic or Latino (of any race)	38.4
Dominican Republic	44.5
Mexican	24.4
Puerto Rican	38.4

Lebanon

Population

Group	Number	%TP[1]	%HP[2]
Total Population	25,477	100.0	–
Hispanic or Latino (of any race)	8,177	32.1	100.0
Central American, ex. Mexican	161	0.6	2.0
Cuban	152	0.6	1.9
Dominican Republic	778	3.1	9.5
Mexican	563	2.2	6.9
Puerto Rican	6,081	23.9	74.4
South American	142	0.6	1.7

Population Growth: 2000–2010

Group	%
Total Population	4.2
Hispanic or Latino (of any race)	103.5
Mexican	149.1
Puerto Rican	99.2

Males per 100 Females

Group	Number
Total Population	93.7
Hispanic or Latino (of any race)	96.6
Central American, ex. Mexican	85.1
Cuban	126.9
Dominican Republic	94.5
Mexican	119.1
Puerto Rican	94.4
South American	102.9

Average Household Size

Group	People
Total Population	2.42
Hispanic or Latino (of any race)	3.19
Central American, ex. Mexican	3.30
Cuban	2.86
Dominican Republic	3.40
Mexican	3.53
Puerto Rican	3.15
South American	3.04

Median Age

Group	Years
Total Population	35.6
Hispanic or Latino (of any race)	23.6
Central American, ex. Mexican	29.9
Cuban	31.8
Dominican Republic	26.5
Mexican	23.9
Puerto Rican	22.9
South American	30.8

High School Graduates
(Universe: Population 25 Years and Over)

Group	Number	%
Total Population	12,560	76.2
Hispanic or Latino (of any race)	1,738	53.1
Puerto Rican	1,347	56.4

Four-Year College Graduates
(Universe: Population 25 Years and Over)

Group	Number	%
Total Population	1,504	9.1
Hispanic or Latino (of any race)	89	2.7
Puerto Rican	84	3.5

Population Age 3–17 Enrolled in Public School
(Universe: Population Age 3–17 Enrolled in School)

Group	Number	%
Total Population	4,530	93.3
Hispanic or Latino (of any race)	2,138	98.3
Puerto Rican	1,551	98.1

Population Age 3–17 Enrolled in Private School
(Universe: Population Age 3–17 Enrolled in School)

Group	Number	%
Total Population	323	6.7
Hispanic or Latino (of any race)	38	1.7
Puerto Rican	30	1.9

Foreign-Born Population

Group	Number	%
Total Population	1,150	4.5
Hispanic or Latino (of any race)	828	11.4
Puerto Rican	0	0.0

Foreign-Born Naturalized U.S. Citizens

Group	Number	%
Total Population	705	61.3
Hispanic or Latino (of any race)	469	56.6
Puerto Rican	0	0.0

Language Spoken at Home: English Only
(Universe: Population 5 Years and Over)

Group	Number	%
Total Population	18,235	77.3
Hispanic or Latino (of any race)	1,556	24.6
Puerto Rican	1,165	24.6

Language Spoken at Home: Spanish
(Universe: Population 5 Years and Over)

Group	Number	%
Total Population	4,957	21.0
Hispanic or Latino (of any race)	4,767	75.4
Puerto Rican	3,578	75.4

Unemployment Rate
(Universe: Population 16 Years and Over)

Group	%
Total Population	11.8
Hispanic or Latino (of any race)	21.3
Puerto Rican	24.9

STATE & PLACE PROFILES

Notes: (1) Percent of total population; (2) Percent of Hispanic/Latino population; Profiles include places with an overall population of at least 125,000, OR an overall population of at least 25,000 where the Hispanic/Latino population is at least 20% of the overall population. In states where less than five places meet either of these criteria, we have included places with at least 10,000 total population with the highest percentage of Hispanic/Latino population. These places are identified with an asterisk (*); Please refer to the User's Guide for a full explanation of data.

Class of Worker: Private Wage and Salary
(Universe: Civilian Employed Population 16 Years and Over)

Group	Number	%
Total Population	9,405	85.3
Hispanic or Latino (of any race)	2,157	95.4
Puerto Rican	1,553	95.0

Class of Worker: Government
(Universe: Civilian Employed Population 16 Years and Over)

Group	Number	%
Total Population	1,224	11.1
Hispanic or Latino (of any race)	103	4.6
Puerto Rican	81	5.0

Means of Transportation to Work: Car, Truck or Van
(Universe: Workers 16 Years and Over)

Group	Number	%
Total Population	9,591	89.1
Hispanic or Latino (of any race)	1,922	88.7
Puerto Rican	1,444	90.2

Means of Transportation to Work: Public Transportation (ex. Taxicab)
(Universe: Workers 16 Years and Over)

Group	Number	%
Total Population	116	1.1
Hispanic or Latino (of any race)	34	1.6
Puerto Rican	34	2.1

Homeownership Rate
(Universe: Occupied Housing Units)

Group	%
Total Population	45.7
Hispanic or Latino (of any race)	25.3
Central American, ex. Mexican	45.3
Cuban	28.6
Dominican Republic	36.3
Mexican	24.1
Puerto Rican	22.9
South American	39.1

Median Home Value

Group	Dollars
Total Population	86,300
Hispanic or Latino (of any race)	79,300
Puerto Rican	81,700

Median Gross Rent

Group	Dollars
Total Population	567
Hispanic or Latino (of any race)	584
Puerto Rican	580

Median Household Income
(2010 Inflation-Adjusted Dollars)

Group	Dollars
Total Population	33,840
Hispanic or Latino (of any race)	27,527
Puerto Rican	21,879

Per Capita Income
(2010 Inflation-Adjusted Dollars)

Group	Dollars
Total Population	18,539
Hispanic or Latino (of any race)	11,124
Puerto Rican	11,046

Households with $100,000+ Income

Group	Number	%
Total Population	611	5.6
Hispanic or Latino (of any race)	70	3.2
Puerto Rican	70	4.2

Households with Food Stamps/SNAP Benefits During Past 12 Months

Group	Number	%
Total Population	2,297	21.1
Hispanic or Latino (of any race)	1,075	48.4
Puerto Rican	947	56.6

Poverty Rate
(Income in Past 12 Months Below Poverty Level)

Group	%
Total Population	22.9
Hispanic or Latino (of any race)	40.9
Puerto Rican	46.0

Norristown

Population

Group	Number	%TP[1]	%HP[2]
Total Population	34,324	100.0	–
Hispanic or Latino (of any race)	9,714	28.3	100.0
Central American, ex. Mexican	349	1.0	3.6
Honduran	126	0.4	1.3
Dominican Republic	136	0.4	1.4
Mexican	7,578	22.1	78.0
Puerto Rican	1,176	3.4	12.1
South American	119	0.3	1.2

Population Growth: 2000–2010

Group	%
Total Population	9.7
Hispanic or Latino (of any race)	196.0
Mexican	292.4
Puerto Rican	35.5

Males per 100 Females

Group	Number
Total Population	99.3
Hispanic or Latino (of any race)	141.8
Central American, ex. Mexican	198.3
Honduran	281.8
Dominican Republic	72.2
Mexican	155.6
Puerto Rican	87.9
South American	95.1

Average Household Size

Group	People
Total Population	2.79
Hispanic or Latino (of any race)	4.42
Central American, ex. Mexican	3.90
Honduran	4.20
Dominican Republic	3.68
Mexican	4.87
Puerto Rican	3.21
South American	2.94

Median Age

Group	Years
Total Population	31.2
Hispanic or Latino (of any race)	25.6
Central American, ex. Mexican	29.1
Honduran	27.7
Dominican Republic	27.4
Mexican	25.6
Puerto Rican	23.6
South American	30.6

High School Graduates
(Universe: Population 25 Years and Over)

Group	Number	%
Total Population	16,283	77.2
Hispanic or Latino (of any race)	2,467	58.3
Mexican	1,836	55.0

Four-Year College Graduates
(Universe: Population 25 Years and Over)

Group	Number	%
Total Population	3,414	16.2
Hispanic or Latino (of any race)	129	3.0
Mexican	14	0.4

Population Age 3–17 Enrolled in Public School
(Universe: Population Age 3–17 Enrolled in School)

Group	Number	%
Total Population	5,008	90.6
Hispanic or Latino (of any race)	1,118	93.6
Mexican	681	93.8

Population Age 3–17 Enrolled in Private School
(Universe: Population Age 3–17 Enrolled in School)

Group	Number	%
Total Population	521	9.4
Hispanic or Latino (of any race)	77	6.4
Mexican	45	6.2

Foreign-Born Population

Group	Number	%
Total Population	6,517	19.3
Hispanic or Latino (of any race)	4,873	58.3
Mexican	4,226	67.6

Foreign-Born Naturalized U.S. Citizens

Group	Number	%
Total Population	891	13.7
Hispanic or Latino (of any race)	349	7.2
Mexican	249	5.9

Language Spoken at Home: English Only
(Universe: Population 5 Years and Over)

Group	Number	%
Total Population	23,348	75.2
Hispanic or Latino (of any race)	1,390	19.3
Mexican	567	10.5

Language Spoken at Home: Spanish
(Universe: Population 5 Years and Over)

Group	Number	%
Total Population	6,008	19.4
Hispanic or Latino (of any race)	5,823	80.7
Mexican	4,841	89.5

Unemployment Rate
(Universe: Population 16 Years and Over)

Group	%
Total Population	8.2
Hispanic or Latino (of any race)	6.7
Mexican	4.3

Class of Worker: Private Wage and Salary
(Universe: Civilian Employed Population 16 Years and Over)

Group	Number	%
Total Population	15,388	87.3
Hispanic or Latino (of any race)	4,884	97.2
Mexican	3,949	98.2

Class of Worker: Government
(Universe: Civilian Employed Population 16 Years and Over)

Group	Number	%
Total Population	1,601	9.1
Hispanic or Latino (of any race)	49	1.0
Mexican	0	0.0

Means of Transportation to Work: Car, Truck or Van
(Universe: Workers 16 Years and Over)

Group	Number	%
Total Population	13,105	76.2
Hispanic or Latino (of any race)	3,247	65.1
Mexican	2,610	65.1

Means of Transportation to Work: Public Transportation (ex. Taxicab)
(Universe: Workers 16 Years and Over)

Group	Number	%
Total Population	1,790	10.4
Hispanic or Latino (of any race)	795	15.9
Mexican	727	18.1

Homeownership Rate
(Universe: Occupied Housing Units)

Group	%
Total Population	41.5
Hispanic or Latino (of any race)	14.2
Central American, ex. Mexican	28.7
Honduran	0.0
Dominican Republic	27.5
Mexican	8.4
Puerto Rican	27.1
South American	47.2

Median Home Value

Group	Dollars
Total Population	153,100
Hispanic or Latino (of any race)	146,300
Mexican	79,500

Median Gross Rent

Group	Dollars
Total Population	937
Hispanic or Latino (of any race)	1,032
Mexican	1,039

Notes: (1) Percent of total population; (2) Percent of Hispanic/Latino population; Profiles include places with an overall population of at least 125,000, OR an overall population of at least 25,000 where the Hispanic/Latino population is at least 20% of the overall population. In states where less than five places meet either of these criteria, we have included places with at least 10,000 total population with the highest percentage of Hispanic/Latino population. These places are identified with an asterisk (*); Please refer to the User's Guide for a full explanation of data.

Median Household Income
(2010 Inflation-Adjusted Dollars)

Group	Dollars
Total Population	43,551
Hispanic or Latino (of any race)	38,867
Mexican	38,053

Per Capita Income
(2010 Inflation-Adjusted Dollars)

Group	Dollars
Total Population	20,123
Hispanic or Latino (of any race)	14,264
Mexican	14,027

Households with $100,000+ Income

Group	Number	%
Total Population	1,370	10.9
Hispanic or Latino (of any race)	263	12.4
Mexican	180	10.6

Households with Food Stamps/SNAP Benefits During Past 12 Months

Group	Number	%
Total Population	1,661	13.2
Hispanic or Latino (of any race)	245	11.5
Mexican	138	8.2

Poverty Rate
(Income in Past 12 Months Below Poverty Level)

Group	%
Total Population	18.0
Hispanic or Latino (of any race)	20.7
Mexican	22.0

Philadelphia

Population

Group	Number	%TP[1]	%HP[2]
Total Population	1,526,006	100.0	–
Hispanic or Latino (of any race)	187,611	12.3	100.0
Central American, ex. Mexican	7,511	0.5	4.0
Costa Rican	903	0.1	0.5
Guatemalan	2,262	0.1	1.2
Honduran	1,642	0.1	0.9
Nicaraguan	874	0.1	0.5
Panamanian	737	<0.1	0.4
Salvadoran	1,049	0.1	0.6
Cuban	3,930	0.3	2.1
Dominican Republic	15,963	1.0	8.5
Mexican	15,531	1.0	8.3
Puerto Rican	121,643	8.0	64.8
South American	9,969	0.7	5.3
Argentinean	1,006	0.1	0.5
Bolivian	112	<0.1	0.1
Chilean	357	<0.1	0.2
Colombian	4,675	0.3	2.5
Ecuadorian	1,542	0.1	0.8
Peruvian	1,085	0.1	0.6
Uruguayan	234	<0.1	0.1
Venezuelan	773	0.1	0.4
Spaniard	1,294	0.1	0.7

Population Growth: 2000–2010

Group	%
Total Population	0.6
Hispanic or Latino (of any race)	45.5
Central American, ex. Mexican	163.9
Costa Rican	80.2
Guatemalan	336.7
Honduran	252.4
Nicaraguan	60.7
Panamanian	95.0
Salvadoran	211.3
Cuban	44.0
Dominican Republic	268.1
Mexican	149.7
Puerto Rican	32.9
South American	109.4
Argentinean	89.5
Chilean	96.2
Colombian	93.7
Ecuadorian	267.1
Peruvian	130.4
Venezuelan	89.0
Spaniard	399.6

Males per 100 Females

Group	Number
Total Population	89.3
Hispanic or Latino (of any race)	98.6
Central American, ex. Mexican	125.6
Costa Rican	133.3
Guatemalan	163.0
Honduran	137.6
Nicaraguan	98.2
Panamanian	71.0
Salvadoran	109.0
Cuban	104.4
Dominican Republic	94.5
Mexican	135.8
Puerto Rican	91.9
South American	96.3
Argentinean	98.8
Bolivian	111.3
Chilean	124.5
Colombian	83.1
Ecuadorian	138.3
Peruvian	93.4
Uruguayan	100.0
Venezuelan	93.3
Spaniard	100.3

Average Household Size

Group	People
Total Population	2.45
Hispanic or Latino (of any race)	3.16
Central American, ex. Mexican	3.40
Costa Rican	3.13
Guatemalan	3.85
Honduran	3.77
Nicaraguan	3.28
Panamanian	2.46
Salvadoran	3.37
Cuban	2.38
Dominican Republic	3.63
Mexican	3.52
Puerto Rican	3.16
South American	2.71
Argentinean	2.28
Bolivian	2.82
Chilean	2.09
Colombian	2.78
Ecuadorian	3.30
Peruvian	2.64
Uruguayan	2.75
Venezuelan	2.53
Spaniard	2.15

Median Age

Group	Years
Total Population	33.5
Hispanic or Latino (of any race)	26.1
Central American, ex. Mexican	28.6
Costa Rican	30.1
Guatemalan	27.3
Honduran	28.4
Nicaraguan	30.4
Panamanian	30.5
Salvadoran	29.6
Cuban	31.4
Dominican Republic	27.3
Mexican	25.6
Puerto Rican	25.2
South American	31.7
Argentinean	34.5
Bolivian	28.0
Chilean	30.2
Colombian	33.2
Ecuadorian	29.6
Peruvian	32.0
Uruguayan	34.0
Venezuelan	29.9
Spaniard	31.0

High School Graduates
(Universe: Population 25 Years and Over)

Group	Number	%
Total Population	766,202	79.4
Hispanic or Latino (of any race)	54,494	60.2
Central American, ex. Mexican	2,398	53.8
Costa Rican	436	59.1
Guatemalan	417	31.2
Honduran	393	54.0
Cuban	1,366	73.7
Dominican Republic	3,538	52.7
Mexican	4,626	62.8
Puerto Rican	34,956	58.2
South American	4,635	85.1
Colombian	2,299	86.1
Ecuadorian	435	65.8
Peruvian	672	88.4
Spaniard	527	87.4

Four-Year College Graduates
(Universe: Population 25 Years and Over)

Group	Number	%
Total Population	214,094	22.2
Hispanic or Latino (of any race)	9,575	10.6
Central American, ex. Mexican	598	13.4
Costa Rican	76	10.3
Guatemalan	137	10.2
Honduran	79	10.9
Cuban	604	32.6
Dominican Republic	749	11.2
Mexican	1,112	15.1
Puerto Rican	3,740	6.2
South American	2,051	37.6
Colombian	949	35.5
Ecuadorian	160	24.2
Peruvian	197	25.9
Spaniard	209	34.7

Population Age 3–17 Enrolled in Public School
(Universe: Population Age 3–17 Enrolled in School)

Group	Number	%
Total Population	198,802	77.0
Hispanic or Latino (of any race)	35,594	84.4
Central American, ex. Mexican	787	75.5
Costa Rican	90	45.5
Guatemalan	93	48.4
Honduran	174	94.1
Cuban	299	90.3
Dominican Republic	2,819	90.2
Mexican	2,037	85.9
Puerto Rican	27,141	85.0
South American	813	66.3
Colombian	448	63.6
Ecuadorian	158	100.0
Peruvian	85	70.8
Spaniard	174	100.0

Population Age 3–17 Enrolled in Private School
(Universe: Population Age 3–17 Enrolled in School)

Group	Number	%
Total Population	59,446	23.0
Hispanic or Latino (of any race)	6,592	15.6
Central American, ex. Mexican	255	24.5
Costa Rican	108	54.5
Guatemalan	99	51.6
Honduran	11	5.9
Cuban	32	9.7
Dominican Republic	307	9.8
Mexican	334	14.1
Puerto Rican	4,776	15.0
South American	413	33.7
Colombian	256	36.4
Ecuadorian	0	0.0
Peruvian	35	29.2
Spaniard	0	0.0

Foreign-Born Population

Group	Number	%
Total Population	172,415	11.5
Hispanic or Latino (of any race)	28,375	16.2
Central American, ex. Mexican	4,791	66.7
Costa Rican	809	65.0
Guatemalan	1,661	76.9
Honduran	811	74.9
Cuban	967	32.6
Dominican Republic	8,402	64.8
Mexican	6,029	45.3
Puerto Rican	1,237	1.0
South American	5,420	63.1

Notes: (1) Percent of total population; (2) Percent of Hispanic/Latino population; Profiles include places with an overall population of at least 125,000, OR an overall population of at least 25,000 where the Hispanic/Latino population is at least 20% of the overall population. In states where less than five places meet either of these criteria, we have included places with at least 10,000 total population with the highest percentage of Hispanic/Latino population. These places are identified with an asterisk (*); Please refer to the User's Guide for a full explanation of data.

Group	Number	%
Colombian	2,675	61.2
Ecuadorian	698	68.2
Peruvian	746	68.1
Spaniard	164	17.7

Foreign-Born Naturalized U.S. Citizens

Group	Number	%
Total Population	80,084	46.4
Hispanic or Latino (of any race)	9,419	33.2
Central American, ex. Mexican	1,362	28.4
Costa Rican	255	31.5
Guatemalan	309	18.6
Honduran	323	39.8
Cuban	740	76.5
Dominican Republic	3,073	36.6
Mexican	1,180	19.6
Puerto Rican	750	60.6
South American	1,748	32.3
Colombian	880	32.9
Ecuadorian	145	20.8
Peruvian	308	41.3
Spaniard	96	58.5

Language Spoken at Home: English Only
(Universe: Population 5 Years and Over)

Group	Number	%
Total Population	1,112,441	79.1
Hispanic or Latino (of any race)	34,936	22.4
Central American, ex. Mexican	1,024	15.4
Costa Rican	106	9.1
Guatemalan	148	7.7
Honduran	187	17.4
Cuban	1,245	46.0
Dominican Republic	817	6.9
Mexican	3,955	33.6
Puerto Rican	23,819	22.2
South American	920	11.6
Colombian	338	8.3
Ecuadorian	64	6.8
Peruvian	117	11.9
Spaniard	488	57.5

Language Spoken at Home: Spanish
(Universe: Population 5 Years and Over)

Group	Number	%
Total Population	136,688	9.7
Hispanic or Latino (of any race)	120,372	77.1
Central American, ex. Mexican	5,595	84.0
Costa Rican	1,052	89.9
Guatemalan	1,762	92.3
Honduran	885	82.6
Cuban	1,422	52.5
Dominican Republic	10,909	92.7
Mexican	7,712	65.5
Puerto Rican	83,249	77.6
South American	6,911	87.4
Colombian	3,717	91.3
Ecuadorian	883	93.2
Peruvian	868	88.1
Spaniard	361	42.5

Unemployment Rate
(Universe: Population 16 Years and Over)

Group	%
Total Population	12.6
Hispanic or Latino (of any race)	16.0
Central American, ex. Mexican	12.2
Costa Rican	26.6
Guatemalan	10.7
Honduran	9.0
Cuban	18.1
Dominican Republic	14.6
Mexican	7.9
Puerto Rican	19.3
South American	7.9
Colombian	10.7
Ecuadorian	7.8
Peruvian	10.6
Spaniard	9.0

Class of Worker: Private Wage and Salary
(Universe: Civilian Employed Population 16 Years and Over)

Group	Number	%
Total Population	508,347	81.9
Hispanic or Latino (of any race)	49,697	85.8
Central American, ex. Mexican	3,382	88.5
Costa Rican	413	77.1
Guatemalan	1,123	91.9
Honduran	513	91.1
Cuban	1,079	93.7
Dominican Republic	4,443	88.6
Mexican	6,289	92.7
Puerto Rican	27,651	83.4
South American	4,036	85.2
Colombian	2,125	86.9
Ecuadorian	486	89.2
Peruvian	306	77.1
Spaniard	430	88.7

Class of Worker: Government
(Universe: Civilian Employed Population 16 Years and Over)

Group	Number	%
Total Population	88,231	14.2
Hispanic or Latino (of any race)	5,785	10.0
Central American, ex. Mexican	143	3.7
Costa Rican	0	0.0
Guatemalan	43	3.5
Honduran	29	5.2
Cuban	32	2.8
Dominican Republic	224	4.5
Mexican	348	5.1
Puerto Rican	4,382	13.2
South American	305	6.4
Colombian	140	5.7
Ecuadorian	14	2.6
Peruvian	12	3.0
Spaniard	55	11.3

Means of Transportation to Work: Car, Truck or Van
(Universe: Workers 16 Years and Over)

Group	Number	%
Total Population	362,927	60.1
Hispanic or Latino (of any race)	35,132	62.2
Central American, ex. Mexican	2,415	64.0
Costa Rican	357	70.7
Guatemalan	795	65.1
Honduran	392	71.8
Cuban	614	56.2
Dominican Republic	3,582	73.3
Mexican	3,230	48.3
Puerto Rican	20,429	63.4
South American	2,965	64.4
Colombian	1,711	71.0
Ecuadorian	326	70.1
Peruvian	221	57.1
Spaniard	215	44.3

Means of Transportation to Work: Public Transportation (ex. Taxicab)
(Universe: Workers 16 Years and Over)

Group	Number	%
Total Population	158,108	26.2
Hispanic or Latino (of any race)	13,424	23.8
Central American, ex. Mexican	878	23.3
Costa Rican	112	22.2
Guatemalan	298	24.4
Honduran	77	14.1
Cuban	249	22.8
Dominican Republic	778	15.9
Mexican	1,308	19.6
Puerto Rican	8,331	25.8
South American	1,018	22.1
Colombian	501	20.8
Ecuadorian	124	26.7
Peruvian	101	26.1
Spaniard	171	35.3

Homeownership Rate
(Universe: Occupied Housing Units)

Group	%
Total Population	54.1
Hispanic or Latino (of any race)	45.9
Central American, ex. Mexican	40.5
Costa Rican	36.0
Guatemalan	25.0
Honduran	38.2
Nicaraguan	59.6
Panamanian	48.3
Salvadoran	51.6
Cuban	46.8
Dominican Republic	47.6
Mexican	24.7
Puerto Rican	48.3
South American	48.8
Argentinean	45.6
Bolivian	44.7
Chilean	36.2
Colombian	56.3
Ecuadorian	40.2
Peruvian	42.9
Uruguayan	44.7
Venezuelan	41.9
Spaniard	50.0

Median Home Value

Group	Dollars
Total Population	135,200
Hispanic or Latino (of any race)	89,500
Central American, ex. Mexican	152,100
Costa Rican	185,000
Guatemalan	141,400
Honduran	121,600
Cuban	107,600
Dominican Republic	108,200
Mexican	138,500
Puerto Rican	81,100
South American	148,600
Colombian	144,500
Ecuadorian	116,400
Peruvian	138,700
Spaniard	171,400

Median Gross Rent

Group	Dollars
Total Population	819
Hispanic or Latino (of any race)	783
Central American, ex. Mexican	899
Costa Rican	872
Guatemalan	798
Honduran	1,096
Cuban	890
Dominican Republic	799
Mexican	824
Puerto Rican	751
South American	867
Colombian	849
Ecuadorian	944
Peruvian	769
Spaniard	950

Median Household Income
(2010 Inflation-Adjusted Dollars)

Group	Dollars
Total Population	36,251
Hispanic or Latino (of any race)	25,029
Central American, ex. Mexican	41,019
Costa Rican	33,750
Guatemalan	33,150
Honduran	63,112
Cuban	35,217
Dominican Republic	25,668
Mexican	31,082
Puerto Rican	21,948
South American	37,684
Colombian	32,325
Ecuadorian	35,701
Peruvian	40,750
Spaniard	53,261

Per Capita Income
(2010 Inflation-Adjusted Dollars)

Group	Dollars
Total Population	21,117
Hispanic or Latino (of any race)	12,214
Central American, ex. Mexican	17,812
Costa Rican	17,743
Guatemalan	15,856
Honduran	18,915
Cuban	21,610
Dominican Republic	11,225
Mexican	15,900
Puerto Rican	10,642
South American	19,011
Colombian	17,623

Notes: (1) Percent of total population; (2) Percent of Hispanic/Latino population; Profiles include places with an overall population of at least 125,000, OR an overall population of at least 25,000 where the Hispanic/Latino population is at least 20% of the overall population. In states where less than five places meet either of these criteria, we have included places with at least 10,000 total population with the highest percentage of Hispanic/Latino population. These places are identified with an asterisk (*); Please refer to the User's Guide for a full explanation of data.

Ecuadorian	14,210	
Peruvian	15,798	
Spaniard	40,822	

Households with $100,000+ Income

Group	Number	%
Total Population	68,151	11.9
Hispanic or Latino (of any race)	3,275	6.3
Central American, ex. Mexican	407	17.6
Costa Rican	71	15.3
Guatemalan	101	14.2
Honduran	42	15.8
Cuban	149	11.8
Dominican Republic	182	5.4
Mexican	389	9.3
Puerto Rican	1,565	4.5
South American	342	11.1
Colombian	156	9.2
Ecuadorian	0	0.0
Peruvian	22	9.6
Spaniard	115	29.6

Households with Food Stamps/SNAP Benefits During Past 12 Months

Group	Number	%
Total Population	101,040	17.6
Hispanic or Latino (of any race)	18,540	35.8
Central American, ex. Mexican	526	22.8
Costa Rican	49	10.5
Guatemalan	189	26.7
Honduran	130	48.9
Cuban	277	22.0
Dominican Republic	1,123	33.6
Mexican	738	17.7
Puerto Rican	14,736	42.6
South American	326	10.6
Colombian	180	10.7
Ecuadorian	15	4.2
Peruvian	34	14.8
Spaniard	33	8.5

Poverty Rate
(Income in Past 12 Months Below Poverty Level)

Group	%
Total Population	25.1
Hispanic or Latino (of any race)	40.1
Central American, ex. Mexican	31.3
Costa Rican	43.4
Guatemalan	41.0
Honduran	34.8
Cuban	30.8
Dominican Republic	37.7
Mexican	27.9
Puerto Rican	43.9
South American	21.4
Colombian	23.5
Ecuadorian	21.1
Peruvian	19.4
Spaniard	6.9

Pittsburgh

Population

Group	Number	%TP[1]	%HP[2]
Total Population	305,704	100.0	–
Hispanic or Latino (of any race)	6,964	2.3	100.0
Central American, ex. Mexican	500	0.2	7.2
Guatemalan	186	0.1	2.7
Cuban	397	0.1	5.7
Dominican Republic	157	0.1	2.3
Mexican	2,292	0.7	32.9
Puerto Rican	1,336	0.4	19.2
South American	1,162	0.4	16.7
Argentinean	244	0.1	3.5
Chilean	139	<0.1	2.0
Colombian	263	0.1	3.8
Peruvian	211	0.1	3.0
Venezuelan	142	<0.1	2.0
Spaniard	310	0.1	4.5

Population Growth: 2000–2010

Group	%
Total Population	-8.6
Hispanic or Latino (of any race)	57.4

Central American, ex. Mexican	194.1	
Cuban	35.0	
Mexican	85.6	
Puerto Rican	65.3	
South American	90.5	
Argentinean	84.8	
Colombian	126.7	
Venezuelan	17.4	

Males per 100 Females

Group	Number
Total Population	94.0
Hispanic or Latino (of any race)	115.7
Central American, ex. Mexican	109.2
Guatemalan	129.6
Cuban	112.3
Dominican Republic	91.5
Mexican	129.0
Puerto Rican	98.8
South American	99.7
Argentinean	98.4
Chilean	101.4
Colombian	93.4
Peruvian	97.2
Venezuelan	111.9
Spaniard	105.3

Average Household Size

Group	People
Total Population	2.07
Hispanic or Latino (of any race)	2.26
Central American, ex. Mexican	2.45
Guatemalan	2.84
Cuban	2.16
Dominican Republic	2.13
Mexican	2.46
Puerto Rican	2.32
South American	2.07
Argentinean	2.04
Chilean	2.33
Colombian	1.93
Peruvian	2.16
Venezuelan	1.98
Spaniard	1.85

Median Age

Group	Years
Total Population	33.2
Hispanic or Latino (of any race)	26.0
Central American, ex. Mexican	23.5
Guatemalan	22.3
Cuban	23.9
Dominican Republic	22.9
Mexican	26.2
Puerto Rican	22.3
South American	28.6
Argentinean	32.2
Chilean	28.5
Colombian	27.6
Peruvian	28.8
Venezuelan	28.9
Spaniard	29.7

High School Graduates
(Universe: Population 25 Years and Over)

Group	Number	%
Total Population	177,924	88.3
Hispanic or Latino (of any race)	3,448	87.8
Mexican	991	84.5
Puerto Rican	847	83.7
South American	529	95.7

Four-Year College Graduates
(Universe: Population 25 Years and Over)

Group	Number	%
Total Population	68,052	33.8
Hispanic or Latino (of any race)	1,505	38.3
Mexican	410	35.0
Puerto Rican	186	18.4
South American	436	78.8

Population Age 3–17 Enrolled in Public School
(Universe: Population Age 3–17 Enrolled in School)

Group	Number	%
Total Population	30,648	76.7
Hispanic or Latino (of any race)	863	72.6
Mexican	235	62.7
Puerto Rican	266	74.7
South American	47	83.9

Population Age 3–17 Enrolled in Private School
(Universe: Population Age 3–17 Enrolled in School)

Group	Number	%
Total Population	9,303	23.3
Hispanic or Latino (of any race)	325	27.4
Mexican	140	37.3
Puerto Rican	90	25.3
South American	9	16.1

Foreign-Born Population

Group	Number	%
Total Population	21,373	6.9
Hispanic or Latino (of any race)	2,142	30.2
Mexican	828	38.5
Puerto Rican	0	0.0
South American	506	63.2

Foreign-Born Naturalized U.S. Citizens

Group	Number	%
Total Population	7,979	37.3
Hispanic or Latino (of any race)	582	27.2
Mexican	23	2.8
Puerto Rican	0	0.0
South American	152	30.0

Language Spoken at Home: English Only
(Universe: Population 5 Years and Over)

Group	Number	%
Total Population	264,035	90.2
Hispanic or Latino (of any race)	3,185	49.7
Mexican	1,090	54.2
Puerto Rican	1,064	59.6
South American	251	32.9

Language Spoken at Home: Spanish
(Universe: Population 5 Years and Over)

Group	Number	%
Total Population	6,219	2.1
Hispanic or Latino (of any race)	3,118	48.6
Mexican	890	44.3
Puerto Rican	667	37.3
South American	511	67.1

Unemployment Rate
(Universe: Population 16 Years and Over)

Group	%
Total Population	8.6
Hispanic or Latino (of any race)	12.6
Mexican	6.1
Puerto Rican	11.9
South American	17.8

Class of Worker: Private Wage and Salary
(Universe: Civilian Employed Population 16 Years and Over)

Group	Number	%
Total Population	122,543	83.9
Hispanic or Latino (of any race)	3,039	86.8
Mexican	1,143	85.8
Puerto Rican	751	87.0
South American	452	90.6

Class of Worker: Government
(Universe: Civilian Employed Population 16 Years and Over)

Group	Number	%
Total Population	17,550	12.0
Hispanic or Latino (of any race)	225	6.4
Mexican	33	2.5
Puerto Rican	102	11.8
South American	47	9.4

Means of Transportation to Work: Car, Truck or Van
(Universe: Workers 16 Years and Over)

Group	Number	%
Total Population	90,542	63.8
Hispanic or Latino (of any race)	1,377	39.8
Mexican	614	46.1
Puerto Rican	266	30.8
South American	167	36.5

Notes: (1) Percent of total population; (2) Percent of Hispanic/Latino population; Profiles include places with an overall population of at least 125,000, OR an overall population of at least 25,000 where the Hispanic/Latino population is at least 20% of the overall population. In states where less than five places meet either of these criteria, we have included places with at least 10,000 total population with the highest percentage of Hispanic/Latino population. These places are identified with an asterisk (*); Please refer to the User's Guide for a full explanation of data.

Means of Transportation to Work: Public Transportation (ex. Taxicab)
(Universe: Workers 16 Years and Over)

Group	Number	%
Total Population	27,665	19.5
Hispanic or Latino (of any race)	998	28.8
Mexican	329	24.7
Puerto Rican	211	24.4
South American	212	46.4

Homeownership Rate
(Universe: Occupied Housing Units)

Group	%
Total Population	47.6
Hispanic or Latino (of any race)	29.3
Central American, ex. Mexican	20.7
Guatemalan	13.6
Cuban	32.3
Dominican Republic	23.2
Mexican	27.5
Puerto Rican	26.9
South American	33.1
Argentinean	47.1
Chilean	29.6
Colombian	20.6
Peruvian	35.5
Venezuelan	35.0
Spaniard	33.3

Median Home Value

Group	Dollars
Total Population	85,200
Hispanic or Latino (of any race)	111,400
Mexican	114,200
Puerto Rican	154,200
South American	159,600

Median Gross Rent

Group	Dollars
Total Population	700
Hispanic or Latino (of any race)	687
Mexican	626
Puerto Rican	774
South American	701

Median Household Income
(2010 Inflation-Adjusted Dollars)

Group	Dollars
Total Population	36,019
Hispanic or Latino (of any race)	32,372
Mexican	31,232
Puerto Rican	33,351
South American	33,655

Per Capita Income
(2010 Inflation-Adjusted Dollars)

Group	Dollars
Total Population	24,833
Hispanic or Latino (of any race)	19,032
Mexican	19,391
Puerto Rican	14,814
South American	33,988

Households with $100,000+ Income

Group	Number	%
Total Population	16,873	12.5
Hispanic or Latino (of any race)	172	6.2
Mexican	36	4.7
Puerto Rican	34	4.3
South American	33	7.3

Households with Food Stamps/SNAP Benefits During Past 12 Months

Group	Number	%
Total Population	18,478	13.7
Hispanic or Latino (of any race)	301	10.9
Mexican	84	11.0
Puerto Rican	97	12.3
South American	0	0.0

Poverty Rate
(Income in Past 12 Months Below Poverty Level)

Group	%
Total Population	21.9
Hispanic or Latino (of any race)	27.3
Mexican	26.5
Puerto Rican	24.6
South American	19.9

Reading

Population

Group	Number	%TP[1]	%HP[2]
Total Population	88,082	100.0	–
Hispanic or Latino (of any race)	51,230	58.2	100.0
Central American, ex. Mexican	1,436	1.6	2.8
Guatemalan	402	0.5	0.8
Honduran	270	0.3	0.5
Salvadoran	637	0.7	1.2
Cuban	360	0.4	0.7
Dominican Republic	8,716	9.9	17.0
Mexican	8,602	9.8	16.8
Puerto Rican	28,160	32.0	55.0
South American	1,240	1.4	2.4
Colombian	612	0.7	1.2
Ecuadorian	409	0.5	0.8

Population Growth: 2000–2010

Group	%
Total Population	8.5
Hispanic or Latino (of any race)	69.1
Central American, ex. Mexican	232.4
Guatemalan	232.2
Salvadoran	270.3
Cuban	65.9
Dominican Republic	413.9
Mexican	56.3
Puerto Rican	47.8
South American	156.7
Colombian	71.9

Males per 100 Females

Group	Number
Total Population	94.3
Hispanic or Latino (of any race)	98.3
Central American, ex. Mexican	119.9
Guatemalan	154.4
Honduran	119.5
Salvadoran	105.5
Cuban	119.5
Dominican Republic	92.9
Mexican	124.0
Puerto Rican	92.1
South American	96.2
Colombian	94.3
Ecuadorian	96.6

Average Household Size

Group	People
Total Population	2.85
Hispanic or Latino (of any race)	3.49
Central American, ex. Mexican	4.01
Guatemalan	4.56
Honduran	3.69
Salvadoran	4.08
Cuban	2.28
Dominican Republic	3.60
Mexican	4.57
Puerto Rican	3.24
South American	3.49
Colombian	3.45
Ecuadorian	3.65

Median Age

Group	Years
Total Population	28.9
Hispanic or Latino (of any race)	23.3
Central American, ex. Mexican	27.3
Guatemalan	25.9
Honduran	29.2
Salvadoran	27.0
Cuban	28.6
Dominican Republic	26.9
Mexican	21.8
Puerto Rican	22.8
South American	32.1
Colombian	33.5
Ecuadorian	29.8

High School Graduates
(Universe: Population 25 Years and Over)

Group	Number	%
Total Population	31,938	64.7
Hispanic or Latino (of any race)	10,897	49.3
Central American, ex. Mexican	196	43.0
Dominican Republic	2,333	56.7
Mexican	677	18.2
Puerto Rican	6,480	54.4
South American	671	57.2

Four-Year College Graduates
(Universe: Population 25 Years and Over)

Group	Number	%
Total Population	4,847	9.8
Hispanic or Latino (of any race)	1,163	5.3
Central American, ex. Mexican	0	0.0
Dominican Republic	413	10.0
Mexican	31	0.8
Puerto Rican	462	3.9
South American	212	18.1

Population Age 3–17 Enrolled in Public School
(Universe: Population Age 3–17 Enrolled in School)

Group	Number	%
Total Population	17,957	94.4
Hispanic or Latino (of any race)	12,933	96.4
Central American, ex. Mexican	264	100.0
Dominican Republic	2,477	96.7
Mexican	2,213	98.0
Puerto Rican	6,833	95.5
South American	355	100.0

Population Age 3–17 Enrolled in Private School
(Universe: Population Age 3–17 Enrolled in School)

Group	Number	%
Total Population	1,074	5.6
Hispanic or Latino (of any race)	477	3.6
Central American, ex. Mexican	0	0.0
Dominican Republic	84	3.3
Mexican	45	2.0
Puerto Rican	324	4.5
South American	0	0.0

Foreign-Born Population

Group	Number	%
Total Population	15,237	17.4
Hispanic or Latino (of any race)	12,208	25.7
Central American, ex. Mexican	586	62.0
Dominican Republic	5,182	62.7
Mexican	4,458	55.7
Puerto Rican	134	0.5
South American	1,423	71.5

Foreign-Born Naturalized U.S. Citizens

Group	Number	%
Total Population	4,486	29.4
Hispanic or Latino (of any race)	2,968	24.3
Central American, ex. Mexican	240	41.0
Dominican Republic	1,817	35.1
Mexican	421	9.4
Puerto Rican	45	33.6
South American	318	22.3

Language Spoken at Home: English Only
(Universe: Population 5 Years and Over)

Group	Number	%
Total Population	41,295	51.9
Hispanic or Latino (of any race)	7,406	17.8
Central American, ex. Mexican	205	22.5
Dominican Republic	479	6.4
Mexican	601	8.7
Puerto Rican	5,482	24.2
South American	168	9.4

Language Spoken at Home: Spanish
(Universe: Population 5 Years and Over)

Group	Number	%
Total Population	35,046	44.1
Hispanic or Latino (of any race)	34,131	82.2
Central American, ex. Mexican	708	77.5
Dominican Republic	7,041	93.5
Mexican	6,275	91.3
Puerto Rican	17,165	75.8
South American	1,614	90.6

Notes: (1) Percent of total population; (2) Percent of Hispanic/Latino population; Profiles include places with an overall population of at least 125,000, OR an overall population of at least 25,000 where the Hispanic/Latino population is at least 20% of the overall population. In states where less than five places meet either of these criteria, we have included places with at least 10,000 total population with the highest percentage of Hispanic/Latino population. These places are identified with an asterisk (*); Please refer to the User's Guide for a full explanation of data.

Unemployment Rate
(Universe: Population 16 Years and Over)

Group	%
Total Population	16.7
Hispanic or Latino (of any race)	20.3
Central American, ex. Mexican	9.0
Dominican Republic	23.8
Mexican	8.7
Puerto Rican	25.2
South American	10.5

Class of Worker: Private Wage and Salary
(Universe: Civilian Employed Population 16 Years and Over)

Group	Number	%
Total Population	28,436	88.3
Hispanic or Latino (of any race)	14,187	92.4
Central American, ex. Mexican	331	94.0
Dominican Republic	2,583	88.7
Mexican	3,085	96.8
Puerto Rican	6,723	92.3
South American	937	89.0

Class of Worker: Government
(Universe: Civilian Employed Population 16 Years and Over)

Group	Number	%
Total Population	2,411	7.5
Hispanic or Latino (of any race)	694	4.5
Central American, ex. Mexican	13	3.7
Dominican Republic	92	3.2
Mexican	22	0.7
Puerto Rican	491	6.7
South American	49	4.7

Means of Transportation to Work: Car, Truck or Van
(Universe: Workers 16 Years and Over)

Group	Number	%
Total Population	24,465	78.6
Hispanic or Latino (of any race)	11,822	79.9
Central American, ex. Mexican	285	81.0
Dominican Republic	2,245	82.6
Mexican	2,625	83.3
Puerto Rican	5,539	79.0
South American	672	67.1

Means of Transportation to Work: Public Transportation (ex. Taxicab)
(Universe: Workers 16 Years and Over)

Group	Number	%
Total Population	2,262	7.3
Hispanic or Latino (of any race)	1,132	7.7
Central American, ex. Mexican	0	0.0
Dominican Republic	201	7.4
Mexican	234	7.4
Puerto Rican	555	7.9
South American	123	12.3

Homeownership Rate
(Universe: Occupied Housing Units)

Group	%
Total Population	42.4
Hispanic or Latino (of any race)	33.7
Central American, ex. Mexican	48.7
Guatemalan	36.5
Honduran	46.7
Salvadoran	54.2
Cuban	31.3
Dominican Republic	48.3
Mexican	43.4
Puerto Rican	25.8
South American	59.6
Colombian	61.5
Ecuadorian	60.9

Median Home Value

Group	Dollars
Total Population	65,500
Hispanic or Latino (of any race)	66,500
Central American, ex. Mexican	81,300
Dominican Republic	70,700
Mexican	52,100
Puerto Rican	66,600
South American	73,500

Median Gross Rent

Group	Dollars
Total Population	653
Hispanic or Latino (of any race)	642
Central American, ex. Mexican	668
Dominican Republic	681
Mexican	641
Puerto Rican	616
South American	768

Median Household Income
(2010 Inflation-Adjusted Dollars)

Group	Dollars
Total Population	28,197
Hispanic or Latino (of any race)	23,914
Central American, ex. Mexican	16,953
Dominican Republic	23,447
Mexican	29,943
Puerto Rican	21,699
South American	32,847

Per Capita Income
(2010 Inflation-Adjusted Dollars)

Group	Dollars
Total Population	13,135
Hispanic or Latino (of any race)	9,048
Central American, ex. Mexican	9,697
Dominican Republic	8,751
Mexican	8,848
Puerto Rican	9,049
South American	11,984

Households with $100,000+ Income

Group	Number	%
Total Population	1,164	3.8
Hispanic or Latino (of any race)	280	2.0
Central American, ex. Mexican	34	15.4
Dominican Republic	0	0.0
Mexican	62	3.5
Puerto Rican	176	2.1
South American	8	1.0

Households with Food Stamps/SNAP Benefits During Past 12 Months

Group	Number	%
Total Population	9,765	31.5
Hispanic or Latino (of any race)	6,473	46.3
Central American, ex. Mexican	108	48.9
Dominican Republic	1,306	52.6
Mexican	502	28.3
Puerto Rican	4,174	50.8
South American	175	21.9

Poverty Rate
(Income in Past 12 Months Below Poverty Level)

Group	%
Total Population	35.0
Hispanic or Latino (of any race)	44.6
Central American, ex. Mexican	33.6
Dominican Republic	42.7
Mexican	30.9
Puerto Rican	52.1
South American	27.8

York

Population

Group	Number	%TP[1]	%HP[2]
Total Population	43,718	100.0	–
Hispanic or Latino (of any race)	12,458	28.5	100.0
Central American, ex. Mexican	282	0.6	2.3
Salvadoran	131	0.3	1.1
Cuban	178	0.4	1.4
Dominican Republic	1,212	2.8	9.7
Mexican	1,482	3.4	11.9
Puerto Rican	8,440	19.3	67.7
South American	135	0.3	1.1

Population Growth: 2000–2010

Group	%
Total Population	7.0
Hispanic or Latino (of any race)	77.3
Dominican Republic	402.9
Mexican	100.8
Puerto Rican	69.6

Males per 100 Females

Group	Number
Total Population	92.9
Hispanic or Latino (of any race)	97.1
Central American, ex. Mexican	104.3
Salvadoran	125.9
Cuban	114.5
Dominican Republic	91.8
Mexican	117.6
Puerto Rican	93.4
South American	98.5

Average Household Size

Group	People
Total Population	2.62
Hispanic or Latino (of any race)	3.44
Central American, ex. Mexican	3.63
Salvadoran	3.74
Cuban	2.57
Dominican Republic	3.56
Mexican	4.21
Puerto Rican	3.37
South American	3.07

Median Age

Group	Years
Total Population	30.1
Hispanic or Latino (of any race)	22.8
Central American, ex. Mexican	26.3
Salvadoran	26.1
Cuban	27.6
Dominican Republic	27.6
Mexican	22.9
Puerto Rican	22.3
South American	30.9

High School Graduates
(Universe: Population 25 Years and Over)

Group	Number	%
Total Population	18,231	73.7
Hispanic or Latino (of any race)	3,088	59.4
Dominican Republic	361	75.7
Mexican	314	53.0
Puerto Rican	2,101	56.7

Four-Year College Graduates
(Universe: Population 25 Years and Over)

Group	Number	%
Total Population	2,521	10.2
Hispanic or Latino (of any race)	208	4.0
Dominican Republic	13	2.7
Mexican	26	4.4
Puerto Rican	146	3.9

Population Age 3–17 Enrolled in Public School
(Universe: Population Age 3–17 Enrolled in School)

Group	Number	%
Total Population	7,393	90.3
Hispanic or Latino (of any race)	3,038	95.4
Dominican Republic	178	100.0
Mexican	455	91.9
Puerto Rican	2,049	95.1

Population Age 3–17 Enrolled in Private School
(Universe: Population Age 3–17 Enrolled in School)

Group	Number	%
Total Population	797	9.7
Hispanic or Latino (of any race)	145	4.6
Dominican Republic	0	0.0
Mexican	40	8.1
Puerto Rican	105	4.9

Foreign-Born Population

Group	Number	%
Total Population	3,600	8.3
Hispanic or Latino (of any race)	1,605	13.7
Dominican Republic	542	53.6
Mexican	641	39.8
Puerto Rican	26	0.3

Foreign-Born Naturalized U.S. Citizens

Group	Number	%
Total Population	1,098	30.5
Hispanic or Latino (of any race)	284	17.7

STATE & PLACE PROFILES

Notes: (1) Percent of total population; (2) Percent of Hispanic/Latino population; Profiles include places with an overall population of at least 125,000, OR an overall population of at least 25,000 where the Hispanic/Latino population is at least 20% of the overall population. In states where less than five places meet either of these criteria, we have included places with at least 10,000 total population with the highest percentage of Hispanic/Latino population. These places are identified with an asterisk (*); Please refer to the User's Guide for a full explanation of data.

Dominican Republic	65	12.0
Mexican	101	15.8
Puerto Rican	10	38.5

Language Spoken at Home: English Only
(Universe: Population 5 Years and Over)

Group	Number	%
Total Population	29,041	73.8
Hispanic or Latino (of any race)	2,333	22.8
Dominican Republic	77	8.4
Mexican	433	31.9
Puerto Rican	1,589	22.8

Language Spoken at Home: Spanish
(Universe: Population 5 Years and Over)

Group	Number	%
Total Population	8,412	21.4
Hispanic or Latino (of any race)	7,864	76.9
Dominican Republic	841	91.6
Mexican	926	68.1
Puerto Rican	5,360	76.8

Unemployment Rate
(Universe: Population 16 Years and Over)

Group	%
Total Population	15.6
Hispanic or Latino (of any race)	23.1
Dominican Republic	31.8
Mexican	19.7
Puerto Rican	24.0

Class of Worker: Private Wage and Salary
(Universe: Civilian Employed Population 16 Years and Over)

Group	Number	%
Total Population	15,182	89.1
Hispanic or Latino (of any race)	2,977	94.4
Dominican Republic	361	100.0
Mexican	384	93.4
Puerto Rican	1,919	94.5

Class of Worker: Government
(Universe: Civilian Employed Population 16 Years and Over)

Group	Number	%
Total Population	1,367	8.0
Hispanic or Latino (of any race)	117	3.7
Dominican Republic	0	0.0
Mexican	27	6.6
Puerto Rican	90	4.4

Means of Transportation to Work: Car, Truck or Van
(Universe: Workers 16 Years and Over)

Group	Number	%
Total Population	13,388	80.9
Hispanic or Latino (of any race)	2,573	83.9
Dominican Republic	317	87.8
Mexican	333	83.3
Puerto Rican	1,602	81.4

Means of Transportation to Work: Public Transportation (ex. Taxicab)
(Universe: Workers 16 Years and Over)

Group	Number	%
Total Population	1,326	8.0
Hispanic or Latino (of any race)	157	5.1
Dominican Republic	29	8.0
Mexican	0	0.0
Puerto Rican	117	5.9

Homeownership Rate
(Universe: Occupied Housing Units)

Group	%
Total Population	41.8
Hispanic or Latino (of any race)	24.6
Central American, ex. Mexican	43.8
Salvadoran	54.3
Cuban	28.3
Dominican Republic	39.0
Mexican	24.7
Puerto Rican	21.5
South American	53.5

Median Home Value

Group	Dollars
Total Population	80,100
Hispanic or Latino (of any race)	74,900
Dominican Republic	92,700
Mexican	82,100
Puerto Rican	67,200

Median Gross Rent

Group	Dollars
Total Population	621
Hispanic or Latino (of any race)	655
Dominican Republic	494
Mexican	633
Puerto Rican	667

Median Household Income
(2010 Inflation-Adjusted Dollars)

Group	Dollars
Total Population	28,583
Hispanic or Latino (of any race)	21,803
Dominican Republic	21,597
Mexican	31,768
Puerto Rican	21,521

Per Capita Income
(2010 Inflation-Adjusted Dollars)

Group	Dollars
Total Population	14,287
Hispanic or Latino (of any race)	8,271
Dominican Republic	11,063
Mexican	7,542
Puerto Rican	7,997

Households with $100,000+ Income

Group	Number	%
Total Population	651	3.9
Hispanic or Latino (of any race)	1	<0.1
Dominican Republic	0	0.0
Mexican	0	0.0
Puerto Rican	1	<0.1

Households with Food Stamps/SNAP Benefits During Past 12 Months

Group	Number	%
Total Population	5,161	30.9
Hispanic or Latino (of any race)	1,846	53.6
Dominican Republic	148	39.5
Mexican	126	47.0
Puerto Rican	1,407	57.5

Poverty Rate
(Income in Past 12 Months Below Poverty Level)

Group	%
Total Population	36.6
Hispanic or Latino (of any race)	49.4
Dominican Republic	40.4
Mexican	39.4
Puerto Rican	50.8

Notes: (1) Percent of total population; (2) Percent of Hispanic/Latino population; Profiles include places with an overall population of at least 125,000, OR an overall population of at least 25,000 where the Hispanic/Latino population is at least 20% of the overall population. In states where less than five places meet either of these criteria, we have included places with at least 10,000 total population with the highest percentage of Hispanic/Latino population. These places are identified with an asterisk (*); Please refer to the User's Guide for a full explanation of data.

Rhode Island

EDITOR'S NOTE: For a place to be included in this edition, it must meet one of two criteria. Either its overall population is at least 125,000, OR its overall population is at least 25,000 and its Hispanic/Latino population is at least 20% of the overall population. In Rhode Island, less than five places meet either of these criteria. In an effort to include at least five places for each state, we have included places with at least 10,000 total population with the highest percentage of Hispanic/Latino population. These places are identified with an asterisk (*). For the state of Rhode Island, the following locations are included:

- Central Falls*
- Cranston*
- Pawtucket*
- Providence
- Woonsocket*

Section Two: State & Place Profiles starts with the state profile, followed by place profiles that meet the criteria above. Places are listed alphabetically within each state. All states, all counties and places that meet the above criteria are ranked and compared in *Section Three: Rankings & Comparisons*, on page 1055.

For a more detailed look at the Hispanic/Latino population in Rhode Island, a companion web site is available at no additional charge with purchase of this print edition. Visit http://gold.greyhouse.com/page/info_hispanic for more information.

The web site includes data for all counties and places in Rhode Island with Hispanic/Latino population, plus ten additional topics: Self Employed Worker; Walked to Work; Worked from Home; Mean Travel Time to Work; Mean Household Income; Households with Cash Public Assistance; Mean Cash Pubic Assistance; Poverty Rates for 18 and Under, 18 to 64, and 65 and Over.

Population

Group	Number	%TP[1]	%HP[2]
Total Population	1,052,567	100.0	–
Hispanic or Latino (of any race)	130,655	12.4	100.0
Central American, ex. Mexican	23,817	2.3	18.2
Costa Rican	242	<0.1	0.2
Guatemalan	18,852	1.8	14.4
Honduran	1,250	0.1	1.0
Nicaraguan	267	<0.1	0.2
Panamanian	359	<0.1	0.3
Salvadoran	2,715	0.3	2.1
Cuban	1,640	0.2	1.3
Dominican Republic	35,008	3.3	26.8
Mexican	9,090	0.9	7.0
Puerto Rican	34,979	3.3	26.8
South American	14,013	1.3	10.7
Argentinean	471	<0.1	0.4
Bolivian	1,912	0.2	1.5
Chilean	312	<0.1	0.2
Colombian	8,283	0.8	6.3
Ecuadorian	1,128	0.1	0.9
Peruvian	1,067	0.1	0.8
Uruguayan	112	<0.1	0.1
Venezuelan	643	0.1	0.5
Spaniard	1,000	0.1	0.8

Population Growth: 2000–2010

Group	%
Total Population	0.4
Hispanic or Latino (of any race)	43.9
Central American, ex. Mexican	110.4
Costa Rican	124.1
Guatemalan	110.7
Honduran	154.6
Nicaraguan	142.7
Panamanian	64.7
Salvadoran	125.1
Cuban	45.4
Dominican Republic	95.6
Mexican	54.6
Puerto Rican	37.6
South American	61.7
Argentinean	90.7
Bolivian	99.0
Chilean	166.7
Colombian	45.2
Ecuadorian	107.4
Peruvian	114.3
Venezuelan	80.1
Spaniard	455.6

Males per 100 Females

Group	Number
Total Population	93.4
Hispanic or Latino (of any race)	97.6
Central American, ex. Mexican	128.0
Costa Rican	74.1
Guatemalan	137.8
Honduran	104.2
Nicaraguan	85.4
Panamanian	70.1
Salvadoran	100.7
Cuban	113.0
Dominican Republic	85.4
Mexican	112.8
Puerto Rican	88.8
South American	87.8
Argentinean	91.5
Bolivian	87.8
Chilean	116.7
Colombian	85.8
Ecuadorian	99.6
Peruvian	86.5
Uruguayan	69.7
Venezuelan	84.8
Spaniard	89.4

Average Household Size

Group	People
Total Population	2.44
Hispanic or Latino (of any race)	3.29
Central American, ex. Mexican	3.89
Costa Rican	2.57
Guatemalan	4.01
Honduran	3.71
Nicaraguan	3.17
Panamanian	2.61
Salvadoran	3.71
Cuban	2.49
Dominican Republic	3.36
Mexican	3.34
Puerto Rican	3.06
South American	3.03
Argentinean	2.56
Bolivian	3.41
Chilean	2.83
Colombian	2.98
Ecuadorian	3.32
Peruvian	3.01
Uruguayan	2.49
Venezuelan	3.02
Spaniard	2.64

Median Age

Group	Years
Total Population	39.4
Hispanic or Latino (of any race)	25.4
Central American, ex. Mexican	28.1
Costa Rican	29.5
Guatemalan	28.0
Honduran	28.1
Nicaraguan	27.8
Panamanian	28.6
Salvadoran	28.8
Cuban	28.1
Dominican Republic	26.7
Mexican	24.3
Puerto Rican	21.5
South American	32.8
Argentinean	35.1
Bolivian	31.0
Chilean	23.7
Colombian	34.4
Ecuadorian	29.7
Peruvian	33.3
Uruguayan	34.4
Venezuelan	28.4
Spaniard	27.8

High School Graduates
(Universe: Population 25 Years and Over)

Group	Number	%
Total Population	592,800	83.7
Hispanic or Latino (of any race)	37,847	60.1
Central American, ex. Mexican	6,038	43.3
Guatemalan	4,274	39.6
Salvadoran	780	39.2
Cuban	841	86.9
Dominican Republic	11,229	61.5
Mexican	2,924	64.1
Puerto Rican	8,391	60.7
South American	6,614	75.3
Bolivian	1,135	94.3
Colombian	3,672	67.8
Ecuadorian	310	57.2
Peruvian	642	93.3

Four-Year College Graduates
(Universe: Population 25 Years and Over)

Group	Number	%
Total Population	214,958	30.3
Hispanic or Latino (of any race)	7,748	12.3
Central American, ex. Mexican	973	7.0
Guatemalan	651	6.0
Salvadoran	128	6.4
Cuban	390	40.3
Dominican Republic	1,848	10.1
Mexican	776	17.0
Puerto Rican	1,361	9.8
South American	1,881	21.4
Bolivian	311	25.9
Colombian	943	17.4
Ecuadorian	151	27.9
Peruvian	113	16.4

Population Age 3–17 Enrolled in Public School
(Universe: Population Age 3–17 Enrolled in School)

Group	Number	%
Total Population	147,085	83.0
Hispanic or Latino (of any race)	28,726	91.1
Central American, ex. Mexican	4,313	90.3
Guatemalan	3,106	89.1
Salvadoran	697	93.7
Cuban	356	72.7
Dominican Republic	9,453	93.3
Mexican	2,157	94.8
Puerto Rican	8,603	91.1
South American	2,671	85.9
Bolivian	446	97.0
Colombian	1,378	85.4
Ecuadorian	181	86.2
Peruvian	330	84.8

Population Age 3–17 Enrolled in Private School
(Universe: Population Age 3–17 Enrolled in School)

Group	Number	%
Total Population	30,089	17.0
Hispanic or Latino (of any race)	2,814	8.9
Central American, ex. Mexican	464	9.7
Guatemalan	379	10.9
Salvadoran	47	6.3
Cuban	134	27.3
Dominican Republic	678	6.7
Mexican	118	5.2
Puerto Rican	839	8.9
South American	438	14.1

Notes: (1) Percent of total population; (2) Percent of Hispanic/Latino population; Profiles include places with an overall population of at least 125,000, OR an overall population of at least 25,000 where the Hispanic/Latino population is at least 20% of the overall population. In states where less than five places meet either of these criteria, we have included places with at least 10,000 total population with the highest percentage of Hispanic/Latino population. These places are identified with an asterisk (*); Please refer to the User's Guide for a full explanation of data.

Bolivian	14	3.0
Colombian	235	14.6
Ecuadorian	29	13.8
Peruvian	59	15.2

Foreign-Born Population

Group	Number	%
Total Population	133,548	12.6
Hispanic or Latino (of any race)	53,630	43.1
Central American, ex. Mexican	17,115	69.9
Guatemalan	13,314	70.6
Salvadoran	2,424	70.3
Cuban	439	21.6
Dominican Republic	20,101	55.4
Mexican	3,663	41.4
Puerto Rican	223	0.7
South American	10,073	66.7
Bolivian	1,309	64.2
Colombian	6,144	69.6
Ecuadorian	638	52.3
Peruvian	828	65.4

Foreign-Born Naturalized U.S. Citizens

Group	Number	%
Total Population	61,936	46.4
Hispanic or Latino (of any race)	16,851	31.4
Central American, ex. Mexican	3,168	18.5
Guatemalan	2,105	15.8
Salvadoran	533	22.0
Cuban	235	53.5
Dominican Republic	7,776	38.7
Mexican	838	22.9
Puerto Rican	136	61.0
South American	3,895	38.7
Bolivian	407	31.1
Colombian	2,795	45.5
Ecuadorian	258	40.4
Peruvian	224	27.1

Language Spoken at Home: English Only
(Universe: Population 5 Years and Over)

Group	Number	%
Total Population	790,382	79.2
Hispanic or Latino (of any race)	16,202	14.5
Central American, ex. Mexican	1,234	5.5
Guatemalan	654	3.8
Salvadoran	156	5.1
Cuban	762	46.7
Dominican Republic	2,001	6.1
Mexican	2,393	30.7
Puerto Rican	6,877	24.7
South American	1,781	12.8
Bolivian	245	13.4
Colombian	795	9.6
Ecuadorian	202	19.9
Peruvian	105	9.5

Language Spoken at Home: Spanish
(Universe: Population 5 Years and Over)

Group	Number	%
Total Population	103,193	10.3
Hispanic or Latino (of any race)	94,647	85.0
Central American, ex. Mexican	21,071	94.2
Guatemalan	16,562	95.9
Salvadoran	2,925	94.7
Cuban	870	53.3
Dominican Republic	30,763	93.6
Mexican	5,311	68.1
Puerto Rican	20,913	75.0
South American	12,046	86.6
Bolivian	1,559	85.1
Colombian	7,483	90.3
Ecuadorian	815	80.1
Peruvian	996	90.5

Unemployment Rate
(Universe: Population 16 Years and Over)

Group	%
Total Population	8.0
Hispanic or Latino (of any race)	13.8
Central American, ex. Mexican	11.9
Guatemalan	12.2
Salvadoran	3.2
Cuban	5.8
Dominican Republic	17.3
Mexican	8.5
Puerto Rican	16.0
South American	10.2
Bolivian	11.3
Colombian	7.6
Ecuadorian	15.3
Peruvian	9.4

Class of Worker: Private Wage and Salary
(Universe: Civilian Employed Population 16 Years and Over)

Group	Number	%
Total Population	416,800	80.8
Hispanic or Latino (of any race)	44,303	88.4
Central American, ex. Mexican	11,711	93.9
Guatemalan	9,387	94.1
Salvadoran	1,662	94.5
Cuban	593	79.0
Dominican Republic	11,587	86.3
Mexican	3,455	91.7
Puerto Rican	8,719	87.2
South American	6,534	85.5
Bolivian	966	89.4
Colombian	4,039	86.1
Ecuadorian	495	90.0
Peruvian	504	95.5

Class of Worker: Government
(Universe: Civilian Employed Population 16 Years and Over)

Group	Number	%
Total Population	68,646	13.3
Hispanic or Latino (of any race)	3,239	6.5
Central American, ex. Mexican	292	2.3
Guatemalan	233	2.3
Salvadoran	36	2.0
Cuban	146	19.4
Dominican Republic	842	6.3
Mexican	216	5.7
Puerto Rican	897	9.0
South American	545	7.1
Bolivian	38	3.5
Colombian	311	6.6
Ecuadorian	55	10.0
Peruvian	14	2.7

Means of Transportation to Work: Car, Truck or Van
(Universe: Workers 16 Years and Over)

Group	Number	%
Total Population	447,281	89.1
Hispanic or Latino (of any race)	39,778	82.2
Central American, ex. Mexican	9,847	80.8
Guatemalan	8,052	82.3
Salvadoran	1,241	72.1
Cuban	660	90.2
Dominican Republic	10,542	84.2
Mexican	2,967	77.7
Puerto Rican	8,246	84.2
South American	5,961	82.3
Bolivian	930	90.9
Colombian	3,597	82.1
Ecuadorian	351	63.8
Peruvian	448	90.5

Means of Transportation to Work: Public Transportation (ex. Taxicab)
(Universe: Workers 16 Years and Over)

Group	Number	%
Total Population	13,602	2.7
Hispanic or Latino (of any race)	2,711	5.6
Central American, ex. Mexican	917	7.5
Guatemalan	784	8.0
Salvadoran	85	4.9
Cuban	13	1.8
Dominican Republic	476	3.8
Mexican	232	6.1
Puerto Rican	547	5.6
South American	218	3.0
Bolivian	0	0.0
Colombian	109	2.5
Ecuadorian	39	7.1
Peruvian	37	7.5

Homeownership Rate
(Universe: Occupied Housing Units)

Group	%
Total Population	60.7
Hispanic or Latino (of any race)	27.2
Central American, ex. Mexican	32.1
Costa Rican	37.3
Guatemalan	30.9
Honduran	31.3
Nicaraguan	22.9
Panamanian	37.2
Salvadoran	39.4
Cuban	41.2
Dominican Republic	27.8
Mexican	28.4
Puerto Rican	17.3
South American	37.8
Argentinean	50.0
Bolivian	42.8
Chilean	42.0
Colombian	35.4
Ecuadorian	38.2
Peruvian	39.0
Uruguayan	46.3
Venezuelan	38.7
Spaniard	52.4

Median Home Value

Group	Dollars
Total Population	279,300
Hispanic or Latino (of any race)	237,900
Central American, ex. Mexican	235,400
Guatemalan	227,800
Salvadoran	244,900
Cuban	292,500
Dominican Republic	222,000
Mexican	266,100
Puerto Rican	233,700
South American	255,300
Bolivian	278,100
Colombian	253,700
Ecuadorian	273,500
Peruvian	219,100

Median Gross Rent

Group	Dollars
Total Population	882
Hispanic or Latino (of any race)	853
Central American, ex. Mexican	934
Guatemalan	939
Salvadoran	854
Cuban	1,017
Dominican Republic	824
Mexican	902
Puerto Rican	775
South American	851
Bolivian	930
Colombian	811
Ecuadorian	715
Peruvian	795

Median Household Income
(2010 Inflation-Adjusted Dollars)

Group	Dollars
Total Population	54,902
Hispanic or Latino (of any race)	33,679
Central American, ex. Mexican	42,078
Guatemalan	41,954
Salvadoran	44,800
Cuban	63,203
Dominican Republic	26,926
Mexican	38,978
Puerto Rican	23,835
South American	46,132
Bolivian	48,255
Colombian	42,427
Ecuadorian	54,952
Peruvian	50,250

Per Capita Income
(2010 Inflation-Adjusted Dollars)

Group	Dollars
Total Population	28,707
Hispanic or Latino (of any race)	13,331
Central American, ex. Mexican	15,264

Notes: (1) Percent of total population; (2) Percent of Hispanic/Latino population; Profiles include places with an overall population of at least 125,000, OR an overall population of at least 25,000 where the Hispanic/Latino population is at least 20% of the overall population. In states where less than five places meet either of these criteria, we have included places with at least 10,000 total population with the highest percentage of Hispanic/Latino population. These places are identified with an asterisk (*); Please refer to the User's Guide for a full explanation of data.

Guatemalan	15,813
Salvadoran	13,384
Cuban	16,288
Dominican Republic	10,909
Mexican	14,070
Puerto Rican	11,312
South American	18,079
Bolivian	21,237
Colombian	17,040
Ecuadorian	18,492
Peruvian	15,110

Households with $100,000+ Income

Group	Number	%
Total Population	92,726	22.6
Hispanic or Latino (of any race)	2,691	7.6
Central American, ex. Mexican	632	9.6
Guatemalan	552	11.0
Salvadoran	19	1.9
Cuban	115	22.1
Dominican Republic	336	3.1
Mexican	337	14.2
Puerto Rican	528	5.6
South American	486	11.2
Bolivian	57	11.2
Colombian	191	7.0
Ecuadorian	19	7.1
Peruvian	43	15.0

Households with Food Stamps/SNAP Benefits During Past 12 Months

Group	Number	%
Total Population	36,921	9.0
Hispanic or Latino (of any race)	10,363	29.4
Central American, ex. Mexican	1,161	17.6
Guatemalan	852	17.0
Salvadoran	118	12.1
Cuban	79	15.2
Dominican Republic	4,205	39.3
Mexican	260	10.9
Puerto Rican	3,701	39.1
South American	746	17.1
Bolivian	78	15.4
Colombian	436	15.9
Ecuadorian	103	38.6
Peruvian	85	29.6

Poverty Rate
(Income in Past 12 Months Below Poverty Level)

Group	%
Total Population	12.2
Hispanic or Latino (of any race)	28.4
Central American, ex. Mexican	16.7
Guatemalan	17.5
Salvadoran	11.5
Cuban	12.0
Dominican Republic	34.5
Mexican	21.8
Puerto Rican	42.2
South American	14.5
Bolivian	8.9
Colombian	13.4
Ecuadorian	26.4
Peruvian	12.6

Central Falls*

Population

Group	Number	%TP[1]	%HP[2]
Total Population	19,376	100.0	–
Hispanic or Latino (of any race)	11,685	60.3	100.0
Central American, ex. Mexican	3,060	15.8	26.2
Guatemalan	2,574	13.3	22.0
Honduran	101	0.5	0.9
Salvadoran	358	1.8	3.1
Dominican Republic	1,237	6.4	10.6
Mexican	1,341	6.9	11.5
Puerto Rican	2,878	14.9	24.6
South American	2,233	11.5	19.1
Colombian	2,018	10.4	17.3

Population Growth: 2000–2010

Group	%
Total Population	2.4
Hispanic or Latino (of any race)	29.2
Central American, ex. Mexican	115.5
Guatemalan	114.1
Salvadoran	129.5
Dominican Republic	115.1
Mexican	98.1
Puerto Rican	28.0
South American	11.7
Colombian	7.2

Males per 100 Females

Group	Number
Total Population	102.8
Hispanic or Latino (of any race)	107.4
Central American, ex. Mexican	132.7
Guatemalan	139.2
Honduran	119.6
Salvadoran	98.9
Dominican Republic	97.9
Mexican	123.1
Puerto Rican	95.1
South American	89.1
Colombian	88.2

Average Household Size

Group	People
Total Population	2.89
Hispanic or Latino (of any race)	3.49
Central American, ex. Mexican	3.97
Guatemalan	4.03
Honduran	3.85
Salvadoran	3.60
Dominican Republic	3.50
Mexican	4.12
Puerto Rican	3.31
South American	2.97
Colombian	2.95

Median Age

Group	Years
Total Population	30.1
Hispanic or Latino (of any race)	26.5
Central American, ex. Mexican	28.3
Guatemalan	28.0
Honduran	29.6
Salvadoran	29.6
Dominican Republic	27.8
Mexican	25.2
Puerto Rican	21.6
South American	38.6
Colombian	39.6

High School Graduates
(Universe: Population 25 Years and Over)

Group	Number	%
Total Population	6,033	51.7
Hispanic or Latino (of any race)	2,501	40.6
Central American, ex. Mexican	506	25.4
Guatemalan	497	26.2
Dominican Republic	270	50.2
Mexican	225	25.8
Puerto Rican	497	49.9
South American	882	56.8
Colombian	702	51.2

Four-Year College Graduates
(Universe: Population 25 Years and Over)

Group	Number	%
Total Population	859	7.4
Hispanic or Latino (of any race)	393	6.4
Central American, ex. Mexican	146	7.3
Guatemalan	146	7.7
Dominican Republic	61	11.3
Mexican	0	0.0
Puerto Rican	45	4.5
South American	117	7.5
Colombian	59	4.3

Population Age 3–17 Enrolled in Public School
(Universe: Population Age 3–17 Enrolled in School)

Group	Number	%
Total Population	3,341	97.0
Hispanic or Latino (of any race)	2,112	98.8
Central American, ex. Mexican	416	100.0
Guatemalan	383	100.0
Dominican Republic	295	100.0
Mexican	414	100.0
Puerto Rican	503	100.0
South American	369	93.7
Colombian	297	92.2

Population Age 3–17 Enrolled in Private School
(Universe: Population Age 3–17 Enrolled in School)

Group	Number	%
Total Population	103	3.0
Hispanic or Latino (of any race)	25	1.2
Central American, ex. Mexican	0	0.0
Guatemalan	0	0.0
Dominican Republic	0	0.0
Mexican	0	0.0
Puerto Rican	0	0.0
South American	25	6.3
Colombian	25	7.8

Foreign-Born Population

Group	Number	%
Total Population	8,102	41.8
Hispanic or Latino (of any race)	5,944	53.2
Central American, ex. Mexican	2,397	70.5
Guatemalan	2,229	70.2
Dominican Republic	612	53.7
Mexican	909	59.1
Puerto Rican	0	0.0
South American	1,812	72.0
Colombian	1,560	74.1

Foreign-Born Naturalized U.S. Citizens

Group	Number	%
Total Population	2,559	31.6
Hispanic or Latino (of any race)	1,395	23.5
Central American, ex. Mexican	241	10.1
Guatemalan	241	10.8
Dominican Republic	274	44.8
Mexican	143	15.7
Puerto Rican	0	0.0
South American	681	37.6
Colombian	623	39.9

Language Spoken at Home: English Only
(Universe: Population 5 Years and Over)

Group	Number	%
Total Population	5,114	29.6
Hispanic or Latino (of any race)	560	5.7
Central American, ex. Mexican	71	2.4
Guatemalan	71	2.6
Dominican Republic	36	3.6
Mexican	55	4.2
Puerto Rican	203	11.0
South American	149	6.4
Colombian	107	5.4

Language Spoken at Home: Spanish
(Universe: Population 5 Years and Over)

Group	Number	%
Total Population	9,459	54.8
Hispanic or Latino (of any race)	9,187	93.8
Central American, ex. Mexican	2,868	96.3
Guatemalan	2,661	96.1
Dominican Republic	951	96.4
Mexican	1,246	95.8
Puerto Rican	1,642	89.0
South American	2,177	93.6
Colombian	1,883	94.6

Unemployment Rate
(Universe: Population 16 Years and Over)

Group	%
Total Population	7.6
Hispanic or Latino (of any race)	7.0
Central American, ex. Mexican	1.8
Guatemalan	1.9
Dominican Republic	9.9
Mexican	0.0
Puerto Rican	13.6
South American	10.7
Colombian	11.3

STATE & PLACE PROFILES

Notes: (1) Percent of total population; (2) Percent of Hispanic/Latino population; Profiles include places with an overall population of at least 125,000, OR an overall population of at least 25,000 where the Hispanic/Latino population is at least 20% of the overall population. In states where less than five places meet either of these criteria, we have included places with at least 10,000 total population with the highest percentage of Hispanic/Latino population. These places are identified with an asterisk (*); Please refer to the User's Guide for a full explanation of data.

Class of Worker: Private Wage and Salary
(Universe: Civilian Employed Population 16 Years and Over)

Group	Number	%
Total Population	7,559	94.1
Hispanic or Latino (of any race)	4,744	97.4
Central American, ex. Mexican	1,792	98.8
Guatemalan	1,676	98.8
Dominican Republic	469	96.9
Mexican	640	97.0
Puerto Rican	536	94.5
South American	1,174	96.8
Colombian	1,020	97.3

Class of Worker: Government
(Universe: Civilian Employed Population 16 Years and Over)

Group	Number	%
Total Population	370	4.6
Hispanic or Latino (of any race)	105	2.2
Central American, ex. Mexican	0	0.0
Guatemalan	0	0.0
Dominican Republic	15	3.1
Mexican	20	3.0
Puerto Rican	31	5.5
South American	39	3.2
Colombian	28	2.7

Means of Transportation to Work: Car, Truck or Van
(Universe: Workers 16 Years and Over)

Group	Number	%
Total Population	6,018	76.2
Hispanic or Latino (of any race)	3,470	72.9
Central American, ex. Mexican	1,366	76.5
Guatemalan	1,281	76.8
Dominican Republic	350	72.3
Mexican	449	68.0
Puerto Rican	453	78.4
South American	699	64.1
Colombian	545	58.9

Means of Transportation to Work: Public Transportation (ex. Taxicab)
(Universe: Workers 16 Years and Over)

Group	Number	%
Total Population	242	3.1
Hispanic or Latino (of any race)	149	3.1
Central American, ex. Mexican	63	3.5
Guatemalan	63	3.8
Dominican Republic	14	2.9
Mexican	0	0.0
Puerto Rican	0	0.0
South American	72	6.6
Colombian	72	7.8

Homeownership Rate
(Universe: Occupied Housing Units)

Group	%
Total Population	22.4
Hispanic or Latino (of any race)	16.1
Central American, ex. Mexican	21.6
Guatemalan	21.2
Honduran	11.1
Salvadoran	28.4
Dominican Republic	18.5
Mexican	10.6
Puerto Rican	6.6
South American	20.9
Colombian	21.2

Median Home Value

Group	Dollars
Total Population	227,200
Hispanic or Latino (of any race)	238,900
Central American, ex. Mexican	221,100
Guatemalan	222,800
Dominican Republic	221,400
Mexican	348,600
Puerto Rican	234,500
South American	231,700
Colombian	241,500

Median Gross Rent

Group	Dollars
Total Population	765
Hispanic or Latino (of any race)	837
Central American, ex. Mexican	877
Guatemalan	870
Dominican Republic	905
Mexican	935
Puerto Rican	791
South American	765
Colombian	734

Median Household Income
(2010 Inflation-Adjusted Dollars)

Group	Dollars
Total Population	34,389
Hispanic or Latino (of any race)	37,905
Central American, ex. Mexican	44,647
Guatemalan	44,808
Dominican Republic	32,390
Mexican	34,167
Puerto Rican	26,587
South American	40,304
Colombian	34,519

Per Capita Income
(2010 Inflation-Adjusted Dollars)

Group	Dollars
Total Population	14,991
Hispanic or Latino (of any race)	13,643
Central American, ex. Mexican	16,677
Guatemalan	17,119
Dominican Republic	11,120
Mexican	10,872
Puerto Rican	9,026
South American	15,685
Colombian	15,579

Households with $100,000+ Income

Group	Number	%
Total Population	470	7.1
Hispanic or Latino (of any race)	272	8.6
Central American, ex. Mexican	128	14.5
Guatemalan	128	16.0
Dominican Republic	4	1.2
Mexican	80	21.6
Puerto Rican	29	4.2
South American	31	4.0
Colombian	20	3.0

Households with Food Stamps/SNAP Benefits During Past 12 Months

Group	Number	%
Total Population	1,589	24.0
Hispanic or Latino (of any race)	859	27.1
Central American, ex. Mexican	230	26.0
Guatemalan	204	25.4
Dominican Republic	127	39.1
Mexican	16	4.3
Puerto Rican	338	49.2
South American	121	15.5
Colombian	121	17.9

Poverty Rate
(Income in Past 12 Months Below Poverty Level)

Group	%
Total Population	25.4
Hispanic or Latino (of any race)	24.6
Central American, ex. Mexican	13.2
Guatemalan	10.0
Dominican Republic	30.2
Mexican	12.8
Puerto Rican	49.6
South American	24.9
Colombian	23.9

Cranston*

Population

Group	Number	%TP[1]	%HP[2]
Total Population	80,387	100.0	–
Hispanic or Latino (of any race)	8,709	10.8	100.0
Central American, ex. Mexican	1,247	1.6	14.3
Guatemalan	998	1.2	11.5
Salvadoran	111	0.1	1.3
Cuban	191	0.2	2.2
Dominican Republic	3,003	3.7	34.5
Mexican	488	0.6	5.6
Puerto Rican	1,638	2.0	18.8
South American	778	1.0	8.9
Bolivian	278	0.3	3.2
Colombian	215	0.3	2.5

Population Growth: 2000–2010

Group	%
Total Population	1.4
Hispanic or Latino (of any race)	141.0
Central American, ex. Mexican	266.8
Guatemalan	275.2
Dominican Republic	309.1
Mexican	163.8
Puerto Rican	73.2
South American	114.3
Colombian	64.1

Males per 100 Females

Group	Number
Total Population	97.7
Hispanic or Latino (of any race)	107.1
Central American, ex. Mexican	107.1
Guatemalan	120.3
Salvadoran	63.2
Cuban	208.1
Dominican Republic	87.6
Mexican	144.0
Puerto Rican	97.3
South American	80.9
Bolivian	89.1
Colombian	68.0

Average Household Size

Group	People
Total Population	2.45
Hispanic or Latino (of any race)	3.38
Central American, ex. Mexican	3.89
Guatemalan	4.01
Salvadoran	3.48
Cuban	2.52
Dominican Republic	3.58
Mexican	2.82
Puerto Rican	3.02
South American	3.24
Bolivian	3.72
Colombian	2.67

Median Age

Group	Years
Total Population	40.8
Hispanic or Latino (of any race)	26.5
Central American, ex. Mexican	28.7
Guatemalan	28.3
Salvadoran	31.3
Cuban	32.5
Dominican Republic	25.9
Mexican	28.5
Puerto Rican	23.3
South American	31.3
Bolivian	30.6
Colombian	31.3

High School Graduates
(Universe: Population 25 Years and Over)

Group	Number	%
Total Population	48,265	85.2
Hispanic or Latino (of any race)	3,425	76.8
Central American, ex. Mexican	485	63.0
Guatemalan	404	60.2
Dominican Republic	1,162	77.5
Puerto Rican	841	73.1
South American	439	100.0

Four-Year College Graduates
(Universe: Population 25 Years and Over)

Group	Number	%
Total Population	16,838	29.7
Hispanic or Latino (of any race)	729	16.3
Central American, ex. Mexican	0	0.0
Guatemalan	0	0.0
Dominican Republic	217	14.5
Puerto Rican	149	13.0
South American	155	35.3

Notes: (1) Percent of total population; (2) Percent of Hispanic/Latino population; Profiles include places with an overall population of at least 125,000, OR an overall population of at least 25,000 where the Hispanic/Latino population is at least 20% of the overall population. In states where less than five places meet either of these criteria, we have included places with at least 10,000 total population with the highest percentage of Hispanic/Latino population. These places are identified with an asterisk (*); Please refer to the User's Guide for a full explanation of data.

Population Age 3–17 Enrolled in Public School
(Universe: Population Age 3–17 Enrolled in School)

Group	Number	%
Total Population	10,700	79.7
Hispanic or Latino (of any race)	1,543	88.8
Central American, ex. Mexican	290	92.9
Guatemalan	280	92.7
Dominican Republic	388	78.5
Puerto Rican	620	92.8
South American	158	89.3

Population Age 3–17 Enrolled in Private School
(Universe: Population Age 3–17 Enrolled in School)

Group	Number	%
Total Population	2,733	20.3
Hispanic or Latino (of any race)	195	11.2
Central American, ex. Mexican	22	7.1
Guatemalan	22	7.3
Dominican Republic	106	21.5
Puerto Rican	48	7.2
South American	19	10.7

Foreign-Born Population

Group	Number	%
Total Population	9,365	11.6
Hispanic or Latino (of any race)	3,044	37.6
Central American, ex. Mexican	825	64.7
Guatemalan	717	65.4
Dominican Republic	1,347	52.8
Puerto Rican	26	1.1
South American	588	60.6

Foreign-Born Naturalized U.S. Citizens

Group	Number	%
Total Population	4,980	53.2
Hispanic or Latino (of any race)	1,235	40.6
Central American, ex. Mexican	224	27.2
Guatemalan	199	27.8
Dominican Republic	695	51.6
Puerto Rican	16	61.5
South American	100	17.0

Language Spoken at Home: English Only
(Universe: Population 5 Years and Over)

Group	Number	%
Total Population	60,006	78.8
Hispanic or Latino (of any race)	1,233	16.6
Central American, ex. Mexican	63	5.3
Guatemalan	38	3.7
Dominican Republic	92	4.0
Puerto Rican	646	29.5
South American	90	10.7

Language Spoken at Home: Spanish
(Universe: Population 5 Years and Over)

Group	Number	%
Total Population	6,748	8.9
Hispanic or Latino (of any race)	6,139	82.7
Central American, ex. Mexican	1,128	94.2
Guatemalan	982	96.3
Dominican Republic	2,235	96.0
Puerto Rican	1,547	70.5
South American	742	87.9

Unemployment Rate
(Universe: Population 16 Years and Over)

Group	%
Total Population	8.1
Hispanic or Latino (of any race)	8.3
Central American, ex. Mexican	15.3
Guatemalan	12.8
Dominican Republic	5.8
Puerto Rican	8.7
South American	9.6

Class of Worker: Private Wage and Salary
(Universe: Civilian Employed Population 16 Years and Over)

Group	Number	%
Total Population	29,662	79.3
Hispanic or Latino (of any race)	2,841	81.8
Central American, ex. Mexican	479	81.5
Guatemalan	479	81.5
Dominican Republic	908	80.1
Puerto Rican	686	81.7
South American	377	86.7

Class of Worker: Government
(Universe: Civilian Employed Population 16 Years and Over)

Group	Number	%
Total Population	5,505	14.7
Hispanic or Latino (of any race)	402	11.6
Central American, ex. Mexican	94	16.0
Guatemalan	94	16.0
Dominican Republic	80	7.1
Puerto Rican	146	17.4
South American	7	1.6

Means of Transportation to Work: Car, Truck or Van
(Universe: Workers 16 Years and Over)

Group	Number	%
Total Population	33,472	93.3
Hispanic or Latino (of any race)	2,743	86.5
Central American, ex. Mexican	549	93.4
Guatemalan	549	93.4
Dominican Republic	761	82.2
Puerto Rican	713	88.2
South American	334	89.1

Means of Transportation to Work: Public Transportation (ex. Taxicab)
(Universe: Workers 16 Years and Over)

Group	Number	%
Total Population	752	2.1
Hispanic or Latino (of any race)	176	5.5
Central American, ex. Mexican	0	0.0
Guatemalan	0	0.0
Dominican Republic	39	4.2
Puerto Rican	34	4.2
South American	14	3.7

Homeownership Rate
(Universe: Occupied Housing Units)

Group	%
Total Population	67.4
Hispanic or Latino (of any race)	44.7
Central American, ex. Mexican	49.5
Guatemalan	47.9
Salvadoran	57.6
Cuban	58.6
Dominican Republic	46.0
Mexican	44.6
Puerto Rican	34.7
South American	51.9
Bolivian	47.6
Colombian	50.9

Median Home Value

Group	Dollars
Total Population	258,900
Hispanic or Latino (of any race)	238,800
Central American, ex. Mexican	246,600
Guatemalan	241,600
Dominican Republic	241,700
Puerto Rican	223,800
South American	215,000

Median Gross Rent

Group	Dollars
Total Population	942
Hispanic or Latino (of any race)	1,032
Central American, ex. Mexican	1,285
Guatemalan	1,285
Dominican Republic	1,092
Puerto Rican	962
South American	996

Median Household Income
(2010 Inflation-Adjusted Dollars)

Group	Dollars
Total Population	57,922
Hispanic or Latino (of any race)	46,088
Central American, ex. Mexican	87,762
Guatemalan	88,314
Dominican Republic	35,313
Puerto Rican	39,142
South American	44,632

Per Capita Income
(2010 Inflation-Adjusted Dollars)

Group	Dollars
Total Population	27,752
Hispanic or Latino (of any race)	14,990
Central American, ex. Mexican	19,556
Guatemalan	20,970
Dominican Republic	13,348
Puerto Rican	11,371
South American	15,647

Households with $100,000+ Income

Group	Number	%
Total Population	6,759	22.2
Hispanic or Latino (of any race)	199	9.8
Central American, ex. Mexican	31	7.9
Guatemalan	31	8.8
Dominican Republic	57	7.5
Puerto Rican	19	4.0
South American	10	6.0

Households with Food Stamps/SNAP Benefits During Past 12 Months

Group	Number	%
Total Population	2,290	7.5
Hispanic or Latino (of any race)	281	13.8
Central American, ex. Mexican	0	0.0
Guatemalan	0	0.0
Dominican Republic	149	19.7
Puerto Rican	110	23.0
South American	14	8.3

Poverty Rate
(Income in Past 12 Months Below Poverty Level)

Group	%
Total Population	8.4
Hispanic or Latino (of any race)	12.7
Central American, ex. Mexican	3.4
Guatemalan	1.4
Dominican Republic	17.1
Puerto Rican	13.8
South American	10.1

Pawtucket*

Population

Group	Number	%TP[1]	%HP[2]
Total Population	71,148	100.0	–
Hispanic or Latino (of any race)	14,042	19.7	100.0
Central American, ex. Mexican	1,909	2.7	13.6
Guatemalan	1,301	1.8	9.3
Honduran	131	0.2	0.9
Salvadoran	344	0.5	2.4
Cuban	113	0.2	0.8
Dominican Republic	1,894	2.7	13.5
Mexican	798	1.1	5.7
Puerto Rican	4,729	6.6	33.7
South American	3,582	5.0	25.5
Colombian	3,056	4.3	21.8
Ecuadorian	116	0.2	0.8
Peruvian	159	0.2	1.1

Population Growth: 2000–2010

Group	%
Total Population	-2.5
Hispanic or Latino (of any race)	38.5
Central American, ex. Mexican	154.9
Guatemalan	110.5
Dominican Republic	135.6
Mexican	37.3
Puerto Rican	43.4
South American	49.4
Colombian	42.6

Males per 100 Females

Group	Number
Total Population	92.0
Hispanic or Latino (of any race)	94.1
Central American, ex. Mexican	116.0
Guatemalan	120.5
Honduran	133.9
Salvadoran	108.5
Cuban	156.8

Notes: (1) Percent of total population; (2) Percent of Hispanic/Latino population; Profiles include places with an overall population of at least 125,000, OR an overall population of at least 25,000 where the Hispanic/Latino population is at least 20% of the overall population. In states where less than five places meet either of these criteria, we have included places with at least 10,000 total population with the highest percentage of Hispanic/Latino population. These places are identified with an asterisk (*); Please refer to the User's Guide for a full explanation of data.

Group	Years
Dominican Republic	90.2
Mexican	124.8
Puerto Rican	85.5
South American	89.4
Colombian	87.5
Ecuadorian	103.5
Peruvian	89.3

Average Household Size

Group	People
Total Population	2.43
Hispanic or Latino (of any race)	3.03
Central American, ex. Mexican	3.43
Guatemalan	3.46
Honduran	3.69
Salvadoran	3.63
Cuban	2.10
Dominican Republic	3.12
Mexican	3.26
Puerto Rican	2.92
South American	3.00
Colombian	2.99
Ecuadorian	3.44
Peruvian	3.25

Median Age

Group	Years
Total Population	36.7
Hispanic or Latino (of any race)	27.6
Central American, ex. Mexican	30.0
Guatemalan	30.5
Honduran	28.6
Salvadoran	26.5
Cuban	36.5
Dominican Republic	25.3
Mexican	27.4
Puerto Rican	23.5
South American	35.5
Colombian	36.6
Ecuadorian	30.0
Peruvian	34.1

High School Graduates
(Universe: Population 25 Years and Over)

Group	Number	%
Total Population	36,563	75.7
Hispanic or Latino (of any race)	3,915	64.4
Central American, ex. Mexican	573	59.7
Guatemalan	289	51.2
Dominican Republic	412	56.0
Puerto Rican	910	60.2
South American	1,396	70.9
Colombian	1,151	68.1

Four-Year College Graduates
(Universe: Population 25 Years and Over)

Group	Number	%
Total Population	9,115	18.9
Hispanic or Latino (of any race)	570	9.4
Central American, ex. Mexican	80	8.3
Guatemalan	66	11.7
Dominican Republic	88	12.0
Puerto Rican	76	5.0
South American	216	11.0
Colombian	198	11.7

Population Age 3–17 Enrolled in Public School
(Universe: Population Age 3–17 Enrolled in School)

Group	Number	%
Total Population	10,077	84.2
Hispanic or Latino (of any race)	2,628	93.0
Central American, ex. Mexican	327	86.7
Guatemalan	142	74.0
Dominican Republic	289	98.6
Puerto Rican	1,221	99.3
South American	562	87.9
Colombian	373	82.9

Population Age 3–17 Enrolled in Private School
(Universe: Population Age 3–17 Enrolled in School)

Group	Number	%
Total Population	1,888	15.8
Hispanic or Latino (of any race)	198	7.0
Central American, ex. Mexican	50	13.3
Guatemalan	50	26.0
Dominican Republic	4	1.4
Puerto Rican	8	0.7
South American	77	12.1
Colombian	77	17.1

Foreign-Born Population

Group	Number	%
Total Population	17,573	24.5
Hispanic or Latino (of any race)	4,997	43.6
Central American, ex. Mexican	908	55.2
Guatemalan	523	59.7
Dominican Republic	975	67.7
Puerto Rican	22	0.6
South American	2,312	70.0
Colombian	1,932	70.6

Foreign-Born Naturalized U.S. Citizens

Group	Number	%
Total Population	8,853	50.4
Hispanic or Latino (of any race)	1,980	39.6
Central American, ex. Mexican	337	37.1
Guatemalan	199	38.0
Dominican Republic	437	44.8
Puerto Rican	22	100.0
South American	943	40.8
Colombian	851	44.0

Language Spoken at Home: English Only
(Universe: Population 5 Years and Over)

Group	Number	%
Total Population	41,223	61.9
Hispanic or Latino (of any race)	1,327	12.8
Central American, ex. Mexican	162	11.2
Guatemalan	41	5.1
Dominican Republic	25	1.8
Puerto Rican	762	24.7
South American	130	4.2
Colombian	102	4.0

Language Spoken at Home: Spanish
(Universe: Population 5 Years and Over)

Group	Number	%
Total Population	10,050	15.1
Hispanic or Latino (of any race)	8,946	86.5
Central American, ex. Mexican	1,280	88.8
Guatemalan	764	94.9
Dominican Republic	1,318	97.3
Puerto Rican	2,283	74.1
South American	2,926	95.2
Colombian	2,434	95.7

Unemployment Rate
(Universe: Population 16 Years and Over)

Group	%
Total Population	9.3
Hispanic or Latino (of any race)	9.2
Central American, ex. Mexican	2.0
Guatemalan	1.0
Dominican Republic	9.2
Puerto Rican	11.2
South American	8.9
Colombian	10.3

Class of Worker: Private Wage and Salary
(Universe: Civilian Employed Population 16 Years and Over)

Group	Number	%
Total Population	30,190	86.3
Hispanic or Latino (of any race)	4,717	88.9
Central American, ex. Mexican	857	95.9
Guatemalan	462	92.6
Dominican Republic	802	94.5
Puerto Rican	825	77.9
South American	1,503	88.2
Colombian	1,277	88.2

Class of Worker: Government
(Universe: Civilian Employed Population 16 Years and Over)

Group	Number	%
Total Population	3,172	9.1
Hispanic or Latino (of any race)	363	6.8
Central American, ex. Mexican	37	4.1
Guatemalan	37	7.4
Dominican Republic	0	0.0
Puerto Rican	198	18.7
South American	98	5.8
Colombian	78	5.4

Means of Transportation to Work: Car, Truck or Van
(Universe: Workers 16 Years and Over)

Group	Number	%
Total Population	30,008	89.5
Hispanic or Latino (of any race)	4,469	89.8
Central American, ex. Mexican	841	98.9
Guatemalan	486	98.2
Dominican Republic	729	93.2
Puerto Rican	848	87.8
South American	1,468	90.9
Colombian	1,268	91.1

Means of Transportation to Work: Public Transportation (ex. Taxicab)
(Universe: Workers 16 Years and Over)

Group	Number	%
Total Population	1,382	4.1
Hispanic or Latino (of any race)	151	3.0
Central American, ex. Mexican	0	0.0
Guatemalan	0	0.0
Dominican Republic	0	0.0
Puerto Rican	74	7.7
South American	31	1.9
Colombian	21	1.5

Homeownership Rate
(Universe: Occupied Housing Units)

Group	%
Total Population	44.9
Hispanic or Latino (of any race)	24.7
Central American, ex. Mexican	36.0
Guatemalan	34.5
Honduran	39.6
Salvadoran	39.1
Cuban	26.8
Dominican Republic	20.4
Mexican	24.8
Puerto Rican	14.6
South American	33.6
Colombian	33.7
Ecuadorian	40.6
Peruvian	25.5

Median Home Value

Group	Dollars
Total Population	228,400
Hispanic or Latino (of any race)	243,100
Central American, ex. Mexican	279,100
Guatemalan	230,900
Dominican Republic	217,000
Puerto Rican	181,000
South American	240,100
Colombian	249,300

Median Gross Rent

Group	Dollars
Total Population	800
Hispanic or Latino (of any race)	764
Central American, ex. Mexican	677
Guatemalan	725
Dominican Republic	859
Puerto Rican	716
South American	779
Colombian	789

Median Household Income
(2010 Inflation-Adjusted Dollars)

Group	Dollars
Total Population	40,198
Hispanic or Latino (of any race)	29,700
Central American, ex. Mexican	36,107
Guatemalan	45,887
Dominican Republic	28,000
Puerto Rican	18,318
South American	37,282
Colombian	37,326

Per Capita Income
(2010 Inflation-Adjusted Dollars)

Group	Dollars
Total Population	21,568
Hispanic or Latino (of any race)	13,480

Notes: (1) Percent of total population; (2) Percent of Hispanic/Latino population; Profiles include places with an overall population of at least 125,000, OR an overall population of at least 25,000 where the Hispanic/Latino population is at least 20% of the overall population. In states where less than five places meet either of these criteria, we have included places with at least 10,000 total population with the highest percentage of Hispanic/Latino population. These places are identified with an asterisk (*); Please refer to the User's Guide for a full explanation of data.

Central American, ex. Mexican	15,033
Guatemalan	15,274
Dominican Republic	13,312
Puerto Rican	11,857
South American	14,982
Colombian	15,773

Households with $100,000+ Income

Group	Number	%
Total Population	3,211	11.1
Hispanic or Latino (of any race)	152	4.1
Central American, ex. Mexican	35	6.4
Guatemalan	0	0.0
Dominican Republic	10	2.0
Puerto Rican	18	1.4
South American	73	7.0
Colombian	51	5.5

Households with Food Stamps/SNAP Benefits During Past 12 Months

Group	Number	%
Total Population	4,449	15.3
Hispanic or Latino (of any race)	974	26.0
Central American, ex. Mexican	92	16.8
Guatemalan	64	23.2
Dominican Republic	138	27.9
Puerto Rican	531	42.6
South American	184	17.7
Colombian	153	16.6

Poverty Rate
(Income in Past 12 Months Below Poverty Level)

Group	%
Total Population	17.8
Hispanic or Latino (of any race)	26.0
Central American, ex. Mexican	6.7
Guatemalan	11.5
Dominican Republic	25.2
Puerto Rican	51.1
South American	13.0
Colombian	10.9

Providence

Population

Group	Number	%TP[1]	%HP[2]
Total Population	178,042	100.0	–
Hispanic or Latino (of any race)	67,835	38.1	100.0
Central American, ex. Mexican	14,630	8.2	21.6
Guatemalan	11,930	6.7	17.6
Honduran	731	0.4	1.1
Nicaraguan	122	0.1	0.2
Panamanian	169	0.1	0.2
Salvadoran	1,503	0.8	2.2
Cuban	538	0.3	0.8
Dominican Republic	25,267	14.2	37.2
Mexican	3,188	1.8	4.7
Puerto Rican	14,847	8.3	21.9
South American	3,544	2.0	5.2
Argentinean	145	0.1	0.2
Bolivian	1,046	0.6	1.5
Colombian	969	0.5	1.4
Ecuadorian	629	0.4	0.9
Peruvian	404	0.2	0.6
Venezuelan	200	0.1	0.3
Spaniard	347	0.2	0.5

Population Growth: 2000–2010

Group	%
Total Population	2.5
Hispanic or Latino (of any race)	30.1
Central American, ex. Mexican	82.6
Guatemalan	86.5
Honduran	105.9
Panamanian	64.1
Salvadoran	72.6
Cuban	15.0
Dominican Republic	72.6
Mexican	42.5
Puerto Rican	16.8
South American	58.1
Bolivian	65.0
Colombian	39.8
Ecuadorian	111.8

Peruvian	66.9
Venezuelan	36.1

Males per 100 Females

Group	Number
Total Population	93.0
Hispanic or Latino (of any race)	96.7
Central American, ex. Mexican	133.0
Guatemalan	143.1
Honduran	103.1
Nicaraguan	96.8
Panamanian	65.7
Salvadoran	99.3
Cuban	108.5
Dominican Republic	83.9
Mexican	109.6
Puerto Rican	87.6
South American	88.7
Argentinean	85.9
Bolivian	86.8
Colombian	82.1
Ecuadorian	107.6
Peruvian	83.6
Venezuelan	104.1
Spaniard	82.6

Average Household Size

Group	People
Total Population	2.60
Hispanic or Latino (of any race)	3.39
Central American, ex. Mexican	4.01
Guatemalan	4.11
Honduran	3.89
Nicaraguan	3.10
Panamanian	2.44
Salvadoran	3.82
Cuban	2.41
Dominican Republic	3.36
Mexican	3.39
Puerto Rican	3.10
South American	3.06
Argentinean	2.48
Bolivian	3.32
Colombian	2.90
Ecuadorian	3.43
Peruvian	2.96
Venezuelan	2.77
Spaniard	2.62

Median Age

Group	Years
Total Population	28.5
Hispanic or Latino (of any race)	25.5
Central American, ex. Mexican	28.2
Guatemalan	28.2
Honduran	27.7
Nicaraguan	29.1
Panamanian	23.5
Salvadoran	28.7
Cuban	25.9
Dominican Republic	27.7
Mexican	23.0
Puerto Rican	21.6
South American	30.5
Argentinean	30.1
Bolivian	32.1
Colombian	29.5
Ecuadorian	30.8
Peruvian	32.9
Venezuelan	25.8
Spaniard	22.7

High School Graduates
(Universe: Population 25 Years and Over)

Group	Number	%
Total Population	72,339	72.7
Hispanic or Latino (of any race)	18,819	54.7
Central American, ex. Mexican	3,574	40.9
Guatemalan	2,538	36.7
Salvadoran	511	44.1
Dominican Republic	8,108	58.3
Mexican	697	51.5
Puerto Rican	3,699	55.4
South American	1,983	76.6
Bolivian	677	90.9

Colombian	607	69.1

Four-Year College Graduates
(Universe: Population 25 Years and Over)

Group	Number	%
Total Population	28,846	29.0
Hispanic or Latino (of any race)	3,126	9.1
Central American, ex. Mexican	416	4.8
Guatemalan	273	3.9
Salvadoran	44	3.8
Dominican Republic	1,175	8.5
Mexican	213	15.7
Puerto Rican	418	6.3
South American	722	27.9
Bolivian	262	35.2
Colombian	279	31.7

Population Age 3–17 Enrolled in Public School
(Universe: Population Age 3–17 Enrolled in School)

Group	Number	%
Total Population	25,839	84.3
Hispanic or Latino (of any race)	15,799	92.5
Central American, ex. Mexican	2,633	89.4
Guatemalan	1,896	88.2
Salvadoran	455	95.4
Dominican Republic	7,537	93.8
Mexican	678	96.3
Puerto Rican	3,571	91.4
South American	817	93.8
Bolivian	222	100.0
Colombian	189	77.8

Population Age 3–17 Enrolled in Private School
(Universe: Population Age 3–17 Enrolled in School)

Group	Number	%
Total Population	4,812	15.7
Hispanic or Latino (of any race)	1,290	7.5
Central American, ex. Mexican	313	10.6
Guatemalan	253	11.8
Salvadoran	22	4.6
Dominican Republic	499	6.2
Mexican	26	3.7
Puerto Rican	334	8.6
South American	54	6.2
Bolivian	0	0.0
Colombian	54	22.2

Foreign-Born Population

Group	Number	%
Total Population	52,077	29.2
Hispanic or Latino (of any race)	32,339	47.5
Central American, ex. Mexican	11,164	72.4
Guatemalan	8,990	73.2
Salvadoran	1,358	70.3
Dominican Republic	15,689	56.8
Mexican	1,412	47.3
Puerto Rican	146	1.0
South American	2,901	66.8
Bolivian	725	64.4
Colombian	957	69.2

Foreign-Born Naturalized U.S. Citizens

Group	Number	%
Total Population	17,610	33.8
Hispanic or Latino (of any race)	9,074	28.1
Central American, ex. Mexican	1,879	16.8
Guatemalan	1,207	13.4
Salvadoran	415	30.6
Dominican Republic	5,525	35.2
Mexican	273	19.3
Puerto Rican	86	58.9
South American	930	32.1
Bolivian	171	23.6
Colombian	521	54.4

Language Spoken at Home: English Only
(Universe: Population 5 Years and Over)

Group	Number	%
Total Population	86,005	51.7
Hispanic or Latino (of any race)	5,300	8.6
Central American, ex. Mexican	329	2.3
Guatemalan	234	2.1
Salvadoran	12	0.7
Dominican Republic	1,099	4.4
Mexican	389	15.0

Notes: (1) Percent of total population; (2) Percent of Hispanic/Latino population; Profiles include places with an overall population of at least 125,000, OR an overall population of at least 25,000 where the Hispanic/Latino population is at least 20% of the overall population. In states where less than five places meet either of these criteria, we have included places with at least 10,000 total population with the highest percentage of Hispanic/Latino population. These places are identified with an asterisk (*); Please refer to the User's Guide for a full explanation of data.

Group	Number	%
Puerto Rican	2,709	20.5
South American	420	10.6
Bolivian	125	12.4
Colombian	26	2.1

Language Spoken at Home: Spanish
(Universe: Population 5 Years and Over)

Group	Number	%
Total Population	58,331	35.1
Hispanic or Latino (of any race)	56,103	91.2
Central American, ex. Mexican	13,900	97.6
Guatemalan	11,089	97.8
Salvadoran	1,770	99.3
Dominican Republic	24,129	95.6
Mexican	2,177	83.9
Puerto Rican	10,497	79.5
South American	3,482	88.3
Bolivian	865	85.9
Colombian	1,239	97.9

Unemployment Rate
(Universe: Population 16 Years and Over)

Group	%
Total Population	12.5
Hispanic or Latino (of any race)	17.6
Central American, ex. Mexican	15.8
Guatemalan	15.6
Salvadoran	4.0
Dominican Republic	19.5
Mexican	12.3
Puerto Rican	20.3
South American	12.3
Bolivian	12.4
Colombian	3.9

Class of Worker: Private Wage and Salary
(Universe: Civilian Employed Population 16 Years and Over)

Group	Number	%
Total Population	67,383	86.3
Hispanic or Latino (of any race)	23,609	89.8
Central American, ex. Mexican	7,356	94.2
Guatemalan	6,188	95.0
Salvadoran	818	89.4
Dominican Republic	8,377	86.2
Mexican	1,166	97.6
Puerto Rican	3,993	90.6
South American	1,789	84.9
Bolivian	610	94.1
Colombian	595	84.0

Class of Worker: Government
(Universe: Civilian Employed Population 16 Years and Over)

Group	Number	%
Total Population	6,843	8.8
Hispanic or Latino (of any race)	1,244	4.7
Central American, ex. Mexican	96	1.2
Guatemalan	48	0.7
Salvadoran	36	3.9
Dominican Republic	614	6.3
Mexican	29	2.4
Puerto Rican	255	5.8
South American	125	5.9
Bolivian	13	2.0
Colombian	60	8.5

Means of Transportation to Work: Car, Truck or Van
(Universe: Workers 16 Years and Over)

Group	Number	%
Total Population	57,716	76.6
Hispanic or Latino (of any race)	20,614	81.4
Central American, ex. Mexican	6,199	81.4
Guatemalan	5,178	81.2
Salvadoran	729	83.1
Dominican Republic	7,681	84.2
Mexican	873	73.1
Puerto Rican	3,478	81.5
South American	1,678	81.0
Bolivian	573	89.3
Colombian	610	90.0

Means of Transportation to Work: Public Transportation (ex. Taxicab)
(Universe: Workers 16 Years and Over)

Group	Number	%
Total Population	5,949	7.9
Hispanic or Latino (of any race)	2,088	8.2
Central American, ex. Mexican	844	11.1
Guatemalan	711	11.1
Salvadoran	85	9.7
Dominican Republic	423	4.6
Mexican	178	14.9
Puerto Rican	385	9.0
South American	51	2.5
Bolivian	0	0.0
Colombian	0	0.0

Homeownership Rate
(Universe: Occupied Housing Units)

Group	%
Total Population	34.9
Hispanic or Latino (of any race)	24.4
Central American, ex. Mexican	30.1
Guatemalan	29.2
Honduran	26.9
Nicaraguan	15.0
Panamanian	30.2
Salvadoran	39.6
Cuban	27.0
Dominican Republic	26.0
Mexican	21.8
Puerto Rican	14.6
South American	35.6
Argentinean	25.0
Bolivian	38.6
Colombian	41.3
Ecuadorian	32.4
Peruvian	34.6
Venezuelan	22.6
Spaniard	34.4

Median Home Value

Group	Dollars
Total Population	243,600
Hispanic or Latino (of any race)	225,300
Central American, ex. Mexican	229,800
Guatemalan	225,600
Salvadoran	227,000
Dominican Republic	211,100
Mexican	225,600
Puerto Rican	230,200
South American	248,300
Bolivian	330,800
Colombian	239,500

Median Gross Rent

Group	Dollars
Total Population	901
Hispanic or Latino (of any race)	856
Central American, ex. Mexican	945
Guatemalan	953
Salvadoran	853
Dominican Republic	790
Mexican	871
Puerto Rican	769
South American	948
Bolivian	697
Colombian	842

Median Household Income
(2010 Inflation-Adjusted Dollars)

Group	Dollars
Total Population	36,925
Hispanic or Latino (of any race)	29,568
Central American, ex. Mexican	40,983
Guatemalan	40,300
Salvadoran	44,100
Dominican Republic	25,461
Mexican	35,540
Puerto Rican	19,701
South American	50,294
Bolivian	31,818
Colombian	53,750

Per Capita Income
(2010 Inflation-Adjusted Dollars)

Group	Dollars
Total Population	20,735
Hispanic or Latino (of any race)	12,167
Central American, ex. Mexican	14,892
Guatemalan	15,282
Salvadoran	13,620
Dominican Republic	10,445
Mexican	9,530
Puerto Rican	9,785
South American	20,346
Bolivian	24,061
Colombian	19,029

Households with $100,000+ Income

Group	Number	%
Total Population	8,497	13.7
Hispanic or Latino (of any race)	1,080	5.5
Central American, ex. Mexican	414	10.2
Guatemalan	369	11.9
Salvadoran	19	3.1
Dominican Republic	203	2.5
Mexican	23	2.6
Puerto Rican	144	3.1
South American	195	15.8
Bolivian	40	13.3
Colombian	56	15.7

Households with Food Stamps/SNAP Benefits During Past 12 Months

Group	Number	%
Total Population	12,651	20.4
Hispanic or Latino (of any race)	6,848	35.0
Central American, ex. Mexican	792	19.5
Guatemalan	555	18.0
Salvadoran	90	14.8
Dominican Republic	3,494	42.3
Mexican	201	22.9
Puerto Rican	1,865	40.1
South American	295	23.9
Bolivian	78	26.0
Colombian	80	22.5

Poverty Rate
(Income in Past 12 Months Below Poverty Level)

Group	%
Total Population	26.3
Hispanic or Latino (of any race)	32.8
Central American, ex. Mexican	20.3
Guatemalan	20.8
Salvadoran	16.9
Dominican Republic	36.9
Mexican	36.3
Puerto Rican	45.6
South American	16.2
Bolivian	7.9
Colombian	10.2

Woonsocket*

Population

Group	Number	%TP[1]	%HP[2]
Total Population	41,186	100.0	–
Hispanic or Latino (of any race)	5,845	14.2	100.0
Central American, ex. Mexican	154	0.4	2.6
Dominican Republic	721	1.8	12.3
Mexican	287	0.7	4.9
Puerto Rican	4,117	10.0	70.4
South American	182	0.4	3.1
Colombian	110	0.3	1.9

Population Growth: 2000–2010

Group	%
Total Population	-4.7
Hispanic or Latino (of any race)	45.0
Dominican Republic	110.2
Mexican	70.8
Puerto Rican	47.1

Males per 100 Females

Group	Number
Total Population	93.8

Notes: (1) Percent of total population; (2) Percent of Hispanic/Latino population; Profiles include places with an overall population of at least 125,000, OR an overall population of at least 25,000 where the Hispanic/Latino population is at least 20% of the overall population. In states where less than five places meet either of these criteria, we have included places with at least 10,000 total population with the highest percentage of Hispanic/Latino population. These places are identified with an asterisk (*); Please refer to the User's Guide for a full explanation of data.

Hispanic or Latino (of any race)	91.3
Central American, ex. Mexican	133.3
Dominican Republic	89.2
Mexican	139.2
Puerto Rican	87.0
South American	95.7
Colombian	103.7

Average Household Size

Group	People
Total Population	2.37
Hispanic or Latino (of any race)	3.12
Central American, ex. Mexican	3.29
Dominican Republic	3.32
Mexican	3.31
Puerto Rican	3.11
South American	2.91
Colombian	3.03

Median Age

Group	Years
Total Population	36.8
Hispanic or Latino (of any race)	20.4
Central American, ex. Mexican	25.7
Dominican Republic	21.2
Mexican	23.6
Puerto Rican	19.6
South American	30.8
Colombian	30.8

High School Graduates
(Universe: Population 25 Years and Over)

Group	Number	%
Total Population	19,835	72.2
Hispanic or Latino (of any race)	1,229	65.8
Puerto Rican	580	53.8

Four-Year College Graduates
(Universe: Population 25 Years and Over)

Group	Number	%
Total Population	3,545	12.9
Hispanic or Latino (of any race)	125	6.7
Puerto Rican	77	7.1

Population Age 3–17 Enrolled in Public School
(Universe: Population Age 3–17 Enrolled in School)

Group	Number	%
Total Population	6,284	90.1
Hispanic or Latino (of any race)	1,485	96.6
Puerto Rican	1,013	99.5

Population Age 3–17 Enrolled in Private School
(Universe: Population Age 3–17 Enrolled in School)

Group	Number	%
Total Population	694	9.9
Hispanic or Latino (of any race)	53	3.4
Puerto Rican	5	0.5

Foreign-Born Population

Group	Number	%
Total Population	3,821	9.2
Hispanic or Latino (of any race)	782	15.6
Puerto Rican	0	0.0

Foreign-Born Naturalized U.S. Citizens

Group	Number	%
Total Population	1,550	40.6
Hispanic or Latino (of any race)	274	35.0
Puerto Rican	0	0.0

Language Spoken at Home: English Only
(Universe: Population 5 Years and Over)

Group	Number	%
Total Population	28,713	75.1
Hispanic or Latino (of any race)	684	16.9
Puerto Rican	342	13.3

Language Spoken at Home: Spanish
(Universe: Population 5 Years and Over)

Group	Number	%
Total Population	3,627	9.5
Hispanic or Latino (of any race)	3,372	83.1
Puerto Rican	2,226	86.7

Unemployment Rate
(Universe: Population 16 Years and Over)

Group	%
Total Population	7.6
Hispanic or Latino (of any race)	5.5
Puerto Rican	7.0

Class of Worker: Private Wage and Salary
(Universe: Civilian Employed Population 16 Years and Over)

Group	Number	%
Total Population	15,973	87.9
Hispanic or Latino (of any race)	1,536	94.5
Puerto Rican	919	94.1

Class of Worker: Government
(Universe: Civilian Employed Population 16 Years and Over)

Group	Number	%
Total Population	1,552	8.5
Hispanic or Latino (of any race)	89	5.5
Puerto Rican	58	5.9

Means of Transportation to Work: Car, Truck or Van
(Universe: Workers 16 Years and Over)

Group	Number	%
Total Population	16,060	91.6
Hispanic or Latino (of any race)	1,411	86.8
Puerto Rican	796	82.3

Means of Transportation to Work: Public Transportation (ex. Taxicab)
(Universe: Workers 16 Years and Over)

Group	Number	%
Total Population	322	1.8
Hispanic or Latino (of any race)	54	3.3
Puerto Rican	54	5.6

Homeownership Rate
(Universe: Occupied Housing Units)

Group	%
Total Population	38.2
Hispanic or Latino (of any race)	11.5
Central American, ex. Mexican	40.5
Dominican Republic	13.4
Mexican	24.0
Puerto Rican	8.4
South American	31.0
Colombian	34.4

Median Home Value

Group	Dollars
Total Population	227,400
Hispanic or Latino (of any race)	228,300
Puerto Rican	252,800

Median Gross Rent

Group	Dollars
Total Population	751
Hispanic or Latino (of any race)	691
Puerto Rican	662

Median Household Income
(2010 Inflation-Adjusted Dollars)

Group	Dollars
Total Population	38,625
Hispanic or Latino (of any race)	23,706
Puerto Rican	21,166

Per Capita Income
(2010 Inflation-Adjusted Dollars)

Group	Dollars
Total Population	20,242
Hispanic or Latino (of any race)	8,667
Puerto Rican	7,862

Households with $100,000+ Income

Group	Number	%
Total Population	1,746	10.5
Hispanic or Latino (of any race)	25	1.7
Puerto Rican	25	2.5

Households with Food Stamps/SNAP Benefits During Past 12 Months

Group	Number	%
Total Population	2,940	17.7
Hispanic or Latino (of any race)	778	52.6
Puerto Rican	603	61.3

Poverty Rate
(Income in Past 12 Months Below Poverty Level)

Group	%
Total Population	22.2
Hispanic or Latino (of any race)	51.0
Puerto Rican	62.8

STATE & PLACE PROFILES

Notes: (1) Percent of total population; (2) Percent of Hispanic/Latino population; Profiles include places with an overall population of at least 125,000, OR an overall population of at least 25,000 where the Hispanic/Latino population is at least 20% of the overall population. In states where less than five places meet either of these criteria, we have included places with at least 10,000 total population with the highest percentage of Hispanic/Latino population. These places are identified with an asterisk (*); Please refer to the User's Guide for a full explanation of data.

South Carolina

EDITOR'S NOTE: For a place to be included in this edition, it must meet one of two criteria. Either its overall population is at least 125,000, OR its overall population is at least 25,000 and its Hispanic/Latino population is at least 20% of the overall population. In South Carolina, less than five places meet either of these criteria. In an effort to include at least five places for each state, we have included places with at least 10,000 total population with the highest percentage of Hispanic/Latino population. These places are identified with an asterisk (*). For the state of South Carolina, the following locations are included:

Berea*
Bluffton*
Columbia
Hilton Head Island*
Parker*

Section Two: State & Place Profiles starts with the state profile, followed by place profiles that meet the criteria above. Places are listed alphabetically within each state. All states, all counties and places that meet the above criteria are ranked and compared in *Section Three: Rankings & Comparisons*, on page 1055.

For a more detailed look at the Hispanic/Latino population in South Carolina, a companion web site is available at no additional charge with purchase of this print edition. Visit http://gold.greyhouse.com/page/info_hispanic for more information.

The web site includes data for all counties and places in South Carolina with Hispanic/Latino population, plus ten additional topics: Self Employed Worker; Walked to Work; Worked from Home; Mean Travel Time to Work; Mean Household Income; Households with Cash Public Assistance; Mean Cash Pubic Assistance; Poverty Rates for 18 and Under, 18 to 64, and 65 and Over.

Population

Group	Number	%TP[1]	%HP[2]
Total Population	4,625,364	100.0	–
Hispanic or Latino (of any race)	235,682	5.1	100.0
Central American, ex. Mexican	26,290	0.6	11.2
Costa Rican	1,943	<0.1	0.8
Guatemalan	8,883	0.2	3.8
Honduran	8,091	0.2	3.4
Nicaraguan	1,303	<0.1	0.6
Panamanian	2,104	<0.1	0.9
Salvadoran	3,830	0.1	1.6
Cuban	5,955	0.1	2.5
Dominican Republic	3,018	0.1	1.3
Mexican	138,358	3.0	58.7
Puerto Rican	26,493	0.6	11.2
South American	17,856	0.4	7.6
Argentinean	1,439	<0.1	0.6
Bolivian	493	<0.1	0.2
Chilean	567	<0.1	0.2
Colombian	9,436	0.2	4.0
Ecuadorian	1,602	<0.1	0.7
Paraguayan	111	<0.1	<0.1
Peruvian	1,908	<0.1	0.8
Uruguayan	853	<0.1	0.4
Venezuelan	1,315	<0.1	0.6
Spaniard	2,867	0.1	1.2

Population Growth: 2000–2010

Group	%
Total Population	15.3
Hispanic or Latino (of any race)	147.9
Central American, ex. Mexican	355.6
Costa Rican	125.7
Guatemalan	483.6
Honduran	501.6
Nicaraguan	291.3
Panamanian	139.9
Salvadoran	500.3
Cuban	107.1
Dominican Republic	318.6
Mexican	161.7
Puerto Rican	117.0
South American	264.6
Argentinean	341.4
Bolivian	336.3
Chilean	198.4
Colombian	242.9
Ecuadorian	396.0
Peruvian	324.9
Venezuelan	226.3
Spaniard	827.8

Males per 100 Females

Group	Number
Total Population	94.7
Hispanic or Latino (of any race)	125.8
Central American, ex. Mexican	135.0
Costa Rican	117.8
Guatemalan	171.2
Honduran	147.4
Nicaraguan	103.0
Panamanian	66.5
Salvadoran	115.2
Cuban	108.7
Dominican Republic	89.9
Mexican	140.1
Puerto Rican	99.6
South American	88.7
Argentinean	98.2
Bolivian	102.0
Chilean	98.3
Colombian	84.9
Ecuadorian	90.5
Paraguayan	109.4
Peruvian	86.1
Uruguayan	108.6
Venezuelan	83.9
Spaniard	98.1

Average Household Size

Group	People
Total Population	2.49
Hispanic or Latino (of any race)	3.59
Central American, ex. Mexican	3.90
Costa Rican	3.28
Guatemalan	4.47
Honduran	4.02
Nicaraguan	3.28
Panamanian	2.79
Salvadoran	3.90
Cuban	2.73
Dominican Republic	3.24
Mexican	3.98
Puerto Rican	2.88
South American	3.03
Argentinean	2.95
Bolivian	3.28
Chilean	2.69
Colombian	3.02
Ecuadorian	3.19
Paraguayan	2.76
Peruvian	3.03
Uruguayan	3.42
Venezuelan	2.90
Spaniard	2.58

Median Age

Group	Years
Total Population	37.9
Hispanic or Latino (of any race)	25.5
Central American, ex. Mexican	27.2
Costa Rican	29.5
Guatemalan	25.4
Honduran	27.9
Nicaraguan	29.6
Panamanian	32.1
Salvadoran	28.0
Cuban	32.0
Dominican Republic	25.3
Mexican	24.4
Puerto Rican	25.7
South American	33.5
Argentinean	33.4
Bolivian	31.9
Chilean	38.4
Colombian	34.3
Ecuadorian	32.5
Paraguayan	19.5
Peruvian	33.2
Uruguayan	32.0
Venezuelan	31.1
Spaniard	34.2

High School Graduates
(Universe: Population 25 Years and Over)

Group	Number	%
Total Population	2,474,880	83.0
Hispanic or Latino (of any race)	63,091	58.8
Central American, ex. Mexican	7,152	53.0
Costa Rican	901	74.8
Guatemalan	1,412	32.1
Honduran	2,304	56.1
Nicaraguan	508	71.5
Panamanian	983	91.2
Salvadoran	1,002	52.4
Cuban	2,323	81.3
Dominican Republic	654	83.8
Mexican	29,709	47.1
Puerto Rican	10,307	86.3
South American	8,538	87.6
Argentinean	693	80.0
Colombian	4,829	87.7
Ecuadorian	690	91.6
Peruvian	934	97.0
Venezuelan	644	89.7
Spaniard	1,619	86.8

Four-Year College Graduates
(Universe: Population 25 Years and Over)

Group	Number	%
Total Population	714,196	24.0
Hispanic or Latino (of any race)	13,330	12.4
Central American, ex. Mexican	1,539	11.4
Costa Rican	438	36.3
Guatemalan	145	3.3
Honduran	382	9.3
Nicaraguan	197	27.7
Panamanian	274	25.4
Salvadoran	94	4.9
Cuban	927	32.4
Dominican Republic	211	27.1
Mexican	4,124	6.5
Puerto Rican	2,296	19.2
South American	2,964	30.4
Argentinean	223	25.8
Colombian	1,570	28.5
Ecuadorian	218	29.0
Peruvian	341	35.4
Venezuelan	296	41.2
Spaniard	565	30.3

Population Age 3–17 Enrolled in Public School
(Universe: Population Age 3–17 Enrolled in School)

Group	Number	%
Total Population	701,256	86.9
Hispanic or Latino (of any race)	41,945	93.5
Central American, ex. Mexican	3,954	90.4
Costa Rican	185	63.6
Guatemalan	1,053	82.5
Honduran	1,152	96.3
Nicaraguan	206	88.4
Panamanian	410	95.1
Salvadoran	865	100.0
Cuban	966	78.2
Dominican Republic	296	84.6
Mexican	26,342	96.5

Notes: (1) Percent of total population; (2) Percent of Hispanic/Latino population; Profiles include places with an overall population of at least 125,000, OR an overall population of at least 25,000 where the Hispanic/Latino population is at least 20% of the overall population. In states where less than five places meet either of these criteria, we have included places with at least 10,000 total population with the highest percentage of Hispanic/Latino population. These places are identified with an asterisk (*); Please refer to the User's Guide for a full explanation of data.

Group	Number	%
Puerto Rican	5,309	90.5
South American	2,929	89.3
Argentinean	238	87.5
Colombian	1,745	93.6
Ecuadorian	197	84.5
Peruvian	281	73.6
Venezuelan	155	100.0
Spaniard	568	79.3

Population Age 3–17 Enrolled in Private School
(Universe: Population Age 3–17 Enrolled in School)

Group	Number	%
Total Population	105,501	13.1
Hispanic or Latino (of any race)	2,892	6.5
Central American, ex. Mexican	422	9.6
Costa Rican	106	36.4
Guatemalan	224	17.5
Honduran	44	3.7
Nicaraguan	27	11.6
Panamanian	21	4.9
Salvadoran	0	0.0
Cuban	269	21.8
Dominican Republic	54	15.4
Mexican	955	3.5
Puerto Rican	558	9.5
South American	350	10.7
Argentinean	34	12.5
Colombian	120	6.4
Ecuadorian	36	15.5
Peruvian	101	26.4
Venezuelan	0	0.0
Spaniard	148	20.7

Foreign-Born Population

Group	Number	%
Total Population	212,259	4.7
Hispanic or Latino (of any race)	106,851	51.2
Central American, ex. Mexican	16,385	66.2
Costa Rican	1,275	66.7
Guatemalan	6,460	74.1
Honduran	5,204	70.3
Nicaraguan	731	67.1
Panamanian	760	40.8
Salvadoran	1,892	52.8
Cuban	1,494	30.1
Dominican Republic	793	53.0
Mexican	73,738	57.3
Puerto Rican	348	1.5
South American	11,390	72.0
Argentinean	1,052	78.2
Colombian	6,327	70.9
Ecuadorian	723	59.4
Peruvian	1,249	78.3
Venezuelan	855	73.0
Spaniard	712	22.9

Foreign-Born Naturalized U.S. Citizens

Group	Number	%
Total Population	66,105	31.1
Hispanic or Latino (of any race)	14,916	14.0
Central American, ex. Mexican	2,836	17.3
Costa Rican	336	26.4
Guatemalan	732	11.3
Honduran	710	13.6
Nicaraguan	265	36.3
Panamanian	396	52.1
Salvadoran	397	21.0
Cuban	1,036	69.3
Dominican Republic	323	40.7
Mexican	5,472	7.4
Puerto Rican	141	40.5
South American	3,981	35.0
Argentinean	188	17.9
Colombian	2,302	36.4
Ecuadorian	259	35.8
Peruvian	494	39.6
Venezuelan	232	27.1
Spaniard	297	41.7

Language Spoken at Home: English Only
(Universe: Population 5 Years and Over)

Group	Number	%
Total Population	3,936,691	93.4
Hispanic or Latino (of any race)	39,723	21.9
Central American, ex. Mexican	2,286	10.7
Costa Rican	244	14.1
Guatemalan	483	6.6
Honduran	527	8.2
Nicaraguan	143	13.7
Panamanian	492	30.6
Salvadoran	336	10.9
Cuban	2,120	47.5
Dominican Republic	314	22.4
Mexican	18,061	16.4
Puerto Rican	10,028	48.4
South American	2,240	15.2
Argentinean	185	15.2
Colombian	917	11.0
Ecuadorian	232	21.7
Peruvian	334	22.2
Venezuelan	257	22.6
Spaniard	1,789	66.4

Language Spoken at Home: Spanish
(Universe: Population 5 Years and Over)

Group	Number	%
Total Population	179,524	4.3
Hispanic or Latino (of any race)	140,720	77.6
Central American, ex. Mexican	18,861	88.6
Costa Rican	1,472	85.2
Guatemalan	6,667	91.7
Honduran	5,862	91.8
Nicaraguan	900	86.3
Panamanian	1,114	69.4
Salvadoran	2,742	88.9
Cuban	2,282	51.1
Dominican Republic	1,079	77.0
Mexican	91,812	83.3
Puerto Rican	10,592	51.1
South American	12,347	84.1
Argentinean	1,026	84.1
Colombian	7,373	88.4
Ecuadorian	836	78.3
Peruvian	1,172	77.8
Venezuelan	864	75.9
Spaniard	855	31.7

Unemployment Rate
(Universe: Population 16 Years and Over)

Group	%
Total Population	9.3
Hispanic or Latino (of any race)	10.2
Central American, ex. Mexican	12.6
Costa Rican	8.4
Guatemalan	13.9
Honduran	14.3
Nicaraguan	19.2
Panamanian	7.1
Salvadoran	8.4
Cuban	5.6
Dominican Republic	22.9
Mexican	10.2
Puerto Rican	10.5
South American	6.2
Argentinean	5.9
Colombian	6.9
Ecuadorian	6.4
Peruvian	4.0
Venezuelan	9.5
Spaniard	14.7

Class of Worker: Private Wage and Salary
(Universe: Civilian Employed Population 16 Years and Over)

Group	Number	%
Total Population	1,564,286	78.1
Hispanic or Latino (of any race)	80,601	88.3
Central American, ex. Mexican	10,345	89.6
Costa Rican	884	88.0
Guatemalan	3,859	94.6
Honduran	3,253	91.8
Nicaraguan	450	96.2
Panamanian	552	68.5
Salvadoran	1,299	82.3
Cuban	1,626	82.7
Dominican Republic	534	87.8
Mexican	51,707	91.5
Puerto Rican	6,564	77.6
South American	7,085	81.7
Argentinean	604	87.3
Colombian	4,022	80.8
Ecuadorian	419	77.7
Peruvian	754	80.0
Venezuelan	583	88.6
Spaniard	774	71.9

Class of Worker: Government
(Universe: Civilian Employed Population 16 Years and Over)

Group	Number	%
Total Population	318,267	15.9
Hispanic or Latino (of any race)	5,903	6.5
Central American, ex. Mexican	570	4.9
Costa Rican	59	5.9
Guatemalan	56	1.4
Honduran	42	1.2
Nicaraguan	11	2.4
Panamanian	224	27.8
Salvadoran	154	9.8
Cuban	212	10.8
Dominican Republic	74	12.2
Mexican	1,742	3.1
Puerto Rican	1,652	19.5
South American	1,033	11.9
Argentinean	71	10.3
Colombian	578	11.6
Ecuadorian	115	21.3
Peruvian	139	14.7
Venezuelan	61	9.3
Spaniard	257	23.9

Means of Transportation to Work: Car, Truck or Van
(Universe: Workers 16 Years and Over)

Group	Number	%
Total Population	1,832,979	92.1
Hispanic or Latino (of any race)	83,305	89.6
Central American, ex. Mexican	10,388	90.5
Costa Rican	976	97.1
Guatemalan	3,572	88.4
Honduran	3,157	90.4
Nicaraguan	402	84.5
Panamanian	765	90.2
Salvadoran	1,435	93.7
Cuban	1,638	79.9
Dominican Republic	642	86.3
Mexican	51,923	90.9
Puerto Rican	7,731	82.3
South American	7,917	93.0
Argentinean	604	94.5
Colombian	4,530	92.3
Ecuadorian	472	93.3
Peruvian	825	94.0
Venezuelan	650	91.3
Spaniard	971	84.4

Means of Transportation to Work: Public Transportation (ex. Taxicab)
(Universe: Workers 16 Years and Over)

Group	Number	%
Total Population	12,642	0.6
Hispanic or Latino (of any race)	589	0.6
Central American, ex. Mexican	13	0.1
Costa Rican	0	0.0
Guatemalan	13	0.3
Honduran	0	0.0
Nicaraguan	0	0.0
Panamanian	0	0.0
Salvadoran	0	0.0
Cuban	0	0.0
Dominican Republic	9	1.2
Mexican	396	0.7
Puerto Rican	81	0.9
South American	53	0.6
Argentinean	0	0.0
Colombian	33	0.7
Ecuadorian	0	0.0
Peruvian	0	0.0
Venezuelan	20	2.8
Spaniard	0	0.0

Homeownership Rate
(Universe: Occupied Housing Units)

Group	%
Total Population	69.3
Hispanic or Latino (of any race)	42.7
Central American, ex. Mexican	37.5

Notes: (1) Percent of total population; (2) Percent of Hispanic/Latino population; Profiles include places with an overall population of at least 125,000, OR an overall population of at least 25,000 where the Hispanic/Latino population is at least 20% of the overall population. In states where less than five places meet either of these criteria, we have included places with at least 10,000 total population with the highest percentage of Hispanic/Latino population. These places are identified with an asterisk (*); Please refer to the User's Guide for a full explanation of data.

Costa Rican	45.7
Guatemalan	24.6
Honduran	32.0
Nicaraguan	43.1
Panamanian	58.6
Salvadoran	51.9
Cuban	63.1
Dominican Republic	50.4
Mexican	35.6
Puerto Rican	52.4
South American	59.8
Argentinean	57.6
Bolivian	62.0
Chilean	64.4
Colombian	61.2
Ecuadorian	63.5
Paraguayan	60.0
Peruvian	57.6
Uruguayan	49.6
Venezuelan	53.4
Spaniard	67.5

Median Home Value

Group	Dollars
Total Population	134,100
Hispanic or Latino (of any race)	126,200
Central American, ex. Mexican	140,400
Costa Rican	137,100
Guatemalan	106,300
Honduran	131,100
Nicaraguan	244,900
Panamanian	173,100
Salvadoran	137,200
Cuban	185,300
Dominican Republic	164,900
Mexican	95,200
Puerto Rican	152,500
South American	143,500
Argentinean	221,400
Colombian	131,900
Ecuadorian	159,200
Peruvian	184,000
Venezuelan	168,300
Spaniard	134,600

Median Gross Rent

Group	Dollars
Total Population	701
Hispanic or Latino (of any race)	701
Central American, ex. Mexican	754
Costa Rican	880
Guatemalan	743
Honduran	756
Nicaraguan	584
Panamanian	684
Salvadoran	780
Cuban	888
Dominican Republic	821
Mexican	661
Puerto Rican	747
South American	816
Argentinean	1,012
Colombian	806
Ecuadorian	1,303
Peruvian	629
Venezuelan	865
Spaniard	831

Median Household Income
(2010 Inflation-Adjusted Dollars)

Group	Dollars
Total Population	43,939
Hispanic or Latino (of any race)	35,843
Central American, ex. Mexican	37,223
Costa Rican	51,026
Guatemalan	30,862
Honduran	32,731
Nicaraguan	32,472
Panamanian	52,955
Salvadoran	32,679
Cuban	46,911
Dominican Republic	48,227
Mexican	32,229
Puerto Rican	43,306
South American	43,208
Argentinean	55,287
Colombian	38,950
Ecuadorian	57,188
Peruvian	43,917
Venezuelan	67,188
Spaniard	41,661

Per Capita Income
(2010 Inflation-Adjusted Dollars)

Group	Dollars
Total Population	23,443
Hispanic or Latino (of any race)	13,290
Central American, ex. Mexican	12,424
Costa Rican	17,067
Guatemalan	9,839
Honduran	11,080
Nicaraguan	17,075
Panamanian	17,910
Salvadoran	14,531
Cuban	22,241
Dominican Republic	17,649
Mexican	11,522
Puerto Rican	17,522
South American	17,927
Argentinean	21,158
Colombian	16,604
Ecuadorian	16,291
Peruvian	17,385
Venezuelan	22,518
Spaniard	15,068

Households with $100,000+ Income

Group	Number	%
Total Population	253,920	14.6
Hispanic or Latino (of any race)	4,225	7.7
Central American, ex. Mexican	427	6.8
Costa Rican	85	13.9
Guatemalan	100	5.7
Honduran	64	3.4
Nicaraguan	15	5.9
Panamanian	75	12.7
Salvadoran	88	8.2
Cuban	327	20.1
Dominican Republic	16	5.1
Mexican	1,896	5.9
Puerto Rican	653	9.3
South American	637	12.2
Argentinean	126	31.0
Colombian	260	8.8
Ecuadorian	33	9.6
Peruvian	22	4.1
Venezuelan	95	29.0
Spaniard	79	7.7

Households with Food Stamps/SNAP Benefits During Past 12 Months

Group	Number	%
Total Population	199,824	11.5
Hispanic or Latino (of any race)	6,699	12.2
Central American, ex. Mexican	745	11.9
Costa Rican	0	0.0
Guatemalan	281	15.9
Honduran	232	12.2
Nicaraguan	48	19.0
Panamanian	14	2.4
Salvadoran	161	14.9
Cuban	164	10.1
Dominican Republic	80	25.4
Mexican	4,148	13.0
Puerto Rican	1,050	14.9
South American	202	3.9
Argentinean	0	0.0
Colombian	185	6.2
Ecuadorian	11	3.2
Peruvian	0	0.0
Venezuelan	0	0.0
Spaniard	143	14.0

Poverty Rate
(Income in Past 12 Months Below Poverty Level)

Group	%
Total Population	16.4
Hispanic or Latino (of any race)	27.7
Central American, ex. Mexican	27.1
Costa Rican	11.2
Guatemalan	34.5
Honduran	30.5
Nicaraguan	31.1
Panamanian	11.2
Salvadoran	17.4
Cuban	13.9
Dominican Republic	9.7
Mexican	32.5
Puerto Rican	21.1
South American	12.1
Argentinean	21.6
Colombian	10.6
Ecuadorian	14.6
Peruvian	14.5
Venezuelan	12.0
Spaniard	20.8

Berea*

Population

Group	Number	%TP[1]	%HP[2]
Total Population	14,295	100.0	–
Hispanic or Latino (of any race)	3,630	25.4	100.0
Central American, ex. Mexican	954	6.7	26.3
Costa Rican	119	0.8	3.3
Guatemalan	248	1.7	6.8
Honduran	455	3.2	12.5
Salvadoran	116	0.8	3.2
Mexican	2,021	14.1	55.7
Puerto Rican	105	0.7	2.9
South American	359	2.5	9.9
Colombian	317	2.2	8.7

Population Growth: 2000–2010

Group	%
Total Population	1.0
Hispanic or Latino (of any race)	90.9
Central American, ex. Mexican	197.2
Costa Rican	0.0
Honduran	333.3
Mexican	183.8
South American	-5.3
Colombian	-12.2

Males per 100 Females

Group	Number
Total Population	94.9
Hispanic or Latino (of any race)	134.0
Central American, ex. Mexican	152.4
Costa Rican	176.7
Guatemalan	198.8
Honduran	143.3
Salvadoran	100.0
Mexican	143.5
Puerto Rican	81.0
South American	93.0
Colombian	87.6

Average Household Size

Group	People
Total Population	2.58
Hispanic or Latino (of any race)	3.71
Central American, ex. Mexican	3.62
Costa Rican	3.05
Guatemalan	4.00
Honduran	3.40
Salvadoran	4.71
Mexican	3.92
Puerto Rican	3.43
South American	3.25
Colombian	3.21

Median Age

Group	Years
Total Population	36.2
Hispanic or Latino (of any race)	26.3
Central American, ex. Mexican	28.6
Costa Rican	31.1
Guatemalan	27.0
Honduran	28.8
Salvadoran	28.0
Mexican	24.4
Puerto Rican	21.8
South American	39.2

Notes: (1) Percent of total population; (2) Percent of Hispanic/Latino population; Profiles include places with an overall population of at least 125,000, OR an overall population of at least 25,000 where the Hispanic/Latino population is at least 20% of the overall population. In states where less than five places meet either of these criteria, we have included places with at least 10,000 total population with the highest percentage of Hispanic/Latino population. These places are identified with an asterisk (*); Please refer to the User's Guide for a full explanation of data.

Colombian		40.6

High School Graduates
(Universe: Population 25 Years and Over)

Group	Number	%
Total Population	6,573	75.4
Hispanic or Latino (of any race)	657	46.4
Mexican	331	39.3

Four-Year College Graduates
(Universe: Population 25 Years and Over)

Group	Number	%
Total Population	747	8.6
Hispanic or Latino (of any race)	13	0.9
Mexican	0	0.0

Population Age 3–17 Enrolled in Public School
(Universe: Population Age 3–17 Enrolled in School)

Group	Number	%
Total Population	2,212	91.8
Hispanic or Latino (of any race)	804	94.9
Mexican	612	100.0

Population Age 3–17 Enrolled in Private School
(Universe: Population Age 3–17 Enrolled in School)

Group	Number	%
Total Population	198	8.2
Hispanic or Latino (of any race)	43	5.1
Mexican	0	0.0

Foreign-Born Population

Group	Number	%
Total Population	1,676	13.0
Hispanic or Latino (of any race)	1,536	55.6
Mexican	967	53.5

Foreign-Born Naturalized U.S. Citizens

Group	Number	%
Total Population	240	14.3
Hispanic or Latino (of any race)	164	10.7
Mexican	34	3.5

Language Spoken at Home: English Only
(Universe: Population 5 Years and Over)

Group	Number	%
Total Population	9,350	77.7
Hispanic or Latino (of any race)	329	12.8
Mexican	260	15.5

Language Spoken at Home: Spanish
(Universe: Population 5 Years and Over)

Group	Number	%
Total Population	2,446	20.3
Hispanic or Latino (of any race)	2,247	87.2
Mexican	1,415	84.5

Unemployment Rate
(Universe: Population 16 Years and Over)

Group	%
Total Population	10.2
Hispanic or Latino (of any race)	7.3
Mexican	6.4

Class of Worker: Private Wage and Salary
(Universe: Civilian Employed Population 16 Years and Over)

Group	Number	%
Total Population	4,803	88.9
Hispanic or Latino (of any race)	1,171	91.9
Mexican	788	100.0

Class of Worker: Government
(Universe: Civilian Employed Population 16 Years and Over)

Group	Number	%
Total Population	396	7.3
Hispanic or Latino (of any race)	68	5.3
Mexican	0	0.0

Means of Transportation to Work: Car, Truck or Van
(Universe: Workers 16 Years and Over)

Group	Number	%
Total Population	4,917	93.6
Hispanic or Latino (of any race)	1,077	91.4
Mexican	734	94.8

Means of Transportation to Work: Public Transportation (ex. Taxicab)
(Universe: Workers 16 Years and Over)

Group	Number	%
Total Population	41	0.8
Hispanic or Latino (of any race)	12	1.0
Mexican	12	1.6

Homeownership Rate
(Universe: Occupied Housing Units)

Group	%
Total Population	60.3
Hispanic or Latino (of any race)	26.9
Central American, ex. Mexican	21.4
Costa Rican	33.3
Guatemalan	15.7
Honduran	14.6
Salvadoran	41.9
Mexican	19.8
Puerto Rican	46.7
South American	58.5
Colombian	61.8

Median Home Value

Group	Dollars
Total Population	103,900
Hispanic or Latino (of any race)	107,100
Mexican	139,100

Median Gross Rent

Group	Dollars
Total Population	550
Hispanic or Latino (of any race)	545
Mexican	568

Median Household Income
(2010 Inflation-Adjusted Dollars)

Group	Dollars
Total Population	32,610
Hispanic or Latino (of any race)	24,042
Mexican	23,720

Per Capita Income
(2010 Inflation-Adjusted Dollars)

Group	Dollars
Total Population	16,571
Hispanic or Latino (of any race)	9,468
Mexican	8,244

Households with $100,000+ Income

Group	Number	%
Total Population	163	3.2
Hispanic or Latino (of any race)	0	0.0
Mexican	0	0.0

Households with Food Stamps/SNAP Benefits During Past 12 Months

Group	Number	%
Total Population	640	12.4
Hispanic or Latino (of any race)	102	11.9
Mexican	70	14.9

Poverty Rate
(Income in Past 12 Months Below Poverty Level)

Group	%
Total Population	23.9
Hispanic or Latino (of any race)	33.6
Mexican	43.0

Bluffton*

Population

Group	Number	%TP[1]	%HP[2]
Total Population	12,530	100.0	–
Hispanic or Latino (of any race)	2,355	18.8	100.0
Central American, ex. Mexican	404	3.2	17.2
Honduran	210	1.7	8.9
Mexican	1,244	9.9	52.8
Puerto Rican	128	1.0	5.4
South American	345	2.8	14.6

Population Growth: 2000–2010

Group	%
Total Population	882.7

Males per 100 Females

Group	Number
Total Population	95.5
Hispanic or Latino (of any race)	113.1
Central American, ex. Mexican	111.5
Honduran	118.8
Mexican	122.1
Puerto Rican	120.7
South American	90.6

Average Household Size

Group	People
Total Population	2.84
Hispanic or Latino (of any race)	4.15
Central American, ex. Mexican	4.03
Honduran	4.35
Mexican	4.75
Puerto Rican	3.26
South American	3.59

Median Age

Group	Years
Total Population	32.7
Hispanic or Latino (of any race)	26.9
Central American, ex. Mexican	29.9
Honduran	29.2
Mexican	24.1
Puerto Rican	27.4
South American	32.1

High School Graduates
(Universe: Population 25 Years and Over)

Group	Number	%
Total Population	6,181	89.1
Hispanic or Latino (of any race)	858	70.7
Mexican	381	60.4

Four-Year College Graduates
(Universe: Population 25 Years and Over)

Group	Number	%
Total Population	2,262	32.6
Hispanic or Latino (of any race)	142	11.7
Mexican	0	0.0

Population Age 3–17 Enrolled in Public School
(Universe: Population Age 3–17 Enrolled in School)

Group	Number	%
Total Population	1,933	86.4
Hispanic or Latino (of any race)	637	100.0
Mexican	404	100.0

Population Age 3–17 Enrolled in Private School
(Universe: Population Age 3–17 Enrolled in School)

Group	Number	%
Total Population	305	13.6
Hispanic or Latino (of any race)	0	0.0
Mexican	0	0.0

Foreign-Born Population

Group	Number	%
Total Population	2,063	19.2
Hispanic or Latino (of any race)	1,544	69.6
Mexican	989	74.9

Foreign-Born Naturalized U.S. Citizens

Group	Number	%
Total Population	440	21.3
Hispanic or Latino (of any race)	317	20.5
Mexican	126	12.7

Language Spoken at Home: English Only
(Universe: Population 5 Years and Over)

Group	Number	%
Total Population	7,077	73.3
Hispanic or Latino (of any race)	25	1.2
Mexican	15	1.2

Language Spoken at Home: Spanish
(Universe: Population 5 Years and Over)

Group	Number	%
Total Population	2,154	22.3
Hispanic or Latino (of any race)	2,001	98.8
Mexican	1,209	98.8

Notes: (1) Percent of total population; (2) Percent of Hispanic/Latino population; Profiles include places with an overall population of at least 125,000, OR an overall population of at least 25,000 where the Hispanic/Latino population is at least 20% of the overall population. In states where less than five places meet either of these criteria, we have included places with at least 10,000 total population with the highest percentage of Hispanic/Latino population. These places are identified with an asterisk (*); Please refer to the User's Guide for a full explanation of data.

Unemployment Rate
(Universe: Population 16 Years and Over)

Group	%
Total Population	10.0
Hispanic or Latino (of any race)	16.3
Mexican	8.5

Class of Worker: Private Wage and Salary
(Universe: Civilian Employed Population 16 Years and Over)

Group	Number	%
Total Population	4,490	82.6
Hispanic or Latino (of any race)	859	86.2
Mexican	578	95.7

Class of Worker: Government
(Universe: Civilian Employed Population 16 Years and Over)

Group	Number	%
Total Population	627	11.5
Hispanic or Latino (of any race)	87	8.7
Mexican	0	0.0

Means of Transportation to Work: Car, Truck or Van
(Universe: Workers 16 Years and Over)

Group	Number	%
Total Population	4,963	92.5
Hispanic or Latino (of any race)	963	100.0
Mexican	604	100.0

Means of Transportation to Work: Public Transportation (ex. Taxicab)
(Universe: Workers 16 Years and Over)

Group	Number	%
Total Population	0	0.0
Hispanic or Latino (of any race)	0	0.0
Mexican	0	0.0

Homeownership Rate
(Universe: Occupied Housing Units)

Group	%
Total Population	74.6
Hispanic or Latino (of any race)	54.4
Central American, ex. Mexican	56.4
Honduran	54.9
Mexican	43.1
Puerto Rican	65.8
South American	74.3

Median Home Value

Group	Dollars
Total Population	240,800
Hispanic or Latino (of any race)	243,600
Mexican	259,100

Median Gross Rent

Group	Dollars
Total Population	1,221
Hispanic or Latino (of any race)	1,213
Mexican	1,244

Median Household Income
(2010 Inflation-Adjusted Dollars)

Group	Dollars
Total Population	55,699
Hispanic or Latino (of any race)	44,167
Mexican	43,423

Per Capita Income
(2010 Inflation-Adjusted Dollars)

Group	Dollars
Total Population	29,008
Hispanic or Latino (of any race)	11,942
Mexican	8,175

Households with $100,000+ Income

Group	Number	%
Total Population	800	20.0
Hispanic or Latino (of any race)	18	3.1
Mexican	0	0.0

Households with Food Stamps/SNAP Benefits During Past 12 Months

Group	Number	%
Total Population	173	4.3
Hispanic or Latino (of any race)	45	7.8
Mexican	45	15.3

Poverty Rate
(Income in Past 12 Months Below Poverty Level)

Group	%
Total Population	15.3
Hispanic or Latino (of any race)	22.9
Mexican	31.8

Columbia

Population

Group	Number	%TP[1]	%HP[2]
Total Population	129,272	100.0	–
Hispanic or Latino (of any race)	5,622	4.3	100.0
Central American, ex. Mexican	473	0.4	8.4
Guatemalan	136	0.1	2.4
Panamanian	132	0.1	2.3
Cuban	208	0.2	3.7
Dominican Republic	154	0.1	2.7
Mexican	2,423	1.9	43.1
Puerto Rican	1,337	1.0	23.8
South American	428	0.3	7.6
Colombian	188	0.1	3.3
Spaniard	180	0.1	3.2

Population Growth: 2000–2010

Group	%
Total Population	11.2
Hispanic or Latino (of any race)	59.7
Central American, ex. Mexican	134.2
Cuban	66.4
Mexican	74.7
Puerto Rican	50.9
South American	90.2

Males per 100 Females

Group	Number
Total Population	106.0
Hispanic or Latino (of any race)	148.3
Central American, ex. Mexican	137.7
Guatemalan	240.0
Panamanian	65.0
Cuban	147.6
Dominican Republic	156.7
Mexican	167.4
Puerto Rican	133.3
South American	115.1
Colombian	104.3
Spaniard	164.7

Average Household Size

Group	People
Total Population	2.18
Hispanic or Latino (of any race)	2.79
Central American, ex. Mexican	3.12
Guatemalan	4.71
Panamanian	2.42
Cuban	2.13
Dominican Republic	2.61
Mexican	3.29
Puerto Rican	2.55
South American	2.47
Colombian	2.26
Spaniard	2.20

Median Age

Group	Years
Total Population	28.1
Hispanic or Latino (of any race)	23.3
Central American, ex. Mexican	25.1
Guatemalan	23.5
Panamanian	27.0
Cuban	24.9
Dominican Republic	23.0
Mexican	22.5
Puerto Rican	23.4
South American	27.1
Colombian	27.3
Spaniard	24.6

High School Graduates
(Universe: Population 25 Years and Over)

Group	Number	%
Total Population	62,388	85.0
Hispanic or Latino (of any race)	1,795	86.6
Mexican	527	75.5
Puerto Rican	634	94.3

Four-Year College Graduates
(Universe: Population 25 Years and Over)

Group	Number	%
Total Population	28,610	39.0
Hispanic or Latino (of any race)	508	24.5
Mexican	73	10.5
Puerto Rican	153	22.8

Population Age 3–17 Enrolled in Public School
(Universe: Population Age 3–17 Enrolled in School)

Group	Number	%
Total Population	12,806	80.4
Hispanic or Latino (of any race)	1,060	95.8
Mexican	323	89.0
Puerto Rican	578	100.0

Population Age 3–17 Enrolled in Private School
(Universe: Population Age 3–17 Enrolled in School)

Group	Number	%
Total Population	3,123	19.6
Hispanic or Latino (of any race)	47	4.2
Mexican	40	11.0
Puerto Rican	0	0.0

Foreign-Born Population

Group	Number	%
Total Population	6,417	5.0
Hispanic or Latino (of any race)	1,200	22.1
Mexican	562	26.6
Puerto Rican	0	0.0

Foreign-Born Naturalized U.S. Citizens

Group	Number	%
Total Population	2,029	31.6
Hispanic or Latino (of any race)	339	28.3
Mexican	92	16.4
Puerto Rican	0	0.0

Language Spoken at Home: English Only
(Universe: Population 5 Years and Over)

Group	Number	%
Total Population	111,302	91.8
Hispanic or Latino (of any race)	1,594	31.5
Mexican	540	28.0
Puerto Rican	601	31.8

Language Spoken at Home: Spanish
(Universe: Population 5 Years and Over)

Group	Number	%
Total Population	4,520	3.7
Hispanic or Latino (of any race)	3,390	66.9
Mexican	1,357	70.4
Puerto Rican	1,275	67.5

Unemployment Rate
(Universe: Population 16 Years and Over)

Group	%
Total Population	10.6
Hispanic or Latino (of any race)	5.2
Mexican	7.5
Puerto Rican	15.1

Class of Worker: Private Wage and Salary
(Universe: Civilian Employed Population 16 Years and Over)

Group	Number	%
Total Population	38,170	71.4
Hispanic or Latino (of any race)	767	68.7
Mexican	369	90.9
Puerto Rican	110	69.6

Class of Worker: Government
(Universe: Civilian Employed Population 16 Years and Over)

Group	Number	%
Total Population	12,286	23.0
Hispanic or Latino (of any race)	288	25.8
Mexican	37	9.1
Puerto Rican	48	30.4

Notes: (1) Percent of total population; (2) Percent of Hispanic/Latino population; Profiles include places with an overall population of at least 125,000, OR an overall population of at least 25,000 where the Hispanic/Latino population is at least 20% of the overall population. In states where less than five places meet either of these criteria, we have included places with at least 10,000 total population with the highest percentage of Hispanic/Latino population. These places are identified with an asterisk (*); Please refer to the User's Guide for a full explanation of data.

Means of Transportation to Work: Car, Truck or Van
(Universe: Workers 16 Years and Over)

Group	Number	%
Total Population	46,670	74.3
Hispanic or Latino (of any race)	1,063	35.7
Mexican	417	32.0
Puerto Rican	225	25.4

Means of Transportation to Work: Public Transportation (ex. Taxicab)
(Universe: Workers 16 Years and Over)

Group	Number	%
Total Population	1,342	2.1
Hispanic or Latino (of any race)	42	1.4
Mexican	24	1.8
Puerto Rican	9	1.0

Homeownership Rate
(Universe: Occupied Housing Units)

Group	%
Total Population	47.4
Hispanic or Latino (of any race)	27.6
Central American, ex. Mexican	30.1
Guatemalan	20.8
Panamanian	41.7
Cuban	47.6
Dominican Republic	21.4
Mexican	20.9
Puerto Rican	29.9
South American	29.8
Colombian	23.1
Spaniard	49.0

Median Home Value

Group	Dollars
Total Population	156,100
Hispanic or Latino (of any race)	169,600
Mexican	213,500
Puerto Rican	172,100

Median Gross Rent

Group	Dollars
Total Population	742
Hispanic or Latino (of any race)	783
Mexican	752
Puerto Rican	771

Median Household Income
(2010 Inflation-Adjusted Dollars)

Group	Dollars
Total Population	38,272
Hispanic or Latino (of any race)	41,780
Mexican	21,518
Puerto Rican	48,750

Per Capita Income
(2010 Inflation-Adjusted Dollars)

Group	Dollars
Total Population	24,221
Hispanic or Latino (of any race)	13,616
Mexican	11,884
Puerto Rican	11,786

Households with $100,000+ Income

Group	Number	%
Total Population	7,164	15.4
Hispanic or Latino (of any race)	57	5.7
Mexican	46	13.0
Puerto Rican	0	0.0

Households with Food Stamps/SNAP Benefits During Past 12 Months

Group	Number	%
Total Population	5,834	12.5
Hispanic or Latino (of any race)	63	6.3
Mexican	51	14.4
Puerto Rican	0	0.0

Poverty Rate
(Income in Past 12 Months Below Poverty Level)

Group	%
Total Population	22.0
Hispanic or Latino (of any race)	21.8
Mexican	42.5
Puerto Rican	11.9

Hilton Head Island*

Population

Group	Number	%TP[1]	%HP[2]
Total Population	37,099	100.0	–
Hispanic or Latino (of any race)	5,861	15.8	100.0
Central American, ex. Mexican	729	2.0	12.4
Costa Rican	108	0.3	1.8
Guatemalan	124	0.3	2.1
Honduran	311	0.8	5.3
Mexican	4,034	10.9	68.8
Puerto Rican	100	0.3	1.7
South American	665	1.8	11.3
Argentinean	221	0.6	3.8
Colombian	121	0.3	2.1
Uruguayan	189	0.5	3.2

Population Growth: 2000–2010

Group	%
Total Population	9.6
Hispanic or Latino (of any race)	50.8
Central American, ex. Mexican	44.4
Costa Rican	-22.9
Honduran	30.1
Mexican	58.0
South American	226.0

Males per 100 Females

Group	Number
Total Population	96.4
Hispanic or Latino (of any race)	136.0
Central American, ex. Mexican	127.8
Costa Rican	77.0
Guatemalan	158.3
Honduran	139.2
Mexican	148.6
Puerto Rican	88.7
South American	109.1
Argentinean	110.5
Colombian	108.6
Uruguayan	112.4

Average Household Size

Group	People
Total Population	2.23
Hispanic or Latino (of any race)	4.16
Central American, ex. Mexican	4.11
Costa Rican	3.21
Guatemalan	5.17
Honduran	4.06
Mexican	4.59
Puerto Rican	2.43
South American	3.17
Argentinean	3.31
Colombian	2.90
Uruguayan	3.48

Median Age

Group	Years
Total Population	50.9
Hispanic or Latino (of any race)	26.8
Central American, ex. Mexican	27.5
Costa Rican	32.8
Guatemalan	25.7
Honduran	27.5
Mexican	25.7
Puerto Rican	35.0
South American	32.1
Argentinean	30.5
Colombian	37.5
Uruguayan	30.5

High School Graduates
(Universe: Population 25 Years and Over)

Group	Number	%
Total Population	26,146	91.8
Hispanic or Latino (of any race)	1,650	58.9
Mexican	952	52.5

Four-Year College Graduates
(Universe: Population 25 Years and Over)

Group	Number	%
Total Population	14,420	50.7
Hispanic or Latino (of any race)	323	11.5
Mexican	141	7.8

Population Age 3–17 Enrolled in Public School
(Universe: Population Age 3–17 Enrolled in School)

Group	Number	%
Total Population	3,502	75.9
Hispanic or Latino (of any race)	1,193	100.0
Mexican	749	100.0

Population Age 3–17 Enrolled in Private School
(Universe: Population Age 3–17 Enrolled in School)

Group	Number	%
Total Population	1,113	24.1
Hispanic or Latino (of any race)	0	0.0
Mexican	0	0.0

Foreign-Born Population

Group	Number	%
Total Population	5,503	15.0
Hispanic or Latino (of any race)	3,672	70.6
Mexican	2,538	73.1

Foreign-Born Naturalized U.S. Citizens

Group	Number	%
Total Population	1,314	23.9
Hispanic or Latino (of any race)	312	8.5
Mexican	162	6.4

Language Spoken at Home: English Only
(Universe: Population 5 Years and Over)

Group	Number	%
Total Population	28,655	81.9
Hispanic or Latino (of any race)	317	6.7
Mexican	145	4.8

Language Spoken at Home: Spanish
(Universe: Population 5 Years and Over)

Group	Number	%
Total Population	5,029	14.4
Hispanic or Latino (of any race)	4,371	92.5
Mexican	2,893	94.9

Unemployment Rate
(Universe: Population 16 Years and Over)

Group	%
Total Population	6.3
Hispanic or Latino (of any race)	8.0
Mexican	4.4

Class of Worker: Private Wage and Salary
(Universe: Civilian Employed Population 16 Years and Over)

Group	Number	%
Total Population	13,783	84.9
Hispanic or Latino (of any race)	2,354	87.9
Mexican	1,675	89.6

Class of Worker: Government
(Universe: Civilian Employed Population 16 Years and Over)

Group	Number	%
Total Population	1,063	6.5
Hispanic or Latino (of any race)	85	3.2
Mexican	38	2.0

Means of Transportation to Work: Car, Truck or Van
(Universe: Workers 16 Years and Over)

Group	Number	%
Total Population	14,097	88.9
Hispanic or Latino (of any race)	2,387	92.5
Mexican	1,669	91.8

Means of Transportation to Work: Public Transportation (ex. Taxicab)
(Universe: Workers 16 Years and Over)

Group	Number	%
Total Population	84	0.5
Hispanic or Latino (of any race)	19	0.7
Mexican	19	1.0

Notes: (1) Percent of total population; (2) Percent of Hispanic/Latino population; Profiles include places with an overall population of at least 125,000, OR an overall population of at least 25,000 where the Hispanic/Latino population is at least 20% of the overall population. In states where less than five places meet either of these criteria, we have included places with at least 10,000 total population with the highest percentage of Hispanic/Latino population. These places are identified with an asterisk (*); Please refer to the User's Guide for a full explanation of data.

Homeownership Rate
(Universe: Occupied Housing Units)

Group	%
Total Population	72.8
Hispanic or Latino (of any race)	20.0
Central American, ex. Mexican	13.6
Costa Rican	12.8
Guatemalan	13.8
Honduran	8.3
Mexican	17.4
Puerto Rican	42.9
South American	25.2
Argentinean	20.9
Colombian	38.8
Uruguayan	14.8

Median Home Value

Group	Dollars
Total Population	500,800
Hispanic or Latino (of any race)	431,600
Mexican	117,000

Median Gross Rent

Group	Dollars
Total Population	1,064
Hispanic or Latino (of any race)	945
Mexican	929

Median Household Income
(2010 Inflation-Adjusted Dollars)

Group	Dollars
Total Population	67,629
Hispanic or Latino (of any race)	42,795
Mexican	41,584

Per Capita Income
(2010 Inflation-Adjusted Dollars)

Group	Dollars
Total Population	45,195
Hispanic or Latino (of any race)	16,839
Mexican	12,621

Households with $100,000+ Income

Group	Number	%
Total Population	5,307	31.6
Hispanic or Latino (of any race)	157	10.7
Mexican	47	5.0

Households with Food Stamps/SNAP Benefits During Past 12 Months

Group	Number	%
Total Population	531	3.2
Hispanic or Latino (of any race)	116	7.9
Mexican	83	8.9

Poverty Rate
(Income in Past 12 Months Below Poverty Level)

Group	%
Total Population	8.9
Hispanic or Latino (of any race)	22.8
Mexican	25.3

Parker*

Population

Group	Number	%TP[1]	%HP[2]
Total Population	11,431	100.0	–
Hispanic or Latino (of any race)	2,373	20.8	100.0
Central American, ex. Mexican	436	3.8	18.4
Guatemalan	245	2.1	10.3
Honduran	101	0.9	4.3
Mexican	1,581	13.8	66.6
South American	154	1.3	6.5
Colombian	143	1.3	6.0

Population Growth: 2000–2010

Group	%
Total Population	6.2
Hispanic or Latino (of any race)	246.9
Mexican	308.5

Males per 100 Females

Group	Number
Total Population	99.4
Hispanic or Latino (of any race)	128.0
Central American, ex. Mexican	140.9
Guatemalan	133.3
Honduran	173.0
Mexican	134.2
South American	92.5
Colombian	88.2

Average Household Size

Group	People
Total Population	2.65
Hispanic or Latino (of any race)	4.12
Central American, ex. Mexican	4.55
Guatemalan	5.11
Honduran	4.04
Mexican	4.30
South American	3.03
Colombian	3.06

Median Age

Group	Years
Total Population	34.0
Hispanic or Latino (of any race)	24.3
Central American, ex. Mexican	26.3
Guatemalan	24.1
Honduran	28.2
Mexican	23.3
South American	37.5
Colombian	38.4

High School Graduates
(Universe: Population 25 Years and Over)

Group	Number	%
Total Population	3,853	58.5
Hispanic or Latino (of any race)	440	41.1
Mexican	304	39.2

Four-Year College Graduates
(Universe: Population 25 Years and Over)

Group	Number	%
Total Population	316	4.8
Hispanic or Latino (of any race)	45	4.2
Mexican	10	1.3

Population Age 3–17 Enrolled in Public School
(Universe: Population Age 3–17 Enrolled in School)

Group	Number	%
Total Population	1,557	100.0
Hispanic or Latino (of any race)	511	100.0
Mexican	312	100.0

Population Age 3–17 Enrolled in Private School
(Universe: Population Age 3–17 Enrolled in School)

Group	Number	%
Total Population	0	0.0
Hispanic or Latino (of any race)	0	0.0
Mexican	0	0.0

Foreign-Born Population

Group	Number	%
Total Population	1,485	14.4
Hispanic or Latino (of any race)	1,406	57.8
Mexican	994	55.4

Foreign-Born Naturalized U.S. Citizens

Group	Number	%
Total Population	122	8.2
Hispanic or Latino (of any race)	92	6.5
Mexican	42	4.2

Language Spoken at Home: English Only
(Universe: Population 5 Years and Over)

Group	Number	%
Total Population	7,035	74.5
Hispanic or Latino (of any race)	0	0.0
Mexican	0	0.0

Language Spoken at Home: Spanish
(Universe: Population 5 Years and Over)

Group	Number	%
Total Population	2,384	25.2
Hispanic or Latino (of any race)	2,076	100.0
Mexican	1,489	100.0

Unemployment Rate
(Universe: Population 16 Years and Over)

Group	%
Total Population	16.2
Hispanic or Latino (of any race)	11.9
Mexican	15.0

Class of Worker: Private Wage and Salary
(Universe: Civilian Employed Population 16 Years and Over)

Group	Number	%
Total Population	3,164	84.4
Hispanic or Latino (of any race)	844	88.7
Mexican	578	84.3

Class of Worker: Government
(Universe: Civilian Employed Population 16 Years and Over)

Group	Number	%
Total Population	302	8.1
Hispanic or Latino (of any race)	14	1.5
Mexican	14	2.0

Means of Transportation to Work: Car, Truck or Van
(Universe: Workers 16 Years and Over)

Group	Number	%
Total Population	3,365	92.0
Hispanic or Latino (of any race)	857	91.8
Mexican	645	95.7

Means of Transportation to Work: Public Transportation (ex. Taxicab)
(Universe: Workers 16 Years and Over)

Group	Number	%
Total Population	90	2.5
Hispanic or Latino (of any race)	0	0.0
Mexican	0	0.0

Homeownership Rate
(Universe: Occupied Housing Units)

Group	%
Total Population	52.7
Hispanic or Latino (of any race)	34.5
Central American, ex. Mexican	27.0
Guatemalan	21.8
Honduran	36.0
Mexican	29.3
South American	69.5
Colombian	69.8

Median Home Value

Group	Dollars
Total Population	68,000
Hispanic or Latino (of any race)	58,800
Mexican	19,500

Median Gross Rent

Group	Dollars
Total Population	656
Hispanic or Latino (of any race)	658
Mexican	671

Median Household Income
(2010 Inflation-Adjusted Dollars)

Group	Dollars
Total Population	22,650
Hispanic or Latino (of any race)	26,333
Mexican	26,521

Per Capita Income
(2010 Inflation-Adjusted Dollars)

Group	Dollars
Total Population	12,464
Hispanic or Latino (of any race)	7,427
Mexican	7,398

Households with $100,000+ Income

Group	Number	%
Total Population	81	2.0
Hispanic or Latino (of any race)	12	2.2
Mexican	12	3.0

Households with Food Stamps/SNAP Benefits During Past 12 Months

Group	Number	%
Total Population	715	18.0
Hispanic or Latino (of any race)	106	19.8

Notes: (1) Percent of total population; (2) Percent of Hispanic/Latino population; Profiles include places with an overall population of at least 125,000, OR an overall population of at least 25,000 where the Hispanic/Latino population is at least 20% of the overall population. In states where less than five places meet either of these criteria, we have included places with at least 10,000 total population with the highest percentage of Hispanic/Latino population. These places are identified with an asterisk (*); Please refer to the User's Guide for a full explanation of data.

Mexican	101	24.9

Poverty Rate
(Income in Past 12 Months Below Poverty Level)

Group	%
Total Population	38.1
Hispanic or Latino (of any race)	47.8
Mexican	46.7

Notes: (1) Percent of total population; (2) Percent of Hispanic/Latino population; Profiles include places with an overall population of at least 125,000, OR an overall population of at least 25,000 where the Hispanic/Latino population is at least 20% of the overall population. In states where less than five places meet either of these criteria, we have included places with at least 10,000 total population with the highest percentage of Hispanic/Latino population. These places are identified with an asterisk (*); Please refer to the User's Guide for a full explanation of data.

South Dakota

EDITOR'S NOTE: For a place to be included in this edition, it must meet one of two criteria. Either its overall population is at least 125,000, OR its overall population is at least 25,000 and its Hispanic/Latino population is at least 20% of the overall population. In South Dakota, less than five places meet either of these criteria. In an effort to include at least five places for each state, we have included places with at least 10,000 total population with the highest percentage of Hispanic/Latino population. These places are identified with an asterisk (*). For the state of South Dakota, the following locations are included:

Huron*
Rapid City*
Sioux Falls
Spearfish*
Yankton*

Section Two: State & Place Profiles starts with the state profile, followed by place profiles that meet the criteria above. Places are listed alphabetically within each state. All states, all counties and places that meet the above criteria are ranked and compared in *Section Three: Rankings & Comparisons*, on page 1055.

For a more detailed look at the Hispanic/Latino population in South Dakota, a companion web site is available at no additional charge with purchase of this print edition. Visit http://gold.greyhouse.com/page/info_hispanic for more information.

The web site includes data for all counties and places in South Dakota with Hispanic/Latino population, plus ten additional topics: Self Employed Worker; Walked to Work; Worked from Home; Mean Travel Time to Work; Mean Household Income; Households with Cash Public Assistance; Mean Cash Pubic Assistance; Poverty Rates for 18 and Under, 18 to 64, and 65 and Over.

Population

Group	Number	%TP[1]	%HP[2]
Total Population	814,180	100.0	–
Hispanic or Latino (of any race)	22,119	2.7	100.0
Central American, ex. Mexican	2,891	0.4	13.1
Guatemalan	1,620	0.2	7.3
Honduran	221	<0.1	1.0
Salvadoran	780	0.1	3.5
Cuban	265	<0.1	1.2
Mexican	13,839	1.7	62.6
Puerto Rican	1,483	0.2	6.7
South American	617	0.1	2.8
Colombian	186	<0.1	0.8
Peruvian	138	<0.1	0.6
Spaniard	496	0.1	2.2

Population Growth: 2000–2010

Group	%
Total Population	7.9
Hispanic or Latino (of any race)	102.9
Central American, ex. Mexican	282.4
Guatemalan	264.0
Salvadoran	642.9
Cuban	62.6
Mexican	117.5
Puerto Rican	132.8
South American	171.8

Males per 100 Females

Group	Number
Total Population	100.1
Hispanic or Latino (of any race)	117.9
Central American, ex. Mexican	121.7
Guatemalan	134.8
Honduran	104.6
Salvadoran	104.7
Cuban	126.5
Mexican	121.5
Puerto Rican	123.3
South American	90.4
Colombian	69.1
Peruvian	97.1
Spaniard	95.3

Average Household Size

Group	People
Total Population	2.42
Hispanic or Latino (of any race)	3.17
Central American, ex. Mexican	3.77
Guatemalan	3.95
Honduran	3.44
Salvadoran	3.69
Cuban	2.50
Mexican	3.22
Puerto Rican	2.62
South American	2.76
Colombian	2.32
Peruvian	2.77
Spaniard	2.55

Median Age

Group	Years
Total Population	36.9
Hispanic or Latino (of any race)	22.3
Central American, ex. Mexican	25.8
Guatemalan	24.7
Honduran	26.9
Salvadoran	28.3
Cuban	26.3
Mexican	21.1
Puerto Rican	21.4
South American	27.2
Colombian	26.4
Peruvian	32.0
Spaniard	31.0

High School Graduates
(Universe: Population 25 Years and Over)

Group	Number	%
Total Population	462,612	89.3
Hispanic or Latino (of any race)	6,428	69.0
Central American, ex. Mexican	507	41.1
Guatemalan	280	36.5
Mexican	4,277	69.7
Puerto Rican	530	89.7

Four-Year College Graduates
(Universe: Population 25 Years and Over)

Group	Number	%
Total Population	131,234	25.3
Hispanic or Latino (of any race)	1,378	14.8
Central American, ex. Mexican	25	2.0
Guatemalan	15	2.0
Mexican	826	13.5
Puerto Rican	174	29.4

Population Age 3–17 Enrolled in Public School
(Universe: Population Age 3–17 Enrolled in School)

Group	Number	%
Total Population	129,565	88.7
Hispanic or Latino (of any race)	5,416	96.5
Central American, ex. Mexican	624	99.8
Guatemalan	423	99.8
Mexican	3,719	97.5
Puerto Rican	333	92.8

Population Age 3–17 Enrolled in Private School
(Universe: Population Age 3–17 Enrolled in School)

Group	Number	%
Total Population	16,552	11.3
Hispanic or Latino (of any race)	198	3.5
Central American, ex. Mexican	1	0.2
Guatemalan	1	0.2
Mexican	95	2.5
Puerto Rican	26	7.2

Foreign-Born Population

Group	Number	%
Total Population	18,663	2.3
Hispanic or Latino (of any race)	5,255	25.7
Central American, ex. Mexican	1,643	63.5
Guatemalan	1,001	58.6
Mexican	3,035	22.4
Puerto Rican	0	0.0

Foreign-Born Naturalized U.S. Citizens

Group	Number	%
Total Population	7,414	39.7
Hispanic or Latino (of any race)	1,437	27.3
Central American, ex. Mexican	246	15.0
Guatemalan	84	8.4
Mexican	932	30.7
Puerto Rican	0	0.0

Language Spoken at Home: English Only
(Universe: Population 5 Years and Over)

Group	Number	%
Total Population	692,504	93.2
Hispanic or Latino (of any race)	8,284	47.4
Central American, ex. Mexican	222	10.1
Guatemalan	33	2.4
Mexican	5,720	48.7
Puerto Rican	722	66.5

Language Spoken at Home: Spanish
(Universe: Population 5 Years and Over)

Group	Number	%
Total Population	14,829	2.0
Hispanic or Latino (of any race)	9,008	51.6
Central American, ex. Mexican	1,979	89.8
Guatemalan	1,312	97.3
Mexican	5,889	50.1
Puerto Rican	363	33.5

Unemployment Rate
(Universe: Population 16 Years and Over)

Group	%
Total Population	4.7
Hispanic or Latino (of any race)	7.3
Central American, ex. Mexican	5.6
Guatemalan	7.7
Mexican	6.5
Puerto Rican	11.8

Class of Worker: Private Wage and Salary
(Universe: Civilian Employed Population 16 Years and Over)

Group	Number	%
Total Population	304,261	74.2
Hispanic or Latino (of any race)	7,001	85.5
Central American, ex. Mexican	1,203	98.5
Guatemalan	659	97.8
Mexican	4,824	87.3
Puerto Rican	282	59.7

Class of Worker: Government
(Universe: Civilian Employed Population 16 Years and Over)

Group	Number	%
Total Population	65,495	16.0
Hispanic or Latino (of any race)	1,048	12.8
Central American, ex. Mexican	18	1.5
Guatemalan	15	2.2
Mexican	617	11.2
Puerto Rican	174	36.9

Means of Transportation to Work: Car, Truck or Van
(Universe: Workers 16 Years and Over)

Group	Number	%
Total Population	354,635	87.5
Hispanic or Latino (of any race)	7,409	89.6
Central American, ex. Mexican	1,047	86.6
Guatemalan	539	82.5
Mexican	5,005	90.5
Puerto Rican	457	87.5

Notes: (1) Percent of total population; (2) Percent of Hispanic/Latino population; Profiles include places with an overall population of at least 125,000, OR an overall population of at least 25,000 where the Hispanic/Latino population is at least 20% of the overall population. In states where less than five places meet either of these criteria, we have included places with at least 10,000 total population with the highest percentage of Hispanic/Latino population. These places are identified with an asterisk (*); Please refer to the User's Guide for a full explanation of data.

Means of Transportation to Work: Public Transportation (ex. Taxicab)
(Universe: Workers 16 Years and Over)

Group	Number	%
Total Population	1,954	0.5
Hispanic or Latino (of any race)	23	0.3
Central American, ex. Mexican	0	0.0
Guatemalan	0	0.0
Mexican	23	0.4
Puerto Rican	0	0.0

Homeownership Rate
(Universe: Occupied Housing Units)

Group	%
Total Population	68.1
Hispanic or Latino (of any race)	41.0
Central American, ex. Mexican	39.3
Guatemalan	35.3
Honduran	38.6
Salvadoran	45.1
Cuban	46.1
Mexican	41.2
Puerto Rican	31.2
South American	46.2
Colombian	36.0
Peruvian	46.5
Spaniard	55.8

Median Home Value

Group	Dollars
Total Population	122,200
Hispanic or Latino (of any race)	100,100
Central American, ex. Mexican	130,200
Guatemalan	136,100
Mexican	89,500
Puerto Rican	59,300

Median Gross Rent

Group	Dollars
Total Population	574
Hispanic or Latino (of any race)	567
Central American, ex. Mexican	499
Guatemalan	547
Mexican	593
Puerto Rican	501

Median Household Income
(2010 Inflation-Adjusted Dollars)

Group	Dollars
Total Population	46,369
Hispanic or Latino (of any race)	36,290
Central American, ex. Mexican	38,393
Guatemalan	36,250
Mexican	37,064
Puerto Rican	27,109

Per Capita Income
(2010 Inflation-Adjusted Dollars)

Group	Dollars
Total Population	24,110
Hispanic or Latino (of any race)	11,907
Central American, ex. Mexican	10,708
Guatemalan	9,714
Mexican	11,696
Puerto Rican	12,138

Households with $100,000+ Income

Group	Number	%
Total Population	41,726	13.2
Hispanic or Latino (of any race)	246	4.9
Central American, ex. Mexican	0	0.0
Guatemalan	0	0.0
Mexican	170	5.0
Puerto Rican	30	8.3

Households with Food Stamps/SNAP Benefits During Past 12 Months

Group	Number	%
Total Population	26,885	8.5
Hispanic or Latino (of any race)	885	17.5
Central American, ex. Mexican	40	6.5
Guatemalan	29	8.4
Mexican	620	18.3
Puerto Rican	88	24.4

Poverty Rate
(Income in Past 12 Months Below Poverty Level)

Group	%
Total Population	13.7
Hispanic or Latino (of any race)	22.3
Central American, ex. Mexican	18.4
Guatemalan	18.1
Mexican	22.8
Puerto Rican	27.1

Huron*

Population

Group	Number	%TP[1]	%HP[2]
Total Population	12,592	100.0	–
Hispanic or Latino (of any race)	1,234	9.8	100.0
Central American, ex. Mexican	241	1.9	19.5
Guatemalan	172	1.4	13.9
Mexican	649	5.2	52.6
Puerto Rican	208	1.7	16.9

Population Growth: 2000–2010

Group	%
Total Population	5.9
Hispanic or Latino (of any race)	762.9

Males per 100 Females

Group	Number
Total Population	97.8
Hispanic or Latino (of any race)	127.3
Central American, ex. Mexican	117.1
Guatemalan	112.3
Mexican	126.9
Puerto Rican	160.0

Average Household Size

Group	People
Total Population	2.27
Hispanic or Latino (of any race)	2.95
Central American, ex. Mexican	3.38
Guatemalan	3.24
Mexican	3.09
Puerto Rican	2.45

Median Age

Group	Years
Total Population	39.8
Hispanic or Latino (of any race)	24.2
Central American, ex. Mexican	27.7
Guatemalan	26.3
Mexican	22.8
Puerto Rican	22.8

High School Graduates
(Universe: Population 25 Years and Over)

Group	Number	%
Total Population	6,763	82.8

Four-Year College Graduates
(Universe: Population 25 Years and Over)

Group	Number	%
Total Population	1,661	20.3

Population Age 3–17 Enrolled in Public School
(Universe: Population Age 3–17 Enrolled in School)

Group	Number	%
Total Population	1,668	84.1

Population Age 3–17 Enrolled in Private School
(Universe: Population Age 3–17 Enrolled in School)

Group	Number	%
Total Population	316	15.9

Foreign-Born Population

Group	Number	%
Total Population	692	5.7

Foreign-Born Naturalized U.S. Citizens

Group	Number	%
Total Population	114	16.5

Language Spoken at Home: English Only
(Universe: Population 5 Years and Over)

Group	Number	%
Total Population	10,408	92.2

Language Spoken at Home: Spanish
(Universe: Population 5 Years and Over)

Group	Number	%
Total Population	668	5.9

Unemployment Rate
(Universe: Population 16 Years and Over)

Group	%
Total Population	4.6

Class of Worker: Private Wage and Salary
(Universe: Civilian Employed Population 16 Years and Over)

Group	Number	%
Total Population	4,881	78.1

Class of Worker: Government
(Universe: Civilian Employed Population 16 Years and Over)

Group	Number	%
Total Population	1,009	16.1

Means of Transportation to Work: Car, Truck or Van
(Universe: Workers 16 Years and Over)

Group	Number	%
Total Population	5,672	92.0

Means of Transportation to Work: Public Transportation (ex. Taxicab)
(Universe: Workers 16 Years and Over)

Group	Number	%
Total Population	43	0.7

Homeownership Rate
(Universe: Occupied Housing Units)

Group	%
Total Population	59.9
Hispanic or Latino (of any race)	18.1
Central American, ex. Mexican	12.1
Guatemalan	13.0
Mexican	19.0
Puerto Rican	13.1

Median Home Value

Group	Dollars
Total Population	79,800

Median Gross Rent

Group	Dollars
Total Population	441

Median Household Income
(2010 Inflation-Adjusted Dollars)

Group	Dollars
Total Population	38,474

Per Capita Income
(2010 Inflation-Adjusted Dollars)

Group	Dollars
Total Population	22,379

Households with $100,000+ Income

Group	Number	%
Total Population	459	8.6

Households with Food Stamps/SNAP Benefits During Past 12 Months

Group	Number	%
Total Population	503	9.5

Poverty Rate
(Income in Past 12 Months Below Poverty Level)

Group	%
Total Population	15.5

Rapid City*

Population

Group	Number	%TP[1]	%HP[2]
Total Population	67,956	100.0	–
Hispanic or Latino (of any race)	2,816	4.1	100.0

STATE & PLACE PROFILES

Notes: (1) Percent of total population; (2) Percent of Hispanic/Latino population; Profiles include places with an overall population of at least 125,000, OR an overall population of at least 25,000 where the Hispanic/Latino population is at least 20% of the overall population. In states where less than five places meet either of these criteria, we have included places with at least 10,000 total population with the highest percentage of Hispanic/Latino population. These places are identified with an asterisk (*); Please refer to the User's Guide for a full explanation of data.

Mexican	1,949	2.9	69.2
Puerto Rican	234	0.3	8.3
Spaniard	123	0.2	4.4

Population Growth: 2000–2010

Group	%
Total Population	14.0
Hispanic or Latino (of any race)	70.7
Mexican	90.9
Puerto Rican	80.0

Males per 100 Females

Group	Number
Total Population	97.8
Hispanic or Latino (of any race)	102.7
Mexican	109.3
Puerto Rican	114.7
Spaniard	92.2

Average Household Size

Group	People
Total Population	2.29
Hispanic or Latino (of any race)	2.73
Mexican	2.78
Puerto Rican	2.43
Spaniard	2.52

Median Age

Group	Years
Total Population	35.6
Hispanic or Latino (of any race)	20.8
Mexican	19.9
Puerto Rican	22.1
Spaniard	28.2

High School Graduates
(Universe: Population 25 Years and Over)

Group	Number	%
Total Population	39,460	91.8
Hispanic or Latino (of any race)	938	77.7
Mexican	691	76.2

Four-Year College Graduates
(Universe: Population 25 Years and Over)

Group	Number	%
Total Population	12,778	29.7
Hispanic or Latino (of any race)	252	20.9
Mexican	164	18.1

Population Age 3–17 Enrolled in Public School
(Universe: Population Age 3–17 Enrolled in School)

Group	Number	%
Total Population	9,642	85.9
Hispanic or Latino (of any race)	571	88.8
Mexican	512	98.5

Population Age 3–17 Enrolled in Private School
(Universe: Population Age 3–17 Enrolled in School)

Group	Number	%
Total Population	1,589	14.1
Hispanic or Latino (of any race)	72	11.2
Mexican	8	1.5

Foreign-Born Population

Group	Number	%
Total Population	1,577	2.4
Hispanic or Latino (of any race)	237	8.7
Mexican	168	8.0

Foreign-Born Naturalized U.S. Citizens

Group	Number	%
Total Population	765	48.5
Hispanic or Latino (of any race)	125	52.7
Mexican	72	42.9

Language Spoken at Home: English Only
(Universe: Population 5 Years and Over)

Group	Number	%
Total Population	57,545	94.1
Hispanic or Latino (of any race)	1,557	70.7
Mexican	1,190	70.1

Language Spoken at Home: Spanish
(Universe: Population 5 Years and Over)

Group	Number	%
Total Population	999	1.6
Hispanic or Latino (of any race)	553	25.1
Mexican	444	26.2

Unemployment Rate
(Universe: Population 16 Years and Over)

Group	%
Total Population	7.1
Hispanic or Latino (of any race)	13.6
Mexican	16.2

Class of Worker: Private Wage and Salary
(Universe: Civilian Employed Population 16 Years and Over)

Group	Number	%
Total Population	25,880	79.0
Hispanic or Latino (of any race)	771	85.6
Mexican	590	90.1

Class of Worker: Government
(Universe: Civilian Employed Population 16 Years and Over)

Group	Number	%
Total Population	4,907	15.0
Hispanic or Latino (of any race)	100	11.1
Mexican	35	5.3

Means of Transportation to Work: Car, Truck or Van
(Universe: Workers 16 Years and Over)

Group	Number	%
Total Population	29,774	91.1
Hispanic or Latino (of any race)	841	90.3
Mexican	600	90.1

Means of Transportation to Work: Public Transportation (ex. Taxicab)
(Universe: Workers 16 Years and Over)

Group	Number	%
Total Population	391	1.2
Hispanic or Latino (of any race)	15	1.6
Mexican	15	2.3

Homeownership Rate
(Universe: Occupied Housing Units)

Group	%
Total Population	57.5
Hispanic or Latino (of any race)	38.2
Mexican	38.9
Puerto Rican	39.8
Spaniard	40.7

Median Home Value

Group	Dollars
Total Population	147,200
Hispanic or Latino (of any race)	119,300
Mexican	119,200

Median Gross Rent

Group	Dollars
Total Population	668
Hispanic or Latino (of any race)	646
Mexican	931

Median Household Income
(2010 Inflation-Adjusted Dollars)

Group	Dollars
Total Population	44,099
Hispanic or Latino (of any race)	26,832
Mexican	23,848

Per Capita Income
(2010 Inflation-Adjusted Dollars)

Group	Dollars
Total Population	25,681
Hispanic or Latino (of any race)	11,315
Mexican	9,433

Households with $100,000+ Income

Group	Number	%
Total Population	3,688	13.3
Hispanic or Latino (of any race)	42	5.5
Mexican	42	7.1

Households with Food Stamps/SNAP Benefits During Past 12 Months

Group	Number	%
Total Population	3,925	14.2
Hispanic or Latino (of any race)	296	39.0
Mexican	242	40.7

Poverty Rate
(Income in Past 12 Months Below Poverty Level)

Group	%
Total Population	16.3
Hispanic or Latino (of any race)	33.6
Mexican	40.8

Sioux Falls

Population

Group	Number	%TP[1]	%HP[2]
Total Population	153,888	100.0	–
Hispanic or Latino (of any race)	6,827	4.4	100.0
Central American, ex. Mexican	1,903	1.2	27.9
Guatemalan	1,063	0.7	15.6
Honduran	119	0.1	1.7
Salvadoran	608	0.4	8.9
Mexican	3,452	2.2	50.6
Puerto Rican	330	0.2	4.8
South American	169	0.1	2.5
Spaniard	107	0.1	1.6

Population Growth: 2000–2010

Group	%
Total Population	24.1
Hispanic or Latino (of any race)	121.2
Central American, ex. Mexican	235.6
Guatemalan	174.7
Mexican	121.7
Puerto Rican	164.0

Males per 100 Females

Group	Number
Total Population	98.3
Hispanic or Latino (of any race)	116.5
Central American, ex. Mexican	119.2
Guatemalan	132.1
Honduran	112.5
Salvadoran	104.0
Mexican	116.3
Puerto Rican	120.0
South American	103.6
Spaniard	105.8

Average Household Size

Group	People
Total Population	2.40
Hispanic or Latino (of any race)	3.46
Central American, ex. Mexican	3.98
Guatemalan	4.16
Honduran	3.64
Salvadoran	3.78
Mexican	3.45
Puerto Rican	2.72
South American	2.83
Spaniard	2.80

Median Age

Group	Years
Total Population	33.6
Hispanic or Latino (of any race)	23.0
Central American, ex. Mexican	26.7
Guatemalan	25.0
Honduran	28.5
Salvadoran	29.0
Mexican	21.2
Puerto Rican	21.6
South American	31.1
Spaniard	33.5

High School Graduates
(Universe: Population 25 Years and Over)

Group	Number	%
Total Population	87,150	90.9
Hispanic or Latino (of any race)	1,634	53.5
Central American, ex. Mexican	330	36.3
Guatemalan	232	34.3
Mexican	918	57.0

Notes: (1) Percent of total population; (2) Percent of Hispanic/Latino population; Profiles include places with an overall population of at least 125,000, OR an overall population of at least 25,000 where the Hispanic/Latino population is at least 20% of the overall population. In states where less than five places meet either of these criteria, we have included places with at least 10,000 total population with the highest percentage of Hispanic/Latino population. These places are identified with an asterisk (*); Please refer to the User's Guide for a full explanation of data.

Four-Year College Graduates (Universe: Population 25 Years and Over)		
Group	Number	%
Total Population	30,571	31.9
Hispanic or Latino (of any race)	201	6.6
Central American, ex. Mexican	0	0.0
Guatemalan	0	0.0
Mexican	83	5.2

Population Age 3–17 Enrolled in Public School (Universe: Population Age 3–17 Enrolled in School)		
Group	Number	%
Total Population	21,360	84.7
Hispanic or Latino (of any race)	1,705	96.8
Central American, ex. Mexican	494	100.0
Guatemalan	399	100.0
Mexican	949	96.2

Population Age 3–17 Enrolled in Private School (Universe: Population Age 3–17 Enrolled in School)		
Group	Number	%
Total Population	3,852	15.3
Hispanic or Latino (of any race)	57	3.2
Central American, ex. Mexican	0	0.0
Guatemalan	0	0.0
Mexican	37	3.8

Foreign-Born Population		
Group	Number	%
Total Population	9,132	6.1
Hispanic or Latino (of any race)	2,682	41.0
Central American, ex. Mexican	1,236	64.2
Guatemalan	867	57.6
Mexican	1,126	32.5

Foreign-Born Naturalized U.S. Citizens		
Group	Number	%
Total Population	3,348	36.7
Hispanic or Latino (of any race)	778	29.0
Central American, ex. Mexican	147	11.9
Guatemalan	48	5.5
Mexican	509	45.2

Language Spoken at Home: English Only (Universe: Population 5 Years and Over)		
Group	Number	%
Total Population	123,415	90.1
Hispanic or Latino (of any race)	1,267	22.7
Central American, ex. Mexican	22	1.4
Guatemalan	0	0.0
Mexican	753	24.9

Language Spoken at Home: Spanish (Universe: Population 5 Years and Over)		
Group	Number	%
Total Population	5,476	4.0
Hispanic or Latino (of any race)	4,311	77.2
Central American, ex. Mexican	1,581	98.6
Guatemalan	1,189	100.0
Mexican	2,271	75.0

Unemployment Rate (Universe: Population 16 Years and Over)	
Group	%
Total Population	4.2
Hispanic or Latino (of any race)	7.6
Central American, ex. Mexican	6.3
Guatemalan	8.2
Mexican	7.1

Class of Worker: Private Wage and Salary (Universe: Civilian Employed Population 16 Years and Over)		
Group	Number	%
Total Population	72,153	86.8
Hispanic or Latino (of any race)	2,669	96.1
Central American, ex. Mexican	832	98.2
Guatemalan	557	97.4
Mexican	1,513	99.0

Class of Worker: Government (Universe: Civilian Employed Population 16 Years and Over)		
Group	Number	%
Total Population	6,959	8.4
Hispanic or Latino (of any race)	71	2.6
Central American, ex. Mexican	15	1.8
Guatemalan	15	2.6
Mexican	0	0.0

Means of Transportation to Work: Car, Truck or Van (Universe: Workers 16 Years and Over)		
Group	Number	%
Total Population	75,823	92.5
Hispanic or Latino (of any race)	2,521	92.8
Central American, ex. Mexican	732	88.6
Guatemalan	480	87.1
Mexican	1,452	97.4

Means of Transportation to Work: Public Transportation (ex. Taxicab) (Universe: Workers 16 Years and Over)		
Group	Number	%
Total Population	705	0.9
Hispanic or Latino (of any race)	0	0.0
Central American, ex. Mexican	0	0.0
Guatemalan	0	0.0
Mexican	0	0.0

Homeownership Rate (Universe: Occupied Housing Units)	
Group	%
Total Population	62.4
Hispanic or Latino (of any race)	42.8
Central American, ex. Mexican	45.9
Guatemalan	42.1
Honduran	48.5
Salvadoran	49.4
Mexican	43.0
Puerto Rican	23.5
South American	43.1
Spaniard	56.1

Median Home Value	
Group	Dollars
Total Population	146,500
Hispanic or Latino (of any race)	128,200
Central American, ex. Mexican	129,300
Guatemalan	136,100
Mexican	110,800

Median Gross Rent	
Group	Dollars
Total Population	669
Hispanic or Latino (of any race)	613
Central American, ex. Mexican	530
Guatemalan	572
Mexican	728

Median Household Income (2010 Inflation-Adjusted Dollars)	
Group	Dollars
Total Population	50,727
Hispanic or Latino (of any race)	41,035
Central American, ex. Mexican	42,008
Guatemalan	39,643
Mexican	45,767

Per Capita Income (2010 Inflation-Adjusted Dollars)	
Group	Dollars
Total Population	27,639
Hispanic or Latino (of any race)	11,967
Central American, ex. Mexican	11,585
Guatemalan	10,060
Mexican	11,955

Households with $100,000+ Income		
Group	Number	%
Total Population	9,508	15.9
Hispanic or Latino (of any race)	41	2.6
Central American, ex. Mexican	0	0.0
Guatemalan	0	0.0
Mexican	14	1.8

Households with Food Stamps/SNAP Benefits During Past 12 Months		
Group	Number	%
Total Population	5,097	8.5
Hispanic or Latino (of any race)	210	13.4
Central American, ex. Mexican	29	6.6
Guatemalan	29	9.3
Mexican	132	17.0

Poverty Rate (Income in Past 12 Months Below Poverty Level)	
Group	%
Total Population	10.2
Hispanic or Latino (of any race)	14.6
Central American, ex. Mexican	15.5
Guatemalan	16.9
Mexican	13.4

Spearfish*

Population			
Group	Number	%TP[1]	%HP[2]
Total Population	10,494	100.0	–
Hispanic or Latino (of any race)	287	2.7	100.0
Mexican	209	2.0	72.8

Population Growth: 2000–2010	
Group	%
Total Population	21.9
Hispanic or Latino (of any race)	92.6

Males per 100 Females	
Group	Number
Total Population	88.9
Hispanic or Latino (of any race)	109.5
Mexican	124.7

Average Household Size	
Group	People
Total Population	2.09
Hispanic or Latino (of any race)	2.44
Mexican	2.52

Median Age	
Group	Years
Total Population	33.2
Hispanic or Latino (of any race)	23.2
Mexican	23.1

High School Graduates (Universe: Population 25 Years and Over)		
Group	Number	%
Total Population	5,834	93.1

Four-Year College Graduates (Universe: Population 25 Years and Over)		
Group	Number	%
Total Population	2,238	35.7

Population Age 3–17 Enrolled in Public School (Universe: Population Age 3–17 Enrolled in School)		
Group	Number	%
Total Population	1,265	93.3

Population Age 3–17 Enrolled in Private School (Universe: Population Age 3–17 Enrolled in School)		
Group	Number	%
Total Population	91	6.7

Foreign-Born Population		
Group	Number	%
Total Population	154	1.5

Foreign-Born Naturalized U.S. Citizens		
Group	Number	%
Total Population	115	74.7

Language Spoken at Home: English Only (Universe: Population 5 Years and Over)		
Group	Number	%
Total Population	9,271	97.3

Language Spoken at Home: Spanish (Universe: Population 5 Years and Over)		
Group	Number	%
Total Population	64	0.7

Unemployment Rate (Universe: Population 16 Years and Over)	
Group	%
Total Population	4.8

Notes: (1) Percent of total population; (2) Percent of Hispanic/Latino population; Profiles include places with an overall population of at least 125,000, OR an overall population of at least 25,000 where the Hispanic/Latino population is at least 20% of the overall population. In states where less than five places meet either of these criteria, we have included places with at least 10,000 total population with the highest percentage of Hispanic/Latino population. These places are identified with an asterisk (*); Please refer to the User's Guide for a full explanation of data.

STATE & PLACE PROFILES

Class of Worker: Private Wage and Salary
(Universe: Civilian Employed Population 16 Years and Over)

Group	Number	%
Total Population	3,903	72.8

Class of Worker: Government
(Universe: Civilian Employed Population 16 Years and Over)

Group	Number	%
Total Population	1,116	20.8

Means of Transportation to Work: Car, Truck or Van
(Universe: Workers 16 Years and Over)

Group	Number	%
Total Population	4,541	86.9

Means of Transportation to Work: Public Transportation (ex. Taxicab)
(Universe: Workers 16 Years and Over)

Group	Number	%
Total Population	33	0.6

Homeownership Rate
(Universe: Occupied Housing Units)

Group	%
Total Population	50.8
Hispanic or Latino (of any race)	38.6
Mexican	40.0

Median Home Value

Group	Dollars
Total Population	161,800

Median Gross Rent

Group	Dollars
Total Population	526

Median Household Income
(2010 Inflation-Adjusted Dollars)

Group	Dollars
Total Population	33,713

Per Capita Income
(2010 Inflation-Adjusted Dollars)

Group	Dollars
Total Population	25,354

Households with $100,000+ Income

Group	Number	%
Total Population	553	11.2

Households with Food Stamps/SNAP Benefits During Past 12 Months

Group	Number	%
Total Population	446	9.0

Poverty Rate
(Income in Past 12 Months Below Poverty Level)

Group	%
Total Population	15.2

Yankton*

Population

Group	Number	%TP[1]	%HP[2]
Total Population	14,454	100.0	–
Hispanic or Latino (of any race)	494	3.4	100.0
Mexican	378	2.6	76.5

Population Growth: 2000–2010

Group	%
Total Population	6.8
Hispanic or Latino (of any race)	48.3
Mexican	50.0

Males per 100 Females

Group	Number
Total Population	102.0
Hispanic or Latino (of any race)	195.8
Mexican	204.8

Average Household Size

Group	People
Total Population	2.17
Hispanic or Latino (of any race)	2.67
Mexican	3.00

Median Age

Group	Years
Total Population	40.4
Hispanic or Latino (of any race)	27.7
Mexican	27.1

High School Graduates
(Universe: Population 25 Years and Over)

Group	Number	%
Total Population	8,768	87.8

Four-Year College Graduates
(Universe: Population 25 Years and Over)

Group	Number	%
Total Population	2,907	29.1

Population Age 3–17 Enrolled in Public School
(Universe: Population Age 3–17 Enrolled in School)

Group	Number	%
Total Population	1,734	83.3

Population Age 3–17 Enrolled in Private School
(Universe: Population Age 3–17 Enrolled in School)

Group	Number	%
Total Population	348	16.7

Foreign-Born Population

Group	Number	%
Total Population	374	2.6

Foreign-Born Naturalized U.S. Citizens

Group	Number	%
Total Population	88	23.5

Language Spoken at Home: English Only
(Universe: Population 5 Years and Over)

Group	Number	%
Total Population	12,341	91.9

Language Spoken at Home: Spanish
(Universe: Population 5 Years and Over)

Group	Number	%
Total Population	491	3.7

Unemployment Rate
(Universe: Population 16 Years and Over)

Group	%
Total Population	2.8

Class of Worker: Private Wage and Salary
(Universe: Civilian Employed Population 16 Years and Over)

Group	Number	%
Total Population	5,726	80.8

Class of Worker: Government
(Universe: Civilian Employed Population 16 Years and Over)

Group	Number	%
Total Population	927	13.1

Means of Transportation to Work: Car, Truck or Van
(Universe: Workers 16 Years and Over)

Group	Number	%
Total Population	6,170	88.4

Means of Transportation to Work: Public Transportation (ex. Taxicab)
(Universe: Workers 16 Years and Over)

Group	Number	%
Total Population	36	0.5

Homeownership Rate
(Universe: Occupied Housing Units)

Group	%
Total Population	61.9
Hispanic or Latino (of any race)	38.4
Mexican	39.1

Median Home Value

Group	Dollars
Total Population	116,700

Median Gross Rent

Group	Dollars
Total Population	504

Median Household Income
(2010 Inflation-Adjusted Dollars)

Group	Dollars
Total Population	42,956

Per Capita Income
(2010 Inflation-Adjusted Dollars)

Group	Dollars
Total Population	25,312

Households with $100,000+ Income

Group	Number	%
Total Population	754	13.2

Households with Food Stamps/SNAP Benefits During Past 12 Months

Group	Number	%
Total Population	519	9.1

Poverty Rate
(Income in Past 12 Months Below Poverty Level)

Group	%
Total Population	12.8

Notes: (1) Percent of total population; (2) Percent of Hispanic/Latino population; Profiles include places with an overall population of at least 125,000, OR an overall population of at least 25,000 where the Hispanic/Latino population is at least 20% of the overall population. In states where less than five places meet either of these criteria, we have included places with at least 10,000 total population with the highest percentage of Hispanic/Latino population. These places are identified with an asterisk (*); Please refer to the User's Guide for a full explanation of data.

Tennessee

EDITOR'S NOTE: For a place to be included in this edition, it must meet one of two criteria. Either its overall population is at least 125,000, OR its overall population is at least 25,000 and its Hispanic/Latino population is at least 20% of the overall population. For the state of Tennessee, the following locations are included:

- Chattanooga
- Clarksville
- Knoxville
- Memphis
- Nashville-Davidson

Section Two: State & Place Profiles starts with the state profile, followed by place profiles that meet the criteria above. Places are listed alphabetically within each state. All states, all counties and places that meet the above criteria are ranked and compared in *Section Three: Rankings & Comparisons*, on page 1055.

For a more detailed look at the Hispanic/Latino population in Tennessee, a companion web site is available at no additional charge with purchase of this print edition. Visit http://gold.greyhouse.com/page/info_hispanic for more information.

The web site includes data for all counties and places in Tennessee with Hispanic/Latino population, plus ten additional topics: Self Employed Worker; Walked to Work; Worked from Home; Mean Travel Time to Work; Mean Household Income; Households with Cash Public Assistance; Mean Cash Pubic Assistance; Poverty Rates for 18 and Under, 18 to 64, and 65 and Over.

Population

Group	Number	%TP[1]	%HP[2]
Total Population	6,346,105	100.0	–
Hispanic or Latino (of any race)	290,059	4.6	100.0
Central American, ex. Mexican	36,856	0.6	12.7
Costa Rican	1,045	<0.1	0.4
Guatemalan	14,323	0.2	4.9
Honduran	9,455	0.1	3.3
Nicaraguan	1,339	<0.1	0.5
Panamanian	1,915	<0.1	0.7
Salvadoran	8,570	0.1	3.0
Cuban	7,773	0.1	2.7
Dominican Republic	2,113	<0.1	0.7
Mexican	186,615	2.9	64.3
Puerto Rican	21,060	0.3	7.3
South American	11,039	0.2	3.8
Argentinean	1,028	<0.1	0.4
Bolivian	351	<0.1	0.1
Chilean	774	<0.1	0.3
Colombian	3,695	0.1	1.3
Ecuadorian	1,151	<0.1	0.4
Paraguayan	108	<0.1	<0.1
Peruvian	1,918	<0.1	0.7
Uruguayan	214	<0.1	0.1
Venezuelan	1,667	<0.1	0.6
Spaniard	3,239	0.1	1.1

Population Growth: 2000–2010

Group	%
Total Population	11.5
Hispanic or Latino (of any race)	134.2
Central American, ex. Mexican	379.0
Costa Rican	150.6
Guatemalan	408.6
Honduran	553.0
Nicaraguan	381.7
Panamanian	121.9
Salvadoran	459.4
Cuban	110.4
Dominican Republic	300.9
Mexican	141.2
Puerto Rican	104.4
South American	218.2
Argentinean	293.9
Bolivian	165.9
Chilean	135.3
Colombian	208.4
Ecuadorian	351.4
Peruvian	318.8
Venezuelan	190.9
Spaniard	699.8

Males per 100 Females

Group	Number
Total Population	95.1
Hispanic or Latino (of any race)	120.1
Central American, ex. Mexican	128.4
Costa Rican	90.7
Guatemalan	151.1
Honduran	133.2
Nicaraguan	102.9
Panamanian	64.7
Salvadoran	118.8
Cuban	103.8
Dominican Republic	91.4
Mexican	126.5
Puerto Rican	98.4
South American	85.9
Argentinean	91.1
Bolivian	90.8
Chilean	84.3
Colombian	76.8
Ecuadorian	86.2
Paraguayan	71.4
Peruvian	89.5
Uruguayan	94.5
Venezuelan	100.6
Spaniard	87.9

Average Household Size

Group	People
Total Population	2.48
Hispanic or Latino (of any race)	3.63
Central American, ex. Mexican	4.09
Costa Rican	3.17
Guatemalan	4.55
Honduran	3.93
Nicaraguan	3.33
Panamanian	2.91
Salvadoran	4.15
Cuban	2.79
Dominican Republic	3.18
Mexican	3.87
Puerto Rican	2.87
South American	2.88
Argentinean	2.82
Bolivian	2.89
Chilean	2.72
Colombian	2.79
Ecuadorian	3.26
Paraguayan	3.36
Peruvian	2.98
Uruguayan	2.96
Venezuelan	2.79
Spaniard	2.63

Median Age

Group	Years
Total Population	38.0
Hispanic or Latino (of any race)	24.7
Central American, ex. Mexican	27.1
Costa Rican	30.5
Guatemalan	25.4
Honduran	27.9
Nicaraguan	29.4
Panamanian	30.5
Salvadoran	28.8
Cuban	32.1
Dominican Republic	26.4
Mexican	23.5
Puerto Rican	25.3
South American	32.4
Argentinean	34.1
Bolivian	28.9
Chilean	33.2
Colombian	32.4
Ecuadorian	30.0
Paraguayan	21.0
Peruvian	34.5
Uruguayan	35.2
Venezuelan	31.2
Spaniard	32.4

High School Graduates

(Universe: Population 25 Years and Over)

Group	Number	%
Total Population	3,428,302	82.5
Hispanic or Latino (of any race)	73,532	56.9
Central American, ex. Mexican	9,560	49.0
Costa Rican	386	85.4
Guatemalan	2,729	42.1
Honduran	2,615	46.1
Nicaraguan	453	83.0
Panamanian	905	88.6
Salvadoran	2,409	46.1
Cuban	3,115	80.6
Dominican Republic	753	87.3
Mexican	40,194	49.4
Puerto Rican	8,492	85.8
South American	5,793	85.1
Argentinean	598	94.5
Chilean	449	87.4
Colombian	1,625	78.9
Ecuadorian	527	81.3
Peruvian	1,122	89.2
Venezuelan	974	91.3
Spaniard	1,664	94.5

Four-Year College Graduates

(Universe: Population 25 Years and Over)

Group	Number	%
Total Population	943,001	22.7
Hispanic or Latino (of any race)	15,536	12.0
Central American, ex. Mexican	1,298	6.6
Costa Rican	111	24.6
Guatemalan	281	4.3
Honduran	180	3.2
Nicaraguan	102	18.7
Panamanian	221	21.6
Salvadoran	403	7.7
Cuban	1,250	32.4
Dominican Republic	455	52.7
Mexican	5,787	7.1
Puerto Rican	2,271	23.0
South American	2,876	42.2
Argentinean	359	56.7
Chilean	231	44.9
Colombian	601	29.2
Ecuadorian	219	33.8
Peruvian	681	54.1
Venezuelan	497	46.6
Spaniard	626	35.5

Population Age 3–17 Enrolled in Public School

(Universe: Population Age 3–17 Enrolled in School)

Group	Number	%
Total Population	955,345	86.1
Hispanic or Latino (of any race)	54,138	91.6
Central American, ex. Mexican	6,506	93.7
Costa Rican	212	66.5
Guatemalan	1,642	93.9
Honduran	1,687	96.3
Nicaraguan	183	83.9
Panamanian	302	71.2
Salvadoran	2,429	100.0
Cuban	1,322	92.3
Dominican Republic	285	66.4
Mexican	36,934	94.0
Puerto Rican	3,968	82.5
South American	1,754	75.9
Argentinean	176	100.0
Chilean	22	20.8
Colombian	761	76.2

Notes: (1) Percent of total population; (2) Percent of Hispanic/Latino population; Profiles include places with an overall population of at least 125,000, OR an overall population of at least 25,000 where the Hispanic/Latino population is at least 20% of the overall population. In states where less than five places meet either of these criteria, we have included places with at least 10,000 total population with the highest percentage of Hispanic/Latino population. These places are identified with an asterisk (*); Please refer to the User's Guide for a full explanation of data.

Ecuadorian	191	92.7
Peruvian	170	69.4
Venezuelan	299	87.2
Spaniard	526	84.8

Population Age 3–17 Enrolled in Private School
(Universe: Population Age 3–17 Enrolled in School)

Group	Number	%
Total Population	154,357	13.9
Hispanic or Latino (of any race)	4,952	8.4
Central American, ex. Mexican	435	6.3
Costa Rican	107	33.5
Guatemalan	106	6.1
Honduran	65	3.7
Nicaraguan	35	16.1
Panamanian	122	28.8
Salvadoran	0	0.0
Cuban	111	7.7
Dominican Republic	144	33.6
Mexican	2,355	6.0
Puerto Rican	839	17.5
South American	558	24.1
Argentinean	0	0.0
Chilean	84	79.2
Colombian	238	23.8
Ecuadorian	15	7.3
Peruvian	75	30.6
Venezuelan	44	12.8
Spaniard	94	15.2

Foreign-Born Population

Group	Number	%
Total Population	273,300	4.4
Hispanic or Latino (of any race)	128,895	49.3
Central American, ex. Mexican	25,117	68.8
Costa Rican	449	45.8
Guatemalan	9,245	74.6
Honduran	7,210	71.6
Nicaraguan	614	66.7
Panamanian	593	33.0
Salvadoran	6,852	67.6
Cuban	2,518	38.2
Dominican Republic	711	37.7
Mexican	90,949	52.7
Puerto Rican	165	0.9
South American	7,203	65.4
Argentinean	768	82.5
Chilean	440	56.6
Colombian	1,877	54.8
Ecuadorian	675	64.7
Peruvian	1,199	59.7
Venezuelan	1,362	78.0
Spaniard	370	12.3

Foreign-Born Naturalized U.S. Citizens

Group	Number	%
Total Population	84,812	31.0
Hispanic or Latino (of any race)	17,421	13.5
Central American, ex. Mexican	3,640	14.5
Costa Rican	180	40.1
Guatemalan	1,166	12.6
Honduran	852	11.8
Nicaraguan	230	37.5
Panamanian	346	58.3
Salvadoran	784	11.4
Cuban	1,271	50.5
Dominican Republic	444	62.4
Mexican	8,877	9.8
Puerto Rican	54	32.7
South American	2,479	34.4
Argentinean	222	28.9
Chilean	220	50.0
Colombian	755	40.2
Ecuadorian	273	40.4
Peruvian	504	42.0
Venezuelan	301	22.1
Spaniard	106	28.6

Language Spoken at Home: English Only
(Universe: Population 5 Years and Over)

Group	Number	%
Total Population	5,469,277	93.8
Hispanic or Latino (of any race)	56,176	25.0
Central American, ex. Mexican	4,159	12.9
Costa Rican	299	33.0
Guatemalan	992	9.3
Honduran	1,249	13.8
Nicaraguan	166	19.5
Panamanian	814	47.6
Salvadoran	620	7.1
Cuban	2,510	41.2
Dominican Republic	599	36.1
Mexican	30,861	21.2
Puerto Rican	8,382	48.8
South American	2,325	22.7
Argentinean	121	13.2
Chilean	208	30.1
Colombian	866	26.5
Ecuadorian	88	9.7
Peruvian	617	33.8
Venezuelan	215	13.7
Spaniard	1,947	70.6

Language Spoken at Home: Spanish
(Universe: Population 5 Years and Over)

Group	Number	%
Total Population	212,404	3.6
Hispanic or Latino (of any race)	167,350	74.6
Central American, ex. Mexican	27,864	86.7
Costa Rican	608	67.0
Guatemalan	9,631	90.1
Honduran	7,797	86.2
Nicaraguan	686	80.5
Panamanian	842	49.2
Salvadoran	8,126	92.9
Cuban	3,530	58.0
Dominican Republic	1,010	61.0
Mexican	114,061	78.5
Puerto Rican	8,765	51.1
South American	7,837	76.7
Argentinean	796	86.8
Chilean	482	69.9
Colombian	2,396	73.5
Ecuadorian	819	90.3
Peruvian	1,202	65.8
Venezuelan	1,359	86.3
Spaniard	764	27.7

Unemployment Rate
(Universe: Population 16 Years and Over)

Group	%
Total Population	8.6
Hispanic or Latino (of any race)	8.6
Central American, ex. Mexican	8.1
Costa Rican	3.9
Guatemalan	4.9
Honduran	11.9
Nicaraguan	17.5
Panamanian	3.9
Salvadoran	8.5
Cuban	15.3
Dominican Republic	1.7
Mexican	8.9
Puerto Rican	7.7
South American	7.8
Argentinean	2.5
Chilean	0.0
Colombian	19.6
Ecuadorian	4.1
Peruvian	4.1
Venezuelan	3.4
Spaniard	3.8

Class of Worker: Private Wage and Salary
(Universe: Civilian Employed Population 16 Years and Over)

Group	Number	%
Total Population	2,199,524	78.1
Hispanic or Latino (of any race)	102,469	89.0
Central American, ex. Mexican	16,968	90.8
Costa Rican	276	62.9
Guatemalan	6,382	93.2
Honduran	4,786	92.7
Nicaraguan	350	84.5
Panamanian	701	80.4
Salvadoran	4,347	90.0
Cuban	2,345	83.5
Dominican Republic	730	85.9
Mexican	67,457	90.7
Puerto Rican	6,567	81.3
South American	4,176	83.8
Argentinean	399	72.8
Chilean	267	81.7
Colombian	1,039	85.8
Ecuadorian	300	70.8
Peruvian	1,002	86.5
Venezuelan	690	92.5
Spaniard	1,143	85.1

Class of Worker: Government
(Universe: Civilian Employed Population 16 Years and Over)

Group	Number	%
Total Population	400,290	14.2
Hispanic or Latino (of any race)	5,420	4.7
Central American, ex. Mexican	632	3.4
Costa Rican	140	31.9
Guatemalan	86	1.3
Honduran	129	2.5
Nicaraguan	21	5.1
Panamanian	98	11.2
Salvadoran	158	3.3
Cuban	313	11.1
Dominican Republic	102	12.0
Mexican	2,258	3.0
Puerto Rican	1,104	13.7
South American	433	8.7
Argentinean	124	22.6
Chilean	36	11.0
Colombian	83	6.9
Ecuadorian	39	9.2
Peruvian	100	8.6
Venezuelan	29	3.9
Spaniard	63	4.7

Means of Transportation to Work: Car, Truck or Van
(Universe: Workers 16 Years and Over)

Group	Number	%
Total Population	2,571,222	93.4
Hispanic or Latino (of any race)	104,089	92.6
Central American, ex. Mexican	17,320	94.7
Costa Rican	429	97.7
Guatemalan	6,549	97.7
Honduran	4,639	93.2
Nicaraguan	351	86.7
Panamanian	813	92.6
Salvadoran	4,413	92.8
Cuban	2,376	88.3
Dominican Republic	850	95.2
Mexican	67,100	92.4
Puerto Rican	7,339	91.5
South American	4,550	94.4
Argentinean	477	98.1
Chilean	315	100.0
Colombian	1,119	89.5
Ecuadorian	394	98.0
Peruvian	1,025	96.1
Venezuelan	705	95.1
Spaniard	1,129	89.0

Means of Transportation to Work: Public Transportation (ex. Taxicab)
(Universe: Workers 16 Years and Over)

Group	Number	%
Total Population	21,318	0.8
Hispanic or Latino (of any race)	1,377	1.2
Central American, ex. Mexican	224	1.2
Costa Rican	0	0.0
Guatemalan	0	0.0
Honduran	31	0.6
Nicaraguan	17	4.2
Panamanian	12	1.4
Salvadoran	164	3.4
Cuban	0	0.0
Dominican Republic	0	0.0
Mexican	1,002	1.4
Puerto Rican	60	0.7
South American	46	1.0
Argentinean	9	1.9
Chilean	0	0.0
Colombian	29	2.3
Ecuadorian	8	2.0
Peruvian	0	0.0
Venezuelan	0	0.0
Spaniard	22	1.7

Notes: (1) Percent of total population; (2) Percent of Hispanic/Latino population; Profiles include places with an overall population of at least 125,000, OR an overall population of at least 25,000 where the Hispanic/Latino population is at least 20% of the overall population. In states where less than five places meet either of these criteria, we have included places with at least 10,000 total population with the highest percentage of Hispanic/Latino population. These places are identified with an asterisk (*); Please refer to the User's Guide for a full explanation of data.

Homeownership Rate
(Universe: Occupied Housing Units)

Group	%
Total Population	68.2
Hispanic or Latino (of any race)	40.0
Central American, ex. Mexican	36.4
Costa Rican	59.1
Guatemalan	22.6
Honduran	28.6
Nicaraguan	48.2
Panamanian	58.7
Salvadoran	52.6
Cuban	57.8
Dominican Republic	45.6
Mexican	35.7
Puerto Rican	50.1
South American	59.2
Argentinean	60.8
Bolivian	64.5
Chilean	64.5
Colombian	61.7
Ecuadorian	58.5
Paraguayan	45.5
Peruvian	57.7
Uruguayan	42.0
Venezuelan	55.5
Spaniard	61.4

Median Home Value

Group	Dollars
Total Population	134,100
Hispanic or Latino (of any race)	129,300
Central American, ex. Mexican	139,700
Costa Rican	224,000
Guatemalan	142,100
Honduran	133,000
Nicaraguan	163,100
Panamanian	140,000
Salvadoran	131,200
Cuban	142,300
Dominican Republic	144,200
Mexican	114,200
Puerto Rican	134,000
South American	167,900
Argentinean	133,500
Chilean	210,800
Colombian	161,400
Ecuadorian	173,400
Peruvian	174,800
Venezuelan	206,300
Spaniard	176,500

Median Gross Rent

Group	Dollars
Total Population	678
Hispanic or Latino (of any race)	698
Central American, ex. Mexican	722
Costa Rican	737
Guatemalan	677
Honduran	753
Nicaraguan	729
Panamanian	806
Salvadoran	805
Cuban	652
Dominican Republic	726
Mexican	690
Puerto Rican	678
South American	773
Argentinean	719
Chilean	292
Colombian	768
Ecuadorian	878
Peruvian	801
Venezuelan	778
Spaniard	953

Median Household Income
(2010 Inflation-Adjusted Dollars)

Group	Dollars
Total Population	43,314
Hispanic or Latino (of any race)	34,606
Central American, ex. Mexican	37,156
Costa Rican	46,250
Guatemalan	41,953
Honduran	30,467
Nicaraguan	42,333
Panamanian	48,689
Salvadoran	36,787
Cuban	37,587
Dominican Republic	25,888
Mexican	32,286
Puerto Rican	38,509
South American	42,404
Argentinean	46,734
Chilean	47,132
Colombian	42,572
Ecuadorian	41,591
Peruvian	37,737
Venezuelan	42,857
Spaniard	64,157

Per Capita Income
(2010 Inflation-Adjusted Dollars)

Group	Dollars
Total Population	23,722
Hispanic or Latino (of any race)	13,494
Central American, ex. Mexican	13,305
Costa Rican	14,518
Guatemalan	13,382
Honduran	12,530
Nicaraguan	19,740
Panamanian	20,284
Salvadoran	11,945
Cuban	27,509
Dominican Republic	24,527
Mexican	11,392
Puerto Rican	16,952
South American	22,070
Argentinean	39,627
Chilean	20,508
Colombian	16,853
Ecuadorian	20,345
Peruvian	24,214
Venezuelan	24,003
Spaniard	30,144

Households with $100,000+ Income

Group	Number	%
Total Population	350,250	14.3
Hispanic or Latino (of any race)	5,984	8.8
Central American, ex. Mexican	718	7.7
Costa Rican	27	9.0
Guatemalan	399	13.7
Honduran	67	2.5
Nicaraguan	53	23.9
Panamanian	96	14.9
Salvadoran	76	3.1
Cuban	411	16.6
Dominican Republic	59	10.2
Mexican	2,772	6.7
Puerto Rican	822	13.5
South American	592	16.0
Argentinean	28	8.9
Chilean	95	40.3
Colombian	76	7.0
Ecuadorian	64	20.4
Peruvian	131	15.8
Venezuelan	115	21.3
Spaniard	269	25.2

Households with Food Stamps/SNAP Benefits During Past 12 Months

Group	Number	%
Total Population	338,254	13.8
Hispanic or Latino (of any race)	14,665	21.6
Central American, ex. Mexican	1,783	19.2
Costa Rican	0	0.0
Guatemalan	458	15.7
Honduran	624	23.3
Nicaraguan	0	0.0
Panamanian	90	14.0
Salvadoran	611	25.0
Cuban	467	18.8
Dominican Republic	93	16.0
Mexican	9,801	23.6
Puerto Rican	1,286	21.1
South American	458	12.4
Argentinean	36	11.5
Chilean	27	11.4
Colombian	160	14.6
Ecuadorian	16	5.1
Peruvian	128	15.4
Venezuelan	69	12.8
Spaniard	137	12.8

Poverty Rate
(Income in Past 12 Months Below Poverty Level)

Group	%
Total Population	16.5
Hispanic or Latino (of any race)	31.0
Central American, ex. Mexican	31.9
Costa Rican	5.8
Guatemalan	34.1
Honduran	33.2
Nicaraguan	24.0
Panamanian	19.2
Salvadoran	33.8
Cuban	15.7
Dominican Republic	20.1
Mexican	34.1
Puerto Rican	24.3
South American	17.2
Argentinean	6.5
Chilean	8.5
Colombian	17.3
Ecuadorian	20.0
Peruvian	12.2
Venezuelan	31.1
Spaniard	16.8

Chattanooga

Population

Group	Number	%TP[1]	%HP[2]
Total Population	167,674	100.0	–
Hispanic or Latino (of any race)	9,225	5.5	100.0
Central American, ex. Mexican	2,990	1.8	32.4
Guatemalan	2,633	1.6	28.5
Honduran	120	0.1	1.3
Salvadoran	146	0.1	1.6
Cuban	266	0.2	2.9
Mexican	4,180	2.5	45.3
Puerto Rican	495	0.3	5.4
South American	344	0.2	3.7
Colombian	117	0.1	1.3

Population Growth: 2000–2010

Group	%
Total Population	7.8
Hispanic or Latino (of any race)	181.2
Central American, ex. Mexican	377.6
Guatemalan	373.6
Cuban	119.8
Mexican	155.3
Puerto Rican	94.1

Males per 100 Females

Group	Number
Total Population	90.7
Hispanic or Latino (of any race)	133.1
Central American, ex. Mexican	144.1
Guatemalan	149.1
Honduran	126.4
Salvadoran	102.8
Cuban	88.7
Mexican	140.2
Puerto Rican	100.4
South American	97.7
Colombian	85.7

Average Household Size

Group	People
Total Population	2.26
Hispanic or Latino (of any race)	3.82
Central American, ex. Mexican	5.10
Guatemalan	5.38
Honduran	3.68
Salvadoran	4.43
Cuban	2.68
Mexican	3.67
Puerto Rican	2.58
South American	2.69
Colombian	2.62

Notes: (1) Percent of total population; (2) Percent of Hispanic/Latino population; Profiles include places with an overall population of at least 125,000, OR an overall population of at least 25,000 where the Hispanic/Latino population is at least 20% of the overall population. In states where less than five places meet either of these criteria, we have included places with at least 10,000 total population with the highest percentage of Hispanic/Latino population. These places are identified with an asterisk (*); Please refer to the User's Guide for a full explanation of data.

Median Age

Group	Years
Total Population	37.3
Hispanic or Latino (of any race)	24.5
Central American, ex. Mexican	24.7
Guatemalan	24.4
Honduran	28.3
Salvadoran	27.4
Cuban	32.8
Mexican	23.5
Puerto Rican	25.5
South American	29.4
Colombian	31.8

High School Graduates
(Universe: Population 25 Years and Over)

Group	Number	%
Total Population	91,954	82.6
Hispanic or Latino (of any race)	2,062	49.9
Central American, ex. Mexican	253	24.1
Guatemalan	123	18.3
Mexican	1,251	52.2

Four-Year College Graduates
(Universe: Population 25 Years and Over)

Group	Number	%
Total Population	27,445	24.7
Hispanic or Latino (of any race)	318	7.7
Central American, ex. Mexican	0	0.0
Guatemalan	0	0.0
Mexican	236	9.8

Population Age 3–17 Enrolled in Public School
(Universe: Population Age 3–17 Enrolled in School)

Group	Number	%
Total Population	20,412	82.2
Hispanic or Latino (of any race)	1,297	87.9
Central American, ex. Mexican	167	82.3
Guatemalan	167	82.3
Mexican	884	91.9

Population Age 3–17 Enrolled in Private School
(Universe: Population Age 3–17 Enrolled in School)

Group	Number	%
Total Population	4,415	17.8
Hispanic or Latino (of any race)	178	12.1
Central American, ex. Mexican	36	17.7
Guatemalan	36	17.7
Mexican	78	8.1

Foreign-Born Population

Group	Number	%
Total Population	8,809	5.4
Hispanic or Latino (of any race)	4,714	54.5
Central American, ex. Mexican	1,607	75.8
Guatemalan	1,168	75.0
Mexican	2,864	55.5

Foreign-Born Naturalized U.S. Citizens

Group	Number	%
Total Population	2,489	28.3
Hispanic or Latino (of any race)	515	10.9
Central American, ex. Mexican	124	7.7
Guatemalan	72	6.2
Mexican	359	12.5

Language Spoken at Home: English Only
(Universe: Population 5 Years and Over)

Group	Number	%
Total Population	143,698	93.2
Hispanic or Latino (of any race)	2,074	28.0
Central American, ex. Mexican	116	6.4
Guatemalan	69	5.3
Mexican	1,116	25.7

Language Spoken at Home: Spanish
(Universe: Population 5 Years and Over)

Group	Number	%
Total Population	6,135	4.0
Hispanic or Latino (of any race)	5,269	71.2
Central American, ex. Mexican	1,637	90.4
Guatemalan	1,188	90.4
Mexican	3,227	74.3

Unemployment Rate
(Universe: Population 16 Years and Over)

Group	%
Total Population	11.0
Hispanic or Latino (of any race)	11.0
Central American, ex. Mexican	6.3
Guatemalan	5.0
Mexican	11.1

Class of Worker: Private Wage and Salary
(Universe: Civilian Employed Population 16 Years and Over)

Group	Number	%
Total Population	61,633	80.8
Hispanic or Latino (of any race)	3,603	91.0
Central American, ex. Mexican	1,159	92.2
Guatemalan	803	89.9
Mexican	1,965	89.8

Class of Worker: Government
(Universe: Civilian Employed Population 16 Years and Over)

Group	Number	%
Total Population	9,884	13.0
Hispanic or Latino (of any race)	54	1.4
Central American, ex. Mexican	0	0.0
Guatemalan	0	0.0
Mexican	35	1.6

Means of Transportation to Work: Car, Truck or Van
(Universe: Workers 16 Years and Over)

Group	Number	%
Total Population	68,434	91.8
Hispanic or Latino (of any race)	3,576	91.7
Central American, ex. Mexican	1,176	96.1
Guatemalan	853	95.5
Mexican	1,908	88.2

Means of Transportation to Work: Public Transportation (ex. Taxicab)
(Universe: Workers 16 Years and Over)

Group	Number	%
Total Population	1,385	1.9
Hispanic or Latino (of any race)	118	3.0
Central American, ex. Mexican	0	0.0
Guatemalan	0	0.0
Mexican	118	5.5

Homeownership Rate
(Universe: Occupied Housing Units)

Group	%
Total Population	52.6
Hispanic or Latino (of any race)	23.7
Central American, ex. Mexican	14.1
Guatemalan	9.6
Honduran	32.0
Salvadoran	27.5
Cuban	44.3
Mexican	21.2
Puerto Rican	38.4
South American	49.6
Colombian	51.3

Median Home Value

Group	Dollars
Total Population	130,600
Hispanic or Latino (of any race)	99,300
Central American, ex. Mexican	64,100
Guatemalan	61,700
Mexican	153,200

Median Gross Rent

Group	Dollars
Total Population	662
Hispanic or Latino (of any race)	668
Central American, ex. Mexican	655
Guatemalan	639
Mexican	685

Median Household Income
(2010 Inflation-Adjusted Dollars)

Group	Dollars
Total Population	36,675
Hispanic or Latino (of any race)	28,069
Central American, ex. Mexican	31,983
Guatemalan	39,514
Mexican	24,433

Per Capita Income
(2010 Inflation-Adjusted Dollars)

Group	Dollars
Total Population	23,434
Hispanic or Latino (of any race)	11,366
Central American, ex. Mexican	10,725
Guatemalan	10,615
Mexican	10,946

Households with $100,000+ Income

Group	Number	%
Total Population	8,167	11.6
Hispanic or Latino (of any race)	193	8.9
Central American, ex. Mexican	58	10.4
Guatemalan	58	13.7
Mexican	112	9.0

Households with Food Stamps/SNAP Benefits During Past 12 Months

Group	Number	%
Total Population	11,559	16.5
Hispanic or Latino (of any race)	623	28.9
Central American, ex. Mexican	202	36.3
Guatemalan	143	33.7
Mexican	368	29.6

Poverty Rate
(Income in Past 12 Months Below Poverty Level)

Group	%
Total Population	21.3
Hispanic or Latino (of any race)	41.1
Central American, ex. Mexican	32.6
Guatemalan	42.7
Mexican	49.1

Clarksville

Population

Group	Number	%TP[1]	%HP[2]
Total Population	132,929	100.0	–
Hispanic or Latino (of any race)	12,302	9.3	100.0
Central American, ex. Mexican	981	0.7	8.0
Honduran	113	0.1	0.9
Panamanian	588	0.4	4.8
Salvadoran	106	0.1	0.9
Cuban	308	0.2	2.5
Dominican Republic	297	0.2	2.4
Mexican	5,425	4.1	44.1
Puerto Rican	3,957	3.0	32.2
South American	402	0.3	3.3
Colombian	166	0.1	1.3
Spaniard	203	0.2	1.7

Population Growth: 2000–2010

Group	%
Total Population	28.5
Hispanic or Latino (of any race)	97.1
Central American, ex. Mexican	102.3
Panamanian	76.6
Cuban	113.9
Mexican	128.4
Puerto Rican	93.5
South American	191.3

Males per 100 Females

Group	Number
Total Population	95.0
Hispanic or Latino (of any race)	103.6
Central American, ex. Mexican	79.0
Honduran	85.2
Panamanian	69.5
Salvadoran	135.6
Cuban	120.0
Dominican Republic	96.7
Mexican	111.2
Puerto Rican	108.3
South American	75.5
Colombian	71.1
Spaniard	82.9

Notes: (1) Percent of total population; (2) Percent of Hispanic/Latino population; Profiles include places with an overall population of at least 125,000, OR an overall population of at least 25,000 where the Hispanic/Latino population is at least 20% of the overall population. In states where less than five places meet either of these criteria, we have included places with at least 10,000 total population with the highest percentage of Hispanic/Latino population. These places are identified with an asterisk (*); Please refer to the User's Guide for a full explanation of data.

Average Household Size

Group	People
Total Population	2.63
Hispanic or Latino (of any race)	3.01
Central American, ex. Mexican	3.08
Honduran	3.32
Panamanian	3.13
Salvadoran	2.73
Cuban	2.71
Dominican Republic	3.24
Mexican	3.06
Puerto Rican	3.00
South American	2.58
Colombian	2.64
Spaniard	2.96

Median Age

Group	Years
Total Population	28.6
Hispanic or Latino (of any race)	23.3
Central American, ex. Mexican	26.4
Honduran	27.6
Panamanian	28.8
Salvadoran	23.5
Cuban	25.4
Dominican Republic	25.6
Mexican	22.1
Puerto Rican	23.9
South American	26.0
Colombian	25.6
Spaniard	25.1

High School Graduates
(Universe: Population 25 Years and Over)

Group	Number	%
Total Population	66,596	91.0
Hispanic or Latino (of any race)	3,994	81.8
Central American, ex. Mexican	326	55.4
Mexican	1,487	81.3
Puerto Rican	1,488	86.0

Four-Year College Graduates
(Universe: Population 25 Years and Over)

Group	Number	%
Total Population	16,016	21.9
Hispanic or Latino (of any race)	912	18.7
Central American, ex. Mexican	37	6.3
Mexican	300	16.4
Puerto Rican	405	23.4

Population Age 3–17 Enrolled in Public School
(Universe: Population Age 3–17 Enrolled in School)

Group	Number	%
Total Population	22,418	90.0
Hispanic or Latino (of any race)	2,394	92.9
Central American, ex. Mexican	419	98.1
Mexican	928	91.7
Puerto Rican	694	88.3

Population Age 3–17 Enrolled in Private School
(Universe: Population Age 3–17 Enrolled in School)

Group	Number	%
Total Population	2,501	10.0
Hispanic or Latino (of any race)	184	7.1
Central American, ex. Mexican	8	1.9
Mexican	84	8.3
Puerto Rican	92	11.7

Foreign-Born Population

Group	Number	%
Total Population	6,661	5.3
Hispanic or Latino (of any race)	1,870	17.8
Central American, ex. Mexican	636	52.1
Mexican	866	19.2
Puerto Rican	0	0.0

Foreign-Born Naturalized U.S. Citizens

Group	Number	%
Total Population	2,918	43.8
Hispanic or Latino (of any race)	404	21.6
Central American, ex. Mexican	94	14.8
Mexican	56	6.5
Puerto Rican	0	0.0

Language Spoken at Home: English Only
(Universe: Population 5 Years and Over)

Group	Number	%
Total Population	103,512	90.3
Hispanic or Latino (of any race)	3,823	42.6
Central American, ex. Mexican	378	33.9
Mexican	2,011	55.0
Puerto Rican	830	28.4

Language Spoken at Home: Spanish
(Universe: Population 5 Years and Over)

Group	Number	%
Total Population	5,993	5.2
Hispanic or Latino (of any race)	4,974	55.5
Central American, ex. Mexican	682	61.2
Mexican	1,566	42.8
Puerto Rican	2,088	71.4

Unemployment Rate
(Universe: Population 16 Years and Over)

Group	%
Total Population	9.7
Hispanic or Latino (of any race)	10.3
Central American, ex. Mexican	0.0
Mexican	12.0
Puerto Rican	9.6

Class of Worker: Private Wage and Salary
(Universe: Civilian Employed Population 16 Years and Over)

Group	Number	%
Total Population	36,177	72.4
Hispanic or Latino (of any race)	2,901	76.9
Central American, ex. Mexican	363	89.9
Mexican	1,256	80.8
Puerto Rican	997	72.7

Class of Worker: Government
(Universe: Civilian Employed Population 16 Years and Over)

Group	Number	%
Total Population	11,317	22.6
Hispanic or Latino (of any race)	725	19.2
Central American, ex. Mexican	41	10.1
Mexican	272	17.5
Puerto Rican	257	18.7

Means of Transportation to Work: Car, Truck or Van
(Universe: Workers 16 Years and Over)

Group	Number	%
Total Population	53,590	94.4
Hispanic or Latino (of any race)	3,977	93.8
Central American, ex. Mexican	444	97.4
Mexican	1,734	98.3
Puerto Rican	1,311	87.8

Means of Transportation to Work: Public Transportation (ex. Taxicab)
(Universe: Workers 16 Years and Over)

Group	Number	%
Total Population	354	0.6
Hispanic or Latino (of any race)	21	0.5
Central American, ex. Mexican	12	2.6
Mexican	0	0.0
Puerto Rican	9	0.6

Homeownership Rate
(Universe: Occupied Housing Units)

Group	%
Total Population	56.1
Hispanic or Latino (of any race)	47.4
Central American, ex. Mexican	58.9
Honduran	58.1
Panamanian	62.3
Salvadoran	50.0
Cuban	49.5
Dominican Republic	47.8
Mexican	41.8
Puerto Rican	51.6
South American	45.0
Colombian	62.2
Spaniard	52.9

Median Home Value

Group	Dollars
Total Population	124,000
Hispanic or Latino (of any race)	130,300
Central American, ex. Mexican	153,100
Mexican	128,700
Puerto Rican	117,100

Median Gross Rent

Group	Dollars
Total Population	735
Hispanic or Latino (of any race)	705
Central American, ex. Mexican	638
Mexican	680
Puerto Rican	834

Median Household Income
(2010 Inflation-Adjusted Dollars)

Group	Dollars
Total Population	46,742
Hispanic or Latino (of any race)	48,190
Central American, ex. Mexican	9,750
Mexican	51,434
Puerto Rican	44,348

Per Capita Income
(2010 Inflation-Adjusted Dollars)

Group	Dollars
Total Population	21,079
Hispanic or Latino (of any race)	15,795
Central American, ex. Mexican	8,671
Mexican	15,233
Puerto Rican	17,900

Households with $100,000+ Income

Group	Number	%
Total Population	5,497	11.8
Hispanic or Latino (of any race)	247	8.2
Central American, ex. Mexican	0	0.0
Mexican	62	5.1
Puerto Rican	119	11.7

Households with Food Stamps/SNAP Benefits During Past 12 Months

Group	Number	%
Total Population	5,090	10.9
Hispanic or Latino (of any race)	300	9.9
Central American, ex. Mexican	22	8.7
Mexican	55	4.5
Puerto Rican	159	15.6

Poverty Rate
(Income in Past 12 Months Below Poverty Level)

Group	%
Total Population	15.6
Hispanic or Latino (of any race)	19.8
Central American, ex. Mexican	48.4
Mexican	15.7
Puerto Rican	19.6

Knoxville

Population

Group	Number	%TP[1]	%HP[2]
Total Population	178,874	100.0	–
Hispanic or Latino (of any race)	8,206	4.6	100.0
Central American, ex. Mexican	1,294	0.7	15.8
Guatemalan	695	0.4	8.5
Honduran	354	0.2	4.3
Salvadoran	129	0.1	1.6
Cuban	248	0.1	3.0
Mexican	4,960	2.8	60.4
Puerto Rican	611	0.3	7.4
South American	390	0.2	4.8
Colombian	150	0.1	1.8

Population Growth: 2000–2010

Group	%
Total Population	2.9
Hispanic or Latino (of any race)	198.3
Central American, ex. Mexican	614.9
Cuban	108.4
Mexican	236.5
Puerto Rican	110.0
South American	170.8

Notes: (1) Percent of total population; (2) Percent of Hispanic/Latino population; Profiles include places with an overall population of at least 125,000, OR an overall population of at least 25,000 where the Hispanic/Latino population is at least 20% of the overall population. In states where less than five places meet either of these criteria, we have included places with at least 10,000 total population with the highest percentage of Hispanic/Latino population. These places are identified with an asterisk (*); Please refer to the User's Guide for a full explanation of data.

Males per 100 Females

Group	Number
Total Population	92.5
Hispanic or Latino (of any race)	127.4
Central American, ex. Mexican	160.9
Guatemalan	152.7
Honduran	221.8
Salvadoran	158.0
Cuban	85.1
Mexican	133.1
Puerto Rican	83.5
South American	107.4
Colombian	80.7

Average Household Size

Group	People
Total Population	2.16
Hispanic or Latino (of any race)	3.23
Central American, ex. Mexican	4.19
Guatemalan	5.11
Honduran	3.74
Salvadoran	3.13
Cuban	2.17
Mexican	3.41
Puerto Rican	2.37
South American	2.29
Colombian	2.56

Median Age

Group	Years
Total Population	32.7
Hispanic or Latino (of any race)	24.5
Central American, ex. Mexican	25.8
Guatemalan	24.5
Honduran	28.2
Salvadoran	27.3
Cuban	28.2
Mexican	23.8
Puerto Rican	23.7
South American	27.9
Colombian	26.3

High School Graduates
(Universe: Population 25 Years and Over)

Group	Number	%
Total Population	94,461	84.2
Hispanic or Latino (of any race)	1,631	57.0
Central American, ex. Mexican	180	29.3
Mexican	818	56.5

Four-Year College Graduates
(Universe: Population 25 Years and Over)

Group	Number	%
Total Population	32,490	29.0
Hispanic or Latino (of any race)	406	14.2
Central American, ex. Mexican	24	3.9
Mexican	86	5.9

Population Age 3–17 Enrolled in Public School
(Universe: Population Age 3–17 Enrolled in School)

Group	Number	%
Total Population	19,815	84.1
Hispanic or Latino (of any race)	1,139	86.6
Central American, ex. Mexican	172	100.0
Mexican	765	100.0

Population Age 3–17 Enrolled in Private School
(Universe: Population Age 3–17 Enrolled in School)

Group	Number	%
Total Population	3,735	15.9
Hispanic or Latino (of any race)	177	13.4
Central American, ex. Mexican	0	0.0
Mexican	0	0.0

Foreign-Born Population

Group	Number	%
Total Population	7,591	4.3
Hispanic or Latino (of any race)	2,535	40.9
Central American, ex. Mexican	889	69.7
Mexican	1,280	36.9

Foreign-Born Naturalized U.S. Citizens

Group	Number	%
Total Population	2,461	32.4
Hispanic or Latino (of any race)	588	23.2
Central American, ex. Mexican	0	0.0
Mexican	330	25.8

Language Spoken at Home: English Only
(Universe: Population 5 Years and Over)

Group	Number	%
Total Population	157,442	94.0
Hispanic or Latino (of any race)	1,425	26.9
Central American, ex. Mexican	87	8.0
Mexican	857	30.2

Language Spoken at Home: Spanish
(Universe: Population 5 Years and Over)

Group	Number	%
Total Population	4,793	2.9
Hispanic or Latino (of any race)	3,825	72.3
Central American, ex. Mexican	989	90.7
Mexican	1,978	69.8

Unemployment Rate
(Universe: Population 16 Years and Over)

Group	%
Total Population	7.1
Hispanic or Latino (of any race)	3.9
Central American, ex. Mexican	1.0
Mexican	5.8

Class of Worker: Private Wage and Salary
(Universe: Civilian Employed Population 16 Years and Over)

Group	Number	%
Total Population	68,257	81.3
Hispanic or Latino (of any race)	2,611	87.4
Central American, ex. Mexican	604	91.2
Mexican	1,295	85.4

Class of Worker: Government
(Universe: Civilian Employed Population 16 Years and Over)

Group	Number	%
Total Population	11,520	13.7
Hispanic or Latino (of any race)	147	4.9
Central American, ex. Mexican	0	0.0
Mexican	113	7.5

Means of Transportation to Work: Car, Truck or Van
(Universe: Workers 16 Years and Over)

Group	Number	%
Total Population	74,606	91.2
Hispanic or Latino (of any race)	2,506	91.3
Central American, ex. Mexican	599	100.0
Mexican	1,197	88.5

Means of Transportation to Work: Public Transportation (ex. Taxicab)
(Universe: Workers 16 Years and Over)

Group	Number	%
Total Population	1,332	1.6
Hispanic or Latino (of any race)	50	1.8
Central American, ex. Mexican	0	0.0
Mexican	50	3.7

Homeownership Rate
(Universe: Occupied Housing Units)

Group	%
Total Population	49.2
Hispanic or Latino (of any race)	22.8
Central American, ex. Mexican	13.8
Guatemalan	9.3
Honduran	13.2
Salvadoran	15.8
Cuban	33.3
Mexican	19.4
Puerto Rican	30.1
South American	43.3
Colombian	44.1

Median Home Value

Group	Dollars
Total Population	111,500
Hispanic or Latino (of any race)	111,800
Central American, ex. Mexican	–
Mexican	107,500

Median Gross Rent

Group	Dollars
Total Population	656
Hispanic or Latino (of any race)	673
Central American, ex. Mexican	673
Mexican	698

Median Household Income
(2010 Inflation-Adjusted Dollars)

Group	Dollars
Total Population	32,756
Hispanic or Latino (of any race)	30,543
Central American, ex. Mexican	26,615
Mexican	35,127

Per Capita Income
(2010 Inflation-Adjusted Dollars)

Group	Dollars
Total Population	21,964
Hispanic or Latino (of any race)	14,722
Central American, ex. Mexican	9,194
Mexican	10,361

Households with $100,000+ Income

Group	Number	%
Total Population	6,551	8.0
Hispanic or Latino (of any race)	121	5.9
Central American, ex. Mexican	34	12.4
Mexican	12	1.2

Households with Food Stamps/SNAP Benefits During Past 12 Months

Group	Number	%
Total Population	11,809	14.4
Hispanic or Latino (of any race)	361	17.7
Central American, ex. Mexican	45	16.4
Mexican	157	16.1

Poverty Rate
(Income in Past 12 Months Below Poverty Level)

Group	%
Total Population	23.4
Hispanic or Latino (of any race)	28.2
Central American, ex. Mexican	43.6
Mexican	25.7

Memphis

Population

Group	Number	%TP[1]	%HP[2]
Total Population	646,889	100.0	–
Hispanic or Latino (of any race)	41,994	6.5	100.0
Central American, ex. Mexican	4,881	0.8	11.6
Guatemalan	1,680	0.3	4.0
Honduran	1,895	0.3	4.5
Nicaraguan	166	<0.1	0.4
Panamanian	147	<0.1	0.4
Salvadoran	902	0.1	2.1
Cuban	679	0.1	1.6
Dominican Republic	182	<0.1	0.4
Mexican	30,799	4.8	73.3
Puerto Rican	1,169	0.2	2.8
South American	1,051	0.2	2.5
Argentinean	125	<0.1	0.3
Colombian	356	0.1	0.8
Peruvian	147	<0.1	0.4
Venezuelan	207	<0.1	0.5
Spaniard	237	<0.1	0.6

Population Growth: 2000–2010

Group	%
Total Population	-0.5
Hispanic or Latino (of any race)	117.4
Central American, ex. Mexican	464.3
Guatemalan	983.9
Honduran	492.2
Salvadoran	379.8
Cuban	30.3
Mexican	118.6
Puerto Rican	57.5
South American	154.5
Colombian	152.5

Males per 100 Females

Group	Number
Total Population	90.3
Hispanic or Latino (of any race)	132.5

Notes: (1) Percent of total population; (2) Percent of Hispanic/Latino population; Profiles include places with an overall population of at least 125,000, OR an overall population of at least 25,000 where the Hispanic/Latino population is at least 20% of the overall population. In states where less than five places meet either of these criteria, we have included places with at least 10,000 total population with the highest percentage of Hispanic/Latino population. These places are identified with an asterisk (*); Please refer to the User's Guide for a full explanation of data.

Group	
Central American, ex. Mexican	139.6
Guatemalan	171.0
Honduran	136.3
Nicaraguan	97.6
Panamanian	47.0
Salvadoran	127.2
Cuban	122.6
Dominican Republic	114.1
Mexican	136.0
Puerto Rican	104.0
South American	99.8
Argentinean	119.3
Colombian	86.4
Peruvian	98.6
Venezuelan	113.4
Spaniard	99.2

Average Household Size

Group	People
Total Population	2.52
Hispanic or Latino (of any race)	3.88
Central American, ex. Mexican	3.96
Guatemalan	4.53
Honduran	3.88
Nicaraguan	3.35
Panamanian	2.70
Salvadoran	3.72
Cuban	2.59
Dominican Republic	3.20
Mexican	4.15
Puerto Rican	2.52
South American	2.72
Argentinean	3.00
Colombian	2.91
Peruvian	2.35
Venezuelan	2.59
Spaniard	2.20

Median Age

Group	Years
Total Population	33.0
Hispanic or Latino (of any race)	25.3
Central American, ex. Mexican	27.4
Guatemalan	25.4
Honduran	28.6
Nicaraguan	27.3
Panamanian	31.5
Salvadoran	29.2
Cuban	37.3
Dominican Republic	26.8
Mexican	24.4
Puerto Rican	27.1
South American	34.0
Argentinean	33.4
Colombian	34.1
Peruvian	36.5
Venezuelan	34.4
Spaniard	30.1

High School Graduates

(Universe: Population 25 Years and Over)

Group	Number	%
Total Population	330,329	81.2
Hispanic or Latino (of any race)	8,986	46.1
Central American, ex. Mexican	961	34.2
Honduran	365	26.6
Mexican	5,908	42.2
Puerto Rican	453	73.8
South American	600	73.3

Four-Year College Graduates

(Universe: Population 25 Years and Over)

Group	Number	%
Total Population	91,523	22.5
Hispanic or Latino (of any race)	1,780	9.1
Central American, ex. Mexican	95	3.4
Honduran	50	3.6
Mexican	724	5.2
Puerto Rican	184	30.0
South American	383	46.8

Population Age 3–17 Enrolled in Public School

(Universe: Population Age 3–17 Enrolled in School)

Group	Number	%
Total Population	110,186	86.7
Hispanic or Latino (of any race)	7,249	93.0
Central American, ex. Mexican	941	94.1
Honduran	508	97.3
Mexican	5,365	94.5
Puerto Rican	258	94.2
South American	98	64.9

Population Age 3–17 Enrolled in Private School

(Universe: Population Age 3–17 Enrolled in School)

Group	Number	%
Total Population	16,875	13.3
Hispanic or Latino (of any race)	547	7.0
Central American, ex. Mexican	59	5.9
Honduran	14	2.7
Mexican	315	5.5
Puerto Rican	16	5.8
South American	53	35.1

Foreign-Born Population

Group	Number	%
Total Population	39,668	6.1
Hispanic or Latino (of any race)	22,867	59.3
Central American, ex. Mexican	3,376	69.8
Honduran	1,564	67.6
Mexican	17,819	61.7
Puerto Rican	44	3.3
South American	885	82.2

Foreign-Born Naturalized U.S. Citizens

Group	Number	%
Total Population	9,543	24.1
Hispanic or Latino (of any race)	3,081	13.5
Central American, ex. Mexican	506	15.0
Honduran	217	13.9
Mexican	2,131	12.0
Puerto Rican	35	79.5
South American	122	13.8

Language Spoken at Home: English Only

(Universe: Population 5 Years and Over)

Group	Number	%
Total Population	553,305	91.4
Hispanic or Latino (of any race)	5,341	16.1
Central American, ex. Mexican	722	16.0
Honduran	404	18.6
Mexican	2,958	12.2
Puerto Rican	585	54.8
South American	185	17.4

Language Spoken at Home: Spanish

(Universe: Population 5 Years and Over)

Group	Number	%
Total Population	34,708	5.7
Hispanic or Latino (of any race)	27,575	83.3
Central American, ex. Mexican	3,790	84.0
Honduran	1,771	81.4
Mexican	21,325	87.8
Puerto Rican	475	44.5
South American	823	77.4

Unemployment Rate

(Universe: Population 16 Years and Over)

Group	%
Total Population	12.5
Hispanic or Latino (of any race)	8.8
Central American, ex. Mexican	8.8
Honduran	16.5
Mexican	9.0
Puerto Rican	13.4
South American	4.2

Class of Worker: Private Wage and Salary

(Universe: Civilian Employed Population 16 Years and Over)

Group	Number	%
Total Population	228,056	80.4
Hispanic or Latino (of any race)	16,643	91.9
Central American, ex. Mexican	2,328	85.1
Honduran	1,063	88.1
Mexican	12,516	93.6
Puerto Rican	450	93.8
South American	462	78.7

Class of Worker: Government

(Universe: Civilian Employed Population 16 Years and Over)

Group	Number	%
Total Population	40,940	14.4
Hispanic or Latino (of any race)	316	1.7
Central American, ex. Mexican	56	2.0
Honduran	32	2.7
Mexican	181	1.4
Puerto Rican	30	6.3
South American	41	7.0

Means of Transportation to Work: Car, Truck or Van

(Universe: Workers 16 Years and Over)

Group	Number	%
Total Population	252,111	91.7
Hispanic or Latino (of any race)	16,910	95.7
Central American, ex. Mexican	2,659	97.8
Honduran	1,175	97.3
Mexican	12,466	95.7
Puerto Rican	433	91.4
South American	524	95.8

Means of Transportation to Work: Public Transportation (ex. Taxicab)

(Universe: Workers 16 Years and Over)

Group	Number	%
Total Population	6,991	2.5
Hispanic or Latino (of any race)	173	1.0
Central American, ex. Mexican	11	0.4
Honduran	11	0.9
Mexican	146	1.1
Puerto Rican	16	3.4
South American	0	0.0

Homeownership Rate

(Universe: Occupied Housing Units)

Group	%
Total Population	51.9
Hispanic or Latino (of any race)	31.1
Central American, ex. Mexican	28.6
Guatemalan	14.5
Honduran	25.6
Nicaraguan	40.7
Panamanian	48.1
Salvadoran	48.4
Cuban	51.9
Dominican Republic	42.4
Mexican	29.3
Puerto Rican	35.9
South American	53.5
Argentinean	56.5
Colombian	61.4
Peruvian	43.9
Venezuelan	54.1
Spaniard	46.2

Median Home Value

Group	Dollars
Total Population	98,300
Hispanic or Latino (of any race)	91,500
Central American, ex. Mexican	96,300
Honduran	109,000
Mexican	84,400
Puerto Rican	139,200
South American	167,000

Median Gross Rent

Group	Dollars
Total Population	758
Hispanic or Latino (of any race)	749
Central American, ex. Mexican	752
Honduran	780
Mexican	719
Puerto Rican	778
South American	845

Median Household Income

(2010 Inflation-Adjusted Dollars)

Group	Dollars
Total Population	36,473
Hispanic or Latino (of any race)	32,020
Central American, ex. Mexican	38,553
Honduran	35,639
Mexican	31,399
Puerto Rican	24,273
South American	41,862

Notes: (1) Percent of total population; (2) Percent of Hispanic/Latino population; Profiles include places with an overall population of at least 125,000, OR an overall population of at least 25,000 where the Hispanic/Latino population is at least 20% of the overall population. In states where less than five places meet either of these criteria, we have included places with at least 10,000 total population with the highest percentage of Hispanic/Latino population. These places are identified with an asterisk (*); Please refer to the User's Guide for a full explanation of data.

Per Capita Income (2010 Inflation-Adjusted Dollars)	
Group	Dollars
Total Population	21,007
Hispanic or Latino (of any race)	12,659
Central American, ex. Mexican	13,029
Honduran	12,188
Mexican	11,375
Puerto Rican	15,397
South American	22,487

Households with $100,000+ Income		
Group	Number	%
Total Population	28,446	11.5
Hispanic or Latino (of any race)	800	8.1
Central American, ex. Mexican	28	2.3
Honduran	0	0.0
Mexican	571	8.3
Puerto Rican	87	18.7
South American	78	16.6

Households with Food Stamps/SNAP Benefits During Past 12 Months		
Group	Number	%
Total Population	52,278	21.2
Hispanic or Latino (of any race)	2,445	24.9
Central American, ex. Mexican	311	26.0
Honduran	178	28.8
Mexican	1,713	24.9
Puerto Rican	152	32.7
South American	89	18.9

Poverty Rate (Income in Past 12 Months Below Poverty Level)	
Group	%
Total Population	25.4
Hispanic or Latino (of any race)	32.5
Central American, ex. Mexican	28.0
Honduran	31.7
Mexican	34.8
Puerto Rican	26.8
South American	6.1

Nashville-Davidson

Population			
Group	Number	%TP[1]	%HP[2]
Total Population	601,222	100.0	–
Hispanic or Latino (of any race)	60,390	10.0	100.0
Central American, ex. Mexican	11,180	1.9	18.5
Costa Rican	252	<0.1	0.4
Guatemalan	3,140	0.5	5.2
Honduran	3,018	0.5	5.0
Nicaraguan	374	0.1	0.6
Panamanian	212	<0.1	0.4
Salvadoran	4,121	0.7	6.8
Cuban	1,716	0.3	2.8
Dominican Republic	355	0.1	0.6
Mexican	36,877	6.1	61.1
Puerto Rican	3,076	0.5	5.1
South American	2,204	0.4	3.6
Argentinean	162	<0.1	0.3
Chilean	160	<0.1	0.3
Colombian	732	0.1	1.2
Ecuadorian	306	0.1	0.5
Peruvian	375	0.1	0.6
Venezuelan	349	0.1	0.6
Spaniard	443	0.1	0.7

Population Growth: 2000–2010	
Group	%
Total Population	10.2
Hispanic or Latino (of any race)	134.3
Central American, ex. Mexican	336.2
Costa Rican	64.7
Guatemalan	362.4
Honduran	464.1
Salvadoran	382.0
Cuban	114.8
Mexican	129.3
Puerto Rican	64.6
South American	171.1
Colombian	167.2
Peruvian	228.9
Venezuelan	111.5

Males per 100 Females	
Group	Number
Total Population	94.0
Hispanic or Latino (of any race)	121.9
Central American, ex. Mexican	133.2
Costa Rican	95.3
Guatemalan	163.2
Honduran	137.5
Nicaraguan	118.7
Panamanian	64.3
Salvadoran	119.4
Cuban	107.7
Dominican Republic	85.9
Mexican	126.3
Puerto Rican	95.1
South American	87.3
Argentinean	97.6
Chilean	107.8
Colombian	79.4
Ecuadorian	83.2
Peruvian	84.7
Venezuelan	99.4
Spaniard	90.9

Average Household Size	
Group	People
Total Population	2.31
Hispanic or Latino (of any race)	3.74
Central American, ex. Mexican	4.11
Costa Rican	3.19
Guatemalan	4.19
Honduran	4.08
Nicaraguan	3.42
Panamanian	2.40
Salvadoran	4.38
Cuban	2.82
Dominican Republic	2.73
Mexican	3.98
Puerto Rican	2.65
South American	2.69
Argentinean	2.44
Chilean	2.48
Colombian	2.54
Ecuadorian	3.46
Peruvian	2.56
Venezuelan	2.75
Spaniard	2.37

Median Age	
Group	Years
Total Population	33.7
Hispanic or Latino (of any race)	25.7
Central American, ex. Mexican	28.4
Costa Rican	31.1
Guatemalan	28.0
Honduran	27.6
Nicaraguan	31.9
Panamanian	32.4
Salvadoran	28.9
Cuban	32.0
Dominican Republic	27.9
Mexican	24.2
Puerto Rican	27.2
South American	32.3
Argentinean	31.4
Chilean	32.8
Colombian	32.0
Ecuadorian	29.9
Peruvian	35.7
Venezuelan	29.7
Spaniard	31.5

High School Graduates (Universe: Population 25 Years and Over)		
Group	Number	%
Total Population	330,760	84.8
Hispanic or Latino (of any race)	13,664	49.1
Central American, ex. Mexican	2,751	45.8
Guatemalan	710	37.7
Honduran	662	41.7
Salvadoran	962	47.5
Cuban	501	64.6
Mexican	7,848	44.2
Puerto Rican	1,033	76.1
South American	782	78.8

Four-Year College Graduates (Universe: Population 25 Years and Over)		
Group	Number	%
Total Population	130,146	33.4
Hispanic or Latino (of any race)	2,481	8.9
Central American, ex. Mexican	348	5.8
Guatemalan	76	4.0
Honduran	35	2.2
Salvadoran	156	7.7
Cuban	161	20.8
Mexican	991	5.6
Puerto Rican	314	23.1
South American	364	36.7

Population Age 3–17 Enrolled in Public School (Universe: Population Age 3–17 Enrolled in School)		
Group	Number	%
Total Population	72,073	79.9
Hispanic or Latino (of any race)	10,208	93.7
Central American, ex. Mexican	1,539	95.5
Guatemalan	248	100.0
Honduran	298	100.0
Salvadoran	965	100.0
Cuban	218	89.7
Mexican	7,193	95.7
Puerto Rican	620	84.2
South American	256	95.9

Population Age 3–17 Enrolled in Private School (Universe: Population Age 3–17 Enrolled in School)		
Group	Number	%
Total Population	18,130	20.1
Hispanic or Latino (of any race)	687	6.3
Central American, ex. Mexican	72	4.5
Guatemalan	0	0.0
Honduran	0	0.0
Salvadoran	0	0.0
Cuban	25	10.3
Mexican	325	4.3
Puerto Rican	116	15.8
South American	11	4.1

Foreign-Born Population		
Group	Number	%
Total Population	68,779	11.7
Hispanic or Latino (of any race)	32,184	59.5
Central American, ex. Mexican	7,779	72.8
Guatemalan	2,591	85.4
Honduran	1,927	70.7
Salvadoran	2,792	66.3
Cuban	636	48.8
Mexican	22,098	61.6
Puerto Rican	48	1.7
South American	1,114	69.8

Foreign-Born Naturalized U.S. Citizens		
Group	Number	%
Total Population	18,912	27.5
Hispanic or Latino (of any race)	2,853	8.9
Central American, ex. Mexican	815	10.5
Guatemalan	162	6.3
Honduran	223	11.6
Salvadoran	272	9.7
Cuban	82	12.9
Mexican	1,490	6.7
Puerto Rican	0	0.0
South American	290	26.0

Language Spoken at Home: English Only (Universe: Population 5 Years and Over)		
Group	Number	%
Total Population	464,107	85.0
Hispanic or Latino (of any race)	6,546	14.1
Central American, ex. Mexican	571	6.2
Guatemalan	184	6.6
Honduran	24	1.1
Salvadoran	175	5.1
Cuban	275	22.1
Mexican	3,363	11.1
Puerto Rican	1,247	50.2
South American	279	19.4

Notes: (1) Percent of total population; (2) Percent of Hispanic/Latino population; Profiles include places with an overall population of at least 125,000, OR an overall population of at least 25,000 where the Hispanic/Latino population is at least 20% of the overall population. In states where less than five places meet either of these criteria, we have included places with at least 10,000 total population with the highest percentage of Hispanic/Latino population. These places are identified with an asterisk (*); Please refer to the User's Guide for a full explanation of data.

Language Spoken at Home: Spanish
(Universe: Population 5 Years and Over)

Group	Number	%
Total Population	44,022	8.1
Hispanic or Latino (of any race)	39,624	85.6
Central American, ex. Mexican	8,589	93.8
Guatemalan	2,612	93.4
Honduran	2,248	98.9
Salvadoran	3,229	94.9
Cuban	967	77.9
Mexican	26,897	88.7
Puerto Rican	1,237	49.8
South American	1,162	80.6

Unemployment Rate
(Universe: Population 16 Years and Over)

Group	%
Total Population	7.6
Hispanic or Latino (of any race)	7.8
Central American, ex. Mexican	7.3
Guatemalan	0.7
Honduran	9.9
Salvadoran	10.3
Cuban	14.0
Mexican	8.4
Puerto Rican	5.4
South American	5.1

Class of Worker: Private Wage and Salary
(Universe: Civilian Employed Population 16 Years and Over)

Group	Number	%
Total Population	243,259	80.9
Hispanic or Latino (of any race)	23,284	91.4
Central American, ex. Mexican	5,431	95.3
Guatemalan	1,923	95.6
Honduran	1,345	96.1
Salvadoran	1,784	93.9
Cuban	544	87.2
Mexican	14,726	91.3
Puerto Rican	1,096	85.3
South American	717	85.0

Class of Worker: Government
(Universe: Civilian Employed Population 16 Years and Over)

Group	Number	%
Total Population	36,423	12.1
Hispanic or Latino (of any race)	647	2.5
Central American, ex. Mexican	103	1.8
Guatemalan	66	3.3
Honduran	14	1.0
Salvadoran	13	0.7
Cuban	57	9.1
Mexican	230	1.4
Puerto Rican	122	9.5
South American	30	3.6

Means of Transportation to Work: Car, Truck or Van
(Universe: Workers 16 Years and Over)

Group	Number	%
Total Population	264,413	90.4
Hispanic or Latino (of any race)	22,656	92.0
Central American, ex. Mexican	5,320	94.9
Guatemalan	1,971	100.0
Honduran	1,239	92.1
Salvadoran	1,760	92.7
Cuban	574	94.3
Mexican	14,173	91.2
Puerto Rican	1,122	91.7
South American	733	90.3

Means of Transportation to Work: Public Transportation (ex. Taxicab)
(Universe: Workers 16 Years and Over)

Group	Number	%
Total Population	6,006	2.1
Hispanic or Latino (of any race)	526	2.1
Central American, ex. Mexican	92	1.6
Guatemalan	0	0.0
Honduran	0	0.0
Salvadoran	92	4.8
Cuban	0	0.0
Mexican	342	2.2
Puerto Rican	19	1.6
South American	37	4.6

Homeownership Rate
(Universe: Occupied Housing Units)

Group	%
Total Population	55.4
Hispanic or Latino (of any race)	33.2
Central American, ex. Mexican	37.2
Costa Rican	58.4
Guatemalan	26.3
Honduran	23.6
Nicaraguan	37.1
Panamanian	45.3
Salvadoran	51.8
Cuban	47.5
Dominican Republic	36.1
Mexican	28.9
Puerto Rican	37.9
South American	50.4
Argentinean	47.5
Chilean	61.7
Colombian	55.6
Ecuadorian	63.6
Peruvian	39.8
Venezuelan	36.4
Spaniard	51.9

Median Home Value

Group	Dollars
Total Population	162,400
Hispanic or Latino (of any race)	137,700
Central American, ex. Mexican	131,400
Guatemalan	136,300
Honduran	136,800
Salvadoran	114,900
Cuban	133,200
Mexican	131,900
Puerto Rican	229,200
South American	166,300

Median Gross Rent

Group	Dollars
Total Population	773
Hispanic or Latino (of any race)	756
Central American, ex. Mexican	730
Guatemalan	671
Honduran	711
Salvadoran	886
Cuban	850
Mexican	760
Puerto Rican	700
South American	772

Median Household Income
(2010 Inflation-Adjusted Dollars)

Group	Dollars
Total Population	45,063
Hispanic or Latino (of any race)	34,307
Central American, ex. Mexican	36,860
Guatemalan	41,490
Honduran	30,273
Salvadoran	36,339
Cuban	26,304
Mexican	32,804
Puerto Rican	32,225
South American	36,591

Per Capita Income
(2010 Inflation-Adjusted Dollars)

Group	Dollars
Total Population	26,550
Hispanic or Latino (of any race)	12,864
Central American, ex. Mexican	12,853
Guatemalan	14,357
Honduran	14,679
Salvadoran	9,972
Cuban	19,080
Mexican	11,113
Puerto Rican	21,187
South American	19,917

Households with $100,000+ Income

Group	Number	%
Total Population	37,855	15.6
Hispanic or Latino (of any race)	938	6.6
Central American, ex. Mexican	88	3.1
Guatemalan	37	4.9
Honduran	17	2.0
Salvadoran	34	3.3
Cuban	60	11.5
Mexican	430	4.8
Puerto Rican	177	21.5
South American	61	12.1

Households with Food Stamps/SNAP Benefits During Past 12 Months

Group	Number	%
Total Population	30,662	12.6
Hispanic or Latino (of any race)	3,555	25.2
Central American, ex. Mexican	639	22.3
Guatemalan	60	7.9
Honduran	233	27.9
Salvadoran	304	29.5
Cuban	164	31.5
Mexican	2,574	29.0
Puerto Rican	108	13.1
South American	40	7.9

Poverty Rate
(Income in Past 12 Months Below Poverty Level)

Group	%
Total Population	17.8
Hispanic or Latino (of any race)	31.9
Central American, ex. Mexican	38.5
Guatemalan	40.7
Honduran	38.0
Salvadoran	41.0
Cuban	24.6
Mexican	32.5
Puerto Rican	22.3
South American	13.5

Notes: (1) Percent of total population; (2) Percent of Hispanic/Latino population; Profiles include places with an overall population of at least 125,000, OR an overall population of at least 25,000 where the Hispanic/Latino population is at least 20% of the overall population. In states where less than five places meet either of these criteria, we have included places with at least 10,000 total population with the highest percentage of Hispanic/Latino population. These places are identified with an asterisk (*); Please refer to the User's Guide for a full explanation of data.

Texas

EDITOR'S NOTE: For a place to be included in this edition, it must meet one of two criteria. Either its overall population is at least 125,000, OR its overall population is at least 25,000 and its Hispanic/Latino population is at least 20% of the overall population. For the state of Texas, the following locations are included:

- Abilene
- Amarillo
- Arlington
- Atascocita
- Austin
- Baytown
- Big Spring
- Brownsville
- Bryan
- Carrollton
- Channelview
- Cleburne
- Conroe
- Corpus Christi
- Dallas
- Deer Park
- Del Rio
- Denton
- Duncanville
- Eagle Pass
- Edinburg
- El Paso
- Farmers Branch
- Fort Hood
- Fort Worth
- Galveston
- Garland
- Georgetown
- Grand Prairie
- Greenville
- Haltom City
- Harlingen
- Houston
- Hurst
- Irving
- Killeen
- Kingsville
- Kyle
- La Porte
- Lake Jackson
- Laredo
- Leander
- Lewisville
- Little Elm
- Lubbock
- Lufkin
- McAllen
- McKinney
- Mesquite
- Midland
- Mission
- Mission Bend
- New Braunfels
- Odessa
- Pasadena
- Pearland
- Pflugerville
- Pharr
- Plano
- Port Arthur
- Rosenberg
- Round Rock
- San Angelo
- San Antonio
- San Juan
- San Marcos
- Schertz
- Seguin
- Sherman
- Socorro
- Spring
- Temple
- Texas City
- The Colony
- Tyler
- Victoria
- Waco
- Waxahachie
- Weslaco

Section Two: State & Place Profiles starts with the state profile, followed by place profiles that meet the criteria above. Places are listed alphabetically within each state. All states, all counties and places that meet the above criteria are ranked and compared in *Section Three: Rankings & Comparisons*, on page 1055.

For a more detailed look at the Hispanic/Latino population in Texas, a companion web site is available at no additional charge with purchase of this print edition. Visit http://gold.greyhouse.com/page/info_hispanic for more information.

The web site includes data for all counties and places in Texas with Hispanic/Latino population, plus ten additional topics: Self Employed Worker; Walked to Work; Worked from Home; Mean Travel Time to Work; Mean Household Income; Households with Cash Public Assistance; Mean Cash Pubic Assistance; Poverty Rates for 18 and Under, 18 to 64, and 65 and Over.

Population

Group	Number	%TP[1]	%HP[2]
Total Population	25,145,561	100.0	–
Hispanic or Latino (of any race)	9,460,921	37.6	100.0
Central American, ex. Mexican	420,683	1.7	4.4
Costa Rican	6,982	<0.1	0.1
Guatemalan	66,244	0.3	0.7
Honduran	88,389	0.4	0.9
Nicaraguan	19,817	0.1	0.2
Panamanian	13,994	0.1	0.1
Salvadoran	222,599	0.9	2.4
Cuban	46,541	0.2	0.5
Dominican Republic	13,353	0.1	0.1
Mexican	7,951,193	31.6	84.0
Puerto Rican	130,576	0.5	1.4
South American	133,808	0.5	1.4
Argentinean	13,831	0.1	0.1
Bolivian	4,913	<0.1	0.1
Chilean	6,282	<0.1	0.1
Colombian	50,810	0.2	0.5
Ecuadorian	10,793	<0.1	0.1
Paraguayan	763	<0.1	<0.1
Peruvian	22,605	0.1	0.2
Uruguayan	2,566	<0.1	<0.1
Venezuelan	20,162	0.1	0.2
Spaniard	65,777	0.3	0.7

Population Growth: 2000–2010

Group	%
Total Population	20.6
Hispanic or Latino (of any race)	41.8
Central American, ex. Mexican	186.7
Costa Rican	111.4
Guatemalan	257.3
Honduran	265.6
Nicaraguan	164.7
Panamanian	97.8
Salvadoran	181.0
Cuban	81.1
Dominican Republic	210.8
Mexican	56.8
Puerto Rican	87.9
South American	160.2
Argentinean	193.6
Bolivian	161.5
Chilean	114.1
Colombian	149.0
Ecuadorian	202.7
Paraguayan	147.7
Peruvian	182.1
Uruguayan	265.0
Venezuelan	219.8
Spaniard	813.3

Males per 100 Females

Group	Number
Total Population	98.4
Hispanic or Latino (of any race)	101.4
Central American, ex. Mexican	112.6
Costa Rican	91.3
Guatemalan	148.7
Honduran	118.1
Nicaraguan	95.8
Panamanian	70.1
Salvadoran	107.1
Cuban	110.2
Dominican Republic	95.2
Mexican	101.2
Puerto Rican	102.9
South American	89.0
Argentinean	104.5
Bolivian	90.3
Chilean	94.2
Colombian	83.9
Ecuadorian	92.8
Paraguayan	80.8
Peruvian	90.0
Uruguayan	104.0
Venezuelan	85.6
Spaniard	91.6

Average Household Size

Group	People
Total Population	2.75
Hispanic or Latino (of any race)	3.46
Central American, ex. Mexican	3.77
Costa Rican	2.91
Guatemalan	3.79
Honduran	3.75
Nicaraguan	3.39
Panamanian	2.67
Salvadoran	3.92
Cuban	2.73
Dominican Republic	3.03
Mexican	3.50
Puerto Rican	2.86
South American	2.88
Argentinean	2.77
Bolivian	2.82
Chilean	2.77
Colombian	2.87
Ecuadorian	3.13
Paraguayan	2.77
Peruvian	2.99
Uruguayan	2.94
Venezuelan	2.83
Spaniard	2.78

Median Age

Group	Years
Total Population	33.6
Hispanic or Latino (of any race)	27.0
Central American, ex. Mexican	30.2
Costa Rican	33.3
Guatemalan	29.3
Honduran	29.0
Nicaraguan	32.7
Panamanian	35.1
Salvadoran	30.7
Cuban	35.4
Dominican Republic	28.6
Mexican	26.6
Puerto Rican	28.2

Notes: (1) Percent of total population; (2) Percent of Hispanic/Latino population; Profiles include places with an overall population of at least 125,000, OR an overall population of at least 25,000 where the Hispanic/Latino population is at least 20% of the overall population. In states where less than five places meet either of these criteria, we have included places with at least 10,000 total population with the highest percentage of Hispanic/Latino population. These places are identified with an asterisk (*); Please refer to the User's Guide for a full explanation of data.

South American	34.6
Argentinean	35.2
Bolivian	34.7
Chilean	36.3
Colombian	34.4
Ecuadorian	33.7
Paraguayan	30.9
Peruvian	35.6
Uruguayan	35.7
Venezuelan	33.5
Spaniard	32.6

High School Graduates
(Universe: Population 25 Years and Over)

Group	Number	%
Total Population	12,095,373	80.0
Hispanic or Latino (of any race)	2,743,095	58.2
Central American, ex. Mexican	105,525	43.5
Costa Rican	3,347	83.7
Guatemalan	15,276	42.1
Honduran	19,747	39.4
Nicaraguan	8,031	73.5
Panamanian	7,379	92.5
Salvadoran	50,150	38.5
Cuban	21,725	83.7
Dominican Republic	5,210	80.0
Mexican	2,289,774	56.9
Puerto Rican	59,700	87.6
South American	73,337	88.0
Argentinean	7,145	86.2
Bolivian	2,531	88.3
Chilean	2,888	88.7
Colombian	26,794	85.4
Ecuadorian	6,372	86.6
Paraguayan	653	88.5
Peruvian	12,789	90.2
Uruguayan	1,051	70.2
Venezuelan	11,526	96.1
Spaniard	31,484	85.7

Four-Year College Graduates
(Universe: Population 25 Years and Over)

Group	Number	%
Total Population	3,894,123	25.8
Hispanic or Latino (of any race)	528,931	11.2
Central American, ex. Mexican	19,614	8.1
Costa Rican	1,021	25.5
Guatemalan	2,969	8.2
Honduran	3,108	6.2
Nicaraguan	2,677	24.5
Panamanian	2,718	34.1
Salvadoran	6,713	5.2
Cuban	8,832	34.0
Dominican Republic	1,841	28.3
Mexican	410,011	10.2
Puerto Rican	19,033	27.9
South American	35,286	42.4
Argentinean	3,241	39.1
Bolivian	1,429	49.8
Chilean	1,158	35.6
Colombian	13,125	41.8
Ecuadorian	2,434	33.1
Paraguayan	204	27.6
Peruvian	5,212	36.8
Uruguayan	415	27.7
Venezuelan	7,108	59.3
Spaniard	9,551	26.0

Population Age 3–17 Enrolled in Public School
(Universe: Population Age 3–17 Enrolled in School)

Group	Number	%
Total Population	4,485,585	90.7
Hispanic or Latino (of any race)	2,154,697	95.4
Central American, ex. Mexican	80,440	96.3
Costa Rican	767	83.8
Guatemalan	9,774	93.1
Honduran	16,005	98.0
Nicaraguan	2,724	90.7
Panamanian	2,384	87.3
Salvadoran	47,593	97.5
Cuban	6,197	87.2
Dominican Republic	2,421	96.9
Mexican	1,900,254	95.8
Puerto Rican	25,167	90.7
South American	21,771	85.7
Argentinean	1,770	83.8
Bolivian	766	91.4
Chilean	699	77.5
Colombian	8,285	84.4
Ecuadorian	2,537	91.0
Paraguayan	40	44.4
Peruvian	4,077	88.8
Uruguayan	433	89.1
Venezuelan	2,802	83.8
Spaniard	10,381	88.6

Population Age 3–17 Enrolled in Private School
(Universe: Population Age 3–17 Enrolled in School)

Group	Number	%
Total Population	461,840	9.3
Hispanic or Latino (of any race)	103,341	4.6
Central American, ex. Mexican	3,130	3.7
Costa Rican	148	16.2
Guatemalan	722	6.9
Honduran	327	2.0
Nicaraguan	280	9.3
Panamanian	348	12.7
Salvadoran	1,208	2.5
Cuban	910	12.8
Dominican Republic	77	3.1
Mexican	84,079	4.2
Puerto Rican	2,594	9.3
South American	3,619	14.3
Argentinean	341	16.2
Bolivian	72	8.6
Chilean	203	22.5
Colombian	1,532	15.6
Ecuadorian	250	9.0
Paraguayan	50	55.6
Peruvian	512	11.2
Uruguayan	53	10.9
Venezuelan	543	16.2
Spaniard	1,341	11.4

Foreign-Born Population

Group	Number	%
Total Population	3,913,577	16.1
Hispanic or Latino (of any race)	2,801,938	31.4
Central American, ex. Mexican	280,630	67.4
Costa Rican	3,769	64.7
Guatemalan	45,118	73.1
Honduran	63,788	72.5
Nicaraguan	10,739	64.3
Panamanian	6,451	49.2
Salvadoran	147,737	65.4
Cuban	20,499	51.8
Dominican Republic	5,334	48.0
Mexican	2,359,804	30.6
Puerto Rican	1,782	1.5
South American	87,667	67.2
Argentinean	8,591	70.2
Bolivian	2,740	62.4
Chilean	3,207	66.3
Colombian	32,905	66.3
Ecuadorian	7,101	58.3
Paraguayan	558	61.2
Peruvian	15,989	71.0
Uruguayan	1,783	72.2
Venezuelan	13,377	71.3
Spaniard	5,484	9.4

Foreign-Born Naturalized U.S. Citizens

Group	Number	%
Total Population	1,245,278	31.8
Hispanic or Latino (of any race)	675,761	24.1
Central American, ex. Mexican	60,381	21.5
Costa Rican	1,896	50.3
Guatemalan	7,995	17.7
Honduran	6,209	9.7
Nicaraguan	4,784	44.5
Panamanian	3,884	60.2
Salvadoran	34,441	23.3
Cuban	10,661	52.0
Dominican Republic	2,762	51.8
Mexican	548,063	23.2
Puerto Rican	837	47.0
South American	33,699	38.4
Argentinean	2,978	34.7
Bolivian	1,086	39.6
Chilean	1,360	42.4
Colombian	13,565	41.2
Ecuadorian	3,292	46.4
Paraguayan	353	63.3
Peruvian	6,357	39.8
Uruguayan	474	26.6
Venezuelan	3,673	27.5
Spaniard	2,822	51.5

Language Spoken at Home: English Only
(Universe: Population 5 Years and Over)

Group	Number	%
Total Population	14,740,304	65.8
Hispanic or Latino (of any race)	1,720,628	21.6
Central American, ex. Mexican	24,886	6.6
Costa Rican	1,294	23.7
Guatemalan	4,162	7.4
Honduran	4,050	5.2
Nicaraguan	2,274	14.8
Panamanian	3,958	32.3
Salvadoran	8,695	4.3
Cuban	10,195	27.7
Dominican Republic	2,269	22.0
Mexican	1,451,001	21.1
Puerto Rican	38,858	35.7
South American	15,980	13.3
Argentinean	1,227	11.0
Bolivian	873	20.6
Chilean	1,109	24.7
Colombian	5,458	11.9
Ecuadorian	1,923	17.2
Paraguayan	290	33.4
Peruvian	2,591	12.4
Uruguayan	308	13.2
Venezuelan	1,852	10.8
Spaniard	30,941	57.0

Language Spoken at Home: Spanish
(Universe: Population 5 Years and Over)

Group	Number	%
Total Population	6,547,178	29.2
Hispanic or Latino (of any race)	6,234,052	78.2
Central American, ex. Mexican	350,597	93.2
Costa Rican	4,170	76.3
Guatemalan	51,761	92.0
Honduran	74,263	94.5
Nicaraguan	13,024	85.0
Panamanian	8,162	66.6
Salvadoran	195,120	95.7
Cuban	26,217	71.2
Dominican Republic	7,956	77.3
Mexican	5,408,330	78.8
Puerto Rican	69,306	63.6
South American	103,715	86.1
Argentinean	9,815	88.3
Bolivian	3,362	79.2
Chilean	3,340	74.3
Colombian	40,137	87.7
Ecuadorian	9,206	82.4
Paraguayan	568	65.4
Peruvian	18,185	87.0
Uruguayan	1,996	85.4
Venezuelan	15,132	88.4
Spaniard	22,484	41.4

Unemployment Rate
(Universe: Population 16 Years and Over)

Group	%
Total Population	7.0
Hispanic or Latino (of any race)	7.9
Central American, ex. Mexican	7.9
Costa Rican	10.1
Guatemalan	5.8
Honduran	10.1
Nicaraguan	9.2
Panamanian	8.0
Salvadoran	7.4
Cuban	8.6
Dominican Republic	7.5
Mexican	7.9
Puerto Rican	8.4
South American	6.3
Argentinean	5.6
Bolivian	9.5
Chilean	4.6
Colombian	6.2

Notes: (1) Percent of total population; (2) Percent of Hispanic/Latino population; Profiles include places with an overall population of at least 125,000, OR an overall population of at least 25,000 where the Hispanic/Latino population is at least 20% of the overall population. In states where less than five places meet either of these criteria, we have included places with at least 10,000 total population with the highest percentage of Hispanic/Latino population. These places are identified with an asterisk (*); Please refer to the User's Guide for a full explanation of data.

Group		%
Ecuadorian		5.2
Paraguayan		11.7
Peruvian		6.6
Uruguayan		0.0
Venezuelan		7.7
Spaniard		6.9

Class of Worker: Private Wage and Salary
(Universe: Civilian Employed Population 16 Years and Over)

Group	Number	%
Total Population	8,667,774	77.9
Hispanic or Latino (of any race)	2,986,048	80.2
Central American, ex. Mexican	186,658	86.2
Costa Rican	2,449	77.2
Guatemalan	31,334	87.9
Honduran	38,249	86.3
Nicaraguan	7,328	82.6
Panamanian	4,479	74.0
Salvadoran	101,115	87.0
Cuban	15,561	81.4
Dominican Republic	4,189	79.7
Mexican	2,532,760	80.0
Puerto Rican	39,994	75.3
South American	51,787	78.1
Argentinean	5,428	83.4
Bolivian	1,724	74.7
Chilean	1,997	81.2
Colombian	18,472	74.7
Ecuadorian	4,556	77.6
Paraguayan	448	83.9
Peruvian	9,175	79.3
Uruguayan	1,118	80.5
Venezuelan	7,880	82.6
Spaniard	21,482	76.2

Class of Worker: Government
(Universe: Civilian Employed Population 16 Years and Over)

Group	Number	%
Total Population	1,633,861	14.7
Hispanic or Latino (of any race)	465,715	12.5
Central American, ex. Mexican	9,952	4.6
Costa Rican	489	15.4
Guatemalan	933	2.6
Honduran	1,273	2.9
Nicaraguan	706	8.0
Panamanian	1,317	21.8
Salvadoran	5,021	4.3
Cuban	2,373	12.4
Dominican Republic	683	13.0
Mexican	401,192	12.7
Puerto Rican	10,996	20.7
South American	8,218	12.4
Argentinean	551	8.5
Bolivian	413	17.9
Chilean	262	10.7
Colombian	3,475	14.0
Ecuadorian	926	15.8
Paraguayan	46	8.6
Peruvian	1,215	10.5
Uruguayan	90	6.5
Venezuelan	1,020	10.7
Spaniard	4,820	17.1

Means of Transportation to Work: Car, Truck or Van
(Universe: Workers 16 Years and Over)

Group	Number	%
Total Population	9,973,640	91.0
Hispanic or Latino (of any race)	3,340,792	91.5
Central American, ex. Mexican	188,288	88.4
Costa Rican	2,897	91.7
Guatemalan	28,149	80.1
Honduran	37,913	87.0
Nicaraguan	7,669	87.3
Panamanian	5,469	90.9
Salvadoran	104,308	91.2
Cuban	17,078	89.2
Dominican Republic	4,699	87.9
Mexican	2,845,613	91.8
Puerto Rican	49,227	89.9
South American	58,280	90.1
Argentinean	5,570	88.2
Bolivian	2,054	90.6
Chilean	2,241	92.9
Colombian	21,665	89.6
Ecuadorian	5,384	93.9
Paraguayan	470	92.7
Peruvian	9,994	88.2
Uruguayan	1,273	93.4
Venezuelan	8,449	91.5
Spaniard	24,989	89.1

Means of Transportation to Work: Public Transportation (ex. Taxicab)
(Universe: Workers 16 Years and Over)

Group	Number	%
Total Population	179,792	1.6
Hispanic or Latino (of any race)	68,121	1.9
Central American, ex. Mexican	8,571	4.0
Costa Rican	43	1.4
Guatemalan	2,494	7.1
Honduran	1,699	3.9
Nicaraguan	180	2.0
Panamanian	57	0.9
Salvadoran	4,053	3.5
Cuban	464	2.4
Dominican Republic	138	2.6
Mexican	52,628	1.7
Puerto Rican	1,023	1.9
South American	1,161	1.8
Argentinean	163	2.6
Bolivian	93	4.1
Chilean	0	0.0
Colombian	357	1.5
Ecuadorian	9	0.2
Paraguayan	0	0.0
Peruvian	367	3.2
Uruguayan	14	1.0
Venezuelan	144	1.6
Spaniard	634	2.3

Homeownership Rate
(Universe: Occupied Housing Units)

Group	%
Total Population	63.7
Hispanic or Latino (of any race)	57.8
Central American, ex. Mexican	46.7
Costa Rican	55.9
Guatemalan	37.7
Honduran	32.4
Nicaraguan	53.3
Panamanian	57.1
Salvadoran	52.9
Cuban	54.3
Dominican Republic	49.2
Mexican	59.1
Puerto Rican	52.7
South American	58.5
Argentinean	58.3
Bolivian	64.4
Chilean	61.7
Colombian	57.8
Ecuadorian	63.4
Paraguayan	64.2
Peruvian	56.2
Uruguayan	55.2
Venezuelan	59.0
Spaniard	61.0

Median Home Value

Group	Dollars
Total Population	123,500
Hispanic or Latino (of any race)	89,800
Central American, ex. Mexican	110,700
Costa Rican	156,100
Guatemalan	113,600
Honduran	103,000
Nicaraguan	119,800
Panamanian	150,600
Salvadoran	108,800
Cuban	147,200
Dominican Republic	139,200
Mexican	86,700
Puerto Rican	140,400
South American	156,600
Argentinean	166,800
Bolivian	160,200
Chilean	146,200
Colombian	149,600
Ecuadorian	142,000
Paraguayan	144,000
Peruvian	154,000
Uruguayan	140,200
Venezuelan	188,100
Spaniard	140,400

Median Gross Rent

Group	Dollars
Total Population	786
Hispanic or Latino (of any race)	709
Central American, ex. Mexican	709
Costa Rican	811
Guatemalan	723
Honduran	701
Nicaraguan	788
Panamanian	809
Salvadoran	694
Cuban	788
Dominican Republic	764
Mexican	700
Puerto Rican	827
South American	861
Argentinean	846
Bolivian	796
Chilean	866
Colombian	852
Ecuadorian	818
Paraguayan	543
Peruvian	859
Uruguayan	745
Venezuelan	988
Spaniard	845

Median Household Income
(2010 Inflation-Adjusted Dollars)

Group	Dollars
Total Population	49,646
Hispanic or Latino (of any race)	37,019
Central American, ex. Mexican	36,441
Costa Rican	48,750
Guatemalan	34,797
Honduran	31,762
Nicaraguan	47,813
Panamanian	45,994
Salvadoran	36,764
Cuban	47,299
Dominican Republic	39,301
Mexican	36,408
Puerto Rican	50,296
South American	54,352
Argentinean	53,299
Bolivian	49,332
Chilean	55,893
Colombian	52,421
Ecuadorian	49,620
Paraguayan	41,818
Peruvian	49,540
Uruguayan	50,511
Venezuelan	78,117
Spaniard	50,301

Per Capita Income
(2010 Inflation-Adjusted Dollars)

Group	Dollars
Total Population	24,870
Hispanic or Latino (of any race)	14,169
Central American, ex. Mexican	14,024
Costa Rican	24,669
Guatemalan	14,407
Honduran	12,330
Nicaraguan	20,778
Panamanian	23,162
Salvadoran	13,251
Cuban	27,544
Dominican Republic	22,529
Mexican	13,653
Puerto Rican	22,499
South American	24,849
Argentinean	30,902
Bolivian	28,200
Chilean	24,208
Colombian	23,281
Ecuadorian	20,236
Paraguayan	27,563
Peruvian	21,597

Notes: (1) Percent of total population; (2) Percent of Hispanic/Latino population; Profiles include places with an overall population of at least 125,000, OR an overall population of at least 25,000 where the Hispanic/Latino population is at least 20% of the overall population. In states where less than five places meet either of these criteria, we have included places with at least 10,000 total population with the highest percentage of Hispanic/Latino population. These places are identified with an asterisk (*); Please refer to the User's Guide for a full explanation of data.

Uruguayan	22,984
Venezuelan	29,850
Spaniard	25,092

Households with $100,000+ Income

Group	Number	%
Total Population	1,699,243	19.9
Hispanic or Latino (of any race)	229,010	9.3
Central American, ex. Mexican	7,707	6.5
Costa Rican	469	21.6
Guatemalan	1,215	6.8
Honduran	1,166	5.0
Nicaraguan	709	13.4
Panamanian	882	19.6
Salvadoran	3,073	4.8
Cuban	3,088	20.5
Dominican Republic	384	10.7
Mexican	183,578	8.8
Puerto Rican	7,316	18.6
South American	9,772	23.0
Argentinean	1,236	25.3
Bolivian	335	20.3
Chilean	375	21.6
Colombian	3,087	20.6
Ecuadorian	650	16.9
Paraguayan	105	26.0
Peruvian	1,281	18.6
Uruguayan	125	14.3
Venezuelan	2,258	37.6
Spaniard	4,469	18.9

Households with Food Stamps/SNAP Benefits During Past 12 Months

Group	Number	%
Total Population	890,215	10.4
Hispanic or Latino (of any race)	444,989	18.2
Central American, ex. Mexican	11,777	9.9
Costa Rican	150	6.9
Guatemalan	1,551	8.7
Honduran	3,182	13.8
Nicaraguan	473	8.9
Panamanian	237	5.3
Salvadoran	6,054	9.4
Cuban	1,701	11.3
Dominican Republic	301	8.4
Mexican	396,528	19.0
Puerto Rican	4,591	11.7
South American	2,288	5.4
Argentinean	268	5.5
Bolivian	54	3.3
Chilean	43	2.5
Colombian	852	5.7
Ecuadorian	358	9.3
Paraguayan	29	7.2
Peruvian	396	5.7
Uruguayan	70	8.0
Venezuelan	161	2.7
Spaniard	2,601	11.0

Poverty Rate
(Income in Past 12 Months Below Poverty Level)

Group	%
Total Population	16.8
Hispanic or Latino (of any race)	25.5
Central American, ex. Mexican	23.5
Costa Rican	12.1
Guatemalan	23.4
Honduran	32.0
Nicaraguan	11.5
Panamanian	14.9
Salvadoran	21.8
Cuban	14.0
Dominican Republic	14.8
Mexican	26.2
Puerto Rican	14.8
South American	11.5
Argentinean	9.0
Bolivian	13.6
Chilean	10.0
Colombian	12.4
Ecuadorian	17.6
Paraguayan	9.0
Peruvian	12.1
Uruguayan	12.2
Venezuelan	7.3

Spaniard	12.7

Abilene

Population

Group	Number	%TP[1]	%HP[2]
Total Population	117,063	100.0	–
Hispanic or Latino (of any race)	28,666	24.5	100.0
Central American, ex. Mexican	394	0.3	1.4
Nicaraguan	119	0.1	0.4
Salvadoran	111	0.1	0.4
Cuban	107	0.1	0.4
Mexican	22,897	19.6	79.9
Puerto Rican	569	0.5	2.0
South American	197	0.2	0.7
Spaniard	319	0.3	1.1

Population Growth: 2000–2010

Group	%
Total Population	1.0
Hispanic or Latino (of any race)	27.1
Central American, ex. Mexican	125.1
Mexican	45.4
Puerto Rican	37.4

Males per 100 Females

Group	Number
Total Population	102.0
Hispanic or Latino (of any race)	108.6
Central American, ex. Mexican	104.1
Nicaraguan	75.0
Salvadoran	164.3
Cuban	127.7
Mexican	99.2
Puerto Rican	121.4
South American	91.3
Spaniard	84.4

Average Household Size

Group	People
Total Population	2.46
Hispanic or Latino (of any race)	3.05
Central American, ex. Mexican	3.27
Nicaraguan	3.40
Salvadoran	3.55
Cuban	2.57
Mexican	3.09
Puerto Rican	2.68
South American	2.61
Spaniard	2.75

Median Age

Group	Years
Total Population	31.7
Hispanic or Latino (of any race)	25.1
Central American, ex. Mexican	29.0
Nicaraguan	33.5
Salvadoran	27.8
Cuban	22.8
Mexican	24.4
Puerto Rican	22.9
South American	26.4
Spaniard	25.8

High School Graduates
(Universe: Population 25 Years and Over)

Group	Number	%
Total Population	57,534	81.4
Hispanic or Latino (of any race)	8,206	58.8
Mexican	6,847	56.8

Four-Year College Graduates
(Universe: Population 25 Years and Over)

Group	Number	%
Total Population	16,237	23.0
Hispanic or Latino (of any race)	990	7.1
Mexican	689	5.7

Population Age 3–17 Enrolled in Public School
(Universe: Population Age 3–17 Enrolled in School)

Group	Number	%
Total Population	17,028	91.9
Hispanic or Latino (of any race)	5,869	95.9
Mexican	4,943	96.1

Population Age 3–17 Enrolled in Private School
(Universe: Population Age 3–17 Enrolled in School)

Group	Number	%
Total Population	1,496	8.1
Hispanic or Latino (of any race)	254	4.1
Mexican	201	3.9

Foreign-Born Population

Group	Number	%
Total Population	6,391	5.5
Hispanic or Latino (of any race)	3,699	13.2
Mexican	3,049	12.8

Foreign-Born Naturalized U.S. Citizens

Group	Number	%
Total Population	2,760	43.2
Hispanic or Latino (of any race)	1,444	39.0
Mexican	1,119	36.7

Language Spoken at Home: English Only
(Universe: Population 5 Years and Over)

Group	Number	%
Total Population	90,564	83.8
Hispanic or Latino (of any race)	11,249	45.3
Mexican	9,482	44.7

Language Spoken at Home: Spanish
(Universe: Population 5 Years and Over)

Group	Number	%
Total Population	14,882	13.8
Hispanic or Latino (of any race)	13,471	54.3
Mexican	11,663	55.0

Unemployment Rate
(Universe: Population 16 Years and Over)

Group	%
Total Population	5.8
Hispanic or Latino (of any race)	6.9
Mexican	7.2

Class of Worker: Private Wage and Salary
(Universe: Civilian Employed Population 16 Years and Over)

Group	Number	%
Total Population	38,738	76.1
Hispanic or Latino (of any race)	8,781	78.1
Mexican	7,553	78.6

Class of Worker: Government
(Universe: Civilian Employed Population 16 Years and Over)

Group	Number	%
Total Population	8,741	17.2
Hispanic or Latino (of any race)	1,827	16.2
Mexican	1,490	15.5

Means of Transportation to Work: Car, Truck or Van
(Universe: Workers 16 Years and Over)

Group	Number	%
Total Population	49,073	91.7
Hispanic or Latino (of any race)	10,707	93.5
Mexican	9,140	94.5

Means of Transportation to Work: Public Transportation (ex. Taxicab)
(Universe: Workers 16 Years and Over)

Group	Number	%
Total Population	233	0.4
Hispanic or Latino (of any race)	94	0.8
Mexican	60	0.6

Homeownership Rate
(Universe: Occupied Housing Units)

Group	%
Total Population	57.2
Hispanic or Latino (of any race)	52.0
Central American, ex. Mexican	59.1
Nicaraguan	61.9
Salvadoran	48.4
Cuban	34.3
Mexican	53.9
Puerto Rican	36.5
South American	42.1
Spaniard	42.7

Notes: (1) Percent of total population; (2) Percent of Hispanic/Latino population; Profiles include places with an overall population of at least 125,000, OR an overall population of at least 25,000 where the Hispanic/Latino population is at least 20% of the overall population. In states where less than five places meet either of these criteria, we have included places with at least 10,000 total population with the highest percentage of Hispanic/Latino population. These places are identified with an asterisk (*); Please refer to the User's Guide for a full explanation of data.

Median Home Value	
Group	Dollars
Total Population	88,400
Hispanic or Latino (of any race)	54,800
Mexican	53,500

Median Gross Rent	
Group	Dollars
Total Population	723
Hispanic or Latino (of any race)	686
Mexican	679

Median Household Income (2010 Inflation-Adjusted Dollars)	
Group	Dollars
Total Population	39,766
Hispanic or Latino (of any race)	33,437
Mexican	33,448

Per Capita Income (2010 Inflation-Adjusted Dollars)	
Group	Dollars
Total Population	20,826
Hispanic or Latino (of any race)	12,712
Mexican	12,594

Households with $100,000+ Income		
Group	Number	%
Total Population	4,957	11.6
Hispanic or Latino (of any race)	434	5.7
Mexican	326	5.1

Households with Food Stamps/SNAP Benefits During Past 12 Months		
Group	Number	%
Total Population	4,644	10.9
Hispanic or Latino (of any race)	1,578	20.7
Mexican	1,370	21.3

Poverty Rate (Income in Past 12 Months Below Poverty Level)	
Group	%
Total Population	17.8
Hispanic or Latino (of any race)	22.2
Mexican	23.5

Amarillo

Population			
Group	Number	%TP[1]	%HP[2]
Total Population	190,695	100.0	–
Hispanic or Latino (of any race)	54,881	28.8	100.0
Central American, ex. Mexican	560	0.3	1.0
Honduran	137	0.1	0.2
Salvadoran	261	0.1	0.5
Cuban	249	0.1	0.5
Mexican	47,195	24.7	86.0
Puerto Rican	318	0.2	0.6
South American	193	0.1	0.4
Spaniard	965	0.5	1.8

Population Growth: 2000–2010	
Group	%
Total Population	9.8
Hispanic or Latino (of any race)	44.6
Central American, ex. Mexican	150.0
Cuban	124.3
Mexican	76.4
Puerto Rican	44.5

Males per 100 Females	
Group	Number
Total Population	94.1
Hispanic or Latino (of any race)	99.1
Central American, ex. Mexican	98.6
Honduran	101.5
Salvadoran	113.9
Cuban	96.1
Mexican	100.1
Puerto Rican	92.7
South American	103.2
Spaniard	98.6

Average Household Size	
Group	People
Total Population	2.55
Hispanic or Latino (of any race)	3.30
Central American, ex. Mexican	3.65
Honduran	3.69
Salvadoran	3.70
Cuban	2.67
Mexican	3.36
Puerto Rican	2.90
South American	2.60
Spaniard	2.78

Median Age	
Group	Years
Total Population	33.4
Hispanic or Latino (of any race)	23.9
Central American, ex. Mexican	31.7
Honduran	32.8
Salvadoran	30.7
Cuban	31.1
Mexican	23.5
Puerto Rican	28.3
South American	35.3
Spaniard	29.3

High School Graduates (Universe: Population 25 Years and Over)		
Group	Number	%
Total Population	96,266	81.7
Hispanic or Latino (of any race)	14,740	57.6
Mexican	12,687	56.2

Four-Year College Graduates (Universe: Population 25 Years and Over)		
Group	Number	%
Total Population	25,656	21.8
Hispanic or Latino (of any race)	1,436	5.6
Mexican	1,058	4.7

Population Age 3–17 Enrolled in Public School (Universe: Population Age 3–17 Enrolled in School)		
Group	Number	%
Total Population	33,434	91.1
Hispanic or Latino (of any race)	13,325	93.3
Mexican	12,329	94.2

Population Age 3–17 Enrolled in Private School (Universe: Population Age 3–17 Enrolled in School)		
Group	Number	%
Total Population	3,259	8.9
Hispanic or Latino (of any race)	950	6.7
Mexican	762	5.8

Foreign-Born Population		
Group	Number	%
Total Population	19,007	10.2
Hispanic or Latino (of any race)	12,739	24.3
Mexican	11,837	25.0

Foreign-Born Naturalized U.S. Citizens		
Group	Number	%
Total Population	5,380	28.3
Hispanic or Latino (of any race)	2,864	22.5
Mexican	2,523	21.3

Language Spoken at Home: English Only (Universe: Population 5 Years and Over)		
Group	Number	%
Total Population	132,849	77.3
Hispanic or Latino (of any race)	15,214	33.1
Mexican	13,267	32.1

Language Spoken at Home: Spanish (Universe: Population 5 Years and Over)		
Group	Number	%
Total Population	32,335	18.8
Hispanic or Latino (of any race)	30,671	66.8
Mexican	28,002	67.8

Unemployment Rate (Universe: Population 16 Years and Over)	
Group	%
Total Population	5.5
Hispanic or Latino (of any race)	7.0
Mexican	6.7

Class of Worker: Private Wage and Salary (Universe: Civilian Employed Population 16 Years and Over)		
Group	Number	%
Total Population	72,806	79.0
Hispanic or Latino (of any race)	19,487	84.9
Mexican	17,622	85.3

Class of Worker: Government (Universe: Civilian Employed Population 16 Years and Over)		
Group	Number	%
Total Population	13,085	14.2
Hispanic or Latino (of any race)	2,180	9.5
Mexican	1,891	9.2

Means of Transportation to Work: Car, Truck or Van (Universe: Workers 16 Years and Over)		
Group	Number	%
Total Population	85,334	94.6
Hispanic or Latino (of any race)	21,310	95.4
Mexican	19,321	95.8

Means of Transportation to Work: Public Transportation (ex. Taxicab) (Universe: Workers 16 Years and Over)		
Group	Number	%
Total Population	668	0.7
Hispanic or Latino (of any race)	237	1.1
Mexican	209	1.0

Homeownership Rate (Universe: Occupied Housing Units)	
Group	%
Total Population	62.6
Hispanic or Latino (of any race)	55.7
Central American, ex. Mexican	67.6
Honduran	68.6
Salvadoran	63.7
Cuban	31.5
Mexican	56.4
Puerto Rican	52.3
South American	66.7
Spaniard	61.7

Median Home Value	
Group	Dollars
Total Population	105,300
Hispanic or Latino (of any race)	70,800
Mexican	69,300

Median Gross Rent	
Group	Dollars
Total Population	670
Hispanic or Latino (of any race)	629
Mexican	617

Median Household Income (2010 Inflation-Adjusted Dollars)	
Group	Dollars
Total Population	43,978
Hispanic or Latino (of any race)	31,995
Mexican	31,694

Per Capita Income (2010 Inflation-Adjusted Dollars)	
Group	Dollars
Total Population	23,149
Hispanic or Latino (of any race)	12,518
Mexican	12,190

Households with $100,000+ Income		
Group	Number	%
Total Population	9,515	13.6
Hispanic or Latino (of any race)	747	5.2
Mexican	611	4.9

Households with Food Stamps/SNAP Benefits During Past 12 Months		
Group	Number	%
Total Population	7,130	10.2
Hispanic or Latino (of any race)	2,377	16.7
Mexican	2,124	17.1

Notes: (1) Percent of total population; (2) Percent of Hispanic/Latino population; Profiles include places with an overall population of at least 125,000, OR an overall population of at least 25,000 where the Hispanic/Latino population is at least 20% of the overall population. In states where less than five places meet either of these criteria, we have included places with at least 10,000 total population with the highest percentage of Hispanic/Latino population. These places are identified with an asterisk (*); Please refer to the User's Guide for a full explanation of data.

Poverty Rate
(Income in Past 12 Months Below Poverty Level)

Group	%
Total Population	16.7
Hispanic or Latino (of any race)	27.6
Mexican	27.9

Arlington

Population

Group	Number	%TP[1]	%HP[2]
Total Population	365,438	100.0	–
Hispanic or Latino (of any race)	100,269	27.4	100.0
Central American, ex. Mexican	5,002	1.4	5.0
Costa Rican	134	<0.1	0.1
Guatemalan	605	0.2	0.6
Honduran	835	0.2	0.8
Nicaraguan	236	0.1	0.2
Panamanian	240	0.1	0.2
Salvadoran	2,938	0.8	2.9
Cuban	532	0.1	0.5
Dominican Republic	323	0.1	0.3
Mexican	82,834	22.7	82.6
Puerto Rican	3,251	0.9	3.2
South American	1,935	0.5	1.9
Argentinean	187	0.1	0.2
Colombian	781	0.2	0.8
Ecuadorian	273	0.1	0.3
Peruvian	383	0.1	0.4
Venezuelan	151	<0.1	0.2
Spaniard	877	0.2	0.9

Population Growth: 2000–2010

Group	%
Total Population	9.8
Hispanic or Latino (of any race)	64.9
Central American, ex. Mexican	234.6
Guatemalan	177.5
Honduran	403.0
Panamanian	96.7
Salvadoran	289.1
Cuban	56.9
Mexican	77.1
Puerto Rican	56.2
South American	114.8
Colombian	97.2
Peruvian	120.1

Males per 100 Females

Group	Number
Total Population	96.3
Hispanic or Latino (of any race)	103.0
Central American, ex. Mexican	109.6
Costa Rican	139.3
Guatemalan	102.3
Honduran	130.0
Nicaraguan	90.3
Panamanian	76.5
Salvadoran	109.6
Cuban	124.5
Dominican Republic	85.6
Mexican	103.6
Puerto Rican	98.7
South American	88.4
Argentinean	107.8
Colombian	82.1
Ecuadorian	85.7
Peruvian	88.7
Venezuelan	67.8
Spaniard	89.8

Average Household Size

Group	People
Total Population	2.72
Hispanic or Latino (of any race)	3.60
Central American, ex. Mexican	3.71
Costa Rican	2.83
Guatemalan	3.58
Honduran	3.65
Nicaraguan	3.46
Panamanian	2.55
Salvadoran	3.96
Cuban	2.58
Dominican Republic	3.13
Mexican	3.69
Puerto Rican	2.99
South American	3.00
Argentinean	2.97
Colombian	2.94
Ecuadorian	3.70
Peruvian	3.02
Venezuelan	2.67
Spaniard	2.75

Median Age

Group	Years
Total Population	32.1
Hispanic or Latino (of any race)	24.5
Central American, ex. Mexican	29.5
Costa Rican	31.1
Guatemalan	31.1
Honduran	28.2
Nicaraguan	30.3
Panamanian	35.2
Salvadoran	28.9
Cuban	33.3
Dominican Republic	27.7
Mexican	23.8
Puerto Rican	26.6
South American	34.0
Argentinean	31.8
Colombian	34.2
Ecuadorian	32.5
Peruvian	36.9
Venezuelan	32.8
Spaniard	30.9

High School Graduates
(Universe: Population 25 Years and Over)

Group	Number	%
Total Population	184,083	84.6
Hispanic or Latino (of any race)	26,634	57.3
Central American, ex. Mexican	1,712	59.1
Salvadoran	1,172	55.6
Mexican	20,435	53.4
Puerto Rican	1,698	93.6
South American	823	78.8

Four-Year College Graduates
(Universe: Population 25 Years and Over)

Group	Number	%
Total Population	62,376	28.7
Hispanic or Latino (of any race)	4,965	10.7
Central American, ex. Mexican	332	11.5
Salvadoran	146	6.9
Mexican	3,018	7.9
Puerto Rican	640	35.3
South American	302	28.9

Population Age 3–17 Enrolled in Public School
(Universe: Population Age 3–17 Enrolled in School)

Group	Number	%
Total Population	68,266	89.9
Hispanic or Latino (of any race)	24,698	95.8
Central American, ex. Mexican	1,037	90.6
Salvadoran	899	89.8
Mexican	21,255	96.8
Puerto Rican	863	88.7
South American	349	100.0

Population Age 3–17 Enrolled in Private School
(Universe: Population Age 3–17 Enrolled in School)

Group	Number	%
Total Population	7,639	10.1
Hispanic or Latino (of any race)	1,072	4.2
Central American, ex. Mexican	108	9.4
Salvadoran	102	10.2
Mexican	712	3.2
Puerto Rican	110	11.3
South American	0	0.0

Foreign-Born Population

Group	Number	%
Total Population	70,346	19.6
Hispanic or Latino (of any race)	38,700	40.5
Central American, ex. Mexican	3,688	64.6
Salvadoran	2,517	58.9
Mexican	32,698	40.7
Puerto Rican	89	2.8
South American	1,198	67.8

Foreign-Born Naturalized U.S. Citizens

Group	Number	%
Total Population	22,824	32.4
Hispanic or Latino (of any race)	6,300	16.3
Central American, ex. Mexican	754	20.4
Salvadoran	411	16.3
Mexican	4,620	14.1
Puerto Rican	75	84.3
South American	402	33.6

Language Spoken at Home: English Only
(Universe: Population 5 Years and Over)

Group	Number	%
Total Population	228,441	69.1
Hispanic or Latino (of any race)	16,860	20.1
Central American, ex. Mexican	245	4.9
Salvadoran	134	3.7
Mexican	13,728	19.6
Puerto Rican	1,177	38.3
South American	288	18.5

Language Spoken at Home: Spanish
(Universe: Population 5 Years and Over)

Group	Number	%
Total Population	70,763	21.4
Hispanic or Latino (of any race)	66,807	79.7
Central American, ex. Mexican	4,792	95.1
Salvadoran	3,532	96.3
Mexican	56,334	80.3
Puerto Rican	1,860	60.6
South American	1,265	81.5

Unemployment Rate
(Universe: Population 16 Years and Over)

Group	%
Total Population	8.1
Hispanic or Latino (of any race)	8.8
Central American, ex. Mexican	8.8
Salvadoran	5.5
Mexican	8.5
Puerto Rican	3.7
South American	10.5

Class of Worker: Private Wage and Salary
(Universe: Civilian Employed Population 16 Years and Over)

Group	Number	%
Total Population	148,061	81.7
Hispanic or Latino (of any race)	37,337	86.2
Central American, ex. Mexican	2,559	86.1
Salvadoran	1,935	90.2
Mexican	31,396	87.2
Puerto Rican	1,235	79.9
South American	725	78.0

Class of Worker: Government
(Universe: Civilian Employed Population 16 Years and Over)

Group	Number	%
Total Population	22,445	12.4
Hispanic or Latino (of any race)	3,449	8.0
Central American, ex. Mexican	202	6.8
Salvadoran	120	5.6
Mexican	2,599	7.2
Puerto Rican	284	18.4
South American	139	14.9

Means of Transportation to Work: Car, Truck or Van
(Universe: Workers 16 Years and Over)

Group	Number	%
Total Population	164,531	93.3
Hispanic or Latino (of any race)	40,062	94.7
Central American, ex. Mexican	2,720	93.7
Salvadoran	1,943	92.4
Mexican	33,411	94.9
Puerto Rican	1,386	94.7
South American	909	97.7

Means of Transportation to Work: Public Transportation (ex. Taxicab)
(Universe: Workers 16 Years and Over)

Group	Number	%
Total Population	409	0.2
Hispanic or Latino (of any race)	117	0.3

Notes: (1) Percent of total population; (2) Percent of Hispanic/Latino population; Profiles include places with an overall population of at least 125,000, OR an overall population of at least 25,000 where the Hispanic/Latino population is at least 20% of the overall population. In states where less than five places meet either of these criteria, we have included places with at least 10,000 total population with the highest percentage of Hispanic/Latino population. These places are identified with an asterisk (*); Please refer to the User's Guide for a full explanation of data.

Central American, ex. Mexican	0	0.0
Salvadoran	0	0.0
Mexican	96	0.3
Puerto Rican	0	0.0
South American	21	2.3

Homeownership Rate
(Universe: Occupied Housing Units)

Group	%
Total Population	57.4
Hispanic or Latino (of any race)	45.9
Central American, ex. Mexican	50.4
Costa Rican	43.5
Guatemalan	53.3
Honduran	36.8
Nicaraguan	52.4
Panamanian	55.4
Salvadoran	52.8
Cuban	54.0
Dominican Republic	52.5
Mexican	45.3
Puerto Rican	52.3
South American	57.2
Argentinean	42.4
Colombian	56.1
Ecuadorian	65.1
Peruvian	51.2
Venezuelan	55.6
Spaniard	54.0

Median Home Value

Group	Dollars
Total Population	132,500
Hispanic or Latino (of any race)	111,800
Central American, ex. Mexican	99,200
Salvadoran	101,500
Mexican	110,300
Puerto Rican	134,000
South American	132,600

Median Gross Rent

Group	Dollars
Total Population	814
Hispanic or Latino (of any race)	736
Central American, ex. Mexican	679
Salvadoran	653
Mexican	732
Puerto Rican	847
South American	785

Median Household Income
(2010 Inflation-Adjusted Dollars)

Group	Dollars
Total Population	52,094
Hispanic or Latino (of any race)	41,512
Central American, ex. Mexican	37,908
Salvadoran	37,318
Mexican	41,140
Puerto Rican	49,347
South American	40,962

Per Capita Income
(2010 Inflation-Adjusted Dollars)

Group	Dollars
Total Population	25,045
Hispanic or Latino (of any race)	14,440
Central American, ex. Mexican	13,467
Salvadoran	13,098
Mexican	13,724
Puerto Rican	24,291
South American	18,289

Households with $100,000+ Income

Group	Number	%
Total Population	26,060	19.8
Hispanic or Latino (of any race)	2,286	9.0
Central American, ex. Mexican	107	6.9
Salvadoran	36	3.1
Mexican	1,804	8.7
Puerto Rican	144	12.4
South American	62	10.9

Households with Food Stamps/SNAP Benefits During Past 12 Months

Group	Number	%
Total Population	11,809	9.0
Hispanic or Latino (of any race)	3,272	12.8
Central American, ex. Mexican	202	13.0
Salvadoran	170	14.8
Mexican	2,738	13.1
Puerto Rican	169	14.6
South American	20	3.5

Poverty Rate
(Income in Past 12 Months Below Poverty Level)

Group	%
Total Population	14.3
Hispanic or Latino (of any race)	20.1
Central American, ex. Mexican	16.8
Salvadoran	18.2
Mexican	20.9
Puerto Rican	22.1
South American	20.5

Atascocita

Population

Group	Number	%TP[1]	%HP[2]
Total Population	65,844	100.0	–
Hispanic or Latino (of any race)	15,027	22.8	100.0
Central American, ex. Mexican	1,072	1.6	7.1
Guatemalan	164	0.2	1.1
Honduran	190	0.3	1.3
Nicaraguan	115	0.2	0.8
Salvadoran	490	0.7	3.3
Cuban	167	0.3	1.1
Mexican	10,663	16.2	71.0
Puerto Rican	500	0.8	3.3
South American	842	1.3	5.6
Colombian	289	0.4	1.9
Ecuadorian	114	0.2	0.8
Peruvian	110	0.2	0.7
Venezuelan	160	0.2	1.1
Spaniard	185	0.3	1.2

Population Growth: 2000–2010

Group	%
Total Population	84.1
Hispanic or Latino (of any race)	249.7
Central American, ex. Mexican	744.1
Mexican	255.2
Puerto Rican	270.4
South American	472.8

Males per 100 Females

Group	Number
Total Population	104.0
Hispanic or Latino (of any race)	103.5
Central American, ex. Mexican	89.1
Guatemalan	97.6
Honduran	93.9
Nicaraguan	64.3
Salvadoran	97.6
Cuban	108.8
Mexican	96.7
Puerto Rican	104.1
South American	79.5
Colombian	79.5
Ecuadorian	75.4
Peruvian	69.2
Venezuelan	79.8
Spaniard	90.7

Average Household Size

Group	People
Total Population	3.02
Hispanic or Latino (of any race)	3.65
Central American, ex. Mexican	3.94
Guatemalan	4.30
Honduran	3.98
Nicaraguan	4.09
Salvadoran	3.88
Cuban	3.13
Mexican	3.73
Puerto Rican	2.99
South American	3.29
Colombian	3.30
Ecuadorian	4.03
Peruvian	3.17
Venezuelan	3.04
Spaniard	2.73

Median Age

Group	Years
Total Population	32.6
Hispanic or Latino (of any race)	27.1
Central American, ex. Mexican	32.6
Guatemalan	32.5
Honduran	32.5
Nicaraguan	34.6
Salvadoran	32.0
Cuban	34.1
Mexican	25.6
Puerto Rican	30.9
South American	34.7
Colombian	34.3
Ecuadorian	33.8
Peruvian	37.5
Venezuelan	32.3
Spaniard	32.6

High School Graduates
(Universe: Population 25 Years and Over)

Group	Number	%
Total Population	34,941	90.7
Hispanic or Latino (of any race)	5,568	72.1
Central American, ex. Mexican	537	69.3
Mexican	4,009	68.3

Four-Year College Graduates
(Universe: Population 25 Years and Over)

Group	Number	%
Total Population	11,785	30.6
Hispanic or Latino (of any race)	1,448	18.7
Central American, ex. Mexican	141	18.2
Mexican	994	16.9

Population Age 3–17 Enrolled in Public School
(Universe: Population Age 3–17 Enrolled in School)

Group	Number	%
Total Population	12,880	90.0
Hispanic or Latino (of any race)	4,388	95.4
Central American, ex. Mexican	480	100.0
Mexican	3,465	95.0

Population Age 3–17 Enrolled in Private School
(Universe: Population Age 3–17 Enrolled in School)

Group	Number	%
Total Population	1,425	10.0
Hispanic or Latino (of any race)	212	4.6
Central American, ex. Mexican	0	0.0
Mexican	183	5.0

Foreign-Born Population

Group	Number	%
Total Population	6,228	10.1
Hispanic or Latino (of any race)	3,829	25.3
Central American, ex. Mexican	743	51.8
Mexican	2,491	21.5

Foreign-Born Naturalized U.S. Citizens

Group	Number	%
Total Population	2,763	44.4
Hispanic or Latino (of any race)	1,324	34.6
Central American, ex. Mexican	226	30.4
Mexican	926	37.2

Language Spoken at Home: English Only
(Universe: Population 5 Years and Over)

Group	Number	%
Total Population	43,952	77.1
Hispanic or Latino (of any race)	4,249	31.1
Central American, ex. Mexican	165	12.3
Mexican	3,567	34.1

Language Spoken at Home: Spanish
(Universe: Population 5 Years and Over)

Group	Number	%
Total Population	10,325	18.1
Hispanic or Latino (of any race)	9,332	68.4
Central American, ex. Mexican	1,180	87.7

Notes: (1) Percent of total population; (2) Percent of Hispanic/Latino population; Profiles include places with an overall population of at least 125,000, OR an overall population of at least 25,000 where the Hispanic/Latino population is at least 20% of the overall population. In states where less than five places meet either of these criteria, we have included places with at least 10,000 total population with the highest percentage of Hispanic/Latino population. These places are identified with an asterisk (*); Please refer to the User's Guide for a full explanation of data.

Group	Number	%
Mexican	6,853	65.5

Unemployment Rate
(Universe: Population 16 Years and Over)

Group	%
Total Population	3.7
Hispanic or Latino (of any race)	4.9
Central American, ex. Mexican	1.6
Mexican	4.0

Class of Worker: Private Wage and Salary
(Universe: Civilian Employed Population 16 Years and Over)

Group	Number	%
Total Population	24,223	78.5
Hispanic or Latino (of any race)	5,403	83.1
Central American, ex. Mexican	393	71.6
Mexican	4,315	84.3

Class of Worker: Government
(Universe: Civilian Employed Population 16 Years and Over)

Group	Number	%
Total Population	4,918	15.9
Hispanic or Latino (of any race)	706	10.9
Central American, ex. Mexican	58	10.6
Mexican	550	10.7

Means of Transportation to Work: Car, Truck or Van
(Universe: Workers 16 Years and Over)

Group	Number	%
Total Population	28,416	94.5
Hispanic or Latino (of any race)	5,821	94.7
Central American, ex. Mexican	502	98.6
Mexican	4,564	94.9

Means of Transportation to Work: Public Transportation (ex. Taxicab)
(Universe: Workers 16 Years and Over)

Group	Number	%
Total Population	288	1.0
Hispanic or Latino (of any race)	37	0.6
Central American, ex. Mexican	0	0.0
Mexican	37	0.8

Homeownership Rate
(Universe: Occupied Housing Units)

Group	%
Total Population	82.5
Hispanic or Latino (of any race)	83.1
Central American, ex. Mexican	80.1
Guatemalan	90.9
Honduran	74.5
Nicaraguan	69.7
Salvadoran	81.0
Cuban	85.0
Mexican	84.6
Puerto Rican	76.6
South American	79.7
Colombian	78.9
Ecuadorian	73.3
Peruvian	86.7
Venezuelan	78.0
Spaniard	77.5

Median Home Value

Group	Dollars
Total Population	150,700
Hispanic or Latino (of any race)	136,100
Central American, ex. Mexican	139,100
Mexican	133,000

Median Gross Rent

Group	Dollars
Total Population	1,162
Hispanic or Latino (of any race)	1,143
Central American, ex. Mexican	1,162
Mexican	1,037

Median Household Income
(2010 Inflation-Adjusted Dollars)

Group	Dollars
Total Population	82,405
Hispanic or Latino (of any race)	65,731
Central American, ex. Mexican	60,938
Mexican	65,734

Per Capita Income
(2010 Inflation-Adjusted Dollars)

Group	Dollars
Total Population	30,809
Hispanic or Latino (of any race)	19,568
Central American, ex. Mexican	16,849
Mexican	18,875

Households with $100,000+ Income

Group	Number	%
Total Population	7,257	37.8
Hispanic or Latino (of any race)	874	25.5
Central American, ex. Mexican	46	14.6
Mexican	665	25.2

Households with Food Stamps/SNAP Benefits During Past 12 Months

Group	Number	%
Total Population	511	2.7
Hispanic or Latino (of any race)	176	5.1
Central American, ex. Mexican	36	11.5
Mexican	98	3.7

Poverty Rate
(Income in Past 12 Months Below Poverty Level)

Group	%
Total Population	4.4
Hispanic or Latino (of any race)	8.2
Central American, ex. Mexican	17.0
Mexican	8.0

Austin

Population

Group	Number	%TP[1]	%HP[2]
Total Population	790,390	100.0	–
Hispanic or Latino (of any race)	277,707	35.1	100.0
Central American, ex. Mexican	13,423	1.7	4.8
Costa Rican	312	<0.1	0.1
Guatemalan	3,007	0.4	1.1
Honduran	4,503	0.6	1.6
Nicaraguan	1,041	0.1	0.4
Panamanian	607	0.1	0.2
Salvadoran	3,811	0.5	1.4
Cuban	3,163	0.4	1.1
Dominican Republic	366	<0.1	0.1
Mexican	229,865	29.1	82.8
Puerto Rican	4,055	0.5	1.5
South American	5,002	0.6	1.8
Argentinean	600	0.1	0.2
Bolivian	244	<0.1	0.1
Chilean	340	<0.1	0.1
Colombian	1,619	0.2	0.6
Ecuadorian	390	<0.1	0.1
Peruvian	804	0.1	0.3
Venezuelan	823	0.1	0.3
Spaniard	2,914	0.4	1.0

Population Growth: 2000–2010

Group	%
Total Population	20.4
Hispanic or Latino (of any race)	38.5
Central American, ex. Mexican	212.9
Costa Rican	132.8
Guatemalan	302.0
Honduran	322.8
Nicaraguan	128.3
Panamanian	75.9
Salvadoran	186.3
Cuban	122.0
Dominican Republic	183.7
Mexican	49.4
Puerto Rican	60.3
South American	131.5
Argentinean	147.9
Bolivian	123.9
Chilean	102.4
Colombian	171.6
Ecuadorian	172.7
Peruvian	124.0
Venezuelan	111.0
Spaniard	834.0

Males per 100 Females

Group	Number
Total Population	102.3
Hispanic or Latino (of any race)	106.7
Central American, ex. Mexican	127.0
Costa Rican	88.0
Guatemalan	165.6
Honduran	132.2
Nicaraguan	107.8
Panamanian	82.3
Salvadoran	114.7
Cuban	118.1
Dominican Republic	97.8
Mexican	106.7
Puerto Rican	106.3
South American	93.4
Argentinean	92.9
Bolivian	108.5
Chilean	113.8
Colombian	88.3
Ecuadorian	94.0
Peruvian	96.6
Venezuelan	90.5
Spaniard	97.0

Average Household Size

Group	People
Total Population	2.37
Hispanic or Latino (of any race)	3.13
Central American, ex. Mexican	3.54
Costa Rican	2.51
Guatemalan	3.89
Honduran	3.79
Nicaraguan	3.11
Panamanian	2.30
Salvadoran	3.51
Cuban	2.55
Dominican Republic	2.51
Mexican	3.21
Puerto Rican	2.36
South American	2.32
Argentinean	2.23
Bolivian	2.38
Chilean	2.20
Colombian	2.30
Ecuadorian	2.69
Peruvian	2.32
Venezuelan	2.31
Spaniard	2.26

Median Age

Group	Years
Total Population	31.0
Hispanic or Latino (of any race)	26.2
Central American, ex. Mexican	28.7
Costa Rican	29.0
Guatemalan	28.0
Honduran	27.8
Nicaraguan	32.4
Panamanian	31.8
Salvadoran	29.3
Cuban	33.1
Dominican Republic	27.7
Mexican	25.8
Puerto Rican	28.7
South American	31.2
Argentinean	33.0
Bolivian	31.8
Chilean	31.3
Colombian	30.6
Ecuadorian	30.2
Peruvian	32.4
Venezuelan	30.2
Spaniard	30.6

High School Graduates
(Universe: Population 25 Years and Over)

Group	Number	%
Total Population	411,598	85.1
Hispanic or Latino (of any race)	85,274	60.8
Central American, ex. Mexican	3,887	46.2
Guatemalan	667	37.5
Honduran	956	34.9
Nicaraguan	480	81.9
Salvadoran	1,060	44.1

STATE & PLACE PROFILES

Notes: (1) Percent of total population; (2) Percent of Hispanic/Latino population; Profiles include places with an overall population of at least 125,000, OR an overall population of at least 25,000 where the Hispanic/Latino population is at least 20% of the overall population. In states where less than five places meet either of these criteria, we have included places with at least 10,000 total population with the highest percentage of Hispanic/Latino population. These places are identified with an asterisk (*); Please refer to the User's Guide for a full explanation of data.

Group	Number	%
Cuban	1,442	87.2
Mexican	68,731	58.9
Puerto Rican	1,881	89.1
South American	2,692	97.0
Colombian	720	95.0
Peruvian	617	95.2
Spaniard	1,828	88.7

Four-Year College Graduates
(Universe: Population 25 Years and Over)

Group	Number	%
Total Population	213,348	44.1
Hispanic or Latino (of any race)	24,770	17.7
Central American, ex. Mexican	1,226	14.6
Guatemalan	322	18.1
Honduran	136	5.0
Nicaraguan	165	28.2
Salvadoran	276	11.5
Cuban	553	33.5
Mexican	18,332	15.7
Puerto Rican	840	39.8
South American	1,746	62.9
Colombian	435	57.4
Peruvian	304	46.9
Spaniard	820	39.8

Population Age 3–17 Enrolled in Public School
(Universe: Population Age 3–17 Enrolled in School)

Group	Number	%
Total Population	105,370	88.2
Hispanic or Latino (of any race)	54,929	95.4
Central American, ex. Mexican	2,160	95.5
Guatemalan	479	96.8
Honduran	622	100.0
Nicaraguan	201	86.3
Salvadoran	698	96.7
Cuban	429	97.1
Mexican	48,573	95.7
Puerto Rican	498	94.1
South American	480	78.6
Colombian	129	64.2
Peruvian	70	100.0
Spaniard	345	79.3

Population Age 3–17 Enrolled in Private School
(Universe: Population Age 3–17 Enrolled in School)

Group	Number	%
Total Population	14,067	11.8
Hispanic or Latino (of any race)	2,662	4.6
Central American, ex. Mexican	101	4.5
Guatemalan	16	3.2
Honduran	0	0.0
Nicaraguan	32	13.7
Salvadoran	24	3.3
Cuban	13	2.9
Mexican	2,185	4.3
Puerto Rican	31	5.9
South American	131	21.4
Colombian	72	35.8
Peruvian	0	0.0
Spaniard	90	20.7

Foreign-Born Population

Group	Number	%
Total Population	148,871	19.5
Hispanic or Latino (of any race)	96,810	36.2
Central American, ex. Mexican	9,904	70.5
Guatemalan	2,387	79.4
Honduran	3,248	75.3
Nicaraguan	680	66.3
Salvadoran	2,865	65.6
Cuban	1,582	56.1
Mexican	81,348	36.0
Puerto Rican	118	3.5
South American	2,408	56.6
Colombian	643	56.7
Peruvian	680	76.7
Spaniard	215	6.6

Foreign-Born Naturalized U.S. Citizens

Group	Number	%
Total Population	33,431	22.5
Hispanic or Latino (of any race)	11,275	11.6
Central American, ex. Mexican	1,380	13.9
Guatemalan	194	8.1
Honduran	109	3.4
Nicaraguan	289	42.5
Salvadoran	456	15.9
Cuban	247	15.6
Mexican	8,196	10.1
Puerto Rican	55	46.6
South American	828	34.4
Colombian	320	49.8
Peruvian	173	25.4
Spaniard	57	26.5

Language Spoken at Home: English Only
(Universe: Population 5 Years and Over)

Group	Number	%
Total Population	467,075	66.0
Hispanic or Latino (of any race)	63,585	26.8
Central American, ex. Mexican	1,081	8.5
Guatemalan	128	4.7
Honduran	190	4.9
Nicaraguan	104	10.7
Salvadoran	170	4.4
Cuban	495	19.3
Mexican	52,577	26.2
Puerto Rican	1,552	50.4
South American	796	20.4
Colombian	214	20.9
Peruvian	137	15.9
Spaniard	1,735	55.9

Language Spoken at Home: Spanish
(Universe: Population 5 Years and Over)

Group	Number	%
Total Population	186,027	26.3
Hispanic or Latino (of any race)	173,237	73.0
Central American, ex. Mexican	11,560	91.3
Guatemalan	2,612	94.9
Honduran	3,678	95.1
Nicaraguan	853	88.1
Salvadoran	3,655	95.6
Cuban	2,072	80.7
Mexican	147,837	73.7
Puerto Rican	1,502	48.8
South American	3,046	78.2
Colombian	811	79.1
Peruvian	726	84.1
Spaniard	1,334	43.0

Unemployment Rate
(Universe: Population 16 Years and Over)

Group	%
Total Population	6.5
Hispanic or Latino (of any race)	8.0
Central American, ex. Mexican	9.6
Guatemalan	1.6
Honduran	10.9
Nicaraguan	21.9
Salvadoran	8.1
Cuban	10.2
Mexican	7.9
Puerto Rican	12.9
South American	8.4
Colombian	2.1
Peruvian	6.8
Spaniard	4.4

Class of Worker: Private Wage and Salary
(Universe: Civilian Employed Population 16 Years and Over)

Group	Number	%
Total Population	317,699	76.0
Hispanic or Latino (of any race)	107,096	81.4
Central American, ex. Mexican	6,852	86.4
Guatemalan	1,722	89.4
Honduran	2,321	92.6
Nicaraguan	406	86.2
Salvadoran	1,859	80.3
Cuban	1,248	78.2
Mexican	89,607	82.0
Puerto Rican	1,344	74.4
South American	1,611	70.2
Colombian	448	69.9
Peruvian	425	75.6
Spaniard	1,715	79.1

Class of Worker: Government
(Universe: Civilian Employed Population 16 Years and Over)

Group	Number	%
Total Population	70,049	16.8
Hispanic or Latino (of any race)	17,184	13.1
Central American, ex. Mexican	489	6.2
Guatemalan	93	4.8
Honduran	77	3.1
Nicaraguan	16	3.4
Salvadoran	169	7.3
Cuban	296	18.6
Mexican	13,592	12.4
Puerto Rican	403	22.3
South American	552	24.1
Colombian	135	21.1
Peruvian	137	24.4
Spaniard	413	19.0

Means of Transportation to Work: Car, Truck or Van
(Universe: Workers 16 Years and Over)

Group	Number	%
Total Population	341,403	83.5
Hispanic or Latino (of any race)	107,514	83.3
Central American, ex. Mexican	5,981	75.7
Guatemalan	1,404	73.7
Honduran	1,842	73.5
Nicaraguan	374	79.4
Salvadoran	1,777	76.7
Cuban	1,168	76.8
Mexican	90,103	84.0
Puerto Rican	1,506	86.4
South American	1,694	78.2
Colombian	531	88.2
Peruvian	289	54.0
Spaniard	1,754	82.3

Means of Transportation to Work: Public Transportation (ex. Taxicab)
(Universe: Workers 16 Years and Over)

Group	Number	%
Total Population	19,640	4.8
Hispanic or Latino (of any race)	7,757	6.0
Central American, ex. Mexican	882	11.2
Guatemalan	426	22.4
Honduran	168	6.7
Nicaraguan	34	7.2
Salvadoran	223	9.6
Cuban	124	8.2
Mexican	6,024	5.6
Puerto Rican	60	3.4
South American	109	5.0
Colombian	10	1.7
Peruvian	83	15.5
Spaniard	171	8.0

Homeownership Rate
(Universe: Occupied Housing Units)

Group	%
Total Population	45.1
Hispanic or Latino (of any race)	34.6
Central American, ex. Mexican	28.0
Costa Rican	35.1
Guatemalan	20.0
Honduran	18.7
Nicaraguan	37.4
Panamanian	37.2
Salvadoran	37.4
Cuban	28.8
Dominican Republic	34.2
Mexican	35.4
Puerto Rican	33.8
South American	42.3
Argentinean	49.6
Bolivian	50.0
Chilean	39.8
Colombian	40.9
Ecuadorian	50.7
Peruvian	36.4
Venezuelan	41.4
Spaniard	41.4

Median Home Value

Group	Dollars
Total Population	200,000

Notes: (1) Percent of total population; (2) Percent of Hispanic/Latino population; Profiles include places with an overall population of at least 125,000, OR an overall population of at least 25,000 where the Hispanic/Latino population is at least 20% of the overall population. In states where less than five places meet either of these criteria, we have included places with at least 10,000 total population with the highest percentage of Hispanic/Latino population. These places are identified with an asterisk (*); Please refer to the User's Guide for a full explanation of data.

Hispanic or Latino (of any race)	142,300
Central American, ex. Mexican	130,300
Guatemalan	149,100
Honduran	93,200
Nicaraguan	140,300
Salvadoran	109,300
Cuban	139,600
Mexican	139,100
Puerto Rican	174,100
South American	200,300
Colombian	226,900
Peruvian	148,900
Spaniard	148,300

Median Gross Rent

Group	Dollars
Total Population	882
Hispanic or Latino (of any race)	825
Central American, ex. Mexican	798
Guatemalan	787
Honduran	802
Nicaraguan	853
Salvadoran	740
Cuban	741
Mexican	820
Puerto Rican	876
South American	964
Colombian	896
Peruvian	913
Spaniard	941

Median Household Income
(2010 Inflation-Adjusted Dollars)

Group	Dollars
Total Population	50,520
Hispanic or Latino (of any race)	39,125
Central American, ex. Mexican	33,336
Guatemalan	34,104
Honduran	31,594
Nicaraguan	32,344
Salvadoran	30,833
Cuban	41,710
Mexican	38,856
Puerto Rican	44,720
South American	55,375
Colombian	52,258
Peruvian	30,278
Spaniard	44,951

Per Capita Income
(2010 Inflation-Adjusted Dollars)

Group	Dollars
Total Population	30,286
Hispanic or Latino (of any race)	15,958
Central American, ex. Mexican	14,074
Guatemalan	13,452
Honduran	12,871
Nicaraguan	14,434
Salvadoran	12,233
Cuban	19,842
Mexican	15,410
Puerto Rican	28,372
South American	23,213
Colombian	22,850
Peruvian	21,304
Spaniard	25,845

Households with $100,000+ Income

Group	Number	%
Total Population	67,283	21.3
Hispanic or Latino (of any race)	7,932	9.6
Central American, ex. Mexican	205	4.7
Guatemalan	46	5.6
Honduran	0	0.0
Nicaraguan	24	8.5
Salvadoran	33	2.5
Cuban	147	12.6
Mexican	6,311	9.4
Puerto Rican	263	18.7
South American	313	20.1
Colombian	80	27.0
Peruvian	28	6.5
Spaniard	189	10.3

Households with Food Stamps/SNAP Benefits During Past 12 Months

Group	Number	%
Total Population	25,116	7.9
Hispanic or Latino (of any race)	13,772	16.7
Central American, ex. Mexican	767	17.6
Guatemalan	20	2.4
Honduran	266	19.3
Nicaraguan	84	29.8
Salvadoran	336	25.6
Cuban	168	14.4
Mexican	11,436	17.0
Puerto Rican	203	14.4
South American	45	2.9
Colombian	0	0.0
Peruvian	23	5.3
Spaniard	163	8.9

Poverty Rate
(Income in Past 12 Months Below Poverty Level)

Group	%
Total Population	18.4
Hispanic or Latino (of any race)	26.4
Central American, ex. Mexican	29.2
Guatemalan	30.5
Honduran	32.8
Nicaraguan	27.3
Salvadoran	29.1
Cuban	21.5
Mexican	26.8
Puerto Rican	17.2
South American	12.0
Colombian	7.6
Peruvian	23.0
Spaniard	19.0

Baytown

Population

Group	Number	%TP[1]	%HP[2]
Total Population	71,802	100.0	
Hispanic or Latino (of any race)	31,156	43.4	100.0
Central American, ex. Mexican	553	0.8	1.8
Guatemalan	120	0.2	0.4
Honduran	146	0.2	0.5
Salvadoran	229	0.3	0.7
Cuban	104	0.1	0.3
Mexican	28,015	39.0	89.9
Puerto Rican	310	0.4	1.0
South American	171	0.2	0.5
Spaniard	126	0.2	0.4

Population Growth: 2000–2010

Group	%
Total Population	8.1
Hispanic or Latino (of any race)	37.0
Central American, ex. Mexican	185.1
Mexican	46.5
Puerto Rican	90.2

Males per 100 Females

Group	Number
Total Population	95.5
Hispanic or Latino (of any race)	103.1
Central American, ex. Mexican	115.2
Guatemalan	160.9
Honduran	89.6
Salvadoran	116.0
Cuban	100.0
Mexican	104.3
Puerto Rican	95.0
South American	78.1
Spaniard	90.9

Average Household Size

Group	People
Total Population	2.85
Hispanic or Latino (of any race)	3.71
Central American, ex. Mexican	3.51
Guatemalan	3.97
Honduran	3.35
Salvadoran	3.71
Cuban	2.92
Mexican	3.77
Puerto Rican	2.71
South American	3.15
Spaniard	3.00

Median Age

Group	Years
Total Population	32.1
Hispanic or Latino (of any race)	25.2
Central American, ex. Mexican	30.6
Guatemalan	26.3
Honduran	30.2
Salvadoran	30.8
Cuban	33.5
Mexican	25.2
Puerto Rican	24.5
South American	29.5
Spaniard	36.5

High School Graduates
(Universe: Population 25 Years and Over)

Group	Number	%
Total Population	32,295	76.2
Hispanic or Latino (of any race)	7,148	52.2
Mexican	6,477	50.3

Four-Year College Graduates
(Universe: Population 25 Years and Over)

Group	Number	%
Total Population	6,018	14.2
Hispanic or Latino (of any race)	701	5.1
Mexican	582	4.5

Population Age 3–17 Enrolled in Public School
(Universe: Population Age 3–17 Enrolled in School)

Group	Number	%
Total Population	14,043	94.1
Hispanic or Latino (of any race)	7,366	96.1
Mexican	7,059	96.6

Population Age 3–17 Enrolled in Private School
(Universe: Population Age 3–17 Enrolled in School)

Group	Number	%
Total Population	877	5.9
Hispanic or Latino (of any race)	295	3.9
Mexican	250	3.4

Foreign-Born Population

Group	Number	%
Total Population	11,442	16.2
Hispanic or Latino (of any race)	9,420	34.0
Mexican	9,002	34.4

Foreign-Born Naturalized U.S. Citizens

Group	Number	%
Total Population	3,149	27.5
Hispanic or Latino (of any race)	2,166	23.0
Mexican	2,010	22.3

Language Spoken at Home: English Only
(Universe: Population 5 Years and Over)

Group	Number	%
Total Population	42,009	65.4
Hispanic or Latino (of any race)	4,430	18.3
Mexican	4,054	17.7

Language Spoken at Home: Spanish
(Universe: Population 5 Years and Over)

Group	Number	%
Total Population	20,463	31.9
Hispanic or Latino (of any race)	19,840	81.7
Mexican	18,876	82.3

Unemployment Rate
(Universe: Population 16 Years and Over)

Group	%
Total Population	9.6
Hispanic or Latino (of any race)	9.8
Mexican	9.8

Class of Worker: Private Wage and Salary
(Universe: Civilian Employed Population 16 Years and Over)

Group	Number	%
Total Population	24,988	84.5
Hispanic or Latino (of any race)	9,822	90.0
Mexican	9,155	89.8

Notes: (1) Percent of total population; (2) Percent of Hispanic/Latino population; Profiles include places with an overall population of at least 125,000, OR an overall population of at least 25,000 where the Hispanic/Latino population is at least 20% of the overall population. In states where less than five places meet either of these criteria, we have included places with at least 10,000 total population with the highest percentage of Hispanic/Latino population. These places are identified with an asterisk (*); Please refer to the User's Guide for a full explanation of data.

Class of Worker: Government
(Universe: Civilian Employed Population 16 Years and Over)

Group	Number	%
Total Population	3,298	11.1
Hispanic or Latino (of any race)	804	7.4
Mexican	764	7.5

Means of Transportation to Work: Car, Truck or Van
(Universe: Workers 16 Years and Over)

Group	Number	%
Total Population	27,272	94.1
Hispanic or Latino (of any race)	9,941	94.3
Mexican	9,261	94.2

Means of Transportation to Work: Public Transportation (ex. Taxicab)
(Universe: Workers 16 Years and Over)

Group	Number	%
Total Population	100	0.3
Hispanic or Latino (of any race)	22	0.2
Mexican	22	0.2

Homeownership Rate
(Universe: Occupied Housing Units)

Group	%
Total Population	60.0
Hispanic or Latino (of any race)	62.3
Central American, ex. Mexican	50.0
Guatemalan	55.6
Honduran	38.8
Salvadoran	54.4
Cuban	50.0
Mexican	64.0
Puerto Rican	49.5
South American	46.3
Spaniard	60.4

Median Home Value

Group	Dollars
Total Population	98,000
Hispanic or Latino (of any race)	80,100
Mexican	77,800

Median Gross Rent

Group	Dollars
Total Population	757
Hispanic or Latino (of any race)	731
Mexican	730

Median Household Income
(2010 Inflation-Adjusted Dollars)

Group	Dollars
Total Population	47,586
Hispanic or Latino (of any race)	41,977
Mexican	41,014

Per Capita Income
(2010 Inflation-Adjusted Dollars)

Group	Dollars
Total Population	21,167
Hispanic or Latino (of any race)	14,649
Mexican	14,535

Households with $100,000+ Income

Group	Number	%
Total Population	3,918	16.5
Hispanic or Latino (of any race)	714	9.6
Mexican	647	9.3

Households with Food Stamps/SNAP Benefits During Past 12 Months

Group	Number	%
Total Population	2,711	11.4
Hispanic or Latino (of any race)	1,140	15.3
Mexican	1,075	15.4

Poverty Rate
(Income in Past 12 Months Below Poverty Level)

Group	%
Total Population	17.0
Hispanic or Latino (of any race)	18.5
Mexican	19.0

Big Spring

Population

Group	Number	%TP[1]	%HP[2]
Total Population	27,282	100.0	–
Hispanic or Latino (of any race)	11,751	43.1	100.0
Mexican	8,291	30.4	70.6

Population Growth: 2000–2010

Group	%
Total Population	8.1
Hispanic or Latino (of any race)	4.3
Mexican	-1.0

Males per 100 Females

Group	Number
Total Population	138.4
Hispanic or Latino (of any race)	140.7
Mexican	112.3

Average Household Size

Group	People
Total Population	2.56
Hispanic or Latino (of any race)	3.09
Mexican	3.11

Median Age

Group	Years
Total Population	36.5
Hispanic or Latino (of any race)	29.9
Mexican	28.0

High School Graduates
(Universe: Population 25 Years and Over)

Group	Number	%
Total Population	12,682	68.1
Hispanic or Latino (of any race)	3,323	45.1
Mexican	2,805	45.2

Four-Year College Graduates
(Universe: Population 25 Years and Over)

Group	Number	%
Total Population	1,746	9.4
Hispanic or Latino (of any race)	184	2.5
Mexican	129	2.1

Population Age 3–17 Enrolled in Public School
(Universe: Population Age 3–17 Enrolled in School)

Group	Number	%
Total Population	4,088	95.8
Hispanic or Latino (of any race)	2,219	97.2
Mexican	1,757	96.5

Population Age 3–17 Enrolled in Private School
(Universe: Population Age 3–17 Enrolled in School)

Group	Number	%
Total Population	180	4.2
Hispanic or Latino (of any race)	64	2.8
Mexican	64	3.5

Foreign-Born Population

Group	Number	%
Total Population	5,151	19.4
Hispanic or Latino (of any race)	4,320	37.5
Mexican	3,851	40.2

Foreign-Born Naturalized U.S. Citizens

Group	Number	%
Total Population	551	10.7
Hispanic or Latino (of any race)	247	5.7
Mexican	217	5.6

Language Spoken at Home: English Only
(Universe: Population 5 Years and Over)

Group	Number	%
Total Population	16,067	64.9
Hispanic or Latino (of any race)	2,803	26.8
Mexican	2,293	26.4

Language Spoken at Home: Spanish
(Universe: Population 5 Years and Over)

Group	Number	%
Total Population	7,950	32.1
Hispanic or Latino (of any race)	7,609	72.8
Mexican	6,360	73.2

Unemployment Rate
(Universe: Population 16 Years and Over)

Group	%
Total Population	9.0
Hispanic or Latino (of any race)	7.4
Mexican	6.0

Class of Worker: Private Wage and Salary
(Universe: Civilian Employed Population 16 Years and Over)

Group	Number	%
Total Population	6,007	68.9
Hispanic or Latino (of any race)	1,977	76.0
Mexican	1,629	74.7

Class of Worker: Government
(Universe: Civilian Employed Population 16 Years and Over)

Group	Number	%
Total Population	2,184	25.1
Hispanic or Latino (of any race)	525	20.2
Mexican	475	21.8

Means of Transportation to Work: Car, Truck or Van
(Universe: Workers 16 Years and Over)

Group	Number	%
Total Population	7,884	92.1
Hispanic or Latino (of any race)	2,421	95.7
Mexican	2,060	96.7

Means of Transportation to Work: Public Transportation (ex. Taxicab)
(Universe: Workers 16 Years and Over)

Group	Number	%
Total Population	0	0.0
Hispanic or Latino (of any race)	0	0.0
Mexican	0	0.0

Homeownership Rate
(Universe: Occupied Housing Units)

Group	%
Total Population	61.3
Hispanic or Latino (of any race)	59.3
Mexican	62.0

Median Home Value

Group	Dollars
Total Population	55,300
Hispanic or Latino (of any race)	28,000
Mexican	32,600

Median Gross Rent

Group	Dollars
Total Population	615
Hispanic or Latino (of any race)	589
Mexican	596

Median Household Income
(2010 Inflation-Adjusted Dollars)

Group	Dollars
Total Population	35,183
Hispanic or Latino (of any race)	29,765
Mexican	30,160

Per Capita Income
(2010 Inflation-Adjusted Dollars)

Group	Dollars
Total Population	15,754
Hispanic or Latino (of any race)	7,629
Mexican	7,718

Households with $100,000+ Income

Group	Number	%
Total Population	851	10.6
Hispanic or Latino (of any race)	85	4.4
Mexican	79	5.2

Households with Food Stamps/SNAP Benefits During Past 12 Months

Group	Number	%
Total Population	1,035	12.9
Hispanic or Latino (of any race)	420	22.0
Mexican	324	21.5

Notes: (1) Percent of total population; (2) Percent of Hispanic/Latino population; Profiles include places with an overall population of at least 125,000, OR an overall population of at least 25,000 where the Hispanic/Latino population is at least 20% of the overall population. In states where less than five places meet either of these criteria, we have included places with at least 10,000 total population with the highest percentage of Hispanic/Latino population. These places are identified with an asterisk (*); Please refer to the User's Guide for a full explanation of data.

Poverty Rate
(Income in Past 12 Months Below Poverty Level)

Group	%
Total Population	20.9
Hispanic or Latino (of any race)	23.9
Mexican	21.7

Brownsville

Population

Group	Number	%TP[1]	%HP[2]
Total Population	175,023	100.0	–
Hispanic or Latino (of any race)	163,109	93.2	100.0
Central American, ex. Mexican	725	0.4	0.4
Honduran	260	0.1	0.2
Nicaraguan	104	0.1	0.1
Salvadoran	222	0.1	0.1
Cuban	240	0.1	0.1
Mexican	150,945	86.2	92.5
Puerto Rican	459	0.3	0.3
South American	363	0.2	0.2
Colombian	124	0.1	0.1
Spaniard	434	0.2	0.3

Population Growth: 2000–2010

Group	%
Total Population	25.3
Hispanic or Latino (of any race)	27.9
Central American, ex. Mexican	86.9
Honduran	113.1
Cuban	50.9
Mexican	46.1
Puerto Rican	113.5
South American	124.1

Males per 100 Females

Group	Number
Total Population	89.5
Hispanic or Latino (of any race)	88.4
Central American, ex. Mexican	104.2
Honduran	98.5
Nicaraguan	96.2
Salvadoran	94.7
Cuban	137.6
Mexican	88.3
Puerto Rican	111.5
South American	92.1
Colombian	72.2
Spaniard	91.2

Average Household Size

Group	People
Total Population	3.48
Hispanic or Latino (of any race)	3.59
Central American, ex. Mexican	3.24
Honduran	3.24
Nicaraguan	3.24
Salvadoran	3.42
Cuban	2.88
Mexican	3.60
Puerto Rican	3.13
South American	2.90
Colombian	2.88
Spaniard	2.94

Median Age

Group	Years
Total Population	29.5
Hispanic or Latino (of any race)	28.5
Central American, ex. Mexican	34.7
Honduran	33.9
Nicaraguan	39.7
Salvadoran	33.1
Cuban	43.2
Mexican	28.7
Puerto Rican	32.8
South American	43.1
Colombian	36.7
Spaniard	40.3

High School Graduates
(Universe: Population 25 Years and Over)

Group	Number	%
Total Population	54,324	59.2
Hispanic or Latino (of any race)	46,578	55.9
Mexican	43,871	55.1

Four-Year College Graduates
(Universe: Population 25 Years and Over)

Group	Number	%
Total Population	14,067	15.3
Hispanic or Latino (of any race)	10,928	13.1
Mexican	10,205	12.8

Population Age 3–17 Enrolled in Public School
(Universe: Population Age 3–17 Enrolled in School)

Group	Number	%
Total Population	42,948	95.2
Hispanic or Latino (of any race)	41,680	95.9
Mexican	40,214	96.1

Population Age 3–17 Enrolled in Private School
(Universe: Population Age 3–17 Enrolled in School)

Group	Number	%
Total Population	2,187	4.8
Hispanic or Latino (of any race)	1,785	4.1
Mexican	1,619	3.9

Foreign-Born Population

Group	Number	%
Total Population	52,339	30.9
Hispanic or Latino (of any race)	50,814	32.2
Mexican	49,356	32.6

Foreign-Born Naturalized U.S. Citizens

Group	Number	%
Total Population	15,930	30.4
Hispanic or Latino (of any race)	15,395	30.3
Mexican	14,793	30.0

Language Spoken at Home: English Only
(Universe: Population 5 Years and Over)

Group	Number	%
Total Population	17,495	11.5
Hispanic or Latino (of any race)	10,213	7.2
Mexican	9,592	7.1

Language Spoken at Home: Spanish
(Universe: Population 5 Years and Over)

Group	Number	%
Total Population	133,839	87.7
Hispanic or Latino (of any race)	131,602	92.7
Mexican	126,294	92.9

Unemployment Rate
(Universe: Population 16 Years and Over)

Group	%
Total Population	8.2
Hispanic or Latino (of any race)	8.5
Mexican	8.3

Class of Worker: Private Wage and Salary
(Universe: Civilian Employed Population 16 Years and Over)

Group	Number	%
Total Population	43,011	69.5
Hispanic or Latino (of any race)	39,668	69.9
Mexican	37,939	69.9

Class of Worker: Government
(Universe: Civilian Employed Population 16 Years and Over)

Group	Number	%
Total Population	13,013	21.0
Hispanic or Latino (of any race)	11,500	20.3
Mexican	10,958	20.2

Means of Transportation to Work: Car, Truck or Van
(Universe: Workers 16 Years and Over)

Group	Number	%
Total Population	54,832	91.2
Hispanic or Latino (of any race)	50,235	91.1
Mexican	48,068	91.1

Means of Transportation to Work: Public Transportation (ex. Taxicab)
(Universe: Workers 16 Years and Over)

Group	Number	%
Total Population	754	1.3
Hispanic or Latino (of any race)	726	1.3
Mexican	700	1.3

Homeownership Rate
(Universe: Occupied Housing Units)

Group	%
Total Population	62.2
Hispanic or Latino (of any race)	61.0
Central American, ex. Mexican	53.5
Honduran	49.4
Nicaraguan	64.9
Salvadoran	49.4
Cuban	66.3
Mexican	61.2
Puerto Rican	53.5
South American	64.7
Colombian	58.3
Spaniard	60.4

Median Home Value

Group	Dollars
Total Population	77,200
Hispanic or Latino (of any race)	75,100
Mexican	74,900

Median Gross Rent

Group	Dollars
Total Population	561
Hispanic or Latino (of any race)	544
Mexican	540

Median Household Income
(2010 Inflation-Adjusted Dollars)

Group	Dollars
Total Population	30,134
Hispanic or Latino (of any race)	28,107
Mexican	27,733

Per Capita Income
(2010 Inflation-Adjusted Dollars)

Group	Dollars
Total Population	12,130
Hispanic or Latino (of any race)	10,854
Mexican	10,583

Households with $100,000+ Income

Group	Number	%
Total Population	3,724	8.1
Hispanic or Latino (of any race)	2,684	6.5
Mexican	2,478	6.3

Households with Food Stamps/SNAP Benefits During Past 12 Months

Group	Number	%
Total Population	13,471	29.3
Hispanic or Latino (of any race)	13,117	31.9
Mexican	12,561	32.0

Poverty Rate
(Income in Past 12 Months Below Poverty Level)

Group	%
Total Population	35.8
Hispanic or Latino (of any race)	37.5
Mexican	38.1

Bryan

Population

Group	Number	%TP[1]	%HP[2]
Total Population	76,201	100.0	–
Hispanic or Latino (of any race)	27,617	36.2	100.0
Central American, ex. Mexican	649	0.9	2.4
Guatemalan	189	0.2	0.7
Honduran	169	0.2	0.6
Salvadoran	241	0.3	0.9
Mexican	24,699	32.4	89.4
Puerto Rican	228	0.3	0.8
South American	189	0.2	0.7
Spaniard	122	0.2	0.4

STATE & PLACE PROFILES

Notes: (1) Percent of total population; (2) Percent of Hispanic/Latino population; Profiles include places with an overall population of at least 125,000, OR an overall population of at least 25,000 where the Hispanic/Latino population is at least 20% of the overall population. In states where less than five places meet either of these criteria, we have included places with at least 10,000 total population with the highest percentage of Hispanic/Latino population. These places are identified with an asterisk (*); Please refer to the User's Guide for a full explanation of data.

Population Growth: 2000–2010

Group	%
Total Population	16.1
Hispanic or Latino (of any race)	51.2
Central American, ex. Mexican	318.7
Mexican	67.4
Puerto Rican	107.3

Males per 100 Females

Group	Number
Total Population	100.8
Hispanic or Latino (of any race)	108.4
Central American, ex. Mexican	151.6
Guatemalan	220.3
Honduran	186.4
Salvadoran	115.2
Mexican	108.0
Puerto Rican	91.6
South American	125.0
Spaniard	96.8

Average Household Size

Group	People
Total Population	2.64
Hispanic or Latino (of any race)	3.57
Central American, ex. Mexican	3.13
Guatemalan	3.54
Honduran	3.17
Salvadoran	3.08
Mexican	3.66
Puerto Rican	2.59
South American	2.03
Spaniard	2.32

Median Age

Group	Years
Total Population	28.5
Hispanic or Latino (of any race)	24.5
Central American, ex. Mexican	28.2
Guatemalan	30.3
Honduran	27.1
Salvadoran	28.3
Mexican	24.2
Puerto Rican	28.2
South American	27.8
Spaniard	28.0

High School Graduates
(Universe: Population 25 Years and Over)

Group	Number	%
Total Population	30,573	76.8
Hispanic or Latino (of any race)	6,281	52.6
Mexican	5,337	50.4

Four-Year College Graduates
(Universe: Population 25 Years and Over)

Group	Number	%
Total Population	10,404	26.2
Hispanic or Latino (of any race)	789	6.6
Mexican	588	5.5

Population Age 3–17 Enrolled in Public School
(Universe: Population Age 3–17 Enrolled in School)

Group	Number	%
Total Population	11,954	93.8
Hispanic or Latino (of any race)	5,595	97.0
Mexican	5,232	97.1

Population Age 3–17 Enrolled in Private School
(Universe: Population Age 3–17 Enrolled in School)

Group	Number	%
Total Population	789	6.2
Hispanic or Latino (of any race)	173	3.0
Mexican	155	2.9

Foreign-Born Population

Group	Number	%
Total Population	9,381	12.8
Hispanic or Latino (of any race)	7,580	30.1
Mexican	6,643	29.4

Foreign-Born Naturalized U.S. Citizens

Group	Number	%
Total Population	1,937	20.6
Hispanic or Latino (of any race)	1,067	14.1
Mexican	861	13.0

Language Spoken at Home: English Only
(Universe: Population 5 Years and Over)

Group	Number	%
Total Population	49,993	74.5
Hispanic or Latino (of any race)	7,103	32.5
Mexican	6,472	33.1

Language Spoken at Home: Spanish
(Universe: Population 5 Years and Over)

Group	Number	%
Total Population	15,677	23.4
Hispanic or Latino (of any race)	14,744	67.5
Mexican	13,096	66.9

Unemployment Rate
(Universe: Population 16 Years and Over)

Group	%
Total Population	7.4
Hispanic or Latino (of any race)	7.5
Mexican	6.9

Class of Worker: Private Wage and Salary
(Universe: Civilian Employed Population 16 Years and Over)

Group	Number	%
Total Population	24,640	70.9
Hispanic or Latino (of any race)	8,970	81.4
Mexican	8,124	82.8

Class of Worker: Government
(Universe: Civilian Employed Population 16 Years and Over)

Group	Number	%
Total Population	7,916	22.8
Hispanic or Latino (of any race)	1,481	13.4
Mexican	1,260	12.8

Means of Transportation to Work: Car, Truck or Van
(Universe: Workers 16 Years and Over)

Group	Number	%
Total Population	31,070	91.0
Hispanic or Latino (of any race)	10,144	92.7
Mexican	9,117	93.2

Means of Transportation to Work: Public Transportation (ex. Taxicab)
(Universe: Workers 16 Years and Over)

Group	Number	%
Total Population	456	1.3
Hispanic or Latino (of any race)	64	0.6
Mexican	64	0.7

Homeownership Rate
(Universe: Occupied Housing Units)

Group	%
Total Population	48.2
Hispanic or Latino (of any race)	47.8
Central American, ex. Mexican	27.9
Guatemalan	24.6
Honduran	13.0
Salvadoran	40.2
Mexican	49.5
Puerto Rican	36.2
South American	21.3
Spaniard	58.9

Median Home Value

Group	Dollars
Total Population	109,300
Hispanic or Latino (of any race)	81,700
Mexican	78,300

Median Gross Rent

Group	Dollars
Total Population	708
Hispanic or Latino (of any race)	676
Mexican	665

Median Household Income
(2010 Inflation-Adjusted Dollars)

Group	Dollars
Total Population	37,077
Hispanic or Latino (of any race)	33,858
Mexican	33,063

Per Capita Income
(2010 Inflation-Adjusted Dollars)

Group	Dollars
Total Population	18,930
Hispanic or Latino (of any race)	11,993
Mexican	11,459

Households with $100,000+ Income

Group	Number	%
Total Population	3,082	11.7
Hispanic or Latino (of any race)	386	5.7
Mexican	258	4.3

Households with Food Stamps/SNAP Benefits During Past 12 Months

Group	Number	%
Total Population	3,944	14.9
Hispanic or Latino (of any race)	1,231	18.1
Mexican	1,109	18.5

Poverty Rate
(Income in Past 12 Months Below Poverty Level)

Group	%
Total Population	27.5
Hispanic or Latino (of any race)	30.1
Mexican	29.8

Carrollton

Population

Group	Number	%TP[1]	%HP[2]
Total Population	119,097	100.0	–
Hispanic or Latino (of any race)	35,710	30.0	100.0
Central American, ex. Mexican	4,295	3.6	12.0
Guatemalan	384	0.3	1.1
Honduran	519	0.4	1.5
Nicaraguan	208	0.2	0.6
Salvadoran	3,034	2.5	8.5
Cuban	372	0.3	1.0
Mexican	27,195	22.8	76.2
Puerto Rican	654	0.5	1.8
South American	1,165	1.0	3.3
Colombian	425	0.4	1.2
Ecuadorian	141	0.1	0.4
Peruvian	287	0.2	0.8
Spaniard	275	0.2	0.8

Population Growth: 2000–2010

Group	%
Total Population	8.7
Hispanic or Latino (of any race)	66.9
Central American, ex. Mexican	200.6
Guatemalan	202.4
Honduran	278.8
Nicaraguan	60.0
Salvadoran	242.8
Cuban	15.9
Mexican	72.7
Puerto Rican	72.1
South American	82.3
Colombian	82.4
Peruvian	75.0

Males per 100 Females

Group	Number
Total Population	95.7
Hispanic or Latino (of any race)	102.2
Central American, ex. Mexican	104.1
Guatemalan	101.0
Honduran	98.9
Nicaraguan	85.7
Salvadoran	107.5
Cuban	93.8
Mexican	103.3
Puerto Rican	101.2
South American	85.2
Colombian	84.8
Ecuadorian	98.6
Peruvian	86.4
Spaniard	71.9

Average Household Size

Group	People
Total Population	2.74

Notes: (1) Percent of total population; (2) Percent of Hispanic/Latino population; Profiles include places with an overall population of at least 125,000, OR an overall population of at least 25,000 where the Hispanic/Latino population is at least 20% of the overall population. In states where less than five places meet either of these criteria, we have included places with at least 10,000 total population with the highest percentage of Hispanic/Latino population. These places are identified with an asterisk (*); Please refer to the User's Guide for a full explanation of data.

Group	
Hispanic or Latino (of any race)	3.70
Central American, ex. Mexican	4.17
Guatemalan	3.67
Honduran	4.02
Nicaraguan	3.51
Salvadoran	4.39
Cuban	2.65
Mexican	3.73
Puerto Rican	2.97
South American	3.14
Colombian	3.14
Ecuadorian	3.55
Peruvian	3.33
Spaniard	2.71

Median Age

Group	Years
Total Population	35.6
Hispanic or Latino (of any race)	26.8
Central American, ex. Mexican	29.9
Guatemalan	30.0
Honduran	29.2
Nicaraguan	40.3
Salvadoran	29.6
Cuban	42.8
Mexican	25.7
Puerto Rican	31.4
South American	36.6
Colombian	37.5
Ecuadorian	35.6
Peruvian	35.3
Spaniard	34.6

High School Graduates
(Universe: Population 25 Years and Over)

Group	Number	%
Total Population	66,556	86.7
Hispanic or Latino (of any race)	10,390	59.7
Central American, ex. Mexican	1,786	67.0
Salvadoran	934	56.8
Mexican	6,627	53.4
South American	574	88.2

Four-Year College Graduates
(Universe: Population 25 Years and Over)

Group	Number	%
Total Population	29,227	38.1
Hispanic or Latino (of any race)	2,605	15.0
Central American, ex. Mexican	394	14.8
Salvadoran	205	12.5
Mexican	1,351	10.9
South American	394	60.5

Population Age 3–17 Enrolled in Public School
(Universe: Population Age 3–17 Enrolled in School)

Group	Number	%
Total Population	21,855	89.8
Hispanic or Latino (of any race)	8,810	96.3
Central American, ex. Mexican	1,231	97.7
Salvadoran	958	100.0
Mexican	6,448	96.9
South American	150	76.9

Population Age 3–17 Enrolled in Private School
(Universe: Population Age 3–17 Enrolled in School)

Group	Number	%
Total Population	2,484	10.2
Hispanic or Latino (of any race)	338	3.7
Central American, ex. Mexican	29	2.3
Salvadoran	0	0.0
Mexican	209	3.1
South American	45	23.1

Foreign-Born Population

Group	Number	%
Total Population	29,104	24.7
Hispanic or Latino (of any race)	15,290	46.5
Central American, ex. Mexican	2,981	62.1
Salvadoran	1,757	55.5
Mexican	10,963	45.6
South American	666	68.4

Foreign-Born Naturalized U.S. Citizens

Group	Number	%
Total Population	11,455	39.4
Hispanic or Latino (of any race)	3,911	25.6
Central American, ex. Mexican	762	25.6
Salvadoran	434	24.7
Mexican	2,452	22.4
South American	355	53.3

Language Spoken at Home: English Only
(Universe: Population 5 Years and Over)

Group	Number	%
Total Population	69,254	63.3
Hispanic or Latino (of any race)	5,142	17.3
Central American, ex. Mexican	389	9.1
Salvadoran	179	6.4
Mexican	3,716	17.2
South American	115	12.6

Language Spoken at Home: Spanish
(Universe: Population 5 Years and Over)

Group	Number	%
Total Population	25,660	23.5
Hispanic or Latino (of any race)	24,463	82.3
Central American, ex. Mexican	3,881	90.9
Salvadoran	2,610	93.6
Mexican	17,824	82.6
South American	800	87.4

Unemployment Rate
(Universe: Population 16 Years and Over)

Group	%
Total Population	5.7
Hispanic or Latino (of any race)	5.7
Central American, ex. Mexican	4.8
Salvadoran	2.1
Mexican	6.1
South American	0.0

Class of Worker: Private Wage and Salary
(Universe: Civilian Employed Population 16 Years and Over)

Group	Number	%
Total Population	53,889	83.2
Hispanic or Latino (of any race)	13,714	86.1
Central American, ex. Mexican	2,154	91.2
Salvadoran	1,532	96.4
Mexican	10,001	86.0
South American	439	72.3

Class of Worker: Government
(Universe: Civilian Employed Population 16 Years and Over)

Group	Number	%
Total Population	6,256	9.7
Hispanic or Latino (of any race)	1,288	8.1
Central American, ex. Mexican	84	3.6
Salvadoran	0	0.0
Mexican	925	8.0
South American	133	21.9

Means of Transportation to Work: Car, Truck or Van
(Universe: Workers 16 Years and Over)

Group	Number	%
Total Population	58,456	92.1
Hispanic or Latino (of any race)	14,920	95.4
Central American, ex. Mexican	2,210	94.7
Salvadoran	1,536	97.5
Mexican	10,873	95.7
South American	576	94.9

Means of Transportation to Work: Public Transportation (ex. Taxicab)
(Universe: Workers 16 Years and Over)

Group	Number	%
Total Population	613	1.0
Hispanic or Latino (of any race)	80	0.5
Central American, ex. Mexican	0	0.0
Salvadoran	0	0.0
Mexican	63	0.6
South American	0	0.0

Homeownership Rate
(Universe: Occupied Housing Units)

Group	%
Total Population	63.1
Hispanic or Latino (of any race)	47.7
Central American, ex. Mexican	54.8
Guatemalan	54.5
Honduran	43.5
Nicaraguan	64.2
Salvadoran	55.7
Cuban	63.9
Mexican	44.7
Puerto Rican	55.9
South American	66.9
Colombian	64.4
Ecuadorian	72.7
Peruvian	73.0
Spaniard	59.4

Median Home Value

Group	Dollars
Total Population	164,300
Hispanic or Latino (of any race)	136,000
Central American, ex. Mexican	133,400
Salvadoran	124,600
Mexican	133,900
South American	176,200

Median Gross Rent

Group	Dollars
Total Population	926
Hispanic or Latino (of any race)	838
Central American, ex. Mexican	895
Salvadoran	827
Mexican	817
South American	793

Median Household Income
(2010 Inflation-Adjusted Dollars)

Group	Dollars
Total Population	69,599
Hispanic or Latino (of any race)	49,684
Central American, ex. Mexican	52,583
Salvadoran	52,667
Mexican	48,625
South American	55,227

Per Capita Income
(2010 Inflation-Adjusted Dollars)

Group	Dollars
Total Population	31,481
Hispanic or Latino (of any race)	18,185
Central American, ex. Mexican	15,958
Salvadoran	14,017
Mexican	17,378
South American	32,747

Households with $100,000+ Income

Group	Number	%
Total Population	13,345	31.5
Hispanic or Latino (of any race)	1,434	16.6
Central American, ex. Mexican	168	13.7
Salvadoran	57	7.4
Mexican	1,050	16.8
South American	97	28.5

Households with Food Stamps/SNAP Benefits During Past 12 Months

Group	Number	%
Total Population	1,254	3.0
Hispanic or Latino (of any race)	427	4.9
Central American, ex. Mexican	41	3.3
Salvadoran	41	5.3
Mexican	339	5.4
South American	0	0.0

Poverty Rate
(Income in Past 12 Months Below Poverty Level)

Group	%
Total Population	8.7
Hispanic or Latino (of any race)	16.8
Central American, ex. Mexican	20.3
Salvadoran	15.0
Mexican	17.6
South American	7.0

Channelview

Population

Group	Number	%TP[1]	%HP[2]
Total Population	38,289	100.0	–
Hispanic or Latino (of any race)	23,100	60.3	100.0

Notes: (1) Percent of total population; (2) Percent of Hispanic/Latino population; Profiles include places with an overall population of at least 125,000, OR an overall population of at least 25,000 where the Hispanic/Latino population is at least 20% of the overall population. In states where less than five places meet either of these criteria, we have included places with at least 10,000 total population with the highest percentage of Hispanic/Latino population. These places are identified with an asterisk (*); Please refer to the User's Guide for a full explanation of data.

Central American, ex. Mexican	1,465	3.8	6.3
Guatemalan	163	0.4	0.7
Honduran	359	0.9	1.6
Salvadoran	888	2.3	3.8
Mexican	19,822	51.8	85.8
Puerto Rican	177	0.5	0.8
South American	159	0.4	0.7
Spaniard	114	0.3	0.5

Population Growth: 2000–2010

Group	%
Total Population	29.0
Hispanic or Latino (of any race)	109.7
Central American, ex. Mexican	383.5
Salvadoran	431.7
Mexican	126.0
Puerto Rican	77.0

Males per 100 Females

Group	Number
Total Population	100.6
Hispanic or Latino (of any race)	105.0
Central American, ex. Mexican	109.6
Guatemalan	120.3
Honduran	109.9
Salvadoran	111.9
Mexican	104.6
Puerto Rican	113.3
South American	109.2
Spaniard	115.1

Average Household Size

Group	People
Total Population	3.45
Hispanic or Latino (of any race)	4.11
Central American, ex. Mexican	4.25
Guatemalan	4.27
Honduran	4.31
Salvadoran	4.29
Mexican	4.14
Puerto Rican	3.81
South American	3.41
Spaniard	3.77

Median Age

Group	Years
Total Population	28.3
Hispanic or Latino (of any race)	24.1
Central American, ex. Mexican	31.0
Guatemalan	34.6
Honduran	30.1
Salvadoran	31.0
Mexican	23.6
Puerto Rican	29.1
South American	33.5
Spaniard	26.5

High School Graduates
(Universe: Population 25 Years and Over)

Group	Number	%
Total Population	14,966	71.5
Hispanic or Latino (of any race)	5,219	52.7
Central American, ex. Mexican	230	32.1
Mexican	4,388	52.3

Four-Year College Graduates
(Universe: Population 25 Years and Over)

Group	Number	%
Total Population	2,131	10.2
Hispanic or Latino (of any race)	813	8.2
Central American, ex. Mexican	11	1.5
Mexican	727	8.7

Population Age 3–17 Enrolled in Public School
(Universe: Population Age 3–17 Enrolled in School)

Group	Number	%
Total Population	9,768	97.2
Hispanic or Latino (of any race)	6,541	98.3
Central American, ex. Mexican	440	100.0
Mexican	5,730	99.0

Population Age 3–17 Enrolled in Private School
(Universe: Population Age 3–17 Enrolled in School)

Group	Number	%
Total Population	285	2.8
Hispanic or Latino (of any race)	113	1.7
Central American, ex. Mexican	0	0.0
Mexican	56	1.0

Foreign-Born Population

Group	Number	%
Total Population	8,656	22.8
Hispanic or Latino (of any race)	8,230	39.2
Central American, ex. Mexican	807	59.1
Mexican	7,019	38.6

Foreign-Born Naturalized U.S. Citizens

Group	Number	%
Total Population	1,964	22.7
Hispanic or Latino (of any race)	1,723	20.9
Central American, ex. Mexican	157	19.5
Mexican	1,375	19.6

Language Spoken at Home: English Only
(Universe: Population 5 Years and Over)

Group	Number	%
Total Population	18,147	52.2
Hispanic or Latino (of any race)	2,726	14.6
Central American, ex. Mexican	17	1.4
Mexican	2,298	14.3

Language Spoken at Home: Spanish
(Universe: Population 5 Years and Over)

Group	Number	%
Total Population	16,104	46.3
Hispanic or Latino (of any race)	15,901	85.4
Central American, ex. Mexican	1,224	98.6
Mexican	13,815	85.7

Unemployment Rate
(Universe: Population 16 Years and Over)

Group	%
Total Population	8.9
Hispanic or Latino (of any race)	6.1
Central American, ex. Mexican	2.1
Mexican	6.2

Class of Worker: Private Wage and Salary
(Universe: Civilian Employed Population 16 Years and Over)

Group	Number	%
Total Population	13,297	81.1
Hispanic or Latino (of any race)	6,944	82.4
Central American, ex. Mexican	540	98.0
Mexican	5,861	80.6

Class of Worker: Government
(Universe: Civilian Employed Population 16 Years and Over)

Group	Number	%
Total Population	2,032	12.4
Hispanic or Latino (of any race)	746	8.9
Central American, ex. Mexican	11	2.0
Mexican	693	9.5

Means of Transportation to Work: Car, Truck or Van
(Universe: Workers 16 Years and Over)

Group	Number	%
Total Population	15,254	96.0
Hispanic or Latino (of any race)	7,801	95.6
Central American, ex. Mexican	526	100.0
Mexican	6,696	95.2

Means of Transportation to Work: Public Transportation (ex. Taxicab)
(Universe: Workers 16 Years and Over)

Group	Number	%
Total Population	44	0.3
Hispanic or Latino (of any race)	0	0.0
Central American, ex. Mexican	0	0.0
Mexican	0	0.0

Homeownership Rate
(Universe: Occupied Housing Units)

Group	%
Total Population	70.1
Hispanic or Latino (of any race)	71.9
Central American, ex. Mexican	73.0
Guatemalan	81.3
Honduran	62.2
Salvadoran	75.8
Mexican	72.6
Puerto Rican	57.4
South American	82.4
Spaniard	61.3

Median Home Value

Group	Dollars
Total Population	93,500
Hispanic or Latino (of any race)	92,200
Central American, ex. Mexican	115,000
Mexican	90,900

Median Gross Rent

Group	Dollars
Total Population	851
Hispanic or Latino (of any race)	810
Central American, ex. Mexican	428
Mexican	834

Median Household Income
(2010 Inflation-Adjusted Dollars)

Group	Dollars
Total Population	50,963
Hispanic or Latino (of any race)	46,845
Central American, ex. Mexican	43,068
Mexican	47,447

Per Capita Income
(2010 Inflation-Adjusted Dollars)

Group	Dollars
Total Population	18,426
Hispanic or Latino (of any race)	13,477
Central American, ex. Mexican	11,429
Mexican	13,442

Households with $100,000+ Income

Group	Number	%
Total Population	1,671	15.3
Hispanic or Latino (of any race)	468	9.1
Central American, ex. Mexican	0	0.0
Mexican	447	10.2

Households with Food Stamps/SNAP Benefits During Past 12 Months

Group	Number	%
Total Population	1,005	9.2
Hispanic or Latino (of any race)	465	9.1
Central American, ex. Mexican	50	12.4
Mexican	402	9.2

Poverty Rate
(Income in Past 12 Months Below Poverty Level)

Group	%
Total Population	16.7
Hispanic or Latino (of any race)	19.6
Central American, ex. Mexican	32.4
Mexican	19.1

Cleburne

Population

Group	Number	%TP[1]	%HP[2]
Total Population	29,337	100.0	–
Hispanic or Latino (of any race)	7,959	27.1	100.0
Central American, ex. Mexican	129	0.4	1.6
Mexican	7,160	24.4	90.0
Puerto Rican	144	0.5	1.8

Population Growth: 2000–2010

Group	%
Total Population	12.8
Hispanic or Latino (of any race)	53.8
Mexican	64.8

Males per 100 Females

Group	Number
Total Population	96.0
Hispanic or Latino (of any race)	110.3
Central American, ex. Mexican	126.3
Mexican	111.3
Puerto Rican	121.5

Average Household Size

Group	People
Total Population	2.73
Hispanic or Latino (of any race)	3.92

Notes: (1) Percent of total population; (2) Percent of Hispanic/Latino population; Profiles include places with an overall population of at least 125,000, OR an overall population of at least 25,000 where the Hispanic/Latino population is at least 20% of the overall population. In states where less than five places meet either of these criteria, we have included places with at least 10,000 total population with the highest percentage of Hispanic/Latino population. These places are identified with an asterisk (*); Please refer to the User's Guide for a full explanation of data.

Central American, ex. Mexican	4.00
Mexican	4.01
Puerto Rican	2.81

Median Age

Group	Years
Total Population	33.9
Hispanic or Latino (of any race)	23.5
Central American, ex. Mexican	35.1
Mexican	23.2
Puerto Rican	23.5

High School Graduates
(Universe: Population 25 Years and Over)

Group	Number	%
Total Population	13,739	75.2
Hispanic or Latino (of any race)	1,456	45.7
Mexican	1,339	44.6

Four-Year College Graduates
(Universe: Population 25 Years and Over)

Group	Number	%
Total Population	2,603	14.2
Hispanic or Latino (of any race)	136	4.3
Mexican	122	4.1

Population Age 3–17 Enrolled in Public School
(Universe: Population Age 3–17 Enrolled in School)

Group	Number	%
Total Population	5,198	94.9
Hispanic or Latino (of any race)	1,669	98.8
Mexican	1,610	100.0

Population Age 3–17 Enrolled in Private School
(Universe: Population Age 3–17 Enrolled in School)

Group	Number	%
Total Population	277	5.1
Hispanic or Latino (of any race)	21	1.2
Mexican	0	0.0

Foreign-Born Population

Group	Number	%
Total Population	2,934	10.1
Hispanic or Latino (of any race)	2,661	41.6
Mexican	2,588	42.6

Foreign-Born Naturalized U.S. Citizens

Group	Number	%
Total Population	665	22.7
Hispanic or Latino (of any race)	608	22.8
Mexican	583	22.5

Language Spoken at Home: English Only
(Universe: Population 5 Years and Over)

Group	Number	%
Total Population	21,470	80.5
Hispanic or Latino (of any race)	996	17.9
Mexican	840	15.9

Language Spoken at Home: Spanish
(Universe: Population 5 Years and Over)

Group	Number	%
Total Population	4,898	18.4
Hispanic or Latino (of any race)	4,577	82.1
Mexican	4,437	84.1

Unemployment Rate
(Universe: Population 16 Years and Over)

Group	%
Total Population	8.0
Hispanic or Latino (of any race)	8.9
Mexican	8.6

Class of Worker: Private Wage and Salary
(Universe: Civilian Employed Population 16 Years and Over)

Group	Number	%
Total Population	9,955	78.9
Hispanic or Latino (of any race)	2,357	86.3
Mexican	2,238	86.2

Class of Worker: Government
(Universe: Civilian Employed Population 16 Years and Over)

Group	Number	%
Total Population	1,834	14.5
Hispanic or Latino (of any race)	256	9.4
Mexican	240	9.2

Means of Transportation to Work: Car, Truck or Van
(Universe: Workers 16 Years and Over)

Group	Number	%
Total Population	11,482	93.2
Hispanic or Latino (of any race)	2,454	94.6
Mexican	2,328	94.4

Means of Transportation to Work: Public Transportation (ex. Taxicab)
(Universe: Workers 16 Years and Over)

Group	Number	%
Total Population	36	0.3
Hispanic or Latino (of any race)	0	0.0
Mexican	0	0.0

Homeownership Rate
(Universe: Occupied Housing Units)

Group	%
Total Population	60.7
Hispanic or Latino (of any race)	56.9
Central American, ex. Mexican	60.0
Mexican	57.7
Puerto Rican	48.8

Median Home Value

Group	Dollars
Total Population	93,100
Hispanic or Latino (of any race)	73,900
Mexican	74,600

Median Gross Rent

Group	Dollars
Total Population	834
Hispanic or Latino (of any race)	733
Mexican	729

Median Household Income
(2010 Inflation-Adjusted Dollars)

Group	Dollars
Total Population	44,844
Hispanic or Latino (of any race)	44,000
Mexican	44,011

Per Capita Income
(2010 Inflation-Adjusted Dollars)

Group	Dollars
Total Population	20,745
Hispanic or Latino (of any race)	16,170
Mexican	16,290

Households with $100,000+ Income

Group	Number	%
Total Population	1,268	12.2
Hispanic or Latino (of any race)	127	8.3
Mexican	127	8.9

Households with Food Stamps/SNAP Benefits During Past 12 Months

Group	Number	%
Total Population	1,592	15.4
Hispanic or Latino (of any race)	364	23.7
Mexican	332	23.3

Poverty Rate
(Income in Past 12 Months Below Poverty Level)

Group	%
Total Population	16.5
Hispanic or Latino (of any race)	19.1
Mexican	18.9

Conroe

Population

Group	Number	%TP[1]	%HP[2]
Total Population	56,207	100.0	–
Hispanic or Latino (of any race)	21,661	38.5	100.0
Central American, ex. Mexican	3,475	6.2	16.0
Guatemalan	178	0.3	0.8
Honduran	1,766	3.1	8.2
Salvadoran	1,415	2.5	6.5
Mexican	16,452	29.3	76.0
Puerto Rican	268	0.5	1.2
South American	233	0.4	1.1
Spaniard	100	0.2	0.5

Population Growth: 2000–2010

Group	%
Total Population	52.7
Hispanic or Latino (of any race)	80.4
Central American, ex. Mexican	294.0
Honduran	314.6
Salvadoran	295.3
Mexican	74.3

Males per 100 Females

Group	Number
Total Population	102.0
Hispanic or Latino (of any race)	122.5
Central American, ex. Mexican	154.0
Guatemalan	169.7
Honduran	152.6
Salvadoran	150.0
Mexican	118.5
Puerto Rican	111.0
South American	117.8
Spaniard	104.1

Average Household Size

Group	People
Total Population	2.69
Hispanic or Latino (of any race)	3.92
Central American, ex. Mexican	4.08
Guatemalan	3.62
Honduran	4.31
Salvadoran	3.93
Mexican	3.98
Puerto Rican	2.90
South American	2.83
Spaniard	2.79

Median Age

Group	Years
Total Population	31.5
Hispanic or Latino (of any race)	25.4
Central American, ex. Mexican	29.8
Guatemalan	28.7
Honduran	28.9
Salvadoran	30.9
Mexican	24.2
Puerto Rican	26.7
South American	33.3
Spaniard	28.0

High School Graduates
(Universe: Population 25 Years and Over)

Group	Number	%
Total Population	24,241	74.6
Hispanic or Latino (of any race)	3,811	39.4
Central American, ex. Mexican	421	31.1
Honduran	258	36.9
Mexican	3,106	39.8

Four-Year College Graduates
(Universe: Population 25 Years and Over)

Group	Number	%
Total Population	5,951	18.3
Hispanic or Latino (of any race)	350	3.6
Central American, ex. Mexican	27	2.0
Honduran	14	2.0
Mexican	254	3.3

Population Age 3–17 Enrolled in Public School
(Universe: Population Age 3–17 Enrolled in School)

Group	Number	%
Total Population	8,510	87.3
Hispanic or Latino (of any race)	4,668	95.8
Central American, ex. Mexican	520	100.0
Honduran	432	100.0
Mexican	3,936	95.0

Population Age 3–17 Enrolled in Private School
(Universe: Population Age 3–17 Enrolled in School)

Group	Number	%
Total Population	1,239	12.7
Hispanic or Latino (of any race)	207	4.2
Central American, ex. Mexican	0	0.0
Honduran	0	0.0
Mexican	207	5.0

Notes: (1) Percent of total population; (2) Percent of Hispanic/Latino population; Profiles include places with an overall population of at least 125,000, OR an overall population of at least 25,000 where the Hispanic/Latino population is at least 20% of the overall population. In states where less than five places meet either of these criteria, we have included places with at least 10,000 total population with the highest percentage of Hispanic/Latino population. These places are identified with an asterisk (*); Please refer to the User's Guide for a full explanation of data.

Foreign-Born Population

Group	Number	%
Total Population	12,464	23.4
Hispanic or Latino (of any race)	10,829	54.1
Central American, ex. Mexican	2,004	79.3
Honduran	1,093	75.0
Mexican	8,472	51.0

Foreign-Born Naturalized U.S. Citizens

Group	Number	%
Total Population	2,419	19.4
Hispanic or Latino (of any race)	1,831	16.9
Central American, ex. Mexican	270	13.5
Honduran	147	13.4
Mexican	1,483	17.5

Language Spoken at Home: English Only
(Universe: Population 5 Years and Over)

Group	Number	%
Total Population	31,128	64.7
Hispanic or Latino (of any race)	2,042	11.9
Central American, ex. Mexican	91	3.9
Honduran	66	5.1
Mexican	1,777	12.7

Language Spoken at Home: Spanish
(Universe: Population 5 Years and Over)

Group	Number	%
Total Population	15,680	32.6
Hispanic or Latino (of any race)	15,050	88.0
Central American, ex. Mexican	2,240	96.1
Honduran	1,220	94.9
Mexican	12,201	87.3

Unemployment Rate
(Universe: Population 16 Years and Over)

Group	%
Total Population	6.6
Hispanic or Latino (of any race)	6.5
Central American, ex. Mexican	4.8
Honduran	9.7
Mexican	6.7

Class of Worker: Private Wage and Salary
(Universe: Civilian Employed Population 16 Years and Over)

Group	Number	%
Total Population	19,722	77.9
Hispanic or Latino (of any race)	7,625	78.9
Central American, ex. Mexican	1,162	78.5
Honduran	497	71.1
Mexican	6,180	79.7

Class of Worker: Government
(Universe: Civilian Employed Population 16 Years and Over)

Group	Number	%
Total Population	3,048	12.0
Hispanic or Latino (of any race)	666	6.9
Central American, ex. Mexican	108	7.3
Honduran	28	4.0
Mexican	501	6.5

Means of Transportation to Work: Car, Truck or Van
(Universe: Workers 16 Years and Over)

Group	Number	%
Total Population	23,194	93.6
Hispanic or Latino (of any race)	9,031	95.1
Central American, ex. Mexican	1,362	93.9
Honduran	580	86.8
Mexican	7,310	95.6

Means of Transportation to Work: Public Transportation (ex. Taxicab)
(Universe: Workers 16 Years and Over)

Group	Number	%
Total Population	122	0.5
Hispanic or Latino (of any race)	21	0.2
Central American, ex. Mexican	11	0.8
Honduran	11	1.6
Mexican	10	0.1

Homeownership Rate
(Universe: Occupied Housing Units)

Group	%
Total Population	49.1
Hispanic or Latino (of any race)	46.8
Central American, ex. Mexican	46.0
Guatemalan	34.0
Honduran	43.1
Salvadoran	51.5
Mexican	48.2
Puerto Rican	34.9
South American	35.2
Spaniard	33.3

Median Home Value

Group	Dollars
Total Population	122,400
Hispanic or Latino (of any race)	80,800
Central American, ex. Mexican	94,400
Honduran	111,700
Mexican	73,600

Median Gross Rent

Group	Dollars
Total Population	771
Hispanic or Latino (of any race)	691
Central American, ex. Mexican	626
Honduran	634
Mexican	699

Median Household Income
(2010 Inflation-Adjusted Dollars)

Group	Dollars
Total Population	45,567
Hispanic or Latino (of any race)	36,806
Central American, ex. Mexican	38,365
Honduran	35,739
Mexican	36,273

Per Capita Income
(2010 Inflation-Adjusted Dollars)

Group	Dollars
Total Population	21,443
Hispanic or Latino (of any race)	11,995
Central American, ex. Mexican	14,198
Honduran	10,481
Mexican	11,290

Households with $100,000+ Income

Group	Number	%
Total Population	2,508	13.4
Hispanic or Latino (of any race)	307	6.1
Central American, ex. Mexican	46	5.8
Honduran	12	3.2
Mexican	219	5.6

Households with Food Stamps/SNAP Benefits During Past 12 Months

Group	Number	%
Total Population	1,472	7.9
Hispanic or Latino (of any race)	613	12.1
Central American, ex. Mexican	109	13.6
Honduran	57	15.3
Mexican	485	12.4

Poverty Rate
(Income in Past 12 Months Below Poverty Level)

Group	%
Total Population	18.9
Hispanic or Latino (of any race)	28.8
Central American, ex. Mexican	24.4
Honduran	31.4
Mexican	29.4

Corpus Christi

Population

Group	Number	%TP[1]	%HP[2]
Total Population	305,215	100.0	–
Hispanic or Latino (of any race)	182,181	59.7	100.0
Central American, ex. Mexican	978	0.3	0.5
Guatemalan	204	0.1	0.1
Honduran	202	0.1	0.1
Panamanian	119	<0.1	0.1
Salvadoran	354	0.1	0.2
Cuban	483	0.2	0.3
Mexican	148,800	48.8	81.7
Puerto Rican	1,248	0.4	0.7
South American	832	0.3	0.5
Colombian	304	0.1	0.2
Peruvian	121	<0.1	0.1
Venezuelan	139	<0.1	0.1
Spaniard	1,878	0.6	1.0

Population Growth: 2000–2010

Group	%
Total Population	10.0
Hispanic or Latino (of any race)	20.9
Central American, ex. Mexican	129.0
Cuban	44.6
Mexican	51.6
Puerto Rican	67.5
South American	102.9
Colombian	111.1
Spaniard	967.0

Males per 100 Females

Group	Number
Total Population	96.2
Hispanic or Latino (of any race)	94.7
Central American, ex. Mexican	107.2
Guatemalan	114.7
Honduran	106.1
Panamanian	67.6
Salvadoran	119.9
Cuban	133.3
Mexican	95.9
Puerto Rican	110.8
South American	92.1
Colombian	75.7
Peruvian	105.1
Venezuelan	110.6
Spaniard	83.0

Average Household Size

Group	People
Total Population	2.66
Hispanic or Latino (of any race)	2.97
Central American, ex. Mexican	3.12
Guatemalan	3.48
Honduran	3.36
Panamanian	2.37
Salvadoran	3.21
Cuban	2.40
Mexican	2.98
Puerto Rican	2.87
South American	2.81
Colombian	2.92
Peruvian	2.98
Venezuelan	2.80
Spaniard	2.73

Median Age

Group	Years
Total Population	34.8
Hispanic or Latino (of any race)	30.6
Central American, ex. Mexican	30.3
Guatemalan	27.3
Honduran	29.8
Panamanian	39.6
Salvadoran	30.3
Cuban	38.7
Mexican	31.3
Puerto Rican	28.7
South American	35.5
Colombian	36.7
Peruvian	40.6
Venezuelan	33.5
Spaniard	33.6

High School Graduates
(Universe: Population 25 Years and Over)

Group	Number	%
Total Population	149,752	79.3
Hispanic or Latino (of any race)	70,880	69.7
Central American, ex. Mexican	480	59.6
Mexican	58,914	69.4
Puerto Rican	634	78.0
South American	530	91.7
Spaniard	846	79.7

Notes: (1) Percent of total population; (2) Percent of Hispanic/Latino population; Profiles include places with an overall population of at least 125,000, OR an overall population of at least 25,000 where the Hispanic/Latino population is at least 20% of the overall population. In states where less than five places meet either of these criteria, we have included places with at least 10,000 total population with the highest percentage of Hispanic/Latino population. These places are identified with an asterisk (*); Please refer to the User's Guide for a full explanation of data.

Four-Year College Graduates
(Universe: Population 25 Years and Over)

Group	Number	%
Total Population	38,842	20.6
Hispanic or Latino (of any race)	11,865	11.7
Central American, ex. Mexican	184	22.9
Mexican	9,663	11.4
Puerto Rican	143	17.6
South American	314	54.3
Spaniard	221	20.8

Population Age 3–17 Enrolled in Public School
(Universe: Population Age 3–17 Enrolled in School)

Group	Number	%
Total Population	53,681	91.5
Hispanic or Latino (of any race)	38,026	93.2
Central American, ex. Mexican	158	90.8
Mexican	30,810	93.2
Puerto Rican	637	98.0
South American	278	93.9
Spaniard	165	78.9

Population Age 3–17 Enrolled in Private School
(Universe: Population Age 3–17 Enrolled in School)

Group	Number	%
Total Population	4,998	8.5
Hispanic or Latino (of any race)	2,756	6.8
Central American, ex. Mexican	16	9.2
Mexican	2,243	6.8
Puerto Rican	13	2.0
South American	18	6.1
Spaniard	44	21.1

Foreign-Born Population

Group	Number	%
Total Population	22,636	7.6
Hispanic or Latino (of any race)	15,223	8.7
Central American, ex. Mexican	649	49.6
Mexican	13,026	9.0
Puerto Rican	34	1.8
South American	623	60.5
Spaniard	93	6.3

Foreign-Born Naturalized U.S. Citizens

Group	Number	%
Total Population	8,843	39.1
Hispanic or Latino (of any race)	5,025	33.0
Central American, ex. Mexican	250	38.5
Mexican	4,079	31.3
Puerto Rican	0	0.0
South American	195	31.3
Spaniard	22	23.7

Language Spoken at Home: English Only
(Universe: Population 5 Years and Over)

Group	Number	%
Total Population	168,881	60.8
Hispanic or Latino (of any race)	62,959	39.2
Central American, ex. Mexican	449	36.3
Mexican	52,961	39.8
Puerto Rican	484	30.1
South American	151	14.7
Spaniard	624	45.7

Language Spoken at Home: Spanish
(Universe: Population 5 Years and Over)

Group	Number	%
Total Population	101,929	36.7
Hispanic or Latino (of any race)	97,328	60.6
Central American, ex. Mexican	787	63.7
Mexican	79,802	60.0
Puerto Rican	1,089	67.8
South American	869	84.4
Spaniard	698	51.2

Unemployment Rate
(Universe: Population 16 Years and Over)

Group	%
Total Population	8.0
Hispanic or Latino (of any race)	9.3
Central American, ex. Mexican	10.9
Mexican	9.0
Puerto Rican	14.2
South American	7.7
Spaniard	11.2

Class of Worker: Private Wage and Salary
(Universe: Civilian Employed Population 16 Years and Over)

Group	Number	%
Total Population	100,968	75.2
Hispanic or Latino (of any race)	57,128	75.9
Central American, ex. Mexican	545	79.2
Mexican	47,089	75.6
Puerto Rican	500	69.7
South American	488	88.1
Spaniard	391	72.4

Class of Worker: Government
(Universe: Civilian Employed Population 16 Years and Over)

Group	Number	%
Total Population	24,160	18.0
Hispanic or Latino (of any race)	13,572	18.0
Central American, ex. Mexican	135	19.6
Mexican	11,257	18.1
Puerto Rican	184	25.7
South American	57	10.3
Spaniard	94	17.4

Means of Transportation to Work: Car, Truck or Van
(Universe: Workers 16 Years and Over)

Group	Number	%
Total Population	121,492	90.7
Hispanic or Latino (of any race)	67,741	92.0
Central American, ex. Mexican	607	85.6
Mexican	55,774	91.7
Puerto Rican	598	79.5
South American	431	77.0
Spaniard	497	93.4

Means of Transportation to Work: Public Transportation (ex. Taxicab)
(Universe: Workers 16 Years and Over)

Group	Number	%
Total Population	2,478	1.9
Hispanic or Latino (of any race)	1,258	1.7
Central American, ex. Mexican	9	1.3
Mexican	1,058	1.7
Puerto Rican	44	5.9
South American	61	10.9
Spaniard	15	2.8

Homeownership Rate
(Universe: Occupied Housing Units)

Group	%
Total Population	59.3
Hispanic or Latino (of any race)	56.3
Central American, ex. Mexican	51.9
Guatemalan	45.9
Honduran	50.0
Panamanian	56.5
Salvadoran	50.0
Cuban	52.4
Mexican	58.6
Puerto Rican	53.8
South American	59.1
Colombian	62.7
Peruvian	52.4
Venezuelan	52.0
Spaniard	60.3

Median Home Value

Group	Dollars
Total Population	107,600
Hispanic or Latino (of any race)	83,900
Central American, ex. Mexican	125,800
Mexican	83,400
Puerto Rican	77,300
South American	252,400
Spaniard	100,400

Median Gross Rent

Group	Dollars
Total Population	796
Hispanic or Latino (of any race)	780
Central American, ex. Mexican	837
Mexican	775
Puerto Rican	857
South American	746
Spaniard	902

Median Household Income
(2010 Inflation-Adjusted Dollars)

Group	Dollars
Total Population	43,457
Hispanic or Latino (of any race)	37,036
Central American, ex. Mexican	52,813
Mexican	37,807
Puerto Rican	34,569
South American	57,083
Spaniard	41,280

Per Capita Income
(2010 Inflation-Adjusted Dollars)

Group	Dollars
Total Population	22,921
Hispanic or Latino (of any race)	16,956
Central American, ex. Mexican	18,422
Mexican	17,173
Puerto Rican	13,312
South American	28,058
Spaniard	24,045

Households with $100,000+ Income

Group	Number	%
Total Population	17,748	16.3
Hispanic or Latino (of any race)	6,429	11.4
Central American, ex. Mexican	94	22.7
Mexican	5,416	11.7
Puerto Rican	9	1.6
South American	96	25.1
Spaniard	55	8.9

Households with Food Stamps/SNAP Benefits During Past 12 Months

Group	Number	%
Total Population	15,760	14.4
Hispanic or Latino (of any race)	11,485	20.4
Central American, ex. Mexican	79	19.1
Mexican	9,307	20.1
Puerto Rican	125	22.9
South American	13	3.4
Spaniard	58	9.4

Poverty Rate
(Income in Past 12 Months Below Poverty Level)

Group	%
Total Population	18.8
Hispanic or Latino (of any race)	23.1
Central American, ex. Mexican	31.7
Mexican	22.5
Puerto Rican	21.5
South American	14.8
Spaniard	20.4

Dallas

Population

Group	Number	%TP[1]	%HP[2]
Total Population	1,197,816	100.0	–
Hispanic or Latino (of any race)	507,309	42.4	100.0
Central American, ex. Mexican	28,798	2.4	5.7
Costa Rican	462	<0.1	0.1
Guatemalan	4,238	0.4	0.8
Honduran	6,890	0.6	1.4
Nicaraguan	816	0.1	0.2
Panamanian	458	<0.1	0.1
Salvadoran	15,696	1.3	3.1
Cuban	2,322	0.2	0.5
Dominican Republic	530	<0.1	0.1
Mexican	439,460	36.7	86.6
Puerto Rican	3,643	0.3	0.7
South American	5,683	0.5	1.1
Argentinean	599	0.1	0.1
Bolivian	301	<0.1	0.1
Chilean	283	<0.1	0.1
Colombian	1,563	0.1	0.3
Ecuadorian	412	<0.1	0.1
Peruvian	1,725	0.1	0.3
Uruguayan	103	<0.1	<0.1
Venezuelan	548	<0.1	0.1
Spaniard	2,468	0.2	0.5

Notes: (1) Percent of total population; (2) Percent of Hispanic/Latino population; Profiles include places with an overall population of at least 125,000, OR an overall population of at least 25,000 where the Hispanic/Latino population is at least 20% of the overall population. In states where less than five places meet either of these criteria, we have included places with at least 10,000 total population with the highest percentage of Hispanic/Latino population. These places are identified with an asterisk (*); Please refer to the User's Guide for a full explanation of data.

Population Growth: 2000–2010

Group	%
Total Population	0.8
Hispanic or Latino (of any race)	20.0
Central American, ex. Mexican	92.3
Costa Rican	10.5
Guatemalan	117.3
Honduran	161.3
Nicaraguan	100.5
Panamanian	43.6
Salvadoran	82.9
Cuban	1.7
Dominican Republic	142.0
Mexican	25.4
Puerto Rican	53.8
South American	96.3
Argentinean	169.8
Bolivian	152.9
Chilean	66.5
Colombian	81.3
Ecuadorian	79.9
Peruvian	102.2
Venezuelan	99.3
Spaniard	482.1

Males per 100 Females

Group	Number
Total Population	100.0
Hispanic or Latino (of any race)	110.9
Central American, ex. Mexican	118.8
Costa Rican	106.3
Guatemalan	141.6
Honduran	126.3
Nicaraguan	100.0
Panamanian	78.9
Salvadoran	113.1
Cuban	123.9
Dominican Republic	84.7
Mexican	111.2
Puerto Rican	103.6
South American	92.1
Argentinean	108.0
Bolivian	90.5
Chilean	99.3
Colombian	86.5
Ecuadorian	88.1
Peruvian	93.4
Uruguayan	87.3
Venezuelan	96.4
Spaniard	105.7

Average Household Size

Group	People
Total Population	2.57
Hispanic or Latino (of any race)	3.70
Central American, ex. Mexican	3.65
Costa Rican	2.52
Guatemalan	3.49
Honduran	3.58
Nicaraguan	2.94
Panamanian	2.33
Salvadoran	3.86
Cuban	2.41
Dominican Republic	2.36
Mexican	3.80
Puerto Rican	2.31
South American	2.42
Argentinean	2.30
Bolivian	2.32
Chilean	2.12
Colombian	2.32
Ecuadorian	2.56
Peruvian	2.68
Uruguayan	2.55
Venezuelan	2.17
Spaniard	2.63

Median Age

Group	Years
Total Population	31.8
Hispanic or Latino (of any race)	25.8
Central American, ex. Mexican	30.1
Costa Rican	33.7
Guatemalan	30.1
Honduran	29.0
Nicaraguan	31.8
Panamanian	37.1
Salvadoran	30.4
Cuban	37.4
Dominican Republic	29.4
Mexican	25.3
Puerto Rican	29.5
South American	35.0
Argentinean	35.1
Bolivian	35.6
Chilean	36.6
Colombian	34.2
Ecuadorian	35.6
Peruvian	35.8
Uruguayan	34.6
Venezuelan	34.3
Spaniard	31.8

High School Graduates

(Universe: Population 25 Years and Over)

Group	Number	%
Total Population	542,917	72.9
Hispanic or Latino (of any race)	104,645	41.5
Central American, ex. Mexican	7,043	35.0
Guatemalan	1,369	40.7
Honduran	1,477	31.1
Salvadoran	3,325	30.7
Cuban	1,125	79.2
Mexican	87,047	39.9
Puerto Rican	1,949	87.7
South American	3,499	82.5
Colombian	1,004	78.8
Peruvian	1,184	82.5
Spaniard	1,158	89.6

Four-Year College Graduates

(Universe: Population 25 Years and Over)

Group	Number	%
Total Population	213,048	28.6
Hispanic or Latino (of any race)	18,907	7.5
Central American, ex. Mexican	1,275	6.3
Guatemalan	242	7.2
Honduran	194	4.1
Salvadoran	506	4.7
Cuban	449	31.6
Mexican	13,583	6.2
Puerto Rican	843	37.9
South American	1,610	38.0
Colombian	618	48.5
Peruvian	417	29.0
Spaniard	499	38.6

Population Age 3–17 Enrolled in Public School

(Universe: Population Age 3–17 Enrolled in School)

Group	Number	%
Total Population	193,204	87.9
Hispanic or Latino (of any race)	115,810	95.8
Central American, ex. Mexican	5,129	96.8
Guatemalan	522	92.9
Honduran	1,132	99.8
Salvadoran	3,181	96.2
Cuban	223	76.6
Mexican	106,752	96.0
Puerto Rican	480	76.6
South American	800	89.2
Colombian	163	74.8
Peruvian	374	97.1
Spaniard	133	81.6

Population Age 3–17 Enrolled in Private School

(Universe: Population Age 3–17 Enrolled in School)

Group	Number	%
Total Population	26,706	12.1
Hispanic or Latino (of any race)	5,139	4.2
Central American, ex. Mexican	167	3.2
Guatemalan	40	7.1
Honduran	2	0.2
Salvadoran	125	3.8
Cuban	68	23.4
Mexican	4,409	4.0
Puerto Rican	147	23.4
South American	97	10.8
Colombian	55	25.2
Peruvian	11	2.9
Spaniard	30	18.4

Foreign-Born Population

Group	Number	%
Total Population	295,137	24.9
Hispanic or Latino (of any race)	238,488	48.3
Central American, ex. Mexican	24,245	71.9
Guatemalan	4,373	78.8
Honduran	5,794	75.1
Salvadoran	12,820	69.3
Cuban	1,206	55.2
Mexican	206,277	47.2
Puerto Rican	111	3.4
South American	4,494	72.6
Colombian	1,217	69.6
Peruvian	1,698	76.4
Spaniard	158	8.7

Foreign-Born Naturalized U.S. Citizens

Group	Number	%
Total Population	60,498	20.5
Hispanic or Latino (of any race)	35,516	14.9
Central American, ex. Mexican	3,243	13.4
Guatemalan	691	15.8
Honduran	207	3.6
Salvadoran	1,888	14.7
Cuban	669	55.5
Mexican	29,649	14.4
Puerto Rican	0	0.0
South American	1,256	27.9
Colombian	325	26.7
Peruvian	442	26.0
Spaniard	59	37.3

Language Spoken at Home: English Only

(Universe: Population 5 Years and Over)

Group	Number	%
Total Population	631,609	58.3
Hispanic or Latino (of any race)	45,278	10.4
Central American, ex. Mexican	1,588	5.2
Guatemalan	362	7.2
Honduran	135	2.0
Salvadoran	754	4.5
Cuban	439	22.8
Mexican	38,771	10.1
Puerto Rican	884	28.5
South American	470	8.3
Colombian	165	10.1
Peruvian	177	8.6
Spaniard	952	55.4

Language Spoken at Home: Spanish

(Universe: Population 5 Years and Over)

Group	Number	%
Total Population	401,858	37.1
Hispanic or Latino (of any race)	388,224	89.5
Central American, ex. Mexican	28,695	94.8
Guatemalan	4,693	92.8
Honduran	6,638	98.0
Salvadoran	15,870	95.5
Cuban	1,487	77.2
Mexican	343,802	89.8
Puerto Rican	2,187	70.4
South American	5,189	91.4
Colombian	1,464	89.9
Peruvian	1,875	91.4
Spaniard	755	43.9

Unemployment Rate

(Universe: Population 16 Years and Over)

Group	%
Total Population	8.2
Hispanic or Latino (of any race)	7.7
Central American, ex. Mexican	8.0
Guatemalan	4.1
Honduran	16.7
Salvadoran	5.3
Cuban	12.0
Mexican	7.7
Puerto Rican	10.3
South American	3.3
Colombian	1.0
Peruvian	2.3
Spaniard	3.0

Notes: (1) Percent of total population; (2) Percent of Hispanic/Latino population; Profiles include places with an overall population of at least 125,000, OR an overall population of at least 25,000 where the Hispanic/Latino population is at least 20% of the overall population. In states where less than five places meet either of these criteria, we have included places with at least 10,000 total population with the highest percentage of Hispanic/Latino population. These places are identified with an asterisk (*); Please refer to the User's Guide for a full explanation of data.

Class of Worker: Private Wage and Salary
(Universe: Civilian Employed Population 16 Years and Over)

Group	Number	%
Total Population	470,631	84.0
Hispanic or Latino (of any race)	191,093	87.8
Central American, ex. Mexican	17,039	91.8
Guatemalan	3,258	90.6
Honduran	3,518	95.2
Salvadoran	9,496	92.1
Cuban	878	80.2
Mexican	164,893	87.9
Puerto Rican	1,371	80.4
South American	3,008	76.7
Colombian	808	70.0
Peruvian	1,205	79.2
Spaniard	970	81.9

Class of Worker: Government
(Universe: Civilian Employed Population 16 Years and Over)

Group	Number	%
Total Population	51,146	9.1
Hispanic or Latino (of any race)	11,813	5.4
Central American, ex. Mexican	434	2.3
Guatemalan	87	2.4
Honduran	17	0.5
Salvadoran	245	2.4
Cuban	86	7.9
Mexican	10,106	5.4
Puerto Rican	238	14.0
South American	395	10.1
Colombian	134	11.6
Peruvian	158	10.4
Spaniard	148	12.5

Means of Transportation to Work: Car, Truck or Van
(Universe: Workers 16 Years and Over)

Group	Number	%
Total Population	488,552	88.9
Hispanic or Latino (of any race)	196,112	91.9
Central American, ex. Mexican	16,637	90.4
Guatemalan	3,076	86.1
Honduran	3,206	88.0
Salvadoran	9,545	93.2
Cuban	847	84.6
Mexican	169,753	92.3
Puerto Rican	1,455	86.0
South American	3,310	88.7
Colombian	993	93.2
Peruvian	1,394	91.7
Spaniard	1,006	86.1

Means of Transportation to Work: Public Transportation (ex. Taxicab)
(Universe: Workers 16 Years and Over)

Group	Number	%
Total Population	23,287	4.2
Hispanic or Latino (of any race)	6,672	3.1
Central American, ex. Mexican	588	3.2
Guatemalan	100	2.8
Honduran	179	4.9
Salvadoran	268	2.6
Cuban	58	5.8
Mexican	5,512	3.0
Puerto Rican	170	10.1
South American	137	3.7
Colombian	16	1.5
Peruvian	98	6.4
Spaniard	72	6.2

Homeownership Rate
(Universe: Occupied Housing Units)

Group	%
Total Population	44.1
Hispanic or Latino (of any race)	40.1
Central American, ex. Mexican	32.3
Costa Rican	37.9
Guatemalan	27.2
Honduran	17.3
Nicaraguan	35.5
Panamanian	39.8
Salvadoran	39.5
Cuban	43.5
Dominican Republic	25.5
Mexican	41.4
Puerto Rican	31.4
South American	34.8
Argentinean	39.1
Bolivian	42.2
Chilean	44.8
Colombian	35.2
Ecuadorian	41.0
Peruvian	30.1
Uruguayan	25.0
Venezuelan	32.1
Spaniard	41.4

Median Home Value

Group	Dollars
Total Population	129,800
Hispanic or Latino (of any race)	89,900
Central American, ex. Mexican	104,100
Guatemalan	121,500
Honduran	113,600
Salvadoran	101,100
Cuban	150,600
Mexican	88,400
Puerto Rican	97,700
South American	136,000
Colombian	125,700
Peruvian	126,300
Spaniard	209,000

Median Gross Rent

Group	Dollars
Total Population	789
Hispanic or Latino (of any race)	723
Central American, ex. Mexican	697
Guatemalan	721
Honduran	674
Salvadoran	696
Cuban	848
Mexican	720
Puerto Rican	786
South American	780
Colombian	740
Peruvian	804
Spaniard	938

Median Household Income
(2010 Inflation-Adjusted Dollars)

Group	Dollars
Total Population	41,682
Hispanic or Latino (of any race)	34,014
Central American, ex. Mexican	31,925
Guatemalan	34,167
Honduran	27,518
Salvadoran	32,163
Cuban	45,518
Mexican	33,725
Puerto Rican	41,331
South American	41,116
Colombian	54,332
Peruvian	51,932
Spaniard	60,197

Per Capita Income
(2010 Inflation-Adjusted Dollars)

Group	Dollars
Total Population	26,716
Hispanic or Latino (of any race)	12,485
Central American, ex. Mexican	13,287
Guatemalan	17,478
Honduran	10,097
Salvadoran	12,640
Cuban	26,042
Mexican	11,967
Puerto Rican	26,423
South American	22,207
Colombian	22,930
Peruvian	20,408
Spaniard	36,979

Households with $100,000+ Income

Group	Number	%
Total Population	78,007	17.4
Hispanic or Latino (of any race)	7,868	6.0
Central American, ex. Mexican	420	4.3
Guatemalan	92	5.6
Honduran	88	4.2
Salvadoran	175	3.4
Cuban	96	12.4
Mexican	6,359	5.7
Puerto Rican	114	9.2
South American	321	14.4
Colombian	105	16.6
Peruvian	84	11.9
Spaniard	287	29.8

Households with Food Stamps/SNAP Benefits During Past 12 Months

Group	Number	%
Total Population	45,268	10.1
Hispanic or Latino (of any race)	14,933	11.4
Central American, ex. Mexican	808	8.2
Guatemalan	71	4.3
Honduran	380	18.0
Salvadoran	333	6.4
Cuban	63	8.2
Mexican	13,312	11.8
Puerto Rican	157	12.7
South American	88	3.9
Colombian	43	6.8
Peruvian	32	4.5
Spaniard	72	7.5

Poverty Rate
(Income in Past 12 Months Below Poverty Level)

Group	%
Total Population	22.3
Hispanic or Latino (of any race)	28.5
Central American, ex. Mexican	27.8
Guatemalan	20.0
Honduran	39.9
Salvadoran	26.1
Cuban	13.1
Mexican	28.8
Puerto Rican	20.3
South American	16.3
Colombian	12.6
Peruvian	13.1
Spaniard	8.6

Deer Park

Population

Group	Number	%TP[1]	%HP[2]
Total Population	32,010	100.0	–
Hispanic or Latino (of any race)	8,418	26.3	100.0
Central American, ex. Mexican	280	0.9	3.3
Salvadoran	144	0.4	1.7
Mexican	7,050	22.0	83.7
Puerto Rican	124	0.4	1.5
South American	111	0.3	1.3

Population Growth: 2000–2010

Group	%
Total Population	12.2
Hispanic or Latino (of any race)	93.9
Mexican	128.7

Males per 100 Females

Group	Number
Total Population	97.1
Hispanic or Latino (of any race)	99.6
Central American, ex. Mexican	110.5
Salvadoran	136.1
Mexican	99.1
Puerto Rican	93.8
South American	98.2

Average Household Size

Group	People
Total Population	2.87
Hispanic or Latino (of any race)	3.59
Central American, ex. Mexican	3.75
Salvadoran	3.81
Mexican	3.65
Puerto Rican	2.90
South American	2.74

Median Age

Group	Years
Total Population	35.3

Group	%
Hispanic or Latino (of any race)	26.1
Central American, ex. Mexican	32.8
Salvadoran	32.0
Mexican	25.8
Puerto Rican	32.6
South American	31.7

High School Graduates
(Universe: Population 25 Years and Over)

Group	Number	%
Total Population	17,123	87.1
Hispanic or Latino (of any race)	2,628	68.4
Mexican	2,244	67.5

Four-Year College Graduates
(Universe: Population 25 Years and Over)

Group	Number	%
Total Population	3,781	19.2
Hispanic or Latino (of any race)	210	5.5
Mexican	155	4.7

Population Age 3–17 Enrolled in Public School
(Universe: Population Age 3–17 Enrolled in School)

Group	Number	%
Total Population	6,034	92.6
Hispanic or Latino (of any race)	2,247	96.8
Mexican	1,952	96.7

Population Age 3–17 Enrolled in Private School
(Universe: Population Age 3–17 Enrolled in School)

Group	Number	%
Total Population	483	7.4
Hispanic or Latino (of any race)	75	3.2
Mexican	66	3.3

Foreign-Born Population

Group	Number	%
Total Population	2,043	6.5
Hispanic or Latino (of any race)	1,470	18.7
Mexican	1,196	17.4

Foreign-Born Naturalized U.S. Citizens

Group	Number	%
Total Population	831	40.7
Hispanic or Latino (of any race)	454	30.9
Mexican	364	30.4

Language Spoken at Home: English Only
(Universe: Population 5 Years and Over)

Group	Number	%
Total Population	23,967	82.5
Hispanic or Latino (of any race)	2,890	41.1
Mexican	2,335	38.6

Language Spoken at Home: Spanish
(Universe: Population 5 Years and Over)

Group	Number	%
Total Population	4,321	14.9
Hispanic or Latino (of any race)	4,055	57.7
Mexican	3,674	60.7

Unemployment Rate
(Universe: Population 16 Years and Over)

Group	%
Total Population	6.6
Hispanic or Latino (of any race)	10.6
Mexican	10.7

Class of Worker: Private Wage and Salary
(Universe: Civilian Employed Population 16 Years and Over)

Group	Number	%
Total Population	12,390	80.2
Hispanic or Latino (of any race)	2,630	82.2
Mexican	2,253	80.6

Class of Worker: Government
(Universe: Civilian Employed Population 16 Years and Over)

Group	Number	%
Total Population	2,363	15.3
Hispanic or Latino (of any race)	518	16.2
Mexican	490	17.5

Means of Transportation to Work: Car, Truck or Van
(Universe: Workers 16 Years and Over)

Group	Number	%
Total Population	14,638	95.8
Hispanic or Latino (of any race)	3,111	97.8
Mexican	2,715	97.8

Means of Transportation to Work: Public Transportation (ex. Taxicab)
(Universe: Workers 16 Years and Over)

Group	Number	%
Total Population	67	0.4
Hispanic or Latino (of any race)	22	0.7
Mexican	22	0.8

Homeownership Rate
(Universe: Occupied Housing Units)

Group	%
Total Population	77.3
Hispanic or Latino (of any race)	68.1
Central American, ex. Mexican	65.8
Salvadoran	76.6
Mexican	69.1
Puerto Rican	63.4
South American	67.6

Median Home Value

Group	Dollars
Total Population	129,600
Hispanic or Latino (of any race)	117,700
Mexican	118,700

Median Gross Rent

Group	Dollars
Total Population	968
Hispanic or Latino (of any race)	846
Mexican	821

Median Household Income
(2010 Inflation-Adjusted Dollars)

Group	Dollars
Total Population	73,820
Hispanic or Latino (of any race)	52,623
Mexican	52,895

Per Capita Income
(2010 Inflation-Adjusted Dollars)

Group	Dollars
Total Population	28,966
Hispanic or Latino (of any race)	17,083
Mexican	16,801

Households with $100,000+ Income

Group	Number	%
Total Population	3,571	34.1
Hispanic or Latino (of any race)	410	22.5
Mexican	347	22.2

Households with Food Stamps/SNAP Benefits During Past 12 Months

Group	Number	%
Total Population	531	5.1
Hispanic or Latino (of any race)	308	16.9
Mexican	299	19.1

Poverty Rate
(Income in Past 12 Months Below Poverty Level)

Group	%
Total Population	8.4
Hispanic or Latino (of any race)	16.6
Mexican	16.3

Del Rio

Population

Group	Number	%TP[1]	%HP[2]
Total Population	35,591	100.0	–
Hispanic or Latino (of any race)	29,927	84.1	100.0
Central American, ex. Mexican	145	0.4	0.5
Mexican	27,626	77.6	92.3
Puerto Rican	184	0.5	0.6

Population Growth: 2000–2010

Group	%
Total Population	5.1
Hispanic or Latino (of any race)	9.0
Mexican	17.7

Males per 100 Females

Group	Number
Total Population	98.7
Hispanic or Latino (of any race)	96.2
Central American, ex. Mexican	314.3
Mexican	96.0
Puerto Rican	148.6

Average Household Size

Group	People
Total Population	2.95
Hispanic or Latino (of any race)	3.13
Central American, ex. Mexican	3.70
Mexican	3.14
Puerto Rican	2.55

Median Age

Group	Years
Total Population	33.4
Hispanic or Latino (of any race)	32.1
Central American, ex. Mexican	32.1
Mexican	32.6
Puerto Rican	30.2

High School Graduates
(Universe: Population 25 Years and Over)

Group	Number	%
Total Population	13,605	63.2
Hispanic or Latino (of any race)	9,637	55.9
Mexican	9,164	55.2

Four-Year College Graduates
(Universe: Population 25 Years and Over)

Group	Number	%
Total Population	3,347	15.6
Hispanic or Latino (of any race)	2,028	11.8
Mexican	1,935	11.6

Population Age 3–17 Enrolled in Public School
(Universe: Population Age 3–17 Enrolled in School)

Group	Number	%
Total Population	7,466	94.9
Hispanic or Latino (of any race)	6,835	95.8
Mexican	6,650	96.3

Population Age 3–17 Enrolled in Private School
(Universe: Population Age 3–17 Enrolled in School)

Group	Number	%
Total Population	398	5.1
Hispanic or Latino (of any race)	302	4.2
Mexican	258	3.7

Foreign-Born Population

Group	Number	%
Total Population	8,175	23.2
Hispanic or Latino (of any race)	7,932	27.0
Mexican	7,746	27.4

Foreign-Born Naturalized U.S. Citizens

Group	Number	%
Total Population	2,981	36.5
Hispanic or Latino (of any race)	2,875	36.2
Mexican	2,793	36.1

Language Spoken at Home: English Only
(Universe: Population 5 Years and Over)

Group	Number	%
Total Population	7,918	24.6
Hispanic or Latino (of any race)	3,248	12.2
Mexican	3,070	11.9

Language Spoken at Home: Spanish
(Universe: Population 5 Years and Over)

Group	Number	%
Total Population	24,154	74.9
Hispanic or Latino (of any race)	23,469	87.8
Mexican	22,663	88.1

Notes: (1) Percent of total population; (2) Percent of Hispanic/Latino population; Profiles include places with an overall population of at least 125,000, OR an overall population of at least 25,000 where the Hispanic/Latino population is at least 20% of the overall population. In states where less than five places meet either of these criteria, we have included places with at least 10,000 total population with the highest percentage of Hispanic/Latino population. These places are identified with an asterisk (*); Please refer to the User's Guide for a full explanation of data.

Unemployment Rate
(Universe: Population 16 Years and Over)

Group	%
Total Population	10.0
Hispanic or Latino (of any race)	11.6
Mexican	11.6

Class of Worker: Private Wage and Salary
(Universe: Civilian Employed Population 16 Years and Over)

Group	Number	%
Total Population	8,587	63.1
Hispanic or Latino (of any race)	7,303	66.9
Mexican	7,055	67.1

Class of Worker: Government
(Universe: Civilian Employed Population 16 Years and Over)

Group	Number	%
Total Population	4,340	31.9
Hispanic or Latino (of any race)	3,094	28.3
Mexican	2,937	27.9

Means of Transportation to Work: Car, Truck or Van
(Universe: Workers 16 Years and Over)

Group	Number	%
Total Population	12,737	93.0
Hispanic or Latino (of any race)	9,938	92.7
Mexican	9,581	92.7

Means of Transportation to Work: Public Transportation (ex. Taxicab)
(Universe: Workers 16 Years and Over)

Group	Number	%
Total Population	45	0.3
Hispanic or Latino (of any race)	37	0.3
Mexican	37	0.4

Homeownership Rate
(Universe: Occupied Housing Units)

Group	%
Total Population	62.6
Hispanic or Latino (of any race)	62.4
Central American, ex. Mexican	50.0
Mexican	63.1
Puerto Rican	36.4

Median Home Value

Group	Dollars
Total Population	82,600
Hispanic or Latino (of any race)	70,200
Mexican	70,200

Median Gross Rent

Group	Dollars
Total Population	563
Hispanic or Latino (of any race)	532
Mexican	526

Median Household Income
(2010 Inflation-Adjusted Dollars)

Group	Dollars
Total Population	34,111
Hispanic or Latino (of any race)	28,729
Mexican	28,906

Per Capita Income
(2010 Inflation-Adjusted Dollars)

Group	Dollars
Total Population	15,677
Hispanic or Latino (of any race)	13,015
Mexican	13,047

Households with $100,000+ Income

Group	Number	%
Total Population	1,045	9.4
Hispanic or Latino (of any race)	637	7.6
Mexican	634	7.8

Households with Food Stamps/SNAP Benefits During Past 12 Months

Group	Number	%
Total Population	2,052	18.4
Hispanic or Latino (of any race)	1,884	22.5
Mexican	1,835	22.7

Poverty Rate
(Income in Past 12 Months Below Poverty Level)

Group	%
Total Population	25.6
Hispanic or Latino (of any race)	28.7
Mexican	28.7

Denton

Population

Group	Number	%TP[1]	%HP[2]
Total Population	113,383	100.0	–
Hispanic or Latino (of any race)	24,071	21.2	100.0
Central American, ex. Mexican	1,336	1.2	5.6
Guatemalan	458	0.4	1.9
Honduran	187	0.2	0.8
Salvadoran	505	0.4	2.1
Cuban	158	0.1	0.7
Mexican	18,766	16.6	78.0
Puerto Rican	621	0.5	2.6
South American	742	0.7	3.1
Colombian	322	0.3	1.3
Peruvian	176	0.2	0.7
Spaniard	320	0.3	1.3

Population Growth: 2000–2010

Group	%
Total Population	40.8
Hispanic or Latino (of any race)	82.5
Central American, ex. Mexican	206.4
Guatemalan	111.1
Salvadoran	346.9
Mexican	81.6
Puerto Rican	230.3
South American	228.3

Males per 100 Females

Group	Number
Total Population	95.4
Hispanic or Latino (of any race)	105.2
Central American, ex. Mexican	93.3
Guatemalan	108.2
Honduran	110.1
Salvadoran	81.7
Cuban	100.0
Mexican	107.3
Puerto Rican	97.1
South American	97.9
Colombian	101.3
Peruvian	91.3
Spaniard	93.9

Average Household Size

Group	People
Total Population	2.45
Hispanic or Latino (of any race)	3.35
Central American, ex. Mexican	3.72
Guatemalan	3.85
Honduran	3.43
Salvadoran	3.79
Cuban	2.34
Mexican	3.44
Puerto Rican	2.75
South American	2.79
Colombian	3.13
Peruvian	2.91
Spaniard	2.54

Median Age

Group	Years
Total Population	27.1
Hispanic or Latino (of any race)	23.2
Central American, ex. Mexican	27.4
Guatemalan	30.3
Honduran	26.6
Salvadoran	25.9
Cuban	24.2
Mexican	23.0
Puerto Rican	23.8
South American	25.8
Colombian	25.8
Peruvian	26.8
Spaniard	25.0

High School Graduates
(Universe: Population 25 Years and Over)

Group	Number	%
Total Population	52,083	86.1
Hispanic or Latino (of any race)	5,586	55.8
Central American, ex. Mexican	277	43.3
Mexican	4,434	52.8

Four-Year College Graduates
(Universe: Population 25 Years and Over)

Group	Number	%
Total Population	21,201	35.1
Hispanic or Latino (of any race)	1,373	13.7
Central American, ex. Mexican	37	5.8
Mexican	1,123	13.4

Population Age 3–17 Enrolled in Public School
(Universe: Population Age 3–17 Enrolled in School)

Group	Number	%
Total Population	14,026	88.4
Hispanic or Latino (of any race)	4,464	93.0
Central American, ex. Mexican	246	100.0
Mexican	3,864	92.7

Population Age 3–17 Enrolled in Private School
(Universe: Population Age 3–17 Enrolled in School)

Group	Number	%
Total Population	1,838	11.6
Hispanic or Latino (of any race)	336	7.0
Central American, ex. Mexican	0	0.0
Mexican	303	7.3

Foreign-Born Population

Group	Number	%
Total Population	13,721	12.6
Hispanic or Latino (of any race)	8,383	38.0
Central American, ex. Mexican	847	63.9
Mexican	7,032	38.3

Foreign-Born Naturalized U.S. Citizens

Group	Number	%
Total Population	3,122	22.8
Hispanic or Latino (of any race)	1,203	14.4
Central American, ex. Mexican	206	24.3
Mexican	874	12.4

Language Spoken at Home: English Only
(Universe: Population 5 Years and Over)

Group	Number	%
Total Population	81,063	78.8
Hispanic or Latino (of any race)	4,970	25.4
Central American, ex. Mexican	186	14.8
Mexican	3,912	24.1

Language Spoken at Home: Spanish
(Universe: Population 5 Years and Over)

Group	Number	%
Total Population	16,429	16.0
Hispanic or Latino (of any race)	14,599	74.5
Central American, ex. Mexican	1,070	85.2
Mexican	12,327	75.9

Unemployment Rate
(Universe: Population 16 Years and Over)

Group	%
Total Population	7.7
Hispanic or Latino (of any race)	9.0
Central American, ex. Mexican	0.8
Mexican	9.3

Class of Worker: Private Wage and Salary
(Universe: Civilian Employed Population 16 Years and Over)

Group	Number	%
Total Population	41,046	74.3
Hispanic or Latino (of any race)	7,601	77.3
Central American, ex. Mexican	761	88.7
Mexican	6,064	76.8

Class of Worker: Government
(Universe: Civilian Employed Population 16 Years and Over)

Group	Number	%
Total Population	11,513	20.8
Hispanic or Latino (of any race)	1,693	17.2
Central American, ex. Mexican	67	7.8
Mexican	1,402	17.8

Notes: (1) Percent of total population; (2) Percent of Hispanic/Latino population; Profiles include places with an overall population of at least 125,000, OR an overall population of at least 25,000 where the Hispanic/Latino population is at least 20% of the overall population. In states where less than five places meet either of these criteria, we have included places with at least 10,000 total population with the highest percentage of Hispanic/Latino population. These places are identified with an asterisk (*); Please refer to the User's Guide for a full explanation of data.

Means of Transportation to Work: Car, Truck or Van
(Universe: Workers 16 Years and Over)

Group	Number	%
Total Population	46,412	87.4
Hispanic or Latino (of any race)	8,245	88.8
Central American, ex. Mexican	574	77.0
Mexican	6,834	90.3

Means of Transportation to Work: Public Transportation (ex. Taxicab)
(Universe: Workers 16 Years and Over)

Group	Number	%
Total Population	648	1.2
Hispanic or Latino (of any race)	69	0.7
Central American, ex. Mexican	28	3.8
Mexican	41	0.5

Homeownership Rate
(Universe: Occupied Housing Units)

Group	%
Total Population	46.4
Hispanic or Latino (of any race)	40.1
Central American, ex. Mexican	54.7
Guatemalan	62.2
Honduran	33.3
Salvadoran	57.1
Cuban	44.6
Mexican	39.5
Puerto Rican	36.3
South American	49.2
Colombian	52.7
Peruvian	66.1
Spaniard	40.2

Median Home Value

Group	Dollars
Total Population	144,700
Hispanic or Latino (of any race)	116,200
Central American, ex. Mexican	119,900
Mexican	111,000

Median Gross Rent

Group	Dollars
Total Population	782
Hispanic or Latino (of any race)	758
Central American, ex. Mexican	761
Mexican	765

Median Household Income
(2010 Inflation-Adjusted Dollars)

Group	Dollars
Total Population	44,415
Hispanic or Latino (of any race)	33,397
Central American, ex. Mexican	30,365
Mexican	33,435

Per Capita Income
(2010 Inflation-Adjusted Dollars)

Group	Dollars
Total Population	22,940
Hispanic or Latino (of any race)	12,049
Central American, ex. Mexican	12,689
Mexican	11,665

Households with $100,000+ Income

Group	Number	%
Total Population	6,433	16.5
Hispanic or Latino (of any race)	349	6.2
Central American, ex. Mexican	27	6.7
Mexican	239	5.2

Households with Food Stamps/SNAP Benefits During Past 12 Months

Group	Number	%
Total Population	2,140	5.5
Hispanic or Latino (of any race)	436	7.7
Central American, ex. Mexican	34	8.4
Mexican	397	8.7

Poverty Rate
(Income in Past 12 Months Below Poverty Level)

Group	%
Total Population	20.3
Hispanic or Latino (of any race)	26.1
Central American, ex. Mexican	22.7
Mexican	26.8

Duncanville

Population

Group	Number	%TP[1]	%HP[2]
Total Population	38,524	100.0	–
Hispanic or Latino (of any race)	13,480	35.0	100.0
Central American, ex. Mexican	604	1.6	4.5
Guatemalan	116	0.3	0.9
Salvadoran	347	0.9	2.6
Mexican	11,972	31.1	88.8
Puerto Rican	135	0.4	1.0
South American	137	0.4	1.0

Population Growth: 2000–2010

Group	%
Total Population	6.8
Hispanic or Latino (of any race)	144.1
Central American, ex. Mexican	364.6
Mexican	183.2

Males per 100 Females

Group	Number
Total Population	90.6
Hispanic or Latino (of any race)	99.5
Central American, ex. Mexican	101.3
Guatemalan	114.8
Salvadoran	99.4
Mexican	98.7
Puerto Rican	114.3
South American	114.1

Average Household Size

Group	People
Total Population	2.89
Hispanic or Latino (of any race)	4.17
Central American, ex. Mexican	4.32
Guatemalan	4.71
Salvadoran	4.39
Mexican	4.21
Puerto Rican	3.27
South American	3.51

Median Age

Group	Years
Total Population	35.4
Hispanic or Latino (of any race)	24.8
Central American, ex. Mexican	29.7
Guatemalan	27.6
Salvadoran	30.8
Mexican	24.4
Puerto Rican	28.1
South American	39.8

High School Graduates
(Universe: Population 25 Years and Over)

Group	Number	%
Total Population	19,667	83.7
Hispanic or Latino (of any race)	3,630	58.2
Mexican	3,183	57.5

Four-Year College Graduates
(Universe: Population 25 Years and Over)

Group	Number	%
Total Population	5,961	25.4
Hispanic or Latino (of any race)	453	7.3
Mexican	326	5.9

Population Age 3–17 Enrolled in Public School
(Universe: Population Age 3–17 Enrolled in School)

Group	Number	%
Total Population	7,314	88.6
Hispanic or Latino (of any race)	3,515	93.2
Mexican	3,193	92.5

Population Age 3–17 Enrolled in Private School
(Universe: Population Age 3–17 Enrolled in School)

Group	Number	%
Total Population	939	11.4
Hispanic or Latino (of any race)	258	6.8
Mexican	258	7.5

Foreign-Born Population

Group	Number	%
Total Population	5,089	13.5
Hispanic or Latino (of any race)	4,184	32.1
Mexican	3,866	32.3

Foreign-Born Naturalized U.S. Citizens

Group	Number	%
Total Population	1,677	33.0
Hispanic or Latino (of any race)	1,156	27.6
Mexican	974	25.2

Language Spoken at Home: English Only
(Universe: Population 5 Years and Over)

Group	Number	%
Total Population	24,566	69.8
Hispanic or Latino (of any race)	2,463	21.8
Mexican	2,182	21.3

Language Spoken at Home: Spanish
(Universe: Population 5 Years and Over)

Group	Number	%
Total Population	9,754	27.7
Hispanic or Latino (of any race)	8,852	78.2
Mexican	8,069	78.7

Unemployment Rate
(Universe: Population 16 Years and Over)

Group	%
Total Population	6.3
Hispanic or Latino (of any race)	7.9
Mexican	8.1

Class of Worker: Private Wage and Salary
(Universe: Civilian Employed Population 16 Years and Over)

Group	Number	%
Total Population	13,978	77.0
Hispanic or Latino (of any race)	4,610	84.7
Mexican	4,265	86.2

Class of Worker: Government
(Universe: Civilian Employed Population 16 Years and Over)

Group	Number	%
Total Population	3,036	16.7
Hispanic or Latino (of any race)	490	9.0
Mexican	367	7.4

Means of Transportation to Work: Car, Truck or Van
(Universe: Workers 16 Years and Over)

Group	Number	%
Total Population	16,593	93.6
Hispanic or Latino (of any race)	4,901	93.6
Mexican	4,459	93.7

Means of Transportation to Work: Public Transportation (ex. Taxicab)
(Universe: Workers 16 Years and Over)

Group	Number	%
Total Population	245	1.4
Hispanic or Latino (of any race)	55	1.1
Mexican	55	1.2

Homeownership Rate
(Universe: Occupied Housing Units)

Group	%
Total Population	68.0
Hispanic or Latino (of any race)	71.6
Central American, ex. Mexican	74.1
Guatemalan	60.7
Salvadoran	81.9
Mexican	71.8
Puerto Rican	62.2
South American	76.9

Median Home Value

Group	Dollars
Total Population	113,800
Hispanic or Latino (of any race)	104,600
Mexican	102,600

Median Gross Rent

Group	Dollars
Total Population	973
Hispanic or Latino (of any race)	973
Mexican	979

Notes: (1) Percent of total population; (2) Percent of Hispanic/Latino population; Profiles include places with an overall population of at least 125,000, OR an overall population of at least 25,000 where the Hispanic/Latino population is at least 20% of the overall population. In states where less than five places meet either of these criteria, we have included places with at least 10,000 total population with the highest percentage of Hispanic/Latino population. These places are identified with an asterisk (*); Please refer to the User's Guide for a full explanation of data.

Median Household Income (2010 Inflation-Adjusted Dollars)	
Group	Dollars
Total Population	52,671
Hispanic or Latino (of any race)	44,729
Mexican	44,688

Per Capita Income (2010 Inflation-Adjusted Dollars)	
Group	Dollars
Total Population	23,852
Hispanic or Latino (of any race)	13,114
Mexican	12,713

Households with $100,000+ Income		
Group	Number	%
Total Population	2,409	18.2
Hispanic or Latino (of any race)	227	7.2
Mexican	206	7.3

Households with Food Stamps/SNAP Benefits During Past 12 Months		
Group	Number	%
Total Population	792	6.0
Hispanic or Latino (of any race)	301	9.5
Mexican	249	8.9

Poverty Rate (Income in Past 12 Months Below Poverty Level)	
Group	%
Total Population	12.6
Hispanic or Latino (of any race)	21.1
Mexican	21.5

Eagle Pass

Population			
Group	Number	%TP[1]	%HP[2]
Total Population	26,248	100.0	–
Hispanic or Latino (of any race)	25,065	95.5	100.0
Mexican	23,574	89.8	94.1
Puerto Rican	106	0.4	0.4

Population Growth: 2000–2010	
Group	%
Total Population	17.1
Hispanic or Latino (of any race)	17.8
Mexican	31.2

Males per 100 Females	
Group	Number
Total Population	90.8
Hispanic or Latino (of any race)	89.8
Mexican	87.8
Puerto Rican	146.5

Average Household Size	
Group	People
Total Population	3.13
Hispanic or Latino (of any race)	3.16
Mexican	3.16
Puerto Rican	2.60

Median Age	
Group	Years
Total Population	33.1
Hispanic or Latino (of any race)	33.1
Mexican	33.6
Puerto Rican	27.0

High School Graduates (Universe: Population 25 Years and Over)		
Group	Number	%
Total Population	9,368	61.2
Hispanic or Latino (of any race)	8,748	59.8
Mexican	8,343	59.7

Four-Year College Graduates (Universe: Population 25 Years and Over)		
Group	Number	%
Total Population	2,986	19.5
Hispanic or Latino (of any race)	2,673	18.3
Mexican	2,570	18.4

Population Age 3–17 Enrolled in Public School (Universe: Population Age 3–17 Enrolled in School)		
Group	Number	%
Total Population	6,062	95.9
Hispanic or Latino (of any race)	5,789	95.9
Mexican	5,513	95.9

Population Age 3–17 Enrolled in Private School (Universe: Population Age 3–17 Enrolled in School)		
Group	Number	%
Total Population	261	4.1
Hispanic or Latino (of any race)	245	4.1
Mexican	234	4.1

Foreign-Born Population		
Group	Number	%
Total Population	8,676	34.1
Hispanic or Latino (of any race)	8,543	35.0
Mexican	8,276	35.5

Foreign-Born Naturalized U.S. Citizens		
Group	Number	%
Total Population	3,583	41.3
Hispanic or Latino (of any race)	3,550	41.6
Mexican	3,373	40.8

Language Spoken at Home: English Only (Universe: Population 5 Years and Over)		
Group	Number	%
Total Population	1,813	7.8
Hispanic or Latino (of any race)	1,238	5.6
Mexican	1,177	5.5

Language Spoken at Home: Spanish (Universe: Population 5 Years and Over)		
Group	Number	%
Total Population	21,372	91.9
Hispanic or Latino (of any race)	20,980	94.4
Mexican	20,079	94.5

Unemployment Rate (Universe: Population 16 Years and Over)	
Group	%
Total Population	9.1
Hispanic or Latino (of any race)	9.3
Mexican	8.9

Class of Worker: Private Wage and Salary (Universe: Civilian Employed Population 16 Years and Over)		
Group	Number	%
Total Population	6,122	63.6
Hispanic or Latino (of any race)	5,868	64.5
Mexican	5,709	65.5

Class of Worker: Government (Universe: Civilian Employed Population 16 Years and Over)		
Group	Number	%
Total Population	2,778	28.9
Hispanic or Latino (of any race)	2,585	28.4
Mexican	2,395	27.5

Means of Transportation to Work: Car, Truck or Van (Universe: Workers 16 Years and Over)		
Group	Number	%
Total Population	8,591	92.3
Hispanic or Latino (of any race)	8,082	91.9
Mexican	7,794	92.3

Means of Transportation to Work: Public Transportation (ex. Taxicab) (Universe: Workers 16 Years and Over)		
Group	Number	%
Total Population	34	0.4
Hispanic or Latino (of any race)	34	0.4
Mexican	12	0.1

Homeownership Rate (Universe: Occupied Housing Units)	
Group	%
Total Population	60.2
Hispanic or Latino (of any race)	61.0
Mexican	61.3
Puerto Rican	26.7

Median Home Value	
Group	Dollars
Total Population	98,300
Hispanic or Latino (of any race)	96,500
Mexican	97,000

Median Gross Rent	
Group	Dollars
Total Population	518
Hispanic or Latino (of any race)	514
Mexican	511

Median Household Income (2010 Inflation-Adjusted Dollars)	
Group	Dollars
Total Population	32,160
Hispanic or Latino (of any race)	29,718
Mexican	29,389

Per Capita Income (2010 Inflation-Adjusted Dollars)	
Group	Dollars
Total Population	15,123
Hispanic or Latino (of any race)	13,886
Mexican	13,848

Households with $100,000+ Income		
Group	Number	%
Total Population	675	8.9
Hispanic or Latino (of any race)	512	7.2
Mexican	492	7.2

Households with Food Stamps/SNAP Benefits During Past 12 Months		
Group	Number	%
Total Population	2,473	32.6
Hispanic or Latino (of any race)	2,453	34.5
Mexican	2,351	34.4

Poverty Rate (Income in Past 12 Months Below Poverty Level)	
Group	%
Total Population	30.1
Hispanic or Latino (of any race)	31.1
Mexican	31.1

Edinburg

Population			
Group	Number	%TP[1]	%HP[2]
Total Population	77,100	100.0	–
Hispanic or Latino (of any race)	67,989	88.2	100.0
Central American, ex. Mexican	365	0.5	0.5
Honduran	106	0.1	0.2
Mexican	63,294	82.1	93.1
Puerto Rican	244	0.3	0.4
South American	243	0.3	0.4
Spaniard	207	0.3	0.3

Population Growth: 2000–2010	
Group	%
Total Population	59.1
Hispanic or Latino (of any race)	58.2
Mexican	82.6

Males per 100 Females	
Group	Number
Total Population	98.9
Hispanic or Latino (of any race)	94.7
Central American, ex. Mexican	102.8
Honduran	130.4
Mexican	95.1
Puerto Rican	136.9
South American	97.6
Spaniard	64.3

Average Household Size	
Group	People
Total Population	3.16
Hispanic or Latino (of any race)	3.26
Central American, ex. Mexican	3.32
Honduran	3.35
Mexican	3.27
Puerto Rican	3.01

STATE & PLACE PROFILES

Notes: (1) Percent of total population; (2) Percent of Hispanic/Latino population; Profiles include places with an overall population of at least 125,000, OR an overall population of at least 25,000 where the Hispanic/Latino population is at least 20% of the overall population. In states where less than five places meet either of these criteria, we have included places with at least 10,000 total population with the highest percentage of Hispanic/Latino population. These places are identified with an asterisk (*); Please refer to the User's Guide for a full explanation of data.

South American	2.91
Spaniard	2.73

Median Age

Group	Years
Total Population	28.0
Hispanic or Latino (of any race)	26.8
Central American, ex. Mexican	27.1
Honduran	23.8
Mexican	26.9
Puerto Rican	27.3
South American	33.6
Spaniard	33.8

High School Graduates
(Universe: Population 25 Years and Over)

Group	Number	%
Total Population	28,936	72.2
Hispanic or Latino (of any race)	23,327	69.0
Mexican	21,956	68.6

Four-Year College Graduates
(Universe: Population 25 Years and Over)

Group	Number	%
Total Population	8,208	20.5
Hispanic or Latino (of any race)	5,873	17.4
Mexican	5,543	17.3

Population Age 3–17 Enrolled in Public School
(Universe: Population Age 3–17 Enrolled in School)

Group	Number	%
Total Population	15,452	93.4
Hispanic or Latino (of any race)	14,682	94.8
Mexican	13,950	94.5

Population Age 3–17 Enrolled in Private School
(Universe: Population Age 3–17 Enrolled in School)

Group	Number	%
Total Population	1,092	6.6
Hispanic or Latino (of any race)	805	5.2
Mexican	805	5.5

Foreign-Born Population

Group	Number	%
Total Population	14,099	19.4
Hispanic or Latino (of any race)	12,294	19.3
Mexican	11,515	19.1

Foreign-Born Naturalized U.S. Citizens

Group	Number	%
Total Population	4,271	30.3
Hispanic or Latino (of any race)	3,635	29.6
Mexican	3,306	28.7

Language Spoken at Home: English Only
(Universe: Population 5 Years and Over)

Group	Number	%
Total Population	15,266	23.2
Hispanic or Latino (of any race)	9,283	16.3
Mexican	8,706	16.1

Language Spoken at Home: Spanish
(Universe: Population 5 Years and Over)

Group	Number	%
Total Population	48,923	74.3
Hispanic or Latino (of any race)	47,756	83.7
Mexican	45,346	83.8

Unemployment Rate
(Universe: Population 16 Years and Over)

Group	%
Total Population	9.2
Hispanic or Latino (of any race)	9.3
Mexican	9.3

Class of Worker: Private Wage and Salary
(Universe: Civilian Employed Population 16 Years and Over)

Group	Number	%
Total Population	19,695	67.4
Hispanic or Latino (of any race)	17,016	66.8
Mexican	16,229	67.1

Class of Worker: Government
(Universe: Civilian Employed Population 16 Years and Over)

Group	Number	%
Total Population	7,019	24.0
Hispanic or Latino (of any race)	6,165	24.2
Mexican	5,748	23.8

Means of Transportation to Work: Car, Truck or Van
(Universe: Workers 16 Years and Over)

Group	Number	%
Total Population	25,456	90.5
Hispanic or Latino (of any race)	22,325	91.2
Mexican	21,165	91.1

Means of Transportation to Work: Public Transportation (ex. Taxicab)
(Universe: Workers 16 Years and Over)

Group	Number	%
Total Population	167	0.6
Hispanic or Latino (of any race)	109	0.4
Mexican	109	0.5

Homeownership Rate
(Universe: Occupied Housing Units)

Group	%
Total Population	56.1
Hispanic or Latino (of any race)	55.4
Central American, ex. Mexican	60.0
Honduran	40.0
Mexican	55.8
Puerto Rican	51.2
South American	52.9
Spaniard	61.2

Median Home Value

Group	Dollars
Total Population	94,600
Hispanic or Latino (of any race)	90,400
Mexican	89,400

Median Gross Rent

Group	Dollars
Total Population	631
Hispanic or Latino (of any race)	628
Mexican	629

Median Household Income
(2010 Inflation-Adjusted Dollars)

Group	Dollars
Total Population	37,176
Hispanic or Latino (of any race)	35,288
Mexican	35,540

Per Capita Income
(2010 Inflation-Adjusted Dollars)

Group	Dollars
Total Population	15,542
Hispanic or Latino (of any race)	14,249
Mexican	14,183

Households with $100,000+ Income

Group	Number	%
Total Population	2,739	12.6
Hispanic or Latino (of any race)	1,952	10.5
Mexican	1,793	10.3

Households with Food Stamps/SNAP Benefits During Past 12 Months

Group	Number	%
Total Population	5,069	23.4
Hispanic or Latino (of any race)	4,859	26.2
Mexican	4,650	26.7

Poverty Rate
(Income in Past 12 Months Below Poverty Level)

Group	%
Total Population	28.0
Hispanic or Latino (of any race)	29.4
Mexican	29.5

El Paso

Population

Group	Number	%TP[1]	%HP[2]
Total Population	649,121	100.0	–
Hispanic or Latino (of any race)	523,721	80.7	100.0
Central American, ex. Mexican	2,313	0.4	0.4
Guatemalan	432	0.1	0.1
Honduran	302	<0.1	0.1
Nicaraguan	288	<0.1	0.1
Panamanian	551	0.1	0.1
Salvadoran	625	0.1	0.1
Cuban	737	0.1	0.1
Dominican Republic	385	0.1	0.1
Mexican	486,186	74.9	92.8
Puerto Rican	5,793	0.9	1.1
South American	1,676	0.3	0.3
Argentinean	240	<0.1	<0.1
Chilean	111	<0.1	<0.1
Colombian	578	0.1	0.1
Ecuadorian	174	<0.1	<0.1
Peruvian	293	<0.1	0.1
Venezuelan	161	<0.1	<0.1
Spaniard	2,020	0.3	0.4

Population Growth: 2000–2010

Group	%
Total Population	15.2
Hispanic or Latino (of any race)	21.3
Central American, ex. Mexican	88.4
Guatemalan	80.8
Honduran	102.7
Nicaraguan	154.9
Panamanian	49.3
Salvadoran	150.0
Cuban	54.8
Dominican Republic	205.6
Mexican	35.2
Puerto Rican	58.3
South American	124.4
Argentinean	79.1
Colombian	156.9
Peruvian	164.0
Spaniard	752.3

Males per 100 Females

Group	Number
Total Population	92.1
Hispanic or Latino (of any race)	88.5
Central American, ex. Mexican	86.8
Guatemalan	90.3
Honduran	79.8
Nicaraguan	116.5
Panamanian	64.0
Salvadoran	95.3
Cuban	149.0
Dominican Republic	110.4
Mexican	88.3
Puerto Rican	122.0
South American	94.2
Argentinean	101.7
Chilean	82.0
Colombian	92.0
Ecuadorian	89.1
Peruvian	92.8
Venezuelan	89.4
Spaniard	87.6

Average Household Size

Group	People
Total Population	2.95
Hispanic or Latino (of any race)	3.14
Central American, ex. Mexican	2.93
Guatemalan	3.13
Honduran	3.50
Nicaraguan	2.87
Panamanian	2.59
Salvadoran	3.04
Cuban	2.79
Dominican Republic	3.15
Mexican	3.15
Puerto Rican	2.85
South American	2.72
Argentinean	2.76
Chilean	2.64
Colombian	2.64
Ecuadorian	3.09
Peruvian	2.97
Venezuelan	2.52
Spaniard	2.59

Notes: (1) Percent of total population; (2) Percent of Hispanic/Latino population; Profiles include places with an overall population of at least 125,000, OR an overall population of at least 25,000 where the Hispanic/Latino population is at least 20% of the overall population. In states where less than five places meet either of these criteria, we have included places with at least 10,000 total population with the highest percentage of Hispanic/Latino population. These places are identified with an asterisk (*); Please refer to the User's Guide for a full explanation of data.

Median Age

Group	Years
Total Population	32.5
Hispanic or Latino (of any race)	30.7
Central American, ex. Mexican	34.7
Guatemalan	35.3
Honduran	28.4
Nicaraguan	35.3
Panamanian	39.2
Salvadoran	33.8
Cuban	37.6
Dominican Republic	26.8
Mexican	30.9
Puerto Rican	29.6
South American	35.2
Argentinean	40.2
Chilean	35.5
Colombian	34.8
Ecuadorian	33.1
Peruvian	34.9
Venezuelan	33.8
Spaniard	41.0

High School Graduates
(Universe: Population 25 Years and Over)

Group	Number	%
Total Population	276,578	73.6
Hispanic or Latino (of any race)	196,406	67.7
Central American, ex. Mexican	1,094	64.0
Mexican	182,764	67.0
Puerto Rican	2,687	88.9
South American	779	74.5
Spaniard	1,187	88.6

Four-Year College Graduates
(Universe: Population 25 Years and Over)

Group	Number	%
Total Population	80,238	21.3
Hispanic or Latino (of any race)	47,994	16.6
Central American, ex. Mexican	371	21.7
Mexican	44,224	16.2
Puerto Rican	775	25.7
South American	417	39.9
Spaniard	505	37.7

Population Age 3–17 Enrolled in Public School
(Universe: Population Age 3–17 Enrolled in School)

Group	Number	%
Total Population	131,638	93.9
Hispanic or Latino (of any race)	115,432	95.0
Central American, ex. Mexican	316	85.4
Mexican	109,328	95.2
Puerto Rican	1,098	90.7
South American	242	77.8
Spaniard	274	84.3

Population Age 3–17 Enrolled in Private School
(Universe: Population Age 3–17 Enrolled in School)

Group	Number	%
Total Population	8,613	6.1
Hispanic or Latino (of any race)	6,098	5.0
Central American, ex. Mexican	54	14.6
Mexican	5,538	4.8
Puerto Rican	112	9.3
South American	69	22.2
Spaniard	51	15.7

Foreign-Born Population

Group	Number	%
Total Population	162,525	25.8
Hispanic or Latino (of any race)	149,454	29.6
Central American, ex. Mexican	1,589	61.0
Mexican	143,944	30.2
Puerto Rican	35	0.7
South American	1,074	73.9
Spaniard	182	10.1

Foreign-Born Naturalized U.S. Citizens

Group	Number	%
Total Population	69,873	43.0
Hispanic or Latino (of any race)	62,101	41.6
Central American, ex. Mexican	748	47.1
Mexican	59,127	41.1
Puerto Rican	14	40.0
South American	584	54.4
Spaniard	126	69.2

Language Spoken at Home: English Only
(Universe: Population 5 Years and Over)

Group	Number	%
Total Population	156,132	27.0
Hispanic or Latino (of any race)	64,206	13.9
Central American, ex. Mexican	357	14.4
Mexican	57,888	13.3
Puerto Rican	1,192	25.5
South American	102	7.3
Spaniard	882	49.9

Language Spoken at Home: Spanish
(Universe: Population 5 Years and Over)

Group	Number	%
Total Population	408,268	70.7
Hispanic or Latino (of any race)	396,529	86.0
Central American, ex. Mexican	2,076	83.6
Mexican	376,553	86.6
Puerto Rican	3,456	74.1
South American	1,288	91.9
Spaniard	872	49.3

Unemployment Rate
(Universe: Population 16 Years and Over)

Group	%
Total Population	7.2
Hispanic or Latino (of any race)	7.4
Central American, ex. Mexican	9.5
Mexican	7.3
Puerto Rican	9.1
South American	5.0
Spaniard	4.2

Class of Worker: Private Wage and Salary
(Universe: Civilian Employed Population 16 Years and Over)

Group	Number	%
Total Population	183,438	72.2
Hispanic or Latino (of any race)	149,492	74.2
Central American, ex. Mexican	914	67.3
Mexican	141,525	74.5
Puerto Rican	1,081	61.3
South American	506	68.6
Spaniard	598	64.1

Class of Worker: Government
(Universe: Civilian Employed Population 16 Years and Over)

Group	Number	%
Total Population	53,794	21.2
Hispanic or Latino (of any race)	38,635	19.2
Central American, ex. Mexican	263	19.4
Mexican	36,077	19.0
Puerto Rican	570	32.3
South American	171	23.2
Spaniard	234	25.1

Means of Transportation to Work: Car, Truck or Van
(Universe: Workers 16 Years and Over)

Group	Number	%
Total Population	232,846	91.1
Hispanic or Latino (of any race)	180,524	90.8
Central American, ex. Mexican	1,155	82.2
Mexican	170,096	91.0
Puerto Rican	1,828	86.7
South American	649	87.7
Spaniard	876	91.4

Means of Transportation to Work: Public Transportation (ex. Taxicab)
(Universe: Workers 16 Years and Over)

Group	Number	%
Total Population	5,332	2.1
Hispanic or Latino (of any race)	4,709	2.4
Central American, ex. Mexican	42	3.0
Mexican	4,468	2.4
Puerto Rican	9	0.4
South American	48	6.5
Spaniard	0	0.0

Homeownership Rate
(Universe: Occupied Housing Units)

Group	%
Total Population	60.4
Hispanic or Latino (of any race)	60.2
Central American, ex. Mexican	55.0
Guatemalan	55.9
Honduran	47.6
Nicaraguan	54.3
Panamanian	57.7
Salvadoran	54.4
Cuban	46.3
Dominican Republic	42.3
Mexican	60.7
Puerto Rican	54.4
South American	55.3
Argentinean	61.5
Chilean	59.0
Colombian	53.6
Ecuadorian	50.0
Peruvian	54.5
Venezuelan	56.5
Spaniard	64.9

Median Home Value

Group	Dollars
Total Population	108,400
Hispanic or Latino (of any race)	99,500
Central American, ex. Mexican	112,400
Mexican	98,900
Puerto Rican	136,600
South American	177,800
Spaniard	154,500

Median Gross Rent

Group	Dollars
Total Population	620
Hispanic or Latino (of any race)	579
Central American, ex. Mexican	749
Mexican	572
Puerto Rican	752
South American	802
Spaniard	810

Median Household Income
(2010 Inflation-Adjusted Dollars)

Group	Dollars
Total Population	37,428
Hispanic or Latino (of any race)	32,762
Central American, ex. Mexican	42,282
Mexican	32,242
Puerto Rican	50,756
South American	68,750
Spaniard	50,435

Per Capita Income
(2010 Inflation-Adjusted Dollars)

Group	Dollars
Total Population	17,812
Hispanic or Latino (of any race)	14,299
Central American, ex. Mexican	17,042
Mexican	14,001
Puerto Rican	25,703
South American	30,302
Spaniard	30,119

Households with $100,000+ Income

Group	Number	%
Total Population	25,114	12.2
Hispanic or Latino (of any race)	13,155	8.6
Central American, ex. Mexican	123	12.7
Mexican	11,873	8.3
Puerto Rican	303	14.7
South American	186	38.1
Spaniard	131	13.7

Households with Food Stamps/SNAP Benefits During Past 12 Months

Group	Number	%
Total Population	39,381	19.1
Hispanic or Latino (of any race)	36,161	23.7
Central American, ex. Mexican	82	8.5
Mexican	34,465	24.2
Puerto Rican	234	11.3
South American	50	10.2
Spaniard	150	15.7

Notes: (1) Percent of total population; (2) Percent of Hispanic/Latino population; Profiles include places with an overall population of at least 125,000, OR an overall population of at least 25,000 where the Hispanic/Latino population is at least 20% of the overall population. In states where less than five places meet either of these criteria, we have included places with at least 10,000 total population with the highest percentage of Hispanic/Latino population. These places are identified with an asterisk (*); Please refer to the User's Guide for a full explanation of data.

Poverty Rate
(Income in Past 12 Months Below Poverty Level)

Group	%
Total Population	24.1
Hispanic or Latino (of any race)	27.2
Central American, ex. Mexican	20.6
Mexican	27.5
Puerto Rican	21.3
South American	8.8
Spaniard	19.9

Farmers Branch

Population

Group	Number	%TP[1]	%HP[2]
Total Population	28,616	100.0	–
Hispanic or Latino (of any race)	12,984	45.4	100.0
Central American, ex. Mexican	1,683	5.9	13.0
Guatemalan	113	0.4	0.9
Honduran	134	0.5	1.0
Salvadoran	1,347	4.7	10.4
Mexican	10,258	35.8	79.0
South American	249	0.9	1.9
Colombian	103	0.4	0.8

Population Growth: 2000–2010

Group	%
Total Population	4.0
Hispanic or Latino (of any race)	26.8
Central American, ex. Mexican	85.1
Salvadoran	94.7
Mexican	30.5
South American	87.2

Males per 100 Females

Group	Number
Total Population	96.8
Hispanic or Latino (of any race)	101.6
Central American, ex. Mexican	109.1
Guatemalan	88.3
Honduran	112.7
Salvadoran	112.8
Mexican	101.5
South American	102.4
Colombian	94.3

Average Household Size

Group	People
Total Population	2.64
Hispanic or Latino (of any race)	4.02
Central American, ex. Mexican	4.43
Guatemalan	4.46
Honduran	4.36
Salvadoran	4.52
Mexican	4.06
South American	3.14
Colombian	3.42

Median Age

Group	Years
Total Population	35.6
Hispanic or Latino (of any race)	26.5
Central American, ex. Mexican	31.9
Guatemalan	28.5
Honduran	29.5
Salvadoran	32.0
Mexican	25.2
South American	39.1
Colombian	36.5

High School Graduates
(Universe: Population 25 Years and Over)

Group	Number	%
Total Population	14,255	77.8
Hispanic or Latino (of any race)	2,854	46.1
Central American, ex. Mexican	327	35.0
Salvadoran	267	33.3
Mexican	2,288	46.2

Four-Year College Graduates
(Universe: Population 25 Years and Over)

Group	Number	%
Total Population	5,452	29.8
Hispanic or Latino (of any race)	425	6.9
Central American, ex. Mexican	0	0.0
Salvadoran	0	0.0
Mexican	362	7.3

Population Age 3–17 Enrolled in Public School
(Universe: Population Age 3–17 Enrolled in School)

Group	Number	%
Total Population	4,904	89.4
Hispanic or Latino (of any race)	3,317	95.0
Central American, ex. Mexican	496	100.0
Salvadoran	476	100.0
Mexican	2,734	94.0

Population Age 3–17 Enrolled in Private School
(Universe: Population Age 3–17 Enrolled in School)

Group	Number	%
Total Population	582	10.6
Hispanic or Latino (of any race)	176	5.0
Central American, ex. Mexican	0	0.0
Salvadoran	0	0.0
Mexican	176	6.0

Foreign-Born Population

Group	Number	%
Total Population	7,143	25.4
Hispanic or Latino (of any race)	5,782	47.4
Central American, ex. Mexican	1,026	60.2
Salvadoran	895	59.3
Mexican	4,618	45.8

Foreign-Born Naturalized U.S. Citizens

Group	Number	%
Total Population	2,139	29.9
Hispanic or Latino (of any race)	1,468	25.4
Central American, ex. Mexican	365	35.6
Salvadoran	330	36.9
Mexican	998	21.6

Language Spoken at Home: English Only
(Universe: Population 5 Years and Over)

Group	Number	%
Total Population	15,748	59.9
Hispanic or Latino (of any race)	1,862	16.9
Central American, ex. Mexican	40	2.5
Salvadoran	40	2.8
Mexican	1,659	18.4

Language Spoken at Home: Spanish
(Universe: Population 5 Years and Over)

Group	Number	%
Total Population	9,286	35.3
Hispanic or Latino (of any race)	9,105	82.7
Central American, ex. Mexican	1,551	97.5
Salvadoran	1,400	97.2
Mexican	7,298	81.1

Unemployment Rate
(Universe: Population 16 Years and Over)

Group	%
Total Population	8.3
Hispanic or Latino (of any race)	6.2
Central American, ex. Mexican	5.5
Salvadoran	4.7
Mexican	6.3

Class of Worker: Private Wage and Salary
(Universe: Civilian Employed Population 16 Years and Over)

Group	Number	%
Total Population	12,417	86.7
Hispanic or Latino (of any race)	5,343	92.8
Central American, ex. Mexican	794	90.7
Salvadoran	686	89.4
Mexican	4,389	93.4

Class of Worker: Government
(Universe: Civilian Employed Population 16 Years and Over)

Group	Number	%
Total Population	909	6.3
Hispanic or Latino (of any race)	210	3.6
Central American, ex. Mexican	0	0.0
Salvadoran	0	0.0
Mexican	186	4.0

Means of Transportation to Work: Car, Truck or Van
(Universe: Workers 16 Years and Over)

Group	Number	%
Total Population	12,847	91.9
Hispanic or Latino (of any race)	5,239	94.6
Central American, ex. Mexican	797	93.3
Salvadoran	698	92.5
Mexican	4,279	94.9

Means of Transportation to Work: Public Transportation (ex. Taxicab)
(Universe: Workers 16 Years and Over)

Group	Number	%
Total Population	210	1.5
Hispanic or Latino (of any race)	93	1.7
Central American, ex. Mexican	57	6.7
Salvadoran	57	7.5
Mexican	36	0.8

Homeownership Rate
(Universe: Occupied Housing Units)

Group	%
Total Population	60.3
Hispanic or Latino (of any race)	56.1
Central American, ex. Mexican	68.5
Guatemalan	89.3
Honduran	63.6
Salvadoran	67.1
Mexican	53.7
South American	57.9
Colombian	55.3

Median Home Value

Group	Dollars
Total Population	141,600
Hispanic or Latino (of any race)	124,100
Central American, ex. Mexican	131,300
Salvadoran	130,700
Mexican	121,900

Median Gross Rent

Group	Dollars
Total Population	967
Hispanic or Latino (of any race)	872
Central American, ex. Mexican	818
Salvadoran	810
Mexican	887

Median Household Income
(2010 Inflation-Adjusted Dollars)

Group	Dollars
Total Population	57,454
Hispanic or Latino (of any race)	44,359
Central American, ex. Mexican	39,418
Salvadoran	39,388
Mexican	45,052

Per Capita Income
(2010 Inflation-Adjusted Dollars)

Group	Dollars
Total Population	28,528
Hispanic or Latino (of any race)	15,441
Central American, ex. Mexican	13,587
Salvadoran	12,941
Mexican	15,037

Households with $100,000+ Income

Group	Number	%
Total Population	2,408	23.2
Hispanic or Latino (of any race)	458	14.3
Central American, ex. Mexican	52	12.8
Salvadoran	33	9.1
Mexican	366	14.3

Households with Food Stamps/SNAP Benefits During Past 12 Months

Group	Number	%
Total Population	347	3.3
Hispanic or Latino (of any race)	217	6.8
Central American, ex. Mexican	41	10.1
Salvadoran	41	11.3
Mexican	150	5.8

Notes: (1) Percent of total population; (2) Percent of Hispanic/Latino population; Profiles include places with an overall population of at least 125,000, OR an overall population of at least 25,000 where the Hispanic/Latino population is at least 20% of the overall population. In states where less than five places meet either of these criteria, we have included places with at least 10,000 total population with the highest percentage of Hispanic/Latino population. These places are identified with an asterisk (*); Please refer to the User's Guide for a full explanation of data.

Poverty Rate
(Income in Past 12 Months Below Poverty Level)

Group	%
Total Population	10.3
Hispanic or Latino (of any race)	15.6
Central American, ex. Mexican	29.7
Salvadoran	33.1
Mexican	13.4

Fort Hood

Population

Group	Number	%TP[1]	%HP[2]
Total Population	29,589	100.0	–
Hispanic or Latino (of any race)	5,923	20.0	100.0
Central American, ex. Mexican	287	1.0	4.8
Mexican	3,613	12.2	61.0
Puerto Rican	1,240	4.2	20.9
South American	180	0.6	3.0
Spaniard	110	0.4	1.9

Population Growth: 2000–2010

Group	%
Total Population	-12.2
Hispanic or Latino (of any race)	5.2
Central American, ex. Mexican	10.4
Mexican	32.5
Puerto Rican	-19.5
South American	6.5

Males per 100 Females

Group	Number
Total Population	137.2
Hispanic or Latino (of any race)	123.8
Central American, ex. Mexican	117.4
Mexican	123.3
Puerto Rican	118.3
South American	143.2
Spaniard	139.1

Average Household Size

Group	People
Total Population	3.66
Hispanic or Latino (of any race)	3.78
Central American, ex. Mexican	3.64
Mexican	3.88
Puerto Rican	3.66
South American	3.24
Spaniard	3.91

Median Age

Group	Years
Total Population	21.9
Hispanic or Latino (of any race)	20.4
Central American, ex. Mexican	22.1
Mexican	19.9
Puerto Rican	21.3
South American	22.9
Spaniard	21.5

High School Graduates
(Universe: Population 25 Years and Over)

Group	Number	%
Total Population	11,402	95.4
Hispanic or Latino (of any race)	2,118	92.8
Mexican	1,241	89.1
Puerto Rican	493	100.0

Four-Year College Graduates
(Universe: Population 25 Years and Over)

Group	Number	%
Total Population	2,072	17.3
Hispanic or Latino (of any race)	251	11.0
Mexican	165	11.8
Puerto Rican	86	17.4

Population Age 3–17 Enrolled in Public School
(Universe: Population Age 3–17 Enrolled in School)

Group	Number	%
Total Population	7,941	98.7
Hispanic or Latino (of any race)	1,914	100.0
Mexican	1,333	100.0
Puerto Rican	223	100.0

Population Age 3–17 Enrolled in Private School
(Universe: Population Age 3–17 Enrolled in School)

Group	Number	%
Total Population	106	1.3
Hispanic or Latino (of any race)	0	0.0
Mexican	0	0.0
Puerto Rican	0	0.0

Foreign-Born Population

Group	Number	%
Total Population	1,793	5.2
Hispanic or Latino (of any race)	682	9.2
Mexican	290	6.3
Puerto Rican	0	0.0

Foreign-Born Naturalized U.S. Citizens

Group	Number	%
Total Population	667	37.2
Hispanic or Latino (of any race)	235	34.5
Mexican	148	51.0
Puerto Rican	0	0.0

Language Spoken at Home: English Only
(Universe: Population 5 Years and Over)

Group	Number	%
Total Population	24,824	82.9
Hispanic or Latino (of any race)	3,080	49.6
Mexican	2,098	54.5
Puerto Rican	363	35.6

Language Spoken at Home: Spanish
(Universe: Population 5 Years and Over)

Group	Number	%
Total Population	3,483	11.6
Hispanic or Latino (of any race)	2,987	48.1
Mexican	1,750	45.5
Puerto Rican	657	64.4

Unemployment Rate
(Universe: Population 16 Years and Over)

Group	%
Total Population	14.1
Hispanic or Latino (of any race)	10.0
Mexican	4.1
Puerto Rican	37.1

Class of Worker: Private Wage and Salary
(Universe: Civilian Employed Population 16 Years and Over)

Group	Number	%
Total Population	2,212	58.0
Hispanic or Latino (of any race)	476	50.6
Mexican	250	43.1
Puerto Rican	79	70.5

Class of Worker: Government
(Universe: Civilian Employed Population 16 Years and Over)

Group	Number	%
Total Population	1,547	40.5
Hispanic or Latino (of any race)	427	45.4
Mexican	293	50.5
Puerto Rican	33	29.5

Means of Transportation to Work: Car, Truck or Van
(Universe: Workers 16 Years and Over)

Group	Number	%
Total Population	11,855	72.0
Hispanic or Latino (of any race)	2,434	75.2
Mexican	1,495	77.8
Puerto Rican	366	62.5

Means of Transportation to Work: Public Transportation (ex. Taxicab)
(Universe: Workers 16 Years and Over)

Group	Number	%
Total Population	23	0.1
Hispanic or Latino (of any race)	13	0.4
Mexican	0	0.0
Puerto Rican	0	0.0

Homeownership Rate
(Universe: Occupied Housing Units)

Group	%
Total Population	0.8
Hispanic or Latino (of any race)	0.5
Central American, ex. Mexican	2.9
Mexican	0.3
Puerto Rican	0.7
South American	0.0
Spaniard	0.0

Median Home Value

Group	Dollars
Total Population	–
Hispanic or Latino (of any race)	–
Mexican	–
Puerto Rican	–

Median Gross Rent

Group	Dollars
Total Population	972
Hispanic or Latino (of any race)	962
Mexican	1,021
Puerto Rican	873

Median Household Income
(2010 Inflation-Adjusted Dollars)

Group	Dollars
Total Population	39,833
Hispanic or Latino (of any race)	37,246
Mexican	40,929
Puerto Rican	32,558

Per Capita Income
(2010 Inflation-Adjusted Dollars)

Group	Dollars
Total Population	14,584
Hispanic or Latino (of any race)	13,167
Mexican	12,945
Puerto Rican	15,115

Households with $100,000+ Income

Group	Number	%
Total Population	192	2.9
Hispanic or Latino (of any race)	0	0.0
Mexican	0	0.0
Puerto Rican	0	0.0

Households with Food Stamps/SNAP Benefits During Past 12 Months

Group	Number	%
Total Population	249	3.7
Hispanic or Latino (of any race)	64	5.2
Mexican	0	0.0
Puerto Rican	0	0.0

Poverty Rate
(Income in Past 12 Months Below Poverty Level)

Group	%
Total Population	19.9
Hispanic or Latino (of any race)	19.8
Mexican	15.3
Puerto Rican	14.7

Fort Worth

Population

Group	Number	%TP[1]	%HP[2]
Total Population	741,206	100.0	–
Hispanic or Latino (of any race)	252,468	34.1	100.0
Central American, ex. Mexican	6,855	0.9	2.7
Costa Rican	183	<0.1	0.1
Guatemalan	1,280	0.2	0.5
Honduran	1,820	0.2	0.7
Nicaraguan	372	0.1	0.1
Panamanian	419	0.1	0.2
Salvadoran	2,729	0.4	1.1
Cuban	1,495	0.2	0.6
Dominican Republic	470	0.1	0.2
Mexican	219,653	29.6	87.0
Puerto Rican	5,650	0.8	2.2
South American	3,014	0.4	1.2
Argentinean	436	0.1	0.2
Chilean	153	<0.1	0.1
Colombian	1,093	0.1	0.4
Ecuadorian	344	<0.1	0.1
Peruvian	473	0.1	0.2
Venezuelan	339	<0.1	0.1
Spaniard	1,631	0.2	0.6

STATE & PLACE PROFILES

Notes: (1) Percent of total population; (2) Percent of Hispanic/Latino population; Profiles include places with an overall population of at least 125,000, OR an overall population of at least 25,000 where the Hispanic/Latino population is at least 20% of the overall population. In states where less than five places meet either of these criteria, we have included places with at least 10,000 total population with the highest percentage of Hispanic/Latino population. These places are identified with an asterisk (*); Please refer to the User's Guide for a full explanation of data.

Population Growth: 2000–2010

Group	%
Total Population	38.6
Hispanic or Latino (of any race)	58.4
Central American, ex. Mexican	333.6
Guatemalan	321.1
Honduran	420.0
Panamanian	193.0
Salvadoran	374.6
Cuban	145.9
Dominican Republic	351.9
Mexican	65.3
Puerto Rican	198.6
South American	233.4
Colombian	204.5
Peruvian	311.3
Venezuelan	130.6
Spaniard	727.9

Males per 100 Females

Group	Number
Total Population	96.4
Hispanic or Latino (of any race)	104.9
Central American, ex. Mexican	103.2
Costa Rican	92.6
Guatemalan	106.5
Honduran	102.0
Nicaraguan	75.5
Panamanian	71.7
Salvadoran	113.0
Cuban	114.2
Dominican Republic	82.9
Mexican	106.0
Puerto Rican	100.9
South American	91.9
Argentinean	127.1
Chilean	96.2
Colombian	84.3
Ecuadorian	100.0
Peruvian	82.6
Venezuelan	83.2
Spaniard	90.8

Average Household Size

Group	People
Total Population	2.77
Hispanic or Latino (of any race)	3.74
Central American, ex. Mexican	3.79
Costa Rican	3.20
Guatemalan	3.80
Honduran	3.97
Nicaraguan	3.14
Panamanian	2.37
Salvadoran	4.06
Cuban	2.90
Dominican Republic	3.22
Mexican	3.81
Puerto Rican	3.07
South American	2.99
Argentinean	3.01
Chilean	3.02
Colombian	2.92
Ecuadorian	3.52
Peruvian	2.83
Venezuelan	3.02
Spaniard	2.98

Median Age

Group	Years
Total Population	31.2
Hispanic or Latino (of any race)	24.9
Central American, ex. Mexican	29.9
Costa Rican	28.5
Guatemalan	29.5
Honduran	28.6
Nicaraguan	31.5
Panamanian	33.5
Salvadoran	30.6
Cuban	32.6
Dominican Republic	26.5
Mexican	24.5
Puerto Rican	28.1
South American	33.8
Argentinean	34.6
Chilean	37.2
Colombian	34.2
Ecuadorian	31.3
Peruvian	35.4
Venezuelan	32.8
Spaniard	30.1

High School Graduates
(Universe: Population 25 Years and Over)

Group	Number	%
Total Population	336,593	78.6
Hispanic or Latino (of any race)	57,760	49.4
Central American, ex. Mexican	1,942	50.2
Guatemalan	349	42.8
Honduran	329	36.2
Salvadoran	815	51.1
Cuban	666	91.9
Mexican	47,382	46.3
Puerto Rican	2,036	86.5
South American	1,751	84.3
Colombian	678	85.0
Spaniard	827	95.2

Four-Year College Graduates
(Universe: Population 25 Years and Over)

Group	Number	%
Total Population	110,127	25.7
Hispanic or Latino (of any race)	10,062	8.6
Central American, ex. Mexican	399	10.3
Guatemalan	96	11.8
Honduran	118	13.0
Salvadoran	100	6.3
Cuban	294	40.6
Mexican	7,329	7.2
Puerto Rican	473	20.1
South American	723	34.8
Colombian	320	40.1
Spaniard	262	30.1

Population Age 3–17 Enrolled in Public School
(Universe: Population Age 3–17 Enrolled in School)

Group	Number	%
Total Population	127,759	88.3
Hispanic or Latino (of any race)	58,266	95.8
Central American, ex. Mexican	984	90.5
Guatemalan	91	74.6
Honduran	161	100.0
Salvadoran	649	94.2
Cuban	132	89.2
Mexican	53,818	96.1
Puerto Rican	609	97.3
South American	441	83.8
Colombian	161	75.6
Spaniard	253	80.8

Population Age 3–17 Enrolled in Private School
(Universe: Population Age 3–17 Enrolled in School)

Group	Number	%
Total Population	16,867	11.7
Hispanic or Latino (of any race)	2,567	4.2
Central American, ex. Mexican	103	9.5
Guatemalan	31	25.4
Honduran	0	0.0
Salvadoran	40	5.8
Cuban	16	10.8
Mexican	2,202	3.9
Puerto Rican	17	2.7
South American	85	16.2
Colombian	52	24.4
Spaniard	60	19.2

Foreign-Born Population

Group	Number	%
Total Population	122,982	17.4
Hispanic or Latino (of any race)	91,820	39.2
Central American, ex. Mexican	4,306	69.6
Guatemalan	889	76.4
Honduran	1,104	82.5
Salvadoran	1,800	60.4
Cuban	702	66.5
Mexican	83,181	39.7
Puerto Rican	0	0.0
South American	1,928	65.7
Colombian	749	67.5
Spaniard	291	20.7

Foreign-Born Naturalized U.S. Citizens

Group	Number	%
Total Population	33,552	27.3
Hispanic or Latino (of any race)	17,668	19.2
Central American, ex. Mexican	1,036	24.1
Guatemalan	208	23.4
Honduran	41	3.7
Salvadoran	504	28.0
Cuban	330	47.0
Mexican	14,685	17.7
Puerto Rican	0	0.0
South American	874	45.3
Colombian	388	51.8
Spaniard	82	28.2

Language Spoken at Home: English Only
(Universe: Population 5 Years and Over)

Group	Number	%
Total Population	436,395	68.1
Hispanic or Latino (of any race)	38,173	18.6
Central American, ex. Mexican	510	9.0
Guatemalan	80	7.0
Honduran	34	2.7
Salvadoran	308	12.0
Cuban	211	21.5
Mexican	32,364	17.7
Puerto Rican	1,053	29.6
South American	259	9.6
Colombian	102	10.1
Spaniard	766	57.9

Language Spoken at Home: Spanish
(Universe: Population 5 Years and Over)

Group	Number	%
Total Population	174,573	27.2
Hispanic or Latino (of any race)	166,640	81.3
Central American, ex. Mexican	5,171	91.0
Guatemalan	1,055	93.0
Honduran	1,239	97.3
Salvadoran	2,257	88.0
Cuban	771	78.5
Mexican	150,409	82.3
Puerto Rican	2,473	69.6
South American	2,432	89.8
Colombian	905	89.9
Spaniard	557	42.1

Unemployment Rate
(Universe: Population 16 Years and Over)

Group	%
Total Population	8.1
Hispanic or Latino (of any race)	9.2
Central American, ex. Mexican	9.8
Guatemalan	17.4
Honduran	5.2
Salvadoran	6.3
Cuban	5.8
Mexican	9.1
Puerto Rican	12.7
South American	10.9
Colombian	6.9
Spaniard	4.7

Class of Worker: Private Wage and Salary
(Universe: Civilian Employed Population 16 Years and Over)

Group	Number	%
Total Population	270,128	82.7
Hispanic or Latino (of any race)	83,776	86.5
Central American, ex. Mexican	2,958	89.8
Guatemalan	669	95.4
Honduran	751	83.9
Salvadoran	1,286	92.1
Cuban	586	90.3
Mexican	73,553	86.5
Puerto Rican	1,709	85.8
South American	1,315	85.2
Colombian	570	87.6
Spaniard	492	80.0

Class of Worker: Government
(Universe: Civilian Employed Population 16 Years and Over)

Group	Number	%
Total Population	37,708	11.5
Hispanic or Latino (of any race)	7,915	8.2
Central American, ex. Mexican	67	2.0

Notes: (1) Percent of total population; (2) Percent of Hispanic/Latino population; Profiles include places with an overall population of at least 125,000, OR an overall population of at least 25,000 where the Hispanic/Latino population is at least 20% of the overall population. In states where less than five places meet either of these criteria, we have included places with at least 10,000 total population with the highest percentage of Hispanic/Latino population. These places are identified with an asterisk (*); Please refer to the User's Guide for a full explanation of data.

Group	Number	%
Guatemalan	10	1.4
Honduran	0	0.0
Salvadoran	36	2.6
Cuban	33	5.1
Mexican	6,813	8.0
Puerto Rican	264	13.3
South American	217	14.1
Colombian	70	10.8
Spaniard	111	18.0

Means of Transportation to Work: Car, Truck or Van

(Universe: Workers 16 Years and Over)

Group	Number	%
Total Population	295,834	92.2
Hispanic or Latino (of any race)	88,379	92.9
Central American, ex. Mexican	3,040	92.6
Guatemalan	648	92.4
Honduran	753	84.1
Salvadoran	1,339	96.5
Cuban	612	96.8
Mexican	77,566	92.9
Puerto Rican	1,808	94.0
South American	1,318	87.7
Colombian	500	76.8
Spaniard	566	92.0

Means of Transportation to Work: Public Transportation (ex. Taxicab)

(Universe: Workers 16 Years and Over)

Group	Number	%
Total Population	4,281	1.3
Hispanic or Latino (of any race)	918	1.0
Central American, ex. Mexican	0	0.0
Guatemalan	0	0.0
Honduran	0	0.0
Salvadoran	0	0.0
Cuban	0	0.0
Mexican	843	1.0
Puerto Rican	13	0.7
South American	10	0.7
Colombian	0	0.0
Spaniard	0	0.0

Homeownership Rate

(Universe: Occupied Housing Units)

Group	%
Total Population	59.2
Hispanic or Latino (of any race)	57.9
Central American, ex. Mexican	54.8
Costa Rican	71.4
Guatemalan	52.8
Honduran	35.3
Nicaraguan	70.6
Panamanian	49.7
Salvadoran	64.6
Cuban	58.1
Dominican Republic	63.1
Mexican	58.4
Puerto Rican	58.5
South American	65.3
Argentinean	60.0
Chilean	71.2
Colombian	65.1
Ecuadorian	74.3
Peruvian	66.0
Venezuelan	66.4
Spaniard	63.1

Median Home Value

Group	Dollars
Total Population	120,300
Hispanic or Latino (of any race)	84,600
Central American, ex. Mexican	106,700
Guatemalan	116,500
Honduran	71,700
Salvadoran	108,900
Cuban	141,000
Mexican	81,400
Puerto Rican	134,900
South American	135,800
Colombian	120,300
Spaniard	143,800

Median Gross Rent

Group	Dollars
Total Population	803
Hispanic or Latino (of any race)	740
Central American, ex. Mexican	675
Guatemalan	732
Honduran	636
Salvadoran	698
Cuban	749
Mexican	740
Puerto Rican	789
South American	750
Colombian	734
Spaniard	746

Median Household Income

(2010 Inflation-Adjusted Dollars)

Group	Dollars
Total Population	49,530
Hispanic or Latino (of any race)	38,297
Central American, ex. Mexican	34,688
Guatemalan	42,000
Honduran	26,633
Salvadoran	35,342
Cuban	45,463
Mexican	37,561
Puerto Rican	46,361
South American	53,630
Colombian	54,356
Spaniard	49,640

Per Capita Income

(2010 Inflation-Adjusted Dollars)

Group	Dollars
Total Population	23,792
Hispanic or Latino (of any race)	13,205
Central American, ex. Mexican	15,453
Guatemalan	15,841
Honduran	13,545
Salvadoran	14,528
Cuban	29,069
Mexican	12,506
Puerto Rican	21,427
South American	24,455
Colombian	27,076
Spaniard	24,096

Households with $100,000+ Income

Group	Number	%
Total Population	45,237	18.0
Hispanic or Latino (of any race)	4,916	8.0
Central American, ex. Mexican	149	7.5
Guatemalan	0	0.0
Honduran	0	0.0
Salvadoran	113	12.7
Cuban	72	15.7
Mexican	3,906	7.3
Puerto Rican	223	14.2
South American	182	18.1
Colombian	87	20.4
Spaniard	114	19.0

Households with Food Stamps/SNAP Benefits During Past 12 Months

Group	Number	%
Total Population	25,755	10.2
Hispanic or Latino (of any race)	8,735	14.2
Central American, ex. Mexican	154	7.8
Guatemalan	11	2.4
Honduran	31	6.3
Salvadoran	112	12.6
Cuban	50	10.9
Mexican	8,010	15.0
Puerto Rican	166	10.6
South American	50	5.0
Colombian	0	0.0
Spaniard	14	2.3

Poverty Rate

(Income in Past 12 Months Below Poverty Level)

Group	%
Total Population	17.0
Hispanic or Latino (of any race)	24.0
Central American, ex. Mexican	21.1
Guatemalan	7.5
Honduran	26.2
Salvadoran	25.3
Cuban	10.0
Mexican	25.2
Puerto Rican	15.2
South American	9.2
Colombian	10.8
Spaniard	4.2

Galveston

Population

Group	Number	%TP[1]	%HP[2]
Total Population	47,743	100.0	–
Hispanic or Latino (of any race)	14,925	31.3	100.0
Central American, ex. Mexican	1,599	3.3	10.7
Guatemalan	271	0.6	1.8
Honduran	438	0.9	2.9
Salvadoran	780	1.6	5.2
Cuban	101	0.2	0.7
Mexican	11,605	24.3	77.8
Puerto Rican	198	0.4	1.3
South American	240	0.5	1.6
Spaniard	109	0.2	0.7

Population Growth: 2000–2010

Group	%
Total Population	-16.6
Hispanic or Latino (of any race)	1.2
Central American, ex. Mexican	145.6
Honduran	165.5
Salvadoran	150.0
Mexican	1.5
Puerto Rican	34.7
South American	61.1

Males per 100 Females

Group	Number
Total Population	104.4
Hispanic or Latino (of any race)	107.8
Central American, ex. Mexican	124.9
Guatemalan	194.6
Honduran	140.7
Salvadoran	105.8
Cuban	140.5
Mexican	104.5
Puerto Rican	125.0
South American	105.1
Spaniard	78.7

Average Household Size

Group	People
Total Population	2.27
Hispanic or Latino (of any race)	2.97
Central American, ex. Mexican	3.46
Guatemalan	3.49
Honduran	3.45
Salvadoran	3.53
Cuban	2.15
Mexican	2.96
Puerto Rican	2.43
South American	2.39
Spaniard	2.32

Median Age

Group	Years
Total Population	38.8
Hispanic or Latino (of any race)	30.1
Central American, ex. Mexican	31.2
Guatemalan	30.1
Honduran	29.3
Salvadoran	32.9
Cuban	47.5
Mexican	29.7
Puerto Rican	29.0
South American	34.4
Spaniard	33.5

High School Graduates

(Universe: Population 25 Years and Over)

Group	Number	%
Total Population	26,469	80.1
Hispanic or Latino (of any race)	5,127	59.5
Central American, ex. Mexican	280	36.1

Notes: (1) Percent of total population; (2) Percent of Hispanic/Latino population; Profiles include places with an overall population of at least 125,000, OR an overall population of at least 25,000 where the Hispanic/Latino population is at least 20% of the overall population. In states where less than five places meet either of these criteria, we have included places with at least 10,000 total population with the highest percentage of Hispanic/Latino population. These places are identified with an asterisk (*); Please refer to the User's Guide for a full explanation of data.

Mexican	4,014	58.0

Four-Year College Graduates
(Universe: Population 25 Years and Over)

Group	Number	%
Total Population	8,791	26.6
Hispanic or Latino (of any race)	956	11.1
Central American, ex. Mexican	12	1.5
Mexican	697	10.1

Population Age 3–17 Enrolled in Public School
(Universe: Population Age 3–17 Enrolled in School)

Group	Number	%
Total Population	6,642	88.8
Hispanic or Latino (of any race)	2,966	92.3
Central American, ex. Mexican	139	71.3
Mexican	2,441	95.2

Population Age 3–17 Enrolled in Private School
(Universe: Population Age 3–17 Enrolled in School)

Group	Number	%
Total Population	840	11.2
Hispanic or Latino (of any race)	249	7.7
Central American, ex. Mexican	56	28.7
Mexican	123	4.8

Foreign-Born Population

Group	Number	%
Total Population	6,744	13.5
Hispanic or Latino (of any race)	4,418	29.5
Central American, ex. Mexican	929	68.3
Mexican	3,300	27.7

Foreign-Born Naturalized U.S. Citizens

Group	Number	%
Total Population	2,226	33.0
Hispanic or Latino (of any race)	1,265	28.6
Central American, ex. Mexican	150	16.1
Mexican	1,089	33.0

Language Spoken at Home: English Only
(Universe: Population 5 Years and Over)

Group	Number	%
Total Population	34,528	73.3
Hispanic or Latino (of any race)	4,595	33.4
Central American, ex. Mexican	12	1.1
Mexican	3,636	33.0

Language Spoken at Home: Spanish
(Universe: Population 5 Years and Over)

Group	Number	%
Total Population	10,173	21.6
Hispanic or Latino (of any race)	9,163	66.5
Central American, ex. Mexican	1,110	98.9
Mexican	7,358	66.8

Unemployment Rate
(Universe: Population 16 Years and Over)

Group	%
Total Population	7.8
Hispanic or Latino (of any race)	6.4
Central American, ex. Mexican	6.8
Mexican	5.3

Class of Worker: Private Wage and Salary
(Universe: Civilian Employed Population 16 Years and Over)

Group	Number	%
Total Population	14,873	63.8
Hispanic or Latino (of any race)	5,297	72.7
Central American, ex. Mexican	731	91.9
Mexican	3,989	69.6

Class of Worker: Government
(Universe: Civilian Employed Population 16 Years and Over)

Group	Number	%
Total Population	6,655	28.6
Hispanic or Latino (of any race)	1,584	21.7
Central American, ex. Mexican	64	8.1
Mexican	1,358	23.7

Means of Transportation to Work: Car, Truck or Van
(Universe: Workers 16 Years and Over)

Group	Number	%
Total Population	18,707	82.2
Hispanic or Latino (of any race)	6,086	85.7
Central American, ex. Mexican	614	79.8
Mexican	4,868	87.5

Means of Transportation to Work: Public Transportation (ex. Taxicab)
(Universe: Workers 16 Years and Over)

Group	Number	%
Total Population	467	2.1
Hispanic or Latino (of any race)	51	0.7
Central American, ex. Mexican	14	1.8
Mexican	37	0.7

Homeownership Rate
(Universe: Occupied Housing Units)

Group	%
Total Population	47.9
Hispanic or Latino (of any race)	45.2
Central American, ex. Mexican	35.5
Guatemalan	25.6
Honduran	18.1
Salvadoran	46.0
Cuban	61.0
Mexican	47.4
Puerto Rican	31.1
South American	31.6
Spaniard	51.2

Median Home Value

Group	Dollars
Total Population	121,500
Hispanic or Latino (of any race)	92,600
Central American, ex. Mexican	85,800
Mexican	89,600

Median Gross Rent

Group	Dollars
Total Population	751
Hispanic or Latino (of any race)	744
Central American, ex. Mexican	588
Mexican	771

Median Household Income
(2010 Inflation-Adjusted Dollars)

Group	Dollars
Total Population	36,165
Hispanic or Latino (of any race)	34,984
Central American, ex. Mexican	31,917
Mexican	37,160

Per Capita Income
(2010 Inflation-Adjusted Dollars)

Group	Dollars
Total Population	23,963
Hispanic or Latino (of any race)	15,556
Central American, ex. Mexican	11,263
Mexican	15,680

Households with $100,000+ Income

Group	Number	%
Total Population	2,727	12.9
Hispanic or Latino (of any race)	327	6.7
Central American, ex. Mexican	10	3.7
Mexican	298	7.4

Households with Food Stamps/SNAP Benefits During Past 12 Months

Group	Number	%
Total Population	2,669	12.6
Hispanic or Latino (of any race)	664	13.6
Central American, ex. Mexican	33	12.3
Mexican	474	11.8

Poverty Rate
(Income in Past 12 Months Below Poverty Level)

Group	%
Total Population	22.5
Hispanic or Latino (of any race)	21.1
Central American, ex. Mexican	27.0
Mexican	20.6

Garland

Population

Group	Number	%TP[1]	%HP[2]
Total Population	226,876	100.0	–
Hispanic or Latino (of any race)	85,784	37.8	100.0
Central American, ex. Mexican	7,792	3.4	9.1
Costa Rican	134	0.1	0.2
Guatemalan	1,656	0.7	1.9
Honduran	1,058	0.5	1.2
Nicaraguan	151	0.1	0.2
Panamanian	113	<0.1	0.1
Salvadoran	4,627	2.0	5.4
Cuban	399	0.2	0.5
Dominican Republic	105	<0.1	0.1
Mexican	70,016	30.9	81.6
Puerto Rican	912	0.4	1.1
South American	1,580	0.7	1.8
Argentinean	128	0.1	0.1
Colombian	576	0.3	0.7
Ecuadorian	146	0.1	0.2
Peruvian	493	0.2	0.6
Spaniard	493	0.2	0.6

Population Growth: 2000–2010

Group	%
Total Population	5.1
Hispanic or Latino (of any race)	55.4
Central American, ex. Mexican	142.6
Guatemalan	103.7
Honduran	245.8
Salvadoran	166.4
Cuban	41.5
Mexican	64.9
Puerto Rican	42.5
South American	124.1
Colombian	80.0
Peruvian	254.7

Males per 100 Females

Group	Number
Total Population	96.1
Hispanic or Latino (of any race)	105.7
Central American, ex. Mexican	108.0
Costa Rican	71.8
Guatemalan	108.6
Honduran	109.9
Nicaraguan	79.8
Panamanian	46.8
Salvadoran	111.6
Cuban	112.2
Dominican Republic	69.4
Mexican	106.3
Puerto Rican	105.4
South American	94.8
Argentinean	116.9
Colombian	77.2
Ecuadorian	108.6
Peruvian	102.0
Spaniard	88.9

Average Household Size

Group	People
Total Population	2.99
Hispanic or Latino (of any race)	4.14
Central American, ex. Mexican	4.24
Costa Rican	2.77
Guatemalan	4.16
Honduran	4.09
Nicaraguan	3.54
Panamanian	3.26
Salvadoran	4.41
Cuban	3.16
Dominican Republic	3.65
Mexican	4.22
Puerto Rican	3.11
South American	3.27
Argentinean	3.39
Colombian	3.16
Ecuadorian	2.96
Peruvian	3.57
Spaniard	2.96

Notes: (1) Percent of total population; (2) Percent of Hispanic/Latino population; Profiles include places with an overall population of at least 125,000, OR an overall population of at least 25,000 where the Hispanic/Latino population is at least 20% of the overall population. In states where less than five places meet either of these criteria, we have included places with at least 10,000 total population with the highest percentage of Hispanic/Latino population. These places are identified with an asterisk (*); Please refer to the User's Guide for a full explanation of data.

Median Age

Group	Years
Total Population	33.7
Hispanic or Latino (of any race)	24.8
Central American, ex. Mexican	31.3
Costa Rican	38.7
Guatemalan	33.6
Honduran	30.6
Nicaraguan	33.1
Panamanian	38.1
Salvadoran	30.5
Cuban	35.7
Dominican Republic	27.5
Mexican	23.8
Puerto Rican	29.4
South American	35.9
Argentinean	31.2
Colombian	38.1
Ecuadorian	32.0
Peruvian	35.8
Spaniard	30.9

High School Graduates

(Universe: Population 25 Years and Over)

Group	Number	%
Total Population	104,744	75.6
Hispanic or Latino (of any race)	18,794	46.0
Central American, ex. Mexican	1,744	35.5
Guatemalan	364	39.4
Honduran	451	52.6
Salvadoran	696	24.8
Mexican	14,397	44.1
Puerto Rican	509	86.6
South American	1,136	85.1
Peruvian	570	84.2

Four-Year College Graduates

(Universe: Population 25 Years and Over)

Group	Number	%
Total Population	30,016	21.7
Hispanic or Latino (of any race)	3,054	7.5
Central American, ex. Mexican	220	4.5
Guatemalan	83	9.0
Honduran	32	3.7
Salvadoran	52	1.9
Mexican	1,996	6.1
Puerto Rican	185	31.5
South American	380	28.5
Peruvian	122	18.0

Population Age 3–17 Enrolled in Public School

(Universe: Population Age 3–17 Enrolled in School)

Group	Number	%
Total Population	43,414	93.0
Hispanic or Latino (of any race)	20,493	96.2
Central American, ex. Mexican	1,927	100.0
Guatemalan	296	100.0
Honduran	373	100.0
Salvadoran	1,237	100.0
Mexican	17,315	96.4
Puerto Rican	332	100.0
South American	345	78.9
Peruvian	192	93.7

Population Age 3–17 Enrolled in Private School

(Universe: Population Age 3–17 Enrolled in School)

Group	Number	%
Total Population	3,262	7.0
Hispanic or Latino (of any race)	807	3.8
Central American, ex. Mexican	0	0.0
Guatemalan	0	0.0
Honduran	0	0.0
Salvadoran	0	0.0
Mexican	651	3.6
Puerto Rican	0	0.0
South American	92	21.1
Peruvian	13	6.3

Foreign-Born Population

Group	Number	%
Total Population	61,010	27.4
Hispanic or Latino (of any race)	38,824	48.4
Central American, ex. Mexican	5,581	65.6
Guatemalan	1,108	77.5
Honduran	878	54.6
Salvadoran	3,356	67.1
Mexican	31,172	47.1
Puerto Rican	11	1.0
South American	1,541	74.2
Peruvian	843	80.3

Foreign-Born Naturalized U.S. Citizens

Group	Number	%
Total Population	19,116	31.3
Hispanic or Latino (of any race)	6,390	16.5
Central American, ex. Mexican	977	17.5
Guatemalan	225	20.3
Honduran	72	8.2
Salvadoran	516	15.4
Mexican	4,674	15.0
Puerto Rican	0	0.0
South American	524	34.0
Peruvian	267	31.7

Language Spoken at Home: English Only

(Universe: Population 5 Years and Over)

Group	Number	%
Total Population	115,607	56.3
Hispanic or Latino (of any race)	8,462	11.9
Central American, ex. Mexican	208	2.7
Guatemalan	63	4.5
Honduran	15	1.1
Salvadoran	109	2.4
Mexican	7,018	12.1
Puerto Rican	355	32.4
South American	61	3.2
Peruvian	43	4.3

Language Spoken at Home: Spanish

(Universe: Population 5 Years and Over)

Group	Number	%
Total Population	65,009	31.7
Hispanic or Latino (of any race)	62,397	87.9
Central American, ex. Mexican	7,411	97.3
Guatemalan	1,333	95.5
Honduran	1,318	98.9
Salvadoran	4,435	97.6
Mexican	51,102	87.8
Puerto Rican	740	67.6
South American	1,863	96.8
Peruvian	946	95.7

Unemployment Rate

(Universe: Population 16 Years and Over)

Group	%
Total Population	8.1
Hispanic or Latino (of any race)	7.2
Central American, ex. Mexican	9.5
Guatemalan	13.4
Honduran	5.7
Salvadoran	9.7
Mexican	6.6
Puerto Rican	12.5
South American	4.0
Peruvian	2.1

Class of Worker: Private Wage and Salary

(Universe: Civilian Employed Population 16 Years and Over)

Group	Number	%
Total Population	89,276	80.7
Hispanic or Latino (of any race)	30,169	80.3
Central American, ex. Mexican	3,558	84.2
Guatemalan	873	100.0
Honduran	587	78.5
Salvadoran	1,883	79.9
Mexican	24,598	80.8
Puerto Rican	511	75.1
South American	740	66.5
Peruvian	349	63.6

Class of Worker: Government

(Universe: Civilian Employed Population 16 Years and Over)

Group	Number	%
Total Population	11,120	10.0
Hispanic or Latino (of any race)	2,175	5.8
Central American, ex. Mexican	151	3.6
Guatemalan	0	0.0
Honduran	39	5.2
Salvadoran	91	3.9
Mexican	1,595	5.2
Puerto Rican	119	17.5
South American	112	10.1
Peruvian	22	4.0

Means of Transportation to Work: Car, Truck or Van

(Universe: Workers 16 Years and Over)

Group	Number	%
Total Population	100,259	92.4
Hispanic or Latino (of any race)	34,473	94.1
Central American, ex. Mexican	3,993	96.0
Guatemalan	806	94.7
Honduran	737	100.0
Salvadoran	2,214	95.3
Mexican	28,144	94.5
Puerto Rican	536	78.8
South American	853	88.9
Peruvian	316	77.3

Means of Transportation to Work: Public Transportation (ex. Taxicab)

(Universe: Workers 16 Years and Over)

Group	Number	%
Total Population	3,071	2.8
Hispanic or Latino (of any race)	886	2.4
Central American, ex. Mexican	91	2.2
Guatemalan	45	5.3
Honduran	0	0.0
Salvadoran	46	2.0
Mexican	617	2.1
Puerto Rican	39	5.7
South American	78	8.1
Peruvian	78	19.1

Homeownership Rate

(Universe: Occupied Housing Units)

Group	%
Total Population	65.2
Hispanic or Latino (of any race)	59.3
Central American, ex. Mexican	65.2
Costa Rican	59.6
Guatemalan	61.7
Honduran	61.4
Nicaraguan	71.7
Panamanian	74.3
Salvadoran	66.9
Cuban	70.2
Dominican Republic	58.1
Mexican	58.9
Puerto Rican	53.4
South American	65.0
Argentinean	71.1
Colombian	64.1
Ecuadorian	76.1
Peruvian	63.5
Spaniard	60.0

Median Home Value

Group	Dollars
Total Population	118,700
Hispanic or Latino (of any race)	104,400
Central American, ex. Mexican	102,200
Guatemalan	104,900
Honduran	110,900
Salvadoran	97,600
Mexican	102,700
Puerto Rican	117,200
South American	131,600
Peruvian	129,900

Median Gross Rent

Group	Dollars
Total Population	890
Hispanic or Latino (of any race)	820
Central American, ex. Mexican	769
Guatemalan	785
Honduran	1,065
Salvadoran	748
Mexican	824
Puerto Rican	996
South American	859
Peruvian	1,115

Notes: (1) Percent of total population; (2) Percent of Hispanic/Latino population; Profiles include places with an overall population of at least 125,000, OR an overall population of at least 25,000 where the Hispanic/Latino population is at least 20% of the overall population. In states where less than five places meet either of these criteria, we have included places with at least 10,000 total population with the highest percentage of Hispanic/Latino population. These places are identified with an asterisk (*); Please refer to the User's Guide for a full explanation of data.

Median Household Income
(2010 Inflation-Adjusted Dollars)

Group	Dollars
Total Population	52,389
Hispanic or Latino (of any race)	44,630
Central American, ex. Mexican	39,266
Guatemalan	35,391
Honduran	44,537
Salvadoran	39,556
Mexican	45,220
Puerto Rican	67,109
South American	49,811
Peruvian	60,442

Per Capita Income
(2010 Inflation-Adjusted Dollars)

Group	Dollars
Total Population	22,071
Hispanic or Latino (of any race)	13,428
Central American, ex. Mexican	13,040
Guatemalan	12,388
Honduran	10,945
Salvadoran	13,348
Mexican	12,891
Puerto Rican	21,424
South American	20,057
Peruvian	13,483

Households with $100,000+ Income

Group	Number	%
Total Population	12,411	17.1
Hispanic or Latino (of any race)	1,544	8.2
Central American, ex. Mexican	150	6.6
Guatemalan	10	2.5
Honduran	10	3.8
Salvadoran	85	6.0
Mexican	1,077	7.2
Puerto Rican	122	32.7
South American	30	5.2
Peruvian	10	4.0

Households with Food Stamps/SNAP Benefits During Past 12 Months

Group	Number	%
Total Population	6,157	8.5
Hispanic or Latino (of any race)	1,856	9.8
Central American, ex. Mexican	163	7.2
Guatemalan	28	7.0
Honduran	73	27.9
Salvadoran	62	4.3
Mexican	1,525	10.2
Puerto Rican	16	4.3
South American	66	11.5
Peruvian	13	5.1

Poverty Rate
(Income in Past 12 Months Below Poverty Level)

Group	%
Total Population	13.4
Hispanic or Latino (of any race)	18.3
Central American, ex. Mexican	14.5
Guatemalan	8.5
Honduran	24.0
Salvadoran	13.2
Mexican	19.9
Puerto Rican	1.5
South American	5.6
Peruvian	1.1

Georgetown

Population

Group	Number	%TP[1]	%HP[2]
Total Population	47,400	100.0	–
Hispanic or Latino (of any race)	10,317	21.8	100.0
Central American, ex. Mexican	192	0.4	1.9
Mexican	8,798	18.6	85.3
Puerto Rican	295	0.6	2.9
South American	185	0.4	1.8
Spaniard	120	0.3	1.2

Population Growth: 2000–2010

Group	%
Total Population	67.3
Hispanic or Latino (of any race)	101.5
Mexican	124.2
Puerto Rican	134.1

Males per 100 Females

Group	Number
Total Population	93.2
Hispanic or Latino (of any race)	108.1
Central American, ex. Mexican	84.6
Mexican	111.9
Puerto Rican	103.4
South American	66.7
Spaniard	84.6

Average Household Size

Group	People
Total Population	2.38
Hispanic or Latino (of any race)	3.52
Central American, ex. Mexican	3.23
Mexican	3.59
Puerto Rican	3.25
South American	2.90
Spaniard	2.76

Median Age

Group	Years
Total Population	44.0
Hispanic or Latino (of any race)	24.9
Central American, ex. Mexican	34.0
Mexican	24.4
Puerto Rican	24.9
South American	34.8
Spaniard	31.5

High School Graduates
(Universe: Population 25 Years and Over)

Group	Number	%
Total Population	26,774	89.3
Hispanic or Latino (of any race)	3,417	63.2
Mexican	2,878	61.3

Four-Year College Graduates
(Universe: Population 25 Years and Over)

Group	Number	%
Total Population	11,194	37.3
Hispanic or Latino (of any race)	435	8.0
Mexican	316	6.7

Population Age 3–17 Enrolled in Public School
(Universe: Population Age 3–17 Enrolled in School)

Group	Number	%
Total Population	6,836	87.3
Hispanic or Latino (of any race)	3,351	94.5
Mexican	2,971	95.4

Population Age 3–17 Enrolled in Private School
(Universe: Population Age 3–17 Enrolled in School)

Group	Number	%
Total Population	994	12.7
Hispanic or Latino (of any race)	196	5.5
Mexican	143	4.6

Foreign-Born Population

Group	Number	%
Total Population	5,089	11.5
Hispanic or Latino (of any race)	3,784	32.6
Mexican	3,643	35.8

Foreign-Born Naturalized U.S. Citizens

Group	Number	%
Total Population	1,517	29.8
Hispanic or Latino (of any race)	548	14.5
Mexican	484	13.3

Language Spoken at Home: English Only
(Universe: Population 5 Years and Over)

Group	Number	%
Total Population	32,956	79.7
Hispanic or Latino (of any race)	3,225	31.0
Mexican	2,690	29.5

Language Spoken at Home: Spanish
(Universe: Population 5 Years and Over)

Group	Number	%
Total Population	7,580	18.3
Hispanic or Latino (of any race)	7,149	68.8
Mexican	6,421	70.4

Unemployment Rate
(Universe: Population 16 Years and Over)

Group	%
Total Population	6.1
Hispanic or Latino (of any race)	6.1
Mexican	7.0

Class of Worker: Private Wage and Salary
(Universe: Civilian Employed Population 16 Years and Over)

Group	Number	%
Total Population	13,464	75.9
Hispanic or Latino (of any race)	4,192	80.5
Mexican	3,632	81.3

Class of Worker: Government
(Universe: Civilian Employed Population 16 Years and Over)

Group	Number	%
Total Population	2,928	16.5
Hispanic or Latino (of any race)	887	17.0
Mexican	711	15.9

Means of Transportation to Work: Car, Truck or Van
(Universe: Workers 16 Years and Over)

Group	Number	%
Total Population	15,906	89.6
Hispanic or Latino (of any race)	4,835	93.5
Mexican	4,182	94.3

Means of Transportation to Work: Public Transportation (ex. Taxicab)
(Universe: Workers 16 Years and Over)

Group	Number	%
Total Population	0	0.0
Hispanic or Latino (of any race)	0	0.0
Mexican	0	0.0

Homeownership Rate
(Universe: Occupied Housing Units)

Group	%
Total Population	72.8
Hispanic or Latino (of any race)	45.4
Central American, ex. Mexican	42.6
Mexican	44.5
Puerto Rican	50.0
South American	60.0
Spaniard	47.6

Median Home Value

Group	Dollars
Total Population	178,100
Hispanic or Latino (of any race)	130,800
Mexican	126,100

Median Gross Rent

Group	Dollars
Total Population	910
Hispanic or Latino (of any race)	908
Mexican	901

Median Household Income
(2010 Inflation-Adjusted Dollars)

Group	Dollars
Total Population	60,888
Hispanic or Latino (of any race)	50,355
Mexican	48,722

Per Capita Income
(2010 Inflation-Adjusted Dollars)

Group	Dollars
Total Population	29,618
Hispanic or Latino (of any race)	14,227
Mexican	13,651

Households with $100,000+ Income

Group	Number	%
Total Population	3,958	23.1
Hispanic or Latino (of any race)	291	10.7
Mexican	212	9.3

Notes: (1) Percent of total population; (2) Percent of Hispanic/Latino population; Profiles include places with an overall population of at least 125,000, OR an overall population of at least 25,000 where the Hispanic/Latino population is at least 20% of the overall population. In states where less than five places meet either of these criteria, we have included places with at least 10,000 total population with the highest percentage of Hispanic/Latino population. These places are identified with an asterisk (*); Please refer to the User's Guide for a full explanation of data.

Households with Food Stamps/SNAP Benefits During Past 12 Months

Group	Number	%
Total Population	774	4.5
Hispanic or Latino (of any race)	374	13.8
Mexican	324	14.2

Poverty Rate
(Income in Past 12 Months Below Poverty Level)

Group	%
Total Population	9.5
Hispanic or Latino (of any race)	21.3
Mexican	21.4

Grand Prairie

Population

Group	Number	%TP[1]	%HP[2]
Total Population	175,396	100.0	–
Hispanic or Latino (of any race)	74,893	42.7	100.0
Central American, ex. Mexican	4,345	2.5	5.8
Guatemalan	377	0.2	0.5
Honduran	484	0.3	0.6
Nicaraguan	242	0.1	0.3
Panamanian	113	0.1	0.2
Salvadoran	3,043	1.7	4.1
Cuban	300	0.2	0.4
Dominican Republic	128	0.1	0.2
Mexican	63,100	36.0	84.3
Puerto Rican	1,500	0.9	2.0
South American	919	0.5	1.2
Argentinean	196	0.1	0.3
Colombian	300	0.2	0.4
Ecuadorian	117	0.1	0.2
Peruvian	177	0.1	0.2
Spaniard	435	0.2	0.6

Population Growth: 2000–2010

Group	%
Total Population	37.6
Hispanic or Latino (of any race)	78.2
Central American, ex. Mexican	376.9
Salvadoran	449.3
Cuban	70.5
Mexican	95.9
Puerto Rican	84.7
South American	231.8

Males per 100 Females

Group	Number
Total Population	95.8
Hispanic or Latino (of any race)	100.2
Central American, ex. Mexican	96.8
Guatemalan	108.3
Honduran	87.6
Nicaraguan	90.6
Panamanian	76.6
Salvadoran	97.6
Cuban	96.1
Dominican Republic	88.2
Mexican	101.4
Puerto Rican	90.8
South American	95.5
Argentinean	115.4
Colombian	78.6
Ecuadorian	112.7
Peruvian	101.1
Spaniard	80.5

Average Household Size

Group	People
Total Population	3.01
Hispanic or Latino (of any race)	3.81
Central American, ex. Mexican	4.16
Guatemalan	3.81
Honduran	4.23
Nicaraguan	3.95
Panamanian	2.76
Salvadoran	4.29
Cuban	2.90
Dominican Republic	2.98
Mexican	3.86
Puerto Rican	3.16
South American	3.39
Argentinean	3.70
Colombian	3.51
Ecuadorian	3.87
Peruvian	3.12
Spaniard	3.29

Median Age

Group	Years
Total Population	31.3
Hispanic or Latino (of any race)	25.0
Central American, ex. Mexican	30.1
Guatemalan	29.6
Honduran	30.3
Nicaraguan	33.0
Panamanian	32.5
Salvadoran	29.9
Cuban	35.3
Dominican Republic	31.5
Mexican	24.5
Puerto Rican	29.0
South American	33.3
Argentinean	29.9
Colombian	32.5
Ecuadorian	29.8
Peruvian	36.5
Spaniard	31.4

High School Graduates
(Universe: Population 25 Years and Over)

Group	Number	%
Total Population	76,703	78.1
Hispanic or Latino (of any race)	19,690	58.2
Central American, ex. Mexican	654	32.8
Salvadoran	304	26.1
Mexican	16,400	57.3
Puerto Rican	474	80.9

Four-Year College Graduates
(Universe: Population 25 Years and Over)

Group	Number	%
Total Population	20,633	21.0
Hispanic or Latino (of any race)	2,471	7.3
Central American, ex. Mexican	79	4.0
Salvadoran	5	0.4
Mexican	1,866	6.5
Puerto Rican	155	26.5

Population Age 3–17 Enrolled in Public School
(Universe: Population Age 3–17 Enrolled in School)

Group	Number	%
Total Population	34,720	92.9
Hispanic or Latino (of any race)	18,321	96.1
Central American, ex. Mexican	839	91.7
Salvadoran	554	96.2
Mexican	16,051	96.6
Puerto Rican	308	87.3

Population Age 3–17 Enrolled in Private School
(Universe: Population Age 3–17 Enrolled in School)

Group	Number	%
Total Population	2,634	7.1
Hispanic or Latino (of any race)	741	3.9
Central American, ex. Mexican	76	8.3
Salvadoran	22	3.8
Mexican	567	3.4
Puerto Rican	45	12.7

Foreign-Born Population

Group	Number	%
Total Population	33,616	20.3
Hispanic or Latino (of any race)	22,432	32.7
Central American, ex. Mexican	2,283	63.0
Salvadoran	1,385	60.0
Mexican	19,037	32.2
Puerto Rican	0	0.0

Foreign-Born Naturalized U.S. Citizens

Group	Number	%
Total Population	11,097	33.0
Hispanic or Latino (of any race)	5,001	22.3
Central American, ex. Mexican	557	24.4
Salvadoran	292	21.1
Mexican	3,778	19.8
Puerto Rican	0	0.0

Language Spoken at Home: English Only
(Universe: Population 5 Years and Over)

Group	Number	%
Total Population	92,109	60.9
Hispanic or Latino (of any race)	14,797	24.5
Central American, ex. Mexican	107	3.2
Salvadoran	13	0.6
Mexican	12,766	24.7
Puerto Rican	216	20.7

Language Spoken at Home: Spanish
(Universe: Population 5 Years and Over)

Group	Number	%
Total Population	47,497	31.4
Hispanic or Latino (of any race)	45,353	75.2
Central American, ex. Mexican	3,206	96.8
Salvadoran	2,060	99.4
Mexican	38,690	75.0
Puerto Rican	830	79.3

Unemployment Rate
(Universe: Population 16 Years and Over)

Group	%
Total Population	8.3
Hispanic or Latino (of any race)	8.5
Central American, ex. Mexican	11.6
Salvadoran	10.6
Mexican	8.5
Puerto Rican	3.1

Class of Worker: Private Wage and Salary
(Universe: Civilian Employed Population 16 Years and Over)

Group	Number	%
Total Population	65,093	81.9
Hispanic or Latino (of any race)	25,859	86.8
Central American, ex. Mexican	1,571	83.8
Salvadoran	1,024	82.3
Mexican	21,983	87.0
Puerto Rican	461	92.9

Class of Worker: Government
(Universe: Civilian Employed Population 16 Years and Over)

Group	Number	%
Total Population	10,215	12.9
Hispanic or Latino (of any race)	2,510	8.4
Central American, ex. Mexican	129	6.9
Salvadoran	104	8.4
Mexican	2,085	8.3
Puerto Rican	13	2.6

Means of Transportation to Work: Car, Truck or Van
(Universe: Workers 16 Years and Over)

Group	Number	%
Total Population	73,769	94.8
Hispanic or Latino (of any race)	27,639	95.8
Central American, ex. Mexican	1,651	95.4
Salvadoran	1,020	92.8
Mexican	23,365	95.6
Puerto Rican	496	100.0

Means of Transportation to Work: Public Transportation (ex. Taxicab)
(Universe: Workers 16 Years and Over)

Group	Number	%
Total Population	280	0.4
Hispanic or Latino (of any race)	73	0.3
Central American, ex. Mexican	0	0.0
Salvadoran	0	0.0
Mexican	63	0.3
Puerto Rican	0	0.0

Homeownership Rate
(Universe: Occupied Housing Units)

Group	%
Total Population	62.8
Hispanic or Latino (of any race)	60.6
Central American, ex. Mexican	72.4
Guatemalan	56.6
Honduran	55.6
Nicaraguan	74.6
Panamanian	76.2
Salvadoran	76.4
Cuban	64.2
Dominican Republic	51.0

Notes: (1) Percent of total population; (2) Percent of Hispanic/Latino population; Profiles include places with an overall population of at least 125,000, OR an overall population of at least 25,000 where the Hispanic/Latino population is at least 20% of the overall population. In states where less than five places meet either of these criteria, we have included places with at least 10,000 total population with the highest percentage of Hispanic/Latino population. These places are identified with an asterisk (*); Please refer to the User's Guide for a full explanation of data.

Mexican	60.4
Puerto Rican	62.1
South American	67.6
Argentinean	85.7
Colombian	62.8
Ecuadorian	74.4
Peruvian	65.5
Spaniard	66.4

Median Home Value

Group	Dollars
Total Population	123,400
Hispanic or Latino (of any race)	103,500
Central American, ex. Mexican	122,300
Salvadoran	118,200
Mexican	99,200
Puerto Rican	158,600

Median Gross Rent

Group	Dollars
Total Population	858
Hispanic or Latino (of any race)	799
Central American, ex. Mexican	942
Salvadoran	880
Mexican	784
Puerto Rican	645

Median Household Income
(2010 Inflation-Adjusted Dollars)

Group	Dollars
Total Population	51,368
Hispanic or Latino (of any race)	42,692
Central American, ex. Mexican	43,611
Salvadoran	43,250
Mexican	41,568
Puerto Rican	51,000

Per Capita Income
(2010 Inflation-Adjusted Dollars)

Group	Dollars
Total Population	21,412
Hispanic or Latino (of any race)	14,030
Central American, ex. Mexican	14,113
Salvadoran	15,182
Mexican	13,562
Puerto Rican	14,462

Households with $100,000+ Income

Group	Number	%
Total Population	9,304	16.9
Hispanic or Latino (of any race)	1,429	7.9
Central American, ex. Mexican	69	6.2
Salvadoran	69	9.8
Mexican	1,074	7.1
Puerto Rican	40	13.3

Households with Food Stamps/SNAP Benefits During Past 12 Months

Group	Number	%
Total Population	5,567	10.1
Hispanic or Latino (of any race)	2,225	12.3
Central American, ex. Mexican	39	3.5
Salvadoran	39	5.5
Mexican	2,023	13.4
Puerto Rican	67	22.3

Poverty Rate
(Income in Past 12 Months Below Poverty Level)

Group	%
Total Population	14.6
Hispanic or Latino (of any race)	19.7
Central American, ex. Mexican	12.5
Salvadoran	16.1
Mexican	20.5
Puerto Rican	29.1

Greenville

Population

Group	Number	%TP[1]	%HP[2]
Total Population	25,557	100.0	–
Hispanic or Latino (of any race)	5,733	22.4	100.0
Central American, ex. Mexican	134	0.5	2.3
Mexican	5,139	20.1	89.6

Population Growth: 2000–2010

Group	%
Total Population	6.7
Hispanic or Latino (of any race)	63.3
Mexican	71.9

Males per 100 Females

Group	Number
Total Population	94.9
Hispanic or Latino (of any race)	115.5
Central American, ex. Mexican	119.7
Mexican	115.6

Average Household Size

Group	People
Total Population	2.56
Hispanic or Latino (of any race)	3.78
Central American, ex. Mexican	4.35
Mexican	3.84

Median Age

Group	Years
Total Population	34.0
Hispanic or Latino (of any race)	23.1
Central American, ex. Mexican	26.2
Mexican	22.8

High School Graduates
(Universe: Population 25 Years and Over)

Group	Number	%
Total Population	12,286	77.1
Hispanic or Latino (of any race)	1,057	39.6
Mexican	943	37.5

Four-Year College Graduates
(Universe: Population 25 Years and Over)

Group	Number	%
Total Population	2,966	18.6
Hispanic or Latino (of any race)	89	3.3
Mexican	63	2.5

Population Age 3–17 Enrolled in Public School
(Universe: Population Age 3–17 Enrolled in School)

Group	Number	%
Total Population	5,064	96.5
Hispanic or Latino (of any race)	1,799	99.6
Mexican	1,653	99.5

Population Age 3–17 Enrolled in Private School
(Universe: Population Age 3–17 Enrolled in School)

Group	Number	%
Total Population	185	3.5
Hispanic or Latino (of any race)	8	0.4
Mexican	8	0.5

Foreign-Born Population

Group	Number	%
Total Population	2,484	9.8
Hispanic or Latino (of any race)	2,025	35.2
Mexican	1,999	37.3

Foreign-Born Naturalized U.S. Citizens

Group	Number	%
Total Population	644	25.9
Hispanic or Latino (of any race)	350	17.3
Mexican	341	17.1

Language Spoken at Home: English Only
(Universe: Population 5 Years and Over)

Group	Number	%
Total Population	18,425	80.2
Hispanic or Latino (of any race)	1,022	20.0
Mexican	864	18.2

Language Spoken at Home: Spanish
(Universe: Population 5 Years and Over)

Group	Number	%
Total Population	4,279	18.6
Hispanic or Latino (of any race)	4,077	80.0
Mexican	3,878	81.8

Unemployment Rate
(Universe: Population 16 Years and Over)

Group	%
Total Population	7.8
Hispanic or Latino (of any race)	9.6
Mexican	9.9

Class of Worker: Private Wage and Salary
(Universe: Civilian Employed Population 16 Years and Over)

Group	Number	%
Total Population	7,739	79.1
Hispanic or Latino (of any race)	2,012	91.1
Mexican	1,940	91.4

Class of Worker: Government
(Universe: Civilian Employed Population 16 Years and Over)

Group	Number	%
Total Population	1,550	15.8
Hispanic or Latino (of any race)	112	5.1
Mexican	112	5.3

Means of Transportation to Work: Car, Truck or Van
(Universe: Workers 16 Years and Over)

Group	Number	%
Total Population	9,195	95.0
Hispanic or Latino (of any race)	2,078	94.3
Mexican	2,006	94.7

Means of Transportation to Work: Public Transportation (ex. Taxicab)
(Universe: Workers 16 Years and Over)

Group	Number	%
Total Population	55	0.6
Hispanic or Latino (of any race)	0	0.0
Mexican	0	0.0

Homeownership Rate
(Universe: Occupied Housing Units)

Group	%
Total Population	52.8
Hispanic or Latino (of any race)	55.6
Central American, ex. Mexican	64.9
Mexican	56.4

Median Home Value

Group	Dollars
Total Population	79,200
Hispanic or Latino (of any race)	44,800
Mexican	43,600

Median Gross Rent

Group	Dollars
Total Population	702
Hispanic or Latino (of any race)	633
Mexican	637

Median Household Income
(2010 Inflation-Adjusted Dollars)

Group	Dollars
Total Population	36,224
Hispanic or Latino (of any race)	29,289
Mexican	29,203

Per Capita Income
(2010 Inflation-Adjusted Dollars)

Group	Dollars
Total Population	19,274
Hispanic or Latino (of any race)	9,695
Mexican	9,869

Households with $100,000+ Income

Group	Number	%
Total Population	975	11.0
Hispanic or Latino (of any race)	65	5.5
Mexican	65	5.8

Households with Food Stamps/SNAP Benefits During Past 12 Months

Group	Number	%
Total Population	1,507	17.0
Hispanic or Latino (of any race)	317	26.6
Mexican	302	26.9

Poverty Rate
(Income in Past 12 Months Below Poverty Level)

Group	%
Total Population	27.1
Hispanic or Latino (of any race)	35.8
Mexican	35.3

Notes: (1) Percent of total population; (2) Percent of Hispanic/Latino population; Profiles include places with an overall population of at least 125,000, OR an overall population of at least 25,000 where the Hispanic/Latino population is at least 20% of the overall population. In states where less than five places meet either of these criteria, we have included places with at least 10,000 total population with the highest percentage of Hispanic/Latino population. These places are identified with an asterisk (*); Please refer to the User's Guide for a full explanation of data.

Haltom City

Population

Group	Number	%TP[1]	%HP[2]
Total Population	42,409	100.0	–
Hispanic or Latino (of any race)	16,515	38.9	100.0
Central American, ex. Mexican	681	1.6	4.1
Honduran	125	0.3	0.8
Salvadoran	422	1.0	2.6
Mexican	14,291	33.7	86.5
Puerto Rican	231	0.5	1.4
South American	131	0.3	0.8

Population Growth: 2000–2010

Group	%
Total Population	8.7
Hispanic or Latino (of any race)	112.5
Central American, ex. Mexican	320.4
Mexican	134.8
Puerto Rican	40.9

Males per 100 Females

Group	Number
Total Population	101.2
Hispanic or Latino (of any race)	107.7
Central American, ex. Mexican	110.8
Honduran	111.9
Salvadoran	105.9
Mexican	108.9
Puerto Rican	84.8
South American	74.7

Average Household Size

Group	People
Total Population	2.77
Hispanic or Latino (of any race)	3.74
Central American, ex. Mexican	3.95
Honduran	4.43
Salvadoran	4.16
Mexican	3.82
Puerto Rican	2.47
South American	2.54

Median Age

Group	Years
Total Population	31.7
Hispanic or Latino (of any race)	23.9
Central American, ex. Mexican	29.0
Honduran	24.9
Salvadoran	28.0
Mexican	23.4
Puerto Rican	27.5
South American	32.3

High School Graduates
(Universe: Population 25 Years and Over)

Group	Number	%
Total Population	19,051	73.5
Hispanic or Latino (of any race)	3,913	53.1
Mexican	3,228	50.8

Four-Year College Graduates
(Universe: Population 25 Years and Over)

Group	Number	%
Total Population	3,584	13.8
Hispanic or Latino (of any race)	671	9.1
Mexican	511	8.0

Population Age 3–17 Enrolled in Public School
(Universe: Population Age 3–17 Enrolled in School)

Group	Number	%
Total Population	7,271	90.4
Hispanic or Latino (of any race)	3,771	97.9
Mexican	3,421	98.6

Population Age 3–17 Enrolled in Private School
(Universe: Population Age 3–17 Enrolled in School)

Group	Number	%
Total Population	772	9.6
Hispanic or Latino (of any race)	82	2.1
Mexican	48	1.4

Foreign-Born Population

Group	Number	%
Total Population	9,486	22.8
Hispanic or Latino (of any race)	6,741	45.1
Mexican	6,215	46.8

Foreign-Born Naturalized U.S. Citizens

Group	Number	%
Total Population	2,560	27.0
Hispanic or Latino (of any race)	879	13.0
Mexican	733	11.8

Language Spoken at Home: English Only
(Universe: Population 5 Years and Over)

Group	Number	%
Total Population	23,450	61.9
Hispanic or Latino (of any race)	1,934	15.1
Mexican	1,643	14.5

Language Spoken at Home: Spanish
(Universe: Population 5 Years and Over)

Group	Number	%
Total Population	11,159	29.5
Hispanic or Latino (of any race)	10,906	84.9
Mexican	9,703	85.5

Unemployment Rate
(Universe: Population 16 Years and Over)

Group	%
Total Population	8.7
Hispanic or Latino (of any race)	6.9
Mexican	6.3

Class of Worker: Private Wage and Salary
(Universe: Civilian Employed Population 16 Years and Over)

Group	Number	%
Total Population	17,519	87.9
Hispanic or Latino (of any race)	6,336	91.7
Mexican	5,638	92.2

Class of Worker: Government
(Universe: Civilian Employed Population 16 Years and Over)

Group	Number	%
Total Population	1,681	8.4
Hispanic or Latino (of any race)	349	5.1
Mexican	268	4.4

Means of Transportation to Work: Car, Truck or Van
(Universe: Workers 16 Years and Over)

Group	Number	%
Total Population	18,181	93.3
Hispanic or Latino (of any race)	6,119	90.2
Mexican	5,386	89.4

Means of Transportation to Work: Public Transportation (ex. Taxicab)
(Universe: Workers 16 Years and Over)

Group	Number	%
Total Population	42	0.2
Hispanic or Latino (of any race)	17	0.3
Mexican	17	0.3

Homeownership Rate
(Universe: Occupied Housing Units)

Group	%
Total Population	55.0
Hispanic or Latino (of any race)	50.0
Central American, ex. Mexican	55.7
Honduran	52.2
Salvadoran	57.1
Mexican	50.8
Puerto Rican	34.9
South American	42.3

Median Home Value

Group	Dollars
Total Population	88,000
Hispanic or Latino (of any race)	82,600
Mexican	82,200

Median Gross Rent

Group	Dollars
Total Population	759
Hispanic or Latino (of any race)	716
Mexican	724

Median Household Income
(2010 Inflation-Adjusted Dollars)

Group	Dollars
Total Population	41,215
Hispanic or Latino (of any race)	35,329
Mexican	36,090

Per Capita Income
(2010 Inflation-Adjusted Dollars)

Group	Dollars
Total Population	19,228
Hispanic or Latino (of any race)	11,823
Mexican	11,403

Households with $100,000+ Income

Group	Number	%
Total Population	1,516	9.9
Hispanic or Latino (of any race)	140	3.3
Mexican	108	3.0

Households with Food Stamps/SNAP Benefits During Past 12 Months

Group	Number	%
Total Population	1,324	8.6
Hispanic or Latino (of any race)	412	9.8
Mexican	337	9.4

Poverty Rate
(Income in Past 12 Months Below Poverty Level)

Group	%
Total Population	17.1
Hispanic or Latino (of any race)	28.5
Mexican	28.6

Harlingen

Population

Group	Number	%TP[1]	%HP[2]
Total Population	64,849	100.0	–
Hispanic or Latino (of any race)	51,581	79.5	100.0
Central American, ex. Mexican	428	0.7	0.8
Salvadoran	166	0.3	0.3
Mexican	45,357	69.9	87.9
Puerto Rican	292	0.5	0.6
South American	187	0.3	0.4
Spaniard	216	0.3	0.4

Population Growth: 2000–2010

Group	%
Total Population	12.7
Hispanic or Latino (of any race)	23.2
Central American, ex. Mexican	170.9
Mexican	42.1
Puerto Rican	21.2

Males per 100 Females

Group	Number
Total Population	91.6
Hispanic or Latino (of any race)	91.0
Central American, ex. Mexican	104.8
Salvadoran	121.3
Mexican	91.1
Puerto Rican	100.0
South American	81.6
Spaniard	72.8

Average Household Size

Group	People
Total Population	2.95
Hispanic or Latino (of any race)	3.24
Central American, ex. Mexican	3.36
Salvadoran	3.45
Mexican	3.24
Puerto Rican	3.01
South American	3.07
Spaniard	3.11

Median Age

Group	Years
Total Population	32.8
Hispanic or Latino (of any race)	28.8
Central American, ex. Mexican	26.0
Salvadoran	23.0
Mexican	29.2

Notes: (1) Percent of total population; (2) Percent of Hispanic/Latino population; Profiles include places with an overall population of at least 125,000, OR an overall population of at least 25,000 where the Hispanic/Latino population is at least 20% of the overall population. In states where less than five places meet either of these criteria, we have included places with at least 10,000 total population with the highest percentage of Hispanic/Latino population. These places are identified with an asterisk (*); Please refer to the User's Guide for a full explanation of data.

Group		%
Puerto Rican		30.5
South American		33.3
Spaniard		31.7

High School Graduates
(Universe: Population 25 Years and Over)

Group	Number	%
Total Population	28,782	72.9
Hispanic or Latino (of any race)	18,754	65.7
Mexican	17,713	65.6

Four-Year College Graduates
(Universe: Population 25 Years and Over)

Group	Number	%
Total Population	7,319	18.5
Hispanic or Latino (of any race)	3,607	12.6
Mexican	3,245	12.0

Population Age 3–17 Enrolled in Public School
(Universe: Population Age 3–17 Enrolled in School)

Group	Number	%
Total Population	13,101	92.8
Hispanic or Latino (of any race)	11,338	96.8
Mexican	10,735	96.9

Population Age 3–17 Enrolled in Private School
(Universe: Population Age 3–17 Enrolled in School)

Group	Number	%
Total Population	1,019	7.2
Hispanic or Latino (of any race)	379	3.2
Mexican	339	3.1

Foreign-Born Population

Group	Number	%
Total Population	10,651	16.6
Hispanic or Latino (of any race)	9,460	19.2
Mexican	8,912	19.1

Foreign-Born Naturalized U.S. Citizens

Group	Number	%
Total Population	4,086	38.4
Hispanic or Latino (of any race)	3,610	38.2
Mexican	3,360	37.7

Language Spoken at Home: English Only
(Universe: Population 5 Years and Over)

Group	Number	%
Total Population	32,240	54.9
Hispanic or Latino (of any race)	19,849	44.4
Mexican	19,166	45.4

Language Spoken at Home: Spanish
(Universe: Population 5 Years and Over)

Group	Number	%
Total Population	25,535	43.5
Hispanic or Latino (of any race)	24,816	55.5
Mexican	23,061	54.6

Unemployment Rate
(Universe: Population 16 Years and Over)

Group	%
Total Population	6.3
Hispanic or Latino (of any race)	7.1
Mexican	6.5

Class of Worker: Private Wage and Salary
(Universe: Civilian Employed Population 16 Years and Over)

Group	Number	%
Total Population	15,977	70.3
Hispanic or Latino (of any race)	12,427	70.6
Mexican	11,713	70.4

Class of Worker: Government
(Universe: Civilian Employed Population 16 Years and Over)

Group	Number	%
Total Population	5,095	22.4
Hispanic or Latino (of any race)	4,019	22.8
Mexican	3,885	23.3

Means of Transportation to Work: Car, Truck or Van
(Universe: Workers 16 Years and Over)

Group	Number	%
Total Population	21,322	95.2
Hispanic or Latino (of any race)	16,469	95.1
Mexican	15,644	95.3

Means of Transportation to Work: Public Transportation (ex. Taxicab)
(Universe: Workers 16 Years and Over)

Group	Number	%
Total Population	12	0.1
Hispanic or Latino (of any race)	12	0.1
Mexican	12	0.1

Homeownership Rate
(Universe: Occupied Housing Units)

Group	%
Total Population	60.4
Hispanic or Latino (of any race)	55.7
Central American, ex. Mexican	50.8
Salvadoran	50.0
Mexican	56.6
Puerto Rican	53.7
South American	51.9
Spaniard	59.7

Median Home Value

Group	Dollars
Total Population	75,500
Hispanic or Latino (of any race)	69,300
Mexican	68,100

Median Gross Rent

Group	Dollars
Total Population	641
Hispanic or Latino (of any race)	622
Mexican	621

Median Household Income
(2010 Inflation-Adjusted Dollars)

Group	Dollars
Total Population	34,748
Hispanic or Latino (of any race)	30,337
Mexican	29,800

Per Capita Income
(2010 Inflation-Adjusted Dollars)

Group	Dollars
Total Population	17,330
Hispanic or Latino (of any race)	13,456
Mexican	13,201

Households with $100,000+ Income

Group	Number	%
Total Population	2,385	11.1
Hispanic or Latino (of any race)	1,240	8.2
Mexican	1,065	7.5

Households with Food Stamps/SNAP Benefits During Past 12 Months

Group	Number	%
Total Population	3,973	18.5
Hispanic or Latino (of any race)	3,676	24.3
Mexican	3,393	23.9

Poverty Rate
(Income in Past 12 Months Below Poverty Level)

Group	%
Total Population	31.1
Hispanic or Latino (of any race)	37.2
Mexican	37.7

Houston

Population

Group	Number	%TP[1]	%HP[2]
Total Population	2,099,451	100.0	–
Hispanic or Latino (of any race)	919,668	43.8	100.0
Central American, ex. Mexican	140,815	6.7	15.3
Costa Rican	923	<0.1	0.1
Guatemalan	25,205	1.2	2.7
Honduran	32,807	1.6	3.6
Nicaraguan	4,226	0.2	0.5
Panamanian	1,076	0.1	0.1
Salvadoran	75,907	3.6	8.3
Cuban	7,663	0.4	0.8
Dominican Republic	1,876	0.1	0.2
Mexican	673,093	32.1	73.2
Puerto Rican	9,290	0.4	1.0
South American	24,040	1.1	2.6
Argentinean	2,440	0.1	0.3
Bolivian	958	<0.1	0.1
Chilean	934	<0.1	0.1
Colombian	10,226	0.5	1.1
Ecuadorian	1,557	0.1	0.2
Paraguayan	119	<0.1	<0.1
Peruvian	3,237	0.2	0.4
Uruguayan	642	<0.1	0.1
Venezuelan	3,770	0.2	0.4
Spaniard	5,674	0.3	0.6

Population Growth: 2000–2010

Group	%
Total Population	7.5
Hispanic or Latino (of any race)	25.8
Central American, ex. Mexican	132.2
Costa Rican	62.8
Guatemalan	249.1
Honduran	219.0
Nicaraguan	92.4
Panamanian	35.9
Salvadoran	106.3
Cuban	54.2
Dominican Republic	89.5
Mexican	27.6
Puerto Rican	34.5
South American	81.9
Argentinean	94.3
Bolivian	99.6
Chilean	58.0
Colombian	75.7
Ecuadorian	80.2
Peruvian	95.5
Uruguayan	179.1
Venezuelan	136.8
Spaniard	422.5

Males per 100 Females

Group	Number
Total Population	100.7
Hispanic or Latino (of any race)	109.1
Central American, ex. Mexican	121.0
Costa Rican	96.8
Guatemalan	185.3
Honduran	123.6
Nicaraguan	105.0
Panamanian	76.7
Salvadoran	106.4
Cuban	110.3
Dominican Republic	95.4
Mexican	108.1
Puerto Rican	98.9
South American	90.2
Argentinean	104.7
Bolivian	89.3
Chilean	102.6
Colombian	85.9
Ecuadorian	97.3
Paraguayan	91.9
Peruvian	95.8
Uruguayan	105.1
Venezuelan	81.4
Spaniard	98.8

Average Household Size

Group	People
Total Population	2.64
Hispanic or Latino (of any race)	3.48
Central American, ex. Mexican	3.67
Costa Rican	2.67
Guatemalan	3.74
Honduran	3.64
Nicaraguan	3.24
Panamanian	2.24
Salvadoran	3.73
Cuban	2.38
Dominican Republic	2.76
Mexican	3.57
Puerto Rican	2.50
South American	2.44
Argentinean	2.31
Bolivian	2.50
Chilean	2.43
Colombian	2.43
Ecuadorian	2.65

Notes: (1) Percent of total population; (2) Percent of Hispanic/Latino population; Profiles include places with an overall population of at least 125,000, OR an overall population of at least 25,000 where the Hispanic/Latino population is at least 20% of the overall population. In states where less than five places meet either of these criteria, we have included places with at least 10,000 total population with the highest percentage of Hispanic/Latino population. These places are identified with an asterisk (*); Please refer to the User's Guide for a full explanation of data.

Paraguayan	2.65
Peruvian	2.56
Uruguayan	2.65
Venezuelan	2.33
Spaniard	2.54

Median Age

Group	Years
Total Population	32.1
Hispanic or Latino (of any race)	27.1
Central American, ex. Mexican	30.2
Costa Rican	33.8
Guatemalan	28.7
Honduran	28.8
Nicaraguan	33.2
Panamanian	37.0
Salvadoran	31.4
Cuban	38.0
Dominican Republic	30.2
Mexican	26.1
Puerto Rican	29.2
South American	35.7
Argentinean	36.9
Bolivian	37.1
Chilean	38.6
Colombian	35.0
Ecuadorian	36.6
Paraguayan	34.8
Peruvian	37.7
Uruguayan	36.0
Venezuelan	34.2
Spaniard	31.7

High School Graduates
(Universe: Population 25 Years and Over)

Group	Number	%
Total Population	964,136	74.0
Hispanic or Latino (of any race)	228,927	48.4
Central American, ex. Mexican	28,945	34.7
Guatemalan	4,771	33.3
Honduran	5,399	30.1
Nicaraguan	1,828	68.6
Panamanian	557	98.2
Salvadoran	15,574	33.4
Cuban	3,705	80.0
Dominican Republic	642	66.9
Mexican	167,887	48.2
Puerto Rican	3,918	82.3
South American	14,007	86.6
Argentinean	1,400	94.7
Colombian	5,507	80.6
Ecuadorian	1,023	77.9
Peruvian	1,989	95.0
Venezuelan	2,587	96.8
Spaniard	2,250	83.9

Four-Year College Graduates
(Universe: Population 25 Years and Over)

Group	Number	%
Total Population	367,369	28.2
Hispanic or Latino (of any race)	44,661	9.4
Central American, ex. Mexican	4,131	5.0
Guatemalan	707	4.9
Honduran	513	2.9
Nicaraguan	545	20.5
Panamanian	308	54.3
Salvadoran	1,997	4.3
Cuban	1,586	34.3
Dominican Republic	212	22.1
Mexican	27,680	7.9
Puerto Rican	1,703	35.8
South American	7,143	44.2
Argentinean	770	52.1
Colombian	2,764	40.5
Ecuadorian	474	36.1
Peruvian	859	41.0
Venezuelan	1,628	60.9
Spaniard	959	35.8

Population Age 3–17 Enrolled in Public School
(Universe: Population Age 3–17 Enrolled in School)

Group	Number	%
Total Population	351,293	90.9
Hispanic or Latino (of any race)	193,971	95.9
Central American, ex. Mexican	25,373	97.5
Guatemalan	3,408	92.8
Honduran	5,193	98.3
Nicaraguan	602	94.5
Panamanian	32	100.0
Salvadoran	15,767	98.9
Cuban	1,001	90.3
Dominican Republic	320	100.0
Mexican	156,603	96.3
Puerto Rican	1,023	84.6
South American	3,440	84.2
Argentinean	123	72.8
Colombian	1,893	85.8
Ecuadorian	124	69.3
Peruvian	460	86.0
Venezuelan	456	82.9
Spaniard	607	88.9

Population Age 3–17 Enrolled in Private School
(Universe: Population Age 3–17 Enrolled in School)

Group	Number	%
Total Population	35,124	9.1
Hispanic or Latino (of any race)	8,229	4.1
Central American, ex. Mexican	639	2.5
Guatemalan	264	7.2
Honduran	88	1.7
Nicaraguan	35	5.5
Panamanian	0	0.0
Salvadoran	174	1.1
Cuban	108	9.7
Dominican Republic	0	0.0
Mexican	6,001	3.7
Puerto Rican	186	15.4
South American	646	15.8
Argentinean	46	27.2
Colombian	314	14.2
Ecuadorian	55	30.7
Peruvian	75	14.0
Venezuelan	94	17.1
Spaniard	76	11.1

Foreign-Born Population

Group	Number	%
Total Population	585,384	28.3
Hispanic or Latino (of any race)	419,487	47.8
Central American, ex. Mexican	101,903	72.1
Guatemalan	18,862	77.1
Honduran	24,490	76.2
Nicaraguan	2,713	71.6
Panamanian	490	64.6
Salvadoran	53,870	69.0
Cuban	4,292	65.5
Dominican Republic	1,022	60.0
Mexican	288,572	43.1
Puerto Rican	224	3.1
South American	16,591	69.9
Argentinean	1,371	74.8
Colombian	7,226	66.9
Ecuadorian	1,145	66.9
Peruvian	2,375	76.5
Venezuelan	2,777	73.7
Spaniard	867	21.0

Foreign-Born Naturalized U.S. Citizens

Group	Number	%
Total Population	157,725	26.9
Hispanic or Latino (of any race)	82,055	19.6
Central American, ex. Mexican	17,203	16.9
Guatemalan	2,455	13.0
Honduran	1,302	5.3
Nicaraguan	897	33.1
Panamanian	360	73.5
Salvadoran	11,623	21.6
Cuban	1,934	45.1
Dominican Republic	376	36.8
Mexican	54,439	18.9
Puerto Rican	84	37.5
South American	5,571	33.6
Argentinean	411	30.0
Colombian	2,843	39.3
Ecuadorian	529	46.2
Peruvian	868	36.5
Venezuelan	408	14.7
Spaniard	362	41.8

Language Spoken at Home: English Only
(Universe: Population 5 Years and Over)

Group	Number	%
Total Population	1,037,557	54.7
Hispanic or Latino (of any race)	101,069	12.9
Central American, ex. Mexican	4,712	3.7
Guatemalan	1,090	4.9
Honduran	828	2.9
Nicaraguan	371	10.5
Panamanian	186	26.5
Salvadoran	2,072	2.9
Cuban	1,038	16.6
Dominican Republic	276	17.7
Mexican	82,309	13.9
Puerto Rican	1,900	28.2
South American	2,481	11.2
Argentinean	113	6.6
Colombian	1,223	11.9
Ecuadorian	246	15.8
Peruvian	256	9.2
Venezuelan	250	7.2
Spaniard	2,030	54.8

Language Spoken at Home: Spanish
(Universe: Population 5 Years and Over)

Group	Number	%
Total Population	705,212	37.2
Hispanic or Latino (of any race)	678,076	86.8
Central American, ex. Mexican	123,434	96.1
Guatemalan	21,165	94.6
Honduran	27,464	96.6
Nicaraguan	3,163	89.5
Panamanian	495	70.6
Salvadoran	69,370	97.1
Cuban	5,182	82.8
Dominican Republic	1,271	81.6
Mexican	507,476	85.9
Puerto Rican	4,779	70.9
South American	19,564	88.2
Argentinean	1,590	93.4
Colombian	9,021	87.6
Ecuadorian	1,302	83.7
Peruvian	2,526	90.5
Venezuelan	3,196	91.8
Spaniard	1,555	42.0

Unemployment Rate
(Universe: Population 16 Years and Over)

Group	%
Total Population	8.0
Hispanic or Latino (of any race)	7.6
Central American, ex. Mexican	8.2
Guatemalan	5.9
Honduran	10.8
Nicaraguan	0.9
Panamanian	7.9
Salvadoran	8.4
Cuban	9.4
Dominican Republic	10.3
Mexican	7.4
Puerto Rican	9.8
South American	5.7
Argentinean	4.1
Colombian	5.7
Ecuadorian	0.0
Peruvian	6.9
Venezuelan	5.8
Spaniard	3.6

Class of Worker: Private Wage and Salary
(Universe: Civilian Employed Population 16 Years and Over)

Group	Number	%
Total Population	814,576	82.3
Hispanic or Latino (of any race)	339,773	85.1
Central American, ex. Mexican	68,699	88.1
Guatemalan	12,750	86.2
Honduran	15,092	88.4
Nicaraguan	2,058	84.8
Panamanian	422	86.3
Salvadoran	37,477	88.8
Cuban	2,734	84.3
Dominican Republic	715	83.2
Mexican	244,474	84.8
Puerto Rican	3,177	82.8
South American	9,922	78.3

Notes: (1) Percent of total population; (2) Percent of Hispanic/Latino population; Profiles include places with an overall population of at least 125,000, OR an overall population of at least 25,000 where the Hispanic/Latino population is at least 20% of the overall population. In states where less than five places meet either of these criteria, we have included places with at least 10,000 total population with the highest percentage of Hispanic/Latino population. These places are identified with an asterisk (*); Please refer to the User's Guide for a full explanation of data.

Argentinean	1,012	80.8
Colombian	3,884	72.7
Ecuadorian	744	85.5
Peruvian	1,384	86.8
Venezuelan	1,852	82.1
Spaniard	1,840	77.8

Class of Worker: Government
(Universe: Civilian Employed Population 16 Years and Over)

Group	Number	%
Total Population	100,160	10.1
Hispanic or Latino (of any race)	23,000	5.8
Central American, ex. Mexican	1,530	2.0
Guatemalan	172	1.2
Honduran	171	1.0
Nicaraguan	129	5.3
Panamanian	57	11.7
Salvadoran	1,001	2.4
Cuban	368	11.3
Dominican Republic	27	3.1
Mexican	18,377	6.4
Puerto Rican	436	11.4
South American	1,311	10.3
Argentinean	76	6.1
Colombian	583	10.9
Ecuadorian	77	8.9
Peruvian	144	9.0
Venezuelan	217	9.6
Spaniard	281	11.9

Means of Transportation to Work: Car, Truck or Van
(Universe: Workers 16 Years and Over)

Group	Number	%
Total Population	849,617	87.7
Hispanic or Latino (of any race)	342,430	87.6
Central American, ex. Mexican	64,555	84.4
Guatemalan	10,723	73.1
Honduran	14,172	85.3
Nicaraguan	2,076	87.6
Panamanian	428	90.3
Salvadoran	36,264	87.7
Cuban	2,922	91.8
Dominican Republic	681	79.8
Mexican	249,848	88.4
Puerto Rican	3,332	88.1
South American	10,895	89.6
Argentinean	1,026	84.5
Colombian	4,468	88.7
Ecuadorian	800	94.1
Peruvian	1,369	87.5
Venezuelan	1,943	91.3
Spaniard	2,160	92.4

Means of Transportation to Work: Public Transportation (ex. Taxicab)
(Universe: Workers 16 Years and Over)

Group	Number	%
Total Population	46,403	4.8
Hispanic or Latino (of any race)	18,986	4.9
Central American, ex. Mexican	5,672	7.4
Guatemalan	1,630	11.1
Honduran	1,024	6.2
Nicaraguan	104	4.4
Panamanian	7	1.5
Salvadoran	2,862	6.9
Cuban	105	3.3
Dominican Republic	48	5.6
Mexican	11,923	4.2
Puerto Rican	138	3.6
South American	290	2.4
Argentinean	80	6.6
Colombian	119	2.4
Ecuadorian	0	0.0
Peruvian	22	1.4
Venezuelan	25	1.2
Spaniard	64	2.7

Homeownership Rate
(Universe: Occupied Housing Units)

Group	%
Total Population	45.4
Hispanic or Latino (of any race)	38.6
Central American, ex. Mexican	29.9
Costa Rican	39.2
Guatemalan	17.9
Honduran	16.8
Nicaraguan	31.2
Panamanian	39.9
Salvadoran	38.6
Cuban	35.8
Dominican Republic	28.6
Mexican	41.4
Puerto Rican	31.8
South American	40.2
Argentinean	45.1
Bolivian	52.2
Chilean	48.8
Colombian	36.4
Ecuadorian	44.0
Paraguayan	58.1
Peruvian	41.6
Uruguayan	33.9
Venezuelan	40.2
Spaniard	44.6

Median Home Value

Group	Dollars
Total Population	123,800
Hispanic or Latino (of any race)	98,200
Central American, ex. Mexican	103,900
Guatemalan	108,400
Honduran	89,800
Nicaraguan	116,200
Panamanian	137,500
Salvadoran	103,300
Cuban	129,300
Dominican Republic	117,400
Mexican	94,800
Puerto Rican	143,500
South American	145,600
Argentinean	164,400
Colombian	130,500
Ecuadorian	138,800
Peruvian	142,400
Venezuelan	216,600
Spaniard	144,700

Median Gross Rent

Group	Dollars
Total Population	793
Hispanic or Latino (of any race)	721
Central American, ex. Mexican	683
Guatemalan	683
Honduran	689
Nicaraguan	741
Panamanian	811
Salvadoran	671
Cuban	702
Dominican Republic	642
Mexican	721
Puerto Rican	848
South American	873
Argentinean	848
Colombian	876
Ecuadorian	744
Peruvian	908
Venezuelan	945
Spaniard	963

Median Household Income
(2010 Inflation-Adjusted Dollars)

Group	Dollars
Total Population	42,962
Hispanic or Latino (of any race)	34,730
Central American, ex. Mexican	31,370
Guatemalan	28,099
Honduran	26,586
Nicaraguan	42,554
Panamanian	41,435
Salvadoran	33,819
Cuban	37,156
Dominican Republic	31,369
Mexican	34,707
Puerto Rican	42,317
South American	45,484
Argentinean	59,286
Colombian	41,973
Ecuadorian	34,762
Peruvian	36,868
Venezuelan	62,761
Spaniard	55,401

Per Capita Income
(2010 Inflation-Adjusted Dollars)

Group	Dollars
Total Population	25,927
Hispanic or Latino (of any race)	13,700
Central American, ex. Mexican	12,571
Guatemalan	12,276
Honduran	11,069
Nicaraguan	19,243
Panamanian	30,034
Salvadoran	12,669
Cuban	27,694
Dominican Republic	19,582
Mexican	13,086
Puerto Rican	25,789
South American	26,140
Argentinean	42,070
Colombian	21,910
Ecuadorian	24,071
Peruvian	25,092
Venezuelan	31,132
Spaniard	29,226

Households with $100,000+ Income

Group	Number	%
Total Population	136,800	17.9
Hispanic or Latino (of any race)	17,779	7.2
Central American, ex. Mexican	1,460	3.5
Guatemalan	278	3.7
Honduran	244	2.8
Nicaraguan	72	5.8
Panamanian	70	15.2
Salvadoran	704	3.0
Cuban	485	17.5
Dominican Republic	36	5.7
Mexican	12,497	6.9
Puerto Rican	562	17.3
South American	1,773	18.9
Argentinean	270	26.1
Colombian	606	16.0
Ecuadorian	117	15.6
Peruvian	154	12.7
Venezuelan	413	29.5
Spaniard	430	23.1

Households with Food Stamps/SNAP Benefits During Past 12 Months

Group	Number	%
Total Population	79,834	10.4
Hispanic or Latino (of any race)	30,923	12.5
Central American, ex. Mexican	3,913	9.3
Guatemalan	709	9.4
Honduran	1,181	13.4
Nicaraguan	110	8.8
Panamanian	49	10.6
Salvadoran	1,801	7.7
Cuban	409	14.8
Dominican Republic	91	14.3
Mexican	24,546	13.5
Puerto Rican	427	13.2
South American	628	6.7
Argentinean	74	7.1
Colombian	265	7.0
Ecuadorian	58	7.8
Peruvian	117	9.7
Venezuelan	50	3.6
Spaniard	157	8.4

Poverty Rate
(Income in Past 12 Months Below Poverty Level)

Group	%
Total Population	21.0
Hispanic or Latino (of any race)	26.6
Central American, ex. Mexican	27.5
Guatemalan	29.9
Honduran	38.7
Nicaraguan	13.3
Panamanian	10.4
Salvadoran	22.7
Cuban	16.5
Dominican Republic	24.0
Mexican	27.3

Notes: (1) Percent of total population; (2) Percent of Hispanic/Latino population; Profiles include places with an overall population of at least 125,000, OR an overall population of at least 25,000 where the Hispanic/Latino population is at least 20% of the overall population. In states where less than five places meet either of these criteria, we have included places with at least 10,000 total population with the highest percentage of Hispanic/Latino population. These places are identified with an asterisk (*); Please refer to the User's Guide for a full explanation of data.

Puerto Rican	15.2
South American	16.4
Argentinean	8.5
Colombian	20.1
Ecuadorian	28.9
Peruvian	15.1
Venezuelan	7.8
Spaniard	7.2

Hurst

Population

Group	Number	%TP[1]	%HP[2]
Total Population	37,337	100.0	–
Hispanic or Latino (of any race)	7,510	20.1	100.0
Central American, ex. Mexican	454	1.2	6.0
Salvadoran	282	0.8	3.8
Mexican	5,899	15.8	78.5
Puerto Rican	328	0.9	4.4
South American	141	0.4	1.9
Spaniard	111	0.3	1.5

Population Growth: 2000–2010

Group	%
Total Population	2.9
Hispanic or Latino (of any race)	87.8
Central American, ex. Mexican	269.1
Mexican	102.6
Puerto Rican	129.4

Males per 100 Females

Group	Number
Total Population	93.3
Hispanic or Latino (of any race)	105.5
Central American, ex. Mexican	109.2
Salvadoran	113.6
Mexican	108.4
Puerto Rican	96.4
South American	78.5
Spaniard	113.5

Average Household Size

Group	People
Total Population	2.53
Hispanic or Latino (of any race)	3.46
Central American, ex. Mexican	3.49
Salvadoran	3.66
Mexican	3.60
Puerto Rican	2.79
South American	2.63
Spaniard	2.74

Median Age

Group	Years
Total Population	38.8
Hispanic or Latino (of any race)	25.5
Central American, ex. Mexican	29.4
Salvadoran	28.7
Mexican	24.5
Puerto Rican	27.8
South American	34.3
Spaniard	31.8

High School Graduates
(Universe: Population 25 Years and Over)

Group	Number	%
Total Population	21,997	88.5
Hispanic or Latino (of any race)	2,025	60.0
Mexican	1,500	55.7

Four-Year College Graduates
(Universe: Population 25 Years and Over)

Group	Number	%
Total Population	6,926	27.9
Hispanic or Latino (of any race)	390	11.5
Mexican	268	10.0

Population Age 3–17 Enrolled in Public School
(Universe: Population Age 3–17 Enrolled in School)

Group	Number	%
Total Population	5,766	87.1
Hispanic or Latino (of any race)	1,965	100.0
Mexican	1,606	100.0

Population Age 3–17 Enrolled in Private School
(Universe: Population Age 3–17 Enrolled in School)

Group	Number	%
Total Population	852	12.9
Hispanic or Latino (of any race)	0	0.0
Mexican	0	0.0

Foreign-Born Population

Group	Number	%
Total Population	5,344	14.4
Hispanic or Latino (of any race)	3,434	44.4
Mexican	3,056	47.0

Foreign-Born Naturalized U.S. Citizens

Group	Number	%
Total Population	1,438	26.9
Hispanic or Latino (of any race)	400	11.6
Mexican	368	12.0

Language Spoken at Home: English Only
(Universe: Population 5 Years and Over)

Group	Number	%
Total Population	27,252	77.8
Hispanic or Latino (of any race)	1,262	19.0
Mexican	950	17.4

Language Spoken at Home: Spanish
(Universe: Population 5 Years and Over)

Group	Number	%
Total Population	6,216	17.7
Hispanic or Latino (of any race)	5,383	81.0
Mexican	4,496	82.6

Unemployment Rate
(Universe: Population 16 Years and Over)

Group	%
Total Population	6.7
Hispanic or Latino (of any race)	8.2
Mexican	9.4

Class of Worker: Private Wage and Salary
(Universe: Civilian Employed Population 16 Years and Over)

Group	Number	%
Total Population	15,309	82.3
Hispanic or Latino (of any race)	3,077	91.0
Mexican	2,345	90.0

Class of Worker: Government
(Universe: Civilian Employed Population 16 Years and Over)

Group	Number	%
Total Population	1,970	10.6
Hispanic or Latino (of any race)	201	5.9
Mexican	167	6.4

Means of Transportation to Work: Car, Truck or Van
(Universe: Workers 16 Years and Over)

Group	Number	%
Total Population	16,867	92.0
Hispanic or Latino (of any race)	3,020	88.6
Mexican	2,330	89.0

Means of Transportation to Work: Public Transportation (ex. Taxicab)
(Universe: Workers 16 Years and Over)

Group	Number	%
Total Population	93	0.5
Hispanic or Latino (of any race)	5	0.1
Mexican	0	0.0

Homeownership Rate
(Universe: Occupied Housing Units)

Group	%
Total Population	64.9
Hispanic or Latino (of any race)	34.7
Central American, ex. Mexican	24.8
Salvadoran	25.0
Mexican	34.8
Puerto Rican	33.9
South American	56.3
Spaniard	61.8

Median Home Value

Group	Dollars
Total Population	137,200
Hispanic or Latino (of any race)	99,500
Mexican	109,500

Median Gross Rent

Group	Dollars
Total Population	758
Hispanic or Latino (of any race)	767
Mexican	771

Median Household Income
(2010 Inflation-Adjusted Dollars)

Group	Dollars
Total Population	52,913
Hispanic or Latino (of any race)	38,910
Mexican	38,241

Per Capita Income
(2010 Inflation-Adjusted Dollars)

Group	Dollars
Total Population	27,744
Hispanic or Latino (of any race)	13,594
Mexican	12,189

Households with $100,000+ Income

Group	Number	%
Total Population	3,384	23.5
Hispanic or Latino (of any race)	221	12.8
Mexican	183	12.6

Households with Food Stamps/SNAP Benefits During Past 12 Months

Group	Number	%
Total Population	774	5.4
Hispanic or Latino (of any race)	244	14.1
Mexican	235	16.2

Poverty Rate
(Income in Past 12 Months Below Poverty Level)

Group	%
Total Population	10.9
Hispanic or Latino (of any race)	23.2
Mexican	26.2

Irving

Population

Group	Number	%TP[1]	%HP[2]
Total Population	216,290	100.0	–
Hispanic or Latino (of any race)	88,967	41.1	100.0
Central American, ex. Mexican	15,203	7.0	17.1
Guatemalan	644	0.3	0.7
Honduran	1,547	0.7	1.7
Nicaraguan	186	0.1	0.2
Panamanian	123	0.1	0.1
Salvadoran	12,544	5.8	14.1
Cuban	359	0.2	0.4
Dominican Republic	196	0.1	0.2
Mexican	64,396	29.8	72.4
Puerto Rican	1,176	0.5	1.3
South American	2,388	1.1	2.7
Argentinean	803	0.4	0.9
Colombian	456	0.2	0.5
Ecuadorian	136	0.1	0.2
Peruvian	538	0.2	0.6
Venezuelan	245	0.1	0.3
Spaniard	563	0.3	0.6

Population Growth: 2000–2010

Group	%
Total Population	12.9
Hispanic or Latino (of any race)	48.7
Central American, ex. Mexican	144.2
Guatemalan	191.4
Honduran	229.1
Salvadoran	145.9
Cuban	32.0
Mexican	52.2
Puerto Rican	73.2
South American	132.3
Argentinean	234.6
Colombian	76.7
Peruvian	197.2
Venezuelan	107.6
Spaniard	446.6

Notes: (1) Percent of total population; (2) Percent of Hispanic/Latino population; Profiles include places with an overall population of at least 125,000, OR an overall population of at least 25,000 where the Hispanic/Latino population is at least 20% of the overall population. In states where less than five places meet either of these criteria, we have included places with at least 10,000 total population with the highest percentage of Hispanic/Latino population. These places are identified with an asterisk (*); Please refer to the User's Guide for a full explanation of data.

Males per 100 Females

Group	Number
Total Population	100.0
Hispanic or Latino (of any race)	104.9
Central American, ex. Mexican	110.4
Guatemalan	128.4
Honduran	123.6
Nicaraguan	91.8
Panamanian	66.2
Salvadoran	109.0
Cuban	99.4
Dominican Republic	83.2
Mexican	104.7
Puerto Rican	95.7
South American	98.5
Argentinean	117.0
Colombian	82.4
Ecuadorian	106.1
Peruvian	93.5
Venezuelan	88.5
Spaniard	99.6

Average Household Size

Group	People
Total Population	2.61
Hispanic or Latino (of any race)	3.54
Central American, ex. Mexican	3.94
Guatemalan	3.92
Honduran	3.78
Nicaraguan	2.68
Panamanian	2.19
Salvadoran	4.03
Cuban	2.42
Dominican Republic	2.43
Mexican	3.56
Puerto Rican	2.39
South American	2.85
Argentinean	3.08
Colombian	2.48
Ecuadorian	2.88
Peruvian	3.06
Venezuelan	2.64
Spaniard	2.66

Median Age

Group	Years
Total Population	31.3
Hispanic or Latino (of any race)	25.9
Central American, ex. Mexican	29.7
Guatemalan	30.9
Honduran	28.9
Nicaraguan	39.5
Panamanian	36.3
Salvadoran	29.5
Cuban	32.9
Dominican Republic	31.0
Mexican	24.8
Puerto Rican	29.2
South American	33.7
Argentinean	33.0
Colombian	33.6
Ecuadorian	36.4
Peruvian	36.2
Venezuelan	32.2
Spaniard	31.5

High School Graduates
(Universe: Population 25 Years and Over)

Group	Number	%
Total Population	102,833	78.3
Hispanic or Latino (of any race)	21,284	50.2
Central American, ex. Mexican	2,647	32.1
Salvadoran	1,875	27.5
Mexican	15,286	50.9
Puerto Rican	571	93.6
South American	1,210	82.5

Four-Year College Graduates
(Universe: Population 25 Years and Over)

Group	Number	%
Total Population	42,750	32.6
Hispanic or Latino (of any race)	4,725	11.1
Central American, ex. Mexican	226	2.7
Salvadoran	112	1.6
Mexican	3,363	11.2
Puerto Rican	308	50.5
South American	475	32.4

Population Age 3–17 Enrolled in Public School
(Universe: Population Age 3–17 Enrolled in School)

Group	Number	%
Total Population	35,748	90.9
Hispanic or Latino (of any race)	21,094	95.5
Central American, ex. Mexican	3,484	96.9
Salvadoran	3,238	97.4
Mexican	16,123	95.4
Puerto Rican	135	100.0
South American	330	97.3

Population Age 3–17 Enrolled in Private School
(Universe: Population Age 3–17 Enrolled in School)

Group	Number	%
Total Population	3,596	9.1
Hispanic or Latino (of any race)	986	4.5
Central American, ex. Mexican	111	3.1
Salvadoran	85	2.6
Mexican	779	4.6
Puerto Rican	0	0.0
South American	9	2.7

Foreign-Born Population

Group	Number	%
Total Population	68,858	32.8
Hispanic or Latino (of any race)	40,533	47.6
Central American, ex. Mexican	10,017	66.0
Salvadoran	8,463	64.8
Mexican	28,020	44.6
Puerto Rican	66	5.5
South American	1,645	73.8

Foreign-Born Naturalized U.S. Citizens

Group	Number	%
Total Population	17,829	25.9
Hispanic or Latino (of any race)	7,332	18.1
Central American, ex. Mexican	1,494	14.9
Salvadoran	1,307	15.4
Mexican	5,072	18.1
Puerto Rican	0	0.0
South American	390	23.7

Language Spoken at Home: English Only
(Universe: Population 5 Years and Over)

Group	Number	%
Total Population	97,019	50.6
Hispanic or Latino (of any race)	10,476	13.9
Central American, ex. Mexican	347	2.6
Salvadoran	276	2.4
Mexican	8,040	14.6
Puerto Rican	228	21.5
South American	145	7.2

Language Spoken at Home: Spanish
(Universe: Population 5 Years and Over)

Group	Number	%
Total Population	66,861	34.9
Hispanic or Latino (of any race)	64,620	86.0
Central American, ex. Mexican	13,225	97.4
Salvadoran	11,441	97.6
Mexican	46,972	85.3
Puerto Rican	832	78.5
South American	1,858	92.8

Unemployment Rate
(Universe: Population 16 Years and Over)

Group	%
Total Population	8.2
Hispanic or Latino (of any race)	7.9
Central American, ex. Mexican	8.7
Salvadoran	9.2
Mexican	7.4
Puerto Rican	6.9
South American	5.9

Class of Worker: Private Wage and Salary
(Universe: Civilian Employed Population 16 Years and Over)

Group	Number	%
Total Population	94,490	87.3
Hispanic or Latino (of any race)	35,720	90.5
Central American, ex. Mexican	7,383	97.2
Salvadoran	6,088	97.0
Mexican	25,419	89.7
Puerto Rican	585	83.1
South American	1,165	84.5

Class of Worker: Government
(Universe: Civilian Employed Population 16 Years and Over)

Group	Number	%
Total Population	8,696	8.0
Hispanic or Latino (of any race)	2,320	5.9
Central American, ex. Mexican	128	1.7
Salvadoran	128	2.0
Mexican	1,747	6.2
Puerto Rican	119	16.9
South American	143	10.4

Means of Transportation to Work: Car, Truck or Van
(Universe: Workers 16 Years and Over)

Group	Number	%
Total Population	96,882	91.7
Hispanic or Latino (of any race)	36,012	93.6
Central American, ex. Mexican	7,058	95.6
Salvadoran	5,896	96.4
Mexican	25,682	93.1
Puerto Rican	593	86.4
South American	1,316	95.5

Means of Transportation to Work: Public Transportation (ex. Taxicab)
(Universe: Workers 16 Years and Over)

Group	Number	%
Total Population	2,138	2.0
Hispanic or Latino (of any race)	556	1.4
Central American, ex. Mexican	106	1.4
Salvadoran	74	1.2
Mexican	410	1.5
Puerto Rican	0	0.0
South American	0	0.0

Homeownership Rate
(Universe: Occupied Housing Units)

Group	%
Total Population	38.4
Hispanic or Latino (of any race)	34.2
Central American, ex. Mexican	37.4
Guatemalan	31.3
Honduran	22.1
Nicaraguan	35.2
Panamanian	24.1
Salvadoran	40.0
Cuban	32.6
Dominican Republic	27.6
Mexican	34.3
Puerto Rican	23.9
South American	33.8
Argentinean	26.3
Colombian	40.0
Ecuadorian	37.5
Peruvian	31.6
Venezuelan	39.6
Spaniard	39.1

Median Home Value

Group	Dollars
Total Population	136,500
Hispanic or Latino (of any race)	113,900
Central American, ex. Mexican	112,700
Salvadoran	111,800
Mexican	113,600
Puerto Rican	117,500
South American	153,700

Median Gross Rent

Group	Dollars
Total Population	847
Hispanic or Latino (of any race)	740
Central American, ex. Mexican	712
Salvadoran	711
Mexican	735
Puerto Rican	863
South American	861

Median Household Income
(2010 Inflation-Adjusted Dollars)

Group	Dollars
Total Population	47,248

Notes: (1) Percent of total population; (2) Percent of Hispanic/Latino population; Profiles include places with an overall population of at least 125,000, OR an overall population of at least 25,000 where the Hispanic/Latino population is at least 20% of the overall population. In states where less than five places meet either of these criteria, we have included places with at least 10,000 total population with the highest percentage of Hispanic/Latino population. These places are identified with an asterisk (*); Please refer to the User's Guide for a full explanation of data.

Group	Dollars
Hispanic or Latino (of any race)	35,859
Central American, ex. Mexican	33,251
Salvadoran	32,105
Mexican	36,212
Puerto Rican	33,958
South American	42,109

Per Capita Income
(2010 Inflation-Adjusted Dollars)

Group	Dollars
Total Population	26,016
Hispanic or Latino (of any race)	14,120
Central American, ex. Mexican	12,132
Salvadoran	11,627
Mexican	13,626
Puerto Rican	20,496
South American	20,134

Households with $100,000+ Income

Group	Number	%
Total Population	13,930	17.3
Hispanic or Latino (of any race)	1,442	6.0
Central American, ex. Mexican	204	4.7
Salvadoran	160	4.3
Mexican	990	5.9
Puerto Rican	58	10.4
South American	92	10.0

Households with Food Stamps/SNAP Benefits During Past 12 Months

Group	Number	%
Total Population	6,996	8.7
Hispanic or Latino (of any race)	3,197	13.4
Central American, ex. Mexican	499	11.5
Salvadoran	432	11.7
Mexican	2,343	13.9
Puerto Rican	158	28.3
South American	75	8.2

Poverty Rate
(Income in Past 12 Months Below Poverty Level)

Group	%
Total Population	16.4
Hispanic or Latino (of any race)	23.7
Central American, ex. Mexican	27.6
Salvadoran	28.7
Mexican	22.9
Puerto Rican	19.1
South American	15.6

Killeen

Population

Group	Number	%TP[1]	%HP[2]
Total Population	127,921	100.0	–
Hispanic or Latino (of any race)	29,345	22.9	100.0
Central American, ex. Mexican	1,758	1.4	6.0
Guatemalan	156	0.1	0.5
Honduran	167	0.1	0.6
Nicaraguan	126	0.1	0.4
Panamanian	998	0.8	3.4
Salvadoran	273	0.2	0.9
Cuban	345	0.3	1.2
Dominican Republic	479	0.4	1.6
Mexican	16,321	12.8	55.6
Puerto Rican	8,117	6.3	27.7
South American	746	0.6	2.5
Colombian	264	0.2	0.9
Ecuadorian	135	0.1	0.5
Peruvian	227	0.2	0.8
Spaniard	389	0.3	1.3

Population Growth: 2000–2010

Group	%
Total Population	47.2
Hispanic or Latino (of any race)	89.7
Central American, ex. Mexican	129.8
Panamanian	67.4
Cuban	197.4
Dominican Republic	195.7
Mexican	120.3
Puerto Rican	80.4
South American	184.7
Colombian	133.6

Males per 100 Females

Group	Number
Total Population	96.1
Hispanic or Latino (of any race)	96.7
Central American, ex. Mexican	74.9
Guatemalan	116.7
Honduran	89.8
Nicaraguan	82.6
Panamanian	59.2
Salvadoran	111.6
Cuban	94.9
Dominican Republic	87.8
Mexican	99.0
Puerto Rican	102.1
South American	82.8
Colombian	89.9
Ecuadorian	92.9
Peruvian	69.4
Spaniard	66.2

Average Household Size

Group	People
Total Population	2.66
Hispanic or Latino (of any race)	2.97
Central American, ex. Mexican	2.86
Guatemalan	3.25
Honduran	2.62
Nicaraguan	2.86
Panamanian	2.80
Salvadoran	2.95
Cuban	2.56
Dominican Republic	2.79
Mexican	3.07
Puerto Rican	2.93
South American	2.81
Colombian	2.84
Ecuadorian	2.88
Peruvian	2.79
Spaniard	2.57

Median Age

Group	Years
Total Population	27.1
Hispanic or Latino (of any race)	24.5
Central American, ex. Mexican	28.3
Guatemalan	25.0
Honduran	28.3
Nicaraguan	26.8
Panamanian	31.6
Salvadoran	24.8
Cuban	25.2
Dominican Republic	26.0
Mexican	23.3
Puerto Rican	26.1
South American	26.9
Colombian	26.6
Ecuadorian	26.1
Peruvian	26.9
Spaniard	26.4

High School Graduates
(Universe: Population 25 Years and Over)

Group	Number	%
Total Population	59,774	90.5
Hispanic or Latino (of any race)	10,959	82.5
Central American, ex. Mexican	790	89.8
Panamanian	559	89.7
Mexican	4,926	76.7
Puerto Rican	3,791	86.2
South American	377	94.7

Four-Year College Graduates
(Universe: Population 25 Years and Over)

Group	Number	%
Total Population	10,768	16.3
Hispanic or Latino (of any race)	1,450	10.9
Central American, ex. Mexican	105	11.9
Panamanian	40	6.4
Mexican	464	7.2
Puerto Rican	626	14.2
South American	88	22.1

Population Age 3–17 Enrolled in Public School
(Universe: Population Age 3–17 Enrolled in School)

Group	Number	%
Total Population	24,661	96.2
Hispanic or Latino (of any race)	7,074	95.5
Central American, ex. Mexican	360	94.0
Panamanian	221	90.6
Mexican	3,855	97.0
Puerto Rican	1,820	92.4
South American	211	95.0

Population Age 3–17 Enrolled in Private School
(Universe: Population Age 3–17 Enrolled in School)

Group	Number	%
Total Population	966	3.8
Hispanic or Latino (of any race)	330	4.5
Central American, ex. Mexican	23	6.0
Panamanian	23	9.4
Mexican	121	3.0
Puerto Rican	149	7.6
South American	11	5.0

Foreign-Born Population

Group	Number	%
Total Population	11,898	9.9
Hispanic or Latino (of any race)	4,295	15.5
Central American, ex. Mexican	936	51.8
Panamanian	656	57.5
Mexican	2,656	18.5
Puerto Rican	69	0.9
South American	334	41.1

Foreign-Born Naturalized U.S. Citizens

Group	Number	%
Total Population	5,806	48.8
Hispanic or Latino (of any race)	1,421	33.1
Central American, ex. Mexican	312	33.3
Panamanian	234	35.7
Mexican	678	25.5
Puerto Rican	58	84.1
South American	203	60.8

Language Spoken at Home: English Only
(Universe: Population 5 Years and Over)

Group	Number	%
Total Population	85,149	79.5
Hispanic or Latino (of any race)	9,284	39.3
Central American, ex. Mexican	386	26.9
Panamanian	240	24.9
Mexican	5,624	46.3
Puerto Rican	1,491	21.1
South American	138	19.6

Language Spoken at Home: Spanish
(Universe: Population 5 Years and Over)

Group	Number	%
Total Population	14,865	13.9
Hispanic or Latino (of any race)	14,175	59.9
Central American, ex. Mexican	989	68.8
Panamanian	712	73.8
Mexican	6,482	53.4
Puerto Rican	5,503	77.8
South American	566	80.4

Unemployment Rate
(Universe: Population 16 Years and Over)

Group	%
Total Population	10.0
Hispanic or Latino (of any race)	8.9
Central American, ex. Mexican	12.4
Panamanian	13.6
Mexican	10.8
Puerto Rican	6.2
South American	19.7

Class of Worker: Private Wage and Salary
(Universe: Civilian Employed Population 16 Years and Over)

Group	Number	%
Total Population	29,638	67.5
Hispanic or Latino (of any race)	6,330	70.6
Central American, ex. Mexican	292	53.1
Panamanian	203	49.2
Mexican	3,406	73.1
Puerto Rican	1,908	69.4
South American	171	75.0

Notes: (1) Percent of total population; (2) Percent of Hispanic/Latino population; Profiles include places with an overall population of at least 125,000, OR an overall population of at least 25,000 where the Hispanic/Latino population is at least 20% of the overall population. In states where less than five places meet either of these criteria, we have included places with at least 10,000 total population with the highest percentage of Hispanic/Latino population. These places are identified with an asterisk (*); Please refer to the User's Guide for a full explanation of data.

Class of Worker: Government
(Universe: Civilian Employed Population 16 Years and Over)

Group	Number	%
Total Population	12,588	28.7
Hispanic or Latino (of any race)	2,137	23.8
Central American, ex. Mexican	213	38.7
Panamanian	165	40.0
Mexican	1,035	22.2
Puerto Rican	709	25.8
South American	47	20.6

Means of Transportation to Work: Car, Truck or Van
(Universe: Workers 16 Years and Over)

Group	Number	%
Total Population	53,907	94.8
Hispanic or Latino (of any race)	10,559	94.2
Central American, ex. Mexican	569	95.0
Panamanian	400	96.9
Mexican	5,566	94.3
Puerto Rican	3,192	96.6
South American	306	100.0

Means of Transportation to Work: Public Transportation (ex. Taxicab)
(Universe: Workers 16 Years and Over)

Group	Number	%
Total Population	236	0.4
Hispanic or Latino (of any race)	99	0.9
Central American, ex. Mexican	0	0.0
Panamanian	0	0.0
Mexican	73	1.2
Puerto Rican	0	0.0
South American	0	0.0

Homeownership Rate
(Universe: Occupied Housing Units)

Group	%
Total Population	48.2
Hispanic or Latino (of any race)	48.8
Central American, ex. Mexican	55.7
Guatemalan	56.6
Honduran	36.2
Nicaraguan	53.5
Panamanian	59.6
Salvadoran	50.0
Cuban	37.9
Dominican Republic	55.4
Mexican	45.7
Puerto Rican	54.4
South American	48.8
Colombian	46.8
Ecuadorian	57.1
Peruvian	54.4
Spaniard	44.8

Median Home Value

Group	Dollars
Total Population	103,900
Hispanic or Latino (of any race)	102,700
Central American, ex. Mexican	116,100
Panamanian	112,000
Mexican	95,400
Puerto Rican	108,500
South American	108,700

Median Gross Rent

Group	Dollars
Total Population	828
Hispanic or Latino (of any race)	806
Central American, ex. Mexican	790
Panamanian	846
Mexican	773
Puerto Rican	800
South American	539

Median Household Income
(2010 Inflation-Adjusted Dollars)

Group	Dollars
Total Population	44,370
Hispanic or Latino (of any race)	41,415
Central American, ex. Mexican	37,500
Panamanian	39,107
Mexican	39,830
Puerto Rican	43,764
South American	40,000

Per Capita Income
(2010 Inflation-Adjusted Dollars)

Group	Dollars
Total Population	20,095
Hispanic or Latino (of any race)	15,152
Central American, ex. Mexican	13,385
Panamanian	14,967
Mexican	14,947
Puerto Rican	16,206
South American	18,872

Households with $100,000+ Income

Group	Number	%
Total Population	4,131	9.6
Hispanic or Latino (of any race)	396	5.1
Central American, ex. Mexican	46	9.0
Panamanian	40	10.7
Mexican	154	3.9
Puerto Rican	143	6.1
South American	53	28.8

Households with Food Stamps/SNAP Benefits During Past 12 Months

Group	Number	%
Total Population	3,839	8.9
Hispanic or Latino (of any race)	748	9.6
Central American, ex. Mexican	34	6.6
Panamanian	25	6.7
Mexican	482	12.1
Puerto Rican	218	9.3
South American	7	3.8

Poverty Rate
(Income in Past 12 Months Below Poverty Level)

Group	%
Total Population	16.4
Hispanic or Latino (of any race)	16.2
Central American, ex. Mexican	17.1
Panamanian	25.3
Mexican	16.6
Puerto Rican	17.8
South American	17.8

Kingsville

Population

Group	Number	%TP[1]	%HP[2]
Total Population	26,213	100.0	–
Hispanic or Latino (of any race)	18,726	71.4	100.0
Mexican	15,711	59.9	83.9
Puerto Rican	150	0.6	0.8
Spaniard	124	0.5	0.7

Population Growth: 2000–2010

Group	%
Total Population	2.5
Hispanic or Latino (of any race)	9.2
Mexican	32.7

Males per 100 Females

Group	Number
Total Population	103.4
Hispanic or Latino (of any race)	98.4
Mexican	98.5
Puerto Rican	167.9
Spaniard	87.9

Average Household Size

Group	People
Total Population	2.69
Hispanic or Latino (of any race)	2.87
Mexican	2.85
Puerto Rican	3.12
Spaniard	2.89

Median Age

Group	Years
Total Population	27.6
Hispanic or Latino (of any race)	26.7
Mexican	27.3
Puerto Rican	24.0
Spaniard	29.0

High School Graduates
(Universe: Population 25 Years and Over)

Group	Number	%
Total Population	10,518	74.7
Hispanic or Latino (of any race)	6,569	68.8
Mexican	5,414	69.9

Four-Year College Graduates
(Universe: Population 25 Years and Over)

Group	Number	%
Total Population	2,904	20.6
Hispanic or Latino (of any race)	1,483	15.5
Mexican	1,322	17.1

Population Age 3–17 Enrolled in Public School
(Universe: Population Age 3–17 Enrolled in School)

Group	Number	%
Total Population	4,333	92.2
Hispanic or Latino (of any race)	3,650	93.0
Mexican	3,197	95.0

Population Age 3–17 Enrolled in Private School
(Universe: Population Age 3–17 Enrolled in School)

Group	Number	%
Total Population	365	7.8
Hispanic or Latino (of any race)	276	7.0
Mexican	169	5.0

Foreign-Born Population

Group	Number	%
Total Population	1,854	7.2
Hispanic or Latino (of any race)	1,080	5.9
Mexican	995	6.7

Foreign-Born Naturalized U.S. Citizens

Group	Number	%
Total Population	350	18.9
Hispanic or Latino (of any race)	168	15.6
Mexican	142	14.3

Language Spoken at Home: English Only
(Universe: Population 5 Years and Over)

Group	Number	%
Total Population	11,377	48.0
Hispanic or Latino (of any race)	5,439	32.6
Mexican	4,628	34.1

Language Spoken at Home: Spanish
(Universe: Population 5 Years and Over)

Group	Number	%
Total Population	11,496	48.5
Hispanic or Latino (of any race)	11,226	67.2
Mexican	8,881	65.5

Unemployment Rate
(Universe: Population 16 Years and Over)

Group	%
Total Population	10.1
Hispanic or Latino (of any race)	11.3
Mexican	10.3

Class of Worker: Private Wage and Salary
(Universe: Civilian Employed Population 16 Years and Over)

Group	Number	%
Total Population	6,524	62.9
Hispanic or Latino (of any race)	4,762	65.2
Mexican	3,722	63.6

Class of Worker: Government
(Universe: Civilian Employed Population 16 Years and Over)

Group	Number	%
Total Population	3,359	32.4
Hispanic or Latino (of any race)	2,361	32.3
Mexican	1,964	33.5

Means of Transportation to Work: Car, Truck or Van
(Universe: Workers 16 Years and Over)

Group	Number	%
Total Population	9,292	90.2
Hispanic or Latino (of any race)	6,411	90.8
Mexican	5,065	90.5

Notes: (1) Percent of total population; (2) Percent of Hispanic/Latino population; Profiles include places with an overall population of at least 125,000, OR an overall population of at least 25,000 where the Hispanic/Latino population is at least 20% of the overall population. In states where less than five places meet either of these criteria, we have included places with at least 10,000 total population with the highest percentage of Hispanic/Latino population. These places are identified with an asterisk (*); Please refer to the User's Guide for a full explanation of data.

Means of Transportation to Work: Public Transportation (ex. Taxicab)
(Universe: Workers 16 Years and Over)

Group	Number	%
Total Population	32	0.3
Hispanic or Latino (of any race)	28	0.4
Mexican	28	0.5

Homeownership Rate
(Universe: Occupied Housing Units)

Group	%
Total Population	51.6
Hispanic or Latino (of any race)	51.6
Mexican	53.3
Puerto Rican	38.8
Spaniard	52.3

Median Home Value

Group	Dollars
Total Population	70,200
Hispanic or Latino (of any race)	62,400
Mexican	61,300

Median Gross Rent

Group	Dollars
Total Population	631
Hispanic or Latino (of any race)	613
Mexican	616

Median Household Income
(2010 Inflation-Adjusted Dollars)

Group	Dollars
Total Population	32,319
Hispanic or Latino (of any race)	30,249
Mexican	30,083

Per Capita Income
(2010 Inflation-Adjusted Dollars)

Group	Dollars
Total Population	17,529
Hispanic or Latino (of any race)	14,033
Mexican	14,039

Households with $100,000+ Income

Group	Number	%
Total Population	724	8.1
Hispanic or Latino (of any race)	294	5.0
Mexican	233	4.8

Households with Food Stamps/SNAP Benefits During Past 12 Months

Group	Number	%
Total Population	1,429	15.9
Hispanic or Latino (of any race)	1,250	21.2
Mexican	1,009	20.9

Poverty Rate
(Income in Past 12 Months Below Poverty Level)

Group	%
Total Population	27.8
Hispanic or Latino (of any race)	27.4
Mexican	28.5

Kyle

Population

Group	Number	%TP[1]	%HP[2]
Total Population	28,016	100.0	–
Hispanic or Latino (of any race)	12,979	46.3	100.0
Central American, ex. Mexican	319	1.1	2.5
Mexican	11,102	39.6	85.5
Puerto Rican	238	0.8	1.8
South American	109	0.4	0.8
Spaniard	135	0.5	1.0

Population Growth: 2000–2010

Group	%
Total Population	427.2
Hispanic or Latino (of any race)	366.9
Mexican	439.5

Males per 100 Females

Group	Number
Total Population	99.0
Hispanic or Latino (of any race)	97.3
Central American, ex. Mexican	93.3
Mexican	98.7
Puerto Rican	85.9
South American	87.9
Spaniard	77.6

Average Household Size

Group	People
Total Population	3.15
Hispanic or Latino (of any race)	3.63
Central American, ex. Mexican	3.82
Mexican	3.66
Puerto Rican	3.43
South American	3.45
Spaniard	2.87

Median Age

Group	Years
Total Population	30.2
Hispanic or Latino (of any race)	26.8
Central American, ex. Mexican	31.5
Mexican	26.6
Puerto Rican	23.5
South American	32.3
Spaniard	33.8

High School Graduates
(Universe: Population 25 Years and Over)

Group	Number	%
Total Population	12,850	88.4
Hispanic or Latino (of any race)	4,897	79.9
Mexican	2,721	83.9

Four-Year College Graduates
(Universe: Population 25 Years and Over)

Group	Number	%
Total Population	3,697	25.4
Hispanic or Latino (of any race)	801	13.1
Mexican	576	17.8

Population Age 3–17 Enrolled in Public School
(Universe: Population Age 3–17 Enrolled in School)

Group	Number	%
Total Population	4,661	88.9
Hispanic or Latino (of any race)	2,586	93.1
Mexican	1,362	94.1

Population Age 3–17 Enrolled in Private School
(Universe: Population Age 3–17 Enrolled in School)

Group	Number	%
Total Population	582	11.1
Hispanic or Latino (of any race)	191	6.9
Mexican	85	5.9

Foreign-Born Population

Group	Number	%
Total Population	1,512	6.3
Hispanic or Latino (of any race)	1,129	10.3
Mexican	599	10.5

Foreign-Born Naturalized U.S. Citizens

Group	Number	%
Total Population	720	47.6
Hispanic or Latino (of any race)	426	37.7
Mexican	287	47.9

Language Spoken at Home: English Only
(Universe: Population 5 Years and Over)

Group	Number	%
Total Population	15,181	71.6
Hispanic or Latino (of any race)	4,045	42.5
Mexican	2,120	42.2

Language Spoken at Home: Spanish
(Universe: Population 5 Years and Over)

Group	Number	%
Total Population	5,615	26.5
Hispanic or Latino (of any race)	5,447	57.3
Mexican	2,896	57.6

Unemployment Rate
(Universe: Population 16 Years and Over)

Group	%
Total Population	5.8
Hispanic or Latino (of any race)	6.1
Mexican	8.9

Class of Worker: Private Wage and Salary
(Universe: Civilian Employed Population 16 Years and Over)

Group	Number	%
Total Population	7,956	68.7
Hispanic or Latino (of any race)	3,478	70.0
Mexican	1,690	64.6

Class of Worker: Government
(Universe: Civilian Employed Population 16 Years and Over)

Group	Number	%
Total Population	3,150	27.2
Hispanic or Latino (of any race)	1,386	27.9
Mexican	828	31.6

Means of Transportation to Work: Car, Truck or Van
(Universe: Workers 16 Years and Over)

Group	Number	%
Total Population	10,798	94.7
Hispanic or Latino (of any race)	4,604	94.7
Mexican	2,358	94.2

Means of Transportation to Work: Public Transportation (ex. Taxicab)
(Universe: Workers 16 Years and Over)

Group	Number	%
Total Population	77	0.7
Hispanic or Latino (of any race)	77	1.6
Mexican	56	2.2

Homeownership Rate
(Universe: Occupied Housing Units)

Group	%
Total Population	80.6
Hispanic or Latino (of any race)	79.5
Central American, ex. Mexican	85.1
Mexican	80.0
Puerto Rican	80.0
South American	87.9
Spaniard	89.1

Median Home Value

Group	Dollars
Total Population	143,800
Hispanic or Latino (of any race)	141,600
Mexican	140,400

Median Gross Rent

Group	Dollars
Total Population	1,218
Hispanic or Latino (of any race)	1,118
Mexican	1,119

Median Household Income
(2010 Inflation-Adjusted Dollars)

Group	Dollars
Total Population	70,166
Hispanic or Latino (of any race)	63,750
Mexican	73,789

Per Capita Income
(2010 Inflation-Adjusted Dollars)

Group	Dollars
Total Population	23,266
Hispanic or Latino (of any race)	18,354
Mexican	18,838

Households with $100,000+ Income

Group	Number	%
Total Population	1,663	22.5
Hispanic or Latino (of any race)	532	18.9
Mexican	320	22.4

Households with Food Stamps/SNAP Benefits During Past 12 Months

Group	Number	%
Total Population	400	5.4
Hispanic or Latino (of any race)	258	9.2
Mexican	128	9.0

Poverty Rate
(Income in Past 12 Months Below Poverty Level)

Group	%
Total Population	7.8

Notes: (1) Percent of total population; (2) Percent of Hispanic/Latino population; Profiles include places with an overall population of at least 125,000, OR an overall population of at least 25,000 where the Hispanic/Latino population is at least 20% of the overall population. In states where less than five places meet either of these criteria, we have included places with at least 10,000 total population with the highest percentage of Hispanic/Latino population. These places are identified with an asterisk (*); Please refer to the User's Guide for a full explanation of data.

Hispanic or Latino (of any race)	11.1
Mexican	11.3

La Porte

Population

Group	Number	%TP[1]	%HP[2]
Total Population	33,800	100.0	–
Hispanic or Latino (of any race)	9,932	29.4	100.0
Central American, ex. Mexican	322	1.0	3.2
Salvadoran	131	0.4	1.3
Cuban	101	0.3	1.0
Mexican	8,230	24.3	82.9
Puerto Rican	175	0.5	1.8
South American	134	0.4	1.3

Population Growth: 2000–2010

Group	%
Total Population	6.0
Hispanic or Latino (of any race)	52.3
Central American, ex. Mexican	190.1
Mexican	78.9
Puerto Rican	17.4

Males per 100 Females

Group	Number
Total Population	98.6
Hispanic or Latino (of any race)	103.3
Central American, ex. Mexican	120.5
Salvadoran	114.8
Cuban	87.0
Mexican	103.5
Puerto Rican	124.4
South American	106.2

Average Household Size

Group	People
Total Population	2.84
Hispanic or Latino (of any race)	3.58
Central American, ex. Mexican	4.12
Salvadoran	4.00
Cuban	2.77
Mexican	3.62
Puerto Rican	2.98
South American	3.39

Median Age

Group	Years
Total Population	34.5
Hispanic or Latino (of any race)	27.1
Central American, ex. Mexican	30.0
Salvadoran	27.6
Cuban	30.5
Mexican	26.9
Puerto Rican	33.6
South American	33.3

High School Graduates
(Universe: Population 25 Years and Over)

Group	Number	%
Total Population	16,933	82.1
Hispanic or Latino (of any race)	2,980	61.8
Mexican	2,371	58.4

Four-Year College Graduates
(Universe: Population 25 Years and Over)

Group	Number	%
Total Population	3,280	15.9
Hispanic or Latino (of any race)	381	7.9
Mexican	275	6.8

Population Age 3–17 Enrolled in Public School
(Universe: Population Age 3–17 Enrolled in School)

Group	Number	%
Total Population	6,647	92.6
Hispanic or Latino (of any race)	2,654	98.2
Mexican	2,276	99.1

Population Age 3–17 Enrolled in Private School
(Universe: Population Age 3–17 Enrolled in School)

Group	Number	%
Total Population	533	7.4
Hispanic or Latino (of any race)	49	1.8
Mexican	20	0.9

Foreign-Born Population

Group	Number	%
Total Population	3,167	9.5
Hispanic or Latino (of any race)	2,283	24.4
Mexican	1,916	24.0

Foreign-Born Naturalized U.S. Citizens

Group	Number	%
Total Population	1,296	40.9
Hispanic or Latino (of any race)	779	34.1
Mexican	645	33.7

Language Spoken at Home: English Only
(Universe: Population 5 Years and Over)

Group	Number	%
Total Population	24,858	80.7
Hispanic or Latino (of any race)	3,572	42.1
Mexican	3,103	42.4

Language Spoken at Home: Spanish
(Universe: Population 5 Years and Over)

Group	Number	%
Total Population	5,373	17.4
Hispanic or Latino (of any race)	4,922	57.9
Mexican	4,209	57.6

Unemployment Rate
(Universe: Population 16 Years and Over)

Group	%
Total Population	6.5
Hispanic or Latino (of any race)	5.6
Mexican	4.3

Class of Worker: Private Wage and Salary
(Universe: Civilian Employed Population 16 Years and Over)

Group	Number	%
Total Population	13,295	80.0
Hispanic or Latino (of any race)	3,523	81.5
Mexican	3,097	82.3

Class of Worker: Government
(Universe: Civilian Employed Population 16 Years and Over)

Group	Number	%
Total Population	2,421	14.6
Hispanic or Latino (of any race)	657	15.2
Mexican	561	14.9

Means of Transportation to Work: Car, Truck or Van
(Universe: Workers 16 Years and Over)

Group	Number	%
Total Population	15,491	95.7
Hispanic or Latino (of any race)	3,931	94.0
Mexican	3,463	93.9

Means of Transportation to Work: Public Transportation (ex. Taxicab)
(Universe: Workers 16 Years and Over)

Group	Number	%
Total Population	37	0.2
Hispanic or Latino (of any race)	0	0.0
Mexican	0	0.0

Homeownership Rate
(Universe: Occupied Housing Units)

Group	%
Total Population	74.8
Hispanic or Latino (of any race)	73.9
Central American, ex. Mexican	69.8
Salvadoran	66.7
Cuban	86.7
Mexican	74.8
Puerto Rican	76.7
South American	77.8

Median Home Value

Group	Dollars
Total Population	118,100
Hispanic or Latino (of any race)	106,900
Mexican	102,500

Median Gross Rent

Group	Dollars
Total Population	990
Hispanic or Latino (of any race)	959
Mexican	966

Median Household Income
(2010 Inflation-Adjusted Dollars)

Group	Dollars
Total Population	66,522
Hispanic or Latino (of any race)	57,124
Mexican	57,621

Per Capita Income
(2010 Inflation-Adjusted Dollars)

Group	Dollars
Total Population	25,604
Hispanic or Latino (of any race)	18,692
Mexican	17,788

Households with $100,000+ Income

Group	Number	%
Total Population	2,907	26.4
Hispanic or Latino (of any race)	448	17.8
Mexican	393	18.4

Households with Food Stamps/SNAP Benefits During Past 12 Months

Group	Number	%
Total Population	576	5.2
Hispanic or Latino (of any race)	83	3.3
Mexican	83	3.9

Poverty Rate
(Income in Past 12 Months Below Poverty Level)

Group	%
Total Population	8.0
Hispanic or Latino (of any race)	9.8
Mexican	7.9

Lake Jackson

Population

Group	Number	%TP[1]	%HP[2]
Total Population	26,849	100.0	–
Hispanic or Latino (of any race)	5,513	20.5	100.0
Central American, ex. Mexican	104	0.4	1.9
Mexican	4,585	17.1	83.2
South American	142	0.5	2.6

Population Growth: 2000–2010

Group	%
Total Population	1.8
Hispanic or Latino (of any race)	42.1
Mexican	63.8

Males per 100 Females

Group	Number
Total Population	96.1
Hispanic or Latino (of any race)	96.8
Central American, ex. Mexican	103.9
Mexican	98.1
South American	77.5

Average Household Size

Group	People
Total Population	2.60
Hispanic or Latino (of any race)	3.09
Central American, ex. Mexican	3.46
Mexican	3.09
South American	3.21

Median Age

Group	Years
Total Population	37.1
Hispanic or Latino (of any race)	26.2
Central American, ex. Mexican	42.5
Mexican	26.0
South American	38.0

High School Graduates
(Universe: Population 25 Years and Over)

Group	Number	%
Total Population	16,207	93.1
Hispanic or Latino (of any race)	2,032	79.2
Mexican	1,703	76.1

Notes: (1) Percent of total population; (2) Percent of Hispanic/Latino population; Profiles include places with an overall population of at least 125,000, OR an overall population of at least 25,000 where the Hispanic/Latino population is at least 20% of the overall population. In states where less than five places meet either of these criteria, we have included places with at least 10,000 total population with the highest percentage of Hispanic/Latino population. These places are identified with an asterisk (*); Please refer to the User's Guide for a full explanation of data.

Four-Year College Graduates
(Universe: Population 25 Years and Over)

Group	Number	%
Total Population	5,409	31.1
Hispanic or Latino (of any race)	388	15.1
Mexican	326	14.6

Population Age 3–17 Enrolled in Public School
(Universe: Population Age 3–17 Enrolled in School)

Group	Number	%
Total Population	5,208	86.9
Hispanic or Latino (of any race)	1,097	91.7
Mexican	1,006	96.1

Population Age 3–17 Enrolled in Private School
(Universe: Population Age 3–17 Enrolled in School)

Group	Number	%
Total Population	786	13.1
Hispanic or Latino (of any race)	99	8.3
Mexican	41	3.9

Foreign-Born Population

Group	Number	%
Total Population	2,060	7.6
Hispanic or Latino (of any race)	868	17.5
Mexican	762	17.9

Foreign-Born Naturalized U.S. Citizens

Group	Number	%
Total Population	843	40.9
Hispanic or Latino (of any race)	213	24.5
Mexican	162	21.3

Language Spoken at Home: English Only
(Universe: Population 5 Years and Over)

Group	Number	%
Total Population	21,495	85.1
Hispanic or Latino (of any race)	1,994	46.2
Mexican	1,728	45.6

Language Spoken at Home: Spanish
(Universe: Population 5 Years and Over)

Group	Number	%
Total Population	2,722	10.8
Hispanic or Latino (of any race)	2,324	53.8
Mexican	2,059	54.4

Unemployment Rate
(Universe: Population 16 Years and Over)

Group	%
Total Population	5.1
Hispanic or Latino (of any race)	3.8
Mexican	3.2

Class of Worker: Private Wage and Salary
(Universe: Civilian Employed Population 16 Years and Over)

Group	Number	%
Total Population	9,914	79.9
Hispanic or Latino (of any race)	1,981	89.4
Mexican	1,767	89.6

Class of Worker: Government
(Universe: Civilian Employed Population 16 Years and Over)

Group	Number	%
Total Population	1,906	15.4
Hispanic or Latino (of any race)	137	6.2
Mexican	106	5.4

Means of Transportation to Work: Car, Truck or Van
(Universe: Workers 16 Years and Over)

Group	Number	%
Total Population	11,989	97.1
Hispanic or Latino (of any race)	2,157	98.3
Mexican	1,899	98.1

Means of Transportation to Work: Public Transportation (ex. Taxicab)
(Universe: Workers 16 Years and Over)

Group	Number	%
Total Population	0	0.0
Hispanic or Latino (of any race)	0	0.0
Mexican	0	0.0

Homeownership Rate
(Universe: Occupied Housing Units)

Group	%
Total Population	69.1
Hispanic or Latino (of any race)	56.7
Central American, ex. Mexican	48.6
Mexican	56.8
South American	73.7

Median Home Value

Group	Dollars
Total Population	134,600
Hispanic or Latino (of any race)	114,100
Mexican	113,000

Median Gross Rent

Group	Dollars
Total Population	846
Hispanic or Latino (of any race)	699
Mexican	657

Median Household Income
(2010 Inflation-Adjusted Dollars)

Group	Dollars
Total Population	72,618
Hispanic or Latino (of any race)	54,375
Mexican	55,655

Per Capita Income
(2010 Inflation-Adjusted Dollars)

Group	Dollars
Total Population	30,279
Hispanic or Latino (of any race)	20,245
Mexican	20,513

Households with $100,000+ Income

Group	Number	%
Total Population	3,132	32.4
Hispanic or Latino (of any race)	320	22.6
Mexican	280	23.3

Households with Food Stamps/SNAP Benefits During Past 12 Months

Group	Number	%
Total Population	326	3.4
Hispanic or Latino (of any race)	76	5.4
Mexican	76	6.3

Poverty Rate
(Income in Past 12 Months Below Poverty Level)

Group	%
Total Population	6.6
Hispanic or Latino (of any race)	12.3
Mexican	14.0

Laredo

Population

Group	Number	%TP[1]	%HP[2]
Total Population	236,091	100.0	–
Hispanic or Latino (of any race)	225,750	95.6	100.0
Central American, ex. Mexican	966	0.4	0.4
Guatemalan	209	0.1	0.1
Honduran	370	0.2	0.2
Salvadoran	261	0.1	0.1
Cuban	223	0.1	0.1
Mexican	205,079	86.9	90.8
Puerto Rican	831	0.4	0.4
South American	332	0.1	0.1
Colombian	106	<0.1	<0.1
Spaniard	439	0.2	0.2

Population Growth: 2000–2010

Group	%
Total Population	33.7
Hispanic or Latino (of any race)	35.8
Central American, ex. Mexican	176.8
Honduran	249.1
Salvadoran	155.9
Cuban	102.7
Mexican	54.0
Puerto Rican	182.7
South American	159.4

Males per 100 Females

Group	Number
Total Population	93.8
Hispanic or Latino (of any race)	92.6
Central American, ex. Mexican	130.0
Guatemalan	115.5
Honduran	116.4
Salvadoran	161.0
Cuban	189.6
Mexican	92.4
Puerto Rican	138.1
South American	110.1
Colombian	73.8
Spaniard	99.5

Average Household Size

Group	People
Total Population	3.66
Hispanic or Latino (of any race)	3.72
Central American, ex. Mexican	3.57
Guatemalan	3.58
Honduran	3.72
Salvadoran	3.64
Cuban	2.91
Mexican	3.72
Puerto Rican	3.11
South American	3.04
Colombian	3.22
Spaniard	2.84

Median Age

Group	Years
Total Population	27.9
Hispanic or Latino (of any race)	27.6
Central American, ex. Mexican	31.6
Guatemalan	31.8
Honduran	29.5
Salvadoran	32.6
Cuban	40.2
Mexican	27.9
Puerto Rican	29.0
South American	37.0
Colombian	38.3
Spaniard	42.9

High School Graduates
(Universe: Population 25 Years and Over)

Group	Number	%
Total Population	77,642	63.8
Hispanic or Latino (of any race)	71,639	62.2
Central American, ex. Mexican	234	40.0
Mexican	67,460	62.0

Four-Year College Graduates
(Universe: Population 25 Years and Over)

Group	Number	%
Total Population	21,078	17.3
Hispanic or Latino (of any race)	18,443	16.0
Central American, ex. Mexican	37	6.3
Mexican	17,366	16.0

Population Age 3–17 Enrolled in Public School
(Universe: Population Age 3–17 Enrolled in School)

Group	Number	%
Total Population	57,631	95.2
Hispanic or Latino (of any race)	55,974	95.5
Central American, ex. Mexican	163	100.0
Mexican	52,754	95.6

Population Age 3–17 Enrolled in Private School
(Universe: Population Age 3–17 Enrolled in School)

Group	Number	%
Total Population	2,900	4.8
Hispanic or Latino (of any race)	2,618	4.5
Central American, ex. Mexican	0	0.0
Mexican	2,429	4.4

Foreign-Born Population

Group	Number	%
Total Population	66,008	29.2
Hispanic or Latino (of any race)	64,030	29.7
Central American, ex. Mexican	795	69.8
Mexican	61,599	30.2

STATE & PLACE PROFILES

Notes: (1) Percent of total population; (2) Percent of Hispanic/Latino population; Profiles include places with an overall population of at least 125,000, OR an overall population of at least 25,000 where the Hispanic/Latino population is at least 20% of the overall population. In states where less than five places meet either of these criteria, we have included places with at least 10,000 total population with the highest percentage of Hispanic/Latino population. These places are identified with an asterisk (*); Please refer to the User's Guide for a full explanation of data.

Foreign-Born Naturalized U.S. Citizens

Group	Number	%
Total Population	18,885	28.6
Hispanic or Latino (of any race)	18,159	28.4
Central American, ex. Mexican	63	7.9
Mexican	17,250	28.0

Language Spoken at Home: English Only
(Universe: Population 5 Years and Over)

Group	Number	%
Total Population	15,499	7.6
Hispanic or Latino (of any race)	10,355	5.4
Central American, ex. Mexican	20	2.0
Mexican	9,302	5.1

Language Spoken at Home: Spanish
(Universe: Population 5 Years and Over)

Group	Number	%
Total Population	185,722	91.6
Hispanic or Latino (of any race)	182,471	94.5
Central American, ex. Mexican	976	98.0
Mexican	172,964	94.8

Unemployment Rate
(Universe: Population 16 Years and Over)

Group	%
Total Population	7.3
Hispanic or Latino (of any race)	7.2
Central American, ex. Mexican	12.1
Mexican	7.1

Class of Worker: Private Wage and Salary
(Universe: Civilian Employed Population 16 Years and Over)

Group	Number	%
Total Population	64,483	70.5
Hispanic or Latino (of any race)	61,437	70.9
Central American, ex. Mexican	386	93.5
Mexican	58,555	71.1

Class of Worker: Government
(Universe: Civilian Employed Population 16 Years and Over)

Group	Number	%
Total Population	19,622	21.5
Hispanic or Latino (of any race)	18,163	21.0
Central American, ex. Mexican	9	2.2
Mexican	16,987	20.6

Means of Transportation to Work: Car, Truck or Van
(Universe: Workers 16 Years and Over)

Group	Number	%
Total Population	81,607	91.6
Hispanic or Latino (of any race)	77,410	91.8
Central American, ex. Mexican	292	70.7
Mexican	73,578	91.8

Means of Transportation to Work: Public Transportation (ex. Taxicab)
(Universe: Workers 16 Years and Over)

Group	Number	%
Total Population	1,662	1.9
Hispanic or Latino (of any race)	1,569	1.9
Central American, ex. Mexican	65	15.7
Mexican	1,453	1.8

Homeownership Rate
(Universe: Occupied Housing Units)

Group	%
Total Population	63.7
Hispanic or Latino (of any race)	64.0
Central American, ex. Mexican	44.4
Guatemalan	43.8
Honduran	46.3
Salvadoran	46.0
Cuban	57.0
Mexican	64.2
Puerto Rican	54.0
South American	67.8
Colombian	77.8
Spaniard	71.0

Median Home Value

Group	Dollars
Total Population	108,300
Hispanic or Latino (of any race)	107,000
Central American, ex. Mexican	203,100
Mexican	106,100

Median Gross Rent

Group	Dollars
Total Population	693
Hispanic or Latino (of any race)	683
Central American, ex. Mexican	756
Mexican	682

Median Household Income
(2010 Inflation-Adjusted Dollars)

Group	Dollars
Total Population	37,245
Hispanic or Latino (of any race)	36,319
Central American, ex. Mexican	21,271
Mexican	36,321

Per Capita Income
(2010 Inflation-Adjusted Dollars)

Group	Dollars
Total Population	14,447
Hispanic or Latino (of any race)	13,770
Central American, ex. Mexican	6,446
Mexican	13,726

Households with $100,000+ Income

Group	Number	%
Total Population	7,230	11.8
Hispanic or Latino (of any race)	6,331	11.0
Central American, ex. Mexican	0	0.0
Mexican	5,946	10.9

Households with Food Stamps/SNAP Benefits During Past 12 Months

Group	Number	%
Total Population	16,446	26.9
Hispanic or Latino (of any race)	16,167	28.0
Central American, ex. Mexican	37	20.2
Mexican	15,406	28.3

Poverty Rate
(Income in Past 12 Months Below Poverty Level)

Group	%
Total Population	29.2
Hispanic or Latino (of any race)	30.0
Central American, ex. Mexican	40.4
Mexican	30.2

Leander

Population

Group	Number	%TP[1]	%HP[2]
Total Population	26,521	100.0	–
Hispanic or Latino (of any race)	6,500	24.5	100.0
Central American, ex. Mexican	249	0.9	3.8
Mexican	5,328	20.1	82.0
Puerto Rican	219	0.8	3.4
South American	131	0.5	2.0

Population Growth: 2000–2010

Group	%
Total Population	249.1
Hispanic or Latino (of any race)	436.7
Mexican	502.7

Males per 100 Females

Group	Number
Total Population	97.1
Hispanic or Latino (of any race)	98.7
Central American, ex. Mexican	72.9
Mexican	99.5
Puerto Rican	123.5
South American	87.1

Average Household Size

Group	People
Total Population	3.10
Hispanic or Latino (of any race)	3.74
Central American, ex. Mexican	3.69
Mexican	3.82
Puerto Rican	3.47
South American	2.94

Median Age

Group	Years
Total Population	31.4
Hispanic or Latino (of any race)	23.9
Central American, ex. Mexican	31.1
Mexican	23.0
Puerto Rican	27.8
South American	32.1

High School Graduates
(Universe: Population 25 Years and Over)

Group	Number	%
Total Population	12,738	91.9
Hispanic or Latino (of any race)	2,367	77.6
Mexican	1,828	74.8

Four-Year College Graduates
(Universe: Population 25 Years and Over)

Group	Number	%
Total Population	4,102	29.6
Hispanic or Latino (of any race)	553	18.1
Mexican	467	19.1

Population Age 3–17 Enrolled in Public School
(Universe: Population Age 3–17 Enrolled in School)

Group	Number	%
Total Population	5,116	89.0
Hispanic or Latino (of any race)	1,735	96.4
Mexican	1,275	95.2

Population Age 3–17 Enrolled in Private School
(Universe: Population Age 3–17 Enrolled in School)

Group	Number	%
Total Population	632	11.0
Hispanic or Latino (of any race)	64	3.6
Mexican	64	4.8

Foreign-Born Population

Group	Number	%
Total Population	1,892	8.1
Hispanic or Latino (of any race)	1,181	20.2
Mexican	1,063	22.8

Foreign-Born Naturalized U.S. Citizens

Group	Number	%
Total Population	807	42.7
Hispanic or Latino (of any race)	303	25.7
Mexican	238	22.4

Language Spoken at Home: English Only
(Universe: Population 5 Years and Over)

Group	Number	%
Total Population	16,990	82.4
Hispanic or Latino (of any race)	2,198	42.8
Mexican	1,593	38.8

Language Spoken at Home: Spanish
(Universe: Population 5 Years and Over)

Group	Number	%
Total Population	3,061	14.8
Hispanic or Latino (of any race)	2,934	57.2
Mexican	2,515	61.2

Unemployment Rate
(Universe: Population 16 Years and Over)

Group	%
Total Population	5.1
Hispanic or Latino (of any race)	4.5
Mexican	3.2

Class of Worker: Private Wage and Salary
(Universe: Civilian Employed Population 16 Years and Over)

Group	Number	%
Total Population	8,734	75.6
Hispanic or Latino (of any race)	1,945	76.9
Mexican	1,618	78.5

Class of Worker: Government
(Universe: Civilian Employed Population 16 Years and Over)

Group	Number	%
Total Population	2,086	18.1
Hispanic or Latino (of any race)	521	20.6
Mexican	403	19.6

Notes: (1) Percent of total population; (2) Percent of Hispanic/Latino population; Profiles include places with an overall population of at least 125,000, OR an overall population of at least 25,000 where the Hispanic/Latino population is at least 20% of the overall population. In states where less than five places meet either of these criteria, we have included places with at least 10,000 total population with the highest percentage of Hispanic/Latino population. These places are identified with an asterisk (*); Please refer to the User's Guide for a full explanation of data.

Means of Transportation to Work: Car, Truck or Van
(Universe: Workers 16 Years and Over)

Group	Number	%
Total Population	10,527	92.4
Hispanic or Latino (of any race)	2,433	97.5
Mexican	1,988	97.8

Means of Transportation to Work: Public Transportation (ex. Taxicab)
(Universe: Workers 16 Years and Over)

Group	Number	%
Total Population	173	1.5
Hispanic or Latino (of any race)	46	1.8
Mexican	28	1.4

Homeownership Rate
(Universe: Occupied Housing Units)

Group	%
Total Population	80.3
Hispanic or Latino (of any race)	76.1
Central American, ex. Mexican	93.8
Mexican	75.2
Puerto Rican	78.3
South American	87.5

Median Home Value

Group	Dollars
Total Population	152,600
Hispanic or Latino (of any race)	143,400
Mexican	138,800

Median Gross Rent

Group	Dollars
Total Population	1,309
Hispanic or Latino (of any race)	1,271
Mexican	1,309

Median Household Income
(2010 Inflation-Adjusted Dollars)

Group	Dollars
Total Population	70,455
Hispanic or Latino (of any race)	58,674
Mexican	59,659

Per Capita Income
(2010 Inflation-Adjusted Dollars)

Group	Dollars
Total Population	25,722
Hispanic or Latino (of any race)	17,711
Mexican	17,199

Households with $100,000+ Income

Group	Number	%
Total Population	1,858	25.3
Hispanic or Latino (of any race)	317	19.4
Mexican	244	19.3

Households with Food Stamps/SNAP Benefits During Past 12 Months

Group	Number	%
Total Population	376	5.1
Hispanic or Latino (of any race)	134	8.2
Mexican	73	5.8

Poverty Rate
(Income in Past 12 Months Below Poverty Level)

Group	%
Total Population	4.7
Hispanic or Latino (of any race)	4.2
Mexican	3.4

Lewisville

Population

Group	Number	%TP[1]	%HP[2]
Total Population	95,290	100.0	–
Hispanic or Latino (of any race)	27,783	29.2	100.0
Central American, ex. Mexican	1,675	1.8	6.0
Guatemalan	239	0.3	0.9
Honduran	271	0.3	1.0
Salvadoran	972	1.0	3.5
Cuban	222	0.2	0.8
Dominican Republic	101	0.1	0.4
Mexican	22,886	24.0	82.4
Puerto Rican	701	0.7	2.5
South American	639	0.7	2.3
Colombian	203	0.2	0.7
Peruvian	138	0.1	0.5
Spaniard	229	0.2	0.8

Population Growth: 2000–2010

Group	%
Total Population	22.6
Hispanic or Latino (of any race)	101.3
Central American, ex. Mexican	264.1
Salvadoran	242.3
Cuban	65.7
Mexican	117.3
Puerto Rican	74.8
South American	145.8

Males per 100 Females

Group	Number
Total Population	97.5
Hispanic or Latino (of any race)	108.5
Central American, ex. Mexican	119.2
Guatemalan	159.8
Honduran	111.7
Salvadoran	123.4
Cuban	98.2
Dominican Republic	77.2
Mexican	111.2
Puerto Rican	79.7
South American	79.0
Colombian	61.1
Peruvian	94.4
Spaniard	87.7

Average Household Size

Group	People
Total Population	2.53
Hispanic or Latino (of any race)	3.59
Central American, ex. Mexican	3.62
Guatemalan	3.68
Honduran	3.81
Salvadoran	3.77
Cuban	2.48
Dominican Republic	2.64
Mexican	3.74
Puerto Rican	2.47
South American	2.66
Colombian	2.57
Peruvian	2.96
Spaniard	2.41

Median Age

Group	Years
Total Population	30.9
Hispanic or Latino (of any race)	25.4
Central American, ex. Mexican	29.7
Guatemalan	28.6
Honduran	29.1
Salvadoran	29.6
Cuban	36.9
Dominican Republic	31.5
Mexican	24.5
Puerto Rican	28.9
South American	35.6
Colombian	34.9
Peruvian	38.0
Spaniard	30.5

High School Graduates
(Universe: Population 25 Years and Over)

Group	Number	%
Total Population	50,848	86.5
Hispanic or Latino (of any race)	7,407	58.1
Central American, ex. Mexican	406	51.1
Salvadoran	257	47.9
Mexican	5,799	55.1

Four-Year College Graduates
(Universe: Population 25 Years and Over)

Group	Number	%
Total Population	17,586	29.9
Hispanic or Latino (of any race)	1,515	11.9
Central American, ex. Mexican	25	3.1
Salvadoran	14	2.6
Mexican	1,067	10.1

Population Age 3–17 Enrolled in Public School
(Universe: Population Age 3–17 Enrolled in School)

Group	Number	%
Total Population	15,270	88.0
Hispanic or Latino (of any race)	5,784	94.6
Central American, ex. Mexican	216	100.0
Salvadoran	203	100.0
Mexican	5,282	94.9

Population Age 3–17 Enrolled in Private School
(Universe: Population Age 3–17 Enrolled in School)

Group	Number	%
Total Population	2,088	12.0
Hispanic or Latino (of any race)	330	5.4
Central American, ex. Mexican	0	0.0
Salvadoran	0	0.0
Mexican	286	5.1

Foreign-Born Population

Group	Number	%
Total Population	19,820	21.3
Hispanic or Latino (of any race)	11,759	47.3
Central American, ex. Mexican	883	60.7
Salvadoran	552	51.9
Mexican	10,195	48.0

Foreign-Born Naturalized U.S. Citizens

Group	Number	%
Total Population	4,620	23.3
Hispanic or Latino (of any race)	1,311	11.1
Central American, ex. Mexican	196	22.2
Salvadoran	183	33.2
Mexican	889	8.7

Language Spoken at Home: English Only
(Universe: Population 5 Years and Over)

Group	Number	%
Total Population	57,426	68.0
Hispanic or Latino (of any race)	3,556	16.4
Central American, ex. Mexican	13	1.1
Salvadoran	0	0.0
Mexican	3,022	16.4

Language Spoken at Home: Spanish
(Universe: Population 5 Years and Over)

Group	Number	%
Total Population	18,594	22.0
Hispanic or Latino (of any race)	17,938	83.0
Central American, ex. Mexican	1,127	93.3
Salvadoran	866	100.0
Mexican	15,369	83.5

Unemployment Rate
(Universe: Population 16 Years and Over)

Group	%
Total Population	6.8
Hispanic or Latino (of any race)	6.5
Central American, ex. Mexican	7.7
Salvadoran	11.4
Mexican	6.7

Class of Worker: Private Wage and Salary
(Universe: Civilian Employed Population 16 Years and Over)

Group	Number	%
Total Population	45,274	85.5
Hispanic or Latino (of any race)	11,002	87.9
Central American, ex. Mexican	628	83.4
Salvadoran	394	80.1
Mexican	9,358	89.6

Class of Worker: Government
(Universe: Civilian Employed Population 16 Years and Over)

Group	Number	%
Total Population	5,369	10.1
Hispanic or Latino (of any race)	869	6.9
Central American, ex. Mexican	11	1.5
Salvadoran	0	0.0
Mexican	631	6.0

Means of Transportation to Work: Car, Truck or Van
(Universe: Workers 16 Years and Over)

Group	Number	%
Total Population	48,248	93.8

Notes: (1) Percent of total population; (2) Percent of Hispanic/Latino population; Profiles include places with an overall population of at least 125,000, OR an overall population of at least 25,000 where the Hispanic/Latino population is at least 20% of the overall population. In states where less than five places meet either of these criteria, we have included places with at least 10,000 total population with the highest percentage of Hispanic/Latino population. These places are identified with an asterisk (*); Please refer to the User's Guide for a full explanation of data.

Group	Number	%
Hispanic or Latino (of any race)	11,440	95.0
Central American, ex. Mexican	753	100.0
Salvadoran	492	100.0
Mexican	9,465	94.5

Means of Transportation to Work: Public Transportation (ex. Taxicab)
(Universe: Workers 16 Years and Over)

Group	Number	%
Total Population	250	0.5
Hispanic or Latino (of any race)	84	0.7
Central American, ex. Mexican	0	0.0
Salvadoran	0	0.0
Mexican	84	0.8

Homeownership Rate
(Universe: Occupied Housing Units)

Group	%
Total Population	45.7
Hispanic or Latino (of any race)	40.0
Central American, ex. Mexican	41.5
Guatemalan	23.1
Honduran	32.0
Salvadoran	48.0
Cuban	45.1
Dominican Republic	17.9
Mexican	40.6
Puerto Rican	33.5
South American	43.8
Colombian	42.0
Peruvian	48.9
Spaniard	41.9

Median Home Value

Group	Dollars
Total Population	149,900
Hispanic or Latino (of any race)	114,700
Central American, ex. Mexican	114,700
Salvadoran	114,100
Mexican	110,900

Median Gross Rent

Group	Dollars
Total Population	887
Hispanic or Latino (of any race)	843
Central American, ex. Mexican	771
Salvadoran	765
Mexican	838

Median Household Income
(2010 Inflation-Adjusted Dollars)

Group	Dollars
Total Population	54,589
Hispanic or Latino (of any race)	42,101
Central American, ex. Mexican	34,933
Salvadoran	40,833
Mexican	42,211

Per Capita Income
(2010 Inflation-Adjusted Dollars)

Group	Dollars
Total Population	27,320
Hispanic or Latino (of any race)	15,043
Central American, ex. Mexican	13,241
Salvadoran	12,430
Mexican	14,363

Households with $100,000+ Income

Group	Number	%
Total Population	6,992	19.3
Hispanic or Latino (of any race)	648	9.2
Central American, ex. Mexican	0	0.0
Salvadoran	0	0.0
Mexican	526	9.0

Households with Food Stamps/SNAP Benefits During Past 12 Months

Group	Number	%
Total Population	2,058	5.7
Hispanic or Latino (of any race)	774	11.0
Central American, ex. Mexican	11	3.0
Salvadoran	0	0.0
Mexican	669	11.5

Poverty Rate
(Income in Past 12 Months Below Poverty Level)

Group	%
Total Population	8.7
Hispanic or Latino (of any race)	17.7
Central American, ex. Mexican	2.1
Salvadoran	2.8
Mexican	19.7

Little Elm

Population

Group	Number	%TP[1]	%HP[2]
Total Population	25,898	100.0	–
Hispanic or Latino (of any race)	6,228	24.0	100.0
Central American, ex. Mexican	807	3.1	13.0
Guatemalan	144	0.6	2.3
Honduran	111	0.4	1.8
Salvadoran	444	1.7	7.1
Cuban	104	0.4	1.7
Mexican	4,208	16.2	67.6
Puerto Rican	261	1.0	4.2
South American	304	1.2	4.9
Colombian	105	0.4	1.7

Population Growth: 2000–2010

Group	%
Total Population	610.3
Hispanic or Latino (of any race)	644.1
Mexican	524.3

Males per 100 Females

Group	Number
Total Population	96.3
Hispanic or Latino (of any race)	98.0
Central American, ex. Mexican	99.8
Guatemalan	97.3
Honduran	113.5
Salvadoran	97.3
Cuban	100.0
Mexican	99.0
Puerto Rican	100.8
South American	92.4
Colombian	59.1

Average Household Size

Group	People
Total Population	3.17
Hispanic or Latino (of any race)	3.96
Central American, ex. Mexican	4.14
Guatemalan	4.41
Honduran	4.26
Salvadoran	4.34
Cuban	3.06
Mexican	4.04
Puerto Rican	3.59
South American	3.64
Colombian	3.71

Median Age

Group	Years
Total Population	30.8
Hispanic or Latino (of any race)	24.9
Central American, ex. Mexican	31.0
Guatemalan	32.3
Honduran	31.5
Salvadoran	29.4
Cuban	36.0
Mexican	23.1
Puerto Rican	29.1
South American	32.2
Colombian	31.2

High School Graduates
(Universe: Population 25 Years and Over)

Group	Number	%
Total Population	11,398	87.6
Hispanic or Latino (of any race)	1,712	66.2
Central American, ex. Mexican	272	65.4
Mexican	1,053	61.8

Four-Year College Graduates
(Universe: Population 25 Years and Over)

Group	Number	%
Total Population	3,855	29.6
Hispanic or Latino (of any race)	418	16.2
Central American, ex. Mexican	31	7.5
Mexican	252	14.8

Population Age 3–17 Enrolled in Public School
(Universe: Population Age 3–17 Enrolled in School)

Group	Number	%
Total Population	5,059	91.0
Hispanic or Latino (of any race)	1,442	94.7
Central American, ex. Mexican	353	100.0
Mexican	946	95.2

Population Age 3–17 Enrolled in Private School
(Universe: Population Age 3–17 Enrolled in School)

Group	Number	%
Total Population	503	9.0
Hispanic or Latino (of any race)	81	5.3
Central American, ex. Mexican	0	0.0
Mexican	48	4.8

Foreign-Born Population

Group	Number	%
Total Population	3,156	14.2
Hispanic or Latino (of any race)	1,938	37.9
Central American, ex. Mexican	438	46.9
Mexican	1,154	34.1

Foreign-Born Naturalized U.S. Citizens

Group	Number	%
Total Population	1,188	37.6
Hispanic or Latino (of any race)	512	26.4
Central American, ex. Mexican	131	29.9
Mexican	228	19.8

Language Spoken at Home: English Only
(Universe: Population 5 Years and Over)

Group	Number	%
Total Population	14,395	74.2
Hispanic or Latino (of any race)	739	16.8
Central American, ex. Mexican	31	3.9
Mexican	582	19.7

Language Spoken at Home: Spanish
(Universe: Population 5 Years and Over)

Group	Number	%
Total Population	3,749	19.3
Hispanic or Latino (of any race)	3,650	83.0
Central American, ex. Mexican	769	96.1
Mexican	2,365	80.3

Unemployment Rate
(Universe: Population 16 Years and Over)

Group	%
Total Population	8.4
Hispanic or Latino (of any race)	10.7
Central American, ex. Mexican	36.7
Mexican	4.2

Class of Worker: Private Wage and Salary
(Universe: Civilian Employed Population 16 Years and Over)

Group	Number	%
Total Population	9,401	85.8
Hispanic or Latino (of any race)	1,929	91.7
Central American, ex. Mexican	206	82.4
Mexican	1,440	95.0

Class of Worker: Government
(Universe: Civilian Employed Population 16 Years and Over)

Group	Number	%
Total Population	1,146	10.5
Hispanic or Latino (of any race)	120	5.7
Central American, ex. Mexican	0	0.0
Mexican	72	4.7

Means of Transportation to Work: Car, Truck or Van
(Universe: Workers 16 Years and Over)

Group	Number	%
Total Population	10,098	94.4
Hispanic or Latino (of any race)	2,025	97.0
Central American, ex. Mexican	199	79.6
Mexican	1,504	99.2

Notes: (1) Percent of total population; (2) Percent of Hispanic/Latino population; Profiles include places with an overall population of at least 125,000, OR an overall population of at least 25,000 where the Hispanic/Latino population is at least 20% of the overall population. In states where less than five places meet either of these criteria, we have included places with at least 10,000 total population with the highest percentage of Hispanic/Latino population. These places are identified with an asterisk (*); Please refer to the User's Guide for a full explanation of data.

Means of Transportation to Work: Public Transportation (ex. Taxicab)
(Universe: Workers 16 Years and Over)

Group	Number	%
Total Population	0	0.0
Hispanic or Latino (of any race)	0	0.0
Central American, ex. Mexican	0	0.0
Mexican	0	0.0

Homeownership Rate
(Universe: Occupied Housing Units)

Group	%
Total Population	82.4
Hispanic or Latino (of any race)	80.6
Central American, ex. Mexican	87.7
Guatemalan	91.2
Honduran	83.9
Salvadoran	87.7
Cuban	82.4
Mexican	79.3
Puerto Rican	82.6
South American	88.9
Colombian	87.5

Median Home Value

Group	Dollars
Total Population	147,200
Hispanic or Latino (of any race)	140,600
Central American, ex. Mexican	147,800
Mexican	142,100

Median Gross Rent

Group	Dollars
Total Population	1,324
Hispanic or Latino (of any race)	780
Central American, ex. Mexican	–
Mexican	770

Median Household Income
(2010 Inflation-Adjusted Dollars)

Group	Dollars
Total Population	77,198
Hispanic or Latino (of any race)	47,314
Central American, ex. Mexican	33,750
Mexican	51,678

Per Capita Income
(2010 Inflation-Adjusted Dollars)

Group	Dollars
Total Population	25,149
Hispanic or Latino (of any race)	14,117
Central American, ex. Mexican	8,309
Mexican	15,472

Households with $100,000+ Income

Group	Number	%
Total Population	1,871	27.1
Hispanic or Latino (of any race)	131	11.0
Central American, ex. Mexican	0	0.0
Mexican	125	15.8

Households with Food Stamps/SNAP Benefits During Past 12 Months

Group	Number	%
Total Population	241	3.5
Hispanic or Latino (of any race)	42	3.5
Central American, ex. Mexican	22	11.2
Mexican	20	2.5

Poverty Rate
(Income in Past 12 Months Below Poverty Level)

Group	%
Total Population	6.8
Hispanic or Latino (of any race)	14.1
Central American, ex. Mexican	17.5
Mexican	14.6

Lubbock

Population

Group	Number	%TP[1]	%HP[2]
Total Population	229,573	100.0	–
Hispanic or Latino (of any race)	73,625	32.1	100.0
Central American, ex. Mexican	490	0.2	0.7
Salvadoran	155	0.1	0.2
Cuban	207	0.1	0.3
Mexican	60,977	26.6	82.8
Puerto Rican	490	0.2	0.7
South American	400	0.2	0.5
Colombian	160	0.1	0.2
Spaniard	830	0.4	1.1

Population Growth: 2000–2010

Group	%
Total Population	15.0
Hispanic or Latino (of any race)	34.4
Central American, ex. Mexican	237.9
Mexican	88.2
Puerto Rican	40.0
South American	89.6

Males per 100 Females

Group	Number
Total Population	96.5
Hispanic or Latino (of any race)	99.6
Central American, ex. Mexican	135.6
Salvadoran	146.0
Cuban	115.6
Mexican	101.2
Puerto Rican	89.9
South American	95.1
Colombian	92.8
Spaniard	90.8

Average Household Size

Group	People
Total Population	2.48
Hispanic or Latino (of any race)	3.06
Central American, ex. Mexican	2.98
Salvadoran	3.18
Cuban	2.92
Mexican	3.07
Puerto Rican	2.56
South American	2.50
Colombian	2.40
Spaniard	2.84

Median Age

Group	Years
Total Population	29.2
Hispanic or Latino (of any race)	25.0
Central American, ex. Mexican	27.7
Salvadoran	25.0
Cuban	25.3
Mexican	25.1
Puerto Rican	23.8
South American	27.8
Colombian	25.8
Spaniard	26.3

High School Graduates
(Universe: Population 25 Years and Over)

Group	Number	%
Total Population	106,910	84.1
Hispanic or Latino (of any race)	22,931	65.8
Central American, ex. Mexican	223	49.0
Mexican	19,783	65.7
Spaniard	547	82.9

Four-Year College Graduates
(Universe: Population 25 Years and Over)

Group	Number	%
Total Population	37,513	29.5
Hispanic or Latino (of any race)	3,522	10.1
Central American, ex. Mexican	60	13.2
Mexican	2,892	9.6
Spaniard	141	21.4

Population Age 3–17 Enrolled in Public School
(Universe: Population Age 3–17 Enrolled in School)

Group	Number	%
Total Population	33,393	91.2
Hispanic or Latino (of any race)	15,628	96.3
Central American, ex. Mexican	265	92.7
Mexican	13,066	96.8
Spaniard	118	77.1

Population Age 3–17 Enrolled in Private School
(Universe: Population Age 3–17 Enrolled in School)

Group	Number	%
Total Population	3,224	8.8
Hispanic or Latino (of any race)	599	3.7
Central American, ex. Mexican	21	7.3
Mexican	437	3.2
Spaniard	35	22.9

Foreign-Born Population

Group	Number	%
Total Population	12,404	5.6
Hispanic or Latino (of any race)	6,724	9.7
Central American, ex. Mexican	506	55.2
Mexican	5,709	9.6
Spaniard	0	0.0

Foreign-Born Naturalized U.S. Citizens

Group	Number	%
Total Population	4,322	34.8
Hispanic or Latino (of any race)	2,071	30.8
Central American, ex. Mexican	170	33.6
Mexican	1,677	29.4
Spaniard	0	0.0

Language Spoken at Home: English Only
(Universe: Population 5 Years and Over)

Group	Number	%
Total Population	160,089	77.8
Hispanic or Latino (of any race)	25,072	40.6
Central American, ex. Mexican	133	15.3
Mexican	21,275	40.3
Spaniard	383	41.3

Language Spoken at Home: Spanish
(Universe: Population 5 Years and Over)

Group	Number	%
Total Population	39,361	19.1
Hispanic or Latino (of any race)	36,591	59.2
Central American, ex. Mexican	735	84.7
Mexican	31,545	59.7
Spaniard	517	55.7

Unemployment Rate
(Universe: Population 16 Years and Over)

Group	%
Total Population	6.2
Hispanic or Latino (of any race)	7.9
Central American, ex. Mexican	7.6
Mexican	7.7
Spaniard	0.0

Class of Worker: Private Wage and Salary
(Universe: Civilian Employed Population 16 Years and Over)

Group	Number	%
Total Population	81,781	75.0
Hispanic or Latino (of any race)	24,959	79.0
Central American, ex. Mexican	318	84.4
Mexican	21,646	78.8
Spaniard	473	88.4

Class of Worker: Government
(Universe: Civilian Employed Population 16 Years and Over)

Group	Number	%
Total Population	20,475	18.8
Hispanic or Latino (of any race)	5,077	16.1
Central American, ex. Mexican	46	12.2
Mexican	4,401	16.0
Spaniard	53	9.9

Means of Transportation to Work: Car, Truck or Van
(Universe: Workers 16 Years and Over)

Group	Number	%
Total Population	98,416	92.4
Hispanic or Latino (of any race)	29,416	94.8
Central American, ex. Mexican	356	100.0
Mexican	25,608	94.9
Spaniard	494	92.3

Means of Transportation to Work: Public Transportation (ex. Taxicab)
(Universe: Workers 16 Years and Over)

Group	Number	%
Total Population	1,231	1.2

STATE & PLACE PROFILES

Notes: (1) Percent of total population; (2) Percent of Hispanic/Latino population; Profiles include places with an overall population of at least 125,000, OR an overall population of at least 25,000 where the Hispanic/Latino population is at least 20% of the overall population. In states where less than five places meet either of these criteria, we have included places with at least 10,000 total population with the highest percentage of Hispanic/Latino population. These places are identified with an asterisk (*); Please refer to the User's Guide for a full explanation of data.

Group	Number	%TP	%HP
Hispanic or Latino (of any race)	179	0.6	
Central American, ex. Mexican	0	0.0	
Mexican	158	0.6	
Spaniard	0	0.0	

Homeownership Rate
(Universe: Occupied Housing Units)

Group	%
Total Population	54.6
Hispanic or Latino (of any race)	47.4
Central American, ex. Mexican	45.9
Salvadoran	47.1
Cuban	43.7
Mexican	48.2
Puerto Rican	35.6
South American	38.8
Colombian	27.3
Spaniard	45.3

Median Home Value

Group	Dollars
Total Population	106,600
Hispanic or Latino (of any race)	74,000
Central American, ex. Mexican	100,300
Mexican	74,000
Spaniard	92,200

Median Gross Rent

Group	Dollars
Total Population	737
Hispanic or Latino (of any race)	686
Central American, ex. Mexican	964
Mexican	679
Spaniard	793

Median Household Income
(2010 Inflation-Adjusted Dollars)

Group	Dollars
Total Population	41,262
Hispanic or Latino (of any race)	33,819
Central American, ex. Mexican	41,472
Mexican	34,310
Spaniard	34,355

Per Capita Income
(2010 Inflation-Adjusted Dollars)

Group	Dollars
Total Population	22,726
Hispanic or Latino (of any race)	13,520
Central American, ex. Mexican	14,668
Mexican	13,494
Spaniard	19,350

Households with $100,000+ Income

Group	Number	%
Total Population	11,817	13.7
Hispanic or Latino (of any race)	1,147	5.4
Central American, ex. Mexican	48	21.5
Mexican	991	5.5
Spaniard	9	2.0

Households with Food Stamps/SNAP Benefits During Past 12 Months

Group	Number	%
Total Population	9,261	10.8
Hispanic or Latino (of any race)	4,543	21.5
Central American, ex. Mexican	76	34.1
Mexican	3,900	21.6
Spaniard	50	10.9

Poverty Rate
(Income in Past 12 Months Below Poverty Level)

Group	%
Total Population	20.4
Hispanic or Latino (of any race)	25.4
Central American, ex. Mexican	33.9
Mexican	25.2
Spaniard	10.7

Lufkin

Population

Group	Number	%TP[1]	%HP[2]
Total Population	35,067	100.0	–
Hispanic or Latino (of any race)	8,464	24.1	100.0
Central American, ex. Mexican	255	0.7	3.0
Salvadoran	190	0.5	2.2
Mexican	7,615	21.7	90.0

Population Growth: 2000–2010

Group	%
Total Population	7.2
Hispanic or Latino (of any race)	47.1
Mexican	59.6

Males per 100 Females

Group	Number
Total Population	89.2
Hispanic or Latino (of any race)	106.8
Central American, ex. Mexican	99.2
Salvadoran	97.9
Mexican	106.9

Average Household Size

Group	People
Total Population	2.62
Hispanic or Latino (of any race)	3.97
Central American, ex. Mexican	4.19
Salvadoran	4.67
Mexican	4.02

Median Age

Group	Years
Total Population	34.0
Hispanic or Latino (of any race)	23.4
Central American, ex. Mexican	28.0
Salvadoran	27.2
Mexican	23.0

High School Graduates
(Universe: Population 25 Years and Over)

Group	Number	%
Total Population	17,113	78.2
Hispanic or Latino (of any race)	1,743	45.9
Mexican	1,405	43.3

Four-Year College Graduates
(Universe: Population 25 Years and Over)

Group	Number	%
Total Population	4,242	19.4
Hispanic or Latino (of any race)	43	1.1
Mexican	28	0.9

Population Age 3–17 Enrolled in Public School
(Universe: Population Age 3–17 Enrolled in School)

Group	Number	%
Total Population	6,430	95.0
Hispanic or Latino (of any race)	2,274	98.1
Mexican	2,186	98.0

Population Age 3–17 Enrolled in Private School
(Universe: Population Age 3–17 Enrolled in School)

Group	Number	%
Total Population	338	5.0
Hispanic or Latino (of any race)	44	1.9
Mexican	44	2.0

Foreign-Born Population

Group	Number	%
Total Population	4,195	12.1
Hispanic or Latino (of any race)	3,721	45.4
Mexican	3,348	45.0

Foreign-Born Naturalized U.S. Citizens

Group	Number	%
Total Population	847	20.2
Hispanic or Latino (of any race)	632	17.0
Mexican	613	18.3

Language Spoken at Home: English Only
(Universe: Population 5 Years and Over)

Group	Number	%
Total Population	24,899	78.4
Hispanic or Latino (of any race)	1,189	17.2
Mexican	1,010	16.2

Language Spoken at Home: Spanish
(Universe: Population 5 Years and Over)

Group	Number	%
Total Population	6,382	20.1
Hispanic or Latino (of any race)	5,738	82.8
Mexican	5,208	83.8

Unemployment Rate
(Universe: Population 16 Years and Over)

Group	%
Total Population	8.3
Hispanic or Latino (of any race)	6.9
Mexican	6.3

Class of Worker: Private Wage and Salary
(Universe: Civilian Employed Population 16 Years and Over)

Group	Number	%
Total Population	11,059	76.8
Hispanic or Latino (of any race)	2,760	88.1
Mexican	2,408	88.6

Class of Worker: Government
(Universe: Civilian Employed Population 16 Years and Over)

Group	Number	%
Total Population	2,377	16.5
Hispanic or Latino (of any race)	259	8.3
Mexican	202	7.4

Means of Transportation to Work: Car, Truck or Van
(Universe: Workers 16 Years and Over)

Group	Number	%
Total Population	13,297	94.8
Hispanic or Latino (of any race)	3,032	98.0
Mexican	2,635	98.3

Means of Transportation to Work: Public Transportation (ex. Taxicab)
(Universe: Workers 16 Years and Over)

Group	Number	%
Total Population	77	0.5
Hispanic or Latino (of any race)	16	0.5
Mexican	0	0.0

Homeownership Rate
(Universe: Occupied Housing Units)

Group	%
Total Population	55.4
Hispanic or Latino (of any race)	58.9
Central American, ex. Mexican	51.4
Salvadoran	59.2
Mexican	60.1

Median Home Value

Group	Dollars
Total Population	87,700
Hispanic or Latino (of any race)	56,700
Mexican	56,000

Median Gross Rent

Group	Dollars
Total Population	681
Hispanic or Latino (of any race)	656
Mexican	666

Median Household Income
(2010 Inflation-Adjusted Dollars)

Group	Dollars
Total Population	35,988
Hispanic or Latino (of any race)	30,918
Mexican	30,176

Per Capita Income
(2010 Inflation-Adjusted Dollars)

Group	Dollars
Total Population	21,473
Hispanic or Latino (of any race)	9,647
Mexican	9,019

Households with $100,000+ Income

Group	Number	%
Total Population	1,679	12.9
Hispanic or Latino (of any race)	68	3.4
Mexican	57	3.2

Households with Food Stamps/SNAP Benefits During Past 12 Months

Group	Number	%
Total Population	1,963	15.1
Hispanic or Latino (of any race)	409	20.6

Notes: (1) Percent of total population; (2) Percent of Hispanic/Latino population; Profiles include places with an overall population of at least 125,000, OR an overall population of at least 25,000 where the Hispanic/Latino population is at least 20% of the overall population. In states where less than five places meet either of these criteria, we have included places with at least 10,000 total population with the highest percentage of Hispanic/Latino population. These places are identified with an asterisk (*); Please refer to the User's Guide for a full explanation of data.

Mexican	328	18.7

Poverty Rate
(Income in Past 12 Months Below Poverty Level)

Group	%
Total Population	20.2
Hispanic or Latino (of any race)	32.5
Mexican	34.2

McAllen

Population

Group	Number	%TP[1]	%HP[2]
Total Population	129,877	100.0	–
Hispanic or Latino (of any race)	109,910	84.6	100.0
Central American, ex. Mexican	609	0.5	0.6
Guatemalan	112	0.1	0.1
Honduran	147	0.1	0.1
Salvadoran	192	0.1	0.2
Cuban	328	0.3	0.3
Dominican Republic	191	0.1	0.2
Mexican	100,963	77.7	91.9
Puerto Rican	574	0.4	0.5
South American	817	0.6	0.7
Argentinean	137	0.1	0.1
Colombian	253	0.2	0.2
Peruvian	161	0.1	0.1
Venezuelan	100	0.1	0.1
Spaniard	403	0.3	0.4

Population Growth: 2000–2010

Group	%
Total Population	22.0
Hispanic or Latino (of any race)	28.7
Central American, ex. Mexican	131.6
Cuban	65.7
Mexican	44.4
Puerto Rican	56.8
South American	132.1
Colombian	138.7

Males per 100 Females

Group	Number
Total Population	91.5
Hispanic or Latino (of any race)	89.8
Central American, ex. Mexican	89.1
Guatemalan	89.8
Honduran	98.6
Salvadoran	95.9
Cuban	120.1
Dominican Republic	91.0
Mexican	89.7
Puerto Rican	115.0
South American	95.9
Argentinean	98.6
Colombian	88.8
Peruvian	91.7
Venezuelan	85.2
Spaniard	86.6

Average Household Size

Group	People
Total Population	3.10
Hispanic or Latino (of any race)	3.26
Central American, ex. Mexican	3.22
Guatemalan	3.60
Honduran	2.81
Salvadoran	3.48
Cuban	2.73
Dominican Republic	3.13
Mexican	3.28
Puerto Rican	2.96
South American	3.02
Argentinean	2.95
Colombian	2.91
Peruvian	2.75
Venezuelan	3.58
Spaniard	2.56

Median Age

Group	Years
Total Population	32.2
Hispanic or Latino (of any race)	30.3
Central American, ex. Mexican	36.1
Guatemalan	37.3
Honduran	28.7
Salvadoran	37.4
Cuban	40.5
Dominican Republic	32.7
Mexican	30.3
Puerto Rican	34.4
South American	37.0
Argentinean	39.3
Colombian	36.3
Peruvian	39.5
Venezuelan	33.0
Spaniard	39.1

High School Graduates
(Universe: Population 25 Years and Over)

Group	Number	%
Total Population	54,464	73.7
Hispanic or Latino (of any race)	41,034	68.8
Mexican	37,859	67.9

Four-Year College Graduates
(Universe: Population 25 Years and Over)

Group	Number	%
Total Population	20,457	27.7
Hispanic or Latino (of any race)	13,601	22.8
Mexican	12,379	22.2

Population Age 3–17 Enrolled in Public School
(Universe: Population Age 3–17 Enrolled in School)

Group	Number	%
Total Population	27,104	93.6
Hispanic or Latino (of any race)	23,687	95.7
Mexican	22,325	95.8

Population Age 3–17 Enrolled in Private School
(Universe: Population Age 3–17 Enrolled in School)

Group	Number	%
Total Population	1,857	6.4
Hispanic or Latino (of any race)	1,075	4.3
Mexican	973	4.2

Foreign-Born Population

Group	Number	%
Total Population	35,637	28.4
Hispanic or Latino (of any race)	32,645	31.3
Mexican	31,009	31.8

Foreign-Born Naturalized U.S. Citizens

Group	Number	%
Total Population	12,144	34.1
Hispanic or Latino (of any race)	10,832	33.2
Mexican	9,922	32.0

Language Spoken at Home: English Only
(Universe: Population 5 Years and Over)

Group	Number	%
Total Population	25,308	22.1
Hispanic or Latino (of any race)	12,095	12.7
Mexican	10,855	12.2

Language Spoken at Home: Spanish
(Universe: Population 5 Years and Over)

Group	Number	%
Total Population	86,519	75.6
Hispanic or Latino (of any race)	82,905	87.3
Mexican	78,101	87.8

Unemployment Rate
(Universe: Population 16 Years and Over)

Group	%
Total Population	6.4
Hispanic or Latino (of any race)	6.7
Mexican	6.8

Class of Worker: Private Wage and Salary
(Universe: Civilian Employed Population 16 Years and Over)

Group	Number	%
Total Population	37,581	71.2
Hispanic or Latino (of any race)	30,820	71.6
Mexican	28,846	72.0

Class of Worker: Government
(Universe: Civilian Employed Population 16 Years and Over)

Group	Number	%
Total Population	9,388	17.8
Hispanic or Latino (of any race)	7,470	17.4
Mexican	6,824	17.0

Means of Transportation to Work: Car, Truck or Van
(Universe: Workers 16 Years and Over)

Group	Number	%
Total Population	46,848	91.2
Hispanic or Latino (of any race)	38,248	91.0
Mexican	35,623	91.0

Means of Transportation to Work: Public Transportation (ex. Taxicab)
(Universe: Workers 16 Years and Over)

Group	Number	%
Total Population	414	0.8
Hispanic or Latino (of any race)	407	1.0
Mexican	389	1.0

Homeownership Rate
(Universe: Occupied Housing Units)

Group	%
Total Population	61.3
Hispanic or Latino (of any race)	59.2
Central American, ex. Mexican	50.0
Guatemalan	44.2
Honduran	41.7
Salvadoran	57.5
Cuban	48.9
Dominican Republic	48.6
Mexican	59.6
Puerto Rican	54.1
South American	61.8
Argentinean	50.9
Colombian	57.4
Peruvian	63.2
Venezuelan	62.5
Spaniard	60.6

Median Home Value

Group	Dollars
Total Population	100,000
Hispanic or Latino (of any race)	94,300
Mexican	93,900

Median Gross Rent

Group	Dollars
Total Population	675
Hispanic or Latino (of any race)	654
Mexican	653

Median Household Income
(2010 Inflation-Adjusted Dollars)

Group	Dollars
Total Population	39,547
Hispanic or Latino (of any race)	34,371
Mexican	33,953

Per Capita Income
(2010 Inflation-Adjusted Dollars)

Group	Dollars
Total Population	19,490
Hispanic or Latino (of any race)	16,441
Mexican	15,867

Households with $100,000+ Income

Group	Number	%
Total Population	5,978	14.9
Hispanic or Latino (of any race)	3,719	11.8
Mexican	3,433	11.7

Households with Food Stamps/SNAP Benefits During Past 12 Months

Group	Number	%
Total Population	8,072	20.1
Hispanic or Latino (of any race)	7,607	24.2
Mexican	7,360	25.1

Poverty Rate
(Income in Past 12 Months Below Poverty Level)

Group	%
Total Population	27.0
Hispanic or Latino (of any race)	30.3
Mexican	31.7

Notes: (1) Percent of total population; (2) Percent of Hispanic/Latino population; Profiles include places with an overall population of at least 125,000, OR an overall population of at least 25,000 where the Hispanic/Latino population is at least 20% of the overall population. In states where less than five places meet either of these criteria, we have included places with at least 10,000 total population with the highest percentage of Hispanic/Latino population. These places are identified with an asterisk (*); Please refer to the User's Guide for a full explanation of data.

McKinney

Population

Group	Number	%TP[1]	%HP[2]
Total Population	131,117	100.0	–
Hispanic or Latino (of any race)	24,406	18.6	100.0
Central American, ex. Mexican	1,270	1.0	5.2
Guatemalan	178	0.1	0.7
Honduran	286	0.2	1.2
Panamanian	106	0.1	0.4
Salvadoran	578	0.4	2.4
Cuban	290	0.2	1.2
Dominican Republic	103	0.1	0.4
Mexican	18,917	14.4	77.5
Puerto Rican	839	0.6	3.4
South American	1,054	0.8	4.3
Colombian	359	0.3	1.5
Ecuadorian	114	0.1	0.5
Peruvian	212	0.2	0.9
Venezuelan	166	0.1	0.7
Spaniard	362	0.3	1.5

Population Growth: 2000–2010

Group	%
Total Population	141.2
Hispanic or Latino (of any race)	147.1
Central American, ex. Mexican	528.7
Mexican	142.9
Puerto Rican	466.9
South American	933.3

Males per 100 Females

Group	Number
Total Population	96.6
Hispanic or Latino (of any race)	106.8
Central American, ex. Mexican	92.1
Guatemalan	74.5
Honduran	101.4
Panamanian	68.3
Salvadoran	99.3
Cuban	116.4
Dominican Republic	77.6
Mexican	110.1
Puerto Rican	106.1
South American	82.0
Colombian	79.5
Ecuadorian	93.2
Peruvian	91.0
Venezuelan	74.7
Spaniard	109.2

Average Household Size

Group	People
Total Population	2.91
Hispanic or Latino (of any race)	3.74
Central American, ex. Mexican	3.87
Guatemalan	3.83
Honduran	4.09
Panamanian	2.89
Salvadoran	4.18
Cuban	2.86
Dominican Republic	3.31
Mexican	3.87
Puerto Rican	3.05
South American	3.43
Colombian	3.27
Ecuadorian	4.15
Peruvian	3.49
Venezuelan	3.40
Spaniard	2.93

Median Age

Group	Years
Total Population	32.7
Hispanic or Latino (of any race)	25.3
Central American, ex. Mexican	30.2
Guatemalan	27.3
Honduran	31.0
Panamanian	29.0
Salvadoran	29.8
Cuban	31.0
Dominican Republic	28.2
Mexican	24.4
Puerto Rican	28.2
South American	32.8
Colombian	32.3
Ecuadorian	29.0
Peruvian	36.3
Venezuelan	34.2
Spaniard	29.4

High School Graduates
(Universe: Population 25 Years and Over)

Group	Number	%
Total Population	66,065	92.2
Hispanic or Latino (of any race)	6,557	65.4
Central American, ex. Mexican	370	70.1
Mexican	4,937	60.6
South American	518	100.0

Four-Year College Graduates
(Universe: Population 25 Years and Over)

Group	Number	%
Total Population	31,554	44.0
Hispanic or Latino (of any race)	2,054	20.5
Central American, ex. Mexican	94	17.8
Mexican	1,385	17.0
South American	200	38.6

Population Age 3–17 Enrolled in Public School
(Universe: Population Age 3–17 Enrolled in School)

Group	Number	%
Total Population	23,864	85.4
Hispanic or Latino (of any race)	4,488	93.0
Central American, ex. Mexican	354	89.4
Mexican	3,720	93.1
South American	121	84.6

Population Age 3–17 Enrolled in Private School
(Universe: Population Age 3–17 Enrolled in School)

Group	Number	%
Total Population	4,078	14.6
Hispanic or Latino (of any race)	340	7.0
Central American, ex. Mexican	42	10.6
Mexican	276	6.9
South American	22	15.4

Foreign-Born Population

Group	Number	%
Total Population	13,891	11.7
Hispanic or Latino (of any race)	7,639	37.2
Central American, ex. Mexican	664	54.4
Mexican	6,220	36.5
South American	571	66.4

Foreign-Born Naturalized U.S. Citizens

Group	Number	%
Total Population	5,250	37.8
Hispanic or Latino (of any race)	1,677	22.0
Central American, ex. Mexican	245	36.9
Mexican	1,087	17.5
South American	223	39.1

Language Spoken at Home: English Only
(Universe: Population 5 Years and Over)

Group	Number	%
Total Population	86,939	81.0
Hispanic or Latino (of any race)	5,137	29.0
Central American, ex. Mexican	200	19.7
Mexican	4,126	28.2
South American	142	18.0

Language Spoken at Home: Spanish
(Universe: Population 5 Years and Over)

Group	Number	%
Total Population	14,267	13.3
Hispanic or Latino (of any race)	12,542	70.7
Central American, ex. Mexican	815	80.3
Mexican	10,495	71.8
South American	648	82.0

Unemployment Rate
(Universe: Population 16 Years and Over)

Group	%
Total Population	4.6
Hispanic or Latino (of any race)	4.9
Central American, ex. Mexican	1.3
Mexican	4.9
South American	0.0

Class of Worker: Private Wage and Salary
(Universe: Civilian Employed Population 16 Years and Over)

Group	Number	%
Total Population	49,098	85.6
Hispanic or Latino (of any race)	8,213	90.0
Central American, ex. Mexican	411	90.7
Mexican	6,778	90.7
South American	484	87.8

Class of Worker: Government
(Universe: Civilian Employed Population 16 Years and Over)

Group	Number	%
Total Population	5,536	9.6
Hispanic or Latino (of any race)	589	6.5
Central American, ex. Mexican	23	5.1
Mexican	502	6.7
South American	12	2.2

Means of Transportation to Work: Car, Truck or Van
(Universe: Workers 16 Years and Over)

Group	Number	%
Total Population	50,177	88.6
Hispanic or Latino (of any race)	7,741	85.4
Central American, ex. Mexican	431	95.1
Mexican	6,324	85.3
South American	505	91.7

Means of Transportation to Work: Public Transportation (ex. Taxicab)
(Universe: Workers 16 Years and Over)

Group	Number	%
Total Population	469	0.8
Hispanic or Latino (of any race)	88	1.0
Central American, ex. Mexican	0	0.0
Mexican	75	1.0
South American	13	2.4

Homeownership Rate
(Universe: Occupied Housing Units)

Group	%
Total Population	71.0
Hispanic or Latino (of any race)	57.3
Central American, ex. Mexican	66.3
Guatemalan	59.5
Honduran	66.2
Panamanian	78.6
Salvadoran	67.3
Cuban	70.4
Dominican Republic	58.6
Mexican	54.6
Puerto Rican	70.3
South American	75.3
Colombian	72.4
Ecuadorian	80.8
Peruvian	74.6
Venezuelan	73.1
Spaniard	73.3

Median Home Value

Group	Dollars
Total Population	185,300
Hispanic or Latino (of any race)	157,400
Central American, ex. Mexican	153,800
Mexican	152,600
South American	171,300

Median Gross Rent

Group	Dollars
Total Population	943
Hispanic or Latino (of any race)	854
Central American, ex. Mexican	995
Mexican	821
South American	1,313

Median Household Income
(2010 Inflation-Adjusted Dollars)

Group	Dollars
Total Population	78,256
Hispanic or Latino (of any race)	44,153
Central American, ex. Mexican	41,944
Mexican	39,534
South American	64,063

Notes: (1) Percent of total population; (2) Percent of Hispanic/Latino population; Profiles include places with an overall population of at least 125,000, OR an overall population of at least 25,000 where the Hispanic/Latino population is at least 20% of the overall population. In states where less than five places meet either of these criteria, we have included places with at least 10,000 total population with the highest percentage of Hispanic/Latino population. These places are identified with an asterisk (*); Please refer to the User's Guide for a full explanation of data.

Per Capita Income
(2010 Inflation-Adjusted Dollars)

Group	Dollars
Total Population	31,635
Hispanic or Latino (of any race)	15,804
Central American, ex. Mexican	11,143
Mexican	14,755
South American	18,392

Households with $100,000+ Income

Group	Number	%
Total Population	14,528	36.7
Hispanic or Latino (of any race)	716	13.9
Central American, ex. Mexican	0	0.0
Mexican	504	12.2
South American	24	8.9

Households with Food Stamps/SNAP Benefits During Past 12 Months

Group	Number	%
Total Population	1,098	2.8
Hispanic or Latino (of any race)	419	8.1
Central American, ex. Mexican	0	0.0
Mexican	350	8.5
South American	7	2.6

Poverty Rate
(Income in Past 12 Months Below Poverty Level)

Group	%
Total Population	10.0
Hispanic or Latino (of any race)	24.1
Central American, ex. Mexican	15.7
Mexican	25.7
South American	26.9

Mesquite

Population

Group	Number	%TP[1]	%HP[2]
Total Population	139,824	100.0	–
Hispanic or Latino (of any race)	44,133	31.6	100.0
Central American, ex. Mexican	2,210	1.6	5.0
Guatemalan	415	0.3	0.9
Honduran	369	0.3	0.8
Salvadoran	1,197	0.9	2.7
Cuban	303	0.2	0.7
Dominican Republic	118	0.1	0.3
Mexican	37,430	26.8	84.8
Puerto Rican	615	0.4	1.4
South American	713	0.5	1.6
Colombian	221	0.2	0.5
Peruvian	262	0.2	0.6
Spaniard	259	0.2	0.6

Population Growth: 2000–2010

Group	%
Total Population	12.3
Hispanic or Latino (of any race)	126.3
Central American, ex. Mexican	477.0
Salvadoran	625.5
Cuban	136.7
Mexican	151.3
Puerto Rican	81.4
South American	202.1

Males per 100 Females

Group	Number
Total Population	91.3
Hispanic or Latino (of any race)	100.3
Central American, ex. Mexican	103.5
Guatemalan	102.4
Honduran	97.3
Salvadoran	108.9
Cuban	94.2
Dominican Republic	114.5
Mexican	100.6
Puerto Rican	103.0
South American	84.2
Colombian	84.2
Peruvian	88.5
Spaniard	96.2

Average Household Size

Group	People
Total Population	2.88
Hispanic or Latino (of any race)	3.81
Central American, ex. Mexican	4.03
Guatemalan	4.00
Honduran	4.06
Salvadoran	4.10
Cuban	3.22
Dominican Republic	3.62
Mexican	3.86
Puerto Rican	2.94
South American	3.49
Colombian	3.41
Peruvian	3.86
Spaniard	3.20

Median Age

Group	Years
Total Population	32.3
Hispanic or Latino (of any race)	24.4
Central American, ex. Mexican	30.9
Guatemalan	32.5
Honduran	30.1
Salvadoran	29.5
Cuban	35.4
Dominican Republic	30.5
Mexican	23.8
Puerto Rican	26.1
South American	35.5
Colombian	37.4
Peruvian	36.1
Spaniard	33.3

High School Graduates
(Universe: Population 25 Years and Over)

Group	Number	%
Total Population	67,045	81.8
Hispanic or Latino (of any race)	11,193	60.1
Central American, ex. Mexican	640	74.4
Salvadoran	226	56.5
Mexican	9,453	57.8

Four-Year College Graduates
(Universe: Population 25 Years and Over)

Group	Number	%
Total Population	15,760	19.2
Hispanic or Latino (of any race)	2,094	11.2
Central American, ex. Mexican	118	13.7
Salvadoran	33	8.3
Mexican	1,571	9.6

Population Age 3–17 Enrolled in Public School
(Universe: Population Age 3–17 Enrolled in School)

Group	Number	%
Total Population	28,739	93.9
Hispanic or Latino (of any race)	9,902	97.2
Central American, ex. Mexican	649	100.0
Salvadoran	443	100.0
Mexican	8,552	97.0

Population Age 3–17 Enrolled in Private School
(Universe: Population Age 3–17 Enrolled in School)

Group	Number	%
Total Population	1,873	6.1
Hispanic or Latino (of any race)	289	2.8
Central American, ex. Mexican	0	0.0
Salvadoran	0	0.0
Mexican	262	3.0

Foreign-Born Population

Group	Number	%
Total Population	20,001	14.7
Hispanic or Latino (of any race)	13,702	36.3
Central American, ex. Mexican	1,062	52.1
Salvadoran	587	54.0
Mexican	11,906	36.1

Foreign-Born Naturalized U.S. Citizens

Group	Number	%
Total Population	6,487	32.4
Hispanic or Latino (of any race)	3,082	22.5
Central American, ex. Mexican	342	32.2
Salvadoran	144	24.5
Mexican	2,587	21.7

Language Spoken at Home: English Only
(Universe: Population 5 Years and Over)

Group	Number	%
Total Population	89,608	71.5
Hispanic or Latino (of any race)	6,308	19.0
Central American, ex. Mexican	141	7.8
Salvadoran	90	9.0
Mexican	5,467	18.9

Language Spoken at Home: Spanish
(Universe: Population 5 Years and Over)

Group	Number	%
Total Population	28,342	22.6
Hispanic or Latino (of any race)	26,826	80.8
Central American, ex. Mexican	1,663	92.2
Salvadoran	914	91.0
Mexican	23,411	81.0

Unemployment Rate
(Universe: Population 16 Years and Over)

Group	%
Total Population	6.8
Hispanic or Latino (of any race)	3.9
Central American, ex. Mexican	4.8
Salvadoran	10.1
Mexican	3.7

Class of Worker: Private Wage and Salary
(Universe: Civilian Employed Population 16 Years and Over)

Group	Number	%
Total Population	55,270	82.2
Hispanic or Latino (of any race)	15,049	87.0
Central American, ex. Mexican	797	87.9
Salvadoran	365	89.5
Mexican	13,211	87.5

Class of Worker: Government
(Universe: Civilian Employed Population 16 Years and Over)

Group	Number	%
Total Population	8,437	12.5
Hispanic or Latino (of any race)	1,324	7.7
Central American, ex. Mexican	59	6.5
Salvadoran	25	6.1
Mexican	1,127	7.5

Means of Transportation to Work: Car, Truck or Van
(Universe: Workers 16 Years and Over)

Group	Number	%
Total Population	63,053	95.4
Hispanic or Latino (of any race)	16,488	96.5
Central American, ex. Mexican	821	93.3
Salvadoran	408	100.0
Mexican	14,451	96.8

Means of Transportation to Work: Public Transportation (ex. Taxicab)
(Universe: Workers 16 Years and Over)

Group	Number	%
Total Population	457	0.7
Hispanic or Latino (of any race)	32	0.2
Central American, ex. Mexican	0	0.0
Salvadoran	0	0.0
Mexican	32	0.2

Homeownership Rate
(Universe: Occupied Housing Units)

Group	%
Total Population	61.4
Hispanic or Latino (of any race)	62.1
Central American, ex. Mexican	70.6
Guatemalan	74.0
Honduran	67.0
Salvadoran	72.0
Cuban	63.8
Dominican Republic	66.7
Mexican	62.5
Puerto Rican	49.0
South American	69.2
Colombian	69.7
Peruvian	73.1
Spaniard	64.5

Notes: (1) Percent of total population; (2) Percent of Hispanic/Latino population; Profiles include places with an overall population of at least 125,000, OR an overall population of at least 25,000 where the Hispanic/Latino population is at least 20% of the overall population. In states where less than five places meet either of these criteria, we have included places with at least 10,000 total population with the highest percentage of Hispanic/Latino population. These places are identified with an asterisk (*); Please refer to the User's Guide for a full explanation of data.

Median Home Value

Group	Dollars
Total Population	113,900
Hispanic or Latino (of any race)	104,800
Central American, ex. Mexican	108,000
Salvadoran	96,600
Mexican	105,100

Median Gross Rent

Group	Dollars
Total Population	895
Hispanic or Latino (of any race)	823
Central American, ex. Mexican	750
Salvadoran	843
Mexican	830

Median Household Income
(2010 Inflation-Adjusted Dollars)

Group	Dollars
Total Population	51,368
Hispanic or Latino (of any race)	45,910
Central American, ex. Mexican	41,394
Salvadoran	41,058
Mexican	45,772

Per Capita Income
(2010 Inflation-Adjusted Dollars)

Group	Dollars
Total Population	22,330
Hispanic or Latino (of any race)	15,316
Central American, ex. Mexican	13,218
Salvadoran	10,413
Mexican	15,247

Households with $100,000+ Income

Group	Number	%
Total Population	8,088	17.3
Hispanic or Latino (of any race)	1,282	13.1
Central American, ex. Mexican	68	13.5
Salvadoran	11	4.2
Mexican	1,119	13.2

Households with Food Stamps/SNAP Benefits During Past 12 Months

Group	Number	%
Total Population	3,051	6.5
Hispanic or Latino (of any race)	570	5.8
Central American, ex. Mexican	34	6.7
Salvadoran	24	9.2
Mexican	462	5.5

Poverty Rate
(Income in Past 12 Months Below Poverty Level)

Group	%
Total Population	11.3
Hispanic or Latino (of any race)	11.5
Central American, ex. Mexican	9.7
Salvadoran	1.1
Mexican	11.8

Midland

Population

Group	Number	%TP[1]	%HP[2]
Total Population	111,147	100.0	–
Hispanic or Latino (of any race)	41,797	37.6	100.0
Central American, ex. Mexican	244	0.2	0.6
Salvadoran	116	0.1	0.3
Mexican	36,996	33.3	88.5
Puerto Rican	257	0.2	0.6
South American	321	0.3	0.8
Spaniard	266	0.2	0.6

Population Growth: 2000–2010

Group	%
Total Population	17.0
Hispanic or Latino (of any race)	51.8
Mexican	78.5

Males per 100 Females

Group	Number
Total Population	94.9
Hispanic or Latino (of any race)	96.6
Central American, ex. Mexican	115.9
Salvadoran	110.9
Mexican	97.6
Puerto Rican	102.4
South American	79.3
Spaniard	77.3

Average Household Size

Group	People
Total Population	2.62
Hispanic or Latino (of any race)	3.25
Central American, ex. Mexican	3.33
Salvadoran	3.65
Mexican	3.28
Puerto Rican	3.05
South American	2.82
Spaniard	2.73

Median Age

Group	Years
Total Population	33.0
Hispanic or Latino (of any race)	25.5
Central American, ex. Mexican	29.0
Salvadoran	31.0
Mexican	25.5
Puerto Rican	26.6
South American	33.8
Spaniard	29.5

High School Graduates
(Universe: Population 25 Years and Over)

Group	Number	%
Total Population	54,249	81.9
Hispanic or Latino (of any race)	11,793	59.1
Mexican	10,917	58.7

Four-Year College Graduates
(Universe: Population 25 Years and Over)

Group	Number	%
Total Population	17,224	26.0
Hispanic or Latino (of any race)	1,335	6.7
Mexican	1,227	6.6

Population Age 3–17 Enrolled in Public School
(Universe: Population Age 3–17 Enrolled in School)

Group	Number	%
Total Population	18,546	84.5
Hispanic or Latino (of any race)	9,971	95.2
Mexican	9,385	95.9

Population Age 3–17 Enrolled in Private School
(Universe: Population Age 3–17 Enrolled in School)

Group	Number	%
Total Population	3,389	15.5
Hispanic or Latino (of any race)	507	4.8
Mexican	405	4.1

Foreign-Born Population

Group	Number	%
Total Population	8,947	8.3
Hispanic or Latino (of any race)	7,452	18.9
Mexican	7,032	19.1

Foreign-Born Naturalized U.S. Citizens

Group	Number	%
Total Population	3,346	37.4
Hispanic or Latino (of any race)	2,606	35.0
Mexican	2,448	34.8

Language Spoken at Home: English Only
(Universe: Population 5 Years and Over)

Group	Number	%
Total Population	70,546	71.3
Hispanic or Latino (of any race)	9,930	28.2
Mexican	9,165	27.9

Language Spoken at Home: Spanish
(Universe: Population 5 Years and Over)

Group	Number	%
Total Population	26,939	27.2
Hispanic or Latino (of any race)	25,297	71.8
Mexican	23,635	72.0

Unemployment Rate
(Universe: Population 16 Years and Over)

Group	%
Total Population	4.1
Hispanic or Latino (of any race)	4.9
Mexican	4.6

Class of Worker: Private Wage and Salary
(Universe: Civilian Employed Population 16 Years and Over)

Group	Number	%
Total Population	42,598	80.1
Hispanic or Latino (of any race)	14,982	81.8
Mexican	14,053	82.0

Class of Worker: Government
(Universe: Civilian Employed Population 16 Years and Over)

Group	Number	%
Total Population	6,052	11.4
Hispanic or Latino (of any race)	2,065	11.3
Mexican	1,905	11.1

Means of Transportation to Work: Car, Truck or Van
(Universe: Workers 16 Years and Over)

Group	Number	%
Total Population	49,838	95.3
Hispanic or Latino (of any race)	17,581	97.0
Mexican	16,452	96.9

Means of Transportation to Work: Public Transportation (ex. Taxicab)
(Universe: Workers 16 Years and Over)

Group	Number	%
Total Population	141	0.3
Hispanic or Latino (of any race)	17	0.1
Mexican	17	0.1

Homeownership Rate
(Universe: Occupied Housing Units)

Group	%
Total Population	65.7
Hispanic or Latino (of any race)	61.0
Central American, ex. Mexican	49.4
Salvadoran	59.5
Mexican	61.7
Puerto Rican	52.5
South American	61.3
Spaniard	57.3

Median Home Value

Group	Dollars
Total Population	126,600
Hispanic or Latino (of any race)	79,200
Mexican	78,800

Median Gross Rent

Group	Dollars
Total Population	786
Hispanic or Latino (of any race)	734
Mexican	735

Median Household Income
(2010 Inflation-Adjusted Dollars)

Group	Dollars
Total Population	53,965
Hispanic or Latino (of any race)	40,238
Mexican	40,047

Per Capita Income
(2010 Inflation-Adjusted Dollars)

Group	Dollars
Total Population	31,592
Hispanic or Latino (of any race)	15,371
Mexican	15,312

Households with $100,000+ Income

Group	Number	%
Total Population	9,751	24.0
Hispanic or Latino (of any race)	1,064	8.6
Mexican	952	8.4

Households with Food Stamps/SNAP Benefits During Past 12 Months

Group	Number	%
Total Population	4,055	10.0
Hispanic or Latino (of any race)	2,275	18.5
Mexican	1,990	17.5

Notes: (1) Percent of total population; (2) Percent of Hispanic/Latino population; Profiles include places with an overall population of at least 125,000, OR an overall population of at least 25,000 where the Hispanic/Latino population is at least 20% of the overall population. In states where less than five places meet either of these criteria, we have included places with at least 10,000 total population with the highest percentage of Hispanic/Latino population. These places are identified with an asterisk (*); Please refer to the User's Guide for a full explanation of data.

Poverty Rate
(Income in Past 12 Months Below Poverty Level)

Group	%
Total Population	12.9
Hispanic or Latino (of any race)	20.3
Mexican	20.4

Mission

Population

Group	Number	%TP[1]	%HP[2]
Total Population	77,058	100.0	–
Hispanic or Latino (of any race)	65,812	85.4	100.0
Central American, ex. Mexican	209	0.3	0.3
Mexican	61,703	80.1	93.8
Puerto Rican	254	0.3	0.4
South American	249	0.3	0.4
Spaniard	138	0.2	0.2

Population Growth: 2000–2010

Group	%
Total Population	69.7
Hispanic or Latino (of any race)	78.9
Mexican	102.3
Puerto Rican	109.9

Males per 100 Females

Group	Number
Total Population	92.6
Hispanic or Latino (of any race)	91.2
Central American, ex. Mexican	85.0
Mexican	91.4
Puerto Rican	111.7
South American	83.1
Spaniard	74.7

Average Household Size

Group	People
Total Population	3.33
Hispanic or Latino (of any race)	3.60
Central American, ex. Mexican	3.59
Mexican	3.62
Puerto Rican	3.46
South American	3.47
Spaniard	2.98

Median Age

Group	Years
Total Population	30.4
Hispanic or Latino (of any race)	27.6
Central American, ex. Mexican	35.4
Mexican	27.5
Puerto Rican	29.4
South American	37.2
Spaniard	41.5

High School Graduates
(Universe: Population 25 Years and Over)

Group	Number	%
Total Population	28,751	69.5
Hispanic or Latino (of any race)	21,113	64.0
Mexican	19,981	63.6

Four-Year College Graduates
(Universe: Population 25 Years and Over)

Group	Number	%
Total Population	8,623	20.8
Hispanic or Latino (of any race)	5,617	17.0
Mexican	5,363	17.1

Population Age 3–17 Enrolled in Public School
(Universe: Population Age 3–17 Enrolled in School)

Group	Number	%
Total Population	18,011	94.8
Hispanic or Latino (of any race)	16,637	95.5
Mexican	16,194	95.6

Population Age 3–17 Enrolled in Private School
(Universe: Population Age 3–17 Enrolled in School)

Group	Number	%
Total Population	991	5.2
Hispanic or Latino (of any race)	779	4.5
Mexican	745	4.4

Foreign-Born Population

Group	Number	%
Total Population	19,076	26.6
Hispanic or Latino (of any race)	17,995	29.4
Mexican	17,578	29.9

Foreign-Born Naturalized U.S. Citizens

Group	Number	%
Total Population	5,557	29.1
Hispanic or Latino (of any race)	5,107	28.4
Mexican	4,981	28.3

Language Spoken at Home: English Only
(Universe: Population 5 Years and Over)

Group	Number	%
Total Population	13,280	20.3
Hispanic or Latino (of any race)	4,814	8.7
Mexican	4,414	8.3

Language Spoken at Home: Spanish
(Universe: Population 5 Years and Over)

Group	Number	%
Total Population	51,410	78.6
Hispanic or Latino (of any race)	50,392	91.3
Mexican	48,558	91.7

Unemployment Rate
(Universe: Population 16 Years and Over)

Group	%
Total Population	7.5
Hispanic or Latino (of any race)	8.3
Mexican	8.2

Class of Worker: Private Wage and Salary
(Universe: Civilian Employed Population 16 Years and Over)

Group	Number	%
Total Population	18,454	69.1
Hispanic or Latino (of any race)	16,222	70.1
Mexican	15,384	69.5

Class of Worker: Government
(Universe: Civilian Employed Population 16 Years and Over)

Group	Number	%
Total Population	4,988	18.7
Hispanic or Latino (of any race)	4,154	17.9
Mexican	4,039	18.3

Means of Transportation to Work: Car, Truck or Van
(Universe: Workers 16 Years and Over)

Group	Number	%
Total Population	23,047	89.0
Hispanic or Latino (of any race)	19,990	88.9
Mexican	19,022	88.5

Means of Transportation to Work: Public Transportation (ex. Taxicab)
(Universe: Workers 16 Years and Over)

Group	Number	%
Total Population	63	0.2
Hispanic or Latino (of any race)	63	0.3
Mexican	63	0.3

Homeownership Rate
(Universe: Occupied Housing Units)

Group	%
Total Population	71.3
Hispanic or Latino (of any race)	68.1
Central American, ex. Mexican	57.5
Mexican	68.2
Puerto Rican	71.3
South American	68.6
Spaniard	84.9

Median Home Value

Group	Dollars
Total Population	88,600
Hispanic or Latino (of any race)	88,200
Mexican	88,600

Median Gross Rent

Group	Dollars
Total Population	642
Hispanic or Latino (of any race)	632
Mexican	632

Median Household Income
(2010 Inflation-Adjusted Dollars)

Group	Dollars
Total Population	40,108
Hispanic or Latino (of any race)	37,089
Mexican	37,164

Per Capita Income
(2010 Inflation-Adjusted Dollars)

Group	Dollars
Total Population	17,574
Hispanic or Latino (of any race)	14,036
Mexican	13,719

Households with $100,000+ Income

Group	Number	%
Total Population	3,023	14.1
Hispanic or Latino (of any race)	1,776	10.7
Mexican	1,652	10.5

Households with Food Stamps/SNAP Benefits During Past 12 Months

Group	Number	%
Total Population	4,489	21.0
Hispanic or Latino (of any race)	4,302	25.9
Mexican	4,080	25.9

Poverty Rate
(Income in Past 12 Months Below Poverty Level)

Group	%
Total Population	24.0
Hispanic or Latino (of any race)	26.8
Mexican	26.9

Mission Bend

Population

Group	Number	%TP[1]	%HP[2]
Total Population	36,501	100.0	–
Hispanic or Latino (of any race)	14,718	40.3	100.0
Central American, ex. Mexican	3,734	10.2	25.4
Guatemalan	407	1.1	2.8
Honduran	405	1.1	2.8
Nicaraguan	181	0.5	1.2
Salvadoran	2,616	7.2	17.8
Cuban	406	1.1	2.8
Mexican	7,899	21.6	53.7
Puerto Rican	301	0.8	2.0
South American	1,243	3.4	8.4
Argentinean	115	0.3	0.8
Colombian	661	1.8	4.5
Peruvian	149	0.4	1.0

Population Growth: 2000–2010

Group	%
Total Population	18.4
Hispanic or Latino (of any race)	76.4
Central American, ex. Mexican	299.4
Guatemalan	257.0
Salvadoran	435.0
Cuban	83.7
Mexican	93.6
Puerto Rican	6.4
South American	57.3
Colombian	44.3

Males per 100 Females

Group	Number
Total Population	94.8
Hispanic or Latino (of any race)	98.3
Central American, ex. Mexican	101.4
Guatemalan	100.5
Honduran	104.5
Nicaraguan	105.7
Salvadoran	101.5
Cuban	100.0
Mexican	97.5
Puerto Rican	92.9
South American	90.9
Argentinean	88.5
Colombian	86.2
Peruvian	96.1

Notes: (1) Percent of total population; (2) Percent of Hispanic/Latino population; Profiles include places with an overall population of at least 125,000, OR an overall population of at least 25,000 where the Hispanic/Latino population is at least 20% of the overall population. In states where less than five places meet either of these criteria, we have included places with at least 10,000 total population with the highest percentage of Hispanic/Latino population. These places are identified with an asterisk (*); Please refer to the User's Guide for a full explanation of data.

Average Household Size

Group	People
Total Population	3.51
Hispanic or Latino (of any race)	4.13
Central American, ex. Mexican	4.30
Guatemalan	4.54
Honduran	4.44
Nicaraguan	4.06
Salvadoran	4.36
Cuban	3.54
Mexican	4.26
Puerto Rican	3.26
South American	3.59
Argentinean	3.88
Colombian	3.55
Peruvian	3.61

Median Age

Group	Years
Total Population	32.9
Hispanic or Latino (of any race)	27.8
Central American, ex. Mexican	33.0
Guatemalan	32.6
Honduran	32.6
Nicaraguan	35.5
Salvadoran	32.8
Cuban	39.2
Mexican	24.6
Puerto Rican	31.1
South American	40.2
Argentinean	38.2
Colombian	41.7
Peruvian	42.8

High School Graduates
(Universe: Population 25 Years and Over)

Group	Number	%
Total Population	18,043	80.0
Hispanic or Latino (of any race)	5,151	62.9
Central American, ex. Mexican	1,608	56.6
Salvadoran	752	44.9
Mexican	2,176	57.6
South American	534	84.1

Four-Year College Graduates
(Universe: Population 25 Years and Over)

Group	Number	%
Total Population	5,601	24.8
Hispanic or Latino (of any race)	1,091	13.3
Central American, ex. Mexican	473	16.6
Salvadoran	36	2.1
Mexican	309	8.2
South American	119	18.7

Population Age 3–17 Enrolled in Public School
(Universe: Population Age 3–17 Enrolled in School)

Group	Number	%
Total Population	8,608	95.9
Hispanic or Latino (of any race)	4,035	98.4
Central American, ex. Mexican	1,091	96.6
Salvadoran	569	100.0
Mexican	2,348	100.0
South American	248	95.8

Population Age 3–17 Enrolled in Private School
(Universe: Population Age 3–17 Enrolled in School)

Group	Number	%
Total Population	371	4.1
Hispanic or Latino (of any race)	66	1.6
Central American, ex. Mexican	38	3.4
Salvadoran	0	0.0
Mexican	0	0.0
South American	11	4.2

Foreign-Born Population

Group	Number	%
Total Population	14,440	38.2
Hispanic or Latino (of any race)	7,582	51.2
Central American, ex. Mexican	3,057	65.9
Salvadoran	1,813	67.1
Mexican	3,020	40.3
South American	842	78.4

Foreign-Born Naturalized U.S. Citizens

Group	Number	%
Total Population	6,349	44.0
Hispanic or Latino (of any race)	2,169	28.6
Central American, ex. Mexican	565	18.5
Salvadoran	288	15.9
Mexican	766	25.4
South American	429	51.0

Language Spoken at Home: English Only
(Universe: Population 5 Years and Over)

Group	Number	%
Total Population	15,116	42.9
Hispanic or Latino (of any race)	1,473	10.8
Central American, ex. Mexican	79	1.8
Salvadoran	0	0.0
Mexican	981	14.4
South American	70	6.7

Language Spoken at Home: Spanish
(Universe: Population 5 Years and Over)

Group	Number	%
Total Population	12,948	36.8
Hispanic or Latino (of any race)	12,179	89.1
Central American, ex. Mexican	4,245	98.2
Salvadoran	2,499	100.0
Mexican	5,798	85.4
South American	975	93.3

Unemployment Rate
(Universe: Population 16 Years and Over)

Group	%
Total Population	6.7
Hispanic or Latino (of any race)	5.2
Central American, ex. Mexican	6.1
Salvadoran	3.9
Mexican	2.3
South American	9.6

Class of Worker: Private Wage and Salary
(Universe: Civilian Employed Population 16 Years and Over)

Group	Number	%
Total Population	14,623	80.6
Hispanic or Latino (of any race)	5,712	81.5
Central American, ex. Mexican	1,914	79.1
Salvadoran	1,188	78.1
Mexican	2,711	83.7
South American	388	66.3

Class of Worker: Government
(Universe: Civilian Employed Population 16 Years and Over)

Group	Number	%
Total Population	2,223	12.3
Hispanic or Latino (of any race)	683	9.8
Central American, ex. Mexican	277	11.4
Salvadoran	153	10.1
Mexican	290	9.0
South American	68	11.6

Means of Transportation to Work: Car, Truck or Van
(Universe: Workers 16 Years and Over)

Group	Number	%
Total Population	16,804	94.3
Hispanic or Latino (of any race)	6,310	92.9
Central American, ex. Mexican	2,200	90.9
Salvadoran	1,474	96.8
Mexican	3,008	94.1
South American	489	89.7

Means of Transportation to Work: Public Transportation (ex. Taxicab)
(Universe: Workers 16 Years and Over)

Group	Number	%
Total Population	314	1.8
Hispanic or Latino (of any race)	142	2.1
Central American, ex. Mexican	101	4.2
Salvadoran	36	2.4
Mexican	35	1.1
South American	6	1.1

Homeownership Rate
(Universe: Occupied Housing Units)

Group	%
Total Population	82.7
Hispanic or Latino (of any race)	84.1
Central American, ex. Mexican	88.1
Guatemalan	83.9
Honduran	86.7
Nicaraguan	79.2
Salvadoran	89.5
Cuban	78.9
Mexican	82.9
Puerto Rican	76.1
South American	82.7
Argentinean	79.4
Colombian	84.1
Peruvian	83.7

Median Home Value

Group	Dollars
Total Population	120,400
Hispanic or Latino (of any race)	111,100
Central American, ex. Mexican	109,500
Salvadoran	108,000
Mexican	110,100
South American	113,600

Median Gross Rent

Group	Dollars
Total Population	1,226
Hispanic or Latino (of any race)	1,042
Central American, ex. Mexican	931
Salvadoran	913
Mexican	1,220
South American	–

Median Household Income
(2010 Inflation-Adjusted Dollars)

Group	Dollars
Total Population	60,491
Hispanic or Latino (of any race)	55,063
Central American, ex. Mexican	49,545
Salvadoran	52,679
Mexican	60,877
South American	36,042

Per Capita Income
(2010 Inflation-Adjusted Dollars)

Group	Dollars
Total Population	21,514
Hispanic or Latino (of any race)	16,026
Central American, ex. Mexican	15,336
Salvadoran	15,097
Mexican	13,946
South American	14,590

Households with $100,000+ Income

Group	Number	%
Total Population	2,494	24.5
Hispanic or Latino (of any race)	535	15.1
Central American, ex. Mexican	156	13.3
Salvadoran	91	13.0
Mexican	185	12.0
South American	39	13.5

Households with Food Stamps/SNAP Benefits During Past 12 Months

Group	Number	%
Total Population	644	6.3
Hispanic or Latino (of any race)	277	7.8
Central American, ex. Mexican	61	5.2
Salvadoran	43	6.1
Mexican	135	8.7
South American	46	15.9

Poverty Rate
(Income in Past 12 Months Below Poverty Level)

Group	%
Total Population	9.8
Hispanic or Latino (of any race)	13.3
Central American, ex. Mexican	7.5
Salvadoran	5.7
Mexican	16.2
South American	25.1

Notes: (1) Percent of total population; (2) Percent of Hispanic/Latino population; Profiles include places with an overall population of at least 125,000, OR an overall population of at least 25,000 where the Hispanic/Latino population is at least 20% of the overall population. In states where less than five places meet either of these criteria, we have included places with at least 10,000 total population with the highest percentage of Hispanic/Latino population. These places are identified with an asterisk (*); Please refer to the User's Guide for a full explanation of data.

New Braunfels

Population

Group	Number	%TP[1]	%HP[2]
Total Population	57,740	100.0	–
Hispanic or Latino (of any race)	20,230	35.0	100.0
Central American, ex. Mexican	257	0.4	1.3
Mexican	17,492	30.3	86.5
Puerto Rican	295	0.5	1.5
South American	120	0.2	0.6
Spaniard	234	0.4	1.2

Population Growth: 2000–2010

Group	%
Total Population	58.2
Hispanic or Latino (of any race)	60.6
Mexican	87.9

Males per 100 Females

Group	Number
Total Population	92.5
Hispanic or Latino (of any race)	97.0
Central American, ex. Mexican	97.7
Mexican	98.5
Puerto Rican	99.3
South American	57.9
Spaniard	105.3

Average Household Size

Group	People
Total Population	2.67
Hispanic or Latino (of any race)	3.38
Central American, ex. Mexican	3.79
Mexican	3.40
Puerto Rican	2.89
South American	3.13
Spaniard	2.81

Median Age

Group	Years
Total Population	35.6
Hispanic or Latino (of any race)	27.9
Central American, ex. Mexican	29.9
Mexican	27.8
Puerto Rican	28.5
South American	35.8
Spaniard	33.0

High School Graduates
(Universe: Population 25 Years and Over)

Group	Number	%
Total Population	30,127	85.0
Hispanic or Latino (of any race)	7,288	69.5
Mexican	5,907	67.9

Four-Year College Graduates
(Universe: Population 25 Years and Over)

Group	Number	%
Total Population	9,855	27.8
Hispanic or Latino (of any race)	1,008	9.6
Mexican	852	9.8

Population Age 3–17 Enrolled in Public School
(Universe: Population Age 3–17 Enrolled in School)

Group	Number	%
Total Population	9,223	87.7
Hispanic or Latino (of any race)	4,428	94.6
Mexican	3,620	96.4

Population Age 3–17 Enrolled in Private School
(Universe: Population Age 3–17 Enrolled in School)

Group	Number	%
Total Population	1,293	12.3
Hispanic or Latino (of any race)	254	5.4
Mexican	135	3.6

Foreign-Born Population

Group	Number	%
Total Population	3,840	7.1
Hispanic or Latino (of any race)	2,893	15.2
Mexican	2,533	15.9

Foreign-Born Naturalized U.S. Citizens

Group	Number	%
Total Population	1,504	39.2
Hispanic or Latino (of any race)	888	30.7
Mexican	737	29.1

Language Spoken at Home: English Only
(Universe: Population 5 Years and Over)

Group	Number	%
Total Population	37,606	75.4
Hispanic or Latino (of any race)	6,868	40.5
Mexican	5,501	38.9

Language Spoken at Home: Spanish
(Universe: Population 5 Years and Over)

Group	Number	%
Total Population	10,659	21.4
Hispanic or Latino (of any race)	10,035	59.2
Mexican	8,596	60.8

Unemployment Rate
(Universe: Population 16 Years and Over)

Group	%
Total Population	5.3
Hispanic or Latino (of any race)	5.1
Mexican	4.6

Class of Worker: Private Wage and Salary
(Universe: Civilian Employed Population 16 Years and Over)

Group	Number	%
Total Population	19,659	77.7
Hispanic or Latino (of any race)	6,680	79.9
Mexican	5,853	81.3

Class of Worker: Government
(Universe: Civilian Employed Population 16 Years and Over)

Group	Number	%
Total Population	3,834	15.1
Hispanic or Latino (of any race)	1,302	15.6
Mexican	992	13.8

Means of Transportation to Work: Car, Truck or Van
(Universe: Workers 16 Years and Over)

Group	Number	%
Total Population	23,038	92.6
Hispanic or Latino (of any race)	7,587	92.9
Mexican	6,543	92.9

Means of Transportation to Work: Public Transportation (ex. Taxicab)
(Universe: Workers 16 Years and Over)

Group	Number	%
Total Population	0	0.0
Hispanic or Latino (of any race)	0	0.0
Mexican	0	0.0

Homeownership Rate
(Universe: Occupied Housing Units)

Group	%
Total Population	66.6
Hispanic or Latino (of any race)	60.3
Central American, ex. Mexican	52.9
Mexican	60.8
Puerto Rican	63.3
South American	74.2
Spaniard	55.6

Median Home Value

Group	Dollars
Total Population	146,500
Hispanic or Latino (of any race)	105,000
Mexican	100,500

Median Gross Rent

Group	Dollars
Total Population	887
Hispanic or Latino (of any race)	827
Mexican	792

Median Household Income
(2010 Inflation-Adjusted Dollars)

Group	Dollars
Total Population	56,334
Hispanic or Latino (of any race)	40,684
Mexican	39,843

Per Capita Income
(2010 Inflation-Adjusted Dollars)

Group	Dollars
Total Population	25,975
Hispanic or Latino (of any race)	16,099
Mexican	15,770

Households with $100,000+ Income

Group	Number	%
Total Population	4,051	20.3
Hispanic or Latino (of any race)	518	9.8
Mexican	468	10.4

Households with Food Stamps/SNAP Benefits During Past 12 Months

Group	Number	%
Total Population	1,569	7.9
Hispanic or Latino (of any race)	630	11.9
Mexican	540	11.9

Poverty Rate
(Income in Past 12 Months Below Poverty Level)

Group	%
Total Population	12.1
Hispanic or Latino (of any race)	19.1
Mexican	20.6

Odessa

Population

Group	Number	%TP[1]	%HP[2]
Total Population	99,940	100.0	–
Hispanic or Latino (of any race)	50,601	50.6	100.0
Central American, ex. Mexican	120	0.1	0.2
Mexican	46,042	46.1	91.0
Puerto Rican	178	0.2	0.4
South American	139	0.1	0.3
Spaniard	282	0.3	0.6

Population Growth: 2000–2010

Group	%
Total Population	9.9
Hispanic or Latino (of any race)	34.3
Mexican	60.1

Males per 100 Females

Group	Number
Total Population	96.0
Hispanic or Latino (of any race)	98.0
Central American, ex. Mexican	103.4
Mexican	98.4
Puerto Rican	147.2
South American	85.3
Spaniard	90.5

Average Household Size

Group	People
Total Population	2.67
Hispanic or Latino (of any race)	3.16
Central American, ex. Mexican	3.26
Mexican	3.18
Puerto Rican	2.83
South American	2.48
Spaniard	2.62

Median Age

Group	Years
Total Population	31.6
Hispanic or Latino (of any race)	25.8
Central American, ex. Mexican	31.3
Mexican	25.8
Puerto Rican	25.4
South American	38.8
Spaniard	34.0

High School Graduates
(Universe: Population 25 Years and Over)

Group	Number	%
Total Population	43,918	75.5
Hispanic or Latino (of any race)	14,682	60.0
Mexican	13,416	58.9

STATE & PLACE PROFILES

Notes: (1) Percent of total population; (2) Percent of Hispanic/Latino population; Profiles include places with an overall population of at least 125,000, OR an overall population of at least 25,000 where the Hispanic/Latino population is at least 20% of the overall population. In states where less than five places meet either of these criteria, we have included places with at least 10,000 total population with the highest percentage of Hispanic/Latino population. These places are identified with an asterisk (*); Please refer to the User's Guide for a full explanation of data.

Four-Year College Graduates
(Universe: Population 25 Years and Over)

Group	Number	%
Total Population	9,405	16.2
Hispanic or Latino (of any race)	1,635	6.7
Mexican	1,481	6.5

Population Age 3–17 Enrolled in Public School
(Universe: Population Age 3–17 Enrolled in School)

Group	Number	%
Total Population	18,887	92.5
Hispanic or Latino (of any race)	11,839	94.2
Mexican	10,943	94.3

Population Age 3–17 Enrolled in Private School
(Universe: Population Age 3–17 Enrolled in School)

Group	Number	%
Total Population	1,539	7.5
Hispanic or Latino (of any race)	726	5.8
Mexican	656	5.7

Foreign-Born Population

Group	Number	%
Total Population	10,734	11.0
Hispanic or Latino (of any race)	9,182	19.0
Mexican	8,910	19.8

Foreign-Born Naturalized U.S. Citizens

Group	Number	%
Total Population	4,090	38.1
Hispanic or Latino (of any race)	3,094	33.7
Mexican	3,024	33.9

Language Spoken at Home: English Only
(Universe: Population 5 Years and Over)

Group	Number	%
Total Population	55,366	61.9
Hispanic or Latino (of any race)	11,634	27.0
Mexican	10,472	26.2

Language Spoken at Home: Spanish
(Universe: Population 5 Years and Over)

Group	Number	%
Total Population	32,401	36.2
Hispanic or Latino (of any race)	31,332	72.8
Mexican	29,502	73.7

Unemployment Rate
(Universe: Population 16 Years and Over)

Group	%
Total Population	5.4
Hispanic or Latino (of any race)	5.9
Mexican	5.7

Class of Worker: Private Wage and Salary
(Universe: Civilian Employed Population 16 Years and Over)

Group	Number	%
Total Population	36,596	79.7
Hispanic or Latino (of any race)	17,696	83.3
Mexican	16,532	83.4

Class of Worker: Government
(Universe: Civilian Employed Population 16 Years and Over)

Group	Number	%
Total Population	6,603	14.4
Hispanic or Latino (of any race)	2,373	11.2
Mexican	2,158	10.9

Means of Transportation to Work: Car, Truck or Van
(Universe: Workers 16 Years and Over)

Group	Number	%
Total Population	42,881	95.3
Hispanic or Latino (of any race)	19,847	94.9
Mexican	18,562	95.1

Means of Transportation to Work: Public Transportation (ex. Taxicab)
(Universe: Workers 16 Years and Over)

Group	Number	%
Total Population	213	0.5
Hispanic or Latino (of any race)	91	0.4
Mexican	91	0.5

Homeownership Rate
(Universe: Occupied Housing Units)

Group	%
Total Population	62.8
Hispanic or Latino (of any race)	60.6
Central American, ex. Mexican	41.0
Mexican	61.7
Puerto Rican	40.0
South American	66.7
Spaniard	65.0

Median Home Value

Group	Dollars
Total Population	86,200
Hispanic or Latino (of any race)	61,500
Mexican	59,900

Median Gross Rent

Group	Dollars
Total Population	660
Hispanic or Latino (of any race)	622
Mexican	627

Median Household Income
(2010 Inflation-Adjusted Dollars)

Group	Dollars
Total Population	47,140
Hispanic or Latino (of any race)	43,438
Mexican	43,365

Per Capita Income
(2010 Inflation-Adjusted Dollars)

Group	Dollars
Total Population	24,422
Hispanic or Latino (of any race)	17,739
Mexican	17,705

Households with $100,000+ Income

Group	Number	%
Total Population	5,876	16.4
Hispanic or Latino (of any race)	1,814	12.1
Mexican	1,653	12.0

Households with Food Stamps/SNAP Benefits During Past 12 Months

Group	Number	%
Total Population	4,406	12.3
Hispanic or Latino (of any race)	2,811	18.8
Mexican	2,507	18.2

Poverty Rate
(Income in Past 12 Months Below Poverty Level)

Group	%
Total Population	16.1
Hispanic or Latino (of any race)	21.1
Mexican	21.1

Pasadena

Population

Group	Number	%TP[1]	%HP[2]
Total Population	149,043	100.0	–
Hispanic or Latino (of any race)	92,692	62.2	100.0
Central American, ex. Mexican	4,703	3.2	5.1
Guatemalan	544	0.4	0.6
Honduran	1,335	0.9	1.4
Nicaraguan	175	0.1	0.2
Salvadoran	2,500	1.7	2.7
Cuban	398	0.3	0.4
Dominican Republic	103	0.1	0.1
Mexican	80,575	54.1	86.9
Puerto Rican	704	0.5	0.8
South American	711	0.5	0.8
Colombian	326	0.2	0.4
Peruvian	116	0.1	0.1
Spaniard	344	0.2	0.4

Population Growth: 2000–2010

Group	%
Total Population	5.2
Hispanic or Latino (of any race)	35.6
Central American, ex. Mexican	147.5
Guatemalan	181.9
Honduran	277.1
Salvadoran	125.4
Cuban	31.4
Mexican	47.2
Puerto Rican	32.8
South American	63.8
Colombian	34.2

Males per 100 Females

Group	Number
Total Population	99.0
Hispanic or Latino (of any race)	102.6
Central American, ex. Mexican	115.0
Guatemalan	174.7
Honduran	112.6
Nicaraguan	96.6
Salvadoran	107.6
Cuban	112.8
Dominican Republic	83.9
Mexican	102.5
Puerto Rican	100.6
South American	104.9
Colombian	110.3
Peruvian	93.3
Spaniard	93.3

Average Household Size

Group	People
Total Population	3.06
Hispanic or Latino (of any race)	3.73
Central American, ex. Mexican	3.81
Guatemalan	3.61
Honduran	3.85
Nicaraguan	3.90
Salvadoran	3.91
Cuban	2.78
Dominican Republic	3.25
Mexican	3.78
Puerto Rican	2.94
South American	3.02
Colombian	3.24
Peruvian	2.86
Spaniard	2.90

Median Age

Group	Years
Total Population	30.7
Hispanic or Latino (of any race)	25.2
Central American, ex. Mexican	31.0
Guatemalan	31.5
Honduran	29.2
Nicaraguan	33.4
Salvadoran	31.8
Cuban	40.0
Dominican Republic	28.6
Mexican	24.6
Puerto Rican	28.9
South American	37.0
Colombian	36.3
Peruvian	40.3
Spaniard	30.6

High School Graduates
(Universe: Population 25 Years and Over)

Group	Number	%
Total Population	58,851	68.8
Hispanic or Latino (of any race)	23,548	52.6
Central American, ex. Mexican	1,281	44.5
Honduran	318	40.3
Salvadoran	627	41.0
Mexican	20,270	52.0

Four-Year College Graduates
(Universe: Population 25 Years and Over)

Group	Number	%
Total Population	11,350	13.3
Hispanic or Latino (of any race)	2,364	5.3
Central American, ex. Mexican	67	2.3
Honduran	0	0.0
Salvadoran	39	2.5
Mexican	1,868	4.8

Population Age 3–17 Enrolled in Public School
(Universe: Population Age 3–17 Enrolled in School)

Group	Number	%
Total Population	32,108	94.5

Notes: (1) Percent of total population; (2) Percent of Hispanic/Latino population; Profiles include places with an overall population of at least 125,000, OR an overall population of at least 25,000 where the Hispanic/Latino population is at least 20% of the overall population. In states where less than five places meet either of these criteria, we have included places with at least 10,000 total population with the highest percentage of Hispanic/Latino population. These places are identified with an asterisk (*); Please refer to the User's Guide for a full explanation of data.

Group	Number	%
Hispanic or Latino (of any race)	23,734	97.5
Central American, ex. Mexican	833	96.2
Honduran	249	98.0
Salvadoran	520	94.9
Mexican	21,644	97.6

Population Age 3–17 Enrolled in Private School
(Universe: Population Age 3–17 Enrolled in School)

Group	Number	%
Total Population	1,865	5.5
Hispanic or Latino (of any race)	605	2.5
Central American, ex. Mexican	33	3.8
Honduran	5	2.0
Salvadoran	28	5.1
Mexican	537	2.4

Foreign-Born Population

Group	Number	%
Total Population	38,733	26.3
Hispanic or Latino (of any race)	35,271	39.6
Central American, ex. Mexican	3,523	70.5
Honduran	989	76.5
Salvadoran	1,841	63.3
Mexican	30,873	39.1

Foreign-Born Naturalized U.S. Citizens

Group	Number	%
Total Population	9,840	25.4
Hispanic or Latino (of any race)	7,552	21.4
Central American, ex. Mexican	803	22.8
Honduran	93	9.4
Salvadoran	424	23.0
Mexican	6,325	20.5

Language Spoken at Home: English Only
(Universe: Population 5 Years and Over)

Group	Number	%
Total Population	63,877	47.5
Hispanic or Latino (of any race)	14,479	18.3
Central American, ex. Mexican	240	5.3
Honduran	129	10.7
Salvadoran	111	4.4
Mexican	12,313	17.6

Language Spoken at Home: Spanish
(Universe: Population 5 Years and Over)

Group	Number	%
Total Population	66,397	49.4
Hispanic or Latino (of any race)	64,466	81.6
Central American, ex. Mexican	4,268	94.1
Honduran	1,054	87.2
Salvadoran	2,420	95.6
Mexican	57,545	82.3

Unemployment Rate
(Universe: Population 16 Years and Over)

Group	%
Total Population	9.1
Hispanic or Latino (of any race)	10.9
Central American, ex. Mexican	7.8
Honduran	9.2
Salvadoran	6.8
Mexican	10.9

Class of Worker: Private Wage and Salary
(Universe: Civilian Employed Population 16 Years and Over)

Group	Number	%
Total Population	53,057	82.9
Hispanic or Latino (of any race)	29,969	84.5
Central American, ex. Mexican	2,485	87.8
Honduran	674	90.0
Salvadoran	1,319	85.9
Mexican	25,635	84.1

Class of Worker: Government
(Universe: Civilian Employed Population 16 Years and Over)

Group	Number	%
Total Population	6,852	10.7
Hispanic or Latino (of any race)	3,039	8.6
Central American, ex. Mexican	102	3.6
Honduran	0	0.0
Salvadoran	97	6.3
Mexican	2,687	8.8

Means of Transportation to Work: Car, Truck or Van
(Universe: Workers 16 Years and Over)

Group	Number	%
Total Population	57,046	91.9
Hispanic or Latino (of any race)	31,334	91.2
Central American, ex. Mexican	2,423	89.0
Honduran	581	80.4
Salvadoran	1,364	93.7
Mexican	26,945	91.1

Means of Transportation to Work: Public Transportation (ex. Taxicab)
(Universe: Workers 16 Years and Over)

Group	Number	%
Total Population	362	0.6
Hispanic or Latino (of any race)	246	0.7
Central American, ex. Mexican	0	0.0
Honduran	0	0.0
Salvadoran	0	0.0
Mexican	237	0.8

Homeownership Rate
(Universe: Occupied Housing Units)

Group	%
Total Population	56.6
Hispanic or Latino (of any race)	49.9
Central American, ex. Mexican	43.6
Guatemalan	45.0
Honduran	29.4
Nicaraguan	48.3
Salvadoran	48.1
Cuban	55.3
Dominican Republic	37.5
Mexican	51.0
Puerto Rican	43.8
South American	60.6
Colombian	64.6
Peruvian	56.8
Spaniard	47.9

Median Home Value

Group	Dollars
Total Population	103,600
Hispanic or Latino (of any race)	90,200
Central American, ex. Mexican	85,800
Honduran	90,000
Salvadoran	83,000
Mexican	90,200

Median Gross Rent

Group	Dollars
Total Population	734
Hispanic or Latino (of any race)	703
Central American, ex. Mexican	674
Honduran	655
Salvadoran	639
Mexican	701

Median Household Income
(2010 Inflation-Adjusted Dollars)

Group	Dollars
Total Population	45,116
Hispanic or Latino (of any race)	36,267
Central American, ex. Mexican	34,949
Honduran	48,800
Salvadoran	33,305
Mexican	36,265

Per Capita Income
(2010 Inflation-Adjusted Dollars)

Group	Dollars
Total Population	19,940
Hispanic or Latino (of any race)	13,236
Central American, ex. Mexican	13,868
Honduran	14,835
Salvadoran	12,532
Mexican	13,021

Households with $100,000+ Income

Group	Number	%
Total Population	7,559	16.0
Hispanic or Latino (of any race)	1,861	7.8
Central American, ex. Mexican	65	4.1
Honduran	11	2.9
Salvadoran	46	5.3
Mexican	1,685	8.3

Households with Food Stamps/SNAP Benefits During Past 12 Months

Group	Number	%
Total Population	6,090	12.9
Hispanic or Latino (of any race)	4,213	17.8
Central American, ex. Mexican	282	17.9
Honduran	39	10.4
Salvadoran	199	23.1
Mexican	3,445	16.9

Poverty Rate
(Income in Past 12 Months Below Poverty Level)

Group	%
Total Population	19.6
Hispanic or Latino (of any race)	25.5
Central American, ex. Mexican	32.2
Honduran	44.7
Salvadoran	33.0
Mexican	25.8

Pearland

Population

Group	Number	%TP[1]	%HP[2]
Total Population	91,252	100.0	–
Hispanic or Latino (of any race)	18,694	20.5	100.0
Central American, ex. Mexican	886	1.0	4.7
Honduran	140	0.2	0.7
Salvadoran	516	0.6	2.8
Cuban	207	0.2	1.1
Mexican	14,879	16.3	79.6
Puerto Rican	544	0.6	2.9
South American	694	0.8	3.7
Colombian	292	0.3	1.6
Venezuelan	116	0.1	0.6
Spaniard	219	0.2	1.2

Population Growth: 2000–2010

Group	%
Total Population	142.4
Hispanic or Latino (of any race)	206.1
Mexican	228.8

Males per 100 Females

Group	Number
Total Population	94.6
Hispanic or Latino (of any race)	98.5
Central American, ex. Mexican	95.2
Honduran	86.7
Salvadoran	103.1
Cuban	97.1
Mexican	99.0
Puerto Rican	103.0
South American	92.2
Colombian	89.6
Venezuelan	107.1
Spaniard	92.1

Average Household Size

Group	People
Total Population	2.91
Hispanic or Latino (of any race)	3.47
Central American, ex. Mexican	3.84
Honduran	3.78
Salvadoran	4.08
Cuban	3.04
Mexican	3.50
Puerto Rican	3.16
South American	3.14
Colombian	3.36
Venezuelan	2.95
Spaniard	2.94

Median Age

Group	Years
Total Population	34.1
Hispanic or Latino (of any race)	27.8
Central American, ex. Mexican	31.7
Honduran	32.0
Salvadoran	29.8
Cuban	34.9

Notes: (1) Percent of total population; (2) Percent of Hispanic/Latino population; Profiles include places with an overall population of at least 125,000, OR an overall population of at least 25,000 where the Hispanic/Latino population is at least 20% of the overall population. In states where less than five places meet either of these criteria, we have included places with at least 10,000 total population with the highest percentage of Hispanic/Latino population. These places are identified with an asterisk (*); Please refer to the User's Guide for a full explanation of data.

Mexican	27.2
Puerto Rican	27.8
South American	34.4
Colombian	31.8
Venezuelan	34.5
Spaniard	33.7

High School Graduates
(Universe: Population 25 Years and Over)

Group	Number	%
Total Population	47,329	92.3
Hispanic or Latino (of any race)	6,508	78.3
Mexican	5,009	75.8

Four-Year College Graduates
(Universe: Population 25 Years and Over)

Group	Number	%
Total Population	22,571	44.0
Hispanic or Latino (of any race)	2,518	30.3
Mexican	1,721	26.1

Population Age 3–17 Enrolled in Public School
(Universe: Population Age 3–17 Enrolled in School)

Group	Number	%
Total Population	15,846	85.3
Hispanic or Latino (of any race)	4,158	89.5
Mexican	3,299	89.9

Population Age 3–17 Enrolled in Private School
(Universe: Population Age 3–17 Enrolled in School)

Group	Number	%
Total Population	2,724	14.7
Hispanic or Latino (of any race)	489	10.5
Mexican	372	10.1

Foreign-Born Population

Group	Number	%
Total Population	11,816	14.3
Hispanic or Latino (of any race)	3,360	20.9
Mexican	2,579	20.0

Foreign-Born Naturalized U.S. Citizens

Group	Number	%
Total Population	6,259	53.0
Hispanic or Latino (of any race)	1,332	39.6
Mexican	981	38.0

Language Spoken at Home: English Only
(Universe: Population 5 Years and Over)

Group	Number	%
Total Population	57,362	76.6
Hispanic or Latino (of any race)	5,759	40.5
Mexican	4,735	41.2

Language Spoken at Home: Spanish
(Universe: Population 5 Years and Over)

Group	Number	%
Total Population	9,204	12.3
Hispanic or Latino (of any race)	8,401	59.1
Mexican	6,705	58.3

Unemployment Rate
(Universe: Population 16 Years and Over)

Group	%
Total Population	4.4
Hispanic or Latino (of any race)	7.3
Mexican	6.8

Class of Worker: Private Wage and Salary
(Universe: Civilian Employed Population 16 Years and Over)

Group	Number	%
Total Population	33,226	78.2
Hispanic or Latino (of any race)	5,763	80.6
Mexican	4,662	81.9

Class of Worker: Government
(Universe: Civilian Employed Population 16 Years and Over)

Group	Number	%
Total Population	7,236	17.0
Hispanic or Latino (of any race)	1,078	15.1
Mexican	790	13.9

Means of Transportation to Work: Car, Truck or Van
(Universe: Workers 16 Years and Over)

Group	Number	%
Total Population	39,618	95.0
Hispanic or Latino (of any race)	6,770	96.5
Mexican	5,413	97.0

Means of Transportation to Work: Public Transportation (ex. Taxicab)
(Universe: Workers 16 Years and Over)

Group	Number	%
Total Population	119	0.3
Hispanic or Latino (of any race)	14	0.2
Mexican	0	0.0

Homeownership Rate
(Universe: Occupied Housing Units)

Group	%
Total Population	79.6
Hispanic or Latino (of any race)	76.5
Central American, ex. Mexican	77.5
Honduran	75.0
Salvadoran	79.2
Cuban	85.4
Mexican	76.5
Puerto Rican	71.0
South American	83.4
Colombian	82.9
Venezuelan	77.5
Spaniard	80.7

Median Home Value

Group	Dollars
Total Population	173,700
Hispanic or Latino (of any race)	168,700
Mexican	163,300

Median Gross Rent

Group	Dollars
Total Population	1,047
Hispanic or Latino (of any race)	927
Mexican	909

Median Household Income
(2010 Inflation-Adjusted Dollars)

Group	Dollars
Total Population	85,452
Hispanic or Latino (of any race)	80,152
Mexican	80,458

Per Capita Income
(2010 Inflation-Adjusted Dollars)

Group	Dollars
Total Population	34,052
Hispanic or Latino (of any race)	24,121
Mexican	23,694

Households with $100,000+ Income

Group	Number	%
Total Population	11,864	41.5
Hispanic or Latino (of any race)	1,538	35.6
Mexican	1,204	34.6

Households with Food Stamps/SNAP Benefits During Past 12 Months

Group	Number	%
Total Population	783	2.7
Hispanic or Latino (of any race)	273	6.3
Mexican	273	7.8

Poverty Rate
(Income in Past 12 Months Below Poverty Level)

Group	%
Total Population	5.1
Hispanic or Latino (of any race)	10.1
Mexican	11.4

Pflugerville

Population

Group	Number	%TP[1]	%HP[2]
Total Population	46,936	100.0	–
Hispanic or Latino (of any race)	13,024	27.7	100.0
Central American, ex. Mexican	497	1.1	3.8
Honduran	100	0.2	0.8
Salvadoran	178	0.4	1.4
Cuban	255	0.5	2.0
Mexican	10,676	22.7	82.0
Puerto Rican	372	0.8	2.9
South American	253	0.5	1.9
Spaniard	179	0.4	1.4

Population Growth: 2000–2010

Group	%
Total Population	187.3
Hispanic or Latino (of any race)	377.6
Mexican	441.9

Males per 100 Females

Group	Number
Total Population	93.9
Hispanic or Latino (of any race)	96.4
Central American, ex. Mexican	98.8
Honduran	96.1
Salvadoran	104.6
Cuban	104.0
Mexican	96.1
Puerto Rican	104.4
South American	109.1
Spaniard	79.0

Average Household Size

Group	People
Total Population	2.96
Hispanic or Latino (of any race)	3.52
Central American, ex. Mexican	3.90
Honduran	3.66
Salvadoran	4.33
Cuban	3.99
Mexican	3.53
Puerto Rican	2.93
South American	3.24
Spaniard	3.16

Median Age

Group	Years
Total Population	33.8
Hispanic or Latino (of any race)	27.3
Central American, ex. Mexican	33.0
Honduran	31.5
Salvadoran	32.5
Cuban	30.9
Mexican	26.7
Puerto Rican	27.8
South American	34.4
Spaniard	29.8

High School Graduates
(Universe: Population 25 Years and Over)

Group	Number	%
Total Population	23,880	92.6
Hispanic or Latino (of any race)	4,986	82.4
Mexican	3,813	79.6

Four-Year College Graduates
(Universe: Population 25 Years and Over)

Group	Number	%
Total Population	8,947	34.7
Hispanic or Latino (of any race)	1,499	24.8
Mexican	1,063	22.2

Population Age 3–17 Enrolled in Public School
(Universe: Population Age 3–17 Enrolled in School)

Group	Number	%
Total Population	9,416	88.5
Hispanic or Latino (of any race)	2,734	86.7
Mexican	2,202	83.9

Population Age 3–17 Enrolled in Private School
(Universe: Population Age 3–17 Enrolled in School)

Group	Number	%
Total Population	1,222	11.5
Hispanic or Latino (of any race)	421	13.3
Mexican	421	16.1

Foreign-Born Population

Group	Number	%
Total Population	5,575	13.0
Hispanic or Latino (of any race)	1,974	18.0

Notes: (1) Percent of total population; (2) Percent of Hispanic/Latino population; Profiles include places with an overall population of at least 125,000, OR an overall population of at least 25,000 where the Hispanic/Latino population is at least 20% of the overall population. In states where less than five places meet either of these criteria, we have included places with at least 10,000 total population with the highest percentage of Hispanic/Latino population. These places are identified with an asterisk (*); Please refer to the User's Guide for a full explanation of data.

Mexican	1,422	16.0

Foreign-Born Naturalized U.S. Citizens

Group	Number	%
Total Population	2,983	53.5
Hispanic or Latino (of any race)	644	32.6
Mexican	448	31.5

Language Spoken at Home: English Only
(Universe: Population 5 Years and Over)

Group	Number	%
Total Population	28,997	74.0
Hispanic or Latino (of any race)	3,881	39.3
Mexican	3,195	40.6

Language Spoken at Home: Spanish
(Universe: Population 5 Years and Over)

Group	Number	%
Total Population	6,404	16.4
Hispanic or Latino (of any race)	5,905	59.9
Mexican	4,656	59.1

Unemployment Rate
(Universe: Population 16 Years and Over)

Group	%
Total Population	6.3
Hispanic or Latino (of any race)	5.6
Mexican	5.7

Class of Worker: Private Wage and Salary
(Universe: Civilian Employed Population 16 Years and Over)

Group	Number	%
Total Population	15,930	73.8
Hispanic or Latino (of any race)	3,970	73.4
Mexican	3,184	75.0

Class of Worker: Government
(Universe: Civilian Employed Population 16 Years and Over)

Group	Number	%
Total Population	4,520	20.9
Hispanic or Latino (of any race)	1,147	21.2
Mexican	815	19.2

Means of Transportation to Work: Car, Truck or Van
(Universe: Workers 16 Years and Over)

Group	Number	%
Total Population	20,108	93.9
Hispanic or Latino (of any race)	5,150	96.9
Mexican	4,037	97.2

Means of Transportation to Work: Public Transportation (ex. Taxicab)
(Universe: Workers 16 Years and Over)

Group	Number	%
Total Population	86	0.4
Hispanic or Latino (of any race)	18	0.3
Mexican	18	0.4

Homeownership Rate
(Universe: Occupied Housing Units)

Group	%
Total Population	77.4
Hispanic or Latino (of any race)	74.0
Central American, ex. Mexican	75.2
Honduran	65.5
Salvadoran	74.1
Cuban	78.6
Mexican	73.8
Puerto Rican	71.9
South American	83.3
Spaniard	79.3

Median Home Value

Group	Dollars
Total Population	160,100
Hispanic or Latino (of any race)	147,600
Mexican	146,800

Median Gross Rent

Group	Dollars
Total Population	1,133
Hispanic or Latino (of any race)	1,100
Mexican	1,089

Median Household Income
(2010 Inflation-Adjusted Dollars)

Group	Dollars
Total Population	73,574
Hispanic or Latino (of any race)	70,514
Mexican	66,211

Per Capita Income
(2010 Inflation-Adjusted Dollars)

Group	Dollars
Total Population	28,217
Hispanic or Latino (of any race)	21,230
Mexican	20,153

Households with $100,000+ Income

Group	Number	%
Total Population	4,649	33.3
Hispanic or Latino (of any race)	878	27.3
Mexican	641	24.9

Households with Food Stamps/SNAP Benefits During Past 12 Months

Group	Number	%
Total Population	844	6.0
Hispanic or Latino (of any race)	322	10.0
Mexican	303	11.8

Poverty Rate
(Income in Past 12 Months Below Poverty Level)

Group	%
Total Population	7.5
Hispanic or Latino (of any race)	11.9
Mexican	14.0

Pharr

Population

Group	Number	%TP[1]	%HP[2]
Total Population	70,400	100.0	–
Hispanic or Latino (of any race)	65,496	93.0	100.0
Central American, ex. Mexican	225	0.3	0.3
Mexican	61,340	87.1	93.7
Puerto Rican	117	0.2	0.2
South American	102	0.1	0.2

Population Growth: 2000–2010

Group	%
Total Population	50.9
Hispanic or Latino (of any race)	54.9
Mexican	67.7

Males per 100 Females

Group	Number
Total Population	92.2
Hispanic or Latino (of any race)	92.2
Central American, ex. Mexican	82.9
Mexican	92.5
Puerto Rican	101.7
South American	117.0

Average Household Size

Group	People
Total Population	3.57
Hispanic or Latino (of any race)	3.78
Central American, ex. Mexican	3.38
Mexican	3.79
Puerto Rican	2.97
South American	2.56

Median Age

Group	Years
Total Population	28.0
Hispanic or Latino (of any race)	26.6
Central American, ex. Mexican	34.8
Mexican	26.7
Puerto Rican	28.8
South American	32.0

High School Graduates
(Universe: Population 25 Years and Over)

Group	Number	%
Total Population	20,988	58.4
Hispanic or Latino (of any race)	17,891	55.2
Mexican	17,025	54.5

Four-Year College Graduates
(Universe: Population 25 Years and Over)

Group	Number	%
Total Population	4,622	12.9
Hispanic or Latino (of any race)	3,691	11.4
Mexican	3,398	10.9

Population Age 3–17 Enrolled in Public School
(Universe: Population Age 3–17 Enrolled in School)

Group	Number	%
Total Population	16,321	98.3
Hispanic or Latino (of any race)	15,822	98.7
Mexican	15,358	99.3

Population Age 3–17 Enrolled in Private School
(Universe: Population Age 3–17 Enrolled in School)

Group	Number	%
Total Population	274	1.7
Hispanic or Latino (of any race)	208	1.3
Mexican	105	0.7

Foreign-Born Population

Group	Number	%
Total Population	21,103	31.9
Hispanic or Latino (of any race)	20,433	33.1
Mexican	20,081	33.8

Foreign-Born Naturalized U.S. Citizens

Group	Number	%
Total Population	4,762	22.6
Hispanic or Latino (of any race)	4,621	22.6
Mexican	4,516	22.5

Language Spoken at Home: English Only
(Universe: Population 5 Years and Over)

Group	Number	%
Total Population	6,477	11.0
Hispanic or Latino (of any race)	3,271	6.0
Mexican	2,926	5.5

Language Spoken at Home: Spanish
(Universe: Population 5 Years and Over)

Group	Number	%
Total Population	52,223	88.4
Hispanic or Latino (of any race)	51,460	94.0
Mexican	49,810	94.4

Unemployment Rate
(Universe: Population 16 Years and Over)

Group	%
Total Population	12.0
Hispanic or Latino (of any race)	12.4
Mexican	12.5

Class of Worker: Private Wage and Salary
(Universe: Civilian Employed Population 16 Years and Over)

Group	Number	%
Total Population	16,420	71.6
Hispanic or Latino (of any race)	15,576	71.8
Mexican	14,783	71.2

Class of Worker: Government
(Universe: Civilian Employed Population 16 Years and Over)

Group	Number	%
Total Population	3,456	15.1
Hispanic or Latino (of any race)	3,200	14.7
Mexican	3,073	14.8

Means of Transportation to Work: Car, Truck or Van
(Universe: Workers 16 Years and Over)

Group	Number	%
Total Population	21,003	94.4
Hispanic or Latino (of any race)	19,915	94.3
Mexican	19,015	94.1

Means of Transportation to Work: Public Transportation (ex. Taxicab)
(Universe: Workers 16 Years and Over)

Group	Number	%
Total Population	32	0.1
Hispanic or Latino (of any race)	32	0.2
Mexican	32	0.2

STATE & PLACE PROFILES

Notes: (1) Percent of total population; (2) Percent of Hispanic/Latino population; Profiles include places with an overall population of at least 125,000, OR an overall population of at least 25,000 where the Hispanic/Latino population is at least 20% of the overall population. In states where less than five places meet either of these criteria, we have included places with at least 10,000 total population with the highest percentage of Hispanic/Latino population. These places are identified with an asterisk (*); Please refer to the User's Guide for a full explanation of data.

Homeownership Rate
(Universe: Occupied Housing Units)

Group	%
Total Population	65.4
Hispanic or Latino (of any race)	64.1
Central American, ex. Mexican	43.7
Mexican	64.5
Puerto Rican	31.4
South American	53.8

Median Home Value

Group	Dollars
Total Population	66,200
Hispanic or Latino (of any race)	68,700
Mexican	68,400

Median Gross Rent

Group	Dollars
Total Population	625
Hispanic or Latino (of any race)	616
Mexican	614

Median Household Income
(2010 Inflation-Adjusted Dollars)

Group	Dollars
Total Population	29,527
Hispanic or Latino (of any race)	27,328
Mexican	26,767

Per Capita Income
(2010 Inflation-Adjusted Dollars)

Group	Dollars
Total Population	11,860
Hispanic or Latino (of any race)	10,884
Mexican	10,670

Households with $100,000+ Income

Group	Number	%
Total Population	1,093	5.9
Hispanic or Latino (of any race)	919	5.6
Mexican	792	5.0

Households with Food Stamps/SNAP Benefits During Past 12 Months

Group	Number	%
Total Population	6,612	35.8
Hispanic or Latino (of any race)	6,510	39.5
Mexican	6,341	40.1

Poverty Rate
(Income in Past 12 Months Below Poverty Level)

Group	%
Total Population	37.3
Hispanic or Latino (of any race)	39.3
Mexican	39.7

Plano

Population

Group	Number	%TP[1]	%HP[2]
Total Population	259,841	100.0	–
Hispanic or Latino (of any race)	38,174	14.7	100.0
Central American, ex. Mexican	3,833	1.5	10.0
Costa Rican	160	0.1	0.4
Guatemalan	1,097	0.4	2.9
Honduran	635	0.2	1.7
Nicaraguan	181	0.1	0.5
Panamanian	153	0.1	0.4
Salvadoran	1,544	0.6	4.0
Cuban	414	0.2	1.1
Dominican Republic	106	<0.1	0.3
Mexican	27,465	10.6	71.9
Puerto Rican	1,217	0.5	3.2
South American	2,248	0.9	5.9
Argentinean	241	0.1	0.6
Chilean	151	0.1	0.4
Colombian	643	0.2	1.7
Ecuadorian	160	0.1	0.4
Peruvian	573	0.2	1.5
Venezuelan	289	0.1	0.8
Spaniard	647	0.2	1.7

Population Growth: 2000–2010

Group	%
Total Population	17.0
Hispanic or Latino (of any race)	70.7
Central American, ex. Mexican	202.0
Guatemalan	368.8
Honduran	194.0
Salvadoran	182.8
Cuban	24.0
Mexican	76.7
Puerto Rican	62.1
South American	149.5
Colombian	140.8
Peruvian	129.2

Males per 100 Females

Group	Number
Total Population	95.7
Hispanic or Latino (of any race)	105.3
Central American, ex. Mexican	112.1
Costa Rican	61.6
Guatemalan	143.2
Honduran	103.5
Nicaraguan	96.7
Panamanian	70.0
Salvadoran	108.4
Cuban	109.1
Dominican Republic	89.3
Mexican	108.0
Puerto Rican	90.5
South American	86.7
Argentinean	117.1
Chilean	91.1
Colombian	76.6
Ecuadorian	92.8
Peruvian	79.6
Venezuelan	76.2
Spaniard	81.7

Average Household Size

Group	People
Total Population	2.61
Hispanic or Latino (of any race)	3.47
Central American, ex. Mexican	3.94
Costa Rican	3.19
Guatemalan	4.28
Honduran	3.88
Nicaraguan	3.48
Panamanian	2.67
Salvadoran	4.13
Cuban	2.68
Dominican Republic	2.75
Mexican	3.60
Puerto Rican	2.50
South American	2.89
Argentinean	2.88
Chilean	3.10
Colombian	2.64
Ecuadorian	3.20
Peruvian	3.09
Venezuelan	2.82
Spaniard	2.61

Median Age

Group	Years
Total Population	37.2
Hispanic or Latino (of any race)	27.2
Central American, ex. Mexican	29.8
Costa Rican	32.6
Guatemalan	28.1
Honduran	29.8
Nicaraguan	32.5
Panamanian	37.2
Salvadoran	30.6
Cuban	35.8
Dominican Republic	31.5
Mexican	25.9
Puerto Rican	30.6
South American	35.2
Argentinean	35.5
Chilean	36.8
Colombian	36.5
Ecuadorian	30.0
Peruvian	36.2
Venezuelan	33.6
Spaniard	34.9

High School Graduates
(Universe: Population 25 Years and Over)

Group	Number	%
Total Population	156,915	92.9
Hispanic or Latino (of any race)	13,417	64.1
Central American, ex. Mexican	598	31.5
Salvadoran	211	30.6
Mexican	9,435	61.4
Puerto Rican	472	100.0
South American	1,440	96.9

Four-Year College Graduates
(Universe: Population 25 Years and Over)

Group	Number	%
Total Population	91,198	54.0
Hispanic or Latino (of any race)	5,009	23.9
Central American, ex. Mexican	194	10.2
Salvadoran	54	7.8
Mexican	3,168	20.6
Puerto Rican	239	50.6
South American	767	51.6

Population Age 3–17 Enrolled in Public School
(Universe: Population Age 3–17 Enrolled in School)

Group	Number	%
Total Population	45,688	84.9
Hispanic or Latino (of any race)	9,347	93.5
Central American, ex. Mexican	692	96.8
Salvadoran	201	100.0
Mexican	7,421	95.1
Puerto Rican	135	62.5
South American	496	89.2

Population Age 3–17 Enrolled in Private School
(Universe: Population Age 3–17 Enrolled in School)

Group	Number	%
Total Population	8,115	15.1
Hispanic or Latino (of any race)	647	6.5
Central American, ex. Mexican	23	3.2
Salvadoran	0	0.0
Mexican	383	4.9
Puerto Rican	81	37.5
South American	60	10.8

Foreign-Born Population

Group	Number	%
Total Population	58,784	23.0
Hispanic or Latino (of any race)	16,719	43.7
Central American, ex. Mexican	2,140	67.3
Salvadoran	710	70.2
Mexican	12,369	42.4
Puerto Rican	0	0.0
South American	1,799	75.5

Foreign-Born Naturalized U.S. Citizens

Group	Number	%
Total Population	24,930	42.4
Hispanic or Latino (of any race)	3,375	20.2
Central American, ex. Mexican	316	14.8
Salvadoran	138	19.4
Mexican	2,070	16.7
Puerto Rican	0	0.0
South American	691	38.4

Language Spoken at Home: English Only
(Universe: Population 5 Years and Over)

Group	Number	%
Total Population	164,037	68.6
Hispanic or Latino (of any race)	7,556	22.0
Central American, ex. Mexican	128	4.5
Salvadoran	10	1.1
Mexican	5,625	21.7
Puerto Rican	210	30.3
South American	291	13.1

Language Spoken at Home: Spanish
(Universe: Population 5 Years and Over)

Group	Number	%
Total Population	29,553	12.4
Hispanic or Latino (of any race)	26,569	77.4
Central American, ex. Mexican	2,695	95.5
Salvadoran	921	98.9
Mexican	20,210	78.0
Puerto Rican	451	65.1

Notes: (1) Percent of total population; (2) Percent of Hispanic/Latino population; Profiles include places with an overall population of at least 125,000, OR an overall population of at least 25,000 where the Hispanic/Latino population is at least 20% of the overall population. In states where less than five places meet either of these criteria, we have included places with at least 10,000 total population with the highest percentage of Hispanic/Latino population. These places are identified with an asterisk (*); Please refer to the User's Guide for a full explanation of data.

South American	1,930	86.9

Unemployment Rate
(Universe: Population 16 Years and Over)

Group	%
Total Population	5.2
Hispanic or Latino (of any race)	4.5
Central American, ex. Mexican	5.2
Salvadoran	2.6
Mexican	4.7
Puerto Rican	7.1
South American	3.8

Class of Worker: Private Wage and Salary
(Universe: Civilian Employed Population 16 Years and Over)

Group	Number	%
Total Population	114,624	84.8
Hispanic or Latino (of any race)	16,030	86.0
Central American, ex. Mexican	1,427	88.2
Salvadoran	582	91.9
Mexican	12,234	86.9
Puerto Rican	256	78.8
South American	1,003	85.4

Class of Worker: Government
(Universe: Civilian Employed Population 16 Years and Over)

Group	Number	%
Total Population	11,527	8.5
Hispanic or Latino (of any race)	1,206	6.5
Central American, ex. Mexican	29	1.8
Salvadoran	6	0.9
Mexican	826	5.9
Puerto Rican	57	17.5
South American	58	4.9

Means of Transportation to Work: Car, Truck or Van
(Universe: Workers 16 Years and Over)

Group	Number	%
Total Population	118,285	89.0
Hispanic or Latino (of any race)	16,333	89.1
Central American, ex. Mexican	1,346	86.7
Salvadoran	560	95.1
Mexican	12,433	89.7
Puerto Rican	267	82.2
South American	1,003	85.7

Means of Transportation to Work: Public Transportation (ex. Taxicab)
(Universe: Workers 16 Years and Over)

Group	Number	%
Total Population	2,195	1.7
Hispanic or Latino (of any race)	179	1.0
Central American, ex. Mexican	31	2.0
Salvadoran	0	0.0
Mexican	144	1.0
Puerto Rican	4	1.2
South American	0	0.0

Homeownership Rate
(Universe: Occupied Housing Units)

Group	%
Total Population	63.0
Hispanic or Latino (of any race)	45.4
Central American, ex. Mexican	41.2
Costa Rican	46.8
Guatemalan	26.3
Honduran	41.2
Nicaraguan	57.7
Panamanian	49.2
Salvadoran	49.0
Cuban	59.3
Dominican Republic	41.7
Mexican	45.0
Puerto Rican	51.0
South American	54.9
Argentinean	62.8
Chilean	66.0
Colombian	57.0
Ecuadorian	55.6
Peruvian	50.9
Venezuelan	47.5
Spaniard	60.3

Median Home Value

Group	Dollars
Total Population	210,500
Hispanic or Latino (of any race)	159,700
Central American, ex. Mexican	126,100
Salvadoran	118,100
Mexican	148,500
Puerto Rican	300,000
South American	260,700

Median Gross Rent

Group	Dollars
Total Population	981
Hispanic or Latino (of any race)	914
Central American, ex. Mexican	834
Salvadoran	908
Mexican	911
Puerto Rican	962
South American	946

Median Household Income
(2010 Inflation-Adjusted Dollars)

Group	Dollars
Total Population	81,822
Hispanic or Latino (of any race)	52,771
Central American, ex. Mexican	41,393
Salvadoran	48,125
Mexican	53,652
Puerto Rican	64,375
South American	55,000

Per Capita Income
(2010 Inflation-Adjusted Dollars)

Group	Dollars
Total Population	40,744
Hispanic or Latino (of any race)	18,970
Central American, ex. Mexican	13,161
Salvadoran	16,189
Mexican	17,900
Puerto Rican	25,974
South American	24,978

Households with $100,000+ Income

Group	Number	%
Total Population	38,877	40.7
Hispanic or Latino (of any race)	2,256	22.0
Central American, ex. Mexican	121	15.3
Salvadoran	44	15.4
Mexican	1,582	21.2
Puerto Rican	70	41.2
South American	207	26.3

Households with Food Stamps/SNAP Benefits During Past 12 Months

Group	Number	%
Total Population	2,237	2.3
Hispanic or Latino (of any race)	622	6.1
Central American, ex. Mexican	45	5.7
Salvadoran	0	0.0
Mexican	458	6.1
Puerto Rican	41	24.1
South American	0	0.0

Poverty Rate
(Income in Past 12 Months Below Poverty Level)

Group	%
Total Population	6.7
Hispanic or Latino (of any race)	15.7
Central American, ex. Mexican	15.8
Salvadoran	18.3
Mexican	15.9
Puerto Rican	8.7
South American	13.9

Port Arthur

Population

Group	Number	%TP[1]	%HP[2]
Total Population	53,818	100.0	–
Hispanic or Latino (of any race)	15,917	29.6	100.0
Central American, ex. Mexican	1,496	2.8	9.4
Honduran	362	0.7	2.3
Nicaraguan	822	1.5	5.2
Salvadoran	231	0.4	1.5
Mexican	13,112	24.4	82.4
Puerto Rican	179	0.3	1.1
South American	116	0.2	0.7
Spaniard	119	0.2	0.7

Population Growth: 2000–2010

Group	%
Total Population	-6.8
Hispanic or Latino (of any race)	57.9
Central American, ex. Mexican	127.4
Nicaraguan	90.3
Mexican	67.5

Males per 100 Females

Group	Number
Total Population	96.9
Hispanic or Latino (of any race)	113.2
Central American, ex. Mexican	107.8
Honduran	135.1
Nicaraguan	99.0
Salvadoran	111.9
Mexican	114.1
Puerto Rican	129.5
South American	87.1
Spaniard	101.7

Average Household Size

Group	People
Total Population	2.63
Hispanic or Latino (of any race)	3.74
Central American, ex. Mexican	3.80
Honduran	3.66
Nicaraguan	3.90
Salvadoran	3.97
Mexican	3.78
Puerto Rican	3.11
South American	2.70
Spaniard	3.35

Median Age

Group	Years
Total Population	35.3
Hispanic or Latino (of any race)	25.1
Central American, ex. Mexican	29.7
Honduran	29.6
Nicaraguan	29.3
Salvadoran	31.9
Mexican	24.4
Puerto Rican	26.8
South American	40.0
Spaniard	24.9

High School Graduates
(Universe: Population 25 Years and Over)

Group	Number	%
Total Population	25,058	74.0
Hispanic or Latino (of any race)	3,059	44.3
Mexican	2,435	42.8

Four-Year College Graduates
(Universe: Population 25 Years and Over)

Group	Number	%
Total Population	3,206	9.5
Hispanic or Latino (of any race)	255	3.7
Mexican	198	3.5

Population Age 3–17 Enrolled in Public School
(Universe: Population Age 3–17 Enrolled in School)

Group	Number	%
Total Population	10,161	94.0
Hispanic or Latino (of any race)	3,660	98.0
Mexican	3,185	99.1

Population Age 3–17 Enrolled in Private School
(Universe: Population Age 3–17 Enrolled in School)

Group	Number	%
Total Population	648	6.0
Hispanic or Latino (of any race)	75	2.0
Mexican	30	0.9

Foreign-Born Population

Group	Number	%
Total Population	9,253	17.2
Hispanic or Latino (of any race)	6,605	46.4
Mexican	5,665	47.6

STATE & PLACE PROFILES

Notes: (1) Percent of total population; (2) Percent of Hispanic/Latino population; Profiles include places with an overall population of at least 125,000, OR an overall population of at least 25,000 where the Hispanic/Latino population is at least 20% of the overall population. In states where less than five places meet either of these criteria, we have included places with at least 10,000 total population with the highest percentage of Hispanic/Latino population. These places are identified with an asterisk (*); Please refer to the User's Guide for a full explanation of data.

Foreign-Born Naturalized U.S. Citizens

Group	Number	%
Total Population	3,009	32.5
Hispanic or Latino (of any race)	1,664	25.2
Mexican	1,373	24.2

Language Spoken at Home: English Only
(Universe: Population 5 Years and Over)

Group	Number	%
Total Population	34,709	69.3
Hispanic or Latino (of any race)	1,630	13.1
Mexican	1,141	10.9

Language Spoken at Home: Spanish
(Universe: Population 5 Years and Over)

Group	Number	%
Total Population	12,031	24.0
Hispanic or Latino (of any race)	10,825	86.9
Mexican	9,322	89.1

Unemployment Rate
(Universe: Population 16 Years and Over)

Group	%
Total Population	11.3
Hispanic or Latino (of any race)	9.4
Mexican	10.9

Class of Worker: Private Wage and Salary
(Universe: Civilian Employed Population 16 Years and Over)

Group	Number	%
Total Population	15,881	79.0
Hispanic or Latino (of any race)	4,512	85.6
Mexican	3,745	85.1

Class of Worker: Government
(Universe: Civilian Employed Population 16 Years and Over)

Group	Number	%
Total Population	2,960	14.7
Hispanic or Latino (of any race)	326	6.2
Mexican	264	6.0

Means of Transportation to Work: Car, Truck or Van
(Universe: Workers 16 Years and Over)

Group	Number	%
Total Population	18,348	94.7
Hispanic or Latino (of any race)	4,732	94.8
Mexican	3,935	94.7

Means of Transportation to Work: Public Transportation (ex. Taxicab)
(Universe: Workers 16 Years and Over)

Group	Number	%
Total Population	95	0.5
Hispanic or Latino (of any race)	7	0.1
Mexican	7	0.2

Homeownership Rate
(Universe: Occupied Housing Units)

Group	%
Total Population	60.1
Hispanic or Latino (of any race)	63.8
Central American, ex. Mexican	61.6
Honduran	48.6
Nicaraguan	66.7
Salvadoran	66.7
Mexican	64.9
Puerto Rican	48.2
South American	60.9
Spaniard	70.0

Median Home Value

Group	Dollars
Total Population	59,000
Hispanic or Latino (of any race)	44,500
Mexican	46,800

Median Gross Rent

Group	Dollars
Total Population	584
Hispanic or Latino (of any race)	629
Mexican	608

Median Household Income
(2010 Inflation-Adjusted Dollars)

Group	Dollars
Total Population	31,245
Hispanic or Latino (of any race)	35,741
Mexican	34,417

Per Capita Income
(2010 Inflation-Adjusted Dollars)

Group	Dollars
Total Population	17,086
Hispanic or Latino (of any race)	12,128
Mexican	11,725

Households with $100,000+ Income

Group	Number	%
Total Population	1,760	8.6
Hispanic or Latino (of any race)	248	6.8
Mexican	228	7.9

Households with Food Stamps/SNAP Benefits During Past 12 Months

Group	Number	%
Total Population	4,349	21.4
Hispanic or Latino (of any race)	788	21.6
Mexican	666	23.2

Poverty Rate
(Income in Past 12 Months Below Poverty Level)

Group	%
Total Population	24.0
Hispanic or Latino (of any race)	27.7
Mexican	27.2

Rosenberg

Population

Group	Number	%TP[1]	%HP[2]
Total Population	30,618	100.0	–
Hispanic or Latino (of any race)	18,470	60.3	100.0
Central American, ex. Mexican	1,180	3.9	6.4
Honduran	109	0.4	0.6
Salvadoran	977	3.2	5.3
Mexican	15,587	50.9	84.4
Puerto Rican	116	0.4	0.6
South American	105	0.3	0.6

Population Growth: 2000–2010

Group	%
Total Population	27.3
Hispanic or Latino (of any race)	39.8
Central American, ex. Mexican	217.2
Salvadoran	189.1
Mexican	57.0

Males per 100 Females

Group	Number
Total Population	94.3
Hispanic or Latino (of any race)	100.4
Central American, ex. Mexican	116.5
Honduran	172.5
Salvadoran	110.1
Mexican	99.4
Puerto Rican	123.1
South American	110.0

Average Household Size

Group	People
Total Population	3.00
Hispanic or Latino (of any race)	3.54
Central American, ex. Mexican	3.78
Honduran	4.03
Salvadoran	3.77
Mexican	3.56
Puerto Rican	3.03
South American	3.61

Median Age

Group	Years
Total Population	30.7
Hispanic or Latino (of any race)	26.9
Central American, ex. Mexican	30.5
Honduran	29.1
Salvadoran	30.9
Mexican	26.7
Puerto Rican	23.7
South American	32.5

High School Graduates
(Universe: Population 25 Years and Over)

Group	Number	%
Total Population	12,481	72.7
Hispanic or Latino (of any race)	5,281	57.0
Mexican	4,631	57.3

Four-Year College Graduates
(Universe: Population 25 Years and Over)

Group	Number	%
Total Population	1,862	10.8
Hispanic or Latino (of any race)	203	2.2
Mexican	159	2.0

Population Age 3–17 Enrolled in Public School
(Universe: Population Age 3–17 Enrolled in School)

Group	Number	%
Total Population	6,070	93.9
Hispanic or Latino (of any race)	4,192	94.7
Mexican	3,916	94.6

Population Age 3–17 Enrolled in Private School
(Universe: Population Age 3–17 Enrolled in School)

Group	Number	%
Total Population	391	6.1
Hispanic or Latino (of any race)	235	5.3
Mexican	224	5.4

Foreign-Born Population

Group	Number	%
Total Population	4,765	16.2
Hispanic or Latino (of any race)	4,562	25.4
Mexican	3,660	23.2

Foreign-Born Naturalized U.S. Citizens

Group	Number	%
Total Population	1,159	24.3
Hispanic or Latino (of any race)	1,024	22.4
Mexican	912	24.9

Language Spoken at Home: English Only
(Universe: Population 5 Years and Over)

Group	Number	%
Total Population	14,783	55.7
Hispanic or Latino (of any race)	4,542	28.8
Mexican	4,173	29.9

Language Spoken at Home: Spanish
(Universe: Population 5 Years and Over)

Group	Number	%
Total Population	11,552	43.6
Hispanic or Latino (of any race)	11,222	71.1
Mexican	9,768	70.0

Unemployment Rate
(Universe: Population 16 Years and Over)

Group	%
Total Population	6.8
Hispanic or Latino (of any race)	6.0
Mexican	4.8

Class of Worker: Private Wage and Salary
(Universe: Civilian Employed Population 16 Years and Over)

Group	Number	%
Total Population	10,160	77.3
Hispanic or Latino (of any race)	6,351	82.6
Mexican	5,565	82.2

Class of Worker: Government
(Universe: Civilian Employed Population 16 Years and Over)

Group	Number	%
Total Population	2,177	16.6
Hispanic or Latino (of any race)	957	12.4
Mexican	831	12.3

Means of Transportation to Work: Car, Truck or Van
(Universe: Workers 16 Years and Over)

Group	Number	%
Total Population	12,297	95.0
Hispanic or Latino (of any race)	7,200	95.1
Mexican	6,312	94.8

Notes: (1) Percent of total population; (2) Percent of Hispanic/Latino population; Profiles include places with an overall population of at least 125,000, OR an overall population of at least 25,000 where the Hispanic/Latino population is at least 20% of the overall population. In states where less than five places meet either of these criteria, we have included places with at least 10,000 total population with the highest percentage of Hispanic/Latino population. These places are identified with an asterisk (*); Please refer to the User's Guide for a full explanation of data.

Means of Transportation to Work: Public Transportation (ex. Taxicab)
(Universe: Workers 16 Years and Over)

Group	Number	%
Total Population	88	0.7
Hispanic or Latino (of any race)	12	0.2
Mexican	12	0.2

Homeownership Rate
(Universe: Occupied Housing Units)

Group	%
Total Population	55.4
Hispanic or Latino (of any race)	52.3
Central American, ex. Mexican	57.5
Honduran	47.1
Salvadoran	60.2
Mexican	52.4
Puerto Rican	39.4
South American	64.3

Median Home Value

Group	Dollars
Total Population	98,100
Hispanic or Latino (of any race)	90,400
Mexican	85,600

Median Gross Rent

Group	Dollars
Total Population	782
Hispanic or Latino (of any race)	749
Mexican	767

Median Household Income
(2010 Inflation-Adjusted Dollars)

Group	Dollars
Total Population	43,120
Hispanic or Latino (of any race)	40,093
Mexican	40,607

Per Capita Income
(2010 Inflation-Adjusted Dollars)

Group	Dollars
Total Population	18,645
Hispanic or Latino (of any race)	14,301
Mexican	14,651

Households with $100,000+ Income

Group	Number	%
Total Population	1,154	12.1
Hispanic or Latino (of any race)	416	8.5
Mexican	348	8.1

Households with Food Stamps/SNAP Benefits During Past 12 Months

Group	Number	%
Total Population	1,151	12.1
Hispanic or Latino (of any race)	833	17.0
Mexican	696	16.2

Poverty Rate
(Income in Past 12 Months Below Poverty Level)

Group	%
Total Population	17.6
Hispanic or Latino (of any race)	21.0
Mexican	18.5

Round Rock

Population

Group	Number	%TP[1]	%HP[2]
Total Population	99,887	100.0	–
Hispanic or Latino (of any race)	28,958	29.0	100.0
Central American, ex. Mexican	1,107	1.1	3.8
Guatemalan	157	0.2	0.5
Honduran	242	0.2	0.8
Panamanian	119	0.1	0.4
Salvadoran	450	0.5	1.6
Cuban	313	0.3	1.1
Mexican	23,361	23.4	80.7
Puerto Rican	880	0.9	3.0
South American	652	0.7	2.3
Colombian	241	0.2	0.8
Peruvian	107	0.1	0.4
Spaniard	370	0.4	1.3

Population Growth: 2000–2010

Group	%
Total Population	63.4
Hispanic or Latino (of any race)	114.3
Central American, ex. Mexican	476.6
Mexican	135.5
Puerto Rican	135.3
South American	413.4

Males per 100 Females

Group	Number
Total Population	96.8
Hispanic or Latino (of any race)	99.4
Central American, ex. Mexican	94.6
Guatemalan	130.9
Honduran	100.0
Panamanian	67.6
Salvadoran	91.5
Cuban	104.6
Mexican	100.8
Puerto Rican	99.5
South American	88.4
Colombian	84.0
Peruvian	84.5
Spaniard	98.9

Average Household Size

Group	People
Total Population	2.84
Hispanic or Latino (of any race)	3.38
Central American, ex. Mexican	3.52
Guatemalan	3.89
Honduran	3.41
Panamanian	2.72
Salvadoran	3.80
Cuban	2.93
Mexican	3.45
Puerto Rican	2.98
South American	3.06
Colombian	3.37
Peruvian	3.06
Spaniard	2.82

Median Age

Group	Years
Total Population	32.0
Hispanic or Latino (of any race)	25.8
Central American, ex. Mexican	30.5
Guatemalan	28.1
Honduran	28.8
Panamanian	33.8
Salvadoran	30.3
Cuban	31.5
Mexican	25.1
Puerto Rican	27.6
South American	33.5
Colombian	30.9
Peruvian	34.5
Spaniard	32.8

High School Graduates
(Universe: Population 25 Years and Over)

Group	Number	%
Total Population	52,682	91.1
Hispanic or Latino (of any race)	10,035	74.6
Mexican	7,795	72.4
Puerto Rican	645	92.5
South American	513	90.6

Four-Year College Graduates
(Universe: Population 25 Years and Over)

Group	Number	%
Total Population	21,279	36.8
Hispanic or Latino (of any race)	2,637	19.6
Mexican	1,650	15.3
Puerto Rican	201	28.8
South American	383	67.7

Population Age 3–17 Enrolled in Public School
(Universe: Population Age 3–17 Enrolled in School)

Group	Number	%
Total Population	18,560	89.0
Hispanic or Latino (of any race)	6,300	95.6
Mexican	5,375	96.7
Puerto Rican	305	84.5
South American	161	87.0

Population Age 3–17 Enrolled in Private School
(Universe: Population Age 3–17 Enrolled in School)

Group	Number	%
Total Population	2,289	11.0
Hispanic or Latino (of any race)	292	4.4
Mexican	186	3.3
Puerto Rican	56	15.5
South American	24	13.0

Foreign-Born Population

Group	Number	%
Total Population	11,737	12.6
Hispanic or Latino (of any race)	6,013	24.1
Mexican	4,522	22.1
Puerto Rican	0	0.0
South American	559	60.1

Foreign-Born Naturalized U.S. Citizens

Group	Number	%
Total Population	3,917	33.4
Hispanic or Latino (of any race)	1,503	25.0
Mexican	972	21.5
Puerto Rican	0	0.0
South American	243	43.5

Language Spoken at Home: English Only
(Universe: Population 5 Years and Over)

Group	Number	%
Total Population	64,745	76.3
Hispanic or Latino (of any race)	8,790	39.8
Mexican	7,335	40.6
Puerto Rican	494	45.3
South American	155	19.2

Language Spoken at Home: Spanish
(Universe: Population 5 Years and Over)

Group	Number	%
Total Population	14,483	17.1
Hispanic or Latino (of any race)	13,185	59.6
Mexican	10,638	58.8
Puerto Rican	596	54.7
South American	652	80.8

Unemployment Rate
(Universe: Population 16 Years and Over)

Group	%
Total Population	7.1
Hispanic or Latino (of any race)	8.9
Mexican	8.1
Puerto Rican	13.1
South American	9.4

Class of Worker: Private Wage and Salary
(Universe: Civilian Employed Population 16 Years and Over)

Group	Number	%
Total Population	39,018	81.1
Hispanic or Latino (of any race)	9,788	81.4
Mexican	8,088	81.6
Puerto Rican	411	77.4
South American	348	78.4

Class of Worker: Government
(Universe: Civilian Employed Population 16 Years and Over)

Group	Number	%
Total Population	6,841	14.2
Hispanic or Latino (of any race)	1,712	14.2
Mexican	1,385	14.0
Puerto Rican	120	22.6
South American	83	18.7

Means of Transportation to Work: Car, Truck or Van
(Universe: Workers 16 Years and Over)

Group	Number	%
Total Population	44,034	92.3
Hispanic or Latino (of any race)	11,359	96.7
Mexican	9,309	96.6
Puerto Rican	531	100.0
South American	444	100.0

Notes: (1) Percent of total population; (2) Percent of Hispanic/Latino population; Profiles include places with an overall population of at least 125,000, OR an overall population of at least 25,000 where the Hispanic/Latino population is at least 20% of the overall population. In states where less than five places meet either of these criteria, we have included places with at least 10,000 total population with the highest percentage of Hispanic/Latino population. These places are identified with an asterisk (*); Please refer to the User's Guide for a full explanation of data.

Means of Transportation to Work: Public Transportation (ex. Taxicab)
(Universe: Workers 16 Years and Over)

Group	Number	%
Total Population	107	0.2
Hispanic or Latino (of any race)	15	0.1
Mexican	15	0.2
Puerto Rican	0	0.0
South American	0	0.0

Homeownership Rate
(Universe: Occupied Housing Units)

Group	%
Total Population	62.1
Hispanic or Latino (of any race)	51.1
Central American, ex. Mexican	53.0
Guatemalan	56.5
Honduran	36.5
Panamanian	61.1
Salvadoran	60.7
Cuban	48.7
Mexican	50.9
Puerto Rican	53.4
South American	70.4
Colombian	76.1
Peruvian	61.8
Spaniard	59.0

Median Home Value

Group	Dollars
Total Population	164,900
Hispanic or Latino (of any race)	144,200
Mexican	138,800
Puerto Rican	195,700
South American	154,700

Median Gross Rent

Group	Dollars
Total Population	985
Hispanic or Latino (of any race)	984
Mexican	976
Puerto Rican	748
South American	1,050

Median Household Income
(2010 Inflation-Adjusted Dollars)

Group	Dollars
Total Population	68,952
Hispanic or Latino (of any race)	55,664
Mexican	54,548
Puerto Rican	59,375
South American	93,125

Per Capita Income
(2010 Inflation-Adjusted Dollars)

Group	Dollars
Total Population	29,929
Hispanic or Latino (of any race)	20,891
Mexican	20,504
Puerto Rican	22,119
South American	24,299

Households with $100,000+ Income

Group	Number	%
Total Population	9,637	29.1
Hispanic or Latino (of any race)	1,290	17.7
Mexican	941	15.9
Puerto Rican	109	28.9
South American	118	44.9

Households with Food Stamps/SNAP Benefits During Past 12 Months

Group	Number	%
Total Population	2,073	6.3
Hispanic or Latino (of any race)	897	12.3
Mexican	781	13.2
Puerto Rican	48	12.7
South American	22	8.4

Poverty Rate
(Income in Past 12 Months Below Poverty Level)

Group	%
Total Population	6.2
Hispanic or Latino (of any race)	8.4
Mexican	8.5
Puerto Rican	12.2
South American	7.7

San Angelo

Population

Group	Number	%TP[1]	%HP[2]
Total Population	93,200	100.0	–
Hispanic or Latino (of any race)	35,862	38.5	100.0
Central American, ex. Mexican	159	0.2	0.4
Mexican	31,960	34.3	89.1
Puerto Rican	466	0.5	1.3
South American	119	0.1	0.3
Spaniard	262	0.3	0.7

Population Growth: 2000–2010

Group	%
Total Population	5.4
Hispanic or Latino (of any race)	22.3
Mexican	43.1
Puerto Rican	67.6

Males per 100 Females

Group	Number
Total Population	94.8
Hispanic or Latino (of any race)	95.7
Central American, ex. Mexican	120.8
Mexican	95.7
Puerto Rican	126.2
South American	88.9
Spaniard	95.5

Average Household Size

Group	People
Total Population	2.45
Hispanic or Latino (of any race)	2.94
Central American, ex. Mexican	2.87
Mexican	2.97
Puerto Rican	2.62
South American	2.47
Spaniard	2.77

Median Age

Group	Years
Total Population	32.8
Hispanic or Latino (of any race)	26.8
Central American, ex. Mexican	26.2
Mexican	26.9
Puerto Rican	24.7
South American	24.6
Spaniard	29.1

High School Graduates
(Universe: Population 25 Years and Over)

Group	Number	%
Total Population	45,534	81.4
Hispanic or Latino (of any race)	11,375	62.1
Mexican	9,866	60.6

Four-Year College Graduates
(Universe: Population 25 Years and Over)

Group	Number	%
Total Population	12,184	21.8
Hispanic or Latino (of any race)	1,560	8.5
Mexican	1,333	8.2

Population Age 3–17 Enrolled in Public School
(Universe: Population Age 3–17 Enrolled in School)

Group	Number	%
Total Population	14,296	93.4
Hispanic or Latino (of any race)	7,551	95.8
Mexican	6,752	95.4

Population Age 3–17 Enrolled in Private School
(Universe: Population Age 3–17 Enrolled in School)

Group	Number	%
Total Population	1,016	6.6
Hispanic or Latino (of any race)	329	4.2
Mexican	329	4.6

Foreign-Born Population

Group	Number	%
Total Population	6,785	7.4
Hispanic or Latino (of any race)	4,904	14.0
Mexican	4,575	14.7

Foreign-Born Naturalized U.S. Citizens

Group	Number	%
Total Population	2,708	39.9
Hispanic or Latino (of any race)	1,587	32.4
Mexican	1,431	31.3

Language Spoken at Home: English Only
(Universe: Population 5 Years and Over)

Group	Number	%
Total Population	61,713	72.9
Hispanic or Latino (of any race)	11,529	36.5
Mexican	9,983	35.8

Language Spoken at Home: Spanish
(Universe: Population 5 Years and Over)

Group	Number	%
Total Population	20,850	24.6
Hispanic or Latino (of any race)	19,936	63.2
Mexican	17,849	64.1

Unemployment Rate
(Universe: Population 16 Years and Over)

Group	%
Total Population	6.8
Hispanic or Latino (of any race)	8.6
Mexican	8.7

Class of Worker: Private Wage and Salary
(Universe: Civilian Employed Population 16 Years and Over)

Group	Number	%
Total Population	30,911	76.2
Hispanic or Latino (of any race)	12,346	81.4
Mexican	11,085	81.8

Class of Worker: Government
(Universe: Civilian Employed Population 16 Years and Over)

Group	Number	%
Total Population	6,941	17.1
Hispanic or Latino (of any race)	1,992	13.1
Mexican	1,751	12.9

Means of Transportation to Work: Car, Truck or Van
(Universe: Workers 16 Years and Over)

Group	Number	%
Total Population	38,326	88.2
Hispanic or Latino (of any race)	13,653	89.0
Mexican	12,055	89.9

Means of Transportation to Work: Public Transportation (ex. Taxicab)
(Universe: Workers 16 Years and Over)

Group	Number	%
Total Population	196	0.5
Hispanic or Latino (of any race)	66	0.4
Mexican	51	0.4

Homeownership Rate
(Universe: Occupied Housing Units)

Group	%
Total Population	61.6
Hispanic or Latino (of any race)	59.0
Central American, ex. Mexican	53.3
Mexican	60.4
Puerto Rican	48.1
South American	53.3
Spaniard	64.3

Median Home Value

Group	Dollars
Total Population	86,900
Hispanic or Latino (of any race)	61,300
Mexican	59,900

Median Gross Rent

Group	Dollars
Total Population	649
Hispanic or Latino (of any race)	638
Mexican	650

Median Household Income
(2010 Inflation-Adjusted Dollars)

Group	Dollars
Total Population	39,616

Notes: (1) Percent of total population; (2) Percent of Hispanic/Latino population; Profiles include places with an overall population of at least 125,000, OR an overall population of at least 25,000 where the Hispanic/Latino population is at least 20% of the overall population. In states where less than five places meet either of these criteria, we have included places with at least 10,000 total population with the highest percentage of Hispanic/Latino population. These places are identified with an asterisk (*); Please refer to the User's Guide for a full explanation of data.

Hispanic or Latino (of any race)	34,051
Mexican	34,245

Per Capita Income
(2010 Inflation-Adjusted Dollars)

Group	Dollars
Total Population	21,827
Hispanic or Latino (of any race)	14,078
Mexican	13,916

Households with $100,000+ Income

Group	Number	%
Total Population	4,300	12.1
Hispanic or Latino (of any race)	566	5.1
Mexican	476	4.8

Households with Food Stamps/SNAP Benefits During Past 12 Months

Group	Number	%
Total Population	3,842	10.8
Hispanic or Latino (of any race)	2,345	20.9
Mexican	2,071	21.0

Poverty Rate
(Income in Past 12 Months Below Poverty Level)

Group	%
Total Population	17.9
Hispanic or Latino (of any race)	24.9
Mexican	23.7

San Antonio

Population

Group	Number	%TP[1]	%HP[2]
Total Population	1,327,407	100.0	–
Hispanic or Latino (of any race)	838,952	63.2	100.0
Central American, ex. Mexican	10,735	0.8	1.3
Costa Rican	364	<0.1	<0.1
Guatemalan	1,848	0.1	0.2
Honduran	2,776	0.2	0.3
Nicaraguan	1,059	0.1	0.1
Panamanian	1,602	0.1	0.2
Salvadoran	2,969	0.2	0.4
Cuban	2,468	0.2	0.3
Dominican Republic	735	0.1	0.1
Mexican	705,530	53.2	84.1
Puerto Rican	13,164	1.0	1.6
South American	5,698	0.4	0.7
Argentinean	488	<0.1	0.1
Bolivian	284	<0.1	<0.1
Chilean	374	<0.1	<0.1
Colombian	2,139	0.2	0.3
Ecuadorian	471	<0.1	0.1
Peruvian	1,258	0.1	0.1
Venezuelan	505	<0.1	0.1
Spaniard	7,388	0.6	0.9

Population Growth: 2000–2010

Group	%
Total Population	16.0
Hispanic or Latino (of any race)	25.0
Central American, ex. Mexican	207.4
Costa Rican	154.5
Guatemalan	216.4
Honduran	333.1
Nicaraguan	168.1
Panamanian	87.8
Salvadoran	346.5
Cuban	65.5
Dominican Republic	175.3
Mexican	49.0
Puerto Rican	69.3
South American	149.0
Argentinean	118.8
Chilean	149.3
Colombian	140.9
Ecuadorian	316.8
Peruvian	167.7
Venezuelan	198.8
Spaniard	874.7

Males per 100 Females

Group	Number
Total Population	95.3
Hispanic or Latino (of any race)	94.9
Central American, ex. Mexican	111.7
Costa Rican	84.8
Guatemalan	122.9
Honduran	155.6
Nicaraguan	86.8
Panamanian	69.2
Salvadoran	112.4
Cuban	111.1
Dominican Republic	105.3
Mexican	95.2
Puerto Rican	99.6
South American	92.5
Argentinean	109.4
Bolivian	89.3
Chilean	103.3
Colombian	86.5
Ecuadorian	88.4
Peruvian	95.3
Venezuelan	88.4
Spaniard	82.8

Average Household Size

Group	People
Total Population	2.71
Hispanic or Latino (of any race)	3.04
Central American, ex. Mexican	3.15
Costa Rican	2.70
Guatemalan	3.31
Honduran	3.32
Nicaraguan	3.08
Panamanian	2.54
Salvadoran	3.34
Cuban	2.61
Dominican Republic	2.71
Mexican	3.06
Puerto Rican	2.73
South American	2.70
Argentinean	2.57
Bolivian	3.07
Chilean	2.75
Colombian	2.63
Ecuadorian	2.92
Peruvian	2.79
Venezuelan	2.49
Spaniard	2.59

Median Age

Group	Years
Total Population	32.7
Hispanic or Latino (of any race)	29.5
Central American, ex. Mexican	31.2
Costa Rican	33.6
Guatemalan	32.0
Honduran	29.3
Nicaraguan	33.3
Panamanian	35.4
Salvadoran	31.1
Cuban	35.0
Dominican Republic	29.2
Mexican	29.8
Puerto Rican	29.2
South American	34.2
Argentinean	35.7
Bolivian	33.1
Chilean	35.8
Colombian	33.9
Ecuadorian	32.4
Peruvian	35.7
Venezuelan	30.2
Spaniard	35.5

High School Graduates
(Universe: Population 25 Years and Over)

Group	Number	%
Total Population	631,190	79.5
Hispanic or Latino (of any race)	320,535	69.9
Central American, ex. Mexican	3,609	60.6
Guatemalan	671	54.5
Honduran	541	50.4
Panamanian	718	93.0
Salvadoran	1,032	49.6
Cuban	1,278	89.4
Mexican	276,044	69.2
Puerto Rican	6,535	89.4
South American	2,987	89.8
Colombian	1,076	91.7
Peruvian	574	88.0
Spaniard	3,303	86.2

Four-Year College Graduates
(Universe: Population 25 Years and Over)

Group	Number	%
Total Population	187,916	23.7
Hispanic or Latino (of any race)	59,647	13.0
Central American, ex. Mexican	905	15.2
Guatemalan	99	8.0
Honduran	49	4.6
Panamanian	268	34.7
Salvadoran	314	15.1
Cuban	458	32.1
Mexican	50,048	12.5
Puerto Rican	2,181	29.8
South American	1,446	43.5
Colombian	649	55.3
Peruvian	187	28.7
Spaniard	812	21.2

Population Age 3–17 Enrolled in Public School
(Universe: Population Age 3–17 Enrolled in School)

Group	Number	%
Total Population	233,119	90.2
Hispanic or Latino (of any race)	171,154	92.4
Central American, ex. Mexican	1,406	87.8
Guatemalan	488	84.6
Honduran	258	100.0
Panamanian	151	81.2
Salvadoran	345	94.8
Cuban	319	100.0
Mexican	149,205	92.7
Puerto Rican	2,254	87.6
South American	874	95.2
Colombian	304	97.4
Peruvian	132	90.4
Spaniard	746	89.7

Population Age 3–17 Enrolled in Private School
(Universe: Population Age 3–17 Enrolled in School)

Group	Number	%
Total Population	25,361	9.8
Hispanic or Latino (of any race)	13,998	7.6
Central American, ex. Mexican	196	12.2
Guatemalan	89	15.4
Honduran	0	0.0
Panamanian	35	18.8
Salvadoran	19	5.2
Cuban	0	0.0
Mexican	11,793	7.3
Puerto Rican	319	12.4
South American	44	4.8
Colombian	8	2.6
Peruvian	14	9.6
Spaniard	86	10.3

Foreign-Born Population

Group	Number	%
Total Population	176,544	13.7
Hispanic or Latino (of any race)	137,973	17.1
Central American, ex. Mexican	6,037	64.8
Guatemalan	1,328	65.0
Honduran	1,302	70.1
Panamanian	615	49.9
Salvadoran	2,056	70.9
Cuban	1,032	51.5
Mexican	123,058	17.5
Puerto Rican	247	2.0
South American	3,240	61.7
Colombian	1,256	65.7
Peruvian	581	59.9
Spaniard	418	7.7

Foreign-Born Naturalized U.S. Citizens

Group	Number	%
Total Population	65,111	36.9
Hispanic or Latino (of any race)	44,485	32.2
Central American, ex. Mexican	2,257	37.4
Guatemalan	446	33.6
Honduran	324	24.9
Panamanian	432	70.2
Salvadoran	749	36.4

Notes: (1) Percent of total population; (2) Percent of Hispanic/Latino population; Profiles include places with an overall population of at least 125,000, OR an overall population of at least 25,000 where the Hispanic/Latino population is at least 20% of the overall population. In states where less than five places meet either of these criteria, we have included places with at least 10,000 total population with the highest percentage of Hispanic/Latino population. These places are identified with an asterisk (*); Please refer to the User's Guide for a full explanation of data.

Group	Number	%
Cuban	670	64.9
Mexican	37,766	30.7
Puerto Rican	173	70.0
South American	1,462	45.1
Colombian	584	46.5
Peruvian	276	47.5
Spaniard	334	79.9

Language Spoken at Home: English Only
(Universe: Population 5 Years and Over)

Group	Number	%
Total Population	634,669	53.2
Hispanic or Latino (of any race)	238,592	32.5
Central American, ex. Mexican	1,157	13.2
Guatemalan	314	16.7
Honduran	137	7.7
Panamanian	299	24.4
Salvadoran	245	9.1
Cuban	527	27.0
Mexican	206,069	32.2
Puerto Rican	3,055	27.6
South American	714	14.7
Colombian	180	10.5
Peruvian	177	19.9
Spaniard	2,528	50.5

Language Spoken at Home: Spanish
(Universe: Population 5 Years and Over)

Group	Number	%
Total Population	516,289	43.3
Hispanic or Latino (of any race)	493,883	67.3
Central American, ex. Mexican	7,576	86.6
Guatemalan	1,569	83.3
Honduran	1,618	91.4
Panamanian	924	75.6
Salvadoran	2,455	90.9
Cuban	1,426	73.0
Mexican	432,159	67.6
Puerto Rican	7,958	71.9
South American	4,122	85.0
Colombian	1,538	89.5
Peruvian	713	80.1
Spaniard	2,345	46.9

Unemployment Rate
(Universe: Population 16 Years and Over)

Group	%
Total Population	7.1
Hispanic or Latino (of any race)	8.1
Central American, ex. Mexican	10.7
Guatemalan	5.7
Honduran	11.5
Panamanian	17.7
Salvadoran	7.8
Cuban	3.0
Mexican	8.3
Puerto Rican	4.6
South American	4.8
Colombian	8.0
Peruvian	5.2
Spaniard	6.7

Class of Worker: Private Wage and Salary
(Universe: Civilian Employed Population 16 Years and Over)

Group	Number	%
Total Population	458,941	79.1
Hispanic or Latino (of any race)	277,671	80.7
Central American, ex. Mexican	4,110	82.2
Guatemalan	944	92.2
Honduran	787	78.9
Panamanian	503	81.1
Salvadoran	1,371	78.8
Cuban	724	78.2
Mexican	243,038	80.7
Puerto Rican	3,987	71.8
South American	2,199	83.5
Colombian	770	84.2
Peruvian	361	79.5
Spaniard	1,905	70.4

Class of Worker: Government
(Universe: Civilian Employed Population 16 Years and Over)

Group	Number	%
Total Population	85,969	14.8
Hispanic or Latino (of any race)	45,694	13.3
Central American, ex. Mexican	422	8.4
Guatemalan	42	4.1
Honduran	67	6.7
Panamanian	105	16.9
Salvadoran	152	8.7
Cuban	134	14.5
Mexican	39,712	13.2
Puerto Rican	1,374	24.7
South American	301	11.4
Colombian	120	13.1
Peruvian	43	9.5
Spaniard	548	20.3

Means of Transportation to Work: Car, Truck or Van
(Universe: Workers 16 Years and Over)

Group	Number	%
Total Population	522,196	90.3
Hispanic or Latino (of any race)	306,460	90.4
Central American, ex. Mexican	4,503	88.2
Guatemalan	903	83.8
Honduran	880	88.2
Panamanian	569	89.9
Salvadoran	1,564	88.8
Cuban	901	98.5
Mexican	268,634	90.6
Puerto Rican	5,287	91.2
South American	2,247	85.0
Colombian	817	85.0
Peruvian	322	73.9
Spaniard	2,392	89.7

Means of Transportation to Work: Public Transportation (ex. Taxicab)
(Universe: Workers 16 Years and Over)

Group	Number	%
Total Population	19,048	3.3
Hispanic or Latino (of any race)	13,005	3.8
Central American, ex. Mexican	252	4.9
Guatemalan	70	6.5
Honduran	39	3.9
Panamanian	0	0.0
Salvadoran	143	8.1
Cuban	0	0.0
Mexican	11,351	3.8
Puerto Rican	164	2.8
South American	37	1.4
Colombian	37	3.9
Peruvian	0	0.0
Spaniard	165	6.2

Homeownership Rate
(Universe: Occupied Housing Units)

Group	%
Total Population	56.5
Hispanic or Latino (of any race)	54.9
Central American, ex. Mexican	45.5
Costa Rican	52.5
Guatemalan	49.6
Honduran	35.0
Nicaraguan	46.4
Panamanian	48.1
Salvadoran	49.1
Cuban	52.3
Dominican Republic	46.0
Mexican	56.5
Puerto Rican	48.9
South American	51.2
Argentinean	52.1
Bolivian	52.2
Chilean	66.9
Colombian	49.0
Ecuadorian	58.4
Peruvian	50.2
Venezuelan	42.1
Spaniard	58.5

Median Home Value

Group	Dollars
Total Population	108,600
Hispanic or Latino (of any race)	87,000
Central American, ex. Mexican	115,500
Guatemalan	152,000
Honduran	109,000
Panamanian	153,000
Salvadoran	102,200
Cuban	132,800
Mexican	86,500
Puerto Rican	137,200
South American	157,600
Colombian	161,000
Peruvian	158,500
Spaniard	128,100

Median Gross Rent

Group	Dollars
Total Population	748
Hispanic or Latino (of any race)	703
Central American, ex. Mexican	718
Guatemalan	905
Honduran	742
Panamanian	830
Salvadoran	628
Cuban	814
Mexican	700
Puerto Rican	855
South American	803
Colombian	945
Peruvian	850
Spaniard	782

Median Household Income
(2010 Inflation-Adjusted Dollars)

Group	Dollars
Total Population	43,152
Hispanic or Latino (of any race)	37,019
Central American, ex. Mexican	40,351
Guatemalan	39,988
Honduran	29,861
Panamanian	37,763
Salvadoran	40,680
Cuban	35,125
Mexican	37,047
Puerto Rican	46,971
South American	48,043
Colombian	56,129
Peruvian	50,045
Spaniard	42,794

Per Capita Income
(2010 Inflation-Adjusted Dollars)

Group	Dollars
Total Population	21,812
Hispanic or Latino (of any race)	15,898
Central American, ex. Mexican	18,678
Guatemalan	19,009
Honduran	13,341
Panamanian	24,203
Salvadoran	18,465
Cuban	28,237
Mexican	15,610
Puerto Rican	25,473
South American	28,232
Colombian	27,883
Peruvian	19,020
Spaniard	26,741

Households with $100,000+ Income

Group	Number	%
Total Population	68,472	14.8
Hispanic or Latino (of any race)	23,285	9.2
Central American, ex. Mexican	399	13.8
Guatemalan	61	11.9
Honduran	33	6.0
Panamanian	102	23.2
Salvadoran	135	14.2
Cuban	165	19.0
Mexican	19,556	8.9
Puerto Rican	889	19.5
South American	408	23.4
Colombian	167	29.3
Peruvian	32	12.0
Spaniard	304	12.8

Households with Food Stamps/SNAP Benefits During Past 12 Months

Group	Number	%
Total Population	57,524	12.5
Hispanic or Latino (of any race)	42,997	17.0
Central American, ex. Mexican	308	10.7

Notes: (1) Percent of total population; (2) Percent of Hispanic/Latino population; Profiles include places with an overall population of at least 125,000, OR an overall population of at least 25,000 where the Hispanic/Latino population is at least 20% of the overall population. In states where less than five places meet either of these criteria, we have included places with at least 10,000 total population with the highest percentage of Hispanic/Latino population. These places are identified with an asterisk (*); Please refer to the User's Guide for a full explanation of data.

Group	Number	%
Guatemalan	62	12.1
Honduran	131	23.7
Panamanian	0	0.0
Salvadoran	98	10.3
Cuban	146	16.8
Mexican	37,093	16.9
Puerto Rican	508	11.1
South American	116	6.7
Colombian	31	5.4
Peruvian	9	3.4
Spaniard	319	13.5

Poverty Rate
(Income in Past 12 Months Below Poverty Level)

Group	%
Total Population	18.9
Hispanic or Latino (of any race)	22.5
Central American, ex. Mexican	14.3
Guatemalan	5.1
Honduran	33.9
Panamanian	9.6
Salvadoran	14.9
Cuban	24.1
Mexican	22.6
Puerto Rican	14.9
South American	12.5
Colombian	3.0
Peruvian	5.2
Spaniard	12.6

San Juan

Population

Group	Number	%TP[1]	%HP[2]
Total Population	33,856	100.0	–
Hispanic or Latino (of any race)	32,734	96.7	100.0
Mexican	31,279	92.4	95.6

Population Growth: 2000–2010

Group	%
Total Population	29.1
Hispanic or Latino (of any race)	31.2
Mexican	41.1

Males per 100 Females

Group	Number
Total Population	93.8
Hispanic or Latino (of any race)	93.7
Mexican	93.7

Average Household Size

Group	People
Total Population	3.80
Hispanic or Latino (of any race)	3.88
Mexican	3.88

Median Age

Group	Years
Total Population	27.7
Hispanic or Latino (of any race)	27.2
Mexican	27.2

High School Graduates
(Universe: Population 25 Years and Over)

Group	Number	%
Total Population	8,707	52.1
Hispanic or Latino (of any race)	7,934	50.3
Mexican	7,524	49.2

Four-Year College Graduates
(Universe: Population 25 Years and Over)

Group	Number	%
Total Population	1,526	9.1
Hispanic or Latino (of any race)	1,364	8.7
Mexican	1,274	8.3

Population Age 3–17 Enrolled in Public School
(Universe: Population Age 3–17 Enrolled in School)

Group	Number	%
Total Population	8,865	99.1
Hispanic or Latino (of any race)	8,604	99.7
Mexican	8,189	99.7

Population Age 3–17 Enrolled in Private School
(Universe: Population Age 3–17 Enrolled in School)

Group	Number	%
Total Population	83	0.9
Hispanic or Latino (of any race)	24	0.3
Mexican	24	0.3

Foreign-Born Population

Group	Number	%
Total Population	10,219	31.4
Hispanic or Latino (of any race)	10,179	32.6
Mexican	10,066	33.5

Foreign-Born Naturalized U.S. Citizens

Group	Number	%
Total Population	2,660	26.0
Hispanic or Latino (of any race)	2,631	25.8
Mexican	2,606	25.9

Language Spoken at Home: English Only
(Universe: Population 5 Years and Over)

Group	Number	%
Total Population	2,501	8.6
Hispanic or Latino (of any race)	1,409	5.1
Mexican	1,241	4.6

Language Spoken at Home: Spanish
(Universe: Population 5 Years and Over)

Group	Number	%
Total Population	26,605	91.3
Hispanic or Latino (of any race)	26,467	94.9
Mexican	25,620	95.4

Unemployment Rate
(Universe: Population 16 Years and Over)

Group	%
Total Population	12.0
Hispanic or Latino (of any race)	11.9
Mexican	12.0

Class of Worker: Private Wage and Salary
(Universe: Civilian Employed Population 16 Years and Over)

Group	Number	%
Total Population	8,527	72.0
Hispanic or Latino (of any race)	8,226	71.6
Mexican	7,928	71.5

Class of Worker: Government
(Universe: Civilian Employed Population 16 Years and Over)

Group	Number	%
Total Population	1,964	16.6
Hispanic or Latino (of any race)	1,940	16.9
Mexican	1,848	16.7

Means of Transportation to Work: Car, Truck or Van
(Universe: Workers 16 Years and Over)

Group	Number	%
Total Population	10,762	93.2
Hispanic or Latino (of any race)	10,460	93.5
Mexican	10,065	93.2

Means of Transportation to Work: Public Transportation (ex. Taxicab)
(Universe: Workers 16 Years and Over)

Group	Number	%
Total Population	21	0.2
Hispanic or Latino (of any race)	21	0.2
Mexican	21	0.2

Homeownership Rate
(Universe: Occupied Housing Units)

Group	%
Total Population	77.4
Hispanic or Latino (of any race)	76.9
Mexican	77.2

Median Home Value

Group	Dollars
Total Population	78,100
Hispanic or Latino (of any race)	79,000
Mexican	78,800

Median Gross Rent

Group	Dollars
Total Population	505
Hispanic or Latino (of any race)	501
Mexican	499

Median Household Income
(2010 Inflation-Adjusted Dollars)

Group	Dollars
Total Population	30,766
Hispanic or Latino (of any race)	30,471
Mexican	30,134

Per Capita Income
(2010 Inflation-Adjusted Dollars)

Group	Dollars
Total Population	10,832
Hispanic or Latino (of any race)	10,423
Mexican	10,397

Households with $100,000+ Income

Group	Number	%
Total Population	463	5.5
Hispanic or Latino (of any race)	424	5.3
Mexican	418	5.4

Households with Food Stamps/SNAP Benefits During Past 12 Months

Group	Number	%
Total Population	2,723	32.2
Hispanic or Latino (of any race)	2,681	33.7
Mexican	2,625	34.2

Poverty Rate
(Income in Past 12 Months Below Poverty Level)

Group	%
Total Population	32.3
Hispanic or Latino (of any race)	33.2
Mexican	33.8

San Marcos

Population

Group	Number	%TP[1]	%HP[2]
Total Population	44,894	100.0	–
Hispanic or Latino (of any race)	16,967	37.8	100.0
Central American, ex. Mexican	214	0.5	1.3
Mexican	14,082	31.4	83.0
Puerto Rican	268	0.6	1.6
South American	210	0.5	1.2
Spaniard	186	0.4	1.1

Population Growth: 2000–2010

Group	%
Total Population	29.3
Hispanic or Latino (of any race)	33.9
Mexican	55.5
Puerto Rican	112.7

Males per 100 Females

Group	Number
Total Population	98.7
Hispanic or Latino (of any race)	97.3
Central American, ex. Mexican	98.1
Mexican	97.6
Puerto Rican	109.4
South American	64.1
Spaniard	84.2

Average Household Size

Group	People
Total Population	2.27
Hispanic or Latino (of any race)	2.74
Central American, ex. Mexican	2.71
Mexican	2.76
Puerto Rican	2.49
South American	2.14
Spaniard	2.31

Median Age

Group	Years
Total Population	23.1
Hispanic or Latino (of any race)	23.2
Central American, ex. Mexican	23.6
Mexican	23.3
Puerto Rican	21.1
South American	22.9

Notes: (1) Percent of total population; (2) Percent of Hispanic/Latino population; Profiles include places with an overall population of at least 125,000, OR an overall population of at least 25,000 where the Hispanic/Latino population is at least 20% of the overall population. In states where less than five places meet either of these criteria, we have included places with at least 10,000 total population with the highest percentage of Hispanic/Latino population. These places are identified with an asterisk (*); Please refer to the User's Guide for a full explanation of data.

Group	Number	%
Spaniard		21.9

High School Graduates
(Universe: Population 25 Years and Over)

Group	Number	%
Total Population	14,509	83.3
Hispanic or Latino (of any race)	5,195	70.4
Mexican	2,678	68.3

Four-Year College Graduates
(Universe: Population 25 Years and Over)

Group	Number	%
Total Population	5,200	29.8
Hispanic or Latino (of any race)	834	11.3
Mexican	512	13.1

Population Age 3–17 Enrolled in Public School
(Universe: Population Age 3–17 Enrolled in School)

Group	Number	%
Total Population	4,378	89.4
Hispanic or Latino (of any race)	3,443	96.7
Mexican	1,374	96.4

Population Age 3–17 Enrolled in Private School
(Universe: Population Age 3–17 Enrolled in School)

Group	Number	%
Total Population	518	10.6
Hispanic or Latino (of any race)	118	3.3
Mexican	52	3.6

Foreign-Born Population

Group	Number	%
Total Population	2,454	5.7
Hispanic or Latino (of any race)	1,608	9.5
Mexican	979	14.2

Foreign-Born Naturalized U.S. Citizens

Group	Number	%
Total Population	774	31.5
Hispanic or Latino (of any race)	400	24.9
Mexican	186	19.0

Language Spoken at Home: English Only
(Universe: Population 5 Years and Over)

Group	Number	%
Total Population	31,228	75.5
Hispanic or Latino (of any race)	7,046	45.3
Mexican	2,474	39.1

Language Spoken at Home: Spanish
(Universe: Population 5 Years and Over)

Group	Number	%
Total Population	9,071	21.9
Hispanic or Latino (of any race)	8,458	54.4
Mexican	3,861	60.9

Unemployment Rate
(Universe: Population 16 Years and Over)

Group	%
Total Population	9.6
Hispanic or Latino (of any race)	6.5
Mexican	4.4

Class of Worker: Private Wage and Salary
(Universe: Civilian Employed Population 16 Years and Over)

Group	Number	%
Total Population	15,173	74.0
Hispanic or Latino (of any race)	6,066	80.3
Mexican	2,413	77.2

Class of Worker: Government
(Universe: Civilian Employed Population 16 Years and Over)

Group	Number	%
Total Population	4,318	21.1
Hispanic or Latino (of any race)	1,246	16.5
Mexican	552	17.7

Means of Transportation to Work: Car, Truck or Van
(Universe: Workers 16 Years and Over)

Group	Number	%
Total Population	17,392	85.8
Hispanic or Latino (of any race)	6,742	90.1
Mexican	2,887	92.7

Means of Transportation to Work: Public Transportation (ex. Taxicab)
(Universe: Workers 16 Years and Over)

Group	Number	%
Total Population	512	2.5
Hispanic or Latino (of any race)	289	3.9
Mexican	63	2.0

Homeownership Rate
(Universe: Occupied Housing Units)

Group	%
Total Population	26.3
Hispanic or Latino (of any race)	31.5
Central American, ex. Mexican	16.4
Mexican	33.9
Puerto Rican	14.6
South American	22.9
Spaniard	21.1

Median Home Value

Group	Dollars
Total Population	121,700
Hispanic or Latino (of any race)	91,400
Mexican	86,400

Median Gross Rent

Group	Dollars
Total Population	765
Hispanic or Latino (of any race)	740
Mexican	723

Median Household Income
(2010 Inflation-Adjusted Dollars)

Group	Dollars
Total Population	26,734
Hispanic or Latino (of any race)	28,773
Mexican	35,030

Per Capita Income
(2010 Inflation-Adjusted Dollars)

Group	Dollars
Total Population	15,021
Hispanic or Latino (of any race)	12,120
Mexican	13,944

Households with $100,000+ Income

Group	Number	%
Total Population	1,077	6.8
Hispanic or Latino (of any race)	264	5.0
Mexican	157	7.2

Households with Food Stamps/SNAP Benefits During Past 12 Months

Group	Number	%
Total Population	1,144	7.2
Hispanic or Latino (of any race)	730	13.8
Mexican	338	15.4

Poverty Rate
(Income in Past 12 Months Below Poverty Level)

Group	%
Total Population	36.9
Hispanic or Latino (of any race)	32.3
Mexican	25.8

Schertz

Population

Group	Number	%TP[1]	%HP[2]
Total Population	31,465	100.0	–
Hispanic or Latino (of any race)	8,099	25.7	100.0
Central American, ex. Mexican	201	0.6	2.5
Mexican	6,228	19.8	76.9
Puerto Rican	493	1.6	6.1
South American	102	0.3	1.3
Spaniard	194	0.6	2.4

Population Growth: 2000–2010

Group	%
Total Population	68.3
Hispanic or Latino (of any race)	122.5
Mexican	154.0
Puerto Rican	180.1

Males per 100 Females

Group	Number
Total Population	93.5
Hispanic or Latino (of any race)	90.3
Central American, ex. Mexican	71.8
Mexican	92.2
Puerto Rican	110.7
South American	72.9
Spaniard	79.6

Average Household Size

Group	People
Total Population	2.75
Hispanic or Latino (of any race)	3.14
Central American, ex. Mexican	3.54
Mexican	3.16
Puerto Rican	3.18
South American	3.07
Spaniard	3.25

Median Age

Group	Years
Total Population	37.8
Hispanic or Latino (of any race)	29.4
Central American, ex. Mexican	33.5
Mexican	29.3
Puerto Rican	32.5
South American	38.0
Spaniard	33.0

High School Graduates
(Universe: Population 25 Years and Over)

Group	Number	%
Total Population	17,302	93.5
Hispanic or Latino (of any race)	3,065	87.4
Mexican	2,600	87.0

Four-Year College Graduates
(Universe: Population 25 Years and Over)

Group	Number	%
Total Population	6,164	33.3
Hispanic or Latino (of any race)	817	23.3
Mexican	654	21.9

Population Age 3–17 Enrolled in Public School
(Universe: Population Age 3–17 Enrolled in School)

Group	Number	%
Total Population	4,960	88.3
Hispanic or Latino (of any race)	1,276	93.6
Mexican	1,069	93.4

Population Age 3–17 Enrolled in Private School
(Universe: Population Age 3–17 Enrolled in School)

Group	Number	%
Total Population	655	11.7
Hispanic or Latino (of any race)	87	6.4
Mexican	76	6.6

Foreign-Born Population

Group	Number	%
Total Population	1,445	5.1
Hispanic or Latino (of any race)	452	7.3
Mexican	293	5.6

Foreign-Born Naturalized U.S. Citizens

Group	Number	%
Total Population	1,040	72.0
Hispanic or Latino (of any race)	268	59.3
Mexican	133	45.4

Language Spoken at Home: English Only
(Universe: Population 5 Years and Over)

Group	Number	%
Total Population	22,563	85.5
Hispanic or Latino (of any race)	3,000	53.1
Mexican	2,509	52.8

Language Spoken at Home: Spanish
(Universe: Population 5 Years and Over)

Group	Number	%
Total Population	3,002	11.4
Hispanic or Latino (of any race)	2,653	46.9
Mexican	2,243	47.2

Notes: (1) Percent of total population; (2) Percent of Hispanic/Latino population; Profiles include places with an overall population of at least 125,000, OR an overall population of at least 25,000 where the Hispanic/Latino population is at least 20% of the overall population. In states where less than five places meet either of these criteria, we have included places with at least 10,000 total population with the highest percentage of Hispanic/Latino population. These places are identified with an asterisk (*); Please refer to the User's Guide for a full explanation of data.

Unemployment Rate
(Universe: Population 16 Years and Over)

Group	%
Total Population	7.1
Hispanic or Latino (of any race)	5.2
Mexican	5.8

Class of Worker: Private Wage and Salary
(Universe: Civilian Employed Population 16 Years and Over)

Group	Number	%
Total Population	8,940	68.6
Hispanic or Latino (of any race)	2,096	72.0
Mexican	1,754	71.4

Class of Worker: Government
(Universe: Civilian Employed Population 16 Years and Over)

Group	Number	%
Total Population	3,412	26.2
Hispanic or Latino (of any race)	686	23.5
Mexican	571	23.2

Means of Transportation to Work: Car, Truck or Van
(Universe: Workers 16 Years and Over)

Group	Number	%
Total Population	12,548	95.3
Hispanic or Latino (of any race)	2,714	95.7
Mexican	2,321	96.9

Means of Transportation to Work: Public Transportation (ex. Taxicab)
(Universe: Workers 16 Years and Over)

Group	Number	%
Total Population	14	0.1
Hispanic or Latino (of any race)	0	0.0
Mexican	0	0.0

Homeownership Rate
(Universe: Occupied Housing Units)

Group	%
Total Population	77.5
Hispanic or Latino (of any race)	71.9
Central American, ex. Mexican	86.0
Mexican	72.0
Puerto Rican	78.2
South American	76.7
Spaniard	83.6

Median Home Value

Group	Dollars
Total Population	159,700
Hispanic or Latino (of any race)	154,100
Mexican	152,400

Median Gross Rent

Group	Dollars
Total Population	913
Hispanic or Latino (of any race)	939
Mexican	970

Median Household Income
(2010 Inflation-Adjusted Dollars)

Group	Dollars
Total Population	73,267
Hispanic or Latino (of any race)	62,339
Mexican	64,643

Per Capita Income
(2010 Inflation-Adjusted Dollars)

Group	Dollars
Total Population	29,824
Hispanic or Latino (of any race)	23,627
Mexican	24,106

Households with $100,000+ Income

Group	Number	%
Total Population	3,084	30.5
Hispanic or Latino (of any race)	484	25.7
Mexican	423	26.8

Households with Food Stamps/SNAP Benefits During Past 12 Months

Group	Number	%
Total Population	314	3.1
Hispanic or Latino (of any race)	111	5.9
Mexican	80	5.1

Poverty Rate
(Income in Past 12 Months Below Poverty Level)

Group	%
Total Population	4.9
Hispanic or Latino (of any race)	8.7
Mexican	7.6

Seguin

Population

Group	Number	%TP[1]	%HP[2]
Total Population	25,175	100.0	–
Hispanic or Latino (of any race)	13,938	55.4	100.0
Central American, ex. Mexican	106	0.4	0.8
Mexican	12,263	48.7	88.0

Population Growth: 2000–2010

Group	%
Total Population	14.4
Hispanic or Latino (of any race)	19.4
Mexican	50.3

Males per 100 Females

Group	Number
Total Population	93.6
Hispanic or Latino (of any race)	97.4
Central American, ex. Mexican	96.3
Mexican	99.1

Average Household Size

Group	People
Total Population	2.68
Hispanic or Latino (of any race)	3.22
Central American, ex. Mexican	3.20
Mexican	3.24

Median Age

Group	Years
Total Population	35.3
Hispanic or Latino (of any race)	28.4
Central American, ex. Mexican	33.0
Mexican	28.4

High School Graduates
(Universe: Population 25 Years and Over)

Group	Number	%
Total Population	11,020	72.7
Hispanic or Latino (of any race)	4,160	57.0
Mexican	3,632	58.5

Four-Year College Graduates
(Universe: Population 25 Years and Over)

Group	Number	%
Total Population	2,540	16.8
Hispanic or Latino (of any race)	362	5.0
Mexican	290	4.7

Population Age 3–17 Enrolled in Public School
(Universe: Population Age 3–17 Enrolled in School)

Group	Number	%
Total Population	5,246	95.6
Hispanic or Latino (of any race)	3,627	97.9
Mexican	2,621	97.1

Population Age 3–17 Enrolled in Private School
(Universe: Population Age 3–17 Enrolled in School)

Group	Number	%
Total Population	243	4.4
Hispanic or Latino (of any race)	78	2.1
Mexican	78	2.9

Foreign-Born Population

Group	Number	%
Total Population	2,169	8.8
Hispanic or Latino (of any race)	1,908	14.0
Mexican	1,849	17.0

Foreign-Born Naturalized U.S. Citizens

Group	Number	%
Total Population	808	37.3
Hispanic or Latino (of any race)	650	34.1
Mexican	627	33.9

Language Spoken at Home: English Only
(Universe: Population 5 Years and Over)

Group	Number	%
Total Population	14,318	62.1
Hispanic or Latino (of any race)	4,304	35.0
Mexican	3,344	33.6

Language Spoken at Home: Spanish
(Universe: Population 5 Years and Over)

Group	Number	%
Total Population	8,283	35.9
Hispanic or Latino (of any race)	7,987	64.9
Mexican	6,600	66.3

Unemployment Rate
(Universe: Population 16 Years and Over)

Group	%
Total Population	6.9
Hispanic or Latino (of any race)	7.0
Mexican	6.8

Class of Worker: Private Wage and Salary
(Universe: Civilian Employed Population 16 Years and Over)

Group	Number	%
Total Population	8,883	81.2
Hispanic or Latino (of any race)	4,895	83.5
Mexican	4,141	82.5

Class of Worker: Government
(Universe: Civilian Employed Population 16 Years and Over)

Group	Number	%
Total Population	1,500	13.7
Hispanic or Latino (of any race)	698	11.9
Mexican	626	12.5

Means of Transportation to Work: Car, Truck or Van
(Universe: Workers 16 Years and Over)

Group	Number	%
Total Population	9,696	90.5
Hispanic or Latino (of any race)	5,400	94.1
Mexican	4,678	95.4

Means of Transportation to Work: Public Transportation (ex. Taxicab)
(Universe: Workers 16 Years and Over)

Group	Number	%
Total Population	0	0.0
Hispanic or Latino (of any race)	0	0.0
Mexican	0	0.0

Homeownership Rate
(Universe: Occupied Housing Units)

Group	%
Total Population	59.4
Hispanic or Latino (of any race)	53.0
Central American, ex. Mexican	54.3
Mexican	53.7

Median Home Value

Group	Dollars
Total Population	92,000
Hispanic or Latino (of any race)	70,500
Mexican	71,400

Median Gross Rent

Group	Dollars
Total Population	706
Hispanic or Latino (of any race)	730
Mexican	714

Median Household Income
(2010 Inflation-Adjusted Dollars)

Group	Dollars
Total Population	40,339
Hispanic or Latino (of any race)	35,960
Mexican	37,600

Per Capita Income
(2010 Inflation-Adjusted Dollars)

Group	Dollars
Total Population	19,851
Hispanic or Latino (of any race)	14,626
Mexican	16,242

Notes: (1) Percent of total population; (2) Percent of Hispanic/Latino population; Profiles include places with an overall population of at least 125,000, OR an overall population of at least 25,000 where the Hispanic/Latino population is at least 20% of the overall population. In states where less than five places meet either of these criteria, we have included places with at least 10,000 total population with the highest percentage of Hispanic/Latino population. These places are identified with an asterisk (*); Please refer to the User's Guide for a full explanation of data.

Households with $100,000+ Income

Group	Number	%
Total Population	878	10.1
Hispanic or Latino (of any race)	233	6.1
Mexican	190	5.9

Households with Food Stamps/SNAP Benefits During Past 12 Months

Group	Number	%
Total Population	1,559	17.9
Hispanic or Latino (of any race)	965	25.2
Mexican	781	24.1

Poverty Rate
(Income in Past 12 Months Below Poverty Level)

Group	%
Total Population	17.6
Hispanic or Latino (of any race)	20.9
Mexican	20.1

Sherman

Population

Group	Number	%TP[1]	%HP[2]
Total Population	38,521	100.0	–
Hispanic or Latino (of any race)	7,881	20.5	100.0
Central American, ex. Mexican	704	1.8	8.9
Salvadoran	625	1.6	7.9
Mexican	6,559	17.0	83.2

Population Growth: 2000–2010

Group	%
Total Population	9.8
Hispanic or Latino (of any race)	85.0
Central American, ex. Mexican	334.6
Salvadoran	366.4
Mexican	86.8

Males per 100 Females

Group	Number
Total Population	91.5
Hispanic or Latino (of any race)	105.2
Central American, ex. Mexican	142.8
Salvadoran	149.0
Mexican	102.6

Average Household Size

Group	People
Total Population	2.51
Hispanic or Latino (of any race)	3.84
Central American, ex. Mexican	3.90
Salvadoran	3.96
Mexican	3.89

Median Age

Group	Years
Total Population	33.2
Hispanic or Latino (of any race)	22.6
Central American, ex. Mexican	28.0
Salvadoran	27.9
Mexican	21.8

High School Graduates
(Universe: Population 25 Years and Over)

Group	Number	%
Total Population	19,773	82.6
Hispanic or Latino (of any race)	1,590	50.6
Mexican	1,315	52.3

Four-Year College Graduates
(Universe: Population 25 Years and Over)

Group	Number	%
Total Population	4,735	19.8
Hispanic or Latino (of any race)	160	5.1
Mexican	107	4.3

Population Age 3–17 Enrolled in Public School
(Universe: Population Age 3–17 Enrolled in School)

Group	Number	%
Total Population	6,413	94.0
Hispanic or Latino (of any race)	1,845	97.4
Mexican	1,758	97.2

Population Age 3–17 Enrolled in Private School
(Universe: Population Age 3–17 Enrolled in School)

Group	Number	%
Total Population	407	6.0
Hispanic or Latino (of any race)	50	2.6
Mexican	50	2.8

Foreign-Born Population

Group	Number	%
Total Population	4,002	10.5
Hispanic or Latino (of any race)	2,882	42.3
Mexican	2,334	39.1

Foreign-Born Naturalized U.S. Citizens

Group	Number	%
Total Population	645	16.1
Hispanic or Latino (of any race)	257	8.9
Mexican	192	8.2

Language Spoken at Home: English Only
(Universe: Population 5 Years and Over)

Group	Number	%
Total Population	28,613	81.2
Hispanic or Latino (of any race)	671	11.3
Mexican	537	10.4

Language Spoken at Home: Spanish
(Universe: Population 5 Years and Over)

Group	Number	%
Total Population	5,558	15.8
Hispanic or Latino (of any race)	5,289	88.7
Mexican	4,618	89.6

Unemployment Rate
(Universe: Population 16 Years and Over)

Group	%
Total Population	9.6
Hispanic or Latino (of any race)	11.3
Mexican	11.2

Class of Worker: Private Wage and Salary
(Universe: Civilian Employed Population 16 Years and Over)

Group	Number	%
Total Population	13,880	82.4
Hispanic or Latino (of any race)	2,618	90.1
Mexican	2,120	89.5

Class of Worker: Government
(Universe: Civilian Employed Population 16 Years and Over)

Group	Number	%
Total Population	1,985	11.8
Hispanic or Latino (of any race)	183	6.3
Mexican	164	6.9

Means of Transportation to Work: Car, Truck or Van
(Universe: Workers 16 Years and Over)

Group	Number	%
Total Population	15,196	92.1
Hispanic or Latino (of any race)	2,742	95.8
Mexican	2,215	95.3

Means of Transportation to Work: Public Transportation (ex. Taxicab)
(Universe: Workers 16 Years and Over)

Group	Number	%
Total Population	181	1.1
Hispanic or Latino (of any race)	16	0.6
Mexican	16	0.7

Homeownership Rate
(Universe: Occupied Housing Units)

Group	%
Total Population	54.8
Hispanic or Latino (of any race)	54.6
Central American, ex. Mexican	59.8
Salvadoran	57.1
Mexican	54.6

Median Home Value

Group	Dollars
Total Population	91,800
Hispanic or Latino (of any race)	60,100
Mexican	56,800

Median Gross Rent

Group	Dollars
Total Population	728
Hispanic or Latino (of any race)	660
Mexican	726

Median Household Income
(2010 Inflation-Adjusted Dollars)

Group	Dollars
Total Population	41,490
Hispanic or Latino (of any race)	37,406
Mexican	35,656

Per Capita Income
(2010 Inflation-Adjusted Dollars)

Group	Dollars
Total Population	20,850
Hispanic or Latino (of any race)	13,017
Mexican	11,932

Households with $100,000+ Income

Group	Number	%
Total Population	1,545	10.6
Hispanic or Latino (of any race)	212	12.4
Mexican	178	12.9

Households with Food Stamps/SNAP Benefits During Past 12 Months

Group	Number	%
Total Population	2,037	13.9
Hispanic or Latino (of any race)	496	29.0
Mexican	472	34.2

Poverty Rate
(Income in Past 12 Months Below Poverty Level)

Group	%
Total Population	17.6
Hispanic or Latino (of any race)	26.0
Mexican	26.8

Socorro

Population

Group	Number	%TP[1]	%HP[2]
Total Population	32,013	100.0	–
Hispanic or Latino (of any race)	30,964	96.7	100.0
Mexican	29,019	90.6	93.7
Spaniard	157	0.5	0.5

Population Growth: 2000–2010

Group	%
Total Population	17.9
Hispanic or Latino (of any race)	18.3
Mexican	29.3

Males per 100 Females

Group	Number
Total Population	93.1
Hispanic or Latino (of any race)	92.4
Mexican	92.4
Spaniard	103.9

Average Household Size

Group	People
Total Population	3.64
Hispanic or Latino (of any race)	3.66
Mexican	3.66
Spaniard	3.60

Median Age

Group	Years
Total Population	29.5
Hispanic or Latino (of any race)	29.4
Mexican	29.7
Spaniard	24.9

High School Graduates
(Universe: Population 25 Years and Over)

Group	Number	%
Total Population	9,442	55.3
Hispanic or Latino (of any race)	9,020	54.6
Mexican	8,602	54.2

Notes: (1) Percent of total population; (2) Percent of Hispanic/Latino population; Profiles include places with an overall population of at least 125,000, OR an overall population of at least 25,000 where the Hispanic/Latino population is at least 20% of the overall population. In states where less than five places meet either of these criteria, we have included places with at least 10,000 total population with the highest percentage of Hispanic/Latino population. These places are identified with an asterisk (*); Please refer to the User's Guide for a full explanation of data.

Four-Year College Graduates
(Universe: Population 25 Years and Over)

Group	Number	%
Total Population	1,288	7.5
Hispanic or Latino (of any race)	1,133	6.9
Mexican	1,047	6.6

Population Age 3–17 Enrolled in Public School
(Universe: Population Age 3–17 Enrolled in School)

Group	Number	%
Total Population	7,430	98.1
Hispanic or Latino (of any race)	7,246	98.1
Mexican	6,807	97.9

Population Age 3–17 Enrolled in Private School
(Universe: Population Age 3–17 Enrolled in School)

Group	Number	%
Total Population	144	1.9
Hispanic or Latino (of any race)	144	1.9
Mexican	144	2.1

Foreign-Born Population

Group	Number	%
Total Population	10,513	33.9
Hispanic or Latino (of any race)	10,494	34.8
Mexican	10,189	35.4

Foreign-Born Naturalized U.S. Citizens

Group	Number	%
Total Population	4,894	46.6
Hispanic or Latino (of any race)	4,875	46.5
Mexican	4,765	46.8

Language Spoken at Home: English Only
(Universe: Population 5 Years and Over)

Group	Number	%
Total Population	2,797	9.8
Hispanic or Latino (of any race)	2,277	8.2
Mexican	2,164	8.2

Language Spoken at Home: Spanish
(Universe: Population 5 Years and Over)

Group	Number	%
Total Population	25,647	90.2
Hispanic or Latino (of any race)	25,384	91.8
Mexican	24,356	91.8

Unemployment Rate
(Universe: Population 16 Years and Over)

Group	%
Total Population	10.9
Hispanic or Latino (of any race)	11.1
Mexican	11.0

Class of Worker: Private Wage and Salary
(Universe: Civilian Employed Population 16 Years and Over)

Group	Number	%
Total Population	8,490	71.6
Hispanic or Latino (of any race)	8,140	71.1
Mexican	7,904	71.5

Class of Worker: Government
(Universe: Civilian Employed Population 16 Years and Over)

Group	Number	%
Total Population	2,412	20.3
Hispanic or Latino (of any race)	2,353	20.6
Mexican	2,249	20.3

Means of Transportation to Work: Car, Truck or Van
(Universe: Workers 16 Years and Over)

Group	Number	%
Total Population	10,394	90.5
Hispanic or Latino (of any race)	10,035	90.4
Mexican	9,662	90.2

Means of Transportation to Work: Public Transportation (ex. Taxicab)
(Universe: Workers 16 Years and Over)

Group	Number	%
Total Population	111	1.0
Hispanic or Latino (of any race)	111	1.0
Mexican	111	1.0

Homeownership Rate
(Universe: Occupied Housing Units)

Group	%
Total Population	77.3
Hispanic or Latino (of any race)	77.4
Mexican	77.2
Spaniard	76.7

Median Home Value

Group	Dollars
Total Population	76,800
Hispanic or Latino (of any race)	76,300
Mexican	75,800

Median Gross Rent

Group	Dollars
Total Population	528
Hispanic or Latino (of any race)	525
Mexican	527

Median Household Income
(2010 Inflation-Adjusted Dollars)

Group	Dollars
Total Population	31,680
Hispanic or Latino (of any race)	31,196
Mexican	31,098

Per Capita Income
(2010 Inflation-Adjusted Dollars)

Group	Dollars
Total Population	11,567
Hispanic or Latino (of any race)	11,162
Mexican	11,254

Households with $100,000+ Income

Group	Number	%
Total Population	401	4.8
Hispanic or Latino (of any race)	327	4.0
Mexican	327	4.2

Households with Food Stamps/SNAP Benefits During Past 12 Months

Group	Number	%
Total Population	2,400	28.5
Hispanic or Latino (of any race)	2,290	28.3
Mexican	2,181	28.0

Poverty Rate
(Income in Past 12 Months Below Poverty Level)

Group	%
Total Population	26.1
Hispanic or Latino (of any race)	26.7
Mexican	25.7

Spring

Population

Group	Number	%TP[1]	%HP[2]
Total Population	54,298	100.0	–
Hispanic or Latino (of any race)	15,445	28.4	100.0
Central American, ex. Mexican	1,747	3.2	11.3
Guatemalan	243	0.4	1.6
Honduran	346	0.6	2.2
Nicaraguan	159	0.3	1.0
Salvadoran	920	1.7	6.0
Cuban	153	0.3	1.0
Mexican	11,023	20.3	71.4
Puerto Rican	468	0.9	3.0
South American	708	1.3	4.6
Argentinean	123	0.2	0.8
Colombian	267	0.5	1.7
Spaniard	151	0.3	1.0

Population Growth: 2000–2010

Group	%
Total Population	49.2
Hispanic or Latino (of any race)	164.3
Central American, ex. Mexican	494.2
Salvadoran	721.4
Mexican	193.8
Puerto Rican	82.1
South American	220.4

Males per 100 Females

Group	Number
Total Population	94.6
Hispanic or Latino (of any race)	96.1
Central American, ex. Mexican	97.2
Guatemalan	107.7
Honduran	80.2
Nicaraguan	74.7
Salvadoran	107.2
Cuban	82.1
Mexican	97.5
Puerto Rican	100.0
South American	85.8
Argentinean	119.6
Colombian	64.8
Spaniard	91.1

Average Household Size

Group	People
Total Population	3.01
Hispanic or Latino (of any race)	3.67
Central American, ex. Mexican	4.19
Guatemalan	3.96
Honduran	4.43
Nicaraguan	4.44
Salvadoran	4.22
Cuban	3.34
Mexican	3.68
Puerto Rican	3.26
South American	3.22
Argentinean	3.82
Colombian	3.16
Spaniard	2.71

Median Age

Group	Years
Total Population	31.9
Hispanic or Latino (of any race)	26.5
Central American, ex. Mexican	31.9
Guatemalan	31.4
Honduran	28.9
Nicaraguan	36.5
Salvadoran	31.6
Cuban	33.3
Mexican	25.3
Puerto Rican	27.4
South American	36.3
Argentinean	34.2
Colombian	38.5
Spaniard	32.9

High School Graduates
(Universe: Population 25 Years and Over)

Group	Number	%
Total Population	28,469	88.3
Hispanic or Latino (of any race)	5,274	76.6
Central American, ex. Mexican	573	70.6
Mexican	3,673	74.7

Four-Year College Graduates
(Universe: Population 25 Years and Over)

Group	Number	%
Total Population	6,736	20.9
Hispanic or Latino (of any race)	751	10.9
Central American, ex. Mexican	164	20.2
Mexican	436	8.9

Population Age 3–17 Enrolled in Public School
(Universe: Population Age 3–17 Enrolled in School)

Group	Number	%
Total Population	11,308	92.0
Hispanic or Latino (of any race)	3,518	92.5
Central American, ex. Mexican	470	97.1
Mexican	2,617	90.6

Population Age 3–17 Enrolled in Private School
(Universe: Population Age 3–17 Enrolled in School)

Group	Number	%
Total Population	986	8.0
Hispanic or Latino (of any race)	284	7.5
Central American, ex. Mexican	14	2.9
Mexican	270	9.4

STATE & PLACE PROFILES

Notes: (1) Percent of total population; (2) Percent of Hispanic/Latino population; Profiles include places with an overall population of at least 125,000, OR an overall population of at least 25,000 where the Hispanic/Latino population is at least 20% of the overall population. In states where less than five places meet either of these criteria, we have included places with at least 10,000 total population with the highest percentage of Hispanic/Latino population. These places are identified with an asterisk (*); Please refer to the User's Guide for a full explanation of data.

Foreign-Born Population		
Group	Number	%
Total Population	5,672	10.7
Hispanic or Latino (of any race)	3,305	25.5
Central American, ex. Mexican	800	54.1
Mexican	1,879	19.7

Foreign-Born Naturalized U.S. Citizens		
Group	Number	%
Total Population	2,633	46.4
Hispanic or Latino (of any race)	1,117	33.8
Central American, ex. Mexican	273	34.1
Mexican	406	21.6

Language Spoken at Home: English Only (Universe: Population 5 Years and Over)		
Group	Number	%
Total Population	37,935	77.8
Hispanic or Latino (of any race)	4,184	35.2
Central American, ex. Mexican	80	5.9
Mexican	3,515	40.7

Language Spoken at Home: Spanish (Universe: Population 5 Years and Over)		
Group	Number	%
Total Population	8,616	17.7
Hispanic or Latino (of any race)	7,674	64.6
Central American, ex. Mexican	1,286	94.1
Mexican	5,115	59.2

Unemployment Rate (Universe: Population 16 Years and Over)	
Group	%
Total Population	7.0
Hispanic or Latino (of any race)	7.0
Central American, ex. Mexican	15.4
Mexican	5.9

Class of Worker: Private Wage and Salary (Universe: Civilian Employed Population 16 Years and Over)		
Group	Number	%
Total Population	21,808	81.7
Hispanic or Latino (of any race)	4,996	87.1
Central American, ex. Mexican	315	74.5
Mexican	3,814	88.2

Class of Worker: Government (Universe: Civilian Employed Population 16 Years and Over)		
Group	Number	%
Total Population	3,568	13.4
Hispanic or Latino (of any race)	509	8.9
Central American, ex. Mexican	100	23.6
Mexican	348	8.0

Means of Transportation to Work: Car, Truck or Van (Universe: Workers 16 Years and Over)		
Group	Number	%
Total Population	24,612	94.1
Hispanic or Latino (of any race)	5,530	96.4
Central American, ex. Mexican	402	95.0
Mexican	4,135	96.3

Means of Transportation to Work: Public Transportation (ex. Taxicab) (Universe: Workers 16 Years and Over)		
Group	Number	%
Total Population	541	2.1
Hispanic or Latino (of any race)	109	1.9
Central American, ex. Mexican	0	0.0
Mexican	88	2.0

Homeownership Rate (Universe: Occupied Housing Units)	
Group	%
Total Population	74.9
Hispanic or Latino (of any race)	77.2
Central American, ex. Mexican	82.7
Guatemalan	82.9
Honduran	81.0
Nicaraguan	75.6
Salvadoran	85.0
Cuban	72.3
Mexican	76.7
Puerto Rican	76.4
South American	79.0
Argentinean	73.7
Colombian	84.0
Spaniard	72.9

Median Home Value	
Group	Dollars
Total Population	113,500
Hispanic or Latino (of any race)	108,400
Central American, ex. Mexican	133,200
Mexican	106,800

Median Gross Rent	
Group	Dollars
Total Population	1,045
Hispanic or Latino (of any race)	983
Central American, ex. Mexican	–
Mexican	975

Median Household Income (2010 Inflation-Adjusted Dollars)	
Group	Dollars
Total Population	67,787
Hispanic or Latino (of any race)	57,692
Central American, ex. Mexican	47,270
Mexican	59,083

Per Capita Income (2010 Inflation-Adjusted Dollars)	
Group	Dollars
Total Population	24,622
Hispanic or Latino (of any race)	17,023
Central American, ex. Mexican	12,624
Mexican	16,964

Households with $100,000+ Income		
Group	Number	%
Total Population	3,797	22.0
Hispanic or Latino (of any race)	453	13.7
Central American, ex. Mexican	30	8.8
Mexican	364	15.0

Households with Food Stamps/SNAP Benefits During Past 12 Months		
Group	Number	%
Total Population	1,465	8.5
Hispanic or Latino (of any race)	361	10.9
Central American, ex. Mexican	16	4.7
Mexican	288	11.9

Poverty Rate (Income in Past 12 Months Below Poverty Level)	
Group	%
Total Population	8.8
Hispanic or Latino (of any race)	11.7
Central American, ex. Mexican	13.5
Mexican	11.6

Temple

Population			
Group	Number	%TP[1]	%HP[2]
Total Population	66,102	100.0	–
Hispanic or Latino (of any race)	15,694	23.7	100.0
Central American, ex. Mexican	267	0.4	1.7
Mexican	13,179	19.9	84.0
Puerto Rican	795	1.2	5.1
South American	125	0.2	0.8
Spaniard	136	0.2	0.9

Population Growth: 2000–2010	
Group	%
Total Population	21.3
Hispanic or Latino (of any race)	61.5
Mexican	81.2
Puerto Rican	110.3

Males per 100 Females	
Group	Number
Total Population	91.7
Hispanic or Latino (of any race)	97.1
Central American, ex. Mexican	108.6
Mexican	96.8
Puerto Rican	112.6
South American	73.6
Spaniard	100.0

Average Household Size	
Group	People
Total Population	2.47
Hispanic or Latino (of any race)	3.19
Central American, ex. Mexican	3.08
Mexican	3.26
Puerto Rican	2.81
South American	2.69
Spaniard	2.67

Median Age	
Group	Years
Total Population	34.6
Hispanic or Latino (of any race)	25.2
Central American, ex. Mexican	32.1
Mexican	24.8
Puerto Rican	26.2
South American	32.8
Spaniard	33.3

High School Graduates (Universe: Population 25 Years and Over)		
Group	Number	%
Total Population	36,447	85.7
Hispanic or Latino (of any race)	4,727	64.6
Mexican	4,025	63.5

Four-Year College Graduates (Universe: Population 25 Years and Over)		
Group	Number	%
Total Population	10,602	24.9
Hispanic or Latino (of any race)	819	11.2
Mexican	624	9.8

Population Age 3–17 Enrolled in Public School (Universe: Population Age 3–17 Enrolled in School)		
Group	Number	%
Total Population	9,503	88.3
Hispanic or Latino (of any race)	3,179	97.3
Mexican	2,655	97.1

Population Age 3–17 Enrolled in Private School (Universe: Population Age 3–17 Enrolled in School)		
Group	Number	%
Total Population	1,254	11.7
Hispanic or Latino (of any race)	87	2.7
Mexican	79	2.9

Foreign-Born Population		
Group	Number	%
Total Population	5,590	8.8
Hispanic or Latino (of any race)	3,832	27.9
Mexican	3,421	28.5

Foreign-Born Naturalized U.S. Citizens		
Group	Number	%
Total Population	2,098	37.5
Hispanic or Latino (of any race)	1,095	28.6
Mexican	820	24.0

Language Spoken at Home: English Only (Universe: Population 5 Years and Over)		
Group	Number	%
Total Population	48,114	81.8
Hispanic or Latino (of any race)	3,847	31.1
Mexican	3,061	28.6

Language Spoken at Home: Spanish (Universe: Population 5 Years and Over)		
Group	Number	%
Total Population	9,271	15.8
Hispanic or Latino (of any race)	8,511	68.9
Mexican	7,629	71.4

Unemployment Rate (Universe: Population 16 Years and Over)	
Group	%
Total Population	4.9
Hispanic or Latino (of any race)	5.1
Mexican	5.5

Notes: (1) Percent of total population; (2) Percent of Hispanic/Latino population; Profiles include places with an overall population of at least 125,000, OR an overall population of at least 25,000 where the Hispanic/Latino population is at least 20% of the overall population. In states where less than five places meet either of these criteria, we have included places with at least 10,000 total population with the highest percentage of Hispanic/Latino population. These places are identified with an asterisk (*); Please refer to the User's Guide for a full explanation of data.

Class of Worker: Private Wage and Salary
(Universe: Civilian Employed Population 16 Years and Over)

Group	Number	%
Total Population	22,578	77.3
Hispanic or Latino (of any race)	4,755	82.7
Mexican	4,140	82.9

Class of Worker: Government
(Universe: Civilian Employed Population 16 Years and Over)

Group	Number	%
Total Population	5,407	18.5
Hispanic or Latino (of any race)	793	13.8
Mexican	684	13.7

Means of Transportation to Work: Car, Truck or Van
(Universe: Workers 16 Years and Over)

Group	Number	%
Total Population	27,644	94.7
Hispanic or Latino (of any race)	5,450	94.4
Mexican	4,725	93.5

Means of Transportation to Work: Public Transportation (ex. Taxicab)
(Universe: Workers 16 Years and Over)

Group	Number	%
Total Population	57	0.2
Hispanic or Latino (of any race)	0	0.0
Mexican	0	0.0

Homeownership Rate
(Universe: Occupied Housing Units)

Group	%
Total Population	55.3
Hispanic or Latino (of any race)	51.8
Central American, ex. Mexican	54.2
Mexican	52.5
Puerto Rican	42.0
South American	50.0
Spaniard	61.5

Median Home Value

Group	Dollars
Total Population	107,100
Hispanic or Latino (of any race)	87,000
Mexican	86,900

Median Gross Rent

Group	Dollars
Total Population	728
Hispanic or Latino (of any race)	641
Mexican	621

Median Household Income
(2010 Inflation-Adjusted Dollars)

Group	Dollars
Total Population	47,240
Hispanic or Latino (of any race)	39,635
Mexican	40,000

Per Capita Income
(2010 Inflation-Adjusted Dollars)

Group	Dollars
Total Population	25,740
Hispanic or Latino (of any race)	14,213
Mexican	13,562

Households with $100,000+ Income

Group	Number	%
Total Population	3,717	15.9
Hispanic or Latino (of any race)	216	6.0
Mexican	171	5.6

Households with Food Stamps/SNAP Benefits During Past 12 Months

Group	Number	%
Total Population	2,140	9.2
Hispanic or Latino (of any race)	634	17.6
Mexican	509	16.6

Poverty Rate
(Income in Past 12 Months Below Poverty Level)

Group	%
Total Population	12.5
Hispanic or Latino (of any race)	22.1
Mexican	20.3

Texas City

Population

Group	Number	%TP[1]	%HP[2]
Total Population	45,099	100.0	–
Hispanic or Latino (of any race)	12,184	27.0	100.0
Central American, ex. Mexican	447	1.0	3.7
Honduran	122	0.3	1.0
Salvadoran	221	0.5	1.8
Mexican	10,307	22.9	84.6
Puerto Rican	226	0.5	1.9

Population Growth: 2000–2010

Group	%
Total Population	8.6
Hispanic or Latino (of any race)	43.0
Central American, ex. Mexican	223.9
Mexican	52.1
Puerto Rican	31.4

Males per 100 Females

Group	Number
Total Population	92.0
Hispanic or Latino (of any race)	99.3
Central American, ex. Mexican	105.0
Honduran	100.0
Salvadoran	118.8
Mexican	101.3
Puerto Rican	78.0

Average Household Size

Group	People
Total Population	2.66
Hispanic or Latino (of any race)	3.22
Central American, ex. Mexican	3.40
Honduran	3.38
Salvadoran	3.51
Mexican	3.23
Puerto Rican	3.22

Median Age

Group	Years
Total Population	35.9
Hispanic or Latino (of any race)	28.1
Central American, ex. Mexican	29.3
Honduran	30.8
Salvadoran	29.2
Mexican	27.9
Puerto Rican	30.5

High School Graduates
(Universe: Population 25 Years and Over)

Group	Number	%
Total Population	24,255	82.4
Hispanic or Latino (of any race)	4,079	64.0
Mexican	3,692	63.8

Four-Year College Graduates
(Universe: Population 25 Years and Over)

Group	Number	%
Total Population	3,717	12.6
Hispanic or Latino (of any race)	484	7.6
Mexican	459	7.9

Population Age 3–17 Enrolled in Public School
(Universe: Population Age 3–17 Enrolled in School)

Group	Number	%
Total Population	7,641	91.0
Hispanic or Latino (of any race)	2,392	88.8
Mexican	2,209	87.9

Population Age 3–17 Enrolled in Private School
(Universe: Population Age 3–17 Enrolled in School)

Group	Number	%
Total Population	757	9.0
Hispanic or Latino (of any race)	303	11.2
Mexican	303	12.1

Foreign-Born Population

Group	Number	%
Total Population	3,474	7.7
Hispanic or Latino (of any race)	2,687	23.2
Mexican	2,374	22.7

Foreign-Born Naturalized U.S. Citizens

Group	Number	%
Total Population	1,032	29.7
Hispanic or Latino (of any race)	684	25.5
Mexican	490	20.6

Language Spoken at Home: English Only
(Universe: Population 5 Years and Over)

Group	Number	%
Total Population	35,331	85.1
Hispanic or Latino (of any race)	4,786	47.9
Mexican	4,428	49.1

Language Spoken at Home: Spanish
(Universe: Population 5 Years and Over)

Group	Number	%
Total Population	5,606	13.5
Hispanic or Latino (of any race)	5,198	52.1
Mexican	4,584	50.9

Unemployment Rate
(Universe: Population 16 Years and Over)

Group	%
Total Population	8.9
Hispanic or Latino (of any race)	10.7
Mexican	11.1

Class of Worker: Private Wage and Salary
(Universe: Civilian Employed Population 16 Years and Over)

Group	Number	%
Total Population	14,795	74.5
Hispanic or Latino (of any race)	4,194	82.8
Mexican	3,742	83.4

Class of Worker: Government
(Universe: Civilian Employed Population 16 Years and Over)

Group	Number	%
Total Population	4,237	21.3
Hispanic or Latino (of any race)	696	13.7
Mexican	579	12.9

Means of Transportation to Work: Car, Truck or Van
(Universe: Workers 16 Years and Over)

Group	Number	%
Total Population	17,945	91.9
Hispanic or Latino (of any race)	4,396	87.6
Mexican	3,894	87.6

Means of Transportation to Work: Public Transportation (ex. Taxicab)
(Universe: Workers 16 Years and Over)

Group	Number	%
Total Population	0	0.0
Hispanic or Latino (of any race)	0	0.0
Mexican	0	0.0

Homeownership Rate
(Universe: Occupied Housing Units)

Group	%
Total Population	60.7
Hispanic or Latino (of any race)	58.7
Central American, ex. Mexican	54.8
Honduran	50.0
Salvadoran	58.8
Mexican	59.0
Puerto Rican	48.5

Median Home Value

Group	Dollars
Total Population	95,200
Hispanic or Latino (of any race)	97,900
Mexican	99,700

Median Gross Rent

Group	Dollars
Total Population	772
Hispanic or Latino (of any race)	757
Mexican	738

Median Household Income
(2010 Inflation-Adjusted Dollars)

Group	Dollars
Total Population	46,496
Hispanic or Latino (of any race)	47,375
Mexican	45,625

STATE & PLACE PROFILES

Notes: (1) Percent of total population; (2) Percent of Hispanic/Latino population; Profiles include places with an overall population of at least 125,000, OR an overall population of at least 25,000 where the Hispanic/Latino population is at least 20% of the overall population. In states where less than five places meet either of these criteria, we have included places with at least 10,000 total population with the highest percentage of Hispanic/Latino population. These places are identified with an asterisk (*); Please refer to the User's Guide for a full explanation of data.

Per Capita Income (2010 Inflation-Adjusted Dollars)	
Group	Dollars
Total Population	21,942
Hispanic or Latino (of any race)	19,234
Mexican	19,476

Households with $100,000+ Income		
Group	Number	%
Total Population	2,395	14.2
Hispanic or Latino (of any race)	363	10.1
Mexican	329	10.1

Households with Food Stamps/SNAP Benefits During Past 12 Months		
Group	Number	%
Total Population	2,604	15.5
Hispanic or Latino (of any race)	521	14.5
Mexican	490	15.1

Poverty Rate (Income in Past 12 Months Below Poverty Level)	
Group	%
Total Population	15.0
Hispanic or Latino (of any race)	16.1
Mexican	17.3

The Colony

Population			
Group	Number	%TP[1]	%HP[2]
Total Population	36,328	100.0	–
Hispanic or Latino (of any race)	7,684	21.2	100.0
Central American, ex. Mexican	638	1.8	8.3
Honduran	137	0.4	1.8
Salvadoran	369	1.0	4.8
Cuban	107	0.3	1.4
Mexican	5,748	15.8	74.8
Puerto Rican	194	0.5	2.5
South American	349	1.0	4.5
Colombian	102	0.3	1.3
Spaniard	107	0.3	1.4

Population Growth: 2000–2010	
Group	%
Total Population	36.9
Hispanic or Latino (of any race)	118.4
Central American, ex. Mexican	309.0
Mexican	145.3
Puerto Rican	64.4

Males per 100 Females	
Group	Number
Total Population	99.5
Hispanic or Latino (of any race)	102.4
Central American, ex. Mexican	93.3
Honduran	85.1
Salvadoran	100.5
Cuban	105.8
Mexican	104.3
Puerto Rican	86.5
South American	84.7
Colombian	45.7
Spaniard	122.9

Average Household Size	
Group	People
Total Population	2.76
Hispanic or Latino (of any race)	3.65
Central American, ex. Mexican	4.13
Honduran	4.46
Salvadoran	4.27
Cuban	2.78
Mexican	3.75
Puerto Rican	2.86
South American	3.15
Colombian	3.22
Spaniard	2.95

Median Age	
Group	Years
Total Population	33.1
Hispanic or Latino (of any race)	26.6
Central American, ex. Mexican	31.0
Honduran	29.5
Salvadoran	30.6
Cuban	36.5
Mexican	25.8
Puerto Rican	28.5
South American	33.7
Colombian	32.5
Spaniard	35.2

High School Graduates (Universe: Population 25 Years and Over)		
Group	Number	%
Total Population	20,551	91.9
Hispanic or Latino (of any race)	2,668	74.4
Mexican	1,705	67.1

Four-Year College Graduates (Universe: Population 25 Years and Over)		
Group	Number	%
Total Population	7,696	34.4
Hispanic or Latino (of any race)	566	15.8
Mexican	326	12.8

Population Age 3–17 Enrolled in Public School (Universe: Population Age 3–17 Enrolled in School)		
Group	Number	%
Total Population	6,847	92.3
Hispanic or Latino (of any race)	2,103	97.8
Mexican	1,620	97.9

Population Age 3–17 Enrolled in Private School (Universe: Population Age 3–17 Enrolled in School)		
Group	Number	%
Total Population	573	7.7
Hispanic or Latino (of any race)	48	2.2
Mexican	35	2.1

Foreign-Born Population		
Group	Number	%
Total Population	5,525	15.8
Hispanic or Latino (of any race)	2,349	33.3
Mexican	1,555	29.9

Foreign-Born Naturalized U.S. Citizens		
Group	Number	%
Total Population	2,208	40.0
Hispanic or Latino (of any race)	706	30.1
Mexican	420	27.0

Language Spoken at Home: English Only (Universe: Population 5 Years and Over)		
Group	Number	%
Total Population	24,735	76.1
Hispanic or Latino (of any race)	1,759	27.8
Mexican	1,230	27.1

Language Spoken at Home: Spanish (Universe: Population 5 Years and Over)		
Group	Number	%
Total Population	4,912	15.1
Hispanic or Latino (of any race)	4,527	71.4
Mexican	3,276	72.1

Unemployment Rate (Universe: Population 16 Years and Over)	
Group	%
Total Population	5.3
Hispanic or Latino (of any race)	3.1
Mexican	3.2

Class of Worker: Private Wage and Salary (Universe: Civilian Employed Population 16 Years and Over)		
Group	Number	%
Total Population	17,280	83.8
Hispanic or Latino (of any race)	2,972	85.7
Mexican	2,082	86.1

Class of Worker: Government (Universe: Civilian Employed Population 16 Years and Over)		
Group	Number	%
Total Population	2,119	10.3
Hispanic or Latino (of any race)	202	5.8
Mexican	128	5.3

Means of Transportation to Work: Car, Truck or Van (Universe: Workers 16 Years and Over)		
Group	Number	%
Total Population	18,710	93.7
Hispanic or Latino (of any race)	3,263	95.5
Mexican	2,231	94.2

Means of Transportation to Work: Public Transportation (ex. Taxicab) (Universe: Workers 16 Years and Over)		
Group	Number	%
Total Population	148	0.7
Hispanic or Latino (of any race)	0	0.0
Mexican	0	0.0

Homeownership Rate (Universe: Occupied Housing Units)	
Group	%
Total Population	68.5
Hispanic or Latino (of any race)	73.4
Central American, ex. Mexican	81.1
Honduran	74.3
Salvadoran	86.9
Cuban	53.3
Mexican	74.5
Puerto Rican	64.1
South American	76.1
Colombian	74.1
Spaniard	73.8

Median Home Value	
Group	Dollars
Total Population	141,200
Hispanic or Latino (of any race)	120,600
Mexican	120,700

Median Gross Rent	
Group	Dollars
Total Population	1,126
Hispanic or Latino (of any race)	1,186
Mexican	1,180

Median Household Income (2010 Inflation-Adjusted Dollars)	
Group	Dollars
Total Population	76,497
Hispanic or Latino (of any race)	58,714
Mexican	60,391

Per Capita Income (2010 Inflation-Adjusted Dollars)	
Group	Dollars
Total Population	32,159
Hispanic or Latino (of any race)	17,913
Mexican	17,625

Households with $100,000+ Income		
Group	Number	%
Total Population	4,334	34.0
Hispanic or Latino (of any race)	321	18.6
Mexican	201	15.8

Households with Food Stamps/SNAP Benefits During Past 12 Months		
Group	Number	%
Total Population	245	1.9
Hispanic or Latino (of any race)	38	2.2
Mexican	38	3.0

Poverty Rate (Income in Past 12 Months Below Poverty Level)	
Group	%
Total Population	4.6
Hispanic or Latino (of any race)	4.0
Mexican	4.5

Tyler

Population			
Group	Number	%TP[1]	%HP[2]
Total Population	96,900	100.0	–
Hispanic or Latino (of any race)	20,511	21.2	100.0
Central American, ex. Mexican	666	0.7	3.2

Notes: (1) Percent of total population; (2) Percent of Hispanic/Latino population; Profiles include places with an overall population of at least 125,000, OR an overall population of at least 25,000 where the Hispanic/Latino population is at least 20% of the overall population. In states where less than five places meet either of these criteria, we have included places with at least 10,000 total population with the highest percentage of Hispanic/Latino population. These places are identified with an asterisk (*); Please refer to the User's Guide for a full explanation of data.

Honduran	119	0.1	0.6
Salvadoran	376	0.4	1.8
Mexican	18,265	18.8	89.0
Puerto Rican	215	0.2	1.0
South American	192	0.2	0.9
Spaniard	105	0.1	0.5

Population Growth: 2000–2010

Group	%
Total Population	15.8
Hispanic or Latino (of any race)	55.0
Central American, ex. Mexican	252.4
Mexican	60.1
Puerto Rican	90.3

Males per 100 Females

Group	Number
Total Population	89.3
Hispanic or Latino (of any race)	106.8
Central American, ex. Mexican	114.1
Honduran	124.5
Salvadoran	125.1
Mexican	107.8
Puerto Rican	85.3
South American	79.4
Spaniard	56.7

Average Household Size

Group	People
Total Population	2.46
Hispanic or Latino (of any race)	3.87
Central American, ex. Mexican	3.85
Honduran	2.92
Salvadoran	4.10
Mexican	3.95
Puerto Rican	2.51
South American	2.64
Spaniard	2.41

Median Age

Group	Years
Total Population	32.8
Hispanic or Latino (of any race)	23.1
Central American, ex. Mexican	30.6
Honduran	32.1
Salvadoran	29.6
Mexican	22.8
Puerto Rican	28.8
South American	33.0
Spaniard	30.6

High School Graduates
(Universe: Population 25 Years and Over)

Group	Number	%
Total Population	48,989	83.7
Hispanic or Latino (of any race)	3,259	37.0
Mexican	2,891	35.4

Four-Year College Graduates
(Universe: Population 25 Years and Over)

Group	Number	%
Total Population	16,956	29.0
Hispanic or Latino (of any race)	499	5.7
Mexican	405	5.0

Population Age 3–17 Enrolled in Public School
(Universe: Population Age 3–17 Enrolled in School)

Group	Number	%
Total Population	14,379	83.7
Hispanic or Latino (of any race)	4,335	94.2
Mexican	4,205	95.0

Population Age 3–17 Enrolled in Private School
(Universe: Population Age 3–17 Enrolled in School)

Group	Number	%
Total Population	2,801	16.3
Hispanic or Latino (of any race)	265	5.8
Mexican	220	5.0

Foreign-Born Population

Group	Number	%
Total Population	10,720	11.3
Hispanic or Latino (of any race)	9,146	49.9
Mexican	8,633	50.0

Foreign-Born Naturalized U.S. Citizens

Group	Number	%
Total Population	2,506	23.4
Hispanic or Latino (of any race)	1,721	18.8
Mexican	1,621	18.8

Language Spoken at Home: English Only
(Universe: Population 5 Years and Over)

Group	Number	%
Total Population	71,531	81.4
Hispanic or Latino (of any race)	1,892	11.8
Mexican	1,670	11.0

Language Spoken at Home: Spanish
(Universe: Population 5 Years and Over)

Group	Number	%
Total Population	14,903	17.0
Hispanic or Latino (of any race)	14,205	88.2
Mexican	13,466	89.0

Unemployment Rate
(Universe: Population 16 Years and Over)

Group	%
Total Population	7.2
Hispanic or Latino (of any race)	6.2
Mexican	6.3

Class of Worker: Private Wage and Salary
(Universe: Civilian Employed Population 16 Years and Over)

Group	Number	%
Total Population	36,584	82.4
Hispanic or Latino (of any race)	7,142	86.2
Mexican	6,801	86.9

Class of Worker: Government
(Universe: Civilian Employed Population 16 Years and Over)

Group	Number	%
Total Population	5,286	11.9
Hispanic or Latino (of any race)	566	6.8
Mexican	539	6.9

Means of Transportation to Work: Car, Truck or Van
(Universe: Workers 16 Years and Over)

Group	Number	%
Total Population	38,941	89.5
Hispanic or Latino (of any race)	6,991	85.7
Mexican	6,575	85.4

Means of Transportation to Work: Public Transportation (ex. Taxicab)
(Universe: Workers 16 Years and Over)

Group	Number	%
Total Population	350	0.8
Hispanic or Latino (of any race)	81	1.0
Mexican	81	1.1

Homeownership Rate
(Universe: Occupied Housing Units)

Group	%
Total Population	53.0
Hispanic or Latino (of any race)	53.9
Central American, ex. Mexican	57.5
Honduran	50.0
Salvadoran	62.9
Mexican	54.7
Puerto Rican	40.5
South American	51.5
Spaniard	38.6

Median Home Value

Group	Dollars
Total Population	123,600
Hispanic or Latino (of any race)	69,100
Mexican	68,500

Median Gross Rent

Group	Dollars
Total Population	748
Hispanic or Latino (of any race)	651
Mexican	642

Median Household Income
(2010 Inflation-Adjusted Dollars)

Group	Dollars
Total Population	41,607
Hispanic or Latino (of any race)	39,681
Mexican	38,385

Per Capita Income
(2010 Inflation-Adjusted Dollars)

Group	Dollars
Total Population	27,169
Hispanic or Latino (of any race)	13,275
Mexican	12,563

Households with $100,000+ Income

Group	Number	%
Total Population	6,382	17.1
Hispanic or Latino (of any race)	306	6.6
Mexican	278	6.5

Households with Food Stamps/SNAP Benefits During Past 12 Months

Group	Number	%
Total Population	4,499	12.0
Hispanic or Latino (of any race)	765	16.5
Mexican	733	17.1

Poverty Rate
(Income in Past 12 Months Below Poverty Level)

Group	%
Total Population	20.2
Hispanic or Latino (of any race)	29.5
Mexican	29.6

Victoria

Population

Group	Number	%TP[1]	%HP[2]
Total Population	62,592	100.0	–
Hispanic or Latino (of any race)	30,220	48.3	100.0
Central American, ex. Mexican	135	0.2	0.4
Mexican	25,500	40.7	84.4
Puerto Rican	215	0.3	0.7
Spaniard	305	0.5	1.0

Population Growth: 2000–2010

Group	%
Total Population	3.3
Hispanic or Latino (of any race)	16.2
Mexican	43.2
Puerto Rican	59.3

Males per 100 Females

Group	Number
Total Population	92.4
Hispanic or Latino (of any race)	96.5
Central American, ex. Mexican	154.7
Mexican	96.4
Puerto Rican	93.7
Spaniard	102.0

Average Household Size

Group	People
Total Population	2.62
Hispanic or Latino (of any race)	3.08
Central American, ex. Mexican	3.30
Mexican	3.09
Puerto Rican	2.64
Spaniard	3.02

Median Age

Group	Years
Total Population	34.9
Hispanic or Latino (of any race)	28.0
Central American, ex. Mexican	34.4
Mexican	28.3
Puerto Rican	29.1
Spaniard	26.6

High School Graduates
(Universe: Population 25 Years and Over)

Group	Number	%
Total Population	30,449	78.6
Hispanic or Latino (of any race)	9,488	62.0
Mexican	8,195	61.2

Notes: (1) Percent of total population; (2) Percent of Hispanic/Latino population; Profiles include places with an overall population of at least 125,000, OR an overall population of at least 25,000 where the Hispanic/Latino population is at least 20% of the overall population. In states where less than five places meet either of these criteria, we have included places with at least 10,000 total population with the highest percentage of Hispanic/Latino population. These places are identified with an asterisk (*); Please refer to the User's Guide for a full explanation of data.

Four-Year College Graduates
(Universe: Population 25 Years and Over)

Group	Number	%
Total Population	6,814	17.6
Hispanic or Latino (of any race)	915	6.0
Mexican	782	5.8

Population Age 3–17 Enrolled in Public School
(Universe: Population Age 3–17 Enrolled in School)

Group	Number	%
Total Population	11,147	87.8
Hispanic or Latino (of any race)	6,421	93.2
Mexican	5,975	93.6

Population Age 3–17 Enrolled in Private School
(Universe: Population Age 3–17 Enrolled in School)

Group	Number	%
Total Population	1,546	12.2
Hispanic or Latino (of any race)	465	6.8
Mexican	409	6.4

Foreign-Born Population

Group	Number	%
Total Population	4,102	6.6
Hispanic or Latino (of any race)	3,004	10.6
Mexican	2,645	10.4

Foreign-Born Naturalized U.S. Citizens

Group	Number	%
Total Population	1,101	26.8
Hispanic or Latino (of any race)	687	22.9
Mexican	587	22.2

Language Spoken at Home: English Only
(Universe: Population 5 Years and Over)

Group	Number	%
Total Population	41,500	72.7
Hispanic or Latino (of any race)	11,755	46.2
Mexican	10,583	46.6

Language Spoken at Home: Spanish
(Universe: Population 5 Years and Over)

Group	Number	%
Total Population	14,383	25.2
Hispanic or Latino (of any race)	13,636	53.6
Mexican	12,113	53.4

Unemployment Rate
(Universe: Population 16 Years and Over)

Group	%
Total Population	7.8
Hispanic or Latino (of any race)	9.7
Mexican	9.6

Class of Worker: Private Wage and Salary
(Universe: Civilian Employed Population 16 Years and Over)

Group	Number	%
Total Population	22,630	80.4
Hispanic or Latino (of any race)	10,024	84.5
Mexican	8,815	85.0

Class of Worker: Government
(Universe: Civilian Employed Population 16 Years and Over)

Group	Number	%
Total Population	3,679	13.1
Hispanic or Latino (of any race)	1,151	9.7
Mexican	960	9.3

Means of Transportation to Work: Car, Truck or Van
(Universe: Workers 16 Years and Over)

Group	Number	%
Total Population	25,537	93.6
Hispanic or Latino (of any race)	10,751	94.8
Mexican	9,401	95.0

Means of Transportation to Work: Public Transportation (ex. Taxicab)
(Universe: Workers 16 Years and Over)

Group	Number	%
Total Population	420	1.5
Hispanic or Latino (of any race)	115	1.0
Mexican	103	1.0

Homeownership Rate
(Universe: Occupied Housing Units)

Group	%
Total Population	59.1
Hispanic or Latino (of any race)	50.4
Central American, ex. Mexican	58.0
Mexican	51.5
Puerto Rican	56.5
Spaniard	53.2

Median Home Value

Group	Dollars
Total Population	97,200
Hispanic or Latino (of any race)	70,500
Mexican	69,500

Median Gross Rent

Group	Dollars
Total Population	679
Hispanic or Latino (of any race)	669
Mexican	666

Median Household Income
(2010 Inflation-Adjusted Dollars)

Group	Dollars
Total Population	44,504
Hispanic or Latino (of any race)	35,820
Mexican	35,000

Per Capita Income
(2010 Inflation-Adjusted Dollars)

Group	Dollars
Total Population	23,176
Hispanic or Latino (of any race)	14,769
Mexican	14,159

Households with $100,000+ Income

Group	Number	%
Total Population	3,457	14.8
Hispanic or Latino (of any race)	676	7.7
Mexican	568	7.4

Households with Food Stamps/SNAP Benefits During Past 12 Months

Group	Number	%
Total Population	3,440	14.7
Hispanic or Latino (of any race)	2,100	24.0
Mexican	1,918	25.1

Poverty Rate
(Income in Past 12 Months Below Poverty Level)

Group	%
Total Population	18.6
Hispanic or Latino (of any race)	27.9
Mexican	28.9

Waco

Population

Group	Number	%TP[1]	%HP[2]
Total Population	124,805	100.0	–
Hispanic or Latino (of any race)	36,947	29.6	100.0
Central American, ex. Mexican	487	0.4	1.3
Honduran	100	0.1	0.3
Salvadoran	225	0.2	0.6
Cuban	114	0.1	0.3
Mexican	33,080	26.5	89.5
Puerto Rican	599	0.5	1.6
South American	236	0.2	0.6
Spaniard	209	0.2	0.6

Population Growth: 2000–2010

Group	%
Total Population	9.7
Hispanic or Latino (of any race)	37.4
Central American, ex. Mexican	141.1
Mexican	54.2
Puerto Rican	126.0
South American	133.7

Males per 100 Females

Group	Number
Total Population	91.8
Hispanic or Latino (of any race)	102.4
Central American, ex. Mexican	104.6
Honduran	112.8
Salvadoran	104.5
Cuban	93.2
Mexican	103.5
Puerto Rican	108.7
South American	62.8
Spaniard	75.6

Average Household Size

Group	People
Total Population	2.52
Hispanic or Latino (of any race)	3.40
Central American, ex. Mexican	3.34
Honduran	3.71
Salvadoran	3.56
Cuban	2.16
Mexican	3.48
Puerto Rican	2.87
South American	2.03
Spaniard	2.62

Median Age

Group	Years
Total Population	28.2
Hispanic or Latino (of any race)	23.6
Central American, ex. Mexican	28.0
Honduran	27.5
Salvadoran	29.3
Cuban	25.6
Mexican	23.5
Puerto Rican	24.0
South American	23.0
Spaniard	24.2

High School Graduates
(Universe: Population 25 Years and Over)

Group	Number	%
Total Population	50,572	75.5
Hispanic or Latino (of any race)	7,957	48.5
Mexican	6,715	45.2

Four-Year College Graduates
(Universe: Population 25 Years and Over)

Group	Number	%
Total Population	13,611	20.3
Hispanic or Latino (of any race)	1,145	7.0
Mexican	868	5.8

Population Age 3–17 Enrolled in Public School
(Universe: Population Age 3–17 Enrolled in School)

Group	Number	%
Total Population	20,014	91.6
Hispanic or Latino (of any race)	8,913	94.8
Mexican	8,356	95.3

Population Age 3–17 Enrolled in Private School
(Universe: Population Age 3–17 Enrolled in School)

Group	Number	%
Total Population	1,842	8.4
Hispanic or Latino (of any race)	490	5.2
Mexican	408	4.7

Foreign-Born Population

Group	Number	%
Total Population	12,893	10.5
Hispanic or Latino (of any race)	10,132	28.7
Mexican	9,479	29.5

Foreign-Born Naturalized U.S. Citizens

Group	Number	%
Total Population	3,119	24.2
Hispanic or Latino (of any race)	1,939	19.1
Mexican	1,757	18.5

Language Spoken at Home: English Only
(Universe: Population 5 Years and Over)

Group	Number	%
Total Population	85,910	76.4
Hispanic or Latino (of any race)	8,684	28.1
Mexican	7,347	26.2

Language Spoken at Home: Spanish
(Universe: Population 5 Years and Over)

Group	Number	%
Total Population	23,563	21.0

Notes: (1) Percent of total population; (2) Percent of Hispanic/Latino population; Profiles include places with an overall population of at least 125,000, OR an overall population of at least 25,000 where the Hispanic/Latino population is at least 20% of the overall population. In states where less than five places meet either of these criteria, we have included places with at least 10,000 total population with the highest percentage of Hispanic/Latino population. These places are identified with an asterisk (*); Please refer to the User's Guide for a full explanation of data.

Hispanic or Latino (of any race)	22,190	71.8
Mexican	20,661	73.8

Unemployment Rate
(Universe: Population 16 Years and Over)

Group	%
Total Population	9.3
Hispanic or Latino (of any race)	9.4
Mexican	9.6

Class of Worker: Private Wage and Salary
(Universe: Civilian Employed Population 16 Years and Over)

Group	Number	%
Total Population	42,374	81.6
Hispanic or Latino (of any race)	12,208	86.2
Mexican	10,884	85.4

Class of Worker: Government
(Universe: Civilian Employed Population 16 Years and Over)

Group	Number	%
Total Population	6,871	13.2
Hispanic or Latino (of any race)	1,243	8.8
Mexican	1,148	9.0

Means of Transportation to Work: Car, Truck or Van
(Universe: Workers 16 Years and Over)

Group	Number	%
Total Population	46,433	91.7
Hispanic or Latino (of any race)	13,271	95.3
Mexican	11,935	95.5

Means of Transportation to Work: Public Transportation (ex. Taxicab)
(Universe: Workers 16 Years and Over)

Group	Number	%
Total Population	382	0.8
Hispanic or Latino (of any race)	97	0.7
Mexican	86	0.7

Homeownership Rate
(Universe: Occupied Housing Units)

Group	%
Total Population	46.3
Hispanic or Latino (of any race)	50.1
Central American, ex. Mexican	52.1
Honduran	32.4
Salvadoran	59.5
Cuban	48.9
Mexican	51.8
Puerto Rican	35.8
South American	18.5
Spaniard	39.0

Median Home Value

Group	Dollars
Total Population	86,600
Hispanic or Latino (of any race)	61,200
Mexican	60,600

Median Gross Rent

Group	Dollars
Total Population	725
Hispanic or Latino (of any race)	661
Mexican	655

Median Household Income
(2010 Inflation-Adjusted Dollars)

Group	Dollars
Total Population	31,288
Hispanic or Latino (of any race)	29,437
Mexican	30,267

Per Capita Income
(2010 Inflation-Adjusted Dollars)

Group	Dollars
Total Population	17,323
Hispanic or Latino (of any race)	10,435
Mexican	10,010

Households with $100,000+ Income

Group	Number	%
Total Population	3,877	8.7
Hispanic or Latino (of any race)	234	2.6
Mexican	212	2.6

Households with Food Stamps/SNAP Benefits During Past 12 Months

Group	Number	%
Total Population	6,974	15.7
Hispanic or Latino (of any race)	1,977	21.8
Mexican	1,825	22.3

Poverty Rate
(Income in Past 12 Months Below Poverty Level)

Group	%
Total Population	28.7
Hispanic or Latino (of any race)	32.0
Mexican	32.4

Waxahachie

Population

Group	Number	%TP[1]	%HP[2]
Total Population	29,621	100.0	–
Hispanic or Latino (of any race)	6,870	23.2	100.0
Central American, ex. Mexican	121	0.4	1.8
Mexican	5,998	20.2	87.3
Puerto Rican	100	0.3	1.5

Population Growth: 2000–2010

Group	%
Total Population	38.2
Hispanic or Latino (of any race)	62.4
Mexican	79.7

Males per 100 Females

Group	Number
Total Population	93.0
Hispanic or Latino (of any race)	103.8
Central American, ex. Mexican	108.6
Mexican	104.4
Puerto Rican	100.0

Average Household Size

Group	People
Total Population	2.72
Hispanic or Latino (of any race)	3.61
Central American, ex. Mexican	3.71
Mexican	3.67
Puerto Rican	2.57

Median Age

Group	Years
Total Population	31.7
Hispanic or Latino (of any race)	23.5
Central American, ex. Mexican	28.8
Mexican	23.4
Puerto Rican	23.7

High School Graduates
(Universe: Population 25 Years and Over)

Group	Number	%
Total Population	13,881	82.7
Hispanic or Latino (of any race)	1,714	56.2
Mexican	1,336	52.5

Four-Year College Graduates
(Universe: Population 25 Years and Over)

Group	Number	%
Total Population	3,866	23.0
Hispanic or Latino (of any race)	248	8.1
Mexican	125	4.9

Population Age 3–17 Enrolled in Public School
(Universe: Population Age 3–17 Enrolled in School)

Group	Number	%
Total Population	5,073	87.2
Hispanic or Latino (of any race)	1,828	91.6
Mexican	1,622	93.9

Population Age 3–17 Enrolled in Private School
(Universe: Population Age 3–17 Enrolled in School)

Group	Number	%
Total Population	745	12.8
Hispanic or Latino (of any race)	167	8.4
Mexican	105	6.1

Foreign-Born Population

Group	Number	%
Total Population	1,802	6.4
Hispanic or Latino (of any race)	1,476	21.5
Mexican	1,366	23.0

Foreign-Born Naturalized U.S. Citizens

Group	Number	%
Total Population	522	29.0
Hispanic or Latino (of any race)	345	23.4
Mexican	304	22.3

Language Spoken at Home: English Only
(Universe: Population 5 Years and Over)

Group	Number	%
Total Population	21,201	82.1
Hispanic or Latino (of any race)	1,831	31.3
Mexican	1,520	30.5

Language Spoken at Home: Spanish
(Universe: Population 5 Years and Over)

Group	Number	%
Total Population	4,193	16.2
Hispanic or Latino (of any race)	4,016	68.7
Mexican	3,464	69.5

Unemployment Rate
(Universe: Population 16 Years and Over)

Group	%
Total Population	7.1
Hispanic or Latino (of any race)	5.3
Mexican	4.3

Class of Worker: Private Wage and Salary
(Universe: Civilian Employed Population 16 Years and Over)

Group	Number	%
Total Population	10,444	80.1
Hispanic or Latino (of any race)	2,405	88.5
Mexican	2,101	90.4

Class of Worker: Government
(Universe: Civilian Employed Population 16 Years and Over)

Group	Number	%
Total Population	1,751	13.4
Hispanic or Latino (of any race)	206	7.6
Mexican	117	5.0

Means of Transportation to Work: Car, Truck or Van
(Universe: Workers 16 Years and Over)

Group	Number	%
Total Population	11,925	93.2
Hispanic or Latino (of any race)	2,477	95.1
Mexican	2,176	95.0

Means of Transportation to Work: Public Transportation (ex. Taxicab)
(Universe: Workers 16 Years and Over)

Group	Number	%
Total Population	21	0.2
Hispanic or Latino (of any race)	0	0.0
Mexican	0	0.0

Homeownership Rate
(Universe: Occupied Housing Units)

Group	%
Total Population	58.4
Hispanic or Latino (of any race)	52.6
Central American, ex. Mexican	61.3
Mexican	53.9
Puerto Rican	35.7

Median Home Value

Group	Dollars
Total Population	128,100
Hispanic or Latino (of any race)	105,200
Mexican	105,900

Median Gross Rent

Group	Dollars
Total Population	862
Hispanic or Latino (of any race)	735
Mexican	731

Notes: (1) Percent of total population; (2) Percent of Hispanic/Latino population; Profiles include places with an overall population of at least 125,000, OR an overall population of at least 25,000 where the Hispanic/Latino population is at least 20% of the overall population. In states where less than five places meet either of these criteria, we have included places with at least 10,000 total population with the highest percentage of Hispanic/Latino population. These places are identified with an asterisk (*); Please refer to the User's Guide for a full explanation of data.

Median Household Income
(2010 Inflation-Adjusted Dollars)

Group	Dollars
Total Population	51,360
Hispanic or Latino (of any race)	31,583
Mexican	32,722

Per Capita Income
(2010 Inflation-Adjusted Dollars)

Group	Dollars
Total Population	21,794
Hispanic or Latino (of any race)	11,985
Mexican	11,250

Households with $100,000+ Income

Group	Number	%
Total Population	1,444	14.5
Hispanic or Latino (of any race)	93	5.1
Mexican	67	4.4

Households with Food Stamps/SNAP Benefits During Past 12 Months

Group	Number	%
Total Population	1,171	11.8
Hispanic or Latino (of any race)	383	21.0
Mexican	344	22.8

Poverty Rate
(Income in Past 12 Months Below Poverty Level)

Group	%
Total Population	16.1
Hispanic or Latino (of any race)	29.1
Mexican	28.4

Weslaco

Population

Group	Number	%TP[1]	%HP[2]
Total Population	35,670	100.0	–
Hispanic or Latino (of any race)	30,312	85.0	100.0
Mexican	27,801	77.9	91.7

Population Growth: 2000–2010

Group	%
Total Population	32.4
Hispanic or Latino (of any race)	34.4
Mexican	53.1

Males per 100 Females

Group	Number
Total Population	90.0
Hispanic or Latino (of any race)	89.8
Mexican	89.8

Average Household Size

Group	People
Total Population	3.12
Hispanic or Latino (of any race)	3.40
Mexican	3.41

Median Age

Group	Years
Total Population	32.5
Hispanic or Latino (of any race)	28.8
Mexican	28.9

High School Graduates
(Universe: Population 25 Years and Over)

Group	Number	%
Total Population	14,173	68.0
Hispanic or Latino (of any race)	9,101	59.5
Mexican	8,558	58.6

Four-Year College Graduates
(Universe: Population 25 Years and Over)

Group	Number	%
Total Population	3,593	17.2
Hispanic or Latino (of any race)	1,807	11.8
Mexican	1,663	11.4

Population Age 3–17 Enrolled in Public School
(Universe: Population Age 3–17 Enrolled in School)

Group	Number	%
Total Population	7,878	97.5
Hispanic or Latino (of any race)	7,210	98.7
Mexican	6,727	98.8

Population Age 3–17 Enrolled in Private School
(Universe: Population Age 3–17 Enrolled in School)

Group	Number	%
Total Population	198	2.5
Hispanic or Latino (of any race)	95	1.3
Mexican	84	1.2

Foreign-Born Population

Group	Number	%
Total Population	7,376	21.4
Hispanic or Latino (of any race)	6,360	22.9
Mexican	6,219	23.7

Foreign-Born Naturalized U.S. Citizens

Group	Number	%
Total Population	2,465	33.4
Hispanic or Latino (of any race)	2,167	34.1
Mexican	2,120	34.1

Language Spoken at Home: English Only
(Universe: Population 5 Years and Over)

Group	Number	%
Total Population	8,102	25.7
Hispanic or Latino (of any race)	2,658	10.7
Mexican	2,495	10.6

Language Spoken at Home: Spanish
(Universe: Population 5 Years and Over)

Group	Number	%
Total Population	22,742	72.0
Hispanic or Latino (of any race)	22,210	89.2
Mexican	21,052	89.3

Unemployment Rate
(Universe: Population 16 Years and Over)

Group	%
Total Population	9.7
Hispanic or Latino (of any race)	11.1
Mexican	10.7

Class of Worker: Private Wage and Salary
(Universe: Civilian Employed Population 16 Years and Over)

Group	Number	%
Total Population	8,812	71.5
Hispanic or Latino (of any race)	7,204	71.7
Mexican	6,906	71.8

Class of Worker: Government
(Universe: Civilian Employed Population 16 Years and Over)

Group	Number	%
Total Population	2,805	22.8
Hispanic or Latino (of any race)	2,214	22.0
Mexican	2,110	21.9

Means of Transportation to Work: Car, Truck or Van
(Universe: Workers 16 Years and Over)

Group	Number	%
Total Population	11,335	94.1
Hispanic or Latino (of any race)	9,321	94.8
Mexican	8,950	94.6

Means of Transportation to Work: Public Transportation (ex. Taxicab)
(Universe: Workers 16 Years and Over)

Group	Number	%
Total Population	0	0.0
Hispanic or Latino (of any race)	0	0.0
Mexican	0	0.0

Homeownership Rate
(Universe: Occupied Housing Units)

Group	%
Total Population	64.5
Hispanic or Latino (of any race)	62.1
Mexican	62.5

Median Home Value

Group	Dollars
Total Population	64,900
Hispanic or Latino (of any race)	67,900
Mexican	68,100

Median Gross Rent

Group	Dollars
Total Population	563
Hispanic or Latino (of any race)	547
Mexican	526

Median Household Income
(2010 Inflation-Adjusted Dollars)

Group	Dollars
Total Population	35,851
Hispanic or Latino (of any race)	28,700
Mexican	28,638

Per Capita Income
(2010 Inflation-Adjusted Dollars)

Group	Dollars
Total Population	15,547
Hispanic or Latino (of any race)	12,673
Mexican	12,638

Households with $100,000+ Income

Group	Number	%
Total Population	1,149	10.5
Hispanic or Latino (of any race)	709	9.0
Mexican	672	9.0

Households with Food Stamps/SNAP Benefits During Past 12 Months

Group	Number	%
Total Population	3,031	27.8
Hispanic or Latino (of any race)	2,944	37.5
Mexican	2,715	36.5

Poverty Rate
(Income in Past 12 Months Below Poverty Level)

Group	%
Total Population	29.2
Hispanic or Latino (of any race)	35.5
Mexican	35.2

Population

Group	Number	%TP[1]	%HP[2]
Total Population	308,745,538	100.0	–
Hispanic or Latino (of any race)	50,477,594	16.3	100.0
Central American, ex. Mexican	3,998,280	1.3	7.9
Costa Rican	126,418	<0.1	0.3
Guatemalan	1,044,209	0.3	2.1
Honduran	633,401	0.2	1.3
Nicaraguan	348,202	0.1	0.7
Panamanian	165,456	0.1	0.3
Salvadoran	1,648,968	0.5	3.3
Cuban	1,785,547	0.6	3.5
Dominican Republic	1,414,703	0.5	2.8
Mexican	31,798,258	10.3	63.0
Puerto Rican	4,623,716	1.5	9.2
South American	2,769,434	0.9	5.5
Argentinean	224,952	0.1	0.4
Bolivian	99,210	<0.1	0.2
Chilean	126,810	<0.1	0.3
Colombian	908,734	0.3	1.8
Ecuadorian	564,631	0.2	1.1
Paraguayan	20,023	<0.1	<0.1
Peruvian	531,358	0.2	1.1
Uruguayan	56,884	<0.1	0.1
Venezuelan	215,023	0.1	0.4
Spaniard	635,253	0.2	1.3

Population Growth: 2000–2010

Group	%
Total Population	9.7
Hispanic or Latino (of any race)	43.0
Central American, ex. Mexican	137.0
Costa Rican	84.3
Guatemalan	180.3
Honduran	191.1
Nicaraguan	96.0
Panamanian	80.4
Salvadoran	151.7
Cuban	43.8
Dominican Republic	84.9
Mexican	54.1
Puerto Rican	35.7
South American	104.6
Argentinean	123.0
Bolivian	135.8

Notes: (1) Percent of total population; (2) Percent of Hispanic/Latino population; Profiles include places with an overall population of at least 125,000, OR an overall population of at least 25,000 where the Hispanic/Latino population is at least 20% of the overall population. In states where less than five places meet either of these criteria, we have included places with at least 10,000 total population with the highest percentage of Hispanic/Latino population. These places are identified with an asterisk (*); Please refer to the User's Guide for a full explanation of data.

Group	Number
Chilean	84.2
Colombian	93.1
Ecuadorian	116.7
Paraguayan	128.3
Peruvian	127.1
Uruguayan	202.5
Venezuelan	135.0
Spaniard	534.4

Males per 100 Females

Group	Number
Total Population	96.7
Hispanic or Latino (of any race)	103.1
Central American, ex. Mexican	108.9
Costa Rican	93.4
Guatemalan	133.7
Honduran	110.9
Nicaraguan	89.4
Panamanian	71.5
Salvadoran	104.7
Cuban	98.8
Dominican Republic	85.3
Mexican	106.2
Puerto Rican	94.1
South American	90.1
Argentinean	99.3
Bolivian	92.6
Chilean	93.0
Colombian	80.5
Ecuadorian	104.8
Paraguayan	85.0
Peruvian	89.0
Uruguayan	101.4
Venezuelan	84.9
Spaniard	91.9

Average Household Size

Group	People
Total Population	2.58
Hispanic or Latino (of any race)	3.52
Central American, ex. Mexican	3.91
Costa Rican	3.02
Guatemalan	4.16
Honduran	3.82
Nicaraguan	3.51
Panamanian	2.69
Salvadoran	4.14
Cuban	2.79
Dominican Republic	3.40
Mexican	3.78
Puerto Rican	2.87
South American	3.10
Argentinean	2.72
Bolivian	3.36
Chilean	2.79
Colombian	2.95
Ecuadorian	3.64
Paraguayan	3.06
Peruvian	3.23
Uruguayan	2.91
Venezuelan	2.86
Spaniard	2.63

Median Age

Group	Years
Total Population	37.2
Hispanic or Latino (of any race)	27.3
Central American, ex. Mexican	30.2
Costa Rican	32.8
Guatemalan	28.5
Honduran	29.6
Nicaraguan	33.8
Panamanian	35.2
Salvadoran	30.6
Cuban	40.1
Dominican Republic	30.0
Mexican	25.5
Puerto Rican	28.0
South American	35.0
Argentinean	36.6
Bolivian	33.9
Chilean	36.6
Colombian	35.6
Ecuadorian	32.9
Paraguayan	30.2
Peruvian	36.4
Uruguayan	36.1
Venezuelan	33.4
Spaniard	35.2

High School Graduates

(Universe: Population 25 Years and Over)

Group	Number	%
Total Population	169,828,176	85.0
Hispanic or Latino (of any race)	15,729,225	61.5
Central American, ex. Mexican	1,229,291	53.1
Costa Rican	62,430	79.4
Guatemalan	261,380	45.5
Honduran	183,875	51.4
Nicaraguan	163,713	73.6
Panamanian	90,726	90.9
Salvadoran	441,975	46.8
Cuban	893,728	76.0
Dominican Republic	487,188	64.6
Mexican	8,617,825	55.5
Puerto Rican	1,792,697	73.4
South American	1,500,164	83.8
Argentinean	131,501	87.7
Bolivian	56,563	88.7
Chilean	73,302	89.2
Colombian	492,011	85.1
Ecuadorian	257,111	70.5
Paraguayan	9,345	81.3
Peruvian	304,661	89.1
Uruguayan	28,000	74.9
Venezuelan	122,521	93.4
Spaniard	311,644	87.7

Four-Year College Graduates

(Universe: Population 25 Years and Over)

Group	Number	%
Total Population	55,726,999	27.9
Hispanic or Latino (of any race)	3,329,326	13.0
Central American, ex. Mexican	259,600	11.2
Costa Rican	19,902	25.3
Guatemalan	49,972	8.7
Honduran	36,825	10.3
Nicaraguan	43,076	19.4
Panamanian	30,742	30.8
Salvadoran	73,221	7.8
Cuban	294,051	25.0
Dominican Republic	114,831	15.2
Mexican	1,421,023	9.1
Puerto Rican	387,923	15.9
South American	547,657	30.6
Argentinean	58,342	38.9
Bolivian	21,696	34.0
Chilean	29,501	35.9
Colombian	180,693	31.3
Ecuadorian	66,496	18.2
Paraguayan	3,321	28.9
Peruvian	104,165	30.5
Uruguayan	7,721	20.6
Venezuelan	65,185	49.7
Spaniard	107,497	30.3

Population Age 3–17 Enrolled in Public School

(Universe: Population Age 3–17 Enrolled in School)

Group	Number	%
Total Population	48,352,782	86.4
Hispanic or Latino (of any race)	10,886,462	93.0
Central American, ex. Mexican	700,787	92.6
Costa Rican	20,289	83.4
Guatemalan	172,787	90.5
Honduran	104,642	94.2
Nicaraguan	52,697	89.2
Panamanian	26,230	87.1
Salvadoran	312,416	95.3
Cuban	219,287	81.2
Dominican Republic	285,040	91.7
Mexican	7,641,087	94.9
Puerto Rican	993,926	90.0
South American	434,809	85.0
Argentinean	28,593	79.6
Bolivian	16,501	83.6
Chilean	18,439	82.0
Colombian	144,999	85.4
Ecuadorian	94,696	88.6
Paraguayan	3,400	77.4
Peruvian	80,130	85.0
Uruguayan	8,612	87.9
Venezuelan	32,485	82.0
Spaniard	86,626	83.5

Population Age 3–17 Enrolled in Private School

(Universe: Population Age 3–17 Enrolled in School)

Group	Number	%
Total Population	7,635,968	13.6
Hispanic or Latino (of any race)	814,030	7.0
Central American, ex. Mexican	55,721	7.4
Costa Rican	4,037	16.6
Guatemalan	18,054	9.5
Honduran	6,435	5.8
Nicaraguan	6,358	10.8
Panamanian	3,884	12.9
Salvadoran	15,573	4.7
Cuban	50,835	18.8
Dominican Republic	25,638	8.3
Mexican	413,757	5.1
Puerto Rican	110,897	10.0
South American	76,510	15.0
Argentinean	7,330	20.4
Bolivian	3,235	16.4
Chilean	4,048	18.0
Colombian	24,831	14.6
Ecuadorian	12,191	11.4
Paraguayan	992	22.6
Peruvian	14,152	15.0
Uruguayan	1,188	12.1
Venezuelan	7,143	18.0
Spaniard	17,167	16.5

Foreign-Born Population

Group	Number	%
Total Population	38,675,012	12.7
Hispanic or Latino (of any race)	18,203,058	38.1
Central American, ex. Mexican	2,581,953	65.6
Costa Rican	74,872	59.5
Guatemalan	704,059	69.3
Honduran	425,875	69.7
Nicaraguan	220,730	64.5
Panamanian	76,484	48.1
Salvadoran	1,040,817	64.5
Cuban	999,690	59.2
Dominican Republic	777,554	58.0
Mexican	11,484,169	37.4
Puerto Rican	50,753	1.1
South American	1,872,507	67.7
Argentinean	146,004	67.5
Bolivian	68,572	66.7
Chilean	78,755	63.2
Colombian	597,006	66.8
Ecuadorian	384,474	66.4
Paraguayan	13,369	68.5
Peruvian	365,695	70.0
Uruguayan	41,778	73.9
Venezuelan	150,031	71.9
Spaniard	80,388	14.6

Foreign-Born Naturalized U.S. Citizens

Group	Number	%
Total Population	16,653,874	43.1
Hispanic or Latino (of any race)	5,226,941	28.7
Central American, ex. Mexican	735,326	28.5
Costa Rican	29,747	39.7
Guatemalan	161,189	22.9
Honduran	87,415	20.5
Nicaraguan	101,087	45.8
Panamanian	47,616	62.3
Salvadoran	292,250	28.1
Cuban	574,825	57.5
Dominican Republic	364,573	46.9
Mexican	2,548,167	22.2
Puerto Rican	25,495	50.2
South American	776,192	41.5
Argentinean	60,178	41.2
Bolivian	27,677	40.4
Chilean	36,557	46.4
Colombian	276,096	46.2
Ecuadorian	147,890	38.5
Paraguayan	6,063	45.4
Peruvian	152,366	41.7
Uruguayan	11,688	28.0
Venezuelan	42,508	28.3
Spaniard	40,848	50.8

Notes: (1) Percent of total population; (2) Percent of Hispanic/Latino population; Profiles include places with an overall population of at least 125,000, OR an overall population of at least 25,000 where the Hispanic/Latino population is at least 20% of the overall population. In states where less than five places meet either of these criteria, we have included places with at least 10,000 total population with the highest percentage of Hispanic/Latino population. These places are identified with an asterisk (*); Please refer to the User's Guide for a full explanation of data.

STATE & PLACE PROFILES

Language Spoken at Home: English Only
(Universe: Population 5 Years and Over)

Group	Number	%
Total Population	226,738,479	79.9
Hispanic or Latino (of any race)	10,070,161	23.6
Central American, ex. Mexican	364,729	10.2
Costa Rican	26,114	22.6
Guatemalan	79,842	8.8
Honduran	46,543	8.5
Nicaraguan	38,709	12.1
Panamanian	53,775	36.4
Salvadoran	111,815	7.6
Cuban	274,415	17.2
Dominican Republic	100,224	8.1
Mexican	6,364,824	23.4
Puerto Rican	1,363,661	33.8
South American	330,673	12.9
Argentinean	32,840	16.3
Bolivian	12,798	13.6
Chilean	25,158	21.6
Colombian	103,982	12.5
Ecuadorian	50,198	9.5
Paraguayan	4,548	25.0
Peruvian	60,210	12.4
Uruguayan	5,142	9.9
Venezuelan	26,260	13.6
Spaniard	329,412	64.3

Language Spoken at Home: Spanish
(Universe: Population 5 Years and Over)

Group	Number	%
Total Population	35,470,765	12.5
Hispanic or Latino (of any race)	32,517,599	76.1
Central American, ex. Mexican	3,189,144	89.4
Costa Rican	89,133	77.0
Guatemalan	825,152	90.5
Honduran	502,536	91.3
Nicaraguan	280,317	87.6
Panamanian	93,044	62.9
Salvadoran	1,348,423	92.2
Cuban	1,309,854	82.3
Dominican Republic	1,126,270	91.5
Mexican	20,807,289	76.4
Puerto Rican	2,652,253	65.8
South American	2,216,454	86.4
Argentinean	164,105	81.7
Bolivian	80,512	85.4
Chilean	89,784	77.0
Colombian	727,528	87.2
Ecuadorian	477,869	90.1
Paraguayan	13,135	72.3
Peruvian	423,220	87.1
Uruguayan	45,802	88.4
Venezuelan	164,193	85.0
Spaniard	170,755	33.3

Unemployment Rate
(Universe: Population 16 Years and Over)

Group	%
Total Population	7.9
Hispanic or Latino (of any race)	9.6
Central American, ex. Mexican	9.1
Costa Rican	9.1
Guatemalan	8.7
Honduran	10.5
Nicaraguan	9.1
Panamanian	8.8
Salvadoran	8.8
Cuban	8.5
Dominican Republic	11.7
Mexican	9.5
Puerto Rican	12.5
South American	7.7
Argentinean	6.4
Bolivian	6.9
Chilean	6.6
Colombian	8.1
Ecuadorian	8.0
Paraguayan	8.1
Peruvian	7.6
Uruguayan	8.1
Venezuelan	7.9
Spaniard	9.2

Class of Worker: Private Wage and Salary
(Universe: Civilian Employed Population 16 Years and Over)

Group	Number	%
Total Population	111,303,933	78.5
Hispanic or Latino (of any race)	16,885,499	83.2
Central American, ex. Mexican	1,735,651	85.8
Costa Rican	50,429	81.1
Guatemalan	459,613	87.0
Honduran	268,965	86.2
Nicaraguan	148,230	83.2
Panamanian	57,807	74.6
Salvadoran	724,552	86.9
Cuban	629,005	80.7
Dominican Republic	488,117	84.4
Mexican	10,604,462	83.9
Puerto Rican	1,356,636	79.9
South American	1,195,277	82.5
Argentinean	92,107	79.3
Bolivian	45,728	82.1
Chilean	50,903	78.9
Colombian	381,844	82.6
Ecuadorian	255,883	85.2
Paraguayan	7,915	77.0
Peruvian	232,048	82.5
Uruguayan	23,505	80.0
Venezuelan	87,720	82.9
Spaniard	189,956	74.8

Class of Worker: Government
(Universe: Civilian Employed Population 16 Years and Over)

Group	Number	%
Total Population	21,024,265	14.8
Hispanic or Latino (of any race)	2,135,316	10.5
Central American, ex. Mexican	120,877	6.0
Costa Rican	6,463	10.4
Guatemalan	21,854	4.1
Honduran	13,908	4.5
Nicaraguan	14,861	8.3
Panamanian	16,015	20.7
Salvadoran	44,561	5.3
Cuban	94,604	12.1
Dominican Republic	55,159	9.5
Mexican	1,262,016	10.0
Puerto Rican	283,831	16.7
South American	131,556	9.1
Argentinean	12,024	10.3
Bolivian	4,998	9.0
Chilean	7,943	12.3
Colombian	44,077	9.5
Ecuadorian	22,643	7.5
Paraguayan	767	7.5
Peruvian	24,716	8.8
Uruguayan	2,129	7.2
Venezuelan	9,240	8.7
Spaniard	46,709	18.4

Means of Transportation to Work: Car, Truck or Van
(Universe: Workers 16 Years and Over)

Group	Number	%
Total Population	120,259,023	86.4
Hispanic or Latino (of any race)	16,597,731	83.4
Central American, ex. Mexican	1,549,435	78.0
Costa Rican	49,391	81.2
Guatemalan	384,713	74.1
Honduran	230,424	75.3
Nicaraguan	142,809	81.5
Panamanian	58,971	76.4
Salvadoran	658,199	80.6
Cuban	671,804	87.7
Dominican Republic	323,251	57.5
Mexican	10,758,657	86.9
Puerto Rican	1,279,483	76.3
South American	1,063,488	75.2
Argentinean	88,574	78.2
Bolivian	44,555	82.2
Chilean	50,425	79.8
Colombian	354,212	78.4
Ecuadorian	180,050	61.3
Paraguayan	6,983	69.7
Peruvian	213,120	77.7
Uruguayan	21,478	75.3
Venezuelan	86,535	83.5
Spaniard	211,423	84.6

Means of Transportation to Work: Public Transportation (ex. Taxicab)
(Universe: Workers 16 Years and Over)

Group	Number	%
Total Population	6,872,730	4.9
Hispanic or Latino (of any race)	1,589,344	8.0
Central American, ex. Mexican	248,277	12.5
Costa Rican	5,006	8.2
Guatemalan	73,231	14.1
Honduran	42,849	14.0
Nicaraguan	18,044	10.3
Panamanian	11,417	14.8
Salvadoran	93,589	11.5
Cuban	32,279	4.2
Dominican Republic	165,574	29.4
Mexican	625,271	5.1
Puerto Rican	243,076	14.5
South American	211,741	15.0
Argentinean	10,827	9.6
Bolivian	5,465	10.1
Chilean	6,026	9.5
Colombian	56,401	12.5
Ecuadorian	82,656	28.1
Paraguayan	1,841	18.4
Peruvian	35,642	13.0
Uruguayan	3,213	11.3
Venezuelan	7,299	7.0
Spaniard	13,801	5.5

Homeownership Rate
(Universe: Occupied Housing Units)

Group	%
Total Population	65.1
Hispanic or Latino (of any race)	47.3
Central American, ex. Mexican	39.7
Costa Rican	46.8
Guatemalan	31.9
Honduran	31.9
Nicaraguan	46.4
Panamanian	48.8
Salvadoran	43.9
Cuban	57.1
Dominican Republic	26.8
Mexican	49.8
Puerto Rican	37.9
South American	48.8
Argentinean	55.0
Bolivian	56.4
Chilean	52.7
Colombian	50.3
Ecuadorian	40.8
Paraguayan	42.7
Peruvian	47.8
Uruguayan	44.1
Venezuelan	52.4
Spaniard	63.7

Median Home Value

Group	Dollars
Total Population	188,400
Hispanic or Latino (of any race)	185,900
Central American, ex. Mexican	244,100
Costa Rican	267,200
Guatemalan	246,100
Honduran	194,200
Nicaraguan	247,100
Panamanian	236,300
Salvadoran	254,000
Cuban	268,500
Dominican Republic	282,200
Mexican	155,200
Puerto Rican	219,100
South American	290,800
Argentinean	323,800
Bolivian	357,200
Chilean	294,700
Colombian	260,900
Ecuadorian	336,100
Paraguayan	285,300
Peruvian	296,500
Uruguayan	271,300
Venezuelan	258,400
Spaniard	241,000

Notes: (1) Percent of total population; (2) Percent of Hispanic/Latino population; Profiles include places with an overall population of at least 125,000, OR an overall population of at least 25,000 where the Hispanic/Latino population is at least 20% of the overall population. In states where less than five places meet either of these criteria, we have included places with at least 10,000 total population with the highest percentage of Hispanic/Latino population. These places are identified with an asterisk (*); Please refer to the User's Guide for a full explanation of data.

Median Gross Rent	
Group	Dollars
Total Population	841
Hispanic or Latino (of any race)	877
Central American, ex. Mexican	944
Costa Rican	1,038
Guatemalan	941
Honduran	886
Nicaraguan	1,022
Panamanian	958
Salvadoran	947
Cuban	920
Dominican Republic	944
Mexican	842
Puerto Rican	864
South American	1,101
Argentinean	1,118
Bolivian	1,240
Chilean	1,120
Colombian	1,092
Ecuadorian	1,102
Paraguayan	1,169
Peruvian	1,081
Uruguayan	1,033
Venezuelan	1,132
Spaniard	959

Median Household Income (2010 Inflation-Adjusted Dollars)	
Group	Dollars
Total Population	51,914
Hispanic or Latino (of any race)	41,534
Central American, ex. Mexican	43,332
Costa Rican	50,197
Guatemalan	41,272
Honduran	37,901
Nicaraguan	49,335
Panamanian	49,834
Salvadoran	44,322
Cuban	43,857
Dominican Republic	34,925
Mexican	40,588
Puerto Rican	38,426
South American	51,747
Argentinean	56,918
Bolivian	61,501
Chilean	58,579
Colombian	50,731
Ecuadorian	49,755
Paraguayan	50,930
Peruvian	50,179
Uruguayan	46,991
Venezuelan	52,435
Spaniard	54,275

Per Capita Income (2010 Inflation-Adjusted Dollars)	
Group	Dollars
Total Population	27,334
Hispanic or Latino (of any race)	15,638
Central American, ex. Mexican	15,838
Costa Rican	20,657
Guatemalan	14,281
Honduran	14,264
Nicaraguan	19,311
Panamanian	23,572
Salvadoran	15,416
Cuban	24,144
Dominican Republic	14,986
Mexican	13,925
Puerto Rican	17,556
South American	22,420
Argentinean	31,616
Bolivian	23,689
Chilean	26,551
Colombian	21,619
Ecuadorian	18,651
Paraguayan	23,507
Peruvian	21,529
Uruguayan	22,297
Venezuelan	24,842
Spaniard	27,912

Households with $100,000+ Income		
Group	Number	%
Total Population	23,850,374	20.9
Hispanic or Latino (of any race)	1,605,309	12.5
Central American, ex. Mexican	126,726	12.0
Costa Rican	6,840	17.7
Guatemalan	26,906	10.5
Honduran	14,741	9.2
Nicaraguan	16,352	16.7
Panamanian	10,050	18.4
Salvadoran	48,507	11.4
Cuban	110,896	18.4
Dominican Republic	37,904	9.5
Mexican	838,495	10.9
Puerto Rican	184,689	13.1
South American	165,425	19.1
Argentinean	21,197	26.5
Bolivian	7,624	25.1
Chilean	9,788	23.5
Colombian	48,775	17.4
Ecuadorian	26,975	16.2
Paraguayan	1,028	18.5
Peruvian	28,095	17.7
Uruguayan	2,905	15.0
Venezuelan	14,836	21.6
Spaniard	48,174	22.1

Households with Food Stamps/SNAP Benefits During Past 12 Months		
Group	Number	%
Total Population	10,583,720	9.3
Hispanic or Latino (of any race)	2,019,816	15.7
Central American, ex. Mexican	111,818	10.6
Costa Rican	3,042	7.9
Guatemalan	27,422	10.7
Honduran	23,632	14.7
Nicaraguan	11,786	12.0
Panamanian	5,602	10.3
Salvadoran	38,438	9.0
Cuban	108,226	17.9
Dominican Republic	121,131	30.4
Mexican	1,155,415	15.1
Puerto Rican	344,445	24.4
South American	70,886	8.2
Argentinean	4,313	5.4
Bolivian	1,103	3.6
Chilean	2,164	5.2
Colombian	24,038	8.6
Ecuadorian	20,562	12.3
Paraguayan	307	5.5
Peruvian	11,947	7.5
Uruguayan	1,378	7.1
Venezuelan	4,390	6.4
Spaniard	18,301	8.4

Poverty Rate (Income in Past 12 Months Below Poverty Level)	
Group	%
Total Population	13.8
Hispanic or Latino (of any race)	22.4
Central American, ex. Mexican	19.8
Costa Rican	14.4
Guatemalan	23.4
Honduran	25.4
Nicaraguan	14.0
Panamanian	14.0
Salvadoran	17.8
Cuban	15.2
Dominican Republic	25.7
Mexican	24.0
Puerto Rican	25.1
South American	12.3
Argentinean	10.7
Bolivian	8.7
Chilean	9.0
Colombian	11.9
Ecuadorian	15.3
Paraguayan	12.3
Peruvian	12.1
Uruguayan	13.5
Venezuelan	12.6
Spaniard	12.2

Notes: (1) Percent of total population; (2) Percent of Hispanic/Latino population; Profiles include places with an overall population of at least 125,000, OR an overall population of at least 25,000 where the Hispanic/Latino population is at least 20% of the overall population. In states where less than five places meet either of these criteria, we have included places with at least 10,000 total population with the highest percentage of Hispanic/Latino population. These places are identified with an asterisk (*); Please refer to the User's Guide for a full explanation of data.

Utah

EDITOR'S NOTE: For a place to be included in this edition, it must meet one of two criteria. Either its overall population is at least 125,000, OR its overall population is at least 25,000 and its Hispanic/Latino population is at least 20% of the overall population. For the state of Utah, the following locations are included:

- Kearns
- Magna
- Midvale
- Ogden
- Salt Lake City
- West Valley City

Section Two: State & Place Profiles starts with the state profile, followed by place profiles that meet the criteria above. Places are listed alphabetically within each state. All states, all counties and places that meet the above criteria are ranked and compared in *Section Three: Rankings & Comparisons*, on page 1055.

For a more detailed look at the Hispanic/Latino population in Utah, a companion web site is available at no additional charge with purchase of this print edition. Visit http://gold.greyhouse.com/page/info_hispanic for more information.

The web site includes data for all counties and places in Utah with Hispanic/Latino population, plus ten additional topics: Self Employed Worker; Walked to Work; Worked from Home; Mean Travel Time to Work; Mean Household Income; Households with Cash Public Assistance; Mean Cash Pubic Assistance; Poverty Rates for 18 and Under, 18 to 64, and 65 and Over.

Population

Group	Number	%TP[1]	%HP[2]
Total Population	2,763,885	100.0	–
Hispanic or Latino (of any race)	358,340	13.0	100.0
Central American, ex. Mexican	20,442	0.7	5.7
Costa Rican	775	<0.1	0.2
Guatemalan	6,877	0.2	1.9
Honduran	2,087	0.1	0.6
Nicaraguan	1,043	<0.1	0.3
Panamanian	531	<0.1	0.1
Salvadoran	8,998	0.3	2.5
Cuban	1,963	0.1	0.5
Dominican Republic	1,252	<0.1	0.3
Mexican	258,905	9.4	72.3
Puerto Rican	7,182	0.3	2.0
South American	26,028	0.9	7.3
Argentinean	4,639	0.2	1.3
Bolivian	969	<0.1	0.3
Chilean	3,364	0.1	0.9
Colombian	3,467	0.1	1.0
Ecuadorian	2,026	0.1	0.6
Paraguayan	158	<0.1	<0.1
Peruvian	7,514	0.3	2.1
Uruguayan	1,011	<0.1	0.3
Venezuelan	2,698	0.1	0.8
Spaniard	8,184	0.3	2.3

Population Growth: 2000–2010

Group	%
Total Population	23.8
Hispanic or Latino (of any race)	77.8
Central American, ex. Mexican	207.6
Costa Rican	90.9
Guatemalan	221.8
Honduran	240.5
Nicaraguan	216.1
Panamanian	128.9
Salvadoran	237.0
Cuban	108.8
Dominican Republic	255.7
Mexican	89.8
Puerto Rican	80.6
South American	170.6
Argentinean	185.3
Bolivian	151.7
Chilean	123.7
Colombian	165.9
Ecuadorian	218.1
Peruvian	230.1
Uruguayan	287.4
Venezuelan	120.4
Spaniard	852.7

Males per 100 Females

Group	Number
Total Population	100.9
Hispanic or Latino (of any race)	106.8
Central American, ex. Mexican	102.1
Costa Rican	79.8
Guatemalan	112.3
Honduran	96.3
Nicaraguan	84.0
Panamanian	87.0
Salvadoran	101.9
Cuban	101.5
Dominican Republic	82.5
Mexican	109.4
Puerto Rican	97.1
South American	89.9
Argentinean	93.4
Bolivian	80.8
Chilean	89.6
Colombian	82.1
Ecuadorian	78.7
Paraguayan	75.6
Peruvian	99.0
Uruguayan	84.8
Venezuelan	84.7
Spaniard	94.4

Average Household Size

Group	People
Total Population	3.10
Hispanic or Latino (of any race)	3.90
Central American, ex. Mexican	4.04
Costa Rican	3.34
Guatemalan	4.21
Honduran	4.01
Nicaraguan	3.72
Panamanian	3.14
Salvadoran	4.10
Cuban	2.94
Dominican Republic	3.36
Mexican	4.11
Puerto Rican	3.09
South American	3.55
Argentinean	3.60
Bolivian	3.43
Chilean	3.41
Colombian	3.30
Ecuadorian	3.64
Paraguayan	3.35
Peruvian	3.71
Uruguayan	3.58
Venezuelan	3.51
Spaniard	3.00

Median Age

Group	Years
Total Population	29.2
Hispanic or Latino (of any race)	23.5
Central American, ex. Mexican	27.8
Costa Rican	26.0
Guatemalan	27.0
Honduran	27.4
Nicaraguan	27.5
Panamanian	28.7
Salvadoran	28.9
Cuban	27.0
Dominican Republic	24.3
Mexican	22.2
Puerto Rican	23.1
South American	29.4
Argentinean	29.6
Bolivian	28.9
Chilean	29.5
Colombian	28.4
Ecuadorian	27.1
Paraguayan	26.6
Peruvian	30.5
Uruguayan	33.0
Venezuelan	28.3
Spaniard	29.4

High School Graduates

(Universe: Population 25 Years and Over)

Group	Number	%
Total Population	1,361,877	90.6
Hispanic or Latino (of any race)	98,125	63.5
Central American, ex. Mexican	6,347	64.8
Guatemalan	2,223	62.7
Honduran	917	71.5
Salvadoran	2,400	60.4
Cuban	1,000	88.5
Dominican Republic	340	86.7
Mexican	64,577	57.3
Puerto Rican	2,580	89.5
South American	11,695	90.1
Argentinean	2,127	83.4
Chilean	1,738	91.9
Colombian	1,357	92.5
Ecuadorian	1,071	98.0
Peruvian	3,465	90.4
Venezuelan	1,252	97.2
Spaniard	2,887	82.0

Four-Year College Graduates

(Universe: Population 25 Years and Over)

Group	Number	%
Total Population	442,289	29.4
Hispanic or Latino (of any race)	17,375	11.2
Central American, ex. Mexican	1,402	14.3
Guatemalan	583	16.5
Honduran	257	20.0
Salvadoran	360	9.1
Cuban	443	39.2
Dominican Republic	115	29.3
Mexican	9,355	8.3
Puerto Rican	672	23.3
South American	3,454	26.6
Argentinean	500	19.6
Chilean	589	31.1
Colombian	475	32.4
Ecuadorian	249	22.8
Peruvian	930	24.3
Venezuelan	398	30.9
Spaniard	636	18.1

Population Age 3–17 Enrolled in Public School

(Universe: Population Age 3–17 Enrolled in School)

Group	Number	%
Total Population	542,234	90.7
Hispanic or Latino (of any race)	83,912	94.4
Central American, ex. Mexican	3,519	90.6
Guatemalan	1,109	90.2
Honduran	522	89.2
Salvadoran	1,708	91.6
Cuban	404	97.1
Dominican Republic	301	91.5
Mexican	65,867	95.0
Puerto Rican	1,895	93.0
South American	5,423	92.7
Argentinean	1,563	95.8
Chilean	512	94.6
Colombian	486	87.9
Ecuadorian	634	95.2
Peruvian	1,310	87.9
Venezuelan	587	95.1
Spaniard	1,509	87.8

Notes: (1) Percent of total population; (2) Percent of Hispanic/Latino population; Profiles include places with an overall population of at least 125,000, OR an overall population of at least 25,000 where the Hispanic/Latino population is at least 20% of the overall population. In states where less than five places meet either of these criteria, we have included places with at least 10,000 total population with the highest percentage of Hispanic/Latino population. These places are identified with an asterisk (*); Please refer to the User's Guide for a full explanation of data.

Population Age 3–17 Enrolled in Private School
(Universe: Population Age 3–17 Enrolled in School)

Group	Number	%
Total Population	55,524	9.3
Hispanic or Latino (of any race)	4,961	5.6
Central American, ex. Mexican	363	9.4
Guatemalan	120	9.8
Honduran	63	10.8
Salvadoran	156	8.4
Cuban	12	2.9
Dominican Republic	28	8.5
Mexican	3,448	5.0
Puerto Rican	143	7.0
South American	428	7.3
Argentinean	69	4.2
Chilean	29	5.4
Colombian	67	12.1
Ecuadorian	32	4.8
Peruvian	180	12.1
Venezuelan	30	4.9
Spaniard	209	12.2

Foreign-Born Population

Group	Number	%
Total Population	218,283	8.2
Hispanic or Latino (of any race)	130,278	39.9
Central American, ex. Mexican	10,831	59.0
Guatemalan	4,097	62.2
Honduran	1,334	59.6
Salvadoran	4,477	56.2
Cuban	609	31.0
Dominican Republic	713	54.3
Mexican	98,988	40.1
Puerto Rican	56	0.9
South American	16,041	65.6
Argentinean	3,327	64.2
Chilean	2,264	64.9
Colombian	1,657	58.0
Ecuadorian	1,359	59.8
Peruvian	4,856	70.6
Venezuelan	1,697	74.2
Spaniard	212	3.3

Foreign-Born Naturalized U.S. Citizens

Group	Number	%
Total Population	71,025	32.5
Hispanic or Latino (of any race)	27,754	21.3
Central American, ex. Mexican	4,121	38.0
Guatemalan	1,462	35.7
Honduran	455	34.1
Salvadoran	1,772	39.6
Cuban	300	49.3
Dominican Republic	265	37.2
Mexican	17,264	17.4
Puerto Rican	41	73.2
South American	4,838	30.2
Argentinean	990	29.8
Chilean	486	21.5
Colombian	727	43.9
Ecuadorian	527	38.8
Peruvian	1,404	28.9
Venezuelan	374	22.0
Spaniard	113	53.3

Language Spoken at Home: English Only
(Universe: Population 5 Years and Over)

Group	Number	%
Total Population	2,061,526	85.8
Hispanic or Latino (of any race)	93,446	32.9
Central American, ex. Mexican	2,556	15.9
Guatemalan	742	13.1
Honduran	157	7.8
Salvadoran	1,198	17.2
Cuban	985	55.7
Dominican Republic	186	16.6
Mexican	66,385	31.1
Puerto Rican	3,118	57.2
South American	3,260	15.1
Argentinean	566	12.4
Chilean	512	17.2
Colombian	381	16.1
Ecuadorian	323	15.7
Peruvian	961	15.4
Venezuelan	220	10.6
Spaniard	4,460	77.7

Language Spoken at Home: Spanish
(Universe: Population 5 Years and Over)

Group	Number	%
Total Population	225,418	9.4
Hispanic or Latino (of any race)	189,589	66.7
Central American, ex. Mexican	13,520	83.9
Guatemalan	4,892	86.5
Honduran	1,860	92.2
Salvadoran	5,744	82.6
Cuban	782	44.3
Dominican Republic	935	83.4
Mexican	146,146	68.6
Puerto Rican	2,327	42.7
South American	18,266	84.4
Argentinean	4,013	87.6
Chilean	2,461	82.4
Colombian	1,938	81.9
Ecuadorian	1,735	84.3
Peruvian	5,252	84.1
Venezuelan	1,855	89.4
Spaniard	1,154	20.1

Unemployment Rate
(Universe: Population 16 Years and Over)

Group	%
Total Population	5.9
Hispanic or Latino (of any race)	8.7
Central American, ex. Mexican	5.2
Guatemalan	2.2
Honduran	5.8
Salvadoran	5.0
Cuban	7.7
Dominican Republic	9.6
Mexican	9.0
Puerto Rican	7.3
South American	9.5
Argentinean	15.0
Chilean	2.0
Colombian	9.6
Ecuadorian	7.2
Peruvian	9.3
Venezuelan	1.2
Spaniard	8.6

Class of Worker: Private Wage and Salary
(Universe: Civilian Employed Population 16 Years and Over)

Group	Number	%
Total Population	972,073	78.6
Hispanic or Latino (of any race)	123,203	88.0
Central American, ex. Mexican	7,957	86.5
Guatemalan	2,976	87.4
Honduran	911	88.5
Salvadoran	3,491	86.6
Cuban	754	73.5
Dominican Republic	245	45.9
Mexican	92,719	89.7
Puerto Rican	1,858	73.4
South American	10,006	87.5
Argentinean	2,077	95.4
Chilean	1,357	81.1
Colombian	1,198	87.5
Ecuadorian	863	80.8
Peruvian	3,058	89.6
Venezuelan	937	87.4
Spaniard	2,244	83.9

Class of Worker: Government
(Universe: Civilian Employed Population 16 Years and Over)

Group	Number	%
Total Population	197,303	16.0
Hispanic or Latino (of any race)	11,192	8.0
Central American, ex. Mexican	499	5.4
Guatemalan	57	1.7
Honduran	50	4.9
Salvadoran	243	6.0
Cuban	229	22.3
Dominican Republic	218	40.8
Mexican	7,055	6.8
Puerto Rican	535	21.1
South American	789	6.9
Argentinean	71	3.3
Chilean	213	12.7
Colombian	107	7.8
Ecuadorian	39	3.7
Peruvian	164	4.8

Venezuelan	123	11.5
Spaniard	365	13.6

Means of Transportation to Work: Car, Truck or Van
(Universe: Workers 16 Years and Over)

Group	Number	%
Total Population	1,071,965	88.1
Hispanic or Latino (of any race)	123,868	89.9
Central American, ex. Mexican	7,985	88.0
Guatemalan	2,818	85.1
Honduran	950	92.3
Salvadoran	3,636	91.7
Cuban	843	82.1
Dominican Republic	363	69.8
Mexican	91,822	90.2
Puerto Rican	2,244	91.1
South American	9,785	87.5
Argentinean	2,027	93.7
Chilean	1,336	83.0
Colombian	1,126	86.0
Ecuadorian	864	82.9
Peruvian	2,884	85.5
Venezuelan	957	92.6
Spaniard	2,508	93.3

Means of Transportation to Work: Public Transportation (ex. Taxicab)
(Universe: Workers 16 Years and Over)

Group	Number	%
Total Population	29,218	2.4
Hispanic or Latino (of any race)	4,396	3.2
Central American, ex. Mexican	293	3.2
Guatemalan	63	1.9
Honduran	0	0.0
Salvadoran	153	3.9
Cuban	25	2.4
Dominican Republic	0	0.0
Mexican	3,496	3.4
Puerto Rican	51	2.1
South American	358	3.2
Argentinean	55	2.5
Chilean	53	3.3
Colombian	46	3.5
Ecuadorian	12	1.2
Peruvian	159	4.7
Venezuelan	23	2.2
Spaniard	9	0.3

Homeownership Rate
(Universe: Occupied Housing Units)

Group	%
Total Population	70.4
Hispanic or Latino (of any race)	50.5
Central American, ex. Mexican	52.5
Costa Rican	47.2
Guatemalan	50.9
Honduran	46.2
Nicaraguan	48.8
Panamanian	61.1
Salvadoran	55.7
Cuban	51.4
Dominican Republic	39.4
Mexican	49.3
Puerto Rican	48.6
South American	54.2
Argentinean	55.7
Bolivian	62.9
Chilean	52.7
Colombian	56.4
Ecuadorian	51.2
Paraguayan	47.1
Peruvian	54.3
Uruguayan	53.4
Venezuelan	50.1
Spaniard	65.4

Median Home Value

Group	Dollars
Total Population	218,100
Hispanic or Latino (of any race)	175,300
Central American, ex. Mexican	205,600
Guatemalan	209,700
Honduran	232,100
Salvadoran	196,600

Notes: (1) Percent of total population; (2) Percent of Hispanic/Latino population; Profiles include places with an overall population of at least 125,000, OR an overall population of at least 25,000 where the Hispanic/Latino population is at least 20% of the overall population. In states where less than five places meet either of these criteria, we have included places with at least 10,000 total population with the highest percentage of Hispanic/Latino population. These places are identified with an asterisk (*); Please refer to the User's Guide for a full explanation of data.

Cuban	265,900
Dominican Republic	202,600
Mexican	169,200
Puerto Rican	210,900
South American	198,200
Argentinean	170,800
Chilean	199,500
Colombian	203,000
Ecuadorian	213,700
Peruvian	203,500
Venezuelan	196,000
Spaniard	182,700

Median Gross Rent

Group	Dollars
Total Population	781
Hispanic or Latino (of any race)	767
Central American, ex. Mexican	780
Guatemalan	781
Honduran	549
Salvadoran	787
Cuban	705
Dominican Republic	759
Mexican	764
Puerto Rican	773
South American	812
Argentinean	813
Chilean	760
Colombian	831
Ecuadorian	861
Peruvian	788
Venezuelan	799
Spaniard	748

Median Household Income
(2010 Inflation-Adjusted Dollars)

Group	Dollars
Total Population	56,330
Hispanic or Latino (of any race)	41,195
Central American, ex. Mexican	40,319
Guatemalan	39,896
Honduran	30,985
Salvadoran	45,980
Cuban	35,575
Dominican Republic	19,516
Mexican	40,181
Puerto Rican	48,750
South American	43,436
Argentinean	42,875
Chilean	56,068
Colombian	36,994
Ecuadorian	39,028
Peruvian	46,865
Venezuelan	36,440
Spaniard	50,625

Per Capita Income
(2010 Inflation-Adjusted Dollars)

Group	Dollars
Total Population	23,139
Hispanic or Latino (of any race)	13,218
Central American, ex. Mexican	14,579
Guatemalan	15,677
Honduran	12,124
Salvadoran	13,558
Cuban	20,432
Dominican Republic	7,075
Mexican	12,168
Puerto Rican	14,140
South American	15,377
Argentinean	12,713
Chilean	19,214
Colombian	14,706
Ecuadorian	13,416
Peruvian	15,972
Venezuelan	14,811
Spaniard	24,056

Households with $100,000+ Income

Group	Number	%
Total Population	171,548	20.0
Hispanic or Latino (of any race)	7,368	9.0
Central American, ex. Mexican	317	6.3
Guatemalan	94	5.1
Honduran	10	2.0
Salvadoran	122	5.7
Cuban	146	17.4
Dominican Republic	0	0.0
Mexican	4,914	8.4
Puerto Rican	98	6.1
South American	672	10.6
Argentinean	86	7.0
Chilean	228	23.1
Colombian	24	2.9
Ecuadorian	31	4.9
Peruvian	165	9.6
Venezuelan	49	8.8
Spaniard	333	15.4

Households with Food Stamps/SNAP Benefits During Past 12 Months

Group	Number	%
Total Population	54,897	6.4
Hispanic or Latino (of any race)	9,697	11.9
Central American, ex. Mexican	583	11.6
Guatemalan	353	19.1
Honduran	56	11.3
Salvadoran	78	3.6
Cuban	123	14.7
Dominican Republic	102	43.6
Mexican	7,063	12.0
Puerto Rican	201	12.5
South American	585	9.2
Argentinean	156	12.8
Chilean	99	10.0
Colombian	145	17.5
Ecuadorian	78	12.2
Peruvian	107	6.2
Venezuelan	0	0.0
Spaniard	203	9.4

Poverty Rate
(Income in Past 12 Months Below Poverty Level)

Group	%
Total Population	10.8
Hispanic or Latino (of any race)	21.4
Central American, ex. Mexican	17.0
Guatemalan	21.0
Honduran	22.2
Salvadoran	11.5
Cuban	29.5
Dominican Republic	34.1
Mexican	23.3
Puerto Rican	10.6
South American	16.3
Argentinean	23.9
Chilean	14.8
Colombian	16.5
Ecuadorian	25.5
Peruvian	11.8
Venezuelan	5.6
Spaniard	9.0

Kearns

Population

Group	Number	%TP[1]	%HP[2]
Total Population	35,731	100.0	–
Hispanic or Latino (of any race)	11,729	32.8	100.0
Central American, ex. Mexican	673	1.9	5.7
Guatemalan	176	0.5	1.5
Salvadoran	396	1.1	3.4
Mexican	9,207	25.8	78.5
Puerto Rican	172	0.5	1.5
South American	527	1.5	4.5
Peruvian	204	0.6	1.7
Spaniard	159	0.4	1.4

Population Growth: 2000–2010

Group	%
Total Population	6.2
Hispanic or Latino (of any race)	77.6
Central American, ex. Mexican	143.8
Salvadoran	209.4
Mexican	102.1
South American	160.9

Males per 100 Females

Group	Number
Total Population	102.3
Hispanic or Latino (of any race)	108.8
Central American, ex. Mexican	107.7
Guatemalan	122.8
Salvadoran	103.1
Mexican	110.6
Puerto Rican	126.3
South American	100.4
Peruvian	108.2
Spaniard	106.5

Average Household Size

Group	People
Total Population	3.65
Hispanic or Latino (of any race)	4.77
Central American, ex. Mexican	4.90
Guatemalan	5.08
Salvadoran	4.80
Mexican	4.94
Puerto Rican	3.67
South American	4.48
Peruvian	4.64
Spaniard	3.29

Median Age

Group	Years
Total Population	28.4
Hispanic or Latino (of any race)	23.5
Central American, ex. Mexican	30.3
Guatemalan	30.7
Salvadoran	31.2
Mexican	22.3
Puerto Rican	24.0
South American	31.1
Peruvian	32.3
Spaniard	30.2

High School Graduates
(Universe: Population 25 Years and Over)

Group	Number	%
Total Population	15,765	81.8
Hispanic or Latino (of any race)	3,071	63.1
Mexican	2,420	59.0

Four-Year College Graduates
(Universe: Population 25 Years and Over)

Group	Number	%
Total Population	2,077	10.8
Hispanic or Latino (of any race)	337	6.9
Mexican	248	6.0

Population Age 3–17 Enrolled in Public School
(Universe: Population Age 3–17 Enrolled in School)

Group	Number	%
Total Population	8,478	96.5
Hispanic or Latino (of any race)	2,893	98.6
Mexican	2,622	98.7

Population Age 3–17 Enrolled in Private School
(Universe: Population Age 3–17 Enrolled in School)

Group	Number	%
Total Population	306	3.5
Hispanic or Latino (of any race)	42	1.4
Mexican	34	1.3

Foreign-Born Population

Group	Number	%
Total Population	5,982	17.2
Hispanic or Latino (of any race)	4,682	44.9
Mexican	4,161	45.5

Foreign-Born Naturalized U.S. Citizens

Group	Number	%
Total Population	1,709	28.6
Hispanic or Latino (of any race)	988	21.1
Mexican	807	19.4

Language Spoken at Home: English Only
(Universe: Population 5 Years and Over)

Group	Number	%
Total Population	22,622	72.5
Hispanic or Latino (of any race)	2,215	24.6
Mexican	1,834	23.3

Notes: (1) Percent of total population; (2) Percent of Hispanic/Latino population; Profiles include places with an overall population of at least 125,000, OR an overall population of at least 25,000 where the Hispanic/Latino population is at least 20% of the overall population. In states where less than five places meet either of these criteria, we have included places with at least 10,000 total population with the highest percentage of Hispanic/Latino population. These places are identified with an asterisk (*); Please refer to the User's Guide for a full explanation of data.

Language Spoken at Home: Spanish
(Universe: Population 5 Years and Over)

Group	Number	%
Total Population	7,020	22.5
Hispanic or Latino (of any race)	6,775	75.2
Mexican	6,026	76.4

Unemployment Rate
(Universe: Population 16 Years and Over)

Group	%
Total Population	6.9
Hispanic or Latino (of any race)	8.8
Mexican	9.1

Class of Worker: Private Wage and Salary
(Universe: Civilian Employed Population 16 Years and Over)

Group	Number	%
Total Population	14,900	87.4
Hispanic or Latino (of any race)	4,409	93.5
Mexican	3,942	95.1

Class of Worker: Government
(Universe: Civilian Employed Population 16 Years and Over)

Group	Number	%
Total Population	1,727	10.1
Hispanic or Latino (of any race)	207	4.4
Mexican	143	3.4

Means of Transportation to Work: Car, Truck or Van
(Universe: Workers 16 Years and Over)

Group	Number	%
Total Population	15,785	94.4
Hispanic or Latino (of any race)	4,421	94.7
Mexican	3,896	94.9

Means of Transportation to Work: Public Transportation (ex. Taxicab)
(Universe: Workers 16 Years and Over)

Group	Number	%
Total Population	390	2.3
Hispanic or Latino (of any race)	120	2.6
Mexican	120	2.9

Homeownership Rate
(Universe: Occupied Housing Units)

Group	%
Total Population	81.8
Hispanic or Latino (of any race)	74.8
Central American, ex. Mexican	83.4
Guatemalan	84.2
Salvadoran	82.4
Mexican	73.8
Puerto Rican	63.6
South American	82.4
Peruvian	78.6
Spaniard	80.4

Median Home Value

Group	Dollars
Total Population	160,700
Hispanic or Latino (of any race)	160,000
Mexican	158,400

Median Gross Rent

Group	Dollars
Total Population	1,043
Hispanic or Latino (of any race)	917
Mexican	928

Median Household Income
(2010 Inflation-Adjusted Dollars)

Group	Dollars
Total Population	52,790
Hispanic or Latino (of any race)	46,630
Mexican	46,590

Per Capita Income
(2010 Inflation-Adjusted Dollars)

Group	Dollars
Total Population	17,483
Hispanic or Latino (of any race)	12,397
Mexican	12,056

Households with $100,000+ Income

Group	Number	%
Total Population	1,112	11.3
Hispanic or Latino (of any race)	239	10.5
Mexican	224	11.5

Households with Food Stamps/SNAP Benefits During Past 12 Months

Group	Number	%
Total Population	652	6.6
Hispanic or Latino (of any race)	181	8.0
Mexican	156	8.0

Poverty Rate
(Income in Past 12 Months Below Poverty Level)

Group	%
Total Population	10.1
Hispanic or Latino (of any race)	13.0
Mexican	13.8

Magna

Population

Group	Number	%TP[1]	%HP[2]
Total Population	26,505	100.0	–
Hispanic or Latino (of any race)	6,188	23.3	100.0
Central American, ex. Mexican	279	1.1	4.5
Salvadoran	126	0.5	2.0
Mexican	4,662	17.6	75.3
South American	287	1.1	4.6
Peruvian	101	0.4	1.6
Spaniard	170	0.6	2.7

Population Growth: 2000–2010

Group	%
Total Population	16.4
Hispanic or Latino (of any race)	81.1
Mexican	111.1
South American	76.1

Males per 100 Females

Group	Number
Total Population	102.1
Hispanic or Latino (of any race)	109.3
Central American, ex. Mexican	116.3
Salvadoran	110.0
Mexican	111.0
South American	96.6
Peruvian	98.0
Spaniard	100.0

Average Household Size

Group	People
Total Population	3.43
Hispanic or Latino (of any race)	4.31
Central American, ex. Mexican	4.46
Salvadoran	4.48
Mexican	4.46
South American	4.26
Peruvian	4.57
Spaniard	3.55

Median Age

Group	Years
Total Population	28.4
Hispanic or Latino (of any race)	23.0
Central American, ex. Mexican	30.7
Salvadoran	31.8
Mexican	21.8
South American	32.3
Peruvian	35.2
Spaniard	28.6

High School Graduates
(Universe: Population 25 Years and Over)

Group	Number	%
Total Population	11,961	83.9
Hispanic or Latino (of any race)	1,459	57.0
Mexican	897	49.6

Four-Year College Graduates
(Universe: Population 25 Years and Over)

Group	Number	%
Total Population	1,734	12.2
Hispanic or Latino (of any race)	133	5.2
Mexican	52	2.9

Population Age 3–17 Enrolled in Public School
(Universe: Population Age 3–17 Enrolled in School)

Group	Number	%
Total Population	6,079	92.7
Hispanic or Latino (of any race)	1,577	94.7
Mexican	1,101	93.5

Population Age 3–17 Enrolled in Private School
(Universe: Population Age 3–17 Enrolled in School)

Group	Number	%
Total Population	479	7.3
Hispanic or Latino (of any race)	89	5.3
Mexican	76	6.5

Foreign-Born Population

Group	Number	%
Total Population	2,699	10.0
Hispanic or Latino (of any race)	2,139	35.8
Mexican	1,695	38.1

Foreign-Born Naturalized U.S. Citizens

Group	Number	%
Total Population	630	23.3
Hispanic or Latino (of any race)	419	19.6
Mexican	359	21.2

Language Spoken at Home: English Only
(Universe: Population 5 Years and Over)

Group	Number	%
Total Population	18,529	77.4
Hispanic or Latino (of any race)	881	17.6
Mexican	530	14.4

Language Spoken at Home: Spanish
(Universe: Population 5 Years and Over)

Group	Number	%
Total Population	4,459	18.6
Hispanic or Latino (of any race)	4,084	81.5
Mexican	3,119	84.6

Unemployment Rate
(Universe: Population 16 Years and Over)

Group	%
Total Population	8.1
Hispanic or Latino (of any race)	10.1
Mexican	9.8

Class of Worker: Private Wage and Salary
(Universe: Civilian Employed Population 16 Years and Over)

Group	Number	%
Total Population	10,836	85.2
Hispanic or Latino (of any race)	2,198	93.8
Mexican	1,636	93.5

Class of Worker: Government
(Universe: Civilian Employed Population 16 Years and Over)

Group	Number	%
Total Population	1,531	12.0
Hispanic or Latino (of any race)	130	5.5
Mexican	98	5.6

Means of Transportation to Work: Car, Truck or Van
(Universe: Workers 16 Years and Over)

Group	Number	%
Total Population	11,737	93.9
Hispanic or Latino (of any race)	2,230	96.4
Mexican	1,690	96.6

Means of Transportation to Work: Public Transportation (ex. Taxicab)
(Universe: Workers 16 Years and Over)

Group	Number	%
Total Population	289	2.3
Hispanic or Latino (of any race)	20	0.9
Mexican	20	1.1

Homeownership Rate
(Universe: Occupied Housing Units)

Group	%
Total Population	78.3
Hispanic or Latino (of any race)	71.5
Central American, ex. Mexican	77.1

STATE & PLACE PROFILES

Notes: (1) Percent of total population; (2) Percent of Hispanic/Latino population; Profiles include places with an overall population of at least 125,000, OR an overall population of at least 25,000 where the Hispanic/Latino population is at least 20% of the overall population. In states where less than five places meet either of these criteria, we have included places with at least 10,000 total population with the highest percentage of Hispanic/Latino population. These places are identified with an asterisk (*); Please refer to the User's Guide for a full explanation of data.

Salvadoran	89.7
Mexican	70.1
South American	82.4
Peruvian	91.3
Spaniard	81.8

Median Home Value

Group	Dollars
Total Population	157,100
Hispanic or Latino (of any race)	156,300
Mexican	155,300

Median Gross Rent

Group	Dollars
Total Population	900
Hispanic or Latino (of any race)	804
Mexican	796

Median Household Income
(2010 Inflation-Adjusted Dollars)

Group	Dollars
Total Population	53,007
Hispanic or Latino (of any race)	40,227
Mexican	35,948

Per Capita Income
(2010 Inflation-Adjusted Dollars)

Group	Dollars
Total Population	17,574
Hispanic or Latino (of any race)	10,903
Mexican	10,861

Households with $100,000+ Income

Group	Number	%
Total Population	1,064	13.9
Hispanic or Latino (of any race)	111	8.1
Mexican	60	6.1

Households with Food Stamps/SNAP Benefits During Past 12 Months

Group	Number	%
Total Population	784	10.2
Hispanic or Latino (of any race)	171	12.4
Mexican	97	9.8

Poverty Rate
(Income in Past 12 Months Below Poverty Level)

Group	%
Total Population	11.6
Hispanic or Latino (of any race)	23.9
Mexican	23.1

Midvale

Population

Group	Number	%TP[1]	%HP[2]
Total Population	27,964	100.0	–
Hispanic or Latino (of any race)	6,795	24.3	100.0
Central American, ex. Mexican	217	0.8	3.2
Mexican	5,342	19.1	78.6
Puerto Rican	132	0.5	1.9
South American	311	1.1	4.6
Peruvian	124	0.4	1.8
Spaniard	140	0.5	2.1

Population Growth: 2000–2010

Group	%
Total Population	3.5
Hispanic or Latino (of any race)	21.1
Mexican	21.4
Puerto Rican	-1.5
South American	132.1

Males per 100 Females

Group	Number
Total Population	97.8
Hispanic or Latino (of any race)	115.2
Central American, ex. Mexican	146.6
Mexican	118.3
Puerto Rican	100.0
South American	96.8
Peruvian	87.9
Spaniard	81.8

Average Household Size

Group	People
Total Population	2.55
Hispanic or Latino (of any race)	3.66
Central American, ex. Mexican	3.10
Mexican	3.95
Puerto Rican	2.52
South American	2.89
Peruvian	3.43
Spaniard	2.42

Median Age

Group	Years
Total Population	30.6
Hispanic or Latino (of any race)	25.3
Central American, ex. Mexican	29.7
Mexican	24.1
Puerto Rican	29.0
South American	33.9
Peruvian	35.0
Spaniard	35.5

High School Graduates
(Universe: Population 25 Years and Over)

Group	Number	%
Total Population	14,019	80.9
Hispanic or Latino (of any race)	1,905	52.5
Mexican	1,388	46.4

Four-Year College Graduates
(Universe: Population 25 Years and Over)

Group	Number	%
Total Population	3,643	21.0
Hispanic or Latino (of any race)	257	7.1
Mexican	160	5.4

Population Age 3–17 Enrolled in Public School
(Universe: Population Age 3–17 Enrolled in School)

Group	Number	%
Total Population	3,988	93.9
Hispanic or Latino (of any race)	1,374	96.4
Mexican	1,235	97.6

Population Age 3–17 Enrolled in Private School
(Universe: Population Age 3–17 Enrolled in School)

Group	Number	%
Total Population	259	6.1
Hispanic or Latino (of any race)	51	3.6
Mexican	31	2.4

Foreign-Born Population

Group	Number	%
Total Population	4,184	15.2
Hispanic or Latino (of any race)	3,359	47.3
Mexican	3,014	49.7

Foreign-Born Naturalized U.S. Citizens

Group	Number	%
Total Population	1,092	26.1
Hispanic or Latino (of any race)	431	12.8
Mexican	353	11.7

Language Spoken at Home: English Only
(Universe: Population 5 Years and Over)

Group	Number	%
Total Population	18,851	75.3
Hispanic or Latino (of any race)	1,350	22.0
Mexican	1,058	20.1

Language Spoken at Home: Spanish
(Universe: Population 5 Years and Over)

Group	Number	%
Total Population	5,025	20.1
Hispanic or Latino (of any race)	4,799	78.0
Mexican	4,200	79.9

Unemployment Rate
(Universe: Population 16 Years and Over)

Group	%
Total Population	7.6
Hispanic or Latino (of any race)	9.7
Mexican	8.2

Class of Worker: Private Wage and Salary
(Universe: Civilian Employed Population 16 Years and Over)

Group	Number	%
Total Population	12,415	86.4
Hispanic or Latino (of any race)	3,362	93.4
Mexican	2,945	94.5

Class of Worker: Government
(Universe: Civilian Employed Population 16 Years and Over)

Group	Number	%
Total Population	1,408	9.8
Hispanic or Latino (of any race)	122	3.4
Mexican	55	1.8

Means of Transportation to Work: Car, Truck or Van
(Universe: Workers 16 Years and Over)

Group	Number	%
Total Population	12,343	87.5
Hispanic or Latino (of any race)	2,983	84.6
Mexican	2,548	83.5

Means of Transportation to Work: Public Transportation (ex. Taxicab)
(Universe: Workers 16 Years and Over)

Group	Number	%
Total Population	826	5.9
Hispanic or Latino (of any race)	384	10.9
Mexican	344	11.3

Homeownership Rate
(Universe: Occupied Housing Units)

Group	%
Total Population	48.4
Hispanic or Latino (of any race)	28.8
Central American, ex. Mexican	23.2
Mexican	26.8
Puerto Rican	35.2
South American	29.5
Peruvian	32.4
Spaniard	59.3

Median Home Value

Group	Dollars
Total Population	199,900
Hispanic or Latino (of any race)	160,300
Mexican	158,900

Median Gross Rent

Group	Dollars
Total Population	800
Hispanic or Latino (of any race)	738
Mexican	734

Median Household Income
(2010 Inflation-Adjusted Dollars)

Group	Dollars
Total Population	44,988
Hispanic or Latino (of any race)	34,085
Mexican	33,883

Per Capita Income
(2010 Inflation-Adjusted Dollars)

Group	Dollars
Total Population	21,358
Hispanic or Latino (of any race)	11,557
Mexican	11,033

Households with $100,000+ Income

Group	Number	%
Total Population	1,193	11.3
Hispanic or Latino (of any race)	64	3.3
Mexican	55	3.4

Households with Food Stamps/SNAP Benefits During Past 12 Months

Group	Number	%
Total Population	865	8.2
Hispanic or Latino (of any race)	299	15.6
Mexican	249	15.4

Poverty Rate
(Income in Past 12 Months Below Poverty Level)

Group	%
Total Population	16.3
Hispanic or Latino (of any race)	29.6

Notes: (1) Percent of total population; (2) Percent of Hispanic/Latino population; Profiles include places with an overall population of at least 125,000, OR an overall population of at least 25,000 where the Hispanic/Latino population is at least 20% of the overall population. In states where less than five places meet either of these criteria, we have included places with at least 10,000 total population with the highest percentage of Hispanic/Latino population. These places are identified with an asterisk (*); Please refer to the User's Guide for a full explanation of data.

Mexican	28.7

Ogden

Population

Group	Number	%TP[1]	%HP[2]
Total Population	82,825	100.0	–
Hispanic or Latino (of any race)	24,940	30.1	100.0
Central American, ex. Mexican	894	1.1	3.6
Guatemalan	179	0.2	0.7
Salvadoran	557	0.7	2.2
Mexican	20,118	24.3	80.7
Puerto Rican	310	0.4	1.2
South American	434	0.5	1.7
Spaniard	435	0.5	1.7

Population Growth: 2000–2010

Group	%
Total Population	7.3
Hispanic or Latino (of any race)	36.6
Central American, ex. Mexican	188.4
Salvadoran	212.9
Mexican	48.8
Puerto Rican	59.8
South American	126.0

Males per 100 Females

Group	Number
Total Population	103.1
Hispanic or Latino (of any race)	107.1
Central American, ex. Mexican	116.5
Guatemalan	115.7
Salvadoran	119.3
Mexican	107.1
Puerto Rican	89.0
South American	94.6
Spaniard	76.1

Average Household Size

Group	People
Total Population	2.73
Hispanic or Latino (of any race)	3.75
Central American, ex. Mexican	3.98
Guatemalan	3.51
Salvadoran	4.20
Mexican	3.93
Puerto Rican	2.78
South American	3.19
Spaniard	2.53

Median Age

Group	Years
Total Population	29.6
Hispanic or Latino (of any race)	23.3
Central American, ex. Mexican	29.9
Guatemalan	31.3
Salvadoran	29.7
Mexican	22.2
Puerto Rican	22.9
South American	30.3
Spaniard	31.5

High School Graduates
(Universe: Population 25 Years and Over)

Group	Number	%
Total Population	38,379	80.8
Hispanic or Latino (of any race)	5,054	47.7
Mexican	4,035	43.9

Four-Year College Graduates
(Universe: Population 25 Years and Over)

Group	Number	%
Total Population	8,482	17.8
Hispanic or Latino (of any race)	678	6.4
Mexican	567	6.2

Population Age 3–17 Enrolled in Public School
(Universe: Population Age 3–17 Enrolled in School)

Group	Number	%
Total Population	14,603	92.1
Hispanic or Latino (of any race)	6,307	96.2
Mexican	5,462	96.2

Population Age 3–17 Enrolled in Private School
(Universe: Population Age 3–17 Enrolled in School)

Group	Number	%
Total Population	1,257	7.9
Hispanic or Latino (of any race)	251	3.8
Mexican	217	3.8

Foreign-Born Population

Group	Number	%
Total Population	11,368	14.0
Hispanic or Latino (of any race)	9,423	41.7
Mexican	8,272	42.1

Foreign-Born Naturalized U.S. Citizens

Group	Number	%
Total Population	1,799	15.8
Hispanic or Latino (of any race)	972	10.3
Mexican	777	9.4

Language Spoken at Home: English Only
(Universe: Population 5 Years and Over)

Group	Number	%
Total Population	57,014	77.7
Hispanic or Latino (of any race)	6,266	31.6
Mexican	5,322	31.0

Language Spoken at Home: Spanish
(Universe: Population 5 Years and Over)

Group	Number	%
Total Population	14,261	19.4
Hispanic or Latino (of any race)	13,543	68.4
Mexican	11,833	69.0

Unemployment Rate
(Universe: Population 16 Years and Over)

Group	%
Total Population	9.8
Hispanic or Latino (of any race)	12.9
Mexican	12.9

Class of Worker: Private Wage and Salary
(Universe: Civilian Employed Population 16 Years and Over)

Group	Number	%
Total Population	28,493	79.6
Hispanic or Latino (of any race)	8,169	90.7
Mexican	6,919	90.6

Class of Worker: Government
(Universe: Civilian Employed Population 16 Years and Over)

Group	Number	%
Total Population	6,224	17.4
Hispanic or Latino (of any race)	628	7.0
Mexican	540	7.1

Means of Transportation to Work: Car, Truck or Van
(Universe: Workers 16 Years and Over)

Group	Number	%
Total Population	31,832	89.4
Hispanic or Latino (of any race)	7,877	89.5
Mexican	6,672	89.0

Means of Transportation to Work: Public Transportation (ex. Taxicab)
(Universe: Workers 16 Years and Over)

Group	Number	%
Total Population	1,182	3.3
Hispanic or Latino (of any race)	459	5.2
Mexican	398	5.3

Homeownership Rate
(Universe: Occupied Housing Units)

Group	%
Total Population	57.7
Hispanic or Latino (of any race)	46.9
Central American, ex. Mexican	57.7
Guatemalan	60.0
Salvadoran	57.9
Mexican	47.6
Puerto Rican	34.9
South American	57.8
Spaniard	52.8

Median Home Value

Group	Dollars
Total Population	133,200
Hispanic or Latino (of any race)	114,600
Mexican	111,100

Median Gross Rent

Group	Dollars
Total Population	655
Hispanic or Latino (of any race)	662
Mexican	665

Median Household Income
(2010 Inflation-Adjusted Dollars)

Group	Dollars
Total Population	41,073
Hispanic or Latino (of any race)	33,203
Mexican	33,246

Per Capita Income
(2010 Inflation-Adjusted Dollars)

Group	Dollars
Total Population	19,548
Hispanic or Latino (of any race)	11,077
Mexican	10,611

Households with $100,000+ Income

Group	Number	%
Total Population	2,781	9.4
Hispanic or Latino (of any race)	247	4.2
Mexican	163	3.2

Households with Food Stamps/SNAP Benefits During Past 12 Months

Group	Number	%
Total Population	4,302	14.5
Hispanic or Latino (of any race)	1,097	18.4
Mexican	1,026	20.1

Poverty Rate
(Income in Past 12 Months Below Poverty Level)

Group	%
Total Population	21.3
Hispanic or Latino (of any race)	31.3
Mexican	31.1

Salt Lake City

Population

Group	Number	%TP[1]	%HP[2]
Total Population	186,440	100.0	–
Hispanic or Latino (of any race)	41,637	22.3	100.0
Central American, ex. Mexican	2,209	1.2	5.3
Guatemalan	1,029	0.6	2.5
Honduran	224	0.1	0.5
Salvadoran	758	0.4	1.8
Cuban	303	0.2	0.7
Dominican Republic	105	0.1	0.3
Mexican	32,094	17.2	77.1
Puerto Rican	655	0.4	1.6
South American	1,976	1.1	4.7
Argentinean	298	0.2	0.7
Chilean	240	0.1	0.6
Colombian	268	0.1	0.6
Ecuadorian	119	0.1	0.3
Peruvian	651	0.3	1.6
Venezuelan	190	0.1	0.5
Spaniard	816	0.4	2.0

Population Growth: 2000–2010

Group	%
Total Population	2.6
Hispanic or Latino (of any race)	21.6
Central American, ex. Mexican	112.2
Guatemalan	134.4
Honduran	113.3
Salvadoran	126.3
Cuban	50.7
Mexican	26.2
Puerto Rican	35.6
South American	64.3
Argentinean	49.0
Chilean	27.7
Colombian	69.6
Peruvian	82.9
Venezuelan	43.9
Spaniard	487.1

STATE & PLACE PROFILES

Notes: (1) Percent of total population; (2) Percent of Hispanic/Latino population; Profiles include places with an overall population of at least 125,000, OR an overall population of at least 25,000 where the Hispanic/Latino population is at least 20% of the overall population. In states where less than five places meet either of these criteria, we have included places with at least 10,000 total population with the highest percentage of Hispanic/Latino population. These places are identified with an asterisk (*); Please refer to the User's Guide for a full explanation of data.

Males per 100 Females

Group	Number
Total Population	105.3
Hispanic or Latino (of any race)	109.2
Central American, ex. Mexican	121.8
Guatemalan	138.2
Honduran	138.3
Salvadoran	111.1
Cuban	104.7
Dominican Republic	84.2
Mexican	110.5
Puerto Rican	96.7
South American	94.7
Argentinean	82.8
Chilean	84.6
Colombian	82.3
Ecuadorian	80.3
Peruvian	110.0
Venezuelan	115.9
Spaniard	95.7

Average Household Size

Group	People
Total Population	2.44
Hispanic or Latino (of any race)	3.66
Central American, ex. Mexican	3.58
Guatemalan	3.99
Honduran	3.51
Salvadoran	3.39
Cuban	2.32
Dominican Republic	2.47
Mexican	4.01
Puerto Rican	2.33
South American	2.60
Argentinean	2.27
Chilean	2.46
Colombian	2.48
Ecuadorian	2.40
Peruvian	2.91
Venezuelan	2.62
Spaniard	2.39

Median Age

Group	Years
Total Population	30.9
Hispanic or Latino (of any race)	24.7
Central American, ex. Mexican	28.5
Guatemalan	27.7
Honduran	27.1
Salvadoran	30.8
Cuban	32.7
Dominican Republic	26.3
Mexican	23.3
Puerto Rican	27.6
South American	32.1
Argentinean	32.0
Chilean	31.7
Colombian	30.7
Ecuadorian	29.4
Peruvian	33.2
Venezuelan	31.1
Spaniard	30.5

High School Graduates
(Universe: Population 25 Years and Over)

Group	Number	%
Total Population	100,489	86.3
Hispanic or Latino (of any race)	10,076	52.6
Central American, ex. Mexican	658	52.6
Guatemalan	342	57.2
Mexican	7,143	47.9
South American	949	88.0
Peruvian	398	87.3

Four-Year College Graduates
(Universe: Population 25 Years and Over)

Group	Number	%
Total Population	46,442	39.9
Hispanic or Latino (of any race)	1,843	9.6
Central American, ex. Mexican	111	8.9
Guatemalan	72	12.0
Mexican	1,037	7.0
South American	354	32.8
Peruvian	113	24.8

Population Age 3–17 Enrolled in Public School
(Universe: Population Age 3–17 Enrolled in School)

Group	Number	%
Total Population	24,495	86.6
Hispanic or Latino (of any race)	8,994	94.4
Central American, ex. Mexican	229	100.0
Guatemalan	111	100.0
Mexican	7,937	94.8
South American	200	91.3
Peruvian	69	78.4

Population Age 3–17 Enrolled in Private School
(Universe: Population Age 3–17 Enrolled in School)

Group	Number	%
Total Population	3,781	13.4
Hispanic or Latino (of any race)	535	5.6
Central American, ex. Mexican	0	0.0
Guatemalan	0	0.0
Mexican	435	5.2
South American	19	8.7
Peruvian	19	21.6

Foreign-Born Population

Group	Number	%
Total Population	33,045	17.9
Hispanic or Latino (of any race)	18,264	46.2
Central American, ex. Mexican	1,422	71.3
Guatemalan	697	75.1
Mexican	14,950	46.3
South American	1,229	71.6
Peruvian	585	78.7

Foreign-Born Naturalized U.S. Citizens

Group	Number	%
Total Population	9,270	28.1
Hispanic or Latino (of any race)	3,367	18.4
Central American, ex. Mexican	390	27.4
Guatemalan	158	22.7
Mexican	2,322	15.5
South American	433	35.2
Peruvian	191	32.6

Language Spoken at Home: English Only
(Universe: Population 5 Years and Over)

Group	Number	%
Total Population	122,652	72.5
Hispanic or Latino (of any race)	7,513	21.9
Central American, ex. Mexican	305	16.4
Guatemalan	63	7.3
Mexican	5,234	18.9
South American	199	12.5
Peruvian	81	11.4

Language Spoken at Home: Spanish
(Universe: Population 5 Years and Over)

Group	Number	%
Total Population	29,525	17.5
Hispanic or Latino (of any race)	26,645	77.8
Central American, ex. Mexican	1,560	83.6
Guatemalan	803	92.7
Mexican	22,366	80.9
South American	1,374	86.4
Peruvian	632	88.6

Unemployment Rate
(Universe: Population 16 Years and Over)

Group	%
Total Population	6.5
Hispanic or Latino (of any race)	7.6
Central American, ex. Mexican	8.8
Guatemalan	1.7
Mexican	7.3
South American	9.7
Peruvian	9.8

Class of Worker: Private Wage and Salary
(Universe: Civilian Employed Population 16 Years and Over)

Group	Number	%
Total Population	75,972	77.9
Hispanic or Latino (of any race)	16,004	89.1
Central American, ex. Mexican	1,038	88.6
Guatemalan	574	97.6
Mexican	12,720	90.0
South American	866	85.8
Peruvian	370	77.7

Class of Worker: Government
(Universe: Civilian Employed Population 16 Years and Over)

Group	Number	%
Total Population	16,162	16.6
Hispanic or Latino (of any race)	1,408	7.8
Central American, ex. Mexican	41	3.5
Guatemalan	0	0.0
Mexican	1,046	7.4
South American	121	12.0
Peruvian	84	17.6

Means of Transportation to Work: Car, Truck or Van
(Universe: Workers 16 Years and Over)

Group	Number	%
Total Population	77,538	81.1
Hispanic or Latino (of any race)	15,365	87.4
Central American, ex. Mexican	948	80.9
Guatemalan	510	86.7
Mexican	12,170	88.0
South American	805	83.4
Peruvian	384	83.8

Means of Transportation to Work: Public Transportation (ex. Taxicab)
(Universe: Workers 16 Years and Over)

Group	Number	%
Total Population	5,411	5.7
Hispanic or Latino (of any race)	809	4.6
Central American, ex. Mexican	14	1.2
Guatemalan	0	0.0
Mexican	670	4.8
South American	59	6.1
Peruvian	28	6.1

Homeownership Rate
(Universe: Occupied Housing Units)

Group	%
Total Population	48.4
Hispanic or Latino (of any race)	37.3
Central American, ex. Mexican	35.0
Guatemalan	31.5
Honduran	40.0
Salvadoran	37.1
Cuban	34.4
Dominican Republic	14.9
Mexican	38.3
Puerto Rican	30.9
South American	36.7
Argentinean	39.6
Chilean	23.1
Colombian	35.6
Ecuadorian	12.0
Peruvian	45.4
Venezuelan	26.9
Spaniard	44.4

Median Home Value

Group	Dollars
Total Population	243,200
Hispanic or Latino (of any race)	170,800
Central American, ex. Mexican	199,100
Guatemalan	135,600
Mexican	164,500
South American	220,500
Peruvian	225,900

Median Gross Rent

Group	Dollars
Total Population	712
Hispanic or Latino (of any race)	719
Central American, ex. Mexican	727
Guatemalan	720
Mexican	718
South American	716
Peruvian	533

Median Household Income
(2010 Inflation-Adjusted Dollars)

Group	Dollars
Total Population	44,223
Hispanic or Latino (of any race)	33,170
Central American, ex. Mexican	38,801
Guatemalan	39,515
Mexican	32,112

Notes: (1) Percent of total population; (2) Percent of Hispanic/Latino population; Profiles include places with an overall population of at least 125,000, OR an overall population of at least 25,000 where the Hispanic/Latino population is at least 20% of the overall population. In states where less than five places meet either of these criteria, we have included places with at least 10,000 total population with the highest percentage of Hispanic/Latino population. These places are identified with an asterisk (*); Please refer to the User's Guide for a full explanation of data.

South American	32,759
Peruvian	45,972

Per Capita Income
(2010 Inflation-Adjusted Dollars)

Group	Dollars
Total Population	26,055
Hispanic or Latino (of any race)	12,868
Central American, ex. Mexican	15,802
Guatemalan	13,137
Mexican	11,626
South American	17,525
Peruvian	18,241

Households with $100,000+ Income

Group	Number	%
Total Population	12,385	16.5
Hispanic or Latino (of any race)	645	5.9
Central American, ex. Mexican	25	3.9
Guatemalan	0	0.0
Mexican	463	5.6
South American	56	10.7
Peruvian	37	20.9

Households with Food Stamps/SNAP Benefits During Past 12 Months

Group	Number	%
Total Population	6,135	8.2
Hispanic or Latino (of any race)	1,616	14.9
Central American, ex. Mexican	52	8.2
Guatemalan	37	11.7
Mexican	1,264	15.3
South American	40	7.6
Peruvian	0	0.0

Poverty Rate
(Income in Past 12 Months Below Poverty Level)

Group	%
Total Population	17.5
Hispanic or Latino (of any race)	27.2
Central American, ex. Mexican	13.4
Guatemalan	12.8
Mexican	28.7
South American	27.6
Peruvian	14.9

West Valley City

Population

Group	Number	%TP[1]	%HP[2]
Total Population	129,480	100.0	–
Hispanic or Latino (of any race)	42,892	33.1	100.0
Central American, ex. Mexican	2,504	1.9	5.8
Guatemalan	767	0.6	1.8
Honduran	261	0.2	0.6
Nicaraguan	131	0.1	0.3
Salvadoran	1,230	0.9	2.9
Cuban	128	0.1	0.3
Mexican	33,620	26.0	78.4
Puerto Rican	525	0.4	1.2
South American	2,126	1.6	5.0
Argentinean	204	0.2	0.5
Chilean	220	0.2	0.5
Colombian	305	0.2	0.7
Ecuadorian	196	0.2	0.5
Peruvian	736	0.6	1.7
Venezuelan	321	0.2	0.7
Spaniard	534	0.4	1.2

Population Growth: 2000–2010

Group	%
Total Population	18.9
Hispanic or Latino (of any race)	113.1
Central American, ex. Mexican	205.0
Guatemalan	178.9
Salvadoran	276.1
Mexican	148.4
Puerto Rican	53.5
South American	143.5
Colombian	160.7
Peruvian	211.9
Venezuelan	58.1

Males per 100 Females

Group	Number
Total Population	101.7
Hispanic or Latino (of any race)	107.2
Central American, ex. Mexican	108.3
Guatemalan	131.0
Honduran	102.3
Nicaraguan	81.9
Salvadoran	105.0
Cuban	128.6
Mexican	109.1
Puerto Rican	110.8
South American	96.3
Argentinean	102.0
Chilean	94.7
Colombian	91.8
Ecuadorian	83.2
Peruvian	108.5
Venezuelan	85.5
Spaniard	88.7

Average Household Size

Group	People
Total Population	3.48
Hispanic or Latino (of any race)	4.49
Central American, ex. Mexican	4.42
Guatemalan	4.58
Honduran	4.40
Nicaraguan	4.06
Salvadoran	4.45
Cuban	3.95
Mexican	4.68
Puerto Rican	3.40
South American	3.91
Argentinean	3.43
Chilean	3.87
Colombian	3.34
Ecuadorian	4.37
Peruvian	4.41
Venezuelan	3.62
Spaniard	3.17

Median Age

Group	Years
Total Population	28.8
Hispanic or Latino (of any race)	23.2
Central American, ex. Mexican	30.8
Guatemalan	30.2
Honduran	30.8
Nicaraguan	28.8
Salvadoran	31.1
Cuban	28.5
Mexican	21.9
Puerto Rican	22.1
South American	32.0
Argentinean	32.1
Chilean	34.8
Colombian	33.5
Ecuadorian	31.5
Peruvian	32.5
Venezuelan	26.8
Spaniard	30.9

High School Graduates
(Universe: Population 25 Years and Over)

Group	Number	%
Total Population	57,431	79.5
Hispanic or Latino (of any race)	10,612	56.0
Central American, ex. Mexican	823	59.9
Guatemalan	192	38.1
Salvadoran	340	66.5
Mexican	7,655	51.8
South American	925	79.4
Peruvian	346	81.2

Four-Year College Graduates
(Universe: Population 25 Years and Over)

Group	Number	%
Total Population	9,282	12.8
Hispanic or Latino (of any race)	1,238	6.5
Central American, ex. Mexican	177	12.9
Guatemalan	34	6.7
Salvadoran	111	21.7
Mexican	733	5.0
South American	186	16.0
Peruvian	49	11.5

Population Age 3–17 Enrolled in Public School
(Universe: Population Age 3–17 Enrolled in School)

Group	Number	%
Total Population	25,493	94.0
Hispanic or Latino (of any race)	10,061	94.4
Central American, ex. Mexican	475	90.6
Guatemalan	121	71.2
Salvadoran	198	100.0
Mexican	8,739	96.2
South American	257	81.6
Peruvian	167	78.4

Population Age 3–17 Enrolled in Private School
(Universe: Population Age 3–17 Enrolled in School)

Group	Number	%
Total Population	1,634	6.0
Hispanic or Latino (of any race)	597	5.6
Central American, ex. Mexican	49	9.4
Guatemalan	49	28.8
Salvadoran	0	0.0
Mexican	341	3.8
South American	58	18.4
Peruvian	46	21.6

Foreign-Born Population

Group	Number	%
Total Population	25,810	20.6
Hispanic or Latino (of any race)	17,365	45.2
Central American, ex. Mexican	1,469	58.7
Guatemalan	666	64.7
Salvadoran	440	51.2
Mexican	13,915	45.1
South American	1,404	72.0
Peruvian	559	70.8

Foreign-Born Naturalized U.S. Citizens

Group	Number	%
Total Population	8,441	32.7
Hispanic or Latino (of any race)	3,947	22.7
Central American, ex. Mexican	560	38.1
Guatemalan	244	36.6
Salvadoran	264	60.0
Mexican	2,627	18.9
South American	436	31.1
Peruvian	187	33.5

Language Spoken at Home: English Only
(Universe: Population 5 Years and Over)

Group	Number	%
Total Population	76,718	68.1
Hispanic or Latino (of any race)	8,234	24.6
Central American, ex. Mexican	91	4.2
Guatemalan	28	3.4
Salvadoran	43	5.7
Mexican	6,400	23.9
South American	162	9.2
Peruvian	90	12.4

Language Spoken at Home: Spanish
(Universe: Population 5 Years and Over)

Group	Number	%
Total Population	26,025	23.1
Hispanic or Latino (of any race)	25,119	75.2
Central American, ex. Mexican	2,093	95.8
Guatemalan	802	96.6
Salvadoran	708	94.3
Mexican	20,392	76.0
South American	1,598	90.8
Peruvian	636	87.6

Unemployment Rate
(Universe: Population 16 Years and Over)

Group	%
Total Population	6.8
Hispanic or Latino (of any race)	7.2
Central American, ex. Mexican	3.6
Guatemalan	6.4
Salvadoran	0.0
Mexican	8.2
South American	4.1
Peruvian	2.4

Notes: (1) Percent of total population; (2) Percent of Hispanic/Latino population; Profiles include places with an overall population of at least 125,000, OR an overall population of at least 25,000 where the Hispanic/Latino population is at least 20% of the overall population. In states where less than five places meet either of these criteria, we have included places with at least 10,000 total population with the highest percentage of Hispanic/Latino population. These places are identified with an asterisk (*); Please refer to the User's Guide for a full explanation of data.

Class of Worker: Private Wage and Salary
(Universe: Civilian Employed Population 16 Years and Over)

Group	Number	%
Total Population	52,649	85.6
Hispanic or Latino (of any race)	15,528	92.5
Central American, ex. Mexican	1,305	93.0
Guatemalan	496	88.6
Salvadoran	481	98.0
Mexican	11,936	93.1
South American	983	88.4
Peruvian	369	83.1

Class of Worker: Government
(Universe: Civilian Employed Population 16 Years and Over)

Group	Number	%
Total Population	6,576	10.7
Hispanic or Latino (of any race)	611	3.6
Central American, ex. Mexican	10	0.7
Guatemalan	10	1.8
Salvadoran	0	0.0
Mexican	474	3.7
South American	0	0.0
Peruvian	0	0.0

Means of Transportation to Work: Car, Truck or Van
(Universe: Workers 16 Years and Over)

Group	Number	%
Total Population	55,522	91.7
Hispanic or Latino (of any race)	15,400	93.3
Central American, ex. Mexican	1,207	89.1
Guatemalan	430	84.1
Salvadoran	481	98.0
Mexican	11,730	93.2
South American	1,015	92.3
Peruvian	366	82.4

Means of Transportation to Work: Public Transportation (ex. Taxicab)
(Universe: Workers 16 Years and Over)

Group	Number	%
Total Population	1,777	2.9
Hispanic or Latino (of any race)	503	3.0
Central American, ex. Mexican	54	4.0
Guatemalan	54	10.6
Salvadoran	0	0.0
Mexican	371	2.9
South American	78	7.1
Peruvian	78	17.6

Homeownership Rate
(Universe: Occupied Housing Units)

Group	%
Total Population	69.9
Hispanic or Latino (of any race)	56.2
Central American, ex. Mexican	61.1
Guatemalan	59.3
Honduran	54.8
Nicaraguan	57.6
Salvadoran	63.8
Cuban	62.2
Mexican	54.7
Puerto Rican	43.3
South American	68.6
Argentinean	70.0
Chilean	74.6
Colombian	72.4
Ecuadorian	64.8
Peruvian	70.1
Venezuelan	57.6
Spaniard	72.8

Median Home Value

Group	Dollars
Total Population	178,500
Hispanic or Latino (of any race)	174,200
Central American, ex. Mexican	209,200
Guatemalan	199,000
Salvadoran	211,700
Mexican	173,700
South American	187,800
Peruvian	171,700

Median Gross Rent

Group	Dollars
Total Population	818
Hispanic or Latino (of any race)	799
Central American, ex. Mexican	749
Guatemalan	795
Salvadoran	773
Mexican	819
South American	723
Peruvian	535

Median Household Income
(2010 Inflation-Adjusted Dollars)

Group	Dollars
Total Population	52,971
Hispanic or Latino (of any race)	42,532
Central American, ex. Mexican	36,677
Guatemalan	35,208
Salvadoran	56,967
Mexican	42,904
South American	40,945
Peruvian	38,264

Per Capita Income
(2010 Inflation-Adjusted Dollars)

Group	Dollars
Total Population	18,353
Hispanic or Latino (of any race)	12,937
Central American, ex. Mexican	13,947
Guatemalan	11,874
Salvadoran	18,600
Mexican	11,876
South American	17,284
Peruvian	14,327

Households with $100,000+ Income

Group	Number	%
Total Population	4,665	12.3
Hispanic or Latino (of any race)	805	8.5
Central American, ex. Mexican	45	5.3
Guatemalan	11	3.6
Salvadoran	5	1.8
Mexican	595	8.3
South American	64	10.9
Peruvian	9	3.5

Households with Food Stamps/SNAP Benefits During Past 12 Months

Group	Number	%
Total Population	3,481	9.2
Hispanic or Latino (of any race)	1,107	11.7
Central American, ex. Mexican	67	7.8
Guatemalan	36	11.8
Salvadoran	0	0.0
Mexican	889	12.4
South American	132	22.6
Peruvian	60	23.2

Poverty Rate
(Income in Past 12 Months Below Poverty Level)

Group	%
Total Population	12.3
Hispanic or Latino (of any race)	20.7
Central American, ex. Mexican	23.9
Guatemalan	27.9
Salvadoran	12.7
Mexican	21.8
South American	15.7
Peruvian	13.4

Notes: (1) Percent of total population; (2) Percent of Hispanic/Latino population; Profiles include places with an overall population of at least 125,000, OR an overall population of at least 25,000 where the Hispanic/Latino population is at least 20% of the overall population. In states where less than five places meet either of these criteria, we have included places with at least 10,000 total population with the highest percentage of Hispanic/Latino population. These places are identified with an asterisk (*); Please refer to the User's Guide for a full explanation of data.

Vermont

EDITOR'S NOTE: For a place to be included in this edition, it must meet one of two criteria. Either its overall population is at least 125,000, OR its overall population is at least 25,000 and its Hispanic/Latino population is at least 20% of the overall population. In Vermont, less than five places meet either of these criteria. In an effort to include at least five places for each state, we have included places with at least 10,000 total population with the highest percentage of Hispanic/Latino population. These places are identified with an asterisk (*). For the state of Vermont, the following locations are included:

Bennington*
Brattleboro*
Burlington*
Essex*
South Burlington*

Section Two: State & Place Profiles starts with the state profile, followed by place profiles that meet the criteria above. Places are listed alphabetically within each state. All states, all counties and places that meet the above criteria are ranked and compared in *Section Three: Rankings & Comparisons*, on page 1055.

For a more detailed look at the Hispanic/Latino population in Vermont, a companion web site is available at no additional charge with purchase of this print edition. Visit http://gold.greyhouse.com/page/info_hispanic for more information.

The web site includes data for all counties and places in Vermont with Hispanic/Latino population, plus ten additional topics: Self Employed Worker; Walked to Work; Worked from Home; Mean Travel Time to Work; Mean Household Income; Households with Cash Public Assistance; Mean Cash Pubic Assistance; Poverty Rates for 18 and Under, 18 to 64, and 65 and Over.

Population

Group	Number	%TP[1]	%HP[2]
Total Population	625,741	100.0	–
Hispanic or Latino (of any race)	9,208	1.5	100.0
Central American, ex. Mexican	671	0.1	7.3
Guatemalan	215	<0.1	2.3
Honduran	109	<0.1	1.2
Salvadoran	116	<0.1	1.3
Cuban	510	0.1	5.5
Dominican Republic	282	<0.1	3.1
Mexican	2,534	0.4	27.5
Puerto Rican	2,261	0.4	24.6
South American	1,204	0.2	13.1
Argentinean	185	<0.1	2.0
Chilean	127	<0.1	1.4
Colombian	327	0.1	3.6
Ecuadorian	125	<0.1	1.4
Peruvian	242	<0.1	2.6
Spaniard	701	0.1	7.6

Population Growth: 2000–2010

Group	%
Total Population	2.8
Hispanic or Latino (of any race)	67.3
Central American, ex. Mexican	172.8
Cuban	64.5
Mexican	115.8
Puerto Rican	64.6
South American	131.5
Colombian	120.9
Spaniard	537.3

Males per 100 Females

Group	Number
Total Population	97.1
Hispanic or Latino (of any race)	101.0
Central American, ex. Mexican	90.6
Guatemalan	97.2
Honduran	62.7
Salvadoran	118.9
Cuban	93.2
Dominican Republic	102.9
Mexican	125.0
Puerto Rican	96.6
South American	83.5
Argentinean	105.6
Chilean	111.7
Colombian	73.9
Ecuadorian	86.6
Peruvian	64.6
Spaniard	84.5

Average Household Size

Group	People
Total Population	2.34
Hispanic or Latino (of any race)	2.49
Central American, ex. Mexican	2.67
Guatemalan	2.72
Honduran	3.09
Salvadoran	2.43
Cuban	2.34
Dominican Republic	2.70
Mexican	2.75
Puerto Rican	2.50
South American	2.48
Argentinean	2.37
Chilean	2.49
Colombian	2.34
Ecuadorian	2.70
Peruvian	2.53
Spaniard	2.15

Median Age

Group	Years
Total Population	41.5
Hispanic or Latino (of any race)	24.6
Central American, ex. Mexican	20.9
Guatemalan	10.8
Honduran	21.6
Salvadoran	22.0
Cuban	26.8
Dominican Republic	20.6
Mexican	23.9
Puerto Rican	22.2
South American	26.4
Argentinean	34.8
Chilean	28.1
Colombian	25.7
Ecuadorian	23.9
Peruvian	26.9
Spaniard	42.4

High School Graduates
(Universe: Population 25 Years and Over)

Group	Number	%
Total Population	386,164	90.6
Hispanic or Latino (of any race)	4,287	91.0
Central American, ex. Mexican	228	76.8
Mexican	1,180	87.9
Puerto Rican	1,012	88.2
South American	560	96.6

Four-Year College Graduates
(Universe: Population 25 Years and Over)

Group	Number	%
Total Population	141,865	33.3
Hispanic or Latino (of any race)	1,741	36.9
Central American, ex. Mexican	59	19.9
Mexican	409	30.5
Puerto Rican	289	25.2
South American	279	48.1

Population Age 3–17 Enrolled in Public School
(Universe: Population Age 3–17 Enrolled in School)

Group	Number	%
Total Population	90,726	87.5
Hispanic or Latino (of any race)	1,903	86.3
Central American, ex. Mexican	277	90.5
Mexican	554	90.2
Puerto Rican	557	93.5
South American	157	78.9

Population Age 3–17 Enrolled in Private School
(Universe: Population Age 3–17 Enrolled in School)

Group	Number	%
Total Population	12,986	12.5
Hispanic or Latino (of any race)	301	13.7
Central American, ex. Mexican	29	9.5
Mexican	60	9.8
Puerto Rican	39	6.5
South American	42	21.1

Foreign-Born Population

Group	Number	%
Total Population	24,837	4.0
Hispanic or Latino (of any race)	1,665	18.2
Central American, ex. Mexican	357	54.6
Mexican	585	21.2
Puerto Rican	0	0.0
South American	497	50.9

Foreign-Born Naturalized U.S. Citizens

Group	Number	%
Total Population	13,586	54.7
Hispanic or Latino (of any race)	840	50.5
Central American, ex. Mexican	206	57.7
Mexican	100	17.1
Puerto Rican	0	0.0
South American	373	75.1

Language Spoken at Home: English Only
(Universe: Population 5 Years and Over)

Group	Number	%
Total Population	560,326	94.6
Hispanic or Latino (of any race)	5,118	61.2
Central American, ex. Mexican	419	66.3
Mexican	1,569	63.1
Puerto Rican	1,102	53.1
South American	349	38.5

Language Spoken at Home: Spanish
(Universe: Population 5 Years and Over)

Group	Number	%
Total Population	6,482	1.1
Hispanic or Latino (of any race)	3,138	37.5
Central American, ex. Mexican	213	33.7
Mexican	911	36.6
Puerto Rican	965	46.5
South American	547	60.3

Unemployment Rate
(Universe: Population 16 Years and Over)

Group	%
Total Population	5.9
Hispanic or Latino (of any race)	5.8
Central American, ex. Mexican	4.1
Mexican	4.8
Puerto Rican	6.7
South American	6.2

Class of Worker: Private Wage and Salary
(Universe: Civilian Employed Population 16 Years and Over)

Group	Number	%
Total Population	246,643	74.8
Hispanic or Latino (of any race)	3,288	74.8
Central American, ex. Mexican	138	58.7
Mexican	1,204	80.4
Puerto Rican	706	72.6
South American	352	66.0

Class of Worker: Government
(Universe: Civilian Employed Population 16 Years and Over)

Group	Number	%
Total Population	48,200	14.6
Hispanic or Latino (of any race)	603	13.7
Central American, ex. Mexican	13	5.5
Mexican	252	16.8
Puerto Rican	147	15.1

STATE & PLACE PROFILES

Notes: (1) Percent of total population; (2) Percent of Hispanic/Latino population; Profiles include places with an overall population of at least 125,000, OR an overall population of at least 25,000 where the Hispanic/Latino population is at least 20% of the overall population. In states where less than five places meet either of these criteria, we have included places with at least 10,000 total population with the highest percentage of Hispanic/Latino population. These places are identified with an asterisk (*); Please refer to the User's Guide for a full explanation of data.

South American	82	15.4

Means of Transportation to Work: Car, Truck or Van
(Universe: Workers 16 Years and Over)

Group	Number	%
Total Population	271,563	84.6
Hispanic or Latino (of any race)	3,162	75.9
Central American, ex. Mexican	162	85.3
Mexican	918	63.8
Puerto Rican	769	85.7
South American	365	72.7

Means of Transportation to Work: Public Transportation (ex. Taxicab)
(Universe: Workers 16 Years and Over)

Group	Number	%
Total Population	3,140	1.0
Hispanic or Latino (of any race)	61	1.5
Central American, ex. Mexican	0	0.0
Mexican	16	1.1
Puerto Rican	37	4.1
South American	0	0.0

Homeownership Rate
(Universe: Occupied Housing Units)

Group	%
Total Population	70.7
Hispanic or Latino (of any race)	50.1
Central American, ex. Mexican	37.0
Guatemalan	40.0
Honduran	40.9
Salvadoran	33.3
Cuban	54.4
Dominican Republic	32.1
Mexican	40.6
Puerto Rican	44.2
South American	56.0
Argentinean	57.6
Chilean	65.7
Colombian	51.3
Ecuadorian	52.5
Peruvian	60.3
Spaniard	75.7

Median Home Value

Group	Dollars
Total Population	208,400
Hispanic or Latino (of any race)	231,500
Central American, ex. Mexican	269,200
Mexican	196,700
Puerto Rican	208,100
South American	171,300

Median Gross Rent

Group	Dollars
Total Population	809
Hispanic or Latino (of any race)	819
Central American, ex. Mexican	483
Mexican	886
Puerto Rican	727
South American	749

Median Household Income
(2010 Inflation-Adjusted Dollars)

Group	Dollars
Total Population	51,841
Hispanic or Latino (of any race)	50,833
Central American, ex. Mexican	15,114
Mexican	54,116
Puerto Rican	36,667
South American	28,370

Per Capita Income
(2010 Inflation-Adjusted Dollars)

Group	Dollars
Total Population	27,478
Hispanic or Latino (of any race)	20,391
Central American, ex. Mexican	7,109
Mexican	17,222
Puerto Rican	18,489
South American	22,211

Households with $100,000+ Income

Group	Number	%
Total Population	45,541	17.7
Hispanic or Latino (of any race)	589	21.9
Central American, ex. Mexican	0	0.0
Mexican	137	18.0
Puerto Rican	136	19.9
South American	50	18.9

Households with Food Stamps/SNAP Benefits During Past 12 Months

Group	Number	%
Total Population	25,957	10.1
Hispanic or Latino (of any race)	350	13.0
Central American, ex. Mexican	54	58.1
Mexican	25	3.3
Puerto Rican	174	25.5
South American	32	12.1

Poverty Rate
(Income in Past 12 Months Below Poverty Level)

Group	%
Total Population	11.1
Hispanic or Latino (of any race)	19.2
Central American, ex. Mexican	43.3
Mexican	11.6
Puerto Rican	28.7
South American	16.9

Bennington*

Population

Group	Number	%TP[1]	%HP[2]
Total Population	15,764	100.0	–
Hispanic or Latino (of any race)	274	1.7	100.0
Puerto Rican	105	0.7	38.3

Population Growth: 2000–2010

Group	%
Total Population	0.2
Hispanic or Latino (of any race)	75.6

Males per 100 Females

Group	Number
Total Population	88.0
Hispanic or Latino (of any race)	67.1
Puerto Rican	61.5

Average Household Size

Group	People
Total Population	2.29
Hispanic or Latino (of any race)	2.61
Puerto Rican	2.68

Median Age

Group	Years
Total Population	40.8
Hispanic or Latino (of any race)	22.6
Puerto Rican	17.8

High School Graduates
(Universe: Population 25 Years and Over)

Group	Number	%
Total Population	8,799	86.6

Four-Year College Graduates
(Universe: Population 25 Years and Over)

Group	Number	%
Total Population	2,321	22.8

Population Age 3–17 Enrolled in Public School
(Universe: Population Age 3–17 Enrolled in School)

Group	Number	%
Total Population	2,231	90.1

Population Age 3–17 Enrolled in Private School
(Universe: Population Age 3–17 Enrolled in School)

Group	Number	%
Total Population	244	9.9

Foreign-Born Population

Group	Number	%
Total Population	425	2.7

Foreign-Born Naturalized U.S. Citizens

Group	Number	%
Total Population	221	52.0

Language Spoken at Home: English Only
(Universe: Population 5 Years and Over)

Group	Number	%
Total Population	14,089	95.9

Language Spoken at Home: Spanish
(Universe: Population 5 Years and Over)

Group	Number	%
Total Population	146	1.0

Unemployment Rate
(Universe: Population 16 Years and Over)

Group	%
Total Population	6.6

Class of Worker: Private Wage and Salary
(Universe: Civilian Employed Population 16 Years and Over)

Group	Number	%
Total Population	5,821	77.9

Class of Worker: Government
(Universe: Civilian Employed Population 16 Years and Over)

Group	Number	%
Total Population	942	12.6

Means of Transportation to Work: Car, Truck or Van
(Universe: Workers 16 Years and Over)

Group	Number	%
Total Population	6,199	85.4

Means of Transportation to Work: Public Transportation (ex. Taxicab)
(Universe: Workers 16 Years and Over)

Group	Number	%
Total Population	27	0.4

Homeownership Rate
(Universe: Occupied Housing Units)

Group	%
Total Population	59.8
Hispanic or Latino (of any race)	43.1
Puerto Rican	27.3

Median Home Value

Group	Dollars
Total Population	160,800

Median Gross Rent

Group	Dollars
Total Population	703

Median Household Income
(2010 Inflation-Adjusted Dollars)

Group	Dollars
Total Population	39,765

Per Capita Income
(2010 Inflation-Adjusted Dollars)

Group	Dollars
Total Population	23,560

Households with $100,000+ Income

Group	Number	%
Total Population	719	11.5

Households with Food Stamps/SNAP Benefits During Past 12 Months

Group	Number	%
Total Population	1,160	18.5

Poverty Rate
(Income in Past 12 Months Below Poverty Level)

Group	%
Total Population	15.1

Brattleboro*

Population

Group	Number	%TP[1]	%HP[2]
Total Population	12,046	100.0	–
Hispanic or Latino (of any race)	322	2.7	100.0
Puerto Rican	118	1.0	36.6

Notes: (1) Percent of total population; (2) Percent of Hispanic/Latino population; Profiles include places with an overall population of at least 125,000, OR an overall population of at least 25,000 where the Hispanic/Latino population is at least 20% of the overall population. In states where less than five places meet either of these criteria, we have included places with at least 10,000 total population with the highest percentage of Hispanic/Latino population. These places are identified with an asterisk (*); Please refer to the User's Guide for a full explanation of data.

Population Growth: 2000–2010	
Group	%
Total Population	0.3
Hispanic or Latino (of any race)	60.2

Males per 100 Females	
Group	Number
Total Population	86.6
Hispanic or Latino (of any race)	119.0
Puerto Rican	122.6

Average Household Size	
Group	People
Total Population	2.09
Hispanic or Latino (of any race)	2.29
Puerto Rican	2.25

Median Age	
Group	Years
Total Population	43.2
Hispanic or Latino (of any race)	25.3
Puerto Rican	23.0

High School Graduates (Universe: Population 25 Years and Over)		
Group	Number	%
Total Population	7,969	90.1

Four-Year College Graduates (Universe: Population 25 Years and Over)		
Group	Number	%
Total Population	3,246	36.7

Population Age 3–17 Enrolled in Public School (Universe: Population Age 3–17 Enrolled in School)		
Group	Number	%
Total Population	1,463	74.4

Population Age 3–17 Enrolled in Private School (Universe: Population Age 3–17 Enrolled in School)		
Group	Number	%
Total Population	504	25.6

Foreign-Born Population		
Group	Number	%
Total Population	632	5.2

Foreign-Born Naturalized U.S. Citizens		
Group	Number	%
Total Population	358	56.6

Language Spoken at Home: English Only (Universe: Population 5 Years and Over)		
Group	Number	%
Total Population	10,749	93.6

Language Spoken at Home: Spanish (Universe: Population 5 Years and Over)		
Group	Number	%
Total Population	301	2.6

Unemployment Rate (Universe: Population 16 Years and Over)	
Group	%
Total Population	7.6

Class of Worker: Private Wage and Salary (Universe: Civilian Employed Population 16 Years and Over)		
Group	Number	%
Total Population	4,865	77.5

Class of Worker: Government (Universe: Civilian Employed Population 16 Years and Over)		
Group	Number	%
Total Population	720	11.5

Means of Transportation to Work: Car, Truck or Van (Universe: Workers 16 Years and Over)		
Group	Number	%
Total Population	4,842	80.1

Means of Transportation to Work: Public Transportation (ex. Taxicab) (Universe: Workers 16 Years and Over)		
Group	Number	%
Total Population	23	0.4

Homeownership Rate (Universe: Occupied Housing Units)	
Group	%
Total Population	51.3
Hispanic or Latino (of any race)	28.9
Puerto Rican	28.6

Median Home Value	
Group	Dollars
Total Population	199,700

Median Gross Rent	
Group	Dollars
Total Population	710

Median Household Income (2010 Inflation-Adjusted Dollars)	
Group	Dollars
Total Population	39,314

Per Capita Income (2010 Inflation-Adjusted Dollars)	
Group	Dollars
Total Population	26,217

Households with $100,000+ Income		
Group	Number	%
Total Population	714	12.1

Households with Food Stamps/SNAP Benefits During Past 12 Months		
Group	Number	%
Total Population	916	15.5

Poverty Rate (Income in Past 12 Months Below Poverty Level)	
Group	%
Total Population	14.2

Burlington*

Population			
Group	Number	%TP[1]	%HP[2]
Total Population	42,417	100.0	–
Hispanic or Latino (of any race)	1,144	2.7	100.0
Central American, ex. Mexican	117	0.3	10.2
Mexican	227	0.5	19.8
Puerto Rican	265	0.6	23.2
South American	197	0.5	17.2

Population Growth: 2000–2010	
Group	%
Total Population	9.1
Hispanic or Latino (of any race)	109.5
Mexican	90.8
Puerto Rican	89.3

Males per 100 Females	
Group	Number
Total Population	94.6
Hispanic or Latino (of any race)	98.3
Central American, ex. Mexican	69.6
Mexican	104.5
Puerto Rican	110.3
South American	80.7

Average Household Size	
Group	People
Total Population	2.19
Hispanic or Latino (of any race)	2.24
Central American, ex. Mexican	2.73
Mexican	2.23
Puerto Rican	2.21
South American	2.15

Median Age	
Group	Years
Total Population	26.5
Hispanic or Latino (of any race)	22.1
Central American, ex. Mexican	21.7
Mexican	25.3
Puerto Rican	21.3
South American	22.2

High School Graduates (Universe: Population 25 Years and Over)		
Group	Number	%
Total Population	21,261	89.9
Hispanic or Latino (of any race)	324	85.3

Four-Year College Graduates (Universe: Population 25 Years and Over)		
Group	Number	%
Total Population	10,127	42.8
Hispanic or Latino (of any race)	168	44.2

Population Age 3–17 Enrolled in Public School (Universe: Population Age 3–17 Enrolled in School)		
Group	Number	%
Total Population	3,756	81.3
Hispanic or Latino (of any race)	84	94.4

Population Age 3–17 Enrolled in Private School (Universe: Population Age 3–17 Enrolled in School)		
Group	Number	%
Total Population	866	18.7
Hispanic or Latino (of any race)	5	5.6

Foreign-Born Population		
Group	Number	%
Total Population	3,686	8.8
Hispanic or Latino (of any race)	95	14.1

Foreign-Born Naturalized U.S. Citizens		
Group	Number	%
Total Population	1,877	50.9
Hispanic or Latino (of any race)	48	50.5

Language Spoken at Home: English Only (Universe: Population 5 Years and Over)		
Group	Number	%
Total Population	36,126	89.6
Hispanic or Latino (of any race)	332	52.2

Language Spoken at Home: Spanish (Universe: Population 5 Years and Over)		
Group	Number	%
Total Population	407	1.0
Hispanic or Latino (of any race)	238	37.4

Unemployment Rate (Universe: Population 16 Years and Over)	
Group	%
Total Population	8.0
Hispanic or Latino (of any race)	6.7

Class of Worker: Private Wage and Salary (Universe: Civilian Employed Population 16 Years and Over)		
Group	Number	%
Total Population	17,705	78.2
Hispanic or Latino (of any race)	180	56.4

Class of Worker: Government (Universe: Civilian Employed Population 16 Years and Over)		
Group	Number	%
Total Population	3,491	15.4
Hispanic or Latino (of any race)	87	27.3

Means of Transportation to Work: Car, Truck or Van (Universe: Workers 16 Years and Over)		
Group	Number	%
Total Population	14,476	66.0
Hispanic or Latino (of any race)	151	50.5

Means of Transportation to Work: Public Transportation (ex. Taxicab) (Universe: Workers 16 Years and Over)		
Group	Number	%
Total Population	1,014	4.6
Hispanic or Latino (of any race)	18	6.0

Notes: (1) Percent of total population; (2) Percent of Hispanic/Latino population; Profiles include places with an overall population of at least 125,000, OR an overall population of at least 25,000 where the Hispanic/Latino population is at least 20% of the overall population. In states where less than five places meet either of these criteria, we have included places with at least 10,000 total population with the highest percentage of Hispanic/Latino population. These places are identified with an asterisk (*); Please refer to the User's Guide for a full explanation of data.

STATE & PLACE PROFILES

Homeownership Rate
(Universe: Occupied Housing Units)

Group	%
Total Population	40.7
Hispanic or Latino (of any race)	21.0
Central American, ex. Mexican	18.2
Mexican	21.6
Puerto Rican	15.8
South American	25.5

Median Home Value

Group	Dollars
Total Population	253,300
Hispanic or Latino (of any race)	331,800

Median Gross Rent

Group	Dollars
Total Population	908
Hispanic or Latino (of any race)	868

Median Household Income
(2010 Inflation-Adjusted Dollars)

Group	Dollars
Total Population	39,185
Hispanic or Latino (of any race)	28,942

Per Capita Income
(2010 Inflation-Adjusted Dollars)

Group	Dollars
Total Population	24,025
Hispanic or Latino (of any race)	26,552

Households with $100,000+ Income

Group	Number	%
Total Population	2,281	13.5
Hispanic or Latino (of any race)	89	31.2

Households with Food Stamps/SNAP Benefits During Past 12 Months

Group	Number	%
Total Population	2,176	12.9
Hispanic or Latino (of any race)	62	21.8

Poverty Rate
(Income in Past 12 Months Below Poverty Level)

Group	%
Total Population	24.2
Hispanic or Latino (of any race)	29.6

Essex*

Population

Group	Number	%TP[1]	%HP[2]
Total Population	19,587	100.0	–
Hispanic or Latino (of any race)	335	1.7	100.0

Population Growth: 2000–2010

Group	%
Total Population	5.2
Hispanic or Latino (of any race)	112.0

Males per 100 Females

Group	Number
Total Population	95.2
Hispanic or Latino (of any race)	87.2

Average Household Size

Group	People
Total Population	2.48
Hispanic or Latino (of any race)	2.64

Median Age

Group	Years
Total Population	39.9
Hispanic or Latino (of any race)	27.1

High School Graduates
(Universe: Population 25 Years and Over)

Group	Number	%
Total Population	12,022	94.1

Four-Year College Graduates
(Universe: Population 25 Years and Over)

Group	Number	%
Total Population	5,795	45.4

Population Age 3–17 Enrolled in Public School
(Universe: Population Age 3–17 Enrolled in School)

Group	Number	%
Total Population	3,619	89.4

Population Age 3–17 Enrolled in Private School
(Universe: Population Age 3–17 Enrolled in School)

Group	Number	%
Total Population	427	10.6

Foreign-Born Population

Group	Number	%
Total Population	1,258	6.5

Foreign-Born Naturalized U.S. Citizens

Group	Number	%
Total Population	668	53.1

Language Spoken at Home: English Only
(Universe: Population 5 Years and Over)

Group	Number	%
Total Population	16,778	91.8

Language Spoken at Home: Spanish
(Universe: Population 5 Years and Over)

Group	Number	%
Total Population	63	0.3

Unemployment Rate
(Universe: Population 16 Years and Over)

Group	%
Total Population	4.0

Class of Worker: Private Wage and Salary
(Universe: Civilian Employed Population 16 Years and Over)

Group	Number	%
Total Population	8,866	79.8

Class of Worker: Government
(Universe: Civilian Employed Population 16 Years and Over)

Group	Number	%
Total Population	1,466	13.2

Means of Transportation to Work: Car, Truck or Van
(Universe: Workers 16 Years and Over)

Group	Number	%
Total Population	9,626	89.3

Means of Transportation to Work: Public Transportation (ex. Taxicab)
(Universe: Workers 16 Years and Over)

Group	Number	%
Total Population	227	2.1

Homeownership Rate
(Universe: Occupied Housing Units)

Group	%
Total Population	75.5
Hispanic or Latino (of any race)	57.0

Median Home Value

Group	Dollars
Total Population	254,900

Median Gross Rent

Group	Dollars
Total Population	1,001

Median Household Income
(2010 Inflation-Adjusted Dollars)

Group	Dollars
Total Population	69,512

Per Capita Income
(2010 Inflation-Adjusted Dollars)

Group	Dollars
Total Population	32,035

Households with $100,000+ Income

Group	Number	%
Total Population	2,038	27.3

Households with Food Stamps/SNAP Benefits During Past 12 Months

Group	Number	%
Total Population	424	5.7

Poverty Rate
(Income in Past 12 Months Below Poverty Level)

Group	%
Total Population	4.5

South Burlington*

Population

Group	Number	%TP[1]	%HP[2]
Total Population	17,904	100.0	–
Hispanic or Latino (of any race)	336	1.9	100.0

Population Growth: 2000–2010

Group	%
Total Population	13.2
Hispanic or Latino (of any race)	75.0

Males per 100 Females

Group	Number
Total Population	89.3
Hispanic or Latino (of any race)	88.8

Average Household Size

Group	People
Total Population	2.19
Hispanic or Latino (of any race)	2.52

Median Age

Group	Years
Total Population	40.6
Hispanic or Latino (of any race)	29.3

High School Graduates
(Universe: Population 25 Years and Over)

Group	Number	%
Total Population	11,334	93.2

Four-Year College Graduates
(Universe: Population 25 Years and Over)

Group	Number	%
Total Population	6,233	51.3

Population Age 3–17 Enrolled in Public School
(Universe: Population Age 3–17 Enrolled in School)

Group	Number	%
Total Population	2,363	88.4

Population Age 3–17 Enrolled in Private School
(Universe: Population Age 3–17 Enrolled in School)

Group	Number	%
Total Population	311	11.6

Foreign-Born Population

Group	Number	%
Total Population	1,636	9.4

Foreign-Born Naturalized U.S. Citizens

Group	Number	%
Total Population	803	49.1

Language Spoken at Home: English Only
(Universe: Population 5 Years and Over)

Group	Number	%
Total Population	14,514	88.0

Language Spoken at Home: Spanish
(Universe: Population 5 Years and Over)

Group	Number	%
Total Population	192	1.2

Unemployment Rate
(Universe: Population 16 Years and Over)

Group	%
Total Population	3.3

Notes: (1) Percent of total population; (2) Percent of Hispanic/Latino population; Profiles include places with an overall population of at least 125,000, OR an overall population of at least 25,000 where the Hispanic/Latino population is at least 20% of the overall population. In states where less than five places meet either of these criteria, we have included places with at least 10,000 total population with the highest percentage of Hispanic/Latino population. These places are identified with an asterisk (*); Please refer to the User's Guide for a full explanation of data.

Class of Worker: Private Wage and Salary (Universe: Civilian Employed Population 16 Years and Over)		
Group	Number	%
Total Population	8,252	82.7

Class of Worker: Government (Universe: Civilian Employed Population 16 Years and Over)		
Group	Number	%
Total Population	988	9.9

Means of Transportation to Work: Car, Truck or Van (Universe: Workers 16 Years and Over)		
Group	Number	%
Total Population	8,247	84.5

Means of Transportation to Work: Public Transportation (ex. Taxicab) (Universe: Workers 16 Years and Over)		
Group	Number	%
Total Population	293	3.0

Homeownership Rate (Universe: Occupied Housing Units)	
Group	%
Total Population	64.9
Hispanic or Latino (of any race)	56.9

Median Home Value	
Group	Dollars
Total Population	252,800

Median Gross Rent	
Group	Dollars
Total Population	1,064

Median Household Income (2010 Inflation-Adjusted Dollars)	
Group	Dollars
Total Population	61,007

Per Capita Income (2010 Inflation-Adjusted Dollars)	
Group	Dollars
Total Population	34,293

Households with $100,000+ Income		
Group	Number	%
Total Population	1,804	23.6

Households with Food Stamps/SNAP Benefits During Past 12 Months		
Group	Number	%
Total Population	508	6.7

Poverty Rate (Income in Past 12 Months Below Poverty Level)	
Group	%
Total Population	4.8

Notes: (1) Percent of total population; (2) Percent of Hispanic/Latino population; Profiles include places with an overall population of at least 125,000, OR an overall population of at least 25,000 where the Hispanic/Latino population is at least 20% of the overall population. In states where less than five places meet either of these criteria, we have included places with at least 10,000 total population with the highest percentage of Hispanic/Latino population. These places are identified with an asterisk (*); Please refer to the User's Guide for a full explanation of data.

Virginia

EDITOR'S NOTE: For a place to be included in this edition, it must meet one of two criteria. Either its overall population is at least 125,000, OR its overall population is at least 25,000 and its Hispanic/Latino population is at least 20% of the overall population. For the state of Virginia, the following locations are included:

- Alexandria
- Annandale
- Arlington
- Chesapeake
- Dale City
- Hampton
- Manassas
- Marumsco
- Newport News
- Norfolk
- Richmond
- Springfield
- Sterling
- Virginia Beach
- West Falls Church

Section Two: State & Place Profiles starts with the state profile, followed by place profiles that meet the criteria above. Places are listed alphabetically within each state. All states, all counties and places that meet the above criteria are ranked and compared in *Section Three: Rankings & Comparisons*, on page 1055.

For a more detailed look at the Hispanic/Latino population in Virginia, a companion web site is available at no additional charge with purchase of this print edition. Visit http://gold.greyhouse.com/page/info_hispanic for more information.

The web site includes data for all counties and places in Virginia with Hispanic/Latino population, plus ten additional topics: Self Employed Worker; Walked to Work; Worked from Home; Mean Travel Time to Work; Mean Household Income; Households with Cash Public Assistance; Mean Cash Pubic Assistance; Poverty Rates for 18 and Under, 18 to 64, and 65 and Over.

Population

Group	Number	%TP[1]	%HP[2]
Total Population	8,001,024	100.0	–
Hispanic or Latino (of any race)	631,825	7.9	100.0
Central American, ex. Mexican	206,568	2.6	32.7
Costa Rican	2,630	<0.1	0.4
Guatemalan	33,556	0.4	5.3
Honduran	30,583	0.4	4.8
Nicaraguan	7,388	0.1	1.2
Panamanian	7,180	0.1	1.1
Salvadoran	123,800	1.5	19.6
Cuban	15,229	0.2	2.4
Dominican Republic	10,504	0.1	1.7
Mexican	155,067	1.9	24.5
Puerto Rican	73,958	0.9	11.7
South American	101,480	1.3	16.1
Argentinean	6,263	0.1	1.0
Bolivian	31,333	0.4	5.0
Chilean	4,195	0.1	0.7
Colombian	15,797	0.2	2.5
Ecuadorian	6,902	0.1	1.1
Paraguayan	924	<0.1	0.1
Peruvian	29,096	0.4	4.6
Uruguayan	1,594	<0.1	0.3
Venezuelan	4,429	0.1	0.7
Spaniard	11,041	0.1	1.7

Population Growth: 2000–2010

Group	%
Total Population	13.0
Hispanic or Latino (of any race)	91.7
Central American, ex. Mexican	182.4
Costa Rican	137.8
Guatemalan	235.6
Honduran	291.1
Nicaraguan	131.5
Panamanian	103.1
Salvadoran	183.6
Cuban	82.8
Dominican Republic	200.4
Mexican	109.6
Puerto Rican	79.8
South American	154.7
Argentinean	201.4
Bolivian	177.9
Chilean	105.6
Colombian	163.6
Ecuadorian	178.0
Paraguayan	154.5
Peruvian	176.4
Uruguayan	230.7
Venezuelan	121.9
Spaniard	459.0

Males per 100 Females

Group	Number
Total Population	96.3
Hispanic or Latino (of any race)	108.6
Central American, ex. Mexican	116.5
Costa Rican	95.0
Guatemalan	147.6
Honduran	134.2
Nicaraguan	89.0
Panamanian	66.0
Salvadoran	111.4
Cuban	96.8
Dominican Republic	92.1
Mexican	121.8
Puerto Rican	96.3
South American	90.7
Argentinean	95.1
Bolivian	102.1
Chilean	85.9
Colombian	79.0
Ecuadorian	87.0
Paraguayan	72.7
Peruvian	88.5
Uruguayan	98.5
Venezuelan	78.7
Spaniard	90.0

Average Household Size

Group	People
Total Population	2.54
Hispanic or Latino (of any race)	3.63
Central American, ex. Mexican	4.40
Costa Rican	2.92
Guatemalan	4.38
Honduran	4.53
Nicaraguan	3.62
Panamanian	2.73
Salvadoran	4.61
Cuban	2.70
Dominican Republic	3.10
Mexican	3.62
Puerto Rican	2.85
South American	3.46
Argentinean	3.09
Bolivian	4.04
Chilean	2.91
Colombian	2.92
Ecuadorian	3.08
Paraguayan	2.99
Peruvian	3.60
Uruguayan	2.90
Venezuelan	2.89
Spaniard	2.67

Median Age

Group	Years
Total Population	37.5
Hispanic or Latino (of any race)	27.3
Central American, ex. Mexican	28.5
Costa Rican	30.4
Guatemalan	27.7
Honduran	28.5
Nicaraguan	31.3
Panamanian	32.2
Salvadoran	28.5
Cuban	30.0
Dominican Republic	26.0
Mexican	24.5
Puerto Rican	25.9
South American	33.5
Argentinean	33.4
Bolivian	32.8
Chilean	35.8
Colombian	32.1
Ecuadorian	32.4
Paraguayan	31.0
Peruvian	35.2
Uruguayan	35.4
Venezuelan	32.8
Spaniard	32.6

High School Graduates

(Universe: Population 25 Years and Over)

Group	Number	%
Total Population	4,483,473	86.1
Hispanic or Latino (of any race)	214,173	68.1
Central American, ex. Mexican	52,408	48.1
Costa Rican	1,026	82.7
Guatemalan	7,402	43.5
Honduran	7,579	49.2
Nicaraguan	3,530	76.1
Panamanian	4,521	94.1
Salvadoran	27,426	42.8
Cuban	7,544	94.1
Dominican Republic	3,859	86.1
Mexican	45,031	62.0
Puerto Rican	31,106	89.1
South American	57,558	88.3
Argentinean	3,204	89.9
Bolivian	18,545	84.4
Chilean	2,393	96.3
Colombian	8,222	88.7
Ecuadorian	3,430	89.2
Peruvian	16,611	90.4
Uruguayan	940	78.4
Venezuelan	2,922	94.0
Spaniard	4,709	91.3

Four-Year College Graduates

(Universe: Population 25 Years and Over)

Group	Number	%
Total Population	1,761,162	33.8
Hispanic or Latino (of any race)	71,415	22.7
Central American, ex. Mexican	12,048	11.1
Costa Rican	532	42.9
Guatemalan	1,305	7.7
Honduran	2,062	13.4
Nicaraguan	819	17.7
Panamanian	1,679	34.9
Salvadoran	5,452	8.5
Cuban	3,627	45.2
Dominican Republic	1,251	27.9
Mexican	13,413	18.5
Puerto Rican	11,246	32.2
South American	23,094	35.4
Argentinean	1,669	46.8
Bolivian	5,567	25.3
Chilean	1,006	40.5
Colombian	4,051	43.7
Ecuadorian	1,612	41.9
Peruvian	6,815	37.1
Uruguayan	266	22.2
Venezuelan	1,553	50.0
Spaniard	2,652	51.4

Notes: (1) Percent of total population; (2) Percent of Hispanic/Latino population; Profiles include places with an overall population of at least 125,000, OR an overall population of at least 25,000 where the Hispanic/Latino population is at least 20% of the overall population. In states where less than five places meet either of these criteria, we have included places with at least 10,000 total population with the highest percentage of Hispanic/Latino population. These places are identified with an asterisk (*); Please refer to the User's Guide for a full explanation of data.

Population Age 3–17 Enrolled in Public School
(Universe: Population Age 3–17 Enrolled in School)

Group	Number	%
Total Population	1,186,616	85.4
Hispanic or Latino (of any race)	111,587	90.2
Central American, ex. Mexican	32,218	93.2
Costa Rican	344	78.4
Guatemalan	3,781	89.0
Honduran	3,795	96.7
Nicaraguan	1,472	91.7
Panamanian	1,156	89.9
Salvadoran	21,099	94.3
Cuban	2,434	77.1
Dominican Republic	1,735	86.3
Mexican	32,131	91.3
Puerto Rican	16,933	90.7
South American	17,365	86.7
Argentinean	902	79.5
Bolivian	6,170	91.8
Chilean	546	78.1
Colombian	2,218	84.0
Ecuadorian	1,239	73.8
Peruvian	4,825	88.2
Uruguayan	336	81.4
Venezuelan	698	87.3
Spaniard	1,075	85.2

Population Age 3–17 Enrolled in Private School
(Universe: Population Age 3–17 Enrolled in School)

Group	Number	%
Total Population	203,166	14.6
Hispanic or Latino (of any race)	12,096	9.8
Central American, ex. Mexican	2,353	6.8
Costa Rican	95	21.6
Guatemalan	468	11.0
Honduran	129	3.3
Nicaraguan	134	8.3
Panamanian	130	10.1
Salvadoran	1,281	5.7
Cuban	724	22.9
Dominican Republic	276	13.7
Mexican	3,063	8.7
Puerto Rican	1,727	9.3
South American	2,661	13.3
Argentinean	233	20.5
Bolivian	549	8.2
Chilean	153	21.9
Colombian	421	16.0
Ecuadorian	441	26.3
Peruvian	643	11.8
Uruguayan	77	18.6
Venezuelan	102	12.8
Spaniard	186	14.8

Foreign-Born Population

Group	Number	%
Total Population	848,087	10.8
Hispanic or Latino (of any race)	285,218	49.6
Central American, ex. Mexican	128,165	67.1
Costa Rican	1,125	53.4
Guatemalan	22,329	72.9
Honduran	19,410	72.6
Nicaraguan	5,109	64.5
Panamanian	3,331	45.0
Salvadoran	74,959	66.1
Cuban	4,570	31.2
Dominican Republic	3,669	40.8
Mexican	61,888	42.2
Puerto Rican	1,040	1.5
South American	73,584	70.4
Argentinean	3,691	65.2
Bolivian	26,612	73.9
Chilean	2,543	66.0
Colombian	9,855	66.5
Ecuadorian	3,454	53.8
Peruvian	20,949	73.4
Uruguayan	1,287	61.4
Venezuelan	3,550	72.9
Spaniard	1,949	24.1

Foreign-Born Naturalized U.S. Citizens

Group	Number	%
Total Population	375,650	44.3
Hispanic or Latino (of any race)	70,616	24.8
Central American, ex. Mexican	26,541	20.7
Costa Rican	460	40.9
Guatemalan	3,847	17.2
Honduran	2,564	13.2
Nicaraguan	2,057	40.3
Panamanian	2,268	68.1
Salvadoran	14,663	19.6
Cuban	2,727	59.7
Dominican Republic	2,032	55.4
Mexican	7,825	12.6
Puerto Rican	551	53.0
South American	25,303	34.4
Argentinean	1,167	31.6
Bolivian	7,448	28.0
Chilean	1,111	43.7
Colombian	4,147	42.1
Ecuadorian	1,955	56.6
Peruvian	7,301	34.9
Uruguayan	430	33.4
Venezuelan	945	26.6
Spaniard	1,018	52.2

Language Spoken at Home: English Only
(Universe: Population 5 Years and Over)

Group	Number	%
Total Population	6,299,127	85.9
Hispanic or Latino (of any race)	116,275	22.7
Central American, ex. Mexican	13,467	7.9
Costa Rican	546	29.7
Guatemalan	2,565	9.4
Honduran	1,424	6.0
Nicaraguan	719	10.0
Panamanian	2,938	42.4
Salvadoran	5,152	5.1
Cuban	5,908	45.7
Dominican Republic	2,537	30.8
Mexican	40,020	31.4
Puerto Rican	29,130	46.9
South American	10,890	11.4
Argentinean	855	16.8
Bolivian	1,742	5.3
Chilean	901	24.2
Colombian	2,410	17.7
Ecuadorian	1,243	21.0
Peruvian	2,421	9.2
Uruguayan	364	19.6
Venezuelan	565	12.5
Spaniard	4,701	63.4

Language Spoken at Home: Spanish
(Universe: Population 5 Years and Over)

Group	Number	%
Total Population	469,303	6.4
Hispanic or Latino (of any race)	391,398	76.6
Central American, ex. Mexican	156,212	91.9
Costa Rican	1,295	70.3
Guatemalan	24,481	90.1
Honduran	22,116	93.9
Nicaraguan	6,434	89.4
Panamanian	3,958	57.1
Salvadoran	95,619	94.8
Cuban	6,912	53.5
Dominican Republic	5,628	68.3
Mexican	86,475	67.8
Puerto Rican	32,560	52.4
South American	84,293	87.9
Argentinean	4,203	82.5
Bolivian	30,750	94.0
Chilean	2,684	72.0
Colombian	11,115	81.8
Ecuadorian	4,650	78.5
Peruvian	23,741	90.4
Uruguayan	1,456	78.5
Venezuelan	3,964	87.5
Spaniard	2,468	33.3

Unemployment Rate
(Universe: Population 16 Years and Over)

Group	%
Total Population	5.9
Hispanic or Latino (of any race)	7.0
Central American, ex. Mexican	8.1
Costa Rican	17.3
Guatemalan	9.0
Honduran	9.0
Nicaraguan	9.1
Panamanian	3.9
Salvadoran	7.8
Cuban	4.4
Dominican Republic	10.5
Mexican	6.7
Puerto Rican	7.1
South American	5.6
Argentinean	3.1
Bolivian	6.1
Chilean	6.9
Colombian	4.9
Ecuadorian	4.9
Peruvian	5.1
Uruguayan	5.9
Venezuelan	10.1
Spaniard	4.1

Class of Worker: Private Wage and Salary
(Universe: Civilian Employed Population 16 Years and Over)

Group	Number	%
Total Population	2,837,211	74.2
Hispanic or Latino (of any race)	233,284	82.0
Central American, ex. Mexican	91,253	87.9
Costa Rican	791	79.4
Guatemalan	15,364	90.0
Honduran	13,921	91.9
Nicaraguan	3,456	76.6
Panamanian	2,654	68.4
Salvadoran	54,279	88.7
Cuban	5,485	77.7
Dominican Republic	2,893	69.0
Mexican	53,524	83.3
Puerto Rican	21,274	69.9
South American	46,515	80.3
Argentinean	2,155	74.6
Bolivian	16,745	82.2
Chilean	1,487	70.3
Colombian	6,638	81.5
Ecuadorian	2,298	77.7
Peruvian	13,063	80.0
Uruguayan	949	88.0
Venezuelan	2,099	76.9
Spaniard	3,266	71.2

Class of Worker: Government
(Universe: Civilian Employed Population 16 Years and Over)

Group	Number	%
Total Population	784,595	20.5
Hispanic or Latino (of any race)	34,166	12.0
Central American, ex. Mexican	6,435	6.2
Costa Rican	109	10.9
Guatemalan	757	4.4
Honduran	457	3.0
Nicaraguan	656	14.5
Panamanian	1,129	29.1
Salvadoran	3,225	5.3
Cuban	1,094	15.5
Dominican Republic	964	23.0
Mexican	7,633	11.9
Puerto Rican	8,306	27.3
South American	6,452	11.1
Argentinean	548	19.0
Bolivian	1,523	7.5
Chilean	360	17.0
Colombian	1,101	13.5
Ecuadorian	466	15.8
Peruvian	1,842	11.3
Uruguayan	104	9.6
Venezuelan	362	13.3
Spaniard	969	21.1

Means of Transportation to Work: Car, Truck or Van
(Universe: Workers 16 Years and Over)

Group	Number	%
Total Population	3,381,246	87.8
Hispanic or Latino (of any race)	240,926	83.4
Central American, ex. Mexican	83,657	81.7
Costa Rican	871	83.6
Guatemalan	12,898	76.6
Honduran	11,270	75.2
Nicaraguan	3,876	86.1
Panamanian	3,293	87.2
Salvadoran	50,551	83.8
Cuban	6,487	88.1

Notes: (1) Percent of total population; (2) Percent of Hispanic/Latino population; Profiles include places with an overall population of at least 125,000, OR an overall population of at least 25,000 where the Hispanic/Latino population is at least 20% of the overall population. In states where less than five places meet either of these criteria, we have included places with at least 10,000 total population with the highest percentage of Hispanic/Latino population. These places are identified with an asterisk (*); Please refer to the User's Guide for a full explanation of data.

Group	Number	%
Dominican Republic	4,009	86.5
Mexican	56,593	83.0
Puerto Rican	27,729	85.5
South American	47,995	84.4
Argentinean	2,143	76.0
Bolivian	16,794	85.1
Chilean	1,790	85.3
Colombian	6,936	84.1
Ecuadorian	2,520	84.4
Peruvian	13,451	83.9
Uruguayan	894	84.7
Venezuelan	2,339	90.6
Spaniard	3,975	83.9

Means of Transportation to Work: Public Transportation (ex. Taxicab)

(Universe: Workers 16 Years and Over)

Group	Number	%
Total Population	164,107	4.3
Hispanic or Latino (of any race)	22,388	7.7
Central American, ex. Mexican	10,301	10.1
Costa Rican	31	3.0
Guatemalan	2,404	14.3
Honduran	2,042	13.6
Nicaraguan	262	5.8
Panamanian	258	6.8
Salvadoran	5,236	8.7
Cuban	314	4.3
Dominican Republic	174	3.8
Mexican	3,462	5.1
Puerto Rican	2,316	7.1
South American	4,796	8.4
Argentinean	317	11.2
Bolivian	1,639	8.3
Chilean	180	8.6
Colombian	639	7.7
Ecuadorian	223	7.5
Peruvian	1,528	9.5
Uruguayan	26	2.5
Venezuelan	161	6.2
Spaniard	304	6.4

Homeownership Rate

(Universe: Occupied Housing Units)

Group	%
Total Population	67.2
Hispanic or Latino (of any race)	46.4
Central American, ex. Mexican	41.8
Costa Rican	46.4
Guatemalan	34.0
Honduran	27.5
Nicaraguan	48.0
Panamanian	54.5
Salvadoran	45.5
Cuban	57.9
Dominican Republic	41.7
Mexican	41.4
Puerto Rican	49.3
South American	55.0
Argentinean	57.8
Bolivian	54.3
Chilean	60.9
Colombian	55.1
Ecuadorian	62.1
Paraguayan	54.3
Peruvian	53.0
Uruguayan	51.1
Venezuelan	54.4
Spaniard	65.4

Median Home Value

Group	Dollars
Total Population	255,100
Hispanic or Latino (of any race)	325,800
Central American, ex. Mexican	326,300
Costa Rican	408,900
Guatemalan	334,300
Honduran	312,400
Nicaraguan	364,800
Panamanian	288,900
Salvadoran	324,300
Cuban	381,000
Dominican Republic	265,500
Mexican	262,800
Puerto Rican	285,100
South American	381,800
Argentinean	453,400
Bolivian	418,400
Chilean	399,700
Colombian	333,000
Ecuadorian	381,600
Peruvian	372,300
Uruguayan	325,200
Venezuelan	309,500
Spaniard	344,100

Median Gross Rent

Group	Dollars
Total Population	970
Hispanic or Latino (of any race)	1,152
Central American, ex. Mexican	1,206
Costa Rican	1,308
Guatemalan	1,141
Honduran	1,223
Nicaraguan	1,264
Panamanian	1,060
Salvadoran	1,225
Cuban	955
Dominican Republic	962
Mexican	972
Puerto Rican	1,063
South American	1,400
Argentinean	1,387
Bolivian	1,496
Chilean	1,405
Colombian	1,310
Ecuadorian	1,169
Peruvian	1,434
Uruguayan	1,008
Venezuelan	1,190
Spaniard	1,219

Median Household Income

(2010 Inflation-Adjusted Dollars)

Group	Dollars
Total Population	61,406
Hispanic or Latino (of any race)	57,793
Central American, ex. Mexican	54,930
Costa Rican	75,563
Guatemalan	46,597
Honduran	51,250
Nicaraguan	61,956
Panamanian	58,877
Salvadoran	55,585
Cuban	71,116
Dominican Republic	55,836
Mexican	50,811
Puerto Rican	61,449
South American	66,410
Argentinean	74,618
Bolivian	67,843
Chilean	74,167
Colombian	73,520
Ecuadorian	59,479
Peruvian	62,451
Uruguayan	53,906
Venezuelan	57,450
Spaniard	81,370

Per Capita Income

(2010 Inflation-Adjusted Dollars)

Group	Dollars
Total Population	32,145
Hispanic or Latino (of any race)	20,949
Central American, ex. Mexican	17,785
Costa Rican	23,031
Guatemalan	16,240
Honduran	15,971
Nicaraguan	23,757
Panamanian	28,368
Salvadoran	17,364
Cuban	36,015
Dominican Republic	21,967
Mexican	18,280
Puerto Rican	24,140
South American	24,354
Argentinean	31,477
Bolivian	21,401
Chilean	27,103
Colombian	27,687
Ecuadorian	25,717
Peruvian	23,740
Uruguayan	19,123
Venezuelan	25,100
Spaniard	40,112

Households with $100,000+ Income

Group	Number	%
Total Population	821,409	27.6
Hispanic or Latino (of any race)	35,206	23.3
Central American, ex. Mexican	8,640	18.9
Costa Rican	280	42.7
Guatemalan	1,092	16.1
Honduran	957	15.1
Nicaraguan	489	24.1
Panamanian	711	29.6
Salvadoran	4,916	18.2
Cuban	1,730	36.7
Dominican Republic	627	25.3
Mexican	7,049	19.5
Puerto Rican	5,231	25.1
South American	8,549	28.5
Argentinean	638	33.2
Bolivian	2,619	28.2
Chilean	495	35.9
Colombian	1,499	33.9
Ecuadorian	559	32.3
Peruvian	2,008	24.2
Uruguayan	161	28.4
Venezuelan	381	22.3
Spaniard	1,236	40.2

Households with Food Stamps/SNAP Benefits During Past 12 Months

Group	Number	%
Total Population	205,190	6.9
Hispanic or Latino (of any race)	9,132	6.1
Central American, ex. Mexican	3,198	7.0
Costa Rican	0	0.0
Guatemalan	564	8.3
Honduran	390	6.1
Nicaraguan	201	9.9
Panamanian	125	5.2
Salvadoran	1,864	6.9
Cuban	242	5.1
Dominican Republic	188	7.6
Mexican	2,488	6.9
Puerto Rican	1,784	8.6
South American	851	2.8
Argentinean	12	0.6
Bolivian	204	2.2
Chilean	26	1.9
Colombian	107	2.4
Ecuadorian	136	7.9
Peruvian	246	3.0
Uruguayan	92	16.3
Venezuelan	28	1.6
Spaniard	39	1.3

Poverty Rate

(Income in Past 12 Months Below Poverty Level)

Group	%
Total Population	10.3
Hispanic or Latino (of any race)	13.9
Central American, ex. Mexican	15.4
Costa Rican	5.9
Guatemalan	21.0
Honduran	18.7
Nicaraguan	5.3
Panamanian	7.5
Salvadoran	14.5
Cuban	7.7
Dominican Republic	12.9
Mexican	19.4
Puerto Rican	12.4
South American	8.0
Argentinean	8.1
Bolivian	7.1
Chilean	8.3
Colombian	8.2
Ecuadorian	4.2
Peruvian	8.8
Uruguayan	12.3
Venezuelan	12.6
Spaniard	4.5

Notes: (1) Percent of total population; (2) Percent of Hispanic/Latino population; Profiles include places with an overall population of at least 125,000, OR an overall population of at least 25,000 where the Hispanic/Latino population is at least 20% of the overall population. In states where less than five places meet either of these criteria, we have included places with at least 10,000 total population with the highest percentage of Hispanic/Latino population. These places are identified with an asterisk (*); Please refer to the User's Guide for a full explanation of data.

Alexandria

Population

Group	Number	%TP[1]	%HP[2]
Total Population	139,966	100.0	–
Hispanic or Latino (of any race)	22,524	16.1	100.0
Central American, ex. Mexican	10,963	7.8	48.7
Guatemalan	1,587	1.1	7.0
Honduran	2,243	1.6	10.0
Nicaraguan	368	0.3	1.6
Panamanian	203	0.1	0.9
Salvadoran	6,436	4.6	28.6
Cuban	399	0.3	1.8
Dominican Republic	302	0.2	1.3
Mexican	2,352	1.7	10.4
Puerto Rican	1,603	1.1	7.1
South American	4,202	3.0	18.7
Argentinean	303	0.2	1.3
Bolivian	1,227	0.9	5.4
Chilean	274	0.2	1.2
Colombian	599	0.4	2.7
Ecuadorian	280	0.2	1.2
Peruvian	1,174	0.8	5.2
Venezuelan	229	0.2	1.0
Spaniard	378	0.3	1.7

Population Growth: 2000–2010

Group	%
Total Population	9.1
Hispanic or Latino (of any race)	19.3
Central American, ex. Mexican	51.4
Guatemalan	146.4
Honduran	69.2
Nicaraguan	53.3
Panamanian	84.5
Salvadoran	43.8
Cuban	42.5
Dominican Republic	81.9
Mexican	28.6
Puerto Rican	43.6
South American	80.7
Bolivian	101.5
Chilean	37.7
Colombian	83.7
Ecuadorian	85.4
Peruvian	81.7
Venezuelan	77.5
Spaniard	274.3

Males per 100 Females

Group	Number
Total Population	92.5
Hispanic or Latino (of any race)	105.5
Central American, ex. Mexican	118.7
Guatemalan	168.1
Honduran	125.0
Nicaraguan	91.7
Panamanian	61.1
Salvadoran	111.3
Cuban	83.0
Dominican Republic	94.8
Mexican	101.7
Puerto Rican	92.9
South American	84.6
Argentinean	95.5
Bolivian	86.8
Chilean	103.0
Colombian	76.2
Ecuadorian	97.2
Peruvian	82.6
Venezuelan	63.6
Spaniard	88.1

Average Household Size

Group	People
Total Population	2.03
Hispanic or Latino (of any race)	3.03
Central American, ex. Mexican	3.92
Guatemalan	4.00
Honduran	4.19
Nicaraguan	3.16
Panamanian	2.02
Salvadoran	4.02
Cuban	1.96
Dominican Republic	2.25
Mexican	2.46
Puerto Rican	1.90
South American	2.64
Argentinean	2.27
Bolivian	3.12
Chilean	2.59
Colombian	2.17
Ecuadorian	2.17
Peruvian	2.85
Venezuelan	2.18
Spaniard	2.03

Median Age

Group	Years
Total Population	35.6
Hispanic or Latino (of any race)	30.0
Central American, ex. Mexican	29.2
Guatemalan	28.1
Honduran	29.4
Nicaraguan	31.5
Panamanian	33.9
Salvadoran	29.2
Cuban	33.6
Dominican Republic	29.0
Mexican	29.4
Puerto Rican	32.3
South American	35.2
Argentinean	36.1
Bolivian	35.3
Chilean	36.2
Colombian	34.4
Ecuadorian	34.2
Peruvian	35.5
Venezuelan	34.6
Spaniard	33.8

High School Graduates
(Universe: Population 25 Years and Over)

Group	Number	%
Total Population	91,856	90.9
Hispanic or Latino (of any race)	8,239	64.8
Central American, ex. Mexican	2,238	38.8
Salvadoran	1,401	34.5
Mexican	1,729	83.6
Puerto Rican	1,344	95.4
South American	2,149	84.4
Peruvian	667	91.7

Four-Year College Graduates
(Universe: Population 25 Years and Over)

Group	Number	%
Total Population	60,977	60.4
Hispanic or Latino (of any race)	3,869	30.5
Central American, ex. Mexican	550	9.5
Salvadoran	321	7.9
Mexican	1,018	49.3
Puerto Rican	853	60.5
South American	961	37.8
Peruvian	331	45.5

Population Age 3–17 Enrolled in Public School
(Universe: Population Age 3–17 Enrolled in School)

Group	Number	%
Total Population	10,773	77.4
Hispanic or Latino (of any race)	2,555	92.8
Central American, ex. Mexican	1,449	94.3
Salvadoran	1,027	94.5
Mexican	188	88.7
Puerto Rican	197	100.0
South American	289	96.3
Peruvian	73	86.9

Population Age 3–17 Enrolled in Private School
(Universe: Population Age 3–17 Enrolled in School)

Group	Number	%
Total Population	3,151	22.6
Hispanic or Latino (of any race)	198	7.2
Central American, ex. Mexican	88	5.7
Salvadoran	60	5.5
Mexican	24	11.3
Puerto Rican	0	0.0
South American	11	3.7
Peruvian	11	13.1

Foreign-Born Population

Group	Number	%
Total Population	32,101	24.0
Hispanic or Latino (of any race)	11,006	54.9
Central American, ex. Mexican	6,886	68.3
Salvadoran	4,695	69.7
Mexican	1,132	40.1
Puerto Rican	21	1.0
South American	2,440	72.9
Peruvian	716	81.6

Foreign-Born Naturalized U.S. Citizens

Group	Number	%
Total Population	11,600	36.1
Hispanic or Latino (of any race)	2,068	18.8
Central American, ex. Mexican	820	11.9
Salvadoran	493	10.5
Mexican	141	12.5
Puerto Rican	0	0.0
South American	814	33.4
Peruvian	257	35.9

Language Spoken at Home: English Only
(Universe: Population 5 Years and Over)

Group	Number	%
Total Population	88,143	71.0
Hispanic or Latino (of any race)	3,019	16.8
Central American, ex. Mexican	309	3.5
Salvadoran	99	1.7
Mexican	1,141	43.8
Puerto Rican	667	37.2
South American	247	8.0
Peruvian	73	8.4

Language Spoken at Home: Spanish
(Universe: Population 5 Years and Over)

Group	Number	%
Total Population	16,156	13.0
Hispanic or Latino (of any race)	14,746	82.0
Central American, ex. Mexican	8,507	95.7
Salvadoran	5,811	97.1
Mexican	1,462	56.2
Puerto Rican	1,111	62.0
South American	2,791	90.5
Peruvian	775	89.6

Unemployment Rate
(Universe: Population 16 Years and Over)

Group	%
Total Population	3.9
Hispanic or Latino (of any race)	6.6
Central American, ex. Mexican	8.4
Salvadoran	7.8
Mexican	1.7
Puerto Rican	10.6
South American	5.5
Peruvian	2.2

Class of Worker: Private Wage and Salary
(Universe: Civilian Employed Population 16 Years and Over)

Group	Number	%
Total Population	59,128	70.9
Hispanic or Latino (of any race)	9,607	80.6
Central American, ex. Mexican	5,230	92.0
Salvadoran	3,575	91.2
Mexican	1,398	71.2
Puerto Rican	637	49.0
South American	1,824	82.1
Peruvian	481	78.5

Class of Worker: Government
(Universe: Civilian Employed Population 16 Years and Over)

Group	Number	%
Total Population	20,637	24.8
Hispanic or Latino (of any race)	1,852	15.5
Central American, ex. Mexican	261	4.6
Salvadoran	199	5.1
Mexican	461	23.5
Puerto Rican	662	51.0
South American	326	14.7
Peruvian	95	15.5

Notes: (1) Percent of total population; (2) Percent of Hispanic/Latino population; Profiles include places with an overall population of at least 125,000, OR an overall population of at least 25,000 where the Hispanic/Latino population is at least 20% of the overall population. In states where less than five places meet either of these criteria, we have included places with at least 10,000 total population with the highest percentage of Hispanic/Latino population. These places are identified with an asterisk (*); Please refer to the User's Guide for a full explanation of data.

Means of Transportation to Work: Car, Truck or Van
(Universe: Workers 16 Years and Over)

Group	Number	%
Total Population	58,087	69.2
Hispanic or Latino (of any race)	7,252	60.6
Central American, ex. Mexican	3,450	61.5
Salvadoran	2,485	64.4
Mexican	1,088	53.2
Puerto Rican	707	55.1
South American	1,387	62.4
Peruvian	439	71.6

Means of Transportation to Work: Public Transportation (ex. Taxicab)
(Universe: Workers 16 Years and Over)

Group	Number	%
Total Population	18,703	22.3
Hispanic or Latino (of any race)	3,710	31.0
Central American, ex. Mexican	1,695	30.2
Salvadoran	996	25.8
Mexican	691	33.8
Puerto Rican	471	36.7
South American	698	31.4
Peruvian	154	25.1

Homeownership Rate
(Universe: Occupied Housing Units)

Group	%
Total Population	43.3
Hispanic or Latino (of any race)	25.0
Central American, ex. Mexican	15.8
Guatemalan	13.6
Honduran	8.5
Nicaraguan	23.8
Panamanian	33.3
Salvadoran	17.0
Cuban	42.1
Dominican Republic	16.3
Mexican	31.3
Puerto Rican	29.6
South American	33.7
Argentinean	39.7
Bolivian	32.5
Chilean	30.5
Colombian	36.0
Ecuadorian	38.9
Peruvian	31.3
Venezuelan	29.6
Spaniard	45.9

Median Home Value

Group	Dollars
Total Population	486,800
Hispanic or Latino (of any race)	353,400
Central American, ex. Mexican	331,200
Salvadoran	337,800
Mexican	369,900
Puerto Rican	406,100
South American	302,800
Peruvian	265,300

Median Gross Rent

Group	Dollars
Total Population	1,330
Hispanic or Latino (of any race)	1,252
Central American, ex. Mexican	1,195
Salvadoran	1,166
Mexican	1,357
Puerto Rican	1,315
South American	1,311
Peruvian	1,281

Median Household Income
(2010 Inflation-Adjusted Dollars)

Group	Dollars
Total Population	80,847
Hispanic or Latino (of any race)	57,795
Central American, ex. Mexican	50,083
Salvadoran	50,413
Mexican	81,250
Puerto Rican	101,394
South American	54,497
Peruvian	54,420

Per Capita Income
(2010 Inflation-Adjusted Dollars)

Group	Dollars
Total Population	54,345
Hispanic or Latino (of any race)	26,134
Central American, ex. Mexican	16,646
Salvadoran	15,843
Mexican	45,466
Puerto Rican	40,030
South American	27,527
Peruvian	26,303

Households with $100,000+ Income

Group	Number	%
Total Population	25,265	39.6
Hispanic or Latino (of any race)	1,520	22.6
Central American, ex. Mexican	257	10.1
Salvadoran	155	8.6
Mexican	411	38.4
Puerto Rican	466	53.3
South American	214	14.1
Peruvian	45	12.4

Households with Food Stamps/SNAP Benefits During Past 12 Months

Group	Number	%
Total Population	2,120	3.3
Hispanic or Latino (of any race)	319	4.7
Central American, ex. Mexican	158	6.2
Salvadoran	54	3.0
Mexican	28	2.6
Puerto Rican	43	4.9
South American	56	3.7
Peruvian	11	3.0

Poverty Rate
(Income in Past 12 Months Below Poverty Level)

Group	%
Total Population	7.8
Hispanic or Latino (of any race)	12.8
Central American, ex. Mexican	18.4
Salvadoran	16.8
Mexican	5.9
Puerto Rican	3.2
South American	5.9
Peruvian	9.1

Annandale

Population

Group	Number	%TP[1]	%HP[2]
Total Population	41,008	100.0	–
Hispanic or Latino (of any race)	11,326	27.6	100.0
Central American, ex. Mexican	4,487	10.9	39.6
Guatemalan	736	1.8	6.5
Honduran	611	1.5	5.4
Nicaraguan	262	0.6	2.3
Salvadoran	2,770	6.8	24.5
Cuban	123	0.3	1.1
Dominican Republic	107	0.3	0.9
Mexican	626	1.5	5.5
Puerto Rican	338	0.8	3.0
South American	4,473	10.9	39.5
Argentinean	313	0.8	2.8
Bolivian	2,740	6.7	24.2
Colombian	196	0.5	1.7
Ecuadorian	118	0.3	1.0
Peruvian	917	2.2	8.1

Population Growth: 2000–2010

Group	%
Total Population	-25.4
Hispanic or Latino (of any race)	42.2
Central American, ex. Mexican	119.0
Guatemalan	273.6
Honduran	362.9
Nicaraguan	123.9
Salvadoran	96.9
Cuban	-38.2
Mexican	6.8
Puerto Rican	-3.4
South American	108.1
Bolivian	184.8
Colombian	37.1
Peruvian	68.3

Males per 100 Females

Group	Number
Total Population	97.7
Hispanic or Latino (of any race)	107.4
Central American, ex. Mexican	120.0
Guatemalan	169.6
Honduran	164.5
Nicaraguan	72.4
Salvadoran	108.6
Cuban	112.1
Dominican Republic	62.1
Mexican	105.2
Puerto Rican	101.2
South American	97.0
Argentinean	101.9
Bolivian	103.6
Colombian	79.8
Ecuadorian	87.3
Peruvian	86.8

Average Household Size

Group	People
Total Population	2.87
Hispanic or Latino (of any race)	4.11
Central American, ex. Mexican	4.55
Guatemalan	4.63
Honduran	4.77
Nicaraguan	4.05
Salvadoran	4.56
Cuban	2.96
Dominican Republic	3.16
Mexican	3.53
Puerto Rican	2.82
South American	4.10
Argentinean	4.41
Bolivian	4.42
Colombian	2.73
Ecuadorian	3.26
Peruvian	3.78

Median Age

Group	Years
Total Population	37.9
Hispanic or Latino (of any race)	30.0
Central American, ex. Mexican	29.0
Guatemalan	29.3
Honduran	28.7
Nicaraguan	33.3
Salvadoran	28.6
Cuban	41.1
Dominican Republic	31.3
Mexican	29.3
Puerto Rican	30.1
South American	33.0
Argentinean	30.3
Bolivian	31.8
Colombian	35.7
Ecuadorian	40.5
Peruvian	37.0

High School Graduates
(Universe: Population 25 Years and Over)

Group	Number	%
Total Population	23,217	85.9
Hispanic or Latino (of any race)	4,537	71.9
Central American, ex. Mexican	840	40.0
Salvadoran	401	34.5
South American	2,627	88.6
Bolivian	1,388	83.9

Four-Year College Graduates
(Universe: Population 25 Years and Over)

Group	Number	%
Total Population	11,541	42.7
Hispanic or Latino (of any race)	1,819	28.8
Central American, ex. Mexican	199	9.5
Salvadoran	107	9.2
South American	1,011	34.1
Bolivian	557	33.7

Notes: (1) Percent of total population; (2) Percent of Hispanic/Latino population; Profiles include places with an overall population of at least 125,000, OR an overall population of at least 25,000 where the Hispanic/Latino population is at least 20% of the overall population. In states where less than five places meet either of these criteria, we have included places with at least 10,000 total population with the highest percentage of Hispanic/Latino population. These places are identified with an asterisk (*); Please refer to the User's Guide for a full explanation of data.

Population Age 3–17 Enrolled in Public School
(Universe: Population Age 3–17 Enrolled in School)

Group	Number	%
Total Population	4,748	79.0
Hispanic or Latino (of any race)	1,375	81.5
Central American, ex. Mexican	319	87.4
Salvadoran	257	87.7
South American	808	83.3
Bolivian	597	86.9

Population Age 3–17 Enrolled in Private School
(Universe: Population Age 3–17 Enrolled in School)

Group	Number	%
Total Population	1,259	21.0
Hispanic or Latino (of any race)	312	18.5
Central American, ex. Mexican	46	12.6
Salvadoran	36	12.3
South American	162	16.7
Bolivian	90	13.1

Foreign-Born Population

Group	Number	%
Total Population	16,324	42.5
Hispanic or Latino (of any race)	6,726	67.1
Central American, ex. Mexican	2,592	77.4
Salvadoran	1,252	66.5
South American	3,417	69.7
Bolivian	2,060	66.6

Foreign-Born Naturalized U.S. Citizens

Group	Number	%
Total Population	7,073	43.3
Hispanic or Latino (of any race)	1,906	28.3
Central American, ex. Mexican	563	21.7
Salvadoran	308	24.6
South American	1,016	29.7
Bolivian	568	27.6

Language Spoken at Home: English Only
(Universe: Population 5 Years and Over)

Group	Number	%
Total Population	16,812	46.9
Hispanic or Latino (of any race)	689	7.6
Central American, ex. Mexican	138	4.5
Salvadoran	101	6.3
South American	109	2.5
Bolivian	32	1.2

Language Spoken at Home: Spanish
(Universe: Population 5 Years and Over)

Group	Number	%
Total Population	9,053	25.3
Hispanic or Latino (of any race)	8,383	91.9
Central American, ex. Mexican	2,901	95.5
Salvadoran	1,507	93.7
South American	4,307	97.5
Bolivian	2,674	98.8

Unemployment Rate
(Universe: Population 16 Years and Over)

Group	%
Total Population	5.1
Hispanic or Latino (of any race)	6.1
Central American, ex. Mexican	8.2
Salvadoran	11.8
South American	5.7
Bolivian	4.8

Class of Worker: Private Wage and Salary
(Universe: Civilian Employed Population 16 Years and Over)

Group	Number	%
Total Population	15,566	72.0
Hispanic or Latino (of any race)	5,076	79.5
Central American, ex. Mexican	2,032	87.5
Salvadoran	936	79.7
South American	2,309	75.4
Bolivian	1,522	82.1

Class of Worker: Government
(Universe: Civilian Employed Population 16 Years and Over)

Group	Number	%
Total Population	4,112	19.0
Hispanic or Latino (of any race)	622	9.7
Central American, ex. Mexican	149	6.4
Salvadoran	129	11.0
South American	330	10.8
Bolivian	132	7.1

Means of Transportation to Work: Car, Truck or Van
(Universe: Workers 16 Years and Over)

Group	Number	%
Total Population	18,525	86.8
Hispanic or Latino (of any race)	5,377	83.2
Central American, ex. Mexican	1,894	81.7
Salvadoran	1,014	87.5
South American	2,516	83.4
Bolivian	1,561	85.1

Means of Transportation to Work: Public Transportation (ex. Taxicab)
(Universe: Workers 16 Years and Over)

Group	Number	%
Total Population	1,532	7.2
Hispanic or Latino (of any race)	666	10.3
Central American, ex. Mexican	261	11.3
Salvadoran	100	8.6
South American	319	10.6
Bolivian	195	10.6

Homeownership Rate
(Universe: Occupied Housing Units)

Group	%
Total Population	60.9
Hispanic or Latino (of any race)	39.1
Central American, ex. Mexican	30.3
Guatemalan	24.3
Honduran	19.8
Nicaraguan	43.8
Salvadoran	32.3
Cuban	72.3
Dominican Republic	34.2
Mexican	38.5
Puerto Rican	54.1
South American	43.6
Argentinean	45.0
Bolivian	43.2
Colombian	52.5
Ecuadorian	66.7
Peruvian	34.0

Median Home Value

Group	Dollars
Total Population	450,000
Hispanic or Latino (of any race)	408,700
Central American, ex. Mexican	444,300
Salvadoran	454,400
South American	392,900
Bolivian	438,600

Median Gross Rent

Group	Dollars
Total Population	1,383
Hispanic or Latino (of any race)	1,422
Central American, ex. Mexican	1,321
Salvadoran	1,331
South American	1,571
Bolivian	1,644

Median Household Income
(2010 Inflation-Adjusted Dollars)

Group	Dollars
Total Population	75,871
Hispanic or Latino (of any race)	64,459
Central American, ex. Mexican	86,815
Salvadoran	85,464
South American	53,333
Bolivian	66,563

Per Capita Income
(2010 Inflation-Adjusted Dollars)

Group	Dollars
Total Population	35,146
Hispanic or Latino (of any race)	22,668
Central American, ex. Mexican	19,583
Salvadoran	18,397
South American	20,780
Bolivian	19,333

Households with $100,000+ Income

Group	Number	%
Total Population	4,926	35.5
Hispanic or Latino (of any race)	593	22.5
Central American, ex. Mexican	177	23.1
Salvadoran	58	11.8
South American	214	17.9
Bolivian	153	22.1

Households with Food Stamps/SNAP Benefits During Past 12 Months

Group	Number	%
Total Population	562	4.0
Hispanic or Latino (of any race)	45	1.7
Central American, ex. Mexican	0	0.0
Salvadoran	0	0.0
South American	14	1.2
Bolivian	14	2.0

Poverty Rate
(Income in Past 12 Months Below Poverty Level)

Group	%
Total Population	7.5
Hispanic or Latino (of any race)	8.7
Central American, ex. Mexican	17.4
Salvadoran	14.5
South American	5.4
Bolivian	3.2

Arlington

Population

Group	Number	%TP[1]	%HP[2]
Total Population	207,627	100.0	–
Hispanic or Latino (of any race)	31,382	15.1	100.0
Central American, ex. Mexican	12,171	5.9	38.8
Costa Rican	185	0.1	0.6
Guatemalan	3,017	1.5	9.6
Honduran	881	0.4	2.8
Nicaraguan	614	0.3	2.0
Panamanian	217	0.1	0.7
Salvadoran	7,088	3.4	22.6
Cuban	699	0.3	2.2
Dominican Republic	348	0.2	1.1
Mexican	3,590	1.7	11.4
Puerto Rican	1,664	0.8	5.3
South American	9,089	4.4	29.0
Argentinean	719	0.3	2.3
Bolivian	4,225	2.0	13.5
Chilean	302	0.1	1.0
Colombian	1,204	0.6	3.8
Ecuadorian	452	0.2	1.4
Paraguayan	113	0.1	0.4
Peruvian	1,531	0.7	4.9
Uruguayan	129	0.1	0.4
Venezuelan	279	0.1	0.9
Spaniard	621	0.3	2.0

Population Growth: 2000–2010

Group	%
Total Population	9.6
Hispanic or Latino (of any race)	-11.0
Central American, ex. Mexican	7.5
Costa Rican	55.5
Guatemalan	77.2
Honduran	28.4
Nicaraguan	27.7
Panamanian	36.5
Salvadoran	-7.1
Cuban	38.1
Dominican Republic	51.3
Mexican	20.8
Puerto Rican	50.9
South American	28.3
Argentinean	88.2
Bolivian	19.6
Chilean	48.0
Colombian	91.1
Ecuadorian	48.2
Peruvian	30.7
Venezuelan	13.0
Spaniard	198.6

STATE & PLACE PROFILES

Notes: (1) Percent of total population; (2) Percent of Hispanic/Latino population; Profiles include places with an overall population of at least 125,000, OR an overall population of at least 25,000 where the Hispanic/Latino population is at least 20% of the overall population. In states where less than five places meet either of these criteria, we have included places with at least 10,000 total population with the highest percentage of Hispanic/Latino population. These places are identified with an asterisk (*); Please refer to the User's Guide for a full explanation of data.

Males per 100 Females

Group	Number
Total Population	99.4
Hispanic or Latino (of any race)	105.7
Central American, ex. Mexican	115.1
Costa Rican	79.6
Guatemalan	157.6
Honduran	112.8
Nicaraguan	82.2
Panamanian	69.5
Salvadoran	107.1
Cuban	102.6
Dominican Republic	103.5
Mexican	105.8
Puerto Rican	89.5
South American	95.8
Argentinean	90.7
Bolivian	114.9
Chilean	68.7
Colombian	73.0
Ecuadorian	73.2
Paraguayan	59.2
Peruvian	90.4
Uruguayan	84.3
Venezuelan	72.2
Spaniard	97.8

Average Household Size

Group	People
Total Population	2.09
Hispanic or Latino (of any race)	3.01
Central American, ex. Mexican	3.83
Costa Rican	1.92
Guatemalan	4.14
Honduran	3.81
Nicaraguan	2.99
Panamanian	1.98
Salvadoran	4.01
Cuban	2.03
Dominican Republic	2.36
Mexican	2.41
Puerto Rican	1.91
South American	2.97
Argentinean	2.65
Bolivian	3.80
Chilean	2.28
Colombian	2.14
Ecuadorian	2.28
Paraguayan	2.64
Peruvian	2.76
Uruguayan	2.22
Venezuelan	1.89
Spaniard	1.97

Median Age

Group	Years
Total Population	33.4
Hispanic or Latino (of any race)	31.0
Central American, ex. Mexican	30.2
Costa Rican	33.1
Guatemalan	28.4
Honduran	30.2
Nicaraguan	35.1
Panamanian	31.1
Salvadoran	30.8
Cuban	32.2
Dominican Republic	30.2
Mexican	29.6
Puerto Rican	32.5
South American	34.8
Argentinean	33.1
Bolivian	34.3
Chilean	35.8
Colombian	33.1
Ecuadorian	37.8
Paraguayan	33.8
Peruvian	39.4
Uruguayan	39.1
Venezuelan	33.7
Spaniard	35.7

High School Graduates
(Universe: Population 25 Years and Over)

Group	Number	%
Total Population	135,378	92.5
Hispanic or Latino (of any race)	12,813	67.9
Central American, ex. Mexican	2,923	42.9
Guatemalan	655	44.4
Salvadoran	1,332	34.1
Mexican	1,992	76.5
Puerto Rican	998	99.0
South American	4,811	79.4
Bolivian	2,197	73.5
Colombian	704	89.8
Peruvian	841	77.7

Four-Year College Graduates
(Universe: Population 25 Years and Over)

Group	Number	%
Total Population	102,687	70.1
Hispanic or Latino (of any race)	6,655	35.3
Central American, ex. Mexican	984	14.4
Guatemalan	330	22.4
Salvadoran	250	6.4
Mexican	1,178	45.2
Puerto Rican	671	66.6
South American	2,606	43.0
Bolivian	876	29.3
Colombian	506	64.5
Peruvian	537	49.6

Population Age 3–17 Enrolled in Public School
(Universe: Population Age 3–17 Enrolled in School)

Group	Number	%
Total Population	17,528	81.4
Hispanic or Latino (of any race)	4,215	88.1
Central American, ex. Mexican	1,547	90.7
Guatemalan	179	87.3
Salvadoran	1,045	94.3
Mexican	548	82.4
Puerto Rican	340	97.1
South American	1,244	85.0
Bolivian	607	83.4
Colombian	125	76.2
Peruvian	339	100.0

Population Age 3–17 Enrolled in Private School
(Universe: Population Age 3–17 Enrolled in School)

Group	Number	%
Total Population	4,015	18.6
Hispanic or Latino (of any race)	567	11.9
Central American, ex. Mexican	159	9.3
Guatemalan	26	12.7
Salvadoran	63	5.7
Mexican	117	17.6
Puerto Rican	10	2.9
South American	220	15.0
Bolivian	121	16.6
Colombian	39	23.8
Peruvian	0	0.0

Foreign-Born Population

Group	Number	%
Total Population	45,654	23.1
Hispanic or Latino (of any race)	17,412	59.3
Central American, ex. Mexican	7,977	69.6
Guatemalan	1,968	80.2
Salvadoran	4,463	67.2
Mexican	1,564	36.9
Puerto Rican	37	2.4
South American	6,471	73.8
Bolivian	3,431	79.3
Colombian	693	63.6
Peruvian	1,234	74.7

Foreign-Born Naturalized U.S. Citizens

Group	Number	%
Total Population	17,778	38.9
Hispanic or Latino (of any race)	4,727	27.1
Central American, ex. Mexican	1,286	16.1
Guatemalan	277	14.1
Salvadoran	536	12.0
Mexican	435	27.8
Puerto Rican	31	83.8
South American	2,168	33.5
Bolivian	1,011	29.5
Colombian	264	38.1
Peruvian	511	41.4

Language Spoken at Home: English Only
(Universe: Population 5 Years and Over)

Group	Number	%
Total Population	132,179	71.0
Hispanic or Latino (of any race)	3,916	14.5
Central American, ex. Mexican	530	5.2
Guatemalan	291	12.6
Salvadoran	80	1.4
Mexican	1,192	31.5
Puerto Rican	564	36.3
South American	705	8.6
Bolivian	165	4.1
Colombian	205	20.4
Peruvian	209	13.1

Language Spoken at Home: Spanish
(Universe: Population 5 Years and Over)

Group	Number	%
Total Population	26,543	14.3
Hispanic or Latino (of any race)	22,772	84.4
Central American, ex. Mexican	9,714	94.8
Guatemalan	2,016	87.4
Salvadoran	5,704	98.6
Mexican	2,546	67.3
Puerto Rican	937	60.3
South American	7,424	90.9
Bolivian	3,818	95.9
Colombian	781	77.6
Peruvian	1,382	86.9

Unemployment Rate
(Universe: Population 16 Years and Over)

Group	%
Total Population	3.2
Hispanic or Latino (of any race)	6.7
Central American, ex. Mexican	8.3
Guatemalan	7.0
Salvadoran	9.7
Mexican	5.1
Puerto Rican	2.3
South American	6.4
Bolivian	9.3
Colombian	3.4
Peruvian	2.8

Class of Worker: Private Wage and Salary
(Universe: Civilian Employed Population 16 Years and Over)

Group	Number	%
Total Population	87,134	69.2
Hispanic or Latino (of any race)	13,589	79.6
Central American, ex. Mexican	5,606	88.4
Guatemalan	1,313	81.4
Salvadoran	3,224	91.5
Mexican	1,900	76.8
Puerto Rican	482	53.6
South American	4,396	80.7
Bolivian	2,055	78.7
Colombian	620	82.7
Peruvian	947	86.7

Class of Worker: Government
(Universe: Civilian Employed Population 16 Years and Over)

Group	Number	%
Total Population	33,529	26.6
Hispanic or Latino (of any race)	2,392	14.0
Central American, ex. Mexican	425	6.7
Guatemalan	132	8.2
Salvadoran	227	6.4
Mexican	479	19.4
Puerto Rican	408	45.3
South American	560	10.3
Bolivian	149	5.7
Colombian	130	17.3
Peruvian	145	13.3

Means of Transportation to Work: Car, Truck or Van
(Universe: Workers 16 Years and Over)

Group	Number	%
Total Population	77,148	60.2
Hispanic or Latino (of any race)	10,348	60.1
Central American, ex. Mexican	3,153	50.4
Guatemalan	647	41.3
Salvadoran	1,952	55.9
Mexican	1,489	56.6

Notes: (1) Percent of total population; (2) Percent of Hispanic/Latino population; Profiles include places with an overall population of at least 125,000, OR an overall population of at least 25,000 where the Hispanic/Latino population is at least 20% of the overall population. In states where less than five places meet either of these criteria, we have included places with at least 10,000 total population with the highest percentage of Hispanic/Latino population. These places are identified with an asterisk (*); Please refer to the User's Guide for a full explanation of data.

Puerto Rican	443	44.8
South American	3,845	71.3
Bolivian	2,064	78.3
Colombian	468	62.4
Peruvian	754	70.3

Means of Transportation to Work: Public Transportation (ex. Taxicab)
(Universe: Workers 16 Years and Over)

Group	Number	%
Total Population	35,101	27.4
Hispanic or Latino (of any race)	4,985	29.0
Central American, ex. Mexican	2,314	37.0
Guatemalan	753	48.1
Salvadoran	1,088	31.2
Mexican	872	33.1
Puerto Rican	392	39.7
South American	1,052	19.5
Bolivian	390	14.8
Colombian	198	26.4
Peruvian	252	23.5

Homeownership Rate
(Universe: Occupied Housing Units)

Group	%
Total Population	43.3
Hispanic or Latino (of any race)	29.1
Central American, ex. Mexican	22.2
Costa Rican	30.6
Guatemalan	15.7
Honduran	18.9
Nicaraguan	21.7
Panamanian	27.6
Salvadoran	25.1
Cuban	42.1
Dominican Republic	30.3
Mexican	29.5
Puerto Rican	27.6
South American	34.4
Argentinean	34.0
Bolivian	34.0
Chilean	39.0
Colombian	32.1
Ecuadorian	41.1
Paraguayan	43.2
Peruvian	33.8
Uruguayan	41.7
Venezuelan	36.7
Spaniard	44.9

Median Home Value

Group	Dollars
Total Population	571,700
Hispanic or Latino (of any race)	459,600
Central American, ex. Mexican	459,500
Guatemalan	450,000
Salvadoran	503,200
Mexican	381,000
Puerto Rican	417,000
South American	498,900
Bolivian	579,600
Colombian	361,500
Peruvian	311,500

Median Gross Rent

Group	Dollars
Total Population	1,519
Hispanic or Latino (of any race)	1,278
Central American, ex. Mexican	1,216
Guatemalan	1,222
Salvadoran	1,225
Mexican	1,222
Puerto Rican	1,289
South American	1,370
Bolivian	1,385
Colombian	1,411
Peruvian	1,296

Median Household Income
(2010 Inflation-Adjusted Dollars)

Group	Dollars
Total Population	94,880
Hispanic or Latino (of any race)	57,953
Central American, ex. Mexican	44,290
Guatemalan	36,734
Salvadoran	42,255
Mexican	51,250
Puerto Rican	71,009
South American	69,078
Bolivian	66,471
Colombian	97,568
Peruvian	54,767

Per Capita Income
(2010 Inflation-Adjusted Dollars)

Group	Dollars
Total Population	57,724
Hispanic or Latino (of any race)	26,374
Central American, ex. Mexican	16,427
Guatemalan	19,811
Salvadoran	14,235
Mexican	29,391
Puerto Rican	58,437
South American	27,476
Bolivian	20,421
Colombian	37,556
Peruvian	29,590

Households with $100,000+ Income

Group	Number	%
Total Population	43,586	47.4
Hispanic or Latino (of any race)	2,372	24.8
Central American, ex. Mexican	437	14.1
Guatemalan	96	13.4
Salvadoran	207	11.9
Mexican	302	21.6
Puerto Rican	194	25.5
South American	880	31.2
Bolivian	340	31.5
Colombian	190	42.0
Peruvian	153	26.4

Households with Food Stamps/SNAP Benefits During Past 12 Months

Group	Number	%
Total Population	1,973	2.1
Hispanic or Latino (of any race)	345	3.6
Central American, ex. Mexican	217	7.0
Guatemalan	14	2.0
Salvadoran	125	7.2
Mexican	10	0.7
Puerto Rican	12	1.6
South American	83	2.9
Bolivian	34	3.2
Colombian	13	2.9
Peruvian	11	1.9

Poverty Rate
(Income in Past 12 Months Below Poverty Level)

Group	%
Total Population	7.0
Hispanic or Latino (of any race)	13.7
Central American, ex. Mexican	17.3
Guatemalan	15.8
Salvadoran	17.9
Mexican	16.7
Puerto Rican	13.1
South American	8.5
Bolivian	7.7
Colombian	9.0
Peruvian	8.5

Chesapeake

Population

Group	Number	%TP[1]	%HP[2]
Total Population	222,209	100.0	–
Hispanic or Latino (of any race)	9,706	4.4	100.0
Central American, ex. Mexican	998	0.4	10.3
Guatemalan	255	0.1	2.6
Honduran	191	0.1	2.0
Panamanian	267	0.1	2.8
Salvadoran	192	0.1	2.0
Cuban	408	0.2	4.2
Dominican Republic	286	0.1	2.9
Mexican	3,579	1.6	36.9
Puerto Rican	2,739	1.2	28.2
South American	710	0.3	7.3
Colombian	266	0.1	2.7
Ecuadorian	103	<0.1	1.1
Peruvian	137	0.1	1.4
Spaniard	346	0.2	3.6

Population Growth: 2000–2010

Group	%
Total Population	11.6
Hispanic or Latino (of any race)	138.1
Central American, ex. Mexican	349.5
Panamanian	154.3
Cuban	101.0
Mexican	197.8
Puerto Rican	114.7
South American	294.4

Males per 100 Females

Group	Number
Total Population	94.7
Hispanic or Latino (of any race)	110.1
Central American, ex. Mexican	133.7
Guatemalan	292.3
Honduran	141.8
Panamanian	81.6
Salvadoran	131.3
Cuban	98.1
Dominican Republic	93.2
Mexican	134.8
Puerto Rican	94.4
South American	83.9
Colombian	77.3
Ecuadorian	102.0
Peruvian	77.9
Spaniard	77.4

Average Household Size

Group	People
Total Population	2.75
Hispanic or Latino (of any race)	3.25
Central American, ex. Mexican	3.61
Guatemalan	4.75
Honduran	3.74
Panamanian	2.87
Salvadoran	3.85
Cuban	2.99
Dominican Republic	3.25
Mexican	3.50
Puerto Rican	3.02
South American	3.15
Colombian	3.25
Ecuadorian	3.10
Peruvian	3.03
Spaniard	2.97

Median Age

Group	Years
Total Population	37.0
Hispanic or Latino (of any race)	24.9
Central American, ex. Mexican	27.8
Guatemalan	26.6
Honduran	28.1
Panamanian	30.6
Salvadoran	26.5
Cuban	28.7
Dominican Republic	24.6
Mexican	23.8
Puerto Rican	24.3
South American	26.4
Colombian	25.5
Ecuadorian	26.5
Peruvian	32.2
Spaniard	28.8

High School Graduates
(Universe: Population 25 Years and Over)

Group	Number	%
Total Population	126,203	89.3
Hispanic or Latino (of any race)	3,346	76.8
Central American, ex. Mexican	559	64.0
Mexican	1,012	68.8
Puerto Rican	711	83.5
South American	388	92.4

STATE & PLACE PROFILES

Notes: (1) Percent of total population; (2) Percent of Hispanic/Latino population; Profiles include places with an overall population of at least 125,000, OR an overall population of at least 25,000 where the Hispanic/Latino population is at least 20% of the overall population. In states where less than five places meet either of these criteria, we have included places with at least 10,000 total population with the highest percentage of Hispanic/Latino population. These places are identified with an asterisk (*); Please refer to the User's Guide for a full explanation of data.

Four-Year College Graduates
(Universe: Population 25 Years and Over)

Group	Number	%
Total Population	39,449	27.9
Hispanic or Latino (of any race)	990	22.7
Central American, ex. Mexican	162	18.6
Mexican	177	12.0
Puerto Rican	233	27.3
South American	132	31.4

Population Age 3–17 Enrolled in Public School
(Universe: Population Age 3–17 Enrolled in School)

Group	Number	%
Total Population	38,352	84.8
Hispanic or Latino (of any race)	1,981	88.0
Central American, ex. Mexican	258	94.5
Mexican	643	81.8
Puerto Rican	657	90.2
South American	171	100.0

Population Age 3–17 Enrolled in Private School
(Universe: Population Age 3–17 Enrolled in School)

Group	Number	%
Total Population	6,889	15.2
Hispanic or Latino (of any race)	269	12.0
Central American, ex. Mexican	15	5.5
Mexican	143	18.2
Puerto Rican	71	9.8
South American	0	0.0

Foreign-Born Population

Group	Number	%
Total Population	9,652	4.4
Hispanic or Latino (of any race)	2,314	26.8
Central American, ex. Mexican	845	55.4
Mexican	854	28.4
Puerto Rican	0	0.0
South American	355	43.1

Foreign-Born Naturalized U.S. Citizens

Group	Number	%
Total Population	5,451	56.5
Hispanic or Latino (of any race)	794	34.3
Central American, ex. Mexican	369	43.7
Mexican	61	7.1
Puerto Rican	0	0.0
South American	181	51.0

Language Spoken at Home: English Only
(Universe: Population 5 Years and Over)

Group	Number	%
Total Population	191,209	93.3
Hispanic or Latino (of any race)	3,469	45.7
Central American, ex. Mexican	331	23.1
Mexican	1,290	47.1
Puerto Rican	833	49.9
South American	208	34.0

Language Spoken at Home: Spanish
(Universe: Population 5 Years and Over)

Group	Number	%
Total Population	6,203	3.0
Hispanic or Latino (of any race)	4,070	53.6
Central American, ex. Mexican	1,102	76.9
Mexican	1,408	51.4
Puerto Rican	836	50.1
South American	404	66.0

Unemployment Rate
(Universe: Population 16 Years and Over)

Group	%
Total Population	4.9
Hispanic or Latino (of any race)	4.9
Central American, ex. Mexican	3.8
Mexican	4.2
Puerto Rican	5.7
South American	3.1

Class of Worker: Private Wage and Salary
(Universe: Civilian Employed Population 16 Years and Over)

Group	Number	%
Total Population	77,441	72.5
Hispanic or Latino (of any race)	2,942	80.2
Central American, ex. Mexican	817	83.8
Mexican	1,094	86.6
Puerto Rican	360	60.1
South American	253	79.8

Class of Worker: Government
(Universe: Civilian Employed Population 16 Years and Over)

Group	Number	%
Total Population	25,305	23.7
Hispanic or Latino (of any race)	678	18.5
Central American, ex. Mexican	158	16.2
Mexican	146	11.6
Puerto Rican	239	39.9
South American	50	15.8

Means of Transportation to Work: Car, Truck or Van
(Universe: Workers 16 Years and Over)

Group	Number	%
Total Population	103,460	93.6
Hispanic or Latino (of any race)	3,719	89.5
Central American, ex. Mexican	924	89.8
Mexican	1,296	87.3
Puerto Rican	637	96.1
South American	338	95.8

Means of Transportation to Work: Public Transportation (ex. Taxicab)
(Universe: Workers 16 Years and Over)

Group	Number	%
Total Population	1,012	0.9
Hispanic or Latino (of any race)	97	2.3
Central American, ex. Mexican	97	9.4
Mexican	0	0.0
Puerto Rican	0	0.0
South American	0	0.0

Homeownership Rate
(Universe: Occupied Housing Units)

Group	%
Total Population	73.0
Hispanic or Latino (of any race)	57.2
Central American, ex. Mexican	50.4
Guatemalan	21.6
Honduran	36.2
Panamanian	74.4
Salvadoran	45.0
Cuban	63.7
Dominican Republic	56.0
Mexican	50.7
Puerto Rican	60.2
South American	67.0
Colombian	56.3
Ecuadorian	73.3
Peruvian	87.1
Spaniard	77.2

Median Home Value

Group	Dollars
Total Population	272,800
Hispanic or Latino (of any race)	257,000
Central American, ex. Mexican	235,300
Mexican	226,600
Puerto Rican	277,000
South American	218,000

Median Gross Rent

Group	Dollars
Total Population	1,005
Hispanic or Latino (of any race)	1,042
Central American, ex. Mexican	1,169
Mexican	892
Puerto Rican	889
South American	933

Median Household Income
(2010 Inflation-Adjusted Dollars)

Group	Dollars
Total Population	67,855
Hispanic or Latino (of any race)	59,934
Central American, ex. Mexican	47,125
Mexican	55,804
Puerto Rican	66,250
South American	63,750

Per Capita Income
(2010 Inflation-Adjusted Dollars)

Group	Dollars
Total Population	29,306
Hispanic or Latino (of any race)	21,513
Central American, ex. Mexican	18,348
Mexican	19,649
Puerto Rican	20,410
South American	21,958

Households with $100,000+ Income

Group	Number	%
Total Population	22,244	28.2
Hispanic or Latino (of any race)	472	19.5
Central American, ex. Mexican	8	1.7
Mexican	144	17.3
Puerto Rican	142	34.0
South American	46	21.5

Households with Food Stamps/SNAP Benefits During Past 12 Months

Group	Number	%
Total Population	4,716	6.0
Hispanic or Latino (of any race)	66	2.7
Central American, ex. Mexican	0	0.0
Mexican	0	0.0
Puerto Rican	66	15.8
South American	0	0.0

Poverty Rate
(Income in Past 12 Months Below Poverty Level)

Group	%
Total Population	6.8
Hispanic or Latino (of any race)	9.1
Central American, ex. Mexican	11.1
Mexican	11.4
Puerto Rican	9.0
South American	0.0

Dale City

Population

Group	Number	%TP[1]	%HP[2]
Total Population	65,969	100.0	–
Hispanic or Latino (of any race)	17,648	26.8	100.0
Central American, ex. Mexican	9,389	14.2	53.2
Guatemalan	833	1.3	4.7
Honduran	925	1.4	5.2
Nicaraguan	282	0.4	1.6
Panamanian	185	0.3	1.0
Salvadoran	7,036	10.7	39.9
Cuban	110	0.2	0.6
Dominican Republic	229	0.3	1.3
Mexican	2,373	3.6	13.4
Puerto Rican	1,504	2.3	8.5
South American	2,142	3.2	12.1
Bolivian	656	1.0	3.7
Colombian	246	0.4	1.4
Ecuadorian	124	0.2	0.7
Peruvian	766	1.2	4.3
Spaniard	122	0.2	0.7

Population Growth: 2000–2010

Group	%
Total Population	17.9
Hispanic or Latino (of any race)	218.9
Central American, ex. Mexican	646.9
Guatemalan	486.6
Panamanian	77.9
Salvadoran	741.6
Mexican	112.6
Puerto Rican	56.5
South American	300.4
Peruvian	263.0

Males per 100 Females

Group	Number
Total Population	97.9
Hispanic or Latino (of any race)	104.1
Central American, ex. Mexican	108.2
Guatemalan	114.7
Honduran	115.1
Nicaraguan	108.9

Notes: (1) Percent of total population; (2) Percent of Hispanic/Latino population; Profiles include places with an overall population of at least 125,000, OR an overall population of at least 25,000 where the Hispanic/Latino population is at least 20% of the overall population. In states where less than five places meet either of these criteria, we have included places with at least 10,000 total population with the highest percentage of Hispanic/Latino population. These places are identified with an asterisk (*); Please refer to the User's Guide for a full explanation of data.

Group	
Panamanian	55.5
Salvadoran	108.2
Cuban	59.4
Dominican Republic	99.1
Mexican	108.5
Puerto Rican	101.6
South American	87.9
Bolivian	93.5
Colombian	85.0
Ecuadorian	90.8
Peruvian	85.0
Spaniard	62.7

Average Household Size

Group	People
Total Population	3.30
Hispanic or Latino (of any race)	4.50
Central American, ex. Mexican	4.95
Guatemalan	4.46
Honduran	5.28
Nicaraguan	4.47
Panamanian	3.31
Salvadoran	5.09
Cuban	3.25
Dominican Republic	3.64
Mexican	4.49
Puerto Rican	3.22
South American	4.13
Bolivian	4.61
Colombian	3.66
Ecuadorian	3.34
Peruvian	4.17
Spaniard	2.97

Median Age

Group	Years
Total Population	32.4
Hispanic or Latino (of any race)	27.1
Central American, ex. Mexican	28.3
Guatemalan	30.1
Honduran	29.4
Nicaraguan	31.4
Panamanian	34.8
Salvadoran	27.6
Cuban	31.0
Dominican Republic	27.4
Mexican	24.5
Puerto Rican	27.8
South American	32.2
Bolivian	30.9
Colombian	30.5
Ecuadorian	34.7
Peruvian	33.4
Spaniard	38.3

High School Graduates
(Universe: Population 25 Years and Over)

Group	Number	%
Total Population	33,108	85.7
Hispanic or Latino (of any race)	5,623	61.5
Central American, ex. Mexican	2,275	46.4
Salvadoran	1,544	44.1
Mexican	845	56.5
Puerto Rican	725	98.1
South American	1,292	90.4
Bolivian	845	96.0

Four-Year College Graduates
(Universe: Population 25 Years and Over)

Group	Number	%
Total Population	10,770	27.9
Hispanic or Latino (of any race)	1,540	16.8
Central American, ex. Mexican	587	12.0
Salvadoran	427	12.2
Mexican	172	11.5
Puerto Rican	230	31.1
South American	396	27.7
Bolivian	156	17.7

Population Age 3–17 Enrolled in Public School
(Universe: Population Age 3–17 Enrolled in School)

Group	Number	%
Total Population	11,884	89.1
Hispanic or Latino (of any race)	3,910	96.4
Central American, ex. Mexican	1,725	95.0
Salvadoran	1,117	94.2
Mexican	806	98.3
Puerto Rican	460	95.6
South American	433	96.0
Bolivian	278	96.5

Population Age 3–17 Enrolled in Private School
(Universe: Population Age 3–17 Enrolled in School)

Group	Number	%
Total Population	1,455	10.9
Hispanic or Latino (of any race)	144	3.6
Central American, ex. Mexican	91	5.0
Salvadoran	69	5.8
Mexican	14	1.7
Puerto Rican	21	4.4
South American	18	4.0
Bolivian	10	3.5

Foreign-Born Population

Group	Number	%
Total Population	17,319	27.2
Hispanic or Latino (of any race)	9,702	56.3
Central American, ex. Mexican	5,711	64.0
Salvadoran	4,155	64.7
Mexican	1,580	48.8
Puerto Rican	39	2.7
South American	1,787	81.1
Bolivian	1,216	84.0

Foreign-Born Naturalized U.S. Citizens

Group	Number	%
Total Population	6,795	39.2
Hispanic or Latino (of any race)	2,256	23.3
Central American, ex. Mexican	1,391	24.4
Salvadoran	973	23.4
Mexican	274	17.3
Puerto Rican	39	100.0
South American	378	21.2
Bolivian	213	17.5

Language Spoken at Home: English Only
(Universe: Population 5 Years and Over)

Group	Number	%
Total Population	35,466	61.3
Hispanic or Latino (of any race)	1,676	11.2
Central American, ex. Mexican	294	3.9
Salvadoran	93	1.7
Mexican	470	17.1
Puerto Rican	579	42.6
South American	129	6.3
Bolivian	35	2.7

Language Spoken at Home: Spanish
(Universe: Population 5 Years and Over)

Group	Number	%
Total Population	14,183	24.5
Hispanic or Latino (of any race)	13,165	88.2
Central American, ex. Mexican	7,275	95.8
Salvadoran	5,241	98.3
Mexican	2,274	82.9
Puerto Rican	763	56.1
South American	1,870	91.9
Bolivian	1,238	94.6

Unemployment Rate
(Universe: Population 16 Years and Over)

Group	%
Total Population	6.0
Hispanic or Latino (of any race)	7.3
Central American, ex. Mexican	10.2
Salvadoran	10.1
Mexican	4.5
Puerto Rican	1.9
South American	0.0
Bolivian	0.0

Class of Worker: Private Wage and Salary
(Universe: Civilian Employed Population 16 Years and Over)

Group	Number	%
Total Population	23,830	70.9
Hispanic or Latino (of any race)	6,790	81.7
Central American, ex. Mexican	3,722	83.3
Salvadoran	2,711	84.8
Mexican	1,217	86.1
Puerto Rican	553	70.6
South American	977	82.1
Bolivian	644	88.0

Class of Worker: Government
(Universe: Civilian Employed Population 16 Years and Over)

Group	Number	%
Total Population	8,001	23.8
Hispanic or Latino (of any race)	789	9.5
Central American, ex. Mexican	299	6.7
Salvadoran	141	4.4
Mexican	116	8.2
Puerto Rican	180	23.0
South American	102	8.6
Bolivian	12	1.6

Means of Transportation to Work: Car, Truck or Van
(Universe: Workers 16 Years and Over)

Group	Number	%
Total Population	29,700	88.9
Hispanic or Latino (of any race)	7,363	90.0
Central American, ex. Mexican	3,936	90.1
Salvadoran	2,788	88.6
Mexican	1,412	95.6
Puerto Rican	696	88.0
South American	933	85.9
Bolivian	545	83.8

Means of Transportation to Work: Public Transportation (ex. Taxicab)
(Universe: Workers 16 Years and Over)

Group	Number	%
Total Population	2,067	6.2
Hispanic or Latino (of any race)	448	5.5
Central American, ex. Mexican	196	4.5
Salvadoran	132	4.2
Mexican	42	2.8
Puerto Rican	95	12.0
South American	77	7.1
Bolivian	29	4.5

Homeownership Rate
(Universe: Occupied Housing Units)

Group	%
Total Population	76.8
Hispanic or Latino (of any race)	73.5
Central American, ex. Mexican	73.1
Guatemalan	77.4
Honduran	68.0
Nicaraguan	74.3
Panamanian	69.5
Salvadoran	73.3
Cuban	71.4
Dominican Republic	72.1
Mexican	73.2
Puerto Rican	68.8
South American	78.8
Bolivian	85.2
Colombian	78.5
Ecuadorian	82.9
Peruvian	80.1
Spaniard	91.4

Median Home Value

Group	Dollars
Total Population	324,500
Hispanic or Latino (of any race)	319,800
Central American, ex. Mexican	303,100
Salvadoran	297,000
Mexican	323,100
Puerto Rican	354,300
South American	339,700
Bolivian	328,400

Median Gross Rent

Group	Dollars
Total Population	1,324
Hispanic or Latino (of any race)	1,399
Central American, ex. Mexican	1,351
Salvadoran	1,346
Mexican	1,661
Puerto Rican	1,422
South American	1,313
Bolivian	2,000+

STATE & PLACE PROFILES

Notes: (1) Percent of total population; (2) Percent of Hispanic/Latino population; Profiles include places with an overall population of at least 125,000, OR an overall population of at least 25,000 where the Hispanic/Latino population is at least 20% of the overall population. In states where less than five places meet either of these criteria, we have included places with at least 10,000 total population with the highest percentage of Hispanic/Latino population. These places are identified with an asterisk (*); Please refer to the User's Guide for a full explanation of data.

Median Household Income
(2010 Inflation-Adjusted Dollars)

Group	Dollars
Total Population	84,471
Hispanic or Latino (of any race)	72,738
Central American, ex. Mexican	63,438
Salvadoran	56,202
Mexican	76,795
Puerto Rican	86,739
South American	79,141
Bolivian	65,517

Per Capita Income
(2010 Inflation-Adjusted Dollars)

Group	Dollars
Total Population	30,065
Hispanic or Latino (of any race)	20,136
Central American, ex. Mexican	18,524
Salvadoran	17,437
Mexican	18,810
Puerto Rican	31,992
South American	23,647
Bolivian	19,027

Households with $100,000+ Income

Group	Number	%
Total Population	7,836	39.8
Hispanic or Latino (of any race)	1,151	29.3
Central American, ex. Mexican	466	22.4
Salvadoran	274	18.6
Mexican	273	35.4
Puerto Rican	172	45.5
South American	202	42.0
Bolivian	92	30.7

Households with Food Stamps/SNAP Benefits During Past 12 Months

Group	Number	%
Total Population	720	3.7
Hispanic or Latino (of any race)	135	3.4
Central American, ex. Mexican	67	3.2
Salvadoran	67	4.5
Mexican	0	0.0
Puerto Rican	52	13.8
South American	0	0.0
Bolivian	0	0.0

Poverty Rate
(Income in Past 12 Months Below Poverty Level)

Group	%
Total Population	6.4
Hispanic or Latino (of any race)	9.9
Central American, ex. Mexican	15.7
Salvadoran	18.0
Mexican	5.1
Puerto Rican	2.3
South American	0.8
Bolivian	0.0

Hampton

Population

Group	Number	%TP[1]	%HP[2]
Total Population	137,436	100.0	–
Hispanic or Latino (of any race)	6,241	4.5	100.0
Central American, ex. Mexican	661	0.5	10.6
Honduran	143	0.1	2.3
Panamanian	319	0.2	5.1
Salvadoran	111	0.1	1.8
Cuban	256	0.2	4.1
Dominican Republic	251	0.2	4.0
Mexican	1,868	1.4	29.9
Puerto Rican	2,339	1.7	37.5
South American	286	0.2	4.6
Colombian	125	0.1	2.0
Spaniard	180	0.1	2.9

Population Growth: 2000–2010

Group	%
Total Population	-6.1
Hispanic or Latino (of any race)	50.3
Central American, ex. Mexican	109.8
Panamanian	61.1
Cuban	71.8
Mexican	65.3
Puerto Rican	59.2
South American	123.4

Males per 100 Females

Group	Number
Total Population	91.7
Hispanic or Latino (of any race)	96.3
Central American, ex. Mexican	87.8
Honduran	186.0
Panamanian	61.1
Salvadoran	94.7
Cuban	100.0
Dominican Republic	97.6
Mexican	100.9
Puerto Rican	98.2
South American	86.9
Colombian	78.6
Spaniard	76.5

Average Household Size

Group	People
Total Population	2.42
Hispanic or Latino (of any race)	2.80
Central American, ex. Mexican	3.09
Honduran	3.59
Panamanian	2.80
Salvadoran	3.74
Cuban	2.49
Dominican Republic	2.64
Mexican	2.88
Puerto Rican	2.87
South American	2.57
Colombian	2.89
Spaniard	2.39

Median Age

Group	Years
Total Population	35.5
Hispanic or Latino (of any race)	24.9
Central American, ex. Mexican	28.1
Honduran	26.6
Panamanian	30.5
Salvadoran	26.6
Cuban	22.9
Dominican Republic	23.9
Mexican	24.4
Puerto Rican	23.6
South American	26.6
Colombian	25.2
Spaniard	30.5

High School Graduates
(Universe: Population 25 Years and Over)

Group	Number	%
Total Population	78,920	88.6
Hispanic or Latino (of any race)	2,740	90.5
Mexican	936	88.1
Puerto Rican	863	91.4

Four-Year College Graduates
(Universe: Population 25 Years and Over)

Group	Number	%
Total Population	19,445	21.8
Hispanic or Latino (of any race)	778	25.7
Mexican	151	14.2
Puerto Rican	186	19.7

Population Age 3–17 Enrolled in Public School
(Universe: Population Age 3–17 Enrolled in School)

Group	Number	%
Total Population	21,374	90.4
Hispanic or Latino (of any race)	1,209	91.6
Mexican	594	87.2
Puerto Rican	341	93.4

Population Age 3–17 Enrolled in Private School
(Universe: Population Age 3–17 Enrolled in School)

Group	Number	%
Total Population	2,257	9.6
Hispanic or Latino (of any race)	111	8.4
Mexican	87	12.8
Puerto Rican	24	6.6

Foreign-Born Population

Group	Number	%
Total Population	7,585	5.5
Hispanic or Latino (of any race)	1,318	22.0
Mexican	337	14.0
Puerto Rican	60	3.5

Foreign-Born Naturalized U.S. Citizens

Group	Number	%
Total Population	4,515	59.5
Hispanic or Latino (of any race)	693	52.6
Mexican	277	82.2
Puerto Rican	38	63.3

Language Spoken at Home: English Only
(Universe: Population 5 Years and Over)

Group	Number	%
Total Population	120,664	92.9
Hispanic or Latino (of any race)	2,636	49.8
Mexican	1,053	51.6
Puerto Rican	912	61.2

Language Spoken at Home: Spanish
(Universe: Population 5 Years and Over)

Group	Number	%
Total Population	3,883	3.0
Hispanic or Latino (of any race)	2,569	48.6
Mexican	975	47.8
Puerto Rican	539	36.2

Unemployment Rate
(Universe: Population 16 Years and Over)

Group	%
Total Population	7.9
Hispanic or Latino (of any race)	12.5
Mexican	6.3
Puerto Rican	15.8

Class of Worker: Private Wage and Salary
(Universe: Civilian Employed Population 16 Years and Over)

Group	Number	%
Total Population	45,261	71.6
Hispanic or Latino (of any race)	1,435	64.2
Mexican	454	60.6
Puerto Rican	438	63.8

Class of Worker: Government
(Universe: Civilian Employed Population 16 Years and Over)

Group	Number	%
Total Population	15,324	24.2
Hispanic or Latino (of any race)	659	29.5
Mexican	278	37.1
Puerto Rican	175	25.5

Means of Transportation to Work: Car, Truck or Van
(Universe: Workers 16 Years and Over)

Group	Number	%
Total Population	61,746	92.6
Hispanic or Latino (of any race)	2,562	95.0
Mexican	965	98.7
Puerto Rican	785	100.0

Means of Transportation to Work: Public Transportation (ex. Taxicab)
(Universe: Workers 16 Years and Over)

Group	Number	%
Total Population	1,428	2.1
Hispanic or Latino (of any race)	92	3.4
Mexican	13	1.3
Puerto Rican	0	0.0

Homeownership Rate
(Universe: Occupied Housing Units)

Group	%
Total Population	58.1
Hispanic or Latino (of any race)	44.7
Central American, ex. Mexican	44.2
Honduran	27.0
Panamanian	55.0
Salvadoran	38.7
Cuban	38.5
Dominican Republic	38.8
Mexican	43.8
Puerto Rican	47.7

Notes: (1) Percent of total population; (2) Percent of Hispanic/Latino population; Profiles include places with an overall population of at least 125,000, OR an overall population of at least 25,000 where the Hispanic/Latino population is at least 20% of the overall population. In states where less than five places meet either of these criteria, we have included places with at least 10,000 total population with the highest percentage of Hispanic/Latino population. These places are identified with an asterisk (*); Please refer to the User's Guide for a full explanation of data.

South American	49.4
Colombian	57.1
Spaniard	45.2

Median Home Value

Group	Dollars
Total Population	191,500
Hispanic or Latino (of any race)	210,400
Mexican	201,700
Puerto Rican	198,700

Median Gross Rent

Group	Dollars
Total Population	923
Hispanic or Latino (of any race)	986
Mexican	911
Puerto Rican	971

Median Household Income
(2010 Inflation-Adjusted Dollars)

Group	Dollars
Total Population	49,815
Hispanic or Latino (of any race)	46,103
Mexican	49,741
Puerto Rican	39,841

Per Capita Income
(2010 Inflation-Adjusted Dollars)

Group	Dollars
Total Population	24,051
Hispanic or Latino (of any race)	19,081
Mexican	17,037
Puerto Rican	17,598

Households with $100,000+ Income

Group	Number	%
Total Population	7,661	14.4
Hispanic or Latino (of any race)	294	14.0
Mexican	98	12.5
Puerto Rican	44	6.2

Households with Food Stamps/SNAP Benefits During Past 12 Months

Group	Number	%
Total Population	4,523	8.5
Hispanic or Latino (of any race)	276	13.1
Mexican	158	20.2
Puerto Rican	118	16.7

Poverty Rate
(Income in Past 12 Months Below Poverty Level)

Group	%
Total Population	12.6
Hispanic or Latino (of any race)	16.3
Mexican	9.0
Puerto Rican	29.7

Manassas

Population

Group	Number	%TP[1]	%HP[2]
Total Population	37,821	100.0	–
Hispanic or Latino (of any race)	11,876	31.4	100.0
Central American, ex. Mexican	5,529	14.6	46.6
Guatemalan	708	1.9	6.0
Honduran	657	1.7	5.5
Nicaraguan	177	0.5	1.5
Salvadoran	3,870	10.2	32.6
Dominican Republic	101	0.3	0.9
Mexican	3,754	9.9	31.6
Puerto Rican	417	1.1	3.5
South American	924	2.4	7.8
Bolivian	233	0.6	2.0
Colombian	122	0.3	1.0
Peruvian	369	1.0	3.1

Population Growth: 2000–2010

Group	%
Total Population	7.6
Hispanic or Latino (of any race)	123.4
Central American, ex. Mexican	292.1
Guatemalan	409.4
Honduran	236.9
Salvadoran	301.9
Mexican	57.7
Puerto Rican	58.0
South American	413.3

Males per 100 Females

Group	Number
Total Population	100.6
Hispanic or Latino (of any race)	113.8
Central American, ex. Mexican	113.6
Guatemalan	123.3
Honduran	125.0
Nicaraguan	105.8
Salvadoran	112.2
Dominican Republic	87.0
Mexican	125.3
Puerto Rican	96.7
South American	89.7
Bolivian	97.5
Colombian	114.0
Peruvian	90.2

Average Household Size

Group	People
Total Population	3.02
Hispanic or Latino (of any race)	4.79
Central American, ex. Mexican	5.10
Guatemalan	5.27
Honduran	5.64
Nicaraguan	4.60
Salvadoran	5.09
Dominican Republic	4.39
Mexican	5.17
Puerto Rican	3.20
South American	3.67
Bolivian	4.35
Colombian	3.23
Peruvian	3.55

Median Age

Group	Years
Total Population	32.1
Hispanic or Latino (of any race)	25.7
Central American, ex. Mexican	28.0
Guatemalan	27.9
Honduran	29.0
Nicaraguan	29.8
Salvadoran	27.7
Dominican Republic	23.8
Mexican	22.8
Puerto Rican	25.4
South American	32.7
Bolivian	29.9
Colombian	32.6
Peruvian	34.5

High School Graduates
(Universe: Population 25 Years and Over)

Group	Number	%
Total Population	17,962	80.6
Hispanic or Latino (of any race)	2,459	44.9
Central American, ex. Mexican	1,156	42.7
Salvadoran	824	39.8
Mexican	691	34.9

Four-Year College Graduates
(Universe: Population 25 Years and Over)

Group	Number	%
Total Population	6,302	28.3
Hispanic or Latino (of any race)	467	8.5
Central American, ex. Mexican	125	4.6
Salvadoran	118	5.7
Mexican	111	5.6

Population Age 3–17 Enrolled in Public School
(Universe: Population Age 3–17 Enrolled in School)

Group	Number	%
Total Population	6,431	89.6
Hispanic or Latino (of any race)	2,351	96.4
Central American, ex. Mexican	1,282	98.3
Salvadoran	1,116	100.0
Mexican	895	97.4

Population Age 3–17 Enrolled in Private School
(Universe: Population Age 3–17 Enrolled in School)

Group	Number	%
Total Population	747	10.4
Hispanic or Latino (of any race)	89	3.6
Central American, ex. Mexican	22	1.7
Salvadoran	0	0.0
Mexican	24	2.6

Foreign-Born Population

Group	Number	%
Total Population	8,894	24.7
Hispanic or Latino (of any race)	6,438	60.2
Central American, ex. Mexican	3,427	61.2
Salvadoran	2,656	58.9
Mexican	2,252	60.3

Foreign-Born Naturalized U.S. Citizens

Group	Number	%
Total Population	2,284	25.7
Hispanic or Latino (of any race)	1,012	15.7
Central American, ex. Mexican	588	17.2
Salvadoran	488	18.4
Mexican	178	7.9

Language Spoken at Home: English Only
(Universe: Population 5 Years and Over)

Group	Number	%
Total Population	21,685	65.9
Hispanic or Latino (of any race)	377	4.1
Central American, ex. Mexican	204	4.2
Salvadoran	177	4.5
Mexican	73	2.2

Language Spoken at Home: Spanish
(Universe: Population 5 Years and Over)

Group	Number	%
Total Population	9,007	27.4
Hispanic or Latino (of any race)	8,806	95.7
Central American, ex. Mexican	4,611	95.8
Salvadoran	3,723	95.5
Mexican	3,181	97.8

Unemployment Rate
(Universe: Population 16 Years and Over)

Group	%
Total Population	6.5
Hispanic or Latino (of any race)	9.9
Central American, ex. Mexican	14.5
Salvadoran	17.4
Mexican	5.1

Class of Worker: Private Wage and Salary
(Universe: Civilian Employed Population 16 Years and Over)

Group	Number	%
Total Population	15,068	79.2
Hispanic or Latino (of any race)	4,559	90.9
Central American, ex. Mexican	2,311	95.9
Salvadoran	1,753	97.1
Mexican	1,764	93.9

Class of Worker: Government
(Universe: Civilian Employed Population 16 Years and Over)

Group	Number	%
Total Population	3,290	17.3
Hispanic or Latino (of any race)	228	4.5
Central American, ex. Mexican	0	0.0
Salvadoran	0	0.0
Mexican	12	0.6

Means of Transportation to Work: Car, Truck or Van
(Universe: Workers 16 Years and Over)

Group	Number	%
Total Population	16,834	90.0
Hispanic or Latino (of any race)	4,277	88.1
Central American, ex. Mexican	2,128	90.6
Salvadoran	1,673	94.5
Mexican	1,531	83.0

Means of Transportation to Work: Public Transportation (ex. Taxicab)
(Universe: Workers 16 Years and Over)

Group	Number	%
Total Population	687	3.7

STATE & PLACE PROFILES

Notes: (1) Percent of total population; (2) Percent of Hispanic/Latino population; Profiles include places with an overall population of at least 125,000, OR an overall population of at least 25,000 where the Hispanic/Latino population is at least 20% of the overall population. In states where less than five places meet either of these criteria, we have included places with at least 10,000 total population with the highest percentage of Hispanic/Latino population. These places are identified with an asterisk (*); Please refer to the User's Guide for a full explanation of data.

Hispanic or Latino (of any race)	115	2.4
Central American, ex. Mexican	45	1.9
Salvadoran	45	2.5
Mexican	48	2.6

Homeownership Rate
(Universe: Occupied Housing Units)

Group	%
Total Population	64.2
Hispanic or Latino (of any race)	47.6
Central American, ex. Mexican	48.4
Guatemalan	51.0
Honduran	37.6
Nicaraguan	59.6
Salvadoran	48.8
Dominican Republic	38.9
Mexican	39.8
Puerto Rican	55.7
South American	61.5
Bolivian	68.3
Colombian	56.8
Peruvian	66.7

Median Home Value

Group	Dollars
Total Population	325,800
Hispanic or Latino (of any race)	236,600
Central American, ex. Mexican	244,100
Salvadoran	243,900
Mexican	192,400

Median Gross Rent

Group	Dollars
Total Population	1,232
Hispanic or Latino (of any race)	1,392
Central American, ex. Mexican	1,229
Salvadoran	1,209
Mexican	1,641

Median Household Income
(2010 Inflation-Adjusted Dollars)

Group	Dollars
Total Population	75,173
Hispanic or Latino (of any race)	51,068
Central American, ex. Mexican	51,250
Salvadoran	53,913
Mexican	38,980

Per Capita Income
(2010 Inflation-Adjusted Dollars)

Group	Dollars
Total Population	28,941
Hispanic or Latino (of any race)	13,472
Central American, ex. Mexican	13,082
Salvadoran	12,286
Mexican	12,514

Households with $100,000+ Income

Group	Number	%
Total Population	4,081	34.8
Hispanic or Latino (of any race)	381	15.8
Central American, ex. Mexican	111	9.0
Salvadoran	105	10.1
Mexican	129	17.1

Households with Food Stamps/SNAP Benefits During Past 12 Months

Group	Number	%
Total Population	767	6.5
Hispanic or Latino (of any race)	217	9.0
Central American, ex. Mexican	112	9.1
Salvadoran	112	10.7
Mexican	79	10.5

Poverty Rate
(Income in Past 12 Months Below Poverty Level)

Group	%
Total Population	13.4
Hispanic or Latino (of any race)	23.7
Central American, ex. Mexican	27.4
Salvadoran	28.6
Mexican	23.0

Marumsco

Population

Group	Number	%TP[1]	%HP[2]
Total Population	35,036	100.0	–
Hispanic or Latino (of any race)	14,372	41.0	100.0
Central American, ex. Mexican	8,223	23.5	57.2
Guatemalan	594	1.7	4.1
Honduran	973	2.8	6.8
Nicaraguan	255	0.7	1.8
Salvadoran	6,261	17.9	43.6
Dominican Republic	137	0.4	1.0
Mexican	2,729	7.8	19.0
Puerto Rican	669	1.9	4.7
South American	1,194	3.4	8.3
Bolivian	327	0.9	2.3
Colombian	111	0.3	0.8
Peruvian	509	1.5	3.5

Population Growth: 2000–2010

Group	%
Total Population	n/a

Males per 100 Females

Group	Number
Total Population	103.7
Hispanic or Latino (of any race)	117.0
Central American, ex. Mexican	116.5
Guatemalan	113.7
Honduran	141.4
Nicaraguan	110.7
Salvadoran	113.5
Dominican Republic	93.0
Mexican	135.7
Puerto Rican	83.3
South American	107.7
Bolivian	113.7
Colombian	76.2
Peruvian	115.7

Average Household Size

Group	People
Total Population	3.17
Hispanic or Latino (of any race)	4.65
Central American, ex. Mexican	5.01
Guatemalan	4.83
Honduran	4.94
Nicaraguan	4.71
Salvadoran	5.08
Dominican Republic	3.34
Mexican	4.78
Puerto Rican	2.89
South American	4.29
Bolivian	4.51
Colombian	3.44
Peruvian	4.42

Median Age

Group	Years
Total Population	30.5
Hispanic or Latino (of any race)	26.6
Central American, ex. Mexican	28.2
Guatemalan	29.9
Honduran	27.6
Nicaraguan	29.3
Salvadoran	28.1
Dominican Republic	26.8
Mexican	25.0
Puerto Rican	26.0
South American	32.6
Bolivian	31.1
Colombian	32.2
Peruvian	35.6

High School Graduates
(Universe: Population 25 Years and Over)

Group	Number	%
Total Population	14,810	74.8
Hispanic or Latino (of any race)	2,952	45.0
Central American, ex. Mexican	1,471	36.2
Salvadoran	860	30.0
Mexican	737	46.7

Four-Year College Graduates
(Universe: Population 25 Years and Over)

Group	Number	%
Total Population	4,099	20.7
Hispanic or Latino (of any race)	310	4.7
Central American, ex. Mexican	96	2.4
Salvadoran	66	2.3
Mexican	77	4.9

Population Age 3–17 Enrolled in Public School
(Universe: Population Age 3–17 Enrolled in School)

Group	Number	%
Total Population	5,908	93.3
Hispanic or Latino (of any race)	2,922	96.9
Central American, ex. Mexican	1,843	97.0
Salvadoran	1,436	98.2
Mexican	680	94.8

Population Age 3–17 Enrolled in Private School
(Universe: Population Age 3–17 Enrolled in School)

Group	Number	%
Total Population	421	6.7
Hispanic or Latino (of any race)	94	3.1
Central American, ex. Mexican	57	3.0
Salvadoran	26	1.8
Mexican	37	5.2

Foreign-Born Population

Group	Number	%
Total Population	10,948	33.8
Hispanic or Latino (of any race)	7,954	63.3
Central American, ex. Mexican	5,244	66.1
Salvadoran	3,726	65.5
Mexican	1,722	57.8

Foreign-Born Naturalized U.S. Citizens

Group	Number	%
Total Population	2,676	24.4
Hispanic or Latino (of any race)	1,378	17.3
Central American, ex. Mexican	925	17.6
Salvadoran	621	16.7
Mexican	214	12.4

Language Spoken at Home: English Only
(Universe: Population 5 Years and Over)

Group	Number	%
Total Population	15,085	51.0
Hispanic or Latino (of any race)	409	3.6
Central American, ex. Mexican	195	2.7
Salvadoran	166	3.2
Mexican	59	2.3

Language Spoken at Home: Spanish
(Universe: Population 5 Years and Over)

Group	Number	%
Total Population	11,552	39.0
Hispanic or Latino (of any race)	10,907	96.4
Central American, ex. Mexican	7,040	97.3
Salvadoran	4,990	96.8
Mexican	2,542	97.7

Unemployment Rate
(Universe: Population 16 Years and Over)

Group	%
Total Population	5.7
Hispanic or Latino (of any race)	6.9
Central American, ex. Mexican	8.3
Salvadoran	8.4
Mexican	4.8

Class of Worker: Private Wage and Salary
(Universe: Civilian Employed Population 16 Years and Over)

Group	Number	%
Total Population	12,089	73.2
Hispanic or Latino (of any race)	5,213	83.9
Central American, ex. Mexican	3,347	84.2
Salvadoran	2,294	86.6
Mexican	1,224	86.9

Class of Worker: Government
(Universe: Civilian Employed Population 16 Years and Over)

Group	Number	%
Total Population	3,458	21.0
Hispanic or Latino (of any race)	491	7.9
Central American, ex. Mexican	206	5.2

Notes: (1) Percent of total population; (2) Percent of Hispanic/Latino population; Profiles include places with an overall population of at least 125,000, OR an overall population of at least 25,000 where the Hispanic/Latino population is at least 20% of the overall population. In states where less than five places meet either of these criteria, we have included places with at least 10,000 total population with the highest percentage of Hispanic/Latino population. These places are identified with an asterisk (*); Please refer to the User's Guide for a full explanation of data.

Salvadoran	161	6.1
Mexican	131	9.3

Means of Transportation to Work: Car, Truck or Van
(Universe: Workers 16 Years and Over)

Group	Number	%
Total Population	14,904	90.0
Hispanic or Latino (of any race)	5,416	89.2
Central American, ex. Mexican	3,354	86.5
Salvadoran	2,193	86.1
Mexican	1,258	94.0

Means of Transportation to Work: Public Transportation (ex. Taxicab)
(Universe: Workers 16 Years and Over)

Group	Number	%
Total Population	799	4.8
Hispanic or Latino (of any race)	203	3.3
Central American, ex. Mexican	133	3.4
Salvadoran	133	5.2
Mexican	53	4.0

Homeownership Rate
(Universe: Occupied Housing Units)

Group	%
Total Population	54.1
Hispanic or Latino (of any race)	46.9
Central American, ex. Mexican	48.8
Guatemalan	60.9
Honduran	35.4
Nicaraguan	41.5
Salvadoran	50.3
Dominican Republic	28.6
Mexican	48.2
Puerto Rican	32.1
South American	52.5
Bolivian	58.2
Colombian	37.5
Peruvian	52.8

Median Home Value

Group	Dollars
Total Population	290,100
Hispanic or Latino (of any race)	306,700
Central American, ex. Mexican	314,300
Salvadoran	321,800
Mexican	313,200

Median Gross Rent

Group	Dollars
Total Population	1,205
Hispanic or Latino (of any race)	1,213
Central American, ex. Mexican	1,302
Salvadoran	1,238
Mexican	1,100

Median Household Income
(2010 Inflation-Adjusted Dollars)

Group	Dollars
Total Population	63,206
Hispanic or Latino (of any race)	59,502
Central American, ex. Mexican	60,234
Salvadoran	66,875
Mexican	69,063

Per Capita Income
(2010 Inflation-Adjusted Dollars)

Group	Dollars
Total Population	25,062
Hispanic or Latino (of any race)	15,291
Central American, ex. Mexican	15,068
Salvadoran	13,784
Mexican	15,655

Households with $100,000+ Income

Group	Number	%
Total Population	2,541	24.1
Hispanic or Latino (of any race)	499	18.0
Central American, ex. Mexican	279	16.5
Salvadoran	234	19.0
Mexican	179	25.8

Households with Food Stamps/SNAP Benefits During Past 12 Months

Group	Number	%
Total Population	526	5.0
Hispanic or Latino (of any race)	166	6.0
Central American, ex. Mexican	132	7.8
Salvadoran	82	6.7
Mexican	21	3.0

Poverty Rate
(Income in Past 12 Months Below Poverty Level)

Group	%
Total Population	9.0
Hispanic or Latino (of any race)	14.8
Central American, ex. Mexican	12.0
Salvadoran	15.0
Mexican	27.4

Newport News

Population

Group	Number	%TP[1]	%HP[2]
Total Population	180,719	100.0	–
Hispanic or Latino (of any race)	13,590	7.5	100.0
Central American, ex. Mexican	1,714	0.9	12.6
Guatemalan	337	0.2	2.5
Honduran	379	0.2	2.8
Panamanian	615	0.3	4.5
Salvadoran	264	0.1	1.9
Cuban	772	0.4	5.7
Dominican Republic	422	0.2	3.1
Mexican	4,473	2.5	32.9
Puerto Rican	4,544	2.5	33.4
South American	607	0.3	4.5
Colombian	225	0.1	1.7
Ecuadorian	112	0.1	0.8
Peruvian	115	0.1	0.8
Spaniard	235	0.1	1.7

Population Growth: 2000–2010

Group	%
Total Population	0.3
Hispanic or Latino (of any race)	78.9
Central American, ex. Mexican	213.9
Panamanian	61.4
Cuban	278.4
Dominican Republic	134.4
Mexican	128.7
Puerto Rican	44.5
South American	105.8
Colombian	108.3

Males per 100 Females

Group	Number
Total Population	93.4
Hispanic or Latino (of any race)	108.8
Central American, ex. Mexican	114.3
Guatemalan	224.0
Honduran	149.3
Panamanian	65.3
Salvadoran	127.6
Cuban	103.2
Dominican Republic	81.9
Mexican	132.7
Puerto Rican	96.8
South American	87.9
Colombian	82.9
Ecuadorian	100.0
Peruvian	62.0
Spaniard	78.0

Average Household Size

Group	People
Total Population	2.45
Hispanic or Latino (of any race)	3.01
Central American, ex. Mexican	3.11
Guatemalan	4.08
Honduran	3.55
Panamanian	2.50
Salvadoran	3.98
Cuban	2.89
Dominican Republic	3.00
Mexican	3.30
Puerto Rican	2.89
South American	2.81
Colombian	2.66
Ecuadorian	3.00
Peruvian	3.22
Spaniard	2.29

Median Age

Group	Years
Total Population	32.3
Hispanic or Latino (of any race)	25.1
Central American, ex. Mexican	28.8
Guatemalan	27.4
Honduran	27.8
Panamanian	32.0
Salvadoran	28.1
Cuban	30.0
Dominican Republic	24.3
Mexican	24.0
Puerto Rican	24.0
South American	28.8
Colombian	29.1
Ecuadorian	27.5
Peruvian	29.2
Spaniard	27.7

High School Graduates
(Universe: Population 25 Years and Over)

Group	Number	%
Total Population	99,623	88.9
Hispanic or Latino (of any race)	5,549	89.8
Central American, ex. Mexican	674	90.3
Mexican	1,821	86.5
Puerto Rican	1,778	87.4

Four-Year College Graduates
(Universe: Population 25 Years and Over)

Group	Number	%
Total Population	26,278	23.5
Hispanic or Latino (of any race)	998	16.2
Central American, ex. Mexican	140	18.8
Mexican	301	14.3
Puerto Rican	237	11.6

Population Age 3–17 Enrolled in Public School
(Universe: Population Age 3–17 Enrolled in School)

Group	Number	%
Total Population	29,127	87.7
Hispanic or Latino (of any race)	2,615	92.8
Central American, ex. Mexican	320	100.0
Mexican	754	88.2
Puerto Rican	1,087	100.0

Population Age 3–17 Enrolled in Private School
(Universe: Population Age 3–17 Enrolled in School)

Group	Number	%
Total Population	4,103	12.3
Hispanic or Latino (of any race)	202	7.2
Central American, ex. Mexican	0	0.0
Mexican	101	11.8
Puerto Rican	0	0.0

Foreign-Born Population

Group	Number	%
Total Population	12,506	6.9
Hispanic or Latino (of any race)	3,550	28.6
Central American, ex. Mexican	791	60.1
Mexican	1,616	34.3
Puerto Rican	42	1.0

Foreign-Born Naturalized U.S. Citizens

Group	Number	%
Total Population	6,138	49.1
Hispanic or Latino (of any race)	993	28.0
Central American, ex. Mexican	219	27.7
Mexican	255	15.8
Puerto Rican	42	100.0

Language Spoken at Home: English Only
(Universe: Population 5 Years and Over)

Group	Number	%
Total Population	152,403	90.6
Hispanic or Latino (of any race)	4,686	43.0
Central American, ex. Mexican	286	23.9
Mexican	1,821	47.8
Puerto Rican	1,639	43.3

Notes: (1) Percent of total population; (2) Percent of Hispanic/Latino population; Profiles include places with an overall population of at least 125,000, OR an overall population of at least 25,000 where the Hispanic/Latino population is at least 20% of the overall population. In states where less than five places meet either of these criteria, we have included places with at least 10,000 total population with the highest percentage of Hispanic/Latino population. These places are identified with an asterisk (*); Please refer to the User's Guide for a full explanation of data.

Language Spoken at Home: Spanish
(Universe: Population 5 Years and Over)

Group	Number	%
Total Population	8,416	5.0
Hispanic or Latino (of any race)	6,058	55.6
Central American, ex. Mexican	910	76.1
Mexican	1,926	50.6
Puerto Rican	2,110	55.7

Unemployment Rate
(Universe: Population 16 Years and Over)

Group	%
Total Population	7.9
Hispanic or Latino (of any race)	8.4
Central American, ex. Mexican	5.3
Mexican	6.7
Puerto Rican	9.6

Class of Worker: Private Wage and Salary
(Universe: Civilian Employed Population 16 Years and Over)

Group	Number	%
Total Population	62,744	75.7
Hispanic or Latino (of any race)	4,377	81.3
Central American, ex. Mexican	513	76.0
Mexican	1,543	86.9
Puerto Rican	1,396	76.0

Class of Worker: Government
(Universe: Civilian Employed Population 16 Years and Over)

Group	Number	%
Total Population	17,543	21.2
Hispanic or Latino (of any race)	812	15.1
Central American, ex. Mexican	125	18.5
Mexican	171	9.6
Puerto Rican	379	20.6

Means of Transportation to Work: Car, Truck or Van
(Universe: Workers 16 Years and Over)

Group	Number	%
Total Population	79,359	87.7
Hispanic or Latino (of any race)	5,167	81.6
Central American, ex. Mexican	522	73.1
Mexican	1,733	73.4
Puerto Rican	1,804	90.7

Means of Transportation to Work: Public Transportation (ex. Taxicab)
(Universe: Workers 16 Years and Over)

Group	Number	%
Total Population	2,797	3.1
Hispanic or Latino (of any race)	229	3.6
Central American, ex. Mexican	73	10.2
Mexican	80	3.4
Puerto Rican	10	0.5

Homeownership Rate
(Universe: Occupied Housing Units)

Group	%
Total Population	51.1
Hispanic or Latino (of any race)	36.4
Central American, ex. Mexican	32.0
Guatemalan	14.1
Honduran	24.7
Panamanian	41.4
Salvadoran	31.3
Cuban	40.1
Dominican Republic	32.5
Mexican	34.1
Puerto Rican	37.7
South American	48.8
Colombian	41.8
Ecuadorian	47.5
Peruvian	62.5
Spaniard	48.6

Median Home Value

Group	Dollars
Total Population	198,500
Hispanic or Latino (of any race)	185,200
Central American, ex. Mexican	149,000
Mexican	217,100
Puerto Rican	173,100

Median Gross Rent

Group	Dollars
Total Population	881
Hispanic or Latino (of any race)	890
Central American, ex. Mexican	845
Mexican	910
Puerto Rican	925

Median Household Income
(2010 Inflation-Adjusted Dollars)

Group	Dollars
Total Population	49,562
Hispanic or Latino (of any race)	53,020
Central American, ex. Mexican	42,520
Mexican	56,581
Puerto Rican	47,105

Per Capita Income
(2010 Inflation-Adjusted Dollars)

Group	Dollars
Total Population	24,249
Hispanic or Latino (of any race)	19,197
Central American, ex. Mexican	18,362
Mexican	19,187
Puerto Rican	18,214

Households with $100,000+ Income

Group	Number	%
Total Population	10,468	14.8
Hispanic or Latino (of any race)	514	15.1
Central American, ex. Mexican	0	0.0
Mexican	221	19.8
Puerto Rican	108	8.1

Households with Food Stamps/SNAP Benefits During Past 12 Months

Group	Number	%
Total Population	6,631	9.4
Hispanic or Latino (of any race)	234	6.9
Central American, ex. Mexican	0	0.0
Mexican	108	9.7
Puerto Rican	108	8.1

Poverty Rate
(Income in Past 12 Months Below Poverty Level)

Group	%
Total Population	13.5
Hispanic or Latino (of any race)	11.8
Central American, ex. Mexican	10.4
Mexican	8.7
Puerto Rican	13.3

Norfolk

Population

Group	Number	%TP[1]	%HP[2]
Total Population	242,803	100.0	–
Hispanic or Latino (of any race)	16,144	6.6	100.0
Central American, ex. Mexican	2,278	0.9	14.1
Guatemalan	211	0.1	1.3
Honduran	856	0.4	5.3
Nicaraguan	141	0.1	0.9
Panamanian	330	0.1	2.0
Salvadoran	676	0.3	4.2
Cuban	623	0.3	3.9
Dominican Republic	795	0.3	4.9
Mexican	5,432	2.2	33.6
Puerto Rican	4,387	1.8	27.2
South American	1,047	0.4	6.5
Colombian	310	0.1	1.9
Ecuadorian	195	0.1	1.2
Peruvian	249	0.1	1.5
Spaniard	398	0.2	2.5

Population Growth: 2000–2010

Group	%
Total Population	3.6
Hispanic or Latino (of any race)	81.1
Central American, ex. Mexican	364.9
Panamanian	123.0
Cuban	111.9
Dominican Republic	263.0
Mexican	107.0
Puerto Rican	50.4
South American	139.0
Colombian	106.7

Males per 100 Females

Group	Number
Total Population	107.5
Hispanic or Latino (of any race)	138.5
Central American, ex. Mexican	156.8
Guatemalan	181.3
Honduran	209.0
Nicaraguan	161.1
Panamanian	94.1
Salvadoran	138.0
Cuban	166.2
Dominican Republic	129.8
Mexican	159.5
Puerto Rican	121.5
South American	127.1
Colombian	162.7
Ecuadorian	129.4
Peruvian	112.8
Spaniard	98.0

Average Household Size

Group	People
Total Population	2.43
Hispanic or Latino (of any race)	2.97
Central American, ex. Mexican	3.59
Guatemalan	3.37
Honduran	4.00
Nicaraguan	3.79
Panamanian	2.42
Salvadoran	3.95
Cuban	2.67
Dominican Republic	2.91
Mexican	3.04
Puerto Rican	2.80
South American	2.72
Colombian	2.49
Ecuadorian	3.08
Peruvian	2.97
Spaniard	2.48

Median Age

Group	Years
Total Population	29.7
Hispanic or Latino (of any race)	23.8
Central American, ex. Mexican	26.8
Guatemalan	27.7
Honduran	27.7
Nicaraguan	24.5
Panamanian	27.8
Salvadoran	25.3
Cuban	24.4
Dominican Republic	23.4
Mexican	23.1
Puerto Rican	23.2
South American	25.3
Colombian	24.4
Ecuadorian	25.7
Peruvian	25.2
Spaniard	25.3

High School Graduates
(Universe: Population 25 Years and Over)

Group	Number	%
Total Population	119,392	83.9
Hispanic or Latino (of any race)	5,318	78.9
Central American, ex. Mexican	740	53.8
Mexican	1,645	85.1
Puerto Rican	1,390	82.8
South American	704	99.2

Four-Year College Graduates
(Universe: Population 25 Years and Over)

Group	Number	%
Total Population	33,730	23.7
Hispanic or Latino (of any race)	1,395	20.7
Central American, ex. Mexican	183	13.3
Mexican	276	14.3
Puerto Rican	358	21.3
South American	250	35.2

Notes: (1) Percent of total population; (2) Percent of Hispanic/Latino population; Profiles include places with an overall population of at least 125,000, OR an overall population of at least 25,000 where the Hispanic/Latino population is at least 20% of the overall population. In states where less than five places meet either of these criteria, we have included places with at least 10,000 total population with the highest percentage of Hispanic/Latino population. These places are identified with an asterisk (*); Please refer to the User's Guide for a full explanation of data.

Population Age 3–17 Enrolled in Public School
(Universe: Population Age 3–17 Enrolled in School)

Group	Number	%
Total Population	32,412	86.1
Hispanic or Latino (of any race)	2,170	84.4
Central American, ex. Mexican	111	63.8
Mexican	739	84.2
Puerto Rican	898	88.3
South American	333	97.4

Population Age 3–17 Enrolled in Private School
(Universe: Population Age 3–17 Enrolled in School)

Group	Number	%
Total Population	5,243	13.9
Hispanic or Latino (of any race)	400	15.6
Central American, ex. Mexican	63	36.2
Mexican	139	15.8
Puerto Rican	119	11.7
South American	9	2.6

Foreign-Born Population

Group	Number	%
Total Population	16,572	6.8
Hispanic or Latino (of any race)	4,287	28.5
Central American, ex. Mexican	1,790	74.0
Mexican	1,224	26.5
Puerto Rican	152	3.4
South American	658	46.3

Foreign-Born Naturalized U.S. Citizens

Group	Number	%
Total Population	7,144	43.1
Hispanic or Latino (of any race)	967	22.6
Central American, ex. Mexican	180	10.1
Mexican	204	16.7
Puerto Rican	102	67.1
South American	237	36.0

Language Spoken at Home: English Only
(Universe: Population 5 Years and Over)

Group	Number	%
Total Population	203,677	90.5
Hispanic or Latino (of any race)	5,112	38.1
Central American, ex. Mexican	359	16.0
Mexican	1,876	45.0
Puerto Rican	1,711	44.5
South American	197	16.0

Language Spoken at Home: Spanish
(Universe: Population 5 Years and Over)

Group	Number	%
Total Population	10,353	4.6
Hispanic or Latino (of any race)	8,191	61.1
Central American, ex. Mexican	1,882	84.0
Mexican	2,263	54.2
Puerto Rican	2,080	54.1
South American	1,034	84.0

Unemployment Rate
(Universe: Population 16 Years and Over)

Group	%
Total Population	9.6
Hispanic or Latino (of any race)	8.5
Central American, ex. Mexican	2.8
Mexican	8.2
Puerto Rican	7.7
South American	5.4

Class of Worker: Private Wage and Salary
(Universe: Civilian Employed Population 16 Years and Over)

Group	Number	%
Total Population	76,128	73.7
Hispanic or Latino (of any race)	4,403	72.2
Central American, ex. Mexican	1,424	81.6
Mexican	1,146	73.4
Puerto Rican	951	63.1
South American	437	77.9

Class of Worker: Government
(Universe: Civilian Employed Population 16 Years and Over)

Group	Number	%
Total Population	23,152	22.4
Hispanic or Latino (of any race)	1,291	21.2
Central American, ex. Mexican	110	6.3
Mexican	340	21.8
Puerto Rican	482	32.0
South American	92	16.4

Means of Transportation to Work: Car, Truck or Van
(Universe: Workers 16 Years and Over)

Group	Number	%
Total Population	98,314	81.2
Hispanic or Latino (of any race)	5,915	75.6
Central American, ex. Mexican	1,489	82.9
Mexican	1,650	70.2
Puerto Rican	1,465	77.6
South American	513	76.7

Means of Transportation to Work: Public Transportation (ex. Taxicab)
(Universe: Workers 16 Years and Over)

Group	Number	%
Total Population	5,121	4.2
Hispanic or Latino (of any race)	459	5.9
Central American, ex. Mexican	211	11.7
Mexican	143	6.1
Puerto Rican	78	4.1
South American	16	2.4

Homeownership Rate
(Universe: Occupied Housing Units)

Group	%
Total Population	45.4
Hispanic or Latino (of any race)	29.7
Central American, ex. Mexican	24.5
Guatemalan	23.3
Honduran	10.2
Nicaraguan	20.8
Panamanian	46.9
Salvadoran	28.0
Cuban	46.8
Dominican Republic	29.5
Mexican	28.2
Puerto Rican	28.3
South American	35.9
Colombian	42.1
Ecuadorian	39.6
Peruvian	33.9
Spaniard	50.5

Median Home Value

Group	Dollars
Total Population	208,400
Hispanic or Latino (of any race)	196,100
Central American, ex. Mexican	165,300
Mexican	166,200
Puerto Rican	195,300
South American	375,000

Median Gross Rent

Group	Dollars
Total Population	845
Hispanic or Latino (of any race)	906
Central American, ex. Mexican	888
Mexican	945
Puerto Rican	944
South American	871

Median Household Income
(2010 Inflation-Adjusted Dollars)

Group	Dollars
Total Population	42,677
Hispanic or Latino (of any race)	42,736
Central American, ex. Mexican	41,083
Mexican	47,109
Puerto Rican	37,817
South American	43,340

Per Capita Income
(2010 Inflation-Adjusted Dollars)

Group	Dollars
Total Population	23,773
Hispanic or Latino (of any race)	16,865
Central American, ex. Mexican	16,628
Mexican	17,128
Puerto Rican	14,506
South American	16,168

Households with $100,000+ Income

Group	Number	%
Total Population	11,159	13.1
Hispanic or Latino (of any race)	183	4.6
Central American, ex. Mexican	19	2.7
Mexican	49	4.5
Puerto Rican	54	4.9
South American	0	0.0

Households with Food Stamps/SNAP Benefits During Past 12 Months

Group	Number	%
Total Population	9,867	11.6
Hispanic or Latino (of any race)	292	7.3
Central American, ex. Mexican	99	14.3
Mexican	17	1.6
Puerto Rican	122	11.1
South American	6	1.4

Poverty Rate
(Income in Past 12 Months Below Poverty Level)

Group	%
Total Population	16.5
Hispanic or Latino (of any race)	14.8
Central American, ex. Mexican	17.9
Mexican	15.8
Puerto Rican	16.6
South American	9.6

Richmond

Population

Group	Number	%TP[1]	%HP[2]
Total Population	204,214	100.0	–
Hispanic or Latino (of any race)	12,803	6.3	100.0
Central American, ex. Mexican	4,382	2.1	34.2
Guatemalan	1,936	0.9	15.1
Honduran	640	0.3	5.0
Salvadoran	1,551	0.8	12.1
Cuban	347	0.2	2.7
Dominican Republic	420	0.2	3.3
Mexican	4,161	2.0	32.5
Puerto Rican	1,486	0.7	11.6
South American	767	0.4	6.0
Bolivian	112	0.1	0.9
Colombian	179	0.1	1.4
Peruvian	170	0.1	1.3
Spaniard	176	0.1	1.4

Population Growth: 2000–2010

Group	%
Total Population	3.2
Hispanic or Latino (of any race)	152.3
Central American, ex. Mexican	352.2
Guatemalan	355.5
Salvadoran	363.0
Cuban	72.6
Mexican	185.6
Puerto Rican	82.3
South American	279.7

Males per 100 Females

Group	Number
Total Population	91.1
Hispanic or Latino (of any race)	128.4
Central American, ex. Mexican	160.4
Guatemalan	202.5
Honduran	150.0
Salvadoran	132.2
Cuban	81.7
Dominican Republic	79.5
Mexican	141.4
Puerto Rican	91.5
South American	87.1
Bolivian	86.7
Colombian	65.7
Peruvian	100.0
Spaniard	79.6

Average Household Size

Group	People
Total Population	2.20
Hispanic or Latino (of any race)	3.15

STATE & PLACE PROFILES

Notes: (1) Percent of total population; (2) Percent of Hispanic/Latino population; Profiles include places with an overall population of at least 125,000, OR an overall population of at least 25,000 where the Hispanic/Latino population is at least 20% of the overall population. In states where less than five places meet either of these criteria, we have included places with at least 10,000 total population with the highest percentage of Hispanic/Latino population. These places are identified with an asterisk (*); Please refer to the User's Guide for a full explanation of data.

Group	
Central American, ex. Mexican	3.65
Guatemalan	3.86
Honduran	3.94
Salvadoran	3.50
Cuban	2.12
Dominican Republic	2.99
Mexican	3.47
Puerto Rican	2.49
South American	2.30
Bolivian	2.31
Colombian	2.14
Peruvian	2.61
Spaniard	2.20

Median Age

Group	Years
Total Population	32.0
Hispanic or Latino (of any race)	25.6
Central American, ex. Mexican	27.4
Guatemalan	27.0
Honduran	28.0
Salvadoran	27.8
Cuban	25.7
Dominican Republic	22.0
Mexican	24.6
Puerto Rican	23.8
South American	25.8
Bolivian	22.4
Colombian	28.2
Peruvian	26.8
Spaniard	25.4

High School Graduates
(Universe: Population 25 Years and Over)

Group	Number	%
Total Population	102,171	80.2
Hispanic or Latino (of any race)	2,450	42.5
Central American, ex. Mexican	566	21.7
Guatemalan	273	18.2
Salvadoran	168	23.6
Mexican	860	46.9

Four-Year College Graduates
(Universe: Population 25 Years and Over)

Group	Number	%
Total Population	41,615	32.6
Hispanic or Latino (of any race)	595	10.3
Central American, ex. Mexican	64	2.5
Guatemalan	6	0.4
Salvadoran	41	5.8
Mexican	83	4.5

Population Age 3–17 Enrolled in Public School
(Universe: Population Age 3–17 Enrolled in School)

Group	Number	%
Total Population	22,810	83.8
Hispanic or Latino (of any race)	1,255	90.0
Central American, ex. Mexican	354	86.8
Guatemalan	107	100.0
Salvadoran	169	75.8
Mexican	673	93.9

Population Age 3–17 Enrolled in Private School
(Universe: Population Age 3–17 Enrolled in School)

Group	Number	%
Total Population	4,412	16.2
Hispanic or Latino (of any race)	139	10.0
Central American, ex. Mexican	54	13.2
Guatemalan	0	0.0
Salvadoran	54	24.2
Mexican	44	6.1

Foreign-Born Population

Group	Number	%
Total Population	14,392	7.1
Hispanic or Latino (of any race)	6,209	55.3
Central American, ex. Mexican	3,397	73.9
Guatemalan	1,941	77.9
Salvadoran	903	72.0
Mexican	2,109	54.8

Foreign-Born Naturalized U.S. Citizens

Group	Number	%
Total Population	3,499	24.3
Hispanic or Latino (of any race)	568	9.1
Central American, ex. Mexican	228	6.7
Guatemalan	19	1.0
Salvadoran	97	10.7
Mexican	101	4.8

Language Spoken at Home: English Only
(Universe: Population 5 Years and Over)

Group	Number	%
Total Population	170,605	90.4
Hispanic or Latino (of any race)	2,137	22.0
Central American, ex. Mexican	452	10.8
Guatemalan	150	6.7
Salvadoran	96	8.0
Mexican	624	19.7

Language Spoken at Home: Spanish
(Universe: Population 5 Years and Over)

Group	Number	%
Total Population	9,815	5.2
Hispanic or Latino (of any race)	7,548	77.7
Central American, ex. Mexican	3,731	89.2
Guatemalan	2,104	93.3
Salvadoran	1,102	92.0
Mexican	2,521	79.7

Unemployment Rate
(Universe: Population 16 Years and Over)

Group	%
Total Population	10.5
Hispanic or Latino (of any race)	16.1
Central American, ex. Mexican	22.4
Guatemalan	24.2
Salvadoran	20.8
Mexican	6.4

Class of Worker: Private Wage and Salary
(Universe: Civilian Employed Population 16 Years and Over)

Group	Number	%
Total Population	76,380	79.1
Hispanic or Latino (of any race)	4,794	92.1
Central American, ex. Mexican	2,255	98.9
Guatemalan	1,271	99.6
Salvadoran	646	100.0
Mexican	1,690	91.2

Class of Worker: Government
(Universe: Civilian Employed Population 16 Years and Over)

Group	Number	%
Total Population	15,960	16.5
Hispanic or Latino (of any race)	246	4.7
Central American, ex. Mexican	19	0.8
Guatemalan	5	0.4
Salvadoran	0	0.0
Mexican	43	2.3

Means of Transportation to Work: Car, Truck or Van
(Universe: Workers 16 Years and Over)

Group	Number	%
Total Population	77,608	82.7
Hispanic or Latino (of any race)	4,504	88.2
Central American, ex. Mexican	2,046	93.0
Guatemalan	1,178	96.8
Salvadoran	543	84.1
Mexican	1,717	92.1

Means of Transportation to Work: Public Transportation (ex. Taxicab)
(Universe: Workers 16 Years and Over)

Group	Number	%
Total Population	6,534	7.0
Hispanic or Latino (of any race)	173	3.4
Central American, ex. Mexican	62	2.8
Guatemalan	23	1.9
Salvadoran	39	6.0
Mexican	35	1.9

Homeownership Rate
(Universe: Occupied Housing Units)

Group	%
Total Population	43.1
Hispanic or Latino (of any race)	21.0
Central American, ex. Mexican	17.6
Guatemalan	11.7
Honduran	12.1
Salvadoran	25.1
Cuban	29.9
Dominican Republic	28.3
Mexican	17.4
Puerto Rican	23.4
South American	32.2
Bolivian	36.1
Colombian	39.7
Peruvian	16.9
Spaniard	35.4

Median Home Value

Group	Dollars
Total Population	201,800
Hispanic or Latino (of any race)	136,300
Central American, ex. Mexican	120,200
Guatemalan	<10,000
Salvadoran	77,300
Mexican	93,800

Median Gross Rent

Group	Dollars
Total Population	805
Hispanic or Latino (of any race)	769
Central American, ex. Mexican	779
Guatemalan	752
Salvadoran	871
Mexican	785

Median Household Income
(2010 Inflation-Adjusted Dollars)

Group	Dollars
Total Population	38,266
Hispanic or Latino (of any race)	32,855
Central American, ex. Mexican	35,634
Guatemalan	45,972
Salvadoran	25,566
Mexican	33,844

Per Capita Income
(2010 Inflation-Adjusted Dollars)

Group	Dollars
Total Population	26,034
Hispanic or Latino (of any race)	13,077
Central American, ex. Mexican	13,353
Guatemalan	13,988
Salvadoran	10,922
Mexican	11,596

Households with $100,000+ Income

Group	Number	%
Total Population	11,346	13.6
Hispanic or Latino (of any race)	265	9.2
Central American, ex. Mexican	108	9.2
Guatemalan	66	12.6
Salvadoran	8	1.9
Mexican	80	9.8

Households with Food Stamps/SNAP Benefits During Past 12 Months

Group	Number	%
Total Population	11,696	14.0
Hispanic or Latino (of any race)	346	12.0
Central American, ex. Mexican	53	4.5
Guatemalan	20	3.8
Salvadoran	25	5.8
Mexican	209	25.5

Poverty Rate
(Income in Past 12 Months Below Poverty Level)

Group	%
Total Population	25.3
Hispanic or Latino (of any race)	38.4
Central American, ex. Mexican	42.9
Guatemalan	39.4
Salvadoran	49.9
Mexican	32.2

Springfield

Population

Group	Number	%TP[1]	%HP[2]
Total Population	30,484	100.0	–
Hispanic or Latino (of any race)	7,766	25.5	100.0
Central American, ex. Mexican	4,125	13.5	53.1

Notes: (1) Percent of total population; (2) Percent of Hispanic/Latino population; Profiles include places with an overall population of at least 125,000, OR an overall population of at least 25,000 where the Hispanic/Latino population is at least 20% of the overall population. In states where less than five places meet either of these criteria, we have included places with at least 10,000 total population with the highest percentage of Hispanic/Latino population. These places are identified with an asterisk (*); Please refer to the User's Guide for a full explanation of data.

Guatemalan	240	0.8	3.1
Honduran	1,759	5.8	22.7
Salvadoran	1,961	6.4	25.3
Mexican	485	1.6	6.2
Puerto Rican	233	0.8	3.0
South American	1,868	6.1	24.1
Argentinean	121	0.4	1.6
Bolivian	855	2.8	11.0
Colombian	110	0.4	1.4
Peruvian	573	1.9	7.4

Population Growth: 2000–2010

Group	%
Total Population	0.2
Hispanic or Latino (of any race)	44.5
Central American, ex. Mexican	102.3
Guatemalan	122.2
Honduran	146.7
Salvadoran	98.1
Mexican	19.8
Puerto Rican	5.4
South American	140.7
Bolivian	228.8
Peruvian	142.8

Males per 100 Females

Group	Number
Total Population	99.1
Hispanic or Latino (of any race)	117.8
Central American, ex. Mexican	129.7
Guatemalan	144.9
Honduran	150.2
Salvadoran	116.9
Mexican	112.7
Puerto Rican	82.0
South American	98.9
Argentinean	105.1
Bolivian	101.2
Colombian	83.3
Peruvian	101.1

Average Household Size

Group	People
Total Population	2.97
Hispanic or Latino (of any race)	4.87
Central American, ex. Mexican	5.49
Guatemalan	4.92
Honduran	5.83
Salvadoran	5.41
Mexican	4.09
Puerto Rican	2.74
South American	4.59
Argentinean	4.30
Bolivian	4.95
Colombian	3.84
Peruvian	4.51

Median Age

Group	Years
Total Population	38.3
Hispanic or Latino (of any race)	29.4
Central American, ex. Mexican	29.3
Guatemalan	31.6
Honduran	29.3
Salvadoran	28.7
Mexican	25.3
Puerto Rican	32.8
South American	34.6
Argentinean	31.8
Bolivian	32.7
Colombian	37.0
Peruvian	38.2

High School Graduates
(Universe: Population 25 Years and Over)

Group	Number	%
Total Population	17,495	83.8
Hispanic or Latino (of any race)	2,652	60.5
Central American, ex. Mexican	1,260	49.2
Honduran	414	53.6
Salvadoran	624	41.4
South American	1,082	76.5
Bolivian	637	81.9

Four-Year College Graduates
(Universe: Population 25 Years and Over)

Group	Number	%
Total Population	8,463	40.5
Hispanic or Latino (of any race)	730	16.6
Central American, ex. Mexican	227	8.9
Honduran	123	15.9
Salvadoran	49	3.2
South American	397	28.1
Bolivian	178	22.9

Population Age 3–17 Enrolled in Public School
(Universe: Population Age 3–17 Enrolled in School)

Group	Number	%
Total Population	4,247	82.5
Hispanic or Latino (of any race)	1,007	86.1
Central American, ex. Mexican	635	85.5
Honduran	114	100.0
Salvadoran	351	76.5
South American	106	77.9
Bolivian	84	73.7

Population Age 3–17 Enrolled in Private School
(Universe: Population Age 3–17 Enrolled in School)

Group	Number	%
Total Population	898	17.5
Hispanic or Latino (of any race)	162	13.9
Central American, ex. Mexican	108	14.5
Honduran	0	0.0
Salvadoran	108	23.5
South American	30	22.1
Bolivian	30	26.3

Foreign-Born Population

Group	Number	%
Total Population	12,470	40.8
Hispanic or Latino (of any race)	5,050	68.2
Central American, ex. Mexican	3,230	71.3
Honduran	1,077	69.2
Salvadoran	1,784	75.1
South American	1,535	85.2
Bolivian	895	83.9

Foreign-Born Naturalized U.S. Citizens

Group	Number	%
Total Population	6,381	51.2
Hispanic or Latino (of any race)	1,538	30.5
Central American, ex. Mexican	632	19.6
Honduran	51	4.7
Salvadoran	491	27.5
South American	705	45.9
Bolivian	227	25.4

Language Spoken at Home: English Only
(Universe: Population 5 Years and Over)

Group	Number	%
Total Population	13,236	47.0
Hispanic or Latino (of any race)	562	8.5
Central American, ex. Mexican	151	3.8
Honduran	0	0.0
Salvadoran	109	5.0
South American	87	5.2
Bolivian	38	4.0

Language Spoken at Home: Spanish
(Universe: Population 5 Years and Over)

Group	Number	%
Total Population	6,643	23.6
Hispanic or Latino (of any race)	6,020	91.3
Central American, ex. Mexican	3,850	96.2
Honduran	1,224	100.0
Salvadoran	2,093	95.0
South American	1,589	94.1
Bolivian	916	96.0

Unemployment Rate
(Universe: Population 16 Years and Over)

Group	%
Total Population	6.9
Hispanic or Latino (of any race)	6.3
Central American, ex. Mexican	7.2
Honduran	7.8
Salvadoran	8.4
South American	4.5
Bolivian	7.6

Class of Worker: Private Wage and Salary
(Universe: Civilian Employed Population 16 Years and Over)

Group	Number	%
Total Population	11,232	73.7
Hispanic or Latino (of any race)	3,500	81.7
Central American, ex. Mexican	2,179	83.7
Honduran	824	92.4
Salvadoran	1,108	80.3
South American	1,034	81.0
Bolivian	611	83.2

Class of Worker: Government
(Universe: Civilian Employed Population 16 Years and Over)

Group	Number	%
Total Population	3,140	20.6
Hispanic or Latino (of any race)	355	8.3
Central American, ex. Mexican	116	4.5
Honduran	40	4.5
Salvadoran	58	4.2
South American	138	10.8
Bolivian	31	4.2

Means of Transportation to Work: Car, Truck or Van
(Universe: Workers 16 Years and Over)

Group	Number	%
Total Population	12,840	85.8
Hispanic or Latino (of any race)	3,629	89.5
Central American, ex. Mexican	2,352	94.3
Honduran	740	89.8
Salvadoran	1,279	95.6
South American	925	79.7
Bolivian	543	81.4

Means of Transportation to Work: Public Transportation (ex. Taxicab)
(Universe: Workers 16 Years and Over)

Group	Number	%
Total Population	1,314	8.8
Hispanic or Latino (of any race)	136	3.4
Central American, ex. Mexican	46	1.8
Honduran	46	5.6
Salvadoran	0	0.0
South American	41	3.5
Bolivian	41	6.1

Homeownership Rate
(Universe: Occupied Housing Units)

Group	%
Total Population	62.3
Hispanic or Latino (of any race)	54.7
Central American, ex. Mexican	46.5
Guatemalan	60.4
Honduran	25.9
Salvadoran	59.4
Mexican	55.8
Puerto Rican	48.7
South American	67.3
Argentinean	69.7
Bolivian	72.2
Colombian	71.0
Peruvian	59.0

Median Home Value

Group	Dollars
Total Population	431,900
Hispanic or Latino (of any race)	428,000
Central American, ex. Mexican	383,600
Honduran	–
Salvadoran	374,600
South American	469,000
Bolivian	461,900

Median Gross Rent

Group	Dollars
Total Population	1,534
Hispanic or Latino (of any race)	1,398
Central American, ex. Mexican	1,418
Honduran	1,368
Salvadoran	1,757
South American	1,230
Bolivian	1,625

Notes: (1) Percent of total population; (2) Percent of Hispanic/Latino population; Profiles include places with an overall population of at least 125,000, OR an overall population of at least 25,000 where the Hispanic/Latino population is at least 20% of the overall population. In states where less than five places meet either of these criteria, we have included places with at least 10,000 total population with the highest percentage of Hispanic/Latino population. These places are identified with an asterisk (*); Please refer to the User's Guide for a full explanation of data.

Median Household Income (2010 Inflation-Adjusted Dollars)	
Group	Dollars
Total Population	84,389
Hispanic or Latino (of any race)	85,270
Central American, ex. Mexican	72,941
Honduran	59,400
Salvadoran	87,466
South American	92,396
Bolivian	92,841

Per Capita Income (2010 Inflation-Adjusted Dollars)	
Group	Dollars
Total Population	36,525
Hispanic or Latino (of any race)	21,272
Central American, ex. Mexican	17,748
Honduran	13,139
Salvadoran	20,372
South American	30,393
Bolivian	28,005

Households with $100,000+ Income		
Group	Number	%
Total Population	4,269	41.7
Hispanic or Latino (of any race)	688	39.8
Central American, ex. Mexican	319	36.4
Honduran	64	26.7
Salvadoran	255	48.0
South American	237	39.3
Bolivian	109	31.8

Households with Food Stamps/SNAP Benefits During Past 12 Months		
Group	Number	%
Total Population	421	4.1
Hispanic or Latino (of any race)	125	7.2
Central American, ex. Mexican	125	14.3
Honduran	52	21.7
Salvadoran	73	13.7
South American	0	0.0
Bolivian	0	0.0

Poverty Rate (Income in Past 12 Months Below Poverty Level)	
Group	%
Total Population	8.7
Hispanic or Latino (of any race)	17.4
Central American, ex. Mexican	24.7
Honduran	40.8
Salvadoran	16.2
South American	4.0
Bolivian	2.2

Sterling

Population			
Group	Number	%TP[1]	%HP[2]
Total Population	27,822	100.0	–
Hispanic or Latino (of any race)	9,230	33.2	100.0
Central American, ex. Mexican	5,227	18.8	56.6
Guatemalan	384	1.4	4.2
Honduran	779	2.8	8.4
Nicaraguan	110	0.4	1.2
Salvadoran	3,903	14.0	42.3
Mexican	803	2.9	8.7
Puerto Rican	285	1.0	3.1
South American	1,597	5.7	17.3
Bolivian	483	1.7	5.2
Colombian	138	0.5	1.5
Ecuadorian	126	0.5	1.4
Peruvian	694	2.5	7.5

Population Growth: 2000–2010	
Group	%
Total Population	n/a

Males per 100 Females	
Group	Number
Total Population	105.3
Hispanic or Latino (of any race)	116.3
Central American, ex. Mexican	123.1
Guatemalan	138.5
Honduran	121.3
Nicaraguan	107.5
Salvadoran	122.0
Mexican	130.7
Puerto Rican	103.6
South American	100.9
Bolivian	106.4
Colombian	84.0
Ecuadorian	121.1
Peruvian	98.9

Average Household Size	
Group	People
Total Population	3.03
Hispanic or Latino (of any race)	4.68
Central American, ex. Mexican	5.21
Guatemalan	5.14
Honduran	5.43
Nicaraguan	3.97
Salvadoran	5.27
Mexican	4.52
Puerto Rican	2.65
South American	4.00
Bolivian	4.36
Colombian	3.44
Ecuadorian	3.82
Peruvian	4.11

Median Age	
Group	Years
Total Population	33.6
Hispanic or Latino (of any race)	28.7
Central American, ex. Mexican	28.6
Guatemalan	29.3
Honduran	28.6
Nicaraguan	35.0
Salvadoran	28.4
Mexican	26.3
Puerto Rican	33.1
South American	34.6
Bolivian	33.3
Colombian	36.3
Ecuadorian	32.5
Peruvian	36.1

High School Graduates (Universe: Population 25 Years and Over)		
Group	Number	%
Total Population	14,639	82.7
Hispanic or Latino (of any race)	2,661	55.9
Central American, ex. Mexican	1,513	45.6
Salvadoran	1,073	48.3
South American	569	90.5

Four-Year College Graduates (Universe: Population 25 Years and Over)		
Group	Number	%
Total Population	6,304	35.6
Hispanic or Latino (of any race)	571	12.0
Central American, ex. Mexican	213	6.4
Salvadoran	150	6.8
South American	220	35.0

Population Age 3–17 Enrolled in Public School (Universe: Population Age 3–17 Enrolled in School)		
Group	Number	%
Total Population	3,051	85.2
Hispanic or Latino (of any race)	1,134	100.0
Central American, ex. Mexican	578	100.0
Salvadoran	390	100.0
South American	246	100.0

Population Age 3–17 Enrolled in Private School (Universe: Population Age 3–17 Enrolled in School)		
Group	Number	%
Total Population	529	14.8
Hispanic or Latino (of any race)	0	0.0
Central American, ex. Mexican	0	0.0
Salvadoran	0	0.0
South American	0	0.0

Foreign-Born Population		
Group	Number	%
Total Population	9,018	35.3
Hispanic or Latino (of any race)	5,479	73.3
Central American, ex. Mexican	3,794	82.5
Salvadoran	2,538	84.2
South American	955	81.0

Foreign-Born Naturalized U.S. Citizens		
Group	Number	%
Total Population	2,729	30.3
Hispanic or Latino (of any race)	764	13.9
Central American, ex. Mexican	642	16.9
Salvadoran	439	17.3
South American	64	6.7

Language Spoken at Home: English Only (Universe: Population 5 Years and Over)		
Group	Number	%
Total Population	13,571	57.3
Hispanic or Latino (of any race)	587	8.5
Central American, ex. Mexican	111	2.6
Salvadoran	98	3.5
South American	96	9.2

Language Spoken at Home: Spanish (Universe: Population 5 Years and Over)		
Group	Number	%
Total Population	6,743	28.5
Hispanic or Latino (of any race)	6,295	91.4
Central American, ex. Mexican	4,150	97.3
Salvadoran	2,719	96.4
South American	949	90.8

Unemployment Rate (Universe: Population 16 Years and Over)	
Group	%
Total Population	4.9
Hispanic or Latino (of any race)	5.9
Central American, ex. Mexican	5.7
Salvadoran	6.2
South American	9.9

Class of Worker: Private Wage and Salary (Universe: Civilian Employed Population 16 Years and Over)		
Group	Number	%
Total Population	12,859	81.2
Hispanic or Latino (of any race)	4,088	86.8
Central American, ex. Mexican	2,735	85.3
Salvadoran	1,728	83.9
South American	476	85.8

Class of Worker: Government (Universe: Civilian Employed Population 16 Years and Over)		
Group	Number	%
Total Population	2,313	14.6
Hispanic or Latino (of any race)	280	5.9
Central American, ex. Mexican	187	5.8
Salvadoran	168	8.2
South American	41	7.4

Means of Transportation to Work: Car, Truck or Van (Universe: Workers 16 Years and Over)		
Group	Number	%
Total Population	14,236	92.4
Hispanic or Latino (of any race)	4,061	91.1
Central American, ex. Mexican	2,720	89.5
Salvadoran	1,827	95.0
South American	472	93.1

Means of Transportation to Work: Public Transportation (ex. Taxicab) (Universe: Workers 16 Years and Over)		
Group	Number	%
Total Population	240	1.6
Hispanic or Latino (of any race)	44	1.0
Central American, ex. Mexican	25	0.8
Salvadoran	25	1.3
South American	19	3.7

Homeownership Rate (Universe: Occupied Housing Units)	
Group	%
Total Population	74.4
Hispanic or Latino (of any race)	59.6
Central American, ex. Mexican	58.8
Guatemalan	48.8
Honduran	39.7
Nicaraguan	71.9
Salvadoran	61.7

Notes: (1) Percent of total population; (2) Percent of Hispanic/Latino population; Profiles include places with an overall population of at least 125,000, OR an overall population of at least 25,000 where the Hispanic/Latino population is at least 20% of the overall population. In states where less than five places meet either of these criteria, we have included places with at least 10,000 total population with the highest percentage of Hispanic/Latino population. These places are identified with an asterisk (*); Please refer to the User's Guide for a full explanation of data.

Mexican	49.1
Puerto Rican	64.0
South American	64.7
Bolivian	73.8
Colombian	74.4
Ecuadorian	73.7
Peruvian	55.3

Median Home Value

Group	Dollars
Total Population	349,900
Hispanic or Latino (of any race)	347,000
Central American, ex. Mexican	334,300
Salvadoran	331,300
South American	331,200

Median Gross Rent

Group	Dollars
Total Population	1,475
Hispanic or Latino (of any race)	1,681
Central American, ex. Mexican	1,709
Salvadoran	1,947
South American	2,000+

Median Household Income
(2010 Inflation-Adjusted Dollars)

Group	Dollars
Total Population	82,997
Hispanic or Latino (of any race)	61,985
Central American, ex. Mexican	64,846
Salvadoran	62,791
South American	41,838

Per Capita Income
(2010 Inflation-Adjusted Dollars)

Group	Dollars
Total Population	34,899
Hispanic or Latino (of any race)	21,632
Central American, ex. Mexican	23,106
Salvadoran	25,746
South American	16,570

Households with $100,000+ Income

Group	Number	%
Total Population	3,491	40.3
Hispanic or Latino (of any race)	321	17.3
Central American, ex. Mexican	253	21.9
Salvadoran	182	24.4
South American	0	0.0

Households with Food Stamps/SNAP Benefits During Past 12 Months

Group	Number	%
Total Population	176	2.0
Hispanic or Latino (of any race)	81	4.4
Central American, ex. Mexican	46	4.0
Salvadoran	46	6.2
South American	35	13.7

Poverty Rate
(Income in Past 12 Months Below Poverty Level)

Group	%
Total Population	5.0
Hispanic or Latino (of any race)	6.7
Central American, ex. Mexican	5.3
Salvadoran	3.5
South American	4.0

Virginia Beach

Population

Group	Number	%TP[1]	%HP[2]
Total Population	437,994	100.0	–
Hispanic or Latino (of any race)	28,987	6.6	100.0
Central American, ex. Mexican	2,755	0.6	9.5
Costa Rican	131	<0.1	0.5
Guatemalan	425	0.1	1.5
Honduran	555	0.1	1.9
Nicaraguan	185	<0.1	0.6
Panamanian	702	0.2	2.4
Salvadoran	741	0.2	2.6
Cuban	1,040	0.2	3.6
Dominican Republic	1,135	0.3	3.9
Mexican	8,528	1.9	29.4
Puerto Rican	9,461	2.2	32.6
South American	2,517	0.6	8.7
Argentinean	127	<0.1	0.4
Chilean	151	<0.1	0.5
Colombian	929	0.2	3.2
Ecuadorian	414	0.1	1.4
Peruvian	609	0.1	2.1
Venezuelan	143	<0.1	0.5
Spaniard	1,363	0.3	4.7

Population Growth: 2000–2010

Group	%
Total Population	3.0
Hispanic or Latino (of any race)	63.1
Central American, ex. Mexican	217.0
Panamanian	66.4
Salvadoran	497.6
Cuban	73.0
Dominican Republic	185.9
Mexican	75.7
Puerto Rican	50.8
South American	152.2
Colombian	136.4
Ecuadorian	174.2
Peruvian	250.0
Spaniard	403.0

Males per 100 Females

Group	Number
Total Population	95.9
Hispanic or Latino (of any race)	96.9
Central American, ex. Mexican	107.5
Costa Rican	87.1
Guatemalan	150.0
Honduran	160.6
Nicaraguan	103.3
Panamanian	67.1
Salvadoran	109.3
Cuban	88.7
Dominican Republic	92.4
Mexican	110.0
Puerto Rican	92.5
South American	80.3
Argentinean	89.6
Chilean	96.1
Colombian	80.4
Ecuadorian	76.9
Peruvian	78.6
Venezuelan	60.7
Spaniard	75.6

Average Household Size

Group	People
Total Population	2.60
Hispanic or Latino (of any race)	3.03
Central American, ex. Mexican	3.32
Costa Rican	2.87
Guatemalan	3.75
Honduran	3.70
Nicaraguan	2.74
Panamanian	2.75
Salvadoran	3.84
Cuban	2.73
Dominican Republic	3.08
Mexican	3.13
Puerto Rican	2.99
South American	3.03
Argentinean	2.73
Chilean	3.40
Colombian	2.81
Ecuadorian	3.31
Peruvian	3.20
Venezuelan	2.90
Spaniard	2.90

Median Age

Group	Years
Total Population	34.9
Hispanic or Latino (of any race)	25.1
Central American, ex. Mexican	26.8
Costa Rican	27.5
Guatemalan	24.2
Honduran	28.0
Nicaraguan	25.6
Panamanian	29.8
Salvadoran	26.2
Cuban	26.1
Dominican Republic	25.3
Mexican	23.4
Puerto Rican	24.6
South American	29.6
Argentinean	37.5
Chilean	32.4
Colombian	28.5
Ecuadorian	26.0
Peruvian	30.5
Venezuelan	31.3
Spaniard	31.0

High School Graduates
(Universe: Population 25 Years and Over)

Group	Number	%
Total Population	260,468	92.5
Hispanic or Latino (of any race)	11,591	86.1
Central American, ex. Mexican	1,375	74.2
Mexican	2,856	82.3
Puerto Rican	3,800	90.2
South American	1,202	86.5
Colombian	480	79.6
Spaniard	724	94.6

Four-Year College Graduates
(Universe: Population 25 Years and Over)

Group	Number	%
Total Population	89,893	31.9
Hispanic or Latino (of any race)	2,538	18.9
Central American, ex. Mexican	139	7.5
Mexican	558	16.1
Puerto Rican	707	16.8
South American	433	31.2
Colombian	110	18.2
Spaniard	277	36.2

Population Age 3–17 Enrolled in Public School
(Universe: Population Age 3–17 Enrolled in School)

Group	Number	%
Total Population	69,947	84.9
Hispanic or Latino (of any race)	6,440	93.1
Central American, ex. Mexican	281	79.8
Mexican	1,738	88.0
Puerto Rican	2,331	95.8
South American	824	98.8
Colombian	253	96.2
Spaniard	294	91.9

Population Age 3–17 Enrolled in Private School
(Universe: Population Age 3–17 Enrolled in School)

Group	Number	%
Total Population	12,401	15.1
Hispanic or Latino (of any race)	481	6.9
Central American, ex. Mexican	71	20.2
Mexican	236	12.0
Puerto Rican	101	4.2
South American	10	1.2
Colombian	10	3.8
Spaniard	26	8.1

Foreign-Born Population

Group	Number	%
Total Population	38,988	8.9
Hispanic or Latino (of any race)	6,697	24.6
Central American, ex. Mexican	1,967	68.0
Mexican	1,682	22.7
Puerto Rican	79	0.9
South American	1,519	58.1
Colombian	670	63.4
Spaniard	395	26.3

Foreign-Born Naturalized U.S. Citizens

Group	Number	%
Total Population	22,755	58.4
Hispanic or Latino (of any race)	2,856	42.6
Central American, ex. Mexican	822	41.8
Mexican	372	22.1
Puerto Rican	16	20.3
South American	667	43.9
Colombian	231	34.5
Spaniard	157	39.7

Notes: (1) Percent of total population; (2) Percent of Hispanic/Latino population; Profiles include places with an overall population of at least 125,000, OR an overall population of at least 25,000 where the Hispanic/Latino population is at least 20% of the overall population. In states where less than five places meet either of these criteria, we have included places with at least 10,000 total population with the highest percentage of Hispanic/Latino population. These places are identified with an asterisk (*); Please refer to the User's Guide for a full explanation of data.

Language Spoken at Home: English Only
(Universe: Population 5 Years and Over)

Group	Number	%
Total Population	358,990	88.3
Hispanic or Latino (of any race)	10,908	45.2
Central American, ex. Mexican	651	25.3
Mexican	3,245	51.0
Puerto Rican	3,781	48.0
South American	505	21.1
Colombian	270	26.9
Spaniard	977	68.6

Language Spoken at Home: Spanish
(Universe: Population 5 Years and Over)

Group	Number	%
Total Population	17,183	4.2
Hispanic or Latino (of any race)	13,006	53.9
Central American, ex. Mexican	1,922	74.7
Mexican	3,104	48.8
Puerto Rican	4,011	51.0
South American	1,847	77.2
Colombian	713	71.0
Spaniard	400	28.1

Unemployment Rate
(Universe: Population 16 Years and Over)

Group	%
Total Population	5.3
Hispanic or Latino (of any race)	5.4
Central American, ex. Mexican	1.4
Mexican	6.2
Puerto Rican	6.2
South American	5.1
Colombian	0.0
Spaniard	0.0

Class of Worker: Private Wage and Salary
(Universe: Civilian Employed Population 16 Years and Over)

Group	Number	%
Total Population	156,788	74.3
Hispanic or Latino (of any race)	8,813	78.0
Central American, ex. Mexican	1,462	85.2
Mexican	2,286	80.9
Puerto Rican	2,715	76.7
South American	582	68.2
Colombian	242	68.2
Spaniard	603	81.4

Class of Worker: Government
(Universe: Civilian Employed Population 16 Years and Over)

Group	Number	%
Total Population	43,794	20.8
Hispanic or Latino (of any race)	2,029	17.9
Central American, ex. Mexican	241	14.0
Mexican	473	16.7
Puerto Rican	772	21.8
South American	113	13.2
Colombian	34	9.6
Spaniard	96	13.0

Means of Transportation to Work: Car, Truck or Van
(Universe: Workers 16 Years and Over)

Group	Number	%
Total Population	211,376	91.3
Hispanic or Latino (of any race)	12,298	91.7
Central American, ex. Mexican	1,597	84.9
Mexican	3,213	90.3
Puerto Rican	3,979	95.3
South American	962	94.4
Colombian	424	94.4
Spaniard	759	92.7

Means of Transportation to Work: Public Transportation (ex. Taxicab)
(Universe: Workers 16 Years and Over)

Group	Number	%
Total Population	2,008	0.9
Hispanic or Latino (of any race)	229	1.7
Central American, ex. Mexican	97	5.2
Mexican	15	0.4
Puerto Rican	61	1.5
South American	56	5.5
Colombian	24	5.3
Spaniard	0	0.0

Homeownership Rate
(Universe: Occupied Housing Units)

Group	%
Total Population	65.3
Hispanic or Latino (of any race)	48.8
Central American, ex. Mexican	42.8
Costa Rican	43.6
Guatemalan	37.9
Honduran	31.1
Nicaraguan	48.3
Panamanian	54.6
Salvadoran	37.2
Cuban	56.4
Dominican Republic	43.9
Mexican	44.7
Puerto Rican	48.5
South American	60.3
Argentinean	53.3
Chilean	71.1
Colombian	59.3
Ecuadorian	66.1
Peruvian	58.0
Venezuelan	57.1
Spaniard	63.7

Median Home Value

Group	Dollars
Total Population	277,400
Hispanic or Latino (of any race)	244,200
Central American, ex. Mexican	245,300
Mexican	268,800
Puerto Rican	234,400
South American	267,000
Colombian	266,500
Spaniard	309,100

Median Gross Rent

Group	Dollars
Total Population	1,143
Hispanic or Latino (of any race)	1,150
Central American, ex. Mexican	1,031
Mexican	1,222
Puerto Rican	1,122
South American	1,248
Colombian	1,130
Spaniard	1,179

Median Household Income
(2010 Inflation-Adjusted Dollars)

Group	Dollars
Total Population	64,618
Hispanic or Latino (of any race)	56,764
Central American, ex. Mexican	42,986
Mexican	57,847
Puerto Rican	53,580
South American	55,188
Colombian	52,250
Spaniard	69,293

Per Capita Income
(2010 Inflation-Adjusted Dollars)

Group	Dollars
Total Population	30,873
Hispanic or Latino (of any race)	19,230
Central American, ex. Mexican	21,243
Mexican	17,495
Puerto Rican	18,702
South American	17,137
Colombian	20,471
Spaniard	20,880

Households with $100,000+ Income

Group	Number	%
Total Population	41,929	25.6
Hispanic or Latino (of any race)	1,451	19.7
Central American, ex. Mexican	170	22.3
Mexican	415	24.2
Puerto Rican	366	13.4
South American	104	16.2
Colombian	30	12.5
Spaniard	194	37.2

Households with Food Stamps/SNAP Benefits During Past 12 Months

Group	Number	%
Total Population	5,574	3.4
Hispanic or Latino (of any race)	372	5.0
Central American, ex. Mexican	62	8.1
Mexican	19	1.1
Puerto Rican	179	6.6
South American	41	6.4
Colombian	20	8.3
Spaniard	13	2.5

Poverty Rate
(Income in Past 12 Months Below Poverty Level)

Group	%
Total Population	6.8
Hispanic or Latino (of any race)	10.8
Central American, ex. Mexican	4.4
Mexican	9.9
Puerto Rican	14.6
South American	13.9
Colombian	1.6
Spaniard	6.8

West Falls Church

Population

Group	Number	%TP[1]	%HP[2]
Total Population	29,207	100.0	–
Hispanic or Latino (of any race)	9,679	33.1	100.0
Central American, ex. Mexican	4,274	14.6	44.2
Guatemalan	845	2.9	8.7
Honduran	441	1.5	4.6
Nicaraguan	180	0.6	1.9
Salvadoran	2,748	9.4	28.4
Mexican	693	2.4	7.2
Puerto Rican	161	0.6	1.7
South American	3,296	11.3	34.1
Argentinean	198	0.7	2.0
Bolivian	2,226	7.6	23.0
Colombian	130	0.4	1.3
Peruvian	480	1.6	5.0

Population Growth: 2000–2010

Group	%
Total Population	n/a

Males per 100 Females

Group	Number
Total Population	101.3
Hispanic or Latino (of any race)	114.1
Central American, ex. Mexican	118.4
Guatemalan	142.8
Honduran	141.0
Nicaraguan	97.8
Salvadoran	111.1
Mexican	124.3
Puerto Rican	114.7
South American	110.2
Argentinean	120.0
Bolivian	120.8
Colombian	78.1
Peruvian	94.3

Average Household Size

Group	People
Total Population	2.86
Hispanic or Latino (of any race)	4.30
Central American, ex. Mexican	4.83
Guatemalan	5.00
Honduran	5.21
Nicaraguan	4.17
Salvadoran	4.84
Mexican	3.80
Puerto Rican	2.42
South American	4.22
Argentinean	3.82
Bolivian	4.59
Colombian	3.14
Peruvian	3.76

Notes: (1) Percent of total population; (2) Percent of Hispanic/Latino population; Profiles include places with an overall population of at least 125,000, OR an overall population of at least 25,000 where the Hispanic/Latino population is at least 20% of the overall population. In states where less than five places meet either of these criteria, we have included places with at least 10,000 total population with the highest percentage of Hispanic/Latino population. These places are identified with an asterisk (*); Please refer to the User's Guide for a full explanation of data.

Median Age	
Group	Years
Total Population	35.4
Hispanic or Latino (of any race)	29.5
Central American, ex. Mexican	29.0
Guatemalan	27.4
Honduran	27.6
Nicaraguan	32.8
Salvadoran	29.8
Mexican	28.1
Puerto Rican	38.1
South American	33.0
Argentinean	32.0
Bolivian	31.6
Colombian	38.7
Peruvian	37.2

High School Graduates (Universe: Population 25 Years and Over)		
Group	Number	%
Total Population	16,896	85.4
Hispanic or Latino (of any race)	3,120	66.8
Central American, ex. Mexican	889	59.3
Salvadoran	374	53.5
South American	1,732	72.5
Bolivian	757	71.4

Four-Year College Graduates (Universe: Population 25 Years and Over)		
Group	Number	%
Total Population	8,795	44.4
Hispanic or Latino (of any race)	760	16.3
Central American, ex. Mexican	135	9.0
Salvadoran	79	11.3
South American	512	21.4
Bolivian	254	24.0

Population Age 3–17 Enrolled in Public School (Universe: Population Age 3–17 Enrolled in School)		
Group	Number	%
Total Population	3,292	77.9
Hispanic or Latino (of any race)	1,148	82.7
Central American, ex. Mexican	404	96.2
Salvadoran	240	100.0
South American	395	77.9
Bolivian	211	83.7

Population Age 3–17 Enrolled in Private School (Universe: Population Age 3–17 Enrolled in School)		
Group	Number	%
Total Population	935	22.1
Hispanic or Latino (of any race)	240	17.3
Central American, ex. Mexican	16	3.8
Salvadoran	0	0.0
South American	112	22.1
Bolivian	41	16.3

Foreign-Born Population		
Group	Number	%
Total Population	11,235	40.7
Hispanic or Latino (of any race)	4,855	63.8
Central American, ex. Mexican	1,788	71.9
Salvadoran	818	64.3
South American	2,621	74.5
Bolivian	1,259	78.2

Foreign-Born Naturalized U.S. Citizens		
Group	Number	%
Total Population	4,933	43.9
Hispanic or Latino (of any race)	1,384	28.5
Central American, ex. Mexican	389	21.8
Salvadoran	199	24.3
South American	869	33.2
Bolivian	362	28.8

Language Spoken at Home: English Only (Universe: Population 5 Years and Over)		
Group	Number	%
Total Population	12,775	49.7
Hispanic or Latino (of any race)	912	13.4
Central American, ex. Mexican	68	3.0
Salvadoran	25	2.1
South American	102	3.3
Bolivian	29	2.0

Language Spoken at Home: Spanish (Universe: Population 5 Years and Over)		
Group	Number	%
Total Population	6,317	24.6
Hispanic or Latino (of any race)	5,819	85.5
Central American, ex. Mexican	2,227	97.0
Salvadoran	1,151	97.9
South American	2,965	94.6
Bolivian	1,448	98.0

Unemployment Rate (Universe: Population 16 Years and Over)	
Group	%
Total Population	4.7
Hispanic or Latino (of any race)	6.6
Central American, ex. Mexican	6.1
Salvadoran	8.4
South American	6.4
Bolivian	11.7

Class of Worker: Private Wage and Salary (Universe: Civilian Employed Population 16 Years and Over)		
Group	Number	%
Total Population	12,475	77.9
Hispanic or Latino (of any race)	3,570	85.6
Central American, ex. Mexican	1,209	92.8
Salvadoran	531	86.5
South American	1,778	83.6
Bolivian	816	85.7

Class of Worker: Government (Universe: Civilian Employed Population 16 Years and Over)		
Group	Number	%
Total Population	2,568	16.0
Hispanic or Latino (of any race)	276	6.6
Central American, ex. Mexican	11	0.8
Salvadoran	0	0.0
South American	108	5.1
Bolivian	26	2.7

Means of Transportation to Work: Car, Truck or Van (Universe: Workers 16 Years and Over)		
Group	Number	%
Total Population	13,120	83.4
Hispanic or Latino (of any race)	3,076	75.3
Central American, ex. Mexican	913	70.4
Salvadoran	424	69.7
South American	1,515	74.6
Bolivian	790	87.4

Means of Transportation to Work: Public Transportation (ex. Taxicab) (Universe: Workers 16 Years and Over)		
Group	Number	%
Total Population	1,410	9.0
Hispanic or Latino (of any race)	622	15.2
Central American, ex. Mexican	218	16.8
Salvadoran	121	19.9
South American	304	15.0
Bolivian	72	8.0

Homeownership Rate (Universe: Occupied Housing Units)	
Group	%
Total Population	65.2
Hispanic or Latino (of any race)	42.9
Central American, ex. Mexican	37.8
Guatemalan	26.5
Honduran	16.3
Nicaraguan	39.1
Salvadoran	43.0
Mexican	40.8
Puerto Rican	46.7
South American	49.1
Argentinean	44.9
Bolivian	46.9
Colombian	52.8
Peruvian	51.4

Median Home Value	
Group	Dollars
Total Population	461,300
Hispanic or Latino (of any race)	445,500
Central American, ex. Mexican	465,600
Salvadoran	450,000
South American	449,700
Bolivian	488,900

Median Gross Rent	
Group	Dollars
Total Population	1,390
Hispanic or Latino (of any race)	1,538
Central American, ex. Mexican	1,714
Salvadoran	1,819
South American	1,325
Bolivian	1,107

Median Household Income (2010 Inflation-Adjusted Dollars)	
Group	Dollars
Total Population	85,744
Hispanic or Latino (of any race)	55,625
Central American, ex. Mexican	58,229
Salvadoran	78,879
South American	63,594
Bolivian	81,250

Per Capita Income (2010 Inflation-Adjusted Dollars)	
Group	Dollars
Total Population	39,389
Hispanic or Latino (of any race)	20,525
Central American, ex. Mexican	16,140
Salvadoran	15,335
South American	20,554
Bolivian	17,925

Households with $100,000+ Income		
Group	Number	%
Total Population	4,185	41.7
Hispanic or Latino (of any race)	423	22.4
Central American, ex. Mexican	83	17.8
Salvadoran	68	27.4
South American	288	28.5
Bolivian	129	32.9

Households with Food Stamps/SNAP Benefits During Past 12 Months		
Group	Number	%
Total Population	342	3.4
Hispanic or Latino (of any race)	151	8.0
Central American, ex. Mexican	58	12.5
Salvadoran	58	23.4
South American	10	1.0
Bolivian	10	2.6

Poverty Rate (Income in Past 12 Months Below Poverty Level)	
Group	%
Total Population	7.6
Hispanic or Latino (of any race)	13.1
Central American, ex. Mexican	19.6
Salvadoran	26.0
South American	4.4
Bolivian	0.0

STATE & PLACE PROFILES

Notes: (1) Percent of total population; (2) Percent of Hispanic/Latino population; Profiles include places with an overall population of at least 125,000, OR an overall population of at least 25,000 where the Hispanic/Latino population is at least 20% of the overall population. In states where less than five places meet either of these criteria, we have included places with at least 10,000 total population with the highest percentage of Hispanic/Latino population. These places are identified with an asterisk (*); Please refer to the User's Guide for a full explanation of data.

Washington

EDITOR'S NOTE: For a place to be included in this edition, it must meet one of two criteria. Either its overall population is at least 125,000, OR its overall population is at least 25,000 and its Hispanic/Latino population is at least 20% of the overall population. For the state of Washington, the following locations are included:

- Burien
- Kennewick
- Mount Vernon
- Pasco
- SeaTac
- Seattle
- Spokane
- Tacoma
- Vancouver
- Walla Walla
- Wenatchee
- Yakima

Section Two: State & Place Profiles starts with the state profile, followed by place profiles that meet the criteria above. Places are listed alphabetically within each state. All states, all counties and places that meet the above criteria are ranked and compared in *Section Three: Rankings & Comparisons*, on page 1055.

For a more detailed look at the Hispanic/Latino population in Washington, a companion web site is available at no additional charge with purchase of this print edition. Visit http://gold.greyhouse.com/page/info_hispanic for more information.

The web site includes data for all counties and places in Washington with Hispanic/Latino population, plus ten additional topics: Self Employed Worker; Walked to Work; Worked from Home; Mean Travel Time to Work; Mean Household Income; Households with Cash Public Assistance; Mean Cash Pubic Assistance; Poverty Rates for 18 and Under, 18 to 64, and 65 and Over.

Population

Group	Number	%TP[1]	%HP[2]
Total Population	6,724,540	100.0	–
Hispanic or Latino (of any race)	755,790	11.2	100.0
Central American, ex. Mexican	33,661	0.5	4.5
Costa Rican	1,563	<0.1	0.2
Guatemalan	9,520	0.1	1.3
Honduran	4,381	0.1	0.6
Nicaraguan	2,313	<0.1	0.3
Panamanian	2,939	<0.1	0.4
Salvadoran	12,637	0.2	1.7
Cuban	6,744	0.1	0.9
Dominican Republic	1,819	<0.1	0.2
Mexican	601,768	8.9	79.6
Puerto Rican	25,838	0.4	3.4
South American	20,742	0.3	2.7
Argentinean	2,376	<0.1	0.3
Bolivian	782	<0.1	0.1
Chilean	2,625	<0.1	0.3
Colombian	5,560	0.1	0.7
Ecuadorian	1,855	<0.1	0.2
Paraguayan	165	<0.1	<0.1
Peruvian	5,276	0.1	0.7
Uruguayan	301	<0.1	<0.1
Venezuelan	1,556	<0.1	0.2
Spaniard	15,567	0.2	2.1

Population Growth: 2000–2010

Group	%
Total Population	14.1
Hispanic or Latino (of any race)	71.2
Central American, ex. Mexican	177.6
Costa Rican	91.1
Guatemalan	243.3
Honduran	229.4
Nicaraguan	165.6
Panamanian	70.4
Salvadoran	217.0
Cuban	49.8
Dominican Republic	175.2
Mexican	82.4
Puerto Rican	60.1
South American	145.3
Argentinean	153.0
Bolivian	125.4
Chilean	113.6
Colombian	154.0
Ecuadorian	191.2
Peruvian	171.7
Uruguayan	171.2
Venezuelan	194.7
Spaniard	704.1

Males per 100 Females

Group	Number
Total Population	99.3
Hispanic or Latino (of any race)	109.0
Central American, ex. Mexican	113.0
Costa Rican	88.8
Guatemalan	133.9
Honduran	118.1
Nicaraguan	94.5
Panamanian	76.8
Salvadoran	114.2
Cuban	111.1
Dominican Republic	99.9
Mexican	110.9
Puerto Rican	105.0
South American	87.4
Argentinean	96.0
Bolivian	82.3
Chilean	88.7
Colombian	80.3
Ecuadorian	98.2
Paraguayan	60.2
Peruvian	86.8
Uruguayan	113.5
Venezuelan	89.5
Spaniard	88.7

Average Household Size

Group	People
Total Population	2.51
Hispanic or Latino (of any race)	3.59
Central American, ex. Mexican	3.55
Costa Rican	2.67
Guatemalan	4.02
Honduran	3.63
Nicaraguan	3.04
Panamanian	2.54
Salvadoran	3.70
Cuban	2.52
Dominican Republic	2.91
Mexican	3.79
Puerto Rican	2.72
South American	2.73
Argentinean	2.70
Bolivian	2.69
Chilean	2.72
Colombian	2.65
Ecuadorian	2.78
Paraguayan	2.53
Peruvian	2.87
Uruguayan	2.47
Venezuelan	2.69
Spaniard	2.58

Median Age

Group	Years
Total Population	37.3
Hispanic or Latino (of any race)	23.7
Central American, ex. Mexican	27.6
Costa Rican	29.1
Guatemalan	25.6
Honduran	27.6
Nicaraguan	29.2
Panamanian	31.2
Salvadoran	28.5
Cuban	28.8
Dominican Republic	24.1
Mexican	22.8
Puerto Rican	24.7
South American	31.9
Argentinean	34.6
Bolivian	31.3
Chilean	34.0
Colombian	30.5
Ecuadorian	30.0
Paraguayan	28.4
Peruvian	32.0
Uruguayan	36.4
Venezuelan	31.0
Spaniard	32.2

High School Graduates
(Universe: Population 25 Years and Over)

Group	Number	%
Total Population	3,905,782	89.6
Hispanic or Latino (of any race)	192,821	58.7
Central American, ex. Mexican	10,337	63.5
Costa Rican	618	97.8
Guatemalan	2,222	49.6
Honduran	1,202	63.1
Nicaraguan	934	90.1
Panamanian	1,526	91.9
Salvadoran	3,600	57.0
Cuban	3,405	84.6
Dominican Republic	491	92.8
Mexican	135,648	52.3
Puerto Rican	10,602	90.9
South American	10,741	92.7
Argentinean	1,346	95.8
Chilean	1,280	92.0
Colombian	2,836	93.8
Ecuadorian	839	87.9
Peruvian	2,543	92.2
Venezuelan	991	99.0
Spaniard	7,461	92.2

Four-Year College Graduates
(Universe: Population 25 Years and Over)

Group	Number	%
Total Population	1,351,723	31.0
Hispanic or Latino (of any race)	40,747	12.4
Central American, ex. Mexican	2,557	15.7
Costa Rican	241	38.1
Guatemalan	413	9.2
Honduran	306	16.1
Nicaraguan	413	39.8
Panamanian	463	27.9
Salvadoran	627	9.9
Cuban	1,332	33.1
Dominican Republic	151	28.5
Mexican	22,558	8.7
Puerto Rican	2,783	23.8
South American	5,116	44.2
Argentinean	738	52.5
Chilean	599	43.0
Colombian	1,578	52.2
Ecuadorian	313	32.8
Peruvian	921	33.4
Venezuelan	531	53.0
Spaniard	2,599	32.1

Population Age 3–17 Enrolled in Public School
(Universe: Population Age 3–17 Enrolled in School)

Group	Number	%
Total Population	1,006,600	86.7
Hispanic or Latino (of any race)	175,489	94.3
Central American, ex. Mexican	6,309	91.2
Costa Rican	406	86.9
Guatemalan	1,811	87.6
Honduran	826	98.8
Nicaraguan	141	52.0
Panamanian	664	93.1

Notes: (1) Percent of total population; (2) Percent of Hispanic/Latino population; Profiles include places with an overall population of at least 125,000, OR an overall population of at least 25,000 where the Hispanic/Latino population is at least 20% of the overall population. In states where less than five places meet either of these criteria, we have included places with at least 10,000 total population with the highest percentage of Hispanic/Latino population. These places are identified with an asterisk (*); Please refer to the User's Guide for a full explanation of data.

Group	Number	%
Salvadoran	2,420	96.7
Cuban	1,414	87.7
Dominican Republic	332	86.5
Mexican	149,771	95.8
Puerto Rican	5,500	86.8
South American	2,852	80.1
Argentinean	178	88.6
Chilean	304	78.1
Colombian	991	87.6
Ecuadorian	158	67.5
Peruvian	691	70.8
Venezuelan	146	85.9
Spaniard	2,110	82.2

Population Age 3–17 Enrolled in Private School
(Universe: Population Age 3–17 Enrolled in School)

Group	Number	%
Total Population	154,151	13.3
Hispanic or Latino (of any race)	10,614	5.7
Central American, ex. Mexican	607	8.8
Costa Rican	61	13.1
Guatemalan	257	12.4
Honduran	10	1.2
Nicaraguan	130	48.0
Panamanian	49	6.9
Salvadoran	82	3.3
Cuban	198	12.3
Dominican Republic	52	13.5
Mexican	6,560	4.2
Puerto Rican	840	13.2
South American	708	19.9
Argentinean	23	11.4
Chilean	85	21.9
Colombian	140	12.4
Ecuadorian	76	32.5
Peruvian	285	29.2
Venezuelan	24	14.1
Spaniard	457	17.8

Foreign-Born Population

Group	Number	%
Total Population	832,746	12.7
Hispanic or Latino (of any race)	258,021	37.3
Central American, ex. Mexican	17,563	56.5
Costa Rican	514	39.6
Guatemalan	5,704	62.8
Honduran	2,406	59.2
Nicaraguan	790	43.5
Panamanian	851	29.0
Salvadoran	7,076	61.4
Cuban	2,190	30.6
Dominican Republic	406	33.5
Mexican	221,385	39.3
Puerto Rican	439	1.8
South American	10,555	55.3
Argentinean	988	52.0
Chilean	1,245	56.4
Colombian	3,090	59.1
Ecuadorian	770	46.8
Peruvian	3,014	61.9
Venezuelan	909	64.1
Spaniard	1,131	8.3

Foreign-Born Naturalized U.S. Citizens

Group	Number	%
Total Population	364,326	43.7
Hispanic or Latino (of any race)	53,266	20.6
Central American, ex. Mexican	5,202	29.6
Costa Rican	126	24.5
Guatemalan	1,466	25.7
Honduran	520	21.6
Nicaraguan	502	63.5
Panamanian	607	71.3
Salvadoran	1,879	26.6
Cuban	1,115	50.9
Dominican Republic	257	63.3
Mexican	38,858	17.6
Puerto Rican	165	37.6
South American	5,250	49.7
Argentinean	476	48.2
Chilean	648	52.0
Colombian	1,530	49.5
Ecuadorian	394	51.2
Peruvian	1,606	53.3
Venezuelan	295	32.5
Spaniard	511	45.2

Language Spoken at Home: English Only
(Universe: Population 5 Years and Over)

Group	Number	%
Total Population	5,060,313	82.5
Hispanic or Latino (of any race)	180,566	30.0
Central American, ex. Mexican	5,967	21.6
Costa Rican	442	37.1
Guatemalan	1,916	24.0
Honduran	712	19.4
Nicaraguan	453	29.0
Panamanian	1,423	52.1
Salvadoran	952	9.4
Cuban	3,481	53.9
Dominican Republic	312	30.4
Mexican	123,951	25.4
Puerto Rican	13,580	64.7
South American	5,746	33.3
Argentinean	546	30.7
Chilean	881	41.1
Colombian	1,484	32.0
Ecuadorian	444	33.5
Peruvian	1,264	28.2
Venezuelan	338	27.1
Spaniard	9,601	78.4

Language Spoken at Home: Spanish
(Universe: Population 5 Years and Over)

Group	Number	%
Total Population	477,752	7.8
Hispanic or Latino (of any race)	418,562	69.4
Central American, ex. Mexican	21,398	77.4
Costa Rican	715	60.0
Guatemalan	6,008	75.1
Honduran	2,873	78.3
Nicaraguan	1,059	67.7
Panamanian	1,299	47.6
Salvadoran	9,180	90.2
Cuban	2,876	44.5
Dominican Republic	694	67.6
Mexican	362,866	74.3
Puerto Rican	7,193	34.3
South American	11,384	65.9
Argentinean	1,202	67.7
Chilean	1,261	58.9
Colombian	3,148	67.8
Ecuadorian	828	62.4
Peruvian	3,221	71.8
Venezuelan	907	72.9
Spaniard	2,150	17.6

Unemployment Rate
(Universe: Population 16 Years and Over)

Group	%
Total Population	7.6
Hispanic or Latino (of any race)	9.9
Central American, ex. Mexican	7.2
Costa Rican	6.7
Guatemalan	9.1
Honduran	5.0
Nicaraguan	3.5
Panamanian	10.0
Salvadoran	6.5
Cuban	11.4
Dominican Republic	6.0
Mexican	9.9
Puerto Rican	13.2
South American	10.2
Argentinean	11.5
Chilean	7.0
Colombian	8.6
Ecuadorian	5.5
Peruvian	12.2
Venezuelan	15.7
Spaniard	10.4

Class of Worker: Private Wage and Salary
(Universe: Civilian Employed Population 16 Years and Over)

Group	Number	%
Total Population	2,399,612	76.8
Hispanic or Latino (of any race)	243,569	86.1
Central American, ex. Mexican	12,849	86.0
Costa Rican	430	88.8
Guatemalan	3,767	87.4
Honduran	1,824	92.5
Nicaraguan	692	76.9
Panamanian	814	64.3
Salvadoran	5,114	88.4
Cuban	2,340	83.1
Dominican Republic	287	65.7
Mexican	199,881	87.5
Puerto Rican	6,482	74.0
South American	7,177	79.1
Argentinean	782	82.9
Chilean	897	70.9
Colombian	1,775	79.6
Ecuadorian	488	67.5
Peruvian	1,863	82.5
Venezuelan	547	82.6
Spaniard	4,680	81.4

Class of Worker: Government
(Universe: Civilian Employed Population 16 Years and Over)

Group	Number	%
Total Population	513,474	16.4
Hispanic or Latino (of any race)	26,778	9.5
Central American, ex. Mexican	1,357	9.1
Costa Rican	54	11.2
Guatemalan	231	5.4
Honduran	85	4.3
Nicaraguan	169	18.8
Panamanian	385	30.4
Salvadoran	415	7.2
Cuban	317	11.3
Dominican Republic	108	24.7
Mexican	18,573	8.1
Puerto Rican	1,943	22.2
South American	1,295	14.3
Argentinean	79	8.4
Chilean	268	21.2
Colombian	271	12.2
Ecuadorian	190	26.3
Peruvian	264	11.7
Venezuelan	76	11.5
Spaniard	903	15.7

Means of Transportation to Work: Car, Truck or Van
(Universe: Workers 16 Years and Over)

Group	Number	%
Total Population	2,595,085	83.9
Hispanic or Latino (of any race)	240,611	85.7
Central American, ex. Mexican	12,085	80.3
Costa Rican	362	71.4
Guatemalan	3,632	84.5
Honduran	1,331	62.6
Nicaraguan	523	59.4
Panamanian	1,163	87.2
Salvadoran	4,844	85.5
Cuban	2,370	79.8
Dominican Republic	316	59.2
Mexican	195,494	86.9
Puerto Rican	7,722	82.1
South American	7,063	78.7
Argentinean	685	73.1
Chilean	848	70.4
Colombian	1,912	84.5
Ecuadorian	511	73.5
Peruvian	1,772	79.3
Venezuelan	545	82.3
Spaniard	4,877	83.0

Means of Transportation to Work: Public Transportation (ex. Taxicab)
(Universe: Workers 16 Years and Over)

Group	Number	%
Total Population	171,774	5.6
Hispanic or Latino (of any race)	14,563	5.2
Central American, ex. Mexican	1,537	10.2
Costa Rican	112	22.1
Guatemalan	197	4.6
Honduran	591	27.8
Nicaraguan	154	17.5
Panamanian	14	1.0
Salvadoran	462	8.2
Cuban	179	6.0
Dominican Republic	54	10.1
Mexican	10,184	4.5
Puerto Rican	593	6.3

Notes: (1) Percent of total population; (2) Percent of Hispanic/Latino population; Profiles include places with an overall population of at least 125,000, OR an overall population of at least 25,000 where the Hispanic/Latino population is at least 20% of the overall population. In states where less than five places meet either of these criteria, we have included places with at least 10,000 total population with the highest percentage of Hispanic/Latino population. These places are identified with an asterisk (*); Please refer to the User's Guide for a full explanation of data.

South American	960	10.7
Argentinean	115	12.3
Chilean	136	11.3
Colombian	169	7.5
Ecuadorian	63	9.1
Peruvian	339	15.2
Venezuelan	42	6.3
Spaniard	303	5.2

Homeownership Rate
(Universe: Occupied Housing Units)

Group	%
Total Population	63.9
Hispanic or Latino (of any race)	42.8
Central American, ex. Mexican	39.8
Costa Rican	54.3
Guatemalan	33.2
Honduran	28.2
Nicaraguan	47.7
Panamanian	49.4
Salvadoran	41.5
Cuban	45.3
Dominican Republic	40.0
Mexican	42.1
Puerto Rican	43.0
South American	51.2
Argentinean	56.0
Bolivian	58.4
Chilean	56.3
Colombian	48.6
Ecuadorian	52.9
Paraguayan	57.8
Peruvian	47.3
Uruguayan	54.2
Venezuelan	50.1
Spaniard	58.2

Median Home Value

Group	Dollars
Total Population	285,400
Hispanic or Latino (of any race)	200,000
Central American, ex. Mexican	255,800
Costa Rican	296,700
Guatemalan	243,800
Honduran	285,100
Nicaraguan	351,400
Panamanian	282,400
Salvadoran	223,600
Cuban	308,500
Dominican Republic	259,800
Mexican	170,400
Puerto Rican	271,500
South American	327,500
Argentinean	321,200
Chilean	309,900
Colombian	341,700
Ecuadorian	320,000
Peruvian	346,200
Venezuelan	311,500
Spaniard	301,700

Median Gross Rent

Group	Dollars
Total Population	882
Hispanic or Latino (of any race)	803
Central American, ex. Mexican	867
Costa Rican	1,080
Guatemalan	823
Honduran	1,054
Nicaraguan	850
Panamanian	857
Salvadoran	892
Cuban	827
Dominican Republic	856
Mexican	776
Puerto Rican	948
South American	996
Argentinean	1,517
Chilean	1,121
Colombian	925
Ecuadorian	985
Peruvian	940
Venezuelan	1,210
Spaniard	893

Median Household Income
(2010 Inflation-Adjusted Dollars)

Group	Dollars
Total Population	57,244
Hispanic or Latino (of any race)	41,284
Central American, ex. Mexican	46,397
Costa Rican	49,028
Guatemalan	35,074
Honduran	34,700
Nicaraguan	49,750
Panamanian	62,070
Salvadoran	47,357
Cuban	53,224
Dominican Republic	35,368
Mexican	39,887
Puerto Rican	49,704
South American	57,543
Argentinean	66,250
Chilean	54,932
Colombian	55,461
Ecuadorian	63,906
Peruvian	56,474
Venezuelan	54,018
Spaniard	52,031

Per Capita Income
(2010 Inflation-Adjusted Dollars)

Group	Dollars
Total Population	29,733
Hispanic or Latino (of any race)	14,668
Central American, ex. Mexican	16,319
Costa Rican	17,451
Guatemalan	13,445
Honduran	14,856
Nicaraguan	20,387
Panamanian	22,866
Salvadoran	16,547
Cuban	29,743
Dominican Republic	15,030
Mexican	13,341
Puerto Rican	19,519
South American	23,447
Argentinean	40,247
Chilean	23,032
Colombian	18,929
Ecuadorian	17,543
Peruvian	21,760
Venezuelan	27,342
Spaniard	27,183

Households with $100,000+ Income

Group	Number	%
Total Population	596,750	23.2
Hispanic or Latino (of any race)	20,456	11.4
Central American, ex. Mexican	1,061	12.7
Costa Rican	73	21.0
Guatemalan	209	10.9
Honduran	112	11.4
Nicaraguan	165	23.1
Panamanian	240	24.2
Salvadoran	252	7.7
Cuban	523	21.7
Dominican Republic	26	7.0
Mexican	13,479	9.7
Puerto Rican	1,276	17.3
South American	1,505	24.1
Argentinean	313	39.2
Chilean	131	17.2
Colombian	383	25.3
Ecuadorian	194	40.2
Peruvian	265	17.4
Venezuelan	108	21.5
Spaniard	1,054	21.5

Households with Food Stamps/SNAP Benefits During Past 12 Months

Group	Number	%
Total Population	252,714	9.8
Hispanic or Latino (of any race)	37,046	20.6
Central American, ex. Mexican	1,368	16.4
Costa Rican	53	15.2
Guatemalan	457	23.8
Honduran	250	25.5
Nicaraguan	20	2.8
Panamanian	114	11.5
Salvadoran	442	13.6
Cuban	343	14.3
Dominican Republic	77	20.8
Mexican	31,512	22.6
Puerto Rican	1,159	15.7
South American	362	5.8
Argentinean	31	3.9
Chilean	45	5.9
Colombian	119	7.9
Ecuadorian	5	1.0
Peruvian	68	4.5
Venezuelan	27	5.4
Spaniard	690	14.1

Poverty Rate
(Income in Past 12 Months Below Poverty Level)

Group	%
Total Population	12.1
Hispanic or Latino (of any race)	25.1
Central American, ex. Mexican	19.1
Costa Rican	1.8
Guatemalan	21.8
Honduran	38.4
Nicaraguan	11.6
Panamanian	8.7
Salvadoran	16.5
Cuban	16.0
Dominican Republic	29.3
Mexican	26.9
Puerto Rican	20.3
South American	11.2
Argentinean	11.4
Chilean	2.8
Colombian	12.4
Ecuadorian	6.9
Peruvian	13.4
Venezuelan	15.1
Spaniard	12.4

Burien

Population

Group	Number	%TP[1]	%HP[2]
Total Population	33,313	100.0	–
Hispanic or Latino (of any race)	6,902	20.7	100.0
Central American, ex. Mexican	823	2.5	11.9
Guatemalan	164	0.5	2.4
Honduran	269	0.8	3.9
Salvadoran	305	0.9	4.4
Mexican	5,136	15.4	74.4
Puerto Rican	132	0.4	1.9
South American	240	0.7	3.5

Population Growth: 2000–2010

Group	%
Total Population	4.5
Hispanic or Latino (of any race)	103.2
Central American, ex. Mexican	311.5
Mexican	108.9
South American	122.2

Males per 100 Females

Group	Number
Total Population	101.3
Hispanic or Latino (of any race)	115.5
Central American, ex. Mexican	133.8
Guatemalan	127.8
Honduran	166.3
Salvadoran	131.1
Mexican	114.4
Puerto Rican	94.1
South American	92.0

Average Household Size

Group	People
Total Population	2.49
Hispanic or Latino (of any race)	3.70
Central American, ex. Mexican	3.90
Guatemalan	3.76
Honduran	4.00
Salvadoran	3.99
Mexican	3.81
Puerto Rican	2.24
South American	3.35

Notes: (1) Percent of total population; (2) Percent of Hispanic/Latino population; Profiles include places with an overall population of at least 125,000, OR an overall population of at least 25,000 where the Hispanic/Latino population is at least 20% of the overall population. In states where less than five places meet either of these criteria, we have included places with at least 10,000 total population with the highest percentage of Hispanic/Latino population. These places are identified with an asterisk (*); Please refer to the User's Guide for a full explanation of data.

Median Age

Group	Years
Total Population	38.5
Hispanic or Latino (of any race)	25.6
Central American, ex. Mexican	29.1
Guatemalan	29.1
Honduran	28.6
Salvadoran	29.7
Mexican	24.4
Puerto Rican	31.3
South American	33.5

High School Graduates
(Universe: Population 25 Years and Over)

Group	Number	%
Total Population	19,646	85.3
Hispanic or Latino (of any race)	1,826	57.2
Mexican	1,324	52.4

Four-Year College Graduates
(Universe: Population 25 Years and Over)

Group	Number	%
Total Population	5,836	25.3
Hispanic or Latino (of any race)	241	7.6
Mexican	103	4.1

Population Age 3–17 Enrolled in Public School
(Universe: Population Age 3–17 Enrolled in School)

Group	Number	%
Total Population	4,163	80.3
Hispanic or Latino (of any race)	1,077	85.9
Mexican	967	89.4

Population Age 3–17 Enrolled in Private School
(Universe: Population Age 3–17 Enrolled in School)

Group	Number	%
Total Population	1,019	19.7
Hispanic or Latino (of any race)	177	14.1
Mexican	115	10.6

Foreign-Born Population

Group	Number	%
Total Population	7,222	22.1
Hispanic or Latino (of any race)	3,361	57.8
Mexican	2,753	57.7

Foreign-Born Naturalized U.S. Citizens

Group	Number	%
Total Population	2,907	40.3
Hispanic or Latino (of any race)	549	16.3
Mexican	434	15.8

Language Spoken at Home: English Only
(Universe: Population 5 Years and Over)

Group	Number	%
Total Population	22,314	72.3
Hispanic or Latino (of any race)	883	17.0
Mexican	644	15.1

Language Spoken at Home: Spanish
(Universe: Population 5 Years and Over)

Group	Number	%
Total Population	4,501	14.6
Hispanic or Latino (of any race)	4,298	83.0
Mexican	3,619	84.9

Unemployment Rate
(Universe: Population 16 Years and Over)

Group	%
Total Population	7.0
Hispanic or Latino (of any race)	5.5
Mexican	3.0

Class of Worker: Private Wage and Salary
(Universe: Civilian Employed Population 16 Years and Over)

Group	Number	%
Total Population	13,852	81.3
Hispanic or Latino (of any race)	2,777	92.7
Mexican	2,247	93.0

Class of Worker: Government
(Universe: Civilian Employed Population 16 Years and Over)

Group	Number	%
Total Population	2,204	12.9
Hispanic or Latino (of any race)	142	4.7
Mexican	92	3.8

Means of Transportation to Work: Car, Truck or Van
(Universe: Workers 16 Years and Over)

Group	Number	%
Total Population	13,977	83.5
Hispanic or Latino (of any race)	2,356	79.0
Mexican	1,856	76.8

Means of Transportation to Work: Public Transportation (ex. Taxicab)
(Universe: Workers 16 Years and Over)

Group	Number	%
Total Population	1,566	9.4
Hispanic or Latino (of any race)	458	15.4
Mexican	391	16.2

Homeownership Rate
(Universe: Occupied Housing Units)

Group	%
Total Population	54.7
Hispanic or Latino (of any race)	24.0
Central American, ex. Mexican	22.3
Guatemalan	11.1
Honduran	8.8
Salvadoran	35.2
Mexican	21.7
Puerto Rican	35.2
South American	48.5

Median Home Value

Group	Dollars
Total Population	333,700
Hispanic or Latino (of any race)	306,100
Mexican	322,100

Median Gross Rent

Group	Dollars
Total Population	870
Hispanic or Latino (of any race)	903
Mexican	917

Median Household Income
(2010 Inflation-Adjusted Dollars)

Group	Dollars
Total Population	51,995
Hispanic or Latino (of any race)	41,165
Mexican	39,778

Per Capita Income
(2010 Inflation-Adjusted Dollars)

Group	Dollars
Total Population	30,648
Hispanic or Latino (of any race)	16,532
Mexican	14,312

Households with $100,000+ Income

Group	Number	%
Total Population	2,745	19.8
Hispanic or Latino (of any race)	242	13.5
Mexican	143	10.3

Households with Food Stamps/SNAP Benefits During Past 12 Months

Group	Number	%
Total Population	1,744	12.6
Hispanic or Latino (of any race)	464	25.8
Mexican	346	25.0

Poverty Rate
(Income in Past 12 Months Below Poverty Level)

Group	%
Total Population	14.6
Hispanic or Latino (of any race)	34.8
Mexican	39.5

Kennewick

Population

Group	Number	%TP[1]	%HP[2]
Total Population	73,917	100.0	–
Hispanic or Latino (of any race)	17,909	24.2	100.0
Central American, ex. Mexican	416	0.6	2.3
Salvadoran	259	0.4	1.4
Cuban	125	0.2	0.7
Mexican	15,887	21.5	88.7
Puerto Rican	160	0.2	0.9
South American	140	0.2	0.8
Spaniard	197	0.3	1.1

Population Growth: 2000–2010

Group	%
Total Population	35.1
Hispanic or Latino (of any race)	110.6
Central American, ex. Mexican	249.6
Mexican	127.3

Males per 100 Females

Group	Number
Total Population	99.7
Hispanic or Latino (of any race)	105.0
Central American, ex. Mexican	114.4
Salvadoran	115.8
Cuban	135.8
Mexican	105.9
Puerto Rican	81.8
South American	89.2
Spaniard	85.8

Average Household Size

Group	People
Total Population	2.67
Hispanic or Latino (of any race)	3.66
Central American, ex. Mexican	3.73
Salvadoran	3.63
Cuban	2.88
Mexican	3.72
Puerto Rican	2.84
South American	3.22
Spaniard	2.65

Median Age

Group	Years
Total Population	32.6
Hispanic or Latino (of any race)	21.3
Central American, ex. Mexican	26.4
Salvadoran	26.6
Cuban	30.5
Mexican	21.1
Puerto Rican	21.5
South American	28.0
Spaniard	32.1

High School Graduates
(Universe: Population 25 Years and Over)

Group	Number	%
Total Population	36,338	84.3
Hispanic or Latino (of any race)	3,506	50.2
Mexican	2,954	47.4

Four-Year College Graduates
(Universe: Population 25 Years and Over)

Group	Number	%
Total Population	9,254	21.5
Hispanic or Latino (of any race)	380	5.4
Mexican	306	4.9

Population Age 3–17 Enrolled in Public School
(Universe: Population Age 3–17 Enrolled in School)

Group	Number	%
Total Population	13,366	91.3
Hispanic or Latino (of any race)	4,771	98.1
Mexican	4,468	98.3

Population Age 3–17 Enrolled in Private School
(Universe: Population Age 3–17 Enrolled in School)

Group	Number	%
Total Population	1,267	8.7
Hispanic or Latino (of any race)	93	1.9
Mexican	78	1.7

Foreign-Born Population

Group	Number	%
Total Population	8,572	12.2
Hispanic or Latino (of any race)	5,704	35.4
Mexican	5,441	37.1

Foreign-Born Naturalized U.S. Citizens

Group	Number	%
Total Population	2,373	27.7
Hispanic or Latino (of any race)	894	15.7

Notes: (1) Percent of total population; (2) Percent of Hispanic/Latino population; Profiles include places with an overall population of at least 125,000, OR an overall population of at least 25,000 where the Hispanic/Latino population is at least 20% of the overall population. In states where less than five places meet either of these criteria, we have included places with at least 10,000 total population with the highest percentage of Hispanic/Latino population. These places are identified with an asterisk (*); Please refer to the User's Guide for a full explanation of data.

Group	Number	%
Mexican	759	13.9

Language Spoken at Home: English Only
(Universe: Population 5 Years and Over)

Group	Number	%
Total Population	50,082	77.3
Hispanic or Latino (of any race)	3,357	24.0
Mexican	2,708	21.3

Language Spoken at Home: Spanish
(Universe: Population 5 Years and Over)

Group	Number	%
Total Population	11,578	17.9
Hispanic or Latino (of any race)	10,585	75.8
Mexican	9,997	78.7

Unemployment Rate
(Universe: Population 16 Years and Over)

Group	%
Total Population	5.9
Hispanic or Latino (of any race)	4.4
Mexican	4.8

Class of Worker: Private Wage and Salary
(Universe: Civilian Employed Population 16 Years and Over)

Group	Number	%
Total Population	25,812	79.0
Hispanic or Latino (of any race)	5,627	89.1
Mexican	5,185	90.4

Class of Worker: Government
(Universe: Civilian Employed Population 16 Years and Over)

Group	Number	%
Total Population	5,403	16.5
Hispanic or Latino (of any race)	521	8.2
Mexican	426	7.4

Means of Transportation to Work: Car, Truck or Van
(Universe: Workers 16 Years and Over)

Group	Number	%
Total Population	29,485	92.6
Hispanic or Latino (of any race)	5,701	93.8
Mexican	5,153	93.4

Means of Transportation to Work: Public Transportation (ex. Taxicab)
(Universe: Workers 16 Years and Over)

Group	Number	%
Total Population	729	2.3
Hispanic or Latino (of any race)	150	2.5
Mexican	150	2.7

Homeownership Rate
(Universe: Occupied Housing Units)

Group	%
Total Population	61.3
Hispanic or Latino (of any race)	37.2
Central American, ex. Mexican	48.1
Salvadoran	45.8
Cuban	31.0
Mexican	36.5
Puerto Rican	35.6
South American	43.5
Spaniard	62.3

Median Home Value

Group	Dollars
Total Population	158,700
Hispanic or Latino (of any race)	123,500
Mexican	118,600

Median Gross Rent

Group	Dollars
Total Population	713
Hispanic or Latino (of any race)	701
Mexican	697

Median Household Income
(2010 Inflation-Adjusted Dollars)

Group	Dollars
Total Population	48,512
Hispanic or Latino (of any race)	29,823
Mexican	29,086

Per Capita Income
(2010 Inflation-Adjusted Dollars)

Group	Dollars
Total Population	23,116
Hispanic or Latino (of any race)	10,496
Mexican	10,075

Households with $100,000+ Income

Group	Number	%
Total Population	4,600	17.8
Hispanic or Latino (of any race)	152	3.6
Mexican	103	2.7

Households with Food Stamps/SNAP Benefits During Past 12 Months

Group	Number	%
Total Population	3,791	14.7
Hispanic or Latino (of any race)	1,442	34.4
Mexican	1,336	35.3

Poverty Rate
(Income in Past 12 Months Below Poverty Level)

Group	%
Total Population	16.2
Hispanic or Latino (of any race)	36.5
Mexican	36.3

Mount Vernon

Population

Group	Number	%TP[1]	%HP[2]
Total Population	31,743	100.0	–
Hispanic or Latino (of any race)	10,686	33.7	100.0
Central American, ex. Mexican	137	0.4	1.3
Mexican	9,651	30.4	90.3
Puerto Rican	107	0.3	1.0

Population Growth: 2000–2010

Group	%
Total Population	21.0
Hispanic or Latino (of any race)	62.2
Mexican	75.4

Males per 100 Females

Group	Number
Total Population	96.2
Hispanic or Latino (of any race)	105.8
Central American, ex. Mexican	132.2
Mexican	106.3
Puerto Rican	132.6

Average Household Size

Group	People
Total Population	2.74
Hispanic or Latino (of any race)	4.33
Central American, ex. Mexican	3.68
Mexican	4.44
Puerto Rican	2.63

Median Age

Group	Years
Total Population	32.3
Hispanic or Latino (of any race)	21.4
Central American, ex. Mexican	28.2
Mexican	21.1
Puerto Rican	28.6

High School Graduates
(Universe: Population 25 Years and Over)

Group	Number	%
Total Population	15,193	80.1
Hispanic or Latino (of any race)	2,160	47.2
Mexican	1,909	45.6

Four-Year College Graduates
(Universe: Population 25 Years and Over)

Group	Number	%
Total Population	3,493	18.4
Hispanic or Latino (of any race)	137	3.0
Mexican	122	2.9

Population Age 3–17 Enrolled in Public School
(Universe: Population Age 3–17 Enrolled in School)

Group	Number	%
Total Population	5,955	94.5
Hispanic or Latino (of any race)	3,192	96.5
Mexican	2,880	97.3

Population Age 3–17 Enrolled in Private School
(Universe: Population Age 3–17 Enrolled in School)

Group	Number	%
Total Population	347	5.5
Hispanic or Latino (of any race)	116	3.5
Mexican	80	2.7

Foreign-Born Population

Group	Number	%
Total Population	6,217	20.0
Hispanic or Latino (of any race)	4,378	41.2
Mexican	4,133	43.0

Foreign-Born Naturalized U.S. Citizens

Group	Number	%
Total Population	1,697	27.3
Hispanic or Latino (of any race)	704	16.1
Mexican	704	17.0

Language Spoken at Home: English Only
(Universe: Population 5 Years and Over)

Group	Number	%
Total Population	19,177	67.9
Hispanic or Latino (of any race)	1,972	21.4
Mexican	1,575	18.8

Language Spoken at Home: Spanish
(Universe: Population 5 Years and Over)

Group	Number	%
Total Population	7,473	26.4
Hispanic or Latino (of any race)	7,264	78.6
Mexican	6,803	81.2

Unemployment Rate
(Universe: Population 16 Years and Over)

Group	%
Total Population	7.3
Hispanic or Latino (of any race)	9.6
Mexican	9.3

Class of Worker: Private Wage and Salary
(Universe: Civilian Employed Population 16 Years and Over)

Group	Number	%
Total Population	10,371	81.2
Hispanic or Latino (of any race)	3,565	91.0
Mexican	3,285	92.0

Class of Worker: Government
(Universe: Civilian Employed Population 16 Years and Over)

Group	Number	%
Total Population	1,713	13.4
Hispanic or Latino (of any race)	243	6.2
Mexican	175	4.9

Means of Transportation to Work: Car, Truck or Van
(Universe: Workers 16 Years and Over)

Group	Number	%
Total Population	11,686	91.9
Hispanic or Latino (of any race)	3,803	97.2
Mexican	3,426	96.9

Means of Transportation to Work: Public Transportation (ex. Taxicab)
(Universe: Workers 16 Years and Over)

Group	Number	%
Total Population	247	1.9
Hispanic or Latino (of any race)	13	0.3
Mexican	13	0.4

Homeownership Rate
(Universe: Occupied Housing Units)

Group	%
Total Population	58.2
Hispanic or Latino (of any race)	36.6
Central American, ex. Mexican	39.5
Mexican	36.5
Puerto Rican	60.0

Notes: (1) Percent of total population; (2) Percent of Hispanic/Latino population; Profiles include places with an overall population of at least 125,000, OR an overall population of at least 25,000 where the Hispanic/Latino population is at least 20% of the overall population. In states where less than five places meet either of these criteria, we have included places with at least 10,000 total population with the highest percentage of Hispanic/Latino population. These places are identified with an asterisk (*); Please refer to the User's Guide for a full explanation of data.

Median Home Value

Group	Dollars
Total Population	233,900
Hispanic or Latino (of any race)	229,100
Mexican	225,600

Median Gross Rent

Group	Dollars
Total Population	837
Hispanic or Latino (of any race)	836
Mexican	837

Median Household Income
(2010 Inflation-Adjusted Dollars)

Group	Dollars
Total Population	45,986
Hispanic or Latino (of any race)	42,604
Mexican	41,230

Per Capita Income
(2010 Inflation-Adjusted Dollars)

Group	Dollars
Total Population	21,791
Hispanic or Latino (of any race)	10,903
Mexican	10,823

Households with $100,000+ Income

Group	Number	%
Total Population	1,446	12.7
Hispanic or Latino (of any race)	215	8.5
Mexican	184	8.1

Households with Food Stamps/SNAP Benefits During Past 12 Months

Group	Number	%
Total Population	1,722	15.1
Hispanic or Latino (of any race)	672	26.6
Mexican	652	28.7

Poverty Rate
(Income in Past 12 Months Below Poverty Level)

Group	%
Total Population	15.5
Hispanic or Latino (of any race)	26.2
Mexican	27.0

Pasco

Population

Group	Number	%TP[1]	%HP[2]
Total Population	59,781	100.0	–
Hispanic or Latino (of any race)	33,314	55.7	100.0
Central American, ex. Mexican	637	1.1	1.9
Guatemalan	139	0.2	0.4
Salvadoran	398	0.7	1.2
Mexican	30,104	50.4	90.4
Puerto Rican	167	0.3	0.5
South American	111	0.2	0.3

Population Growth: 2000–2010

Group	%
Total Population	86.4
Hispanic or Latino (of any race)	84.7
Central American, ex. Mexican	105.5
Salvadoran	88.6
Mexican	97.3

Males per 100 Females

Group	Number
Total Population	102.6
Hispanic or Latino (of any race)	106.4
Central American, ex. Mexican	100.9
Guatemalan	167.3
Salvadoran	88.6
Mexican	107.2
Puerto Rican	92.0
South American	94.7

Average Household Size

Group	People
Total Population	3.30
Hispanic or Latino (of any race)	4.17
Central American, ex. Mexican	4.09
Guatemalan	3.56
Salvadoran	4.46
Mexican	4.18
Puerto Rican	3.85
South American	3.17

Median Age

Group	Years
Total Population	27.3
Hispanic or Latino (of any race)	21.6
Central American, ex. Mexican	30.0
Guatemalan	29.5
Salvadoran	29.9
Mexican	21.5
Puerto Rican	19.5
South American	34.1

High School Graduates
(Universe: Population 25 Years and Over)

Group	Number	%
Total Population	18,833	64.5
Hispanic or Latino (of any race)	4,983	37.4
Mexican	4,487	36.1

Four-Year College Graduates
(Universe: Population 25 Years and Over)

Group	Number	%
Total Population	4,166	14.3
Hispanic or Latino (of any race)	538	4.0
Mexican	331	2.7

Population Age 3–17 Enrolled in Public School
(Universe: Population Age 3–17 Enrolled in School)

Group	Number	%
Total Population	11,277	91.1
Hispanic or Latino (of any race)	8,176	98.8
Mexican	7,741	99.2

Population Age 3–17 Enrolled in Private School
(Universe: Population Age 3–17 Enrolled in School)

Group	Number	%
Total Population	1,105	8.9
Hispanic or Latino (of any race)	96	1.2
Mexican	62	0.8

Foreign-Born Population

Group	Number	%
Total Population	15,827	29.2
Hispanic or Latino (of any race)	13,919	46.3
Mexican	13,211	46.7

Foreign-Born Naturalized U.S. Citizens

Group	Number	%
Total Population	3,192	20.2
Hispanic or Latino (of any race)	2,133	15.3
Mexican	1,954	14.8

Language Spoken at Home: English Only
(Universe: Population 5 Years and Over)

Group	Number	%
Total Population	22,216	46.5
Hispanic or Latino (of any race)	3,207	12.3
Mexican	2,749	11.3

Language Spoken at Home: Spanish
(Universe: Population 5 Years and Over)

Group	Number	%
Total Population	23,287	48.7
Hispanic or Latino (of any race)	22,786	87.7
Mexican	21,614	88.7

Unemployment Rate
(Universe: Population 16 Years and Over)

Group	%
Total Population	8.8
Hispanic or Latino (of any race)	9.9
Mexican	9.5

Class of Worker: Private Wage and Salary
(Universe: Civilian Employed Population 16 Years and Over)

Group	Number	%
Total Population	18,460	81.8
Hispanic or Latino (of any race)	10,272	88.1
Mexican	9,646	88.6

Class of Worker: Government
(Universe: Civilian Employed Population 16 Years and Over)

Group	Number	%
Total Population	2,756	12.2
Hispanic or Latino (of any race)	666	5.7
Mexican	537	4.9

Means of Transportation to Work: Car, Truck or Van
(Universe: Workers 16 Years and Over)

Group	Number	%
Total Population	19,835	90.4
Hispanic or Latino (of any race)	10,256	91.1
Mexican	9,506	90.7

Means of Transportation to Work: Public Transportation (ex. Taxicab)
(Universe: Workers 16 Years and Over)

Group	Number	%
Total Population	448	2.0
Hispanic or Latino (of any race)	298	2.6
Mexican	286	2.7

Homeownership Rate
(Universe: Occupied Housing Units)

Group	%
Total Population	64.9
Hispanic or Latino (of any race)	53.0
Central American, ex. Mexican	58.8
Guatemalan	44.2
Salvadoran	63.8
Mexican	52.8
Puerto Rican	65.9
South American	58.6

Median Home Value

Group	Dollars
Total Population	143,100
Hispanic or Latino (of any race)	121,900
Mexican	121,700

Median Gross Rent

Group	Dollars
Total Population	688
Hispanic or Latino (of any race)	657
Mexican	656

Median Household Income
(2010 Inflation-Adjusted Dollars)

Group	Dollars
Total Population	44,659
Hispanic or Latino (of any race)	35,548
Mexican	34,846

Per Capita Income
(2010 Inflation-Adjusted Dollars)

Group	Dollars
Total Population	17,374
Hispanic or Latino (of any race)	10,840
Mexican	10,347

Households with $100,000+ Income

Group	Number	%
Total Population	1,952	12.0
Hispanic or Latino (of any race)	430	6.1
Mexican	365	5.6

Households with Food Stamps/SNAP Benefits During Past 12 Months

Group	Number	%
Total Population	3,065	18.8
Hispanic or Latino (of any race)	1,903	27.1
Mexican	1,861	28.4

Poverty Rate
(Income in Past 12 Months Below Poverty Level)

Group	%
Total Population	21.5
Hispanic or Latino (of any race)	30.0
Mexican	30.9

Notes: (1) Percent of total population; (2) Percent of Hispanic/Latino population; Profiles include places with an overall population of at least 125,000, OR an overall population of at least 25,000 where the Hispanic/Latino population is at least 20% of the overall population. In states where less than five places meet either of these criteria, we have included places with at least 10,000 total population with the highest percentage of Hispanic/Latino population. These places are identified with an asterisk (*); Please refer to the User's Guide for a full explanation of data.

SeaTac

Population

Group	Number	%TP[1]	%HP[2]
Total Population	26,909	100.0	–
Hispanic or Latino (of any race)	5,474	20.3	100.0
Central American, ex. Mexican	620	2.3	11.3
Guatemalan	144	0.5	2.6
Honduran	164	0.6	3.0
Salvadoran	278	1.0	5.1
Mexican	4,172	15.5	76.2
South American	102	0.4	1.9

Population Growth: 2000–2010

Group	%
Total Population	5.5
Hispanic or Latino (of any race)	65.8
Central American, ex. Mexican	211.6
Mexican	73.5

Males per 100 Females

Group	Number
Total Population	110.1
Hispanic or Latino (of any race)	128.9
Central American, ex. Mexican	130.5
Guatemalan	161.8
Honduran	141.2
Salvadoran	113.8
Mexican	132.6
South American	96.2

Average Household Size

Group	People
Total Population	2.72
Hispanic or Latino (of any race)	3.99
Central American, ex. Mexican	4.00
Guatemalan	4.14
Honduran	4.18
Salvadoran	3.96
Mexican	4.20
South American	2.74

Median Age

Group	Years
Total Population	34.5
Hispanic or Latino (of any race)	26.1
Central American, ex. Mexican	29.8
Guatemalan	28.9
Honduran	28.7
Salvadoran	30.0
Mexican	25.0
South American	37.3

High School Graduates
(Universe: Population 25 Years and Over)

Group	Number	%
Total Population	14,225	80.8
Hispanic or Latino (of any race)	1,542	52.8
Mexican	1,301	54.0

Four-Year College Graduates
(Universe: Population 25 Years and Over)

Group	Number	%
Total Population	2,697	15.3
Hispanic or Latino (of any race)	254	8.7
Mexican	216	9.0

Population Age 3–17 Enrolled in Public School
(Universe: Population Age 3–17 Enrolled in School)

Group	Number	%
Total Population	3,027	90.6
Hispanic or Latino (of any race)	931	97.7
Mexican	775	97.2

Population Age 3–17 Enrolled in Private School
(Universe: Population Age 3–17 Enrolled in School)

Group	Number	%
Total Population	315	9.4
Hispanic or Latino (of any race)	22	2.3
Mexican	22	2.8

Foreign-Born Population

Group	Number	%
Total Population	8,183	31.0
Hispanic or Latino (of any race)	2,985	55.0
Mexican	2,487	54.0

Foreign-Born Naturalized U.S. Citizens

Group	Number	%
Total Population	3,297	40.3
Hispanic or Latino (of any race)	465	15.6
Mexican	361	14.5

Language Spoken at Home: English Only
(Universe: Population 5 Years and Over)

Group	Number	%
Total Population	14,544	60.2
Hispanic or Latino (of any race)	1,001	20.7
Mexican	828	20.3

Language Spoken at Home: Spanish
(Universe: Population 5 Years and Over)

Group	Number	%
Total Population	4,042	16.7
Hispanic or Latino (of any race)	3,819	79.1
Mexican	3,258	79.7

Unemployment Rate
(Universe: Population 16 Years and Over)

Group	%
Total Population	5.4
Hispanic or Latino (of any race)	0.8
Mexican	0.5

Class of Worker: Private Wage and Salary
(Universe: Civilian Employed Population 16 Years and Over)

Group	Number	%
Total Population	11,378	85.1
Hispanic or Latino (of any race)	2,567	89.8
Mexican	2,336	92.1

Class of Worker: Government
(Universe: Civilian Employed Population 16 Years and Over)

Group	Number	%
Total Population	1,250	9.3
Hispanic or Latino (of any race)	138	4.8
Mexican	108	4.3

Means of Transportation to Work: Car, Truck or Van
(Universe: Workers 16 Years and Over)

Group	Number	%
Total Population	10,853	83.5
Hispanic or Latino (of any race)	2,257	81.4
Mexican	1,978	80.9

Means of Transportation to Work: Public Transportation (ex. Taxicab)
(Universe: Workers 16 Years and Over)

Group	Number	%
Total Population	1,292	9.9
Hispanic or Latino (of any race)	416	15.0
Mexican	366	15.0

Homeownership Rate
(Universe: Occupied Housing Units)

Group	%
Total Population	52.6
Hispanic or Latino (of any race)	34.9
Central American, ex. Mexican	24.1
Guatemalan	5.7
Honduran	12.8
Salvadoran	35.4
Mexican	36.2
South American	57.1

Median Home Value

Group	Dollars
Total Population	271,600
Hispanic or Latino (of any race)	244,400
Mexican	237,600

Median Gross Rent

Group	Dollars
Total Population	836
Hispanic or Latino (of any race)	893
Mexican	869

Median Household Income
(2010 Inflation-Adjusted Dollars)

Group	Dollars
Total Population	48,341
Hispanic or Latino (of any race)	44,754
Mexican	43,438

Per Capita Income
(2010 Inflation-Adjusted Dollars)

Group	Dollars
Total Population	22,661
Hispanic or Latino (of any race)	15,773
Mexican	15,344

Households with $100,000+ Income

Group	Number	%
Total Population	1,506	14.6
Hispanic or Latino (of any race)	198	12.2
Mexican	129	9.4

Households with Food Stamps/SNAP Benefits During Past 12 Months

Group	Number	%
Total Population	1,430	13.9
Hispanic or Latino (of any race)	284	17.6
Mexican	205	14.9

Poverty Rate
(Income in Past 12 Months Below Poverty Level)

Group	%
Total Population	13.3
Hispanic or Latino (of any race)	12.9
Mexican	10.3

Seattle

Population

Group	Number	%TP[1]	%HP[2]
Total Population	608,660	100.0	–
Hispanic or Latino (of any race)	40,329	6.6	100.0
Central American, ex. Mexican	3,740	0.6	9.3
Costa Rican	166	<0.1	0.4
Guatemalan	1,056	0.2	2.6
Honduran	633	0.1	1.6
Nicaraguan	299	<0.1	0.7
Panamanian	231	<0.1	0.6
Salvadoran	1,322	0.2	3.3
Cuban	1,068	0.2	2.6
Dominican Republic	200	<0.1	0.5
Mexican	24,800	4.1	61.5
Puerto Rican	2,127	0.3	5.3
South American	3,346	0.5	8.3
Argentinean	505	0.1	1.3
Bolivian	150	<0.1	0.4
Chilean	438	0.1	1.1
Colombian	784	0.1	1.9
Ecuadorian	309	0.1	0.8
Peruvian	774	0.1	1.9
Venezuelan	267	<0.1	0.7
Spaniard	1,799	0.3	4.5

Population Growth: 2000–2010

Group	%
Total Population	8.0
Hispanic or Latino (of any race)	35.7
Central American, ex. Mexican	88.2
Guatemalan	140.5
Honduran	90.7
Nicaraguan	112.1
Panamanian	48.1
Salvadoran	91.6
Cuban	40.7
Dominican Republic	68.1
Mexican	38.7
Puerto Rican	45.1
South American	100.6
Argentinean	147.5
Chilean	66.5
Colombian	119.6
Ecuadorian	178.4
Peruvian	83.0
Venezuelan	151.9
Spaniard	544.8

Notes: (1) Percent of total population; (2) Percent of Hispanic/Latino population; Profiles include places with an overall population of at least 125,000, OR an overall population of at least 25,000 where the Hispanic/Latino population is at least 20% of the overall population. In states where less than five places meet either of these criteria, we have included places with at least 10,000 total population with the highest percentage of Hispanic/Latino population. These places are identified with an asterisk (*); Please refer to the User's Guide for a full explanation of data.

Males per 100 Females

Group	Number
Total Population	99.8
Hispanic or Latino (of any race)	117.1
Central American, ex. Mexican	130.6
Costa Rican	104.9
Guatemalan	164.7
Honduran	153.2
Nicaraguan	100.7
Panamanian	99.1
Salvadoran	117.8
Cuban	131.2
Dominican Republic	112.8
Mexican	121.6
Puerto Rican	109.1
South American	91.0
Argentinean	93.5
Bolivian	76.5
Chilean	85.6
Colombian	90.3
Ecuadorian	90.7
Peruvian	90.2
Venezuelan	102.3
Spaniard	94.3

Average Household Size

Group	People
Total Population	2.06
Hispanic or Latino (of any race)	2.47
Central American, ex. Mexican	2.90
Costa Rican	2.03
Guatemalan	3.27
Honduran	3.20
Nicaraguan	2.43
Panamanian	1.85
Salvadoran	3.15
Cuban	1.96
Dominican Republic	2.11
Mexican	2.64
Puerto Rican	2.09
South American	2.15
Argentinean	2.18
Bolivian	2.27
Chilean	2.26
Colombian	2.01
Ecuadorian	2.35
Peruvian	2.27
Venezuelan	1.97
Spaniard	2.00

Median Age

Group	Years
Total Population	36.1
Hispanic or Latino (of any race)	29.1
Central American, ex. Mexican	29.1
Costa Rican	30.6
Guatemalan	27.4
Honduran	28.6
Nicaraguan	29.0
Panamanian	32.5
Salvadoran	30.0
Cuban	33.0
Dominican Republic	28.8
Mexican	28.1
Puerto Rican	29.0
South American	32.4
Argentinean	33.6
Bolivian	33.2
Chilean	33.1
Colombian	31.0
Ecuadorian	30.1
Peruvian	33.2
Venezuelan	33.1
Spaniard	32.9

High School Graduates
(Universe: Population 25 Years and Over)

Group	Number	%
Total Population	401,142	92.4
Hispanic or Latino (of any race)	16,968	75.7
Central American, ex. Mexican	1,379	65.2
Cuban	635	90.2
Mexican	9,301	68.5
Puerto Rican	1,132	88.2
South American	2,055	93.2
Spaniard	990	97.8

Four-Year College Graduates
(Universe: Population 25 Years and Over)

Group	Number	%
Total Population	239,356	55.1
Hispanic or Latino (of any race)	7,695	34.3
Central American, ex. Mexican	519	24.6
Cuban	340	48.3
Mexican	3,691	27.2
Puerto Rican	493	38.4
South American	1,436	65.2
Spaniard	446	44.1

Population Age 3–17 Enrolled in Public School
(Universe: Population Age 3–17 Enrolled in School)

Group	Number	%
Total Population	46,658	71.4
Hispanic or Latino (of any race)	4,828	83.9
Central American, ex. Mexican	783	81.3
Cuban	108	81.8
Mexican	3,420	91.2
Puerto Rican	197	55.2
South American	183	61.0
Spaniard	54	53.5

Population Age 3–17 Enrolled in Private School
(Universe: Population Age 3–17 Enrolled in School)

Group	Number	%
Total Population	18,679	28.6
Hispanic or Latino (of any race)	924	16.1
Central American, ex. Mexican	180	18.7
Cuban	24	18.2
Mexican	328	8.8
Puerto Rican	160	44.8
South American	117	39.0
Spaniard	47	46.5

Foreign-Born Population

Group	Number	%
Total Population	103,173	17.3
Hispanic or Latino (of any race)	14,084	38.6
Central American, ex. Mexican	2,037	53.5
Cuban	326	33.4
Mexican	9,243	39.8
Puerto Rican	71	3.6
South American	1,888	60.4
Spaniard	199	15.7

Foreign-Born Naturalized U.S. Citizens

Group	Number	%
Total Population	53,454	51.8
Hispanic or Latino (of any race)	3,696	26.2
Central American, ex. Mexican	679	33.3
Cuban	198	60.7
Mexican	1,524	16.5
Puerto Rican	37	52.1
South American	1,001	53.0
Spaniard	63	31.7

Language Spoken at Home: English Only
(Universe: Population 5 Years and Over)

Group	Number	%
Total Population	444,476	78.7
Hispanic or Latino (of any race)	12,919	38.6
Central American, ex. Mexican	763	22.9
Cuban	404	46.3
Mexican	7,887	36.9
Puerto Rican	995	55.6
South American	763	26.1
Spaniard	756	63.7

Language Spoken at Home: Spanish
(Universe: Population 5 Years and Over)

Group	Number	%
Total Population	25,708	4.5
Hispanic or Latino (of any race)	20,024	59.8
Central American, ex. Mexican	2,567	77.1
Cuban	421	48.2
Mexican	13,260	62.0
Puerto Rican	759	42.4
South American	2,072	70.9
Spaniard	370	31.2

Unemployment Rate
(Universe: Population 16 Years and Over)

Group	%
Total Population	6.3
Hispanic or Latino (of any race)	9.3
Central American, ex. Mexican	3.4
Cuban	16.8
Mexican	9.7
Puerto Rican	9.3
South American	10.6
Spaniard	8.5

Class of Worker: Private Wage and Salary
(Universe: Civilian Employed Population 16 Years and Over)

Group	Number	%
Total Population	269,137	77.5
Hispanic or Latino (of any race)	17,592	86.6
Central American, ex. Mexican	1,947	89.5
Cuban	403	85.6
Mexican	11,173	87.6
Puerto Rican	785	76.3
South American	1,532	86.1
Spaniard	752	91.9

Class of Worker: Government
(Universe: Civilian Employed Population 16 Years and Over)

Group	Number	%
Total Population	54,063	15.6
Hispanic or Latino (of any race)	2,005	9.9
Central American, ex. Mexican	97	4.5
Cuban	49	10.4
Mexican	1,206	9.5
Puerto Rican	131	12.7
South American	226	12.7
Spaniard	42	5.1

Means of Transportation to Work: Car, Truck or Van
(Universe: Workers 16 Years and Over)

Group	Number	%
Total Population	213,548	62.9
Hispanic or Latino (of any race)	12,062	60.5
Central American, ex. Mexican	1,203	57.7
Cuban	243	53.4
Mexican	7,625	60.4
Puerto Rican	538	53.6
South American	1,051	60.5
Spaniard	644	78.7

Means of Transportation to Work: Public Transportation (ex. Taxicab)
(Universe: Workers 16 Years and Over)

Group	Number	%
Total Population	63,741	18.8
Hispanic or Latino (of any race)	4,971	24.9
Central American, ex. Mexican	677	32.5
Cuban	98	21.5
Mexican	3,111	24.7
Puerto Rican	264	26.3
South American	383	22.1
Spaniard	77	9.4

Homeownership Rate
(Universe: Occupied Housing Units)

Group	%
Total Population	48.1
Hispanic or Latino (of any race)	27.2
Central American, ex. Mexican	23.9
Costa Rican	40.0
Guatemalan	18.1
Honduran	11.6
Nicaraguan	35.0
Panamanian	35.8
Salvadoran	23.8
Cuban	33.1
Dominican Republic	15.0
Mexican	23.5
Puerto Rican	29.1
South American	38.4
Argentinean	45.9
Bolivian	50.9
Chilean	42.3
Colombian	33.0
Ecuadorian	33.0
Peruvian	35.7

Notes: (1) Percent of total population; (2) Percent of Hispanic/Latino population; Profiles include places with an overall population of at least 125,000, OR an overall population of at least 25,000 where the Hispanic/Latino population is at least 20% of the overall population. In states where less than five places meet either of these criteria, we have included places with at least 10,000 total population with the highest percentage of Hispanic/Latino population. These places are identified with an asterisk (*); Please refer to the User's Guide for a full explanation of data.

Venezuelan	37.5
Spaniard	40.9

Median Home Value

Group	Dollars
Total Population	456,200
Hispanic or Latino (of any race)	383,900
Central American, ex. Mexican	300,000
Cuban	453,800
Mexican	398,500
Puerto Rican	394,900
South American	402,000
Spaniard	383,500

Median Gross Rent

Group	Dollars
Total Population	958
Hispanic or Latino (of any race)	893
Central American, ex. Mexican	894
Cuban	830
Mexican	870
Puerto Rican	960
South American	1,069
Spaniard	963

Median Household Income
(2010 Inflation-Adjusted Dollars)

Group	Dollars
Total Population	60,665
Hispanic or Latino (of any race)	47,701
Central American, ex. Mexican	47,589
Cuban	38,026
Mexican	46,234
Puerto Rican	57,625
South American	59,598
Spaniard	30,074

Per Capita Income
(2010 Inflation-Adjusted Dollars)

Group	Dollars
Total Population	40,868
Hispanic or Latino (of any race)	23,303
Central American, ex. Mexican	18,333
Cuban	34,208
Mexican	21,266
Puerto Rican	28,393
South American	27,687
Spaniard	34,330

Households with $100,000+ Income

Group	Number	%
Total Population	78,839	28.1
Hispanic or Latino (of any race)	2,092	16.0
Central American, ex. Mexican	166	14.2
Cuban	103	19.7
Mexican	1,107	14.3
Puerto Rican	201	27.1
South American	291	22.8
Spaniard	88	15.2

Households with Food Stamps/SNAP Benefits During Past 12 Months

Group	Number	%
Total Population	19,340	6.9
Hispanic or Latino (of any race)	1,332	10.2
Central American, ex. Mexican	112	9.6
Cuban	93	17.7
Mexican	929	12.0
Puerto Rican	38	5.1
South American	74	5.8
Spaniard	41	7.1

Poverty Rate
(Income in Past 12 Months Below Poverty Level)

Group	%
Total Population	12.7
Hispanic or Latino (of any race)	19.0
Central American, ex. Mexican	19.1
Cuban	18.2
Mexican	21.0
Puerto Rican	14.7
South American	15.1
Spaniard	9.1

Spokane

Population

Group	Number	%TP[1]	%HP[2]
Total Population	208,916	100.0	–
Hispanic or Latino (of any race)	10,467	5.0	100.0
Central American, ex. Mexican	464	0.2	4.4
Guatemalan	119	0.1	1.1
Salvadoran	196	0.1	1.9
Cuban	333	0.2	3.2
Mexican	7,006	3.4	66.9
Puerto Rican	651	0.3	6.2
South American	348	0.2	3.3
Colombian	116	0.1	1.1
Spaniard	485	0.2	4.6

Population Growth: 2000–2010

Group	%
Total Population	6.8
Hispanic or Latino (of any race)	78.7
Central American, ex. Mexican	126.3
Cuban	134.5
Mexican	97.2
Puerto Rican	41.2
South American	159.7

Males per 100 Females

Group	Number
Total Population	95.1
Hispanic or Latino (of any race)	104.7
Central American, ex. Mexican	90.2
Guatemalan	80.3
Salvadoran	84.9
Cuban	113.5
Mexican	107.7
Puerto Rican	102.8
South American	95.5
Colombian	93.3
Spaniard	83.0

Average Household Size

Group	People
Total Population	2.31
Hispanic or Latino (of any race)	2.80
Central American, ex. Mexican	3.36
Guatemalan	3.43
Salvadoran	4.07
Cuban	2.94
Mexican	2.90
Puerto Rican	2.45
South American	2.71
Colombian	2.67
Spaniard	2.44

Median Age

Group	Years
Total Population	35.0
Hispanic or Latino (of any race)	22.8
Central American, ex. Mexican	22.3
Guatemalan	21.2
Salvadoran	21.0
Cuban	30.9
Mexican	21.7
Puerto Rican	24.0
South American	25.5
Colombian	23.5
Spaniard	29.4

High School Graduates
(Universe: Population 25 Years and Over)

Group	Number	%
Total Population	122,364	91.1
Hispanic or Latino (of any race)	3,460	80.0
Mexican	2,229	79.1

Four-Year College Graduates
(Universe: Population 25 Years and Over)

Group	Number	%
Total Population	37,899	28.2
Hispanic or Latino (of any race)	899	20.8
Mexican	491	17.4

Population Age 3–17 Enrolled in Public School
(Universe: Population Age 3–17 Enrolled in School)

Group	Number	%
Total Population	28,888	84.9
Hispanic or Latino (of any race)	2,667	88.5
Mexican	1,744	90.2

Population Age 3–17 Enrolled in Private School
(Universe: Population Age 3–17 Enrolled in School)

Group	Number	%
Total Population	5,155	15.1
Hispanic or Latino (of any race)	345	11.5
Mexican	190	9.8

Foreign-Born Population

Group	Number	%
Total Population	12,348	6.0
Hispanic or Latino (of any race)	1,527	14.9
Mexican	879	12.8

Foreign-Born Naturalized U.S. Citizens

Group	Number	%
Total Population	4,917	39.8
Hispanic or Latino (of any race)	244	16.0
Mexican	124	14.1

Language Spoken at Home: English Only
(Universe: Population 5 Years and Over)

Group	Number	%
Total Population	177,080	92.1
Hispanic or Latino (of any race)	6,023	67.8
Mexican	4,102	68.7

Language Spoken at Home: Spanish
(Universe: Population 5 Years and Over)

Group	Number	%
Total Population	4,304	2.2
Hispanic or Latino (of any race)	2,772	31.2
Mexican	1,821	30.5

Unemployment Rate
(Universe: Population 16 Years and Over)

Group	%
Total Population	8.7
Hispanic or Latino (of any race)	12.2
Mexican	10.6

Class of Worker: Private Wage and Salary
(Universe: Civilian Employed Population 16 Years and Over)

Group	Number	%
Total Population	76,062	79.8
Hispanic or Latino (of any race)	3,092	84.5
Mexican	2,261	85.4

Class of Worker: Government
(Universe: Civilian Employed Population 16 Years and Over)

Group	Number	%
Total Population	13,780	14.5
Hispanic or Latino (of any race)	533	14.6
Mexican	361	13.6

Means of Transportation to Work: Car, Truck or Van
(Universe: Workers 16 Years and Over)

Group	Number	%
Total Population	80,143	86.1
Hispanic or Latino (of any race)	3,195	90.0
Mexican	2,243	88.2

Means of Transportation to Work: Public Transportation (ex. Taxicab)
(Universe: Workers 16 Years and Over)

Group	Number	%
Total Population	4,057	4.4
Hispanic or Latino (of any race)	113	3.2
Mexican	97	3.8

Homeownership Rate
(Universe: Occupied Housing Units)

Group	%
Total Population	57.6
Hispanic or Latino (of any race)	40.6
Central American, ex. Mexican	52.6
Guatemalan	42.9
Salvadoran	61.4
Cuban	36.2

Notes: (1) Percent of total population; (2) Percent of Hispanic/Latino population; Profiles include places with an overall population of at least 125,000, OR an overall population of at least 25,000 where the Hispanic/Latino population is at least 20% of the overall population. In states where less than five places meet either of these criteria, we have included places with at least 10,000 total population with the highest percentage of Hispanic/Latino population. These places are identified with an asterisk (*); Please refer to the User's Guide for a full explanation of data.

Mexican	39.8
Puerto Rican	36.2
South American	46.5
Colombian	59.3
Spaniard	55.2

Median Home Value

Group	Dollars
Total Population	161,200
Hispanic or Latino (of any race)	150,500
Mexican	141,300

Median Gross Rent

Group	Dollars
Total Population	677
Hispanic or Latino (of any race)	730
Mexican	758

Median Household Income
(2010 Inflation-Adjusted Dollars)

Group	Dollars
Total Population	40,367
Hispanic or Latino (of any race)	40,327
Mexican	42,336

Per Capita Income
(2010 Inflation-Adjusted Dollars)

Group	Dollars
Total Population	23,408
Hispanic or Latino (of any race)	13,109
Mexican	13,634

Households with $100,000+ Income

Group	Number	%
Total Population	9,702	11.1
Hispanic or Latino (of any race)	164	5.8
Mexican	114	5.7

Households with Food Stamps/SNAP Benefits During Past 12 Months

Group	Number	%
Total Population	14,877	17.0
Hispanic or Latino (of any race)	890	31.3
Mexican	507	25.5

Poverty Rate
(Income in Past 12 Months Below Poverty Level)

Group	%
Total Population	18.7
Hispanic or Latino (of any race)	30.1
Mexican	30.9

Tacoma

Population

Group	Number	%TP[1]	%HP[2]
Total Population	198,397	100.0	–
Hispanic or Latino (of any race)	22,390	11.3	100.0
Central American, ex. Mexican	1,322	0.7	5.9
Guatemalan	246	0.1	1.1
Honduran	134	0.1	0.6
Panamanian	263	0.1	1.2
Salvadoran	565	0.3	2.5
Cuban	319	0.2	1.4
Dominican Republic	101	0.1	0.5
Mexican	16,145	8.1	72.1
Puerto Rican	1,964	1.0	8.8
South American	585	0.3	2.6
Colombian	168	0.1	0.8
Peruvian	224	0.1	1.0
Spaniard	470	0.2	2.1

Population Growth: 2000–2010

Group	%
Total Population	2.5
Hispanic or Latino (of any race)	68.8
Central American, ex. Mexican	152.3
Panamanian	43.7
Salvadoran	217.4
Cuban	76.2
Mexican	87.8
Puerto Rican	35.7
South American	92.4
Peruvian	86.7

Males per 100 Females

Group	Number
Total Population	97.5
Hispanic or Latino (of any race)	112.2
Central American, ex. Mexican	115.0
Guatemalan	182.8
Honduran	112.7
Panamanian	75.3
Salvadoran	122.4
Cuban	127.9
Dominican Republic	98.0
Mexican	114.6
Puerto Rican	115.8
South American	91.8
Colombian	86.7
Peruvian	93.1
Spaniard	63.2

Average Household Size

Group	People
Total Population	2.44
Hispanic or Latino (of any race)	3.46
Central American, ex. Mexican	3.37
Guatemalan	3.74
Honduran	3.00
Panamanian	2.57
Salvadoran	3.97
Cuban	2.28
Dominican Republic	2.53
Mexican	3.78
Puerto Rican	2.78
South American	2.85
Colombian	3.00
Peruvian	2.94
Spaniard	2.47

Median Age

Group	Years
Total Population	35.1
Hispanic or Latino (of any race)	24.1
Central American, ex. Mexican	28.4
Guatemalan	26.2
Honduran	26.5
Panamanian	30.8
Salvadoran	29.0
Cuban	25.4
Dominican Republic	25.9
Mexican	23.1
Puerto Rican	23.7
South American	33.5
Colombian	32.2
Peruvian	34.7
Spaniard	29.7

High School Graduates
(Universe: Population 25 Years and Over)

Group	Number	%
Total Population	114,096	87.3
Hispanic or Latino (of any race)	6,171	64.2
Central American, ex. Mexican	843	73.4
Salvadoran	276	59.1
Mexican	3,597	55.5
Puerto Rican	622	89.4

Four-Year College Graduates
(Universe: Population 25 Years and Over)

Group	Number	%
Total Population	30,984	23.7
Hispanic or Latino (of any race)	866	9.0
Central American, ex. Mexican	40	3.5
Salvadoran	4	0.9
Mexican	388	6.0
Puerto Rican	135	19.4

Population Age 3–17 Enrolled in Public School
(Universe: Population Age 3–17 Enrolled in School)

Group	Number	%
Total Population	28,624	87.1
Hispanic or Latino (of any race)	5,009	95.6
Central American, ex. Mexican	465	100.0
Salvadoran	269	100.0
Mexican	3,541	96.1
Puerto Rican	480	94.3

Population Age 3–17 Enrolled in Private School
(Universe: Population Age 3–17 Enrolled in School)

Group	Number	%
Total Population	4,239	12.9
Hispanic or Latino (of any race)	228	4.4
Central American, ex. Mexican	0	0.0
Salvadoran	0	0.0
Mexican	142	3.9
Puerto Rican	29	5.7

Foreign-Born Population

Group	Number	%
Total Population	25,248	12.7
Hispanic or Latino (of any race)	7,700	38.1
Central American, ex. Mexican	1,094	51.1
Salvadoran	592	59.6
Mexican	6,102	43.1
Puerto Rican	17	1.0

Foreign-Born Naturalized U.S. Citizens

Group	Number	%
Total Population	12,121	48.0
Hispanic or Latino (of any race)	1,823	23.7
Central American, ex. Mexican	433	39.6
Salvadoran	120	20.3
Mexican	1,179	19.3
Puerto Rican	0	0.0

Language Spoken at Home: English Only
(Universe: Population 5 Years and Over)

Group	Number	%
Total Population	151,138	81.6
Hispanic or Latino (of any race)	6,000	33.6
Central American, ex. Mexican	356	18.1
Salvadoran	22	2.5
Mexican	3,579	29.2
Puerto Rican	1,003	64.8

Language Spoken at Home: Spanish
(Universe: Population 5 Years and Over)

Group	Number	%
Total Population	13,919	7.5
Hispanic or Latino (of any race)	11,756	65.7
Central American, ex. Mexican	1,611	81.9
Salvadoran	857	97.5
Mexican	8,634	70.5
Puerto Rican	525	33.9

Unemployment Rate
(Universe: Population 16 Years and Over)

Group	%
Total Population	9.3
Hispanic or Latino (of any race)	7.9
Central American, ex. Mexican	3.4
Salvadoran	0.0
Mexican	6.3
Puerto Rican	23.8

Class of Worker: Private Wage and Salary
(Universe: Civilian Employed Population 16 Years and Over)

Group	Number	%
Total Population	69,950	78.1
Hispanic or Latino (of any race)	7,224	88.9
Central American, ex. Mexican	909	93.3
Salvadoran	378	95.7
Mexican	5,216	92.7
Puerto Rican	439	78.0

Class of Worker: Government
(Universe: Civilian Employed Population 16 Years and Over)

Group	Number	%
Total Population	14,877	16.6
Hispanic or Latino (of any race)	637	7.8
Central American, ex. Mexican	65	6.7
Salvadoran	17	4.3
Mexican	236	4.2
Puerto Rican	110	19.5

Means of Transportation to Work: Car, Truck or Van
(Universe: Workers 16 Years and Over)

Group	Number	%
Total Population	77,207	86.8
Hispanic or Latino (of any race)	7,019	87.1
Central American, ex. Mexican	854	90.6

Notes: (1) Percent of total population; (2) Percent of Hispanic/Latino population; Profiles include places with an overall population of at least 125,000, OR an overall population of at least 25,000 where the Hispanic/Latino population is at least 20% of the overall population. In states where less than five places meet either of these criteria, we have included places with at least 10,000 total population with the highest percentage of Hispanic/Latino population. These places are identified with an asterisk (*); Please refer to the User's Guide for a full explanation of data.

Salvadoran	350	95.4
Mexican	4,894	87.5
Puerto Rican	451	80.1

Means of Transportation to Work: Public Transportation (ex. Taxicab)
(Universe: Workers 16 Years and Over)

Group	Number	%
Total Population	4,526	5.1
Hispanic or Latino (of any race)	357	4.4
Central American, ex. Mexican	0	0.0
Salvadoran	0	0.0
Mexican	299	5.3
Puerto Rican	56	9.9

Homeownership Rate
(Universe: Occupied Housing Units)

Group	%
Total Population	53.9
Hispanic or Latino (of any race)	39.0
Central American, ex. Mexican	45.8
Guatemalan	51.7
Honduran	30.3
Panamanian	48.9
Salvadoran	48.7
Cuban	37.7
Dominican Republic	40.0
Mexican	38.5
Puerto Rican	37.1
South American	52.2
Colombian	65.9
Peruvian	51.4
Spaniard	43.6

Median Home Value

Group	Dollars
Total Population	241,300
Hispanic or Latino (of any race)	219,300
Central American, ex. Mexican	215,300
Salvadoran	173,800
Mexican	211,700
Puerto Rican	234,200

Median Gross Rent

Group	Dollars
Total Population	818
Hispanic or Latino (of any race)	759
Central American, ex. Mexican	685
Salvadoran	756
Mexican	742
Puerto Rican	866

Median Household Income
(2010 Inflation-Adjusted Dollars)

Group	Dollars
Total Population	47,862
Hispanic or Latino (of any race)	38,258
Central American, ex. Mexican	31,446
Salvadoran	63,182
Mexican	39,977
Puerto Rican	30,778

Per Capita Income
(2010 Inflation-Adjusted Dollars)

Group	Dollars
Total Population	25,377
Hispanic or Latino (of any race)	13,779
Central American, ex. Mexican	13,678
Salvadoran	11,718
Mexican	12,999
Puerto Rican	13,647

Households with $100,000+ Income

Group	Number	%
Total Population	13,263	16.6
Hispanic or Latino (of any race)	585	11.3
Central American, ex. Mexican	56	10.4
Salvadoran	0	0.0
Mexican	335	10.2
Puerto Rican	68	11.7

Households with Food Stamps/SNAP Benefits During Past 12 Months

Group	Number	%
Total Population	11,229	14.0
Hispanic or Latino (of any race)	1,080	20.8
Central American, ex. Mexican	74	13.8
Salvadoran	5	2.9
Mexican	716	21.8
Puerto Rican	136	23.4

Poverty Rate
(Income in Past 12 Months Below Poverty Level)

Group	%
Total Population	17.1
Hispanic or Latino (of any race)	25.8
Central American, ex. Mexican	30.7
Salvadoran	48.8
Mexican	26.0
Puerto Rican	26.0

Vancouver

Population

Group	Number	%TP[1]	%HP[2]
Total Population	161,791	100.0	–
Hispanic or Latino (of any race)	16,756	10.4	100.0
Central American, ex. Mexican	698	0.4	4.2
Guatemalan	240	0.1	1.4
Honduran	104	0.1	0.6
Salvadoran	189	0.1	1.1
Cuban	193	0.1	1.2
Mexican	13,240	8.2	79.0
Puerto Rican	553	0.3	3.3
South American	465	0.3	2.8
Peruvian	138	0.1	0.8
Spaniard	342	0.2	2.0

Population Growth: 2000–2010

Group	%
Total Population	12.7
Hispanic or Latino (of any race)	85.5
Central American, ex. Mexican	148.4
Cuban	50.8
Mexican	101.9
Puerto Rican	85.6
South American	198.1

Males per 100 Females

Group	Number
Total Population	95.1
Hispanic or Latino (of any race)	104.4
Central American, ex. Mexican	96.1
Guatemalan	140.0
Honduran	85.7
Salvadoran	85.3
Cuban	135.4
Mexican	106.7
Puerto Rican	96.1
South American	83.1
Peruvian	109.1
Spaniard	90.0

Average Household Size

Group	People
Total Population	2.43
Hispanic or Latino (of any race)	3.40
Central American, ex. Mexican	3.02
Guatemalan	3.33
Honduran	3.27
Salvadoran	2.88
Cuban	2.72
Mexican	3.60
Puerto Rican	2.60
South American	2.81
Peruvian	3.03
Spaniard	2.46

Median Age

Group	Years
Total Population	35.9
Hispanic or Latino (of any race)	23.5
Central American, ex. Mexican	28.6
Guatemalan	27.5
Honduran	20.0
Salvadoran	30.7
Cuban	25.6
Mexican	22.5
Puerto Rican	23.8
South American	30.7
Peruvian	26.7
Spaniard	32.0

High School Graduates
(Universe: Population 25 Years and Over)

Group	Number	%
Total Population	94,757	88.8
Hispanic or Latino (of any race)	4,984	64.6
Mexican	3,281	55.7

Four-Year College Graduates
(Universe: Population 25 Years and Over)

Group	Number	%
Total Population	24,969	23.4
Hispanic or Latino (of any race)	887	11.5
Mexican	529	9.0

Population Age 3–17 Enrolled in Public School
(Universe: Population Age 3–17 Enrolled in School)

Group	Number	%
Total Population	25,583	90.8
Hispanic or Latino (of any race)	4,255	96.7
Mexican	3,666	96.4

Population Age 3–17 Enrolled in Private School
(Universe: Population Age 3–17 Enrolled in School)

Group	Number	%
Total Population	2,600	9.2
Hispanic or Latino (of any race)	145	3.3
Mexican	136	3.6

Foreign-Born Population

Group	Number	%
Total Population	19,943	12.4
Hispanic or Latino (of any race)	5,920	38.0
Mexican	5,003	39.3

Foreign-Born Naturalized U.S. Citizens

Group	Number	%
Total Population	8,326	41.7
Hispanic or Latino (of any race)	1,107	18.7
Mexican	850	17.0

Language Spoken at Home: English Only
(Universe: Population 5 Years and Over)

Group	Number	%
Total Population	123,665	82.8
Hispanic or Latino (of any race)	4,841	35.4
Mexican	3,418	30.9

Language Spoken at Home: Spanish
(Universe: Population 5 Years and Over)

Group	Number	%
Total Population	9,735	6.5
Hispanic or Latino (of any race)	8,780	64.2
Mexican	7,638	69.0

Unemployment Rate
(Universe: Population 16 Years and Over)

Group	%
Total Population	10.5
Hispanic or Latino (of any race)	15.5
Mexican	13.2

Class of Worker: Private Wage and Salary
(Universe: Civilian Employed Population 16 Years and Over)

Group	Number	%
Total Population	60,451	81.8
Hispanic or Latino (of any race)	5,221	88.7
Mexican	4,285	90.9

Class of Worker: Government
(Universe: Civilian Employed Population 16 Years and Over)

Group	Number	%
Total Population	8,969	12.1
Hispanic or Latino (of any race)	323	5.5
Mexican	179	3.8

Means of Transportation to Work: Car, Truck or Van
(Universe: Workers 16 Years and Over)

Group	Number	%
Total Population	63,289	88.0
Hispanic or Latino (of any race)	4,963	87.2
Mexican	4,073	88.9

Notes: (1) Percent of total population; (2) Percent of Hispanic/Latino population; Profiles include places with an overall population of at least 125,000, OR an overall population of at least 25,000 where the Hispanic/Latino population is at least 20% of the overall population. In states where less than five places meet either of these criteria, we have included places with at least 10,000 total population with the highest percentage of Hispanic/Latino population. These places are identified with an asterisk (*); Please refer to the User's Guide for a full explanation of data.

Means of Transportation to Work: Public Transportation (ex. Taxicab)
(Universe: Workers 16 Years and Over)

Group	Number	%
Total Population	2,318	3.2
Hispanic or Latino (of any race)	217	3.8
Mexican	145	3.2

Homeownership Rate
(Universe: Occupied Housing Units)

Group	%
Total Population	50.9
Hispanic or Latino (of any race)	29.5
Central American, ex. Mexican	36.2
Guatemalan	22.9
Honduran	26.9
Salvadoran	38.3
Cuban	33.8
Mexican	26.7
Puerto Rican	31.1
South American	46.5
Peruvian	38.5
Spaniard	51.5

Median Home Value

Group	Dollars
Total Population	234,500
Hispanic or Latino (of any race)	218,400
Mexican	218,200

Median Gross Rent

Group	Dollars
Total Population	833
Hispanic or Latino (of any race)	816
Mexican	790

Median Household Income
(2010 Inflation-Adjusted Dollars)

Group	Dollars
Total Population	48,875
Hispanic or Latino (of any race)	39,542
Mexican	36,031

Per Capita Income
(2010 Inflation-Adjusted Dollars)

Group	Dollars
Total Population	25,792
Hispanic or Latino (of any race)	13,631
Mexican	11,924

Households with $100,000+ Income

Group	Number	%
Total Population	9,649	14.8
Hispanic or Latino (of any race)	419	9.1
Mexican	274	7.7

Households with Food Stamps/SNAP Benefits During Past 12 Months

Group	Number	%
Total Population	9,346	14.3
Hispanic or Latino (of any race)	834	18.1
Mexican	723	20.4

Poverty Rate
(Income in Past 12 Months Below Poverty Level)

Group	%
Total Population	14.8
Hispanic or Latino (of any race)	31.8
Mexican	35.4

Walla Walla

Population

Group	Number	%TP[1]	%HP[2]
Total Population	31,731	100.0	–
Hispanic or Latino (of any race)	6,970	22.0	100.0
Central American, ex. Mexican	150	0.5	2.2
Mexican	6,300	19.9	90.4

Population Growth: 2000–2010

Group	%
Total Population	6.9
Hispanic or Latino (of any race)	34.8
Mexican	48.6

Males per 100 Females

Group	Number
Total Population	108.0
Hispanic or Latino (of any race)	109.9
Central American, ex. Mexican	85.2
Mexican	114.1

Average Household Size

Group	People
Total Population	2.43
Hispanic or Latino (of any race)	3.71
Central American, ex. Mexican	3.41
Mexican	3.79

Median Age

Group	Years
Total Population	34.4
Hispanic or Latino (of any race)	23.0
Central American, ex. Mexican	24.7
Mexican	23.0

High School Graduates
(Universe: Population 25 Years and Over)

Group	Number	%
Total Population	17,392	85.7
Hispanic or Latino (of any race)	1,509	46.5
Mexican	1,279	43.6

Four-Year College Graduates
(Universe: Population 25 Years and Over)

Group	Number	%
Total Population	4,328	21.3
Hispanic or Latino (of any race)	116	3.6
Mexican	87	3.0

Population Age 3–17 Enrolled in Public School
(Universe: Population Age 3–17 Enrolled in School)

Group	Number	%
Total Population	4,370	88.4
Hispanic or Latino (of any race)	1,391	93.8
Mexican	1,363	98.1

Population Age 3–17 Enrolled in Private School
(Universe: Population Age 3–17 Enrolled in School)

Group	Number	%
Total Population	576	11.6
Hispanic or Latino (of any race)	92	6.2
Mexican	26	1.9

Foreign-Born Population

Group	Number	%
Total Population	3,706	11.9
Hispanic or Latino (of any race)	2,985	47.0
Mexican	2,829	49.2

Foreign-Born Naturalized U.S. Citizens

Group	Number	%
Total Population	1,254	33.8
Hispanic or Latino (of any race)	923	30.9
Mexican	856	30.3

Language Spoken at Home: English Only
(Universe: Population 5 Years and Over)

Group	Number	%
Total Population	22,919	78.1
Hispanic or Latino (of any race)	685	12.2
Mexican	427	8.4

Language Spoken at Home: Spanish
(Universe: Population 5 Years and Over)

Group	Number	%
Total Population	5,387	18.4
Hispanic or Latino (of any race)	4,910	87.6
Mexican	4,645	91.6

Unemployment Rate
(Universe: Population 16 Years and Over)

Group	%
Total Population	9.1
Hispanic or Latino (of any race)	21.8
Mexican	22.4

Class of Worker: Private Wage and Salary
(Universe: Civilian Employed Population 16 Years and Over)

Group	Number	%
Total Population	9,113	72.3
Hispanic or Latino (of any race)	1,855	87.9
Mexican	1,672	87.6

Class of Worker: Government
(Universe: Civilian Employed Population 16 Years and Over)

Group	Number	%
Total Population	2,533	20.1
Hispanic or Latino (of any race)	110	5.2
Mexican	110	5.8

Means of Transportation to Work: Car, Truck or Van
(Universe: Workers 16 Years and Over)

Group	Number	%
Total Population	10,475	84.6
Hispanic or Latino (of any race)	1,795	86.5
Mexican	1,639	87.4

Means of Transportation to Work: Public Transportation (ex. Taxicab)
(Universe: Workers 16 Years and Over)

Group	Number	%
Total Population	140	1.1
Hispanic or Latino (of any race)	0	0.0
Mexican	0	0.0

Homeownership Rate
(Universe: Occupied Housing Units)

Group	%
Total Population	56.8
Hispanic or Latino (of any race)	46.2
Central American, ex. Mexican	58.8
Mexican	46.8

Median Home Value

Group	Dollars
Total Population	182,200
Hispanic or Latino (of any race)	116,100
Mexican	113,600

Median Gross Rent

Group	Dollars
Total Population	666
Hispanic or Latino (of any race)	610
Mexican	617

Median Household Income
(2010 Inflation-Adjusted Dollars)

Group	Dollars
Total Population	39,397
Hispanic or Latino (of any race)	25,893
Mexican	25,022

Per Capita Income
(2010 Inflation-Adjusted Dollars)

Group	Dollars
Total Population	20,324
Hispanic or Latino (of any race)	10,092
Mexican	9,814

Households with $100,000+ Income

Group	Number	%
Total Population	1,284	11.0
Hispanic or Latino (of any race)	30	2.0
Mexican	30	2.2

Households with Food Stamps/SNAP Benefits During Past 12 Months

Group	Number	%
Total Population	1,809	15.4
Hispanic or Latino (of any race)	589	39.7
Mexican	572	41.0

Poverty Rate
(Income in Past 12 Months Below Poverty Level)

Group	%
Total Population	22.2
Hispanic or Latino (of any race)	41.3
Mexican	42.7

Notes: (1) Percent of total population; (2) Percent of Hispanic/Latino population; Profiles include places with an overall population of at least 125,000, OR an overall population of at least 25,000 where the Hispanic/Latino population is at least 20% of the overall population. In states where less than five places meet either of these criteria, we have included places with at least 10,000 total population with the highest percentage of Hispanic/Latino population. These places are identified with an asterisk (*); Please refer to the User's Guide for a full explanation of data.

Wenatchee

Population

Group	Number	%TP[1]	%HP[2]
Total Population	31,925	100.0	–
Hispanic or Latino (of any race)	9,388	29.4	100.0
Central American, ex. Mexican	307	1.0	3.3
Salvadoran	178	0.6	1.9
Mexican	8,567	26.8	91.3

Population Growth: 2000–2010

Group	%
Total Population	14.6
Hispanic or Latino (of any race)	56.6
Central American, ex. Mexican	104.7
Mexican	68.9

Males per 100 Females

Group	Number
Total Population	95.7
Hispanic or Latino (of any race)	107.5
Central American, ex. Mexican	129.1
Salvadoran	114.5
Mexican	106.0

Average Household Size

Group	People
Total Population	2.53
Hispanic or Latino (of any race)	3.99
Central American, ex. Mexican	3.75
Salvadoran	3.98
Mexican	4.06

Median Age

Group	Years
Total Population	35.2
Hispanic or Latino (of any race)	22.3
Central American, ex. Mexican	25.5
Salvadoran	24.8
Mexican	22.2

High School Graduates
(Universe: Population 25 Years and Over)

Group	Number	%
Total Population	16,460	81.3
Hispanic or Latino (of any race)	1,901	47.5
Mexican	1,477	42.5

Four-Year College Graduates
(Universe: Population 25 Years and Over)

Group	Number	%
Total Population	4,451	22.0
Hispanic or Latino (of any race)	407	10.2
Mexican	301	8.7

Population Age 3–17 Enrolled in Public School
(Universe: Population Age 3–17 Enrolled in School)

Group	Number	%
Total Population	5,306	90.1
Hispanic or Latino (of any race)	2,274	98.3
Mexican	2,033	98.4

Population Age 3–17 Enrolled in Private School
(Universe: Population Age 3–17 Enrolled in School)

Group	Number	%
Total Population	586	9.9
Hispanic or Latino (of any race)	40	1.7
Mexican	33	1.6

Foreign-Born Population

Group	Number	%
Total Population	3,775	12.1
Hispanic or Latino (of any race)	3,100	35.8
Mexican	2,867	37.4

Foreign-Born Naturalized U.S. Citizens

Group	Number	%
Total Population	1,272	33.7
Hispanic or Latino (of any race)	882	28.5
Mexican	833	29.1

Language Spoken at Home: English Only
(Universe: Population 5 Years and Over)

Group	Number	%
Total Population	21,960	75.3
Hispanic or Latino (of any race)	1,365	17.9
Mexican	893	13.2

Language Spoken at Home: Spanish
(Universe: Population 5 Years and Over)

Group	Number	%
Total Population	6,683	22.9
Hispanic or Latino (of any race)	6,282	82.1
Mexican	5,866	86.8

Unemployment Rate
(Universe: Population 16 Years and Over)

Group	%
Total Population	7.2
Hispanic or Latino (of any race)	6.1
Mexican	6.5

Class of Worker: Private Wage and Salary
(Universe: Civilian Employed Population 16 Years and Over)

Group	Number	%
Total Population	10,598	76.6
Hispanic or Latino (of any race)	3,517	86.0
Mexican	3,150	86.4

Class of Worker: Government
(Universe: Civilian Employed Population 16 Years and Over)

Group	Number	%
Total Population	2,379	17.2
Hispanic or Latino (of any race)	347	8.5
Mexican	305	8.4

Means of Transportation to Work: Car, Truck or Van
(Universe: Workers 16 Years and Over)

Group	Number	%
Total Population	12,277	89.7
Hispanic or Latino (of any race)	3,606	90.8
Mexican	3,232	91.6

Means of Transportation to Work: Public Transportation (ex. Taxicab)
(Universe: Workers 16 Years and Over)

Group	Number	%
Total Population	203	1.5
Hispanic or Latino (of any race)	16	0.4
Mexican	16	0.5

Homeownership Rate
(Universe: Occupied Housing Units)

Group	%
Total Population	55.3
Hispanic or Latino (of any race)	39.5
Central American, ex. Mexican	42.0
Salvadoran	45.7
Mexican	39.8

Median Home Value

Group	Dollars
Total Population	196,900
Hispanic or Latino (of any race)	185,200
Mexican	180,100

Median Gross Rent

Group	Dollars
Total Population	688
Hispanic or Latino (of any race)	707
Mexican	692

Median Household Income
(2010 Inflation-Adjusted Dollars)

Group	Dollars
Total Population	44,156
Hispanic or Latino (of any race)	43,106
Mexican	41,177

Per Capita Income
(2010 Inflation-Adjusted Dollars)

Group	Dollars
Total Population	22,942
Hispanic or Latino (of any race)	15,800
Mexican	15,723

Households with $100,000+ Income

Group	Number	%
Total Population	1,627	13.6
Hispanic or Latino (of any race)	312	14.6
Mexican	296	15.9

Households with Food Stamps/SNAP Benefits During Past 12 Months

Group	Number	%
Total Population	1,281	10.7
Hispanic or Latino (of any race)	348	16.3
Mexican	333	17.9

Poverty Rate
(Income in Past 12 Months Below Poverty Level)

Group	%
Total Population	12.8
Hispanic or Latino (of any race)	16.2
Mexican	16.6

Yakima

Population

Group	Number	%TP[1]	%HP[2]
Total Population	91,067	100.0	–
Hispanic or Latino (of any race)	37,587	41.3	100.0
Central American, ex. Mexican	338	0.4	0.9
Salvadoran	162	0.2	0.4
Mexican	34,697	38.1	92.3
Puerto Rican	232	0.3	0.6
South American	149	0.2	0.4
Spaniard	196	0.2	0.5

Population Growth: 2000–2010

Group	%
Total Population	26.8
Hispanic or Latino (of any race)	55.2
Central American, ex. Mexican	141.4
Mexican	66.6
Puerto Rican	100.0

Males per 100 Females

Group	Number
Total Population	97.1
Hispanic or Latino (of any race)	105.7
Central American, ex. Mexican	119.5
Salvadoran	131.4
Mexican	105.4
Puerto Rican	100.0
South American	122.4
Spaniard	90.3

Average Household Size

Group	People
Total Population	2.68
Hispanic or Latino (of any race)	3.85
Central American, ex. Mexican	4.02
Salvadoran	4.17
Mexican	3.90
Puerto Rican	2.77
South American	3.26
Spaniard	2.61

Median Age

Group	Years
Total Population	32.7
Hispanic or Latino (of any race)	22.1
Central American, ex. Mexican	29.4
Salvadoran	29.3
Mexican	21.8
Puerto Rican	26.8
South American	28.5
Spaniard	30.3

High School Graduates
(Universe: Population 25 Years and Over)

Group	Number	%
Total Population	40,733	74.1
Hispanic or Latino (of any race)	6,203	42.8
Mexican	5,428	40.2

Four-Year College Graduates
(Universe: Population 25 Years and Over)

Group	Number	%
Total Population	10,487	19.1
Hispanic or Latino (of any race)	862	5.9
Mexican	588	4.3

Notes: (1) Percent of total population; (2) Percent of Hispanic/Latino population; Profiles include places with an overall population of at least 125,000, OR an overall population of at least 25,000 where the Hispanic/Latino population is at least 20% of the overall population. In states where less than five places meet either of these criteria, we have included places with at least 10,000 total population with the highest percentage of Hispanic/Latino population. These places are identified with an asterisk (*); Please refer to the User's Guide for a full explanation of data.

Population Age 3–17 Enrolled in Public School
(Universe: Population Age 3–17 Enrolled in School)

Group	Number	%
Total Population	14,897	90.8
Hispanic or Latino (of any race)	8,630	96.2
Mexican	8,281	96.1

Population Age 3–17 Enrolled in Private School
(Universe: Population Age 3–17 Enrolled in School)

Group	Number	%
Total Population	1,509	9.2
Hispanic or Latino (of any race)	341	3.8
Mexican	333	3.9

Foreign-Born Population

Group	Number	%
Total Population	14,601	16.5
Hispanic or Latino (of any race)	13,152	38.9
Mexican	12,630	39.6

Foreign-Born Naturalized U.S. Citizens

Group	Number	%
Total Population	3,615	24.8
Hispanic or Latino (of any race)	2,890	22.0
Mexican	2,699	21.4

Language Spoken at Home: English Only
(Universe: Population 5 Years and Over)

Group	Number	%
Total Population	54,288	67.6
Hispanic or Latino (of any race)	5,049	17.8
Mexican	4,515	16.8

Language Spoken at Home: Spanish
(Universe: Population 5 Years and Over)

Group	Number	%
Total Population	24,570	30.6
Hispanic or Latino (of any race)	23,332	82.2
Mexican	22,317	83.2

Unemployment Rate
(Universe: Population 16 Years and Over)

Group	%
Total Population	11.1
Hispanic or Latino (of any race)	12.7
Mexican	12.9

Class of Worker: Private Wage and Salary
(Universe: Civilian Employed Population 16 Years and Over)

Group	Number	%
Total Population	30,401	82.5
Hispanic or Latino (of any race)	12,047	90.9
Mexican	11,528	92.4

Class of Worker: Government
(Universe: Civilian Employed Population 16 Years and Over)

Group	Number	%
Total Population	4,824	13.1
Hispanic or Latino (of any race)	962	7.3
Mexican	697	5.6

Means of Transportation to Work: Car, Truck or Van
(Universe: Workers 16 Years and Over)

Group	Number	%
Total Population	32,842	91.1
Hispanic or Latino (of any race)	11,730	90.9
Mexican	11,132	91.4

Means of Transportation to Work: Public Transportation (ex. Taxicab)
(Universe: Workers 16 Years and Over)

Group	Number	%
Total Population	804	2.2
Hispanic or Latino (of any race)	518	4.0
Mexican	487	4.0

Homeownership Rate
(Universe: Occupied Housing Units)

Group	%
Total Population	54.1
Hispanic or Latino (of any race)	41.6
Central American, ex. Mexican	47.3
Salvadoran	51.9
Mexican	41.7
Puerto Rican	31.5
South American	58.1
Spaniard	43.4

Median Home Value

Group	Dollars
Total Population	152,800
Hispanic or Latino (of any race)	112,700
Mexican	110,400

Median Gross Rent

Group	Dollars
Total Population	649
Hispanic or Latino (of any race)	621
Mexican	618

Median Household Income
(2010 Inflation-Adjusted Dollars)

Group	Dollars
Total Population	39,706
Hispanic or Latino (of any race)	34,795
Mexican	33,096

Per Capita Income
(2010 Inflation-Adjusted Dollars)

Group	Dollars
Total Population	20,771
Hispanic or Latino (of any race)	10,754
Mexican	10,307

Households with $100,000+ Income

Group	Number	%
Total Population	3,990	12.2
Hispanic or Latino (of any race)	348	4.0
Mexican	340	4.2

Households with Food Stamps/SNAP Benefits During Past 12 Months

Group	Number	%
Total Population	6,807	20.8
Hispanic or Latino (of any race)	2,758	31.5
Mexican	2,619	32.6

Poverty Rate
(Income in Past 12 Months Below Poverty Level)

Group	%
Total Population	21.3
Hispanic or Latino (of any race)	35.0
Mexican	35.7

STATE & PLACE PROFILES

Notes: (1) Percent of total population; (2) Percent of Hispanic/Latino population; Profiles include places with an overall population of at least 125,000, OR an overall population of at least 25,000 where the Hispanic/Latino population is at least 20% of the overall population. In states where less than five places meet either of these criteria, we have included places with at least 10,000 total population with the highest percentage of Hispanic/Latino population. These places are identified with an asterisk (*); Please refer to the User's Guide for a full explanation of data.

West Virginia

EDITOR'S NOTE: For a place to be included in this edition, it must meet one of two criteria. Either its overall population is at least 125,000, OR its overall population is at least 25,000 and its Hispanic/Latino population is at least 20% of the overall population. In West Virginia, less than five places meet either of these criteria. In an effort to include at least five places for each state, we have included places with at least 10,000 total population with the highest percentage of Hispanic/Latino population. These places are identified with an asterisk (*). For the state of West Virginia, the following locations are included:

Beckley*
Clarksburg*
Huntington*
Martinsburg*
Morgantown*

Section Two: State & Place Profiles starts with the state profile, followed by place profiles that meet the criteria above. Places are listed alphabetically within each state. All states, all counties and places that meet the above criteria are ranked and compared in *Section Three: Rankings & Comparisons*, on page 1055.

For a more detailed look at the Hispanic/Latino population in West Virginia, a companion web site is available at no additional charge with purchase of this print edition. Visit http://gold.greyhouse.com/page/info_hispanic for more information.

The web site includes data for all counties and places in West Virginia with Hispanic/Latino population, plus ten additional topics: Self Employed Worker; Walked to Work; Worked from Home; Mean Travel Time to Work; Mean Household Income; Households with Cash Public Assistance; Mean Cash Pubic Assistance; Poverty Rates for 18 and Under, 18 to 64, and 65 and Over.

Population

Group	Number	%TP[1]	%HP[2]
Total Population	1,852,994	100.0	–
Hispanic or Latino (of any race)	22,268	1.2	100.0
Central American, ex. Mexican	2,081	0.1	9.3
Guatemalan	347	<0.1	1.6
Honduran	333	<0.1	1.5
Nicaraguan	162	<0.1	0.7
Panamanian	261	<0.1	1.2
Salvadoran	893	<0.1	4.0
Cuban	764	<0.1	3.4
Dominican Republic	363	<0.1	1.6
Mexican	9,704	0.5	43.6
Puerto Rican	3,701	0.2	16.6
South American	1,700	0.1	7.6
Argentinean	165	<0.1	0.7
Bolivian	139	<0.1	0.6
Chilean	110	<0.1	0.5
Colombian	483	<0.1	2.2
Ecuadorian	155	<0.1	0.7
Peruvian	444	<0.1	2.0
Venezuelan	142	<0.1	0.6
Spaniard	970	0.1	4.4

Population Growth: 2000–2010

Group	%
Total Population	2.5
Hispanic or Latino (of any race)	81.4
Central American, ex. Mexican	467.0
Cuban	68.7
Mexican	123.2
Puerto Rican	130.0
South American	210.8
Colombian	150.3
Spaniard	758.4

Males per 100 Females

Group	Number
Total Population	97.3
Hispanic or Latino (of any race)	117.3
Central American, ex. Mexican	111.1
Guatemalan	115.5
Honduran	143.1
Nicaraguan	100.0
Panamanian	91.9
Salvadoran	110.1
Cuban	117.7
Dominican Republic	113.5
Mexican	133.2
Puerto Rican	117.8
South American	88.9
Argentinean	91.9
Bolivian	117.2
Chilean	89.7
Colombian	80.2
Ecuadorian	86.7
Peruvian	85.8
Venezuelan	102.9
Spaniard	91.7

Average Household Size

Group	People
Total Population	2.36
Hispanic or Latino (of any race)	2.79
Central American, ex. Mexican	3.50
Guatemalan	3.80
Honduran	3.12
Nicaraguan	3.14
Panamanian	2.72
Salvadoran	3.98
Cuban	2.68
Dominican Republic	3.05
Mexican	2.97
Puerto Rican	2.81
South American	2.70
Argentinean	2.82
Bolivian	2.72
Chilean	2.51
Colombian	2.55
Ecuadorian	2.90
Peruvian	2.98
Venezuelan	2.29
Spaniard	2.29

Median Age

Group	Years
Total Population	41.3
Hispanic or Latino (of any race)	26.3
Central American, ex. Mexican	23.6
Guatemalan	13.1
Honduran	25.7
Nicaraguan	24.4
Panamanian	23.7
Salvadoran	24.9
Cuban	29.9
Dominican Republic	25.5
Mexican	24.5
Puerto Rican	23.9
South American	30.2
Argentinean	34.5
Bolivian	31.5
Chilean	29.5
Colombian	29.1
Ecuadorian	27.5
Peruvian	32.2
Venezuelan	28.0
Spaniard	40.1

High School Graduates
(Universe: Population 25 Years and Over)

Group	Number	%
Total Population	1,050,620	81.9
Hispanic or Latino (of any race)	8,139	73.2
Central American, ex. Mexican	521	64.9
Cuban	448	84.1
Mexican	2,955	64.7
Puerto Rican	1,158	82.1
South American	931	86.1
Spaniard	688	82.7

Four-Year College Graduates
(Universe: Population 25 Years and Over)

Group	Number	%
Total Population	221,274	17.3
Hispanic or Latino (of any race)	2,145	19.3
Central American, ex. Mexican	163	20.3
Cuban	131	24.6
Mexican	614	13.5
Puerto Rican	277	19.6
South American	435	40.2
Spaniard	236	28.4

Population Age 3–17 Enrolled in Public School
(Universe: Population Age 3–17 Enrolled in School)

Group	Number	%
Total Population	265,963	91.6
Hispanic or Latino (of any race)	4,107	88.7
Central American, ex. Mexican	461	92.2
Cuban	186	94.9
Mexican	1,841	89.8
Puerto Rican	623	81.8
South American	296	100.0
Spaniard	197	73.8

Population Age 3–17 Enrolled in Private School
(Universe: Population Age 3–17 Enrolled in School)

Group	Number	%
Total Population	24,290	8.4
Hispanic or Latino (of any race)	525	11.3
Central American, ex. Mexican	39	7.8
Cuban	10	5.1
Mexican	209	10.2
Puerto Rican	139	18.2
South American	0	0.0
Spaniard	70	26.2

Foreign-Born Population

Group	Number	%
Total Population	23,917	1.3
Hispanic or Latino (of any race)	4,687	22.4
Central American, ex. Mexican	925	50.4
Cuban	305	33.2
Mexican	1,870	20.5
Puerto Rican	0	0.0
South American	1,089	59.3
Spaniard	133	10.0

Foreign-Born Naturalized U.S. Citizens

Group	Number	%
Total Population	11,568	48.4
Hispanic or Latino (of any race)	1,832	39.1
Central American, ex. Mexican	420	45.4
Cuban	253	83.0
Mexican	526	28.1
Puerto Rican	0	0.0
South American	380	34.9
Spaniard	99	74.4

Language Spoken at Home: English Only
(Universe: Population 5 Years and Over)

Group	Number	%
Total Population	1,697,042	97.7
Hispanic or Latino (of any race)	11,522	60.9
Central American, ex. Mexican	409	25.6
Cuban	461	56.4
Mexican	5,544	67.9
Puerto Rican	1,484	58.5
South American	551	31.3
Spaniard	914	76.7

Language Spoken at Home: Spanish
(Universe: Population 5 Years and Over)

Group	Number	%
Total Population	17,860	1.0
Hispanic or Latino (of any race)	7,272	38.4
Central American, ex. Mexican	1,169	73.2
Cuban	356	43.6

Notes: (1) Percent of total population; (2) Percent of Hispanic/Latino population; Profiles include places with an overall population of at least 125,000, OR an overall population of at least 25,000 where the Hispanic/Latino population is at least 20% of the overall population. In states where less than five places meet either of these criteria, we have included places with at least 10,000 total population with the highest percentage of Hispanic/Latino population. These places are identified with an asterisk (*); Please refer to the User's Guide for a full explanation of data.

Mexican	2,619	32.1
Puerto Rican	1,051	41.5
South American	1,192	67.7
Spaniard	254	21.3

Unemployment Rate
(Universe: Population 16 Years and Over)

Group	%
Total Population	7.1
Hispanic or Latino (of any race)	7.0
Central American, ex. Mexican	0.9
Cuban	7.8
Mexican	7.6
Puerto Rican	8.6
South American	8.7
Spaniard	1.5

Class of Worker: Private Wage and Salary
(Universe: Civilian Employed Population 16 Years and Over)

Group	Number	%
Total Population	578,396	75.7
Hispanic or Latino (of any race)	5,813	77.2
Central American, ex. Mexican	433	75.7
Cuban	244	70.9
Mexican	2,544	81.2
Puerto Rican	915	82.4
South American	513	68.2
Spaniard	478	81.3

Class of Worker: Government
(Universe: Civilian Employed Population 16 Years and Over)

Group	Number	%
Total Population	142,964	18.7
Hispanic or Latino (of any race)	1,161	15.4
Central American, ex. Mexican	89	15.6
Cuban	43	12.5
Mexican	322	10.3
Puerto Rican	175	15.8
South American	182	24.2
Spaniard	76	12.9

Means of Transportation to Work: Car, Truck or Van
(Universe: Workers 16 Years and Over)

Group	Number	%
Total Population	685,640	92.2
Hispanic or Latino (of any race)	6,393	87.1
Central American, ex. Mexican	528	97.6
Cuban	286	83.1
Mexican	2,722	88.1
Puerto Rican	853	80.5
South American	596	83.1
Spaniard	530	90.6

Means of Transportation to Work: Public Transportation (ex. Taxicab)
(Universe: Workers 16 Years and Over)

Group	Number	%
Total Population	6,770	0.9
Hispanic or Latino (of any race)	173	2.4
Central American, ex. Mexican	13	2.4
Cuban	0	0.0
Mexican	30	1.0
Puerto Rican	25	2.4
South American	20	2.8
Spaniard	0	0.0

Homeownership Rate
(Universe: Occupied Housing Units)

Group	%
Total Population	73.4
Hispanic or Latino (of any race)	53.2
Central American, ex. Mexican	58.5
Guatemalan	55.0
Honduran	42.6
Nicaraguan	56.8
Panamanian	57.4
Salvadoran	63.7
Cuban	54.1
Dominican Republic	45.9
Mexican	47.7
Puerto Rican	47.1
South American	56.9
Argentinean	68.4
Bolivian	67.4
Chilean	65.7
Colombian	47.5
Ecuadorian	46.2
Peruvian	58.3
Venezuelan	52.9
Spaniard	74.7

Median Home Value

Group	Dollars
Total Population	94,500
Hispanic or Latino (of any race)	124,500
Central American, ex. Mexican	233,300
Cuban	143,800
Mexican	99,100
Puerto Rican	132,700
South American	254,500
Spaniard	173,000

Median Gross Rent

Group	Dollars
Total Population	549
Hispanic or Latino (of any race)	593
Central American, ex. Mexican	627
Cuban	387
Mexican	633
Puerto Rican	735
South American	685
Spaniard	439

Median Household Income
(2010 Inflation-Adjusted Dollars)

Group	Dollars
Total Population	38,380
Hispanic or Latino (of any race)	36,002
Central American, ex. Mexican	61,615
Cuban	14,769
Mexican	32,054
Puerto Rican	40,482
South American	50,938
Spaniard	47,442

Per Capita Income
(2010 Inflation-Adjusted Dollars)

Group	Dollars
Total Population	21,232
Hispanic or Latino (of any race)	18,275
Central American, ex. Mexican	12,995
Cuban	22,252
Mexican	13,873
Puerto Rican	19,449
South American	20,296
Spaniard	25,778

Households with $100,000+ Income

Group	Number	%
Total Population	78,855	10.6
Hispanic or Latino (of any race)	675	10.9
Central American, ex. Mexican	0	0.0
Cuban	30	10.6
Mexican	272	10.6
Puerto Rican	116	13.9
South American	115	19.4
Spaniard	31	6.2

Households with Food Stamps/SNAP Benefits During Past 12 Months

Group	Number	%
Total Population	97,779	13.2
Hispanic or Latino (of any race)	1,047	16.9
Central American, ex. Mexican	7	2.3
Cuban	117	41.3
Mexican	624	24.3
Puerto Rican	122	14.6
South American	0	0.0
Spaniard	26	5.2

Poverty Rate
(Income in Past 12 Months Below Poverty Level)

Group	%
Total Population	17.4
Hispanic or Latino (of any race)	23.2
Central American, ex. Mexican	16.5
Cuban	35.1
Mexican	28.4
Puerto Rican	19.6
South American	20.4
Spaniard	16.6

Beckley*

Population

Group	Number	%TP[1]	%HP[2]
Total Population	17,614	100.0	–
Hispanic or Latino (of any race)	265	1.5	100.0
Mexican	111	0.6	41.9

Population Growth: 2000–2010

Group	%
Total Population	2.1
Hispanic or Latino (of any race)	107.0

Males per 100 Females

Group	Number
Total Population	87.1
Hispanic or Latino (of any race)	132.5
Mexican	131.3

Average Household Size

Group	People
Total Population	2.17
Hispanic or Latino (of any race)	2.45
Mexican	2.77

Median Age

Group	Years
Total Population	41.6
Hispanic or Latino (of any race)	26.5
Mexican	21.5

High School Graduates
(Universe: Population 25 Years and Over)

Group	Number	%
Total Population	9,949	82.6

Four-Year College Graduates
(Universe: Population 25 Years and Over)

Group	Number	%
Total Population	2,700	22.4

Population Age 3–17 Enrolled in Public School
(Universe: Population Age 3–17 Enrolled in School)

Group	Number	%
Total Population	2,370	92.3

Population Age 3–17 Enrolled in Private School
(Universe: Population Age 3–17 Enrolled in School)

Group	Number	%
Total Population	199	7.7

Foreign-Born Population

Group	Number	%
Total Population	573	3.3

Foreign-Born Naturalized U.S. Citizens

Group	Number	%
Total Population	349	60.9

Language Spoken at Home: English Only
(Universe: Population 5 Years and Over)

Group	Number	%
Total Population	15,548	94.9

Language Spoken at Home: Spanish
(Universe: Population 5 Years and Over)

Group	Number	%
Total Population	266	1.6

Unemployment Rate
(Universe: Population 16 Years and Over)

Group	%
Total Population	8.2

Class of Worker: Private Wage and Salary
(Universe: Civilian Employed Population 16 Years and Over)

Group	Number	%
Total Population	5,415	76.2

Notes: (1) Percent of total population; (2) Percent of Hispanic/Latino population; Profiles include places with an overall population of at least 125,000, OR an overall population of at least 25,000 where the Hispanic/Latino population is at least 20% of the overall population. In states where less than five places meet either of these criteria, we have included places with at least 10,000 total population with the highest percentage of Hispanic/Latino population. These places are identified with an asterisk (*); Please refer to the User's Guide for a full explanation of data.

Class of Worker: Government
(Universe: Civilian Employed Population 16 Years and Over)

Group	Number	%
Total Population	1,419	20.0

Means of Transportation to Work: Car, Truck or Van
(Universe: Workers 16 Years and Over)

Group	Number	%
Total Population	6,163	88.7

Means of Transportation to Work: Public Transportation (ex. Taxicab)
(Universe: Workers 16 Years and Over)

Group	Number	%
Total Population	43	0.6

Homeownership Rate
(Universe: Occupied Housing Units)

Group	%
Total Population	59.9
Hispanic or Latino (of any race)	39.2
Mexican	46.7

Median Home Value

Group	Dollars
Total Population	95,400

Median Gross Rent

Group	Dollars
Total Population	526

Median Household Income
(2010 Inflation-Adjusted Dollars)

Group	Dollars
Total Population	31,480

Per Capita Income
(2010 Inflation-Adjusted Dollars)

Group	Dollars
Total Population	22,122

Households with $100,000+ Income

Group	Number	%
Total Population	786	10.3

Households with Food Stamps/SNAP Benefits During Past 12 Months

Group	Number	%
Total Population	1,318	17.3

Poverty Rate
(Income in Past 12 Months Below Poverty Level)

Group	%
Total Population	25.0

Clarksburg*

Population

Group	Number	%TP[1]	%HP[2]
Total Population	16,578	100.0	–
Hispanic or Latino (of any race)	269	1.6	100.0

Population Growth: 2000–2010

Group	%
Total Population	-1.0
Hispanic or Latino (of any race)	52.0

Males per 100 Females

Group	Number
Total Population	92.2
Hispanic or Latino (of any race)	99.3

Average Household Size

Group	People
Total Population	2.25
Hispanic or Latino (of any race)	2.22

Median Age

Group	Years
Total Population	39.5
Hispanic or Latino (of any race)	26.6

High School Graduates
(Universe: Population 25 Years and Over)

Group	Number	%
Total Population	9,170	82.8

Four-Year College Graduates
(Universe: Population 25 Years and Over)

Group	Number	%
Total Population	1,738	15.7

Population Age 3–17 Enrolled in Public School
(Universe: Population Age 3–17 Enrolled in School)

Group	Number	%
Total Population	2,594	95.3

Population Age 3–17 Enrolled in Private School
(Universe: Population Age 3–17 Enrolled in School)

Group	Number	%
Total Population	127	4.7

Foreign-Born Population

Group	Number	%
Total Population	111	0.7

Foreign-Born Naturalized U.S. Citizens

Group	Number	%
Total Population	80	72.1

Language Spoken at Home: English Only
(Universe: Population 5 Years and Over)

Group	Number	%
Total Population	15,080	98.2

Language Spoken at Home: Spanish
(Universe: Population 5 Years and Over)

Group	Number	%
Total Population	158	1.0

Unemployment Rate
(Universe: Population 16 Years and Over)

Group	%
Total Population	9.1

Class of Worker: Private Wage and Salary
(Universe: Civilian Employed Population 16 Years and Over)

Group	Number	%
Total Population	5,119	78.1

Class of Worker: Government
(Universe: Civilian Employed Population 16 Years and Over)

Group	Number	%
Total Population	1,083	16.5

Means of Transportation to Work: Car, Truck or Van
(Universe: Workers 16 Years and Over)

Group	Number	%
Total Population	5,845	91.2

Means of Transportation to Work: Public Transportation (ex. Taxicab)
(Universe: Workers 16 Years and Over)

Group	Number	%
Total Population	149	2.3

Homeownership Rate
(Universe: Occupied Housing Units)

Group	%
Total Population	60.3
Hispanic or Latino (of any race)	48.0

Median Home Value

Group	Dollars
Total Population	78,100

Median Gross Rent

Group	Dollars
Total Population	555

Median Household Income
(2010 Inflation-Adjusted Dollars)

Group	Dollars
Total Population	32,078

Per Capita Income
(2010 Inflation-Adjusted Dollars)

Group	Dollars
Total Population	17,367

Households with $100,000+ Income

Group	Number	%
Total Population	460	6.7

Households with Food Stamps/SNAP Benefits During Past 12 Months

Group	Number	%
Total Population	1,501	22.0

Poverty Rate
(Income in Past 12 Months Below Poverty Level)

Group	%
Total Population	27.7

Huntington*

Population

Group	Number	%TP[1]	%HP[2]
Total Population	49,138	100.0	–
Hispanic or Latino (of any race)	685	1.4	100.0
Mexican	338	0.7	49.3

Population Growth: 2000–2010

Group	%
Total Population	-4.5
Hispanic or Latino (of any race)	56.8
Mexican	80.7

Males per 100 Females

Group	Number
Total Population	94.7
Hispanic or Latino (of any race)	121.7
Mexican	134.7

Average Household Size

Group	People
Total Population	2.12
Hispanic or Latino (of any race)	2.39
Mexican	2.52

Median Age

Group	Years
Total Population	35.4
Hispanic or Latino (of any race)	24.4
Mexican	22.0

High School Graduates
(Universe: Population 25 Years and Over)

Group	Number	%
Total Population	27,279	85.9

Four-Year College Graduates
(Universe: Population 25 Years and Over)

Group	Number	%
Total Population	7,609	24.0

Population Age 3–17 Enrolled in Public School
(Universe: Population Age 3–17 Enrolled in School)

Group	Number	%
Total Population	5,736	87.8

Population Age 3–17 Enrolled in Private School
(Universe: Population Age 3–17 Enrolled in School)

Group	Number	%
Total Population	800	12.2

Foreign-Born Population

Group	Number	%
Total Population	938	1.9

Foreign-Born Naturalized U.S. Citizens

Group	Number	%
Total Population	296	31.6

Language Spoken at Home: English Only
(Universe: Population 5 Years and Over)

Group	Number	%
Total Population	44,994	96.7

Notes: (1) Percent of total population; (2) Percent of Hispanic/Latino population; Profiles include places with an overall population of at least 125,000, OR an overall population of at least 25,000 where the Hispanic/Latino population is at least 20% of the overall population. In states where less than five places meet either of these criteria, we have included places with at least 10,000 total population with the highest percentage of Hispanic/Latino population. These places are identified with an asterisk (*); Please refer to the User's Guide for a full explanation of data.

Language Spoken at Home: Spanish (Universe: Population 5 Years and Over)		
Group	Number	%
Total Population	510	1.1

Unemployment Rate (Universe: Population 16 Years and Over)	
Group	%
Total Population	7.7

Class of Worker: Private Wage and Salary (Universe: Civilian Employed Population 16 Years and Over)		
Group	Number	%
Total Population	16,316	78.3

Class of Worker: Government (Universe: Civilian Employed Population 16 Years and Over)		
Group	Number	%
Total Population	3,559	17.1

Means of Transportation to Work: Car, Truck or Van (Universe: Workers 16 Years and Over)		
Group	Number	%
Total Population	17,241	85.3

Means of Transportation to Work: Public Transportation (ex. Taxicab) (Universe: Workers 16 Years and Over)		
Group	Number	%
Total Population	460	2.3

Homeownership Rate (Universe: Occupied Housing Units)	
Group	%
Total Population	52.3
Hispanic or Latino (of any race)	34.3
Mexican	29.5

Median Home Value	
Group	Dollars
Total Population	81,500

Median Gross Rent	
Group	Dollars
Total Population	579

Median Household Income (2010 Inflation-Adjusted Dollars)	
Group	Dollars
Total Population	27,858

Per Capita Income (2010 Inflation-Adjusted Dollars)	
Group	Dollars
Total Population	19,648

Households with $100,000+ Income		
Group	Number	%
Total Population	1,740	8.1

Households with Food Stamps/SNAP Benefits During Past 12 Months		
Group	Number	%
Total Population	4,092	18.9

Poverty Rate (Income in Past 12 Months Below Poverty Level)	
Group	%
Total Population	29.4

Martinsburg*

Population			
Group	Number	%TP[1]	%HP[2]
Total Population	17,227	100.0	–
Hispanic or Latino (of any race)	1,069	6.2	100.0
Central American, ex. Mexican	133	0.8	12.4
Mexican	600	3.5	56.1
Puerto Rican	181	1.1	16.9

Population Growth: 2000–2010	
Group	%
Total Population	15.1
Hispanic or Latino (of any race)	145.2
Mexican	106.9

Males per 100 Females	
Group	Number
Total Population	95.3
Hispanic or Latino (of any race)	125.5
Central American, ex. Mexican	95.6
Mexican	147.9
Puerto Rican	105.7

Average Household Size	
Group	People
Total Population	2.32
Hispanic or Latino (of any race)	3.57
Central American, ex. Mexican	4.13
Mexican	3.85
Puerto Rican	3.02

Median Age	
Group	Years
Total Population	37.0
Hispanic or Latino (of any race)	22.6
Central American, ex. Mexican	24.3
Mexican	22.2
Puerto Rican	20.8

High School Graduates (Universe: Population 25 Years and Over)		
Group	Number	%
Total Population	9,619	82.8

Four-Year College Graduates (Universe: Population 25 Years and Over)		
Group	Number	%
Total Population	2,445	21.1

Population Age 3–17 Enrolled in Public School (Universe: Population Age 3–17 Enrolled in School)		
Group	Number	%
Total Population	2,370	85.9

Population Age 3–17 Enrolled in Private School (Universe: Population Age 3–17 Enrolled in School)		
Group	Number	%
Total Population	389	14.1

Foreign-Born Population		
Group	Number	%
Total Population	1,059	6.2

Foreign-Born Naturalized U.S. Citizens		
Group	Number	%
Total Population	323	30.5

Language Spoken at Home: English Only (Universe: Population 5 Years and Over)		
Group	Number	%
Total Population	14,359	93.2

Language Spoken at Home: Spanish (Universe: Population 5 Years and Over)		
Group	Number	%
Total Population	644	4.2

Unemployment Rate (Universe: Population 16 Years and Over)	
Group	%
Total Population	9.6

Class of Worker: Private Wage and Salary (Universe: Civilian Employed Population 16 Years and Over)		
Group	Number	%
Total Population	5,372	71.2

Class of Worker: Government (Universe: Civilian Employed Population 16 Years and Over)		
Group	Number	%
Total Population	1,800	23.9

Means of Transportation to Work: Car, Truck or Van (Universe: Workers 16 Years and Over)		
Group	Number	%
Total Population	6,391	85.1

Means of Transportation to Work: Public Transportation (ex. Taxicab) (Universe: Workers 16 Years and Over)		
Group	Number	%
Total Population	260	3.5

Homeownership Rate (Universe: Occupied Housing Units)	
Group	%
Total Population	49.9
Hispanic or Latino (of any race)	31.2
Central American, ex. Mexican	51.6
Mexican	19.7
Puerto Rican	38.0

Median Home Value	
Group	Dollars
Total Population	178,400

Median Gross Rent	
Group	Dollars
Total Population	665

Median Household Income (2010 Inflation-Adjusted Dollars)	
Group	Dollars
Total Population	34,799

Per Capita Income (2010 Inflation-Adjusted Dollars)	
Group	Dollars
Total Population	23,511

Households with $100,000+ Income		
Group	Number	%
Total Population	779	10.1

Households with Food Stamps/SNAP Benefits During Past 12 Months		
Group	Number	%
Total Population	1,142	14.9

Poverty Rate (Income in Past 12 Months Below Poverty Level)	
Group	%
Total Population	18.8

Morgantown*

Population			
Group	Number	%TP[1]	%HP[2]
Total Population	29,660	100.0	–
Hispanic or Latino (of any race)	765	2.6	100.0
Mexican	252	0.8	32.9
Puerto Rican	127	0.4	16.6
South American	181	0.6	23.7

Population Growth: 2000–2010	
Group	%
Total Population	10.6
Hispanic or Latino (of any race)	85.7
Mexican	123.0

Males per 100 Females	
Group	Number
Total Population	114.9
Hispanic or Latino (of any race)	127.0
Mexican	129.1
Puerto Rican	135.2
South American	120.7

Average Household Size	
Group	People
Total Population	2.05
Hispanic or Latino (of any race)	2.34
Mexican	2.40
Puerto Rican	2.26
South American	2.38

Median Age	
Group	Years
Total Population	22.6
Hispanic or Latino (of any race)	21.7
Mexican	21.8

STATE & PLACE PROFILES

Notes: (1) Percent of total population; (2) Percent of Hispanic/Latino population; Profiles include places with an overall population of at least 125,000, OR an overall population of at least 25,000 where the Hispanic/Latino population is at least 20% of the overall population. In states where less than five places meet either of these criteria, we have included places with at least 10,000 total population with the highest percentage of Hispanic/Latino population. These places are identified with an asterisk (*); Please refer to the User's Guide for a full explanation of data.

Puerto Rican		20.7
South American		22.9

High School Graduates
(Universe: Population 25 Years and Over)

Group	Number	%
Total Population	10,238	90.3
Hispanic or Latino (of any race)	251	86.6

Four-Year College Graduates
(Universe: Population 25 Years and Over)

Group	Number	%
Total Population	5,193	45.8
Hispanic or Latino (of any race)	163	56.2

Population Age 3–17 Enrolled in Public School
(Universe: Population Age 3–17 Enrolled in School)

Group	Number	%
Total Population	1,970	93.5
Hispanic or Latino (of any race)	94	100.0

Population Age 3–17 Enrolled in Private School
(Universe: Population Age 3–17 Enrolled in School)

Group	Number	%
Total Population	138	6.5
Hispanic or Latino (of any race)	0	0.0

Foreign-Born Population

Group	Number	%
Total Population	1,353	4.7
Hispanic or Latino (of any race)	200	28.0

Foreign-Born Naturalized U.S. Citizens

Group	Number	%
Total Population	457	33.8
Hispanic or Latino (of any race)	91	45.5

Language Spoken at Home: English Only
(Universe: Population 5 Years and Over)

Group	Number	%
Total Population	26,646	93.6
Hispanic or Latino (of any race)	374	52.9

Language Spoken at Home: Spanish
(Universe: Population 5 Years and Over)

Group	Number	%
Total Population	495	1.7
Hispanic or Latino (of any race)	333	47.1

Unemployment Rate
(Universe: Population 16 Years and Over)

Group	%
Total Population	9.1
Hispanic or Latino (of any race)	2.7

Class of Worker: Private Wage and Salary
(Universe: Civilian Employed Population 16 Years and Over)

Group	Number	%
Total Population	8,372	66.7
Hispanic or Latino (of any race)	227	69.0

Class of Worker: Government
(Universe: Civilian Employed Population 16 Years and Over)

Group	Number	%
Total Population	3,935	31.3
Hispanic or Latino (of any race)	102	31.0

Means of Transportation to Work: Car, Truck or Van
(Universe: Workers 16 Years and Over)

Group	Number	%
Total Population	9,143	75.2
Hispanic or Latino (of any race)	157	56.7

Means of Transportation to Work: Public Transportation (ex. Taxicab)
(Universe: Workers 16 Years and Over)

Group	Number	%
Total Population	339	2.8
Hispanic or Latino (of any race)	15	5.4

Homeownership Rate
(Universe: Occupied Housing Units)

Group	%
Total Population	37.3
Hispanic or Latino (of any race)	22.3

Mexican	25.0
Puerto Rican	20.0
South American	25.8

Median Home Value

Group	Dollars
Total Population	157,600
Hispanic or Latino (of any race)	167,700

Median Gross Rent

Group	Dollars
Total Population	598
Hispanic or Latino (of any race)	510

Median Household Income
(2010 Inflation-Adjusted Dollars)

Group	Dollars
Total Population	25,495
Hispanic or Latino (of any race)	22,344

Per Capita Income
(2010 Inflation-Adjusted Dollars)

Group	Dollars
Total Population	17,122
Hispanic or Latino (of any race)	17,215

Households with $100,000+ Income

Group	Number	%
Total Population	1,182	12.6
Hispanic or Latino (of any race)	13	5.2

Households with Food Stamps/SNAP Benefits During Past 12 Months

Group	Number	%
Total Population	420	4.5
Hispanic or Latino (of any race)	16	6.5

Poverty Rate
(Income in Past 12 Months Below Poverty Level)

Group	%
Total Population	37.5
Hispanic or Latino (of any race)	26.6

Notes: (1) Percent of total population; (2) Percent of Hispanic/Latino population; Profiles include places with an overall population of at least 125,000, OR an overall population of at least 25,000 where the Hispanic/Latino population is at least 20% of the overall population. In states where less than five places meet either of these criteria, we have included places with at least 10,000 total population with the highest percentage of Hispanic/Latino population. These places are identified with an asterisk (*); Please refer to the User's Guide for a full explanation of data.

Wisconsin

EDITOR'S NOTE: For a place to be included in this edition, it must meet one of two criteria. Either its overall population is at least 125,000, OR its overall population is at least 25,000 and its Hispanic/Latino population is at least 20% of the overall population. In Wisconsin, less than five places meet either of these criteria. In an effort to include at least five places for each state, we have included places with at least 10,000 total population with the highest percentage of Hispanic/Latino population. These places are identified with an asterisk (*). For the state of Wisconsin, the following locations are included:

- Beloit*
- Fitchburg*
- Madison
- Milwaukee
- Racine

Section Two: State & Place Profiles starts with the state profile, followed by place profiles that meet the criteria above. Places are listed alphabetically within each state. All states, all counties and places that meet the above criteria are ranked and compared in *Section Three: Rankings & Comparisons*, on page 1055.

For a more detailed look at the Hispanic/Latino population in Wisconsin, a companion web site is available at no additional charge with purchase of this print edition. Visit http://gold.greyhouse.com/page/info_hispanic for more information.

The web site includes data for all counties and places in Wisconsin with Hispanic/Latino population, plus ten additional topics: Self Employed Worker; Walked to Work; Worked from Home; Mean Travel Time to Work; Mean Household Income; Households with Cash Public Assistance; Mean Cash Pubic Assistance; Poverty Rates for 18 and Under, 18 to 64, and 65 and Over.

Population

Group	Number	%TP[1]	%HP[2]
Total Population	5,686,986	100.0	–
Hispanic or Latino (of any race)	336,056	5.9	100.0
Central American, ex. Mexican	10,616	0.2	3.2
Costa Rican	779	<0.1	0.2
Guatemalan	3,037	0.1	0.9
Honduran	2,402	<0.1	0.7
Nicaraguan	1,624	<0.1	0.5
Panamanian	822	<0.1	0.2
Salvadoran	1,867	<0.1	0.6
Cuban	3,696	0.1	1.1
Dominican Republic	1,786	<0.1	0.5
Mexican	244,248	4.3	72.7
Puerto Rican	46,323	0.8	13.8
South American	9,675	0.2	2.9
Argentinean	1,065	<0.1	0.3
Bolivian	430	<0.1	0.1
Chilean	815	<0.1	0.2
Colombian	2,941	0.1	0.9
Ecuadorian	886	<0.1	0.3
Paraguayan	176	<0.1	0.1
Peruvian	2,029	<0.1	0.6
Uruguayan	338	<0.1	0.1
Venezuelan	868	<0.1	0.3
Spaniard	3,220	0.1	1.0

Population Growth: 2000–2010

Group	%
Total Population	6.0
Hispanic or Latino (of any race)	74.2
Central American, ex. Mexican	164.1
Costa Rican	87.7
Guatemalan	279.2
Honduran	207.2
Nicaraguan	114.5
Panamanian	106.5
Salvadoran	178.2
Cuban	48.4
Dominican Republic	191.8
Mexican	92.7
Puerto Rican	53.0
South American	138.7
Argentinean	194.2
Bolivian	132.4
Chilean	83.6
Colombian	122.3
Ecuadorian	214.2
Paraguayan	22.2
Peruvian	198.4
Venezuelan	130.9
Spaniard	580.8

Males per 100 Females

Group	Number
Total Population	98.5
Hispanic or Latino (of any race)	110.1
Central American, ex. Mexican	99.9
Costa Rican	91.4
Guatemalan	102.9
Honduran	106.9
Nicaraguan	92.2
Panamanian	68.4
Salvadoran	114.1
Cuban	116.3
Dominican Republic	96.9
Mexican	114.5
Puerto Rican	97.6
South American	88.8
Argentinean	87.5
Bolivian	79.9
Chilean	86.1
Colombian	85.2
Ecuadorian	108.0
Paraguayan	97.8
Peruvian	86.1
Uruguayan	102.4
Venezuelan	88.3
Spaniard	96.3

Average Household Size

Group	People
Total Population	2.43
Hispanic or Latino (of any race)	3.43
Central American, ex. Mexican	3.28
Costa Rican	2.85
Guatemalan	3.33
Honduran	3.50
Nicaraguan	3.13
Panamanian	2.80
Salvadoran	3.48
Cuban	2.60
Dominican Republic	3.14
Mexican	3.62
Puerto Rican	3.06
South American	2.74
Argentinean	2.73
Bolivian	2.87
Chilean	2.43
Colombian	2.63
Ecuadorian	2.88
Paraguayan	2.61
Peruvian	2.83
Uruguayan	3.29
Venezuelan	2.74
Spaniard	2.62

Median Age

Group	Years
Total Population	38.5
Hispanic or Latino (of any race)	23.4
Central American, ex. Mexican	25.0
Costa Rican	27.6
Guatemalan	13.4
Honduran	27.2
Nicaraguan	29.0
Panamanian	30.6
Salvadoran	28.7
Cuban	25.5
Dominican Republic	24.7
Mexican	23.1
Puerto Rican	22.9
South American	29.6
Argentinean	33.2
Bolivian	31.3
Chilean	27.1
Colombian	28.1
Ecuadorian	29.4
Paraguayan	19.1
Peruvian	30.6
Uruguayan	31.5
Venezuelan	32.1
Spaniard	29.4

High School Graduates
(Universe: Population 25 Years and Over)

Group	Number	%
Total Population	3,343,833	89.4
Hispanic or Latino (of any race)	90,761	61.7
Central American, ex. Mexican	3,795	71.9
Costa Rican	338	90.6
Guatemalan	510	68.4
Honduran	919	69.7
Nicaraguan	1,043	81.9
Panamanian	434	90.6
Salvadoran	515	49.5
Cuban	1,330	77.4
Dominican Republic	483	71.1
Mexican	61,441	57.0
Puerto Rican	13,506	69.7
South American	4,892	85.0
Argentinean	794	91.3
Chilean	514	80.6
Colombian	1,261	86.9
Ecuadorian	349	74.9
Peruvian	1,215	90.3
Venezuelan	483	89.4
Spaniard	1,232	96.3

Four-Year College Graduates
(Universe: Population 25 Years and Over)

Group	Number	%
Total Population	964,412	25.8
Hispanic or Latino (of any race)	16,037	10.9
Central American, ex. Mexican	1,143	21.7
Costa Rican	140	37.5
Guatemalan	167	22.4
Honduran	234	17.8
Nicaraguan	326	25.6
Panamanian	121	25.3
Salvadoran	144	13.8
Cuban	506	29.5
Dominican Republic	107	15.8
Mexican	8,417	7.8
Puerto Rican	2,368	12.2
South American	2,089	36.3
Argentinean	356	40.9
Chilean	161	25.2
Colombian	604	41.6
Ecuadorian	147	31.5
Peruvian	443	32.9
Venezuelan	271	50.2
Spaniard	485	37.9

Population Age 3–17 Enrolled in Public School
(Universe: Population Age 3–17 Enrolled in School)

Group	Number	%
Total Population	864,985	84.8
Hispanic or Latino (of any race)	77,073	89.1
Central American, ex. Mexican	2,304	80.9
Costa Rican	144	71.3
Guatemalan	646	70.1
Honduran	565	100.0
Nicaraguan	517	83.8
Panamanian	152	73.1
Salvadoran	280	85.6
Cuban	660	78.4

Notes: (1) Percent of total population; (2) Percent of Hispanic/Latino population; Profiles include places with an overall population of at least 125,000, OR an overall population of at least 25,000 where the Hispanic/Latino population is at least 20% of the overall population. In states where less than five places meet either of these criteria, we have included places with at least 10,000 total population with the highest percentage of Hispanic/Latino population. These places are identified with an asterisk (*); Please refer to the User's Guide for a full explanation of data.

Group	Number	%
Dominican Republic	348	83.5
Mexican	57,450	89.9
Puerto Rican	11,069	93.0
South American	1,916	74.0
Argentinean	214	71.6
Chilean	242	92.4
Colombian	425	75.5
Ecuadorian	170	87.2
Peruvian	435	54.5
Venezuelan	181	86.2
Spaniard	491	79.4

Population Age 3–17 Enrolled in Private School
(Universe: Population Age 3–17 Enrolled in School)

Group	Number	%
Total Population	155,517	15.2
Hispanic or Latino (of any race)	9,433	10.9
Central American, ex. Mexican	544	19.1
Costa Rican	58	28.7
Guatemalan	275	29.9
Honduran	0	0.0
Nicaraguan	100	16.2
Panamanian	56	26.9
Salvadoran	47	14.4
Cuban	182	21.6
Dominican Republic	69	16.5
Mexican	6,473	10.1
Puerto Rican	833	7.0
South American	673	26.0
Argentinean	85	28.4
Chilean	20	7.6
Colombian	138	24.5
Ecuadorian	25	12.8
Peruvian	363	45.5
Venezuelan	29	13.8
Spaniard	127	20.6

Foreign-Born Population

Group	Number	%
Total Population	257,987	4.6
Hispanic or Latino (of any race)	104,809	33.7
Central American, ex. Mexican	5,986	57.7
Costa Rican	366	55.6
Guatemalan	1,497	61.8
Honduran	1,572	65.8
Nicaraguan	1,193	50.7
Panamanian	255	30.9
Salvadoran	1,038	64.4
Cuban	729	23.7
Dominican Republic	793	51.2
Mexican	89,062	38.8
Puerto Rican	177	0.4
South American	6,154	57.5
Argentinean	928	70.7
Chilean	612	49.4
Colombian	1,575	57.6
Ecuadorian	502	60.1
Peruvian	1,409	51.3
Venezuelan	544	58.4
Spaniard	469	19.5

Foreign-Born Naturalized U.S. Citizens

Group	Number	%
Total Population	105,865	41.0
Hispanic or Latino (of any race)	21,838	20.8
Central American, ex. Mexican	2,746	45.9
Costa Rican	169	46.2
Guatemalan	965	64.5
Honduran	437	27.8
Nicaraguan	671	56.2
Panamanian	102	40.0
Salvadoran	349	33.6
Cuban	448	61.5
Dominican Republic	243	30.6
Mexican	15,380	17.3
Puerto Rican	83	46.9
South American	2,104	34.2
Argentinean	192	20.7
Chilean	211	34.5
Colombian	760	48.3
Ecuadorian	155	30.9
Peruvian	489	34.7
Venezuelan	80	14.7
Spaniard	200	42.6

Language Spoken at Home: English Only
(Universe: Population 5 Years and Over)

Group	Number	%
Total Population	4,838,913	91.6
Hispanic or Latino (of any race)	85,842	31.8
Central American, ex. Mexican	2,495	28.6
Costa Rican	129	20.0
Guatemalan	814	47.1
Honduran	405	18.9
Nicaraguan	495	25.1
Panamanian	414	56.1
Salvadoran	187	13.2
Cuban	1,651	57.4
Dominican Republic	374	27.5
Mexican	58,114	29.3
Puerto Rican	13,159	35.9
South American	2,879	30.1
Argentinean	225	18.6
Chilean	444	42.0
Colombian	696	28.4
Ecuadorian	147	20.4
Peruvian	968	39.5
Venezuelan	95	11.1
Spaniard	1,474	64.5

Language Spoken at Home: Spanish
(Universe: Population 5 Years and Over)

Group	Number	%
Total Population	234,062	4.4
Hispanic or Latino (of any race)	182,656	67.8
Central American, ex. Mexican	6,244	71.4
Costa Rican	516	80.0
Guatemalan	916	52.9
Honduran	1,741	81.1
Nicaraguan	1,480	74.9
Panamanian	324	43.9
Salvadoran	1,230	86.8
Cuban	1,112	38.7
Dominican Republic	987	72.5
Mexican	139,615	70.4
Puerto Rican	23,289	63.5
South American	6,656	69.5
Argentinean	968	80.2
Chilean	614	58.0
Colombian	1,742	71.0
Ecuadorian	572	79.6
Peruvian	1,480	60.5
Venezuelan	746	87.3
Spaniard	750	32.8

Unemployment Rate
(Universe: Population 16 Years and Over)

Group	%
Total Population	6.7
Hispanic or Latino (of any race)	10.0
Central American, ex. Mexican	10.2
Costa Rican	1.1
Guatemalan	7.4
Honduran	12.4
Nicaraguan	13.1
Panamanian	2.4
Salvadoran	10.1
Cuban	9.0
Dominican Republic	2.8
Mexican	9.3
Puerto Rican	16.0
South American	4.5
Argentinean	2.3
Chilean	3.3
Colombian	5.6
Ecuadorian	5.8
Peruvian	3.0
Venezuelan	7.7
Spaniard	10.0

Class of Worker: Private Wage and Salary
(Universe: Civilian Employed Population 16 Years and Over)

Group	Number	%
Total Population	2,340,886	81.6
Hispanic or Latino (of any race)	114,493	89.1
Central American, ex. Mexican	3,680	84.0
Costa Rican	295	83.1
Guatemalan	701	93.6
Honduran	963	85.0
Nicaraguan	746	78.2
Panamanian	301	72.7
Salvadoran	674	88.2
Cuban	956	77.2
Dominican Republic	529	81.1
Mexican	88,235	90.9
Puerto Rican	12,394	85.8
South American	4,357	81.3
Argentinean	579	79.5
Chilean	453	86.6
Colombian	1,131	79.1
Ecuadorian	269	83.3
Peruvian	1,252	85.0
Venezuelan	349	78.4
Spaniard	898	79.8

Class of Worker: Government
(Universe: Civilian Employed Population 16 Years and Over)

Group	Number	%
Total Population	356,366	12.4
Hispanic or Latino (of any race)	9,348	7.3
Central American, ex. Mexican	518	11.8
Costa Rican	42	11.8
Guatemalan	48	6.4
Honduran	118	10.4
Nicaraguan	136	14.3
Panamanian	77	18.6
Salvadoran	86	11.3
Cuban	214	17.3
Dominican Republic	23	3.5
Mexican	5,580	5.7
Puerto Rican	1,591	11.0
South American	689	12.8
Argentinean	119	16.3
Chilean	65	12.4
Colombian	215	15.0
Ecuadorian	34	10.5
Peruvian	154	10.5
Venezuelan	55	12.4
Spaniard	167	14.8

Means of Transportation to Work: Car, Truck or Van
(Universe: Workers 16 Years and Over)

Group	Number	%
Total Population	2,507,722	89.2
Hispanic or Latino (of any race)	111,517	88.8
Central American, ex. Mexican	3,979	93.7
Costa Rican	322	92.3
Guatemalan	632	88.8
Honduran	1,080	96.3
Nicaraguan	874	96.4
Panamanian	364	95.3
Salvadoran	696	91.1
Cuban	962	79.4
Dominican Republic	471	80.1
Mexican	84,892	89.3
Puerto Rican	12,224	86.6
South American	4,487	86.1
Argentinean	617	89.3
Chilean	484	95.1
Colombian	1,279	91.8
Ecuadorian	253	88.2
Peruvian	1,138	78.9
Venezuelan	411	92.4
Spaniard	866	81.7

Means of Transportation to Work: Public Transportation (ex. Taxicab)
(Universe: Workers 16 Years and Over)

Group	Number	%
Total Population	50,545	1.8
Hispanic or Latino (of any race)	4,312	3.4
Central American, ex. Mexican	40	0.9
Costa Rican	0	0.0
Guatemalan	0	0.0
Honduran	34	3.0
Nicaraguan	0	0.0
Panamanian	0	0.0
Salvadoran	6	0.8
Cuban	108	8.9
Dominican Republic	16	2.7
Mexican	2,805	2.9
Puerto Rican	884	6.3
South American	254	4.9
Argentinean	47	6.8

Notes: (1) Percent of total population; (2) Percent of Hispanic/Latino population; Profiles include places with an overall population of at least 125,000, OR an overall population of at least 25,000 where the Hispanic/Latino population is at least 20% of the overall population. In states where less than five places meet either of these criteria, we have included places with at least 10,000 total population with the highest percentage of Hispanic/Latino population. These places are identified with an asterisk (*); Please refer to the User's Guide for a full explanation of data.

Chilean	14	2.8
Colombian	47	3.4
Ecuadorian	10	3.5
Peruvian	119	8.3
Venezuelan	0	0.0
Spaniard	64	6.0

Homeownership Rate
(Universe: Occupied Housing Units)

Group	%
Total Population	68.1
Hispanic or Latino (of any race)	40.9
Central American, ex. Mexican	42.4
Costa Rican	52.6
Guatemalan	41.1
Honduran	29.1
Nicaraguan	42.9
Panamanian	54.8
Salvadoran	51.2
Cuban	40.5
Dominican Republic	39.1
Mexican	41.7
Puerto Rican	35.0
South American	49.8
Argentinean	51.0
Bolivian	65.9
Chilean	48.3
Colombian	50.8
Ecuadorian	46.0
Paraguayan	46.4
Peruvian	45.6
Uruguayan	46.3
Venezuelan	54.8
Spaniard	54.0

Median Home Value

Group	Dollars
Total Population	169,000
Hispanic or Latino (of any race)	142,900
Central American, ex. Mexican	147,800
Costa Rican	171,700
Guatemalan	210,300
Honduran	127,900
Nicaraguan	169,400
Panamanian	143,800
Salvadoran	147,000
Cuban	148,800
Dominican Republic	135,100
Mexican	139,000
Puerto Rican	142,600
South American	202,800
Argentinean	254,500
Chilean	190,700
Colombian	234,500
Ecuadorian	129,800
Peruvian	184,400
Venezuelan	193,900
Spaniard	208,300

Median Gross Rent

Group	Dollars
Total Population	713
Hispanic or Latino (of any race)	709
Central American, ex. Mexican	688
Costa Rican	719
Guatemalan	613
Honduran	687
Nicaraguan	752
Panamanian	894
Salvadoran	720
Cuban	731
Dominican Republic	680
Mexican	702
Puerto Rican	731
South American	722
Argentinean	776
Chilean	668
Colombian	751
Ecuadorian	690
Peruvian	706
Venezuelan	811
Spaniard	796

Median Household Income
(2010 Inflation-Adjusted Dollars)

Group	Dollars
Total Population	51,598
Hispanic or Latino (of any race)	37,787
Central American, ex. Mexican	47,688
Costa Rican	52,778
Guatemalan	53,750
Honduran	32,750
Nicaraguan	53,145
Panamanian	48,125
Salvadoran	49,613
Cuban	43,846
Dominican Republic	21,635
Mexican	37,705
Puerto Rican	31,861
South American	51,475
Argentinean	32,813
Chilean	71,389
Colombian	64,464
Ecuadorian	22,292
Peruvian	51,259
Venezuelan	60,682
Spaniard	44,107

Per Capita Income
(2010 Inflation-Adjusted Dollars)

Group	Dollars
Total Population	26,624
Hispanic or Latino (of any race)	13,670
Central American, ex. Mexican	15,104
Costa Rican	19,115
Guatemalan	9,975
Honduran	14,076
Nicaraguan	16,130
Panamanian	19,445
Salvadoran	19,154
Cuban	20,006
Dominican Republic	14,085
Mexican	13,190
Puerto Rican	12,666
South American	22,694
Argentinean	25,591
Chilean	19,033
Colombian	25,388
Ecuadorian	11,029
Peruvian	22,499
Venezuelan	32,441
Spaniard	20,887

Households with $100,000+ Income

Group	Number	%
Total Population	392,928	17.3
Hispanic or Latino (of any race)	6,573	8.1
Central American, ex. Mexican	244	9.4
Costa Rican	20	13.5
Guatemalan	30	8.5
Honduran	35	5.3
Nicaraguan	23	3.5
Panamanian	64	29.8
Salvadoran	72	13.7
Cuban	150	14.7
Dominican Republic	53	11.5
Mexican	4,477	7.7
Puerto Rican	738	6.3
South American	543	17.4
Argentinean	73	16.9
Chilean	40	14.6
Colombian	162	22.4
Ecuadorian	22	8.7
Peruvian	92	12.0
Venezuelan	110	29.7
Spaniard	75	9.9

Households with Food Stamps/SNAP Benefits During Past 12 Months

Group	Number	%
Total Population	174,348	7.7
Hispanic or Latino (of any race)	14,607	18.0
Central American, ex. Mexican	388	15.0
Costa Rican	0	0.0
Guatemalan	34	9.6
Honduran	103	15.7
Nicaraguan	97	14.9
Panamanian	60	27.9
Salvadoran	69	13.1
Cuban	329	32.2
Dominican Republic	102	22.1
Mexican	9,632	16.6
Puerto Rican	3,366	28.6
South American	195	6.3
Argentinean	21	4.9
Chilean	8	2.9
Colombian	83	11.5
Ecuadorian	10	4.0
Peruvian	21	2.7
Venezuelan	25	6.8
Spaniard	7	0.9

Poverty Rate
(Income in Past 12 Months Below Poverty Level)

Group	%
Total Population	11.6
Hispanic or Latino (of any race)	24.0
Central American, ex. Mexican	14.9
Costa Rican	0.0
Guatemalan	9.8
Honduran	25.0
Nicaraguan	11.9
Panamanian	16.5
Salvadoran	16.2
Cuban	26.6
Dominican Republic	36.0
Mexican	23.3
Puerto Rican	33.3
South American	11.7
Argentinean	10.9
Chilean	6.9
Colombian	10.6
Ecuadorian	24.0
Peruvian	11.4
Venezuelan	9.5
Spaniard	13.5

Beloit*

Population

Group	Number	%TP[1]	%HP[2]
Total Population	36,966	100.0	–
Hispanic or Latino (of any race)	6,332	17.1	100.0
Dominican Republic	103	0.3	1.6
Mexican	5,522	14.9	87.2
Puerto Rican	190	0.5	3.0

Population Growth: 2000–2010

Group	%
Total Population	3.3
Hispanic or Latino (of any race)	94.4
Mexican	97.9

Males per 100 Females

Group	Number
Total Population	91.9
Hispanic or Latino (of any race)	106.7
Dominican Republic	98.1
Mexican	109.0
Puerto Rican	81.0

Average Household Size

Group	People
Total Population	2.57
Hispanic or Latino (of any race)	3.99
Dominican Republic	3.82
Mexican	4.11
Puerto Rican	3.25

Median Age

Group	Years
Total Population	33.1
Hispanic or Latino (of any race)	21.0
Dominican Republic	25.6
Mexican	20.8
Puerto Rican	19.1

High School Graduates
(Universe: Population 25 Years and Over)

Group	Number	%
Total Population	17,949	80.1
Hispanic or Latino (of any race)	1,267	49.3

Notes: (1) Percent of total population; (2) Percent of Hispanic/Latino population; Profiles include places with an overall population of at least 125,000, OR an overall population of at least 25,000 where the Hispanic/Latino population is at least 20% of the overall population. In states where less than five places meet either of these criteria, we have included places with at least 10,000 total population with the highest percentage of Hispanic/Latino population. These places are identified with an asterisk (*); Please refer to the User's Guide for a full explanation of data.

Mexican	920	43.0

Four-Year College Graduates
(Universe: Population 25 Years and Over)

Group	Number	%
Total Population	3,407	15.2
Hispanic or Latino (of any race)	160	6.2
Mexican	65	3.0

Population Age 3–17 Enrolled in Public School
(Universe: Population Age 3–17 Enrolled in School)

Group	Number	%
Total Population	7,182	96.6
Hispanic or Latino (of any race)	1,898	95.9
Mexican	1,715	96.0

Population Age 3–17 Enrolled in Private School
(Universe: Population Age 3–17 Enrolled in School)

Group	Number	%
Total Population	250	3.4
Hispanic or Latino (of any race)	82	4.1
Mexican	71	4.0

Foreign-Born Population

Group	Number	%
Total Population	3,056	8.3
Hispanic or Latino (of any race)	2,427	39.7
Mexican	2,108	40.5

Foreign-Born Naturalized U.S. Citizens

Group	Number	%
Total Population	888	29.1
Hispanic or Latino (of any race)	539	22.2
Mexican	432	20.5

Language Spoken at Home: English Only
(Universe: Population 5 Years and Over)

Group	Number	%
Total Population	28,835	84.0
Hispanic or Latino (of any race)	752	14.4
Mexican	582	12.8

Language Spoken at Home: Spanish
(Universe: Population 5 Years and Over)

Group	Number	%
Total Population	4,735	13.8
Hispanic or Latino (of any race)	4,436	84.9
Mexican	3,949	87.2

Unemployment Rate
(Universe: Population 16 Years and Over)

Group	%
Total Population	13.8
Hispanic or Latino (of any race)	15.1
Mexican	13.9

Class of Worker: Private Wage and Salary
(Universe: Civilian Employed Population 16 Years and Over)

Group	Number	%
Total Population	13,409	84.3
Hispanic or Latino (of any race)	2,136	90.4
Mexican	1,842	90.4

Class of Worker: Government
(Universe: Civilian Employed Population 16 Years and Over)

Group	Number	%
Total Population	1,699	10.7
Hispanic or Latino (of any race)	121	5.1
Mexican	100	4.9

Means of Transportation to Work: Car, Truck or Van
(Universe: Workers 16 Years and Over)

Group	Number	%
Total Population	13,822	88.8
Hispanic or Latino (of any race)	2,082	92.0
Mexican	1,778	91.1

Means of Transportation to Work: Public Transportation (ex. Taxicab)
(Universe: Workers 16 Years and Over)

Group	Number	%
Total Population	157	1.0
Hispanic or Latino (of any race)	69	3.0
Mexican	60	3.1

Homeownership Rate
(Universe: Occupied Housing Units)

Group	%
Total Population	59.1
Hispanic or Latino (of any race)	54.7
Dominican Republic	35.7
Mexican	56.5
Puerto Rican	43.1

Median Home Value

Group	Dollars
Total Population	89,800
Hispanic or Latino (of any race)	78,300
Mexican	77,000

Median Gross Rent

Group	Dollars
Total Population	679
Hispanic or Latino (of any race)	678
Mexican	654

Median Household Income
(2010 Inflation-Adjusted Dollars)

Group	Dollars
Total Population	37,102
Hispanic or Latino (of any race)	31,265
Mexican	30,982

Per Capita Income
(2010 Inflation-Adjusted Dollars)

Group	Dollars
Total Population	18,145
Hispanic or Latino (of any race)	10,524
Mexican	10,422

Households with $100,000+ Income

Group	Number	%
Total Population	1,068	7.6
Hispanic or Latino (of any race)	23	1.5
Mexican	0	0.0

Households with Food Stamps/SNAP Benefits During Past 12 Months

Group	Number	%
Total Population	2,564	18.1
Hispanic or Latino (of any race)	487	32.3
Mexican	433	34.1

Poverty Rate
(Income in Past 12 Months Below Poverty Level)

Group	%
Total Population	21.5
Hispanic or Latino (of any race)	30.7
Mexican	27.9

Fitchburg*

Population

Group	Number	%TP[1]	%HP[2]
Total Population	25,260	100.0	–
Hispanic or Latino (of any race)	4,341	17.2	100.0
Central American, ex. Mexican	170	0.7	3.9
Mexican	3,508	13.9	80.8
Puerto Rican	193	0.8	4.4
South American	248	1.0	5.7

Population Growth: 2000–2010

Group	%
Total Population	23.2
Hispanic or Latino (of any race)	226.6
Mexican	310.8

Males per 100 Females

Group	Number
Total Population	106.7
Hispanic or Latino (of any race)	117.2
Central American, ex. Mexican	93.2
Mexican	123.9
Puerto Rican	103.2
South American	81.0

Average Household Size

Group	People
Total Population	2.45
Hispanic or Latino (of any race)	3.59
Central American, ex. Mexican	3.28
Mexican	3.74
Puerto Rican	3.10
South American	2.94

Median Age

Group	Years
Total Population	32.9
Hispanic or Latino (of any race)	24.4
Central American, ex. Mexican	26.3
Mexican	24.0
Puerto Rican	24.2
South American	30.0

High School Graduates
(Universe: Population 25 Years and Over)

Group	Number	%
Total Population	15,457	93.9
Hispanic or Latino (of any race)	1,559	84.1
Mexican	1,155	81.1

Four-Year College Graduates
(Universe: Population 25 Years and Over)

Group	Number	%
Total Population	7,448	45.2
Hispanic or Latino (of any race)	211	11.4
Mexican	69	4.8

Population Age 3–17 Enrolled in Public School
(Universe: Population Age 3–17 Enrolled in School)

Group	Number	%
Total Population	2,974	78.1
Hispanic or Latino (of any race)	455	88.2
Mexican	219	93.2

Population Age 3–17 Enrolled in Private School
(Universe: Population Age 3–17 Enrolled in School)

Group	Number	%
Total Population	835	21.9
Hispanic or Latino (of any race)	61	11.8
Mexican	16	6.8

Foreign-Born Population

Group	Number	%
Total Population	3,334	13.6
Hispanic or Latino (of any race)	1,908	56.0
Mexican	1,503	58.6

Foreign-Born Naturalized U.S. Citizens

Group	Number	%
Total Population	1,068	32.0
Hispanic or Latino (of any race)	217	11.4
Mexican	121	8.1

Language Spoken at Home: English Only
(Universe: Population 5 Years and Over)

Group	Number	%
Total Population	17,905	80.0
Hispanic or Latino (of any race)	304	10.9
Mexican	226	11.0

Language Spoken at Home: Spanish
(Universe: Population 5 Years and Over)

Group	Number	%
Total Population	2,816	12.6
Hispanic or Latino (of any race)	2,486	89.1
Mexican	1,829	89.0

Unemployment Rate
(Universe: Population 16 Years and Over)

Group	%
Total Population	4.7
Hispanic or Latino (of any race)	0.0
Mexican	0.0

Class of Worker: Private Wage and Salary
(Universe: Civilian Employed Population 16 Years and Over)

Group	Number	%
Total Population	10,713	78.7
Hispanic or Latino (of any race)	1,828	91.1
Mexican	1,561	97.6

Notes: (1) Percent of total population; (2) Percent of Hispanic/Latino population; Profiles include places with an overall population of at least 125,000, OR an overall population of at least 25,000 where the Hispanic/Latino population is at least 20% of the overall population. In states where less than five places meet either of these criteria, we have included places with at least 10,000 total population with the highest percentage of Hispanic/Latino population. These places are identified with an asterisk (*); Please refer to the User's Guide for a full explanation of data.

Class of Worker: Government (Universe: Civilian Employed Population 16 Years and Over)		
Group	Number	%
Total Population	2,389	17.5
Hispanic or Latino (of any race)	164	8.2
Mexican	23	1.4

Means of Transportation to Work: Car, Truck or Van (Universe: Workers 16 Years and Over)		
Group	Number	%
Total Population	12,234	91.3
Hispanic or Latino (of any race)	1,809	92.9
Mexican	1,451	92.1

Means of Transportation to Work: Public Transportation (ex. Taxicab) (Universe: Workers 16 Years and Over)		
Group	Number	%
Total Population	311	2.3
Hispanic or Latino (of any race)	76	3.9
Mexican	76	4.8

Homeownership Rate (Universe: Occupied Housing Units)	
Group	%
Total Population	53.0
Hispanic or Latino (of any race)	12.3
Central American, ex. Mexican	6.5
Mexican	8.9
Puerto Rican	27.5
South American	33.3

Median Home Value	
Group	Dollars
Total Population	270,800
Hispanic or Latino (of any race)	195,800
Mexican	99,600

Median Gross Rent	
Group	Dollars
Total Population	799
Hispanic or Latino (of any race)	763
Mexican	753

Median Household Income (2010 Inflation-Adjusted Dollars)	
Group	Dollars
Total Population	63,050
Hispanic or Latino (of any race)	41,735
Mexican	41,250

Per Capita Income (2010 Inflation-Adjusted Dollars)	
Group	Dollars
Total Population	35,096
Hispanic or Latino (of any race)	13,504
Mexican	12,612

Households with $100,000+ Income		
Group	Number	%
Total Population	2,571	27.4
Hispanic or Latino (of any race)	64	6.7
Mexican	27	3.7

Households with Food Stamps/SNAP Benefits During Past 12 Months		
Group	Number	%
Total Population	749	8.0
Hispanic or Latino (of any race)	162	17.0
Mexican	115	15.9

Poverty Rate (Income in Past 12 Months Below Poverty Level)	
Group	%
Total Population	10.4
Hispanic or Latino (of any race)	21.9
Mexican	20.4

Madison

Population			
Group	Number	%TP[1]	%HP[2]
Total Population	233,209	100.0	–
Hispanic or Latino (of any race)	15,948	6.8	100.0
Central American, ex. Mexican	980	0.4	6.1
Guatemalan	167	0.1	1.0
Honduran	350	0.2	2.2
Nicaraguan	179	0.1	1.1
Salvadoran	163	0.1	1.0
Cuban	299	0.1	1.9
Dominican Republic	155	0.1	1.0
Mexican	10,558	4.5	66.2
Puerto Rican	1,165	0.5	7.3
South American	1,740	0.7	10.9
Argentinean	219	0.1	1.4
Bolivian	100	<0.1	0.6
Chilean	167	0.1	1.0
Colombian	512	0.2	3.2
Ecuadorian	184	0.1	1.2
Peruvian	295	0.1	1.8
Venezuelan	156	0.1	1.0
Spaniard	288	0.1	1.8

Population Growth: 2000–2010	
Group	%
Total Population	12.1
Hispanic or Latino (of any race)	87.4
Central American, ex. Mexican	116.8
Honduran	173.4
Cuban	58.2
Mexican	104.5
Puerto Rican	63.9
South American	123.4
Chilean	65.3
Colombian	117.9
Peruvian	154.3

Males per 100 Females	
Group	Number
Total Population	97.0
Hispanic or Latino (of any race)	110.9
Central American, ex. Mexican	95.6
Guatemalan	103.7
Honduran	93.4
Nicaraguan	103.4
Salvadoran	123.3
Cuban	133.6
Dominican Republic	103.9
Mexican	119.0
Puerto Rican	92.2
South American	90.0
Argentinean	84.0
Bolivian	92.3
Chilean	75.8
Colombian	88.2
Ecuadorian	121.7
Peruvian	96.7
Venezuelan	69.6
Spaniard	100.0

Average Household Size	
Group	People
Total Population	2.17
Hispanic or Latino (of any race)	3.07
Central American, ex. Mexican	3.08
Guatemalan	3.03
Honduran	3.38
Nicaraguan	2.98
Salvadoran	3.25
Cuban	2.11
Dominican Republic	2.93
Mexican	3.39
Puerto Rican	2.50
South American	2.50
Argentinean	2.73
Bolivian	2.97
Chilean	1.95
Colombian	2.49
Ecuadorian	2.58
Peruvian	2.38
Venezuelan	2.63
Spaniard	2.23

Median Age	
Group	Years
Total Population	30.9
Hispanic or Latino (of any race)	24.8
Central American, ex. Mexican	25.9
Guatemalan	18.1
Honduran	27.6
Nicaraguan	28.8
Salvadoran	23.7
Cuban	25.0
Dominican Republic	24.1
Mexican	23.9
Puerto Rican	24.0
South American	29.5
Argentinean	29.5
Bolivian	35.0
Chilean	28.5
Colombian	28.5
Ecuadorian	30.7
Peruvian	31.4
Venezuelan	28.8
Spaniard	29.3

High School Graduates (Universe: Population 25 Years and Over)		
Group	Number	%
Total Population	132,469	94.1
Hispanic or Latino (of any race)	5,298	75.5
Mexican	3,002	69.2
Puerto Rican	506	84.9
South American	813	85.4

Four-Year College Graduates (Universe: Population 25 Years and Over)		
Group	Number	%
Total Population	73,542	52.2
Hispanic or Latino (of any race)	1,788	25.5
Mexican	761	17.5
Puerto Rican	288	48.3
South American	335	35.2

Population Age 3–17 Enrolled in Public School (Universe: Population Age 3–17 Enrolled in School)		
Group	Number	%
Total Population	24,385	83.5
Hispanic or Latino (of any race)	2,867	90.4
Mexican	2,049	93.6
Puerto Rican	290	82.4
South American	189	71.6

Population Age 3–17 Enrolled in Private School (Universe: Population Age 3–17 Enrolled in School)		
Group	Number	%
Total Population	4,822	16.5
Hispanic or Latino (of any race)	306	9.6
Mexican	139	6.4
Puerto Rican	62	17.6
South American	75	28.4

Foreign-Born Population		
Group	Number	%
Total Population	23,334	10.2
Hispanic or Latino (of any race)	5,904	40.8
Mexican	3,970	43.9
Puerto Rican	0	0.0
South American	1,131	60.3

Foreign-Born Naturalized U.S. Citizens		
Group	Number	%
Total Population	7,615	32.6
Hispanic or Latino (of any race)	1,242	21.0
Mexican	589	14.8
Puerto Rican	0	0.0
South American	341	30.2

Language Spoken at Home: English Only (Universe: Population 5 Years and Over)		
Group	Number	%
Total Population	184,088	85.2
Hispanic or Latino (of any race)	3,898	30.7
Mexican	2,279	28.6
Puerto Rican	433	36.4
South American	439	26.3

Language Spoken at Home: Spanish (Universe: Population 5 Years and Over)		
Group	Number	%
Total Population	11,724	5.4
Hispanic or Latino (of any race)	8,692	68.5
Mexican	5,683	71.3
Puerto Rican	756	63.6

Notes: (1) Percent of total population; (2) Percent of Hispanic/Latino population; Profiles include places with an overall population of at least 125,000, OR an overall population of at least 25,000 where the Hispanic/Latino population is at least 20% of the overall population. In states where less than five places meet either of these criteria, we have included places with at least 10,000 total population with the highest percentage of Hispanic/Latino population. These places are identified with an asterisk (*); Please refer to the User's Guide for a full explanation of data.

South American	1,231	73.7

Unemployment Rate
(Universe: Population 16 Years and Over)

Group	%
Total Population	5.6
Hispanic or Latino (of any race)	6.1
Mexican	5.5
Puerto Rican	6.2
South American	7.6

Class of Worker: Private Wage and Salary
(Universe: Civilian Employed Population 16 Years and Over)

Group	Number	%
Total Population	92,274	69.6
Hispanic or Latino (of any race)	6,052	79.5
Mexican	4,008	86.2
Puerto Rican	508	68.0
South American	905	78.4

Class of Worker: Government
(Universe: Civilian Employed Population 16 Years and Over)

Group	Number	%
Total Population	35,086	26.5
Hispanic or Latino (of any race)	1,394	18.3
Mexican	612	13.2
Puerto Rican	233	31.2
South American	236	20.5

Means of Transportation to Work: Car, Truck or Van
(Universe: Workers 16 Years and Over)

Group	Number	%
Total Population	95,662	73.8
Hispanic or Latino (of any race)	5,860	78.6
Mexican	3,755	82.2
Puerto Rican	548	75.1
South American	773	69.0

Means of Transportation to Work: Public Transportation (ex. Taxicab)
(Universe: Workers 16 Years and Over)

Group	Number	%
Total Population	10,977	8.5
Hispanic or Latino (of any race)	664	8.9
Mexican	322	7.0
Puerto Rican	40	5.5
South American	188	16.8

Homeownership Rate
(Universe: Occupied Housing Units)

Group	%
Total Population	49.3
Hispanic or Latino (of any race)	31.9
Central American, ex. Mexican	33.2
Guatemalan	42.1
Honduran	25.5
Nicaraguan	28.6
Salvadoran	39.2
Cuban	21.2
Dominican Republic	40.9
Mexican	30.6
Puerto Rican	30.7
South American	39.5
Argentinean	40.8
Bolivian	69.0
Chilean	31.0
Colombian	36.0
Ecuadorian	36.4
Peruvian	40.5
Venezuelan	46.3
Spaniard	40.9

Median Home Value

Group	Dollars
Total Population	220,200
Hispanic or Latino (of any race)	201,800
Mexican	195,000
Puerto Rican	238,300
South American	177,100

Median Gross Rent

Group	Dollars
Total Population	847
Hispanic or Latino (of any race)	799
Mexican	813
Puerto Rican	840
South American	780

Median Household Income
(2010 Inflation-Adjusted Dollars)

Group	Dollars
Total Population	52,550
Hispanic or Latino (of any race)	48,488
Mexican	47,308
Puerto Rican	73,175
South American	43,750

Per Capita Income
(2010 Inflation-Adjusted Dollars)

Group	Dollars
Total Population	29,782
Hispanic or Latino (of any race)	16,952
Mexican	15,079
Puerto Rican	18,108
South American	21,885

Households with $100,000+ Income

Group	Number	%
Total Population	19,374	19.7
Hispanic or Latino (of any race)	396	10.3
Mexican	246	10.8
Puerto Rican	58	16.6
South American	45	8.2

Households with Food Stamps/SNAP Benefits During Past 12 Months

Group	Number	%
Total Population	6,742	6.9
Hispanic or Latino (of any race)	497	12.9
Mexican	359	15.8
Puerto Rican	13	3.7
South American	21	3.8

Poverty Rate
(Income in Past 12 Months Below Poverty Level)

Group	%
Total Population	17.9
Hispanic or Latino (of any race)	16.4
Mexican	15.0
Puerto Rican	24.4
South American	13.5

Milwaukee

Population

Group	Number	%TP[1]	%HP[2]
Total Population	594,833	100.0	–
Hispanic or Latino (of any race)	103,007	17.3	100.0
Central American, ex. Mexican	1,962	0.3	1.9
Costa Rican	210	<0.1	0.2
Guatemalan	432	0.1	0.4
Honduran	282	<0.1	0.3
Nicaraguan	397	0.1	0.4
Panamanian	150	<0.1	0.1
Salvadoran	473	0.1	0.5
Cuban	866	0.1	0.8
Dominican Republic	720	0.1	0.7
Mexican	69,680	11.7	67.6
Puerto Rican	24,672	4.1	24.0
South American	1,299	0.2	1.3
Chilean	115	<0.1	0.1
Colombian	440	0.1	0.4
Ecuadorian	112	<0.1	0.1
Peruvian	307	0.1	0.3
Venezuelan	137	<0.1	0.1
Spaniard	372	0.1	0.4

Population Growth: 2000–2010

Group	%
Total Population	-0.4
Hispanic or Latino (of any race)	43.8
Central American, ex. Mexican	61.9
Costa Rican	30.4
Guatemalan	152.6
Honduran	86.8
Nicaraguan	24.8
Salvadoran	74.5
Cuban	35.9
Dominican Republic	136.1
Mexican	60.9
Puerto Rican	25.8
South American	100.8
Colombian	84.1
Peruvian	176.6

Males per 100 Females

Group	Number
Total Population	93.2
Hispanic or Latino (of any race)	107.1
Central American, ex. Mexican	92.5
Costa Rican	101.9
Guatemalan	96.4
Honduran	102.9
Nicaraguan	73.4
Panamanian	76.5
Salvadoran	102.1
Cuban	119.8
Dominican Republic	84.1
Mexican	113.1
Puerto Rican	94.7
South American	99.5
Chilean	144.7
Colombian	91.3
Ecuadorian	128.6
Peruvian	91.9
Venezuelan	95.7
Spaniard	89.8

Average Household Size

Group	People
Total Population	2.50
Hispanic or Latino (of any race)	3.54
Central American, ex. Mexican	3.38
Costa Rican	3.03
Guatemalan	3.54
Honduran	3.31
Nicaraguan	3.35
Panamanian	2.80
Salvadoran	3.70
Cuban	2.75
Dominican Republic	3.26
Mexican	3.79
Puerto Rican	3.14
South American	2.49
Chilean	2.30
Colombian	2.37
Ecuadorian	2.77
Peruvian	2.88
Venezuelan	2.29
Spaniard	2.41

Median Age

Group	Years
Total Population	30.3
Hispanic or Latino (of any race)	24.4
Central American, ex. Mexican	28.4
Costa Rican	27.1
Guatemalan	27.4
Honduran	26.6
Nicaraguan	28.8
Panamanian	35.0
Salvadoran	29.2
Cuban	26.8
Dominican Republic	26.3
Mexican	24.3
Puerto Rican	23.8
South American	31.6
Chilean	30.1
Colombian	31.0
Ecuadorian	33.3
Peruvian	33.2
Venezuelan	31.7
Spaniard	29.2

High School Graduates
(Universe: Population 25 Years and Over)

Group	Number	%
Total Population	282,117	80.4
Hispanic or Latino (of any race)	25,117	53.3
Central American, ex. Mexican	771	55.8
Cuban	381	79.5
Mexican	15,501	48.3
Puerto Rican	6,488	61.7
South American	814	76.2

Notes: (1) Percent of total population; (2) Percent of Hispanic/Latino population; Profiles include places with an overall population of at least 125,000, OR an overall population of at least 25,000 where the Hispanic/Latino population is at least 20% of the overall population. In states where less than five places meet either of these criteria, we have included places with at least 10,000 total population with the highest percentage of Hispanic/Latino population. These places are identified with an asterisk (*); Please refer to the User's Guide for a full explanation of data.

Four-Year College Graduates
(Universe: Population 25 Years and Over)

Group	Number	%
Total Population	73,670	21.0
Hispanic or Latino (of any race)	3,427	7.3
Central American, ex. Mexican	216	15.6
Cuban	150	31.3
Mexican	1,733	5.4
Puerto Rican	779	7.4
South American	321	30.1

Population Age 3–17 Enrolled in Public School
(Universe: Population Age 3–17 Enrolled in School)

Group	Number	%
Total Population	96,445	80.9
Hispanic or Latino (of any race)	21,852	84.9
Central American, ex. Mexican	548	86.0
Cuban	121	64.7
Mexican	14,017	82.6
Puerto Rican	6,040	93.4
South American	286	76.1

Population Age 3–17 Enrolled in Private School
(Universe: Population Age 3–17 Enrolled in School)

Group	Number	%
Total Population	22,763	19.1
Hispanic or Latino (of any race)	3,876	15.1
Central American, ex. Mexican	89	14.0
Cuban	66	35.3
Mexican	2,944	17.4
Puerto Rican	430	6.6
South American	90	23.9

Foreign-Born Population

Group	Number	%
Total Population	57,108	9.7
Hispanic or Latino (of any race)	34,194	35.4
Central American, ex. Mexican	1,390	57.2
Cuban	231	26.4
Mexican	30,801	46.8
Puerto Rican	29	0.1
South American	924	54.8

Foreign-Born Naturalized U.S. Citizens

Group	Number	%
Total Population	17,556	30.7
Hispanic or Latino (of any race)	5,794	16.9
Central American, ex. Mexican	543	39.1
Cuban	131	56.7
Mexican	4,530	14.7
Puerto Rican	8	27.6
South American	336	36.4

Language Spoken at Home: English Only
(Universe: Population 5 Years and Over)

Group	Number	%
Total Population	439,508	81.0
Hispanic or Latino (of any race)	16,472	19.5
Central American, ex. Mexican	314	14.3
Cuban	272	34.6
Mexican	9,913	17.5
Puerto Rican	4,312	21.7
South American	338	21.7

Language Spoken at Home: Spanish
(Universe: Population 5 Years and Over)

Group	Number	%
Total Population	73,301	13.5
Hispanic or Latino (of any race)	67,784	80.2
Central American, ex. Mexican	1,878	85.7
Cuban	498	63.4
Mexican	46,610	82.1
Puerto Rican	15,552	78.2
South American	1,217	78.3

Unemployment Rate
(Universe: Population 16 Years and Over)

Group	%
Total Population	11.6
Hispanic or Latino (of any race)	13.1
Central American, ex. Mexican	9.2
Cuban	13.3
Mexican	11.3
Puerto Rican	19.9
South American	5.9

Class of Worker: Private Wage and Salary
(Universe: Civilian Employed Population 16 Years and Over)

Group	Number	%
Total Population	218,658	83.4
Hispanic or Latino (of any race)	33,949	89.1
Central American, ex. Mexican	986	89.2
Cuban	279	80.6
Mexican	24,734	90.7
Puerto Rican	6,266	85.8
South American	711	83.5

Class of Worker: Government
(Universe: Civilian Employed Population 16 Years and Over)

Group	Number	%
Total Population	34,563	13.2
Hispanic or Latino (of any race)	2,791	7.3
Central American, ex. Mexican	112	10.1
Cuban	67	19.4
Mexican	1,564	5.7
Puerto Rican	813	11.1
South American	74	8.7

Means of Transportation to Work: Car, Truck or Van
(Universe: Workers 16 Years and Over)

Group	Number	%
Total Population	213,524	83.0
Hispanic or Latino (of any race)	32,657	87.6
Central American, ex. Mexican	1,019	93.5
Cuban	231	68.5
Mexican	23,717	89.0
Puerto Rican	5,943	82.7
South American	689	85.2

Means of Transportation to Work: Public Transportation (ex. Taxicab)
(Universe: Workers 16 Years and Over)

Group	Number	%
Total Population	21,809	8.5
Hispanic or Latino (of any race)	2,514	6.7
Central American, ex. Mexican	34	3.1
Cuban	58	17.2
Mexican	1,592	6.0
Puerto Rican	738	10.3
South American	40	4.9

Homeownership Rate
(Universe: Occupied Housing Units)

Group	%
Total Population	43.6
Hispanic or Latino (of any race)	37.1
Central American, ex. Mexican	46.2
Costa Rican	44.1
Guatemalan	38.2
Honduran	24.0
Nicaraguan	48.1
Panamanian	55.4
Salvadoran	62.2
Cuban	27.2
Dominican Republic	38.3
Mexican	39.7
Puerto Rican	31.2
South American	44.0
Chilean	47.5
Colombian	42.7
Ecuadorian	53.8
Peruvian	43.3
Venezuelan	49.0
Spaniard	37.8

Median Home Value

Group	Dollars
Total Population	140,000
Hispanic or Latino (of any race)	128,100
Central American, ex. Mexican	132,200
Cuban	118,900
Mexican	128,700
Puerto Rican	120,000
South American	157,600

Median Gross Rent

Group	Dollars
Total Population	736
Hispanic or Latino (of any race)	713
Central American, ex. Mexican	720
Cuban	698
Mexican	714
Puerto Rican	708
South American	727

Median Household Income
(2010 Inflation-Adjusted Dollars)

Group	Dollars
Total Population	35,921
Hispanic or Latino (of any race)	33,921
Central American, ex. Mexican	47,417
Cuban	39,309
Mexican	34,909
Puerto Rican	28,709
South American	38,077

Per Capita Income
(2010 Inflation-Adjusted Dollars)

Group	Dollars
Total Population	18,884
Hispanic or Latino (of any race)	11,784
Central American, ex. Mexican	14,328
Cuban	20,095
Mexican	11,700
Puerto Rican	11,041
South American	16,898

Households with $100,000+ Income

Group	Number	%
Total Population	20,412	8.9
Hispanic or Latino (of any race)	1,338	5.1
Central American, ex. Mexican	50	7.2
Cuban	92	25.6
Mexican	956	5.6
Puerto Rican	141	2.1
South American	60	8.8

Households with Food Stamps/SNAP Benefits During Past 12 Months

Group	Number	%
Total Population	40,250	17.5
Hispanic or Latino (of any race)	6,024	22.8
Central American, ex. Mexican	152	21.9
Cuban	150	41.7
Mexican	3,333	19.7
Puerto Rican	2,137	31.5
South American	100	14.6

Poverty Rate
(Income in Past 12 Months Below Poverty Level)

Group	%
Total Population	26.3
Hispanic or Latino (of any race)	28.3
Central American, ex. Mexican	10.9
Cuban	46.2
Mexican	26.3
Puerto Rican	37.3
South American	16.7

Racine

Population

Group	Number	%TP[1]	%HP[2]
Total Population	78,860	100.0	–
Hispanic or Latino (of any race)	16,309	20.7	100.0
Central American, ex. Mexican	213	0.3	1.3
Mexican	13,731	17.4	84.2
Puerto Rican	1,224	1.6	7.5

Population Growth: 2000–2010

Group	%
Total Population	-3.7
Hispanic or Latino (of any race)	42.8
Mexican	53.6
Puerto Rican	63.2

Males per 100 Females

Group	Number
Total Population	95.2
Hispanic or Latino (of any race)	105.2
Central American, ex. Mexican	136.7
Mexican	106.9
Puerto Rican	91.0

Notes: (1) Percent of total population; (2) Percent of Hispanic/Latino population; Profiles include places with an overall population of at least 125,000, OR an overall population of at least 25,000 where the Hispanic/Latino population is at least 20% of the overall population. In states where less than five places meet either of these criteria, we have included places with at least 10,000 total population with the highest percentage of Hispanic/Latino population. These places are identified with an asterisk (*); Please refer to the User's Guide for a full explanation of data.

Average Household Size

Group	People
Total Population	2.53
Hispanic or Latino (of any race)	3.54
Central American, ex. Mexican	3.66
Mexican	3.62
Puerto Rican	3.13

Median Age

Group	Years
Total Population	33.0
Hispanic or Latino (of any race)	23.3
Central American, ex. Mexican	30.5
Mexican	23.2
Puerto Rican	22.2

High School Graduates
(Universe: Population 25 Years and Over)

Group	Number	%
Total Population	40,478	82.3
Hispanic or Latino (of any race)	4,201	57.6
Mexican	3,443	54.9

Four-Year College Graduates
(Universe: Population 25 Years and Over)

Group	Number	%
Total Population	8,445	17.2
Hispanic or Latino (of any race)	478	6.6
Mexican	353	5.6

Population Age 3–17 Enrolled in Public School
(Universe: Population Age 3–17 Enrolled in School)

Group	Number	%
Total Population	14,651	88.5
Hispanic or Latino (of any race)	4,339	94.8
Mexican	3,941	94.6

Population Age 3–17 Enrolled in Private School
(Universe: Population Age 3–17 Enrolled in School)

Group	Number	%
Total Population	1,904	11.5
Hispanic or Latino (of any race)	239	5.2
Mexican	227	5.4

Foreign-Born Population

Group	Number	%
Total Population	5,945	7.5
Hispanic or Latino (of any race)	4,328	27.2
Mexican	3,946	28.0

Foreign-Born Naturalized U.S. Citizens

Group	Number	%
Total Population	2,038	34.3
Hispanic or Latino (of any race)	1,141	26.4
Mexican	1,029	26.1

Language Spoken at Home: English Only
(Universe: Population 5 Years and Over)

Group	Number	%
Total Population	61,574	84.5
Hispanic or Latino (of any race)	5,084	37.3
Mexican	4,154	34.6

Language Spoken at Home: Spanish
(Universe: Population 5 Years and Over)

Group	Number	%
Total Population	9,244	12.7
Hispanic or Latino (of any race)	8,509	62.5
Mexican	7,841	65.4

Unemployment Rate
(Universe: Population 16 Years and Over)

Group	%
Total Population	10.6
Hispanic or Latino (of any race)	10.7
Mexican	11.2

Class of Worker: Private Wage and Salary
(Universe: Civilian Employed Population 16 Years and Over)

Group	Number	%
Total Population	29,718	85.1
Hispanic or Latino (of any race)	5,431	90.7
Mexican	4,842	91.8

Class of Worker: Government
(Universe: Civilian Employed Population 16 Years and Over)

Group	Number	%
Total Population	4,109	11.8
Hispanic or Latino (of any race)	466	7.8
Mexican	365	6.9

Means of Transportation to Work: Car, Truck or Van
(Universe: Workers 16 Years and Over)

Group	Number	%
Total Population	30,945	91.1
Hispanic or Latino (of any race)	5,402	91.9
Mexican	4,783	92.1

Means of Transportation to Work: Public Transportation (ex. Taxicab)
(Universe: Workers 16 Years and Over)

Group	Number	%
Total Population	1,099	3.2
Hispanic or Latino (of any race)	139	2.4
Mexican	139	2.7

Homeownership Rate
(Universe: Occupied Housing Units)

Group	%
Total Population	56.6
Hispanic or Latino (of any race)	46.8
Central American, ex. Mexican	50.0
Mexican	48.6
Puerto Rican	34.0

Median Home Value

Group	Dollars
Total Population	129,300
Hispanic or Latino (of any race)	113,700
Mexican	116,700

Median Gross Rent

Group	Dollars
Total Population	677
Hispanic or Latino (of any race)	672
Mexican	657

Median Household Income
(2010 Inflation-Adjusted Dollars)

Group	Dollars
Total Population	38,550
Hispanic or Latino (of any race)	34,011
Mexican	33,493

Per Capita Income
(2010 Inflation-Adjusted Dollars)

Group	Dollars
Total Population	19,980
Hispanic or Latino (of any race)	13,008
Mexican	12,689

Households with $100,000+ Income

Group	Number	%
Total Population	2,937	9.3
Hispanic or Latino (of any race)	257	6.0
Mexican	229	6.1

Households with Food Stamps/SNAP Benefits During Past 12 Months

Group	Number	%
Total Population	4,453	14.1
Hispanic or Latino (of any race)	940	21.8
Mexican	878	23.5

Poverty Rate
(Income in Past 12 Months Below Poverty Level)

Group	%
Total Population	18.9
Hispanic or Latino (of any race)	23.9
Mexican	24.0

Notes: (1) Percent of total population; (2) Percent of Hispanic/Latino population; Profiles include places with an overall population of at least 125,000, OR an overall population of at least 25,000 where the Hispanic/Latino population is at least 20% of the overall population. In states where less than five places meet either of these criteria, we have included places with at least 10,000 total population with the highest percentage of Hispanic/Latino population. These places are identified with an asterisk (*); Please refer to the User's Guide for a full explanation of data.

Wyoming

EDITOR'S NOTE: For a place to be included in this edition, it must meet one of two criteria. Either its overall population is at least 125,000, OR its overall population is at least 25,000 and its Hispanic/Latino population is at least 20% of the overall population. In Wyoming, less than five places meet either of these criteria. In an effort to include at least five places for each state, we have included places with at least 10,000 total population with the highest percentage of Hispanic/Latino population. These places are identified with an asterisk (*). For the state of Wyoming, the following locations are included:

Cheyenne*
Evanston*
Gillette*
Green River*
Rock Springs*

Section Two: State & Place Profiles starts with the state profile, followed by place profiles that meet the criteria above. Places are listed alphabetically within each state. All states, all counties and places that meet the above criteria are ranked and compared in *Section Three: Rankings & Comparisons*, on page 1055.

For a more detailed look at the Hispanic/Latino population in Wyoming, a companion web site is available at no additional charge with purchase of this print edition. Visit http://gold.greyhouse.com/page/info_hispanic for more information.

The web site includes data for all counties and places in Wyoming with Hispanic/Latino population, plus ten additional topics: Self Employed Worker; Walked to Work; Worked from Home; Mean Travel Time to Work; Mean Household Income; Households with Cash Public Assistance; Mean Cash Pubic Assistance; Poverty Rates for 18 and Under, 18 to 64, and 65 and Over.

Population

Group	Number	%TP[1]	%HP[2]
Total Population	563,626	100.0	–
Hispanic or Latino (of any race)	50,231	8.9	100.0
Central American, ex. Mexican	977	0.2	1.9
Guatemalan	418	0.1	0.8
Honduran	145	<0.1	0.3
Salvadoran	198	<0.1	0.4
Cuban	275	<0.1	0.5
Mexican	37,719	6.7	75.1
Puerto Rican	1,026	0.2	2.0
South American	852	0.2	1.7
Colombian	178	<0.1	0.4
Peruvian	305	0.1	0.6
Spaniard	1,972	0.3	3.9

Population Growth: 2000–2010

Group	%
Total Population	14.1
Hispanic or Latino (of any race)	58.6
Central American, ex. Mexican	419.7
Cuban	71.9
Mexican	88.9
Puerto Rican	78.4
South American	226.4
Spaniard	1,393.9

Males per 100 Females

Group	Number
Total Population	104.1
Hispanic or Latino (of any race)	111.1
Central American, ex. Mexican	149.9
Guatemalan	202.9
Honduran	141.7
Salvadoran	120.0
Cuban	113.2
Mexican	115.1
Puerto Rican	103.6
South American	99.5
Colombian	56.1
Peruvian	167.5
Spaniard	100.6

Average Household Size

Group	People
Total Population	2.42
Hispanic or Latino (of any race)	2.93
Central American, ex. Mexican	3.37
Guatemalan	3.50
Honduran	3.97
Salvadoran	3.37
Cuban	2.53
Mexican	3.05
Puerto Rican	2.67
South American	2.63
Colombian	2.44
Peruvian	2.82
Spaniard	2.43

Median Age

Group	Years
Total Population	36.8
Hispanic or Latino (of any race)	25.9
Central American, ex. Mexican	28.0
Guatemalan	28.9
Honduran	25.8
Salvadoran	28.6
Cuban	28.3
Mexican	24.8
Puerto Rican	23.1
South American	31.5
Colombian	28.3
Peruvian	35.5
Spaniard	34.8

High School Graduates
(Universe: Population 25 Years and Over)

Group	Number	%
Total Population	326,862	91.3
Hispanic or Latino (of any race)	17,802	74.2
Central American, ex. Mexican	428	65.5
Mexican	11,568	69.9
Puerto Rican	307	83.4
South American	784	98.9
Spaniard	969	83.6

Four-Year College Graduates
(Universe: Population 25 Years and Over)

Group	Number	%
Total Population	84,326	23.6
Hispanic or Latino (of any race)	2,298	9.6
Central American, ex. Mexican	148	22.7
Mexican	1,268	7.7
Puerto Rican	90	24.5
South American	268	33.8
Spaniard	94	8.1

Population Age 3–17 Enrolled in Public School
(Universe: Population Age 3–17 Enrolled in School)

Group	Number	%
Total Population	88,071	91.6
Hispanic or Latino (of any race)	10,392	92.2
Central American, ex. Mexican	239	100.0
Mexican	7,786	90.4
Puerto Rican	109	100.0
South American	103	100.0
Spaniard	649	96.6

Population Age 3–17 Enrolled in Private School
(Universe: Population Age 3–17 Enrolled in School)

Group	Number	%
Total Population	8,086	8.4
Hispanic or Latino (of any race)	876	7.8
Central American, ex. Mexican	0	0.0
Mexican	830	9.6
Puerto Rican	0	0.0
South American	0	0.0
Spaniard	23	3.4

Foreign-Born Population

Group	Number	%
Total Population	16,712	3.1
Hispanic or Latino (of any race)	9,461	20.7
Central American, ex. Mexican	721	66.1
Mexican	7,568	23.0
Puerto Rican	0	0.0
South American	718	61.6
Spaniard	75	3.4

Foreign-Born Naturalized U.S. Citizens

Group	Number	%
Total Population	5,936	35.5
Hispanic or Latino (of any race)	2,175	23.0
Central American, ex. Mexican	64	8.9
Mexican	1,646	21.7
Puerto Rican	0	0.0
South American	251	35.0
Spaniard	0	0.0

Language Spoken at Home: English Only
(Universe: Population 5 Years and Over)

Group	Number	%
Total Population	474,343	93.3
Hispanic or Latino (of any race)	22,412	55.1
Central American, ex. Mexican	88	9.5
Mexican	15,076	51.9
Puerto Rican	465	73.3
South American	256	22.0
Spaniard	1,684	82.6

Language Spoken at Home: Spanish
(Universe: Population 5 Years and Over)

Group	Number	%
Total Population	23,489	4.6
Hispanic or Latino (of any race)	18,173	44.7
Central American, ex. Mexican	825	89.0
Mexican	13,952	48.0
Puerto Rican	162	25.6
South American	910	78.0
Spaniard	335	16.4

Unemployment Rate
(Universe: Population 16 Years and Over)

Group	%
Total Population	4.4
Hispanic or Latino (of any race)	6.6
Central American, ex. Mexican	11.3
Mexican	6.3
Puerto Rican	15.7
South American	7.7
Spaniard	7.2

Class of Worker: Private Wage and Salary
(Universe: Civilian Employed Population 16 Years and Over)

Group	Number	%
Total Population	204,935	72.1
Hispanic or Latino (of any race)	16,780	80.6
Central American, ex. Mexican	517	91.5
Mexican	12,404	84.6
Puerto Rican	127	52.7
South American	643	84.3
Spaniard	617	67.4

Class of Worker: Government
(Universe: Civilian Employed Population 16 Years and Over)

Group	Number	%
Total Population	56,225	19.8
Hispanic or Latino (of any race)	3,107	14.9
Central American, ex. Mexican	33	5.8
Mexican	1,898	12.9
Puerto Rican	99	41.1
South American	53	6.9
Spaniard	253	27.7

Notes: (1) Percent of total population; (2) Percent of Hispanic/Latino population; Profiles include places with an overall population of at least 125,000, OR an overall population of at least 25,000 where the Hispanic/Latino population is at least 20% of the overall population. In states where less than five places meet either of these criteria, we have included places with at least 10,000 total population with the highest percentage of Hispanic/Latino population. These places are identified with an asterisk (*); Please refer to the User's Guide for a full explanation of data.

Means of Transportation to Work: Car, Truck or Van
(Universe: Workers 16 Years and Over)

Group	Number	%
Total Population	245,433	87.7
Hispanic or Latino (of any race)	18,739	91.0
Central American, ex. Mexican	555	98.2
Mexican	13,249	91.3
Puerto Rican	267	92.4
South American	640	92.5
Spaniard	853	96.4

Means of Transportation to Work: Public Transportation (ex. Taxicab)
(Universe: Workers 16 Years and Over)

Group	Number	%
Total Population	3,842	1.4
Hispanic or Latino (of any race)	178	0.9
Central American, ex. Mexican	10	1.8
Mexican	111	0.8
Puerto Rican	22	7.6
South American	24	3.5
Spaniard	3	0.3

Homeownership Rate
(Universe: Occupied Housing Units)

Group	%
Total Population	69.2
Hispanic or Latino (of any race)	53.5
Central American, ex. Mexican	35.3
Guatemalan	32.2
Honduran	37.9
Salvadoran	31.5
Cuban	53.2
Mexican	52.4
Puerto Rican	39.9
South American	43.7
Colombian	43.8
Peruvian	51.2
Spaniard	69.5

Median Home Value

Group	Dollars
Total Population	174,000
Hispanic or Latino (of any race)	128,900
Central American, ex. Mexican	20,500
Mexican	117,300
Puerto Rican	194,900
South American	198,600
Spaniard	166,300

Median Gross Rent

Group	Dollars
Total Population	666
Hispanic or Latino (of any race)	716
Central American, ex. Mexican	778
Mexican	715
Puerto Rican	919
South American	797
Spaniard	436

Median Household Income
(2010 Inflation-Adjusted Dollars)

Group	Dollars
Total Population	53,802
Hispanic or Latino (of any race)	45,256
Central American, ex. Mexican	49,676
Mexican	44,616
Puerto Rican	54,091
South American	51,964
Spaniard	46,953

Per Capita Income
(2010 Inflation-Adjusted Dollars)

Group	Dollars
Total Population	27,860
Hispanic or Latino (of any race)	17,276
Central American, ex. Mexican	14,985
Mexican	16,570
Puerto Rican	17,414
South American	27,523
Spaniard	17,665

Households with $100,000+ Income

Group	Number	%
Total Population	41,945	19.3
Hispanic or Latino (of any race)	1,637	12.1
Central American, ex. Mexican	25	10.5
Mexican	1,049	11.9
Puerto Rican	46	20.4
South American	86	27.4
Spaniard	110	14.0

Households with Food Stamps/SNAP Benefits During Past 12 Months

Group	Number	%
Total Population	10,764	4.9
Hispanic or Latino (of any race)	1,347	9.9
Central American, ex. Mexican	58	24.3
Mexican	742	8.4
Puerto Rican	0	0.0
South American	25	8.0
Spaniard	55	7.0

Poverty Rate
(Income in Past 12 Months Below Poverty Level)

Group	%
Total Population	9.8
Hispanic or Latino (of any race)	15.5
Central American, ex. Mexican	24.8
Mexican	17.2
Puerto Rican	12.6
South American	0.0
Spaniard	9.4

Cheyenne*

Population

Group	Number	%TP[1]	%HP[2]
Total Population	59,466	100.0	–
Hispanic or Latino (of any race)	8,594	14.5	100.0
Mexican	5,803	9.8	67.5
Puerto Rican	267	0.4	3.1
South American	105	0.2	1.2
Spaniard	495	0.8	5.8

Population Growth: 2000–2010

Group	%
Total Population	12.2
Hispanic or Latino (of any race)	29.3
Mexican	66.9
Puerto Rican	59.9

Males per 100 Females

Group	Number
Total Population	97.3
Hispanic or Latino (of any race)	100.3
Mexican	104.5
Puerto Rican	132.2
South American	105.9
Spaniard	88.9

Average Household Size

Group	People
Total Population	2.29
Hispanic or Latino (of any race)	2.62
Mexican	2.70
Puerto Rican	2.74
South American	2.62
Spaniard	2.42

Median Age

Group	Years
Total Population	36.5
Hispanic or Latino (of any race)	27.3
Mexican	26.2
Puerto Rican	24.2
South American	30.6
Spaniard	35.8

High School Graduates
(Universe: Population 25 Years and Over)

Group	Number	%
Total Population	34,678	92.4
Hispanic or Latino (of any race)	3,300	79.9
Mexican	1,719	77.1

Four-Year College Graduates
(Universe: Population 25 Years and Over)

Group	Number	%
Total Population	8,889	23.7
Hispanic or Latino (of any race)	470	11.4
Mexican	290	13.0

Population Age 3–17 Enrolled in Public School
(Universe: Population Age 3–17 Enrolled in School)

Group	Number	%
Total Population	9,533	89.7
Hispanic or Latino (of any race)	1,893	92.6
Mexican	1,214	88.9

Population Age 3–17 Enrolled in Private School
(Universe: Population Age 3–17 Enrolled in School)

Group	Number	%
Total Population	1,093	10.3
Hispanic or Latino (of any race)	151	7.4
Mexican	151	11.1

Foreign-Born Population

Group	Number	%
Total Population	1,560	2.7
Hispanic or Latino (of any race)	437	5.2
Mexican	373	7.5

Foreign-Born Naturalized U.S. Citizens

Group	Number	%
Total Population	1,021	65.4
Hispanic or Latino (of any race)	241	55.1
Mexican	177	47.5

Language Spoken at Home: English Only
(Universe: Population 5 Years and Over)

Group	Number	%
Total Population	48,972	91.5
Hispanic or Latino (of any race)	5,061	68.8
Mexican	2,853	65.7

Language Spoken at Home: Spanish
(Universe: Population 5 Years and Over)

Group	Number	%
Total Population	3,118	5.8
Hispanic or Latino (of any race)	2,294	31.2
Mexican	1,490	34.3

Unemployment Rate
(Universe: Population 16 Years and Over)

Group	%
Total Population	5.0
Hispanic or Latino (of any race)	5.7
Mexican	6.6

Class of Worker: Private Wage and Salary
(Universe: Civilian Employed Population 16 Years and Over)

Group	Number	%
Total Population	19,695	68.6
Hispanic or Latino (of any race)	2,568	72.5
Mexican	1,458	79.3

Class of Worker: Government
(Universe: Civilian Employed Population 16 Years and Over)

Group	Number	%
Total Population	7,706	26.8
Hispanic or Latino (of any race)	860	24.3
Mexican	375	20.4

Means of Transportation to Work: Car, Truck or Van
(Universe: Workers 16 Years and Over)

Group	Number	%
Total Population	27,730	93.2
Hispanic or Latino (of any race)	3,454	95.4
Mexican	1,870	96.8

Means of Transportation to Work: Public Transportation (ex. Taxicab)
(Universe: Workers 16 Years and Over)

Group	Number	%
Total Population	264	0.9
Hispanic or Latino (of any race)	5	0.1
Mexican	0	0.0

Notes: (1) Percent of total population; (2) Percent of Hispanic/Latino population; Profiles include places with an overall population of at least 125,000, OR an overall population of at least 25,000 where the Hispanic/Latino population is at least 20% of the overall population. In states where less than five places meet either of these criteria, we have included places with at least 10,000 total population with the highest percentage of Hispanic/Latino population. These places are identified with an asterisk (*); Please refer to the User's Guide for a full explanation of data.

Homeownership Rate (Universe: Occupied Housing Units)	
Group	%
Total Population	63.8
Hispanic or Latino (of any race)	55.6
Mexican	55.6
Puerto Rican	38.4
South American	45.9
Spaniard	65.9

Median Home Value	
Group	Dollars
Total Population	165,300
Hispanic or Latino (of any race)	139,600
Mexican	138,100

Median Gross Rent	
Group	Dollars
Total Population	662
Hispanic or Latino (of any race)	647
Mexican	728

Median Household Income (2010 Inflation-Adjusted Dollars)	
Group	Dollars
Total Population	50,535
Hispanic or Latino (of any race)	41,875
Mexican	43,108

Per Capita Income (2010 Inflation-Adjusted Dollars)	
Group	Dollars
Total Population	27,107
Hispanic or Latino (of any race)	16,499
Mexican	15,860

Households with $100,000+ Income		
Group	Number	%
Total Population	3,718	15.5
Hispanic or Latino (of any race)	286	10.6
Mexican	163	12.5

Households with Food Stamps/SNAP Benefits During Past 12 Months		
Group	Number	%
Total Population	1,449	6.1
Hispanic or Latino (of any race)	267	9.9
Mexican	71	5.5

Poverty Rate (Income in Past 12 Months Below Poverty Level)	
Group	%
Total Population	9.3
Hispanic or Latino (of any race)	10.0
Mexican	11.4

Evanston*

Population			
Group	Number	%TP[1]	%HP[2]
Total Population	12,359	100.0	–
Hispanic or Latino (of any race)	1,526	12.3	100.0
Mexican	1,241	10.0	81.3

Population Growth: 2000–2010	
Group	%
Total Population	7.4
Hispanic or Latino (of any race)	81.9
Mexican	126.0

Males per 100 Females	
Group	Number
Total Population	100.0
Hispanic or Latino (of any race)	104.3
Mexican	108.6

Average Household Size	
Group	People
Total Population	2.67
Hispanic or Latino (of any race)	3.62
Mexican	3.89

Median Age	
Group	Years
Total Population	32.7
Hispanic or Latino (of any race)	23.7
Mexican	21.5

High School Graduates (Universe: Population 25 Years and Over)		
Group	Number	%
Total Population	6,517	87.5
Hispanic or Latino (of any race)	550	79.4
Mexican	301	70.2

Four-Year College Graduates (Universe: Population 25 Years and Over)		
Group	Number	%
Total Population	1,479	19.8
Hispanic or Latino (of any race)	123	17.7
Mexican	62	14.5

Population Age 3–17 Enrolled in Public School (Universe: Population Age 3–17 Enrolled in School)		
Group	Number	%
Total Population	2,573	95.7
Hispanic or Latino (of any race)	445	100.0
Mexican	438	100.0

Population Age 3–17 Enrolled in Private School (Universe: Population Age 3–17 Enrolled in School)		
Group	Number	%
Total Population	116	4.3
Hispanic or Latino (of any race)	0	0.0
Mexican	0	0.0

Foreign-Born Population		
Group	Number	%
Total Population	525	4.4
Hispanic or Latino (of any race)	463	34.7
Mexican	269	26.9

Foreign-Born Naturalized U.S. Citizens		
Group	Number	%
Total Population	165	31.4
Hispanic or Latino (of any race)	135	29.2
Mexican	87	32.3

Language Spoken at Home: English Only (Universe: Population 5 Years and Over)		
Group	Number	%
Total Population	10,295	93.4
Hispanic or Latino (of any race)	628	50.5
Mexican	535	58.1

Language Spoken at Home: Spanish (Universe: Population 5 Years and Over)		
Group	Number	%
Total Population	639	5.8
Hispanic or Latino (of any race)	616	49.5
Mexican	386	41.9

Unemployment Rate (Universe: Population 16 Years and Over)	
Group	%
Total Population	6.6
Hispanic or Latino (of any race)	14.8
Mexican	13.1

Class of Worker: Private Wage and Salary (Universe: Civilian Employed Population 16 Years and Over)		
Group	Number	%
Total Population	4,820	77.2
Hispanic or Latino (of any race)	586	90.2
Mexican	362	91.2

Class of Worker: Government (Universe: Civilian Employed Population 16 Years and Over)		
Group	Number	%
Total Population	1,125	18.0
Hispanic or Latino (of any race)	64	9.8
Mexican	35	8.8

Means of Transportation to Work: Car, Truck or Van (Universe: Workers 16 Years and Over)		
Group	Number	%
Total Population	5,483	90.7
Hispanic or Latino (of any race)	623	97.8
Mexican	384	100.0

Means of Transportation to Work: Public Transportation (ex. Taxicab) (Universe: Workers 16 Years and Over)		
Group	Number	%
Total Population	45	0.7
Hispanic or Latino (of any race)	0	0.0
Mexican	0	0.0

Homeownership Rate (Universe: Occupied Housing Units)	
Group	%
Total Population	68.8
Hispanic or Latino (of any race)	56.9
Mexican	58.3

Median Home Value	
Group	Dollars
Total Population	180,200
Hispanic or Latino (of any race)	202,400
Mexican	200,400

Median Gross Rent	
Group	Dollars
Total Population	543
Hispanic or Latino (of any race)	538
Mexican	481

Median Household Income (2010 Inflation-Adjusted Dollars)	
Group	Dollars
Total Population	53,032
Hispanic or Latino (of any race)	61,071
Mexican	61,488

Per Capita Income (2010 Inflation-Adjusted Dollars)	
Group	Dollars
Total Population	24,320
Hispanic or Latino (of any race)	21,687
Mexican	19,936

Households with $100,000+ Income		
Group	Number	%
Total Population	911	21.1
Hispanic or Latino (of any race)	95	26.0
Mexican	60	22.6

Households with Food Stamps/SNAP Benefits During Past 12 Months		
Group	Number	%
Total Population	351	8.1
Hispanic or Latino (of any race)	33	9.0
Mexican	33	12.5

Poverty Rate (Income in Past 12 Months Below Poverty Level)	
Group	%
Total Population	11.5
Hispanic or Latino (of any race)	20.6
Mexican	26.9

Gillette*

Population			
Group	Number	%TP[1]	%HP[2]
Total Population	29,087	100.0	–
Hispanic or Latino (of any race)	2,764	9.5	100.0
Central American, ex. Mexican	155	0.5	5.6
Mexican	2,163	7.4	78.3

Population Growth: 2000–2010	
Group	%
Total Population	48.1
Hispanic or Latino (of any race)	257.1
Mexican	327.5

Males per 100 Females	
Group	Number
Total Population	109.6
Hispanic or Latino (of any race)	129.4
Central American, ex. Mexican	216.3

STATE & PLACE PROFILES

Notes: (1) Percent of total population; (2) Percent of Hispanic/Latino population; Profiles include places with an overall population of at least 125,000, OR an overall population of at least 25,000 where the Hispanic/Latino population is at least 20% of the overall population. In states where less than five places meet either of these criteria, we have included places with at least 10,000 total population with the highest percentage of Hispanic/Latino population. These places are identified with an asterisk (*); Please refer to the User's Guide for a full explanation of data.

Mexican	129.9

Average Household Size

Group	People
Total Population	2.61
Hispanic or Latino (of any race)	3.40
Central American, ex. Mexican	3.50
Mexican	3.55

Median Age

Group	Years
Total Population	30.6
Hispanic or Latino (of any race)	24.2
Central American, ex. Mexican	27.9
Mexican	23.0

High School Graduates
(Universe: Population 25 Years and Over)

Group	Number	%
Total Population	15,098	91.0
Hispanic or Latino (of any race)	608	58.8
Mexican	410	50.1

Four-Year College Graduates
(Universe: Population 25 Years and Over)

Group	Number	%
Total Population	3,294	19.9
Hispanic or Latino (of any race)	142	13.7
Mexican	72	8.8

Population Age 3–17 Enrolled in Public School
(Universe: Population Age 3–17 Enrolled in School)

Group	Number	%
Total Population	5,048	96.8
Hispanic or Latino (of any race)	556	97.5
Mexican	397	96.6

Population Age 3–17 Enrolled in Private School
(Universe: Population Age 3–17 Enrolled in School)

Group	Number	%
Total Population	166	3.2
Hispanic or Latino (of any race)	14	2.5
Mexican	14	3.4

Foreign-Born Population

Group	Number	%
Total Population	1,042	3.8
Hispanic or Latino (of any race)	779	35.3
Mexican	704	38.8

Foreign-Born Naturalized U.S. Citizens

Group	Number	%
Total Population	200	19.2
Hispanic or Latino (of any race)	81	10.4
Mexican	81	11.5

Language Spoken at Home: English Only
(Universe: Population 5 Years and Over)

Group	Number	%
Total Population	22,861	92.9
Hispanic or Latino (of any race)	710	38.6
Mexican	510	34.7

Language Spoken at Home: Spanish
(Universe: Population 5 Years and Over)

Group	Number	%
Total Population	1,293	5.3
Hispanic or Latino (of any race)	1,131	61.4
Mexican	958	65.3

Unemployment Rate
(Universe: Population 16 Years and Over)

Group	%
Total Population	4.1
Hispanic or Latino (of any race)	2.0
Mexican	2.4

Class of Worker: Private Wage and Salary
(Universe: Civilian Employed Population 16 Years and Over)

Group	Number	%
Total Population	12,300	78.7
Hispanic or Latino (of any race)	754	86.0
Mexican	627	86.8

Class of Worker: Government
(Universe: Civilian Employed Population 16 Years and Over)

Group	Number	%
Total Population	2,353	15.1
Hispanic or Latino (of any race)	90	10.3
Mexican	77	10.7

Means of Transportation to Work: Car, Truck or Van
(Universe: Workers 16 Years and Over)

Group	Number	%
Total Population	13,934	91.4
Hispanic or Latino (of any race)	800	93.2
Mexican	645	91.7

Means of Transportation to Work: Public Transportation (ex. Taxicab)
(Universe: Workers 16 Years and Over)

Group	Number	%
Total Population	460	3.0
Hispanic or Latino (of any race)	0	0.0
Mexican	0	0.0

Homeownership Rate
(Universe: Occupied Housing Units)

Group	%
Total Population	67.7
Hispanic or Latino (of any race)	39.0
Central American, ex. Mexican	14.3
Mexican	39.7

Median Home Value

Group	Dollars
Total Population	189,500
Hispanic or Latino (of any race)	164,200
Mexican	154,200

Median Gross Rent

Group	Dollars
Total Population	772
Hispanic or Latino (of any race)	810
Mexican	794

Median Household Income
(2010 Inflation-Adjusted Dollars)

Group	Dollars
Total Population	72,697
Hispanic or Latino (of any race)	63,750
Mexican	48,302

Per Capita Income
(2010 Inflation-Adjusted Dollars)

Group	Dollars
Total Population	31,918
Hispanic or Latino (of any race)	19,993
Mexican	15,632

Households with $100,000+ Income

Group	Number	%
Total Population	3,345	32.4
Hispanic or Latino (of any race)	130	19.6
Mexican	36	7.3

Households with Food Stamps/SNAP Benefits During Past 12 Months

Group	Number	%
Total Population	354	3.4
Hispanic or Latino (of any race)	16	2.4
Mexican	16	3.3

Poverty Rate
(Income in Past 12 Months Below Poverty Level)

Group	%
Total Population	8.1
Hispanic or Latino (of any race)	16.4
Mexican	20.0

Green River*

Population

Group	Number	%TP[1]	%HP[2]
Total Population	12,515	100.0	–
Hispanic or Latino (of any race)	1,682	13.4	100.0
Mexican	1,296	10.4	77.1
Spaniard	114	0.9	6.8

Population Growth: 2000–2010

Group	%
Total Population	6.0
Hispanic or Latino (of any race)	39.5
Mexican	85.9

Males per 100 Females

Group	Number
Total Population	106.7
Hispanic or Latino (of any race)	117.6
Mexican	124.2
Spaniard	128.0

Average Household Size

Group	People
Total Population	2.68
Hispanic or Latino (of any race)	2.86
Mexican	2.97
Spaniard	2.59

Median Age

Group	Years
Total Population	33.9
Hispanic or Latino (of any race)	28.5
Mexican	27.6
Spaniard	38.0

High School Graduates
(Universe: Population 25 Years and Over)

Group	Number	%
Total Population	6,418	90.1
Hispanic or Latino (of any race)	585	82.0
Mexican	348	73.1

Four-Year College Graduates
(Universe: Population 25 Years and Over)

Group	Number	%
Total Population	1,280	18.0
Hispanic or Latino (of any race)	16	2.2
Mexican	0	0.0

Population Age 3–17 Enrolled in Public School
(Universe: Population Age 3–17 Enrolled in School)

Group	Number	%
Total Population	2,536	89.2
Hispanic or Latino (of any race)	377	92.6
Mexican	240	88.9

Population Age 3–17 Enrolled in Private School
(Universe: Population Age 3–17 Enrolled in School)

Group	Number	%
Total Population	306	10.8
Hispanic or Latino (of any race)	30	7.4
Mexican	30	11.1

Foreign-Born Population

Group	Number	%
Total Population	465	3.8
Hispanic or Latino (of any race)	268	19.1
Mexican	191	20.5

Foreign-Born Naturalized U.S. Citizens

Group	Number	%
Total Population	128	27.5
Hispanic or Latino (of any race)	70	26.1
Mexican	61	31.9

Language Spoken at Home: English Only
(Universe: Population 5 Years and Over)

Group	Number	%
Total Population	10,370	93.8
Hispanic or Latino (of any race)	760	59.0
Mexican	515	57.8

Language Spoken at Home: Spanish
(Universe: Population 5 Years and Over)

Group	Number	%
Total Population	600	5.4
Hispanic or Latino (of any race)	529	41.0
Mexican	376	42.2

Notes: (1) Percent of total population; (2) Percent of Hispanic/Latino population; Profiles include places with an overall population of at least 125,000, OR an overall population of at least 25,000 where the Hispanic/Latino population is at least 20% of the overall population. In states where less than five places meet either of these criteria, we have included places with at least 10,000 total population with the highest percentage of Hispanic/Latino population. These places are identified with an asterisk (*); Please refer to the User's Guide for a full explanation of data.

Unemployment Rate (Universe: Population 16 Years and Over)	
Group	%
Total Population	3.1
Hispanic or Latino (of any race)	1.9
Mexican	2.8

Class of Worker: Private Wage and Salary (Universe: Civilian Employed Population 16 Years and Over)		
Group	Number	%
Total Population	4,610	77.5
Hispanic or Latino (of any race)	492	87.4
Mexican	370	96.1

Class of Worker: Government (Universe: Civilian Employed Population 16 Years and Over)		
Group	Number	%
Total Population	1,122	18.9
Hispanic or Latino (of any race)	64	11.4
Mexican	15	3.9

Means of Transportation to Work: Car, Truck or Van (Universe: Workers 16 Years and Over)		
Group	Number	%
Total Population	5,397	92.6
Hispanic or Latino (of any race)	538	98.0
Mexican	374	97.1

Means of Transportation to Work: Public Transportation (ex. Taxicab) (Universe: Workers 16 Years and Over)		
Group	Number	%
Total Population	217	3.7
Hispanic or Latino (of any race)	11	2.0
Mexican	11	2.9

Homeownership Rate (Universe: Occupied Housing Units)	
Group	%
Total Population	74.4
Hispanic or Latino (of any race)	66.2
Mexican	64.5
Spaniard	81.8

Median Home Value	
Group	Dollars
Total Population	195,400
Hispanic or Latino (of any race)	158,300
Mexican	151,400

Median Gross Rent	
Group	Dollars
Total Population	790
Hispanic or Latino (of any race)	694
Mexican	555

Median Household Income (2010 Inflation-Adjusted Dollars)	
Group	Dollars
Total Population	71,502
Hispanic or Latino (of any race)	62,188
Mexican	60,781

Per Capita Income (2010 Inflation-Adjusted Dollars)	
Group	Dollars
Total Population	28,265
Hispanic or Latino (of any race)	19,259
Mexican	21,720

Households with $100,000+ Income		
Group	Number	%
Total Population	1,284	29.0
Hispanic or Latino (of any race)	115	28.3
Mexican	81	31.8

Households with Food Stamps/SNAP Benefits During Past 12 Months		
Group	Number	%
Total Population	109	2.5
Hispanic or Latino (of any race)	5	1.2
Mexican	5	2.0

Poverty Rate (Income in Past 12 Months Below Poverty Level)	
Group	%
Total Population	8.0
Hispanic or Latino (of any race)	6.0
Mexican	9.1

Rock Springs*

Population			
Group	Number	%TP[1]	%HP[2]
Total Population	23,036	100.0	–
Hispanic or Latino (of any race)	3,771	16.4	100.0
Central American, ex. Mexican	152	0.7	4.0
Mexican	2,819	12.2	74.8
Spaniard	150	0.7	4.0

Population Growth: 2000–2010	
Group	%
Total Population	23.1
Hispanic or Latino (of any race)	125.0
Mexican	183.9

Males per 100 Females	
Group	Number
Total Population	108.8
Hispanic or Latino (of any race)	114.3
Central American, ex. Mexican	198.0
Mexican	115.5
Spaniard	117.4

Average Household Size	
Group	People
Total Population	2.57
Hispanic or Latino (of any race)	3.16
Central American, ex. Mexican	3.65
Mexican	3.40
Spaniard	2.32

Median Age	
Group	Years
Total Population	31.5
Hispanic or Latino (of any race)	25.1
Central American, ex. Mexican	29.2
Mexican	23.9
Spaniard	31.7

High School Graduates (Universe: Population 25 Years and Over)		
Group	Number	%
Total Population	12,670	90.8
Hispanic or Latino (of any race)	1,274	75.0
Mexican	923	69.3

Four-Year College Graduates (Universe: Population 25 Years and Over)		
Group	Number	%
Total Population	2,435	17.5
Hispanic or Latino (of any race)	44	2.6
Mexican	39	2.9

Population Age 3–17 Enrolled in Public School (Universe: Population Age 3–17 Enrolled in School)		
Group	Number	%
Total Population	3,356	88.4
Hispanic or Latino (of any race)	757	90.2
Mexican	713	90.8

Population Age 3–17 Enrolled in Private School (Universe: Population Age 3–17 Enrolled in School)		
Group	Number	%
Total Population	441	11.6
Hispanic or Latino (of any race)	82	9.8
Mexican	72	9.2

Foreign-Born Population		
Group	Number	%
Total Population	1,437	6.5
Hispanic or Latino (of any race)	1,215	35.7
Mexican	1,033	36.9

Foreign-Born Naturalized U.S. Citizens		
Group	Number	%
Total Population	267	18.6
Hispanic or Latino (of any race)	179	14.7
Mexican	168	16.3

Language Spoken at Home: English Only (Universe: Population 5 Years and Over)		
Group	Number	%
Total Population	18,208	90.1
Hispanic or Latino (of any race)	1,335	46.0
Mexican	1,087	45.5

Language Spoken at Home: Spanish (Universe: Population 5 Years and Over)		
Group	Number	%
Total Population	1,691	8.4
Hispanic or Latino (of any race)	1,568	54.0
Mexican	1,301	54.5

Unemployment Rate (Universe: Population 16 Years and Over)	
Group	%
Total Population	6.1
Hispanic or Latino (of any race)	2.9
Mexican	2.9

Class of Worker: Private Wage and Salary (Universe: Civilian Employed Population 16 Years and Over)		
Group	Number	%
Total Population	9,489	80.2
Hispanic or Latino (of any race)	1,286	85.1
Mexican	961	84.3

Class of Worker: Government (Universe: Civilian Employed Population 16 Years and Over)		
Group	Number	%
Total Population	1,803	15.2
Hispanic or Latino (of any race)	147	9.7
Mexican	128	11.2

Means of Transportation to Work: Car, Truck or Van (Universe: Workers 16 Years and Over)		
Group	Number	%
Total Population	10,548	91.4
Hispanic or Latino (of any race)	1,354	91.9
Mexican	1,016	92.2

Means of Transportation to Work: Public Transportation (ex. Taxicab) (Universe: Workers 16 Years and Over)		
Group	Number	%
Total Population	421	3.6
Hispanic or Latino (of any race)	24	1.6
Mexican	7	0.6

Homeownership Rate (Universe: Occupied Housing Units)	
Group	%
Total Population	67.9
Hispanic or Latino (of any race)	53.1
Central American, ex. Mexican	32.6
Mexican	53.6
Spaniard	71.2

Median Home Value	
Group	Dollars
Total Population	170,600
Hispanic or Latino (of any race)	80,000
Mexican	53,700

Median Gross Rent	
Group	Dollars
Total Population	818
Hispanic or Latino (of any race)	721
Mexican	703

Median Household Income (2010 Inflation-Adjusted Dollars)	
Group	Dollars
Total Population	69,351
Hispanic or Latino (of any race)	56,000
Mexican	58,462

Per Capita Income (2010 Inflation-Adjusted Dollars)	
Group	Dollars
Total Population	31,105

Notes: (1) Percent of total population; (2) Percent of Hispanic/Latino population; Profiles include places with an overall population of at least 125,000, OR an overall population of at least 25,000 where the Hispanic/Latino population is at least 20% of the overall population. In states where less than five places meet either of these criteria, we have included places with at least 10,000 total population with the highest percentage of Hispanic/Latino population. These places are identified with an asterisk (*); Please refer to the User's Guide for a full explanation of data.

Hispanic or Latino (of any race)	17,818	
Mexican	16,105	

Households with $100,000+ Income

Group	Number	%
Total Population	2,351	26.6
Hispanic or Latino (of any race)	200	18.3
Mexican	161	19.8

Households with Food Stamps/SNAP Benefits During Past 12 Months

Group	Number	%
Total Population	243	2.8
Hispanic or Latino (of any race)	43	3.9
Mexican	43	5.3

Poverty Rate
(Income in Past 12 Months Below Poverty Level)

Group	%
Total Population	8.2
Hispanic or Latino (of any race)	16.9
Mexican	20.6

Notes: (1) Percent of total population; (2) Percent of Hispanic/Latino population; Profiles include places with an overall population of at least 125,000, OR an overall population of at least 25,000 where the Hispanic/Latino population is at least 20% of the overall population. In states where less than five places meet either of these criteria, we have included places with at least 10,000 total population with the highest percentage of Hispanic/Latino population. These places are identified with an asterisk (*); Please refer to the User's Guide for a full explanation of data.

SECTION THREE:
Rankings & Comparisons

Population

Total Population

Top 10 States, Counties, and Places[1]

Sorted by Number in Descending Order — U.S. = 308,745,538

State	Number	County	Number	Place	Number
California	37,253,956	Los Angeles County, CA	9,818,605	**New York, NY** (city)	8,175,133
Texas	25,145,561	Cook County, IL	5,194,675	**Los Angeles, CA** (city) Los Angeles County	3,792,621
New York	19,378,102	Harris County, TX	4,092,459	**Chicago, IL** (city) Cook County	2,695,598
Florida	18,801,310	Maricopa County, AZ	3,817,117	**Brooklyn, NY** (borough) Kings County	2,504,700
Illinois	12,830,632	San Diego County, CA	3,095,313	**Queens, NY** (borough) Queens County	2,230,722
Pennsylvania	12,702,379	Orange County, CA	3,010,232	**Houston, TX** (city) Harris County	2,099,451
Ohio	11,536,504	Kings County, NY	2,504,700	**Manhattan, NY** (borough) New York County	1,585,873
Michigan	9,883,640	Miami-Dade County, FL	2,496,435	**Philadelphia, PA** (city) Philadelphia County	1,526,006
Georgia	9,687,653	Dallas County, TX	2,368,139	**Phoenix, AZ** (city) Maricopa County	1,445,632
North Carolina	9,535,483	Queens County, NY	2,230,722	**Bronx, NY** (borough) Bronx County	1,385,108

Sorted by Number in Ascending Order — U.S. = 308,745,538

State	Number	County	Number	Place	Number
Wyoming	563,626	Kenedy County, TX	416	**Mayfield*, KY** (city) Graves County	10,024
District of Columbia	601,723	Harding County, NM	695	**Warr Acres*, OK** (city) Oklahoma County	10,043
Vermont	625,741	McMullen County, TX	707	**Hope*, AR** (city) Hempstead County	10,095
North Dakota	672,591	Esmeralda County, NV	783	**Lexington*, NE** (city) Dawson County	10,230
Alaska	710,231	Kent County, TX	808	**Burley*, ID** (city) Cassia County	10,345
South Dakota	814,180	Clark County, ID	982	**Spearfish*, SD** (city) Lawrence County	10,494
Delaware	897,934	Terrell County, TX	984	**Storm Lake*, IA** (city) Buena Vista County	10,600
Montana	989,415	Sterling County, TX	1,143	**Jerome*, ID** (city) Jerome County	10,890
Rhode Island	1,052,567	Motley County, TX	1,210	**Hanover*, NH** (town) Grafton County	11,260
New Hampshire	1,316,470	Glasscock County, TX	1,226	**Hawaiian Paradise Park*, HI** (cdp) Hawaii County	11,404

RANKINGS & COMPARISONS

Note: (1) Ranking tables cover all states and counties, and places with an overall population of at least 125,000, OR an overall population of at least 25,000 where the Hispanic/Latino population is at least 20% of the overall population. In states where less than five places meet either of these criteria, we have included places with at least 10,000 total population with the highest percentage of Hispanic/Latino population. These places are identified with an asterisk (*); Please refer to the User's Guide for a full explanation of data.

Population

Hispanic or Latino (of any race)

Top 10 States, Counties, and Places[1]

Sorted by Number in Descending Order — U.S. = 50,477,594

State	Number	County	Number	Place	Number
California	14,013,719	Los Angeles County, CA	4,687,889	**New York, NY** (city)	2,336,076
Texas	9,460,921	Harris County, TX	1,671,540	**Los Angeles, CA** (city) Los Angeles County	1,838,822
Florida	4,223,806	Miami-Dade County, FL	1,623,859	**Houston, TX** (city) Harris County	919,668
New York	3,416,922	Cook County, IL	1,244,762	**San Antonio, TX** (city) Bexar County	838,952
Illinois	2,027,578	Maricopa County, AZ	1,128,741	**Chicago, IL** (city) Cook County	778,862
Arizona	1,895,149	Orange County, CA	1,012,973	**Bronx, NY** (borough) Bronx County	741,413
New Jersey	1,555,144	Bexar County, TX	1,006,958	**Queens, NY** (borough) Queens County	613,750
Colorado	1,038,687	San Bernardino County, CA	1,001,145	**Phoenix, AZ** (city) Maricopa County	589,877
New Mexico	953,403	Riverside County, CA	995,257	**El Paso, TX** (city) El Paso County	523,721
Georgia	853,689	San Diego County, CA	991,348	**Dallas, TX** (city) Dallas County	507,309

Sorted by Number in Ascending Order — U.S. = 50,477,594

State	Number	County	Number	Place	Number
Vermont	9,208	Chase County, KS	100	**Beckley*, WV** (city) Raleigh County	265
North Dakota	13,467	Dickey County, ND	100	**Clarksburg*, WV** (city) Harrison County	269
Maine	16,935	Edmonson County, KY	100	**Bennington*, VT** (town) Bennington County	274
South Dakota	22,119	Ida County, IA	100	**Spearfish*, SD** (city) Lawrence County	287
West Virginia	22,268	Adair County, IA	101	**Brattleboro*, VT** (town) Windham County	322
Montana	28,565	Aurora County, SD	101	**Williston*, ND** (city) Williams County	328
New Hampshire	36,704	Bath County, VA	101	**Essex*, VT** (town) Chittenden County	335
Alaska	39,249	Estill County, KY	101	**South Burlington*, VT** (city) Chittenden County	336
Wyoming	50,231	Jefferson Davis County, MS	101	**Waterville*, ME** (city) Kennebec County	374
District of Columbia	54,749	Red Lake County, MN	101	**Dickinson*, ND** (city) Stark County	382

Sorted by Percent of Total Population in Descending Order — U.S. = 16.3%

State	Percent	County	Percent	Place	Percent
New Mexico	46.3	Maverick County, TX	95.7	**San Luis, AZ** (city) Yuma County	98.7
California	37.6	Starr County, TX	95.7	**Maywood, CA** (city) Los Angeles County	97.4
Texas	37.6	Webb County, TX	95.7	**East Los Angeles, CA** (cdp) Los Angeles County	97.1
Arizona	29.6	Zavala County, TX	93.9	**Huntington Park, CA** (city) Los Angeles County	97.1
Nevada	26.5	Zapata County, TX	93.3	**Calexico, CA** (city) Imperial County	96.8
Florida	22.5	Jim Hogg County, TX	92.6	**San Juan, TX** (city) Hidalgo County	96.7
Colorado	20.7	Brooks County, TX	91.2	**Socorro, TX** (city) El Paso County	96.7
New Jersey	17.7	Hidalgo County, TX	90.6	**Coachella, CA** (city) Riverside County	96.4
New York	17.6	Duval County, TX	88.5	**Bell Gardens, CA** (city) Los Angeles County	95.7
Illinois	15.8	Cameron County, TX	88.1	**Laredo, TX** (city) Webb County	95.6

Sorted by Percent of Total Population in Ascending Order — U.S. = 16.3%

State	Percent	County	Percent	Place	Percent
West Virginia	1.2	Mason County, WV	0.4	**Huntington*, WV** (city) Cabell County	1.4
Maine	1.3	Mingo County, WV	0.4	**Beckley*, WV** (city) Raleigh County	1.5
Vermont	1.5	Wyoming County, WV	0.4	**Clarksburg*, WV** (city) Harrison County	1.6
North Dakota	2.0	Armstrong County, PA	0.5	**Jackson, MS** (city) Hinds County	1.6
Mississippi	2.7	Johnson County, KY	0.5	**Bennington*, VT** (town) Bennington County	1.7
South Dakota	2.7	Letcher County, KY	0.5	**Essex*, VT** (town) Chittenden County	1.7
New Hampshire	2.8	Meigs County, OH	0.5	**South Burlington*, VT** (city) Chittenden County	1.9
Montana	2.9	Perry County, OH	0.5	**Sterling Heights, MI** (city) Macomb County	1.9
Kentucky	3.1	Scott County, TN	0.5	**Lewiston*, ME** (city) Androscoggin County	2.0
Ohio	3.1	Wayne County, WV	0.5	**Akron, OH** (city) Summit County	2.1

Note: (1) Ranking tables cover all states and counties, and places with an overall population of at least 125,000, OR an overall population of at least 25,000 where the Hispanic/Latino population is at least 20% of the overall population. In states where less than five places meet either of these criteria, we have included places with at least 10,000 total population with the highest percentage of Hispanic/Latino population. These places are identified with an asterisk (*); Please refer to the User's Guide for a full explanation of data.

Population

Central American, excluding Mexican

Top 10 States, Counties, and Places[1]

Sorted by Number in Descending Order — U.S. = 3,998,280

State	Number	County	Number	Place	Number
California	1,132,520	Los Angeles County, CA	675,832	**Los Angeles, CA** (city) Los Angeles County	415,913
Florida	432,665	Harris County, TX	217,624	**New York, NY** (city)	151,378
Texas	420,683	Miami-Dade County, FL	212,542	**Houston, TX** (city) Harris County	140,815
New York	353,589	Montgomery County, MD	78,327	**Miami, FL** (city) Miami-Dade County	62,995
Virginia	206,568	Suffolk County, NY	77,117	**Queens, NY** (borough) Queens County	52,509
Maryland	195,692	Fairfax County, VA	70,485	**Hempstead (town), NY** (town) Nassau County	49,236
New Jersey	176,611	Prince George's County, MD	70,237	**Brooklyn, NY** (borough) Kings County	46,119
Georgia	106,987	Nassau County, NY	69,816	**Islip, NY** (town) Suffolk County	38,530
North Carolina	105,066	Dallas County, TX	66,163	**Bronx, NY** (borough) Bronx County	34,492
Massachusetts	96,958	San Bernardino County, CA	53,571	**San Francisco, CA** (city) San Francisco County	33,834

Sorted by Number in Ascending Order — U.S. = 3,998,280

State	Number	County	Number	Place	Number
North Dakota	452	Jefferson County, WI	100	**Billings*, MT** (city) Yellowstone County	103
Vermont	671	Monongalia County, WV	100	**Fort Campbell North*, KY** (cdp) Christian County	103
Montana	735	Harrison County, TX	101	**Horn Lake*, MS** (city) DeSoto County	103
Wyoming	977	Lincoln Parish, LA	101	**West Chicago, IL** (city) DuPage County	103
Maine	1,708	Madison County, ID	101	**Lake Jackson, TX** (city) Brazoria County	104
West Virginia	2,081	Northumberland County, PA	101	**Brighton, CO** (city) Adams County	105
Alaska	2,509	Rogers County, OK	101	**Seguin, TX** (city) Guadalupe County	106
New Hampshire	2,731	Sauk County, WI	101	**Drexel Heights, AZ** (cdp) Pima County	108
South Dakota	2,891	Blaine County, ID	102	**Middle*, DE** (town) New Castle County	108
Hawaii	2,962	McDowell County, NC	102	**Burlington*, VT** (city) Chittenden County	117

Sorted by Percent of Total Population in Descending Order — U.S. = 1.3%

State	Percent	County	Percent	Place	Percent
District of Columbia	3.9	Colfax County, NE	11.1	**Chelsea, MA** (city) Suffolk County	36.1
Maryland	3.4	Prince William County, VA	9.5	**Brentwood, NY** (cdp) Suffolk County	32.9
California	3.0	Miami-Dade County, FL	8.5	**Hempstead (village), NY** (village) Nassau County	30.0
Virginia	2.6	Montgomery County, MD	8.1	**Chillum, MD** (cdp) Prince George's County	29.4
Florida	2.3	Prince George's County, MD	8.1	**Wheaton, MD** (cdp) Montgomery County	25.0
Rhode Island	2.3	Nobles County, MN	7.8	**Central Islip, NY** (cdp) Suffolk County	24.6
Nevada	2.1	Los Angeles County, CA	6.9	**Marumsco, VA** (cdp) Prince William County	23.5
New Jersey	2.0	Stewart County, GA	6.7	**Huntington Station, NY** (cdp) Suffolk County	22.3
New York	1.8	Fairfax County, VA	6.5	**Plainfield, NJ** (city) Union County	19.7
Texas	1.7	Nantucket County, MA	6.3	**Sterling, VA** (cdp) Loudoun County	18.8

Sorted by Percent of Total Population in Ascending Order — U.S. = 1.3%

State	Percent	County	Percent	Place	Percent
Maine	0.1	Allegan County, MI	0.1	**Billings*, MT** (city) Yellowstone County	0.1
Montana	0.1	Allegheny County, PA	0.1	**Buffalo, NY** (city) Erie County	0.1
North Dakota	0.1	Ashtabula County, OH	0.1	**Odessa, TX** (city) Ector County	0.1
Vermont	0.1	Beaver County, PA	0.1	**Toledo, OH** (city) Lucas County	0.1
West Virginia	0.1	Butler County, PA	0.1	**Akron, OH** (city) Summit County	0.2
Hawaii	0.2	Cass County, ND	0.1	**Boise City, ID** (city) Ada County	0.2
Idaho	0.2	Chautauqua County, NY	0.1	**Dayton, OH** (city) Montgomery County	0.2
Michigan	0.2	Chemung County, NY	0.1	**Jackson, MS** (city) Hinds County	0.2
New Hampshire	0.2	Clark County, OH	0.1	**Las Cruces, NM** (city) Dona Ana County	0.2
Ohio	0.2	Clermont County, OH	0.1	**Lorain, OH** (city) Lorain County	0.2

Note: (1) Ranking tables cover all states and counties, and places with an overall population of at least 125,000, OR an overall population of at least 25,000 where the Hispanic/Latino population is at least 20% of the overall population. In states where less than five places meet either of these criteria, we have included places with at least 10,000 total population with the highest percentage of Hispanic/Latino population. These places are identified with an asterisk (*); Please refer to the User's Guide for a full explanation of data.

Sorted by Percent of Hispanic Population in Descending Order — U.S. = 7.9%

State	Percent	County	Percent	Place	Percent
District of Columbia	42.7	Nantucket County, MA	67.4	**Chillum, MD** (cdp) Prince George's County	70.0
Maryland	41.6	Prince George's County, MD	54.5	**Hempstead (village), NY** (village) Nassau County	67.9
Virginia	32.7	Jefferson Parish, LA	48.7	**Silver Spring, MD** (cdp) Montgomery County	61.2
Louisiana	26.9	Montgomery County, MD	47.4	**Huntington Station, NY** (cdp) Suffolk County	60.9
Rhode Island	18.2	Prince William County, VA	46.8	**Wheaton, MD** (cdp) Montgomery County	59.9
Massachusetts	15.4	Saline County, MO	45.0	**Chelsea, MA** (city) Suffolk County	58.0
North Carolina	13.1	Burke County, NC	42.7	**Kenner, LA** (city) Jefferson Parish	57.9
South Dakota	13.1	Caroline County, MD	41.9	**Marumsco, VA** (cdp) Prince William County	57.2
Tennessee	12.7	Fairfax County, VA	41.8	**Sterling, VA** (cdp) Loudoun County	56.6
Arkansas	12.5	Tuscarawas County, OH	41.4	**Carthage*, MO** (city) Jasper County	55.9

Sorted by Percent of Hispanic Population in Ascending Order — U.S. = 7.9%

State	Percent	County	Percent	Place	Percent
New Mexico	0.7	Ector County, TX	0.2	**Odessa, TX** (city) Ector County	0.2
Arizona	1.9	Valencia County, NM	0.2	**Mission, TX** (city) Hidalgo County	0.3
Wyoming	1.9	Doña Ana County, NM	0.3	**Pharr, TX** (city) Hidalgo County	0.3
Idaho	2.0	Hidalgo County, TX	0.3	**Brownsville, TX** (city) Cameron County	0.4
Hawaii	2.5	El Paso County, TX	0.4	**El Centro, CA** (city) Imperial County	0.4
Montana	2.6	Tom Green County, TX	0.4	**El Paso, TX** (city) El Paso County	0.4
Colorado	2.8	Val Verde County, TX	0.4	**Laredo, TX** (city) Webb County	0.4
Wisconsin	3.2	Victoria County, TX	0.4	**Las Cruces, NM** (city) Dona Ana County	0.4
North Dakota	3.4	Webb County, TX	0.4	**Pueblo, CO** (city) Pueblo County	0.4
Illinois	3.5	Imperial County, CA	0.5	**San Angelo, TX** (city) Tom Green County	0.4

Note: (1) Ranking tables cover all states and counties, and places with an overall population of at least 125,000, OR an overall population of at least 25,000 where the Hispanic/Latino population is at least 20% of the overall population. In states where less than five places meet either of these criteria, we have included places with at least 10,000 total population with the highest percentage of Hispanic/Latino population. These places are identified with an asterisk (*); Please refer to the User's Guide for a full explanation of data.

Population

Central American: Costa Rican

Top 10 States, Counties, and Places[1]

Sorted by Number in Descending Order — U.S. = 126,418

State	Number	County	Number	Place	Number
California	22,469	Los Angeles County, CA	9,365	**New York, NY** (city)	6,673
Florida	20,761	Miami-Dade County, FL	6,736	**Los Angeles, CA** (city) Los Angeles County	3,182
New Jersey	19,933	Somerset County, NJ	4,034	**Brooklyn, NY** (borough) Kings County	2,576
New York	11,576	Union County, NJ	3,200	**Queens, NY** (borough) Queens County	1,749
Texas	6,982	Broward County, FL	3,014	**Trenton, NJ** (city) Mercer County	1,279
North Carolina	4,658	Kings County, NY	2,576	**Paterson, NJ** (city) Passaic County	1,241
Georgia	3,114	Passaic County, NJ	2,065	**Miami, FL** (city) Miami-Dade County	1,197
Pennsylvania	3,048	Harris County, TX	2,063	**Bronx, NY** (borough) Bronx County	1,095
Massachusetts	2,951	Fairfield County, CT	2,025	**Norwalk, CT** (city/town) Fairfield County	1,024
Connecticut	2,767	Orange County, CA	2,006	**Manhattan, NY** (borough) New York County	987

Sorted by Number in Ascending Order — U.S. = 126,418

State	Number	County	Number	Place	Number
Maine	105	Galveston County, TX	101	**Kendall West, FL** (cdp) Miami-Dade County	100
Alaska	140	Sumner County, TN	101	**Oyster Bay, NY** (town) Nassau County	101
Nebraska	166	Escambia County, FL	102	**Tulsa, OK** (city) Tulsa County	101
Idaho	230	San Luis Obispo County, CA	102	**North Las Vegas, NV** (city) Clark County	102
New Hampshire	233	Jefferson County, CO	103	**Rialto, CA** (city) San Bernardino County	102
Rhode Island	242	Wayne County, MI	105	**Ramapo, NY** (town) Rockland County	103
Delaware	243	York County, SC	106	**Westchester, FL** (cdp) Miami-Dade County	103
Kentucky	253	Bristol County, MA	108	**Colorado Springs, CO** (city) El Paso County	104
Iowa	255	Clackamas County, OR	108	**Richmond West, FL** (cdp) Miami-Dade County	105
District of Columbia	258	Cuyahoga County, OH	108	**Weston, FL** (city) Broward County	105

Sorted by Percent of Total Population in Descending Order — U.S. < 0.1%

State	Percent	County	Percent	Place	Percent
New Jersey	0.2	Lincoln County, NC	1.3	**Trenton, NJ** (city) Mercer County	1.5
California	0.1	Somerset County, NJ	1.2	**Norwalk, CT** (city/town) Fairfield County	1.2
Connecticut	0.1	Union County, NJ	0.6	**Berea*, SC** (cdp) Greenville County	0.8
Florida	0.1	Mercer County, NJ	0.5	**Paterson, NJ** (city) Passaic County	0.8
Nevada	0.1	Passaic County, NJ	0.4	**Bloomfield, NJ** (township) Essex County	0.7
New York	0.1	Hunterdon County, NJ	0.3	**Chelsea, MA** (city) Suffolk County	0.5
Alabama	0.0	Miami-Dade County, FL	0.3	**Elizabeth, NJ** (city) Union County	0.5
Alaska	0.0	Montgomery County, NY	0.3	**Country Club, FL** (cdp) Miami-Dade County	0.4
Arizona	0.0	Morris County, NJ	0.3	**Doral, FL** (city) Miami-Dade County	0.4
Arkansas	0.0	Warren County, NJ	0.3	**Fountainebleau, FL** (cdp) Miami-Dade County	0.4

Sorted by Percent of Total Population in Ascending Order — U.S. < 0.1%

State	Percent	County	Percent	Place	Percent
Alabama	0.0	Alameda County, CA	0.0	**Albuquerque, NM** (city) Bernalillo County	0.0
Alaska	0.0	Allegheny County, PA	0.0	**Arlington, TX** (city) Tarrant County	0.0
Arizona	0.0	Anne Arundel County, MD	0.0	**Atlanta, GA** (city) Fulton County	0.0
Arkansas	0.0	Arapahoe County, CO	0.0	**Austin, TX** (city) Travis County	0.0
Colorado	0.0	Baltimore County, MD	0.0	**Bakersfield, CA** (city) Kern County	0.0
Delaware	0.0	Bernalillo County, NM	0.0	**Brookhaven, NY** (town) Suffolk County	0.0
District of Columbia	0.0	Bexar County, TX	0.0	**Chicago, IL** (city) Cook County	0.0
Georgia	0.0	Bristol County, MA	0.0	**Colorado Springs, CO** (city) El Paso County	0.0
Hawaii	0.0	Burlington County, NJ	0.0	**Columbus, OH** (city) Franklin County	0.0
Idaho	0.0	Camden County, NJ	0.0	**Dallas, TX** (city) Dallas County	0.0

Note: (1) Ranking tables cover all states and counties, and places with an overall population of at least 125,000, OR an overall population of at least 25,000 where the Hispanic/Latino population is at least 20% of the overall population. In states where less than five places meet either of these criteria, we have included places with at least 10,000 total population with the highest percentage of Hispanic/Latino population. These places are identified with an asterisk (*); Please refer to the User's Guide for a full explanation of data.

Sorted by Percent of Hispanic Population in Descending Order — U.S. = 0.3%

State	Percent	County	Percent	Place	Percent
New Jersey	1.3	Lincoln County, NC	19.8	**Norwalk, CT** (city/town) Fairfield County	4.9
South Carolina	0.8	Somerset County, NJ	9.6	**Trenton, NJ** (city) Mercer County	4.5
Connecticut	0.6	Hunterdon County, NJ	4.8	**Berea*, SC** (cdp) Greenville County	3.3
Louisiana	0.6	Warren County, NJ	3.7	**Bloomfield, NJ** (township) Essex County	2.7
Maine	0.6	Aiken County, SC	3.4	**Hilton Head Island*, SC** (town) Beaufort County	1.8
New Hampshire	0.6	Mercer County, NJ	3.3	**Paterson, NJ** (city) Passaic County	1.5
North Carolina	0.6	Catawba County, NC	2.9	**Kenner, LA** (city) Jefferson Parish	1.1
District of Columbia	0.5	Montgomery County, NY	2.3	**Linden, NJ** (city) Union County	1.1
Florida	0.5	Morris County, NJ	2.3	**Metairie, LA** (cdp) Jefferson Parish	1.1
Maryland	0.5	Union County, NJ	2.2	**Bridgeport, CT** (city/town) Fairfield County	0.9

Sorted by Percent of Hispanic Population in Ascending Order — U.S. = 0.3%

State	Percent	County	Percent	Place	Percent
New Mexico	0.0	Bernalillo County, NM	0.0	**San Antonio, TX** (city) Bexar County	0.0
Arizona	0.1	El Paso County, TX	0.0	**Santa Ana, CA** (city) Orange County	0.0
Colorado	0.1	Fresno County, CA	0.0	**Albuquerque, NM** (city) Bernalillo County	0.1
Idaho	0.1	Arapahoe County, CO	0.1	**Arlington, TX** (city) Tarrant County	0.1
Illinois	0.1	Bexar County, TX	0.1	**Austin, TX** (city) Travis County	0.1
Kansas	0.1	Bronx County, NY	0.1	**Bakersfield, CA** (city) Kern County	0.1
Nebraska	0.1	Cook County, IL	0.1	**Bronx, NY** (borough) Bronx County	0.1
Oklahoma	0.1	Dallas County, TX	0.1	**Chicago, IL** (city) Cook County	0.1
Texas	0.1	Denver County, CO	0.1	**Chula Vista, CA** (city) San Diego County	0.1
Arkansas	0.2	DuPage County, IL	0.1	**Dallas, TX** (city) Dallas County	0.1

Note: (1) Ranking tables cover all states and counties, and places with an overall population of at least 125,000, OR an overall population of at least 25,000 where the Hispanic/Latino population is at least 20% of the overall population. In states where less than five places meet either of these criteria, we have included places with at least 10,000 total population with the highest percentage of Hispanic/Latino population. These places are identified with an asterisk (*); Please refer to the User's Guide for a full explanation of data.

Population

Central American: Guatemalan

Top 10 States, Counties, and Places[1]

Sorted by Number in Descending Order — U.S. = 1,044,209

State	Number	County	Number	Place	Number
California	332,737	Los Angeles County, CA	214,939	**Los Angeles, CA** (city) Los Angeles County	138,139
Florida	83,882	Harris County, TX	34,117	**New York, NY** (city)	30,420
New York	73,806	Cook County, IL	24,931	**Houston, TX** (city) Harris County	25,205
Texas	66,244	Palm Beach County, FL	20,080	**Chicago, IL** (city) Cook County	17,973
New Jersey	48,869	Miami-Dade County, FL	19,771	**Queens, NY** (borough) Queens County	13,700
Georgia	36,874	Providence County, RI	17,907	**Providence, RI** (city) Providence County	11,930
Illinois	35,321	Orange County, CA	16,365	**Brooklyn, NY** (borough) Kings County	9,160
Maryland	34,491	Riverside County, CA	14,388	**Trenton, NJ** (city) Mercer County	8,691
Virginia	33,556	San Bernardino County, CA	14,338	**Stamford, CT** (city/town) Fairfield County	7,707
Massachusetts	32,812	Prince George's County, MD	13,818	**Phoenix, AZ** (city) Maricopa County	6,722

Sorted by Number in Ascending Order — U.S. = 1,044,209

State	Number	County	Number	Place	Number
North Dakota	134	Delaware County, OH	100	**University, FL** (cdp) Hillsborough County	100
Montana	200	Lorain County, OH	100	**Urban Honolulu, HI** (cdp) Honolulu County	100
Vermont	215	Bay County, FL	101	**National City, CA** (city) San Diego County	101
West Virginia	347	Chelan County, WA	101	**Lancaster, PA** (city) Lancaster County	103
Wyoming	418	Hendricks County, IN	101	**Madera, CA** (city) Madera County	104
Maine	457	Middlesex County, CT	101	**Bergenfield, NJ** (borough) Bergen County	105
Alaska	508	Schenectady County, NY	101	**Brea, CA** (city) Orange County	105
Hawaii	565	Yuma County, AZ	101	**Ceres, CA** (city) Stanislaus County	105
New Hampshire	743	Jasper County, SC	102	**Laguna Hills, CA** (city) Orange County	106
Idaho	1,168	Lubbock County, TX	102	**North Highlands, CA** (cdp) Sacramento County	106

Sorted by Percent of Total Population in Descending Order — U.S. = 0.3%

State	Percent	County	Percent	Place	Percent
Rhode Island	1.8	Colfax County, NE	8.4	**Central Falls*, RI** (city) Providence County	13.3
California	0.9	Franklin County, AL	4.6	**Carthage*, MO** (city) Jasper County	12.8
Delaware	0.6	Dawson County, NE	4.4	**Lake Worth, FL** (city) Palm Beach County	12.7
Maryland	0.6	Nobles County, MN	4.3	**Spring Valley, NY** (village) Rockland County	10.4
New Jersey	0.6	Saline County, NE	3.9	**San Rafael, CA** (city) Marin County	10.2
Connecticut	0.5	Saluda County, SC	3.9	**Trenton, NJ** (city) Mercer County	10.2
Massachusetts	0.5	Texas County, OK	3.5	**Lexington*, NE** (city) Dawson County	8.7
Nebraska	0.5	Martin County, FL	3.4	**Plainfield, NJ** (city) Union County	8.6
Nevada	0.5	Mercer County, NJ	3.4	**Port Chester, NY** (village) Westchester County	8.4
District of Columbia	0.4	Seward County, KS	3.4	**Albertville*, AL** (city) Marshall County	8.2

Sorted by Percent of Total Population in Ascending Order — U.S. = 0.3%

State	Percent	County	Percent	Place	Percent
Hawaii	0.0	Albany County, NY	0.0	**Saint Louis, MO** (independent city)	0.0
Maine	0.0	Allegheny County, PA	0.0	**Urban Honolulu, HI** (cdp) Honolulu County	0.0
Montana	0.0	Erie County, NY	0.0	**Albuquerque, NM** (city) Bernalillo County	0.1
North Dakota	0.0	Honolulu County, HI	0.0	**Anchorage, AK** (municipality)	0.1
Vermont	0.0	Lorain County, OH	0.0	**Atlanta, GA** (city) Fulton County	0.1
West Virginia	0.0	Lubbock County, TX	0.0	**Baton Rouge, LA** (city) East Baton Rouge Parish	0.1
Alaska	0.1	Lucas County, OH	0.0	**Boise City, ID** (city) Ada County	0.1
Colorado	0.1	Luzerne County, PA	0.0	**Cedar Rapids, IA** (city) Linn County	0.1
Idaho	0.1	Macomb County, MI	0.0	**Chesapeake, VA** (independent city)	0.1
Indiana	0.1	Monroe County, NY	0.0	**Chula Vista, CA** (city) San Diego County	0.1

Note: (1) Ranking tables cover all states and counties, and places with an overall population of at least 125,000, OR an overall population of at least 25,000 where the Hispanic/Latino population is at least 20% of the overall population. In states where less than five places meet either of these criteria, we have included places with at least 10,000 total population with the highest percentage of Hispanic/Latino population. These places are identified with an asterisk (*); Please refer to the User's Guide for a full explanation of data.

Sorted by Percent of Hispanic Population in Descending Order — U.S. = 2.1%

State	Percent	County	Percent	Place	Percent
Rhode Island	14.4	Tuscarawas County, OH	39.1	**Carthage*, MO** (city) Jasper County	49.9
Alabama	7.7	Burke County, NC	37.1	**San Rafael, CA** (city) Marin County	34.1
Maryland	7.3	Caroline County, MD	36.0	**Spring Valley, NY** (village) Rockland County	34.1
South Dakota	7.3	Franklin County, AL	31.0	**Lake Worth, FL** (city) Palm Beach County	32.0
Delaware	7.1	Chattooga County, GA	30.9	**Trenton, NJ** (city) Mercer County	30.4
Virginia	5.3	Floyd County, GA	30.5	**Albertville*, AL** (city) Marshall County	29.5
Massachusetts	5.2	Leake County, MS	30.2	**Chattanooga, TN** (city) Hamilton County	28.5
Nebraska	5.1	Gilmer County, GA	29.4	**Stamford, CT** (city/town) Fairfield County	26.4
Tennessee	4.9	Martin County, FL	27.8	**Ramapo, NY** (town) Rockland County	23.5
District of Columbia	4.8	Jasper County, MO	27.2	**Central Falls*, RI** (city) Providence County	22.0

Sorted by Percent of Hispanic Population in Ascending Order — U.S. = 2.1%

State	Percent	County	Percent	Place	Percent
New Mexico	0.3	Cameron County, TX	0.1	**Corpus Christi, TX** (city) Nueces County	0.1
Hawaii	0.5	Doña Ana County, NM	0.1	**El Paso, TX** (city) El Paso County	0.1
Arizona	0.7	El Paso County, TX	0.1	**Laredo, TX** (city) Webb County	0.1
Colorado	0.7	Hidalgo County, TX	0.1	**McAllen, TX** (city) Hidalgo County	0.1
Idaho	0.7	Lubbock County, TX	0.1	**Chula Vista, CA** (city) San Diego County	0.2
Montana	0.7	Nueces County, TX	0.1	**Madera, CA** (city) Madera County	0.2
Texas	0.7	Webb County, TX	0.1	**Salinas, CA** (city) Monterey County	0.2
Wyoming	0.8	Yakima County, WA	0.1	**San Antonio, TX** (city) Bexar County	0.2
Wisconsin	0.9	Yuma County, AZ	0.1	**Albuquerque, NM** (city) Bernalillo County	0.3
North Dakota	1.0	Bexar County, TX	0.2	**Delano, CA** (city) Kern County	0.3

Note: (1) Ranking tables cover all states and counties, and places with an overall population of at least 125,000, OR an overall population of at least 25,000 where the Hispanic/Latino population is at least 20% of the overall population. In states where less than five places meet either of these criteria, we have included places with at least 10,000 total population with the highest percentage of Hispanic/Latino population. These places are identified with an asterisk (*); Please refer to the User's Guide for a full explanation of data.

Population

Central American: Honduran

Top 10 States, Counties, and Places[1]

Sorted by Number in Descending Order — U.S. = 633,401

State	Number	County	Number	Place	Number
Florida	107,302	Miami-Dade County, FL	54,192	**New York, NY** (city)	42,400
Texas	88,389	Harris County, TX	47,067	**Houston, TX** (city) Harris County	32,807
California	72,795	Los Angeles County, CA	42,901	**Los Angeles, CA** (city) Los Angeles County	23,919
New York	71,919	Bronx County, NY	17,990	**Miami, FL** (city) Miami-Dade County	23,209
New Jersey	36,556	Jefferson Parish, LA	17,056	**Bronx, NY** (borough) Bronx County	17,990
North Carolina	30,900	Broward County, FL	11,667	**Brooklyn, NY** (borough) Kings County	10,071
Louisiana	30,617	Fairfax County, VA	11,418	**Queens, NY** (borough) Queens County	8,546
Virginia	30,583	Dallas County, TX	11,384	**Hempstead (town), NY** (town) Nassau County	7,842
Georgia	20,577	Nassau County, NY	11,051	**Charlotte, NC** (city) Mecklenburg County	7,557
Maryland	20,576	Kings County, NY	10,071	**Dallas, TX** (city) Dallas County	6,890

Sorted by Number in Ascending Order — U.S. = 633,401

State	Number	County	Number	Place	Number
Vermont	109	Bartow County, GA	100	**Culver City, CA** (city) Los Angeles County	100
Wyoming	145	Ada County, ID	101	**Pflugerville, TX** (city) Travis County	100
South Dakota	221	Coffee County, AL	101	**Waco, TX** (city) McLennan County	100
Alaska	272	Hendricks County, IN	103	**Central Falls*, RI** (city) Providence County	101
Maine	280	Sumner County, TN	103	**Dalton, GA** (city) Whitfield County	101
West Virginia	333	Glynn County, GA	104	**Escondido, CA** (city) San Diego County	101
Hawaii	390	Kent County, DE	104	**Parker*, SC** (cdp) Greenville County	101
Idaho	461	Sarpy County, NE	104	**Rubidoux, CA** (cdp) Riverside County	101
New Hampshire	506	Bibb County, GA	105	**Whitney, NV** (cdp) Clark County	101
New Mexico	657	Charles County, MD	105	**Ossining, NY** (village) Westchester County	102

Sorted by Percent of Total Population in Descending Order — U.S. = 0.2%

State	Percent	County	Percent	Place	Percent
Louisiana	0.7	Jefferson Parish, LA	3.9	**Chelsea, MA** (city) Suffolk County	8.4
Florida	0.6	Duplin County, NC	3.8	**Kenner, LA** (city) Jefferson Parish	8.3
District of Columbia	0.4	Stewart County, GA	2.7	**Hempstead (village), NY** (village) Nassau County	7.0
Maryland	0.4	Miami-Dade County, FL	2.2	**Miami, FL** (city) Miami-Dade County	5.8
New Jersey	0.4	Frio County, TX	1.9	**Springfield, VA** (cdp) Fairfax County	5.8
New York	0.4	Saint Bernard Parish, LA	1.7	**West Little River, FL** (cdp) Miami-Dade County	5.5
Texas	0.4	Sampson County, NC	1.6	**Newburgh, NY** (city) Orange County	5.4
Virginia	0.4	Hudson County, NJ	1.4	**New Brunswick, NJ** (city) Middlesex County	5.0
North Carolina	0.3	Bronx County, NY	1.3	**Metairie, LA** (cdp) Jefferson Parish	4.1
California	0.2	Durham County, NC	1.3	**Huntington Station, NY** (cdp) Suffolk County	3.8

Sorted by Percent of Total Population in Ascending Order — U.S. = 0.2%

State	Percent	County	Percent	Place	Percent
Alaska	0.0	Ada County, ID	0.0	**Albuquerque, NM** (city) Bernalillo County	0.0
Hawaii	0.0	Albany County, NY	0.0	**El Paso, TX** (city) El Paso County	0.0
Idaho	0.0	Allegheny County, PA	0.0	**Milwaukee, WI** (city) Milwaukee County	0.0
Kentucky	0.0	Allen County, IN	0.0	**Amarillo, TX** (city) Potter County	0.1
Maine	0.0	Anoka County, MN	0.0	**Anchorage, AK** (municipality)	0.1
Michigan	0.0	Bernalillo County, NM	0.0	**Antioch, CA** (city) Contra Costa County	0.1
New Hampshire	0.0	Boulder County, CO	0.0	**Atlanta, GA** (city) Fulton County	0.1
New Mexico	0.0	Caddo Parish, LA	0.0	**Augusta-Richmond County, GA** (consolidated govt) Richmond County	0.1
Ohio	0.0	Chester County, PA	0.0	**Aurora, IL** (city) Kane County	0.1
Oregon	0.0	Clackamas County, OR	0.0	**Birmingham, AL** (city) Jefferson County	0.1

Note: (1) Ranking tables cover all states and counties, and places with an overall population of at least 125,000, OR an overall population of at least 25,000 where the Hispanic/Latino population is at least 20% of the overall population. In states where less than five places meet either of these criteria, we have included places with at least 10,000 total population with the highest percentage of Hispanic/Latino population. These places are identified with an asterisk (*); Please refer to the User's Guide for a full explanation of data.

Sorted by Percent of Hispanic Population in Descending Order — U.S. = 0.7%

State	Percent	County	Percent	Place	Percent
Louisiana	3.3	Monroe County, FL	6.9	**Fountainebleau, FL** (cdp) Miami-Dade County	12.3
Florida	3.2	Jefferson Parish, LA	6.6	**West Little River, FL** (cdp) Miami-Dade County	12.0
Maryland	1.7	Miami-Dade County, FL	6.5	**Daly City, CA** (city) San Mateo County	11.6
District of Columbia	1.6	San Francisco County, CA	6.2	**Miami, FL** (city) Miami-Dade County	10.2
Virginia	1.2	Orleans Parish, LA	5.4	**Miami Gardens, FL** (city) Miami-Dade County	9.0
Mississippi	0.9	Saint Charles Parish, LA	5.2	**Kenner, LA** (city) Jefferson Parish	8.8
California	0.7	San Mateo County, CA	4.8	**Metairie, LA** (cdp) Jefferson Parish	8.4
West Virginia	0.7	Saint Bernard Parish, LA	4.4	**Richmond West, FL** (cdp) Miami-Dade County	8.1
Georgia	0.6	Saint Tammany Parish, LA	3.5	**South San Francisco, CA** (city) San Mateo County	7.6
Nevada	0.6	Carroll County, GA	3.1	**Kendale Lakes, FL** (cdp) Miami-Dade County	7.3

Sorted by Percent of Hispanic Population in Ascending Order — U.S. = 0.7%

State	Percent	County	Percent	Place	Percent
Arizona	0.1	El Paso County, TX	0.0	**Albuquerque, NM** (city) Bernalillo County	0.1
Colorado	0.1	Hidalgo County, TX	0.0	**Brownsville, TX** (city) Cameron County	0.1
Idaho	0.1	Adams County, CO	0.1	**Cicero, IL** (town) Cook County	0.1
New Mexico	0.1	Bernalillo County, NM	0.1	**Denver, CO** (city) Denver County	0.1
Oklahoma	0.1	Bexar County, TX	0.1	**El Paso, TX** (city) El Paso County	0.1
Illinois	0.2	Cameron County, TX	0.1	**Fort Worth, TX** (city) Tarrant County	0.1
Kansas	0.2	Denver County, CO	0.1	**Fresno, CA** (city) Fresno County	0.1
Michigan	0.2	DuPage County, IL	0.1	**Oklahoma City, OK** (city) Oklahoma County	0.1
Nebraska	0.2	Fresno County, CA	0.1	**Oxnard, CA** (city) Ventura County	0.1
Oregon	0.2	Kane County, IL	0.1	**San Antonio, TX** (city) Bexar County	0.1

Note: (1) Ranking tables cover all states and counties, and places with an overall population of at least 125,000, OR an overall population of at least 25,000 where the Hispanic/Latino population is at least 20% of the overall population. In states where less than five places meet either of these criteria, we have included places with at least 10,000 total population with the highest percentage of Hispanic/Latino population. These places are identified with an asterisk (*); Please refer to the User's Guide for a full explanation of data.

Population

Central American: Panamanian

Top 10 States, Counties, and Places[1]

Sorted by Number in Descending Order — U.S. = 165,456

State	Number	County	Number	Place	Number
Florida	28,741	Kings County, NY	13,681	**New York, NY** (city)	22,353
New York	28,200	Miami-Dade County, FL	8,188	**Brooklyn, NY** (borough) Kings County	13,681
California	17,768	Los Angeles County, CA	5,402	**Queens, NY** (borough) Queens County	3,977
Texas	13,994	Broward County, FL	4,256	**Bronx, NY** (borough) Bronx County	2,372
Georgia	8,678	Queens County, NY	3,977	**Los Angeles, CA** (city) Los Angeles County	2,131
Virginia	7,180	Hillsborough County, FL	2,495	**Manhattan, NY** (borough) New York County	1,716
North Carolina	5,708	Orange County, FL	2,457	**San Antonio, TX** (city) Bexar County	1,602
New Jersey	5,431	Bronx County, NY	2,372	**Jacksonville, FL** (city) Duval County	1,165
Maryland	5,341	Bexar County, TX	2,357	**Hempstead (town), NY** (town) Nassau County	1,163
Pennsylvania	3,234	Harris County, TX	2,327	**Fayetteville, NC** (city) Cumberland County	1,154

Sorted by Number in Ascending Order — U.S. = 165,456

State	Number	County	Number	Place	Number
North Dakota	100	Jones County, MS	100	**Anaheim, CA** (city) Orange County	100
Montana	131	Kane County, IL	100	**Aspen Hill, MD** (cdp) Montgomery County	100
Maine	141	Macomb County, MI	100	**Gaithersburg, MD** (city) Montgomery County	100
New Hampshire	214	Citrus County, FL	101	**Hayward, CA** (city) Alameda County	100
Idaho	223	Lexington County, SC	101	**Meadow Woods, FL** (cdp) Orange County	100
West Virginia	261	James City County, VA	102	**Rancho Cucamonga, CA** (city) San Bernardino County	100
Rhode Island	359	Pinal County, AZ	102	**North Miami Beach, FL** (city) Miami-Dade County	101
Nebraska	398	Butler County, OH	103	**Ontario, CA** (city) San Bernardino County	102
Iowa	413	Dakota County, MN	104	**McKinney, TX** (city) Collin County	106
Alaska	446	Knox County, TN	106	**Victorville, CA** (city) San Bernardino County	106

Sorted by Percent of Total Population in Descending Order — U.S. = 0.1%

State	Percent	County	Percent	Place	Percent
Florida	0.2	Cumberland County, NC	0.5	**Doral, FL** (city) Miami-Dade County	0.8
Alaska	0.1	Kings County, NY	0.5	**Killeen, TX** (city) Bell County	0.8
Delaware	0.1	Liberty County, GA	0.5	**Fayetteville, NC** (city) Cumberland County	0.6
District of Columbia	0.1	Bell County, TX	0.4	**Miramar, FL** (city) Broward County	0.6
Georgia	0.1	Geary County, KS	0.4	**Richmond West, FL** (cdp) Miami-Dade County	0.6
Maryland	0.1	Hoke County, NC	0.4	**The Hammocks, FL** (cdp) Miami-Dade County	0.6
Nevada	0.1	Montgomery County, TN	0.4	**Brooklyn, NY** (borough) Kings County	0.5
New Jersey	0.1	Muscogee County, GA	0.4	**Country Club, FL** (cdp) Miami-Dade County	0.5
New York	0.1	Clayton County, GA	0.3	**Cutler Bay, FL** (town) Miami-Dade County	0.5
North Carolina	0.1	Coryell County, TX	0.3	**Fontainebleau, FL** (cdp) Miami-Dade County	0.5

Sorted by Percent of Total Population in Ascending Order — U.S. = 0.1%

State	Percent	County	Percent	Place	Percent
Alabama	0.0	Adams County, CO	0.0	**Anaheim, CA** (city) Orange County	0.0
Arizona	0.0	Albany County, NY	0.0	**Baltimore, MD** (independent city)	0.0
Arkansas	0.0	Allegheny County, PA	0.0	**Chicago, IL** (city) Cook County	0.0
California	0.0	Atlantic County, NJ	0.0	**Columbus, OH** (city) Franklin County	0.0
Colorado	0.0	Bergen County, NJ	0.0	**Corpus Christi, TX** (city) Nueces County	0.0
Connecticut	0.0	Berks County, PA	0.0	**Dallas, TX** (city) Dallas County	0.0
Hawaii	0.0	Brazoria County, TX	0.0	**Denver, CO** (city) Denver County	0.0
Idaho	0.0	Bucks County, PA	0.0	**Detroit, MI** (city) Wayne County	0.0
Illinois	0.0	Butler County, OH	0.0	**Fresno, CA** (city) Fresno County	0.0
Indiana	0.0	Charleston County, SC	0.0	**Garland, TX** (city) Dallas County	0.0

Note: (1) Ranking tables cover all states and counties, and places with an overall population of at least 125,000, OR an overall population of at least 25,000 where the Hispanic/Latino population is at least 20% of the overall population. In states where less than five places meet either of these criteria, we have included places with at least 10,000 total population with the highest percentage of Hispanic/Latino population. These places are identified with an asterisk (*); Please refer to the User's Guide for a full explanation of data.

Sorted by Percent of Hispanic Population in Descending Order — U.S. = 0.3%

State	Percent	County	Percent	Place	Percent
District of Columbia	1.4	Muscogee County, GA	5.7	**Columbus, GA** (city) Muscogee County	5.7
West Virginia	1.2	Cumberland County, NC	5.3	**Fayetteville, NC** (city) Cumberland County	5.7
Alaska	1.1	Liberty County, GA	5.2	**Hampton, VA** (independent city)	5.1
Maryland	1.1	Richmond County, GA	4.8	**Augusta-Richmond County, GA** (consolidated govt) Richmond County	4.8
Virginia	1.1	Montgomery County, TN	4.5	**Clarksville, TN** (city) Montgomery County	4.8
Georgia	1.0	Dale County, AL	4.4	**Newport News, VA** (independent city)	4.5
South Carolina	0.9	Columbia County, GA	4.1	**Killeen, TX** (city) Bell County	3.4
Alabama	0.8	Hardin County, KY	3.9	**Brooklyn, NY** (borough) Kings County	2.8
Kentucky	0.8	Richland County, SC	3.7	**Chesapeake, VA** (independent city)	2.8
Maine	0.8	James City County, VA	3.4	**Savannah, GA** (city) Chatham County	2.6

Sorted by Percent of Hispanic Population in Ascending Order — U.S. = 0.3%

State	Percent	County	Percent	Place	Percent
Arizona	0.1	Fresno County, CA	0.0	**Fresno, CA** (city) Fresno County	0.0
California	0.1	Hidalgo County, TX	0.0	**Albuquerque, NM** (city) Bernalillo County	0.1
Idaho	0.1	Kern County, CA	0.0	**Anaheim, CA** (city) Orange County	0.1
Illinois	0.1	Adams County, CO	0.1	**Chicago, IL** (city) Cook County	0.1
New Mexico	0.1	Bernalillo County, NM	0.1	**Chula Vista, CA** (city) San Diego County	0.1
Texas	0.1	Brazoria County, TX	0.1	**Corpus Christi, TX** (city) Nueces County	0.1
Utah	0.1	Cook County, IL	0.1	**Dallas, TX** (city) Dallas County	0.1
Colorado	0.2	Dallas County, TX	0.1	**Denver, CO** (city) Denver County	0.1
Nebraska	0.2	Denver County, CO	0.1	**El Paso, TX** (city) El Paso County	0.1
Nevada	0.2	El Paso County, TX	0.1	**Fontana, CA** (city) San Bernardino County	0.1

Note: (1) Ranking tables cover all states and counties, and places with an overall population of at least 125,000, OR an overall population of at least 25,000 where the Hispanic/Latino population is at least 20% of the overall population. In states where less than five places meet either of these criteria, we have included places with at least 10,000 total population with the highest percentage of Hispanic/Latino population. These places are identified with an asterisk (*); Please refer to the User's Guide for a full explanation of data.

Population

Central American: Salvadoran

Top 10 States, Counties, and Places[1]

Sorted by Number in Descending Order — U.S. = 1,648,968

State	Number	County	Number	Place	Number
California	573,956	Los Angeles County, CA	358,825	**Los Angeles, CA** (city) Los Angeles County	228,990
Texas	222,599	Harris County, TX	123,049	**Houston, TX** (city) Harris County	75,907
New York	152,130	Montgomery County, MD	52,615	**New York, NY** (city)	38,559
Virginia	123,800	Suffolk County, NY	52,315	**Hempstead (town), NY** (town) Nassau County	32,681
Maryland	123,789	Prince George's County, MD	47,355	**Islip, NY** (town) Suffolk County	29,849
New Jersey	56,532	Nassau County, NY	47,180	**Queens, NY** (borough) Queens County	21,342
Florida	55,144	Fairfax County, VA	43,566	**San Francisco, CA** (city) San Francisco County	16,165
Massachusetts	43,400	Dallas County, TX	42,345	**Brentwood, NY** (cdp) Suffolk County	15,946
North Carolina	37,778	Prince William County, VA	27,269	**Dallas, TX** (city) Dallas County	15,696
Georgia	32,107	San Bernardino County, CA	25,056	**Irving, TX** (city) Dallas County	12,544

Sorted by Number in Ascending Order — U.S. = 1,648,968

State	Number	County	Number	Place	Number
Vermont	116	Craighead County, AR	100	**Rockford, IL** (city) Winnebago County	100
Montana	140	Loudon County, TN	100	**Commerce City, CO** (city) Adams County	101
Wyoming	198	Houston County, GA	101	**Mobile, AL** (city) Mobile County	101
Maine	618	Wicomico County, MD	101	**Middletown, NY** (city) Orange County	104
South Dakota	780	Onondaga County, NY	102	**North Chicago, IL** (city) Lake County	104
Hawaii	801	Orange County, VA	102	**Porterville, CA** (city) Tulare County	104
New Hampshire	823	Doña Ana County, NM	103	**Birmingham, AL** (city) Jefferson County	106
West Virginia	893	Nevada County, CA	103	**Clarksville, TN** (city) Montgomery County	106
Alaska	938	Titus County, TX	103	**Joliet, IL** (city) Will County	109
Idaho	1,159	Monroe County, FL	105	**Abilene, TX** (city) Taylor County	111

Sorted by Percent of Total Population in Descending Order — U.S. = 0.5%

State	Percent	County	Percent	Place	Percent
District of Columbia	2.8	Prince William County, VA	6.8	**Brentwood, NY** (cdp) Suffolk County	26.3
Maryland	2.1	Nantucket County, MA	5.5	**Chillum, MD** (cdp) Prince George's County	21.8
California	1.5	Prince George's County, MD	5.5	**Hempstead (village), NY** (village) Nassau County	19.9
Virginia	1.5	Montgomery County, MD	5.4	**Central Islip, NY** (cdp) Suffolk County	18.5
Nevada	1.1	Fairfax County, VA	4.0	**Wheaton, MD** (cdp) Montgomery County	18.5
Texas	0.9	Los Angeles County, CA	3.7	**Chelsea, MA** (city) Suffolk County	18.2
New York	0.8	Crawford County, IA	3.6	**Marumsco, VA** (cdp) Prince William County	17.9
Massachusetts	0.7	Nassau County, NY	3.5	**Huntington Station, NY** (cdp) Suffolk County	15.8
New Jersey	0.6	Suffolk County, NY	3.5	**Sterling, VA** (cdp) Loudoun County	14.0
Arkansas	0.5	Arlington County, VA	3.4	**Dale City, VA** (cdp) Prince William County	10.7

Sorted by Percent of Total Population in Ascending Order — U.S. = 0.5%

State	Percent	County	Percent	Place	Percent
Maine	0.0	Allegheny County, PA	0.0	**Birmingham, AL** (city) Jefferson County	0.0
Michigan	0.0	Chester County, PA	0.0	**Cincinnati, OH** (city) Hamilton County	0.0
Mississippi	0.0	Cumberland County, PA	0.0	**Saint Louis, MO** (independent city)	0.0
Montana	0.0	Dane County, WI	0.0	**Urban Honolulu, HI** (cdp) Honolulu County	0.0
Ohio	0.0	Dauphin County, PA	0.0	**Abilene, TX** (city) Taylor County	0.1
Vermont	0.0	Delaware County, PA	0.0	**Albuquerque, NM** (city) Bernalillo County	0.1
West Virginia	0.0	Doña Ana County, NM	0.0	**Amarillo, TX** (city) Potter County	0.1
Wisconsin	0.0	Erie County, NY	0.0	**Atlanta, GA** (city) Fulton County	0.1
Wyoming	0.0	Erie County, PA	0.0	**Aurora, IL** (city) Kane County	0.1
Alabama	0.1	Gloucester County, NJ	0.0	**Boise City, ID** (city) Ada County	0.1

Note: (1) Ranking tables cover all states and counties, and places with an overall population of at least 125,000, OR an overall population of at least 25,000 where the Hispanic/Latino population is at least 20% of the overall population. In states where less than five places meet either of these criteria, we have included places with at least 10,000 total population with the highest percentage of Hispanic/Latino population. These places are identified with an asterisk (*); Please refer to the User's Guide for a full explanation of data.

Sorted by Percent of Hispanic Population in Descending Order — U.S. = 3.3%

State	Percent	County	Percent	Place	Percent
District of Columbia	30.3	Nantucket County, MA	58.4	**Chillum, MD** (cdp) Prince George's County	51.9
Maryland	26.3	Saline County, MO	41.3	**Hempstead (village), NY** (village) Nassau County	44.9
Virginia	19.6	Prince George's County, MD	36.7	**Everett, MA** (city) Middlesex County	44.3
Arkansas	8.1	Prince William County, VA	33.5	**Wheaton, MD** (cdp) Montgomery County	44.2
Massachusetts	6.9	Dubois County, IN	32.6	**Marumsco, VA** (cdp) Prince William County	43.6
North Carolina	4.7	Montgomery County, MD	31.8	**Huntington Station, NY** (cdp) Suffolk County	43.2
New York	4.5	Crawford County, AR	27.7	**Sterling, VA** (cdp) Loudoun County	42.3
Nevada	4.2	Loudoun County, VA	27.1	**Dale City, VA** (cdp) Prince William County	39.9
California	4.1	Fairfax County, VA	25.9	**Brentwood, NY** (cdp) Suffolk County	38.4
West Virginia	4.0	Nassau County, NY	24.2	**Silver Spring, MD** (cdp) Montgomery County	37.9

Sorted by Percent of Hispanic Population in Ascending Order — U.S. = 3.3%

State	Percent	County	Percent	Place	Percent
New Mexico	0.2	Doña Ana County, NM	0.1	**Brownsville, TX** (city) Cameron County	0.1
Wyoming	0.4	El Paso County, TX	0.1	**El Paso, TX** (city) El Paso County	0.1
Montana	0.5	Hidalgo County, TX	0.1	**Laredo, TX** (city) Webb County	0.1
Arizona	0.6	Webb County, TX	0.1	**Corpus Christi, TX** (city) Nueces County	0.2
Wisconsin	0.6	Cameron County, TX	0.2	**Lubbock, TX** (city) Lubbock County	0.2
Hawaii	0.7	Lubbock County, TX	0.2	**McAllen, TX** (city) Hidalgo County	0.2
Idaho	0.7	Nueces County, TX	0.2	**Albuquerque, NM** (city) Bernalillo County	0.3
Illinois	0.7	Bernalillo County, NM	0.3	**Chula Vista, CA** (city) San Diego County	0.3
Michigan	0.8	Imperial County, CA	0.3	**Harlingen, TX** (city) Cameron County	0.3
Oklahoma	0.8	Midland County, TX	0.3	**Joliet, IL** (city) Will County	0.3

Note: (1) Ranking tables cover all states and counties, and places with an overall population of at least 125,000, OR an overall population of at least 25,000 where the Hispanic/Latino population is at least 20% of the overall population. In states where less than five places meet either of these criteria, we have included places with at least 10,000 total population with the highest percentage of Hispanic/Latino population. These places are identified with an asterisk (*); Please refer to the User's Guide for a full explanation of data.

Population

Cuban

Top 10 States, Counties, and Places[1]

Sorted by Number in Descending Order — U.S. = 1,785,547

State	Number	County	Number	Place	Number
Florida	1,213,438	Miami-Dade County, FL	856,007	**Hialeah, FL** (city) Miami-Dade County	164,717
California	88,607	Broward County, FL	83,713	**Miami, FL** (city) Miami-Dade County	137,301
New Jersey	83,362	Hillsborough County, FL	65,451	**New York, NY** (city)	40,840
New York	70,803	Palm Beach County, FL	43,038	**Tamiami, FL** (cdp) Miami-Dade County	36,180
Texas	46,541	Los Angeles County, CA	41,350	**Kendale Lakes, FL** (cdp) Miami-Dade County	29,095
Georgia	25,048	Hudson County, NJ	28,652	**Fountainebleau, FL** (cdp) Miami-Dade County	27,798
Illinois	22,541	Orange County, FL	22,528	**Kendall, FL** (cdp) Miami-Dade County	24,533
Nevada	21,459	Clark County, NV	20,569	**Westchester, FL** (cdp) Miami-Dade County	21,391
North Carolina	18,079	Lee County, FL	20,253	**Tampa, FL** (city) Hillsborough County	21,295
Pennsylvania	17,930	Collier County, FL	17,179	**Pembroke Pines, FL** (city) Broward County	19,826

Sorted by Number in Ascending Order — U.S. = 1,785,547

State	Number	County	Number	Place	Number
North Dakota	260	Chautauqua County, NY	101	**Camarillo, CA** (city) Ventura County	100
South Dakota	265	Jackson County, OR	101	**Stanton, CA** (city) Orange County	100
Wyoming	275	Hanover County, VA	102	**Birmingham, AL** (city) Jefferson County	101
Montana	421	Saint Louis County, MN	102	**Galveston, TX** (city) Galveston County	101
Vermont	510	Kenton County, KY	103	**La Porte, TX** (city) Harris County	101
West Virginia	764	Spalding County, GA	103	**Pennsauken, NJ** (township) Camden County	101
Maine	783	Bradley County, TN	104	**Goodyear, AZ** (city) Maricopa County	102
Idaho	825	Gadsden County, FL	104	**Greeley, CO** (city) Weld County	103
Alaska	927	Haywood County, NC	104	**Long Branch, NJ** (city) Monmouth County	103
Iowa	1,226	Madison County, IL	104	**Baytown, TX** (city) Harris County	104

Sorted by Percent of Total Population in Descending Order — U.S. = 0.6%

State	Percent	County	Percent	Place	Percent
Florida	6.5	Miami-Dade County, FL	34.3	**Hialeah, FL** (city) Miami-Dade County	73.3
New Jersey	0.9	Monroe County, FL	11.3	**Westchester, FL** (cdp) Miami-Dade County	71.6
Nevada	0.8	Hendry County, FL	7.0	**Tamiami, FL** (cdp) Miami-Dade County	65.5
New York	0.4	Collier County, FL	5.3	**University Park, FL** (cdp) Miami-Dade County	63.5
Connecticut	0.3	Hillsborough County, FL	5.3	**Miami Lakes, FL** (town) Miami-Dade County	57.1
District of Columbia	0.3	Broward County, FL	4.8	**Kendale Lakes, FL** (cdp) Miami-Dade County	51.8
Georgia	0.3	Hudson County, NJ	4.5	**Fountainebleau, FL** (cdp) Miami-Dade County	46.5
Arizona	0.2	Lee County, FL	3.3	**Kendall West, FL** (cdp) Miami-Dade County	44.6
California	0.2	Palm Beach County, FL	3.3	**Richmond West, FL** (cdp) Miami-Dade County	40.1
Delaware	0.2	Union County, NJ	2.1	**South Miami Heights, FL** (cdp) Miami-Dade County	37.7

Sorted by Percent of Total Population in Ascending Order — U.S. = 0.6%

State	Percent	County	Percent	Place	Percent
Iowa	0.0	Anoka County, MN	0.0	**Birmingham, AL** (city) Jefferson County	0.0
Montana	0.0	Davis County, UT	0.0	**Abilene, TX** (city) Taylor County	0.1
North Dakota	0.0	Jackson County, OR	0.0	**Akron, OH** (city) Summit County	0.1
South Dakota	0.0	Lake County, OH	0.0	**Amarillo, TX** (city) Potter County	0.1
West Virginia	0.0	Madison County, IL	0.0	**Arlington, TX** (city) Tarrant County	0.1
Wyoming	0.0	Stark County, OH	0.0	**Augusta-Richmond County, GA** (consolidated govt) Richmond County	0.1
Alabama	0.1	Weber County, UT	0.0	**Bakersfield, CA** (city) Kern County	0.1
Alaska	0.1	Westmoreland County, PA	0.0	**Baltimore, MD** (independent city)	0.1
Arkansas	0.1	Yakima County, WA	0.0	**Baytown, TX** (city) Harris County	0.1
Colorado	0.1	Ada County, ID	0.1	**Boise City, ID** (city) Ada County	0.1

Note: (1) Ranking tables cover all states and counties, and places with an overall population of at least 125,000, OR an overall population of at least 25,000 where the Hispanic/Latino population is at least 20% of the overall population. In states where less than five places meet either of these criteria, we have included places with at least 10,000 total population with the highest percentage of Hispanic/Latino population. These places are identified with an asterisk (*); Please refer to the User's Guide for a full explanation of data.

Sorted by Percent of Hispanic Population in Descending Order U.S. = 3.5%

State	Percent	County	Percent	Place	Percent
Florida	28.7	Monroe County, FL	55.0	**Westchester, FL** (cdp) Miami-Dade County	78.6
Kentucky	7.0	Miami-Dade County, FL	52.7	**Hialeah, FL** (city) Miami-Dade County	77.4
Vermont	5.5	Jefferson County, KY	21.9	**University Park, FL** (cdp) Miami-Dade County	74.8
Louisiana	5.4	Hillsborough County, FL	21.3	**Tamiami, FL** (cdp) Miami-Dade County	70.6
New Jersey	5.4	Alachua County, FL	20.8	**Miami Lakes, FL** (town) Miami-Dade County	70.3
Maine	4.6	Collier County, FL	20.7	**Kendale Lakes, FL** (cdp) Miami-Dade County	59.9
New Hampshire	3.7	Broward County, FL	19.1	**Coral Gables, FL** (city) Miami-Dade County	58.5
West Virginia	3.4	Leon County, FL	18.7	**South Miami Heights, FL** (cdp) Miami-Dade County	55.5
District of Columbia	3.3	Union County, FL	18.2	**Kendall, FL** (cdp) Miami-Dade County	51.1
Nevada	3.0	Lee County, FL	17.9	**Richmond West, FL** (cdp) Miami-Dade County	51.0

Sorted by Percent of Hispanic Population in Ascending Order U.S. = 3.5%

State	Percent	County	Percent	Place	Percent
Idaho	0.5	Cameron County, TX	0.1	**Brownsville, TX** (city) Cameron County	0.1
New Mexico	0.5	Doña Ana County, NM	0.1	**East Los Angeles, CA** (cdp) Los Angeles County	0.1
Texas	0.5	El Paso County, TX	0.1	**El Paso, TX** (city) El Paso County	0.1
Utah	0.5	Fresno County, CA	0.1	**Laredo, TX** (city) Webb County	0.1
Wyoming	0.5	Hidalgo County, TX	0.1	**Oxnard, CA** (city) Ventura County	0.1
Arizona	0.6	Imperial County, CA	0.1	**Cicero, IL** (town) Cook County	0.2
California	0.6	Merced County, CA	0.1	**Escondido, CA** (city) San Diego County	0.2
Colorado	0.6	Tulare County, CA	0.1	**Fresno, CA** (city) Fresno County	0.2
Arkansas	0.8	Webb County, TX	0.1	**Las Cruces, NM** (city) Dona Ana County	0.2
Iowa	0.8	Yakima County, WA	0.1	**Lynwood, CA** (city) Los Angeles County	0.2

Note: (1) Ranking tables cover all states and counties, and places with an overall population of at least 125,000, OR an overall population of at least 25,000 where the Hispanic/Latino population is at least 20% of the overall population. In states where less than five places meet either of these criteria, we have included places with at least 10,000 total population with the highest percentage of Hispanic/Latino population. These places are identified with an asterisk (*); Please refer to the User's Guide for a full explanation of data.

Population

Dominican Republic

Top 10 States, Counties, and Places[1]

Sorted by Number in Descending Order — U.S. = 1,414,703

State	Number	County	Number	Place	Number
New York	674,787	Bronx County, NY	240,987	**New York, NY** (city)	576,701
New Jersey	197,922	New York County, NY	155,971	**Bronx, NY** (borough) Bronx County	240,987
Florida	172,451	Queens County, NY	88,061	**Manhattan, NY** (borough) New York County	155,971
Massachusetts	103,292	Kings County, NY	86,764	**Queens, NY** (borough) Queens County	88,061
Pennsylvania	62,348	Miami-Dade County, FL	57,999	**Brooklyn, NY** (borough) Kings County	86,764
Rhode Island	35,008	Essex County, MA	53,520	**Lawrence, MA** (city) Essex County	30,243
Connecticut	26,093	Passaic County, NJ	47,433	**Paterson, NJ** (city) Passaic County	27,426
North Carolina	15,225	Hudson County, NJ	41,174	**Boston, MA** (city) Suffolk County	25,648
Georgia	14,941	Providence County, RI	33,551	**Providence, RI** (city) Providence County	25,267
Maryland	14,873	Broward County, FL	27,775	**Hempstead (town), NY** (town) Nassau County	16,914

Sorted by Number in Ascending Order — U.S. = 1,414,703

State	Number	County	Number	Place	Number
Idaho	185	Chemung County, NY	100	**Lewisville, TX** (city) Denton County	101
Vermont	282	Fairfield County, OH	101	**Manassas, VA** (independent city)	101
Nebraska	358	Northumberland County, PA	101	**Tacoma, WA** (city) Pierce County	101
West Virginia	363	Harnett County, NC	102	**Beloit*, WI** (city) Rock County	103
Arkansas	384	Merrimack County, NH	102	**McKinney, TX** (city) Collin County	103
Iowa	429	Washington County, OR	102	**Pasadena, TX** (city) Harris County	103
New Mexico	492	Ingham County, MI	103	**Waukegan, IL** (city) Lake County	103
Oregon	574	Christian County, KY	105	**Huntsville, AL** (city) Madison County	104
Hawaii	600	Sedgwick County, KS	105	**Garland, TX** (city) Dallas County	105
Maine	610	Jefferson County, CO	106	**Salt Lake City, UT** (city) Salt Lake County	105

Sorted by Percent of Total Population in Descending Order — U.S. = 0.5%

State	Percent	County	Percent	Place	Percent
New York	3.5	Bronx County, NY	17.4	**Lawrence, MA** (city) Essex County	39.6
Rhode Island	3.3	New York County, NY	9.8	**Perth Amboy, NJ** (city) Middlesex County	29.1
New Jersey	2.3	Passaic County, NJ	9.5	**Hazleton, PA** (city) Luzerne County	21.0
Massachusetts	1.6	Essex County, MA	7.2	**Paterson, NJ** (city) Passaic County	18.8
Florida	0.9	Hudson County, NJ	6.5	**Passaic, NJ** (city) Passaic County	17.7
Connecticut	0.7	Providence County, RI	5.4	**Bronx, NY** (borough) Bronx County	17.4
Pennsylvania	0.5	Queens County, NY	3.9	**Haverstraw, NY** (town) Rockland County	17.1
District of Columbia	0.4	Osceola County, FL	3.8	**Union City, NJ** (city) Hudson County	15.1
Alaska	0.3	Suffolk County, MA	3.8	**Providence, RI** (city) Providence County	14.2
Maryland	0.3	Kings County, NY	3.5	**Freeport, NY** (village) Nassau County	12.9

Sorted by Percent of Total Population in Ascending Order — U.S. = 0.5%

State	Percent	County	Percent	Place	Percent
Alabama	0.0	Adams County, CO	0.0	**Albuquerque, NM** (city) Bernalillo County	0.0
Arizona	0.0	Alameda County, CA	0.0	**Anaheim, CA** (city) Orange County	0.0
Arkansas	0.0	Allegheny County, PA	0.0	**Austin, TX** (city) Travis County	0.0
California	0.0	Bernalillo County, NM	0.0	**Cincinnati, OH** (city) Hamilton County	0.0
Colorado	0.0	Brazoria County, TX	0.0	**Dallas, TX** (city) Dallas County	0.0
Hawaii	0.0	Cameron County, TX	0.0	**Denver, CO** (city) Denver County	0.0
Idaho	0.0	Contra Costa County, CA	0.0	**Garland, TX** (city) Dallas County	0.0
Illinois	0.0	Dakota County, MN	0.0	**Long Beach, CA** (city) Los Angeles County	0.0
Indiana	0.0	Dane County, WI	0.0	**Los Angeles, CA** (city) Los Angeles County	0.0
Iowa	0.0	Denver County, CO	0.0	**Louisville-Jefferson County, KY** (metropolitan govt) Jefferson County	0.0

RANKINGS & COMPARISONS

Note: (1) Ranking tables cover all states and counties, and places with an overall population of at least 125,000, OR an overall population of at least 25,000 where the Hispanic/Latino population is at least 20% of the overall population. In states where less than five places meet either of these criteria, we have included places with at least 10,000 total population with the highest percentage of Hispanic/Latino population. These places are identified with an asterisk (*); Please refer to the User's Guide for a full explanation of data.

Sorted by Percent of Hispanic Population in Descending Order — U.S. = 2.8%

State	Percent	County	Percent	Place	Percent
Rhode Island	26.8	Essex County, MA	43.6	**Hazleton, PA** (city) Luzerne County	56.3
New York	19.7	New York County, NY	38.6	**Lawrence, MA** (city) Essex County	53.7
Massachusetts	16.5	Luzerne County, PA	35.9	**Haverstraw, NY** (town) Rockland County	41.8
New Jersey	12.7	Bronx County, NY	32.5	**Manhattan, NY** (borough) New York County	38.6
New Hampshire	12.2	Providence County, RI	28.5	**Perth Amboy, NJ** (city) Middlesex County	37.2
Pennsylvania	8.7	Passaic County, NJ	25.5	**Providence, RI** (city) Providence County	37.2
Connecticut	5.4	Suffolk County, MA	18.9	**Cranston*, RI** (city) Providence County	34.5
Alaska	4.9	Clearfield County, PA	18.7	**Lynn, MA** (city) Essex County	32.8
District of Columbia	4.6	Rockland County, NY	18.7	**Paterson, NJ** (city) Passaic County	32.6
Florida	4.1	Middlesex County, NJ	18.3	**Bronx, NY** (borough) Bronx County	32.5

Sorted by Percent of Hispanic Population in Ascending Order — U.S. = 2.8%

State	Percent	County	Percent	Place	Percent
California	0.1	Cameron County, TX	0.0	**Albuquerque, NM** (city) Bernalillo County	0.1
Idaho	0.1	Fresno County, CA	0.0	**Anaheim, CA** (city) Orange County	0.1
New Mexico	0.1	Kern County, CA	0.0	**Aurora, IL** (city) Kane County	0.1
Oregon	0.1	Adams County, CO	0.1	**Austin, TX** (city) Travis County	0.1
Texas	0.1	Alameda County, CA	0.1	**Chula Vista, CA** (city) San Diego County	0.1
Arizona	0.2	Bernalillo County, NM	0.1	**Dallas, TX** (city) Dallas County	0.1
Arkansas	0.2	Bexar County, TX	0.1	**Denver, CO** (city) Denver County	0.1
Colorado	0.2	Brazoria County, TX	0.1	**El Paso, TX** (city) El Paso County	0.1
Nebraska	0.2	Contra Costa County, CA	0.1	**Garland, TX** (city) Dallas County	0.1
Oklahoma	0.2	Dallas County, TX	0.1	**Long Beach, CA** (city) Los Angeles County	0.1

Note: (1) Ranking tables cover all states and counties, and places with an overall population of at least 125,000, OR an overall population of at least 25,000 where the Hispanic/Latino population is at least 20% of the overall population. In states where less than five places meet either of these criteria, we have included places with at least 10,000 total population with the highest percentage of Hispanic/Latino population. These places are identified with an asterisk (*); Please refer to the User's Guide for a full explanation of data.

Population

Mexican

Top 10 States, Counties, and Places[1]

Sorted by Number in Descending Order — U.S. = 31,798,258

State	Number	County	Number	Place	Number
California	11,423,146	Los Angeles County, CA	3,510,677	**Los Angeles, CA** (city) Los Angeles County	1,209,573
Texas	7,951,193	Harris County, TX	1,250,401	**San Antonio, TX** (city) Bexar County	705,530
Arizona	1,657,668	Maricopa County, AZ	975,622	**Houston, TX** (city) Harris County	673,093
Illinois	1,602,403	Cook County, IL	961,963	**Chicago, IL** (city) Cook County	578,100
Colorado	757,181	San Diego County, CA	869,868	**Phoenix, AZ** (city) Maricopa County	519,635
Florida	629,718	Riverside County, CA	865,117	**El Paso, TX** (city) El Paso County	486,186
Washington	601,768	Orange County, CA	858,068	**Dallas, TX** (city) Dallas County	439,460
New Mexico	590,890	San Bernardino County, CA	848,541	**San Diego, CA** (city) San Diego County	325,812
Nevada	540,978	Bexar County, TX	843,619	**New York, NY** (city)	319,263
Georgia	519,502	Dallas County, TX	762,168	**San Jose, CA** (city) Santa Clara County	268,538

Sorted by Number in Ascending Order — U.S. = 31,798,258

State	Number	County	Number	Place	Number
Vermont	2,534	Cedar County, NE	100	**Waterville*, ME** (city) Kennebec County	101
Maine	5,134	Claiborne Parish, LA	100	**Beckley*, WV** (city) Raleigh County	111
New Hampshire	7,822	Holmes County, OH	100	**Hanover*, NH** (town) Grafton County	111
District of Columbia	8,507	Rolette County, ND	100	**South Portland*, ME** (city) Cumberland County	122
Rhode Island	9,090	Trigg County, KY	100	**Derry*, NH** (cdp) Rockingham County	124
North Dakota	9,223	Butler County, AL	101	**Holyoke, MA** (city) Hampden County	167
West Virginia	9,704	Nemaha County, NE	102	**Spearfish*, SD** (city) Lawrence County	209
South Dakota	13,839	Terrell County, GA	102	**Cooper City, FL** (city) Broward County	212
Montana	20,048	Wabash County, IL	102	**Williston*, ND** (city) Williams County	213
Alaska	21,642	Wilkin County, MN	102	**Brunswick*, ME** (town) Cumberland County	215

Sorted by Percent of Total Population in Descending Order — U.S. = 10.3%

State	Percent	County	Percent	Place	Percent
Texas	31.6	Maverick County, TX	92.3	**San Luis, AZ** (city) Yuma County	96.2
California	30.7	Starr County, TX	92.3	**Calexico, CA** (city) Imperial County	94.5
New Mexico	28.7	Zapata County, TX	88.1	**San Juan, TX** (city) Hidalgo County	92.4
Arizona	25.9	Webb County, TX	87.1	**Coachella, CA** (city) Riverside County	91.6
Nevada	20.0	Zavala County, TX	85.8	**Socorro, TX** (city) El Paso County	90.6
Colorado	15.1	Hidalgo County, TX	85.3	**Eagle Pass, TX** (city) Maverick County	89.8
Illinois	12.5	Jim Hogg County, TX	81.3	**East Los Angeles, CA** (cdp) Los Angeles County	88.1
Oregon	9.7	Cameron County, TX	80.5	**Pharr, TX** (city) Hidalgo County	87.1
Idaho	9.5	Presidio County, TX	79.5	**Laredo, TX** (city) Webb County	86.9
Utah	9.4	Santa Cruz County, AZ	78.1	**Brownsville, TX** (city) Cameron County	86.2

Sorted by Percent of Total Population in Ascending Order — U.S. = 10.3%

State	Percent	County	Percent	Place	Percent
Maine	0.4	Armstrong County, PA	0.2	**Holyoke, MA** (city) Hampden County	0.4
Vermont	0.4	Aroostook County, ME	0.2	**Miami Gardens, FL** (city) Miami-Dade County	0.4
West Virginia	0.5	Belmont County, OH	0.2	**Babylon, NY** (town) Suffolk County	0.5
Massachusetts	0.6	Carroll County, NH	0.2	**Buffalo, NY** (city) Erie County	0.5
New Hampshire	0.6	Fulton County, NY	0.2	**Burlington*, VT** (city) Chittenden County	0.5
Rhode Island	0.9	Holmes County, OH	0.2	**Oyster Bay, NY** (town) Nassau County	0.5
Pennsylvania	1.0	Jefferson County, PA	0.2	**South Portland*, ME** (city) Cumberland County	0.5
Connecticut	1.4	Rutland County, VT	0.2	**Beckley*, WV** (city) Raleigh County	0.6
District of Columbia	1.4	Bedford County, PA	0.3	**Cranston*, RI** (city) Providence County	0.6
North Dakota	1.4	Belknap County, NH	0.3	**Derry*, NH** (cdp) Rockingham County	0.6

RANKINGS & COMPARISONS

Note: (1) Ranking tables cover all states and counties, and places with an overall population of at least 125,000, OR an overall population of at least 25,000 where the Hispanic/Latino population is at least 20% of the overall population. In states where less than five places meet either of these criteria, we have included places with at least 10,000 total population with the highest percentage of Hispanic/Latino population. These places are identified with an asterisk (*); Please refer to the User's Guide for a full explanation of data.

Sorted by Percent of Hispanic Population in Descending Order — U.S. = 63.0%

State	Percent	County	Percent	Place	Percent
Arizona	87.5	Glasscock County, TX	96.8	**Calexico, CA** (city) Imperial County	97.6
Idaho	84.7	Ness County, KS	96.5	**San Luis, AZ** (city) Yuma County	97.5
Texas	84.0	Starr County, TX	96.5	**El Centro, CA** (city) Imperial County	95.6
Kansas	82.4	Maverick County, TX	96.4	**San Juan, TX** (city) Hidalgo County	95.6
Oregon	82.2	Sterling County, TX	96.2	**Coachella, CA** (city) Riverside County	94.9
California	81.5	Imperial County, CA	96.1	**Santa Paula, CA** (city) Ventura County	94.8
Oklahoma	80.4	Ochiltree County, TX	96.0	**Madera, CA** (city) Madera County	94.4
Washington	79.6	Adams County, WA	95.9	**Eagle Pass, TX** (city) Maverick County	94.1
Illinois	79.0	Hansford County, TX	95.8	**Oxnard, CA** (city) Ventura County	94.1
Iowa	77.3	Edwards County, KS	95.7	**Mission, TX** (city) Hidalgo County	93.8

Sorted by Percent of Hispanic Population in Ascending Order — U.S. = 63.0%

State	Percent	County	Percent	Place	Percent
Massachusetts	6.1	Hampden County, MA	2.6	**Hialeah, FL** (city) Miami-Dade County	0.9
Rhode Island	7.0	Miami-Dade County, FL	3.2	**Holyoke, MA** (city) Hampden County	0.9
Connecticut	10.6	Essex County, MA	3.6	**Tamiami, FL** (cdp) Miami-Dade County	0.9
New York	13.4	Montgomery County, NY	3.9	**Fountainebleau, FL** (cdp) Miami-Dade County	1.0
New Jersey	14.0	Monroe County, PA	4.9	**Lawrence, MA** (city) Essex County	1.0
Florida	14.9	Nassau County, NY	5.4	**Miami Lakes, FL** (town) Miami-Dade County	1.0
District of Columbia	15.5	Pike County, PA	5.4	**University Park, FL** (cdp) Miami-Dade County	1.1
Pennsylvania	18.0	Hartford County, CT	5.5	**Westchester, FL** (cdp) Miami-Dade County	1.1
Maryland	18.7	Suffolk County, MA	5.6	**Kendall West, FL** (cdp) Miami-Dade County	1.2
New Hampshire	21.3	Essex County, NJ	5.7	**Country Club, FL** (cdp) Miami-Dade County	1.3

Note: (1) Ranking tables cover all states and counties, and places with an overall population of at least 125,000, OR an overall population of at least 25,000 where the Hispanic/Latino population is at least 20% of the overall population. In states where less than five places meet either of these criteria, we have included places with at least 10,000 total population with the highest percentage of Hispanic/Latino population. These places are identified with an asterisk (*); Please refer to the User's Guide for a full explanation of data.

Population

Puerto Rican

Top 10 States, Counties, and Places[1]

Sorted by Number in Descending Order — U.S. = 4,623,716

State	Number	County	Number	Place	Number
New York	1,070,558	Bronx County, NY	298,921	**New York, NY** (city)	723,621
Florida	847,550	Kings County, NY	176,528	**Bronx, NY** (borough) Bronx County	298,921
New Jersey	434,092	Orange County, FL	149,457	**Brooklyn, NY** (borough) Kings County	176,528
Pennsylvania	366,082	Cook County, IL	133,882	**Philadelphia, PA** (city) Philadelphia County	121,643
Massachusetts	266,125	Philadelphia County, PA	121,643	**Manhattan, NY** (borough) New York County	107,774
Connecticut	252,972	New York County, NY	107,774	**Queens, NY** (borough) Queens County	102,881
California	189,945	Queens County, NY	102,881	**Chicago, IL** (city) Cook County	102,703
Illinois	182,989	Hartford County, CT	95,964	**Springfield, MA** (city) Hampden County	50,798
Texas	130,576	Miami-Dade County, FL	92,358	**Hartford, CT** (city/town) Hartford County	41,995
Ohio	94,965	Hillsborough County, FL	91,476	**Staten Island, NY** (borough) Richmond County	37,517

Sorted by Number in Ascending Order — U.S. = 4,623,716

State	Number	County	Number	Place	Number
North Dakota	987	Chambers County, TX	100	**Hilton Head Island*, SC** (town) Beaufort County	100
Wyoming	1,026	Adams County, WI	101	**Waxahachie, TX** (city) Ellis County	100
South Dakota	1,483	Dyer County, TN	101	**Windsor, CA** (town) Sonoma County	100
Montana	1,491	Freeborn County, MN	101	**Brighton, CO** (city) Adams County	103
Vermont	2,261	McDonough County, IL	101	**Norco, CA** (city) Riverside County	103
Idaho	2,910	Polk County, TX	101	**Bennington*, VT** (town) Bennington County	105
District of Columbia	3,129	Powhatan County, VA	101	**Berea*, SC** (cdp) Greenville County	105
Nebraska	3,242	Clinton County, MI	102	**Muscatine*, IA** (city) Muscatine County	105
West Virginia	3,701	Liberty County, TX	102	**Eagle Pass, TX** (city) Maverick County	106
Maine	4,377	Somerset County, MD	102	**Altus*, OK** (city) Jackson County	107

Sorted by Percent of Total Population in Descending Order — U.S. = 1.5%

State	Percent	County	Percent	Place	Percent
Connecticut	7.1	Osceola County, FL	27.2	**Holyoke, MA** (city) Hampden County	44.7
New York	5.5	Bronx County, NY	21.6	**Buenaventura Lakes, FL** (cdp) Osceola County	44.5
New Jersey	4.9	Hampden County, MA	17.9	**Poinciana, FL** (cdp) Osceola County	35.8
Florida	4.5	Cumberland County, NJ	14.7	**Meadow Woods, FL** (cdp) Orange County	35.1
Massachusetts	4.1	Orange County, FL	13.0	**Hartford, CT** (city/town) Hartford County	33.7
Rhode Island	3.3	Lehigh County, PA	10.9	**Springfield, MA** (city) Hampden County	33.2
Hawaii	3.2	Hartford County, CT	10.7	**Kissimmee, FL** (city) Osceola County	33.1
Pennsylvania	2.9	New Haven County, CT	9.0	**Reading, PA** (city) Berks County	32.0
Delaware	2.5	Hudson County, NJ	8.9	**Camden, NJ** (city) Camden County	30.7
Illinois	1.4	Berks County, PA	8.8	**New Britain, CT** (city/town) Hartford County	29.9

Sorted by Percent of Total Population in Ascending Order — U.S. = 1.5%

State	Percent	County	Percent	Place	Percent
North Dakota	0.1	Bonneville County, ID	0.1	**Fargo*, ND** (city) Cass County	0.1
Arkansas	0.2	Cabell County, WV	0.1	**Jackson, MS** (city) Hinds County	0.1
Idaho	0.2	Cache County, UT	0.1	**Amarillo, TX** (city) Potter County	0.2
Iowa	0.2	Cape Girardeau County, MO	0.1	**Baton Rouge, LA** (city) East Baton Rouge Parish	0.2
Minnesota	0.2	Carver County, MN	0.1	**Billings*, MT** (city) Yellowstone County	0.2
Mississippi	0.2	Cass County, ND	0.1	**Birmingham, AL** (city) Jefferson County	0.2
Missouri	0.2	Clark County, OH	0.1	**Boise City, ID** (city) Ada County	0.2
Montana	0.2	Clinton County, MI	0.1	**Cedar Rapids, IA** (city) Linn County	0.2
Nebraska	0.2	Cole County, MO	0.1	**Compton, CA** (city) Los Angeles County	0.2
Oregon	0.2	Craighead County, AR	0.1	**East Los Angeles, CA** (cdp) Los Angeles County	0.2

Note: (1) Ranking tables cover all states and counties, and places with an overall population of at least 125,000, OR an overall population of at least 25,000 where the Hispanic/Latino population is at least 20% of the overall population. In states where less than five places meet either of these criteria, we have included places with at least 10,000 total population with the highest percentage of Hispanic/Latino population. These places are identified with an asterisk (*); Please refer to the User's Guide for a full explanation of data.

Sorted by Percent of Hispanic Population in Descending Order U.S. = 9.2%

State	Percent	County	Percent	Place	Percent
Connecticut	52.8	Hampden County, MA	85.6	**Holyoke, MA** (city) Hampden County	92.3
Pennsylvania	50.9	Chautauqua County, NY	77.7	**Springfield, MA** (city) Hampden County	85.4
Massachusetts	42.4	Montgomery County, NY	76.6	**New Britain, CT** (city/town) Hartford County	81.4
Hawaii	36.5	Monroe County, NY	72.0	**Rochester, NY** (city) Monroe County	80.5
New Hampshire	32.0	Lebanon County, PA	71.7	**Buffalo, NY** (city) Erie County	80.2
New York	31.3	Erie County, NY	70.5	**Hartford, CT** (city/town) Hartford County	77.5
Delaware	30.8	Hartford County, CT	70.2	**Lorain, OH** (city) Lorain County	76.7
New Jersey	27.9	Lorain County, OH	69.5	**Bethlehem, PA** (city) Northampton County	75.1
Ohio	26.8	Lancaster County, PA	67.7	**Lebanon, PA** (city) Lebanon County	74.4
Rhode Island	26.8	Windham County, CT	65.6	**Lancaster, PA** (city) Lancaster County	74.3

Sorted by Percent of Hispanic Population in Ascending Order U.S. = 9.2%

State	Percent	County	Percent	Place	Percent
New Mexico	0.8	Hidalgo County, TX	0.2	**East Los Angeles, CA** (cdp) Los Angeles County	0.2
California	1.4	Cameron County, TX	0.3	**Pharr, TX** (city) Hidalgo County	0.2
Texas	1.4	Ector County, TX	0.3	**Bell Gardens, CA** (city) Los Angeles County	0.3
Idaho	1.7	Imperial County, CA	0.3	**Brownsville, TX** (city) Cameron County	0.3
Arizona	1.8	Maverick County, TX	0.3	**Compton, CA** (city) Los Angeles County	0.3
Nebraska	1.9	Grant County, WA	0.4	**El Monte, CA** (city) Los Angeles County	0.3
Oregon	2.0	Potter County, TX	0.4	**Florence-Graham, CA** (cdp) Los Angeles County	0.3
Utah	2.0	Santa Cruz County, AZ	0.4	**Huntington Park, CA** (city) Los Angeles County	0.3
Wyoming	2.0	Webb County, TX	0.4	**Lynwood, CA** (city) Los Angeles County	0.3
Colorado	2.2	Yakima County, WA	0.4	**Santa Ana, CA** (city) Orange County	0.3

Note: (1) Ranking tables cover all states and counties, and places with an overall population of at least 125,000, OR an overall population of at least 25,000 where the Hispanic/Latino population is at least 20% of the overall population. In states where less than five places meet either of these criteria, we have included places with at least 10,000 total population with the highest percentage of Hispanic/Latino population. These places are identified with an asterisk (*); Please refer to the User's Guide for a full explanation of data.

Population

South American

Top 10 States, Counties, and Places[1]

Sorted by Number in Descending Order — U.S. = 2,769,434

State	Number	County	Number	Place	Number
Florida	674,542	Miami-Dade County, FL	273,542	**New York, NY** (city)	343,468
New York	513,417	Queens County, NY	214,022	**Queens, NY** (borough) Queens County	214,022
New Jersey	325,179	Broward County, FL	146,063	**Los Angeles, CA** (city) Los Angeles County	49,352
California	293,880	Los Angeles County, CA	118,776	**Brooklyn, NY** (borough) Kings County	49,003
Texas	133,808	Hudson County, NJ	65,513	**Manhattan, NY** (borough) New York County	36,748
Virginia	101,480	Harris County, TX	50,955	**Bronx, NY** (borough) Bronx County	35,463
Connecticut	71,355	Westchester County, NY	50,521	**Miami, FL** (city) Miami-Dade County	34,718
Illinois	67,862	Palm Beach County, FL	50,419	**Chicago, IL** (city) Cook County	32,129
Maryland	61,400	Kings County, NY	49,003	**Elizabeth, NJ** (city) Union County	25,649
Georgia	57,707	Cook County, IL	47,583	**Houston, TX** (city) Harris County	24,040

Sorted by Number in Ascending Order — U.S. = 2,769,434

State	Number	County	Number	Place	Number
North Dakota	539	Robeson County, NC	100	**Commerce City, CO** (city) Adams County	100
South Dakota	617	San Patricio County, TX	100	**Pharr, TX** (city) Hidalgo County	102
Wyoming	852	Androscoggin County, ME	101	**Schertz, TX** (city) Guadalupe County	102
Montana	997	Jackson County, MI	101	**SeaTac, WA** (city) King County	102
Vermont	1,204	Bryan County, GA	102	**Dalton, GA** (city) Whitfield County	103
Maine	1,515	Livingston County, NY	102	**South Portland*, ME** (city) Cumberland County	103
West Virginia	1,700	Natrona County, WY	102	**Bozeman*, MT** (city) Gallatin County	104
Alaska	2,345	Campbell County, KY	103	**Fallbrook, CA** (cdp) San Diego County	104
Nebraska	2,824	Lenawee County, MI	103	**Cheyenne*, WY** (city) Laramie County	105
Mississippi	2,833	Platte County, NE	103	**Rosenberg, TX** (city) Fort Bend County	105

Sorted by Percent of Total Population in Descending Order — U.S. = 0.9%

State	Percent	County	Percent	Place	Percent
New Jersey	3.7	Miami-Dade County, FL	11.0	**Doral, FL** (city) Miami-Dade County	46.1
Florida	3.6	Hudson County, NJ	10.3	**Weston, FL** (city) Broward County	27.9
New York	2.6	Queens County, NY	9.6	**The Hammocks, FL** (cdp) Miami-Dade County	27.1
Connecticut	2.0	Broward County, FL	8.4	**Ossining, NY** (village) Westchester County	25.7
District of Columbia	1.3	Union County, NJ	8.4	**Aventura, FL** (city) Miami-Dade County	22.7
Rhode Island	1.3	Passaic County, NJ	7.7	**Country Club, FL** (cdp) Miami-Dade County	21.6
Virginia	1.3	Osceola County, FL	5.6	**North Bergen, NJ** (township) Hudson County	21.4
Maryland	1.1	Essex County, NJ	5.4	**Kendall West, FL** (cdp) Miami-Dade County	21.3
Utah	0.9	Westchester County, NY	5.3	**Union City, NJ** (city) Hudson County	21.0
California	0.8	Bergen County, NJ	4.9	**Elizabeth, NJ** (city) Union County	20.5

Sorted by Percent of Total Population in Ascending Order — U.S. = 0.9%

State	Percent	County	Percent	Place	Percent
Alabama	0.1	Aiken County, SC	0.1	**Detroit, MI** (city) Wayne County	0.0
Arkansas	0.1	Androscoggin County, ME	0.1	**Akron, OH** (city) Summit County	0.1
Iowa	0.1	Bastrop County, TX	0.1	**Amarillo, TX** (city) Potter County	0.1
Kentucky	0.1	Beaver County, PA	0.1	**Augusta-Richmond County, GA** (consolidated govt) Richmond County	0.1
Maine	0.1	Bibb County, GA	0.1	**Birmingham, AL** (city) Jefferson County	0.1
Michigan	0.1	Black Hawk County, IA	0.1	**Cedar Rapids, IA** (city) Linn County	0.1
Mississippi	0.1	Blair County, PA	0.1	**Fargo*, ND** (city) Cass County	0.1
Missouri	0.1	Blount County, TN	0.1	**Laredo, TX** (city) Webb County	0.1
Montana	0.1	Bossier Parish, LA	0.1	**Montgomery, AL** (city) Montgomery County	0.1
North Dakota	0.1	Brown County, WI	0.1	**Odessa, TX** (city) Ector County	0.1

Note: (1) Ranking tables cover all states and counties, and places with an overall population of at least 125,000, OR an overall population of at least 25,000 where the Hispanic/Latino population is at least 20% of the overall population. In states where less than five places meet either of these criteria, we have included places with at least 10,000 total population with the highest percentage of Hispanic/Latino population. These places are identified with an asterisk (*); Please refer to the User's Guide for a full explanation of data.

Sorted by Percent of Hispanic Population in Descending Order — U.S. = 5.5%

State	Percent	County	Percent	Place	Percent
New Jersey	20.9	Morris County, NJ	35.6	**Aventura, FL** (city) Miami-Dade County	63.4
Virginia	16.1	Queens County, NY	34.9	**Ossining, NY** (village) Westchester County	62.1
Florida	16.0	Broward County, FL	33.3	**Weston, FL** (city) Broward County	62.1
New York	15.0	Union County, NJ	30.8	**Ossining, NY** (town) Westchester County	59.9
Connecticut	14.9	Bergen County, NJ	30.3	**Doral, FL** (city) Miami-Dade County	58.0
District of Columbia	14.0	Arlington County, VA	29.0	**Hackensack, NJ** (city) Bergen County	45.5
Vermont	13.1	Fairfax County, VA	27.3	**Tamarac, FL** (city) Broward County	44.9
Maryland	13.0	Somerset County, NJ	26.5	**Kearny, NJ** (town) Hudson County	43.2
New Hampshire	11.6	Essex County, NJ	26.4	**Sunrise, FL** (city) Broward County	42.6
Rhode Island	10.7	Loudoun County, VA	24.8	**Hallandale Beach, FL** (city) Broward County	41.6

Sorted by Percent of Hispanic Population in Ascending Order — U.S. = 5.5%

State	Percent	County	Percent	Place	Percent
New Mexico	0.5	Webb County, TX	0.1	**Laredo, TX** (city) Webb County	0.1
Arizona	1.2	Cameron County, TX	0.2	**Brownsville, TX** (city) Cameron County	0.2
Texas	1.4	Ector County, TX	0.2	**Florence-Graham, CA** (cdp) Los Angeles County	0.2
Arkansas	1.6	Hidalgo County, TX	0.2	**Pharr, TX** (city) Hidalgo County	0.2
Nebraska	1.7	Imperial County, CA	0.2	**Pueblo, CO** (city) Pueblo County	0.2
Wyoming	1.7	Tulare County, CA	0.2	**Compton, CA** (city) Los Angeles County	0.3
Colorado	1.8	Doña Ana County, NM	0.3	**El Paso, TX** (city) El Paso County	0.3
Kansas	1.9	El Paso County, TX	0.3	**Odessa, TX** (city) Ector County	0.3
California	2.1	Franklin County, WA	0.3	**Pasco, WA** (city) Franklin County	0.3
Idaho	2.1	Grant County, WA	0.3	**San Angelo, TX** (city) Tom Green County	0.3

Note: (1) Ranking tables cover all states and counties, and places with an overall population of at least 125,000, OR an overall population of at least 25,000 where the Hispanic/Latino population is at least 20% of the overall population. In states where less than five places meet either of these criteria, we have included places with at least 10,000 total population with the highest percentage of Hispanic/Latino population. These places are identified with an asterisk (*); Please refer to the User's Guide for a full explanation of data.

Population

South American: Argentinean

Top 10 States, Counties, and Places[1]

Sorted by Number in Descending Order — U.S. = 224,952

State	Number	County	Number	Place	Number
Florida	56,260	Miami-Dade County, FL	28,612	**New York, NY** (city)	15,169
California	44,410	Los Angeles County, CA	19,540	**Los Angeles, CA** (city) Los Angeles County	8,570
New York	24,969	Broward County, FL	10,708	**Queens, NY** (borough) Queens County	6,345
New Jersey	14,272	Queens County, NY	6,345	**Miami, FL** (city) Miami-Dade County	4,891
Texas	13,831	Orange County, CA	5,566	**Manhattan, NY** (borough) New York County	4,339
Virginia	6,263	Harris County, TX	4,700	**Miami Beach, FL** (city) Miami-Dade County	4,030
Illinois	5,294	Palm Beach County, FL	4,683	**Brooklyn, NY** (borough) Kings County	2,760
Maryland	5,138	New York County, NY	4,339	**Houston, TX** (city) Harris County	2,440
Utah	4,639	Cook County, IL	3,380	**Chicago, IL** (city) Cook County	1,743
Pennsylvania	4,269	Clark County, NV	3,122	**Hollywood, FL** (city) Broward County	1,626

Sorted by Number in Ascending Order — U.S. = 224,952

State	Number	County	Number	Place	Number
Montana	115	Tulare County, CA	100	**Metairie, LA** (cdp) Jefferson Parish	100
Alaska	149	Lake County, IN	103	**El Monte, CA** (city) Los Angeles County	103
Maine	149	Marion County, OR	103	**Fremont, CA** (city) Alameda County	103
West Virginia	165	Buncombe County, NC	105	**Kansas City, MO** (city) Jackson County	103
Vermont	185	Tompkins County, NY	105	**Louisville-Jefferson County, KY** (metropolitan govt) Jefferson County	103
Nebraska	243	Charlotte County, FL	106	**Brandon, FL** (cdp) Hillsborough County	105
Mississippi	276	Tippecanoe County, IN	106	**Oxnard, CA** (city) Ventura County	105
New Hampshire	322	Adams County, CO	107	**Montebello, CA** (city) Los Angeles County	106
Arkansas	338	Harford County, MD	107	**Fort Collins, CO** (city) Larimer County	108
Iowa	344	Hunterdon County, NJ	107	**Naperville, IL** (city) DuPage County	111

Sorted by Percent of Total Population in Descending Order — U.S. = 0.1%

State	Percent	County	Percent	Place	Percent
Florida	0.3	Miami-Dade County, FL	1.1	**Miami Beach, FL** (city) Miami-Dade County	4.6
District of Columbia	0.2	Broward County, FL	0.6	**Aventura, FL** (city) Miami-Dade County	4.4
New Jersey	0.2	Hudson County, NJ	0.4	**Doral, FL** (city) Miami-Dade County	2.4
Utah	0.2	Palm Beach County, FL	0.4	**Hallandale Beach, FL** (city) Broward County	2.0
California	0.1	Utah County, UT	0.4	**North Miami Beach, FL** (city) Miami-Dade County	1.7
Connecticut	0.1	Arlington County, VA	0.3	**Weston, FL** (city) Broward County	1.4
Maryland	0.1	Beaufort County, SC	0.3	**Fountainebleau, FL** (cdp) Miami-Dade County	1.3
Massachusetts	0.1	Montgomery County, MD	0.3	**The Hammocks, FL** (cdp) Miami-Dade County	1.3
Nevada	0.1	New York County, NY	0.3	**Coral Gables, FL** (city) Miami-Dade County	1.2
New York	0.1	Osceola County, FL	0.3	**Hollywood, FL** (city) Broward County	1.2

Sorted by Percent of Total Population in Ascending Order — U.S. = 0.1%

State	Percent	County	Percent	Place	Percent
Alabama	0.0	Ada County, ID	0.0	**Albuquerque, NM** (city) Bernalillo County	0.0
Alaska	0.0	Adams County, CO	0.0	**Aurora, CO** (city) Arapahoe County	0.0
Arizona	0.0	Albany County, NY	0.0	**Baltimore, MD** (independent city)	0.0
Arkansas	0.0	Allegheny County, PA	0.0	**Buffalo, NY** (city) Erie County	0.0
Colorado	0.0	Anne Arundel County, MD	0.0	**Colorado Springs, CO** (city) El Paso County	0.0
Delaware	0.0	Bernalillo County, NM	0.0	**Columbus, OH** (city) Franklin County	0.0
Georgia	0.0	Bexar County, TX	0.0	**Denver, CO** (city) Denver County	0.0
Hawaii	0.0	Brazoria County, TX	0.0	**El Paso, TX** (city) El Paso County	0.0
Idaho	0.0	Bristol County, MA	0.0	**Fremont, CA** (city) Alameda County	0.0
Illinois	0.0	Bucks County, PA	0.0	**Fresno, CA** (city) Fresno County	0.0

Note: (1) Ranking tables cover all states and counties, and places with an overall population of at least 125,000, OR an overall population of at least 25,000 where the Hispanic/Latino population is at least 20% of the overall population. In states where less than five places meet either of these criteria, we have included places with at least 10,000 total population with the highest percentage of Hispanic/Latino population. These places are identified with an asterisk (*); Please refer to the User's Guide for a full explanation of data.

Sorted by Percent of Hispanic Population in Descending Order — U.S. = 0.4%

State	Percent	County	Percent	Place	Percent
District of Columbia	2.1	Utah County, UT	3.8	**Aventura, FL** (city) Miami-Dade County	12.3
Vermont	2.0	Allegheny County, PA	2.5	**Miami Beach, FL** (city) Miami-Dade County	8.7
Florida	1.3	Tompkins County, NY	2.5	**Hallandale Beach, FL** (city) Broward County	6.1
Utah	1.3	Broward County, FL	2.4	**North Miami Beach, FL** (city) Miami-Dade County	4.6
Maryland	1.1	Arlington County, VA	2.3	**Dania Beach, FL** (city) Broward County	4.0
Virginia	1.0	Norfolk County, MA	2.3	**North Miami, FL** (city) Miami-Dade County	3.9
Maine	0.9	Beaufort County, SC	2.2	**Hilton Head Island*, SC** (town) Beaufort County	3.8
New Hampshire	0.9	Palm Beach County, FL	1.9	**Hollywood, FL** (city) Broward County	3.5
New Jersey	0.9	Sarasota County, FL	1.9	**Pittsburgh, PA** (city) Allegheny County	3.5
Connecticut	0.8	Sussex County, NJ	1.9	**Weston, FL** (city) Broward County	3.2

Sorted by Percent of Hispanic Population in Ascending Order — U.S. = 0.4%

State	Percent	County	Percent	Place	Percent
Arizona	0.1	El Paso County, TX	0.0	**El Paso, TX** (city) El Paso County	0.0
Nebraska	0.1	Fresno County, CA	0.0	**Albuquerque, NM** (city) Bernalillo County	0.1
New Mexico	0.1	Hidalgo County, TX	0.0	**Bakersfield, CA** (city) Kern County	0.1
Texas	0.1	Tulare County, CA	0.0	**Chula Vista, CA** (city) San Diego County	0.1
Arkansas	0.2	Adams County, CO	0.1	**Dallas, TX** (city) Dallas County	0.1
Colorado	0.2	Bernalillo County, NM	0.1	**Denver, CO** (city) Denver County	0.1
Idaho	0.2	Bexar County, TX	0.1	**El Monte, CA** (city) Los Angeles County	0.1
Iowa	0.2	Denver County, CO	0.1	**Fresno, CA** (city) Fresno County	0.1
Kansas	0.2	Kane County, IL	0.1	**Garland, TX** (city) Dallas County	0.1
Oklahoma	0.2	Kern County, CA	0.1	**Glendale, AZ** (city) Maricopa County	0.1

Note: (1) Ranking tables cover all states and counties, and places with an overall population of at least 125,000, OR an overall population of at least 25,000 where the Hispanic/Latino population is at least 20% of the overall population. In states where less than five places meet either of these criteria, we have included places with at least 10,000 total population with the highest percentage of Hispanic/Latino population. These places are identified with an asterisk (*); Please refer to the User's Guide for a full explanation of data.

Population

South American: Bolivian

Top 10 States, Counties, and Places[1]

Sorted by Number in Descending Order — U.S. = 99,210

State	Number	County	Number	Place	Number
Virginia	31,333	Fairfax County, VA	18,785	**New York, NY** (city)	4,488
California	13,351	Montgomery County, MD	5,356	**Arlington, VA** (cdp) Arlington County	4,225
Florida	10,938	Los Angeles County, CA	4,857	**Queens, NY** (borough) Queens County	3,268
Maryland	7,496	Arlington County, VA	4,225	**Annandale, VA** (cdp) Fairfax County	2,740
New York	7,122	Miami-Dade County, FL	4,198	**Los Angeles, CA** (city) Los Angeles County	2,561
Texas	4,913	Queens County, NY	3,268	**West Falls Church, VA** (cdp) Fairfax County	2,226
New Jersey	3,361	Prince William County, VA	2,747	**Alexandria, VA** (independent city)	1,227
Illinois	2,304	Orange County, CA	2,211	**Providence, RI** (city) Providence County	1,046
Rhode Island	1,912	Loudoun County, VA	1,906	**Houston, TX** (city) Harris County	958
Massachusetts	1,401	Providence County, RI	1,769	**Springfield, VA** (cdp) Fairfax County	855

Sorted by Number in Ascending Order — U.S. = 99,210

State	Number	County	Number	Place	Number
Delaware	112	Allegheny County, PA	100	**Kendall West, FL** (cdp) Miami-Dade County	100
Idaho	122	Snohomish County, WA	104	**Madison, WI** (city) Dane County	100
Hawaii	131	Washoe County, NV	109	**Pasadena, CA** (city) Los Angeles County	101
West Virginia	139	Charleston County, SC	111	**Garfield, NJ** (city) Bergen County	102
Iowa	171	Montgomery County, TX	111	**Riverside, CA** (city) Riverside County	102
Kentucky	227	Philadelphia County, PA	112	**Tucson, AZ** (city) Pima County	103
New Mexico	229	San Joaquin County, CA	112	**Newark, NJ** (city) Essex County	105
Arkansas	260	Will County, IL	113	**Orlando, FL** (city) Orange County	108
Alabama	292	Williamson County, TX	114	**Garden Grove, CA** (city) Orange County	110
Louisiana	295	Worcester County, MA	115	**Oyster Bay, NY** (town) Nassau County	110

Sorted by Percent of Total Population in Descending Order — U.S. < 0.1%

State	Percent	County	Percent	Place	Percent
Virginia	0.4	Arlington County, VA	2.0	**West Falls Church, VA** (cdp) Fairfax County	7.6
Rhode Island	0.2	Fairfax County, VA	1.7	**Annandale, VA** (cdp) Fairfax County	6.7
District of Columbia	0.1	Prince William County, VA	0.7	**Springfield, VA** (cdp) Fairfax County	2.8
Florida	0.1	Loudoun County, VA	0.6	**Arlington, VA** (cdp) Arlington County	2.0
Maryland	0.1	Montgomery County, MD	0.6	**Sterling, VA** (cdp) Loudoun County	1.7
Alabama	0.0	Collier County, FL	0.4	**Port Chester, NY** (village) Westchester County	1.2
Arizona	0.0	Providence County, RI	0.3	**Aspen Hill, MD** (cdp) Montgomery County	1.1
Arkansas	0.0	Miami-Dade County, FL	0.2	**Dale City, VA** (cdp) Prince William County	1.0
California	0.0	Stafford County, VA	0.2	**Wheaton, MD** (cdp) Montgomery County	1.0
Colorado	0.0	Beaufort County, SC	0.1	**Alexandria, VA** (independent city)	0.9

Sorted by Percent of Total Population in Ascending Order — U.S. < 0.1%

State	Percent	County	Percent	Place	Percent
Alabama	0.0	Alameda County, CA	0.0	**Austin, TX** (city) Travis County	0.0
Arizona	0.0	Allegheny County, PA	0.0	**Boston, MA** (city) Suffolk County	0.0
Arkansas	0.0	Anne Arundel County, MD	0.0	**Bronx, NY** (borough) Bronx County	0.0
California	0.0	Arapahoe County, CO	0.0	**Brookhaven, NY** (town) Suffolk County	0.0
Colorado	0.0	Baltimore County, MD	0.0	**Brooklyn, NY** (borough) Kings County	0.0
Connecticut	0.0	Bexar County, TX	0.0	**Charlotte, NC** (city) Mecklenburg County	0.0
Delaware	0.0	Bronx County, NY	0.0	**Chicago, IL** (city) Cook County	0.0
Georgia	0.0	Charleston County, SC	0.0	**Chula Vista, CA** (city) San Diego County	0.0
Hawaii	0.0	Clark County, NV	0.0	**Dallas, TX** (city) Dallas County	0.0
Idaho	0.0	Cobb County, GA	0.0	**Denver, CO** (city) Denver County	0.0

RANKINGS & COMPARISONS

Note: (1) Ranking tables cover all states and counties, and places with an overall population of at least 125,000, OR an overall population of at least 25,000 where the Hispanic/Latino population is at least 20% of the overall population. In states where less than five places meet either of these criteria, we have included places with at least 10,000 total population with the highest percentage of Hispanic/Latino population. These places are identified with an asterisk (*); Please refer to the User's Guide for a full explanation of data.

Sorted by Percent of Hispanic Population in Descending Order — U.S. = 0.2%

State	Percent	County	Percent	Place	Percent
Virginia	5.0	Arlington County, VA	13.5	**Annandale, VA** (cdp) Fairfax County	24.2
Maryland	1.6	Fairfax County, VA	11.1	**West Falls Church, VA** (cdp) Fairfax County	23.0
Rhode Island	1.5	Loudoun County, VA	4.9	**Arlington, VA** (cdp) Arlington County	13.5
District of Columbia	1.1	Prince William County, VA	3.4	**Springfield, VA** (cdp) Fairfax County	11.0
West Virginia	0.6	Montgomery County, MD	3.2	**Alexandria, VA** (independent city)	5.4
Florida	0.3	Stafford County, VA	2.0	**Sterling, VA** (cdp) Loudoun County	5.2
Utah	0.3	Frederick County, MD	1.7	**Aspen Hill, MD** (cdp) Montgomery County	3.8
Alabama	0.2	Providence County, RI	1.5	**Dale City, VA** (cdp) Prince William County	3.7
Connecticut	0.2	Collier County, FL	1.4	**Cranston*, RI** (city) Providence County	3.2
Delaware	0.2	Howard County, MD	1.2	**Gaithersburg, MD** (city) Montgomery County	3.1

Sorted by Percent of Hispanic Population in Ascending Order — U.S. = 0.2%

State	Percent	County	Percent	Place	Percent
Arizona	0.0	Bexar County, TX	0.0	**Bronx, NY** (borough) Bronx County	0.0
New Mexico	0.0	Bronx County, NY	0.0	**Phoenix, AZ** (city) Maricopa County	0.0
Arkansas	0.1	Maricopa County, AZ	0.0	**San Antonio, TX** (city) Bexar County	0.0
California	0.1	Pima County, AZ	0.0	**Tucson, AZ** (city) Pima County	0.0
Colorado	0.1	San Bernardino County, CA	0.0	**Anaheim, CA** (city) Orange County	0.1
Georgia	0.1	San Joaquin County, CA	0.0	**Austin, TX** (city) Travis County	0.1
Hawaii	0.1	Tarrant County, TX	0.0	**Brooklyn, NY** (borough) Kings County	0.1
Idaho	0.1	Arapahoe County, CO	0.1	**Charlotte, NC** (city) Mecklenburg County	0.1
Illinois	0.1	Clark County, NV	0.1	**Chicago, IL** (city) Cook County	0.1
Indiana	0.1	Cook County, IL	0.1	**Chula Vista, CA** (city) San Diego County	0.1

Note: (1) Ranking tables cover all states and counties, and places with an overall population of at least 125,000, OR an overall population of at least 25,000 where the Hispanic/Latino population is at least 20% of the overall population. In states where less than five places meet either of these criteria, we have included places with at least 10,000 total population with the highest percentage of Hispanic/Latino population. These places are identified with an asterisk (*); Please refer to the User's Guide for a full explanation of data.

Population

South American: Chilean

Top 10 States, Counties, and Places[1]

Sorted by Number in Descending Order — U.S. = 126,810

State	Number	County	Number	Place	Number
California	24,006	Miami-Dade County, FL	11,452	**New York, NY** (city)	7,026
Florida	23,549	Los Angeles County, CA	8,573	**Los Angeles, CA** (city) Los Angeles County	4,112
New York	15,050	Broward County, FL	4,054	**Queens, NY** (borough) Queens County	3,184
New Jersey	8,100	Queens County, NY	3,184	**Manhattan, NY** (borough) New York County	1,824
Texas	6,282	Nassau County, NY	2,945	**Miami, FL** (city) Miami-Dade County	1,427
Virginia	4,195	Montgomery County, MD	2,407	**Hempstead (town), NY** (town) Nassau County	1,415
Maryland	4,146	Hudson County, NJ	2,012	**Brooklyn, NY** (borough) Kings County	1,026
Utah	3,364	Harris County, TX	1,987	**Houston, TX** (city) Harris County	934
Massachusetts	3,045	Orange County, CA	1,898	**Chicago, IL** (city) Cook County	876
Illinois	2,753	New York County, NY	1,824	**San Diego, CA** (city) San Diego County	876

Sorted by Number in Ascending Order — U.S. = 126,810

State	Number	County	Number	Place	Number
Montana	105	Kent County, MI	100	**Concord, CA** (city) Contra Costa County	101
West Virginia	110	Leon County, FL	101	**Greenacres, FL** (city) Palm Beach County	101
Vermont	127	Atlantic County, NJ	102	**Paterson, NJ** (city) Passaic County	101
Mississippi	146	Jefferson Parish, LA	102	**Greensboro, NC** (city) Guilford County	102
Maine	166	Ottawa County, MI	102	**Worcester, MA** (city) Worcester County	102
Arkansas	219	Bucks County, PA	103	**University Park, FL** (cdp) Miami-Dade County	104
Alaska	223	Dakota County, MN	103	**Colorado Springs, CO** (city) El Paso County	105
New Hampshire	224	Hamilton County, OH	103	**Bridgeport, CT** (city/town) Fairfield County	107
Nebraska	228	Johnson County, KS	103	**Montgomery Village, MD** (cdp) Montgomery County	108
Oklahoma	289	Ada County, ID	104	**Chandler, AZ** (city) Maricopa County	110

Sorted by Percent of Total Population in Descending Order — U.S. < 0.1%

State	Percent	County	Percent	Place	Percent
California	0.1	Miami-Dade County, FL	0.5	**Doral, FL** (city) Miami-Dade County	1.4
Connecticut	0.1	Hudson County, NJ	0.3	**The Hammocks, FL** (cdp) Miami-Dade County	1.1
District of Columbia	0.1	Broward County, FL	0.2	**Fountainebleau, FL** (cdp) Miami-Dade County	0.9
Florida	0.1	Fairfax County, VA	0.2	**Glen Cove, NY** (city) Nassau County	0.8
Maryland	0.1	Montgomery County, MD	0.2	**Kendale Lakes, FL** (cdp) Miami-Dade County	0.8
Nevada	0.1	Morris County, NJ	0.2	**Kendall, FL** (cdp) Miami-Dade County	0.8
New Jersey	0.1	Nassau County, NY	0.2	**Kendall West, FL** (cdp) Miami-Dade County	0.8
New York	0.1	Utah County, UT	0.2	**Miami Beach, FL** (city) Miami-Dade County	0.8
Utah	0.1	Westchester County, NY	0.2	**North Bergen, NJ** (township) Hudson County	0.8
Virginia	0.1	Alachua County, FL	0.1	**Ossining, NY** (village) Westchester County	0.7

Sorted by Percent of Total Population in Ascending Order — U.S. < 0.1%

State	Percent	County	Percent	Place	Percent
Alabama	0.0	Ada County, ID	0.0	**Anchorage, AK** (municipality)	0.0
Alaska	0.0	Allegheny County, PA	0.0	**Atlanta, GA** (city) Fulton County	0.0
Arizona	0.0	Anne Arundel County, MD	0.0	**Austin, TX** (city) Travis County	0.0
Arkansas	0.0	Atlantic County, NJ	0.0	**Baltimore, MD** (independent city)	0.0
Colorado	0.0	Baltimore County, MD	0.0	**Bronx, NY** (borough) Bronx County	0.0
Delaware	0.0	Bernalillo County, NM	0.0	**Brooklyn, NY** (borough) Kings County	0.0
Georgia	0.0	Bexar County, TX	0.0	**Chandler, AZ** (city) Maricopa County	0.0
Hawaii	0.0	Brevard County, FL	0.0	**Chicago, IL** (city) Cook County	0.0
Idaho	0.0	Bronx County, NY	0.0	**Colorado Springs, CO** (city) El Paso County	0.0
Illinois	0.0	Bucks County, PA	0.0	**Columbus, OH** (city) Franklin County	0.0

Note: (1) Ranking tables cover all states and counties, and places with an overall population of at least 125,000, OR an overall population of at least 25,000 where the Hispanic/Latino population is at least 20% of the overall population. In states where less than five places meet either of these criteria, we have included places with at least 10,000 total population with the highest percentage of Hispanic/Latino population. These places are identified with an asterisk (*); Please refer to the User's Guide for a full explanation of data.

Sorted by Percent of Hispanic Population in Descending Order — U.S. = 0.3%

State	Percent	County	Percent	Place	Percent
Vermont	1.4	Utah County, UT	2.0	**Glen Cove, NY** (city) Nassau County	2.9
District of Columbia	1.3	Morris County, NJ	1.7	**Oyster Bay, NY** (town) Nassau County	2.6
Maine	1.0	Norfolk County, MA	1.6	**Valley Stream, NY** (village) Nassau County	2.5
Maryland	0.9	Sussex County, NJ	1.6	**North Hempstead, NY** (town) Nassau County	2.3
Utah	0.9	Allegheny County, PA	1.5	**Pittsburgh, PA** (city) Allegheny County	2.0
Virginia	0.7	Montgomery County, MD	1.5	**Doral, FL** (city) Miami-Dade County	1.7
Alaska	0.6	Nassau County, NY	1.5	**Ossining, NY** (town) Westchester County	1.7
Florida	0.6	Davis County, UT	1.3	**Aspen Hill, MD** (cdp) Montgomery County	1.6
New Hampshire	0.6	Frederick County, MD	1.3	**Elmont, NY** (cdp) Nassau County	1.6
Connecticut	0.5	Howard County, MD	1.3	**Miami Beach, FL** (city) Miami-Dade County	1.6

Sorted by Percent of Hispanic Population in Ascending Order — U.S. = 0.3%

State	Percent	County	Percent	Place	Percent
Arizona	0.1	Bexar County, TX	0.0	**El Paso, TX** (city) El Paso County	0.0
Arkansas	0.1	El Paso County, TX	0.0	**Fresno, CA** (city) Fresno County	0.0
Illinois	0.1	Fresno County, CA	0.0	**San Antonio, TX** (city) Bexar County	0.0
Kansas	0.1	Hidalgo County, TX	0.0	**Albuquerque, NM** (city) Bernalillo County	0.1
Nebraska	0.1	Kern County, CA	0.0	**Anaheim, CA** (city) Orange County	0.1
New Mexico	0.1	Bernalillo County, NM	0.1	**Austin, TX** (city) Travis County	0.1
Oklahoma	0.1	Bronx County, NY	0.1	**Bronx, NY** (borough) Bronx County	0.1
Texas	0.1	Cook County, IL	0.1	**Chicago, IL** (city) Cook County	0.1
Alabama	0.2	Dallas County, TX	0.1	**Chula Vista, CA** (city) San Diego County	0.1
California	0.2	Denver County, CO	0.1	**Dallas, TX** (city) Dallas County	0.1

Note: (1) Ranking tables cover all states and counties, and places with an overall population of at least 125,000, OR an overall population of at least 25,000 where the Hispanic/Latino population is at least 20% of the overall population. In states where less than five places meet either of these criteria, we have included places with at least 10,000 total population with the highest percentage of Hispanic/Latino population. These places are identified with an asterisk (*); Please refer to the User's Guide for a full explanation of data.

Population

South American: Colombian

Top 10 States, Counties, and Places[1]

Sorted by Number in Descending Order — U.S. = 908,734

State	Number	County	Number	Place	Number
Florida	300,414	Miami-Dade County, FL	114,701	**New York, NY** (city)	94,723
New York	141,879	Queens County, NY	70,290	**Queens, NY** (borough) Queens County	70,290
New Jersey	101,593	Broward County, FL	66,517	**Miami, FL** (city) Miami-Dade County	12,966
California	64,416	Los Angeles County, CA	25,272	**Elizabeth, NJ** (city) Union County	10,692
Texas	50,810	Palm Beach County, FL	22,980	**Houston, TX** (city) Harris County	10,226
Georgia	26,013	Orange County, FL	22,668	**Pembroke Pines, FL** (city) Broward County	9,937
Massachusetts	23,843	Harris County, TX	22,342	**Los Angeles, CA** (city) Los Angeles County	9,766
Connecticut	20,048	Bergen County, NJ	18,486	**Brooklyn, NY** (borough) Kings County	8,861
Illinois	19,345	Union County, NJ	17,750	**Hempstead (town), NY** (town) Nassau County	8,522
North Carolina	17,648	Hudson County, NJ	16,743	**Manhattan, NY** (borough) New York County	8,411

Sorted by Number in Ascending Order — U.S. = 908,734

State	Number	County	Number	Place	Number
Wyoming	178	James City County, VA	100	**Montclair, CA** (city) San Bernardino County	100
South Dakota	186	Maui County, HI	100	**Akron, OH** (city) Summit County	101
North Dakota	244	York County, ME	100	**Detroit, MI** (city) Wayne County	101
Montana	288	Kenosha County, WI	101	**Hemet, CA** (city) Riverside County	101
Vermont	327	Benton County, WA	102	**Moorpark, CA** (city) Ventura County	102
West Virginia	483	Niagara County, NY	104	**The Colony, TX** (city) Denton County	102
Maine	496	Rensselaer County, NY	104	**Farmers Branch, TX** (city) Dallas County	103
Idaho	734	Rockdale County, GA	104	**Mundelein, IL** (village) Lake County	103
Alaska	867	Saint Mary's County, MD	104	**Novato, CA** (city) Marin County	103
Arkansas	888	Sumner County, TN	104	**Little Elm, TX** (city) Denton County	105

Sorted by Percent of Total Population in Descending Order — U.S. = 0.3%

State	Percent	County	Percent	Place	Percent
Florida	1.6	Miami-Dade County, FL	4.6	**Doral, FL** (city) Miami-Dade County	14.7
New Jersey	1.2	Broward County, FL	3.8	**Country Club, FL** (cdp) Miami-Dade County	13.7
Rhode Island	0.8	Union County, NJ	3.3	**The Hammocks, FL** (cdp) Miami-Dade County	13.5
New York	0.7	Queens County, NY	3.2	**Weston, FL** (city) Broward County	11.7
Connecticut	0.6	Osceola County, FL	2.8	**Central Falls*, RI** (city) Providence County	10.4
Massachusetts	0.4	Hudson County, NJ	2.6	**Kendall West, FL** (cdp) Miami-Dade County	10.4
District of Columbia	0.3	Passaic County, NJ	2.3	**Aventura, FL** (city) Miami-Dade County	9.2
Georgia	0.3	Morris County, NJ	2.2	**Meadow Woods, FL** (cdp) Orange County	8.7
California	0.2	Bergen County, NJ	2.0	**Elizabeth, NJ** (city) Union County	8.6
Illinois	0.2	Orange County, FL	2.0	**Englewood, NJ** (city) Bergen County	8.5

Sorted by Percent of Total Population in Ascending Order — U.S. = 0.3%

State	Percent	County	Percent	Place	Percent
Alabama	0.0	Brown County, WI	0.0	**Detroit, MI** (city) Wayne County	0.0
Arkansas	0.0	Erie County, PA	0.0	**Laredo, TX** (city) Webb County	0.0
Idaho	0.0	Genesee County, MI	0.0	**Akron, OH** (city) Summit County	0.1
Indiana	0.0	Greene County, MO	0.0	**Albuquerque, NM** (city) Bernalillo County	0.1
Iowa	0.0	Lake County, IN	0.0	**Augusta-Richmond County, GA** (consolidated govt) Richmond County	0.1
Kentucky	0.0	Lorain County, OH	0.0	**Aurora, CO** (city) Arapahoe County	0.1
Maine	0.0	Macomb County, MI	0.0	**Bakersfield, CA** (city) Kern County	0.1
Michigan	0.0	Marion County, OR	0.0	**Baltimore, MD** (independent city)	0.1
Mississippi	0.0	Montgomery County, OH	0.0	**Baton Rouge, LA** (city) East Baton Rouge Parish	0.1
Missouri	0.0	Niagara County, NY	0.0	**Boise City, ID** (city) Ada County	0.1

Note: (1) Ranking tables cover all states and counties, and places with an overall population of at least 125,000, OR an overall population of at least 25,000 where the Hispanic/Latino population is at least 20% of the overall population. In states where less than five places meet either of these criteria, we have included places with at least 10,000 total population with the highest percentage of Hispanic/Latino population. These places are identified with an asterisk (*); Please refer to the User's Guide for a full explanation of data.

Sorted by Percent of Hispanic Population in Descending Order					U.S. = 1.8%
State	**Percent**	**County**	**Percent**	**Place**	**Percent**
Florida	7.1	Morris County, NJ	19.4	**Englewood, NJ** (city) Bergen County	30.9
New Jersey	6.5	Telfair County, GA	16.6	**Weston, FL** (city) Broward County	26.0
Rhode Island	6.3	Broward County, FL	15.2	**Aventura, FL** (city) Miami-Dade County	25.7
New Hampshire	5.2	Greenville County, SC	13.5	**Tamarac, FL** (city) Broward County	25.6
Connecticut	4.2	Bergen County, NJ	12.7	**Bergenfield, NJ** (borough) Bergen County	22.1
New York	4.2	Union County, NJ	12.1	**Pawtucket*, RI** (city) Providence County	21.8
South Carolina	4.0	Queens County, NY	11.5	**Sunrise, FL** (city) Broward County	21.2
Massachusetts	3.8	Clearfield County, PA	9.4	**Revere, MA** (city) Suffolk County	20.0
District of Columbia	3.6	Palm Beach County, FL	9.2	**Coral Springs, FL** (city) Broward County	19.4
Vermont	3.6	Gaston County, NC	8.7	**Margate, FL** (city) Broward County	18.7

Sorted by Percent of Hispanic Population in Ascending Order					U.S. = 1.8%
State	**Percent**	**County**	**Percent**	**Place**	**Percent**
New Mexico	0.1	Tulare County, CA	0.0	**Laredo, TX** (city) Webb County	0.0
Arizona	0.4	Webb County, TX	0.0	**Brownsville, TX** (city) Cameron County	0.1
Idaho	0.4	Cameron County, TX	0.1	**El Paso, TX** (city) El Paso County	0.1
Wyoming	0.4	Doña Ana County, NM	0.1	**Fresno, CA** (city) Fresno County	0.1
Arkansas	0.5	El Paso County, TX	0.1	**Oxnard, CA** (city) Ventura County	0.1
California	0.5	Fresno County, CA	0.1	**Albuquerque, NM** (city) Bernalillo County	0.2
Colorado	0.5	Hidalgo County, TX	0.1	**Baldwin Park, CA** (city) Los Angeles County	0.2
Oregon	0.5	Marion County, OR	0.1	**Cicero, IL** (town) Cook County	0.2
Texas	0.5	Monterey County, CA	0.1	**Corpus Christi, TX** (city) Nueces County	0.2
Kansas	0.6	Nueces County, TX	0.1	**Detroit, MI** (city) Wayne County	0.2

Note: (1) Ranking tables cover all states and counties, and places with an overall population of at least 125,000, OR an overall population of at least 25,000 where the Hispanic/Latino population is at least 20% of the overall population. In states where less than five places meet either of these criteria, we have included places with at least 10,000 total population with the highest percentage of Hispanic/Latino population. These places are identified with an asterisk (*); Please refer to the User's Guide for a full explanation of data.

Population

South American: Ecuadorian

Top 10 States, Counties, and Places[1]

Sorted by Number in Descending Order — U.S. = 564,631

State	Number	County	Number	Place	Number
New York	228,216	Queens County, NY	98,512	**New York, NY** (city)	167,209
New Jersey	100,480	Kings County, NY	28,684	**Queens, NY** (borough) Queens County	98,512
Florida	60,574	Hudson County, NJ	26,650	**Brooklyn, NY** (borough) Kings County	28,684
California	35,750	Essex County, NJ	25,169	**Bronx, NY** (borough) Bronx County	23,206
Connecticut	23,677	Bronx County, NY	23,206	**Newark, NJ** (city) Essex County	16,847
Illinois	22,816	Westchester County, NY	22,460	**Chicago, IL** (city) Cook County	15,466
Texas	10,793	Miami-Dade County, FL	19,832	**Manhattan, NY** (borough) New York County	14,132
Pennsylvania	10,680	Los Angeles County, CA	19,588	**Los Angeles, CA** (city) Los Angeles County	7,314
North Carolina	8,110	Cook County, IL	19,450	**Brookhaven, NY** (town) Suffolk County	6,437
Massachusetts	7,592	Suffolk County, NY	17,638	**Union City, NJ** (city) Hudson County	6,135

Sorted by Number in Ascending Order — U.S. = 564,631

State	Number	County	Number	Place	Number
Vermont	125	Hidalgo County, TX	100	**La Habra, CA** (city) Orange County	101
West Virginia	155	Kent County, MI	100	**Syracuse, NY** (city) Onondaga County	101
Maine	178	Berkeley County, SC	102	**El Monte, CA** (city) Los Angeles County	102
Alaska	189	Yolo County, CA	103	**Chesapeake, VA** (independent city)	103
Nebraska	233	Boulder County, CO	104	**Monterey Park, CA** (city) Los Angeles County	103
Idaho	274	Escambia County, FL	104	**Inglewood, CA** (city) Los Angeles County	105
Mississippi	298	Beaufort County, SC	106	**Buffalo, NY** (city) Erie County	106
Arkansas	302	Clayton County, GA	106	**Fitchburg, MA** (city) Worcester County	106
Hawaii	362	Harford County, MD	106	**Kenner, LA** (city) Jefferson Parish	106
Alabama	466	Sedgwick County, KS	107	**San Bernardino, CA** (city) San Bernardino County	106

Sorted by Percent of Total Population in Descending Order — U.S. = 0.2%

State	Percent	County	Percent	Place	Percent
New York	1.2	Queens County, NY	4.4	**Ossining, NY** (village) Westchester County	19.3
New Jersey	1.1	Hudson County, NJ	4.2	**Ossining, NY** (town) Westchester County	13.2
Connecticut	0.7	Essex County, NJ	3.2	**Hackensack, NJ** (city) Bergen County	10.0
Florida	0.3	Westchester County, NY	2.4	**Port Chester, NY** (village) Westchester County	9.6
Illinois	0.2	Union County, NJ	2.0	**Union City, NJ** (city) Hudson County	9.2
California	0.1	Bronx County, NY	1.7	**Spring Valley, NY** (village) Rockland County	8.6
Delaware	0.1	Rockland County, NY	1.6	**North Bergen, NJ** (township) Hudson County	8.3
District of Columbia	0.1	Fairfield County, CT	1.5	**Belleville, NJ** (township) Essex County	7.9
Georgia	0.1	Bergen County, NJ	1.4	**Danbury, CT** (city/town) Fairfield County	7.6
Maryland	0.1	Mercer County, NJ	1.2	**West New York, NJ** (town) Hudson County	6.7

Sorted by Percent of Total Population in Ascending Order — U.S. = 0.2%

State	Percent	County	Percent	Place	Percent
Alabama	0.0	Adams County, CO	0.0	**Anchorage, AK** (municipality)	0.0
Alaska	0.0	Alameda County, CA	0.0	**Atlanta, GA** (city) Fulton County	0.0
Arizona	0.0	Allegheny County, PA	0.0	**Aurora, CO** (city) Arapahoe County	0.0
Arkansas	0.0	Allen County, IN	0.0	**Austin, TX** (city) Travis County	0.0
Colorado	0.0	Arapahoe County, CO	0.0	**Bakersfield, CA** (city) Kern County	0.0
Hawaii	0.0	Bexar County, TX	0.0	**Buffalo, NY** (city) Erie County	0.0
Idaho	0.0	Boulder County, CO	0.0	**Chandler, AZ** (city) Maricopa County	0.0
Indiana	0.0	Brazoria County, TX	0.0	**Chesapeake, VA** (independent city)	0.0
Iowa	0.0	Butler County, OH	0.0	**Cleveland, OH** (city) Cuyahoga County	0.0
Kansas	0.0	Clayton County, GA	0.0	**Colorado Springs, CO** (city) El Paso County	0.0

Note: (1) Ranking tables cover all states and counties, and places with an overall population of at least 125,000, OR an overall population of at least 25,000 where the Hispanic/Latino population is at least 20% of the overall population. In states where less than five places meet either of these criteria, we have included places with at least 10,000 total population with the highest percentage of Hispanic/Latino population. These places are identified with an asterisk (*); Please refer to the User's Guide for a full explanation of data.

Sorted by Percent of Hispanic Population in Descending Order — U.S. = 1.1%

State	Percent	County	Percent	Place	Percent
New York	6.7	Queens County, NY	16.1	**Ossining, NY** (village) Westchester County	46.7
New Jersey	6.5	Essex County, NJ	15.8	**Ossining, NY** (town) Westchester County	43.7
Connecticut	4.9	Litchfield County, CT	12.1	**Danbury, CT** (city/town) Fairfield County	30.3
Minnesota	2.9	Westchester County, NY	10.8	**Hackensack, NJ** (city) Bergen County	28.3
New Hampshire	1.6	Rockland County, NY	10.1	**Spring Valley, NY** (village) Rockland County	28.0
Maryland	1.5	Hudson County, NJ	9.9	**Belleville, NJ** (township) Essex County	20.0
Pennsylvania	1.5	Bergen County, NJ	8.7	**City of Orange, NJ** (township) Essex County	18.5
Florida	1.4	Fairfield County, CT	8.6	**Newark, NJ** (city) Essex County	18.0
Vermont	1.4	Somerset County, NJ	8.1	**Ramapo, NY** (town) Rockland County	16.9
District of Columbia	1.3	Mercer County, NJ	7.7	**Port Chester, NY** (village) Westchester County	16.1

Sorted by Percent of Hispanic Population in Ascending Order — U.S. = 1.1%

State	Percent	County	Percent	Place	Percent
Arizona	0.1	El Paso County, TX	0.0	**El Paso, TX** (city) El Paso County	0.0
Colorado	0.1	Fresno County, CA	0.0	**Albuquerque, NM** (city) Bernalillo County	0.1
Nebraska	0.1	Hidalgo County, TX	0.0	**Aurora, CO** (city) Arapahoe County	0.1
New Mexico	0.1	Monterey County, CA	0.0	**Austin, TX** (city) Travis County	0.1
Oklahoma	0.1	Adams County, CO	0.1	**Bakersfield, CA** (city) Kern County	0.1
Texas	0.1	Bernalillo County, NM	0.1	**Chula Vista, CA** (city) San Diego County	0.1
Arkansas	0.2	Bexar County, TX	0.1	**Dallas, TX** (city) Dallas County	0.1
Idaho	0.2	Dallas County, TX	0.1	**Denver, CO** (city) Denver County	0.1
Kansas	0.2	Denver County, CO	0.1	**East Los Angeles, CA** (cdp) Los Angeles County	0.1
Oregon	0.2	Kern County, CA	0.1	**El Monte, CA** (city) Los Angeles County	0.1

Note: (1) Ranking tables cover all states and counties, and places with an overall population of at least 125,000, OR an overall population of at least 25,000 where the Hispanic/Latino population is at least 20% of the overall population. In states where less than five places meet either of these criteria, we have included places with at least 10,000 total population with the highest percentage of Hispanic/Latino population. These places are identified with an asterisk (*); Please refer to the User's Guide for a full explanation of data.

Population

South American: Paraguayan

Top 10 States, Counties, and Places[1]

Sorted by Number in Descending Order — U.S. = 20,023

State	Number	County	Number	Place	Number
New York	5,940	Queens County, NY	2,775	**New York, NY** (city)	3,534
Florida	2,222	Westchester County, NY	1,328	**Queens, NY** (borough) Queens County	2,775
New Jersey	1,964	Somerset County, NJ	1,073	**Manhattan, NY** (borough) New York County	268
California	1,228	Miami-Dade County, FL	900	**White Plains, NY** (city) Westchester County	260
Maryland	1,161	Montgomery County, MD	828	**Brooklyn, NY** (borough) Kings County	230
Virginia	924	Los Angeles County, CA	413	**Bronx, NY** (borough) Bronx County	223
Texas	763	Nassau County, NY	406	**Hempstead (town), NY** (town) Nassau County	185
Pennsylvania	500	Fairfield County, CT	336	**Los Angeles, CA** (city) Los Angeles County	180
Connecticut	494	Broward County, FL	325	**North Hempstead, NY** (town) Nassau County	140
Illinois	423	Fairfax County, VA	318	**Miami, FL** (city) Miami-Dade County	131

Sorted by Number in Ascending Order — U.S. = 20,023

State	Number	County	Number	Place	Number
Tennessee	108	San Diego County, CA	100	**Chicago, IL** (city) Cook County	101
South Carolina	111	Clark County, NV	109	**Rye, NY** (town) Westchester County	102
Oregon	112	Dallas County, TX	109	**Arlington, VA** (cdp) Arlington County	113
Nevada	116	Maricopa County, AZ	112	**Houston, TX** (city) Harris County	119
Alabama	121	Arlington County, VA	113	**Miami, FL** (city) Miami-Dade County	131
Missouri	128	Gwinnett County, GA	117	**North Hempstead, NY** (town) Nassau County	140
Utah	158	Middlesex County, MA	123	**Los Angeles, CA** (city) Los Angeles County	180
District of Columbia	161	Prince George's County, MD	123	**Hempstead (town), NY** (town) Nassau County	185
Washington	165	Harris County, TX	205	**Bronx, NY** (borough) Bronx County	223
Arizona	175	Bronx County, NY	223	**Brooklyn, NY** (borough) Kings County	230

Sorted by Percent of Total Population in Descending Order — U.S. < 0.1%

State	Percent	County	Percent	Place	Percent
Alabama	0.0	Somerset County, NJ	0.3	**White Plains, NY** (city) Westchester County	0.5
Arizona	0.0	Arlington County, VA	0.1	**Rye, NY** (town) Westchester County	0.2
California	0.0	Montgomery County, MD	0.1	**Arlington, VA** (cdp) Arlington County	0.1
Colorado	0.0	Queens County, NY	0.1	**North Hempstead, NY** (town) Nassau County	0.1
Connecticut	0.0	Westchester County, NY	0.1	**Queens, NY** (borough) Queens County	0.1
District of Columbia	0.0	Bronx County, NY	0.0	**Bronx, NY** (borough) Bronx County	0.0
Florida	0.0	Broward County, FL	0.0	**Brooklyn, NY** (borough) Kings County	0.0
Georgia	0.0	Clark County, NV	0.0	**Chicago, IL** (city) Cook County	0.0
Illinois	0.0	Cook County, IL	0.0	**Hempstead (town), NY** (town) Nassau County	0.0
Kansas	0.0	Dallas County, TX	0.0	**Houston, TX** (city) Harris County	0.0

Sorted by Percent of Total Population in Ascending Order — U.S. < 0.1%

State	Percent	County	Percent	Place	Percent
Alabama	0.0	Bronx County, NY	0.0	**Bronx, NY** (borough) Bronx County	0.0
Arizona	0.0	Broward County, FL	0.0	**Brooklyn, NY** (borough) Kings County	0.0
California	0.0	Clark County, NV	0.0	**Chicago, IL** (city) Cook County	0.0
Colorado	0.0	Cook County, IL	0.0	**Hempstead (town), NY** (town) Nassau County	0.0
Connecticut	0.0	Dallas County, TX	0.0	**Houston, TX** (city) Harris County	0.0
District of Columbia	0.0	Fairfax County, VA	0.0	**Los Angeles, CA** (city) Los Angeles County	0.0
Florida	0.0	Fairfield County, CT	0.0	**Manhattan, NY** (borough) New York County	0.0
Georgia	0.0	Gwinnett County, GA	0.0	**Miami, FL** (city) Miami-Dade County	0.0
Illinois	0.0	Harris County, TX	0.0	**New York, NY** (city)	0.0
Kansas	0.0	Kings County, NY	0.0	**Arlington, VA** (cdp) Arlington County	0.1

Note: (1) Ranking tables cover all states and counties, and places with an overall population of at least 125,000, OR an overall population of at least 25,000 where the Hispanic/Latino population is at least 20% of the overall population. In states where less than five places meet either of these criteria, we have included places with at least 10,000 total population with the highest percentage of Hispanic/Latino population. These places are identified with an asterisk (*); Please refer to the User's Guide for a full explanation of data.

Sorted by Percent of Hispanic Population in Descending Order — U.S. < 0.1%

State	Percent	County	Percent	Place	Percent
District of Columbia	0.3	Somerset County, NJ	2.5	**White Plains, NY** (city) Westchester County	1.5
Maryland	0.2	Westchester County, NY	0.6	**North Hempstead, NY** (town) Nassau County	0.5
New York	0.2	Montgomery County, MD	0.5	**Queens, NY** (borough) Queens County	0.5
Alabama	0.1	Queens County, NY	0.5	**Rye, NY** (town) Westchester County	0.5
Connecticut	0.1	Arlington County, VA	0.4	**Arlington, VA** (cdp) Arlington County	0.4
Florida	0.1	Morris County, NJ	0.4	**New York, NY** (city)	0.2
Kansas	0.1	Fairfax County, VA	0.2	**Hempstead (town), NY** (town) Nassau County	0.1
Massachusetts	0.1	Fairfield County, CT	0.2	**Manhattan, NY** (borough) New York County	0.1
Michigan	0.1	Nassau County, NY	0.2	**Bronx, NY** (borough) Bronx County	0.0
Minnesota	0.1	Broward County, FL	0.1	**Brooklyn, NY** (borough) Kings County	0.0

Sorted by Percent of Hispanic Population in Ascending Order — U.S. < 0.1%

State	Percent	County	Percent	Place	Percent
Arizona	0.0	Bronx County, NY	0.0	**Bronx, NY** (borough) Bronx County	0.0
California	0.0	Clark County, NV	0.0	**Brooklyn, NY** (borough) Kings County	0.0
Colorado	0.0	Cook County, IL	0.0	**Chicago, IL** (city) Cook County	0.0
Georgia	0.0	Dallas County, TX	0.0	**Houston, TX** (city) Harris County	0.0
Illinois	0.0	Harris County, TX	0.0	**Los Angeles, CA** (city) Los Angeles County	0.0
Nevada	0.0	Kings County, NY	0.0	**Miami, FL** (city) Miami-Dade County	0.0
North Carolina	0.0	Los Angeles County, CA	0.0	**Hempstead (town), NY** (town) Nassau County	0.1
Oregon	0.0	Maricopa County, AZ	0.0	**Manhattan, NY** (borough) New York County	0.1
South Carolina	0.0	San Diego County, CA	0.0	**New York, NY** (city)	0.2
Tennessee	0.0	Broward County, FL	0.1	**Arlington, VA** (cdp) Arlington County	0.4

Note: (1) Ranking tables cover all states and counties, and places with an overall population of at least 125,000, OR an overall population of at least 25,000 where the Hispanic/Latino population is at least 20% of the overall population. In states where less than five places meet either of these criteria, we have included places with at least 10,000 total population with the highest percentage of Hispanic/Latino population. These places are identified with an asterisk (*); Please refer to the User's Guide for a full explanation of data.

Population

South American: Peruvian

Top 10 States, Counties, and Places[1]

Sorted by Number in Descending Order — U.S. = 531,358

State	Number	County	Number	Place	Number
Florida	100,965	Miami-Dade County, FL	40,701	**New York, NY** (city)	36,018
California	91,511	Los Angeles County, CA	34,135	**Queens, NY** (borough) Queens County	22,886
New Jersey	75,869	Broward County, FL	23,600	**Los Angeles, CA** (city) Los Angeles County	14,033
New York	66,318	Queens County, NY	22,886	**Paterson, NJ** (city) Passaic County	9,943
Virginia	29,096	Passaic County, NJ	19,696	**Elizabeth, NJ** (city) Union County	5,419
Texas	22,605	Hudson County, NJ	13,533	**Miami, FL** (city) Miami-Dade County	4,946
Maryland	18,229	Fairfax County, VA	12,922	**Hempstead (town), NY** (town) Nassau County	4,510
Connecticut	16,424	Montgomery County, MD	12,005	**Clifton, NJ** (city) Passaic County	4,473
Georgia	10,570	Westchester County, NY	9,774	**Brooklyn, NY** (borough) Kings County	4,222
Illinois	10,213	Union County, NJ	9,446	**Chicago, IL** (city) Cook County	4,075

Sorted by Number in Ascending Order — U.S. = 531,358

State	Number	County	Number	Place	Number
South Dakota	138	Horry County, SC	100	**East Los Angeles, CA** (cdp) Los Angeles County	100
Montana	237	Gaston County, NC	102	**Lake Worth, FL** (city) Palm Beach County	100
Vermont	242	Whatcom County, WA	102	**Lawrence, MA** (city) Essex County	100
Maine	272	Chittenden County, VT	103	**University, FL** (cdp) Orange County	100
Wyoming	305	Yakima County, WA	103	**Winter Garden, FL** (city) Orange County	100
West Virginia	444	Windham County, CT	104	**Magna, UT** (cdp) Salt Lake County	101
New Hampshire	471	Montgomery County, VA	105	**Casselberry, FL** (city) Seminole County	102
Mississippi	473	Wicomico County, MD	105	**Joliet, IL** (city) Will County	102
Iowa	607	Yavapai County, AZ	105	**Marietta, GA** (city) Cobb County	103
Alaska	611	Lebanon County, PA	106	**Buffalo, NY** (city) Erie County	105

Sorted by Percent of Total Population in Descending Order — U.S. = 0.2%

State	Percent	County	Percent	Place	Percent
New Jersey	0.9	Passaic County, NJ	3.9	**Kearny, NJ** (town) Hudson County	8.1
Connecticut	0.5	Hudson County, NJ	2.1	**Paterson, NJ** (city) Passaic County	6.8
Florida	0.5	Blaine County, ID	1.9	**Clifton, NJ** (city) Passaic County	5.3
Virginia	0.4	Union County, NJ	1.8	**Port Chester, NY** (village) Westchester County	5.1
Maryland	0.3	Miami-Dade County, FL	1.6	**Garfield, NJ** (city) Bergen County	4.8
New York	0.3	Broward County, FL	1.4	**The Hammocks, FL** (cdp) Miami-Dade County	4.7
Utah	0.3	Loudoun County, VA	1.3	**Union City, NJ** (city) Hudson County	4.7
California	0.2	Fairfax County, VA	1.2	**Elizabeth, NJ** (city) Union County	4.3
District of Columbia	0.2	Montgomery County, MD	1.2	**White Plains, NY** (city) Westchester County	4.0
Nevada	0.2	Prince William County, VA	1.0	**Perth Amboy, NJ** (city) Middlesex County	3.9

Sorted by Percent of Total Population in Ascending Order — U.S. = 0.2%

State	Percent	County	Percent	Place	Percent
Alabama	0.0	Allegheny County, PA	0.0	**Buffalo, NY** (city) Erie County	0.0
Arkansas	0.0	Allen County, IN	0.0	**Cincinnati, OH** (city) Hamilton County	0.0
Indiana	0.0	Anoka County, MN	0.0	**Corpus Christi, TX** (city) Nueces County	0.0
Iowa	0.0	Bristol County, MA	0.0	**El Paso, TX** (city) El Paso County	0.0
Kansas	0.0	Cameron County, TX	0.0	**Kansas City, MO** (city) Jackson County	0.0
Kentucky	0.0	Charleston County, SC	0.0	**Louisville-Jefferson County, KY** (metropolitan govt) Jefferson County	0.0
Louisiana	0.0	Chester County, PA	0.0	**Memphis, TN** (city) Shelby County	0.0
Maine	0.0	Dakota County, MN	0.0	**New Orleans, LA** (city) Orleans Parish	0.0
Michigan	0.0	Douglas County, NE	0.0	**Omaha, NE** (city) Douglas County	0.0
Minnesota	0.0	East Baton Rouge Parish, LA	0.0	**Saint Louis, MO** (independent city)	0.0

Note: (1) Ranking tables cover all states and counties, and places with an overall population of at least 125,000, OR an overall population of at least 25,000 where the Hispanic/Latino population is at least 20% of the overall population. In states where less than five places meet either of these criteria, we have included places with at least 10,000 total population with the highest percentage of Hispanic/Latino population. These places are identified with an asterisk (*); Please refer to the User's Guide for a full explanation of data.

Sorted by Percent of Hispanic Population in Descending Order — U.S. = 1.1%

State	Percent	County	Percent	Place	Percent
New Jersey	4.9	Loudoun County, VA	10.9	**Kearny, NJ** (town) Hudson County	20.4
Virginia	4.6	Passaic County, NJ	10.6	**Clifton, NJ** (city) Passaic County	16.7
Maryland	3.9	Blaine County, ID	9.7	**Garfield, NJ** (city) Bergen County	14.9
Connecticut	3.4	Jefferson County, WV	8.1	**White Plains, NY** (city) Westchester County	13.4
District of Columbia	2.7	Fairfax County, VA	7.7	**Glen Cove, NY** (city) Nassau County	11.8
Vermont	2.6	Montgomery County, MD	7.3	**Paterson, NJ** (city) Passaic County	11.8
Florida	2.4	Dare County, NC	6.9	**Montgomery Village, MD** (cdp) Montgomery County	10.8
Utah	2.1	Union County, NJ	6.4	**Rahway, NJ** (city) Union County	10.0
West Virginia	2.0	New London County, CT	6.2	**Linden, NJ** (city) Union County	9.0
New York	1.9	Broward County, FL	5.4	**Hallandale Beach, FL** (city) Broward County	8.9

Sorted by Percent of Hispanic Population in Ascending Order — U.S. = 1.1%

State	Percent	County	Percent	Place	Percent
New Mexico	0.1	Cameron County, TX	0.0	**Corpus Christi, TX** (city) Nueces County	0.1
Arizona	0.2	El Paso County, TX	0.0	**East Los Angeles, CA** (cdp) Los Angeles County	0.1
Texas	0.2	Hidalgo County, TX	0.0	**El Paso, TX** (city) El Paso County	0.1
Arkansas	0.3	Bernalillo County, NM	0.1	**Fresno, CA** (city) Fresno County	0.1
Iowa	0.4	Fresno County, CA	0.1	**McAllen, TX** (city) Hidalgo County	0.1
Kansas	0.4	Merced County, CA	0.1	**Oxnard, CA** (city) Ventura County	0.1
Nebraska	0.4	Nueces County, TX	0.1	**Pasadena, TX** (city) Harris County	0.1
Illinois	0.5	Tulare County, CA	0.1	**San Antonio, TX** (city) Bexar County	0.1
Michigan	0.5	Yakima County, WA	0.1	**Albuquerque, NM** (city) Bernalillo County	0.2
Oklahoma	0.5	Bexar County, TX	0.2	**Aurora, IL** (city) Kane County	0.2

Note: (1) Ranking tables cover all states and counties, and places with an overall population of at least 125,000, OR an overall population of at least 25,000 where the Hispanic/Latino population is at least 20% of the overall population. In states where less than five places meet either of these criteria, we have included places with at least 10,000 total population with the highest percentage of Hispanic/Latino population. These places are identified with an asterisk (*); Please refer to the User's Guide for a full explanation of data.

Population

South American: Uruguayan

Top 10 States, Counties, and Places[1]

Sorted by Number in Descending Order — U.S. = 56,884

State	Number	County	Number	Place	Number
Florida	14,542	Miami-Dade County, FL	5,855	**New York, NY** (city)	3,004
New Jersey	10,902	Union County, NJ	3,482	**Elizabeth, NJ** (city) Union County	2,553
New York	6,021	Broward County, FL	3,266	**Queens, NY** (borough) Queens County	1,743
California	4,110	Essex County, NJ	2,334	**Miami, FL** (city) Miami-Dade County	1,040
Georgia	2,708	Palm Beach County, FL	1,960	**Miami Beach, FL** (city) Miami-Dade County	958
Texas	2,566	Queens County, NY	1,743	**Los Angeles, CA** (city) Los Angeles County	697
Massachusetts	2,317	Worcester County, MA	1,673	**Fitchburg, MA** (city) Worcester County	650
Virginia	1,594	Los Angeles County, CA	1,628	**Houston, TX** (city) Harris County	642
Connecticut	1,294	Hudson County, NJ	1,373	**Newark, NJ** (city) Essex County	634
Maryland	1,282	Harris County, TX	1,324	**Manhattan, NY** (borough) New York County	549

Sorted by Number in Ascending Order — U.S. = 56,884

State	Number	County	Number	Place	Number
Louisiana	109	Henry County, GA	103	**Country Club, FL** (cdp) Miami-Dade County	100
Rhode Island	112	Cuyahoga County, OH	105	**Port Saint Lucie, FL** (city) Saint Lucie County	102
Alabama	129	Baltimore County, MD	106	**Dallas, TX** (city) Dallas County	103
Oregon	132	Polk County, FL	109	**Phoenix, AZ** (city) Maricopa County	106
Indiana	150	San Mateo County, CA	109	**Bloomfield, NJ** (township) Essex County	108
Missouri	179	Suffolk County, MA	112	**Bridgeport, CT** (city/town) Fairfield County	110
Tennessee	214	Bexar County, TX	113	**Plantation, FL** (city) Broward County	115
District of Columbia	216	Mercer County, NJ	115	**Las Vegas, NV** (city) Clark County	117
Minnesota	223	Collin County, TX	116	**San Francisco, CA** (city) San Francisco County	118
Colorado	224	Contra Costa County, CA	117	**Belleville, NJ** (township) Essex County	119

Sorted by Percent of Total Population in Descending Order — U.S. < 0.1%

State	Percent	County	Percent	Place	Percent
Florida	0.1	Union County, NJ	0.6	**Elizabeth, NJ** (city) Union County	2.0
New Jersey	0.1	Beaufort County, SC	0.3	**Fitchburg, MA** (city) Worcester County	1.6
Alabama	0.0	Essex County, NJ	0.3	**City of Orange, NJ** (township) Essex County	1.5
Arizona	0.0	Broward County, FL	0.2	**Miami Beach, FL** (city) Miami-Dade County	1.1
California	0.0	Hudson County, NJ	0.2	**Kearny, NJ** (town) Hudson County	1.0
Colorado	0.0	Miami-Dade County, FL	0.2	**Ossining, NY** (village) Westchester County	0.9
Connecticut	0.0	Morris County, NJ	0.2	**Ossining, NY** (town) Westchester County	0.7
District of Columbia	0.0	Worcester County, MA	0.2	**Hallandale Beach, FL** (city) Broward County	0.6
Georgia	0.0	Arlington County, VA	0.1	**Hilton Head Island*, SC** (town) Beaufort County	0.5
Illinois	0.0	Bergen County, NJ	0.1	**Linden, NJ** (city) Union County	0.5

Sorted by Percent of Total Population in Ascending Order — U.S. < 0.1%

State	Percent	County	Percent	Place	Percent
Alabama	0.0	Alameda County, CA	0.0	**Bronx, NY** (borough) Bronx County	0.0
Arizona	0.0	Baltimore County, MD	0.0	**Brooklyn, NY** (borough) Kings County	0.0
California	0.0	Bexar County, TX	0.0	**Charlotte, NC** (city) Mecklenburg County	0.0
Colorado	0.0	Bronx County, NY	0.0	**Chicago, IL** (city) Cook County	0.0
Connecticut	0.0	Clark County, NV	0.0	**Dallas, TX** (city) Dallas County	0.0
District of Columbia	0.0	Cobb County, GA	0.0	**Hempstead (town), NY** (town) Nassau County	0.0
Georgia	0.0	Collin County, TX	0.0	**Houston, TX** (city) Harris County	0.0
Illinois	0.0	Contra Costa County, CA	0.0	**Jacksonville, FL** (city) Duval County	0.0
Indiana	0.0	Cook County, IL	0.0	**Las Vegas, NV** (city) Clark County	0.0
Louisiana	0.0	Cuyahoga County, OH	0.0	**Los Angeles, CA** (city) Los Angeles County	0.0

Note: (1) Ranking tables cover all states and counties, and places with an overall population of at least 125,000, OR an overall population of at least 25,000 where the Hispanic/Latino population is at least 20% of the overall population. In states where less than five places meet either of these criteria, we have included places with at least 10,000 total population with the highest percentage of Hispanic/Latino population. These places are identified with an asterisk (*); Please refer to the User's Guide for a full explanation of data.

Sorted by Percent of Hispanic Population in Descending Order U.S. = 0.1%

State	Percent	County	Percent	Place	Percent
New Hampshire	1.0	Union County, NJ	2.4	**Fitchburg, MA** (city) Worcester County	7.4
New Jersey	0.7	Worcester County, MA	2.2	**City of Orange, NJ** (township) Essex County	6.8
District of Columbia	0.4	Beaufort County, SC	2.1	**Elizabeth, NJ** (city) Union County	3.4
Massachusetts	0.4	Morris County, NJ	1.6	**Hilton Head Island*, SC** (town) Beaufort County	3.2
South Carolina	0.4	Essex County, NJ	1.5	**Kearny, NJ** (town) Hudson County	2.6
Connecticut	0.3	Sussex County, NJ	1.4	**Manchester*, NH** (city) Hillsborough County	2.4
Florida	0.3	Lackawanna County, PA	1.3	**Ossining, NY** (town) Westchester County	2.4
Georgia	0.3	Hillsborough County, NH	1.2	**Ossining, NY** (village) Westchester County	2.2
Maryland	0.3	Henry County, GA	0.9	**Linden, NJ** (city) Union County	2.1
Utah	0.3	Clayton County, GA	0.8	**Miami Beach, FL** (city) Miami-Dade County	2.1

Sorted by Percent of Hispanic Population in Ascending Order U.S. = 0.1%

State	Percent	County	Percent	Place	Percent
Arizona	0.0	Alameda County, CA	0.0	**Bronx, NY** (borough) Bronx County	0.0
California	0.0	Bexar County, TX	0.0	**Chicago, IL** (city) Cook County	0.0
Colorado	0.0	Bronx County, NY	0.0	**Dallas, TX** (city) Dallas County	0.0
Illinois	0.0	Contra Costa County, CA	0.0	**Los Angeles, CA** (city) Los Angeles County	0.0
Indiana	0.0	Cook County, IL	0.0	**Phoenix, AZ** (city) Maricopa County	0.0
Oregon	0.0	Dallas County, TX	0.0	**San Diego, CA** (city) San Diego County	0.0
Texas	0.0	Los Angeles County, CA	0.0	**Brooklyn, NY** (borough) Kings County	0.1
Washington	0.0	Maricopa County, AZ	0.0	**Hialeah, FL** (city) Miami-Dade County	0.1
Alabama	0.1	Orange County, CA	0.0	**Houston, TX** (city) Harris County	0.1
Louisiana	0.1	Riverside County, CA	0.0	**Las Vegas, NV** (city) Clark County	0.1

Note: (1) Ranking tables cover all states and counties, and places with an overall population of at least 125,000, OR an overall population of at least 25,000 where the Hispanic/Latino population is at least 20% of the overall population. In states where less than five places meet either of these criteria, we have included places with at least 10,000 total population with the highest percentage of Hispanic/Latino population. These places are identified with an asterisk (*); Please refer to the User's Guide for a full explanation of data.

Population

South American: Venezuelan

Top 10 States, Counties, and Places[1]

Sorted by Number in Descending Order — U.S. = 215,023

State	Number	County	Number	Place	Number
Florida	102,116	Miami-Dade County, FL	46,851	**New York, NY** (city)	9,619
Texas	20,162	Broward County, FL	23,343	**Doral, FL** (city) Miami-Dade County	9,423
New York	13,910	Harris County, TX	8,012	**Weston, FL** (city) Broward County	6,360
California	11,100	Orange County, FL	7,968	**Miami, FL** (city) Miami-Dade County	5,770
New Jersey	6,950	Palm Beach County, FL	5,041	**Houston, TX** (city) Harris County	3,770
Georgia	6,289	Queens County, NY	3,580	**Queens, NY** (borough) Queens County	3,580
Virginia	4,429	Hillsborough County, FL	3,349	**Pembroke Pines, FL** (city) Broward County	2,937
North Carolina	4,070	Los Angeles County, CA	3,279	**Miramar, FL** (city) Broward County	2,594
Massachusetts	3,982	Fort Bend County, TX	3,082	**Manhattan, NY** (borough) New York County	2,573
Maryland	3,328	New York County, NY	2,573	**Fountainebleau, FL** (cdp) Miami-Dade County	2,334

Sorted by Number in Ascending Order — U.S. = 215,023

State	Number	County	Number	Place	Number
Alaska	140	Orange County, NC	100	**McAllen, TX** (city) Hidalgo County	100
West Virginia	142	Marin County, CA	103	**Pasadena, CA** (city) Los Angeles County	100
Maine	146	Onondaga County, NY	103	**Kenner, LA** (city) Jefferson Parish	101
Idaho	200	Hernando County, FL	104	**Chandler, AZ** (city) Maricopa County	103
New Hampshire	243	Butler County, OH	105	**Babylon, NY** (town) Suffolk County	104
Hawaii	287	Santa Barbara County, CA	107	**Kearny, NJ** (town) Hudson County	104
Arkansas	300	Jefferson County, TX	109	**Ocoee, FL** (city) Orange County	105
Iowa	310	Kent County, MI	109	**Cincinnati, OH** (city) Hamilton County	107
Nebraska	319	Monroe County, FL	114	**Naperville, IL** (city) DuPage County	108
Delaware	389	Cumberland County, NC	115	**University, FL** (cdp) Orange County	109

Sorted by Percent of Total Population in Descending Order — U.S. = 0.1%

State	Percent	County	Percent	Place	Percent
Florida	0.5	Miami-Dade County, FL	1.9	**Doral, FL** (city) Miami-Dade County	20.6
Connecticut	0.1	Broward County, FL	1.3	**Weston, FL** (city) Broward County	9.7
District of Columbia	0.1	Osceola County, FL	0.8	**Aventura, FL** (city) Miami-Dade County	4.9
Georgia	0.1	Orange County, FL	0.7	**The Hammocks, FL** (cdp) Miami-Dade County	4.0
Maryland	0.1	Fort Bend County, TX	0.5	**Fountainebleau, FL** (cdp) Miami-Dade County	3.9
Massachusetts	0.1	Alachua County, FL	0.4	**Kendall West, FL** (cdp) Miami-Dade County	3.1
New Jersey	0.1	Palm Beach County, FL	0.4	**Coral Gables, FL** (city) Miami-Dade County	2.6
New York	0.1	Seminole County, FL	0.4	**Meadow Woods, FL** (cdp) Orange County	2.6
Rhode Island	0.1	Hillsborough County, FL	0.3	**Country Club, FL** (cdp) Miami-Dade County	2.5
Texas	0.1	Collier County, FL	0.2	**Kendall, FL** (cdp) Miami-Dade County	2.1

Sorted by Percent of Total Population in Ascending Order — U.S. = 0.1%

State	Percent	County	Percent	Place	Percent
Alabama	0.0	Adams County, CO	0.0	**Albuquerque, NM** (city) Bernalillo County	0.0
Alaska	0.0	Alameda County, CA	0.0	**Arlington, TX** (city) Tarrant County	0.0
Arizona	0.0	Allegheny County, PA	0.0	**Aurora, CO** (city) Arapahoe County	0.0
Arkansas	0.0	Anne Arundel County, MD	0.0	**Babylon, NY** (town) Suffolk County	0.0
California	0.0	Baltimore County, MD	0.0	**Baltimore, MD** (independent city)	0.0
Colorado	0.0	Bernalillo County, NM	0.0	**Chandler, AZ** (city) Maricopa County	0.0
Delaware	0.0	Bexar County, TX	0.0	**Chicago, IL** (city) Cook County	0.0
Hawaii	0.0	Bristol County, MA	0.0	**Cincinnati, OH** (city) Hamilton County	0.0
Idaho	0.0	Bucks County, PA	0.0	**Colorado Springs, CO** (city) El Paso County	0.0
Illinois	0.0	Burlington County, NJ	0.0	**Columbus, OH** (city) Franklin County	0.0

Note: (1) Ranking tables cover all states and counties, and places with an overall population of at least 125,000, OR an overall population of at least 25,000 where the Hispanic/Latino population is at least 20% of the overall population. In states where less than five places meet either of these criteria, we have included places with at least 10,000 total population with the highest percentage of Hispanic/Latino population. These places are identified with an asterisk (*); Please refer to the User's Guide for a full explanation of data.

Sorted by Percent of Hispanic Population in Descending Order — U.S. = 0.4%

State	Percent	County	Percent	Place	Percent
Florida	2.4	Broward County, FL	5.3	**Doral, FL** (city) Miami-Dade County	25.9
District of Columbia	1.1	Alachua County, FL	4.3	**Weston, FL** (city) Broward County	21.7
Maine	0.9	Warren County, OH	4.3	**Aventura, FL** (city) Miami-Dade County	13.8
Louisiana	0.8	Hamilton County, IN	2.9	**Miramar, FL** (city) Broward County	5.8
Utah	0.8	Miami-Dade County, FL	2.9	**Sunrise, FL** (city) Broward County	5.7
Georgia	0.7	Lafayette Parish, LA	2.7	**The Hammocks, FL** (cdp) Miami-Dade County	5.3
Maryland	0.7	Orange County, FL	2.6	**Coral Springs, FL** (city) Broward County	5.0
New Hampshire	0.7	Seminole County, FL	2.4	**Coconut Creek, FL** (city) Broward County	4.9
Virginia	0.7	Fort Bend County, TX	2.2	**Coral Gables, FL** (city) Miami-Dade County	4.8
Massachusetts	0.6	Leon County, FL	2.2	**Plantation, FL** (city) Broward County	4.8

Sorted by Percent of Hispanic Population in Ascending Order — U.S. = 0.4%

State	Percent	County	Percent	Place	Percent
New Mexico	0.0	El Paso County, TX	0.0	**El Paso, TX** (city) El Paso County	0.0
Arizona	0.1	Hidalgo County, TX	0.0	**Albuquerque, NM** (city) Bernalillo County	0.1
California	0.1	San Bernardino County, CA	0.0	**Chicago, IL** (city) Cook County	0.1
Idaho	0.1	San Joaquin County, CA	0.0	**Corpus Christi, TX** (city) Nueces County	0.1
Nevada	0.1	Adams County, CO	0.1	**Dallas, TX** (city) Dallas County	0.1
Arkansas	0.2	Bernalillo County, NM	0.1	**Denver, CO** (city) Denver County	0.1
Colorado	0.2	Bexar County, TX	0.1	**Fort Worth, TX** (city) Tarrant County	0.1
Hawaii	0.2	Clark County, NV	0.1	**Las Vegas, NV** (city) Clark County	0.1
Illinois	0.2	Cook County, IL	0.1	**Long Beach, CA** (city) Los Angeles County	0.1
Iowa	0.2	Dallas County, TX	0.1	**Los Angeles, CA** (city) Los Angeles County	0.1

Note: (1) Ranking tables cover all states and counties, and places with an overall population of at least 125,000, OR an overall population of at least 25,000 where the Hispanic/Latino population is at least 20% of the overall population. In states where less than five places meet either of these criteria, we have included places with at least 10,000 total population with the highest percentage of Hispanic/Latino population. These places are identified with an asterisk (*); Please refer to the User's Guide for a full explanation of data.

Population

Spaniard

Top 10 States, Counties, and Places[1]

Sorted by Number in Descending Order — U.S. = 635,253

State	Number	County	Number	Place	Number
California	142,194	Los Angeles County, CA	30,356	**Albuquerque, NM** (city) Bernalillo County	23,386
Texas	65,777	Bernalillo County, NM	27,920	**New York, NY** (city)	17,793
New Mexico	65,045	Maricopa County, AZ	13,365	**Los Angeles, CA** (city) Los Angeles County	11,211
Florida	48,815	Miami-Dade County, FL	12,050	**San Antonio, TX** (city) Bexar County	7,388
Colorado	41,960	San Diego County, CA	11,623	**Houston, TX** (city) Harris County	5,674
New York	35,571	Harris County, TX	10,904	**Manhattan, NY** (borough) New York County	5,629
New Jersey	21,791	Orange County, CA	9,842	**Queens, NY** (borough) Queens County	5,485
Arizona	21,561	Bexar County, TX	9,360	**Denver, CO** (city) Denver County	5,269
Washington	15,567	San Bernardino County, CA	8,380	**San Diego, CA** (city) San Diego County	4,921
Illinois	11,666	Hillsborough County, FL	8,202	**Phoenix, AZ** (city) Maricopa County	4,863

Sorted by Number in Ascending Order — U.S. = 635,253

State	Number	County	Number	Place	Number
North Dakota	381	Teller County, CO	100	**Conroe, TX** (city) Montgomery County	100
South Dakota	496	Wayne County, NC	100	**Fallbrook, CA** (cdp) San Diego County	100
Maine	672	Cass County, MO	101	**Montgomery, AL** (city) Montgomery County	100
Vermont	701	Kent County, RI	101	**Altadena, CA** (cdp) Los Angeles County	101
Delaware	850	Liberty County, TX	101	**Sahuarita, AZ** (town) Pima County	101
West Virginia	970	Monroe County, MI	101	**Rowland Heights, CA** (cdp) Los Angeles County	102
Rhode Island	1,000	Sumner County, TN	101	**Lynn, MA** (city) Essex County	103
New Hampshire	1,032	Walla Walla County, WA	101	**Central Islip, NY** (cdp) Suffolk County	104
Mississippi	1,353	Montgomery County, AL	102	**Revere, MA** (city) Suffolk County	104
Montana	1,360	Warren County, OH	102	**Waterbury, CT** (city/town) New Haven County	104

Sorted by Percent of Total Population in Descending Order — U.S. = 0.2%

State	Percent	County	Percent	Place	Percent
New Mexico	3.2	Socorro County, NM	7.0	**Santa Fe, NM** (city) Santa Fe County	5.9
Colorado	0.8	San Miguel County, NM	6.4	**South Valley, NM** (cdp) Bernalillo County	4.6
Hawaii	0.8	Rio Arriba County, NM	6.2	**Rio Rancho, NM** (city) Sandoval County	4.4
California	0.4	Mora County, NM	5.8	**Albuquerque, NM** (city) Bernalillo County	4.3
Nevada	0.4	Santa Fe County, NM	5.5	**Pueblo, CO** (city) Pueblo County	2.5
Arizona	0.3	Valencia County, NM	5.5	**Farmington, NM** (city) San Juan County	2.4
Florida	0.3	Conejos County, CO	5.4	**Kearny, NJ** (town) Hudson County	2.2
Texas	0.3	Taos County, NM	5.3	**Pueblo West, CO** (cdp) Pueblo County	1.9
Utah	0.3	Colfax County, NM	4.7	**Makakilo*, HI** (cdp) Honolulu County	1.7
Wyoming	0.3	Guadalupe County, NM	4.4	**Northglenn, CO** (city) Adams County	1.7

Sorted by Percent of Total Population in Ascending Order — U.S. = 0.2%

State	Percent	County	Percent	Place	Percent
Alabama	0.0	Anoka County, MN	0.0	**Cleveland, OH** (city) Cuyahoga County	0.0
Kentucky	0.0	Brown County, WI	0.0	**Detroit, MI** (city) Wayne County	0.0
Mississippi	0.0	Butler County, OH	0.0	**Louisville-Jefferson County, KY** (metropolitan govt) Jefferson County	0.0
Arkansas	0.1	Clayton County, GA	0.0	**Memphis, TN** (city) Shelby County	0.0
Delaware	0.1	Erie County, PA	0.0	**Montgomery, AL** (city) Montgomery County	0.0
Georgia	0.1	Jefferson County, AL	0.0	**Akron, OH** (city) Summit County	0.1
Illinois	0.1	Jefferson County, KY	0.0	**Allentown, PA** (city) Lehigh County	0.1
Indiana	0.1	Montgomery County, AL	0.0	**Atlanta, GA** (city) Fulton County	0.1
Iowa	0.1	Spartanburg County, SC	0.0	**Augusta-Richmond County, GA** (consolidated govt) Richmond County	0.1
Kansas	0.1	Warren County, OH	0.0	**Aurora, IL** (city) Kane County	0.1

Note: (1) Ranking tables cover all states and counties, and places with an overall population of at least 125,000, OR an overall population of at least 25,000 where the Hispanic/Latino population is at least 20% of the overall population. In states where less than five places meet either of these criteria, we have included places with at least 10,000 total population with the highest percentage of Hispanic/Latino population. These places are identified with an asterisk (*); Please refer to the User's Guide for a full explanation of data.

Sorted by Percent of Hispanic Population in Descending Order U.S. = 1.3%

State	Percent	County	Percent	Place	Percent
Hawaii	8.5	Los Alamos County, NM	18.7	**Makakilo*, HI** (cdp) Honolulu County	13.0
Vermont	7.6	Harrison County, WV	17.2	**Rio Rancho, NM** (city) Sandoval County	12.1
New Mexico	6.8	Washington County, VT	14.6	**Santa Fe, NM** (city) Santa Fe County	12.1
Montana	4.8	Socorro County, NM	14.4	**Farmington, NM** (city) San Juan County	10.5
West Virginia	4.4	Saint Bernard Parish, LA	12.6	**Urban Honolulu, HI** (cdp) Honolulu County	9.9
Colorado	4.0	La Plata County, CO	11.5	**Albuquerque, NM** (city) Bernalillo County	9.2
Maine	4.0	Huerfano County, CO	11.3	**Pueblo West, CO** (cdp) Pueblo County	8.3
Alaska	3.9	Santa Fe County, NM	10.9	**Green River*, WY** (city) Sweetwater County	6.8
Wyoming	3.9	Cibola County, NM	10.8	**Missoula*, MT** (city) Missoula County	6.0
Louisiana	3.1	Sandoval County, NM	10.8	**Waianae*, HI** (cdp) Honolulu County	5.9

Sorted by Percent of Hispanic Population in Ascending Order U.S. = 1.3%

State	Percent	County	Percent	Place	Percent
Illinois	0.6	Hidalgo County, TX	0.2	**Aurora, IL** (city) Kane County	0.2
Texas	0.7	Imperial County, CA	0.2	**Compton, CA** (city) Los Angeles County	0.2
Rhode Island	0.8	Webb County, TX	0.2	**East Los Angeles, CA** (cdp) Los Angeles County	0.2
Georgia	0.9	Bronx County, NY	0.3	**Florence-Graham, CA** (cdp) Los Angeles County	0.2
Indiana	0.9	Cameron County, TX	0.3	**Hartford, CT** (city/town) Hartford County	0.2
North Carolina	0.9	Clayton County, GA	0.3	**Huntington Park, CA** (city) Los Angeles County	0.2
Arkansas	1.0	Cumberland County, NJ	0.3	**Laredo, TX** (city) Webb County	0.2
California	1.0	Franklin County, WA	0.3	**Mission, TX** (city) Hidalgo County	0.2
Iowa	1.0	Hall County, GA	0.3	**Paterson, NJ** (city) Passaic County	0.2
Kansas	1.0	Berks County, PA	0.4	**Santa Ana, CA** (city) Orange County	0.2

Note: (1) Ranking tables cover all states and counties, and places with an overall population of at least 125,000, OR an overall population of at least 25,000 where the Hispanic/Latino population is at least 20% of the overall population. In states where less than five places meet either of these criteria, we have included places with at least 10,000 total population with the highest percentage of Hispanic/Latino population. These places are identified with an asterisk (*); Please refer to the User's Guide for a full explanation of data.

Population Growth: 2000–2010

Total Population

Top 10 States, Counties, and Places[1]

Sorted by Percent in Descending Order — U.S. = 9.7%

State	Percent	County	Percent	Place	Percent
Nevada	35.1	Kendall County, IL	110.4	**Maricopa, AZ** (city) Pinal County	4,081.0
Arizona	24.6	Pinal County, AZ	109.1	**Bluffton*, SC** (town) Beaufort County	882.7
Utah	23.8	Flagler County, FL	92.0	**Sahuarita, AZ** (town) Pima County	679.1
Idaho	21.1	Lincoln County, SD	85.8	**Buckeye, AZ** (town) Maricopa County	678.3
Texas	20.6	Loudoun County, VA	84.1	**Wesley Chapel, FL** (cdp) Pasco County	674.8
North Carolina	18.5	Rockwall County, TX	81.8	**Little Elm, TX** (city) Denton County	610.3
Georgia	18.3	Forsyth County, GA	78.4	**Riverview, FL** (cdp) Hillsborough County	490.4
Florida	17.6	Sumter County, FL	75.1	**Kyle, TX** (city) Hays County	427.2
Colorado	16.9	Paulding County, GA	74.3	**El Mirage, AZ** (city) Maricopa County	317.9
South Carolina	15.3	Sublette County, WY	73.1	**Poinciana, FL** (cdp) Osceola County	289.8

Sorted by Percent in Ascending Order — U.S. = 9.7%

State	Percent	County	Percent	Place	Percent
Michigan	-0.6	Saint Bernard Parish, LA	-46.6	**Goleta, CA** (city) Santa Barbara County	-45.9
Rhode Island	0.4	Cameron Parish, LA	-31.5	**New Orleans, LA** (city) Orleans Parish	-29.1
Louisiana	1.4	Orleans Parish, LA	-29.1	**Annandale, VA** (cdp) Fairfax County	-25.4
Ohio	1.6	Chattahoochee County, GA	-24.3	**Detroit, MI** (city) Wayne County	-25.0
New York	2.1	Cimarron County, OK	-21.4	**Cleveland, OH** (city) Cuyahoga County	-17.1
West Virginia	2.5	Cottle County, TX	-21.0	**Galveston, TX** (city) Galveston County	-16.6
Vermont	2.8	Monroe County, AR	-20.5	**Montgomery Village, MD** (cdp) Montgomery County	-15.8
Massachusetts	3.1	Culberson County, TX	-19.4	**Dayton, OH** (city) Montgomery County	-14.8
Illinois	3.3	Esmeralda County, NV	-19.4	**Alamogordo, NM** (city) Otero County	-14.6
Pennsylvania	3.4	Washington County, MS	-18.8	**Pascagoula*, MS** (city) Jackson County	-14.5

Note: (1) Ranking tables cover all states and counties, and places with an overall population of at least 125,000, OR an overall population of at least 25,000 where the Hispanic/Latino population is at least 20% of the overall population. In states where less than five places meet either of these criteria, we have included places with at least 10,000 total population with the highest percentage of Hispanic/Latino population. These places are identified with an asterisk (*); Please refer to the User's Guide for a full explanation of data.

Population Growth: 2000–2010

Hispanic or Latino (of any race)

Top 10 States, Counties, and Places[1]

Sorted by Percent in Descending Order — U.S. = 43.0%

State	Percent	County	Percent	Place	Percent
South Carolina	147.9	Telfair County, GA	842.3	**Maricopa, AZ** (city) Pinal County	1,350.4
Alabama	144.8	Beadle County, SD	762.6	**Riverview, FL** (cdp) Hillsborough County	1,277.5
Tennessee	134.2	Adams County, MS	687.5	**Wesley Chapel, FL** (cdp) Pasco County	1,214.2
Kentucky	121.6	Trempealeau County, WI	594.6	**Sahuarita, AZ** (town) Pima County	930.2
Arkansas	114.2	Sublette County, WY	535.7	**Huron*, SD** (city) Beadle County	762.9
North Carolina	111.1	Tallahatchie County, MS	532.1	**Hazleton, PA** (city) Luzerne County	735.2
Maryland	106.5	Luzerne County, PA	478.8	**Buckeye, AZ** (town) Maricopa County	713.4
Mississippi	105.9	Sevier County, TN	441.5	**Little Elm, TX** (city) Denton County	644.1
South Dakota	102.9	Paulding County, GA	419.6	**Lehigh Acres, FL** (cdp) Lee County	567.2
Delaware	96.4	Frederick County, VA	414.7	**Leander, TX** (city) Williamson County	436.7

Sorted by Percent in Ascending Order — U.S. = 43.0%

State	Percent	County	Percent	Place	Percent
New York	19.2	Allen Parish, LA	-70.2	**Goleta, CA** (city) Santa Barbara County	-20.3
District of Columbia	21.8	Seminole County, GA	-41.2	**Alamogordo, NM** (city) Otero County	-18.6
New Mexico	24.6	Webster County, MS	-40.2	**Rosemead, CA** (city) Los Angeles County	-17.9
California	27.8	Lee County, AR	-39.1	**San Gabriel, CA** (city) Los Angeles County	-16.6
Illinois	32.5	Madison Parish, LA	-34.7	**Glendale, CA** (city) Los Angeles County	-13.1
Michigan	34.7	Holmes County, MS	-30.9	**Arlington, VA** (cdp) Arlington County	-11.0
Hawaii	37.8	Concordia Parish, LA	-30.3	**East Chicago, IN** (city) Lake County	-9.7
New Jersey	39.2	Foard County, TX	-29.4	**El Monte, CA** (city) Los Angeles County	-6.7
Colorado	41.2	Newton County, TX	-29.4	**Monterey Park, CA** (city) Los Angeles County	-6.6
Texas	41.8	Cameron Parish, LA	-28.4	**Alhambra, CA** (city) Los Angeles County	-6.1

Note: (1) Ranking tables cover all states and counties, and places with an overall population of at least 125,000, OR an overall population of at least 25,000 where the Hispanic/Latino population is at least 20% of the overall population. In states where less than five places meet either of these criteria, we have included places with at least 10,000 total population with the highest percentage of Hispanic/Latino population. These places are identified with an asterisk (*); Please refer to the User's Guide for a full explanation of data.

Population Growth: 2000–2010

Central American, excluding Mexican

Top 10 States, Counties, and Places[1]

Sorted by Percent in Descending Order — U.S. = 137.0%

State	Percent	County	Percent	Place	Percent
West Virginia	467.0	Douglas County, GA	1,127.9	**Lehigh Acres, FL** (cdp) Lee County	1,824.4
Wyoming	419.7	Frederick County, VA	1,123.6	**Port Saint Lucie, FL** (city) Saint Lucie County	757.4
Mississippi	390.5	Shelby County, AL	888.1	**Atascocita, TX** (cdp) Harris County	744.1
Alabama	380.8	Fauquier County, VA	843.1	**Avondale, AZ** (city) Maricopa County	705.7
Tennessee	379.0	Spotsylvania County, VA	839.3	**Brentwood, CA** (city) Contra Costa County	691.5
South Carolina	355.6	Stafford County, VA	836.2	**Dale City, VA** (cdp) Prince William County	646.9
Arkansas	303.5	Lexington County, SC	787.7	**Manteca, CA** (city) San Joaquin County	628.9
South Dakota	282.4	Frederick County, MD	774.6	**Knoxville, TN** (city) Knox County	614.9
Kentucky	268.4	Berkeley County, SC	730.5	**Poinciana, FL** (cdp) Osceola County	608.7
Indiana	260.8	Rutherford County, TN	706.8	**Lawrenceville, GA** (city) Gwinnett County	603.8

Sorted by Percent in Ascending Order — U.S. = 137.0%

State	Percent	County	Percent	Place	Percent
District of Columbia	47.8	Marion County, GA	-24.6	**Florence, AZ** (town) Pinal County	-48.3
Illinois	77.8	Liberty County, GA	6.0	**Fort Campbell North*, KY** (cdp) Christian County	-18.9
New York	94.4	Arlington County, VA	7.5	**El Centro, CA** (city) Imperial County	-13.3
California	96.5	Christian County, KY	10.1	**Arlington, VA** (cdp) Arlington County	7.5
Alaska	108.9	Lincoln County, NC	10.9	**Goleta, CA** (city) Santa Barbara County	9.8
Rhode Island	110.4	Vernon Parish, LA	22.6	**Fort Hood, TX** (cdp) Bell County	10.4
Florida	113.4	Gilmer County, GA	23.7	**North Atlanta, GA** (cdp) DeKalb County	15.6
New Jersey	119.4	Montgomery County, NY	26.3	**Fort Leonard Wood*, MO** (cdp) Pulaski County	16.2
Oregon	128.7	Coryell County, TX	33.3	**Hialeah, FL** (city) Miami-Dade County	18.0
Hawaii	133.4	Kings County, NY	43.6	**Fountainebleau, FL** (cdp) Miami-Dade County	24.0

Note: (1) Ranking tables cover all states and counties, and places with an overall population of at least 125,000, OR an overall population of at least 25,000 where the Hispanic/Latino population is at least 20% of the overall population. In states where less than five places meet either of these criteria, we have included places with at least 10,000 total population with the highest percentage of Hispanic/Latino population. These places are identified with an asterisk (*); Please refer to the User's Guide for a full explanation of data.

Population Growth: 2000–2010

Central American: Costa Rican

Top 10 States, Counties, and Places[1]

Sorted by Percent in Descending Order — U.S. = 84.3%

State	Percent	County	Percent	Place	Percent
Hawaii	175.2	Bucks County, PA	314.7	**Miramar, FL** (city) Broward County	158.2
Pennsylvania	173.1	Lee County, FL	214.2	**San Antonio, TX** (city) Bexar County	154.5
Georgia	160.6	Cobb County, GA	195.8	**Charlotte, NC** (city) Mecklenburg County	137.0
Tennessee	150.6	Bexar County, TX	193.4	**Rancho Cucamonga, CA** (city) San Bernardino County	133.3
Arkansas	150.4	Gwinnett County, GA	176.1	**Austin, TX** (city) Travis County	132.8
Missouri	142.6	Polk County, FL	173.7	**Jacksonville, FL** (city) Duval County	109.3
New Mexico	140.8	Collin County, TX	172.3	**Orlando, FL** (city) Orange County	105.9
Virginia	137.8	Hunterdon County, NJ	152.3	**Elizabeth, NJ** (city) Union County	104.3
Colorado	135.4	Riverside County, CA	138.0	**Bridgeport, CT** (city/town) Fairfield County	94.3
Maryland	133.7	New Haven County, CT	137.1	**Las Vegas, NV** (city) Clark County	84.8

Sorted by Percent in Ascending Order — U.S. = 84.3%

State	Percent	County	Percent	Place	Percent
New York	47.6	Lincoln County, NC	-9.0	**Hilton Head Island*, SC** (town) Beaufort County	-22.9
Illinois	49.0	Montgomery County, NY	-8.4	**Kendall West, FL** (cdp) Miami-Dade County	-4.8
District of Columbia	54.5	Orleans Parish, LA	20.5	**Berea*, SC** (cdp) Greenville County	0.0
Oklahoma	60.1	Richmond County, NY	22.6	**Hialeah, FL** (city) Miami-Dade County	0.6
Michigan	66.0	Queens County, NY	28.0	**Miami Beach, FL** (city) Miami-Dade County	1.7
Massachusetts	68.0	Cook County, IL	28.5	**Glendale, CA** (city) Los Angeles County	3.6
California	69.8	Bronx County, NY	29.4	**Chelsea, MA** (city) Suffolk County	4.5
Connecticut	74.4	Rockland County, NY	32.3	**Dallas, TX** (city) Dallas County	10.5
North Carolina	77.5	Hudson County, NJ	38.9	**Chicago, IL** (city) Cook County	11.8
New Jersey	78.4	Dallas County, TX	39.3	**Yonkers, NY** (city) Westchester County	15.6

Note: (1) Ranking tables cover all states and counties, and places with an overall population of at least 125,000, OR an overall population of at least 25,000 where the Hispanic/Latino population is at least 20% of the overall population. In states where less than five places meet either of these criteria, we have included places with at least 10,000 total population with the highest percentage of Hispanic/Latino population. These places are identified with an asterisk (*); Please refer to the User's Guide for a full explanation of data.

Population Growth: 2000–2010

Central American: Guatemalan

Top 10 States, Counties, and Places[1]

Sorted by Percent in Descending Order — U.S. = 180.3%

State	Percent	County	Percent	Place	Percent
Mississippi	778.5	Shelby County, TN	921.8	**Memphis, TN** (city) Shelby County	983.9
South Carolina	483.6	Frederick County, MD	813.7	**Worthington*, MN** (city) Nobles County	630.6
Alabama	482.2	Hamilton County, OH	759.6	**Dodge City, KS** (city) Ford County	619.3
Ohio	426.7	Anne Arundel County, MD	750.2	**Victorville, CA** (city) San Bernardino County	610.9
Kansas	412.8	Horry County, SC	717.6	**Baltimore, MD** (independent city)	559.3
Tennessee	408.6	Rutherford County, TN	695.0	**Port Saint Lucie, FL** (city) Saint Lucie County	547.3
Pennsylvania	393.6	Pulaski County, AR	694.9	**Indianapolis, IN** (city) Marion County	546.4
Kentucky	379.9	Baltimore County, MD	635.6	**Lancaster, CA** (city) Los Angeles County	510.3
Arkansas	334.2	Nobles County, MN	632.5	**Perris, CA** (city) Riverside County	506.9
Oklahoma	332.8	Hampden County, MA	618.3	**Cincinnati, OH** (city) Hamilton County	495.7

Sorted by Percent in Ascending Order — U.S. = 180.3%

State	Percent	County	Percent	Place	Percent
Illinois	78.5	Finney County, KS	4.5	**Garden City, KS** (city) Finney County	2.1
District of Columbia	95.2	Gilmer County, GA	22.0	**Goleta, CA** (city) Santa Barbara County	7.8
Rhode Island	110.7	Maui County, HI	34.7	**Culver City, CA** (city) Los Angeles County	17.4
Hawaii	112.4	Cook County, IL	48.4	**Union City, CA** (city) Alameda County	28.0
Oregon	119.3	Alamosa County, CO	58.3	**Chicago, IL** (city) Cook County	32.1
California	131.9	Carroll County, AR	64.8	**Cicero, IL** (town) Cook County	36.0
New York	153.9	Burke County, NC	66.3	**Hialeah, FL** (city) Miami-Dade County	36.1
Michigan	175.5	Arlington County, VA	77.2	**Fountainebleau, FL** (cdp) Miami-Dade County	43.8
Alaska	180.7	Dallas County, IA	79.0	**Kendall, FL** (cdp) Miami-Dade County	45.2
Massachusetts	186.9	New York County, NY	79.0	**Hillsboro, OR** (city) Washington County	46.6

Note: (1) Ranking tables cover all states and counties, and places with an overall population of at least 125,000, OR an overall population of at least 25,000 where the Hispanic/Latino population is at least 20% of the overall population. In states where less than five places meet either of these criteria, we have included places with at least 10,000 total population with the highest percentage of Hispanic/Latino population. These places are identified with an asterisk (*); Please refer to the User's Guide for a full explanation of data.

Population Growth: 2000–2010

Central American: Honduran

Top 10 States, Counties, and Places[1]

Sorted by Percent in Descending Order — U.S. = 191.1%

State	Percent	County	Percent	Place	Percent
Tennessee	553.0	Loudoun County, VA	1,212.9	**Baltimore, MD** (independent city)	758.3
Alabama	513.1	Prince William County, VA	933.6	**Jacksonville, FL** (city) Duval County	642.7
South Carolina	501.6	Baltimore County, MD	751.7	**Brookhaven, NY** (town) Suffolk County	628.7
Delaware	440.0	Saint Lucie County, FL	675.9	**Columbus, OH** (city) Franklin County	625.9
Mississippi	429.9	Bristol County, MA	672.8	**Aspen Hill, MD** (cdp) Montgomery County	494.5
Maryland	405.9	Duval County, FL	622.1	**Memphis, TN** (city) Shelby County	492.2
Arkansas	323.7	Denton County, TX	606.6	**Nashville-Davidson, TN** (metropolitan govt) Davidson County	464.1
Kentucky	320.9	Polk County, FL	584.9	**Baton Rouge, LA** (city) East Baton Rouge Parish	444.8
Kansas	309.3	Gwinnett County, GA	573.3	**Trenton, NJ** (city) Mercer County	443.0
Pennsylvania	306.4	Lee County, FL	573.2	**Tulsa, OK** (city) Tulsa County	428.3

Sorted by Percent in Ascending Order — U.S. = 191.1%

State	Percent	County	Percent	Place	Percent
Alaska	90.2	Burke County, NC	-5.2	**North Atlanta, GA** (cdp) DeKalb County	5.4
Illinois	100.7	Arlington County, VA	28.4	**Arlington, VA** (cdp) Arlington County	28.4
New York	104.7	Kings County, NY	47.3	**Hilton Head Island*, SC** (town) Beaufort County	30.1
New Jersey	136.9	New York County, NY	48.9	**Jersey City, NJ** (city) Hudson County	38.7
California	139.7	Hudson County, NJ	65.7	**Miami Beach, FL** (city) Miami-Dade County	39.6
Massachusetts	144.5	Queens County, NY	70.2	**Glendale, CA** (city) Los Angeles County	41.7
District of Columbia	150.8	Bronx County, NY	76.3	**Hialeah, FL** (city) Miami-Dade County	44.4
Oregon	151.4	Cook County, IL	78.0	**Brooklyn, NY** (borough) Kings County	47.3
Rhode Island	154.6	DeKalb County, GA	83.8	**Manhattan, NY** (borough) New York County	48.9
Michigan	159.8	El Paso County, TX	89.9	**Tamiami, FL** (cdp) Miami-Dade County	50.8

Note: (1) Ranking tables cover all states and counties, and places with an overall population of at least 125,000, OR an overall population of at least 25,000 where the Hispanic/Latino population is at least 20% of the overall population. In states where less than five places meet either of these criteria, we have included places with at least 10,000 total population with the highest percentage of Hispanic/Latino population. These places are identified with an asterisk (*); Please refer to the User's Guide for a full explanation of data.

Population Growth: 2000–2010

Central American: Nicaraguan

Top 10 States, Counties, and Places[1]

Sorted by Percent in Descending Order — U.S. = 96.0%

State	Percent	County	Percent	Place	Percent
Tennessee	381.7	Lee County, FL	917.0	**Homestead, FL** (city) Miami-Dade County	493.9
Alabama	310.6	Fort Bend County, TX	400.0	**Antioch, CA** (city) Contra Costa County	279.9
Arkansas	304.6	Prince William County, VA	373.1	**Hempstead (town), NY** (town) Nassau County	250.8
Mississippi	295.5	Gwinnett County, GA	359.8	**North Las Vegas, NV** (city) Clark County	244.0
South Carolina	291.3	San Joaquin County, CA	359.7	**Jacksonville, FL** (city) Duval County	243.0
Kentucky	267.8	Wake County, NC	343.6	**Sunrise Manor, NV** (cdp) Clark County	239.3
Georgia	243.4	Denton County, TX	330.8	**Stockton, CA** (city) San Joaquin County	238.8
North Carolina	242.6	Collin County, TX	314.4	**Rancho Cucamonga, CA** (city) San Bernardino County	234.1
Arizona	232.1	Polk County, FL	298.2	**Riverside, CA** (city) Riverside County	226.1
Colorado	231.1	Maricopa County, AZ	268.4	**Orlando, FL** (city) Orange County	206.5

Sorted by Percent in Ascending Order — U.S. = 96.0%

State	Percent	County	Percent	Place	Percent
District of Columbia	44.6	Kings County, NY	19.0	**New Brunswick, NJ** (city) Middlesex County	-5.4
New York	61.9	Arlington County, VA	27.7	**San Gabriel, CA** (city) Los Angeles County	-3.9
Florida	69.9	Cuyahoga County, OH	32.7	**Miami Beach, FL** (city) Miami-Dade County	0.8
New Jersey	87.5	San Francisco County, CA	39.3	**Rosemead, CA** (city) Los Angeles County	10.0
California	96.3	Bronx County, NY	41.4	**Hialeah, FL** (city) Miami-Dade County	13.0
Illinois	105.2	Wayne County, MI	44.0	**Brooklyn, NY** (borough) Kings County	19.0
Michigan	112.7	Milwaukee County, WI	46.8	**Fountainebleau, FL** (cdp) Miami-Dade County	19.8
Connecticut	113.3	Carson City, NV	48.1	**Silver Spring, MD** (cdp) Montgomery County	22.0
Wisconsin	114.5	New York County, NY	49.9	**Milwaukee, WI** (city) Milwaukee County	24.8
Louisiana	127.9	Miami-Dade County, FL	52.3	**Bell Gardens, CA** (city) Los Angeles County	27.4

RANKINGS & COMPARISONS

Note: (1) Ranking tables cover all states and counties, and places with an overall population of at least 125,000, OR an overall population of at least 25,000 where the Hispanic/Latino population is at least 20% of the overall population. In states where less than five places meet either of these criteria, we have included places with at least 10,000 total population with the highest percentage of Hispanic/Latino population. These places are identified with an asterisk (*); Please refer to the User's Guide for a full explanation of data.

Population Growth: 2000–2010

Central American: Panamanian

Top 10 States, Counties, and Places[1]

Sorted by Percent in Descending Order — U.S. = 80.4%

State	Percent	County	Percent	Place	Percent
Nevada	141.4	Gwinnett County, GA	329.1	**Charlotte, NC** (city) Mecklenburg County	357.1
South Carolina	139.9	Mecklenburg County, NC	324.6	**Atlanta, GA** (city) Fulton County	216.0
Georgia	131.7	Pasco County, FL	320.5	**Fort Worth, TX** (city) Tarrant County	193.0
Pennsylvania	131.5	Williamson County, TX	300.0	**Raleigh, NC** (city) Wake County	174.6
Utah	128.9	Polk County, FL	215.8	**Orlando, FL** (city) Orange County	159.1
Tennessee	121.9	Wake County, NC	214.4	**Baltimore, MD** (independent city)	156.2
Maryland	115.0	Collin County, TX	212.7	**Chesapeake, VA** (independent city)	154.3
Indiana	113.7	Baltimore County, MD	209.7	**Jacksonville, FL** (city) Duval County	152.7
Delaware	111.4	Fort Bend County, TX	206.7	**Brandon, FL** (cdp) Hillsborough County	141.0
Colorado	109.9	Fulton County, GA	205.4	**Fayetteville, NC** (city) Cumberland County	138.9

Sorted by Percent in Ascending Order — U.S. = 80.4%

State	Percent	County	Percent	Place	Percent
Hawaii	31.4	Liberty County, GA	-11.5	**Kendale Lakes, FL** (cdp) Miami-Dade County	-9.0
New York	40.6	Vernon Parish, LA	2.7	**Fountainebleau, FL** (cdp) Miami-Dade County	-7.2
Oklahoma	52.7	Coryell County, TX	6.2	**Richmond West, FL** (cdp) Miami-Dade County	-1.4
New Hampshire	62.1	Comanche County, OK	10.2	**Hialeah, FL** (city) Miami-Dade County	3.2
Rhode Island	64.7	Orleans Parish, LA	13.0	**Country Club, FL** (cdp) Miami-Dade County	3.8
California	66.2	Jefferson County, NY	14.4	**Miami Beach, FL** (city) Miami-Dade County	7.1
New Mexico	66.7	Geary County, KS	17.3	**Brentwood, NY** (cdp) Suffolk County	8.0
Louisiana	67.7	Pulaski County, MO	19.8	**New Orleans, LA** (city) Orleans Parish	13.0
District of Columbia	69.8	Queens County, NY	24.2	**Kendall West, FL** (cdp) Miami-Dade County	13.3
Washington	70.4	Cumberland County, NC	28.1	**Hempstead (village), NY** (village) Nassau County	16.0

Note: (1) Ranking tables cover all states and counties, and places with an overall population of at least 125,000, OR an overall population of at least 25,000 where the Hispanic/Latino population is at least 20% of the overall population. In states where less than five places meet either of these criteria, we have included places with at least 10,000 total population with the highest percentage of Hispanic/Latino population. These places are identified with an asterisk (*); Please refer to the User's Guide for a full explanation of data.

Population Growth: 2000–2010

Central American: Salvadoran

Top 10 States, Counties, and Places[1]

Sorted by Percent in Descending Order — U.S. = 151.7%

State	Percent	County	Percent	Place	Percent
South Dakota	642.9	Frederick County, MD	986.9	**Lynn, MA** (city) Essex County	832.7
South Carolina	500.3	Spotsylvania County, VA	913.1	**Dale City, VA** (cdp) Prince William County	741.6
Mississippi	484.1	Baltimore County, MD	878.6	**Hesperia, CA** (city) San Bernardino County	728.6
Tennessee	459.4	Rutherford County, TN	790.2	**Spring, TX** (cdp) Harris County	721.4
Delaware	423.8	Essex County, MA	705.4	**Victorville, CA** (city) San Bernardino County	689.9
Alabama	421.3	East Baton Rouge Parish, LA	618.0	**Mesquite, TX** (city) Dallas County	625.5
Oklahoma	421.1	Loudoun County, VA	573.1	**Whitney, NV** (cdp) Clark County	595.0
Louisiana	354.3	Prince William County, VA	560.4	**Revere, MA** (city) Suffolk County	587.3
Indiana	341.3	Williamson County, TX	559.3	**Baton Rouge, LA** (city) East Baton Rouge Parish	547.0
Idaho	340.7	Garfield County, CO	535.2	**Tracy, CA** (city) San Joaquin County	537.4

Sorted by Percent in Ascending Order — U.S. = 151.7%

State	Percent	County	Percent	Place	Percent
District of Columbia	41.5	Arlington County, VA	-7.1	**North Atlanta, GA** (cdp) DeKalb County	-12.0
Illinois	100.7	DeKalb County, GA	19.9	**Arlington, VA** (cdp) Arlington County	-7.1
New York	109.2	Umatilla County, OR	49.2	**Mundelein, IL** (village) Lake County	7.5
Alaska	109.8	San Francisco County, CA	51.7	**Kendall, FL** (cdp) Miami-Dade County	26.4
California	110.2	Kings County, NY	52.2	**Kendall West, FL** (cdp) Miami-Dade County	26.5
New Jersey	124.1	Queens County, NY	54.7	**Culver City, CA** (city) Los Angeles County	30.5
Rhode Island	125.1	Hendry County, FL	56.7	**Atlanta, GA** (city) Fulton County	33.1
Florida	166.4	New York County, NY	57.3	**Round Lake Beach, IL** (village) Lake County	33.6
Oregon	171.2	Yell County, AR	59.9	**Glendale, CA** (city) Los Angeles County	35.8
Massachusetts	173.0	Bronx County, NY	67.0	**Miami Beach, FL** (city) Miami-Dade County	36.3

Note: (1) Ranking tables cover all states and counties, and places with an overall population of at least 125,000, OR an overall population of at least 25,000 where the Hispanic/Latino population is at least 20% of the overall population. In states where less than five places meet either of these criteria, we have included places with at least 10,000 total population with the highest percentage of Hispanic/Latino population. These places are identified with an asterisk (*); Please refer to the User's Guide for a full explanation of data.

Population Growth: 2000–2010

Cuban

Top 10 States, Counties, and Places[1]

Sorted by Percent in Descending Order — U.S. = 43.8%

State	Percent	County	Percent	Place	Percent
Kentucky	165.2	Lee County, FL	611.1	**Lehigh Acres, FL** (cdp) Lee County	2,622.2
Nebraska	150.5	Forsyth County, GA	394.9	**Riverview, FL** (cdp) Hillsborough County	1,015.4
North Carolina	144.7	Cabarrus County, NC	392.7	**Poinciana, FL** (cdp) Osceola County	751.9
Hawaii	117.2	Colquitt County, GA	361.9	**Cape Coral, FL** (city) Lee County	599.1
Tennessee	110.4	Saint Lucie County, FL	350.4	**Port Saint Lucie, FL** (city) Saint Lucie County	424.2
Utah	108.8	Hernando County, FL	337.5	**Homestead, FL** (city) Miami-Dade County	338.7
South Carolina	107.1	Lake County, FL	292.3	**Fayetteville, NC** (city) Cumberland County	301.5
Arizona	102.8	Pinal County, AZ	276.7	**Apopka, FL** (city) Orange County	288.2
Idaho	102.2	Williamson County, TX	275.3	**Glendale, AZ** (city) Maricopa County	278.7
Georgia	99.8	Pasco County, FL	273.1	**Newport News, VA** (independent city)	278.4

Sorted by Percent in Ascending Order — U.S. = 43.8%

State	Percent	County	Percent	Place	Percent
North Dakota	4.0	Scott County, MS	-30.2	**Annandale, VA** (cdp) Fairfax County	-38.2
New Jersey	7.8	Hamilton County, FL	-29.4	**Huntington Park, CA** (city) Los Angeles County	-35.8
New York	13.1	Madera County, CA	-26.6	**Melrose Park, IL** (village) Cook County	-31.3
Illinois	22.3	Orleans Parish, LA	-20.4	**Union City, NJ** (city) Hudson County	-27.1
Louisiana	22.3	Saint Bernard Parish, LA	-19.7	**Passaic, NJ** (city) Passaic County	-26.5
California	22.6	Hudson County, NJ	-15.5	**Newark, NJ** (city) Essex County	-24.3
Massachusetts	27.5	Queens County, NY	-13.9	**Port Chester, NY** (village) Westchester County	-22.8
Connecticut	33.6	Oneida County, NY	-10.1	**Lawndale, CA** (city) Los Angeles County	-21.6
Mississippi	36.8	New York County, NY	-2.7	**Hawthorne, CA** (city) Los Angeles County	-21.2
Michigan	37.4	Jackson County, FL	-1.9	**Rosemead, CA** (city) Los Angeles County	-20.7

Note: (1) Ranking tables cover all states and counties, and places with an overall population of at least 125,000, OR an overall population of at least 25,000 where the Hispanic/Latino population is at least 20% of the overall population. In states where less than five places meet either of these criteria, we have included places with at least 10,000 total population with the highest percentage of Hispanic/Latino population. These places are identified with an asterisk (*); Please refer to the User's Guide for a full explanation of data.

Population Growth: 2000–2010

Dominican Republic

Top 10 States, Counties, and Places[1]

Sorted by Percent in Descending Order — U.S. = 84.9%

State	Percent	County	Percent	Place	Percent
North Carolina	431.4	Luzerne County, PA	1,908.9	**Hazleton, PA** (city) Luzerne County	1,519.1
Pennsylvania	411.6	Lake County, FL	1,139.2	**Port Saint Lucie, FL** (city) Saint Lucie County	773.6
Georgia	362.1	Pasco County, FL	961.1	**Poinciana, FL** (cdp) Osceola County	744.7
South Carolina	318.6	Saint Lucie County, FL	684.0	**Raleigh, NC** (city) Wake County	647.8
Tennessee	300.9	Polk County, FL	671.6	**Meadow Woods, FL** (cdp) Orange County	624.1
Mississippi	285.8	Wake County, NC	632.1	**Charlotte, NC** (city) Mecklenburg County	594.9
Kansas	278.2	Mecklenburg County, NC	628.0	**Brandon, FL** (cdp) Hillsborough County	475.4
Indiana	262.8	Lebanon County, PA	577.1	**Fayetteville, NC** (city) Cumberland County	470.3
Utah	255.7	Gwinnett County, GA	566.4	**Greensboro, NC** (city) Guilford County	462.4
Arizona	247.9	Northampton County, PA	549.6	**Allentown, PA** (city) Lehigh County	440.2

Sorted by Percent in Ascending Order — U.S. = 84.9%

State	Percent	County	Percent	Place	Percent
New York	48.3	Franklin County, NY	-22.6	**Hialeah, FL** (city) Miami-Dade County	2.4
District of Columbia	67.6	Greene County, NY	-13.5	**Kendall West, FL** (cdp) Miami-Dade County	8.4
New Jersey	92.9	Saint Lawrence County, NY	-8.9	**Miami Beach, FL** (city) Miami-Dade County	11.8
Illinois	94.0	Jefferson County, NY	-2.7	**University Park, FL** (cdp) Miami-Dade County	13.2
Rhode Island	95.6	Chautauqua County, NY	7.7	**Manhattan, NY** (borough) New York County	14.4
Massachusetts	106.9	Washington County, NY	7.7	**Fountainebleau, FL** (cdp) Miami-Dade County	16.0
Alaska	117.7	New York County, NY	14.4	**South Miami Heights, FL** (cdp) Miami-Dade County	16.1
Michigan	124.2	Clinton County, NY	23.2	**Tamiami, FL** (cdp) Miami-Dade County	17.8
California	127.0	Queens County, NY	26.0	**Westchester, FL** (cdp) Miami-Dade County	20.5
Florida	143.0	Kings County, NY	32.1	**Silver Spring, MD** (cdp) Montgomery County	23.9

RANKINGS & COMPARISONS

Note: (1) Ranking tables cover all states and counties, and places with an overall population of at least 125,000, OR an overall population of at least 25,000 where the Hispanic/Latino population is at least 20% of the overall population. In states where less than five places meet either of these criteria, we have included places with at least 10,000 total population with the highest percentage of Hispanic/Latino population. These places are identified with an asterisk (*); Please refer to the User's Guide for a full explanation of data.

Population Growth: 2000–2010

Mexican

Top 10 States, Counties, and Places[1]

Sorted by Percent in Descending Order — U.S. = 54.1%

State	Percent	County	Percent	Place	Percent
Alabama	176.1	Adams County, MS	1,359.8	**Riverview, FL** (cdp) Hillsborough County	1,660.0
South Carolina	161.7	Trempealeau County, WI	723.5	**Maricopa, AZ** (city) Pinal County	1,207.7
Kentucky	161.6	Grant Parish, LA	661.0	**Sahuarita, AZ** (town) Pima County	933.9
Louisiana	143.7	Telfair County, GA	619.1	**Buckeye, AZ** (town) Maricopa County	785.4
Mississippi	142.7	Macon County, NC	582.0	**Bear*, DE** (cdp) New Castle County	708.2
Tennessee	141.2	Tallapoosa County, AL	522.1	**Lehigh Acres, FL** (cdp) Lee County	670.3
Pennsylvania	134.8	Luzerne County, PA	481.8	**Poinciana, FL** (cdp) Osceola County	581.6
Delaware	133.2	Paulding County, GA	459.7	**Port Saint Lucie, FL** (city) Saint Lucie County	569.0
Arkansas	125.8	Pasquotank County, NC	438.5	**Little Elm, TX** (city) Denton County	524.3
West Virginia	123.2	Saline County, AR	416.8	**Leander, TX** (city) Williamson County	502.7

Sorted by Percent in Ascending Order — U.S. = 54.1%

State	Percent	County	Percent	Place	Percent
California	35.1	Seminole County, GA	-56.1	**Goleta, CA** (city) Santa Barbara County	-16.0
Illinois	40.0	Madison Parish, LA	-44.1	**Rosemead, CA** (city) Los Angeles County	-13.4
Michigan	44.0	Lee County, AR	-28.6	**Kendall West, FL** (cdp) Miami-Dade County	-11.9
Rhode Island	54.6	Winston County, MS	-21.7	**San Gabriel, CA** (city) Los Angeles County	-11.8
Arizona	55.6	Cameron Parish, LA	-18.2	**Alamogordo, NM** (city) Otero County	-10.7
Texas	56.8	Phillips County, AR	-15.2	**Glendale, CA** (city) Los Angeles County	-8.1
Alaska	62.3	Crawford County, GA	-14.2	**Atlanta, GA** (city) Fulton County	-7.0
Kansas	66.8	Culberson County, TX	-12.7	**East Chicago, IN** (city) Lake County	-3.5
District of Columbia	66.9	Carbon County, MT	-11.8	**Monterey Park, CA** (city) Los Angeles County	-3.3
Colorado	68.0	Foard County, TX	-10.9	**Alhambra, CA** (city) Los Angeles County	-3.1

Note: (1) Ranking tables cover all states and counties, and places with an overall population of at least 125,000, OR an overall population of at least 25,000 where the Hispanic/Latino population is at least 20% of the overall population. In states where less than five places meet either of these criteria, we have included places with at least 10,000 total population with the highest percentage of Hispanic/Latino population. These places are identified with an asterisk (*); Please refer to the User's Guide for a full explanation of data.

Population Growth: 2000–2010

Puerto Rican

Top 10 States, Counties, and Places[1]

Sorted by Percent in Descending Order — U.S. = 35.7%

State	Percent	County	Percent	Place	Percent
South Dakota	132.8	Pinal County, AZ	601.8	**Riverview, FL** (cdp) Hillsborough County	1,303.3
North Carolina	130.7	Union County, NC	469.5	**Wesley Chapel, FL** (cdp) Pasco County	1,221.1
West Virginia	130.0	Kendall County, IL	406.6	**Pascagoula*, MS** (city) Jackson County	580.5
South Carolina	117.0	Paulding County, GA	393.5	**Hazleton, PA** (city) Luzerne County	526.9
Mississippi	104.4	Forsyth County, GA	390.7	**McKinney, TX** (city) Collin County	466.9
Tennessee	104.4	Union County, PA	390.1	**Poinciana, FL** (cdp) Osceola County	402.9
Georgia	102.6	Johnston County, NC	375.7	**Elk Grove, CA** (city) Sacramento County	350.8
Nevada	98.3	Jackson County, MS	367.1	**Murrieta, CA** (city) Riverside County	306.7
Arizona	97.8	Coweta County, GA	350.4	**Saint Cloud, FL** (city) Osceola County	297.7
North Dakota	94.7	Luzerne County, PA	337.5	**Lehigh Acres, FL** (cdp) Lee County	274.8

Sorted by Percent in Ascending Order — U.S. = 35.7%

State	Percent	County	Percent	Place	Percent
New York	1.9	Franklin County, NY	-36.6	**San Pablo, CA** (city) Contra Costa County	-27.7
Illinois	15.9	Wyoming County, NY	-28.2	**Brentwood, NY** (cdp) Suffolk County	-25.8
New Jersey	18.3	Orleans County, NY	-23.1	**Kendall West, FL** (cdp) Miami-Dade County	-24.3
Connecticut	30.1	Chattahoochee County, GA	-22.8	**Hialeah, FL** (city) Miami-Dade County	-23.6
Massachusetts	33.6	Kings County, NY	-17.1	**La Puente, CA** (city) Los Angeles County	-23.0
District of Columbia	34.4	Washington County, NY	-17.0	**Bell, CA** (city) Los Angeles County	-22.8
California	35.1	New York County, NY	-10.0	**Stanton, CA** (city) Orange County	-22.8
Rhode Island	37.6	Saint Lawrence County, NY	-9.3	**Long Branch, NJ** (city) Monmouth County	-21.3
Michigan	38.3	Mercer County, PA	-8.6	**Chillum, MD** (cdp) Prince George's County	-20.8
Ohio	43.3	Orleans Parish, LA	-8.1	**Huntington Park, CA** (city) Los Angeles County	-19.7

Note: (1) Ranking tables cover all states and counties, and places with an overall population of at least 125,000, OR an overall population of at least 25,000 where the Hispanic/Latino population is at least 20% of the overall population. In states where less than five places meet either of these criteria, we have included places with at least 10,000 total population with the highest percentage of Hispanic/Latino population. These places are identified with an asterisk (*); Please refer to the User's Guide for a full explanation of data.

Population Growth: 2000–2010

South American

Top 10 States, Counties, and Places[1]

Sorted by Percent in Descending Order — U.S. = 104.6%

State	Percent	County	Percent	Place	Percent
South Carolina	264.6	Cabarrus County, NC	940.6	**McKinney, TX** (city) Collin County	933.3
North Carolina	257.4	Pinal County, AZ	918.8	**Lehigh Acres, FL** (cdp) Lee County	907.9
Wyoming	226.4	Cherokee County, GA	686.6	**Winter Garden, FL** (city) Orange County	784.1
Montana	223.7	Paulding County, GA	655.2	**Homestead, FL** (city) Miami-Dade County	738.6
Tennessee	218.2	Union County, NC	634.1	**Port Saint Lucie, FL** (city) Saint Lucie County	713.4
West Virginia	210.8	Pasco County, FL	614.3	**Saint Cloud, FL** (city) Osceola County	514.0
Georgia	196.0	Forsyth County, GA	601.6	**Poinciana, FL** (cdp) Osceola County	495.0
Alabama	184.9	Saint Lucie County, FL	581.8	**Atascocita, TX** (cdp) Harris County	472.8
Arkansas	183.3	Rutherford County, TN	558.3	**Royal Palm Beach, FL** (village) Palm Beach County	465.4
Idaho	181.0	Lake County, FL	533.5	**Meadow Woods, FL** (cdp) Orange County	458.7

Sorted by Percent in Ascending Order — U.S. = 104.6%

State	Percent	County	Percent	Place	Percent
New York	61.3	Sumter County, FL	-39.6	**Berea*, SC** (cdp) Greenville County	-5.3
Rhode Island	61.7	Etowah County, AL	-10.3	**Chelsea, MA** (city) Suffolk County	-2.3
Illinois	75.5	Arlington County, VA	28.3	**Goleta, CA** (city) Santa Barbara County	3.6
California	81.6	Leavenworth County, KS	30.4	**Fort Hood, TX** (cdp) Bell County	6.5
New Jersey	83.7	Union County, PA	38.8	**Huntington Park, CA** (city) Los Angeles County	6.7
Michigan	92.8	Queens County, NY	40.2	**Kendall West, FL** (cdp) Miami-Dade County	9.1
Massachusetts	94.0	Jefferson County, TX	40.5	**Hialeah, FL** (city) Miami-Dade County	10.6
Alaska	104.8	New York County, NY	45.9	**Central Falls*, RI** (city) Providence County	11.7
District of Columbia	105.3	Kings County, NY	46.5	**South Gate, CA** (city) Los Angeles County	12.3
Iowa	111.9	Black Hawk County, IA	48.1	**Detroit, MI** (city) Wayne County	17.0

Note: (1) Ranking tables cover all states and counties, and places with an overall population of at least 125,000, OR an overall population of at least 25,000 where the Hispanic/Latino population is at least 20% of the overall population. In states where less than five places meet either of these criteria, we have included places with at least 10,000 total population with the highest percentage of Hispanic/Latino population. These places are identified with an asterisk (*); Please refer to the User's Guide for a full explanation of data.

Population Growth: 2000–2010

South American: Argentinean

Top 10 States, Counties, and Places[1]

Sorted by Percent in Descending Order — U.S. = 123.0%

State	Percent	County	Percent	Place	Percent
South Carolina	341.4	Lee County, FL	378.6	**Charlotte, NC** (city) Mecklenburg County	317.9
Tennessee	293.9	Collier County, FL	375.0	**Doral, FL** (city) Miami-Dade County	313.0
New Mexico	281.9	Wake County, NC	374.4	**Miramar, FL** (city) Broward County	274.5
Hawaii	269.8	Denton County, TX	369.2	**Aventura, FL** (city) Miami-Dade County	272.4
North Carolina	255.1	Tarrant County, TX	366.5	**Hollywood, FL** (city) Broward County	256.6
Georgia	226.9	Collin County, TX	359.7	**Irving, TX** (city) Dallas County	234.6
Alabama	213.9	Montgomery County, TX	335.0	**Jacksonville, FL** (city) Duval County	230.8
Virginia	201.4	Fort Bend County, TX	318.3	**Tamarac, FL** (city) Broward County	230.4
Oregon	200.9	Mecklenburg County, NC	312.7	**Tampa, FL** (city) Hillsborough County	229.9
Idaho	200.0	Osceola County, FL	298.2	**Weston, FL** (city) Broward County	209.2

Sorted by Percent in Ascending Order — U.S. = 123.0%

State	Percent	County	Percent	Place	Percent
New York	73.3	Queens County, NY	40.0	**El Monte, CA** (city) Los Angeles County	-1.9
Massachusetts	78.9	Hudson County, NJ	43.4	**South Gate, CA** (city) Los Angeles County	6.7
New Jersey	83.1	Suffolk County, MA	47.0	**Union City, NJ** (city) Hudson County	10.9
Rhode Island	90.7	Los Angeles County, CA	67.1	**Garfield, NJ** (city) Bergen County	18.0
California	91.3	Passaic County, NJ	67.7	**West Covina, CA** (city) Los Angeles County	18.4
Michigan	96.6	New York County, NY	67.9	**North Bergen, NJ** (township) Hudson County	19.3
Illinois	110.7	Nassau County, NY	68.1	**Downey, CA** (city) Los Angeles County	22.6
District of Columbia	122.4	Mercer County, NJ	72.9	**Glendale, CA** (city) Los Angeles County	32.1
Maryland	125.3	Middlesex County, MA	74.0	**Covina, CA** (city) Los Angeles County	33.0
Pennsylvania	126.5	Bronx County, NY	74.3	**Kendall, FL** (cdp) Miami-Dade County	38.8

RANKINGS & COMPARISONS

Note: (1) Ranking tables cover all states and counties, and places with an overall population of at least 125,000, OR an overall population of at least 25,000 where the Hispanic/Latino population is at least 20% of the overall population. In states where less than five places meet either of these criteria, we have included places with at least 10,000 total population with the highest percentage of Hispanic/Latino population. These places are identified with an asterisk (*); Please refer to the User's Guide for a full explanation of data.

Population Growth: 2000–2010

South American: Bolivian

Top 10 States, Counties, and Places[1]

Sorted by Percent in Descending Order — U.S. = 135.8%

State	Percent	County	Percent	Place	Percent
South Carolina	336.3	Loudoun County, VA	1,014.6	**Springfield, VA** (cdp) Fairfax County	228.8
Nevada	291.1	Prince William County, VA	606.2	**Annandale, VA** (cdp) Fairfax County	184.8
Arizona	190.7	Collier County, FL	456.8	**Dallas, TX** (city) Dallas County	152.9
Virginia	177.9	Fairfax County, VA	212.3	**Gaithersburg, MD** (city) Montgomery County	135.6
Minnesota	173.9	Palm Beach County, FL	185.0	**Boston, MA** (city) Suffolk County	128.7
Pennsylvania	173.7	Salt Lake County, UT	184.7	**San Diego, CA** (city) San Diego County	124.0
Tennessee	165.9	Riverside County, CA	181.3	**Austin, TX** (city) Travis County	123.9
North Carolina	164.5	Prince George's County, MD	179.7	**Hempstead (town), NY** (town) Nassau County	116.7
Colorado	162.7	Maricopa County, AZ	178.8	**Clifton, NJ** (city) Passaic County	116.1
Texas	161.5	Suffolk County, MA	150.4	**Port Chester, NY** (village) Westchester County	114.7

Sorted by Percent in Ascending Order — U.S. = 135.8%

State	Percent	County	Percent	Place	Percent
New York	68.7	Arlington County, VA	19.6	**Arlington, VA** (cdp) Arlington County	19.6
Illinois	89.3	Queens County, NY	41.0	**Miami Beach, FL** (city) Miami-Dade County	19.9
District of Columbia	90.6	Richmond County, NY	49.1	**Silver Spring, MD** (cdp) Montgomery County	21.3
New Jersey	91.5	Passaic County, NJ	57.8	**Hollywood, FL** (city) Broward County	30.0
Rhode Island	99.0	Cook County, IL	58.3	**Burbank, CA** (city) Los Angeles County	30.8
California	101.7	Bergen County, NJ	60.8	**Passaic, NJ** (city) Passaic County	35.0
Ohio	117.1	San Francisco County, CA	61.2	**Elizabeth, NJ** (city) Union County	35.5
Connecticut	118.2	Kings County, NY	69.4	**Jersey City, NJ** (city) Hudson County	38.1
Kentucky	118.3	Middlesex County, MA	72.5	**Fountainebleau, FL** (cdp) Miami-Dade County	40.5
Oklahoma	120.6	Miami-Dade County, FL	73.6	**Queens, NY** (borough) Queens County	41.0

Note: (1) Ranking tables cover all states and counties, and places with an overall population of at least 125,000, OR an overall population of at least 25,000 where the Hispanic/Latino population is at least 20% of the overall population. In states where less than five places meet either of these criteria, we have included places with at least 10,000 total population with the highest percentage of Hispanic/Latino population. These places are identified with an asterisk (*); Please refer to the User's Guide for a full explanation of data.

Population Growth: 2000–2010

South American: Chilean

Top 10 States, Counties, and Places[1]

Sorted by Percent in Descending Order — U.S. = 84.2%

State	Percent	County	Percent	Place	Percent
Hawaii	209.1	Wake County, NC	283.2	**Doral, FL** (city) Miami-Dade County	177.7
South Carolina	198.4	Prince William County, VA	201.7	**Weston, FL** (city) Broward County	163.8
Alabama	194.8	Osceola County, FL	189.2	**Charlotte, NC** (city) Mecklenburg County	162.9
Kentucky	179.0	Fulton County, GA	175.2	**Santa Clarita, CA** (city) Los Angeles County	158.2
North Carolina	173.3	Collin County, TX	170.2	**Phoenix, AZ** (city) Maricopa County	154.0
Rhode Island	166.7	Hillsborough County, FL	169.4	**San Antonio, TX** (city) Bexar County	149.3
Georgia	157.9	Riverside County, CA	169.3	**Portland, OR** (city) Multnomah County	147.6
Arizona	147.2	Seminole County, FL	164.0	**Jacksonville, FL** (city) Duval County	145.3
Nevada	141.5	Maricopa County, AZ	162.4	**Las Vegas, NV** (city) Clark County	142.0
Indiana	136.1	Mecklenburg County, NC	159.8	**Miramar, FL** (city) Broward County	137.8

Sorted by Percent in Ascending Order — U.S. = 84.2%

State	Percent	County	Percent	Place	Percent
New York	51.5	Cuyahoga County, OH	19.5	**North Miami Beach, FL** (city) Miami-Dade County	-14.0
New Jersey	57.9	Prince George's County, MD	24.7	**Hialeah, FL** (city) Miami-Dade County	-1.5
Illinois	59.4	Queens County, NY	24.8	**Fountainebleau, FL** (cdp) Miami-Dade County	-0.2
Ohio	72.9	Marin County, CA	25.4	**Elizabeth, NJ** (city) Union County	1.4
Massachusetts	74.0	Bronx County, NY	30.8	**Union City, NJ** (city) Hudson County	5.7
Iowa	74.1	Suffolk County, MA	31.7	**Kendall West, FL** (cdp) Miami-Dade County	10.8
Nebraska	75.4	Hudson County, NJ	31.8	**Port Chester, NY** (village) Westchester County	10.8
Florida	75.7	Union County, NJ	41.0	**Elmont, NY** (cdp) Nassau County	11.2
Michigan	75.8	Westchester County, NY	41.0	**Ossining, NY** (village) Westchester County	11.2
California	77.4	Cook County, IL	43.6	**Lancaster, CA** (city) Los Angeles County	12.5

Note: (1) Ranking tables cover all states and counties, and places with an overall population of at least 125,000, OR an overall population of at least 25,000 where the Hispanic/Latino population is at least 20% of the overall population. In states where less than five places meet either of these criteria, we have included places with at least 10,000 total population with the highest percentage of Hispanic/Latino population. These places are identified with an asterisk (*); Please refer to the User's Guide for a full explanation of data.

Population Growth: 2000–2010

South American: Colombian

Top 10 States, Counties, and Places[1]

Sorted by Percent in Descending Order — U.S. = 93.1%

State	Percent	County	Percent	Place	Percent
North Carolina	254.0	Cherokee County, GA	743.5	**Port Saint Lucie, FL** (city) Saint Lucie County	799.3
South Carolina	242.9	Pasco County, FL	702.0	**Homestead, FL** (city) Miami-Dade County	689.7
Tennessee	208.4	Saint Lucie County, FL	673.5	**Poinciana, FL** (cdp) Osceola County	463.3
Idaho	197.2	Union County, NC	641.7	**Royal Palm Beach, FL** (village) Palm Beach County	445.8
Kentucky	194.5	Lake County, FL	553.6	**Meadow Woods, FL** (cdp) Orange County	445.6
Nevada	187.2	Polk County, FL	552.9	**Sanford, FL** (city) Seminole County	377.1
Georgia	186.4	Loudoun County, VA	503.3	**Fayetteville, NC** (city) Cumberland County	339.3
Colorado	181.8	Frederick County, MD	442.2	**Revere, MA** (city) Suffolk County	305.1
Arizona	175.2	Forsyth County, GA	437.9	**Cape Coral, FL** (city) Lee County	301.6
Arkansas	165.9	Williamson County, TX	409.9	**Charlotte, NC** (city) Mecklenburg County	299.8

Sorted by Percent in Ascending Order — U.S. = 93.1%

State	Percent	County	Percent	Place	Percent
New York	36.2	Sumter County, FL	-55.2	**Detroit, MI** (city) Wayne County	-22.9
Rhode Island	45.2	Jefferson County, TX	-6.6	**Chelsea, MA** (city) Suffolk County	-15.8
New Jersey	56.1	Queens County, NY	16.6	**Cicero, IL** (town) Cook County	-15.2
Illinois	63.2	Sullivan County, NY	25.6	**Berea*, SC** (cdp) Greenville County	-12.2
Connecticut	82.7	Ulster County, NY	26.2	**Hialeah, FL** (city) Miami-Dade County	-4.9
Massachusetts	86.4	Kings County, NY	27.1	**Passaic, NJ** (city) Passaic County	-0.7
Michigan	90.7	Passaic County, NJ	29.5	**Kendall West, FL** (cdp) Miami-Dade County	-0.2
California	93.6	Hudson County, NJ	30.4	**Huntington Park, CA** (city) Los Angeles County	0.0
Alaska	97.0	DeKalb County, GA	38.5	**Paterson, NJ** (city) Passaic County	1.8
New Hampshire	102.0	Providence County, RI	40.4	**Port Chester, NY** (village) Westchester County	4.0

Note: (1) Ranking tables cover all states and counties, and places with an overall population of at least 125,000, OR an overall population of at least 25,000 where the Hispanic/Latino population is at least 20% of the overall population. In states where less than five places meet either of these criteria, we have included places with at least 10,000 total population with the highest percentage of Hispanic/Latino population. These places are identified with an asterisk (*); Please refer to the User's Guide for a full explanation of data.

Population Growth: 2000–2010

South American: Ecuadorian

Top 10 States, Counties, and Places[1]

Sorted by Percent in Descending Order — U.S. = 116.7%

State	Percent	County	Percent	Place	Percent
South Carolina	396.0	Delaware County, PA	694.9	**Port Saint Lucie, FL** (city) Saint Lucie County	541.1
Tennessee	351.4	Pasco County, FL	610.3	**Baltimore, MD** (independent city)	467.7
Pennsylvania	334.3	Polk County, FL	511.2	**Spring Valley, NY** (village) Rockland County	436.2
North Carolina	332.8	Loudoun County, VA	491.1	**Doral, FL** (city) Miami-Dade County	417.8
Georgia	242.2	Saint Lucie County, FL	471.1	**Linden, NJ** (city) Union County	407.2
Arizona	231.1	Monroe County, PA	469.9	**Ramapo, NY** (town) Rockland County	362.0
Minnesota	228.2	Litchfield County, CT	456.5	**Bridgeport, CT** (city/town) Fairfield County	333.3
Nevada	226.7	Wake County, NC	415.1	**City of Orange, NJ** (township) Essex County	317.2
Utah	218.1	Tarrant County, TX	414.1	**San Antonio, TX** (city) Bexar County	316.8
Colorado	214.6	Fort Bend County, TX	405.2	**Waterbury, CT** (city/town) New Haven County	308.4

Sorted by Percent in Ascending Order — U.S. = 116.7%

State	Percent	County	Percent	Place	Percent
New York	84.8	New York County, NY	37.3	**Baldwin Park, CA** (city) Los Angeles County	-6.6
Oklahoma	87.4	Arlington County, VA	48.2	**Kendall West, FL** (cdp) Miami-Dade County	16.8
Illinois	89.2	Kings County, NY	51.4	**Huntington Park, CA** (city) Los Angeles County	19.3
California	97.4	Orleans Parish, LA	55.2	**Silver Spring, MD** (cdp) Montgomery County	26.7
District of Columbia	103.2	Onslow County, NC	61.0	**Glendale, CA** (city) Los Angeles County	31.9
Rhode Island	107.4	Lake County, IL	67.0	**Burbank, CA** (city) Los Angeles County	37.2
Kansas	111.8	Queens County, NY	70.7	**Manhattan, NY** (borough) New York County	37.3
New Jersey	121.4	Los Angeles County, CA	71.3	**Hialeah, FL** (city) Miami-Dade County	38.6
Louisiana	123.6	Hudson County, NJ	73.1	**West Covina, CA** (city) Los Angeles County	39.2
Iowa	141.6	Jackson County, MO	73.3	**Huntington Station, NY** (cdp) Suffolk County	41.1

RANKINGS & COMPARISONS

Note: (1) Ranking tables cover all states and counties, and places with an overall population of at least 125,000, OR an overall population of at least 25,000 where the Hispanic/Latino population is at least 20% of the overall population. In states where less than five places meet either of these criteria, we have included places with at least 10,000 total population with the highest percentage of Hispanic/Latino population. These places are identified with an asterisk (*); Please refer to the User's Guide for a full explanation of data.

Population Growth: 2000–2010

South American: Paraguayan

Top 10 States, Counties, and Places[1]

Sorted by Percent in Descending Order — U.S. = 128.3%

State	Percent	County	Percent	Place	Percent
Maryland	157.4	Somerset County, NJ	173.0	**Brooklyn, NY** (borough) Kings County	119.0
Virginia	154.5	Palm Beach County, FL	168.4	**Manhattan, NY** (borough) New York County	117.9
Texas	147.7	Montgomery County, MD	160.4	**New York, NY** (city)	113.1
New Jersey	144.6	Nassau County, NY	155.3	**Queens, NY** (borough) Queens County	112.2
Florida	144.4	Suffolk County, NY	145.2	**Bronx, NY** (borough) Bronx County	100.9
Pennsylvania	141.5	Broward County, FL	144.4	**Los Angeles, CA** (city) Los Angeles County	71.4
New York	122.6	Fairfax County, VA	137.3	**White Plains, NY** (city) Westchester County	52.0
Georgia	120.9	Westchester County, NY	130.6		
California	109.6	Kings County, NY	119.0		
Massachusetts	106.5	New York County, NY	117.9		

Sorted by Percent in Ascending Order — U.S. = 128.3%

State	Percent	County	Percent	Place	Percent
Wisconsin	22.2	Cook County, IL	42.6	**White Plains, NY** (city) Westchester County	52.0
Minnesota	45.7	Fairfield County, CT	83.6	**Los Angeles, CA** (city) Los Angeles County	71.4
Illinois	53.8	Los Angeles County, CA	92.1	**Bronx, NY** (borough) Bronx County	100.9
Kansas	81.2	Bronx County, NY	100.9	**Queens, NY** (borough) Queens County	112.2
Ohio	86.4	Miami-Dade County, FL	107.4	**New York, NY** (city)	113.1
Connecticut	91.5	Queens County, NY	112.2	**Manhattan, NY** (borough) New York County	117.9
Michigan	97.4	New York County, NY	117.9	**Brooklyn, NY** (borough) Kings County	119.0
Massachusetts	106.5	Kings County, NY	119.0		
California	109.6	Westchester County, NY	130.6		
Georgia	120.9	Fairfax County, VA	137.3		

Note: (1) Ranking tables cover all states and counties, and places with an overall population of at least 125,000, OR an overall population of at least 25,000 where the Hispanic/Latino population is at least 20% of the overall population. In states where less than five places meet either of these criteria, we have included places with at least 10,000 total population with the highest percentage of Hispanic/Latino population. These places are identified with an asterisk (*); Please refer to the User's Guide for a full explanation of data.

Population Growth: 2000–2010

South American: Peruvian

Top 10 States, Counties, and Places[1]

Sorted by Percent in Descending Order — U.S. = 127.1%

State	Percent	County	Percent	Place	Percent
South Carolina	324.9	Pasco County, FL	867.6	**Charlotte, NC** (city) Mecklenburg County	422.1
Tennessee	318.8	Saint Lucie County, FL	613.1	**Cape Coral, FL** (city) Lee County	402.7
North Carolina	315.9	Loudoun County, VA	576.6	**Norwalk, CT** (city/town) Fairfield County	331.7
Alabama	269.5	Polk County, FL	512.8	**Jacksonville, FL** (city) Duval County	323.1
Mississippi	261.1	Lee County, FL	493.3	**Antioch, CA** (city) Contra Costa County	322.6
Arkansas	240.3	Northampton County, PA	441.0	**Fort Worth, TX** (city) Tarrant County	311.3
Delaware	240.1	Mecklenburg County, NC	401.5	**Spring Valley, NV** (cdp) Clark County	306.0
Indiana	238.7	Fort Bend County, TX	376.0	**Raleigh, NC** (city) Wake County	305.0
Kentucky	237.4	Lake County, FL	362.3	**Henderson, NV** (city) Clark County	297.6
Georgia	234.4	Denton County, TX	355.3	**Colorado Springs, CO** (city) El Paso County	283.5

Sorted by Percent in Ascending Order — U.S. = 127.1%

State	Percent	County	Percent	Place	Percent
New York	77.6	Arlington County, VA	30.7	**South Gate, CA** (city) Los Angeles County	13.4
Illinois	85.3	Queens County, NY	43.4	**San Rafael, CA** (city) Marin County	23.0
New Jersey	101.4	Ramsey County, MN	50.0	**City of Orange, NJ** (township) Essex County	25.6
California	107.0	New York County, NY	54.9	**Kendall West, FL** (cdp) Miami-Dade County	26.3
Hawaii	109.0	Kings County, NY	56.6	**Kendale Lakes, FL** (cdp) Miami-Dade County	27.3
District of Columbia	109.3	Monterey County, CA	61.5	**Glendale, CA** (city) Los Angeles County	27.5
Rhode Island	114.3	Cook County, IL	63.0	**Miami Beach, FL** (city) Miami-Dade County	28.3
Alaska	119.8	Passaic County, NJ	70.6	**Arlington, VA** (cdp) Arlington County	30.7
Michigan	121.0	Miami-Dade County, FL	74.5	**Tamiami, FL** (cdp) Miami-Dade County	32.5
Massachusetts	122.4	Saint Louis County, MO	78.0	**Glen Cove, NY** (city) Nassau County	34.0

Note: (1) Ranking tables cover all states and counties, and places with an overall population of at least 125,000, OR an overall population of at least 25,000 where the Hispanic/Latino population is at least 20% of the overall population. In states where less than five places meet either of these criteria, we have included places with at least 10,000 total population with the highest percentage of Hispanic/Latino population. These places are identified with an asterisk (*); Please refer to the User's Guide for a full explanation of data.

Population Growth: 2000–2010

South American: Uruguayan

Top 10 States, Counties, and Places[1]

Sorted by Percent in Descending Order U.S. = 202.5%

State	Percent	County	Percent	Place	Percent
North Carolina	636.8	Gwinnett County, GA	481.2	**Miami, FL** (city) Miami-Dade County	370.6
Georgia	476.2	Orange County, FL	319.1	**Fitchburg, MA** (city) Worcester County	357.7
Pennsylvania	359.5	Palm Beach County, FL	275.5	**Hollywood, FL** (city) Broward County	340.7
Utah	287.4	Worcester County, MA	264.5	**Miami Beach, FL** (city) Miami-Dade County	331.5
Texas	265.0	Harris County, TX	247.5	**Elizabeth, NJ** (city) Union County	230.7
Florida	259.5	Fairfield County, CT	230.4	**Houston, TX** (city) Harris County	179.1
Massachusetts	234.8	Passaic County, NJ	227.0	**Stamford, CT** (city/town) Fairfield County	168.8
Connecticut	230.9	Miami-Dade County, FL	220.1	**Newark, NJ** (city) Essex County	165.3
Virginia	230.7	Broward County, FL	219.3	**Hialeah, FL** (city) Miami-Dade County	146.6
Maryland	199.5	Union County, NJ	213.7	**City of Orange, NJ** (township) Essex County	134.2

Sorted by Percent in Ascending Order U.S. = 202.5%

State	Percent	County	Percent	Place	Percent
New York	78.9	Queens County, NY	38.9	**Ossining, NY** (village) Westchester County	28.5
New Hampshire	96.1	Westchester County, NY	81.3	**Ossining, NY** (town) Westchester County	33.2
District of Columbia	116.0	Suffolk County, NY	90.4	**Queens, NY** (borough) Queens County	38.9
Illinois	129.6	Cook County, IL	98.1	**New York, NY** (city)	57.5
California	150.8	Hillsborough County, NH	98.5	**Kendale Lakes, FL** (cdp) Miami-Dade County	61.0
New Jersey	167.3	New York County, NY	98.9	**Rye, NY** (town) Westchester County	73.0
Washington	171.2	Kings County, NY	99.2	**Manchester*, NH** (city) Hillsborough County	74.4
Arizona	189.0	Nassau County, NY	103.2	**Union City, NJ** (city) Hudson County	81.0
Maryland	199.5	San Diego County, CA	106.6	**North Bergen, NJ** (township) Hudson County	93.3
Virginia	230.7	Bergen County, NJ	112.7	**Hempstead (town), NY** (town) Nassau County	94.1

Note: (1) Ranking tables cover all states and counties, and places with an overall population of at least 125,000, OR an overall population of at least 25,000 where the Hispanic/Latino population is at least 20% of the overall population. In states where less than five places meet either of these criteria, we have included places with at least 10,000 total population with the highest percentage of Hispanic/Latino population. These places are identified with an asterisk (*); Please refer to the User's Guide for a full explanation of data.

Population Growth: 2000–2010

South American: Venezuelan

Top 10 States, Counties, and Places[1]

Sorted by Percent in Descending Order — U.S. = 135.0%

State	Percent	County	Percent	Place	Percent
Nevada	259.8	Fort Bend County, TX	809.1	**Doral, FL** (city) Miami-Dade County	460.9
North Carolina	232.8	Montgomery County, TX	549.3	**Aventura, FL** (city) Miami-Dade County	433.2
South Carolina	226.3	Lee County, FL	499.4	**Miramar, FL** (city) Broward County	419.8
Texas	219.8	Denton County, TX	380.6	**Raleigh, NC** (city) Wake County	311.7
Washington	194.7	Collin County, TX	339.1	**Jacksonville, FL** (city) Duval County	259.3
Tennessee	190.9	Polk County, FL	330.0	**Charlotte, NC** (city) Mecklenburg County	255.7
Georgia	180.3	Prince William County, VA	273.8	**Tamarac, FL** (city) Broward County	229.7
Arkansas	177.8	Wake County, NC	267.9	**Davie, FL** (town) Broward County	216.5
New Mexico	171.7	Clark County, NV	262.4	**Weston, FL** (city) Broward County	214.9
Alabama	166.5	Sarasota County, FL	259.3	**Orlando, FL** (city) Orange County	208.0

Sorted by Percent in Ascending Order — U.S. = 135.0%

State	Percent	County	Percent	Place	Percent
Iowa	49.0	Arlington County, VA	13.0	**Kendall West, FL** (cdp) Miami-Dade County	10.1
New York	57.6	Sedgwick County, KS	19.4	**Paterson, NJ** (city) Passaic County	10.1
Mississippi	62.2	Queens County, NY	22.4	**Arlington, VA** (cdp) Arlington County	13.0
Michigan	72.5	Ramsey County, MN	40.9	**Miami Beach, FL** (city) Miami-Dade County	14.6
New Jersey	75.4	Essex County, NJ	43.4	**University Park, FL** (cdp) Miami-Dade County	15.9
Kansas	78.5	Cuyahoga County, OH	49.5	**Pittsburgh, PA** (city) Allegheny County	17.4
Rhode Island	80.1	Bronx County, NY	49.8	**Newark, NJ** (city) Essex County	21.5
Massachusetts	83.8	Saint Joseph County, IN	50.0	**Union City, NJ** (city) Hudson County	22.0
New Hampshire	88.4	Union County, NJ	50.4	**Queens, NY** (borough) Queens County	22.4
Idaho	90.5	Passaic County, NJ	50.6	**Kendale Lakes, FL** (cdp) Miami-Dade County	23.7

Note: (1) Ranking tables cover all states and counties, and places with an overall population of at least 125,000, OR an overall population of at least 25,000 where the Hispanic/Latino population is at least 20% of the overall population. In states where less than five places meet either of these criteria, we have included places with at least 10,000 total population with the highest percentage of Hispanic/Latino population. These places are identified with an asterisk (*); Please refer to the User's Guide for a full explanation of data.

Population Growth: 2000–2010

Spaniard

Top 10 States, Counties, and Places[1]

Sorted by Percent in Descending Order — U.S. = 534.4%

State	Percent	County	Percent	Place	Percent
New Mexico	3,178.5	Sandoval County, NM	4,375.7	**Albuquerque, NM** (city) Bernalillo County	3,193.8
Colorado	1,754.2	Santa Fe County, NM	3,259.2	**Santa Fe, NM** (city) Santa Fe County	2,612.8
Wyoming	1,393.9	Bernalillo County, NM	3,026.5	**Pueblo, CO** (city) Pueblo County	2,581.2
Kansas	1,089.8	Pueblo County, CO	2,900.8	**Colorado Springs, CO** (city) El Paso County	1,495.7
Arkansas	1,025.4	Adams County, CO	2,187.4	**Denver, CO** (city) Denver County	1,312.6
Hawaii	978.3	Doña Ana County, NM	1,987.4	**Aurora, CO** (city) Arapahoe County	1,019.8
Oklahoma	913.5	Jefferson County, CO	1,891.8	**Corpus Christi, TX** (city) Nueces County	967.0
Montana	900.0	El Paso County, CO	1,484.4	**Riverside, CA** (city) Riverside County	879.5
Iowa	888.5	Arapahoe County, CO	1,461.9	**San Antonio, TX** (city) Bexar County	874.7
Arizona	869.5	Denver County, CO	1,312.6	**Henderson, NV** (city) Clark County	853.0

Sorted by Percent in Ascending Order — U.S. = 534.4%

State	Percent	County	Percent	Place	Percent
New Jersey	137.3	Essex County, NJ	51.7	**Newark, NJ** (city) Essex County	3.9
New York	173.3	Hudson County, NJ	57.5	**Fountainebleau, FL** (cdp) Miami-Dade County	6.6
District of Columbia	234.4	Queens County, NY	63.5	**Union City, NJ** (city) Hudson County	20.0
Florida	246.0	Bronx County, NY	96.0	**University Park, FL** (cdp) Miami-Dade County	22.9
Connecticut	300.2	Miami-Dade County, FL	100.0	**Kearny, NJ** (town) Hudson County	36.1
Massachusetts	319.7	Passaic County, NJ	108.6	**Hialeah, FL** (city) Miami-Dade County	37.7
Maryland	362.2	Bergen County, NJ	124.3	**Tamiami, FL** (cdp) Miami-Dade County	39.6
New Hampshire	448.9	Union County, NJ	135.9	**Westchester, FL** (cdp) Miami-Dade County	41.0
Rhode Island	455.6	Kings County, NY	139.4	**Kendall West, FL** (cdp) Miami-Dade County	44.2
Virginia	459.0	Elko County, NV	148.0	**Elizabeth, NJ** (city) Union County	44.3

Note: (1) Ranking tables cover all states and counties, and places with an overall population of at least 125,000, OR an overall population of at least 25,000 where the Hispanic/Latino population is at least 20% of the overall population. In states where less than five places meet either of these criteria, we have included places with at least 10,000 total population with the highest percentage of Hispanic/Latino population. These places are identified with an asterisk (*); Please refer to the User's Guide for a full explanation of data.

Males per 100 Females

Total Population

Top 10 States, Counties, and Places[1]

Sorted by Percent in Descending Order — U.S. = 96.7

State	Number	County	Number	Place	Number
Alaska	108.5	Crowley County, CO	258.6	**Florence, AZ** (town) Pinal County	457.2
Wyoming	104.1	Concho County, TX	215.8	**Fort Leonard Wood*, MO** (cdp) Pulaski County	255.9
North Dakota	102.1	Forest County, PA	202.4	**Soledad, CA** (city) Monterey County	235.5
Nevada	102.0	Bent County, CO	191.6	**Wasco, CA** (city) Kern County	160.3
Utah	100.9	West Feliciana Parish, LA	190.8	**Fort Campbell North*, KY** (cdp) Christian County	154.7
Montana	100.8	Union County, FL	183.0	**North Chicago, IL** (city) Lake County	152.9
Colorado	100.5	Lassen County, CA	179.6	**Delano, CA** (city) Kern County	149.1
Idaho	100.4	Brown County, IL	178.9	**Big Spring, TX** (city) Howard County	138.4
Hawaii	100.3	Lake County, TN	175.3	**Schofield Barracks*, HI** (cdp) Honolulu County	137.5
South Dakota	100.1	Garza County, TX	172.7	**Fort Hood, TX** (cdp) Bell County	137.2

Sorted by Percent in Ascending Order — U.S. = 96.7

State	Number	County	Number	Place	Number
District of Columbia	89.5	Pulaski County, GA	76.1	**Tamarac, FL** (city) Broward County	80.3
Rhode Island	93.4	Livingston County, MO	81.0	**Aventura, FL** (city) Miami-Dade County	84.6
Maryland	93.6	Summers County, WV	81.4	**Pembroke Pines, FL** (city) Broward County	85.9
Massachusetts	93.7	Marion County, SC	84.2	**Fountainebleau, FL** (cdp) Miami-Dade County	86.2
New York	93.8	Macon County, AL	84.5	**Hope*, AR** (city) Hempstead County	86.3
Delaware	93.9	Coahoma County, MS	84.8	**Brattleboro*, VT** (town) Windham County	86.6
Alabama	94.3	Fluvanna County, VA	85.0	**Country Club, FL** (cdp) Miami-Dade County	86.6
Mississippi	94.4	Randolph County, GA	85.2	**Kendall, FL** (cdp) Miami-Dade County	86.6
South Carolina	94.7	Audrain County, MO	85.9	**Dover*, DE** (city) Kent County	86.7
Connecticut	94.8	Dallas County, AL	85.9	**Jackson, MS** (city) Hinds County	86.8

Note: (1) Ranking tables cover all states and counties, and places with an overall population of at least 125,000, OR an overall population of at least 25,000 where the Hispanic/Latino population is at least 20% of the overall population. In states where less than five places meet either of these criteria, we have included places with at least 10,000 total population with the highest percentage of Hispanic/Latino population. These places are identified with an asterisk (*); Please refer to the User's Guide for a full explanation of data.

Males per 100 Females

Hispanic or Latino (of any race)

Top 10 States, Counties, and Places[1]

Sorted by Percent in Descending Order — U.S. = 103.1

State	Number	County	Number	Place	Number
Mississippi	141.1	Stewart County, GA	2,867.3	**Florence, AZ** (town) Pinal County	603.5
Kentucky	126.9	Brown County, IL	2,264.7	**Fort Leonard Wood*, MO** (cdp) Pulaski County	248.1
Alabama	126.8	Tallahatchie County, MS	2,065.0	**Yankton*, SD** (city) Yankton County	195.8
South Carolina	125.8	Martin County, KY	1,285.7	**Laurel*, MS** (city) Jones County	173.3
Louisiana	123.5	Adams County, MS	1,235.4	**Soledad, CA** (city) Monterey County	169.8
Tennessee	120.1	Yazoo County, MS	1,175.5	**Norco, CA** (city) Riverside County	150.3
South Dakota	117.9	Gilmer County, WV	1,073.8	**Birmingham, AL** (city) Jefferson County	150.2
West Virginia	117.3	Forest County, PA	971.8	**Columbia, SC** (city) Richland County	148.3
Georgia	117.1	McCreary County, KY	811.6	**Biloxi*, MS** (city) Harrison County	145.5
North Carolina	114.9	Telfair County, GA	780.9	**Lake Worth, FL** (city) Palm Beach County	145.2

Sorted by Percent in Ascending Order — U.S. = 103.1

State	Number	County	Number	Place	Number
Massachusetts	96.4	Summers County, WV	33.1	**Bennington*, VT** (town) Bennington County	67.1
New York	97.2	Waseca County, MN	59.6	**Aventura, FL** (city) Miami-Dade County	80.6
Rhode Island	97.6	Carter County, MO	60.0	**Coral Gables, FL** (city) Miami-Dade County	82.5
Florida	97.7	Iron County, MI	62.6	**Kendall, FL** (cdp) Miami-Dade County	83.0
New Mexico	98.4	Crook County, WY	64.0	**Fountainebleau, FL** (cdp) Miami-Dade County	84.1
Connecticut	99.9	Oregon County, MO	70.1	**Goodyear, AZ** (city) Maricopa County	85.1
New Hampshire	100.4	Morgan County, UT	71.2	**Cooper City, FL** (city) Broward County	85.2
Arizona	100.9	Otsego County, MI	71.8	**Kendale Lakes, FL** (cdp) Miami-Dade County	85.6
Vermont	101.0	Monroe County, IA	72.4	**Pembroke Pines, FL** (city) Broward County	85.6
Maine	101.2	Holmes County, MS	74.0	**Plantation, FL** (city) Broward County	85.6

Note: (1) Ranking tables cover all states and counties, and places with an overall population of at least 125,000, OR an overall population of at least 25,000 where the Hispanic/Latino population is at least 20% of the overall population. In states where less than five places meet either of these criteria, we have included places with at least 10,000 total population with the highest percentage of Hispanic/Latino population. These places are identified with an asterisk (*); Please refer to the User's Guide for a full explanation of data.

Males per 100 Females

Central American, excluding Mexican

Top 10 States, Counties, and Places[1]

Sorted by Percent in Descending Order — U.S. = 108.9

State	Number	County	Number	Place	Number
Wyoming	149.9	Stewart County, GA	20,050.0	**Florence, AZ** (town) Pinal County	771.4
Mississippi	147.8	Frio County, TX	3,800.0	**Del Rio, TX** (city) Val Verde County	314.3
Alabama	141.8	Telfair County, GA	2,333.3	**Windham, CT** (town) Windham County	255.7
South Carolina	135.0	Union County, PA	971.4	**Fort Leonard Wood*, MO** (cdp) Pulaski County	248.6
Kentucky	134.1	Franklin County, NY	668.8	**Gillette*, WY** (city) Campbell County	216.3
Connecticut	132.1	Adams County, MS	428.6	**Mayfield*, KY** (city) Graves County	202.1
Oklahoma	131.3	Washington County, NY	400.0	**Norristown, PA** (borough) Montgomery County	198.3
Tennessee	128.4	Parmer County, TX	396.8	**Rock Springs*, WY** (city) Sweetwater County	198.0
Rhode Island	128.0	Atkinson County, GA	331.0	**El Centro, CA** (city) Imperial County	197.9
Georgia	126.3	Willacy County, TX	327.5	**Guymon*, OK** (city) Texas County	195.2

Sorted by Percent in Ascending Order — U.S. = 108.9

State	Number	County	Number	Place	Number
Montana	80.1	Otero County, NM	58.5	**Coral Gables, FL** (city) Miami-Dade County	63.8
Vermont	90.6	Licking County, OH	61.8	**Billings*, MT** (city) Yellowstone County	66.1
North Dakota	94.0	Geary County, KS	62.3	**Hanford, CA** (city) Kings County	66.9
Idaho	96.3	Liberty County, GA	63.7	**Burlington*, VT** (city) Chittenden County	69.6
California	97.8	Kerr County, TX	66.1	**Miami Lakes, FL** (town) Miami-Dade County	70.1
Alaska	99.4	Saint Clair County, MI	66.2	**Marana, AZ** (town) Pima County	71.1
Wisconsin	99.9	Cochise County, AZ	68.5	**Schertz, TX** (city) Guadalupe County	71.8
Illinois	101.2	Plaquemines Parish, LA	69.0	**Aventura, FL** (city) Miami-Dade County	72.4
Nevada	101.7	Iron County, UT	69.1	**Toledo, OH** (city) Lucas County	72.7
Florida	101.9	Randall County, TX	69.5	**Leander, TX** (city) Williamson County	72.9

RANKINGS & COMPARISONS

Note: (1) Ranking tables cover all states and counties, and places with an overall population of at least 125,000, OR an overall population of at least 25,000 where the Hispanic/Latino population is at least 20% of the overall population. In states where less than five places meet either of these criteria, we have included places with at least 10,000 total population with the highest percentage of Hispanic/Latino population. These places are identified with an asterisk (*); Please refer to the User's Guide for a full explanation of data.

Males per 100 Females

Central American: Costa Rican

Top 10 States, Counties, and Places[1]

Sorted by Percent in Descending Order — U.S. = 93.4

State	Number	County	Number	Place	Number
New Jersey	133.9	Hunterdon County, NJ	201.9	**Berea*, SC** (cdp) Greenville County	176.7
South Carolina	117.8	Greenville County, SC	176.0	**Bloomfield, NJ** (township) Essex County	168.1
Pennsylvania	114.6	Warren County, NJ	159.1	**Trenton, NJ** (city) Mercer County	165.9
Iowa	112.5	Essex County, NJ	158.8	**Paterson, NJ** (city) Passaic County	165.2
Connecticut	111.5	Northampton County, PA	155.4	**Elizabeth, NJ** (city) Union County	154.8
Minnesota	102.8	Chesterfield County, VA	154.3	**Linden, NJ** (city) Union County	142.2
Kentucky	102.4	Montgomery County, OH	152.3	**Arlington, TX** (city) Tarrant County	139.3
North Carolina	97.1	Mercer County, NJ	151.9	**Philadelphia, PA** (city) Philadelphia County	133.3
Georgia	96.6	Morris County, NJ	146.4	**Lehigh Acres, FL** (cdp) Lee County	125.9
Arkansas	95.9	Passaic County, NJ	143.5	**Norwalk, CT** (city/town) Fairfield County	124.6

Sorted by Percent in Ascending Order — U.S. = 93.4

State	Number	County	Number	Place	Number
Rhode Island	74.1	Larimer County, CO	49.4	**Yonkers, NY** (city) Westchester County	52.9
Oregon	79.0	Sumner County, TN	60.3	**Babylon, NY** (town) Suffolk County	53.7
Colorado	79.5	Westchester County, NY	60.9	**Miami Gardens, FL** (city) Miami-Dade County	53.8
Utah	79.8	Oakland County, MI	64.2	**Kendale Lakes, FL** (cdp) Miami-Dade County	54.5
Alabama	80.0	Kings County, NY	64.7	**Country Club, FL** (cdp) Miami-Dade County	54.9
Arizona	80.0	Brevard County, FL	64.9	**Richmond West, FL** (cdp) Miami-Dade County	56.7
New Mexico	80.0	Providence County, RI	66.4	**Alhambra, CA** (city) Los Angeles County	59.4
New York	80.0	Dane County, WI	67.6	**South Miami Heights, FL** (cdp) Miami-Dade County	60.6
Mississippi	80.1	Sarasota County, FL	69.5	**Plano, TX** (city) Collin County	61.6
Michigan	80.2	Arapahoe County, CO	69.8	**Hialeah, FL** (city) Miami-Dade County	62.5

Note: (1) Ranking tables cover all states and counties, and places with an overall population of at least 125,000, OR an overall population of at least 25,000 where the Hispanic/Latino population is at least 20% of the overall population. In states where less than five places meet either of these criteria, we have included places with at least 10,000 total population with the highest percentage of Hispanic/Latino population. These places are identified with an asterisk (*); Please refer to the User's Guide for a full explanation of data.

Males per 100 Females

Central American: Guatemalan

Top 10 States, Counties, and Places[1]

Sorted by Percent in Descending Order — U.S. = 133.7

State	Number	County	Number	Place	Number
Wyoming	202.9	Willacy County, TX	486.0	**Windham, CT** (town) Windham County	456.3
Mississippi	178.8	Faulkner County, AR	484.2	**Miami Beach, FL** (city) Miami-Dade County	388.7
South Carolina	171.2	Parmer County, TX	479.2	**City of Orange, NJ** (township) Essex County	317.3
Georgia	169.9	Okeechobee County, FL	403.7	**Chesapeake, VA** (independent city)	292.3
Alabama	167.6	Pontotoc County, MS	345.5	**Birmingham, AL** (city) Jefferson County	267.8
New Jersey	165.5	Cayuga County, NY	344.6	**Homestead, FL** (city) Miami-Dade County	242.9
District of Columbia	159.1	New London County, CT	302.9	**Passaic, NJ** (city) Passaic County	240.8
Florida	159.0	Columbia County, NY	273.3	**Columbia, SC** (city) Richland County	240.0
Connecticut	158.9	Mobile County, AL	273.2	**Margate, FL** (city) Broward County	238.2
Kentucky	158.1	Coffee County, AL	272.8	**North Bergen, NJ** (township) Hudson County	236.0

Sorted by Percent in Ascending Order — U.S. = 133.7

State	Number	County	Number	Place	Number
Montana	83.5	Guadalupe County, TX	67.8	**Brea, CA** (city) Orange County	56.7
Vermont	97.2	Kendall County, IL	77.3	**Menifee, CA** (city) Riverside County	73.2
Idaho	101.0	Carver County, MN	78.1	**San Gabriel, CA** (city) Los Angeles County	73.2
Wisconsin	102.9	DeKalb County, IL	78.7	**Coral Gables, FL** (city) Miami-Dade County	74.3
Illinois	108.0	Olmsted County, MN	79.3	**McKinney, TX** (city) Collin County	74.5
Alaska	109.9	Douglas County, CO	80.2	**Irvine, CA** (city) Orange County	76.7
Nevada	112.2	Calcasieu Parish, LA	80.6	**Alafaya, FL** (cdp) Orange County	77.3
California	112.3	Lucas County, OH	81.0	**Chino, CA** (city) San Bernardino County	77.8
Utah	112.3	El Dorado County, CA	83.5	**San Buenaventura (Ventura), CA** (city) Ventura County	78.7
New Hampshire	115.4	Albany County, NY	85.7	**Culver City, CA** (city) Los Angeles County	79.2

Note: (1) Ranking tables cover all states and counties, and places with an overall population of at least 125,000, OR an overall population of at least 25,000 where the Hispanic/Latino population is at least 20% of the overall population. In states where less than five places meet either of these criteria, we have included places with at least 10,000 total population with the highest percentage of Hispanic/Latino population. These places are identified with an asterisk (*); Please refer to the User's Guide for a full explanation of data.

Males per 100 Females

Central American: Honduran

Top 10 States, Counties, and Places[1]

Sorted by Percent in Descending Order — U.S. = 110.9

State	Number	County	Number	Place	Number
Mississippi	164.6	Stewart County, GA	16,000.0	**Norristown, PA** (borough) Montgomery County	281.8
District of Columbia	155.6	Frio County, TX	11,033.3	**Jackson, MS** (city) Hinds County	252.3
Kentucky	148.1	Willacy County, TX	396.4	**City of Orange, NJ** (township) Essex County	242.9
South Carolina	147.4	Spalding County, GA	288.9	**Fort Pierce, FL** (city) Saint Lucie County	235.0
West Virginia	143.1	Bossier Parish, LA	274.0	**Knoxville, TN** (city) Knox County	221.8
Wyoming	141.7	Saint Mary Parish, LA	272.2	**Santa Maria, CA** (city) Santa Barbara County	210.8
Alabama	137.7	Jackson County, MS	238.5	**Norfolk, VA** (independent city)	209.0
Oklahoma	136.4	Craven County, NC	234.2	**Bryan, TX** (city) Brazos County	186.4
Maryland	134.3	Kershaw County, SC	230.0	**Hampton, VA** (independent city)	186.0
Virginia	134.2	Aiken County, SC	227.7	**North Atlanta, GA** (cdp) DeKalb County	182.0

Sorted by Percent in Ascending Order — U.S. = 110.9

State	Number	County	Number	Place	Number
Vermont	62.7	Plaquemines Parish, LA	48.6	**Coral Gables, FL** (city) Miami-Dade County	46.2
Alaska	76.6	Norfolk County, MA	71.0	**Lawndale, CA** (city) Los Angeles County	50.4
California	92.3	Kenosha County, WI	71.6	**Huntington Beach, CA** (city) Orange County	55.1
Arizona	93.9	Charles County, MD	72.1	**Wesley Chapel, FL** (cdp) Pasco County	56.3
Nevada	94.4	Henry County, GA	72.1	**Upland, CA** (city) San Bernardino County	57.5
Idaho	96.2	Albany County, NY	72.7	**Bellflower, CA** (city) Los Angeles County	60.0
Utah	96.3	Hernando County, FL	73.0	**Glendale, CA** (city) Los Angeles County	61.7
Oregon	96.7	Monroe County, PA	73.8	**Burbank, CA** (city) Los Angeles County	63.4
Florida	97.4	Putnam County, NY	76.1	**Bloomfield, NJ** (township) Essex County	64.3
New Mexico	99.1	Pasco County, FL	77.2	**Westchester, FL** (cdp) Miami-Dade County	64.6

Note: (1) Ranking tables cover all states and counties, and places with an overall population of at least 125,000, OR an overall population of at least 25,000 where the Hispanic/Latino population is at least 20% of the overall population. In states where less than five places meet either of these criteria, we have included places with at least 10,000 total population with the highest percentage of Hispanic/Latino population. These places are identified with an asterisk (*); Please refer to the User's Guide for a full explanation of data.

Males per 100 Females

Central American: Nicaraguan

Top 10 States, Counties, and Places[1]

Sorted by Percent in Descending Order — U.S. = 89.4

State	Number	County	Number	Place	Number
Arkansas	108.9	Onslow County, NC	159.3	**Norfolk, VA** (independent city)	161.1
Hawaii	108.7	Saint Bernard Parish, LA	141.7	**Bridgeport, CT** (city/town) Fairfield County	156.3
Louisiana	105.1	San Luis Obispo County, CA	129.7	**Minneapolis, MN** (city) Hennepin County	145.2
Missouri	104.1	Orleans Parish, LA	128.6	**Saint Louis, MO** (independent city)	135.6
South Carolina	103.0	Gaston County, NC	127.8	**Babylon, NY** (town) Suffolk County	133.3
Tennessee	102.9	Beaufort County, SC	127.1	**New Orleans, LA** (city) Orleans Parish	128.6
Colorado	101.8	Mercer County, NJ	126.9	**North Atlanta, GA** (cdp) DeKalb County	125.9
Iowa	101.7	Adams County, CO	124.6	**Union City, NJ** (city) Hudson County	124.4
Minnesota	101.7	Harrison County, MS	122.5	**Nashville-Davidson, TN** (metropolitan govt) Davidson County	118.7
Mississippi	100.6	Ramsey County, MN	121.1	**Paterson, NJ** (city) Passaic County	117.3

Sorted by Percent in Ascending Order — U.S. = 89.4

State	Number	County	Number	Place	Number
New Hampshire	77.6	Baltimore County, MD	59.1	**Hacienda Heights, CA** (cdp) Los Angeles County	58.6
District of Columbia	83.2	El Dorado County, CA	63.2	**Carson, CA** (city) Los Angeles County	63.8
Utah	84.0	New Castle County, DE	65.4	**Greensboro, NC** (city) Guilford County	63.9
Rhode Island	85.4	Dakota County, MN	66.7	**Dania Beach, FL** (city) Broward County	64.2
Oregon	85.5	Guilford County, NC	67.2	**Atascocita, TX** (cdp) Harris County	64.3
Alabama	85.7	Yolo County, CA	67.2	**Gilbert, AZ** (town) Maricopa County	65.3
California	86.2	Sedgwick County, KS	70.0	**Royal Palm Beach, FL** (village) Palm Beach County	65.8
Maryland	87.6	Volusia County, FL	70.3	**East Los Angeles, CA** (cdp) Los Angeles County	66.5
Illinois	87.9	Kenosha County, WI	71.7	**Riverview, FL** (cdp) Hillsborough County	66.7
New York	87.9	Santa Cruz County, CA	71.8	**Coral Gables, FL** (city) Miami-Dade County	67.4

Note: (1) Ranking tables cover all states and counties, and places with an overall population of at least 125,000, OR an overall population of at least 25,000 where the Hispanic/Latino population is at least 20% of the overall population. In states where less than five places meet either of these criteria, we have included places with at least 10,000 total population with the highest percentage of Hispanic/Latino population. These places are identified with an asterisk (*); Please refer to the User's Guide for a full explanation of data.

Males per 100 Females

Central American: Panamanian

Top 10 States, Counties, and Places[1]

Sorted by Percent in Descending Order — U.S. = 71.5

State	Number	County	Number	Place	Number
West Virginia	91.9	Ulster County, NY	165.0	**Urban Honolulu, HI** (cdp) Honolulu County	114.5
Idaho	90.6	Utah County, UT	140.0	**Victorville, CA** (city) San Bernardino County	112.0
Utah	87.0	Jones County, MS	122.2	**Seattle, WA** (city) King County	99.1
Hawaii	86.2	Tulsa County, OK	110.4	**San Francisco, CA** (city) San Francisco County	98.5
Mississippi	82.6	Monroe County, PA	105.3	**Atlanta, GA** (city) Fulton County	97.9
Connecticut	81.4	Spokane County, WA	103.3	**Norfolk, VA** (independent city)	94.1
Oregon	78.6	Orange County, NY	101.1	**Tulsa, OK** (city) Tulsa County	93.7
Pennsylvania	78.1	Chester County, PA	100.0	**Allentown, PA** (city) Lehigh County	93.2
Nebraska	77.7	Pulaski County, AR	100.0	**Brookhaven, NY** (town) Suffolk County	92.7
Oklahoma	77.3	Saint Charles County, MO	100.0	**Brentwood, NY** (cdp) Suffolk County	92.2

Sorted by Percent in Ascending Order — U.S. = 71.5

State	Number	County	Number	Place	Number
New Mexico	56.6	Geary County, KS	38.7	**Garland, TX** (city) Dallas County	46.8
Delaware	59.6	Albany County, NY	41.2	**Memphis, TN** (city) Shelby County	47.0
Arkansas	63.9	Fayette County, GA	41.6	**Huntsville, AL** (city) Madison County	47.2
North Dakota	63.9	Spotsylvania County, VA	43.0	**Poinciana, FL** (cdp) Osceola County	50.7
North Carolina	64.1	Liberty County, GA	46.4	**Columbus, GA** (city) Muscogee County	53.0
Alabama	64.2	Madison County, AL	47.8	**Fayetteville, NC** (city) Cumberland County	54.3
Tennessee	64.7	Pinal County, AZ	47.8	**Detroit, MI** (city) Wayne County	55.0
Georgia	65.9	Hoke County, NC	48.7	**Palmdale, CA** (city) Los Angeles County	55.0
Virginia	66.0	Hernando County, FL	49.6	**Dale City, VA** (cdp) Prince William County	55.5
South Carolina	66.5	Hidalgo County, TX	50.7	**Albuquerque, NM** (city) Bernalillo County	56.9

Note: (1) Ranking tables cover all states and counties, and places with an overall population of at least 125,000, OR an overall population of at least 25,000 where the Hispanic/Latino population is at least 20% of the overall population. In states where less than five places meet either of these criteria, we have included places with at least 10,000 total population with the highest percentage of Hispanic/Latino population. These places are identified with an asterisk (*); Please refer to the User's Guide for a full explanation of data.

Males per 100 Females

Central American: Salvadoran

Top 10 States, Counties, and Places[1]

Sorted by Percent in Descending Order — U.S. = 104.7

State	Number	County	Number	Place	Number
Mississippi	151.9	Frio County, TX	5,133.3	**Atlanta, GA** (city) Fulton County	178.2
Maine	128.0	Willacy County, TX	246.1	**Abilene, TX** (city) Taylor County	164.3
Louisiana	126.4	Lewis County, WA	211.9	**Laredo, TX** (city) Webb County	161.0
Kentucky	125.8	Grays Harbor County, WA	206.3	**Knoxville, TN** (city) Knox County	158.0
Oklahoma	125.2	Imperial County, CA	182.4	**Lompoc, CA** (city) Santa Barbara County	154.2
Ohio	122.9	Harrison County, MS	171.4	**Storm Lake*, IA** (city) Buena Vista County	154.2
Alaska	121.7	Taylor County, TX	171.4	**Bethlehem, PA** (city) Northampton County	152.2
Alabama	121.3	Webb County, TX	161.5	**East Hartford, CT** (cdp/town) Hartford County	150.7
New Hampshire	120.1	Yuma County, AZ	161.3	**Columbus, GA** (city) Muscogee County	150.0
Wyoming	120.0	Lafayette Parish, LA	159.4	**Conroe, TX** (city) Montgomery County	150.0

Sorted by Percent in Ascending Order — U.S. = 104.7

State	Number	County	Number	Place	Number
California	94.2	Tehama County, CA	65.4	**Cranston*, RI** (city) Providence County	63.2
Idaho	95.1	Murray County, GA	66.3	**San Juan Capistrano, CA** (city) Orange County	63.8
Oregon	96.5	Pettis County, MO	73.1	**San Dimas, CA** (city) Los Angeles County	64.4
Montana	97.2	Oconee County, SC	74.2	**Santa Paula, CA** (city) Ventura County	64.4
Illinois	100.4	Umatilla County, OR	74.3	**North Miami, FL** (city) Miami-Dade County	68.5
Arizona	100.5	Charleston County, SC	76.9	**Irvine, CA** (city) Orange County	72.1
Rhode Island	100.7	Mobile County, AL	77.4	**Laguna Hills, CA** (city) Orange County	72.7
Utah	101.9	Franklin County, AL	79.2	**Kendale Lakes, FL** (cdp) Miami-Dade County	72.8
Nevada	102.2	Hays County, TX	79.3	**Monrovia, CA** (city) Los Angeles County	73.5
South Dakota	104.7	Yolo County, CA	80.4	**Torrance, CA** (city) Los Angeles County	74.6

Note: (1) Ranking tables cover all states and counties, and places with an overall population of at least 125,000, OR an overall population of at least 25,000 where the Hispanic/Latino population is at least 20% of the overall population. In states where less than five places meet either of these criteria, we have included places with at least 10,000 total population with the highest percentage of Hispanic/Latino population. These places are identified with an asterisk (*); Please refer to the User's Guide for a full explanation of data.

Males per 100 Females

Cuban

Top 10 States, Counties, and Places[1]

Sorted by Percent in Descending Order — U.S. = 98.8

State	Number	County	Number	Place	Number
Nebraska	141.5	Telfair County, GA	10,100.0	**Grand Island, NE** (city) Hall County	210.6
Mississippi	127.7	Adams County, MS	2,850.0	**Cranston*, RI** (city) Providence County	208.1
Arkansas	127.6	Granville County, NC	900.0	**Yuma, AZ** (city) Yuma County	191.7
South Dakota	126.5	Calhoun County, FL	606.3	**Laredo, TX** (city) Webb County	189.6
North Dakota	124.1	Wayne County, GA	535.3	**Palm Springs, CA** (city) Riverside County	182.2
West Virginia	117.7	Union County, FL	513.6	**Norfolk, VA** (independent city)	166.2
Kansas	117.0	Taylor County, FL	416.7	**Pawtucket*, RI** (city) Providence County	156.8
Wisconsin	116.3	Bradford County, FL	305.6	**Livermore, CA** (city) Alameda County	156.1
Minnesota	115.7	Jackson County, FL	254.8	**Dodge City, KS** (city) Ford County	152.2
Oklahoma	115.1	Hardee County, FL	220.9	**Vista, CA** (city) San Diego County	151.9

Sorted by Percent in Ascending Order — U.S. = 98.8

State	Number	County	Number	Place	Number
Delaware	87.4	Caldwell County, NC	66.3	**Santa Barbara, CA** (city) Santa Barbara County	51.4
Vermont	93.2	Roanoke County, VA	69.6	**Dale City, VA** (cdp) Prince William County	59.4
New Hampshire	93.8	Hancock County, MS	69.7	**Wallkill, NY** (town) Orange County	62.3
New Jersey	94.4	Fauquier County, VA	69.9	**Gardena, CA** (city) Los Angeles County	63.0
Montana	94.9	Davis County, UT	70.0	**North Highlands, CA** (cdp) Sacramento County	63.4
Massachusetts	95.2	Pitt County, NC	70.3	**Akron, OH** (city) Summit County	70.1
District of Columbia	95.3	Merrimack County, NH	70.6	**Wilmington*, DE** (city) New Castle County	73.1
Maryland	95.7	Calvert County, MD	74.0	**Joliet, IL** (city) Will County	73.6
Virginia	96.8	DeKalb County, IL	75.0	**Placentia, CA** (city) Orange County	73.7
Florida	97.4	Santa Fe County, NM	75.5	**Moorpark, CA** (city) Ventura County	74.2

Note: (1) Ranking tables cover all states and counties, and places with an overall population of at least 125,000, OR an overall population of at least 25,000 where the Hispanic/Latino population is at least 20% of the overall population. In states where less than five places meet either of these criteria, we have included places with at least 10,000 total population with the highest percentage of Hispanic/Latino population. These places are identified with an asterisk (*); Please refer to the User's Guide for a full explanation of data.

Males per 100 Females

Dominican Republic

Top 10 States, Counties, and Places[1]

Sorted by Percent in Descending Order — U.S. = 85.3

State	Number	County	Number	Place	Number
Mississippi	134.2	Telfair County, GA	15,100.0	**Columbia, SC** (city) Richland County	156.7
Hawaii	123.9	Clearfield County, PA	11,800.0	**Urban Honolulu, HI** (cdp) Honolulu County	146.3
Louisiana	114.9	Franklin County, NY	2,512.5	**Huntsville, AL** (city) Madison County	136.4
West Virginia	113.5	Union County, PA	1,211.8	**Tucson, AZ** (city) Pima County	134.7
Arizona	110.2	Washington County, NY	833.3	**Portland, OR** (city) Multnomah County	130.0
Oklahoma	106.5	Greene County, NY	428.6	**Pascagoula*, MS** (city) Jackson County	129.9
Vermont	102.9	Mahoning County, OH	417.7	**Norfolk, VA** (independent city)	129.8
Iowa	102.4	Saint Lawrence County, NY	302.0	**San Diego, CA** (city) San Diego County	121.9
Kentucky	101.7	Chemung County, NY	300.0	**San Francisco, CA** (city) San Francisco County	120.6
Kansas	101.6	Clinton County, NY	276.4	**Chula Vista, CA** (city) San Diego County	119.3

Sorted by Percent in Ascending Order — U.S. = 85.3

State	Number	County	Number	Place	Number
District of Columbia	79.7	Dorchester County, SC	57.1	**Annandale, VA** (cdp) Fairfax County	62.1
Utah	82.5	Hampshire County, MA	61.3	**Westchester, FL** (cdp) Miami-Dade County	62.6
New York	83.0	Lincoln County, NC	62.1	**Aventura, FL** (city) Miami-Dade County	65.5
Massachusetts	83.5	Charleston County, SC	63.6	**Coral Gables, FL** (city) Miami-Dade County	65.5
Florida	84.2	Horry County, SC	67.1	**University Park, FL** (cdp) Miami-Dade County	66.0
Idaho	85.0	Salt Lake County, UT	70.3	**Lawrenceville, GA** (city) Gwinnett County	67.0
Connecticut	85.2	Chesterfield County, VA	71.6	**Spring Valley, NY** (village) Rockland County	68.8
Rhode Island	85.4	Oklahoma County, OK	72.0	**Garland, TX** (city) Dallas County	69.4
Georgia	85.7	Jefferson County, AL	72.5	**Minneapolis, MN** (city) Hennepin County	71.8
Delaware	86.2	Clayton County, GA	72.6	**Norristown, PA** (borough) Montgomery County	72.2

Note: (1) Ranking tables cover all states and counties, and places with an overall population of at least 125,000, OR an overall population of at least 25,000 where the Hispanic/Latino population is at least 20% of the overall population. In states where less than five places meet either of these criteria, we have included places with at least 10,000 total population with the highest percentage of Hispanic/Latino population. These places are identified with an asterisk (*); Please refer to the User's Guide for a full explanation of data.

Males per 100 Females

Mexican

Top 10 States, Counties, and Places[1]

Sorted by Percent in Descending Order — U.S. = 106.2

State	Number	County	Number	Place	Number
Mississippi	153.1	Stewart County, GA	4,200.0	**Florence, AZ** (town) Pinal County	609.0
South Carolina	140.1	Tallahatchie County, MS	2,662.5	**Fort Leonard Wood*, MO** (cdp) Pulaski County	240.1
Louisiana	139.1	Martin County, KY	2,071.4	**Yankton*, SD** (city) Yankton County	204.8
Kentucky	135.5	Gilmer County, WV	1,829.4	**University, FL** (cdp) Hillsborough County	184.7
West Virginia	133.2	Adams County, MS	1,695.4	**Bergenfield, NJ** (borough) Bergen County	184.0
Alabama	133.0	Yazoo County, MS	1,568.4	**Laurel*, MS** (city) Jones County	180.7
Pennsylvania	130.4	Union County, PA	1,193.8	**Columbia, SC** (city) Richland County	167.4
New York	128.1	Brown County, IL	930.8	**Spring Valley, NY** (village) Rockland County	165.8
New Jersey	127.0	Essex County, NY	810.3	**New Orleans, LA** (city) Orleans Parish	165.3
Tennessee	126.5	Marlboro County, SC	757.1	**Birmingham, AL** (city) Jefferson County	164.5

Sorted by Percent in Ascending Order — U.S. = 106.2

State	Number	County	Number	Place	Number
Maine	99.0	Waseca County, MN	61.4	**Cooper City, FL** (city) Broward County	75.2
New Mexico	100.7	Iron County, MI	62.2	**Syracuse, NY** (city) Onondaga County	81.8
Texas	101.2	Jefferson County, PA	62.7	**Goodyear, AZ** (city) Maricopa County	82.8
Arizona	101.4	Wright County, MO	67.4	**Richmond West, FL** (cdp) Miami-Dade County	85.2
California	103.0	Crook County, WY	69.4	**Eagle Pass, TX** (city) Maverick County	87.8
Michigan	105.1	Morgan County, UT	70.7	**The Hammocks, FL** (cdp) Miami-Dade County	88.0
Nevada	105.9	Hampshire County, MA	70.8	**Brownsville, TX** (city) Cameron County	88.3
Montana	106.0	Jefferson County, OH	71.0	**El Paso, TX** (city) El Paso County	88.3
Colorado	107.5	Otsego County, MI	74.2	**Calexico, CA** (city) Imperial County	88.4
New Hampshire	107.9	Livingston County, MO	79.3	**Plantation, FL** (city) Broward County	88.7

Note: (1) Ranking tables cover all states and counties, and places with an overall population of at least 125,000, OR an overall population of at least 25,000 where the Hispanic/Latino population is at least 20% of the overall population. In states where less than five places meet either of these criteria, we have included places with at least 10,000 total population with the highest percentage of Hispanic/Latino population. These places are identified with an asterisk (*); Please refer to the User's Guide for a full explanation of data.

Males per 100 Females

Puerto Rican

Top 10 States, Counties, and Places[1]

Sorted by Percent in Descending Order — U.S. = 94.1

State	Number	County	Number	Place	Number
South Dakota	123.3	Yazoo County, MS	846.2	**Florence, AZ** (town) Pinal County	804.8
West Virginia	117.8	Wyoming County, NY	709.2	**Fort Leonard Wood*, MO** (cdp) Pulaski County	240.9
North Dakota	116.9	Franklin County, NY	529.3	**National City, CA** (city) San Diego County	191.1
Mississippi	111.8	Taylor County, FL	460.0	**El Centro, CA** (city) Imperial County	170.6
Alaska	110.6	Bee County, TX	372.7	**Kingsville, TX** (city) Kleberg County	167.9
Maine	108.7	Essex County, NY	362.5	**Muscatine*, IA** (city) Muscatine County	162.5
Kentucky	108.6	Edgefield County, SC	351.7	**Huron*, SD** (city) Beadle County	160.0
Nebraska	107.3	Union County, PA	328.2	**Del Rio, TX** (city) Val Verde County	148.6
Louisiana	107.1	Gulf County, FL	328.1	**Odessa, TX** (city) Ector County	147.2
Missouri	106.4	McKean County, PA	300.0	**Eagle Pass, TX** (city) Maverick County	146.5

Sorted by Percent in Ascending Order — U.S. = 94.1

State	Number	County	Number	Place	Number
Rhode Island	88.8	Fluvanna County, VA	61.7	**Bennington*, VT** (town) Bennington County	61.5
New York	89.6	Butler County, KS	64.2	**Petaluma, CA** (city) Sonoma County	70.8
Connecticut	90.2	Gilmer County, GA	65.1	**Rogers, AR** (city) Benton County	73.1
Massachusetts	91.0	Somerset County, MD	67.2	**Englewood, NJ** (city) Bergen County	73.2
Maryland	92.5	Gila County, AZ	67.7	**La Mirada, CA** (city) Los Angeles County	73.5
Georgia	93.6	Cherokee County, NC	69.4	**Orange, CA** (city) Orange County	73.7
New Jersey	93.9	Caldwell County, TX	70.2	**Aloha, OR** (cdp) Washington County	73.8
Florida	94.5	Spalding County, GA	70.5	**Westmont, CA** (cdp) Los Angeles County	74.7
Oregon	94.5	Putnam County, TN	70.6	**Brunswick*, ME** (town) Cumberland County	75.3
Illinois	95.1	Etowah County, AL	70.7	**Salem, OR** (city) Marion County	76.7

Note: (1) Ranking tables cover all states and counties, and places with an overall population of at least 125,000, OR an overall population of at least 25,000 where the Hispanic/Latino population is at least 20% of the overall population. In states where less than five places meet either of these criteria, we have included places with at least 10,000 total population with the highest percentage of Hispanic/Latino population. These places are identified with an asterisk (*); Please refer to the User's Guide for a full explanation of data.

Males per 100 Females

South American

Top 10 States, Counties, and Places[1]

Sorted by Percent in Descending Order — U.S. = 90.1

State	Number	County	Number	Place	Number
Idaho	103.7	Telfair County, GA	18,550.0	**Fort Leonard Wood*, MO** (cdp) Pulaski County	284.4
Minnesota	103.6	Adams County, MS	1,950.0	**North Chicago, IL** (city) Lake County	179.7
Mississippi	100.2	Clearfield County, PA	1,121.1	**National City, CA** (city) San Diego County	148.2
Connecticut	100.0	Chattahoochee County, GA	402.6	**Fort Hood, TX** (cdp) Bell County	143.2
Wyoming	99.5	Union County, PA	248.8	**Spring Valley, NY** (village) Rockland County	138.1
Iowa	98.4	Sumter County, FL	220.0	**Danbury, CT** (city/town) Fairfield County	132.6
New York	98.0	Mahoning County, OH	182.7	**City of Orange, NJ** (township) Essex County	132.4
Hawaii	96.8	Granville County, NC	166.7	**Minneapolis, MN** (city) Hennepin County	131.1
New Jersey	94.8	Pulaski County, MO	156.0	**Ossining, NY** (village) Westchester County	128.6
Illinois	94.4	Saint Lawrence County, NY	153.7	**Newark, NJ** (city) Essex County	127.7

Sorted by Percent in Ascending Order — U.S. = 90.1

State	Number	County	Number	Place	Number
Maine	81.0	Rogers County, OK	46.2	**Sahuarita, AZ** (town) Pima County	53.3
Alaska	82.3	Calvert County, MD	55.5	**New Braunfels, TX** (city) Comal County	57.9
Montana	82.3	Harnett County, NC	56.5	**Waco, TX** (city) McLennan County	62.8
Florida	82.7	Bryan County, GA	56.9	**San Marcos, TX** (city) Hays County	64.1
New Hampshire	82.8	Portage County, OH	58.2	**Casa Grande, AZ** (city) Pinal County	64.2
New Mexico	83.0	Eagle County, CO	59.7	**Suisun City, CA** (city) Solano County	65.0
District of Columbia	83.1	Gallatin County, MT	60.2	**Woodland, CA** (city) Yolo County	65.3
Oklahoma	83.5	Jackson County, MI	60.3	**Georgetown, TX** (city) Williamson County	66.7
Vermont	83.5	Platte County, NE	60.9	**Bozeman*, MT** (city) Gallatin County	67.7
Arizona	84.3	Linn County, OR	61.4	**Fayetteville, NC** (city) Cumberland County	68.5

Note: (1) Ranking tables cover all states and counties, and places with an overall population of at least 125,000, OR an overall population of at least 25,000 where the Hispanic/Latino population is at least 20% of the overall population. In states where less than five places meet either of these criteria, we have included places with at least 10,000 total population with the highest percentage of Hispanic/Latino population. These places are identified with an asterisk (*); Please refer to the User's Guide for a full explanation of data.

Males per 100 Females

South American: Argentinean

Top 10 States, Counties, and Places[1]

Sorted by Percent in Descending Order — U.S. = 99.3

State	Number	County	Number	Place	Number
Nebraska	133.7	Maui County, HI	190.9	**Alafaya, FL** (cdp) Orange County	160.0
Hawaii	126.2	Leon County, FL	143.3	**Tallahassee, FL** (city) Leon County	152.1
Mississippi	117.3	Tulsa County, OK	138.1	**Oxnard, CA** (city) Ventura County	144.2
Oklahoma	113.8	Onondaga County, NY	129.8	**Tulsa, OK** (city) Tulsa County	142.9
Iowa	106.0	Snohomish County, WA	125.8	**San Bernardino, CA** (city) San Bernardino County	140.0
Indiana	105.8	Williamson County, TX	125.5	**Town 'n' Country, FL** (cdp) Hillsborough County	137.9
Vermont	105.6	Clackamas County, OR	124.3	**South Gate, CA** (city) Los Angeles County	133.3
Texas	104.5	Marion County, FL	122.8	**Altadena, CA** (cdp) Los Angeles County	132.7
Alaska	104.1	Will County, IL	120.9	**Belleville, NJ** (township) Essex County	132.7
Delaware	103.4	Oklahoma County, OK	120.0	**Scottsdale, AZ** (city) Maricopa County	132.4

Sorted by Percent in Ascending Order — U.S. = 99.3

State	Number	County	Number	Place	Number
Maine	60.2	Orange County, NC	64.1	**Lehigh Acres, FL** (cdp) Lee County	64.9
Alabama	79.7	Union County, NC	64.1	**Kansas City, MO** (city) Jackson County	68.9
New Hampshire	85.1	Bristol County, MA	65.2	**Altamonte Springs, FL** (city) Seminole County	76.3
Minnesota	86.7	Bucks County, PA	69.7	**Saint Petersburg, FL** (city) Pinellas County	76.6
Wisconsin	87.5	Pierce County, WA	74.5	**Simi Valley, CA** (city) Ventura County	78.2
Missouri	88.0	Chester County, PA	76.3	**Culver City, CA** (city) Los Angeles County	79.2
Montana	88.5	Sonoma County, CA	76.3	**Chino Hills, CA** (city) San Bernardino County	79.6
Colorado	88.8	Charlotte County, FL	76.7	**Cary, NC** (town) Wake County	79.7
Tennessee	91.1	Charleston County, SC	76.9	**Norwalk, CT** (city/town) Fairfield County	80.0
Rhode Island	91.5	Marion County, OR	77.6	**Chino, CA** (city) San Bernardino County	80.3

RANKINGS & COMPARISONS

Note: (1) Ranking tables cover all states and counties, and places with an overall population of at least 125,000, OR an overall population of at least 25,000 where the Hispanic/Latino population is at least 20% of the overall population. In states where less than five places meet either of these criteria, we have included places with at least 10,000 total population with the highest percentage of Hispanic/Latino population. These places are identified with an asterisk (*); Please refer to the User's Guide for a full explanation of data.

Males per 100 Females

South American: Bolivian

Top 10 States, Counties, and Places[1]

Sorted by Percent in Descending Order — U.S. = 92.6

State	Number	County	Number	Place	Number
Delaware	124.0	Charleston County, SC	152.3	**Wheaton, MD** (cdp) Montgomery County	122.4
West Virginia	117.2	Collin County, TX	115.1	**West Falls Church, VA** (cdp) Fairfax County	120.8
Iowa	111.1	Arlington County, VA	114.9	**Charlotte, NC** (city) Mecklenburg County	119.0
Alabama	105.6	Mecklenburg County, NC	112.3	**Port Chester, NY** (village) Westchester County	117.4
Virginia	102.1	Prince George's County, MD	112.1	**Arlington, VA** (cdp) Arlington County	114.9
South Carolina	102.0	Philadelphia County, PA	111.3	**Rye, NY** (town) Westchester County	114.3
Louisiana	99.3	Travis County, TX	111.0	**Marumsco, VA** (cdp) Prince William County	113.7
Minnesota	99.1	Arapahoe County, CO	109.0	**Philadelphia, PA** (city) Philadelphia County	111.3
Colorado	98.2	Middlesex County, NJ	108.5	**Newark, NJ** (city) Essex County	110.0
Michigan	97.7	Fairfax County, VA	102.0	**Austin, TX** (city) Travis County	108.5

Sorted by Percent in Ascending Order — U.S. = 92.6

State	Number	County	Number	Place	Number
Idaho	71.8	Hillsborough County, FL	70.5	**Glendale, CA** (city) Los Angeles County	66.7
New Mexico	72.2	Utah County, UT	71.1	**Hollywood, FL** (city) Broward County	66.7
Arkansas	78.1	Norfolk County, MA	71.3	**Tampa, FL** (city) Hillsborough County	67.3
Hawaii	79.5	Sacramento County, CA	73.2	**San Mateo, CA** (city) San Mateo County	67.9
Wisconsin	79.9	New York County, NY	75.2	**Fountainebleau, FL** (cdp) Miami-Dade County	70.6
Utah	80.8	Baltimore County, MD	75.3	**Brookhaven, NY** (town) Suffolk County	72.1
Washington	82.3	Kane County, IL	75.3	**The Hammocks, FL** (cdp) Miami-Dade County	73.3
Kansas	82.4	Snohomish County, WA	76.3	**Oyster Bay, NY** (town) Nassau County	74.6
Ohio	83.3	Dane County, WI	78.8	**Manhattan, NY** (borough) New York County	75.2
Indiana	84.8	Richmond County, NY	78.9	**Kendall West, FL** (cdp) Miami-Dade County	75.4

Note: (1) Ranking tables cover all states and counties, and places with an overall population of at least 125,000, OR an overall population of at least 25,000 where the Hispanic/Latino population is at least 20% of the overall population. In states where less than five places meet either of these criteria, we have included places with at least 10,000 total population with the highest percentage of Hispanic/Latino population. These places are identified with an asterisk (*); Please refer to the User's Guide for a full explanation of data.

Males per 100 Females

South American: Chilean

Top 10 States, Counties, and Places[1]

Sorted by Percent in Descending Order — U.S. = 93.0

State	Number	County	Number	Place	Number
Rhode Island	116.7	Lane County, OR	136.2	**Elmont, NY** (cdp) Nassau County	230.6
Vermont	111.7	Milwaukee County, WI	128.1	**Milwaukee, WI** (city) Milwaukee County	144.7
Delaware	108.1	Mobile County, AL	126.4	**Bridgeport, CT** (city/town) Fairfield County	143.2
Maine	107.5	Philadelphia County, PA	124.5	**Ossining, NY** (village) Westchester County	141.4
Pennsylvania	106.8	Leon County, FL	119.6	**Brentwood, NY** (cdp) Suffolk County	139.1
Alabama	105.0	Atlantic County, NJ	117.0	**Port Chester, NY** (village) Westchester County	136.5
Alaska	102.7	Lehigh County, PA	117.0	**Baltimore, MD** (independent city)	136.2
New York	101.5	Kings County, NY	115.5	**Ossining, NY** (town) Westchester County	134.6
Kansas	101.2	Chester County, PA	113.7	**Homestead, FL** (city) Miami-Dade County	129.8
Idaho	100.0	New Castle County, DE	113.3	**Union City, NJ** (city) Hudson County	128.2

Sorted by Percent in Ascending Order — U.S. = 93.0

State	Number	County	Number	Place	Number
Arizona	78.2	Douglas County, CO	66.2	**Mesa, AZ** (city) Maricopa County	46.9
District of Columbia	80.6	Dutchess County, NY	67.3	**Aventura, FL** (city) Miami-Dade County	63.0
Oklahoma	80.6	Washoe County, NV	68.6	**Concord, CA** (city) Contra Costa County	65.6
Nebraska	82.4	Arlington County, VA	68.7	**Arlington, VA** (cdp) Arlington County	68.7
Ohio	83.9	Lake County, IL	68.9	**Columbus, OH** (city) Franklin County	69.7
Tennessee	84.3	Solano County, CA	69.3	**Phoenix, AZ** (city) Maricopa County	71.1
Virginia	85.9	Franklin County, OH	71.0	**Corona, CA** (city) Riverside County	72.8
Wisconsin	86.1	Anne Arundel County, MD	71.2	**Reno, NV** (city) Washoe County	74.2
Maryland	86.5	Somerset County, NJ	71.9	**Madison, WI** (city) Dane County	75.8
New Mexico	86.6	Maricopa County, AZ	74.8	**Babylon, NY** (town) Suffolk County	76.6

Note: (1) Ranking tables cover all states and counties, and places with an overall population of at least 125,000, OR an overall population of at least 25,000 where the Hispanic/Latino population is at least 20% of the overall population. In states where less than five places meet either of these criteria, we have included places with at least 10,000 total population with the highest percentage of Hispanic/Latino population. These places are identified with an asterisk (*); Please refer to the User's Guide for a full explanation of data.

Males per 100 Females

South American: Colombian

Top 10 States, Counties, and Places[1]

Sorted by Percent in Descending Order — U.S. = 80.5

State	Number	County	Number	Place	Number
Mississippi	113.5	Telfair County, GA	16,750.0	**Norfolk, VA** (independent city)	162.7
North Dakota	93.7	Adams County, MS	4,400.0	**Mundelein, IL** (village) Lake County	119.1
Iowa	91.1	Clearfield County, PA	2,471.4	**Hesperia, CA** (city) San Bernardino County	114.0
Massachusetts	88.3	Mahoning County, OH	441.7	**Manassas, VA** (independent city)	114.0
Arkansas	87.7	Sumter County, FL	341.5	**Rochester, NY** (city) Monroe County	111.6
Minnesota	87.6	Craven County, NC	162.7	**Baltimore, MD** (independent city)	110.3
Indiana	87.0	Centre County, PA	160.5	**Pasadena, TX** (city) Harris County	110.3
Missouri	87.0	Oneida County, NY	142.2	**Hilton Head Island*, SC** (town) Beaufort County	108.6
Ohio	86.6	Onslow County, NC	137.7	**Stockton, CA** (city) San Joaquin County	106.9
Rhode Island	85.8	Tippecanoe County, IN	134.8	**Boston, MA** (city) Suffolk County	105.9

Sorted by Percent in Ascending Order — U.S. = 80.5

State	Number	County	Number	Place	Number
Wyoming	56.1	Smith County, TX	50.7	**Redwood City, CA** (city) San Mateo County	44.6
Montana	67.4	Johnston County, NC	54.1	**The Colony, TX** (city) Denton County	45.7
South Dakota	69.1	Harnett County, NC	58.2	**San Rafael, CA** (city) Marin County	53.4
New Mexico	71.4	Marin County, CA	58.4	**Culver City, CA** (city) Los Angeles County	56.3
Vermont	73.9	Highlands County, FL	59.0	**Temecula, CA** (city) Riverside County	58.7
Nebraska	74.2	Anderson County, SC	59.1	**Little Elm, TX** (city) Denton County	59.1
Alaska	74.8	Rockdale County, GA	60.0	**Reno, NV** (city) Washoe County	59.6
Arizona	75.8	Clark County, WA	61.1	**Lewisville, TX** (city) Denton County	61.1
Nevada	76.3	Doña Ana County, NM	61.3	**Gardena, CA** (city) Los Angeles County	62.7
Idaho	76.4	Berrien County, MI	63.0	**Petaluma, CA** (city) Sonoma County	62.7

Note: (1) Ranking tables cover all states and counties, and places with an overall population of at least 125,000, OR an overall population of at least 25,000 where the Hispanic/Latino population is at least 20% of the overall population. In states where less than five places meet either of these criteria, we have included places with at least 10,000 total population with the highest percentage of Hispanic/Latino population. These places are identified with an asterisk (*); Please refer to the User's Guide for a full explanation of data.

Males per 100 Females

South American: Ecuadorian

Top 10 States, Counties, and Places[1]

Sorted by Percent in Descending Order — U.S. = 104.8

State	Number	County	Number	Place	Number
Minnesota	131.9	Middlesex County, CT	155.0	**Dayton, OH** (city) Montgomery County	180.5
Connecticut	128.0	Litchfield County, CT	151.2	**New London, CT** (city/town) New London County	167.8
Hawaii	116.8	Bucks County, PA	150.3	**Middletown, NY** (city) Orange County	165.1
Iowa	116.6	Honolulu County, HI	150.0	**New Haven, CT** (city/town) New Haven County	157.2
New York	113.3	New London County, CT	144.5	**Bakersfield, CA** (city) Kern County	156.6
Illinois	113.1	Hennepin County, MN	139.9	**Haverstraw, NY** (town) Rockland County	155.3
Pennsylvania	112.6	Delaware County, PA	138.8	**City of Orange, NJ** (township) Essex County	154.2
New Jersey	108.2	Rockland County, NY	138.4	**Danbury, CT** (city/town) Fairfield County	151.4
Wisconsin	108.0	Philadelphia County, PA	138.3	**Port Chester, NY** (village) Westchester County	147.7
Ohio	107.1	Burlington County, NJ	136.8	**Spring Valley, NY** (village) Rockland County	144.4

Sorted by Percent in Ascending Order — U.S. = 104.8

State	Number	County	Number	Place	Number
District of Columbia	70.4	Davis County, UT	60.4	**Glen Cove, NY** (city) Nassau County	61.2
Oklahoma	74.3	Jefferson County, CO	62.0	**Cary, NC** (town) Wake County	64.7
Alaska	78.3	Leon County, FL	65.1	**Chandler, AZ** (city) Maricopa County	64.7
Utah	78.7	Denver County, CO	67.0	**Coral Gables, FL** (city) Miami-Dade County	65.6
Florida	82.9	Rutherford County, TN	67.1	**Wesley Chapel, FL** (cdp) Pasco County	65.8
Colorado	84.3	Hernando County, FL	67.2	**East Los Angeles, CA** (cdp) Los Angeles County	66.3
Kentucky	85.2	Oklahoma County, OK	68.5	**Denver, CO** (city) Denver County	67.0
Nevada	85.2	Henrico County, VA	69.6	**West Palm Beach, FL** (city) Palm Beach County	67.3
Tennessee	86.2	Harford County, MD	71.0	**Glendale, AZ** (city) Maricopa County	68.2
Arizona	86.4	Iredell County, NC	71.4	**Saint Cloud, FL** (city) Osceola County	68.3

RANKINGS & COMPARISONS

Note: (1) Ranking tables cover all states and counties, and places with an overall population of at least 125,000, OR an overall population of at least 25,000 where the Hispanic/Latino population is at least 20% of the overall population. In states where less than five places meet either of these criteria, we have included places with at least 10,000 total population with the highest percentage of Hispanic/Latino population. These places are identified with an asterisk (*); Please refer to the User's Guide for a full explanation of data.

Males per 100 Females

South American: Paraguayan

Top 10 States, Counties, and Places[1]

Sorted by Percent in Descending Order — U.S. = 85.0

State	Number	County	Number	Place	Number
South Carolina	109.4	Somerset County, NJ	106.7	**White Plains, NY** (city) Westchester County	104.7
New Jersey	98.6	Suffolk County, NY	102.9	**Rye, NY** (town) Westchester County	100.0
Alabama	98.4	Middlesex County, MA	101.6	**Queens, NY** (borough) Queens County	96.0
Kansas	98.1	Morris County, NJ	100.9	**New York, NY** (city)	92.5
Wisconsin	97.8	Westchester County, NY	98.5	**Houston, TX** (city) Harris County	91.9
Pennsylvania	93.1	Queens County, NY	96.0	**Hempstead (town), NY** (town) Nassau County	90.7
New York	92.1	Harris County, TX	93.4	**Brooklyn, NY** (borough) Kings County	84.0
Minnesota	91.3	Maricopa County, AZ	93.1	**Bronx, NY** (borough) Bronx County	82.8
Georgia	90.5	Cook County, IL	84.8	**Miami, FL** (city) Miami-Dade County	81.9
Illinois	88.0	Kings County, NY	84.0	**Manhattan, NY** (borough) New York County	81.1

Sorted by Percent in Ascending Order — U.S. = 85.0

State	Number	County	Number	Place	Number
Washington	60.2	Arlington County, VA	59.2	**Arlington, VA** (cdp) Arlington County	59.2
Oregon	69.7	Broward County, FL	63.3	**Los Angeles, CA** (city) Los Angeles County	59.3
Colorado	69.8	Miami-Dade County, FL	69.8	**Chicago, IL** (city) Cook County	65.6
Nevada	70.6	Palm Beach County, FL	71.9	**North Hempstead, NY** (town) Nassau County	77.2
Tennessee	71.4	Clark County, NV	73.0	**Manhattan, NY** (borough) New York County	81.1
Virginia	72.7	Fairfax County, VA	74.7	**Miami, FL** (city) Miami-Dade County	81.9
Florida	72.8	Los Angeles County, CA	75.0	**Bronx, NY** (borough) Bronx County	82.8
California	74.2	Dallas County, TX	75.8	**Brooklyn, NY** (borough) Kings County	84.0
Utah	75.6	Fairfield County, CT	75.9	**Hempstead (town), NY** (town) Nassau County	90.7
District of Columbia	76.9	Prince George's County, MD	80.9	**Houston, TX** (city) Harris County	91.9

Note: (1) Ranking tables cover all states and counties, and places with an overall population of at least 125,000, OR an overall population of at least 25,000 where the Hispanic/Latino population is at least 20% of the overall population. In states where less than five places meet either of these criteria, we have included places with at least 10,000 total population with the highest percentage of Hispanic/Latino population. These places are identified with an asterisk (*); Please refer to the User's Guide for a full explanation of data.

Males per 100 Females

South American: Peruvian

Top 10 States, Counties, and Places[1]

Sorted by Percent in Descending Order — U.S. = 89.0

State	Number	County	Number	Place	Number
Wyoming	167.5	Orleans Parish, LA	144.1	**Lancaster, PA** (city) Lancaster County	151.2
Idaho	134.6	Catawba County, NC	128.0	**New Orleans, LA** (city) Orleans Parish	144.1
Utah	99.0	Kern County, CA	126.4	**Longmont, CO** (city) Boulder County	141.7
Delaware	98.3	Canyon County, ID	124.6	**Bell, CA** (city) Los Angeles County	140.8
South Dakota	97.1	Centre County, PA	122.6	**Tempe, AZ** (city) Maricopa County	135.0
New Jersey	94.7	Dare County, NC	121.7	**North Atlanta, GA** (cdp) DeKalb County	132.6
Nevada	93.9	Cache County, UT	119.7	**Lynwood, CA** (city) Los Angeles County	132.2
Connecticut	93.5	Allen County, IN	119.1	**Hempstead (village), NY** (village) Nassau County	128.7
Kentucky	93.1	Blaine County, ID	119.0	**Hesperia, CA** (city) San Bernardino County	128.6
Louisiana	92.9	Boulder County, CO	118.8	**West Little River, FL** (cdp) Miami-Dade County	125.0

Sorted by Percent in Ascending Order — U.S. = 89.0

State	Number	County	Number	Place	Number
Vermont	64.6	Winnebago County, IL	54.9	**Winter Garden, FL** (city) Orange County	53.8
Maine	76.6	Frederick County, VA	58.0	**Placentia, CA** (city) Orange County	58.4
Mississippi	77.8	Monroe County, FL	60.0	**San Marcos, CA** (city) San Diego County	61.5
Oklahoma	78.7	Tulsa County, OK	63.2	**Newport News, VA** (independent city)	62.0
New Hampshire	79.1	Chittenden County, VT	63.5	**San Dimas, CA** (city) Los Angeles County	62.3
Missouri	79.9	Carroll County, MD	65.2	**La Habra, CA** (city) Orange County	62.4
Alaska	81.8	Martin County, FL	65.6	**San Buenaventura (Ventura), CA** (city) Ventura County	64.9
Florida	82.0	Charles County, MD	67.0	**Coral Gables, FL** (city) Miami-Dade County	65.6
Ohio	82.7	Kane County, IL	67.1	**La Mesa, CA** (city) San Diego County	66.2
Iowa	82.8	Middlesex County, CT	67.6	**Tulsa, OK** (city) Tulsa County	66.2

Note: (1) Ranking tables cover all states and counties, and places with an overall population of at least 125,000, OR an overall population of at least 25,000 where the Hispanic/Latino population is at least 20% of the overall population. In states where less than five places meet either of these criteria, we have included places with at least 10,000 total population with the highest percentage of Hispanic/Latino population. These places are identified with an asterisk (*); Please refer to the User's Guide for a full explanation of data.

Males per 100 Females

South American: Uruguayan

Top 10 States, Counties, and Places[1]

Sorted by Percent in Descending Order — U.S. = 101.4

State	Number	County	Number	Place	Number
Missouri	121.0	San Bernardino County, CA	157.3	**Bridgeport, CT** (city/town) Fairfield County	161.9
Washington	113.5	Volusia County, FL	155.7	**Jacksonville, FL** (city) Duval County	158.0
Connecticut	109.0	Duval County, FL	151.9	**North Bergen, NJ** (township) Hudson County	142.2
North Carolina	109.0	Cobb County, GA	134.4	**Raleigh, NC** (city) Wake County	139.3
South Carolina	108.6	King County, WA	129.2	**Weston, FL** (city) Broward County	133.3
Georgia	107.4	Suffolk County, MA	128.6	**Plantation, FL** (city) Broward County	130.0
New York	105.5	Polk County, FL	127.1	**Cape Coral, FL** (city) Lee County	128.3
Texas	104.0	Clayton County, GA	125.8	**Doral, FL** (city) Miami-Dade County	127.8
Florida	103.6	San Francisco County, CA	122.6	**Tamarac, FL** (city) Broward County	127.3
Oregon	103.1	Bexar County, TX	121.6	**San Francisco, CA** (city) San Francisco County	122.6

Sorted by Percent in Ascending Order — U.S. = 101.4

State	Number	County	Number	Place	Number
Rhode Island	69.7	Pinellas County, FL	78.0	**West New York, NJ** (town) Hudson County	71.6
Colorado	80.6	Lackawanna County, PA	80.0	**Kendall West, FL** (cdp) Miami-Dade County	79.0
District of Columbia	83.1	Saint Lucie County, FL	80.0	**Linden, NJ** (city) Union County	80.2
New Hampshire	84.7	Salt Lake County, UT	83.9	**Kissimmee, FL** (city) Osceola County	82.2
Utah	84.8	Cuyahoga County, OH	84.2	**Fort Lauderdale, FL** (city) Broward County	83.2
Minnesota	85.8	Arlington County, VA	84.3	**Coral Gables, FL** (city) Miami-Dade County	83.8
Arizona	86.7	San Mateo County, CA	84.7	**Arlington, VA** (cdp) Arlington County	84.3
Indiana	87.5	Hillsborough County, NH	85.6	**Manchester*, NH** (city) Hillsborough County	85.1
Louisiana	87.9	Henry County, GA	87.3	**Port Saint Lucie, FL** (city) Saint Lucie County	85.5
Michigan	88.2	Montgomery County, MD	87.4	**Dallas, TX** (city) Dallas County	87.3

Note: (1) Ranking tables cover all states and counties, and places with an overall population of at least 125,000, OR an overall population of at least 25,000 where the Hispanic/Latino population is at least 20% of the overall population. In states where less than five places meet either of these criteria, we have included places with at least 10,000 total population with the highest percentage of Hispanic/Latino population. These places are identified with an asterisk (*); Please refer to the User's Guide for a full explanation of data.

Males per 100 Females

South American: Venezuelan

Top 10 States, Counties, and Places[1]

Sorted by Percent in Descending Order — U.S. = 84.9

State	Number	County	Number	Place	Number
Iowa	110.9	Hamilton County, TN	132.7	**Denver, CO** (city) Denver County	130.9
West Virginia	102.9	Denver County, CO	130.9	**Atlanta, GA** (city) Fulton County	130.3
Tennessee	100.6	Orleans Parish, LA	129.9	**New Orleans, LA** (city) Orleans Parish	129.9
Indiana	99.4	San Francisco County, CA	125.5	**San Francisco, CA** (city) San Francisco County	125.5
Arizona	94.9	Erie County, NY	119.4	**Chandler, AZ** (city) Maricopa County	123.9
Arkansas	94.8	Hampden County, MA	116.9	**Cincinnati, OH** (city) Hamilton County	122.9
Minnesota	93.3	Rockland County, NY	112.5	**Minneapolis, MN** (city) Hennepin County	121.9
Missouri	92.9	Nueces County, TX	110.4	**Salt Lake City, UT** (city) Salt Lake County	115.9
Hawaii	92.6	Richland County, SC	109.8	**Paradise, NV** (cdp) Clark County	113.5
Pennsylvania	92.6	San Joaquin County, CA	109.1	**Memphis, TN** (city) Shelby County	113.4

Sorted by Percent in Ascending Order — U.S. = 84.9

State	Number	County	Number	Place	Number
Alaska	62.8	Marin County, CA	49.3	**Virginia Beach, VA** (independent city)	60.7
New Hampshire	65.3	Cumberland County, NC	55.4	**Winston-Salem, NC** (city) Forsyth County	63.1
Maine	78.0	Macomb County, MI	55.9	**Alexandria, VA** (independent city)	63.6
Idaho	78.6	Monroe County, FL	58.3	**West New York, NJ** (town) Hudson County	64.2
Virginia	78.7	Chesterfield County, VA	60.2	**New Rochelle, NY** (city) Westchester County	65.8
Maryland	79.2	Frederick County, MD	60.7	**Arlington, TX** (city) Tarrant County	67.8
New Jersey	79.6	Orange County, NC	61.3	**Clifton, NJ** (city) Passaic County	68.1
Delaware	80.1	Orange County, NY	61.7	**Baton Rouge, LA** (city) East Baton Rouge Parish	69.5
Nebraska	80.2	Martin County, FL	64.8	**Madison, WI** (city) Dane County	69.6
Nevada	81.8	Hernando County, FL	65.1	**Oyster Bay, NY** (town) Nassau County	69.7

Note: (1) Ranking tables cover all states and counties, and places with an overall population of at least 125,000, OR an overall population of at least 25,000 where the Hispanic/Latino population is at least 20% of the overall population. In states where less than five places meet either of these criteria, we have included places with at least 10,000 total population with the highest percentage of Hispanic/Latino population. These places are identified with an asterisk (*); Please refer to the User's Guide for a full explanation of data.

Males per 100 Females

Spaniard

Top 10 States, Counties, and Places[1]

Sorted by Percent in Descending Order — U.S. = 91.9

State	Number	County	Number	Place	Number
Louisiana	104.3	Oneida County, NY	150.0	**Plainfield, NJ** (city) Union County	182.5
Wyoming	100.6	Westmoreland County, PA	142.2	**Columbia, SC** (city) Richland County	164.7
Kentucky	100.0	Iberia Parish, LA	140.4	**Chelsea, MA** (city) Suffolk County	157.4
New Jersey	100.0	Olmsted County, MN	139.2	**North Miami, FL** (city) Miami-Dade County	143.8
Mississippi	99.0	Ascension Parish, LA	139.1	**Union City, NJ** (city) Hudson County	142.2
District of Columbia	98.7	Richland County, SC	138.1	**Fort Hood, TX** (cdp) Bell County	139.1
North Dakota	98.4	Campbell County, WY	135.6	**Hobbs, NM** (city) Lea County	135.9
South Carolina	98.1	Saint Bernard Parish, LA	132.4	**Freeport, NY** (village) Nassau County	135.2
Connecticut	97.1	Saguache County, CO	129.1	**Stanton, CA** (city) Orange County	129.8
New York	96.3	Livingston County, MI	127.8	**Yucaipa, CA** (city) San Bernardino County	128.3

Sorted by Percent in Ascending Order — U.S. = 91.9

State	Number	County	Number	Place	Number
Maine	77.8	Clayton County, GA	55.1	**Tyler, TX** (city) Smith County	56.7
Vermont	84.5	Walla Walla County, WA	57.8	**Bolingbrook, IL** (village) Will County	59.1
Ohio	86.6	Clay County, FL	63.4	**Florin, CA** (cdp) Sacramento County	61.2
Hawaii	86.7	Kent County, DE	65.3	**Naperville, IL** (city) DuPage County	62.4
Tennessee	87.9	Stafford County, VA	66.1	**Dale City, VA** (cdp) Prince William County	62.7
Oklahoma	88.1	Greene County, OH	67.4	**Tacoma, WA** (city) Pierce County	63.2
Washington	88.7	Northampton County, PA	69.1	**Edinburg, TX** (city) Hidalgo County	64.3
Rhode Island	89.4	Saint Mary's County, MD	69.1	**North Highlands, CA** (cdp) Sacramento County	64.9
Iowa	89.7	Skagit County, WA	69.2	**Azusa, CA** (city) Los Angeles County	65.9
Alaska	89.8	Hampshire County, MA	69.6	**Killeen, TX** (city) Bell County	66.2

Note: (1) Ranking tables cover all states and counties, and places with an overall population of at least 125,000, OR an overall population of at least 25,000 where the Hispanic/Latino population is at least 20% of the overall population. In states where less than five places meet either of these criteria, we have included places with at least 10,000 total population with the highest percentage of Hispanic/Latino population. These places are identified with an asterisk (*); Please refer to the User's Guide for a full explanation of data.

Average Household Size

Total Population

Top 10 States, Counties, and Places[1]

Sorted by Percent in Descending Order — U.S. = 2.58

State	Number	County	Number	Place	Number
Utah	3.10	Shannon County, SD	4.29	**Lynwood, CA** (city) Los Angeles County	4.57
California	2.90	Webb County, TX	3.68	**Florence-Graham, CA** (cdp) Los Angeles County	4.56
Hawaii	2.89	Utah County, UT	3.57	**Coachella, CA** (city) Riverside County	4.52
Texas	2.75	Hidalgo County, TX	3.55	**Santa Ana, CA** (city) Orange County	4.37
New Jersey	2.68	Starr County, TX	3.54	**Baldwin Park, CA** (city) Los Angeles County	4.36
Idaho	2.66	Todd County, SD	3.45	**Brentwood, NY** (cdp) Suffolk County	4.35
Alaska	2.65	Madison County, ID	3.44	**Bell Gardens, CA** (city) Los Angeles County	4.31
Nevada	2.65	Maverick County, TX	3.42	**Soledad, CA** (city) Monterey County	4.27
Arizona	2.63	Cameron County, TX	3.36	**Waianae*, HI** (cdp) Honolulu County	4.25
Georgia	2.63	Morgan County, UT	3.36	**La Puente, CA** (city) Los Angeles County	4.21

Sorted by Percent in Ascending Order — U.S. = 2.58

State	Number	County	Number	Place	Number
District of Columbia	2.11	Sierra County, NM	1.98	**Miami Beach, FL** (city) Miami-Dade County	1.84
North Dakota	2.30	Harding County, NM	1.99	**Palm Springs, CA** (city) Riverside County	1.93
Maine	2.32	New York County, NY	1.99	**Aventura, FL** (city) Miami-Dade County	1.99
Vermont	2.34	Esmeralda County, NV	2.01	**Manhattan, NY** (borough) New York County	1.99
Montana	2.35	Catron County, NM	2.03	**Hallandale Beach, FL** (city) Broward County	2.02
West Virginia	2.36	Sumter County, FL	2.04	**Alexandria, VA** (independent city)	2.03
Iowa	2.41	San Juan County, WA	2.05	**Morgantown*, WV** (city) Monongalia County	2.05
South Dakota	2.42	Iron County, MI	2.06	**Seattle, WA** (city) King County	2.06
Wyoming	2.42	Forest County, PA	2.08	**Pittsburgh, PA** (city) Allegheny County	2.07
Wisconsin	2.43	Jefferson County, WA	2.08	**Portland*, ME** (city) Cumberland County	2.07

Note: (1) Ranking tables cover all states and counties, and places with an overall population of at least 125,000, OR an overall population of at least 25,000 where the Hispanic/Latino population is at least 20% of the overall population. In states where less than five places meet either of these criteria, we have included places with at least 10,000 total population with the highest percentage of Hispanic/Latino population. These places are identified with an asterisk (*); Please refer to the User's Guide for a full explanation of data.

Average Household Size

Hispanic or Latino (of any race)

Top 10 States, Counties, and Places[1]

Sorted by Percent in Descending Order — U.S. = 3.52

State	Number	County	Number	Place	Number
California	3.93	Marshall County, SD	6.43	**Willowbrook, CA** (cdp) Los Angeles County	5.40
Utah	3.90	Lawrence County, MS	4.82	**Bridgeton, NJ** (city) Cumberland County	5.30
Maryland	3.87	Colfax County, NE	4.70	**Compton, CA** (city) Los Angeles County	5.30
Georgia	3.85	Hall County, GA	4.69	**East Palo Alto, CA** (city) San Mateo County	5.21
Illinois	3.78	Caroline County, MD	4.68	**Santa Ana, CA** (city) Orange County	5.19
Arkansas	3.72	Candler County, GA	4.65	**Brentwood, NY** (cdp) Suffolk County	5.13
Delaware	3.70	Polk County, GA	4.65	**Huntington Station, NY** (cdp) Suffolk County	5.10
North Carolina	3.70	Thurston County, NE	4.64	**San Juan Capistrano, CA** (city) Orange County	5.02
Oregon	3.68	Calhoun County, GA	4.63	**Hempstead (village), NY** (village) Nassau County	5.00
Nevada	3.66	Wasatch County, UT	4.63	**Central Islip, NY** (cdp) Suffolk County	4.99

Sorted by Percent in Ascending Order — U.S. = 3.52

State	Number	County	Number	Place	Number
Vermont	2.49	Harding County, NM	1.88	**Miami Beach, FL** (city) Miami-Dade County	1.94
Montana	2.70	Crawford County, WI	2.00	**Clarksburg*, WV** (city) Harrison County	2.22
Maine	2.74	Caldwell County, MO	2.05	**Burlington*, VT** (city) Chittenden County	2.24
District of Columbia	2.79	Catron County, NM	2.07	**Pittsburgh, PA** (city) Allegheny County	2.26
West Virginia	2.79	Hancock County, GA	2.12	**Brattleboro*, VT** (town) Windham County	2.29
North Dakota	2.82	Taylor County, GA	2.13	**Aventura, FL** (city) Miami-Dade County	2.34
New Mexico	2.87	Marion County, WV	2.18	**Morgantown*, WV** (city) Monongalia County	2.34
Wyoming	2.93	Clear Creek County, CO	2.20	**Hallandale Beach, FL** (city) Broward County	2.35
Alaska	2.98	Fergus County, MT	2.20	**Minot*, ND** (city) Ward County	2.35
Ohio	3.03	Deer Lodge County, MT	2.21	**Huntington*, WV** (city) Cabell County	2.39

Note: (1) Ranking tables cover all states and counties, and places with an overall population of at least 125,000, OR an overall population of at least 25,000 where the Hispanic/Latino population is at least 20% of the overall population. In states where less than five places meet either of these criteria, we have included places with at least 10,000 total population with the highest percentage of Hispanic/Latino population. These places are identified with an asterisk (*); Please refer to the User's Guide for a full explanation of data.

Average Household Size

Central American, excluding Mexican

Top 10 States, Counties, and Places[1]

Sorted by Percent in Descending Order — U.S. = 3.91

State	Number	County	Number	Place	Number
Delaware	4.78	Mason County, WA	5.97	**Central Islip, NY** (cdp) Suffolk County	6.24
Maryland	4.65	Sussex County, DE	5.76	**Brentwood, NY** (cdp) Suffolk County	5.95
Virginia	4.40	Caroline County, MD	5.66	**Bridgeton, NJ** (city) Cumberland County	5.89
Nebraska	4.15	Suffolk County, NY	5.60	**Huntington Station, NY** (cdp) Suffolk County	5.88
Alabama	4.13	Bedford County, TN	5.39	**Islip, NY** (town) Suffolk County	5.85
Georgia	4.10	Polk County, GA	5.38	**Huntington, NY** (town) Suffolk County	5.66
Tennessee	4.09	Habersham County, GA	5.37	**Babylon, NY** (town) Suffolk County	5.64
New York	4.06	Greene County, VA	5.36	**Hempstead (village), NY** (village) Nassau County	5.53
Utah	4.04	Nassau County, NY	5.20	**Springfield, VA** (cdp) Fairfax County	5.49
New Jersey	4.00	DeKalb County, AL	5.19	**Wheaton, MD** (cdp) Montgomery County	5.35

Sorted by Percent in Ascending Order — U.S. = 3.91

State	Number	County	Number	Place	Number
North Dakota	2.55	Franklin County, NY	2.00	**Aventura, FL** (city) Miami-Dade County	2.21
Montana	2.65	Stewart County, GA	2.00	**Urban Honolulu, HI** (cdp) Honolulu County	2.34
Vermont	2.67	Monroe County, IN	2.19	**Pittsburgh, PA** (city) Allegheny County	2.45
Hawaii	3.01	Grafton County, NH	2.25	**Las Cruces, NM** (city) Dona Ana County	2.49
Alaska	3.23	Cass County, ND	2.29	**Coral Gables, FL** (city) Miami-Dade County	2.52
Wisconsin	3.28	Ingham County, MI	2.36	**Miami Beach, FL** (city) Miami-Dade County	2.52
Louisiana	3.32	Centre County, PA	2.39	**Billings*, MT** (city) Yellowstone County	2.53
New Mexico	3.32	Missoula County, MT	2.42	**Manhattan, NY** (borough) New York County	2.55
Maine	3.37	Penobscot County, ME	2.45	**Tallahassee, FL** (city) Leon County	2.55
Wyoming	3.37	Tompkins County, NY	2.48	**Buffalo, NY** (city) Erie County	2.60

Note: (1) Ranking tables cover all states and counties, and places with an overall population of at least 125,000, OR an overall population of at least 25,000 where the Hispanic/Latino population is at least 20% of the overall population. In states where less than five places meet either of these criteria, we have included places with at least 10,000 total population with the highest percentage of Hispanic/Latino population. These places are identified with an asterisk (*); Please refer to the User's Guide for a full explanation of data.

Average Household Size

Central American: Costa Rican

Top 10 States, Counties, and Places[1]

Sorted by Percent in Descending Order — U.S. = 3.02

State	Number	County	Number	Place	Number
New Jersey	3.63	Ocean County, NJ	4.09	**Palmdale, CA** (city) Los Angeles County	4.20
Utah	3.34	Frederick County, MD	4.08	**Moreno Valley, CA** (city) Riverside County	4.12
South Carolina	3.28	Stanislaus County, CA	4.00	**Islip, NY** (town) Suffolk County	4.10
New Hampshire	3.24	Somerset County, NJ	3.88	**Fontana, CA** (city) San Bernardino County	4.09
Pennsylvania	3.21	Union County, NC	3.87	**Trenton, NJ** (city) Mercer County	3.92
Tennessee	3.17	Suffolk County, NY	3.83	**Babylon, NY** (town) Suffolk County	3.85
North Carolina	3.13	Union County, NJ	3.79	**Weston, FL** (city) Broward County	3.81
Maryland	3.11	Mercer County, NJ	3.77	**Victorville, CA** (city) San Bernardino County	3.80
Nevada	3.06	Morris County, NJ	3.72	**Plainfield, NJ** (city) Union County	3.79
Delaware	3.05	Sussex County, NJ	3.64	**Norwalk, CA** (city) Los Angeles County	3.77

Sorted by Percent in Ascending Order — U.S. = 3.02

State	Number	County	Number	Place	Number
District of Columbia	1.94	Arlington County, VA	1.92	**Atlanta, GA** (city) Fulton County	1.81
Kentucky	2.50	New York County, NY	2.03	**Arlington, VA** (cdp) Arlington County	1.92
Maine	2.53	Orleans Parish, LA	2.07	**Portland, OR** (city) Multnomah County	2.00
Rhode Island	2.57	Denver County, CO	2.12	**Manhattan, NY** (borough) New York County	2.03
New Mexico	2.60	Fulton County, GA	2.17	**Seattle, WA** (city) King County	2.03
Hawaii	2.63	Multnomah County, OR	2.19	**New Orleans, LA** (city) Orleans Parish	2.07
Nebraska	2.63	Dane County, WI	2.31	**Denver, CO** (city) Denver County	2.12
Colorado	2.66	Brevard County, FL	2.36	**Miami Beach, FL** (city) Miami-Dade County	2.18
Alaska	2.67	Alachua County, FL	2.40	**Minneapolis, MN** (city) Hennepin County	2.33
Washington	2.67	Marin County, CA	2.42	**Fort Lauderdale, FL** (city) Broward County	2.34

Note: (1) Ranking tables cover all states and counties, and places with an overall population of at least 125,000, OR an overall population of at least 25,000 where the Hispanic/Latino population is at least 20% of the overall population. In states where less than five places meet either of these criteria, we have included places with at least 10,000 total population with the highest percentage of Hispanic/Latino population. These places are identified with an asterisk (*); Please refer to the User's Guide for a full explanation of data.

Average Household Size

Central American: Guatemalan

Top 10 States, Counties, and Places[1]

Sorted by Percent in Descending Order — U.S. = 4.16

State	Number	County	Number	Place	Number
Delaware	5.79	Sussex County, DE	6.21	**Bridgeton, NJ** (city) Cumberland County	6.67
Alabama	4.69	Mason County, WA	6.20	**Lake Forest, CA** (city) Orange County	5.74
Georgia	4.59	Caroline County, MD	5.89	**Springfield, MA** (city) Hampden County	5.65
Maryland	4.59	Jasper County, SC	5.81	**Brentwood, NY** (cdp) Suffolk County	5.50
Mississippi	4.55	Habersham County, GA	5.78	**Huntington Station, NY** (cdp) Suffolk County	5.50
Tennessee	4.55	Cumberland County, NJ	5.72	**Huntington, NY** (town) Suffolk County	5.46
South Carolina	4.47	Madison County, MS	5.72	**Gainesville, GA** (city) Hall County	5.39
Nebraska	4.45	Bedford County, TN	5.67	**Chattanooga, TN** (city) Hamilton County	5.38
Virginia	4.38	Murray County, GA	5.65	**Ramapo, NY** (town) Rockland County	5.38
Connecticut	4.35	Clallam County, WA	5.61	**Hempstead (village), NY** (village) Nassau County	5.36

Sorted by Percent in Ascending Order — U.S. = 4.16

State	Number	County	Number	Place	Number
Montana	2.58	Albany County, NY	1.83	**Urban Honolulu, HI** (cdp) Honolulu County	2.35
Vermont	2.72	Ingham County, MI	2.35	**Hallandale Beach, FL** (city) Broward County	2.39
North Dakota	2.81	New York County, NY	2.56	**Saint Petersburg, FL** (city) Pinellas County	2.39
Hawaii	3.26	Erie County, NY	2.65	**Coral Gables, FL** (city) Miami-Dade County	2.50
Wisconsin	3.33	Calcasieu Parish, LA	2.67	**Saint Louis, MO** (independent city)	2.53
Louisiana	3.34	Pinellas County, FL	2.71	**Manhattan, NY** (borough) New York County	2.56
New Hampshire	3.44	Orleans Parish, LA	2.78	**Kendall, FL** (cdp) Miami-Dade County	2.73
Alaska	3.46	Allegheny County, PA	2.80	**University, FL** (cdp) Hillsborough County	2.74
Wyoming	3.50	Humboldt County, CA	2.80	**New Orleans, LA** (city) Orleans Parish	2.78
Maine	3.55	Honolulu County, HI	2.89	**Wheeling, IL** (village) Cook County	2.80

RANKINGS & COMPARISONS

Note: (1) Ranking tables cover all states and counties, and places with an overall population of at least 125,000, OR an overall population of at least 25,000 where the Hispanic/Latino population is at least 20% of the overall population. In states where less than five places meet either of these criteria, we have included places with at least 10,000 total population with the highest percentage of Hispanic/Latino population. These places are identified with an asterisk (*); Please refer to the User's Guide for a full explanation of data.

Average Household Size

Central American: Honduran

Top 10 States, Counties, and Places[1]

Sorted by Percent in Descending Order — U.S. = 3.82

State	Number	County	Number	Place	Number
Maryland	4.62	Suffolk County, NY	5.48	**Central Islip, NY** (cdp) Suffolk County	6.14
Virginia	4.53	Nassau County, NY	5.37	**Huntington Station, NY** (cdp) Suffolk County	6.04
Georgia	4.08	Robertson County, TN	5.20	**Springfield, VA** (cdp) Fairfax County	5.83
Connecticut	4.03	Culpeper County, VA	5.02	**Brentwood, NY** (cdp) Suffolk County	5.72
South Carolina	4.02	Loudoun County, VA	5.01	**Huntington, NY** (town) Suffolk County	5.69
California	4.01	Prince William County, VA	4.93	**Willowbrook, CA** (cdp) Los Angeles County	5.68
New Jersey	4.01	Fairfax County, VA	4.92	**Islip, NY** (town) Suffolk County	5.64
Utah	4.01	Hall County, GA	4.91	**Manassas, VA** (independent city)	5.64
North Carolina	3.97	Montgomery County, MD	4.79	**North Hempstead, NY** (town) Nassau County	5.64
Wyoming	3.97	Charles County, MD	4.76	**Babylon, NY** (town) Suffolk County	5.54

Sorted by Percent in Ascending Order — U.S. = 3.82

State	Number	County	Number	Place	Number
Vermont	3.09	Albany County, NY	2.37	**Augusta-Richmond County, GA** (consolidated govt) Richmond County	2.49
West Virginia	3.12	Richmond County, GA	2.49	**Tallahassee, FL** (city) Leon County	2.56
New Mexico	3.16	Frio County, TX	2.50	**Killeen, TX** (city) Bell County	2.62
Hawaii	3.24	Onondaga County, NY	2.75	**Coral Gables, FL** (city) Miami-Dade County	2.64
Alaska	3.29	Leon County, FL	2.76	**Shreveport, LA** (city) Caddo Parish	2.66
Ohio	3.37	Allegheny County, PA	2.78	**Huntington Beach, CA** (city) Orange County	2.67
Louisiana	3.41	Caddo Parish, LA	2.79	**Miami Beach, FL** (city) Miami-Dade County	2.68
South Dakota	3.44	Alachua County, FL	2.80	**Albuquerque, NM** (city) Bernalillo County	2.72
Iowa	3.49	Citrus County, FL	2.82	**Mobile, AL** (city) Mobile County	2.80
Oregon	3.49	New York County, NY	2.84	**McAllen, TX** (city) Hidalgo County	2.81

Note: (1) Ranking tables cover all states and counties, and places with an overall population of at least 125,000, OR an overall population of at least 25,000 where the Hispanic/Latino population is at least 20% of the overall population. In states where less than five places meet either of these criteria, we have included places with at least 10,000 total population with the highest percentage of Hispanic/Latino population. These places are identified with an asterisk (*); Please refer to the User's Guide for a full explanation of data.

Average Household Size

Central American: Nicaraguan

Top 10 States, Counties, and Places[1]

Sorted by Percent in Descending Order — U.S. = 3.51

State	Number	County	Number	Place	Number
Maryland	3.88	Nassau County, NY	4.56	**Compton, CA** (city) Los Angeles County	5.21
Utah	3.72	Davis County, UT	4.36	**Perris, CA** (city) Riverside County	4.94
Connecticut	3.67	Prince William County, VA	4.36	**New Brunswick, NJ** (city) Middlesex County	4.92
Virginia	3.62	Suffolk County, NY	4.34	**Eastvale, CA** (cdp) Riverside County	4.72
Florida	3.61	Utah County, UT	4.28	**Marumsco, VA** (cdp) Prince William County	4.71
New Jersey	3.59	Benton County, AR	4.21	**North Hempstead, NY** (town) Nassau County	4.67
Arkansas	3.56	San Bernardino County, CA	4.14	**Manassas, VA** (independent city)	4.60
Nevada	3.56	Stafford County, VA	4.10	**Islip, NY** (town) Suffolk County	4.59
California	3.55	Prince George's County, MD	4.08	**Fontana, CA** (city) San Bernardino County	4.54
Georgia	3.47	Fairfield County, CT	4.05	**Palmdale, CA** (city) Los Angeles County	4.53

Sorted by Percent in Ascending Order — U.S. = 3.51

State	Number	County	Number	Place	Number
District of Columbia	2.68	Oakland County, MI	2.38	**Atlanta, GA** (city) Fulton County	2.17
New Mexico	2.80	Escambia County, FL	2.46	**Aventura, FL** (city) Miami-Dade County	2.20
Michigan	2.83	New York County, NY	2.47	**Miami Beach, FL** (city) Miami-Dade County	2.28
Hawaii	2.94	Leon County, FL	2.48	**Tallahassee, FL** (city) Leon County	2.38
Kentucky	2.94	Alachua County, FL	2.55	**Seattle, WA** (city) King County	2.43
Oklahoma	3.03	Waukesha County, WI	2.56	**Baton Rouge, LA** (city) East Baton Rouge Parish	2.46
Washington	3.04	Butte County, CA	2.63	**Manhattan, NY** (borough) New York County	2.47
Colorado	3.06	Bernalillo County, NM	2.66	**Aurora, CO** (city) Arapahoe County	2.51
Oregon	3.07	Arapahoe County, CO	2.68	**Coral Gables, FL** (city) Miami-Dade County	2.51
Alabama	3.08	Franklin County, OH	2.71	**Irvine, CA** (city) Orange County	2.56

Note: (1) Ranking tables cover all states and counties, and places with an overall population of at least 125,000, OR an overall population of at least 25,000 where the Hispanic/Latino population is at least 20% of the overall population. In states where less than five places meet either of these criteria, we have included places with at least 10,000 total population with the highest percentage of Hispanic/Latino population. These places are identified with an asterisk (*); Please refer to the User's Guide for a full explanation of data.

Average Household Size

Central American: Panamanian

Top 10 States, Counties, and Places[1]

Sorted by Percent in Descending Order — U.S. = 2.69

State	Number	County	Number	Place	Number
Utah	3.14	Newton County, GA	4.13	**Brentwood, NY** (cdp) Suffolk County	4.51
Tennessee	2.91	Dorchester County, SC	3.55	**Elmont, NY** (cdp) Nassau County	3.98
Arkansas	2.84	Utah County, UT	3.55	**Fontana, CA** (city) San Bernardino County	3.78
Kansas	2.84	Jones County, MS	3.52	**Islip, NY** (town) Suffolk County	3.69
Minnesota	2.84	Spotsylvania County, VA	3.43	**South Miami Heights, FL** (cdp) Miami-Dade County	3.65
Hawaii	2.82	Nassau County, NY	3.42	**Hempstead (town), NY** (town) Nassau County	3.52
Nevada	2.82	Geary County, KS	3.35	**Moreno Valley, CA** (city) Riverside County	3.49
Maryland	2.81	Guadalupe County, TX	3.35	**Freeport, NY** (village) Nassau County	3.47
Wisconsin	2.80	Douglas County, GA	3.31	**Meadow Woods, FL** (cdp) Orange County	3.46
South Carolina	2.79	Lehigh County, PA	3.31	**Aspen Hill, MD** (cdp) Montgomery County	3.41

Sorted by Percent in Ascending Order — U.S. = 2.69

State	Number	County	Number	Place	Number
District of Columbia	2.09	New York County, NY	1.97	**Miami Beach, FL** (city) Miami-Dade County	1.77
North Dakota	2.32	Arlington County, VA	1.98	**Seattle, WA** (city) King County	1.85
New Mexico	2.44	Brazos County, TX	2.00	**Manhattan, NY** (borough) New York County	1.97
Maine	2.45	San Francisco County, CA	2.02	**Arlington, VA** (cdp) Arlington County	1.98
Delaware	2.48	Clark County, WA	2.17	**Atlanta, GA** (city) Fulton County	1.98
Alaska	2.50	Denver County, CO	2.18	**Alexandria, VA** (independent city)	2.02
New Hampshire	2.52	Orleans Parish, LA	2.21	**San Francisco, CA** (city) San Francisco County	2.02
Nebraska	2.53	Hernando County, FL	2.25	**Oakland, CA** (city) Alameda County	2.13
Arizona	2.54	Onondaga County, NY	2.26	**Denver, CO** (city) Denver County	2.18
Washington	2.54	Fulton County, GA	2.27	**Irving, TX** (city) Dallas County	2.19

Note: (1) Ranking tables cover all states and counties, and places with an overall population of at least 125,000, OR an overall population of at least 25,000 where the Hispanic/Latino population is at least 20% of the overall population. In states where less than five places meet either of these criteria, we have included places with at least 10,000 total population with the highest percentage of Hispanic/Latino population. These places are identified with an asterisk (*); Please refer to the User's Guide for a full explanation of data.

Average Household Size

Central American: Salvadoran

Top 10 States, Counties, and Places[1]

Sorted by Percent in Descending Order — U.S. = 4.14

State	Number	County	Number	Place	Number
Maryland	4.90	Suffolk County, NY	5.93	**Central Islip, NY** (cdp) Suffolk County	6.54
New York	4.87	Greene County, VA	5.81	**Brentwood, NY** (cdp) Suffolk County	6.08
Virginia	4.61	Nassau County, NY	5.43	**Islip, NY** (town) Suffolk County	6.05
Georgia	4.35	Nobles County, MN	5.39	**Babylon, NY** (town) Suffolk County	5.99
Delaware	4.21	Culpeper County, VA	5.32	**Huntington Station, NY** (cdp) Suffolk County	5.95
Massachusetts	4.20	White County, IN	5.30	**Huntington, NY** (town) Suffolk County	5.79
Tennessee	4.15	Eagle County, CO	5.29	**Brookhaven, NY** (town) Suffolk County	5.72
New Jersey	4.14	Charles County, MD	5.28	**San Juan Capistrano, CA** (city) Orange County	5.70
Nebraska	4.11	Robertson County, TN	5.15	**Hempstead (village), NY** (village) Nassau County	5.63
District of Columbia	4.10	Prince George's County, MD	5.07	**North Hempstead, NY** (town) Nassau County	5.53

Sorted by Percent in Ascending Order — U.S. = 4.14

State	Number	County	Number	Place	Number
Vermont	2.43	Frio County, TX	2.67	**Miami Beach, FL** (city) Miami-Dade County	2.01
Montana	2.97	Honolulu County, HI	2.78	**Urban Honolulu, HI** (cdp) Honolulu County	2.25
Hawaii	3.05	Alachua County, FL	2.80	**Hallandale Beach, FL** (city) Broward County	2.46
Idaho	3.36	Kitsap County, WA	2.80	**Atlanta, GA** (city) Fulton County	2.55
Wyoming	3.37	Humboldt County, CA	2.81	**Coral Gables, FL** (city) Miami-Dade County	2.66
New Mexico	3.41	Escambia County, FL	2.86	**Clarksville, TN** (city) Montgomery County	2.73
Oklahoma	3.45	Montgomery County, TN	2.86	**Manhattan, NY** (borough) New York County	2.86
Louisiana	3.47	New York County, NY	2.86	**Columbus, GA** (city) Muscogee County	2.88
Wisconsin	3.48	Muscogee County, GA	2.88	**Vancouver, WA** (city) Clark County	2.88
Ohio	3.53	Allegheny County, PA	2.93	**Tempe, AZ** (city) Maricopa County	2.89

RANKINGS & COMPARISONS

Note: (1) Ranking tables cover all states and counties, and places with an overall population of at least 125,000, OR an overall population of at least 25,000 where the Hispanic/Latino population is at least 20% of the overall population. In states where less than five places meet either of these criteria, we have included places with at least 10,000 total population with the highest percentage of Hispanic/Latino population. These places are identified with an asterisk (*); Please refer to the User's Guide for a full explanation of data.

Average Household Size

Cuban

Top 10 States, Counties, and Places[1]

Sorted by Percent in Descending Order — U.S. = 2.79

State	Number	County	Number	Place	Number
Utah	2.94	Marshall County, AL	5.56	**Eastvale, CA** (cdp) Riverside County	4.03
Kentucky	2.90	Union County, FL	3.75	**Pflugerville, TX** (city) Travis County	3.99
Nevada	2.90	Wayne County, GA	3.63	**West Valley City, UT** (city) Salt Lake County	3.95
Florida	2.87	Williamson County, TN	3.58	**Highland, CA** (city) San Bernardino County	3.89
Georgia	2.80	Wilson County, TN	3.53	**Lynwood, CA** (city) Los Angeles County	3.68
Alaska	2.79	Coryell County, TX	3.52	**Colton, CA** (city) San Bernardino County	3.66
Idaho	2.79	Calvert County, MD	3.51	**Perris, CA** (city) Riverside County	3.63
Tennessee	2.79	Union County, NC	3.51	**Apple Valley, CA** (town) San Bernardino County	3.60
Mississippi	2.74	Berkeley County, WV	3.47	**Richmond West, FL** (cdp) Miami-Dade County	3.60
Arizona	2.73	Utah County, UT	3.44	**West Little River, FL** (cdp) Miami-Dade County	3.56

Sorted by Percent in Ascending Order — U.S. = 2.79

State	Number	County	Number	Place	Number
District of Columbia	1.92	Telfair County, GA	1.00	**Palm Springs, CA** (city) Riverside County	1.67
Montana	2.28	New York County, NY	1.82	**Miami Beach, FL** (city) Miami-Dade County	1.81
North Dakota	2.32	Pueblo County, CO	1.88	**Manhattan, NY** (borough) New York County	1.82
Vermont	2.34	Montgomery County, VA	2.00	**Wilmington*, DE** (city) New Castle County	1.92
New York	2.35	Oneida County, NY	2.00	**Alexandria, VA** (independent city)	1.96
Maine	2.45	Santa Fe County, NM	2.00	**Seattle, WA** (city) King County	1.96
Massachusetts	2.47	Champaign County, IL	2.02	**Aventura, FL** (city) Miami-Dade County	1.97
Rhode Island	2.49	Arlington County, VA	2.03	**Birmingham, AL** (city) Jefferson County	1.98
South Dakota	2.50	San Francisco County, CA	2.09	**Santa Barbara, CA** (city) Santa Barbara County	1.98
Washington	2.52	Watauga County, NC	2.09	**Arlington, VA** (cdp) Arlington County	2.03

Note: (1) Ranking tables cover all states and counties, and places with an overall population of at least 125,000, OR an overall population of at least 25,000 where the Hispanic/Latino population is at least 20% of the overall population. In states where less than five places meet either of these criteria, we have included places with at least 10,000 total population with the highest percentage of Hispanic/Latino population. These places are identified with an asterisk (*); Please refer to the User's Guide for a full explanation of data.

Average Household Size

Dominican Republic

Top 10 States, Counties, and Places[1]

Sorted by Percent in Descending Order — U.S. = 3.40

State	Number	County	Number	Place	Number
New Jersey	3.66	Clearfield County, PA	5.00	**Huntington Station, NY** (cdp) Suffolk County	5.11
Pennsylvania	3.65	Suffolk County, NY	4.76	**Babylon, NY** (town) Suffolk County	5.05
Maryland	3.55	Nassau County, NY	4.26	**Brentwood, NY** (cdp) Suffolk County	4.97
Alaska	3.49	Walton County, GA	4.26	**Islip, NY** (town) Suffolk County	4.74
Delaware	3.49	Hendricks County, IN	4.13	**Central Islip, NY** (cdp) Suffolk County	4.66
Connecticut	3.45	Franklin County, PA	4.12	**Freeport, NY** (village) Nassau County	4.61
New York	3.42	San Joaquin County, CA	4.12	**Brookhaven, NY** (town) Suffolk County	4.58
Rhode Island	3.36	Pinal County, AZ	4.08	**Huntington, NY** (town) Suffolk County	4.52
Utah	3.36	Somerset County, NJ	4.07	**Plainfield, NJ** (city) Union County	4.45
North Carolina	3.32	Rockland County, NY	4.05	**Manassas, VA** (independent city)	4.39

Sorted by Percent in Ascending Order — U.S. = 3.40

State	Number	County	Number	Place	Number
Vermont	2.70	Centre County, PA	2.00	**Atlanta, GA** (city) Fulton County	1.96
Oregon	2.72	San Francisco County, CA	2.06	**Miami Beach, FL** (city) Miami-Dade County	2.05
California	2.75	Kalamazoo County, MI	2.21	**San Francisco, CA** (city) San Francisco County	2.06
New Mexico	2.83	Chemung County, NY	2.25	**Seattle, WA** (city) King County	2.11
Hawaii	2.84	Chittenden County, VT	2.33	**Pittsburgh, PA** (city) Allegheny County	2.13
Arkansas	2.85	Arlington County, VA	2.36	**Alexandria, VA** (independent city)	2.25
Colorado	2.89	Alameda County, CA	2.43	**Oakland, CA** (city) Alameda County	2.27
Alabama	2.90	Ingham County, MI	2.45	**Los Angeles, CA** (city) Los Angeles County	2.35
Illinois	2.90	Chautauqua County, NY	2.48	**Arlington, VA** (cdp) Arlington County	2.36
Iowa	2.91	Washtenaw County, MI	2.49	**Dallas, TX** (city) Dallas County	2.36

Note: (1) Ranking tables cover all states and counties, and places with an overall population of at least 125,000, OR an overall population of at least 25,000 where the Hispanic/Latino population is at least 20% of the overall population. In states where less than five places meet either of these criteria, we have included places with at least 10,000 total population with the highest percentage of Hispanic/Latino population. These places are identified with an asterisk (*); Please refer to the User's Guide for a full explanation of data.

Average Household Size

Mexican

Top 10 States, Counties, and Places[1]

Sorted by Percent in Descending Order — U.S. = 3.78

State	Number	County	Number	Place	Number
New Jersey	4.64	Marshall County, SD	7.03	**Bridgeton, NJ** (city) Cumberland County	6.12
Delaware	4.36	Cumberland County, NJ	5.65	**New Brunswick, NJ** (city) Middlesex County	6.08
New York	4.34	Ocean County, NJ	5.58	**North Hempstead, NY** (town) Nassau County	5.55
Georgia	4.28	Middlesex County, NJ	5.19	**Willowbrook, CA** (cdp) Los Angeles County	5.46
Utah	4.11	Lawrence County, MS	5.17	**Central Islip, NY** (cdp) Suffolk County	5.40
California	4.06	McCreary County, KY	5.14	**Compton, CA** (city) Los Angeles County	5.35
North Carolina	4.03	Calhoun County, GA	5.09	**Passaic, NJ** (city) Passaic County	5.35
Illinois	4.02	Passaic County, NJ	5.09	**East Palo Alto, CA** (city) San Mateo County	5.31
Maryland	3.98	Switzerland County, IN	5.00	**Brentwood, NY** (cdp) Suffolk County	5.30
South Carolina	3.98	Jasper County, GA	4.95	**Santa Ana, CA** (city) Orange County	5.28

Sorted by Percent in Ascending Order — U.S. = 3.78

State	Number	County	Number	Place	Number
District of Columbia	2.42	Harding County, NM	1.77	**Miami Beach, FL** (city) Miami-Dade County	1.92
Vermont	2.75	Taylor County, GA	1.92	**Burlington*, VT** (city) Chittenden County	2.23
Maine	2.76	Deer Lodge County, MT	1.96	**Portland*, ME** (city) Cumberland County	2.25
Montana	2.83	Fulton County, NY	2.14	**Morgantown*, WV** (city) Monongalia County	2.40
North Dakota	2.97	Madison County, MT	2.16	**Arlington, VA** (cdp) Arlington County	2.41
West Virginia	2.97	Martin County, KY	2.20	**Boston, MA** (city) Suffolk County	2.43
Massachusetts	2.99	Catron County, NM	2.24	**Syracuse, NY** (city) Onondaga County	2.45
Alaska	3.02	Tompkins County, NY	2.24	**Alexandria, VA** (independent city)	2.46
Wyoming	3.05	Clear Creek County, CO	2.25	**Pittsburgh, PA** (city) Allegheny County	2.46
Hawaii	3.08	Nemaha County, NE	2.30	**Urban Honolulu, HI** (cdp) Honolulu County	2.49

Note: (1) Ranking tables cover all states and counties, and places with an overall population of at least 125,000, OR an overall population of at least 25,000 where the Hispanic/Latino population is at least 20% of the overall population. In states where less than five places meet either of these criteria, we have included places with at least 10,000 total population with the highest percentage of Hispanic/Latino population. These places are identified with an asterisk (*); Please refer to the User's Guide for a full explanation of data.

Average Household Size

Puerto Rican

Top 10 States, Counties, and Places[1]

Sorted by Percent in Descending Order — U.S. = 2.87

State	Number	County	Number	Place	Number
Hawaii	3.30	Wakulla County, FL	3.93	**Wasco, CA** (city) Kern County	4.11
Pennsylvania	3.14	Ford County, KS	3.79	**Florence-Graham, CA** (cdp) Los Angeles County	4.09
Delaware	3.12	Franklin County, WA	3.78	**Fort Campbell North*, KY** (cdp) Christian County	4.08
Utah	3.09	Taylor County, FL	3.78	**Waianae*, HI** (cdp) Honolulu County	4.07
Rhode Island	3.06	Stephenson County, IL	3.74	**San Jacinto, CA** (city) Riverside County	3.92
Wisconsin	3.06	Utah County, UT	3.68	**Caldwell, ID** (city) Canyon County	3.88
New Hampshire	2.99	Cache County, UT	3.62	**Montclair, CA** (city) San Bernardino County	3.88
Connecticut	2.98	Ware County, GA	3.62	**Dodge City, KS** (city) Ford County	3.86
Kansas	2.97	Wyoming County, PA	3.62	**Pasco, WA** (city) Franklin County	3.85
Michigan	2.96	Bladen County, NC	3.61	**Eastvale, CA** (cdp) Riverside County	3.83

Sorted by Percent in Ascending Order — U.S. = 2.87

State	Number	County	Number	Place	Number
District of Columbia	1.87	Arlington County, VA	1.91	**Palm Springs, CA** (city) Riverside County	1.79
Vermont	2.50	Hancock County, OH	1.95	**Miami Beach, FL** (city) Miami-Dade County	1.81
North Dakota	2.57	San Francisco County, CA	2.06	**Alexandria, VA** (independent city)	1.90
Oregon	2.58	Tuscaloosa County, AL	2.06	**Arlington, VA** (cdp) Arlington County	1.91
South Dakota	2.62	Orleans Parish, LA	2.09	**Atlanta, GA** (city) Fulton County	1.91
Montana	2.65	Santa Fe County, NM	2.09	**Santa Fe, NM** (city) Santa Fe County	1.93
New Mexico	2.65	Forrest County, MS	2.16	**Silver Spring, MD** (cdp) Montgomery County	1.96
Wyoming	2.67	Addison County, VT	2.17	**Aventura, FL** (city) Miami-Dade County	1.99
New York	2.68	Jackson County, NC	2.19	**San Francisco, CA** (city) San Francisco County	2.06
Louisiana	2.69	Coos County, OR	2.20	**New Orleans, LA** (city) Orleans Parish	2.09

Note: (1) Ranking tables cover all states and counties, and places with an overall population of at least 125,000, OR an overall population of at least 25,000 where the Hispanic/Latino population is at least 20% of the overall population. In states where less than five places meet either of these criteria, we have included places with at least 10,000 total population with the highest percentage of Hispanic/Latino population. These places are identified with an asterisk (*); Please refer to the User's Guide for a full explanation of data.

Average Household Size

South American

Top 10 States, Counties, and Places[1]

Sorted by Percent in Descending Order — U.S. = 3.10

State	Number	County	Number	Place	Number
Utah	3.55	Rockland County, NY	4.46	**Spring Valley, NY** (village) Rockland County	5.51
Virginia	3.46	Suffolk County, NY	4.31	**Brentwood, NY** (cdp) Suffolk County	4.98
New Jersey	3.41	Culpeper County, VA	4.05	**Ramapo, NY** (town) Rockland County	4.98
Connecticut	3.38	Iron County, UT	4.04	**Springfield, VA** (cdp) Fairfax County	4.59
New York	3.38	Prince William County, VA	3.97	**Islip, NY** (town) Suffolk County	4.55
Minnesota	3.37	Tooele County, UT	3.94	**Compton, CA** (city) Los Angeles County	4.54
Maryland	3.28	Warren County, VA	3.91	**Central Islip, NY** (cdp) Suffolk County	4.53
Idaho	3.09	Utah County, UT	3.88	**Lynwood, CA** (city) Los Angeles County	4.53
Georgia	3.08	Anoka County, MN	3.83	**Kearns, UT** (cdp) Salt Lake County	4.48
Illinois	3.07	Mercer County, NJ	3.80	**Bay Shore, NY** (cdp) Suffolk County	4.35

Sorted by Percent in Ascending Order — U.S. = 3.10

State	Number	County	Number	Place	Number
District of Columbia	2.03	Sumter County, FL	1.96	**Atlanta, GA** (city) Fulton County	1.92
Vermont	2.48	Tuscaloosa County, AL	2.12	**Cincinnati, OH** (city) Hamilton County	1.95
North Dakota	2.49	Jackson County, IL	2.15	**Saint Louis, MO** (independent city)	2.02
New Mexico	2.51	Monroe County, IN	2.16	**Bryan, TX** (city) Brazos County	2.03
Montana	2.53	Kanawha County, WV	2.17	**Waco, TX** (city) McLennan County	2.03
Louisiana	2.63	Orleans Parish, LA	2.17	**Miami Beach, FL** (city) Miami-Dade County	2.04
Michigan	2.63	Saint Lawrence County, NY	2.17	**Pittsburgh, PA** (city) Allegheny County	2.07
Wyoming	2.63	La Crosse County, WI	2.18	**Santa Fe, NM** (city) Santa Fe County	2.09
Arkansas	2.65	Bastrop County, TX	2.19	**San Marcos, TX** (city) Hays County	2.14
Missouri	2.68	Champaign County, IL	2.19	**Burlington*, VT** (city) Chittenden County	2.15

Note: (1) Ranking tables cover all states and counties, and places with an overall population of at least 125,000, OR an overall population of at least 25,000 where the Hispanic/Latino population is at least 20% of the overall population. In states where less than five places meet either of these criteria, we have included places with at least 10,000 total population with the highest percentage of Hispanic/Latino population. These places are identified with an asterisk (*); Please refer to the User's Guide for a full explanation of data.

Average Household Size

South American: Argentinean

Top 10 States, Counties, and Places[1]

Sorted by Percent in Descending Order — U.S. = 2.72

State	Number	County	Number	Place	Number
Utah	3.60	Utah County, UT	3.89	**Annandale, VA** (cdp) Fairfax County	4.41
Virginia	3.09	Davis County, UT	3.86	**Brentwood, NY** (cdp) Suffolk County	4.37
Indiana	2.96	Orange County, NY	3.86	**Springfield, VA** (cdp) Fairfax County	4.30
Mississippi	2.95	Prince William County, VA	3.79	**Mission Bend, TX** (cdp) Fort Bend County	3.88
South Carolina	2.95	Stafford County, VA	3.59	**Norwalk, CA** (city) Los Angeles County	3.87
Connecticut	2.94	Chesterfield County, VA	3.54	**Spring, TX** (cdp) Harris County	3.82
Idaho	2.91	Union County, NC	3.51	**West Falls Church, VA** (cdp) Fairfax County	3.82
Georgia	2.89	Beaufort County, SC	3.45	**Grand Prairie, TX** (city) Dallas County	3.70
Maryland	2.89	Martin County, FL	3.41	**Moreno Valley, CA** (city) Riverside County	3.69
New Jersey	2.89	Loudoun County, VA	3.40	**San Bernardino, CA** (city) San Bernardino County	3.67

Sorted by Percent in Ascending Order — U.S. = 2.72

State	Number	County	Number	Place	Number
District of Columbia	1.97	New York County, NY	1.91	**Manhattan, NY** (borough) New York County	1.91
Vermont	2.37	Hampshire County, MA	1.95	**Atlanta, GA** (city) Fulton County	1.97
Maine	2.41	San Francisco County, CA	2.07	**Miami Beach, FL** (city) Miami-Dade County	2.04
Louisiana	2.42	Orange County, NC	2.16	**Pittsburgh, PA** (city) Allegheny County	2.04
Montana	2.42	Orleans Parish, LA	2.17	**Minneapolis, MN** (city) Hennepin County	2.05
Iowa	2.43	Denver County, CO	2.19	**San Francisco, CA** (city) San Francisco County	2.07
Alaska	2.44	Santa Fe County, NM	2.22	**Pasadena, CA** (city) Los Angeles County	2.12
New Mexico	2.52	Albany County, NY	2.24	**New Orleans, LA** (city) Orleans Parish	2.17
Massachusetts	2.55	Alachua County, FL	2.27	**Chicago, IL** (city) Cook County	2.18
Arizona	2.56	Monroe County, NY	2.28	**Seattle, WA** (city) King County	2.18

Note: (1) Ranking tables cover all states and counties, and places with an overall population of at least 125,000, OR an overall population of at least 25,000 where the Hispanic/Latino population is at least 20% of the overall population. In states where less than five places meet either of these criteria, we have included places with at least 10,000 total population with the highest percentage of Hispanic/Latino population. These places are identified with an asterisk (*); Please refer to the User's Guide for a full explanation of data.

Average Household Size

South American: Bolivian

Top 10 States, Counties, and Places[1]

Sorted by Percent in Descending Order — U.S. = 3.36

State	Number	County	Number	Place	Number
Virginia	4.04	Prince William County, VA	4.27	**Springfield, VA** (cdp) Fairfax County	4.95
Maryland	3.67	Stafford County, VA	4.27	**Islip, NY** (town) Suffolk County	4.63
Utah	3.43	Suffolk County, NY	4.26	**Dale City, VA** (cdp) Prince William County	4.61
Rhode Island	3.41	Fairfax County, VA	4.19	**West Falls Church, VA** (cdp) Fairfax County	4.59
Connecticut	3.35	Loudoun County, VA	4.00	**Marumsco, VA** (cdp) Prince William County	4.51
New Jersey	3.34	Frederick County, MD	3.84	**Annandale, VA** (cdp) Fairfax County	4.42
Delaware	3.33	Arlington County, VA	3.80	**Sterling, VA** (cdp) Loudoun County	4.36
South Carolina	3.28	Anne Arundel County, MD	3.79	**Manassas, VA** (independent city)	4.35
California	3.17	Westchester County, NY	3.77	**Wheaton, MD** (cdp) Montgomery County	4.19
New York	3.14	Utah County, UT	3.76	**Aspen Hill, MD** (cdp) Montgomery County	4.11

Sorted by Percent in Ascending Order — U.S. = 3.36

State	Number	County	Number	Place	Number
District of Columbia	2.03	New York County, NY	2.06	**Manhattan, NY** (borough) New York County	2.06
New Mexico	2.24	Hennepin County, MN	2.36	**Miami Beach, FL** (city) Miami-Dade County	2.14
Oklahoma	2.62	Kings County, NY	2.36	**Seattle, WA** (city) King County	2.27
Minnesota	2.65	San Francisco County, CA	2.37	**Richmond, VA** (independent city)	2.31
Hawaii	2.66	Travis County, TX	2.45	**Dallas, TX** (city) Dallas County	2.32
Washington	2.69	Allegheny County, PA	2.48	**Brooklyn, NY** (borough) Kings County	2.36
Missouri	2.70	Denver County, CO	2.48	**San Francisco, CA** (city) San Francisco County	2.37
Oregon	2.71	Fulton County, GA	2.50	**Austin, TX** (city) Travis County	2.38
Kentucky	2.72	Washington County, AR	2.50	**Chicago, IL** (city) Cook County	2.44
West Virginia	2.72	King County, WA	2.55	**Denver, CO** (city) Denver County	2.48

Note: (1) Ranking tables cover all states and counties, and places with an overall population of at least 125,000, OR an overall population of at least 25,000 where the Hispanic/Latino population is at least 20% of the overall population. In states where less than five places meet either of these criteria, we have included places with at least 10,000 total population with the highest percentage of Hispanic/Latino population. These places are identified with an asterisk (*); Please refer to the User's Guide for a full explanation of data.

Average Household Size

South American: Chilean

Top 10 States, Counties, and Places[1]

Sorted by Percent in Descending Order — U.S. = 2.79

State	Number	County	Number	Place	Number
Utah	3.41	Utah County, UT	3.74	**Brentwood, NY** (cdp) Suffolk County	4.15
Maryland	2.98	Suffolk County, NY	3.62	**Palmdale, CA** (city) Los Angeles County	4.00
New Jersey	2.97	Davis County, UT	3.59	**Islip, NY** (town) Suffolk County	3.91
Nebraska	2.94	Prince William County, VA	3.55	**West Valley City, UT** (city) Salt Lake County	3.87
Connecticut	2.92	Kern County, CA	3.48	**Huntington, NY** (town) Suffolk County	3.86
Virginia	2.91	Fort Bend County, TX	3.47	**Wheaton, MD** (cdp) Montgomery County	3.84
North Carolina	2.89	Frederick County, MD	3.47	**Chula Vista, CA** (city) San Diego County	3.76
Georgia	2.86	Osceola County, FL	3.47	**Oyster Bay, NY** (town) Nassau County	3.73
Kansas	2.85	Nassau County, NY	3.46	**Fontana, CA** (city) San Bernardino County	3.70
Hawaii	2.83	Lake County, FL	3.42	**Richmond West, FL** (cdp) Miami-Dade County	3.64

Sorted by Percent in Ascending Order — U.S. = 2.79

State	Number	County	Number	Place	Number
District of Columbia	1.94	New York County, NY	1.93	**Atlanta, GA** (city) Fulton County	1.67
Montana	2.25	Denver County, CO	2.01	**Miami Beach, FL** (city) Miami-Dade County	1.92
New Mexico	2.37	Philadelphia County, PA	2.09	**Manhattan, NY** (borough) New York County	1.93
Wisconsin	2.43	Dane County, WI	2.10	**Madison, WI** (city) Dane County	1.95
Kentucky	2.44	San Francisco County, CA	2.11	**Denver, CO** (city) Denver County	2.01
Vermont	2.49	Hamilton County, OH	2.26	**Philadelphia, PA** (city) Philadelphia County	2.09
Louisiana	2.51	Arlington County, VA	2.28	**San Francisco, CA** (city) San Francisco County	2.11
West Virginia	2.51	Erie County, NY	2.30	**Dallas, TX** (city) Dallas County	2.12
Arkansas	2.52	Milwaukee County, WI	2.31	**Fort Lauderdale, FL** (city) Broward County	2.14
Colorado	2.53	Travis County, TX	2.31	**Minneapolis, MN** (city) Hennepin County	2.15

Note: (1) Ranking tables cover all states and counties, and places with an overall population of at least 125,000, OR an overall population of at least 25,000 where the Hispanic/Latino population is at least 20% of the overall population. In states where less than five places meet either of these criteria, we have included places with at least 10,000 total population with the highest percentage of Hispanic/Latino population. These places are identified with an asterisk (*); Please refer to the User's Guide for a full explanation of data.

Average Household Size

South American: Colombian

Top 10 States, Counties, and Places[1]

Sorted by Percent in Descending Order — U.S. = 2.95

State	Number	County	Number	Place	Number
Utah	3.30	Suffolk County, NY	3.93	**Brentwood, NY** (cdp) Suffolk County	4.67
New Jersey	3.19	Spotsylvania County, VA	3.84	**Central Islip, NY** (cdp) Suffolk County	4.32
New Hampshire	3.09	Paulding County, GA	3.78	**Hacienda Heights, CA** (cdp) Los Angeles County	4.28
Connecticut	3.06	Utah County, UT	3.74	**Islip, NY** (town) Suffolk County	4.19
Delaware	3.03	Barrow County, GA	3.73	**Fontana, CA** (city) San Bernardino County	4.08
Georgia	3.03	Tulare County, CA	3.67	**Eastvale, CA** (cdp) Riverside County	4.06
South Carolina	3.02	Kendall County, IL	3.66	**Elmont, NY** (cdp) Nassau County	4.04
Maryland	3.01	Harnett County, NC	3.63	**Murrieta, CA** (city) Riverside County	3.98
Idaho	2.99	Nassau County, NY	3.61	**Bay Shore, NY** (cdp) Suffolk County	3.97
New York	2.99	Pike County, PA	3.56	**Montclair, CA** (city) San Bernardino County	3.96

Sorted by Percent in Ascending Order — U.S. = 2.95

State	Number	County	Number	Place	Number
District of Columbia	2.00	Monroe County, IN	1.82	**Cincinnati, OH** (city) Hamilton County	1.88
Montana	2.29	Adams County, MS	2.00	**Pittsburgh, PA** (city) Allegheny County	1.93
South Dakota	2.32	Champaign County, IL	2.01	**Atlanta, GA** (city) Fulton County	1.94
Vermont	2.34	New York County, NY	2.02	**Miami Beach, FL** (city) Miami-Dade County	1.98
North Dakota	2.40	Santa Fe County, NM	2.02	**San Rafael, CA** (city) Marin County	2.00
Wyoming	2.44	Orleans Parish, LA	2.05	**Seattle, WA** (city) King County	2.01
New Mexico	2.51	Tippecanoe County, IN	2.06	**Huntsville, AL** (city) Madison County	2.02
Hawaii	2.52	Denver County, CO	2.08	**Manhattan, NY** (borough) New York County	2.02
Michigan	2.55	Cumberland County, ME	2.10	**New Orleans, LA** (city) Orleans Parish	2.05
West Virginia	2.55	Albemarle County, VA	2.12	**Denver, CO** (city) Denver County	2.08

Note: (1) Ranking tables cover all states and counties, and places with an overall population of at least 125,000, OR an overall population of at least 25,000 where the Hispanic/Latino population is at least 20% of the overall population. In states where less than five places meet either of these criteria, we have included places with at least 10,000 total population with the highest percentage of Hispanic/Latino population. These places are identified with an asterisk (*); Please refer to the User's Guide for a full explanation of data.

Average Household Size

South American: Ecuadorian

Top 10 States, Counties, and Places[1]

Sorted by Percent in Descending Order — U.S. = 3.64

State	Number	County	Number	Place	Number
Minnesota	4.44	Rockland County, NY	5.34	**Ramapo, NY** (town) Rockland County	5.76
Connecticut	3.96	Suffolk County, NY	4.92	**Spring Valley, NY** (village) Rockland County	5.76
New York	3.96	Barnstable County, MA	4.88	**Brentwood, NY** (cdp) Suffolk County	5.25
New Jersey	3.75	Plymouth County, MA	4.74	**Brookhaven, NY** (town) Suffolk County	5.06
Illinois	3.66	Hennepin County, MN	4.57	**Islip, NY** (town) Suffolk County	4.94
Utah	3.64	Anoka County, MN	4.56	**Central Islip, NY** (cdp) Suffolk County	4.92
Pennsylvania	3.62	Mercer County, NJ	4.42	**Trenton, NJ** (city) Mercer County	4.91
Maryland	3.47	Dakota County, MN	4.32	**Middletown, NY** (city) Orange County	4.77
Delaware	3.37	Washington County, MD	4.31	**Bay Shore, NY** (cdp) Suffolk County	4.76
Iowa	3.36	Nassau County, NY	4.26	**Plainfield, NJ** (city) Union County	4.75

Sorted by Percent in Ascending Order — U.S. = 3.64

State	Number	County	Number	Place	Number
District of Columbia	2.05	Orleans Parish, LA	2.23	**Atlanta, GA** (city) Fulton County	2.12
New Mexico	2.59	Arlington County, VA	2.28	**Alexandria, VA** (independent city)	2.17
Michigan	2.63	Alachua County, FL	2.37	**Miami Beach, FL** (city) Miami-Dade County	2.18
Oklahoma	2.65	Allegheny County, PA	2.38	**New Orleans, LA** (city) Orleans Parish	2.23
Alaska	2.68	Oakland County, MI	2.42	**Arlington, VA** (cdp) Arlington County	2.28
Louisiana	2.69	San Francisco County, CA	2.42	**Fort Lauderdale, FL** (city) Broward County	2.28
Oregon	2.69	Marion County, IN	2.48	**Seattle, WA** (city) King County	2.35
Vermont	2.70	Tulsa County, OK	2.48	**Oakland, CA** (city) Alameda County	2.38
Hawaii	2.72	Denver County, CO	2.49	**Salt Lake City, UT** (city) Salt Lake County	2.40
Missouri	2.76	Saint Louis County, MO	2.51	**Sacramento, CA** (city) Sacramento County	2.42

Note: (1) Ranking tables cover all states and counties, and places with an overall population of at least 125,000, OR an overall population of at least 25,000 where the Hispanic/Latino population is at least 20% of the overall population. In states where less than five places meet either of these criteria, we have included places with at least 10,000 total population with the highest percentage of Hispanic/Latino population. These places are identified with an asterisk (*); Please refer to the User's Guide for a full explanation of data.

Average Household Size

South American: Paraguayan

Top 10 States, Counties, and Places[1]

Sorted by Percent in Descending Order — U.S. = 3.06

State	Number	County	Number	Place	Number
New Jersey	3.58	Suffolk County, NY	4.12	**North Hempstead, NY** (town) Nassau County	4.34
Colorado	3.53	Nassau County, NY	3.95	**Hempstead (town), NY** (town) Nassau County	4.14
Tennessee	3.36	Somerset County, NJ	3.88	**White Plains, NY** (city) Westchester County	3.88
Utah	3.35	Morris County, NJ	3.70	**Queens, NY** (borough) Queens County	3.32
New York	3.31	Gwinnett County, GA	3.54	**New York, NY** (city)	3.15
Maryland	3.29	Westchester County, NY	3.53	**Bronx, NY** (borough) Bronx County	3.12
Connecticut	3.17	Prince George's County, MD	3.50	**Rye, NY** (town) Westchester County	3.06
Georgia	3.01	Montgomery County, MD	3.38	**Brooklyn, NY** (borough) Kings County	2.89
Ohio	3.00	Queens County, NY	3.32	**Los Angeles, CA** (city) Los Angeles County	2.74
Virginia	2.99	Fairfield County, CT	3.30	**Houston, TX** (city) Harris County	2.65

Sorted by Percent in Ascending Order — U.S. = 3.06

State	Number	County	Number	Place	Number
District of Columbia	2.23	New York County, NY	1.89	**Manhattan, NY** (borough) New York County	1.89
Michigan	2.37	San Diego County, CA	2.30	**Chicago, IL** (city) Cook County	2.14
Alabama	2.40	Dallas County, TX	2.50	**Miami, FL** (city) Miami-Dade County	2.28
Arizona	2.44	Cook County, IL	2.51	**Arlington, VA** (cdp) Arlington County	2.64
Kansas	2.49	Maricopa County, AZ	2.56	**Houston, TX** (city) Harris County	2.65
Illinois	2.51	Arlington County, VA	2.64	**Los Angeles, CA** (city) Los Angeles County	2.74
Washington	2.53	Middlesex County, MA	2.65	**Brooklyn, NY** (borough) Kings County	2.89
Oregon	2.55	Broward County, FL	2.68	**Rye, NY** (town) Westchester County	3.06
Wisconsin	2.61	Harris County, TX	2.68	**Bronx, NY** (borough) Bronx County	3.12
Massachusetts	2.70	Miami-Dade County, FL	2.79	**New York, NY** (city)	3.15

Note: (1) Ranking tables cover all states and counties, and places with an overall population of at least 125,000, OR an overall population of at least 25,000 where the Hispanic/Latino population is at least 20% of the overall population. In states where less than five places meet either of these criteria, we have included places with at least 10,000 total population with the highest percentage of Hispanic/Latino population. These places are identified with an asterisk (*); Please refer to the User's Guide for a full explanation of data.

Average Household Size

South American: Peruvian

Top 10 States, Counties, and Places[1]

Sorted by Percent in Descending Order — U.S. = 3.23

State	Number	County	Number	Place	Number
Utah	3.71	Culpeper County, VA	4.63	**Brentwood, NY** (cdp) Suffolk County	5.30
Virginia	3.60	Suffolk County, NY	4.50	**Lynwood, CA** (city) Los Angeles County	5.13
Maryland	3.57	Frederick County, VA	4.39	**Islip, NY** (town) Suffolk County	4.93
New Jersey	3.57	Spotsylvania County, VA	4.25	**Central Islip, NY** (cdp) Suffolk County	4.85
New York	3.35	Utah County, UT	4.15	**Hempstead (village), NY** (village) Nassau County	4.68
Connecticut	3.34	Prince William County, VA	4.11	**Babylon, NY** (town) Suffolk County	4.67
Idaho	3.28	Nassau County, NY	3.97	**Kearns, UT** (cdp) Salt Lake County	4.64
Georgia	3.26	Union County, NC	3.92	**Magna, UT** (cdp) Salt Lake County	4.57
California	3.25	Loudoun County, VA	3.91	**Springfield, VA** (cdp) Fairfax County	4.51
Delaware	3.21	Stafford County, VA	3.87	**Marumsco, VA** (cdp) Prince William County	4.42

Sorted by Percent in Ascending Order — U.S. = 3.23

State	Number	County	Number	Place	Number
District of Columbia	2.24	New York County, NY	2.12	**Atlanta, GA** (city) Fulton County	1.89
Vermont	2.53	Champaign County, IL	2.15	**Saint Louis, MO** (independent city)	1.92
Michigan	2.62	Washtenaw County, MI	2.20	**Cincinnati, OH** (city) Hamilton County	2.02
New Mexico	2.62	Brazos County, TX	2.26	**Miami Beach, FL** (city) Miami-Dade County	2.09
Louisiana	2.73	Alachua County, FL	2.28	**Manhattan, NY** (borough) New York County	2.12
Missouri	2.73	Orleans Parish, LA	2.29	**Pittsburgh, PA** (city) Allegheny County	2.16
Arkansas	2.74	Centre County, PA	2.32	**Minneapolis, MN** (city) Hennepin County	2.22
Oregon	2.76	Leon County, FL	2.37	**Tempe, AZ** (city) Maricopa County	2.23
South Dakota	2.77	East Baton Rouge Parish, LA	2.40	**Tallahassee, FL** (city) Leon County	2.24
Iowa	2.80	Cleveland County, OK	2.41	**Tucson, AZ** (city) Pima County	2.25

Note: (1) Ranking tables cover all states and counties, and places with an overall population of at least 125,000, OR an overall population of at least 25,000 where the Hispanic/Latino population is at least 20% of the overall population. In states where less than five places meet either of these criteria, we have included places with at least 10,000 total population with the highest percentage of Hispanic/Latino population. These places are identified with an asterisk (*); Please refer to the User's Guide for a full explanation of data.

Average Household Size

South American: Uruguayan

Top 10 States, Counties, and Places[1]

Sorted by Percent in Descending Order — U.S. = 2.91

State	Number	County	Number	Place	Number
Utah	3.58	Henry County, GA	4.04	**Islip, NY** (town) Suffolk County	4.20
South Carolina	3.42	Clayton County, GA	3.85	**Oyster Bay, NY** (town) Nassau County	3.80
Missouri	3.41	Prince William County, VA	3.84	**Kissimmee, FL** (city) Osceola County	3.74
Georgia	3.33	Beaufort County, SC	3.72	**Weston, FL** (city) Broward County	3.59
Wisconsin	3.29	Utah County, UT	3.59	**Port Saint Lucie, FL** (city) Saint Lucie County	3.53
North Carolina	3.09	Suffolk County, NY	3.56	**Hilton Head Island*, SC** (town) Beaufort County	3.48
New Jersey	3.05	Saint Lucie County, FL	3.55	**Paterson, NJ** (city) Passaic County	3.42
Indiana	3.02	Gwinnett County, GA	3.48	**Bloomfield, NJ** (township) Essex County	3.34
Massachusetts	3.00	Polk County, FL	3.47	**Fitchburg, MA** (city) Worcester County	3.33
Connecticut	2.99	Salt Lake County, UT	3.47	**Kendall West, FL** (cdp) Miami-Dade County	3.33

Sorted by Percent in Ascending Order — U.S. = 2.91

State	Number	County	Number	Place	Number
District of Columbia	1.89	San Francisco County, CA	1.89	**San Francisco, CA** (city) San Francisco County	1.89
Washington	2.47	New York County, NY	1.95	**Manhattan, NY** (borough) New York County	1.95
Rhode Island	2.49	Bronx County, NY	2.11	**Bronx, NY** (borough) Bronx County	2.11
Oregon	2.51	Pinellas County, FL	2.16	**West Palm Beach, FL** (city) Palm Beach County	2.12
Alabama	2.52	Arlington County, VA	2.22	**Arlington, VA** (cdp) Arlington County	2.22
Michigan	2.60	King County, WA	2.35	**West New York, NJ** (town) Hudson County	2.27
Ohio	2.66	Santa Clara County, CA	2.36	**Miami Beach, FL** (city) Miami-Dade County	2.31
California	2.70	Duval County, FL	2.46	**Aventura, FL** (city) Miami-Dade County	2.44
Louisiana	2.73	Alameda County, CA	2.47	**San Diego, CA** (city) San Diego County	2.46
Nevada	2.73	Cuyahoga County, OH	2.50	**Fort Lauderdale, FL** (city) Broward County	2.50

Note: (1) Ranking tables cover all states and counties, and places with an overall population of at least 125,000, OR an overall population of at least 25,000 where the Hispanic/Latino population is at least 20% of the overall population. In states where less than five places meet either of these criteria, we have included places with at least 10,000 total population with the highest percentage of Hispanic/Latino population. These places are identified with an asterisk (*); Please refer to the User's Guide for a full explanation of data.

Average Household Size

South American: Venezuelan

Top 10 States, Counties, and Places[1]

Sorted by Percent in Descending Order — U.S. = 2.86

State	Number	County	Number	Place	Number
Utah	3.51	Chesterfield County, VA	3.90	**Brentwood, NY** (cdp) Suffolk County	4.61
Maine	3.18	Davis County, UT	3.67	**Islip, NY** (town) Suffolk County	4.17
Idaho	3.10	Hamilton County, IN	3.67	**Saint Cloud, FL** (city) Osceola County	3.93
Connecticut	3.05	Union County, NC	3.67	**Tamiami, FL** (cdp) Miami-Dade County	3.79
Rhode Island	3.02	Utah County, UT	3.65	**Richmond West, FL** (cdp) Miami-Dade County	3.78
Maryland	2.98	Forsyth County, GA	3.58	**Naperville, IL** (city) DuPage County	3.64
Nebraska	2.98	Will County, IL	3.57	**West Valley City, UT** (city) Salt Lake County	3.62
Georgia	2.95	Nassau County, NY	3.56	**Royal Palm Beach, FL** (village) Palm Beach County	3.60
New Jersey	2.95	Hidalgo County, TX	3.54	**McAllen, TX** (city) Hidalgo County	3.58
Florida	2.93	Mercer County, NJ	3.52	**Hempstead (town), NY** (town) Nassau County	3.51

Sorted by Percent in Ascending Order — U.S. = 2.86

State	Number	County	Number	Place	Number
District of Columbia	1.84	Arlington County, VA	1.89	**Cincinnati, OH** (city) Hamilton County	1.81
West Virginia	2.29	New York County, NY	1.90	**Arlington, VA** (cdp) Arlington County	1.89
Hawaii	2.51	San Francisco County, CA	2.02	**Manhattan, NY** (borough) New York County	1.90
Massachusetts	2.51	Denver County, CO	2.12	**Atlanta, GA** (city) Fulton County	1.95
Arkansas	2.52	Jefferson County, TX	2.12	**Miami Beach, FL** (city) Miami-Dade County	1.97
Kentucky	2.61	Multnomah County, OR	2.13	**Seattle, WA** (city) King County	1.97
New Mexico	2.61	Suffolk County, MA	2.15	**Pittsburgh, PA** (city) Allegheny County	1.98
New York	2.63	Orleans Parish, LA	2.19	**San Francisco, CA** (city) San Francisco County	2.02
Colorado	2.64	Marin County, CA	2.28	**Portland, OR** (city) Multnomah County	2.08
Oregon	2.64	Durham County, NC	2.34	**Denver, CO** (city) Denver County	2.12

RANKINGS & COMPARISONS

Note: (1) Ranking tables cover all states and counties, and places with an overall population of at least 125,000, OR an overall population of at least 25,000 where the Hispanic/Latino population is at least 20% of the overall population. In states where less than five places meet either of these criteria, we have included places with at least 10,000 total population with the highest percentage of Hispanic/Latino population. These places are identified with an asterisk (*); Please refer to the User's Guide for a full explanation of data.

Average Household Size

Spaniard

Top 10 States, Counties, and Places[1]

Sorted by Percent in Descending Order U.S. = 2.63

State	Number	County	Number	Place	Number
Hawaii	3.18	Clayton County, GA	3.83	**Waianae*, HI** (cdp) Honolulu County	4.78
Utah	3.00	Tulare County, CA	3.49	**Delano, CA** (city) Kern County	4.66
Alaska	2.79	Elkhart County, IN	3.47	**Florence-Graham, CA** (cdp) Los Angeles County	4.31
Nebraska	2.79	Fauquier County, VA	3.46	**Perris, CA** (city) Riverside County	4.18
Texas	2.78	Johnston County, NC	3.44	**Madera, CA** (city) Madera County	4.06
Arkansas	2.77	Cabarrus County, NC	3.43	**Compton, CA** (city) Los Angeles County	4.05
Iowa	2.76	Ellis County, TX	3.42	**Fort Hood, TX** (cdp) Bell County	3.91
Kansas	2.74	Utah County, UT	3.42	**Tulare, CA** (city) Tulare County	3.90
Georgia	2.72	Hall County, GA	3.36	**Adelanto, CA** (city) San Bernardino County	3.89
Oklahoma	2.72	Calvert County, MD	3.32	**Rialto, CA** (city) San Bernardino County	3.86

Sorted by Percent in Ascending Order U.S. = 2.63

State	Number	County	Number	Place	Number
District of Columbia	1.96	New York County, NY	1.79	**Manhattan, NY** (borough) New York County	1.79
Vermont	2.15	Washington County, VT	1.82	**Pittsburgh, PA** (city) Allegheny County	1.85
West Virginia	2.29	Hampshire County, MA	1.87	**Atlanta, GA** (city) Fulton County	1.86
Maine	2.35	Arlington County, VA	1.97	**University, FL** (cdp) Hillsborough County	1.87
Montana	2.39	Orleans Parish, LA	1.98	**Baton Rouge, LA** (city) East Baton Rouge Parish	1.88
Louisiana	2.41	Costilla County, CO	2.00	**Shreveport, LA** (city) Caddo Parish	1.90
Florida	2.43	San Francisco County, CA	2.00	**Baltimore, MD** (independent city)	1.92
Wyoming	2.43	Caddo Parish, LA	2.04	**Miami Beach, FL** (city) Miami-Dade County	1.92
New York	2.44	Siskiyou County, CA	2.08	**Palm Desert, CA** (city) Riverside County	1.95
Pennsylvania	2.44	Montgomery County, VA	2.09	**Lynn, MA** (city) Essex County	1.96

Note: (1) Ranking tables cover all states and counties, and places with an overall population of at least 125,000, OR an overall population of at least 25,000 where the Hispanic/Latino population is at least 20% of the overall population. In states where less than five places meet either of these criteria, we have included places with at least 10,000 total population with the highest percentage of Hispanic/Latino population. These places are identified with an asterisk (*); Please refer to the User's Guide for a full explanation of data.

Median Age

Total Population

Top 10 States, Counties, and Places[1]

Sorted by Percent in Descending Order — U.S. = 37.2

State	Years	County	Years	Place	Years
Maine	42.7	Sumter County, FL	62.7	**Fortuna Foothills, AZ** (cdp) Yuma County	59.4
Vermont	41.5	Charlotte County, FL	55.9	**Bonita Springs, FL** (city) Lee County	55.2
West Virginia	41.3	Harding County, NM	55.9	**Palm Desert, CA** (city) Riverside County	53.0
New Hampshire	41.1	Catron County, NM	55.8	**Palm Springs, CA** (city) Riverside County	51.6
Florida	40.7	Alcona County, MI	55.2	**Hilton Head Island*, SC** (town) Beaufort County	50.9
Pennsylvania	40.1	Llano County, TX	55.0	**Bullhead City, AZ** (city) Mohave County	48.2
Connecticut	40.0	Sierra County, NM	54.5	**Tamarac, FL** (city) Broward County	47.1
Montana	39.8	Lancaster County, VA	54.1	**Hallandale Beach, FL** (city) Broward County	46.7
Rhode Island	39.4	Citrus County, FL	54.0	**Aventura, FL** (city) Miami-Dade County	46.1
Massachusetts	39.1	Jefferson County, WA	53.9	**La Quinta, CA** (city) Riverside County	45.6

Sorted by Percent in Ascending Order — U.S. = 37.2

State	Years	County	Years	Place	Years
Utah	29.2	Madison County, ID	22.6	**University, FL** (cdp) Orange County	21.1
Texas	33.6	Shannon County, SD	23.5	**Fort Leonard Wood*, MO** (cdp) Pulaski County	21.2
Alaska	33.8	Chattahoochee County, GA	24.0	**Fort Campbell North*, KY** (cdp) Christian County	21.3
District of Columbia	33.8	Todd County, SD	24.0	**Fort Hood, TX** (cdp) Bell County	21.9
Idaho	34.6	Riley County, KS	24.3	**Schofield Barracks*, HI** (cdp) Honolulu County	22.0
California	35.2	Whitman County, WA	24.4	**Morgantown*, WV** (city) Monongalia County	22.6
Georgia	35.3	Brazos County, TX	24.5	**North Chicago, IL** (city) Lake County	22.8
Louisiana	35.8	Utah County, UT	24.6	**Hanover*, NH** (town) Grafton County	23.0
Arizona	35.9	Clay County, SD	25.0	**San Marcos, TX** (city) Hays County	23.1
Kansas	36.0	Isabella County, MI	25.1	**New Brunswick, NJ** (city) Middlesex County	23.3

Note: (1) Ranking tables cover all states and counties, and places with an overall population of at least 125,000, OR an overall population of at least 25,000 where the Hispanic/Latino population is at least 20% of the overall population. In states where less than five places meet either of these criteria, we have included places with at least 10,000 total population with the highest percentage of Hispanic/Latino population. These places are identified with an asterisk (*); Please refer to the User's Guide for a full explanation of data.

Median Age

Hispanic or Latino (of any race)

Top 10 States, Counties, and Places[1]

Sorted by Percent in Descending Order — U.S. = 27.3

State	Years	County	Years	Place	Years
Florida	33.6	Harding County, NM	52.4	**Westchester, FL** (cdp) Miami-Dade County	45.7
New York	30.3	Catron County, NM	50.1	**University Park, FL** (cdp) Miami-Dade County	44.5
District of Columbia	30.1	Costilla County, CO	43.4	**Tamiami, FL** (cdp) Miami-Dade County	43.1
New Jersey	30.0	Huerfano County, CO	43.0	**Hialeah, FL** (city) Miami-Dade County	42.8
New Mexico	29.8	Mora County, NM	42.9	**Miami Beach, FL** (city) Miami-Dade County	41.5
Louisiana	28.9	Kenedy County, TX	42.4	**Coral Gables, FL** (city) Miami-Dade County	41.3
Maryland	27.8	Jeff Davis County, TX	40.6	**Kendale Lakes, FL** (cdp) Miami-Dade County	41.0
Connecticut	27.4	De Baca County, NM	40.2	**Fountainebleau, FL** (cdp) Miami-Dade County	40.8
Virginia	27.3	Terrell County, TX	40.2	**Miami, FL** (city) Miami-Dade County	40.6
California	27.1	Miami-Dade County, FL	39.2	**Hallandale Beach, FL** (city) Broward County	39.8

Sorted by Percent in Ascending Order — U.S. = 27.3

State	Years	County	Years	Place	Years
North Dakota	21.9	Cedar County, NE	12.4	**Waianae*, HI** (cdp) Honolulu County	19.5
Iowa	22.2	Knox County, NE	13.5	**Schofield Barracks*, HI** (cdp) Honolulu County	19.8
South Dakota	22.3	Corson County, SD	14.3	**Fort Campbell North*, KY** (cdp) Christian County	19.9
Idaho	22.5	Sheridan County, NE	14.4	**Marshalltown, IA** (city) Marshall County	20.1
Nebraska	22.8	Thurston County, NE	14.4	**Fort Hood, TX** (cdp) Bell County	20.4
Kansas	23.3	Clearwater County, MN	14.6	**Woonsocket*, RI** (city) Providence County	20.4
Oklahoma	23.4	Menominee County, WI	14.7	**Brunswick*, ME** (town) Cumberland County	20.6
Wisconsin	23.4	Grundy County, IA	14.9	**Hanover*, NH** (town) Grafton County	20.7
Arkansas	23.5	Merrick County, NE	14.9	**Rapid City*, SD** (city) Pennington County	20.8
Minnesota	23.5	Rolette County, ND	15.3	**Fort Leonard Wood*, MO** (cdp) Pulaski County	20.9

Note: (1) Ranking tables cover all states and counties, and places with an overall population of at least 125,000, OR an overall population of at least 25,000 where the Hispanic/Latino population is at least 20% of the overall population. In states where less than five places meet either of these criteria, we have included places with at least 10,000 total population with the highest percentage of Hispanic/Latino population. These places are identified with an asterisk (*); Please refer to the User's Guide for a full explanation of data.

Median Age

Central American, excluding Mexican

Top 10 States, Counties, and Places[1]

Sorted by Percent in Descending Order — U.S. = 30.2

State	Years	County	Years	Place	Years
California	32.7	Calaveras County, CA	42.0	**Lake Jackson, TX** (city) Brazoria County	42.5
Florida	31.8	Kerr County, TX	37.8	**Drexel Heights, AZ** (cdp) Pima County	40.3
New Mexico	31.4	Adams County, MS	37.5	**Tamiami, FL** (cdp) Miami-Dade County	39.4
Louisiana	30.8	Blaine County, ID	37.0	**Aventura, FL** (city) Miami-Dade County	39.1
Nevada	30.8	Colusa County, CA	36.8	**Kendale Lakes, FL** (cdp) Miami-Dade County	39.0
Illinois	30.7	Charlotte County, FL	36.4	**Coral Gables, FL** (city) Miami-Dade County	38.5
Arizona	30.6	Madera County, CA	36.2	**Culver City, CA** (city) Los Angeles County	38.2
New York	30.4	Doña Ana County, NM	36.1	**Diamond Bar, CA** (city) Los Angeles County	38.0
Texas	30.2	Valencia County, NM	36.0	**San Gabriel, CA** (city) Los Angeles County	37.6
District of Columbia	30.1	Nye County, NV	35.7	**Bullhead City, AZ** (city) Mohave County	37.5

Sorted by Percent in Ascending Order — U.S. = 30.2

State	Years	County	Years	Place	Years
Vermont	20.9	Washington County, WI	10.0	**Schofield Barracks*, HI** (cdp) Honolulu County	14.8
Montana	21.9	Medina County, OH	13.5	**Billings*, MT** (city) Yellowstone County	14.9
North Dakota	22.3	Ozaukee County, WI	14.3	**Fort Campbell North*, KY** (cdp) Christian County	20.2
Maine	22.7	Merrimack County, NH	14.6	**Syracuse, NY** (city) Onondaga County	20.9
West Virginia	23.6	Saint Croix County, WI	15.0	**Fort Leonard Wood*, MO** (cdp) Pulaski County	21.2
Michigan	24.6	Saginaw County, MI	15.3	**Burlington*, VT** (city) Chittenden County	21.7
Ohio	24.8	Saint Louis County, MN	15.6	**Fort Hood, TX** (cdp) Bell County	22.1
Wisconsin	25.0	Kanawha County, WV	15.8	**Spokane, WA** (city) Spokane County	22.3
Missouri	25.1	Jefferson County, MO	16.0	**Fairbanks*, AK** (city) Fairbanks North Star Borough	22.6
Kentucky	25.2	Boone County, IN	16.3	**Twentynine Palms, CA** (city) San Bernardino County	23.1

RANKINGS & COMPARISONS

Note: (1) Ranking tables cover all states and counties, and places with an overall population of at least 125,000, OR an overall population of at least 25,000 where the Hispanic/Latino population is at least 20% of the overall population. In states where less than five places meet either of these criteria, we have included places with at least 10,000 total population with the highest percentage of Hispanic/Latino population. These places are identified with an asterisk (*); Please refer to the User's Guide for a full explanation of data.

Median Age

Central American: Costa Rican

Top 10 States, Counties, and Places[1]

Sorted by Percent in Descending Order — U.S. = 32.8

State	Years	County	Years	Place	Years
New York	36.9	Kings County, NY	43.1	**Alhambra, CA** (city) Los Angeles County	52.0
California	36.2	Richmond County, NY	40.5	**Burbank, CA** (city) Los Angeles County	45.1
Louisiana	35.5	Queens County, NY	39.7	**Freeport, NY** (village) Nassau County	44.0
Florida	34.8	Los Angeles County, CA	39.2	**Pasadena, CA** (city) Los Angeles County	44.0
New Mexico	34.8	Nassau County, NY	39.2	**San Jose, CA** (city) Santa Clara County	43.2
Mississippi	34.6	Bronx County, NY	39.1	**Brooklyn, NY** (borough) Kings County	43.1
District of Columbia	34.3	San Mateo County, CA	38.3	**South Miami Heights, FL** (cdp) Miami-Dade County	42.5
Texas	33.3	Jefferson Parish, LA	38.2	**Yonkers, NY** (city) Westchester County	42.2
Nevada	33.0	Polk County, FL	38.0	**North Hempstead, NY** (town) Nassau County	42.0
Connecticut	32.9	San Francisco County, CA	37.7	**Rialto, CA** (city) San Bernardino County	41.5

Sorted by Percent in Ascending Order — U.S. = 32.8

State	Years	County	Years	Place	Years
Iowa	24.8	Allegheny County, PA	23.0	**Colorado Springs, CO** (city) El Paso County	25.4
Arkansas	25.9	Utah County, UT	24.0	**Atlanta, GA** (city) Fulton County	26.6
Utah	26.0	Alachua County, FL	24.4	**Lehigh Acres, FL** (cdp) Lee County	27.0
New Hampshire	26.1	Larimer County, CO	24.8	**Milwaukee, WI** (city) Milwaukee County	27.1
Alaska	26.5	El Paso County, CO	25.4	**Virginia Beach, VA** (independent city)	27.5
Maine	26.8	Escambia County, FL	25.5	**Indianapolis, IN** (city) Marion County	28.2
Idaho	27.3	Pierce County, WA	25.8	**Fort Worth, TX** (city) Tarrant County	28.5
Minnesota	27.6	Oklahoma County, OK	25.9	**Worcester, MA** (city) Worcester County	28.6
Wisconsin	27.6	Saint Louis County, MO	26.3	**Austin, TX** (city) Travis County	29.0
Kentucky	27.7	San Luis Obispo County, CA	26.5	**Brandon, FL** (cdp) Hillsborough County	29.0

Note: (1) Ranking tables cover all states and counties, and places with an overall population of at least 125,000, OR an overall population of at least 25,000 where the Hispanic/Latino population is at least 20% of the overall population. In states where less than five places meet either of these criteria, we have included places with at least 10,000 total population with the highest percentage of Hispanic/Latino population. These places are identified with an asterisk (*); Please refer to the User's Guide for a full explanation of data.

Median Age

Central American: Guatemalan

Top 10 States, Counties, and Places[1]

Sorted by Percent in Descending Order — U.S. = 28.5

State	Years	County	Years	Place	Years
California	31.4	Guadalupe County, TX	37.0	**Kendale Lakes, FL** (cdp) Miami-Dade County	39.7
Illinois	30.6	Madera County, CA	36.1	**Richmond West, FL** (cdp) Miami-Dade County	39.0
New Mexico	30.6	Sandoval County, NM	35.5	**West Whittier-Los Nietos, CA** (cdp) Los Angeles County	39.0
Nevada	30.3	Johnson County, TX	35.3	**North Miami, FL** (city) Miami-Dade County	38.8
Texas	29.3	Mohave County, AZ	35.3	**Pico Rivera, CA** (city) Los Angeles County	38.8
Louisiana	29.2	Tulare County, CA	35.2	**Alhambra, CA** (city) Los Angeles County	38.7
District of Columbia	29.0	Saint John the Baptist Parish, LA	34.8	**Diamond Bar, CA** (city) Los Angeles County	38.3
Arizona	28.9	Hidalgo County, TX	33.3	**Rosemead, CA** (city) Los Angeles County	38.0
New York	28.9	Osceola County, FL	33.3	**Culver City, CA** (city) Los Angeles County	37.8
Wyoming	28.9	Doña Ana County, NM	33.2	**Glendora, CA** (city) Los Angeles County	37.8

Sorted by Percent in Ascending Order — U.S. = 28.5

State	Years	County	Years	Place	Years
Vermont	10.8	Delaware County, OH	8.2	**Madison, WI** (city) Dane County	18.1
Montana	12.0	Waukesha County, WI	8.5	**Saint Louis, MO** (independent city)	19.5
West Virginia	13.1	Washington County, MN	9.1	**Syracuse, NY** (city) Onondaga County	20.5
Wisconsin	13.4	Calcasieu Parish, LA	9.7	**Spokane, WA** (city) Spokane County	21.2
Maine	14.4	Dane County, WI	9.9	**Cedar Rapids, IA** (city) Linn County	21.9
North Dakota	15.4	Lucas County, OH	10.0	**Pittsburgh, PA** (city) Allegheny County	22.3
New Hampshire	20.0	Warren County, OH	10.0	**Mobile, AL** (city) Mobile County	22.8
Michigan	20.6	Summit County, OH	10.3	**Lexington-Fayette, KY** (consolidated govt) Fayette County	23.1
Minnesota	21.4	Macomb County, MI	10.4	**Saint Paul, MN** (city) Ramsey County	23.3
Missouri	21.4	Daviess County, KY	11.0	**Topeka, KS** (city) Shawnee County	23.3

Note: (1) Ranking tables cover all states and counties, and places with an overall population of at least 125,000, OR an overall population of at least 25,000 where the Hispanic/Latino population is at least 20% of the overall population. In states where less than five places meet either of these criteria, we have included places with at least 10,000 total population with the highest percentage of Hispanic/Latino population. These places are identified with an asterisk (*); Please refer to the User's Guide for a full explanation of data.

Median Age

Central American: Honduran

Top 10 States, Counties, and Places[1]

Sorted by Percent in Descending Order — U.S. = 29.6

State	Years	County	Years	Place	Years
Florida	31.4	Highlands County, FL	38.0	**Adelanto, CA** (city) San Bernardino County	39.7
California	31.3	Winnebago County, IL	36.0	**Tamiami, FL** (cdp) Miami-Dade County	38.8
New Mexico	30.9	New York County, NY	34.7	**Coral Gables, FL** (city) Miami-Dade County	38.6
Louisiana	30.5	Bergen County, NJ	34.0	**Culver City, CA** (city) Los Angeles County	38.0
Nevada	30.5	Tulare County, CA	33.5	**Redwood City, CA** (city) San Mateo County	37.8
Illinois	30.4	San Joaquin County, CA	33.3	**Glendale, CA** (city) Los Angeles County	36.8
New York	30.4	Miami-Dade County, FL	33.0	**Carrollwood, FL** (cdp) Hillsborough County	36.3
Arizona	30.2	Saint John the Baptist Parish, LA	33.0	**Tamarac, FL** (city) Broward County	36.3
New Jersey	30.0	Will County, IL	32.9	**Alhambra, CA** (city) Los Angeles County	36.2
Connecticut	29.5	Kings County, NY	32.8	**Corona, CA** (city) Riverside County	35.9

Sorted by Percent in Ascending Order — U.S. = 29.6

State	Years	County	Years	Place	Years
Maine	20.7	Ottawa County, MI	22.0	**Vancouver, WA** (city) Clark County	20.0
Vermont	21.6	Saint Joseph County, IN	22.1	**Worthington*, MN** (city) Nobles County	21.8
Hawaii	24.9	Erie County, NY	22.2	**Springfield, MO** (city) Greene County	22.6
Minnesota	25.3	Nobles County, MN	22.3	**Edinburg, TX** (city) Hidalgo County	23.8
West Virginia	25.7	Allegheny County, PA	22.6	**Savannah, GA** (city) Chatham County	24.0
Ohio	25.8	Albany County, NY	22.7	**Grand Rapids, MI** (city) Kent County	24.3
Wyoming	25.8	Greene County, MO	22.7	**Willmar*, MN** (city) Kandiyohi County	24.4
Idaho	26.0	Anoka County, MN	22.8	**Tallahassee, FL** (city) Leon County	24.6
Iowa	26.2	Onslow County, NC	22.9	**Worcester, MA** (city) Worcester County	24.8
Alaska	26.3	Davis County, UT	23.5	**Haltom City, TX** (city) Tarrant County	24.9

Note: (1) Ranking tables cover all states and counties, and places with an overall population of at least 125,000, OR an overall population of at least 25,000 where the Hispanic/Latino population is at least 20% of the overall population. In states where less than five places meet either of these criteria, we have included places with at least 10,000 total population with the highest percentage of Hispanic/Latino population. These places are identified with an asterisk (*); Please refer to the User's Guide for a full explanation of data.

Median Age

Central American: Nicaraguan

Top 10 States, Counties, and Places[1]

Sorted by Percent in Descending Order — U.S. = 33.8

State	Years	County	Years	Place	Years
District of Columbia	36.6	El Dorado County, CA	42.0	**Monterey Park, CA** (city) Los Angeles County	45.5
California	35.1	San Francisco County, CA	40.5	**Rosemead, CA** (city) Los Angeles County	45.1
Florida	35.0	Hendry County, FL	40.2	**San Gabriel, CA** (city) Los Angeles County	45.0
New York	34.7	New York County, NY	38.5	**Pico Rivera, CA** (city) Los Angeles County	42.9
Louisiana	34.5	Mobile County, AL	37.5	**Glendale, CA** (city) Los Angeles County	42.2
New Jersey	33.1	Saint Tammany Parish, LA	37.5	**La Puente, CA** (city) Los Angeles County	42.0
Nevada	32.8	Westchester County, NY	37.4	**Hacienda Heights, CA** (cdp) Los Angeles County	41.1
Texas	32.7	Bergen County, NJ	36.9	**San Francisco, CA** (city) San Francisco County	40.5
New Mexico	32.6	Hall County, GA	36.9	**Carrollton, TX** (city) Denton County	40.3
Arizona	32.2	Marin County, CA	36.8	**Union City, NJ** (city) Hudson County	40.2

Sorted by Percent in Ascending Order — U.S. = 33.8

State	Years	County	Years	Place	Years
West Virginia	24.4	Leon County, FL	22.6	**Tallahassee, FL** (city) Leon County	22.5
Alaska	25.6	Alachua County, FL	23.0	**Norfolk, VA** (independent city)	24.5
Hawaii	26.6	Onslow County, NC	23.6	**Sparks, NV** (city) Washoe County	24.7
Iowa	27.0	Lane County, OR	23.7	**Anchorage, AK** (municipality)	25.0
Missouri	27.1	Davis County, UT	24.0	**Virginia Beach, VA** (independent city)	25.6
Utah	27.5	Yolo County, CA	24.2	**Killeen, TX** (city) Bell County	26.8
Rhode Island	27.8	Burlington County, NJ	25.5	**Irvine, CA** (city) Orange County	27.0
Kansas	27.9	Utah County, UT	25.5	**Fayetteville, NC** (city) Cumberland County	27.3
Kentucky	28.1	Santa Barbara County, CA	25.6	**Memphis, TN** (city) Shelby County	27.3
Nebraska	28.1	Kent County, MI	25.7	**Manteca, CA** (city) San Joaquin County	27.5

Note: (1) Ranking tables cover all states and counties, and places with an overall population of at least 125,000, OR an overall population of at least 25,000 where the Hispanic/Latino population is at least 20% of the overall population. In states where less than five places meet either of these criteria, we have included places with at least 10,000 total population with the highest percentage of Hispanic/Latino population. These places are identified with an asterisk (*); Please refer to the User's Guide for a full explanation of data.

Median Age

Central American: Panamanian

Top 10 States, Counties, and Places[1]

Sorted by Percent in Descending Order — U.S. = 35.2

State	Years	County	Years	Place	Years
New York	40.4	Charlotte County, FL	50.3	**Bayonne, NJ** (city) Hudson County	49.1
Florida	38.0	Queens County, NY	43.7	**Central Islip, NY** (cdp) Suffolk County	47.0
New Jersey	37.3	Citrus County, FL	43.1	**Inglewood, CA** (city) Los Angeles County	46.5
California	37.0	Kings County, NY	43.1	**Moreno Valley, CA** (city) Riverside County	46.3
New Mexico	36.3	Hidalgo County, TX	42.0	**Kendale Lakes, FL** (cdp) Miami-Dade County	45.1
Louisiana	35.3	Sarasota County, FL	41.6	**Queens, NY** (borough) Queens County	43.7
Delaware	35.2	Middlesex County, NJ	41.4	**Sunrise, FL** (city) Broward County	43.2
Texas	35.1	Hernando County, FL	41.3	**Brooklyn, NY** (borough) Kings County	43.1
District of Columbia	35.0	Jefferson Parish, LA	40.9	**Tamarac, FL** (city) Broward County	43.0
New Hampshire	34.5	Sonoma County, CA	40.8	**Tamiami, FL** (cdp) Miami-Dade County	42.5

Sorted by Percent in Ascending Order — U.S. = 35.2

State	Years	County	Years	Place	Years
North Dakota	22.8	Brazos County, TX	23.3	**Tallahassee, FL** (city) Leon County	22.5
West Virginia	23.7	Leon County, FL	23.3	**Providence, RI** (city) Providence County	23.5
Maine	25.5	Spokane County, WA	24.3	**Savannah, GA** (city) Chatham County	23.9
Idaho	25.6	Dakota County, MN	25.0	**Rochester, NY** (city) Monroe County	25.5
Alaska	26.5	Saint Charles County, MO	25.0	**Greensboro, NC** (city) Guilford County	26.2
Montana	26.5	Alachua County, FL	25.1	**Columbia, SC** (city) Richland County	27.0
Iowa	27.5	Jefferson County, NY	25.3	**Allentown, PA** (city) Lehigh County	27.1
Missouri	27.7	Washtenaw County, MI	25.6	**Kansas City, MO** (city) Jackson County	27.2
Kansas	27.9	Erie County, NY	25.7	**Raleigh, NC** (city) Wake County	27.2
Rhode Island	28.6	Coryell County, TX	25.8	**North Las Vegas, NV** (city) Clark County	27.3

Note: (1) Ranking tables cover all states and counties, and places with an overall population of at least 125,000, OR an overall population of at least 25,000 where the Hispanic/Latino population is at least 20% of the overall population. In states where less than five places meet either of these criteria, we have included places with at least 10,000 total population with the highest percentage of Hispanic/Latino population. These places are identified with an asterisk (*); Please refer to the User's Guide for a full explanation of data.

Median Age

Central American: Salvadoran

Top 10 States, Counties, and Places[1]

Sorted by Percent in Descending Order — U.S. = 30.6

State	Years	County	Years	Place	Years
California	33.2	Doña Ana County, NM	36.5	**Coral Gables, FL** (city) Miami-Dade County	40.1
Arizona	32.0	Madera County, CA	36.3	**Culver City, CA** (city) Los Angeles County	39.6
Florida	31.1	San Francisco County, CA	36.3	**Kendall, FL** (cdp) Miami-Dade County	39.5
New Mexico	31.0	Hernando County, FL	35.8	**North Miami, FL** (city) Miami-Dade County	39.3
Illinois	30.8	Hidalgo County, TX	35.7	**Kendale Lakes, FL** (cdp) Miami-Dade County	38.7
Texas	30.7	Douglas County, NV	35.5	**San Dimas, CA** (city) Los Angeles County	38.6
Nevada	30.6	Fayette County, GA	35.4	**McAllen, TX** (city) Hidalgo County	37.4
District of Columbia	30.2	Titus County, TX	35.3	**Palm Springs, CA** (city) Riverside County	37.4
New Jersey	30.2	Yavapai County, AZ	35.2	**Deltona, FL** (city) Volusia County	37.3
Louisiana	30.1	Guadalupe County, TX	34.4	**Country Club, FL** (cdp) Miami-Dade County	37.2

Sorted by Percent in Ascending Order — U.S. = 30.6

State	Years	County	Years	Place	Years
Vermont	22.0	Onondaga County, NY	20.4	**Spokane, WA** (city) Spokane County	21.0
Montana	22.8	Craven County, NC	21.3	**Harlingen, TX** (city) Cameron County	23.0
Hawaii	24.4	Columbia County, PA	21.5	**Clarksville, TN** (city) Montgomery County	23.5
West Virginia	24.9	White County, IN	21.7	**Madison, WI** (city) Dane County	23.7
Alaska	25.8	Tooele County, UT	21.8	**Cincinnati, OH** (city) Hamilton County	24.8
Ohio	26.6	Onslow County, NC	22.1	**Killeen, TX** (city) Bell County	24.8
Indiana	27.1	Lackawanna County, PA	22.3	**Wenatchee, WA** (city) Chelan County	24.8
Kentucky	27.1	Spokane County, WA	22.4	**Lubbock, TX** (city) Lubbock County	25.0
Maine	27.1	Albany County, NY	22.8	**Anchorage, AK** (municipality)	25.1
New Hampshire	27.3	Brazos County, TX	22.9	**Fayetteville, NC** (city) Cumberland County	25.1

RANKINGS & COMPARISONS

Note: (1) Ranking tables cover all states and counties, and places with an overall population of at least 125,000, OR an overall population of at least 25,000 where the Hispanic/Latino population is at least 20% of the overall population. In states where less than five places meet either of these criteria, we have included places with at least 10,000 total population with the highest percentage of Hispanic/Latino population. These places are identified with an asterisk (*); Please refer to the User's Guide for a full explanation of data.

Median Age

Cuban

Top 10 States, Counties, and Places[1]

Sorted by Percent in Descending Order — U.S. = 40.1

State	Years	County	Years	Place	Years
New Jersey	42.3	Granville County, NC	55.5	**Huntington Park, CA** (city) Los Angeles County	60.7
Florida	42.0	Hudson County, NJ	48.7	**Bell, CA** (city) Los Angeles County	56.9
New York	39.3	Union County, FL	48.4	**Rosemead, CA** (city) Los Angeles County	55.8
Louisiana	37.7	Santa Fe County, NM	47.0	**Maywood, CA** (city) Los Angeles County	54.5
California	37.3	Sumter County, FL	47.0	**West New York, NJ** (town) Hudson County	53.8
Nevada	37.1	Queens County, NY	46.6	**Miami Beach, FL** (city) Miami-Dade County	52.5
Texas	35.4	New York County, NY	45.5	**Aventura, FL** (city) Miami-Dade County	51.8
New Mexico	35.2	Mohave County, AZ	45.1	**San Gabriel, CA** (city) Los Angeles County	51.3
Mississippi	34.5	Miami-Dade County, FL	43.9	**Union City, NJ** (city) Hudson County	50.9
Kentucky	34.3	Scott County, MS	43.9	**Port Chester, NY** (village) Westchester County	50.3

Sorted by Percent in Ascending Order — U.S. = 40.1

State	Years	County	Years	Place	Years
North Dakota	25.0	Brown County, WI	19.8	**Highland, CA** (city) San Bernardino County	19.5
Wisconsin	25.5	Saint Louis County, MN	19.8	**University, FL** (cdp) Orange County	21.1
Idaho	25.7	Peoria County, IL	19.9	**Tallahassee, FL** (city) Leon County	22.1
Alaska	26.1	Coryell County, TX	20.3	**Bethlehem, PA** (city) Northampton County	22.3
South Dakota	26.3	Erie County, PA	20.3	**Abilene, TX** (city) Taylor County	22.8
Hawaii	26.4	Windham County, CT	20.8	**New Brunswick, NJ** (city) Middlesex County	22.8
Minnesota	26.6	Berkshire County, MA	20.9	**Hampton, VA** (independent city)	22.9
Vermont	26.8	Anoka County, MN	21.0	**Tempe, AZ** (city) Maricopa County	23.0
Kansas	27.0	Tompkins County, NY	21.0	**San Tan Valley, AZ** (cdp) Pinal County	23.3
Utah	27.0	Davis County, UT	21.1	**Pittsburgh, PA** (city) Allegheny County	23.9

Note: (1) Ranking tables cover all states and counties, and places with an overall population of at least 125,000, OR an overall population of at least 25,000 where the Hispanic/Latino population is at least 20% of the overall population. In states where less than five places meet either of these criteria, we have included places with at least 10,000 total population with the highest percentage of Hispanic/Latino population. These places are identified with an asterisk (*); Please refer to the User's Guide for a full explanation of data.

Median Age

Dominican Republic

Top 10 States, Counties, and Places[1]

Sorted by Percent in Descending Order — U.S. = 30.0

State	Years	County	Years	Place	Years
Florida	32.3	Telfair County, GA	42.3	**Tamiami, FL** (cdp) Miami-Dade County	40.6
New York	31.4	Clearfield County, PA	41.2	**Westchester, FL** (cdp) Miami-Dade County	40.1
District of Columbia	30.7	Highlands County, FL	39.5	**West Little River, FL** (cdp) Miami-Dade County	38.9
Louisiana	30.3	Union County, PA	38.1	**South Miami Heights, FL** (cdp) Miami-Dade County	38.3
New Jersey	29.9	Citrus County, FL	37.5	**Miami Beach, FL** (city) Miami-Dade County	38.2
Mississippi	29.7	Mahoning County, OH	37.4	**Hialeah, FL** (city) Miami-Dade County	36.6
California	28.9	New York County, NY	36.0	**Kendale Lakes, FL** (cdp) Miami-Dade County	36.6
Nevada	28.9	Miami-Dade County, FL	35.1	**Coral Gables, FL** (city) Miami-Dade County	36.4
Illinois	28.7	Forsyth County, GA	35.0	**Miami, FL** (city) Miami-Dade County	36.3
New Mexico	28.6	Fayette County, GA	34.0	**Hallandale Beach, FL** (city) Broward County	36.2

Sorted by Percent in Ascending Order — U.S. = 30.0

State	Years	County	Years	Place	Years
Vermont	20.6	Thurston County, WA	16.9	**Syracuse, NY** (city) Onondaga County	20.8
Idaho	21.6	Merrimack County, NH	19.0	**Woonsocket*, RI** (city) Providence County	21.2
Maine	21.8	Erie County, PA	19.1	**Richmond, VA** (independent city)	22.0
Iowa	22.2	Newport County, RI	19.7	**Tallahassee, FL** (city) Leon County	22.0
Oklahoma	22.8	Sedgwick County, KS	19.8	**University, FL** (cdp) Orange County	22.3
Hawaii	23.2	Washington County, RI	19.8	**Buffalo, NY** (city) Erie County	22.4
Kansas	23.8	Ontario County, NY	19.9	**Newburgh, NY** (city) Orange County	22.6
Alaska	23.9	Geary County, KS	20.0	**Oklahoma City, OK** (city) Oklahoma County	22.8
Washington	24.1	Berkshire County, MA	20.6	**Greensboro, NC** (city) Guilford County	22.9
Missouri	24.2	Fairfield County, OH	20.6	**Pittsburgh, PA** (city) Allegheny County	22.9

RANKINGS & COMPARISONS

Note: (1) Ranking tables cover all states and counties, and places with an overall population of at least 125,000, OR an overall population of at least 25,000 where the Hispanic/Latino population is at least 20% of the overall population. In states where less than five places meet either of these criteria, we have included places with at least 10,000 total population with the highest percentage of Hispanic/Latino population. These places are identified with an asterisk (*); Please refer to the User's Guide for a full explanation of data.

Median Age

Mexican

Top 10 States, Counties, and Places[1]

Sorted by Percent in Descending Order — U.S. = 25.5

State	Years	County	Years	Place	Years
District of Columbia	28.6	Harding County, NM	53.8	**Monterey Park, CA** (city) Los Angeles County	34.8
New Mexico	28.1	Catron County, NM	46.6	**Aventura, FL** (city) Miami-Dade County	34.4
Texas	26.6	Huerfano County, CO	43.3	**Eagle Pass, TX** (city) Maverick County	33.6
California	26.2	Kenedy County, TX	42.4	**Kendall, FL** (cdp) Miami-Dade County	33.4
Louisiana	26.2	Terrell County, TX	41.3	**Miami Beach, FL** (city) Miami-Dade County	33.4
Connecticut	25.7	Guadalupe County, NM	41.1	**San Gabriel, CA** (city) Los Angeles County	33.3
Maryland	25.7	Jeff Davis County, TX	40.2	**Alhambra, CA** (city) Los Angeles County	33.2
Massachusetts	25.7	Mora County, NM	40.2	**Coral Gables, FL** (city) Miami-Dade County	32.8
Illinois	25.6	De Baca County, NM	40.1	**Del Rio, TX** (city) Val Verde County	32.6
New York	25.6	Alfalfa County, OK	39.2	**Diamond Bar, CA** (city) Los Angeles County	32.6

Sorted by Percent in Ascending Order — U.S. = 25.5

State	Years	County	Years	Place	Years
North Dakota	21.0	Knox County, NE	11.9	**Carthage*, MO** (city) Jasper County	18.3
South Dakota	21.1	Cedar County, NE	12.8	**Waianae*, HI** (cdp) Honolulu County	18.5
Iowa	21.4	Rolette County, ND	13.0	**Schofield Barracks*, HI** (cdp) Honolulu County	19.4
Idaho	21.9	Sheridan County, NE	14.6	**Fort Campbell North*, KY** (cdp) Christian County	19.8
Nebraska	21.9	Merrick County, NE	14.8	**Marshalltown, IA** (city) Marshall County	19.8
Utah	22.2	Thurston County, NE	14.8	**Fort Hood, TX** (cdp) Bell County	19.9
Arkansas	22.3	Dickinson County, MI	15.0	**Hanover*, NH** (town) Grafton County	19.9
Montana	22.4	Mason County, KY	15.0	**Rapid City*, SD** (city) Pennington County	19.9
Minnesota	22.6	Menominee County, WI	15.0	**Waterville*, ME** (city) Kennebec County	20.1
Oklahoma	22.7	Redwood County, MN	15.0	**Grand Island, NE** (city) Hall County	20.2

Note: (1) Ranking tables cover all states and counties, and places with an overall population of at least 125,000, OR an overall population of at least 25,000 where the Hispanic/Latino population is at least 20% of the overall population. In states where less than five places meet either of these criteria, we have included places with at least 10,000 total population with the highest percentage of Hispanic/Latino population. These places are identified with an asterisk (*); Please refer to the User's Guide for a full explanation of data.

Median Age

Puerto Rican

Top 10 States, Counties, and Places[1]

Sorted by Percent in Descending Order — U.S. = 28.0

State	Years	County	Years	Place	Years
New York	31.1	Wilson County, TX	43.6	**Palm Springs, CA** (city) Riverside County	45.0
Florida	30.9	New York County, NY	38.8	**Westchester, FL** (cdp) Miami-Dade County	42.6
District of Columbia	30.0	Sumter County, FL	38.5	**Monterey Park, CA** (city) Los Angeles County	42.0
New Jersey	29.2	Santa Fe County, NM	38.3	**Hacienda Heights, CA** (cdp) Los Angeles County	41.1
California	28.9	Calaveras County, CA	37.5	**Cathedral City, CA** (city) Riverside County	40.0
New Mexico	28.8	Citrus County, FL	37.3	**Aventura, FL** (city) Miami-Dade County	39.8
Illinois	28.6	Wyoming County, NY	37.0	**Santa Fe, NM** (city) Santa Fe County	39.1
Texas	28.2	Medina County, TX	36.5	**Manhattan, NY** (borough) New York County	38.8
Nevada	28.1	Starke County, IN	36.5	**Tamiami, FL** (cdp) Miami-Dade County	38.7
Arizona	27.7	Siskiyou County, CA	36.0	**Bullhead City, AZ** (city) Mohave County	38.5

Sorted by Percent in Ascending Order — U.S. = 28.0

State	Years	County	Years	Place	Years
Maine	21.4	Mifflin County, PA	14.3	**Bennington*, VT** (town) Bennington County	17.8
South Dakota	21.4	Meade County, KY	15.4	**Fort Campbell North*, KY** (cdp) Christian County	18.3
Rhode Island	21.5	Muskingum County, OH	16.5	**Waianae*, HI** (cdp) Honolulu County	18.8
Iowa	21.9	Saint Croix County, WI	16.7	**Beloit*, WI** (city) Rock County	19.1
New Hampshire	21.9	Crawford County, PA	17.0	**Hazleton, PA** (city) Luzerne County	19.4
Vermont	22.2	Waldo County, ME	17.0	**Schofield Barracks*, HI** (cdp) Honolulu County	19.4
Kansas	22.4	Franklin County, VT	17.3	**Hawaiian Paradise Park*, HI** (cdp) Hawaii County	19.5
Nebraska	22.4	Sherburne County, MN	17.3	**Pasco, WA** (city) Franklin County	19.5
North Dakota	22.4	Dodge County, WI	17.5	**Woonsocket*, RI** (city) Providence County	19.6
Alaska	22.7	Manitowoc County, WI	17.5	**Dodge City, KS** (city) Ford County	19.7

RANKINGS & COMPARISONS

Note: (1) Ranking tables cover all states and counties, and places with an overall population of at least 125,000, OR an overall population of at least 25,000 where the Hispanic/Latino population is at least 20% of the overall population. In states where less than five places meet either of these criteria, we have included places with at least 10,000 total population with the highest percentage of Hispanic/Latino population. These places are identified with an asterisk (*); Please refer to the User's Guide for a full explanation of data.

Median Age

South American

Top 10 States, Counties, and Places[1]

Sorted by Percent in Descending Order — U.S. = 35.0

State	Years	County	Years	Place	Years
California	37.4	Sumter County, FL	50.8	**Huntington Park, CA** (city) Los Angeles County	48.3
Florida	37.2	Hendry County, FL	46.8	**Winchester, NV** (cdp) Clark County	46.4
Nevada	36.3	Mohave County, AZ	46.5	**Palm Springs, CA** (city) Riverside County	46.3
New Jersey	35.2	Highlands County, FL	44.5	**San Gabriel, CA** (city) Los Angeles County	44.8
New York	35.0	Clearfield County, PA	44.4	**San Juan Capistrano, CA** (city) Orange County	44.4
New Mexico	34.9	Citrus County, FL	44.2	**San Dimas, CA** (city) Los Angeles County	43.8
Maryland	34.7	Telfair County, GA	43.2	**East Los Angeles, CA** (cdp) Los Angeles County	43.7
Arizona	34.6	Adams County, MS	42.7	**Yucaipa, CA** (city) San Bernardino County	43.6
Texas	34.6	Charlotte County, FL	42.5	**Florence-Graham, CA** (cdp) Los Angeles County	43.5
District of Columbia	34.1	Levy County, FL	42.5	**South Gate, CA** (city) Los Angeles County	43.5

Sorted by Percent in Ascending Order — U.S. = 35.0

State	Years	County	Years	Place	Years
North Dakota	25.7	Madison County, NY	20.3	**Hanover*, NH** (town) Grafton County	21.2
Vermont	26.4	Saint Louis County, MN	20.3	**Fort Leonard Wood*, MO** (cdp) Pulaski County	21.5
Montana	26.5	Niagara County, NY	20.4	**Syracuse, NY** (city) Onondaga County	22.1
South Dakota	27.2	Livingston County, NY	20.5	**Burlington*, VT** (city) Chittenden County	22.2
Maine	27.8	Rice County, MN	20.6	**University, FL** (cdp) Orange County	22.2
Minnesota	27.8	Eau Claire County, WI	21.0	**Twentynine Palms, CA** (city) San Bernardino County	22.5
Iowa	29.2	Addison County, VT	21.1	**Tallahassee, FL** (city) Leon County	22.6
Idaho	29.4	Stearns County, MN	21.1	**Fort Hood, TX** (cdp) Bell County	22.9
Utah	29.4	Cheshire County, NH	21.3	**Morgantown*, WV** (city) Monongalia County	22.9
Wisconsin	29.6	Oswego County, NY	21.4	**San Marcos, TX** (city) Hays County	22.9

Note: (1) Ranking tables cover all states and counties, and places with an overall population of at least 125,000, OR an overall population of at least 25,000 where the Hispanic/Latino population is at least 20% of the overall population. In states where less than five places meet either of these criteria, we have included places with at least 10,000 total population with the highest percentage of Hispanic/Latino population. These places are identified with an asterisk (*); Please refer to the User's Guide for a full explanation of data.

Median Age

South American: Argentinean

Top 10 States, Counties, and Places[1]

Sorted by Percent in Descending Order — U.S. = 36.6

State	Years	County	Years	Place	Years
Arizona	39.4	Charlotte County, FL	45.5	**Hacienda Heights, CA** (cdp) Los Angeles County	51.8
California	39.1	Solano County, CA	44.7	**Fremont, CA** (city) Alameda County	49.4
Nevada	38.2	Putnam County, NY	43.7	**Scottsdale, AZ** (city) Maricopa County	49.3
New York	37.9	Baltimore County, MD	43.4	**La Verne, CA** (city) Los Angeles County	48.5
New Mexico	37.8	Santa Cruz County, CA	43.4	**San Dimas, CA** (city) Los Angeles County	48.5
New Jersey	37.3	Marion County, FL	43.3	**Margate, FL** (city) Broward County	46.9
Florida	37.1	Marin County, CA	42.6	**Glendale, CA** (city) Los Angeles County	46.8
Louisiana	37.0	Brevard County, FL	42.1	**Culver City, CA** (city) Los Angeles County	45.8
Michigan	36.9	Ventura County, CA	42.0	**South Gate, CA** (city) Los Angeles County	45.5
Maine	36.3	Nassau County, NY	41.8	**Concord, CA** (city) Contra Costa County	44.5

Sorted by Percent in Ascending Order — U.S. = 36.6

State	Years	County	Years	Place	Years
Utah	29.6	Stafford County, VA	22.0	**Tallahassee, FL** (city) Leon County	22.1
Idaho	30.9	Leon County, FL	22.4	**Columbus, OH** (city) Franklin County	29.3
Oklahoma	31.5	Tompkins County, NY	22.4	**Buffalo, NY** (city) Erie County	29.5
Hawaii	31.8	Alachua County, FL	26.1	**Madison, WI** (city) Dane County	29.5
Alabama	32.4	Hampshire County, MA	26.3	**San Bernardino, CA** (city) San Bernardino County	29.5
Montana	32.5	Utah County, UT	27.4	**Grand Prairie, TX** (city) Dallas County	29.9
New Hampshire	32.8	Weber County, UT	29.0	**Providence, RI** (city) Providence County	30.1
Wisconsin	33.2	Harford County, MD	29.3	**Annandale, VA** (cdp) Fairfax County	30.3
Oregon	33.4	Franklin County, OH	29.7	**Brandon, FL** (cdp) Hillsborough County	30.3
South Carolina	33.4	Oklahoma County, OK	29.7	**Tempe, AZ** (city) Maricopa County	30.4

RANKINGS & COMPARISONS

Note: (1) Ranking tables cover all states and counties, and places with an overall population of at least 125,000, OR an overall population of at least 25,000 where the Hispanic/Latino population is at least 20% of the overall population. In states where less than five places meet either of these criteria, we have included places with at least 10,000 total population with the highest percentage of Hispanic/Latino population. These places are identified with an asterisk (*); Please refer to the User's Guide for a full explanation of data.

Median Age

South American: Bolivian

Top 10 States, Counties, and Places[1]

Sorted by Percent in Descending Order — U.S. = 33.9

State	Years	County	Years	Place	Years
New Mexico	38.6	Ventura County, CA	44.1	**Santa Clarita, CA** (city) Los Angeles County	45.2
California	37.6	Osceola County, FL	41.9	**Glendale, CA** (city) Los Angeles County	43.5
New Jersey	37.0	Queens County, NY	40.5	**Pasadena, CA** (city) Los Angeles County	42.3
New York	36.7	Contra Costa County, CA	40.4	**Chula Vista, CA** (city) San Diego County	41.5
Nevada	35.5	Pinellas County, FL	39.5	**Kendall West, FL** (cdp) Miami-Dade County	41.5
District of Columbia	35.3	Richmond County, NY	39.5	**Queens, NY** (borough) Queens County	40.5
Florida	35.2	Montgomery County, TX	39.4	**Irvine, CA** (city) Orange County	39.8
Texas	34.7	Union County, NJ	39.0	**Elizabeth, NJ** (city) Union County	39.6
Maryland	34.6	Los Angeles County, CA	38.9	**Fountainebleau, FL** (cdp) Miami-Dade County	39.6
Illinois	34.5	Santa Clara County, CA	38.6	**Los Angeles, CA** (city) Los Angeles County	39.5

Sorted by Percent in Ascending Order — U.S. = 33.9

State	Years	County	Years	Place	Years
Arkansas	23.1	Washington County, AR	22.5	**Richmond, VA** (independent city)	22.4
Idaho	24.4	Utah County, UT	25.8	**Philadelphia, PA** (city) Philadelphia County	28.0
Michigan	24.6	Kane County, IL	27.4	**Tucson, AZ** (city) Pima County	29.5
Hawaii	27.9	Hartford County, CT	27.5	**Manassas, VA** (independent city)	29.9
Indiana	28.2	Philadelphia County, PA	28.0	**Jacksonville, FL** (city) Duval County	30.1
Minnesota	28.3	Wake County, NC	28.1	**Cranston*, RI** (city) Providence County	30.6
Alabama	28.4	Will County, IL	28.3	**Boston, MA** (city) Suffolk County	30.7
Iowa	28.5	Baltimore County, MD	29.3	**Dale City, VA** (cdp) Prince William County	30.9
Tennessee	28.9	Norfolk County, MA	29.3	**Brookhaven, NY** (town) Suffolk County	31.0
Utah	28.9	Snohomish County, WA	29.3	**Marumsco, VA** (cdp) Prince William County	31.1

Note: (1) Ranking tables cover all states and counties, and places with an overall population of at least 125,000, OR an overall population of at least 25,000 where the Hispanic/Latino population is at least 20% of the overall population. In states where less than five places meet either of these criteria, we have included places with at least 10,000 total population with the highest percentage of Hispanic/Latino population. These places are identified with an asterisk (*); Please refer to the User's Guide for a full explanation of data.

Median Age

South American: Chilean

Top 10 States, Counties, and Places[1]

Sorted by Percent in Descending Order — U.S. = 36.6

State	Years	County	Years	Place	Years
Florida	40.3	Jefferson Parish, LA	47.0	**Hallandale Beach, FL** (city) Broward County	50.3
New Jersey	38.5	Sarasota County, FL	45.0	**Paterson, NJ** (city) Passaic County	48.8
South Carolina	38.4	Rockland County, NY	43.5	**Tamiami, FL** (cdp) Miami-Dade County	47.9
California	38.1	San Mateo County, CA	43.3	**Kendale Lakes, FL** (cdp) Miami-Dade County	47.8
New York	37.9	Queens County, NY	42.9	**North Miami Beach, FL** (city) Miami-Dade County	47.4
Nevada	37.8	Ulster County, NY	42.5	**San Mateo, CA** (city) San Mateo County	46.5
Texas	36.3	Bronx County, NY	41.7	**Port Chester, NY** (village) Westchester County	46.2
Louisiana	36.2	Polk County, FL	41.5	**Elizabeth, NJ** (city) Union County	45.6
Maryland	36.1	Miami-Dade County, FL	41.3	**Tamarac, FL** (city) Broward County	45.5
New Mexico	36.1	Palm Beach County, FL	41.2	**Fountainebleau, FL** (cdp) Miami-Dade County	45.0

Sorted by Percent in Ascending Order — U.S. = 36.6

State	Years	County	Years	Place	Years
Rhode Island	23.7	Ada County, ID	24.0	**Fontana, CA** (city) San Bernardino County	26.5
Idaho	25.6	Alachua County, FL	25.0	**Minneapolis, MN** (city) Hennepin County	27.9
Iowa	26.7	Providence County, RI	25.3	**Madison, WI** (city) Dane County	28.5
Wisconsin	27.1	Leon County, FL	25.5	**Pittsburgh, PA** (city) Allegheny County	28.5
Montana	27.8	Pierce County, WA	25.5	**New Haven, CT** (city/town) New Haven County	28.9
New Hampshire	27.9	Kent County, MI	26.5	**Milwaukee, WI** (city) Milwaukee County	30.1
Oklahoma	28.0	Wayne County, MI	26.8	**Philadelphia, PA** (city) Philadelphia County	30.2
Vermont	28.1	Dakota County, MN	26.9	**Colorado Springs, CO** (city) El Paso County	30.3
Maine	28.7	Utah County, UT	27.5	**Baltimore, MD** (independent city)	30.6
Minnesota	28.7	Washtenaw County, MI	28.3	**Austin, TX** (city) Travis County	31.3

Note: (1) Ranking tables cover all states and counties, and places with an overall population of at least 125,000, OR an overall population of at least 25,000 where the Hispanic/Latino population is at least 20% of the overall population. In states where less than five places meet either of these criteria, we have included places with at least 10,000 total population with the highest percentage of Hispanic/Latino population. These places are identified with an asterisk (*); Please refer to the User's Guide for a full explanation of data.

Median Age

South American: Colombian

Top 10 States, Counties, and Places[1]

Sorted by Percent in Descending Order — U.S. = 35.6

State	Years	County	Years	Place	Years
Florida	37.7	Sumter County, FL	49.4	**Huntington Park, CA** (city) Los Angeles County	49.1
New York	37.4	Hendry County, FL	47.9	**Palm Desert, CA** (city) Riverside County	46.5
New Jersey	36.4	Highlands County, FL	46.8	**West Little River, FL** (cdp) Miami-Dade County	46.5
California	35.7	Citrus County, FL	45.5	**Laguna Hills, CA** (city) Orange County	45.4
Louisiana	35.0	Clearfield County, PA	44.9	**Kenner, LA** (city) Jefferson Parish	45.3
Nevada	34.8	Rockdale County, GA	44.2	**Diamond Bar, CA** (city) Los Angeles County	44.3
Connecticut	34.6	Charlotte County, FL	43.7	**Hialeah, FL** (city) Miami-Dade County	44.3
Mississippi	34.6	Adams County, MS	43.4	**Atlantic City, NJ** (city) Atlantic County	43.8
New Mexico	34.4	Mahoning County, OH	43.2	**San Rafael, CA** (city) Marin County	43.8
Rhode Island	34.4	Telfair County, GA	43.0	**Westchester, FL** (cdp) Miami-Dade County	43.2

Sorted by Percent in Ascending Order — U.S. = 35.6

State	Years	County	Years	Place	Years
Minnesota	22.3	Niagara County, NY	14.0	**Syracuse, NY** (city) Onondaga County	21.8
North Dakota	24.2	Scott County, MN	14.0	**University, FL** (cdp) Orange County	22.3
Montana	24.6	Anoka County, MN	17.5	**Saint Paul, MN** (city) Ramsey County	22.6
Vermont	25.7	Erie County, NY	19.8	**Tallahassee, FL** (city) Leon County	22.7
South Dakota	26.4	Onondaga County, NY	21.3	**Eugene, OR** (city) Lane County	23.3
Idaho	26.9	Centre County, PA	21.6	**Spokane, WA** (city) Spokane County	23.5
Maine	27.7	Washington County, MN	21.6	**Buffalo, NY** (city) Erie County	24.4
Wisconsin	28.1	Washington County, RI	21.6	**Norfolk, VA** (independent city)	24.4
Hawaii	28.3	Broome County, NY	21.8	**University, FL** (cdp) Hillsborough County	24.7
Wyoming	28.3	Dakota County, MN	21.9	**New Brunswick, NJ** (city) Middlesex County	24.8

Note: (1) Ranking tables cover all states and counties, and places with an overall population of at least 125,000, OR an overall population of at least 25,000 where the Hispanic/Latino population is at least 20% of the overall population. In states where less than five places meet either of these criteria, we have included places with at least 10,000 total population with the highest percentage of Hispanic/Latino population. These places are identified with an asterisk (*); Please refer to the User's Guide for a full explanation of data.

Median Age

South American: Ecuadorian

Top 10 States, Counties, and Places[1]

Sorted by Percent in Descending Order — U.S. = 32.9

State	Years	County	Years	Place	Years
California	38.2	Sarasota County, FL	42.9	**Huntington Park, CA** (city) Los Angeles County	51.0
Florida	37.4	Hernando County, FL	41.4	**Victorville, CA** (city) San Bernardino County	48.3
New Mexico	34.5	Charlotte County, FL	41.2	**La Puente, CA** (city) Los Angeles County	47.5
Nevada	34.2	Los Angeles County, CA	40.6	**El Monte, CA** (city) Los Angeles County	46.5
Texas	33.7	Indian River County, FL	40.5	**East Los Angeles, CA** (cdp) Los Angeles County	45.5
Louisiana	33.2	Jefferson Parish, LA	40.4	**Rowland Heights, CA** (cdp) Los Angeles County	45.5
Maryland	33.2	Marion County, FL	39.2	**Baldwin Park, CA** (city) Los Angeles County	44.9
New Jersey	32.9	Pinellas County, FL	38.9	**Santa Ana, CA** (city) Orange County	44.6
New York	32.7	Brevard County, FL	38.7	**Westchester, FL** (cdp) Miami-Dade County	44.3
South Carolina	32.5	Hidalgo County, TX	38.5	**South Gate, CA** (city) Los Angeles County	44.2

Sorted by Percent in Ascending Order — U.S. = 32.9

State	Years	County	Years	Place	Years
Maine	22.8	Broome County, NY	20.4	**Syracuse, NY** (city) Onondaga County	21.1
Idaho	23.7	Cumberland County, PA	21.7	**Tallahassee, FL** (city) Leon County	22.4
Vermont	23.9	Alachua County, FL	22.0	**Saint Paul, MN** (city) Ramsey County	24.0
Alaska	26.9	Champaign County, IL	22.2	**Dayton, OH** (city) Montgomery County	25.3
Utah	27.1	Onslow County, NC	22.3	**Norfolk, VA** (independent city)	25.7
Michigan	27.3	Washtenaw County, MI	22.4	**Virginia Beach, VA** (independent city)	26.0
Missouri	27.3	Leon County, FL	22.9	**Killeen, TX** (city) Bell County	26.1
West Virginia	27.5	Hampshire County, MA	23.1	**University, FL** (cdp) Orange County	26.3
Alabama	28.2	Johnston County, NC	23.5	**Chesapeake, VA** (independent city)	26.5
Minnesota	28.2	Chatham County, GA	23.9	**Lancaster, PA** (city) Lancaster County	26.6

Note: (1) Ranking tables cover all states and counties, and places with an overall population of at least 125,000, OR an overall population of at least 25,000 where the Hispanic/Latino population is at least 20% of the overall population. In states where less than five places meet either of these criteria, we have included places with at least 10,000 total population with the highest percentage of Hispanic/Latino population. These places are identified with an asterisk (*); Please refer to the User's Guide for a full explanation of data.

Median Age

South American: Paraguayan

Top 10 States, Counties, and Places[1]

Sorted by Percent in Descending Order — U.S. = 30.2

State	Years	County	Years	Place	Years
Nevada	43.0	Clark County, NV	43.5	**Rye, NY** (town) Westchester County	40.0
Florida	34.9	Harris County, TX	36.9	**White Plains, NY** (city) Westchester County	37.5
New York	33.6	Broward County, FL	36.5	**North Hempstead, NY** (town) Nassau County	36.5
California	33.3	Montgomery County, MD	36.4	**Los Angeles, CA** (city) Los Angeles County	35.7
District of Columbia	33.1	Los Angeles County, CA	36.2	**Brooklyn, NY** (borough) Kings County	35.3
New Jersey	33.0	Miami-Dade County, FL	35.9	**Queens, NY** (borough) Queens County	35.2
Maryland	32.4	Westchester County, NY	35.5	**Houston, TX** (city) Harris County	34.8
Virginia	31.0	Kings County, NY	35.3	**New York, NY** (city)	34.6
Texas	30.9	Queens County, NY	35.2	**Arlington, VA** (cdp) Arlington County	33.8
Oregon	28.5	Dallas County, TX	34.8	**Miami, FL** (city) Miami-Dade County	32.9

Sorted by Percent in Ascending Order — U.S. = 30.2

State	Years	County	Years	Place	Years
Minnesota	18.2	Middlesex County, MA	20.4	**Chicago, IL** (city) Cook County	27.4
Wisconsin	19.1	Cook County, IL	25.9	**Hempstead (town), NY** (town) Nassau County	28.8
South Carolina	19.5	Maricopa County, AZ	26.3	**Manhattan, NY** (borough) New York County	29.8
Alabama	20.3	New York County, NY	29.8	**Bronx, NY** (borough) Bronx County	32.3
Ohio	20.4	Prince George's County, MD	29.8	**Miami, FL** (city) Miami-Dade County	32.9
Tennessee	21.0	Suffolk County, NY	29.8	**Arlington, VA** (cdp) Arlington County	33.8
Massachusetts	21.1	Fairfield County, CT	30.5	**New York, NY** (city)	34.6
Michigan	21.7	Morris County, NJ	31.1	**Houston, TX** (city) Harris County	34.8
Pennsylvania	21.9	San Diego County, CA	32.0	**Queens, NY** (borough) Queens County	35.2
Illinois	22.0	Bronx County, NY	32.3	**Brooklyn, NY** (borough) Kings County	35.3

Note: (1) Ranking tables cover all states and counties, and places with an overall population of at least 125,000, OR an overall population of at least 25,000 where the Hispanic/Latino population is at least 20% of the overall population. In states where less than five places meet either of these criteria, we have included places with at least 10,000 total population with the highest percentage of Hispanic/Latino population. These places are identified with an asterisk (*); Please refer to the User's Guide for a full explanation of data.

Median Age

South American: Peruvian

Top 10 States, Counties, and Places[1]

Sorted by Percent in Descending Order — U.S. = 36.4

State	Years	County	Years	Place	Years
Florida	38.7	Cameron County, TX	43.8	**Huntington Park, CA** (city) Los Angeles County	46.5
California	37.7	Hernando County, FL	42.9	**Palm Springs, CA** (city) Riverside County	46.3
New York	37.7	Flagler County, FL	40.7	**Westchester, FL** (cdp) Miami-Dade County	45.9
Nevada	36.8	Miami-Dade County, FL	40.4	**San Dimas, CA** (city) Los Angeles County	45.0
New Jersey	36.5	Nueces County, TX	40.3	**South Gate, CA** (city) Los Angeles County	44.3
District of Columbia	36.4	Queens County, NY	40.3	**Salinas, CA** (city) Monterey County	44.1
Connecticut	35.8	Martin County, FL	39.5	**Carson, CA** (city) Los Angeles County	43.6
Delaware	35.6	Arlington County, VA	39.4	**Glendale, CA** (city) Los Angeles County	43.3
Texas	35.6	Monterey County, CA	39.4	**Glendora, CA** (city) Los Angeles County	43.3
Wyoming	35.5	Los Angeles County, CA	39.3	**Margate, FL** (city) Broward County	43.3

Sorted by Percent in Ascending Order — U.S. = 36.4

State	Years	County	Years	Place	Years
Vermont	26.9	Centre County, PA	21.3	**University, FL** (cdp) Orange County	21.5
Montana	27.1	Hampshire County, MA	21.7	**Tallahassee, FL** (city) Leon County	22.8
Alaska	28.4	Montgomery County, VA	21.7	**Norfolk, VA** (independent city)	25.2
New Hampshire	28.4	Tompkins County, NY	22.3	**Vancouver, WA** (city) Clark County	26.7
Maine	29.6	Alachua County, FL	22.9	**Denton, TX** (city) Denton County	26.8
Iowa	30.0	Leon County, FL	23.5	**Richmond, VA** (independent city)	26.8
Missouri	30.1	Onslow County, NC	23.8	**Killeen, TX** (city) Bell County	26.9
Kansas	30.3	Saint Charles County, MO	24.5	**Salem, OR** (city) Marion County	27.0
Utah	30.5	Whatcom County, WA	24.5	**University, FL** (cdp) Hillsborough County	27.8
Wisconsin	30.6	Larimer County, CO	25.0	**Fayetteville, NC** (city) Cumberland County	28.6

Note: (1) Ranking tables cover all states and counties, and places with an overall population of at least 125,000, OR an overall population of at least 25,000 where the Hispanic/Latino population is at least 20% of the overall population. In states where less than five places meet either of these criteria, we have included places with at least 10,000 total population with the highest percentage of Hispanic/Latino population. These places are identified with an asterisk (*); Please refer to the User's Guide for a full explanation of data.

Median Age

South American: Uruguayan

Top 10 States, Counties, and Places[1]

Sorted by Percent in Descending Order — U.S. = 36.1

State	Years	County	Years	Place	Years
Arizona	39.9	Pinellas County, FL	51.0	**Oyster Bay, NY** (town) Nassau County	46.0
California	39.8	Santa Clara County, CA	43.6	**Sunrise, FL** (city) Broward County	45.5
New York	39.4	Nassau County, NY	43.3	**The Hammocks, FL** (cdp) Miami-Dade County	45.2
New Hampshire	38.6	Ocean County, NJ	43.1	**Aventura, FL** (city) Miami-Dade County	42.0
Louisiana	38.4	Monmouth County, NJ	41.5	**Hempstead (town), NY** (town) Nassau County	41.9
Colorado	38.3	Queens County, NY	41.5	**Queens, NY** (borough) Queens County	41.5
Florida	37.3	Bergen County, NJ	41.3	**Bronx, NY** (borough) Bronx County	41.0
Nevada	37.1	Bronx County, NY	41.0	**Manchester*, NH** (city) Hillsborough County	40.7
District of Columbia	37.0	Riverside County, CA	40.8	**Weston, FL** (city) Broward County	40.7
Oregon	37.0	San Bernardino County, CA	40.8	**West New York, NJ** (town) Hudson County	40.5

Sorted by Percent in Ascending Order — U.S. = 36.1

State	Years	County	Years	Place	Years
Missouri	29.8	Clayton County, GA	28.6	**Charlotte, NC** (city) Mecklenburg County	30.5
Wisconsin	31.5	Utah County, UT	29.5	**Hilton Head Island*, SC** (town) Beaufort County	30.5
South Carolina	32.0	Lackawanna County, PA	29.8	**Fitchburg, MA** (city) Worcester County	31.3
North Carolina	32.4	Wake County, NC	30.4	**Raleigh, NC** (city) Wake County	31.5
Massachusetts	32.6	Beaufort County, SC	30.5	**Kearny, NJ** (town) Hudson County	32.8
Minnesota	32.6	Dane County, WI	30.5	**Jacksonville, FL** (city) Duval County	33.3
Georgia	33.0	Mecklenburg County, NC	30.6	**Orlando, FL** (city) Orange County	33.3
Utah	33.0	Henry County, GA	31.1	**Elizabeth, NJ** (city) Union County	33.4
Pennsylvania	33.3	Fulton County, GA	31.8	**Bloomfield, NJ** (township) Essex County	33.6
Rhode Island	34.4	Worcester County, MA	31.9	**Philadelphia, PA** (city) Philadelphia County	34.0

Note: (1) Ranking tables cover all states and counties, and places with an overall population of at least 125,000, OR an overall population of at least 25,000 where the Hispanic/Latino population is at least 20% of the overall population. In states where less than five places meet either of these criteria, we have included places with at least 10,000 total population with the highest percentage of Hispanic/Latino population. These places are identified with an asterisk (*); Please refer to the User's Guide for a full explanation of data.

Median Age

South American: Venezuelan

Top 10 States, Counties, and Places[1]

Sorted by Percent in Descending Order U.S. = 33.4

State	Years	County	Years	Place	Years
Nevada	35.1	Marin County, CA	38.6	**Oyster Bay, NY** (town) Nassau County	40.1
New Hampshire	35.1	Monroe County, FL	38.0	**Oakland Park, FL** (city) Broward County	39.6
Florida	34.5	Rockland County, NY	37.4	**Hallandale Beach, FL** (city) Broward County	38.1
Delaware	34.1	Pinellas County, FL	36.6	**Miami Beach, FL** (city) Miami-Dade County	37.6
New Mexico	34.0	Cobb County, GA	36.3	**Kendall, FL** (cdp) Miami-Dade County	37.4
California	33.9	Ocean County, NJ	36.0	**Ocoee, FL** (city) Orange County	37.3
Texas	33.5	San Joaquin County, CA	35.9	**Cooper City, FL** (city) Broward County	37.1
Maryland	33.4	Fayette County, KY	35.8	**Las Vegas, NV** (city) Clark County	37.0
Georgia	33.2	Broward County, FL	35.5	**Coral Gables, FL** (city) Miami-Dade County	36.7
District of Columbia	32.8	Hamilton County, IN	35.5	**Pembroke Pines, FL** (city) Broward County	36.7

Sorted by Percent in Ascending Order U.S. = 33.4

State	Years	County	Years	Place	Years
Maine	26.0	Brazos County, TX	22.3	**University, FL** (cdp) Orange County	22.2
Idaho	26.3	Alachua County, FL	22.7	**Tallahassee, FL** (city) Leon County	22.3
West Virginia	28.0	Leon County, FL	23.3	**Providence, RI** (city) Providence County	25.8
Iowa	28.2	Orange County, NC	24.0	**Baton Rouge, LA** (city) East Baton Rouge Parish	26.6
Utah	28.3	Utah County, UT	26.5	**West Valley City, UT** (city) Salt Lake County	26.8
Rhode Island	28.4	Butler County, OH	27.6	**Boston, MA** (city) Suffolk County	27.5
Arkansas	28.8	Cleveland County, OK	27.8	**Clifton, NJ** (city) Passaic County	27.5
Kansas	29.8	East Baton Rouge Parish, LA	27.8	**Colorado Springs, CO** (city) El Paso County	27.9
Massachusetts	29.9	Suffolk County, MA	27.9	**Tucson, AZ** (city) Pima County	27.9
Nebraska	30.4	Providence County, RI	28.1	**Brentwood, NY** (cdp) Suffolk County	28.1

Note: (1) Ranking tables cover all states and counties, and places with an overall population of at least 125,000, OR an overall population of at least 25,000 where the Hispanic/Latino population is at least 20% of the overall population. In states where less than five places meet either of these criteria, we have included places with at least 10,000 total population with the highest percentage of Hispanic/Latino population. These places are identified with an asterisk (*); Please refer to the User's Guide for a full explanation of data.

Median Age

Spaniard

Top 10 States, Counties, and Places[1]

Sorted by Percent in Descending Order — U.S. = 35.2

State	Years	County	Years	Place	Years
Vermont	42.4	Charlotte County, FL	57.2	**Westchester, FL** (cdp) Miami-Dade County	60.9
Florida	41.6	Washington County, VT	55.6	**University Park, FL** (cdp) Miami-Dade County	58.3
Louisiana	41.0	Citrus County, FL	55.1	**Hallandale Beach, FL** (city) Broward County	54.0
West Virginia	40.1	Flagler County, FL	54.8	**Egypt Lake-Leto, FL** (cdp) Hillsborough County	53.7
New Jersey	39.6	Calaveras County, CA	53.2	**Fountainebleau, FL** (cdp) Miami-Dade County	53.2
Maine	38.9	Gila County, AZ	52.6	**Hialeah, FL** (city) Miami-Dade County	52.8
New York	37.3	Costilla County, CO	52.5	**Tamiami, FL** (cdp) Miami-Dade County	51.5
California	36.8	Chaffee County, CO	51.5	**New Britain, CT** (city/town) Hartford County	50.8
Nevada	36.2	Harrison County, WV	51.0	**Montebello, CA** (city) Los Angeles County	50.5
Connecticut	35.8	Iberia Parish, LA	50.8	**Kendale Lakes, FL** (cdp) Miami-Dade County	49.6

Sorted by Percent in Ascending Order — U.S. = 35.2

State	Years	County	Years	Place	Years
North Dakota	24.9	Pulaski County, MO	21.4	**Hempstead (village), NY** (village) Nassau County	18.5
Iowa	27.2	Brazos County, TX	21.9	**Trenton, NJ** (city) Mercer County	19.8
Rhode Island	27.8	Montgomery County, VA	21.9	**Chelsea, MA** (city) Suffolk County	20.5
Nebraska	27.9	McLean County, IL	22.3	**Waianae*, HI** (cdp) Honolulu County	21.0
Oklahoma	28.3	Centre County, PA	22.5	**New Brunswick, NJ** (city) Middlesex County	21.1
Kansas	28.5	Payne County, OK	22.6	**Fort Hood, TX** (cdp) Bell County	21.5
Hawaii	29.0	Onslow County, NC	22.8	**Rogers, AR** (city) Benton County	21.8
Utah	29.4	Tompkins County, NY	23.0	**San Marcos, TX** (city) Hays County	21.9
Wisconsin	29.4	Clayton County, GA	23.1	**Providence, RI** (city) Providence County	22.7
Alaska	29.6	Saint Joseph County, IN	23.1	**Lincoln, NE** (city) Lancaster County	23.3

Note: (1) Ranking tables cover all states and counties, and places with an overall population of at least 125,000, OR an overall population of at least 25,000 where the Hispanic/Latino population is at least 20% of the overall population. In states where less than five places meet either of these criteria, we have included places with at least 10,000 total population with the highest percentage of Hispanic/Latino population. These places are identified with an asterisk (*); Please refer to the User's Guide for a full explanation of data.

High School Graduates

(Universe: Population 25 Years and Over)

Total Population

Top 10 States, Counties, and Places[1]

Sorted by Number in Descending Order — U.S. = 169,828,176

State	Number	County	Number	Place	Number
California	18,958,197	Los Angeles County, CA	4,757,060	**New York, NY** (city)	4,314,755
Texas	12,095,373	Cook County, IL	2,840,274	**Los Angeles, CA** (city) Los Angeles County	1,809,429
Florida	10,908,069	Maricopa County, AZ	2,033,854	**Chicago, IL** (city) Cook County	1,403,628
New York	10,905,648	Harris County, TX	1,889,271	**Brooklyn, NY** (borough) Kings County	1,254,863
Pennsylvania	7,481,469	San Diego County, CA	1,659,690	**Queens, NY** (borough) Queens County	1,221,800
Illinois	7,194,979	Orange County, CA	1,608,460	**Manhattan, NY** (borough) New York County	987,572
Ohio	6,693,408	Miami-Dade County, FL	1,274,809	**Houston, TX** (city) Harris County	964,136
Michigan	5,776,855	Kings County, NY	1,254,863	**Philadelphia, PA** (city) Philadelphia County	766,202
New Jersey	5,139,449	Queens County, NY	1,221,800	**San Diego, CA** (city) San Diego County	721,897
North Carolina	5,115,556	King County, WA	1,194,622	**Phoenix, AZ** (city) Maricopa County	706,360

Sorted by Number in Ascending Order — U.S. = 169,828,176

State	Number	County	Number	Place	Number
Wyoming	326,862	Kenedy County, TX	110	**Lexington*, NE** (city) Dawson County	3,149
District of Columbia	345,504	Clark County, ID	392	**Parker*, SC** (cdp) Greenville County	3,853
North Dakota	383,914	Terrell County, TX	508	**Jerome*, ID** (city) Jerome County	3,873
Vermont	386,164	Harding County, NM	509	**Storm Lake*, IA** (city) Buena Vista County	3,982
Alaska	390,034	Kent County, TX	510	**Burley*, ID** (city) Cassia County	4,228
South Dakota	462,612	McMullen County, TX	510	**Hope*, AR** (city) Hempstead County	4,262
Delaware	511,757	Sterling County, TX	581	**Fort Leonard Wood*, MO** (cdp) Pulaski County	4,362
Rhode Island	592,800	Glasscock County, TX	600	**Fort Campbell North*, KY** (cdp) Christian County	4,400
Montana	594,992	Esmeralda County, NV	638	**Guymon*, OK** (city) Texas County	4,550
Hawaii	811,365	Motley County, TX	664	**Schofield Barracks*, HI** (cdp) Honolulu County	4,645

Sorted by Percent in Descending Order — U.S. = 85.0%

State	Percent	County	Percent	Place	Percent
Minnesota	91.3	Los Alamos County, NM	99.3	**Bozeman*, MT** (city) Gallatin County	97.2
Wyoming	91.3	Douglas County, CO	97.6	**Hanover*, NH** (town) Grafton County	97.1
Montana	91.0	Clear Creek County, CO	96.9	**Schofield Barracks*, HI** (cdp) Honolulu County	97.0
New Hampshire	90.9	Morgan County, UT	96.9	**Naperville, IL** (city) DuPage County	96.6
Alaska	90.7	Routt County, CO	96.8	**Overland Park, KS** (city) Johnson County	96.5
Utah	90.6	Elbert County, CO	96.1	**Irvine, CA** (city) Orange County	96.4
Vermont	90.6	Hamilton County, IN	96.1	**Sahuarita, AZ** (town) Pima County	96.4
Nebraska	90.0	Pitkin County, CO	96.1	**Fort Leonard Wood*, MO** (cdp) Pulaski County	96.0
Iowa	89.9	Gallatin County, MT	96.0	**Weston, FL** (city) Broward County	95.9
Hawaii	89.8	Washington County, MN	95.7	**Scottsdale, AZ** (city) Maricopa County	95.6

Sorted by Percent in Ascending Order — U.S. = 85.0%

State	Percent	County	Percent	Place	Percent
Mississippi	79.6	Starr County, TX	47.9	**Florence-Graham, CA** (cdp) Los Angeles County	40.5
Texas	80.0	Hudspeth County, TX	50.5	**Maywood, CA** (city) Los Angeles County	40.9
California	80.7	Reeves County, TX	52.8	**Bell Gardens, CA** (city) Los Angeles County	42.1
Kentucky	81.0	Brooks County, TX	53.7	**Huntington Park, CA** (city) Los Angeles County	42.2
Louisiana	81.0	Presidio County, TX	53.7	**Bell, CA** (city) Los Angeles County	42.3
Alabama	81.4	Maverick County, TX	55.2	**East Los Angeles, CA** (cdp) Los Angeles County	44.3
Arkansas	81.9	Holmes County, OH	56.3	**Coachella, CA** (city) Riverside County	45.3
West Virginia	81.9	Zapata County, TX	56.7	**San Luis, AZ** (city) Yuma County	45.3
Tennessee	82.5	Willacy County, TX	57.4	**Lynwood, CA** (city) Los Angeles County	49.7
New Mexico	82.7	Clinton County, KY	57.5	**Delano, CA** (city) Kern County	50.6

Note: (1) Ranking tables cover all states and counties, and places with an overall population of at least 125,000, OR an overall population of at least 25,000 where the Hispanic/Latino population is at least 20% of the overall population. In states where less than five places meet either of these criteria, we have included places with at least 10,000 total population with the highest percentage of Hispanic/Latino population. These places are identified with an asterisk (*); Please refer to the User's Guide for a full explanation of data.

High School Graduates

(Universe: Population 25 Years and Over)

Hispanic or Latino (of any race)

Top 10 States, Counties, and Places[1]

Sorted by Number in Descending Order — U.S. = 15,729,225

State	Number	County	Number	Place	Number
California	4,060,139	Los Angeles County, CA	1,384,409	**New York, NY** (city)	867,402
Texas	2,743,095	Miami-Dade County, FL	809,256	**Los Angeles, CA** (city) Los Angeles County	493,910
Florida	1,853,026	Harris County, TX	432,430	**San Antonio, TX** (city) Bexar County	320,535
New York	1,250,438	Bexar County, TX	385,169	**Queens, NY** (borough) Queens County	258,592
Illinois	602,728	Cook County, IL	381,481	**Bronx, NY** (borough) Bronx County	241,009
New Jersey	597,803	Maricopa County, AZ	314,345	**Chicago, IL** (city) Cook County	235,015
Arizona	565,554	San Diego County, CA	306,278	**Houston, TX** (city) Harris County	228,927
New Mexico	364,439	San Bernardino County, CA	292,100	**El Paso, TX** (city) El Paso County	196,406
Colorado	331,389	Orange County, CA	291,128	**Brooklyn, NY** (borough) Kings County	171,983
Georgia	223,237	Riverside County, CA	272,294	**Manhattan, NY** (borough) New York County	162,831

Sorted by Number in Ascending Order — U.S. = 15,729,225

State	Number	County	Number	Place	Number
Vermont	4,287	Thurston County, NE	26	**Morgantown*, WV** (city) Monongalia County	251
North Dakota	4,411	Mahaska County, IA	34	**Mayfield*, KY** (city) Graves County	288
South Dakota	6,428	Yellow Medicine County, MN	34	**Brookside*, DE** (cdp) New Castle County	315
Maine	6,558	Benzie County, MI	36	**Albertville*, AL** (city) Marshall County	319
West Virginia	8,139	Hughes County, OK	36	**College*, AK** (cdp) Fairbanks North Star Borough	323
Montana	10,670	Buffalo County, WI	37	**Burlington*, VT** (city) Chittenden County	324
New Hampshire	13,823	West Carroll Parish, LA	45	**Shelbyville*, KY** (city) Shelby County	354
Alaska	14,451	Iowa County, WI	48	**Storm Lake*, IA** (city) Buena Vista County	355
Wyoming	17,802	Jackson County, MN	48	**Jerome*, ID** (city) Jerome County	366
Delaware	19,189	Lafayette County, WI	49	**Warr Acres*, OK** (city) Oklahoma County	388

Sorted by Percent in Descending Order — U.S. = 61.5%

State	Percent	County	Percent	Place	Percent
Vermont	91.0	Orleans County, VT	100.0	**Fort Leonard Wood*, MO** (cdp) Pulaski County	100.0
Hawaii	86.8	Warren County, PA	100.0	**Makakilo*, HI** (cdp) Honolulu County	97.0
Montana	83.3	Nodaway County, MO	99.2	**Bozeman*, MT** (city) Gallatin County	96.9
Maine	81.9	McDonough County, IL	99.0	**Schofield Barracks*, HI** (cdp) Honolulu County	96.2
New Hampshire	79.8	Meade County, SD	98.9	**Weston, FL** (city) Broward County	95.4
North Dakota	77.4	Washington County, VT	98.8	**Doral, FL** (city) Miami-Dade County	95.0
Alaska	76.7	Woodford County, IL	98.5	**Fort Campbell North*, KY** (cdp) Christian County	94.5
Wyoming	74.2	Jackson County, KS	98.2	**Missoula*, MT** (city) Missoula County	94.3
Florida	73.9	Elbert County, CO	97.1	**Coconut Creek, FL** (city) Broward County	93.5
West Virginia	73.2	Cabell County, WV	97.0	**Coral Gables, FL** (city) Miami-Dade County	92.9

Sorted by Percent in Ascending Order — U.S. = 61.5%

State	Percent	County	Percent	Place	Percent
Arkansas	49.0	Hughes County, OK	14.4	**Albertville*, AL** (city) Marshall County	16.2
Nebraska	51.8	Evans County, GA	14.6	**Carthage*, MO** (city) Jasper County	21.8
Idaho	53.1	Camp County, TX	15.2	**Storm Lake*, IA** (city) Buena Vista County	22.5
North Carolina	53.2	Ashe County, NC	16.3	**Jerome*, ID** (city) Jerome County	25.3
Oregon	55.1	Todd County, MN	17.0	**Worthington*, MN** (city) Nobles County	28.9
Alabama	55.5	Harmon County, OK	18.7	**Lexington*, NE** (city) Dawson County	29.5
Iowa	55.5	Berrien County, GA	18.8	**Dalton, GA** (city) Whitfield County	32.2
Georgia	56.1	Bradley County, AR	19.0	**Florence-Graham, CA** (cdp) Los Angeles County	34.3
Oklahoma	56.1	Fremont County, ID	19.5	**Sanford, NC** (city) Lee County	34.4
Tennessee	56.9	Cuming County, NE	19.9	**Bridgeton, NJ** (city) Cumberland County	34.8

Note: (1) Ranking tables cover all states and counties, and places with an overall population of at least 125,000, OR an overall population of at least 25,000 where the Hispanic/Latino population is at least 20% of the overall population. In states where less than five places meet either of these criteria, we have included places with at least 10,000 total population with the highest percentage of Hispanic/Latino population. These places are identified with an asterisk (*); Please refer to the User's Guide for a full explanation of data.

High School Graduates

(Universe: Population 25 Years and Over)

Central American, excluding Mexican

Top 10 States, Counties, and Places[1]

Sorted by Number in Descending Order — U.S. = 1,229,291

State	Number	County	Number	Place	Number
California	383,210	Los Angeles County, CA	217,040	**Los Angeles, CA** (city) Los Angeles County	117,139
Florida	171,797	Miami-Dade County, FL	96,036	**New York, NY** (city)	61,977
New York	114,288	Harris County, TX	47,883	**Houston, TX** (city) Harris County	28,945
Texas	105,525	Montgomery County, MD	21,985	**Miami, FL** (city) Miami-Dade County	24,251
New Jersey	54,395	Queens County, NY	20,671	**Queens, NY** (borough) Queens County	20,671
Virginia	52,408	Kings County, NY	19,854	**Brooklyn, NY** (borough) Kings County	19,854
Maryland	48,867	San Bernardino County, CA	19,459	**San Francisco, CA** (city) San Francisco County	13,429
Massachusetts	29,733	Suffolk County, NY	19,337	**Bronx, NY** (borough) Bronx County	12,583
Georgia	26,215	Broward County, FL	18,069	**Hempstead (town), NY** (town) Nassau County	11,974
Illinois	26,021	Cook County, IL	17,981	**Chicago, IL** (city) Cook County	11,674

Sorted by Number in Ascending Order — U.S. = 1,229,291

State	Number	County	Number	Place	Number
Vermont	228	Caroline County, MD	17	**Albertville*, AL** (city) Marshall County	59
Maine	296	Colfax County, NE	19	**Worthington*, MN** (city) Nobles County	79
Wyoming	428	Cass County, IN	32	**Garden City, KS** (city) Finney County	82
South Dakota	507	Gilmer County, GA	38	**Lexington*, NE** (city) Dawson County	86
West Virginia	521	Franklin County, AL	62	**Carthage*, MO** (city) Jasper County	118
Alaska	862	Carroll County, AR	70	**Cincinnati, OH** (city) Hamilton County	125
New Hampshire	994	Nobles County, MN	79	**Gainesville, GA** (city) Hall County	158
Idaho	1,099	Finney County, KS	82	**Santa Maria, CA** (city) Santa Barbara County	169
Hawaii	1,140	Wapello County, IA	83	**Palm Springs, CA** (city) Riverside County	172
Delaware	1,431	Madera County, CA	105	**Knoxville, TN** (city) Knox County	180

Sorted by Percent in Descending Order — U.S. = 53.1%

State	Percent	County	Percent	Place	Percent
Hawaii	80.3	Douglas County, CO	95.7	**Fayetteville, NC** (city) Cumberland County	95.3
Vermont	76.8	Kitsap County, WA	91.3	**Doral, FL** (city) Miami-Dade County	94.9
Wisconsin	71.9	Dane County, WI	89.3	**Weston, FL** (city) Broward County	94.5
New Mexico	66.7	Allegheny County, PA	89.0	**Miami Lakes, FL** (town) Miami-Dade County	94.0
Louisiana	66.5	Honolulu County, HI	88.9	**Plantation, FL** (city) Broward County	93.2
New Hampshire	65.5	Thurston County, WA	87.4	**Murrieta, CA** (city) Riverside County	92.1
Wyoming	65.5	Clay County, FL	86.4	**Coral Springs, FL** (city) Broward County	90.9
West Virginia	64.9	Bell County, TX	86.3	**Coral Gables, FL** (city) Miami-Dade County	90.4
Utah	64.8	Clark County, WA	85.3	**Newport News, VA** (independent city)	90.3
Illinois	64.4	Saint Louis County, MO	85.1	**Killeen, TX** (city) Bell County	89.8

Sorted by Percent in Ascending Order — U.S. = 53.1%

State	Percent	County	Percent	Place	Percent
Arkansas	33.9	Colfax County, NE	5.9	**Albertville*, AL** (city) Marshall County	7.8
Nebraska	35.6	Caroline County, MD	7.4	**Gainesville, GA** (city) Hall County	11.8
Delaware	38.1	Cass County, IN	9.5	**Carthage*, MO** (city) Jasper County	13.2
District of Columbia	38.6	Franklin County, AL	10.5	**Worthington*, MN** (city) Nobles County	13.9
Iowa	40.3	Gilmer County, GA	11.7	**Garden City, KS** (city) Finney County	14.3
Alabama	41.1	Nobles County, MN	13.1	**Cincinnati, OH** (city) Hamilton County	14.5
South Dakota	41.1	Finney County, KS	13.9	**Lexington*, NE** (city) Dawson County	15.3
Rhode Island	43.3	Jasper County, MO	14.3	**Grand Rapids, MI** (city) Kent County	18.3
Texas	43.5	Madera County, CA	14.7	**Richmond, VA** (independent city)	21.7
Georgia	44.1	Carroll County, AR	19.9	**Springdale, AR** (city) Washington County	22.0

Note: (1) Ranking tables cover all states and counties, and places with an overall population of at least 125,000, OR an overall population of at least 25,000 where the Hispanic/Latino population is at least 20% of the overall population. In states where less than five places meet either of these criteria, we have included places with at least 10,000 total population with the highest percentage of Hispanic/Latino population. These places are identified with an asterisk (*); Please refer to the User's Guide for a full explanation of data.

High School Graduates

(Universe: Population 25 Years and Over)

Central American: Costa Rican

Top 10 States, Counties, and Places[1]

Sorted by Number in Descending Order — U.S. = 62,430

State	Number	County	Number	Place	Number
California	12,067	Los Angeles County, CA	5,228	**New York, NY** (city)	3,473
Florida	10,447	Miami-Dade County, FL	4,127	**Los Angeles, CA** (city) Los Angeles County	1,650
New Jersey	7,825	Union County, NJ	1,714	**Brooklyn, NY** (borough) Kings County	1,249
New York	6,045	Broward County, FL	1,510	**Queens, NY** (borough) Queens County	1,051
Texas	3,347	Kings County, NY	1,249	**Miami, FL** (city) Miami-Dade County	830
Massachusetts	2,193	Orange County, CA	1,181	**Philadelphia, PA** (city) Philadelphia County	436
North Carolina	2,123	Queens County, NY	1,051	**Bronx, NY** (borough) Bronx County	423
Pennsylvania	1,751	Harris County, TX	1,008		
Georgia	1,681	Somerset County, NJ	989		
Maryland	1,381	Bergen County, NJ	964		

Sorted by Number in Ascending Order — U.S. = 62,430

State	Number	County	Number	Place	Number
Michigan	328	Mercer County, NJ	290	**Bronx, NY** (borough) Bronx County	423
Wisconsin	338	Bronx County, NY	423	**Philadelphia, PA** (city) Philadelphia County	436
Tennessee	386	Philadelphia County, PA	436	**Miami, FL** (city) Miami-Dade County	830
Oregon	436	Orange County, FL	460	**Queens, NY** (borough) Queens County	1,051
Minnesota	489	Clark County, NV	545	**Brooklyn, NY** (borough) Kings County	1,249
Colorado	544	Nassau County, NY	578	**Los Angeles, CA** (city) Los Angeles County	1,650
Washington	618	Contra Costa County, CA	596	**New York, NY** (city)	3,473
Louisiana	779	Essex County, NJ	625		
Nevada	806	Fairfield County, CT	657		
Arizona	863	Maricopa County, AZ	676		

Sorted by Percent in Descending Order — U.S. = 79.4%

State	Percent	County	Percent	Place	Percent
Washington	97.8	Contra Costa County, CA	100.0	**Los Angeles, CA** (city) Los Angeles County	83.8
Minnesota	94.2	Maricopa County, AZ	96.6	**Miami, FL** (city) Miami-Dade County	81.5
Arizona	92.6	Riverside County, CA	91.8	**New York, NY** (city)	76.6
Wisconsin	90.6	San Diego County, CA	88.4	**Brooklyn, NY** (borough) Kings County	74.6
Massachusetts	88.6	Orange County, CA	87.0	**Queens, NY** (borough) Queens County	74.6
Maryland	86.3	Harris County, TX	83.7	**Bronx, NY** (borough) Bronx County	65.8
Tennessee	85.4	Suffolk County, NY	83.7	**Philadelphia, PA** (city) Philadelphia County	59.1
California	85.2	Broward County, FL	83.1		
Colorado	85.1	Miami-Dade County, FL	82.8		
Michigan	84.8	Los Angeles County, CA	82.4		

Sorted by Percent in Ascending Order — U.S. = 79.4%

State	Percent	County	Percent	Place	Percent
New Jersey	64.6	Mercer County, NJ	34.7	**Philadelphia, PA** (city) Philadelphia County	59.1
Connecticut	74.0	Essex County, NJ	55.3	**Bronx, NY** (borough) Bronx County	65.8
Georgia	74.4	Philadelphia County, PA	59.1	**Brooklyn, NY** (borough) Kings County	74.6
North Carolina	74.6	Morris County, NJ	59.2	**Queens, NY** (borough) Queens County	74.6
Nevada	74.8	Orange County, FL	62.4	**New York, NY** (city)	76.6
South Carolina	74.8	Bronx County, NY	65.8	**Miami, FL** (city) Miami-Dade County	81.5
Louisiana	76.1	Palm Beach County, FL	66.8	**Los Angeles, CA** (city) Los Angeles County	83.8
Pennsylvania	77.0	Somerset County, NJ	69.0		
New York	78.4	Union County, NJ	70.2		
Florida	80.0	Passaic County, NJ	73.2		

Note: (1) Ranking tables cover all states and counties, and places with an overall population of at least 125,000, OR an overall population of at least 25,000 where the Hispanic/Latino population is at least 20% of the overall population. In states where less than five places meet either of these criteria, we have included places with at least 10,000 total population with the highest percentage of Hispanic/Latino population. These places are identified with an asterisk (*); Please refer to the User's Guide for a full explanation of data.

High School Graduates

(Universe: Population 25 Years and Over)

Central American: Guatemalan

Top 10 States, Counties, and Places[1]

Sorted by Number in Descending Order — U.S. = 261,380

State	Number	County	Number	Place	Number
California	94,581	Los Angeles County, CA	60,346	**Los Angeles, CA** (city) Los Angeles County	34,064
Florida	20,888	Cook County, IL	9,999	**New York, NY** (city)	9,562
New York	20,327	Harris County, TX	6,867	**Chicago, IL** (city) Cook County	6,593
Texas	15,276	Miami-Dade County, FL	6,798	**Houston, TX** (city) Harris County	4,771
Illinois	12,956	San Bernardino County, CA	4,641	**Queens, NY** (borough) Queens County	4,273
New Jersey	12,135	Orange County, CA	4,632	**Providence, RI** (city) Providence County	2,538
Massachusetts	9,635	Queens County, NY	4,273	**Stamford, CT** (city/town) Fairfield County	2,464
Maryland	7,824	Providence County, RI	4,130	**Brooklyn, NY** (borough) Kings County	2,459
Virginia	7,402	Clark County, NV	4,081	**San Francisco, CA** (city) San Francisco County	2,136
Georgia	6,233	Riverside County, CA	4,037	**Miami, FL** (city) Miami-Dade County	1,805

Sorted by Number in Ascending Order — U.S. = 261,380

State	Number	County	Number	Place	Number
New Hampshire	205	Caroline County, MD	12	**Lexington*, NE** (city) Dawson County	41
Idaho	263	Nobles County, MN	21	**Albertville*, AL** (city) Marshall County	46
South Dakota	280	Gilmer County, GA	38	**Cincinnati, OH** (city) Hamilton County	61
Mississippi	327	Franklin County, AL	62	**Carthage*, MO** (city) Jasper County	87
Wisconsin	510	Dawson County, NE	68	**Durham, NC** (city) Durham County	89
District of Columbia	543	Durham County, NC	89	**Chattanooga, TN** (city) Hamilton County	123
Kentucky	565	DeKalb County, AL	94	**Omaha, NE** (city) Douglas County	128
Missouri	611	Pinal County, AZ	95	**Westmont, CA** (cdp) Los Angeles County	150
Kansas	697	Jasper County, MO	96	**Cathedral City, CA** (city) Riverside County	171
Delaware	721	Lee County, AL	107	**Mesa, AZ** (city) Maricopa County	183

Sorted by Percent in Descending Order — U.S. = 45.5%

State	Percent	County	Percent	Place	Percent
Wisconsin	68.4	Osceola County, FL	81.6	**Burbank, CA** (city) Los Angeles County	79.9
Louisiana	65.8	Morris County, NJ	74.9	**Downey, CA** (city) Los Angeles County	79.1
New Mexico	64.6	Norfolk County, MA	72.0	**Garden Grove, CA** (city) Orange County	75.9
Illinois	64.1	Loudoun County, VA	71.7	**Brookhaven, NY** (town) Suffolk County	75.3
Utah	62.7	Stanislaus County, CA	71.6	**Minneapolis, MN** (city) Hennepin County	73.9
Nevada	57.3	Solano County, CA	69.6	**Norwalk, CA** (city) Los Angeles County	71.5
Massachusetts	52.4	Worcester County, MA	69.3	**Central Islip, NY** (cdp) Suffolk County	71.4
New Hampshire	52.3	Arapahoe County, CO	68.6	**West Covina, CA** (city) Los Angeles County	70.6
New York	51.5	Jefferson Parish, LA	66.8	**Bakersfield, CA** (city) Kern County	67.9
District of Columbia	50.7	Orange County, FL	65.6	**Corona, CA** (city) Riverside County	66.1

Sorted by Percent in Ascending Order — U.S. = 45.5%

State	Percent	County	Percent	Place	Percent
Alabama	24.2	Nobles County, MN	5.3	**Albertville*, AL** (city) Marshall County	6.2
Nebraska	26.4	Caroline County, MD	6.3	**Cincinnati, OH** (city) Hamilton County	9.0
Delaware	27.4	Franklin County, AL	10.5	**Lexington*, NE** (city) Dawson County	11.1
Missouri	27.6	Gilmer County, GA	11.7	**Carthage*, MO** (city) Jasper County	11.3
Oklahoma	29.8	Jasper County, MO	11.9	**Grand Rapids, MI** (city) Kent County	13.3
South Carolina	32.1	Durham County, NC	13.7	**Durham, NC** (city) Durham County	14.4
Georgia	32.9	DeKalb County, AL	14.4	**Portland, OR** (city) Multnomah County	15.2
Mississippi	33.6	Douglas County, NE	15.5	**Lynn, MA** (city) Essex County	15.7
Kansas	33.8	Dawson County, NE	16.0	**Omaha, NE** (city) Douglas County	17.0
Iowa	34.5	Kent County, MI	16.8	**Homestead, FL** (city) Miami-Dade County	17.5

RANKINGS & COMPARISONS

Note: (1) Ranking tables cover all states and counties, and places with an overall population of at least 125,000, OR an overall population of at least 25,000 where the Hispanic/Latino population is at least 20% of the overall population. In states where less than five places meet either of these criteria, we have included places with at least 10,000 total population with the highest percentage of Hispanic/Latino population. These places are identified with an asterisk (*); Please refer to the User's Guide for a full explanation of data.

High School Graduates

(Universe: Population 25 Years and Over)

Central American: Honduran

Top 10 States, Counties, and Places[1]

Sorted by Number in Descending Order — U.S. = 183,875

State	Number	County	Number	Place	Number
Florida	38,858	Miami-Dade County, FL	19,946	**New York, NY** (city)	15,213
New York	22,455	Los Angeles County, CA	11,832	**Miami, FL** (city) Miami-Dade County	6,986
California	20,622	Harris County, TX	8,919	**Los Angeles, CA** (city) Los Angeles County	6,028
Texas	19,747	Jefferson Parish, LA	6,151	**Bronx, NY** (borough) Bronx County	5,968
Louisiana	11,172	Bronx County, NY	5,968	**Houston, TX** (city) Harris County	5,399
New Jersey	11,067	Broward County, FL	4,459	**Queens, NY** (borough) Queens County	3,700
Virginia	7,579	Queens County, NY	3,700	**Brooklyn, NY** (borough) Kings County	3,550
North Carolina	6,318	Kings County, NY	3,550	**Kenner, LA** (city) Jefferson Parish	2,405
Georgia	4,995	Hudson County, NJ	3,350	**Hialeah, FL** (city) Miami-Dade County	2,120
Maryland	4,935	Dallas County, TX	3,111	**Metairie, LA** (cdp) Jefferson Parish	1,890

Sorted by Number in Ascending Order — U.S. = 183,875

State	Number	County	Number	Place	Number
Nebraska	354	Hall County, GA	110	**Aurora, CO** (city) Arapahoe County	214
Iowa	364	New Haven County, CT	151	**Conroe, TX** (city) Montgomery County	258
Kentucky	391	Sampson County, NC	168	**Pasadena, CA** (city) Los Angeles County	283
District of Columbia	433	Arapahoe County, CO	188	**Oklahoma City, OK** (city) Oklahoma County	304
Arkansas	590	Kern County, CA	192	**Pasadena, TX** (city) Harris County	318
Mississippi	628	Elkhart County, IN	219	**Fort Worth, TX** (city) Tarrant County	329
Oregon	647	Clayton County, GA	221	**Newark, NJ** (city) Essex County	350
Michigan	688	Galveston County, TX	234	**Brentwood, NY** (cdp) Suffolk County	351
Alabama	745	Johnston County, NC	244	**Newburgh, NY** (city) Orange County	358
Ohio	766	Fresno County, CA	260	**Memphis, TN** (city) Shelby County	365

Sorted by Percent in Descending Order — U.S. = 51.4%

State	Percent	County	Percent	Place	Percent
Utah	71.5	Middlesex County, MA	82.0	**North Miami, FL** (city) Miami-Dade County	75.9
Wisconsin	69.7	Bergen County, NJ	81.1	**North Miami Beach, FL** (city) Miami-Dade County	71.6
Massachusetts	68.3	East Baton Rouge Parish, LA	79.7	**Kenner, LA** (city) Jefferson Parish	69.9
Arkansas	67.2	Osceola County, FL	79.1	**Huntington Station, NY** (cdp) Suffolk County	69.6
Michigan	66.4	Fort Bend County, TX	75.9	**Boston, MA** (city) Suffolk County	69.1
Louisiana	64.5	Salt Lake County, UT	72.9	**South Miami Heights, FL** (cdp) Miami-Dade County	68.3
Washington	63.1	Atlantic County, NJ	72.2	**Huntington, NY** (town) Suffolk County	68.2
Illinois	61.9	Denton County, TX	71.2	**Yonkers, NY** (city) Westchester County	67.9
Iowa	60.3	Jefferson Parish, LA	66.2	**Hialeah, FL** (city) Miami-Dade County	67.5
Oregon	59.6	Essex County, MA	65.5	**Metairie, LA** (cdp) Jefferson Parish	67.0

Sorted by Percent in Ascending Order — U.S. = 51.4%

State	Percent	County	Percent	Place	Percent
District of Columbia	36.8	Hall County, GA	17.5	**Aurora, CO** (city) Arapahoe County	23.9
North Carolina	39.2	Duplin County, NC	21.2	**Memphis, TN** (city) Shelby County	26.6
Texas	39.4	Clayton County, GA	22.9	**Brentwood, NY** (cdp) Suffolk County	29.1
Nebraska	40.2	Arapahoe County, CO	25.1	**Houston, TX** (city) Harris County	30.1
Georgia	42.5	Loudoun County, VA	25.3	**Dallas, TX** (city) Dallas County	31.1
Indiana	44.3	Sampson County, NC	27.9	**Indianapolis, IN** (city) Marion County	32.9
Kentucky	44.4	Marion County, IN	30.6	**Charlotte, NC** (city) Mecklenburg County	33.1
Colorado	45.6	Montgomery County, TX	33.5	**Durham, NC** (city) Durham County	33.5
Tennessee	46.1	Prince George's County, MD	33.5	**Austin, TX** (city) Travis County	34.9
Maryland	46.5	Durham County, NC	34.1	**Pasadena, CA** (city) Los Angeles County	35.0

Note: (1) Ranking tables cover all states and counties, and places with an overall population of at least 125,000, OR an overall population of at least 25,000 where the Hispanic/Latino population is at least 20% of the overall population. In states where less than five places meet either of these criteria, we have included places with at least 10,000 total population with the highest percentage of Hispanic/Latino population. These places are identified with an asterisk (*); Please refer to the User's Guide for a full explanation of data.

High School Graduates

(Universe: Population 25 Years and Over)

Central American: Nicaraguan

Top 10 States, Counties, and Places[1]

Sorted by Number in Descending Order — U.S. = 163,713

State	Number	County	Number	Place	Number
Florida	68,327	Miami-Dade County, FL	54,046	**Miami, FL** (city) Miami-Dade County	12,823
California	46,811	Los Angeles County, CA	17,584	**Los Angeles, CA** (city) Los Angeles County	7,804
Texas	8,031	San Mateo County, CA	5,229	**Hialeah, FL** (city) Miami-Dade County	5,710
New York	6,397	Broward County, FL	4,246	**New York, NY** (city)	4,910
New Jersey	3,754	San Bernardino County, CA	3,375	**Fountainebleau, FL** (cdp) Miami-Dade County	4,177
Louisiana	3,692	Contra Costa County, CA	3,371	**San Francisco, CA** (city) San Francisco County	3,221
Virginia	3,530	San Francisco County, CA	3,221	**Daly City, CA** (city) San Mateo County	2,445
Maryland	3,092	Harris County, TX	3,092	**Tamiami, FL** (cdp) Miami-Dade County	2,404
North Carolina	2,271	Alameda County, CA	2,803	**Houston, TX** (city) Harris County	1,828
Nevada	1,765	Jefferson Parish, LA	2,142	**Kendale Lakes, FL** (cdp) Miami-Dade County	1,815

Sorted by Number in Ascending Order — U.S. = 163,713

State	Number	County	Number	Place	Number
Minnesota	329	Gwinnett County, GA	272	**South Gate, CA** (city) Los Angeles County	347
Oregon	376	King County, WA	392	**Las Vegas, NV** (city) Clark County	432
District of Columbia	428	Camden County, NJ	404	**San Diego, CA** (city) San Diego County	432
Missouri	443	Collier County, FL	538	**Austin, TX** (city) Travis County	480
Michigan	452	Stanislaus County, CA	546	**Sacramento, CA** (city) Sacramento County	483
Tennessee	453	Sonoma County, CA	608	**South Miami Heights, FL** (cdp) Miami-Dade County	484
Connecticut	469	Bexar County, TX	617	**Oakland, CA** (city) Alameda County	487
South Carolina	508	Lee County, FL	617	**Fontana, CA** (city) San Bernardino County	497
Indiana	547	Prince George's County, MD	654	**South San Francisco, CA** (city) San Mateo County	530
Colorado	644	Travis County, TX	654	**Metairie, LA** (cdp) Jefferson Parish	558

Sorted by Percent in Descending Order — U.S. = 73.6%

State	Percent	County	Percent	Place	Percent
Connecticut	96.7	Sonoma County, CA	90.5	**The Hammocks, FL** (cdp) Miami-Dade County	90.5
Michigan	95.0	Lee County, FL	89.2	**Hollywood, FL** (city) Broward County	88.4
Washington	90.1	Collier County, FL	87.5	**Homestead, FL** (city) Miami-Dade County	88.0
Ohio	89.8	Travis County, TX	85.0	**Daly City, CA** (city) San Mateo County	86.3
Missouri	83.0	Maricopa County, AZ	83.5	**Tamiami, FL** (cdp) Miami-Dade County	85.9
Tennessee	83.0	Contra Costa County, CA	82.7	**Kendall, FL** (cdp) Miami-Dade County	83.1
Massachusetts	82.4	Duval County, FL	82.7	**Jacksonville, FL** (city) Duval County	82.7
Wisconsin	81.9	San Joaquin County, CA	82.7	**Richmond West, FL** (cdp) Miami-Dade County	82.2
North Carolina	81.8	San Mateo County, CA	82.6	**Austin, TX** (city) Travis County	81.9
Pennsylvania	81.3	Orange County, FL	82.5	**Pembroke Pines, FL** (city) Broward County	81.8

Sorted by Percent in Ascending Order — U.S. = 73.6%

State	Percent	County	Percent	Place	Percent
Minnesota	56.5	Gwinnett County, GA	45.3	**Metairie, LA** (cdp) Jefferson Parish	45.9
District of Columbia	58.6	Camden County, NJ	54.7	**West Little River, FL** (cdp) Miami-Dade County	56.8
Maryland	69.8	Prince George's County, MD	63.9	**Miami, FL** (city) Miami-Dade County	59.8
Indiana	71.2	Kings County, NY	65.3	**South Miami Heights, FL** (cdp) Miami-Dade County	60.4
Louisiana	71.3	Jefferson Parish, LA	65.9	**South Gate, CA** (city) Los Angeles County	60.6
South Carolina	71.5	Montgomery County, MD	67.5	**Fontana, CA** (city) San Bernardino County	62.4
Georgia	71.6	Los Angeles County, CA	68.8	**North Miami, FL** (city) Miami-Dade County	65.0
New York	71.9	Harris County, TX	69.2	**Brooklyn, NY** (borough) Kings County	65.3
Florida	72.4	San Francisco County, CA	69.4	**Miami Gardens, FL** (city) Miami-Dade County	67.1
New Jersey	72.9	Bronx County, NY	70.3	**Los Angeles, CA** (city) Los Angeles County	67.3

Note: (1) Ranking tables cover all states and counties, and places with an overall population of at least 125,000, OR an overall population of at least 25,000 where the Hispanic/Latino population is at least 20% of the overall population. In states where less than five places meet either of these criteria, we have included places with at least 10,000 total population with the highest percentage of Hispanic/Latino population. These places are identified with an asterisk (*); Please refer to the User's Guide for a full explanation of data.

High School Graduates

(Universe: Population 25 Years and Over)

Central American: Panamanian

Top 10 States, Counties, and Places[1]

Sorted by Number in Descending Order — U.S. = 90,726

State	Number	County	Number	Place	Number
New York	17,562	Kings County, NY	8,385	**New York, NY** (city)	14,030
Florida	15,244	Miami-Dade County, FL	4,933	**Brooklyn, NY** (borough) Kings County	8,385
California	10,269	Los Angeles County, CA	3,316	**Queens, NY** (borough) Queens County	2,665
Texas	7,379	Queens County, NY	2,665	**Manhattan, NY** (borough) New York County	1,440
Virginia	4,521	Broward County, FL	2,368	**Los Angeles, CA** (city) Los Angeles County	1,306
Georgia	4,226	Orange County, FL	1,456	**Bronx, NY** (borough) Bronx County	1,298
New Jersey	3,515	San Diego County, CA	1,449	**Hempstead (town), NY** (town) Nassau County	911
North Carolina	2,995	New York County, NY	1,440	**San Antonio, TX** (city) Bexar County	718
Maryland	2,875	Hillsborough County, FL	1,334	**Fayetteville, NC** (city) Cumberland County	706
Massachusetts	1,565	Bronx County, NY	1,298	**San Diego, CA** (city) San Diego County	688

Sorted by Number in Ascending Order — U.S. = 90,726

State	Number	County	Number	Place	Number
Minnesota	343	Pierce County, WA	446	**Miami, FL** (city) Miami-Dade County	537
New Mexico	344	Sacramento County, CA	492	**Houston, TX** (city) Harris County	557
Mississippi	382	Palm Beach County, FL	523	**Killeen, TX** (city) Bell County	559
Wisconsin	434	Orange County, CA	542	**Jacksonville, FL** (city) Duval County	664
Indiana	533	Dallas County, TX	553	**San Diego, CA** (city) San Diego County	688
Oklahoma	592	Hudson County, NJ	554	**Fayetteville, NC** (city) Cumberland County	706
Connecticut	650	Montgomery County, MD	557	**San Antonio, TX** (city) Bexar County	718
Michigan	669	Bell County, TX	629	**Hempstead (town), NY** (town) Nassau County	911
Missouri	676	Clark County, NV	633	**Bronx, NY** (borough) Bronx County	1,298
Nevada	712	Essex County, NJ	640	**Los Angeles, CA** (city) Los Angeles County	1,306

Sorted by Percent in Descending Order — U.S. = 90.9%

State	Percent	County	Percent	Place	Percent
Minnesota	100.0	Harris County, TX	99.2	**Fayetteville, NC** (city) Cumberland County	98.9
Connecticut	98.0	Prince George's County, MD	98.5	**Houston, TX** (city) Harris County	98.2
Oklahoma	96.3	Cumberland County, NC	97.3	**Hempstead (town), NY** (town) Nassau County	96.5
North Carolina	95.2	Pierce County, WA	96.7	**Manhattan, NY** (borough) New York County	93.4
Kentucky	94.3	Nassau County, NY	96.6	**Queens, NY** (borough) Queens County	93.4
Virginia	94.1	Fairfax County, VA	96.5	**San Antonio, TX** (city) Bexar County	93.0
Colorado	94.0	Palm Beach County, FL	96.5	**Jacksonville, FL** (city) Duval County	92.7
Illinois	93.9	Prince William County, VA	95.8	**Los Angeles, CA** (city) Los Angeles County	91.6
Mississippi	93.9	Essex County, NJ	94.8	**Killeen, TX** (city) Bell County	89.7
Pennsylvania	93.7	Bexar County, TX	94.2	**New York, NY** (city)	89.3

Sorted by Percent in Ascending Order — U.S. = 90.9%

State	Percent	County	Percent	Place	Percent
Massachusetts	80.3	Montgomery County, MD	81.1	**Miami, FL** (city) Miami-Dade County	73.5
New Mexico	81.9	Bronx County, NY	81.6	**Bronx, NY** (borough) Bronx County	81.6
Ohio	86.7	Suffolk County, NY	83.7	**San Diego, CA** (city) San Diego County	84.2
Indiana	87.8	San Bernardino County, CA	85.8	**Brooklyn, NY** (borough) Kings County	88.8
Tennessee	88.6	Brevard County, FL	86.7	**New York, NY** (city)	89.3
Missouri	89.5	Riverside County, CA	86.7	**Killeen, TX** (city) Bell County	89.7
California	89.6	Sacramento County, CA	86.9	**Los Angeles, CA** (city) Los Angeles County	91.6
New York	89.6	San Diego County, CA	87.8	**Jacksonville, FL** (city) Duval County	92.7
Florida	89.9	Cook County, IL	88.1	**San Antonio, TX** (city) Bexar County	93.0
Alabama	90.3	Kings County, NY	88.8	**Manhattan, NY** (borough) New York County	93.4

Note: (1) Ranking tables cover all states and counties, and places with an overall population of at least 125,000, OR an overall population of at least 25,000 where the Hispanic/Latino population is at least 20% of the overall population. In states where less than five places meet either of these criteria, we have included places with at least 10,000 total population with the highest percentage of Hispanic/Latino population. These places are identified with an asterisk (*); Please refer to the User's Guide for a full explanation of data.

High School Graduates

(Universe: Population 25 Years and Over)

Central American: Salvadoran

Top 10 States, Counties, and Places[1]

Sorted by Number in Descending Order — U.S. = 441,975

State	Number	County	Number	Place	Number
California	187,315	Los Angeles County, CA	112,182	**Los Angeles, CA** (city) Los Angeles County	63,380
Texas	50,150	Harris County, TX	26,230	**Houston, TX** (city) Harris County	15,574
New York	39,207	Montgomery County, MD	14,067	**New York, NY** (city)	13,447
Maryland	27,841	Suffolk County, NY	11,455	**Queens, NY** (borough) Queens County	7,232
Virginia	27,426	Nassau County, NY	10,728	**Hempstead (town), NY** (town) Nassau County	7,216
Florida	16,296	Fairfax County, VA	9,911	**Islip, NY** (town) Suffolk County	6,173
New Jersey	15,483	Prince George's County, MD	8,764	**San Francisco, CA** (city) San Francisco County	6,146
Massachusetts	9,844	San Bernardino County, CA	8,090	**Dallas, TX** (city) Dallas County	3,325
Georgia	7,168	San Mateo County, CA	8,054	**San Jose, CA** (city) Santa Clara County	3,320
Nevada	7,038	Orange County, CA	7,683	**Palmdale, CA** (city) Los Angeles County	3,266

Sorted by Number in Ascending Order — U.S. = 441,975

State	Number	County	Number	Place	Number
Idaho	300	Sebastian County, AR	118	**Gainesville, GA** (city) Hall County	72
Alaska	334	Crawford County, AR	130	**Greensboro, NC** (city) Guilford County	129
Hawaii	421	Henrico County, VA	177	**Lake Worth, FL** (city) Palm Beach County	136
Kentucky	489	Santa Cruz County, CA	190	**Richmond, VA** (independent city)	168
Wisconsin	515	Buncombe County, NC	198	**Bridgeport, CT** (city/town) Fairfield County	182
Alabama	595	Guilford County, NC	198	**Des Moines, IA** (city) Polk County	190
New Mexico	595	Polk County, IA	214	**Willowbrook, CA** (cdp) Los Angeles County	203
Michigan	735	Adams County, CO	216	**Salinas, CA** (city) Monterey County	207
Oklahoma	741	Hartford County, CT	216	**Plano, TX** (city) Collin County	211
Rhode Island	780	El Paso County, TX	227	**Mesquite, TX** (city) Dallas County	226

Sorted by Percent in Descending Order — U.S. = 46.8%

State	Percent	County	Percent	Place	Percent
Hawaii	84.7	Solano County, CA	72.3	**Fairfield, CA** (city) Solano County	95.0
Oregon	60.6	Washington County, OR	70.5	**Whittier, CA** (city) Los Angeles County	87.0
Utah	60.4	Sonoma County, CA	70.4	**San Bruno, CA** (city) San Mateo County	86.3
Washington	57.0	Passaic County, NJ	69.3	**Fremont, CA** (city) Alameda County	79.9
Louisiana	56.9	Pierce County, WA	68.8	**Antioch, CA** (city) Contra Costa County	78.6
Illinois	56.6	Napa County, CA	68.6	**San Diego, CA** (city) San Diego County	77.4
Alabama	55.6	Santa Clara County, CA	68.1	**West Covina, CA** (city) Los Angeles County	75.8
Oklahoma	54.4	San Diego County, CA	67.8	**Corona, CA** (city) Riverside County	75.0
New Mexico	53.5	San Mateo County, CA	67.1	**Rancho Cucamonga, CA** (city) San Bernardino County	74.8
Alaska	53.4	Contra Costa County, CA	66.8	**Simi Valley, CA** (city) Ventura County	73.6

Sorted by Percent in Ascending Order — U.S. = 46.8%

State	Percent	County	Percent	Place	Percent
Arkansas	25.6	Washington County, AR	16.9	**Gainesville, GA** (city) Hall County	8.6
District of Columbia	32.4	Sebastian County, AR	21.0	**Springdale, AR** (city) Washington County	15.8
Iowa	33.9	Guilford County, NC	22.0	**Greensboro, NC** (city) Guilford County	16.8
Nebraska	34.5	Henrico County, VA	22.5	**Des Moines, IA** (city) Polk County	22.7
Indiana	36.1	Crawford County, AR	23.6	**Richmond, VA** (independent city)	23.6
Kansas	36.3	Douglas County, NE	23.9	**Revere, MA** (city) Suffolk County	23.7
Georgia	37.6	Polk County, IA	24.6	**Omaha, NE** (city) Douglas County	23.8
North Carolina	37.6	Hall County, GA	24.8	**Garland, TX** (city) Dallas County	24.8
Kentucky	38.4	DeKalb County, GA	26.6	**Homestead, FL** (city) Miami-Dade County	25.0
Texas	38.5	Franklin County, OH	27.0	**Lake Worth, FL** (city) Palm Beach County	25.1

Note: (1) Ranking tables cover all states and counties, and places with an overall population of at least 125,000, OR an overall population of at least 25,000 where the Hispanic/Latino population is at least 20% of the overall population. In states where less than five places meet either of these criteria, we have included places with at least 10,000 total population with the highest percentage of Hispanic/Latino population. These places are identified with an asterisk (*); Please refer to the User's Guide for a full explanation of data.

High School Graduates

(Universe: Population 25 Years and Over)

Cuban

Top 10 States, Counties, and Places[1]

Sorted by Number in Descending Order — U.S. = 893,728

State	Number	County	Number	Place	Number
Florida	612,769	Miami-Dade County, FL	432,463	**Hialeah, FL** (city) Miami-Dade County	78,697
California	45,039	Broward County, FL	45,142	**Miami, FL** (city) Miami-Dade County	70,004
New Jersey	45,025	Hillsborough County, FL	31,542	**New York, NY** (city)	23,866
New York	39,584	Los Angeles County, CA	22,257	**Tamiami, FL** (cdp) Miami-Dade County	19,234
Texas	21,725	Palm Beach County, FL	21,261	**Kendale Lakes, FL** (cdp) Miami-Dade County	15,138
Georgia	12,762	Hudson County, NJ	15,993	**Kendall, FL** (cdp) Miami-Dade County	14,297
Illinois	10,644	Orange County, FL	10,712	**Fountainebleau, FL** (cdp) Miami-Dade County	13,979
Nevada	9,258	Lee County, FL	9,020	**Westchester, FL** (cdp) Miami-Dade County	11,588
North Carolina	8,437	Clark County, NV	8,672	**Miami Beach, FL** (city) Miami-Dade County	10,535
Virginia	7,544	Collier County, FL	7,557	**Tampa, FL** (city) Hillsborough County	10,304

Sorted by Number in Ascending Order — U.S. = 893,728

State	Number	County	Number	Place	Number
Arkansas	318	Hampden County, MA	274	**Linden, NJ** (city) Union County	326
West Virginia	448	Saint Tammany Parish, LA	291	**Columbus, OH** (city) Franklin County	331
Maine	470	Kern County, CA	293	**Bell, CA** (city) Los Angeles County	341
Iowa	526	Hamilton County, OH	297	**Milwaukee, WI** (city) Milwaukee County	381
Nebraska	527	Pierce County, WA	302	**Kearny, NJ** (town) Hudson County	434
New Hampshire	718	Arapahoe County, CO	307	**Riverside, CA** (city) Riverside County	436
Hawaii	721	Berks County, PA	313	**Santa Clarita, CA** (city) Los Angeles County	466
Mississippi	731	Forsyth County, NC	332	**Rochester, NY** (city) Monroe County	470
Delaware	777	Sussex County, NJ	408	**Nashville-Davidson, TN** (metropolitan govt) Davidson County	501
Rhode Island	841	Salt Lake County, UT	416	**New Orleans, LA** (city) Orleans Parish	512

Sorted by Percent in Descending Order — U.S. = 76.0%

State	Percent	County	Percent	Place	Percent
Hawaii	96.3	Bucks County, PA	100.0	**Oyster Bay, NY** (town) Nassau County	97.4
District of Columbia	95.1	Norfolk County, MA	100.0	**Coconut Creek, FL** (city) Broward County	96.8
Maine	94.6	Oakland County, MI	100.0	**New Orleans, LA** (city) Orleans Parish	96.4
Virginia	94.1	Honolulu County, HI	99.4	**Tamarac, FL** (city) Broward County	94.7
Delaware	91.4	Ventura County, CA	99.1	**Atlanta, GA** (city) Fulton County	94.0
Maryland	89.9	San Mateo County, CA	98.3	**Staten Island, NY** (borough) Richmond County	94.0
Colorado	89.2	Baltimore County, MD	98.1	**Brookhaven, NY** (town) Suffolk County	93.5
Iowa	88.6	Dutchess County, NY	97.0	**Islip, NY** (town) Suffolk County	93.0
Utah	88.5	Prince William County, VA	96.9	**Carrollwood, FL** (cdp) Hillsborough County	92.6
Kansas	88.3	Orleans Parish, LA	96.4	**Santa Clarita, CA** (city) Los Angeles County	92.5

Sorted by Percent in Ascending Order — U.S. = 76.0%

State	Percent	County	Percent	Place	Percent
Nebraska	57.8	Burlington County, NJ	43.5	**Bell, CA** (city) Los Angeles County	47.5
Arkansas	63.5	Kern County, CA	53.6	**West Little River, FL** (cdp) Miami-Dade County	54.6
Mississippi	63.7	Hendry County, FL	58.3	**Sunrise Manor, NV** (cdp) Clark County	59.2
Florida	73.9	Hampden County, MA	61.9	**Newark, NJ** (city) Essex County	61.6
Nevada	74.0	Davidson County, TN	64.6	**Union City, NJ** (city) Hudson County	62.2
New Mexico	75.1	Erie County, NY	64.8	**West New York, NJ** (town) Hudson County	62.3
New Jersey	75.4	Pierce County, WA	65.7	**Miami Gardens, FL** (city) Miami-Dade County	63.7
Oklahoma	77.0	Hudson County, NJ	66.5	**Miami, FL** (city) Miami-Dade County	64.1
Wisconsin	77.4	Clay County, FL	67.3	**Nashville-Davidson, TN** (metropolitan govt) Davidson County	64.6
Alabama	77.7	Bronx County, NY	68.4	**Hialeah, FL** (city) Miami-Dade County	64.9

Note: (1) Ranking tables cover all states and counties, and places with an overall population of at least 125,000, OR an overall population of at least 25,000 where the Hispanic/Latino population is at least 20% of the overall population. In states where less than five places meet either of these criteria, we have included places with at least 10,000 total population with the highest percentage of Hispanic/Latino population. These places are identified with an asterisk (*); Please refer to the User's Guide for a full explanation of data.

High School Graduates

(Universe: Population 25 Years and Over)

Dominican Republic

Top 10 States, Counties, and Places[1]

Sorted by Number in Descending Order — U.S. = 487,188

State	Number	County	Number	Place	Number
New York	228,846	Bronx County, NY	73,799	**New York, NY** (city)	193,362
Florida	73,772	New York County, NY	56,697	**Bronx, NY** (borough) Bronx County	73,799
New Jersey	67,302	Queens County, NY	34,443	**Manhattan, NY** (borough) New York County	56,697
Massachusetts	31,681	Kings County, NY	26,567	**Queens, NY** (borough) Queens County	34,443
Pennsylvania	16,131	Miami-Dade County, FL	25,680	**Brooklyn, NY** (borough) Kings County	26,567
Rhode Island	11,229	Hudson County, NJ	15,525	**Lawrence, MA** (city) Essex County	8,188
Connecticut	7,871	Essex County, MA	14,944	**Paterson, NJ** (city) Passaic County	8,123
Georgia	5,559	Passaic County, NJ	14,075	**Providence, RI** (city) Providence County	8,108
Texas	5,210	Broward County, FL	13,490	**Boston, MA** (city) Suffolk County	7,516
California	4,937	Providence County, RI	10,599	**Hempstead (town), NY** (town) Nassau County	6,251

Sorted by Number in Ascending Order — U.S. = 487,188

State	Number	County	Number	Place	Number
Minnesota	310	Lackawanna County, PA	155	**Central Falls*, RI** (city) Providence County	270
Utah	340	Ulster County, NY	201	**Syracuse, NY** (city) Onondaga County	273
Alabama	345	Litchfield County, CT	252	**Chelsea, MA** (city) Suffolk County	277
Delaware	409	Sullivan County, NY	304	**Plainfield, NJ** (city) Union County	289
Wisconsin	483	New Castle County, DE	306	**Bethlehem, PA** (city) Northampton County	337
Washington	491	Oneida County, NY	377	**New Haven, CT** (city/town) New Haven County	337
Missouri	605	Tarrant County, TX	404	**Tamiami, FL** (cdp) Miami-Dade County	339
Alaska	610	Albany County, NY	436	**Kearny, NJ** (town) Hudson County	343
South Carolina	654	Kent County, MI	442	**Elmont, NY** (cdp) Nassau County	353
Colorado	674	Erie County, NY	447	**West Little River, FL** (cdp) Miami-Dade County	356

Sorted by Percent in Descending Order — U.S. = 64.6%

State	Percent	County	Percent	Place	Percent
Washington	92.8	Fulton County, GA	98.0	**Alafaya, FL** (cdp) Orange County	95.8
Arizona	91.7	Bexar County, TX	96.3	**Doral, FL** (city) Miami-Dade County	93.9
Alabama	90.1	San Diego County, CA	92.2	**Davie, FL** (town) Broward County	92.6
California	87.6	Maricopa County, AZ	91.7	**Kendall, FL** (cdp) Miami-Dade County	91.0
Tennessee	87.3	Collier County, FL	88.8	**Richmond West, FL** (cdp) Miami-Dade County	90.5
Utah	86.7	Onondaga County, NY	85.8	**The Hammocks, FL** (cdp) Miami-Dade County	88.8
Virginia	86.1	Seminole County, FL	85.8	**Kendale Lakes, FL** (cdp) Miami-Dade County	88.5
South Carolina	83.8	Burlington County, NJ	85.6	**Weston, FL** (city) Broward County	88.1
New Hampshire	82.3	Marion County, FL	85.4	**Columbus, OH** (city) Franklin County	87.9
Missouri	81.6	Monroe County, PA	84.7	**Kendall West, FL** (cdp) Miami-Dade County	87.7

Sorted by Percent in Ascending Order — U.S. = 64.6%

State	Percent	County	Percent	Place	Percent
Delaware	57.7	Lackawanna County, PA	42.8	**Freeport, NY** (village) Nassau County	44.3
New York	59.3	Bristol County, MA	47.1	**Pennsauken, NJ** (township) Camden County	45.4
Massachusetts	61.0	Luzerne County, PA	50.1	**Elmont, NY** (cdp) Nassau County	45.6
Rhode Island	61.5	Volusia County, FL	52.6	**Hazleton, PA** (city) Luzerne County	46.6
Pennsylvania	61.6	Philadelphia County, PA	52.7	**Plainfield, NJ** (city) Union County	48.2
Connecticut	66.1	Litchfield County, CT	53.6	**Central Falls*, RI** (city) Providence County	50.2
New Jersey	66.8	New York County, NY	54.8	**Hartford, CT** (city/town) Hartford County	52.7
Wisconsin	71.1	Camden County, NJ	55.2	**Philadelphia, PA** (city) Philadelphia County	52.7
Louisiana	72.0	Kings County, NY	55.5	**Perth Amboy, NJ** (city) Middlesex County	52.8
District of Columbia	72.7	Berks County, PA	57.3	**Deltona, FL** (city) Volusia County	53.1

Note: (1) Ranking tables cover all states and counties, and places with an overall population of at least 125,000, OR an overall population of at least 25,000 where the Hispanic/Latino population is at least 20% of the overall population. In states where less than five places meet either of these criteria, we have included places with at least 10,000 total population with the highest percentage of Hispanic/Latino population. These places are identified with an asterisk (*); Please refer to the User's Guide for a full explanation of data.

High School Graduates

(Universe: Population 25 Years and Over)

Mexican

Top 10 States, Counties, and Places[1]

Sorted by Number in Descending Order — U.S. = 8,617,825

State	Number	County	Number	Place	Number
California	3,146,911	Los Angeles County, CA	991,950	**Los Angeles, CA** (city) Los Angeles County	309,521
Texas	2,289,774	Bexar County, TX	329,234	**San Antonio, TX** (city) Bexar County	276,044
Arizona	484,752	Harris County, TX	318,465	**El Paso, TX** (city) El Paso County	182,764
Illinois	430,416	Cook County, IL	264,756	**Houston, TX** (city) Harris County	167,887
Colorado	218,728	Maricopa County, AZ	264,419	**Chicago, IL** (city) Cook County	153,063
New Mexico	176,406	San Diego County, CA	259,179	**Phoenix, AZ** (city) Maricopa County	132,117
Florida	145,292	San Bernardino County, CA	240,368	**San Diego, CA** (city) San Diego County	99,171
Washington	135,648	Orange County, CA	230,892	**Dallas, TX** (city) Dallas County	87,047
Nevada	135,593	Riverside County, CA	227,722	**San Jose, CA** (city) Santa Clara County	84,633
New York	110,889	El Paso County, TX	215,534	**New York, NY** (city)	73,096

Sorted by Number in Ascending Order — U.S. = 8,617,825

State	Number	County	Number	Place	Number
Vermont	1,180	Benzie County, MI	21	**Fort Leonard Wood*, MO** (cdp) Pulaski County	115
Maine	2,007	Yellow Medicine County, MN	24	**Hazleton, PA** (city) Luzerne County	128
New Hampshire	2,429	Buffalo County, WI	25	**Carthage*, MO** (city) Jasper County	176
Rhode Island	2,924	Marshall County, MN	31	**Fort Campbell North*, KY** (cdp) Christian County	184
West Virginia	2,955	Antrim County, MI	35	**Laurel*, MS** (city) Jones County	184
North Dakota	3,000	Berrien County, GA	39	**Albertville*, AL** (city) Marshall County	214
District of Columbia	3,168	Cottle County, TX	40	**Central Falls*, RI** (city) Providence County	225
South Dakota	4,277	Sedgwick County, CO	40	**Mayfield*, KY** (city) Graves County	230
Delaware	5,727	Todd County, MN	42	**Windham, CT** (town) Windham County	234
Montana	7,316	Washington County, CO	42	**Storm Lake*, IA** (city) Buena Vista County	238

Sorted by Percent in Descending Order — U.S. = 55.5%

State	Percent	County	Percent	Place	Percent
Vermont	87.9	Tompkins County, NY	100.0	**Fort Campbell North*, KY** (cdp) Christian County	100.0
Hawaii	87.4	Los Alamos County, NM	98.6	**Fort Leonard Wood*, MO** (cdp) Pulaski County	100.0
Montana	81.4	McDonough County, IL	98.4	**Weston, FL** (city) Broward County	100.0
Maine	80.8	Ogemaw County, MI	98.1	**Alafaya, FL** (cdp) Orange County	97.9
North Dakota	74.7	Elbert County, CO	97.6	**Schofield Barracks*, HI** (cdp) Honolulu County	96.7
Massachusetts	74.6	Trinity County, CA	96.3	**Coral Gables, FL** (city) Miami-Dade County	93.6
Alaska	73.2	Menominee County, MI	95.9	**Casas Adobes, AZ** (cdp) Pima County	93.2
Wyoming	69.9	York County, ME	94.6	**Doral, FL** (city) Miami-Dade County	92.8
South Dakota	69.7	Latah County, ID	94.2	**Sahuarita, AZ** (town) Pima County	91.8
New Hampshire	68.0	Chittenden County, VT	93.0	**Urban Honolulu, HI** (cdp) Honolulu County	89.6

Sorted by Percent in Ascending Order — U.S. = 55.5%

State	Percent	County	Percent	Place	Percent
North Carolina	41.9	Ashe County, NC	9.5	**Reading, PA** (city) Berks County	18.2
Delaware	42.9	Evans County, GA	9.6	**Storm Lake*, IA** (city) Buena Vista County	18.3
Georgia	45.6	Todd County, MN	11.8	**Albertville*, AL** (city) Marshall County	18.9
Arkansas	46.0	Camp County, TX	13.8	**Carthage*, MO** (city) Jasper County	20.5
South Carolina	47.1	Obion County, TN	14.0	**Jerome*, ID** (city) Jerome County	23.7
Mississippi	48.0	Berrien County, GA	14.3	**Sanford, NC** (city) Lee County	23.8
Alabama	48.7	Glades County, FL	14.3	**Central Falls*, RI** (city) Providence County	25.8
Idaho	48.8	Habersham County, GA	15.0	**Bridgeton, NJ** (city) Cumberland County	26.4
Tennessee	49.4	Saluda County, SC	16.6	**Hazleton, PA** (city) Luzerne County	26.9
Florida	49.7	Montgomery County, NC	17.1	**Dalton, GA** (city) Whitfield County	29.7

Note: (1) Ranking tables cover all states and counties, and places with an overall population of at least 125,000, OR an overall population of at least 25,000 where the Hispanic/Latino population is at least 20% of the overall population. In states where less than five places meet either of these criteria, we have included places with at least 10,000 total population with the highest percentage of Hispanic/Latino population. These places are identified with an asterisk (*); Please refer to the User's Guide for a full explanation of data.

High School Graduates

(Universe: Population 25 Years and Over)

Puerto Rican

Top 10 States, Counties, and Places[1]

Sorted by Number in Descending Order — U.S. = 1,792,697

State	Number	County	Number	Place	Number
New York	432,536	Bronx County, NY	110,615	**New York, NY** (city)	299,268
Florida	371,118	Kings County, NY	70,656	**Bronx, NY** (borough) Bronx County	110,615
New Jersey	170,525	Orange County, FL	65,106	**Brooklyn, NY** (borough) Kings County	70,656
Pennsylvania	109,792	Queens County, NY	53,155	**Queens, NY** (borough) Queens County	53,155
California	83,784	Cook County, IL	51,185	**Manhattan, NY** (borough) New York County	47,722
Connecticut	81,699	Miami-Dade County, FL	49,220	**Chicago, IL** (city) Cook County	41,080
Massachusetts	76,444	New York County, NY	47,722	**Philadelphia, PA** (city) Philadelphia County	34,956
Illinois	70,993	Hillsborough County, FL	37,770	**Staten Island, NY** (borough) Richmond County	17,120
Texas	59,700	Broward County, FL	37,626	**Springfield, MA** (city) Hampden County	13,156
Ohio	31,143	Philadelphia County, PA	34,956	**Newark, NJ** (city) Essex County	12,738

Sorted by Number in Ascending Order — U.S. = 1,792,697

State	Number	County	Number	Place	Number
Wyoming	307	Perry County, PA	54	**Akron, OH** (city) Summit County	240
North Dakota	315	Grafton County, NH	102	**Hazleton, PA** (city) Luzerne County	246
South Dakota	530	Chenango County, NY	133	**West Covina, CA** (city) Los Angeles County	283
Montana	617	Sampson County, NC	154	**Omaha, NE** (city) Douglas County	292
Vermont	1,012	Lowndes County, GA	163	**Waianae*, HI** (cdp) Honolulu County	327
Nebraska	1,098	Schoharie County, NY	165	**Montgomery, AL** (city) Montgomery County	329
West Virginia	1,158	DeKalb County, IL	170	**Cooper City, FL** (city) Broward County	331
Idaho	1,162	Butte County, CA	188	**Palmdale, CA** (city) Los Angeles County	364
Alaska	1,598	Oswego County, NY	194	**Rockford, IL** (city) Winnebago County	389
Maine	1,698	Seneca County, NY	200	**Wichita, KS** (city) Sedgwick County	397

Sorted by Percent in Descending Order — U.S. = 73.4%

State	Percent	County	Percent	Place	Percent
North Dakota	100.0	Camden County, GA	100.0	**Fort Hood, TX** (cdp) Bell County	100.0
District of Columbia	96.1	Forsyth County, GA	100.0	**Plano, TX** (city) Collin County	100.0
Washington	90.9	Hamilton County, IN	100.0	**Temecula, CA** (city) Riverside County	100.0
South Dakota	89.7	Henry County, GA	100.0	**Arlington, VA** (cdp) Arlington County	99.0
Missouri	89.6	Arlington County, VA	99.0	**Dale City, VA** (cdp) Prince William County	98.1
Utah	89.5	Spotsylvania County, VA	99.0	**Oceanside, CA** (city) San Diego County	98.1
Colorado	89.3	Harrison County, MS	98.5	**Elmont, NY** (cdp) Nassau County	97.5
Virginia	89.1	New Hanover County, NC	98.5	**Huntington Beach, CA** (city) Orange County	96.5
Maryland	88.6	Frederick County, MD	97.7	**Weston, FL** (city) Broward County	96.5
Mississippi	88.6	Collin County, TX	97.0	**Kansas City, MO** (city) Jackson County	96.1

Sorted by Percent in Ascending Order — U.S. = 73.4%

State	Percent	County	Percent	Place	Percent
Rhode Island	60.7	Sampson County, NC	44.5	**Bridgeton, NJ** (city) Cumberland County	41.5
Massachusetts	62.5	Perry County, PA	47.0	**Central Falls*, RI** (city) Providence County	49.9
Pennsylvania	64.5	Montgomery County, NY	48.4	**Camden, NJ** (city) Camden County	50.1
Connecticut	65.0	Chenango County, NY	49.1	**West Little River, FL** (cdp) Miami-Dade County	50.6
New York	67.3	Hendry County, FL	49.2	**Holyoke, MA** (city) Hampden County	51.0
Wisconsin	69.7	Chautauqua County, NY	51.0	**Hartford, CT** (city/town) Hartford County	52.0
Delaware	70.5	Livingston County, NY	51.5	**Windham, CT** (town) Windham County	52.5
Illinois	70.8	Oswego County, NY	51.5	**Woonsocket*, RI** (city) Providence County	53.8
New Jersey	71.7	Bristol County, MA	53.1	**Wilmington*, DE** (city) New Castle County	54.0
Ohio	71.9	Wyoming County, NY	53.8	**Reading, PA** (city) Berks County	54.4

Note: (1) Ranking tables cover all states and counties, and places with an overall population of at least 125,000, OR an overall population of at least 25,000 where the Hispanic/Latino population is at least 20% of the overall population. In states where less than five places meet either of these criteria, we have included places with at least 10,000 total population with the highest percentage of Hispanic/Latino population. These places are identified with an asterisk (*); Please refer to the User's Guide for a full explanation of data.

High School Graduates

(Universe: Population 25 Years and Over)

South American

Top 10 States, Counties, and Places[1]

Sorted by Number in Descending Order — U.S. = 1,500,164

State	Number	County	Number	Place	Number
Florida	392,267	Miami-Dade County, FL	163,049	**New York, NY** (city)	176,213
New York	258,050	Queens County, NY	107,662	**Queens, NY** (borough) Queens County	107,662
New Jersey	171,877	Broward County, FL	86,058	**Los Angeles, CA** (city) Los Angeles County	31,585
California	170,801	Los Angeles County, CA	72,448	**Brooklyn, NY** (borough) Kings County	23,400
Texas	73,337	Hudson County, NJ	35,704	**Manhattan, NY** (borough) New York County	21,239
Virginia	57,558	Palm Beach County, FL	27,687	**Miami, FL** (city) Miami-Dade County	19,085
Illinois	38,751	Harris County, TX	27,327	**Bronx, NY** (borough) Bronx County	18,567
Connecticut	34,231	Fairfax County, VA	26,922	**Chicago, IL** (city) Cook County	17,075
Maryland	32,896	Orange County, FL	26,638	**Houston, TX** (city) Harris County	14,007
Georgia	30,406	Cook County, IL	26,483	**Hempstead (town), NY** (town) Nassau County	13,467

Sorted by Number in Ascending Order — U.S. = 1,500,164

State	Number	County	Number	Place	Number
North Dakota	352	Cache County, UT	276	**Palm Springs, CA** (city) Riverside County	255
Montana	461	Oneida County, NY	279	**Lynn, MA** (city) Essex County	350
Vermont	560	Schenectady County, NY	294	**Modesto, CA** (city) Stanislaus County	370
Maine	563	Tolland County, CT	294	**Killeen, TX** (city) Bell County	377
Wyoming	784	Washington County, MN	318	**Chesapeake, VA** (independent city)	388
West Virginia	931	Spokane County, WA	326	**New Brunswick, NJ** (city) Middlesex County	426
Alaska	1,194	Spartanburg County, SC	328	**Cranston*, RI** (city) Providence County	439
Nebraska	1,465	Polk County, IA	342	**New London, CT** (city/town) New London County	440
Idaho	1,513	Anoka County, MN	349	**Montebello, CA** (city) Los Angeles County	443
Iowa	1,793	San Luis Obispo County, CA	351	**Glendora, CA** (city) Los Angeles County	470

Sorted by Percent in Descending Order — U.S. = 83.8%

State	Percent	County	Percent	Place	Percent
Wyoming	98.9	Douglas County, CO	100.0	**Chandler, AZ** (city) Maricopa County	100.0
Vermont	96.6	Durham County, NC	100.0	**Cranston*, RI** (city) Providence County	100.0
Maine	95.9	Hamilton County, IN	100.0	**Durham, NC** (city) Durham County	100.0
Hawaii	95.8	Tompkins County, NY	100.0	**McKinney, TX** (city) Collin County	100.0
Missouri	95.7	Washington County, MN	100.0	**Scottsdale, AZ** (city) Maricopa County	100.0
New Mexico	95.0	Davis County, UT	99.1	**Norfolk, VA** (independent city)	99.2
Mississippi	94.0	Galveston County, TX	99.0	**Huntington Beach, CA** (city) Orange County	99.0
North Dakota	93.9	Oakland County, MI	98.6	**Overland Park, KS** (city) Johnson County	98.1
Arkansas	93.6	Orange County, NC	98.6	**Sanford, FL** (city) Seminole County	97.9
Kansas	93.3	Boulder County, CO	98.4	**Corona, CA** (city) Riverside County	97.8

Sorted by Percent in Ascending Order — U.S. = 83.8%

State	Percent	County	Percent	Place	Percent
Minnesota	69.4	Hennepin County, MN	54.4	**Minneapolis, MN** (city) Hennepin County	45.6
New York	73.6	Oneida County, NY	61.6	**Ossining, NY** (village) Westchester County	47.7
Rhode Island	75.3	Berks County, PA	64.5	**Ossining, NY** (town) Westchester County	49.8
Connecticut	79.7	Kings County, NY	64.9	**Spring Valley, NY** (village) Rockland County	51.4
New Jersey	79.9	Rockland County, NY	66.0	**Central Falls*, RI** (city) Providence County	56.8
Massachusetts	82.0	Bronx County, NY	66.5	**Reading, PA** (city) Berks County	57.2
Illinois	82.9	Spartanburg County, SC	69.3	**Danbury, CT** (city/town) Fairfield County	58.0
Pennsylvania	82.9	Essex County, NJ	69.7	**Ramapo, NY** (town) Rockland County	60.6
Alaska	84.0	Marion County, FL	69.7	**Newark, NJ** (city) Essex County	61.2
Delaware	84.0	Westchester County, NY	70.4	**Meriden, CT** (city/town) New Haven County	62.3

Note: (1) Ranking tables cover all states and counties, and places with an overall population of at least 125,000, OR an overall population of at least 25,000 where the Hispanic/Latino population is at least 20% of the overall population. In states where less than five places meet either of these criteria, we have included places with at least 10,000 total population with the highest percentage of Hispanic/Latino population. These places are identified with an asterisk (*); Please refer to the User's Guide for a full explanation of data.

High School Graduates

(Universe: Population 25 Years and Over)

South American: Argentinean

Top 10 States, Counties, and Places[1]

Sorted by Number in Descending Order — U.S. = 131,501

State	Number	County	Number	Place	Number
Florida	32,662	Miami-Dade County, FL	17,332	**New York, NY** (city)	9,198
California	26,641	Los Angeles County, CA	11,977	**Los Angeles, CA** (city) Los Angeles County	5,440
New York	14,984	Broward County, FL	6,067	**Queens, NY** (borough) Queens County	3,476
New Jersey	7,976	Orange County, CA	3,590	**Miami, FL** (city) Miami-Dade County	3,236
Texas	7,145	Queens County, NY	3,476	**Manhattan, NY** (borough) New York County	3,029
Illinois	3,751	New York County, NY	3,029	**Miami Beach, FL** (city) Miami-Dade County	2,975
Maryland	3,546	Harris County, TX	2,424	**Brooklyn, NY** (borough) Kings County	1,540
Virginia	3,204	Cook County, IL	2,321	**Houston, TX** (city) Harris County	1,400
Massachusetts	2,501	Palm Beach County, FL	2,276	**Chicago, IL** (city) Cook County	1,095
Connecticut	2,446	Montgomery County, MD	1,911	**San Francisco, CA** (city) San Francisco County	973

Sorted by Number in Ascending Order — U.S. = 131,501

State	Number	County	Number	Place	Number
Missouri	546	Tarrant County, TX	373	**San Jose, CA** (city) Santa Clara County	462
Minnesota	564	Montgomery County, TX	484	**San Diego, CA** (city) San Diego County	551
Louisiana	566	Oakland County, MI	510	**Doral, FL** (city) Miami-Dade County	674
Tennessee	598	Travis County, TX	526	**Hempstead (town), NY** (town) Nassau County	680
Indiana	650	Contra Costa County, CA	553	**Coral Springs, FL** (city) Broward County	685
South Carolina	693	Orange County, NY	569	**Hialeah, FL** (city) Miami-Dade County	685
Wisconsin	794	Bexar County, TX	580	**Pembroke Pines, FL** (city) Broward County	692
Oregon	821	Salt Lake County, UT	596	**Bronx, NY** (borough) Bronx County	735
District of Columbia	830	Union County, NJ	603	**Hollywood, FL** (city) Broward County	829
Colorado	1,066	New Haven County, CT	671	**Aventura, FL** (city) Miami-Dade County	902

Sorted by Percent in Descending Order — U.S. = 87.7%

State	Percent	County	Percent	Place	Percent
Minnesota	98.8	Travis County, TX	98.3	**Doral, FL** (city) Miami-Dade County	97.8
Oregon	97.7	Oakland County, MI	97.5	**Aventura, FL** (city) Miami-Dade County	95.6
District of Columbia	96.7	Fairfield County, CT	96.7	**Manhattan, NY** (borough) New York County	95.2
Colorado	96.6	Ventura County, CA	96.7	**Houston, TX** (city) Harris County	94.7
Washington	95.8	King County, WA	96.4	**San Diego, CA** (city) San Diego County	93.5
Georgia	95.1	New York County, NY	95.2	**Coral Springs, FL** (city) Broward County	93.1
Tennessee	94.5	Orange County, CA	93.5	**San Francisco, CA** (city) San Francisco County	93.1
Louisiana	94.0	San Francisco County, CA	93.1	**Pembroke Pines, FL** (city) Broward County	89.8
Michigan	93.9	Middlesex County, MA	92.9	**Miami Beach, FL** (city) Miami-Dade County	88.1
Connecticut	93.4	Hillsborough County, FL	91.7	**Los Angeles, CA** (city) Los Angeles County	86.4

Sorted by Percent in Ascending Order — U.S. = 87.7%

State	Percent	County	Percent	Place	Percent
South Carolina	80.0	Union County, NJ	66.2	**Hialeah, FL** (city) Miami-Dade County	74.9
New Jersey	82.0	Montgomery County, TX	72.7	**Hempstead (town), NY** (town) Nassau County	75.8
Nevada	82.2	San Bernardino County, CA	72.9	**San Jose, CA** (city) Santa Clara County	77.6
Utah	83.4	Salt Lake County, UT	74.3	**Hollywood, FL** (city) Broward County	78.1
New York	85.9	Dallas County, TX	77.2	**Bronx, NY** (borough) Bronx County	78.4
Texas	86.2	Hudson County, NJ	78.3	**Queens, NY** (borough) Queens County	79.4
Florida	86.3	Bronx County, NY	78.4	**Miami, FL** (city) Miami-Dade County	82.6
California	87.4	Queens County, NY	79.4	**Brooklyn, NY** (borough) Kings County	84.1
Ohio	88.1	Utah County, UT	80.7	**New York, NY** (city)	85.1
Virginia	89.9	Clark County, NV	81.7	**Chicago, IL** (city) Cook County	86.2

Note: (1) Ranking tables cover all states and counties, and places with an overall population of at least 125,000, OR an overall population of at least 25,000 where the Hispanic/Latino population is at least 20% of the overall population. In states where less than five places meet either of these criteria, we have included places with at least 10,000 total population with the highest percentage of Hispanic/Latino population. These places are identified with an asterisk (*); Please refer to the User's Guide for a full explanation of data.

High School Graduates

(Universe: Population 25 Years and Over)

South American: Bolivian

Top 10 States, Counties, and Places[1]

Sorted by Number in Descending Order — U.S. = 56,563

State	Number	County	Number	Place	Number
Virginia	18,545	Fairfax County, VA	10,171	**New York, NY** (city)	2,995
California	8,377	Los Angeles County, CA	3,497	**Los Angeles, CA** (city) Los Angeles County	2,279
Florida	5,830	Montgomery County, MD	3,019	**Arlington, VA** (cdp) Arlington County	2,197
New York	4,655	Prince William County, VA	2,429	**Queens, NY** (borough) Queens County	1,855
Maryland	4,035	Arlington County, VA	2,197	**Annandale, VA** (cdp) Fairfax County	1,388
Texas	2,531	Queens County, NY	1,855	**Dale City, VA** (cdp) Prince William County	845
New Jersey	2,360	Miami-Dade County, FL	1,769	**West Falls Church, VA** (cdp) Fairfax County	757
Illinois	1,171	Loudoun County, VA	1,241	**Providence, RI** (city) Providence County	677
Rhode Island	1,135	Providence County, RI	1,135	**Springfield, VA** (cdp) Fairfax County	637
Massachusetts	962	Broward County, FL	933		

Sorted by Number in Ascending Order — U.S. = 56,563

State	Number	County	Number	Place	Number
North Carolina	391	Cook County, IL	523	**Springfield, VA** (cdp) Fairfax County	637
Pennsylvania	425	Prince George's County, MD	562	**Providence, RI** (city) Providence County	677
Massachusetts	962	San Diego County, CA	589	**West Falls Church, VA** (cdp) Fairfax County	757
Rhode Island	1,135	Palm Beach County, FL	664	**Dale City, VA** (cdp) Prince William County	845
Illinois	1,171	Harris County, TX	742	**Annandale, VA** (cdp) Fairfax County	1,388
New Jersey	2,360	Santa Clara County, CA	755	**Queens, NY** (borough) Queens County	1,855
Texas	2,531	Orange County, CA	904	**Arlington, VA** (cdp) Arlington County	2,197
Maryland	4,035	Broward County, FL	933	**Los Angeles, CA** (city) Los Angeles County	2,279
New York	4,655	Providence County, RI	1,135	**New York, NY** (city)	2,995
Florida	5,830	Loudoun County, VA	1,241		

Sorted by Percent in Descending Order — U.S. = 88.7%

State	Percent	County	Percent	Place	Percent
Pennsylvania	99.3	Santa Clara County, CA	97.8	**Dale City, VA** (cdp) Prince William County	96.0
North Carolina	98.2	Loudoun County, VA	96.2	**Los Angeles, CA** (city) Los Angeles County	91.6
Illinois	95.6	Providence County, RI	94.3	**Providence, RI** (city) Providence County	90.9
Rhode Island	94.3	Cook County, IL	94.1	**Annandale, VA** (cdp) Fairfax County	83.9
California	92.8	San Diego County, CA	92.9	**New York, NY** (city)	83.8
Florida	91.5	Los Angeles County, CA	92.8	**Queens, NY** (borough) Queens County	82.8
Massachusetts	91.4	Montgomery County, MD	92.5	**Springfield, VA** (cdp) Fairfax County	81.9
Maryland	90.5	Miami-Dade County, FL	90.6	**Arlington, VA** (cdp) Arlington County	73.5
Texas	88.3	Palm Beach County, FL	90.0	**West Falls Church, VA** (cdp) Fairfax County	71.4
New York	87.8	Orange County, CA	87.6		

Sorted by Percent in Ascending Order — U.S. = 88.7%

State	Percent	County	Percent	Place	Percent
New Jersey	83.8	Arlington County, VA	73.5	**West Falls Church, VA** (cdp) Fairfax County	71.4
Virginia	84.4	Prince George's County, MD	76.5	**Arlington, VA** (cdp) Arlington County	73.5
New York	87.8	Harris County, TX	78.0	**Springfield, VA** (cdp) Fairfax County	81.9
Texas	88.3	Queens County, NY	82.8	**Queens, NY** (borough) Queens County	82.8
Maryland	90.5	Fairfax County, VA	85.1	**New York, NY** (city)	83.8
Massachusetts	91.4	Broward County, FL	87.2	**Annandale, VA** (cdp) Fairfax County	83.9
Florida	91.5	Prince William County, VA	87.3	**Providence, RI** (city) Providence County	90.9
California	92.8	Orange County, CA	87.6	**Los Angeles, CA** (city) Los Angeles County	91.6
Rhode Island	94.3	Palm Beach County, FL	90.0	**Dale City, VA** (cdp) Prince William County	96.0
Illinois	95.6	Miami-Dade County, FL	90.6		

Note: (1) Ranking tables cover all states and counties, and places with an overall population of at least 125,000, OR an overall population of at least 25,000 where the Hispanic/Latino population is at least 20% of the overall population. In states where less than five places meet either of these criteria, we have included places with at least 10,000 total population with the highest percentage of Hispanic/Latino population. These places are identified with an asterisk (*); Please refer to the User's Guide for a full explanation of data.

High School Graduates

(Universe: Population 25 Years and Over)

South American: Chilean

Top 10 States, Counties, and Places[1]

Sorted by Number in Descending Order — U.S. = 73,302

State	Number	County	Number	Place	Number
Florida	15,216	Miami-Dade County, FL	7,895	**New York, NY** (city)	4,535
California	14,285	Los Angeles County, CA	5,444	**Los Angeles, CA** (city) Los Angeles County	2,846
New York	8,932	Broward County, FL	2,499	**Queens, NY** (borough) Queens County	2,344
New Jersey	4,908	Queens County, NY	2,344	**Manhattan, NY** (borough) New York County	961
Texas	2,888	Nassau County, NY	1,427	**Miami, FL** (city) Miami-Dade County	842
Virginia	2,393	Hudson County, NJ	1,335	**Brooklyn, NY** (borough) Kings County	799
Maryland	2,293	Montgomery County, MD	1,288	**Hempstead (town), NY** (town) Nassau County	635
Massachusetts	2,053	Westchester County, NY	1,245	**Chicago, IL** (city) Cook County	580
Utah	1,738	Fairfax County, VA	1,038	**Kendall, FL** (cdp) Miami-Dade County	471
Illinois	1,657	Santa Clara County, CA	1,005		

Sorted by Number in Ascending Order — U.S. = 73,302

State	Number	County	Number	Place	Number
Minnesota	364	San Mateo County, CA	559	**Kendall, FL** (cdp) Miami-Dade County	471
Tennessee	449	Riverside County, CA	581	**Chicago, IL** (city) Cook County	580
Wisconsin	514	Maricopa County, AZ	603	**Hempstead (town), NY** (town) Nassau County	635
Ohio	529	Bergen County, NJ	628	**Brooklyn, NY** (borough) Kings County	799
Missouri	540	Clark County, NV	638	**Miami, FL** (city) Miami-Dade County	842
Michigan	591	Salt Lake County, UT	645	**Manhattan, NY** (borough) New York County	961
Oregon	655	San Bernardino County, CA	666	**Queens, NY** (borough) Queens County	2,344
Colorado	662	Alameda County, CA	671	**Los Angeles, CA** (city) Los Angeles County	2,846
Nevada	820	Utah County, UT	676	**New York, NY** (city)	4,535
Connecticut	862	Suffolk County, NY	775		

Sorted by Percent in Descending Order — U.S. = 89.2%

State	Percent	County	Percent	Place	Percent
Missouri	100.0	Alameda County, CA	100.0	**Manhattan, NY** (borough) New York County	92.2
Michigan	98.0	Bergen County, NJ	100.0	**Miami, FL** (city) Miami-Dade County	90.2
Pennsylvania	96.3	Middlesex County, MA	98.7	**Chicago, IL** (city) Cook County	90.1
Virginia	96.3	Utah County, UT	96.3	**Kendall, FL** (cdp) Miami-Dade County	88.2
Massachusetts	95.4	Suffolk County, NY	95.1	**Los Angeles, CA** (city) Los Angeles County	86.7
North Carolina	95.2	Fairfax County, VA	94.1	**Queens, NY** (borough) Queens County	83.8
Ohio	94.6	Palm Beach County, FL	93.9	**New York, NY** (city)	82.5
Georgia	94.0	Riverside County, CA	93.6	**Brooklyn, NY** (borough) Kings County	76.4
Arizona	92.7	Cook County, IL	92.2	**Hempstead (town), NY** (town) Nassau County	73.0
Washington	92.0	New York County, NY	92.2		

Sorted by Percent in Ascending Order — U.S. = 89.2%

State	Percent	County	Percent	Place	Percent
Colorado	78.1	Kings County, NY	76.4	**Hempstead (town), NY** (town) Nassau County	73.0
Wisconsin	80.6	Nassau County, NY	78.5	**Brooklyn, NY** (borough) Kings County	76.4
Connecticut	82.2	Westchester County, NY	80.3	**New York, NY** (city)	82.5
New York	83.5	Hudson County, NJ	83.2	**Queens, NY** (borough) Queens County	83.8
Maryland	84.4	Queens County, NY	83.8	**Los Angeles, CA** (city) Los Angeles County	86.7
New Jersey	85.6	Harris County, TX	85.1	**Kendall, FL** (cdp) Miami-Dade County	88.2
Illinois	86.3	Los Angeles County, CA	85.4	**Chicago, IL** (city) Cook County	90.1
Tennessee	87.4	Montgomery County, MD	86.6	**Miami, FL** (city) Miami-Dade County	90.2
Texas	88.7	Santa Clara County, CA	86.6	**Manhattan, NY** (borough) New York County	92.2
California	89.8	Salt Lake County, UT	87.4		

Note: (1) Ranking tables cover all states and counties, and places with an overall population of at least 125,000, OR an overall population of at least 25,000 where the Hispanic/Latino population is at least 20% of the overall population. In states where less than five places meet either of these criteria, we have included places with at least 10,000 total population with the highest percentage of Hispanic/Latino population. These places are identified with an asterisk (*); Please refer to the User's Guide for a full explanation of data.

High School Graduates

(Universe: Population 25 Years and Over)

South American: Colombian

Top 10 States, Counties, and Places[1]

Sorted by Number in Descending Order — U.S. = 492,011

State	Number	County	Number	Place	Number
Florida	169,402	Miami-Dade County, FL	66,988	**New York, NY** (city)	54,227
New York	79,976	Queens County, NY	39,054	**Queens, NY** (borough) Queens County	39,054
New Jersey	53,579	Broward County, FL	36,718	**Miami, FL** (city) Miami-Dade County	6,471
California	35,056	Los Angeles County, CA	15,027	**Pembroke Pines, FL** (city) Broward County	6,146
Texas	26,794	Orange County, FL	13,553	**Los Angeles, CA** (city) Los Angeles County	5,792
Georgia	13,161	Palm Beach County, FL	12,038	**Elizabeth, NJ** (city) Union County	5,660
Massachusetts	12,220	Harris County, TX	11,410	**Brooklyn, NY** (borough) Kings County	5,586
Illinois	11,181	Bergen County, NJ	10,424	**Houston, TX** (city) Harris County	5,507
Connecticut	10,671	Hudson County, NJ	9,059	**Hempstead (town), NY** (town) Nassau County	5,166
North Carolina	8,792	Hillsborough County, FL	8,694	**Manhattan, NY** (borough) New York County	5,093

Sorted by Number in Ascending Order — U.S. = 492,011

State	Number	County	Number	Place	Number
Nebraska	472	Dane County, WI	224	**Anaheim, CA** (city) Orange County	347
Alaska	475	Luzerne County, PA	272	**Tallahassee, FL** (city) Leon County	355
Kentucky	524	Ulster County, NY	296	**Long Beach, CA** (city) Los Angeles County	366
Iowa	574	Erie County, NY	344	**Royal Palm Beach, FL** (village) Palm Beach County	368
Delaware	608	Leon County, FL	376	**Indianapolis, IN** (city) Marion County	373
Arkansas	639	Will County, IL	382	**Garfield, NJ** (city) Bergen County	404
New Mexico	671	Lancaster County, PA	395	**Raleigh, NC** (city) Wake County	457
Oregon	871	Burlington County, NJ	407	**Elmont, NY** (cdp) Nassau County	460
Oklahoma	886	Forsyth County, GA	417	**Worcester, MA** (city) Worcester County	471
Kansas	1,069	Milwaukee County, WI	420	**Virginia Beach, VA** (independent city)	480

Sorted by Percent in Descending Order — U.S. = 85.1%

State	Percent	County	Percent	Place	Percent
Minnesota	99.1	Franklin County, OH	100.0	**Coconut Creek, FL** (city) Broward County	100.0
Ohio	98.6	Oakland County, MI	100.0	**Raleigh, NC** (city) Wake County	98.1
Indiana	96.1	Hennepin County, MN	99.5	**Indianapolis, IN** (city) Marion County	97.4
Missouri	96.1	Collin County, TX	98.7	**Doral, FL** (city) Miami-Dade County	97.0
Arkansas	95.7	Loudoun County, VA	98.4	**Aventura, FL** (city) Miami-Dade County	96.7
Iowa	94.6	Marion County, IN	97.8	**Downey, CA** (city) Los Angeles County	96.7
Washington	93.8	Saint Louis County, MO	97.6	**Huntington, NY** (town) Suffolk County	96.0
Alabama	93.3	Montgomery County, PA	97.5	**Linden, NJ** (city) Union County	95.2
Colorado	93.3	Baltimore County, MD	97.2	**Austin, TX** (city) Travis County	95.0
Utah	92.5	Cuyahoga County, OH	96.6	**Egypt Lake-Leto, FL** (cdp) Hillsborough County	94.8

Sorted by Percent in Ascending Order — U.S. = 85.1%

State	Percent	County	Percent	Place	Percent
Rhode Island	67.8	Providence County, RI	65.4	**Central Falls*, RI** (city) Providence County	51.2
Alaska	73.8	Suffolk County, MA	66.1	**Revere, MA** (city) Suffolk County	57.3
Massachusetts	76.7	Erie County, NY	69.2	**Garfield, NJ** (city) Bergen County	60.1
Tennessee	78.9	Forsyth County, GA	72.5	**Bergenfield, NJ** (borough) Bergen County	65.8
New York	80.4	Ulster County, NY	72.7	**Boston, MA** (city) Suffolk County	67.1
New Jersey	82.3	Bronx County, NY	72.9	**Brandon, FL** (cdp) Hillsborough County	67.9
Nebraska	83.7	Marion County, FL	72.9	**Pawtucket*, RI** (city) Providence County	68.1
Connecticut	83.9	Lancaster County, PA	73.6	**Providence, RI** (city) Providence County	69.1
Kentucky	84.5	Dutchess County, NY	74.1	**Hartford, CT** (city/town) Hartford County	70.5
North Carolina	84.8	Dallas County, TX	74.9	**Newark, NJ** (city) Essex County	70.9

Note: (1) Ranking tables cover all states and counties, and places with an overall population of at least 125,000, OR an overall population of at least 25,000 where the Hispanic/Latino population is at least 20% of the overall population. In states where less than five places meet either of these criteria, we have included places with at least 10,000 total population with the highest percentage of Hispanic/Latino population. These places are identified with an asterisk (*); Please refer to the User's Guide for a full explanation of data.

High School Graduates

(Universe: Population 25 Years and Over)

South American: Ecuadorian

Top 10 States, Counties, and Places[1]

Sorted by Number in Descending Order — U.S. = 257,111

State	Number	County	Number	Place	Number
New York	90,710	Queens County, NY	39,905	**New York, NY** (city)	69,184
New Jersey	47,037	Hudson County, NJ	13,632	**Queens, NY** (borough) Queens County	39,905
Florida	34,652	Miami-Dade County, FL	12,315	**Bronx, NY** (borough) Bronx County	10,841
California	20,416	Los Angeles County, CA	10,916	**Brooklyn, NY** (borough) Kings County	10,288
Illinois	11,067	Bronx County, NY	10,841	**Chicago, IL** (city) Cook County	6,873
Connecticut	9,045	Kings County, NY	10,288	**Manhattan, NY** (borough) New York County	6,643
Texas	6,372	Essex County, NJ	9,135	**Newark, NJ** (city) Essex County	5,290
North Carolina	4,749	Cook County, IL	8,967	**Los Angeles, CA** (city) Los Angeles County	4,173
Pennsylvania	4,431	Broward County, FL	7,708	**Jersey City, NJ** (city) Hudson County	3,531
Maryland	3,501	New York County, NY	6,643	**Hempstead (town), NY** (town) Nassau County	2,923

Sorted by Number in Ascending Order — U.S. = 257,111

State	Number	County	Number	Place	Number
Iowa	300	Providence County, RI	264	**White Plains, NY** (city) Westchester County	231
Rhode Island	310	Putnam County, NY	315	**City of Orange, NJ** (township) Essex County	232
Wisconsin	349	Baltimore County, MD	316	**Downey, CA** (city) Los Angeles County	293
Missouri	361	Ocean County, NJ	366	**Central Islip, NY** (cdp) Suffolk County	333
Oregon	363	Pinellas County, FL	370	**Norwalk, CT** (city/town) Fairfield County	377
Kansas	413	Delaware County, PA	379	**Philadelphia, PA** (city) Philadelphia County	435
Oklahoma	488	Prince George's County, MD	380	**Miramar, FL** (city) Broward County	440
Tennessee	527	Berks County, PA	408	**Plainfield, NJ** (city) Union County	478
Indiana	533	Santa Clara County, CA	411	**Country Club, FL** (cdp) Miami-Dade County	487
Louisiana	554	Philadelphia County, PA	435	**Spring Valley, NY** (village) Rockland County	505

Sorted by Percent in Descending Order — U.S. = 70.5%

State	Percent	County	Percent	Place	Percent
Oklahoma	100.0	Utah County, UT	100.0	**Doral, FL** (city) Miami-Dade County	97.9
Michigan	98.8	Maricopa County, AZ	95.8	**Sunrise, FL** (city) Broward County	95.5
Utah	98.0	Dallas County, TX	93.9	**Coral Springs, FL** (city) Broward County	91.2
Louisiana	97.4	Baltimore County, MD	92.4	**Paterson, NJ** (city) Passaic County	91.0
Kansas	95.8	Orange County, CA	92.0	**Oyster Bay, NY** (town) Nassau County	89.9
Colorado	95.4	Will County, IL	91.9	**Country Club, FL** (cdp) Miami-Dade County	88.2
Arizona	93.0	Clark County, NV	91.3	**Kearny, NJ** (town) Hudson County	85.6
Nevada	92.1	Palm Beach County, FL	90.7	**Clifton, NJ** (city) Passaic County	84.9
South Carolina	91.6	Hillsborough County, FL	89.1	**Pembroke Pines, FL** (city) Broward County	84.3
Missouri	89.8	Lee County, FL	88.3	**Babylon, NY** (town) Suffolk County	84.1

Sorted by Percent in Ascending Order — U.S. = 70.5%

State	Percent	County	Percent	Place	Percent
Minnesota	40.4	Hennepin County, MN	33.8	**Minneapolis, MN** (city) Hennepin County	33.3
Rhode Island	57.2	Berks County, PA	48.5	**White Plains, NY** (city) Westchester County	34.0
Oregon	59.9	Delaware County, PA	49.9	**Ossining, NY** (village) Westchester County	36.0
New York	61.3	Westchester County, NY	50.5	**Ossining, NY** (town) Westchester County	37.6
Connecticut	64.5	Providence County, RI	53.2	**Port Chester, NY** (village) Westchester County	41.1
Pennsylvania	68.1	Ocean County, NJ	53.9	**Rye, NY** (town) Westchester County	43.3
Iowa	70.3	Kings County, NY	54.3	**City of Orange, NJ** (township) Essex County	43.7
Illinois	70.4	Rockland County, NY	54.7	**Spring Valley, NY** (village) Rockland County	45.3
New Jersey	71.2	New York County, NY	59.7	**Norwalk, CT** (city/town) Fairfield County	48.5
Indiana	73.0	Orange County, NY	60.9	**Central Islip, NY** (cdp) Suffolk County	49.7

Note: (1) Ranking tables cover all states and counties, and places with an overall population of at least 125,000, OR an overall population of at least 25,000 where the Hispanic/Latino population is at least 20% of the overall population. In states where less than five places meet either of these criteria, we have included places with at least 10,000 total population with the highest percentage of Hispanic/Latino population. These places are identified with an asterisk (*); Please refer to the User's Guide for a full explanation of data.

High School Graduates

(Universe: Population 25 Years and Over)

South American: Paraguayan

Top 10 States, Counties, and Places[1]

Sorted by Number in Descending Order — U.S. = 9,345

State	Number	County	Number	Place	Number
New York	3,487	Queens County, NY	1,367	**New York, NY** (city)	1,859
Florida	882	Westchester County, NY	874	**Queens, NY** (borough) Queens County	1,367
New Jersey	859				
Texas	653				
Maryland	621				
California	558				

Sorted by Number in Ascending Order — U.S. = 9,345

State	Number	County	Number	Place	Number
California	558	Westchester County, NY	874	**Queens, NY** (borough) Queens County	1,367
Maryland	621	Queens County, NY	1,367	**New York, NY** (city)	1,859
Texas	653				
New Jersey	859				
Florida	882				
New York	3,487				

Sorted by Percent in Descending Order — U.S. = 81.3%

State	Percent	County	Percent	Place	Percent
California	94.4	Queens County, NY	78.7	**Queens, NY** (borough) Queens County	78.7
Maryland	90.5	Westchester County, NY	75.5	**New York, NY** (city)	77.0
Texas	88.5				
Florida	83.4				
New York	78.5				
New Jersey	70.4				

Sorted by Percent in Ascending Order — U.S. = 81.3%

State	Percent	County	Percent	Place	Percent
New Jersey	70.4	Westchester County, NY	75.5	**New York, NY** (city)	77.0
New York	78.5	Queens County, NY	78.7	**Queens, NY** (borough) Queens County	78.7
Florida	83.4				
Texas	88.5				
Maryland	90.5				
California	94.4				

Note: (1) Ranking tables cover all states and counties, and places with an overall population of at least 125,000, OR an overall population of at least 25,000 where the Hispanic/Latino population is at least 20% of the overall population. In states where less than five places meet either of these criteria, we have included places with at least 10,000 total population with the highest percentage of Hispanic/Latino population. These places are identified with an asterisk (*); Please refer to the User's Guide for a full explanation of data.

High School Graduates

(Universe: Population 25 Years and Over)

South American: Peruvian

Top 10 States, Counties, and Places[1]

Sorted by Number in Descending Order — U.S. = 304,661

State	Number	County	Number	Place	Number
Florida	62,583	Miami-Dade County, FL	23,926	**New York, NY** (city)	24,192
California	50,156	Los Angeles County, CA	19,187	**Queens, NY** (borough) Queens County	15,519
New Jersey	44,452	Broward County, FL	15,669	**Los Angeles, CA** (city) Los Angeles County	8,664
New York	40,332	Queens County, NY	15,519	**Paterson, NJ** (city) Passaic County	5,774
Virginia	16,611	Passaic County, NJ	12,032	**Clifton, NJ** (city) Passaic County	3,263
Texas	12,789	Fairfax County, VA	8,306	**Elizabeth, NJ** (city) Union County	3,236
Maryland	9,352	Hudson County, NJ	8,046	**Manhattan, NY** (borough) New York County	2,794
Connecticut	8,657	Montgomery County, MD	6,127	**Chicago, IL** (city) Cook County	2,760
Illinois	6,260	Union County, NJ	5,688	**Miami, FL** (city) Miami-Dade County	2,736
Georgia	5,610	Westchester County, NY	5,602	**Brooklyn, NY** (borough) Kings County	2,682

Sorted by Number in Ascending Order — U.S. = 304,661

State	Number	County	Number	Place	Number
Kansas	562	Denver County, CO	314	**Denver, CO** (city) Denver County	314
Kentucky	624	Lake County, IL	318	**West Valley City, UT** (city) Salt Lake County	346
Rhode Island	642	Baltimore County, MD	347	**Cape Coral, FL** (city) Lee County	398
Hawaii	646	Solano County, CA	376	**Salt Lake City, UT** (city) Salt Lake County	398
Delaware	678	Fort Bend County, TX	438	**Belleville, NJ** (township) Essex County	431
District of Columbia	697	Ocean County, NJ	467	**Torrance, CA** (city) Los Angeles County	450
New Mexico	705	Franklin County, OH	471	**Santa Ana, CA** (city) Orange County	465
Idaho	733	Wake County, NC	505	**Tampa, FL** (city) Hillsborough County	489
Alabama	740	Lehigh County, PA	532	**Phoenix, AZ** (city) Maricopa County	505
Missouri	786	San Joaquin County, CA	538	**Bridgeport, CT** (city/town) Fairfield County	506

Sorted by Percent in Descending Order — U.S. = 89.1%

State	Percent	County	Percent	Place	Percent
New Mexico	100.0	San Joaquin County, CA	99.1	**Doral, FL** (city) Miami-Dade County	100.0
Kentucky	98.0	Utah County, UT	98.0	**Downey, CA** (city) Los Angeles County	100.0
South Carolina	97.0	Franklin County, OH	97.1	**San Mateo, CA** (city) San Mateo County	100.0
Michigan	96.6	Fort Bend County, TX	96.7	**Oyster Bay, NY** (town) Nassau County	98.7
Hawaii	96.4	Collin County, TX	96.3	**Weston, FL** (city) Broward County	98.3
Louisiana	96.3	Lee County, FL	96.3	**Phoenix, AZ** (city) Maricopa County	98.1
Minnesota	95.3	Broward County, FL	95.8	**Las Vegas, NV** (city) Clark County	97.7
Ohio	94.4	Hillsborough County, FL	95.7	**Pembroke Pines, FL** (city) Broward County	97.4
Missouri	93.9	Mecklenburg County, NC	94.7	**Davie, FL** (town) Broward County	97.3
Alabama	93.8	Travis County, TX	94.5	**Coral Springs, FL** (city) Broward County	97.1

Sorted by Percent in Ascending Order — U.S. = 89.1%

State	Percent	County	Percent	Place	Percent
Delaware	68.8	Prince George's County, MD	70.2	**Belleville, NJ** (township) Essex County	70.2
District of Columbia	79.2	Kings County, NY	77.1	**West New York, NJ** (town) Hudson County	75.1
New York	86.0	Solano County, CA	77.4	**Brooklyn, NY** (borough) Kings County	77.1
Indiana	86.8	Arlington County, VA	77.7	**Newark, NJ** (city) Essex County	77.1
Idaho	87.0	Atlantic County, NJ	80.5	**Arlington, VA** (cdp) Arlington County	77.7
Massachusetts	87.1	Ocean County, NJ	81.1	**Santa Clarita, CA** (city) Los Angeles County	79.1
Maryland	87.2	Baltimore County, MD	81.5	**West Valley City, UT** (city) Salt Lake County	81.2
New Jersey	87.3	Bronx County, NY	81.6	**Bronx, NY** (borough) Bronx County	81.6
California	87.6	Collier County, FL	82.9	**Dallas, TX** (city) Dallas County	82.5
Tennessee	89.2	Essex County, NJ	82.9	**Union City, NJ** (city) Hudson County	83.4

Note: (1) Ranking tables cover all states and counties, and places with an overall population of at least 125,000, OR an overall population of at least 25,000 where the Hispanic/Latino population is at least 20% of the overall population. In states where less than five places meet either of these criteria, we have included places with at least 10,000 total population with the highest percentage of Hispanic/Latino population. These places are identified with an asterisk (*); Please refer to the User's Guide for a full explanation of data.

High School Graduates

(Universe: Population 25 Years and Over)

South American: Uruguayan

Top 10 States, Counties, and Places[1]

Sorted by Number in Descending Order — U.S. = 28,000

State	Number	County	Number	Place	Number
Florida	7,810	Miami-Dade County, FL	3,524	**New York, NY** (city)	1,651
New Jersey	5,695	Broward County, FL	2,129	**Elizabeth, NJ** (city) Union County	1,090
New York	3,008	Union County, NJ	1,739	**Queens, NY** (borough) Queens County	802
California	1,711	Essex County, NJ	1,109		
Georgia	1,593	Palm Beach County, FL	829		
Texas	1,051	Queens County, NY	802		
Massachusetts	999	Los Angeles County, CA	646		
Virginia	940	Hudson County, NJ	610		
Maryland	816	Gwinnett County, GA	575		
Pennsylvania	502	Middlesex County, NJ	498		

Sorted by Number in Ascending Order — U.S. = 28,000

State	Number	County	Number	Place	Number
Pennsylvania	502	Morris County, NJ	421	**Queens, NY** (borough) Queens County	802
Maryland	816	Westchester County, NY	460	**Elizabeth, NJ** (city) Union County	1,090
Virginia	940	Worcester County, MA	489	**New York, NY** (city)	1,651
Massachusetts	999	Harris County, TX	494		
Texas	1,051	Middlesex County, NJ	498		
Georgia	1,593	Gwinnett County, GA	575		
California	1,711	Hudson County, NJ	610		
New York	3,008	Los Angeles County, CA	646		
New Jersey	5,695	Queens County, NY	802		
Florida	7,810	Palm Beach County, FL	829		

Sorted by Percent in Descending Order — U.S. = 74.9%

State	Percent	County	Percent	Place	Percent
Georgia	81.3	Middlesex County, NJ	89.7	**New York, NY** (city)	76.3
Maryland	80.6	Broward County, FL	85.8	**Queens, NY** (borough) Queens County	71.5
Virginia	78.4	Palm Beach County, FL	79.0	**Elizabeth, NJ** (city) Union County	63.6
Florida	77.9	Los Angeles County, CA	76.1		
California	74.7	Miami-Dade County, FL	75.4		
New York	73.3	Gwinnett County, GA	75.0		
New Jersey	70.7	Queens County, NY	71.5		
Texas	70.2	Essex County, NJ	66.2		
Pennsylvania	68.9	Union County, NJ	65.7		
Massachusetts	60.8	Hudson County, NJ	64.3		

Sorted by Percent in Ascending Order — U.S. = 74.9%

State	Percent	County	Percent	Place	Percent
Massachusetts	60.8	Westchester County, NY	57.4	**Elizabeth, NJ** (city) Union County	63.6
Pennsylvania	68.9	Worcester County, MA	58.7	**Queens, NY** (borough) Queens County	71.5
Texas	70.2	Morris County, NJ	60.3	**New York, NY** (city)	76.3
New Jersey	70.7	Harris County, TX	62.5		
New York	73.3	Hudson County, NJ	64.3		
California	74.7	Union County, NJ	65.7		
Florida	77.9	Essex County, NJ	66.2		
Virginia	78.4	Queens County, NY	71.5		
Maryland	80.6	Gwinnett County, GA	75.0		
Georgia	81.3	Miami-Dade County, FL	75.4		

Note: (1) Ranking tables cover all states and counties, and places with an overall population of at least 125,000, OR an overall population of at least 25,000 where the Hispanic/Latino population is at least 20% of the overall population. In states where less than five places meet either of these criteria, we have included places with at least 10,000 total population with the highest percentage of Hispanic/Latino population. These places are identified with an asterisk (*); Please refer to the User's Guide for a full explanation of data.

High School Graduates

(Universe: Population 25 Years and Over)

South American: Venezuelan

Top 10 States, Counties, and Places[1]

Sorted by Number in Descending Order — U.S. = 122,521

State	Number	County	Number	Place	Number
Florida	59,352	Miami-Dade County, FL	27,562	**New York, NY** (city)	6,148
Texas	11,526	Broward County, FL	13,567	**Doral, FL** (city) Miami-Dade County	4,260
New York	8,255	Harris County, TX	4,573	**Weston, FL** (city) Broward County	3,689
California	7,118	Orange County, FL	4,341	**Miami, FL** (city) Miami-Dade County	3,558
Georgia	4,006	Palm Beach County, FL	2,517	**Houston, TX** (city) Harris County	2,587
New Jersey	3,566	Los Angeles County, CA	2,469	**Queens, NY** (borough) Queens County	2,419
Virginia	2,922	Queens County, NY	2,419	**Fontainebleau, FL** (cdp) Miami-Dade County	2,234
North Carolina	2,324	Osceola County, FL	1,639	**Manhattan, NY** (borough) New York County	1,627
Massachusetts	1,974	New York County, NY	1,627	**Pembroke Pines, FL** (city) Broward County	1,516
Illinois	1,896	Hillsborough County, FL	1,621	**Miami Beach, FL** (city) Miami-Dade County	1,279

Sorted by Number in Ascending Order — U.S. = 122,521

State	Number	County	Number	Place	Number
Missouri	430	Tarrant County, TX	391	**Coral Springs, FL** (city) Broward County	622
Wisconsin	483	Suffolk County, MA	470	**Kendall West, FL** (cdp) Miami-Dade County	700
Michigan	559	Travis County, TX	526	**Bronx, NY** (borough) Bronx County	704
Minnesota	599	Collin County, TX	530	**Hialeah, FL** (city) Miami-Dade County	747
South Carolina	644	Fulton County, GA	556	**Davie, FL** (town) Broward County	783
Indiana	678	San Diego County, CA	572	**Tamiami, FL** (cdp) Miami-Dade County	828
Arizona	748	King County, WA	626	**Aventura, FL** (city) Miami-Dade County	877
Oklahoma	755	Montgomery County, TX	634	**Los Angeles, CA** (city) Los Angeles County	888
Colorado	941	Fairfield County, CT	644	**Country Club, FL** (cdp) Miami-Dade County	891
Tennessee	974	Bronx County, NY	704	**Miramar, FL** (city) Broward County	911

Sorted by Percent in Descending Order — U.S. = 93.4%

State	Percent	County	Percent	Place	Percent
Colorado	100.0	Fulton County, GA	100.0	**Weston, FL** (city) Broward County	98.8
Washington	99.0	King County, WA	100.0	**Davie, FL** (town) Broward County	98.4
Louisiana	98.6	San Diego County, CA	100.0	**Orlando, FL** (city) Orange County	98.4
Indiana	98.5	Travis County, TX	100.0	**Coral Springs, FL** (city) Broward County	98.0
Utah	97.2	Fort Bend County, TX	99.2	**Fontainebleau, FL** (cdp) Miami-Dade County	97.0
Missouri	96.4	Fairfax County, VA	98.9	**Houston, TX** (city) Harris County	96.8
Texas	96.1	Seminole County, FL	98.6	**Doral, FL** (city) Miami-Dade County	96.6
California	95.0	Montgomery County, MD	98.5	**The Hammocks, FL** (cdp) Miami-Dade County	96.5
Maryland	94.6	Orange County, CA	98.5	**Kendall West, FL** (cdp) Miami-Dade County	95.6
Georgia	94.5	Harris County, TX	97.2	**Miami Beach, FL** (city) Miami-Dade County	95.4

Sorted by Percent in Ascending Order — U.S. = 93.4%

State	Percent	County	Percent	Place	Percent
Michigan	81.5	Kings County, NY	78.5	**Brooklyn, NY** (borough) Kings County	78.5
Arizona	82.4	Queens County, NY	82.7	**Queens, NY** (borough) Queens County	82.7
New York	86.5	Suffolk County, MA	83.6	**Bronx, NY** (borough) Bronx County	83.7
Pennsylvania	88.5	Bronx County, NY	83.7	**New York, NY** (city)	83.7
Wisconsin	89.4	Gwinnett County, GA	84.5	**Hialeah, FL** (city) Miami-Dade County	83.8
South Carolina	89.7	New York County, NY	89.1	**Pembroke Pines, FL** (city) Broward County	85.7
Tennessee	91.3	Hudson County, NJ	90.6	**Country Club, FL** (cdp) Miami-Dade County	85.8
Massachusetts	91.4	Fairfield County, CT	92.1	**Tamiami, FL** (cdp) Miami-Dade County	87.2
New Jersey	91.7	Dallas County, TX	92.6	**Los Angeles, CA** (city) Los Angeles County	88.7
Oklahoma	93.0	Pinellas County, FL	92.6	**Manhattan, NY** (borough) New York County	89.1

Note: (1) Ranking tables cover all states and counties, and places with an overall population of at least 125,000, OR an overall population of at least 25,000 where the Hispanic/Latino population is at least 20% of the overall population. In states where less than five places meet either of these criteria, we have included places with at least 10,000 total population with the highest percentage of Hispanic/Latino population. These places are identified with an asterisk (*); Please refer to the User's Guide for a full explanation of data.

High School Graduates

(Universe: Population 25 Years and Over)

Spaniard

Top 10 States, Counties, and Places[1]

Sorted by Number in Descending Order — U.S. = 311,644

State	Number	County	Number	Place	Number
California	65,718	Los Angeles County, CA	13,493	**New York, NY** (city)	11,402
Texas	31,484	Bernalillo County, NM	9,533	**Albuquerque, NM** (city) Bernalillo County	7,891
New Mexico	26,977	Miami-Dade County, FL	6,176	**Los Angeles, CA** (city) Los Angeles County	4,624
Florida	26,133	San Diego County, CA	6,076	**Queens, NY** (borough) Queens County	3,341
Colorado	22,418	Maricopa County, AZ	5,781	**San Antonio, TX** (city) Bexar County	3,303
New York	21,247	Harris County, TX	4,888	**Manhattan, NY** (borough) New York County	3,017
New Jersey	11,999	Hillsborough County, FL	4,836	**Denver, CO** (city) Denver County	3,015
Arizona	10,019	Orange County, CA	4,413	**San Diego, CA** (city) San Diego County	2,916
Washington	7,461	Bexar County, TX	4,157	**Brooklyn, NY** (borough) Kings County	2,313
Illinois	6,092	Riverside County, CA	3,905	**Houston, TX** (city) Harris County	2,250

Sorted by Number in Ascending Order — U.S. = 311,644

State	Number	County	Number	Place	Number
Iowa	444	Las Animas County, CO	214	**San Bernardino, CA** (city) San Bernardino County	370
Maine	631	Tulare County, CA	229	**Las Cruces, NM** (city) Dona Ana County	386
New Hampshire	657	La Plata County, CO	263	**Fort Collins, CO** (city) Larimer County	395
Mississippi	671	Butte County, CA	310	**Anchorage, AK** (municipality)	436
West Virginia	688	Utah County, UT	317	**Riverside, CA** (city) Riverside County	462
Montana	748	Milwaukee County, WI	340	**Kearny, NJ** (town) Hudson County	473
Nebraska	777	Douglas County, NE	343	**Fresno, CA** (city) Fresno County	483
District of Columbia	841	Colfax County, NM	349	**Glendale, AZ** (city) Maricopa County	493
Alaska	855	Rio Arriba County, NM	350	**Oyster Bay, NY** (town) Nassau County	514
Wyoming	969	Weber County, UT	383	**Philadelphia, PA** (city) Philadelphia County	527

Sorted by Percent in Descending Order — U.S. = 87.7%

State	Percent	County	Percent	Place	Percent
New Hampshire	96.9	Denton County, TX	100.0	**Anchorage, AK** (municipality)	100.0
Alaska	96.6	Milwaukee County, WI	100.0	**Seattle, WA** (city) King County	97.8
Wisconsin	96.3	Washington County, OR	99.2	**Portland, OR** (city) Multnomah County	97.3
Kansas	95.4	Fairfield County, CT	98.7	**San Francisco, CA** (city) San Francisco County	95.8
Maine	95.2	Collin County, TX	98.6	**Rio Rancho, NM** (city) Sandoval County	95.7
Connecticut	94.9	Douglas County, CO	97.8	**Fort Worth, TX** (city) Tarrant County	95.2
Tennessee	94.5	King County, WA	97.8	**Staten Island, NY** (borough) Richmond County	94.7
Maryland	93.5	Montgomery County, PA	97.4	**Virginia Beach, VA** (independent city)	94.6
Hawaii	92.9	Taos County, NM	96.6	**Aurora, CO** (city) Arapahoe County	94.1
Pennsylvania	92.6	Middlesex County, MA	96.5	**Brookhaven, NY** (town) Suffolk County	93.9

Sorted by Percent in Ascending Order — U.S. = 87.7%

State	Percent	County	Percent	Place	Percent
Mississippi	74.4	Fresno County, CA	69.3	**Newark, NJ** (city) Essex County	58.0
Nebraska	81.0	La Plata County, CO	70.3	**Kearny, NJ** (town) Hudson County	58.7
Utah	82.0	Tulare County, CA	70.5	**Fresno, CA** (city) Fresno County	63.6
Louisiana	82.6	Hudson County, NJ	71.4	**South Valley, NM** (cdp) Bernalillo County	70.3
New Jersey	82.6	Essex County, NJ	71.5	**Pueblo, CO** (city) Pueblo County	74.8
West Virginia	82.7	Passaic County, NJ	72.5	**Stockton, CA** (city) San Joaquin County	77.5
Alabama	83.5	Las Animas County, CO	73.5	**San Bernardino, CA** (city) San Bernardino County	79.2
Wyoming	83.6	Utah County, UT	74.4	**Corpus Christi, TX** (city) Nueces County	79.7
Oklahoma	84.1	Union County, NJ	74.5	**Riverside, CA** (city) Riverside County	81.2
Indiana	84.3	Douglas County, NE	76.1	**Henderson, NV** (city) Clark County	82.2

Note: (1) Ranking tables cover all states and counties, and places with an overall population of at least 125,000, OR an overall population of at least 25,000 where the Hispanic/Latino population is at least 20% of the overall population. In states where less than five places meet either of these criteria, we have included places with at least 10,000 total population with the highest percentage of Hispanic/Latino population. These places are identified with an asterisk (*); Please refer to the User's Guide for a full explanation of data.

Four-Year College Graduates

(Universe: Population 25 Years and Over)

Total Population

Top 10 States, Counties, and Places[1]

Sorted by Number in Descending Order — U.S. = 55,726,999

State	Number	County	Number	Place	Number
California	7,063,690	Los Angeles County, CA	1,816,606	**New York, NY** (city)	1,816,233
New York	4,149,168	Cook County, IL	1,131,925	**Los Angeles, CA** (city) Los Angeles County	742,172
Texas	3,894,123	Orange County, CA	693,883	**Manhattan, NY** (borough) New York County	665,064
Florida	3,313,411	Maricopa County, AZ	689,976	**Chicago, IL** (city) Cook County	570,134
Illinois	2,526,884	Harris County, TX	674,371	**Brooklyn, NY** (borough) Kings County	463,908
Pennsylvania	2,258,056	New York County, NY	665,064	**Queens, NY** (borough) Queens County	450,252
New Jersey	2,037,395	San Diego County, CA	663,054	**Houston, TX** (city) Harris County	367,369
Ohio	1,848,454	King County, WA	587,701	**San Diego, CA** (city) San Diego County	340,907
Virginia	1,761,162	Santa Clara County, CA	525,838	**San Francisco, CA** (city) San Francisco County	311,713
Massachusetts	1,678,209	Middlesex County, MA	502,407	**Seattle, WA** (city) King County	239,356

Sorted by Number in Ascending Order — U.S. = 55,726,999

State	Number	County	Number	Place	Number
Wyoming	84,326	Clark County, ID	30	**Fort Campbell North*, KY** (cdp) Christian County	262
North Dakota	112,977	Kenedy County, TX	33	**Parker*, SC** (cdp) Greenville County	316
Alaska	116,112	McMullen County, TX	68	**Jerome*, ID** (city) Jerome County	429
South Dakota	131,234	Harding County, NM	103	**Lexington*, NE** (city) Dawson County	536
Vermont	141,865	Kent County, TX	109	**Maywood, CA** (city) Los Angeles County	539
Delaware	162,651	Glasscock County, TX	126	**Wasco, CA** (city) Kern County	634
Montana	182,330	Terrell County, TX	131	**Waianae*, HI** (cdp) Honolulu County	654
District of Columbia	196,513	Echols County, GA	144	**Hope*, AR** (city) Hempstead County	679
Rhode Island	214,958	Motley County, TX	145	**Berea*, SC** (cdp) Greenville County	747
West Virginia	221,274	Foard County, TX	150	**Bell, CA** (city) Los Angeles County	754

Sorted by Percent in Descending Order — U.S. = 27.9%

State	Percent	County	Percent	Place	Percent
District of Columbia	49.2	Arlington County, VA	70.1	**Hanover*, NH** (town) Grafton County	82.4
Massachusetts	38.3	Los Alamos County, NM	64.0	**Arlington, VA** (cdp) Arlington County	70.1
Colorado	35.9	Pitkin County, CO	59.7	**Irvine, CA** (city) Orange County	65.5
Maryland	35.7	Howard County, MD	58.3	**Naperville, IL** (city) DuPage County	65.1
Connecticut	35.2	Fairfax County, VA	58.0	**Coral Gables, FL** (city) Miami-Dade County	63.7
New Jersey	34.6	Loudoun County, VA	57.2	**Cary, NC** (town) Wake County	62.3
Virginia	33.8	Boulder County, CO	57.0	**Alexandria, VA** (independent city)	60.4
Vermont	33.3	New York County, NY	57.0	**Mountain View, CA** (city) Santa Clara County	58.7
New Hampshire	32.9	Montgomery County, MD	56.7	**Weston, FL** (city) Broward County	58.5
New York	32.1	Douglas County, CO	54.4	**Manhattan, NY** (borough) New York County	57.0

Sorted by Percent in Ascending Order — U.S. = 27.9%

State	Percent	County	Percent	Place	Percent
West Virginia	17.3	Clinton County, KY	3.7	**Maywood, CA** (city) Los Angeles County	3.6
Arkansas	19.1	Brantley County, GA	4.9	**Bell, CA** (city) Los Angeles County	3.8
Mississippi	19.5	Lake County, TN	5.2	**Florence-Graham, CA** (cdp) Los Angeles County	3.8
Kentucky	20.3	Clark County, ID	5.3	**Bell Gardens, CA** (city) Los Angeles County	4.5
Louisiana	20.9	Greensville County, VA	5.5	**Wasco, CA** (city) Kern County	4.6
Alabama	21.7	Pulaski County, GA	5.6	**Coachella, CA** (city) Riverside County	4.7
Nevada	21.8	Echols County, GA	6.1	**Lynwood, CA** (city) Los Angeles County	4.7
Indiana	22.4	Baker County, FL	6.2	**Parker*, SC** (cdp) Greenville County	4.8
Oklahoma	22.6	Dixie County, FL	6.2	**Florence, AZ** (town) Pinal County	4.9
Tennessee	22.7	Morgan County, TN	6.3	**Soledad, CA** (city) Monterey County	5.3

Note: (1) Ranking tables cover all states and counties, and places with an overall population of at least 125,000, OR an overall population of at least 25,000 where the Hispanic/Latino population is at least 20% of the overall population. In states where less than five places meet either of these criteria, we have included places with at least 10,000 total population with the highest percentage of Hispanic/Latino population. These places are identified with an asterisk (*); Please refer to the User's Guide for a full explanation of data.

Four-Year College Graduates

(Universe: Population 25 Years and Over)

Hispanic or Latino (of any race)

Top 10 States, Counties, and Places[1]

Sorted by Number in Descending Order — U.S. = 3,329,326

State	Number	County	Number	Place	Number
California	730,285	Miami-Dade County, FL	259,134	**New York, NY** (city)	206,669
Florida	532,242	Los Angeles County, CA	246,860	**Los Angeles, CA** (city) Los Angeles County	92,069
Texas	528,931	Harris County, TX	80,525	**Queens, NY** (borough) Queens County	59,895
New York	304,711	Cook County, IL	75,164	**San Antonio, TX** (city) Bexar County	59,647
New Jersey	134,127	Bexar County, TX	74,832	**Manhattan, NY** (borough) New York County	55,322
Illinois	119,375	Broward County, FL	73,459	**El Paso, TX** (city) El Paso County	47,994
Arizona	93,714	San Diego County, CA	71,064	**Chicago, IL** (city) Cook County	46,857
Virginia	71,415	Orange County, CA	61,560	**Bronx, NY** (borough) Bronx County	46,757
New Mexico	66,753	Queens County, NY	59,895	**Houston, TX** (city) Harris County	44,661
Colorado	61,984	New York County, NY	55,322	**Miami, FL** (city) Miami-Dade County	38,521

Sorted by Number in Ascending Order — U.S. = 3,329,326

State	Number	County	Number	Place	Number
North Dakota	915	Adams County, IN	0	**Berea*, SC** (cdp) Greenville County	13
South Dakota	1,378	Becker County, MN	0	**Green River*, WY** (city) Sweetwater County	16
Maine	1,631	Cass County, IL	0	**Warr Acres*, OK** (city) Oklahoma County	17
Vermont	1,741	Choctaw County, OK	0	**Waianae*, HI** (cdp) Honolulu County	20
West Virginia	2,145	Clark County, ID	0	**Albertville*, AL** (city) Marshall County	21
Wyoming	2,298	Coke County, TX	0	**Mayfield*, KY** (city) Graves County	23
Montana	2,412	Cuming County, NE	0	**Jerome*, ID** (city) Jerome County	29
Alaska	3,433	Dickens County, TX	0	**Willmar*, MN** (city) Kandiyohi County	32
Mississippi	4,110	Evans County, GA	0	**Muscatine*, IA** (city) Muscatine County	36
Delaware	4,163	Franklin County, IA	0	**Middle*, DE** (town) New Castle County	37

Sorted by Percent in Descending Order — U.S. = 13.0%

State	Percent	County	Percent	Place	Percent
Vermont	36.9	Athens County, OH	56.7	**Coral Gables, FL** (city) Miami-Dade County	59.4
District of Columbia	35.9	Tompkins County, NY	51.8	**Weston, FL** (city) Broward County	57.5
New Hampshire	25.5	Story County, IA	50.4	**Morgantown*, WV** (city) Monongalia County	56.2
Virginia	22.7	Windham County, VT	50.4	**Doral, FL** (city) Miami-Dade County	54.3
Florida	21.2	Monongalia County, WV	49.0	**Aventura, FL** (city) Miami-Dade County	53.2
Maine	20.4	Chittenden County, VT	46.1	**Burlington*, VT** (city) Chittenden County	44.2
Maryland	20.0	York County, VA	43.9	**Tallahassee, FL** (city) Leon County	41.1
West Virginia	19.3	Ashland County, OH	43.1	**Irvine, CA** (city) Orange County	40.7
Montana	18.8	Alachua County, FL	43.0	**Plantation, FL** (city) Broward County	40.6
Alaska	18.2	Whitman County, WA	41.1	**Bozeman*, MT** (city) Gallatin County	38.6

Sorted by Percent in Ascending Order — U.S. = 13.0%

State	Percent	County	Percent	Place	Percent
Idaho	7.8	Adams County, IN	0.0	**Berea*, SC** (cdp) Greenville County	0.9
Nevada	8.4	Becker County, MN	0.0	**Albertville*, AL** (city) Marshall County	1.1
Arkansas	8.9	Cass County, IL	0.0	**Lufkin, TX** (city) Angelina County	1.1
Oklahoma	9.5	Choctaw County, OK	0.0	**Florence, AZ** (town) Pinal County	1.4
Wyoming	9.6	Clark County, ID	0.0	**Willowbrook, CA** (cdp) Los Angeles County	1.7
Nebraska	9.9	Coke County, TX	0.0	**Jerome*, ID** (city) Jerome County	2.0
California	10.2	Cuming County, NE	0.0	**Willmar*, MN** (city) Kandiyohi County	2.0
Arizona	10.3	Dickens County, TX	0.0	**Green River*, WY** (city) Sweetwater County	2.2
Iowa	10.9	Evans County, GA	0.0	**Lexington*, NE** (city) Dawson County	2.2
Oregon	10.9	Franklin County, IA	0.0	**Rosenberg, TX** (city) Fort Bend County	2.2

Note: (1) Ranking tables cover all states and counties, and places with an overall population of at least 125,000, OR an overall population of at least 25,000 where the Hispanic/Latino population is at least 20% of the overall population. In states where less than five places meet either of these criteria, we have included places with at least 10,000 total population with the highest percentage of Hispanic/Latino population. These places are identified with an asterisk (*); Please refer to the User's Guide for a full explanation of data.

Four-Year College Graduates

(Universe: Population 25 Years and Over)

Central American, excluding Mexican

Top 10 States, Counties, and Places[1]

Sorted by Number in Descending Order — U.S. = 259,600

State	Number	County	Number	Place	Number
California	76,505	Los Angeles County, CA	38,699	**Los Angeles, CA** (city) Los Angeles County	19,863
Florida	41,173	Miami-Dade County, FL	22,957	**New York, NY** (city)	14,636
New York	23,946	Harris County, TX	7,260	**Miami, FL** (city) Miami-Dade County	4,876
Texas	19,614	Queens County, NY	4,720	**Queens, NY** (borough) Queens County	4,720
Virginia	12,048	Broward County, FL	4,672	**Houston, TX** (city) Harris County	4,131
New Jersey	9,872	Fairfax County, VA	4,462	**Brooklyn, NY** (borough) Kings County	3,974
Maryland	9,206	Cook County, IL	4,170	**San Francisco, CA** (city) San Francisco County	3,119
Illinois	6,639	Kings County, NY	3,974	**Manhattan, NY** (borough) New York County	2,882
Massachusetts	6,214	Montgomery County, MD	3,974	**Chicago, IL** (city) Cook County	2,774
Georgia	5,694	Orange County, CA	3,874	**Bronx, NY** (borough) Bronx County	2,558

Sorted by Number in Ascending Order — U.S. = 259,600

State	Number	County	Number	Place	Number
South Dakota	25	Carroll County, AR	0	**Albertville*, AL** (city) Marshall County	0
Maine	38	Colfax County, NE	0	**Chattanooga, TN** (city) Hamilton County	0
Vermont	59	Crawford County, AR	0	**Cincinnati, OH** (city) Hamilton County	0
New Hampshire	112	Dawson County, NE	0	**Cranston*, RI** (city) Providence County	0
Idaho	145	Etowah County, AL	0	**Farmers Branch, TX** (city) Dallas County	0
Wyoming	148	Finney County, KS	0	**Gainesville, GA** (city) Hall County	0
West Virginia	163	Franklin County, AL	0	**Garden City, KS** (city) Finney County	0
Alaska	275	Hamilton County, TN	0	**Lexington*, NE** (city) Dawson County	0
Delaware	392	Hendry County, FL	0	**Reading, PA** (city) Berks County	0
Hawaii	408	Lee County, NC	0	**Sanford, NC** (city) Lee County	0

Sorted by Percent in Descending Order — U.S. = 11.2%

State	Percent	County	Percent	Place	Percent
Hawaii	28.8	Douglas County, CO	52.3	**Doral, FL** (city) Miami-Dade County	53.6
Wyoming	22.7	Saint Louis County, MO	42.7	**Coral Gables, FL** (city) Miami-Dade County	49.4
Wisconsin	21.7	Hamilton County, IN	41.3	**Weston, FL** (city) Broward County	47.0
Alaska	20.5	Norfolk County, MA	40.3	**Irvine, CA** (city) Orange County	46.7
West Virginia	20.3	Allegheny County, PA	39.1	**Chino Hills, CA** (city) San Bernardino County	39.1
Vermont	19.9	Alachua County, FL	38.9	**Mountain View, CA** (city) Santa Clara County	35.9
New Mexico	19.2	New Castle County, DE	36.9	**University Park, FL** (cdp) Miami-Dade County	34.3
Ohio	16.7	Lane County, OR	36.3	**Lake Forest, CA** (city) Orange County	34.0
Missouri	16.6	Leon County, FL	32.8	**The Hammocks, FL** (cdp) Miami-Dade County	33.3
Illinois	16.4	Lake County, IN	32.7	**Plantation, FL** (city) Broward County	32.9

Sorted by Percent in Ascending Order — U.S. = 11.2%

State	Percent	County	Percent	Place	Percent
South Dakota	2.0	Carroll County, AR	0.0	**Albertville*, AL** (city) Marshall County	0.0
Nebraska	5.8	Colfax County, NE	0.0	**Chattanooga, TN** (city) Hamilton County	0.0
Arkansas	6.1	Crawford County, AR	0.0	**Cincinnati, OH** (city) Hamilton County	0.0
Maine	6.1	Dawson County, NE	0.0	**Cranston*, RI** (city) Providence County	0.0
Iowa	6.5	Etowah County, AL	0.0	**Farmers Branch, TX** (city) Dallas County	0.0
Tennessee	6.6	Finney County, KS	0.0	**Gainesville, GA** (city) Hall County	0.0
Nevada	7.0	Franklin County, AL	0.0	**Garden City, KS** (city) Finney County	0.0
Rhode Island	7.0	Hamilton County, TN	0.0	**Lexington*, NE** (city) Dawson County	0.0
New Hampshire	7.4	Hendry County, FL	0.0	**Reading, PA** (city) Berks County	0.0
Idaho	7.8	Lee County, NC	0.0	**Sanford, NC** (city) Lee County	0.0

Note: (1) Ranking tables cover all states and counties, and places with an overall population of at least 125,000, OR an overall population of at least 25,000 where the Hispanic/Latino population is at least 20% of the overall population. In states where less than five places meet either of these criteria, we have included places with at least 10,000 total population with the highest percentage of Hispanic/Latino population. These places are identified with an asterisk (*); Please refer to the User's Guide for a full explanation of data.

Four-Year College Graduates

(Universe: Population 25 Years and Over)

Central American: Costa Rican

Top 10 States, Counties, and Places[1]

Sorted by Number in Descending Order U.S. = 19,902

State	Number	County	Number	Place	Number
California	4,180	Los Angeles County, CA	1,663	**New York, NY** (city)	1,096
Florida	3,142	Miami-Dade County, FL	1,217	**Los Angeles, CA** (city) Los Angeles County	458
New York	1,683	Broward County, FL	598	**Brooklyn, NY** (borough) Kings County	380
New Jersey	1,380	Orange County, CA	410	**Queens, NY** (borough) Queens County	373
Texas	1,021	Kings County, NY	380	**Miami, FL** (city) Miami-Dade County	176
North Carolina	720	Queens County, NY	373	**Bronx, NY** (borough) Bronx County	82
Maryland	648	Cook County, IL	334	**Philadelphia, PA** (city) Philadelphia County	76
Massachusetts	631	San Bernardino County, CA	257		
Illinois	619	Union County, NJ	244		
Georgia	562	Contra Costa County, CA	232		

Sorted by Number in Ascending Order U.S. = 19,902

State	Number	County	Number	Place	Number
Tennessee	111	Mercer County, NJ	11	**Philadelphia, PA** (city) Philadelphia County	76
Michigan	112	Fairfield County, CT	67	**Bronx, NY** (borough) Bronx County	82
Wisconsin	140	Nassau County, NY	76	**Miami, FL** (city) Miami-Dade County	176
Oregon	161	Philadelphia County, PA	76	**Queens, NY** (borough) Queens County	373
Nevada	167	Bronx County, NY	82	**Brooklyn, NY** (borough) Kings County	380
Connecticut	199	Orange County, FL	99	**Los Angeles, CA** (city) Los Angeles County	458
Louisiana	226	Clark County, NV	133	**New York, NY** (city)	1,096
Washington	241	Passaic County, NJ	143		
Minnesota	269	Palm Beach County, FL	145		
Arizona	287	Essex County, NJ	150		

Sorted by Percent in Descending Order U.S. = 25.3%

State	Percent	County	Percent	Place	Percent
Colorado	55.2	Contra Costa County, CA	38.9	**Queens, NY** (borough) Queens County	26.5
Minnesota	51.8	Cook County, IL	34.4	**New York, NY** (city)	24.2
Illinois	43.6	Broward County, FL	32.9	**Los Angeles, CA** (city) Los Angeles County	23.3
Virginia	42.9	Orange County, CA	30.2	**Brooklyn, NY** (borough) Kings County	22.7
Maryland	40.5	Maricopa County, AZ	30.1	**Miami, FL** (city) Miami-Dade County	17.3
Washington	38.1	Queens County, NY	26.5	**Bronx, NY** (borough) Bronx County	12.8
Wisconsin	37.5	Los Angeles County, CA	26.2	**Philadelphia, PA** (city) Philadelphia County	10.3
South Carolina	36.3	Riverside County, CA	25.8		
Arizona	30.8	Hillsborough County, FL	25.6		
Oregon	30.6	San Diego County, CA	24.8		

Sorted by Percent in Ascending Order U.S. = 25.3%

State	Percent	County	Percent	Place	Percent
New Jersey	11.4	Mercer County, NJ	1.3	**Philadelphia, PA** (city) Philadelphia County	10.3
Connecticut	15.1	Fairfield County, CT	8.1	**Bronx, NY** (borough) Bronx County	12.8
Nevada	15.5	Union County, NJ	10.0	**Miami, FL** (city) Miami-Dade County	17.3
Pennsylvania	16.5	Nassau County, NY	10.3	**Brooklyn, NY** (borough) Kings County	22.7
New York	21.8	Philadelphia County, PA	10.3	**Los Angeles, CA** (city) Los Angeles County	23.3
Louisiana	22.1	Morris County, NJ	12.5	**New York, NY** (city)	24.2
Florida	24.1	Bronx County, NY	12.8	**Queens, NY** (borough) Queens County	26.5
Tennessee	24.6	Passaic County, NJ	12.9		
Georgia	24.9	Essex County, NJ	13.3		
North Carolina	25.3	Orange County, FL	13.4		

Note: (1) Ranking tables cover all states and counties, and places with an overall population of at least 125,000, OR an overall population of at least 25,000 where the Hispanic/Latino population is at least 20% of the overall population. In states where less than five places meet either of these criteria, we have included places with at least 10,000 total population with the highest percentage of Hispanic/Latino population. These places are identified with an asterisk (*); Please refer to the User's Guide for a full explanation of data.

Four-Year College Graduates

(Universe: Population 25 Years and Over)

Central American: Guatemalan

Top 10 States, Counties, and Places[1]

Sorted by Number in Descending Order — U.S. = 49,972

State	Number	County	Number	Place	Number
California	18,216	Los Angeles County, CA	10,806	**Los Angeles, CA** (city) Los Angeles County	6,163
Florida	4,295	Cook County, IL	1,973	**New York, NY** (city)	2,061
New York	3,731	Miami-Dade County, FL	1,709	**Chicago, IL** (city) Cook County	1,435
Texas	2,969	Harris County, TX	1,084	**Queens, NY** (borough) Queens County	872
Illinois	2,877	San Bernardino County, CA	992	**Houston, TX** (city) Harris County	707
Massachusetts	2,052	Orange County, CA	919	**San Francisco, CA** (city) San Francisco County	561
New Jersey	2,046	Queens County, NY	872	**Brooklyn, NY** (borough) Kings County	471
Maryland	1,355	Middlesex County, MA	707	**Boston, MA** (city) Suffolk County	452
Virginia	1,305	Montgomery County, MD	702	**Manhattan, NY** (borough) New York County	418
Georgia	970	Palm Beach County, FL	669	**Miami, FL** (city) Miami-Dade County	331

Sorted by Number in Ascending Order — U.S. = 49,972

State	Number	County	Number	Place	Number
South Dakota	15	Adams County, CO	0	**Albertville*, AL** (city) Marshall County	0
New Hampshire	17	Dawson County, NE	0	**Bell, CA** (city) Los Angeles County	0
Idaho	29	Franklin County, AL	0	**Cathedral City, CA** (city) Riverside County	0
Mississippi	64	Hamilton County, TN	0	**Chattanooga, TN** (city) Hamilton County	0
Missouri	119	Lee County, AL	0	**Chelsea, MA** (city) Suffolk County	0
South Carolina	145	Marshall County, AL	0	**Cincinnati, OH** (city) Hamilton County	0
Arkansas	158	Minnehaha County, SD	0	**Cranston*, RI** (city) Providence County	0
Wisconsin	167	Murray County, GA	0	**Gardena, CA** (city) Los Angeles County	0
Delaware	168	Nobles County, MN	0	**Lexington*, NE** (city) Dawson County	0
Kansas	178	Rutherford County, TN	0	**North Las Vegas, NV** (city) Clark County	0

Sorted by Percent in Descending Order — U.S. = 8.7%

State	Percent	County	Percent	Place	Percent
Wisconsin	22.4	Utah County, UT	27.0	**Minneapolis, MN** (city) Hennepin County	32.0
Louisiana	17.5	New York County, NY	26.0	**West Covina, CA** (city) Los Angeles County	27.4
District of Columbia	17.1	Osceola County, FL	25.1	**Manhattan, NY** (borough) New York County	26.0
Utah	16.5	Lake County, IL	23.0	**Garden Grove, CA** (city) Orange County	25.3
New Mexico	15.6	Arlington County, VA	22.4	**San Diego, CA** (city) San Diego County	25.1
Kentucky	15.1	Santa Barbara County, CA	22.0	**Sacramento, CA** (city) Sacramento County	23.0
Illinois	14.2	Santa Clara County, CA	21.8	**Arlington, VA** (cdp) Arlington County	22.4
Pennsylvania	13.4	Worcester County, MA	21.3	**San Jose, CA** (city) Santa Clara County	22.2
Ohio	12.6	Stanislaus County, CA	21.1	**Charlotte, NC** (city) Mecklenburg County	21.3
Minnesota	12.4	Mecklenburg County, NC	21.0	**Winston-Salem, NC** (city) Forsyth County	19.5

Sorted by Percent in Ascending Order — U.S. = 8.7%

State	Percent	County	Percent	Place	Percent
South Dakota	2.0	Adams County, CO	0.0	**Albertville*, AL** (city) Marshall County	0.0
Alabama	3.3	Dawson County, NE	0.0	**Bell, CA** (city) Los Angeles County	0.0
South Carolina	3.3	Franklin County, AL	0.0	**Cathedral City, CA** (city) Riverside County	0.0
New Hampshire	4.3	Hamilton County, TN	0.0	**Chattanooga, TN** (city) Hamilton County	0.0
Tennessee	4.3	Lee County, AL	0.0	**Chelsea, MA** (city) Suffolk County	0.0
Nevada	4.7	Marshall County, AL	0.0	**Cincinnati, OH** (city) Hamilton County	0.0
Idaho	4.8	Minnehaha County, SD	0.0	**Cranston*, RI** (city) Providence County	0.0
Nebraska	4.8	Murray County, GA	0.0	**Gardena, CA** (city) Los Angeles County	0.0
Georgia	5.1	Nobles County, MN	0.0	**Lexington*, NE** (city) Dawson County	0.0
Missouri	5.4	Rutherford County, TN	0.0	**North Las Vegas, NV** (city) Clark County	0.0

RANKINGS & COMPARISONS

Note: (1) Ranking tables cover all states and counties, and places with an overall population of at least 125,000, OR an overall population of at least 25,000 where the Hispanic/Latino population is at least 20% of the overall population. In states where less than five places meet either of these criteria, we have included places with at least 10,000 total population with the highest percentage of Hispanic/Latino population. These places are identified with an asterisk (*); Please refer to the User's Guide for a full explanation of data.

Four-Year College Graduates

(Universe: Population 25 Years and Over)

Central American: Honduran

Top 10 States, Counties, and Places[1]

Sorted by Number in Descending Order — U.S. = 36,825

State	Number	County	Number	Place	Number
Florida	7,496	Miami-Dade County, FL	3,302	**New York, NY** (city)	3,421
New York	4,937	Los Angeles County, CA	2,007	**Bronx, NY** (borough) Bronx County	1,147
California	3,804	Broward County, FL	1,176	**Los Angeles, CA** (city) Los Angeles County	1,102
Texas	3,108	Bronx County, NY	1,147	**Miami, FL** (city) Miami-Dade County	1,093
Louisiana	2,178	Harris County, TX	1,114	**Brooklyn, NY** (borough) Kings County	879
Virginia	2,062	Jefferson Parish, LA	1,042	**Queens, NY** (borough) Queens County	816
New Jersey	1,949	Kings County, NY	879	**Houston, TX** (city) Harris County	513
Massachusetts	1,284	Queens County, NY	816	**Metairie, LA** (cdp) Jefferson Parish	507
Maryland	1,262	Hudson County, NJ	762	**Boston, MA** (city) Suffolk County	439
North Carolina	1,124	Fairfax County, VA	691	**Manhattan, NY** (borough) New York County	412

Sorted by Number in Ascending Order — U.S. = 36,825

State	Number	County	Number	Place	Number
Nebraska	69	Sampson County, NC	7	**Pasadena, TX** (city) Harris County	0
Arkansas	82	Johnston County, NC	10	**Conroe, TX** (city) Montgomery County	14
Iowa	84	New Haven County, CT	10	**Elizabeth, NJ** (city) Union County	14
Kentucky	125	Clayton County, GA	11	**Newark, NJ** (city) Essex County	21
Oklahoma	128	Hall County, GA	21	**Garland, TX** (city) Dallas County	32
Oregon	146	Elkhart County, IN	22	**Pasadena, CA** (city) Los Angeles County	32
Michigan	151	Davidson County, TN	35	**Aurora, CO** (city) Arapahoe County	33
Alabama	162	Durham County, NC	38	**Waukegan, IL** (city) Lake County	33
Mississippi	162	Atlantic County, NJ	43	**San Jose, CA** (city) Santa Clara County	34
District of Columbia	179	Kern County, CA	44	**Nashville-Davidson, TN** (metropolitan govt) Davidson County	35

Sorted by Percent in Descending Order — U.S. = 10.3%

State	Percent	County	Percent	Place	Percent
Utah	20.0	Fort Bend County, TX	30.4	**South Miami Heights, FL** (cdp) Miami-Dade County	23.8
Massachusetts	18.8	Baltimore County, MD	24.5	**Raleigh, NC** (city) Wake County	21.5
Wisconsin	17.8	Essex County, MA	24.5	**Staten Island, NY** (borough) Richmond County	20.8
Ohio	17.7	Salt Lake County, UT	24.5	**Boston, MA** (city) Suffolk County	20.6
Washington	16.1	Osceola County, FL	22.7	**Phoenix, AZ** (city) Maricopa County	19.0
District of Columbia	15.2	Hartford County, CT	22.4	**Metairie, LA** (cdp) Jefferson Parish	18.0
Michigan	14.6	Westchester County, NY	21.8	**Miramar, FL** (city) Broward County	16.9
Connecticut	14.3	East Baton Rouge Parish, LA	21.1	**Yonkers, NY** (city) Westchester County	16.8
Kentucky	14.2	Richmond County, NY	20.8	**Jersey City, NJ** (city) Hudson County	16.5
Iowa	13.9	Wake County, NC	20.0	**Springfield, VA** (cdp) Fairfax County	15.9

Sorted by Percent in Ascending Order — U.S. = 10.3%

State	Percent	County	Percent	Place	Percent
Tennessee	3.2	Clayton County, GA	1.1	**Pasadena, TX** (city) Harris County	0.0
Texas	6.2	Sampson County, NC	1.2	**Elizabeth, NJ** (city) Union County	1.2
North Carolina	7.0	Johnston County, NC	1.6	**Durham, NC** (city) Durham County	1.7
Nevada	7.6	Durham County, NC	1.7	**Conroe, TX** (city) Montgomery County	2.0
Nebraska	7.8	Davidson County, TN	2.2	**Long Beach, CA** (city) Los Angeles County	2.2
Oklahoma	8.5	New Haven County, CT	2.9	**Nashville-Davidson, TN** (metropolitan govt) Davidson County	2.2
Colorado	8.8	Hall County, GA	3.3	**Newark, NJ** (city) Essex County	2.4
California	8.9	Elkhart County, IN	3.7	**Waukegan, IL** (city) Lake County	2.5
Arkansas	9.3	Marion County, IN	3.7	**New Brunswick, NJ** (city) Middlesex County	2.8
Georgia	9.3	Duplin County, NC	3.9	**San Jose, CA** (city) Santa Clara County	2.8

Note: (1) Ranking tables cover all states and counties, and places with an overall population of at least 125,000, OR an overall population of at least 25,000 where the Hispanic/Latino population is at least 20% of the overall population. In states where less than five places meet either of these criteria, we have included places with at least 10,000 total population with the highest percentage of Hispanic/Latino population. These places are identified with an asterisk (*); Please refer to the User's Guide for a full explanation of data.

Four-Year College Graduates

(Universe: Population 25 Years and Over)

Central American: Nicaraguan

Top 10 States, Counties, and Places[1]

Sorted by Number in Descending Order — U.S. = 43,076

State	Number	County	Number	Place	Number
Florida	16,845	Miami-Dade County, FL	13,426	**Miami, FL** (city) Miami-Dade County	2,947
California	11,875	Los Angeles County, CA	3,795	**New York, NY** (city)	1,442
Texas	2,677	San Mateo County, CA	1,365	**Los Angeles, CA** (city) Los Angeles County	1,435
New York	2,054	Broward County, FL	1,039	**Fountainebleau, FL** (cdp) Miami-Dade County	1,007
Louisiana	1,265	Contra Costa County, CA	973	**Hialeah, FL** (city) Miami-Dade County	895
New Jersey	867	Jefferson Parish, LA	936	**The Hammocks, FL** (cdp) Miami-Dade County	736
Virginia	819	Harris County, TX	919	**San Francisco, CA** (city) San Francisco County	701
Maryland	732	San Bernardino County, CA	857	**Tamiami, FL** (cdp) Miami-Dade County	694
North Carolina	712	Alameda County, CA	779	**Kendale Lakes, FL** (cdp) Miami-Dade County	645
Georgia	452	San Francisco County, CA	701	**Houston, TX** (city) Harris County	545

Sorted by Number in Ascending Order — U.S. = 43,076

State	Number	County	Number	Place	Number
Tennessee	102	Camden County, NJ	45	**North Miami, FL** (city) Miami-Dade County	46
Oregon	123	Collier County, FL	53	**Las Vegas, NV** (city) Clark County	49
District of Columbia	139	Prince William County, VA	59	**Fontana, CA** (city) San Bernardino County	55
Colorado	153	San Joaquin County, CA	67	**Sacramento, CA** (city) Sacramento County	59
Minnesota	173	Prince George's County, MD	75	**Chicago, IL** (city) Cook County	80
Massachusetts	189	Sonoma County, CA	92	**South Gate, CA** (city) Los Angeles County	88
Connecticut	190	Gwinnett County, GA	104	**South San Francisco, CA** (city) San Mateo County	88
Missouri	191	Duval County, FL	115	**Richmond, CA** (city) Contra Costa County	91
South Carolina	197	Cook County, IL	175	**Antioch, CA** (city) Contra Costa County	95
Arizona	238	Lee County, FL	180	**South Miami Heights, FL** (cdp) Miami-Dade County	95

Sorted by Percent in Descending Order — U.S. = 19.4%

State	Percent	County	Percent	Place	Percent
Michigan	56.9	King County, WA	56.6	**The Hammocks, FL** (cdp) Miami-Dade County	37.1
Washington	39.8	Stanislaus County, CA	37.2	**Kenner, LA** (city) Jefferson Parish	32.9
Connecticut	39.2	New York County, NY	30.4	**Kendall West, FL** (cdp) Miami-Dade County	32.5
Missouri	35.8	Jefferson Parish, LA	28.8	**Richmond West, FL** (cdp) Miami-Dade County	31.1
Ohio	34.6	Orange County, CA	28.5	**Manhattan, NY** (borough) New York County	30.4
Indiana	31.0	Dallas County, TX	27.5	**University Park, FL** (cdp) Miami-Dade County	28.3
Minnesota	29.7	Bexar County, TX	27.3	**Austin, TX** (city) Travis County	28.2
South Carolina	27.7	Santa Clara County, CA	26.6	**Pembroke Pines, FL** (city) Broward County	28.2
Oregon	26.1	Travis County, TX	26.1	**Kendale Lakes, FL** (cdp) Miami-Dade County	27.2
Pennsylvania	26.1	Lee County, FL	26.0	**San Diego, CA** (city) San Diego County	25.4

Sorted by Percent in Ascending Order — U.S. = 19.4%

State	Percent	County	Percent	Place	Percent
Nevada	10.1	Prince William County, VA	5.1	**North Miami, FL** (city) Miami-Dade County	4.5
Maryland	16.5	Camden County, NJ	6.1	**Fontana, CA** (city) San Bernardino County	6.9
Massachusetts	16.6	Prince George's County, MD	7.3	**West Little River, FL** (cdp) Miami-Dade County	7.4
New Jersey	16.8	San Joaquin County, CA	7.3	**Las Vegas, NV** (city) Clark County	7.8
Illinois	17.6	Collier County, FL	8.6	**Antioch, CA** (city) Contra Costa County	9.0
Colorado	17.7	Clark County, NV	11.7	**Sacramento, CA** (city) Sacramento County	9.8
Virginia	17.7	Bronx County, NY	13.5	**Hollywood, FL** (city) Broward County	10.5
Florida	17.8	Sonoma County, CA	13.7	**Chicago, IL** (city) Cook County	10.8
Tennessee	18.7	Cook County, IL	14.1	**Country Club, FL** (cdp) Miami-Dade County	11.2
Arizona	18.8	Duval County, FL	14.4	**Hialeah, FL** (city) Miami-Dade County	11.5

Note: (1) Ranking tables cover all states and counties, and places with an overall population of at least 125,000, OR an overall population of at least 25,000 where the Hispanic/Latino population is at least 20% of the overall population. In states where less than five places meet either of these criteria, we have included places with at least 10,000 total population with the highest percentage of Hispanic/Latino population. These places are identified with an asterisk (*); Please refer to the User's Guide for a full explanation of data.

Four-Year College Graduates

(Universe: Population 25 Years and Over)

Central American: Panamanian

Top 10 States, Counties, and Places[1]

Sorted by Number in Descending Order — U.S. = 30,742

State	Number	County	Number	Place	Number
Florida	5,339	Miami-Dade County, FL	1,618	**New York, NY** (city)	3,453
New York	4,790	Kings County, NY	1,384	**Brooklyn, NY** (borough) Kings County	1,384
California	3,739	Los Angeles County, CA	1,116	**Queens, NY** (borough) Queens County	785
Texas	2,718	Broward County, FL	843	**Manhattan, NY** (borough) New York County	758
Virginia	1,679	Queens County, NY	785	**Los Angeles, CA** (city) Los Angeles County	514
Georgia	1,346	New York County, NY	758	**Bronx, NY** (borough) Bronx County	408
Maryland	1,340	Harris County, TX	582	**Hempstead (town), NY** (town) Nassau County	377
New Jersey	1,340	Orange County, FL	570	**San Diego, CA** (city) San Diego County	333
Illinois	774	San Diego County, CA	569	**Houston, TX** (city) Harris County	308
North Carolina	680	Bexar County, TX	477	**San Antonio, TX** (city) Bexar County	268

Sorted by Number in Ascending Order — U.S. = 30,742

State	Number	County	Number	Place	Number
New Mexico	104	Bell County, TX	58	**Killeen, TX** (city) Bell County	40
Minnesota	105	Pierce County, WA	89	**Fayetteville, NC** (city) Cumberland County	99
Wisconsin	121	Sacramento County, CA	104	**Miami, FL** (city) Miami-Dade County	111
Mississippi	131	Cumberland County, NC	108	**Jacksonville, FL** (city) Duval County	241
Alabama	143	Clark County, NV	135	**San Antonio, TX** (city) Bexar County	268
Nevada	163	San Bernardino County, CA	136	**Houston, TX** (city) Harris County	308
Indiana	203	Dallas County, TX	151	**San Diego, CA** (city) San Diego County	333
Michigan	205	Essex County, NJ	192	**Hempstead (town), NY** (town) Nassau County	377
Oklahoma	211	Maricopa County, AZ	217	**Bronx, NY** (borough) Bronx County	408
Tennessee	221	Riverside County, CA	228	**Los Angeles, CA** (city) Los Angeles County	514

Sorted by Percent in Descending Order — U.S. = 30.8%

State	Percent	County	Percent	Place	Percent
Illinois	51.8	Cook County, IL	55.9	**Houston, TX** (city) Harris County	54.3
Maryland	43.5	Fairfax County, VA	55.7	**Manhattan, NY** (borough) New York County	49.2
Missouri	42.4	Harris County, TX	49.2	**San Diego, CA** (city) San Diego County	40.8
Connecticut	40.7	New York County, NY	49.2	**Hempstead (town), NY** (town) Nassau County	39.9
Louisiana	38.9	Palm Beach County, FL	45.9	**Los Angeles, CA** (city) Los Angeles County	36.0
Pennsylvania	37.0	Nassau County, NY	41.1	**San Antonio, TX** (city) Bexar County	34.7
Ohio	36.9	Orange County, CA	39.7	**Jacksonville, FL** (city) Duval County	33.7
New Jersey	35.6	Brevard County, FL	39.6	**Queens, NY** (borough) Queens County	27.5
Virginia	34.9	Bexar County, TX	39.4	**Bronx, NY** (borough) Bronx County	25.7
Oklahoma	34.3	Hudson County, NJ	38.5	**New York, NY** (city)	22.0

Sorted by Percent in Ascending Order — U.S. = 30.8%

State	Percent	County	Percent	Place	Percent
Alabama	16.1	Bell County, TX	8.2	**Killeen, TX** (city) Bell County	6.4
Nevada	21.3	Cumberland County, NC	11.0	**Fayetteville, NC** (city) Cumberland County	13.9
North Carolina	21.6	Kings County, NY	14.7	**Brooklyn, NY** (borough) Kings County	14.7
Tennessee	21.6	San Bernardino County, CA	16.5	**Miami, FL** (city) Miami-Dade County	15.2
Arizona	22.6	Sacramento County, CA	18.4	**New York, NY** (city)	22.0
New York	24.4	Pierce County, WA	19.3	**Bronx, NY** (borough) Bronx County	25.7
New Mexico	24.8	Clark County, NV	19.7	**Queens, NY** (borough) Queens County	27.5
Wisconsin	25.3	Dallas County, TX	24.8	**Jacksonville, FL** (city) Duval County	33.7
South Carolina	25.4	Riverside County, CA	25.0	**San Antonio, TX** (city) Bexar County	34.7
Washington	27.9	Suffolk County, NY	25.0	**Los Angeles, CA** (city) Los Angeles County	36.0

Note: (1) Ranking tables cover all states and counties, and places with an overall population of at least 125,000, OR an overall population of at least 25,000 where the Hispanic/Latino population is at least 20% of the overall population. In states where less than five places meet either of these criteria, we have included places with at least 10,000 total population with the highest percentage of Hispanic/Latino population. These places are identified with an asterisk (*); Please refer to the User's Guide for a full explanation of data.

Four-Year College Graduates

(Universe: Population 25 Years and Over)

Central American: Salvadoran

Top 10 States, Counties, and Places[1]

Sorted by Number in Descending Order — U.S. = 73,221

State	Number	County	Number	Place	Number
California	32,428	Los Angeles County, CA	18,168	**Los Angeles, CA** (city) Los Angeles County	9,646
Texas	6,713	Harris County, TX	3,279	**New York, NY** (city)	2,734
New York	6,214	Fairfax County, VA	2,279	**Houston, TX** (city) Harris County	1,997
Virginia	5,452	San Mateo County, CA	1,699	**Queens, NY** (borough) Queens County	1,397
Florida	3,581	Montgomery County, MD	1,643	**San Francisco, CA** (city) San Francisco County	1,240
Maryland	3,520	Nassau County, NY	1,581	**Hempstead (town), NY** (town) Nassau County	917
New Jersey	2,119	Alameda County, CA	1,463	**San Jose, CA** (city) Santa Clara County	680
Georgia	1,248	Miami-Dade County, FL	1,430	**Long Beach, CA** (city) Los Angeles County	601
Massachusetts	1,151	Orange County, CA	1,400	**Palmdale, CA** (city) Los Angeles County	590
North Carolina	1,110	Queens County, NY	1,397	**Islip, NY** (town) Suffolk County	568

Sorted by Number in Ascending Order — U.S. = 73,221

State	Number	County	Number	Place	Number
Idaho	46	Alamance County, NC	0	**Farmers Branch, TX** (city) Dallas County	0
Kentucky	54	Crawford County, AR	0	**Gainesville, GA** (city) Hall County	0
Nebraska	55	Forsyth County, NC	0	**Grand Island, NE** (city) Hall County	0
Alabama	60	Galveston County, TX	0	**Greensboro, NC** (city) Guilford County	0
South Carolina	94	Hall County, NE	0	**Hialeah, FL** (city) Miami-Dade County	0
Iowa	96	Sebastian County, AR	0	**Lake Worth, FL** (city) Palm Beach County	0
Alaska	101	Tulare County, CA	0	**Revere, MA** (city) Suffolk County	0
Kansas	108	Douglas County, NE	5	**Saint Paul, MN** (city) Ramsey County	0
Michigan	113	Ramsey County, MN	10	**Willowbrook, CA** (cdp) Los Angeles County	0
Hawaii	123	Yolo County, CA	11	**Winston-Salem, NC** (city) Forsyth County	0

Sorted by Percent in Descending Order — U.S. = 7.8%

State	Percent	County	Percent	Place	Percent
Hawaii	24.7	Pima County, AZ	26.0	**San Diego, CA** (city) San Diego County	25.1
Alaska	16.2	New York County, NY	23.1	**Alhambra, CA** (city) Los Angeles County	24.8
Oklahoma	16.1	Placer County, CA	20.9	**Rancho Cucamonga, CA** (city) San Bernardino County	24.3
Missouri	13.9	San Diego County, CA	20.4	**Manhattan, NY** (borough) New York County	23.1
Wisconsin	13.8	Cuyahoga County, OH	19.6	**Sacramento, CA** (city) Sacramento County	22.2
Illinois	12.9	Fairfield County, CT	17.9	**West Valley City, UT** (city) Salt Lake County	21.7
New Mexico	12.8	Rutherford County, TN	17.4	**Fremont, CA** (city) Alameda County	21.0
Connecticut	11.9	Buncombe County, NC	17.1	**Corona, CA** (city) Riverside County	20.7
Arizona	11.4	Brazoria County, TX	17.0	**Portland, OR** (city) Multnomah County	20.0
Florida	10.9	Santa Clara County, CA	16.8	**La Puente, CA** (city) Los Angeles County	18.6

Sorted by Percent in Ascending Order — U.S. = 7.8%

State	Percent	County	Percent	Place	Percent
Nebraska	1.8	Alamance County, NC	0.0	**Farmers Branch, TX** (city) Dallas County	0.0
Arkansas	2.8	Crawford County, AR	0.0	**Gainesville, GA** (city) Hall County	0.0
Iowa	3.5	Forsyth County, NC	0.0	**Grand Island, NE** (city) Hall County	0.0
Kansas	4.0	Galveston County, TX	0.0	**Greensboro, NC** (city) Guilford County	0.0
Kentucky	4.2	Hall County, NE	0.0	**Hialeah, FL** (city) Miami-Dade County	0.0
South Carolina	4.9	Sebastian County, AR	0.0	**Lake Worth, FL** (city) Palm Beach County	0.0
Texas	5.2	Tulare County, CA	0.0	**Revere, MA** (city) Suffolk County	0.0
Maryland	5.3	Douglas County, NE	0.4	**Saint Paul, MN** (city) Ramsey County	0.0
Massachusetts	5.4	Ramsey County, MN	0.8	**Willowbrook, CA** (cdp) Los Angeles County	0.0
Alabama	5.6	Guilford County, NC	1.3	**Winston-Salem, NC** (city) Forsyth County	0.0

Note: (1) Ranking tables cover all states and counties, and places with an overall population of at least 125,000, OR an overall population of at least 25,000 where the Hispanic/Latino population is at least 20% of the overall population. In states where less than five places meet either of these criteria, we have included places with at least 10,000 total population with the highest percentage of Hispanic/Latino population. These places are identified with an asterisk (*); Please refer to the User's Guide for a full explanation of data.

Four-Year College Graduates

(Universe: Population 25 Years and Over)

Cuban

Top 10 States, Counties, and Places[1]

Sorted by Number in Descending Order — U.S. = 294,051

State	Number	County	Number	Place	Number
Florida	185,277	Miami-Dade County, FL	133,961	**Miami, FL** (city) Miami-Dade County	20,224
California	16,535	Broward County, FL	14,338	**Hialeah, FL** (city) Miami-Dade County	16,643
New Jersey	16,445	Hillsborough County, FL	7,722	**New York, NY** (city)	9,192
New York	15,508	Los Angeles County, CA	7,703	**Tamiami, FL** (cdp) Miami-Dade County	6,724
Texas	8,832	Palm Beach County, FL	6,703	**Kendall, FL** (cdp) Miami-Dade County	6,385
Georgia	5,150	Hudson County, NJ	5,154	**Coral Gables, FL** (city) Miami-Dade County	6,072
Illinois	4,742	Orange County, FL	3,498	**Kendale Lakes, FL** (cdp) Miami-Dade County	5,489
Virginia	3,627	New York County, NY	3,254	**Fountainebleau, FL** (cdp) Miami-Dade County	5,164
North Carolina	3,524	Bergen County, NJ	3,040	**Miami Beach, FL** (city) Miami-Dade County	4,238
Pennsylvania	3,124	Cook County, IL	2,955	**University Park, FL** (cdp) Miami-Dade County	3,377

Sorted by Number in Ascending Order — U.S. = 294,051

State	Number	County	Number	Place	Number
West Virginia	131	Kern County, CA	36	**Bell, CA** (city) Los Angeles County	13
Arkansas	142	Hampden County, MA	54	**Linden, NJ** (city) Union County	55
Maine	189	Berks County, PA	79	**University, FL** (cdp) Hillsborough County	55
Nebraska	201	Sumter County, FL	86	**Oakland Park, FL** (city) Broward County	68
New Hampshire	251	Arapahoe County, CO	95	**Henderson, NV** (city) Clark County	85
Iowa	262	Citrus County, FL	96	**Syracuse, NY** (city) Onondaga County	86
Hawaii	269	Pierce County, WA	101	**Metairie, LA** (cdp) Jefferson Parish	88
Mississippi	293	Jackson County, MO	102	**Rochester, NY** (city) Monroe County	96
Oklahoma	294	Indian River County, FL	127	**Deltona, FL** (city) Volusia County	98
Delaware	335	Saint Tammany Parish, LA	127	**Lake Magdalene, FL** (cdp) Hillsborough County	110

Sorted by Percent in Descending Order — U.S. = 25.0%

State	Percent	County	Percent	Place	Percent
District of Columbia	58.1	Orleans Parish, LA	63.3	**Atlanta, GA** (city) Fulton County	65.1
Virginia	45.2	Oakland County, MI	61.8	**Tallahassee, FL** (city) Leon County	65.0
Colorado	44.9	Fairfax County, VA	61.0	**New Orleans, LA** (city) Orleans Parish	63.3
Iowa	44.1	Loudoun County, VA	60.5	**North Hempstead, NY** (town) Nassau County	62.5
Massachusetts	42.1	Somerset County, NJ	60.5	**Coral Gables, FL** (city) Miami-Dade County	57.3
Maryland	41.7	Guilford County, NC	58.3	**San Diego, CA** (city) San Diego County	54.0
Rhode Island	40.3	Chester County, PA	56.7	**Boston, MA** (city) Suffolk County	52.6
Delaware	39.4	DeKalb County, GA	54.7	**Weston, FL** (city) Broward County	52.0
Utah	39.2	Leon County, FL	53.8	**Coconut Creek, FL** (city) Broward County	48.8
Maine	38.0	Morris County, NJ	52.4	**Seattle, WA** (city) King County	48.3

Sorted by Percent in Ascending Order — U.S. = 25.0%

State	Percent	County	Percent	Place	Percent
Nevada	15.6	Kern County, CA	6.6	**Bell, CA** (city) Los Angeles County	1.8
Nebraska	22.0	Hendry County, FL	8.2	**West Little River, FL** (cdp) Miami-Dade County	4.0
Florida	22.3	Hampden County, MA	12.2	**Henderson, NV** (city) Clark County	6.6
Kentucky	23.6	Sumter County, FL	13.3	**Oakland Park, FL** (city) Broward County	7.1
Oregon	24.5	Highlands County, FL	13.6	**Deltona, FL** (city) Volusia County	7.2
West Virginia	24.6	Richmond County, NY	13.8	**Newark, NJ** (city) Essex County	7.8
Louisiana	25.2	Collier County, FL	14.5	**University, FL** (cdp) Hillsborough County	7.8
Mississippi	25.5	Marion County, FL	14.7	**Elizabeth, NJ** (city) Union County	11.2
New Mexico	26.5	Monroe County, FL	14.7	**Metairie, LA** (cdp) Jefferson Parish	11.3
Oklahoma	26.6	Clark County, NV	14.9	**Town 'n' Country, FL** (cdp) Hillsborough County	12.8

Note: (1) Ranking tables cover all states and counties, and places with an overall population of at least 125,000, OR an overall population of at least 25,000 where the Hispanic/Latino population is at least 20% of the overall population. In states where less than five places meet either of these criteria, we have included places with at least 10,000 total population with the highest percentage of Hispanic/Latino population. These places are identified with an asterisk (*); Please refer to the User's Guide for a full explanation of data.

Four-Year College Graduates

(Universe: Population 25 Years and Over)

Dominican Republic

Top 10 States, Counties, and Places[1]

Sorted by Number in Descending Order — U.S. = 114,831

State	Number	County	Number	Place	Number
New York	53,405	New York County, NY	15,202	**New York, NY** (city)	43,952
Florida	19,808	Bronx County, NY	14,961	**Manhattan, NY** (borough) New York County	15,202
New Jersey	14,486	Queens County, NY	7,876	**Bronx, NY** (borough) Bronx County	14,961
Massachusetts	5,306	Miami-Dade County, FL	7,343	**Queens, NY** (borough) Queens County	7,876
Pennsylvania	2,898	Kings County, NY	5,338	**Brooklyn, NY** (borough) Kings County	5,338
Georgia	1,884	Broward County, FL	4,073	**Hempstead (town), NY** (town) Nassau County	1,540
Rhode Island	1,848	Hudson County, NJ	3,371	**Yonkers, NY** (city) Westchester County	1,385
Texas	1,841	Bergen County, NJ	2,942	**Paterson, NJ** (city) Passaic County	1,245
California	1,638	Westchester County, NY	2,531	**Providence, RI** (city) Providence County	1,175
Connecticut	1,458	Passaic County, NJ	2,413	**Boston, MA** (city) Suffolk County	1,099

Sorted by Number in Ascending Order — U.S. = 114,831

State	Number	County	Number	Place	Number
Alaska	52	Sullivan County, NY	19	**Chelsea, MA** (city) Suffolk County	0
Delaware	91	Jefferson Parish, LA	31	**New Haven, CT** (city/town) New Haven County	0
Minnesota	105	Ulster County, NY	33	**Plainfield, NJ** (city) Union County	0
Wisconsin	107	Lackawanna County, PA	42	**Anchorage, AK** (municipality)	10
Utah	115	Pinellas County, FL	44	**Atlantic City, NJ** (city) Atlantic County	11
Alabama	120	Litchfield County, CT	54	**Lancaster, PA** (city) Lancaster County	11
Missouri	140	Cumberland County, NJ	55	**New London, CT** (city/town) New London County	11
Washington	151	Cuyahoga County, OH	60	**York, PA** (city) York County	13
Colorado	193	Oneida County, NY	63	**Cleveland, OH** (city) Cuyahoga County	14
South Carolina	211	New Castle County, DE	64	**Buenaventura Lakes, FL** (cdp) Osceola County	16

Sorted by Percent in Descending Order — U.S. = 15.2%

State	Percent	County	Percent	Place	Percent
Tennessee	52.7	Morris County, NJ	48.3	**Doral, FL** (city) Miami-Dade County	52.6
Alabama	31.3	Fairfax County, VA	47.7	**Weston, FL** (city) Broward County	46.8
Illinois	29.8	Bexar County, TX	44.5	**Ramapo, NY** (town) Rockland County	44.3
Utah	29.3	Fulton County, GA	39.8	**Kendall, FL** (cdp) Miami-Dade County	39.4
California	29.1	Cobb County, GA	34.9	**North Hempstead, NY** (town) Nassau County	32.2
Washington	28.5	Seminole County, FL	32.8	**Country Club, FL** (cdp) Miami-Dade County	30.1
District of Columbia	28.3	Tarrant County, TX	32.2	**The Hammocks, FL** (cdp) Miami-Dade County	29.9
Texas	28.3	Albany County, NY	31.7	**Miramar, FL** (city) Broward County	28.3
Indiana	28.1	Norfolk County, MA	31.1	**Plantation, FL** (city) Broward County	28.3
Virginia	27.9	Onondaga County, NY	30.3	**Fountainebleau, FL** (cdp) Miami-Dade County	27.6

Sorted by Percent in Ascending Order — U.S. = 15.2%

State	Percent	County	Percent	Place	Percent
Alaska	6.2	Luzerne County, PA	2.8	**Chelsea, MA** (city) Suffolk County	0.0
Rhode Island	10.1	Sullivan County, NY	4.2	**New Haven, CT** (city/town) New Haven County	0.0
Massachusetts	10.2	Jefferson Parish, LA	4.4	**Plainfield, NJ** (city) Union County	0.0
Pennsylvania	11.1	Lancaster County, PA	6.5	**Anchorage, AK** (municipality)	1.5
Connecticut	12.2	Cumberland County, NJ	6.8	**Atlantic City, NJ** (city) Atlantic County	1.5
Delaware	12.8	Pinellas County, FL	6.9	**Lancaster, PA** (city) Lancaster County	1.5
New York	13.8	Cuyahoga County, OH	7.7	**Buenaventura Lakes, FL** (cdp) Osceola County	1.7
New Jersey	14.4	Essex County, MA	7.9	**New London, CT** (city/town) New London County	1.9
Wisconsin	15.8	Lehigh County, PA	8.1	**South Miami Heights, FL** (cdp) Miami-Dade County	2.2
Ohio	17.5	Atlantic County, NJ	8.3	**Cleveland, OH** (city) Cuyahoga County	2.4

RANKINGS & COMPARISONS

Note: (1) Ranking tables cover all states and counties, and places with an overall population of at least 125,000, OR an overall population of at least 25,000 where the Hispanic/Latino population is at least 20% of the overall population. In states where less than five places meet either of these criteria, we have included places with at least 10,000 total population with the highest percentage of Hispanic/Latino population. These places are identified with an asterisk (*); Please refer to the User's Guide for a full explanation of data.

Four-Year College Graduates

(Universe: Population 25 Years and Over)

Mexican

Top 10 States, Counties, and Places[1]

Sorted by Number in Descending Order — U.S. = 1,421,023

State	Number	County	Number	Place	Number
California	488,479	Los Angeles County, CA	153,381	**San Antonio, TX** (city) Bexar County	50,048
Texas	410,011	Bexar County, TX	61,841	**Los Angeles, CA** (city) Los Angeles County	49,079
Arizona	71,755	San Diego County, CA	53,976	**El Paso, TX** (city) El Paso County	44,224
Illinois	67,905	Harris County, TX	49,464	**Houston, TX** (city) Harris County	27,680
Colorado	36,138	El Paso County, TX	48,227	**Chicago, IL** (city) Cook County	25,648
New Mexico	32,193	Cook County, IL	43,030	**San Diego, CA** (city) San Diego County	23,145
Florida	26,766	Orange County, CA	42,526	**Austin, TX** (city) Travis County	18,332
New York	23,114	Maricopa County, AZ	40,667	**Laredo, TX** (city) Webb County	17,366
Washington	22,558	Hidalgo County, TX	39,753	**Phoenix, AZ** (city) Maricopa County	17,197
Nevada	16,078	Riverside County, CA	28,565	**New York, NY** (city)	15,604

Sorted by Number in Ascending Order — U.S. = 1,421,023

State	Number	County	Number	Place	Number
Vermont	409	Adams County, IN	0	**Albertville*, AL** (city) Marshall County	0
Maine	427	Alexander County, NC	0	**Berea*, SC** (cdp) Greenville County	0
North Dakota	432	Ashe County, NC	0	**Bluffton*, SC** (town) Beaufort County	0
West Virginia	614	Becker County, MN	0	**Central Falls*, RI** (city) Providence County	0
Rhode Island	776	Berrien County, GA	0	**Fort Campbell North*, KY** (cdp) Christian County	0
South Dakota	826	Bladen County, NC	0	**Green River*, WY** (city) Sweetwater County	0
New Hampshire	841	Blount County, AL	0	**Hazleton, PA** (city) Luzerne County	0
Delaware	929	Box Butte County, NE	0	**Muscatine*, IA** (city) Muscatine County	0
Wyoming	1,268	Bradley County, AR	0	**Pascagoula*, MS** (city) Jackson County	0
Mississippi	1,378	Bulloch County, GA	0	**Springfield, MA** (city) Hampden County	9

Sorted by Percent in Descending Order — U.S. = 9.1%

State	Percent	County	Percent	Place	Percent
District of Columbia	44.2	McDonough County, IL	53.2	**Doral, FL** (city) Miami-Dade County	70.4
Vermont	30.5	Tompkins County, NY	52.2	**Weston, FL** (city) Broward County	67.6
Massachusetts	28.9	Los Alamos County, NM	49.9	**Coral Gables, FL** (city) Miami-Dade County	59.6
New Hampshire	23.5	Arlington County, VA	45.2	**Alexandria, VA** (independent city)	49.3
Hawaii	19.1	Henry County, TN	44.0	**Miramar, FL** (city) Broward County	48.5
Virginia	18.5	Middlesex County, MA	43.7	**Arlington, VA** (cdp) Arlington County	45.2
Maryland	17.9	Norfolk County, MA	42.9	**Pittsburgh, PA** (city) Allegheny County	35.0
Maine	17.2	Chittenden County, VT	38.3	**Irvine, CA** (city) Orange County	34.5
Rhode Island	17.0	Onondaga County, NY	38.2	**Alafaya, FL** (cdp) Orange County	33.2
Montana	16.9	Whitman County, WA	37.7	**Sterling Heights, MI** (city) Macomb County	32.8

Sorted by Percent in Ascending Order — U.S. = 9.1%

State	Percent	County	Percent	Place	Percent
North Carolina	5.7	Adams County, IN	0.0	**Albertville*, AL** (city) Marshall County	0.0
Arkansas	6.1	Alexander County, NC	0.0	**Berea*, SC** (cdp) Greenville County	0.0
Mississippi	6.2	Ashe County, NC	0.0	**Bluffton*, SC** (town) Beaufort County	0.0
Georgia	6.3	Becker County, MN	0.0	**Central Falls*, RI** (city) Providence County	0.0
Idaho	6.3	Berrien County, GA	0.0	**Fort Campbell North*, KY** (cdp) Christian County	0.0
Nevada	6.3	Bladen County, NC	0.0	**Green River*, WY** (city) Sweetwater County	0.0
South Carolina	6.5	Blount County, AL	0.0	**Hazleton, PA** (city) Luzerne County	0.0
Delaware	7.0	Box Butte County, NE	0.0	**Muscatine*, IA** (city) Muscatine County	0.0
Oklahoma	7.0	Bradley County, AR	0.0	**Pascagoula*, MS** (city) Jackson County	0.0
Tennessee	7.1	Bulloch County, GA	0.0	**Norristown, PA** (borough) Montgomery County	0.4

Note: (1) Ranking tables cover all states and counties, and places with an overall population of at least 125,000, OR an overall population of at least 25,000 where the Hispanic/Latino population is at least 20% of the overall population. In states where less than five places meet either of these criteria, we have included places with at least 10,000 total population with the highest percentage of Hispanic/Latino population. These places are identified with an asterisk (*); Please refer to the User's Guide for a full explanation of data.

Four-Year College Graduates

(Universe: Population 25 Years and Over)

Puerto Rican

Top 10 States, Counties, and Places[1]

Sorted by Number in Descending Order — U.S. = 387,923

State	Number	County	Number	Place	Number
New York	90,126	Bronx County, NY	20,122	**New York, NY** (city)	59,035
Florida	84,335	Orange County, FL	15,666	**Bronx, NY** (borough) Bronx County	20,122
New Jersey	30,343	Miami-Dade County, FL	14,669	**Brooklyn, NY** (borough) Kings County	12,006
California	22,404	Kings County, NY	12,006	**Manhattan, NY** (borough) New York County	11,948
Texas	19,033	New York County, NY	11,948	**Queens, NY** (borough) Queens County	11,554
Illinois	14,343	Queens County, NY	11,554	**Chicago, IL** (city) Cook County	7,101
Pennsylvania	14,317	Broward County, FL	10,103	**Philadelphia, PA** (city) Philadelphia County	3,740
Massachusetts	12,570	Cook County, IL	9,513	**Staten Island, NY** (borough) Richmond County	3,405
Virginia	11,246	Hillsborough County, FL	7,790	**Orlando, FL** (city) Orange County	2,718
Connecticut	10,906	Westchester County, NY	6,711	**Hempstead (town), NY** (town) Nassau County	2,710

Sorted by Number in Ascending Order — U.S. = 387,923

State	Number	County	Number	Place	Number
Wyoming	90	Chenango County, NY	0	**Palmdale, CA** (city) Los Angeles County	0
North Dakota	93	Grafton County, NH	2	**Waianae*, HI** (cdp) Honolulu County	0
Montana	137	Sampson County, NC	4	**Bridgeton, NJ** (city) Cumberland County	11
South Dakota	174	Adams County, PA	5	**Akron, OH** (city) Summit County	21
Idaho	190	Perry County, PA	5	**Moreno Valley, CA** (city) Riverside County	27
West Virginia	277	Otsego County, NY	8	**Hazleton, PA** (city) Luzerne County	38
Vermont	289	Ashtabula County, OH	13	**Rockford, IL** (city) Winnebago County	42
Maine	292	Lycoming County, PA	13	**Atlantic City, NJ** (city) Atlantic County	44
Alaska	322	Washington County, NY	13	**East Chicago, IN** (city) Lake County	44
Mississippi	357	Wyoming County, NY	16	**Central Falls*, RI** (city) Providence County	45

Sorted by Percent in Descending Order — U.S. = 15.9%

State	Percent	County	Percent	Place	Percent
District of Columbia	61.2	Arlington County, VA	66.6	**Coral Gables, FL** (city) Miami-Dade County	67.8
Maryland	36.8	Butler County, OH	55.0	**Arlington, VA** (cdp) Arlington County	66.6
Minnesota	34.1	Forsyth County, GA	52.6	**Alexandria, VA** (independent city)	60.5
Virginia	32.2	Loudoun County, VA	52.3	**Weston, FL** (city) Broward County	59.9
Alabama	31.5	Howard County, MD	50.4	**Atlanta, GA** (city) Fulton County	55.5
North Dakota	29.5	Fairfax County, VA	50.3	**Doral, FL** (city) Miami-Dade County	53.7
South Dakota	29.4	Hamilton County, IN	48.1	**Plano, TX** (city) Collin County	50.6
Missouri	29.1	Montgomery County, MD	47.9	**Irving, TX** (city) Dallas County	50.5
Louisiana	29.0	Washtenaw County, MI	47.1	**Madison, WI** (city) Dane County	48.3
Nebraska	29.0	Fulton County, GA	47.0	**Oakland, CA** (city) Alameda County	45.5

Sorted by Percent in Ascending Order — U.S. = 15.9%

State	Percent	County	Percent	Place	Percent
Pennsylvania	8.4	Chenango County, NY	0.0	**Palmdale, CA** (city) Los Angeles County	0.0
Connecticut	8.7	Grafton County, NH	1.2	**Waianae*, HI** (cdp) Honolulu County	0.0
Rhode Island	9.8	Sampson County, NC	1.2	**Bridgeton, NJ** (city) Cumberland County	1.0
Massachusetts	10.3	Adams County, PA	1.8	**Atlantic City, NJ** (city) Atlantic County	2.7
Hawaii	11.2	Ashtabula County, OH	2.2	**Camden, NJ** (city) Camden County	2.7
Delaware	11.5	Rensselaer County, NY	2.3	**Paterson, NJ** (city) Passaic County	2.8
Wisconsin	12.2	Washington County, NY	2.6	**East Chicago, IN** (city) Lake County	3.2
New Jersey	12.8	Otsego County, NY	2.7	**Allentown, PA** (city) Lehigh County	3.4
Idaho	13.8	Wyoming County, NY	2.7	**Lebanon, PA** (city) Lebanon County	3.5
Maine	13.9	Clearfield County, PA	3.4	**Fitchburg, MA** (city) Worcester County	3.8

Note: (1) Ranking tables cover all states and counties, and places with an overall population of at least 125,000, OR an overall population of at least 25,000 where the Hispanic/Latino population is at least 20% of the overall population. In states where less than five places meet either of these criteria, we have included places with at least 10,000 total population with the highest percentage of Hispanic/Latino population. These places are identified with an asterisk (*); Please refer to the User's Guide for a full explanation of data.

Four-Year College Graduates

(Universe: Population 25 Years and Over)

South American

Top 10 States, Counties, and Places[1]

Sorted by Number in Descending Order — U.S. = 547,657

State	Number	County	Number	Place	Number
Florida	145,912	Miami-Dade County, FL	63,955	**New York, NY** (city)	49,250
New York	74,214	Broward County, FL	33,949	**Queens, NY** (borough) Queens County	25,844
California	66,592	Los Angeles County, CA	26,151	**Los Angeles, CA** (city) Los Angeles County	11,822
New Jersey	42,235	Queens County, NY	25,844	**Manhattan, NY** (borough) New York County	10,701
Texas	35,286	Harris County, TX	12,588	**Miami, FL** (city) Miami-Dade County	8,074
Virginia	23,094	New York County, NY	10,701	**Houston, TX** (city) Harris County	7,143
Illinois	16,393	Fairfax County, VA	10,700	**Brooklyn, NY** (borough) Kings County	7,039
Maryland	14,018	Cook County, IL	10,388	**Chicago, IL** (city) Cook County	6,498
Georgia	13,915	Palm Beach County, FL	9,620	**Doral, FL** (city) Miami-Dade County	6,088
Massachusetts	11,844	Hudson County, NJ	9,354	**Weston, FL** (city) Broward County	5,823

Sorted by Number in Ascending Order — U.S. = 547,657

State	Number	County	Number	Place	Number
North Dakota	139	Sullivan County, NY	40	**City of Orange, NJ** (township) Essex County	45
Montana	160	Spartanburg County, SC	55	**Lynn, MA** (city) Essex County	70
Maine	180	Oneida County, NY	60	**East Hartford, CT** (cdp/town) Hartford County	72
Wyoming	268	Cache County, UT	65	**Meriden, CT** (city/town) New Haven County	76
Vermont	279	Anoka County, MN	79	**Killeen, TX** (city) Bell County	88
West Virginia	435	Weber County, UT	98	**Moreno Valley, CA** (city) Riverside County	97
Idaho	511	Spokane County, WA	102	**Modesto, CA** (city) Stanislaus County	108
Alaska	662	Onslow County, NC	108	**Stockton, CA** (city) San Joaquin County	112
Hawaii	847	Tolland County, CT	110	**Glendora, CA** (city) Los Angeles County	114
Nebraska	855	Hall County, GA	120	**Central Falls*, RI** (city) Providence County	117

Sorted by Percent in Descending Order — U.S. = 30.6%

State	Percent	County	Percent	Place	Percent
District of Columbia	68.7	Champaign County, IL	85.4	**Lexington-Fayette, KY** (consolidated govt) Fayette County	82.4
Missouri	59.1	Fayette County, KY	82.4	**Pittsburgh, PA** (city) Allegheny County	78.8
Iowa	54.9	Washtenaw County, MI	80.1	**Saint Paul, MN** (city) Ramsey County	71.4
Nebraska	53.3	Cleveland County, OK	74.9	**Overland Park, KS** (city) Johnson County	68.5
Arkansas	52.7	Washington County, MN	73.0	**Round Rock, TX** (city) Williamson County	67.7
Michigan	52.4	Saint Louis County, MO	71.4	**Durham, NC** (city) Durham County	67.5
Ohio	48.2	Ramsey County, MN	70.3	**Coral Gables, FL** (city) Miami-Dade County	66.7
Kansas	48.1	Oakland County, MI	68.9	**Scottsdale, AZ** (city) Maricopa County	65.8
Vermont	48.1	Allegheny County, PA	67.0	**Seattle, WA** (city) King County	65.2
Colorado	47.7	East Baton Rouge Parish, LA	65.6	**Atlanta, GA** (city) Fulton County	65.1

Sorted by Percent in Ascending Order — U.S. = 30.6%

State	Percent	County	Percent	Place	Percent
New Jersey	19.6	Sullivan County, NY	5.5	**City of Orange, NJ** (township) Essex County	3.0
New York	21.2	Spartanburg County, SC	11.6	**Central Falls*, RI** (city) Providence County	7.5
Rhode Island	21.4	Union County, NJ	13.0	**East Hartford, CT** (cdp/town) Hartford County	7.6
Nevada	23.6	Oneida County, NY	13.2	**Freeport, NY** (village) Nassau County	9.5
Connecticut	24.4	Cumberland County, NJ	13.4	**Meriden, CT** (city/town) New Haven County	9.5
Utah	26.6	Atlantic County, NJ	14.7	**Elizabeth, NJ** (city) Union County	9.7
Idaho	29.8	Bronx County, NY	14.9	**Newark, NJ** (city) Essex County	11.0
Delaware	30.4	Essex County, NJ	15.1	**Pawtucket*, RI** (city) Providence County	11.0
South Carolina	30.4	Weber County, UT	16.0	**Port Chester, NY** (village) Westchester County	11.0
Maine	30.7	Anoka County, MN	16.4	**Plainfield, NJ** (city) Union County	11.1

Note: (1) Ranking tables cover all states and counties, and places with an overall population of at least 125,000, OR an overall population of at least 25,000 where the Hispanic/Latino population is at least 20% of the overall population. In states where less than five places meet either of these criteria, we have included places with at least 10,000 total population with the highest percentage of Hispanic/Latino population. These places are identified with an asterisk (*); Please refer to the User's Guide for a full explanation of data.

Four-Year College Graduates

(Universe: Population 25 Years and Over)

South American: Argentinean

Top 10 States, Counties, and Places[1]

Sorted by Number in Descending Order — U.S. = 58,342

State	Number	County	Number	Place	Number
Florida	11,879	Miami-Dade County, FL	6,372	**New York, NY** (city)	4,274
California	11,467	Los Angeles County, CA	4,649	**Los Angeles, CA** (city) Los Angeles County	2,294
New York	6,987	Broward County, FL	2,625	**Manhattan, NY** (borough) New York County	2,173
Texas	3,241	New York County, NY	2,173	**Miami, FL** (city) Miami-Dade County	1,202
New Jersey	2,501	Orange County, CA	1,434	**Miami Beach, FL** (city) Miami-Dade County	1,058
Maryland	2,127	Montgomery County, MD	1,235	**Queens, NY** (borough) Queens County	937
Illinois	2,093	Harris County, TX	1,185	**Houston, TX** (city) Harris County	770
Virginia	1,669	Cook County, IL	1,183	**Brooklyn, NY** (borough) Kings County	733
Massachusetts	1,475	Queens County, NY	937	**San Francisco, CA** (city) San Francisco County	673
Connecticut	1,335	Fairfax County, VA	875	**Chicago, IL** (city) Cook County	656

Sorted by Number in Ascending Order — U.S. = 58,342

State	Number	County	Number	Place	Number
South Carolina	223	Passaic County, NJ	111	**Hialeah, FL** (city) Miami-Dade County	154
Nevada	253	Salt Lake County, UT	155	**San Jose, CA** (city) Santa Clara County	248
Minnesota	298	Tarrant County, TX	160	**Hollywood, FL** (city) Broward County	268
Louisiana	333	Middlesex County, NJ	168	**Bronx, NY** (borough) Bronx County	274
Indiana	343	Union County, NJ	173	**Pembroke Pines, FL** (city) Broward County	275
Wisconsin	356	Dallas County, TX	180	**Hempstead (town), NY** (town) Nassau County	320
Tennessee	359	Orange County, NY	201	**San Diego, CA** (city) San Diego County	326
Missouri	434	Utah County, UT	203	**Coral Springs, FL** (city) Broward County	380
Oregon	443	Riverside County, CA	230	**Aventura, FL** (city) Miami-Dade County	434
Utah	500	Montgomery County, TX	232	**Doral, FL** (city) Miami-Dade County	446

Sorted by Percent in Descending Order — U.S. = 38.9%

State	Percent	County	Percent	Place	Percent
District of Columbia	85.3	Middlesex County, MA	69.1	**Manhattan, NY** (borough) New York County	68.3
Missouri	74.1	New York County, NY	68.3	**Doral, FL** (city) Miami-Dade County	64.7
Michigan	61.3	Oakland County, MI	65.0	**San Francisco, CA** (city) San Francisco County	64.4
Colorado	58.1	San Francisco County, CA	64.4	**San Diego, CA** (city) San Diego County	55.3
Tennessee	56.7	Alameda County, CA	62.0	**Houston, TX** (city) Harris County	52.1
Louisiana	55.3	Travis County, TX	61.7	**Chicago, IL** (city) Cook County	51.6
Georgia	54.2	Montgomery County, MD	59.1	**Coral Springs, FL** (city) Broward County	51.6
Massachusetts	54.2	Fairfield County, CT	58.3	**Aventura, FL** (city) Miami-Dade County	46.0
Maryland	54.1	Santa Clara County, CA	55.5	**San Jose, CA** (city) Santa Clara County	41.7
North Carolina	53.2	New Haven County, CT	54.1	**Brooklyn, NY** (borough) Kings County	40.0

Sorted by Percent in Ascending Order — U.S. = 38.9%

State	Percent	County	Percent	Place	Percent
Nevada	13.9	Clark County, NV	14.3	**Hialeah, FL** (city) Miami-Dade County	16.8
Utah	19.6	Middlesex County, NJ	14.4	**Queens, NY** (borough) Queens County	21.4
New Jersey	25.7	Passaic County, NJ	14.4	**Hollywood, FL** (city) Broward County	25.2
South Carolina	25.8	Riverside County, CA	15.9	**Bronx, NY** (borough) Bronx County	29.2
Florida	31.4	Dallas County, TX	16.4	**Miami, FL** (city) Miami-Dade County	30.7
California	37.6	Union County, NJ	19.0	**Miami Beach, FL** (city) Miami-Dade County	31.3
Texas	39.1	Salt Lake County, UT	19.3	**Hempstead (town), NY** (town) Nassau County	35.7
New York	40.1	Utah County, UT	19.7	**Pembroke Pines, FL** (city) Broward County	35.7
Arizona	40.8	Queens County, NY	21.4	**Los Angeles, CA** (city) Los Angeles County	36.4
Wisconsin	40.9	Palm Beach County, FL	23.8	**New York, NY** (city)	39.6

Note: (1) Ranking tables cover all states and counties, and places with an overall population of at least 125,000, OR an overall population of at least 25,000 where the Hispanic/Latino population is at least 20% of the overall population. In states where less than five places meet either of these criteria, we have included places with at least 10,000 total population with the highest percentage of Hispanic/Latino population. These places are identified with an asterisk (*); Please refer to the User's Guide for a full explanation of data.

Four-Year College Graduates

(Universe: Population 25 Years and Over)

South American: Bolivian

Top 10 States, Counties, and Places[1]

Sorted by Number in Descending Order — U.S. = 21,696

State	Number	County	Number	Place	Number
Virginia	5,567	Fairfax County, VA	2,861	**New York, NY** (city)	976
California	3,277	Los Angeles County, CA	1,231	**Arlington, VA** (cdp) Arlington County	876
Florida	2,334	Montgomery County, MD	1,087	**Los Angeles, CA** (city) Los Angeles County	737
New York	1,599	Arlington County, VA	876	**Queens, NY** (borough) Queens County	566
Maryland	1,525	Miami-Dade County, FL	772	**Annandale, VA** (cdp) Fairfax County	557
Texas	1,429	Queens County, NY	566	**Providence, RI** (city) Providence County	262
New Jersey	765	Loudoun County, VA	546	**West Falls Church, VA** (cdp) Fairfax County	254
Illinois	627	Prince William County, VA	528	**Springfield, VA** (cdp) Fairfax County	178
Massachusetts	358	Broward County, FL	424	**Dale City, VA** (cdp) Prince William County	156
Rhode Island	311	San Diego County, CA	419		

Sorted by Number in Ascending Order — U.S. = 21,696

State	Number	County	Number	Place	Number
North Carolina	176	Santa Clara County, CA	142	**Dale City, VA** (cdp) Prince William County	156
Pennsylvania	178	Orange County, CA	261	**Springfield, VA** (cdp) Fairfax County	178
Rhode Island	311	Prince George's County, MD	289	**West Falls Church, VA** (cdp) Fairfax County	254
Massachusetts	358	Palm Beach County, FL	296	**Providence, RI** (city) Providence County	262
Illinois	627	Harris County, TX	304	**Annandale, VA** (cdp) Fairfax County	557
New Jersey	765	Providence County, RI	311	**Queens, NY** (borough) Queens County	566
Texas	1,429	Cook County, IL	350	**Los Angeles, CA** (city) Los Angeles County	737
Maryland	1,525	San Diego County, CA	419	**Arlington, VA** (cdp) Arlington County	876
New York	1,599	Broward County, FL	424	**New York, NY** (city)	976
Florida	2,334	Prince William County, VA	528		

Sorted by Percent in Descending Order — U.S. = 34.0%

State	Percent	County	Percent	Place	Percent
Illinois	51.2	San Diego County, CA	66.1	**Providence, RI** (city) Providence County	35.2
Texas	49.8	Cook County, IL	62.9	**Annandale, VA** (cdp) Fairfax County	33.7
North Carolina	44.2	Loudoun County, VA	42.3	**Los Angeles, CA** (city) Los Angeles County	29.6
Pennsylvania	41.6	Palm Beach County, FL	40.1	**Arlington, VA** (cdp) Arlington County	29.3
Florida	36.6	Broward County, FL	39.6	**New York, NY** (city)	27.3
California	36.3	Miami-Dade County, FL	39.5	**Queens, NY** (borough) Queens County	25.3
Maryland	34.2	Prince George's County, MD	39.3	**West Falls Church, VA** (cdp) Fairfax County	24.0
Massachusetts	34.0	Montgomery County, MD	33.3	**Springfield, VA** (cdp) Fairfax County	22.9
New York	30.2	Los Angeles County, CA	32.7	**Dale City, VA** (cdp) Prince William County	17.7
New Jersey	27.2	Harris County, TX	32.0		

Sorted by Percent in Ascending Order — U.S. = 34.0%

State	Percent	County	Percent	Place	Percent
Virginia	25.3	Santa Clara County, CA	18.4	**Dale City, VA** (cdp) Prince William County	17.7
Rhode Island	25.9	Prince William County, VA	19.0	**Springfield, VA** (cdp) Fairfax County	22.9
New Jersey	27.2	Fairfax County, VA	23.9	**West Falls Church, VA** (cdp) Fairfax County	24.0
New York	30.2	Orange County, CA	25.3	**Queens, NY** (borough) Queens County	25.3
Massachusetts	34.0	Queens County, NY	25.3	**New York, NY** (city)	27.3
Maryland	34.2	Providence County, RI	25.9	**Arlington, VA** (cdp) Arlington County	29.3
California	36.3	Arlington County, VA	29.3	**Los Angeles, CA** (city) Los Angeles County	29.6
Florida	36.6	Harris County, TX	32.0	**Annandale, VA** (cdp) Fairfax County	33.7
Pennsylvania	41.6	Los Angeles County, CA	32.7	**Providence, RI** (city) Providence County	35.2
North Carolina	44.2	Montgomery County, MD	33.3		

Note: (1) Ranking tables cover all states and counties, and places with an overall population of at least 125,000, OR an overall population of at least 25,000 where the Hispanic/Latino population is at least 20% of the overall population. In states where less than five places meet either of these criteria, we have included places with at least 10,000 total population with the highest percentage of Hispanic/Latino population. These places are identified with an asterisk (*); Please refer to the User's Guide for a full explanation of data.

Four-Year College Graduates

(Universe: Population 25 Years and Over)

South American: Chilean

Top 10 States, Counties, and Places[1]

Sorted by Number in Descending Order — U.S. = 29,501

State	Number	County	Number	Place	Number
Florida	5,646	Miami-Dade County, FL	2,968	**New York, NY** (city)	2,006
California	5,323	Los Angeles County, CA	1,625	**Los Angeles, CA** (city) Los Angeles County	878
New York	3,361	Broward County, FL	1,002	**Queens, NY** (borough) Queens County	690
New Jersey	1,477	Queens County, NY	690	**Manhattan, NY** (borough) New York County	680
Texas	1,158	New York County, NY	680	**Brooklyn, NY** (borough) Kings County	441
Maryland	1,027	Santa Clara County, CA	546	**Miami, FL** (city) Miami-Dade County	403
Virginia	1,006	Montgomery County, MD	517	**Chicago, IL** (city) Cook County	315
Massachusetts	947	Westchester County, NY	510	**Kendall, FL** (cdp) Miami-Dade County	214
Illinois	873	Cook County, IL	492	**Hempstead (town), NY** (town) Nassau County	63
Pennsylvania	646	Hudson County, NJ	478		

Sorted by Number in Ascending Order — U.S. = 29,501

State	Number	County	Number	Place	Number
Wisconsin	161	Bergen County, NJ	79	**Hempstead (town), NY** (town) Nassau County	63
Tennessee	231	San Bernardino County, CA	123	**Kendall, FL** (cdp) Miami-Dade County	214
Minnesota	237	Nassau County, NY	165	**Chicago, IL** (city) Cook County	315
Michigan	254	Utah County, UT	184	**Miami, FL** (city) Miami-Dade County	403
Oregon	282	San Mateo County, CA	188	**Brooklyn, NY** (borough) Kings County	441
Colorado	291	Clark County, NV	190	**Manhattan, NY** (borough) New York County	680
Connecticut	314	Riverside County, CA	191	**Queens, NY** (borough) Queens County	690
Nevada	330	Salt Lake County, UT	207	**Los Angeles, CA** (city) Los Angeles County	878
Missouri	335	Maricopa County, AZ	227	**New York, NY** (city)	2,006
Ohio	371	Suffolk County, NY	238		

Sorted by Percent in Descending Order — U.S. = 35.9%

State	Percent	County	Percent	Place	Percent
Ohio	66.4	New York County, NY	65.3	**Manhattan, NY** (borough) New York County	65.3
Missouri	62.0	Middlesex County, MA	55.0	**Chicago, IL** (city) Cook County	48.9
Minnesota	59.1	Cook County, IL	50.9	**Miami, FL** (city) Miami-Dade County	43.2
Pennsylvania	49.2	Alameda County, CA	47.4	**Brooklyn, NY** (borough) Kings County	42.2
Illinois	45.5	San Diego County, CA	47.0	**Kendall, FL** (cdp) Miami-Dade County	40.1
Tennessee	44.9	Santa Clara County, CA	47.0	**New York, NY** (city)	36.5
Massachusetts	44.0	Orange County, CA	42.7	**Los Angeles, CA** (city) Los Angeles County	26.8
Washington	43.0	Kings County, NY	42.2	**Queens, NY** (borough) Queens County	24.7
Michigan	42.1	Broward County, FL	35.7	**Hempstead (town), NY** (town) Nassau County	7.2
Virginia	40.5	Fairfax County, VA	35.7		

Sorted by Percent in Ascending Order — U.S. = 35.9%

State	Percent	County	Percent	Place	Percent
Wisconsin	25.2	Nassau County, NY	9.1	**Hempstead (town), NY** (town) Nassau County	7.2
New Jersey	25.8	Bergen County, NJ	12.6	**Queens, NY** (borough) Queens County	24.7
Connecticut	29.9	San Bernardino County, CA	16.8	**Los Angeles, CA** (city) Los Angeles County	26.8
Utah	31.1	Queens County, NY	24.7	**New York, NY** (city)	36.5
New York	31.4	Los Angeles County, CA	25.5	**Kendall, FL** (cdp) Miami-Dade County	40.1
Florida	33.3	Clark County, NV	26.2	**Brooklyn, NY** (borough) Kings County	42.2
California	33.5	Utah County, UT	26.2	**Miami, FL** (city) Miami-Dade County	43.2
Colorado	34.3	Salt Lake County, UT	28.0	**Chicago, IL** (city) Cook County	48.9
Texas	35.6	Palm Beach County, FL	28.3	**Manhattan, NY** (borough) New York County	65.3
Nevada	36.4	Suffolk County, NY	29.2		

Note: (1) Ranking tables cover all states and counties, and places with an overall population of at least 125,000, OR an overall population of at least 25,000 where the Hispanic/Latino population is at least 20% of the overall population. In states where less than five places meet either of these criteria, we have included places with at least 10,000 total population with the highest percentage of Hispanic/Latino population. These places are identified with an asterisk (*); Please refer to the User's Guide for a full explanation of data.

Four-Year College Graduates

(Universe: Population 25 Years and Over)

South American: Colombian

Top 10 States, Counties, and Places[1]

Sorted by Number in Descending Order — U.S. = 180,693

State	Number	County	Number	Place	Number
Florida	59,383	Miami-Dade County, FL	24,855	**New York, NY** (city)	16,235
New York	24,135	Broward County, FL	13,851	**Queens, NY** (borough) Queens County	10,132
California	15,073	Queens County, NY	10,132	**Houston, TX** (city) Harris County	2,764
New Jersey	14,548	Los Angeles County, CA	5,953	**Miami, FL** (city) Miami-Dade County	2,707
Texas	13,125	Harris County, TX	5,272	**Manhattan, NY** (borough) New York County	2,622
Georgia	6,057	Palm Beach County, FL	4,019	**Pembroke Pines, FL** (city) Broward County	2,352
Illinois	4,876	Orange County, FL	3,871	**Los Angeles, CA** (city) Los Angeles County	2,187
Massachusetts	4,317	Bergen County, NJ	3,561	**Weston, FL** (city) Broward County	2,047
Virginia	4,051	Cook County, IL	3,121	**Brooklyn, NY** (borough) Kings County	2,039
North Carolina	3,523	Hillsborough County, FL	2,747	**Chicago, IL** (city) Cook County	1,986

Sorted by Number in Ascending Order — U.S. = 180,693

State	Number	County	Number	Place	Number
Delaware	231	Ulster County, NY	72	**Elmont, NY** (cdp) Nassau County	34
Alaska	254	Will County, IL	91	**Garfield, NJ** (city) Bergen County	44
Nebraska	259	Dane County, WI	101	**Central Falls*, RI** (city) Providence County	59
Kentucky	312	Hall County, GA	102	**Miami Gardens, FL** (city) Miami-Dade County	62
Iowa	313	Burlington County, NJ	114	**New Rochelle, NY** (city) Westchester County	80
New Mexico	325	Luzerne County, PA	125	**North Lauderdale, FL** (city) Broward County	106
Oklahoma	338	Hampden County, MA	129	**Passaic, NJ** (city) Passaic County	109
Oregon	413	Berks County, PA	134	**Newark, NJ** (city) Essex County	110
Arkansas	427	Erie County, NY	136	**Virginia Beach, VA** (independent city)	110
New Hampshire	427	Lehigh County, PA	143	**Royal Palm Beach, FL** (village) Palm Beach County	113

Sorted by Percent in Descending Order — U.S. = 31.3%

State	Percent	County	Percent	Place	Percent
District of Columbia	67.1	Oakland County, MI	80.8	**San Francisco, CA** (city) San Francisco County	64.6
Arkansas	63.9	San Francisco County, CA	64.6	**Arlington, VA** (cdp) Arlington County	64.5
Indiana	61.4	Arlington County, VA	64.5	**Coral Gables, FL** (city) Miami-Dade County	62.5
Alabama	57.6	Marion County, IN	63.7	**Austin, TX** (city) Travis County	57.4
Michigan	56.4	Alachua County, FL	63.5	**Weston, FL** (city) Broward County	57.2
Ohio	56.3	Loudoun County, VA	63.1	**Indianapolis, IN** (city) Marion County	55.9
Missouri	55.2	Norfolk County, MA	62.0	**San Antonio, TX** (city) Bexar County	55.3
Washington	52.2	Fulton County, GA	61.5	**Doral, FL** (city) Miami-Dade County	51.0
Iowa	51.6	King County, WA	59.5	**Dallas, TX** (city) Dallas County	48.5
Colorado	50.9	Travis County, TX	59.1	**Aventura, FL** (city) Miami-Dade County	48.1

Sorted by Percent in Ascending Order — U.S. = 31.3%

State	Percent	County	Percent	Place	Percent
Rhode Island	17.4	Atlantic County, NJ	14.5	**Central Falls*, RI** (city) Providence County	4.3
New Jersey	22.4	Union County, NJ	14.8	**Elmont, NY** (cdp) Nassau County	6.5
New York	24.3	Providence County, RI	15.9	**Garfield, NJ** (city) Bergen County	6.5
Connecticut	24.5	Greenville County, SC	17.2	**Miami Gardens, FL** (city) Miami-Dade County	8.2
Nevada	24.5	Lake County, FL	17.3	**New Rochelle, NY** (city) Westchester County	9.7
Massachusetts	27.1	Volusia County, FL	17.4	**Newark, NJ** (city) Essex County	10.6
South Carolina	28.5	Ulster County, NY	17.7	**North Lauderdale, FL** (city) Broward County	10.8
Tennessee	29.2	Suffolk County, MA	18.0	**Passaic, NJ** (city) Passaic County	10.8
Florida	30.5	Essex County, MA	18.4	**Bridgeport, CT** (city/town) Fairfield County	10.9
Utah	32.4	Lehigh County, PA	18.7	**Elizabeth, NJ** (city) Union County	11.4

Note: (1) Ranking tables cover all states and counties, and places with an overall population of at least 125,000, OR an overall population of at least 25,000 where the Hispanic/Latino population is at least 20% of the overall population. In states where less than five places meet either of these criteria, we have included places with at least 10,000 total population with the highest percentage of Hispanic/Latino population. These places are identified with an asterisk (*); Please refer to the User's Guide for a full explanation of data.

Four-Year College Graduates

(Universe: Population 25 Years and Over)

South American: Ecuadorian

Top 10 States, Counties, and Places[1]

Sorted by Number in Descending Order — U.S. = 66,496

State	Number	County	Number	Place	Number
New York	18,419	Queens County, NY	7,132	**New York, NY** (city)	13,070
Florida	10,254	Miami-Dade County, FL	4,144	**Queens, NY** (borough) Queens County	7,132
New Jersey	10,105	Los Angeles County, CA	3,548	**Brooklyn, NY** (borough) Kings County	1,953
California	7,042	Hudson County, NJ	3,315	**Bronx, NY** (borough) Bronx County	1,939
Illinois	3,205	Broward County, FL	2,504	**Chicago, IL** (city) Cook County	1,769
Texas	2,434	Cook County, IL	2,274	**Manhattan, NY** (borough) New York County	1,762
Connecticut	1,788	Kings County, NY	1,953	**Los Angeles, CA** (city) Los Angeles County	1,602
Virginia	1,612	Bronx County, NY	1,939	**Newark, NJ** (city) Essex County	971
Maryland	1,264	New York County, NY	1,762	**Jersey City, NJ** (city) Hudson County	875
Pennsylvania	1,168	Suffolk County, NY	1,625	**Hempstead (town), NY** (town) Nassau County	816

Sorted by Number in Ascending Order — U.S. = 66,496

State	Number	County	Number	Place	Number
Iowa	146	Putnam County, NY	24	**White Plains, NY** (city) Westchester County	0
Wisconsin	147	Dutchess County, NY	41	**City of Orange, NJ** (township) Essex County	5
Rhode Island	151	Delaware County, PA	48	**Bridgeport, CT** (city/town) Fairfield County	27
Oklahoma	153	Berks County, PA	65	**Port Chester, NY** (village) Westchester County	58
Nevada	178	Ocean County, NJ	69	**Plainfield, NJ** (city) Union County	62
Oregon	187	Pinellas County, FL	75	**Rye, NY** (town) Westchester County	71
Missouri	197	Hartford County, CT	101	**New Haven, CT** (city/town) New Haven County	77
South Carolina	218	Baltimore County, MD	103	**Allentown, PA** (city) Lehigh County	89
Tennessee	219	Camden County, NJ	113	**Central Islip, NY** (cdp) Suffolk County	95
Indiana	229	Seminole County, FL	113	**Clifton, NJ** (city) Passaic County	98

Sorted by Percent in Descending Order — U.S. = 18.2%

State	Percent	County	Percent	Place	Percent
Colorado	60.5	Fairfax County, VA	50.0	**Doral, FL** (city) Miami-Dade County	53.5
Kansas	58.5	Maricopa County, AZ	48.5	**Coral Springs, FL** (city) Broward County	38.2
Louisiana	50.1	King County, WA	43.9	**Houston, TX** (city) Harris County	36.1
Missouri	49.0	Santa Clara County, CA	42.5	**Miami, FL** (city) Miami-Dade County	35.7
Michigan	43.0	Monmouth County, NJ	41.4	**Country Club, FL** (cdp) Miami-Dade County	34.6
Virginia	41.9	Utah County, UT	37.6	**Oyster Bay, NY** (town) Nassau County	34.0
Arizona	39.2	Orange County, CA	35.5	**Sunrise, FL** (city) Broward County	31.4
Georgia	34.4	San Diego County, CA	34.5	**Los Angeles, CA** (city) Los Angeles County	30.7
Iowa	34.2	Harris County, TX	32.2	**Miramar, FL** (city) Broward County	27.4
Tennessee	33.8	Gwinnett County, GA	31.7	**Downey, CA** (city) Los Angeles County	24.5

Sorted by Percent in Ascending Order — U.S. = 18.2%

State	Percent	County	Percent	Place	Percent
Minnesota	12.4	Dutchess County, NY	5.4	**White Plains, NY** (city) Westchester County	0.0
New York	12.5	Putnam County, NY	6.0	**City of Orange, NJ** (township) Essex County	0.9
Connecticut	12.8	Delaware County, PA	6.3	**Bridgeport, CT** (city/town) Fairfield County	2.3
New Jersey	15.3	Berks County, PA	7.7	**Port Chester, NY** (village) Westchester County	4.6
Nevada	17.8	Mercer County, NJ	8.8	**Rye, NY** (town) Westchester County	5.4
Pennsylvania	17.9	Hennepin County, MN	9.0	**Plainfield, NJ** (city) Union County	7.2
Illinois	20.4	Rockland County, NY	9.2	**Elizabeth, NJ** (city) Union County	7.3
North Carolina	20.7	Union County, NJ	9.7	**Minneapolis, MN** (city) Hennepin County	7.7
Utah	22.8	Ocean County, NJ	10.2	**New Haven, CT** (city/town) New Haven County	8.3
Massachusetts	24.5	Kings County, NY	10.3	**Allentown, PA** (city) Lehigh County	9.0

Note: (1) Ranking tables cover all states and counties, and places with an overall population of at least 125,000, OR an overall population of at least 25,000 where the Hispanic/Latino population is at least 20% of the overall population. In states where less than five places meet either of these criteria, we have included places with at least 10,000 total population with the highest percentage of Hispanic/Latino population. These places are identified with an asterisk (*); Please refer to the User's Guide for a full explanation of data.

Four-Year College Graduates

(Universe: Population 25 Years and Over)

South American: Paraguayan

Top 10 States, Counties, and Places[1]

Sorted by Number in Descending Order — U.S. = 3,321

State	Number	County	Number	Place	Number
New York	841	Queens County, NY	420	**New York, NY** (city)	578
Florida	421	Westchester County, NY	67	**Queens, NY** (borough) Queens County	420
California	301				
Texas	204				
Maryland	203				
New Jersey	133				

Sorted by Number in Ascending Order — U.S. = 3,321

State	Number	County	Number	Place	Number
New Jersey	133	Westchester County, NY	67	**Queens, NY** (borough) Queens County	420
Maryland	203	Queens County, NY	420	**New York, NY** (city)	578
Texas	204				
California	301				
Florida	421				
New York	841				

Sorted by Percent in Descending Order — U.S. = 28.9%

State	Percent	County	Percent	Place	Percent
California	50.9	Queens County, NY	24.2	**Queens, NY** (borough) Queens County	24.2
Florida	39.8	Westchester County, NY	5.8	**New York, NY** (city)	24.0
Maryland	29.6				
Texas	27.6				
New York	18.9				
New Jersey	10.9				

Sorted by Percent in Ascending Order — U.S. = 28.9%

State	Percent	County	Percent	Place	Percent
New Jersey	10.9	Westchester County, NY	5.8	**New York, NY** (city)	24.0
New York	18.9	Queens County, NY	24.2	**Queens, NY** (borough) Queens County	24.2
Texas	27.6				
Maryland	29.6				
Florida	39.8				
California	50.9				

Note: (1) Ranking tables cover all states and counties, and places with an overall population of at least 125,000, OR an overall population of at least 25,000 where the Hispanic/Latino population is at least 20% of the overall population. In states where less than five places meet either of these criteria, we have included places with at least 10,000 total population with the highest percentage of Hispanic/Latino population. These places are identified with an asterisk (*); Please refer to the User's Guide for a full explanation of data.

Four-Year College Graduates

(Universe: Population 25 Years and Over)

South American: Peruvian

Top 10 States, Counties, and Places[1]

Sorted by Number in Descending Order — U.S. = 104,165

State	Number	County	Number	Place	Number
Florida	22,300	Miami-Dade County, FL	8,761	**New York, NY** (city)	7,990
California	16,885	Los Angeles County, CA	6,332	**Queens, NY** (borough) Queens County	4,652
New York	12,593	Broward County, FL	5,201	**Los Angeles, CA** (city) Los Angeles County	3,088
New Jersey	9,924	Queens County, NY	4,652	**Manhattan, NY** (borough) New York County	1,672
Virginia	6,815	Fairfax County, VA	3,220	**Chicago, IL** (city) Cook County	1,145
Texas	5,212	Passaic County, NJ	2,451	**Clifton, NJ** (city) Passaic County	1,126
Maryland	3,593	Montgomery County, MD	2,239	**Hempstead (town), NY** (town) Nassau County	941
Illinois	2,967	Cook County, IL	1,923	**Paterson, NJ** (city) Passaic County	879
Connecticut	2,587	Palm Beach County, FL	1,832	**Houston, TX** (city) Harris County	859
Georgia	2,519	Orange County, CA	1,815	**Miami, FL** (city) Miami-Dade County	854

Sorted by Number in Ascending Order — U.S. = 104,165

State	Number	County	Number	Place	Number
Rhode Island	113	San Joaquin County, CA	38	**West Valley City, UT** (city) Salt Lake County	49
Kentucky	173	Ocean County, NJ	50	**Belleville, NJ** (township) Essex County	82
Idaho	193	Osceola County, FL	89	**Downey, CA** (city) Los Angeles County	82
Delaware	217	Solano County, CA	93	**Bloomfield, NJ** (township) Essex County	107
New Mexico	239	Denver County, CO	110	**Denver, CO** (city) Denver County	110
Hawaii	250	Duval County, FL	141	**Linden, NJ** (city) Union County	112
Alabama	287	Lake County, IL	153	**Salt Lake City, UT** (city) Salt Lake County	113
Oklahoma	330	Monmouth County, NJ	166	**Concord, CA** (city) Contra Costa County	116
South Carolina	341	Baltimore County, MD	174	**Santa Ana, CA** (city) Orange County	117
Indiana	376	Fort Bend County, TX	177	**Port Chester, NY** (village) Westchester County	121

Sorted by Percent in Descending Order — U.S. = 30.5%

State	Percent	County	Percent	Place	Percent
Kansas	64.7	Fulton County, GA	59.9	**Doral, FL** (city) Miami-Dade County	69.7
Missouri	54.4	New York County, NY	51.7	**Weston, FL** (city) Broward County	54.7
Tennessee	54.1	Arlington County, VA	49.6	**Manhattan, NY** (borough) New York County	51.7
Minnesota	49.1	Seminole County, FL	47.9	**Arlington, VA** (cdp) Arlington County	49.6
District of Columbia	47.8	Maricopa County, AZ	45.9	**Phoenix, AZ** (city) Maricopa County	49.3
Ohio	43.9	Franklin County, OH	45.8	**Austin, TX** (city) Travis County	46.9
Arizona	43.6	Collin County, TX	44.6	**San Jose, CA** (city) Santa Clara County	45.7
Illinois	42.6	San Diego County, CA	43.7	**Tampa, FL** (city) Hillsborough County	45.6
Georgia	40.5	Lake County, IL	42.5	**Alexandria, VA** (independent city)	45.5
Oregon	40.0	Travis County, TX	41.8	**Fort Lauderdale, FL** (city) Broward County	44.8

Sorted by Percent in Ascending Order — U.S. = 30.5%

State	Percent	County	Percent	Place	Percent
Rhode Island	16.4	San Joaquin County, CA	7.0	**Passaic, NJ** (city) Passaic County	8.7
New Jersey	19.5	Ocean County, NJ	8.7	**Port Chester, NY** (village) Westchester County	10.2
Delaware	22.0	Osceola County, FL	9.2	**Elizabeth, NJ** (city) Union County	11.5
Idaho	22.9	Union County, NJ	14.8	**West Valley City, UT** (city) Salt Lake County	11.5
Utah	24.3	Bronx County, NY	16.6	**White Plains, NY** (city) Westchester County	11.5
Connecticut	26.7	Essex County, NJ	17.5	**Rye, NY** (town) Westchester County	11.6
New York	26.9	Contra Costa County, CA	17.7	**Brentwood, NY** (cdp) Suffolk County	11.9
Kentucky	27.2	Passaic County, NJ	17.9	**Paterson, NJ** (city) Passaic County	12.8
Indiana	27.6	Atlantic County, NJ	18.3	**Belleville, NJ** (township) Essex County	13.4
Nevada	28.5	Hudson County, NJ	19.1	**Newark, NJ** (city) Essex County	14.3

Note: (1) Ranking tables cover all states and counties, and places with an overall population of at least 125,000, OR an overall population of at least 25,000 where the Hispanic/Latino population is at least 20% of the overall population. In states where less than five places meet either of these criteria, we have included places with at least 10,000 total population with the highest percentage of Hispanic/Latino population. These places are identified with an asterisk (*); Please refer to the User's Guide for a full explanation of data.

Four-Year College Graduates

(Universe: Population 25 Years and Over)

South American: Uruguayan

Top 10 States, Counties, and Places[1]

Sorted by Number in Descending Order — U.S. = 7,721

State	Number	County	Number	Place	Number
Florida	1,942	Miami-Dade County, FL	1,012	**New York, NY** (city)	572
New York	976	Broward County, FL	396	**Queens, NY** (borough) Queens County	157
New Jersey	916	Los Angeles County, CA	342	**Elizabeth, NJ** (city) Union County	108
California	637	Harris County, TX	236		
Texas	415	Union County, NJ	211		
Maryland	372	Essex County, NJ	206		
Massachusetts	271	Palm Beach County, FL	174		
Virginia	266	Queens County, NY	157		
Georgia	259	Westchester County, NY	147		
Pennsylvania	179	Gwinnett County, GA	146		

Sorted by Number in Ascending Order — U.S. = 7,721

State	Number	County	Number	Place	Number
Pennsylvania	179	Morris County, NJ	42	**Elizabeth, NJ** (city) Union County	108
Georgia	259	Worcester County, MA	47	**Queens, NY** (borough) Queens County	157
Virginia	266	Hudson County, NJ	50	**New York, NY** (city)	572
Massachusetts	271	Middlesex County, NJ	144		
Maryland	372	Gwinnett County, GA	146		
Texas	415	Westchester County, NY	147		
California	637	Queens County, NY	157		
New Jersey	916	Palm Beach County, FL	174		
New York	976	Essex County, NJ	206		
Florida	1,942	Union County, NJ	211		

Sorted by Percent in Descending Order — U.S. = 20.6%

State	Percent	County	Percent	Place	Percent
Maryland	36.7	Los Angeles County, CA	40.3	**New York, NY** (city)	26.4
California	27.8	Harris County, TX	29.8	**Queens, NY** (borough) Queens County	14.0
Texas	27.7	Middlesex County, NJ	25.9	**Elizabeth, NJ** (city) Union County	6.3
Pennsylvania	24.6	Miami-Dade County, FL	21.7		
New York	23.8	Gwinnett County, GA	19.0		
Virginia	22.2	Westchester County, NY	18.4		
Florida	19.4	Palm Beach County, FL	16.6		
Massachusetts	16.5	Broward County, FL	16.0		
Georgia	13.2	Queens County, NY	14.0		
New Jersey	11.4	Essex County, NJ	12.3		

Sorted by Percent in Ascending Order — U.S. = 20.6%

State	Percent	County	Percent	Place	Percent
New Jersey	11.4	Hudson County, NJ	5.3	**Elizabeth, NJ** (city) Union County	6.3
Georgia	13.2	Worcester County, MA	5.6	**Queens, NY** (borough) Queens County	14.0
Massachusetts	16.5	Morris County, NJ	6.0	**New York, NY** (city)	26.4
Florida	19.4	Union County, NJ	8.0		
Virginia	22.2	Essex County, NJ	12.3		
New York	23.8	Queens County, NY	14.0		
Pennsylvania	24.6	Broward County, FL	16.0		
Texas	27.7	Palm Beach County, FL	16.6		
California	27.8	Westchester County, NY	18.4		
Maryland	36.7	Gwinnett County, GA	19.0		

Note: (1) Ranking tables cover all states and counties, and places with an overall population of at least 125,000, OR an overall population of at least 25,000 where the Hispanic/Latino population is at least 20% of the overall population. In states where less than five places meet either of these criteria, we have included places with at least 10,000 total population with the highest percentage of Hispanic/Latino population. These places are identified with an asterisk (*); Please refer to the User's Guide for a full explanation of data.

Four-Year College Graduates

(Universe: Population 25 Years and Over)

South American: Venezuelan

Top 10 States, Counties, and Places[1]

Sorted by Number in Descending Order — U.S. = 65,185

State	Number	County	Number	Place	Number
Florida	30,191	Miami-Dade County, FL	14,301	**Doral, FL** (city) Miami-Dade County	2,797
Texas	7,108	Broward County, FL	7,598	**New York, NY** (city)	2,740
California	3,934	Harris County, TX	2,592	**Weston, FL** (city) Broward County	2,461
New York	3,883	Orange County, FL	1,955	**Miami, FL** (city) Miami-Dade County	1,870
Georgia	2,325	Palm Beach County, FL	1,301	**Houston, TX** (city) Harris County	1,628
Virginia	1,553	Los Angeles County, CA	1,275	**Manhattan, NY** (borough) New York County	1,076
Massachusetts	1,523	Fort Bend County, TX	1,105	**Fountainebleau, FL** (cdp) Miami-Dade County	927
New Jersey	1,460	New York County, NY	1,076	**Queens, NY** (borough) Queens County	861
North Carolina	1,248	Queens County, NY	861	**Pembroke Pines, FL** (city) Broward County	782
Illinois	1,076	Middlesex County, MA	815	**Aventura, FL** (city) Miami-Dade County	720

Sorted by Number in Ascending Order — U.S. = 65,185

State	Number	County	Number	Place	Number
Wisconsin	271	Tarrant County, TX	178	**Bronx, NY** (borough) Bronx County	208
Missouri	288	Bronx County, NY	208	**Kendall West, FL** (cdp) Miami-Dade County	280
South Carolina	296	Salt Lake County, UT	281	**Tamiami, FL** (cdp) Miami-Dade County	282
Arizona	363	Travis County, TX	305	**Hialeah, FL** (city) Miami-Dade County	285
Oklahoma	364	Suffolk County, MA	340	**Coral Springs, FL** (city) Broward County	286
Indiana	366	Lee County, FL	370	**Country Club, FL** (cdp) Miami-Dade County	337
Utah	398	King County, WA	376	**Los Angeles, CA** (city) Los Angeles County	355
Michigan	428	Collin County, TX	379	**Sunrise, FL** (city) Broward County	394
Minnesota	482	San Diego County, CA	396	**Davie, FL** (town) Broward County	433
Tennessee	497	Hudson County, NJ	409	**Hollywood, FL** (city) Broward County	464

Sorted by Percent in Descending Order — U.S. = 49.7%

State	Percent	County	Percent	Place	Percent
Minnesota	76.0	Fulton County, GA	86.5	**Aventura, FL** (city) Miami-Dade County	76.5
Massachusetts	70.5	Middlesex County, MA	84.1	**Weston, FL** (city) Broward County	65.9
Missouri	64.6	Montgomery County, TX	78.4	**Doral, FL** (city) Miami-Dade County	63.4
Ohio	64.5	Fort Bend County, TX	69.9	**Houston, TX** (city) Harris County	60.9
Michigan	62.4	San Diego County, CA	69.2	**The Hammocks, FL** (cdp) Miami-Dade County	59.9
Colorado	60.5	Collin County, TX	68.5	**Manhattan, NY** (borough) New York County	58.9
Texas	59.3	Fairfax County, VA	67.0	**Kendall, FL** (cdp) Miami-Dade County	58.4
Connecticut	54.8	Seminole County, FL	63.0	**Davie, FL** (town) Broward County	54.4
Georgia	54.8	Orange County, CA	62.1	**Miramar, FL** (city) Broward County	52.9
Louisiana	54.0	Dallas County, TX	61.1	**Miami, FL** (city) Miami-Dade County	49.9

Sorted by Percent in Ascending Order — U.S. = 49.7%

State	Percent	County	Percent	Place	Percent
Utah	30.9	Osceola County, FL	24.4	**Bronx, NY** (borough) Bronx County	24.7
New Jersey	37.6	Bronx County, NY	24.7	**Queens, NY** (borough) Queens County	29.4
Arizona	40.0	Queens County, NY	29.4	**Tamiami, FL** (cdp) Miami-Dade County	29.7
New York	40.7	Kings County, NY	34.1	**Hialeah, FL** (city) Miami-Dade County	32.0
South Carolina	41.2	Lee County, FL	34.5	**Country Club, FL** (cdp) Miami-Dade County	32.4
Oklahoma	44.8	Salt Lake County, UT	36.3	**Sunrise, FL** (city) Broward County	32.5
Tennessee	46.6	Orange County, FL	42.2	**Brooklyn, NY** (borough) Kings County	34.1
Pennsylvania	47.2	Tarrant County, TX	42.4	**Los Angeles, CA** (city) Los Angeles County	35.5
Florida	47.7	Hillsborough County, FL	44.0	**New York, NY** (city)	37.3
Virginia	50.0	Pinellas County, FL	44.0	**Kendall West, FL** (cdp) Miami-Dade County	38.3

Note: (1) Ranking tables cover all states and counties, and places with an overall population of at least 125,000, OR an overall population of at least 25,000 where the Hispanic/Latino population is at least 20% of the overall population. In states where less than five places meet either of these criteria, we have included places with at least 10,000 total population with the highest percentage of Hispanic/Latino population. These places are identified with an asterisk (*); Please refer to the User's Guide for a full explanation of data.

Four-Year College Graduates

(Universe: Population 25 Years and Over)

Spaniard

Top 10 States, Counties, and Places[1]

Sorted by Number in Descending Order — U.S. = 107,497

State	Number	County	Number	Place	Number
California	21,279	Los Angeles County, CA	4,604	**New York, NY** (city)	6,057
Florida	10,995	Miami-Dade County, FL	3,281	**Albuquerque, NM** (city) Bernalillo County	2,256
New York	10,157	San Diego County, CA	2,732	**Manhattan, NY** (borough) New York County	2,248
Texas	9,551	Bernalillo County, NM	2,558	**Los Angeles, CA** (city) Los Angeles County	1,850
New Mexico	5,922	New York County, NY	2,248	**San Diego, CA** (city) San Diego County	1,371
New Jersey	5,457	Hillsborough County, FL	1,711	**Queens, NY** (borough) Queens County	1,262
Colorado	4,739	Santa Clara County, CA	1,692	**San Francisco, CA** (city) San Francisco County	1,105
Illinois	2,841	Maricopa County, AZ	1,635	**Brooklyn, NY** (borough) Kings County	1,073
Virginia	2,652	Orange County, CA	1,633	**Houston, TX** (city) Harris County	959
Arizona	2,608	Harris County, TX	1,513	**Bronx, NY** (borough) Bronx County	852

Sorted by Number in Ascending Order — U.S. = 107,497

State	Number	County	Number	Place	Number
Wyoming	94	Las Animas County, CO	6	**San Bernardino, CA** (city) San Bernardino County	36
Montana	150	Colfax County, NM	23	**Glendale, AZ** (city) Maricopa County	44
Mississippi	157	Weber County, UT	26	**Thornton, CO** (city) Adams County	47
Iowa	197	Hawaii County, HI	61	**South Valley, NM** (cdp) Bernalillo County	81
West Virginia	236	Rio Arriba County, NM	62	**Anchorage, AK** (municipality)	93
Alaska	241	La Plata County, CO	65	**Las Cruces, NM** (city) Dona Ana County	100
New Hampshire	252	Tulare County, CA	76	**Mesa, AZ** (city) Maricopa County	100
Arkansas	262	San Juan County, NM	86	**Kearny, NJ** (town) Hudson County	101
Maine	268	Mesa County, CO	90	**Westminster, CO** (city) Adams County	102
Idaho	338	Weld County, CO	99	**Bakersfield, CA** (city) Kern County	108

Sorted by Percent in Descending Order — U.S. = 30.3%

State	Percent	County	Percent	Place	Percent
District of Columbia	76.2	New York County, NY	67.0	**Manhattan, NY** (borough) New York County	67.0
Virginia	51.4	Middlesex County, MA	64.2	**San Francisco, CA** (city) San Francisco County	54.4
Massachusetts	47.4	Hennepin County, MN	60.6	**Staten Island, NY** (borough) Richmond County	50.8
Maryland	46.7	DuPage County, IL	60.2	**Chicago, IL** (city) Cook County	49.9
Connecticut	46.5	Montgomery County, MD	58.3	**Portland, OR** (city) Multnomah County	48.9
Georgia	44.8	Fairfield County, CT	57.2	**Bronx, NY** (borough) Bronx County	46.6
Illinois	42.6	Montgomery County, PA	56.5	**New York, NY** (city)	46.5
Minnesota	42.6	Morris County, NJ	56.2	**Miami, FL** (city) Miami-Dade County	46.1
New York	42.2	San Francisco County, CA	54.4	**Seattle, WA** (city) King County	44.1
Pennsylvania	42.1	Collin County, TX	53.2	**San Diego, CA** (city) San Diego County	43.5

Sorted by Percent in Ascending Order — U.S. = 30.3%

State	Percent	County	Percent	Place	Percent
Wyoming	8.1	Las Animas County, CO	2.1	**Thornton, CO** (city) Adams County	6.6
Mississippi	17.4	Cibola County, NM	4.5	**Glendale, AZ** (city) Maricopa County	7.5
Colorado	18.0	Colfax County, NM	5.1	**San Bernardino, CA** (city) San Bernardino County	7.7
Utah	18.1	Weber County, UT	6.4	**Pueblo, CO** (city) Pueblo County	8.5
Montana	18.5	Weld County, CO	7.8	**Newark, NJ** (city) Essex County	9.5
New Mexico	18.8	Adams County, CO	9.4	**South Valley, NM** (cdp) Bernalillo County	10.5
Idaho	19.3	Pueblo County, CO	10.1	**Kearny, NJ** (town) Hudson County	12.5
Oklahoma	20.4	San Miguel County, NM	10.7	**Mesa, AZ** (city) Maricopa County	12.6
Hawaii	21.6	San Juan County, NM	12.1	**Westminster, CO** (city) Adams County	14.2
Arkansas	22.3	Hawaii County, HI	12.2	**Stockton, CA** (city) San Joaquin County	15.9

Note: (1) Ranking tables cover all states and counties, and places with an overall population of at least 125,000, OR an overall population of at least 25,000 where the Hispanic/Latino population is at least 20% of the overall population. In states where less than five places meet either of these criteria, we have included places with at least 10,000 total population with the highest percentage of Hispanic/Latino population. These places are identified with an asterisk (*); Please refer to the User's Guide for a full explanation of data.

Population Age 3–17 Enrolled in Public School

(Universe: Population Age 3–17 Enrolled in School)

Total Population

Top 10 States, Counties, and Places[1]

Sorted by Number in Descending Order — U.S. = 48,352,782

State	Number	County	Number	Place	Number
California	6,273,823	Los Angeles County, CA	1,670,003	**New York, NY** (city)	1,047,997
Texas	4,485,585	Cook County, IL	797,509	**Los Angeles, CA** (city) Los Angeles County	589,068
New York	2,813,896	Harris County, TX	741,629	**Chicago, IL** (city) Cook County	395,453
Florida	2,575,757	Maricopa County, AZ	652,531	**Houston, TX** (city) Harris County	351,293
Illinois	2,074,471	Orange County, CA	491,025	**Brooklyn, NY** (borough) Kings County	338,020
Pennsylvania	1,767,108	San Diego County, CA	483,386	**Queens, NY** (borough) Queens County	281,512
Ohio	1,766,122	San Bernardino County, CA	420,665	**Phoenix, AZ** (city) Maricopa County	267,314
Michigan	1,645,770	Riverside County, CA	420,401	**Bronx, NY** (borough) Bronx County	241,152
Georgia	1,616,006	Dallas County, TX	415,879	**San Antonio, TX** (city) Bexar County	233,119
North Carolina	1,465,699	Miami-Dade County, FL	342,082	**Philadelphia, PA** (city) Philadelphia County	198,802

Sorted by Number in Ascending Order — U.S. = 48,352,782

State	Number	County	Number	Place	Number
District of Columbia	60,279	Esmeralda County, NV	81	**Florence, AZ** (town) Pinal County	754
Wyoming	88,071	McMullen County, TX	90	**Spearfish*, SD** (city) Lawrence County	1,265
Vermont	90,726	Kent County, TX	129	**Hanover*, NH** (town) Grafton County	1,407
North Dakota	95,224	Clark County, ID	149	**Hawaiian Paradise Park*, HI** (cdp) Hawaii County	1,445
Alaska	121,462	Motley County, TX	156	**Brattleboro*, VT** (town) Windham County	1,463
Delaware	122,713	Terrell County, TX	161	**Warr Acres*, OK** (city) Oklahoma County	1,539
South Dakota	129,565	Sterling County, TX	180	**Parker*, SC** (cdp) Greenville County	1,557
Montana	144,534	Harding County, NM	205	**Waterville*, ME** (city) Kennebec County	1,658
Rhode Island	147,085	Foard County, TX	213	**Huron*, SD** (city) Beadle County	1,668
Hawaii	173,945	Greeley County, KS	235	**Yankton*, SD** (city) Yankton County	1,734

Sorted by Percent in Descending Order — U.S. = 86.4%

State	Percent	County	Percent	Place	Percent
Nevada	92.5	Armstrong County, TX	100.0	**Parker*, SC** (cdp) Greenville County	100.0
West Virginia	91.6	Atkinson County, GA	100.0	**San Luis, AZ** (city) Yuma County	99.3
Wyoming	91.6	Baker County, GA	100.0	**Bell, CA** (city) Los Angeles County	99.1
Oklahoma	91.1	Baylor County, TX	100.0	**San Juan, TX** (city) Hidalgo County	99.1
Arizona	90.8	Carter County, MO	100.0	**Coachella, CA** (city) Riverside County	99.0
Texas	90.7	Clark County, ID	100.0	**Fort Hood, TX** (cdp) Bell County	98.7
Utah	90.7	Clay County, IL	100.0	**Delano, CA** (city) Kern County	98.4
Arkansas	90.4	Cleveland County, AR	100.0	**Pharr, TX** (city) Hidalgo County	98.3
Alaska	90.0	Costilla County, CO	100.0	**Maywood, CA** (city) Los Angeles County	98.2
New Mexico	89.8	Cottle County, TX	100.0	**Lexington*, NE** (city) Dawson County	98.1

Sorted by Percent in Ascending Order — U.S. = 86.4%

State	Percent	County	Percent	Place	Percent
Hawaii	76.9	Fayette County, TN	61.1	**Coral Gables, FL** (city) Miami-Dade County	35.1
District of Columbia	78.8	Jefferson Parish, LA	63.0	**Ramapo, NY** (town) Rockland County	38.8
Delaware	79.5	Rockland County, NY	63.4	**Metairie, LA** (cdp) Jefferson Parish	41.8
Louisiana	80.5	Pointe Coupee Parish, LA	64.6	**Altadena, CA** (cdp) Los Angeles County	60.5
Maryland	80.8	Sioux County, IA	64.6	**Miami Beach, FL** (city) Miami-Dade County	61.8
Pennsylvania	81.9	Holmes County, OH	66.3	**Spring Valley, NY** (village) Rockland County	62.6
New York	82.7	Piute County, UT	66.5	**Englewood, NJ** (city) Bergen County	64.7
Rhode Island	83.0	Jefferson County, FL	66.6	**Kenner, LA** (city) Jefferson Parish	65.3
New Jersey	83.3	LaGrange County, IN	66.6	**Plantation, FL** (city) Broward County	68.7
Missouri	83.9	Amite County, MS	67.7	**Manhattan, NY** (borough) New York County	69.6

RANKINGS & COMPARISONS

Note: (1) Ranking tables cover all states and counties, and places with an overall population of at least 125,000, OR an overall population of at least 25,000 where the Hispanic/Latino population is at least 20% of the overall population. In states where less than five places meet either of these criteria, we have included places with at least 10,000 total population with the highest percentage of Hispanic/Latino population. These places are identified with an asterisk (*); Please refer to the User's Guide for a full explanation of data.

Population Age 3–17 Enrolled in Public School

(Universe: Population Age 3–17 Enrolled in School)

Hispanic or Latino (of any race)

Top 10 States, Counties, and Places[1]

Sorted by Number in Descending Order — U.S. = 10,886,462

State	Number	County	Number	Place	Number
California	3,257,353	Los Angeles County, CA	1,068,643	**New York, NY** (city)	416,151
Texas	2,154,697	Harris County, TX	372,277	**Los Angeles, CA** (city) Los Angeles County	411,269
Florida	674,661	Maricopa County, AZ	275,770	**Houston, TX** (city) Harris County	193,971
New York	633,498	Cook County, IL	270,781	**San Antonio, TX** (city) Bexar County	171,154
Illinois	458,353	San Bernardino County, CA	256,301	**Chicago, IL** (city) Cook County	161,362
Arizona	450,245	Riverside County, CA	250,287	**Phoenix, AZ** (city) Maricopa County	148,255
New Jersey	293,234	Orange County, CA	233,447	**Bronx, NY** (borough) Bronx County	146,210
Colorado	232,114	San Diego County, CA	223,383	**Dallas, TX** (city) Dallas County	115,810
New Mexico	194,883	Dallas County, TX	211,025	**El Paso, TX** (city) El Paso County	115,432
Washington	175,489	Bexar County, TX	208,094	**Queens, NY** (borough) Queens County	96,682

Sorted by Number in Ascending Order — U.S. = 10,886,462

State	Number	County	Number	Place	Number
Vermont	1,903	Evangeline Parish, LA	13	**Burlington*, VT** (city) Chittenden County	84
North Dakota	3,102	Buffalo County, WI	16	**Morgantown*, WV** (city) Monongalia County	94
Maine	3,992	Perry County, IL	19	**College*, AK** (cdp) Fairbanks North Star Borough	97
West Virginia	4,107	Johnson County, NE	20	**Bozeman*, MT** (city) Gallatin County	99
South Dakota	5,416	Telfair County, GA	20	**Grand Forks*, ND** (city) Grand Forks County	143
Montana	6,595	Marlboro County, SC	23	**Laurel*, MS** (city) Jones County	165
District of Columbia	6,884	Wakulla County, FL	31	**Jackson, MS** (city) Hinds County	180
Alaska	8,441	Hampton County, SC	36	**Biloxi*, MS** (city) Harrison County	208
New Hampshire	8,597	Yazoo County, MS	39	**Fort Leonard Wood*, MO** (cdp) Pulaski County	245
Wyoming	10,392	Union County, FL	41	**Salem*, NH** (town) Rockingham County	268

Sorted by Percent in Descending Order — U.S. = 93.0%

State	Percent	County	Percent	Place	Percent
Nevada	96.5	Accomack County, VA	100.0	**Albertville*, AL** (city) Marshall County	100.0
South Dakota	96.5	Adair County, OK	100.0	**Asheboro, NC** (city) Randolph County	100.0
Arizona	95.4	Adams County, WI	100.0	**Bluffton*, SC** (town) Beaufort County	100.0
Texas	95.4	Alexander County, NC	100.0	**Bozeman*, MT** (city) Gallatin County	100.0
Oklahoma	95.2	Alleghany County, NC	100.0	**Butte-Silver Bow*, MT** (consolidated govt) Silver Bow County	100.0
North Carolina	95.1	Allen Parish, LA	100.0	**Evanston*, WY** (city) Uinta County	100.0
Arkansas	95.0	Anderson County, TN	100.0	**Fitchburg, MA** (city) Worcester County	100.0
Oregon	94.6	Antrim County, MI	100.0	**Fort Campbell North*, KY** (cdp) Christian County	100.0
Iowa	94.4	Archer County, TX	100.0	**Fort Hood, TX** (cdp) Bell County	100.0
Utah	94.4	Ashe County, NC	100.0	**Fort Leonard Wood*, MO** (cdp) Pulaski County	100.0

Sorted by Percent in Ascending Order — U.S. = 93.0%

State	Percent	County	Percent	Place	Percent
Louisiana	80.2	Wakulla County, FL	23.5	**Coral Gables, FL** (city) Miami-Dade County	34.9
Hawaii	84.0	Putnam County, IN	33.1	**Mobile, AL** (city) Mobile County	54.6
Maine	85.1	Bristol County, RI	41.5	**Metairie, LA** (cdp) Jefferson Parish	57.0
Ohio	85.2	Sullivan County, TN	50.2	**Plantation, FL** (city) Broward County	63.0
District of Columbia	85.5	Geauga County, OH	52.3	**New Orleans, LA** (city) Orleans Parish	64.8
Vermont	86.3	Hampton County, SC	53.7	**Jackson, MS** (city) Hinds County	65.2
Missouri	87.9	Addison County, VT	55.4	**Salem*, NH** (town) Rockingham County	65.5
Florida	88.0	Johnson County, NE	55.6	**Grand Forks*, ND** (city) Grand Forks County	65.9
Maryland	88.3	Lee County, IA	56.1	**Missoula*, MT** (city) Missoula County	69.6
New Hampshire	88.6	Centre County, PA	56.5	**Kendall, FL** (cdp) Miami-Dade County	69.9

Note: (1) Ranking tables cover all states and counties, and places with an overall population of at least 125,000, OR an overall population of at least 25,000 where the Hispanic/Latino population is at least 20% of the overall population. In states where less than five places meet either of these criteria, we have included places with at least 10,000 total population with the highest percentage of Hispanic/Latino population. These places are identified with an asterisk (*); Please refer to the User's Guide for a full explanation of data.

Population Age 3–17 Enrolled in Public School

(Universe: Population Age 3–17 Enrolled in School)

Central American, excluding Mexican

Top 10 States, Counties, and Places[1]

Sorted by Number in Descending Order — U.S. = 700,787

State	Number	County	Number	Place	Number
California	210,194	Los Angeles County, CA	129,016	**Los Angeles, CA** (city) Los Angeles County	77,465
Texas	80,440	Harris County, TX	40,096	**Houston, TX** (city) Harris County	25,373
Florida	67,854	Miami-Dade County, FL	33,213	**New York, NY** (city)	24,068
New York	58,166	Dallas County, TX	14,262	**Miami, FL** (city) Miami-Dade County	9,987
Maryland	32,896	Montgomery County, MD	13,989	**Hempstead (town), NY** (town) Nassau County	8,198
Virginia	32,218	Suffolk County, NY	12,682	**Queens, NY** (borough) Queens County	7,897
New Jersey	27,936	Nassau County, NY	12,219	**Brooklyn, NY** (borough) Kings County	7,062
North Carolina	19,863	Prince George's County, MD	12,217	**Islip, NY** (town) Suffolk County	6,852
Georgia	18,077	San Bernardino County, CA	11,465	**Bronx, NY** (borough) Bronx County	6,418
Massachusetts	17,793	Fairfax County, VA	9,626	**Dallas, TX** (city) Dallas County	5,129

Sorted by Number in Ascending Order — U.S. = 700,787

State	Number	County	Number	Place	Number
Wyoming	239	Lee County, AL	32	**Atlanta, GA** (city) Fulton County	0
Vermont	277	Harrison County, MS	43	**Baton Rouge, LA** (city) East Baton Rouge Parish	52
Alaska	331	Kings County, CA	48	**Palm Springs, CA** (city) Riverside County	55
Idaho	455	Madison County, AL	52	**Coral Gables, FL** (city) Miami-Dade County	61
West Virginia	461	El Dorado County, CA	63	**Danbury, CT** (city/town) Fairfield County	63
Hawaii	549	York County, PA	70	**Rohnert Park, CA** (city) Sonoma County	70
South Dakota	624	Weber County, UT	79	**Irvine, CA** (city) Orange County	92
New Hampshire	659	Garfield County, CO	80	**Delano, CA** (city) Kern County	97
Maine	730	Montgomery County, AL	108	**Hackensack, NJ** (city) Bergen County	107
Mississippi	959	Allegheny County, PA	110	**Montgomery, AL** (city) Montgomery County	108

Sorted by Percent in Descending Order — U.S. = 92.6%

State	Percent	County	Percent	Place	Percent
Wyoming	100.0	Albany County, NY	100.0	**Adelanto, CA** (city) San Bernardino County	100.0
South Dakota	99.8	Berks County, PA	100.0	**Albertville*, AL** (city) Marshall County	100.0
Iowa	98.9	Butte County, CA	100.0	**Atascocita, TX** (cdp) Harris County	100.0
Texas	96.3	Caroline County, MD	100.0	**Avondale, AZ** (city) Maricopa County	100.0
Nebraska	96.1	Carroll County, AR	100.0	**Bell Gardens, CA** (city) Los Angeles County	100.0
Oregon	96.1	Carroll County, GA	100.0	**Belleville, NJ** (township) Essex County	100.0
Nevada	96.0	Cass County, IN	100.0	**Bellflower, CA** (city) Los Angeles County	100.0
Oklahoma	95.4	Chatham County, GA	100.0	**Bridgeport, CT** (city/town) Fairfield County	100.0
Arizona	95.1	Chatham County, NC	100.0	**Buenaventura Lakes, FL** (cdp) Osceola County	100.0
Delaware	94.3	Clark County, WA	100.0	**Cathedral City, CA** (city) Riverside County	100.0

Sorted by Percent in Ascending Order — U.S. = 92.6%

State	Percent	County	Percent	Place	Percent
Alaska	68.4	York County, PA	36.3	**Atlanta, GA** (city) Fulton County	0.0
Hawaii	71.4	Madison County, AL	38.8	**Coral Gables, FL** (city) Miami-Dade County	55.5
Louisiana	74.5	Allegheny County, PA	51.9	**Metairie, LA** (cdp) Jefferson Parish	59.1
Ohio	77.4	Jefferson County, AL	53.2	**Murrieta, CA** (city) Riverside County	59.9
Mississippi	80.0	Erie County, NY	54.1	**Rohnert Park, CA** (city) Sonoma County	61.4
Wisconsin	80.9	McHenry County, IL	54.7	**Baton Rouge, LA** (city) East Baton Rouge Parish	61.9
Pennsylvania	81.7	Charles County, MD	55.8	**Norfolk, VA** (independent city)	63.8
Michigan	83.1	Honolulu County, HI	58.9	**Cleveland, OH** (city) Cuyahoga County	64.6
Indiana	83.9	Saint Louis County, MO	60.3	**Alhambra, CA** (city) Los Angeles County	64.9
Alabama	84.3	Cuyahoga County, OH	60.4	**Chino Hills, CA** (city) San Bernardino County	66.2

Note: (1) Ranking tables cover all states and counties, and places with an overall population of at least 125,000, OR an overall population of at least 25,000 where the Hispanic/Latino population is at least 20% of the overall population. In states where less than five places meet either of these criteria, we have included places with at least 10,000 total population with the highest percentage of Hispanic/Latino population. These places are identified with an asterisk (*); Please refer to the User's Guide for a full explanation of data.

Population Age 3–17 Enrolled in Public School

(Universe: Population Age 3–17 Enrolled in School)

Central American: Costa Rican

Top 10 States, Counties, and Places[1]

Sorted by Number in Descending Order U.S. = 20,289

State	Number	County	Number	Place	Number
California	3,417	Los Angeles County, CA	1,147	**New York, NY** (city)	782
Florida	3,227	Miami-Dade County, FL	968	**Los Angeles, CA** (city) Los Angeles County	445
New Jersey	2,919	Union County, NJ	632	**Brooklyn, NY** (borough) Kings County	417
New York	1,691	Broward County, FL	467	**Queens, NY** (borough) Queens County	213
North Carolina	1,154	Kings County, NY	417	**Miami, FL** (city) Miami-Dade County	109
Texas	767	Essex County, NJ	405	**Philadelphia, PA** (city) Philadelphia County	90
Pennsylvania	749	Suffolk County, NY	356	**Bronx, NY** (borough) Bronx County	25
Massachusetts	501	Palm Beach County, FL	351		
Illinois	419	Passaic County, NJ	334		
Georgia	418	Orange County, CA	331		

Sorted by Number in Ascending Order U.S. = 20,289

State	Number	County	Number	Place	Number
Louisiana	97	Bronx County, NY	25	**Bronx, NY** (borough) Bronx County	25
Oregon	103	Mercer County, NJ	84	**Philadelphia, PA** (city) Philadelphia County	90
Wisconsin	144	Philadelphia County, PA	90	**Miami, FL** (city) Miami-Dade County	109
South Carolina	185	Clark County, NV	145	**Queens, NY** (borough) Queens County	213
Minnesota	205	Harris County, TX	151	**Brooklyn, NY** (borough) Kings County	417
Michigan	208	Hillsborough County, FL	179	**Los Angeles, CA** (city) Los Angeles County	445
Tennessee	212	Riverside County, CA	192	**New York, NY** (city)	782
Nevada	266	San Diego County, CA	202		
Connecticut	313	Morris County, NJ	210		
Arizona	327	Fairfield County, CT	213		

Sorted by Percent in Descending Order U.S. = 83.4%

State	Percent	County	Percent	Place	Percent
Michigan	93.7	Bronx County, NY	100.0	**Bronx, NY** (borough) Bronx County	100.0
Colorado	92.5	Clark County, NV	100.0	**New York, NY** (city)	93.0
North Carolina	92.3	Essex County, NJ	100.0	**Brooklyn, NY** (borough) Kings County	91.4
Nevada	92.0	Fairfield County, CT	100.0	**Queens, NY** (borough) Queens County	91.4
New York	90.8	Orange County, FL	100.0	**Miami, FL** (city) Miami-Dade County	83.8
New Jersey	89.3	San Diego County, CA	100.0	**Los Angeles, CA** (city) Los Angeles County	77.3
Florida	87.6	Somerset County, NJ	100.0	**Philadelphia, PA** (city) Philadelphia County	45.5
Oregon	87.3	Suffolk County, NY	100.0		
Arizona	87.2	Contra Costa County, CA	95.1		
Washington	86.9	Morris County, NJ	93.3		

Sorted by Percent in Ascending Order U.S. = 83.4%

State	Percent	County	Percent	Place	Percent
Maryland	59.7	Philadelphia County, PA	45.5	**Philadelphia, PA** (city) Philadelphia County	45.5
South Carolina	63.6	Los Angeles County, CA	68.1	**Los Angeles, CA** (city) Los Angeles County	77.3
Tennessee	66.5	Cook County, IL	73.5	**Miami, FL** (city) Miami-Dade County	83.8
Massachusetts	66.7	Hillsborough County, FL	75.2	**Brooklyn, NY** (borough) Kings County	91.4
Minnesota	69.3	Union County, NJ	78.7	**Queens, NY** (borough) Queens County	91.4
Wisconsin	71.3	Broward County, FL	82.9	**New York, NY** (city)	93.0
Pennsylvania	76.1	Harris County, TX	84.8	**Bronx, NY** (borough) Bronx County	100.0
Illinois	77.2	Maricopa County, AZ	85.3		
Virginia	78.4	Nassau County, NY	85.9		
California	80.0	Mercer County, NJ	86.6		

Note: (1) Ranking tables cover all states and counties, and places with an overall population of at least 125,000, OR an overall population of at least 25,000 where the Hispanic/Latino population is at least 20% of the overall population. In states where less than five places meet either of these criteria, we have included places with at least 10,000 total population with the highest percentage of Hispanic/Latino population. These places are identified with an asterisk (*); Please refer to the User's Guide for a full explanation of data.

Population Age 3–17 Enrolled in Public School

(Universe: Population Age 3–17 Enrolled in School)

Central American: Guatemalan

Top 10 States, Counties, and Places[1]

Sorted by Number in Descending Order — U.S. = 172,787

State	Number	County	Number	Place	Number
California	60,983	Los Angeles County, CA	40,131	**Los Angeles, CA** (city) Los Angeles County	24,804
Florida	12,110	Harris County, TX	4,855	**New York, NY** (city)	3,485
New York	10,696	Cook County, IL	4,431	**Houston, TX** (city) Harris County	3,408
Texas	9,774	Palm Beach County, FL	3,510	**Chicago, IL** (city) Cook County	2,886
New Jersey	6,866	San Bernardino County, CA	3,361	**Providence, RI** (city) Providence County	1,896
Massachusetts	6,450	Providence County, RI	2,998	**Queens, NY** (borough) Queens County	1,863
Illinois	6,050	Orange County, CA	2,864	**Phoenix, AZ** (city) Maricopa County	1,176
Georgia	5,646	Riverside County, CA	2,839	**Lynn, MA** (city) Essex County	1,119
Maryland	4,661	Miami-Dade County, FL	2,697	**Trenton, NJ** (city) Mercer County	1,119
Virginia	3,781	Maricopa County, AZ	2,148	**Long Beach, CA** (city) Los Angeles County	1,114

Sorted by Number in Ascending Order — U.S. = 172,787

State	Number	County	Number	Place	Number
District of Columbia	142	Lee County, AL	12	**Newark, NJ** (city) Essex County	42
Idaho	215	Fulton County, GA	52	**West New York, NJ** (town) Hudson County	59
Mississippi	229	Morris County, NJ	61	**Paramount, CA** (city) Los Angeles County	76
New Hampshire	236	Burke County, NC	73	**Ontario, CA** (city) San Bernardino County	79
New Mexico	409	Pinal County, AZ	82	**Marietta, GA** (city) Cobb County	84
South Dakota	423	Jefferson Parish, LA	93	**Fort Worth, TX** (city) Tarrant County	91
Wisconsin	646	Philadelphia County, PA	93	**Philadelphia, PA** (city) Philadelphia County	93
Louisiana	683	Nobles County, MN	96	**Montebello, CA** (city) Los Angeles County	104
Arkansas	744	Anne Arundel County, MD	120	**Richmond, VA** (independent city)	107
Delaware	1,035	Marion County, IN	120	**Salt Lake City, UT** (city) Salt Lake County	111

Sorted by Percent in Descending Order — U.S. = 90.5%

State	Percent	County	Percent	Place	Percent
South Dakota	99.8	Burke County, NC	100.0	**Albertville*, AL** (city) Marshall County	100.0
Iowa	98.1	Caroline County, MD	100.0	**Alhambra, CA** (city) Los Angeles County	100.0
Oregon	96.9	Davidson County, TN	100.0	**Bell Gardens, CA** (city) Los Angeles County	100.0
Nebraska	96.3	DeKalb County, AL	100.0	**Bell, CA** (city) Los Angeles County	100.0
Oklahoma	96.2	Douglas County, NE	100.0	**Burbank, CA** (city) Los Angeles County	100.0
California	94.9	Floyd County, GA	100.0	**Cathedral City, CA** (city) Riverside County	100.0
Maryland	93.9	Fort Bend County, TX	100.0	**Central Falls*, RI** (city) Providence County	100.0
Tennessee	93.9	Franklin County, AL	100.0	**Chillum, MD** (cdp) Prince George's County	100.0
Nevada	93.2	Fresno County, CA	100.0	**Elizabeth, NJ** (city) Union County	100.0
Texas	93.1	Gilmer County, GA	100.0	**Gardena, CA** (city) Los Angeles County	100.0

Sorted by Percent in Ascending Order — U.S. = 90.5%

State	Percent	County	Percent	Place	Percent
District of Columbia	38.4	Fulton County, GA	33.8	**Philadelphia, PA** (city) Philadelphia County	48.4
Louisiana	61.3	Jefferson Parish, LA	33.8	**Columbus, OH** (city) Franklin County	59.6
Wisconsin	70.1	Philadelphia County, PA	48.4	**Indianapolis, IN** (city) Marion County	61.1
Pennsylvania	70.7	Morris County, NJ	50.8	**Downey, CA** (city) Los Angeles County	65.2
Mississippi	70.9	Manatee County, FL	56.6	**Central Islip, NY** (cdp) Suffolk County	70.4
Indiana	71.6	Cuyahoga County, OH	57.5	**West Valley City, UT** (city) Salt Lake County	71.2
Ohio	72.7	Marion County, IN	58.5	**Charlotte, NC** (city) Mecklenburg County	72.5
New Mexico	78.4	Franklin County, OH	60.6	**Pawtucket*, RI** (city) Providence County	74.0
Michigan	79.1	Somerset County, NJ	63.9	**Fort Worth, TX** (city) Tarrant County	74.6
Minnesota	80.8	Anne Arundel County, MD	66.3	**Paramount, CA** (city) Los Angeles County	75.2

Note: (1) Ranking tables cover all states and counties, and places with an overall population of at least 125,000, OR an overall population of at least 25,000 where the Hispanic/Latino population is at least 20% of the overall population. In states where less than five places meet either of these criteria, we have included places with at least 10,000 total population with the highest percentage of Hispanic/Latino population. These places are identified with an asterisk (*); Please refer to the User's Guide for a full explanation of data.

Population Age 3–17 Enrolled in Public School

(Universe: Population Age 3–17 Enrolled in School)

Central American: Honduran

Top 10 States, Counties, and Places[1]

Sorted by Number in Descending Order — U.S. = 104,642

State	Number	County	Number	Place	Number
Florida	17,916	Miami-Dade County, FL	9,629	**New York, NY** (city)	8,119
Texas	16,005	Los Angeles County, CA	8,805	**Houston, TX** (city) Harris County	5,193
California	13,954	Harris County, TX	8,002	**Los Angeles, CA** (city) Los Angeles County	4,463
New York	11,871	Bronx County, NY	3,593	**Miami, FL** (city) Miami-Dade County	4,010
North Carolina	5,589	Dallas County, TX	2,379	**Bronx, NY** (borough) Bronx County	3,593
New Jersey	5,411	Kings County, NY	2,080	**Brooklyn, NY** (borough) Kings County	2,080
Virginia	3,795	Jefferson Parish, LA	2,010	**Charlotte, NC** (city) Mecklenburg County	1,538
Louisiana	3,486	Mecklenburg County, NC	1,649	**Queens, NY** (borough) Queens County	1,511
Georgia	3,193	Queens County, NY	1,511	**Dallas, TX** (city) Dallas County	1,132
Massachusetts	2,947	Broward County, FL	1,421	**Hempstead (town), NY** (town) Nassau County	994

Sorted by Number in Ascending Order — U.S. = 104,642

State	Number	County	Number	Place	Number
Mississippi	248	Richmond County, NY	89	**Baltimore, MD** (independent city)	82
District of Columbia	312	Johnston County, NC	91	**Miami Beach, FL** (city) Miami-Dade County	87
Alabama	333	Osceola County, FL	129	**Staten Island, NY** (borough) Richmond County	89
Iowa	342	Fulton County, GA	133	**Raleigh, NC** (city) Wake County	100
Nebraska	346	Polk County, FL	146	**Las Vegas, NV** (city) Clark County	104
Kansas	359	Fresno County, CA	155	**Springfield, VA** (cdp) Fairfax County	114
Oregon	372	Arapahoe County, CO	159	**Brentwood, NY** (cdp) Suffolk County	125
Kentucky	408	Philadelphia County, PA	174	**Wheaton, MD** (cdp) Montgomery County	128
Arkansas	453	Hall County, GA	179	**Yonkers, NY** (city) Westchester County	142
Oklahoma	465	Hartford County, CT	182	**Newburgh, NY** (city) Orange County	152

Sorted by Percent in Descending Order — U.S. = 94.2%

State	Percent	County	Percent	Place	Percent
Oregon	100.0	Arapahoe County, CO	100.0	**Austin, TX** (city) Travis County	100.0
Wisconsin	100.0	Atlantic County, NJ	100.0	**Chelsea, MA** (city) Suffolk County	100.0
Washington	98.8	Beaufort County, SC	100.0	**Conroe, TX** (city) Montgomery County	100.0
Iowa	98.3	Bexar County, TX	100.0	**Durham, NC** (city) Durham County	100.0
Texas	98.0	Clark County, NV	100.0	**Fort Worth, TX** (city) Tarrant County	100.0
Arizona	97.3	Cobb County, GA	100.0	**Garland, TX** (city) Dallas County	100.0
Georgia	96.9	Davidson County, TN	100.0	**Hempstead (village), NY** (village) Nassau County	100.0
Virginia	96.7	DeKalb County, GA	100.0	**Huntington Station, NY** (cdp) Suffolk County	100.0
Oklahoma	96.5	Denton County, TX	100.0	**Huntington, NY** (town) Suffolk County	100.0
South Carolina	96.3	Duplin County, NC	100.0	**Las Vegas, NV** (city) Clark County	100.0

Sorted by Percent in Ascending Order — U.S. = 94.2%

State	Percent	County	Percent	Place	Percent
Mississippi	70.7	East Baton Rouge Parish, LA	57.8	**Aurora, CO** (city) Arapahoe County	67.8
Louisiana	80.5	Osceola County, FL	63.5	**Metairie, LA** (cdp) Jefferson Parish	70.8
Ohio	83.1	San Francisco County, CA	75.7	**Miami Beach, FL** (city) Miami-Dade County	71.3
Colorado	88.2	Saint Tammany Parish, LA	76.0	**San Francisco, CA** (city) San Francisco County	75.7
Arkansas	88.5	Fresno County, CA	77.1	**Boston, MA** (city) Suffolk County	81.7
Missouri	88.8	Jefferson Parish, LA	80.9	**Indianapolis, IN** (city) Marion County	82.8
Utah	89.2	Fulton County, GA	83.1	**Staten Island, NY** (borough) Richmond County	84.0
Indiana	89.7	Fort Bend County, TX	83.3	**North Miami, FL** (city) Miami-Dade County	84.2
Massachusetts	91.3	Marion County, IN	83.9	**Union City, NJ** (city) Hudson County	84.8
Nebraska	91.3	Richmond County, NY	84.0	**Oakland, CA** (city) Alameda County	85.0

Note: (1) Ranking tables cover all states and counties, and places with an overall population of at least 125,000, OR an overall population of at least 25,000 where the Hispanic/Latino population is at least 20% of the overall population. In states where less than five places meet either of these criteria, we have included places with at least 10,000 total population with the highest percentage of Hispanic/Latino population. These places are identified with an asterisk (*); Please refer to the User's Guide for a full explanation of data.

Population Age 3–17 Enrolled in Public School

(Universe: Population Age 3–17 Enrolled in School)

Central American: Nicaraguan

Top 10 States, Counties, and Places[1]

Sorted by Number in Descending Order — U.S. = 52,697

State	Number	County	Number	Place	Number
Florida	21,488	Miami-Dade County, FL	16,552	**Miami, FL** (city) Miami-Dade County	4,567
California	14,956	Los Angeles County, CA	5,733	**Los Angeles, CA** (city) Los Angeles County	2,452
Texas	2,724	Contra Costa County, CA	1,274	**Hialeah, FL** (city) Miami-Dade County	1,733
New York	1,702	San Mateo County, CA	1,148	**New York, NY** (city)	1,281
Virginia	1,472	Alameda County, CA	1,109	**Fountainebleau, FL** (cdp) Miami-Dade County	926
New Jersey	1,340	Broward County, FL	954	**San Francisco, CA** (city) San Francisco County	758
Maryland	770	Harris County, TX	881	**Tamiami, FL** (cdp) Miami-Dade County	637
Nevada	732	San Bernardino County, CA	805	**Houston, TX** (city) Harris County	602
North Carolina	608	San Francisco County, CA	758	**Kendale Lakes, FL** (cdp) Miami-Dade County	601
Wisconsin	517	Riverside County, CA	733	**Daly City, CA** (city) San Mateo County	600

Sorted by Number in Ascending Order — U.S. = 52,697

State	Number	County	Number	Place	Number
Oregon	115	King County, WA	55	**Metairie, LA** (cdp) Jefferson Parish	22
District of Columbia	118	Duval County, FL	151	**Pembroke Pines, FL** (city) Broward County	70
Washington	141	Camden County, NJ	182	**South Gate, CA** (city) Los Angeles County	99
Indiana	163	San Joaquin County, CA	186	**Chicago, IL** (city) Cook County	102
Tennessee	183	Fairfax County, VA	197	**Fontana, CA** (city) San Bernardino County	105
Ohio	187	Gwinnett County, GA	199	**University Park, FL** (cdp) Miami-Dade County	113
Colorado	200	Hudson County, NJ	200	**Richmond, CA** (city) Contra Costa County	137
Connecticut	203	Lee County, FL	208	**Las Vegas, NV** (city) Clark County	140
South Carolina	206	Stanislaus County, CA	219	**Kendall West, FL** (cdp) Miami-Dade County	145
Michigan	210	Mecklenburg County, NC	231	**San Diego, CA** (city) San Diego County	145

Sorted by Percent in Descending Order — U.S. = 89.2%

State	Percent	County	Percent	Place	Percent
Arizona	100.0	Collier County, FL	100.0	**Brooklyn, NY** (borough) Kings County	100.0
District of Columbia	100.0	Gwinnett County, GA	100.0	**Charlotte, NC** (city) Mecklenburg County	100.0
New Jersey	96.1	Hudson County, NJ	100.0	**Fontana, CA** (city) San Bernardino County	100.0
Minnesota	94.6	Kings County, NY	100.0	**Hayward, CA** (city) Alameda County	100.0
Nevada	94.3	Maricopa County, AZ	100.0	**Oakland, CA** (city) Alameda County	100.0
Missouri	93.5	Mecklenburg County, NC	100.0	**Pembroke Pines, FL** (city) Broward County	100.0
Florida	93.0	Orange County, FL	100.0	**San Diego, CA** (city) San Diego County	100.0
Massachusetts	93.0	San Diego County, CA	100.0	**South Miami Heights, FL** (cdp) Miami-Dade County	100.0
Michigan	91.7	Stanislaus County, CA	100.0	**West Little River, FL** (cdp) Miami-Dade County	100.0
Virginia	91.7	Hillsborough County, FL	97.8	**Miramar, FL** (city) Broward County	97.7

Sorted by Percent in Ascending Order — U.S. = 89.2%

State	Percent	County	Percent	Place	Percent
Washington	52.0	King County, WA	34.4	**Metairie, LA** (cdp) Jefferson Parish	12.7
Ohio	53.9	Jefferson Parish, LA	54.3	**The Hammocks, FL** (cdp) Miami-Dade County	62.5
Louisiana	55.6	Prince George's County, MD	76.6	**Bronx, NY** (borough) Bronx County	77.7
Colorado	70.2	Bronx County, NY	77.7	**Richmond, CA** (city) Contra Costa County	77.8
Indiana	74.4	Sonoma County, CA	77.7	**Chicago, IL** (city) Cook County	79.1
Pennsylvania	76.5	San Mateo County, CA	80.7	**Hollywood, FL** (city) Broward County	81.4
Illinois	76.6	Montgomery County, MD	81.1	**South San Francisco, CA** (city) San Mateo County	81.6
Oregon	77.2	Orange County, CA	82.8	**University Park, FL** (cdp) Miami-Dade County	81.9
Maryland	78.4	San Bernardino County, CA	83.0	**Las Vegas, NV** (city) Clark County	83.3
North Carolina	82.8	Riverside County, CA	84.6	**Daly City, CA** (city) San Mateo County	85.7

Note: (1) Ranking tables cover all states and counties, and places with an overall population of at least 125,000, OR an overall population of at least 25,000 where the Hispanic/Latino population is at least 20% of the overall population. In states where less than five places meet either of these criteria, we have included places with at least 10,000 total population with the highest percentage of Hispanic/Latino population. These places are identified with an asterisk (*); Please refer to the User's Guide for a full explanation of data.

Population Age 3–17 Enrolled in Public School

(Universe: Population Age 3–17 Enrolled in School)

Central American: Panamanian

Top 10 States, Counties, and Places[1]

Sorted by Number in Descending Order — U.S. = 26,230

State	Number	County	Number	Place	Number
New York	4,466	Kings County, NY	2,204	**New York, NY** (city)	3,406
Florida	3,981	Miami-Dade County, FL	927	**Brooklyn, NY** (borough) Kings County	2,204
California	2,525	San Bernardino County, CA	560	**Bronx, NY** (borough) Bronx County	515
Texas	2,384	Hillsborough County, FL	555	**San Diego, CA** (city) San Diego County	354
Georgia	1,349	San Diego County, CA	534	**Queens, NY** (borough) Queens County	334
Virginia	1,156	Cumberland County, NC	530	**Hempstead (town), NY** (town) Nassau County	257
North Carolina	1,090	Los Angeles County, CA	520	**Manhattan, NY** (borough) New York County	251
New Jersey	954	Bronx County, NY	515	**Killeen, TX** (city) Bell County	221
Pennsylvania	747	Orange County, FL	512	**Fayetteville, NC** (city) Cumberland County	215
Washington	664	Bexar County, TX	382	**Jacksonville, FL** (city) Duval County	191

Sorted by Number in Ascending Order — U.S. = 26,230

State	Number	County	Number	Place	Number
Louisiana	82	Orange County, CA	59	**Houston, TX** (city) Harris County	32
Oklahoma	91	Brevard County, FL	60	**Los Angeles, CA** (city) Los Angeles County	77
Mississippi	92	Prince George's County, MD	68	**Miami, FL** (city) Miami-Dade County	127
Kentucky	98	Montgomery County, MD	73	**San Antonio, TX** (city) Bexar County	151
Indiana	112	Hudson County, NJ	83	**Jacksonville, FL** (city) Duval County	191
Minnesota	137	Essex County, NJ	90	**Fayetteville, NC** (city) Cumberland County	215
Wisconsin	152	Fairfax County, VA	95	**Killeen, TX** (city) Bell County	221
Alabama	224	Riverside County, CA	98	**Manhattan, NY** (borough) New York County	251
Nevada	240	Cook County, IL	100	**Hempstead (town), NY** (town) Nassau County	257
Connecticut	242	Dallas County, TX	130	**Queens, NY** (borough) Queens County	334

Sorted by Percent in Descending Order — U.S. = 87.1%

State	Percent	County	Percent	Place	Percent
Arizona	100.0	Duval County, FL	100.0	**Houston, TX** (city) Harris County	100.0
Minnesota	100.0	Maricopa County, AZ	100.0	**Jacksonville, FL** (city) Duval County	100.0
Mississippi	100.0	Montgomery County, MD	100.0	**Manhattan, NY** (borough) New York County	100.0
New Mexico	96.8	New York County, NY	100.0	**Miami, FL** (city) Miami-Dade County	100.0
Michigan	96.3	Pierce County, WA	100.0	**San Diego, CA** (city) San Diego County	98.3
South Carolina	95.1	Sacramento County, CA	100.0	**Brooklyn, NY** (borough) Kings County	93.0
Connecticut	93.1	Orange County, FL	97.3	**New York, NY** (city)	93.0
Washington	93.1	Harris County, TX	95.8	**Bronx, NY** (borough) Bronx County	92.5
Pennsylvania	92.5	Riverside County, CA	93.3	**Killeen, TX** (city) Bell County	90.6
North Carolina	91.8	Kings County, NY	93.0	**Queens, NY** (borough) Queens County	87.2

Sorted by Percent in Ascending Order — U.S. = 87.1%

State	Percent	County	Percent	Place	Percent
Kentucky	57.6	Hudson County, NJ	63.8	**Los Angeles, CA** (city) Los Angeles County	71.3
Oklahoma	64.1	Brevard County, FL	65.2	**Hempstead (town), NY** (town) Nassau County	74.9
Louisiana	66.7	Orange County, CA	68.6	**San Antonio, TX** (city) Bexar County	81.2
Maryland	67.3	Cook County, IL	69.9	**Fayetteville, NC** (city) Cumberland County	85.7
Illinois	71.2	Los Angeles County, CA	72.5	**Queens, NY** (borough) Queens County	87.2
Tennessee	71.2	Nassau County, NY	74.9	**Killeen, TX** (city) Bell County	90.6
Wisconsin	73.1	Palm Beach County, FL	80.1	**Bronx, NY** (borough) Bronx County	92.5
Ohio	75.0	Prince George's County, MD	82.9	**Brooklyn, NY** (borough) Kings County	93.0
Alabama	77.2	Dallas County, TX	83.3	**New York, NY** (city)	93.0
Colorado	78.2	Bexar County, TX	85.7	**San Diego, CA** (city) San Diego County	98.3

Note: (1) Ranking tables cover all states and counties, and places with an overall population of at least 125,000, OR an overall population of at least 25,000 where the Hispanic/Latino population is at least 20% of the overall population. In states where less than five places meet either of these criteria, we have included places with at least 10,000 total population with the highest percentage of Hispanic/Latino population. These places are identified with an asterisk (*); Please refer to the User's Guide for a full explanation of data.

Population Age 3–17 Enrolled in Public School

(Universe: Population Age 3–17 Enrolled in School)

Central American: Salvadoran

Top 10 States, Counties, and Places[1]

Sorted by Number in Descending Order — U.S. = 312,416

State	Number	County	Number	Place	Number
California	109,836	Los Angeles County, CA	70,392	**Los Angeles, CA** (city) Los Angeles County	44,067
Texas	47,593	Harris County, TX	25,298	**Houston, TX** (city) Harris County	15,767
New York	26,608	Montgomery County, MD	10,918	**New York, NY** (city)	6,450
Maryland	23,815	Dallas County, TX	10,144	**Hempstead (town), NY** (town) Nassau County	5,655
Virginia	21,099	Prince George's County, MD	9,171	**Islip, NY** (town) Suffolk County	5,188
New Jersey	10,056	Suffolk County, NY	8,943	**Queens, NY** (borough) Queens County	3,483
North Carolina	8,436	Nassau County, NY	8,646	**Irving, TX** (city) Dallas County	3,238
Florida	8,435	Fairfax County, VA	6,700	**Dallas, TX** (city) Dallas County	3,181
Georgia	6,741	San Bernardino County, CA	5,418	**Palmdale, CA** (city) Los Angeles County	2,878
Massachusetts	6,609	Clark County, NV	5,242	**Brentwood, NY** (cdp) Suffolk County	2,547

Sorted by Number in Ascending Order — U.S. = 312,416

State	Number	County	Number	Place	Number
Idaho	56	Jefferson Parish, LA	57	**Bridgeport, CT** (city/town) Fairfield County	42
Alaska	151	Monmouth County, NJ	89	**Fullerton, CA** (city) Orange County	62
Hawaii	188	Santa Cruz County, CA	91	**San Bruno, CA** (city) San Mateo County	90
New Mexico	240	Williamson County, TX	100	**Chino, CA** (city) San Bernardino County	93
Wisconsin	280	El Paso County, TX	106	**Jersey City, NJ** (city) Hudson County	93
Alabama	306	Cuyahoga County, OH	143	**Corona, CA** (city) Riverside County	99
Michigan	411	Fulton County, GA	143	**Spring Valley, NV** (cdp) Clark County	100
Louisiana	476	Hartford County, CT	145	**Whittier, CA** (city) Los Angeles County	118
Oklahoma	560	Duval County, FL	155	**Portland, OR** (city) Multnomah County	129
Rhode Island	697	Sedgwick County, KS	165	**Lake Worth, FL** (city) Palm Beach County	140

Sorted by Percent in Descending Order — U.S. = 95.3%

State	Percent	County	Percent	Place	Percent
Idaho	100.0	Alamance County, NC	100.0	**Anaheim, CA** (city) Orange County	100.0
Iowa	100.0	Atlantic County, NJ	100.0	**Bakersfield, CA** (city) Kern County	100.0
Kentucky	100.0	Benton County, AR	100.0	**Bell Gardens, CA** (city) Los Angeles County	100.0
South Carolina	100.0	Cache County, UT	100.0	**Bellflower, CA** (city) Los Angeles County	100.0
Tennessee	100.0	Cobb County, GA	100.0	**Bridgeport, CT** (city/town) Fairfield County	100.0
Minnesota	99.2	Crawford County, AR	100.0	**Carrollton, TX** (city) Denton County	100.0
Kansas	99.1	Dakota County, MN	100.0	**Carson, CA** (city) Los Angeles County	100.0
Arkansas	98.7	Davidson County, TN	100.0	**Chillum, MD** (cdp) Prince George's County	100.0
Nevada	98.3	DeKalb County, GA	100.0	**Corona, CA** (city) Riverside County	100.0
North Carolina	98.2	Douglas County, NE	100.0	**Costa Mesa, CA** (city) Orange County	100.0

Sorted by Percent in Ascending Order — U.S. = 95.3%

State	Percent	County	Percent	Place	Percent
Alabama	61.8	Lake County, IL	73.5	**Fullerton, CA** (city) Orange County	49.2
Michigan	77.5	Hartford County, CT	74.4	**Paterson, NJ** (city) Passaic County	65.8
Louisiana	79.6	Passaic County, NJ	78.9	**Alhambra, CA** (city) Los Angeles County	68.4
Hawaii	82.1	Stafford County, VA	79.7	**Concord, CA** (city) Contra Costa County	73.5
Alaska	83.0	San Mateo County, CA	82.8	**San Diego, CA** (city) San Diego County	73.6
Missouri	84.6	Utah County, UT	83.9	**Baltimore, MD** (independent city)	75.0
Wisconsin	85.6	Camden County, NJ	84.6	**Richmond, VA** (independent city)	75.8
Connecticut	87.2	Kings County, NY	84.9	**Springfield, VA** (cdp) Fairfax County	76.5
Illinois	89.0	Sonoma County, CA	84.9	**San Mateo, CA** (city) San Mateo County	78.0
Utah	91.6	New York County, NY	85.5	**Whittier, CA** (city) Los Angeles County	79.7

Note: (1) Ranking tables cover all states and counties, and places with an overall population of at least 125,000, OR an overall population of at least 25,000 where the Hispanic/Latino population is at least 20% of the overall population. In states where less than five places meet either of these criteria, we have included places with at least 10,000 total population with the highest percentage of Hispanic/Latino population. These places are identified with an asterisk (*); Please refer to the User's Guide for a full explanation of data.

Population Age 3–17 Enrolled in Public School

(Universe: Population Age 3–17 Enrolled in School)

Cuban

Top 10 States, Counties, and Places[1]

Sorted by Number in Descending Order — U.S. = 219,287

State	Number	County	Number	Place	Number
Florida	139,006	Miami-Dade County, FL	86,664	**Hialeah, FL** (city) Miami-Dade County	17,734
New Jersey	11,440	Broward County, FL	12,342	**Miami, FL** (city) Miami-Dade County	11,256
California	10,858	Hillsborough County, FL	9,704	**Tamiami, FL** (cdp) Miami-Dade County	4,225
New York	7,604	Palm Beach County, FL	5,070	**New York, NY** (city)	3,386
Texas	6,197	Los Angeles County, CA	4,473	**Kendale Lakes, FL** (cdp) Miami-Dade County	3,098
Georgia	4,236	Lee County, FL	3,438	**Tampa, FL** (city) Hillsborough County	3,084
Illinois	3,619	Clark County, NV	2,898	**Pembroke Pines, FL** (city) Broward County	2,889
Pennsylvania	3,370	Hudson County, NJ	2,706	**Fountainebleau, FL** (cdp) Miami-Dade County	2,471
Nevada	3,266	Orange County, FL	2,672	**Miramar, FL** (city) Broward County	2,309
North Carolina	2,790	Collier County, FL	2,642	**Kendall, FL** (cdp) Miami-Dade County	2,274

Sorted by Number in Ascending Order — U.S. = 219,287

State	Number	County	Number	Place	Number
District of Columbia	116	Orleans Parish, LA	0	**Metairie, LA** (cdp) Jefferson Parish	0
Arkansas	119	Forsyth County, NC	51	**New Orleans, LA** (city) Orleans Parish	0
Maine	127	El Paso County, TX	57	**Bell, CA** (city) Los Angeles County	38
Delaware	167	Prince George's County, MD	70	**Atlanta, GA** (city) Fulton County	39
West Virginia	186	Saint Johns County, FL	71	**Newark, NJ** (city) Essex County	43
New Hampshire	190	East Baton Rouge Parish, LA	87	**Glendale, CA** (city) Los Angeles County	58
Oklahoma	208	Hampden County, MA	88	**Alafaya, FL** (cdp) Orange County	63
Hawaii	237	San Francisco County, CA	91	**Carrollwood, FL** (cdp) Hillsborough County	84
Iowa	246	New Castle County, DE	103	**Kenner, LA** (city) Jefferson Parish	88
Nebraska	283	Sussex County, NJ	106	**San Francisco, CA** (city) San Francisco County	91

Sorted by Percent in Descending Order — U.S. = 81.2%

State	Percent	County	Percent	Place	Percent
Arkansas	100.0	Clay County, FL	100.0	**Atlanta, GA** (city) Fulton County	100.0
Utah	97.1	Clay County, MO	100.0	**Bell, CA** (city) Los Angeles County	100.0
West Virginia	94.9	Henry County, GA	100.0	**Boston, MA** (city) Suffolk County	100.0
Missouri	94.0	Indian River County, FL	100.0	**Columbus, OH** (city) Franklin County	100.0
Kentucky	93.6	Kern County, CA	100.0	**Greenacres, FL** (city) Palm Beach County	100.0
Tennessee	92.3	Lancaster County, PA	100.0	**Kearny, NJ** (town) Hudson County	100.0
Nevada	90.6	Lehigh County, PA	100.0	**Newark, NJ** (city) Essex County	100.0
Arizona	90.4	Pierce County, WA	100.0	**San Antonio, TX** (city) Bexar County	100.0
Nebraska	90.4	Suffolk County, MA	100.0	**Syracuse, NY** (city) Onondaga County	100.0
Pennsylvania	90.4	Franklin County, OH	98.8	**University, FL** (cdp) Hillsborough County	100.0

Sorted by Percent in Ascending Order — U.S. = 81.2%

State	Percent	County	Percent	Place	Percent
Delaware	46.9	Orleans Parish, LA	0.0	**Metairie, LA** (cdp) Jefferson Parish	0.0
District of Columbia	56.0	Saint Johns County, FL	35.5	**New Orleans, LA** (city) Orleans Parish	0.0
Louisiana	59.3	New Castle County, DE	36.1	**Glendale, CA** (city) Los Angeles County	27.4
Oklahoma	65.4	DeKalb County, GA	39.5	**Carrollwood, FL** (cdp) Hillsborough County	29.5
Maryland	66.3	Prince George's County, MD	40.2	**Coral Gables, FL** (city) Miami-Dade County	35.5
Maine	68.6	East Baton Rouge Parish, LA	40.5	**Kenner, LA** (city) Jefferson Parish	43.1
Indiana	71.3	Jefferson Parish, LA	41.8	**Royal Palm Beach, FL** (village) Palm Beach County	45.1
Rhode Island	72.7	Lake County, FL	49.0	**Baltimore, MD** (independent city)	51.2
Iowa	73.9	Queens County, NY	54.7	**Tallahassee, FL** (city) Leon County	51.3
New York	75.3	Essex County, NJ	57.1	**North Hempstead, NY** (town) Nassau County	54.3

Note: (1) Ranking tables cover all states and counties, and places with an overall population of at least 125,000, OR an overall population of at least 25,000 where the Hispanic/Latino population is at least 20% of the overall population. In states where less than five places meet either of these criteria, we have included places with at least 10,000 total population with the highest percentage of Hispanic/Latino population. These places are identified with an asterisk (*); Please refer to the User's Guide for a full explanation of data.

Population Age 3–17 Enrolled in Public School

(Universe: Population Age 3–17 Enrolled in School)

Dominican Republic

Top 10 States, Counties, and Places[1]

Sorted by Number in Descending Order — U.S. = 285,040

State	Number	County	Number	Place	Number
New York	136,948	Bronx County, NY	49,492	**New York, NY** (city)	114,782
New Jersey	39,691	New York County, NY	28,643	**Bronx, NY** (borough) Bronx County	49,492
Florida	30,110	Kings County, NY	18,633	**Manhattan, NY** (borough) New York County	28,643
Massachusetts	24,312	Queens County, NY	17,002	**Brooklyn, NY** (borough) Kings County	18,633
Pennsylvania	13,333	Essex County, MA	11,575	**Queens, NY** (borough) Queens County	17,002
Rhode Island	9,453	Passaic County, NJ	10,266	**Providence, RI** (city) Providence County	7,537
Connecticut	5,666	Providence County, RI	9,109	**Lawrence, MA** (city) Essex County	6,507
Georgia	3,710	Miami-Dade County, FL	8,437	**Paterson, NJ** (city) Passaic County	5,852
North Carolina	3,041	Hudson County, NJ	7,672	**Boston, MA** (city) Suffolk County	5,269
Maryland	2,840	Broward County, FL	5,841	**Hempstead (town), NY** (town) Nassau County	4,120

Sorted by Number in Ascending Order — U.S. = 285,040

State	Number	County	Number	Place	Number
Minnesota	69	Ulster County, NY	48	**West Little River, FL** (cdp) Miami-Dade County	65
Alabama	175	Pasco County, FL	148	**North Miami, FL** (city) Miami-Dade County	79
Delaware	235	Volusia County, FL	177	**Kendale Lakes, FL** (cdp) Miami-Dade County	84
Tennessee	285	Pinellas County, FL	178	**Richmond West, FL** (cdp) Miami-Dade County	87
South Carolina	296	San Diego County, CA	178	**Los Angeles, CA** (city) Los Angeles County	125
Utah	301	Sullivan County, NY	189	**Tamiami, FL** (cdp) Miami-Dade County	128
Colorado	318	Tarrant County, TX	215	**Oyster Bay, NY** (town) Nassau County	136
Missouri	324	New Castle County, DE	216	**Linden, NJ** (city) Union County	137
Washington	332	Marion County, FL	220	**Deltona, FL** (city) Volusia County	142
Wisconsin	348	Jefferson Parish, LA	222	**Fountainebleau, FL** (cdp) Miami-Dade County	152

Sorted by Percent in Descending Order — U.S. = 91.7%

State	Percent	County	Percent	Place	Percent
Alaska	98.5	Atlantic County, NJ	100.0	**Alafaya, FL** (cdp) Orange County	100.0
Texas	96.9	Bexar County, TX	100.0	**Anchorage, AK** (municipality)	100.0
Delaware	95.9	Lackawanna County, PA	100.0	**Atlantic City, NJ** (city) Atlantic County	100.0
Missouri	95.6	Marion County, FL	100.0	**Bayonne, NJ** (city) Hudson County	100.0
North Carolina	94.6	Mercer County, NJ	100.0	**Bethlehem, PA** (city) Northampton County	100.0
Pennsylvania	94.3	Monroe County, PA	100.0	**Buenaventura Lakes, FL** (cdp) Osceola County	100.0
Georgia	93.6	New London County, CT	100.0	**Cape Coral, FL** (city) Lee County	100.0
Connecticut	93.3	Oneida County, NY	100.0	**Central Falls*, RI** (city) Providence County	100.0
New Jersey	93.3	Plymouth County, MA	100.0	**Columbus, OH** (city) Franklin County	100.0
Rhode Island	93.3	Sullivan County, NY	100.0	**Country Club, FL** (cdp) Miami-Dade County	100.0

Sorted by Percent in Ascending Order — U.S. = 91.7%

State	Percent	County	Percent	Place	Percent
Tennessee	66.4	Pasco County, FL	61.7	**North Hempstead, NY** (town) Nassau County	62.7
Michigan	76.5	Erie County, NY	62.8	**Grand Rapids, MI** (city) Kent County	70.3
Minnesota	76.7	Ulster County, NY	68.6	**Plantation, FL** (city) Broward County	71.3
Nevada	79.1	Kent County, MI	73.4	**Richmond West, FL** (cdp) Miami-Dade County	77.0
Indiana	80.4	Clark County, NV	75.3	**West New York, NJ** (town) Hudson County	77.7
Louisiana	81.4	Fairfax County, VA	76.8	**Cranston*, RI** (city) Providence County	78.5
New Hampshire	82.3	Ocean County, NJ	77.6	**Pennsauken, NJ** (township) Camden County	79.3
Wisconsin	83.5	Duval County, FL	79.7	**Jacksonville, FL** (city) Duval County	79.7
South Carolina	84.6	Orange County, NY	80.0	**Garfield, NJ** (city) Bergen County	79.8
Virginia	86.3	San Diego County, CA	82.4	**Ramapo, NY** (town) Rockland County	80.0

Note: (1) Ranking tables cover all states and counties, and places with an overall population of at least 125,000, OR an overall population of at least 25,000 where the Hispanic/Latino population is at least 20% of the overall population. In states where less than five places meet either of these criteria, we have included places with at least 10,000 total population with the highest percentage of Hispanic/Latino population. These places are identified with an asterisk (*); Please refer to the User's Guide for a full explanation of data.

Population Age 3–17 Enrolled in Public School

(Universe: Population Age 3–17 Enrolled in School)

Mexican

Top 10 States, Counties, and Places[1]

Sorted by Number in Descending Order — U.S. = 7,641,087

State	Number	County	Number	Place	Number
California	2,846,741	Los Angeles County, CA	875,964	**Los Angeles, CA** (city) Los Angeles County	311,583
Texas	1,900,254	Harris County, TX	304,702	**Houston, TX** (city) Harris County	156,603
Arizona	413,039	Maricopa County, AZ	251,223	**San Antonio, TX** (city) Bexar County	149,205
Illinois	378,866	San Bernardino County, CA	227,806	**Phoenix, AZ** (city) Maricopa County	138,159
Colorado	182,908	Riverside County, CA	225,808	**Chicago, IL** (city) Cook County	126,765
Washington	149,771	Cook County, IL	220,232	**El Paso, TX** (city) El Paso County	109,328
Florida	134,304	Orange County, CA	210,682	**Dallas, TX** (city) Dallas County	106,752
Nevada	134,216	San Diego County, CA	207,013	**San Diego, CA** (city) San Diego County	77,245
New Mexico	122,200	Dallas County, TX	186,032	**New York, NY** (city)	64,969
Georgia	115,462	Bexar County, TX	181,087	**San Jose, CA** (city) Santa Clara County	60,399

Sorted by Number in Ascending Order — U.S. = 7,641,087

State	Number	County	Number	Place	Number
Vermont	554	Union County, PA	3	**Coral Gables, FL** (city) Miami-Dade County	45
Maine	1,092	Buffalo County, WI	7	**Fort Leonard Wood*, MO** (cdp) Pulaski County	82
District of Columbia	1,139	Telfair County, GA	12	**Grand Forks*, ND** (city) Grand Forks County	84
West Virginia	1,841	Evangeline Parish, LA	13	**Mobile, AL** (city) Mobile County	91
New Hampshire	1,901	Saint Mary Parish, LA	18	**Laurel*, MS** (city) Jones County	105
Rhode Island	2,157	Johnson County, NE	20	**Lancaster, PA** (city) Lancaster County	114
North Dakota	2,396	Sedgwick County, CO	31	**Bayonne, NJ** (city) Hudson County	124
South Dakota	3,719	Tompkins County, NY	36	**Biloxi*, MS** (city) Harrison County	152
Alaska	4,595	Yazoo County, MS	39	**Kenner, LA** (city) Jefferson Parish	170
Montana	4,917	Swift County, MN	40	**Kendall, FL** (cdp) Miami-Dade County	175

Sorted by Percent in Descending Order — U.S. = 94.9%

State	Percent	County	Percent	Place	Percent
South Dakota	97.5	Accomack County, VA	100.0	**Albertville*, AL** (city) Marshall County	100.0
Nevada	97.2	Adair County, OK	100.0	**Allentown, PA** (city) Lehigh County	100.0
North Carolina	97.0	Adams County, NE	100.0	**Altus*, OK** (city) Jackson County	100.0
Georgia	96.5	Adams County, WI	100.0	**Apopka, FL** (city) Orange County	100.0
South Carolina	96.5	Aiken County, SC	100.0	**Asheboro, NC** (city) Randolph County	100.0
Arkansas	96.0	Alexander County, NC	100.0	**Aspen Hill, MD** (cdp) Montgomery County	100.0
Arizona	95.8	Allen Parish, LA	100.0	**Bayonne, NJ** (city) Hudson County	100.0
Oklahoma	95.8	Anderson County, TN	100.0	**Berea*, SC** (cdp) Greenville County	100.0
Texas	95.8	Andrews County, TX	100.0	**Biloxi*, MS** (city) Harrison County	100.0
Washington	95.8	Antrim County, MI	100.0	**Bluffton*, SC** (town) Beaufort County	100.0

Sorted by Percent in Ascending Order — U.S. = 94.9%

State	Percent	County	Percent	Place	Percent
District of Columbia	83.1	Union County, PA	12.0	**Coral Gables, FL** (city) Miami-Dade County	27.6
Hawaii	85.1	Saint Mary Parish, LA	21.4	**Mobile, AL** (city) Mobile County	51.1
Ohio	87.5	Johnson County, NE	55.6	**Cleveland, OH** (city) Cuyahoga County	60.2
Maryland	88.6	Midland County, MI	60.3	**Pittsburgh, PA** (city) Allegheny County	62.7
Montana	88.9	Douglas County, KS	61.3	**Grand Forks*, ND** (city) Grand Forks County	66.7
Alaska	89.2	Tompkins County, NY	62.1	**Kenner, LA** (city) Jefferson Parish	66.9
Louisiana	89.4	Buffalo County, WI	63.6	**Weston, FL** (city) Broward County	68.8
Massachusetts	89.7	Menominee County, MI	64.6	**Metairie, LA** (cdp) Jefferson Parish	71.1
Pennsylvania	89.8	Webster County, IA	65.6	**Ramapo, NY** (town) Rockland County	71.2
West Virginia	89.8	Lee County, IA	65.9	**Great Falls*, MT** (city) Cascade County	71.7

Note: (1) Ranking tables cover all states and counties, and places with an overall population of at least 125,000, OR an overall population of at least 25,000 where the Hispanic/Latino population is at least 20% of the overall population. In states where less than five places meet either of these criteria, we have included places with at least 10,000 total population with the highest percentage of Hispanic/Latino population. These places are identified with an asterisk (*); Please refer to the User's Guide for a full explanation of data.

Population Age 3–17 Enrolled in Public School

(Universe: Population Age 3–17 Enrolled in School)

Puerto Rican

Top 10 States, Counties, and Places[1]

Sorted by Number in Descending Order — U.S. = 993,926

State	Number	County	Number	Place	Number
New York	227,352	Bronx County, NY	62,973	**New York, NY** (city)	144,445
Florida	162,696	Kings County, NY	34,910	**Bronx, NY** (borough) Bronx County	62,973
New Jersey	97,767	Orange County, FL	29,808	**Brooklyn, NY** (borough) Kings County	34,910
Pennsylvania	85,190	Philadelphia County, PA	27,141	**Philadelphia, PA** (city) Philadelphia County	27,141
Massachusetts	69,229	Hartford County, CT	25,744	**Queens, NY** (borough) Queens County	20,208
Connecticut	65,958	Cook County, IL	23,849	**Chicago, IL** (city) Cook County	18,100
Illinois	35,277	Hampden County, MA	22,321	**Manhattan, NY** (borough) New York County	17,989
California	32,394	New Haven County, CT	20,423	**Springfield, MA** (city) Hampden County	13,616
Texas	25,167	Queens County, NY	20,208	**Hartford, CT** (city/town) Hartford County	11,069
Ohio	20,453	Hillsborough County, FL	18,834	**Newark, NJ** (city) Essex County	9,535

Sorted by Number in Ascending Order — U.S. = 993,926

State	Number	County	Number	Place	Number
Wyoming	109	Madera County, CA	46	**Rio Rancho, NM** (city) Sandoval County	106
North Dakota	268	Sumter County, FL	83	**Bergenfield, NJ** (borough) Bergen County	110
District of Columbia	293	Warren County, OH	89	**Freeport, NY** (village) Nassau County	112
South Dakota	333	Perry County, PA	93	**Coral Gables, FL** (city) Miami-Dade County	117
Montana	367	DeKalb County, IL	94	**Montgomery, AL** (city) Montgomery County	124
Vermont	557	Saint Mary's County, MD	98	**Tallahassee, FL** (city) Leon County	130
West Virginia	623	Monroe County, FL	99	**Irving, TX** (city) Dallas County	135
Idaho	631	Lowndes County, GA	100	**Plano, TX** (city) Collin County	135
Nebraska	716	Washington County, NY	106	**Huntsville, AL** (city) Madison County	136
Iowa	1,061	Wyoming County, NY	106	**Atlanta, GA** (city) Fulton County	137

Sorted by Percent in Descending Order — U.S. = 90.0%

State	Percent	County	Percent	Place	Percent
Montana	100.0	Adams County, CO	100.0	**Akron, OH** (city) Summit County	100.0
Wyoming	100.0	Butte County, CA	100.0	**Alexandria, VA** (independent city)	100.0
Alaska	99.2	Cecil County, MD	100.0	**Central Falls*, RI** (city) Providence County	100.0
Idaho	99.1	Charleston County, SC	100.0	**Columbia, SC** (city) Richland County	100.0
Iowa	96.5	Christian County, KY	100.0	**Elmont, NY** (cdp) Nassau County	100.0
Massachusetts	94.8	Cochise County, AZ	100.0	**Fairfield, CA** (city) Solano County	100.0
Connecticut	94.5	Columbia County, FL	100.0	**Fitchburg, MA** (city) Worcester County	100.0
Nevada	94.3	Coryell County, TX	100.0	**Fort Hood, TX** (cdp) Bell County	100.0
Arizona	93.7	Craven County, NC	100.0	**Fontainebleau, FL** (cdp) Miami-Dade County	100.0
Vermont	93.5	Dale County, AL	100.0	**Fresno, CA** (city) Fresno County	100.0

Sorted by Percent in Ascending Order — U.S. = 90.0%

State	Percent	County	Percent	Place	Percent
Louisiana	72.2	Adams County, PA	43.9	**Coral Gables, FL** (city) Miami-Dade County	42.5
North Dakota	72.2	Harrison County, MS	46.7	**Seattle, WA** (city) King County	55.2
Maine	76.2	Marion County, OR	53.0	**Kendale Lakes, FL** (cdp) Miami-Dade County	56.9
District of Columbia	78.3	Saint Mary's County, MD	54.4	**Tamiami, FL** (cdp) Miami-Dade County	57.6
New Mexico	79.5	Lowndes County, GA	56.5	**Huntsville, AL** (city) Madison County	60.7
Nebraska	81.4	Carroll County, MD	57.1	**Dania Beach, FL** (city) Broward County	61.3
West Virginia	81.8	Butler County, OH	60.8	**Plano, TX** (city) Collin County	62.5
Tennessee	82.5	Jefferson Parish, LA	62.1	**Montgomery, AL** (city) Montgomery County	62.6
Oregon	82.9	Montgomery County, AL	62.6	**Fort Lauderdale, FL** (city) Broward County	64.7
Mississippi	83.4	Newport County, RI	62.8	**Lancaster, CA** (city) Los Angeles County	65.5

Note: (1) Ranking tables cover all states and counties, and places with an overall population of at least 125,000, OR an overall population of at least 25,000 where the Hispanic/Latino population is at least 20% of the overall population. In states where less than five places meet either of these criteria, we have included places with at least 10,000 total population with the highest percentage of Hispanic/Latino population. These places are identified with an asterisk (*); Please refer to the User's Guide for a full explanation of data.

Population Age 3–17 Enrolled in Public School

(Universe: Population Age 3–17 Enrolled in School)

South American

Top 10 States, Counties, and Places[1]

Sorted by Number in Descending Order — U.S. = 434,809

State	Number	County	Number	Place	Number
Florida	101,499	Miami-Dade County, FL	35,506	**New York, NY** (city)	47,573
New York	76,902	Queens County, NY	29,543	**Queens, NY** (borough) Queens County	29,543
New Jersey	54,000	Broward County, FL	22,247	**Brooklyn, NY** (borough) Kings County	8,420
California	42,840	Los Angeles County, CA	16,936	**Los Angeles, CA** (city) Los Angeles County	6,117
Texas	21,771	Hudson County, NJ	10,404	**Elizabeth, NJ** (city) Union County	5,028
Virginia	17,365	Westchester County, NY	8,524	**Bronx, NY** (borough) Bronx County	4,955
Illinois	12,044	Kings County, NY	8,420	**Chicago, IL** (city) Cook County	4,767
Connecticut	10,960	Orange County, FL	8,121	**Weston, FL** (city) Broward County	3,891
Maryland	9,628	Palm Beach County, FL	7,826	**Hempstead (town), NY** (town) Nassau County	3,644
Georgia	9,603	Suffolk County, NY	7,700	**Newark, NJ** (city) Essex County	3,543

Sorted by Number in Ascending Order — U.S. = 434,809

State	Number	County	Number	Place	Number
Wyoming	103	East Baton Rouge Parish, LA	48	**Tallahassee, FL** (city) Leon County	43
North Dakota	127	Tompkins County, NY	63	**Pittsburgh, PA** (city) Allegheny County	47
Montana	152	Kent County, MI	71	**Riverview, FL** (cdp) Hillsborough County	48
Vermont	157	Douglas County, NE	72	**Scottsdale, AZ** (city) Maricopa County	69
West Virginia	296	Leon County, FL	76	**Fullerton, CA** (city) Orange County	73
Nebraska	334	Placer County, CA	76	**Lake Forest, CA** (city) Orange County	75
Mississippi	363	Cameron County, TX	77	**Springfield, MA** (city) Hampden County	77
Hawaii	409	Orange County, NC	86	**North Las Vegas, NV** (city) Clark County	79
Maine	431	Tolland County, CT	86	**Vineland, NJ** (city) Cumberland County	80
District of Columbia	486	Santa Cruz County, CA	88	**Overland Park, KS** (city) Johnson County	92

Sorted by Percent in Descending Order — U.S. = 85.0%

State	Percent	County	Percent	Place	Percent
West Virginia	100.0	Adams County, CO	100.0	**Arlington, TX** (city) Tarrant County	100.0
Wyoming	100.0	Butler County, OH	100.0	**Aspen Hill, MD** (cdp) Montgomery County	100.0
Alaska	93.6	Cache County, UT	100.0	**Bay Shore, NY** (cdp) Suffolk County	100.0
Utah	92.7	Cherokee County, GA	100.0	**Brandon, FL** (cdp) Hillsborough County	100.0
Montana	92.1	Clark County, WA	100.0	**Chesapeake, VA** (independent city)	100.0
Iowa	90.2	Clarke County, GA	100.0	**Daly City, CA** (city) San Mateo County	100.0
New Mexico	90.1	Cumberland County, NJ	100.0	**Deltona, FL** (city) Volusia County	100.0
Oklahoma	90.0	Gaston County, NC	100.0	**Fremont, CA** (city) Alameda County	100.0
New Jersey	89.8	Hampshire County, MA	100.0	**Garfield, NJ** (city) Bergen County	100.0
Maine	89.4	Macomb County, MI	100.0	**Glendale, AZ** (city) Maricopa County	100.0

Sorted by Percent in Ascending Order — U.S. = 85.0%

State	Percent	County	Percent	Place	Percent
Louisiana	64.2	Leon County, FL	25.8	**Tallahassee, FL** (city) Leon County	23.1
Hawaii	67.9	East Baton Rouge Parish, LA	31.0	**Coral Gables, FL** (city) Miami-Dade County	37.1
Missouri	70.5	Kent County, MI	54.2	**Pasadena, CA** (city) Los Angeles County	39.6
Kansas	70.7	Hamilton County, TN	54.6	**Overland Park, KS** (city) Johnson County	49.5
Ohio	71.2	Erie County, NY	54.9	**Rahway, NJ** (city) Union County	55.5
Kentucky	72.6	Allegheny County, PA	55.9	**New Orleans, LA** (city) Orleans Parish	57.1
Arkansas	73.2	Orange County, NC	56.6	**Plantation, FL** (city) Broward County	60.0
Wisconsin	74.0	Orleans Parish, LA	57.1	**Atlanta, GA** (city) Fulton County	60.1
District of Columbia	75.7	San Luis Obispo County, CA	57.1	**Springfield, MA** (city) Hampden County	60.6
Tennessee	75.9	Jefferson County, KY	58.0	**Metairie, LA** (cdp) Jefferson Parish	61.0

Note: (1) Ranking tables cover all states and counties, and places with an overall population of at least 125,000, OR an overall population of at least 25,000 where the Hispanic/Latino population is at least 20% of the overall population. In states where less than five places meet either of these criteria, we have included places with at least 10,000 total population with the highest percentage of Hispanic/Latino population. These places are identified with an asterisk (*); Please refer to the User's Guide for a full explanation of data.

Population Age 3–17 Enrolled in Public School

(Universe: Population Age 3–17 Enrolled in School)

South American: Argentinean

Top 10 States, Counties, and Places[1]

Sorted by Number in Descending Order — U.S. = 28,593

State	Number	County	Number	Place	Number
Florida	6,712	Miami-Dade County, FL	3,224	**New York, NY** (city)	1,312
California	5,239	Los Angeles County, CA	2,292	**Los Angeles, CA** (city) Los Angeles County	960
New York	2,515	Broward County, FL	1,377	**Miami, FL** (city) Miami-Dade County	822
New Jersey	1,785	Orange County, CA	603	**Queens, NY** (borough) Queens County	595
Texas	1,770	Queens County, NY	595	**Miami Beach, FL** (city) Miami-Dade County	536
Utah	1,563	Palm Beach County, FL	565	**Brooklyn, NY** (borough) Kings County	383
Illinois	1,145	San Bernardino County, CA	527	**Doral, FL** (city) Miami-Dade County	238
Virginia	902	Fairfax County, VA	466	**Aventura, FL** (city) Miami-Dade County	236
Maryland	853	Salt Lake County, UT	460	**Coral Springs, FL** (city) Broward County	226
North Carolina	646	Clark County, NV	386	**Hollywood, FL** (city) Broward County	180

Sorted by Number in Ascending Order — U.S. = 28,593

State	Number	County	Number	Place	Number
District of Columbia	21	New Haven County, CT	48	**San Diego, CA** (city) San Diego County	38
Missouri	93	Oakland County, MI	61	**San Francisco, CA** (city) San Francisco County	67
Louisiana	94	San Francisco County, CA	67	**Bronx, NY** (borough) Bronx County	82
Ohio	107	Bronx County, NY	82	**San Jose, CA** (city) Santa Clara County	99
Minnesota	125	Bexar County, TX	106	**Hempstead (town), NY** (town) Nassau County	114
Oregon	161	San Diego County, CA	108	**Houston, TX** (city) Harris County	123
Tennessee	176	King County, WA	126	**Pembroke Pines, FL** (city) Broward County	131
Washington	178	Orange County, NY	132	**Hialeah, FL** (city) Miami-Dade County	140
Colorado	197	Travis County, TX	133	**Chicago, IL** (city) Cook County	174
Michigan	206	Riverside County, CA	140	**Hollywood, FL** (city) Broward County	180

Sorted by Percent in Descending Order — U.S. = 79.6%

State	Percent	County	Percent	Place	Percent
Missouri	100.0	Dallas County, TX	100.0	**Coral Springs, FL** (city) Broward County	100.0
Tennessee	100.0	Montgomery County, TX	100.0	**Hialeah, FL** (city) Miami-Dade County	100.0
Utah	95.8	Orange County, NY	100.0	**Miami Beach, FL** (city) Miami-Dade County	97.5
Nevada	92.6	Passaic County, NJ	100.0	**Miami, FL** (city) Miami-Dade County	93.1
North Carolina	92.6	Utah County, UT	97.0	**Queens, NY** (borough) Queens County	90.2
Indiana	89.9	Alameda County, CA	96.0	**Bronx, NY** (borough) Bronx County	85.4
Washington	88.6	Lee County, FL	94.7	**Hollywood, FL** (city) Broward County	82.9
Illinois	88.1	Ventura County, CA	94.4	**Doral, FL** (city) Miami-Dade County	82.6
South Carolina	87.5	Suffolk County, NY	94.2	**Los Angeles, CA** (city) Los Angeles County	81.4
Connecticut	86.2	Travis County, TX	93.0	**Hempstead (town), NY** (town) Nassau County	79.2

Sorted by Percent in Ascending Order — U.S. = 79.6%

State	Percent	County	Percent	Place	Percent
District of Columbia	23.9	New York County, NY	49.6	**Manhattan, NY** (borough) New York County	49.6
Georgia	59.4	Maricopa County, AZ	57.6	**San Diego, CA** (city) San Diego County	69.1
Arizona	62.2	San Diego County, CA	58.7	**Pembroke Pines, FL** (city) Broward County	69.3
Minnesota	63.5	New Haven County, CT	60.8	**Houston, TX** (city) Harris County	72.8
Massachusetts	64.7	Montgomery County, MD	61.8	**Brooklyn, NY** (borough) Kings County	73.1
Louisiana	67.6	Riverside County, CA	62.8	**Chicago, IL** (city) Cook County	74.0
Maryland	69.6	Hudson County, NJ	64.0	**New York, NY** (city)	76.0
Wisconsin	71.6	Santa Clara County, CA	65.2	**San Jose, CA** (city) Santa Clara County	77.3
Michigan	73.0	Hillsborough County, FL	67.6	**Aventura, FL** (city) Miami-Dade County	78.7
Oregon	74.5	Fairfax County, VA	69.8	**San Francisco, CA** (city) San Francisco County	78.8

Note: (1) Ranking tables cover all states and counties, and places with an overall population of at least 125,000, OR an overall population of at least 25,000 where the Hispanic/Latino population is at least 20% of the overall population. In states where less than five places meet either of these criteria, we have included places with at least 10,000 total population with the highest percentage of Hispanic/Latino population. These places are identified with an asterisk (*); Please refer to the User's Guide for a full explanation of data.

Population Age 3–17 Enrolled in Public School

(Universe: Population Age 3–17 Enrolled in School)

South American: Bolivian

Top 10 States, Counties, and Places[1]

Sorted by Number in Descending Order — U.S. = 16,501

State	Number	County	Number	Place	Number
Virginia	6,170	Fairfax County, VA	3,257	**Arlington, VA** (cdp) Arlington County	607
California	1,981	Prince William County, VA	1,150	**Annandale, VA** (cdp) Fairfax County	597
Florida	1,635	Montgomery County, MD	829	**Los Angeles, CA** (city) Los Angeles County	538
Maryland	1,056	Los Angeles County, CA	695	**New York, NY** (city)	437
New York	881	Arlington County, VA	607	**Queens, NY** (borough) Queens County	311
Texas	766	Providence County, RI	446	**Dale City, VA** (cdp) Prince William County	278
New Jersey	502	Broward County, FL	443	**Providence, RI** (city) Providence County	222
Rhode Island	446	Loudoun County, VA	412	**West Falls Church, VA** (cdp) Fairfax County	211
Illinois	379	Miami-Dade County, FL	393	**Springfield, VA** (cdp) Fairfax County	84
Massachusetts	318	Queens County, NY	311		

Sorted by Number in Ascending Order — U.S. = 16,501

State	Number	County	Number	Place	Number
Pennsylvania	73	San Diego County, CA	86	**Springfield, VA** (cdp) Fairfax County	84
North Carolina	75	Cook County, IL	110	**West Falls Church, VA** (cdp) Fairfax County	211
Massachusetts	318	Prince George's County, MD	126	**Providence, RI** (city) Providence County	222
Illinois	379	Palm Beach County, FL	127	**Dale City, VA** (cdp) Prince William County	278
Rhode Island	446	Santa Clara County, CA	237	**Queens, NY** (borough) Queens County	311
New Jersey	502	Harris County, TX	257	**New York, NY** (city)	437
Texas	766	Orange County, CA	281	**Los Angeles, CA** (city) Los Angeles County	538
New York	881	Queens County, NY	311	**Annandale, VA** (cdp) Fairfax County	597
Maryland	1,056	Miami-Dade County, FL	393	**Arlington, VA** (cdp) Arlington County	607
Florida	1,635	Loudoun County, VA	412		

Sorted by Percent in Descending Order — U.S. = 83.6%

State	Percent	County	Percent	Place	Percent
Rhode Island	97.0	Broward County, FL	100.0	**Providence, RI** (city) Providence County	100.0
New Jersey	96.9	Cook County, IL	100.0	**Dale City, VA** (cdp) Prince William County	96.5
Virginia	91.8	Harris County, TX	100.0	**Los Angeles, CA** (city) Los Angeles County	92.4
Texas	91.4	Palm Beach County, FL	100.0	**Annandale, VA** (cdp) Fairfax County	86.9
Florida	88.6	Prince William County, VA	97.6	**West Falls Church, VA** (cdp) Fairfax County	83.7
Maryland	88.1	Providence County, RI	97.0	**Arlington, VA** (cdp) Arlington County	83.4
California	81.2	Montgomery County, MD	93.8	**Springfield, VA** (cdp) Fairfax County	73.7
Illinois	76.0	Fairfax County, VA	92.8	**New York, NY** (city)	48.9
Pennsylvania	76.0	Santa Clara County, CA	88.8	**Queens, NY** (borough) Queens County	42.7
Massachusetts	71.8	Loudoun County, VA	88.0		

Sorted by Percent in Ascending Order — U.S. = 83.6%

State	Percent	County	Percent	Place	Percent
North Carolina	57.7	Queens County, NY	42.7	**Queens, NY** (borough) Queens County	42.7
New York	61.4	Prince George's County, MD	71.6	**New York, NY** (city)	48.9
Massachusetts	71.8	San Diego County, CA	76.1	**Springfield, VA** (cdp) Fairfax County	73.7
Illinois	76.0	Los Angeles County, CA	79.4	**Arlington, VA** (cdp) Arlington County	83.4
Pennsylvania	76.0	Miami-Dade County, FL	82.0	**West Falls Church, VA** (cdp) Fairfax County	83.7
California	81.2	Orange County, CA	82.2	**Annandale, VA** (cdp) Fairfax County	86.9
Maryland	88.1	Arlington County, VA	83.4	**Los Angeles, CA** (city) Los Angeles County	92.4
Florida	88.6	Loudoun County, VA	88.0	**Dale City, VA** (cdp) Prince William County	96.5
Texas	91.4	Santa Clara County, CA	88.8	**Providence, RI** (city) Providence County	100.0
Virginia	91.8	Fairfax County, VA	92.8		

Note: (1) Ranking tables cover all states and counties, and places with an overall population of at least 125,000, OR an overall population of at least 25,000 where the Hispanic/Latino population is at least 20% of the overall population. In states where less than five places meet either of these criteria, we have included places with at least 10,000 total population with the highest percentage of Hispanic/Latino population. These places are identified with an asterisk (*); Please refer to the User's Guide for a full explanation of data.

Population Age 3–17 Enrolled in Public School

(Universe: Population Age 3–17 Enrolled in School)

South American: Chilean

Top 10 States, Counties, and Places[1]

Sorted by Number in Descending Order — U.S. = 18,439

State	Number	County	Number	Place	Number
California	3,404	Miami-Dade County, FL	1,229	**New York, NY** (city)	651
Florida	2,664	Los Angeles County, CA	954	**Los Angeles, CA** (city) Los Angeles County	520
New York	2,161	Westchester County, NY	407	**Queens, NY** (borough) Queens County	244
New Jersey	1,066	Nassau County, NY	403	**Brooklyn, NY** (borough) Kings County	239
Maryland	835	Montgomery County, MD	394	**Kendall, FL** (cdp) Miami-Dade County	238
Georgia	822	Palm Beach County, FL	392	**Hempstead (town), NY** (town) Nassau County	180
Texas	699	Broward County, FL	354	**Miami, FL** (city) Miami-Dade County	114
Virginia	546	Utah County, UT	346	**Manhattan, NY** (borough) New York County	90
Illinois	536	Suffolk County, NY	300	**Chicago, IL** (city) Cook County	34
Massachusetts	515	San Bernardino County, CA	280		

Sorted by Number in Ascending Order — U.S. = 18,439

State	Number	County	Number	Place	Number
Tennessee	22	Maricopa County, AZ	75	**Chicago, IL** (city) Cook County	34
Ohio	122	New York County, NY	90	**Manhattan, NY** (borough) New York County	90
Oregon	147	Cook County, IL	96	**Miami, FL** (city) Miami-Dade County	114
Arizona	150	San Mateo County, CA	106	**Hempstead (town), NY** (town) Nassau County	180
Minnesota	165	Bergen County, NJ	127	**Kendall, FL** (cdp) Miami-Dade County	238
Missouri	198	Harris County, TX	127	**Brooklyn, NY** (borough) Kings County	239
Wisconsin	242	Clark County, NV	142	**Queens, NY** (borough) Queens County	244
Nevada	250	Salt Lake County, UT	147	**Los Angeles, CA** (city) Los Angeles County	520
Michigan	260	Santa Clara County, CA	168	**New York, NY** (city)	651
Colorado	269	Middlesex County, MA	206		

Sorted by Percent in Descending Order — U.S. = 82.0%

State	Percent	County	Percent	Place	Percent
Oregon	100.0	Salt Lake County, UT	100.0	**Los Angeles, CA** (city) Los Angeles County	95.1
Utah	94.6	San Mateo County, CA	100.0	**Kendall, FL** (cdp) Miami-Dade County	93.7
Wisconsin	92.4	Nassau County, NY	96.6	**Hempstead (town), NY** (town) Nassau County	92.8
Connecticut	91.9	Suffolk County, NY	94.6	**Brooklyn, NY** (borough) Kings County	90.5
Massachusetts	90.5	Riverside County, CA	94.0	**Miami, FL** (city) Miami-Dade County	82.6
Minnesota	89.7	Alameda County, CA	93.5	**New York, NY** (city)	71.9
Maryland	89.0	Santa Clara County, CA	92.8	**Manhattan, NY** (borough) New York County	67.2
Georgia	88.6	Utah County, UT	92.3	**Chicago, IL** (city) Cook County	61.8
New York	85.6	Montgomery County, MD	90.6	**Queens, NY** (borough) Queens County	59.4
Missouri	83.9	Kings County, NY	90.5		

Sorted by Percent in Ascending Order — U.S. = 82.0%

State	Percent	County	Percent	Place	Percent
Tennessee	20.8	San Diego County, CA	48.7	**Queens, NY** (borough) Queens County	59.4
Arizona	58.8	Bergen County, NJ	55.9	**Chicago, IL** (city) Cook County	61.8
Ohio	63.2	Queens County, NY	59.4	**Manhattan, NY** (borough) New York County	67.2
New Jersey	74.1	Maricopa County, AZ	60.0	**New York, NY** (city)	71.9
Texas	77.5	Harris County, TX	62.9	**Miami, FL** (city) Miami-Dade County	82.6
Virginia	78.1	New York County, NY	67.2	**Brooklyn, NY** (borough) Kings County	90.5
Washington	78.1	Cook County, IL	70.6	**Hempstead (town), NY** (town) Nassau County	92.8
North Carolina	78.7	San Bernardino County, CA	71.4	**Kendall, FL** (cdp) Miami-Dade County	93.7
California	81.0	Broward County, FL	72.2	**Los Angeles, CA** (city) Los Angeles County	95.1
Illinois	81.8	Hudson County, NJ	72.8		

RANKINGS & COMPARISONS

Note: (1) Ranking tables cover all states and counties, and places with an overall population of at least 125,000, OR an overall population of at least 25,000 where the Hispanic/Latino population is at least 20% of the overall population. In states where less than five places meet either of these criteria, we have included places with at least 10,000 total population with the highest percentage of Hispanic/Latino population. These places are identified with an asterisk (*); Please refer to the User's Guide for a full explanation of data.

Population Age 3–17 Enrolled in Public School

(Universe: Population Age 3–17 Enrolled in School)

South American: Colombian

Top 10 States, Counties, and Places[1]

Sorted by Number in Descending Order — U.S. = 144,999

State	Number	County	Number	Place	Number
Florida	47,135	Miami-Dade County, FL	15,148	**New York, NY** (city)	12,612
New York	21,434	Broward County, FL	9,755	**Queens, NY** (borough) Queens County	9,549
New Jersey	17,076	Queens County, NY	9,549	**Houston, TX** (city) Harris County	1,893
California	9,202	Orange County, FL	4,667	**Brooklyn, NY** (borough) Kings County	1,745
Texas	8,285	Harris County, TX	3,944	**Elizabeth, NJ** (city) Union County	1,706
Massachusetts	4,106	Los Angeles County, CA	3,644	**Weston, FL** (city) Broward County	1,505
Georgia	4,098	Palm Beach County, FL	3,601	**Pembroke Pines, FL** (city) Broward County	1,352
Illinois	3,865	Bergen County, NJ	3,339	**Hempstead (town), NY** (town) Nassau County	1,262
Connecticut	3,288	Hillsborough County, FL	2,999	**Boston, MA** (city) Suffolk County	1,149
Pennsylvania	2,785	Suffolk County, NY	2,658	**Hialeah, FL** (city) Miami-Dade County	1,145

Sorted by Number in Ascending Order — U.S. = 144,999

State	Number	County	Number	Place	Number
Alaska	116	Sacramento County, CA	11	**North Miami Beach, FL** (city) Miami-Dade County	7
Nebraska	121	Leon County, FL	31	**Tallahassee, FL** (city) Leon County	10
New Mexico	123	Hampden County, MA	45	**San Jose, CA** (city) Santa Clara County	30
Delaware	134	San Francisco County, CA	74	**Glendale, CA** (city) Los Angeles County	46
District of Columbia	145	DeKalb County, GA	83	**San Francisco, CA** (city) San Francisco County	74
Oklahoma	145	Franklin County, OH	110	**Coral Gables, FL** (city) Miami-Dade County	88
Arkansas	156	Dane County, WI	111	**Anaheim, CA** (city) Orange County	93
Kentucky	203	Luzerne County, PA	118	**Brandon, FL** (cdp) Hillsborough County	101
Iowa	213	Pima County, AZ	121	**Elmont, NY** (cdp) Nassau County	105
Kansas	287	Arlington County, VA	125	**Raleigh, NC** (city) Wake County	118

Sorted by Percent in Descending Order — U.S. = 85.4%

State	Percent	County	Percent	Place	Percent
Delaware	100.0	Burlington County, NJ	100.0	**Bergenfield, NJ** (borough) Bergen County	100.0
Oklahoma	96.7	Cherokee County, GA	100.0	**Brandon, FL** (cdp) Hillsborough County	100.0
South Carolina	93.6	Lehigh County, PA	100.0	**Burbank, CA** (city) Los Angeles County	100.0
New Hampshire	93.3	Northampton County, PA	100.0	**Deltona, FL** (city) Volusia County	100.0
Arizona	92.9	Sacramento County, CA	100.0	**Egypt Lake-Leto, FL** (cdp) Hillsborough County	100.0
New Jersey	91.1	Sarasota County, FL	100.0	**Garfield, NJ** (city) Bergen County	100.0
Nevada	88.6	Ulster County, NY	100.0	**Hackensack, NJ** (city) Bergen County	100.0
Utah	87.9	Volusia County, FL	100.0	**Hallandale Beach, FL** (city) Broward County	100.0
Washington	87.6	Middlesex County, NJ	98.3	**Hartford, CT** (city/town) Hartford County	100.0
Connecticut	87.5	Greenville County, SC	98.1	**Long Beach, CA** (city) Los Angeles County	100.0

Sorted by Percent in Ascending Order — U.S. = 85.4%

State	Percent	County	Percent	Place	Percent
Kentucky	55.9	Leon County, FL	18.7	**Tallahassee, FL** (city) Leon County	6.9
Alabama	64.0	Hampden County, MA	32.4	**Coral Gables, FL** (city) Miami-Dade County	28.8
Nebraska	64.0	New York County, NY	49.9	**North Miami Beach, FL** (city) Miami-Dade County	43.8
Ohio	64.0	Richmond County, NY	52.4	**West Palm Beach, FL** (city) Palm Beach County	46.4
Louisiana	65.1	DeKalb County, GA	60.1	**Manhattan, NY** (borough) New York County	49.9
Arkansas	67.2	Erie County, NY	60.4	**Staten Island, NY** (borough) Richmond County	52.4
Missouri	71.5	Bucks County, PA	61.7	**Anaheim, CA** (city) Orange County	55.7
Indiana	72.5	Philadelphia County, PA	63.6	**Downey, CA** (city) Los Angeles County	62.3
Michigan	74.0	San Francisco County, CA	63.8	**Las Vegas, NV** (city) Clark County	63.5
Pennsylvania	74.7	Fulton County, GA	67.9	**Philadelphia, PA** (city) Philadelphia County	63.6

Note: (1) Ranking tables cover all states and counties, and places with an overall population of at least 125,000, OR an overall population of at least 25,000 where the Hispanic/Latino population is at least 20% of the overall population. In states where less than five places meet either of these criteria, we have included places with at least 10,000 total population with the highest percentage of Hispanic/Latino population. These places are identified with an asterisk (*); Please refer to the User's Guide for a full explanation of data.

Population Age 3–17 Enrolled in Public School

(Universe: Population Age 3–17 Enrolled in School)

South American: Ecuadorian

Top 10 States, Counties, and Places[1]

Sorted by Number in Descending Order — U.S. = 94,696

State	Number	County	Number	Place	Number
New York	35,430	Queens County, NY	14,377	**New York, NY** (city)	25,362
New Jersey	18,098	Hudson County, NJ	4,917	**Queens, NY** (borough) Queens County	14,377
Florida	9,793	Kings County, NY	4,900	**Brooklyn, NY** (borough) Kings County	4,900
California	5,514	Essex County, NJ	4,107	**Bronx, NY** (borough) Bronx County	3,513
Illinois	3,970	Westchester County, NY	3,953	**Chicago, IL** (city) Cook County	2,729
Connecticut	3,537	Bronx County, NY	3,513	**Newark, NJ** (city) Essex County	2,546
Texas	2,537	Cook County, IL	3,124	**Manhattan, NY** (borough) New York County	2,135
Pennsylvania	2,257	Suffolk County, NY	2,861	**Islip, NY** (town) Suffolk County	1,229
North Carolina	1,814	Miami-Dade County, FL	2,811	**Elizabeth, NJ** (city) Union County	1,205
Maryland	1,542	Los Angeles County, CA	2,788	**North Bergen, NJ** (township) Hudson County	1,145

Sorted by Number in Ascending Order — U.S. = 94,696

State	Number	County	Number	Place	Number
Louisiana	27	King County, WA	27	**Downey, CA** (city) Los Angeles County	46
Oregon	31	Prince George's County, MD	125	**City of Orange, NJ** (township) Essex County	72
Kansas	130	Santa Clara County, CA	126	**Hollywood, FL** (city) Broward County	77
Missouri	130	Lee County, FL	145	**Paterson, NJ** (city) Passaic County	113
Iowa	131	Putnam County, NY	152	**Houston, TX** (city) Harris County	124
Washington	158	Philadelphia County, PA	158	**Miami, FL** (city) Miami-Dade County	142
Wisconsin	170	Orange County, NY	160	**Oyster Bay, NY** (town) Nassau County	156
Rhode Island	181	Monmouth County, NJ	161	**Philadelphia, PA** (city) Philadelphia County	158
Tennessee	191	Providence County, RI	169	**Country Club, FL** (cdp) Miami-Dade County	167
South Carolina	197	Clark County, NV	206	**Norwalk, CT** (city/town) Fairfield County	169

Sorted by Percent in Descending Order — U.S. = 88.6%

State	Percent	County	Percent	Place	Percent
Colorado	100.0	Berks County, PA	100.0	**Allentown, PA** (city) Lehigh County	100.0
Missouri	100.0	Burlington County, NJ	100.0	**Babylon, NY** (town) Suffolk County	100.0
North Carolina	97.3	Dallas County, TX	100.0	**Charlotte, NC** (city) Mecklenburg County	100.0
Michigan	96.6	Lehigh County, PA	100.0	**City of Orange, NJ** (township) Essex County	100.0
Utah	95.2	Mecklenburg County, NC	100.0	**Clifton, NJ** (city) Passaic County	100.0
Ohio	95.0	Mercer County, NJ	100.0	**Kearny, NJ** (town) Hudson County	100.0
Iowa	94.9	Osceola County, FL	100.0	**Miami, FL** (city) Miami-Dade County	100.0
Massachusetts	92.9	Philadelphia County, PA	100.0	**Miramar, FL** (city) Broward County	100.0
Tennessee	92.7	Pinellas County, FL	100.0	**New Haven, CT** (city/town) New Haven County	100.0
New Jersey	91.8	Riverside County, CA	100.0	**Paterson, NJ** (city) Passaic County	100.0

Sorted by Percent in Ascending Order — U.S. = 88.6%

State	Percent	County	Percent	Place	Percent
Louisiana	22.3	King County, WA	41.5	**Hollywood, FL** (city) Broward County	51.0
Oregon	29.5	Dutchess County, NY	71.4	**Yonkers, NY** (city) Westchester County	62.5
Washington	67.5	Fairfax County, VA	72.2	**Downey, CA** (city) Los Angeles County	63.9
Kansas	67.7	Richmond County, NY	75.3	**Oyster Bay, NY** (town) Nassau County	66.1
Virginia	73.8	Prince George's County, MD	75.8	**Houston, TX** (city) Harris County	69.3
Indiana	74.0	Maricopa County, AZ	78.8	**Staten Island, NY** (borough) Richmond County	75.3
Illinois	82.8	Bronx County, NY	81.5	**Bronx, NY** (borough) Bronx County	81.5
California	83.7	Orange County, NY	81.6	**Pembroke Pines, FL** (city) Broward County	81.8
Nevada	83.7	Worcester County, MA	81.6	**Central Islip, NY** (cdp) Suffolk County	82.6
Oklahoma	84.5	Cook County, IL	82.0	**Brentwood, NY** (cdp) Suffolk County	82.9

Note: (1) Ranking tables cover all states and counties, and places with an overall population of at least 125,000, OR an overall population of at least 25,000 where the Hispanic/Latino population is at least 20% of the overall population. In states where less than five places meet either of these criteria, we have included places with at least 10,000 total population with the highest percentage of Hispanic/Latino population. These places are identified with an asterisk (*); Please refer to the User's Guide for a full explanation of data.

Population Age 3–17 Enrolled in Public School

(Universe: Population Age 3–17 Enrolled in School)

South American: Paraguayan

Top 10 States, Counties, and Places[1]

Sorted by Number in Descending Order — U.S. = 3,400

State	Number	County	Number	Place	Number
New York	1,199	Westchester County, NY	427	**New York, NY** (city)	473
New Jersey	323	Queens County, NY	323	**Queens, NY** (borough) Queens County	323
Maryland	223				
California	151				
Florida	133				
Texas	40				

Sorted by Number in Ascending Order — U.S. = 3,400

State	Number	County	Number	Place	Number
Texas	40	Queens County, NY	323	**Queens, NY** (borough) Queens County	323
Florida	133	Westchester County, NY	427	**New York, NY** (city)	473
California	151				
Maryland	223				
New Jersey	323				
New York	1,199				

Sorted by Percent in Descending Order — U.S. = 77.4%

State	Percent	County	Percent	Place	Percent
California	95.0	Westchester County, NY	97.0	**New York, NY** (city)	87.9
Maryland	93.7	Queens County, NY	85.7	**Queens, NY** (borough) Queens County	85.7
New York	93.3				
New Jersey	74.3				
Florida	47.7				
Texas	44.4				

Sorted by Percent in Ascending Order — U.S. = 77.4%

State	Percent	County	Percent	Place	Percent
Texas	44.4	Queens County, NY	85.7	**Queens, NY** (borough) Queens County	85.7
Florida	47.7	Westchester County, NY	97.0	**New York, NY** (city)	87.9
New Jersey	74.3				
New York	93.3				
Maryland	93.7				
California	95.0				

Note: (1) Ranking tables cover all states and counties, and places with an overall population of at least 125,000, OR an overall population of at least 25,000 where the Hispanic/Latino population is at least 20% of the overall population. In states where less than five places meet either of these criteria, we have included places with at least 10,000 total population with the highest percentage of Hispanic/Latino population. These places are identified with an asterisk (*); Please refer to the User's Guide for a full explanation of data.

Population Age 3–17 Enrolled in Public School

(Universe: Population Age 3–17 Enrolled in School)

South American: Peruvian

Top 10 States, Counties, and Places[1]

Sorted by Number in Descending Order — U.S. = 80,130

State	Number	County	Number	Place	Number
Florida	13,819	Los Angeles County, CA	5,059	**New York, NY** (city)	4,961
California	13,526	Miami-Dade County, FL	4,807	**Queens, NY** (borough) Queens County	3,417
New Jersey	11,885	Queens County, NY	3,417	**Los Angeles, CA** (city) Los Angeles County	1,985
New York	9,662	Broward County, FL	3,236	**Paterson, NJ** (city) Passaic County	1,540
Virginia	4,825	Passaic County, NJ	2,836	**Elizabeth, NJ** (city) Union County	1,061
Texas	4,077	Fairfax County, VA	2,182	**Hempstead (town), NY** (town) Nassau County	671
Connecticut	2,313	Hudson County, NJ	1,935	**Islip, NY** (town) Suffolk County	624
Maryland	2,300	Union County, NJ	1,717	**Brooklyn, NY** (borough) Kings County	622
Georgia	1,459	Montgomery County, MD	1,522	**Kearny, NJ** (town) Hudson County	553
Illinois	1,391	Orange County, CA	1,428	**Hollywood, FL** (city) Broward County	532

Sorted by Number in Ascending Order — U.S. = 80,130

State	Number	County	Number	Place	Number
District of Columbia	121	Duval County, FL	20	**Jacksonville, FL** (city) Duval County	20
Kentucky	123	Lehigh County, PA	55	**Orlando, FL** (city) Orange County	61
Kansas	134	Travis County, TX	70	**Salt Lake City, UT** (city) Salt Lake County	69
Hawaii	135	Philadelphia County, PA	85	**Austin, TX** (city) Travis County	70
Missouri	167	Baltimore County, MD	98	**Alexandria, VA** (independent city)	73
Tennessee	170	Denver County, CO	102	**Philadelphia, PA** (city) Philadelphia County	85
Louisiana	204	Ocean County, NJ	102	**Fort Lauderdale, FL** (city) Broward County	87
Alabama	232	Lake County, IL	103	**Tampa, FL** (city) Hillsborough County	88
Michigan	251	Franklin County, OH	104	**Denver, CO** (city) Denver County	102
Minnesota	266	Solano County, CA	110	**Santa Ana, CA** (city) Orange County	107

Sorted by Percent in Descending Order — U.S. = 85.0%

State	Percent	County	Percent	Place	Percent
Delaware	100.0	Arlington County, VA	100.0	**Anaheim, CA** (city) Orange County	100.0
Louisiana	97.6	Collier County, FL	100.0	**Arlington, VA** (cdp) Arlington County	100.0
Arizona	96.2	Denver County, CO	100.0	**Austin, TX** (city) Travis County	100.0
New Mexico	94.9	Maricopa County, AZ	100.0	**Brentwood, NY** (cdp) Suffolk County	100.0
Nevada	93.0	Mecklenburg County, NC	100.0	**Cape Coral, FL** (city) Lee County	100.0
Alabama	92.4	Osceola County, FL	100.0	**Charlotte, NC** (city) Mecklenburg County	100.0
North Carolina	90.9	Travis County, TX	100.0	**Denver, CO** (city) Denver County	100.0
Colorado	90.7	Gwinnett County, GA	98.2	**Downey, CA** (city) Los Angeles County	100.0
Massachusetts	90.4	Collin County, TX	98.0	**Fort Lauderdale, FL** (city) Broward County	100.0
Idaho	90.0	Atlantic County, NJ	97.6	**Kendall West, FL** (cdp) Miami-Dade County	100.0

Sorted by Percent in Ascending Order — U.S. = 85.0%

State	Percent	County	Percent	Place	Percent
Missouri	43.4	Duval County, FL	22.5	**Jacksonville, FL** (city) Duval County	27.4
Wisconsin	54.5	Baltimore County, MD	45.6	**Orlando, FL** (city) Orange County	40.4
Kansas	60.6	New Haven County, CT	48.1	**Port Chester, NY** (village) Westchester County	54.2
Illinois	68.1	Seminole County, FL	60.6	**Concord, CA** (city) Contra Costa County	56.1
Tennessee	69.4	Contra Costa County, CA	61.1	**Rye, NY** (town) Westchester County	58.6
Washington	70.8	New York County, NY	66.2	**Davie, FL** (town) Broward County	64.2
South Carolina	73.6	Morris County, NJ	66.7	**Manhattan, NY** (borough) New York County	66.2
Hawaii	74.2	Lake County, IL	69.6	**Miami Beach, FL** (city) Miami-Dade County	69.0
Kentucky	76.9	New London County, CT	69.8	**Doral, FL** (city) Miami-Dade County	69.3
Maryland	77.4	Philadelphia County, PA	70.8	**Tampa, FL** (city) Hillsborough County	70.4

Note: (1) Ranking tables cover all states and counties, and places with an overall population of at least 125,000, OR an overall population of at least 25,000 where the Hispanic/Latino population is at least 20% of the overall population. In states where less than five places meet either of these criteria, we have included places with at least 10,000 total population with the highest percentage of Hispanic/Latino population. These places are identified with an asterisk (*); Please refer to the User's Guide for a full explanation of data.

Population Age 3–17 Enrolled in Public School

(Universe: Population Age 3–17 Enrolled in School)

South American: Uruguayan

Top 10 States, Counties, and Places[1]

Sorted by Number in Descending Order — U.S. = 8,612

State	Number	County	Number	Place	Number
Florida	2,204	Miami-Dade County, FL	1,115	**Elizabeth, NJ** (city) Union County	752
New Jersey	1,982	Union County, NJ	830	**New York, NY** (city)	200
New York	711	Palm Beach County, FL	360	**Queens, NY** (borough) Queens County	77
Georgia	477	Broward County, FL	336		
Texas	433	Essex County, NJ	320		
California	393	Worcester County, MA	299		
Massachusetts	342	Harris County, TX	297		
Virginia	336	Westchester County, NY	214		
Maryland	246	Morris County, NJ	180		
Pennsylvania	199	Gwinnett County, GA	177		

Sorted by Number in Ascending Order — U.S. = 8,612

State	Number	County	Number	Place	Number
Pennsylvania	199	Hudson County, NJ	66	**Queens, NY** (borough) Queens County	77
Maryland	246	Queens County, NY	77	**New York, NY** (city)	200
Virginia	336	Los Angeles County, CA	136	**Elizabeth, NJ** (city) Union County	752
Massachusetts	342	Middlesex County, NJ	166		
California	393	Gwinnett County, GA	177		
Texas	433	Morris County, NJ	180		
Georgia	477	Westchester County, NY	214		
New York	711	Harris County, TX	297		
New Jersey	1,982	Worcester County, MA	299		
Florida	2,204	Essex County, NJ	320		

Sorted by Percent in Descending Order — U.S. = 87.9%

State	Percent	County	Percent	Place	Percent
Pennsylvania	100.0	Broward County, FL	100.0	**Elizabeth, NJ** (city) Union County	100.0
Georgia	98.4	Gwinnett County, GA	100.0	**Queens, NY** (borough) Queens County	65.8
Maryland	95.0	Hudson County, NJ	100.0	**New York, NY** (city)	58.7
Florida	94.2	Union County, NJ	100.0		
New Jersey	93.8	Palm Beach County, FL	96.0		
Texas	89.1	Morris County, NJ	95.2		
Virginia	81.4	Miami-Dade County, FL	94.1		
Massachusetts	80.5	Essex County, NJ	92.5		
California	80.0	Worcester County, MA	92.3		
New York	74.3	Harris County, TX	90.0		

Sorted by Percent in Ascending Order — U.S. = 87.9%

State	Percent	County	Percent	Place	Percent
New York	74.3	Los Angeles County, CA	61.3	**New York, NY** (city)	58.7
California	80.0	Queens County, NY	65.8	**Queens, NY** (borough) Queens County	65.8
Massachusetts	80.5	Westchester County, NY	70.2	**Elizabeth, NJ** (city) Union County	100.0
Virginia	81.4	Middlesex County, NJ	79.4		
Texas	89.1	Harris County, TX	90.0		
New Jersey	93.8	Worcester County, MA	92.3		
Florida	94.2	Essex County, NJ	92.5		
Maryland	95.0	Miami-Dade County, FL	94.1		
Georgia	98.4	Morris County, NJ	95.2		
Pennsylvania	100.0	Palm Beach County, FL	96.0		

Note: (1) Ranking tables cover all states and counties, and places with an overall population of at least 125,000, OR an overall population of at least 25,000 where the Hispanic/Latino population is at least 20% of the overall population. In states where less than five places meet either of these criteria, we have included places with at least 10,000 total population with the highest percentage of Hispanic/Latino population. These places are identified with an asterisk (*); Please refer to the User's Guide for a full explanation of data.

Population Age 3–17 Enrolled in Public School

(Universe: Population Age 3–17 Enrolled in School)

South American: Venezuelan

Top 10 States, Counties, and Places[1]

Sorted by Number in Descending Order — U.S. = 32,485

State	Number	County	Number	Place	Number
Florida	16,411	Miami-Dade County, FL	6,556	**Weston, FL** (city) Broward County	1,774
Texas	2,802	Broward County, FL	4,411	**Doral, FL** (city) Miami-Dade County	1,375
New York	1,902	Orange County, FL	1,258	**New York, NY** (city)	1,100
California	1,657	Harris County, TX	853	**Fountainebleau, FL** (cdp) Miami-Dade County	599
Georgia	1,110	Fort Bend County, TX	768	**Queens, NY** (borough) Queens County	507
New Jersey	866	Palm Beach County, FL	597	**Miami, FL** (city) Miami-Dade County	472
Virginia	698	Seminole County, FL	548	**Houston, TX** (city) Harris County	456
North Carolina	616	Osceola County, FL	522	**Pembroke Pines, FL** (city) Broward County	363
Utah	587	Hillsborough County, FL	516	**Davie, FL** (town) Broward County	322
Pennsylvania	532	Queens County, NY	507	**Country Club, FL** (cdp) Miami-Dade County	307

Sorted by Number in Ascending Order — U.S. = 32,485

State	Number	County	Number	Place	Number
Ohio	103	Montgomery County, MD	44	**Hollywood, FL** (city) Broward County	95
Colorado	117	San Diego County, CA	52	**Los Angeles, CA** (city) Los Angeles County	103
Washington	146	Dallas County, TX	54	**Miami Beach, FL** (city) Miami-Dade County	107
Indiana	150	Tarrant County, TX	89	**Tamiami, FL** (cdp) Miami-Dade County	113
South Carolina	155	King County, WA	103	**Manhattan, NY** (borough) New York County	149
Minnesota	159	Suffolk County, MA	105	**Aventura, FL** (city) Miami-Dade County	153
Wisconsin	181	Travis County, TX	140	**Bronx, NY** (borough) Bronx County	198
Arizona	202	New York County, NY	149	**Kendall, FL** (cdp) Miami-Dade County	216
Maryland	202	Montgomery County, TX	152	**The Hammocks, FL** (cdp) Miami-Dade County	224
Michigan	216	Fairfax County, VA	161	**Brooklyn, NY** (borough) Kings County	244

Sorted by Percent in Descending Order — U.S. = 82.0%

State	Percent	County	Percent	Place	Percent
South Carolina	100.0	King County, WA	100.0	**Country Club, FL** (cdp) Miami-Dade County	100.0
Oklahoma	95.9	Orange County, CA	100.0	**Bronx, NY** (borough) Bronx County	95.2
Utah	95.1	Salt Lake County, UT	96.6	**Coral Springs, FL** (city) Broward County	95.2
California	87.5	Seminole County, FL	96.6	**Tamiami, FL** (cdp) Miami-Dade County	94.2
Virginia	87.3	Lee County, FL	96.4	**Pembroke Pines, FL** (city) Broward County	93.3
Tennessee	87.2	Bronx County, NY	95.2	**Kendall West, FL** (cdp) Miami-Dade County	92.7
Pennsylvania	86.4	Fort Bend County, TX	94.7	**Miramar, FL** (city) Broward County	92.5
Wisconsin	86.2	Travis County, TX	94.0	**Hollywood, FL** (city) Broward County	92.2
Washington	85.9	Hillsborough County, FL	92.3	**Davie, FL** (town) Broward County	91.0
New Jersey	84.9	Fulton County, GA	91.4	**Fountainebleau, FL** (cdp) Miami-Dade County	86.8

Sorted by Percent in Ascending Order — U.S. = 82.0%

State	Percent	County	Percent	Place	Percent
Ohio	36.1	San Diego County, CA	57.8	**Miami Beach, FL** (city) Miami-Dade County	44.4
Maryland	51.5	Montgomery County, MD	58.7	**Aventura, FL** (city) Miami-Dade County	67.7
Indiana	64.4	Fairfield County, CT	65.2	**Los Angeles, CA** (city) Los Angeles County	72.0
Connecticut	68.2	Dallas County, TX	66.7	**The Hammocks, FL** (cdp) Miami-Dade County	75.9
Louisiana	68.5	Fairfax County, VA	69.4	**Manhattan, NY** (borough) New York County	77.2
Colorado	74.5	Cobb County, GA	73.2	**Kendall, FL** (cdp) Miami-Dade County	78.3
Michigan	74.7	Tarrant County, TX	74.2	**Doral, FL** (city) Miami-Dade County	79.5
Illinois	77.4	Middlesex County, MA	74.5	**Miami, FL** (city) Miami-Dade County	81.0
Georgia	78.3	New York County, NY	77.2	**Houston, TX** (city) Harris County	82.9
Arizona	79.2	Collin County, TX	78.7	**Orlando, FL** (city) Orange County	83.3

RANKINGS & COMPARISONS

Note: (1) Ranking tables cover all states and counties, and places with an overall population of at least 125,000, OR an overall population of at least 25,000 where the Hispanic/Latino population is at least 20% of the overall population. In states where less than five places meet either of these criteria, we have included places with at least 10,000 total population with the highest percentage of Hispanic/Latino population. These places are identified with an asterisk (*); Please refer to the User's Guide for a full explanation of data.

Population Age 3–17 Enrolled in Public School

(Universe: Population Age 3–17 Enrolled in School)

Spaniard

Top 10 States, Counties, and Places[1]

Sorted by Number in Descending Order — U.S. = 86,626

State	Number	County	Number	Place	Number
California	15,355	Bernalillo County, NM	2,592	**Albuquerque, NM** (city) Bernalillo County	2,269
Texas	10,381	Los Angeles County, CA	2,518	**New York, NY** (city)	1,129
Colorado	8,306	Harris County, TX	1,513	**Denver, CO** (city) Denver County	1,032
New Mexico	7,834	Maricopa County, AZ	1,457	**Pueblo, CO** (city) Pueblo County	785
Florida	5,225	San Bernardino County, CA	1,422	**San Antonio, TX** (city) Bexar County	746
New York	3,620	Riverside County, CA	1,369	**Rio Rancho, NM** (city) Sandoval County	654
New Jersey	2,825	San Diego County, CA	1,357	**Houston, TX** (city) Harris County	607
Arizona	2,652	Honolulu County, HI	1,194	**Los Angeles, CA** (city) Los Angeles County	604
Washington	2,110	Pueblo County, CO	1,186	**Phoenix, AZ** (city) Maricopa County	543
Hawaii	2,022	Miami-Dade County, FL	1,160	**San Diego, CA** (city) San Diego County	448

Sorted by Number in Ascending Order — U.S. = 86,626

State	Number	County	Number	Place	Number
District of Columbia	11	Duval County, FL	33	**Miami, FL** (city) Miami-Dade County	28
Maine	102	Rio Arriba County, NM	44	**Jacksonville, FL** (city) Duval County	33
Mississippi	103	Oakland County, MI	54	**Riverside, CA** (city) Riverside County	43
Iowa	109	Jefferson Parish, LA	56	**Seattle, WA** (city) King County	54
Montana	139	Hidalgo County, TX	61	**Tucson, AZ** (city) Pima County	54
Kentucky	183	Butte County, CA	76	**Glendale, AZ** (city) Maricopa County	68
West Virginia	197	Santa Barbara County, CA	83	**South Valley, NM** (cdp) Bernalillo County	76
New Hampshire	206	Tulare County, CA	84	**Fresno, CA** (city) Fresno County	89
Arkansas	254	New York County, NY	90	**Manhattan, NY** (borough) New York County	90
Alabama	261	San Francisco County, CA	92	**Aurora, CO** (city) Arapahoe County	92

Sorted by Percent in Descending Order — U.S. = 83.5%

State	Percent	County	Percent	Place	Percent
District of Columbia	100.0	Boulder County, CO	100.0	**Bakersfield, CA** (city) Kern County	100.0
Kentucky	100.0	Colfax County, NM	100.0	**Fort Collins, CO** (city) Larimer County	100.0
Maine	100.0	Doña Ana County, NM	100.0	**Glendale, AZ** (city) Maricopa County	100.0
Alaska	97.6	Erie County, NY	100.0	**Henderson, NV** (city) Clark County	100.0
Wyoming	96.6	Hidalgo County, TX	100.0	**Las Cruces, NM** (city) Dona Ana County	100.0
Alabama	96.0	Las Animas County, CO	100.0	**Miami, FL** (city) Miami-Dade County	100.0
Oklahoma	95.2	Mesa County, CO	100.0	**North Las Vegas, NV** (city) Clark County	100.0
Idaho	93.6	Milwaukee County, WI	100.0	**Oklahoma City, OK** (city) Oklahoma County	100.0
Montana	93.3	Oklahoma County, OK	100.0	**Paradise, NV** (cdp) Clark County	100.0
New Hampshire	91.2	Passaic County, NJ	100.0	**Philadelphia, PA** (city) Philadelphia County	100.0

Sorted by Percent in Ascending Order — U.S. = 83.5%

State	Percent	County	Percent	Place	Percent
Mississippi	52.6	Jefferson Parish, LA	35.0	**San Francisco, CA** (city) San Francisco County	35.0
Louisiana	66.9	San Francisco County, CA	35.0	**Queens, NY** (borough) Queens County	46.7
Maryland	68.2	Queens County, NY	46.7	**Tucson, AZ** (city) Pima County	50.9
Florida	73.1	New York County, NY	55.9	**Seattle, WA** (city) King County	53.5
New York	73.4	Montgomery County, MD	61.6	**Hempstead (town), NY** (town) Nassau County	55.2
West Virginia	73.8	Duval County, FL	62.3	**Manhattan, NY** (borough) New York County	55.9
Pennsylvania	77.2	Placer County, CA	62.7	**Long Beach, CA** (city) Los Angeles County	57.8
Ohio	77.3	Santa Barbara County, CA	62.9	**Jacksonville, FL** (city) Duval County	62.3
Minnesota	77.4	Miami-Dade County, FL	64.7	**New York, NY** (city)	63.7
North Carolina	77.6	Solano County, CA	65.7	**Reno, NV** (city) Washoe County	65.2

Note: (1) Ranking tables cover all states and counties, and places with an overall population of at least 125,000, OR an overall population of at least 25,000 where the Hispanic/Latino population is at least 20% of the overall population. In states where less than five places meet either of these criteria, we have included places with at least 10,000 total population with the highest percentage of Hispanic/Latino population. These places are identified with an asterisk (*); Please refer to the User's Guide for a full explanation of data.

Population Age 3–17 Enrolled in Private School

(Universe: Population Age 3–17 Enrolled in School)

Total Population

Top 10 States, Counties, and Places[1]

Sorted by Number in Descending Order — U.S. = 7,635,968

State	Number	County	Number	Place	Number
California	842,757	Los Angeles County, CA	230,524	**New York, NY** (city)	298,131
New York	589,586	Cook County, IL	151,665	**Brooklyn, NY** (borough) Kings County	112,797
Florida	471,003	Kings County, NY	112,797	**Los Angeles, CA** (city) Los Angeles County	94,921
Texas	461,840	Orange County, CA	79,928	**Chicago, IL** (city) Cook County	78,750
Pennsylvania	391,562	Harris County, TX	74,052	**Queens, NY** (borough) Queens County	67,374
Illinois	351,622	Miami-Dade County, FL	70,244	**Philadelphia, PA** (city) Philadelphia County	59,446
Ohio	335,092	Maricopa County, AZ	68,346	**Manhattan, NY** (borough) New York County	53,919
New Jersey	272,484	Queens County, NY	67,374	**Bronx, NY** (borough) Bronx County	41,583
Georgia	239,640	San Diego County, CA	61,383	**Houston, TX** (city) Harris County	35,124
Michigan	222,360	Philadelphia County, PA	59,446	**Jacksonville, FL** (city) Duval County	29,315

Sorted by Number in Ascending Order — U.S. = 7,635,968

State	Number	County	Number	Place	Number
Wyoming	8,086	Armstrong County, TX	0	**Parker*, SC** (cdp) Greenville County	0
North Dakota	10,789	Atkinson County, GA	0	**Lexington*, NE** (city) Dawson County	46
Vermont	12,986	Baker County, GA	0	**San Luis, AZ** (city) Yuma County	47
Alaska	13,425	Baylor County, TX	0	**Florence, AZ** (town) Pinal County	52
District of Columbia	16,239	Carter County, MO	0	**Mayfield*, KY** (city) Graves County	58
South Dakota	16,552	Clark County, ID	0	**Fort Campbell North*, KY** (cdp) Christian County	61
Montana	19,268	Clay County, IL	0	**Bell, CA** (city) Los Angeles County	79
West Virginia	24,290	Cleveland County, AR	0	**San Juan, TX** (city) Hidalgo County	83
Maine	26,425	Costilla County, CO	0	**Storm Lake*, IA** (city) Buena Vista County	87
Rhode Island	30,089	Cottle County, TX	0	**Spearfish*, SD** (city) Lawrence County	91

Sorted by Percent in Descending Order — U.S. = 13.6%

State	Percent	County	Percent	Place	Percent
Hawaii	23.1	Fayette County, TN	38.9	**Coral Gables, FL** (city) Miami-Dade County	64.9
District of Columbia	21.2	Jefferson Parish, LA	37.0	**Ramapo, NY** (town) Rockland County	61.2
Delaware	20.5	Rockland County, NY	36.6	**Metairie, LA** (cdp) Jefferson Parish	58.2
Louisiana	19.5	Pointe Coupee Parish, LA	35.4	**Altadena, CA** (cdp) Los Angeles County	39.5
Maryland	19.2	Sioux County, IA	35.4	**Miami Beach, FL** (city) Miami-Dade County	38.2
Pennsylvania	18.1	Holmes County, OH	33.7	**Spring Valley, NY** (village) Rockland County	37.4
New York	17.3	Piute County, UT	33.5	**Englewood, NJ** (city) Bergen County	35.3
Rhode Island	17.0	Jefferson County, FL	33.4	**Kenner, LA** (city) Jefferson Parish	34.7
New Jersey	16.7	LaGrange County, IN	33.4	**Plantation, FL** (city) Broward County	31.3
Missouri	16.1	Amite County, MS	32.3	**Manhattan, NY** (borough) New York County	30.4

Sorted by Percent in Ascending Order — U.S. = 13.6%

State	Percent	County	Percent	Place	Percent
Nevada	7.5	Armstrong County, TX	0.0	**Parker*, SC** (cdp) Greenville County	0.0
West Virginia	8.4	Atkinson County, GA	0.0	**San Luis, AZ** (city) Yuma County	0.7
Wyoming	8.4	Baker County, GA	0.0	**Bell, CA** (city) Los Angeles County	0.9
Oklahoma	8.9	Baylor County, TX	0.0	**San Juan, TX** (city) Hidalgo County	0.9
Arizona	9.2	Carter County, MO	0.0	**Coachella, CA** (city) Riverside County	1.0
Texas	9.3	Clark County, ID	0.0	**Fort Hood, TX** (cdp) Bell County	1.3
Utah	9.3	Clay County, IL	0.0	**Delano, CA** (city) Kern County	1.6
Arkansas	9.6	Cleveland County, AR	0.0	**Pharr, TX** (city) Hidalgo County	1.7
Alaska	10.0	Costilla County, CO	0.0	**Maywood, CA** (city) Los Angeles County	1.8
New Mexico	10.2	Cottle County, TX	0.0	**Lexington*, NE** (city) Dawson County	1.9

Note: (1) Ranking tables cover all states and counties, and places with an overall population of at least 125,000, OR an overall population of at least 25,000 where the Hispanic/Latino population is at least 20% of the overall population. In states where less than five places meet either of these criteria, we have included places with at least 10,000 total population with the highest percentage of Hispanic/Latino population. These places are identified with an asterisk (*); Please refer to the User's Guide for a full explanation of data.

Population Age 3–17 Enrolled in Private School

(Universe: Population Age 3–17 Enrolled in School)

Hispanic or Latino (of any race)

Top 10 States, Counties, and Places[1]

Sorted by Number in Descending Order — U.S. = 814,030

State	Number	County	Number	Place	Number
California	200,929	Los Angeles County, CA	72,837	**New York, NY** (city)	52,952
Texas	103,341	Miami-Dade County, FL	38,722	**Los Angeles, CA** (city) Los Angeles County	24,443
Florida	92,190	Cook County, IL	27,739	**Bronx, NY** (borough) Bronx County	19,548
New York	73,986	Bronx County, NY	19,548	**Chicago, IL** (city) Cook County	17,855
Illinois	42,799	Bexar County, TX	17,850	**Queens, NY** (borough) Queens County	14,385
New Jersey	29,098	Harris County, TX	15,736	**San Antonio, TX** (city) Bexar County	13,998
Arizona	21,910	Orange County, CA	15,198	**Manhattan, NY** (borough) New York County	8,751
Pennsylvania	18,544	San Diego County, CA	14,808	**Houston, TX** (city) Harris County	8,229
New Mexico	15,603	Queens County, NY	14,385	**Brooklyn, NY** (borough) Kings County	7,046
Colorado	14,463	Broward County, FL	12,923	**Philadelphia, PA** (city) Philadelphia County	6,592

Sorted by Number in Ascending Order — U.S. = 814,030

State	Number	County	Number	Place	Number
South Dakota	198	Accomack County, VA	0	**Albertville*, AL** (city) Marshall County	0
Vermont	301	Adair County, OK	0	**Asheboro, NC** (city) Randolph County	0
North Dakota	309	Adams County, WI	0	**Bluffton*, SC** (town) Beaufort County	0
West Virginia	525	Alexander County, NC	0	**Bozeman*, MT** (city) Gallatin County	0
Maine	700	Alleghany County, NC	0	**Butte-Silver Bow*, MT** (consolidated govt) Silver Bow County	0
Montana	730	Allen Parish, LA	0	**Evanston*, WY** (city) Uinta County	0
Wyoming	876	Anderson County, TN	0	**Fitchburg, MA** (city) Worcester County	0
Alaska	917	Antrim County, MI	0	**Fort Campbell North*, KY** (cdp) Christian County	0
New Hampshire	1,102	Archer County, TX	0	**Fort Hood, TX** (cdp) Bell County	0
District of Columbia	1,169	Ashe County, NC	0	**Fort Leonard Wood*, MO** (cdp) Pulaski County	0

Sorted by Percent in Descending Order — U.S. = 7.0%

State	Percent	County	Percent	Place	Percent
Louisiana	19.8	Wakulla County, FL	76.5	**Coral Gables, FL** (city) Miami-Dade County	65.1
Hawaii	16.0	Putnam County, IN	66.9	**Mobile, AL** (city) Mobile County	45.4
Maine	14.9	Bristol County, RI	58.5	**Metairie, LA** (cdp) Jefferson Parish	43.0
Ohio	14.8	Sullivan County, TN	49.8	**Plantation, FL** (city) Broward County	37.0
District of Columbia	14.5	Geauga County, OH	47.7	**New Orleans, LA** (city) Orleans Parish	35.2
Vermont	13.7	Hampton County, SC	46.3	**Jackson, MS** (city) Hinds County	34.8
Missouri	12.1	Addison County, VT	44.6	**Salem*, NH** (town) Rockingham County	34.5
Florida	12.0	Johnson County, NE	44.4	**Grand Forks*, ND** (city) Grand Forks County	34.1
Maryland	11.7	Lee County, IA	43.9	**Missoula*, MT** (city) Missoula County	30.4
New Hampshire	11.4	Centre County, PA	43.5	**Kendall, FL** (cdp) Miami-Dade County	30.1

Sorted by Percent in Ascending Order — U.S. = 7.0%

State	Percent	County	Percent	Place	Percent
Nevada	3.5	Accomack County, VA	0.0	**Albertville*, AL** (city) Marshall County	0.0
South Dakota	3.5	Adair County, OK	0.0	**Asheboro, NC** (city) Randolph County	0.0
Arizona	4.6	Adams County, WI	0.0	**Bluffton*, SC** (town) Beaufort County	0.0
Texas	4.6	Alexander County, NC	0.0	**Bozeman*, MT** (city) Gallatin County	0.0
Oklahoma	4.8	Alleghany County, NC	0.0	**Butte-Silver Bow*, MT** (consolidated govt) Silver Bow County	0.0
North Carolina	4.9	Allen Parish, LA	0.0	**Evanston*, WY** (city) Uinta County	0.0
Arkansas	5.0	Anderson County, TN	0.0	**Fitchburg, MA** (city) Worcester County	0.0
Oregon	5.4	Antrim County, MI	0.0	**Fort Campbell North*, KY** (cdp) Christian County	0.0
Iowa	5.6	Archer County, TX	0.0	**Fort Hood, TX** (cdp) Bell County	0.0
Utah	5.6	Ashe County, NC	0.0	**Fort Leonard Wood*, MO** (cdp) Pulaski County	0.0

Note: (1) Ranking tables cover all states and counties, and places with an overall population of at least 125,000, OR an overall population of at least 25,000 where the Hispanic/Latino population is at least 20% of the overall population. In states where less than five places meet either of these criteria, we have included places with at least 10,000 total population with the highest percentage of Hispanic/Latino population. These places are identified with an asterisk (*); Please refer to the User's Guide for a full explanation of data.

Population Age 3–17 Enrolled in Private School

(Universe: Population Age 3–17 Enrolled in School)

Central American, excluding Mexican

Top 10 States, Counties, and Places[1]

Sorted by Number in Descending Order — U.S. = 55,721

State	Number	County	Number	Place	Number
California	14,916	Los Angeles County, CA	7,792	**Los Angeles, CA** (city) Los Angeles County	4,073
Florida	5,478	Miami-Dade County, FL	2,460	**New York, NY** (city)	2,430
New York	4,313	Cook County, IL	1,227	**San Francisco, CA** (city) San Francisco County	836
Texas	3,130	Harris County, TX	981	**Bronx, NY** (borough) Bronx County	708
Virginia	2,353	Jefferson Parish, LA	950	**Queens, NY** (borough) Queens County	702
Maryland	2,260	San Mateo County, CA	892	**Chicago, IL** (city) Cook County	652
New Jersey	2,228	San Francisco County, CA	836	**Houston, TX** (city) Harris County	639
Illinois	1,925	Fairfax County, VA	758	**Brooklyn, NY** (borough) Kings County	615
Louisiana	1,851	Montgomery County, MD	746	**Hempstead (town), NY** (town) Nassau County	491
Massachusetts	1,480	Bronx County, NY	708	**Metairie, LA** (cdp) Jefferson Parish	448

Sorted by Number in Ascending Order — U.S. = 55,721

State	Number	County	Number	Place	Number
Wyoming	0	Albany County, NY	0	**Adelanto, CA** (city) San Bernardino County	0
South Dakota	1	Berks County, PA	0	**Albertville*, AL** (city) Marshall County	0
Vermont	29	Butte County, CA	0	**Atascocita, TX** (cdp) Harris County	0
Iowa	31	Caroline County, MD	0	**Avondale, AZ** (city) Maricopa County	0
West Virginia	39	Carroll County, AR	0	**Bell Gardens, CA** (city) Los Angeles County	0
Idaho	61	Carroll County, GA	0	**Belleville, NJ** (township) Essex County	0
New Hampshire	65	Cass County, IN	0	**Bellflower, CA** (city) Los Angeles County	0
Maine	70	Chatham County, GA	0	**Bridgeport, CT** (city/town) Fairfield County	0
Delaware	95	Chatham County, NC	0	**Buenaventura Lakes, FL** (cdp) Osceola County	0
Oklahoma	129	Clark County, WA	0	**Cathedral City, CA** (city) Riverside County	0

Sorted by Percent in Descending Order — U.S. = 7.4%

State	Percent	County	Percent	Place	Percent
Alaska	31.6	York County, PA	63.7	**Atlanta, GA** (city) Fulton County	100.0
Hawaii	28.6	Madison County, AL	61.2	**Coral Gables, FL** (city) Miami-Dade County	44.5
Louisiana	25.5	Allegheny County, PA	48.1	**Metairie, LA** (cdp) Jefferson Parish	40.9
Ohio	22.6	Jefferson County, AL	46.8	**Murrieta, CA** (city) Riverside County	40.1
Mississippi	20.0	Erie County, NY	45.9	**Rohnert Park, CA** (city) Sonoma County	38.6
Wisconsin	19.1	McHenry County, IL	45.3	**Baton Rouge, LA** (city) East Baton Rouge Parish	38.1
Pennsylvania	18.3	Charles County, MD	44.2	**Norfolk, VA** (independent city)	36.2
Michigan	16.9	Honolulu County, HI	41.1	**Cleveland, OH** (city) Cuyahoga County	35.4
Indiana	16.1	Saint Louis County, MO	39.7	**Alhambra, CA** (city) Los Angeles County	35.1
Alabama	15.7	Cuyahoga County, OH	39.6	**Chino Hills, CA** (city) San Bernardino County	33.8

Sorted by Percent in Ascending Order — U.S. = 7.4%

State	Percent	County	Percent	Place	Percent
Wyoming	0.0	Albany County, NY	0.0	**Adelanto, CA** (city) San Bernardino County	0.0
South Dakota	0.2	Berks County, PA	0.0	**Albertville*, AL** (city) Marshall County	0.0
Iowa	1.1	Butte County, CA	0.0	**Atascocita, TX** (cdp) Harris County	0.0
Texas	3.7	Caroline County, MD	0.0	**Avondale, AZ** (city) Maricopa County	0.0
Nebraska	3.9	Carroll County, AR	0.0	**Bell Gardens, CA** (city) Los Angeles County	0.0
Oregon	3.9	Carroll County, GA	0.0	**Belleville, NJ** (township) Essex County	0.0
Nevada	4.0	Cass County, IN	0.0	**Bellflower, CA** (city) Los Angeles County	0.0
Oklahoma	4.6	Chatham County, GA	0.0	**Bridgeport, CT** (city/town) Fairfield County	0.0
Arizona	4.9	Chatham County, NC	0.0	**Buenaventura Lakes, FL** (cdp) Osceola County	0.0
Delaware	5.7	Clark County, WA	0.0	**Cathedral City, CA** (city) Riverside County	0.0

Note: (1) Ranking tables cover all states and counties, and places with an overall population of at least 125,000, OR an overall population of at least 25,000 where the Hispanic/Latino population is at least 20% of the overall population. In states where less than five places meet either of these criteria, we have included places with at least 10,000 total population with the highest percentage of Hispanic/Latino population. These places are identified with an asterisk (*); Please refer to the User's Guide for a full explanation of data.

Population Age 3–17 Enrolled in Private School

(Universe: Population Age 3–17 Enrolled in School)

Central American: Costa Rican

Top 10 States, Counties, and Places[1]

Sorted by Number in Descending Order — U.S. = 4,037

State	Number	County	Number	Place	Number
California	856	Los Angeles County, CA	538	**Los Angeles, CA** (city) Los Angeles County	131
Florida	456	Union County, NJ	171	**Philadelphia, PA** (city) Philadelphia County	108
New Jersey	349	Miami-Dade County, FL	132	**New York, NY** (city)	59
Massachusetts	250	Philadelphia County, PA	108	**Brooklyn, NY** (borough) Kings County	39
Maryland	244	Broward County, FL	96	**Miami, FL** (city) Miami-Dade County	21
Pennsylvania	235	Cook County, IL	78	**Queens, NY** (borough) Queens County	20
New York	171	Hillsborough County, FL	59	**Bronx, NY** (borough) Bronx County	0
Texas	148	Nassau County, NY	53		
Illinois	124	Passaic County, NJ	49		
Tennessee	107	Maricopa County, AZ	48		

Sorted by Number in Ascending Order — U.S. = 4,037

State	Number	County	Number	Place	Number
Michigan	14	Bronx County, NY	0	**Bronx, NY** (borough) Bronx County	0
Oregon	15	Clark County, NV	0	**Queens, NY** (borough) Queens County	20
Louisiana	20	Essex County, NJ	0	**Miami, FL** (city) Miami-Dade County	21
Nevada	23	Fairfield County, CT	0	**Brooklyn, NY** (borough) Kings County	39
Colorado	30	Orange County, FL	0	**New York, NY** (city)	59
Arizona	48	San Diego County, CA	0	**Philadelphia, PA** (city) Philadelphia County	108
Connecticut	52	Somerset County, NJ	0	**Los Angeles, CA** (city) Los Angeles County	131
Wisconsin	58	Suffolk County, NY	0		
Washington	61	Mercer County, NJ	13		
Georgia	88	Contra Costa County, CA	14		

Sorted by Percent in Descending Order — U.S. = 16.6%

State	Percent	County	Percent	Place	Percent
Maryland	40.3	Philadelphia County, PA	54.5	**Philadelphia, PA** (city) Philadelphia County	54.5
South Carolina	36.4	Los Angeles County, CA	31.9	**Los Angeles, CA** (city) Los Angeles County	22.7
Tennessee	33.5	Cook County, IL	26.5	**Miami, FL** (city) Miami-Dade County	16.2
Massachusetts	33.3	Hillsborough County, FL	24.8	**Brooklyn, NY** (borough) Kings County	8.6
Minnesota	30.7	Union County, NJ	21.3	**Queens, NY** (borough) Queens County	8.6
Wisconsin	28.7	Broward County, FL	17.1	**New York, NY** (city)	7.0
Pennsylvania	23.9	Harris County, TX	15.2	**Bronx, NY** (borough) Bronx County	0.0
Illinois	22.8	Maricopa County, AZ	14.7		
Virginia	21.6	Nassau County, NY	14.1		
California	20.0	Mercer County, NJ	13.4		

Sorted by Percent in Ascending Order — U.S. = 16.6%

State	Percent	County	Percent	Place	Percent
Michigan	6.3	Bronx County, NY	0.0	**Bronx, NY** (borough) Bronx County	0.0
Colorado	7.5	Clark County, NV	0.0	**New York, NY** (city)	7.0
North Carolina	7.7	Essex County, NJ	0.0	**Brooklyn, NY** (borough) Kings County	8.6
Nevada	8.0	Fairfield County, CT	0.0	**Queens, NY** (borough) Queens County	8.6
New York	9.2	Orange County, FL	0.0	**Miami, FL** (city) Miami-Dade County	16.2
New Jersey	10.7	San Diego County, CA	0.0	**Los Angeles, CA** (city) Los Angeles County	22.7
Florida	12.4	Somerset County, NJ	0.0	**Philadelphia, PA** (city) Philadelphia County	54.5
Oregon	12.7	Suffolk County, NY	0.0		
Arizona	12.8	Contra Costa County, CA	4.9		
Washington	13.1	Morris County, NJ	6.7		

Note: (1) Ranking tables cover all states and counties, and places with an overall population of at least 125,000, OR an overall population of at least 25,000 where the Hispanic/Latino population is at least 20% of the overall population. In states where less than five places meet either of these criteria, we have included places with at least 10,000 total population with the highest percentage of Hispanic/Latino population. These places are identified with an asterisk (*); Please refer to the User's Guide for a full explanation of data.

Population Age 3–17 Enrolled in Private School

(Universe: Population Age 3–17 Enrolled in School)

Central American: Guatemalan

Top 10 States, Counties, and Places[1]

Sorted by Number in Descending Order — U.S. = 18,054

State	Number	County	Number	Place	Number
California	3,289	Los Angeles County, CA	1,916	**Los Angeles, CA** (city) Los Angeles County	1,102
Florida	1,556	Cook County, IL	858	**Chicago, IL** (city) Cook County	429
Illinois	1,122	Providence County, RI	369	**New York, NY** (city)	411
New York	1,008	Harris County, TX	300	**Houston, TX** (city) Harris County	264
New Jersey	813	Miami-Dade County, FL	282	**Providence, RI** (city) Providence County	253
Texas	722	Suffolk County, NY	262	**Queens, NY** (borough) Queens County	228
Pennsylvania	712	Queens County, NY	228	**San Francisco, CA** (city) San Francisco County	197
Ohio	577	San Francisco County, CA	197	**Islip, NY** (town) Suffolk County	142
Michigan	563	Contra Costa County, CA	192	**Phoenix, AZ** (city) Maricopa County	121
Georgia	552	Maricopa County, AZ	188	**Las Vegas, NV** (city) Clark County	107

Sorted by Number in Ascending Order — U.S. = 18,054

State	Number	County	Number	Place	Number
South Dakota	1	Burke County, NC	0	**Albertville*, AL** (city) Marshall County	0
New Hampshire	18	Caroline County, MD	0	**Alhambra, CA** (city) Los Angeles County	0
Iowa	25	Davidson County, TN	0	**Bell Gardens, CA** (city) Los Angeles County	0
Oklahoma	45	DeKalb County, AL	0	**Bell, CA** (city) Los Angeles County	0
Idaho	48	Douglas County, NE	0	**Burbank, CA** (city) Los Angeles County	0
Nebraska	62	Floyd County, GA	0	**Cathedral City, CA** (city) Riverside County	0
Oregon	70	Fort Bend County, TX	0	**Central Falls*, RI** (city) Providence County	0
Delaware	81	Franklin County, AL	0	**Chillum, MD** (cdp) Prince George's County	0
Mississippi	94	Fresno County, CA	0	**Elizabeth, NJ** (city) Union County	0
Colorado	100	Gilmer County, GA	0	**Gardena, CA** (city) Los Angeles County	0

Sorted by Percent in Descending Order — U.S. = 9.5%

State	Percent	County	Percent	Place	Percent
District of Columbia	61.6	Fulton County, GA	66.2	**Philadelphia, PA** (city) Philadelphia County	51.6
Louisiana	38.7	Jefferson Parish, LA	66.2	**Columbus, OH** (city) Franklin County	40.4
Wisconsin	29.9	Philadelphia County, PA	51.6	**Indianapolis, IN** (city) Marion County	38.9
Pennsylvania	29.3	Morris County, NJ	49.2	**Downey, CA** (city) Los Angeles County	34.8
Mississippi	29.1	Manatee County, FL	43.4	**Central Islip, NY** (cdp) Suffolk County	29.6
Indiana	28.4	Cuyahoga County, OH	42.5	**West Valley City, UT** (city) Salt Lake County	28.8
Ohio	27.3	Marion County, IN	41.5	**Charlotte, NC** (city) Mecklenburg County	27.5
New Mexico	21.6	Franklin County, OH	39.4	**Pawtucket*, RI** (city) Providence County	26.0
Michigan	20.9	Somerset County, NJ	36.1	**Fort Worth, TX** (city) Tarrant County	25.4
Minnesota	19.2	Anne Arundel County, MD	33.7	**Paramount, CA** (city) Los Angeles County	24.8

Sorted by Percent in Ascending Order — U.S. = 9.5%

State	Percent	County	Percent	Place	Percent
South Dakota	0.2	Burke County, NC	0.0	**Albertville*, AL** (city) Marshall County	0.0
Iowa	1.9	Caroline County, MD	0.0	**Alhambra, CA** (city) Los Angeles County	0.0
Oregon	3.1	Davidson County, TN	0.0	**Bell Gardens, CA** (city) Los Angeles County	0.0
Nebraska	3.7	DeKalb County, AL	0.0	**Bell, CA** (city) Los Angeles County	0.0
Oklahoma	3.8	Douglas County, NE	0.0	**Burbank, CA** (city) Los Angeles County	0.0
California	5.1	Floyd County, GA	0.0	**Cathedral City, CA** (city) Riverside County	0.0
Maryland	6.1	Fort Bend County, TX	0.0	**Central Falls*, RI** (city) Providence County	0.0
Tennessee	6.1	Franklin County, AL	0.0	**Chillum, MD** (cdp) Prince George's County	0.0
Nevada	6.8	Fresno County, CA	0.0	**Elizabeth, NJ** (city) Union County	0.0
Texas	6.9	Gilmer County, GA	0.0	**Gardena, CA** (city) Los Angeles County	0.0

Note: (1) Ranking tables cover all states and counties, and places with an overall population of at least 125,000, OR an overall population of at least 25,000 where the Hispanic/Latino population is at least 20% of the overall population. In states where less than five places meet either of these criteria, we have included places with at least 10,000 total population with the highest percentage of Hispanic/Latino population. These places are identified with an asterisk (*); Please refer to the User's Guide for a full explanation of data.

Population Age 3–17 Enrolled in Private School

(Universe: Population Age 3–17 Enrolled in School)

Central American: Honduran

Top 10 States, Counties, and Places[1]

Sorted by Number in Descending Order — U.S. = 6,435

State	Number	County	Number	Place	Number
New York	1,029	Jefferson Parish, LA	475	**New York, NY** (city)	822
Florida	863	Miami-Dade County, FL	422	**Bronx, NY** (borough) Bronx County	411
Louisiana	842	Bronx County, NY	411	**Los Angeles, CA** (city) Los Angeles County	231
California	704	Los Angeles County, CA	341	**Metairie, LA** (cdp) Jefferson Parish	226
Texas	327	Suffolk County, MA	165	**Boston, MA** (city) Suffolk County	165
Massachusetts	281	Mecklenburg County, NC	158	**Manhattan, NY** (borough) New York County	138
New Jersey	248	East Baton Rouge Parish, LA	148	**Brooklyn, NY** (borough) Kings County	133
North Carolina	233	New York County, NY	138	**Charlotte, NC** (city) Mecklenburg County	128
Virginia	129	Kings County, NY	133	**Queens, NY** (borough) Queens County	123
Indiana	111	Queens County, NY	123	**Miami, FL** (city) Miami-Dade County	116

Sorted by Number in Ascending Order — U.S. = 6,435

State	Number	County	Number	Place	Number
Oregon	0	Arapahoe County, CO	0	**Austin, TX** (city) Travis County	0
Wisconsin	0	Atlantic County, NJ	0	**Chelsea, MA** (city) Suffolk County	0
Iowa	6	Beaufort County, SC	0	**Conroe, TX** (city) Montgomery County	0
Washington	10	Bexar County, TX	0	**Durham, NC** (city) Durham County	0
Kentucky	16	Clark County, NV	0	**Fort Worth, TX** (city) Tarrant County	0
Oklahoma	17	Cobb County, GA	0	**Garland, TX** (city) Dallas County	0
Alabama	18	Davidson County, TN	0	**Hempstead (village), NY** (village) Nassau County	0
Arizona	19	DeKalb County, GA	0	**Huntington Station, NY** (cdp) Suffolk County	0
Michigan	23	Denton County, TX	0	**Huntington, NY** (town) Suffolk County	0
District of Columbia	26	Duplin County, NC	0	**Las Vegas, NV** (city) Clark County	0

Sorted by Percent in Descending Order — U.S. = 5.8%

State	Percent	County	Percent	Place	Percent
Mississippi	29.3	East Baton Rouge Parish, LA	42.2	**Aurora, CO** (city) Arapahoe County	32.2
Louisiana	19.5	Osceola County, FL	36.5	**Metairie, LA** (cdp) Jefferson Parish	29.2
Ohio	16.9	San Francisco County, CA	24.3	**Miami Beach, FL** (city) Miami-Dade County	28.7
Colorado	11.8	Saint Tammany Parish, LA	24.0	**San Francisco, CA** (city) San Francisco County	24.3
Arkansas	11.5	Fresno County, CA	22.9	**Boston, MA** (city) Suffolk County	18.3
Missouri	11.2	Jefferson Parish, LA	19.1	**Indianapolis, IN** (city) Marion County	17.2
Utah	10.8	Fulton County, GA	16.9	**Staten Island, NY** (borough) Richmond County	16.0
Indiana	10.3	Fort Bend County, TX	16.7	**North Miami, FL** (city) Miami-Dade County	15.8
Massachusetts	8.7	Marion County, IN	16.1	**Union City, NJ** (city) Hudson County	15.2
Nebraska	8.7	Richmond County, NY	16.0	**Oakland, CA** (city) Alameda County	15.0

Sorted by Percent in Ascending Order — U.S. = 5.8%

State	Percent	County	Percent	Place	Percent
Oregon	0.0	Arapahoe County, CO	0.0	**Austin, TX** (city) Travis County	0.0
Wisconsin	0.0	Atlantic County, NJ	0.0	**Chelsea, MA** (city) Suffolk County	0.0
Washington	1.2	Beaufort County, SC	0.0	**Conroe, TX** (city) Montgomery County	0.0
Iowa	1.7	Bexar County, TX	0.0	**Durham, NC** (city) Durham County	0.0
Texas	2.0	Clark County, NV	0.0	**Fort Worth, TX** (city) Tarrant County	0.0
Arizona	2.7	Cobb County, GA	0.0	**Garland, TX** (city) Dallas County	0.0
Georgia	3.1	Davidson County, TN	0.0	**Hempstead (village), NY** (village) Nassau County	0.0
Virginia	3.3	DeKalb County, GA	0.0	**Huntington Station, NY** (cdp) Suffolk County	0.0
Oklahoma	3.5	Denton County, TX	0.0	**Huntington, NY** (town) Suffolk County	0.0
South Carolina	3.7	Duplin County, NC	0.0	**Las Vegas, NV** (city) Clark County	0.0

Note: (1) Ranking tables cover all states and counties, and places with an overall population of at least 125,000, OR an overall population of at least 25,000 where the Hispanic/Latino population is at least 20% of the overall population. In states where less than five places meet either of these criteria, we have included places with at least 10,000 total population with the highest percentage of Hispanic/Latino population. These places are identified with an asterisk (*); Please refer to the User's Guide for a full explanation of data.

Population Age 3–17 Enrolled in Private School

(Universe: Population Age 3–17 Enrolled in School)

Central American: Nicaraguan

Top 10 States, Counties, and Places[1]

Sorted by Number in Descending Order — U.S. = 6,358

State	Number	County	Number	Place	Number
California	2,146	Miami-Dade County, FL	1,253	**Los Angeles, CA** (city) Los Angeles County	289
Florida	1,623	Los Angeles County, CA	750	**Miami, FL** (city) Miami-Dade County	242
Louisiana	363	San Mateo County, CA	274	**The Hammocks, FL** (cdp) Miami-Dade County	235
Texas	280	Jefferson Parish, LA	268	**Metairie, LA** (cdp) Jefferson Parish	151
Maryland	212	San Bernardino County, CA	165	**New York, NY** (city)	149
New York	181	Riverside County, CA	133	**San Francisco, CA** (city) San Francisco County	118
Ohio	160	Contra Costa County, CA	120	**Hialeah, FL** (city) Miami-Dade County	116
Virginia	134	Orange County, CA	118	**Daly City, CA** (city) San Mateo County	100
Washington	130	San Francisco County, CA	118	**Bronx, NY** (borough) Bronx County	94
North Carolina	126	King County, WA	105	**Fountainebleau, FL** (cdp) Miami-Dade County	76

Sorted by Number in Ascending Order — U.S. = 6,358

State	Number	County	Number	Place	Number
Arizona	0	Collier County, FL	0	**Brooklyn, NY** (borough) Kings County	0
District of Columbia	0	Gwinnett County, GA	0	**Charlotte, NC** (city) Mecklenburg County	0
Minnesota	15	Hudson County, NJ	0	**Fontana, CA** (city) San Bernardino County	0
Missouri	16	Kings County, NY	0	**Hayward, CA** (city) Alameda County	0
Michigan	19	Maricopa County, AZ	0	**Oakland, CA** (city) Alameda County	0
South Carolina	27	Mecklenburg County, NC	0	**Pembroke Pines, FL** (city) Broward County	0
Connecticut	29	Orange County, FL	0	**San Diego, CA** (city) San Diego County	0
Massachusetts	31	San Diego County, CA	0	**South Miami Heights, FL** (cdp) Miami-Dade County	0
Oregon	34	Stanislaus County, CA	0	**West Little River, FL** (cdp) Miami-Dade County	0
Tennessee	35	Hillsborough County, FL	11	**Miramar, FL** (city) Broward County	6

Sorted by Percent in Descending Order — U.S. = 10.8%

State	Percent	County	Percent	Place	Percent
Washington	48.0	King County, WA	65.6	**Metairie, LA** (cdp) Jefferson Parish	87.3
Ohio	46.1	Jefferson Parish, LA	45.7	**The Hammocks, FL** (cdp) Miami-Dade County	37.5
Louisiana	44.4	Prince George's County, MD	23.4	**Bronx, NY** (borough) Bronx County	22.3
Colorado	29.8	Bronx County, NY	22.3	**Richmond, CA** (city) Contra Costa County	22.2
Indiana	25.6	Sonoma County, CA	22.3	**Chicago, IL** (city) Cook County	20.9
Pennsylvania	23.5	San Mateo County, CA	19.3	**Hollywood, FL** (city) Broward County	18.6
Illinois	23.4	Montgomery County, MD	18.9	**South San Francisco, CA** (city) San Mateo County	18.4
Oregon	22.8	Orange County, CA	17.2	**University Park, FL** (cdp) Miami-Dade County	18.1
Maryland	21.6	San Bernardino County, CA	17.0	**Las Vegas, NV** (city) Clark County	16.7
North Carolina	17.2	Riverside County, CA	15.4	**Daly City, CA** (city) San Mateo County	14.3

Sorted by Percent in Ascending Order — U.S. = 10.8%

State	Percent	County	Percent	Place	Percent
Arizona	0.0	Collier County, FL	0.0	**Brooklyn, NY** (borough) Kings County	0.0
District of Columbia	0.0	Gwinnett County, GA	0.0	**Charlotte, NC** (city) Mecklenburg County	0.0
New Jersey	3.9	Hudson County, NJ	0.0	**Fontana, CA** (city) San Bernardino County	0.0
Minnesota	5.4	Kings County, NY	0.0	**Hayward, CA** (city) Alameda County	0.0
Nevada	5.7	Maricopa County, AZ	0.0	**Oakland, CA** (city) Alameda County	0.0
Missouri	6.5	Mecklenburg County, NC	0.0	**Pembroke Pines, FL** (city) Broward County	0.0
Florida	7.0	Orange County, FL	0.0	**San Diego, CA** (city) San Diego County	0.0
Massachusetts	7.0	San Diego County, CA	0.0	**South Miami Heights, FL** (cdp) Miami-Dade County	0.0
Michigan	8.3	Stanislaus County, CA	0.0	**West Little River, FL** (cdp) Miami-Dade County	0.0
Virginia	8.3	Hillsborough County, FL	2.2	**Miramar, FL** (city) Broward County	2.3

Note: (1) Ranking tables cover all states and counties, and places with an overall population of at least 125,000, OR an overall population of at least 25,000 where the Hispanic/Latino population is at least 20% of the overall population. In states where less than five places meet either of these criteria, we have included places with at least 10,000 total population with the highest percentage of Hispanic/Latino population. These places are identified with an asterisk (*); Please refer to the User's Guide for a full explanation of data.

Population Age 3–17 Enrolled in Private School

(Universe: Population Age 3–17 Enrolled in School)

Central American: Panamanian

Top 10 States, Counties, and Places[1]

Sorted by Number in Descending Order — U.S. = 3,884

State	Number	County	Number	Place	Number
California	487	Los Angeles County, CA	197	**New York, NY** (city)	257
Florida	446	Kings County, NY	166	**Brooklyn, NY** (borough) Kings County	166
New York	442	Miami-Dade County, FL	141	**Hempstead (town), NY** (town) Nassau County	86
Texas	348	Nassau County, NY	86	**Queens, NY** (borough) Queens County	49
Maryland	256	Hillsborough County, FL	71	**Bronx, NY** (borough) Bronx County	42
New Jersey	229	Bexar County, TX	64	**Fayetteville, NC** (city) Cumberland County	36
Georgia	185	San Bernardino County, CA	52	**San Antonio, TX** (city) Bexar County	35
Illinois	153	Queens County, NY	49	**Los Angeles, CA** (city) Los Angeles County	31
Ohio	131	Hudson County, NJ	47	**Killeen, TX** (city) Bell County	23
Virginia	130	Cumberland County, NC	44	**San Diego, CA** (city) San Diego County	6

Sorted by Number in Ascending Order — U.S. = 3,884

State	Number	County	Number	Place	Number
Arizona	0	Duval County, FL	0	**Houston, TX** (city) Harris County	0
Minnesota	0	Maricopa County, AZ	0	**Jacksonville, FL** (city) Duval County	0
Mississippi	0	Montgomery County, MD	0	**Manhattan, NY** (borough) New York County	0
New Mexico	9	New York County, NY	0	**Miami, FL** (city) Miami-Dade County	0
Indiana	12	Pierce County, WA	0	**San Diego, CA** (city) San Diego County	6
Michigan	14	Sacramento County, CA	0	**Killeen, TX** (city) Bell County	23
Connecticut	18	Riverside County, CA	7	**Los Angeles, CA** (city) Los Angeles County	31
South Carolina	21	Harris County, TX	11	**San Antonio, TX** (city) Bexar County	35
Nevada	26	Essex County, NJ	13	**Fayetteville, NC** (city) Cumberland County	36
Louisiana	41	Fairfax County, VA	14	**Bronx, NY** (borough) Bronx County	42

Sorted by Percent in Descending Order — U.S. = 12.9%

State	Percent	County	Percent	Place	Percent
Kentucky	42.4	Hudson County, NJ	36.2	**Los Angeles, CA** (city) Los Angeles County	28.7
Oklahoma	35.9	Brevard County, FL	34.8	**Hempstead (town), NY** (town) Nassau County	25.1
Louisiana	33.3	Orange County, CA	31.4	**San Antonio, TX** (city) Bexar County	18.8
Maryland	32.7	Cook County, IL	30.1	**Fayetteville, NC** (city) Cumberland County	14.3
Illinois	28.8	Los Angeles County, CA	27.5	**Queens, NY** (borough) Queens County	12.8
Tennessee	28.8	Nassau County, NY	25.1	**Killeen, TX** (city) Bell County	9.4
Wisconsin	26.9	Palm Beach County, FL	19.9	**Bronx, NY** (borough) Bronx County	7.5
Ohio	25.0	Prince George's County, MD	17.1	**Brooklyn, NY** (borough) Kings County	7.0
Alabama	22.8	Dallas County, TX	16.7	**New York, NY** (city)	7.0
Colorado	21.8	Bexar County, TX	14.3	**San Diego, CA** (city) San Diego County	1.7

Sorted by Percent in Ascending Order — U.S. = 12.9%

State	Percent	County	Percent	Place	Percent
Arizona	0.0	Duval County, FL	0.0	**Houston, TX** (city) Harris County	0.0
Minnesota	0.0	Maricopa County, AZ	0.0	**Jacksonville, FL** (city) Duval County	0.0
Mississippi	0.0	Montgomery County, MD	0.0	**Manhattan, NY** (borough) New York County	0.0
New Mexico	3.2	New York County, NY	0.0	**Miami, FL** (city) Miami-Dade County	0.0
Michigan	3.7	Pierce County, WA	0.0	**San Diego, CA** (city) San Diego County	1.7
South Carolina	4.9	Sacramento County, CA	0.0	**Brooklyn, NY** (borough) Kings County	7.0
Connecticut	6.9	Orange County, FL	2.7	**New York, NY** (city)	7.0
Washington	6.9	Harris County, TX	4.2	**Bronx, NY** (borough) Bronx County	7.5
Pennsylvania	7.5	Riverside County, CA	6.7	**Killeen, TX** (city) Bell County	9.4
North Carolina	8.2	Kings County, NY	7.0	**Queens, NY** (borough) Queens County	12.8

Note: (1) Ranking tables cover all states and counties, and places with an overall population of at least 125,000, OR an overall population of at least 25,000 where the Hispanic/Latino population is at least 20% of the overall population. In states where less than five places meet either of these criteria, we have included places with at least 10,000 total population with the highest percentage of Hispanic/Latino population. These places are identified with an asterisk (*); Please refer to the User's Guide for a full explanation of data.

Population Age 3–17 Enrolled in Private School

(Universe: Population Age 3–17 Enrolled in School)

Central American: Salvadoran

Top 10 States, Counties, and Places[1]

Sorted by Number in Descending Order U.S. = 15,573

State	Number	County	Number	Place	Number
California	6,816	Los Angeles County, CA	3,798	**Los Angeles, CA** (city) Los Angeles County	2,169
New York	1,445	San Mateo County, CA	521	**New York, NY** (city)	709
Virginia	1,281	Fairfax County, VA	427	**San Francisco, CA** (city) San Francisco County	348
Texas	1,208	Harris County, TX	419	**Hempstead (town), NY** (town) Nassau County	263
Maryland	1,105	Montgomery County, MD	416	**Queens, NY** (borough) Queens County	255
New Jersey	522	San Francisco County, CA	348	**Brooklyn, NY** (borough) Kings County	235
Florida	460	Orange County, CA	338	**Houston, TX** (city) Harris County	174
Illinois	258	Prince George's County, MD	325	**Islip, NY** (town) Suffolk County	143
Massachusetts	232	Contra Costa County, CA	322	**Hawthorne, CA** (city) Los Angeles County	134
Alabama	189	Nassau County, NY	295	**Brookhaven, NY** (town) Suffolk County	126

Sorted by Number in Ascending Order U.S. = 15,573

State	Number	County	Number	Place	Number
Idaho	0	Alamance County, NC	0	**Anaheim, CA** (city) Orange County	0
Iowa	0	Atlantic County, NJ	0	**Bakersfield, CA** (city) Kern County	0
Kentucky	0	Benton County, AR	0	**Bell Gardens, CA** (city) Los Angeles County	0
South Carolina	0	Cache County, UT	0	**Bellflower, CA** (city) Los Angeles County	0
Tennessee	0	Cobb County, GA	0	**Bridgeport, CT** (city/town) Fairfield County	0
Kansas	8	Crawford County, AR	0	**Carrollton, TX** (city) Denton County	0
New Mexico	9	Dakota County, MN	0	**Carson, CA** (city) Los Angeles County	0
Minnesota	14	Davidson County, TN	0	**Chillum, MD** (cdp) Prince George's County	0
Oklahoma	16	DeKalb County, GA	0	**Corona, CA** (city) Riverside County	0
Nebraska	26	Douglas County, NE	0	**Costa Mesa, CA** (city) Orange County	0

Sorted by Percent in Descending Order U.S. = 4.7%

State	Percent	County	Percent	Place	Percent
Alabama	38.2	Lake County, IL	26.5	**Fullerton, CA** (city) Orange County	50.8
Michigan	22.5	Hartford County, CT	25.6	**Paterson, NJ** (city) Passaic County	34.2
Louisiana	20.4	Passaic County, NJ	21.1	**Alhambra, CA** (city) Los Angeles County	31.6
Hawaii	17.9	Stafford County, VA	20.3	**Concord, CA** (city) Contra Costa County	26.5
Alaska	17.0	San Mateo County, CA	17.2	**San Diego, CA** (city) San Diego County	26.4
Missouri	15.4	Utah County, UT	16.1	**Baltimore, MD** (independent city)	25.0
Wisconsin	14.4	Camden County, NJ	15.4	**Richmond, VA** (independent city)	24.2
Connecticut	12.8	Kings County, NY	15.1	**Springfield, VA** (cdp) Fairfax County	23.5
Illinois	11.0	Sonoma County, CA	15.1	**San Mateo, CA** (city) San Mateo County	22.0
Utah	8.4	New York County, NY	14.5	**Whittier, CA** (city) Los Angeles County	20.3

Sorted by Percent in Ascending Order U.S. = 4.7%

State	Percent	County	Percent	Place	Percent
Idaho	0.0	Alamance County, NC	0.0	**Anaheim, CA** (city) Orange County	0.0
Iowa	0.0	Atlantic County, NJ	0.0	**Bakersfield, CA** (city) Kern County	0.0
Kentucky	0.0	Benton County, AR	0.0	**Bell Gardens, CA** (city) Los Angeles County	0.0
South Carolina	0.0	Cache County, UT	0.0	**Bellflower, CA** (city) Los Angeles County	0.0
Tennessee	0.0	Cobb County, GA	0.0	**Bridgeport, CT** (city/town) Fairfield County	0.0
Minnesota	0.8	Crawford County, AR	0.0	**Carrollton, TX** (city) Denton County	0.0
Kansas	0.9	Dakota County, MN	0.0	**Carson, CA** (city) Los Angeles County	0.0
Arkansas	1.3	Davidson County, TN	0.0	**Chillum, MD** (cdp) Prince George's County	0.0
Nevada	1.7	DeKalb County, GA	0.0	**Corona, CA** (city) Riverside County	0.0
North Carolina	1.8	Douglas County, NE	0.0	**Costa Mesa, CA** (city) Orange County	0.0

Note: (1) Ranking tables cover all states and counties, and places with an overall population of at least 125,000, OR an overall population of at least 25,000 where the Hispanic/Latino population is at least 20% of the overall population. In states where less than five places meet either of these criteria, we have included places with at least 10,000 total population with the highest percentage of Hispanic/Latino population. These places are identified with an asterisk (*); Please refer to the User's Guide for a full explanation of data.

Population Age 3–17 Enrolled in Private School

(Universe: Population Age 3–17 Enrolled in School)

Cuban

Top 10 States, Counties, and Places[1]

Sorted by Number in Descending Order U.S. = 50,835

State	Number	County	Number	Place	Number
Florida	32,539	Miami-Dade County, FL	21,244	**Miami, FL** (city) Miami-Dade County	2,002
California	3,062	Broward County, FL	3,686	**Kendall, FL** (cdp) Miami-Dade County	1,690
New York	2,500	Hillsborough County, FL	1,721	**Coral Gables, FL** (city) Miami-Dade County	1,592
New Jersey	2,310	Los Angeles County, CA	1,306	**Hialeah, FL** (city) Miami-Dade County	1,386
Illinois	1,141	Palm Beach County, FL	1,265	**New York, NY** (city)	1,357
Georgia	997	Queens County, NY	798	**Tamiami, FL** (cdp) Miami-Dade County	828
Texas	910	Brevard County, FL	473	**Queens, NY** (borough) Queens County	798
Virginia	724	DuPage County, IL	470	**Kendale Lakes, FL** (cdp) Miami-Dade County	763
Louisiana	673	Hudson County, NJ	469	**Pembroke Pines, FL** (city) Broward County	679
Maryland	600	Orange County, FL	464	**Miami Lakes, FL** (town) Miami-Dade County	612

Sorted by Number in Ascending Order U.S. = 50,835

State	Number	County	Number	Place	Number
Arkansas	0	Clay County, FL	0	**Atlanta, GA** (city) Fulton County	0
West Virginia	10	Clay County, MO	0	**Bell, CA** (city) Los Angeles County	0
Utah	12	Henry County, GA	0	**Boston, MA** (city) Suffolk County	0
Nebraska	30	Indian River County, FL	0	**Columbus, OH** (city) Franklin County	0
Hawaii	40	Kern County, CA	0	**Greenacres, FL** (city) Palm Beach County	0
Missouri	43	Lancaster County, PA	0	**Kearny, NJ** (town) Hudson County	0
New Hampshire	46	Lehigh County, PA	0	**Newark, NJ** (city) Essex County	0
Kansas	57	Pierce County, WA	0	**San Antonio, TX** (city) Bexar County	0
Maine	58	Suffolk County, MA	0	**Syracuse, NY** (city) Onondaga County	0
Mississippi	70	Franklin County, OH	4	**University, FL** (cdp) Hillsborough County	0

Sorted by Percent in Descending Order U.S. = 18.8%

State	Percent	County	Percent	Place	Percent
Delaware	53.1	Orleans Parish, LA	100.0	**Metairie, LA** (cdp) Jefferson Parish	100.0
District of Columbia	44.0	Saint Johns County, FL	64.5	**New Orleans, LA** (city) Orleans Parish	100.0
Louisiana	40.7	New Castle County, DE	63.9	**Glendale, CA** (city) Los Angeles County	72.6
Oklahoma	34.6	DeKalb County, GA	60.5	**Carrollwood, FL** (cdp) Hillsborough County	70.5
Maryland	33.7	Prince George's County, MD	59.8	**Coral Gables, FL** (city) Miami-Dade County	64.5
Maine	31.4	East Baton Rouge Parish, LA	59.5	**Kenner, LA** (city) Jefferson Parish	56.9
Indiana	28.7	Jefferson Parish, LA	58.2	**Royal Palm Beach, FL** (village) Palm Beach County	54.9
Rhode Island	27.3	Lake County, FL	51.0	**Baltimore, MD** (independent city)	48.8
Iowa	26.1	Queens County, NY	45.3	**Tallahassee, FL** (city) Leon County	48.7
New York	24.7	Essex County, NJ	42.9	**North Hempstead, NY** (town) Nassau County	45.7

Sorted by Percent in Ascending Order U.S. = 18.8%

State	Percent	County	Percent	Place	Percent
Arkansas	0.0	Clay County, FL	0.0	**Atlanta, GA** (city) Fulton County	0.0
Utah	2.9	Clay County, MO	0.0	**Bell, CA** (city) Los Angeles County	0.0
West Virginia	5.1	Henry County, GA	0.0	**Boston, MA** (city) Suffolk County	0.0
Missouri	6.0	Indian River County, FL	0.0	**Columbus, OH** (city) Franklin County	0.0
Kentucky	6.4	Kern County, CA	0.0	**Greenacres, FL** (city) Palm Beach County	0.0
Tennessee	7.7	Lancaster County, PA	0.0	**Kearny, NJ** (town) Hudson County	0.0
Nevada	9.4	Lehigh County, PA	0.0	**Newark, NJ** (city) Essex County	0.0
Arizona	9.6	Pierce County, WA	0.0	**San Antonio, TX** (city) Bexar County	0.0
Nebraska	9.6	Suffolk County, MA	0.0	**Syracuse, NY** (city) Onondaga County	0.0
Pennsylvania	9.6	Franklin County, OH	1.2	**University, FL** (cdp) Hillsborough County	0.0

Note: (1) Ranking tables cover all states and counties, and places with an overall population of at least 125,000, OR an overall population of at least 25,000 where the Hispanic/Latino population is at least 20% of the overall population. In states where less than five places meet either of these criteria, we have included places with at least 10,000 total population with the highest percentage of Hispanic/Latino population. These places are identified with an asterisk (*); Please refer to the User's Guide for a full explanation of data.

Population Age 3–17 Enrolled in Private School

(Universe: Population Age 3–17 Enrolled in School)

Dominican Republic

Top 10 States, Counties, and Places[1]

Sorted by Number in Descending Order — U.S. = 25,638

State	Number	County	Number	Place	Number
New York	13,728	Bronx County, NY	5,824	**New York, NY** (city)	11,724
New Jersey	2,829	New York County, NY	2,865	**Bronx, NY** (borough) Bronx County	5,824
Florida	2,461	Queens County, NY	1,945	**Manhattan, NY** (borough) New York County	2,865
Massachusetts	1,924	Essex County, MA	958	**Queens, NY** (borough) Queens County	1,945
Pennsylvania	808	Kings County, NY	875	**Brooklyn, NY** (borough) Kings County	875
Rhode Island	678	Miami-Dade County, FL	815	**Lawrence, MA** (city) Essex County	689
Connecticut	410	Hudson County, NJ	727	**Boston, MA** (city) Suffolk County	611
Virginia	276	Suffolk County, MA	669	**Providence, RI** (city) Providence County	499
Maryland	261	Providence County, RI	609	**Hempstead (town), NY** (town) Nassau County	358
Georgia	252	Nassau County, NY	548	**Philadelphia, PA** (city) Philadelphia County	307

Sorted by Number in Ascending Order — U.S. = 25,638

State	Number	County	Number	Place	Number
Alaska	6	Atlantic County, NJ	0	**Alafaya, FL** (cdp) Orange County	0
Delaware	10	Bexar County, TX	0	**Anchorage, AK** (municipality)	0
Missouri	15	Lackawanna County, PA	0	**Atlantic City, NJ** (city) Atlantic County	0
Minnesota	21	Marion County, FL	0	**Bayonne, NJ** (city) Hudson County	0
Alabama	23	Mercer County, NJ	0	**Bethlehem, PA** (city) Northampton County	0
Utah	28	Monroe County, PA	0	**Buenaventura Lakes, FL** (cdp) Osceola County	0
Colorado	29	New London County, CT	0	**Cape Coral, FL** (city) Lee County	0
Washington	52	Oneida County, NY	0	**Central Falls*, RI** (city) Providence County	0
South Carolina	54	Plymouth County, MA	0	**Columbus, OH** (city) Franklin County	0
District of Columbia	64	Sullivan County, NY	0	**Country Club, FL** (cdp) Miami-Dade County	0

Sorted by Percent in Descending Order — U.S. = 8.3%

State	Percent	County	Percent	Place	Percent
Tennessee	33.6	Pasco County, FL	38.3	**North Hempstead, NY** (town) Nassau County	37.3
Michigan	23.5	Erie County, NY	37.2	**Grand Rapids, MI** (city) Kent County	29.7
Minnesota	23.3	Ulster County, NY	31.4	**Plantation, FL** (city) Broward County	28.7
Nevada	20.9	Kent County, MI	26.6	**Richmond West, FL** (cdp) Miami-Dade County	23.0
Indiana	19.6	Clark County, NV	24.7	**West New York, NJ** (town) Hudson County	22.3
Louisiana	18.6	Fairfax County, VA	23.2	**Cranston*, RI** (city) Providence County	21.5
New Hampshire	17.7	Ocean County, NJ	22.4	**Pennsauken, NJ** (township) Camden County	20.7
Wisconsin	16.5	Duval County, FL	20.3	**Jacksonville, FL** (city) Duval County	20.3
South Carolina	15.4	Orange County, NY	20.0	**Garfield, NJ** (city) Bergen County	20.2
Virginia	13.7	San Diego County, CA	17.6	**Ramapo, NY** (town) Rockland County	20.0

Sorted by Percent in Ascending Order — U.S. = 8.3%

State	Percent	County	Percent	Place	Percent
Alaska	1.5	Atlantic County, NJ	0.0	**Alafaya, FL** (cdp) Orange County	0.0
Texas	3.1	Bexar County, TX	0.0	**Anchorage, AK** (municipality)	0.0
Delaware	4.1	Lackawanna County, PA	0.0	**Atlantic City, NJ** (city) Atlantic County	0.0
Missouri	4.4	Marion County, FL	0.0	**Bayonne, NJ** (city) Hudson County	0.0
North Carolina	5.4	Mercer County, NJ	0.0	**Bethlehem, PA** (city) Northampton County	0.0
Pennsylvania	5.7	Monroe County, PA	0.0	**Buenaventura Lakes, FL** (cdp) Osceola County	0.0
Georgia	6.4	New London County, CT	0.0	**Cape Coral, FL** (city) Lee County	0.0
Connecticut	6.7	Oneida County, NY	0.0	**Central Falls*, RI** (city) Providence County	0.0
New Jersey	6.7	Plymouth County, MA	0.0	**Columbus, OH** (city) Franklin County	0.0
Rhode Island	6.7	Sullivan County, NY	0.0	**Country Club, FL** (cdp) Miami-Dade County	0.0

Note: (1) Ranking tables cover all states and counties, and places with an overall population of at least 125,000, OR an overall population of at least 25,000 where the Hispanic/Latino population is at least 20% of the overall population. In states where less than five places meet either of these criteria, we have included places with at least 10,000 total population with the highest percentage of Hispanic/Latino population. These places are identified with an asterisk (*); Please refer to the User's Guide for a full explanation of data.

Population Age 3–17 Enrolled in Private School

(Universe: Population Age 3–17 Enrolled in School)

Mexican

Top 10 States, Counties, and Places[1]

Sorted by Number in Descending Order — U.S. = 413,757

State	Number	County	Number	Place	Number
California	153,722	Los Angeles County, CA	53,683	**Los Angeles, CA** (city) Los Angeles County	16,393
Texas	84,079	Cook County, IL	19,754	**Chicago, IL** (city) Cook County	12,445
Illinois	29,575	Bexar County, TX	15,020	**San Antonio, TX** (city) Bexar County	11,793
Arizona	18,276	San Diego County, CA	12,592	**Houston, TX** (city) Harris County	6,001
Colorado	9,321	Orange County, CA	11,893	**El Paso, TX** (city) El Paso County	5,538
Florida	7,718	Harris County, TX	11,750	**Phoenix, AZ** (city) Maricopa County	4,469
New Mexico	7,519	Riverside County, CA	9,768	**Dallas, TX** (city) Dallas County	4,409
Michigan	6,677	San Bernardino County, CA	9,673	**San Diego, CA** (city) San Diego County	3,986
Indiana	6,592	Maricopa County, AZ	9,645	**San Jose, CA** (city) Santa Clara County	3,763
Washington	6,560	Dallas County, TX	8,070	**Chula Vista, CA** (city) San Diego County	3,383

Sorted by Number in Ascending Order — U.S. = 413,757

State	Number	County	Number	Place	Number
Vermont	60	Accomack County, VA	0	**Albertville*, AL** (city) Marshall County	0
South Dakota	95	Adair County, OK	0	**Allentown, PA** (city) Lehigh County	0
Maine	115	Adams County, NE	0	**Altus*, OK** (city) Jackson County	0
Rhode Island	118	Adams County, WI	0	**Apopka, FL** (city) Orange County	0
North Dakota	148	Aiken County, SC	0	**Asheboro, NC** (city) Randolph County	0
New Hampshire	167	Alexander County, NC	0	**Aspen Hill, MD** (cdp) Montgomery County	0
West Virginia	209	Allen Parish, LA	0	**Bayonne, NJ** (city) Hudson County	0
District of Columbia	232	Anderson County, TN	0	**Berea*, SC** (cdp) Greenville County	0
Delaware	328	Andrews County, TX	0	**Biloxi*, MS** (city) Harrison County	0
Alaska	554	Antrim County, MI	0	**Bluffton*, SC** (town) Beaufort County	0

Sorted by Percent in Descending Order — U.S. = 5.1%

State	Percent	County	Percent	Place	Percent
District of Columbia	16.9	Union County, PA	88.0	**Coral Gables, FL** (city) Miami-Dade County	72.4
Hawaii	14.9	Saint Mary Parish, LA	78.6	**Mobile, AL** (city) Mobile County	48.9
Ohio	12.5	Johnson County, NE	44.4	**Cleveland, OH** (city) Cuyahoga County	39.8
Maryland	11.4	Midland County, MI	39.7	**Pittsburgh, PA** (city) Allegheny County	37.3
Montana	11.1	Douglas County, KS	38.7	**Grand Forks*, ND** (city) Grand Forks County	33.3
Alaska	10.8	Tompkins County, NY	37.9	**Kenner, LA** (city) Jefferson Parish	33.1
Louisiana	10.6	Buffalo County, WI	36.4	**Weston, FL** (city) Broward County	31.2
Massachusetts	10.3	Menominee County, MI	35.4	**Metairie, LA** (cdp) Jefferson Parish	28.9
Pennsylvania	10.2	Webster County, IA	34.4	**Ramapo, NY** (town) Rockland County	28.8
West Virginia	10.2	Lee County, IA	34.1	**Great Falls*, MT** (city) Cascade County	28.3

Sorted by Percent in Ascending Order — U.S. = 5.1%

State	Percent	County	Percent	Place	Percent
South Dakota	2.5	Accomack County, VA	0.0	**Albertville*, AL** (city) Marshall County	0.0
Nevada	2.8	Adair County, OK	0.0	**Allentown, PA** (city) Lehigh County	0.0
North Carolina	3.0	Adams County, NE	0.0	**Altus*, OK** (city) Jackson County	0.0
Georgia	3.5	Adams County, WI	0.0	**Apopka, FL** (city) Orange County	0.0
South Carolina	3.5	Aiken County, SC	0.0	**Asheboro, NC** (city) Randolph County	0.0
Arkansas	4.0	Alexander County, NC	0.0	**Aspen Hill, MD** (cdp) Montgomery County	0.0
Arizona	4.2	Allen Parish, LA	0.0	**Bayonne, NJ** (city) Hudson County	0.0
Oklahoma	4.2	Anderson County, TN	0.0	**Berea*, SC** (cdp) Greenville County	0.0
Texas	4.2	Andrews County, TX	0.0	**Biloxi*, MS** (city) Harrison County	0.0
Washington	4.2	Antrim County, MI	0.0	**Bluffton*, SC** (town) Beaufort County	0.0

Note: (1) Ranking tables cover all states and counties, and places with an overall population of at least 125,000, OR an overall population of at least 25,000 where the Hispanic/Latino population is at least 20% of the overall population. In states where less than five places meet either of these criteria, we have included places with at least 10,000 total population with the highest percentage of Hispanic/Latino population. These places are identified with an asterisk (*); Please refer to the User's Guide for a full explanation of data.

Population Age 3–17 Enrolled in Private School

(Universe: Population Age 3–17 Enrolled in School)

Puerto Rican

Top 10 States, Counties, and Places[1]

Sorted by Number in Descending Order — U.S. = 110,897

State	Number	County	Number	Place	Number
New York	29,255	Bronx County, NY	9,726	**New York, NY** (city)	21,204
Florida	17,370	Philadelphia County, PA	4,776	**Bronx, NY** (borough) Bronx County	9,726
New Jersey	10,630	Queens County, NY	3,876	**Philadelphia, PA** (city) Philadelphia County	4,776
Pennsylvania	9,707	Cook County, IL	3,392	**Queens, NY** (borough) Queens County	3,876
Illinois	4,796	Kings County, NY	3,038	**Brooklyn, NY** (borough) Kings County	3,038
California	4,770	Miami-Dade County, FL	2,854	**Chicago, IL** (city) Cook County	2,750
Connecticut	3,829	New York County, NY	2,670	**Manhattan, NY** (borough) New York County	2,670
Massachusetts	3,784	Orange County, FL	2,645	**Staten Island, NY** (borough) Richmond County	1,894
Ohio	3,740	Broward County, FL	2,331	**Cleveland, OH** (city) Cuyahoga County	1,306
Texas	2,594	Richmond County, NY	1,894	**Boston, MA** (city) Suffolk County	857

Sorted by Number in Ascending Order — U.S. = 110,897

State	Number	County	Number	Place	Number
Montana	0	Adams County, CO	0	**Akron, OH** (city) Summit County	0
Wyoming	0	Butte County, CA	0	**Alexandria, VA** (independent city)	0
Idaho	6	Cecil County, MD	0	**Central Falls*, RI** (city) Providence County	0
Alaska	11	Charleston County, SC	0	**Columbia, SC** (city) Richland County	0
South Dakota	26	Christian County, KY	0	**Elmont, NY** (cdp) Nassau County	0
Iowa	39	Cochise County, AZ	0	**Fairfield, CA** (city) Solano County	0
Vermont	39	Columbia County, FL	0	**Fitchburg, MA** (city) Worcester County	0
District of Columbia	81	Coryell County, TX	0	**Fort Hood, TX** (cdp) Bell County	0
Arkansas	102	Craven County, NC	0	**Fountainebleau, FL** (cdp) Miami-Dade County	0
North Dakota	103	Dale County, AL	0	**Fresno, CA** (city) Fresno County	0

Sorted by Percent in Descending Order — U.S. = 10.0%

State	Percent	County	Percent	Place	Percent
Louisiana	27.8	Adams County, PA	56.1	**Coral Gables, FL** (city) Miami-Dade County	57.5
North Dakota	27.8	Harrison County, MS	53.3	**Seattle, WA** (city) King County	44.8
Maine	23.8	Marion County, OR	47.0	**Kendale Lakes, FL** (cdp) Miami-Dade County	43.1
District of Columbia	21.7	Saint Mary's County, MD	45.6	**Tamiami, FL** (cdp) Miami-Dade County	42.4
New Mexico	20.5	Lowndes County, GA	43.5	**Huntsville, AL** (city) Madison County	39.3
Nebraska	18.6	Carroll County, MD	42.9	**Dania Beach, FL** (city) Broward County	38.7
West Virginia	18.2	Butler County, OH	39.2	**Plano, TX** (city) Collin County	37.5
Tennessee	17.5	Jefferson Parish, LA	37.9	**Montgomery, AL** (city) Montgomery County	37.4
Oregon	17.1	Montgomery County, AL	37.4	**Fort Lauderdale, FL** (city) Broward County	35.3
Mississippi	16.6	Newport County, RI	37.2	**Lancaster, CA** (city) Los Angeles County	34.5

Sorted by Percent in Ascending Order — U.S. = 10.0%

State	Percent	County	Percent	Place	Percent
Montana	0.0	Adams County, CO	0.0	**Akron, OH** (city) Summit County	0.0
Wyoming	0.0	Butte County, CA	0.0	**Alexandria, VA** (independent city)	0.0
Alaska	0.8	Cecil County, MD	0.0	**Central Falls*, RI** (city) Providence County	0.0
Idaho	0.9	Charleston County, SC	0.0	**Columbia, SC** (city) Richland County	0.0
Iowa	3.5	Christian County, KY	0.0	**Elmont, NY** (cdp) Nassau County	0.0
Massachusetts	5.2	Cochise County, AZ	0.0	**Fairfield, CA** (city) Solano County	0.0
Connecticut	5.5	Columbia County, FL	0.0	**Fitchburg, MA** (city) Worcester County	0.0
Nevada	5.7	Coryell County, TX	0.0	**Fort Hood, TX** (cdp) Bell County	0.0
Arizona	6.3	Craven County, NC	0.0	**Fountainebleau, FL** (cdp) Miami-Dade County	0.0
Vermont	6.5	Dale County, AL	0.0	**Fresno, CA** (city) Fresno County	0.0

Note: (1) Ranking tables cover all states and counties, and places with an overall population of at least 125,000, OR an overall population of at least 25,000 where the Hispanic/Latino population is at least 20% of the overall population. In states where less than five places meet either of these criteria, we have included places with at least 10,000 total population with the highest percentage of Hispanic/Latino population. These places are identified with an asterisk (*); Please refer to the User's Guide for a full explanation of data.

Population Age 3–17 Enrolled in Private School

(Universe: Population Age 3–17 Enrolled in School)

South American

Top 10 States, Counties, and Places[1]

Sorted by Number in Descending Order — U.S. = 76,510

State	Number	County	Number	Place	Number
Florida	16,816	Miami-Dade County, FL	6,344	**New York, NY** (city)	8,828
New York	12,804	Queens County, NY	5,027	**Queens, NY** (borough) Queens County	5,027
California	9,105	Broward County, FL	4,172	**Manhattan, NY** (borough) New York County	1,245
New Jersey	6,109	Los Angeles County, CA	3,508	**Los Angeles, CA** (city) Los Angeles County	1,171
Texas	3,619	Cook County, IL	1,486	**Bronx, NY** (borough) Bronx County	1,019
Illinois	2,799	Westchester County, NY	1,304	**Brooklyn, NY** (borough) Kings County	979
Virginia	2,661	Palm Beach County, FL	1,280	**Chicago, IL** (city) Cook County	830
Maryland	2,196	New York County, NY	1,245	**Doral, FL** (city) Miami-Dade County	806
Georgia	2,005	Fairfax County, VA	1,214	**Weston, FL** (city) Broward County	706
Pennsylvania	1,742	Harris County, TX	1,210	**Houston, TX** (city) Harris County	646

Sorted by Number in Ascending Order — U.S. = 76,510

State	Number	County	Number	Place	Number
West Virginia	0	Adams County, CO	0	**Arlington, TX** (city) Tarrant County	0
Wyoming	0	Butler County, OH	0	**Aspen Hill, MD** (cdp) Montgomery County	0
Montana	13	Cache County, UT	0	**Bay Shore, NY** (cdp) Suffolk County	0
North Dakota	16	Cherokee County, GA	0	**Brandon, FL** (cdp) Hillsborough County	0
Alaska	39	Clark County, WA	0	**Chesapeake, VA** (independent city)	0
Vermont	42	Clarke County, GA	0	**Daly City, CA** (city) San Mateo County	0
Maine	51	Cumberland County, NJ	0	**Deltona, FL** (city) Volusia County	0
Iowa	76	Gaston County, NC	0	**Fremont, CA** (city) Alameda County	0
Mississippi	86	Hampshire County, MA	0	**Garfield, NJ** (city) Bergen County	0
New Mexico	95	Macomb County, MI	0	**Glendale, AZ** (city) Maricopa County	0

Sorted by Percent in Descending Order — U.S. = 15.0%

State	Percent	County	Percent	Place	Percent
Louisiana	35.8	Leon County, FL	74.2	**Tallahassee, FL** (city) Leon County	76.9
Hawaii	32.1	East Baton Rouge Parish, LA	69.0	**Coral Gables, FL** (city) Miami-Dade County	62.9
Missouri	29.5	Kent County, MI	45.8	**Pasadena, CA** (city) Los Angeles County	60.4
Kansas	29.3	Hamilton County, TN	45.4	**Overland Park, KS** (city) Johnson County	50.5
Ohio	28.8	Erie County, NY	45.1	**Rahway, NJ** (city) Union County	44.5
Kentucky	27.4	Allegheny County, PA	44.1	**New Orleans, LA** (city) Orleans Parish	42.9
Arkansas	26.8	Orange County, NC	43.4	**Plantation, FL** (city) Broward County	40.0
Wisconsin	26.0	Orleans Parish, LA	42.9	**Atlanta, GA** (city) Fulton County	39.9
District of Columbia	24.3	San Luis Obispo County, CA	42.9	**Springfield, MA** (city) Hampden County	39.4
Tennessee	24.1	Jefferson County, KY	42.0	**Metairie, LA** (cdp) Jefferson Parish	39.0

Sorted by Percent in Ascending Order — U.S. = 15.0%

State	Percent	County	Percent	Place	Percent
West Virginia	0.0	Adams County, CO	0.0	**Arlington, TX** (city) Tarrant County	0.0
Wyoming	0.0	Butler County, OH	0.0	**Aspen Hill, MD** (cdp) Montgomery County	0.0
Alaska	6.4	Cache County, UT	0.0	**Bay Shore, NY** (cdp) Suffolk County	0.0
Utah	7.3	Cherokee County, GA	0.0	**Brandon, FL** (cdp) Hillsborough County	0.0
Montana	7.9	Clark County, WA	0.0	**Chesapeake, VA** (independent city)	0.0
Iowa	9.8	Clarke County, GA	0.0	**Daly City, CA** (city) San Mateo County	0.0
New Mexico	9.9	Cumberland County, NJ	0.0	**Deltona, FL** (city) Volusia County	0.0
Oklahoma	10.0	Gaston County, NC	0.0	**Fremont, CA** (city) Alameda County	0.0
New Jersey	10.2	Hampshire County, MA	0.0	**Garfield, NJ** (city) Bergen County	0.0
Maine	10.6	Macomb County, MI	0.0	**Glendale, AZ** (city) Maricopa County	0.0

Note: (1) Ranking tables cover all states and counties, and places with an overall population of at least 125,000, OR an overall population of at least 25,000 where the Hispanic/Latino population is at least 20% of the overall population. In states where less than five places meet either of these criteria, we have included places with at least 10,000 total population with the highest percentage of Hispanic/Latino population. These places are identified with an asterisk (*); Please refer to the User's Guide for a full explanation of data.

Population Age 3–17 Enrolled in Private School

(Universe: Population Age 3–17 Enrolled in School)

South American: Argentinean

Top 10 States, Counties, and Places[1]

Sorted by Number in Descending Order — U.S. = 7,330

State	Number	County	Number	Place	Number
California	1,577	Miami-Dade County, FL	774	**New York, NY** (city)	415
Florida	1,511	Los Angeles County, CA	503	**Los Angeles, CA** (city) Los Angeles County	220
New York	709	Broward County, FL	357	**Manhattan, NY** (borough) New York County	183
New Jersey	586	Montgomery County, MD	207	**Brooklyn, NY** (borough) Kings County	141
Maryland	373	Fairfax County, VA	202	**Queens, NY** (borough) Queens County	65
Texas	341	New York County, NY	183	**Aventura, FL** (city) Miami-Dade County	64
Georgia	276	Hudson County, NJ	144	**Chicago, IL** (city) Cook County	61
Virginia	233	Kings County, NY	141	**Miami, FL** (city) Miami-Dade County	61
Massachusetts	228	Maricopa County, AZ	134	**Pembroke Pines, FL** (city) Broward County	58
Arizona	167	Orange County, CA	127	**Doral, FL** (city) Miami-Dade County	50

Sorted by Number in Ascending Order — U.S. = 7,330

State	Number	County	Number	Place	Number
Missouri	0	Dallas County, TX	0	**Coral Springs, FL** (city) Broward County	0
Tennessee	0	Montgomery County, TX	0	**Hialeah, FL** (city) Miami-Dade County	0
Washington	23	Orange County, NY	0	**Bronx, NY** (borough) Bronx County	14
Indiana	26	Passaic County, NJ	0	**Miami Beach, FL** (city) Miami-Dade County	14
Ohio	28	Alameda County, CA	10	**San Diego, CA** (city) San Diego County	17
Nevada	32	Travis County, TX	10	**San Francisco, CA** (city) San Francisco County	18
South Carolina	34	Bexar County, TX	12	**San Jose, CA** (city) Santa Clara County	29
Louisiana	45	Utah County, UT	12	**Hempstead (town), NY** (town) Nassau County	30
North Carolina	52	King County, WA	13	**Hollywood, FL** (city) Broward County	37
Colorado	53	Bronx County, NY	14	**Houston, TX** (city) Harris County	46

Sorted by Percent in Descending Order — U.S. = 20.4%

State	Percent	County	Percent	Place	Percent
District of Columbia	76.1	New York County, NY	50.4	**Manhattan, NY** (borough) New York County	50.4
Georgia	40.6	Maricopa County, AZ	42.4	**San Diego, CA** (city) San Diego County	30.9
Arizona	37.8	San Diego County, CA	41.3	**Pembroke Pines, FL** (city) Broward County	30.7
Minnesota	36.5	New Haven County, CT	39.2	**Houston, TX** (city) Harris County	27.2
Massachusetts	35.3	Montgomery County, MD	38.2	**Brooklyn, NY** (borough) Kings County	26.9
Louisiana	32.4	Riverside County, CA	37.2	**Chicago, IL** (city) Cook County	26.0
Maryland	30.4	Hudson County, NJ	36.0	**New York, NY** (city)	24.0
Wisconsin	28.4	Santa Clara County, CA	34.8	**San Jose, CA** (city) Santa Clara County	22.7
Michigan	27.0	Hillsborough County, FL	32.4	**Aventura, FL** (city) Miami-Dade County	21.3
Oregon	25.5	Fairfax County, VA	30.2	**San Francisco, CA** (city) San Francisco County	21.2

Sorted by Percent in Ascending Order — U.S. = 20.4%

State	Percent	County	Percent	Place	Percent
Missouri	0.0	Dallas County, TX	0.0	**Coral Springs, FL** (city) Broward County	0.0
Tennessee	0.0	Montgomery County, TX	0.0	**Hialeah, FL** (city) Miami-Dade County	0.0
Utah	4.2	Orange County, NY	0.0	**Miami Beach, FL** (city) Miami-Dade County	2.5
Nevada	7.4	Passaic County, NJ	0.0	**Miami, FL** (city) Miami-Dade County	6.9
North Carolina	7.4	Utah County, UT	3.0	**Queens, NY** (borough) Queens County	9.8
Indiana	10.1	Alameda County, CA	4.0	**Bronx, NY** (borough) Bronx County	14.6
Washington	11.4	Lee County, FL	5.3	**Hollywood, FL** (city) Broward County	17.1
Illinois	11.9	Ventura County, CA	5.6	**Doral, FL** (city) Miami-Dade County	17.4
South Carolina	12.5	Suffolk County, NY	5.8	**Los Angeles, CA** (city) Los Angeles County	18.6
Connecticut	13.8	Travis County, TX	7.0	**Hempstead (town), NY** (town) Nassau County	20.8

Note: (1) Ranking tables cover all states and counties, and places with an overall population of at least 125,000, OR an overall population of at least 25,000 where the Hispanic/Latino population is at least 20% of the overall population. In states where less than five places meet either of these criteria, we have included places with at least 10,000 total population with the highest percentage of Hispanic/Latino population. These places are identified with an asterisk (*); Please refer to the User's Guide for a full explanation of data.

Population Age 3–17 Enrolled in Private School

(Universe: Population Age 3–17 Enrolled in School)

South American: Bolivian

Top 10 States, Counties, and Places[1]

Sorted by Number in Descending Order — U.S. = 3,235

State	Number	County	Number	Place	Number
New York	554	Queens County, NY	417	**New York, NY** (city)	457
Virginia	549	Fairfax County, VA	252	**Queens, NY** (borough) Queens County	417
California	459	Los Angeles County, CA	180	**Arlington, VA** (cdp) Arlington County	121
Florida	211	Arlington County, VA	121	**Annandale, VA** (cdp) Fairfax County	90
Maryland	142	Miami-Dade County, FL	86	**Los Angeles, CA** (city) Los Angeles County	44
Massachusetts	125	Orange County, CA	61	**West Falls Church, VA** (cdp) Fairfax County	41
Illinois	120	Loudoun County, VA	56	**Springfield, VA** (cdp) Fairfax County	30
Texas	72	Montgomery County, MD	55	**Dale City, VA** (cdp) Prince William County	10
North Carolina	55	Prince George's County, MD	50	**Providence, RI** (city) Providence County	0
Pennsylvania	23	Santa Clara County, CA	30		

Sorted by Number in Ascending Order — U.S. = 3,235

State	Number	County	Number	Place	Number
Rhode Island	14	Broward County, FL	0	**Providence, RI** (city) Providence County	0
New Jersey	16	Cook County, IL	0	**Dale City, VA** (cdp) Prince William County	10
Pennsylvania	23	Harris County, TX	0	**Springfield, VA** (cdp) Fairfax County	30
North Carolina	55	Palm Beach County, FL	0	**West Falls Church, VA** (cdp) Fairfax County	41
Texas	72	Providence County, RI	14	**Los Angeles, CA** (city) Los Angeles County	44
Illinois	120	San Diego County, CA	27	**Annandale, VA** (cdp) Fairfax County	90
Massachusetts	125	Prince William County, VA	28	**Arlington, VA** (cdp) Arlington County	121
Maryland	142	Santa Clara County, CA	30	**Queens, NY** (borough) Queens County	417
Florida	211	Prince George's County, MD	50	**New York, NY** (city)	457
California	459	Montgomery County, MD	55		

Sorted by Percent in Descending Order — U.S. = 16.4%

State	Percent	County	Percent	Place	Percent
North Carolina	42.3	Queens County, NY	57.3	**Queens, NY** (borough) Queens County	57.3
New York	38.6	Prince George's County, MD	28.4	**New York, NY** (city)	51.1
Massachusetts	28.2	San Diego County, CA	23.9	**Springfield, VA** (cdp) Fairfax County	26.3
Illinois	24.0	Los Angeles County, CA	20.6	**Arlington, VA** (cdp) Arlington County	16.6
Pennsylvania	24.0	Miami-Dade County, FL	18.0	**West Falls Church, VA** (cdp) Fairfax County	16.3
California	18.8	Orange County, CA	17.8	**Annandale, VA** (cdp) Fairfax County	13.1
Maryland	11.9	Arlington County, VA	16.6	**Los Angeles, CA** (city) Los Angeles County	7.6
Florida	11.4	Loudoun County, VA	12.0	**Dale City, VA** (cdp) Prince William County	3.5
Texas	8.6	Santa Clara County, CA	11.2	**Providence, RI** (city) Providence County	0.0
Virginia	8.2	Fairfax County, VA	7.2		

Sorted by Percent in Ascending Order — U.S. = 16.4%

State	Percent	County	Percent	Place	Percent
Rhode Island	3.0	Broward County, FL	0.0	**Providence, RI** (city) Providence County	0.0
New Jersey	3.1	Cook County, IL	0.0	**Dale City, VA** (cdp) Prince William County	3.5
Virginia	8.2	Harris County, TX	0.0	**Los Angeles, CA** (city) Los Angeles County	7.6
Texas	8.6	Palm Beach County, FL	0.0	**Annandale, VA** (cdp) Fairfax County	13.1
Florida	11.4	Prince William County, VA	2.4	**West Falls Church, VA** (cdp) Fairfax County	16.3
Maryland	11.9	Providence County, RI	3.0	**Arlington, VA** (cdp) Arlington County	16.6
California	18.8	Montgomery County, MD	6.2	**Springfield, VA** (cdp) Fairfax County	26.3
Illinois	24.0	Fairfax County, VA	7.2	**New York, NY** (city)	51.1
Pennsylvania	24.0	Santa Clara County, CA	11.2	**Queens, NY** (borough) Queens County	57.3
Massachusetts	28.2	Loudoun County, VA	12.0		

Note: (1) Ranking tables cover all states and counties, and places with an overall population of at least 125,000, OR an overall population of at least 25,000 where the Hispanic/Latino population is at least 20% of the overall population. In states where less than five places meet either of these criteria, we have included places with at least 10,000 total population with the highest percentage of Hispanic/Latino population. These places are identified with an asterisk (*); Please refer to the User's Guide for a full explanation of data.

Population Age 3–17 Enrolled in Private School

(Universe: Population Age 3–17 Enrolled in School)

South American: Chilean

Top 10 States, Counties, and Places[1]

Sorted by Number in Descending Order — U.S. = 4,048

State	Number	County	Number	Place	Number
California	801	San Diego County, CA	285	**New York, NY** (city)	254
Florida	552	Miami-Dade County, FL	249	**Queens, NY** (borough) Queens County	167
New Jersey	373	Los Angeles County, CA	169	**Manhattan, NY** (borough) New York County	44
New York	363	Queens County, NY	167	**Los Angeles, CA** (city) Los Angeles County	27
Texas	203	Broward County, FL	136	**Brooklyn, NY** (borough) Kings County	25
Virginia	153	San Bernardino County, CA	112	**Miami, FL** (city) Miami-Dade County	24
Illinois	119	Bergen County, NJ	100	**Chicago, IL** (city) Cook County	21
Georgia	106	Hudson County, NJ	95	**Kendall, FL** (cdp) Miami-Dade County	16
Arizona	105	Harris County, TX	75	**Hempstead (town), NY** (town) Nassau County	14
Maryland	103	Maricopa County, AZ	50		

Sorted by Number in Ascending Order — U.S. = 4,048

State	Number	County	Number	Place	Number
Oregon	0	Salt Lake County, UT	0	**Hempstead (town), NY** (town) Nassau County	14
Minnesota	19	San Mateo County, CA	0	**Kendall, FL** (cdp) Miami-Dade County	16
Wisconsin	20	Santa Clara County, CA	13	**Chicago, IL** (city) Cook County	21
Connecticut	25	Nassau County, NY	14	**Miami, FL** (city) Miami-Dade County	24
Utah	29	Riverside County, CA	14	**Brooklyn, NY** (borough) Kings County	25
Missouri	38	Alameda County, CA	16	**Los Angeles, CA** (city) Los Angeles County	27
Colorado	52	Clark County, NV	17	**Manhattan, NY** (borough) New York County	44
Massachusetts	54	Suffolk County, NY	17	**Queens, NY** (borough) Queens County	167
Michigan	54	Kings County, NY	25	**New York, NY** (city)	254
Nevada	54	Utah County, UT	29		

Sorted by Percent in Descending Order — U.S. = 18.0%

State	Percent	County	Percent	Place	Percent
Tennessee	79.2	San Diego County, CA	51.3	**Queens, NY** (borough) Queens County	40.6
Arizona	41.2	Bergen County, NJ	44.1	**Chicago, IL** (city) Cook County	38.2
Ohio	36.8	Queens County, NY	40.6	**Manhattan, NY** (borough) New York County	32.8
New Jersey	25.9	Maricopa County, AZ	40.0	**New York, NY** (city)	28.1
Texas	22.5	Harris County, TX	37.1	**Miami, FL** (city) Miami-Dade County	17.4
Virginia	21.9	New York County, NY	32.8	**Brooklyn, NY** (borough) Kings County	9.5
Washington	21.9	Cook County, IL	29.4	**Hempstead (town), NY** (town) Nassau County	7.2
North Carolina	21.3	San Bernardino County, CA	28.6	**Kendall, FL** (cdp) Miami-Dade County	6.3
California	19.0	Broward County, FL	27.8	**Los Angeles, CA** (city) Los Angeles County	4.9
Illinois	18.2	Hudson County, NJ	27.2		

Sorted by Percent in Ascending Order — U.S. = 18.0%

State	Percent	County	Percent	Place	Percent
Oregon	0.0	Salt Lake County, UT	0.0	**Los Angeles, CA** (city) Los Angeles County	4.9
Utah	5.4	San Mateo County, CA	0.0	**Kendall, FL** (cdp) Miami-Dade County	6.3
Wisconsin	7.6	Nassau County, NY	3.4	**Hempstead (town), NY** (town) Nassau County	7.2
Connecticut	8.1	Suffolk County, NY	5.4	**Brooklyn, NY** (borough) Kings County	9.5
Massachusetts	9.5	Riverside County, CA	6.0	**Miami, FL** (city) Miami-Dade County	17.4
Minnesota	10.3	Alameda County, CA	6.5	**New York, NY** (city)	28.1
Maryland	11.0	Santa Clara County, CA	7.2	**Manhattan, NY** (borough) New York County	32.8
Georgia	11.4	Utah County, UT	7.7	**Chicago, IL** (city) Cook County	38.2
New York	14.4	Montgomery County, MD	9.4	**Queens, NY** (borough) Queens County	40.6
Missouri	16.1	Kings County, NY	9.5		

Note: (1) Ranking tables cover all states and counties, and places with an overall population of at least 125,000, OR an overall population of at least 25,000 where the Hispanic/Latino population is at least 20% of the overall population. In states where less than five places meet either of these criteria, we have included places with at least 10,000 total population with the highest percentage of Hispanic/Latino population. These places are identified with an asterisk (*); Please refer to the User's Guide for a full explanation of data.

Population Age 3–17 Enrolled in Private School

(Universe: Population Age 3–17 Enrolled in School)

South American: Colombian

Top 10 States, Counties, and Places[1]

Sorted by Number in Descending Order — U.S. = 24,831

State	Number	County	Number	Place	Number
Florida	7,037	Miami-Dade County, FL	2,395	**New York, NY** (city)	2,591
New York	3,619	Broward County, FL	1,880	**Queens, NY** (borough) Queens County	1,513
California	1,921	Queens County, NY	1,513	**Manhattan, NY** (borough) New York County	395
New Jersey	1,669	Los Angeles County, CA	911	**Houston, TX** (city) Harris County	314
Texas	1,532	Palm Beach County, FL	664	**Staten Island, NY** (borough) Richmond County	314
Pennsylvania	943	Harris County, TX	605	**Pembroke Pines, FL** (city) Broward County	308
Georgia	842	Orange County, FL	521	**Doral, FL** (city) Miami-Dade County	273
Massachusetts	722	New York County, NY	395	**Weston, FL** (city) Broward County	258
Illinois	631	Hudson County, NJ	338	**Philadelphia, PA** (city) Philadelphia County	256
Ohio	559	Nassau County, NY	317	**Brooklyn, NY** (borough) Kings County	255

Sorted by Number in Ascending Order — U.S. = 24,831

State	Number	County	Number	Place	Number
Delaware	0	Burlington County, NJ	0	**Bergenfield, NJ** (borough) Bergen County	0
Oklahoma	5	Cherokee County, GA	0	**Brandon, FL** (cdp) Hillsborough County	0
Alaska	18	Lehigh County, PA	0	**Burbank, CA** (city) Los Angeles County	0
New Mexico	18	Northampton County, PA	0	**Deltona, FL** (city) Volusia County	0
Iowa	36	Sacramento County, CA	0	**Egypt Lake-Leto, FL** (cdp) Hillsborough County	0
District of Columbia	45	Sarasota County, FL	0	**Garfield, NJ** (city) Bergen County	0
New Hampshire	54	Ulster County, NY	0	**Hackensack, NJ** (city) Bergen County	0
Utah	67	Volusia County, FL	0	**Hallandale Beach, FL** (city) Broward County	0
Nebraska	68	Dane County, WI	4	**Hartford, CT** (city/town) Hartford County	0
Arkansas	76	Luzerne County, PA	10	**Long Beach, CA** (city) Los Angeles County	0

Sorted by Percent in Descending Order — U.S. = 14.6%

State	Percent	County	Percent	Place	Percent
Kentucky	44.1	Leon County, FL	81.3	**Tallahassee, FL** (city) Leon County	93.1
Alabama	36.0	Hampden County, MA	67.6	**Coral Gables, FL** (city) Miami-Dade County	71.2
Nebraska	36.0	New York County, NY	50.1	**North Miami Beach, FL** (city) Miami-Dade County	56.3
Ohio	36.0	Richmond County, NY	47.6	**West Palm Beach, FL** (city) Palm Beach County	53.6
Louisiana	34.9	DeKalb County, GA	39.9	**Manhattan, NY** (borough) New York County	50.1
Arkansas	32.8	Erie County, NY	39.6	**Staten Island, NY** (borough) Richmond County	47.6
Missouri	28.5	Bucks County, PA	38.3	**Anaheim, CA** (city) Orange County	44.3
Indiana	27.5	Philadelphia County, PA	36.4	**Downey, CA** (city) Los Angeles County	37.7
Michigan	26.0	San Francisco County, CA	36.2	**Las Vegas, NV** (city) Clark County	36.5
Pennsylvania	25.3	Fulton County, GA	32.1	**Philadelphia, PA** (city) Philadelphia County	36.4

Sorted by Percent in Ascending Order — U.S. = 14.6%

State	Percent	County	Percent	Place	Percent
Delaware	0.0	Burlington County, NJ	0.0	**Bergenfield, NJ** (borough) Bergen County	0.0
Oklahoma	3.3	Cherokee County, GA	0.0	**Brandon, FL** (cdp) Hillsborough County	0.0
South Carolina	6.4	Lehigh County, PA	0.0	**Burbank, CA** (city) Los Angeles County	0.0
New Hampshire	6.7	Northampton County, PA	0.0	**Deltona, FL** (city) Volusia County	0.0
Arizona	7.1	Sacramento County, CA	0.0	**Egypt Lake-Leto, FL** (cdp) Hillsborough County	0.0
New Jersey	8.9	Sarasota County, FL	0.0	**Garfield, NJ** (city) Bergen County	0.0
Nevada	11.4	Ulster County, NY	0.0	**Hackensack, NJ** (city) Bergen County	0.0
Utah	12.1	Volusia County, FL	0.0	**Hallandale Beach, FL** (city) Broward County	0.0
Washington	12.4	Middlesex County, NJ	1.7	**Hartford, CT** (city/town) Hartford County	0.0
Connecticut	12.5	Greenville County, SC	1.9	**Long Beach, CA** (city) Los Angeles County	0.0

Note: (1) Ranking tables cover all states and counties, and places with an overall population of at least 125,000, OR an overall population of at least 25,000 where the Hispanic/Latino population is at least 20% of the overall population. In states where less than five places meet either of these criteria, we have included places with at least 10,000 total population with the highest percentage of Hispanic/Latino population. These places are identified with an asterisk (*); Please refer to the User's Guide for a full explanation of data.

Population Age 3–17 Enrolled in Private School

(Universe: Population Age 3–17 Enrolled in School)

South American: Ecuadorian

Top 10 States, Counties, and Places[1]

Sorted by Number in Descending Order — U.S. = 12,191

State	Number	County	Number	Place	Number
New York	4,778	Queens County, NY	1,740	**New York, NY** (city)	3,347
New Jersey	1,617	Bronx County, NY	796	**Queens, NY** (borough) Queens County	1,740
California	1,070	Cook County, IL	685	**Bronx, NY** (borough) Bronx County	796
Florida	1,067	Essex County, NJ	567	**Newark, NJ** (city) Essex County	421
Illinois	822	Los Angeles County, CA	530	**Chicago, IL** (city) Cook County	388
Virginia	441	Suffolk County, NY	406	**Manhattan, NY** (borough) New York County	371
Connecticut	370	Westchester County, NY	404	**Brooklyn, NY** (borough) Kings County	297
Texas	250	New York County, NY	371	**Yonkers, NY** (city) Westchester County	264
Pennsylvania	238	Broward County, FL	328	**Islip, NY** (town) Suffolk County	189
Maryland	194	Miami-Dade County, FL	326	**Hempstead (town), NY** (town) Nassau County	180

Sorted by Number in Ascending Order — U.S. = 12,191

State	Number	County	Number	Place	Number
Colorado	0	Berks County, PA	0	**Allentown, PA** (city) Lehigh County	0
Missouri	0	Burlington County, NJ	0	**Babylon, NY** (town) Suffolk County	0
Iowa	7	Dallas County, TX	0	**Charlotte, NC** (city) Mecklenburg County	0
Michigan	10	Lehigh County, PA	0	**City of Orange, NJ** (township) Essex County	0
Tennessee	15	Mecklenburg County, NC	0	**Clifton, NJ** (city) Passaic County	0
Ohio	23	Mercer County, NJ	0	**Kearny, NJ** (town) Hudson County	0
Wisconsin	25	Osceola County, FL	0	**Miami, FL** (city) Miami-Dade County	0
Rhode Island	29	Philadelphia County, PA	0	**Miramar, FL** (city) Broward County	0
Utah	32	Pinellas County, FL	0	**New Haven, CT** (city/town) New Haven County	0
South Carolina	36	Riverside County, CA	0	**Paterson, NJ** (city) Passaic County	0

Sorted by Percent in Descending Order — U.S. = 11.4%

State	Percent	County	Percent	Place	Percent
Louisiana	77.7	King County, WA	58.5	**Hollywood, FL** (city) Broward County	49.0
Oregon	70.5	Dutchess County, NY	28.6	**Yonkers, NY** (city) Westchester County	37.5
Washington	32.5	Fairfax County, VA	27.8	**Downey, CA** (city) Los Angeles County	36.1
Kansas	32.3	Richmond County, NY	24.7	**Oyster Bay, NY** (town) Nassau County	33.9
Virginia	26.3	Prince George's County, MD	24.2	**Houston, TX** (city) Harris County	30.7
Indiana	26.0	Maricopa County, AZ	21.2	**Staten Island, NY** (borough) Richmond County	24.7
Illinois	17.2	Bronx County, NY	18.5	**Bronx, NY** (borough) Bronx County	18.5
California	16.3	Orange County, NY	18.4	**Pembroke Pines, FL** (city) Broward County	18.2
Nevada	16.3	Worcester County, MA	18.4	**Central Islip, NY** (cdp) Suffolk County	17.4
Oklahoma	15.5	Cook County, IL	18.0	**Brentwood, NY** (cdp) Suffolk County	17.1

Sorted by Percent in Ascending Order — U.S. = 11.4%

State	Percent	County	Percent	Place	Percent
Colorado	0.0	Berks County, PA	0.0	**Allentown, PA** (city) Lehigh County	0.0
Missouri	0.0	Burlington County, NJ	0.0	**Babylon, NY** (town) Suffolk County	0.0
North Carolina	2.7	Dallas County, TX	0.0	**Charlotte, NC** (city) Mecklenburg County	0.0
Michigan	3.4	Lehigh County, PA	0.0	**City of Orange, NJ** (township) Essex County	0.0
Utah	4.8	Mecklenburg County, NC	0.0	**Clifton, NJ** (city) Passaic County	0.0
Ohio	5.0	Mercer County, NJ	0.0	**Kearny, NJ** (town) Hudson County	0.0
Iowa	5.1	Osceola County, FL	0.0	**Miami, FL** (city) Miami-Dade County	0.0
Massachusetts	7.1	Philadelphia County, PA	0.0	**Miramar, FL** (city) Broward County	0.0
Tennessee	7.3	Pinellas County, FL	0.0	**New Haven, CT** (city/town) New Haven County	0.0
New Jersey	8.2	Riverside County, CA	0.0	**Paterson, NJ** (city) Passaic County	0.0

Note: (1) Ranking tables cover all states and counties, and places with an overall population of at least 125,000, OR an overall population of at least 25,000 where the Hispanic/Latino population is at least 20% of the overall population. In states where less than five places meet either of these criteria, we have included places with at least 10,000 total population with the highest percentage of Hispanic/Latino population. These places are identified with an asterisk (*); Please refer to the User's Guide for a full explanation of data.

Population Age 3–17 Enrolled in Private School

(Universe: Population Age 3–17 Enrolled in School)

South American: Paraguayan

Top 10 States, Counties, and Places[1]

Sorted by Number in Descending Order — U.S. = 992

State	Number	County	Number	Place	Number
Florida	146	Queens County, NY	54	**New York, NY** (city)	65
New Jersey	112	Westchester County, NY	13	**Queens, NY** (borough) Queens County	54
New York	86				
Texas	50				
Maryland	15				
California	8				

Sorted by Number in Ascending Order — U.S. = 992

State	Number	County	Number	Place	Number
California	8	Westchester County, NY	13	**Queens, NY** (borough) Queens County	54
Maryland	15	Queens County, NY	54	**New York, NY** (city)	65
Texas	50				
New York	86				
New Jersey	112				
Florida	146				

Sorted by Percent in Descending Order — U.S. = 22.6%

State	Percent	County	Percent	Place	Percent
Texas	55.6	Queens County, NY	14.3	**Queens, NY** (borough) Queens County	14.3
Florida	52.3	Westchester County, NY	3.0	**New York, NY** (city)	12.1
New Jersey	25.7				
New York	6.7				
Maryland	6.3				
California	5.0				

Sorted by Percent in Ascending Order — U.S. = 22.6%

State	Percent	County	Percent	Place	Percent
California	5.0	Westchester County, NY	3.0	**New York, NY** (city)	12.1
Maryland	6.3	Queens County, NY	14.3	**Queens, NY** (borough) Queens County	14.3
New York	6.7				
New Jersey	25.7				
Florida	52.3				
Texas	55.6				

Note: (1) Ranking tables cover all states and counties, and places with an overall population of at least 125,000, OR an overall population of at least 25,000 where the Hispanic/Latino population is at least 20% of the overall population. In states where less than five places meet either of these criteria, we have included places with at least 10,000 total population with the highest percentage of Hispanic/Latino population. These places are identified with an asterisk (*); Please refer to the User's Guide for a full explanation of data.

Population Age 3–17 Enrolled in Private School

(Universe: Population Age 3–17 Enrolled in School)

South American: Peruvian

Top 10 States, Counties, and Places[1]

Sorted by Number in Descending Order — U.S. = 14,152

State	Number	County	Number	Place	Number
California	2,665	Los Angeles County, CA	914	**New York, NY** (city)	1,233
Florida	2,397	Queens County, NY	855	**Queens, NY** (borough) Queens County	855
New York	1,783	Miami-Dade County, FL	682	**Los Angeles, CA** (city) Los Angeles County	314
New Jersey	1,382	Passaic County, NJ	591	**Chicago, IL** (city) Cook County	203
Maryland	672	Broward County, FL	544	**Paterson, NJ** (city) Passaic County	179
Illinois	651	Contra Costa County, CA	411	**Brooklyn, NY** (borough) Kings County	171
Virginia	643	Fairfax County, VA	333	**Clifton, NJ** (city) Passaic County	132
Texas	512	Westchester County, NY	264	**Port Chester, NY** (village) Westchester County	108
Connecticut	467	Montgomery County, MD	254	**Rye, NY** (town) Westchester County	108
Wisconsin	363	Cook County, IL	238	**Concord, CA** (city) Contra Costa County	101

Sorted by Number in Ascending Order — U.S. = 14,152

State	Number	County	Number	Place	Number
Delaware	0	Arlington County, VA	0	**Anaheim, CA** (city) Orange County	0
Louisiana	5	Collier County, FL	0	**Arlington, VA** (cdp) Arlington County	0
Alabama	19	Denver County, CO	0	**Austin, TX** (city) Travis County	0
District of Columbia	19	Maricopa County, AZ	0	**Brentwood, NY** (cdp) Suffolk County	0
New Mexico	21	Mecklenburg County, NC	0	**Cape Coral, FL** (city) Lee County	0
Kentucky	37	Osceola County, FL	0	**Charlotte, NC** (city) Mecklenburg County	0
Arizona	38	Travis County, TX	0	**Denver, CO** (city) Denver County	0
Hawaii	47	Collin County, TX	8	**Downey, CA** (city) Los Angeles County	0
Idaho	49	Prince George's County, MD	9	**Fort Lauderdale, FL** (city) Broward County	0
Michigan	50	Atlantic County, NJ	11	**Kendall West, FL** (cdp) Miami-Dade County	0

Sorted by Percent in Descending Order — U.S. = 15.0%

State	Percent	County	Percent	Place	Percent
Missouri	56.6	Duval County, FL	77.5	**Jacksonville, FL** (city) Duval County	72.6
Wisconsin	45.5	Baltimore County, MD	54.4	**Orlando, FL** (city) Orange County	59.6
Kansas	39.4	New Haven County, CT	51.9	**Port Chester, NY** (village) Westchester County	45.8
Illinois	31.9	Seminole County, FL	39.4	**Concord, CA** (city) Contra Costa County	43.9
Tennessee	30.6	Contra Costa County, CA	38.9	**Rye, NY** (town) Westchester County	41.4
Washington	29.2	New York County, NY	33.8	**Davie, FL** (town) Broward County	35.8
South Carolina	26.4	Morris County, NJ	33.3	**Manhattan, NY** (borough) New York County	33.8
Hawaii	25.8	Lake County, IL	30.4	**Miami Beach, FL** (city) Miami-Dade County	31.0
Kentucky	23.1	New London County, CT	30.2	**Doral, FL** (city) Miami-Dade County	30.7
Maryland	22.6	Philadelphia County, PA	29.2	**Tampa, FL** (city) Hillsborough County	29.6

Sorted by Percent in Ascending Order — U.S. = 15.0%

State	Percent	County	Percent	Place	Percent
Delaware	0.0	Arlington County, VA	0.0	**Anaheim, CA** (city) Orange County	0.0
Louisiana	2.4	Collier County, FL	0.0	**Arlington, VA** (cdp) Arlington County	0.0
Arizona	3.8	Denver County, CO	0.0	**Austin, TX** (city) Travis County	0.0
New Mexico	5.1	Maricopa County, AZ	0.0	**Brentwood, NY** (cdp) Suffolk County	0.0
Nevada	7.0	Mecklenburg County, NC	0.0	**Cape Coral, FL** (city) Lee County	0.0
Alabama	7.6	Osceola County, FL	0.0	**Charlotte, NC** (city) Mecklenburg County	0.0
North Carolina	9.1	Travis County, TX	0.0	**Denver, CO** (city) Denver County	0.0
Colorado	9.3	Gwinnett County, GA	1.8	**Downey, CA** (city) Los Angeles County	0.0
Massachusetts	9.6	Collin County, TX	2.0	**Fort Lauderdale, FL** (city) Broward County	0.0
Idaho	10.0	Atlantic County, NJ	2.4	**Kendall West, FL** (cdp) Miami-Dade County	0.0

Note: (1) Ranking tables cover all states and counties, and places with an overall population of at least 125,000, OR an overall population of at least 25,000 where the Hispanic/Latino population is at least 20% of the overall population. In states where less than five places meet either of these criteria, we have included places with at least 10,000 total population with the highest percentage of Hispanic/Latino population. These places are identified with an asterisk (*); Please refer to the User's Guide for a full explanation of data.

Population Age 3–17 Enrolled in Private School

(Universe: Population Age 3–17 Enrolled in School)

South American: Uruguayan

Top 10 States, Counties, and Places[1]

Sorted by Number in Descending Order — U.S. = 1,188

State	Number	County	Number	Place	Number
New York	246	Westchester County, NY	91	**New York, NY** (city)	141
Florida	135	Los Angeles County, CA	86	**Queens, NY** (borough) Queens County	40
New Jersey	132	Miami-Dade County, FL	70	**Elizabeth, NJ** (city) Union County	0
California	98	Middlesex County, NJ	43		
Massachusetts	83	Queens County, NY	40		
Virginia	77	Harris County, TX	33		
Texas	53	Essex County, NJ	26		
Maryland	13	Worcester County, MA	25		
Georgia	8	Palm Beach County, FL	15		
Pennsylvania	0	Morris County, NJ	9		

Sorted by Number in Ascending Order — U.S. = 1,188

State	Number	County	Number	Place	Number
Pennsylvania	0	Broward County, FL	0	**Elizabeth, NJ** (city) Union County	0
Georgia	8	Gwinnett County, GA	0	**Queens, NY** (borough) Queens County	40
Maryland	13	Hudson County, NJ	0	**New York, NY** (city)	141
Texas	53	Union County, NJ	0		
Virginia	77	Morris County, NJ	9		
Massachusetts	83	Palm Beach County, FL	15		
California	98	Worcester County, MA	25		
New Jersey	132	Essex County, NJ	26		
Florida	135	Harris County, TX	33		
New York	246	Queens County, NY	40		

Sorted by Percent in Descending Order — U.S. = 12.1%

State	Percent	County	Percent	Place	Percent
New York	25.7	Los Angeles County, CA	38.7	**New York, NY** (city)	41.3
California	20.0	Queens County, NY	34.2	**Queens, NY** (borough) Queens County	34.2
Massachusetts	19.5	Westchester County, NY	29.8	**Elizabeth, NJ** (city) Union County	0.0
Virginia	18.6	Middlesex County, NJ	20.6		
Texas	10.9	Harris County, TX	10.0		
New Jersey	6.2	Worcester County, MA	7.7		
Florida	5.8	Essex County, NJ	7.5		
Maryland	5.0	Miami-Dade County, FL	5.9		
Georgia	1.6	Morris County, NJ	4.8		
Pennsylvania	0.0	Palm Beach County, FL	4.0		

Sorted by Percent in Ascending Order — U.S. = 12.1%

State	Percent	County	Percent	Place	Percent
Pennsylvania	0.0	Broward County, FL	0.0	**Elizabeth, NJ** (city) Union County	0.0
Georgia	1.6	Gwinnett County, GA	0.0	**Queens, NY** (borough) Queens County	34.2
Maryland	5.0	Hudson County, NJ	0.0	**New York, NY** (city)	41.3
Florida	5.8	Union County, NJ	0.0		
New Jersey	6.2	Palm Beach County, FL	4.0		
Texas	10.9	Morris County, NJ	4.8		
Virginia	18.6	Miami-Dade County, FL	5.9		
Massachusetts	19.5	Essex County, NJ	7.5		
California	20.0	Worcester County, MA	7.7		
New York	25.7	Harris County, TX	10.0		

Note: (1) Ranking tables cover all states and counties, and places with an overall population of at least 125,000, OR an overall population of at least 25,000 where the Hispanic/Latino population is at least 20% of the overall population. In states where less than five places meet either of these criteria, we have included places with at least 10,000 total population with the highest percentage of Hispanic/Latino population. These places are identified with an asterisk (*); Please refer to the User's Guide for a full explanation of data.

Population Age 3–17 Enrolled in Private School

(Universe: Population Age 3–17 Enrolled in School)

South American: Venezuelan

Top 10 States, Counties, and Places[1]

Sorted by Number in Descending Order — U.S. = 7,143

State	Number	County	Number	Place	Number
Florida	3,460	Miami-Dade County, FL	1,706	**Doral, FL** (city) Miami-Dade County	355
Texas	543	Broward County, FL	751	**Weston, FL** (city) Broward County	296
New York	372	Orange County, FL	206	**New York, NY** (city)	215
Georgia	307	Harris County, TX	203	**Miami Beach, FL** (city) Miami-Dade County	134
California	237	Palm Beach County, FL	143	**Miami, FL** (city) Miami-Dade County	111
Maryland	190	Cobb County, GA	135	**Queens, NY** (borough) Queens County	102
Ohio	182	Fairfield County, CT	132	**Houston, TX** (city) Harris County	94
Connecticut	180	Osceola County, FL	120	**Fountainebleau, FL** (cdp) Miami-Dade County	91
Louisiana	169	Queens County, NY	102	**Aventura, FL** (city) Miami-Dade County	73
New Jersey	154	Los Angeles County, CA	87	**The Hammocks, FL** (cdp) Miami-Dade County	71

Sorted by Number in Ascending Order — U.S. = 7,143

State	Number	County	Number	Place	Number
South Carolina	0	King County, WA	0	**Country Club, FL** (cdp) Miami-Dade County	0
Oklahoma	15	Orange County, CA	0	**Tamiami, FL** (cdp) Miami-Dade County	7
Washington	24	Travis County, TX	9	**Hollywood, FL** (city) Broward County	8
Wisconsin	29	Bronx County, NY	10	**Bronx, NY** (borough) Bronx County	10
Utah	30	Lee County, FL	15	**Coral Springs, FL** (city) Broward County	15
Colorado	40	Fulton County, GA	16	**Kendall West, FL** (cdp) Miami-Dade County	23
Minnesota	41	Salt Lake County, UT	16	**Miramar, FL** (city) Broward County	23
Tennessee	44	Seminole County, FL	19	**Pembroke Pines, FL** (city) Broward County	26
Arizona	53	Suffolk County, MA	22	**Davie, FL** (town) Broward County	32
Missouri	57	Dallas County, TX	27	**Los Angeles, CA** (city) Los Angeles County	40

Sorted by Percent in Descending Order — U.S. = 18.0%

State	Percent	County	Percent	Place	Percent
Ohio	63.9	San Diego County, CA	42.2	**Miami Beach, FL** (city) Miami-Dade County	55.6
Maryland	48.5	Montgomery County, MD	41.3	**Aventura, FL** (city) Miami-Dade County	32.3
Indiana	35.6	Fairfield County, CT	34.8	**Los Angeles, CA** (city) Los Angeles County	28.0
Connecticut	31.8	Dallas County, TX	33.3	**The Hammocks, FL** (cdp) Miami-Dade County	24.1
Louisiana	31.5	Fairfax County, VA	30.6	**Manhattan, NY** (borough) New York County	22.8
Colorado	25.5	Cobb County, GA	26.8	**Kendall, FL** (cdp) Miami-Dade County	21.7
Michigan	25.3	Tarrant County, TX	25.8	**Doral, FL** (city) Miami-Dade County	20.5
Illinois	22.6	Middlesex County, MA	25.5	**Miami, FL** (city) Miami-Dade County	19.0
Georgia	21.7	New York County, NY	22.8	**Houston, TX** (city) Harris County	17.1
Arizona	20.8	Collin County, TX	21.3	**Orlando, FL** (city) Orange County	16.7

Sorted by Percent in Ascending Order — U.S. = 18.0%

State	Percent	County	Percent	Place	Percent
South Carolina	0.0	King County, WA	0.0	**Country Club, FL** (cdp) Miami-Dade County	0.0
Oklahoma	4.1	Orange County, CA	0.0	**Bronx, NY** (borough) Bronx County	4.8
Utah	4.9	Salt Lake County, UT	3.4	**Coral Springs, FL** (city) Broward County	4.8
California	12.5	Seminole County, FL	3.4	**Tamiami, FL** (cdp) Miami-Dade County	5.8
Tennessee	12.8	Lee County, FL	3.6	**Pembroke Pines, FL** (city) Broward County	6.7
Virginia	12.8	Bronx County, NY	4.8	**Kendall West, FL** (cdp) Miami-Dade County	7.3
Pennsylvania	13.6	Fort Bend County, TX	5.3	**Miramar, FL** (city) Broward County	7.5
Wisconsin	13.8	Travis County, TX	6.0	**Hollywood, FL** (city) Broward County	7.8
Washington	14.1	Hillsborough County, FL	7.7	**Davie, FL** (town) Broward County	9.0
New Jersey	15.1	Fulton County, GA	8.6	**Fountainebleau, FL** (cdp) Miami-Dade County	13.2

RANKINGS & COMPARISONS

Note: (1) Ranking tables cover all states and counties, and places with an overall population of at least 125,000, OR an overall population of at least 25,000 where the Hispanic/Latino population is at least 20% of the overall population. In states where less than five places meet either of these criteria, we have included places with at least 10,000 total population with the highest percentage of Hispanic/Latino population. These places are identified with an asterisk (*); Please refer to the User's Guide for a full explanation of data.

Population Age 3–17 Enrolled in Private School

(Universe: Population Age 3–17 Enrolled in School)

Spaniard

Top 10 States, Counties, and Places[1]

Sorted by Number in Descending Order — U.S. = 17,167

State	Number	County	Number	Place	Number
California	3,219	Los Angeles County, CA	961	**New York, NY** (city)	642
Florida	1,920	Miami-Dade County, FL	632	**Albuquerque, NM** (city) Bernalillo County	467
Texas	1,341	Bernalillo County, NM	549	**Queens, NY** (borough) Queens County	327
New York	1,312	Honolulu County, HI	365	**Los Angeles, CA** (city) Los Angeles County	288
Colorado	1,067	Hillsborough County, FL	332	**Hempstead (town), NY** (town) Nassau County	214
New Mexico	987	Queens County, NY	327	**Denver, CO** (city) Denver County	172
New Jersey	807	Maricopa County, AZ	252	**San Francisco, CA** (city) San Francisco County	171
Washington	457	San Diego County, CA	241	**Tampa, FL** (city) Hillsborough County	135
Maryland	443	Nassau County, NY	234	**Rio Rancho, NM** (city) Sandoval County	127
Hawaii	438	Montgomery County, MD	218	**Phoenix, AZ** (city) Maricopa County	114

Sorted by Number in Ascending Order — U.S. = 17,167

State	Number	County	Number	Place	Number
District of Columbia	0	Boulder County, CO	0	**Bakersfield, CA** (city) Kern County	0
Kentucky	0	Colfax County, NM	0	**Fort Collins, CO** (city) Larimer County	0
Maine	0	Doña Ana County, NM	0	**Glendale, AZ** (city) Maricopa County	0
Montana	10	Erie County, NY	0	**Henderson, NV** (city) Clark County	0
Alabama	11	Hidalgo County, TX	0	**Las Cruces, NM** (city) Dona Ana County	0
Alaska	11	Las Animas County, CO	0	**Miami, FL** (city) Miami-Dade County	0
New Hampshire	20	Mesa County, CO	0	**North Las Vegas, NV** (city) Clark County	0
Wyoming	23	Milwaukee County, WI	0	**Oklahoma City, OK** (city) Oklahoma County	0
Iowa	24	Oklahoma County, OK	0	**Paradise, NV** (cdp) Clark County	0
Idaho	47	Passaic County, NJ	0	**Philadelphia, PA** (city) Philadelphia County	0

Sorted by Percent in Descending Order — U.S. = 16.5%

State	Percent	County	Percent	Place	Percent
Mississippi	47.4	Jefferson Parish, LA	65.0	**San Francisco, CA** (city) San Francisco County	65.0
Louisiana	33.1	San Francisco County, CA	65.0	**Queens, NY** (borough) Queens County	53.3
Maryland	31.8	Queens County, NY	53.3	**Tucson, AZ** (city) Pima County	49.1
Florida	26.9	New York County, NY	44.1	**Seattle, WA** (city) King County	46.5
New York	26.6	Montgomery County, MD	38.4	**Hempstead (town), NY** (town) Nassau County	44.8
West Virginia	26.2	Duval County, FL	37.7	**Manhattan, NY** (borough) New York County	44.1
Pennsylvania	22.8	Placer County, CA	37.3	**Long Beach, CA** (city) Los Angeles County	42.2
Ohio	22.7	Santa Barbara County, CA	37.1	**Jacksonville, FL** (city) Duval County	37.7
Minnesota	22.6	Miami-Dade County, FL	35.3	**New York, NY** (city)	36.3
North Carolina	22.4	Solano County, CA	34.3	**Reno, NV** (city) Washoe County	34.8

Sorted by Percent in Ascending Order — U.S. = 16.5%

State	Percent	County	Percent	Place	Percent
District of Columbia	0.0	Boulder County, CO	0.0	**Bakersfield, CA** (city) Kern County	0.0
Kentucky	0.0	Colfax County, NM	0.0	**Fort Collins, CO** (city) Larimer County	0.0
Maine	0.0	Doña Ana County, NM	0.0	**Glendale, AZ** (city) Maricopa County	0.0
Alaska	2.4	Erie County, NY	0.0	**Henderson, NV** (city) Clark County	0.0
Wyoming	3.4	Hidalgo County, TX	0.0	**Las Cruces, NM** (city) Dona Ana County	0.0
Alabama	4.0	Las Animas County, CO	0.0	**Miami, FL** (city) Miami-Dade County	0.0
Oklahoma	4.8	Mesa County, CO	0.0	**North Las Vegas, NV** (city) Clark County	0.0
Idaho	6.4	Milwaukee County, WI	0.0	**Oklahoma City, OK** (city) Oklahoma County	0.0
Montana	6.7	Oklahoma County, OK	0.0	**Paradise, NV** (cdp) Clark County	0.0
New Hampshire	8.8	Passaic County, NJ	0.0	**Philadelphia, PA** (city) Philadelphia County	0.0

Note: (1) Ranking tables cover all states and counties, and places with an overall population of at least 125,000, OR an overall population of at least 25,000 where the Hispanic/Latino population is at least 20% of the overall population. In states where less than five places meet either of these criteria, we have included places with at least 10,000 total population with the highest percentage of Hispanic/Latino population. These places are identified with an asterisk (*); Please refer to the User's Guide for a full explanation of data.

Foreign-Born Population

Total Population

Top 10 States, Counties, and Places[1]

Sorted by Number in Descending Order — U.S. = 38,675,012

State	Number	County	Number	Place	Number
California	9,962,472	Los Angeles County, CA	3,477,823	**New York, NY** (city)	2,971,143
New York	4,180,075	Miami-Dade County, FL	1,248,803	**Los Angeles, CA** (city) Los Angeles County	1,494,946
Texas	3,913,577	Cook County, IL	1,086,881	**Queens, NY** (borough) Queens County	1,057,296
Florida	3,549,510	Queens County, NY	1,057,296	**Brooklyn, NY** (borough) Kings County	921,519
New Jersey	1,773,859	Harris County, TX	987,697	**Houston, TX** (city) Harris County	585,384
Illinois	1,736,696	Kings County, NY	921,519	**Chicago, IL** (city) Cook County	570,543
Massachusetts	942,255	Orange County, CA	903,037	**Manhattan, NY** (borough) New York County	452,102
Georgia	909,022	San Diego County, CA	698,486	**Bronx, NY** (borough) Bronx County	443,968
Arizona	884,625	Santa Clara County, CA	643,430	**San Jose, CA** (city) Santa Clara County	357,333
Virginia	848,087	Maricopa County, AZ	596,802	**San Diego, CA** (city) San Diego County	332,084

Sorted by Number in Ascending Order — U.S. = 38,675,012

State	Number	County	Number	Place	Number
North Dakota	15,807	Baker County, GA	0	**Clarksburg*, WV** (city) Harrison County	111
Wyoming	16,712	Pendleton County, KY	0	**Spearfish*, SD** (city) Lawrence County	154
South Dakota	18,663	Conecuh County, AL	6	**Williston*, ND** (city) Williams County	302
Montana	19,119	Kenedy County, TX	6	**Yankton*, SD** (city) Yankton County	374
West Virginia	23,917	Oneida County, ID	6	**Dickinson*, ND** (city) Stark County	381
Vermont	24,837	Dundy County, NE	7	**Bennington*, VT** (town) Bennington County	425
Maine	43,911	Menominee County, WI	7	**Green River*, WY** (city) Sweetwater County	465
Alaska	49,762	Stonewall County, TX	9	**Evanston*, WY** (city) Uinta County	525
Mississippi	63,518	Piute County, UT	10	**Badger*, AK** (cdp) Fairbanks North Star Borough	528
New Hampshire	68,999	Kent County, TX	11	**Fort Campbell North*, KY** (cdp) Christian County	535

Sorted by Percent in Descending Order — U.S. = 12.7%

State	Percent	County	Percent	Place	Percent
California	27.2	Miami-Dade County, FL	51.1	**Fountainebleau, FL** (cdp) Miami-Dade County	74.1
New York	21.7	Queens County, NY	48.1	**Hialeah, FL** (city) Miami-Dade County	73.2
New Jersey	20.3	Hudson County, NJ	40.6	**University Park, FL** (cdp) Miami-Dade County	66.7
Nevada	19.3	Concho County, TX	38.5	**Westchester, FL** (cdp) Miami-Dade County	65.3
Florida	19.2	Kings County, NY	37.4	**Tamiami, FL** (cdp) Miami-Dade County	65.0
Hawaii	17.7	Santa Clara County, CA	37.0	**West New York, NJ** (town) Hudson County	60.7
Texas	16.1	Los Angeles County, CA	35.6	**Doral, FL** (city) Miami-Dade County	60.5
Massachusetts	14.5	San Francisco County, CA	35.6	**Kendall West, FL** (cdp) Miami-Dade County	59.7
Arizona	14.2	Maverick County, TX	34.2	**Miami, FL** (city) Miami-Dade County	58.1
Illinois	13.6	San Mateo County, CA	34.0	**Rosemead, CA** (city) Los Angeles County	57.4

Sorted by Percent in Ascending Order — U.S. = 12.7%

State	Percent	County	Percent	Place	Percent
West Virginia	1.3	Baker County, GA	0.0	**Clarksburg*, WV** (city) Harrison County	0.7
Montana	2.0	Conecuh County, AL	0.0	**Spearfish*, SD** (city) Lawrence County	1.5
Mississippi	2.2	Pendleton County, KY	0.0	**Billings*, MT** (city) Yellowstone County	1.8
South Dakota	2.3	Franklin Parish, LA	0.1	**Jackson, MS** (city) Hinds County	1.8
North Dakota	2.4	Hamilton County, IL	0.1	**Huntington*, WV** (city) Cabell County	1.9
Kentucky	3.1	Lincoln County, KY	0.1	**Butte-Silver Bow*, MT** (consolidated govt) Silver Bow County	2.2
Wyoming	3.1	Macon County, MO	0.1	**Dickinson*, ND** (city) Stark County	2.2
Maine	3.3	Madison Parish, LA	0.1	**Pueblo West, CO** (cdp) Pueblo County	2.2
Alabama	3.4	Martin County, KY	0.1	**Williston*, ND** (city) Williams County	2.2
Louisiana	3.6	Oneida County, ID	0.1	**Great Falls*, MT** (city) Cascade County	2.4

Note: (1) Ranking tables cover all states and counties, and places with an overall population of at least 125,000, OR an overall population of at least 25,000 where the Hispanic/Latino population is at least 20% of the overall population. In states where less than five places meet either of these criteria, we have included places with at least 10,000 total population with the highest percentage of Hispanic/Latino population. These places are identified with an asterisk (*); Please refer to the User's Guide for a full explanation of data.

Foreign-Born Population

Hispanic or Latino (of any race)

Top 10 States, Counties, and Places[1]

Sorted by Number in Descending Order — U.S. = 18,203,058

State	Number	County	Number	Place	Number
California	5,324,223	Los Angeles County, CA	2,017,569	**New York, NY** (city)	939,329
Texas	2,801,938	Miami-Dade County, FL	1,031,874	**Los Angeles, CA** (city) Los Angeles County	922,507
Florida	2,007,233	Harris County, TX	690,695	**Houston, TX** (city) Harris County	419,487
New York	1,310,773	Cook County, IL	508,896	**Chicago, IL** (city) Cook County	314,643
Illinois	802,182	Orange County, CA	430,162	**Queens, NY** (borough) Queens County	314,615
New Jersey	652,005	Dallas County, TX	391,384	**Bronx, NY** (borough) Bronx County	247,987
Arizona	594,658	Maricopa County, AZ	388,736	**Dallas, TX** (city) Dallas County	238,488
Georgia	413,757	San Diego County, CA	358,462	**Phoenix, AZ** (city) Maricopa County	238,167
North Carolina	378,127	Riverside County, CA	335,689	**Miami, FL** (city) Miami-Dade County	201,058
Nevada	290,989	Queens County, NY	314,615	**Brooklyn, NY** (borough) Kings County	180,828

Sorted by Number in Ascending Order — U.S. = 18,203,058

State	Number	County	Number	Place	Number
North Dakota	1,441	Clare County, MI	0	**Waianae*, HI** (cdp) Honolulu County	14
Vermont	1,665	Wabaunsee County, KS	4	**Bozeman*, MT** (city) Gallatin County	40
Montana	2,335	Jackson County, KS	6	**Pueblo West, CO** (cdp) Pueblo County	60
Maine	3,165	Phelps County, MO	6	**Butte-Silver Bow*, MT** (consolidated govt) Silver Bow County	63
West Virginia	4,687	Warren County, PA	11	**Great Falls*, MT** (city) Cascade County	75
South Dakota	5,255	Harding County, NM	12	**Fort Campbell North*, KY** (cdp) Christian County	90
Alaska	8,643	Jackson County, IA	12	**Burlington*, VT** (city) Chittenden County	95
Wyoming	9,461	Thurston County, NE	12	**Grand Forks*, ND** (city) Grand Forks County	149
New Hampshire	10,019	Ogemaw County, MI	13	**Schofield Barracks*, HI** (cdp) Honolulu County	152
Hawaii	12,312	Norman County, MN	19	**Billings*, MT** (city) Yellowstone County	199

Sorted by Percent in Descending Order — U.S. = 38.1%

State	Percent	County	Percent	Place	Percent
District of Columbia	55.1	Alleghany County, NC	91.2	**Fountainebleau, FL** (cdp) Miami-Dade County	76.4
Maryland	53.7	Evangeline Parish, LA	82.3	**Hialeah, FL** (city) Miami-Dade County	75.6
Georgia	52.7	Telfair County, GA	80.2	**Sterling, VA** (cdp) Loudoun County	73.3
North Carolina	52.3	Logan County, KY	80.1	**Miami, FL** (city) Miami-Dade County	73.0
South Carolina	51.2	Northampton County, VA	75.3	**Aventura, FL** (city) Miami-Dade County	72.6
Florida	50.2	DeKalb County, TN	74.4	**Miami Beach, FL** (city) Miami-Dade County	72.5
Alabama	50.0	Concho County, TX	72.3	**Hallandale Beach, FL** (city) Broward County	71.0
Virginia	49.6	Hertford County, NC	71.3	**University Park, FL** (cdp) Miami-Dade County	71.0
Tennessee	49.3	Loudon County, TN	68.1	**Hilton Head Island*, SC** (town) Beaufort County	70.6
Arkansas	46.5	Edgefield County, SC	68.0	**Westchester, FL** (cdp) Miami-Dade County	70.5

Sorted by Percent in Ascending Order — U.S. = 38.1%

State	Percent	County	Percent	Place	Percent
Montana	8.6	Clare County, MI	0.0	**Waianae*, HI** (cdp) Honolulu County	0.9
Hawaii	10.7	Phelps County, MO	0.6	**Pueblo West, CO** (cdp) Pueblo County	1.0
North Dakota	11.2	Jackson County, KS	1.5	**Holyoke, MA** (city) Hampden County	3.3
New Mexico	16.7	Mora County, NM	1.6	**Billings*, MT** (city) Yellowstone County	4.0
Vermont	18.2	Wabaunsee County, KS	2.3	**Bozeman*, MT** (city) Gallatin County	4.1
Maine	18.6	White Pine County, NV	2.6	**Carlsbad, NM** (city) Eddy County	4.7
Wyoming	20.7	Ravalli County, MT	2.8	**Great Falls*, MT** (city) Cascade County	4.7
Pennsylvania	22.4	Archuleta County, CO	2.9	**Fort Campbell North*, KY** (cdp) Christian County	5.0
West Virginia	22.4	Harding County, NM	3.4	**Pueblo, CO** (city) Pueblo County	5.0
Alaska	22.5	Warren County, PA	3.8	**Butte-Silver Bow*, MT** (consolidated govt) Silver Bow County	5.2

Note: (1) Ranking tables cover all states and counties, and places with an overall population of at least 125,000, OR an overall population of at least 25,000 where the Hispanic/Latino population is at least 20% of the overall population. In states where less than five places meet either of these criteria, we have included places with at least 10,000 total population with the highest percentage of Hispanic/Latino population. These places are identified with an asterisk (*); Please refer to the User's Guide for a full explanation of data.

Foreign-Born Population

Central American, excluding Mexican

Top 10 States, Counties, and Places[1]

Sorted by Number in Descending Order — U.S. = 2,581,953

State	Number	County	Number	Place	Number
California	730,456	Los Angeles County, CA	457,560	**Los Angeles, CA** (city) Los Angeles County	285,693
Florida	312,198	Miami-Dade County, FL	165,128	**Houston, TX** (city) Harris County	101,903
Texas	280,630	Harris County, TX	146,053	**New York, NY** (city)	101,164
New York	219,846	Montgomery County, MD	51,071	**Miami, FL** (city) Miami-Dade County	53,612
Virginia	128,165	Prince George's County, MD	49,067	**Queens, NY** (borough) Queens County	35,711
Maryland	127,841	Dallas County, TX	48,229	**Brooklyn, NY** (borough) Kings County	30,208
New Jersey	117,023	Suffolk County, NY	44,747	**Hempstead (town), NY** (town) Nassau County	28,711
Georgia	72,140	Fairfax County, VA	42,540	**Dallas, TX** (city) Dallas County	24,245
North Carolina	67,743	Nassau County, NY	40,574	**Bronx, NY** (borough) Bronx County	23,521
Massachusetts	62,302	Queens County, NY	35,711	**Islip, NY** (town) Suffolk County	22,031

Sorted by Number in Ascending Order — U.S. = 2,581,953

State	Number	County	Number	Place	Number
Vermont	357	Oneida County, NY	271	**Murrieta, CA** (city) Riverside County	293
Wyoming	721	Thurston County, WA	299	**Palm Springs, CA** (city) Riverside County	305
Maine	876	Caroline County, MD	325	**Clovis, CA** (city) Fresno County	339
West Virginia	925	Gilmer County, GA	390	**Lake Forest, CA** (city) Orange County	408
Alaska	1,069	Clay County, FL	416	**Rohnert Park, CA** (city) Sonoma County	423
Hawaii	1,185	El Dorado County, CA	440	**Delano, CA** (city) Kern County	434
South Dakota	1,643	Shasta County, CA	445	**Little Elm, TX** (city) Denton County	438
New Hampshire	1,739	Carroll County, AR	449	**Rochester, NY** (city) Monroe County	456
Idaho	2,021	Hays County, TX	458	**Woodland, CA** (city) Yolo County	475
New Mexico	3,894	Kings County, CA	472	**Linden, NJ** (city) Union County	480

Sorted by Percent in Descending Order — U.S. = 65.6%

State	Percent	County	Percent	Place	Percent
Connecticut	72.7	Lee County, AL	82.9	**Oakland Park, FL** (city) Broward County	88.9
New Jersey	70.9	Morris County, NJ	81.4	**Miami Beach, FL** (city) Miami-Dade County	87.8
Florida	70.4	Santa Fe County, NM	80.2	**Marietta, GA** (city) Cobb County	86.7
Rhode Island	69.9	DeKalb County, GA	78.5	**Port Chester, NY** (village) Westchester County	85.7
District of Columbia	69.5	Collier County, FL	78.1	**Rye, NY** (town) Westchester County	85.3
Tennessee	68.8	Duplin County, NC	76.2	**Union City, CA** (city) Alameda County	83.7
Georgia	68.3	Fairfield County, CT	75.8	**Hackensack, NJ** (city) Bergen County	83.3
Maryland	67.6	Canyon County, ID	75.7	**Plainfield, NJ** (city) Union County	83.3
North Carolina	67.5	Wapello County, IA	75.6	**Cary, NC** (town) Wake County	83.0
Texas	67.4	Sampson County, NC	75.3	**Sterling, VA** (cdp) Loudoun County	82.5

Sorted by Percent in Ascending Order — U.S. = 65.6%

State	Percent	County	Percent	Place	Percent
Hawaii	39.4	Thurston County, WA	27.8	**Murrieta, CA** (city) Riverside County	26.3
Alaska	43.3	Honolulu County, HI	36.8	**Clovis, CA** (city) Fresno County	39.6
Maine	49.5	San Luis Obispo County, CA	40.7	**Apple Valley, CA** (town) San Bernardino County	39.9
West Virginia	50.4	Butte County, CA	41.0	**Elk Grove, CA** (city) Sacramento County	40.5
Vermont	54.6	Jefferson County, TX	44.2	**Chino Hills, CA** (city) San Bernardino County	42.0
Washington	56.5	Clay County, FL	45.4	**Riverview, FL** (cdp) Hillsborough County	42.1
Kentucky	56.7	Clackamas County, OR	46.3	**Anchorage, AK** (municipality)	42.2
Wisconsin	57.7	Ulster County, NY	46.6	**Lake Forest, CA** (city) Orange County	42.7
Oregon	58.2	Gilmer County, GA	46.9	**Fremont, CA** (city) Alameda County	45.1
Utah	59.0	Davis County, UT	47.0	**Rubidoux, CA** (cdp) Riverside County	45.3

Note: (1) Ranking tables cover all states and counties, and places with an overall population of at least 125,000, OR an overall population of at least 25,000 where the Hispanic/Latino population is at least 20% of the overall population. In states where less than five places meet either of these criteria, we have included places with at least 10,000 total population with the highest percentage of Hispanic/Latino population. These places are identified with an asterisk (*); Please refer to the User's Guide for a full explanation of data.

Foreign-Born Population

Central American: Costa Rican

Top 10 States, Counties, and Places[1]

Sorted by Number in Descending Order — U.S. = 74,872

State	Number	County	Number	Place	Number
New Jersey	14,658	Miami-Dade County, FL	5,069	**New York, NY** (city)	3,891
Florida	13,246	Los Angeles County, CA	4,874	**Los Angeles, CA** (city) Los Angeles County	1,615
California	10,754	Union County, NJ	2,851	**Brooklyn, NY** (borough) Kings County	1,444
New York	6,617	Broward County, FL	1,933	**Queens, NY** (borough) Queens County	1,260
Texas	3,769	Somerset County, NJ	1,859	**Miami, FL** (city) Miami-Dade County	1,167
North Carolina	3,467	Essex County, NJ	1,710	**Philadelphia, PA** (city) Philadelphia County	809
Pennsylvania	2,324	Morris County, NJ	1,509	**Bronx, NY** (borough) Bronx County	425
Massachusetts	2,122	Bergen County, NJ	1,473		
Georgia	1,975	Kings County, NY	1,444		
Maryland	1,596	Passaic County, NJ	1,312		

Sorted by Number in Ascending Order — U.S. = 74,872

State	Number	County	Number	Place	Number
Oregon	358	Bronx County, NY	425	**Bronx, NY** (borough) Bronx County	425
Wisconsin	366	Contra Costa County, CA	442	**Philadelphia, PA** (city) Philadelphia County	809
Tennessee	449	Maricopa County, AZ	535	**Miami, FL** (city) Miami-Dade County	1,167
Michigan	474	Nassau County, NY	581	**Queens, NY** (borough) Queens County	1,260
Minnesota	479	San Diego County, CA	623	**Brooklyn, NY** (borough) Kings County	1,444
Washington	514	Clark County, NV	656	**Los Angeles, CA** (city) Los Angeles County	1,615
Colorado	521	Riverside County, CA	666	**New York, NY** (city)	3,891
Arizona	704	Hillsborough County, FL	744		
Louisiana	848	Orange County, FL	764		
Virginia	1,125	Fairfield County, CT	789		

Sorted by Percent in Descending Order — U.S. = 59.5%

State	Percent	County	Percent	Place	Percent
New Jersey	77.9	Morris County, NJ	86.9	**Miami, FL** (city) Miami-Dade County	73.7
South Carolina	66.7	Essex County, NJ	84.9	**Queens, NY** (borough) Queens County	65.9
North Carolina	66.2	Somerset County, NJ	83.9	**Philadelphia, PA** (city) Philadelphia County	65.0
Florida	65.9	Mercer County, NJ	83.5	**New York, NY** (city)	61.6
Nevada	65.9	Bergen County, NJ	79.3	**Brooklyn, NY** (borough) Kings County	57.5
Texas	64.7	Union County, NJ	72.0	**Bronx, NY** (borough) Bronx County	53.9
Louisiana	59.0	Passaic County, NJ	71.7	**Los Angeles, CA** (city) Los Angeles County	53.7
New York	58.4	Suffolk County, NY	70.6		
Georgia	56.9	Orange County, FL	69.7		
Maryland	56.9	Broward County, FL	69.5		

Sorted by Percent in Ascending Order — U.S. = 59.5%

State	Percent	County	Percent	Place	Percent
Washington	39.6	Contra Costa County, CA	36.0	**Los Angeles, CA** (city) Los Angeles County	53.7
Arizona	42.3	Maricopa County, AZ	42.2	**Bronx, NY** (borough) Bronx County	53.9
Colorado	43.0	Nassau County, NY	43.7	**Brooklyn, NY** (borough) Kings County	57.5
Tennessee	45.8	Orange County, CA	46.8	**New York, NY** (city)	61.6
Minnesota	46.8	Riverside County, CA	50.5	**Philadelphia, PA** (city) Philadelphia County	65.0
Oregon	47.0	Los Angeles County, CA	50.9	**Queens, NY** (borough) Queens County	65.9
California	48.3	San Diego County, CA	52.1	**Miami, FL** (city) Miami-Dade County	73.7
Illinois	51.4	Bronx County, NY	53.9		
Connecticut	52.4	Fairfield County, CT	53.9		
Virginia	53.4	Kings County, NY	57.5		

Note: (1) Ranking tables cover all states and counties, and places with an overall population of at least 125,000, OR an overall population of at least 25,000 where the Hispanic/Latino population is at least 20% of the overall population. In states where less than five places meet either of these criteria, we have included places with at least 10,000 total population with the highest percentage of Hispanic/Latino population. These places are identified with an asterisk (*); Please refer to the User's Guide for a full explanation of data.

Foreign-Born Population

Central American: Guatemalan

Top 10 States, Counties, and Places[1]

Sorted by Number in Descending Order — U.S. = 704,059

State	Number	County	Number	Place	Number
California	223,690	Los Angeles County, CA	150,730	**Los Angeles, CA** (city) Los Angeles County	98,505
Florida	62,889	Harris County, TX	23,238	**New York, NY** (city)	19,805
New York	47,347	Palm Beach County, FL	17,055	**Houston, TX** (city) Harris County	18,862
Texas	45,118	Miami-Dade County, FL	16,496	**Chicago, IL** (city) Cook County	10,501
New Jersey	33,789	Cook County, IL	15,220	**Providence, RI** (city) Providence County	8,990
Maryland	26,430	Providence County, RI	13,073	**Queens, NY** (borough) Queens County	8,898
Georgia	25,942	Prince George's County, MD	12,534	**Stamford, CT** (city/town) Fairfield County	7,314
Massachusetts	22,715	Orange County, CA	9,955	**Trenton, NJ** (city) Mercer County	6,456
Virginia	22,329	Fairfield County, CT	9,635	**Brooklyn, NY** (borough) Kings County	5,111
Illinois	20,779	San Bernardino County, CA	9,092	**Dallas, TX** (city) Dallas County	4,373

Sorted by Number in Ascending Order — U.S. = 704,059

State	Number	County	Number	Place	Number
New Hampshire	603	Caroline County, MD	291	**Lexington*, NE** (city) Dawson County	480
Idaho	839	Gilmer County, GA	390	**Victorville, CA** (city) San Bernardino County	488
South Dakota	1,001	Sonoma County, CA	511	**West Covina, CA** (city) Los Angeles County	488
Wisconsin	1,497	Pinal County, AZ	532	**Bell, CA** (city) Los Angeles County	502
District of Columbia	1,553	Milwaukee County, WI	547	**Alhambra, CA** (city) Los Angeles County	518
Mississippi	1,676	Dawson County, NE	592	**Pawtucket*, RI** (city) Providence County	523
New Mexico	1,900	Arapahoe County, CO	603	**Sacramento, CA** (city) Sacramento County	582
Kentucky	3,063	Loudoun County, VA	616	**Hesperia, CA** (city) San Bernardino County	615
Arkansas	3,125	Denton County, TX	617	**Minneapolis, MN** (city) Hennepin County	641
Kansas	3,289	Cuyahoga County, OH	633	**Lake Elsinore, CA** (city) Riverside County	642

Sorted by Percent in Descending Order — U.S. = 69.3%

State	Percent	County	Percent	Place	Percent
Mississippi	83.5	Lee County, AL	90.7	**Port Chester, NY** (village) Westchester County	93.4
District of Columbia	82.7	Adams County, CO	88.0	**Rye, NY** (town) Westchester County	92.4
Connecticut	79.3	Davidson County, TN	85.5	**Union City, NJ** (city) Hudson County	90.4
Maryland	76.1	Morris County, NJ	84.2	**West New York, NJ** (town) Hudson County	89.3
Tennessee	74.6	Broward County, FL	81.1	**Marietta, GA** (city) Cobb County	88.7
Arkansas	74.5	DeKalb County, GA	81.1	**Bonita Springs, FL** (city) Lee County	86.2
New Jersey	74.1	Baltimore County, MD	81.0	**Plainfield, NJ** (city) Union County	85.7
South Carolina	74.1	Westchester County, NY	81.0	**Nashville-Davidson, TN** (metropolitan govt) Davidson County	85.4
Florida	73.1	Collier County, FL	80.8	**Oakland, CA** (city) Alameda County	82.7
Texas	73.1	Fairfield County, CT	80.3	**Silver Spring, MD** (cdp) Montgomery County	82.3

Sorted by Percent in Ascending Order — U.S. = 69.3%

State	Percent	County	Percent	Place	Percent
South Dakota	58.6	Gilmer County, GA	46.9	**West Covina, CA** (city) Los Angeles County	39.7
Nebraska	60.9	Sonoma County, CA	53.3	**Pasadena, CA** (city) Los Angeles County	45.0
Louisiana	61.2	Arapahoe County, CO	55.5	**Sacramento, CA** (city) Sacramento County	46.6
Wisconsin	61.8	Stanislaus County, CA	55.7	**Victorville, CA** (city) San Bernardino County	47.8
Utah	62.2	Hillsborough County, FL	56.5	**Westmont, CA** (cdp) Los Angeles County	53.6
Illinois	62.6	Caroline County, MD	56.9	**Paterson, NJ** (city) Passaic County	55.1
Washington	62.8	San Joaquin County, CA	56.9	**North Hempstead, NY** (town) Nassau County	55.3
Oregon	63.3	Forsyth County, NC	57.0	**Lynwood, CA** (city) Los Angeles County	56.2
Missouri	63.9	Sacramento County, CA	57.0	**Downey, CA** (city) Los Angeles County	56.4
Kentucky	64.9	Minnehaha County, SD	57.3	**Corona, CA** (city) Riverside County	56.5

RANKINGS & COMPARISONS

Note: (1) Ranking tables cover all states and counties, and places with an overall population of at least 125,000, OR an overall population of at least 25,000 where the Hispanic/Latino population is at least 20% of the overall population. In states where less than five places meet either of these criteria, we have included places with at least 10,000 total population with the highest percentage of Hispanic/Latino population. These places are identified with an asterisk (*); Please refer to the User's Guide for a full explanation of data.

Foreign-Born Population

Central American: Honduran

Top 10 States, Counties, and Places[1]

Sorted by Number in Descending Order — U.S. = 425,875

State	Number	County	Number	Place	Number
Florida	80,349	Miami-Dade County, FL	42,820	**New York, NY** (city)	29,387
Texas	63,788	Harris County, TX	33,861	**Houston, TX** (city) Harris County	24,490
California	48,622	Los Angeles County, CA	28,870	**Miami, FL** (city) Miami-Dade County	20,934
New York	45,894	Bronx County, NY	12,830	**Los Angeles, CA** (city) Los Angeles County	15,802
New Jersey	24,143	Jefferson Parish, LA	9,982	**Bronx, NY** (borough) Bronx County	12,830
North Carolina	21,477	Dallas County, TX	9,601	**Brooklyn, NY** (borough) Kings County	6,710
Virginia	19,410	Broward County, FL	8,338	**Queens, NY** (borough) Queens County	6,137
Louisiana	18,614	Palm Beach County, FL	6,811	**Dallas, TX** (city) Dallas County	5,794
Georgia	14,948	Kings County, NY	6,710	**Charlotte, NC** (city) Mecklenburg County	5,615
Maryland	12,263	Fairfax County, VA	6,527	**Hempstead (town), NY** (town) Nassau County	5,069

Sorted by Number in Ascending Order — U.S. = 425,875

State	Number	County	Number	Place	Number
Iowa	685	New Haven County, CT	368	**Miramar, FL** (city) Broward County	612
Oregon	1,016	Kern County, CA	461	**North Miami Beach, FL** (city) Miami-Dade County	687
Kentucky	1,044	Fresno County, CA	601	**South Miami Heights, FL** (cdp) Miami-Dade County	703
Michigan	1,191	Elkhart County, IN	645	**Oklahoma City, OK** (city) Oklahoma County	739
Arkansas	1,208	Hall County, GA	725	**Pasadena, CA** (city) Los Angeles County	770
Nebraska	1,221	Johnston County, NC	731	**Staten Island, NY** (borough) Richmond County	782
District of Columbia	1,319	Salt Lake County, UT	774	**Philadelphia, PA** (city) Philadelphia County	811
Utah	1,334	Richmond County, NY	782	**Oakland, CA** (city) Alameda County	846
Mississippi	1,527	Osceola County, FL	807	**Las Vegas, NV** (city) Clark County	860
Wisconsin	1,572	Philadelphia County, PA	811	**Yonkers, NY** (city) Westchester County	874

Sorted by Percent in Descending Order — U.S. = 69.7%

State	Percent	County	Percent	Place	Percent
Georgia	75.1	Morris County, NJ	86.2	**Miami Beach, FL** (city) Miami-Dade County	90.6
New Jersey	74.7	Essex County, NJ	84.4	**Plainfield, NJ** (city) Union County	87.1
Kansas	72.7	DeKalb County, GA	82.9	**Fort Worth, TX** (city) Tarrant County	82.5
Virginia	72.6	Union County, NJ	82.5	**West Little River, FL** (cdp) Miami-Dade County	82.3
Texas	72.5	Collier County, FL	82.3	**Newark, NJ** (city) Essex County	81.6
Connecticut	72.3	Tarrant County, TX	81.6	**Brentwood, NY** (cdp) Suffolk County	80.8
Florida	72.0	Polk County, FL	80.9	**Union City, NJ** (city) Hudson County	80.2
Maryland	71.7	Ventura County, CA	80.9	**Elizabeth, NJ** (city) Union County	77.9
Tennessee	71.6	Sampson County, NC	79.2	**Indianapolis, IN** (city) Marion County	77.8
North Carolina	71.5	Arapahoe County, CO	78.9	**Wheaton, MD** (cdp) Montgomery County	77.3

Sorted by Percent in Ascending Order — U.S. = 69.7%

State	Percent	County	Percent	Place	Percent
Iowa	50.7	New Haven County, CT	45.9	**Garland, TX** (city) Dallas County	54.6
Oregon	57.3	Elkhart County, IN	52.0	**Phoenix, AZ** (city) Maricopa County	56.5
Kentucky	59.1	Atlantic County, NJ	54.4	**North Miami, FL** (city) Miami-Dade County	57.6
Washington	59.2	Middlesex County, MA	55.5	**Boston, MA** (city) Suffolk County	61.8
Utah	59.6	Salt Lake County, UT	57.0	**Oakland, CA** (city) Alameda County	63.0
Michigan	59.9	Baltimore County, MD	58.4	**Brooklyn, NY** (borough) Kings County	63.9
Arizona	60.3	Riverside County, CA	60.3	**North Miami Beach, FL** (city) Miami-Dade County	64.2
Massachusetts	60.8	King County, WA	60.7	**Long Beach, CA** (city) Los Angeles County	65.1
Ohio	61.0	Maricopa County, AZ	60.9	**Manhattan, NY** (borough) New York County	65.4
Arkansas	64.6	Kern County, CA	61.6	**Staten Island, NY** (borough) Richmond County	65.6

Note: (1) Ranking tables cover all states and counties, and places with an overall population of at least 125,000, OR an overall population of at least 25,000 where the Hispanic/Latino population is at least 20% of the overall population. In states where less than five places meet either of these criteria, we have included places with at least 10,000 total population with the highest percentage of Hispanic/Latino population. These places are identified with an asterisk (*); Please refer to the User's Guide for a full explanation of data.

Foreign-Born Population

Central American: Nicaraguan

Top 10 States, Counties, and Places[1]

Sorted by Number in Descending Order — U.S. = 220,730

State	Number	County	Number	Place	Number
Florida	101,602	Miami-Dade County, FL	82,561	**Miami, FL** (city) Miami-Dade County	24,045
California	56,218	Los Angeles County, CA	24,333	**Los Angeles, CA** (city) Los Angeles County	11,404
Texas	10,739	San Mateo County, CA	5,286	**Hialeah, FL** (city) Miami-Dade County	8,292
New York	7,978	Broward County, FL	5,229	**New York, NY** (city)	6,398
Virginia	5,109	Harris County, TX	4,371	**Fountainebleau, FL** (cdp) Miami-Dade County	5,785
Louisiana	4,807	San Bernardino County, CA	4,001	**San Francisco, CA** (city) San Francisco County	3,799
New Jersey	4,697	San Francisco County, CA	3,799	**Houston, TX** (city) Harris County	2,713
Maryland	4,262	Contra Costa County, CA	3,539	**Tamiami, FL** (cdp) Miami-Dade County	2,709
North Carolina	3,131	Alameda County, CA	3,530	**Kendale Lakes, FL** (cdp) Miami-Dade County	2,475
Nevada	2,684	Jefferson Parish, LA	3,117	**Kendall, FL** (cdp) Miami-Dade County	2,412

Sorted by Number in Ascending Order — U.S. = 220,730

State	Number	County	Number	Place	Number
Michigan	353	King County, WA	382	**Sacramento, CA** (city) Sacramento County	376
Oregon	427	Sonoma County, CA	514	**San Diego, CA** (city) San Diego County	423
Missouri	437	Gwinnett County, GA	656	**South Gate, CA** (city) Los Angeles County	597
Connecticut	476	Stanislaus County, CA	668	**Las Vegas, NV** (city) Clark County	661
Ohio	538	Bexar County, TX	709	**Austin, TX** (city) Travis County	680
Tennessee	614	Camden County, NJ	723	**Richmond, CA** (city) Contra Costa County	680
District of Columbia	630	Lee County, FL	734	**Oakland, CA** (city) Alameda County	737
Minnesota	658	Duval County, FL	745	**Jacksonville, FL** (city) Duval County	745
Colorado	662	Maricopa County, AZ	796	**Chicago, IL** (city) Cook County	777
South Carolina	731	Collier County, FL	801	**Homestead, FL** (city) Miami-Dade County	815

Sorted by Percent in Descending Order — U.S. = 64.5%

State	Percent	County	Percent	Place	Percent
Indiana	71.7	Fairfax County, VA	75.9	**Fontana, CA** (city) San Bernardino County	81.6
Florida	71.5	Mecklenburg County, NC	75.4	**Kenner, LA** (city) Jefferson Parish	81.5
Louisiana	69.5	Montgomery County, MD	73.9	**Pembroke Pines, FL** (city) Broward County	80.0
North Carolina	68.8	Collier County, FL	73.6	**Chicago, IL** (city) Cook County	79.1
South Carolina	67.1	Miami-Dade County, FL	73.2	**Kendall, FL** (cdp) Miami-Dade County	79.1
Tennessee	66.7	Jefferson Parish, LA	72.8	**Kendall West, FL** (cdp) Miami-Dade County	74.8
Nevada	65.3	Gwinnett County, GA	71.5	**University Park, FL** (cdp) Miami-Dade County	74.8
Virginia	64.5	Broward County, FL	70.7	**Fountainebleau, FL** (cdp) Miami-Dade County	74.6
Texas	64.3	Harris County, TX	70.0	**Charlotte, NC** (city) Mecklenburg County	74.5
Maryland	64.0	Cook County, IL	69.7	**Miami, FL** (city) Miami-Dade County	74.4

Sorted by Percent in Ascending Order — U.S. = 64.5%

State	Percent	County	Percent	Place	Percent
Ohio	36.0	San Diego County, CA	42.7	**Sacramento, CA** (city) Sacramento County	34.8
Oregon	43.0	Sonoma County, CA	43.8	**San Diego, CA** (city) San Diego County	42.7
Washington	43.5	Sacramento County, CA	44.7	**San Jose, CA** (city) Santa Clara County	51.8
Michigan	44.6	King County, WA	45.2	**Oakland, CA** (city) Alameda County	54.0
Missouri	46.1	Orange County, CA	45.2	**Antioch, CA** (city) Contra Costa County	55.6
Colorado	48.8	Orange County, FL	48.5	**Daly City, CA** (city) San Mateo County	58.6
Connecticut	50.5	Santa Clara County, CA	51.1	**San Francisco, CA** (city) San Francisco County	58.8
Wisconsin	50.7	Riverside County, CA	52.4	**South Gate, CA** (city) Los Angeles County	60.0
Pennsylvania	57.0	Contra Costa County, CA	53.3	**Bronx, NY** (borough) Bronx County	62.4
Arizona	57.2	Bexar County, TX	55.5	**Jacksonville, FL** (city) Duval County	62.4

Note: (1) Ranking tables cover all states and counties, and places with an overall population of at least 125,000, OR an overall population of at least 25,000 where the Hispanic/Latino population is at least 20% of the overall population. In states where less than five places meet either of these criteria, we have included places with at least 10,000 total population with the highest percentage of Hispanic/Latino population. These places are identified with an asterisk (*); Please refer to the User's Guide for a full explanation of data.

Foreign-Born Population

Central American: Panamanian

Top 10 States, Counties, and Places[1]

Sorted by Number in Descending Order — U.S. = 76,484

State	Number	County	Number	Place	Number
New York	15,743	Kings County, NY	8,428	**New York, NY** (city)	12,919
Florida	14,859	Miami-Dade County, FL	4,829	**Brooklyn, NY** (borough) Kings County	8,428
California	8,236	Los Angeles County, CA	2,498	**Queens, NY** (borough) Queens County	2,235
Texas	6,451	Queens County, NY	2,235	**Bronx, NY** (borough) Bronx County	1,259
Georgia	3,674	Broward County, FL	2,155	**Los Angeles, CA** (city) Los Angeles County	911
Virginia	3,331	Orange County, FL	1,467	**Manhattan, NY** (borough) New York County	891
New Jersey	3,043	San Diego County, CA	1,320	**San Diego, CA** (city) San Diego County	766
North Carolina	2,494	Bronx County, NY	1,259	**Hempstead (town), NY** (town) Nassau County	675
Maryland	2,216	Hillsborough County, FL	1,173	**Killeen, TX** (city) Bell County	656
Massachusetts	1,693	Harris County, TX	1,116	**San Antonio, TX** (city) Bexar County	615

Sorted by Number in Ascending Order — U.S. = 76,484

State	Number	County	Number	Place	Number
Minnesota	126	Pierce County, WA	192	**Houston, TX** (city) Harris County	490
New Mexico	248	Orange County, CA	366	**Fayetteville, NC** (city) Cumberland County	529
Wisconsin	255	Montgomery County, MD	465	**Miami, FL** (city) Miami-Dade County	563
Mississippi	293	Hudson County, NJ	467	**Jacksonville, FL** (city) Duval County	607
Oklahoma	397	Sacramento County, CA	472	**San Antonio, TX** (city) Bexar County	615
Indiana	413	Fairfax County, VA	480	**Killeen, TX** (city) Bell County	656
Connecticut	448	Clark County, NV	494	**Hempstead (town), NY** (town) Nassau County	675
Missouri	470	Palm Beach County, FL	516	**San Diego, CA** (city) San Diego County	766
Michigan	476	Essex County, NJ	544	**Manhattan, NY** (borough) New York County	891
Kentucky	493	Dallas County, TX	548	**Los Angeles, CA** (city) Los Angeles County	911

Sorted by Percent in Descending Order — U.S. = 48.1%

State	Percent	County	Percent	Place	Percent
Florida	56.7	Harris County, TX	66.4	**Houston, TX** (city) Harris County	64.6
New York	53.1	Brevard County, FL	66.1	**Brooklyn, NY** (borough) Kings County	59.5
New Jersey	52.4	Broward County, FL	64.9	**Queens, NY** (borough) Queens County	57.8
Massachusetts	50.4	Essex County, NJ	64.0	**Killeen, TX** (city) Bell County	57.5
Texas	49.2	Prince George's County, MD	63.6	**Los Angeles, CA** (city) Los Angeles County	56.3
Georgia	49.0	Suffolk County, NY	61.4	**New York, NY** (city)	55.1
Maryland	48.6	Kings County, NY	59.5	**Jacksonville, FL** (city) Duval County	51.9
California	47.9	Riverside County, CA	59.3	**San Diego, CA** (city) San Diego County	51.8
Illinois	47.1	Miami-Dade County, FL	59.2	**San Antonio, TX** (city) Bexar County	49.9
North Carolina	46.5	Palm Beach County, FL	58.1	**Miami, FL** (city) Miami-Dade County	49.1

Sorted by Percent in Ascending Order — U.S. = 48.1%

State	Percent	County	Percent	Place	Percent
Minnesota	17.1	Pierce County, WA	21.9	**Manhattan, NY** (borough) New York County	38.3
Washington	29.0	New York County, NY	38.3	**Fayetteville, NC** (city) Cumberland County	47.0
New Mexico	30.2	Clark County, NV	39.6	**Hempstead (town), NY** (town) Nassau County	47.0
Wisconsin	30.9	Cumberland County, NC	42.0	**Bronx, NY** (borough) Bronx County	47.9
Tennessee	33.0	Maricopa County, AZ	44.9	**Miami, FL** (city) Miami-Dade County	49.1
Mississippi	33.1	San Diego County, CA	45.9	**San Antonio, TX** (city) Bexar County	49.9
Michigan	33.5	Hillsborough County, FL	46.1	**San Diego, CA** (city) San Diego County	51.8
Missouri	34.4	Orange County, CA	46.2	**Jacksonville, FL** (city) Duval County	51.9
Pennsylvania	37.9	Bexar County, TX	47.6	**New York, NY** (city)	55.1
Colorado	38.0	Bronx County, NY	47.9	**Los Angeles, CA** (city) Los Angeles County	56.3

Note: (1) Ranking tables cover all states and counties, and places with an overall population of at least 125,000, OR an overall population of at least 25,000 where the Hispanic/Latino population is at least 20% of the overall population. In states where less than five places meet either of these criteria, we have included places with at least 10,000 total population with the highest percentage of Hispanic/Latino population. These places are identified with an asterisk (*); Please refer to the User's Guide for a full explanation of data.

Foreign-Born Population

Central American: Salvadoran

Top 10 States, Counties, and Places[1]

Sorted by Number in Descending Order — U.S. = 1,040,817

State	Number	County	Number	Place	Number
California	366,066	Los Angeles County, CA	235,329	**Los Angeles, CA** (city) Los Angeles County	151,631
Texas	147,737	Harris County, TX	80,978	**Houston, TX** (city) Harris County	53,870
New York	93,381	Montgomery County, MD	34,432	**New York, NY** (city)	27,115
Maryland	79,178	Prince George's County, MD	30,745	**Hempstead (town), NY** (town) Nassau County	19,577
Virginia	74,959	Suffolk County, NY	29,414	**Islip, NY** (town) Suffolk County	16,070
Florida	36,518	Dallas County, TX	29,107	**Queens, NY** (borough) Queens County	14,762
New Jersey	35,700	Nassau County, NY	28,526	**Dallas, TX** (city) Dallas County	12,820
Massachusetts	25,363	Fairfax County, VA	25,555	**San Francisco, CA** (city) San Francisco County	10,068
North Carolina	22,911	Prince William County, VA	15,710	**Irving, TX** (city) Dallas County	8,463
Georgia	22,873	Orange County, CA	15,131	**Boston, MA** (city) Suffolk County	7,055

Sorted by Number in Ascending Order — U.S. = 1,040,817

State	Number	County	Number	Place	Number
Hawaii	414	Placer County, CA	509	**West Valley City, UT** (city) Salt Lake County	440
Alaska	465	Duval County, FL	541	**Spring Valley, NV** (cdp) Clark County	536
Idaho	569	Cache County, UT	544	**Willowbrook, CA** (cdp) Los Angeles County	537
Alabama	1,013	Williamson County, TX	570	**Jacksonville, FL** (city) Duval County	541
Wisconsin	1,038	Cuyahoga County, OH	577	**Fremont, CA** (city) Alameda County	542
New Mexico	1,123	Napa County, CA	618	**Santa Rosa, CA** (city) Sonoma County	548
Kentucky	1,266	Pima County, AZ	620	**Lewisville, TX** (city) Denton County	552
Oklahoma	1,351	Buncombe County, NC	622	**Fairfield, CA** (city) Solano County	563
Michigan	1,803	Sedgwick County, KS	650	**Carson, CA** (city) Los Angeles County	572
South Carolina	1,892	Ocean County, NJ	665	**Hesperia, CA** (city) San Bernardino County	579

Sorted by Percent in Descending Order — U.S. = 64.5%

State	Percent	County	Percent	Place	Percent
Connecticut	73.6	Santa Cruz County, CA	89.2	**Bridgeport, CT** (city/town) Fairfield County	86.5
Louisiana	70.4	Fulton County, GA	85.8	**Sterling, VA** (cdp) Loudoun County	84.2
Rhode Island	70.3	Jefferson Parish, LA	81.7	**San Rafael, CA** (city) Marin County	81.5
New Mexico	69.5	New Haven County, CT	80.7	**Greensboro, NC** (city) Guilford County	78.5
District of Columbia	68.8	Hennepin County, MN	77.6	**Portland, OR** (city) Multnomah County	78.0
Florida	68.7	Monmouth County, NJ	77.6	**Salinas, CA** (city) Monterey County	77.3
Massachusetts	68.2	Guilford County, NC	75.6	**Plainfield, NJ** (city) Union County	76.8
Iowa	67.9	Broward County, FL	74.6	**Boston, MA** (city) Suffolk County	76.6
Tennessee	67.6	Osceola County, FL	74.5	**Reno, NV** (city) Washoe County	75.6
Georgia	67.5	Atlantic County, NJ	74.4	**San Mateo, CA** (city) San Mateo County	75.5

Sorted by Percent in Ascending Order — U.S. = 64.5%

State	Percent	County	Percent	Place	Percent
Alaska	43.8	El Paso County, CO	41.0	**Fremont, CA** (city) Alameda County	36.8
Hawaii	45.5	Sacramento County, CA	50.1	**Antioch, CA** (city) Contra Costa County	39.5
Alabama	49.7	Pima County, AZ	50.4	**San Diego, CA** (city) San Diego County	46.8
Kentucky	52.0	Stanislaus County, CA	50.7	**Lancaster, CA** (city) Los Angeles County	47.2
South Carolina	52.8	San Diego County, CA	50.9	**Bellflower, CA** (city) Los Angeles County	47.7
Utah	56.2	Denton County, TX	51.0	**San Bernardino, CA** (city) San Bernardino County	49.7
Oklahoma	56.8	Merced County, CA	51.2	**Modesto, CA** (city) Stanislaus County	50.9
Oregon	57.3	Brazoria County, TX	51.8	**Fairfield, CA** (city) Solano County	51.0
Indiana	58.0	Walker County, TX	51.8	**Rancho Cucamonga, CA** (city) San Bernardino County	51.1
Pennsylvania	60.8	Galveston County, TX	53.3	**West Valley City, UT** (city) Salt Lake County	51.2

Note: (1) Ranking tables cover all states and counties, and places with an overall population of at least 125,000, OR an overall population of at least 25,000 where the Hispanic/Latino population is at least 20% of the overall population. In states where less than five places meet either of these criteria, we have included places with at least 10,000 total population with the highest percentage of Hispanic/Latino population. These places are identified with an asterisk (*); Please refer to the User's Guide for a full explanation of data.

Foreign-Born Population

Cuban

Top 10 States, Counties, and Places[1]

Sorted by Number in Descending Order — U.S. = 999,690

State	Number	County	Number	Place	Number
Florida	761,873	Miami-Dade County, FL	573,973	**Hialeah, FL** (city) Miami-Dade County	127,836
New Jersey	48,138	Broward County, FL	41,180	**Miami, FL** (city) Miami-Dade County	107,047
California	37,420	Hillsborough County, FL	34,941	**Tamiami, FL** (cdp) Miami-Dade County	24,933
New York	30,152	Palm Beach County, FL	23,893	**Fountainebleau, FL** (cdp) Miami-Dade County	19,915
Texas	20,499	Hudson County, NJ	22,479	**New York, NY** (city)	19,341
Nevada	11,998	Los Angeles County, CA	21,430	**Kendale Lakes, FL** (cdp) Miami-Dade County	18,745
Georgia	9,584	Lee County, FL	12,524	**Westchester, FL** (cdp) Miami-Dade County	14,922
Illinois	8,255	Orange County, FL	11,375	**Kendall, FL** (cdp) Miami-Dade County	13,384
North Carolina	5,892	Clark County, NV	11,316	**Miami Beach, FL** (city) Miami-Dade County	12,742
Kentucky	5,599	Collier County, FL	10,295	**University Park, FL** (cdp) Miami-Dade County	12,545

Sorted by Number in Ascending Order — U.S. = 999,690

State	Number	County	Number	Place	Number
Maine	231	Berks County, PA	135	**Islip, NY** (town) Suffolk County	199
Arkansas	288	Oakland County, MI	163	**New Orleans, LA** (city) Orleans Parish	229
Hawaii	296	Arapahoe County, CO	168	**Milwaukee, WI** (city) Milwaukee County	231
West Virginia	305	Hamilton County, OH	171	**North Hempstead, NY** (town) Nassau County	268
Iowa	346	Cuyahoga County, OH	212	**Baltimore, MD** (independent city)	292
New Hampshire	414	Pierce County, WA	224	**Atlanta, GA** (city) Fulton County	301
Delaware	425	Orleans Parish, LA	229	**Columbus, OH** (city) Franklin County	307
Rhode Island	439	Prince William County, VA	250	**Coconut Creek, FL** (city) Broward County	309
District of Columbia	576	Loudoun County, VA	256	**Brookhaven, NY** (town) Suffolk County	323
Nebraska	607	Sussex County, NJ	259	**Seattle, WA** (city) King County	326

Sorted by Percent in Descending Order — U.S. = 59.2%

State	Percent	County	Percent	Place	Percent
Kentucky	68.5	Jefferson County, KY	80.5	**Syracuse, NY** (city) Onondaga County	88.8
Florida	66.0	Clay County, MO	78.7	**Bell, CA** (city) Los Angeles County	85.5
Nevada	62.4	Onondaga County, NY	74.5	**Union City, NJ** (city) Hudson County	81.2
New Jersey	56.9	Hudson County, NJ	74.1	**Fountainebleau, FL** (cdp) Miami-Dade County	81.1
New Mexico	52.9	Ingham County, MI	73.0	**West New York, NJ** (town) Hudson County	81.0
Texas	51.8	Sarasota County, FL	71.4	**Louisville-Jefferson County, KY** (metropolitan govt) Jefferson County	80.9
Missouri	50.7	Miami-Dade County, FL	70.8	**Hialeah, FL** (city) Miami-Dade County	79.8
Arizona	49.0	Lee County, FL	67.5	**Miami, FL** (city) Miami-Dade County	79.2
California	45.2	Collier County, FL	66.1	**Hallandale Beach, FL** (city) Broward County	78.4
Louisiana	45.2	Salt Lake County, UT	64.7	**Miami Beach, FL** (city) Miami-Dade County	77.2

Sorted by Percent in Ascending Order — U.S. = 59.2%

State	Percent	County	Percent	Place	Percent
Hawaii	20.0	Berks County, PA	14.6	**Tallahassee, FL** (city) Leon County	17.2
Rhode Island	21.6	Hamilton County, OH	18.8	**Islip, NY** (town) Suffolk County	18.6
Wisconsin	23.7	Honolulu County, HI	21.0	**Brookhaven, NY** (town) Suffolk County	21.6
Colorado	24.2	Prince William County, VA	21.6	**San Diego, CA** (city) San Diego County	22.0
Ohio	25.1	Arapahoe County, CO	22.1	**New Orleans, LA** (city) Orleans Parish	26.2
Iowa	26.7	Providence County, RI	22.5	**Milwaukee, WI** (city) Milwaukee County	26.4
District of Columbia	28.2	Wayne County, MI	22.8	**North Hempstead, NY** (town) Nassau County	26.4
Maine	28.9	Cuyahoga County, OH	22.9	**San Jose, CA** (city) Santa Clara County	27.0
Delaware	29.4	Leon County, FL	23.0	**Baltimore, MD** (independent city)	29.0
New Hampshire	29.7	Oakland County, MI	23.4	**Philadelphia, PA** (city) Philadelphia County	32.6

Note: (1) Ranking tables cover all states and counties, and places with an overall population of at least 125,000, OR an overall population of at least 25,000 where the Hispanic/Latino population is at least 20% of the overall population. In states where less than five places meet either of these criteria, we have included places with at least 10,000 total population with the highest percentage of Hispanic/Latino population. These places are identified with an asterisk (*); Please refer to the User's Guide for a full explanation of data.

Foreign-Born Population

Dominican Republic

Top 10 States, Counties, and Places[1]

Sorted by Number in Descending Order — U.S. = 777,554

State	Number	County	Number	Place	Number
New York	400,918	Bronx County, NY	140,358	**New York, NY** (city)	347,933
New Jersey	105,062	New York County, NY	103,506	**Bronx, NY** (borough) Bronx County	140,358
Florida	91,878	Kings County, NY	51,531	**Manhattan, NY** (borough) New York County	103,506
Massachusetts	59,684	Queens County, NY	50,658	**Brooklyn, NY** (borough) Kings County	51,531
Pennsylvania	30,579	Miami-Dade County, FL	33,735	**Queens, NY** (borough) Queens County	50,658
Rhode Island	20,101	Essex County, MA	29,867	**Lawrence, MA** (city) Essex County	18,145
Connecticut	12,570	Hudson County, NJ	24,608	**Providence, RI** (city) Providence County	15,689
Georgia	6,820	Passaic County, NJ	23,290	**Boston, MA** (city) Suffolk County	15,035
Maryland	6,482	Providence County, RI	19,382	**Paterson, NJ** (city) Passaic County	12,075
North Carolina	5,778	Broward County, FL	15,841	**Hempstead (town), NY** (town) Nassau County	11,343

Sorted by Number in Ascending Order — U.S. = 777,554

State	Number	County	Number	Place	Number
Alabama	346	Ulster County, NY	247	**Los Angeles, CA** (city) Los Angeles County	308
Minnesota	368	Fulton County, GA	362	**Syracuse, NY** (city) Onondaga County	384
Washington	406	Lackawanna County, PA	389	**Ramapo, NY** (town) Rockland County	431
Colorado	664	Sullivan County, NY	406	**Cleveland, OH** (city) Cuyahoga County	434
Missouri	683	Dallas County, TX	407	**Englewood, NJ** (city) Bergen County	484
Tennessee	711	Baltimore County, MD	439	**Chelsea, MA** (city) Suffolk County	509
Utah	713	Tarrant County, TX	481	**Valley Stream, NY** (village) Nassau County	510
South Carolina	793	Marion County, FL	486	**Bethlehem, PA** (city) Northampton County	513
Wisconsin	793	Oneida County, NY	514	**Weston, FL** (city) Broward County	514
Delaware	805	Bexar County, TX	568	**Grand Rapids, MI** (city) Kent County	515

Sorted by Percent in Descending Order — U.S. = 58.0%

State	Percent	County	Percent	Place	Percent
Louisiana	64.9	Plymouth County, MA	69.1	**Fountainebleau, FL** (cdp) Miami-Dade County	84.6
New York	59.7	Luzerne County, PA	68.9	**West Little River, FL** (cdp) Miami-Dade County	74.0
New Jersey	58.7	Collier County, FL	68.5	**The Hammocks, FL** (cdp) Miami-Dade County	72.3
Massachusetts	58.6	Jefferson Parish, LA	67.0	**Hialeah, FL** (city) Miami-Dade County	72.0
Pennsylvania	58.2	Pasco County, FL	66.4	**Atlantic City, NJ** (city) Atlantic County	71.1
Florida	57.9	Prince George's County, MD	65.4	**Hazleton, PA** (city) Luzerne County	70.4
Nevada	56.7	Philadelphia County, PA	64.8	**New London, CT** (city/town) New London County	70.2
Illinois	56.0	Miami-Dade County, FL	64.4	**Camden, NJ** (city) Camden County	69.9
Connecticut	55.5	Hudson County, NJ	64.3	**Linden, NJ** (city) Union County	69.8
Rhode Island	55.4	Gwinnett County, GA	64.1	**Union City, NJ** (city) Hudson County	69.8

Sorted by Percent in Ascending Order — U.S. = 58.0%

State	Percent	County	Percent	Place	Percent
Washington	33.5	Fulton County, GA	30.6	**Los Angeles, CA** (city) Los Angeles County	26.2
Tennessee	37.7	Monroe County, PA	34.6	**Syracuse, NY** (city) Onondaga County	34.3
Arizona	38.3	Baltimore County, MD	35.6	**Coral Springs, FL** (city) Broward County	37.5
Virginia	40.8	Maricopa County, AZ	37.8	**Cleveland, OH** (city) Cuyahoga County	38.5
California	42.0	Cumberland County, NJ	38.1	**Homestead, FL** (city) Miami-Dade County	39.9
Colorado	45.0	Cobb County, GA	38.8	**Cape Coral, FL** (city) Lee County	41.0
Michigan	45.3	Erie County, NY	40.2	**Staten Island, NY** (borough) Richmond County	42.1
Ohio	45.9	Dutchess County, NY	40.4	**Ramapo, NY** (town) Rockland County	43.5
Minnesota	46.6	Fairfax County, VA	40.6	**Alafaya, FL** (cdp) Orange County	44.3
Alabama	47.5	Dallas County, TX	40.8	**Chelsea, MA** (city) Suffolk County	44.4

Note: (1) Ranking tables cover all states and counties, and places with an overall population of at least 125,000, OR an overall population of at least 25,000 where the Hispanic/Latino population is at least 20% of the overall population. In states where less than five places meet either of these criteria, we have included places with at least 10,000 total population with the highest percentage of Hispanic/Latino population. These places are identified with an asterisk (*); Please refer to the User's Guide for a full explanation of data.

Foreign-Born Population

Mexican

Top 10 States, Counties, and Places[1]

Sorted by Number in Descending Order — U.S. = 11,484,169

State	Number	County	Number	Place	Number
California	4,282,066	Los Angeles County, CA	1,425,053	**Los Angeles, CA** (city) Los Angeles County	579,073
Texas	2,359,804	Harris County, TX	489,460	**Houston, TX** (city) Harris County	288,572
Illinois	690,885	Cook County, IL	431,386	**Chicago, IL** (city) Cook County	262,573
Arizona	546,405	Orange County, CA	370,976	**Phoenix, AZ** (city) Maricopa County	221,549
Florida	284,472	Maricopa County, AZ	354,590	**Dallas, TX** (city) Dallas County	206,277
Georgia	279,228	Dallas County, TX	327,633	**New York, NY** (city)	175,988
North Carolina	262,895	San Diego County, CA	326,914	**El Paso, TX** (city) El Paso County	143,944
New York	239,451	Riverside County, CA	296,064	**San Diego, CA** (city) San Diego County	124,528
Colorado	230,622	San Bernardino County, CA	258,498	**San Antonio, TX** (city) Bexar County	123,058
Nevada	226,405	Hidalgo County, TX	201,373	**Santa Ana, CA** (city) Orange County	122,934

Sorted by Number in Ascending Order — U.S. = 11,484,169

State	Number	County	Number	Place	Number
Vermont	585	Becker County, MN	7	**Schofield Barracks*, HI** (cdp) Honolulu County	17
North Dakota	801	Ogemaw County, MI	9	**Fort Campbell North*, KY** (cdp) Christian County	47
Maine	812	Trumbull County, OH	10	**Pueblo West, CO** (cdp) Pueblo County	52
Montana	1,347	Cass County, MN	11	**Grand Forks*, ND** (city) Grand Forks County	56
West Virginia	1,870	Aroostook County, ME	14	**Billings*, MT** (city) Yellowstone County	68
New Hampshire	2,375	De Baca County, NM	19	**Great Falls*, MT** (city) Cascade County	68
South Dakota	3,035	Norman County, MN	19	**Warren, MI** (city) Macomb County	121
Rhode Island	3,663	Beaver County, PA	22	**Fort Leonard Wood*, MO** (cdp) Pulaski County	137
District of Columbia	3,697	Burleigh County, ND	23	**Royal Palm Beach, FL** (village) Palm Beach County	138
Alaska	4,438	Lewis and Clark County, MT	23	**Rapid City*, SD** (city) Pennington County	168

Sorted by Percent in Descending Order — U.S. = 37.4%

State	Percent	County	Percent	Place	Percent
New Jersey	60.6	Telfair County, GA	80.6	**Ramapo, NY** (town) Rockland County	76.1
North Carolina	57.3	Evangeline Parish, LA	78.6	**Laurel*, MS** (city) Jones County	76.0
South Carolina	57.3	Scott County, MS	76.8	**Trenton, NJ** (city) Mercer County	75.7
Georgia	56.9	Concho County, TX	73.9	**Bluffton*, SC** (town) Beaufort County	74.9
New York	56.7	Loudon County, TN	72.9	**Union City, NJ** (city) Hudson County	73.8
Delaware	56.3	Somerset County, NJ	71.5	**Marietta, GA** (city) Cobb County	73.3
Alabama	54.7	Dare County, NC	71.4	**Hilton Head Island*, SC** (town) Beaufort County	73.1
Tennessee	52.7	Edgefield County, SC	70.7	**Miami Beach, FL** (city) Miami-Dade County	72.7
Connecticut	52.0	Tuscaloosa County, AL	68.7	**Doral, FL** (city) Miami-Dade County	72.0
Mississippi	48.5	Gilmer County, GA	68.5	**University, FL** (cdp) Hillsborough County	72.0

Sorted by Percent in Ascending Order — U.S. = 37.4%

State	Percent	County	Percent	Place	Percent
Montana	6.9	Trumbull County, OH	0.8	**Schofield Barracks*, HI** (cdp) Honolulu County	1.2
North Dakota	8.6	Becker County, MN	2.3	**Pueblo West, CO** (cdp) Pueblo County	1.4
Hawaii	16.0	Lewis and Clark County, MT	2.3	**Billings*, MT** (city) Yellowstone County	1.7
Maine	16.6	Beaver County, PA	2.6	**Schertz, TX** (city) Guadalupe County	5.6
Alaska	20.1	Burleigh County, ND	2.8	**Carlsbad, NM** (city) Eddy County	5.9
West Virginia	20.5	White Pine County, NV	2.9	**Fort Campbell North*, KY** (cdp) Christian County	6.0
Vermont	21.2	Saginaw County, MI	3.2	**Grand Forks*, ND** (city) Grand Forks County	6.1
South Dakota	22.4	Ward County, ND	3.2	**Fort Hood, TX** (cdp) Bell County	6.3
Wyoming	23.0	Archuleta County, CO	3.4	**Pueblo, CO** (city) Pueblo County	6.5
Michigan	25.3	Sanilac County, MI	3.5	**Warren, MI** (city) Macomb County	6.6

Note: (1) Ranking tables cover all states and counties, and places with an overall population of at least 125,000, OR an overall population of at least 25,000 where the Hispanic/Latino population is at least 20% of the overall population. In states where less than five places meet either of these criteria, we have included places with at least 10,000 total population with the highest percentage of Hispanic/Latino population. These places are identified with an asterisk (*); Please refer to the User's Guide for a full explanation of data.

Foreign-Born Population

Puerto Rican

Top 10 States, Counties, and Places[1]

Sorted by Number in Descending Order — U.S. = 50,753

State	Number	County	Number	Place	Number
New York	11,935	Bronx County, NY	2,988	**New York, NY** (city)	8,982
Florida	8,908	Kings County, NY	2,444	**Bronx, NY** (borough) Bronx County	2,988
New Jersey	5,642	Miami-Dade County, FL	2,155	**Brooklyn, NY** (borough) Kings County	2,444
California	4,401	Queens County, NY	2,151	**Queens, NY** (borough) Queens County	2,151
Pennsylvania	2,634	Cook County, IL	1,555	**Chicago, IL** (city) Cook County	1,389
Massachusetts	2,235	Orange County, FL	1,480	**Philadelphia, PA** (city) Philadelphia County	1,237
Illinois	1,981	Philadelphia County, PA	1,237	**Manhattan, NY** (borough) New York County	1,165
Texas	1,782	Los Angeles County, CA	1,198	**Los Angeles, CA** (city) Los Angeles County	539
Connecticut	1,635	Broward County, FL	1,181	**Bridgeport, CT** (city/town) Fairfield County	469
Virginia	1,040	New York County, NY	1,165	**Alafaya, FL** (cdp) Orange County	468

Sorted by Number in Ascending Order — U.S. = 50,753

State	Number	County	Number	Place	Number
Montana	0	Adams County, CO	0	**Akron, OH** (city) Summit County	0
North Dakota	0	Adams County, PA	0	**Altamonte Springs, FL** (city) Seminole County	0
South Dakota	0	Allen County, IN	0	**Aurora, CO** (city) Arapahoe County	0
Vermont	0	Broome County, NY	0	**Aurora, IL** (city) Kane County	0
West Virginia	0	Camden County, GA	0	**Belleville, NJ** (township) Essex County	0
Wyoming	0	Cameron County, TX	0	**Berwyn, IL** (city) Cook County	0
Idaho	4	Carbon County, PA	0	**Bolingbrook, IL** (village) Will County	0
Nebraska	21	Carroll County, MD	0	**Bridgeton, NJ** (city) Cumberland County	0
Alaska	41	Cattaraugus County, NY	0	**Central Falls*, RI** (city) Providence County	0
Utah	56	Cecil County, MD	0	**Chandler, AZ** (city) Maricopa County	0

Sorted by Percent in Descending Order — U.S. = 1.1%

State	Percent	County	Percent	Place	Percent
District of Columbia	5.7	Kings County, CA	24.3	**Anaheim, CA** (city) Orange County	9.1
Louisiana	3.5	Washoe County, NV	12.2	**Portland, OR** (city) Multnomah County	7.3
Arkansas	3.3	Butte County, CA	9.2	**Glendale, AZ** (city) Maricopa County	7.0
Nevada	3.1	Hendry County, FL	7.2	**Elk Grove, CA** (city) Sacramento County	6.7
California	2.5	Horry County, SC	6.3	**Tamiami, FL** (cdp) Miami-Dade County	6.7
Oregon	2.0	Lexington County, SC	6.3	**Vallejo, CA** (city) Solano County	6.7
Iowa	1.9	Northumberland County, PA	6.1	**Waukegan, IL** (city) Lake County	5.7
Mississippi	1.9	Multnomah County, OR	6.0	**Irving, TX** (city) Dallas County	5.5
Arizona	1.8	Okaloosa County, FL	5.3	**New Brunswick, NJ** (city) Middlesex County	5.4
Missouri	1.8	Sampson County, NC	5.1	**Lancaster, CA** (city) Los Angeles County	4.9

Sorted by Percent in Ascending Order — U.S. = 1.1%

State	Percent	County	Percent	Place	Percent
Montana	0.0	Adams County, CO	0.0	**Akron, OH** (city) Summit County	0.0
North Dakota	0.0	Adams County, PA	0.0	**Altamonte Springs, FL** (city) Seminole County	0.0
South Dakota	0.0	Allen County, IN	0.0	**Aurora, CO** (city) Arapahoe County	0.0
Vermont	0.0	Broome County, NY	0.0	**Aurora, IL** (city) Kane County	0.0
West Virginia	0.0	Camden County, GA	0.0	**Belleville, NJ** (township) Essex County	0.0
Wyoming	0.0	Cameron County, TX	0.0	**Berwyn, IL** (city) Cook County	0.0
Idaho	0.1	Carbon County, PA	0.0	**Bolingbrook, IL** (village) Will County	0.0
Hawaii	0.4	Carroll County, MD	0.0	**Bridgeton, NJ** (city) Cumberland County	0.0
Wisconsin	0.4	Cattaraugus County, NY	0.0	**Central Falls*, RI** (city) Providence County	0.0
New Hampshire	0.5	Cecil County, MD	0.0	**Chandler, AZ** (city) Maricopa County	0.0

Note: (1) Ranking tables cover all states and counties, and places with an overall population of at least 125,000, OR an overall population of at least 25,000 where the Hispanic/Latino population is at least 20% of the overall population. In states where less than five places meet either of these criteria, we have included places with at least 10,000 total population with the highest percentage of Hispanic/Latino population. These places are identified with an asterisk (*); Please refer to the User's Guide for a full explanation of data.

Foreign-Born Population

South American

Top 10 States, Counties, and Places[1]

Sorted by Number in Descending Order — U.S. = 1,872,507

State	Number	County	Number	Place	Number
Florida	487,765	Miami-Dade County, FL	203,776	**New York, NY** (city)	252,750
New York	361,188	Queens County, NY	155,649	**Queens, NY** (borough) Queens County	155,649
New Jersey	228,358	Broward County, FL	108,647	**Brooklyn, NY** (borough) Kings County	37,242
California	177,838	Los Angeles County, CA	77,513	**Los Angeles, CA** (city) Los Angeles County	33,578
Texas	87,667	Hudson County, NJ	49,903	**Bronx, NY** (borough) Bronx County	28,607
Virginia	73,584	Kings County, NY	37,242	**Manhattan, NY** (borough) New York County	25,484
Connecticut	46,908	Westchester County, NY	36,203	**Miami, FL** (city) Miami-Dade County	25,437
Illinois	44,861	Fairfax County, VA	34,722	**Chicago, IL** (city) Cook County	22,774
Maryland	40,434	Palm Beach County, FL	34,310	**Elizabeth, NJ** (city) Union County	20,447
Massachusetts	38,895	Harris County, TX	33,439	**Houston, TX** (city) Harris County	16,591

Sorted by Number in Ascending Order — U.S. = 1,872,507

State	Number	County	Number	Place	Number
North Dakota	417	Clark County, WA	271	**Placentia, CA** (city) Orange County	307
Vermont	497	San Luis Obispo County, CA	288	**Killeen, TX** (city) Bell County	334
Montana	522	Spokane County, WA	319	**Chesapeake, VA** (independent city)	355
Maine	700	Tolland County, CT	342	**Palm Springs, CA** (city) Riverside County	359
Wyoming	718	Saint Tammany Parish, LA	346	**Lancaster, CA** (city) Los Angeles County	368
West Virginia	1,089	Tompkins County, NY	366	**Glendora, CA** (city) Los Angeles County	428
Alaska	1,612	Ada County, ID	374	**Modesto, CA** (city) Stanislaus County	439
Nebraska	1,851	Schenectady County, NY	387	**Pomona, CA** (city) Los Angeles County	448
Hawaii	1,871	Williamson County, TN	393	**Chino Hills, CA** (city) San Bernardino County	449
Idaho	1,909	Hampshire County, MA	410	**Chino, CA** (city) San Bernardino County	456

Sorted by Percent in Descending Order — U.S. = 67.7%

State	Percent	County	Percent	Place	Percent
Florida	73.5	Fayette County, KY	80.2	**Hallandale Beach, FL** (city) Broward County	91.0
South Carolina	72.0	Guilford County, NC	80.2	**North Miami Beach, FL** (city) Miami-Dade County	89.6
Iowa	71.0	Clayton County, GA	79.6	**Gaithersburg, MD** (city) Montgomery County	88.2
Virginia	70.4	Shelby County, TN	79.6	**Springfield, VA** (cdp) Fairfax County	85.2
Nebraska	70.0	Sussex County, DE	79.0	**Miami Beach, FL** (city) Miami-Dade County	85.0
Connecticut	69.7	Middlesex County, CT	78.2	**Aspen Hill, MD** (cdp) Montgomery County	84.0
Massachusetts	69.7	Manatee County, FL	77.5	**Port Chester, NY** (village) Westchester County	83.2
Mississippi	69.4	Charleston County, SC	77.4	**Fountainebleau, FL** (cdp) Miami-Dade County	83.0
New Jersey	69.3	Beaufort County, SC	77.1	**Bayonne, NJ** (city) Hudson County	82.3
New York	67.8	Hidalgo County, TX	76.6	**Coconut Creek, FL** (city) Broward County	82.3

Sorted by Percent in Ascending Order — U.S. = 67.7%

State	Percent	County	Percent	Place	Percent
Maine	50.1	San Luis Obispo County, CA	28.4	**Lancaster, CA** (city) Los Angeles County	33.3
Montana	50.3	Ada County, ID	33.2	**Placentia, CA** (city) Orange County	34.4
Vermont	50.9	Clark County, WA	34.8	**Chino Hills, CA** (city) San Bernardino County	40.3
Hawaii	53.6	Saint Tammany Parish, LA	38.3	**Killeen, TX** (city) Bell County	41.1
Idaho	54.2	Santa Cruz County, CA	39.4	**Pomona, CA** (city) Los Angeles County	42.3
North Dakota	54.4	Tompkins County, NY	40.1	**Chesapeake, VA** (independent city)	43.1
New Hampshire	55.3	Yolo County, CA	41.4	**Norfolk, VA** (independent city)	46.3
Washington	55.3	Saint Johns County, FL	43.2	**Gilbert, AZ** (town) Maricopa County	46.9
Alabama	55.7	Douglas County, CO	43.5	**Torrance, CA** (city) Los Angeles County	47.0
Louisiana	56.7	Pierce County, WA	44.6	**Fresno, CA** (city) Fresno County	47.3

Note: (1) Ranking tables cover all states and counties, and places with an overall population of at least 125,000, OR an overall population of at least 25,000 where the Hispanic/Latino population is at least 20% of the overall population. In states where less than five places meet either of these criteria, we have included places with at least 10,000 total population with the highest percentage of Hispanic/Latino population. These places are identified with an asterisk (*); Please refer to the User's Guide for a full explanation of data.

Foreign-Born Population

South American: Argentinean

Top 10 States, Counties, and Places[1]

Sorted by Number in Descending Order — U.S. = 146,004

State	Number	County	Number	Place	Number
Florida	41,829	Miami-Dade County, FL	22,445	**New York, NY** (city)	9,405
California	26,865	Los Angeles County, CA	12,425	**Los Angeles, CA** (city) Los Angeles County	5,757
New York	15,765	Broward County, FL	7,764	**Miami, FL** (city) Miami-Dade County	4,708
New Jersey	9,279	Queens County, NY	4,044	**Queens, NY** (borough) Queens County	4,044
Texas	8,591	Orange County, CA	3,300	**Miami Beach, FL** (city) Miami-Dade County	3,821
Maryland	3,845	Palm Beach County, FL	3,105	**Manhattan, NY** (borough) New York County	2,465
Virginia	3,691	Harris County, TX	2,752	**Brooklyn, NY** (borough) Kings County	1,764
Illinois	3,365	New York County, NY	2,465	**Hollywood, FL** (city) Broward County	1,380
Utah	3,327	Cook County, IL	2,124	**Houston, TX** (city) Harris County	1,371
Massachusetts	2,592	Montgomery County, MD	2,033	**Hialeah, FL** (city) Miami-Dade County	1,121

Sorted by Number in Ascending Order — U.S. = 146,004

State	Number	County	Number	Place	Number
Louisiana	411	Travis County, TX	483	**San Diego, CA** (city) San Diego County	560
Minnesota	580	Tarrant County, TX	485	**San Jose, CA** (city) Santa Clara County	582
Missouri	618	Contra Costa County, CA	525	**Pembroke Pines, FL** (city) Broward County	698
Oregon	681	Oakland County, MI	538	**Coral Springs, FL** (city) Broward County	730
District of Columbia	685	King County, WA	585	**San Francisco, CA** (city) San Francisco County	737
Tennessee	768	Orange County, NY	602	**Bronx, NY** (borough) Bronx County	818
Colorado	872	Bexar County, TX	633	**Doral, FL** (city) Miami-Dade County	858
Indiana	877	New Haven County, CT	688	**Hempstead (town), NY** (town) Nassau County	887
Wisconsin	928	Ventura County, CA	688	**Chicago, IL** (city) Cook County	984
Washington	988	San Francisco County, CA	737	**Aventura, FL** (city) Miami-Dade County	1,120

Sorted by Percent in Descending Order — U.S. = 67.5%

State	Percent	County	Percent	Place	Percent
Missouri	83.9	Orange County, FL	82.2	**Miami Beach, FL** (city) Miami-Dade County	87.8
Tennessee	82.5	Miami-Dade County, FL	81.2	**Aventura, FL** (city) Miami-Dade County	86.4
South Carolina	78.2	Dallas County, TX	80.5	**Hollywood, FL** (city) Broward County	85.4
Florida	78.1	Palm Beach County, FL	78.4	**Doral, FL** (city) Miami-Dade County	85.0
Wisconsin	70.7	Harris County, TX	78.2	**Hialeah, FL** (city) Miami-Dade County	81.7
Indiana	70.6	Montgomery County, TX	77.8	**Miami, FL** (city) Miami-Dade County	81.1
Nevada	70.5	Westchester County, NY	77.2	**Houston, TX** (city) Harris County	74.8
Texas	70.2	Broward County, FL	75.5	**Bronx, NY** (borough) Bronx County	72.8
Massachusetts	67.8	Oakland County, MI	75.5	**Coral Springs, FL** (city) Broward County	72.2
District of Columbia	67.0	Utah County, UT	75.4	**Queens, NY** (borough) Queens County	70.8

Sorted by Percent in Ascending Order — U.S. = 67.5%

State	Percent	County	Percent	Place	Percent
Louisiana	46.4	Contra Costa County, CA	50.5	**San Francisco, CA** (city) San Francisco County	55.7
Washington	52.0	Travis County, TX	52.2	**Chicago, IL** (city) Cook County	57.2
Illinois	55.0	San Francisco County, CA	55.7	**Pembroke Pines, FL** (city) Broward County	61.8
Oregon	55.1	King County, WA	57.6	**Brooklyn, NY** (borough) Kings County	63.5
Colorado	59.5	Alameda County, CA	57.9	**Manhattan, NY** (borough) New York County	63.6
North Carolina	59.6	San Bernardino County, CA	57.9	**San Diego, CA** (city) San Diego County	65.3
Georgia	60.9	San Diego County, CA	58.6	**New York, NY** (city)	66.6
California	62.1	Salt Lake County, UT	59.2	**Los Angeles, CA** (city) Los Angeles County	66.9
Maryland	62.4	Ventura County, CA	59.6	**San Jose, CA** (city) Santa Clara County	68.2
Pennsylvania	62.4	Fairfield County, CT	60.2	**Hempstead (town), NY** (town) Nassau County	69.0

Note: (1) Ranking tables cover all states and counties, and places with an overall population of at least 125,000, OR an overall population of at least 25,000 where the Hispanic/Latino population is at least 20% of the overall population. In states where less than five places meet either of these criteria, we have included places with at least 10,000 total population with the highest percentage of Hispanic/Latino population. These places are identified with an asterisk (*); Please refer to the User's Guide for a full explanation of data.

Foreign-Born Population

South American: Bolivian

Top 10 States, Counties, and Places[1]

Sorted by Number in Descending Order — U.S. = 68,572

State	Number	County	Number	Place	Number
Virginia	26,612	Fairfax County, VA	14,562	**Arlington, VA** (cdp) Arlington County	3,431
California	8,322	Montgomery County, MD	3,717	**New York, NY** (city)	3,316
Florida	6,890	Los Angeles County, CA	3,541	**Los Angeles, CA** (city) Los Angeles County	2,395
Maryland	5,193	Prince William County, VA	3,443	**Queens, NY** (borough) Queens County	2,116
New York	5,137	Arlington County, VA	3,431	**Annandale, VA** (cdp) Fairfax County	2,060
New Jersey	3,251	Miami-Dade County, FL	2,286	**West Falls Church, VA** (cdp) Fairfax County	1,259
Texas	2,740	Queens County, NY	2,116	**Dale City, VA** (cdp) Prince William County	1,216
Rhode Island	1,309	Loudoun County, VA	1,845	**Springfield, VA** (cdp) Fairfax County	895
Massachusetts	1,157	Providence County, RI	1,309	**Providence, RI** (city) Providence County	725
Illinois	1,031	Broward County, FL	1,179		

Sorted by Number in Ascending Order — U.S. = 68,572

State	Number	County	Number	Place	Number
North Carolina	401	Cook County, IL	447	**Providence, RI** (city) Providence County	725
Pennsylvania	404	San Diego County, CA	469	**Springfield, VA** (cdp) Fairfax County	895
Illinois	1,031	Palm Beach County, FL	743	**Dale City, VA** (cdp) Prince William County	1,216
Massachusetts	1,157	Santa Clara County, CA	776	**West Falls Church, VA** (cdp) Fairfax County	1,259
Rhode Island	1,309	Harris County, TX	885	**Annandale, VA** (cdp) Fairfax County	2,060
Texas	2,740	Prince George's County, MD	986	**Queens, NY** (borough) Queens County	2,116
New Jersey	3,251	Orange County, CA	1,069	**Los Angeles, CA** (city) Los Angeles County	2,395
New York	5,137	Broward County, FL	1,179	**New York, NY** (city)	3,316
Maryland	5,193	Providence County, RI	1,309	**Arlington, VA** (cdp) Arlington County	3,431
Florida	6,890	Loudoun County, VA	1,845		

Sorted by Percent in Descending Order — U.S. = 66.7%

State	Percent	County	Percent	Place	Percent
New Jersey	75.2	Prince George's County, MD	88.8	**Dale City, VA** (cdp) Prince William County	84.0
Virginia	73.9	Palm Beach County, FL	81.7	**Springfield, VA** (cdp) Fairfax County	83.9
Maryland	73.3	Arlington County, VA	79.3	**Arlington, VA** (cdp) Arlington County	79.3
Florida	68.3	Fairfax County, VA	74.8	**West Falls Church, VA** (cdp) Fairfax County	78.2
New York	65.6	Loudoun County, VA	71.7	**New York, NY** (city)	67.6
Rhode Island	64.2	Montgomery County, MD	71.7	**Los Angeles, CA** (city) Los Angeles County	66.9
Texas	62.4	Prince William County, VA	71.7	**Annandale, VA** (cdp) Fairfax County	66.6
Pennsylvania	60.7	Miami-Dade County, FL	69.4	**Providence, RI** (city) Providence County	64.4
California	60.6	Orange County, CA	68.0	**Queens, NY** (borough) Queens County	63.8
Massachusetts	60.3	Harris County, TX	66.2		

Sorted by Percent in Ascending Order — U.S. = 66.7%

State	Percent	County	Percent	Place	Percent
Illinois	48.4	San Diego County, CA	55.0	**Queens, NY** (borough) Queens County	63.8
North Carolina	58.9	Cook County, IL	62.3	**Providence, RI** (city) Providence County	64.4
Massachusetts	60.3	Broward County, FL	63.5	**Annandale, VA** (cdp) Fairfax County	66.6
California	60.6	Queens County, NY	63.8	**Los Angeles, CA** (city) Los Angeles County	66.9
Pennsylvania	60.7	Providence County, RI	64.2	**New York, NY** (city)	67.6
Texas	62.4	Santa Clara County, CA	65.3	**West Falls Church, VA** (cdp) Fairfax County	78.2
Rhode Island	64.2	Los Angeles County, CA	65.7	**Arlington, VA** (cdp) Arlington County	79.3
New York	65.6	Harris County, TX	66.2	**Springfield, VA** (cdp) Fairfax County	83.9
Florida	68.3	Orange County, CA	68.0	**Dale City, VA** (cdp) Prince William County	84.0
Maryland	73.3	Miami-Dade County, FL	69.4		

Note: (1) Ranking tables cover all states and counties, and places with an overall population of at least 125,000, OR an overall population of at least 25,000 where the Hispanic/Latino population is at least 20% of the overall population. In states where less than five places meet either of these criteria, we have included places with at least 10,000 total population with the highest percentage of Hispanic/Latino population. These places are identified with an asterisk (*); Please refer to the User's Guide for a full explanation of data.

Foreign-Born Population

South American: Chilean

Top 10 States, Counties, and Places[1]

Sorted by Number in Descending Order — U.S. = 78,755

State	Number	County	Number	Place	Number
Florida	17,172	Miami-Dade County, FL	8,923	**New York, NY** (city)	4,981
California	12,916	Los Angeles County, CA	5,315	**Los Angeles, CA** (city) Los Angeles County	2,663
New York	10,100	Broward County, FL	2,974	**Queens, NY** (borough) Queens County	2,617
New Jersey	5,732	Queens County, NY	2,617	**Hempstead (town), NY** (town) Nassau County	920
Texas	3,207	Nassau County, NY	1,777	**Brooklyn, NY** (borough) Kings County	901
Maryland	3,053	Montgomery County, MD	1,741	**Manhattan, NY** (borough) New York County	897
Virginia	2,543	Hudson County, NJ	1,731	**Miami, FL** (city) Miami-Dade County	896
Utah	2,264	Westchester County, NY	1,644	**Kendall, FL** (cdp) Miami-Dade County	599
Massachusetts	2,053	Palm Beach County, FL	1,255	**Chicago, IL** (city) Cook County	515
Illinois	1,680	Fairfax County, VA	1,193		

Sorted by Number in Ascending Order — U.S. = 78,755

State	Number	County	Number	Place	Number
Tennessee	440	San Mateo County, CA	443	**Chicago, IL** (city) Cook County	515
Missouri	479	Alameda County, CA	488	**Kendall, FL** (cdp) Miami-Dade County	599
Minnesota	511	Bergen County, NJ	514	**Miami, FL** (city) Miami-Dade County	896
Ohio	539	San Bernardino County, CA	560	**Manhattan, NY** (borough) New York County	897
Wisconsin	612	Riverside County, CA	575	**Brooklyn, NY** (borough) Kings County	901
Michigan	625	Maricopa County, AZ	584	**Hempstead (town), NY** (town) Nassau County	920
Oregon	758	Clark County, NV	600	**Queens, NY** (borough) Queens County	2,617
Arizona	868	Orange County, CA	663	**Los Angeles, CA** (city) Los Angeles County	2,663
Colorado	880	Salt Lake County, UT	698	**New York, NY** (city)	4,981
Nevada	906	Suffolk County, NY	733		

Sorted by Percent in Descending Order — U.S. = 63.2%

State	Percent	County	Percent	Place	Percent
Florida	74.7	Palm Beach County, FL	80.6	**Miami, FL** (city) Miami-Dade County	76.0
Connecticut	72.5	Hudson County, NJ	79.8	**Hempstead (town), NY** (town) Nassau County	70.9
Maryland	69.2	Fairfax County, VA	76.0	**Queens, NY** (borough) Queens County	69.4
Oregon	69.1	Miami-Dade County, FL	76.0	**New York, NY** (city)	65.1
New Jersey	67.2	Broward County, FL	75.9	**Kendall, FL** (cdp) Miami-Dade County	61.7
Texas	66.3	Harris County, TX	72.3	**Brooklyn, NY** (borough) Kings County	59.5
Virginia	66.0	Montgomery County, MD	71.6	**Los Angeles, CA** (city) Los Angeles County	59.2
New York	64.9	Westchester County, NY	70.3	**Chicago, IL** (city) Cook County	58.9
Utah	64.9	Queens County, NY	69.4	**Manhattan, NY** (borough) New York County	58.2
Minnesota	64.8	Middlesex County, MA	68.6		

Sorted by Percent in Ascending Order — U.S. = 63.2%

State	Percent	County	Percent	Place	Percent
Arizona	46.9	Alameda County, CA	42.2	**Manhattan, NY** (borough) New York County	58.2
Wisconsin	49.4	San Diego County, CA	42.2	**Chicago, IL** (city) Cook County	58.9
Georgia	51.3	San Bernardino County, CA	43.0	**Los Angeles, CA** (city) Los Angeles County	59.2
Pennsylvania	52.2	Orange County, CA	48.0	**Brooklyn, NY** (borough) Kings County	59.5
Michigan	52.3	Bergen County, NJ	50.5	**Kendall, FL** (cdp) Miami-Dade County	61.7
Missouri	53.0	San Mateo County, CA	50.5	**New York, NY** (city)	65.1
Illinois	53.4	Maricopa County, AZ	52.7	**Queens, NY** (borough) Queens County	69.4
California	55.1	Riverside County, CA	57.4	**Hempstead (town), NY** (town) Nassau County	70.9
Washington	56.4	Clark County, NV	58.0	**Miami, FL** (city) Miami-Dade County	76.0
North Carolina	56.6	New York County, NY	58.2		

Note: (1) Ranking tables cover all states and counties, and places with an overall population of at least 125,000, OR an overall population of at least 25,000 where the Hispanic/Latino population is at least 20% of the overall population. In states where less than five places meet either of these criteria, we have included places with at least 10,000 total population with the highest percentage of Hispanic/Latino population. These places are identified with an asterisk (*); Please refer to the User's Guide for a full explanation of data.

Foreign-Born Population

South American: Colombian

Top 10 States, Counties, and Places[1]

Sorted by Number in Descending Order — U.S. = 597,006

State	Number	County	Number	Place	Number
Florida	209,877	Miami-Dade County, FL	82,845	**New York, NY** (city)	67,316
New York	96,977	Queens County, NY	49,800	**Queens, NY** (borough) Queens County	49,800
New Jersey	68,227	Broward County, FL	46,011	**Miami, FL** (city) Miami-Dade County	8,512
California	34,995	Orange County, FL	16,993	**Pembroke Pines, FL** (city) Broward County	8,022
Texas	32,905	Los Angeles County, CA	15,290	**Elizabeth, NJ** (city) Union County	7,765
Massachusetts	17,987	Palm Beach County, FL	14,916	**Houston, TX** (city) Harris County	7,226
Georgia	15,746	Harris County, TX	14,746	**Brooklyn, NY** (borough) Kings County	7,193
Connecticut	13,434	Bergen County, NJ	13,131	**Boston, MA** (city) Suffolk County	6,382
Illinois	12,270	Hudson County, NJ	12,251	**Hialeah, FL** (city) Miami-Dade County	6,096
North Carolina	10,142	Union County, NJ	10,992	**Los Angeles, CA** (city) Los Angeles County	5,889

Sorted by Number in Ascending Order — U.S. = 597,006

State	Number	County	Number	Place	Number
Kentucky	594	Luzerne County, PA	218	**Long Beach, CA** (city) Los Angeles County	431
New Mexico	598	Will County, IL	324	**Royal Palm Beach, FL** (village) Palm Beach County	444
Alaska	660	Milwaukee County, WI	383	**Indianapolis, IN** (city) Marion County	458
Iowa	752	Oakland County, MI	412	**Raleigh, NC** (city) Wake County	459
Arkansas	784	Franklin County, OH	436	**Anaheim, CA** (city) Orange County	503
Delaware	811	Ulster County, NY	439	**San Jose, CA** (city) Santa Clara County	506
Nebraska	841	Burlington County, NJ	442	**Deltona, FL** (city) Volusia County	542
Oregon	845	Cuyahoga County, OH	461	**Glendale, CA** (city) Los Angeles County	548
Oklahoma	983	Hampden County, MA	475	**Cooper City, FL** (city) Broward County	578
District of Columbia	1,150	Hall County, GA	498	**Tallahassee, FL** (city) Leon County	592

Sorted by Percent in Descending Order — U.S. = 66.8%

State	Percent	County	Percent	Place	Percent
Nebraska	81.4	Morris County, NJ	79.2	**North Miami Beach, FL** (city) Miami-Dade County	94.1
Delaware	74.1	Collier County, FL	78.0	**Hallandale Beach, FL** (city) Broward County	94.0
Florida	71.5	Fort Bend County, TX	77.8	**Miami Beach, FL** (city) Miami-Dade County	83.4
South Carolina	70.9	Atlantic County, NJ	77.5	**Englewood, NJ** (city) Bergen County	83.3
Massachusetts	70.8	Manatee County, FL	77.2	**Hollywood, FL** (city) Broward County	82.6
Rhode Island	69.6	Essex County, MA	76.4	**Fountainebleau, FL** (cdp) Miami-Dade County	81.7
New Jersey	68.5	Suffolk County, MA	75.8	**Union City, NJ** (city) Hudson County	80.3
Connecticut	68.3	Greenville County, SC	75.3	**Aventura, FL** (city) Miami-Dade County	80.0
Arkansas	67.4	Dallas County, TX	74.3	**Miami, FL** (city) Miami-Dade County	79.8
Alaska	66.5	Broward County, FL	74.0	**Egypt Lake-Leto, FL** (cdp) Hillsborough County	78.2

Sorted by Percent in Ascending Order — U.S. = 66.8%

State	Percent	County	Percent	Place	Percent
Kentucky	45.4	Will County, IL	38.6	**Babylon, NY** (town) Suffolk County	45.4
Indiana	49.5	Luzerne County, PA	39.1	**San Diego, CA** (city) San Diego County	46.4
Oregon	51.7	Alachua County, FL	48.0	**Staten Island, NY** (borough) Richmond County	49.0
Alabama	52.5	Riverside County, CA	48.0	**Deltona, FL** (city) Volusia County	50.1
Ohio	52.6	Richmond County, NY	49.0	**Burbank, CA** (city) Los Angeles County	50.2
New Mexico	53.2	Bucks County, PA	50.2	**Brookhaven, NY** (town) Suffolk County	51.5
Louisiana	54.8	Milwaukee County, WI	50.2	**Indianapolis, IN** (city) Marion County	52.1
Tennessee	54.8	Hall County, GA	50.8	**Phoenix, AZ** (city) Maricopa County	54.3
Michigan	55.2	Burlington County, NJ	51.1	**Tallahassee, FL** (city) Leon County	54.3
New Hampshire	55.2	Ulster County, NY	51.4	**Long Beach, CA** (city) Los Angeles County	54.6

Note: (1) Ranking tables cover all states and counties, and places with an overall population of at least 125,000, OR an overall population of at least 25,000 where the Hispanic/Latino population is at least 20% of the overall population. In states where less than five places meet either of these criteria, we have included places with at least 10,000 total population with the highest percentage of Hispanic/Latino population. These places are identified with an asterisk (*); Please refer to the User's Guide for a full explanation of data.

Foreign-Born Population

South American: Ecuadorian

Top 10 States, Counties, and Places[1]

Sorted by Number in Descending Order — U.S. = 384,474

State	Number	County	Number	Place	Number
New York	161,322	Queens County, NY	71,111	**New York, NY** (city)	124,046
New Jersey	71,934	Kings County, NY	20,919	**Queens, NY** (borough) Queens County	71,111
Florida	40,792	Hudson County, NJ	20,563	**Brooklyn, NY** (borough) Kings County	20,919
California	20,712	Bronx County, NY	18,700	**Bronx, NY** (borough) Bronx County	18,700
Connecticut	16,378	Essex County, NJ	16,956	**Chicago, IL** (city) Cook County	11,820
Illinois	15,953	Westchester County, NY	15,216	**Manhattan, NY** (borough) New York County	11,301
Pennsylvania	7,478	Miami-Dade County, FL	14,932	**Newark, NJ** (city) Essex County	11,029
Texas	7,101	Cook County, IL	14,202	**Jersey City, NJ** (city) Hudson County	5,748
Minnesota	5,701	Los Angeles County, CA	11,594	**Danbury, CT** (city/town) Fairfield County	5,288
North Carolina	5,608	New York County, NY	11,301	**Elizabeth, NJ** (city) Union County	4,770

Sorted by Number in Ascending Order — U.S. = 384,474

State	Number	County	Number	Place	Number
Missouri	312	Santa Clara County, CA	356	**Downey, CA** (city) Los Angeles County	452
Colorado	408	Baltimore County, MD	404	**Country Club, FL** (cdp) Miami-Dade County	510
Kansas	409	Putnam County, NY	404	**Oyster Bay, NY** (town) Nassau County	549
Louisiana	460	King County, WA	440	**Miramar, FL** (city) Broward County	597
Iowa	495	Monmouth County, NJ	469	**Hollywood, FL** (city) Broward County	619
Wisconsin	502	Will County, IL	479	**Coral Springs, FL** (city) Broward County	657
Oregon	536	Pinellas County, FL	523	**Philadelphia, PA** (city) Philadelphia County	698
Michigan	577	Providence County, RI	567	**Clifton, NJ** (city) Passaic County	748
Oklahoma	623	Camden County, NJ	589	**Central Islip, NY** (cdp) Suffolk County	791
Rhode Island	638	Prince George's County, MD	595	**City of Orange, NJ** (township) Essex County	813

Sorted by Percent in Descending Order — U.S. = 66.4%

State	Percent	County	Percent	Place	Percent
Connecticut	71.5	Morris County, NJ	81.0	**Doral, FL** (city) Miami-Dade County	85.5
Minnesota	69.5	Delaware County, PA	75.5	**Port Chester, NY** (village) Westchester County	84.7
New Jersey	69.4	Utah County, UT	74.6	**City of Orange, NJ** (township) Essex County	84.1
New York	68.8	Rockland County, NY	74.3	**Union City, NJ** (city) Hudson County	81.4
Florida	67.1	Fairfield County, CT	74.2	**Sunrise, FL** (city) Broward County	80.7
Iowa	66.5	Hennepin County, MN	72.9	**White Plains, NY** (city) Westchester County	78.4
Maryland	65.1	Miami-Dade County, FL	72.4	**Stamford, CT** (city/town) Fairfield County	78.3
Oklahoma	64.7	Hudson County, NJ	72.0	**Danbury, CT** (city/town) Fairfield County	78.0
Tennessee	64.7	Mercer County, NJ	71.9	**Miami, FL** (city) Miami-Dade County	77.5
Pennsylvania	63.9	Montgomery County, MD	71.6	**Rye, NY** (town) Westchester County	77.5

Sorted by Percent in Ascending Order — U.S. = 66.4%

State	Percent	County	Percent	Place	Percent
Missouri	36.2	Maricopa County, AZ	44.9	**Babylon, NY** (town) Suffolk County	50.4
Colorado	40.0	Santa Clara County, CA	48.8	**Oyster Bay, NY** (town) Nassau County	50.8
Kansas	41.2	Clark County, NV	51.8	**Brentwood, NY** (cdp) Suffolk County	54.3
Washington	46.8	Camden County, NJ	52.1	**Brookhaven, NY** (town) Suffolk County	55.4
Arizona	50.2	Monmouth County, NJ	52.3	**Orlando, FL** (city) Orange County	56.6
Nevada	50.3	Will County, IL	52.5	**Country Club, FL** (cdp) Miami-Dade County	57.0
Michigan	51.7	San Bernardino County, CA	53.1	**Islip, NY** (town) Suffolk County	57.3
Rhode Island	52.3	Providence County, RI	53.3	**Central Islip, NY** (cdp) Suffolk County	60.2
Virginia	53.8	Orange County, CA	53.7	**Coral Springs, FL** (city) Broward County	60.5
Louisiana	54.9	Baltimore County, MD	54.2	**North Bergen, NJ** (township) Hudson County	62.2

Note: (1) Ranking tables cover all states and counties, and places with an overall population of at least 125,000, OR an overall population of at least 25,000 where the Hispanic/Latino population is at least 20% of the overall population. In states where less than five places meet either of these criteria, we have included places with at least 10,000 total population with the highest percentage of Hispanic/Latino population. These places are identified with an asterisk (*); Please refer to the User's Guide for a full explanation of data.

Foreign-Born Population

South American: Paraguayan

Top 10 States, Counties, and Places[1]

Sorted by Number in Descending Order — U.S. = 13,369

State	Number	County	Number	Place	Number
New York	4,864	Queens County, NY	1,916	**New York, NY** (city)	2,465
New Jersey	1,293	Westchester County, NY	1,265	**Queens, NY** (borough) Queens County	1,916
Florida	1,196				
Maryland	876				
California	575				
Texas	558				

Sorted by Number in Ascending Order — U.S. = 13,369

State	Number	County	Number	Place	Number
Texas	558	Westchester County, NY	1,265	**Queens, NY** (borough) Queens County	1,916
California	575	Queens County, NY	1,916	**New York, NY** (city)	2,465
Maryland	876				
Florida	1,196				
New Jersey	1,293				
New York	4,864				

Sorted by Percent in Descending Order — U.S. = 68.5%

State	Percent	County	Percent	Place	Percent
Maryland	73.9	Queens County, NY	76.3	**Queens, NY** (borough) Queens County	76.3
New York	73.3	Westchester County, NY	73.9	**New York, NY** (city)	70.7
Florida	70.6				
California	67.5				
New Jersey	66.9				
Texas	61.2				

Sorted by Percent in Ascending Order — U.S. = 68.5%

State	Percent	County	Percent	Place	Percent
Texas	61.2	Westchester County, NY	73.9	**New York, NY** (city)	70.7
New Jersey	66.9	Queens County, NY	76.3	**Queens, NY** (borough) Queens County	76.3
California	67.5				
Florida	70.6				
New York	73.3				
Maryland	73.9				

Note: (1) Ranking tables cover all states and counties, and places with an overall population of at least 125,000, OR an overall population of at least 25,000 where the Hispanic/Latino population is at least 20% of the overall population. In states where less than five places meet either of these criteria, we have included places with at least 10,000 total population with the highest percentage of Hispanic/Latino population. These places are identified with an asterisk (*); Please refer to the User's Guide for a full explanation of data.

Foreign-Born Population

South American: Peruvian

Top 10 States, Counties, and Places[1]

Sorted by Number in Descending Order — U.S. = 365,695

State	Number	County	Number	Place	Number
Florida	76,605	Miami-Dade County, FL	29,394	**New York, NY** (city)	28,844
California	57,694	Los Angeles County, CA	22,677	**Queens, NY** (borough) Queens County	18,474
New Jersey	53,643	Broward County, FL	19,296	**Los Angeles, CA** (city) Los Angeles County	9,988
New York	48,639	Queens County, NY	18,474	**Paterson, NJ** (city) Passaic County	6,028
Virginia	20,949	Passaic County, NJ	13,116	**Elizabeth, NJ** (city) Union County	4,244
Texas	15,989	Fairfax County, VA	10,637	**Miami, FL** (city) Miami-Dade County	3,807
Maryland	11,551	Hudson County, NJ	10,569	**Clifton, NJ** (city) Passaic County	3,728
Connecticut	10,488	Montgomery County, MD	7,926	**Brooklyn, NY** (borough) Kings County	3,631
Illinois	6,713	Union County, NJ	7,446	**Islip, NY** (town) Suffolk County	3,165
Georgia	6,662	Westchester County, NY	7,179	**Hollywood, FL** (city) Broward County	3,124

Sorted by Number in Ascending Order — U.S. = 365,695

State	Number	County	Number	Place	Number
Hawaii	611	Lake County, IL	304	**Denver, CO** (city) Denver County	349
Kansas	611	Denver County, CO	349	**Torrance, CA** (city) Los Angeles County	487
New Mexico	667	Baltimore County, MD	411	**Phoenix, AZ** (city) Maricopa County	497
Kentucky	692	Solano County, CA	452	**West Valley City, UT** (city) Salt Lake County	559
District of Columbia	800	Fort Bend County, TX	459	**Bridgeport, CT** (city/town) Fairfield County	579
Missouri	817	Franklin County, OH	510	**San Antonio, TX** (city) Bexar County	581
Rhode Island	828	Ocean County, NJ	550	**Salt Lake City, UT** (city) Salt Lake County	585
Alabama	856	Wake County, NC	579	**Santa Ana, CA** (city) Orange County	587
Idaho	947	San Joaquin County, CA	615	**Long Beach, CA** (city) Los Angeles County	610
Minnesota	1,089	Lehigh County, PA	617	**Concord, CA** (city) Contra Costa County	648

Sorted by Percent in Descending Order — U.S. = 70.0%

State	Percent	County	Percent	Place	Percent
Louisiana	78.9	Middlesex County, MA	82.9	**Sunrise, FL** (city) Broward County	90.3
South Carolina	78.3	Arapahoe County, CO	82.3	**Port Chester, NY** (village) Westchester County	88.2
Florida	76.6	Lee County, FL	81.9	**Rye, NY** (town) Westchester County	87.8
Virginia	73.4	Atlantic County, NJ	81.8	**Hollywood, FL** (city) Broward County	85.6
Massachusetts	72.8	Broward County, FL	81.6	**Miami Beach, FL** (city) Miami-Dade County	85.6
Texas	71.0	Travis County, TX	81.1	**Weston, FL** (city) Broward County	84.0
Connecticut	70.7	Hudson County, NJ	80.8	**Cape Coral, FL** (city) Lee County	83.5
New York	70.7	New London County, CT	80.3	**Fountainebleau, FL** (cdp) Miami-Dade County	83.2
Utah	70.6	Prince George's County, MD	78.6	**Alexandria, VA** (independent city)	81.6
Maryland	70.5	Palm Beach County, FL	78.4	**Union City, NJ** (city) Hudson County	81.3

Sorted by Percent in Ascending Order — U.S. = 70.0%

State	Percent	County	Percent	Place	Percent
New Mexico	50.6	Lake County, IL	46.8	**Phoenix, AZ** (city) Maricopa County	54.6
Wisconsin	51.3	Sacramento County, CA	48.5	**Torrance, CA** (city) Los Angeles County	55.1
Missouri	52.3	Baltimore County, MD	50.9	**Orlando, FL** (city) Orange County	57.1
Hawaii	54.3	San Joaquin County, CA	52.5	**Oyster Bay, NY** (town) Nassau County	59.4
Oklahoma	56.8	Solano County, CA	55.5	**Paterson, NJ** (city) Passaic County	59.6
Tennessee	59.7	Ocean County, NJ	57.7	**San Antonio, TX** (city) Bexar County	59.9
Kentucky	60.8	Maricopa County, AZ	60.2	**Staten Island, NY** (borough) Richmond County	60.4
North Carolina	61.2	Richmond County, NY	60.4	**Long Beach, CA** (city) Los Angeles County	61.1
Idaho	61.9	Bexar County, TX	60.9	**Concord, CA** (city) Contra Costa County	61.8
Washington	61.9	San Bernardino County, CA	61.7	**Las Vegas, NV** (city) Clark County	62.4

Note: (1) Ranking tables cover all states and counties, and places with an overall population of at least 125,000, OR an overall population of at least 25,000 where the Hispanic/Latino population is at least 20% of the overall population. In states where less than five places meet either of these criteria, we have included places with at least 10,000 total population with the highest percentage of Hispanic/Latino population. These places are identified with an asterisk (*); Please refer to the User's Guide for a full explanation of data.

Foreign-Born Population

South American: Uruguayan

Top 10 States, Counties, and Places[1]

Sorted by Number in Descending Order U.S. = 41,778

State	Number	County	Number	Place	Number
Florida	11,512	Miami-Dade County, FL	5,793	**Elizabeth, NJ** (city) Union County	2,494
New Jersey	9,222	Union County, NJ	3,417	**New York, NY** (city)	2,131
New York	4,174	Broward County, FL	2,723	**Queens, NY** (borough) Queens County	1,059
Georgia	2,343	Essex County, NJ	1,927		
California	2,143	Palm Beach County, FL	1,131		
Massachusetts	1,905	Queens County, NY	1,059		
Texas	1,783	Harris County, TX	1,008		
Virginia	1,287	Worcester County, MA	998		
Maryland	1,049	Hudson County, NJ	992		
Pennsylvania	838	Westchester County, NY	921		

Sorted by Number in Ascending Order U.S. = 41,778

State	Number	County	Number	Place	Number
Pennsylvania	838	Middlesex County, NJ	568	**Queens, NY** (borough) Queens County	1,059
Maryland	1,049	Los Angeles County, CA	611	**New York, NY** (city)	2,131
Virginia	1,287	Morris County, NJ	794	**Elizabeth, NJ** (city) Union County	2,494
Texas	1,783	Gwinnett County, GA	917		
Massachusetts	1,905	Westchester County, NY	921		
California	2,143	Hudson County, NJ	992		
Georgia	2,343	Worcester County, MA	998		
New York	4,174	Harris County, TX	1,008		
New Jersey	9,222	Queens County, NY	1,059		
Florida	11,512	Palm Beach County, FL	1,131		

Sorted by Percent in Descending Order U.S. = 73.9%

State	Percent	County	Percent	Place	Percent
Georgia	80.3	Hudson County, NJ	85.7	**Elizabeth, NJ** (city) Union County	77.6
Massachusetts	78.9	Miami-Dade County, FL	85.3	**Queens, NY** (borough) Queens County	75.0
Florida	78.8	Broward County, FL	83.8	**New York, NY** (city)	72.3
New Jersey	76.0	Union County, NJ	79.9		
Maryland	72.5	Gwinnett County, GA	79.7		
Texas	72.2	Morris County, NJ	79.2		
New York	68.7	Essex County, NJ	76.6		
California	67.4	Queens County, NY	75.0		
Pennsylvania	64.2	Worcester County, MA	74.0		
Virginia	61.4	Harris County, TX	71.5		

Sorted by Percent in Ascending Order U.S. = 73.9%

State	Percent	County	Percent	Place	Percent
Virginia	61.4	Los Angeles County, CA	49.5	**New York, NY** (city)	72.3
Pennsylvania	64.2	Palm Beach County, FL	65.4	**Queens, NY** (borough) Queens County	75.0
California	67.4	Westchester County, NY	66.5	**Elizabeth, NJ** (city) Union County	77.6
New York	68.7	Middlesex County, NJ	67.7		
Texas	72.2	Harris County, TX	71.5		
Maryland	72.5	Worcester County, MA	74.0		
New Jersey	76.0	Queens County, NY	75.0		
Florida	78.8	Essex County, NJ	76.6		
Massachusetts	78.9	Morris County, NJ	79.2		
Georgia	80.3	Gwinnett County, GA	79.7		

Note: (1) Ranking tables cover all states and counties, and places with an overall population of at least 125,000, OR an overall population of at least 25,000 where the Hispanic/Latino population is at least 20% of the overall population. In states where less than five places meet either of these criteria, we have included places with at least 10,000 total population with the highest percentage of Hispanic/Latino population. These places are identified with an asterisk (*); Please refer to the User's Guide for a full explanation of data.

Foreign-Born Population

South American: Venezuelan

Top 10 States, Counties, and Places[1]

Sorted by Number in Descending Order — U.S. = 150,031

State	Number	County	Number	Place	Number
Florida	77,464	Miami-Dade County, FL	35,303	**New York, NY** (city)	7,323
Texas	13,377	Broward County, FL	18,868	**Weston, FL** (city) Broward County	5,959
New York	9,586	Orange County, FL	5,675	**Doral, FL** (city) Miami-Dade County	5,576
California	7,482	Harris County, TX	5,245	**Miami, FL** (city) Miami-Dade County	4,408
Georgia	4,621	Queens County, NY	3,219	**Queens, NY** (borough) Queens County	3,219
New Jersey	4,189	Palm Beach County, FL	3,028	**Fountainebleau, FL** (cdp) Miami-Dade County	2,983
Virginia	3,550	Los Angeles County, CA	2,826	**Houston, TX** (city) Harris County	2,777
Massachusetts	2,658	Osceola County, FL	2,365	**Pembroke Pines, FL** (city) Broward County	2,309
North Carolina	2,637	Fort Bend County, TX	2,035	**Manhattan, NY** (borough) New York County	1,732
Illinois	2,008	Hillsborough County, FL	1,880	**Miami Beach, FL** (city) Miami-Dade County	1,475

Sorted by Number in Ascending Order — U.S. = 150,031

State	Number	County	Number	Place	Number
Missouri	521	Tarrant County, TX	444	**Kendall West, FL** (cdp) Miami-Dade County	852
Wisconsin	544	Travis County, TX	483	**Coral Springs, FL** (city) Broward County	877
Michigan	667	San Diego County, CA	610	**Aventura, FL** (city) Miami-Dade County	910
Minnesota	682	King County, WA	621	**Bronx, NY** (borough) Bronx County	917
Indiana	786	Fairfield County, CT	666	**Hollywood, FL** (city) Broward County	959
Colorado	837	Collin County, TX	667	**Hialeah, FL** (city) Miami-Dade County	1,028
South Carolina	855	Fulton County, GA	699	**Los Angeles, CA** (city) Los Angeles County	1,060
Oklahoma	882	Montgomery County, TX	715	**Tamiami, FL** (cdp) Miami-Dade County	1,075
Washington	909	Orange County, CA	720	**The Hammocks, FL** (cdp) Miami-Dade County	1,106
Louisiana	911	Dallas County, TX	760	**Sunrise, FL** (city) Broward County	1,167

Sorted by Percent in Descending Order — U.S. = 71.9%

State	Percent	County	Percent	Place	Percent
Tennessee	78.0	Broward County, FL	81.4	**Pembroke Pines, FL** (city) Broward County	90.4
Florida	77.2	Fairfax County, VA	80.5	**Miramar, FL** (city) Broward County	89.2
Utah	74.2	Los Angeles County, CA	80.1	**Fountainebleau, FL** (cdp) Miami-Dade County	87.5
South Carolina	73.0	Miami-Dade County, FL	77.9	**Weston, FL** (city) Broward County	86.2
Virginia	72.9	Salt Lake County, UT	77.5	**Miami, FL** (city) Miami-Dade County	82.9
Massachusetts	72.3	Collin County, TX	76.8	**Davie, FL** (town) Broward County	82.6
Indiana	71.4	Osceola County, FL	76.8	**Los Angeles, CA** (city) Los Angeles County	81.9
Texas	71.3	Orange County, FL	76.5	**Miami Beach, FL** (city) Miami-Dade County	80.2
New Jersey	68.8	Gwinnett County, GA	76.1	**Tamiami, FL** (cdp) Miami-Dade County	78.1
Georgia	68.7	Montgomery County, TX	76.1	**Coral Springs, FL** (city) Broward County	77.9

Sorted by Percent in Ascending Order — U.S. = 71.9%

State	Percent	County	Percent	Place	Percent
Louisiana	46.2	Fairfield County, CT	55.8	**Brooklyn, NY** (borough) Kings County	61.9
Michigan	51.9	Orange County, CA	58.3	**Bronx, NY** (borough) Bronx County	66.9
Colorado	53.7	Tarrant County, TX	60.5	**Kendall West, FL** (cdp) Miami-Dade County	67.5
Wisconsin	58.4	Travis County, TX	61.5	**New York, NY** (city)	69.1
Oklahoma	59.0	Kings County, NY	61.9	**Manhattan, NY** (borough) New York County	69.5
Maryland	59.6	Cook County, IL	62.2	**Sunrise, FL** (city) Broward County	71.3
Connecticut	60.6	Hudson County, NJ	64.1	**Hialeah, FL** (city) Miami-Dade County	72.4
Ohio	60.8	Hillsborough County, FL	65.8	**Houston, TX** (city) Harris County	73.7
Minnesota	61.9	Bronx County, NY	66.9	**Aventura, FL** (city) Miami-Dade County	74.3
Pennsylvania	62.3	Montgomery County, MD	67.6	**Queens, NY** (borough) Queens County	74.6

RANKINGS & COMPARISONS

Note: (1) Ranking tables cover all states and counties, and places with an overall population of at least 125,000, OR an overall population of at least 25,000 where the Hispanic/Latino population is at least 20% of the overall population. In states where less than five places meet either of these criteria, we have included places with at least 10,000 total population with the highest percentage of Hispanic/Latino population. These places are identified with an asterisk (*); Please refer to the User's Guide for a full explanation of data.

Foreign-Born Population

Spaniard

Top 10 States, Counties, and Places[1]

Sorted by Number in Descending Order — U.S. = 80,388

State	Number	County	Number	Place	Number
Florida	13,997	Miami-Dade County, FL	6,446	**New York, NY** (city)	6,388
California	13,031	Los Angeles County, CA	3,669	**Queens, NY** (borough) Queens County	2,266
New York	9,837	Queens County, NY	2,266	**Manhattan, NY** (borough) New York County	2,024
New Jersey	7,008	Broward County, FL	2,089	**Los Angeles, CA** (city) Los Angeles County	1,502
Texas	5,484	New York County, NY	2,024	**Bronx, NY** (borough) Bronx County	1,010
Illinois	2,275	Hudson County, NJ	1,635	**Houston, TX** (city) Harris County	867
Virginia	1,949	Harris County, TX	1,407	**Brooklyn, NY** (borough) Kings County	865
Maryland	1,886	Essex County, NJ	1,357	**Newark, NJ** (city) Essex County	843
Pennsylvania	1,626	San Diego County, CA	1,353	**Miami, FL** (city) Miami-Dade County	806
North Carolina	1,478	Cook County, IL	1,241	**Kearny, NJ** (town) Hudson County	739

Sorted by Number in Ascending Order — U.S. = 80,388

State	Number	County	Number	Place	Number
Alaska	54	Colfax County, NM	0	**Lakewood, CO** (city) Jefferson County	0
Wyoming	75	La Plata County, CO	0	**Las Cruces, NM** (city) Dona Ana County	0
Montana	126	Las Animas County, CO	0	**Lubbock, TX** (city) Lubbock County	0
West Virginia	133	Lubbock County, TX	0	**South Valley, NM** (cdp) Bernalillo County	0
Iowa	144	Rio Arriba County, NM	0	**Westminster, CO** (city) Adams County	0
New Hampshire	174	Taos County, NM	0	**Pueblo, CO** (city) Pueblo County	11
Arkansas	194	Conejos County, CO	3	**Fort Collins, CO** (city) Larimer County	23
Mississippi	204	Butte County, CA	12	**Rio Rancho, NM** (city) Sandoval County	30
Utah	212	Douglas County, CO	16	**Thornton, CO** (city) Adams County	31
Idaho	213	Clark County, WA	17	**Anchorage, AK** (municipality)	35

Sorted by Percent in Descending Order — U.S. = 14.6%

State	Percent	County	Percent	Place	Percent
District of Columbia	48.9	Miami-Dade County, FL	62.3	**Miami, FL** (city) Miami-Dade County	74.3
Florida	33.0	Hudson County, NJ	59.0	**Kearny, NJ** (town) Hudson County	58.5
New Jersey	32.8	New York County, NY	52.8	**Newark, NJ** (city) Essex County	55.0
Kentucky	29.2	Montgomery County, MD	47.3	**Manhattan, NY** (borough) New York County	52.8
New York	29.2	Essex County, NJ	46.1	**Queens, NY** (borough) Queens County	45.5
Massachusetts	29.1	Queens County, NY	45.5	**Bronx, NY** (borough) Bronx County	41.2
Maryland	28.8	Broward County, FL	43.8	**New York, NY** (city)	38.9
Connecticut	26.5	Westchester County, NY	42.3	**Brooklyn, NY** (borough) Kings County	26.7
Maine	24.7	Bronx County, NY	41.2	**Chicago, IL** (city) Cook County	26.5
Virginia	24.1	Montgomery County, PA	39.8	**Virginia Beach, VA** (independent city)	26.3

Sorted by Percent in Ascending Order — U.S. = 14.6%

State	Percent	County	Percent	Place	Percent
New Mexico	1.7	Colfax County, NM	0.0	**Lakewood, CO** (city) Jefferson County	0.0
Colorado	2.4	La Plata County, CO	0.0	**Las Cruces, NM** (city) Dona Ana County	0.0
Alaska	3.0	Las Animas County, CO	0.0	**Lubbock, TX** (city) Lubbock County	0.0
Utah	3.3	Lubbock County, TX	0.0	**South Valley, NM** (cdp) Bernalillo County	0.0
Wyoming	3.4	Rio Arriba County, NM	0.0	**Westminster, CO** (city) Adams County	0.0
Oregon	6.4	Taos County, NM	0.0	**Pueblo, CO** (city) Pueblo County	0.3
Idaho	7.1	Conejos County, CO	0.3	**Rio Rancho, NM** (city) Sandoval County	1.3
Arizona	7.9	Pueblo County, CO	0.4	**Las Vegas, NV** (city) Clark County	2.3
Washington	8.3	Valencia County, NM	0.7	**Denver, CO** (city) Denver County	2.4
Arkansas	8.4	Sandoval County, NM	0.8	**Santa Fe, NM** (city) Santa Fe County	2.4

Note: (1) Ranking tables cover all states and counties, and places with an overall population of at least 125,000, OR an overall population of at least 25,000 where the Hispanic/Latino population is at least 20% of the overall population. In states where less than five places meet either of these criteria, we have included places with at least 10,000 total population with the highest percentage of Hispanic/Latino population. These places are identified with an asterisk (*); Please refer to the User's Guide for a full explanation of data.

Foreign-Born Naturalized Citizens

Total Population

Top 10 States, Counties, and Places[1]

Sorted by Number in Descending Order — U.S. = 16,653,874

State	Number	County	Number	Place	Number
California	4,472,020	Los Angeles County, CA	1,558,091	**New York, NY** (city)	1,528,135
New York	2,170,747	Miami-Dade County, FL	607,927	**Los Angeles, CA** (city) Los Angeles County	592,483
Florida	1,667,068	Queens County, NY	560,466	**Queens, NY** (borough) Queens County	560,466
Texas	1,245,278	Kings County, NY	509,392	**Brooklyn, NY** (borough) Kings County	509,392
New Jersey	882,018	Cook County, IL	485,662	**Chicago, IL** (city) Cook County	230,492
Illinois	769,086	Orange County, CA	423,722	**Manhattan, NY** (borough) New York County	204,851
Massachusetts	455,803	Santa Clara County, CA	323,435	**Bronx, NY** (borough) Bronx County	193,010
Virginia	375,650	San Diego County, CA	323,236	**San Jose, CA** (city) Santa Clara County	183,707
Washington	364,326	Harris County, TX	307,066	**San Francisco, CA** (city) San Francisco County	173,639
Pennsylvania	346,978	Broward County, FL	263,466	**San Diego, CA** (city) San Diego County	161,050

Sorted by Number in Ascending Order — U.S. = 16,653,874

State	Number	County	Number	Place	Number
Wyoming	5,936	Baker County, GA	0	**Dickinson*, ND** (city) Stark County	59
North Dakota	6,157	Bear Lake County, ID	0	**Mayfield*, KY** (city) Graves County	79
South Dakota	7,414	Cameron Parish, LA	0	**Clarksburg*, WV** (city) Harrison County	80
Montana	10,366	Clay County, IL	0	**Laurel*, MS** (city) Jones County	85
West Virginia	11,568	Clinch County, GA	0	**Yankton*, SD** (city) Yankton County	88
Vermont	13,586	Custer County, ID	0	**Huron*, SD** (city) Beadle County	114
Mississippi	20,476	Dallas County, AR	0	**Spearfish*, SD** (city) Lawrence County	115
Maine	24,092	Dundy County, NE	0	**Parker*, SC** (cdp) Greenville County	122
Alaska	24,772	Echols County, GA	0	**Hope*, AR** (city) Hempstead County	127
District of Columbia	27,350	Estill County, KY	0	**Green River*, WY** (city) Sweetwater County	128

Sorted by Percent in Descending Order — U.S. = 43.1%

State	Percent	County	Percent	Place	Percent
Hawaii	56.4	Bienville Parish, LA	100.0	**Spearfish*, SD** (city) Lawrence County	74.7
Maine	54.9	Carroll County, MS	100.0	**Clarksburg*, WV** (city) Harrison County	72.1
Vermont	54.7	Clay County, MS	100.0	**Schertz, TX** (city) Guadalupe County	72.0
Montana	54.2	Conecuh County, AL	100.0	**Oyster Bay, NY** (town) Nassau County	70.8
New York	51.9	Cross County, AR	100.0	**San Dimas, CA** (city) Los Angeles County	69.7
New Hampshire	51.2	Custer County, NE	100.0	**Elk Grove, CA** (city) Sacramento County	68.9
Alaska	49.8	Fall River County, SD	100.0	**Coral Gables, FL** (city) Miami-Dade County	68.5
New Jersey	49.7	Greenwood County, KS	100.0	**Miami Lakes, FL** (town) Miami-Dade County	68.4
Pennsylvania	49.3	Jackson County, WV	100.0	**Cooper City, FL** (city) Broward County	68.1
Massachusetts	48.4	Jefferson County, NE	100.0	**Diamond Bar, CA** (city) Los Angeles County	67.7

Sorted by Percent in Ascending Order — U.S. = 43.1%

State	Percent	County	Percent	Place	Percent
Arkansas	28.4	Bear Lake County, ID	0.0	**Albertville*, AL** (city) Marshall County	7.2
North Carolina	28.7	Cameron Parish, LA	0.0	**Monroe, NC** (city) Union County	7.5
Alabama	28.8	Clay County, IL	0.0	**Laurel*, MS** (city) Jones County	7.7
Tennessee	31.0	Clinch County, GA	0.0	**Parker*, SC** (cdp) Greenville County	8.2
South Carolina	31.1	Custer County, ID	0.0	**Carthage*, MO** (city) Jasper County	8.5
New Mexico	31.8	Dallas County, AR	0.0	**Gainesville, GA** (city) Hall County	9.1
Texas	31.8	Dundy County, NE	0.0	**Mayfield*, KY** (city) Graves County	9.2
Mississippi	32.2	Echols County, GA	0.0	**Pascagoula*, MS** (city) Jackson County	9.9
Oklahoma	32.2	Estill County, KY	0.0	**Big Spring, TX** (city) Howard County	10.7
Utah	32.5	Grant County, SD	0.0	**Sanford, NC** (city) Lee County	10.8

RANKINGS & COMPARISONS

Note: (1) Ranking tables cover all states and counties, and places with an overall population of at least 125,000, OR an overall population of at least 25,000 where the Hispanic/Latino population is at least 20% of the overall population. In states where less than five places meet either of these criteria, we have included places with at least 10,000 total population with the highest percentage of Hispanic/Latino population. These places are identified with an asterisk (*); Please refer to the User's Guide for a full explanation of data.

Foreign-Born Naturalized Citizens

Hispanic or Latino (of any race)

Top 10 States, Counties, and Places[1]

Sorted by Number in Descending Order — U.S. = 5,226,941

State	Number	County	Number	Place	Number
California	1,594,493	Los Angeles County, CA	652,538	**New York, NY** (city)	361,223
Florida	850,115	Miami-Dade County, FL	497,907	**Los Angeles, CA** (city) Los Angeles County	256,256
Texas	675,761	Harris County, TX	153,365	**Queens, NY** (borough) Queens County	125,497
New York	488,365	Cook County, IL	153,164	**Chicago, IL** (city) Cook County	93,768
New Jersey	234,840	Queens County, NY	125,497	**Bronx, NY** (borough) Bronx County	87,550
Illinois	229,654	San Diego County, CA	115,024	**Miami, FL** (city) Miami-Dade County	83,296
Arizona	139,783	Orange County, CA	110,660	**Houston, TX** (city) Harris County	82,055
Nevada	73,584	Riverside County, CA	108,937	**Manhattan, NY** (borough) New York County	75,859
Virginia	70,616	San Bernardino County, CA	103,611	**Hialeah, FL** (city) Miami-Dade County	71,449
Massachusetts	68,055	Broward County, FL	99,976	**Brooklyn, NY** (borough) Kings County	65,078

Sorted by Number in Ascending Order — U.S. = 5,226,941

State	Number	County	Number	Place	Number
North Dakota	632	Brown County, KS	0	**Pueblo West, CO** (cdp) Pueblo County	3
Vermont	840	Clare County, MI	0	**Great Falls*, MT** (city) Cascade County	7
Maine	1,276	Clinton County, MO	0	**Middle*, DE** (town) New Castle County	10
Montana	1,287	Colleton County, SC	0	**Waianae*, HI** (cdp) Honolulu County	14
South Dakota	1,437	DeKalb County, IN	0	**Fort Campbell North*, KY** (cdp) Christian County	27
West Virginia	1,832	Gibson County, TN	0	**Bozeman*, MT** (city) Gallatin County	33
Wyoming	2,175	Greer County, OK	0	**Burlington*, VT** (city) Chittenden County	48
Alaska	3,649	Hancock County, MS	0	**Mayfield*, KY** (city) Graves County	56
New Hampshire	4,314	Huron County, MI	0	**Grand Forks*, ND** (city) Grand Forks County	57
Mississippi	4,915	Lawrence County, TN	0	**Laurel*, MS** (city) Jones County	61

Sorted by Percent in Descending Order — U.S. = 28.7%

State	Percent	County	Percent	Place	Percent
Montana	55.1	Phelps County, MO	100.0	**Butte-Silver Bow*, MT** (consolidated govt) Silver Bow County	100.0
Hawaii	54.6	Ravalli County, MT	100.0	**Waianae*, HI** (cdp) Honolulu County	100.0
Vermont	50.5	Redwood County, MN	100.0	**Bozeman*, MT** (city) Gallatin County	82.5
North Dakota	43.9	Silver Bow County, MT	100.0	**Billings*, MT** (city) Yellowstone County	81.9
New Hampshire	43.1	Wabaunsee County, KS	100.0	**Diamond Bar, CA** (city) Los Angeles County	77.7
Florida	42.4	Windham County, VT	97.6	**Cooper City, FL** (city) Broward County	77.1
Alaska	42.2	Elbert County, CO	95.4	**San Dimas, CA** (city) Los Angeles County	73.9
Maine	40.3	Rutland County, VT	93.1	**Schofield Barracks*, HI** (cdp) Honolulu County	73.0
West Virginia	39.1	Bedford County, PA	93.0	**Coral Gables, FL** (city) Miami-Dade County	72.9
New York	37.3	Carlton County, MN	91.8	**College*, AK** (cdp) Fairbanks North Star Borough	71.7

Sorted by Percent in Ascending Order — U.S. = 28.7%

State	Percent	County	Percent	Place	Percent
Alabama	12.4	Brown County, KS	0.0	**North Atlanta, GA** (cdp) DeKalb County	2.8
North Carolina	13.1	Clinton County, MO	0.0	**Middle*, DE** (town) New Castle County	3.0
Tennessee	13.5	Colleton County, SC	0.0	**Carthage*, MO** (city) Jasper County	3.9
South Carolina	14.0	DeKalb County, IN	0.0	**Albertville*, AL** (city) Marshall County	4.5
Georgia	15.2	Gibson County, TN	0.0	**Pueblo West, CO** (cdp) Pueblo County	5.0
Mississippi	15.5	Greer County, OK	0.0	**Monroe, NC** (city) Union County	5.3
Oregon	16.3	Hancock County, MS	0.0	**Big Spring, TX** (city) Howard County	5.7
Kentucky	16.5	Huron County, MI	0.0	**Gainesville, GA** (city) Hall County	6.1
Colorado	17.3	Lawrence County, TN	0.0	**Laurel*, MS** (city) Jones County	6.2
Arkansas	17.4	Logan County, KY	0.0	**Biloxi*, MS** (city) Harrison County	6.3

Note: (1) Ranking tables cover all states and counties, and places with an overall population of at least 125,000, OR an overall population of at least 25,000 where the Hispanic/Latino population is at least 20% of the overall population. In states where less than five places meet either of these criteria, we have included places with at least 10,000 total population with the highest percentage of Hispanic/Latino population. These places are identified with an asterisk (*); Please refer to the User's Guide for a full explanation of data.

Foreign-Born Naturalized Citizens

Central American, excluding Mexican

Top 10 States, Counties, and Places[1]

Sorted by Number in Descending Order — U.S. = 735,326

State	Number	County	Number	Place	Number
California	259,341	Los Angeles County, CA	156,705	**Los Angeles, CA** (city) Los Angeles County	85,881
Florida	100,490	Miami-Dade County, FL	57,421	**New York, NY** (city)	41,687
New York	70,817	Harris County, TX	29,256	**Houston, TX** (city) Harris County	17,203
Texas	60,381	San Bernardino County, CA	14,002	**Brooklyn, NY** (borough) Kings County	13,606
New Jersey	28,632	Kings County, NY	13,606	**Queens, NY** (borough) Queens County	13,289
Virginia	26,541	Queens County, NY	13,289	**Miami, FL** (city) Miami-Dade County	10,363
Maryland	25,923	Montgomery County, MD	11,646	**Bronx, NY** (borough) Bronx County	8,996
Illinois	16,209	Cook County, IL	11,298	**San Francisco, CA** (city) San Francisco County	8,937
Massachusetts	15,807	Nassau County, NY	10,916	**Chicago, IL** (city) Cook County	7,644
Louisiana	11,905	Broward County, FL	10,775	**Hempstead (town), NY** (town) Nassau County	7,522

Sorted by Number in Ascending Order — U.S. = 735,326

State	Number	County	Number	Place	Number
Wyoming	64	Cass County, IN	0	**Knoxville, TN** (city) Knox County	0
Vermont	206	Gilmer County, GA	13	**Albertville*, AL** (city) Marshall County	11
South Dakota	246	Colfax County, NE	17	**Gainesville, GA** (city) Hall County	36
Maine	272	Warren County, KY	26	**Delano, CA** (city) Kern County	43
West Virginia	420	DeKalb County, AL	32	**Worthington*, MN** (city) Nobles County	49
Delaware	443	Carroll County, AR	34	**Laredo, TX** (city) Webb County	63
Alaska	510	Hendry County, FL	34	**Detroit, MI** (city) Wayne County	68
Hawaii	531	Pitt County, NC	35	**Carthage*, MO** (city) Jasper County	70
Idaho	663	Lee County, AL	39	**Marietta, GA** (city) Cobb County	80
Mississippi	767	Caroline County, MD	40	**Bonita Springs, FL** (city) Lee County	81

Sorted by Percent in Descending Order — U.S. = 28.5%

State	Percent	County	Percent	Place	Percent
Vermont	57.7	Thurston County, WA	73.2	**Alafaya, FL** (cdp) Orange County	85.4
Alaska	47.7	Lake County, IN	65.6	**Chino Hills, CA** (city) San Bernardino County	84.2
New Hampshire	47.4	Monroe County, PA	62.6	**Eastvale, CA** (cdp) Riverside County	79.9
Wisconsin	45.9	Macomb County, MI	60.8	**West Covina, CA** (city) Los Angeles County	75.2
West Virginia	45.4	Allegheny County, PA	58.2	**Monterey Park, CA** (city) Los Angeles County	72.6
Hawaii	44.8	Muscogee County, GA	57.4	**San Bruno, CA** (city) San Mateo County	71.9
Illinois	39.6	Richmond County, NY	56.6	**Pembroke Pines, FL** (city) Broward County	69.1
Utah	38.0	Pierce County, WA	56.3	**Torrance, CA** (city) Los Angeles County	68.9
Louisiana	37.6	Honolulu County, HI	53.6	**Burbank, CA** (city) Los Angeles County	67.5
California	35.5	Clackamas County, OR	53.5	**Linden, NJ** (city) Union County	67.5

Sorted by Percent in Ascending Order — U.S. = 28.5%

State	Percent	County	Percent	Place	Percent
Wyoming	8.9	Cass County, IN	0.0	**Knoxville, TN** (city) Knox County	0.0
Delaware	9.5	Colfax County, NE	3.2	**Albertville*, AL** (city) Marshall County	1.0
Tennessee	14.5	DeKalb County, AL	3.2	**Gainesville, GA** (city) Hall County	2.0
South Dakota	15.0	Warren County, KY	3.2	**Marietta, GA** (city) Cobb County	3.2
Georgia	16.1	Gilmer County, GA	3.3	**Lake Worth, FL** (city) Palm Beach County	3.6
Mississippi	16.2	Burke County, NC	3.6	**Bonita Springs, FL** (city) Lee County	4.7
North Carolina	17.1	Lee County, AL	4.4	**Detroit, MI** (city) Wayne County	5.4
Alabama	17.2	Franklin County, AL	4.8	**Carthage*, MO** (city) Jasper County	5.6
South Carolina	17.3	Hendry County, FL	5.1	**Worthington*, MN** (city) Nobles County	5.8
Arkansas	18.5	Sussex County, DE	5.1	**Spring Valley, NY** (village) Rockland County	6.3

Note: (1) Ranking tables cover all states and counties, and places with an overall population of at least 125,000, OR an overall population of at least 25,000 where the Hispanic/Latino population is at least 20% of the overall population. In states where less than five places meet either of these criteria, we have included places with at least 10,000 total population with the highest percentage of Hispanic/Latino population. These places are identified with an asterisk (*); Please refer to the User's Guide for a full explanation of data.

Foreign-Born Naturalized Citizens

Central American: Costa Rican

Top 10 States, Counties, and Places[1]

Sorted by Number in Descending Order — U.S. = 29,747

State	Number	County	Number	Place	Number
California	6,207	Los Angeles County, CA	2,883	**New York, NY** (city)	2,832
Florida	5,682	Miami-Dade County, FL	2,230	**Queens, NY** (borough) Queens County	1,033
New York	4,238	Queens County, NY	1,033	**Brooklyn, NY** (borough) Kings County	990
New Jersey	2,462	Kings County, NY	990	**Los Angeles, CA** (city) Los Angeles County	885
Texas	1,896	Broward County, FL	681	**Bronx, NY** (borough) Bronx County	320
Massachusetts	987	Orange County, CA	675	**Miami, FL** (city) Miami-Dade County	280
North Carolina	881	San Bernardino County, CA	502	**Philadelphia, PA** (city) Philadelphia County	255
Georgia	648	Harris County, TX	501		
Maryland	638	Palm Beach County, FL	499		
Pennsylvania	617	Bergen County, NJ	443		

Sorted by Number in Ascending Order — U.S. = 29,747

State	Number	County	Number	Place	Number
Washington	126	Essex County, NJ	144	**Philadelphia, PA** (city) Philadelphia County	255
Minnesota	142	Contra Costa County, CA	150	**Miami, FL** (city) Miami-Dade County	280
Wisconsin	169	Fairfield County, CT	181	**Bronx, NY** (borough) Bronx County	320
Oregon	171	Morris County, NJ	192	**Los Angeles, CA** (city) Los Angeles County	885
Tennessee	180	Mercer County, NJ	222	**Brooklyn, NY** (borough) Kings County	990
Michigan	191	Orange County, FL	228	**Queens, NY** (borough) Queens County	1,033
Colorado	192	Philadelphia County, PA	255	**New York, NY** (city)	2,832
Connecticut	270	Passaic County, NJ	259		
South Carolina	336	Somerset County, NJ	275		
Arizona	396	Maricopa County, AZ	279		

Sorted by Percent in Descending Order — U.S. = 39.7%

State	Percent	County	Percent	Place	Percent
New York	64.0	Queens County, NY	82.0	**Queens, NY** (borough) Queens County	82.0
California	57.7	Bronx County, NY	75.3	**Bronx, NY** (borough) Bronx County	75.3
Arizona	56.3	Nassau County, NY	74.0	**New York, NY** (city)	72.8
Louisiana	52.0	Orange County, CA	71.0	**Brooklyn, NY** (borough) Kings County	68.6
Texas	50.3	Kings County, NY	68.6	**Los Angeles, CA** (city) Los Angeles County	54.8
Oregon	47.8	Riverside County, CA	62.9	**Philadelphia, PA** (city) Philadelphia County	31.5
Massachusetts	46.5	Los Angeles County, CA	59.2	**Miami, FL** (city) Miami-Dade County	24.0
Wisconsin	46.2	Clark County, NV	57.9		
Florida	42.9	San Bernardino County, CA	52.6		
Nevada	42.9	Maricopa County, AZ	52.1		

Sorted by Percent in Ascending Order — U.S. = 39.7%

State	Percent	County	Percent	Place	Percent
New Jersey	16.8	Essex County, NJ	8.4	**Miami, FL** (city) Miami-Dade County	24.0
Connecticut	21.8	Morris County, NJ	12.7	**Philadelphia, PA** (city) Philadelphia County	31.5
Washington	24.5	Union County, NJ	12.9	**Los Angeles, CA** (city) Los Angeles County	54.8
North Carolina	25.4	Somerset County, NJ	14.8	**Brooklyn, NY** (borough) Kings County	68.6
South Carolina	26.4	Passaic County, NJ	19.7	**New York, NY** (city)	72.8
Pennsylvania	26.5	Mercer County, NJ	22.7	**Bronx, NY** (borough) Bronx County	75.3
Minnesota	29.6	Fairfield County, CT	22.9	**Queens, NY** (borough) Queens County	82.0
Georgia	32.8	Orange County, FL	29.8		
Colorado	36.9	Bergen County, NJ	30.1		
Illinois	37.8	Suffolk County, NY	31.3		

Note: (1) Ranking tables cover all states and counties, and places with an overall population of at least 125,000, OR an overall population of at least 25,000 where the Hispanic/Latino population is at least 20% of the overall population. In states where less than five places meet either of these criteria, we have included places with at least 10,000 total population with the highest percentage of Hispanic/Latino population. These places are identified with an asterisk (*); Please refer to the User's Guide for a full explanation of data.

Foreign-Born Naturalized Citizens

Central American: Guatemalan

Top 10 States, Counties, and Places[1]

Sorted by Number in Descending Order — U.S. = 161,189

State	Number	County	Number	Place	Number
California	60,691	Los Angeles County, CA	39,529	**Los Angeles, CA** (city) Los Angeles County	21,360
New York	12,186	Cook County, IL	6,205	**New York, NY** (city)	6,347
Florida	11,910	Miami-Dade County, FL	4,715	**Chicago, IL** (city) Cook County	4,350
Illinois	8,820	Harris County, TX	3,542	**Queens, NY** (borough) Queens County	2,673
Texas	7,995	San Bernardino County, CA	3,489	**Houston, TX** (city) Harris County	2,455
New Jersey	6,211	Riverside County, CA	2,831	**Bronx, NY** (borough) Bronx County	1,433
Massachusetts	5,542	Orange County, CA	2,737	**San Francisco, CA** (city) San Francisco County	1,415
Maryland	4,450	Queens County, NY	2,673	**Brooklyn, NY** (borough) Kings County	1,309
Virginia	3,847	Providence County, RI	1,996	**Boston, MA** (city) Suffolk County	1,254
Georgia	2,873	Suffolk County, NY	1,860	**Providence, RI** (city) Providence County	1,207

Sorted by Number in Ascending Order — U.S. = 161,189

State	Number	County	Number	Place	Number
South Dakota	84	Burke County, NC	0	**Marietta, GA** (city) Cobb County	0
Mississippi	132	Gilmer County, GA	13	**Albertville*, AL** (city) Marshall County	11
Delaware	181	Caroline County, MD	22	**Richmond, VA** (independent city)	19
Idaho	252	Floyd County, GA	30	**West Palm Beach, FL** (city) Palm Beach County	35
District of Columbia	273	Lee County, AL	31	**Cincinnati, OH** (city) Hamilton County	43
New Hampshire	279	DeKalb County, AL	32	**West New York, NJ** (town) Hudson County	45
Iowa	484	Knox County, TN	39	**Carthage*, MO** (city) Jasper County	46
Oklahoma	517	Franklin County, AL	43	**Lexington*, NE** (city) Dawson County	46
New Mexico	535	Nobles County, MN	45	**Sioux Falls, SD** (city) Minnehaha County	48
Kansas	665	Jasper County, MO	46	**Yonkers, NY** (city) Westchester County	49

Sorted by Percent in Descending Order — U.S. = 22.9%

State	Percent	County	Percent	Place	Percent
Wisconsin	64.5	Milwaukee County, WI	65.3	**Burbank, CA** (city) Los Angeles County	69.1
New Hampshire	46.3	Lake County, IL	60.9	**West Covina, CA** (city) Los Angeles County	67.0
Louisiana	44.0	Utah County, UT	51.6	**Central Islip, NY** (cdp) Suffolk County	63.4
Illinois	42.4	Sonoma County, CA	50.3	**Downey, CA** (city) Los Angeles County	62.8
Minnesota	38.7	Osceola County, FL	48.3	**Gardena, CA** (city) Los Angeles County	59.5
Utah	35.7	Stanislaus County, CA	45.4	**Corona, CA** (city) Riverside County	57.9
Pennsylvania	33.0	New York County, NY	44.3	**Norwalk, CA** (city) Los Angeles County	57.6
Indiana	32.8	Will County, IL	43.4	**Montebello, CA** (city) Los Angeles County	54.5
Idaho	30.0	Hartford County, CT	42.5	**North Hempstead, NY** (town) Nassau County	53.2
New Mexico	28.2	Jefferson Parish, LA	41.1	**Alhambra, CA** (city) Los Angeles County	51.5

Sorted by Percent in Ascending Order — U.S. = 22.9%

State	Percent	County	Percent	Place	Percent
Delaware	5.2	Burke County, NC	0.0	**Marietta, GA** (city) Cobb County	0.0
Mississippi	7.9	Floyd County, GA	2.4	**Albertville*, AL** (city) Marshall County	1.0
South Dakota	8.4	Gilmer County, GA	3.3	**Richmond, VA** (independent city)	1.0
Oklahoma	9.8	Knox County, TN	3.4	**West Palm Beach, FL** (city) Palm Beach County	1.0
Alabama	10.8	DeKalb County, AL	3.9	**Lake Worth, FL** (city) Palm Beach County	1.7
Georgia	11.1	Jasper County, MO	4.0	**West New York, NJ** (town) Hudson County	3.2
South Carolina	11.3	DeKalb County, GA	4.1	**Spring Valley, NY** (village) Rockland County	3.3
Tennessee	12.6	Sussex County, DE	4.4	**Plainfield, NJ** (city) Union County	3.4
Connecticut	13.3	Franklin County, AL	4.8	**Carthage*, MO** (city) Jasper County	4.1
Iowa	13.6	Lee County, AL	4.8	**Cincinnati, OH** (city) Hamilton County	4.3

Note: (1) Ranking tables cover all states and counties, and places with an overall population of at least 125,000, OR an overall population of at least 25,000 where the Hispanic/Latino population is at least 20% of the overall population. In states where less than five places meet either of these criteria, we have included places with at least 10,000 total population with the highest percentage of Hispanic/Latino population. These places are identified with an asterisk (*); Please refer to the User's Guide for a full explanation of data.

Foreign-Born Naturalized Citizens

Central American: Honduran

Top 10 States, Counties, and Places[1]

Sorted by Number in Descending Order — U.S. = 87,415

State	Number	County	Number	Place	Number
Florida	19,483	Miami-Dade County, FL	10,113	**New York, NY** (city)	10,554
New York	13,337	Los Angeles County, CA	6,973	**Bronx, NY** (borough) Bronx County	4,562
California	12,171	Bronx County, NY	4,562	**Los Angeles, CA** (city) Los Angeles County	3,600
Texas	6,209	Jefferson Parish, LA	3,690	**Miami, FL** (city) Miami-Dade County	2,916
New Jersey	5,872	Harris County, TX	2,798	**Brooklyn, NY** (borough) Kings County	2,620
Louisiana	5,857	Kings County, NY	2,620	**Queens, NY** (borough) Queens County	2,055
Virginia	2,564	Broward County, FL	2,617	**Houston, TX** (city) Harris County	1,302
Massachusetts	2,460	Hudson County, NJ	2,410	**Jersey City, NJ** (city) Hudson County	1,215
Illinois	2,360	Queens County, NY	2,055	**Metairie, LA** (cdp) Jefferson Parish	1,163
Georgia	1,804	Cook County, IL	1,526	**Kenner, LA** (city) Jefferson Parish	1,040

Sorted by Number in Ascending Order — U.S. = 87,415

State	Number	County	Number	Place	Number
Arkansas	130	Sampson County, NC	28	**Hempstead (village), NY** (village) Nassau County	27
Kentucky	135	Durham County, NC	32	**Durham, NC** (city) Durham County	32
Iowa	155	Galveston County, TX	33	**Aurora, CO** (city) Arapahoe County	36
Mississippi	189	Arapahoe County, CO	36	**Fort Worth, TX** (city) Tarrant County	41
District of Columbia	208	Elkhart County, IN	41	**Raleigh, NC** (city) Wake County	47
Oregon	247	Johnston County, NC	47	**Springfield, VA** (cdp) Fairfax County	51
Michigan	288	Loudoun County, VA	52	**Garland, TX** (city) Dallas County	72
Alabama	345	Hall County, GA	55	**Miami Beach, FL** (city) Miami-Dade County	75
Minnesota	411	Polk County, FL	59	**Wheaton, MD** (cdp) Montgomery County	78
Wisconsin	437	Duplin County, NC	89	**Newburgh, NY** (city) Orange County	89

Sorted by Percent in Descending Order — U.S. = 20.5%

State	Percent	County	Percent	Place	Percent
Nebraska	36.1	Middlesex County, MA	55.9	**Miramar, FL** (city) Broward County	62.6
Utah	34.1	Richmond County, NY	54.2	**South Miami Heights, FL** (cdp) Miami-Dade County	61.6
Ohio	33.1	Philadelphia County, PA	39.8	**Staten Island, NY** (borough) Richmond County	54.2
Missouri	32.8	Kings County, NY	39.0	**Jersey City, NJ** (city) Hudson County	51.0
Illinois	32.5	Bergen County, NJ	38.1	**North Miami Beach, FL** (city) Miami-Dade County	43.2
Louisiana	31.5	Hudson County, NJ	37.6	**Philadelphia, PA** (city) Philadelphia County	39.8
Massachusetts	31.3	Jefferson Parish, LA	37.0	**Brooklyn, NY** (borough) Kings County	39.0
New York	29.1	Riverside County, CA	36.6	**Metairie, LA** (cdp) Jefferson Parish	38.2
Pennsylvania	28.6	Cook County, IL	36.2	**New York, NY** (city)	35.9
Wisconsin	27.8	Bronx County, NY	35.6	**Bronx, NY** (borough) Bronx County	35.6

Sorted by Percent in Ascending Order — U.S. = 20.5%

State	Percent	County	Percent	Place	Percent
North Carolina	6.5	Durham County, NC	1.2	**Hempstead (village), NY** (village) Nassau County	0.9
Texas	9.7	Sampson County, NC	2.9	**Durham, NC** (city) Durham County	1.2
Arkansas	10.8	Mecklenburg County, NC	3.1	**Charlotte, NC** (city) Mecklenburg County	2.3
Tennessee	11.8	Travis County, TX	3.2	**Aurora, CO** (city) Arapahoe County	3.2
Georgia	12.1	Galveston County, TX	3.5	**Austin, TX** (city) Travis County	3.4
Indiana	12.3	Loudoun County, VA	3.5	**Dallas, TX** (city) Dallas County	3.6
Mississippi	12.4	Arapahoe County, CO	3.8	**Fort Worth, TX** (city) Tarrant County	3.7
Kentucky	12.9	Duplin County, NC	4.7	**Raleigh, NC** (city) Wake County	3.8
Maryland	13.0	Tarrant County, TX	5.6	**Springfield, VA** (cdp) Fairfax County	4.7
Virginia	13.2	Dallas County, TX	6.0	**Miami Beach, FL** (city) Miami-Dade County	5.2

Note: (1) Ranking tables cover all states and counties, and places with an overall population of at least 125,000, OR an overall population of at least 25,000 where the Hispanic/Latino population is at least 20% of the overall population. In states where less than five places meet either of these criteria, we have included places with at least 10,000 total population with the highest percentage of Hispanic/Latino population. These places are identified with an asterisk (*); Please refer to the User's Guide for a full explanation of data.

Foreign-Born Naturalized Citizens

Central American: Nicaraguan

Top 10 States, Counties, and Places[1]

Sorted by Number in Descending Order — U.S. = 101,087

State	Number	County	Number	Place	Number
Florida	42,772	Miami-Dade County, FL	34,046	**Miami, FL** (city) Miami-Dade County	5,657
California	30,262	Los Angeles County, CA	11,827	**Los Angeles, CA** (city) Los Angeles County	4,899
Texas	4,784	San Mateo County, CA	3,288	**New York, NY** (city)	3,161
New York	3,837	Broward County, FL	2,714	**Hialeah, FL** (city) Miami-Dade County	3,151
Louisiana	2,562	Contra Costa County, CA	2,330	**Fountainebleau, FL** (cdp) Miami-Dade County	2,623
New Jersey	2,064	San Francisco County, CA	2,292	**San Francisco, CA** (city) San Francisco County	2,292
Virginia	2,057	San Bernardino County, CA	2,176	**Tamiami, FL** (cdp) Miami-Dade County	1,776
Maryland	1,841	Harris County, TX	1,654	**Daly City, CA** (city) San Mateo County	1,618
North Carolina	1,475	Alameda County, CA	1,576	**The Hammocks, FL** (cdp) Miami-Dade County	1,489
Nevada	916	Jefferson Parish, LA	1,573	**Kendale Lakes, FL** (cdp) Miami-Dade County	1,289

Sorted by Number in Ascending Order — U.S. = 101,087

State	Number	County	Number	Place	Number
Michigan	132	Gwinnett County, GA	58	**Sacramento, CA** (city) Sacramento County	141
Minnesota	142	King County, WA	147	**San Diego, CA** (city) San Diego County	206
Oregon	188	Camden County, NJ	260	**Charlotte, NC** (city) Mecklenburg County	244
Connecticut	204	Duval County, FL	297	**Fontana, CA** (city) San Bernardino County	258
Colorado	217	Stanislaus County, CA	322	**Las Vegas, NV** (city) Clark County	287
Tennessee	230	Prince George's County, MD	333	**South Gate, CA** (city) Los Angeles County	287
Missouri	234	Sonoma County, CA	352	**Austin, TX** (city) Travis County	289
Indiana	240	Bexar County, TX	385	**Oakland, CA** (city) Alameda County	290
South Carolina	265	Lee County, FL	393	**Jacksonville, FL** (city) Duval County	297
District of Columbia	289	Collier County, FL	420	**Homestead, FL** (city) Miami-Dade County	346

Sorted by Percent in Descending Order — U.S. = 45.8%

State	Percent	County	Percent	Place	Percent
Washington	63.5	Sonoma County, CA	68.5	**Pembroke Pines, FL** (city) Broward County	83.2
Ohio	60.6	Santa Clara County, CA	66.8	**The Hammocks, FL** (cdp) Miami-Dade County	71.4
Illinois	58.2	Contra Costa County, CA	65.8	**Antioch, CA** (city) Contra Costa County	68.3
Wisconsin	56.2	San Joaquin County, CA	64.4	**Daly City, CA** (city) San Mateo County	67.4
Arizona	56.1	San Mateo County, CA	62.2	**Tamiami, FL** (cdp) Miami-Dade County	65.6
California	53.8	San Francisco County, CA	60.3	**Richmond, CA** (city) Contra Costa County	64.9
Missouri	53.5	New York County, NY	58.9	**University Park, FL** (cdp) Miami-Dade County	62.6
Louisiana	53.3	Orange County, CA	58.1	**Richmond West, FL** (cdp) Miami-Dade County	61.6
Massachusetts	49.0	Riverside County, CA	57.9	**San Francisco, CA** (city) San Francisco County	60.3
New York	48.1	Cook County, IL	56.2	**Manhattan, NY** (borough) New York County	58.9

Sorted by Percent in Ascending Order — U.S. = 45.8%

State	Percent	County	Percent	Place	Percent
Minnesota	21.6	Gwinnett County, GA	8.8	**Miami, FL** (city) Miami-Dade County	23.5
Indiana	29.8	Prince George's County, MD	31.4	**Charlotte, NC** (city) Mecklenburg County	25.4
Georgia	30.0	Mecklenburg County, NC	35.0	**Fontana, CA** (city) San Bernardino County	30.1
Colorado	32.8	Prince William County, VA	35.2	**Houston, TX** (city) Harris County	33.1
Nevada	34.1	Camden County, NJ	36.0	**West Little River, FL** (cdp) Miami-Dade County	35.8
South Carolina	36.3	Clark County, NV	36.9	**Sacramento, CA** (city) Sacramento County	37.5
Michigan	37.4	Harris County, TX	37.8	**Hialeah, FL** (city) Miami-Dade County	38.0
Tennessee	37.5	King County, WA	38.5	**Oakland, CA** (city) Alameda County	39.3
Virginia	40.3	Duval County, FL	39.9	**Jacksonville, FL** (city) Duval County	39.9
Florida	42.1	Miami-Dade County, FL	41.2	**Queens, NY** (borough) Queens County	41.3

Note: (1) Ranking tables cover all states and counties, and places with an overall population of at least 125,000, OR an overall population of at least 25,000 where the Hispanic/Latino population is at least 20% of the overall population. In states where less than five places meet either of these criteria, we have included places with at least 10,000 total population with the highest percentage of Hispanic/Latino population. These places are identified with an asterisk (*); Please refer to the User's Guide for a full explanation of data.

Foreign-Born Naturalized Citizens

Central American: Panamanian

Top 10 States, Counties, and Places[1]

Sorted by Number in Descending Order — U.S. = 47,616

State	Number	County	Number	Place	Number
New York	10,494	Kings County, NY	5,613	**New York, NY** (city)	8,531
Florida	9,372	Miami-Dade County, FL	3,133	**Brooklyn, NY** (borough) Kings County	5,613
California	5,482	Los Angeles County, CA	1,810	**Queens, NY** (borough) Queens County	1,629
Texas	3,884	Queens County, NY	1,629	**Los Angeles, CA** (city) Los Angeles County	714
Virginia	2,268	Broward County, FL	1,516	**Hempstead (town), NY** (town) Nassau County	620
Georgia	2,177	Orange County, FL	818	**Manhattan, NY** (borough) New York County	609
New Jersey	1,725	San Diego County, CA	757	**Bronx, NY** (borough) Bronx County	596
North Carolina	1,573	Hillsborough County, FL	741	**Jacksonville, FL** (city) Duval County	455
Maryland	1,428	Bexar County, TX	680	**San Antonio, TX** (city) Bexar County	432
Massachusetts	934	Harris County, TX	658	**Fayetteville, NC** (city) Cumberland County	366

Sorted by Number in Ascending Order — U.S. = 47,616

State	Number	County	Number	Place	Number
Minnesota	26	Pierce County, WA	188	**Killeen, TX** (city) Bell County	234
Wisconsin	102	Fairfax County, VA	210	**Miami, FL** (city) Miami-Dade County	314
New Mexico	148	Orange County, CA	212	**Houston, TX** (city) Harris County	360
Mississippi	160	Maricopa County, AZ	213	**San Diego, CA** (city) San Diego County	361
Oklahoma	199	Palm Beach County, FL	226	**Fayetteville, NC** (city) Cumberland County	366
Indiana	248	Hudson County, NJ	228	**San Antonio, TX** (city) Bexar County	432
Michigan	250	Dallas County, TX	231	**Jacksonville, FL** (city) Duval County	455
Connecticut	279	Montgomery County, MD	242	**Bronx, NY** (borough) Bronx County	596
Alabama	294	Essex County, NJ	249	**Manhattan, NY** (borough) New York County	609
Missouri	326	Sacramento County, CA	282	**Hempstead (town), NY** (town) Nassau County	620

Sorted by Percent in Descending Order — U.S. = 62.3%

State	Percent	County	Percent	Place	Percent
Nevada	79.3	Pierce County, WA	97.9	**Hempstead (town), NY** (town) Nassau County	91.9
Kentucky	76.9	Nassau County, NY	88.3	**Los Angeles, CA** (city) Los Angeles County	78.4
Colorado	71.8	Clark County, NV	77.3	**Jacksonville, FL** (city) Duval County	75.0
Washington	71.3	Duval County, FL	75.0	**Houston, TX** (city) Harris County	73.5
Missouri	69.4	Prince William County, VA	73.1	**Queens, NY** (borough) Queens County	72.9
Virginia	68.1	Bexar County, TX	72.9	**San Antonio, TX** (city) Bexar County	70.2
Louisiana	67.6	Queens County, NY	72.9	**Fayetteville, NC** (city) Cumberland County	69.2
New York	66.7	Cumberland County, NC	72.7	**Manhattan, NY** (borough) New York County	68.4
California	66.6	Los Angeles County, CA	72.5	**Brooklyn, NY** (borough) Kings County	66.6
Maryland	64.4	Broward County, FL	70.3	**New York, NY** (city)	66.0

Sorted by Percent in Ascending Order — U.S. = 62.3%

State	Percent	County	Percent	Place	Percent
Minnesota	20.6	Maricopa County, AZ	37.4	**Killeen, TX** (city) Bell County	35.7
Wisconsin	40.0	Bell County, TX	41.2	**San Diego, CA** (city) San Diego County	47.1
Illinois	40.3	Dallas County, TX	42.2	**Bronx, NY** (borough) Bronx County	47.3
Alabama	41.5	Fairfax County, VA	43.8	**Miami, FL** (city) Miami-Dade County	55.8
Pennsylvania	43.1	Palm Beach County, FL	43.8	**New York, NY** (city)	66.0
Ohio	48.0	Suffolk County, NY	44.4	**Brooklyn, NY** (borough) Kings County	66.6
Oklahoma	50.1	Essex County, NJ	45.8	**Manhattan, NY** (borough) New York County	68.4
Arizona	51.9	Bronx County, NY	47.3	**Fayetteville, NC** (city) Cumberland County	69.2
South Carolina	52.1	Hudson County, NJ	48.8	**San Antonio, TX** (city) Bexar County	70.2
Michigan	52.5	Montgomery County, MD	52.0	**Queens, NY** (borough) Queens County	72.9

Note: (1) Ranking tables cover all states and counties, and places with an overall population of at least 125,000, OR an overall population of at least 25,000 where the Hispanic/Latino population is at least 20% of the overall population. In states where less than five places meet either of these criteria, we have included places with at least 10,000 total population with the highest percentage of Hispanic/Latino population. These places are identified with an asterisk (*); Please refer to the User's Guide for a full explanation of data.

Foreign-Born Naturalized Citizens

Central American: Salvadoran

Top 10 States, Counties, and Places[1]

Sorted by Number in Descending Order — U.S. = 292,250

State	Number	County	Number	Place	Number
California	137,025	Los Angeles County, CA	88,780	**Los Angeles, CA** (city) Los Angeles County	52,085
Texas	34,441	Harris County, TX	19,683	**Houston, TX** (city) Harris County	11,623
New York	25,137	Montgomery County, MD	7,695	**New York, NY** (city)	9,290
Maryland	15,589	Nassau County, NY	7,416	**Hempstead (town), NY** (town) Nassau County	5,126
Virginia	14,663	Suffolk County, NY	6,332	**Queens, NY** (borough) Queens County	4,862
Florida	10,143	San Bernardino County, CA	6,066	**San Francisco, CA** (city) San Francisco County	4,546
New Jersey	9,992	Prince George's County, MD	5,227	**Islip, NY** (town) Suffolk County	3,523
Nevada	5,324	Fairfax County, VA	5,140	**Palmdale, CA** (city) Los Angeles County	2,347
Massachusetts	4,858	San Mateo County, CA	5,096	**Brooklyn, NY** (borough) Kings County	2,224
North Carolina	3,580	Orange County, CA	5,031	**Dallas, TX** (city) Dallas County	1,888

Sorted by Number in Ascending Order — U.S. = 292,250

State	Number	County	Number	Place	Number
Alaska	149	Sebastian County, AR	8	**Gainesville, GA** (city) Hall County	14
Kentucky	207	Polk County, IA	44	**Des Moines, IA** (city) Polk County	27
Idaho	212	Hartford County, CT	58	**Greensboro, NC** (city) Guilford County	48
Hawaii	275	Dakota County, MN	83	**Salinas, CA** (city) Monterey County	88
Michigan	306	Guilford County, NC	83	**Denver, CO** (city) Denver County	94
Alabama	325	Denver County, CO	94	**Richmond, VA** (independent city)	97
New Mexico	346	Camden County, NJ	99	**Hialeah, FL** (city) Miami-Dade County	103
Wisconsin	349	Rutherford County, TN	104	**Homestead, FL** (city) Miami-Dade County	104
Oklahoma	363	Ocean County, NJ	115	**Lake Worth, FL** (city) Palm Beach County	116
South Carolina	397	Santa Cruz County, CA	119	**Tacoma, WA** (city) Pierce County	120

Sorted by Percent in Descending Order — U.S. = 28.1%

State	Percent	County	Percent	Place	Percent
Hawaii	66.4	Cache County, UT	57.7	**Rancho Cucamonga, CA** (city) San Bernardino County	77.4
Utah	39.6	New York County, NY	50.2	**Burbank, CA** (city) Los Angeles County	76.5
California	37.4	Polk County, FL	50.2	**West Covina, CA** (city) Los Angeles County	75.9
Idaho	37.3	Ventura County, CA	49.1	**Fremont, CA** (city) Alameda County	75.6
Illinois	35.7	El Paso County, TX	47.0	**Pittsburg, CA** (city) Contra Costa County	74.2
Pennsylvania	34.4	San Diego County, CA	46.7	**La Puente, CA** (city) Los Angeles County	69.7
Wisconsin	33.6	Contra Costa County, CA	45.5	**Carson, CA** (city) Los Angeles County	67.3
Alabama	32.1	Middlesex County, NJ	45.5	**San Bruno, CA** (city) San Mateo County	67.0
Alaska	32.0	San Francisco County, CA	45.2	**Whittier, CA** (city) Los Angeles County	66.4
Nevada	31.0	Stanislaus County, CA	43.3	**Alhambra, CA** (city) Los Angeles County	65.5

Sorted by Percent in Ascending Order — U.S. = 28.1%

State	Percent	County	Percent	Place	Percent
Tennessee	11.4	Sebastian County, AR	1.2	**Gainesville, GA** (city) Hall County	1.2
Colorado	13.1	Polk County, IA	4.7	**Des Moines, IA** (city) Polk County	3.0
Georgia	14.6	Hartford County, CT	5.5	**Greensboro, NC** (city) Guilford County	5.5
North Carolina	15.6	Cobb County, GA	7.8	**Glen Cove, NY** (city) Nassau County	6.8
Kentucky	16.4	Guilford County, NC	8.1	**Homestead, FL** (city) Miami-Dade County	7.5
Arkansas	16.9	Camden County, NJ	8.3	**Lynn, MA** (city) Essex County	8.2
Michigan	17.0	Davidson County, TN	9.0	**Denver, CO** (city) Denver County	9.1
Iowa	17.8	Washington County, AR	9.0	**Springdale, AR** (city) Washington County	9.2
District of Columbia	18.4	Dakota County, MN	9.1	**San Rafael, CA** (city) Marin County	9.4
Minnesota	18.9	Denver County, CO	9.1	**Nashville-Davidson, TN** (metropolitan govt) Davidson County	9.7

Note: (1) Ranking tables cover all states and counties, and places with an overall population of at least 125,000, OR an overall population of at least 25,000 where the Hispanic/Latino population is at least 20% of the overall population. In states where less than five places meet either of these criteria, we have included places with at least 10,000 total population with the highest percentage of Hispanic/Latino population. These places are identified with an asterisk (*); Please refer to the User's Guide for a full explanation of data.

Foreign-Born Naturalized Citizens

Cuban

Top 10 States, Counties, and Places[1]

Sorted by Number in Descending Order — U.S. = 574,825

State	Number	County	Number	Place	Number
Florida	424,455	Miami-Dade County, FL	324,394	**Miami, FL** (city) Miami-Dade County	59,628
New Jersey	35,071	Broward County, FL	27,603	**Hialeah, FL** (city) Miami-Dade County	58,060
California	27,376	Los Angeles County, CA	15,835	**Tamiami, FL** (cdp) Miami-Dade County	15,632
New York	21,842	Hudson County, NJ	15,658	**New York, NY** (city)	14,271
Texas	10,661	Hillsborough County, FL	15,554	**Kendale Lakes, FL** (cdp) Miami-Dade County	11,758
Georgia	6,125	Palm Beach County, FL	13,114	**Fountainebleau, FL** (cdp) Miami-Dade County	11,242
Illinois	5,793	Orange County, FL	5,492	**Kendall, FL** (cdp) Miami-Dade County	9,695
Nevada	4,931	Bergen County, NJ	4,982	**Miami Beach, FL** (city) Miami-Dade County	9,241
North Carolina	3,484	Queens County, NY	4,919	**Westchester, FL** (cdp) Miami-Dade County	9,000
Pennsylvania	3,250	Clark County, NV	4,758	**University Park, FL** (cdp) Miami-Dade County	8,171

Sorted by Number in Ascending Order — U.S. = 574,825

State	Number	County	Number	Place	Number
Maine	133	Pierce County, WA	59	**Nashville-Davidson, TN** (metropolitan govt) Davidson County	82
Iowa	206	Berks County, PA	65	**Milwaukee, WI** (city) Milwaukee County	131
Rhode Island	235	Davidson County, TN	82	**Syracuse, NY** (city) Onondaga County	148
Arkansas	237	Hamilton County, OH	92	**Tallahassee, FL** (city) Leon County	154
West Virginia	253	Oakland County, MI	105	**Rochester, NY** (city) Monroe County	158
Hawaii	266	Arapahoe County, CO	116	**Baltimore, MD** (independent city)	168
Oklahoma	299	Lehigh County, PA	123	**Columbus, OH** (city) Franklin County	178
Utah	300	Jackson County, MO	124	**New Orleans, LA** (city) Orleans Parish	192
New Hampshire	302	Prince William County, VA	131	**Seattle, WA** (city) King County	198
Kansas	309	Hennepin County, MN	139	**Islip, NY** (town) Suffolk County	199

Sorted by Percent in Descending Order — U.S. = 57.5%

State	Percent	County	Percent	Place	Percent
Delaware	93.6	Baltimore County, MD	97.6	**Burbank, CA** (city) Los Angeles County	100.0
Hawaii	89.9	Ventura County, CA	96.5	**Islip, NY** (town) Suffolk County	100.0
West Virginia	83.0	Bucks County, PA	96.2	**North Hempstead, NY** (town) Nassau County	100.0
Arkansas	82.3	San Mateo County, CA	95.9	**Cooper City, FL** (city) Broward County	93.6
District of Columbia	79.7	New Castle County, DE	95.1	**Oyster Bay, NY** (town) Nassau County	92.3
Colorado	76.3	Montgomery County, TX	90.8	**Coral Gables, FL** (city) Miami-Dade County	89.6
Connecticut	74.9	Nassau County, NY	90.4	**Glendale, CA** (city) Los Angeles County	88.7
Maryland	74.6	Ocean County, NJ	90.3	**Hempstead (town), NY** (town) Nassau County	87.6
California	73.2	Fort Bend County, TX	89.1	**Brookhaven, NY** (town) Suffolk County	87.0
New Hampshire	72.9	Honolulu County, HI	88.8	**Tamarac, FL** (city) Broward County	86.2

Sorted by Percent in Ascending Order — U.S. = 57.5%

State	Percent	County	Percent	Place	Percent
Kentucky	19.4	Davidson County, TN	12.9	**Nashville-Davidson, TN** (metropolitan govt) Davidson County	12.9
New Mexico	23.9	Travis County, TX	15.2	**Austin, TX** (city) Travis County	15.6
Arizona	34.2	Burlington County, NJ	15.7	**Syracuse, NY** (city) Onondaga County	15.6
Alabama	37.6	Jefferson County, KY	17.6	**Louisville-Jefferson County, KY** (metropolitan govt) Jefferson County	17.1
Mississippi	38.0	Jackson County, MO	19.1	**Phoenix, AZ** (city) Maricopa County	21.2
Nevada	41.1	Bernalillo County, NM	21.4	**Albuquerque, NM** (city) Bernalillo County	22.4
Missouri	41.4	Onondaga County, NY	22.5	**Lehigh Acres, FL** (cdp) Lee County	24.5
Michigan	41.9	Multnomah County, OR	26.1	**Rochester, NY** (city) Monroe County	29.9
Oregon	43.0	Pierce County, WA	26.3	**Portland, OR** (city) Multnomah County	31.3
Kansas	46.1	Clay County, MO	26.7	**Kissimmee, FL** (city) Osceola County	32.0

Note: (1) Ranking tables cover all states and counties, and places with an overall population of at least 125,000, OR an overall population of at least 25,000 where the Hispanic/Latino population is at least 20% of the overall population. In states where less than five places meet either of these criteria, we have included places with at least 10,000 total population with the highest percentage of Hispanic/Latino population. These places are identified with an asterisk (*); Please refer to the User's Guide for a full explanation of data.

Foreign-Born Naturalized Citizens

Dominican Republic

Top 10 States, Counties, and Places[1]

Sorted by Number in Descending Order — U.S. = 364,573

State	Number	County	Number	Place	Number
New York	183,124	Bronx County, NY	56,919	**New York, NY** (city)	156,979
Florida	52,088	New York County, NY	48,373	**Bronx, NY** (borough) Bronx County	56,919
New Jersey	48,516	Queens County, NY	26,741	**Manhattan, NY** (borough) New York County	48,373
Massachusetts	27,150	Kings County, NY	23,845	**Queens, NY** (borough) Queens County	26,741
Pennsylvania	12,125	Miami-Dade County, FL	18,421	**Brooklyn, NY** (borough) Kings County	23,845
Rhode Island	7,776	Essex County, MA	13,540	**Lawrence, MA** (city) Essex County	7,371
Connecticut	5,269	Hudson County, NJ	12,442	**Boston, MA** (city) Suffolk County	6,204
Maryland	3,051	Broward County, FL	10,047	**Hempstead (town), NY** (town) Nassau County	5,875
Georgia	2,818	Passaic County, NJ	9,510	**Providence, RI** (city) Providence County	5,525
Texas	2,762	Providence County, RI	7,301	**Paterson, NJ** (city) Passaic County	5,238

Sorted by Number in Ascending Order — U.S. = 364,573

State	Number	County	Number	Place	Number
Alabama	126	Ulster County, NY	101	**York, PA** (city) York County	65
Minnesota	221	Oneida County, NY	152	**Raleigh, NC** (city) Wake County	86
Wisconsin	243	York County, PA	186	**Plainfield, NJ** (city) Union County	127
Washington	257	Marion County, FL	195	**Bethlehem, PA** (city) Northampton County	162
Utah	265	Dallas County, TX	204	**Syracuse, NY** (city) Onondaga County	182
South Carolina	323	Plymouth County, MA	204	**Los Angeles, CA** (city) Los Angeles County	189
Missouri	372	Sullivan County, NY	228	**Atlantic City, NJ** (city) Atlantic County	190
Delaware	428	Fulton County, GA	230	**Weston, FL** (city) Broward County	231
Colorado	431	Lackawanna County, PA	240	**Huntington, NY** (town) Suffolk County	237
Tennessee	444	Litchfield County, CT	245	**Grand Rapids, MI** (city) Kent County	238

Sorted by Percent in Descending Order — U.S. = 46.9%

State	Percent	County	Percent	Place	Percent
Alaska	69.7	Tarrant County, TX	85.7	**Richmond West, FL** (cdp) Miami-Dade County	88.9
Colorado	64.9	Volusia County, FL	73.4	**North Hempstead, NY** (town) Nassau County	81.7
Arizona	63.5	Maricopa County, AZ	71.9	**Poinciana, FL** (cdp) Osceola County	81.7
Washington	63.3	Orange County, NY	69.7	**Ramapo, NY** (town) Rockland County	80.3
California	63.0	Lee County, FL	66.1	**Anchorage, AK** (municipality)	77.2
Tennessee	62.4	Bergen County, NJ	65.1	**Deltona, FL** (city) Volusia County	74.1
Nevada	60.4	Burlington County, NJ	64.7	**Pembroke Pines, FL** (city) Broward County	73.4
Illinois	60.3	Fairfax County, VA	63.7	**Coral Springs, FL** (city) Broward County	72.3
Minnesota	60.1	Fulton County, GA	63.5	**North Miami Beach, FL** (city) Miami-Dade County	72.0
Florida	56.7	Broward County, FL	63.4	**Sunrise, FL** (city) Broward County	70.6

Sorted by Percent in Ascending Order — U.S. = 46.9%

State	Percent	County	Percent	Place	Percent
Wisconsin	30.6	Gwinnett County, GA	25.8	**York, PA** (city) York County	12.0
Alabama	36.4	York County, PA	26.3	**Raleigh, NC** (city) Wake County	12.8
Utah	37.2	Wake County, NC	26.5	**Atlantic City, NJ** (city) Atlantic County	21.5
Rhode Island	38.7	Plymouth County, MA	28.6	**Plainfield, NJ** (city) Union County	21.7
Louisiana	39.7	Oneida County, NY	29.6	**New Brunswick, NJ** (city) Middlesex County	23.3
Pennsylvania	39.7	Mecklenburg County, NC	32.5	**Hartford, CT** (city/town) Hartford County	28.0
South Carolina	40.7	Camden County, NJ	34.3	**Camden, NJ** (city) Camden County	28.5
Georgia	41.3	Litchfield County, CT	35.5	**Charlotte, NC** (city) Mecklenburg County	28.8
Connecticut	41.9	Morris County, NJ	36.0	**Passaic, NJ** (city) Passaic County	30.0
North Carolina	42.7	Philadelphia County, PA	36.6	**Newark, NJ** (city) Essex County	30.3

Note: (1) Ranking tables cover all states and counties, and places with an overall population of at least 125,000, OR an overall population of at least 25,000 where the Hispanic/Latino population is at least 20% of the overall population. In states where less than five places meet either of these criteria, we have included places with at least 10,000 total population with the highest percentage of Hispanic/Latino population. These places are identified with an asterisk (*); Please refer to the User's Guide for a full explanation of data.

Foreign-Born Naturalized Citizens

Mexican

Top 10 States, Counties, and Places[1]

Sorted by Number in Descending Order — U.S. = 2,548,167

State	Number	County	Number	Place	Number
California	1,165,060	Los Angeles County, CA	420,890	**Los Angeles, CA** (city) Los Angeles County	141,307
Texas	548,063	Cook County, IL	117,977	**Chicago, IL** (city) Cook County	71,170
Illinois	178,596	Harris County, TX	102,337	**El Paso, TX** (city) El Paso County	59,127
Arizona	120,171	San Diego County, CA	99,078	**Houston, TX** (city) Harris County	54,439
Nevada	49,065	Riverside County, CA	90,151	**San Diego, CA** (city) San Diego County	38,196
Florida	43,750	Orange County, CA	84,481	**San Antonio, TX** (city) Bexar County	37,766
Washington	38,858	San Bernardino County, CA	80,875	**Phoenix, AZ** (city) Maricopa County	35,120
Colorado	35,073	El Paso County, TX	74,728	**Dallas, TX** (city) Dallas County	29,649
New Mexico	31,737	Maricopa County, AZ	63,759	**Santa Ana, CA** (city) Orange County	24,841
New York	27,058	Dallas County, TX	51,808	**San Jose, CA** (city) Santa Clara County	23,489

Sorted by Number in Ascending Order — U.S. = 2,548,167

State	Number	County	Number	Place	Number
Vermont	100	Bay County, MI	0	**Bethlehem, PA** (city) Northampton County	0
Maine	243	Becker County, MN	0	**Grand Forks*, ND** (city) Grand Forks County	0
North Dakota	289	Benzie County, MI	0	**Great Falls*, MT** (city) Cascade County	0
District of Columbia	470	Brown County, KS	0	**Waterbury, CT** (city/town) New Haven County	0
New Hampshire	509	Cascade County, MT	0	**Pueblo West, CO** (cdp) Pueblo County	3
West Virginia	526	Cerro Gordo County, IA	0	**Warren, MI** (city) Macomb County	8
Montana	628	Chisago County, MN	0	**Biloxi*, MS** (city) Harrison County	13
Rhode Island	838	Clinton County, IL	0	**Hazleton, PA** (city) Luzerne County	13
South Dakota	932	Culpeper County, VA	0	**Schofield Barracks*, HI** (cdp) Honolulu County	17
Alaska	1,428	Cumberland County, ME	0	**Carthage*, MO** (city) Jasper County	18

Sorted by Percent in Descending Order — U.S. = 22.2%

State	Percent	County	Percent	Place	Percent
Montana	46.6	Cass County, MN	100.0	**Schofield Barracks*, HI** (cdp) Honolulu County	100.0
Hawaii	41.4	Kanawha County, WV	100.0	**Hampton, VA** (independent city)	82.2
North Dakota	36.1	Lewis and Clark County, MT	100.0	**Diamond Bar, CA** (city) Los Angeles County	80.1
Alaska	32.2	Trumbull County, OH	100.0	**Billings*, MT** (city) Yellowstone County	67.6
South Dakota	30.7	Flathead County, MT	97.5	**San Dimas, CA** (city) Los Angeles County	64.2
Maine	29.9	Elbert County, CO	94.4	**La Verne, CA** (city) Los Angeles County	61.9
West Virginia	28.1	Stevens County, WA	91.9	**Maricopa, AZ** (city) Pinal County	59.8
California	27.2	Adams County, IN	88.5	**Alamogordo, NM** (city) Otero County	57.5
Illinois	25.9	Dickinson County, KS	83.7	**Fort Campbell North*, KY** (cdp) Christian County	57.4
New Mexico	23.9	Jackson County, IL	79.1	**Hacienda Heights, CA** (cdp) Los Angeles County	56.8

Sorted by Percent in Ascending Order — U.S. = 22.2%

State	Percent	County	Percent	Place	Percent
North Carolina	7.2	Bay County, MI	0.0	**Bethlehem, PA** (city) Northampton County	0.0
South Carolina	7.4	Becker County, MN	0.0	**Grand Forks*, ND** (city) Grand Forks County	0.0
Alabama	8.5	Benzie County, MI	0.0	**Great Falls*, MT** (city) Cascade County	0.0
Georgia	9.6	Brown County, KS	0.0	**Waterbury, CT** (city/town) New Haven County	0.0
New Jersey	9.6	Cascade County, MT	0.0	**Biloxi*, MS** (city) Harrison County	1.1
Tennessee	9.8	Cerro Gordo County, IA	0.0	**North Atlanta, GA** (cdp) DeKalb County	1.7
Connecticut	10.9	Chisago County, MN	0.0	**Carthage*, MO** (city) Jasper County	1.8
Mississippi	10.9	Clinton County, IL	0.0	**Monroe, NC** (city) Union County	2.3
New York	11.3	Culpeper County, VA	0.0	**Hazleton, PA** (city) Luzerne County	2.6
Kentucky	12.0	Cumberland County, ME	0.0	**Long Branch, NJ** (city) Monmouth County	2.7

Note: (1) Ranking tables cover all states and counties, and places with an overall population of at least 125,000, OR an overall population of at least 25,000 where the Hispanic/Latino population is at least 20% of the overall population. In states where less than five places meet either of these criteria, we have included places with at least 10,000 total population with the highest percentage of Hispanic/Latino population. These places are identified with an asterisk (*); Please refer to the User's Guide for a full explanation of data.

Foreign-Born Naturalized Citizens

Puerto Rican

Top 10 States, Counties, and Places[1]

Sorted by Number in Descending Order — U.S. = 25,495

State	Number	County	Number	Place	Number
New York	6,428	Bronx County, NY	1,595	**New York, NY** (city)	5,061
Florida	4,667	Queens County, NY	1,427	**Bronx, NY** (borough) Bronx County	1,595
New Jersey	2,951	Kings County, NY	1,318	**Queens, NY** (borough) Queens County	1,427
California	2,266	Miami-Dade County, FL	980	**Brooklyn, NY** (borough) Kings County	1,318
Pennsylvania	1,306	Cook County, IL	813	**Philadelphia, PA** (city) Philadelphia County	750
Massachusetts	1,069	Philadelphia County, PA	750	**Chicago, IL** (city) Cook County	673
Connecticut	969	Los Angeles County, CA	678	**Manhattan, NY** (borough) New York County	656
Illinois	952	New York County, NY	656	**Los Angeles, CA** (city) Los Angeles County	265
Texas	837	Broward County, FL	641	**Bridgeport, CT** (city/town) Fairfield County	237
Virginia	551	Orange County, FL	598	**Yonkers, NY** (city) Westchester County	230

Sorted by Number in Ascending Order — U.S. = 25,495

State	Number	County	Number	Place	Number
Idaho	0	Adams County, CO	0	**Akron, OH** (city) Summit County	0
Maine	0	Adams County, PA	0	**Alafaya, FL** (cdp) Orange County	0
Montana	0	Albany County, NY	0	**Albuquerque, NM** (city) Bernalillo County	0
Nebraska	0	Allen County, IN	0	**Alexandria, VA** (independent city)	0
New Mexico	0	Beaufort County, SC	0	**Altamonte Springs, FL** (city) Seminole County	0
North Dakota	0	Bernalillo County, NM	0	**Atlanta, GA** (city) Fulton County	0
South Dakota	0	Berrien County, MI	0	**Augusta-Richmond County, GA** (consolidated govt) Richmond County	0
Vermont	0	Broome County, NY	0	**Aurora, CO** (city) Arapahoe County	0
West Virginia	0	Brown County, WI	0	**Aurora, IL** (city) Kane County	0
Wyoming	0	Camden County, GA	0	**Bakersfield, CA** (city) Kern County	0

Sorted by Percent in Descending Order — U.S. = 50.2%

State	Percent	County	Percent	Place	Percent
Delaware	92.6	Anne Arundel County, MD	100.0	**Anchorage, AK** (municipality)	100.0
Hawaii	83.2	Arapahoe County, CO	100.0	**Bayonne, NJ** (city) Hudson County	100.0
Alaska	75.6	Bay County, FL	100.0	**Bergenfield, NJ** (borough) Bergen County	100.0
Utah	73.2	Cabarrus County, NC	100.0	**Bethlehem, PA** (city) Northampton County	100.0
Maryland	62.9	Clay County, FL	100.0	**Bloomfield, NJ** (township) Essex County	100.0
Rhode Island	61.0	Clayton County, GA	100.0	**Carrollwood, FL** (cdp) Hillsborough County	100.0
Connecticut	59.3	Cochise County, AZ	100.0	**Chula Vista, CA** (city) San Diego County	100.0
New York	53.9	Collier County, FL	100.0	**Dale City, VA** (cdp) Prince William County	100.0
Virginia	53.0	Coryell County, TX	100.0	**Davie, FL** (town) Broward County	100.0
Florida	52.4	DuPage County, IL	100.0	**Detroit, MI** (city) Wayne County	100.0

Sorted by Percent in Ascending Order — U.S. = 50.2%

State	Percent	County	Percent	Place	Percent
Idaho	0.0	Albany County, NY	0.0	**Alafaya, FL** (cdp) Orange County	0.0
Maine	0.0	Beaufort County, SC	0.0	**Albuquerque, NM** (city) Bernalillo County	0.0
Nebraska	0.0	Bernalillo County, NM	0.0	**Alexandria, VA** (independent city)	0.0
New Mexico	0.0	Berrien County, MI	0.0	**Atlanta, GA** (city) Fulton County	0.0
District of Columbia	8.8	Brown County, WI	0.0	**Augusta-Richmond County, GA** (consolidated govt) Richmond County	0.0
Iowa	9.2	Cape May County, NJ	0.0	**Bakersfield, CA** (city) Kern County	0.0
Missouri	15.6	Cayuga County, NY	0.0	**Bay Shore, NY** (cdp) Suffolk County	0.0
Oregon	16.8	Centre County, PA	0.0	**Cincinnati, OH** (city) Hamilton County	0.0
Indiana	21.0	Chatham County, GA	0.0	**Colorado Springs, CO** (city) El Paso County	0.0
Alabama	31.5	Chemung County, NY	0.0	**Corpus Christi, TX** (city) Nueces County	0.0

Note: (1) Ranking tables cover all states and counties, and places with an overall population of at least 125,000, OR an overall population of at least 25,000 where the Hispanic/Latino population is at least 20% of the overall population. In states where less than five places meet either of these criteria, we have included places with at least 10,000 total population with the highest percentage of Hispanic/Latino population. These places are identified with an asterisk (*); Please refer to the User's Guide for a full explanation of data.

Foreign-Born Naturalized Citizens

South American

Top 10 States, Counties, and Places[1]

Sorted by Number in Descending Order — U.S. = 776,192

State	Number	County	Number	Place	Number
Florida	193,942	Miami-Dade County, FL	77,831	**New York, NY** (city)	106,999
New York	154,121	Queens County, NY	66,201	**Queens, NY** (borough) Queens County	66,201
New Jersey	95,248	Broward County, FL	42,511	**Los Angeles, CA** (city) Los Angeles County	16,684
California	92,923	Los Angeles County, CA	41,003	**Brooklyn, NY** (borough) Kings County	14,910
Texas	33,699	Hudson County, NJ	19,998	**Bronx, NY** (borough) Bronx County	11,426
Virginia	25,303	Bergen County, NJ	15,534	**Manhattan, NY** (borough) New York County	11,255
Illinois	20,365	Kings County, NY	14,910	**Hempstead (town), NY** (town) Nassau County	9,205
Connecticut	16,620	Nassau County, NY	14,355	**Chicago, IL** (city) Cook County	9,169
Maryland	16,161	Cook County, IL	14,114	**Miami, FL** (city) Miami-Dade County	7,634
Massachusetts	14,203	Palm Beach County, FL	13,808	**Pembroke Pines, FL** (city) Broward County	6,961

Sorted by Number in Ascending Order — U.S. = 776,192

State	Number	County	Number	Place	Number
North Dakota	224	Weber County, UT	104	**Sterling, VA** (cdp) Loudoun County	64
Wyoming	251	Hamilton County, IN	121	**Cranston*, RI** (city) Providence County	100
Montana	328	Tompkins County, NY	121	**Spring Valley, NY** (village) Rockland County	107
Vermont	373	Cabarrus County, NC	135	**New London, CT** (city/town) New London County	118
West Virginia	380	Cleveland County, OK	141	**Memphis, TN** (city) Shelby County	122
Maine	452	Clark County, WA	144	**Placentia, CA** (city) Orange County	147
Nebraska	585	San Luis Obispo County, CA	144	**Pittsburgh, PA** (city) Allegheny County	152
Arkansas	739	Saint Tammany Parish, LA	145	**Mountain View, CA** (city) Santa Clara County	171
Mississippi	743	Saint Joseph County, IN	149	**Modesto, CA** (city) Stanislaus County	176
Alaska	760	Spokane County, WA	151	**Chesapeake, VA** (independent city)	181

Sorted by Percent in Descending Order — U.S. = 41.5%

State	Percent	County	Percent	Place	Percent
Vermont	75.1	Rockingham County, NH	82.6	**Chino Hills, CA** (city) San Bernardino County	75.3
Hawaii	69.1	Douglas County, CO	81.5	**Gilbert, AZ** (town) Maricopa County	71.3
Maine	64.6	Honolulu County, HI	79.5	**West Covina, CA** (city) Los Angeles County	70.5
Montana	62.8	Pierce County, WA	74.3	**Aurora, IL** (city) Kane County	69.6
New Hampshire	55.6	Saint Johns County, FL	74.2	**Oyster Bay, NY** (town) Nassau County	68.6
Arizona	54.6	Martin County, FL	72.6	**Hayward, CA** (city) Alameda County	68.3
North Dakota	53.7	Putnam County, NY	70.8	**Chino, CA** (city) San Bernardino County	68.0
California	52.3	Erie County, NY	69.8	**Palm Springs, CA** (city) Riverside County	67.4
Washington	49.7	Ada County, ID	69.5	**Cooper City, FL** (city) Broward County	66.8
Michigan	49.2	Kent County, MI	67.4	**Hawthorne, CA** (city) Los Angeles County	66.7

Sorted by Percent in Ascending Order — U.S. = 41.5%

State	Percent	County	Percent	Place	Percent
Utah	30.2	Weber County, UT	11.8	**Spring Valley, NY** (village) Rockland County	5.8
Nebraska	31.6	Beaufort County, SC	17.9	**Sterling, VA** (cdp) Loudoun County	6.7
Alabama	32.6	Hamilton County, IN	21.1	**City of Orange, NJ** (township) Essex County	10.5
Kansas	32.6	Cabarrus County, NC	21.3	**Danbury, CT** (city/town) Fairfield County	13.5
Indiana	32.7	Shelby County, TN	21.7	**Memphis, TN** (city) Shelby County	13.8
Mississippi	32.7	Saint Joseph County, IN	22.9	**Ossining, NY** (village) Westchester County	15.7
Arkansas	33.9	Suffolk County, MA	23.9	**New London, CT** (city/town) New London County	16.0
Wisconsin	34.2	Hennepin County, MN	24.1	**Cranston*, RI** (city) Providence County	17.0
Tennessee	34.4	Henrico County, VA	24.3	**Ossining, NY** (town) Westchester County	18.2
Virginia	34.4	Gaston County, NC	24.4	**Mountain View, CA** (city) Santa Clara County	18.8

Note: (1) Ranking tables cover all states and counties, and places with an overall population of at least 125,000, OR an overall population of at least 25,000 where the Hispanic/Latino population is at least 20% of the overall population. In states where less than five places meet either of these criteria, we have included places with at least 10,000 total population with the highest percentage of Hispanic/Latino population. These places are identified with an asterisk (*); Please refer to the User's Guide for a full explanation of data.

Foreign-Born Naturalized Citizens

South American: Argentinean

Top 10 States, Counties, and Places[1]

Sorted by Number in Descending Order — U.S. = 60,178

State	Number	County	Number	Place	Number
California	14,447	Los Angeles County, CA	6,579	**New York, NY** (city)	4,053
Florida	13,253	Miami-Dade County, FL	6,072	**Los Angeles, CA** (city) Los Angeles County	2,855
New York	7,503	Broward County, FL	3,031	**Queens, NY** (borough) Queens County	1,981
New Jersey	4,338	Queens County, NY	1,981	**Miami, FL** (city) Miami-Dade County	827
Texas	2,978	Orange County, CA	1,538	**Manhattan, NY** (borough) New York County	745
Illinois	1,717	Cook County, IL	1,143	**Brooklyn, NY** (borough) Kings County	732
Maryland	1,449	Nassau County, NY	1,075	**Hempstead (town), NY** (town) Nassau County	612
Massachusetts	1,325	San Bernardino County, CA	1,026	**Miami Beach, FL** (city) Miami-Dade County	495
Virginia	1,167	Palm Beach County, FL	987	**Pembroke Pines, FL** (city) Broward County	475
Arizona	1,147	Harris County, TX	955	**Chicago, IL** (city) Cook County	442

Sorted by Number in Ascending Order — U.S. = 60,178

State	Number	County	Number	Place	Number
Louisiana	183	Lee County, FL	95	**Doral, FL** (city) Miami-Dade County	167
South Carolina	188	Dallas County, TX	186	**San Jose, CA** (city) Santa Clara County	180
Wisconsin	192	Tarrant County, TX	189	**Coral Springs, FL** (city) Broward County	221
Missouri	204	Travis County, TX	191	**Hialeah, FL** (city) Miami-Dade County	299
Tennessee	222	Oakland County, MI	195	**San Diego, CA** (city) San Diego County	308
District of Columbia	232	Orange County, NY	219	**Bronx, NY** (borough) Bronx County	354
Minnesota	259	Montgomery County, TX	220	**Hollywood, FL** (city) Broward County	379
Indiana	291	King County, WA	254	**San Francisco, CA** (city) San Francisco County	399
Oregon	364	Bexar County, TX	276	**Houston, TX** (city) Harris County	411
Ohio	460	Salt Lake County, UT	282	**Aventura, FL** (city) Miami-Dade County	435

Sorted by Percent in Descending Order — U.S. = 41.2%

State	Percent	County	Percent	Place	Percent
Arizona	69.1	Bergen County, NJ	72.5	**Hempstead (town), NY** (town) Nassau County	69.0
California	53.8	Maricopa County, AZ	68.2	**Pembroke Pines, FL** (city) Broward County	68.1
Oregon	53.5	Suffolk County, NY	66.4	**San Diego, CA** (city) San Diego County	55.0
Colorado	53.3	San Bernardino County, CA	65.6	**San Francisco, CA** (city) San Francisco County	54.1
Massachusetts	51.1	Ventura County, CA	65.4	**Los Angeles, CA** (city) Los Angeles County	49.6
Illinois	51.0	Alameda County, CA	61.4	**Queens, NY** (borough) Queens County	49.0
Washington	48.2	Nassau County, NY	60.1	**Chicago, IL** (city) Cook County	44.9
New York	47.6	Riverside County, CA	56.1	**Bronx, NY** (borough) Bronx County	43.3
North Carolina	47.4	Contra Costa County, CA	54.5	**New York, NY** (city)	43.1
New Jersey	46.8	San Francisco County, CA	54.1	**Brooklyn, NY** (borough) Kings County	41.5

Sorted by Percent in Ascending Order — U.S. = 41.2%

State	Percent	County	Percent	Place	Percent
South Carolina	17.9	Lee County, FL	9.3	**Miami Beach, FL** (city) Miami-Dade County	13.0
Wisconsin	20.7	Dallas County, TX	15.4	**Miami, FL** (city) Miami-Dade County	17.6
Tennessee	28.9	Montgomery County, TX	24.6	**Doral, FL** (city) Miami-Dade County	19.5
Utah	29.8	Miami-Dade County, FL	27.1	**Hialeah, FL** (city) Miami-Dade County	26.7
Virginia	31.6	Salt Lake County, UT	29.3	**Hollywood, FL** (city) Broward County	27.5
Florida	31.7	New York County, NY	30.2	**Houston, TX** (city) Harris County	30.0
Missouri	33.0	Palm Beach County, FL	31.8	**Manhattan, NY** (borough) New York County	30.2
Indiana	33.2	Montgomery County, MD	32.0	**Coral Springs, FL** (city) Broward County	30.3
District of Columbia	33.9	Essex County, NJ	32.8	**San Jose, CA** (city) Santa Clara County	30.9
Georgia	33.9	Union County, NJ	34.6	**Aventura, FL** (city) Miami-Dade County	38.8

Note: (1) Ranking tables cover all states and counties, and places with an overall population of at least 125,000, OR an overall population of at least 25,000 where the Hispanic/Latino population is at least 20% of the overall population. In states where less than five places meet either of these criteria, we have included places with at least 10,000 total population with the highest percentage of Hispanic/Latino population. These places are identified with an asterisk (*); Please refer to the User's Guide for a full explanation of data.

Foreign-Born Naturalized Citizens

South American: Bolivian

Top 10 States, Counties, and Places[1]

Sorted by Number in Descending Order — U.S. = 27,677

State	Number	County	Number	Place	Number
Virginia	7,448	Fairfax County, VA	4,476	**New York, NY** (city)	2,014
California	5,040	Los Angeles County, CA	2,042	**Los Angeles, CA** (city) Los Angeles County	1,377
Florida	3,159	Montgomery County, MD	1,952	**Queens, NY** (borough) Queens County	1,221
New York	2,747	Queens County, NY	1,221	**Arlington, VA** (cdp) Arlington County	1,011
Maryland	2,436	Arlington County, VA	1,011	**Annandale, VA** (cdp) Fairfax County	568
Texas	1,086	Prince William County, VA	894	**West Falls Church, VA** (cdp) Fairfax County	362
New Jersey	1,069	Miami-Dade County, FL	886	**Springfield, VA** (cdp) Fairfax County	227
Illinois	588	Broward County, FL	604	**Dale City, VA** (cdp) Prince William County	213
Massachusetts	429	Orange County, CA	559	**Providence, RI** (city) Providence County	171
Rhode Island	407	Santa Clara County, CA	458		

Sorted by Number in Ascending Order — U.S. = 27,677

State	Number	County	Number	Place	Number
North Carolina	156	Prince George's County, MD	235	**Providence, RI** (city) Providence County	171
Pennsylvania	236	Palm Beach County, FL	260	**Dale City, VA** (cdp) Prince William County	213
Rhode Island	407	Cook County, IL	280	**Springfield, VA** (cdp) Fairfax County	227
Massachusetts	429	Harris County, TX	303	**West Falls Church, VA** (cdp) Fairfax County	362
Illinois	588	Providence County, RI	407	**Annandale, VA** (cdp) Fairfax County	568
New Jersey	1,069	Loudoun County, VA	412	**Arlington, VA** (cdp) Arlington County	1,011
Texas	1,086	San Diego County, CA	416	**Queens, NY** (borough) Queens County	1,221
Maryland	2,436	Santa Clara County, CA	458	**Los Angeles, CA** (city) Los Angeles County	1,377
New York	2,747	Orange County, CA	559	**New York, NY** (city)	2,014
Florida	3,159	Broward County, FL	604		

Sorted by Percent in Descending Order — U.S. = 40.4%

State	Percent	County	Percent	Place	Percent
California	60.6	San Diego County, CA	88.7	**New York, NY** (city)	60.7
Pennsylvania	58.4	Cook County, IL	62.6	**Queens, NY** (borough) Queens County	57.7
Illinois	57.0	Santa Clara County, CA	59.0	**Los Angeles, CA** (city) Los Angeles County	57.5
New York	53.5	Los Angeles County, CA	57.7	**Arlington, VA** (cdp) Arlington County	29.5
Maryland	46.9	Queens County, NY	57.7	**West Falls Church, VA** (cdp) Fairfax County	28.8
Florida	45.8	Montgomery County, MD	52.5	**Annandale, VA** (cdp) Fairfax County	27.6
Texas	39.6	Orange County, CA	52.3	**Springfield, VA** (cdp) Fairfax County	25.4
North Carolina	38.9	Broward County, FL	51.2	**Providence, RI** (city) Providence County	23.6
Massachusetts	37.1	Miami-Dade County, FL	38.8	**Dale City, VA** (cdp) Prince William County	17.5
New Jersey	32.9	Palm Beach County, FL	35.0		

Sorted by Percent in Ascending Order — U.S. = 40.4%

State	Percent	County	Percent	Place	Percent
Virginia	28.0	Loudoun County, VA	22.3	**Dale City, VA** (cdp) Prince William County	17.5
Rhode Island	31.1	Prince George's County, MD	23.8	**Providence, RI** (city) Providence County	23.6
New Jersey	32.9	Prince William County, VA	26.0	**Springfield, VA** (cdp) Fairfax County	25.4
Massachusetts	37.1	Arlington County, VA	29.5	**Annandale, VA** (cdp) Fairfax County	27.6
North Carolina	38.9	Fairfax County, VA	30.7	**West Falls Church, VA** (cdp) Fairfax County	28.8
Texas	39.6	Providence County, RI	31.1	**Arlington, VA** (cdp) Arlington County	29.5
Florida	45.8	Harris County, TX	34.2	**Los Angeles, CA** (city) Los Angeles County	57.5
Maryland	46.9	Palm Beach County, FL	35.0	**Queens, NY** (borough) Queens County	57.7
New York	53.5	Miami-Dade County, FL	38.8	**New York, NY** (city)	60.7
Illinois	57.0	Broward County, FL	51.2		

Note: (1) Ranking tables cover all states and counties, and places with an overall population of at least 125,000, OR an overall population of at least 25,000 where the Hispanic/Latino population is at least 20% of the overall population. In states where less than five places meet either of these criteria, we have included places with at least 10,000 total population with the highest percentage of Hispanic/Latino population. These places are identified with an asterisk (*); Please refer to the User's Guide for a full explanation of data.

Foreign-Born Naturalized Citizens

South American: Chilean

Top 10 States, Counties, and Places[1]

Sorted by Number in Descending Order — U.S. = 36,557

State	Number	County	Number	Place	Number
Florida	8,310	Miami-Dade County, FL	4,575	**New York, NY** (city)	2,679
California	6,860	Los Angeles County, CA	2,897	**Los Angeles, CA** (city) Los Angeles County	1,485
New York	4,981	Queens County, NY	1,390	**Queens, NY** (borough) Queens County	1,390
New Jersey	2,872	Broward County, FL	1,215	**Miami, FL** (city) Miami-Dade County	539
Texas	1,360	Nassau County, NY	940	**Brooklyn, NY** (borough) Kings County	470
Maryland	1,325	Montgomery County, MD	742	**Manhattan, NY** (borough) New York County	468
Virginia	1,111	Hudson County, NJ	701	**Kendall, FL** (cdp) Miami-Dade County	405
Massachusetts	798	Santa Clara County, CA	641	**Hempstead (town), NY** (town) Nassau County	357
Illinois	796	Westchester County, NY	589	**Chicago, IL** (city) Cook County	301
Georgia	735	Harris County, TX	479		

Sorted by Number in Ascending Order — U.S. = 36,557

State	Number	County	Number	Place	Number
Missouri	192	Salt Lake County, UT	172	**Chicago, IL** (city) Cook County	301
Wisconsin	211	Alameda County, CA	174	**Hempstead (town), NY** (town) Nassau County	357
Tennessee	220	Utah County, UT	198	**Kendall, FL** (cdp) Miami-Dade County	405
Minnesota	230	San Bernardino County, CA	220	**Manhattan, NY** (borough) New York County	468
Ohio	237	Maricopa County, AZ	230	**Brooklyn, NY** (borough) Kings County	470
Oregon	278	Middlesex County, MA	272	**Miami, FL** (city) Miami-Dade County	539
Michigan	287	San Mateo County, CA	274	**Queens, NY** (borough) Queens County	1,390
Colorado	298	Riverside County, CA	322	**Los Angeles, CA** (city) Los Angeles County	1,485
Pennsylvania	383	Palm Beach County, FL	324	**New York, NY** (city)	2,679
Arizona	420	Suffolk County, NY	331		

Sorted by Percent in Descending Order — U.S. = 46.4%

State	Percent	County	Percent	Place	Percent
California	53.1	Bergen County, NJ	71.8	**Kendall, FL** (cdp) Miami-Dade County	67.6
Washington	52.0	Orange County, CA	71.5	**Miami, FL** (city) Miami-Dade County	60.2
New Jersey	50.1	San Mateo County, CA	61.9	**Chicago, IL** (city) Cook County	58.4
Tennessee	50.0	Santa Clara County, CA	61.6	**Los Angeles, CA** (city) Los Angeles County	55.8
New York	49.3	Clark County, NV	59.7	**New York, NY** (city)	53.8
Arizona	48.4	Riverside County, CA	56.0	**Queens, NY** (borough) Queens County	53.1
Florida	48.4	Los Angeles County, CA	54.5	**Brooklyn, NY** (borough) Kings County	52.2
Georgia	48.0	San Diego County, CA	54.1	**Manhattan, NY** (borough) New York County	52.2
Nevada	47.9	Cook County, IL	53.5	**Hempstead (town), NY** (town) Nassau County	38.8
Illinois	47.4	Queens County, NY	53.1		

Sorted by Percent in Ascending Order — U.S. = 46.4%

State	Percent	County	Percent	Place	Percent
Utah	21.5	Utah County, UT	19.1	**Hempstead (town), NY** (town) Nassau County	38.8
Pennsylvania	32.8	Salt Lake County, UT	24.6	**Brooklyn, NY** (borough) Kings County	52.2
Colorado	33.9	Palm Beach County, FL	25.8	**Manhattan, NY** (borough) New York County	52.2
Wisconsin	34.5	Fairfax County, VA	29.8	**Queens, NY** (borough) Queens County	53.1
Oregon	36.7	Middlesex County, MA	33.0	**New York, NY** (city)	53.8
North Carolina	37.5	Alameda County, CA	35.7	**Los Angeles, CA** (city) Los Angeles County	55.8
Massachusetts	38.9	Westchester County, NY	35.8	**Chicago, IL** (city) Cook County	58.4
Missouri	40.1	San Bernardino County, CA	39.3	**Miami, FL** (city) Miami-Dade County	60.2
Texas	42.4	Maricopa County, AZ	39.4	**Kendall, FL** (cdp) Miami-Dade County	67.6
Maryland	43.4	Hudson County, NJ	40.5		

Note: (1) Ranking tables cover all states and counties, and places with an overall population of at least 125,000, OR an overall population of at least 25,000 where the Hispanic/Latino population is at least 20% of the overall population. In states where less than five places meet either of these criteria, we have included places with at least 10,000 total population with the highest percentage of Hispanic/Latino population. These places are identified with an asterisk (*); Please refer to the User's Guide for a full explanation of data.

Foreign-Born Naturalized Citizens

South American: Colombian

Top 10 States, Counties, and Places[1]

Sorted by Number in Descending Order — U.S. = 276,096

State	Number	County	Number	Place	Number
Florida	90,541	Miami-Dade County, FL	35,806	**New York, NY** (city)	35,981
New York	53,144	Queens County, NY	26,543	**Queens, NY** (borough) Queens County	26,543
New Jersey	32,432	Broward County, FL	19,305	**Hempstead (town), NY** (town) Nassau County	3,804
California	18,599	Los Angeles County, CA	8,255	**Brooklyn, NY** (borough) Kings County	3,624
Texas	13,565	Orange County, FL	7,232	**Miami, FL** (city) Miami-Dade County	3,386
Illinois	6,397	Bergen County, NJ	7,194	**Pembroke Pines, FL** (city) Broward County	3,209
Connecticut	6,351	Palm Beach County, FL	6,181	**Elizabeth, NJ** (city) Union County	3,205
Massachusetts	6,225	Harris County, TX	5,846	**Houston, TX** (city) Harris County	2,843
Georgia	5,969	Nassau County, NY	5,786	**Manhattan, NY** (borough) New York County	2,736
Pennsylvania	4,581	Union County, NJ	5,171	**Los Angeles, CA** (city) Los Angeles County	2,688

Sorted by Number in Ascending Order — U.S. = 276,096

State	Number	County	Number	Place	Number
Nebraska	168	Luzerne County, PA	131	**Long Beach, CA** (city) Los Angeles County	123
Delaware	227	Sacramento County, CA	161	**Brandon, FL** (cdp) Hillsborough County	152
Arkansas	239	Will County, IL	163	**Anaheim, CA** (city) Orange County	156
New Mexico	248	Oakland County, MI	173	**Tallahassee, FL** (city) Leon County	167
Kentucky	259	Saint Louis County, MO	175	**Royal Palm Beach, FL** (village) Palm Beach County	183
District of Columbia	347	Dane County, WI	184	**Indianapolis, IN** (city) Marion County	194
Oklahoma	377	Leon County, FL	190	**Raleigh, NC** (city) Wake County	200
Iowa	381	Hall County, GA	199	**Hartford, CT** (city/town) Hartford County	211
Alaska	389	Alachua County, FL	217	**Virginia Beach, VA** (independent city)	231
Kansas	416	Marion County, IN	221	**West Palm Beach, FL** (city) Palm Beach County	254

Sorted by Percent in Descending Order — U.S. = 46.2%

State	Percent	County	Percent	Place	Percent
Minnesota	66.2	Erie County, NY	85.7	**Staten Island, NY** (borough) Richmond County	81.4
Alaska	58.9	Richmond County, NY	81.4	**Linden, NJ** (city) Union County	77.6
Arizona	56.7	Norfolk County, MA	66.4	**Oyster Bay, NY** (town) Nassau County	72.2
New York	54.8	Nassau County, NY	66.0	**Glendale, CA** (city) Los Angeles County	68.1
Oregon	54.8	Mercer County, NJ	65.4	**Downey, CA** (city) Los Angeles County	67.8
New Hampshire	53.6	Alameda County, CA	65.0	**Hempstead (town), NY** (town) Nassau County	65.0
California	53.1	Dutchess County, NY	64.9	**Cooper City, FL** (city) Broward County	64.5
Nevada	53.0	Hennepin County, MN	64.4	**Englewood, NJ** (city) Bergen County	63.4
Illinois	52.1	Marion County, FL	64.4	**Miami Lakes, FL** (town) Miami-Dade County	62.6
Ohio	51.5	San Mateo County, CA	64.0	**Clifton, NJ** (city) Passaic County	62.4

Sorted by Percent in Ascending Order — U.S. = 46.2%

State	Percent	County	Percent	Place	Percent
Nebraska	20.0	Suffolk County, MA	21.0	**Brandon, FL** (cdp) Hillsborough County	17.6
Delaware	28.0	Dallas County, TX	26.8	**Kissimmee, FL** (city) Osceola County	19.9
District of Columbia	30.2	Saint Louis County, MO	27.1	**Revere, MA** (city) Suffolk County	20.3
Arkansas	30.5	Loudoun County, VA	27.4	**Boston, MA** (city) Suffolk County	20.6
Massachusetts	34.6	Leon County, FL	27.5	**Hartford, CT** (city/town) Hartford County	20.6
Kansas	36.0	Prince William County, VA	27.8	**West Palm Beach, FL** (city) Palm Beach County	21.0
South Carolina	36.4	Alachua County, FL	29.4	**Dallas, TX** (city) Dallas County	26.7
Georgia	37.9	Mecklenburg County, NC	29.7	**Tallahassee, FL** (city) Leon County	28.2
Oklahoma	38.4	Sacramento County, CA	31.1	**Long Beach, CA** (city) Los Angeles County	28.5
North Carolina	38.6	Gwinnett County, GA	32.5	**Town 'n' Country, FL** (cdp) Hillsborough County	29.8

Note: (1) Ranking tables cover all states and counties, and places with an overall population of at least 125,000, OR an overall population of at least 25,000 where the Hispanic/Latino population is at least 20% of the overall population. In states where less than five places meet either of these criteria, we have included places with at least 10,000 total population with the highest percentage of Hispanic/Latino population. These places are identified with an asterisk (*); Please refer to the User's Guide for a full explanation of data.

Foreign-Born Naturalized Citizens

South American: Ecuadorian

Top 10 States, Counties, and Places[1]

Sorted by Number in Descending Order — U.S. = 147,890

State	Number	County	Number	Place	Number
New York	54,428	Queens County, NY	23,288	**New York, NY** (city)	42,633
New Jersey	26,848	Hudson County, NJ	8,412	**Queens, NY** (borough) Queens County	23,288
Florida	21,522	Los Angeles County, CA	7,489	**Bronx, NY** (borough) Bronx County	6,849
California	12,516	Miami-Dade County, FL	7,387	**Brooklyn, NY** (borough) Kings County	6,795
Illinois	6,228	Bronx County, NY	6,849	**Manhattan, NY** (borough) New York County	4,855
Connecticut	3,628	Kings County, NY	6,795	**Chicago, IL** (city) Cook County	3,987
Texas	3,292	Cook County, IL	5,168	**Los Angeles, CA** (city) Los Angeles County	2,882
Pennsylvania	2,420	New York County, NY	4,855	**Jersey City, NJ** (city) Hudson County	2,706
North Carolina	2,161	Broward County, FL	4,839	**Newark, NJ** (city) Essex County	2,392
Maryland	1,982	Essex County, NJ	4,507	**Hempstead (town), NY** (town) Nassau County	1,997

Sorted by Number in Ascending Order — U.S. = 147,890

State	Number	County	Number	Place	Number
Kansas	82	Philadelphia County, PA	145	**Spring Valley, NY** (village) Rockland County	33
Wisconsin	155	Prince George's County, MD	149	**White Plains, NY** (city) Westchester County	52
Indiana	158	Baltimore County, MD	167	**City of Orange, NJ** (township) Essex County	92
Iowa	175	Gwinnett County, GA	173	**Ramapo, NY** (town) Rockland County	135
Missouri	175	Providence County, RI	187	**Philadelphia, PA** (city) Philadelphia County	145
Colorado	211	Utah County, UT	195	**Coral Springs, FL** (city) Broward County	175
Oklahoma	212	Delaware County, PA	201	**New Haven, CT** (city/town) New Haven County	184
Louisiana	216	Ocean County, NJ	203	**Norwalk, CT** (city/town) Fairfield County	185
Rhode Island	258	Burlington County, NJ	212	**Central Islip, NY** (cdp) Suffolk County	207
South Carolina	259	Putnam County, NY	225	**Orlando, FL** (city) Orange County	220

Sorted by Percent in Descending Order — U.S. = 38.5%

State	Percent	County	Percent	Place	Percent
Arizona	62.1	Santa Clara County, CA	82.6	**Hollywood, FL** (city) Broward County	79.0
California	60.4	Maricopa County, AZ	70.6	**Country Club, FL** (cdp) Miami-Dade County	74.1
Virginia	56.6	San Diego County, CA	69.5	**Hialeah, FL** (city) Miami-Dade County	66.0
Missouri	56.1	Pinellas County, FL	69.0	**Los Angeles, CA** (city) Los Angeles County	64.8
Florida	52.8	Riverside County, CA	68.7	**Oyster Bay, NY** (town) Nassau County	64.7
Nevada	52.5	Hillsborough County, FL	64.7	**Miramar, FL** (city) Broward County	63.5
Colorado	51.7	Dallas County, TX	64.6	**Downey, CA** (city) Los Angeles County	58.6
Washington	51.2	Los Angeles County, CA	64.6	**Paterson, NJ** (city) Passaic County	58.6
Oregon	48.5	Osceola County, FL	63.6	**Pembroke Pines, FL** (city) Broward County	56.2
Louisiana	47.0	Orange County, NY	60.9	**Hempstead (town), NY** (town) Nassau County	55.5

Sorted by Percent in Ascending Order — U.S. = 38.5%

State	Percent	County	Percent	Place	Percent
Minnesota	14.5	Hennepin County, MN	10.2	**Spring Valley, NY** (village) Rockland County	2.0
Indiana	18.8	Rockland County, NY	11.1	**White Plains, NY** (city) Westchester County	5.7
Kansas	20.0	Mercer County, NJ	17.5	**Ramapo, NY** (town) Rockland County	6.6
Connecticut	22.2	Delaware County, PA	20.3	**Minneapolis, MN** (city) Hennepin County	11.0
Wisconsin	30.9	Fairfield County, CT	20.3	**City of Orange, NJ** (township) Essex County	11.3
Pennsylvania	32.4	Philadelphia County, PA	20.8	**Danbury, CT** (city/town) Fairfield County	12.0
New York	33.7	Westchester County, NY	22.9	**Ossining, NY** (village) Westchester County	13.6
Oklahoma	34.0	Prince George's County, MD	25.0	**Ossining, NY** (town) Westchester County	13.9
Ohio	34.3	Essex County, NJ	26.6	**New Haven, CT** (city/town) New Haven County	15.8
Iowa	35.4	Gwinnett County, GA	26.7	**Norwalk, CT** (city/town) Fairfield County	20.5

Note: (1) Ranking tables cover all states and counties, and places with an overall population of at least 125,000, OR an overall population of at least 25,000 where the Hispanic/Latino population is at least 20% of the overall population. In states where less than five places meet either of these criteria, we have included places with at least 10,000 total population with the highest percentage of Hispanic/Latino population. These places are identified with an asterisk (*); Please refer to the User's Guide for a full explanation of data.

Foreign-Born Naturalized Citizens

South American: Paraguayan

Top 10 States, Counties, and Places[1]

Sorted by Number in Descending Order — U.S. = 6,063

State	Number	County	Number	Place	Number
New York	1,167	Queens County, NY	335	**New York, NY** (city)	623
Florida	695	Westchester County, NY	112	**Queens, NY** (borough) Queens County	335
New Jersey	426				
California	372				
Maryland	357				
Texas	353				

Sorted by Number in Ascending Order — U.S. = 6,063

State	Number	County	Number	Place	Number
Texas	353	Westchester County, NY	112	**Queens, NY** (borough) Queens County	335
Maryland	357	Queens County, NY	335	**New York, NY** (city)	623
California	372				
New Jersey	426				
Florida	695				
New York	1,167				

Sorted by Percent in Descending Order — U.S. = 45.4%

State	Percent	County	Percent	Place	Percent
California	64.7	Queens County, NY	17.5	**New York, NY** (city)	25.3
Texas	63.3	Westchester County, NY	8.9	**Queens, NY** (borough) Queens County	17.5
Florida	58.1				
Maryland	40.8				
New Jersey	32.9				
New York	24.0				

Sorted by Percent in Ascending Order — U.S. = 45.4%

State	Percent	County	Percent	Place	Percent
New York	24.0	Westchester County, NY	8.9	**Queens, NY** (borough) Queens County	17.5
New Jersey	32.9	Queens County, NY	17.5	**New York, NY** (city)	25.3
Maryland	40.8				
Florida	58.1				
Texas	63.3				
California	64.7				

Note: (1) Ranking tables cover all states and counties, and places with an overall population of at least 125,000, OR an overall population of at least 25,000 where the Hispanic/Latino population is at least 20% of the overall population. In states where less than five places meet either of these criteria, we have included places with at least 10,000 total population with the highest percentage of Hispanic/Latino population. These places are identified with an asterisk (*); Please refer to the User's Guide for a full explanation of data.

Foreign-Born Naturalized Citizens

South American: Peruvian

Top 10 States, Counties, and Places[1]

Sorted by Number in Descending Order — U.S. = 152,366

State	Number	County	Number	Place	Number
Florida	31,754	Miami-Dade County, FL	12,286	**New York, NY** (city)	13,991
California	26,944	Los Angeles County, CA	10,098	**Queens, NY** (borough) Queens County	9,140
New York	22,582	Queens County, NY	9,140	**Los Angeles, CA** (city) Los Angeles County	4,182
New Jersey	21,772	Broward County, FL	8,193	**Paterson, NJ** (city) Passaic County	2,242
Virginia	7,301	Passaic County, NJ	5,239	**Brooklyn, NY** (borough) Kings County	1,893
Texas	6,357	Hudson County, NJ	3,899	**Hempstead (town), NY** (town) Nassau County	1,679
Connecticut	3,840	Fairfax County, VA	3,589	**Clifton, NJ** (city) Passaic County	1,518
Maryland	3,782	Orange County, CA	3,018	**Manhattan, NY** (borough) New York County	1,463
Illinois	2,751	Westchester County, NY	2,702	**Chicago, IL** (city) Cook County	1,451
Georgia	2,410	Union County, NJ	2,668	**Hollywood, FL** (city) Broward County	1,395

Sorted by Number in Ascending Order — U.S. = 152,366

State	Number	County	Number	Place	Number
Louisiana	168	Franklin County, OH	100	**Denver, CO** (city) Denver County	112
Kansas	216	Denver County, CO	112	**Bridgeport, CT** (city/town) Fairfield County	167
Rhode Island	224	Lake County, IL	130	**Doral, FL** (city) Miami-Dade County	170
Alabama	258	Baltimore County, MD	140	**Austin, TX** (city) Travis County	173
Kentucky	330	Wake County, NC	184	**West Valley City, UT** (city) Salt Lake County	187
New Mexico	335	Ocean County, NJ	189	**Salt Lake City, UT** (city) Salt Lake County	191
Idaho	338	Solano County, CA	220	**Cape Coral, FL** (city) Lee County	205
District of Columbia	371	Sarasota County, FL	233	**Belleville, NJ** (township) Essex County	211
Indiana	390	New London County, CT	239	**Las Vegas, NV** (city) Clark County	211
Missouri	407	Fort Bend County, TX	252	**Torrance, CA** (city) Los Angeles County	229

Sorted by Percent in Descending Order — U.S. = 41.7%

State	Percent	County	Percent	Place	Percent
Hawaii	86.9	San Joaquin County, CA	62.4	**San Diego, CA** (city) San Diego County	67.3
Michigan	64.1	San Diego County, CA	58.9	**Miramar, FL** (city) Broward County	64.1
Washington	53.3	Lehigh County, PA	58.8	**Oyster Bay, NY** (town) Nassau County	62.5
Minnesota	52.7	Nassau County, NY	56.0	**Kendale Lakes, FL** (cdp) Miami-Dade County	61.6
New Mexico	50.2	Fort Bend County, TX	54.9	**Pembroke Pines, FL** (city) Broward County	61.2
Missouri	49.8	San Francisco County, CA	54.9	**Hempstead (town), NY** (town) Nassau County	58.5
Pennsylvania	49.8	Morris County, NJ	54.4	**Long Beach, CA** (city) Los Angeles County	55.6
Kentucky	47.7	Bergen County, NJ	54.3	**North Bergen, NJ** (township) Hudson County	55.0
California	46.7	New Haven County, CT	54.2	**San Francisco, CA** (city) San Francisco County	54.9
Oregon	46.7	Riverside County, CA	53.4	**Anaheim, CA** (city) Orange County	54.2

Sorted by Percent in Ascending Order — U.S. = 41.7%

State	Percent	County	Percent	Place	Percent
Louisiana	15.0	Franklin County, OH	19.6	**Stamford, CT** (city/town) Fairfield County	16.2
Indiana	25.1	Sarasota County, FL	22.6	**Sunrise, FL** (city) Broward County	20.8
Rhode Island	27.1	Osceola County, FL	23.2	**Kendall West, FL** (cdp) Miami-Dade County	21.0
Utah	28.9	New London County, CT	23.8	**Union City, NJ** (city) Hudson County	23.9
Alabama	30.1	Loudoun County, VA	24.8	**Port Chester, NY** (village) Westchester County	25.3
Maryland	32.7	Atlantic County, NJ	27.9	**Austin, TX** (city) Travis County	25.4
Massachusetts	33.2	Fairfield County, CT	28.1	**Rye, NY** (town) Westchester County	25.5
Wisconsin	34.7	Middlesex County, MA	28.3	**Doral, FL** (city) Miami-Dade County	25.9
Virginia	34.9	Salt Lake County, UT	28.9	**Dallas, TX** (city) Dallas County	26.0
Kansas	35.4	Prince William County, VA	30.2	**Miami, FL** (city) Miami-Dade County	26.0

RANKINGS & COMPARISONS

Note: (1) Ranking tables cover all states and counties, and places with an overall population of at least 125,000, OR an overall population of at least 25,000 where the Hispanic/Latino population is at least 20% of the overall population. In states where less than five places meet either of these criteria, we have included places with at least 10,000 total population with the highest percentage of Hispanic/Latino population. These places are identified with an asterisk (*); Please refer to the User's Guide for a full explanation of data.

Foreign-Born Naturalized Citizens

South American: Uruguayan

Top 10 States, Counties, and Places[1]

Sorted by Number in Descending Order — U.S. = 11,688

State	Number	County	Number	Place	Number
Florida	3,202	Miami-Dade County, FL	1,273	**New York, NY** (city)	841
New Jersey	2,640	Broward County, FL	805	**Queens, NY** (borough) Queens County	508
New York	1,694	Union County, NJ	539	**Elizabeth, NJ** (city) Union County	248
California	974	Queens County, NY	508		
Texas	474	Essex County, NJ	443		
Virginia	430	Palm Beach County, FL	433		
Massachusetts	380	Morris County, NJ	395		
Georgia	259	Los Angeles County, CA	358		
Maryland	239	Westchester County, NY	301		
Pennsylvania	149	Middlesex County, NJ	252		

Sorted by Number in Ascending Order — U.S. = 11,688

State	Number	County	Number	Place	Number
Pennsylvania	149	Worcester County, MA	79	**Elizabeth, NJ** (city) Union County	248
Maryland	239	Harris County, TX	145	**Queens, NY** (borough) Queens County	508
Georgia	259	Gwinnett County, GA	170	**New York, NY** (city)	841
Massachusetts	380	Hudson County, NJ	193		
Virginia	430	Middlesex County, NJ	252		
Texas	474	Westchester County, NY	301		
California	974	Los Angeles County, CA	358		
New York	1,694	Morris County, NJ	395		
New Jersey	2,640	Palm Beach County, FL	433		
Florida	3,202	Essex County, NJ	443		

Sorted by Percent in Descending Order — U.S. = 28.0%

State	Percent	County	Percent	Place	Percent
California	45.5	Los Angeles County, CA	58.6	**Queens, NY** (borough) Queens County	48.0
New York	40.6	Morris County, NJ	49.7	**New York, NY** (city)	39.5
Virginia	33.4	Queens County, NY	48.0	**Elizabeth, NJ** (city) Union County	9.9
New Jersey	28.6	Middlesex County, NJ	44.4		
Florida	27.8	Palm Beach County, FL	38.3		
Texas	26.6	Westchester County, NY	32.7		
Maryland	22.8	Broward County, FL	29.6		
Massachusetts	19.9	Essex County, NJ	23.0		
Pennsylvania	17.8	Miami-Dade County, FL	22.0		
Georgia	11.1	Hudson County, NJ	19.5		

Sorted by Percent in Ascending Order — U.S. = 28.0%

State	Percent	County	Percent	Place	Percent
Georgia	11.1	Worcester County, MA	7.9	**Elizabeth, NJ** (city) Union County	9.9
Pennsylvania	17.8	Harris County, TX	14.4	**New York, NY** (city)	39.5
Massachusetts	19.9	Union County, NJ	15.8	**Queens, NY** (borough) Queens County	48.0
Maryland	22.8	Gwinnett County, GA	18.5		
Texas	26.6	Hudson County, NJ	19.5		
Florida	27.8	Miami-Dade County, FL	22.0		
New Jersey	28.6	Essex County, NJ	23.0		
Virginia	33.4	Broward County, FL	29.6		
New York	40.6	Westchester County, NY	32.7		
California	45.5	Palm Beach County, FL	38.3		

Note: (1) Ranking tables cover all states and counties, and places with an overall population of at least 125,000, OR an overall population of at least 25,000 where the Hispanic/Latino population is at least 20% of the overall population. In states where less than five places meet either of these criteria, we have included places with at least 10,000 total population with the highest percentage of Hispanic/Latino population. These places are identified with an asterisk (*); Please refer to the User's Guide for a full explanation of data.

Foreign-Born Naturalized Citizens

South American: Venezuelan

Top 10 States, Counties, and Places[1]

Sorted by Number in Descending Order — U.S. = 42,508

State	Number	County	Number	Place	Number
Florida	19,191	Miami-Dade County, FL	8,704	**New York, NY** (city)	2,273
Texas	3,673	Broward County, FL	4,034	**Doral, FL** (city) Miami-Dade County	1,033
New York	3,145	Harris County, TX	1,235	**Queens, NY** (borough) Queens County	908
California	3,111	Los Angeles County, CA	1,071	**Weston, FL** (city) Broward County	819
New Jersey	1,830	Palm Beach County, FL	1,054	**Miami, FL** (city) Miami-Dade County	733
Georgia	1,152	Orange County, FL	946	**Pembroke Pines, FL** (city) Broward County	733
Massachusetts	990	Queens County, NY	908	**Miami Beach, FL** (city) Miami-Dade County	601
Virginia	945	Hillsborough County, FL	625	**Manhattan, NY** (borough) New York County	569
North Carolina	937	New York County, NY	569	**The Hammocks, FL** (cdp) Miami-Dade County	512
Illinois	764	Seminole County, FL	531	**Brooklyn, NY** (borough) Kings County	499

Sorted by Number in Ascending Order — U.S. = 42,508

State	Number	County	Number	Place	Number
Wisconsin	80	Fulton County, GA	92	**Orlando, FL** (city) Orange County	87
Oklahoma	139	Fairfield County, CT	132	**Country Club, FL** (cdp) Miami-Dade County	105
Missouri	146	Collin County, TX	148	**Miramar, FL** (city) Broward County	178
Minnesota	197	King County, WA	149	**Aventura, FL** (city) Miami-Dade County	196
Indiana	202	Suffolk County, MA	167	**Hialeah, FL** (city) Miami-Dade County	215
South Carolina	232	Lee County, FL	187	**Davie, FL** (town) Broward County	253
Colorado	261	Travis County, TX	202	**Kendall West, FL** (cdp) Miami-Dade County	254
Michigan	287	Cobb County, GA	204	**Hollywood, FL** (city) Broward County	259
Washington	295	Montgomery County, MD	209	**Sunrise, FL** (city) Broward County	259
Tennessee	301	Dallas County, TX	217	**Bronx, NY** (borough) Bronx County	284

Sorted by Percent in Descending Order — U.S. = 28.3%

State	Percent	County	Percent	Place	Percent
New Jersey	43.7	Tarrant County, TX	54.7	**The Hammocks, FL** (cdp) Miami-Dade County	46.3
Michigan	43.0	San Diego County, CA	53.1	**Miami Beach, FL** (city) Miami-Dade County	40.7
California	41.6	Orange County, CA	51.7	**Brooklyn, NY** (borough) Kings County	36.5
Illinois	38.0	Middlesex County, MA	48.7	**Coral Springs, FL** (city) Broward County	33.8
Pennsylvania	37.9	Hudson County, NJ	43.4	**Manhattan, NY** (borough) New York County	32.9
Massachusetts	37.2	Travis County, TX	41.8	**Pembroke Pines, FL** (city) Broward County	31.7
Connecticut	36.9	Seminole County, FL	39.8	**Bronx, NY** (borough) Bronx County	31.0
Arizona	36.7	Los Angeles County, CA	37.9	**New York, NY** (city)	31.0
Ohio	35.8	Cook County, IL	36.5	**Tamiami, FL** (cdp) Miami-Dade County	30.6
North Carolina	35.5	Kings County, NY	36.5	**Kendall West, FL** (cdp) Miami-Dade County	29.8

Sorted by Percent in Ascending Order — U.S. = 28.3%

State	Percent	County	Percent	Place	Percent
Wisconsin	14.7	Fulton County, GA	13.2	**Orlando, FL** (city) Orange County	6.2
Oklahoma	15.8	Lee County, FL	15.2	**Country Club, FL** (cdp) Miami-Dade County	8.6
Utah	22.0	Orange County, FL	16.7	**Miramar, FL** (city) Broward County	12.7
Tennessee	22.1	Cobb County, GA	17.4	**Weston, FL** (city) Broward County	13.7
Florida	24.8	Gwinnett County, GA	19.7	**Houston, TX** (city) Harris County	14.7
Georgia	24.9	Osceola County, FL	19.7	**Fountainebleau, FL** (cdp) Miami-Dade County	16.2
Indiana	25.7	Fairfield County, CT	19.8	**Miami, FL** (city) Miami-Dade County	16.6
Virginia	26.6	Suffolk County, MA	20.6	**Doral, FL** (city) Miami-Dade County	18.5
South Carolina	27.1	Fort Bend County, TX	20.7	**Hialeah, FL** (city) Miami-Dade County	20.9
Texas	27.5	Broward County, FL	21.4	**Aventura, FL** (city) Miami-Dade County	21.5

Note: (1) Ranking tables cover all states and counties, and places with an overall population of at least 125,000, OR an overall population of at least 25,000 where the Hispanic/Latino population is at least 20% of the overall population. In states where less than five places meet either of these criteria, we have included places with at least 10,000 total population with the highest percentage of Hispanic/Latino population. These places are identified with an asterisk (*); Please refer to the User's Guide for a full explanation of data.

Foreign-Born Naturalized Citizens

Spaniard

Top 10 States, Counties, and Places[1]

Sorted by Number in Descending Order U.S. = 40,848

State	Number	County	Number	Place	Number
Florida	7,678	Miami-Dade County, FL	3,708	**New York, NY** (city)	2,876
California	7,564	Los Angeles County, CA	2,267	**Queens, NY** (borough) Queens County	1,339
New York	4,500	Queens County, NY	1,339	**Los Angeles, CA** (city) Los Angeles County	675
New Jersey	3,744	Broward County, FL	1,097	**Manhattan, NY** (borough) New York County	559
Texas	2,822	Hudson County, NJ	847	**Brooklyn, NY** (borough) Kings County	437
Illinois	1,122	Essex County, NJ	749	**Bronx, NY** (borough) Bronx County	406
Maryland	1,048	Harris County, TX	735	**Newark, NJ** (city) Essex County	391
Virginia	1,018	San Diego County, CA	627	**Houston, TX** (city) Harris County	362
Arizona	814	Cook County, IL	626	**Chicago, IL** (city) Cook County	352
Georgia	776	Riverside County, CA	566	**Hempstead (town), NY** (town) Nassau County	335

Sorted by Number in Ascending Order U.S. = 40,848

State	Number	County	Number	Place	Number
Wyoming	0	Adams County, CO	0	**Lakewood, CO** (city) Jefferson County	0
Alaska	9	Clark County, WA	0	**Las Cruces, NM** (city) Dona Ana County	0
Iowa	32	Colfax County, NM	0	**Lubbock, TX** (city) Lubbock County	0
Kansas	52	Conejos County, CO	0	**South Valley, NM** (cdp) Bernalillo County	0
Montana	58	Doña Ana County, NM	0	**Thornton, CO** (city) Adams County	0
Arkansas	69	Jefferson County, CO	0	**Westminster, CO** (city) Adams County	0
Kentucky	76	La Plata County, CO	0	**Anchorage, AK** (municipality)	4
New Hampshire	79	Las Animas County, CO	0	**San Bernardino, CA** (city) San Bernardino County	9
West Virginia	99	Lubbock County, TX	0	**Pueblo, CO** (city) Pueblo County	11
Tennessee	106	Mesa County, CO	0	**Fort Collins, CO** (city) Larimer County	12

Sorted by Percent in Descending Order U.S. = 50.8%

State	Percent	County	Percent	Place	Percent
Mississippi	77.0	Butte County, CA	100.0	**Pueblo, CO** (city) Pueblo County	100.0
West Virginia	74.4	Douglas County, CO	100.0	**Mesa, AZ** (city) Maricopa County	87.1
Hawaii	69.5	Pueblo County, CO	100.0	**Reno, NV** (city) Washoe County	86.3
Nevada	58.2	San Luis Obispo County, CA	100.0	**Tampa, FL** (city) Hillsborough County	83.3
Minnesota	58.1	Tulare County, CA	100.0	**San Antonio, TX** (city) Bexar County	79.9
California	58.0	Valencia County, NM	100.0	**Long Beach, CA** (city) Los Angeles County	78.4
Idaho	57.3	Santa Cruz County, CA	89.7	**Urban Honolulu, HI** (cdp) Honolulu County	76.3
Arizona	57.0	Pinellas County, FL	85.0	**Las Vegas, NV** (city) Clark County	72.2
Georgia	55.8	Riverside County, CA	84.9	**Hempstead (town), NY** (town) Nassau County	71.1
Maryland	55.6	San Miguel County, NM	84.7	**El Paso, TX** (city) El Paso County	69.2

Sorted by Percent in Ascending Order U.S. = 50.8%

State	Percent	County	Percent	Place	Percent
Wyoming	0.0	Adams County, CO	0.0	**Thornton, CO** (city) Adams County	0.0
Kentucky	16.1	Clark County, WA	0.0	**Anchorage, AK** (municipality)	11.4
Alaska	16.7	Conejos County, CO	0.0	**Denver, CO** (city) Denver County	16.1
Kansas	20.8	Doña Ana County, NM	0.0	**Paradise, NV** (cdp) Clark County	17.6
Iowa	22.2	Jefferson County, CO	0.0	**San Bernardino, CA** (city) San Bernardino County	18.4
Tennessee	28.6	Mesa County, CO	0.0	**Corpus Christi, TX** (city) Nueces County	23.7
Missouri	33.6	Pinal County, AZ	0.0	**Oyster Bay, NY** (town) Nassau County	23.8
Arkansas	35.6	San Juan County, NM	0.0	**Austin, TX** (city) Travis County	26.5
Michigan	37.1	Cibola County, NM	12.7	**Sacramento, CA** (city) Sacramento County	26.8
Oklahoma	37.1	Boulder County, CO	14.8	**Manhattan, NY** (borough) New York County	27.6

Note: (1) Ranking tables cover all states and counties, and places with an overall population of at least 125,000, OR an overall population of at least 25,000 where the Hispanic/Latino population is at least 20% of the overall population. In states where less than five places meet either of these criteria, we have included places with at least 10,000 total population with the highest percentage of Hispanic/Latino population. These places are identified with an asterisk (*); Please refer to the User's Guide for a full explanation of data.

Language Spoken at Home: English Only

(Universe: Population 5 Years and Over)

Total Population

Top 10 States, Counties, and Places[1]

Sorted by Number in Descending Order — U.S. = 226,738,479

State	Number	County	Number	Place	Number
California	19,429,309	Los Angeles County, CA	3,966,317	**New York, NY** (city)	3,910,650
Texas	14,740,304	Cook County, IL	3,200,754	**Chicago, IL** (city) Cook County	1,627,190
New York	12,788,323	Maricopa County, AZ	2,540,515	**Los Angeles, CA** (city) Los Angeles County	1,415,116
Florida	12,786,704	Harris County, TX	2,108,762	**Brooklyn, NY** (borough) Kings County	1,240,416
Pennsylvania	10,710,239	San Diego County, CA	1,796,039	**Philadelphia, PA** (city) Philadelphia County	1,112,441
Ohio	10,104,160	Orange County, CA	1,541,000	**Houston, TX** (city) Harris County	1,037,557
Illinois	9,315,206	Wayne County, MI	1,535,700	**Queens, NY** (borough) Queens County	905,890
Michigan	8,507,947	King County, WA	1,334,375	**Manhattan, NY** (borough) New York County	902,267
North Carolina	7,750,904	Dallas County, TX	1,301,633	**Phoenix, AZ** (city) Maricopa County	837,361
Georgia	7,666,663	Kings County, NY	1,240,416	**San Diego, CA** (city) San Diego County	736,035

Sorted by Number in Ascending Order — U.S. = 226,738,479

State	Number	County	Number	Place	Number
District of Columbia	471,292	Kenedy County, TX	145	**Eagle Pass, TX** (city) Maverick County	1,813
Wyoming	474,343	Terrell County, TX	383	**University Park, FL** (cdp) Miami-Dade County	2,007
Alaska	534,077	Harding County, NM	416	**Maywood, CA** (city) Los Angeles County	2,017
Vermont	560,326	Clark County, ID	432	**Calexico, CA** (city) Imperial County	2,035
North Dakota	584,946	McMullen County, TX	479	**Westchester, FL** (cdp) Miami-Dade County	2,321
South Dakota	692,504	Kent County, TX	685	**Fountainebleau, FL** (cdp) Miami-Dade County	2,399
Delaware	724,189	Hudspeth County, TX	708	**San Juan, TX** (city) Hidalgo County	2,501
Rhode Island	790,382	Jim Hogg County, TX	735	**Bell Gardens, CA** (city) Los Angeles County	2,551
Montana	871,548	Esmeralda County, NV	737	**San Luis, AZ** (city) Yuma County	2,636
Hawaii	929,303	Culberson County, TX	767	**Socorro, TX** (city) El Paso County	2,797

Sorted by Percent in Descending Order — U.S. = 79.9%

State	Percent	County	Percent	Place	Percent
West Virginia	97.7	Perry County, MS	99.8	**Clarksburg*, WV** (city) Harrison County	98.2
Mississippi	96.2	Rockcastle County, KY	99.8	**Spearfish*, SD** (city) Lawrence County	97.3
Kentucky	95.4	Baker County, GA	99.7	**Huntington*, WV** (city) Cabell County	96.7
Montana	95.4	Iron County, MO	99.6	**Jackson, MS** (city) Hinds County	96.7
Alabama	95.1	Johnson County, KY	99.6	**Williston*, ND** (city) Williams County	96.7
North Dakota	94.6	Carter County, KY	99.5	**Dayton, OH** (city) Montgomery County	96.1
Vermont	94.6	Clay County, TN	99.5	**Bennington*, VT** (town) Bennington County	95.9
Missouri	94.1	Grayson County, KY	99.4	**Shreveport, LA** (city) Caddo Parish	95.6
Tennessee	93.8	Nicholas County, WV	99.4	**Billings*, MT** (city) Yellowstone County	95.3
Ohio	93.7	Powell County, KY	99.4	**Great Falls*, MT** (city) Cascade County	95.1

Sorted by Percent in Ascending Order — U.S. = 79.9%

State	Percent	County	Percent	Place	Percent
California	57.0	Starr County, TX	4.0	**Fountainebleau, FL** (cdp) Miami-Dade County	4.3
New Mexico	64.0	Maverick County, TX	6.2	**Hialeah, FL** (city) Miami-Dade County	5.8
Texas	65.8	Webb County, TX	7.6	**Huntington Park, CA** (city) Los Angeles County	5.8
New York	70.8	Zapata County, TX	12.3	**Calexico, CA** (city) Imperial County	6.1
New Jersey	71.3	Hidalgo County, TX	15.2	**Tamiami, FL** (cdp) Miami-Dade County	6.2
Nevada	71.8	Jim Hogg County, TX	15.4	**Bell Gardens, CA** (city) Los Angeles County	6.6
Arizona	72.9	Presidio County, TX	15.4	**Laredo, TX** (city) Webb County	7.6
Florida	73.4	Santa Cruz County, AZ	18.9	**Eagle Pass, TX** (city) Maverick County	7.8
Hawaii	74.5	Hudspeth County, TX	22.1	**Maywood, CA** (city) Los Angeles County	8.1
Illinois	78.3	Reeves County, TX	23.7	**Westchester, FL** (cdp) Miami-Dade County	8.3

Note: (1) Ranking tables cover all states and counties, and places with an overall population of at least 125,000, OR an overall population of at least 25,000 where the Hispanic/Latino population is at least 20% of the overall population. In states where less than five places meet either of these criteria, we have included places with at least 10,000 total population with the highest percentage of Hispanic/Latino population. These places are identified with an asterisk (*); Please refer to the User's Guide for a full explanation of data.

Language Spoken at Home: English Only

(Universe: Population 5 Years and Over)

Hispanic or Latino (of any race)

Top 10 States, Counties, and Places[1]

Sorted by Number in Descending Order — U.S. = 10,070,161

State	Number	County	Number	Place	Number
California	2,790,012	Los Angeles County, CA	703,104	**New York, NY** (city)	310,498
Texas	1,720,628	Bexar County, TX	292,844	**San Antonio, TX** (city) Bexar County	238,592
New York	559,145	Maricopa County, AZ	277,779	**Los Angeles, CA** (city) Los Angeles County	180,050
Florida	516,481	San Bernardino County, CA	261,949	**Phoenix, AZ** (city) Maricopa County	111,030
Arizona	478,652	Harris County, TX	217,963	**Albuquerque, NM** (city) Bernalillo County	105,387
Colorado	386,966	Riverside County, CA	215,319	**Houston, TX** (city) Harris County	101,069
New Mexico	327,541	San Diego County, CA	197,728	**Chicago, IL** (city) Cook County	94,770
Illinois	316,369	Orange County, CA	179,308	**Bronx, NY** (borough) Bronx County	85,678
New Jersey	228,792	Cook County, IL	157,888	**Brooklyn, NY** (borough) Kings County	75,575
Washington	180,566	Fresno County, CA	133,237	**San Diego, CA** (city) San Diego County	74,786

Sorted by Number in Ascending Order — U.S. = 10,070,161

State	Number	County	Number	Place	Number
Vermont	5,118	Clark County, ID	14	**Parker*, SC** (cdp) Greenville County	0
North Dakota	6,965	Harper County, OK	14	**Bluffton*, SC** (town) Beaufort County	25
South Dakota	8,284	Hertford County, NC	16	**Hope*, AR** (city) Hempstead County	118
Maine	8,888	Cuming County, NE	17	**Mayfield*, KY** (city) Graves County	123
West Virginia	11,522	Alleghany County, NC	30	**Storm Lake*, IA** (city) Buena Vista County	128
New Hampshire	12,770	Bradley County, AR	35	**Warr Acres*, OK** (city) Oklahoma County	189
Delaware	14,807	Crockett County, TN	37	**Carthage*, MO** (city) Jasper County	214
District of Columbia	15,718	Calhoun County, MS	39	**Worthington*, MN** (city) Nobles County	228
Rhode Island	16,202	Evans County, GA	46	**Lexington*, NE** (city) Dawson County	236
Alaska	17,168	Hamilton County, KS	47	**Monroe, NC** (city) Union County	244

Sorted by Percent in Descending Order — U.S. = 23.6%

State	Percent	County	Percent	Place	Percent
Montana	77.8	Wabaunsee County, KS	90.5	**Waianae*, HI** (cdp) Honolulu County	94.0
Hawaii	74.9	Dickinson County, KS	90.0	**Bozeman*, MT** (city) Gallatin County	87.4
North Dakota	61.9	Flathead County, MT	87.3	**Makakilo*, HI** (cdp) Honolulu County	82.4
Vermont	61.2	Nodaway County, MO	86.7	**Billings*, MT** (city) Yellowstone County	81.8
West Virginia	60.9	Washington County, VT	86.4	**Pueblo West, CO** (cdp) Pueblo County	79.5
Maine	58.7	Marquette County, MI	86.3	**Missoula*, MT** (city) Missoula County	78.2
Wyoming	55.1	Jackson County, IA	85.4	**Butte-Silver Bow*, MT** (consolidated govt) Silver Bow County	76.2
Alaska	51.1	Jackson County, KS	85.4	**Pueblo, CO** (city) Pueblo County	71.5
South Dakota	47.4	White Pine County, NV	84.8	**Great Falls*, MT** (city) Cascade County	70.8
Michigan	45.5	Cass County, NE	84.2	**Rapid City*, SD** (city) Pennington County	70.7

Sorted by Percent in Ascending Order — U.S. = 23.6%

State	Percent	County	Percent	Place	Percent
Florida	14.0	Cuming County, NE	2.7	**Parker*, SC** (cdp) Greenville County	0.0
Rhode Island	14.5	Hertford County, NC	2.8	**Bluffton*, SC** (town) Beaufort County	1.2
Georgia	16.8	Harper County, OK	2.9	**Fountainebleau, FL** (cdp) Miami-Dade County	1.6
North Carolina	16.8	Alleghany County, NC	3.0	**Tamiami, FL** (cdp) Miami-Dade County	3.1
New Jersey	17.1	Bradley County, AR	3.0	**West Little River, FL** (cdp) Miami-Dade County	3.1
Illinois	18.3	Presidio County, TX	3.2	**Monroe, NC** (city) Union County	3.3
New York	18.6	Starr County, TX	3.3	**Westchester, FL** (cdp) Miami-Dade County	3.5
Massachusetts	21.1	Crockett County, TN	3.8	**Hialeah, FL** (city) Miami-Dade County	3.6
Texas	21.6	Santa Cruz County, AZ	3.8	**Kendall West, FL** (cdp) Miami-Dade County	3.6
South Carolina	21.9	Maverick County, TX	4.1	**Marumsco, VA** (cdp) Prince William County	3.6

Note: (1) Ranking tables cover all states and counties, and places with an overall population of at least 125,000, OR an overall population of at least 25,000 where the Hispanic/Latino population is at least 20% of the overall population. In states where less than five places meet either of these criteria, we have included places with at least 10,000 total population with the highest percentage of Hispanic/Latino population. These places are identified with an asterisk (*); Please refer to the User's Guide for a full explanation of data.

Language Spoken at Home: English Only

(Universe: Population 5 Years and Over)

Central American, excluding Mexican

Top 10 States, Counties, and Places[1]

Sorted by Number in Descending Order — U.S. = 364,729

State	Number	County	Number	Place	Number
California	92,079	Los Angeles County, CA	36,261	**New York, NY** (city)	17,920
New York	31,856	Prince George's County, MD	14,819	**Los Angeles, CA** (city) Los Angeles County	15,256
Florida	28,089	Harris County, TX	8,311	**Brooklyn, NY** (borough) Kings County	6,641
Maryland	25,449	Miami-Dade County, FL	6,725	**Houston, TX** (city) Harris County	4,712
Texas	24,886	Kings County, NY	6,641	**Queens, NY** (borough) Queens County	4,508
Virginia	13,467	San Bernardino County, CA	5,575	**San Francisco, CA** (city) San Francisco County	3,430
New Jersey	12,862	Orange County, CA	4,893	**Bronx, NY** (borough) Bronx County	3,091
Massachusetts	9,127	Contra Costa County, CA	4,876	**Manhattan, NY** (borough) New York County	2,946
Georgia	8,986	Clark County, NV	4,625	**Hempstead (town), NY** (town) Nassau County	2,835
Illinois	8,193	Riverside County, CA	4,516	**Chicago, IL** (city) Cook County	2,517

Sorted by Number in Ascending Order — U.S. = 364,729

State	Number	County	Number	Place	Number
Wyoming	88	Cass County, IN	0	**Bonita Springs, FL** (city) Lee County	0
South Dakota	222	Finney County, KS	0	**Gainesville, GA** (city) Hall County	0
West Virginia	409	Colfax County, NE	8	**Garden City, KS** (city) Finney County	0
Vermont	419	Wyandotte County, KS	8	**Kearny, NJ** (town) Hudson County	0
New Hampshire	609	Franklin County, AL	13	**Long Branch, NJ** (city) Monmouth County	0
Alaska	633	Duplin County, NC	14	**Hallandale Beach, FL** (city) Broward County	6
Idaho	671	Dawson County, NE	16	**Kansas City, KS** (city) Wyandotte County	8
Maine	819	Frederick County, VA	17	**Delano, CA** (city) Kern County	10
Delaware	907	Wayne County, NC	20	**Greenacres, FL** (city) Palm Beach County	10
Hawaii	1,182	Minnehaha County, SD	22	**Galveston, TX** (city) Galveston County	12

Sorted by Percent in Descending Order — U.S. = 10.2%

State	Percent	County	Percent	Place	Percent
Vermont	66.3	Allegheny County, PA	55.8	**Rochester, NY** (city) Monroe County	45.4
Maine	50.7	Macomb County, MI	51.4	**Colorado Springs, CO** (city) El Paso County	39.4
Hawaii	47.7	Charles County, MD	50.6	**Irvine, CA** (city) Orange County	39.4
District of Columbia	31.7	Saint Louis County, MO	45.5	**Murrieta, CA** (city) Riverside County	38.2
Alaska	30.0	New Castle County, DE	45.4	**Corpus Christi, TX** (city) Nueces County	36.3
Wisconsin	28.6	El Dorado County, CA	43.7	**Clarksville, TN** (city) Montgomery County	33.9
West Virginia	25.6	Thurston County, WA	43.6	**Chino Hills, CA** (city) San Bernardino County	33.3
Kentucky	25.1	Honolulu County, HI	41.8	**Henderson, NV** (city) Clark County	32.8
Michigan	25.0	Erie County, NY	40.2	**Anchorage, AK** (municipality)	32.3
Ohio	24.7	Shasta County, CA	39.8	**Huntington Beach, CA** (city) Orange County	31.7

Sorted by Percent in Ascending Order — U.S. = 10.2%

State	Percent	County	Percent	Place	Percent
Rhode Island	5.5	Cass County, IN	0.0	**Bonita Springs, FL** (city) Lee County	0.0
Texas	6.6	Finney County, KS	0.0	**Gainesville, GA** (city) Hall County	0.0
Florida	6.9	Wyandotte County, KS	0.3	**Garden City, KS** (city) Finney County	0.0
Virginia	7.9	Duplin County, NC	0.4	**Kearny, NJ** (town) Hudson County	0.0
New Jersey	8.5	Franklin County, AL	1.1	**Long Branch, NJ** (city) Monmouth County	0.0
California	8.6	Colfax County, NE	1.2	**Kansas City, KS** (city) Wyandotte County	0.3
North Carolina	9.2	Dawson County, NE	1.3	**Greenacres, FL** (city) Palm Beach County	0.4
Wyoming	9.5	Frederick County, VA	1.3	**Hallandale Beach, FL** (city) Broward County	0.4
Georgia	9.7	Minnehaha County, SD	1.4	**The Hammocks, FL** (cdp) Miami-Dade County	0.6
Nebraska	9.8	Alamance County, NC	1.5	**Huntington Station, NY** (cdp) Suffolk County	1.0

Note: (1) Ranking tables cover all states and counties, and places with an overall population of at least 125,000, OR an overall population of at least 25,000 where the Hispanic/Latino population is at least 20% of the overall population. In states where less than five places meet either of these criteria, we have included places with at least 10,000 total population with the highest percentage of Hispanic/Latino population. These places are identified with an asterisk (*); Please refer to the User's Guide for a full explanation of data.

Language Spoken at Home: English Only

(Universe: Population 5 Years and Over)

Central American: Costa Rican

Top 10 States, Counties, and Places[1]

Sorted by Number in Descending Order U.S. = 26,114

State	Number	County	Number	Place	Number
California	5,737	Los Angeles County, CA	2,319	**New York, NY** (city)	1,378
New York	2,674	Kings County, NY	663	**Los Angeles, CA** (city) Los Angeles County	767
Florida	2,671	Miami-Dade County, FL	621	**Brooklyn, NY** (borough) Kings County	663
Texas	1,294	Maricopa County, AZ	537	**Queens, NY** (borough) Queens County	380
New Jersey	1,260	Contra Costa County, CA	515	**Bronx, NY** (borough) Bronx County	170
Georgia	888	Orange County, CA	475	**Philadelphia, PA** (city) Philadelphia County	106
Pennsylvania	806	Queens County, NY	380	**Miami, FL** (city) Miami-Dade County	42
Illinois	737	San Diego County, CA	377		
North Carolina	723	Broward County, FL	347		
Massachusetts	722	Suffolk County, NY	335		

Sorted by Number in Ascending Order U.S. = 26,114

State	Number	County	Number	Place	Number
Wisconsin	129	Morris County, NJ	46	**Miami, FL** (city) Miami-Dade County	42
Michigan	182	Mercer County, NJ	73	**Philadelphia, PA** (city) Philadelphia County	106
South Carolina	244	Somerset County, NJ	93	**Bronx, NY** (borough) Bronx County	170
Minnesota	294	Philadelphia County, PA	106	**Queens, NY** (borough) Queens County	380
Tennessee	299	Bergen County, NJ	131	**Brooklyn, NY** (borough) Kings County	663
Louisiana	303	Essex County, NJ	137	**Los Angeles, CA** (city) Los Angeles County	767
Oregon	331	Orange County, FL	138	**New York, NY** (city)	1,378
Nevada	373	Passaic County, NJ	143		
Washington	442	Bronx County, NY	170		
Connecticut	529	San Bernardino County, CA	198		

Sorted by Percent in Descending Order U.S. = 22.6%

State	Percent	County	Percent	Place	Percent
Colorado	53.1	Contra Costa County, CA	47.0	**Brooklyn, NY** (borough) Kings County	28.8
Oregon	46.0	Maricopa County, AZ	44.0	**Los Angeles, CA** (city) Los Angeles County	26.2
Arizona	44.9	San Diego County, CA	32.8	**New York, NY** (city)	22.9
Washington	37.1	Clark County, NV	31.4	**Bronx, NY** (borough) Bronx County	22.3
Illinois	34.0	Kings County, NY	28.8	**Queens, NY** (borough) Queens County	20.1
Tennessee	33.0	Los Angeles County, CA	25.8	**Philadelphia, PA** (city) Philadelphia County	9.1
Minnesota	30.6	Orange County, CA	24.7	**Miami, FL** (city) Miami-Dade County	3.1
Virginia	29.7	Suffolk County, NY	22.5		
Maryland	28.0	Bronx County, NY	22.3		
California	27.9	Hillsborough County, FL	21.8		

Sorted by Percent in Ascending Order U.S. = 22.6%

State	Percent	County	Percent	Place	Percent
New Jersey	7.3	Morris County, NJ	2.9	**Miami, FL** (city) Miami-Dade County	3.1
South Carolina	14.1	Somerset County, NJ	4.6	**Philadelphia, PA** (city) Philadelphia County	9.1
Florida	14.2	Union County, NJ	6.0	**Queens, NY** (borough) Queens County	20.1
North Carolina	15.6	Essex County, NJ	6.8	**Bronx, NY** (borough) Bronx County	22.3
Wisconsin	20.0	Mercer County, NJ	6.8	**New York, NY** (city)	22.9
Massachusetts	20.8	Bergen County, NJ	7.6	**Los Angeles, CA** (city) Los Angeles County	26.2
Pennsylvania	20.8	Passaic County, NJ	8.2	**Brooklyn, NY** (borough) Kings County	28.8
Louisiana	22.6	Philadelphia County, PA	9.1		
Nevada	23.5	Miami-Dade County, FL	9.2		
Texas	23.7	Orange County, FL	13.0		

Note: (1) Ranking tables cover all states and counties, and places with an overall population of at least 125,000, OR an overall population of at least 25,000 where the Hispanic/Latino population is at least 20% of the overall population. In states where less than five places meet either of these criteria, we have included places with at least 10,000 total population with the highest percentage of Hispanic/Latino population. These places are identified with an asterisk (*); Please refer to the User's Guide for a full explanation of data.

Language Spoken at Home: English Only

(Universe: Population 5 Years and Over)

Central American: Guatemalan

Top 10 States, Counties, and Places[1]

Sorted by Number in Descending Order — U.S. = 79,842

State	Number	County	Number	Place	Number
California	18,550	Los Angeles County, CA	8,881	**Los Angeles, CA** (city) Los Angeles County	3,718
Maryland	5,086	Prince George's County, MD	3,542	**New York, NY** (city)	2,087
New York	5,045	Cook County, IL	2,204	**Chicago, IL** (city) Cook County	1,468
Florida	4,223	Harris County, TX	1,688	**Houston, TX** (city) Harris County	1,090
Texas	4,162	Riverside County, CA	1,074	**Queens, NY** (borough) Queens County	916
Illinois	3,665	San Bernardino County, CA	995	**Trenton, NJ** (city) Mercer County	593
New Jersey	3,459	Clark County, NV	958	**Manhattan, NY** (borough) New York County	438
Virginia	2,565	Orange County, CA	946	**Boston, MA** (city) Suffolk County	415
Massachusetts	2,403	Queens County, NY	916	**Las Vegas, NV** (city) Clark County	411
Georgia	2,180	Maricopa County, AZ	887	**Brooklyn, NY** (borough) Kings County	407

Sorted by Number in Ascending Order — U.S. = 79,842

State	Number	County	Number	Place	Number
South Dakota	33	Burke County, NC	0	**Bonita Springs, FL** (city) Lee County	0
Idaho	128	Dawson County, NE	0	**Cathedral City, CA** (city) Riverside County	0
Mississippi	160	Minnehaha County, SD	0	**Lexington*, NE** (city) Dawson County	0
New Hampshire	212	Franklin County, AL	13	**Lynwood, CA** (city) Los Angeles County	0
Delaware	225	Murray County, GA	13	**Montebello, CA** (city) Los Angeles County	0
New Mexico	403	Santa Fe County, NM	14	**Newark, NJ** (city) Essex County	0
Kansas	423	Gordon County, GA	17	**San Rafael, CA** (city) Marin County	0
Arkansas	437	Martin County, FL	19	**Sioux Falls, SD** (city) Minnehaha County	0
South Carolina	483	Lee County, AL	22	**Wheaton, MD** (cdp) Montgomery County	4
Nebraska	486	Nobles County, MN	37	**West Palm Beach, FL** (city) Palm Beach County	9

Sorted by Percent in Descending Order — U.S. = 8.8%

State	Percent	County	Percent	Place	Percent
Wisconsin	47.1	Lake County, IL	34.3	**Minneapolis, MN** (city) Hennepin County	31.5
New Hampshire	30.3	Norfolk County, MA	32.7	**Lancaster, CA** (city) Los Angeles County	23.6
District of Columbia	29.7	Hartford County, CT	31.6	**La Puente, CA** (city) Los Angeles County	22.0
Minnesota	25.2	Hennepin County, MN	29.7	**Sacramento, CA** (city) Sacramento County	21.7
Washington	24.0	Pima County, AZ	27.4	**North Las Vegas, NV** (city) Clark County	21.1
Pennsylvania	23.2	Milwaukee County, WI	25.0	**Manhattan, NY** (borough) New York County	17.7
Kentucky	22.7	Prince George's County, MD	25.0	**San Antonio, TX** (city) Bexar County	16.7
Michigan	22.4	Sonoma County, CA	23.5	**West New York, NJ** (town) Hudson County	16.6
Indiana	20.7	Sacramento County, CA	21.6	**Santa Clarita, CA** (city) Los Angeles County	16.3
Missouri	19.5	King County, WA	21.5	**Corona, CA** (city) Riverside County	15.4

Sorted by Percent in Ascending Order — U.S. = 8.8%

State	Percent	County	Percent	Place	Percent
South Dakota	2.4	Burke County, NC	0.0	**Bonita Springs, FL** (city) Lee County	0.0
Rhode Island	3.8	Dawson County, NE	0.0	**Cathedral City, CA** (city) Riverside County	0.0
Delaware	5.2	Minnehaha County, SD	0.0	**Lexington*, NE** (city) Dawson County	0.0
Florida	5.4	Martin County, FL	0.5	**Lynwood, CA** (city) Los Angeles County	0.0
California	6.0	Marin County, CA	0.9	**Montebello, CA** (city) Los Angeles County	0.0
South Carolina	6.6	Franklin County, AL	1.1	**Newark, NJ** (city) Essex County	0.0
Georgia	7.0	Gordon County, GA	1.1	**San Rafael, CA** (city) Marin County	0.0
Connecticut	7.4	Santa Fe County, NM	1.2	**Sioux Falls, SD** (city) Minnehaha County	0.0
Nebraska	7.4	Murray County, GA	1.3	**West Palm Beach, FL** (city) Palm Beach County	0.2
Texas	7.4	Rockland County, NY	2.1	**Lake Worth, FL** (city) Palm Beach County	0.3

Note: (1) Ranking tables cover all states and counties, and places with an overall population of at least 125,000, OR an overall population of at least 25,000 where the Hispanic/Latino population is at least 20% of the overall population. In states where less than five places meet either of these criteria, we have included places with at least 10,000 total population with the highest percentage of Hispanic/Latino population. These places are identified with an asterisk (*); Please refer to the User's Guide for a full explanation of data.

Language Spoken at Home: English Only

(Universe: Population 5 Years and Over)

Central American: Honduran

Top 10 States, Counties, and Places[1]

Sorted by Number in Descending Order — U.S. = 46,543

State	Number	County	Number	Place	Number
Florida	5,345	Los Angeles County, CA	1,704	**New York, NY** (city)	3,248
New York	5,282	Jefferson Parish, LA	1,687	**Bronx, NY** (borough) Bronx County	1,208
California	4,584	Harris County, TX	1,568	**Houston, TX** (city) Harris County	828
Texas	4,050	Miami-Dade County, FL	1,286	**Queens, NY** (borough) Queens County	695
Louisiana	3,924	Bronx County, NY	1,208	**Brooklyn, NY** (borough) Kings County	682
Maryland	2,221	Prince George's County, MD	1,069	**Los Angeles, CA** (city) Los Angeles County	590
Massachusetts	1,851	Queens County, NY	695	**Kenner, LA** (city) Jefferson Parish	575
New Jersey	1,718	Kings County, NY	682	**New Orleans, LA** (city) Orleans Parish	538
Virginia	1,424	Suffolk County, MA	590	**Boston, MA** (city) Suffolk County	511
Georgia	1,256	Broward County, FL	580	**Metairie, LA** (cdp) Jefferson Parish	500

Sorted by Number in Ascending Order — U.S. = 46,543

State	Number	County	Number	Place	Number
Kansas	123	Hall County, GA	0	**Aurora, CO** (city) Arapahoe County	0
Utah	157	Atlantic County, NJ	9	**Brentwood, NY** (cdp) Suffolk County	0
Oklahoma	164	Duplin County, NC	14	**Pasadena, CA** (city) Los Angeles County	0
Iowa	205	Loudoun County, VA	15	**Springfield, VA** (cdp) Fairfax County	0
Nebraska	212	Davidson County, TN	24	**Wheaton, MD** (cdp) Montgomery County	0
Missouri	313	Johnston County, NC	26	**Miami Beach, FL** (city) Miami-Dade County	12
Michigan	330	Kern County, CA	27	**North Miami Beach, FL** (city) Miami-Dade County	13
Kentucky	369	Sampson County, NC	33	**Plainfield, NJ** (city) Union County	13
Indiana	392	Morris County, NJ	36	**Garland, TX** (city) Dallas County	15
Wisconsin	405	Arapahoe County, CO	38	**Durham, NC** (city) Durham County	17

Sorted by Percent in Descending Order — U.S. = 8.5%

State	Percent	County	Percent	Place	Percent
District of Columbia	50.1	Saint Tammany Parish, LA	26.8	**Las Vegas, NV** (city) Clark County	21.5
Oregon	29.1	Prince George's County, MD	26.7	**Phoenix, AZ** (city) Maricopa County	21.0
Arkansas	27.4	Baltimore County, MD	22.6	**Memphis, TN** (city) Shelby County	18.6
Kentucky	25.0	New Haven County, CT	19.9	**Staten Island, NY** (borough) Richmond County	18.0
Ohio	23.7	Maricopa County, AZ	18.7	**Philadelphia, PA** (city) Philadelphia County	17.4
Mississippi	21.5	Richmond County, NY	18.0	**Baltimore, MD** (independent city)	16.1
Washington	19.4	Philadelphia County, PA	17.4	**New Orleans, LA** (city) Orleans Parish	15.6
Arizona	19.1	Shelby County, TN	17.2	**Boston, MA** (city) Suffolk County	13.9
Alabama	18.9	King County, WA	17.0	**Metairie, LA** (cdp) Jefferson Parish	12.4
Pennsylvania	18.9	Orleans Parish, LA	15.6	**Kenner, LA** (city) Jefferson Parish	11.9

Sorted by Percent in Ascending Order — U.S. = 8.5%

State	Percent	County	Percent	Place	Percent
North Carolina	4.1	Hall County, GA	0.0	**Aurora, CO** (city) Arapahoe County	0.0
Kansas	4.6	Atlantic County, NJ	0.6	**Brentwood, NY** (cdp) Suffolk County	0.0
Florida	5.2	Duplin County, NC	0.6	**Pasadena, CA** (city) Los Angeles County	0.0
Texas	5.2	Loudoun County, VA	0.9	**Springfield, VA** (cdp) Fairfax County	0.0
New Jersey	5.7	Davidson County, TN	1.1	**Wheaton, MD** (cdp) Montgomery County	0.0
Virginia	6.0	Durham County, NC	1.3	**Durham, NC** (city) Durham County	0.5
Oklahoma	6.5	Morris County, NJ	1.5	**Plainfield, NJ** (city) Union County	0.6
California	6.9	Dallas County, TX	1.8	**Miami Beach, FL** (city) Miami-Dade County	0.8
Georgia	7.1	Union County, NJ	2.2	**New Brunswick, NJ** (city) Middlesex County	0.9
Indiana	7.7	Fairfax County, VA	2.4	**Waukegan, IL** (city) Lake County	0.9

Note: (1) Ranking tables cover all states and counties, and places with an overall population of at least 125,000, OR an overall population of at least 25,000 where the Hispanic/Latino population is at least 20% of the overall population. In states where less than five places meet either of these criteria, we have included places with at least 10,000 total population with the highest percentage of Hispanic/Latino population. These places are identified with an asterisk (*); Please refer to the User's Guide for a full explanation of data.

Language Spoken at Home: English Only

(Universe: Population 5 Years and Over)

Central American: Nicaraguan

Top 10 States, Counties, and Places[1]

Sorted by Number in Descending Order — U.S. = 38,709

State	Number	County	Number	Place	Number
California	14,189	Los Angeles County, CA	3,570	**Los Angeles, CA** (city) Los Angeles County	1,358
Florida	6,479	Miami-Dade County, FL	2,916	**New York, NY** (city)	1,175
Texas	2,274	San Mateo County, CA	1,525	**San Francisco, CA** (city) San Francisco County	921
New York	1,687	Contra Costa County, CA	1,079	**Miami, FL** (city) Miami-Dade County	700
New Jersey	1,374	San Francisco County, CA	921	**San Jose, CA** (city) Santa Clara County	483
Maryland	946	Riverside County, CA	760	**Daly City, CA** (city) San Mateo County	397
Louisiana	846	Santa Clara County, CA	739	**Queens, NY** (borough) Queens County	395
North Carolina	776	Harris County, TX	714	**Houston, TX** (city) Harris County	371
Virginia	719	San Bernardino County, CA	697	**San Diego, CA** (city) San Diego County	327
Georgia	693	Orange County, CA	691	**Brooklyn, NY** (borough) Kings County	321

Sorted by Number in Ascending Order — U.S. = 38,709

State	Number	County	Number	Place	Number
District of Columbia	102	Lee County, FL	37	**Kendale Lakes, FL** (cdp) Miami-Dade County	0
Indiana	121	Collier County, FL	38	**The Hammocks, FL** (cdp) Miami-Dade County	0
South Carolina	143	Gwinnett County, GA	42	**South Gate, CA** (city) Los Angeles County	8
Tennessee	166	Prince William County, VA	73	**University Park, FL** (cdp) Miami-Dade County	8
Connecticut	184	Stanislaus County, CA	73	**Richmond West, FL** (cdp) Miami-Dade County	13
Minnesota	194	Travis County, TX	104	**Oakland, CA** (city) Alameda County	30
Missouri	283	Bronx County, NY	113	**Fontana, CA** (city) San Bernardino County	41
Michigan	308	Montgomery County, MD	115	**Country Club, FL** (cdp) Miami-Dade County	44
Oregon	349	San Joaquin County, CA	132	**Hollywood, FL** (city) Broward County	57
Colorado	438	King County, WA	154	**Kendall, FL** (cdp) Miami-Dade County	57

Sorted by Percent in Descending Order — U.S. = 12.1%

State	Percent	County	Percent	Place	Percent
Ohio	44.5	Sonoma County, CA	42.4	**San Diego, CA** (city) San Diego County	36.3
Michigan	41.0	San Diego County, CA	33.8	**Sacramento, CA** (city) Sacramento County	34.4
Oregon	39.0	Maricopa County, AZ	29.5	**San Jose, CA** (city) Santa Clara County	25.4
Missouri	34.9	Prince George's County, MD	27.1	**Jacksonville, FL** (city) Duval County	22.9
Colorado	34.8	Riverside County, CA	24.2	**Metairie, LA** (cdp) Jefferson Parish	18.2
Massachusetts	29.2	Sacramento County, CA	24.1	**Pembroke Pines, FL** (city) Broward County	17.8
Washington	29.0	Orange County, CA	23.9	**Brooklyn, NY** (borough) Kings County	16.3
Arizona	28.4	Santa Clara County, CA	23.1	**San Francisco, CA** (city) San Francisco County	15.0
Illinois	26.2	Bexar County, TX	22.9	**Antioch, CA** (city) Contra Costa County	14.8
Wisconsin	25.1	Duval County, FL	22.9	**Manhattan, NY** (borough) New York County	14.7

Sorted by Percent in Ascending Order — U.S. = 12.1%

State	Percent	County	Percent	Place	Percent
Florida	4.8	Miami-Dade County, FL	2.7	**Kendale Lakes, FL** (cdp) Miami-Dade County	0.0
Virginia	10.0	Collier County, FL	3.6	**The Hammocks, FL** (cdp) Miami-Dade County	0.0
Indiana	11.7	Lee County, FL	3.6	**Richmond West, FL** (cdp) Miami-Dade County	0.6
District of Columbia	11.8	Montgomery County, MD	3.8	**University Park, FL** (cdp) Miami-Dade County	0.8
Louisiana	13.2	Prince William County, VA	4.0	**South Gate, CA** (city) Los Angeles County	0.9
South Carolina	13.7	Bronx County, NY	4.4	**Fontainebleau, FL** (cdp) Miami-Dade County	1.1
New York	13.8	Gwinnett County, GA	5.0	**Hialeah, FL** (city) Miami-Dade County	1.4
Texas	14.8	Stanislaus County, CA	7.6	**Kendall, FL** (cdp) Miami-Dade County	1.9
Maryland	15.0	Palm Beach County, FL	8.5	**Miami, FL** (city) Miami-Dade County	2.3
Nevada	15.3	Travis County, TX	8.5	**Oakland, CA** (city) Alameda County	2.3

Note: (1) Ranking tables cover all states and counties, and places with an overall population of at least 125,000, OR an overall population of at least 25,000 where the Hispanic/Latino population is at least 20% of the overall population. In states where less than five places meet either of these criteria, we have included places with at least 10,000 total population with the highest percentage of Hispanic/Latino population. These places are identified with an asterisk (*); Please refer to the User's Guide for a full explanation of data.

Language Spoken at Home: English Only

(Universe: Population 5 Years and Over)

Central American: Panamanian

Top 10 States, Counties, and Places[1]

Sorted by Number in Descending Order — U.S. = 53,775

State	Number	County	Number	Place	Number
New York	10,034	Kings County, NY	4,028	**New York, NY** (city)	7,412
California	6,274	Los Angeles County, CA	1,684	**Brooklyn, NY** (borough) Kings County	4,028
Florida	4,830	New York County, NY	1,305	**Manhattan, NY** (borough) New York County	1,305
Texas	3,958	Queens County, NY	951	**Queens, NY** (borough) Queens County	951
Virginia	2,938	Bronx County, NY	947	**Bronx, NY** (borough) Bronx County	947
Georgia	2,380	San Diego County, CA	853	**Hempstead (town), NY** (town) Nassau County	568
New Jersey	2,055	Hillsborough County, FL	810	**San Diego, CA** (city) San Diego County	426
Maryland	1,783	San Bernardino County, CA	576	**Los Angeles, CA** (city) Los Angeles County	399
North Carolina	1,735	Nassau County, NY	568	**Fayetteville, NC** (city) Cumberland County	346
Washington	1,423	Clark County, NV	520	**Jacksonville, FL** (city) Duval County	338

Sorted by Number in Ascending Order — U.S. = 53,775

State	Number	County	Number	Place	Number
Mississippi	188	Palm Beach County, FL	134	**Miami, FL** (city) Miami-Dade County	16
Minnesota	280	Hudson County, NJ	192	**Houston, TX** (city) Harris County	186
Kentucky	370	Harris County, TX	221	**Killeen, TX** (city) Bell County	240
Wisconsin	414	Riverside County, CA	222	**San Antonio, TX** (city) Bexar County	299
Indiana	441	Dallas County, TX	229	**Jacksonville, FL** (city) Duval County	338
Connecticut	456	Brevard County, FL	237	**Fayetteville, NC** (city) Cumberland County	346
New Mexico	473	Orange County, CA	237	**Los Angeles, CA** (city) Los Angeles County	399
South Carolina	492	Montgomery County, MD	269	**San Diego, CA** (city) San Diego County	426
Oklahoma	509	Cook County, IL	293	**Hempstead (town), NY** (town) Nassau County	568
Louisiana	550	Fairfax County, VA	309	**Bronx, NY** (borough) Bronx County	947

Sorted by Percent in Descending Order — U.S. = 36.4%

State	Percent	County	Percent	Place	Percent
New Mexico	62.6	New York County, NY	58.0	**Manhattan, NY** (borough) New York County	58.0
Michigan	57.6	Sacramento County, CA	53.0	**Hempstead (town), NY** (town) Nassau County	41.6
Wisconsin	56.1	Pierce County, WA	52.8	**Bronx, NY** (borough) Bronx County	37.5
Oklahoma	54.3	Clark County, NV	44.9	**New York, NY** (city)	33.4
Ohio	54.1	Nassau County, NY	40.1	**Fayetteville, NC** (city) Cumberland County	32.4
Missouri	53.5	Maricopa County, AZ	39.8	**San Diego, CA** (city) San Diego County	31.3
Washington	52.1	Prince George's County, MD	39.0	**Jacksonville, FL** (city) Duval County	31.2
Indiana	50.7	San Bernardino County, CA	38.7	**Brooklyn, NY** (borough) Kings County	30.1
Alabama	48.9	Prince William County, VA	38.3	**Houston, TX** (city) Harris County	26.5
Tennessee	47.6	Bronx County, NY	37.5	**Queens, NY** (borough) Queens County	26.4

Sorted by Percent in Ascending Order — U.S. = 36.4%

State	Percent	County	Percent	Place	Percent
Florida	19.6	Miami-Dade County, FL	6.7	**Miami, FL** (city) Miami-Dade County	1.5
Mississippi	28.5	Broward County, FL	12.2	**San Antonio, TX** (city) Bexar County	24.4
South Carolina	30.6	Harris County, TX	13.7	**Killeen, TX** (city) Bell County	24.9
Texas	32.3	Palm Beach County, FL	15.5	**Los Angeles, CA** (city) Los Angeles County	25.4
North Carolina	34.3	Orange County, FL	20.1	**Queens, NY** (borough) Queens County	26.4
Georgia	34.9	Riverside County, CA	20.1	**Houston, TX** (city) Harris County	26.5
Kentucky	35.0	Dallas County, TX	22.1	**Brooklyn, NY** (borough) Kings County	30.1
New York	35.9	Bexar County, TX	23.1	**Jacksonville, FL** (city) Duval County	31.2
New Jersey	36.9	Cumberland County, NC	23.6	**San Diego, CA** (city) San Diego County	31.3
California	39.0	Hudson County, NJ	24.3	**Fayetteville, NC** (city) Cumberland County	32.4

Note: (1) Ranking tables cover all states and counties, and places with an overall population of at least 125,000, OR an overall population of at least 25,000 where the Hispanic/Latino population is at least 20% of the overall population. In states where less than five places meet either of these criteria, we have included places with at least 10,000 total population with the highest percentage of Hispanic/Latino population. These places are identified with an asterisk (*); Please refer to the User's Guide for a full explanation of data.

Language Spoken at Home: English Only

(Universe: Population 5 Years and Over)

Central American: Salvadoran

Top 10 States, Counties, and Places[1]

Sorted by Number in Descending Order — U.S. = 111,815

State	Number	County	Number	Place	Number
California	39,579	Los Angeles County, CA	17,091	**Los Angeles, CA** (city) Los Angeles County	7,989
Maryland	14,531	Prince George's County, MD	9,231	**New York, NY** (city)	2,191
Texas	8,695	Harris County, TX	3,799	**Houston, TX** (city) Harris County	2,072
New York	6,337	San Bernardino County, CA	2,504	**San Francisco, CA** (city) San Francisco County	1,353
Virginia	5,152	Contra Costa County, CA	2,067	**Queens, NY** (borough) Queens County	1,135
District of Columbia	5,116	Orange County, CA	1,999	**Hempstead (town), NY** (town) Nassau County	1,124
Florida	4,036	Montgomery County, MD	1,975	**Palmdale, CA** (city) Los Angeles County	880
New Jersey	2,694	Riverside County, CA	1,897	**Lancaster, CA** (city) Los Angeles County	816
Nevada	2,285	Clark County, NV	1,834	**Las Vegas, NV** (city) Clark County	793
North Carolina	2,282	Nassau County, NY	1,812	**Dallas, TX** (city) Dallas County	754

Sorted by Number in Ascending Order — U.S. = 111,815

State	Number	County	Number	Place	Number
Idaho	114	Alamance County, NC	0	**Gainesville, GA** (city) Hall County	0
New Mexico	133	Camden County, NJ	0	**Lake Worth, FL** (city) Palm Beach County	0
Alaska	136	Rutherford County, TN	0	**Lewisville, TX** (city) Denton County	0
Rhode Island	156	Santa Cruz County, CA	0	**Mission Bend, TX** (cdp) Fort Bend County	0
Wisconsin	187	El Paso County, TX	14	**Montgomery Village, MD** (cdp) Montgomery County	0
Kansas	205	Durham County, NC	26	**Plano, TX** (city) Collin County	10
Iowa	253	New Haven County, CT	26	**Des Moines, IA** (city) Polk County	11
Oklahoma	307	Hall County, GA	27	**Providence, RI** (city) Providence County	12
Michigan	324	Sebastian County, AR	33	**Grand Prairie, TX** (city) Dallas County	13
South Carolina	336	DeKalb County, GA	43	**La Puente, CA** (city) Los Angeles County	14

Sorted by Percent in Descending Order — U.S. = 7.6%

State	Percent	County	Percent	Place	Percent
Hawaii	44.6	Duval County, FL	34.3	**Jacksonville, FL** (city) Duval County	34.3
District of Columbia	32.0	El Paso County, CO	29.5	**San Diego, CA** (city) San Diego County	28.5
Alabama	22.0	Baltimore County, MD	25.9	**Antioch, CA** (city) Contra Costa County	25.9
Pennsylvania	21.0	Napa County, CA	24.9	**Lancaster, CA** (city) Los Angeles County	23.9
Missouri	17.4	Pima County, AZ	24.8	**Santa Clarita, CA** (city) Los Angeles County	23.7
Oregon	17.4	Prince George's County, MD	22.6	**Fairfield, CA** (city) Solano County	22.6
Utah	17.2	Multnomah County, OR	22.3	**Corona, CA** (city) Riverside County	22.1
Idaho	16.1	San Diego County, CA	22.0	**Burbank, CA** (city) Los Angeles County	20.7
Kentucky	15.7	Frederick County, MD	20.9	**Simi Valley, CA** (city) Ventura County	19.3
Ohio	15.7	Anne Arundel County, MD	20.5	**Jersey City, NJ** (city) Hudson County	19.0

Sorted by Percent in Ascending Order — U.S. = 7.6%

State	Percent	County	Percent	Place	Percent
Texas	4.3	Alamance County, NC	0.0	**Gainesville, GA** (city) Hall County	0.0
Kansas	4.9	Camden County, NJ	0.0	**Lake Worth, FL** (city) Palm Beach County	0.0
New York	5.0	Rutherford County, TN	0.0	**Lewisville, TX** (city) Denton County	0.0
Rhode Island	5.1	Santa Cruz County, CA	0.0	**Mission Bend, TX** (cdp) Fort Bend County	0.0
Virginia	5.1	Hall County, GA	1.0	**Montgomery Village, MD** (cdp) Montgomery County	0.0
Georgia	5.2	Durham County, NC	1.2	**Grand Prairie, TX** (city) Dallas County	0.6
New Jersey	5.6	Arlington County, VA	1.4	**Norwalk, CA** (city) Los Angeles County	0.6
Iowa	5.8	El Paso County, TX	1.5	**Plainfield, NJ** (city) Union County	0.6
Arkansas	6.0	Gwinnett County, GA	1.5	**Huntington Station, NY** (cdp) Suffolk County	0.7
Connecticut	6.4	DeKalb County, GA	1.9	**Providence, RI** (city) Providence County	0.7

Note: (1) Ranking tables cover all states and counties, and places with an overall population of at least 125,000, OR an overall population of at least 25,000 where the Hispanic/Latino population is at least 20% of the overall population. In states where less than five places meet either of these criteria, we have included places with at least 10,000 total population with the highest percentage of Hispanic/Latino population. These places are identified with an asterisk (*); Please refer to the User's Guide for a full explanation of data.

Language Spoken at Home: English Only

(Universe: Population 5 Years and Over)

Cuban

Top 10 States, Counties, and Places[1]

Sorted by Number in Descending Order — U.S. = 274,415

State	Number	County	Number	Place	Number
Florida	99,353	Miami-Dade County, FL	33,459	**New York, NY** (city)	11,879
California	26,026	Broward County, FL	13,459	**Hialeah, FL** (city) Miami-Dade County	5,236
New York	23,509	Hillsborough County, FL	12,334	**Tampa, FL** (city) Hillsborough County	3,974
New Jersey	17,008	Los Angeles County, CA	8,530	**Miami, FL** (city) Miami-Dade County	3,799
Texas	10,195	Palm Beach County, FL	5,595	**Queens, NY** (borough) Queens County	3,180
Illinois	8,049	Cook County, IL	4,486	**Manhattan, NY** (borough) New York County	2,892
Georgia	7,919	Bergen County, NJ	3,711	**Pembroke Pines, FL** (city) Broward County	2,699
Pennsylvania	7,095	Orange County, FL	3,559	**Los Angeles, CA** (city) Los Angeles County	2,606
Virginia	5,908	Queens County, NY	3,180	**Brooklyn, NY** (borough) Kings County	2,528
North Carolina	5,329	Pinellas County, FL	3,100	**Bronx, NY** (borough) Bronx County	2,279

Sorted by Number in Ascending Order — U.S. = 274,415

State	Number	County	Number	Place	Number
Arkansas	355	Clay County, MO	26	**Bell, CA** (city) Los Angeles County	30
West Virginia	461	Forsyth County, NC	60	**Syracuse, NY** (city) Onondaga County	46
Nebraska	542	El Paso County, TX	63	**Linden, NJ** (city) Union County	73
Maine	544	Ingham County, MI	157	**Glendale, CA** (city) Los Angeles County	82
Hawaii	617	Onondaga County, NY	184	**Oakland Park, FL** (city) Broward County	86
Iowa	630	Salt Lake County, UT	190	**North Miami, FL** (city) Miami-Dade County	109
Delaware	756	Indian River County, FL	209	**Lehigh Acres, FL** (cdp) Lee County	130
New Hampshire	759	Sumter County, FL	218	**West Little River, FL** (cdp) Miami-Dade County	135
Rhode Island	762	Hampden County, MA	219	**Kissimmee, FL** (city) Osceola County	137
Mississippi	796	Highlands County, FL	242	**Rochester, NY** (city) Monroe County	146

Sorted by Percent in Descending Order — U.S. = 17.2%

State	Percent	County	Percent	Place	Percent
Maine	68.5	Cuyahoga County, OH	70.7	**Brookhaven, NY** (town) Suffolk County	65.1
Colorado	62.1	Hamilton County, OH	67.8	**Staten Island, NY** (borough) Richmond County	56.9
New Hampshire	58.7	New Castle County, DE	67.0	**Islip, NY** (town) Suffolk County	56.5
Ohio	57.5	Dutchess County, NY	62.4	**San Jose, CA** (city) Santa Clara County	55.2
Delaware	57.4	Arapahoe County, CO	62.3	**Oyster Bay, NY** (town) Nassau County	53.2
Wisconsin	57.4	Suffolk County, NY	59.8	**Santa Clarita, CA** (city) Los Angeles County	52.2
West Virginia	56.4	New Haven County, CT	58.3	**San Diego, CA** (city) San Diego County	51.6
Utah	55.7	Pierce County, WA	57.2	**North Hempstead, NY** (town) Nassau County	49.0
Iowa	55.0	Richmond County, NY	56.9	**Anaheim, CA** (city) Orange County	48.7
Washington	53.9	Sacramento County, CA	56.2	**Riverside, CA** (city) Riverside County	47.8

Sorted by Percent in Ascending Order — U.S. = 17.2%

State	Percent	County	Percent	Place	Percent
Florida	9.1	Clay County, MO	2.7	**Fontainebleau, FL** (cdp) Miami-Dade County	1.5
Nevada	17.3	Miami-Dade County, FL	4.3	**Tamiami, FL** (cdp) Miami-Dade County	2.0
New Jersey	21.2	Hudson County, NJ	8.0	**Lehigh Acres, FL** (cdp) Lee County	2.3
Kentucky	23.0	El Paso County, TX	8.7	**University Park, FL** (cdp) Miami-Dade County	2.4
New Mexico	24.8	Lee County, FL	9.0	**West Little River, FL** (cdp) Miami-Dade County	2.4
Texas	27.7	Jefferson County, KY	11.3	**Union City, NJ** (city) Hudson County	2.6
California	33.5	Forsyth County, NC	11.5	**Miami, FL** (city) Miami-Dade County	2.9
Missouri	34.1	Ingham County, MI	11.8	**Kendall West, FL** (cdp) Miami-Dade County	3.0
Arizona	34.5	Highlands County, FL	12.3	**North Miami, FL** (city) Miami-Dade County	3.1
Louisiana	35.2	Polk County, FL	13.3	**Westchester, FL** (cdp) Miami-Dade County	3.1

Note: (1) Ranking tables cover all states and counties, and places with an overall population of at least 125,000, OR an overall population of at least 25,000 where the Hispanic/Latino population is at least 20% of the overall population. In states where less than five places meet either of these criteria, we have included places with at least 10,000 total population with the highest percentage of Hispanic/Latino population. These places are identified with an asterisk (*); Please refer to the User's Guide for a full explanation of data.

Language Spoken at Home: English Only

(Universe: Population 5 Years and Over)

Dominican Republic

Top 10 States, Counties, and Places[1]

Sorted by Number in Descending Order — U.S. = 100,224

State	Number	County	Number	Place	Number
New York	34,632	Bronx County, NY	6,989	**New York, NY** (city)	23,599
Florida	14,625	New York County, NY	5,414	**Bronx, NY** (borough) Bronx County	6,989
New Jersey	11,120	Queens County, NY	5,405	**Manhattan, NY** (borough) New York County	5,414
Massachusetts	6,068	Kings County, NY	4,981	**Queens, NY** (borough) Queens County	5,405
Pennsylvania	4,814	Suffolk County, NY	2,509	**Brooklyn, NY** (borough) Kings County	4,981
California	3,013	Broward County, FL	2,417	**Hempstead (town), NY** (town) Nassau County	1,605
Georgia	2,826	Hudson County, NJ	2,414	**Providence, RI** (city) Providence County	1,099
Connecticut	2,750	Miami-Dade County, FL	2,190	**Islip, NY** (town) Suffolk County	865
Virginia	2,537	Essex County, MA	1,920	**Boston, MA** (city) Suffolk County	839
Texas	2,269	Nassau County, NY	1,855	**Philadelphia, PA** (city) Philadelphia County	817

Sorted by Number in Ascending Order — U.S. = 100,224

State	Number	County	Number	Place	Number
Minnesota	148	Jefferson Parish, LA	54	**Doral, FL** (city) Miami-Dade County	0
Alabama	155	Tarrant County, TX	66	**Plainfield, NJ** (city) Union County	0
Alaska	158	Ocean County, NJ	73	**Atlantic City, NJ** (city) Atlantic County	4
Utah	186	Lancaster County, PA	74	**West Little River, FL** (cdp) Miami-Dade County	11
Delaware	207	Ulster County, NY	92	**Elmont, NY** (cdp) Nassau County	17
Missouri	277	Kent County, MI	95	**Englewood, NJ** (city) Bergen County	20
Louisiana	283	Franklin County, OH	99	**Kendale Lakes, FL** (cdp) Miami-Dade County	20
Colorado	310	Sullivan County, NY	109	**Kendall West, FL** (cdp) Miami-Dade County	24
Washington	312	Dallas County, TX	115	**Lancaster, PA** (city) Lancaster County	25
South Carolina	314	Oneida County, NY	118	**Pawtucket*, RI** (city) Providence County	25

Sorted by Percent in Descending Order — U.S. = 8.1%

State	Percent	County	Percent	Place	Percent
Tennessee	36.1	Fulton County, GA	42.8	**Alafaya, FL** (cdp) Orange County	35.9
California	34.9	San Diego County, CA	33.0	**Los Angeles, CA** (city) Los Angeles County	28.6
Virginia	30.8	Cobb County, GA	31.8	**Town 'n' Country, FL** (cdp) Hillsborough County	23.9
Washington	30.4	Maricopa County, AZ	31.7	**Deltona, FL** (city) Volusia County	23.2
Arizona	29.6	Volusia County, FL	30.9	**Waterbury, CT** (city/town) New Haven County	21.5
Wisconsin	27.5	New London County, CT	29.7	**Homestead, FL** (city) Miami-Dade County	21.3
Michigan	25.8	Monmouth County, NJ	28.9	**Coral Springs, FL** (city) Broward County	20.8
Alabama	23.9	Fairfax County, VA	28.2	**Staten Island, NY** (borough) Richmond County	20.8
Missouri	23.0	Baltimore County, MD	27.5	**Ramapo, NY** (town) Rockland County	20.3
Minnesota	22.9	Los Angeles County, CA	25.0	**Houston, TX** (city) Harris County	17.7

Sorted by Percent in Ascending Order — U.S. = 8.1%

State	Percent	County	Percent	Place	Percent
New York	5.6	Bronx County, NY	3.3	**Doral, FL** (city) Miami-Dade County	0.0
Rhode Island	6.1	New York County, NY	3.5	**Plainfield, NJ** (city) Union County	0.0
Massachusetts	6.6	Union County, NJ	3.5	**Atlantic City, NJ** (city) Atlantic County	0.4
New Jersey	6.8	Passaic County, NJ	3.6	**Elmont, NY** (cdp) Nassau County	1.3
Alaska	9.4	Lancaster County, PA	3.8	**West Little River, FL** (cdp) Miami-Dade County	1.3
Florida	9.9	Essex County, MA	4.2	**Fountainebleau, FL** (cdp) Miami-Dade County	1.4
Pennsylvania	10.2	Miami-Dade County, FL	4.4	**Lawrence, MA** (city) Essex County	1.4
New Hampshire	11.9	Suffolk County, MA	4.4	**Kendall West, FL** (cdp) Miami-Dade County	1.7
Louisiana	12.0	Atlantic County, NJ	4.9	**New Brunswick, NJ** (city) Middlesex County	1.8
Connecticut	13.4	Jefferson Parish, LA	5.0	**Pawtucket*, RI** (city) Providence County	1.8

Note: (1) Ranking tables cover all states and counties, and places with an overall population of at least 125,000, OR an overall population of at least 25,000 where the Hispanic/Latino population is at least 20% of the overall population. In states where less than five places meet either of these criteria, we have included places with at least 10,000 total population with the highest percentage of Hispanic/Latino population. These places are identified with an asterisk (*); Please refer to the User's Guide for a full explanation of data.

Language Spoken at Home: English Only

(Universe: Population 5 Years and Over)

Mexican

Top 10 States, Counties, and Places[1]

Sorted by Number in Descending Order — U.S. = 6,364,824

State	Number	County	Number	Place	Number
California	2,272,329	Los Angeles County, CA	566,837	**San Antonio, TX** (city) Bexar County	206,069
Texas	1,451,001	Bexar County, TX	251,651	**Los Angeles, CA** (city) Los Angeles County	135,186
Arizona	403,596	Maricopa County, AZ	232,641	**Phoenix, AZ** (city) Maricopa County	95,214
Colorado	249,112	San Bernardino County, CA	226,446	**Houston, TX** (city) Harris County	82,309
Illinois	210,250	Riverside County, CA	182,502	**Fresno, CA** (city) Fresno County	66,311
New Mexico	148,120	Harris County, TX	177,762	**San Diego, CA** (city) San Diego County	59,397
Washington	123,951	San Diego County, CA	161,602	**San Jose, CA** (city) Santa Clara County	58,922
Michigan	123,917	Orange County, CA	142,375	**El Paso, TX** (city) El Paso County	57,888
Nevada	99,741	Fresno County, CA	122,830	**Chicago, IL** (city) Cook County	56,338
Florida	95,279	Cook County, IL	99,912	**Corpus Christi, TX** (city) Nueces County	52,961

Sorted by Number in Ascending Order — U.S. = 6,364,824

State	Number	County	Number	Place	Number
Vermont	1,569	Calhoun County, MS	6	**Parker*, SC** (cdp) Greenville County	0
Rhode Island	2,393	Hertford County, NC	6	**Windham, CT** (town) Windham County	11
Maine	2,635	Clark County, ID	14	**Bluffton*, SC** (town) Beaufort County	15
New Hampshire	3,051	Harper County, OK	14	**Central Falls*, RI** (city) Providence County	55
District of Columbia	3,725	Ashe County, NC	16	**Plainfield, NJ** (city) Union County	55
Delaware	4,175	Cuming County, NE	17	**Garfield, NJ** (city) Bergen County	56
North Dakota	4,893	Buffalo County, WI	22	**Marumsco, VA** (cdp) Prince William County	59
West Virginia	5,544	Sedgwick County, CO	22	**Carthage*, MO** (city) Jasper County	70
South Dakota	5,720	Brown County, MN	24	**Manassas, VA** (independent city)	73
Connecticut	8,946	Bradley County, AR	25	**Doral, FL** (city) Miami-Dade County	83

Sorted by Percent in Descending Order — U.S. = 23.4%

State	Percent	County	Percent	Place	Percent
Montana	79.4	Lewis and Clark County, MT	91.8	**Billings*, MT** (city) Yellowstone County	83.8
West Virginia	67.9	Flathead County, MT	91.3	**Fort Campbell North*, KY** (cdp) Christian County	79.1
Vermont	63.1	White Pine County, NV	90.0	**Great Falls*, MT** (city) Cascade County	73.8
Hawaii	61.6	Dickinson County, KS	89.4	**Pueblo West, CO** (cdp) Pueblo County	73.2
Maine	60.4	Kanawha County, WV	86.6	**Warren, MI** (city) Macomb County	72.9
North Dakota	60.4	Trumbull County, OH	86.6	**Pueblo, CO** (city) Pueblo County	70.6
Alaska	55.4	Merrimack County, NH	86.5	**Rapid City*, SD** (city) Pennington County	70.1
Wyoming	51.9	Missoula County, MT	83.4	**Spokane, WA** (city) Spokane County	68.7
District of Columbia	48.8	Becker County, MN	83.1	**Toledo, OH** (city) Lucas County	66.0
South Dakota	48.7	Grand Traverse County, MI	82.6	**Schofield Barracks*, HI** (cdp) Honolulu County	65.9

Sorted by Percent in Ascending Order — U.S. = 23.4%

State	Percent	County	Percent	Place	Percent
New Jersey	11.1	Calhoun County, MS	1.2	**Parker*, SC** (cdp) Greenville County	0.0
North Carolina	11.8	Ashe County, NC	1.7	**Windham, CT** (town) Windham County	0.7
Georgia	11.9	Hertford County, NC	1.9	**Bluffton*, SC** (town) Beaufort County	1.2
New York	12.5	Bradley County, AR	2.4	**New Brunswick, NJ** (city) Middlesex County	1.6
Illinois	15.4	Cuming County, NE	2.8	**Manassas, VA** (independent city)	2.2
South Carolina	16.4	Harper County, OK	3.0	**Marumsco, VA** (cdp) Prince William County	2.3
Delaware	17.0	Edgefield County, SC	3.1	**Monroe, NC** (city) Union County	2.3
Florida	18.4	Glades County, FL	3.2	**White Plains, NY** (city) Westchester County	2.5
Alabama	20.1	Starr County, TX	3.2	**Plainfield, NJ** (city) Union County	2.6
Texas	21.1	Presidio County, TX	3.5	**Elizabeth, NJ** (city) Union County	2.7

Note: (1) Ranking tables cover all states and counties, and places with an overall population of at least 125,000, OR an overall population of at least 25,000 where the Hispanic/Latino population is at least 20% of the overall population. In states where less than five places meet either of these criteria, we have included places with at least 10,000 total population with the highest percentage of Hispanic/Latino population. These places are identified with an asterisk (*); Please refer to the User's Guide for a full explanation of data.

Language Spoken at Home: English Only

(Universe: Population 5 Years and Over)

Puerto Rican

Top 10 States, Counties, and Places[1]

Sorted by Number in Descending Order — U.S. = 1,363,661

State	Number	County	Number	Place	Number
New York	324,593	Bronx County, NY	64,033	**New York, NY** (city)	189,308
Florida	178,395	Kings County, NY	44,763	**Bronx, NY** (borough) Bronx County	64,033
New Jersey	116,903	Queens County, NY	34,012	**Brooklyn, NY** (borough) Kings County	44,763
Pennsylvania	95,744	Cook County, IL	32,149	**Queens, NY** (borough) Queens County	34,012
California	86,652	Suffolk County, NY	31,347	**Manhattan, NY** (borough) New York County	27,248
Massachusetts	59,673	New York County, NY	27,248	**Chicago, IL** (city) Cook County	23,986
Connecticut	59,045	Philadelphia County, PA	23,819	**Philadelphia, PA** (city) Philadelphia County	23,819
Illinois	52,026	Orange County, FL	22,081	**Staten Island, NY** (borough) Richmond County	19,252
Texas	38,858	New Haven County, CT	20,213	**Brookhaven, NY** (town) Suffolk County	11,488
Ohio	30,942	Hillsborough County, FL	19,416	**Islip, NY** (town) Suffolk County	11,119

Sorted by Number in Ascending Order — U.S. = 1,363,661

State	Number	County	Number	Place	Number
Wyoming	465	Perry County, PA	112	**Fountainebleau, FL** (cdp) Miami-Dade County	21
North Dakota	634	Dale County, AL	125	**West Little River, FL** (cdp) Miami-Dade County	49
South Dakota	722	Hendry County, FL	127	**Plant City, FL** (city) Hillsborough County	139
Montana	1,062	Sampson County, NC	148	**Akron, OH** (city) Summit County	195
Vermont	1,102	Christian County, KY	162	**Hallandale Beach, FL** (city) Broward County	199
District of Columbia	1,391	Chenango County, NY	181	**Central Falls*, RI** (city) Providence County	203
West Virginia	1,484	Hall County, GA	188	**Plano, TX** (city) Collin County	210
Nebraska	1,549	Lowndes County, GA	212	**Grand Prairie, TX** (city) Dallas County	216
Idaho	1,776	Tulare County, CA	226	**Irving, TX** (city) Dallas County	228
Mississippi	2,059	Cameron County, TX	232	**Plainfield, NJ** (city) Union County	235

Sorted by Percent in Descending Order — U.S. = 33.8%

State	Percent	County	Percent	Place	Percent
Hawaii	87.3	Maui County, HI	96.1	**Waianae*, HI** (cdp) Honolulu County	99.6
Wyoming	73.3	Kauai County, HI	94.8	**Makakilo*, HI** (cdp) Honolulu County	97.1
North Dakota	71.5	Hawaii County, HI	89.5	**Urban Honolulu, HI** (cdp) Honolulu County	87.9
Montana	70.7	Clark County, WA	88.7	**Vallejo, CA** (city) Solano County	75.7
Oregon	68.4	Honolulu County, HI	84.0	**Modesto, CA** (city) Stanislaus County	72.3
Idaho	67.7	Butte County, CA	83.2	**Kansas City, MO** (city) Jackson County	70.0
South Dakota	66.5	Sonoma County, CA	77.6	**Fremont, CA** (city) Alameda County	69.3
Washington	64.7	Wichita County, TX	77.6	**Wichita, KS** (city) Sedgwick County	68.7
Nebraska	63.2	York County, SC	77.4	**Louisville-Jefferson County, KY** (metropolitan govt) Jefferson County	68.6
Missouri	59.9	Jackson County, MO	77.0	**Stockton, CA** (city) San Joaquin County	67.3

Sorted by Percent in Ascending Order — U.S. = 33.8%

State	Percent	County	Percent	Place	Percent
Florida	24.5	Hendry County, FL	11.4	**Fountainebleau, FL** (cdp) Miami-Dade County	1.1
Rhode Island	24.7	Osceola County, FL	13.3	**West Little River, FL** (cdp) Miami-Dade County	4.3
Massachusetts	26.4	Miami-Dade County, FL	14.8	**Doral, FL** (city) Miami-Dade County	8.5
Connecticut	26.5	Dale County, AL	15.6	**Plant City, FL** (city) Hillsborough County	9.1
New Jersey	30.3	Orange County, FL	17.3	**Meadow Woods, FL** (cdp) Orange County	9.2
Pennsylvania	31.0	Passaic County, NJ	17.4	**Buenaventura Lakes, FL** (cdp) Osceola County	9.4
New York	32.0	Polk County, FL	17.4	**Passaic, NJ** (city) Passaic County	9.9
Illinois	32.5	Christian County, KY	17.8	**Hialeah, FL** (city) Miami-Dade County	10.8
Texas	35.7	Essex County, NJ	18.7	**The Hammocks, FL** (cdp) Miami-Dade County	10.8
Wisconsin	35.9	Essex County, MA	19.4	**Central Falls*, RI** (city) Providence County	11.0

Note: (1) Ranking tables cover all states and counties, and places with an overall population of at least 125,000, OR an overall population of at least 25,000 where the Hispanic/Latino population is at least 20% of the overall population. In states where less than five places meet either of these criteria, we have included places with at least 10,000 total population with the highest percentage of Hispanic/Latino population. These places are identified with an asterisk (*); Please refer to the User's Guide for a full explanation of data.

Language Spoken at Home: English Only

(Universe: Population 5 Years and Over)

South American

Top 10 States, Counties, and Places[1]

Sorted by Number in Descending Order — U.S. = 330,673

State	Number	County	Number	Place	Number
California	51,942	Los Angeles County, CA	17,165	**New York, NY** (city)	25,561
New York	48,893	Queens County, NY	12,113	**Queens, NY** (borough) Queens County	12,113
Florida	45,654	Miami-Dade County, FL	8,301	**Los Angeles, CA** (city) Los Angeles County	6,614
New Jersey	26,263	Broward County, FL	8,228	**Brooklyn, NY** (borough) Kings County	5,365
Texas	15,980	Orange County, CA	5,804	**Manhattan, NY** (borough) New York County	4,004
Illinois	11,240	Suffolk County, NY	5,522	**Chicago, IL** (city) Cook County	3,101
Virginia	10,890	Nassau County, NY	5,369	**Hempstead (town), NY** (town) Nassau County	2,965
Maryland	9,713	Kings County, NY	5,365	**Houston, TX** (city) Harris County	2,481
Pennsylvania	8,590	Cook County, IL	5,348	**Bronx, NY** (borough) Bronx County	2,343
Georgia	8,580	Harris County, TX	4,551	**San Diego, CA** (city) San Diego County	2,269

Sorted by Number in Ascending Order — U.S. = 330,673

State	Number	County	Number	Place	Number
Wyoming	256	Clayton County, GA	52	**South Gate, CA** (city) Los Angeles County	0
North Dakota	266	Horry County, SC	64	**Spring Valley, NY** (village) Rockland County	8
Vermont	349	Sussex County, DE	66	**Richmond, CA** (city) Contra Costa County	13
Alaska	361	Beaufort County, SC	69	**Poinciana, FL** (cdp) Osceola County	15
Montana	467	Spartanburg County, SC	70	**Montebello, CA** (city) Los Angeles County	21
Nebraska	524	York County, SC	82	**Westchester, FL** (cdp) Miami-Dade County	25
West Virginia	551	Hamilton County, IN	114	**Lynn, MA** (city) Essex County	29
Mississippi	566	El Paso County, TX	115	**North Miami, FL** (city) Miami-Dade County	32
Maine	582	Iredell County, NC	119	**Rahway, NJ** (city) Union County	33
Delaware	849	Macomb County, MI	125	**Hempstead (village), NY** (village) Nassau County	36

Sorted by Percent in Descending Order — U.S. = 12.9%

State	Percent	County	Percent	Place	Percent
Montana	47.8	Clark County, WA	61.5	**Lancaster, CA** (city) Los Angeles County	60.6
North Dakota	44.7	Ada County, ID	56.1	**Overland Park, KS** (city) Johnson County	38.9
Maine	44.1	San Luis Obispo County, CA	55.9	**Saint Paul, MN** (city) Ramsey County	37.6
Vermont	38.5	Erie County, NY	54.2	**Columbus, OH** (city) Franklin County	37.0
Hawaii	38.4	Tolland County, CT	54.2	**Glendora, CA** (city) Los Angeles County	36.1
Idaho	33.3	Pierce County, WA	51.0	**Portland, OR** (city) Multnomah County	35.7
Washington	33.3	Rockingham County, NH	50.2	**Scottsdale, AZ** (city) Maricopa County	35.0
Michigan	32.3	Saint Johns County, FL	50.0	**Thousand Oaks, CA** (city) Ventura County	34.3
Missouri	32.2	Placer County, CA	44.5	**Chesapeake, VA** (independent city)	34.0
Kentucky	31.6	Bucks County, PA	41.0	**Placentia, CA** (city) Orange County	33.7

Sorted by Percent in Ascending Order — U.S. = 12.9%

State	Percent	County	Percent	Place	Percent
Florida	7.3	Miami-Dade County, FL	3.3	**South Gate, CA** (city) Los Angeles County	0.0
New Jersey	8.6	Beaufort County, SC	4.6	**Spring Valley, NY** (village) Rockland County	0.4
New York	9.9	Clayton County, GA	4.9	**Poinciana, FL** (cdp) Osceola County	1.0
Virginia	11.4	Polk County, FL	4.9	**Richmond, CA** (city) Contra Costa County	1.0
Connecticut	11.7	Union County, NJ	5.2	**Aventura, FL** (city) Miami-Dade County	1.1
Rhode Island	12.8	Hudson County, NJ	5.9	**North Miami, FL** (city) Miami-Dade County	1.1
Texas	13.3	Passaic County, NJ	5.9	**Fountainebleau, FL** (cdp) Miami-Dade County	1.2
Alaska	15.0	Queens County, NY	5.9	**Doral, FL** (city) Miami-Dade County	1.3
Utah	15.1	Broward County, FL	6.1	**Tamiami, FL** (cdp) Miami-Dade County	1.3
South Carolina	15.2	Osceola County, FL	6.1	**Kendall West, FL** (cdp) Miami-Dade County	1.5

Note: (1) Ranking tables cover all states and counties, and places with an overall population of at least 125,000, OR an overall population of at least 25,000 where the Hispanic/Latino population is at least 20% of the overall population. In states where less than five places meet either of these criteria, we have included places with at least 10,000 total population with the highest percentage of Hispanic/Latino population. These places are identified with an asterisk (*); Please refer to the User's Guide for a full explanation of data.

Language Spoken at Home: English Only

(Universe: Population 5 Years and Over)

South American: Argentinean

Top 10 States, Counties, and Places[1]

Sorted by Number in Descending Order — U.S. = 32,840

State	Number	County	Number	Place	Number
California	7,979	Los Angeles County, CA	2,508	**New York, NY** (city)	2,051
New York	3,910	Orange County, CA	1,291	**Los Angeles, CA** (city) Los Angeles County	1,136
Florida	3,454	Miami-Dade County, FL	713	**Queens, NY** (borough) Queens County	704
New Jersey	2,173	Queens County, NY	704	**Manhattan, NY** (borough) New York County	645
Illinois	1,351	San Bernardino County, CA	695	**Brooklyn, NY** (borough) Kings County	423
Texas	1,227	Broward County, FL	662	**San Diego, CA** (city) San Diego County	277
Maryland	1,183	New York County, NY	645	**Hempstead (town), NY** (town) Nassau County	236
Pennsylvania	890	Cook County, IL	640	**San Francisco, CA** (city) San Francisco County	234
Virginia	855	Riverside County, CA	602	**Chicago, IL** (city) Cook County	217
Connecticut	811	San Diego County, CA	579	**Miami, FL** (city) Miami-Dade County	191

Sorted by Number in Ascending Order — U.S. = 32,840

State	Number	County	Number	Place	Number
Tennessee	121	Montgomery County, TX	7	**Aventura, FL** (city) Miami-Dade County	0
District of Columbia	165	Oakland County, MI	55	**Hialeah, FL** (city) Miami-Dade County	0
Missouri	168	Union County, NJ	62	**Doral, FL** (city) Miami-Dade County	12
Minnesota	180	Travis County, TX	72	**Miami Beach, FL** (city) Miami-Dade County	24
South Carolina	185	Lee County, FL	80	**Hollywood, FL** (city) Broward County	106
Indiana	223	Dallas County, TX	86	**Pembroke Pines, FL** (city) Broward County	110
Colorado	224	Salt Lake County, UT	103	**Houston, TX** (city) Harris County	113
Wisconsin	225	Bronx County, NY	118	**Bronx, NY** (borough) Bronx County	118
Louisiana	289	New Haven County, CT	138	**San Jose, CA** (city) Santa Clara County	123
Ohio	415	Tarrant County, TX	138	**Coral Springs, FL** (city) Broward County	190

Sorted by Percent in Descending Order — U.S. = 16.3%

State	Percent	County	Percent	Place	Percent
Oregon	38.5	Riverside County, CA	32.5	**San Diego, CA** (city) San Diego County	33.3
Louisiana	38.4	Ventura County, CA	31.7	**Hempstead (town), NY** (town) Nassau County	19.6
Washington	30.7	Fairfield County, CT	29.7	**Coral Springs, FL** (city) Broward County	18.8
Ohio	28.4	San Diego County, CA	27.9	**San Francisco, CA** (city) San Francisco County	18.6
Arizona	28.1	San Bernardino County, CA	26.5	**Manhattan, NY** (borough) New York County	17.7
Georgia	28.0	Bexar County, TX	25.8	**Brooklyn, NY** (borough) Kings County	17.1
Pennsylvania	25.3	Orange County, CA	25.5	**New York, NY** (city)	15.6
Illinois	24.1	Maricopa County, AZ	23.7	**San Jose, CA** (city) Santa Clara County	14.9
Connecticut	23.5	Essex County, NJ	21.7	**Chicago, IL** (city) Cook County	14.1
Missouri	23.3	Tarrant County, TX	21.3	**Los Angeles, CA** (city) Los Angeles County	14.1

Sorted by Percent in Ascending Order — U.S. = 16.3%

State	Percent	County	Percent	Place	Percent
Florida	6.9	Montgomery County, TX	0.7	**Aventura, FL** (city) Miami-Dade County	0.0
Texas	11.0	Miami-Dade County, FL	2.8	**Hialeah, FL** (city) Miami-Dade County	0.0
Utah	12.4	Union County, NJ	4.8	**Miami Beach, FL** (city) Miami-Dade County	0.6
Tennessee	13.2	Lee County, FL	6.2	**Doral, FL** (city) Miami-Dade County	1.2
South Carolina	15.2	Dallas County, TX	6.3	**Miami, FL** (city) Miami-Dade County	3.6
Colorado	16.7	Broward County, FL	6.9	**Houston, TX** (city) Harris County	6.6
Massachusetts	16.7	Salt Lake County, UT	7.1	**Hollywood, FL** (city) Broward County	6.9
Virginia	16.8	Hudson County, NJ	8.1	**Pembroke Pines, FL** (city) Broward County	10.5
New Jersey	16.9	Oakland County, MI	8.3	**Bronx, NY** (borough) Bronx County	11.2
District of Columbia	17.4	Palm Beach County, FL	8.7	**Queens, NY** (borough) Queens County	13.0

RANKINGS & COMPARISONS

Note: (1) Ranking tables cover all states and counties, and places with an overall population of at least 125,000, OR an overall population of at least 25,000 where the Hispanic/Latino population is at least 20% of the overall population. In states where less than five places meet either of these criteria, we have included places with at least 10,000 total population with the highest percentage of Hispanic/Latino population. These places are identified with an asterisk (*); Please refer to the User's Guide for a full explanation of data.

Language Spoken at Home: English Only

(Universe: Population 5 Years and Over)

South American: Bolivian

Top 10 States, Counties, and Places[1]

Sorted by Number in Descending Order — U.S. = 12,798

State	Number	County	Number	Place	Number
California	2,316	Fairfax County, VA	534	**New York, NY** (city)	529
Virginia	1,742	Los Angeles County, CA	529	**Queens, NY** (borough) Queens County	270
Texas	873	Montgomery County, MD	493	**Los Angeles, CA** (city) Los Angeles County	195
New York	855	Prince William County, VA	395	**Arlington, VA** (cdp) Arlington County	165
Maryland	828	Orange County, CA	296	**Providence, RI** (city) Providence County	125
Florida	680	Queens County, NY	270	**Springfield, VA** (cdp) Fairfax County	38
Illinois	359	Providence County, RI	245	**Dale City, VA** (cdp) Prince William County	35
New Jersey	352	San Diego County, CA	245	**Annandale, VA** (cdp) Fairfax County	32
Pennsylvania	268	Harris County, TX	212	**West Falls Church, VA** (cdp) Fairfax County	29
Massachusetts	251	Loudoun County, VA	200		

Sorted by Number in Ascending Order — U.S. = 12,798

State	Number	County	Number	Place	Number
North Carolina	196	Miami-Dade County, FL	69	**West Falls Church, VA** (cdp) Fairfax County	29
Rhode Island	245	Palm Beach County, FL	114	**Annandale, VA** (cdp) Fairfax County	32
Massachusetts	251	Cook County, IL	126	**Dale City, VA** (cdp) Prince William County	35
Pennsylvania	268	Santa Clara County, CA	146	**Springfield, VA** (cdp) Fairfax County	38
New Jersey	352	Broward County, FL	148	**Providence, RI** (city) Providence County	125
Illinois	359	Prince George's County, MD	158	**Arlington, VA** (cdp) Arlington County	165
Florida	680	Arlington County, VA	165	**Los Angeles, CA** (city) Los Angeles County	195
Maryland	828	Loudoun County, VA	200	**Queens, NY** (borough) Queens County	270
New York	855	Harris County, TX	212	**New York, NY** (city)	529
Texas	873	Providence County, RI	245		

Sorted by Percent in Descending Order — U.S. = 13.6%

State	Percent	County	Percent	Place	Percent
Pennsylvania	42.9	San Diego County, CA	31.4	**Providence, RI** (city) Providence County	12.4
North Carolina	33.4	Orange County, CA	21.0	**New York, NY** (city)	11.3
Texas	20.6	Cook County, IL	18.4	**Queens, NY** (borough) Queens County	8.6
Illinois	19.6	Harris County, TX	16.1	**Los Angeles, CA** (city) Los Angeles County	5.6
California	18.1	Prince George's County, MD	14.3	**Arlington, VA** (cdp) Arlington County	4.1
Massachusetts	14.1	Providence County, RI	13.4	**Springfield, VA** (cdp) Fairfax County	4.0
Rhode Island	13.4	Santa Clara County, CA	12.9	**Dale City, VA** (cdp) Prince William County	2.7
Maryland	12.7	Palm Beach County, FL	12.7	**West Falls Church, VA** (cdp) Fairfax County	2.0
New York	11.8	Montgomery County, MD	10.5	**Annandale, VA** (cdp) Fairfax County	1.2
New Jersey	9.0	Los Angeles County, CA	10.2		

Sorted by Percent in Ascending Order — U.S. = 13.6%

State	Percent	County	Percent	Place	Percent
Virginia	5.3	Miami-Dade County, FL	2.2	**Annandale, VA** (cdp) Fairfax County	1.2
Florida	7.4	Fairfax County, VA	3.0	**West Falls Church, VA** (cdp) Fairfax County	2.0
New Jersey	9.0	Arlington County, VA	4.1	**Dale City, VA** (cdp) Prince William County	2.7
New York	11.8	Queens County, NY	8.6	**Springfield, VA** (cdp) Fairfax County	4.0
Maryland	12.7	Prince William County, VA	9.1	**Arlington, VA** (cdp) Arlington County	4.1
Rhode Island	13.4	Broward County, FL	9.2	**Los Angeles, CA** (city) Los Angeles County	5.6
Massachusetts	14.1	Loudoun County, VA	9.2	**Queens, NY** (borough) Queens County	8.6
California	18.1	Los Angeles County, CA	10.2	**New York, NY** (city)	11.3
Illinois	19.6	Montgomery County, MD	10.5	**Providence, RI** (city) Providence County	12.4
Texas	20.6	Palm Beach County, FL	12.7		

Note: (1) Ranking tables cover all states and counties, and places with an overall population of at least 125,000, OR an overall population of at least 25,000 where the Hispanic/Latino population is at least 20% of the overall population. In states where less than five places meet either of these criteria, we have included places with at least 10,000 total population with the highest percentage of Hispanic/Latino population. These places are identified with an asterisk (*); Please refer to the User's Guide for a full explanation of data.

Language Spoken at Home: English Only

(Universe: Population 5 Years and Over)

South American: Chilean

Top 10 States, Counties, and Places[1]

Sorted by Number in Descending Order — U.S. = 25,158

State	Number	County	Number	Place	Number
California	4,999	Los Angeles County, CA	1,269	**New York, NY** (city)	1,150
New York	2,814	Suffolk County, NY	556	**Los Angeles, CA** (city) Los Angeles County	734
Florida	1,979	San Diego County, CA	528	**Manhattan, NY** (borough) New York County	387
New Jersey	1,406	Miami-Dade County, FL	518	**Brooklyn, NY** (borough) Kings County	361
Texas	1,109	Orange County, CA	474	**Queens, NY** (borough) Queens County	250
Illinois	1,077	New York County, NY	387	**Chicago, IL** (city) Cook County	159
Virginia	901	Kings County, NY	361	**Miami, FL** (city) Miami-Dade County	139
Washington	881	Alameda County, CA	356	**Hempstead (town), NY** (town) Nassau County	111
Maryland	861	Clark County, NV	305	**Kendall, FL** (cdp) Miami-Dade County	91
Pennsylvania	779	Middlesex County, MA	290		

Sorted by Number in Ascending Order — U.S. = 25,158

State	Number	County	Number	Place	Number
Oregon	187	Palm Beach County, FL	90	**Kendall, FL** (cdp) Miami-Dade County	91
Tennessee	208	Salt Lake County, UT	95	**Hempstead (town), NY** (town) Nassau County	111
Missouri	233	Hudson County, NJ	98	**Miami, FL** (city) Miami-Dade County	139
Connecticut	251	Bergen County, NJ	142	**Chicago, IL** (city) Cook County	159
Minnesota	288	San Bernardino County, CA	178	**Queens, NY** (borough) Queens County	250
Colorado	312	Harris County, TX	201	**Brooklyn, NY** (borough) Kings County	361
Michigan	357	Montgomery County, MD	203	**Manhattan, NY** (borough) New York County	387
Ohio	364	San Mateo County, CA	207	**Los Angeles, CA** (city) Los Angeles County	734
Nevada	394	Riverside County, CA	216	**New York, NY** (city)	1,150
North Carolina	419	Fairfax County, VA	220		

Sorted by Percent in Descending Order — U.S. = 21.6%

State	Percent	County	Percent	Place	Percent
Ohio	42.8	Suffolk County, NY	45.2	**Manhattan, NY** (borough) New York County	27.1
Wisconsin	42.0	Orange County, CA	36.1	**Brooklyn, NY** (borough) Kings County	26.6
Minnesota	41.6	Alameda County, CA	32.8	**Chicago, IL** (city) Cook County	20.1
Washington	41.1	Clark County, NV	31.2	**Los Angeles, CA** (city) Los Angeles County	17.6
Pennsylvania	38.3	San Diego County, CA	30.2	**New York, NY** (city)	15.8
Illinois	36.9	New York County, NY	27.1	**Miami, FL** (city) Miami-Dade County	12.0
Michigan	35.8	Kings County, NY	26.6	**Kendall, FL** (cdp) Miami-Dade County	9.5
Arizona	30.4	San Mateo County, CA	25.5	**Hempstead (town), NY** (town) Nassau County	8.7
Nevada	30.1	Middlesex County, MA	25.1	**Queens, NY** (borough) Queens County	6.8
Tennessee	30.1	Maricopa County, AZ	24.3		

Sorted by Percent in Ascending Order — U.S. = 21.6%

State	Percent	County	Percent	Place	Percent
Florida	9.0	Miami-Dade County, FL	4.6	**Queens, NY** (borough) Queens County	6.8
Connecticut	16.8	Hudson County, NJ	4.7	**Hempstead (town), NY** (town) Nassau County	8.7
Utah	17.2	Palm Beach County, FL	5.9	**Kendall, FL** (cdp) Miami-Dade County	9.5
New Jersey	17.7	Broward County, FL	6.5	**Miami, FL** (city) Miami-Dade County	12.0
New York	19.0	Queens County, NY	6.8	**New York, NY** (city)	15.8
Oregon	19.3	Nassau County, NY	8.8	**Los Angeles, CA** (city) Los Angeles County	17.6
North Carolina	20.4	Montgomery County, MD	9.5	**Chicago, IL** (city) Cook County	20.1
Maryland	21.1	Salt Lake County, UT	10.0	**Brooklyn, NY** (borough) Kings County	26.6
California	22.5	Westchester County, NY	12.4	**Manhattan, NY** (borough) New York County	27.1
Colorado	24.2	Fairfax County, VA	14.4		

Note: (1) Ranking tables cover all states and counties, and places with an overall population of at least 125,000, OR an overall population of at least 25,000 where the Hispanic/Latino population is at least 20% of the overall population. In states where less than five places meet either of these criteria, we have included places with at least 10,000 total population with the highest percentage of Hispanic/Latino population. These places are identified with an asterisk (*); Please refer to the User's Guide for a full explanation of data.

Language Spoken at Home: English Only

(Universe: Population 5 Years and Over)

South American: Colombian

Top 10 States, Counties, and Places[1]

Sorted by Number in Descending Order U.S. = 103,982

State	Number	County	Number	Place	Number
Florida	19,067	Los Angeles County, CA	3,997	**New York, NY** (city)	7,299
New York	15,856	Queens County, NY	3,482	**Queens, NY** (borough) Queens County	3,482
California	10,802	Miami-Dade County, FL	3,391	**Brooklyn, NY** (borough) Kings County	1,482
New Jersey	8,437	Broward County, FL	3,354	**Hempstead (town), NY** (town) Nassau County	1,279
Texas	5,458	Nassau County, NY	2,129	**Houston, TX** (city) Harris County	1,223
Illinois	3,863	Suffolk County, NY	1,838	**Los Angeles, CA** (city) Los Angeles County	1,198
Georgia	3,236	Harris County, TX	1,803	**Chicago, IL** (city) Cook County	1,070
Massachusetts	3,197	Hillsborough County, FL	1,733	**Manhattan, NY** (borough) New York County	1,005
Pennsylvania	2,939	Orange County, FL	1,714	**San Diego, CA** (city) San Diego County	809
North Carolina	2,629	Cook County, IL	1,706	**Staten Island, NY** (borough) Richmond County	709

Sorted by Number in Ascending Order U.S. = 103,982

State	Number	County	Number	Place	Number
Nebraska	81	Dutchess County, NY	41	**Richmond West, FL** (cdp) Miami-Dade County	0
Delaware	87	Pima County, AZ	52	**Hallandale Beach, FL** (city) Broward County	10
Alaska	173	Polk County, FL	66	**North Miami, FL** (city) Miami-Dade County	13
Arkansas	201	Montgomery County, TX	82	**Meadow Woods, FL** (cdp) Orange County	14
New Mexico	207	Ulster County, NY	85	**Miami Gardens, FL** (city) Miami-Dade County	16
District of Columbia	257	Dane County, WI	96	**Passaic, NJ** (city) Passaic County	19
Kansas	312	Hampden County, MA	102	**Elmont, NY** (cdp) Nassau County	21
Iowa	372	Collier County, FL	107	**Providence, RI** (city) Providence County	26
Utah	381	Luzerne County, PA	112	**San Jose, CA** (city) Santa Clara County	26
Oklahoma	413	Forsyth County, GA	117	**Aventura, FL** (city) Miami-Dade County	27

Sorted by Percent in Descending Order U.S. = 12.5%

State	Percent	County	Percent	Place	Percent
Minnesota	60.3	Erie County, NY	66.4	**San Diego, CA** (city) San Diego County	34.3
Michigan	38.1	Hennepin County, MN	63.9	**Tallahassee, FL** (city) Leon County	28.3
Kentucky	36.6	Bucks County, PA	49.0	**Cooper City, FL** (city) Broward County	27.6
Iowa	35.6	Burlington County, NJ	38.0	**Babylon, NY** (town) Suffolk County	26.9
Missouri	35.1	Oakland County, MI	36.2	**Virginia Beach, VA** (independent city)	26.9
Oregon	34.3	Baltimore County, MD	35.5	**Staten Island, NY** (borough) Richmond County	26.0
Washington	32.0	Saint Louis County, MO	32.9	**Royal Palm Beach, FL** (village) Palm Beach County	25.9
Ohio	31.2	Sacramento County, CA	32.5	**Huntington, NY** (town) Suffolk County	23.9
Alabama	29.0	Franklin County, OH	32.1	**San Francisco, CA** (city) San Francisco County	23.3
Oklahoma	28.5	Will County, IL	31.9	**Deltona, FL** (city) Volusia County	21.9

Sorted by Percent in Ascending Order U.S. = 12.5%

State	Percent	County	Percent	Place	Percent
Florida	6.9	Miami-Dade County, FL	3.2	**Richmond West, FL** (cdp) Miami-Dade County	0.0
Delaware	8.4	Collier County, FL	3.3	**Hallandale Beach, FL** (city) Broward County	0.6
Nebraska	8.7	Polk County, FL	3.6	**Meadow Woods, FL** (cdp) Orange County	0.6
New Jersey	9.0	Somerset County, NJ	3.9	**Aventura, FL** (city) Miami-Dade County	0.9
Rhode Island	9.6	Dutchess County, NY	4.2	**North Miami, FL** (city) Miami-Dade County	1.0
South Carolina	11.0	Pima County, AZ	4.6	**Fountainebleau, FL** (cdp) Miami-Dade County	1.4
Connecticut	11.5	Union County, NJ	4.6	**Passaic, NJ** (city) Passaic County	1.4
New York	11.5	Montgomery County, TX	4.7	**Stamford, CT** (city/town) Fairfield County	1.4
Texas	11.9	Fort Bend County, TX	4.8	**Miami Gardens, FL** (city) Miami-Dade County	1.5
Massachusetts	13.6	Gwinnett County, GA	4.9	**Tamiami, FL** (cdp) Miami-Dade County	1.5

Note: (1) Ranking tables cover all states and counties, and places with an overall population of at least 125,000, OR an overall population of at least 25,000 where the Hispanic/Latino population is at least 20% of the overall population. In states where less than five places meet either of these criteria, we have included places with at least 10,000 total population with the highest percentage of Hispanic/Latino population. These places are identified with an asterisk (*); Please refer to the User's Guide for a full explanation of data.

Language Spoken at Home: English Only

(Universe: Population 5 Years and Over)

South American: Ecuadorian

Top 10 States, Counties, and Places[1]

Sorted by Number in Descending Order (U.S. = 50,198)

State	Number	County	Number	Place	Number
New York	12,114	Queens County, NY	3,901	**New York, NY** (city)	7,260
New Jersey	6,583	Los Angeles County, CA	2,753	**Queens, NY** (borough) Queens County	3,901
California	6,526	Suffolk County, NY	1,600	**Brooklyn, NY** (borough) Kings County	1,570
Florida	5,489	Kings County, NY	1,570	**Bronx, NY** (borough) Bronx County	926
Texas	1,923	Hudson County, NJ	1,549	**Los Angeles, CA** (city) Los Angeles County	833
Illinois	1,889	Cook County, IL	1,198	**Chicago, IL** (city) Cook County	820
Connecticut	1,717	Nassau County, NY	967	**Brookhaven, NY** (town) Suffolk County	724
Pennsylvania	1,430	Essex County, NJ	959	**Manhattan, NY** (borough) New York County	685
Virginia	1,243	Westchester County, NY	937	**Hempstead (town), NY** (town) Nassau County	634
Massachusetts	1,225	Bronx County, NY	926	**Charlotte, NC** (city) Mecklenburg County	474

Sorted by Number in Ascending Order (U.S. = 50,198)

State	Number	County	Number	Place	Number
Tennessee	88	Putnam County, NY	42	**Spring Valley, NY** (village) Rockland County	0
Wisconsin	147	Rockland County, NY	49	**White Plains, NY** (city) Westchester County	0
Iowa	166	Philadelphia County, PA	64	**New Haven, CT** (city/town) New Haven County	9
Louisiana	185	Will County, IL	76	**Central Islip, NY** (cdp) Suffolk County	10
Indiana	186	Delaware County, PA	84	**Doral, FL** (city) Miami-Dade County	17
Rhode Island	202	Osceola County, FL	99	**Brentwood, NY** (cdp) Suffolk County	21
Oregon	209	Utah County, UT	103	**Bloomfield, NJ** (township) Essex County	22
South Carolina	232	Orange County, NY	104	**Ramapo, NY** (town) Rockland County	23
Kansas	240	Prince George's County, MD	105	**Country Club, FL** (cdp) Miami-Dade County	24
Michigan	250	Berks County, PA	106	**Downey, CA** (city) Los Angeles County	31

Sorted by Percent in Descending Order (U.S. = 9.5%)

State	Percent	County	Percent	Place	Percent
Missouri	60.7	Dutchess County, NY	38.3	**Oyster Bay, NY** (town) Nassau County	24.8
Colorado	44.8	Burlington County, NJ	37.1	**Brookhaven, NY** (town) Suffolk County	17.5
Oklahoma	43.2	Baltimore County, MD	36.4	**Babylon, NY** (town) Suffolk County	16.4
Washington	33.5	Santa Clara County, CA	28.8	**Houston, TX** (city) Harris County	15.8
Kansas	31.6	Lee County, FL	28.4	**Charlotte, NC** (city) Mecklenburg County	14.6
Nevada	30.8	Ocean County, NJ	26.0	**Los Angeles, CA** (city) Los Angeles County	12.9
Oregon	27.7	Camden County, NJ	25.1	**West New York, NJ** (town) Hudson County	12.4
Ohio	24.8	San Bernardino County, CA	24.4	**Hempstead (town), NY** (town) Nassau County	11.8
Iowa	24.7	Clark County, NV	24.3	**Paterson, NJ** (city) Passaic County	10.9
Michigan	24.7	Worcester County, MA	24.2	**Yonkers, NY** (city) Westchester County	10.6

Sorted by Percent in Ascending Order (U.S. = 9.5%)

State	Percent	County	Percent	Place	Percent
New York	5.7	Rockland County, NY	1.3	**Spring Valley, NY** (village) Rockland County	0.0
New Jersey	6.9	Hennepin County, MN	3.2	**White Plains, NY** (city) Westchester County	0.0
Minnesota	7.1	Bronx County, NY	3.7	**New Haven, CT** (city/town) New Haven County	0.7
Illinois	8.2	Miami-Dade County, FL	4.2	**Central Islip, NY** (cdp) Suffolk County	0.8
Connecticut	8.4	Queens County, NY	4.3	**Brentwood, NY** (cdp) Suffolk County	1.0
Florida	9.6	Essex County, NJ	4.4	**Ramapo, NY** (town) Rockland County	1.0
Tennessee	9.7	New York County, NY	4.5	**Doral, FL** (city) Miami-Dade County	1.3
North Carolina	13.4	Westchester County, NY	4.9	**Hackensack, NJ** (city) Bergen County	1.3
Pennsylvania	13.4	Union County, NJ	5.0	**Bloomfield, NJ** (township) Essex County	1.7
Maryland	14.1	Kings County, NY	5.7	**Union City, NJ** (city) Hudson County	2.5

Note: (1) Ranking tables cover all states and counties, and places with an overall population of at least 125,000, OR an overall population of at least 25,000 where the Hispanic/Latino population is at least 20% of the overall population. In states where less than five places meet either of these criteria, we have included places with at least 10,000 total population with the highest percentage of Hispanic/Latino population. These places are identified with an asterisk (*); Please refer to the User's Guide for a full explanation of data.

Language Spoken at Home: English Only

(Universe: Population 5 Years and Over)

South American: Paraguayan

Top 10 States, Counties, and Places[1]

Sorted by Number in Descending Order — U.S. = 4,548

State	Number	County	Number	Place	Number
New York	591	Westchester County, NY	118	**New York, NY** (city)	254
California	298	Queens County, NY	75	**Queens, NY** (borough) Queens County	75
Texas	290				
Florida	214				
New Jersey	208				
Maryland	138				

Sorted by Number in Ascending Order — U.S. = 4,548

State	Number	County	Number	Place	Number
Maryland	138	Queens County, NY	75	**Queens, NY** (borough) Queens County	75
New Jersey	208	Westchester County, NY	118	**New York, NY** (city)	254
Florida	214				
Texas	290				
California	298				
New York	591				

Sorted by Percent in Descending Order — U.S. = 25.0%

State	Percent	County	Percent	Place	Percent
California	36.4	Westchester County, NY	7.2	**New York, NY** (city)	7.8
Texas	33.4	Queens County, NY	3.2	**Queens, NY** (borough) Queens County	3.2
Florida	14.2				
Maryland	13.0				
New Jersey	12.1				
New York	9.5				

Sorted by Percent in Ascending Order — U.S. = 25.0%

State	Percent	County	Percent	Place	Percent
New York	9.5	Queens County, NY	3.2	**Queens, NY** (borough) Queens County	3.2
New Jersey	12.1	Westchester County, NY	7.2	**New York, NY** (city)	7.8
Maryland	13.0				
Florida	14.2				
Texas	33.4				
California	36.4				

Note: (1) Ranking tables cover all states and counties, and places with an overall population of at least 125,000, OR an overall population of at least 25,000 where the Hispanic/Latino population is at least 20% of the overall population. In states where less than five places meet either of these criteria, we have included places with at least 10,000 total population with the highest percentage of Hispanic/Latino population. These places are identified with an asterisk (*); Please refer to the User's Guide for a full explanation of data.

Language Spoken at Home: English Only

(Universe: Population 5 Years and Over)

South American: Peruvian

Top 10 States, Counties, and Places[1]

Sorted by Number in Descending Order — U.S. = 60,210

State	Number	County	Number	Place	Number
California	13,297	Los Angeles County, CA	3,970	**New York, NY** (city)	3,494
Florida	6,916	Queens County, NY	2,046	**Queens, NY** (borough) Queens County	2,046
New York	6,852	Orange County, CA	1,484	**Los Angeles, CA** (city) Los Angeles County	1,744
New Jersey	4,857	Broward County, FL	1,472	**Manhattan, NY** (borough) New York County	664
Texas	2,591	Miami-Dade County, FL	1,078	**Chicago, IL** (city) Cook County	597
Virginia	2,421	Cook County, IL	946	**San Francisco, CA** (city) San Francisco County	500
Maryland	2,198	Nassau County, NY	923	**Oyster Bay, NY** (town) Nassau County	483
Illinois	1,757	Passaic County, NJ	917	**Paterson, NJ** (city) Passaic County	430
Connecticut	1,479	Riverside County, CA	881	**San Diego, CA** (city) San Diego County	427
Georgia	1,400	San Diego County, CA	798	**Brooklyn, NY** (borough) Kings County	362

Sorted by Number in Ascending Order — U.S. = 60,210

State	Number	County	Number	Place	Number
Delaware	105	Arapahoe County, CO	50	**Fountainebleau, FL** (cdp) Miami-Dade County	0
Rhode Island	105	Lehigh County, PA	52	**Kendall West, FL** (cdp) Miami-Dade County	0
Kansas	158	Osceola County, FL	62	**Doral, FL** (city) Miami-Dade County	5
Alabama	180	Sarasota County, FL	73	**Kendall, FL** (cdp) Miami-Dade County	6
Kentucky	226	Duval County, FL	81	**Linden, NJ** (city) Union County	8
Louisiana	249	Fort Bend County, TX	90	**North Bergen, NJ** (township) Hudson County	15
District of Columbia	287	Lake County, IL	96	**West New York, NJ** (town) Hudson County	21
Idaho	310	Denton County, TX	103	**Santa Ana, CA** (city) Orange County	32
Indiana	323	Lee County, FL	107	**Bloomfield, NJ** (township) Essex County	33
South Carolina	334	Seminole County, FL	107	**Cape Coral, FL** (city) Lee County	33

Sorted by Percent in Descending Order — U.S. = 12.4%

State	Percent	County	Percent	Place	Percent
Hawaii	41.3	Prince George's County, MD	35.4	**Oyster Bay, NY** (town) Nassau County	40.8
Wisconsin	39.5	San Joaquin County, CA	31.1	**San Diego, CA** (city) San Diego County	31.5
New Mexico	36.5	Sacramento County, CA	30.4	**Concord, CA** (city) Contra Costa County	28.2
Tennessee	33.8	Solano County, CA	27.2	**Fort Lauderdale, FL** (city) Broward County	22.2
Oklahoma	31.2	Baltimore County, MD	26.8	**Denver, CO** (city) Denver County	21.9
Washington	28.2	San Diego County, CA	26.2	**San Antonio, TX** (city) Bexar County	19.9
Missouri	26.5	King County, WA	23.9	**San Francisco, CA** (city) San Francisco County	19.7
Michigan	26.0	Ocean County, NJ	22.9	**Boston, MA** (city) Suffolk County	19.1
Arizona	24.8	Denver County, CO	21.9	**Phoenix, AZ** (city) Maricopa County	18.0
District of Columbia	24.8	Utah County, UT	21.7	**Manhattan, NY** (borough) New York County	17.2

Sorted by Percent in Ascending Order — U.S. = 12.4%

State	Percent	County	Percent	Place	Percent
Delaware	6.8	Miami-Dade County, FL	3.0	**Fountainebleau, FL** (cdp) Miami-Dade County	0.0
New Jersey	6.9	Prince William County, VA	3.3	**Kendall West, FL** (cdp) Miami-Dade County	0.0
Florida	7.4	Osceola County, FL	4.0	**Kendall, FL** (cdp) Miami-Dade County	0.3
Virginia	9.2	Hudson County, NJ	4.1	**Doral, FL** (city) Miami-Dade County	0.6
Rhode Island	9.5	Bronx County, NY	4.3	**Linden, NJ** (city) Union County	0.7
New York	10.6	Arapahoe County, CO	4.8	**North Bergen, NJ** (township) Hudson County	1.0
Connecticut	11.0	Passaic County, NJ	5.0	**Hialeah, FL** (city) Miami-Dade County	1.9
Texas	12.4	Gwinnett County, GA	5.1	**Elizabeth, NJ** (city) Union County	2.2
Nevada	13.8	Union County, NJ	5.1	**Stamford, CT** (city/town) Fairfield County	2.4
Maryland	14.5	Montgomery County, MD	5.3	**West New York, NJ** (town) Hudson County	2.4

Note: (1) Ranking tables cover all states and counties, and places with an overall population of at least 125,000, OR an overall population of at least 25,000 where the Hispanic/Latino population is at least 20% of the overall population. In states where less than five places meet either of these criteria, we have included places with at least 10,000 total population with the highest percentage of Hispanic/Latino population. These places are identified with an asterisk (*); Please refer to the User's Guide for a full explanation of data.

Language Spoken at Home: English Only

(Universe: Population 5 Years and Over)

South American: Uruguayan

Top 10 States, Counties, and Places[1]

Sorted by Number in Descending Order — U.S. = 5,142

State	Number	County	Number	Place	Number
California	824	Los Angeles County, CA	546	**New York, NY** (city)	227
Florida	754	Palm Beach County, FL	252	**Queens, NY** (borough) Queens County	80
New Jersey	669	Harris County, TX	194	**Elizabeth, NJ** (city) Union County	69
New York	654	Westchester County, NY	133		
Virginia	364	Union County, NJ	112		
Texas	308	Broward County, FL	111		
Pennsylvania	242	Middlesex County, NJ	100		
Massachusetts	216	Morris County, NJ	100		
Georgia	189	Queens County, NY	80		
Maryland	64	Essex County, NJ	78		

Sorted by Number in Ascending Order — U.S. = 5,142

State	Number	County	Number	Place	Number
Maryland	64	Hudson County, NJ	38	**Elizabeth, NJ** (city) Union County	69
Georgia	189	Miami-Dade County, FL	40	**Queens, NY** (borough) Queens County	80
Massachusetts	216	Worcester County, MA	45	**New York, NY** (city)	227
Pennsylvania	242	Essex County, NJ	78		
Texas	308	Gwinnett County, GA	78		
Virginia	364	Queens County, NY	80		
New York	654	Middlesex County, NJ	100		
New Jersey	669	Morris County, NJ	100		
Florida	754	Broward County, FL	111		
California	824	Union County, NJ	112		

Sorted by Percent in Descending Order — U.S. = 9.9%

State	Percent	County	Percent	Place	Percent
California	26.7	Los Angeles County, CA	45.7	**New York, NY** (city)	8.3
Pennsylvania	20.6	Palm Beach County, FL	15.2	**Queens, NY** (borough) Queens County	6.2
Virginia	19.6	Harris County, TX	14.9	**Elizabeth, NJ** (city) Union County	2.5
Texas	13.2	Middlesex County, NJ	13.0		
New York	11.6	Westchester County, NY	10.8		
Massachusetts	10.0	Morris County, NJ	10.4		
Georgia	6.9	Gwinnett County, GA	7.3		
New Jersey	6.0	Queens County, NY	6.2		
Florida	5.6	Worcester County, MA	3.8		
Maryland	4.8	Broward County, FL	3.7		

Sorted by Percent in Ascending Order — U.S. = 9.9%

State	Percent	County	Percent	Place	Percent
Maryland	4.8	Miami-Dade County, FL	0.6	**Elizabeth, NJ** (city) Union County	2.5
Florida	5.6	Union County, NJ	2.9	**Queens, NY** (borough) Queens County	6.2
New Jersey	6.0	Hudson County, NJ	3.3	**New York, NY** (city)	8.3
Georgia	6.9	Essex County, NJ	3.4		
Massachusetts	10.0	Broward County, FL	3.7		
New York	11.6	Worcester County, MA	3.8		
Texas	13.2	Queens County, NY	6.2		
Virginia	19.6	Gwinnett County, GA	7.3		
Pennsylvania	20.6	Morris County, NJ	10.4		
California	26.7	Westchester County, NY	10.8		

Note: (1) Ranking tables cover all states and counties, and places with an overall population of at least 125,000, OR an overall population of at least 25,000 where the Hispanic/Latino population is at least 20% of the overall population. In states where less than five places meet either of these criteria, we have included places with at least 10,000 total population with the highest percentage of Hispanic/Latino population. These places are identified with an asterisk (*); Please refer to the User's Guide for a full explanation of data.

Language Spoken at Home: English Only

(Universe: Population 5 Years and Over)

South American: Venezuelan

Top 10 States, Counties, and Places[1]

Sorted by Number in Descending Order — U.S. = 26,260

State	Number	County	Number	Place	Number
Florida	6,273	Miami-Dade County, FL	1,358	**New York, NY** (city)	2,082
New York	3,258	Broward County, FL	1,212	**Brooklyn, NY** (borough) Kings County	798
California	2,065	Kings County, NY	798	**Queens, NY** (borough) Queens County	640
Texas	1,852	Orange County, FL	717	**Manhattan, NY** (borough) New York County	367
Georgia	1,250	Queens County, NY	640	**Sunrise, FL** (city) Broward County	349
New Jersey	1,120	Harris County, TX	536	**Orlando, FL** (city) Orange County	291
North Carolina	922	Hillsborough County, FL	535	**Houston, TX** (city) Harris County	250
Pennsylvania	872	Palm Beach County, FL	447	**Bronx, NY** (borough) Bronx County	228
Maryland	638	New York County, NY	367	**Los Angeles, CA** (city) Los Angeles County	141
Illinois	637	Los Angeles County, CA	357	**The Hammocks, FL** (cdp) Miami-Dade County	139

Sorted by Number in Ascending Order — U.S. = 26,260

State	Number	County	Number	Place	Number
Wisconsin	95	Tarrant County, TX	52	**Aventura, FL** (city) Miami-Dade County	0
Indiana	96	Collin County, TX	64	**Kendall West, FL** (cdp) Miami-Dade County	0
Oklahoma	147	Fairfax County, VA	69	**Country Club, FL** (cdp) Miami-Dade County	8
Missouri	170	Osceola County, FL	78	**Tamiami, FL** (cdp) Miami-Dade County	11
Tennessee	215	Travis County, TX	95	**Fountainebleau, FL** (cdp) Miami-Dade County	22
Utah	220	Montgomery County, TX	99	**Pembroke Pines, FL** (city) Broward County	23
South Carolina	257	Dallas County, TX	119	**Davie, FL** (town) Broward County	24
Arizona	323	Suffolk County, MA	121	**Hialeah, FL** (city) Miami-Dade County	35
Washington	338	King County, WA	131	**Doral, FL** (city) Miami-Dade County	40
Colorado	345	Montgomery County, MD	143	**Hollywood, FL** (city) Broward County	43

Sorted by Percent in Descending Order — U.S. = 13.6%

State	Percent	County	Percent	Place	Percent
Minnesota	42.8	Kings County, NY	39.1	**Brooklyn, NY** (borough) Kings County	39.1
Michigan	37.1	San Diego County, CA	25.1	**Sunrise, FL** (city) Broward County	22.6
Louisiana	35.2	Orange County, CA	25.0	**New York, NY** (city)	20.9
Pennsylvania	32.2	Cobb County, GA	21.7	**Bronx, NY** (borough) Bronx County	17.5
Maryland	28.2	Hillsborough County, FL	20.0	**Orlando, FL** (city) Orange County	17.0
Washington	27.1	Cook County, IL	19.2	**Manhattan, NY** (borough) New York County	16.0
Ohio	26.9	Fulton County, GA	19.0	**Queens, NY** (borough) Queens County	15.4
North Carolina	26.0	Middlesex County, MA	18.6	**Coral Springs, FL** (city) Broward County	12.0
Colorado	25.6	Pinellas County, FL	17.6	**Los Angeles, CA** (city) Los Angeles County	11.1
Arizona	24.7	Bronx County, NY	17.5	**The Hammocks, FL** (cdp) Miami-Dade County	9.5

Sorted by Percent in Ascending Order — U.S. = 13.6%

State	Percent	County	Percent	Place	Percent
Florida	6.7	Osceola County, FL	2.9	**Aventura, FL** (city) Miami-Dade County	0.0
Indiana	10.1	Miami-Dade County, FL	3.2	**Kendall West, FL** (cdp) Miami-Dade County	0.0
Oklahoma	10.3	Fairfax County, VA	5.2	**Country Club, FL** (cdp) Miami-Dade County	0.5
Utah	10.6	Broward County, FL	5.5	**Doral, FL** (city) Miami-Dade County	0.6
Texas	10.8	Collin County, TX	8.2	**Fountainebleau, FL** (cdp) Miami-Dade County	0.7
Wisconsin	11.1	Harris County, TX	8.4	**Tamiami, FL** (cdp) Miami-Dade County	0.8
Virginia	12.5	Tarrant County, TX	8.7	**Weston, FL** (city) Broward County	0.8
Tennessee	13.7	Orange County, FL	10.3	**Pembroke Pines, FL** (city) Broward County	0.9
Massachusetts	14.9	Los Angeles County, CA	10.8	**Miami, FL** (city) Miami-Dade County	1.1
New Jersey	19.6	Montgomery County, TX	11.6	**Davie, FL** (town) Broward County	1.7

Note: (1) Ranking tables cover all states and counties, and places with an overall population of at least 125,000, OR an overall population of at least 25,000 where the Hispanic/Latino population is at least 20% of the overall population. In states where less than five places meet either of these criteria, we have included places with at least 10,000 total population with the highest percentage of Hispanic/Latino population. These places are identified with an asterisk (*); Please refer to the User's Guide for a full explanation of data.

Language Spoken at Home: English Only

(Universe: Population 5 Years and Over)

Spaniard

Top 10 States, Counties, and Places[1]

Sorted by Number in Descending Order — U.S. = 329,412

State	Number	County	Number	Place	Number
California	74,570	Los Angeles County, CA	13,144	**Albuquerque, NM** (city) Bernalillo County	9,506
Texas	30,941	Bernalillo County, NM	10,960	**New York, NY** (city)	6,036
Colorado	30,428	Maricopa County, AZ	6,420	**Denver, CO** (city) Denver County	4,234
New Mexico	25,405	San Diego County, CA	6,058	**Los Angeles, CA** (city) Los Angeles County	3,564
Florida	17,938	Orange County, CA	5,042	**Pueblo, CO** (city) Pueblo County	2,586
New York	15,949	San Bernardino County, CA	4,875	**San Antonio, TX** (city) Bexar County	2,528
Arizona	11,081	Honolulu County, HI	4,834	**San Diego, CA** (city) San Diego County	2,492
Washington	9,601	Riverside County, CA	4,641	**Houston, TX** (city) Harris County	2,030
New Jersey	9,229	Harris County, TX	4,337	**Phoenix, AZ** (city) Maricopa County	2,020
Hawaii	6,980	Denver County, CO	4,234	**Austin, TX** (city) Travis County	1,735

Sorted by Number in Ascending Order — U.S. = 329,412

State	Number	County	Number	Place	Number
District of Columbia	296	Cameron County, TX	160	**Miami, FL** (city) Miami-Dade County	72
Maine	493	Rio Arriba County, NM	165	**Kearny, NJ** (town) Hudson County	240
Iowa	590	Taos County, NM	172	**Newark, NJ** (city) Essex County	289
New Hampshire	661	Colfax County, NM	259	**Lubbock, TX** (city) Lubbock County	383
Montana	839	Passaic County, NJ	263	**South Valley, NM** (cdp) Bernalillo County	444
West Virginia	914	Hidalgo County, TX	267	**Henderson, NV** (city) Clark County	461
Kentucky	923	Las Animas County, CO	331	**San Bernardino, CA** (city) San Bernardino County	463
Mississippi	963	Fort Bend County, TX	393	**Las Cruces, NM** (city) Dona Ana County	466
Alaska	1,205	Hennepin County, MN	396	**Philadelphia, PA** (city) Philadelphia County	488
Nebraska	1,229	Tulare County, CA	399	**Oyster Bay, NY** (town) Nassau County	525

Sorted by Percent in Descending Order — U.S. = 64.3%

State	Percent	County	Percent	Place	Percent
Idaho	86.6	Butte County, CA	96.9	**Fort Collins, CO** (city) Larimer County	92.1
Hawaii	85.2	Clark County, WA	93.2	**Westminster, CO** (city) Adams County	87.9
Oregon	83.4	San Luis Obispo County, CA	93.1	**Thornton, CO** (city) Adams County	87.2
Wyoming	82.6	Ocean County, NJ	89.9	**Portland, OR** (city) Multnomah County	86.5
Montana	82.3	Pierce County, WA	87.7	**Reno, NV** (city) Washoe County	85.2
Ohio	78.5	Washington County, OR	87.7	**Urban Honolulu, HI** (cdp) Honolulu County	83.9
Washington	78.4	Maui County, HI	87.3	**Lakewood, CO** (city) Jefferson County	83.6
Mississippi	78.2	Multnomah County, OR	87.2	**Rio Rancho, NM** (city) Sandoval County	83.4
Alaska	77.7	Santa Cruz County, CA	86.6	**Pueblo, CO** (city) Pueblo County	81.2
Utah	77.7	Weber County, UT	86.2	**Denver, CO** (city) Denver County	80.9

Sorted by Percent in Ascending Order — U.S. = 64.3%

State	Percent	County	Percent	Place	Percent
District of Columbia	29.4	Miami-Dade County, FL	12.9	**Miami, FL** (city) Miami-Dade County	6.8
Florida	44.7	Hudson County, NJ	19.2	**Kearny, NJ** (town) Hudson County	19.6
New Jersey	46.2	Cameron County, TX	22.3	**Newark, NJ** (city) Essex County	20.8
New York	50.3	Taos County, NM	22.8	**Bronx, NY** (borough) Bronx County	29.2
Maryland	53.2	Passaic County, NJ	24.4	**Queens, NY** (borough) Queens County	31.3
New Mexico	56.8	Bronx County, NY	29.2	**Manhattan, NY** (borough) New York County	32.0
Texas	57.0	Union County, NJ	30.2	**New York, NY** (city)	38.4
Massachusetts	57.1	Queens County, NY	31.3	**Lubbock, TX** (city) Lubbock County	41.3
Maine	58.9	Montgomery County, MD	31.8	**Brooklyn, NY** (borough) Kings County	42.3
Kentucky	59.2	San Miguel County, NM	31.8	**Corpus Christi, TX** (city) Nueces County	45.7

Note: (1) Ranking tables cover all states and counties, and places with an overall population of at least 125,000, OR an overall population of at least 25,000 where the Hispanic/Latino population is at least 20% of the overall population. In states where less than five places meet either of these criteria, we have included places with at least 10,000 total population with the highest percentage of Hispanic/Latino population. These places are identified with an asterisk (*); Please refer to the User's Guide for a full explanation of data.

Language Spoken at Home: Spanish

(Universe: Population 5 Years and Over)

Total Population

Top 10 States, Counties, and Places[1]

Sorted by Number in Descending Order U.S. = 35,470,765

State	Number	County	Number	Place	Number
California	9,706,949	Los Angeles County, CA	3,582,992	**New York, NY** (city)	1,861,885
Texas	6,547,178	Miami-Dade County, FL	1,462,668	**Los Angeles, CA** (city) Los Angeles County	1,515,409
Florida	3,408,312	Harris County, TX	1,219,646	**Houston, TX** (city) Harris County	705,212
New York	2,613,816	Cook County, IL	964,747	**Chicago, IL** (city) Cook County	608,618
Illinois	1,517,245	Orange County, CA	724,555	**Bronx, NY** (borough) Bronx County	584,463
Arizona	1,199,689	Maricopa County, AZ	716,739	**San Antonio, TX** (city) Bexar County	516,289
New Jersey	1,191,818	San Diego County, CA	688,962	**Queens, NY** (borough) Queens County	493,462
Georgia	652,397	Dallas County, TX	684,808	**Phoenix, AZ** (city) Maricopa County	411,840
North Carolina	601,101	Riverside County, CA	645,829	**El Paso, TX** (city) El Paso County	408,268
Colorado	542,257	San Bernardino County, CA	620,276	**Dallas, TX** (city) Dallas County	401,858

Sorted by Number in Ascending Order U.S. = 35,470,765

State	Number	County	Number	Place	Number
Vermont	6,482	Baker County, GA	0	**Waianae*, HI** (cdp) Honolulu County	11
North Dakota	8,183	McKenzie County, ND	4	**Essex*, VT** (town) Chittenden County	63
Montana	12,822	Perry County, TN	5	**Spearfish*, SD** (city) Lawrence County	64
Maine	13,017	Broadwater County, MT	6	**Williston*, ND** (city) Williams County	108
South Dakota	14,829	Stewart County, GA	6	**Bennington*, VT** (town) Bennington County	146
West Virginia	17,860	Perry County, MS	7	**Clarksburg*, WV** (city) Harrison County	158
Alaska	22,447	Dundy County, NE	9	**South Portland*, ME** (city) Cumberland County	171
Wyoming	23,489	Blaine County, MT	13	**Dickinson*, ND** (city) Stark County	179
Hawaii	25,285	Carroll County, MS	16	**South Burlington*, VT** (city) Chittenden County	192
New Hampshire	26,623	Johnson County, KY	16	**Badger*, AK** (cdp) Fairbanks North Star Borough	195

Sorted by Percent in Descending Order U.S. = 12.5%

State	Percent	County	Percent	Place	Percent
Texas	29.2	Starr County, TX	95.7	**Hialeah, FL** (city) Miami-Dade County	93.8
California	28.5	Maverick County, TX	92.7	**Huntington Park, CA** (city) Los Angeles County	93.1
New Mexico	28.5	Webb County, TX	91.7	**Fontainebleau, FL** (cdp) Miami-Dade County	92.9
Arizona	20.7	Zapata County, TX	87.7	**Tamiami, FL** (cdp) Miami-Dade County	92.4
Florida	19.6	Hidalgo County, TX	83.8	**Bell Gardens, CA** (city) Los Angeles County	92.2
Nevada	19.6	Presidio County, TX	83.8	**Calexico, CA** (city) Imperial County	92.0
New Jersey	14.6	Jim Hogg County, TX	83.7	**Eagle Pass, TX** (city) Maverick County	91.9
New York	14.5	Santa Cruz County, AZ	80.2	**Laredo, TX** (city) Webb County	91.6
Illinois	12.7	Hudspeth County, TX	76.5	**San Juan, TX** (city) Hidalgo County	91.3
Colorado	11.9	Reeves County, TX	75.4	**Maywood, CA** (city) Los Angeles County	91.1

Sorted by Percent in Ascending Order U.S. = 12.5%

State	Percent	County	Percent	Place	Percent
Maine	1.0	Baker County, GA	0.0	**Waianae*, HI** (cdp) Honolulu County	0.1
West Virginia	1.0	Broadwater County, MT	0.1	**Essex*, VT** (town) Chittenden County	0.3
Vermont	1.1	Johnson County, KY	0.1	**South Portland*, ME** (city) Cumberland County	0.7
North Dakota	1.3	McKenzie County, ND	0.1	**Spearfish*, SD** (city) Lawrence County	0.7
Montana	1.4	Perry County, MS	0.1	**Williston*, ND** (city) Williams County	0.8
Hawaii	2.0	Perry County, TN	0.1	**Bennington*, VT** (town) Bennington County	1.0
South Dakota	2.0	Russell County, VA	0.1	**Burlington*, VT** (city) Chittenden County	1.0
New Hampshire	2.1	Stewart County, GA	0.1	**Clarksburg*, WV** (city) Harrison County	1.0
Ohio	2.2	Blaine County, MT	0.2	**Warren, MI** (city) Macomb County	1.0
Mississippi	2.3	Carroll County, MS	0.2	**Dickinson*, ND** (city) Stark County	1.1

Note: (1) Ranking tables cover all states and counties, and places with an overall population of at least 125,000, OR an overall population of at least 25,000 where the Hispanic/Latino population is at least 20% of the overall population. In states where less than five places meet either of these criteria, we have included places with at least 10,000 total population with the highest percentage of Hispanic/Latino population. These places are identified with an asterisk (*); Please refer to the User's Guide for a full explanation of data.

Language Spoken at Home: Spanish

(Universe: Population 5 Years and Over)

Hispanic or Latino (of any race)

Top 10 States, Counties, and Places[1]

Sorted by Number in Descending Order — U.S. = 32,517,599

State	Number	County	Number	Place	Number
California	9,296,159	Los Angeles County, CA	3,470,946	**New York, NY** (city)	1,780,137
Texas	6,234,052	Miami-Dade County, FL	1,396,060	**Los Angeles, CA** (city) Los Angeles County	1,465,019
Florida	3,154,843	Harris County, TX	1,166,842	**Houston, TX** (city) Harris County	678,076
New York	2,435,438	Cook County, IL	917,288	**Chicago, IL** (city) Cook County	582,240
Illinois	1,407,288	Orange County, CA	695,223	**Bronx, NY** (borough) Bronx County	569,607
Arizona	1,125,650	Maricopa County, AZ	675,397	**San Antonio, TX** (city) Bexar County	493,883
New Jersey	1,097,492	Dallas County, TX	657,202	**Queens, NY** (borough) Queens County	474,977
Georgia	562,423	San Diego County, CA	647,751	**El Paso, TX** (city) El Paso County	396,529
North Carolina	515,742	Riverside County, CA	618,917	**Phoenix, AZ** (city) Maricopa County	395,689
New Mexico	500,159	San Bernardino County, CA	598,881	**Dallas, TX** (city) Dallas County	388,224

Sorted by Number in Ascending Order — U.S. = 32,517,599

State	Number	County	Number	Place	Number
Vermont	3,138	Jackson County, KS	12	**Waianae*, HI** (cdp) Honolulu County	11
North Dakota	4,202	Wabaunsee County, KS	14	**Bozeman*, MT** (city) Gallatin County	107
Montana	5,102	Jackson County, IA	26	**Butte-Silver Bow*, MT** (consolidated govt) Silver Bow County	228
Maine	5,936	Thurston County, NE	30	**Burlington*, VT** (city) Chittenden County	238
West Virginia	7,272	Mercer County, IL	33	**Morgantown*, WV** (city) Monongalia County	333
South Dakota	9,008	Burnett County, WI	43	**Missoula*, MT** (city) Missoula County	349
Alaska	15,583	Nodaway County, MO	51	**College*, AK** (cdp) Fairbanks North Star Borough	361
Wyoming	18,173	Osage County, KS	51	**Makakilo*, HI** (cdp) Honolulu County	374
New Hampshire	18,342	Clinton County, MO	58	**Great Falls*, MT** (city) Cascade County	377
Hawaii	19,184	Dickinson County, KS	61	**Grand Forks*, ND** (city) Grand Forks County	440

Sorted by Percent in Descending Order — U.S. = 76.1%

State	Percent	County	Percent	Place	Percent
Florida	85.5	Cuming County, NE	97.3	**Parker*, SC** (cdp) Greenville County	100.0
Rhode Island	85.0	Hertford County, NC	97.2	**Bluffton*, SC** (town) Beaufort County	98.8
North Carolina	82.8	Harper County, OK	97.1	**Fountainebleau, FL** (cdp) Miami-Dade County	98.2
Georgia	82.6	Alleghany County, NC	97.0	**Tamiami, FL** (cdp) Miami-Dade County	96.8
New Jersey	82.3	Bradley County, AR	97.0	**West Little River, FL** (cdp) Miami-Dade County	96.6
Illinois	81.4	Presidio County, TX	96.8	**Marumsco, VA** (cdp) Prince William County	96.4
New York	80.9	Starr County, TX	96.7	**Westchester, FL** (cdp) Miami-Dade County	96.4
Texas	78.2	Crockett County, TN	96.2	**Hialeah, FL** (city) Miami-Dade County	96.3
Massachusetts	77.6	Santa Cruz County, AZ	96.1	**Kendall West, FL** (cdp) Miami-Dade County	96.3
South Carolina	77.6	Evans County, GA	95.8	**University Park, FL** (cdp) Miami-Dade County	96.3

Sorted by Percent in Ascending Order — U.S. = 76.1%

State	Percent	County	Percent	Place	Percent
Hawaii	19.1	Jackson County, KS	3.7	**Waianae*, HI** (cdp) Honolulu County	0.8
Montana	21.3	Dickinson County, KS	9.3	**Bozeman*, MT** (city) Gallatin County	12.6
North Dakota	37.3	Wabaunsee County, KS	9.5	**Makakilo*, HI** (cdp) Honolulu County	17.6
Vermont	37.5	Kauai County, HI	11.9	**Billings*, MT** (city) Yellowstone County	17.9
West Virginia	38.4	Flathead County, MT	12.4	**Pueblo West, CO** (cdp) Pueblo County	19.6
Maine	39.2	Nodaway County, MO	13.3	**Missoula*, MT** (city) Missoula County	19.9
Wyoming	44.7	Washington County, VT	13.6	**Butte-Silver Bow*, MT** (consolidated govt) Silver Bow County	20.1
Alaska	46.4	Marquette County, MI	13.7	**Urban Honolulu, HI** (cdp) Honolulu County	22.5
South Dakota	51.6	Jackson County, IA	14.6	**Rapid City*, SD** (city) Pennington County	25.1
Michigan	53.8	White Pine County, NV	15.2	**Great Falls*, MT** (city) Cascade County	26.7

Note: (1) Ranking tables cover all states and counties, and places with an overall population of at least 125,000, OR an overall population of at least 25,000 where the Hispanic/Latino population is at least 20% of the overall population. In states where less than five places meet either of these criteria, we have included places with at least 10,000 total population with the highest percentage of Hispanic/Latino population. These places are identified with an asterisk (*); Please refer to the User's Guide for a full explanation of data.

Language Spoken at Home: Spanish

(Universe: Population 5 Years and Over)

Central American, excluding Mexican

Top 10 States, Counties, and Places[1]

Sorted by Number in Descending Order — U.S. = 3,189,144

State	Number	County	Number	Place	Number
California	977,048	Los Angeles County, CA	618,956	**Los Angeles, CA** (city) Los Angeles County	380,800
Florida	378,865	Miami-Dade County, FL	206,144	**New York, NY** (city)	125,825
Texas	350,597	Harris County, TX	180,635	**Houston, TX** (city) Harris County	123,434
New York	272,361	Montgomery County, MD	64,709	**Miami, FL** (city) Miami-Dade County	64,627
Virginia	156,212	Dallas County, TX	61,124	**Queens, NY** (borough) Queens County	44,604
Maryland	142,172	Suffolk County, NY	56,474	**Brooklyn, NY** (borough) Kings County	36,285
New Jersey	138,128	Fairfax County, VA	52,281	**Hempstead (town), NY** (town) Nassau County	36,069
Georgia	83,233	Nassau County, NY	51,098	**Bronx, NY** (borough) Bronx County	30,248
North Carolina	79,119	Prince George's County, MD	47,911	**Islip, NY** (town) Suffolk County	28,770
Massachusetts	75,443	San Bernardino County, CA	45,469	**Dallas, TX** (city) Dallas County	28,695

Sorted by Number in Ascending Order — U.S. = 3,189,144

State	Number	County	Number	Place	Number
Vermont	213	Macomb County, MI	330	**Palm Springs, CA** (city) Riverside County	378
Maine	796	Allegheny County, PA	366	**Rohnert Park, CA** (city) Sonoma County	426
Wyoming	825	Oneida County, NY	395	**Rochester, NY** (city) Monroe County	439
West Virginia	1,169	Caroline County, MD	418	**Montgomery, AL** (city) Montgomery County	447
Hawaii	1,238	El Dorado County, CA	444	**Worthington*, MN** (city) Nobles County	459
Alaska	1,471	Charles County, MD	470	**Clovis, CA** (city) Fresno County	496
New Hampshire	1,864	Shasta County, CA	494	**Murrieta, CA** (city) Riverside County	517
South Dakota	1,979	Nobles County, MN	497	**Lake Forest, CA** (city) Orange County	611
Idaho	2,072	New Castle County, DE	501	**Weston, FL** (city) Broward County	645
New Mexico	4,556	New London County, CT	506	**Delano, CA** (city) Kern County	648

Sorted by Percent in Descending Order — U.S. = 89.4%

State	Percent	County	Percent	Place	Percent
Rhode Island	94.2	Finney County, KS	100.0	**Gainesville, GA** (city) Hall County	100.0
Texas	93.2	Wyandotte County, KS	99.7	**Garden City, KS** (city) Finney County	100.0
Florida	92.6	Duplin County, NC	99.6	**Kearny, NJ** (town) Hudson County	100.0
Virginia	91.9	Franklin County, AL	98.9	**Long Branch, NJ** (city) Monmouth County	100.0
California	91.2	Colfax County, NE	98.8	**Kansas City, KS** (city) Wyandotte County	99.7
New Jersey	91.2	Dawson County, NE	98.7	**Greenacres, FL** (city) Palm Beach County	99.6
North Carolina	90.5	Frederick County, VA	98.7	**Hallandale Beach, FL** (city) Broward County	99.6
Arkansas	90.0	Minnehaha County, SD	98.6	**Bonita Springs, FL** (city) Lee County	99.4
Nebraska	90.0	Alamance County, NC	98.5	**The Hammocks, FL** (cdp) Miami-Dade County	99.2
South Dakota	89.8	Wayne County, NC	98.3	**Wheaton, MD** (cdp) Montgomery County	99.0

Sorted by Percent in Ascending Order — U.S. = 89.4%

State	Percent	County	Percent	Place	Percent
Vermont	33.7	Allegheny County, PA	44.2	**Worthington*, MN** (city) Nobles County	45.4
Maine	49.3	Nobles County, MN	47.2	**Rochester, NY** (city) Monroe County	54.6
Hawaii	49.9	Macomb County, MI	48.6	**Murrieta, CA** (city) Riverside County	57.7
District of Columbia	68.1	Charles County, MD	49.4	**Colorado Springs, CO** (city) El Paso County	59.5
Alaska	69.8	New Castle County, DE	50.0	**Montgomery, AL** (city) Montgomery County	60.5
Wisconsin	71.4	Saint Louis County, MO	54.5	**Irvine, CA** (city) Orange County	60.6
West Virginia	73.2	Honolulu County, HI	55.3	**Clarksville, TN** (city) Montgomery County	61.2
Michigan	74.1	El Dorado County, CA	56.3	**Corpus Christi, TX** (city) Nueces County	63.7
Kentucky	74.2	Thurston County, WA	56.4	**Chino Hills, CA** (city) San Bernardino County	66.7
Idaho	74.5	Montgomery County, TN	59.4	**Henderson, NV** (city) Clark County	67.2

RANKINGS & COMPARISONS

Note: (1) Ranking tables cover all states and counties, and places with an overall population of at least 125,000, OR an overall population of at least 25,000 where the Hispanic/Latino population is at least 20% of the overall population. In states where less than five places meet either of these criteria, we have included places with at least 10,000 total population with the highest percentage of Hispanic/Latino population. These places are identified with an asterisk (*); Please refer to the User's Guide for a full explanation of data.

Language Spoken at Home: Spanish

(Universe: Population 5 Years and Over)

Central American: Costa Rican

Top 10 States, Counties, and Places[1]

Sorted by Number in Descending Order — U.S. = 89,133

State	Number	County	Number	Place	Number
Florida	15,998	Los Angeles County, CA	6,612	**New York, NY** (city)	4,637
New Jersey	15,798	Miami-Dade County, FL	6,121	**Los Angeles, CA** (city) Los Angeles County	2,114
California	14,732	Union County, NJ	3,151	**Brooklyn, NY** (borough) Kings County	1,628
New York	7,977	Broward County, FL	2,236	**Queens, NY** (borough) Queens County	1,508
Texas	4,170	Somerset County, NJ	1,918	**Miami, FL** (city) Miami-Dade County	1,315
North Carolina	3,915	Essex County, NJ	1,853	**Philadelphia, PA** (city) Philadelphia County	1,052
Pennsylvania	3,054	Kings County, NY	1,628	**Bronx, NY** (borough) Bronx County	593
Massachusetts	2,739	Bergen County, NJ	1,572		
Georgia	2,299	Passaic County, NJ	1,536		
Maryland	1,782	Morris County, NJ	1,524		

Sorted by Number in Ascending Order — U.S. = 89,133

State	Number	County	Number	Place	Number
Oregon	388	Contra Costa County, CA	580	**Bronx, NY** (borough) Bronx County	593
Wisconsin	516	Bronx County, NY	593	**Philadelphia, PA** (city) Philadelphia County	1,052
Colorado	518	Clark County, NV	634	**Miami, FL** (city) Miami-Dade County	1,315
Michigan	553	Maricopa County, AZ	683	**Queens, NY** (borough) Queens County	1,508
Tennessee	608	San Diego County, CA	772	**Brooklyn, NY** (borough) Kings County	1,628
Minnesota	667	Orange County, FL	920	**Los Angeles, CA** (city) Los Angeles County	2,114
Washington	715	Hillsborough County, FL	927	**New York, NY** (city)	4,637
Arizona	868	Nassau County, NY	957		
Louisiana	1,026	Riverside County, CA	957		
Nevada	1,213	Cook County, IL	989		

Sorted by Percent in Descending Order — U.S. = 77.0%

State	Percent	County	Percent	Place	Percent
New Jersey	91.9	Morris County, NJ	97.1	**Miami, FL** (city) Miami-Dade County	96.9
Florida	85.3	Somerset County, NJ	95.4	**Philadelphia, PA** (city) Philadelphia County	89.9
South Carolina	85.2	Union County, NJ	94.0	**Queens, NY** (borough) Queens County	79.9
North Carolina	84.4	Mercer County, NJ	93.2	**Bronx, NY** (borough) Bronx County	77.7
Wisconsin	80.0	Essex County, NJ	92.0	**New York, NY** (city)	77.0
Massachusetts	78.9	Bergen County, NJ	90.8	**Los Angeles, CA** (city) Los Angeles County	72.1
Pennsylvania	78.7	Miami-Dade County, FL	90.4	**Brooklyn, NY** (borough) Kings County	70.8
Louisiana	76.7	Philadelphia County, PA	89.9		
Nevada	76.5	Passaic County, NJ	88.2		
Texas	76.3	Orange County, FL	87.0		

Sorted by Percent in Ascending Order — U.S. = 77.0%

State	Percent	County	Percent	Place	Percent
Colorado	44.5	Contra Costa County, CA	53.0	**Brooklyn, NY** (borough) Kings County	70.8
Oregon	54.0	Maricopa County, AZ	56.0	**Los Angeles, CA** (city) Los Angeles County	72.1
Arizona	55.1	San Diego County, CA	67.2	**New York, NY** (city)	77.0
Washington	60.0	Clark County, NV	68.6	**Bronx, NY** (borough) Bronx County	77.7
Illinois	64.8	Kings County, NY	70.8	**Queens, NY** (borough) Queens County	79.9
Tennessee	67.0	Los Angeles County, CA	73.6	**Philadelphia, PA** (city) Philadelphia County	89.9
Minnesota	69.4	Orange County, CA	75.3	**Miami, FL** (city) Miami-Dade County	96.9
Virginia	70.3	Cook County, IL	76.9		
Maryland	71.4	Suffolk County, NY	77.5		
California	71.6	Bronx County, NY	77.7		

Note: (1) Ranking tables cover all states and counties, and places with an overall population of at least 125,000, OR an overall population of at least 25,000 where the Hispanic/Latino population is at least 20% of the overall population. In states where less than five places meet either of these criteria, we have included places with at least 10,000 total population with the highest percentage of Hispanic/Latino population. These places are identified with an asterisk (*); Please refer to the User's Guide for a full explanation of data.

Language Spoken at Home: Spanish

(Universe: Population 5 Years and Over)

Central American: Guatemalan

Top 10 States, Counties, and Places[1]

Sorted by Number in Descending Order — U.S. = 825,152

State	Number	County	Number	Place	Number
California	290,126	Los Angeles County, CA	198,085	**Los Angeles, CA** (city) Los Angeles County	126,587
Florida	72,017	Harris County, TX	26,596	**New York, NY** (city)	23,942
New York	55,259	Cook County, IL	20,572	**Houston, TX** (city) Harris County	21,165
Texas	51,761	Miami-Dade County, FL	20,204	**Chicago, IL** (city) Cook County	14,303
New Jersey	37,719	Palm Beach County, FL	19,189	**Providence, RI** (city) Providence County	11,089
Georgia	28,609	Providence County, RI	16,308	**Queens, NY** (borough) Queens County	11,060
Massachusetts	26,881	Orange County, CA	12,985	**Stamford, CT** (city/town) Fairfield County	8,083
Illinois	26,500	San Bernardino County, CA	12,382	**Trenton, NJ** (city) Mercer County	7,148
Maryland	25,911	Queens County, NY	11,060	**Brooklyn, NY** (borough) Kings County	5,946
Virginia	24,481	Riverside County, CA	10,836	**Phoenix, AZ** (city) Maricopa County	5,257

Sorted by Number in Ascending Order — U.S. = 825,152

State	Number	County	Number	Place	Number
New Hampshire	488	Nobles County, MN	240	**Minneapolis, MN** (city) Hennepin County	499
Idaho	823	Caroline County, MD	367	**Alhambra, CA** (city) Los Angeles County	645
Wisconsin	916	Milwaukee County, WI	455	**Lexington*, NE** (city) Dawson County	646
District of Columbia	1,207	Norfolk County, MA	533	**Bell, CA** (city) Los Angeles County	729
South Dakota	1,312	Pinal County, AZ	535	**North Las Vegas, NV** (city) Clark County	751
Mississippi	1,613	Gilmer County, GA	604	**Pawtucket*, RI** (city) Providence County	764
New Mexico	2,159	Sonoma County, CA	635	**Victorville, CA** (city) San Bernardino County	792
Kentucky	2,576	Lee County, AL	646	**West Valley City, UT** (city) Salt Lake County	802
Minnesota	3,059	Loudoun County, VA	659	**Salt Lake City, UT** (city) Salt Lake County	803
Arkansas	3,153	Monterey County, CA	659	**Lake Elsinore, CA** (city) Riverside County	830

Sorted by Percent in Descending Order — U.S. = 90.5%

State	Percent	County	Percent	Place	Percent
South Dakota	97.3	Burke County, NC	100.0	**Cathedral City, CA** (city) Riverside County	100.0
Rhode Island	95.9	Dawson County, NE	100.0	**Lexington*, NE** (city) Dawson County	100.0
California	93.7	Minnehaha County, SD	100.0	**Lynwood, CA** (city) Los Angeles County	100.0
Florida	92.7	Marin County, CA	99.1	**Montebello, CA** (city) Los Angeles County	100.0
Nebraska	92.5	Franklin County, AL	98.9	**Newark, NJ** (city) Essex County	100.0
Connecticut	92.4	Gordon County, GA	98.9	**San Rafael, CA** (city) Marin County	100.0
Delaware	92.3	Santa Fe County, NM	98.8	**Sioux Falls, SD** (city) Minnehaha County	100.0
Texas	92.0	Murray County, GA	98.7	**West Palm Beach, FL** (city) Palm Beach County	99.8
Georgia	91.9	Rockland County, NY	97.9	**Wheaton, MD** (cdp) Montgomery County	99.6
South Carolina	91.7	Oklahoma County, OK	97.6	**Lawrence, MA** (city) Essex County	99.4

Sorted by Percent in Ascending Order — U.S. = 90.5%

State	Percent	County	Percent	Place	Percent
Wisconsin	52.9	Nobles County, MN	31.0	**Minneapolis, MN** (city) Hennepin County	68.5
Minnesota	63.8	Lake County, IL	65.7	**Lancaster, CA** (city) Los Angeles County	76.4
New Hampshire	69.7	Norfolk County, MA	67.2	**La Puente, CA** (city) Los Angeles County	78.0
District of Columbia	70.3	Hartford County, CT	68.4	**Sacramento, CA** (city) Sacramento County	78.3
Washington	75.1	Hennepin County, MN	70.3	**North Las Vegas, NV** (city) Clark County	78.9
Kentucky	75.6	Pima County, AZ	70.9	**Manhattan, NY** (borough) New York County	82.3
Michigan	76.0	Sonoma County, CA	72.6	**San Antonio, TX** (city) Bexar County	83.3
Pennsylvania	76.4	Prince George's County, MD	74.5	**West New York, NJ** (town) Hudson County	83.4
Indiana	78.8	Milwaukee County, WI	75.0	**Santa Clarita, CA** (city) Los Angeles County	83.7
Missouri	79.1	Sacramento County, CA	78.4	**Bakersfield, CA** (city) Kern County	84.6

Note: (1) Ranking tables cover all states and counties, and places with an overall population of at least 125,000, OR an overall population of at least 25,000 where the Hispanic/Latino population is at least 20% of the overall population. In states where less than five places meet either of these criteria, we have included places with at least 10,000 total population with the highest percentage of Hispanic/Latino population. These places are identified with an asterisk (*); Please refer to the User's Guide for a full explanation of data.

RANKINGS & COMPARISONS

Language Spoken at Home: Spanish

(Universe: Population 5 Years and Over)

Central American: Honduran

Top 10 States, Counties, and Places[1]

Sorted by Number in Descending Order — U.S. = 502,536

State	Number	County	Number	Place	Number
Florida	96,470	Miami-Dade County, FL	53,037	**New York, NY** (city)	37,303
Texas	74,263	Harris County, TX	38,291	**Houston, TX** (city) Harris County	27,464
California	61,440	Los Angeles County, CA	37,716	**Miami, FL** (city) Miami-Dade County	24,330
New York	56,980	Bronx County, NY	16,117	**Los Angeles, CA** (city) Los Angeles County	20,561
New Jersey	28,360	Jefferson Parish, LA	11,788	**Bronx, NY** (borough) Bronx County	16,117
North Carolina	24,760	Dallas County, TX	11,700	**Brooklyn, NY** (borough) Kings County	8,908
Virginia	22,116	Broward County, FL	9,526	**Queens, NY** (borough) Queens County	7,607
Louisiana	21,313	Kings County, NY	8,908	**Dallas, TX** (city) Dallas County	6,638
Georgia	16,352	Hudson County, NJ	7,898	**Charlotte, NC** (city) Mecklenburg County	6,336
Maryland	13,124	Palm Beach County, FL	7,749	**Hempstead (town), NY** (town) Nassau County	5,830

Sorted by Number in Ascending Order — U.S. = 502,536

State	Number	County	Number	Place	Number
District of Columbia	882	New Haven County, CT	572	**Miramar, FL** (city) Broward County	839
Iowa	906	Kern County, CA	656	**Oklahoma City, OK** (city) Oklahoma County	884
Kentucky	1,109	Fresno County, CA	784	**Philadelphia, PA** (city) Philadelphia County	885
Oregon	1,121	Johnston County, NC	803	**Staten Island, NY** (borough) Richmond County	940
Arkansas	1,137	Hall County, GA	865	**South Miami Heights, FL** (cdp) Miami-Dade County	943
Nebraska	1,376	Philadelphia County, PA	885	**Las Vegas, NV** (city) Clark County	981
Michigan	1,491	Elkhart County, IN	940	**Newburgh, NY** (city) Orange County	1,008
Mississippi	1,569	Richmond County, NY	940	**North Miami Beach, FL** (city) Miami-Dade County	1,033
Wisconsin	1,741	Hartford County, CT	953	**Pasadena, TX** (city) Harris County	1,054
Utah	1,860	Polk County, FL	993	**Yonkers, NY** (city) Westchester County	1,089

Sorted by Percent in Descending Order — U.S. = 91.3%

State	Percent	County	Percent	Place	Percent
North Carolina	95.7	Hall County, GA	100.0	**Aurora, CO** (city) Arapahoe County	100.0
Kansas	95.4	Atlantic County, NJ	99.4	**Brentwood, NY** (cdp) Suffolk County	100.0
Florida	94.7	Duplin County, NC	99.4	**Pasadena, CA** (city) Los Angeles County	100.0
Texas	94.5	Loudoun County, VA	99.1	**Springfield, VA** (cdp) Fairfax County	100.0
New Jersey	94.1	Davidson County, TN	98.9	**Wheaton, MD** (cdp) Montgomery County	100.0
Virginia	93.9	Durham County, NC	98.7	**Durham, NC** (city) Durham County	99.5
Oklahoma	93.5	Morris County, NJ	98.5	**Plainfield, NJ** (city) Union County	99.4
California	92.8	Dallas County, TX	98.2	**Miami Beach, FL** (city) Miami-Dade County	99.2
Georgia	92.6	Union County, NJ	97.8	**New Brunswick, NJ** (city) Middlesex County	99.1
Indiana	92.3	Fairfax County, VA	97.6	**Waukegan, IL** (city) Lake County	99.1

Sorted by Percent in Ascending Order — U.S. = 91.3%

State	Percent	County	Percent	Place	Percent
District of Columbia	49.9	Saint Tammany Parish, LA	73.2	**Las Vegas, NV** (city) Clark County	78.5
Oregon	70.9	Prince George's County, MD	73.3	**Phoenix, AZ** (city) Maricopa County	79.0
Arkansas	72.6	Baltimore County, MD	77.4	**Memphis, TN** (city) Shelby County	81.4
Kentucky	75.0	King County, WA	79.6	**Staten Island, NY** (borough) Richmond County	82.0
Ohio	76.3	New Haven County, CT	80.1	**Philadelphia, PA** (city) Philadelphia County	82.6
Mississippi	78.0	Middlesex County, MA	81.1	**Baltimore, MD** (independent city)	83.9
Washington	78.3	Maricopa County, AZ	81.3	**New Orleans, LA** (city) Orleans Parish	84.4
Arizona	80.9	Richmond County, NY	82.0	**Boston, MA** (city) Suffolk County	84.7
Pennsylvania	80.9	Philadelphia County, PA	82.6	**Pasadena, TX** (city) Harris County	87.2
Alabama	81.1	Shelby County, TN	82.8	**Metairie, LA** (cdp) Jefferson Parish	87.6

Note: (1) Ranking tables cover all states and counties, and places with an overall population of at least 125,000, OR an overall population of at least 25,000 where the Hispanic/Latino population is at least 20% of the overall population. In states where less than five places meet either of these criteria, we have included places with at least 10,000 total population with the highest percentage of Hispanic/Latino population. These places are identified with an asterisk (*); Please refer to the User's Guide for a full explanation of data.

Language Spoken at Home: Spanish

(Universe: Population 5 Years and Over)

Central American: Nicaraguan

Top 10 States, Counties, and Places[1]

Sorted by Number in Descending Order — U.S. = 280,317

State	Number	County	Number	Place	Number
Florida	127,100	Miami-Dade County, FL	103,198	**Miami, FL** (city) Miami-Dade County	29,513
California	76,400	Los Angeles County, CA	32,749	**Los Angeles, CA** (city) Los Angeles County	14,751
Texas	13,024	San Mateo County, CA	6,984	**Hialeah, FL** (city) Miami-Dade County	10,566
New York	10,433	Broward County, FL	6,081	**New York, NY** (city)	8,209
Virginia	6,434	San Bernardino County, CA	5,330	**Fountainebleau, FL** (cdp) Miami-Dade County	7,020
New Jersey	5,863	San Francisco County, CA	5,206	**San Francisco, CA** (city) San Francisco County	5,206
Louisiana	5,562	Harris County, TX	5,194	**Tamiami, FL** (cdp) Miami-Dade County	3,674
Maryland	5,367	Contra Costa County, CA	5,002	**Kendale Lakes, FL** (cdp) Miami-Dade County	3,401
North Carolina	3,311	Alameda County, CA	4,913	**Daly City, CA** (city) San Mateo County	3,393
Nevada	3,298	Jefferson Parish, LA	3,570	**Houston, TX** (city) Harris County	3,163

Sorted by Number in Ascending Order — U.S. = 280,317

State	Number	County	Number	Place	Number
Michigan	430	King County, WA	509	**San Diego, CA** (city) San Diego County	575
Oregon	526	Sonoma County, CA	608	**Sacramento, CA** (city) Sacramento County	607
Missouri	528	Gwinnett County, GA	792	**Jacksonville, FL** (city) Duval County	839
Connecticut	644	Maricopa County, AZ	809	**Richmond, CA** (city) Contra Costa County	839
Tennessee	686	Duval County, FL	839	**Austin, TX** (city) Travis County	853
Ohio	727	Camden County, NJ	859	**South Gate, CA** (city) Los Angeles County	859
District of Columbia	761	Stanislaus County, CA	893	**Chicago, IL** (city) Cook County	891
Colorado	792	Bexar County, TX	899	**Pembroke Pines, FL** (city) Broward County	891
Minnesota	820	Lee County, FL	983	**Las Vegas, NV** (city) Clark County	907
South Carolina	900	Collier County, FL	1,020	**Homestead, FL** (city) Miami-Dade County	912

Sorted by Percent in Descending Order — U.S. = 87.6%

State	Percent	County	Percent	Place	Percent
Florida	95.0	Miami-Dade County, FL	97.2	**Kendale Lakes, FL** (cdp) Miami-Dade County	100.0
Virginia	89.4	Collier County, FL	96.4	**The Hammocks, FL** (cdp) Miami-Dade County	100.0
Indiana	88.3	Lee County, FL	96.4	**Richmond West, FL** (cdp) Miami-Dade County	99.4
District of Columbia	88.2	Montgomery County, MD	96.2	**South Gate, CA** (city) Los Angeles County	99.1
Louisiana	86.8	Bronx County, NY	95.3	**Fountainebleau, FL** (cdp) Miami-Dade County	98.7
South Carolina	86.3	Gwinnett County, GA	95.0	**Hialeah, FL** (city) Miami-Dade County	98.6
New York	85.5	Prince William County, VA	94.5	**Kendall, FL** (cdp) Miami-Dade County	98.1
Maryland	85.0	Stanislaus County, CA	92.4	**Oakland, CA** (city) Alameda County	97.7
Texas	85.0	Palm Beach County, FL	91.5	**Miami, FL** (city) Miami-Dade County	97.6
Nevada	84.7	Hillsborough County, FL	91.1	**West Little River, FL** (cdp) Miami-Dade County	97.5

Sorted by Percent in Ascending Order — U.S. = 87.6%

State	Percent	County	Percent	Place	Percent
Ohio	55.5	Sonoma County, CA	57.6	**San Diego, CA** (city) San Diego County	63.7
Michigan	57.3	Maricopa County, AZ	65.9	**Sacramento, CA** (city) Sacramento County	65.6
Oregon	58.7	San Diego County, CA	66.2	**San Jose, CA** (city) Santa Clara County	73.6
Colorado	63.0	King County, WA	71.2	**Jacksonville, FL** (city) Duval County	77.1
Missouri	65.1	Prince George's County, MD	72.9	**Metairie, LA** (cdp) Jefferson Parish	81.8
Washington	67.7	Riverside County, CA	75.4	**Pembroke Pines, FL** (city) Broward County	82.2
Arizona	68.7	Sacramento County, CA	75.9	**Manhattan, NY** (borough) New York County	82.4
Illinois	69.6	Orange County, CA	76.1	**Brooklyn, NY** (borough) Kings County	83.3
Massachusetts	69.9	Santa Clara County, CA	76.1	**San Francisco, CA** (city) San Francisco County	84.8
Pennsylvania	74.5	Bexar County, TX	77.1	**Antioch, CA** (city) Contra Costa County	85.2

Note: (1) Ranking tables cover all states and counties, and places with an overall population of at least 125,000, OR an overall population of at least 25,000 where the Hispanic/Latino population is at least 20% of the overall population. In states where less than five places meet either of these criteria, we have included places with at least 10,000 total population with the highest percentage of Hispanic/Latino population. These places are identified with an asterisk (*); Please refer to the User's Guide for a full explanation of data.

Language Spoken at Home: Spanish

(Universe: Population 5 Years and Over)

Central American: Panamanian

Top 10 States, Counties, and Places[1]

Sorted by Number in Descending Order — U.S. = 93,044

State	Number	County	Number	Place	Number
Florida	19,667	Kings County, NY	9,334	**New York, NY** (city)	14,650
New York	17,740	Miami-Dade County, FL	7,038	**Brooklyn, NY** (borough) Kings County	9,334
California	9,593	Los Angeles County, CA	3,000	**Queens, NY** (borough) Queens County	2,625
Texas	8,162	Broward County, FL	2,819	**Bronx, NY** (borough) Bronx County	1,544
Georgia	4,408	Queens County, NY	2,625	**Los Angeles, CA** (city) Los Angeles County	1,153
Virginia	3,958	Orange County, FL	2,008	**Miami, FL** (city) Miami-Dade County	1,055
New Jersey	3,439	San Diego County, CA	1,583	**San Antonio, TX** (city) Bexar County	924
North Carolina	3,325	Hillsborough County, FL	1,564	**San Diego, CA** (city) San Diego County	921
Maryland	2,437	Bronx County, NY	1,544	**Manhattan, NY** (borough) New York County	897
Massachusetts	1,820	Bexar County, TX	1,415	**Hempstead (town), NY** (town) Nassau County	797

Sorted by Number in Ascending Order — U.S. = 93,044

State	Number	County	Number	Place	Number
New Mexico	283	Pierce County, WA	362	**Houston, TX** (city) Harris County	495
Wisconsin	324	Sacramento County, CA	443	**Killeen, TX** (city) Bell County	712
Minnesota	377	Essex County, NJ	473	**Fayetteville, NC** (city) Cumberland County	721
Indiana	409	Orange County, CA	479	**Jacksonville, FL** (city) Duval County	744
Oklahoma	428	Montgomery County, MD	544	**Hempstead (town), NY** (town) Nassau County	797
Mississippi	472	Hudson County, NJ	599	**Manhattan, NY** (borough) New York County	897
Missouri	534	Fairfax County, VA	602	**San Diego, CA** (city) San Diego County	921
Michigan	559	Clark County, NV	639	**San Antonio, TX** (city) Bexar County	924
Connecticut	565	Brevard County, FL	671	**Miami, FL** (city) Miami-Dade County	1,055
Louisiana	669	Maricopa County, AZ	698	**Los Angeles, CA** (city) Los Angeles County	1,153

Sorted by Percent in Descending Order — U.S. = 62.9%

State	Percent	County	Percent	Place	Percent
Florida	80.0	Miami-Dade County, FL	93.1	**Miami, FL** (city) Miami-Dade County	98.5
Mississippi	71.5	Broward County, FL	87.8	**San Antonio, TX** (city) Bexar County	75.6
South Carolina	69.4	Harris County, TX	85.1	**Killeen, TX** (city) Bell County	73.8
Texas	66.6	Palm Beach County, FL	82.2	**Los Angeles, CA** (city) Los Angeles County	73.4
North Carolina	65.7	Riverside County, CA	79.9	**Queens, NY** (borough) Queens County	73.0
Kentucky	65.0	Orange County, FL	78.7	**Houston, TX** (city) Harris County	70.6
Georgia	64.5	Dallas County, TX	77.9	**Brooklyn, NY** (borough) Kings County	69.7
New York	63.5	Cumberland County, NC	76.4	**Jacksonville, FL** (city) Duval County	68.8
New Jersey	61.8	Hudson County, NJ	75.7	**San Diego, CA** (city) San Diego County	67.7
Massachusetts	59.7	Brevard County, FL	73.9	**Fayetteville, NC** (city) Cumberland County	67.6

Sorted by Percent in Ascending Order — U.S. = 62.9%

State	Percent	County	Percent	Place	Percent
New Mexico	37.4	New York County, NY	39.9	**Manhattan, NY** (borough) New York County	39.9
Michigan	42.4	Sacramento County, CA	47.0	**Hempstead (town), NY** (town) Nassau County	58.4
Missouri	43.7	Pierce County, WA	47.2	**Bronx, NY** (borough) Bronx County	61.1
Wisconsin	43.9	Clark County, NV	55.1	**New York, NY** (city)	66.0
Ohio	45.7	Essex County, NJ	56.2	**Fayetteville, NC** (city) Cumberland County	67.6
Oklahoma	45.7	San Bernardino County, CA	58.9	**San Diego, CA** (city) San Diego County	67.7
Indiana	47.1	Maricopa County, AZ	59.1	**Jacksonville, FL** (city) Duval County	68.8
Washington	47.6	Nassau County, NY	59.9	**Brooklyn, NY** (borough) Kings County	69.7
Tennessee	49.2	Prince George's County, MD	61.0	**Houston, TX** (city) Harris County	70.6
Alabama	51.1	Bronx County, NY	61.1	**Queens, NY** (borough) Queens County	73.0

Note: (1) Ranking tables cover all states and counties, and places with an overall population of at least 125,000, OR an overall population of at least 25,000 where the Hispanic/Latino population is at least 20% of the overall population. In states where less than five places meet either of these criteria, we have included places with at least 10,000 total population with the highest percentage of Hispanic/Latino population. These places are identified with an asterisk (*); Please refer to the User's Guide for a full explanation of data.

Language Spoken at Home: Spanish

(Universe: Population 5 Years and Over)

Central American: Salvadoran

Top 10 States, Counties, and Places[1]

Sorted by Number in Descending Order — U.S. = 1,348,423

State	Number
California	501,736
Texas	195,120
New York	120,051
Virginia	95,619
Maryland	91,150
New Jersey	45,720
Florida	44,454
Massachusetts	30,923
North Carolina	28,854
Georgia	28,352

County	Number
Los Angeles County, CA	326,209
Harris County, TX	105,917
Montgomery County, MD	44,872
Suffolk County, NY	38,381
Dallas County, TX	38,375
Nassau County, NY	36,272
Fairfax County, VA	32,650
Prince George's County, MD	31,610
San Bernardino County, CA	21,183
Prince William County, VA	20,365

Place	Number
Los Angeles, CA (city) Los Angeles County	208,046
Houston, TX (city) Harris County	69,370
New York, NY (city)	34,872
Hempstead (town), NY (town) Nassau County	25,024
Islip, NY (town) Suffolk County	21,682
Queens, NY (borough) Queens County	18,878
Dallas, TX (city) Dallas County	15,870
San Francisco, CA (city) San Francisco County	13,133
Irving, TX (city) Dallas County	11,441
Brentwood, NY (cdp) Suffolk County	9,797

Sorted by Number in Ascending Order — U.S. = 1,348,423

State	Number
Hawaii	446
Idaho	594
Alaska	752
Wisconsin	1,230
Alabama	1,323
New Mexico	1,360
Kentucky	1,814
Oklahoma	1,933
Michigan	2,217
South Carolina	2,742

County	Number
Duval County, FL	518
Placer County, CA	619
Cuyahoga County, OH	635
Cache County, UT	688
Williamson County, TX	695
Buncombe County, NC	744
Pima County, AZ	814
Monmouth County, NJ	829
Napa County, CA	831
Ocean County, NJ	837

Place	Number
Jacksonville, FL (city) Duval County	518
Corona, CA (city) Riverside County	644
Spring Valley, NV (cdp) Clark County	688
West Valley City, UT (city) Salt Lake County	708
Bridgeport, CT (city/town) Fairfield County	713
Santa Rosa, CA (city) Sonoma County	737
Jersey City, NJ (city) Hudson County	748
Willowbrook, CA (cdp) Los Angeles County	755
Lake Worth, FL (city) Palm Beach County	787
Hesperia, CA (city) San Bernardino County	792

Sorted by Percent in Descending Order — U.S. = 92.2%

State	Percent
Texas	95.7
Kansas	95.0
Virginia	94.8
Rhode Island	94.7
New York	94.6
Georgia	94.5
New Jersey	94.4
Iowa	94.2
Arkansas	94.0
Connecticut	93.4

County	Percent
Alamance County, NC	100.0
Camden County, NJ	100.0
Rutherford County, TN	100.0
Santa Cruz County, CA	100.0
Hall County, GA	99.0
Arlington County, VA	98.6
El Paso County, TX	98.5
Gwinnett County, GA	98.3
DeKalb County, GA	98.1
New Haven County, CT	97.9

Place	Percent
Gainesville, GA (city) Hall County	100.0
Lewisville, TX (city) Denton County	100.0
Mission Bend, TX (cdp) Fort Bend County	100.0
Montgomery Village, MD (cdp) Montgomery County	100.0
Grand Prairie, TX (city) Dallas County	99.4
Norwalk, CA (city) Los Angeles County	99.4
Plainfield, NJ (city) Union County	99.4
Providence, RI (city) Providence County	99.3
Westmont, CA (cdp) Los Angeles County	99.3
Chelsea, MA (city) Suffolk County	99.1

Sorted by Percent in Ascending Order — U.S. = 92.2%

State	Percent
Hawaii	54.3
District of Columbia	67.8
Alabama	76.8
Pennsylvania	78.8
Missouri	82.6
Oregon	82.6
Utah	82.6
Idaho	83.9
Ohio	84.0
Kentucky	84.1

County	Percent
Duval County, FL	65.7
El Paso County, CO	70.5
Baltimore County, MD	74.1
Napa County, CA	75.1
Pima County, AZ	75.2
Prince George's County, MD	77.4
Multnomah County, OR	77.7
San Diego County, CA	77.8
Frederick County, MD	79.1
Sonoma County, CA	79.1

Place	Percent
Jacksonville, FL (city) Duval County	65.7
San Diego, CA (city) San Diego County	71.5
Antioch, CA (city) Contra Costa County	74.1
Santa Clarita, CA (city) Los Angeles County	75.9
Lancaster, CA (city) Los Angeles County	76.1
Fairfield, CA (city) Solano County	77.4
Corona, CA (city) Riverside County	77.9
Burbank, CA (city) Los Angeles County	79.3
Simi Valley, CA (city) Ventura County	80.7
Jersey City, NJ (city) Hudson County	81.0

Note: (1) Ranking tables cover all states and counties, and places with an overall population of at least 125,000, OR an overall population of at least 25,000 where the Hispanic/Latino population is at least 20% of the overall population. In states where less than five places meet either of these criteria, we have included places with at least 10,000 total population with the highest percentage of Hispanic/Latino population. These places are identified with an asterisk (*); Please refer to the User's Guide for a full explanation of data.

Language Spoken at Home: Spanish

(Universe: Population 5 Years and Over)

Cuban

Top 10 States, Counties, and Places[1]

Sorted by Number in Descending Order — U.S. = 1,309,854

State	Number	County	Number	Place	Number
Florida	990,912	Miami-Dade County, FL	737,241	**Hialeah, FL** (city) Miami-Dade County	148,189
New Jersey	62,508	Broward County, FL	60,746	**Miami, FL** (city) Miami-Dade County	126,813
California	50,832	Hillsborough County, FL	45,672	**Tamiami, FL** (cdp) Miami-Dade County	32,575
New York	42,031	Palm Beach County, FL	29,695	**New York, NY** (city)	27,567
Texas	26,217	Los Angeles County, CA	29,135	**Kendale Lakes, FL** (cdp) Miami-Dade County	24,774
Nevada	14,664	Hudson County, NJ	26,882	**Fountainebleau, FL** (cdp) Miami-Dade County	23,229
Georgia	13,333	Orange County, FL	15,855	**Kendall, FL** (cdp) Miami-Dade County	21,254
Illinois	11,773	Lee County, FL	15,449	**Westchester, FL** (cdp) Miami-Dade County	19,578
North Carolina	8,974	Clark County, NV	13,887	**Tampa, FL** (city) Hillsborough County	16,068
Pennsylvania	7,847	Collier County, FL	12,449	**University Park, FL** (cdp) Miami-Dade County	16,013

Sorted by Number in Ascending Order — U.S. = 1,309,854

State	Number	County	Number	Place	Number
Maine	250	Hamilton County, OH	255	**Columbus, OH** (city) Franklin County	373
Arkansas	325	Arapahoe County, CO	269	**Santa Clarita, CA** (city) Los Angeles County	390
West Virginia	356	Cuyahoga County, OH	269	**Seattle, WA** (city) King County	421
Hawaii	445	Dutchess County, NY	332	**Brookhaven, NY** (town) Suffolk County	435
Iowa	493	New Castle County, DE	342	**North Hempstead, NY** (town) Nassau County	436
New Hampshire	535	Oakland County, MI	343	**Anaheim, CA** (city) Orange County	440
Delaware	562	Shelby County, TN	351	**Atlanta, GA** (city) Fulton County	443
Utah	782	Baltimore County, MD	354	**Islip, NY** (town) Suffolk County	446
Rhode Island	870	Sussex County, NJ	356	**Riverside, CA** (city) Riverside County	450
Nebraska	872	Pierce County, WA	361	**New Orleans, LA** (city) Orleans Parish	479

Sorted by Percent in Descending Order — U.S. = 82.3%

State	Percent	County	Percent	Place	Percent
Florida	90.7	Clay County, MO	97.3	**Fountainebleau, FL** (cdp) Miami-Dade County	98.2
Nevada	82.1	Miami-Dade County, FL	95.5	**Tamiami, FL** (cdp) Miami-Dade County	97.8
New Jersey	78.1	Hudson County, NJ	91.6	**Lehigh Acres, FL** (cdp) Lee County	97.7
Kentucky	77.0	El Paso County, TX	91.3	**University Park, FL** (cdp) Miami-Dade County	97.6
New Mexico	75.0	Lee County, FL	90.7	**West Little River, FL** (cdp) Miami-Dade County	97.6
Texas	71.2	Jefferson County, KY	88.7	**Kendall West, FL** (cdp) Miami-Dade County	97.0
California	65.5	Forsyth County, NC	88.5	**Miami, FL** (city) Miami-Dade County	97.0
Missouri	65.4	Ingham County, MI	88.2	**Union City, NJ** (city) Hudson County	97.0
Arizona	64.9	Highlands County, FL	87.7	**North Miami, FL** (city) Miami-Dade County	96.9
Louisiana	64.2	Polk County, FL	86.7	**Westchester, FL** (cdp) Miami-Dade County	96.8

Sorted by Percent in Ascending Order — U.S. = 82.3%

State	Percent	County	Percent	Place	Percent
Maine	31.5	Cuyahoga County, OH	29.3	**Brookhaven, NY** (town) Suffolk County	32.6
Colorado	37.5	Hamilton County, OH	30.8	**Staten Island, NY** (borough) Richmond County	42.4
Hawaii	38.7	New Castle County, DE	33.0	**Islip, NY** (town) Suffolk County	43.5
Wisconsin	38.7	Dutchess County, NY	37.6	**San Jose, CA** (city) Santa Clara County	43.6
New Hampshire	41.3	Arapahoe County, CO	37.7	**Oyster Bay, NY** (town) Nassau County	46.8
Ohio	41.9	Suffolk County, NY	38.0	**Santa Clarita, CA** (city) Los Angeles County	47.8
Delaware	42.6	Baltimore County, MD	39.5	**San Diego, CA** (city) San Diego County	47.9
Iowa	43.0	New Haven County, CT	40.1	**North Hempstead, NY** (town) Nassau County	48.1
West Virginia	43.6	Shelby County, TN	41.0	**Seattle, WA** (city) King County	48.2
Utah	44.3	San Mateo County, CA	42.1	**Riverside, CA** (city) Riverside County	49.1

Note: (1) Ranking tables cover all states and counties, and places with an overall population of at least 125,000, OR an overall population of at least 25,000 where the Hispanic/Latino population is at least 20% of the overall population. In states where less than five places meet either of these criteria, we have included places with at least 10,000 total population with the highest percentage of Hispanic/Latino population. These places are identified with an asterisk (*); Please refer to the User's Guide for a full explanation of data.

Language Spoken at Home: Spanish

(Universe: Population 5 Years and Over)

Dominican Republic

Top 10 States, Counties, and Places[1]

Sorted by Number in Descending Order — U.S. = 1,126,270

State	Number	County	Number	Place	Number
New York	584,085	Bronx County, NY	202,708	**New York, NY** (city)	504,900
New Jersey	151,709	New York County, NY	149,472	**Bronx, NY** (borough) Bronx County	202,708
Florida	132,272	Queens County, NY	76,867	**Manhattan, NY** (borough) New York County	149,472
Massachusetts	85,406	Kings County, NY	72,792	**Queens, NY** (borough) Queens County	76,867
Pennsylvania	42,254	Miami-Dade County, FL	47,405	**Brooklyn, NY** (borough) Kings County	72,792
Rhode Island	30,763	Essex County, MA	43,331	**Lawrence, MA** (city) Essex County	25,695
Connecticut	17,749	Passaic County, NJ	36,805	**Providence, RI** (city) Providence County	24,129
Georgia	9,783	Hudson County, NJ	33,149	**Paterson, NJ** (city) Passaic County	21,779
North Carolina	9,043	Providence County, RI	29,882	**Boston, MA** (city) Suffolk County	21,095
Maryland	8,793	Broward County, FL	23,427	**Hempstead (town), NY** (town) Nassau County	15,625

Sorted by Number in Ascending Order — U.S. = 1,126,270

State	Number	County	Number	Place	Number
Alabama	494	Ulster County, NY	478	**Ramapo, NY** (town) Rockland County	697
Minnesota	497	Lackawanna County, PA	536	**Los Angeles, CA** (city) Los Angeles County	763
Washington	694	Fulton County, GA	607	**Valley Stream, NY** (village) Nassau County	774
Missouri	886	Sullivan County, NY	620	**Deltona, FL** (city) Volusia County	784
Utah	935	Marion County, FL	726	**Cleveland, OH** (city) Cuyahoga County	799
Wisconsin	987	Pinellas County, FL	771	**North Miami, FL** (city) Miami-Dade County	802
Tennessee	1,010	Bexar County, TX	798	**Tamiami, FL** (cdp) Miami-Dade County	805
Colorado	1,053	Dallas County, TX	816	**West Little River, FL** (cdp) Miami-Dade County	805
South Carolina	1,079	Baltimore County, MD	817	**Syracuse, NY** (city) Onondaga County	813
Delaware	1,103	Plymouth County, MA	825	**Bethlehem, PA** (city) Northampton County	831

Sorted by Percent in Descending Order — U.S. = 91.5%

State	Percent	County	Percent	Place	Percent
New York	94.2	Bronx County, NY	96.6	**Plainfield, NJ** (city) Union County	100.0
Rhode Island	93.6	Passaic County, NJ	96.4	**Atlantic City, NJ** (city) Atlantic County	99.6
New Jersey	93.0	New York County, NY	96.3	**Doral, FL** (city) Miami-Dade County	99.5
Massachusetts	92.7	Lancaster County, PA	96.2	**Elmont, NY** (cdp) Nassau County	98.7
Florida	89.6	Union County, NJ	96.2	**Fountainebleau, FL** (cdp) Miami-Dade County	98.6
Pennsylvania	89.6	Essex County, MA	95.7	**Lawrence, MA** (city) Essex County	98.5
New Hampshire	88.1	Miami-Dade County, FL	95.3	**Kendall West, FL** (cdp) Miami-Dade County	98.3
Louisiana	87.6	Atlantic County, NJ	95.1	**New Brunswick, NJ** (city) Middlesex County	98.2
Alaska	87.4	Providence County, RI	94.8	**Danbury, CT** (city/town) Fairfield County	98.1
Connecticut	86.3	Lehigh County, PA	94.7	**Kendale Lakes, FL** (cdp) Miami-Dade County	98.1

Sorted by Percent in Ascending Order — U.S. = 91.5%

State	Percent	County	Percent	Place	Percent
Tennessee	61.0	Fulton County, GA	57.2	**Alafaya, FL** (cdp) Orange County	64.1
California	63.3	San Diego County, CA	67.0	**Los Angeles, CA** (city) Los Angeles County	67.5
Washington	67.6	Volusia County, FL	67.6	**Deltona, FL** (city) Volusia County	74.8
Virginia	68.3	Baltimore County, MD	67.9	**Coral Springs, FL** (city) Broward County	75.2
Arizona	70.4	Cobb County, GA	68.2	**Town 'n' Country, FL** (cdp) Hillsborough County	76.1
Wisconsin	72.5	Maricopa County, AZ	68.3	**Ramapo, NY** (town) Rockland County	77.8
Michigan	73.2	Fairfax County, VA	69.6	**Waterbury, CT** (city/town) New Haven County	78.5
Missouri	73.6	New London County, CT	70.3	**Homestead, FL** (city) Miami-Dade County	78.7
Alabama	76.1	Monmouth County, NJ	71.1	**Staten Island, NY** (borough) Richmond County	78.7
South Carolina	77.0	Los Angeles County, CA	72.1	**Huntington, NY** (town) Suffolk County	81.0

Note: (1) Ranking tables cover all states and counties, and places with an overall population of at least 125,000, OR an overall population of at least 25,000 where the Hispanic/Latino population is at least 20% of the overall population. In states where less than five places meet either of these criteria, we have included places with at least 10,000 total population with the highest percentage of Hispanic/Latino population. These places are identified with an asterisk (*); Please refer to the User's Guide for a full explanation of data.

Language Spoken at Home: Spanish

(Universe: Population 5 Years and Over)

Mexican

Top 10 States, Counties, and Places[1]

Sorted by Number in Descending Order — U.S. = 20,807,289

State	Number	County	Number	Place	Number
California	7,774,326	Los Angeles County, CA	2,628,596	**Los Angeles, CA** (city) Los Angeles County	991,579
Texas	5,408,330	Harris County, TX	892,826	**Houston, TX** (city) Harris County	507,476
Illinois	1,148,007	Cook County, IL	727,984	**Chicago, IL** (city) Cook County	441,756
Arizona	1,036,366	Maricopa County, AZ	616,917	**San Antonio, TX** (city) Bexar County	432,159
Florida	421,502	Orange County, CA	613,644	**El Paso, TX** (city) El Paso County	376,553
Colorado	397,122	San Diego County, CA	596,054	**Phoenix, AZ** (city) Maricopa County	367,728
Georgia	367,995	Dallas County, TX	563,162	**Dallas, TX** (city) Dallas County	343,802
Washington	362,866	Riverside County, CA	554,295	**New York, NY** (city)	237,363
Nevada	359,796	Hidalgo County, TX	525,236	**San Diego, CA** (city) San Diego County	228,478
North Carolina	341,134	San Bernardino County, CA	516,405	**Santa Ana, CA** (city) Orange County	195,855

Sorted by Number in Ascending Order — U.S. = 20,807,289

State	Number	County	Number	Place	Number
Vermont	911	Becker County, MN	40	**Fort Campbell North*, KY** (cdp) Christian County	112
Maine	1,673	Aroostook County, ME	42	**Great Falls*, MT** (city) Cascade County	193
West Virginia	2,619	Beltrami County, MN	54	**Babylon, NY** (town) Suffolk County	346
North Dakota	3,147	Gladwin County, MI	55	**Grand Forks*, ND** (city) Grand Forks County	350
Montana	3,359	Dickinson County, KS	56	**Schofield Barracks*, HI** (cdp) Honolulu County	371
New Hampshire	3,463	Ogemaw County, MI	60	**Green River*, WY** (city) Sweetwater County	376
District of Columbia	3,835	Trumbull County, OH	64	**Evanston*, WY** (city) Uinta County	386
Rhode Island	5,311	Merrimack County, NH	65	**Juneau*, AK** (borough) Juneau City and Borough	427
South Dakota	5,889	Lewis and Clark County, MT	66	**Warren, MI** (city) Macomb County	431
Alaska	8,129	Menominee County, MI	70	**Rapid City*, SD** (city) Pennington County	444

Sorted by Percent in Descending Order — U.S. = 76.4%

State	Percent	County	Percent	Place	Percent
New Jersey	88.3	Calhoun County, MS	98.8	**Parker*, SC** (cdp) Greenville County	100.0
North Carolina	88.0	Ashe County, NC	98.3	**Windham, CT** (town) Windham County	99.3
Georgia	87.9	Hertford County, NC	98.1	**Bluffton*, SC** (town) Beaufort County	98.8
New York	86.8	Bradley County, AR	97.6	**New Brunswick, NJ** (city) Middlesex County	98.4
Illinois	84.3	Cuming County, NE	97.2	**Manassas, VA** (independent city)	97.8
South Carolina	83.3	Harper County, OK	97.0	**Marumsco, VA** (cdp) Prince William County	97.7
Delaware	82.8	Edgefield County, SC	96.9	**Plainfield, NJ** (city) Union County	97.4
Florida	81.2	Glades County, FL	96.8	**Monroe, NC** (city) Union County	97.0
Alabama	79.8	Starr County, TX	96.8	**White Plains, NY** (city) Westchester County	97.0
Texas	78.8	Presidio County, TX	96.5	**Bridgeton, NJ** (city) Cumberland County	96.8

Sorted by Percent in Ascending Order — U.S. = 76.4%

State	Percent	County	Percent	Place	Percent
Montana	19.9	Trumbull County, OH	5.8	**Billings*, MT** (city) Yellowstone County	16.2
West Virginia	32.1	Lewis and Clark County, MT	8.2	**Fort Campbell North*, KY** (cdp) Christian County	17.0
Hawaii	34.9	Flathead County, MT	8.7	**Great Falls*, MT** (city) Cascade County	22.2
Vermont	36.6	Dickinson County, KS	9.7	**Pueblo West, CO** (cdp) Pueblo County	26.2
Maine	38.3	White Pine County, NV	10.0	**Rapid City*, SD** (city) Pennington County	26.2
North Dakota	38.8	Kanawha County, WV	13.4	**Warren, MI** (city) Macomb County	27.1
Alaska	42.8	Merrimack County, NH	13.5	**Pueblo, CO** (city) Pueblo County	29.4
Wyoming	48.0	Beltrami County, MN	14.4	**Spokane, WA** (city) Spokane County	30.5
South Dakota	50.1	Mecosta County, MI	15.7	**Toledo, OH** (city) Lucas County	33.9
District of Columbia	50.2	Missoula County, MT	16.6	**Schofield Barracks*, HI** (cdp) Honolulu County	34.1

Note: (1) Ranking tables cover all states and counties, and places with an overall population of at least 125,000, OR an overall population of at least 25,000 where the Hispanic/Latino population is at least 20% of the overall population. In states where less than five places meet either of these criteria, we have included places with at least 10,000 total population with the highest percentage of Hispanic/Latino population. These places are identified with an asterisk (*); Please refer to the User's Guide for a full explanation of data.

Language Spoken at Home: Spanish

(Universe: Population 5 Years and Over)

Puerto Rican

Top 10 States, Counties, and Places[1]

Sorted by Number in Descending Order — U.S. = 2,652,253

State	Number	County	Number	Place	Number
New York	685,246	Bronx County, NY	222,629	**New York, NY** (city)	515,835
Florida	546,296	Kings County, NY	128,440	**Bronx, NY** (borough) Bronx County	222,629
New Jersey	268,351	Orange County, FL	105,379	**Brooklyn, NY** (borough) Kings County	128,440
Pennsylvania	212,573	Philadelphia County, PA	83,249	**Philadelphia, PA** (city) Philadelphia County	83,249
Massachusetts	165,348	Cook County, IL	82,984	**Manhattan, NY** (borough) New York County	81,318
Connecticut	163,422	New York County, NY	81,318	**Chicago, IL** (city) Cook County	68,943
Illinois	107,333	Miami-Dade County, FL	79,156	**Queens, NY** (borough) Queens County	67,873
California	70,874	Queens County, NY	67,873	**Hartford, CT** (city/town) Hartford County	33,165
Texas	69,306	Hartford County, CT	65,334	**Newark, NJ** (city) Essex County	31,455
Ohio	45,619	Hillsborough County, FL	58,359	**Springfield, MA** (city) Hampden County	30,711

Sorted by Number in Ascending Order — U.S. = 2,652,253

State	Number	County	Number	Place	Number
Wyoming	162	Kauai County, HI	60	**Waianae*, HI** (cdp) Honolulu County	0
North Dakota	253	Maui County, HI	88	**Makakilo*, HI** (cdp) Honolulu County	27
South Dakota	363	Clark County, WA	93	**Vallejo, CA** (city) Solano County	193
Montana	440	Butte County, CA	97	**West Covina, CA** (city) Los Angeles County	245
Idaho	831	Marion County, OR	126	**Kansas City, MO** (city) Jackson County	282
Nebraska	891	Wichita County, TX	146	**Wichita, KS** (city) Sedgwick County	284
Vermont	965	Perry County, PA	156	**Montgomery, AL** (city) Montgomery County	291
West Virginia	1,051	Schoharie County, NY	170	**Oceanside, CA** (city) San Diego County	296
Alaska	1,529	Adams County, PA	180	**Omaha, NE** (city) Douglas County	299
District of Columbia	1,669	Genesee County, MI	181	**Fremont, CA** (city) Alameda County	311

Sorted by Percent in Descending Order — U.S. = 65.8%

State	Percent	County	Percent	Place	Percent
Florida	75.2	Hendry County, FL	88.6	**Fountainebleau, FL** (cdp) Miami-Dade County	98.9
Rhode Island	75.0	Osceola County, FL	86.5	**West Little River, FL** (cdp) Miami-Dade County	95.7
Connecticut	73.2	Miami-Dade County, FL	85.0	**Doral, FL** (city) Miami-Dade County	91.5
Massachusetts	73.2	Orange County, FL	82.5	**Plant City, FL** (city) Hillsborough County	90.9
New Jersey	69.4	Polk County, FL	82.5	**Buenaventura Lakes, FL** (cdp) Osceola County	90.6
Pennsylvania	68.8	Passaic County, NJ	82.4	**Meadow Woods, FL** (cdp) Orange County	90.4
New York	67.6	Christian County, KY	82.2	**Passaic, NJ** (city) Passaic County	90.1
Illinois	67.1	Dale County, AL	81.5	**Central Falls*, RI** (city) Providence County	89.0
Texas	63.6	Essex County, NJ	81.0	**Hialeah, FL** (city) Miami-Dade County	88.6
Wisconsin	63.5	Windham County, CT	80.6	**The Hammocks, FL** (cdp) Miami-Dade County	88.6

Sorted by Percent in Ascending Order — U.S. = 65.8%

State	Percent	County	Percent	Place	Percent
Hawaii	9.3	Maui County, HI	1.8	**Waianae*, HI** (cdp) Honolulu County	0.0
Wyoming	25.6	Kauai County, HI	3.8	**Makakilo*, HI** (cdp) Honolulu County	2.9
North Dakota	28.5	Hawaii County, HI	5.5	**Urban Honolulu, HI** (cdp) Honolulu County	11.5
Montana	29.3	Clark County, WA	10.2	**Vallejo, CA** (city) Solano County	21.3
Oregon	30.0	Honolulu County, HI	12.7	**Modesto, CA** (city) Stanislaus County	27.7
Idaho	31.7	Butte County, CA	14.4	**Kansas City, MO** (city) Jackson County	29.0
South Dakota	33.5	Marion County, OR	20.2	**Fremont, CA** (city) Alameda County	30.7
Washington	34.3	Wichita County, TX	20.8	**Wichita, KS** (city) Sedgwick County	31.3
Nebraska	36.4	Sonoma County, CA	21.7	**Louisville-Jefferson County, KY** (metropolitan govt) Jefferson County	31.4
Alaska	38.7	York County, SC	22.6	**Fresno, CA** (city) Fresno County	31.8

Note: (1) Ranking tables cover all states and counties, and places with an overall population of at least 125,000, OR an overall population of at least 25,000 where the Hispanic/Latino population is at least 20% of the overall population. In states where less than five places meet either of these criteria, we have included places with at least 10,000 total population with the highest percentage of Hispanic/Latino population. These places are identified with an asterisk (*); Please refer to the User's Guide for a full explanation of data.

Language Spoken at Home: Spanish

(Universe: Population 5 Years and Over)

South American

Top 10 States, Counties, and Places[1]

Sorted by Number in Descending Order — U.S. = 2,216,454

State	Number	County	Number	Place	Number
Florida	574,071	Miami-Dade County, FL	242,415	**New York, NY** (city)	310,678
New York	441,267	Queens County, NY	191,527	**Queens, NY** (borough) Queens County	191,527
New Jersey	276,900	Broward County, FL	124,754	**Brooklyn, NY** (borough) Kings County	45,190
California	217,643	Los Angeles County, CA	96,403	**Los Angeles, CA** (city) Los Angeles County	40,710
Texas	103,715	Hudson County, NJ	59,019	**Bronx, NY** (borough) Bronx County	35,612
Virginia	84,293	Kings County, NY	45,190	**Manhattan, NY** (borough) New York County	31,303
Illinois	56,517	Westchester County, NY	42,833	**Chicago, IL** (city) Cook County	28,855
Connecticut	53,927	Cook County, IL	40,651	**Miami, FL** (city) Miami-Dade County	28,252
Maryland	44,836	Fairfax County, VA	40,115	**Elizabeth, NJ** (city) Union County	24,765
Massachusetts	42,946	Palm Beach County, FL	40,057	**Houston, TX** (city) Harris County	19,564

Sorted by Number in Ascending Order — U.S. = 2,216,454

State	Number	County	Number	Place	Number
North Dakota	329	Clark County, WA	248	**Chesapeake, VA** (independent city)	404
Montana	494	Tolland County, CT	332	**Lancaster, CA** (city) Los Angeles County	418
Vermont	547	Placer County, CA	341	**Palm Springs, CA** (city) Riverside County	432
Maine	716	San Luis Obispo County, CA	370	**Glendora, CA** (city) Los Angeles County	441
Wyoming	910	Ada County, ID	387	**Overland Park, KS** (city) Johnson County	444
West Virginia	1,192	Washington County, MN	398	**Pittsburgh, PA** (city) Allegheny County	511
Alaska	1,842	Rockingham County, NH	403	**Killeen, TX** (city) Bell County	566
Hawaii	1,852	Spokane County, WA	420	**Placentia, CA** (city) Orange County	567
Nebraska	1,889	Schenectady County, NY	421	**Sanford, FL** (city) Seminole County	611
Idaho	2,041	Williamson County, TN	454	**Springfield, MA** (city) Hampden County	617

Sorted by Percent in Descending Order — U.S. = 86.4%

State	Percent	County	Percent	Place	Percent
Florida	92.0	Miami-Dade County, FL	96.2	**South Gate, CA** (city) Los Angeles County	100.0
New Jersey	90.8	Clayton County, GA	95.1	**Spring Valley, NY** (village) Rockland County	99.6
New York	89.5	Polk County, FL	94.9	**Richmond, CA** (city) Contra Costa County	99.0
Virginia	87.9	Union County, NJ	94.3	**Fountainebleau, FL** (cdp) Miami-Dade County	98.8
Connecticut	87.6	Beaufort County, SC	94.1	**Doral, FL** (city) Miami-Dade County	98.5
Rhode Island	86.6	Queens County, NY	93.6	**Westchester, FL** (cdp) Miami-Dade County	98.5
Texas	86.1	Bronx County, NY	93.5	**Aventura, FL** (city) Miami-Dade County	98.4
Utah	84.4	Passaic County, NJ	93.5	**Poinciana, FL** (cdp) Osceola County	98.4
South Carolina	84.1	Hudson County, NJ	93.4	**Kendall West, FL** (cdp) Miami-Dade County	98.3
Illinois	83.0	Montgomery County, TX	93.4	**Tamiami, FL** (cdp) Miami-Dade County	98.3

Sorted by Percent in Ascending Order — U.S. = 86.4%

State	Percent	County	Percent	Place	Percent
Montana	50.5	Clark County, WA	38.5	**Lancaster, CA** (city) Los Angeles County	38.3
Maine	54.3	Ada County, ID	42.0	**Overland Park, KS** (city) Johnson County	58.3
North Dakota	55.3	San Luis Obispo County, CA	42.5	**Glendora, CA** (city) Los Angeles County	61.9
Hawaii	56.5	Erie County, NY	45.8	**Saint Paul, MN** (city) Ramsey County	62.4
Vermont	60.3	Tolland County, CT	45.8	**Columbus, OH** (city) Franklin County	62.5
Michigan	65.9	Saint Johns County, FL	48.3	**Scottsdale, AZ** (city) Maricopa County	62.8
Washington	65.9	Pierce County, WA	48.7	**Portland, OR** (city) Multnomah County	63.0
Idaho	66.1	Rockingham County, NH	49.2	**Fullerton, CA** (city) Orange County	65.3
Missouri	66.7	Placer County, CA	54.0	**Thousand Oaks, CA** (city) Ventura County	65.7
West Virginia	67.7	Bucks County, PA	59.0	**Chesapeake, VA** (independent city)	66.0

Note: (1) Ranking tables cover all states and counties, and places with an overall population of at least 125,000, OR an overall population of at least 25,000 where the Hispanic/Latino population is at least 20% of the overall population. In states where less than five places meet either of these criteria, we have included places with at least 10,000 total population with the highest percentage of Hispanic/Latino population. These places are identified with an asterisk (*); Please refer to the User's Guide for a full explanation of data.

Language Spoken at Home: Spanish

(Universe: Population 5 Years and Over)

South American: Argentinean

Top 10 States, Counties, and Places[1]

Sorted by Number in Descending Order — U.S. = 164,105

State	Number	County	Number	Place	Number
Florida	45,838	Miami-Dade County, FL	24,933	**New York, NY** (city)	10,797
California	31,738	Los Angeles County, CA	15,017	**Los Angeles, CA** (city) Los Angeles County	6,722
New York	17,818	Broward County, FL	8,623	**Miami, FL** (city) Miami-Dade County	5,174
New Jersey	10,330	Queens County, NY	4,572	**Queens, NY** (borough) Queens County	4,572
Texas	9,815	Orange County, CA	3,666	**Miami Beach, FL** (city) Miami-Dade County	4,046
Maryland	4,266	Palm Beach County, FL	3,204	**Manhattan, NY** (borough) New York County	2,943
Illinois	4,236	Harris County, TX	3,039	**Brooklyn, NY** (borough) Kings County	1,970
Virginia	4,203	New York County, NY	2,943	**Houston, TX** (city) Harris County	1,590
Utah	4,013	Cook County, IL	2,471	**Hollywood, FL** (city) Broward County	1,412
Massachusetts	2,802	Hudson County, NJ	2,203	**Chicago, IL** (city) Cook County	1,322

Sorted by Number in Ascending Order — U.S. = 164,105

State	Number	County	Number	Place	Number
Louisiana	449	Tarrant County, TX	510	**San Diego, CA** (city) San Diego County	555
Missouri	552	Travis County, TX	588	**San Jose, CA** (city) Santa Clara County	704
Minnesota	625	Oakland County, MI	595	**Coral Springs, FL** (city) Broward County	782
Oregon	632	Orange County, NY	603	**Hempstead (town), NY** (town) Nassau County	908
District of Columbia	786	Bexar County, TX	630	**Bronx, NY** (borough) Bronx County	928
Tennessee	796	Ventura County, CA	722	**Pembroke Pines, FL** (city) Broward County	933
Indiana	963	King County, WA	726	**Doral, FL** (city) Miami-Dade County	973
Wisconsin	968	New Haven County, CT	733	**San Francisco, CA** (city) San Francisco County	997
Ohio	1,013	Contra Costa County, CA	806	**Aventura, FL** (city) Miami-Dade County	1,237
South Carolina	1,026	Alameda County, CA	885	**Hialeah, FL** (city) Miami-Dade County	1,239

Sorted by Percent in Descending Order — U.S. = 81.7%

State	Percent	County	Percent	Place	Percent
Florida	91.4	Montgomery County, TX	99.3	**Aventura, FL** (city) Miami-Dade County	100.0
Texas	88.3	Miami-Dade County, FL	96.3	**Miami Beach, FL** (city) Miami-Dade County	98.6
Utah	87.6	Union County, NJ	95.2	**Hialeah, FL** (city) Miami-Dade County	98.2
Tennessee	86.8	Lee County, FL	93.8	**Doral, FL** (city) Miami-Dade County	97.5
South Carolina	84.1	Dallas County, TX	93.7	**Miami, FL** (city) Miami-Dade County	96.2
Colorado	83.3	Salt Lake County, UT	92.9	**Houston, TX** (city) Harris County	93.4
District of Columbia	82.6	Harris County, TX	90.7	**Hollywood, FL** (city) Broward County	91.6
Virginia	82.5	Broward County, FL	90.5	**Pembroke Pines, FL** (city) Broward County	89.5
Indiana	80.5	Oakland County, MI	89.9	**Bronx, NY** (borough) Bronx County	88.0
New Jersey	80.4	Middlesex County, NJ	89.6	**Chicago, IL** (city) Cook County	85.9

Sorted by Percent in Ascending Order — U.S. = 81.7%

State	Percent	County	Percent	Place	Percent
Oregon	55.5	Ventura County, CA	65.1	**San Diego, CA** (city) San Diego County	66.7
Louisiana	59.6	Riverside County, CA	67.5	**Hempstead (town), NY** (town) Nassau County	75.2
Georgia	66.5	San Diego County, CA	68.8	**Coral Springs, FL** (city) Broward County	77.3
Washington	67.7	Fairfield County, CT	69.7	**San Francisco, CA** (city) San Francisco County	79.3
Pennsylvania	68.2	Orange County, CA	72.5	**Brooklyn, NY** (borough) Kings County	79.7
Ohio	69.2	Bexar County, TX	72.7	**Manhattan, NY** (borough) New York County	80.8
Arizona	71.0	San Bernardino County, CA	73.5	**New York, NY** (city)	82.1
Michigan	73.9	Nassau County, NY	75.4	**Los Angeles, CA** (city) Los Angeles County	83.5
Illinois	75.7	Maricopa County, AZ	76.0	**Queens, NY** (borough) Queens County	84.6
Maryland	75.9	Essex County, NJ	76.1	**San Jose, CA** (city) Santa Clara County	85.1

Note: (1) Ranking tables cover all states and counties, and places with an overall population of at least 125,000, OR an overall population of at least 25,000 where the Hispanic/Latino population is at least 20% of the overall population. In states where less than five places meet either of these criteria, we have included places with at least 10,000 total population with the highest percentage of Hispanic/Latino population. These places are identified with an asterisk (*); Please refer to the User's Guide for a full explanation of data.

Language Spoken at Home: Spanish

(Universe: Population 5 Years and Over)

South American: Bolivian

Top 10 States, Counties, and Places[1]

Sorted by Number in Descending Order — U.S. = 80,512

State	Number	County	Number	Place	Number
Virginia	30,750	Fairfax County, VA	17,223	**New York, NY** (city)	4,154
California	10,281	Los Angeles County, CA	4,540	**Arlington, VA** (cdp) Arlington County	3,818
Florida	8,373	Montgomery County, MD	4,111	**Los Angeles, CA** (city) Los Angeles County	3,257
New York	6,410	Prince William County, VA	3,934	**Queens, NY** (borough) Queens County	2,869
Maryland	5,508	Arlington County, VA	3,818	**Annandale, VA** (cdp) Fairfax County	2,674
New Jersey	3,533	Miami-Dade County, FL	2,988	**West Falls Church, VA** (cdp) Fairfax County	1,448
Texas	3,362	Queens County, NY	2,869	**Dale City, VA** (cdp) Prince William County	1,238
Rhode Island	1,559	Loudoun County, VA	1,966	**Springfield, VA** (cdp) Fairfax County	916
Massachusetts	1,524	Providence County, RI	1,559	**Providence, RI** (city) Providence County	865
Illinois	1,464	Broward County, FL	1,343		

Sorted by Number in Ascending Order — U.S. = 80,512

State	Number	County	Number	Place	Number
Pennsylvania	357	San Diego County, CA	536	**Providence, RI** (city) Providence County	865
North Carolina	379	Cook County, IL	557	**Springfield, VA** (cdp) Fairfax County	916
Illinois	1,464	Palm Beach County, FL	782	**Dale City, VA** (cdp) Prince William County	1,238
Massachusetts	1,524	Prince George's County, MD	882	**West Falls Church, VA** (cdp) Fairfax County	1,448
Rhode Island	1,559	Santa Clara County, CA	990	**Annandale, VA** (cdp) Fairfax County	2,674
Texas	3,362	Harris County, TX	1,092	**Queens, NY** (borough) Queens County	2,869
New Jersey	3,533	Orange County, CA	1,114	**Los Angeles, CA** (city) Los Angeles County	3,257
Maryland	5,508	Broward County, FL	1,343	**Arlington, VA** (cdp) Arlington County	3,818
New York	6,410	Providence County, RI	1,559	**New York, NY** (city)	4,154
Florida	8,373	Loudoun County, VA	1,966		

Sorted by Percent in Descending Order — U.S. = 85.4%

State	Percent	County	Percent	Place	Percent
Virginia	94.0	Miami-Dade County, FL	96.4	**Annandale, VA** (cdp) Fairfax County	98.8
Florida	90.6	Fairfax County, VA	96.3	**West Falls Church, VA** (cdp) Fairfax County	98.0
New Jersey	90.4	Arlington County, VA	95.9	**Springfield, VA** (cdp) Fairfax County	96.0
New York	88.1	Queens County, NY	91.4	**Arlington, VA** (cdp) Arlington County	95.9
Massachusetts	85.7	Loudoun County, VA	90.8	**Dale City, VA** (cdp) Prince William County	94.6
Rhode Island	85.1	Prince William County, VA	90.1	**Los Angeles, CA** (city) Los Angeles County	94.2
Maryland	84.6	Los Angeles County, CA	87.7	**Queens, NY** (borough) Queens County	91.4
California	80.5	Palm Beach County, FL	87.3	**New York, NY** (city)	88.7
Illinois	79.8	Montgomery County, MD	87.2	**Providence, RI** (city) Providence County	85.9
Texas	79.2	Santa Clara County, CA	87.1		

Sorted by Percent in Ascending Order — U.S. = 85.4%

State	Percent	County	Percent	Place	Percent
Pennsylvania	57.1	San Diego County, CA	68.6	**Providence, RI** (city) Providence County	85.9
North Carolina	64.7	Orange County, CA	79.0	**New York, NY** (city)	88.7
Texas	79.2	Prince George's County, MD	80.0	**Queens, NY** (borough) Queens County	91.4
Illinois	79.8	Cook County, IL	81.6	**Los Angeles, CA** (city) Los Angeles County	94.2
California	80.5	Harris County, TX	83.1	**Dale City, VA** (cdp) Prince William County	94.6
Maryland	84.6	Broward County, FL	83.8	**Arlington, VA** (cdp) Arlington County	95.9
Rhode Island	85.1	Providence County, RI	85.1	**Springfield, VA** (cdp) Fairfax County	96.0
Massachusetts	85.7	Santa Clara County, CA	87.1	**West Falls Church, VA** (cdp) Fairfax County	98.0
New York	88.1	Montgomery County, MD	87.2	**Annandale, VA** (cdp) Fairfax County	98.8
New Jersey	90.4	Palm Beach County, FL	87.3		

Note: (1) Ranking tables cover all states and counties, and places with an overall population of at least 125,000, OR an overall population of at least 25,000 where the Hispanic/Latino population is at least 20% of the overall population. In states where less than five places meet either of these criteria, we have included places with at least 10,000 total population with the highest percentage of Hispanic/Latino population. These places are identified with an asterisk (*); Please refer to the User's Guide for a full explanation of data.

Language Spoken at Home: Spanish

(Universe: Population 5 Years and Over)

South American: Chilean

Top 10 States, Counties, and Places[1]

Sorted by Number in Descending Order — U.S. = 89,784

State	Number	County	Number	Place	Number
Florida	19,696	Miami-Dade County, FL	10,620	**New York, NY** (city)	6,045
California	16,892	Los Angeles County, CA	6,531	**Queens, NY** (borough) Queens County	3,428
New York	11,859	Queens County, NY	3,428	**Los Angeles, CA** (city) Los Angeles County	3,391
New Jersey	6,463	Broward County, FL	3,420	**Hempstead (town), NY** (town) Nassau County	1,172
Texas	3,340	Nassau County, NY	2,319	**Manhattan, NY** (borough) New York County	1,027
Maryland	3,175	Hudson County, NJ	1,975	**Miami, FL** (city) Miami-Dade County	1,024
Virginia	2,684	Montgomery County, MD	1,945	**Brooklyn, NY** (borough) Kings County	965
Utah	2,461	Westchester County, NY	1,837	**Kendall, FL** (cdp) Miami-Dade County	862
Massachusetts	2,083	Palm Beach County, FL	1,334	**Chicago, IL** (city) Cook County	631
Georgia	1,927	Santa Clara County, CA	1,257		

Sorted by Number in Ascending Order — U.S. = 89,784

State	Number	County	Number	Place	Number
Minnesota	384	San Mateo County, CA	576	**Chicago, IL** (city) Cook County	631
Ohio	482	Clark County, NV	673	**Kendall, FL** (cdp) Miami-Dade County	862
Tennessee	482	Suffolk County, NY	675	**Brooklyn, NY** (borough) Kings County	965
Missouri	562	Riverside County, CA	689	**Miami, FL** (city) Miami-Dade County	1,024
Wisconsin	614	Alameda County, CA	728	**Manhattan, NY** (borough) New York County	1,027
Michigan	623	Bergen County, NJ	754	**Hempstead (town), NY** (town) Nassau County	1,172
Oregon	771	Middlesex County, MA	795	**Los Angeles, CA** (city) Los Angeles County	3,391
Nevada	915	Maricopa County, AZ	797	**Queens, NY** (borough) Queens County	3,428
Colorado	977	Orange County, CA	839	**New York, NY** (city)	6,045
Arizona	1,224	Salt Lake County, UT	847		

Sorted by Percent in Descending Order — U.S. = 77.0%

State	Percent	County	Percent	Place	Percent
Florida	89.5	Hudson County, NJ	95.3	**Queens, NY** (borough) Queens County	93.0
Connecticut	83.2	Miami-Dade County, FL	95.1	**Hempstead (town), NY** (town) Nassau County	91.3
Utah	82.4	Queens County, NY	93.0	**Kendall, FL** (cdp) Miami-Dade County	90.5
New Jersey	81.4	Broward County, FL	91.7	**Miami, FL** (city) Miami-Dade County	88.0
New York	80.2	Nassau County, NY	91.2	**New York, NY** (city)	83.2
North Carolina	79.6	Montgomery County, MD	90.5	**Los Angeles, CA** (city) Los Angeles County	81.3
Oregon	79.4	Salt Lake County, UT	88.8	**Chicago, IL** (city) Cook County	79.9
Maryland	77.8	Palm Beach County, FL	87.9	**Manhattan, NY** (borough) New York County	71.9
California	76.2	Westchester County, NY	85.8	**Brooklyn, NY** (borough) Kings County	71.2
Colorado	75.8	San Bernardino County, CA	84.9		

Sorted by Percent in Ascending Order — U.S. = 77.0%

State	Percent	County	Percent	Place	Percent
Minnesota	55.5	Suffolk County, NY	54.8	**Brooklyn, NY** (borough) Kings County	71.2
Ohio	56.7	Orange County, CA	63.9	**Manhattan, NY** (borough) New York County	71.9
Wisconsin	58.0	Alameda County, CA	67.2	**Chicago, IL** (city) Cook County	79.9
Washington	58.9	Clark County, NV	68.8	**Los Angeles, CA** (city) Los Angeles County	81.3
Pennsylvania	60.2	Middlesex County, MA	68.8	**New York, NY** (city)	83.2
Illinois	62.4	San Diego County, CA	69.8	**Miami, FL** (city) Miami-Dade County	88.0
Michigan	62.6	San Mateo County, CA	70.8	**Kendall, FL** (cdp) Miami-Dade County	90.5
Arizona	69.2	Kings County, NY	71.2	**Hempstead (town), NY** (town) Nassau County	91.3
Nevada	69.9	New York County, NY	71.9	**Queens, NY** (borough) Queens County	93.0
Tennessee	69.9	Maricopa County, AZ	75.0		

Note: (1) Ranking tables cover all states and counties, and places with an overall population of at least 125,000, OR an overall population of at least 25,000 where the Hispanic/Latino population is at least 20% of the overall population. In states where less than five places meet either of these criteria, we have included places with at least 10,000 total population with the highest percentage of Hispanic/Latino population. These places are identified with an asterisk (*); Please refer to the User's Guide for a full explanation of data.

Language Spoken at Home: Spanish

(Universe: Population 5 Years and Over)

South American: Colombian

Top 10 States, Counties, and Places[1]

Sorted by Number in Descending Order — U.S. = 727,528

State	Number	County	Number	Place	Number
Florida	257,524	Miami-Dade County, FL	102,563	**New York, NY** (city)	85,166
New York	121,384	Queens County, NY	63,166	**Queens, NY** (borough) Queens County	63,166
New Jersey	84,740	Broward County, FL	55,067	**Miami, FL** (city) Miami-Dade County	9,783
California	44,728	Orange County, FL	21,198	**Elizabeth, NJ** (city) Union County	9,567
Texas	40,137	Los Angeles County, CA	19,859	**Pembroke Pines, FL** (city) Broward County	9,417
Massachusetts	20,302	Palm Beach County, FL	18,664	**Houston, TX** (city) Harris County	9,021
Georgia	18,450	Harris County, TX	18,331	**Brooklyn, NY** (borough) Kings County	8,926
Connecticut	16,289	Bergen County, NJ	16,053	**Hialeah, FL** (city) Miami-Dade County	7,472
Illinois	15,516	Hudson County, NJ	14,961	**Los Angeles, CA** (city) Los Angeles County	7,363
Pennsylvania	12,524	Hillsborough County, FL	13,625	**Boston, MA** (city) Suffolk County	7,178

Sorted by Number in Ascending Order — U.S. = 727,528

State	Number	County	Number	Place	Number
Iowa	672	Erie County, NY	286	**Raleigh, NC** (city) Wake County	542
Alaska	715	Luzerne County, PA	374	**Royal Palm Beach, FL** (village) Palm Beach County	556
Kentucky	731	Oakland County, MI	401	**Anaheim, CA** (city) Orange County	573
New Mexico	783	Hennepin County, MN	436	**Long Beach, CA** (city) Los Angeles County	598
Nebraska	850	Burlington County, NJ	474	**Indianapolis, IN** (city) Marion County	600
Arkansas	863	Milwaukee County, WI	494	**Cooper City, FL** (city) Broward County	615
Oregon	896	Bucks County, PA	508	**San Jose, CA** (city) Santa Clara County	654
Delaware	946	Franklin County, OH	512	**Glendale, CA** (city) Los Angeles County	712
Oklahoma	1,036	Sacramento County, CA	541	**Virginia Beach, VA** (independent city)	713
Kansas	1,368	Dane County, WI	557	**Huntington, NY** (town) Suffolk County	728

Sorted by Percent in Descending Order — U.S. = 87.2%

State	Percent	County	Percent	Place	Percent
Florida	92.8	Miami-Dade County, FL	96.5	**Richmond West, FL** (cdp) Miami-Dade County	99.5
Delaware	91.6	Polk County, FL	96.4	**Hallandale Beach, FL** (city) Broward County	99.4
Nebraska	91.3	Collier County, FL	96.3	**Aventura, FL** (city) Miami-Dade County	99.1
New Jersey	90.8	Somerset County, NJ	96.1	**North Miami, FL** (city) Miami-Dade County	99.0
Rhode Island	90.3	Dutchess County, NY	95.8	**Fountainebleau, FL** (cdp) Miami-Dade County	98.6
South Carolina	88.4	Pima County, AZ	95.4	**Passaic, NJ** (city) Passaic County	98.6
Connecticut	88.2	Union County, NJ	95.4	**Stamford, CT** (city/town) Fairfield County	98.6
New York	88.1	Montgomery County, TX	95.3	**Miami Gardens, FL** (city) Miami-Dade County	98.5
Texas	87.7	Gwinnett County, GA	94.9	**Tamiami, FL** (cdp) Miami-Dade County	98.5
Massachusetts	86.1	Fort Bend County, TX	94.8	**Doral, FL** (city) Miami-Dade County	98.3

Sorted by Percent in Ascending Order — U.S. = 87.2%

State	Percent	County	Percent	Place	Percent
Minnesota	39.6	Erie County, NY	33.6	**San Diego, CA** (city) San Diego County	62.6
Michigan	60.1	Hennepin County, MN	36.1	**Virginia Beach, VA** (independent city)	71.0
Oregon	63.3	Bucks County, PA	51.0	**Tallahassee, FL** (city) Leon County	71.7
Kentucky	63.4	Burlington County, NJ	62.0	**Cooper City, FL** (city) Broward County	72.4
Missouri	63.9	Oakland County, MI	62.6	**Babylon, NY** (town) Suffolk County	73.1
Iowa	64.4	Baltimore County, MD	64.5	**Staten Island, NY** (borough) Richmond County	74.0
Washington	67.8	Norfolk County, MA	67.1	**Royal Palm Beach, FL** (village) Palm Beach County	74.1
Ohio	68.7	Saint Louis County, MO	67.1	**San Francisco, CA** (city) San Francisco County	74.4
Alabama	70.2	Alameda County, CA	67.3	**Huntington, NY** (town) Suffolk County	76.1
Indiana	70.8	Sacramento County, CA	67.5	**Phoenix, AZ** (city) Maricopa County	77.3

Note: (1) Ranking tables cover all states and counties, and places with an overall population of at least 125,000, OR an overall population of at least 25,000 where the Hispanic/Latino population is at least 20% of the overall population. In states where less than five places meet either of these criteria, we have included places with at least 10,000 total population with the highest percentage of Hispanic/Latino population. These places are identified with an asterisk (*); Please refer to the User's Guide for a full explanation of data.

Language Spoken at Home: Spanish

(Universe: Population 5 Years and Over)

South American: Ecuadorian

Top 10 States, Counties, and Places[1]

Sorted by Number in Descending Order — U.S. = 477,869

State	Number	County	Number	Place	Number
New York	201,260	Queens County, NY	87,572	**New York, NY** (city)	154,541
New Jersey	88,079	Kings County, NY	25,982	**Queens, NY** (borough) Queens County	87,572
Florida	51,104	Hudson County, NJ	24,681	**Brooklyn, NY** (borough) Kings County	25,982
California	27,617	Bronx County, NY	23,929	**Bronx, NY** (borough) Bronx County	23,929
Illinois	20,909	Essex County, NJ	20,952	**Chicago, IL** (city) Cook County	15,059
Connecticut	18,631	Miami-Dade County, FL	18,512	**Manhattan, NY** (borough) New York County	14,578
Texas	9,206	Westchester County, NY	18,236	**Newark, NJ** (city) Essex County	13,623
Pennsylvania	9,084	Cook County, IL	18,046	**Jersey City, NJ** (city) Hudson County	6,804
North Carolina	7,122	Los Angeles County, CA	15,637	**Elizabeth, NJ** (city) Union County	5,836
Minnesota	6,527	New York County, NY	14,578	**Danbury, CT** (city/town) Fairfield County	5,750

Sorted by Number in Ascending Order — U.S. = 477,869

State	Number	County	Number	Place	Number
Missouri	259	Baltimore County, MD	360	**Downey, CA** (city) Los Angeles County	505
Oklahoma	499	Santa Clara County, CA	417	**Oyster Bay, NY** (town) Nassau County	712
Iowa	506	King County, WA	442	**Country Club, FL** (cdp) Miami-Dade County	774
Kansas	519	Putnam County, NY	541	**City of Orange, NJ** (township) Essex County	798
Colorado	523	Burlington County, NJ	633	**Coral Springs, FL** (city) Broward County	810
Oregon	532	Pinellas County, FL	678	**Miramar, FL** (city) Broward County	822
Louisiana	565	Prince George's County, MD	705	**Hollywood, FL** (city) Broward County	877
Wisconsin	572	Lee County, FL	709	**Philadelphia, PA** (city) Philadelphia County	883
Michigan	762	Monmouth County, NJ	709	**Clifton, NJ** (city) Passaic County	1,053
Rhode Island	815	Will County, IL	735	**Norwalk, CT** (city/town) Fairfield County	1,053

Sorted by Percent in Descending Order — U.S. = 90.1%

State	Percent	County	Percent	Place	Percent
New York	94.1	Rockland County, NY	98.7	**Spring Valley, NY** (village) Rockland County	100.0
Minnesota	92.9	Hennepin County, MN	96.8	**New Haven, CT** (city/town) New Haven County	99.3
New Jersey	92.5	Bronx County, NY	96.1	**Central Islip, NY** (cdp) Suffolk County	99.2
Connecticut	91.5	Queens County, NY	95.5	**Brentwood, NY** (cdp) Suffolk County	99.0
Illinois	91.0	Essex County, NJ	95.4	**Ramapo, NY** (town) Rockland County	99.0
Tennessee	90.3	New York County, NY	95.4	**Doral, FL** (city) Miami-Dade County	98.7
Florida	89.7	Miami-Dade County, FL	95.3	**White Plains, NY** (city) Westchester County	98.7
North Carolina	86.3	Westchester County, NY	94.7	**Bloomfield, NJ** (township) Essex County	98.3
Pennsylvania	85.4	Kings County, NY	93.9	**Hackensack, NJ** (city) Bergen County	98.3
Maryland	84.9	Union County, NJ	93.9	**Union City, NJ** (city) Hudson County	97.5

Sorted by Percent in Ascending Order — U.S. = 90.1%

State	Percent	County	Percent	Place	Percent
Missouri	39.3	Baltimore County, MD	53.7	**Oyster Bay, NY** (town) Nassau County	75.2
Colorado	53.6	Dutchess County, NY	61.7	**Brookhaven, NY** (town) Suffolk County	82.5
Oklahoma	56.8	Burlington County, NJ	61.8	**Babylon, NY** (town) Suffolk County	83.6
Washington	62.4	Santa Clara County, CA	65.4	**Houston, TX** (city) Harris County	83.7
Kansas	68.4	King County, WA	68.3	**Charlotte, NC** (city) Mecklenburg County	85.4
Nevada	68.5	Lee County, FL	68.5	**Los Angeles, CA** (city) Los Angeles County	86.7
Oregon	70.5	Maricopa County, AZ	73.1	**Allentown, PA** (city) Lehigh County	87.1
Louisiana	74.0	Ocean County, NJ	74.0	**West New York, NJ** (town) Hudson County	87.6
Ohio	75.2	San Bernardino County, CA	74.8	**Hempstead (town), NY** (town) Nassau County	88.2
Iowa	75.3	Camden County, NJ	74.9	**Kearny, NJ** (town) Hudson County	88.3

Note: (1) Ranking tables cover all states and counties, and places with an overall population of at least 125,000, OR an overall population of at least 25,000 where the Hispanic/Latino population is at least 20% of the overall population. In states where less than five places meet either of these criteria, we have included places with at least 10,000 total population with the highest percentage of Hispanic/Latino population. These places are identified with an asterisk (*); Please refer to the User's Guide for a full explanation of data.

Language Spoken at Home: Spanish

(Universe: Population 5 Years and Over)

South American: Paraguayan

Top 10 States, Counties, and Places[1]

Sorted by Number in Descending Order — U.S. = 13,135

State	Number	County	Number	Place	Number
New York	5,456	Queens County, NY	2,166	**New York, NY** (city)	2,844
New Jersey	1,504	Westchester County, NY	1,512	**Queens, NY** (borough) Queens County	2,166
Florida	1,280				
Maryland	916				
Texas	568				
California	497				

Sorted by Number in Ascending Order — U.S. = 13,135

State	Number	County	Number	Place	Number
California	497	Westchester County, NY	1,512	**Queens, NY** (borough) Queens County	2,166
Texas	568	Queens County, NY	2,166	**New York, NY** (city)	2,844
Maryland	916				
Florida	1,280				
New Jersey	1,504				
New York	5,456				

Sorted by Percent in Descending Order — U.S. = 72.3%

State	Percent	County	Percent	Place	Percent
New York	87.5	Westchester County, NY	92.0	**Queens, NY** (borough) Queens County	91.6
New Jersey	87.4	Queens County, NY	91.6	**New York, NY** (city)	86.9
Maryland	86.3				
Florida	84.9				
Texas	65.4				
California	60.7				

Sorted by Percent in Ascending Order — U.S. = 72.3%

State	Percent	County	Percent	Place	Percent
California	60.7	Queens County, NY	91.6	**New York, NY** (city)	86.9
Texas	65.4	Westchester County, NY	92.0	**Queens, NY** (borough) Queens County	91.6
Florida	84.9				
Maryland	86.3				
New Jersey	87.4				
New York	87.5				

Note: (1) Ranking tables cover all states and counties, and places with an overall population of at least 125,000, OR an overall population of at least 25,000 where the Hispanic/Latino population is at least 20% of the overall population. In states where less than five places meet either of these criteria, we have included places with at least 10,000 total population with the highest percentage of Hispanic/Latino population. These places are identified with an asterisk (*); Please refer to the User's Guide for a full explanation of data.

Language Spoken at Home: Spanish

(Universe: Population 5 Years and Over)

South American: Peruvian

Top 10 States, Counties, and Places[1]

Sorted by Number in Descending Order — U.S. = 423,220

State	Number	County	Number	Place	Number
Florida	86,611	Miami-Dade County, FL	34,325	**New York, NY** (city)	34,062
California	68,483	Los Angeles County, CA	27,264	**Queens, NY** (borough) Queens County	22,007
New Jersey	65,644	Queens County, NY	22,007	**Los Angeles, CA** (city) Los Angeles County	11,626
New York	57,434	Broward County, FL	20,734	**Paterson, NJ** (city) Passaic County	9,025
Virginia	23,741	Passaic County, NJ	17,585	**Elizabeth, NJ** (city) Union County	5,291
Texas	18,185	Fairfax County, VA	12,146	**Brooklyn, NY** (borough) Kings County	4,285
Maryland	12,826	Hudson County, NJ	11,855	**Clifton, NJ** (city) Passaic County	4,275
Connecticut	11,803	Union County, NJ	9,130	**Miami, FL** (city) Miami-Dade County	3,977
Illinois	8,012	Montgomery County, MD	8,992	**Hempstead (town), NY** (town) Nassau County	3,928
Georgia	7,513	Westchester County, NY	8,198	**Islip, NY** (town) Suffolk County	3,874

Sorted by Number in Ascending Order — U.S. = 423,220

State	Number	County	Number	Place	Number
Hawaii	611	Denver County, CO	399	**Denver, CO** (city) Denver County	399
Kansas	697	Lake County, IL	437	**Phoenix, AZ** (city) Maricopa County	563
New Mexico	717	Baltimore County, MD	518	**Bridgeport, CT** (city/town) Fairfield County	577
Kentucky	729	Solano County, CA	551	**Oyster Bay, NY** (town) Nassau County	616
District of Columbia	851	Franklin County, OH	583	**Salt Lake City, UT** (city) Salt Lake County	632
Missouri	968	Fort Bend County, TX	596	**West Valley City, UT** (city) Salt Lake County	636
Rhode Island	996	Ocean County, NJ	609	**Concord, CA** (city) Contra Costa County	684
Idaho	1,044	Wake County, NC	627	**Fort Lauderdale, FL** (city) Broward County	699
Alabama	1,053	Duval County, FL	761	**San Antonio, TX** (city) Bexar County	713
Louisiana	1,089	Lehigh County, PA	768	**Santa Ana, CA** (city) Orange County	714

Sorted by Percent in Descending Order — U.S. = 87.1%

State	Percent	County	Percent	Place	Percent
Delaware	93.2	Miami-Dade County, FL	96.7	**Fountainebleau, FL** (cdp) Miami-Dade County	100.0
New Jersey	92.7	Prince William County, VA	96.7	**Kendall West, FL** (cdp) Miami-Dade County	100.0
Florida	92.2	Osceola County, FL	96.0	**Kendall, FL** (cdp) Miami-Dade County	99.7
Rhode Island	90.5	Hudson County, NJ	95.7	**Linden, NJ** (city) Union County	99.3
Virginia	90.4	Arapahoe County, CO	95.2	**North Bergen, NJ** (township) Hudson County	99.0
New York	88.9	Passaic County, NJ	95.0	**Hialeah, FL** (city) Miami-Dade County	98.1
Connecticut	87.5	Gwinnett County, GA	94.9	**Elizabeth, NJ** (city) Union County	97.8
Texas	87.0	Bronx County, NY	94.7	**West New York, NJ** (town) Hudson County	97.6
Nevada	86.0	Sarasota County, FL	94.7	**Sunrise, FL** (city) Broward County	97.5
Alabama	85.4	Union County, NJ	94.3	**Doral, FL** (city) Miami-Dade County	97.1

Sorted by Percent in Ascending Order — U.S. = 87.1%

State	Percent	County	Percent	Place	Percent
Hawaii	58.7	Prince George's County, MD	64.6	**Oyster Bay, NY** (town) Nassau County	52.1
Wisconsin	60.5	San Joaquin County, CA	68.9	**San Diego, CA** (city) San Diego County	66.5
New Mexico	63.5	Sacramento County, CA	69.6	**Concord, CA** (city) Contra Costa County	71.8
Tennessee	65.8	Solano County, CA	71.3	**Bridgeport, CT** (city/town) Fairfield County	73.4
Oklahoma	68.8	San Diego County, CA	72.6	**Boston, MA** (city) Suffolk County	77.8
Washington	71.8	Baltimore County, MD	73.2	**Fort Lauderdale, FL** (city) Broward County	77.8
Missouri	72.1	King County, WA	76.1	**San Francisco, CA** (city) San Francisco County	77.9
District of Columbia	73.6	Ocean County, NJ	77.1	**Denver, CO** (city) Denver County	78.1
Michigan	73.9	San Francisco County, CA	77.9	**San Antonio, TX** (city) Bexar County	80.1
Arizona	74.6	Denver County, CO	78.1	**Manhattan, NY** (borough) New York County	81.8

Note: (1) Ranking tables cover all states and counties, and places with an overall population of at least 125,000, OR an overall population of at least 25,000 where the Hispanic/Latino population is at least 20% of the overall population. In states where less than five places meet either of these criteria, we have included places with at least 10,000 total population with the highest percentage of Hispanic/Latino population. These places are identified with an asterisk (*); Please refer to the User's Guide for a full explanation of data.

Language Spoken at Home: Spanish

(Universe: Population 5 Years and Over)

South American: Uruguayan

Top 10 States, Counties, and Places[1]

Sorted by Number in Descending Order — U.S. = 45,802

State	Number	County	Number	Place	Number
Florida	12,449	Miami-Dade County, FL	6,249	**Elizabeth, NJ** (city) Union County	2,734
New Jersey	10,371	Union County, NJ	3,701	**New York, NY** (city)	2,427
New York	4,809	Broward County, FL	2,814	**Queens, NY** (borough) Queens County	1,171
Georgia	2,559	Essex County, NJ	2,192		
California	2,228	Palm Beach County, FL	1,382		
Texas	1,996	Queens County, NY	1,171		
Massachusetts	1,904	Harris County, TX	1,112		
Virginia	1,456	Hudson County, NJ	1,106		
Maryland	1,051	Worcester County, MA	1,081		
Pennsylvania	875	Westchester County, NY	1,062		

Sorted by Number in Ascending Order — U.S. = 45,802

State	Number	County	Number	Place	Number
Pennsylvania	875	Middlesex County, NJ	646	**Queens, NY** (borough) Queens County	1,171
Maryland	1,051	Los Angeles County, CA	649	**New York, NY** (city)	2,427
Virginia	1,456	Morris County, NJ	866	**Elizabeth, NJ** (city) Union County	2,734
Massachusetts	1,904	Gwinnett County, GA	992		
Texas	1,996	Westchester County, NY	1,062		
California	2,228	Worcester County, MA	1,081		
Georgia	2,559	Hudson County, NJ	1,106		
New York	4,809	Harris County, TX	1,112		
New Jersey	10,371	Queens County, NY	1,171		
Florida	12,449	Palm Beach County, FL	1,382		

Sorted by Percent in Descending Order — U.S. = 88.4%

State	Percent	County	Percent	Place	Percent
New Jersey	93.3	Miami-Dade County, FL	99.1	**Elizabeth, NJ** (city) Union County	97.2
Florida	93.1	Union County, NJ	96.8	**Queens, NY** (borough) Queens County	90.4
Georgia	93.1	Hudson County, NJ	96.7	**New York, NY** (city)	88.5
Massachusetts	88.0	Essex County, NJ	96.2		
New York	85.4	Broward County, FL	93.3		
Texas	85.4	Gwinnett County, GA	92.7		
Maryland	79.4	Worcester County, MA	92.5		
Virginia	78.5	Queens County, NY	90.4		
Pennsylvania	74.5	Morris County, NJ	89.6		
California	72.3	Westchester County, NY	86.5		

Sorted by Percent in Ascending Order — U.S. = 88.4%

State	Percent	County	Percent	Place	Percent
California	72.3	Los Angeles County, CA	54.3	**New York, NY** (city)	88.5
Pennsylvania	74.5	Palm Beach County, FL	83.5	**Queens, NY** (borough) Queens County	90.4
Virginia	78.5	Middlesex County, NJ	84.0	**Elizabeth, NJ** (city) Union County	97.2
Maryland	79.4	Harris County, TX	85.1		
New York	85.4	Westchester County, NY	86.5		
Texas	85.4	Morris County, NJ	89.6		
Massachusetts	88.0	Queens County, NY	90.4		
Florida	93.1	Worcester County, MA	92.5		
Georgia	93.1	Gwinnett County, GA	92.7		
New Jersey	93.3	Broward County, FL	93.3		

Note: (1) Ranking tables cover all states and counties, and places with an overall population of at least 125,000, OR an overall population of at least 25,000 where the Hispanic/Latino population is at least 20% of the overall population. In states where less than five places meet either of these criteria, we have included places with at least 10,000 total population with the highest percentage of Hispanic/Latino population. These places are identified with an asterisk (*); Please refer to the User's Guide for a full explanation of data.

Language Spoken at Home: Spanish

(Universe: Population 5 Years and Over)

South American: Venezuelan

Top 10 States, Counties, and Places[1]

Sorted by Number in Descending Order — U.S. = 164,193

State	Number	County	Number	Place	Number
Florida	86,173	Miami-Dade County, FL	40,151	**New York, NY** (city)	7,701
Texas	15,132	Broward County, FL	20,342	**Doral, FL** (city) Miami-Dade County	6,458
New York	10,031	Orange County, FL	6,197	**Weston, FL** (city) Broward County	6,358
California	8,129	Harris County, TX	5,785	**Miami, FL** (city) Miami-Dade County	4,808
Georgia	4,943	Queens County, NY	3,473	**Queens, NY** (borough) Queens County	3,473
New Jersey	4,335	Palm Beach County, FL	3,263	**Fountainebleau, FL** (cdp) Miami-Dade County	3,237
Virginia	3,964	Los Angeles County, CA	2,947	**Houston, TX** (city) Harris County	3,196
Massachusetts	2,812	Osceola County, FL	2,580	**Pembroke Pines, FL** (city) Broward County	2,432
North Carolina	2,599	Fort Bend County, TX	2,250	**Manhattan, NY** (borough) New York County	1,841
Illinois	2,221	Hillsborough County, FL	2,105	**Miami Beach, FL** (city) Miami-Dade County	1,673

Sorted by Number in Ascending Order — U.S. = 164,193

State	Number	County	Number	Place	Number
Missouri	553	Tarrant County, TX	525	**Coral Springs, FL** (city) Broward County	964
Minnesota	586	San Diego County, CA	631	**Hollywood, FL** (city) Broward County	1,042
Michigan	675	King County, WA	636	**Bronx, NY** (borough) Bronx County	1,077
Wisconsin	746	Travis County, TX	638	**Kendall West, FL** (cdp) Miami-Dade County	1,103
Indiana	854	Collin County, TX	713	**Aventura, FL** (city) Miami-Dade County	1,127
South Carolina	864	Montgomery County, TX	756	**Los Angeles, CA** (city) Los Angeles County	1,134
Washington	907	Fulton County, GA	769	**Sunrise, FL** (city) Broward County	1,192
Arizona	938	Dallas County, TX	846	**Brooklyn, NY** (borough) Kings County	1,195
Colorado	977	Suffolk County, MA	875	**The Hammocks, FL** (cdp) Miami-Dade County	1,314
Louisiana	1,119	Fairfield County, CT	889	**Hialeah, FL** (city) Miami-Dade County	1,325

Sorted by Percent in Descending Order — U.S. = 85.0%

State	Percent	County	Percent	Place	Percent
Florida	92.3	Miami-Dade County, FL	96.0	**Country Club, FL** (cdp) Miami-Dade County	99.5
Indiana	89.9	Osceola County, FL	95.8	**Doral, FL** (city) Miami-Dade County	99.4
Oklahoma	89.7	Fairfax County, VA	94.8	**Fountainebleau, FL** (cdp) Miami-Dade County	99.3
Utah	89.4	Broward County, FL	93.0	**Tamiami, FL** (cdp) Miami-Dade County	99.2
Texas	88.4	Collin County, TX	91.8	**Pembroke Pines, FL** (city) Broward County	99.1
Virginia	87.5	Harris County, TX	91.0	**Aventura, FL** (city) Miami-Dade County	98.9
Wisconsin	87.3	Orange County, FL	89.1	**Kendall West, FL** (cdp) Miami-Dade County	98.7
Tennessee	86.3	Los Angeles County, CA	88.9	**Weston, FL** (city) Broward County	97.5
Massachusetts	82.1	Montgomery County, TX	88.4	**Hialeah, FL** (city) Miami-Dade County	97.4
Georgia	78.9	Lee County, FL	88.2	**Davie, FL** (town) Broward County	97.3

Sorted by Percent in Ascending Order — U.S. = 85.0%

State	Percent	County	Percent	Place	Percent
Minnesota	57.2	Kings County, NY	58.6	**Brooklyn, NY** (borough) Kings County	58.6
Michigan	60.8	San Diego County, CA	73.2	**New York, NY** (city)	77.3
Louisiana	64.8	Orange County, CA	73.9	**Sunrise, FL** (city) Broward County	77.4
Pennsylvania	65.2	Cobb County, GA	75.8	**Manhattan, NY** (borough) New York County	80.5
Ohio	67.2	Middlesex County, MA	76.6	**Orlando, FL** (city) Orange County	82.0
Maryland	69.8	Cook County, IL	78.1	**Bronx, NY** (borough) Bronx County	82.5
Arizona	71.7	Hillsborough County, FL	78.5	**Queens, NY** (borough) Queens County	83.4
Colorado	72.6	Fulton County, GA	79.0	**Coral Springs, FL** (city) Broward County	88.0
Washington	72.9	New York County, NY	80.5	**Los Angeles, CA** (city) Los Angeles County	88.9
Missouri	73.0	Pinellas County, FL	82.4	**The Hammocks, FL** (cdp) Miami-Dade County	89.9

RANKINGS & COMPARISONS

Note: (1) Ranking tables cover all states and counties, and places with an overall population of at least 125,000, OR an overall population of at least 25,000 where the Hispanic/Latino population is at least 20% of the overall population. In states where less than five places meet either of these criteria, we have included places with at least 10,000 total population with the highest percentage of Hispanic/Latino population. These places are identified with an asterisk (*); Please refer to the User's Guide for a full explanation of data.

Language Spoken at Home: Spanish

(Universe: Population 5 Years and Over)

Spaniard

Top 10 States, Counties, and Places[1]

Sorted by Number in Descending Order — U.S. = 170,755

State	Number	County	Number	Place	Number
California	26,342	Miami-Dade County, FL	8,465	**New York, NY** (city)	9,061
Texas	22,484	Los Angeles County, CA	7,481	**Albuquerque, NM** (city) Bernalillo County	3,726
Florida	21,571	Bernalillo County, NM	4,860	**Queens, NY** (borough) Queens County	3,116
New Mexico	19,240	San Miguel County, NM	3,787	**Los Angeles, CA** (city) Los Angeles County	3,072
New York	14,658	Harris County, TX	3,660	**San Antonio, TX** (city) Bexar County	2,345
New Jersey	10,188	Queens County, NY	3,116	**Manhattan, NY** (borough) New York County	2,267
Colorado	9,162	Hillsborough County, FL	2,901	**Brooklyn, NY** (borough) Kings County	1,692
Arizona	5,093	San Diego County, CA	2,884	**Bronx, NY** (borough) Bronx County	1,662
Illinois	3,312	Bexar County, TX	2,780	**Houston, TX** (city) Harris County	1,555
Maryland	2,553	Broward County, FL	2,711	**San Diego, CA** (city) San Diego County	1,347

Sorted by Number in Ascending Order — U.S. = 170,755

State	Number	County	Number	Place	Number
Montana	132	Butte County, CA	20	**Fort Collins, CO** (city) Larimer County	66
Iowa	202	Maui County, HI	36	**Urban Honolulu, HI** (cdp) Honolulu County	78
West Virginia	254	Clark County, WA	54	**Portland, OR** (city) Multnomah County	130
Maine	259	Washington County, OR	74	**Westminster, CO** (city) Adams County	140
Mississippi	269	Hawaii County, HI	76	**Thornton, CO** (city) Adams County	141
New Hampshire	302	Weber County, UT	88	**Reno, NV** (city) Washoe County	148
Alaska	333	Las Animas County, CO	90	**Stockton, CA** (city) San Joaquin County	167
Wyoming	335	Tulare County, CA	94	**Glendale, AZ** (city) Maricopa County	169
Idaho	352	San Luis Obispo County, CA	98	**Lakewood, CO** (city) Jefferson County	201
Nebraska	389	Snohomish County, WA	107	**Anchorage, AK** (municipality)	210

Sorted by Percent in Descending Order — U.S. = 33.3%

State	Percent	County	Percent	Place	Percent
District of Columbia	67.6	Miami-Dade County, FL	85.8	**Miami, FL** (city) Miami-Dade County	93.2
Florida	53.7	Hudson County, NJ	80.8	**Kearny, NJ** (town) Hudson County	80.4
New Jersey	51.0	Taos County, NM	77.1	**Newark, NJ** (city) Essex County	77.0
New York	46.3	Passaic County, NJ	75.6	**Bronx, NY** (borough) Bronx County	70.2
New Mexico	43.0	Cameron County, TX	71.6	**Queens, NY** (borough) Queens County	65.4
Maryland	41.6	Bronx County, NY	70.2	**Manhattan, NY** (borough) New York County	60.8
Texas	41.4	San Miguel County, NM	68.2	**New York, NY** (city)	57.6
Kentucky	39.2	Rio Arriba County, NM	67.9	**Lubbock, TX** (city) Lubbock County	55.7
Connecticut	37.4	Union County, NJ	67.0	**Brooklyn, NY** (borough) Kings County	53.5
North Carolina	36.8	Hidalgo County, TX	66.7	**South Valley, NM** (cdp) Bernalillo County	51.8

Sorted by Percent in Ascending Order — U.S. = 33.3%

State	Percent	County	Percent	Place	Percent
Hawaii	5.1	Butte County, CA	3.1	**Urban Honolulu, HI** (cdp) Honolulu County	6.1
Idaho	12.7	Maui County, HI	3.4	**Fort Collins, CO** (city) Larimer County	7.9
Montana	12.9	Honolulu County, HI	4.6	**Portland, OR** (city) Multnomah County	11.6
Oregon	15.8	Clark County, WA	5.5	**Westminster, CO** (city) Adams County	12.1
Wyoming	16.4	San Luis Obispo County, CA	6.4	**Stockton, CA** (city) San Joaquin County	12.8
Louisiana	16.8	Snohomish County, WA	8.2	**Thornton, CO** (city) Adams County	12.8
Washington	17.6	Hawaii County, HI	8.3	**Reno, NV** (city) Washoe County	14.8
Utah	20.1	Washington County, OR	9.6	**Lakewood, CO** (city) Jefferson County	16.4
Kansas	20.3	Ocean County, NJ	10.1	**Rio Rancho, NM** (city) Sandoval County	16.6
Ohio	20.8	San Joaquin County, CA	10.9	**Glendale, AZ** (city) Maricopa County	17.5

Note: (1) Ranking tables cover all states and counties, and places with an overall population of at least 125,000, OR an overall population of at least 25,000 where the Hispanic/Latino population is at least 20% of the overall population. In states where less than five places meet either of these criteria, we have included places with at least 10,000 total population with the highest percentage of Hispanic/Latino population. These places are identified with an asterisk (*); Please refer to the User's Guide for a full explanation of data.

Unemployment Rate

(Universe: Population 16 Years and Over)

Total Population

Top 10 States, Counties, and Places[1]

Sorted by Percent in Descending Order — U.S. = 7.9%

State	Percent	County	Percent	Place	Percent
Michigan	11.5	Clay County, KY	23.0	**Detroit, MI** (city) Wayne County	24.8
Mississippi	9.6	Todd County, SD	22.7	**Schofield Barracks*, HI** (cdp) Honolulu County	22.5
District of Columbia	9.4	Menominee County, WI	21.4	**Bridgeton, NJ** (city) Cumberland County	20.4
South Carolina	9.3	Humphreys County, MS	20.2	**Fort Campbell North*, KY** (cdp) Christian County	20.2
California	9.0	Washington County, MS	20.2	**Adelanto, CA** (city) San Bernardino County	19.7
Nevada	9.0	Shannon County, SD	20.1	**San Luis, AZ** (city) Yuma County	19.5
Florida	8.9	Corson County, SD	19.8	**Camden, NJ** (city) Camden County	19.3
Georgia	8.8	Holmes County, MS	19.7	**Cleveland, OH** (city) Cuyahoga County	17.8
North Carolina	8.8	Leflore County, MS	19.5	**Hartford, CT** (city/town) Hartford County	17.3
Alabama	8.7	Lee County, SC	18.5	**San Jacinto, CA** (city) Riverside County	16.9

Sorted by Percent in Ascending Order — U.S. = 7.9%

State	Percent	County	Percent	Place	Percent
North Dakota	3.6	Reagan County, TX	0.3	**Williston*, ND** (city) Williams County	1.4
Wyoming	4.4	Scott County, KS	0.8	**Hanover*, NH** (town) Grafton County	1.8
South Dakota	4.7	Barber County, KS	1.1	**Yankton*, SD** (city) Yankton County	2.8
Nebraska	5.1	Greeley County, KS	1.2	**Dickinson*, ND** (city) Stark County	3.0
Iowa	5.3	Hemphill County, TX	1.3	**Warr Acres*, OK** (city) Oklahoma County	3.0
Hawaii	5.6	Hutchinson County, SD	1.3	**Green River*, WY** (city) Sweetwater County	3.1
Montana	5.7	Russell County, KS	1.3	**Minot*, ND** (city) Ward County	3.1
New Hampshire	5.9	York County, NE	1.3	**Arlington, VA** (cdp) Arlington County	3.2
Utah	5.9	Cottle County, TX	1.4	**South Burlington*, VT** (city) Chittenden County	3.3
Vermont	5.9	Dickens County, TX	1.4	**Atascocita, TX** (cdp) Harris County	3.7

Note: (1) Ranking tables cover all states and counties, and places with an overall population of at least 125,000, OR an overall population of at least 25,000 where the Hispanic/Latino population is at least 20% of the overall population. In states where less than five places meet either of these criteria, we have included places with at least 10,000 total population with the highest percentage of Hispanic/Latino population. These places are identified with an asterisk (*); Please refer to the User's Guide for a full explanation of data.

Unemployment Rate

(Universe: Population 16 Years and Over)

Hispanic or Latino (of any race)

Top 10 States, Counties, and Places[1]

Sorted by Percent in Descending Order — U.S. = 9.6%

State	Percent	County	Percent	Place	Percent
Michigan	15.1	Gulf County, FL	64.2	**Mayfield*, KY** (city) Graves County	37.7
Rhode Island	13.8	Colleton County, SC	44.1	**Schofield Barracks*, HI** (cdp) Honolulu County	36.2
Connecticut	13.2	Brown County, MN	43.2	**Middle*, DE** (town) New Castle County	24.2
Pennsylvania	12.8	Price County, WI	40.3	**Holyoke, MA** (city) Hampden County	24.0
Massachusetts	12.4	Saint Joseph County, MI	38.6	**Fort Leonard Wood*, MO** (cdp) Pulaski County	23.1
Ohio	11.7	Gage County, NE	38.1	**York, PA** (city) York County	23.1
Maine	11.1	Wexford County, MI	33.8	**Walla Walla, WA** (city) Walla Walla County	21.8
New Hampshire	11.1	Wright County, IA	31.8	**Carthage*, MO** (city) Jasper County	21.4
Indiana	11.0	Evangeline Parish, LA	31.3	**Lebanon, PA** (city) Lebanon County	21.3
California	10.6	Halifax County, NC	31.0	**Hartford, CT** (city/town) Hartford County	21.2

Sorted by Percent in Ascending Order — U.S. = 9.6%

State	Percent	County	Percent	Place	Percent
Vermont	5.8	Madison County, TX	0.3	**Jerome*, ID** (city) Jerome County	0.8
Oklahoma	6.5	Mercer County, PA	0.3	**SeaTac, WA** (city) King County	0.8
Wyoming	6.6	Hamilton County, KS	0.4	**Green River*, WY** (city) Sweetwater County	1.9
Virginia	7.0	Rice County, KS	0.4	**Warr Acres*, OK** (city) Oklahoma County	1.9
West Virginia	7.0	Franklin County, ID	0.5	**Gillette*, WY** (city) Campbell County	2.0
District of Columbia	7.1	Kingfisher County, OK	0.5	**Grand Forks*, ND** (city) Grand Forks County	2.4
South Dakota	7.3	Grand County, CO	0.6	**Shelbyville*, KY** (city) Shelby County	2.6
Louisiana	7.4	Pottawatomie County, KS	0.6	**Morgantown*, WV** (city) Monongalia County	2.7
Arkansas	7.5	Redwood County, MN	0.6	**Rock Springs*, WY** (city) Sweetwater County	2.9
North Dakota	7.6	Custer County, OK	0.7	**Pascagoula*, MS** (city) Jackson County	3.0

Note: (1) Ranking tables cover all states and counties, and places with an overall population of at least 125,000, OR an overall population of at least 25,000 where the Hispanic/Latino population is at least 20% of the overall population. In states where less than five places meet either of these criteria, we have included places with at least 10,000 total population with the highest percentage of Hispanic/Latino population. These places are identified with an asterisk (*); Please refer to the User's Guide for a full explanation of data.

Unemployment Rate

(Universe: Population 16 Years and Over)

Central American, excluding Mexican

Top 10 States, Counties, and Places[1]

Sorted by Percent in Descending Order — U.S. = 9.1%

State	Percent	County	Percent	Place	Percent
New Hampshire	18.4	Madera County, CA	41.7	**Little Elm, TX** (city) Denton County	36.7
Indiana	15.9	Rowan County, NC	31.7	**University, FL** (cdp) Hillsborough County	24.9
Connecticut	12.8	Lee County, AL	30.3	**Mountain View, CA** (city) Santa Clara County	24.8
Michigan	12.7	New London County, CT	29.7	**Waterbury, CT** (city/town) New Haven County	23.2
South Carolina	12.6	Burke County, NC	28.2	**Richmond, VA** (independent city)	22.4
Rhode Island	11.9	Cass County, IN	27.3	**Indianapolis, IN** (city) Marion County	21.0
Maine	11.4	Clark County, WA	25.4	**San Pablo, CA** (city) Contra Costa County	20.6
North Carolina	11.3	Etowah County, AL	20.7	**Montclair, CA** (city) San Bernardino County	19.8
Wyoming	11.3	Carroll County, GA	20.6	**Hesperia, CA** (city) San Bernardino County	19.7
Minnesota	10.9	Marion County, IN	20.5	**Springfield, MA** (city) Hampden County	19.7

Sorted by Percent in Ascending Order — U.S. = 9.1%

State	Percent	County	Percent	Place	Percent
West Virginia	0.9	Johnson County, KS	0.2	**Denton, TX** (city) Denton County	0.8
Alaska	1.5	New Castle County, DE	0.4	**La Habra, CA** (city) Orange County	0.8
New Mexico	2.8	Knox County, TN	0.6	**Knoxville, TN** (city) Knox County	1.0
Vermont	4.1	Snohomish County, WA	0.6	**Hackensack, NJ** (city) Bergen County	1.1
Arkansas	4.8	Walker County, TX	0.7	**Valley Stream, NY** (village) Nassau County	1.1
Oklahoma	5.2	Davis County, UT	1.2	**McKinney, TX** (city) Collin County	1.3
Utah	5.2	Thurston County, WA	1.2	**Oakland Park, FL** (city) Broward County	1.4
Hawaii	5.6	Sarasota County, FL	1.5	**Virginia Beach, VA** (independent city)	1.4
South Dakota	5.6	Weld County, CO	1.6	**Atascocita, TX** (cdp) Harris County	1.6
Idaho	6.0	Ocean County, NJ	2.2	**Chandler, AZ** (city) Maricopa County	1.6

RANKINGS & COMPARISONS

Note: (1) Ranking tables cover all states and counties, and places with an overall population of at least 125,000, OR an overall population of at least 25,000 where the Hispanic/Latino population is at least 20% of the overall population. In states where less than five places meet either of these criteria, we have included places with at least 10,000 total population with the highest percentage of Hispanic/Latino population. These places are identified with an asterisk (*); Please refer to the User's Guide for a full explanation of data.

Unemployment Rate

(Universe: Population 16 Years and Over)

Central American: Costa Rican

Top 10 States, Counties, and Places[1]

Sorted by Percent in Descending Order — U.S. = 9.1%

State	Percent	County	Percent	Place	Percent
Virginia	17.3	Philadelphia County, PA	26.6	**Philadelphia, PA** (city) Philadelphia County	26.6
Illinois	16.6	Hillsborough County, FL	21.9	**Queens, NY** (borough) Queens County	10.3
Michigan	15.8	Cook County, IL	17.5	**New York, NY** (city)	8.0
Oregon	15.2	San Diego County, CA	15.4	**Brooklyn, NY** (borough) Kings County	6.9
Minnesota	14.7	Essex County, NJ	15.2	**Los Angeles, CA** (city) Los Angeles County	6.3
Pennsylvania	14.1	Suffolk County, NY	14.3	**Miami, FL** (city) Miami-Dade County	2.6
Nevada	13.8	Palm Beach County, FL	12.7		
North Carolina	12.5	Orange County, CA	11.3		
Georgia	10.9	Queens County, NY	10.3		
Texas	10.1	Somerset County, NJ	10.3		

Sorted by Percent in Ascending Order — U.S. = 9.1%

State	Percent	County	Percent	Place	Percent
Wisconsin	1.1	Clark County, NV	1.2	**Miami, FL** (city) Miami-Dade County	2.6
Louisiana	1.5	Mercer County, NJ	1.2	**Los Angeles, CA** (city) Los Angeles County	6.3
Tennessee	3.9	Maricopa County, AZ	1.4	**Brooklyn, NY** (borough) Kings County	6.9
Massachusetts	5.0	Orange County, FL	3.4	**New York, NY** (city)	8.0
Arizona	5.1	Morris County, NJ	3.9	**Queens, NY** (borough) Queens County	10.3
Colorado	5.7	Bergen County, NJ	4.4	**Philadelphia, PA** (city) Philadelphia County	26.6
Washington	6.7	Riverside County, CA	5.1		
New Jersey	8.0	Harris County, TX	6.1		
California	8.1	Broward County, FL	6.2		
South Carolina	8.4	Kings County, NY	6.9		

Note: (1) Ranking tables cover all states and counties, and places with an overall population of at least 125,000, OR an overall population of at least 25,000 where the Hispanic/Latino population is at least 20% of the overall population. In states where less than five places meet either of these criteria, we have included places with at least 10,000 total population with the highest percentage of Hispanic/Latino population. These places are identified with an asterisk (*); Please refer to the User's Guide for a full explanation of data.

Unemployment Rate

(Universe: Population 16 Years and Over)

Central American: Guatemalan

Top 10 States, Counties, and Places[1]

Sorted by Percent in Descending Order — U.S. = 8.7%

State	Percent	County	Percent	Place	Percent
Michigan	14.0	Lee County, AL	44.5	**Ontario, CA** (city) San Bernardino County	26.1
South Carolina	13.9	Burke County, NC	29.0	**Chillum, MD** (cdp) Prince George's County	25.0
Alabama	13.7	Cherokee County, GA	24.0	**Richmond, VA** (independent city)	24.2
Connecticut	12.6	Rutherford County, TN	22.9	**Hesperia, CA** (city) San Bernardino County	22.6
Rhode Island	12.2	Norfolk County, MA	22.8	**Cincinnati, OH** (city) Hamilton County	20.9
Kansas	11.9	DeKalb County, AL	20.6	**San Bernardino, CA** (city) San Bernardino County	20.6
Delaware	11.7	Kern County, CA	20.5	**Lake Worth, FL** (city) Palm Beach County	19.8
Kentucky	10.9	San Joaquin County, CA	20.1	**West Covina, CA** (city) Los Angeles County	19.4
North Carolina	10.9	Ventura County, CA	17.6	**Corona, CA** (city) Riverside County	17.6
Indiana	9.8	Nobles County, MN	16.8	**Fort Worth, TX** (city) Tarrant County	17.4

Sorted by Percent in Ascending Order — U.S. = 8.7%

State	Percent	County	Percent	Place	Percent
New Mexico	2.2	Fulton County, GA	0.4	**Oklahoma City, OK** (city) Oklahoma County	0.4
Utah	2.2	Passaic County, NJ	0.5	**Nashville-Davidson, TN** (metropolitan govt) Davidson County	0.7
New Hampshire	2.3	Collier County, FL	0.7	**Pawtucket*, RI** (city) Providence County	1.0
Arkansas	3.2	Davidson County, TN	0.7	**Homestead, FL** (city) Miami-Dade County	1.4
Oklahoma	3.8	Knox County, TN	0.8	**Austin, TX** (city) Travis County	1.6
Missouri	4.4	Oklahoma County, OK	0.8	**Salt Lake City, UT** (city) Salt Lake County	1.7
Arizona	4.7	Milwaukee County, WI	1.0	**Yonkers, NY** (city) Westchester County	1.7
Mississippi	4.7	Somerset County, NJ	1.5	**Bonita Springs, FL** (city) Lee County	1.8
Tennessee	4.9	Travis County, TX	1.6	**Central Falls*, RI** (city) Providence County	1.9
Colorado	5.4	Floyd County, GA	1.9	**Reno, NV** (city) Washoe County	2.5

Note: (1) Ranking tables cover all states and counties, and places with an overall population of at least 125,000, OR an overall population of at least 25,000 where the Hispanic/Latino population is at least 20% of the overall population. In states where less than five places meet either of these criteria, we have included places with at least 10,000 total population with the highest percentage of Hispanic/Latino population. These places are identified with an asterisk (*); Please refer to the User's Guide for a full explanation of data.

Unemployment Rate

(Universe: Population 16 Years and Over)

Central American: Honduran

Top 10 States, Counties, and Places[1]

Sorted by Percent in Descending Order — U.S. = 10.5%

State	Percent	County	Percent	Place	Percent
Oregon	22.8	Hartford County, CT	33.2	**Indianapolis, IN** (city) Marion County	24.2
Connecticut	20.7	Elkhart County, IN	28.6	**Boston, MA** (city) Suffolk County	19.9
Indiana	19.8	Marion County, IN	23.4	**Long Beach, CA** (city) Los Angeles County	19.9
Ohio	15.9	Kern County, CA	23.0	**West Little River, FL** (cdp) Miami-Dade County	18.8
South Carolina	14.3	Lee County, FL	21.1	**New Brunswick, NJ** (city) Middlesex County	18.2
North Carolina	14.0	Beaufort County, SC	19.2	**Phoenix, AZ** (city) Maricopa County	17.1
Illinois	12.8	Fort Bend County, TX	17.8	**Dallas, TX** (city) Dallas County	16.7
Wisconsin	12.4	Riverside County, CA	17.2	**Memphis, TN** (city) Shelby County	16.5
Tennessee	11.9	Polk County, FL	16.8	**Raleigh, NC** (city) Wake County	15.9
Florida	11.4	Fairfield County, CT	16.7	**San Jose, CA** (city) Santa Clara County	15.7

Sorted by Percent in Ascending Order — U.S. = 10.5%

State	Percent	County	Percent	Place	Percent
District of Columbia	2.1	Atlantic County, NJ	0.6	**Newburgh, NY** (city) Orange County	2.7
Arkansas	2.5	Galveston County, TX	1.5	**Elizabeth, NJ** (city) Union County	4.3
Alabama	3.0	Hall County, GA	2.2	**Hempstead (village), NY** (village) Nassau County	4.3
Colorado	3.9	Middlesex County, MA	3.0	**Miami Beach, FL** (city) Miami-Dade County	4.3
Oklahoma	5.0	Arapahoe County, CO	3.2	**Aurora, CO** (city) Arapahoe County	4.4
Washington	5.0	Cobb County, GA	3.6	**Staten Island, NY** (borough) Richmond County	5.0
Minnesota	5.3	Baltimore County, MD	4.0	**Fort Worth, TX** (city) Tarrant County	5.2
Utah	5.8	Essex County, MA	4.6	**Hempstead (town), NY** (town) Nassau County	5.4
Mississippi	6.6	Orange County, CA	4.6	**Hialeah, FL** (city) Miami-Dade County	5.4
Nebraska	6.6	Bergen County, NJ	5.0	**Garland, TX** (city) Dallas County	5.7

Note: (1) Ranking tables cover all states and counties, and places with an overall population of at least 125,000, OR an overall population of at least 25,000 where the Hispanic/Latino population is at least 20% of the overall population. In states where less than five places meet either of these criteria, we have included places with at least 10,000 total population with the highest percentage of Hispanic/Latino population. These places are identified with an asterisk (*); Please refer to the User's Guide for a full explanation of data.

Unemployment Rate

(Universe: Population 16 Years and Over)

Central American: Nicaraguan

Top 10 States, Counties, and Places[1]

Sorted by Percent in Descending Order — U.S. = 9.1%

State	Percent	County	Percent	Place	Percent
South Carolina	19.2	Gwinnett County, GA	41.0	**San Diego, CA** (city) San Diego County	23.9
Indiana	19.1	Lee County, FL	28.9	**Austin, TX** (city) Travis County	21.9
Tennessee	17.5	Bexar County, TX	26.8	**Manhattan, NY** (borough) New York County	21.2
Georgia	16.6	New York County, NY	21.2	**Homestead, FL** (city) Miami-Dade County	20.0
Michigan	16.3	Camden County, NJ	20.1	**South Gate, CA** (city) Los Angeles County	19.3
Massachusetts	15.5	Travis County, TX	17.3	**Hollywood, FL** (city) Broward County	17.8
Minnesota	14.6	Stanislaus County, CA	17.0	**Sacramento, CA** (city) Sacramento County	17.5
Wisconsin	13.1	San Diego County, CA	15.2	**Las Vegas, NV** (city) Clark County	17.0
Missouri	12.8	Prince William County, VA	13.8	**North Miami, FL** (city) Miami-Dade County	15.6
District of Columbia	12.3	Contra Costa County, CA	12.1	**Antioch, CA** (city) Contra Costa County	15.5

Sorted by Percent in Ascending Order — U.S. = 9.1%

State	Percent	County	Percent	Place	Percent
Washington	3.5	King County, WA	3.5	**Kenner, LA** (city) Jefferson Parish	0.7
Connecticut	4.9	Jefferson Parish, LA	4.0	**Houston, TX** (city) Harris County	0.9
Oregon	5.2	Collier County, FL	4.1	**Kendall West, FL** (cdp) Miami-Dade County	2.7
Louisiana	5.8	Harris County, TX	4.5	**Kendale Lakes, FL** (cdp) Miami-Dade County	3.7
Pennsylvania	7.2	Fairfax County, VA	4.6	**Fontana, CA** (city) San Bernardino County	4.8
Maryland	7.4	Sonoma County, CA	4.6	**Bronx, NY** (borough) Bronx County	4.9
North Carolina	8.1	Bronx County, NY	4.9	**Oakland, CA** (city) Alameda County	5.1
California	8.8	San Joaquin County, CA	5.0	**South Miami Heights, FL** (cdp) Miami-Dade County	5.1
Florida	8.8	Orange County, FL	5.8	**Kendall, FL** (cdp) Miami-Dade County	5.2
Virginia	9.1	Orange County, CA	7.3	**Country Club, FL** (cdp) Miami-Dade County	6.2

Note: (1) Ranking tables cover all states and counties, and places with an overall population of at least 125,000, OR an overall population of at least 25,000 where the Hispanic/Latino population is at least 20% of the overall population. In states where less than five places meet either of these criteria, we have included places with at least 10,000 total population with the highest percentage of Hispanic/Latino population. These places are identified with an asterisk (*); Please refer to the User's Guide for a full explanation of data.

Unemployment Rate

(Universe: Population 16 Years and Over)

Central American: Panamanian

Top 10 States, Counties, and Places[1]

Sorted by Percent in Descending Order — U.S. = 8.8%

State	Percent	County	Percent	Place	Percent
Mississippi	40.3	Sacramento County, CA	23.4	**San Antonio, TX** (city) Bexar County	17.7
North Carolina	13.9	Riverside County, CA	17.4	**Manhattan, NY** (borough) New York County	16.4
Pennsylvania	13.4	Pierce County, WA	16.9	**Bronx, NY** (borough) Bronx County	14.6
Arizona	12.7	New York County, NY	16.4	**Killeen, TX** (city) Bell County	13.6
Minnesota	12.2	Orange County, FL	14.8	**Los Angeles, CA** (city) Los Angeles County	12.5
Colorado	11.7	Bronx County, NY	14.6	**Queens, NY** (borough) Queens County	11.3
Connecticut	11.7	Bexar County, TX	14.1	**New York, NY** (city)	9.7
Nevada	10.4	Cumberland County, NC	12.7	**Hempstead (town), NY** (town) Nassau County	8.0
Washington	10.0	San Bernardino County, CA	12.0	**Houston, TX** (city) Harris County	7.9
Massachusetts	9.7	Palm Beach County, FL	11.7	**Miami, FL** (city) Miami-Dade County	7.8

Sorted by Percent in Ascending Order — U.S. = 8.8%

State	Percent	County	Percent	Place	Percent
Wisconsin	2.4	Prince George's County, MD	1.1	**Jacksonville, FL** (city) Duval County	6.2
Indiana	2.7	Essex County, NJ	2.1	**Fayetteville, NC** (city) Cumberland County	7.0
Ohio	3.2	Dallas County, TX	2.2	**San Diego, CA** (city) San Diego County	7.2
Alabama	3.3	Broward County, FL	3.7	**Brooklyn, NY** (borough) Kings County	7.3
Tennessee	3.9	Suffolk County, NY	3.8	**Miami, FL** (city) Miami-Dade County	7.8
Virginia	3.9	Prince William County, VA	4.0	**Houston, TX** (city) Harris County	7.9
New Mexico	5.5	Fairfax County, VA	4.7	**Hempstead (town), NY** (town) Nassau County	8.0
Illinois	6.0	San Diego County, CA	5.3	**New York, NY** (city)	9.7
Missouri	6.8	Duval County, FL	6.2	**Queens, NY** (borough) Queens County	11.3
Oklahoma	7.0	Hillsborough County, FL	6.4	**Los Angeles, CA** (city) Los Angeles County	12.5

Note: (1) Ranking tables cover all states and counties, and places with an overall population of at least 125,000, OR an overall population of at least 25,000 where the Hispanic/Latino population is at least 20% of the overall population. In states where less than five places meet either of these criteria, we have included places with at least 10,000 total population with the highest percentage of Hispanic/Latino population. These places are identified with an asterisk (*); Please refer to the User's Guide for a full explanation of data.

Unemployment Rate

(Universe: Population 16 Years and Over)

Central American: Salvadoran

Top 10 States, Counties, and Places[1]

Sorted by Percent in Descending Order — U.S. = 8.8%

State	Percent	County	Percent	Place	Percent
Indiana	19.2	Marion County, IN	27.9	**Indianapolis, IN** (city) Marion County	29.4
Minnesota	12.6	Dakota County, MN	23.4	**Downey, CA** (city) Los Angeles County	22.9
Michigan	11.9	Yolo County, CA	20.7	**San Rafael, CA** (city) Marin County	22.5
Alabama	11.1	Essex County, MA	18.4	**Lake Worth, FL** (city) Palm Beach County	20.9
Kentucky	11.1	Polk County, FL	18.3	**Richmond, VA** (independent city)	20.8
Florida	10.2	Marin County, CA	16.7	**Antioch, CA** (city) Contra Costa County	20.7
Iowa	10.1	San Diego County, CA	16.1	**Ontario, CA** (city) San Bernardino County	20.0
Wisconsin	10.1	Hall County, GA	15.9	**San Pablo, CA** (city) Contra Costa County	20.0
Connecticut	10.0	Guilford County, NC	15.3	**Hesperia, CA** (city) San Bernardino County	19.7
Georgia	10.0	Hall County, NE	15.3	**San Diego, CA** (city) San Diego County	19.5

Sorted by Percent in Ascending Order — U.S. = 8.8%

State	Percent	County	Percent	Place	Percent
New Mexico	3.2	Walker County, TX	0.8	**San Bruno, CA** (city) San Mateo County	1.0
Rhode Island	3.2	Hartford County, CT	1.0	**Hawthorne, CA** (city) Los Angeles County	1.2
Arkansas	4.3	Arapahoe County, CO	1.1	**Rogers, AR** (city) Benton County	1.3
Illinois	4.9	Ocean County, NJ	1.6	**Portland, OR** (city) Multnomah County	1.4
Ohio	5.0	Stafford County, VA	2.3	**Vallejo, CA** (city) Solano County	1.7
Utah	5.0	Pierce County, WA	2.7	**Carrollton, TX** (city) Denton County	2.1
Pennsylvania	5.1	Benton County, AR	2.8	**Glen Cove, NY** (city) Nassau County	2.2
Colorado	6.1	Pima County, AZ	2.8	**Plano, TX** (city) Collin County	2.6
Washington	6.5	Collin County, TX	3.2	**Mesa, AZ** (city) Maricopa County	3.0
Kansas	6.6	San Joaquin County, CA	3.5	**Newark, NJ** (city) Essex County	3.2

Note: (1) Ranking tables cover all states and counties, and places with an overall population of at least 125,000, OR an overall population of at least 25,000 where the Hispanic/Latino population is at least 20% of the overall population. In states where less than five places meet either of these criteria, we have included places with at least 10,000 total population with the highest percentage of Hispanic/Latino population. These places are identified with an asterisk (*); Please refer to the User's Guide for a full explanation of data.

Unemployment Rate

(Universe: Population 16 Years and Over)

Cuban

Top 10 States, Counties, and Places[1]

Sorted by Percent in Descending Order — U.S. = 8.5%

State	Percent	County	Percent	Place	Percent
Kentucky	19.4	Worcester County, MA	24.6	**Lake Worth, FL** (city) Palm Beach County	22.3
Iowa	17.0	Charlotte County, FL	21.9	**Louisville-Jefferson County, KY** (metropolitan govt) Jefferson County	22.1
Indiana	16.3	Jefferson County, KY	21.2	**Carrollwood, FL** (cdp) Hillsborough County	21.3
Oklahoma	16.0	Bronx County, NY	21.0	**Bronx, NY** (borough) Bronx County	21.0
Tennessee	15.3	Hampden County, MA	21.0	**Cape Coral, FL** (city) Lee County	20.8
Michigan	14.6	Hamilton County, OH	20.5	**Riverside, CA** (city) Riverside County	19.0
Hawaii	13.7	Lake County, IL	19.2	**Lehigh Acres, FL** (cdp) Lee County	18.3
Mississippi	13.2	Forsyth County, GA	18.7	**Philadelphia, PA** (city) Philadelphia County	18.1
Maine	12.4	El Paso County, TX	18.6	**Lake Magdalene, FL** (cdp) Hillsborough County	17.0
Massachusetts	11.6	Philadelphia County, PA	18.1	**Seattle, WA** (city) King County	16.8

Sorted by Percent in Ascending Order — U.S. = 8.5%

State	Percent	County	Percent	Place	Percent
New Hampshire	4.0	Fairfax County, VA	0.7	**Brookhaven, NY** (town) Suffolk County	0.5
Virginia	4.4	Montgomery County, PA	0.7	**Santa Clarita, CA** (city) Los Angeles County	0.9
Colorado	4.9	Pierce County, WA	0.9	**Tamarac, FL** (city) Broward County	2.3
District of Columbia	4.9	Berks County, PA	1.2	**Rochester, NY** (city) Monroe County	2.4
Maryland	4.9	Monroe County, NY	1.3	**Islip, NY** (town) Suffolk County	2.5
South Carolina	5.6	Providence County, RI	1.3	**Cooper City, FL** (city) Broward County	2.7
Rhode Island	5.8	Ocean County, NJ	1.4	**Glendale, CA** (city) Los Angeles County	2.9
New Mexico	5.9	Allegheny County, PA	1.5	**Charlotte, NC** (city) Mecklenburg County	3.0
California	7.6	Norfolk County, MA	2.0	**San Antonio, TX** (city) Bexar County	3.0
Utah	7.7	Gwinnett County, GA	2.2	**University Park, FL** (cdp) Miami-Dade County	3.2

Note: (1) Ranking tables cover all states and counties, and places with an overall population of at least 125,000, OR an overall population of at least 25,000 where the Hispanic/Latino population is at least 20% of the overall population. In states where less than five places meet either of these criteria, we have included places with at least 10,000 total population with the highest percentage of Hispanic/Latino population. These places are identified with an asterisk (*); Please refer to the User's Guide for a full explanation of data.

Unemployment Rate

(Universe: Population 16 Years and Over)

Dominican Republic

Top 10 States, Counties, and Places[1]

Sorted by Percent in Descending Order — U.S. = 11.7%

State	Percent	County	Percent	Place	Percent
Alaska	23.3	Cobb County, GA	37.2	**York, PA** (city) York County	31.8
South Carolina	22.9	Erie County, NY	36.6	**Raleigh, NC** (city) Wake County	27.9
Georgia	17.3	Litchfield County, CT	34.1	**New London, CT** (city/town) New London County	27.3
Rhode Island	17.3	Brevard County, FL	28.0	**Syracuse, NY** (city) Onondaga County	26.0
Pennsylvania	17.1	San Diego County, CA	27.0	**Anchorage, AK** (municipality)	25.4
North Carolina	16.4	Wake County, NC	24.0	**Reading, PA** (city) Berks County	23.8
Delaware	15.7	York County, PA	22.8	**Alafaya, FL** (cdp) Orange County	22.4
Connecticut	15.2	Berks County, PA	22.0	**Lancaster, PA** (city) Lancaster County	22.4
Michigan	14.8	New London County, CT	21.3	**Hempstead (village), NY** (village) Nassau County	21.5
Illinois	13.4	Lee County, FL	20.9	**Poinciana, FL** (cdp) Osceola County	21.5

Sorted by Percent in Ascending Order — U.S. = 11.7%

State	Percent	County	Percent	Place	Percent
Tennessee	1.7	Fairfax County, VA	1.7	**Oyster Bay, NY** (town) Nassau County	1.5
Wisconsin	2.8	Albany County, NY	2.1	**North Miami Beach, FL** (city) Miami-Dade County	2.0
Indiana	4.4	Bexar County, TX	2.7	**Belleville, NJ** (township) Essex County	2.3
Alabama	5.0	Tarrant County, TX	3.4	**Pennsauken, NJ** (township) Camden County	2.3
Washington	6.0	Dallas County, TX	4.5	**Buenaventura Lakes, FL** (cdp) Osceola County	2.8
Missouri	6.1	Baltimore County, MD	4.6	**Columbus, OH** (city) Franklin County	3.0
Arizona	7.2	Monmouth County, NJ	5.1	**Ramapo, NY** (town) Rockland County	3.3
Texas	7.5	Monroe County, PA	5.2	**Stamford, CT** (city/town) Fairfield County	3.3
Minnesota	7.7	Camden County, NJ	5.6	**Richmond West, FL** (cdp) Miami-Dade County	3.5
New Jersey	9.1	Somerset County, NJ	5.7	**South Miami Heights, FL** (cdp) Miami-Dade County	3.5

RANKINGS & COMPARISONS

Note: (1) Ranking tables cover all states and counties, and places with an overall population of at least 125,000, OR an overall population of at least 25,000 where the Hispanic/Latino population is at least 20% of the overall population. In states where less than five places meet either of these criteria, we have included places with at least 10,000 total population with the highest percentage of Hispanic/Latino population. These places are identified with an asterisk (*); Please refer to the User's Guide for a full explanation of data.

Unemployment Rate

(Universe: Population 16 Years and Over)

Mexican

Top 10 States, Counties, and Places[1]

Sorted by Percent in Descending Order — U.S. = 9.5%

State	Percent	County	Percent	Place	Percent
Michigan	15.3	Brown County, MN	48.3	**Fort Leonard Wood*, MO** (cdp) Pulaski County	46.4
Massachusetts	11.6	Saint Joseph County, MI	42.4	**Fort Campbell North*, KY** (cdp) Christian County	44.3
Ohio	11.3	Huerfano County, CO	41.7	**Springfield, MA** (city) Hampden County	36.2
California	10.9	Orleans County, NY	39.5	**Carthage*, MO** (city) Jasper County	31.5
New Hampshire	10.9	Sumter County, SC	33.4	**Port Saint Lucie, FL** (city) Saint Lucie County	24.5
Indiana	10.7	Wright County, IA	33.4	**Worcester, MA** (city) Worcester County	24.2
Idaho	10.2	Jefferson County, IL	31.1	**Walla Walla, WA** (city) Walla Walla County	22.4
Nevada	10.2	Neosho County, KS	29.9	**Alafaya, FL** (cdp) Orange County	21.3
South Carolina	10.2	McDonough County, IL	29.3	**San Luis, AZ** (city) Yuma County	19.7
Oregon	10.1	Hampden County, MA	29.0	**York, PA** (city) York County	19.7

Sorted by Percent in Ascending Order — U.S. = 9.5%

State	Percent	County	Percent	Place	Percent
Vermont	4.8	Madison County, TX	0.3	**North Hempstead, NY** (town) Nassau County	0.3
Louisiana	5.9	Washington County, OK	0.3	**SeaTac, WA** (city) King County	0.5
District of Columbia	6.0	Hamilton County, KS	0.4	**Jerome*, ID** (city) Jerome County	0.8
Oklahoma	6.1	Rice County, KS	0.5	**Albertville*, AL** (city) Marshall County	1.1
Maryland	6.3	Kingfisher County, OK	0.6	**Oyster Bay, NY** (town) Nassau County	1.2
Wyoming	6.3	Saint Mary Parish, LA	0.6	**Alexandria, VA** (independent city)	1.7
South Dakota	6.5	Eau Claire County, WI	0.7	**Bethlehem, PA** (city) Northampton County	1.8
New York	6.7	Franklin County, ID	0.7	**Grand Forks*, ND** (city) Grand Forks County	1.8
Virginia	6.7	Lafayette County, MO	0.7	**Warren, MI** (city) Macomb County	2.2
Delaware	6.8	Albemarle County, VA	0.8	**Mission Bend, TX** (cdp) Fort Bend County	2.3

Note: (1) Ranking tables cover all states and counties, and places with an overall population of at least 125,000, OR an overall population of at least 25,000 where the Hispanic/Latino population is at least 20% of the overall population. In states where less than five places meet either of these criteria, we have included places with at least 10,000 total population with the highest percentage of Hispanic/Latino population. These places are identified with an asterisk (*); Please refer to the User's Guide for a full explanation of data.

Unemployment Rate

(Universe: Population 16 Years and Over)

Puerto Rican

Top 10 States, Counties, and Places[1]

Sorted by Percent in Descending Order — U.S. = 12.5%

State	Percent	County	Percent	Place	Percent
Michigan	18.7	Kings County, CA	40.0	**Bridgeton, NJ** (city) Cumberland County	42.8
Pennsylvania	16.4	Gaston County, NC	36.9	**Fort Hood, TX** (cdp) Bell County	37.1
Connecticut	16.2	Salem County, NJ	36.9	**Toledo, OH** (city) Lucas County	36.0
Massachusetts	16.2	Clinton County, NY	34.8	**Rockford, IL** (city) Winnebago County	35.3
Rhode Island	16.0	Ottawa County, MI	33.6	**Wichita, KS** (city) Sedgwick County	28.4
Wisconsin	16.0	Lucas County, OH	32.9	**Casselberry, FL** (city) Seminole County	26.2
Alaska	15.8	Washington County, NY	31.8	**Grand Rapids, MI** (city) Kent County	26.2
Wyoming	15.7	Dale County, AL	31.5	**Lake Worth, FL** (city) Palm Beach County	26.0
Ohio	15.0	Columbia County, NY	30.6	**North Miami Beach, FL** (city) Miami-Dade County	25.6
Illinois	13.7	Jefferson County, NY	29.9	**Camden, NJ** (city) Camden County	25.5

Sorted by Percent in Ascending Order — U.S. = 12.5%

State	Percent	County	Percent	Place	Percent
North Dakota	2.6	Cayuga County, NY	0.5	**Country Club, FL** (cdp) Miami-Dade County	0.6
New Mexico	3.5	Spotsylvania County, VA	0.7	**Greenacres, FL** (city) Palm Beach County	1.4
Montana	4.2	Stafford County, VA	0.7	**Richmond West, FL** (cdp) Miami-Dade County	1.6
Arizona	6.6	Grafton County, NH	1.0	**Kansas City, MO** (city) Jackson County	1.8
Vermont	6.7	Loudoun County, VA	1.5	**Dale City, VA** (cdp) Prince William County	1.9
Arkansas	6.8	Jackson County, MO	1.6	**Arlington, VA** (cdp) Arlington County	2.3
Nevada	6.8	Barnstable County, MA	1.8	**Las Vegas, NV** (city) Clark County	2.4
Mississippi	7.1	Douglas County, CO	1.8	**Hackensack, NJ** (city) Bergen County	2.5
Virginia	7.1	Prince William County, VA	1.8	**Oklahoma City, OK** (city) Oklahoma County	2.6
District of Columbia	7.3	Union County, NC	1.8	**Henderson, NV** (city) Clark County	2.9

Note: (1) Ranking tables cover all states and counties, and places with an overall population of at least 125,000, OR an overall population of at least 25,000 where the Hispanic/Latino population is at least 20% of the overall population. In states where less than five places meet either of these criteria, we have included places with at least 10,000 total population with the highest percentage of Hispanic/Latino population. These places are identified with an asterisk (*); Please refer to the User's Guide for a full explanation of data.

Unemployment Rate

(Universe: Population 16 Years and Over)

South American

Top 10 States, Counties, and Places[1]

Sorted by Percent in Descending Order — U.S. = 7.7%

State	Percent	County	Percent	Place	Percent
North Dakota	15.8	Cameron County, TX	30.0	**Poinciana, FL** (cdp) Osceola County	23.8
Montana	11.9	Pierce County, WA	23.0	**Rahway, NJ** (city) Union County	20.6
Rhode Island	10.2	Hamilton County, TN	21.0	**Killeen, TX** (city) Bell County	19.7
Washington	10.2	Clayton County, GA	20.4	**Port Saint Lucie, FL** (city) Saint Lucie County	19.1
Delaware	10.1	Saint Lucie County, FL	20.4	**Plainfield, NJ** (city) Union County	18.2
Alaska	9.8	Rockingham County, NH	20.3	**Pittsburgh, PA** (city) Allegheny County	17.8
Massachusetts	9.8	Henry County, GA	19.9	**Tamarac, FL** (city) Broward County	17.4
North Carolina	9.6	Clark County, WA	18.6	**Henderson, NV** (city) Clark County	16.3
Nevada	9.5	Tolland County, CT	18.5	**Belleville, NJ** (township) Essex County	15.6
Utah	9.5	Iredell County, NC	18.4	**New Haven, CT** (city/town) New Haven County	15.1

Sorted by Percent in Ascending Order — U.S. = 7.7%

State	Percent	County	Percent	Place	Percent
Maine	2.1	Gloucester County, NJ	0.8	**Palm Springs, CA** (city) Riverside County	0.8
Arkansas	3.1	Frederick County, MD	1.0	**Aurora, CO** (city) Arapahoe County	0.9
New Mexico	3.7	Indian River County, FL	1.0	**Bakersfield, CA** (city) Kern County	1.1
Missouri	3.8	Tompkins County, NY	1.2	**Orange, CA** (city) Orange County	1.1
District of Columbia	4.1	Williamson County, TN	1.2	**Bay Shore, NY** (cdp) Suffolk County	1.4
Wisconsin	4.5	Douglas County, NE	1.9	**Lake Forest, CA** (city) Orange County	1.6
Nebraska	5.0	Orange County, NC	1.9	**Oklahoma City, OK** (city) Oklahoma County	1.6
Arizona	5.4	Chester County, PA	2.1	**Daly City, CA** (city) San Mateo County	1.7
Oklahoma	5.4	Collin County, TX	2.1	**Montgomery Village, MD** (cdp) Montgomery County	1.7
Indiana	5.5	Winnebago County, IL	2.1	**Covina, CA** (city) Los Angeles County	1.8

Note: (1) Ranking tables cover all states and counties, and places with an overall population of at least 125,000, OR an overall population of at least 25,000 where the Hispanic/Latino population is at least 20% of the overall population. In states where less than five places meet either of these criteria, we have included places with at least 10,000 total population with the highest percentage of Hispanic/Latino population. These places are identified with an asterisk (*); Please refer to the User's Guide for a full explanation of data.

Unemployment Rate

(Universe: Population 16 Years and Over)

South American: Argentinean

Top 10 States, Counties, and Places[1]

Sorted by Percent in Descending Order — U.S. = 6.4%

State	Percent	County	Percent	Place	Percent
Utah	15.0	Salt Lake County, UT	23.7	**Coral Springs, FL** (city) Broward County	16.9
Louisiana	14.4	Orange County, NY	15.6	**San Diego, CA** (city) San Diego County	14.7
Ohio	12.8	Riverside County, CA	11.6	**Miami Beach, FL** (city) Miami-Dade County	11.8
Washington	11.5	Orange County, FL	10.2	**Brooklyn, NY** (borough) Kings County	9.3
Massachusetts	10.1	Dallas County, TX	9.9	**Bronx, NY** (borough) Bronx County	7.9
Indiana	9.1	Utah County, UT	9.8	**Aventura, FL** (city) Miami-Dade County	7.4
North Carolina	8.5	Kings County, NY	9.3	**Manhattan, NY** (borough) New York County	6.7
Michigan	7.2	San Bernardino County, CA	9.2	**New York, NY** (city)	6.2
Florida	7.1	Union County, NJ	9.2	**Hollywood, FL** (city) Broward County	6.0
Nevada	6.1	San Diego County, CA	8.7	**San Jose, CA** (city) Santa Clara County	4.9

Sorted by Percent in Ascending Order — U.S. = 6.4%

State	Percent	County	Percent	Place	Percent
Wisconsin	2.3	Nassau County, NY	1.2	**Chicago, IL** (city) Cook County	0.8
Tennessee	2.5	Bergen County, NJ	1.3	**Hempstead (town), NY** (town) Nassau County	1.0
Pennsylvania	2.6	New Haven County, CT	1.6	**Hialeah, FL** (city) Miami-Dade County	2.2
Virginia	3.1	Fairfax County, VA	2.3	**Los Angeles, CA** (city) Los Angeles County	3.3
Georgia	3.3	Hudson County, NJ	2.7	**Pembroke Pines, FL** (city) Broward County	3.3
District of Columbia	3.4	Bexar County, TX	3.1	**Houston, TX** (city) Harris County	4.1
Colorado	4.3	Cook County, IL	3.8	**Miami, FL** (city) Miami-Dade County	4.5
Connecticut	4.6	Suffolk County, NY	3.8	**Queens, NY** (borough) Queens County	4.7
New Jersey	4.9	Tarrant County, TX	4.0	**San Jose, CA** (city) Santa Clara County	4.9
Missouri	5.0	Essex County, NJ	4.1	**Hollywood, FL** (city) Broward County	6.0

RANKINGS & COMPARISONS

Note: (1) Ranking tables cover all states and counties, and places with an overall population of at least 125,000, OR an overall population of at least 25,000 where the Hispanic/Latino population is at least 20% of the overall population. In states where less than five places meet either of these criteria, we have included places with at least 10,000 total population with the highest percentage of Hispanic/Latino population. These places are identified with an asterisk (*); Please refer to the User's Guide for a full explanation of data.

Unemployment Rate

(Universe: Population 16 Years and Over)

South American: Bolivian

Top 10 States, Counties, and Places[1]

Sorted by Percent in Descending Order — U.S. = 6.9%

State	Percent	County	Percent	Place	Percent
Illinois	12.0	Palm Beach County, FL	23.7	**Queens, NY** (borough) Queens County	14.3
North Carolina	11.7	Queens County, NY	14.3	**Los Angeles, CA** (city) Los Angeles County	14.2
Rhode Island	11.3	Broward County, FL	12.5	**Providence, RI** (city) Providence County	12.4
Pennsylvania	10.1	Harris County, TX	12.3	**West Falls Church, VA** (cdp) Fairfax County	11.7
Florida	9.8	Providence County, RI	11.3	**New York, NY** (city)	9.9
Texas	9.5	Los Angeles County, CA	11.2	**Arlington, VA** (cdp) Arlington County	9.3
New York	7.3	Cook County, IL	10.5	**Springfield, VA** (cdp) Fairfax County	7.6
California	6.7	Arlington County, VA	9.3	**Annandale, VA** (cdp) Fairfax County	4.8
Virginia	6.1	Miami-Dade County, FL	7.3		
Maryland	4.2	Loudoun County, VA	6.9		

Sorted by Percent in Ascending Order — U.S. = 6.9%

State	Percent	County	Percent	Place	Percent
New Jersey	1.4	Montgomery County, MD	3.1	**Annandale, VA** (cdp) Fairfax County	4.8
Maryland	4.2	Orange County, CA	3.3	**Springfield, VA** (cdp) Fairfax County	7.6
Massachusetts	4.2	Prince William County, VA	5.2	**Arlington, VA** (cdp) Arlington County	9.3
Virginia	6.1	Santa Clara County, CA	5.4	**New York, NY** (city)	9.9
California	6.7	San Diego County, CA	5.6	**West Falls Church, VA** (cdp) Fairfax County	11.7
New York	7.3	Prince George's County, MD	5.7	**Providence, RI** (city) Providence County	12.4
Texas	9.5	Fairfax County, VA	6.4	**Los Angeles, CA** (city) Los Angeles County	14.2
Florida	9.8	Loudoun County, VA	6.9	**Queens, NY** (borough) Queens County	14.3
Pennsylvania	10.1	Miami-Dade County, FL	7.3		
Rhode Island	11.3	Arlington County, VA	9.3		

Note: (1) Ranking tables cover all states and counties, and places with an overall population of at least 125,000, OR an overall population of at least 25,000 where the Hispanic/Latino population is at least 20% of the overall population. In states where less than five places meet either of these criteria, we have included places with at least 10,000 total population with the highest percentage of Hispanic/Latino population. These places are identified with an asterisk (*); Please refer to the User's Guide for a full explanation of data.

Unemployment Rate

(Universe: Population 16 Years and Over)

South American: Chilean

Top 10 States, Counties, and Places[1]

Sorted by Percent in Descending Order — U.S. = 6.6%

State	Percent	County	Percent	Place	Percent
Illinois	13.0	San Bernardino County, CA	17.2	**Hempstead (town), NY** (town) Nassau County	10.4
North Carolina	8.7	Riverside County, CA	16.1	**Los Angeles, CA** (city) Los Angeles County	9.0
California	7.8	Orange County, CA	10.5	**New York, NY** (city)	8.8
New York	7.4	San Diego County, CA	9.6	**Queens, NY** (borough) Queens County	8.8
Georgia	7.0	Hudson County, NJ	9.2	**Brooklyn, NY** (borough) Kings County	7.8
Washington	7.0	Fairfax County, VA	8.9	**Chicago, IL** (city) Cook County	6.7
Virginia	6.9	Queens County, NY	8.8	**Manhattan, NY** (borough) New York County	5.0
Oregon	6.8	Cook County, IL	8.2	**Kendall, FL** (cdp) Miami-Dade County	3.5
Florida	6.4	Kings County, NY	7.8		
Nevada	6.1	Los Angeles County, CA	7.1		

Sorted by Percent in Ascending Order — U.S. = 6.6%

State	Percent	County	Percent	Place	Percent
Utah	2.0	Westchester County, NY	1.4	**Kendall, FL** (cdp) Miami-Dade County	3.5
Arizona	2.6	Bergen County, NJ	2.0	**Manhattan, NY** (borough) New York County	5.0
Missouri	2.6	Middlesex County, MA	2.9	**Chicago, IL** (city) Cook County	6.7
Connecticut	2.9	Harris County, TX	3.3	**Brooklyn, NY** (borough) Kings County	7.8
Michigan	3.1	Salt Lake County, UT	4.4	**New York, NY** (city)	8.8
Wisconsin	3.3	Palm Beach County, FL	4.6	**Queens, NY** (borough) Queens County	8.8
Pennsylvania	4.1	Montgomery County, MD	4.9	**Los Angeles, CA** (city) Los Angeles County	9.0
Minnesota	4.4	New York County, NY	5.0	**Hempstead (town), NY** (town) Nassau County	10.4
Texas	4.6	Alameda County, CA	5.2		
Ohio	4.7	Broward County, FL	5.3		

RANKINGS & COMPARISONS

Note: (1) Ranking tables cover all states and counties, and places with an overall population of at least 125,000, OR an overall population of at least 25,000 where the Hispanic/Latino population is at least 20% of the overall population. In states where less than five places meet either of these criteria, we have included places with at least 10,000 total population with the highest percentage of Hispanic/Latino population. These places are identified with an asterisk (*); Please refer to the User's Guide for a full explanation of data.

Unemployment Rate

(Universe: Population 16 Years and Over)

South American: Colombian

Top 10 States, Counties, and Places[1]

Sorted by Percent in Descending Order — U.S. = 8.1%

State	Percent	County	Percent	Place	Percent
Kentucky	21.5	Saint Lucie County, FL	27.0	**Las Vegas, NV** (city) Clark County	28.2
Tennessee	19.6	Erie County, NY	18.2	**Worcester, MA** (city) Worcester County	23.2
Nevada	13.8	Ulster County, NY	17.8	**Port Saint Lucie, FL** (city) Saint Lucie County	23.0
North Carolina	9.6	Worcester County, MA	17.4	**Margate, FL** (city) Broward County	21.1
Utah	9.6	Hall County, GA	17.2	**Tallahassee, FL** (city) Leon County	19.6
Michigan	9.5	Leon County, FL	16.7	**Passaic, NJ** (city) Passaic County	18.6
Connecticut	9.4	Clark County, NV	15.4	**Cutler Bay, FL** (town) Miami-Dade County	17.4
Georgia	9.4	Fulton County, GA	15.4	**Tamarac, FL** (city) Broward County	16.4
Massachusetts	9.2	New Haven County, CT	14.4	**Stamford, CT** (city/town) Fairfield County	15.4
New Hampshire	9.2	San Bernardino County, CA	13.8	**Charlotte, NC** (city) Mecklenburg County	13.7

Sorted by Percent in Ascending Order — U.S. = 8.1%

State	Percent	County	Percent	Place	Percent
District of Columbia	1.4	Saint Louis County, MO	0.8	**Dallas, TX** (city) Dallas County	1.0
Arkansas	1.7	Collin County, TX	1.0	**White Plains, NY** (city) Westchester County	1.0
Alaska	2.7	Loudoun County, VA	1.0	**Kissimmee, FL** (city) Osceola County	1.8
Kansas	3.7	DuPage County, IL	1.2	**Revere, MA** (city) Suffolk County	2.0
Missouri	4.0	Prince William County, VA	1.2	**Austin, TX** (city) Travis County	2.1
Colorado	4.1	Dallas County, TX	1.4	**Glendale, CA** (city) Los Angeles County	2.2
Virginia	4.9	Lake County, FL	1.4	**Hallandale Beach, FL** (city) Broward County	2.2
Ohio	5.1	Montgomery County, PA	1.5	**Linden, NJ** (city) Union County	2.4
Indiana	5.6	Orange County, NY	1.7	**Phoenix, AZ** (city) Maricopa County	2.5
Wisconsin	5.6	Sacramento County, CA	2.1	**Brandon, FL** (cdp) Hillsborough County	2.7

Note: (1) Ranking tables cover all states and counties, and places with an overall population of at least 125,000, OR an overall population of at least 25,000 where the Hispanic/Latino population is at least 20% of the overall population. In states where less than five places meet either of these criteria, we have included places with at least 10,000 total population with the highest percentage of Hispanic/Latino population. These places are identified with an asterisk (*); Please refer to the User's Guide for a full explanation of data.

Unemployment Rate

(Universe: Population 16 Years and Over)

South American: Ecuadorian

Top 10 States, Counties, and Places[1]

Sorted by Percent in Descending Order — U.S. = 8.0%

State	Percent	County	Percent	Place	Percent
Rhode Island	15.3	Berks County, PA	19.7	**New Haven, CT** (city/town) New Haven County	20.2
Massachusetts	14.4	Worcester County, MA	18.9	**Plainfield, NJ** (city) Union County	18.6
Michigan	14.3	Providence County, RI	16.4	**Country Club, FL** (cdp) Miami-Dade County	17.0
North Carolina	10.9	Camden County, NJ	16.2	**Miramar, FL** (city) Broward County	15.9
Ohio	10.9	New Haven County, CT	15.5	**Allentown, PA** (city) Lehigh County	14.5
Nevada	9.6	Seminole County, FL	15.0	**Orlando, FL** (city) Orange County	12.9
Georgia	9.4	Union County, NJ	14.3	**Elizabeth, NJ** (city) Union County	12.6
Connecticut	9.0	Lehigh County, PA	12.8	**Kearny, NJ** (town) Hudson County	12.6
Florida	9.0	Pinellas County, FL	11.8	**Bridgeport, CT** (city/town) Fairfield County	12.3
New Jersey	9.0	Bronx County, NY	11.3	**Charlotte, NC** (city) Mecklenburg County	12.3

Sorted by Percent in Ascending Order — U.S. = 8.0%

State	Percent	County	Percent	Place	Percent
Oklahoma	1.7	Burlington County, NJ	0.5	**Downey, CA** (city) Los Angeles County	0.7
Kansas	2.7	Richmond County, NY	1.8	**City of Orange, NJ** (township) Essex County	0.8
Arizona	3.0	Lee County, FL	1.9	**Brookhaven, NY** (town) Suffolk County	1.3
Missouri	3.2	Monmouth County, NJ	1.9	**Norwalk, CT** (city/town) Fairfield County	1.8
Tennessee	4.1	Utah County, UT	2.3	**Staten Island, NY** (borough) Richmond County	1.8
Virginia	4.9	Mercer County, NJ	2.6	**Sunrise, FL** (city) Broward County	2.9
Minnesota	5.1	Morris County, NJ	2.8	**Oyster Bay, NY** (town) Nassau County	3.4
Texas	5.2	Orange County, NY	2.8	**Stamford, CT** (city/town) Fairfield County	3.4
Maryland	5.4	Maricopa County, AZ	3.6	**Hempstead (town), NY** (town) Nassau County	3.6
Washington	5.5	Dallas County, TX	3.8	**Doral, FL** (city) Miami-Dade County	3.8

Note: (1) Ranking tables cover all states and counties, and places with an overall population of at least 125,000, OR an overall population of at least 25,000 where the Hispanic/Latino population is at least 20% of the overall population. In states where less than five places meet either of these criteria, we have included places with at least 10,000 total population with the highest percentage of Hispanic/Latino population. These places are identified with an asterisk (*); Please refer to the User's Guide for a full explanation of data.

Unemployment Rate

(Universe: Population 16 Years and Over)

South American: Paraguayan

Top 10 States, Counties, and Places[1]

Sorted by Percent in Descending Order — U.S. = 8.1%

State	Percent	County	Percent	Place	Percent
New Jersey	18.7	Queens County, NY	10.5	**Queens, NY** (borough) Queens County	10.5
Texas	11.7	Westchester County, NY	6.2	**New York, NY** (city)	7.8
Florida	8.2				
New York	6.4				
California	6.3				
Maryland	2.4				

Sorted by Percent in Ascending Order — U.S. = 8.1%

State	Percent	County	Percent	Place	Percent
Maryland	2.4	Westchester County, NY	6.2	**New York, NY** (city)	7.8
California	6.3	Queens County, NY	10.5	**Queens, NY** (borough) Queens County	10.5
New York	6.4				
Florida	8.2				
Texas	11.7				
New Jersey	18.7				

Note: (1) Ranking tables cover all states and counties, and places with an overall population of at least 125,000, OR an overall population of at least 25,000 where the Hispanic/Latino population is at least 20% of the overall population. In states where less than five places meet either of these criteria, we have included places with at least 10,000 total population with the highest percentage of Hispanic/Latino population. These places are identified with an asterisk (*); Please refer to the User's Guide for a full explanation of data.

Unemployment Rate

(Universe: Population 16 Years and Over)

South American: Peruvian

Top 10 States, Counties, and Places[1]

Sorted by Percent in Descending Order — U.S. = 7.6%

State	Percent	County	Percent	Place	Percent
Delaware	21.4	Santa Clara County, CA	16.4	**Belleville, NJ** (township) Essex County	29.0
Washington	12.2	Osceola County, FL	16.3	**Sunrise, FL** (city) Broward County	22.5
Georgia	9.8	Denver County, CO	14.5	**Tampa, FL** (city) Hillsborough County	20.4
Pennsylvania	9.7	Bexar County, TX	14.1	**Torrance, CA** (city) Los Angeles County	20.0
North Carolina	9.6	New Haven County, CT	13.9	**Hollywood, FL** (city) Broward County	19.1
Rhode Island	9.4	Bronx County, NY	13.8	**Kendale Lakes, FL** (cdp) Miami-Dade County	18.7
Utah	9.3	Gwinnett County, GA	13.3	**Anaheim, CA** (city) Orange County	17.3
Florida	8.9	Morris County, NJ	13.3	**Fountainebleau, FL** (cdp) Miami-Dade County	16.4
Nevada	8.6	Alameda County, CA	13.1	**North Bergen, NJ** (township) Hudson County	15.4
Indiana	8.3	Collier County, FL	13.0	**Denver, CO** (city) Denver County	14.5

Sorted by Percent in Ascending Order — U.S. = 7.6%

State	Percent	County	Percent	Place	Percent
Oklahoma	0.9	Middlesex County, MA	0.6	**Doral, FL** (city) Miami-Dade County	0.9
Louisiana	1.0	Prince William County, VA	1.6	**Bloomfield, NJ** (township) Essex County	2.0
Minnesota	1.4	Ocean County, NJ	1.7	**Garland, TX** (city) Dallas County	2.1
Alabama	2.0	Richmond County, NY	2.2	**Alexandria, VA** (independent city)	2.2
Idaho	2.2	Franklin County, OH	2.3	**Staten Island, NY** (borough) Richmond County	2.2
Hawaii	2.9	Arlington County, VA	2.8	**Dallas, TX** (city) Dallas County	2.3
Wisconsin	3.0	San Mateo County, CA	2.8	**Weston, FL** (city) Broward County	2.3
Missouri	3.8	Loudoun County, VA	3.0	**West Valley City, UT** (city) Salt Lake County	2.4
Kentucky	3.9	Denton County, TX	3.1	**Arlington, VA** (cdp) Arlington County	2.8
South Carolina	4.0	Ventura County, CA	3.1	**Jersey City, NJ** (city) Hudson County	2.8

RANKINGS & COMPARISONS

Note: (1) Ranking tables cover all states and counties, and places with an overall population of at least 125,000, OR an overall population of at least 25,000 where the Hispanic/Latino population is at least 20% of the overall population. In states where less than five places meet either of these criteria, we have included places with at least 10,000 total population with the highest percentage of Hispanic/Latino population. These places are identified with an asterisk (*); Please refer to the User's Guide for a full explanation of data.

Unemployment Rate

(Universe: Population 16 Years and Over)

South American: Uruguayan

Top 10 States, Counties, and Places[1]

Sorted by Percent in Descending Order — U.S. = 8.1%

State	Percent	County	Percent	Place	Percent
Massachusetts	18.3	Worcester County, MA	21.7	**Elizabeth, NJ** (city) Union County	8.6
Florida	9.9	Palm Beach County, FL	20.0	**Queens, NY** (borough) Queens County	6.7
California	9.8	Los Angeles County, CA	14.5	**New York, NY** (city)	5.1
Pennsylvania	7.3	Middlesex County, NJ	12.6		
New Jersey	7.1	Westchester County, NY	11.8		
New York	6.3	Broward County, FL	10.2		
Virginia	5.9	Hudson County, NJ	8.6		
Maryland	3.5	Essex County, NJ	8.1		
Georgia	2.4	Union County, NJ	7.8		
		Miami-Dade County, FL	7.5		

Sorted by Percent in Ascending Order — U.S. = 8.1%

State	Percent	County	Percent	Place	Percent
Georgia	2.4	Morris County, NJ	5.5	**New York, NY** (city)	5.1
Maryland	3.5	Queens County, NY	6.7	**Queens, NY** (borough) Queens County	6.7
Virginia	5.9	Miami-Dade County, FL	7.5	**Elizabeth, NJ** (city) Union County	8.6
New York	6.3	Union County, NJ	7.8		
New Jersey	7.1	Essex County, NJ	8.1		
Pennsylvania	7.3	Hudson County, NJ	8.6		
California	9.8	Broward County, FL	10.2		
Florida	9.9	Westchester County, NY	11.8		
Massachusetts	18.3	Middlesex County, NJ	12.6		
		Los Angeles County, CA	14.5		

Note: (1) Ranking tables cover all states and counties, and places with an overall population of at least 125,000, OR an overall population of at least 25,000 where the Hispanic/Latino population is at least 20% of the overall population. In states where less than five places meet either of these criteria, we have included places with at least 10,000 total population with the highest percentage of Hispanic/Latino population. These places are identified with an asterisk (*); Please refer to the User's Guide for a full explanation of data.

Unemployment Rate

(Universe: Population 16 Years and Over)

South American: Venezuelan

Top 10 States, Counties, and Places[1]

Sorted by Percent in Descending Order — U.S. = 7.9%

State	Percent	County	Percent	Place	Percent
Washington	15.7	Bronx County, NY	19.9	**Bronx, NY** (borough) Bronx County	19.9
Minnesota	15.4	King County, WA	14.9	**Hollywood, FL** (city) Broward County	17.6
Massachusetts	11.2	Travis County, TX	14.7	**Los Angeles, CA** (city) Los Angeles County	14.0
Oklahoma	11.1	Montgomery County, TX	13.7	**Sunrise, FL** (city) Broward County	12.5
New York	10.7	Tarrant County, TX	13.7	**Queens, NY** (borough) Queens County	12.2
Virginia	10.1	Lee County, FL	12.4	**Kendall West, FL** (cdp) Miami-Dade County	11.8
South Carolina	9.5	Queens County, NY	12.2	**New York, NY** (city)	11.5
Connecticut	9.0	Orange County, FL	11.5	**Manhattan, NY** (borough) New York County	11.2
Maryland	8.3	Seminole County, FL	11.3	**Pembroke Pines, FL** (city) Broward County	8.9
New Jersey	8.3	New York County, NY	11.2	**Tamiami, FL** (cdp) Miami-Dade County	8.3

Sorted by Percent in Ascending Order — U.S. = 7.9%

State	Percent	County	Percent	Place	Percent
Utah	1.2	San Diego County, CA	0.8	**Fountainebleau, FL** (cdp) Miami-Dade County	2.4
Indiana	2.4	Collin County, TX	3.1	**Hialeah, FL** (city) Miami-Dade County	2.6
Tennessee	3.4	Dallas County, TX	3.3	**Weston, FL** (city) Broward County	2.8
Ohio	3.5	Harris County, TX	3.8	**Miami Beach, FL** (city) Miami-Dade County	3.0
Colorado	3.6	Orange County, CA	3.8	**Coral Springs, FL** (city) Broward County	3.2
Missouri	4.9	Cobb County, GA	4.4	**Davie, FL** (town) Broward County	3.6
Louisiana	5.2	Gwinnett County, GA	4.4	**Country Club, FL** (cdp) Miami-Dade County	3.8
Arizona	5.9	Fort Bend County, TX	4.6	**Aventura, FL** (city) Miami-Dade County	4.5
Pennsylvania	6.4	Hillsborough County, FL	4.6	**The Hammocks, FL** (cdp) Miami-Dade County	4.9
Michigan	6.5	Pinellas County, FL	5.1	**Houston, TX** (city) Harris County	5.8

Note: (1) Ranking tables cover all states and counties, and places with an overall population of at least 125,000, OR an overall population of at least 25,000 where the Hispanic/Latino population is at least 20% of the overall population. In states where less than five places meet either of these criteria, we have included places with at least 10,000 total population with the highest percentage of Hispanic/Latino population. These places are identified with an asterisk (*); Please refer to the User's Guide for a full explanation of data.

Unemployment Rate

(Universe: Population 16 Years and Over)

Spaniard

Top 10 States, Counties, and Places[1]

Sorted by Percent in Descending Order — U.S. = 9.2%

State	Percent	County	Percent	Place	Percent
Maine	31.2	Mesa County, CO	31.3	**Glendale, AZ** (city) Maricopa County	40.1
New Hampshire	17.3	Butte County, CA	27.1	**Stockton, CA** (city) San Joaquin County	21.8
Kentucky	16.6	Clark County, WA	24.3	**Anchorage, AK** (municipality)	19.3
Arkansas	16.0	Monmouth County, NJ	23.5	**Miami, FL** (city) Miami-Dade County	18.0
Idaho	14.9	Pinellas County, FL	19.9	**Henderson, NV** (city) Clark County	17.7
Missouri	14.8	Larimer County, CO	19.8	**Long Beach, CA** (city) Los Angeles County	17.6
South Carolina	14.7	Westchester County, NY	19.6	**Lakewood, CO** (city) Jefferson County	17.5
Oregon	14.6	Milwaukee County, WI	18.3	**San Jose, CA** (city) Santa Clara County	16.9
Alaska	14.1	Cibola County, NM	17.5	**Kearny, NJ** (town) Hudson County	16.6
Michigan	13.1	Ada County, ID	17.4	**Jacksonville, FL** (city) Duval County	16.5

Sorted by Percent in Ascending Order — U.S. = 9.2%

State	Percent	County	Percent	Place	Percent
Mississippi	0.7	Montgomery County, MD	0.8	**Newark, NJ** (city) Essex County	2.9
West Virginia	1.5	Middlesex County, MA	1.0	**Dallas, TX** (city) Dallas County	3.0
Montana	3.0	Jefferson Parish, LA	1.5	**Brookhaven, NY** (town) Suffolk County	3.2
Tennessee	3.8	Pasco County, FL	1.6	**Phoenix, AZ** (city) Maricopa County	3.4
Virginia	4.1	Bergen County, NJ	1.8	**Houston, TX** (city) Harris County	3.6
Maryland	4.4	Ocean County, NJ	1.9	**Paradise, NV** (cdp) Clark County	3.6
Massachusetts	4.6	Montgomery County, PA	2.5	**Reno, NV** (city) Washoe County	3.8
Alabama	5.1	Doña Ana County, NM	2.8	**El Paso, TX** (city) El Paso County	4.2
Georgia	6.0	Monterey County, CA	2.9	**Riverside, CA** (city) Riverside County	4.2
Minnesota	6.3	Brazoria County, TX	3.0	**Austin, TX** (city) Travis County	4.4

Note: (1) Ranking tables cover all states and counties, and places with an overall population of at least 125,000, OR an overall population of at least 25,000 where the Hispanic/Latino population is at least 20% of the overall population. In states where less than five places meet either of these criteria, we have included places with at least 10,000 total population with the highest percentage of Hispanic/Latino population. These places are identified with an asterisk (*); Please refer to the User's Guide for a full explanation of data.

Class of Worker: Private Wage and Salary

(Universe: Civilian Employed Population 16 Years and Over)

Total Population

Top 10 States, Counties, and Places[1]

Sorted by Number in Descending Order — U.S. = 111,303,933

State	Number	County	Number	Place	Number
California	12,729,790	Los Angeles County, CA	3,538,618	**New York, NY** (city)	2,940,465
Texas	8,667,774	Cook County, IL	2,024,074	**Los Angeles, CA** (city) Los Angeles County	1,414,430
New York	6,951,209	Harris County, TX	1,552,189	**Chicago, IL** (city) Cook County	1,024,780
Florida	6,703,300	Maricopa County, AZ	1,426,153	**Queens, NY** (borough) Queens County	844,822
Illinois	4,965,671	Orange County, CA	1,163,250	**Brooklyn, NY** (borough) Kings County	835,561
Pennsylvania	4,896,263	San Diego County, CA	1,052,879	**Houston, TX** (city) Harris County	814,576
Ohio	4,377,198	Dallas County, TX	919,398	**Manhattan, NY** (borough) New York County	696,866
Michigan	3,593,359	Miami-Dade County, FL	903,980	**Phoenix, AZ** (city) Maricopa County	560,126
New Jersey	3,400,308	Queens County, NY	844,822	**Philadelphia, PA** (city) Philadelphia County	508,347
Georgia	3,362,548	Kings County, NY	835,561	**San Diego, CA** (city) San Diego County	472,754

Sorted by Number in Ascending Order — U.S. = 111,303,933

State	Number	County	Number	Place	Number
District of Columbia	203,846	Kenedy County, TX	76	**Schofield Barracks*, HI** (cdp) Honolulu County	564
Wyoming	204,935	Harding County, NM	126	**Fort Leonard Wood*, MO** (cdp) Pulaski County	769
Alaska	222,955	Terrell County, TX	179	**Fort Campbell North*, KY** (cdp) Christian County	811
Vermont	246,643	Esmeralda County, NV	202	**Florence, AZ** (town) Pinal County	876
North Dakota	258,494	Kent County, TX	211	**Fort Hood, TX** (cdp) Bell County	2,212
South Dakota	304,261	Clark County, ID	215	**Hawaiian Paradise Park*, HI** (cdp) Hawaii County	2,451
Montana	336,831	Motley County, TX	257	**Mayfield*, KY** (city) Graves County	2,608
Delaware	339,582	McMullen County, TX	309	**Hope*, AR** (city) Hempstead County	2,704
Rhode Island	416,800	Piute County, UT	312	**Twentynine Palms, CA** (city) San Bernardino County	2,826
Hawaii	455,520	Stonewall County, TX	343	**Burley*, ID** (city) Cassia County	2,982

Sorted by Percent in Descending Order — U.S. = 78.5%

State	Percent	County	Percent	Place	Percent
Indiana	83.1	Vanderburgh County, IN	87.2	**Central Falls*, RI** (city) Providence County	94.1
Nevada	82.6	Saint Charles County, MO	87.1	**Four Corners, FL** (cdp) Lake County	91.0
Pennsylvania	82.4	Washington County, WI	87.0	**Streamwood, IL** (village) Cook County	90.8
Michigan	82.2	Huntington County, IN	86.8	**Bell Gardens, CA** (city) Los Angeles County	90.4
Illinois	81.9	Elk County, PA	86.6	**Holland, MI** (charter township) Ottawa County	90.4
Wisconsin	81.6	Elkhart County, IN	86.6	**Passaic, NJ** (city) Passaic County	90.3
Ohio	81.5	Gibson County, IN	86.6	**Cicero, IL** (town) Cook County	90.0
Minnesota	81.2	Sheboygan County, WI	86.6	**Lexington*, NE** (city) Dawson County	90.0
Delaware	81.0	Whitley County, IN	86.6	**West Chicago, IL** (city) DuPage County	90.0
Rhode Island	80.8	Dearborn County, IN	86.5	**Glendale Heights, IL** (village) DuPage County	89.7

Sorted by Percent in Ascending Order — U.S. = 78.5%

State	Percent	County	Percent	Place	Percent
Alaska	67.1	Shannon County, SD	27.0	**Schofield Barracks*, HI** (cdp) Honolulu County	44.7
District of Columbia	68.6	Todd County, SD	32.2	**Twentynine Palms, CA** (city) San Bernardino County	46.2
New Mexico	69.9	Harding County, NM	37.6	**Fort Leonard Wood*, MO** (cdp) Pulaski County	46.5
Montana	70.7	Pawnee County, KS	39.5	**Juneau*, AK** (borough) Juneau City and Borough	52.7
Hawaii	71.6	Corson County, SD	41.6	**Florence, AZ** (town) Pinal County	54.7
Wyoming	72.1	Mora County, NM	42.2	**Fort Hood, TX** (cdp) Bell County	58.0
Maryland	72.6	Roosevelt County, MT	42.6	**College*, AK** (cdp) Fairbanks North Star Borough	60.2
North Dakota	73.4	Blaine County, MT	42.7	**Fort Campbell North*, KY** (cdp) Christian County	62.6
South Dakota	74.2	Glacier County, MT	43.3	**Kingsville, TX** (city) Kleberg County	62.9
Virginia	74.2	Stonewall County, TX	46.0	**Del Rio, TX** (city) Val Verde County	63.1

Note: (1) Ranking tables cover all states and counties, and places with an overall population of at least 125,000, OR an overall population of at least 25,000 where the Hispanic/Latino population is at least 20% of the overall population. In states where less than five places meet either of these criteria, we have included places with at least 10,000 total population with the highest percentage of Hispanic/Latino population. These places are identified with an asterisk (*); Please refer to the User's Guide for a full explanation of data.

Class of Worker: Private Wage and Salary

(Universe: Civilian Employed Population 16 Years and Over)

Hispanic or Latino (of any race)

Top 10 States, Counties, and Places[1]

Sorted by Number in Descending Order — U.S. = 16,885,499

State	Number	County	Number	Place	Number
California	4,575,525	Los Angeles County, CA	1,632,331	**New York, NY** (city)	783,992
Texas	2,986,048	Miami-Dade County, FL	617,518	**Los Angeles, CA** (city) Los Angeles County	665,476
Florida	1,561,438	Harris County, TX	586,711	**Houston, TX** (city) Harris County	339,773
New York	1,155,761	Cook County, IL	467,850	**Chicago, IL** (city) Cook County	288,186
Illinois	756,887	Orange County, CA	379,538	**San Antonio, TX** (city) Bexar County	277,671
New Jersey	604,565	Maricopa County, AZ	369,963	**Queens, NY** (borough) Queens County	247,108
Arizona	581,032	Dallas County, TX	332,039	**Bronx, NY** (borough) Bronx County	214,697
Colorado	342,940	Bexar County, TX	328,170	**Dallas, TX** (city) Dallas County	191,093
Georgia	301,842	San Diego County, CA	308,814	**Phoenix, AZ** (city) Maricopa County	190,920
North Carolina	276,119	San Bernardino County, CA	296,655	**Brooklyn, NY** (borough) Kings County	160,451

Sorted by Number in Ascending Order — U.S. = 16,885,499

State	Number	County	Number	Place	Number
Vermont	3,288	Gulf County, FL	15	**Schofield Barracks*, HI** (cdp) Honolulu County	68
North Dakota	4,216	Thurston County, NE	18	**Fort Leonard Wood*, MO** (cdp) Pulaski County	79
Maine	5,600	Grant Parish, LA	20	**Fort Campbell North*, KY** (cdp) Christian County	85
West Virginia	5,813	Evangeline Parish, LA	22	**Burlington*, VT** (city) Chittenden County	180
South Dakota	7,001	West Carroll Parish, LA	30	**Morgantown*, WV** (city) Monongalia County	227
Montana	8,352	Allen Parish, LA	37	**Florence, AZ** (town) Pinal County	253
Alaska	12,743	Harding County, NM	37	**Waianae*, HI** (cdp) Honolulu County	308
New Hampshire	12,835	Perry County, IL	40	**Middle*, DE** (town) New Castle County	318
Wyoming	16,780	Price County, WI	43	**Mayfield*, KY** (city) Graves County	325
District of Columbia	23,614	Chippewa County, MI	44	**Juneau*, AK** (borough) Juneau City and Borough	365

Sorted by Percent in Descending Order — U.S. = 83.2%

State	Percent	County	Percent	Place	Percent
Indiana	90.5	Acadia Parish, LA	100.0	**Brookside*, DE** (cdp) New Castle County	100.0
Nevada	90.4	Atkinson County, GA	100.0	**Willmar*, MN** (city) Kandiyohi County	98.3
North Carolina	90.3	Beaver County, UT	100.0	**Elkhart, IN** (city) Elkhart County	97.9
Minnesota	90.1	Calhoun County, FL	100.0	**Storm Lake*, IA** (city) Buena Vista County	97.6
Delaware	89.8	Champaign County, OH	100.0	**Asheboro, NC** (city) Randolph County	97.4
Nebraska	89.5	Chippewa County, WI	100.0	**Central Falls*, RI** (city) Providence County	97.4
Illinois	89.4	Choctaw County, OK	100.0	**Jerome*, ID** (city) Jerome County	97.4
Alabama	89.1	Clark County, ID	100.0	**Norristown, PA** (borough) Montgomery County	97.2
Wisconsin	89.1	Columbiana County, OH	100.0	**West Chicago, IL** (city) DuPage County	97.1
Tennessee	89.0	Evangeline Parish, LA	100.0	**Laurel*, MS** (city) Jones County	97.0

Sorted by Percent in Ascending Order — U.S. = 83.2%

State	Percent	County	Percent	Place	Percent
New Mexico	71.8	Harding County, NM	21.5	**Schofield Barracks*, HI** (cdp) Honolulu County	28.6
Hawaii	74.3	Grant Parish, LA	33.9	**Florence, AZ** (town) Pinal County	45.0
Vermont	74.8	Allen Parish, LA	39.4	**Juneau*, AK** (borough) Juneau City and Borough	48.7
Alaska	76.2	Mora County, NM	40.6	**Fort Hood, TX** (cdp) Bell County	50.6
West Virginia	77.2	Athens County, OH	42.8	**Fort Leonard Wood*, MO** (cdp) Pulaski County	51.6
Montana	78.9	Latah County, ID	45.4	**Burlington*, VT** (city) Chittenden County	56.4
North Dakota	79.4	Rutland County, VT	45.4	**Twentynine Palms, CA** (city) San Bernardino County	59.7
Texas	80.2	Terrell County, TX	47.5	**Elk Grove, CA** (city) Sacramento County	62.5
Wyoming	80.6	Lassen County, CA	50.7	**Waianae*, HI** (cdp) Honolulu County	63.1
Arizona	81.2	San Miguel County, NM	51.3	**Hampton, VA** (independent city)	64.2

Note: (1) Ranking tables cover all states and counties, and places with an overall population of at least 125,000, OR an overall population of at least 25,000 where the Hispanic/Latino population is at least 20% of the overall population. In states where less than five places meet either of these criteria, we have included places with at least 10,000 total population with the highest percentage of Hispanic/Latino population. These places are identified with an asterisk (*); Please refer to the User's Guide for a full explanation of data.

Class of Worker: Private Wage and Salary

(Universe: Civilian Employed Population 16 Years and Over)

Central American, excluding Mexican

Top 10 States, Counties, and Places[1]

Sorted by Number in Descending Order U.S. = 1,735,651

State	Number	County	Number	Place	Number
California	478,921	Los Angeles County, CA	295,421	**Los Angeles, CA** (city) Los Angeles County	181,928
Florida	197,680	Miami-Dade County, FL	99,196	**Houston, TX** (city) Harris County	68,699
Texas	186,658	Harris County, TX	97,624	**New York, NY** (city)	64,881
New York	147,505	Montgomery County, MD	36,707	**Miami, FL** (city) Miami-Dade County	26,462
Maryland	92,265	Prince George's County, MD	35,775	**Queens, NY** (borough) Queens County	23,638
Virginia	91,253	Dallas County, TX	33,840	**Hempstead (town), NY** (town) Nassau County	20,767
New Jersey	84,382	Suffolk County, NY	31,707	**Brooklyn, NY** (borough) Kings County	18,842
Georgia	47,142	Fairfax County, VA	31,026	**Dallas, TX** (city) Dallas County	17,039
Massachusetts	46,404	Nassau County, NY	28,736	**Islip, NY** (town) Suffolk County	16,411
North Carolina	43,297	Queens County, NY	23,638	**Bronx, NY** (borough) Bronx County	13,923

Sorted by Number in Ascending Order U.S. = 1,735,651

State	Number	County	Number	Place	Number
Vermont	138	Oneida County, NY	168	**Delano, CA** (city) Kern County	152
West Virginia	433	Kings County, CA	176	**Murrieta, CA** (city) Riverside County	200
Wyoming	517	Cass County, IN	178	**Little Elm, TX** (city) Denton County	206
Maine	520	Caroline County, MD	188	**La Mirada, CA** (city) Los Angeles County	231
Hawaii	757	Macomb County, MI	193	**Palm Springs, CA** (city) Riverside County	239
Alaska	950	Thurston County, WA	212	**Apple Valley, CA** (town) San Bernardino County	260
New Hampshire	1,016	Carroll County, AR	218	**Clovis, CA** (city) Fresno County	272
South Dakota	1,203	Imperial County, CA	218	**Adelanto, CA** (city) San Bernardino County	279
Idaho	1,518	Gilmer County, GA	227	**Killeen, TX** (city) Bell County	292
New Mexico	2,692	Weld County, CO	248	**Rochester, NY** (city) Monroe County	303

Sorted by Percent in Descending Order U.S. = 85.8%

State	Percent	County	Percent	Place	Percent
South Dakota	98.5	Burke County, NC	100.0	**Albertville*, AL** (city) Marshall County	100.0
Delaware	94.3	Cass County, IN	100.0	**Bonita Springs, FL** (city) Lee County	100.0
Rhode Island	93.9	Colfax County, NE	100.0	**Elkhart, IN** (city) Elkhart County	100.0
Nebraska	92.8	Crawford County, AR	100.0	**Kearny, NJ** (town) Hudson County	100.0
Massachusetts	92.4	Elkhart County, IN	100.0	**Passaic, NJ** (city) Passaic County	100.0
Iowa	92.2	Franklin County, AL	100.0	**Worthington*, MN** (city) Nobles County	100.0
Nevada	92.0	Gilmer County, GA	100.0	**Garden City, KS** (city) Finney County	99.1
District of Columbia	91.8	Nobles County, MN	100.0	**Richmond, VA** (independent city)	98.9
Indiana	91.8	Pitt County, NC	100.0	**Central Falls*, RI** (city) Providence County	98.8
New Jersey	91.6	Etowah County, AL	99.2	**Carthage*, MO** (city) Jasper County	98.7

Sorted by Percent in Ascending Order U.S. = 85.8%

State	Percent	County	Percent	Place	Percent
Vermont	58.7	Thurston County, WA	52.2	**Murrieta, CA** (city) Riverside County	51.8
Hawaii	67.5	Dane County, WI	58.4	**La Mirada, CA** (city) Los Angeles County	52.9
Alaska	69.9	Imperial County, CA	61.4	**Killeen, TX** (city) Bell County	53.1
West Virginia	75.7	Rockwall County, TX	65.5	**Anchorage, AK** (municipality)	56.3
New Mexico	80.0	Smith County, TX	66.3	**Fayetteville, NC** (city) Cumberland County	64.4
California	81.7	Oneida County, NY	66.4	**Covina, CA** (city) Los Angeles County	65.0
Connecticut	83.2	Bell County, TX	66.5	**Irvine, CA** (city) Orange County	67.1
Wisconsin	84.0	San Luis Obispo County, CA	66.5	**El Paso, TX** (city) El Paso County	67.3
Louisiana	84.1	El Paso County, TX	68.4	**Apple Valley, CA** (town) San Bernardino County	68.2
Florida	84.2	Cumberland County, NC	68.8	**Burbank, CA** (city) Los Angeles County	69.0

Note: (1) Ranking tables cover all states and counties, and places with an overall population of at least 125,000, OR an overall population of at least 25,000 where the Hispanic/Latino population is at least 20% of the overall population. In states where less than five places meet either of these criteria, we have included places with at least 10,000 total population with the highest percentage of Hispanic/Latino population. These places are identified with an asterisk (*); Please refer to the User's Guide for a full explanation of data.

Class of Worker: Private Wage and Salary

(Universe: Civilian Employed Population 16 Years and Over)

Central American: Costa Rican

Top 10 States, Counties, and Places[1]

Sorted by Number in Descending Order — U.S. = 50,429

State	Number	County	Number	Place	Number
New Jersey	9,174	Los Angeles County, CA	3,528	**New York, NY** (city)	2,167
Florida	8,326	Miami-Dade County, FL	2,971	**Los Angeles, CA** (city) Los Angeles County	1,033
California	8,003	Union County, NJ	1,633	**Brooklyn, NY** (borough) Kings County	779
New York	3,944	Broward County, FL	1,337	**Queens, NY** (borough) Queens County	648
Texas	2,449	Somerset County, NJ	1,143	**Miami, FL** (city) Miami-Dade County	512
North Carolina	2,114	Essex County, NJ	993	**Philadelphia, PA** (city) Philadelphia County	413
Massachusetts	1,673	Bergen County, NJ	942	**Bronx, NY** (borough) Bronx County	330
Pennsylvania	1,478	Morris County, NJ	882		
Georgia	1,473	Harris County, TX	868		
Maryland	1,095	Passaic County, NJ	857		

Sorted by Number in Ascending Order — U.S. = 50,429

State	Number	County	Number	Place	Number
Michigan	246	San Diego County, CA	270	**Bronx, NY** (borough) Bronx County	330
Tennessee	276	Bronx County, NY	330	**Philadelphia, PA** (city) Philadelphia County	413
Wisconsin	295	Riverside County, CA	398	**Miami, FL** (city) Miami-Dade County	512
Oregon	341	Philadelphia County, PA	413	**Queens, NY** (borough) Queens County	648
Minnesota	361	Clark County, NV	438	**Brooklyn, NY** (borough) Kings County	779
Washington	430	Hillsborough County, FL	501	**Los Angeles, CA** (city) Los Angeles County	1,033
Colorado	606	Contra Costa County, CA	512	**New York, NY** (city)	2,167
Nevada	672	Nassau County, NY	514		
Louisiana	692	Suffolk County, NY	515		
Arizona	751	Cook County, IL	560		

Sorted by Percent in Descending Order — U.S. = 81.1%

State	Percent	County	Percent	Place	Percent
Colorado	89.1	Essex County, NJ	92.5	**Bronx, NY** (borough) Bronx County	84.4
Washington	88.8	Bergen County, NJ	91.2	**Philadelphia, PA** (city) Philadelphia County	77.1
South Carolina	88.0	Morris County, NJ	90.1	**New York, NY** (city)	73.9
New Jersey	87.7	Clark County, NV	89.2	**Miami, FL** (city) Miami-Dade County	70.9
Louisiana	87.0	Passaic County, NJ	88.1	**Brooklyn, NY** (borough) Kings County	70.7
Georgia	86.7	Nassau County, NY	87.6	**Queens, NY** (borough) Queens County	70.3
North Carolina	86.0	Fairfield County, CT	86.8	**Los Angeles, CA** (city) Los Angeles County	67.2
Florida	83.7	Harris County, TX	86.5		
Illinois	83.6	Orange County, FL	86.4		
Maryland	83.5	Somerset County, NJ	86.4		

Sorted by Percent in Ascending Order — U.S. = 81.1%

State	Percent	County	Percent	Place	Percent
Tennessee	62.9	San Diego County, CA	63.7	**Los Angeles, CA** (city) Los Angeles County	67.2
Michigan	68.7	Riverside County, CA	68.6	**Queens, NY** (borough) Queens County	70.3
California	75.0	Queens County, NY	70.3	**Brooklyn, NY** (borough) Kings County	70.7
New York	76.0	San Bernardino County, CA	70.3	**Miami, FL** (city) Miami-Dade County	70.9
Texas	77.2	Kings County, NY	70.7	**New York, NY** (city)	73.9
Virginia	79.4	Contra Costa County, CA	72.9	**Philadelphia, PA** (city) Philadelphia County	77.1
Pennsylvania	79.8	Los Angeles County, CA	75.9	**Bronx, NY** (borough) Bronx County	84.4
Massachusetts	80.2	Orange County, CA	76.9		
Oregon	80.6	Philadelphia County, PA	77.1		
Arizona	81.5	Suffolk County, NY	78.7		

Note: (1) Ranking tables cover all states and counties, and places with an overall population of at least 125,000, OR an overall population of at least 25,000 where the Hispanic/Latino population is at least 20% of the overall population. In states where less than five places meet either of these criteria, we have included places with at least 10,000 total population with the highest percentage of Hispanic/Latino population. These places are identified with an asterisk (*); Please refer to the User's Guide for a full explanation of data.

Class of Worker: Private Wage and Salary

(Universe: Civilian Employed Population 16 Years and Over)

Central American: Guatemalan

Top 10 States, Counties, and Places[1]

Sorted by Number in Descending Order — U.S. = 459,613

State	Number	County	Number	Place	Number
California	140,058	Los Angeles County, CA	94,327	**Los Angeles, CA** (city) Los Angeles County	61,246
Florida	42,259	Harris County, TX	15,799	**New York, NY** (city)	13,502
Texas	31,334	Palm Beach County, FL	11,764	**Houston, TX** (city) Harris County	12,750
New York	31,052	Miami-Dade County, FL	10,761	**Chicago, IL** (city) Cook County	7,754
New Jersey	24,995	Cook County, IL	10,716	**Providence, RI** (city) Providence County	6,188
Maryland	19,100	Prince George's County, MD	9,235	**Queens, NY** (borough) Queens County	6,003
Georgia	16,395	Providence County, RI	9,217	**Trenton, NJ** (city) Mercer County	5,044
Massachusetts	15,798	Orange County, CA	6,962	**Stamford, CT** (city/town) Fairfield County	4,441
Virginia	15,364	Mercer County, NJ	6,515	**Brooklyn, NY** (borough) Kings County	3,588
Illinois	14,177	Queens County, NY	6,003	**Dallas, TX** (city) Dallas County	3,258

Sorted by Number in Ascending Order — U.S. = 459,613

State	Number	County	Number	Place	Number
New Hampshire	302	Pinal County, AZ	96	**Alhambra, CA** (city) Los Angeles County	241
Idaho	545	Caroline County, MD	154	**Lexington*, NE** (city) Dawson County	269
South Dakota	659	Gilmer County, GA	227	**Bell, CA** (city) Los Angeles County	285
Wisconsin	701	Norfolk County, MA	295	**Victorville, CA** (city) San Bernardino County	308
District of Columbia	890	Lee County, AL	312	**Cincinnati, OH** (city) Hamilton County	354
Mississippi	1,120	Murray County, GA	315	**Minneapolis, MN** (city) Hennepin County	354
New Mexico	1,227	Hartford County, CT	339	**Montebello, CA** (city) Los Angeles County	368
Kentucky	1,463	Dawson County, NE	346	**West Covina, CA** (city) Los Angeles County	369
Kansas	1,730	Nobles County, MN	385	**Hesperia, CA** (city) San Bernardino County	378
Arkansas	1,894	Utah County, UT	395	**San Bernardino, CA** (city) San Bernardino County	408

Sorted by Percent in Descending Order — U.S. = 87.0%

State	Percent	County	Percent	Place	Percent
New Hampshire	100.0	Burke County, NC	100.0	**Albertville*, AL** (city) Marshall County	100.0
South Dakota	97.8	Franklin County, AL	100.0	**Bonita Springs, FL** (city) Lee County	100.0
Delaware	96.7	Gilmer County, GA	100.0	**Carthage*, MO** (city) Jasper County	100.0
Alabama	95.0	Jasper County, MO	100.0	**Garland, TX** (city) Dallas County	100.0
Kentucky	94.9	Nobles County, MN	100.0	**Reno, NV** (city) Washoe County	100.0
Mississippi	94.6	Worcester County, MA	100.0	**Richmond, VA** (independent city)	99.6
South Carolina	94.6	Chesterfield County, VA	99.5	**Paterson, NJ** (city) Passaic County	99.2
Nebraska	94.2	Somerset County, NJ	99.1	**West New York, NJ** (town) Hudson County	99.1
Rhode Island	94.1	Arapahoe County, CO	99.0	**Central Falls*, RI** (city) Providence County	98.8
Michigan	93.9	Mecklenburg County, NC	98.8	**Charlotte, NC** (city) Mecklenburg County	98.8

Sorted by Percent in Ascending Order — U.S. = 87.0%

State	Percent	County	Percent	Place	Percent
Louisiana	80.4	Santa Barbara County, CA	71.8	**Burbank, CA** (city) Los Angeles County	59.8
Connecticut	80.9	Santa Fe County, NM	71.8	**Alhambra, CA** (city) Los Angeles County	65.8
California	81.3	Hartford County, CT	73.2	**Cincinnati, OH** (city) Hamilton County	65.9
New Mexico	82.3	Nassau County, NY	73.9	**La Puente, CA** (city) Los Angeles County	67.0
Arkansas	83.3	Solano County, CA	75.3	**North Hempstead, NY** (town) Nassau County	67.1
Arizona	85.5	Alameda County, CA	76.2	**Miami, FL** (city) Miami-Dade County	70.9
New York	85.6	San Diego County, CA	76.5	**Norwalk, CA** (city) Los Angeles County	70.9
Minnesota	85.7	Pima County, AZ	77.0	**Bakersfield, CA** (city) Kern County	72.8
Illinois	86.8	Middlesex County, NJ	77.2	**San Mateo, CA** (city) San Mateo County	72.9
Utah	87.4	Fulton County, GA	78.0	**Huntington Park, CA** (city) Los Angeles County	75.0

Note: (1) Ranking tables cover all states and counties, and places with an overall population of at least 125,000, OR an overall population of at least 25,000 where the Hispanic/Latino population is at least 20% of the overall population. In states where less than five places meet either of these criteria, we have included places with at least 10,000 total population with the highest percentage of Hispanic/Latino population. These places are identified with an asterisk (*); Please refer to the User's Guide for a full explanation of data.

Class of Worker: Private Wage and Salary

(Universe: Civilian Employed Population 16 Years and Over)

Central American: Honduran

Top 10 States, Counties, and Places[1]

Sorted by Number in Descending Order — U.S. = 268,965

State	Number	County	Number	Place	Number
Florida	46,172	Miami-Dade County, FL	23,198	**New York, NY** (city)	17,820
Texas	38,249	Harris County, TX	20,451	**Houston, TX** (city) Harris County	15,092
New York	30,343	Los Angeles County, CA	17,217	**Los Angeles, CA** (city) Los Angeles County	9,597
California	29,091	Bronx County, NY	7,086	**Miami, FL** (city) Miami-Dade County	9,566
New Jersey	17,071	Jefferson Parish, LA	6,319	**Bronx, NY** (borough) Bronx County	7,086
Virginia	13,921	Dallas County, TX	6,114	**Brooklyn, NY** (borough) Kings County	4,328
North Carolina	13,156	Fairfax County, VA	4,895	**Hempstead (town), NY** (town) Nassau County	4,253
Louisiana	12,196	Nassau County, NY	4,884	**Queens, NY** (borough) Queens County	4,048
Georgia	9,357	Broward County, FL	4,867	**Dallas, TX** (city) Dallas County	3,518
Maryland	8,832	Hudson County, NJ	4,349	**Charlotte, NC** (city) Mecklenburg County	3,408

Sorted by Number in Ascending Order — U.S. = 268,965

State	Number	County	Number	Place	Number
Iowa	491	Kern County, CA	131	**Miramar, FL** (city) Broward County	337
Nebraska	590	New Haven County, CT	210	**South Miami Heights, FL** (cdp) Miami-Dade County	360
Oregon	739	Elkhart County, IN	340	**Pasadena, CA** (city) Los Angeles County	407
Kentucky	756	Fresno County, CA	404	**North Miami Beach, FL** (city) Miami-Dade County	469
Arkansas	762	Polk County, FL	455	**Conroe, TX** (city) Montgomery County	497
Michigan	879	Hartford County, CT	471	**Yonkers, NY** (city) Westchester County	498
Utah	911	Galveston County, TX	473	**Philadelphia, PA** (city) Philadelphia County	513
Mississippi	944	Johnston County, NC	491	**Oklahoma City, OK** (city) Oklahoma County	531
Wisconsin	963	Hall County, GA	493	**Garland, TX** (city) Dallas County	587
Ohio	1,117	Philadelphia County, PA	513	**West Little River, FL** (cdp) Miami-Dade County	592

Sorted by Percent in Descending Order — U.S. = 86.2%

State	Percent	County	Percent	Place	Percent
Oklahoma	96.4	Beaufort County, SC	100.0	**Huntington Station, NY** (cdp) Suffolk County	100.0
Ohio	96.1	Elkhart County, IN	100.0	**Plainfield, NJ** (city) Union County	99.3
Michigan	95.4	Denton County, TX	97.1	**Huntington, NY** (town) Suffolk County	98.7
Kentucky	95.1	Jackson County, MO	97.1	**Wheaton, MD** (cdp) Montgomery County	98.4
District of Columbia	95.0	Sampson County, NC	96.7	**Hempstead (village), NY** (village) Nassau County	98.1
Iowa	94.4	Atlantic County, NJ	96.6	**Chelsea, MA** (city) Suffolk County	98.0
Missouri	94.0	Collier County, FL	96.6	**Durham, NC** (city) Durham County	96.6
Kansas	93.8	Davidson County, TN	96.1	**Charlotte, NC** (city) Mecklenburg County	96.1
Pennsylvania	93.8	Mecklenburg County, NC	96.1	**Nashville-Davidson, TN** (metropolitan govt) Davidson County	96.1
North Carolina	92.9	Durham County, NC	95.9	**Waukegan, IL** (city) Lake County	96.0

Sorted by Percent in Ascending Order — U.S. = 86.2%

State	Percent	County	Percent	Place	Percent
Florida	79.4	Kern County, CA	66.2	**Pasadena, CA** (city) Los Angeles County	59.2
Connecticut	82.0	Galveston County, TX	66.5	**West Little River, FL** (cdp) Miami-Dade County	64.4
Nebraska	82.4	Miami-Dade County, FL	73.8	**Miami, FL** (city) Miami-Dade County	65.4
California	82.6	Montgomery County, TX	74.6	**Conroe, TX** (city) Montgomery County	71.1
Wisconsin	85.0	New Haven County, CT	74.7	**North Miami Beach, FL** (city) Miami-Dade County	72.3
Arkansas	85.1	Osceola County, FL	78.3	**Miramar, FL** (city) Broward County	74.2
Arizona	85.2	Westchester County, NY	78.4	**Yonkers, NY** (city) Westchester County	74.4
Louisiana	85.3	Bexar County, TX	78.7	**Hialeah, FL** (city) Miami-Dade County	76.1
New York	85.9	Arapahoe County, CO	79.5	**Garland, TX** (city) Dallas County	78.5
Illinois	86.0	Riverside County, CA	80.7	**San Antonio, TX** (city) Bexar County	78.9

Note: (1) Ranking tables cover all states and counties, and places with an overall population of at least 125,000, OR an overall population of at least 25,000 where the Hispanic/Latino population is at least 20% of the overall population. In states where less than five places meet either of these criteria, we have included places with at least 10,000 total population with the highest percentage of Hispanic/Latino population. These places are identified with an asterisk (*); Please refer to the User's Guide for a full explanation of data.

Class of Worker: Private Wage and Salary

(Universe: Civilian Employed Population 16 Years and Over)

Central American: Nicaraguan

Top 10 States, Counties, and Places[1]

Sorted by Number in Descending Order — U.S. = 148,230

State	Number	County	Number	Place	Number
Florida	63,882	Miami-Dade County, FL	50,572	**Miami, FL** (city) Miami-Dade County	12,392
California	39,062	Los Angeles County, CA	15,578	**Los Angeles, CA** (city) Los Angeles County	6,905
Texas	7,328	San Mateo County, CA	3,898	**Hialeah, FL** (city) Miami-Dade County	5,241
New York	5,709	Broward County, FL	3,563	**New York, NY** (city)	4,319
New Jersey	3,854	Harris County, TX	3,248	**Fountainebleau, FL** (cdp) Miami-Dade County	3,270
Louisiana	3,687	San Bernardino County, CA	2,818	**San Francisco, CA** (city) San Francisco County	2,561
Virginia	3,456	Alameda County, CA	2,811	**Tamiami, FL** (cdp) Miami-Dade County	2,081
Maryland	3,404	San Francisco County, CA	2,561	**Houston, TX** (city) Harris County	2,058
Nevada	1,879	Jefferson Parish, LA	2,269	**Kendale Lakes, FL** (cdp) Miami-Dade County	1,910
North Carolina	1,813	Contra Costa County, CA	2,240	**Daly City, CA** (city) San Mateo County	1,572

Sorted by Number in Ascending Order — U.S. = 148,230

State	Number	County	Number	Place	Number
Missouri	227	Gwinnett County, GA	195	**South Gate, CA** (city) Los Angeles County	252
Michigan	261	King County, WA	303	**San Diego, CA** (city) San Diego County	315
Indiana	297	Lee County, FL	368	**Sacramento, CA** (city) Sacramento County	338
Connecticut	333	Bexar County, TX	372	**Austin, TX** (city) Travis County	406
Tennessee	350	Camden County, NJ	433	**Richmond, CA** (city) Contra Costa County	459
Oregon	396	Stanislaus County, CA	462	**Las Vegas, NV** (city) Clark County	460
South Carolina	450	Duval County, FL	463	**Jacksonville, FL** (city) Duval County	463
District of Columbia	477	Travis County, TX	488	**South San Francisco, CA** (city) San Mateo County	472
Ohio	497	San Joaquin County, CA	510	**Oakland, CA** (city) Alameda County	520
Minnesota	500	Sonoma County, CA	529	**Chicago, IL** (city) Cook County	526

Sorted by Percent in Descending Order — U.S. = 83.2%

State	Percent	County	Percent	Place	Percent
South Carolina	96.2	Collier County, FL	96.4	**Richmond West, FL** (cdp) Miami-Dade County	98.3
Massachusetts	94.9	Sonoma County, CA	93.8	**North Miami, FL** (city) Miami-Dade County	94.7
New Jersey	89.9	Hudson County, NJ	91.3	**Kenner, LA** (city) Jefferson Parish	94.1
Illinois	89.6	New York County, NY	89.3	**Country Club, FL** (cdp) Miami-Dade County	93.8
Minnesota	89.0	Clark County, NV	88.6	**Tamiami, FL** (cdp) Miami-Dade County	93.4
Louisiana	88.6	Cook County, IL	88.5	**Kendall West, FL** (cdp) Miami-Dade County	92.7
Nevada	87.6	Jefferson Parish, LA	88.5	**Homestead, FL** (city) Miami-Dade County	92.1
District of Columbia	85.6	Stanislaus County, CA	88.5	**Metairie, LA** (cdp) Jefferson Parish	91.6
Florida	85.4	Alameda County, CA	88.2	**Fontana, CA** (city) San Bernardino County	91.0
Arizona	85.3	Santa Clara County, CA	88.0	**Kendale Lakes, FL** (cdp) Miami-Dade County	91.0

Sorted by Percent in Ascending Order — U.S. = 83.2%

State	Percent	County	Percent	Place	Percent
Missouri	69.4	Gwinnett County, GA	62.9	**Daly City, CA** (city) San Mateo County	74.5
Connecticut	75.3	Prince William County, VA	66.9	**San Diego, CA** (city) San Diego County	74.5
Indiana	75.6	Prince George's County, MD	68.7	**Antioch, CA** (city) Contra Costa County	74.6
Ohio	75.6	Contra Costa County, CA	69.2	**South San Francisco, CA** (city) San Mateo County	75.5
Maryland	76.6	San Diego County, CA	73.9	**Jacksonville, FL** (city) Duval County	75.7
Virginia	76.6	Sacramento County, CA	74.9	**Richmond, CA** (city) Contra Costa County	76.8
Michigan	76.8	Duval County, FL	75.7	**Charlotte, NC** (city) Mecklenburg County	77.3
Washington	76.9	Travis County, TX	77.1	**Kendall, FL** (cdp) Miami-Dade County	77.7
Wisconsin	78.2	Fairfax County, VA	77.5	**Miami, FL** (city) Miami-Dade County	77.9
North Carolina	79.8	Kings County, NY	78.2	**Brooklyn, NY** (borough) Kings County	78.2

Note: (1) Ranking tables cover all states and counties, and places with an overall population of at least 125,000, OR an overall population of at least 25,000 where the Hispanic/Latino population is at least 20% of the overall population. In states where less than five places meet either of these criteria, we have included places with at least 10,000 total population with the highest percentage of Hispanic/Latino population. These places are identified with an asterisk (*); Please refer to the User's Guide for a full explanation of data.

Class of Worker: Private Wage and Salary

(Universe: Civilian Employed Population 16 Years and Over)

Central American: Panamanian

Top 10 States, Counties, and Places[1]

Sorted by Number in Descending Order — U.S. = 57,807

State	Number	County	Number	Place	Number
Florida	10,353	Kings County, NY	4,834	**New York, NY** (city)	7,998
New York	10,076	Miami-Dade County, FL	3,234	**Brooklyn, NY** (borough) Kings County	4,834
California	6,157	Los Angeles County, CA	2,004	**Queens, NY** (borough) Queens County	1,294
Texas	4,479	Broward County, FL	1,595	**Manhattan, NY** (borough) New York County	920
Virginia	2,654	Queens County, NY	1,294	**Bronx, NY** (borough) Bronx County	762
Georgia	2,591	Orange County, FL	1,170	**Los Angeles, CA** (city) Los Angeles County	672
New Jersey	2,203	Hillsborough County, FL	1,076	**Hempstead (town), NY** (town) Nassau County	549
North Carolina	1,694	New York County, NY	920	**Jacksonville, FL** (city) Duval County	549
Maryland	1,639	San Diego County, CA	907	**San Antonio, TX** (city) Bexar County	503
Massachusetts	1,479	Bronx County, NY	762	**San Diego, CA** (city) San Diego County	446

Sorted by Number in Ascending Order — U.S. = 57,807

State	Number	County	Number	Place	Number
Mississippi	98	Sacramento County, CA	210	**Killeen, TX** (city) Bell County	203
New Mexico	215	Pierce County, WA	262	**Miami, FL** (city) Miami-Dade County	318
Wisconsin	301	Hudson County, NJ	304	**Fayetteville, NC** (city) Cumberland County	339
Minnesota	381	Bell County, TX	308	**Houston, TX** (city) Harris County	422
Connecticut	388	Orange County, CA	320	**San Diego, CA** (city) San Diego County	446
Oklahoma	446	San Bernardino County, CA	340	**San Antonio, TX** (city) Bexar County	503
Indiana	455	Palm Beach County, FL	352	**Hempstead (town), NY** (town) Nassau County	549
Kentucky	478	Fairfax County, VA	374	**Jacksonville, FL** (city) Duval County	549
Michigan	511	Montgomery County, MD	388	**Los Angeles, CA** (city) Los Angeles County	672
Nevada	532	Riverside County, CA	390	**Bronx, NY** (borough) Bronx County	762

Sorted by Percent in Descending Order — U.S. = 74.6%

State	Percent	County	Percent	Place	Percent
Minnesota	89.6	Dallas County, TX	94.0	**Houston, TX** (city) Harris County	86.3
Ohio	89.4	Maricopa County, AZ	88.1	**San Diego, CA** (city) San Diego County	84.0
Illinois	88.7	Clark County, NV	86.7	**San Antonio, TX** (city) Bexar County	81.1
Kentucky	85.8	Orange County, FL	84.8	**Manhattan, NY** (borough) New York County	77.8
Indiana	85.0	Cook County, IL	83.4	**Jacksonville, FL** (city) Duval County	75.2
Massachusetts	84.8	Hudson County, NJ	81.9	**Los Angeles, CA** (city) Los Angeles County	74.5
Pennsylvania	82.9	Pierce County, WA	79.6	**Brooklyn, NY** (borough) Kings County	70.5
Alabama	80.5	Essex County, NJ	79.0	**New York, NY** (city)	70.3
Nevada	80.5	Palm Beach County, FL	78.0	**Hempstead (town), NY** (town) Nassau County	70.0
Tennessee	80.4	New York County, NY	77.8	**Bronx, NY** (borough) Bronx County	69.3

Sorted by Percent in Ascending Order — U.S. = 74.6%

State	Percent	County	Percent	Place	Percent
Mississippi	55.7	Bell County, TX	59.5	**Killeen, TX** (city) Bell County	49.2
Washington	64.3	Sacramento County, CA	59.5	**Fayetteville, NC** (city) Cumberland County	62.5
Maryland	67.7	Prince William County, VA	60.2	**Queens, NY** (borough) Queens County	65.1
Connecticut	68.3	San Bernardino County, CA	62.5	**Miami, FL** (city) Miami-Dade County	68.8
Virginia	68.4	Cumberland County, NC	62.6	**Bronx, NY** (borough) Bronx County	69.3
South Carolina	68.5	Queens County, NY	65.1	**Hempstead (town), NY** (town) Nassau County	70.0
North Carolina	69.1	Suffolk County, NY	66.2	**New York, NY** (city)	70.3
New York	69.7	Orange County, CA	66.9	**Brooklyn, NY** (borough) Kings County	70.5
Colorado	70.3	Fairfax County, VA	68.1	**Los Angeles, CA** (city) Los Angeles County	74.5
Wisconsin	72.7	Bronx County, NY	69.3	**Jacksonville, FL** (city) Duval County	75.2

Note: (1) Ranking tables cover all states and counties, and places with an overall population of at least 125,000, OR an overall population of at least 25,000 where the Hispanic/Latino population is at least 20% of the overall population. In states where less than five places meet either of these criteria, we have included places with at least 10,000 total population with the highest percentage of Hispanic/Latino population. These places are identified with an asterisk (*); Please refer to the User's Guide for a full explanation of data.

Class of Worker: Private Wage and Salary

(Universe: Civilian Employed Population 16 Years and Over)

Central American: Salvadoran

Top 10 States, Counties, and Places[1]

Sorted by Number in Descending Order — U.S. = 724,552

State	Number	County	Number	Place	Number
California	244,392	Los Angeles County, CA	155,274	**Los Angeles, CA** (city) Los Angeles County	98,612
Texas	101,115	Harris County, TX	55,819	**Houston, TX** (city) Harris County	37,477
New York	64,284	Montgomery County, MD	24,990	**New York, NY** (city)	17,926
Maryland	57,041	Prince George's County, MD	22,548	**Hempstead (town), NY** (town) Nassau County	13,774
Virginia	54,279	Suffolk County, NY	21,343	**Islip, NY** (town) Suffolk County	11,965
New Jersey	26,413	Dallas County, TX	20,562	**Queens, NY** (borough) Queens County	10,086
Florida	25,024	Nassau County, NY	19,966	**Dallas, TX** (city) Dallas County	9,496
Massachusetts	19,698	Fairfax County, VA	18,593	**San Francisco, CA** (city) San Francisco County	6,090
North Carolina	15,759	Clark County, NV	11,515	**Irving, TX** (city) Dallas County	6,088
Georgia	15,669	Prince William County, VA	11,168	**Boston, MA** (city) Suffolk County	5,403

Sorted by Number in Ascending Order — U.S. = 724,552

State	Number	County	Number	Place	Number
Hawaii	350	Polk County, FL	271	**Santa Rosa, CA** (city) Sonoma County	319
Idaho	399	Yolo County, CA	308	**Hesperia, CA** (city) San Bernardino County	320
Alaska	535	Duval County, FL	352	**Victorville, CA** (city) San Bernardino County	350
Wisconsin	674	Cache County, UT	361	**Jacksonville, FL** (city) Duval County	352
Kentucky	779	Williamson County, TX	376	**Mesquite, TX** (city) Dallas County	365
New Mexico	814	El Paso County, TX	379	**Tacoma, WA** (city) Pierce County	378
Alabama	991	Buncombe County, NC	383	**East Palo Alto, CA** (city) San Mateo County	381
Oklahoma	1,035	Placer County, CA	385	**Bridgeport, CT** (city/town) Fairfield County	387
South Carolina	1,299	Merced County, CA	387	**Lewisville, TX** (city) Denton County	394
Michigan	1,534	El Paso County, CO	400	**Willowbrook, CA** (cdp) Los Angeles County	400

Sorted by Percent in Descending Order — U.S. = 86.9%

State	Percent	County	Percent	Place	Percent
Indiana	98.0	Crawford County, AR	100.0	**Revere, MA** (city) Suffolk County	100.0
Minnesota	95.7	Fulton County, GA	100.0	**Richmond, VA** (independent city)	100.0
Massachusetts	95.6	Henrico County, VA	100.0	**Salinas, CA** (city) Monterey County	100.0
Pennsylvania	95.3	Hall County, NE	99.7	**Winston-Salem, NC** (city) Forsyth County	100.0
Nebraska	95.0	Osceola County, FL	99.1	**Grand Island, NE** (city) Hall County	99.7
Rhode Island	94.5	Forsyth County, NC	98.9	**Everett, MA** (city) Middlesex County	99.2
Alabama	93.4	Ramsey County, MN	98.8	**Greensboro, NC** (city) Guilford County	99.0
Nevada	93.2	Worcester County, MA	98.8	**Saint Paul, MN** (city) Ramsey County	98.6
New Jersey	92.9	Marion County, IN	98.4	**Worcester, MA** (city) Worcester County	98.4
District of Columbia	92.8	Guilford County, NC	97.9	**Indianapolis, IN** (city) Marion County	98.3

Sorted by Percent in Ascending Order — U.S. = 86.9%

State	Percent	County	Percent	Place	Percent
Louisiana	75.0	Yolo County, CA	67.7	**East Palo Alto, CA** (city) San Mateo County	60.4
New Mexico	78.0	Jackson County, MO	68.9	**Glendale, CA** (city) Los Angeles County	67.4
Alaska	81.3	Merced County, CA	68.9	**Redwood City, CA** (city) San Mateo County	70.9
South Carolina	82.3	Brazoria County, TX	73.4	**Homestead, FL** (city) Miami-Dade County	72.0
California	82.4	Napa County, CA	74.0	**Santa Rosa, CA** (city) Sonoma County	72.5
Oregon	83.9	Multnomah County, OR	75.2	**Vallejo, CA** (city) Solano County	72.6
Oklahoma	84.8	Solano County, CA	76.8	**Portland, OR** (city) Multnomah County	72.8
Missouri	86.1	Walker County, TX	76.8	**Santa Clarita, CA** (city) Los Angeles County	74.1
Utah	86.6	Sonoma County, CA	77.0	**Whittier, CA** (city) Los Angeles County	74.2
Florida	86.9	Williamson County, TX	77.0	**Antioch, CA** (city) Contra Costa County	74.6

Note: (1) Ranking tables cover all states and counties, and places with an overall population of at least 125,000, OR an overall population of at least 25,000 where the Hispanic/Latino population is at least 20% of the overall population. In states where less than five places meet either of these criteria, we have included places with at least 10,000 total population with the highest percentage of Hispanic/Latino population. These places are identified with an asterisk (*); Please refer to the User's Guide for a full explanation of data.

Class of Worker: Private Wage and Salary

(Universe: Civilian Employed Population 16 Years and Over)

Cuban

Top 10 States, Counties, and Places[1]

Sorted by Number in Descending Order — U.S. = 629,005

State	Number	County	Number	Place	Number
Florida	435,092	Miami-Dade County, FL	302,737	**Hialeah, FL** (city) Miami-Dade County	58,490
New Jersey	30,328	Broward County, FL	33,048	**Miami, FL** (city) Miami-Dade County	45,421
California	28,815	Hillsborough County, FL	24,238	**New York, NY** (city)	13,846
New York	23,863	Los Angeles County, CA	13,846	**Tamiami, FL** (cdp) Miami-Dade County	13,574
Texas	15,561	Palm Beach County, FL	13,715	**Kendale Lakes, FL** (cdp) Miami-Dade County	11,167
Nevada	8,472	Hudson County, NJ	9,988	**Fountainebleau, FL** (cdp) Miami-Dade County	10,316
Georgia	8,399	Orange County, FL	8,825	**Kendall, FL** (cdp) Miami-Dade County	9,679
Illinois	7,820	Clark County, NV	7,991	**Westchester, FL** (cdp) Miami-Dade County	8,336
North Carolina	5,900	Lee County, FL	6,452	**Tampa, FL** (city) Hillsborough County	7,984
Pennsylvania	5,894	Collier County, FL	6,411	**Pembroke Pines, FL** (city) Broward County	6,733

Sorted by Number in Ascending Order — U.S. = 629,005

State	Number	County	Number	Place	Number
Arkansas	190	Hampden County, MA	123	**Riverside, CA** (city) Riverside County	212
Maine	236	Sumter County, FL	149	**Santa Clarita, CA** (city) Los Angeles County	257
West Virginia	244	Berks County, PA	156	**Bell, CA** (city) Los Angeles County	259
Iowa	410	Saint Tammany Parish, LA	214	**Columbus, OH** (city) Franklin County	278
Delaware	411	El Paso County, TX	221	**Milwaukee, WI** (city) Milwaukee County	279
Hawaii	459	Kern County, CA	228	**Kearny, NJ** (town) Hudson County	288
Mississippi	493	Forsyth County, GA	236	**Oyster Bay, NY** (town) Nassau County	313
New Hampshire	562	Oakland County, MI	243	**Baltimore, MD** (independent city)	323
Rhode Island	593	Pierce County, WA	249	**Linden, NJ** (city) Union County	323
District of Columbia	652	Worcester County, MA	256	**Rochester, NY** (city) Monroe County	326

Sorted by Percent in Descending Order — U.S. = 80.7%

State	Percent	County	Percent	Place	Percent
Nebraska	94.1	Clay County, MO	98.0	**Oakland Park, FL** (city) Broward County	97.6
Kansas	92.4	Lancaster County, PA	96.1	**Kansas City, MO** (city) Jackson County	95.7
Minnesota	90.5	Essex County, MA	94.8	**Syracuse, NY** (city) Onondaga County	95.4
Missouri	89.7	Lake County, IL	93.9	**Spring Valley, NV** (cdp) Clark County	95.1
Nevada	88.5	Philadelphia County, PA	93.7	**Islip, NY** (town) Suffolk County	94.7
Kentucky	88.2	Cuyahoga County, OH	92.7	**Philadelphia, PA** (city) Philadelphia County	93.7
Oklahoma	85.7	Hernando County, FL	92.5	**Coconut Creek, FL** (city) Broward County	93.1
Pennsylvania	85.4	Chester County, PA	92.3	**Hallandale Beach, FL** (city) Broward County	92.2
Indiana	84.0	El Paso County, TX	92.1	**Lake Magdalene, FL** (cdp) Hillsborough County	92.0
Hawaii	83.8	Jackson County, MO	92.0	**Louisville-Jefferson County, KY** (metropolitan govt) Jefferson County	91.7

Sorted by Percent in Ascending Order — U.S. = 80.7%

State	Percent	County	Percent	Place	Percent
District of Columbia	65.1	Mercer County, NJ	56.3	**Oyster Bay, NY** (town) Nassau County	52.6
Maryland	69.8	Hampden County, MA	62.8	**Carrollwood, FL** (cdp) Hillsborough County	59.2
West Virginia	70.9	Berks County, PA	63.2	**Greenacres, FL** (city) Palm Beach County	63.7
Maine	72.8	Rockland County, NY	64.2	**Riverside, CA** (city) Riverside County	67.1
Arkansas	73.1	Forsyth County, GA	64.7	**Bronx, NY** (borough) Bronx County	67.2
Utah	73.5	Dutchess County, NY	65.5	**Tallahassee, FL** (city) Leon County	69.9
California	76.0	Hamilton County, OH	65.8	**Long Beach, CA** (city) Los Angeles County	70.2
Colorado	77.1	Monroe County, FL	65.9	**Columbus, OH** (city) Franklin County	70.7
Wisconsin	77.2	Montgomery County, MD	65.9	**New Orleans, LA** (city) Orleans Parish	71.6
North Carolina	77.3	Alameda County, CA	66.4	**Tamarac, FL** (city) Broward County	72.4

Note: (1) Ranking tables cover all states and counties, and places with an overall population of at least 125,000, OR an overall population of at least 25,000 where the Hispanic/Latino population is at least 20% of the overall population. In states where less than five places meet either of these criteria, we have included places with at least 10,000 total population with the highest percentage of Hispanic/Latino population. These places are identified with an asterisk (*); Please refer to the User's Guide for a full explanation of data.

Class of Worker: Private Wage and Salary

(Universe: Civilian Employed Population 16 Years and Over)

Dominican Republic

Top 10 States, Counties, and Places[1]

Sorted by Number in Descending Order — U.S. = 488,117

State	Number	County	Number	Place	Number
New York	232,067	Bronx County, NY	76,765	**New York, NY** (city)	196,541
New Jersey	74,139	New York County, NY	55,100	**Bronx, NY** (borough) Bronx County	76,765
Florida	63,927	Queens County, NY	35,131	**Manhattan, NY** (borough) New York County	55,100
Massachusetts	37,941	Kings County, NY	28,398	**Queens, NY** (borough) Queens County	35,131
Pennsylvania	17,769	Miami-Dade County, FL	21,994	**Brooklyn, NY** (borough) Kings County	28,398
Rhode Island	11,587	Essex County, MA	18,941	**Lawrence, MA** (city) Essex County	10,671
Connecticut	8,673	Passaic County, NJ	16,640	**Paterson, NJ** (city) Passaic County	9,620
Georgia	4,471	Hudson County, NJ	16,048	**Boston, MA** (city) Suffolk County	9,474
Maryland	4,418	Broward County, FL	11,363	**Providence, RI** (city) Providence County	8,377
Texas	4,189	Providence County, RI	11,123	**Hempstead (town), NY** (town) Nassau County	7,649

Sorted by Number in Ascending Order — U.S. = 488,117

State	Number	County	Number	Place	Number
Utah	245	Ulster County, NY	88	**Syracuse, NY** (city) Onondaga County	260
Washington	287	Sullivan County, NY	200	**Deltona, FL** (city) Volusia County	277
Alabama	314	San Diego County, CA	236	**North Miami, FL** (city) Miami-Dade County	281
Minnesota	345	Burlington County, NJ	263	**Bethlehem, PA** (city) Northampton County	322
Wisconsin	529	Erie County, NY	264	**Grand Rapids, MI** (city) Kent County	329
Delaware	531	Oneida County, NY	269	**Ramapo, NY** (town) Rockland County	335
South Carolina	534	Lackawanna County, PA	277	**North Hempstead, NY** (town) Nassau County	337
Colorado	574	Marion County, FL	278	**Englewood, NJ** (city) Bergen County	340
Missouri	621	Bexar County, TX	285	**Weston, FL** (city) Broward County	346
Alaska	684	Litchfield County, CT	307	**New Haven, CT** (city/town) New Haven County	354

Sorted by Percent in Descending Order — U.S. = 84.4%

State	Percent	County	Percent	Place	Percent
Missouri	94.4	Hillsborough County, NH	98.6	**New London, CT** (city/town) New London County	100.0
Alabama	91.3	Atlantic County, NJ	96.0	**Stamford, CT** (city/town) Fairfield County	100.0
Ohio	90.2	Lackawanna County, PA	95.8	**York, PA** (city) York County	100.0
Pennsylvania	89.8	Luzerne County, PA	95.7	**The Hammocks, FL** (cdp) Miami-Dade County	99.1
Massachusetts	89.1	Wake County, NC	94.7	**Hazleton, PA** (city) Luzerne County	98.2
New Jersey	89.0	Kent County, MI	94.6	**Nashua*, NH** (city) Hillsborough County	98.0
District of Columbia	88.8	Polk County, FL	94.3	**Hartford, CT** (city/town) Hartford County	97.1
Indiana	88.6	Northampton County, PA	94.2	**Central Falls*, RI** (city) Providence County	96.9
North Carolina	88.1	York County, PA	93.8	**Tamiami, FL** (cdp) Miami-Dade County	95.7
New Hampshire	87.9	Cuyahoga County, OH	93.6	**Hackensack, NJ** (city) Bergen County	95.5

Sorted by Percent in Ascending Order — U.S. = 84.4%

State	Percent	County	Percent	Place	Percent
Utah	45.9	San Diego County, CA	50.6	**North Miami, FL** (city) Miami-Dade County	59.5
Washington	65.7	Onondaga County, NY	61.9	**Deltona, FL** (city) Volusia County	68.1
Virginia	69.0	Bexar County, TX	64.9	**Syracuse, NY** (city) Onondaga County	70.8
California	73.6	Sullivan County, NY	67.1	**South Miami Heights, FL** (cdp) Miami-Dade County	71.5
Colorado	77.2	Fairfax County, VA	71.0	**Pennsauken, NJ** (township) Camden County	74.2
Maryland	77.4	Fulton County, GA	72.3	**Brookhaven, NY** (town) Suffolk County	75.0
Nevada	78.5	Erie County, NY	72.7	**Town 'n' Country, FL** (cdp) Hillsborough County	76.2
Georgia	78.9	Volusia County, FL	73.7	**Jacksonville, FL** (city) Duval County	76.4
Texas	79.7	Orange County, NY	74.3	**Cape Coral, FL** (city) Lee County	76.6
Wisconsin	81.1	Litchfield County, CT	74.9	**West Little River, FL** (cdp) Miami-Dade County	77.0

Note: (1) Ranking tables cover all states and counties, and places with an overall population of at least 125,000, OR an overall population of at least 25,000 where the Hispanic/Latino population is at least 20% of the overall population. In states where less than five places meet either of these criteria, we have included places with at least 10,000 total population with the highest percentage of Hispanic/Latino population. These places are identified with an asterisk (*); Please refer to the User's Guide for a full explanation of data.

Class of Worker: Private Wage and Salary

(Universe: Civilian Employed Population 16 Years and Over)

Mexican

Top 10 States, Counties, and Places[1]

Sorted by Number in Descending Order — U.S. = 10,604,462

State	Number	County	Number	Place	Number
California	3,738,169	Los Angeles County, CA	1,211,426	**Los Angeles, CA** (city) Los Angeles County	433,709
Texas	2,532,760	Harris County, TX	435,580	**Houston, TX** (city) Harris County	244,474
Illinois	607,733	Cook County, IL	367,165	**San Antonio, TX** (city) Bexar County	243,038
Arizona	515,641	Orange County, CA	326,619	**Chicago, IL** (city) Cook County	216,191
Colorado	259,064	Maricopa County, AZ	325,712	**Phoenix, AZ** (city) Maricopa County	172,512
Florida	235,105	Bexar County, TX	286,158	**Dallas, TX** (city) Dallas County	164,893
Nevada	201,580	Dallas County, TX	278,898	**El Paso, TX** (city) El Paso County	141,525
Washington	199,881	San Diego County, CA	275,902	**New York, NY** (city)	123,977
Georgia	190,012	San Bernardino County, CA	254,655	**San Diego, CA** (city) San Diego County	105,128
North Carolina	177,908	Riverside County, CA	253,881	**San Jose, CA** (city) Santa Clara County	97,717

Sorted by Number in Ascending Order — U.S. = 10,604,462

State	Number	County	Number	Place	Number
Vermont	1,204	Evangeline Parish, LA	16	**Schofield Barracks*, HI** (cdp) Honolulu County	8
Maine	1,676	Allen Parish, LA	17	**Fort Leonard Wood*, MO** (cdp) Pulaski County	11
West Virginia	2,544	Fulton County, IL	27	**Fort Campbell North*, KY** (cdp) Christian County	34
New Hampshire	2,815	Union County, PA	28	**Florence, AZ** (town) Pinal County	229
North Dakota	3,069	Swift County, MN	36	**Great Falls*, MT** (city) Cascade County	238
Rhode Island	3,455	Yazoo County, MS	45	**Juneau*, AK** (borough) Juneau City and Borough	240
District of Columbia	3,682	Aroostook County, ME	46	**Fort Hood, TX** (cdp) Bell County	250
South Dakota	4,824	Sedgwick County, CO	46	**Mayfield*, KY** (city) Graves County	260
Montana	5,962	Adams County, WI	54	**Miramar, FL** (city) Broward County	293
Alaska	7,623	Cottle County, TX	56	**Fairbanks*, AK** (city) Fairbanks North Star Borough	302

Sorted by Percent in Descending Order — U.S. = 83.9%

State	Percent	County	Percent	Place	Percent
New Hampshire	94.4	Alexander County, NC	100.0	**Berea*, SC** (cdp) Greenville County	100.0
New Jersey	94.1	Atkinson County, GA	100.0	**Fort Campbell North*, KY** (cdp) Christian County	100.0
North Carolina	93.7	Beaver County, UT	100.0	**Hazleton, PA** (city) Luzerne County	100.0
Delaware	92.9	Brunswick County, NC	100.0	**Kendall, FL** (cdp) Miami-Dade County	100.0
Pennsylvania	92.2	Chippewa County, WI	100.0	**Ocoee, FL** (city) Orange County	100.0
Alabama	92.0	Clark County, ID	100.0	**Sanford, NC** (city) Lee County	100.0
Indiana	91.9	Evangeline Parish, LA	100.0	**Springfield, MA** (city) Hampden County	100.0
Rhode Island	91.7	Franklin County, IA	100.0	**New Brunswick, NJ** (city) Middlesex County	99.8
South Carolina	91.5	Gladwin County, MI	100.0	**Asheboro, NC** (city) Randolph County	99.0
Minnesota	91.4	Greene County, TN	100.0	**Sioux Falls, SD** (city) Minnehaha County	99.0

Sorted by Percent in Ascending Order — U.S. = 83.9%

State	Percent	County	Percent	Place	Percent
New Mexico	74.4	Allen Parish, LA	30.4	**Schofield Barracks*, HI** (cdp) Honolulu County	10.7
Hawaii	74.9	Latah County, ID	40.6	**Fort Leonard Wood*, MO** (cdp) Pulaski County	36.7
District of Columbia	76.5	Oneida County, NY	42.5	**Fort Hood, TX** (cdp) Bell County	43.1
Texas	80.0	Prince George County, VA	45.5	**Florence, AZ** (town) Pinal County	43.5
Alaska	80.1	Crowley County, CO	46.0	**Twentynine Palms, CA** (city) San Bernardino County	51.6
North Dakota	80.3	Osage County, OK	46.7	**Juneau*, AK** (borough) Juneau City and Borough	51.8
Vermont	80.4	Terrell County, TX	48.4	**Hampton, VA** (independent city)	60.6
Montana	80.9	Lassen County, CA	51.2	**Elk Grove, CA** (city) Sacramento County	60.9
West Virginia	81.2	Jeff Davis County, TX	53.2	**Fayetteville, NC** (city) Cumberland County	61.7
Arizona	81.4	Whitman County, WA	54.5	**Kingsville, TX** (city) Kleberg County	63.6

Note: (1) Ranking tables cover all states and counties, and places with an overall population of at least 125,000, OR an overall population of at least 25,000 where the Hispanic/Latino population is at least 20% of the overall population. In states where less than five places meet either of these criteria, we have included places with at least 10,000 total population with the highest percentage of Hispanic/Latino population. These places are identified with an asterisk (*); Please refer to the User's Guide for a full explanation of data.

Class of Worker: Private Wage and Salary

(Universe: Civilian Employed Population 16 Years and Over)

Puerto Rican

Top 10 States, Counties, and Places[1]

Sorted by Number in Descending Order — U.S. = 1,356,636

State	Number	County	Number	Place	Number
New York	298,358	Bronx County, NY	73,471	**New York, NY** (city)	197,991
Florida	275,879	Orange County, FL	50,154	**Bronx, NY** (borough) Bronx County	73,471
New Jersey	140,728	Kings County, NY	46,956	**Brooklyn, NY** (borough) Kings County	46,956
Pennsylvania	95,154	Cook County, IL	40,429	**Queens, NY** (borough) Queens County	37,791
Connecticut	76,263	Queens County, NY	37,791	**Chicago, IL** (city) Cook County	31,946
Massachusetts	66,457	Miami-Dade County, FL	35,761	**Manhattan, NY** (borough) New York County	28,459
California	57,170	Hillsborough County, FL	29,783	**Philadelphia, PA** (city) Philadelphia County	27,651
Illinois	57,118	Broward County, FL	28,962	**Staten Island, NY** (borough) Richmond County	11,314
Texas	39,994	New York County, NY	28,459	**Hartford, CT** (city/town) Hartford County	11,086
Ohio	27,062	Hartford County, CT	27,728	**Springfield, MA** (city) Hampden County	11,029

Sorted by Number in Ascending Order — U.S. = 1,356,636

State	Number	County	Number	Place	Number
Wyoming	127	Wyoming County, NY	12	**Fort Hood, TX** (cdp) Bell County	79
North Dakota	226	Christian County, KY	42	**Columbia, SC** (city) Richland County	110
South Dakota	282	Chemung County, NY	52	**San Bernardino, CA** (city) San Bernardino County	197
Montana	406	Schoharie County, NY	53	**West Covina, CA** (city) Los Angeles County	202
Vermont	706	Dale County, AL	65	**Waianae*, HI** (cdp) Honolulu County	207
West Virginia	915	Washington County, NY	68	**Montgomery, AL** (city) Montgomery County	208
Alaska	1,048	Seneca County, NY	72	**Bridgeton, NJ** (city) Cumberland County	214
Nebraska	1,048	Perry County, PA	74	**Hazleton, PA** (city) Luzerne County	222
Idaho	1,057	Lowndes County, GA	86	**Cooper City, FL** (city) Broward County	238
District of Columbia	1,348	Delaware County, NY	114	**Vallejo, CA** (city) Solano County	242

Sorted by Percent in Descending Order — U.S. = 79.9%

State	Percent	County	Percent	Place	Percent
Iowa	88.1	Clearfield County, PA	100.0	**Hackensack, NJ** (city) Bergen County	98.5
New Hampshire	87.8	Carroll County, MD	97.2	**Spring Valley, NV** (cdp) Clark County	97.6
Rhode Island	87.2	Warren County, OH	97.1	**Fort Wayne, IN** (city) Allen County	97.4
Delaware	87.1	Lake County, OH	96.7	**Rockford, IL** (city) Winnebago County	97.4
Pennsylvania	86.2	Lycoming County, PA	96.7	**Coconut Creek, FL** (city) Broward County	96.5
Maine	85.8	Sussex County, DE	96.5	**Atlantic City, NJ** (city) Atlantic County	95.0
Wisconsin	85.8	Ashtabula County, OH	96.1	**Lebanon, PA** (city) Lebanon County	95.0
Minnesota	84.8	Allen County, IN	95.5	**Miami Beach, FL** (city) Miami-Dade County	94.7
Michigan	84.5	Medina County, OH	95.0	**Casselberry, FL** (city) Seminole County	94.6
Indiana	84.4	Sampson County, NC	94.9	**Central Falls*, RI** (city) Providence County	94.5

Sorted by Percent in Ascending Order — U.S. = 79.9%

State	Percent	County	Percent	Place	Percent
Wyoming	52.7	Chemung County, NY	21.4	**Alexandria, VA** (independent city)	49.0
South Dakota	59.7	Dale County, AL	37.8	**Arlington, VA** (cdp) Arlington County	53.6
District of Columbia	65.7	Delaware County, NY	42.2	**San Bernardino, CA** (city) San Bernardino County	53.7
North Dakota	67.5	Christian County, KY	44.7	**Chesapeake, VA** (independent city)	60.1
Maryland	67.9	Marin County, CA	46.2	**Modesto, CA** (city) Stanislaus County	61.0
Alabama	69.4	Greene County, NY	47.2	**Hempstead (village), NY** (village) Nassau County	61.1
Virginia	69.9	Pulaski County, MO	47.9	**El Paso, TX** (city) El Paso County	61.3
Alaska	70.1	Lee County, AL	50.9	**Chula Vista, CA** (city) San Diego County	62.4
Montana	70.9	Thurston County, WA	51.4	**Moreno Valley, CA** (city) Riverside County	62.4
New Mexico	72.3	Tulare County, CA	51.9	**Augusta-Richmond County, GA** (consolidated govt) Richmond County	63.0

Note: (1) Ranking tables cover all states and counties, and places with an overall population of at least 125,000, OR an overall population of at least 25,000 where the Hispanic/Latino population is at least 20% of the overall population. In states where less than five places meet either of these criteria, we have included places with at least 10,000 total population with the highest percentage of Hispanic/Latino population. These places are identified with an asterisk (*); Please refer to the User's Guide for a full explanation of data.

Class of Worker: Private Wage and Salary

(Universe: Civilian Employed Population 16 Years and Over)

South American

Top 10 States, Counties, and Places[1]

Sorted by Number in Descending Order — U.S. = 1,195,277

State	Number	County	Number	Place	Number
Florida	292,915	Miami-Dade County, FL	119,593	**New York, NY** (city)	159,054
New York	232,734	Queens County, NY	99,210	**Queens, NY** (borough) Queens County	99,210
New Jersey	156,639	Broward County, FL	63,679	**Brooklyn, NY** (borough) Kings County	22,841
California	114,081	Los Angeles County, CA	49,560	**Los Angeles, CA** (city) Los Angeles County	21,538
Texas	51,787	Hudson County, NJ	32,737	**Manhattan, NY** (borough) New York County	17,747
Virginia	46,515	Westchester County, NY	23,596	**Chicago, IL** (city) Cook County	16,741
Illinois	32,544	Cook County, IL	23,327	**Bronx, NY** (borough) Bronx County	15,828
Connecticut	30,940	Kings County, NY	22,841	**Miami, FL** (city) Miami-Dade County	14,718
Massachusetts	26,943	Orange County, FL	22,324	**Elizabeth, NJ** (city) Union County	13,595
Maryland	24,981	Fairfax County, VA	21,726	**Newark, NJ** (city) Essex County	10,666

Sorted by Number in Ascending Order — U.S. = 1,195,277

State	Number	County	Number	Place	Number
North Dakota	242	Oneida County, NY	142	**Killeen, TX** (city) Bell County	171
Vermont	352	Onslow County, NC	148	**Palm Springs, CA** (city) Riverside County	224
Montana	396	Schenectady County, NY	180	**Lexington-Fayette, KY** (consolidated govt) Fayette County	251
West Virginia	513	Spokane County, WA	184	**Chesapeake, VA** (independent city)	253
Maine	579	Washington County, MN	190	**Placentia, CA** (city) Orange County	259
Wyoming	643	Clark County, WA	199	**Inglewood, CA** (city) Los Angeles County	261
Alaska	903	Sussex County, DE	214	**Covina, CA** (city) Los Angeles County	283
Mississippi	908	Hampshire County, MA	249	**Stockton, CA** (city) San Joaquin County	292
Hawaii	1,143	Cache County, UT	250	**Glendora, CA** (city) Los Angeles County	293
Nebraska	1,187	Cleveland County, OK	250	**Sanford, FL** (city) Seminole County	300

Sorted by Percent in Descending Order — U.S. = 82.5%

State	Percent	County	Percent	Place	Percent
Maine	88.8	Kent County, MI	97.7	**New London, CT** (city/town) New London County	100.0
New Hampshire	88.5	Anoka County, MN	96.4	**New Haven, CT** (city/town) New Haven County	97.6
Minnesota	88.4	Cherokee County, GA	96.3	**Central Falls*, RI** (city) Providence County	96.8
Massachusetts	88.1	Douglas County, CO	95.7	**Poinciana, FL** (cdp) Osceola County	96.8
Nevada	88.1	Luzerne County, PA	95.4	**Buenaventura Lakes, FL** (cdp) Osceola County	96.7
New Jersey	87.9	York County, PA	94.8	**New Brunswick, NJ** (city) Middlesex County	96.3
Utah	87.5	Washoe County, NV	94.4	**Lawrence, MA** (city) Essex County	96.1
Idaho	87.2	Oakland County, MI	93.8	**City of Orange, NJ** (township) Essex County	94.9
Pennsylvania	86.0	Saint Louis County, MO	93.6	**Dania Beach, FL** (city) Broward County	94.3
Rhode Island	85.5	Weber County, UT	93.3	**Minneapolis, MN** (city) Hennepin County	94.2

Sorted by Percent in Ascending Order — U.S. = 82.5%

State	Percent	County	Percent	Place	Percent
Mississippi	55.1	Schenectady County, NY	49.5	**Albuquerque, NM** (city) Bernalillo County	51.0
New Mexico	55.6	Bernalillo County, NM	53.5	**Corona, CA** (city) Riverside County	57.5
Vermont	66.0	Brazos County, TX	55.3	**Placentia, CA** (city) Orange County	58.2
Alaska	66.9	El Paso County, TX	56.0	**Inglewood, CA** (city) Los Angeles County	61.4
District of Columbia	67.9	Richland County, SC	57.0	**Rahway, NJ** (city) Union County	63.1
West Virginia	68.2	Hampshire County, MA	57.6	**Silver Spring, MD** (cdp) Montgomery County	63.8
Hawaii	69.9	Cleveland County, OK	58.8	**Hawthorne, CA** (city) Los Angeles County	64.4
Iowa	71.9	Sussex County, DE	60.1	**Covina, CA** (city) Los Angeles County	64.5
North Dakota	72.0	Jefferson County, AL	61.0	**Moreno Valley, CA** (city) Riverside County	65.5
Oregon	75.0	Onslow County, NC	61.2	**Lexington-Fayette, KY** (consolidated govt) Fayette County	65.7

Note: (1) Ranking tables cover all states and counties, and places with an overall population of at least 125,000, OR an overall population of at least 25,000 where the Hispanic/Latino population is at least 20% of the overall population. In states where less than five places meet either of these criteria, we have included places with at least 10,000 total population with the highest percentage of Hispanic/Latino population. These places are identified with an asterisk (*); Please refer to the User's Guide for a full explanation of data.

Class of Worker: Private Wage and Salary

(Universe: Civilian Employed Population 16 Years and Over)

South American: Argentinean

Top 10 States, Counties, and Places[1]

Sorted by Number in Descending Order — U.S. = 92,107

State	Number	County	Number	Place	Number
Florida	24,346	Miami-Dade County, FL	13,182	**New York, NY** (city)	6,786
California	17,066	Los Angeles County, CA	8,113	**Los Angeles, CA** (city) Los Angeles County	3,768
New York	10,907	Broward County, FL	4,640	**Queens, NY** (borough) Queens County	2,688
New Jersey	6,235	Queens County, NY	2,688	**Miami, FL** (city) Miami-Dade County	2,510
Texas	5,428	Orange County, CA	2,328	**Miami Beach, FL** (city) Miami-Dade County	2,197
Illinois	2,384	New York County, NY	2,151	**Manhattan, NY** (borough) New York County	2,151
Virginia	2,155	Harris County, TX	1,830	**Brooklyn, NY** (borough) Kings County	1,207
Utah	2,077	Palm Beach County, FL	1,686	**Houston, TX** (city) Harris County	1,012
Maryland	2,057	Cook County, IL	1,444	**Chicago, IL** (city) Cook County	773
Pennsylvania	2,004	Hudson County, NJ	1,343	**Hollywood, FL** (city) Broward County	746

Sorted by Number in Ascending Order — U.S. = 92,107

State	Number	County	Number	Place	Number
Louisiana	230	Travis County, TX	200	**Coral Springs, FL** (city) Broward County	353
Tennessee	399	Tarrant County, TX	318	**San Diego, CA** (city) San Diego County	390
Missouri	416	Orange County, NY	347	**San Jose, CA** (city) Santa Clara County	413
District of Columbia	451	Montgomery County, TX	377	**Hialeah, FL** (city) Miami-Dade County	420
Oregon	456	Oakland County, MI	398	**San Francisco, CA** (city) San Francisco County	462
Indiana	520	King County, WA	420	**Bronx, NY** (borough) Bronx County	508
Minnesota	537	Contra Costa County, CA	425	**Hempstead (town), NY** (town) Nassau County	560
Wisconsin	579	Ventura County, CA	442	**Doral, FL** (city) Miami-Dade County	566
Colorado	580	Bexar County, TX	456	**Aventura, FL** (city) Miami-Dade County	675
South Carolina	604	Alameda County, CA	459	**Pembroke Pines, FL** (city) Broward County	689

Sorted by Percent in Descending Order — U.S. = 79.3%

State	Percent	County	Percent	Place	Percent
Utah	95.4	Oakland County, MI	100.0	**Aventura, FL** (city) Miami-Dade County	93.4
Minnesota	91.2	Salt Lake County, UT	97.1	**Pembroke Pines, FL** (city) Broward County	93.1
Nevada	87.6	Utah County, UT	96.0	**Doral, FL** (city) Miami-Dade County	91.7
South Carolina	87.3	Hillsborough County, FL	93.8	**Manhattan, NY** (borough) New York County	88.8
New Jersey	85.5	Dallas County, TX	92.1	**Brooklyn, NY** (borough) Kings County	88.2
Massachusetts	84.9	New Haven County, CT	91.7	**San Diego, CA** (city) San Diego County	87.2
Missouri	83.5	Hudson County, NJ	90.6	**New York, NY** (city)	85.7
Texas	83.4	Bergen County, NJ	90.0	**Queens, NY** (borough) Queens County	84.0
Washington	82.9	Middlesex County, NJ	89.5	**Miami Beach, FL** (city) Miami-Dade County	83.6
Florida	82.7	New York County, NY	88.8	**Bronx, NY** (borough) Bronx County	82.5

Sorted by Percent in Ascending Order — U.S. = 79.3%

State	Percent	County	Percent	Place	Percent
Louisiana	59.4	Travis County, TX	55.6	**San Francisco, CA** (city) San Francisco County	58.7
Oregon	62.4	Riverside County, CA	57.0	**Hialeah, FL** (city) Miami-Dade County	68.0
Maryland	64.1	San Francisco County, CA	58.7	**Coral Springs, FL** (city) Broward County	74.8
District of Columbia	64.2	Montgomery County, MD	58.8	**Los Angeles, CA** (city) Los Angeles County	75.5
Arizona	72.6	Fairfax County, VA	64.3	**Miami, FL** (city) Miami-Dade County	75.8
Tennessee	72.8	San Bernardino County, CA	66.3	**Hollywood, FL** (city) Broward County	76.0
California	73.1	Maricopa County, AZ	69.5	**Hempstead (town), NY** (town) Nassau County	77.6
Colorado	74.6	Fairfield County, CT	70.8	**Houston, TX** (city) Harris County	80.8
Virginia	74.6	Suffolk County, NY	71.9	**Chicago, IL** (city) Cook County	81.0
Georgia	76.4	Orange County, CA	72.6	**San Jose, CA** (city) Santa Clara County	82.3

Note: (1) Ranking tables cover all states and counties, and places with an overall population of at least 125,000, OR an overall population of at least 25,000 where the Hispanic/Latino population is at least 20% of the overall population. In states where less than five places meet either of these criteria, we have included places with at least 10,000 total population with the highest percentage of Hispanic/Latino population. These places are identified with an asterisk (*); Please refer to the User's Guide for a full explanation of data.

Class of Worker: Private Wage and Salary

(Universe: Civilian Employed Population 16 Years and Over)

South American: Bolivian

Top 10 States, Counties, and Places[1]

Sorted by Number in Descending Order — U.S. = 45,728

State	Number	County	Number	Place	Number
Virginia	16,745	Fairfax County, VA	9,498	**New York, NY** (city)	2,154
California	5,882	Montgomery County, MD	2,347	**Arlington, VA** (cdp) Arlington County	2,055
Florida	4,530	Los Angeles County, CA	2,281	**Annandale, VA** (cdp) Fairfax County	1,522
New York	3,463	Arlington County, VA	2,055	**Queens, NY** (borough) Queens County	1,461
Maryland	3,333	Prince William County, VA	1,923	**Los Angeles, CA** (city) Los Angeles County	1,340
New Jersey	2,265	Miami-Dade County, FL	1,558	**West Falls Church, VA** (cdp) Fairfax County	816
Texas	1,724	Queens County, NY	1,461	**Dale City, VA** (cdp) Prince William County	644
Massachusetts	995	Loudoun County, VA	1,130	**Springfield, VA** (cdp) Fairfax County	611
Rhode Island	966	Providence County, RI	966	**Providence, RI** (city) Providence County	610
Illinois	699	Broward County, FL	740		

Sorted by Number in Ascending Order — U.S. = 45,728

State	Number	County	Number	Place	Number
North Carolina	194	Cook County, IL	284	**Providence, RI** (city) Providence County	610
Pennsylvania	258	San Diego County, CA	309	**Springfield, VA** (cdp) Fairfax County	611
Illinois	699	Palm Beach County, FL	313	**Dale City, VA** (cdp) Prince William County	644
Rhode Island	966	Santa Clara County, CA	544	**West Falls Church, VA** (cdp) Fairfax County	816
Massachusetts	995	Harris County, TX	553	**Los Angeles, CA** (city) Los Angeles County	1,340
Texas	1,724	Prince George's County, MD	600	**Queens, NY** (borough) Queens County	1,461
New Jersey	2,265	Orange County, CA	635	**Annandale, VA** (cdp) Fairfax County	1,522
Maryland	3,333	Broward County, FL	740	**Arlington, VA** (cdp) Arlington County	2,055
New York	3,463	Providence County, RI	966	**New York, NY** (city)	2,154
Florida	4,530	Loudoun County, VA	1,130		

Sorted by Percent in Descending Order — U.S. = 82.1%

State	Percent	County	Percent	Place	Percent
Massachusetts	92.6	Prince George's County, MD	90.4	**Providence, RI** (city) Providence County	94.1
New Jersey	89.8	Providence County, RI	89.4	**Queens, NY** (borough) Queens County	88.8
Rhode Island	89.4	Queens County, NY	88.8	**Dale City, VA** (cdp) Prince William County	88.0
New York	85.5	Santa Clara County, CA	86.3	**West Falls Church, VA** (cdp) Fairfax County	85.7
Pennsylvania	85.4	Broward County, FL	85.9	**New York, NY** (city)	84.5
Florida	84.0	Loudoun County, VA	85.1	**Springfield, VA** (cdp) Fairfax County	83.2
Virginia	82.2	Prince William County, VA	84.9	**Annandale, VA** (cdp) Fairfax County	82.1
Maryland	80.5	Miami-Dade County, FL	84.6	**Arlington, VA** (cdp) Arlington County	78.7
California	78.4	Fairfax County, VA	83.1	**Los Angeles, CA** (city) Los Angeles County	72.7
North Carolina	77.6	Harris County, TX	82.4		

Sorted by Percent in Ascending Order — U.S. = 82.1%

State	Percent	County	Percent	Place	Percent
Illinois	74.5	Palm Beach County, FL	59.1	**Los Angeles, CA** (city) Los Angeles County	72.7
Texas	74.7	San Diego County, CA	66.0	**Arlington, VA** (cdp) Arlington County	78.7
North Carolina	77.6	Cook County, IL	70.8	**Annandale, VA** (cdp) Fairfax County	82.1
California	78.4	Montgomery County, MD	76.9	**Springfield, VA** (cdp) Fairfax County	83.2
Maryland	80.5	Orange County, CA	77.8	**New York, NY** (city)	84.5
Virginia	82.2	Arlington County, VA	78.7	**West Falls Church, VA** (cdp) Fairfax County	85.7
Florida	84.0	Los Angeles County, CA	79.2	**Dale City, VA** (cdp) Prince William County	88.0
Pennsylvania	85.4	Harris County, TX	82.4	**Queens, NY** (borough) Queens County	88.8
New York	85.5	Fairfax County, VA	83.1	**Providence, RI** (city) Providence County	94.1
Rhode Island	89.4	Miami-Dade County, FL	84.6		

Note: (1) Ranking tables cover all states and counties, and places with an overall population of at least 125,000, OR an overall population of at least 25,000 where the Hispanic/Latino population is at least 20% of the overall population. In states where less than five places meet either of these criteria, we have included places with at least 10,000 total population with the highest percentage of Hispanic/Latino population. These places are identified with an asterisk (*); Please refer to the User's Guide for a full explanation of data.

Class of Worker: Private Wage and Salary

(Universe: Civilian Employed Population 16 Years and Over)

South American: Chilean

Top 10 States, Counties, and Places[1]

Sorted by Number in Descending Order — U.S. = 50,903

State	Number	County	Number	Place	Number
Florida	10,566	Miami-Dade County, FL	5,296	**New York, NY** (city)	2,986
California	8,790	Los Angeles County, CA	3,457	**Los Angeles, CA** (city) Los Angeles County	1,710
New York	6,546	Broward County, FL	2,017	**Queens, NY** (borough) Queens County	1,599
New Jersey	4,092	Queens County, NY	1,599	**Hempstead (town), NY** (town) Nassau County	747
Texas	1,997	Nassau County, NY	1,445	**Miami, FL** (city) Miami-Dade County	613
Maryland	1,718	Westchester County, NY	989	**Manhattan, NY** (borough) New York County	568
Massachusetts	1,509	Hudson County, NJ	984	**Brooklyn, NY** (borough) Kings County	511
Virginia	1,487	Montgomery County, MD	865	**Kendall, FL** (cdp) Miami-Dade County	453
Utah	1,357	Fairfax County, VA	734	**Chicago, IL** (city) Cook County	375
Illinois	1,192	Santa Clara County, CA	734		

Sorted by Number in Ascending Order — U.S. = 50,903

State	Number	County	Number	Place	Number
Minnesota	146	San Bernardino County, CA	331	**Chicago, IL** (city) Cook County	375
Tennessee	267	Alameda County, CA	346	**Kendall, FL** (cdp) Miami-Dade County	453
Ohio	369	Riverside County, CA	351	**Brooklyn, NY** (borough) Kings County	511
Michigan	379	San Mateo County, CA	351	**Manhattan, NY** (borough) New York County	568
Oregon	379	Utah County, UT	418	**Miami, FL** (city) Miami-Dade County	613
Missouri	401	Suffolk County, NY	438	**Hempstead (town), NY** (town) Nassau County	747
Wisconsin	453	Clark County, NV	478	**Queens, NY** (borough) Queens County	1,599
Colorado	631	Maricopa County, AZ	490	**Los Angeles, CA** (city) Los Angeles County	1,710
Nevada	645	Salt Lake County, UT	493	**New York, NY** (city)	2,986
Connecticut	708	Bergen County, NJ	501		

Sorted by Percent in Descending Order — U.S. = 78.9%

State	Percent	County	Percent	Place	Percent
Missouri	90.7	Bergen County, NJ	92.4	**Kendall, FL** (cdp) Miami-Dade County	85.3
New Jersey	87.4	Orange County, CA	88.7	**Hempstead (town), NY** (town) Nassau County	83.9
Georgia	87.1	Hudson County, NJ	87.8	**Manhattan, NY** (borough) New York County	80.6
Wisconsin	86.6	Nassau County, NY	85.0	**Miami, FL** (city) Miami-Dade County	79.3
Michigan	85.9	Middlesex County, MA	84.7	**Los Angeles, CA** (city) Los Angeles County	74.2
Florida	84.7	Broward County, FL	84.5	**New York, NY** (city)	72.3
Nevada	83.9	Miami-Dade County, FL	84.0	**Chicago, IL** (city) Cook County	70.9
Massachusetts	83.4	Harris County, TX	83.9	**Brooklyn, NY** (borough) Kings County	70.8
Arizona	82.4	Santa Clara County, CA	83.0	**Queens, NY** (borough) Queens County	69.0
Colorado	82.1	Palm Beach County, FL	81.8		

Sorted by Percent in Ascending Order — U.S. = 78.9%

State	Percent	County	Percent	Place	Percent
Minnesota	60.8	Suffolk County, NY	57.0	**Queens, NY** (borough) Queens County	69.0
Virginia	70.3	Alameda County, CA	63.4	**Brooklyn, NY** (borough) Kings County	70.8
Washington	70.9	San Bernardino County, CA	68.2	**Chicago, IL** (city) Cook County	70.9
Oregon	72.6	Queens County, NY	69.0	**New York, NY** (city)	72.3
California	73.8	Kings County, NY	70.8	**Los Angeles, CA** (city) Los Angeles County	74.2
North Carolina	74.4	Montgomery County, MD	70.8	**Miami, FL** (city) Miami-Dade County	79.3
New York	75.2	Cook County, IL	73.2	**Manhattan, NY** (borough) New York County	80.6
Maryland	75.7	Riverside County, CA	73.4	**Hempstead (town), NY** (town) Nassau County	83.9
Pennsylvania	77.0	Fairfax County, VA	73.6	**Kendall, FL** (cdp) Miami-Dade County	85.3
Connecticut	78.9	San Diego County, CA	75.2		

Note: (1) Ranking tables cover all states and counties, and places with an overall population of at least 125,000, OR an overall population of at least 25,000 where the Hispanic/Latino population is at least 20% of the overall population. In states where less than five places meet either of these criteria, we have included places with at least 10,000 total population with the highest percentage of Hispanic/Latino population. These places are identified with an asterisk (*); Please refer to the User's Guide for a full explanation of data.

Class of Worker: Private Wage and Salary

(Universe: Civilian Employed Population 16 Years and Over)

South American: Colombian

Top 10 States, Counties, and Places[1]

Sorted by Number in Descending Order — U.S. = 381,844

State	Number	County	Number	Place	Number
Florida	130,006	Miami-Dade County, FL	50,126	**New York, NY** (city)	42,355
New York	62,595	Queens County, NY	30,951	**Queens, NY** (borough) Queens County	30,951
New Jersey	46,212	Broward County, FL	27,685	**Miami, FL** (city) Miami-Dade County	5,446
California	22,924	Orange County, FL	11,790	**Elizabeth, NJ** (city) Union County	4,993
Texas	18,472	Los Angeles County, CA	10,172	**Boston, MA** (city) Suffolk County	4,722
Massachusetts	12,818	Palm Beach County, FL	9,802	**Pembroke Pines, FL** (city) Broward County	4,665
Georgia	10,210	Bergen County, NJ	8,906	**Brooklyn, NY** (borough) Kings County	4,237
Illinois	8,811	Harris County, TX	7,988	**Manhattan, NY** (borough) New York County	4,058
Connecticut	8,754	Hudson County, NJ	7,758	**Los Angeles, CA** (city) Los Angeles County	4,000
Pennsylvania	7,041	Hillsborough County, FL	7,345	**Houston, TX** (city) Harris County	3,884

Sorted by Number in Ascending Order — U.S. = 381,844

State	Number	County	Number	Place	Number
Iowa	328	Luzerne County, PA	238	**Tallahassee, FL** (city) Leon County	242
Arkansas	377	Burlington County, NJ	242	**Virginia Beach, VA** (independent city)	242
New Mexico	378	Leon County, FL	270	**Raleigh, NC** (city) Wake County	284
Kentucky	410	Oakland County, MI	276	**Royal Palm Beach, FL** (village) Palm Beach County	284
Alaska	424	Ulster County, NY	280	**Long Beach, CA** (city) Los Angeles County	292
Delaware	512	Cuyahoga County, OH	296	**Anaheim, CA** (city) Orange County	301
Nebraska	522	Dane County, WI	302	**Indianapolis, IN** (city) Marion County	302
Oregon	615	Will County, IL	336	**Miami Gardens, FL** (city) Miami-Dade County	306
Oklahoma	652	Forsyth County, GA	344	**Worcester, MA** (city) Worcester County	311
Alabama	738	Milwaukee County, WI	344	**Downey, CA** (city) Los Angeles County	341

Sorted by Percent in Descending Order — U.S. = 82.6%

State	Percent	County	Percent	Place	Percent
Delaware	95.0	Luzerne County, PA	100.0	**Central Falls*, RI** (city) Providence County	97.3
Massachusetts	90.2	Cherokee County, GA	98.9	**Garfield, NJ** (city) Bergen County	97.1
Pennsylvania	87.5	Forsyth County, GA	97.7	**Coconut Creek, FL** (city) Broward County	96.4
Utah	87.5	Lancaster County, PA	96.1	**Buenaventura Lakes, FL** (cdp) Osceola County	95.7
Michigan	86.6	Saint Louis County, MO	95.8	**Egypt Lake-Leto, FL** (cdp) Hillsborough County	94.6
Rhode Island	86.1	Hall County, GA	94.5	**Charlotte, NC** (city) Mecklenburg County	94.4
Tennessee	85.8	Manatee County, FL	93.6	**Union City, NJ** (city) Hudson County	94.4
Missouri	85.6	Oakland County, MI	93.6	**Revere, MA** (city) Suffolk County	94.3
New Jersey	85.3	Suffolk County, MA	93.6	**Cooper City, FL** (city) Broward County	93.4
New Hampshire	85.2	Lehigh County, PA	92.9	**Orlando, FL** (city) Orange County	93.4

Sorted by Percent in Ascending Order — U.S. = 82.6%

State	Percent	County	Percent	Place	Percent
Iowa	60.1	Prince George's County, MD	62.1	**Downey, CA** (city) Los Angeles County	56.9
District of Columbia	65.0	Leon County, FL	62.2	**San Francisco, CA** (city) San Francisco County	67.4
New Mexico	69.7	Pima County, AZ	66.1	**Yonkers, NY** (city) Westchester County	67.5
Alaska	70.4	San Francisco County, CA	67.4	**Tallahassee, FL** (city) Leon County	67.8
Arkansas	73.6	Denton County, TX	68.0	**Virginia Beach, VA** (independent city)	68.2
Maryland	74.6	Sarasota County, FL	68.9	**Austin, TX** (city) Travis County	69.9
Oklahoma	74.6	Alameda County, CA	69.4	**Dallas, TX** (city) Dallas County	70.0
Texas	74.7	San Mateo County, CA	69.6	**Cape Coral, FL** (city) Lee County	70.2
Arizona	75.2	Orange County, NY	70.4	**Deltona, FL** (city) Volusia County	72.7
Kentucky	76.1	San Diego County, CA	70.9	**Houston, TX** (city) Harris County	72.7

Note: (1) Ranking tables cover all states and counties, and places with an overall population of at least 125,000, OR an overall population of at least 25,000 where the Hispanic/Latino population is at least 20% of the overall population. In states where less than five places meet either of these criteria, we have included places with at least 10,000 total population with the highest percentage of Hispanic/Latino population. These places are identified with an asterisk (*); Please refer to the User's Guide for a full explanation of data.

Class of Worker: Private Wage and Salary

(Universe: Civilian Employed Population 16 Years and Over)

South American: Ecuadorian

Top 10 States, Counties, and Places[1]

Sorted by Number in Descending Order — U.S. = 255,883

State	Number	County	Number	Place	Number
New York	103,600	Queens County, NY	46,799	**New York, NY** (city)	77,920
New Jersey	50,224	Hudson County, NJ	13,585	**Queens, NY** (borough) Queens County	46,799
Florida	26,088	Kings County, NY	12,753	**Brooklyn, NY** (borough) Kings County	12,753
California	13,967	Essex County, NJ	11,679	**Bronx, NY** (borough) Bronx County	10,232
Illinois	12,057	Cook County, IL	10,561	**Chicago, IL** (city) Cook County	8,810
Connecticut	10,964	Bronx County, NY	10,232	**Newark, NJ** (city) Essex County	7,931
Pennsylvania	4,862	Westchester County, NY	9,962	**Manhattan, NY** (borough) New York County	7,119
Texas	4,556	Miami-Dade County, FL	8,762	**Jersey City, NJ** (city) Hudson County	3,778
Minnesota	4,542	Los Angeles County, CA	7,629	**Danbury, CT** (city/town) Fairfield County	3,534
North Carolina	3,985	Suffolk County, NY	7,568	**Elizabeth, NJ** (city) Union County	3,195

Sorted by Number in Ascending Order — U.S. = 255,883

State	Number	County	Number	Place	Number
Missouri	195	Putnam County, NY	237	**Downey, CA** (city) Los Angeles County	229
Wisconsin	269	Santa Clara County, CA	264	**Miramar, FL** (city) Broward County	309
Oregon	290	Pinellas County, FL	266	**Oyster Bay, NY** (town) Nassau County	380
Louisiana	291	King County, WA	267	**Country Club, FL** (cdp) Miami-Dade County	381
Tennessee	300	Baltimore County, MD	286	**Coral Springs, FL** (city) Broward County	393
Oklahoma	327	Utah County, UT	370	**Clifton, NJ** (city) Passaic County	422
Kansas	338	Monmouth County, NJ	378	**Philadelphia, PA** (city) Philadelphia County	486
Iowa	340	Camden County, NJ	399	**Hialeah, FL** (city) Miami-Dade County	506
South Carolina	419	Will County, IL	445	**Central Islip, NY** (cdp) Suffolk County	545
Colorado	460	Prince George's County, MD	455	**Hollywood, FL** (city) Broward County	546

Sorted by Percent in Descending Order — U.S. = 85.2%

State	Percent	County	Percent	Place	Percent
Minnesota	95.5	Hennepin County, MN	97.2	**Plainfield, NJ** (city) Union County	100.0
Nevada	95.2	Will County, IL	97.2	**New Haven, CT** (city/town) New Haven County	97.1
Michigan	91.1	Mercer County, NJ	96.1	**Minneapolis, MN** (city) Hennepin County	96.4
New Jersey	90.1	Clark County, NV	94.6	**Hackensack, NJ** (city) Bergen County	96.0
Rhode Island	90.0	Somerset County, NJ	94.4	**Country Club, FL** (cdp) Miami-Dade County	95.0
Illinois	87.6	Lee County, FL	94.3	**City of Orange, NJ** (township) Essex County	93.9
Connecticut	86.6	Santa Clara County, CA	94.0	**Sunrise, FL** (city) Broward County	93.8
Pennsylvania	86.5	Camden County, NJ	93.9	**North Bergen, NJ** (township) Hudson County	93.3
North Carolina	86.3	Ocean County, NJ	93.4	**West New York, NJ** (town) Hudson County	93.3
New York	85.1	Delaware County, PA	93.2	**Kearny, NJ** (town) Hudson County	92.8

Sorted by Percent in Ascending Order — U.S. = 85.2%

State	Percent	County	Percent	Place	Percent
Washington	67.5	Richmond County, NY	71.3	**Hialeah, FL** (city) Miami-Dade County	63.0
Louisiana	68.3	Orange County, CA	72.0	**Spring Valley, NY** (village) Rockland County	66.5
Tennessee	70.8	King County, WA	72.6	**Staten Island, NY** (borough) Richmond County	71.3
Arizona	71.7	Putnam County, NY	72.7	**Stamford, CT** (city/town) Fairfield County	71.7
Missouri	72.5	Monmouth County, NJ	73.7	**White Plains, NY** (city) Westchester County	72.3
Ohio	72.7	Maricopa County, AZ	74.1	**Ramapo, NY** (town) Rockland County	74.6
Oregon	75.3	Dallas County, TX	74.9	**Yonkers, NY** (city) Westchester County	75.6
California	76.8	Dutchess County, NY	75.2	**Ossining, NY** (village) Westchester County	76.0
Colorado	77.1	Los Angeles County, CA	75.4	**Los Angeles, CA** (city) Los Angeles County	76.6
Georgia	77.3	Orange County, NY	76.0	**Ossining, NY** (town) Westchester County	77.6

Note: (1) Ranking tables cover all states and counties, and places with an overall population of at least 125,000, OR an overall population of at least 25,000 where the Hispanic/Latino population is at least 20% of the overall population. In states where less than five places meet either of these criteria, we have included places with at least 10,000 total population with the highest percentage of Hispanic/Latino population. These places are identified with an asterisk (*); Please refer to the User's Guide for a full explanation of data.

Class of Worker: Private Wage and Salary

(Universe: Civilian Employed Population 16 Years and Over)

South American: Paraguayan

Top 10 States, Counties, and Places[1]

Sorted by Number in Descending Order — U.S. = 7,915

State	Number	County	Number	Place	Number
New York	3,054	Queens County, NY	1,238	**New York, NY** (city)	1,682
New Jersey	732	Westchester County, NY	759	**Queens, NY** (borough) Queens County	1,238
Florida	689				
Maryland	449				
Texas	448				
California	350				

Sorted by Number in Ascending Order — U.S. = 7,915

State	Number	County	Number	Place	Number
California	350	Westchester County, NY	759	**Queens, NY** (borough) Queens County	1,238
Texas	448	Queens County, NY	1,238	**New York, NY** (city)	1,682
Maryland	449				
Florida	689				
New Jersey	732				
New York	3,054				

Sorted by Percent in Descending Order — U.S. = 77.0%

State	Percent	County	Percent	Place	Percent
Texas	83.9	Queens County, NY	78.4	**Queens, NY** (borough) Queens County	78.4
California	81.2	Westchester County, NY	74.4	**New York, NY** (city)	77.1
New Jersey	80.4				
Florida	77.8				
New York	76.8				
Maryland	60.2				

Sorted by Percent in Ascending Order — U.S. = 77.0%

State	Percent	County	Percent	Place	Percent
Maryland	60.2	Westchester County, NY	74.4	**New York, NY** (city)	77.1
New York	76.8	Queens County, NY	78.4	**Queens, NY** (borough) Queens County	78.4
Florida	77.8				
New Jersey	80.4				
California	81.2				
Texas	83.9				

Note: (1) Ranking tables cover all states and counties, and places with an overall population of at least 125,000, OR an overall population of at least 25,000 where the Hispanic/Latino population is at least 20% of the overall population. In states where less than five places meet either of these criteria, we have included places with at least 10,000 total population with the highest percentage of Hispanic/Latino population. These places are identified with an asterisk (*); Please refer to the User's Guide for a full explanation of data.

Class of Worker: Private Wage and Salary

(Universe: Civilian Employed Population 16 Years and Over)

South American: Peruvian

Top 10 States, Counties, and Places[1]

Sorted by Number in Descending Order — U.S. = 232,048

State	Number	County	Number	Place	Number
Florida	45,134	Miami-Dade County, FL	17,003	**New York, NY** (city)	17,421
New Jersey	37,447	Los Angeles County, CA	14,215	**Queens, NY** (borough) Queens County	11,206
California	35,206	Queens County, NY	11,206	**Los Angeles, CA** (city) Los Angeles County	6,478
New York	30,771	Broward County, FL	10,903	**Paterson, NJ** (city) Passaic County	4,626
Virginia	13,063	Passaic County, NJ	9,335	**Elizabeth, NJ** (city) Union County	3,327
Texas	9,175	Hudson County, NJ	7,239	**Clifton, NJ** (city) Passaic County	2,421
Maryland	7,281	Fairfax County, VA	6,502	**Chicago, IL** (city) Cook County	2,373
Connecticut	7,260	Union County, NJ	5,507	**Islip, NY** (town) Suffolk County	2,194
Illinois	4,998	Westchester County, NY	4,761	**Union City, NJ** (city) Hudson County	2,081
Georgia	3,961	Montgomery County, MD	4,549	**Manhattan, NY** (borough) New York County	2,055

Sorted by Number in Ascending Order — U.S. = 232,048

State	Number	County	Number	Place	Number
New Mexico	307	Solano County, CA	200	**Denver, CO** (city) Denver County	213
Hawaii	367	Denver County, CO	213	**Torrance, CA** (city) Los Angeles County	250
Kentucky	374	Lake County, IL	217	**Belleville, NJ** (township) Essex County	252
Kansas	414	Fort Bend County, TX	274	**Cape Coral, FL** (city) Lee County	305
Delaware	452	Baltimore County, MD	280	**Philadelphia, PA** (city) Philadelphia County	306
Alabama	458	San Joaquin County, CA	284	**Garland, TX** (city) Dallas County	349
Rhode Island	504	Philadelphia County, PA	306	**San Antonio, TX** (city) Bexar County	361
District of Columbia	574	Wake County, NC	307	**West Valley City, UT** (city) Salt Lake County	369
Louisiana	626	Ocean County, NJ	321	**Bridgeport, CT** (city/town) Fairfield County	370
Idaho	664	Bexar County, TX	425	**Salt Lake City, UT** (city) Salt Lake County	370

Sorted by Percent in Descending Order — U.S. = 82.5%

State	Percent	County	Percent	Place	Percent
Rhode Island	95.5	Duval County, FL	97.6	**West New York, NJ** (town) Hudson County	98.4
Oklahoma	92.5	Atlantic County, NJ	95.5	**Kearny, NJ** (town) Hudson County	97.8
Utah	89.6	Lehigh County, PA	94.9	**Tampa, FL** (city) Hillsborough County	97.6
New Jersey	89.4	Franklin County, OH	94.2	**Jacksonville, FL** (city) Duval County	97.5
Pennsylvania	89.3	New Haven County, CT	93.8	**Port Chester, NY** (village) Westchester County	96.9
Nevada	89.0	Osceola County, FL	93.7	**Clifton, NJ** (city) Passaic County	96.1
Indiana	88.8	Arapahoe County, CO	92.6	**Doral, FL** (city) Miami-Dade County	94.7
Minnesota	88.2	King County, WA	92.5	**Rye, NY** (town) Westchester County	94.0
Idaho	88.1	Tarrant County, TX	92.4	**Aurora, CO** (city) Arapahoe County	93.4
Ohio	87.8	Orange County, NY	92.1	**Elizabeth, NJ** (city) Union County	93.3

Sorted by Percent in Ascending Order — U.S. = 82.5%

State	Percent	County	Percent	Place	Percent
New Mexico	44.2	Solano County, CA	46.6	**Garland, TX** (city) Dallas County	63.6
Hawaii	63.4	Baltimore County, MD	67.5	**Miramar, FL** (city) Broward County	67.0
Alabama	70.8	Riverside County, CA	68.2	**Miami, FL** (city) Miami-Dade County	68.2
Louisiana	72.0	Denton County, TX	68.7	**San Jose, CA** (city) Santa Clara County	70.3
Michigan	72.7	Travis County, TX	69.4	**Hempstead (town), NY** (town) Nassau County	71.6
Delaware	74.8	Sacramento County, CA	69.8	**Torrance, CA** (city) Los Angeles County	72.5
District of Columbia	75.6	Ocean County, NJ	69.9	**Miami Beach, FL** (city) Miami-Dade County	73.6
Kentucky	76.2	Alameda County, CA	70.9	**Oyster Bay, NY** (town) Nassau County	74.2
Maryland	76.4	Nassau County, NY	73.4	**Staten Island, NY** (borough) Richmond County	74.2
California	76.9	Richmond County, NY	74.2	**Stamford, CT** (city/town) Fairfield County	75.2

Note: (1) Ranking tables cover all states and counties, and places with an overall population of at least 125,000, OR an overall population of at least 25,000 where the Hispanic/Latino population is at least 20% of the overall population. In states where less than five places meet either of these criteria, we have included places with at least 10,000 total population with the highest percentage of Hispanic/Latino population. These places are identified with an asterisk (*); Please refer to the User's Guide for a full explanation of data.

Class of Worker: Private Wage and Salary

(Universe: Civilian Employed Population 16 Years and Over)

South American: Uruguayan

Top 10 States, Counties, and Places[1]

Sorted by Number in Descending Order — U.S. = 23,505

State	Number	County	Number	Place	Number
Florida	5,888	Miami-Dade County, FL	2,599	**Elizabeth, NJ** (city) Union County	1,393
New Jersey	5,539	Union County, NJ	1,942	**New York, NY** (city)	1,198
New York	2,602	Broward County, FL	1,416	**Queens, NY** (borough) Queens County	606
Georgia	1,335	Essex County, NJ	1,194		
Massachusetts	1,178	Palm Beach County, FL	621		
California	1,160	Queens County, NY	606		
Texas	1,118	Worcester County, MA	593		
Virginia	949	Westchester County, NY	589		
Maryland	530	Harris County, TX	568		
Pennsylvania	380	Hudson County, NJ	544		

Sorted by Number in Ascending Order — U.S. = 23,505

State	Number	County	Number	Place	Number
Pennsylvania	380	Middlesex County, NJ	364	**Queens, NY** (borough) Queens County	606
Maryland	530	Los Angeles County, CA	431	**New York, NY** (city)	1,198
Virginia	949	Morris County, NJ	453	**Elizabeth, NJ** (city) Union County	1,393
Texas	1,118	Gwinnett County, GA	498		
California	1,160	Hudson County, NJ	544		
Massachusetts	1,178	Harris County, TX	568		
Georgia	1,335	Westchester County, NY	589		
New York	2,602	Worcester County, MA	593		
New Jersey	5,539	Queens County, NY	606		
Florida	5,888	Palm Beach County, FL	621		

Sorted by Percent in Descending Order — U.S. = 80.0%

State	Percent	County	Percent	Place	Percent
Massachusetts	92.0	Queens County, NY	92.0	**Queens, NY** (borough) Queens County	92.0
Virginia	88.0	Morris County, NJ	88.0	**Elizabeth, NJ** (city) Union County	87.5
New Jersey	86.1	Middlesex County, NJ	87.7	**New York, NY** (city)	80.7
New York	81.4	Essex County, NJ	87.6		
Texas	80.5	Worcester County, MA	85.7		
Georgia	80.1	Harris County, TX	85.3		
Florida	77.7	Union County, NJ	85.0		
Pennsylvania	76.9	Westchester County, NY	81.1		
California	69.5	Palm Beach County, FL	80.0		
Maryland	62.0	Hudson County, NJ	78.8		

Sorted by Percent in Ascending Order — U.S. = 80.0%

State	Percent	County	Percent	Place	Percent
Maryland	62.0	Los Angeles County, CA	66.9	**New York, NY** (city)	80.7
California	69.5	Gwinnett County, GA	72.6	**Elizabeth, NJ** (city) Union County	87.5
Pennsylvania	76.9	Miami-Dade County, FL	73.1	**Queens, NY** (borough) Queens County	92.0
Florida	77.7	Broward County, FL	76.1		
Georgia	80.1	Hudson County, NJ	78.8		
Texas	80.5	Palm Beach County, FL	80.0		
New York	81.4	Westchester County, NY	81.1		
New Jersey	86.1	Union County, NJ	85.0		
Virginia	88.0	Harris County, TX	85.3		
Massachusetts	92.0	Worcester County, MA	85.7		

Note: (1) Ranking tables cover all states and counties, and places with an overall population of at least 125,000, OR an overall population of at least 25,000 where the Hispanic/Latino population is at least 20% of the overall population. In states where less than five places meet either of these criteria, we have included places with at least 10,000 total population with the highest percentage of Hispanic/Latino population. These places are identified with an asterisk (*); Please refer to the User's Guide for a full explanation of data.

Class of Worker: Private Wage and Salary

(Universe: Civilian Employed Population 16 Years and Over)

South American: Venezuelan

Top 10 States, Counties, and Places[1]

Sorted by Number in Descending Order — U.S. = 87,720

State	Number	County	Number	Place	Number
Florida	43,032	Miami-Dade County, FL	19,772	**New York, NY** (city)	4,886
Texas	7,880	Broward County, FL	9,871	**Doral, FL** (city) Miami-Dade County	2,831
New York	6,411	Orange County, FL	3,389	**Miami, FL** (city) Miami-Dade County	2,671
California	4,503	Harris County, TX	3,262	**Weston, FL** (city) Broward County	2,327
New Jersey	2,699	Queens County, NY	2,043	**Queens, NY** (borough) Queens County	2,043
Georgia	2,508	Palm Beach County, FL	1,763	**Houston, TX** (city) Harris County	1,852
Virginia	2,099	Los Angeles County, CA	1,337	**Fountainebleau, FL** (cdp) Miami-Dade County	1,719
North Carolina	1,537	Osceola County, FL	1,332	**Pembroke Pines, FL** (city) Broward County	1,400
Massachusetts	1,434	Hillsborough County, FL	1,293	**Manhattan, NY** (borough) New York County	1,135
Pennsylvania	1,319	Fort Bend County, TX	1,220	**Miami Beach, FL** (city) Miami-Dade County	1,125

Sorted by Number in Ascending Order — U.S. = 87,720

State	Number	County	Number	Place	Number
Missouri	280	Tarrant County, TX	252	**Aventura, FL** (city) Miami-Dade County	325
Wisconsin	349	Travis County, TX	300	**Los Angeles, CA** (city) Los Angeles County	446
Minnesota	403	Collin County, TX	338	**Kendall West, FL** (cdp) Miami-Dade County	532
Oklahoma	501	Fulton County, GA	355	**Coral Springs, FL** (city) Broward County	538
Indiana	505	King County, WA	368	**Bronx, NY** (borough) Bronx County	548
Michigan	511	Montgomery County, TX	377	**Hollywood, FL** (city) Broward County	630
Washington	547	Fairfield County, CT	387	**Davie, FL** (town) Broward County	643
South Carolina	583	San Diego County, CA	420	**Tamiami, FL** (cdp) Miami-Dade County	644
Arizona	584	Suffolk County, MA	435	**Kendall, FL** (cdp) Miami-Dade County	647
Tennessee	690	Dallas County, TX	442	**Miramar, FL** (city) Broward County	698

Sorted by Percent in Descending Order — U.S. = 82.9%

State	Percent	County	Percent	Place	Percent
Tennessee	92.5	Osceola County, FL	95.9	**Aventura, FL** (city) Miami-Dade County	96.7
Michigan	90.6	Pinellas County, FL	95.0	**Miami Beach, FL** (city) Miami-Dade County	96.0
Indiana	90.5	Fairfield County, CT	93.7	**Fountainebleau, FL** (cdp) Miami-Dade County	95.9
Louisiana	89.8	Salt Lake County, UT	92.4	**Hollywood, FL** (city) Broward County	94.9
South Carolina	88.6	Hillsborough County, FL	90.7	**Pembroke Pines, FL** (city) Broward County	94.7
Colorado	88.2	Fort Bend County, TX	90.1	**Kendall West, FL** (cdp) Miami-Dade County	92.4
Pennsylvania	87.7	Collin County, TX	89.2	**Miramar, FL** (city) Broward County	90.6
Utah	87.4	King County, WA	87.4	**Hialeah, FL** (city) Miami-Dade County	90.4
Florida	86.0	Orange County, FL	87.4	**Country Club, FL** (cdp) Miami-Dade County	90.1
New Jersey	84.9	New York County, NY	86.8	**Tamiami, FL** (cdp) Miami-Dade County	88.2

Sorted by Percent in Ascending Order — U.S. = 82.9%

State	Percent	County	Percent	Place	Percent
Oklahoma	69.7	Travis County, TX	67.9	**Los Angeles, CA** (city) Los Angeles County	71.4
Minnesota	71.2	Dallas County, TX	68.2	**Brooklyn, NY** (borough) Kings County	75.6
Ohio	71.9	Fairfax County, VA	70.2	**Weston, FL** (city) Broward County	80.3
North Carolina	74.7	San Diego County, CA	70.6	**Coral Springs, FL** (city) Broward County	80.4
California	75.3	Orange County, CA	72.5	**New York, NY** (city)	81.4
Arizona	75.4	Cobb County, GA	75.1	**Bronx, NY** (borough) Bronx County	82.0
Maryland	76.9	Kings County, NY	75.6	**Houston, TX** (city) Harris County	82.1
Virginia	76.9	Montgomery County, MD	76.0	**Queens, NY** (borough) Queens County	82.2
Georgia	77.1	Hudson County, NJ	76.4	**Davie, FL** (town) Broward County	83.6
Illinois	77.9	Los Angeles County, CA	76.8	**Sunrise, FL** (city) Broward County	84.6

Note: (1) Ranking tables cover all states and counties, and places with an overall population of at least 125,000, OR an overall population of at least 25,000 where the Hispanic/Latino population is at least 20% of the overall population. In states where less than five places meet either of these criteria, we have included places with at least 10,000 total population with the highest percentage of Hispanic/Latino population. These places are identified with an asterisk (*); Please refer to the User's Guide for a full explanation of data.

Class of Worker: Private Wage and Salary

(Universe: Civilian Employed Population 16 Years and Over)

Spaniard

Top 10 States, Counties, and Places[1]

Sorted by Number in Descending Order — U.S. = 189,956

State	Number	County	Number	Place	Number
California	35,546	Los Angeles County, CA	8,006	**New York, NY** (city)	6,510
Texas	21,482	Bernalillo County, NM	5,872	**Albuquerque, NM** (city) Bernalillo County	4,985
Florida	14,889	Maricopa County, AZ	4,086	**Los Angeles, CA** (city) Los Angeles County	2,808
Colorado	14,692	Miami-Dade County, FL	3,887	**Queens, NY** (borough) Queens County	2,056
New Mexico	13,943	Harris County, TX	3,542	**San Antonio, TX** (city) Bexar County	1,905
New York	12,762	San Diego County, CA	3,264	**Houston, TX** (city) Harris County	1,840
New Jersey	8,325	Hillsborough County, FL	2,672	**Manhattan, NY** (borough) New York County	1,787
Arizona	6,768	Orange County, CA	2,603	**Austin, TX** (city) Travis County	1,715
Washington	4,680	Adams County, CO	2,587	**Denver, CO** (city) Denver County	1,629
Illinois	4,460	Bexar County, TX	2,326	**San Diego, CA** (city) San Diego County	1,440

Sorted by Number in Ascending Order — U.S. = 189,956

State	Number	County	Number	Place	Number
Maine	222	Las Animas County, CO	98	**San Bernardino, CA** (city) San Bernardino County	181
Iowa	279	Tulare County, CA	104	**Anchorage, AK** (municipality)	227
Mississippi	348	Butte County, CA	106	**South Valley, NM** (cdp) Bernalillo County	265
New Hampshire	352	Conejos County, CO	149	**Henderson, NV** (city) Clark County	282
Montana	405	Rio Arriba County, NM	155	**Glendale, AZ** (city) Maricopa County	296
District of Columbia	442	La Plata County, CO	170	**Tucson, AZ** (city) Pima County	299
West Virginia	478	Taos County, NM	189	**Las Cruces, NM** (city) Dona Ana County	301
Alaska	498	Colfax County, NM	198	**Fort Collins, CO** (city) Larimer County	310
Kentucky	542	Hidalgo County, TX	203	**North Las Vegas, NV** (city) Clark County	316
Alabama	544	Hawaii County, HI	227	**Oyster Bay, NY** (town) Nassau County	322

Sorted by Percent in Descending Order — U.S. = 74.8%

State	Percent	County	Percent	Place	Percent
Missouri	88.9	Maui County, HI	95.3	**Thornton, CO** (city) Adams County	93.4
Nebraska	86.2	Utah County, UT	95.3	**Seattle, WA** (city) King County	91.9
New Hampshire	85.6	Morris County, NJ	94.6	**Kearny, NJ** (town) Hudson County	89.8
Tennessee	85.1	DuPage County, IL	93.0	**Jacksonville, FL** (city) Duval County	89.3
Pennsylvania	84.7	Salt Lake County, UT	91.7	**Philadelphia, PA** (city) Philadelphia County	88.7
Kansas	84.1	New Haven County, CT	91.6	**Fresno, CA** (city) Fresno County	88.6
Utah	83.9	Milwaukee County, WI	91.5	**Lubbock, TX** (city) Lubbock County	88.4
Illinois	83.4	Douglas County, CO	90.1	**Las Cruces, NM** (city) Dona Ana County	88.0
Ohio	82.5	Duval County, FL	90.0	**Hempstead (town), NY** (town) Nassau County	87.3
Connecticut	82.3	Monmouth County, NJ	89.0	**Westminster, CO** (city) Adams County	86.2

Sorted by Percent in Ascending Order — U.S. = 74.8%

State	Percent	County	Percent	Place	Percent
Mississippi	58.6	Conejos County, CO	39.8	**Santa Fe, NM** (city) Santa Fe County	54.5
Alabama	63.0	San Miguel County, NM	43.5	**Stockton, CA** (city) San Joaquin County	56.9
Alaska	64.9	Tulare County, CA	51.5	**Staten Island, NY** (borough) Richmond County	58.7
New Mexico	65.6	Taos County, NM	55.4	**Anchorage, AK** (municipality)	59.0
Iowa	66.9	Santa Fe County, NM	56.8	**Sacramento, CA** (city) Sacramento County	61.5
Wyoming	67.4	Hidalgo County, TX	58.3	**El Paso, TX** (city) El Paso County	64.1
Maryland	68.8	Richmond County, NY	58.7	**Long Beach, CA** (city) Los Angeles County	65.0
Kentucky	69.6	Brevard County, FL	58.8	**Pueblo, CO** (city) Pueblo County	66.6
Montana	69.7	Erie County, NY	58.8	**Denver, CO** (city) Denver County	66.9
California	71.1	Valencia County, NM	58.8	**Lakewood, CO** (city) Jefferson County	67.7

Note: (1) Ranking tables cover all states and counties, and places with an overall population of at least 125,000, OR an overall population of at least 25,000 where the Hispanic/Latino population is at least 20% of the overall population. In states where less than five places meet either of these criteria, we have included places with at least 10,000 total population with the highest percentage of Hispanic/Latino population. These places are identified with an asterisk (*); Please refer to the User's Guide for a full explanation of data.

Class of Worker: Government

(Universe: Civilian Employed Population 16 Years and Over)

Total Population

Top 10 States, Counties, and Places[1]

Sorted by Number in Descending Order — U.S. = 21,024,265

State	Number	County	Number	Place	Number
California	2,425,341	Los Angeles County, CA	555,466	**New York, NY** (city)	557,478
Texas	1,633,861	Cook County, IL	299,378	**Brooklyn, NY** (borough) Kings County	181,256
New York	1,520,566	San Diego County, CA	212,024	**Los Angeles, CA** (city) Los Angeles County	180,342
Florida	1,098,322	Maricopa County, AZ	211,125	**Chicago, IL** (city) Cook County	167,678
Virginia	784,595	Harris County, TX	201,997	**Queens, NY** (borough) Queens County	154,944
Illinois	780,081	Kings County, NY	181,256	**Houston, TX** (city) Harris County	100,160
Pennsylvania	694,589	Orange County, CA	159,346	**Bronx, NY** (borough) Bronx County	95,095
Ohio	693,114	Queens County, NY	154,944	**San Diego, CA** (city) San Diego County	93,883
Georgia	675,962	San Bernardino County, CA	142,710	**Philadelphia, PA** (city) Philadelphia County	88,231
Maryland	643,957	Sacramento County, CA	141,189	**San Antonio, TX** (city) Bexar County	85,969

Sorted by Number in Ascending Order — U.S. = 21,024,265

State	Number	County	Number	Place	Number
Vermont	48,200	Kenedy County, TX	36	**Lexington*, NE** (city) Dawson County	214
Wyoming	56,225	McMullen County, TX	58	**Parker*, SC** (cdp) Greenville County	302
North Dakota	60,231	Sterling County, TX	83	**Central Falls*, RI** (city) Providence County	370
Delaware	60,859	Motley County, TX	116	**Mayfield*, KY** (city) Graves County	390
South Dakota	65,495	Glasscock County, TX	118	**Berea*, SC** (cdp) Greenville County	396
Rhode Island	68,646	Irion County, TX	124	**Jerome*, ID** (city) Jerome County	402
District of Columbia	78,192	Harding County, NM	129	**Carthage*, MO** (city) Jasper County	439
Alaska	84,606	Foard County, TX	132	**Fort Campbell North*, KY** (cdp) Christian County	449
Montana	88,177	Briscoe County, TX	137	**Hanover*, NH** (town) Grafton County	458
New Hampshire	92,838	Clark County, ID	137	**Burley*, ID** (city) Cassia County	530

Sorted by Percent in Descending Order — U.S. = 14.8%

State	Percent	County	Percent	Place	Percent
District of Columbia	26.3	Shannon County, SD	65.4	**Fort Leonard Wood*, MO** (cdp) Pulaski County	49.6
Alaska	25.5	Todd County, SD	64.0	**Twentynine Palms, CA** (city) San Bernardino County	48.0
New Mexico	22.3	Pawnee County, KS	49.6	**Schofield Barracks*, HI** (cdp) Honolulu County	45.4
Maryland	22.2	Apache County, AZ	45.9	**Florence, AZ** (town) Pinal County	42.8
Virginia	20.5	Lassen County, CA	44.9	**Fort Hood, TX** (cdp) Bell County	40.5
Hawaii	20.2	Glacier County, MT	44.4	**Juneau*, AK** (borough) Juneau City and Borough	39.9
Wyoming	19.8	Roosevelt County, MT	43.8	**Fort Campbell North*, KY** (cdp) Christian County	34.6
Mississippi	18.8	Kent County, TX	42.0	**College*, AK** (cdp) Fairbanks North Star Borough	34.2
West Virginia	18.7	Mora County, NM	41.7	**Tallahassee, FL** (city) Leon County	32.5
Montana	18.5	Big Horn County, MT	41.5	**Kingsville, TX** (city) Kleberg County	32.4

Sorted by Percent in Ascending Order — U.S. = 14.8%

State	Percent	County	Percent	Place	Percent
Indiana	11.7	Kewaunee County, WI	7.0	**Lexington*, NE** (city) Dawson County	4.4
Pennsylvania	11.7	Sioux County, IA	7.2	**Central Falls*, RI** (city) Providence County	4.6
Michigan	12.1	LaGrange County, IN	7.5	**Bell Gardens, CA** (city) Los Angeles County	5.3
Minnesota	12.3	Nantucket County, MA	7.5	**Four Corners, FL** (cdp) Lake County	5.5
Nevada	12.4	Eagle County, CO	7.6	**Holland, MI** (charter township) Ottawa County	5.9
Wisconsin	12.4	Adams County, IN	7.9	**Hialeah, FL** (city) Miami-Dade County	6.1
Illinois	12.9	Dearborn County, IN	8.0	**Bonita Springs, FL** (city) Lee County	6.2
Ohio	12.9	Washington County, WI	8.0	**Maywood, CA** (city) Los Angeles County	6.2
Massachusetts	13.0	McDonald County, MO	8.2	**Farmers Branch, TX** (city) Dallas County	6.3
Florida	13.2	Elk County, PA	8.3	**Miami Beach, FL** (city) Miami-Dade County	6.3

Note: (1) Ranking tables cover all states and counties, and places with an overall population of at least 125,000, OR an overall population of at least 25,000 where the Hispanic/Latino population is at least 20% of the overall population. In states where less than five places meet either of these criteria, we have included places with at least 10,000 total population with the highest percentage of Hispanic/Latino population. These places are identified with an asterisk (*); Please refer to the User's Guide for a full explanation of data.

Class of Worker: Government

(Universe: Civilian Employed Population 16 Years and Over)

Hispanic or Latino (of any race)

Top 10 States, Counties, and Places[1]

Sorted by Number in Descending Order — U.S. = 2,135,316

State	Number	County	Number	Place	Number
California	612,035	Los Angeles County, CA	192,529	**New York, NY** (city)	119,303
Texas	465,715	Miami-Dade County, FL	64,328	**Los Angeles, CA** (city) Los Angeles County	59,643
New York	175,155	Bexar County, TX	56,278	**San Antonio, TX** (city) Bexar County	45,694
Florida	161,482	San Diego County, CA	49,542	**Bronx, NY** (borough) Bronx County	38,665
Arizona	91,951	Harris County, TX	46,725	**El Paso, TX** (city) El Paso County	38,635
New Mexico	82,406	El Paso County, TX	46,245	**Queens, NY** (borough) Queens County	28,618
New Jersey	62,732	San Bernardino County, CA	45,765	**Chicago, IL** (city) Cook County	26,839
Illinois	61,733	Hidalgo County, TX	41,880	**Brooklyn, NY** (borough) Kings County	26,534
Colorado	46,861	Maricopa County, AZ	41,605	**Houston, TX** (city) Harris County	23,000
Virginia	34,166	Cook County, IL	40,632	**Albuquerque, NM** (city) Bernalillo County	20,088

Sorted by Number in Ascending Order — U.S. = 2,135,316

State	Number	County	Number	Place	Number
Vermont	603	Acadia Parish, LA	0	**Brookside*, DE** (cdp) New Castle County	0
Maine	706	Atkinson County, GA	0	**Carthage*, MO** (city) Jasper County	0
North Dakota	831	Beaver County, UT	0	**Mayfield*, KY** (city) Graves County	0
South Dakota	1,048	Belknap County, NH	0	**Warr Acres*, OK** (city) Oklahoma County	0
West Virginia	1,161	Boone County, AR	0	**Parker*, SC** (cdp) Greenville County	14
New Hampshire	1,179	Brown County, MN	0	**Storm Lake*, IA** (city) Buena Vista County	17
Montana	1,622	Burnett County, WI	0	**Laurel*, MS** (city) Jones County	21
Delaware	2,055	Calhoun County, FL	0	**Willmar*, MN** (city) Kandiyohi County	23
Mississippi	2,561	Calloway County, KY	0	**Jerome*, ID** (city) Jerome County	24
Alaska	3,096	Calumet County, WI	0	**Albertville*, AL** (city) Marshall County	25

Sorted by Percent in Descending Order — U.S. = 10.5%

State	Percent	County	Percent	Place	Percent
New Mexico	21.7	Athens County, OH	57.2	**Schofield Barracks*, HI** (cdp) Honolulu County	54.6
Hawaii	18.7	Grant Parish, LA	54.2	**Florence, AZ** (town) Pinal County	53.7
Alaska	18.5	Terrell County, TX	52.5	**Fort Leonard Wood*, MO** (cdp) Pulaski County	46.4
North Dakota	15.7	Chattahoochee County, GA	48.2	**Fort Hood, TX** (cdp) Bell County	45.4
West Virginia	15.4	Mora County, NM	46.9	**Juneau*, AK** (borough) Juneau City and Borough	41.2
Montana	15.3	Latah County, ID	44.7	**Twentynine Palms, CA** (city) San Bernardino County	37.0
Wyoming	14.9	Meade County, SD	44.7	**Waianae*, HI** (cdp) Honolulu County	33.8
District of Columbia	14.5	Lassen County, CA	43.2	**Kingsville, TX** (city) Kleberg County	32.3
Vermont	13.7	Hardeman County, TX	42.5	**Fort Campbell North*, KY** (cdp) Christian County	31.5
Arizona	12.9	San Miguel County, NM	40.8	**Morgantown*, WV** (city) Monongalia County	31.0

Sorted by Percent in Ascending Order — U.S. = 10.5%

State	Percent	County	Percent	Place	Percent
Tennessee	4.7	Acadia Parish, LA	0.0	**Brookside*, DE** (cdp) New Castle County	0.0
North Carolina	5.2	Atkinson County, GA	0.0	**Carthage*, MO** (city) Jasper County	0.0
Arkansas	5.5	Beaver County, UT	0.0	**Mayfield*, KY** (city) Graves County	0.0
Georgia	5.5	Belknap County, NH	0.0	**Warr Acres*, OK** (city) Oklahoma County	0.0
Alabama	5.8	Boone County, AR	0.0	**Lawrenceville, GA** (city) Gwinnett County	1.0
Nevada	5.9	Brown County, MN	0.0	**Norristown, PA** (borough) Montgomery County	1.0
Indiana	6.0	Burnett County, WI	0.0	**Albertville*, AL** (city) Marshall County	1.1
Minnesota	6.0	Calhoun County, FL	0.0	**North Atlanta, GA** (cdp) DeKalb County	1.1
Nebraska	6.5	Calloway County, KY	0.0	**Storm Lake*, IA** (city) Buena Vista County	1.1
Rhode Island	6.5	Calumet County, WI	0.0	**Asheboro, NC** (city) Randolph County	1.4

Note: (1) Ranking tables cover all states and counties, and places with an overall population of at least 125,000, OR an overall population of at least 25,000 where the Hispanic/Latino population is at least 20% of the overall population. In states where less than five places meet either of these criteria, we have included places with at least 10,000 total population with the highest percentage of Hispanic/Latino population. These places are identified with an asterisk (*); Please refer to the User's Guide for a full explanation of data.

Class of Worker: Government

(Universe: Civilian Employed Population 16 Years and Over)

Central American, excluding Mexican

Top 10 States, Counties, and Places[1]

Sorted by Number in Descending Order — U.S. = 120,877

State	Number	County	Number	Place	Number
California	44,417	Los Angeles County, CA	23,349	**Los Angeles, CA** (city) Los Angeles County	12,259
New York	13,564	Miami-Dade County, FL	5,210	**New York, NY** (city)	8,273
Florida	11,561	Harris County, TX	3,351	**Brooklyn, NY** (borough) Kings County	3,094
Texas	9,952	Kings County, NY	3,094	**Queens, NY** (borough) Queens County	2,515
Virginia	6,435	Fairfax County, VA	2,553	**San Francisco, CA** (city) San Francisco County	1,904
Maryland	5,322	Queens County, NY	2,515	**Bronx, NY** (borough) Bronx County	1,718
New Jersey	3,721	San Bernardino County, CA	2,387	**Houston, TX** (city) Harris County	1,530
Illinois	2,299	San Mateo County, CA	2,217	**Hempstead (town), NY** (town) Nassau County	1,296
North Carolina	2,230	Montgomery County, MD	2,183	**Chicago, IL** (city) Cook County	1,078
Georgia	2,024	Contra Costa County, CA	2,107	**San Jose, CA** (city) Santa Clara County	842

Sorted by Number in Ascending Order — U.S. = 120,877

State	Number	County	Number	Place	Number
Vermont	13	Burke County, NC	0	**Albertville*, AL** (city) Marshall County	0
South Dakota	18	Cass County, IN	0	**Bonita Springs, FL** (city) Lee County	0
Maine	29	Clackamas County, OR	0	**Carthage*, MO** (city) Jasper County	0
Wyoming	33	Colfax County, NE	0	**Cary, NC** (town) Wake County	0
New Hampshire	60	Crawford County, AR	0	**Central Falls*, RI** (city) Providence County	0
West Virginia	89	Dawson County, NE	0	**Chattanooga, TN** (city) Hamilton County	0
Delaware	108	DeKalb County, AL	0	**Danbury, CT** (city/town) Fairfield County	0
Idaho	132	Delaware County, PA	0	**Delano, CA** (city) Kern County	0
Hawaii	153	Elkhart County, IN	0	**Desert Hot Springs, CA** (city) Riverside County	0
Mississippi	160	Finney County, KS	0	**Elkhart, IN** (city) Elkhart County	0

Sorted by Percent in Descending Order — U.S. = 6.0%

State	Percent	County	Percent	Place	Percent
Alaska	20.1	Thurston County, WA	45.3	**Killeen, TX** (city) Bell County	38.7
West Virginia	15.6	San Luis Obispo County, CA	30.6	**La Mirada, CA** (city) Los Angeles County	30.0
Hawaii	13.6	Dane County, WI	28.8	**Fayetteville, NC** (city) Cumberland County	29.2
Wisconsin	11.8	Bell County, TX	27.2	**Anchorage, AK** (municipality)	26.2
Arizona	9.2	Cumberland County, NC	26.2	**Spring, TX** (cdp) Harris County	23.6
Washington	9.1	Yolo County, CA	24.4	**Chula Vista, CA** (city) San Diego County	23.4
New Mexico	9.0	Leon County, FL	23.5	**Murrieta, CA** (city) Riverside County	22.8
New York	7.8	Oneida County, NY	22.9	**Burbank, CA** (city) Los Angeles County	22.3
Idaho	7.7	Macomb County, MI	21.0	**Irvine, CA** (city) Orange County	20.1
California	7.6	Alachua County, FL	20.9	**Corpus Christi, TX** (city) Nueces County	19.6

Sorted by Percent in Ascending Order — U.S. = 6.0%

State	Percent	County	Percent	Place	Percent
South Dakota	1.5	Burke County, NC	0.0	**Albertville*, AL** (city) Marshall County	0.0
Rhode Island	2.3	Cass County, IN	0.0	**Bonita Springs, FL** (city) Lee County	0.0
Arkansas	2.8	Clackamas County, OR	0.0	**Carthage*, MO** (city) Jasper County	0.0
Delaware	3.1	Colfax County, NE	0.0	**Cary, NC** (town) Wake County	0.0
Tennessee	3.4	Crawford County, AR	0.0	**Central Falls*, RI** (city) Providence County	0.0
Connecticut	3.7	Dawson County, NE	0.0	**Chattanooga, TN** (city) Hamilton County	0.0
Georgia	3.8	DeKalb County, AL	0.0	**Danbury, CT** (city/town) Fairfield County	0.0
Minnesota	3.9	Delaware County, PA	0.0	**Delano, CA** (city) Kern County	0.0
Nebraska	3.9	Elkhart County, IN	0.0	**Desert Hot Springs, CA** (city) Riverside County	0.0
Pennsylvania	3.9	Finney County, KS	0.0	**Elkhart, IN** (city) Elkhart County	0.0

Note: (1) Ranking tables cover all states and counties, and places with an overall population of at least 125,000, OR an overall population of at least 25,000 where the Hispanic/Latino population is at least 20% of the overall population. In states where less than five places meet either of these criteria, we have included places with at least 10,000 total population with the highest percentage of Hispanic/Latino population. These places are identified with an asterisk (*); Please refer to the User's Guide for a full explanation of data.

Class of Worker: Government

(Universe: Civilian Employed Population 16 Years and Over)

Central American: Costa Rican

Top 10 States, Counties, and Places[1]

Sorted by Number in Descending Order — U.S. = 6,463

State	Number	County	Number	Place	Number
California	1,643	Los Angeles County, CA	535	**New York, NY** (city)	559
Florida	884	Miami-Dade County, FL	270	**Brooklyn, NY** (borough) Kings County	232
New York	862	Kings County, NY	232	**Queens, NY** (borough) Queens County	230
Texas	489	Queens County, NY	230	**Los Angeles, CA** (city) Los Angeles County	217
New Jersey	301	Riverside County, CA	182	**Bronx, NY** (borough) Bronx County	40
Massachusetts	268	San Bernardino County, CA	151	**Miami, FL** (city) Miami-Dade County	17
Maryland	173	Orange County, CA	135	**Philadelphia, PA** (city) Philadelphia County	0
Tennessee	140	San Diego County, CA	129		
North Carolina	130	Contra Costa County, CA	128		
Arizona	112	Palm Beach County, FL	121		

Sorted by Number in Ascending Order — U.S. = 6,463

State	Number	County	Number	Place	Number
Minnesota	12	Philadelphia County, PA	0	**Philadelphia, PA** (city) Philadelphia County	0
Colorado	35	Union County, NJ	6	**Miami, FL** (city) Miami-Dade County	17
Michigan	37	Passaic County, NJ	9	**Bronx, NY** (borough) Bronx County	40
Wisconsin	42	Morris County, NJ	11	**Los Angeles, CA** (city) Los Angeles County	217
Louisiana	45	Orange County, FL	14	**Queens, NY** (borough) Queens County	230
Washington	54	Clark County, NV	19	**Brooklyn, NY** (borough) Kings County	232
South Carolina	59	Essex County, NJ	23	**New York, NY** (city)	559
Illinois	72	Somerset County, NJ	23		
Connecticut	79	Suffolk County, NY	26		
Nevada	81	Fairfield County, CT	36		

Sorted by Percent in Descending Order — U.S. = 10.4%

State	Percent	County	Percent	Place	Percent
Tennessee	31.9	Riverside County, CA	31.4	**Queens, NY** (borough) Queens County	24.9
Oregon	19.4	San Diego County, CA	30.4	**Brooklyn, NY** (borough) Kings County	21.1
New York	16.6	Queens County, NY	24.9	**New York, NY** (city)	19.1
California	15.4	Kings County, NY	21.1	**Los Angeles, CA** (city) Los Angeles County	14.1
Texas	15.4	Contra Costa County, CA	18.2	**Bronx, NY** (borough) Bronx County	10.2
Maryland	13.2	San Bernardino County, CA	17.7	**Miami, FL** (city) Miami-Dade County	2.4
Massachusetts	12.8	Palm Beach County, FL	16.1	**Philadelphia, PA** (city) Philadelphia County	0.0
Arizona	12.2	Maricopa County, AZ	15.5		
Wisconsin	11.8	Orange County, CA	12.7		
Washington	11.2	Nassau County, NY	12.4		

Sorted by Percent in Ascending Order — U.S. = 10.4%

State	Percent	County	Percent	Place	Percent
Minnesota	2.7	Philadelphia County, PA	0.0	**Philadelphia, PA** (city) Philadelphia County	0.0
New Jersey	2.9	Union County, NJ	0.3	**Miami, FL** (city) Miami-Dade County	2.4
Pennsylvania	4.4	Passaic County, NJ	0.9	**Bronx, NY** (borough) Bronx County	10.2
Colorado	5.1	Morris County, NJ	1.1	**Los Angeles, CA** (city) Los Angeles County	14.1
North Carolina	5.3	Somerset County, NJ	1.7	**New York, NY** (city)	19.1
Georgia	5.7	Essex County, NJ	2.1	**Brooklyn, NY** (borough) Kings County	21.1
Louisiana	5.7	Orange County, FL	2.1	**Queens, NY** (borough) Queens County	24.9
South Carolina	5.9	Clark County, NV	3.9		
Illinois	6.9	Suffolk County, NY	4.0		
Connecticut	7.1	Fairfield County, CT	5.2		

Note: (1) Ranking tables cover all states and counties, and places with an overall population of at least 125,000, OR an overall population of at least 25,000 where the Hispanic/Latino population is at least 20% of the overall population. In states where less than five places meet either of these criteria, we have included places with at least 10,000 total population with the highest percentage of Hispanic/Latino population. These places are identified with an asterisk (*); Please refer to the User's Guide for a full explanation of data.

Class of Worker: Government

(Universe: Civilian Employed Population 16 Years and Over)

Central American: Guatemalan

Top 10 States, Counties, and Places[1]

Sorted by Number in Descending Order — U.S. = 21,854

State	Number	County	Number	Place	Number
California	9,925	Los Angeles County, CA	6,331	**Los Angeles, CA** (city) Los Angeles County	3,022
New York	1,885	Cook County, IL	868	**New York, NY** (city)	1,013
Florida	1,453	Miami-Dade County, FL	591	**Chicago, IL** (city) Cook County	630
Illinois	1,217	San Bernardino County, CA	488	**Queens, NY** (borough) Queens County	426
Texas	933	Fairfax County, VA	431	**Brooklyn, NY** (borough) Kings County	311
Virginia	757	Queens County, NY	426	**Burbank, CA** (city) Los Angeles County	234
Maryland	718	Harris County, TX	364	**Bakersfield, CA** (city) Kern County	182
New Jersey	547	Orange County, CA	361	**Houston, TX** (city) Harris County	172
Massachusetts	486	Riverside County, CA	314	**Inglewood, CA** (city) Los Angeles County	172
Arizona	423	Kings County, NY	311	**Phoenix, AZ** (city) Maricopa County	172

Sorted by Number in Ascending Order — U.S. = 21,854

State	Number	County	Number	Place	Number
New Hampshire	0	Adams County, CO	0	**Albertville*, AL** (city) Marshall County	0
Delaware	7	Baltimore County, MD	0	**Bonita Springs, FL** (city) Lee County	0
Idaho	11	Burke County, NC	0	**Brookhaven, NY** (town) Suffolk County	0
Kansas	13	Cherokee County, GA	0	**Carthage*, MO** (city) Jasper County	0
South Dakota	15	Dawson County, NE	0	**Central Falls*, RI** (city) Providence County	0
Arkansas	29	DeKalb County, AL	0	**Chattanooga, TN** (city) Hamilton County	0
Mississippi	34	Denton County, TX	0	**Columbus, OH** (city) Franklin County	0
Wisconsin	48	Fort Bend County, TX	0	**Elizabeth, NJ** (city) Union County	0
South Carolina	56	Franklin County, AL	0	**Garland, TX** (city) Dallas County	0
Utah	57	Franklin County, OH	0	**Grand Rapids, MI** (city) Kent County	0

Sorted by Percent in Descending Order — U.S. = 4.1%

State	Percent	County	Percent	Place	Percent
District of Columbia	9.9	Hartford County, CT	16.0	**Burbank, CA** (city) Los Angeles County	33.3
Indiana	7.6	Santa Barbara County, CA	14.0	**West Covina, CA** (city) Los Angeles County	21.2
Illinois	7.5	Kern County, CA	13.4	**Bakersfield, CA** (city) Kern County	20.9
Arizona	6.5	Santa Clara County, CA	12.8	**Cranston*, RI** (city) Providence County	16.0
Wisconsin	6.4	Sonoma County, CA	12.2	**Alhambra, CA** (city) Los Angeles County	15.6
California	5.8	Pima County, AZ	11.9	**North Hempstead, NY** (town) Nassau County	14.7
Washington	5.4	Pinal County, AZ	11.9	**Norwalk, CA** (city) Los Angeles County	14.6
New York	5.2	Bristol County, MA	11.3	**Montebello, CA** (city) Los Angeles County	12.8
Louisiana	4.7	Loudoun County, VA	10.7	**San Jose, CA** (city) Santa Clara County	11.5
Minnesota	4.5	Will County, IL	10.3	**Fontana, CA** (city) San Bernardino County	11.3

Sorted by Percent in Ascending Order — U.S. = 4.1%

State	Percent	County	Percent	Place	Percent
New Hampshire	0.0	Adams County, CO	0.0	**Albertville*, AL** (city) Marshall County	0.0
Delaware	0.3	Baltimore County, MD	0.0	**Bonita Springs, FL** (city) Lee County	0.0
Kansas	0.7	Burke County, NC	0.0	**Brookhaven, NY** (town) Suffolk County	0.0
Arkansas	1.3	Cherokee County, GA	0.0	**Carthage*, MO** (city) Jasper County	0.0
Tennessee	1.3	Dawson County, NE	0.0	**Central Falls*, RI** (city) Providence County	0.0
South Carolina	1.4	DeKalb County, AL	0.0	**Chattanooga, TN** (city) Hamilton County	0.0
Georgia	1.5	Denton County, TX	0.0	**Columbus, OH** (city) Franklin County	0.0
Alabama	1.7	Fort Bend County, TX	0.0	**Elizabeth, NJ** (city) Union County	0.0
Utah	1.7	Franklin County, AL	0.0	**Garland, TX** (city) Dallas County	0.0
Idaho	1.8	Franklin County, OH	0.0	**Grand Rapids, MI** (city) Kent County	0.0

Note: (1) Ranking tables cover all states and counties, and places with an overall population of at least 125,000, OR an overall population of at least 25,000 where the Hispanic/Latino population is at least 20% of the overall population. In states where less than five places meet either of these criteria, we have included places with at least 10,000 total population with the highest percentage of Hispanic/Latino population. These places are identified with an asterisk (*); Please refer to the User's Guide for a full explanation of data.

Class of Worker: Government

(Universe: Civilian Employed Population 16 Years and Over)

Central American: Honduran

Top 10 States, Counties, and Places[1]

Sorted by Number in Descending Order — U.S. = 13,908

State	Number	County	Number	Place	Number
New York	2,745	Los Angeles County, CA	980	**New York, NY** (city)	2,078
Florida	2,065	Bronx County, NY	829	**Bronx, NY** (borough) Bronx County	829
California	1,903	Miami-Dade County, FL	766	**Brooklyn, NY** (borough) Kings County	563
Texas	1,273	Kings County, NY	563	**Los Angeles, CA** (city) Los Angeles County	525
New Jersey	690	Queens County, NY	444	**Queens, NY** (borough) Queens County	444
Louisiana	616	Harris County, TX	400	**Boston, MA** (city) Suffolk County	232
Georgia	504	Jefferson Parish, LA	295	**Manhattan, NY** (borough) New York County	195
Maryland	483	Broward County, FL	250	**Miami, FL** (city) Miami-Dade County	184
Massachusetts	478	Fairfax County, VA	247	**Houston, TX** (city) Harris County	171
Virginia	457	Hudson County, NJ	232	**Yonkers, NY** (city) Westchester County	135

Sorted by Number in Ascending Order — U.S. = 13,908

State	Number	County	Number	Place	Number
Mississippi	6	Beaufort County, SC	0	**Chelsea, MA** (city) Suffolk County	0
Kentucky	13	Elkhart County, IN	0	**Fort Worth, TX** (city) Tarrant County	0
Kansas	16	Fulton County, GA	0	**Hempstead (village), NY** (village) Nassau County	0
Michigan	20	Johnston County, NC	0	**Huntington Station, NY** (cdp) Suffolk County	0
Oklahoma	22	Kern County, CA	0	**Pasadena, TX** (city) Harris County	0
Iowa	24	Loudoun County, VA	0	**Plainfield, NJ** (city) Union County	0
Alabama	30	Polk County, FL	0	**Waukegan, IL** (city) Lake County	0
Minnesota	31	Sampson County, NC	0	**West Little River, FL** (cdp) Miami-Dade County	8
South Carolina	42	Duplin County, NC	3	**North Miami, FL** (city) Miami-Dade County	10
Ohio	45	King County, WA	9	**San Jose, CA** (city) Santa Clara County	12

Sorted by Percent in Descending Order — U.S. = 4.5%

State	Percent	County	Percent	Place	Percent
Nebraska	13.3	Westchester County, NY	15.5	**Miramar, FL** (city) Broward County	22.5
Arizona	12.0	Fresno County, CA	13.4	**Yonkers, NY** (city) Westchester County	20.2
Wisconsin	10.4	Manatee County, FL	12.5	**Phoenix, AZ** (city) Maricopa County	16.8
Colorado	8.6	Maricopa County, AZ	12.4	**Boston, MA** (city) Suffolk County	12.3
Oregon	8.1	Riverside County, CA	11.8	**Brooklyn, NY** (borough) Kings County	10.8
New York	7.8	Cobb County, GA	11.5	**San Diego, CA** (city) San Diego County	10.5
Massachusetts	7.3	Kings County, NY	10.8	**South Miami Heights, FL** (cdp) Miami-Dade County	10.2
Illinois	7.2	Lake County, IL	10.6	**Manhattan, NY** (borough) New York County	9.9
Arkansas	5.5	Fort Bend County, TX	10.5	**Newark, NJ** (city) Essex County	9.8
Indiana	5.5	Arapahoe County, CO	10.2	**New York, NY** (city)	9.7

Sorted by Percent in Ascending Order — U.S. = 4.5%

State	Percent	County	Percent	Place	Percent
Mississippi	0.6	Beaufort County, SC	0.0	**Chelsea, MA** (city) Suffolk County	0.0
Kansas	0.9	Elkhart County, IN	0.0	**Fort Worth, TX** (city) Tarrant County	0.0
South Carolina	1.2	Fulton County, GA	0.0	**Hempstead (village), NY** (village) Nassau County	0.0
Oklahoma	1.4	Johnston County, NC	0.0	**Huntington Station, NY** (cdp) Suffolk County	0.0
Kentucky	1.6	Kern County, CA	0.0	**Pasadena, TX** (city) Harris County	0.0
Alabama	2.1	Loudoun County, VA	0.0	**Plainfield, NJ** (city) Union County	0.0
Minnesota	2.1	Polk County, FL	0.0	**Waukegan, IL** (city) Lake County	0.0
Michigan	2.2	Sampson County, NC	0.0	**Dallas, TX** (city) Dallas County	0.5
Tennessee	2.5	Duplin County, NC	0.3	**Hempstead (town), NY** (town) Nassau County	0.6
North Carolina	2.6	Prince William County, VA	0.6	**Hialeah, FL** (city) Miami-Dade County	0.8

Note: (1) Ranking tables cover all states and counties, and places with an overall population of at least 125,000, OR an overall population of at least 25,000 where the Hispanic/Latino population is at least 20% of the overall population. In states where less than five places meet either of these criteria, we have included places with at least 10,000 total population with the highest percentage of Hispanic/Latino population. These places are identified with an asterisk (*); Please refer to the User's Guide for a full explanation of data.

Class of Worker: Government

(Universe: Civilian Employed Population 16 Years and Over)

Central American: Nicaraguan

Top 10 States, Counties, and Places[1]

Sorted by Number in Descending Order — U.S. = 14,861

State	Number	County	Number	Place	Number
California	6,062	Miami-Dade County, FL	2,341	**Los Angeles, CA** (city) Los Angeles County	824
Florida	3,418	Los Angeles County, CA	1,886	**New York, NY** (city)	542
New York	707	San Mateo County, CA	847	**San Francisco, CA** (city) San Francisco County	517
Texas	706	Contra Costa County, CA	719	**Daly City, CA** (city) San Mateo County	424
Virginia	656	San Francisco County, CA	517	**Miami, FL** (city) Miami-Dade County	378
Maryland	594	San Bernardino County, CA	484	**Bronx, NY** (borough) Bronx County	211
New Jersey	282	Broward County, FL	259	**Fountainebleau, FL** (cdp) Miami-Dade County	204
North Carolina	250	Montgomery County, MD	255	**Queens, NY** (borough) Queens County	202
Louisiana	246	Fairfax County, VA	250	**Antioch, CA** (city) Contra Costa County	201
Nevada	203	Prince George's County, MD	220	**Hialeah, FL** (city) Miami-Dade County	200

Sorted by Number in Ascending Order — U.S. = 14,861

State	Number	County	Number	Place	Number
Minnesota	9	New York County, NY	0	**Manhattan, NY** (borough) New York County	0
South Carolina	11	Orange County, FL	10	**Kenner, LA** (city) Jefferson Parish	8
Massachusetts	17	Sonoma County, CA	13	**West Little River, FL** (cdp) Miami-Dade County	9
Tennessee	21	Hudson County, NJ	16	**Las Vegas, NV** (city) Clark County	10
Missouri	33	Gwinnett County, GA	19	**Richmond West, FL** (cdp) Miami-Dade County	13
Oregon	36	Collier County, FL	23	**Austin, TX** (city) Travis County	16
Indiana	46	Bexar County, TX	30	**North Miami, FL** (city) Miami-Dade County	19
Colorado	51	Camden County, NJ	47	**Metairie, LA** (cdp) Jefferson Parish	20
District of Columbia	63	Stanislaus County, CA	60	**South Gate, CA** (city) Los Angeles County	20
Connecticut	64	San Joaquin County, CA	61	**Country Club, FL** (cdp) Miami-Dade County	25

Sorted by Percent in Descending Order — U.S. = 8.3%

State	Percent	County	Percent	Place	Percent
Michigan	22.6	Contra Costa County, CA	22.2	**Antioch, CA** (city) Contra Costa County	23.1
Ohio	22.2	San Diego County, CA	21.5	**Richmond, CA** (city) Contra Costa County	21.7
Washington	18.8	King County, WA	21.1	**Daly City, CA** (city) San Mateo County	20.1
Connecticut	14.5	Prince George's County, MD	18.9	**Sacramento, CA** (city) Sacramento County	17.5
Virginia	14.5	Sacramento County, CA	18.2	**Charlotte, NC** (city) Mecklenburg County	17.0
Wisconsin	14.3	Fairfax County, VA	17.7	**San Francisco, CA** (city) San Francisco County	15.8
Maryland	13.4	Lee County, FL	17.7	**South San Francisco, CA** (city) San Mateo County	15.5
California	12.4	San Mateo County, CA	17.0	**San Diego, CA** (city) San Diego County	15.4
Arizona	11.8	San Francisco County, CA	15.8	**Chicago, IL** (city) Cook County	14.6
Indiana	11.7	Maricopa County, AZ	14.6	**Bronx, NY** (borough) Bronx County	14.3

Sorted by Percent in Ascending Order — U.S. = 8.3%

State	Percent	County	Percent	Place	Percent
Minnesota	1.6	New York County, NY	0.0	**Manhattan, NY** (borough) New York County	0.0
Massachusetts	1.9	Orange County, FL	1.0	**West Little River, FL** (cdp) Miami-Dade County	0.6
South Carolina	2.4	Hudson County, NJ	1.6	**Kenner, LA** (city) Jefferson Parish	0.8
Florida	4.6	Sonoma County, CA	2.3	**Richmond West, FL** (cdp) Miami-Dade County	0.9
Tennessee	5.1	Collier County, FL	3.6	**Las Vegas, NV** (city) Clark County	1.9
Louisiana	5.9	Miami-Dade County, FL	3.9	**Metairie, LA** (cdp) Jefferson Parish	2.4
New Jersey	6.6	Jefferson Parish, LA	5.3	**Miami, FL** (city) Miami-Dade County	2.4
Pennsylvania	7.0	Harris County, TX	5.5	**Country Club, FL** (cdp) Miami-Dade County	2.5
Colorado	7.3	Gwinnett County, GA	6.1	**Tamiami, FL** (cdp) Miami-Dade County	2.6
Oregon	7.6	Broward County, FL	6.2	**North Miami, FL** (city) Miami-Dade County	2.8

RANKINGS & COMPARISONS

Note: (1) Ranking tables cover all states and counties, and places with an overall population of at least 125,000, OR an overall population of at least 25,000 where the Hispanic/Latino population is at least 20% of the overall population. In states where less than five places meet either of these criteria, we have included places with at least 10,000 total population with the highest percentage of Hispanic/Latino population. These places are identified with an asterisk (*); Please refer to the User's Guide for a full explanation of data.

Class of Worker: Government

(Universe: Civilian Employed Population 16 Years and Over)

Central American: Panamanian

Top 10 States, Counties, and Places[1]

Sorted by Number in Descending Order — U.S. = 16,015

State	Number	County	Number	Place	Number
New York	3,641	Kings County, NY	1,586	**New York, NY** (city)	2,699
Florida	2,488	Miami-Dade County, FL	752	**Brooklyn, NY** (borough) Kings County	1,586
California	1,634	Queens County, NY	549	**Queens, NY** (borough) Queens County	549
Texas	1,317	Los Angeles County, CA	430	**Bronx, NY** (borough) Bronx County	286
Virginia	1,129	Broward County, FL	417	**Hempstead (town), NY** (town) Nassau County	223
Georgia	670	Hillsborough County, FL	288	**Manhattan, NY** (borough) New York County	220
North Carolina	619	Bronx County, NY	286	**Fayetteville, NC** (city) Cumberland County	175
Maryland	608	Cumberland County, NC	252	**Killeen, TX** (city) Bell County	165
New Jersey	579	Prince William County, VA	239	**Jacksonville, FL** (city) Duval County	138
Washington	385	San Diego County, CA	234	**San Antonio, TX** (city) Bexar County	105

Sorted by Number in Ascending Order — U.S. = 16,015

State	Number	County	Number	Place	Number
Minnesota	40	Dallas County, TX	24	**Miami, FL** (city) Miami-Dade County	29
New Mexico	60	Maricopa County, AZ	36	**Houston, TX** (city) Harris County	57
Indiana	70	Hudson County, NJ	43	**San Diego, CA** (city) San Diego County	70
Kentucky	70	Palm Beach County, FL	63	**Los Angeles, CA** (city) Los Angeles County	102
Mississippi	76	Pierce County, WA	67	**San Antonio, TX** (city) Bexar County	105
Wisconsin	77	Clark County, NV	80	**Jacksonville, FL** (city) Duval County	138
Ohio	78	Cook County, IL	80	**Killeen, TX** (city) Bell County	165
Tennessee	98	Montgomery County, MD	95	**Fayetteville, NC** (city) Cumberland County	175
Nevada	108	Riverside County, CA	97	**Manhattan, NY** (borough) New York County	220
Missouri	111	Essex County, NJ	119	**Hempstead (town), NY** (town) Nassau County	223

Sorted by Percent in Descending Order — U.S. = 20.7%

State	Percent	County	Percent	Place	Percent
Mississippi	43.2	Sacramento County, CA	37.4	**Killeen, TX** (city) Bell County	40.0
Washington	30.4	Prince William County, VA	34.7	**Fayetteville, NC** (city) Cumberland County	32.3
Virginia	29.1	Cumberland County, NC	33.7	**Hempstead (town), NY** (town) Nassau County	28.4
South Carolina	27.8	Bell County, TX	31.9	**Queens, NY** (borough) Queens County	27.6
Connecticut	27.6	Suffolk County, NY	30.6	**Bronx, NY** (borough) Bronx County	26.0
North Carolina	25.3	Orange County, CA	29.1	**New York, NY** (city)	23.7
New York	25.2	Nassau County, NY	28.4	**Brooklyn, NY** (borough) Kings County	23.1
Maryland	25.1	Queens County, NY	27.6	**Jacksonville, FL** (city) Duval County	18.9
Oklahoma	22.3	Bronx County, NY	26.0	**Manhattan, NY** (borough) New York County	18.6
New Mexico	21.8	San Bernardino County, CA	25.2	**San Antonio, TX** (city) Bexar County	16.9

Sorted by Percent in Ascending Order — U.S. = 20.7%

State	Percent	County	Percent	Place	Percent
Ohio	7.7	Dallas County, TX	3.9	**Miami, FL** (city) Miami-Dade County	6.3
Minnesota	9.4	Maricopa County, AZ	5.5	**Los Angeles, CA** (city) Los Angeles County	11.3
Illinois	10.0	Hudson County, NJ	11.6	**Houston, TX** (city) Harris County	11.7
Pennsylvania	10.4	Orange County, FL	12.3	**San Diego, CA** (city) San Diego County	13.2
Tennessee	11.2	Clark County, NV	13.3	**San Antonio, TX** (city) Bexar County	16.9
Massachusetts	11.7	Cook County, IL	13.7	**Manhattan, NY** (borough) New York County	18.6
Kentucky	12.6	Palm Beach County, FL	14.0	**Jacksonville, FL** (city) Duval County	18.9
Indiana	13.1	Los Angeles County, CA	16.5	**Brooklyn, NY** (borough) Kings County	23.1
Missouri	15.0	Miami-Dade County, FL	17.8	**New York, NY** (city)	23.7
Nevada	16.3	Riverside County, CA	17.9	**Bronx, NY** (borough) Bronx County	26.0

Note: (1) Ranking tables cover all states and counties, and places with an overall population of at least 125,000, OR an overall population of at least 25,000 where the Hispanic/Latino population is at least 20% of the overall population. In states where less than five places meet either of these criteria, we have included places with at least 10,000 total population with the highest percentage of Hispanic/Latino population. These places are identified with an asterisk (*); Please refer to the User's Guide for a full explanation of data.

Class of Worker: Government

(Universe: Civilian Employed Population 16 Years and Over)

Central American: Salvadoran

Top 10 States, Counties, and Places[1]

Sorted by Number in Descending Order — U.S. = 44,561

State	Number	County	Number	Place	Number
California	21,912	Los Angeles County, CA	12,539	**Los Angeles, CA** (city) Los Angeles County	7,268
Texas	5,021	Harris County, TX	2,115	**New York, NY** (city)	1,205
New York	3,432	Fairfax County, VA	1,403	**San Francisco, CA** (city) San Francisco County	1,037
Virginia	3,225	Montgomery County, MD	1,204	**Houston, TX** (city) Harris County	1,001
Maryland	2,642	Nassau County, NY	1,127	**Hempstead (town), NY** (town) Nassau County	854
New Jersey	1,176	San Francisco County, CA	1,037	**Queens, NY** (borough) Queens County	642
Florida	948	San Mateo County, CA	1,034	**San Jose, CA** (city) Santa Clara County	523
North Carolina	554	Contra Costa County, CA	986	**Long Beach, CA** (city) Los Angeles County	326
Nevada	517	Prince George's County, MD	953	**Islip, NY** (town) Suffolk County	315
Arizona	444	San Bernardino County, CA	908	**Silver Spring, MD** (cdp) Montgomery County	265

Sorted by Number in Ascending Order — U.S. = 44,561

State	Number	County	Number	Place	Number
Hawaii	0	Crawford County, AR	0	**Bridgeport, CT** (city/town) Fairfield County	0
Kentucky	16	DeKalb County, GA	0	**Carrollton, TX** (city) Denton County	0
Indiana	17	Douglas County, NE	0	**Columbus, OH** (city) Franklin County	0
Rhode Island	36	Forsyth County, NC	0	**Farmers Branch, TX** (city) Dallas County	0
Idaho	40	Franklin County, OH	0	**Fullerton, CA** (city) Orange County	0
Alabama	47	Fulton County, GA	0	**Gardena, CA** (city) Los Angeles County	0
Louisiana	55	Hall County, NE	0	**Grand Island, NE** (city) Hall County	0
Ohio	55	Henrico County, VA	0	**Lake Worth, FL** (city) Palm Beach County	0
Michigan	58	New Haven County, CT	0	**Lewisville, TX** (city) Denton County	0
Alaska	61	Worcester County, MA	0	**Manassas, VA** (independent city)	0

Sorted by Percent in Descending Order — U.S. = 5.3%

State	Percent	County	Percent	Place	Percent
Wisconsin	11.3	Yolo County, CA	32.3	**Santa Rosa, CA** (city) Sonoma County	21.6
South Carolina	9.8	Santa Barbara County, CA	18.7	**Whittier, CA** (city) Los Angeles County	20.9
Alaska	9.3	Jackson County, MO	17.7	**West Covina, CA** (city) Los Angeles County	19.8
Idaho	9.1	Multnomah County, OR	17.4	**Portland, OR** (city) Multnomah County	19.2
Oklahoma	8.8	Pima County, AZ	15.6	**Rancho Cucamonga, CA** (city) San Bernardino County	18.4
Oregon	8.3	Solano County, CA	14.2	**Baldwin Park, CA** (city) Los Angeles County	17.8
New Mexico	7.8	San Francisco County, CA	13.4	**Paramount, CA** (city) Los Angeles County	17.8
California	7.4	Galveston County, TX	12.8	**Pittsburg, CA** (city) Contra Costa County	16.2
Washington	7.2	Brazoria County, TX	12.3	**Antioch, CA** (city) Contra Costa County	15.8
Arizona	7.0	Sonoma County, CA	12.0	**Montebello, CA** (city) Los Angeles County	15.1

Sorted by Percent in Ascending Order — U.S. = 5.3%

State	Percent	County	Percent	Place	Percent
Hawaii	0.0	Crawford County, AR	0.0	**Bridgeport, CT** (city/town) Fairfield County	0.0
Indiana	0.6	DeKalb County, GA	0.0	**Carrollton, TX** (city) Denton County	0.0
Massachusetts	1.8	Douglas County, NE	0.0	**Columbus, OH** (city) Franklin County	0.0
Kentucky	1.9	Forsyth County, NC	0.0	**Farmers Branch, TX** (city) Dallas County	0.0
Connecticut	2.0	Franklin County, OH	0.0	**Fullerton, CA** (city) Orange County	0.0
Rhode Island	2.0	Fulton County, GA	0.0	**Gardena, CA** (city) Los Angeles County	0.0
Georgia	2.1	Hall County, NE	0.0	**Grand Island, NE** (city) Hall County	0.0
Ohio	2.1	Henrico County, VA	0.0	**Lake Worth, FL** (city) Palm Beach County	0.0
Louisiana	2.2	New Haven County, CT	0.0	**Lewisville, TX** (city) Denton County	0.0
Arkansas	2.7	Worcester County, MA	0.0	**Manassas, VA** (independent city)	0.0

Note: (1) Ranking tables cover all states and counties, and places with an overall population of at least 125,000, OR an overall population of at least 25,000 where the Hispanic/Latino population is at least 20% of the overall population. In states where less than five places meet either of these criteria, we have included places with at least 10,000 total population with the highest percentage of Hispanic/Latino population. These places are identified with an asterisk (*); Please refer to the User's Guide for a full explanation of data.

Class of Worker: Government

(Universe: Civilian Employed Population 16 Years and Over)

Cuban

Top 10 States, Counties, and Places[1]

Sorted by Number in Descending Order — U.S. = 94,604

State	Number	County	Number	Place	Number
Florida	58,500	Miami-Dade County, FL	39,277	**Miami, FL** (city) Miami-Dade County	6,006
New Jersey	6,855	Broward County, FL	5,442	**Hialeah, FL** (city) Miami-Dade County	4,424
California	6,410	Hillsborough County, FL	3,311	**New York, NY** (city)	2,666
New York	5,457	Los Angeles County, CA	2,992	**Tamiami, FL** (cdp) Miami-Dade County	2,320
Texas	2,373	Hudson County, NJ	2,428	**Pembroke Pines, FL** (city) Broward County	1,910
Georgia	1,420	Palm Beach County, FL	2,371	**Kendale Lakes, FL** (cdp) Miami-Dade County	1,635
Illinois	1,258	Bergen County, NJ	1,275	**Kendall, FL** (cdp) Miami-Dade County	1,371
North Carolina	1,129	Orange County, FL	902	**Fountainebleau, FL** (cdp) Miami-Dade County	1,182
Virginia	1,094	Union County, NJ	849	**Tampa, FL** (city) Hillsborough County	1,137
Maryland	1,031	Queens County, NY	812	**University Park, FL** (cdp) Miami-Dade County	1,087

Sorted by Number in Ascending Order — U.S. = 94,604

State	Number	County	Number	Place	Number
Nebraska	11	Montgomery County, TX	0	**Kenner, LA** (city) Jefferson Parish	0
Hawaii	29	Lancaster County, PA	4	**Oakland Park, FL** (city) Broward County	0
Mississippi	40	Lehigh County, PA	7	**Spring Valley, NV** (cdp) Clark County	15
West Virginia	43	Worcester County, MA	10	**Islip, NY** (town) Suffolk County	25
Arkansas	46	Clay County, MO	11	**Syracuse, NY** (city) Onondaga County	27
Kansas	63	El Paso County, TX	12	**Philadelphia, PA** (city) Philadelphia County	32
Maine	72	Chester County, PA	14	**Fort Worth, TX** (city) Tarrant County	33
Delaware	81	Cuyahoga County, OH	15	**Kansas City, MO** (city) Jackson County	34
Minnesota	84	Shelby County, TN	15	**Lake Magdalene, FL** (cdp) Hillsborough County	35
Oklahoma	86	Lake County, IL	16	**Burbank, CA** (city) Los Angeles County	36

Sorted by Percent in Descending Order — U.S. = 12.1%

State	Percent	County	Percent	Place	Percent
District of Columbia	29.9	Rockland County, NY	35.8	**Oyster Bay, NY** (town) Nassau County	43.2
Maryland	22.8	Forsyth County, GA	35.3	**Tallahassee, FL** (city) Leon County	30.1
Utah	22.3	Mercer County, NJ	34.6	**Bronx, NY** (borough) Bronx County	28.2
Maine	22.2	Hamilton County, OH	30.3	**Riverside, CA** (city) Riverside County	26.9
Rhode Island	19.4	Dutchess County, NY	28.4	**Columbus, OH** (city) Franklin County	26.5
Iowa	19.1	Bronx County, NY	28.2	**Long Beach, CA** (city) Los Angeles County	24.3
Arizona	17.7	Montgomery County, MD	28.2	**Hempstead (town), NY** (town) Nassau County	23.1
Arkansas	17.7	Leon County, FL	27.8	**Baltimore, MD** (independent city)	22.8
New Jersey	17.7	Pima County, AZ	27.2	**Cooper City, FL** (city) Broward County	22.6
New York	17.7	San Mateo County, CA	27.1	**Greenacres, FL** (city) Palm Beach County	22.5

Sorted by Percent in Ascending Order — U.S. = 12.1%

State	Percent	County	Percent	Place	Percent
Nebraska	1.4	Montgomery County, TX	0.0	**Kenner, LA** (city) Jefferson Parish	0.0
Hawaii	5.3	Lancaster County, PA	0.7	**Oakland Park, FL** (city) Broward County	0.0
Kansas	6.0	Lehigh County, PA	1.7	**Spring Valley, NV** (cdp) Clark County	1.2
Minnesota	6.2	Clay County, MO	2.0	**Philadelphia, PA** (city) Philadelphia County	2.8
Mississippi	6.3	Chester County, PA	2.6	**Las Vegas, NV** (city) Clark County	3.0
Nevada	6.8	Lake County, IL	2.6	**West Little River, FL** (cdp) Miami-Dade County	3.5
Kentucky	6.9	Philadelphia County, PA	2.8	**Louisville-Jefferson County, KY** (metropolitan govt) Jefferson County	3.6
Pennsylvania	7.2	Hernando County, FL	3.0	**Kansas City, MO** (city) Jackson County	4.3
Missouri	7.3	Fulton County, GA	3.4	**Miami Gardens, FL** (city) Miami-Dade County	4.4
New Mexico	8.8	Worcester County, MA	3.4	**Hallandale Beach, FL** (city) Broward County	4.6

Note: (1) Ranking tables cover all states and counties, and places with an overall population of at least 125,000, OR an overall population of at least 25,000 where the Hispanic/Latino population is at least 20% of the overall population. In states where less than five places meet either of these criteria, we have included places with at least 10,000 total population with the highest percentage of Hispanic/Latino population. These places are identified with an asterisk (*); Please refer to the User's Guide for a full explanation of data.

Class of Worker: Government

(Universe: Civilian Employed Population 16 Years and Over)

Dominican Republic

Top 10 States, Counties, and Places[1]

Sorted by Number in Descending Order — U.S. = 55,159

State	Number	County	Number	Place	Number
New York	30,265	Bronx County, NY	9,388	**New York, NY** (city)	24,833
Florida	6,544	New York County, NY	7,222	**Bronx, NY** (borough) Bronx County	9,388
New Jersey	5,873	Queens County, NY	4,626	**Manhattan, NY** (borough) New York County	7,222
Massachusetts	2,802	Kings County, NY	3,330	**Queens, NY** (borough) Queens County	4,626
Pennsylvania	1,020	Miami-Dade County, FL	1,781	**Brooklyn, NY** (borough) Kings County	3,330
Virginia	964	Hudson County, NJ	1,660	**Lawrence, MA** (city) Essex County	831
Maryland	952	Suffolk County, NY	1,385	**Boston, MA** (city) Suffolk County	774
Rhode Island	842	Broward County, FL	1,306	**Hempstead (town), NY** (town) Nassau County	747
California	764	Westchester County, NY	1,301	**Yonkers, NY** (city) Westchester County	728
Connecticut	743	Essex County, MA	1,258	**Providence, RI** (city) Providence County	614

Sorted by Number in Ascending Order — U.S. = 55,159

State	Number	County	Number	Place	Number
Minnesota	15	Volusia County, FL	0	**Atlantic City, NJ** (city) Atlantic County	0
Wisconsin	23	Lackawanna County, PA	12	**Bethlehem, PA** (city) Northampton County	0
Alabama	30	Cuyahoga County, OH	13	**Deltona, FL** (city) Volusia County	0
Missouri	37	Jefferson Parish, LA	13	**Englewood, NJ** (city) Bergen County	0
Louisiana	56	Oneida County, NY	13	**Kendall West, FL** (cdp) Miami-Dade County	0
Delaware	62	Bristol County, MA	15	**New London, CT** (city/town) New London County	0
District of Columbia	70	Hillsborough County, NH	15	**North Miami Beach, FL** (city) Miami-Dade County	0
South Carolina	74	Kent County, MI	16	**Pawtucket*, RI** (city) Providence County	0
Michigan	84	New Castle County, DE	19	**Stamford, CT** (city/town) Fairfield County	0
Alaska	92	Ulster County, NY	21	**Weston, FL** (city) Broward County	0

Sorted by Percent in Descending Order — U.S. = 9.5%

State	Percent	County	Percent	Place	Percent
Utah	40.8	San Diego County, CA	44.6	**North Miami, FL** (city) Miami-Dade County	40.5
Washington	24.7	Onondaga County, NY	25.9	**Brookhaven, NY** (town) Suffolk County	23.5
Virginia	23.0	Bexar County, TX	20.5	**Poinciana, FL** (cdp) Osceola County	21.0
California	18.3	Ulster County, NY	19.3	**Staten Island, NY** (borough) Richmond County	18.6
Maryland	16.7	Burlington County, NJ	19.1	**Town 'n' Country, FL** (cdp) Hillsborough County	17.5
Colorado	15.6	Orange County, NY	19.1	**New Haven, CT** (city/town) New Haven County	16.8
Texas	13.0	Montgomery County, MD	18.9	**Linden, NJ** (city) Union County	15.8
Georgia	12.6	Richmond County, NY	18.6	**North Hempstead, NY** (town) Nassau County	15.2
South Carolina	12.2	Litchfield County, CT	16.6	**Kendale Lakes, FL** (cdp) Miami-Dade County	14.9
New Hampshire	12.1	Rockland County, NY	15.7	**Pembroke Pines, FL** (city) Broward County	14.9

Sorted by Percent in Ascending Order — U.S. = 9.5%

State	Percent	County	Percent	Place	Percent
Wisconsin	3.5	Volusia County, FL	0.0	**Atlantic City, NJ** (city) Atlantic County	0.0
Minnesota	3.6	Atlantic County, NJ	0.9	**Bethlehem, PA** (city) Northampton County	0.0
Louisiana	4.9	Luzerne County, PA	1.3	**Deltona, FL** (city) Volusia County	0.0
Pennsylvania	5.2	Hillsborough County, NH	1.4	**Englewood, NJ** (city) Bergen County	0.0
District of Columbia	5.3	Bristol County, MA	1.8	**Kendall West, FL** (cdp) Miami-Dade County	0.0
Ohio	5.4	Cuyahoga County, OH	2.1	**New London, CT** (city/town) New London County	0.0
Missouri	5.6	Lehigh County, PA	2.5	**North Miami Beach, FL** (city) Miami-Dade County	0.0
Rhode Island	6.3	Jefferson Parish, LA	2.6	**Pawtucket*, RI** (city) Providence County	0.0
Massachusetts	6.6	Duval County, FL	2.7	**Stamford, CT** (city/town) Fairfield County	0.0
New Jersey	7.1	Gwinnett County, GA	2.8	**Weston, FL** (city) Broward County	0.0

Note: (1) Ranking tables cover all states and counties, and places with an overall population of at least 125,000, OR an overall population of at least 25,000 where the Hispanic/Latino population is at least 20% of the overall population. In states where less than five places meet either of these criteria, we have included places with at least 10,000 total population with the highest percentage of Hispanic/Latino population. These places are identified with an asterisk (*); Please refer to the User's Guide for a full explanation of data.

Class of Worker: Government

(Universe: Civilian Employed Population 16 Years and Over)

Mexican

Top 10 States, Counties, and Places[1]

Sorted by Number in Descending Order — U.S. = 1,262,016

State	Number	County	Number	Place	Number
California	494,871	Los Angeles County, CA	147,950	**Los Angeles, CA** (city) Los Angeles County	40,703
Texas	401,192	Bexar County, TX	48,352	**San Antonio, TX** (city) Bexar County	39,712
Arizona	79,898	El Paso County, TX	43,183	**El Paso, TX** (city) El Paso County	36,077
New Mexico	40,434	San Diego County, CA	42,350	**Houston, TX** (city) Harris County	18,377
Illinois	39,356	Hidalgo County, TX	39,871	**Laredo, TX** (city) Webb County	16,987
Colorado	29,701	San Bernardino County, CA	38,109	**Phoenix, AZ** (city) Maricopa County	15,834
Washington	18,573	Harris County, TX	36,529	**San Diego, CA** (city) San Diego County	15,701
Florida	11,704	Maricopa County, AZ	35,007	**Chicago, IL** (city) Cook County	15,358
Nevada	11,377	Riverside County, CA	33,734	**Austin, TX** (city) Travis County	13,592
Oregon	10,490	Orange County, CA	28,843	**Tucson, AZ** (city) Pima County	12,777

Sorted by Number in Ascending Order — U.S. = 1,262,016

State	Number	County	Number	Place	Number
New Hampshire	115	Alexander County, NC	0	**Albertville*, AL** (city) Marshall County	0
Maine	185	Atkinson County, GA	0	**Asheboro, NC** (city) Randolph County	0
Rhode Island	216	Barbour County, AL	0	**Atlantic City, NJ** (city) Atlantic County	0
Vermont	252	Beaver County, UT	0	**Berea*, SC** (cdp) Greenville County	0
West Virginia	322	Brown County, MN	0	**Biloxi*, MS** (city) Harrison County	0
Delaware	410	Brunswick County, NC	0	**Bluffton*, SC** (town) Beaufort County	0
South Dakota	617	Buffalo County, WI	0	**Carthage*, MO** (city) Jasper County	0
North Dakota	621	Bulloch County, GA	0	**Chelsea, MA** (city) Suffolk County	0
Mississippi	935	Calumet County, WI	0	**Clifton, NJ** (city) Passaic County	0
District of Columbia	1,008	Cape May County, NJ	0	**Danbury, CT** (city/town) Fairfield County	0

Sorted by Percent in Descending Order — U.S. = 10.0%

State	Percent	County	Percent	Place	Percent
District of Columbia	20.9	Oneida County, NY	55.6	**Fort Leonard Wood*, MO** (cdp) Pulaski County	63.3
New Mexico	18.9	Terrell County, TX	51.6	**Florence, AZ** (town) Pinal County	55.1
Hawaii	17.7	Prince George County, VA	50.9	**Fort Hood, TX** (cdp) Bell County	50.5
Vermont	16.8	Latah County, ID	47.6	**Twentynine Palms, CA** (city) San Bernardino County	44.9
North Dakota	16.3	Osage County, OK	45.3	**Hampton, VA** (independent city)	37.1
Alaska	15.8	Crowley County, CO	44.8	**Fayetteville, NC** (city) Cumberland County	36.0
Montana	15.0	Lassen County, CA	42.6	**Schofield Barracks*, HI** (cdp) Honolulu County	36.0
Wyoming	12.9	Yazoo County, MS	42.3	**Kingsville, TX** (city) Kleberg County	33.5
Texas	12.7	Whitman County, WA	40.2	**Juneau*, AK** (borough) Juneau City and Borough	31.7
Arizona	12.6	De Baca County, NM	39.4	**Kyle, TX** (city) Hays County	31.6

Sorted by Percent in Ascending Order — U.S. = 10.0%

State	Percent	County	Percent	Place	Percent
New Jersey	2.3	Alexander County, NC	0.0	**Albertville*, AL** (city) Marshall County	0.0
North Carolina	2.6	Atkinson County, GA	0.0	**Asheboro, NC** (city) Randolph County	0.0
Alabama	3.0	Barbour County, AL	0.0	**Atlantic City, NJ** (city) Atlantic County	0.0
Georgia	3.0	Beaver County, UT	0.0	**Berea*, SC** (cdp) Greenville County	0.0
Tennessee	3.0	Brown County, MN	0.0	**Biloxi*, MS** (city) Harrison County	0.0
South Carolina	3.1	Brunswick County, NC	0.0	**Bluffton*, SC** (town) Beaufort County	0.0
Delaware	3.4	Buffalo County, WI	0.0	**Carthage*, MO** (city) Jasper County	0.0
New Hampshire	3.9	Bulloch County, GA	0.0	**Chelsea, MA** (city) Suffolk County	0.0
New York	3.9	Calumet County, WI	0.0	**Clifton, NJ** (city) Passaic County	0.0
Pennsylvania	3.9	Cape May County, NJ	0.0	**Danbury, CT** (city/town) Fairfield County	0.0

Note: (1) Ranking tables cover all states and counties, and places with an overall population of at least 125,000, OR an overall population of at least 25,000 where the Hispanic/Latino population is at least 20% of the overall population. In states where less than five places meet either of these criteria, we have included places with at least 10,000 total population with the highest percentage of Hispanic/Latino population. These places are identified with an asterisk (*); Please refer to the User's Guide for a full explanation of data.

Class of Worker: Government

(Universe: Civilian Employed Population 16 Years and Over)

Puerto Rican

Top 10 States, Counties, and Places[1]

Sorted by Number in Descending Order — U.S. = 283,831

State	Number	County	Number	Place	Number
New York	85,316	Bronx County, NY	22,716	**New York, NY** (city)	58,826
Florida	42,344	Kings County, NY	15,111	**Bronx, NY** (borough) Bronx County	22,716
New Jersey	27,853	Queens County, NY	9,473	**Brooklyn, NY** (borough) Kings County	15,111
California	13,637	Cook County, IL	8,793	**Queens, NY** (borough) Queens County	9,473
Connecticut	13,141	New York County, NY	7,640	**Manhattan, NY** (borough) New York County	7,640
Pennsylvania	12,301	Orange County, FL	6,720	**Chicago, IL** (city) Cook County	7,339
Illinois	11,952	Miami-Dade County, FL	6,220	**Philadelphia, PA** (city) Philadelphia County	4,382
Texas	10,996	Suffolk County, NY	5,679	**Staten Island, NY** (borough) Richmond County	3,886
Massachusetts	10,624	Hartford County, CT	4,548	**Brookhaven, NY** (town) Suffolk County	2,377
Virginia	8,306	Broward County, FL	4,415	**Islip, NY** (town) Suffolk County	2,197

Sorted by Number in Ascending Order — U.S. = 283,831

State	Number	County	Number	Place	Number
North Dakota	66	Clearfield County, PA	0	**Lake Magdalene, FL** (cdp) Hillsborough County	0
Wyoming	99	Carroll County, MD	6	**Omaha, NE** (city) Douglas County	0
Nebraska	131	Wyoming County, NY	6	**Rockford, IL** (city) Winnebago County	0
Montana	141	Perry County, PA	8	**Spring Valley, NV** (cdp) Clark County	10
Vermont	147	Warren County, OH	9	**Murrieta, CA** (city) Riverside County	12
South Dakota	174	Douglas County, NE	10	**Bridgeton, NJ** (city) Cumberland County	13
West Virginia	175	Lake County, OH	10	**Grand Prairie, TX** (city) Dallas County	13
Maine	194	Lycoming County, PA	10	**Fort Wayne, IN** (city) Allen County	15
Idaho	212	Butte County, CA	11	**Casselberry, FL** (city) Seminole County	17
Iowa	236	Camden County, GA	11	**Hackensack, NJ** (city) Bergen County	19

Sorted by Percent in Descending Order — U.S. = 16.7%

State	Percent	County	Percent	Place	Percent
Wyoming	41.1	Dale County, AL	62.2	**Alexandria, VA** (independent city)	51.0
South Dakota	36.9	Chemung County, NY	57.6	**Arlington, VA** (cdp) Arlington County	45.3
District of Columbia	31.4	Christian County, KY	55.3	**Chesapeake, VA** (independent city)	39.9
Maryland	29.1	Greene County, NY	52.8	**Augusta-Richmond County, GA** (consolidated govt) Richmond County	35.4
Virginia	27.3	Pulaski County, MO	52.1	**Chula Vista, CA** (city) San Diego County	34.2
Montana	24.6	Delaware County, NY	49.3	**Waianae*, HI** (cdp) Honolulu County	33.2
Alabama	24.2	Lee County, AL	47.3	**San Bernardino, CA** (city) San Bernardino County	32.4
Alaska	22.3	Coryell County, TX	45.8	**Wallkill, NY** (town) Orange County	32.4
Oklahoma	22.3	Arlington County, VA	45.3	**El Paso, TX** (city) El Paso County	32.3
Washington	22.2	Jefferson County, NY	44.9	**Norfolk, VA** (independent city)	32.0

Sorted by Percent in Ascending Order — U.S. = 16.7%

State	Percent	County	Percent	Place	Percent
New Hampshire	8.4	Clearfield County, PA	0.0	**Lake Magdalene, FL** (cdp) Hillsborough County	0.0
Rhode Island	9.0	Lake County, OH	1.7	**Omaha, NE** (city) Douglas County	0.0
Maine	10.4	Allen County, IN	2.3	**Rockford, IL** (city) Winnebago County	0.0
Nebraska	10.5	Sussex County, DE	2.4	**Spring Valley, NV** (cdp) Clark County	1.0
Minnesota	10.6	Douglas County, NE	2.7	**Hackensack, NJ** (city) Bergen County	1.5
Wisconsin	11.0	Carroll County, MD	2.8	**Casselberry, FL** (city) Seminole County	1.9
Pennsylvania	11.1	Warren County, OH	2.9	**Coconut Creek, FL** (city) Broward County	2.4
Michigan	11.6	Medina County, OH	3.0	**Murrieta, CA** (city) Riverside County	2.4
Iowa	11.9	Ontario County, NY	3.0	**Fort Wayne, IN** (city) Allen County	2.6
Delaware	12.1	Hunterdon County, NJ	3.3	**Grand Prairie, TX** (city) Dallas County	2.6

Note: (1) Ranking tables cover all states and counties, and places with an overall population of at least 125,000, OR an overall population of at least 25,000 where the Hispanic/Latino population is at least 20% of the overall population. In states where less than five places meet either of these criteria, we have included places with at least 10,000 total population with the highest percentage of Hispanic/Latino population. These places are identified with an asterisk (*); Please refer to the User's Guide for a full explanation of data.

Class of Worker: Government

(Universe: Civilian Employed Population 16 Years and Over)

South American

Top 10 States, Counties, and Places[1]

Sorted by Number in Descending Order — U.S. = 131,556

State	Number	County	Number	Place	Number
New York	23,561	Queens County, NY	8,654	**New York, NY** (city)	15,171
Florida	21,696	Miami-Dade County, FL	8,193	**Queens, NY** (borough) Queens County	8,654
California	19,382	Los Angeles County, CA	7,389	**Los Angeles, CA** (city) Los Angeles County	2,450
New Jersey	11,995	Broward County, FL	4,187	**Bronx, NY** (borough) Bronx County	2,436
Texas	8,218	Fairfax County, VA	2,916	**Brooklyn, NY** (borough) Kings County	1,814
Virginia	6,452	Montgomery County, MD	2,858	**Manhattan, NY** (borough) New York County	1,622
Maryland	4,884	Bronx County, NY	2,436	**Chicago, IL** (city) Cook County	1,540
Illinois	3,642	Harris County, TX	2,371	**Hempstead (town), NY** (town) Nassau County	1,424
Georgia	2,522	Hudson County, NJ	2,367	**Houston, TX** (city) Harris County	1,311
North Carolina	2,339	Westchester County, NY	2,241	**Miami, FL** (city) Miami-Dade County	877

Sorted by Number in Ascending Order — U.S. = 131,556

State	Number	County	Number	Place	Number
North Dakota	40	Luzerne County, PA	0	**Dania Beach, FL** (city) Broward County	0
Maine	43	McHenry County, IL	0	**New London, CT** (city/town) New London County	0
Montana	48	Cherokee County, GA	3	**Newburgh, NY** (city) Orange County	0
Wyoming	53	Douglas County, CO	3	**Oceanside, CA** (city) San Diego County	0
Vermont	82	Kent County, MI	11	**West Valley City, UT** (city) Salt Lake County	0
Idaho	144	Weber County, UT	12	**Poinciana, FL** (cdp) Osceola County	5
West Virginia	182	Anoka County, MN	13	**Cranston*, RI** (city) Providence County	7
New Hampshire	193	Hall County, GA	13	**City of Orange, NJ** (township) Essex County	9
Nebraska	252	Hamilton County, TN	14	**Palm Springs, CA** (city) Riverside County	9
Kentucky	274	Escambia County, FL	16	**Egypt Lake-Leto, FL** (cdp) Hillsborough County	10

Sorted by Percent in Descending Order — U.S. = 9.1%

State	Percent	County	Percent	Place	Percent
Mississippi	32.7	Brazos County, TX	42.6	**Albuquerque, NM** (city) Bernalillo County	41.3
New Mexico	29.9	Richland County, SC	39.5	**Hawthorne, CA** (city) Los Angeles County	31.5
Alaska	27.0	Bernalillo County, NM	39.2	**Lexington-Fayette, KY** (consolidated govt) Fayette County	30.9
District of Columbia	25.9	Onslow County, NC	38.8	**Alhambra, CA** (city) Los Angeles County	24.9
West Virginia	24.2	East Baton Rouge Parish, LA	35.0	**Rahway, NJ** (city) Union County	24.5
Iowa	22.5	Hampshire County, MA	34.5	**Austin, TX** (city) Travis County	24.1
Hawaii	20.2	Yolo County, CA	33.5	**El Paso, TX** (city) El Paso County	23.2
Arkansas	18.2	Champaign County, IL	33.0	**Placentia, CA** (city) Orange County	22.9
Ohio	18.1	Tompkins County, NY	32.9	**Fullerton, CA** (city) Orange County	22.1
Alabama	17.2	El Paso County, TX	31.9	**Hayward, CA** (city) Alameda County	22.1

Sorted by Percent in Ascending Order — U.S. = 9.1%

State	Percent	County	Percent	Place	Percent
Connecticut	6.1	Luzerne County, PA	0.0	**Dania Beach, FL** (city) Broward County	0.0
Florida	6.3	McHenry County, IL	0.0	**New London, CT** (city/town) New London County	0.0
Maine	6.6	Cherokee County, GA	0.2	**Newburgh, NY** (city) Orange County	0.0
New Jersey	6.7	Douglas County, CO	0.6	**Oceanside, CA** (city) San Diego County	0.0
Utah	6.9	Kent County, MI	2.3	**West Valley City, UT** (city) Salt Lake County	0.0
Wyoming	6.9	Weber County, UT	2.3	**City of Orange, NJ** (township) Essex County	0.6
Nevada	7.1	Hall County, GA	2.5	**Poinciana, FL** (cdp) Osceola County	0.7
Rhode Island	7.1	Atlantic County, NJ	2.8	**Egypt Lake-Leto, FL** (cdp) Hillsborough County	1.1
Pennsylvania	7.3	Escambia County, FL	2.8	**Four Corners, FL** (cdp) Lake County	1.2
Massachusetts	7.4	Horry County, SC	2.9	**Danbury, CT** (city/town) Fairfield County	1.5

Note: (1) Ranking tables cover all states and counties, and places with an overall population of at least 125,000, OR an overall population of at least 25,000 where the Hispanic/Latino population is at least 20% of the overall population. In states where less than five places meet either of these criteria, we have included places with at least 10,000 total population with the highest percentage of Hispanic/Latino population. These places are identified with an asterisk (*); Please refer to the User's Guide for a full explanation of data.

Class of Worker: Government

(Universe: Civilian Employed Population 16 Years and Over)

South American: Argentinean

Top 10 States, Counties, and Places[1]

Sorted by Number in Descending Order — U.S. = 12,024

State	Number	County	Number	Place	Number
California	2,902	Los Angeles County, CA	1,088	**New York, NY** (city)	476
Florida	1,490	Miami-Dade County, FL	695	**Los Angeles, CA** (city) Los Angeles County	437
New York	1,197	Montgomery County, MD	427	**San Francisco, CA** (city) San Francisco County	219
Maryland	805	Fairfax County, VA	316	**Manhattan, NY** (borough) New York County	208
New Jersey	586	Cook County, IL	297	**Queens, NY** (borough) Queens County	180
Texas	551	Orange County, CA	287	**Miami, FL** (city) Miami-Dade County	167
Virginia	548	Broward County, FL	251	**Chicago, IL** (city) Cook County	119
Illinois	515	San Bernardino County, CA	242	**Hempstead (town), NY** (town) Nassau County	105
District of Columbia	215	San Francisco County, CA	219	**San Jose, CA** (city) Santa Clara County	89
Arizona	212	New York County, NY	208	**Houston, TX** (city) Harris County	76

Sorted by Number in Ascending Order — U.S. = 12,024

State	Number	County	Number	Place	Number
Minnesota	31	Oakland County, MI	0	**Aventura, FL** (city) Miami-Dade County	11
Missouri	59	Lee County, FL	9	**Doral, FL** (city) Miami-Dade County	18
South Carolina	71	Hillsborough County, FL	10	**Bronx, NY** (borough) Bronx County	23
Utah	71	Utah County, UT	12	**Coral Springs, FL** (city) Broward County	25
Washington	79	Dallas County, TX	15	**Miami Beach, FL** (city) Miami-Dade County	31
Nevada	100	New Haven County, CT	15	**Brooklyn, NY** (borough) Kings County	41
Michigan	107	Salt Lake County, UT	19	**Hialeah, FL** (city) Miami-Dade County	43
Wisconsin	119	Hudson County, NJ	20	**Pembroke Pines, FL** (city) Broward County	51
Oregon	123	Bexar County, TX	22	**San Diego, CA** (city) San Diego County	57
Tennessee	124	Bronx County, NY	23	**Hollywood, FL** (city) Broward County	61

Sorted by Percent in Descending Order — U.S. = 10.3%

State	Percent	County	Percent	Place	Percent
Louisiana	35.7	Travis County, TX	44.4	**San Francisco, CA** (city) San Francisco County	27.8
District of Columbia	30.6	San Francisco County, CA	27.8	**San Jose, CA** (city) Santa Clara County	17.7
Maryland	25.1	Montgomery County, MD	27.2	**Hempstead (town), NY** (town) Nassau County	14.5
Colorado	22.8	Fairfax County, VA	25.1	**San Diego, CA** (city) San Diego County	12.8
Tennessee	22.6	San Bernardino County, CA	19.2	**Chicago, IL** (city) Cook County	12.5
Ohio	20.5	Montgomery County, TX	18.4	**Los Angeles, CA** (city) Los Angeles County	8.8
Indiana	19.9	Westchester County, NY	18.4	**Manhattan, NY** (borough) New York County	8.6
Virginia	19.0	Tarrant County, TX	17.2	**Hialeah, FL** (city) Miami-Dade County	7.0
Oregon	16.8	Contra Costa County, CA	16.7	**Pembroke Pines, FL** (city) Broward County	6.9
Illinois	16.6	Suffolk County, NY	16.0	**Hollywood, FL** (city) Broward County	6.2

Sorted by Percent in Ascending Order — U.S. = 10.3%

State	Percent	County	Percent	Place	Percent
Utah	3.3	Oakland County, MI	0.0	**Miami Beach, FL** (city) Miami-Dade County	1.2
Florida	5.1	Hillsborough County, FL	1.2	**Aventura, FL** (city) Miami-Dade County	1.5
Minnesota	5.3	Hudson County, NJ	1.3	**Doral, FL** (city) Miami-Dade County	2.9
Massachusetts	6.6	Lee County, FL	1.3	**Brooklyn, NY** (borough) Kings County	3.0
Nevada	7.5	Utah County, UT	1.4	**Bronx, NY** (borough) Bronx County	3.7
New Jersey	8.0	Dallas County, TX	1.5	**Miami, FL** (city) Miami-Dade County	5.0
Pennsylvania	8.1	New Haven County, CT	2.7	**Coral Springs, FL** (city) Broward County	5.3
Washington	8.4	Orange County, FL	2.8	**Queens, NY** (borough) Queens County	5.6
Texas	8.5	Salt Lake County, UT	2.9	**New York, NY** (city)	6.0
New York	9.0	Kings County, NY	3.0	**Houston, TX** (city) Harris County	6.1

Note: (1) Ranking tables cover all states and counties, and places with an overall population of at least 125,000, OR an overall population of at least 25,000 where the Hispanic/Latino population is at least 20% of the overall population. In states where less than five places meet either of these criteria, we have included places with at least 10,000 total population with the highest percentage of Hispanic/Latino population. These places are identified with an asterisk (*); Please refer to the User's Guide for a full explanation of data.

Class of Worker: Government

(Universe: Civilian Employed Population 16 Years and Over)

South American: Bolivian

Top 10 States, Counties, and Places[1]

Sorted by Number in Descending Order — U.S. = 4,998

State	Number	County	Number	Place	Number
Virginia	1,523	Fairfax County, VA	945	**Los Angeles, CA** (city) Los Angeles County	173
California	808	Montgomery County, MD	420	**Arlington, VA** (cdp) Arlington County	149
Maryland	471	Los Angeles County, CA	243	**New York, NY** (city)	148
Texas	413	Arlington County, VA	149	**Annandale, VA** (cdp) Fairfax County	132
Florida	361	San Diego County, CA	130	**Queens, NY** (borough) Queens County	96
New York	190	Loudoun County, VA	103	**Springfield, VA** (cdp) Fairfax County	31
New Jersey	147	Queens County, NY	96	**West Falls Church, VA** (cdp) Fairfax County	26
Illinois	122	Palm Beach County, FL	93	**Providence, RI** (city) Providence County	13
Massachusetts	72	Orange County, CA	89	**Dale City, VA** (cdp) Prince William County	12
North Carolina	56	Prince William County, VA	71		

Sorted by Number in Ascending Order — U.S. = 4,998

State	Number	County	Number	Place	Number
Rhode Island	38	Cook County, IL	0	**Dale City, VA** (cdp) Prince William County	12
Pennsylvania	39	Prince George's County, MD	25	**Providence, RI** (city) Providence County	13
North Carolina	56	Santa Clara County, CA	35	**West Falls Church, VA** (cdp) Fairfax County	26
Massachusetts	72	Providence County, RI	38	**Springfield, VA** (cdp) Fairfax County	31
Illinois	122	Broward County, FL	49	**Queens, NY** (borough) Queens County	96
New Jersey	147	Miami-Dade County, FL	56	**Annandale, VA** (cdp) Fairfax County	132
New York	190	Harris County, TX	59	**New York, NY** (city)	148
Florida	361	Prince William County, VA	71	**Arlington, VA** (cdp) Arlington County	149
Texas	413	Orange County, CA	89	**Los Angeles, CA** (city) Los Angeles County	173
Maryland	471	Palm Beach County, FL	93		

Sorted by Percent in Descending Order — U.S. = 9.0%

State	Percent	County	Percent	Place	Percent
North Carolina	22.4	San Diego County, CA	27.8	**Los Angeles, CA** (city) Los Angeles County	9.4
Texas	17.9	Palm Beach County, FL	17.5	**Annandale, VA** (cdp) Fairfax County	7.1
Illinois	13.0	Montgomery County, MD	13.8	**New York, NY** (city)	5.8
Pennsylvania	12.9	Orange County, CA	10.9	**Queens, NY** (borough) Queens County	5.8
Maryland	11.4	Harris County, TX	8.8	**Arlington, VA** (cdp) Arlington County	5.7
California	10.8	Los Angeles County, CA	8.4	**Springfield, VA** (cdp) Fairfax County	4.2
Virginia	7.5	Fairfax County, VA	8.3	**West Falls Church, VA** (cdp) Fairfax County	2.7
Florida	6.7	Loudoun County, VA	7.8	**Providence, RI** (city) Providence County	2.0
Massachusetts	6.7	Queens County, NY	5.8	**Dale City, VA** (cdp) Prince William County	1.6
New Jersey	5.8	Arlington County, VA	5.7		

Sorted by Percent in Ascending Order — U.S. = 9.0%

State	Percent	County	Percent	Place	Percent
Rhode Island	3.5	Cook County, IL	0.0	**Dale City, VA** (cdp) Prince William County	1.6
New York	4.7	Miami-Dade County, FL	3.0	**Providence, RI** (city) Providence County	2.0
New Jersey	5.8	Prince William County, VA	3.1	**West Falls Church, VA** (cdp) Fairfax County	2.7
Florida	6.7	Providence County, RI	3.5	**Springfield, VA** (cdp) Fairfax County	4.2
Massachusetts	6.7	Prince George's County, MD	3.8	**Arlington, VA** (cdp) Arlington County	5.7
Virginia	7.5	Santa Clara County, CA	5.6	**New York, NY** (city)	5.8
California	10.8	Arlington County, VA	5.7	**Queens, NY** (borough) Queens County	5.8
Maryland	11.4	Broward County, FL	5.7	**Annandale, VA** (cdp) Fairfax County	7.1
Pennsylvania	12.9	Queens County, NY	5.8	**Los Angeles, CA** (city) Los Angeles County	9.4
Illinois	13.0	Loudoun County, VA	7.8		

Note: (1) Ranking tables cover all states and counties, and places with an overall population of at least 125,000, OR an overall population of at least 25,000 where the Hispanic/Latino population is at least 20% of the overall population. In states where less than five places meet either of these criteria, we have included places with at least 10,000 total population with the highest percentage of Hispanic/Latino population. These places are identified with an asterisk (*); Please refer to the User's Guide for a full explanation of data.

Class of Worker: Government

(Universe: Civilian Employed Population 16 Years and Over)

South American: Chilean

Top 10 States, Counties, and Places[1]

Sorted by Number in Descending Order — U.S. = 7,943

State	Number	County	Number	Place	Number
California	1,692	Miami-Dade County, FL	675	**New York, NY** (city)	524
Florida	1,140	Los Angeles County, CA	541	**Queens, NY** (borough) Queens County	285
New York	1,074	Queens County, NY	285	**Los Angeles, CA** (city) Los Angeles County	220
Maryland	380	Suffolk County, NY	253	**Miami, FL** (city) Miami-Dade County	121
Virginia	360	Montgomery County, MD	208	**Brooklyn, NY** (borough) Kings County	93
Washington	268	Broward County, FL	186	**Manhattan, NY** (borough) New York County	85
Texas	262	Cook County, IL	132	**Chicago, IL** (city) Cook County	79
New Jersey	249	San Diego County, CA	129	**Kendall, FL** (cdp) Miami-Dade County	78
Utah	213	Maricopa County, AZ	114	**Hempstead (town), NY** (town) Nassau County	48
North Carolina	210	Fairfax County, VA	102		

Sorted by Number in Ascending Order — U.S. = 7,943

State	Number	County	Number	Place	Number
Missouri	35	Bergen County, NJ	9	**Hempstead (town), NY** (town) Nassau County	48
Tennessee	36	Middlesex County, MA	21	**Kendall, FL** (cdp) Miami-Dade County	78
Minnesota	46	Orange County, CA	37	**Chicago, IL** (city) Cook County	79
Connecticut	50	Utah County, UT	39	**Manhattan, NY** (borough) New York County	85
Michigan	62	Palm Beach County, FL	42	**Brooklyn, NY** (borough) Kings County	93
Wisconsin	65	Harris County, TX	51	**Miami, FL** (city) Miami-Dade County	121
Ohio	68	San Mateo County, CA	55	**Los Angeles, CA** (city) Los Angeles County	220
Nevada	76	San Bernardino County, CA	58	**Queens, NY** (borough) Queens County	285
Oregon	92	Hudson County, NJ	65	**New York, NY** (city)	524
Colorado	99	Clark County, NV	76		

Sorted by Percent in Descending Order — U.S. = 12.3%

State	Percent	County	Percent	Place	Percent
Washington	21.2	Suffolk County, NY	32.9	**Miami, FL** (city) Miami-Dade County	15.7
North Carolina	19.9	Maricopa County, AZ	18.9	**Chicago, IL** (city) Cook County	14.9
Minnesota	19.2	Riverside County, CA	17.6	**Kendall, FL** (cdp) Miami-Dade County	14.7
Arizona	17.6	Cook County, IL	17.1	**Brooklyn, NY** (borough) Kings County	12.9
Oregon	17.6	Montgomery County, MD	17.0	**New York, NY** (city)	12.7
Virginia	17.0	Salt Lake County, UT	16.5	**Queens, NY** (borough) Queens County	12.3
Maryland	16.7	San Diego County, CA	16.4	**Manhattan, NY** (borough) New York County	12.1
Ohio	14.7	Alameda County, CA	15.0	**Los Angeles, CA** (city) Los Angeles County	9.5
California	14.2	Kings County, NY	12.9	**Hempstead (town), NY** (town) Nassau County	5.4
Michigan	14.1	Clark County, NV	12.6		

Sorted by Percent in Ascending Order — U.S. = 12.3%

State	Percent	County	Percent	Place	Percent
New Jersey	5.3	Bergen County, NJ	1.7	**Hempstead (town), NY** (town) Nassau County	5.4
Connecticut	5.6	Middlesex County, MA	3.0	**Los Angeles, CA** (city) Los Angeles County	9.5
Missouri	7.9	Orange County, CA	5.4	**Manhattan, NY** (borough) New York County	12.1
Florida	9.1	Palm Beach County, FL	5.6	**Queens, NY** (borough) Queens County	12.3
Georgia	9.1	Hudson County, NJ	5.8	**New York, NY** (city)	12.7
Massachusetts	9.3	Nassau County, NY	5.8	**Brooklyn, NY** (borough) Kings County	12.9
Nevada	9.9	Harris County, TX	6.8	**Kendall, FL** (cdp) Miami-Dade County	14.7
Texas	10.7	Westchester County, NY	7.1	**Chicago, IL** (city) Cook County	14.9
Tennessee	11.0	Utah County, UT	7.4	**Miami, FL** (city) Miami-Dade County	15.7
New York	12.3	Broward County, FL	7.8		

RANKINGS & COMPARISONS

Note: (1) Ranking tables cover all states and counties, and places with an overall population of at least 125,000, OR an overall population of at least 25,000 where the Hispanic/Latino population is at least 20% of the overall population. In states where less than five places meet either of these criteria, we have included places with at least 10,000 total population with the highest percentage of Hispanic/Latino population. These places are identified with an asterisk (*); Please refer to the User's Guide for a full explanation of data.

Class of Worker: Government

(Universe: Civilian Employed Population 16 Years and Over)

South American: Colombian

Top 10 States, Counties, and Places[1]

Sorted by Number in Descending Order U.S. = 44,077

State	Number	County	Number	Place	Number
Florida	10,392	Miami-Dade County, FL	3,715	**New York, NY** (city)	4,745
New York	7,343	Queens County, NY	3,304	**Queens, NY** (borough) Queens County	3,304
New Jersey	4,723	Broward County, FL	2,111	**Houston, TX** (city) Harris County	583
California	3,994	Los Angeles County, CA	1,515	**Brooklyn, NY** (borough) Kings County	496
Texas	3,475	Harris County, TX	1,202	**Elizabeth, NJ** (city) Union County	472
Illinois	1,145	Palm Beach County, FL	800	**Hempstead (town), NY** (town) Nassau County	439
Maryland	1,105	Bergen County, NJ	783	**Chicago, IL** (city) Cook County	437
Virginia	1,101	Hillsborough County, FL	779	**Bronx, NY** (borough) Bronx County	422
Massachusetts	970	Union County, NJ	775	**Manhattan, NY** (borough) New York County	361
North Carolina	941	Hudson County, NJ	728	**Pembroke Pines, FL** (city) Broward County	333

Sorted by Number in Ascending Order U.S. = 44,077

State	Number	County	Number	Place	Number
Delaware	27	Forsyth County, GA	0	**Anaheim, CA** (city) Orange County	0
Tennessee	83	Luzerne County, PA	0	**Egypt Lake-Leto, FL** (cdp) Hillsborough County	0
Nebraska	97	Saint Louis County, MO	0	**Elmont, NY** (cdp) Nassau County	12
Kansas	102	Cherokee County, GA	3	**Huntington, NY** (town) Suffolk County	14
Utah	107	Manatee County, FL	10	**Coconut Creek, FL** (city) Broward County	15
Arkansas	114	Hall County, GA	13	**Brandon, FL** (cdp) Hillsborough County	16
Kentucky	114	Lehigh County, PA	18	**Coral Gables, FL** (city) Miami-Dade County	16
New Hampshire	116	Oakland County, MI	19	**New Rochelle, NY** (city) Westchester County	16
Alaska	118	Lancaster County, PA	24	**Royal Palm Beach, FL** (village) Palm Beach County	16
Michigan	126	Erie County, NY	25	**Garfield, NJ** (city) Bergen County	19

Sorted by Percent in Descending Order U.S. = 9.5%

State	Percent	County	Percent	Place	Percent
Iowa	37.4	Prince George's County, MD	32.1	**Tallahassee, FL** (city) Leon County	32.2
District of Columbia	32.8	Leon County, FL	29.3	**Yonkers, NY** (city) Westchester County	23.2
New Mexico	23.6	Cuyahoga County, OH	24.9	**Downey, CA** (city) Los Angeles County	22.7
Arkansas	22.3	Pima County, AZ	24.0	**Carrollwood, FL** (cdp) Hillsborough County	21.6
Kentucky	21.2	Sacramento County, CA	23.9	**Austin, TX** (city) Travis County	21.1
Ohio	19.7	Dane County, WI	22.4	**Miami Gardens, FL** (city) Miami-Dade County	19.8
Alaska	19.6	DeKalb County, GA	20.5	**Cape Coral, FL** (city) Lee County	18.0
Louisiana	18.7	Lake County, IL	19.6	**Worcester, MA** (city) Worcester County	17.5
Oregon	18.6	Ulster County, NY	19.2	**Arlington, VA** (cdp) Arlington County	17.3
Colorado	18.4	Alachua County, FL	18.5	**Las Vegas, NV** (city) Clark County	17.1

Sorted by Percent in Ascending Order U.S. = 9.5%

State	Percent	County	Percent	Place	Percent
Delaware	5.0	Forsyth County, GA	0.0	**Anaheim, CA** (city) Orange County	0.0
Rhode Island	6.6	Luzerne County, PA	0.0	**Egypt Lake-Leto, FL** (cdp) Hillsborough County	0.0
Florida	6.8	Saint Louis County, MO	0.0	**Meadow Woods, FL** (cdp) Orange County	2.0
Massachusetts	6.8	Cherokee County, GA	0.4	**Coconut Creek, FL** (city) Broward County	2.1
Tennessee	6.9	Manatee County, FL	1.7	**Coral Gables, FL** (city) Miami-Dade County	2.1
Georgia	7.2	Lehigh County, PA	2.8	**Elmont, NY** (cdp) Nassau County	2.1
Pennsylvania	7.5	Hall County, GA	3.1	**New Rochelle, NY** (city) Westchester County	2.1
Utah	7.8	Polk County, FL	3.4	**Huntington, NY** (town) Suffolk County	2.3
Connecticut	8.6	Fulton County, GA	3.5	**Bridgeport, CT** (city/town) Fairfield County	2.6
New Jersey	8.7	DuPage County, IL	3.8	**Central Falls*, RI** (city) Providence County	2.7

Note: (1) Ranking tables cover all states and counties, and places with an overall population of at least 125,000, OR an overall population of at least 25,000 where the Hispanic/Latino population is at least 20% of the overall population. In states where less than five places meet either of these criteria, we have included places with at least 10,000 total population with the highest percentage of Hispanic/Latino population. These places are identified with an asterisk (*); Please refer to the User's Guide for a full explanation of data.

Class of Worker: Government

(Universe: Civilian Employed Population 16 Years and Over)

South American: Ecuadorian

Top 10 States, Counties, and Places[1]

Sorted by Number in Descending Order — U.S. = 22,643

State	Number	County	Number	Place	Number
New York	8,157	Queens County, NY	2,747	**New York, NY** (city)	5,822
New Jersey	3,019	Los Angeles County, CA	1,592	**Queens, NY** (borough) Queens County	2,747
California	2,921	Bronx County, NY	1,577	**Bronx, NY** (borough) Bronx County	1,577
Florida	2,232	Hudson County, NJ	935	**Manhattan, NY** (borough) New York County	630
Texas	926	Miami-Dade County, FL	800	**Brooklyn, NY** (borough) Kings County	583
Illinois	736	Westchester County, NY	642	**Chicago, IL** (city) Cook County	513
Virginia	466	New York County, NY	630	**Los Angeles, CA** (city) Los Angeles County	502
Maryland	437	Cook County, IL	590	**Hempstead (town), NY** (town) Nassau County	449
Massachusetts	390	Kings County, NY	583	**Jersey City, NJ** (city) Hudson County	361
Pennsylvania	340	Nassau County, NY	566	**Staten Island, NY** (borough) Richmond County	285

Sorted by Number in Ascending Order — U.S. = 22,643

State	Number	County	Number	Place	Number
Kansas	31	Delaware County, PA	0	**City of Orange, NJ** (township) Essex County	0
Michigan	33	Somerset County, NJ	0	**Norwalk, CT** (city/town) Fairfield County	0
Wisconsin	34	Utah County, UT	5	**Plainfield, NJ** (city) Union County	0
Iowa	37	Camden County, NJ	6	**Sunrise, FL** (city) Broward County	0
Nevada	38	Will County, IL	13	**Coral Springs, FL** (city) Broward County	11
Tennessee	39	Philadelphia County, PA	14	**Country Club, FL** (cdp) Miami-Dade County	11
Utah	39	Santa Clara County, CA	17	**New Haven, CT** (city/town) New Haven County	14
Oklahoma	54	Baltimore County, MD	21	**Philadelphia, PA** (city) Philadelphia County	14
Rhode Island	55	Lehigh County, PA	22	**Brentwood, NY** (cdp) Suffolk County	21
Missouri	74	Mercer County, NJ	29	**Allentown, PA** (city) Lehigh County	22

Sorted by Percent in Descending Order — U.S. = 7.5%

State	Percent	County	Percent	Place	Percent
Missouri	27.5	King County, WA	22.8	**Clifton, NJ** (city) Passaic County	21.0
Washington	26.3	Orange County, CA	22.5	**Staten Island, NY** (borough) Richmond County	20.0
Oregon	24.7	Tarrant County, TX	21.0	**Central Islip, NY** (cdp) Suffolk County	14.3
South Carolina	21.3	Richmond County, NY	20.0	**Hempstead (town), NY** (town) Nassau County	13.9
Indiana	21.0	Dallas County, TX	16.2	**Los Angeles, CA** (city) Los Angeles County	13.3
Ohio	20.8	Los Angeles County, CA	15.7	**Pembroke Pines, FL** (city) Broward County	12.9
Louisiana	20.0	San Bernardino County, CA	15.7	**Bronx, NY** (borough) Bronx County	12.2
Arizona	17.3	San Diego County, CA	15.6	**Belleville, NJ** (township) Essex County	12.0
Colorado	17.1	Maricopa County, AZ	15.4	**Babylon, NY** (town) Suffolk County	10.9
California	16.1	Montgomery County, MD	14.8	**Oyster Bay, NY** (town) Nassau County	10.7

Sorted by Percent in Ascending Order — U.S. = 7.5%

State	Percent	County	Percent	Place	Percent
Minnesota	1.9	Delaware County, PA	0.0	**City of Orange, NJ** (township) Essex County	0.0
Connecticut	2.6	Somerset County, NJ	0.0	**Norwalk, CT** (city/town) Fairfield County	0.0
Utah	3.7	Mercer County, NJ	1.1	**Plainfield, NJ** (city) Union County	0.0
Nevada	4.8	Utah County, UT	1.1	**Sunrise, FL** (city) Broward County	0.0
Illinois	5.3	Hennepin County, MN	1.2	**Danbury, CT** (city/town) Fairfield County	1.3
New Jersey	5.4	Camden County, NJ	1.4	**Elizabeth, NJ** (city) Union County	1.5
Pennsylvania	6.0	Fairfield County, CT	2.3	**Minneapolis, MN** (city) Hennepin County	1.5
Michigan	6.4	Philadelphia County, PA	2.6	**New Haven, CT** (city/town) New Haven County	1.7
North Carolina	6.4	Lehigh County, PA	2.7	**Newark, NJ** (city) Essex County	1.9
New York	6.7	Will County, IL	2.8	**Stamford, CT** (city/town) Fairfield County	1.9

Note: (1) Ranking tables cover all states and counties, and places with an overall population of at least 125,000, OR an overall population of at least 25,000 where the Hispanic/Latino population is at least 20% of the overall population. In states where less than five places meet either of these criteria, we have included places with at least 10,000 total population with the highest percentage of Hispanic/Latino population. These places are identified with an asterisk (*); Please refer to the User's Guide for a full explanation of data.

Class of Worker: Government

(Universe: Civilian Employed Population 16 Years and Over)

South American: Paraguayan

Top 10 States, Counties, and Places[1]

Sorted by Number in Descending Order — U.S. = 767

State	Number	County	Number	Place	Number
Maryland	130	Queens County, NY	42	**New York, NY** (city)	61
New York	117	Westchester County, NY	32	**Queens, NY** (borough) Queens County	42
Texas	46				
Florida	36				
California	33				
New Jersey	7				

Sorted by Number in Ascending Order — U.S. = 767

State	Number	County	Number	Place	Number
New Jersey	7	Westchester County, NY	32	**Queens, NY** (borough) Queens County	42
California	33	Queens County, NY	42	**New York, NY** (city)	61
Florida	36				
Texas	46				
New York	117				
Maryland	130				

Sorted by Percent in Descending Order — U.S. = 7.5%

State	Percent	County	Percent	Place	Percent
Maryland	17.4	Westchester County, NY	3.1	**New York, NY** (city)	2.8
Texas	8.6	Queens County, NY	2.7	**Queens, NY** (borough) Queens County	2.7
California	7.7				
Florida	4.1				
New York	2.9				
New Jersey	0.8				

Sorted by Percent in Ascending Order — U.S. = 7.5%

State	Percent	County	Percent	Place	Percent
New Jersey	0.8	Queens County, NY	2.7	**Queens, NY** (borough) Queens County	2.7
New York	2.9	Westchester County, NY	3.1	**New York, NY** (city)	2.8
Florida	4.1				
California	7.7				
Texas	8.6				
Maryland	17.4				

Note: (1) Ranking tables cover all states and counties, and places with an overall population of at least 125,000, OR an overall population of at least 25,000 where the Hispanic/Latino population is at least 20% of the overall population. In states where less than five places meet either of these criteria, we have included places with at least 10,000 total population with the highest percentage of Hispanic/Latino population. These places are identified with an asterisk (*); Please refer to the User's Guide for a full explanation of data.

Class of Worker: Government

(Universe: Civilian Employed Population 16 Years and Over)

South American: Peruvian

Top 10 States, Counties, and Places[1]

Sorted by Number in Descending Order — U.S. = 24,716

State	Number	County	Number	Place	Number
California	5,042	Los Angeles County, CA	1,605	**New York, NY** (city)	2,212
New York	3,629	Queens County, NY	1,472	**Queens, NY** (borough) Queens County	1,472
Florida	3,040	Miami-Dade County, FL	1,074	**Los Angeles, CA** (city) Los Angeles County	558
New Jersey	2,504	Fairfax County, VA	897	**Chicago, IL** (city) Cook County	342
Virginia	1,842	Montgomery County, MD	709	**Brooklyn, NY** (borough) Kings County	295
Texas	1,215	Broward County, FL	594	**Hempstead (town), NY** (town) Nassau County	287
Maryland	1,105	Passaic County, NJ	524	**San Jose, CA** (city) Santa Clara County	219
Illinois	625	Cook County, IL	464	**Bronx, NY** (borough) Bronx County	212
Georgia	525	Hudson County, NJ	429	**Paterson, NJ** (city) Passaic County	206
Connecticut	516	Orange County, CA	422	**Newark, NJ** (city) Essex County	192

Sorted by Number in Ascending Order — U.S. = 24,716

State	Number	County	Number	Place	Number
Rhode Island	14	Osceola County, FL	0	**Davie, FL** (town) Broward County	0
Oklahoma	21	Sarasota County, FL	8	**San Mateo, CA** (city) San Mateo County	0
Indiana	48	Duval County, FL	12	**Stamford, CT** (city/town) Fairfield County	0
Kentucky	57	Philadelphia County, PA	12	**Sunrise, FL** (city) Broward County	0
Minnesota	59	Suffolk County, MA	12	**West Valley City, UT** (city) Salt Lake County	0
Kansas	79	Collin County, TX	15	**Hialeah, FL** (city) Miami-Dade County	7
Missouri	84	Lehigh County, PA	17	**West New York, NJ** (town) Hudson County	8
Idaho	90	Atlantic County, NJ	18	**Port Chester, NY** (village) Westchester County	10
Louisiana	90	Arapahoe County, CO	19	**Tampa, FL** (city) Hillsborough County	10
Tennessee	100	Denver County, CO	19	**Boston, MA** (city) Suffolk County	12

Sorted by Percent in Descending Order — U.S. = 8.8%

State	Percent	County	Percent	Place	Percent
Alabama	27.2	Sacramento County, CA	20.6	**Austin, TX** (city) Travis County	24.4
New Mexico	26.9	Travis County, TX	20.0	**San Jose, CA** (city) Santa Clara County	21.1
Delaware	20.5	Alameda County, CA	18.8	**Salt Lake City, UT** (city) Salt Lake County	17.6
Michigan	20.5	Denton County, TX	17.2	**Alexandria, VA** (independent city)	15.5
District of Columbia	20.2	Santa Clara County, CA	14.6	**North Bergen, NJ** (township) Hudson County	15.0
Hawaii	19.0	Prince George's County, MD	14.2	**Phoenix, AZ** (city) Maricopa County	14.3
Kansas	15.3	Prince William County, VA	13.7	**Arlington, VA** (cdp) Arlington County	13.3
South Carolina	14.7	Baltimore County, MD	13.5	**Chicago, IL** (city) Cook County	12.3
Arizona	14.1	Seminole County, FL	13.5	**Downey, CA** (city) Los Angeles County	12.3
Idaho	11.9	Riverside County, CA	13.4	**Miramar, FL** (city) Broward County	12.0

Sorted by Percent in Ascending Order — U.S. = 8.8%

State	Percent	County	Percent	Place	Percent
Oklahoma	1.9	Osceola County, FL	0.0	**Davie, FL** (town) Broward County	0.0
Rhode Island	2.7	Sarasota County, FL	1.1	**San Mateo, CA** (city) San Mateo County	0.0
Utah	4.8	Suffolk County, MA	1.4	**Stamford, CT** (city/town) Fairfield County	0.0
Indiana	4.9	Atlantic County, NJ	1.6	**Sunrise, FL** (city) Broward County	0.0
Florida	5.6	Collin County, TX	1.6	**West Valley City, UT** (city) Salt Lake County	0.0
Nevada	5.7	Duval County, FL	2.4	**Hialeah, FL** (city) Miami-Dade County	0.5
Connecticut	6.0	Fairfield County, CT	2.6	**Port Chester, NY** (village) Westchester County	0.9
New Jersey	6.0	Arapahoe County, CO	3.0	**West New York, NJ** (town) Hudson County	1.6
Pennsylvania	6.1	Philadelphia County, PA	3.0	**Kearny, NJ** (town) Hudson County	1.7
Massachusetts	7.3	Hillsborough County, FL	3.1	**Kendall West, FL** (cdp) Miami-Dade County	1.7

Note: (1) Ranking tables cover all states and counties, and places with an overall population of at least 125,000, OR an overall population of at least 25,000 where the Hispanic/Latino population is at least 20% of the overall population. In states where less than five places meet either of these criteria, we have included places with at least 10,000 total population with the highest percentage of Hispanic/Latino population. These places are identified with an asterisk (*); Please refer to the User's Guide for a full explanation of data.

Class of Worker: Government

(Universe: Civilian Employed Population 16 Years and Over)

South American: Uruguayan

Top 10 States, Counties, and Places[1]

Sorted by Number in Descending Order (U.S. = 2,129)

State	Number	County	Number	Place	Number
New Jersey	321	Union County, NJ	132	**New York, NY** (city)	99
New York	311	Los Angeles County, CA	128	**Elizabeth, NJ** (city) Union County	36
Florida	309	Palm Beach County, FL	107	**Queens, NY** (borough) Queens County	13
California	223	Gwinnett County, GA	103		
Maryland	153	Miami-Dade County, FL	90		
Georgia	119	Westchester County, NY	86		
Virginia	104	Broward County, FL	54		
Texas	90	Worcester County, MA	41		
Massachusetts	44	Harris County, TX	34		
Pennsylvania	37	Middlesex County, NJ	32		

Sorted by Number in Ascending Order (U.S. = 2,129)

State	Number	County	Number	Place	Number
Pennsylvania	37	Queens County, NY	13	**Queens, NY** (borough) Queens County	13
Massachusetts	44	Morris County, NJ	19	**Elizabeth, NJ** (city) Union County	36
Texas	90	Essex County, NJ	26	**New York, NY** (city)	99
Virginia	104	Hudson County, NJ	27		
Georgia	119	Middlesex County, NJ	32		
Maryland	153	Harris County, TX	34		
California	223	Worcester County, MA	41		
Florida	309	Broward County, FL	54		
New York	311	Westchester County, NY	86		
New Jersey	321	Miami-Dade County, FL	90		

Sorted by Percent in Descending Order (U.S. = 7.2%)

State	Percent	County	Percent	Place	Percent
Maryland	17.9	Los Angeles County, CA	19.9	**New York, NY** (city)	6.7
California	13.4	Gwinnett County, GA	15.0	**Elizabeth, NJ** (city) Union County	2.3
New York	9.7	Palm Beach County, FL	13.8	**Queens, NY** (borough) Queens County	2.0
Virginia	9.6	Westchester County, NY	11.8		
Pennsylvania	7.5	Middlesex County, NJ	7.7		
Georgia	7.1	Worcester County, MA	5.9		
Texas	6.5	Union County, NJ	5.8		
New Jersey	5.0	Harris County, TX	5.1		
Florida	4.1	Hudson County, NJ	3.9		
Massachusetts	3.4	Morris County, NJ	3.7		

Sorted by Percent in Ascending Order (U.S. = 7.2%)

State	Percent	County	Percent	Place	Percent
Massachusetts	3.4	Essex County, NJ	1.9	**Queens, NY** (borough) Queens County	2.0
Florida	4.1	Queens County, NY	2.0	**Elizabeth, NJ** (city) Union County	2.3
New Jersey	5.0	Miami-Dade County, FL	2.5	**New York, NY** (city)	6.7
Texas	6.5	Broward County, FL	2.9		
Georgia	7.1	Morris County, NJ	3.7		
Pennsylvania	7.5	Hudson County, NJ	3.9		
Virginia	9.6	Harris County, TX	5.1		
New York	9.7	Union County, NJ	5.8		
California	13.4	Worcester County, MA	5.9		
Maryland	17.9	Middlesex County, NJ	7.7		

Note: (1) Ranking tables cover all states and counties, and places with an overall population of at least 125,000, OR an overall population of at least 25,000 where the Hispanic/Latino population is at least 20% of the overall population. In states where less than five places meet either of these criteria, we have included places with at least 10,000 total population with the highest percentage of Hispanic/Latino population. These places are identified with an asterisk (*); Please refer to the User's Guide for a full explanation of data.

Class of Worker: Government

(Universe: Civilian Employed Population 16 Years and Over)

South American: Venezuelan

Top 10 States, Counties, and Places[1]

Sorted by Number in Descending Order — U.S. = 9,240

State	Number	County	Number	Place	Number
Florida	2,454	Miami-Dade County, FL	1,009	**New York, NY** (city)	680
Texas	1,020	Broward County, FL	494	**Queens, NY** (borough) Queens County	287
New York	959	Harris County, TX	313	**Houston, TX** (city) Harris County	217
California	810	Queens County, NY	287	**Brooklyn, NY** (borough) Kings County	180
Georgia	449	Los Angeles County, CA	199	**Weston, FL** (city) Broward County	176
Virginia	362	Kings County, NY	180	**Doral, FL** (city) Miami-Dade County	165
North Carolina	347	Palm Beach County, FL	166	**Miami, FL** (city) Miami-Dade County	132
New Jersey	323	Dallas County, TX	150	**Bronx, NY** (borough) Bronx County	112
Ohio	277	Seminole County, FL	136	**Manhattan, NY** (borough) New York County	72
Maryland	238	Fairfax County, VA	134	**Sunrise, FL** (city) Broward County	67

Sorted by Number in Ascending Order — U.S. = 9,240

State	Number	County	Number	Place	Number
Tennessee	29	Collin County, TX	12	**Aventura, FL** (city) Miami-Dade County	0
Missouri	36	Hillsborough County, FL	12	**Hollywood, FL** (city) Broward County	0
Indiana	37	Osceola County, FL	16	**Coral Springs, FL** (city) Broward County	9
Oklahoma	38	Suffolk County, MA	17	**Kendall West, FL** (cdp) Miami-Dade County	20
Louisiana	44	Fairfield County, CT	26	**Miramar, FL** (city) Broward County	20
Michigan	46	Lee County, FL	29	**Orlando, FL** (city) Orange County	20
Wisconsin	55	King County, WA	44	**Country Club, FL** (cdp) Miami-Dade County	21
South Carolina	61	Middlesex County, MA	44	**Davie, FL** (town) Broward County	22
Arizona	72	Pinellas County, FL	44	**Kendall, FL** (cdp) Miami-Dade County	23
Washington	76	Fulton County, GA	48	**Fountainebleau, FL** (cdp) Miami-Dade County	24

Sorted by Percent in Descending Order — U.S. = 8.7%

State	Percent	County	Percent	Place	Percent
Ohio	26.8	Travis County, TX	29.0	**Bronx, NY** (borough) Bronx County	16.8
Minnesota	26.3	Dallas County, TX	23.1	**Brooklyn, NY** (borough) Kings County	12.5
North Carolina	16.9	Orange County, CA	18.8	**Queens, NY** (borough) Queens County	11.6
Maryland	16.6	Tarrant County, TX	18.1	**New York, NY** (city)	11.3
Georgia	13.8	Bronx County, NY	16.8	**Houston, TX** (city) Harris County	9.6
California	13.5	Fairfax County, VA	16.0	**The Hammocks, FL** (cdp) Miami-Dade County	7.7
Connecticut	13.3	Seminole County, FL	14.8	**Los Angeles, CA** (city) Los Angeles County	7.2
Virginia	13.3	Montgomery County, MD	14.0	**Sunrise, FL** (city) Broward County	6.8
Wisconsin	12.4	Hudson County, NJ	13.2	**Tamiami, FL** (cdp) Miami-Dade County	6.2
New York	12.1	Kings County, NY	12.5	**Weston, FL** (city) Broward County	6.1

Sorted by Percent in Ascending Order — U.S. = 8.7%

State	Percent	County	Percent	Place	Percent
Tennessee	3.9	Hillsborough County, FL	0.8	**Aventura, FL** (city) Miami-Dade County	0.0
Louisiana	4.6	Osceola County, FL	1.2	**Hollywood, FL** (city) Broward County	0.0
Florida	4.9	Orange County, FL	3.0	**Coral Springs, FL** (city) Broward County	1.3
Oklahoma	5.3	Suffolk County, MA	3.1	**Fountainebleau, FL** (cdp) Miami-Dade County	1.3
Indiana	6.6	Collin County, TX	3.2	**Orlando, FL** (city) Orange County	1.9
Pennsylvania	6.6	Lee County, FL	3.9	**Country Club, FL** (cdp) Miami-Dade County	2.3
Massachusetts	6.7	Pinellas County, FL	3.9	**Miramar, FL** (city) Broward County	2.6
Michigan	8.2	Broward County, FL	4.2	**Davie, FL** (town) Broward County	2.9
Arizona	9.3	Miami-Dade County, FL	4.4	**Kendall, FL** (cdp) Miami-Dade County	3.1
South Carolina	9.3	New York County, NY	5.5	**Miami Beach, FL** (city) Miami-Dade County	3.2

Note: (1) Ranking tables cover all states and counties, and places with an overall population of at least 125,000, OR an overall population of at least 25,000 where the Hispanic/Latino population is at least 20% of the overall population. In states where less than five places meet either of these criteria, we have included places with at least 10,000 total population with the highest percentage of Hispanic/Latino population. These places are identified with an asterisk (*); Please refer to the User's Guide for a full explanation of data.

Class of Worker: Government

(Universe: Civilian Employed Population 16 Years and Over)

Spaniard

Top 10 States, Counties, and Places[1]

Sorted by Number in Descending Order — U.S. = 46,709

State	Number	County	Number	Place	Number
California	9,844	Los Angeles County, CA	1,773	**New York, NY** (city)	1,887
New Mexico	5,722	Bernalillo County, NM	1,761	**Albuquerque, NM** (city) Bernalillo County	1,558
Texas	4,820	San Miguel County, NM	1,038	**Los Angeles, CA** (city) Los Angeles County	595
New York	3,703	San Diego County, CA	945	**Denver, CO** (city) Denver County	568
Colorado	3,584	Santa Fe County, NM	800	**San Antonio, TX** (city) Bexar County	548
Florida	3,250	Bexar County, TX	769	**San Diego, CA** (city) San Diego County	480
New Jersey	1,576	Maricopa County, AZ	742	**Queens, NY** (borough) Queens County	478
Arizona	1,293	Hillsborough County, FL	724	**Austin, TX** (city) Travis County	413
Virginia	969	San Bernardino County, CA	717	**Santa Fe, NM** (city) Santa Fe County	408
Washington	903	Harris County, TX	644	**Brooklyn, NY** (borough) Kings County	388

Sorted by Number in Ascending Order — U.S. = 46,709

State	Number	County	Number	Place	Number
New Hampshire	49	Utah County, UT	14	**Jacksonville, FL** (city) Duval County	18
Maine	59	Duval County, FL	18	**Fort Collins, CO** (city) Larimer County	20
Tennessee	63	Milwaukee County, WI	18	**Paradise, NV** (cdp) Clark County	21
West Virginia	76	Maui County, HI	20	**Kearny, NJ** (town) Hudson County	22
Montana	79	Clark County, WA	22	**South Valley, NM** (cdp) Bernalillo County	29
Nebraska	91	New Haven County, CT	22	**Las Cruces, NM** (city) Dona Ana County	34
Iowa	116	Passaic County, NJ	22	**San Bernardino, CA** (city) San Bernardino County	35
Missouri	135	Mecklenburg County, NC	23	**Thornton, CO** (city) Adams County	41
Kansas	163	Butte County, CA	26	**Seattle, WA** (city) King County	42
Indiana	165	DuPage County, IL	27	**Tucson, AZ** (city) Pima County	44

Sorted by Percent in Descending Order — U.S. = 18.4%

State	Percent	County	Percent	Place	Percent
Mississippi	28.8	Conejos County, CO	57.0	**Staten Island, NY** (borough) Richmond County	38.2
Iowa	27.8	San Miguel County, NM	48.2	**Stockton, CA** (city) San Joaquin County	38.0
Wyoming	27.7	Erie County, NY	38.4	**Sacramento, CA** (city) Sacramento County	35.8
District of Columbia	27.2	Richmond County, NY	38.2	**Santa Fe, NM** (city) Santa Fe County	35.3
New Mexico	26.9	Santa Fe County, NM	35.7	**Long Beach, CA** (city) Los Angeles County	26.0
South Carolina	23.9	Tulare County, CA	33.7	**Oyster Bay, NY** (town) Nassau County	25.5
Kentucky	23.6	La Plata County, CO	33.3	**El Paso, TX** (city) El Paso County	25.1
Alaska	23.5	Cibola County, NM	33.2	**North Las Vegas, NV** (city) Clark County	24.9
Maryland	23.0	Sacramento County, CA	32.9	**Bakersfield, CA** (city) Kern County	24.8
New York	21.4	San Joaquin County, CA	32.8	**Lakewood, CO** (city) Jefferson County	24.8

Sorted by Percent in Ascending Order — U.S. = 18.4%

State	Percent	County	Percent	Place	Percent
Tennessee	4.7	Duval County, FL	3.5	**Paradise, NV** (cdp) Clark County	3.2
Missouri	7.3	New Haven County, CT	3.9	**Jacksonville, FL** (city) Duval County	3.8
Pennsylvania	9.3	Morris County, NJ	4.0	**Kearny, NJ** (town) Hudson County	4.2
Nebraska	11.8	Mecklenburg County, NC	4.1	**Seattle, WA** (city) King County	5.1
New Hampshire	11.9	Passaic County, NJ	4.5	**Fort Collins, CO** (city) Larimer County	5.5
Illinois	12.4	Maui County, HI	4.7	**Thornton, CO** (city) Adams County	6.6
West Virginia	12.9	Utah County, UT	4.7	**South Valley, NM** (cdp) Bernalillo County	8.7
Montana	13.6	DuPage County, IL	4.8	**Miami, FL** (city) Miami-Dade County	9.3
Utah	13.6	Clark County, WA	5.6	**Las Cruces, NM** (city) Dona Ana County	9.9
Indiana	13.8	Milwaukee County, WI	6.1	**Lubbock, TX** (city) Lubbock County	9.9

Note: (1) Ranking tables cover all states and counties, and places with an overall population of at least 125,000, OR an overall population of at least 25,000 where the Hispanic/Latino population is at least 20% of the overall population. In states where less than five places meet either of these criteria, we have included places with at least 10,000 total population with the highest percentage of Hispanic/Latino population. These places are identified with an asterisk (*); Please refer to the User's Guide for a full explanation of data.

Means of Transportation to Work: Car, Truck or Van

(Universe: Civilian Employed Population 16 Years and Over)

Total Population

Top 10 States, Counties, and Places[1]

Sorted by Number in Descending Order — U.S. = 120,259,023

State	Number	County	Number	Place	Number
California	13,810,537	Los Angeles County, CA	3,671,019	**Los Angeles, CA** (city) Los Angeles County	1,364,484
Texas	9,973,640	Cook County, IL	1,727,215	**New York, NY** (city)	1,033,954
Florida	7,334,876	Harris County, TX	1,664,024	**Houston, TX** (city) Harris County	849,617
New York	5,422,644	Maricopa County, AZ	1,508,200	**Chicago, IL** (city) Cook County	743,458
Pennsylvania	4,979,288	Orange County, CA	1,249,365	**Phoenix, AZ** (city) Maricopa County	582,095
Illinois	4,906,968	San Diego County, CA	1,220,376	**San Diego, CA** (city) San Diego County	530,301
Ohio	4,795,529	Dallas County, TX	986,949	**San Antonio, TX** (city) Bexar County	522,196
Michigan	3,907,914	Miami-Dade County, FL	956,248	**Dallas, TX** (city) Dallas County	488,552
North Carolina	3,866,995	Clark County, NV	802,880	**Queens, NY** (borough) Queens County	407,032
Georgia	3,811,245	Tarrant County, TX	771,328	**San Jose, CA** (city) Santa Clara County	384,601

Sorted by Number in Ascending Order — U.S. = 120,259,023

State	Number	County	Number	Place	Number
District of Columbia	124,251	Kenedy County, TX	104	**Florence, AZ** (town) Pinal County	1,350
Wyoming	245,433	Esmeralda County, NV	266	**Hanover*, NH** (town) Grafton County	2,319
Alaska	268,281	Harding County, NM	304	**Fort Leonard Wood*, MO** (cdp) Pulaski County	2,487
Vermont	271,563	Terrell County, TX	316	**Hawaiian Paradise Park*, HI** (cdp) Hawaii County	3,148
North Dakota	309,234	Clark County, ID	351	**Mayfield*, KY** (city) Graves County	3,171
South Dakota	354,635	Motley County, TX	365	**Hope*, AR** (city) Hempstead County	3,335
Delaware	369,627	Kent County, TX	376	**Parker*, SC** (cdp) Greenville County	3,365
Montana	396,379	McMullen County, TX	395	**Burley*, ID** (city) Cassia County	3,437
Rhode Island	447,281	Sterling County, TX	410	**Schofield Barracks*, HI** (cdp) Honolulu County	3,732
Hawaii	538,308	Piute County, UT	441	**Fort Campbell North*, KY** (cdp) Christian County	3,971

Sorted by Percent in Descending Order — U.S. = 86.4%

State	Percent	County	Percent	Place	Percent
Alabama	94.7	Conecuh County, AL	99.1	**Lake Jackson, TX** (city) Brazoria County	97.1
Mississippi	94.1	Terry County, TX	98.4	**Mayfield*, KY** (city) Graves County	96.4
Tennessee	93.4	Crawford County, GA	98.3	**Albertville*, AL** (city) Marshall County	96.3
Arkansas	93.0	Liberty County, FL	97.8	**Sterling Heights, MI** (city) Macomb County	96.3
Kentucky	92.5	Lake County, TN	97.6	**Horn Lake*, MS** (city) DeSoto County	96.2
Louisiana	92.5	Northampton County, NC	97.6	**Asheboro, NC** (city) Randolph County	96.1
Oklahoma	92.4	Murray County, GA	97.5	**Pascagoula*, MS** (city) Jackson County	96.1
Indiana	92.2	Somervell County, TX	97.4	**Channelview, TX** (cdp) Harris County	96.0
West Virginia	92.2	Worth County, GA	97.4	**Holland, MI** (charter township) Ottawa County	96.0
South Carolina	92.1	Humphreys County, TN	97.3	**Deer Park, TX** (city) Harris County	95.8

Sorted by Percent in Ascending Order — U.S. = 86.4%

State	Percent	County	Percent	Place	Percent
District of Columbia	42.4	New York County, NY	9.1	**Manhattan, NY** (borough) New York County	9.1
New York	61.5	Kings County, NY	25.0	**Fort Leonard Wood*, MO** (cdp) Pulaski County	22.2
Alaska	80.3	Bronx County, NY	30.5	**Brooklyn, NY** (borough) Kings County	25.0
New Jersey	80.6	Queens County, NY	39.5	**New York, NY** (city)	28.4
Massachusetts	80.8	San Francisco County, CA	46.1	**Bronx, NY** (borough) Bronx County	30.5
Hawaii	81.8	Hudson County, NJ	48.5	**Queens, NY** (borough) Queens County	39.5
Illinois	82.7	Suffolk County, MA	49.4	**Jersey City, NJ** (city) Hudson County	41.6
Oregon	82.7	Chattahoochee County, GA	55.1	**Union City, NJ** (city) Hudson County	43.7
Maryland	83.8	San Miguel County, CO	58.9	**West New York, NJ** (town) Hudson County	44.9
Washington	83.9	Philadelphia County, PA	60.1	**San Francisco, CA** (city) San Francisco County	46.1

RANKINGS & COMPARISONS

Note: (1) Ranking tables cover all states and counties, and places with an overall population of at least 125,000, OR an overall population of at least 25,000 where the Hispanic/Latino population is at least 20% of the overall population. In states where less than five places meet either of these criteria, we have included places with at least 10,000 total population with the highest percentage of Hispanic/Latino population. These places are identified with an asterisk (*); Please refer to the User's Guide for a full explanation of data.

Means of Transportation to Work: Car, Truck or Van

(Universe: Civilian Employed Population 16 Years and Over)

Hispanic or Latino (of any race)

Top 10 States, Counties, and Places[1]

Sorted by Number in Descending Order — U.S. = 16,597,731

State	Number	County	Number	Place	Number
California	4,640,511	Los Angeles County, CA	1,578,914	**Los Angeles, CA** (city) Los Angeles County	582,673
Texas	3,340,792	Miami-Dade County, FL	649,683	**Houston, TX** (city) Harris County	342,430
Florida	1,617,886	Harris County, TX	609,314	**San Antonio, TX** (city) Bexar County	306,460
Illinois	681,523	Cook County, IL	397,623	**New York, NY** (city)	229,103
Arizona	628,658	Maricopa County, AZ	383,362	**Chicago, IL** (city) Cook County	227,492
New York	565,551	Orange County, CA	375,497	**Dallas, TX** (city) Dallas County	196,112
New Jersey	474,013	Bexar County, TX	367,251	**Phoenix, AZ** (city) Maricopa County	195,495
Colorado	354,205	Dallas County, TX	346,696	**El Paso, TX** (city) El Paso County	180,524
New Mexico	343,729	San Diego County, CA	338,637	**San Diego, CA** (city) San Diego County	125,971
Georgia	288,827	San Bernardino County, CA	327,541	**San Jose, CA** (city) Santa Clara County	111,222

Sorted by Number in Ascending Order — U.S. = 16,597,731

State	Number	County	Number	Place	Number
Vermont	3,162	Thurston County, NE	16	**Burlington*, VT** (city) Chittenden County	151
North Dakota	5,110	Gulf County, FL	19	**Morgantown*, WV** (city) Monongalia County	157
Maine	5,367	Evangeline Parish, LA	22	**Fort Leonard Wood*, MO** (cdp) Pulaski County	287
West Virginia	6,393	West Carroll Parish, LA	30	**Mayfield*, KY** (city) Graves County	352
South Dakota	7,409	Price County, WI	32	**Middle*, DE** (town) New Castle County	376
Montana	9,260	Montour County, PA	33	**Waianae*, HI** (cdp) Honolulu County	390
District of Columbia	10,025	Swift County, MN	33	**Brookside*, DE** (cdp) New Castle County	416
New Hampshire	12,403	Antrim County, MI	37	**College*, AK** (cdp) Fairbanks North Star Borough	427
Alaska	13,500	Fulton County, IL	37	**Bozeman*, MT** (city) Gallatin County	428
Wyoming	18,739	Burnett County, WI	40	**Florence, AZ** (town) Pinal County	464

Sorted by Percent in Descending Order — U.S. = 83.4%

State	Percent	County	Percent	Place	Percent
Alabama	94.7	Alexander County, NC	100.0	**Bluffton*, SC** (town) Beaufort County	100.0
Oklahoma	93.2	Belknap County, NH	100.0	**Pascagoula*, MS** (city) Jackson County	100.0
Tennessee	92.6	Berrien County, GA	100.0	**Salem*, NH** (town) Rockingham County	100.0
Kansas	92.5	Bullitt County, KY	100.0	**Glendale Heights, IL** (village) DuPage County	98.4
Arkansas	92.2	Carroll County, IL	100.0	**Muscatine*, IA** (city) Muscatine County	98.4
New Mexico	92.2	Carroll County, TN	100.0	**Lake Jackson, TX** (city) Brazoria County	98.3
Nebraska	92.1	Cass County, NE	100.0	**Willmar*, MN** (city) Kandiyohi County	98.2
North Carolina	92.0	Charlevoix County, MI	100.0	**Green River*, WY** (city) Sweetwater County	98.0
Indiana	91.7	Coleman County, TX	100.0	**Jerome*, ID** (city) Jerome County	98.0
Texas	91.5	Collingsworth County, TX	100.0	**Lufkin, TX** (city) Angelina County	98.0

Sorted by Percent in Ascending Order — U.S. = 83.4%

State	Percent	County	Percent	Place	Percent
District of Columbia	35.5	New York County, NY	11.2	**Manhattan, NY** (borough) New York County	11.2
New York	41.0	Kings County, NY	20.4	**Fort Leonard Wood*, MO** (cdp) Pulaski County	17.8
New Jersey	69.8	Antrim County, MI	24.3	**Brooklyn, NY** (borough) Kings County	20.4
Massachusetts	72.3	Bronx County, NY	26.4	**New York, NY** (city)	24.5
Vermont	75.9	Clearfield County, PA	26.4	**Bronx, NY** (borough) Bronx County	26.4
Alaska	77.3	Allamakee County, IA	28.1	**Queens, NY** (borough) Queens County	30.0
Pennsylvania	78.4	Lauderdale County, MS	29.4	**Columbia, SC** (city) Richland County	35.7
Maryland	79.1	Queens County, NY	30.0	**Pittsburgh, PA** (city) Allegheny County	39.8
Maine	81.6	Pittsylvania County, VA	34.0	**San Francisco, CA** (city) San Francisco County	42.4
Connecticut	81.8	Mecklenburg County, VA	36.7	**Union City, NJ** (city) Hudson County	44.4

Note: (1) Ranking tables cover all states and counties, and places with an overall population of at least 125,000, OR an overall population of at least 25,000 where the Hispanic/Latino population is at least 20% of the overall population. In states where less than five places meet either of these criteria, we have included places with at least 10,000 total population with the highest percentage of Hispanic/Latino population. These places are identified with an asterisk (*); Please refer to the User's Guide for a full explanation of data.

Means of Transportation to Work: Car, Truck or Van

(Universe: Civilian Employed Population 16 Years and Over)

Central American, excluding Mexican

Top 10 States, Counties, and Places[1]

Sorted by Number in Descending Order — U.S. = 1,549,435

State	Number	County	Number	Place	Number
California	445,021	Los Angeles County, CA	266,353	**Los Angeles, CA** (city) Los Angeles County	151,658
Florida	191,898	Miami-Dade County, FL	96,107	**Houston, TX** (city) Harris County	64,555
Texas	188,288	Harris County, TX	95,636	**Miami, FL** (city) Miami-Dade County	27,070
New York	86,484	Dallas County, TX	33,793	**New York, NY** (city)	17,723
Virginia	83,657	Montgomery County, MD	30,651	**Hempstead (town), NY** (town) Nassau County	16,935
Maryland	78,535	Prince George's County, MD	29,865	**Dallas, TX** (city) Dallas County	16,637
New Jersey	56,541	Suffolk County, NY	29,811	**Islip, NY** (town) Suffolk County	15,252
North Carolina	43,164	Fairfax County, VA	27,501	**Chicago, IL** (city) Cook County	10,746
Georgia	42,952	Nassau County, NY	23,117	**Charlotte, NC** (city) Mecklenburg County	9,714
Massachusetts	33,012	San Bernardino County, CA	22,492	**Queens, NY** (borough) Queens County	8,809

Sorted by Number in Ascending Order — U.S. = 1,549,435

State	Number	County	Number	Place	Number
Vermont	162	Caroline County, MD	128	**Rochester, NY** (city) Monroe County	147
Maine	439	Cass County, IN	131	**Delano, CA** (city) Kern County	149
West Virginia	528	Onondaga County, NY	150	**Little Elm, TX** (city) Denton County	199
Wyoming	555	Madera County, CA	176	**Palm Springs, CA** (city) Riverside County	219
New Hampshire	859	Hendry County, FL	188	**Adelanto, CA** (city) San Bernardino County	264
Alaska	1,018	Macomb County, MI	210	**Reading, PA** (city) Berks County	285
South Dakota	1,047	Oneida County, NY	220	**Linden, NJ** (city) Union County	291
Hawaii	1,067	Gilmer County, GA	221	**Laredo, TX** (city) Webb County	292
Idaho	1,515	Delaware County, PA	223	**Riverview, FL** (cdp) Hillsborough County	317
Delaware	2,688	Carroll County, AR	228	**Long Branch, NJ** (city) Monmouth County	323

Sorted by Percent in Descending Order — U.S. = 78.0%

State	Percent	County	Percent	Place	Percent
Wyoming	98.2	Allen County, IN	100.0	**Alafaya, FL** (cdp) Orange County	100.0
West Virginia	97.6	Cache County, UT	100.0	**Brandon, FL** (cdp) Hillsborough County	100.0
Alabama	95.1	Charles County, MD	100.0	**Channelview, TX** (cdp) Harris County	100.0
Indiana	95.1	Etowah County, AL	100.0	**Chula Vista, CA** (city) San Diego County	100.0
Nebraska	94.8	Franklin County, AL	100.0	**Clovis, CA** (city) Fresno County	100.0
Tennessee	94.7	Gilmer County, GA	100.0	**Eastvale, CA** (cdp) Riverside County	100.0
Arkansas	93.7	Hamilton County, IN	100.0	**Fort Wayne, IN** (city) Allen County	100.0
Wisconsin	93.7	Harnett County, NC	100.0	**Hacienda Heights, CA** (cdp) Los Angeles County	100.0
Oklahoma	93.6	Kings County, CA	100.0	**Knoxville, TN** (city) Knox County	100.0
Michigan	92.0	Lake County, IN	100.0	**Lewisville, TX** (city) Denton County	100.0

Sorted by Percent in Ascending Order — U.S. = 78.0%

State	Percent	County	Percent	Place	Percent
District of Columbia	35.2	New York County, NY	7.1	**Manhattan, NY** (borough) New York County	7.1
New York	50.9	Kings County, NY	18.5	**Brooklyn, NY** (borough) Kings County	18.5
New Jersey	62.7	Bronx County, NY	19.5	**Bronx, NY** (borough) Bronx County	19.5
Massachusetts	67.0	Queens County, NY	31.8	**Miami Beach, FL** (city) Miami-Dade County	22.5
Alaska	70.7	Onondaga County, NY	36.4	**New York, NY** (city)	22.8
Connecticut	74.1	Richmond County, NY	39.2	**Queens, NY** (borough) Queens County	31.8
Hawaii	74.8	Delaware County, PA	43.9	**Port Chester, NY** (village) Westchester County	35.8
Pennsylvania	75.9	San Francisco County, CA	46.9	**Rye, NY** (town) Westchester County	37.1
Maine	77.3	Bergen County, NJ	48.3	**Staten Island, NY** (borough) Richmond County	39.2
Maryland	77.3	Westchester County, NY	49.5	**Rochester, NY** (city) Monroe County	41.2

Note: (1) Ranking tables cover all states and counties, and places with an overall population of at least 125,000, OR an overall population of at least 25,000 where the Hispanic/Latino population is at least 20% of the overall population. In states where less than five places meet either of these criteria, we have included places with at least 10,000 total population with the highest percentage of Hispanic/Latino population. These places are identified with an asterisk (*); Please refer to the User's Guide for a full explanation of data.

Means of Transportation to Work: Car, Truck or Van

(Universe: Civilian Employed Population 16 Years and Over)

Central American: Costa Rican

Top 10 States, Counties, and Places[1]

Sorted by Number in Descending Order — U.S. = 49,391

State	Number	County	Number	Place	Number
California	9,007	Los Angeles County, CA	3,886	**Los Angeles, CA** (city) Los Angeles County	1,323
Florida	8,547	Miami-Dade County, FL	2,888	**New York, NY** (city)	647
New Jersey	6,917	Union County, NJ	1,479	**Miami, FL** (city) Miami-Dade County	470
Texas	2,897	Broward County, FL	1,220	**Philadelphia, PA** (city) Philadelphia County	357
New York	2,583	Orange County, CA	938	**Queens, NY** (borough) Queens County	249
North Carolina	2,371	Harris County, TX	917	**Brooklyn, NY** (borough) Kings County	203
Massachusetts	1,557	Somerset County, NJ	893	**Bronx, NY** (borough) Bronx County	87
Pennsylvania	1,482	Morris County, NJ	703		
Georgia	1,479	San Bernardino County, CA	688		
Maryland	1,175	Palm Beach County, FL	667		

Sorted by Number in Ascending Order — U.S. = 49,391

State	Number	County	Number	Place	Number
Michigan	246	Bronx County, NY	87	**Bronx, NY** (borough) Bronx County	87
Wisconsin	322	Kings County, NY	203	**Brooklyn, NY** (borough) Kings County	203
Oregon	334	Queens County, NY	249	**Queens, NY** (borough) Queens County	249
Minnesota	342	Philadelphia County, PA	357	**Philadelphia, PA** (city) Philadelphia County	357
Washington	362	Clark County, NV	399	**Miami, FL** (city) Miami-Dade County	470
Tennessee	429	San Diego County, CA	445	**New York, NY** (city)	647
Colorado	496	Nassau County, NY	486	**Los Angeles, CA** (city) Los Angeles County	1,323
Nevada	720	Riverside County, CA	536		
Louisiana	723	Cook County, IL	545		
Arizona	806	Passaic County, NJ	549		

Sorted by Percent in Descending Order — U.S. = 81.2%

State	Percent	County	Percent	Place	Percent
Tennessee	97.7	Hillsborough County, FL	98.5	**Los Angeles, CA** (city) Los Angeles County	87.4
South Carolina	97.1	San Diego County, CA	98.0	**Philadelphia, PA** (city) Philadelphia County	70.7
North Carolina	95.3	Riverside County, CA	97.6	**Miami, FL** (city) Miami-Dade County	67.1
Maryland	93.8	Fairfield County, CT	95.8	**Queens, NY** (borough) Queens County	28.9
Connecticut	93.3	Suffolk County, NY	94.5	**New York, NY** (city)	23.0
Louisiana	92.9	Harris County, TX	91.4	**Bronx, NY** (borough) Bronx County	22.3
Wisconsin	92.3	Orange County, FL	91.1	**Brooklyn, NY** (borough) Kings County	18.7
Texas	91.7	Nassau County, NY	91.0		
Nevada	88.7	Maricopa County, AZ	90.1		
Florida	88.6	Palm Beach County, FL	88.6		

Sorted by Percent in Ascending Order — U.S. = 81.2%

State	Percent	County	Percent	Place	Percent
New York	51.8	Kings County, NY	18.7	**Brooklyn, NY** (borough) Kings County	18.7
New Jersey	68.2	Bronx County, NY	22.3	**Bronx, NY** (borough) Bronx County	22.3
Washington	71.4	Queens County, NY	28.9	**New York, NY** (city)	23.0
Colorado	72.9	Bergen County, NJ	55.7	**Queens, NY** (borough) Queens County	28.9
Michigan	75.5	Passaic County, NJ	59.9	**Miami, FL** (city) Miami-Dade County	67.1
Massachusetts	77.5	Essex County, NJ	62.5	**Philadelphia, PA** (city) Philadelphia County	70.7
Minnesota	79.0	Philadelphia County, PA	70.7	**Los Angeles, CA** (city) Los Angeles County	87.4
Oregon	82.7	Morris County, NJ	71.8		
Illinois	83.1	Somerset County, NJ	72.6		
Virginia	83.6	Union County, NJ	72.9		

Note: (1) Ranking tables cover all states and counties, and places with an overall population of at least 125,000, OR an overall population of at least 25,000 where the Hispanic/Latino population is at least 20% of the overall population. In states where less than five places meet either of these criteria, we have included places with at least 10,000 total population with the highest percentage of Hispanic/Latino population. These places are identified with an asterisk (*); Please refer to the User's Guide for a full explanation of data.

Means of Transportation to Work: Car, Truck or Van

(Universe: Civilian Employed Population 16 Years and Over)

Central American: Guatemalan

Top 10 States, Counties, and Places[1]

Sorted by Number in Descending Order — U.S. = 384,713

State	Number	County	Number	Place	Number
California	120,308	Los Angeles County, CA	77,618	**Los Angeles, CA** (city) Los Angeles County	44,727
Florida	37,147	Harris County, TX	13,529	**Houston, TX** (city) Harris County	10,723
Texas	28,149	Palm Beach County, FL	10,575	**Chicago, IL** (city) Cook County	5,975
New York	15,739	Cook County, IL	9,007	**Providence, RI** (city) Providence County	5,178
Maryland	15,570	Miami-Dade County, FL	8,776	**Trenton, NJ** (city) Mercer County	3,561
New Jersey	14,941	Providence County, RI	7,904	**Stamford, CT** (city/town) Fairfield County	3,470
Georgia	14,230	Prince George's County, MD	7,312	**New York, NY** (city)	3,285
Virginia	12,898	Orange County, CA	6,428	**Dallas, TX** (city) Dallas County	3,076
Illinois	12,417	San Bernardino County, CA	5,961	**Lake Worth, FL** (city) Palm Beach County	2,776
Massachusetts	11,983	Clark County, NV	5,329	**Phoenix, AZ** (city) Maricopa County	2,498

Sorted by Number in Ascending Order — U.S. = 384,713

State	Number	County	Number	Place	Number
New Hampshire	173	New York County, NY	62	**Manhattan, NY** (borough) New York County	62
District of Columbia	314	Pinal County, AZ	96	**Yonkers, NY** (city) Westchester County	149
Idaho	428	Caroline County, MD	107	**Bell, CA** (city) Los Angeles County	255
South Dakota	539	Norfolk County, MA	166	**Lexington*, NE** (city) Dawson County	269
Wisconsin	632	Gilmer County, GA	221	**Elizabeth, NJ** (city) Union County	282
Mississippi	1,073	Monmouth County, NJ	282	**North Bergen, NJ** (township) Hudson County	293
Kentucky	1,254	Lee County, AL	317	**Alhambra, CA** (city) Los Angeles County	299
New Mexico	1,318	Murray County, GA	331	**Minneapolis, MN** (city) Hennepin County	303
Kansas	1,635	Putnam County, NY	340	**Victorville, CA** (city) San Bernardino County	325
Missouri	1,641	Dawson County, NE	356	**Westmont, CA** (cdp) Los Angeles County	333

Sorted by Percent in Descending Order — U.S. = 74.1%

State	Percent	County	Percent	Place	Percent
Tennessee	97.7	Davidson County, TN	100.0	**Columbus, OH** (city) Franklin County	100.0
Alabama	97.0	Durham County, NC	100.0	**Corona, CA** (city) Riverside County	100.0
Nebraska	96.8	Franklin County, AL	100.0	**Durham, NC** (city) Durham County	100.0
Oklahoma	95.5	Franklin County, OH	100.0	**Nashville-Davidson, TN** (metropolitan govt) Davidson County	100.0
Indiana	95.4	Gilmer County, GA	100.0	**North Las Vegas, NV** (city) Clark County	100.0
Mississippi	94.8	Knox County, TN	100.0	**San Bernardino, CA** (city) San Bernardino County	100.0
Michigan	91.2	Lee County, AL	100.0	**Spring Valley, NV** (cdp) Clark County	100.0
North Carolina	89.6	Murray County, GA	100.0	**Albertville*, AL** (city) Marshall County	99.1
Arkansas	88.8	Rutherford County, TN	100.0	**Central Islip, NY** (cdp) Suffolk County	98.6
Wisconsin	88.8	Chesterfield County, VA	99.0	**Pawtucket*, RI** (city) Providence County	98.2

Sorted by Percent in Ascending Order — U.S. = 74.1%

State	Percent	County	Percent	Place	Percent
District of Columbia	30.9	New York County, NY	4.2	**Manhattan, NY** (borough) New York County	4.2
New York	44.0	Bronx County, NY	15.1	**Bronx, NY** (borough) Bronx County	15.1
New Jersey	57.0	Kings County, NY	16.1	**Brooklyn, NY** (borough) Kings County	16.1
New Hampshire	65.3	Queens County, NY	29.2	**New York, NY** (city)	21.0
Missouri	70.4	Bergen County, NJ	32.5	**Yonkers, NY** (city) Westchester County	24.3
Idaho	70.6	San Francisco County, CA	39.4	**Queens, NY** (borough) Queens County	29.2
Massachusetts	71.1	Arlington County, VA	41.3	**Port Chester, NY** (village) Westchester County	34.1
Connecticut	71.3	Westchester County, NY	41.8	**Rye, NY** (town) Westchester County	35.2
California	71.4	Monmouth County, NJ	42.9	**Homestead, FL** (city) Miami-Dade County	35.3
Pennsylvania	75.5	Union County, NJ	45.0	**Union City, NJ** (city) Hudson County	37.7

RANKINGS & COMPARISONS

Note: (1) Ranking tables cover all states and counties, and places with an overall population of at least 125,000, OR an overall population of at least 25,000 where the Hispanic/Latino population is at least 20% of the overall population. In states where less than five places meet either of these criteria, we have included places with at least 10,000 total population with the highest percentage of Hispanic/Latino population. These places are identified with an asterisk (*); Please refer to the User's Guide for a full explanation of data.

Means of Transportation to Work: Car, Truck or Van

(Universe: Civilian Employed Population 16 Years and Over)

Central American: Honduran

Top 10 States, Counties, and Places[1]

Sorted by Number in Descending Order — U.S. = 230,424

State	Number	County	Number	Place	Number
Florida	45,180	Miami-Dade County, FL	22,904	**Houston, TX** (city) Harris County	14,172
Texas	37,913	Harris County, TX	19,904	**Miami, FL** (city) Miami-Dade County	10,555
California	25,687	Los Angeles County, CA	14,842	**Los Angeles, CA** (city) Los Angeles County	7,879
New York	13,063	Jefferson Parish, LA	6,334	**New York, NY** (city)	3,672
North Carolina	12,461	Dallas County, TX	6,009	**Dallas, TX** (city) Dallas County	3,206
Louisiana	12,155	Broward County, FL	5,082	**Charlotte, NC** (city) Mecklenburg County	3,020
New Jersey	11,555	Palm Beach County, FL	3,968	**Hempstead (town), NY** (town) Nassau County	2,446
Virginia	11,270	Suffolk County, NY	3,776	**Kenner, LA** (city) Jefferson Parish	2,300
Georgia	8,600	Fairfax County, VA	3,515	**Metairie, LA** (cdp) Jefferson Parish	1,851
Maryland	6,504	Mecklenburg County, NC	3,165	**Austin, TX** (city) Travis County	1,842

Sorted by Number in Ascending Order — U.S. = 230,424

State	Number	County	Number	Place	Number
District of Columbia	382	New York County, NY	79	**Manhattan, NY** (borough) New York County	79
Iowa	460	Kern County, CA	102	**Miami Beach, FL** (city) Miami-Dade County	199
Nebraska	548	New Haven County, CT	281	**Pasadena, CA** (city) Los Angeles County	347
Oregon	668	Elkhart County, IN	305	**Staten Island, NY** (borough) Richmond County	347
Kentucky	703	Hartford County, CT	332	**Yonkers, NY** (city) Westchester County	359
Michigan	866	Richmond County, NY	347	**South Miami Heights, FL** (cdp) Miami-Dade County	389
Arkansas	894	Polk County, FL	357	**Philadelphia, PA** (city) Philadelphia County	392
Utah	950	Johnston County, NC	370	**Newark, NJ** (city) Essex County	421
Mississippi	1,009	Philadelphia County, PA	392	**Miramar, FL** (city) Broward County	437
Ohio	1,021	Fresno County, CA	402	**Wheaton, MD** (cdp) Montgomery County	443

Sorted by Percent in Descending Order — U.S. = 75.3%

State	Percent	County	Percent	Place	Percent
Arkansas	99.9	New Haven County, CT	100.0	**Garland, TX** (city) Dallas County	100.0
Michigan	99.5	Sampson County, NC	99.1	**Memphis, TN** (city) Shelby County	97.3
Wisconsin	96.3	Beaufort County, SC	99.0	**Miramar, FL** (city) Broward County	96.3
Alabama	95.8	Shelby County, TN	97.7	**Durham, NC** (city) Durham County	94.4
Mississippi	94.2	Ventura County, CA	97.0	**Indianapolis, IN** (city) Marion County	93.0
Indiana	94.1	East Baton Rouge Parish, LA	96.6	**Las Vegas, NV** (city) Clark County	92.4
Tennessee	93.2	Fresno County, CA	95.7	**Kenner, LA** (city) Jefferson Parish	92.3
Utah	92.3	Clayton County, GA	95.2	**Nashville-Davidson, TN** (metropolitan govt) Davidson County	92.1
Kansas	90.7	Durham County, NC	94.6	**South Miami Heights, FL** (cdp) Miami-Dade County	91.3
Iowa	90.6	Jackson County, MO	93.6	**Oklahoma City, OK** (city) Oklahoma County	90.7

Sorted by Percent in Ascending Order — U.S. = 75.3%

State	Percent	County	Percent	Place	Percent
District of Columbia	31.5	New York County, NY	4.2	**Manhattan, NY** (borough) New York County	4.2
New York	37.9	Kings County, NY	14.7	**Miami Beach, FL** (city) Miami-Dade County	14.6
Washington	62.6	Bronx County, NY	16.1	**Brooklyn, NY** (borough) Kings County	14.7
New Jersey	63.3	Queens County, NY	23.7	**Bronx, NY** (borough) Bronx County	16.1
Maryland	66.1	San Francisco County, CA	40.3	**New York, NY** (city)	17.5
Massachusetts	71.1	Richmond County, NY	41.6	**Queens, NY** (borough) Queens County	23.7
Pennsylvania	72.9	Union County, NJ	43.0	**Plainfield, NJ** (city) Union County	39.6
California	74.4	King County, WA	46.8	**San Francisco, CA** (city) San Francisco County	40.3
Virginia	75.2	Hudson County, NJ	51.9	**Wheaton, MD** (cdp) Montgomery County	41.2
Connecticut	78.3	Baltimore County, MD	52.9	**Staten Island, NY** (borough) Richmond County	41.6

Note: (1) Ranking tables cover all states and counties, and places with an overall population of at least 125,000, OR an overall population of at least 25,000 where the Hispanic/Latino population is at least 20% of the overall population. In states where less than five places meet either of these criteria, we have included places with at least 10,000 total population with the highest percentage of Hispanic/Latino population. These places are identified with an asterisk (*); Please refer to the User's Guide for a full explanation of data.

Means of Transportation to Work: Car, Truck or Van

(Universe: Civilian Employed Population 16 Years and Over)

Central American: Nicaraguan

Top 10 States, Counties, and Places[1]

Sorted by Number in Descending Order — U.S. = 142,809

State	Number	County	Number	Place	Number
Florida	62,540	Miami-Dade County, FL	49,314	**Miami, FL** (city) Miami-Dade County	11,964
California	38,619	Los Angeles County, CA	15,075	**Los Angeles, CA** (city) Los Angeles County	5,984
Texas	7,669	San Mateo County, CA	3,854	**Hialeah, FL** (city) Miami-Dade County	4,906
Virginia	3,876	Broward County, FL	3,634	**Fountainebleau, FL** (cdp) Miami-Dade County	3,409
Louisiana	3,840	Harris County, TX	3,346	**Houston, TX** (city) Harris County	2,076
New Jersey	3,153	San Bernardino County, CA	3,100	**Kendale Lakes, FL** (cdp) Miami-Dade County	1,967
Maryland	2,867	Alameda County, CA	2,788	**Tamiami, FL** (cdp) Miami-Dade County	1,942
North Carolina	2,223	Contra Costa County, CA	2,400	**San Francisco, CA** (city) San Francisco County	1,631
New York	2,145	Jefferson Parish, LA	2,348	**Daly City, CA** (city) San Mateo County	1,582
Nevada	1,882	Palm Beach County, FL	1,775	**Kendall, FL** (cdp) Miami-Dade County	1,395

Sorted by Number in Ascending Order — U.S. = 142,809

State	Number	County	Number	Place	Number
District of Columbia	213	New York County, NY	69	**Manhattan, NY** (borough) New York County	69
Michigan	307	Kings County, NY	128	**Brooklyn, NY** (borough) Kings County	128
Oregon	334	King County, WA	165	**South Gate, CA** (city) Los Angeles County	252
Missouri	337	Gwinnett County, GA	211	**Queens, NY** (borough) Queens County	299
Tennessee	351	Queens County, NY	299	**South San Francisco, CA** (city) San Mateo County	373
Minnesota	356	Camden County, NJ	395	**Austin, TX** (city) Travis County	374
Indiana	357	Lee County, FL	397	**San Diego, CA** (city) San Diego County	389
Connecticut	396	Bexar County, TX	415	**Sacramento, CA** (city) Sacramento County	406
South Carolina	402	Stanislaus County, CA	454	**Las Vegas, NV** (city) Clark County	462
Washington	523	Bronx County, NY	463	**Bronx, NY** (borough) Bronx County	463

Sorted by Percent in Descending Order — U.S. = 81.5%

State	Percent	County	Percent	Place	Percent
Indiana	100.0	Collier County, FL	100.0	**Charlotte, NC** (city) Mecklenburg County	100.0
Michigan	99.0	Hillsborough County, FL	97.2	**Miami Gardens, FL** (city) Miami-Dade County	100.0
Wisconsin	96.4	Mecklenburg County, NC	95.6	**Miramar, FL** (city) Broward County	98.4
Louisiana	94.8	Riverside County, CA	95.0	**Hollywood, FL** (city) Broward County	98.2
North Carolina	94.6	Duval County, FL	93.9	**Sacramento, CA** (city) Sacramento County	97.1
Missouri	93.4	Jefferson Parish, LA	93.7	**Richmond West, FL** (cdp) Miami-Dade County	96.8
Pennsylvania	91.0	Sonoma County, CA	93.5	**Kendale Lakes, FL** (cdp) Miami-Dade County	95.0
Connecticut	89.6	Sacramento County, CA	90.6	**North Miami, FL** (city) Miami-Dade County	94.5
Nevada	88.7	San Bernardino County, CA	90.3	**Country Club, FL** (cdp) Miami-Dade County	94.4
Georgia	88.4	Orange County, CA	90.0	**The Hammocks, FL** (cdp) Miami-Dade County	94.4

Sorted by Percent in Ascending Order — U.S. = 81.5%

State	Percent	County	Percent	Place	Percent
New York	31.7	New York County, NY	7.0	**Manhattan, NY** (borough) New York County	7.0
District of Columbia	42.3	Kings County, NY	11.8	**Brooklyn, NY** (borough) Kings County	11.8
Washington	59.4	Queens County, NY	19.4	**New York, NY** (city)	18.6
Massachusetts	61.7	Bronx County, NY	31.3	**Queens, NY** (borough) Queens County	19.4
Minnesota	64.6	King County, WA	43.0	**Bronx, NY** (borough) Bronx County	31.3
Maryland	66.3	San Francisco County, CA	50.2	**San Francisco, CA** (city) San Francisco County	50.2
Oregon	72.6	Montgomery County, MD	59.8	**South San Francisco, CA** (city) San Mateo County	63.7
New Jersey	75.3	Hudson County, NJ	64.4	**Los Angeles, CA** (city) Los Angeles County	71.6
Arizona	78.2	Gwinnett County, GA	68.1	**Daly City, CA** (city) San Mateo County	75.1
Colorado	79.1	Prince George's County, MD	68.9	**Miami, FL** (city) Miami-Dade County	76.3

RANKINGS & COMPARISONS

Note: (1) Ranking tables cover all states and counties, and places with an overall population of at least 125,000, OR an overall population of at least 25,000 where the Hispanic/Latino population is at least 20% of the overall population. In states where less than five places meet either of these criteria, we have included places with at least 10,000 total population with the highest percentage of Hispanic/Latino population. These places are identified with an asterisk (*); Please refer to the User's Guide for a full explanation of data.

Means of Transportation to Work: Car, Truck or Van

(Universe: Civilian Employed Population 16 Years and Over)

Central American: Panamanian

Top 10 States, Counties, and Places[1]

Sorted by Number in Descending Order — U.S. = 58,971

State	Number	County	Number	Place	Number
Florida	12,070	Miami-Dade County, FL	3,699	**New York, NY** (city)	2,604
California	6,649	Broward County, FL	1,924	**Brooklyn, NY** (borough) Kings County	1,295
Texas	5,469	Los Angeles County, CA	1,916	**Queens, NY** (borough) Queens County	775
New York	4,807	Hillsborough County, FL	1,430	**Jacksonville, FL** (city) Duval County	649
Virginia	3,293	Kings County, NY	1,295	**San Antonio, TX** (city) Bexar County	569
Georgia	3,048	Orange County, FL	1,068	**Hempstead (town), NY** (town) Nassau County	564
North Carolina	2,213	San Diego County, CA	1,009	**Los Angeles, CA** (city) Los Angeles County	527
New Jersey	2,060	Bexar County, TX	820	**Fayetteville, NC** (city) Cumberland County	514
Maryland	1,961	Queens County, NY	775	**San Diego, CA** (city) San Diego County	474
Washington	1,163	Harris County, TX	747	**Houston, TX** (city) Harris County	428

Sorted by Number in Ascending Order — U.S. = 58,971

State	Number	County	Number	Place	Number
Mississippi	176	New York County, NY	127	**Manhattan, NY** (borough) New York County	127
New Mexico	293	Hudson County, NJ	179	**Miami, FL** (city) Miami-Dade County	315
Wisconsin	364	Essex County, NJ	300	**Bronx, NY** (borough) Bronx County	322
Minnesota	400	Bronx County, NY	322	**Killeen, TX** (city) Bell County	400
Kentucky	487	Fairfax County, VA	325	**Houston, TX** (city) Harris County	428
Indiana	498	Orange County, CA	333	**San Diego, CA** (city) San Diego County	474
Connecticut	543	Sacramento County, CA	338	**Fayetteville, NC** (city) Cumberland County	514
Alabama	587	Pierce County, WA	365	**Los Angeles, CA** (city) Los Angeles County	527
Michigan	587	San Bernardino County, CA	405	**Hempstead (town), NY** (town) Nassau County	564
Oklahoma	598	Palm Beach County, FL	407	**San Antonio, TX** (city) Bexar County	569

Sorted by Percent in Descending Order — U.S. = 76.4%

State	Percent	County	Percent	Place	Percent
New Mexico	100.0	Clark County, NV	99.2	**Fayetteville, NC** (city) Cumberland County	97.0
Oklahoma	98.0	Cumberland County, NC	97.9	**Killeen, TX** (city) Bell County	96.9
Nevada	96.1	Bell County, TX	97.5	**Jacksonville, FL** (city) Duval County	93.1
Wisconsin	95.3	Hillsborough County, FL	97.1	**Houston, TX** (city) Harris County	90.3
Minnesota	94.1	Sacramento County, CA	95.8	**San Antonio, TX** (city) Bexar County	89.9
Louisiana	93.7	Broward County, FL	93.7	**San Diego, CA** (city) San Diego County	84.3
Indiana	92.9	Dallas County, TX	93.7	**Hempstead (town), NY** (town) Nassau County	74.1
Tennessee	92.6	Duval County, FL	93.1	**Miami, FL** (city) Miami-Dade County	68.2
North Carolina	92.2	Harris County, TX	92.9	**Los Angeles, CA** (city) Los Angeles County	60.4
Michigan	92.0	Palm Beach County, FL	91.5	**Queens, NY** (borough) Queens County	39.6

Sorted by Percent in Ascending Order — U.S. = 76.4%

State	Percent	County	Percent	Place	Percent
New York	33.6	New York County, NY	10.9	**Manhattan, NY** (borough) New York County	10.9
Massachusetts	64.8	Kings County, NY	19.2	**Brooklyn, NY** (borough) Kings County	19.2
Pennsylvania	68.6	Bronx County, NY	29.3	**New York, NY** (city)	23.2
New Jersey	72.9	Queens County, NY	39.6	**Bronx, NY** (borough) Bronx County	29.3
Maryland	80.2	Hudson County, NJ	48.2	**Queens, NY** (borough) Queens County	39.6
California	80.5	Essex County, NJ	52.9	**Los Angeles, CA** (city) Los Angeles County	60.4
Mississippi	84.2	Prince George's County, MD	69.2	**Miami, FL** (city) Miami-Dade County	68.2
Alabama	85.4	Orange County, CA	69.7	**Hempstead (town), NY** (town) Nassau County	74.1
Ohio	85.5	San Bernardino County, CA	73.1	**San Diego, CA** (city) San Diego County	84.3
Illinois	86.9	Nassau County, NY	74.2	**San Antonio, TX** (city) Bexar County	89.9

Note: (1) Ranking tables cover all states and counties, and places with an overall population of at least 125,000, OR an overall population of at least 25,000 where the Hispanic/Latino population is at least 20% of the overall population. In states where less than five places meet either of these criteria, we have included places with at least 10,000 total population with the highest percentage of Hispanic/Latino population. These places are identified with an asterisk (*); Please refer to the User's Guide for a full explanation of data.

Means of Transportation to Work: Car, Truck or Van

(Universe: Civilian Employed Population 16 Years and Over)

Central American: Salvadoran

Top 10 States, Counties, and Places[1]

Sorted by Number in Descending Order — U.S. = 658,199

State	Number	County	Number	Place	Number
California	232,885	Los Angeles County, CA	145,884	**Los Angeles, CA** (city) Los Angeles County	87,916
Texas	104,308	Harris County, TX	56,405	**Houston, TX** (city) Harris County	36,264
Virginia	50,551	Montgomery County, MD	21,448	**Hempstead (town), NY** (town) Nassau County	11,948
Maryland	49,399	Dallas County, TX	20,938	**Islip, NY** (town) Suffolk County	10,945
New York	46,970	Suffolk County, NY	20,071	**Dallas, TX** (city) Dallas County	9,545
Florida	24,540	Prince George's County, MD	18,980	**New York, NY** (city)	6,281
New Jersey	17,318	Fairfax County, VA	17,407	**Irving, TX** (city) Dallas County	5,896
North Carolina	15,482	Nassau County, NY	16,579	**Brentwood, NY** (cdp) Suffolk County	4,718
Georgia	13,827	Prince William County, VA	11,245	**Charlotte, NC** (city) Mecklenburg County	4,469
Massachusetts	12,513	Orange County, CA	10,859	**Queens, NY** (borough) Queens County	4,220

Sorted by Number in Ascending Order — U.S. = 658,199

State	Number	County	Number	Place	Number
Hawaii	317	New York County, NY	144	**Manhattan, NY** (borough) New York County	144
Alaska	424	Polk County, FL	312	**Jersey City, NJ** (city) Hudson County	247
Idaho	462	Yolo County, CA	319	**Tacoma, WA** (city) Pierce County	350
Wisconsin	696	Duval County, FL	368	**Bridgeport, CT** (city/town) Fairfield County	355
Kentucky	858	Cache County, UT	376	**Hesperia, CA** (city) San Bernardino County	355
New Mexico	1,029	Placer County, CA	385	**Jacksonville, FL** (city) Duval County	368
Alabama	1,058	Hidalgo County, TX	395	**Santa Rosa, CA** (city) Sonoma County	372
Oklahoma	1,102	El Paso County, TX	403	**Spring Valley, NV** (cdp) Clark County	391
Rhode Island	1,241	Merced County, CA	405	**Victorville, CA** (city) San Bernardino County	395
South Carolina	1,435	Buncombe County, NC	417	**Mesquite, TX** (city) Dallas County	408

Sorted by Percent in Descending Order — U.S. = 80.6%

State	Percent	County	Percent	Place	Percent
Idaho	100.0	Cache County, UT	100.0	**Lake Worth, FL** (city) Palm Beach County	100.0
Indiana	95.2	Shelby County, TN	98.8	**Lewisville, TX** (city) Denton County	100.0
Alabama	95.1	Sebastian County, AR	98.2	**Mesquite, TX** (city) Dallas County	100.0
Arkansas	95.0	Montgomery County, TX	98.1	**Greensboro, NC** (city) Guilford County	98.9
New Mexico	94.8	Washington County, AR	98.1	**Springdale, AR** (city) Washington County	98.9
Nebraska	94.1	Polk County, IA	97.8	**West Valley City, UT** (city) Salt Lake County	98.0
South Carolina	93.7	Durham County, NC	97.7	**Fullerton, CA** (city) Orange County	97.8
Iowa	93.5	Brazoria County, TX	97.5	**Des Moines, IA** (city) Polk County	97.7
Tennessee	92.8	Denton County, TX	97.5	**Carrollton, TX** (city) Denton County	97.5
Kansas	92.6	Pierce County, WA	97.3	**Durham, NC** (city) Durham County	97.5

Sorted by Percent in Ascending Order — U.S. = 80.6%

State	Percent	County	Percent	Place	Percent
District of Columbia	35.1	New York County, NY	9.7	**Manhattan, NY** (borough) New York County	9.7
Alaska	61.1	Bronx County, NY	23.2	**Bronx, NY** (borough) Bronx County	23.2
Massachusetts	62.2	Kings County, NY	24.7	**Brooklyn, NY** (borough) Kings County	24.7
New Jersey	62.4	Queens County, NY	37.8	**New York, NY** (city)	30.9
New York	66.0	Hartford County, CT	44.8	**Queens, NY** (borough) Queens County	37.8
Connecticut	66.5	Suffolk County, MA	49.7	**West New York, NJ** (town) Hudson County	44.0
Pennsylvania	71.4	San Francisco County, CA	50.3	**Boston, MA** (city) Suffolk County	44.1
Rhode Island	72.1	Hudson County, NJ	51.4	**Jersey City, NJ** (city) Hudson County	44.8
Hawaii	75.3	Bergen County, NJ	51.6	**Union City, NJ** (city) Hudson County	48.8
Maryland	79.5	Union County, NJ	55.2	**San Francisco, CA** (city) San Francisco County	50.3

Note: (1) Ranking tables cover all states and counties, and places with an overall population of at least 125,000, OR an overall population of at least 25,000 where the Hispanic/Latino population is at least 20% of the overall population. In states where less than five places meet either of these criteria, we have included places with at least 10,000 total population with the highest percentage of Hispanic/Latino population. These places are identified with an asterisk (*); Please refer to the User's Guide for a full explanation of data.

Means of Transportation to Work: Car, Truck or Van

(Universe: Civilian Employed Population 16 Years and Over)

Cuban

Top 10 States, Counties, and Places[1]

Sorted by Number in Descending Order — U.S. = 671,804

State	Number	County	Number	Place	Number
Florida	480,493	Miami-Dade County, FL	335,037	**Hialeah, FL** (city) Miami-Dade County	61,022
California	31,650	Broward County, FL	36,176	**Miami, FL** (city) Miami-Dade County	50,465
New Jersey	28,411	Hillsborough County, FL	26,471	**Tamiami, FL** (cdp) Miami-Dade County	15,892
Texas	17,078	Palm Beach County, FL	16,098	**Kendale Lakes, FL** (cdp) Miami-Dade County	12,945
New York	15,877	Los Angeles County, CA	15,053	**Fountainebleau, FL** (cdp) Miami-Dade County	11,232
Georgia	9,358	Orange County, FL	9,169	**Kendall, FL** (cdp) Miami-Dade County	10,475
Nevada	8,223	Hudson County, NJ	7,831	**Westchester, FL** (cdp) Miami-Dade County	9,158
Illinois	7,298	Clark County, NV	7,819	**Tampa, FL** (city) Hillsborough County	8,647
North Carolina	6,828	Collier County, FL	7,078	**Pembroke Pines, FL** (city) Broward County	8,336
Virginia	6,487	Lee County, FL	6,929	**University Park, FL** (cdp) Miami-Dade County	7,657

Sorted by Number in Ascending Order — U.S. = 671,804

State	Number	County	Number	Place	Number
Arkansas	253	Berks County, PA	154	**Santa Clarita, CA** (city) Los Angeles County	220
West Virginia	286	Hampden County, MA	192	**Bell, CA** (city) Los Angeles County	230
Maine	291	Sumter County, FL	208	**Linden, NJ** (city) Union County	230
District of Columbia	315	Worcester County, MA	223	**Milwaukee, WI** (city) Milwaukee County	231
Delaware	416	Kern County, CA	261	**Seattle, WA** (city) King County	243
Iowa	426	Forsyth County, NC	283	**Baltimore, MD** (independent city)	301
Hawaii	547	Cuyahoga County, OH	285	**Riverside, CA** (city) Riverside County	304
Mississippi	559	Pierce County, WA	289	**Kearny, NJ** (town) Hudson County	335
New Hampshire	651	Shelby County, TN	289	**Burbank, CA** (city) Los Angeles County	355
Rhode Island	660	El Paso County, TX	292	**Columbus, OH** (city) Franklin County	369

Sorted by Percent in Descending Order — U.S. = 87.7%

State	Percent	County	Percent	Place	Percent
Arkansas	97.3	Henry County, GA	100.0	**Deltona, FL** (city) Volusia County	100.0
New Hampshire	95.9	Clay County, MO	98.7	**Riverview, FL** (cdp) Hillsborough County	100.0
Nebraska	95.4	Saint Tammany Parish, LA	97.6	**Spring Valley, NV** (cdp) Clark County	100.0
Mississippi	93.8	Franklin County, OH	97.5	**Doral, FL** (city) Miami-Dade County	99.6
Florida	91.4	DuPage County, IL	97.4	**Kissimmee, FL** (city) Osceola County	98.7
Indiana	91.0	Volusia County, FL	97.3	**Greenacres, FL** (city) Palm Beach County	98.5
Michigan	90.9	Bernalillo County, NM	97.2	**Kenner, LA** (city) Jefferson Parish	98.5
Rhode Island	90.2	Indian River County, FL	97.2	**Lehigh Acres, FL** (cdp) Lee County	98.5
Kentucky	89.9	Guilford County, NC	97.1	**San Antonio, TX** (city) Bexar County	98.5
Missouri	89.9	Wayne County, MI	97.1	**Coconut Creek, FL** (city) Broward County	98.3

Sorted by Percent in Ascending Order — U.S. = 87.7%

State	Percent	County	Percent	Place	Percent
District of Columbia	32.0	New York County, NY	12.0	**Manhattan, NY** (borough) New York County	12.0
New York	52.6	Kings County, NY	24.8	**Brooklyn, NY** (borough) Kings County	24.8
Massachusetts	70.9	Burlington County, NJ	34.7	**New York, NY** (city)	29.6
New Jersey	74.8	Bronx County, NY	39.7	**Bronx, NY** (borough) Bronx County	39.7
Hawaii	77.4	Queens County, NY	41.0	**Queens, NY** (borough) Queens County	41.0
Oregon	78.0	San Francisco County, CA	41.1	**San Francisco, CA** (city) San Francisco County	41.1
Maryland	78.8	Suffolk County, MA	44.1	**Boston, MA** (city) Suffolk County	46.1
Colorado	79.0	Richmond County, NY	51.3	**Jersey City, NJ** (city) Hudson County	47.6
Wisconsin	79.4	Philadelphia County, PA	56.2	**Union City, NJ** (city) Hudson County	50.2
Minnesota	79.6	Alameda County, CA	57.3	**Staten Island, NY** (borough) Richmond County	51.3

Note: (1) Ranking tables cover all states and counties, and places with an overall population of at least 125,000, OR an overall population of at least 25,000 where the Hispanic/Latino population is at least 20% of the overall population. In states where less than five places meet either of these criteria, we have included places with at least 10,000 total population with the highest percentage of Hispanic/Latino population. These places are identified with an asterisk (*); Please refer to the User's Guide for a full explanation of data.

Means of Transportation to Work: Car, Truck or Van

(Universe: Civilian Employed Population 16 Years and Over)

Dominican Republic

Top 10 States, Counties, and Places[1]

Sorted by Number in Descending Order — U.S. = 323,251

State	Number	County	Number	Place	Number
New York	87,909	Bronx County, NY	24,125	**New York, NY** (city)	56,389
Florida	67,218	Miami-Dade County, FL	22,447	**Bronx, NY** (borough) Bronx County	24,125
New Jersey	58,159	Essex County, MA	17,075	**Queens, NY** (borough) Queens County	14,424
Massachusetts	30,795	Queens County, NY	14,424	**Manhattan, NY** (borough) New York County	10,292
Pennsylvania	15,846	Passaic County, NJ	13,275	**Lawrence, MA** (city) Essex County	9,762
Rhode Island	10,542	Broward County, FL	12,417	**Paterson, NJ** (city) Passaic County	8,124
Connecticut	7,445	New York County, NY	10,292	**Providence, RI** (city) Providence County	7,681
Texas	4,699	Providence County, RI	10,121	**Brooklyn, NY** (borough) Kings County	6,890
Georgia	4,689	Hudson County, NJ	9,594	**Hempstead (town), NY** (town) Nassau County	6,276
Maryland	4,544	Middlesex County, NJ	9,288	**Boston, MA** (city) Suffolk County	5,537

Sorted by Number in Ascending Order — U.S. = 323,251

State	Number	County	Number	Place	Number
Minnesota	277	Ulster County, NY	97	**Syracuse, NY** (city) Onondaga County	168
Washington	316	Sullivan County, NY	211	**Atlantic City, NJ** (city) Atlantic County	244
Alabama	345	Oneida County, NY	235	**Chelsea, MA** (city) Suffolk County	246
Utah	363	Erie County, NY	242	**Elmont, NY** (cdp) Nassau County	275
Wisconsin	471	Lackawanna County, PA	264	**Kearny, NJ** (town) Hudson County	277
Delaware	555	Plymouth County, MA	300	**Ramapo, NY** (town) Rockland County	290
District of Columbia	558	Jefferson Parish, LA	322	**Bethlehem, PA** (city) Northampton County	291
Missouri	620	Burlington County, NJ	333	**New Haven, CT** (city/town) New Haven County	295
South Carolina	642	Onondaga County, NY	340	**North Hempstead, NY** (town) Nassau County	299
Colorado	668	Marion County, FL	350	**Englewood, NJ** (city) Bergen County	312

Sorted by Percent in Descending Order — U.S. = 57.5%

State	Percent	County	Percent	Place	Percent
Indiana	97.9	Collier County, FL	98.5	**Deltona, FL** (city) Volusia County	100.0
Nevada	95.6	Burlington County, NJ	96.5	**Kendale Lakes, FL** (cdp) Miami-Dade County	100.0
Tennessee	95.2	Tarrant County, TX	96.5	**Kendall West, FL** (cdp) Miami-Dade County	100.0
Alabama	94.5	Marion County, FL	96.2	**Plantation, FL** (city) Broward County	100.0
Arizona	93.8	Pasco County, FL	95.8	**Miami Gardens, FL** (city) Miami-Dade County	98.0
Alaska	93.5	Polk County, FL	95.8	**Poinciana, FL** (cdp) Osceola County	97.5
New Hampshire	92.9	Clark County, NV	95.5	**Country Club, FL** (cdp) Miami-Dade County	96.9
Michigan	91.6	Brevard County, FL	95.4	**Pembroke Pines, FL** (city) Broward County	96.8
North Carolina	90.9	Volusia County, FL	95.4	**Brookhaven, NY** (town) Suffolk County	96.1
Florida	90.7	Broward County, FL	95.1	**Town 'n' Country, FL** (cdp) Hillsborough County	95.8

Sorted by Percent in Ascending Order — U.S. = 57.5%

State	Percent	County	Percent	Place	Percent
New York	32.5	New York County, NY	16.3	**Manhattan, NY** (borough) New York County	16.3
District of Columbia	43.4	Kings County, NY	20.7	**Brooklyn, NY** (borough) Kings County	20.7
Washington	59.2	Bronx County, NY	26.6	**New York, NY** (city)	24.7
Utah	69.8	Queens County, NY	36.2	**Bronx, NY** (borough) Bronx County	26.6
New Jersey	71.3	Richmond County, NY	51.9	**Queens, NY** (borough) Queens County	36.2
Massachusetts	74.6	Hudson County, NJ	52.9	**Atlantic City, NJ** (city) Atlantic County	43.5
Minnesota	75.7	Suffolk County, MA	53.5	**Syracuse, NY** (city) Onondaga County	45.8
Illinois	77.8	Westchester County, NY	60.0	**Jersey City, NJ** (city) Hudson County	47.0
Connecticut	78.3	Monmouth County, NJ	61.8	**Union City, NJ** (city) Hudson County	48.7
California	79.5	Onondaga County, NY	63.1	**Hackensack, NJ** (city) Bergen County	50.9

Note: (1) Ranking tables cover all states and counties, and places with an overall population of at least 125,000, OR an overall population of at least 25,000 where the Hispanic/Latino population is at least 20% of the overall population. In states where less than five places meet either of these criteria, we have included places with at least 10,000 total population with the highest percentage of Hispanic/Latino population. These places are identified with an asterisk (*); Please refer to the User's Guide for a full explanation of data.

Means of Transportation to Work: Car, Truck or Van

(Universe: Civilian Employed Population 16 Years and Over)

Mexican

Top 10 States, Counties, and Places[1]

Sorted by Number in Descending Order — U.S. = 10,758,657

State	Number	County	Number	Place	Number
California	3,803,879	Los Angeles County, CA	1,180,137	**Los Angeles, CA** (city) Los Angeles County	381,413
Texas	2,845,613	Harris County, TX	455,891	**San Antonio, TX** (city) Bexar County	268,634
Arizona	557,098	Maricopa County, AZ	336,772	**Houston, TX** (city) Harris County	249,848
Illinois	546,009	Bexar County, TX	320,262	**Phoenix, AZ** (city) Maricopa County	176,260
Colorado	262,955	Orange County, CA	319,309	**Chicago, IL** (city) Cook County	170,874
Florida	215,701	Cook County, IL	312,527	**El Paso, TX** (city) El Paso County	170,096
Washington	195,494	San Diego County, CA	299,764	**Dallas, TX** (city) Dallas County	169,753
New Mexico	193,570	Dallas County, TX	291,826	**San Diego, CA** (city) San Diego County	110,599
Nevada	192,464	San Bernardino County, CA	280,274	**San Jose, CA** (city) Santa Clara County	95,275
North Carolina	176,134	Riverside County, CA	278,279	**Austin, TX** (city) Travis County	90,103

Sorted by Number in Ascending Order — U.S. = 10,758,657

State	Number	County	Number	Place	Number
Vermont	918	Union County, PA	15	**Fort Leonard Wood*, MO** (cdp) Pulaski County	124
District of Columbia	1,612	Antrim County, MI	16	**Fort Campbell North*, KY** (cdp) Christian County	185
Maine	1,643	Evangeline Parish, LA	16	**Lancaster, PA** (city) Lancaster County	234
New Hampshire	2,336	Swift County, MN	19	**Schofield Barracks*, HI** (cdp) Honolulu County	236
West Virginia	2,722	Fulton County, IL	24	**Juneau*, AK** (borough) Juneau City and Borough	238
Rhode Island	2,967	Sedgwick County, CO	45	**Coral Gables, FL** (city) Miami-Dade County	250
North Dakota	3,651	Emmet County, MI	46	**Babylon, NY** (town) Suffolk County	251
South Dakota	5,005	Allen Parish, LA	52	**Huntington, NY** (town) Suffolk County	274
Montana	6,533	Hertford County, NC	54	**Mayfield*, KY** (city) Graves County	287
Alaska	7,166	Adams County, WI	55	**Oyster Bay, NY** (town) Nassau County	303

Sorted by Percent in Descending Order — U.S. = 86.9%

State	Percent	County	Percent	Place	Percent
Alabama	95.3	Alexander County, NC	100.0	**Bluffton*, SC** (town) Beaufort County	100.0
Mississippi	93.8	Ashtabula County, OH	100.0	**Evanston*, WY** (city) Uinta County	100.0
Oklahoma	93.8	Beckham County, OK	100.0	**Hazleton, PA** (city) Luzerne County	100.0
Kansas	93.0	Berrien County, GA	100.0	**Pascagoula*, MS** (city) Jackson County	100.0
North Carolina	92.7	Blount County, TN	100.0	**Little Elm, TX** (city) Denton County	99.2
Tennessee	92.4	Cass County, IL	100.0	**Glendale Heights, IL** (village) DuPage County	99.1
New Mexico	92.3	Chisago County, MN	100.0	**Hampton, VA** (independent city)	98.7
Arkansas	92.2	Churchill County, NV	100.0	**Suisun City, CA** (city) Solano County	98.4
Nebraska	92.0	Citrus County, FL	100.0	**Clarksville, TN** (city) Montgomery County	98.3
Texas	91.8	Cole County, MO	100.0	**Lufkin, TX** (city) Angelina County	98.3

Sorted by Percent in Ascending Order — U.S. = 86.9%

State	Percent	County	Percent	Place	Percent
New York	26.3	New York County, NY	3.4	**Manhattan, NY** (borough) New York County	3.4
District of Columbia	34.3	Bronx County, NY	10.1	**Bronx, NY** (borough) Bronx County	10.1
New Jersey	56.0	Queens County, NY	11.3	**New York, NY** (city)	10.8
Massachusetts	63.5	Kings County, NY	12.4	**Queens, NY** (borough) Queens County	11.3
Vermont	63.8	Antrim County, MI	12.5	**Brooklyn, NY** (borough) Kings County	12.4
Connecticut	71.8	Richmond County, NY	28.2	**Fort Leonard Wood*, MO** (cdp) Pulaski County	13.7
Alaska	73.1	Tompkins County, NY	30.8	**West New York, NJ** (town) Hudson County	19.1
Pennsylvania	76.1	Hudson County, NJ	31.2	**Passaic, NJ** (city) Passaic County	22.3
Hawaii	77.6	Pittsylvania County, VA	32.1	**Union City, NJ** (city) Hudson County	25.9
Rhode Island	77.7	Emmet County, MI	36.2	**Staten Island, NY** (borough) Richmond County	28.2

Note: (1) Ranking tables cover all states and counties, and places with an overall population of at least 125,000, OR an overall population of at least 25,000 where the Hispanic/Latino population is at least 20% of the overall population. In states where less than five places meet either of these criteria, we have included places with at least 10,000 total population with the highest percentage of Hispanic/Latino population. These places are identified with an asterisk (*); Please refer to the User's Guide for a full explanation of data.

Means of Transportation to Work: Car, Truck or Van

(Universe: Civilian Employed Population 16 Years and Over)

Puerto Rican

Top 10 States, Counties, and Places[1]

Sorted by Number in Descending Order — U.S. = 1,279,483

State	Number	County	Number	Place	Number
Florida	296,182	Orange County, FL	52,671	**New York, NY** (city)	76,655
New York	180,027	Miami-Dade County, FL	37,866	**Bronx, NY** (borough) Bronx County	30,775
New Jersey	131,504	Cook County, IL	35,058	**Chicago, IL** (city) Cook County	26,734
Pennsylvania	83,703	Hillsborough County, FL	31,862	**Philadelphia, PA** (city) Philadelphia County	20,429
Connecticut	74,938	Bronx County, NY	30,775	**Queens, NY** (borough) Queens County	17,513
California	64,118	Broward County, FL	30,538	**Brooklyn, NY** (borough) Kings County	15,894
Massachusetts	61,733	Hartford County, CT	26,026	**Springfield, MA** (city) Hampden County	11,191
Illinois	53,224	Osceola County, FL	24,375	**Orlando, FL** (city) Orange County	9,835
Texas	49,227	Suffolk County, NY	23,861	**Bridgeport, CT** (city/town) Fairfield County	9,646
Ohio	28,180	New Haven County, CT	23,562	**Islip, NY** (town) Suffolk County	9,580

Sorted by Number in Ascending Order — U.S. = 1,279,483

State	Number	County	Number	Place	Number
Wyoming	267	Clearfield County, PA	13	**Bridgeton, NJ** (city) Cumberland County	179
North Dakota	396	Wyoming County, NY	16	**West Covina, CA** (city) Los Angeles County	189
South Dakota	457	Perry County, PA	71	**Akron, OH** (city) Summit County	200
Montana	522	Schoharie County, NY	75	**Columbia, SC** (city) Richland County	225
Vermont	769	Washington County, NY	78	**Waianae*, HI** (cdp) Honolulu County	252
West Virginia	853	Seneca County, NY	80	**Montgomery, AL** (city) Montgomery County	254
District of Columbia	891	Cayuga County, NY	117	**Cooper City, FL** (city) Broward County	265
Nebraska	1,117	Livingston County, NY	126	**Pittsburgh, PA** (city) Allegheny County	266
Idaho	1,267	Saint Lawrence County, NY	144	**Plano, TX** (city) Collin County	267
Alaska	1,486	Chenango County, NY	145	**Hempstead (village), NY** (village) Nassau County	269

Sorted by Percent in Descending Order — U.S. = 76.3%

State	Percent	County	Percent	Place	Percent
North Dakota	95.2	Adams County, PA	100.0	**Gilbert, AZ** (town) Maricopa County	100.0
Alabama	94.2	Ashtabula County, OH	100.0	**Grand Prairie, TX** (city) Dallas County	100.0
Idaho	93.9	Bay County, FL	100.0	**Hampton, VA** (independent city)	100.0
Indiana	93.0	Berrien County, MI	100.0	**Hazleton, PA** (city) Luzerne County	100.0
Wyoming	92.4	Cabarrus County, NC	100.0	**Henderson, NV** (city) Clark County	100.0
Louisiana	92.2	Cameron County, TX	100.0	**Huntington Beach, CA** (city) Orange County	100.0
New Mexico	92.1	Chenango County, NY	100.0	**Huntsville, AL** (city) Madison County	100.0
Tennessee	91.5	Davis County, UT	100.0	**Montgomery, AL** (city) Montgomery County	100.0
Florida	91.3	Douglas County, NE	100.0	**North Miami Beach, FL** (city) Miami-Dade County	100.0
Utah	91.1	Fulton County, NY	100.0	**Omaha, NE** (city) Douglas County	100.0

Sorted by Percent in Ascending Order — U.S. = 76.3%

State	Percent	County	Percent	Place	Percent
District of Columbia	44.5	Clearfield County, PA	4.9	**Manhattan, NY** (borough) New York County	9.6
New York	46.7	New York County, NY	9.6	**Brooklyn, NY** (borough) Kings County	25.2
Oregon	75.9	Kings County, NY	25.2	**Columbia, SC** (city) Richland County	25.4
Illinois	76.7	Tompkins County, NY	31.1	**New York, NY** (city)	29.7
New Jersey	78.2	Bronx County, NY	31.9	**Pittsburgh, PA** (city) Allegheny County	30.8
Pennsylvania	78.2	Queens County, NY	37.3	**Bronx, NY** (borough) Bronx County	31.9
Massachusetts	80.1	San Francisco County, CA	39.1	**Queens, NY** (borough) Queens County	37.3
West Virginia	80.5	Arlington County, VA	44.8	**San Francisco, CA** (city) San Francisco County	39.1
Washington	82.1	Pulaski County, MO	52.3	**West New York, NJ** (town) Hudson County	42.4
South Carolina	82.3	Hudson County, NJ	53.5	**Arlington, VA** (cdp) Arlington County	44.8

Note: (1) Ranking tables cover all states and counties, and places with an overall population of at least 125,000, OR an overall population of at least 25,000 where the Hispanic/Latino population is at least 20% of the overall population. In states where less than five places meet either of these criteria, we have included places with at least 10,000 total population with the highest percentage of Hispanic/Latino population. These places are identified with an asterisk (*); Please refer to the User's Guide for a full explanation of data.

Means of Transportation to Work: Car, Truck or Van

(Universe: Civilian Employed Population 16 Years and Over)

South American

Top 10 States, Counties, and Places[1]

Sorted by Number in Descending Order — U.S. = 1,063,488

State	Number	County	Number	Place	Number
Florida	301,004	Miami-Dade County, FL	120,111	**New York, NY** (city)	49,482
California	122,542	Broward County, FL	65,820	**Queens, NY** (borough) Queens County	34,211
New Jersey	122,128	Los Angeles County, CA	52,247	**Los Angeles, CA** (city) Los Angeles County	21,400
New York	116,193	Queens County, NY	34,211	**Miami, FL** (city) Miami-Dade County	14,093
Texas	58,280	Fairfax County, VA	22,597	**Chicago, IL** (city) Cook County	11,873
Virginia	47,995	Palm Beach County, FL	22,528	**Houston, TX** (city) Harris County	10,895
Connecticut	30,438	Orange County, FL	22,461	**Pembroke Pines, FL** (city) Broward County	9,878
Illinois	28,180	Harris County, TX	21,656	**Hempstead (town), NY** (town) Nassau County	9,877
Maryland	26,660	Suffolk County, NY	19,251	**Elizabeth, NJ** (city) Union County	9,535
Georgia	23,677	Cook County, IL	18,684	**Doral, FL** (city) Miami-Dade County	7,396

Sorted by Number in Ascending Order — U.S. = 1,063,488

State	Number	County	Number	Place	Number
North Dakota	271	Oneida County, NY	148	**Pittsburgh, PA** (city) Allegheny County	167
Vermont	365	Spokane County, WA	177	**Palm Springs, CA** (city) Riverside County	241
Montana	450	Clark County, WA	193	**Sanford, FL** (city) Seminole County	303
Maine	478	Washington County, MN	243	**Glendora, CA** (city) Los Angeles County	306
West Virginia	596	San Luis Obispo County, CA	252	**Killeen, TX** (city) Bell County	306
Wyoming	640	Hampshire County, MA	277	**Stockton, CA** (city) San Joaquin County	307
Alaska	1,201	Tolland County, CT	297	**Lexington-Fayette, KY** (consolidated govt) Fayette County	319
Nebraska	1,250	Macomb County, MI	302	**Cranston*, RI** (city) Providence County	334
Idaho	1,270	Polk County, IA	308	**Lynn, MA** (city) Essex County	334
Mississippi	1,373	Washtenaw County, MI	313	**Chesapeake, VA** (independent city)	338

Sorted by Percent in Descending Order — U.S. = 75.2%

State	Percent	County	Percent	Place	Percent
Tennessee	94.4	Gaston County, NC	100.0	**Chandler, AZ** (city) Maricopa County	100.0
South Carolina	93.0	Hamilton County, IN	100.0	**Henderson, NV** (city) Clark County	100.0
Alabama	92.6	Harford County, MD	100.0	**Kansas City, MO** (city) Jackson County	100.0
Wyoming	92.5	Hernando County, FL	100.0	**Killeen, TX** (city) Bell County	100.0
Kansas	92.2	Macomb County, MI	100.0	**Round Rock, TX** (city) Williamson County	100.0
North Carolina	91.7	Sussex County, DE	100.0	**Saint Cloud, FL** (city) Osceola County	100.0
Kentucky	90.8	Washington County, MN	100.0	**North Lauderdale, FL** (city) Broward County	99.2
Nevada	90.7	Guilford County, NC	99.2	**Bakersfield, CA** (city) Kern County	98.9
New Mexico	90.7	York County, SC	99.0	**Lehigh Acres, FL** (cdp) Lee County	98.9
Louisiana	90.3	Greenville County, SC	98.4	**Chino, CA** (city) San Bernardino County	98.7

Sorted by Percent in Ascending Order — U.S. = 75.2%

State	Percent	County	Percent	Place	Percent
District of Columbia	35.0	New York County, NY	8.7	**Manhattan, NY** (borough) New York County	8.7
New York	42.5	Kings County, NY	22.1	**Brooklyn, NY** (borough) Kings County	22.1
Massachusetts	63.2	Bronx County, NY	27.0	**New York, NY** (city)	26.6
New Jersey	70.3	Queens County, NY	29.6	**Bronx, NY** (borough) Bronx County	27.0
Vermont	72.7	Suffolk County, MA	34.6	**Boston, MA** (city) Suffolk County	29.4
Illinois	74.3	San Francisco County, CA	39.9	**Queens, NY** (borough) Queens County	29.6
Minnesota	75.0	Hudson County, NJ	50.3	**Pittsburgh, PA** (city) Allegheny County	36.5
Maine	76.6	Richmond County, NY	53.6	**San Francisco, CA** (city) San Francisco County	39.9
Washington	78.7	Allegheny County, PA	55.4	**Union City, NJ** (city) Hudson County	43.1
Hawaii	79.9	Norfolk County, MA	62.9	**Spring Valley, NY** (village) Rockland County	45.4

Note: (1) Ranking tables cover all states and counties, and places with an overall population of at least 125,000, OR an overall population of at least 25,000 where the Hispanic/Latino population is at least 20% of the overall population. In states where less than five places meet either of these criteria, we have included places with at least 10,000 total population with the highest percentage of Hispanic/Latino population. These places are identified with an asterisk (*); Please refer to the User's Guide for a full explanation of data.

Means of Transportation to Work: Car, Truck or Van

(Universe: Civilian Employed Population 16 Years and Over)

South American: Argentinean

Top 10 States, Counties, and Places[1]

Sorted by Number in Descending Order — U.S. = 88,574

State	Number	County	Number	Place	Number
Florida	24,104	Miami-Dade County, FL	12,558	**Los Angeles, CA** (city) Los Angeles County	4,022
California	19,011	Los Angeles County, CA	8,767	**Miami, FL** (city) Miami-Dade County	2,412
New York	5,771	Broward County, FL	4,928	**New York, NY** (city)	1,699
Texas	5,570	Orange County, CA	2,586	**Miami Beach, FL** (city) Miami-Dade County	1,452
New Jersey	5,225	Harris County, TX	1,846	**Houston, TX** (city) Harris County	1,026
Maryland	2,493	Palm Beach County, FL	1,647	**Queens, NY** (borough) Queens County	963
Illinois	2,253	Cook County, IL	1,229	**Hollywood, FL** (city) Broward County	819
Virginia	2,143	Clark County, NV	1,153	**Aventura, FL** (city) Miami-Dade County	705
Utah	2,027	Montgomery County, MD	1,136	**Pembroke Pines, FL** (city) Broward County	633
Connecticut	1,569	San Bernardino County, CA	1,128	**Doral, FL** (city) Miami-Dade County	549

Sorted by Number in Ascending Order — U.S. = 88,574

State	Number	County	Number	Place	Number
District of Columbia	185	New York County, NY	126	**Manhattan, NY** (borough) New York County	126
Louisiana	379	Kings County, NY	161	**Brooklyn, NY** (borough) Kings County	161
Missouri	393	Bronx County, NY	289	**Bronx, NY** (borough) Bronx County	289
Tennessee	477	Travis County, TX	309	**San Jose, CA** (city) Santa Clara County	360
Minnesota	543	Bexar County, TX	322	**San Francisco, CA** (city) San Francisco County	367
Indiana	564	Tarrant County, TX	334	**Coral Springs, FL** (city) Broward County	400
Colorado	598	Orange County, NY	335	**San Diego, CA** (city) San Diego County	423
Oregon	602	King County, WA	365	**Hialeah, FL** (city) Miami-Dade County	471
South Carolina	604	San Francisco County, CA	367	**Chicago, IL** (city) Cook County	500
Wisconsin	617	Oakland County, MI	378	**Hempstead (town), NY** (town) Nassau County	540

Sorted by Percent in Descending Order — U.S. = 78.2%

State	Percent	County	Percent	Place	Percent
Minnesota	98.9	Montgomery County, TX	100.0	**Aventura, FL** (city) Miami-Dade County	97.5
Tennessee	98.1	Oakland County, MI	100.0	**Doral, FL** (city) Miami-Dade County	94.3
Louisiana	97.2	Salt Lake County, UT	100.0	**San Diego, CA** (city) San Diego County	94.0
North Carolina	96.2	Tarrant County, TX	96.0	**Hollywood, FL** (city) Broward County	90.3
Ohio	94.9	San Bernardino County, CA	95.8	**Pembroke Pines, FL** (city) Broward County	87.6
South Carolina	94.5	Dallas County, TX	93.8	**Coral Springs, FL** (city) Broward County	84.7
Utah	93.7	Clark County, NV	93.1	**Houston, TX** (city) Harris County	84.5
Nevada	93.2	Riverside County, CA	93.1	**Los Angeles, CA** (city) Los Angeles County	81.6
Michigan	90.4	San Diego County, CA	91.1	**Hempstead (town), NY** (town) Nassau County	76.6
Wisconsin	89.3	Broward County, FL	90.7	**Hialeah, FL** (city) Miami-Dade County	76.2

Sorted by Percent in Ascending Order — U.S. = 78.2%

State	Percent	County	Percent	Place	Percent
District of Columbia	28.7	New York County, NY	5.3	**Manhattan, NY** (borough) New York County	5.3
New York	45.3	Kings County, NY	12.1	**Brooklyn, NY** (borough) Kings County	12.1
Pennsylvania	64.7	Queens County, NY	31.5	**New York, NY** (city)	22.2
Massachusetts	70.9	San Francisco County, CA	46.6	**Queens, NY** (borough) Queens County	31.5
Washington	73.1	Bronx County, NY	48.0	**San Francisco, CA** (city) San Francisco County	46.6
New Jersey	73.9	Hudson County, NJ	51.5	**Bronx, NY** (borough) Bronx County	48.0
Illinois	75.1	Union County, NJ	55.3	**Chicago, IL** (city) Cook County	56.7
Virginia	76.0	Westchester County, NY	64.4	**Miami Beach, FL** (city) Miami-Dade County	58.9
Colorado	77.0	Bexar County, TX	66.8	**Miami, FL** (city) Miami-Dade County	74.1
Missouri	78.9	Cook County, IL	67.2	**San Jose, CA** (city) Santa Clara County	75.5

Note: (1) Ranking tables cover all states and counties, and places with an overall population of at least 125,000, OR an overall population of at least 25,000 where the Hispanic/Latino population is at least 20% of the overall population. In states where less than five places meet either of these criteria, we have included places with at least 10,000 total population with the highest percentage of Hispanic/Latino population. These places are identified with an asterisk (*); Please refer to the User's Guide for a full explanation of data.

Means of Transportation to Work: Car, Truck or Van

(Universe: Civilian Employed Population 16 Years and Over)

South American: Bolivian

Top 10 States, Counties, and Places[1]

Sorted by Number in Descending Order — U.S. = 44,555

State	Number	County	Number	Place	Number
Virginia	16,794	Fairfax County, VA	9,441	**Arlington, VA** (cdp) Arlington County	2,064
California	6,334	Montgomery County, MD	2,618	**Annandale, VA** (cdp) Fairfax County	1,561
Florida	4,847	Los Angeles County, CA	2,313	**Los Angeles, CA** (city) Los Angeles County	1,358
Maryland	3,490	Arlington County, VA	2,064	**New York, NY** (city)	853
Texas	2,054	Prince William County, VA	1,979	**West Falls Church, VA** (cdp) Fairfax County	790
New York	1,937	Miami-Dade County, FL	1,582	**Providence, RI** (city) Providence County	573
New Jersey	1,543	Loudoun County, VA	1,062	**Dale City, VA** (cdp) Prince William County	545
Rhode Island	930	Providence County, RI	930	**Springfield, VA** (cdp) Fairfax County	543
Illinois	883	Broward County, FL	819	**Queens, NY** (borough) Queens County	507
Massachusetts	757	Orange County, CA	758		

Sorted by Number in Ascending Order — U.S. = 44,555

State	Number	County	Number	Place	Number
North Carolina	232	Cook County, IL	369	**Queens, NY** (borough) Queens County	507
Pennsylvania	254	San Diego County, CA	446	**Springfield, VA** (cdp) Fairfax County	543
Massachusetts	757	Prince George's County, MD	479	**Dale City, VA** (cdp) Prince William County	545
Illinois	883	Palm Beach County, FL	505	**Providence, RI** (city) Providence County	573
Rhode Island	930	Queens County, NY	507	**West Falls Church, VA** (cdp) Fairfax County	790
New Jersey	1,543	Santa Clara County, CA	566	**New York, NY** (city)	853
New York	1,937	Harris County, TX	574	**Los Angeles, CA** (city) Los Angeles County	1,358
Texas	2,054	Orange County, CA	758	**Annandale, VA** (cdp) Fairfax County	1,561
Maryland	3,490	Broward County, FL	819	**Arlington, VA** (cdp) Arlington County	2,064
Florida	4,847	Providence County, RI	930		

Sorted by Percent in Descending Order — U.S. = 82.2%

State	Percent	County	Percent	Place	Percent
Illinois	94.8	San Diego County, CA	97.4	**Providence, RI** (city) Providence County	89.3
Florida	92.7	Palm Beach County, FL	95.3	**West Falls Church, VA** (cdp) Fairfax County	87.4
Rhode Island	90.9	Cook County, IL	93.7	**Annandale, VA** (cdp) Fairfax County	85.1
Texas	90.6	Orange County, CA	93.7	**Dale City, VA** (cdp) Prince William County	83.8
Pennsylvania	90.1	Broward County, FL	93.6	**Springfield, VA** (cdp) Fairfax County	81.4
North Carolina	89.9	Prince William County, VA	92.3	**Arlington, VA** (cdp) Arlington County	78.3
California	86.0	Providence County, RI	90.9	**Los Angeles, CA** (city) Los Angeles County	73.7
Maryland	85.8	Miami-Dade County, FL	89.8	**New York, NY** (city)	34.3
Virginia	85.1	Santa Clara County, CA	89.8	**Queens, NY** (borough) Queens County	31.1
Massachusetts	77.2	Montgomery County, MD	87.4		

Sorted by Percent in Ascending Order — U.S. = 82.2%

State	Percent	County	Percent	Place	Percent
New York	49.6	Queens County, NY	31.1	**Queens, NY** (borough) Queens County	31.1
New Jersey	62.2	Prince George's County, MD	73.4	**New York, NY** (city)	34.3
Massachusetts	77.2	Arlington County, VA	78.3	**Los Angeles, CA** (city) Los Angeles County	73.7
Virginia	85.1	Los Angeles County, CA	80.9	**Arlington, VA** (cdp) Arlington County	78.3
Maryland	85.8	Loudoun County, VA	81.9	**Springfield, VA** (cdp) Fairfax County	81.4
California	86.0	Harris County, TX	85.5	**Dale City, VA** (cdp) Prince William County	83.8
North Carolina	89.9	Fairfax County, VA	86.1	**Annandale, VA** (cdp) Fairfax County	85.1
Pennsylvania	90.1	Montgomery County, MD	87.4	**West Falls Church, VA** (cdp) Fairfax County	87.4
Texas	90.6	Miami-Dade County, FL	89.8	**Providence, RI** (city) Providence County	89.3
Rhode Island	90.9	Santa Clara County, CA	89.8		

Note: (1) Ranking tables cover all states and counties, and places with an overall population of at least 125,000, OR an overall population of at least 25,000 where the Hispanic/Latino population is at least 20% of the overall population. In states where less than five places meet either of these criteria, we have included places with at least 10,000 total population with the highest percentage of Hispanic/Latino population. These places are identified with an asterisk (*); Please refer to the User's Guide for a full explanation of data.

Means of Transportation to Work: Car, Truck or Van

(Universe: Civilian Employed Population 16 Years and Over)

South American: Chilean

Top 10 States, Counties, and Places[1]

Sorted by Number in Descending Order — U.S. = 50,425

State	Number	County	Number	Place	Number
Florida	11,075	Miami-Dade County, FL	5,455	**Los Angeles, CA** (city) Los Angeles County	1,685
California	9,092	Los Angeles County, CA	3,391	**New York, NY** (city)	1,033
New York	4,474	Broward County, FL	2,125	**Queens, NY** (borough) Queens County	757
New Jersey	3,567	Nassau County, NY	1,233	**Miami, FL** (city) Miami-Dade County	682
Texas	2,241	Montgomery County, MD	1,068	**Hempstead (town), NY** (town) Nassau County	591
Maryland	1,916	Fairfax County, VA	878	**Kendall, FL** (cdp) Miami-Dade County	445
Virginia	1,790	Westchester County, NY	872	**Chicago, IL** (city) Cook County	232
Utah	1,336	Queens County, NY	757	**Manhattan, NY** (borough) New York County	76
Massachusetts	1,322	Harris County, TX	722	**Brooklyn, NY** (borough) Kings County	33
Georgia	1,076	Santa Clara County, CA	693		

Sorted by Number in Ascending Order — U.S. = 50,425

State	Number	County	Number	Place	Number
Minnesota	213	Kings County, NY	33	**Brooklyn, NY** (borough) Kings County	33
Tennessee	315	New York County, NY	76	**Manhattan, NY** (borough) New York County	76
Missouri	348	Alameda County, CA	324	**Chicago, IL** (city) Cook County	232
Ohio	386	Utah County, UT	360	**Kendall, FL** (cdp) Miami-Dade County	445
Michigan	398	San Mateo County, CA	417	**Hempstead (town), NY** (town) Nassau County	591
Wisconsin	484	Riverside County, CA	428	**Miami, FL** (city) Miami-Dade County	682
Oregon	500	San Bernardino County, CA	443	**Queens, NY** (borough) Queens County	757
Colorado	627	Cook County, IL	457	**New York, NY** (city)	1,033
Nevada	645	Bergen County, NJ	503	**Los Angeles, CA** (city) Los Angeles County	1,685
Pennsylvania	685	Middlesex County, MA	503		

Sorted by Percent in Descending Order — U.S. = 79.8%

State	Percent	County	Percent	Place	Percent
Tennessee	100.0	Harris County, TX	96.1	**Miami, FL** (city) Miami-Dade County	90.0
Oregon	95.8	Riverside County, CA	95.7	**Kendall, FL** (cdp) Miami-Dade County	83.8
Wisconsin	95.1	San Bernardino County, CA	94.9	**Los Angeles, CA** (city) Los Angeles County	75.6
Georgia	93.5	Salt Lake County, UT	94.0	**Hempstead (town), NY** (town) Nassau County	67.2
Texas	92.9	Bergen County, NJ	92.8	**Chicago, IL** (city) Cook County	44.8
Michigan	90.2	Broward County, FL	90.8	**Queens, NY** (borough) Queens County	33.0
Florida	90.1	Suffolk County, NY	89.9	**New York, NY** (city)	25.5
North Carolina	89.6	San Mateo County, CA	89.7	**Manhattan, NY** (borough) New York County	11.2
Minnesota	88.8	Miami-Dade County, FL	88.4	**Brooklyn, NY** (borough) Kings County	4.8
Arizona	88.1	Fairfax County, VA	88.1		

Sorted by Percent in Ascending Order — U.S. = 79.8%

State	Percent	County	Percent	Place	Percent
New York	52.5	Kings County, NY	4.8	**Brooklyn, NY** (borough) Kings County	4.8
Pennsylvania	68.9	New York County, NY	11.2	**Manhattan, NY** (borough) New York County	11.2
Washington	70.4	Queens County, NY	33.0	**New York, NY** (city)	25.5
Massachusetts	73.9	Alameda County, CA	59.3	**Queens, NY** (borough) Queens County	33.0
Illinois	74.1	Cook County, IL	60.1	**Chicago, IL** (city) Cook County	44.8
New Jersey	78.0	Hudson County, NJ	61.9	**Hempstead (town), NY** (town) Nassau County	67.2
California	79.2	Utah County, UT	71.7	**Los Angeles, CA** (city) Los Angeles County	75.6
Utah	83.0	Westchester County, NY	72.8	**Kendall, FL** (cdp) Miami-Dade County	83.8
Ohio	83.4	Nassau County, NY	72.9	**Miami, FL** (city) Miami-Dade County	90.0
Maryland	83.6	Middlesex County, MA	75.0		

RANKINGS & COMPARISONS

Note: (1) Ranking tables cover all states and counties, and places with an overall population of at least 125,000, OR an overall population of at least 25,000 where the Hispanic/Latino population is at least 20% of the overall population. In states where less than five places meet either of these criteria, we have included places with at least 10,000 total population with the highest percentage of Hispanic/Latino population. These places are identified with an asterisk (*); Please refer to the User's Guide for a full explanation of data.

Means of Transportation to Work: Car, Truck or Van

(Universe: Civilian Employed Population 16 Years and Over)

South American: Colombian

Top 10 States, Counties, and Places[1]

Sorted by Number in Descending Order — U.S. = 354,212

State	Number	County	Number	Place	Number
Florida	133,818	Miami-Dade County, FL	50,721	**New York, NY** (city)	15,327
New Jersey	39,550	Broward County, FL	28,388	**Queens, NY** (borough) Queens County	11,948
New York	34,299	Queens County, NY	11,948	**Miami, FL** (city) Miami-Dade County	4,871
California	24,536	Orange County, FL	11,864	**Pembroke Pines, FL** (city) Broward County	4,851
Texas	21,665	Los Angeles County, CA	10,390	**Houston, TX** (city) Harris County	4,468
Georgia	10,521	Palm Beach County, FL	10,331	**Elizabeth, NJ** (city) Union County	4,106
Connecticut	9,144	Harris County, TX	9,268	**Hialeah, FL** (city) Miami-Dade County	3,492
Illinois	8,555	Hillsborough County, FL	7,869	**Los Angeles, CA** (city) Los Angeles County	3,482
Massachusetts	7,603	Bergen County, NJ	7,754	**Hempstead (town), NY** (town) Nassau County	3,211
North Carolina	7,276	Union County, NJ	6,231	**The Hammocks, FL** (cdp) Miami-Dade County	3,073

Sorted by Number in Ascending Order — U.S. = 354,212

State	Number	County	Number	Place	Number
Iowa	388	Luzerne County, PA	191	**Tallahassee, FL** (city) Leon County	268
Arkansas	479	Burlington County, NJ	258	**Raleigh, NC** (city) Wake County	274
Nebraska	484	Dane County, WI	277	**San Francisco, CA** (city) San Francisco County	285
Kentucky	486	San Francisco County, CA	285	**Royal Palm Beach, FL** (village) Palm Beach County	302
Delaware	493	Ulster County, NY	291	**Anaheim, CA** (city) Orange County	310
District of Columbia	497	Oakland County, MI	295	**Indianapolis, IN** (city) Marion County	312
New Mexico	502	Leon County, FL	308	**Long Beach, CA** (city) Los Angeles County	327
Alaska	576	Forsyth County, GA	314	**Worcester, MA** (city) Worcester County	351
Oregon	625	Cuyahoga County, OH	334	**Manhattan, NY** (borough) New York County	360
Kansas	896	Hampden County, MA	340	**Miami Gardens, FL** (city) Miami-Dade County	370

Sorted by Percent in Descending Order — U.S. = 78.4%

State	Percent	County	Percent	Place	Percent
Oklahoma	97.2	Milwaukee County, WI	100.0	**Buenaventura Lakes, FL** (cdp) Osceola County	100.0
New Mexico	96.7	Oakland County, MI	100.0	**Miami Gardens, FL** (city) Miami-Dade County	100.0
Nevada	96.1	Lake County, FL	98.5	**San Jose, CA** (city) Santa Clara County	100.0
Alaska	95.2	Manatee County, FL	98.2	**North Lauderdale, FL** (city) Broward County	98.7
Delaware	94.3	Greenville County, SC	98.1	**Phoenix, AZ** (city) Maricopa County	98.4
Missouri	94.2	Hillsborough County, NH	98.1	**Alafaya, FL** (cdp) Orange County	97.9
Arkansas	93.6	Fort Bend County, TX	97.9	**Town 'n' Country, FL** (cdp) Hillsborough County	97.9
New Hampshire	92.9	Saint Louis County, MO	96.9	**Brandon, FL** (cdp) Hillsborough County	97.7
Louisiana	92.6	Saint Lucie County, FL	96.7	**Homestead, FL** (city) Miami-Dade County	97.5
South Carolina	92.3	Clark County, NV	96.0	**Meadow Woods, FL** (cdp) Orange County	96.4

Sorted by Percent in Ascending Order — U.S. = 78.4%

State	Percent	County	Percent	Place	Percent
District of Columbia	41.1	New York County, NY	7.9	**Manhattan, NY** (borough) New York County	7.9
New York	45.8	Kings County, NY	24.1	**Brooklyn, NY** (borough) Kings County	24.1
Massachusetts	55.1	San Francisco County, CA	30.0	**Boston, MA** (city) Suffolk County	24.6
Iowa	74.0	Suffolk County, MA	30.4	**San Francisco, CA** (city) San Francisco County	30.0
New Jersey	75.0	Queens County, NY	32.2	**New York, NY** (city)	30.2
Nebraska	80.5	Bronx County, NY	40.6	**Queens, NY** (borough) Queens County	32.2
Illinois	80.7	Hudson County, NJ	46.7	**Bronx, NY** (borough) Bronx County	40.6
Pennsylvania	81.3	Richmond County, NY	54.1	**Revere, MA** (city) Suffolk County	41.3
Oregon	81.4	Arlington County, VA	62.4	**Jersey City, NJ** (city) Hudson County	42.5
Rhode Island	82.1	Atlantic County, NJ	64.2	**Union City, NJ** (city) Hudson County	44.7

Note: (1) Ranking tables cover all states and counties, and places with an overall population of at least 125,000, OR an overall population of at least 25,000 where the Hispanic/Latino population is at least 20% of the overall population. In states where less than five places meet either of these criteria, we have included places with at least 10,000 total population with the highest percentage of Hispanic/Latino population. These places are identified with an asterisk (*); Please refer to the User's Guide for a full explanation of data.

Means of Transportation to Work: Car, Truck or Van

(Universe: Civilian Employed Population 16 Years and Over)

South American: Ecuadorian

Top 10 States, Counties, and Places[1]

Sorted by Number in Descending Order — U.S. = 180,050

State	Number	County	Number	Place	Number
New York	44,494	Queens County, NY	14,276	**New York, NY** (city)	22,012
New Jersey	35,696	Miami-Dade County, FL	9,388	**Queens, NY** (borough) Queens County	14,276
Florida	27,485	Los Angeles County, CA	8,617	**Chicago, IL** (city) Cook County	5,522
California	15,076	Essex County, NJ	7,900	**Newark, NJ** (city) Essex County	4,883
Connecticut	10,065	Hudson County, NJ	7,663	**Brooklyn, NY** (borough) Kings County	3,167
Illinois	8,734	Westchester County, NY	7,619	**Danbury, CT** (city/town) Fairfield County	2,973
Texas	5,384	Suffolk County, NY	7,392	**Los Angeles, CA** (city) Los Angeles County	2,960
Pennsylvania	4,619	Cook County, IL	7,320	**Bronx, NY** (borough) Bronx County	2,775
North Carolina	4,310	Broward County, FL	6,024	**Brookhaven, NY** (town) Suffolk County	2,495
Maryland	3,218	Fairfield County, CT	5,796	**Hempstead (town), NY** (town) Nassau County	2,413

Sorted by Number in Ascending Order — U.S. = 180,050

State	Number	County	Number	Place	Number
Missouri	217	King County, WA	166	**White Plains, NY** (city) Westchester County	172
Wisconsin	253	Santa Clara County, CA	255	**Downey, CA** (city) Los Angeles County	281
Oregon	336	Baltimore County, MD	271	**Miramar, FL** (city) Broward County	288
Rhode Island	351	Pinellas County, FL	273	**Philadelphia, PA** (city) Philadelphia County	326
Louisiana	379	Putnam County, NY	288	**Oyster Bay, NY** (town) Nassau County	360
Michigan	379	Providence County, RI	305	**City of Orange, NJ** (township) Essex County	380
Kansas	381	Philadelphia County, PA	326	**Country Club, FL** (cdp) Miami-Dade County	387
Tennessee	394	Monmouth County, NJ	333	**Clifton, NJ** (city) Passaic County	401
Colorado	395	Camden County, NJ	338	**Spring Valley, NY** (village) Rockland County	436
Iowa	404	Utah County, UT	354	**Plainfield, NJ** (city) Union County	444

Sorted by Percent in Descending Order — U.S. = 61.3%

State	Percent	County	Percent	Place	Percent
Iowa	100.0	Will County, IL	98.5	**Coral Springs, FL** (city) Broward County	100.0
Tennessee	98.0	Osceola County, FL	97.8	**Central Islip, NY** (cdp) Suffolk County	97.1
Oklahoma	97.6	Tarrant County, TX	96.9	**Country Club, FL** (cdp) Miami-Dade County	96.5
Texas	93.9	Putnam County, NY	95.7	**Downey, CA** (city) Los Angeles County	95.6
Indiana	93.5	Orange County, FL	95.4	**New Haven, CT** (city/town) New Haven County	94.5
South Carolina	93.3	Harris County, TX	94.3	**Houston, TX** (city) Harris County	94.1
Kansas	92.5	New Haven County, CT	93.0	**Orlando, FL** (city) Orange County	93.2
North Carolina	91.5	Dallas County, TX	92.5	**Brookhaven, NY** (town) Suffolk County	93.0
Arizona	90.4	San Diego County, CA	92.3	**Sunrise, FL** (city) Broward County	92.6
Florida	90.3	Lee County, FL	92.2	**Brentwood, NY** (cdp) Suffolk County	92.1

Sorted by Percent in Ascending Order — U.S. = 61.3%

State	Percent	County	Percent	Place	Percent
New York	37.4	New York County, NY	11.8	**Manhattan, NY** (borough) New York County	11.8
Rhode Island	63.8	Bronx County, NY	22.2	**Bronx, NY** (borough) Bronx County	22.2
Illinois	64.9	Kings County, NY	22.3	**Brooklyn, NY** (borough) Kings County	22.3
New Jersey	65.7	Queens County, NY	27.2	**White Plains, NY** (city) Westchester County	22.8
Colorado	66.5	King County, WA	51.2	**New York, NY** (city)	24.9
Minnesota	66.9	Hudson County, NJ	51.7	**Queens, NY** (borough) Queens County	27.2
Massachusetts	69.7	Worcester County, MA	55.8	**Union City, NJ** (city) Hudson County	40.1
Washington	73.5	Rockland County, NY	58.3	**Spring Valley, NY** (village) Rockland County	40.7
Michigan	76.0	Providence County, RI	60.5	**Hackensack, NJ** (city) Bergen County	42.2
Maryland	76.3	Richmond County, NY	60.9	**Jersey City, NJ** (city) Hudson County	47.3

Note: (1) Ranking tables cover all states and counties, and places with an overall population of at least 125,000, OR an overall population of at least 25,000 where the Hispanic/Latino population is at least 20% of the overall population. In states where less than five places meet either of these criteria, we have included places with at least 10,000 total population with the highest percentage of Hispanic/Latino population. These places are identified with an asterisk (*); Please refer to the User's Guide for a full explanation of data.

Means of Transportation to Work: Car, Truck or Van

(Universe: Civilian Employed Population 16 Years and Over)

South American: Paraguayan

Top 10 States, Counties, and Places[1]

Sorted by Number in Descending Order — U.S. = 6,983

State	Number	County	Number	Place	Number
New York	2,195	Westchester County, NY	712	**New York, NY** (city)	800
Florida	676	Queens County, NY	497	**Queens, NY** (borough) Queens County	497
New Jersey	664				
Maryland	628				
Texas	470				
California	388				

Sorted by Number in Ascending Order — U.S. = 6,983

State	Number	County	Number	Place	Number
California	388	Queens County, NY	497	**Queens, NY** (borough) Queens County	497
Texas	470	Westchester County, NY	712	**New York, NY** (city)	800
Maryland	628				
New Jersey	664				
Florida	676				
New York	2,195				

Sorted by Percent in Descending Order — U.S. = 69.7%

State	Percent	County	Percent	Place	Percent
Texas	92.7	Westchester County, NY	72.0	**New York, NY** (city)	36.8
California	90.0	Queens County, NY	31.6	**Queens, NY** (borough) Queens County	31.6
Maryland	87.8				
Florida	79.2				
New Jersey	73.5				
New York	56.0				

Sorted by Percent in Ascending Order — U.S. = 69.7%

State	Percent	County	Percent	Place	Percent
New York	56.0	Queens County, NY	31.6	**Queens, NY** (borough) Queens County	31.6
New Jersey	73.5	Westchester County, NY	72.0	**New York, NY** (city)	36.8
Florida	79.2				
Maryland	87.8				
California	90.0				
Texas	92.7				

Note: (1) Ranking tables cover all states and counties, and places with an overall population of at least 125,000, OR an overall population of at least 25,000 where the Hispanic/Latino population is at least 20% of the overall population. In states where less than five places meet either of these criteria, we have included places with at least 10,000 total population with the highest percentage of Hispanic/Latino population. These places are identified with an asterisk (*); Please refer to the User's Guide for a full explanation of data.

Means of Transportation to Work: Car, Truck or Van

(Universe: Civilian Employed Population 16 Years and Over)

South American: Peruvian

Top 10 States, Counties, and Places[1]

Sorted by Number in Descending Order — U.S. = 213,120

State	Number	County	Number	Place	Number
Florida	46,777	Miami-Dade County, FL	17,256	**Los Angeles, CA** (city) Los Angeles County	6,352
California	37,084	Los Angeles County, CA	14,563	**New York, NY** (city)	5,616
New Jersey	28,370	Broward County, FL	11,378	**Queens, NY** (borough) Queens County	4,171
New York	17,174	Fairfax County, VA	6,882	**Paterson, NJ** (city) Passaic County	2,989
Virginia	13,451	Passaic County, NJ	6,710	**Elizabeth, NJ** (city) Union County	2,190
Texas	9,994	Montgomery County, MD	4,604	**Islip, NY** (town) Suffolk County	2,130
Maryland	7,487	Palm Beach County, FL	4,468	**Hempstead (town), NY** (town) Nassau County	2,037
Connecticut	7,070	Queens County, NY	4,171	**Chicago, IL** (city) Cook County	1,832
Illinois	4,513	Orange County, CA	4,071	**Miami, FL** (city) Miami-Dade County	1,702
Georgia	4,276	Hudson County, NJ	3,953	**Clifton, NJ** (city) Passaic County	1,669

Sorted by Number in Ascending Order — U.S. = 213,120

State	Number	County	Number	Place	Number
District of Columbia	335	New York County, NY	144	**Boston, MA** (city) Suffolk County	116
Delaware	407	Denver County, CO	199	**Manhattan, NY** (borough) New York County	144
Rhode Island	448	Lake County, IL	214	**Denver, CO** (city) Denver County	199
Kentucky	474	Philadelphia County, PA	221	**Philadelphia, PA** (city) Philadelphia County	221
Kansas	516	Suffolk County, MA	250	**West New York, NJ** (town) Hudson County	248
Hawaii	529	Richmond County, NY	301	**Belleville, NJ** (township) Essex County	263
New Mexico	570	San Joaquin County, CA	318	**Austin, TX** (city) Travis County	289
Alabama	606	Wake County, NC	324	**Jersey City, NJ** (city) Hudson County	291
Idaho	609	Fort Bend County, TX	325	**Cape Coral, FL** (city) Lee County	296
Minnesota	649	Baltimore County, MD	377	**Torrance, CA** (city) Los Angeles County	298

Sorted by Percent in Descending Order — U.S. = 77.7%

State	Percent	County	Percent	Place	Percent
Kansas	100.0	Denton County, TX	100.0	**Kendale Lakes, FL** (cdp) Miami-Dade County	100.0
Kentucky	98.5	Fort Bend County, TX	100.0	**Torrance, CA** (city) Los Angeles County	100.0
Alabama	97.7	Lehigh County, PA	100.0	**Doral, FL** (city) Miami-Dade County	97.6
Missouri	97.6	Ocean County, NJ	98.7	**Concord, CA** (city) Contra Costa County	97.0
Tennessee	96.1	Seminole County, FL	96.2	**Sunrise, FL** (city) Broward County	96.8
Indiana	94.2	Hillsborough County, FL	95.5	**Tampa, FL** (city) Hillsborough County	96.7
South Carolina	94.0	Solano County, CA	95.5	**Charlotte, NC** (city) Mecklenburg County	95.4
North Carolina	91.9	New London County, CT	94.3	**Miramar, FL** (city) Broward County	94.9
Nevada	91.0	San Bernardino County, CA	94.0	**Davie, FL** (town) Broward County	94.8
Rhode Island	90.5	Tarrant County, TX	94.0	**Santa Clarita, CA** (city) Los Angeles County	94.7

Sorted by Percent in Ascending Order — U.S. = 77.7%

State	Percent	County	Percent	Place	Percent
District of Columbia	43.5	New York County, NY	6.3	**Manhattan, NY** (borough) New York County	6.3
New York	47.2	Kings County, NY	19.4	**Brooklyn, NY** (borough) Kings County	19.4
Massachusetts	62.3	Suffolk County, MA	29.9	**Boston, MA** (city) Suffolk County	23.0
New Jersey	69.6	Bronx County, NY	30.2	**New York, NY** (city)	27.1
Delaware	74.4	Queens County, NY	31.1	**Bronx, NY** (borough) Bronx County	30.2
Colorado	76.3	Richmond County, NY	37.0	**Queens, NY** (borough) Queens County	31.1
Oregon	78.7	San Francisco County, CA	42.8	**Staten Island, NY** (borough) Richmond County	37.0
Wisconsin	78.9	Middlesex County, MA	50.1	**Jersey City, NJ** (city) Hudson County	41.3
Washington	79.3	Hudson County, NJ	51.0	**Port Chester, NY** (village) Westchester County	42.3
Oklahoma	80.6	Philadelphia County, PA	57.1	**San Francisco, CA** (city) San Francisco County	42.8

Note: (1) Ranking tables cover all states and counties, and places with an overall population of at least 125,000, OR an overall population of at least 25,000 where the Hispanic/Latino population is at least 20% of the overall population. In states where less than five places meet either of these criteria, we have included places with at least 10,000 total population with the highest percentage of Hispanic/Latino population. These places are identified with an asterisk (*); Please refer to the User's Guide for a full explanation of data.

Means of Transportation to Work: Car, Truck or Van

(Universe: Civilian Employed Population 16 Years and Over)

South American: Uruguayan

Top 10 States, Counties, and Places[1]

Sorted by Number in Descending Order — U.S. = 21,478

State	Number	County	Number	Place	Number
Florida	5,792	Miami-Dade County, FL	2,309	**Elizabeth, NJ** (city) Union County	706
New Jersey	4,221	Broward County, FL	1,599	**New York, NY** (city)	219
New York	1,498	Union County, NJ	1,138	**Queens, NY** (borough) Queens County	166
California	1,422	Essex County, NJ	1,065		
Georgia	1,410	Palm Beach County, FL	695		
Texas	1,273	Harris County, TX	666		
Virginia	894	Worcester County, MA	589		
Massachusetts	883	Gwinnett County, GA	535		
Maryland	632	Westchester County, NY	532		
Pennsylvania	400	Los Angeles County, CA	503		

Sorted by Number in Ascending Order — U.S. = 21,478

State	Number	County	Number	Place	Number
Pennsylvania	400	Queens County, NY	166	**Queens, NY** (borough) Queens County	166
Maryland	632	Hudson County, NJ	241	**New York, NY** (city)	219
Massachusetts	883	Middlesex County, NJ	304	**Elizabeth, NJ** (city) Union County	706
Virginia	894	Morris County, NJ	501		
Texas	1,273	Los Angeles County, CA	503		
Georgia	1,410	Westchester County, NY	532		
California	1,422	Gwinnett County, GA	535		
New York	1,498	Worcester County, MA	589		
New Jersey	4,221	Harris County, TX	666		
Florida	5,792	Palm Beach County, FL	695		

Sorted by Percent in Descending Order — U.S. = 75.3%

State	Percent	County	Percent	Place	Percent
Texas	93.4	Harris County, TX	100.0	**Elizabeth, NJ** (city) Union County	44.3
Georgia	91.4	Morris County, NJ	100.0	**Queens, NY** (borough) Queens County	25.2
California	86.4	Palm Beach County, FL	95.7	**New York, NY** (city)	14.9
Virginia	84.7	Gwinnett County, GA	95.2		
Pennsylvania	81.0	Worcester County, MA	95.0		
Maryland	80.7	Broward County, FL	86.6		
Florida	79.5	Middlesex County, NJ	84.2		
Massachusetts	73.1	Essex County, NJ	81.6		
New Jersey	67.0	Los Angeles County, CA	78.1		
New York	47.1	Westchester County, NY	73.3		

Sorted by Percent in Ascending Order — U.S. = 75.3%

State	Percent	County	Percent	Place	Percent
New York	47.1	Queens County, NY	25.2	**New York, NY** (city)	14.9
New Jersey	67.0	Hudson County, NJ	34.9	**Queens, NY** (borough) Queens County	25.2
Massachusetts	73.1	Union County, NJ	49.8	**Elizabeth, NJ** (city) Union County	44.3
Florida	79.5	Miami-Dade County, FL	68.8		
Maryland	80.7	Westchester County, NY	73.3		
Pennsylvania	81.0	Los Angeles County, CA	78.1		
Virginia	84.7	Essex County, NJ	81.6		
California	86.4	Middlesex County, NJ	84.2		
Georgia	91.4	Broward County, FL	86.6		
Texas	93.4	Worcester County, MA	95.0		

Note: (1) Ranking tables cover all states and counties, and places with an overall population of at least 125,000, OR an overall population of at least 25,000 where the Hispanic/Latino population is at least 20% of the overall population. In states where less than five places meet either of these criteria, we have included places with at least 10,000 total population with the highest percentage of Hispanic/Latino population. These places are identified with an asterisk (*); Please refer to the User's Guide for a full explanation of data.

Means of Transportation to Work: Car, Truck or Van

(Universe: Civilian Employed Population 16 Years and Over)

South American: Venezuelan

Top 10 States, Counties, and Places[1]

Sorted by Number in Descending Order — U.S. = 86,535

State	Number	County	Number	Place	Number
Florida	43,787	Miami-Dade County, FL	19,776	**Doral, FL** (city) Miami-Dade County	2,995
Texas	8,449	Broward County, FL	9,992	**Weston, FL** (city) Broward County	2,654
California	4,710	Orange County, FL	3,447	**Miami, FL** (city) Miami-Dade County	2,533
Georgia	2,967	Harris County, TX	3,365	**Houston, TX** (city) Harris County	1,943
New York	2,735	Palm Beach County, FL	1,929	**Fountainebleau, FL** (cdp) Miami-Dade County	1,656
Virginia	2,339	Hillsborough County, FL	1,364	**Pembroke Pines, FL** (city) Broward County	1,381
New Jersey	2,129	Fort Bend County, TX	1,270	**New York, NY** (city)	1,356
North Carolina	1,900	Los Angeles County, CA	1,268	**Miami Beach, FL** (city) Miami-Dade County	966
Massachusetts	1,208	Osceola County, FL	1,228	**Orlando, FL** (city) Orange County	961
Maryland	1,097	Pinellas County, FL	916	**Country Club, FL** (cdp) Miami-Dade County	891

Sorted by Number in Ascending Order — U.S. = 86,535

State	Number	County	Number	Place	Number
Missouri	312	New York County, NY	36	**Manhattan, NY** (borough) New York County	36
Wisconsin	411	Suffolk County, MA	224	**Aventura, FL** (city) Miami-Dade County	261
Minnesota	424	Kings County, NY	297	**Brooklyn, NY** (borough) Kings County	297
Michigan	530	Tarrant County, TX	324	**Bronx, NY** (borough) Bronx County	385
Washington	545	Collin County, TX	326	**Los Angeles, CA** (city) Los Angeles County	433
Indiana	567	King County, WA	332	**Kendall West, FL** (cdp) Miami-Dade County	526
Oklahoma	643	Fairfield County, CT	336	**Queens, NY** (borough) Queens County	573
South Carolina	650	Travis County, TX	366	**Davie, FL** (town) Broward County	590
Tennessee	705	Hudson County, NJ	368	**Hollywood, FL** (city) Broward County	621
Colorado	719	Bronx County, NY	385	**Kendall, FL** (cdp) Miami-Dade County	624

Sorted by Percent in Descending Order — U.S. = 83.5%

State	Percent	County	Percent	Place	Percent
Indiana	98.4	Montgomery County, TX	100.0	**Pembroke Pines, FL** (city) Broward County	98.2
Arizona	96.9	Tarrant County, TX	98.2	**Coral Springs, FL** (city) Broward County	97.7
Tennessee	95.1	Lee County, FL	97.9	**Kendall West, FL** (cdp) Miami-Dade County	97.0
Louisiana	95.0	Seminole County, FL	97.7	**The Hammocks, FL** (cdp) Miami-Dade County	96.3
Michigan	94.3	Orange County, CA	96.8	**Country Club, FL** (cdp) Miami-Dade County	95.7
North Carolina	93.0	Hillsborough County, FL	95.7	**Hialeah, FL** (city) Miami-Dade County	94.8
Utah	92.6	Cobb County, GA	94.1	**Hollywood, FL** (city) Broward County	94.8
Wisconsin	92.4	Salt Lake County, UT	94.1	**Tamiami, FL** (cdp) Miami-Dade County	93.4
Georgia	91.7	Palm Beach County, FL	94.0	**Orlando, FL** (city) Orange County	92.8
Oklahoma	91.5	Fort Bend County, TX	93.8	**Fountainebleau, FL** (cdp) Miami-Dade County	92.6

Sorted by Percent in Ascending Order — U.S. = 83.5%

State	Percent	County	Percent	Place	Percent
New York	35.8	New York County, NY	2.8	**Manhattan, NY** (borough) New York County	2.8
Illinois	68.8	Kings County, NY	21.0	**Brooklyn, NY** (borough) Kings County	21.0
New Jersey	68.9	Queens County, NY	24.0	**New York, NY** (city)	23.2
Pennsylvania	72.2	Suffolk County, MA	47.6	**Queens, NY** (borough) Queens County	24.0
Massachusetts	75.7	Hudson County, NJ	49.7	**Bronx, NY** (borough) Bronx County	58.4
California	79.6	Bronx County, NY	58.4	**Los Angeles, CA** (city) Los Angeles County	69.3
Maryland	79.8	Cook County, IL	66.0	**Davie, FL** (town) Broward County	76.7
Minnesota	79.8	Los Angeles County, CA	72.8	**Aventura, FL** (city) Miami-Dade County	77.7
Washington	82.3	King County, WA	78.9	**Miami, FL** (city) Miami-Dade County	81.8
Colorado	85.2	Pinellas County, FL	82.3	**Sunrise, FL** (city) Broward County	82.0

Note: (1) Ranking tables cover all states and counties, and places with an overall population of at least 125,000, OR an overall population of at least 25,000 where the Hispanic/Latino population is at least 20% of the overall population. In states where less than five places meet either of these criteria, we have included places with at least 10,000 total population with the highest percentage of Hispanic/Latino population. These places are identified with an asterisk (*); Please refer to the User's Guide for a full explanation of data.

Means of Transportation to Work: Car, Truck or Van

(Universe: Civilian Employed Population 16 Years and Over)

Spaniard

Top 10 States, Counties, and Places[1]

Sorted by Number in Descending Order U.S. = 211,423

State	Number	County	Number	Place	Number
California	41,707	Los Angeles County, CA	9,102	**Albuquerque, NM** (city) Bernalillo County	6,277
Texas	24,989	Bernalillo County, NM	7,368	**Los Angeles, CA** (city) Los Angeles County	3,089
New Mexico	19,132	Maricopa County, AZ	4,443	**New York, NY** (city)	2,742
Florida	17,253	Miami-Dade County, FL	4,360	**San Antonio, TX** (city) Bexar County	2,392
Colorado	16,739	Harris County, TX	4,008	**Houston, TX** (city) Harris County	2,160
New York	9,626	San Diego County, CA	3,765	**Denver, CO** (city) Denver County	1,938
New Jersey	7,670	Hillsborough County, FL	3,159	**Austin, TX** (city) Travis County	1,754
Arizona	7,516	Orange County, CA	3,069	**San Diego, CA** (city) San Diego County	1,640
Washington	4,877	Bexar County, TX	3,008	**Phoenix, AZ** (city) Maricopa County	1,469
Illinois	4,221	Riverside County, CA	2,660	**Queens, NY** (borough) Queens County	1,198

Sorted by Number in Ascending Order U.S. = 211,423

State	Number	County	Number	Place	Number
District of Columbia	88	New York County, NY	74	**Manhattan, NY** (borough) New York County	74
Maine	209	Las Animas County, CO	131	**San Bernardino, CA** (city) San Bernardino County	120
Iowa	341	Tulare County, CA	144	**Philadelphia, PA** (city) Philadelphia County	215
New Hampshire	358	Butte County, CA	153	**Las Cruces, NM** (city) Dona Ana County	279
Mississippi	453	Philadelphia County, PA	215	**Fort Collins, CO** (city) Larimer County	301
Montana	477	Rio Arriba County, NM	217	**Henderson, NV** (city) Clark County	308
West Virginia	530	La Plata County, CO	236	**South Valley, NM** (cdp) Bernalillo County	317
Kentucky	608	Colfax County, NM	239	**Anchorage, AK** (municipality)	327
Alaska	636	Hennepin County, MN	239	**Brooklyn, NY** (borough) Kings County	328
Nebraska	742	Milwaukee County, WI	242	**Tucson, AZ** (city) Pima County	343

Sorted by Percent in Descending Order U.S. = 84.6%

State	Percent	County	Percent	Place	Percent
Nebraska	97.5	Butte County, CA	100.0	**Oklahoma City, OK** (city) Oklahoma County	100.0
Wyoming	96.4	Oakland County, MI	100.0	**Bakersfield, CA** (city) Kern County	97.8
Oklahoma	96.2	Passaic County, NJ	100.0	**Glendale, AZ** (city) Maricopa County	97.0
Kansas	95.9	Yolo County, CA	99.1	**Jacksonville, FL** (city) Duval County	96.9
Missouri	93.4	San Miguel County, NM	98.6	**Sacramento, CA** (city) Sacramento County	96.7
Utah	93.3	Oklahoma County, OK	98.4	**Pueblo, CO** (city) Pueblo County	96.6
New Mexico	92.5	Cibola County, NM	98.3	**North Las Vegas, NV** (city) Clark County	95.5
Arkansas	91.8	Weld County, CO	98.1	**Santa Fe, NM** (city) Santa Fe County	95.2
Florida	90.9	Denton County, TX	97.8	**Las Cruces, NM** (city) Dona Ana County	94.9
Michigan	90.8	Pueblo County, CO	97.4	**Stockton, CA** (city) San Joaquin County	94.8

Sorted by Percent in Ascending Order U.S. = 84.6%

State	Percent	County	Percent	Place	Percent
District of Columbia	13.7	New York County, NY	3.4	**Manhattan, NY** (borough) New York County	3.4
New York	56.5	Kings County, NY	19.8	**Brooklyn, NY** (borough) Kings County	19.8
Massachusetts	67.5	Bronx County, NY	37.2	**New York, NY** (city)	32.1
Indiana	75.8	Philadelphia County, PA	44.3	**Bronx, NY** (borough) Bronx County	37.2
New Jersey	77.2	Queens County, NY	48.3	**Philadelphia, PA** (city) Philadelphia County	44.3
Kentucky	77.9	San Francisco County, CA	53.6	**Chicago, IL** (city) Cook County	47.7
Illinois	78.0	Middlesex County, MA	62.0	**Queens, NY** (borough) Queens County	48.3
Minnesota	79.2	Hudson County, NJ	62.3	**San Francisco, CA** (city) San Francisco County	53.6
Pennsylvania	80.2	Multnomah County, OR	62.8	**Newark, NJ** (city) Essex County	59.9
Maine	81.0	Erie County, NY	66.0	**Portland, OR** (city) Multnomah County	66.3

Note: (1) Ranking tables cover all states and counties, and places with an overall population of at least 125,000, OR an overall population of at least 25,000 where the Hispanic/Latino population is at least 20% of the overall population. In states where less than five places meet either of these criteria, we have included places with at least 10,000 total population with the highest percentage of Hispanic/Latino population. These places are identified with an asterisk (*); Please refer to the User's Guide for a full explanation of data.

Means of Transportation to Work: Public Transportation

(Universe: Civilian Employed Population 16 Years and Over)

Total Population

Top 10 States, Counties, and Places[1]

Sorted by Number in Descending Order — U.S. = 6,872,730

State	Number	County	Number	Place	Number
New York	2,338,345	Kings County, NY	641,106	**New York, NY** (city)	2,008,737
California	834,363	Queens County, NY	526,040	**Brooklyn, NY** (borough) Kings County	641,106
Illinois	515,963	New York County, NY	480,415	**Queens, NY** (borough) Queens County	526,040
New Jersey	438,293	Cook County, IL	420,092	**Manhattan, NY** (borough) New York County	480,415
Pennsylvania	312,308	Los Angeles County, CA	311,701	**Chicago, IL** (city) Cook County	324,247
Massachusetts	289,058	Bronx County, NY	297,629	**Bronx, NY** (borough) Bronx County	297,629
Maryland	248,485	Philadelphia County, PA	158,108	**Los Angeles, CA** (city) Los Angeles County	192,261
Texas	179,792	San Francisco County, CA	141,169	**Philadelphia, PA** (city) Philadelphia County	158,108
Washington	171,774	Hudson County, NJ	121,259	**San Francisco, CA** (city) San Francisco County	141,169
Virginia	164,107	Suffolk County, MA	112,626	**Boston, MA** (city) Suffolk County	101,584

Sorted by Number in Ascending Order — U.S. = 6,872,730

State	Number	County	Number	Place	Number
South Dakota	1,954	Alamosa County, CO	0	**Albertville*, AL** (city) Marshall County	0
North Dakota	2,003	Alfalfa County, OK	0	**Altus*, OK** (city) Jackson County	0
Vermont	3,140	Alleghany County, NC	0	**Big Spring, TX** (city) Howard County	0
Wyoming	3,842	Amite County, MS	0	**Bluffton*, SC** (town) Beaufort County	0
Maine	4,107	Anderson County, KS	0	**Burley*, ID** (city) Cassia County	0
Alaska	4,446	Antelope County, NE	0	**Dodge City, KS** (city) Ford County	0
Montana	4,722	Appomattox County, VA	0	**Florence, AZ** (town) Pinal County	0
Mississippi	4,913	Aransas County, TX	0	**Fort Campbell North*, KY** (cdp) Christian County	0
New Hampshire	5,050	Archer County, TX	0	**Georgetown, TX** (city) Williamson County	0
Arkansas	5,321	Armstrong County, TX	0	**Hobbs, NM** (city) Lea County	0

Sorted by Percent in Descending Order — U.S. = 4.9%

State	Percent	County	Percent	Place	Percent
District of Columbia	37.6	Kings County, NY	60.5	**Brooklyn, NY** (borough) Kings County	60.5
New York	26.5	New York County, NY	58.1	**Manhattan, NY** (borough) New York County	58.1
New Jersey	10.6	Bronx County, NY	57.4	**Bronx, NY** (borough) Bronx County	57.4
Massachusetts	9.1	Queens County, NY	51.0	**New York, NY** (city)	55.2
Illinois	8.7	Hudson County, NJ	38.7	**Queens, NY** (borough) Queens County	51.0
Maryland	8.7	San Francisco County, CA	32.6	**Jersey City, NJ** (city) Hudson County	45.9
Hawaii	6.0	Suffolk County, MA	31.7	**West New York, NJ** (town) Hudson County	39.5
Washington	5.6	Richmond County, NY	31.1	**Union City, NJ** (city) Hudson County	38.9
Pennsylvania	5.4	Arlington County, VA	27.4	**Boston, MA** (city) Suffolk County	32.9
California	5.1	Philadelphia County, PA	26.2	**San Francisco, CA** (city) San Francisco County	32.6

Sorted by Percent in Ascending Order — U.S. = 4.9%

State	Percent	County	Percent	Place	Percent
Arkansas	0.4	Alamosa County, CO	0.0	**Albertville*, AL** (city) Marshall County	0.0
Mississippi	0.4	Alfalfa County, OK	0.0	**Altus*, OK** (city) Jackson County	0.0
Alabama	0.5	Alleghany County, NC	0.0	**Big Spring, TX** (city) Howard County	0.0
Kansas	0.5	Amite County, MS	0.0	**Bluffton*, SC** (town) Beaufort County	0.0
Oklahoma	0.5	Anderson County, KS	0.0	**Burley*, ID** (city) Cassia County	0.0
South Dakota	0.5	Antelope County, NE	0.0	**Dickinson*, ND** (city) Stark County	0.0
Maine	0.6	Appomattox County, VA	0.0	**Dodge City, KS** (city) Ford County	0.0
North Dakota	0.6	Aransas County, TX	0.0	**Florence, AZ** (town) Pinal County	0.0
South Carolina	0.6	Archer County, TX	0.0	**Fort Campbell North*, KY** (cdp) Christian County	0.0
Nebraska	0.7	Armstrong County, TX	0.0	**Georgetown, TX** (city) Williamson County	0.0

RANKINGS & COMPARISONS

Note: (1) Ranking tables cover all states and counties, and places with an overall population of at least 125,000, OR an overall population of at least 25,000 where the Hispanic/Latino population is at least 20% of the overall population. In states where less than five places meet either of these criteria, we have included places with at least 10,000 total population with the highest percentage of Hispanic/Latino population. These places are identified with an asterisk (*); Please refer to the User's Guide for a full explanation of data.

Means of Transportation to Work: Public Transportation

(Universe: Civilian Employed Population 16 Years and Over)

Hispanic or Latino (of any race)

Top 10 States, Counties, and Places[1]

Sorted by Number in Descending Order — U.S. = 1,589,344

State	Number	County	Number	Place	Number
New York	619,743	Los Angeles County, CA	209,563	**New York, NY** (city)	566,320
California	364,353	Queens County, NY	171,290	**Queens, NY** (borough) Queens County	171,290
New Jersey	106,979	Bronx County, NY	156,329	**Bronx, NY** (borough) Bronx County	156,329
Illinois	82,573	Kings County, NY	122,814	**Los Angeles, CA** (city) Los Angeles County	139,486
Texas	68,121	New York County, NY	102,770	**Brooklyn, NY** (borough) Kings County	122,814
Florida	62,006	Cook County, IL	75,663	**Manhattan, NY** (borough) New York County	102,770
Massachusetts	37,272	Hudson County, NJ	42,332	**Chicago, IL** (city) Cook County	63,634
Maryland	29,662	Miami-Dade County, FL	34,844	**San Francisco, CA** (city) San Francisco County	23,773
Pennsylvania	24,353	Orange County, CA	28,212	**Houston, TX** (city) Harris County	18,986
Virginia	22,388	San Francisco County, CA	23,773	**Boston, MA** (city) Suffolk County	17,493

Sorted by Number in Ascending Order — U.S. = 1,589,344

State	Number	County	Number	Place	Number
South Dakota	23	Acadia Parish, LA	0	**Alamogordo, NM** (city) Otero County	0
Maine	33	Accomack County, VA	0	**Albertville*, AL** (city) Marshall County	0
North Dakota	60	Adams County, IN	0	**Altus*, OK** (city) Jackson County	0
Vermont	61	Adams County, NE	0	**Belvidere, IL** (city) Boone County	0
Mississippi	135	Adams County, PA	0	**Big Spring, TX** (city) Howard County	0
Montana	160	Adams County, WI	0	**Biloxi*, MS** (city) Harrison County	0
West Virginia	173	Addison County, VT	0	**Bluffton*, SC** (town) Beaufort County	0
Wyoming	178	Aiken County, SC	0	**Bozeman*, MT** (city) Gallatin County	0
New Hampshire	188	Alamance County, NC	0	**Burley*, ID** (city) Cassia County	0
Alabama	198	Alamosa County, CO	0	**Butte-Silver Bow*, MT** (consolidated govt) Silver Bow County	0

Sorted by Percent in Descending Order — U.S. = 8.0%

State	Percent	County	Percent	Place	Percent
District of Columbia	45.5	New York County, NY	64.3	**Manhattan, NY** (borough) New York County	64.3
New York	44.9	Kings County, NY	62.7	**Brooklyn, NY** (borough) Kings County	62.7
Massachusetts	16.1	Queens County, NY	59.8	**New York, NY** (city)	60.6
New Jersey	15.8	Bronx County, NY	59.7	**Queens, NY** (borough) Queens County	59.8
Maryland	13.6	Richmond County, NY	42.1	**Bronx, NY** (borough) Bronx County	59.7
Pennsylvania	10.3	San Francisco County, CA	38.3	**Revere, MA** (city) Suffolk County	43.4
Illinois	10.0	Suffolk County, MA	37.9	**Staten Island, NY** (borough) Richmond County	42.1
Connecticut	8.3	San Miguel County, CO	36.8	**Jersey City, NJ** (city) Hudson County	39.5
Virginia	7.7	Hudson County, NJ	34.3	**Boston, MA** (city) Suffolk County	39.1
Minnesota	7.0	DeSoto County, FL	33.4	**San Francisco, CA** (city) San Francisco County	38.3

Sorted by Percent in Ascending Order — U.S. = 8.0%

State	Percent	County	Percent	Place	Percent
Alabama	0.3	Acadia Parish, LA	0.0	**Alamogordo, NM** (city) Otero County	0.0
South Dakota	0.3	Accomack County, VA	0.0	**Albertville*, AL** (city) Marshall County	0.0
Arkansas	0.5	Adams County, IN	0.0	**Altus*, OK** (city) Jackson County	0.0
Maine	0.5	Adams County, NE	0.0	**Belvidere, IL** (city) Boone County	0.0
Mississippi	0.5	Adams County, PA	0.0	**Big Spring, TX** (city) Howard County	0.0
Kansas	0.6	Adams County, WI	0.0	**Biloxi*, MS** (city) Harrison County	0.0
South Carolina	0.6	Addison County, VT	0.0	**Bluffton*, SC** (town) Beaufort County	0.0
Oklahoma	0.7	Aiken County, SC	0.0	**Bozeman*, MT** (city) Gallatin County	0.0
Idaho	0.9	Alamance County, NC	0.0	**Burley*, ID** (city) Cassia County	0.0
Wyoming	0.9	Alamosa County, CO	0.0	**Butte-Silver Bow*, MT** (consolidated govt) Silver Bow County	0.0

Note: (1) Ranking tables cover all states and counties, and places with an overall population of at least 125,000, OR an overall population of at least 25,000 where the Hispanic/Latino population is at least 20% of the overall population. In states where less than five places meet either of these criteria, we have included places with at least 10,000 total population with the highest percentage of Hispanic/Latino population. These places are identified with an asterisk (*); Please refer to the User's Guide for a full explanation of data.

Means of Transportation to Work: Public Transportation

(Universe: Civilian Employed Population 16 Years and Over)

Central American, excluding Mexican

Top 10 States, Counties, and Places[1]

Sorted by Number in Descending Order — U.S. = 248,277

State	Number	County	Number	Place	Number
California	80,674	Los Angeles County, CA	59,746	**Los Angeles, CA** (city) Los Angeles County	49,746
New York	61,068	Kings County, NY	15,612	**New York, NY** (city)	49,267
Maryland	17,181	Queens County, NY	15,582	**Brooklyn, NY** (borough) Kings County	15,612
Florida	16,228	Miami-Dade County, FL	12,615	**Queens, NY** (borough) Queens County	15,582
New Jersey	15,478	Bronx County, NY	11,298	**Bronx, NY** (borough) Bronx County	11,298
Massachusetts	10,687	Montgomery County, MD	8,503	**San Francisco, CA** (city) San Francisco County	6,703
Virginia	10,301	Prince George's County, MD	7,320	**Miami, FL** (city) Miami-Dade County	6,547
Texas	8,571	Suffolk County, MA	6,984	**Houston, TX** (city) Harris County	5,672
District of Columbia	6,566	San Francisco County, CA	6,703	**Manhattan, NY** (borough) New York County	5,635
Illinois	3,541	Hudson County, NJ	6,474	**Hempstead (town), NY** (town) Nassau County	4,353

Sorted by Number in Ascending Order — U.S. = 248,277

State	Number	County	Number	Place	Number
Idaho	0	Alamance County, NC	0	**Alafaya, FL** (cdp) Orange County	0
Maine	0	Allen County, IN	0	**Albertville*, AL** (city) Marshall County	0
South Dakota	0	Beaufort County, SC	0	**Albuquerque, NM** (city) Bernalillo County	0
Vermont	0	Bell County, TX	0	**Allentown, PA** (city) Lehigh County	0
Wyoming	10	Benton County, AR	0	**Anchorage, AK** (municipality)	0
Alaska	12	Berks County, PA	0	**Arlington, TX** (city) Tarrant County	0
New Hampshire	12	Bernalillo County, NM	0	**Atascocita, TX** (cdp) Harris County	0
Mississippi	13	Brazoria County, TX	0	**Avondale, AZ** (city) Maricopa County	0
South Carolina	13	Brown County, WI	0	**Brandon, FL** (cdp) Hillsborough County	0
West Virginia	13	Burke County, NC	0	**Carrollton, TX** (city) Denton County	0

Sorted by Percent in Descending Order — U.S. = 12.5%

State	Percent	County	Percent	Place	Percent
District of Columbia	51.1	New York County, NY	72.2	**Manhattan, NY** (borough) New York County	72.2
New York	35.9	Bronx County, NY	67.3	**Bronx, NY** (borough) Bronx County	67.3
Massachusetts	21.7	Kings County, NY	67.0	**Brooklyn, NY** (borough) Kings County	67.0
New Jersey	17.2	Richmond County, NY	56.5	**New York, NY** (city)	63.5
Maryland	16.9	Queens County, NY	56.3	**Staten Island, NY** (borough) Richmond County	56.5
California	14.1	San Francisco County, CA	40.4	**Queens, NY** (borough) Queens County	56.3
Connecticut	11.5	Arlington County, VA	37.0	**Revere, MA** (city) Suffolk County	44.1
Illinois	11.1	Suffolk County, MA	36.7	**West New York, NJ** (town) Hudson County	40.5
Washington	10.2	Hudson County, NJ	34.2	**San Francisco, CA** (city) San Francisco County	40.4
Virginia	10.1	Essex County, NJ	27.6	**Boston, MA** (city) Suffolk County	38.3

Sorted by Percent in Ascending Order — U.S. = 12.5%

State	Percent	County	Percent	Place	Percent
Idaho	0.0	Alamance County, NC	0.0	**Alafaya, FL** (cdp) Orange County	0.0
Maine	0.0	Allen County, IN	0.0	**Albertville*, AL** (city) Marshall County	0.0
South Dakota	0.0	Beaufort County, SC	0.0	**Albuquerque, NM** (city) Bernalillo County	0.0
Vermont	0.0	Bell County, TX	0.0	**Allentown, PA** (city) Lehigh County	0.0
South Carolina	0.1	Benton County, AR	0.0	**Anchorage, AK** (municipality)	0.0
Arkansas	0.2	Berks County, PA	0.0	**Arlington, TX** (city) Tarrant County	0.0
Kansas	0.3	Bernalillo County, NM	0.0	**Atascocita, TX** (cdp) Harris County	0.0
Mississippi	0.4	Brazoria County, TX	0.0	**Avondale, AZ** (city) Maricopa County	0.0
Oklahoma	0.5	Brown County, WI	0.0	**Brandon, FL** (cdp) Hillsborough County	0.0
Alabama	0.6	Burke County, NC	0.0	**Carrollton, TX** (city) Denton County	0.0

Note: (1) Ranking tables cover all states and counties, and places with an overall population of at least 125,000, OR an overall population of at least 25,000 where the Hispanic/Latino population is at least 20% of the overall population. In states where less than five places meet either of these criteria, we have included places with at least 10,000 total population with the highest percentage of Hispanic/Latino population. These places are identified with an asterisk (*); Please refer to the User's Guide for a full explanation of data.

Means of Transportation to Work: Public Transportation

(Universe: Civilian Employed Population 16 Years and Over)

Central American: Costa Rican

Top 10 States, Counties, and Places[1]

Sorted by Number in Descending Order — U.S. = 5,006

State	Number	County	Number	Place	Number
New York	2,102	Kings County, NY	840	**New York, NY** (city)	2,008
New Jersey	895	Queens County, NY	600	**Brooklyn, NY** (borough) Kings County	840
California	533	Bronx County, NY	278	**Queens, NY** (borough) Queens County	600
Florida	377	Miami-Dade County, FL	256	**Bronx, NY** (borough) Bronx County	278
Massachusetts	280	Essex County, NJ	255	**Philadelphia, PA** (city) Philadelphia County	112
Colorado	131	Los Angeles County, CA	215	**Miami, FL** (city) Miami-Dade County	63
Pennsylvania	114	Bergen County, NJ	130	**Los Angeles, CA** (city) Los Angeles County	18
Washington	112	Union County, NJ	125		
Illinois	60	Mercer County, NJ	114		
Maryland	58	Philadelphia County, PA	112		

Sorted by Number in Ascending Order — U.S. = 5,006

State	Number	County	Number	Place	Number
Michigan	0	Clark County, NV	0	**Los Angeles, CA** (city) Los Angeles County	18
Nevada	0	Harris County, TX	0	**Miami, FL** (city) Miami-Dade County	63
Oregon	0	Hillsborough County, FL	0	**Philadelphia, PA** (city) Philadelphia County	112
South Carolina	0	Maricopa County, AZ	0	**Bronx, NY** (borough) Bronx County	278
Tennessee	0	Orange County, FL	0	**Queens, NY** (borough) Queens County	600
Wisconsin	0	Riverside County, CA	0	**Brooklyn, NY** (borough) Kings County	840
Minnesota	6	San Bernardino County, CA	0	**New York, NY** (city)	2,008
Connecticut	9	Fairfield County, CT	9		
North Carolina	11	San Diego County, CA	9		
Arizona	16	Orange County, CA	11		

Sorted by Percent in Descending Order — U.S. = 8.2%

State	Percent	County	Percent	Place	Percent
New York	42.2	Kings County, NY	77.6	**Brooklyn, NY** (borough) Kings County	77.6
Washington	22.1	Bronx County, NY	71.1	**New York, NY** (city)	71.4
Colorado	19.3	Queens County, NY	69.7	**Bronx, NY** (borough) Bronx County	71.1
Massachusetts	13.9	Essex County, NJ	24.0	**Queens, NY** (borough) Queens County	69.7
New Jersey	8.8	Philadelphia County, PA	22.2	**Philadelphia, PA** (city) Philadelphia County	22.2
Pennsylvania	6.5	Mercer County, NJ	15.3	**Miami, FL** (city) Miami-Dade County	9.0
Illinois	6.0	Bergen County, NJ	12.7	**Los Angeles, CA** (city) Los Angeles County	1.2
California	5.1	Contra Costa County, CA	12.3		
Louisiana	4.9	Passaic County, NJ	10.2		
Maryland	4.6	Nassau County, NY	9.0		

Sorted by Percent in Ascending Order — U.S. = 8.2%

State	Percent	County	Percent	Place	Percent
Michigan	0.0	Clark County, NV	0.0	**Los Angeles, CA** (city) Los Angeles County	1.2
Nevada	0.0	Harris County, TX	0.0	**Miami, FL** (city) Miami-Dade County	9.0
Oregon	0.0	Hillsborough County, FL	0.0	**Philadelphia, PA** (city) Philadelphia County	22.2
South Carolina	0.0	Maricopa County, AZ	0.0	**Queens, NY** (borough) Queens County	69.7
Tennessee	0.0	Orange County, FL	0.0	**Bronx, NY** (borough) Bronx County	71.1
Wisconsin	0.0	Riverside County, CA	0.0	**New York, NY** (city)	71.4
North Carolina	0.4	San Bernardino County, CA	0.0	**Brooklyn, NY** (borough) Kings County	77.6
Connecticut	0.8	Orange County, CA	1.0		
Minnesota	1.4	Fairfield County, CT	1.3		
Texas	1.4	Somerset County, NJ	1.7		

Note: (1) Ranking tables cover all states and counties, and places with an overall population of at least 125,000, OR an overall population of at least 25,000 where the Hispanic/Latino population is at least 20% of the overall population. In states where less than five places meet either of these criteria, we have included places with at least 10,000 total population with the highest percentage of Hispanic/Latino population. These places are identified with an asterisk (*); Please refer to the User's Guide for a full explanation of data.

Means of Transportation to Work: Public Transportation

(Universe: Civilian Employed Population 16 Years and Over)

Central American: Guatemalan

Top 10 States, Counties, and Places[1]

Sorted by Number in Descending Order — U.S. = 73,231

State	Number	County	Number	Place	Number
California	31,511	Los Angeles County, CA	25,789	**Los Angeles, CA** (city) Los Angeles County	22,504
New York	13,455	Queens County, NY	4,160	**New York, NY** (city)	10,068
New Jersey	5,209	Kings County, NY	2,680	**Queens, NY** (borough) Queens County	4,160
Maryland	3,421	Cook County, IL	2,171	**Brooklyn, NY** (borough) Kings County	2,680
Florida	2,980	Bronx County, NY	2,042	**Bronx, NY** (borough) Bronx County	2,042
Massachusetts	2,607	Prince George's County, MD	1,926	**Chicago, IL** (city) Cook County	2,000
Texas	2,494	Hudson County, NJ	1,804	**Houston, TX** (city) Harris County	1,630
Virginia	2,404	Harris County, TX	1,756	**San Francisco, CA** (city) San Francisco County	1,446
Illinois	2,270	Westchester County, NY	1,692	**Stamford, CT** (city/town) Fairfield County	1,012
Connecticut	1,232	Miami-Dade County, FL	1,678	**Manhattan, NY** (borough) New York County	996

Sorted by Number in Ascending Order — U.S. = 73,231

State	Number	County	Number	Place	Number
Arkansas	0	Burke County, NC	0	**Albertville*, AL** (city) Marshall County	0
Idaho	0	Caroline County, MD	0	**Chattanooga, TN** (city) Hamilton County	0
Kansas	0	Cherokee County, GA	0	**Columbus, OH** (city) Franklin County	0
Mississippi	0	Chesterfield County, VA	0	**Corona, CA** (city) Riverside County	0
South Dakota	0	Collin County, TX	0	**Cranston*, RI** (city) Providence County	0
Tennessee	0	Davidson County, TN	0	**Downey, CA** (city) Los Angeles County	0
Wisconsin	0	Dawson County, NE	0	**Durham, NC** (city) Durham County	0
New Hampshire	12	Douglas County, NE	0	**Fontana, CA** (city) San Bernardino County	0
South Carolina	13	Durham County, NC	0	**Fort Worth, TX** (city) Tarrant County	0
Delaware	18	Forsyth County, NC	0	**Grand Rapids, MI** (city) Kent County	0

Sorted by Percent in Descending Order — U.S. = 14.1%

State	Percent	County	Percent	Place	Percent
District of Columbia	48.2	Bronx County, NY	74.7	**Bronx, NY** (borough) Bronx County	74.7
New York	37.6	New York County, NY	66.8	**Yonkers, NY** (city) Westchester County	70.4
New Jersey	19.9	Kings County, NY	65.2	**Manhattan, NY** (borough) New York County	66.8
California	18.7	Queens County, NY	59.5	**Brooklyn, NY** (borough) Kings County	65.2
Maryland	16.9	Arlington County, VA	48.1	**New York, NY** (city)	64.3
Massachusetts	15.5	San Francisco County, CA	45.5	**Queens, NY** (borough) Queens County	59.5
Illinois	14.3	Bergen County, NJ	40.1	**Union City, NJ** (city) Hudson County	53.0
Virginia	14.3	Hudson County, NJ	38.0	**Arlington, VA** (cdp) Arlington County	48.1
Connecticut	14.1	Suffolk County, MA	33.1	**Silver Spring, MD** (cdp) Montgomery County	47.5
Kentucky	12.1	Norfolk County, MA	28.5	**West New York, NJ** (town) Hudson County	47.3

Sorted by Percent in Ascending Order — U.S. = 14.1%

State	Percent	County	Percent	Place	Percent
Arkansas	0.0	Burke County, NC	0.0	**Albertville*, AL** (city) Marshall County	0.0
Idaho	0.0	Caroline County, MD	0.0	**Chattanooga, TN** (city) Hamilton County	0.0
Kansas	0.0	Cherokee County, GA	0.0	**Columbus, OH** (city) Franklin County	0.0
Mississippi	0.0	Chesterfield County, VA	0.0	**Corona, CA** (city) Riverside County	0.0
South Dakota	0.0	Collin County, TX	0.0	**Cranston*, RI** (city) Providence County	0.0
Tennessee	0.0	Davidson County, TN	0.0	**Downey, CA** (city) Los Angeles County	0.0
Wisconsin	0.0	Dawson County, NE	0.0	**Durham, NC** (city) Durham County	0.0
South Carolina	0.3	Douglas County, NE	0.0	**Fontana, CA** (city) San Bernardino County	0.0
Alabama	0.6	Durham County, NC	0.0	**Fort Worth, TX** (city) Tarrant County	0.0
Oklahoma	0.6	Forsyth County, NC	0.0	**Grand Rapids, MI** (city) Kent County	0.0

Note: (1) Ranking tables cover all states and counties, and places with an overall population of at least 125,000, OR an overall population of at least 25,000 where the Hispanic/Latino population is at least 20% of the overall population. In states where less than five places meet either of these criteria, we have included places with at least 10,000 total population with the highest percentage of Hispanic/Latino population. These places are identified with an asterisk (*); Please refer to the User's Guide for a full explanation of data.

Means of Transportation to Work: Public Transportation

(Universe: Civilian Employed Population 16 Years and Over)

Central American: Honduran

Top 10 States, Counties, and Places[1]

Sorted by Number in Descending Order — U.S. = 42,849

State	Number	County	Number	Place	Number
New York	16,408	Bronx County, NY	5,725	**New York, NY** (city)	14,078
Florida	5,465	Miami-Dade County, FL	4,509	**Bronx, NY** (borough) Bronx County	5,725
California	5,427	Los Angeles County, CA	3,876	**Brooklyn, NY** (borough) Kings County	3,253
New Jersey	3,373	Kings County, NY	3,253	**Queens, NY** (borough) Queens County	3,132
Maryland	2,440	Queens County, NY	3,132	**Miami, FL** (city) Miami-Dade County	2,794
Virginia	2,042	Nassau County, NY	1,680	**Los Angeles, CA** (city) Los Angeles County	2,631
Texas	1,699	Hudson County, NJ	1,665	**Manhattan, NY** (borough) New York County	1,524
Massachusetts	1,261	New York County, NY	1,524	**Hempstead (town), NY** (town) Nassau County	1,425
Louisiana	758	Montgomery County, MD	1,509	**Houston, TX** (city) Harris County	1,024
District of Columbia	632	Harris County, TX	1,087	**Hempstead (village), NY** (village) Nassau County	873

Sorted by Number in Ascending Order — U.S. = 42,849

State	Number	County	Number	Place	Number
Arkansas	0	Beaufort County, SC	0	**Fort Worth, TX** (city) Tarrant County	0
Kansas	0	Clayton County, GA	0	**Garland, TX** (city) Dallas County	0
Michigan	0	Davidson County, TN	0	**Indianapolis, IN** (city) Marion County	0
Oklahoma	0	Duplin County, NC	0	**Miramar, FL** (city) Broward County	0
South Carolina	0	Fresno County, CA	0	**Nashville-Davidson, TN** (metropolitan govt) Davidson County	0
Utah	0	Galveston County, TX	0	**Newburgh, NY** (city) Orange County	0
Alabama	5	Hall County, GA	0	**Oklahoma City, OK** (city) Oklahoma County	0
Mississippi	13	Johnston County, NC	0	**Pasadena, TX** (city) Harris County	0
Kentucky	25	Loudoun County, VA	0	**Conroe, TX** (city) Montgomery County	11
Nebraska	25	Manatee County, FL	0	**Memphis, TN** (city) Shelby County	11

Sorted by Percent in Descending Order — U.S. = 14.0%

State	Percent	County	Percent	Place	Percent
District of Columbia	52.1	New York County, NY	80.6	**Manhattan, NY** (borough) New York County	80.6
New York	47.6	Bronx County, NY	68.9	**Bronx, NY** (borough) Bronx County	68.9
Washington	27.8	Queens County, NY	64.3	**New York, NY** (city)	67.0
Maryland	24.8	Kings County, NY	63.7	**Queens, NY** (borough) Queens County	64.3
Massachusetts	19.5	Richmond County, NY	53.2	**Brooklyn, NY** (borough) Kings County	63.7
New Jersey	18.5	King County, WA	44.7	**Wheaton, MD** (cdp) Montgomery County	58.8
Colorado	17.3	San Francisco County, CA	44.3	**Staten Island, NY** (borough) Richmond County	53.2
California	15.7	Montgomery County, MD	36.8	**San Francisco, CA** (city) San Francisco County	44.3
Virginia	13.6	Bergen County, NJ	35.9	**Jersey City, NJ** (city) Hudson County	38.7
Florida	9.5	Hudson County, NJ	34.1	**Hempstead (village), NY** (village) Nassau County	36.7

Sorted by Percent in Ascending Order — U.S. = 14.0%

State	Percent	County	Percent	Place	Percent
Arkansas	0.0	Beaufort County, SC	0.0	**Fort Worth, TX** (city) Tarrant County	0.0
Kansas	0.0	Clayton County, GA	0.0	**Garland, TX** (city) Dallas County	0.0
Michigan	0.0	Davidson County, TN	0.0	**Indianapolis, IN** (city) Marion County	0.0
Oklahoma	0.0	Duplin County, NC	0.0	**Miramar, FL** (city) Broward County	0.0
South Carolina	0.0	Fresno County, CA	0.0	**Nashville-Davidson, TN** (metropolitan govt) Davidson County	0.0
Utah	0.0	Galveston County, TX	0.0	**Newburgh, NY** (city) Orange County	0.0
Alabama	0.4	Hall County, GA	0.0	**Oklahoma City, OK** (city) Oklahoma County	0.0
Tennessee	0.6	Johnston County, NC	0.0	**Pasadena, TX** (city) Harris County	0.0
Indiana	1.2	Loudoun County, VA	0.0	**Memphis, TN** (city) Shelby County	0.9
Mississippi	1.2	Manatee County, FL	0.0	**Metairie, LA** (cdp) Jefferson Parish	1.2

Note: (1) Ranking tables cover all states and counties, and places with an overall population of at least 125,000, OR an overall population of at least 25,000 where the Hispanic/Latino population is at least 20% of the overall population. In states where less than five places meet either of these criteria, we have included places with at least 10,000 total population with the highest percentage of Hispanic/Latino population. These places are identified with an asterisk (*); Please refer to the User's Guide for a full explanation of data.

Means of Transportation to Work: Public Transportation

(Universe: Civilian Employed Population 16 Years and Over)

Central American: Nicaraguan

Top 10 States, Counties, and Places[1]

Sorted by Number in Descending Order — U.S. = 18,044

State	Number	County	Number	Place	Number
Florida	5,512	Miami-Dade County, FL	5,120	**New York, NY** (city)	3,296
California	5,369	Los Angeles County, CA	2,175	**Miami, FL** (city) Miami-Dade County	2,770
New York	3,628	San Francisco County, CA	1,288	**Los Angeles, CA** (city) Los Angeles County	1,598
Maryland	1,010	Queens County, NY	932	**San Francisco, CA** (city) San Francisco County	1,288
New Jersey	652	Kings County, NY	797	**Queens, NY** (borough) Queens County	932
Virginia	262	New York County, NY	786	**Brooklyn, NY** (borough) Kings County	797
Massachusetts	212	San Mateo County, CA	778	**Manhattan, NY** (borough) New York County	786
Texas	180	Bronx County, NY	745	**Bronx, NY** (borough) Bronx County	745
Washington	154	Montgomery County, MD	602	**Daly City, CA** (city) San Mateo County	432
Arizona	141	Contra Costa County, CA	458	**Fountainebleau, FL** (cdp) Miami-Dade County	296

Sorted by Number in Ascending Order — U.S. = 18,044

State	Number	County	Number	Place	Number
Indiana	0	Bexar County, TX	0	**Charlotte, NC** (city) Mecklenburg County	0
Michigan	0	Collier County, FL	0	**Jacksonville, FL** (city) Duval County	0
Missouri	0	Dallas County, TX	0	**Miami Gardens, FL** (city) Miami-Dade County	0
South Carolina	0	Duval County, FL	0	**Miramar, FL** (city) Broward County	0
Wisconsin	0	Gwinnett County, GA	0	**Pembroke Pines, FL** (city) Broward County	0
North Carolina	11	Hillsborough County, FL	0	**Sacramento, CA** (city) Sacramento County	0
Connecticut	14	Lee County, FL	0	**San Diego, CA** (city) San Diego County	0
Tennessee	17	Mecklenburg County, NC	0	**Hayward, CA** (city) Alameda County	10
Georgia	27	Orange County, FL	0	**Hollywood, FL** (city) Broward County	13
Pennsylvania	40	Prince William County, VA	0	**Country Club, FL** (cdp) Miami-Dade County	14

Sorted by Percent in Descending Order — U.S. = 10.3%

State	Percent	County	Percent	Place	Percent
New York	53.6	New York County, NY	79.7	**Manhattan, NY** (borough) New York County	79.7
Minnesota	24.7	Kings County, NY	73.3	**Brooklyn, NY** (borough) Kings County	73.3
Massachusetts	24.1	Queens County, NY	60.6	**New York, NY** (city)	64.0
Maryland	23.3	Bronx County, NY	50.4	**Queens, NY** (borough) Queens County	60.6
District of Columbia	19.7	San Francisco County, CA	39.6	**Bronx, NY** (borough) Bronx County	50.4
Oregon	18.0	King County, WA	36.7	**San Francisco, CA** (city) San Francisco County	39.6
Colorado	17.7	Hudson County, NJ	32.7	**South San Francisco, CA** (city) San Mateo County	22.2
Washington	17.5	Prince George's County, MD	27.8	**Daly City, CA** (city) San Mateo County	20.5
New Jersey	15.6	Montgomery County, MD	26.2	**Los Angeles, CA** (city) Los Angeles County	19.1
Arizona	12.8	San Mateo County, CA	15.8	**Miami, FL** (city) Miami-Dade County	17.7

Sorted by Percent in Ascending Order — U.S. = 10.3%

State	Percent	County	Percent	Place	Percent
Indiana	0.0	Bexar County, TX	0.0	**Charlotte, NC** (city) Mecklenburg County	0.0
Michigan	0.0	Collier County, FL	0.0	**Jacksonville, FL** (city) Duval County	0.0
Missouri	0.0	Dallas County, TX	0.0	**Miami Gardens, FL** (city) Miami-Dade County	0.0
South Carolina	0.0	Duval County, FL	0.0	**Miramar, FL** (city) Broward County	0.0
Wisconsin	0.0	Gwinnett County, GA	0.0	**Pembroke Pines, FL** (city) Broward County	0.0
North Carolina	0.5	Hillsborough County, FL	0.0	**Sacramento, CA** (city) Sacramento County	0.0
Louisiana	1.0	Lee County, FL	0.0	**San Diego, CA** (city) San Diego County	0.0
Georgia	1.7	Mecklenburg County, NC	0.0	**Hayward, CA** (city) Alameda County	1.3
Texas	2.0	Orange County, FL	0.0	**Country Club, FL** (cdp) Miami-Dade County	1.4
Pennsylvania	3.1	Prince William County, VA	0.0	**Richmond West, FL** (cdp) Miami-Dade County	1.5

Note: (1) Ranking tables cover all states and counties, and places with an overall population of at least 125,000, OR an overall population of at least 25,000 where the Hispanic/Latino population is at least 20% of the overall population. In states where less than five places meet either of these criteria, we have included places with at least 10,000 total population with the highest percentage of Hispanic/Latino population. These places are identified with an asterisk (*); Please refer to the User's Guide for a full explanation of data.

Means of Transportation to Work: Public Transportation

(Universe: Civilian Employed Population 16 Years and Over)

Central American: Panamanian

Top 10 States, Counties, and Places[1]

Sorted by Number in Descending Order — U.S. = 11,417

State	Number	County	Number	Place	Number
New York	8,036	Kings County, NY	4,890	**New York, NY** (city)	7,511
California	717	Queens County, NY	977	**Brooklyn, NY** (borough) Kings County	4,890
New Jersey	589	New York County, NY	793	**Queens, NY** (borough) Queens County	977
Florida	362	Bronx County, NY	690	**Manhattan, NY** (borough) New York County	793
Massachusetts	362	Los Angeles County, CA	299	**Bronx, NY** (borough) Bronx County	690
Virginia	258	Essex County, NJ	226	**Hempstead (town), NY** (town) Nassau County	153
Pennsylvania	209	Hudson County, NJ	177	**Los Angeles, CA** (city) Los Angeles County	122
Maryland	207	Prince George's County, MD	156	**Miami, FL** (city) Miami-Dade County	35
Georgia	116	Nassau County, NY	153	**Houston, TX** (city) Harris County	7
Illinois	65	Miami-Dade County, FL	133	**Fayetteville, NC** (city) Cumberland County	0

Sorted by Number in Ascending Order — U.S. = 11,417

State	Number	County	Number	Place	Number
Alabama	0	Bell County, TX	0	**Fayetteville, NC** (city) Cumberland County	0
Indiana	0	Bexar County, TX	0	**Jacksonville, FL** (city) Duval County	0
Louisiana	0	Cumberland County, NC	0	**Killeen, TX** (city) Bell County	0
Mississippi	0	Duval County, FL	0	**San Antonio, TX** (city) Bexar County	0
New Mexico	0	Hillsborough County, FL	0	**San Diego, CA** (city) San Diego County	0
North Carolina	0	Pierce County, WA	0	**Houston, TX** (city) Harris County	7
Oklahoma	0	Sacramento County, CA	0	**Miami, FL** (city) Miami-Dade County	35
South Carolina	0	Palm Beach County, FL	1	**Los Angeles, CA** (city) Los Angeles County	122
Wisconsin	0	Clark County, NV	5	**Hempstead (town), NY** (town) Nassau County	153
Missouri	8	Harris County, TX	7	**Bronx, NY** (borough) Bronx County	690

Sorted by Percent in Descending Order — U.S. = 14.8%

State	Percent	County	Percent	Place	Percent
New York	56.2	Kings County, NY	72.3	**Brooklyn, NY** (borough) Kings County	72.3
Massachusetts	21.2	New York County, NY	67.9	**Manhattan, NY** (borough) New York County	67.9
New Jersey	20.8	Bronx County, NY	62.8	**New York, NY** (city)	66.9
Pennsylvania	14.6	Queens County, NY	49.9	**Bronx, NY** (borough) Bronx County	62.8
California	8.7	Hudson County, NJ	47.7	**Queens, NY** (borough) Queens County	49.9
Maryland	8.5	Essex County, NJ	39.9	**Hempstead (town), NY** (town) Nassau County	20.1
Virginia	6.8	Fairfax County, VA	23.0	**Los Angeles, CA** (city) Los Angeles County	14.0
Connecticut	5.0	Prince George's County, MD	21.5	**Miami, FL** (city) Miami-Dade County	7.6
Illinois	5.0	Nassau County, NY	20.1	**Houston, TX** (city) Harris County	1.5
Kentucky	4.6	Orange County, CA	19.2	**Fayetteville, NC** (city) Cumberland County	0.0

Sorted by Percent in Ascending Order — U.S. = 14.8%

State	Percent	County	Percent	Place	Percent
Alabama	0.0	Bell County, TX	0.0	**Fayetteville, NC** (city) Cumberland County	0.0
Indiana	0.0	Bexar County, TX	0.0	**Jacksonville, FL** (city) Duval County	0.0
Louisiana	0.0	Cumberland County, NC	0.0	**Killeen, TX** (city) Bell County	0.0
Mississippi	0.0	Duval County, FL	0.0	**San Antonio, TX** (city) Bexar County	0.0
New Mexico	0.0	Hillsborough County, FL	0.0	**San Diego, CA** (city) San Diego County	0.0
North Carolina	0.0	Pierce County, WA	0.0	**Houston, TX** (city) Harris County	1.5
Oklahoma	0.0	Sacramento County, CA	0.0	**Miami, FL** (city) Miami-Dade County	7.6
South Carolina	0.0	Palm Beach County, FL	0.2	**Los Angeles, CA** (city) Los Angeles County	14.0
Wisconsin	0.0	Clark County, NV	0.8	**Hempstead (town), NY** (town) Nassau County	20.1
Ohio	0.9	Harris County, TX	0.9	**Queens, NY** (borough) Queens County	49.9

Note: (1) Ranking tables cover all states and counties, and places with an overall population of at least 125,000, OR an overall population of at least 25,000 where the Hispanic/Latino population is at least 20% of the overall population. In states where less than five places meet either of these criteria, we have included places with at least 10,000 total population with the highest percentage of Hispanic/Latino population. These places are identified with an asterisk (*); Please refer to the User's Guide for a full explanation of data.

Means of Transportation to Work: Public Transportation

(Universe: Civilian Employed Population 16 Years and Over)

Central American: Salvadoran

Top 10 States, Counties, and Places[1]

Sorted by Number in Descending Order — U.S. = 93,589

State	Number	County	Number	Place	Number
California	35,329	Los Angeles County, CA	26,118	**Los Angeles, CA** (city) Los Angeles County	21,876
New York	16,274	Queens County, NY	5,571	**New York, NY** (city)	11,265
Maryland	9,883	Montgomery County, MD	4,960	**Queens, NY** (borough) Queens County	5,571
Massachusetts	5,581	Prince George's County, MD	4,336	**Houston, TX** (city) Harris County	2,862
Virginia	5,236	Suffolk County, MA	4,044	**Brooklyn, NY** (borough) Kings County	2,851
District of Columbia	5,135	Nassau County, NY	3,351	**San Francisco, CA** (city) San Francisco County	2,796
New Jersey	4,578	Harris County, TX	3,155	**Boston, MA** (city) Suffolk County	2,386
Texas	4,053	Kings County, NY	2,851	**Hempstead (town), NY** (town) Nassau County	2,275
Florida	1,497	San Francisco County, CA	2,796	**Bronx, NY** (borough) Bronx County	1,676
Nevada	1,175	Hudson County, NJ	2,394	**Wheaton, MD** (cdp) Montgomery County	1,184

Sorted by Number in Ascending Order — U.S. = 93,589

State	Number	County	Number	Place	Number
Alabama	0	Alamance County, NC	0	**Arlington, TX** (city) Tarrant County	0
Idaho	0	Benton County, AR	0	**Carrollton, TX** (city) Denton County	0
Iowa	0	Brazoria County, TX	0	**Des Moines, IA** (city) Polk County	0
Missouri	0	Buncombe County, NC	0	**East Palo Alto, CA** (city) San Mateo County	0
New Mexico	0	Cache County, UT	0	**Fort Worth, TX** (city) Tarrant County	0
Oklahoma	0	Chesterfield County, VA	0	**Gainesville, GA** (city) Hall County	0
South Carolina	0	Crawford County, AR	0	**Grand Prairie, TX** (city) Dallas County	0
Wisconsin	6	Dakota County, MN	0	**Greensboro, NC** (city) Guilford County	0
Kentucky	8	El Paso County, CO	0	**Indianapolis, IN** (city) Marion County	0
Alaska	12	Forsyth County, NC	0	**La Puente, CA** (city) Los Angeles County	0

Sorted by Percent in Descending Order — U.S. = 11.5%

State	Percent	County	Percent	Place	Percent
District of Columbia	53.8	Bronx County, NY	65.7	**Bronx, NY** (borough) Bronx County	65.7
Massachusetts	27.7	New York County, NY	64.7	**Manhattan, NY** (borough) New York County	64.7
New York	22.9	Kings County, NY	60.1	**Brooklyn, NY** (borough) Kings County	60.1
New Jersey	16.5	Queens County, NY	49.9	**New York, NY** (city)	55.5
Maryland	15.9	Suffolk County, MA	39.4	**Queens, NY** (borough) Queens County	49.9
Connecticut	13.0	San Francisco County, CA	36.5	**Jersey City, NJ** (city) Hudson County	46.6
California	12.2	Hudson County, NJ	32.9	**Boston, MA** (city) Suffolk County	43.4
Pennsylvania	10.6	Arlington County, VA	31.2	**San Francisco, CA** (city) San Francisco County	36.5
Oregon	10.3	Multnomah County, OR	26.3	**West New York, NJ** (town) Hudson County	35.4
Virginia	8.7	Middlesex County, MA	24.4	**Chelsea, MA** (city) Suffolk County	35.2

Sorted by Percent in Ascending Order — U.S. = 11.5%

State	Percent	County	Percent	Place	Percent
Alabama	0.0	Alamance County, NC	0.0	**Arlington, TX** (city) Tarrant County	0.0
Idaho	0.0	Benton County, AR	0.0	**Carrollton, TX** (city) Denton County	0.0
Iowa	0.0	Brazoria County, TX	0.0	**Des Moines, IA** (city) Polk County	0.0
Missouri	0.0	Buncombe County, NC	0.0	**East Palo Alto, CA** (city) San Mateo County	0.0
New Mexico	0.0	Cache County, UT	0.0	**Fort Worth, TX** (city) Tarrant County	0.0
Oklahoma	0.0	Chesterfield County, VA	0.0	**Gainesville, GA** (city) Hall County	0.0
South Carolina	0.0	Crawford County, AR	0.0	**Grand Prairie, TX** (city) Dallas County	0.0
Arkansas	0.3	Dakota County, MN	0.0	**Greensboro, NC** (city) Guilford County	0.0
Kansas	0.5	El Paso County, CO	0.0	**Indianapolis, IN** (city) Marion County	0.0
Kentucky	0.8	Forsyth County, NC	0.0	**La Puente, CA** (city) Los Angeles County	0.0

Note: (1) Ranking tables cover all states and counties, and places with an overall population of at least 125,000, OR an overall population of at least 25,000 where the Hispanic/Latino population is at least 20% of the overall population. In states where less than five places meet either of these criteria, we have included places with at least 10,000 total population with the highest percentage of Hispanic/Latino population. These places are identified with an asterisk (*); Please refer to the User's Guide for a full explanation of data.

Means of Transportation to Work: Public Transportation

(Universe: Civilian Employed Population 16 Years and Over)

Cuban

Top 10 States, Counties, and Places[1]

Sorted by Number in Descending Order — U.S. = 32,279

State	Number	County	Number	Place	Number
New York	10,189	Miami-Dade County, FL	7,943	**New York, NY** (city)	8,988
Florida	9,559	New York County, NY	2,814	**Manhattan, NY** (borough) New York County	2,814
New Jersey	4,865	Queens County, NY	2,687	**Queens, NY** (borough) Queens County	2,687
California	1,798	Hudson County, NJ	2,465	**Miami, FL** (city) Miami-Dade County	2,604
Illinois	933	Kings County, NY	2,078	**Brooklyn, NY** (borough) Kings County	2,078
Massachusetts	664	Bronx County, NY	1,097	**Hialeah, FL** (city) Miami-Dade County	1,397
Pennsylvania	498	Bergen County, NJ	1,052	**Bronx, NY** (borough) Bronx County	1,097
Maryland	478	Los Angeles County, CA	797	**Union City, NJ** (city) Hudson County	844
Texas	464	Cook County, IL	796	**Chicago, IL** (city) Cook County	706
District of Columbia	405	San Francisco County, CA	527	**San Francisco, CA** (city) San Francisco County	527

Sorted by Number in Ascending Order — U.S. = 32,279

State	Number	County	Number	Place	Number
Arkansas	0	Alachua County, FL	0	**Alafaya, FL** (cdp) Orange County	0
Hawaii	0	Brevard County, FL	0	**Brandon, FL** (cdp) Hillsborough County	0
Maine	0	Charlotte County, FL	0	**Burbank, CA** (city) Los Angeles County	0
Michigan	0	Citrus County, FL	0	**Cape Coral, FL** (city) Lee County	0
Mississippi	0	Clay County, FL	0	**Carrollwood, FL** (cdp) Hillsborough County	0
Oklahoma	0	Collin County, TX	0	**Coconut Creek, FL** (city) Broward County	0
South Carolina	0	Davidson County, TN	0	**Columbus, OH** (city) Franklin County	0
Tennessee	0	Denton County, TX	0	**Cooper City, FL** (city) Broward County	0
West Virginia	0	DuPage County, IL	0	**Coral Springs, FL** (city) Broward County	0
Alabama	2	East Baton Rouge Parish, LA	0	**Deltona, FL** (city) Volusia County	0

Sorted by Percent in Descending Order — U.S. = 4.2%

State	Percent	County	Percent	Place	Percent
District of Columbia	41.2	Kings County, NY	59.9	**Brooklyn, NY** (borough) Kings County	59.9
New York	33.8	New York County, NY	56.7	**Manhattan, NY** (borough) New York County	56.7
Massachusetts	14.5	Queens County, NY	50.7	**New York, NY** (city)	52.7
New Jersey	12.8	San Francisco County, CA	47.9	**Queens, NY** (borough) Queens County	50.7
Maryland	10.9	Bronx County, NY	44.2	**San Francisco, CA** (city) San Francisco County	47.9
Illinois	10.3	Richmond County, NY	37.2	**Bronx, NY** (borough) Bronx County	44.2
Wisconsin	8.9	Suffolk County, MA	34.0	**Jersey City, NJ** (city) Hudson County	39.6
Minnesota	8.2	Philadelphia County, PA	22.8	**Staten Island, NY** (borough) Richmond County	37.2
Pennsylvania	7.4	Prince George's County, MD	21.7	**Boston, MA** (city) Suffolk County	30.8
Washington	6.0	Westchester County, NY	20.8	**Yonkers, NY** (city) Westchester County	25.8

Sorted by Percent in Ascending Order — U.S. = 4.2%

State	Percent	County	Percent	Place	Percent
Arkansas	0.0	Alachua County, FL	0.0	**Alafaya, FL** (cdp) Orange County	0.0
Hawaii	0.0	Brevard County, FL	0.0	**Brandon, FL** (cdp) Hillsborough County	0.0
Maine	0.0	Charlotte County, FL	0.0	**Burbank, CA** (city) Los Angeles County	0.0
Michigan	0.0	Citrus County, FL	0.0	**Cape Coral, FL** (city) Lee County	0.0
Mississippi	0.0	Clay County, FL	0.0	**Carrollwood, FL** (cdp) Hillsborough County	0.0
Oklahoma	0.0	Collin County, TX	0.0	**Coconut Creek, FL** (city) Broward County	0.0
South Carolina	0.0	Davidson County, TN	0.0	**Columbus, OH** (city) Franklin County	0.0
Tennessee	0.0	Denton County, TX	0.0	**Cooper City, FL** (city) Broward County	0.0
West Virginia	0.0	DuPage County, IL	0.0	**Coral Springs, FL** (city) Broward County	0.0
Alabama	0.1	East Baton Rouge Parish, LA	0.0	**Deltona, FL** (city) Volusia County	0.0

Note: (1) Ranking tables cover all states and counties, and places with an overall population of at least 125,000, OR an overall population of at least 25,000 where the Hispanic/Latino population is at least 20% of the overall population. In states where less than five places meet either of these criteria, we have included places with at least 10,000 total population with the highest percentage of Hispanic/Latino population. These places are identified with an asterisk (*); Please refer to the User's Guide for a full explanation of data.

Means of Transportation to Work: Public Transportation

(Universe: Civilian Employed Population 16 Years and Over)

Dominican Republic

Top 10 States, Counties, and Places[1]

Sorted by Number in Descending Order — U.S. = 165,574

State	Number	County	Number	Place	Number
New York	138,155	Bronx County, NY	52,459	**New York, NY** (city)	132,556
New Jersey	13,367	New York County, NY	39,192	**Bronx, NY** (borough) Bronx County	52,459
Massachusetts	5,563	Queens County, NY	20,289	**Manhattan, NY** (borough) New York County	39,192
Florida	2,292	Kings County, NY	20,156	**Queens, NY** (borough) Queens County	20,289
Pennsylvania	1,671	Hudson County, NJ	5,815	**Brooklyn, NY** (borough) Kings County	20,156
Maryland	807	Suffolk County, MA	3,833	**Boston, MA** (city) Suffolk County	3,650
Connecticut	651	Westchester County, NY	2,408	**Jersey City, NJ** (city) Hudson County	1,916
District of Columbia	632	Bergen County, NJ	1,763	**Yonkers, NY** (city) Westchester County	1,770
Rhode Island	476	Passaic County, NJ	1,674	**Union City, NJ** (city) Hudson County	1,435
California	460	Nassau County, NY	1,627	**Hempstead (town), NY** (town) Nassau County	1,317

Sorted by Number in Ascending Order — U.S. = 165,574

State	Number	County	Number	Place	Number
Delaware	0	Bexar County, TX	0	**Alafaya, FL** (cdp) Orange County	0
Indiana	0	Brevard County, FL	0	**Cape Coral, FL** (city) Lee County	0
Michigan	0	Burlington County, NJ	0	**Coral Springs, FL** (city) Broward County	0
Missouri	0	Collier County, FL	0	**Deltona, FL** (city) Volusia County	0
New Hampshire	0	Fulton County, GA	0	**Doral, FL** (city) Miami-Dade County	0
Tennessee	0	Hillsborough County, NH	0	**Grand Rapids, MI** (city) Kent County	0
Utah	0	Kent County, MI	0	**Homestead, FL** (city) Miami-Dade County	0
Alabama	5	Lee County, FL	0	**Kendale Lakes, FL** (cdp) Miami-Dade County	0
South Carolina	9	Litchfield County, CT	0	**Kendall West, FL** (cdp) Miami-Dade County	0
Alaska	16	Marion County, FL	0	**Miramar, FL** (city) Broward County	0

Sorted by Percent in Descending Order — U.S. = 29.4%

State	Percent	County	Percent	Place	Percent
New York	51.1	New York County, NY	62.1	**Manhattan, NY** (borough) New York County	62.1
District of Columbia	49.2	Kings County, NY	60.7	**Brooklyn, NY** (borough) Kings County	60.7
New Jersey	16.4	Bronx County, NY	57.9	**New York, NY** (city)	58.1
Louisiana	15.7	Queens County, NY	50.9	**Bronx, NY** (borough) Bronx County	57.9
Illinois	14.6	Richmond County, NY	36.3	**Queens, NY** (borough) Queens County	50.9
Maryland	14.1	Suffolk County, MA	35.3	**Staten Island, NY** (borough) Richmond County	36.3
Massachusetts	13.5	Jefferson Parish, LA	33.1	**Jersey City, NJ** (city) Hudson County	35.7
Minnesota	12.3	Hudson County, NJ	32.0	**Boston, MA** (city) Suffolk County	35.2
California	10.4	Norfolk County, MA	25.9	**Union City, NJ** (city) Hudson County	34.6
Washington	10.1	Essex County, NJ	23.6	**Bayonne, NJ** (city) Hudson County	33.4

Sorted by Percent in Ascending Order — U.S. = 29.4%

State	Percent	County	Percent	Place	Percent
Delaware	0.0	Bexar County, TX	0.0	**Alafaya, FL** (cdp) Orange County	0.0
Indiana	0.0	Brevard County, FL	0.0	**Cape Coral, FL** (city) Lee County	0.0
Michigan	0.0	Burlington County, NJ	0.0	**Coral Springs, FL** (city) Broward County	0.0
Missouri	0.0	Collier County, FL	0.0	**Deltona, FL** (city) Volusia County	0.0
New Hampshire	0.0	Fulton County, GA	0.0	**Doral, FL** (city) Miami-Dade County	0.0
Tennessee	0.0	Hillsborough County, NH	0.0	**Grand Rapids, MI** (city) Kent County	0.0
Utah	0.0	Kent County, MI	0.0	**Homestead, FL** (city) Miami-Dade County	0.0
South Carolina	1.2	Lee County, FL	0.0	**Kendale Lakes, FL** (cdp) Miami-Dade County	0.0
Alabama	1.4	Litchfield County, CT	0.0	**Kendall West, FL** (cdp) Miami-Dade County	0.0
Nevada	1.5	Marion County, FL	0.0	**Miramar, FL** (city) Broward County	0.0

Note: (1) Ranking tables cover all states and counties, and places with an overall population of at least 125,000, OR an overall population of at least 25,000 where the Hispanic/Latino population is at least 20% of the overall population. In states where less than five places meet either of these criteria, we have included places with at least 10,000 total population with the highest percentage of Hispanic/Latino population. These places are identified with an asterisk (*); Please refer to the User's Guide for a full explanation of data.

Means of Transportation to Work: Public Transportation

(Universe: Civilian Employed Population 16 Years and Over)

Mexican

Top 10 States, Counties, and Places[1]

Sorted by Number in Descending Order — U.S. = 625,271

State	Number	County	Number	Place	Number
California	257,943	Los Angeles County, CA	139,616	**New York, NY** (city)	96,792
New York	105,149	Cook County, IL	53,412	**Los Angeles, CA** (city) Los Angeles County	83,927
Illinois	58,514	Queens County, NY	30,390	**Chicago, IL** (city) Cook County	43,929
Texas	52,628	Kings County, NY	26,499	**Queens, NY** (borough) Queens County	30,390
Arizona	18,231	Orange County, CA	25,301	**Brooklyn, NY** (borough) Kings County	26,499
New Jersey	17,055	Bronx County, NY	22,432	**Bronx, NY** (borough) Bronx County	22,432
Colorado	15,443	San Diego County, CA	18,287	**Manhattan, NY** (borough) New York County	14,321
Florida	13,724	New York County, NY	14,321	**San Francisco, CA** (city) San Francisco County	12,573
Nevada	11,057	Harris County, TX	13,951	**Houston, TX** (city) Harris County	11,923
Washington	10,184	Maricopa County, AZ	13,059	**San Antonio, TX** (city) Bexar County	11,351

Sorted by Number in Ascending Order — U.S. = 625,271

State	Number	County	Number	Place	Number
Maine	6	Accomack County, VA	0	**Alamogordo, NM** (city) Otero County	0
Vermont	16	Adams County, IN	0	**Albertville*, AL** (city) Marshall County	0
South Dakota	23	Adams County, NE	0	**Altus*, OK** (city) Jackson County	0
West Virginia	30	Adams County, PA	0	**Belvidere, IL** (city) Boone County	0
North Dakota	42	Adams County, WI	0	**Big Spring, TX** (city) Howard County	0
Alabama	50	Aiken County, SC	0	**Biloxi*, MS** (city) Harrison County	0
Alaska	96	Alamance County, NC	0	**Bluffton*, SC** (town) Beaufort County	0
New Hampshire	104	Alamosa County, CO	0	**Brandon, FL** (cdp) Hillsborough County	0
Wyoming	111	Albemarle County, VA	0	**Burley*, ID** (city) Cassia County	0
Mississippi	119	Alexander County, NC	0	**Camarillo, CA** (city) Ventura County	0

Sorted by Percent in Descending Order — U.S. = 5.1%

State	Percent	County	Percent	Place	Percent
New York	54.8	Queens County, NY	77.2	**Queens, NY** (borough) Queens County	77.2
District of Columbia	37.1	Bronx County, NY	74.4	**Bronx, NY** (borough) Bronx County	74.4
Massachusetts	20.2	New York County, NY	68.8	**New York, NY** (city)	71.8
New Jersey	17.8	Kings County, NY	67.2	**Manhattan, NY** (borough) New York County	68.8
Connecticut	13.4	Richmond County, NY	61.7	**Brooklyn, NY** (borough) Kings County	67.2
Maryland	11.0	Hudson County, NJ	47.0	**Staten Island, NY** (borough) Richmond County	61.7
Illinois	9.0	Suffolk County, MA	40.4	**West New York, NJ** (town) Hudson County	60.9
Pennsylvania	8.6	San Francisco County, CA	37.7	**Yonkers, NY** (city) Westchester County	49.8
Delaware	8.0	DeSoto County, FL	37.6	**Jersey City, NJ** (city) Hudson County	49.0
Rhode Island	6.1	Arlington County, VA	33.1	**Union City, NJ** (city) Hudson County	45.5

Sorted by Percent in Ascending Order — U.S. = 5.1%

State	Percent	County	Percent	Place	Percent
Alabama	0.1	Accomack County, VA	0.0	**Alamogordo, NM** (city) Otero County	0.0
Maine	0.3	Adams County, IN	0.0	**Albertville*, AL** (city) Marshall County	0.0
South Dakota	0.4	Adams County, NE	0.0	**Altus*, OK** (city) Jackson County	0.0
Arkansas	0.5	Adams County, PA	0.0	**Belvidere, IL** (city) Boone County	0.0
Mississippi	0.6	Adams County, WI	0.0	**Big Spring, TX** (city) Howard County	0.0
Oklahoma	0.6	Aiken County, SC	0.0	**Biloxi*, MS** (city) Harrison County	0.0
Kansas	0.7	Alamance County, NC	0.0	**Bluffton*, SC** (town) Beaufort County	0.0
South Carolina	0.7	Alamosa County, CO	0.0	**Brandon, FL** (cdp) Hillsborough County	0.0
Wyoming	0.8	Albemarle County, VA	0.0	**Burley*, ID** (city) Cassia County	0.0
Idaho	0.9	Alexander County, NC	0.0	**Camarillo, CA** (city) Ventura County	0.0

Note: (1) Ranking tables cover all states and counties, and places with an overall population of at least 125,000, OR an overall population of at least 25,000 where the Hispanic/Latino population is at least 20% of the overall population. In states where less than five places meet either of these criteria, we have included places with at least 10,000 total population with the highest percentage of Hispanic/Latino population. These places are identified with an asterisk (*); Please refer to the User's Guide for a full explanation of data.

Means of Transportation to Work: Public Transportation

(Universe: Civilian Employed Population 16 Years and Over)

Puerto Rican

Top 10 States, Counties, and Places[1]

Sorted by Number in Descending Order — U.S. = 243,076

State	Number	County	Number	Place	Number
New York	157,980	Bronx County, NY	53,480	**New York, NY** (city)	144,786
New Jersey	21,714	Kings County, NY	37,387	**Bronx, NY** (borough) Bronx County	53,480
Pennsylvania	12,925	Queens County, NY	25,067	**Brooklyn, NY** (borough) Kings County	37,387
Illinois	10,531	New York County, NY	23,306	**Queens, NY** (borough) Queens County	25,067
Massachusetts	7,951	Cook County, IL	9,895	**Manhattan, NY** (borough) New York County	23,306
Florida	7,290	Philadelphia County, PA	8,331	**Chicago, IL** (city) Cook County	8,770
Connecticut	6,530	Hudson County, NJ	7,407	**Philadelphia, PA** (city) Philadelphia County	8,331
California	4,192	Richmond County, NY	5,546	**Staten Island, NY** (borough) Richmond County	5,546
Virginia	2,316	Westchester County, NY	4,183	**Jersey City, NJ** (city) Hudson County	3,770
Maryland	1,782	Essex County, NJ	3,840	**Boston, MA** (city) Suffolk County	3,428

Sorted by Number in Ascending Order — U.S. = 243,076

State	Number	County	Number	Place	Number
Kansas	0	Adams County, PA	0	**Alafaya, FL** (cdp) Orange County	0
Montana	0	Allen County, IN	0	**Albuquerque, NM** (city) Bernalillo County	0
Nebraska	0	Ashtabula County, OH	0	**Arlington, TX** (city) Tarrant County	0
North Dakota	0	Barnstable County, MA	0	**Brandon, FL** (cdp) Hillsborough County	0
South Dakota	0	Bay County, FL	0	**Carrollwood, FL** (cdp) Hillsborough County	0
Mississippi	3	Beaufort County, SC	0	**Central Falls*, RI** (city) Providence County	0
Arkansas	5	Bell County, TX	0	**Central Islip, NY** (cdp) Suffolk County	0
Alabama	13	Berkeley County, SC	0	**Chesapeake, VA** (independent city)	0
Idaho	17	Bernalillo County, NM	0	**Coconut Creek, FL** (city) Broward County	0
Oklahoma	17	Berrien County, MI	0	**Cooper City, FL** (city) Broward County	0

Sorted by Percent in Descending Order — U.S. = 14.5%

State	Percent	County	Percent	Place	Percent
New York	41.0	New York County, NY	64.9	**Manhattan, NY** (borough) New York County	64.9
District of Columbia	37.6	Kings County, NY	59.2	**Brooklyn, NY** (borough) Kings County	59.2
Illinois	15.2	Bronx County, NY	55.4	**New York, NY** (city)	56.2
New Jersey	12.9	Queens County, NY	53.4	**Bronx, NY** (borough) Bronx County	55.4
Pennsylvania	12.1	Arlington County, VA	39.7	**Queens, NY** (borough) Queens County	53.4
Massachusetts	10.3	Richmond County, NY	36.4	**Atlantic City, NJ** (city) Atlantic County	44.9
Oregon	9.7	San Francisco County, CA	35.9	**West New York, NJ** (town) Hudson County	43.1
Maryland	9.4	Hudson County, NJ	33.5	**Hackensack, NJ** (city) Bergen County	41.5
Wyoming	7.6	Suffolk County, MA	31.7	**Arlington, VA** (cdp) Arlington County	39.7
Connecticut	7.4	Tompkins County, NY	30.3	**Union City, NJ** (city) Hudson County	37.6

Sorted by Percent in Ascending Order — U.S. = 14.5%

State	Percent	County	Percent	Place	Percent
Kansas	0.0	Adams County, PA	0.0	**Alafaya, FL** (cdp) Orange County	0.0
Montana	0.0	Allen County, IN	0.0	**Albuquerque, NM** (city) Bernalillo County	0.0
Nebraska	0.0	Ashtabula County, OH	0.0	**Arlington, TX** (city) Tarrant County	0.0
North Dakota	0.0	Barnstable County, MA	0.0	**Brandon, FL** (cdp) Hillsborough County	0.0
South Dakota	0.0	Bay County, FL	0.0	**Carrollwood, FL** (cdp) Hillsborough County	0.0
Mississippi	0.1	Beaufort County, SC	0.0	**Central Falls*, RI** (city) Providence County	0.0
Alabama	0.3	Bell County, TX	0.0	**Central Islip, NY** (cdp) Suffolk County	0.0
Arkansas	0.3	Berkeley County, SC	0.0	**Chesapeake, VA** (independent city)	0.0
Oklahoma	0.4	Bernalillo County, NM	0.0	**Coconut Creek, FL** (city) Broward County	0.0
Kentucky	0.5	Berrien County, MI	0.0	**Cooper City, FL** (city) Broward County	0.0

Note: (1) Ranking tables cover all states and counties, and places with an overall population of at least 125,000, OR an overall population of at least 25,000 where the Hispanic/Latino population is at least 20% of the overall population. In states where less than five places meet either of these criteria, we have included places with at least 10,000 total population with the highest percentage of Hispanic/Latino population. These places are identified with an asterisk (*); Please refer to the User's Guide for a full explanation of data.

Means of Transportation to Work: Public Transportation

(Universe: Civilian Employed Population 16 Years and Over)

South American

Top 10 States, Counties, and Places[1]

Sorted by Number in Descending Order — U.S. = 211,741

State	Number	County	Number	Place	Number
New York	125,110	Queens County, NY	70,847	**New York, NY** (city)	114,075
New Jersey	29,800	Kings County, NY	16,540	**Queens, NY** (borough) Queens County	70,847
Florida	11,384	Hudson County, NJ	13,723	**Brooklyn, NY** (borough) Kings County	16,540
California	9,505	New York County, NY	12,895	**Manhattan, NY** (borough) New York County	12,895
Massachusetts	7,243	Bronx County, NY	11,941	**Bronx, NY** (borough) Bronx County	11,941
Illinois	6,188	Miami-Dade County, FL	8,015	**Chicago, IL** (city) Cook County	5,319
Virginia	4,796	Cook County, IL	5,727	**Boston, MA** (city) Suffolk County	3,931
Maryland	3,271	Suffolk County, MA	5,314	**Union City, NJ** (city) Hudson County	3,302
Connecticut	2,614	Westchester County, NY	5,162	**Jersey City, NJ** (city) Hudson County	3,087
Pennsylvania	2,143	Los Angeles County, CA	3,984	**Newark, NJ** (city) Essex County	2,586

Sorted by Number in Ascending Order — U.S. = 211,741

State	Number	County	Number	Place	Number
Indiana	0	Ada County, ID	0	**Alafaya, FL** (cdp) Orange County	0
Maine	0	Anne Arundel County, MD	0	**Albuquerque, NM** (city) Bernalillo County	0
Mississippi	0	Beaufort County, SC	0	**Altamonte Springs, FL** (city) Seminole County	0
Montana	0	Bell County, TX	0	**Apopka, FL** (city) Orange County	0
North Dakota	0	Bernalillo County, NM	0	**Aurora, IL** (city) Kane County	0
Vermont	0	Brazoria County, TX	0	**Aventura, FL** (city) Miami-Dade County	0
New Mexico	11	Butler County, OH	0	**Cape Coral, FL** (city) Lee County	0
Kansas	12	Cabarrus County, NC	0	**Carrollton, TX** (city) Denton County	0
New Hampshire	19	Cache County, UT	0	**Chandler, AZ** (city) Maricopa County	0
West Virginia	20	Cameron County, TX	0	**Chesapeake, VA** (independent city)	0

Sorted by Percent in Descending Order — U.S. = 15.0%

State	Percent	County	Percent	Place	Percent
New York	45.7	New York County, NY	64.4	**Manhattan, NY** (borough) New York County	64.4
District of Columbia	40.0	Kings County, NY	62.5	**Brooklyn, NY** (borough) Kings County	62.5
Massachusetts	24.4	Bronx County, NY	61.4	**Bronx, NY** (borough) Bronx County	61.4
Minnesota	17.3	Queens County, NY	61.4	**New York, NY** (city)	61.4
New Jersey	17.2	Suffolk County, MA	51.8	**Queens, NY** (borough) Queens County	61.4
Illinois	16.3	San Francisco County, CA	41.6	**Boston, MA** (city) Suffolk County	54.0
Washington	10.7	Richmond County, NY	41.1	**Revere, MA** (city) Suffolk County	47.9
Maryland	10.1	Hudson County, NJ	37.8	**Pittsburgh, PA** (city) Allegheny County	46.4
Pennsylvania	9.5	Allegheny County, PA	34.4	**Jersey City, NJ** (city) Hudson County	44.7
Virginia	8.4	Hennepin County, MN	26.1	**Union City, NJ** (city) Hudson County	43.7

Sorted by Percent in Ascending Order — U.S. = 15.0%

State	Percent	County	Percent	Place	Percent
Indiana	0.0	Ada County, ID	0.0	**Alafaya, FL** (cdp) Orange County	0.0
Maine	0.0	Anne Arundel County, MD	0.0	**Albuquerque, NM** (city) Bernalillo County	0.0
Mississippi	0.0	Beaufort County, SC	0.0	**Altamonte Springs, FL** (city) Seminole County	0.0
Montana	0.0	Bell County, TX	0.0	**Apopka, FL** (city) Orange County	0.0
North Dakota	0.0	Bernalillo County, NM	0.0	**Aurora, IL** (city) Kane County	0.0
Vermont	0.0	Brazoria County, TX	0.0	**Aventura, FL** (city) Miami-Dade County	0.0
Kansas	0.4	Butler County, OH	0.0	**Cape Coral, FL** (city) Lee County	0.0
New Mexico	0.5	Cabarrus County, NC	0.0	**Carrollton, TX** (city) Denton County	0.0
South Carolina	0.6	Cache County, UT	0.0	**Chandler, AZ** (city) Maricopa County	0.0
New Hampshire	0.8	Cameron County, TX	0.0	**Chesapeake, VA** (independent city)	0.0

Note: (1) Ranking tables cover all states and counties, and places with an overall population of at least 125,000, OR an overall population of at least 25,000 where the Hispanic/Latino population is at least 20% of the overall population. In states where less than five places meet either of these criteria, we have included places with at least 10,000 total population with the highest percentage of Hispanic/Latino population. These places are identified with an asterisk (*); Please refer to the User's Guide for a full explanation of data.

Means of Transportation to Work: Public Transportation

(Universe: Civilian Employed Population 16 Years and Over)

South American: Argentinean

Top 10 States, Counties, and Places[1]

Sorted by Number in Descending Order — U.S. = 10,827

State	Number	County	Number	Place	Number
New York	4,785	Queens County, NY	1,659	**New York, NY** (city)	4,395
Florida	1,343	New York County, NY	1,462	**Queens, NY** (borough) Queens County	1,659
New Jersey	1,031	Miami-Dade County, FL	1,134	**Manhattan, NY** (borough) New York County	1,462
California	971	Kings County, NY	1,003	**Brooklyn, NY** (borough) Kings County	1,003
Maryland	381	Hudson County, NJ	579	**Miami, FL** (city) Miami-Dade County	449
Illinois	341	Los Angeles County, CA	406	**Los Angeles, CA** (city) Los Angeles County	314
Pennsylvania	341	Cook County, IL	315	**San Francisco, CA** (city) San Francisco County	279
Virginia	317	San Francisco County, CA	279	**Miami Beach, FL** (city) Miami-Dade County	264
District of Columbia	297	Montgomery County, MD	273	**Chicago, IL** (city) Cook County	224
Massachusetts	288	Westchester County, NY	193	**Bronx, NY** (borough) Bronx County	156

Sorted by Number in Ascending Order — U.S. = 10,827

State	Number	County	Number	Place	Number
Indiana	0	Bexar County, TX	0	**Aventura, FL** (city) Miami-Dade County	0
Minnesota	0	Dallas County, TX	0	**Doral, FL** (city) Miami-Dade County	0
North Carolina	0	Lee County, FL	0	**Hollywood, FL** (city) Broward County	0
South Carolina	0	Middlesex County, NJ	0	**Pembroke Pines, FL** (city) Broward County	0
Nevada	9	Montgomery County, TX	0	**Coral Springs, FL** (city) Broward County	12
Tennessee	9	Oakland County, MI	0	**San Diego, CA** (city) San Diego County	14
Ohio	10	Orange County, NY	0	**San Jose, CA** (city) Santa Clara County	35
Louisiana	11	Riverside County, CA	0	**Hialeah, FL** (city) Miami-Dade County	50
Missouri	17	Salt Lake County, UT	0	**Houston, TX** (city) Harris County	80
Arizona	18	Tarrant County, TX	0	**Hempstead (town), NY** (town) Nassau County	83

Sorted by Percent in Descending Order — U.S. = 9.6%

State	Percent	County	Percent	Place	Percent
District of Columbia	46.1	Kings County, NY	75.5	**Brooklyn, NY** (borough) Kings County	75.5
New York	37.6	New York County, NY	61.5	**Manhattan, NY** (borough) New York County	61.5
New Jersey	14.6	Queens County, NY	54.3	**New York, NY** (city)	57.4
Pennsylvania	14.2	Hudson County, NJ	39.0	**Queens, NY** (borough) Queens County	54.3
Massachusetts	13.7	San Francisco County, CA	35.5	**San Francisco, CA** (city) San Francisco County	35.5
Washington	12.3	Bronx County, NY	25.9	**Bronx, NY** (borough) Bronx County	25.9
Maryland	12.1	King County, WA	18.1	**Chicago, IL** (city) Cook County	25.4
Illinois	11.4	Essex County, NJ	17.8	**Miami, FL** (city) Miami-Dade County	13.8
Virginia	11.2	Montgomery County, MD	17.8	**Hempstead (town), NY** (town) Nassau County	11.8
Wisconsin	6.8	Westchester County, NY	17.4	**Miami Beach, FL** (city) Miami-Dade County	10.7

Sorted by Percent in Ascending Order — U.S. = 9.6%

State	Percent	County	Percent	Place	Percent
Indiana	0.0	Bexar County, TX	0.0	**Aventura, FL** (city) Miami-Dade County	0.0
Minnesota	0.0	Dallas County, TX	0.0	**Doral, FL** (city) Miami-Dade County	0.0
North Carolina	0.0	Lee County, FL	0.0	**Hollywood, FL** (city) Broward County	0.0
South Carolina	0.0	Middlesex County, NJ	0.0	**Pembroke Pines, FL** (city) Broward County	0.0
Nevada	0.7	Montgomery County, TX	0.0	**Coral Springs, FL** (city) Broward County	2.5
Arizona	1.3	Oakland County, MI	0.0	**San Diego, CA** (city) San Diego County	3.1
Ohio	1.3	Orange County, NY	0.0	**Los Angeles, CA** (city) Los Angeles County	6.4
Tennessee	1.9	Riverside County, CA	0.0	**Houston, TX** (city) Harris County	6.6
Georgia	2.2	Salt Lake County, UT	0.0	**San Jose, CA** (city) Santa Clara County	7.3
Utah	2.5	Tarrant County, TX	0.0	**Hialeah, FL** (city) Miami-Dade County	8.1

RANKINGS & COMPARISONS

Note: (1) Ranking tables cover all states and counties, and places with an overall population of at least 125,000, OR an overall population of at least 25,000 where the Hispanic/Latino population is at least 20% of the overall population. In states where less than five places meet either of these criteria, we have included places with at least 10,000 total population with the highest percentage of Hispanic/Latino population. These places are identified with an asterisk (*); Please refer to the User's Guide for a full explanation of data.

Means of Transportation to Work: Public Transportation

(Universe: Civilian Employed Population 16 Years and Over)

South American: Bolivian

Top 10 States, Counties, and Places[1]

Sorted by Number in Descending Order — U.S. = 5,465

State	Number	County	Number	Place	Number
Virginia	1,639	Queens County, NY	950	**New York, NY** (city)	1,299
New York	1,552	Fairfax County, VA	893	**Queens, NY** (borough) Queens County	950
New Jersey	595	Arlington County, VA	390	**Arlington, VA** (cdp) Arlington County	390
California	580	Los Angeles County, CA	336	**Los Angeles, CA** (city) Los Angeles County	315
Maryland	418	Montgomery County, MD	266	**Annandale, VA** (cdp) Fairfax County	195
Texas	93	Prince George's County, MD	138	**West Falls Church, VA** (cdp) Fairfax County	72
Massachusetts	84	Harris County, TX	74	**Springfield, VA** (cdp) Fairfax County	41
Florida	76	Miami-Dade County, FL	57	**Dale City, VA** (cdp) Prince William County	29
Pennsylvania	15	Santa Clara County, CA	47	**Providence, RI** (city) Providence County	0
Illinois	0	Orange County, CA	45		

Sorted by Number in Ascending Order — U.S. = 5,465

State	Number	County	Number	Place	Number
Illinois	0	Broward County, FL	0	**Providence, RI** (city) Providence County	0
North Carolina	0	Cook County, IL	0	**Dale City, VA** (cdp) Prince William County	29
Rhode Island	0	Providence County, RI	0	**Springfield, VA** (cdp) Fairfax County	41
Pennsylvania	15	San Diego County, CA	11	**West Falls Church, VA** (cdp) Fairfax County	72
Florida	76	Palm Beach County, FL	19	**Annandale, VA** (cdp) Fairfax County	195
Massachusetts	84	Loudoun County, VA	22	**Los Angeles, CA** (city) Los Angeles County	315
Texas	93	Prince William County, VA	44	**Arlington, VA** (cdp) Arlington County	390
Maryland	418	Orange County, CA	45	**Queens, NY** (borough) Queens County	950
California	580	Santa Clara County, CA	47	**New York, NY** (city)	1,299
New Jersey	595	Miami-Dade County, FL	57		

Sorted by Percent in Descending Order — U.S. = 10.1%

State	Percent	County	Percent	Place	Percent
New York	39.8	Queens County, NY	58.3	**Queens, NY** (borough) Queens County	58.3
New Jersey	24.0	Prince George's County, MD	21.1	**New York, NY** (city)	52.2
Maryland	10.3	Arlington County, VA	14.8	**Los Angeles, CA** (city) Los Angeles County	17.1
Massachusetts	8.6	Los Angeles County, CA	11.7	**Arlington, VA** (cdp) Arlington County	14.8
Virginia	8.3	Harris County, TX	11.0	**Annandale, VA** (cdp) Fairfax County	10.6
California	7.9	Montgomery County, MD	8.9	**West Falls Church, VA** (cdp) Fairfax County	8.0
Pennsylvania	5.3	Fairfax County, VA	8.1	**Springfield, VA** (cdp) Fairfax County	6.1
Texas	4.1	Santa Clara County, CA	7.5	**Dale City, VA** (cdp) Prince William County	4.5
Florida	1.5	Orange County, CA	5.6	**Providence, RI** (city) Providence County	0.0
Illinois	0.0	Palm Beach County, FL	3.6		

Sorted by Percent in Ascending Order — U.S. = 10.1%

State	Percent	County	Percent	Place	Percent
Illinois	0.0	Broward County, FL	0.0	**Providence, RI** (city) Providence County	0.0
North Carolina	0.0	Cook County, IL	0.0	**Dale City, VA** (cdp) Prince William County	4.5
Rhode Island	0.0	Providence County, RI	0.0	**Springfield, VA** (cdp) Fairfax County	6.1
Florida	1.5	Loudoun County, VA	1.7	**West Falls Church, VA** (cdp) Fairfax County	8.0
Texas	4.1	Prince William County, VA	2.1	**Annandale, VA** (cdp) Fairfax County	10.6
Pennsylvania	5.3	San Diego County, CA	2.4	**Arlington, VA** (cdp) Arlington County	14.8
California	7.9	Miami-Dade County, FL	3.2	**Los Angeles, CA** (city) Los Angeles County	17.1
Virginia	8.3	Palm Beach County, FL	3.6	**New York, NY** (city)	52.2
Massachusetts	8.6	Orange County, CA	5.6	**Queens, NY** (borough) Queens County	58.3
Maryland	10.3	Santa Clara County, CA	7.5		

Note: (1) Ranking tables cover all states and counties, and places with an overall population of at least 125,000, OR an overall population of at least 25,000 where the Hispanic/Latino population is at least 20% of the overall population. In states where less than five places meet either of these criteria, we have included places with at least 10,000 total population with the highest percentage of Hispanic/Latino population. These places are identified with an asterisk (*); Please refer to the User's Guide for a full explanation of data.

Means of Transportation to Work: Public Transportation

(Universe: Civilian Employed Population 16 Years and Over)

South American: Chilean

Top 10 States, Counties, and Places[1]

Sorted by Number in Descending Order — U.S. = 6,026

State	Number	County	Number	Place	Number
New York	2,763	Queens County, NY	1,328	**New York, NY** (city)	2,336
California	799	Kings County, NY	515	**Queens, NY** (borough) Queens County	1,328
New Jersey	515	Los Angeles County, CA	403	**Brooklyn, NY** (borough) Kings County	515
Florida	427	New York County, NY	382	**Manhattan, NY** (borough) New York County	382
Massachusetts	288	Miami-Dade County, FL	345	**Los Angeles, CA** (city) Los Angeles County	141
Virginia	180	Hudson County, NJ	242	**Chicago, IL** (city) Cook County	133
Pennsylvania	175	Nassau County, NY	213	**Hempstead (town), NY** (town) Nassau County	122
Maryland	159	Westchester County, NY	196	**Kendall, FL** (cdp) Miami-Dade County	79
Illinois	147	Cook County, IL	133	**Miami, FL** (city) Miami-Dade County	54
Washington	136	Montgomery County, MD	111		

Sorted by Number in Ascending Order — U.S. = 6,026

State	Number	County	Number	Place	Number
Michigan	0	Harris County, TX	0	**Miami, FL** (city) Miami-Dade County	54
North Carolina	0	Palm Beach County, FL	0	**Kendall, FL** (cdp) Miami-Dade County	79
Tennessee	0	Riverside County, CA	0	**Hempstead (town), NY** (town) Nassau County	122
Texas	0	San Bernardino County, CA	0	**Chicago, IL** (city) Cook County	133
Minnesota	2	San Mateo County, CA	0	**Los Angeles, CA** (city) Los Angeles County	141
Missouri	6	Suffolk County, NY	0	**Manhattan, NY** (borough) New York County	382
Oregon	8	Santa Clara County, CA	7	**Brooklyn, NY** (borough) Kings County	515
Ohio	12	Orange County, CA	8	**Queens, NY** (borough) Queens County	1,328
Colorado	14	Bergen County, NJ	12	**New York, NY** (city)	2,336
Wisconsin	14	Broward County, FL	26		

Sorted by Percent in Descending Order — U.S. = 9.5%

State	Percent	County	Percent	Place	Percent
New York	32.4	Kings County, NY	74.6	**Brooklyn, NY** (borough) Kings County	74.6
Pennsylvania	17.6	Queens County, NY	57.8	**Queens, NY** (borough) Queens County	57.8
Massachusetts	16.1	New York County, NY	56.5	**New York, NY** (city)	57.7
Nevada	11.7	Hudson County, NJ	21.8	**Manhattan, NY** (borough) New York County	56.5
New Jersey	11.3	Cook County, IL	17.5	**Chicago, IL** (city) Cook County	25.7
Washington	11.3	Westchester County, NY	16.4	**Kendall, FL** (cdp) Miami-Dade County	14.9
Illinois	10.3	Clark County, NV	13.1	**Hempstead (town), NY** (town) Nassau County	13.9
Virginia	8.6	Nassau County, NY	12.6	**Miami, FL** (city) Miami-Dade County	7.1
California	7.0	Fairfax County, VA	10.7	**Los Angeles, CA** (city) Los Angeles County	6.3
Maryland	6.9	Alameda County, CA	10.1		

Sorted by Percent in Ascending Order — U.S. = 9.5%

State	Percent	County	Percent	Place	Percent
Michigan	0.0	Harris County, TX	0.0	**Los Angeles, CA** (city) Los Angeles County	6.3
North Carolina	0.0	Palm Beach County, FL	0.0	**Miami, FL** (city) Miami-Dade County	7.1
Tennessee	0.0	Riverside County, CA	0.0	**Hempstead (town), NY** (town) Nassau County	13.9
Texas	0.0	San Bernardino County, CA	0.0	**Kendall, FL** (cdp) Miami-Dade County	14.9
Minnesota	0.8	San Mateo County, CA	0.0	**Chicago, IL** (city) Cook County	25.7
Georgia	1.3	Suffolk County, NY	0.0	**Manhattan, NY** (borough) New York County	56.5
Missouri	1.5	Santa Clara County, CA	0.8	**New York, NY** (city)	57.7
Oregon	1.5	Broward County, FL	1.1	**Queens, NY** (borough) Queens County	57.8
Colorado	1.9	Orange County, CA	1.3	**Brooklyn, NY** (borough) Kings County	74.6
Ohio	2.6	Bergen County, NJ	2.2		

Note: (1) Ranking tables cover all states and counties, and places with an overall population of at least 125,000, OR an overall population of at least 25,000 where the Hispanic/Latino population is at least 20% of the overall population. In states where less than five places meet either of these criteria, we have included places with at least 10,000 total population with the highest percentage of Hispanic/Latino population. These places are identified with an asterisk (*); Please refer to the User's Guide for a full explanation of data.

Means of Transportation to Work: Public Transportation

(Universe: Civilian Employed Population 16 Years and Over)

South American: Colombian

Top 10 States, Counties, and Places[1]

Sorted by Number in Descending Order — U.S. = 56,401

State	Number	County	Number	Place	Number
New York	32,425	Queens County, NY	21,739	**New York, NY** (city)	29,650
New Jersey	7,168	Suffolk County, MA	4,023	**Queens, NY** (borough) Queens County	21,739
Massachusetts	4,662	Hudson County, NJ	3,362	**Brooklyn, NY** (borough) Kings County	3,263
Florida	4,271	Kings County, NY	3,263	**Boston, MA** (city) Suffolk County	2,980
California	1,824	New York County, NY	2,794	**Manhattan, NY** (borough) New York County	2,794
Illinois	1,136	Miami-Dade County, FL	2,759	**Bronx, NY** (borough) Bronx County	1,297
Pennsylvania	792	Bergen County, NJ	1,441	**North Bergen, NJ** (township) Hudson County	856
Connecticut	749	Bronx County, NY	1,297	**Chicago, IL** (city) Cook County	835
Virginia	639	Nassau County, NY	1,170	**Revere, MA** (city) Suffolk County	830
Maryland	485	Westchester County, NY	1,079	**Miami, FL** (city) Miami-Dade County	756

Sorted by Number in Ascending Order — U.S. = 56,401

State	Number	County	Number	Place	Number
Alaska	0	Cherokee County, GA	0	**Alafaya, FL** (cdp) Orange County	0
Arizona	0	Collier County, FL	0	**Anaheim, CA** (city) Orange County	0
Arkansas	0	Collin County, TX	0	**Aventura, FL** (city) Miami-Dade County	0
Delaware	0	Contra Costa County, CA	0	**Brandon, FL** (cdp) Hillsborough County	0
Indiana	0	Denton County, TX	0	**Buenaventura Lakes, FL** (cdp) Osceola County	0
Kansas	0	Duval County, FL	0	**Cape Coral, FL** (city) Lee County	0
Michigan	0	Forsyth County, GA	0	**Charlotte, NC** (city) Mecklenburg County	0
New Mexico	0	Greenville County, SC	0	**Coconut Creek, FL** (city) Broward County	0
Oklahoma	0	Hall County, GA	0	**Cooper City, FL** (city) Broward County	0
New Hampshire	7	Lake County, FL	0	**Davie, FL** (town) Broward County	0

Sorted by Percent in Descending Order — U.S. = 12.5%

State	Percent	County	Percent	Place	Percent
New York	43.3	Kings County, NY	64.5	**Brooklyn, NY** (borough) Kings County	64.5
District of Columbia	39.3	New York County, NY	61.5	**Manhattan, NY** (borough) New York County	61.5
Massachusetts	33.8	Queens County, NY	58.6	**Boston, MA** (city) Suffolk County	60.2
New Jersey	13.6	Suffolk County, MA	56.7	**Queens, NY** (borough) Queens County	58.6
Illinois	10.7	Bronx County, NY	49.7	**New York, NY** (city)	58.5
Pennsylvania	10.1	San Francisco County, CA	42.7	**Revere, MA** (city) Suffolk County	51.0
Maryland	8.0	Richmond County, NY	40.5	**Bronx, NY** (borough) Bronx County	49.7
Virginia	7.7	Hudson County, NJ	37.9	**San Francisco, CA** (city) San Francisco County	42.7
Washington	7.5	Arlington County, VA	26.4	**Jersey City, NJ** (city) Hudson County	42.4
Connecticut	7.1	Atlantic County, NJ	23.7	**Staten Island, NY** (borough) Richmond County	40.5

Sorted by Percent in Ascending Order — U.S. = 12.5%

State	Percent	County	Percent	Place	Percent
Alaska	0.0	Cherokee County, GA	0.0	**Alafaya, FL** (cdp) Orange County	0.0
Arizona	0.0	Collier County, FL	0.0	**Anaheim, CA** (city) Orange County	0.0
Arkansas	0.0	Collin County, TX	0.0	**Aventura, FL** (city) Miami-Dade County	0.0
Delaware	0.0	Contra Costa County, CA	0.0	**Brandon, FL** (cdp) Hillsborough County	0.0
Indiana	0.0	Denton County, TX	0.0	**Buenaventura Lakes, FL** (cdp) Osceola County	0.0
Kansas	0.0	Duval County, FL	0.0	**Cape Coral, FL** (city) Lee County	0.0
Michigan	0.0	Forsyth County, GA	0.0	**Charlotte, NC** (city) Mecklenburg County	0.0
New Mexico	0.0	Greenville County, SC	0.0	**Coconut Creek, FL** (city) Broward County	0.0
Oklahoma	0.0	Hall County, GA	0.0	**Cooper City, FL** (city) Broward County	0.0
Nevada	0.4	Lake County, FL	0.0	**Davie, FL** (town) Broward County	0.0

Note: (1) Ranking tables cover all states and counties, and places with an overall population of at least 125,000, OR an overall population of at least 25,000 where the Hispanic/Latino population is at least 20% of the overall population. In states where less than five places meet either of these criteria, we have included places with at least 10,000 total population with the highest percentage of Hispanic/Latino population. These places are identified with an asterisk (*); Please refer to the User's Guide for a full explanation of data.

Means of Transportation to Work: Public Transportation

(Universe: Civilian Employed Population 16 Years and Over)

South American: Ecuadorian

Top 10 States, Counties, and Places[1]

Sorted by Number in Descending Order — U.S. = 82,656

State	Number	County	Number	Place	Number
New York	60,827	Queens County, NY	33,747	**New York, NY** (city)	56,594
New Jersey	11,572	Kings County, NY	8,549	**Queens, NY** (borough) Queens County	33,747
Illinois	3,565	Bronx County, NY	8,385	**Brooklyn, NY** (borough) Kings County	8,549
Minnesota	1,299	Hudson County, NJ	5,691	**Bronx, NY** (borough) Bronx County	8,385
California	1,169	New York County, NY	5,430	**Manhattan, NY** (borough) New York County	5,430
Connecticut	1,009	Cook County, IL	3,503	**Chicago, IL** (city) Cook County	3,361
Florida	837	Essex County, NJ	2,495	**Newark, NJ** (city) Essex County	1,833
Maryland	651	Westchester County, NY	2,153	**Jersey City, NJ** (city) Hudson County	1,760
Massachusetts	467	Bergen County, NJ	1,472	**Union City, NJ** (city) Hudson County	1,450
Pennsylvania	442	Hennepin County, MN	1,299	**Minneapolis, MN** (city) Hennepin County	1,211

Sorted by Number in Ascending Order — U.S. = 82,656

State	Number	County	Number	Place	Number
Georgia	0	Gwinnett County, GA	0	**Coral Springs, FL** (city) Broward County	0
Indiana	0	Harris County, TX	0	**Doral, FL** (city) Miami-Dade County	0
Iowa	0	Lee County, FL	0	**Downey, CA** (city) Los Angeles County	0
Kansas	0	Ocean County, NJ	0	**Houston, TX** (city) Harris County	0
Louisiana	0	Osceola County, FL	0	**New Haven, CT** (city/town) New Haven County	0
Missouri	0	Pinellas County, FL	0	**Paterson, NJ** (city) Passaic County	0
Oklahoma	0	Putnam County, NY	0	**Allentown, PA** (city) Lehigh County	8
South Carolina	0	Santa Clara County, CA	0	**Clifton, NJ** (city) Passaic County	12
Tennessee	8	Tarrant County, TX	0	**Hollywood, FL** (city) Broward County	13
Texas	9	Utah County, UT	0	**Country Club, FL** (cdp) Miami-Dade County	14

Sorted by Percent in Descending Order — U.S. = 28.1%

State	Percent	County	Percent	Place	Percent
New York	51.2	New York County, NY	67.8	**Manhattan, NY** (borough) New York County	67.8
Minnesota	27.7	Bronx County, NY	67.0	**Bronx, NY** (borough) Bronx County	67.0
Illinois	26.5	Queens County, NY	64.4	**Queens, NY** (borough) Queens County	64.4
New Jersey	21.3	Kings County, NY	60.1	**New York, NY** (city)	63.9
Maryland	15.4	Hudson County, NJ	38.4	**Brooklyn, NY** (borough) Kings County	60.1
Massachusetts	14.5	Richmond County, NY	34.5	**Union City, NJ** (city) Hudson County	48.6
Michigan	11.8	Hennepin County, MN	33.2	**White Plains, NY** (city) Westchester County	45.7
Nevada	11.5	Monmouth County, NJ	31.2	**Spring Valley, NY** (village) Rockland County	44.8
Colorado	9.3	Rockland County, NY	30.2	**Jersey City, NJ** (city) Hudson County	42.5
Washington	9.1	Cook County, IL	29.9	**Minneapolis, MN** (city) Hennepin County	39.1

Sorted by Percent in Ascending Order — U.S. = 28.1%

State	Percent	County	Percent	Place	Percent
Georgia	0.0	Gwinnett County, GA	0.0	**Coral Springs, FL** (city) Broward County	0.0
Indiana	0.0	Harris County, TX	0.0	**Doral, FL** (city) Miami-Dade County	0.0
Iowa	0.0	Lee County, FL	0.0	**Downey, CA** (city) Los Angeles County	0.0
Kansas	0.0	Ocean County, NJ	0.0	**Houston, TX** (city) Harris County	0.0
Louisiana	0.0	Osceola County, FL	0.0	**New Haven, CT** (city/town) New Haven County	0.0
Missouri	0.0	Pinellas County, FL	0.0	**Paterson, NJ** (city) Passaic County	0.0
Oklahoma	0.0	Putnam County, NY	0.0	**Allentown, PA** (city) Lehigh County	1.2
South Carolina	0.0	Santa Clara County, CA	0.0	**Pembroke Pines, FL** (city) Broward County	1.7
Texas	0.2	Tarrant County, TX	0.0	**Charlotte, NC** (city) Mecklenburg County	2.1
Arizona	0.9	Utah County, UT	0.0	**Hialeah, FL** (city) Miami-Dade County	2.2

Note: (1) Ranking tables cover all states and counties, and places with an overall population of at least 125,000, OR an overall population of at least 25,000 where the Hispanic/Latino population is at least 20% of the overall population. In states where less than five places meet either of these criteria, we have included places with at least 10,000 total population with the highest percentage of Hispanic/Latino population. These places are identified with an asterisk (*); Please refer to the User's Guide for a full explanation of data.

Means of Transportation to Work: Public Transportation

(Universe: Civilian Employed Population 16 Years and Over)

South American: Paraguayan

Top 10 States, Counties, and Places[1]

Sorted by Number in Descending Order — U.S. = 1,841

State	Number	County	Number	Place	Number
New York	1,371	Queens County, NY	978	**New York, NY** (city)	1,189
Florida	105	Westchester County, NY	144	**Queens, NY** (borough) Queens County	978
New Jersey	101				
Maryland	35				
California	19				
Texas	0				

Sorted by Number in Ascending Order — U.S. = 1,841

State	Number	County	Number	Place	Number
Texas	0	Westchester County, NY	144	**Queens, NY** (borough) Queens County	978
California	19	Queens County, NY	978	**New York, NY** (city)	1,189
Maryland	35				
New Jersey	101				
Florida	105				
New York	1,371				

Sorted by Percent in Descending Order — U.S. = 18.4%

State	Percent	County	Percent	Place	Percent
New York	35.0	Queens County, NY	62.2	**Queens, NY** (borough) Queens County	62.2
Florida	12.3	Westchester County, NY	14.6	**New York, NY** (city)	54.7
New Jersey	11.2				
Maryland	4.9				
California	4.4				
Texas	0.0				

Sorted by Percent in Ascending Order — U.S. = 18.4%

State	Percent	County	Percent	Place	Percent
Texas	0.0	Westchester County, NY	14.6	**New York, NY** (city)	54.7
California	4.4	Queens County, NY	62.2	**Queens, NY** (borough) Queens County	62.2
Maryland	4.9				
New Jersey	11.2				
Florida	12.3				
New York	35.0				

Note: (1) Ranking tables cover all states and counties, and places with an overall population of at least 125,000, OR an overall population of at least 25,000 where the Hispanic/Latino population is at least 20% of the overall population. In states where less than five places meet either of these criteria, we have included places with at least 10,000 total population with the highest percentage of Hispanic/Latino population. These places are identified with an asterisk (*); Please refer to the User's Guide for a full explanation of data.

Means of Transportation to Work: Public Transportation

(Universe: Civilian Employed Population 16 Years and Over)

South American: Peruvian

Top 10 States, Counties, and Places[1]

Sorted by Number in Descending Order — U.S. = 35,642

State	Number	County	Number	Place	Number
New York	14,980	Queens County, NY	8,182	**New York, NY** (city)	12,774
New Jersey	7,133	Hudson County, NJ	2,988	**Queens, NY** (borough) Queens County	8,182
California	3,511	Miami-Dade County, FL	1,907	**Brooklyn, NY** (borough) Kings County	1,603
Florida	2,446	Kings County, NY	1,603	**Manhattan, NY** (borough) New York County	1,457
Virginia	1,528	Passaic County, NJ	1,599	**Bronx, NY** (borough) Bronx County	1,069
Massachusetts	1,053	New York County, NY	1,457	**Paterson, NJ** (city) Passaic County	1,043
Maryland	968	Los Angeles County, CA	1,344	**Union City, NJ** (city) Hudson County	967
Illinois	722	Westchester County, NY	1,078	**Los Angeles, CA** (city) Los Angeles County	760
Connecticut	617	Bronx County, NY	1,069	**San Francisco, CA** (city) San Francisco County	691
Texas	367	Fairfax County, VA	842	**Chicago, IL** (city) Cook County	614

Sorted by Number in Ascending Order — U.S. = 35,642

State	Number	County	Number	Place	Number
Indiana	0	Baltimore County, MD	0	**Cape Coral, FL** (city) Lee County	0
Kansas	0	Bexar County, TX	0	**Charlotte, NC** (city) Mecklenburg County	0
Kentucky	0	Collier County, FL	0	**Davie, FL** (town) Broward County	0
Missouri	0	Denton County, TX	0	**Doral, FL** (city) Miami-Dade County	0
South Carolina	0	Fort Bend County, TX	0	**Fort Lauderdale, FL** (city) Broward County	0
Tennessee	0	Fulton County, GA	0	**Kendale Lakes, FL** (cdp) Miami-Dade County	0
New Mexico	11	Lee County, FL	0	**Linden, NJ** (city) Union County	0
North Carolina	11	Lehigh County, PA	0	**Phoenix, AZ** (city) Maricopa County	0
Alabama	14	Orange County, NY	0	**San Antonio, TX** (city) Bexar County	0
Rhode Island	37	San Joaquin County, CA	0	**Sunrise, FL** (city) Broward County	0

Sorted by Percent in Descending Order — U.S. = 13.0%

State	Percent	County	Percent	Place	Percent
New York	41.2	Kings County, NY	65.9	**Brooklyn, NY** (borough) Kings County	65.9
District of Columbia	30.9	New York County, NY	64.0	**Manhattan, NY** (borough) New York County	64.0
Massachusetts	24.1	Bronx County, NY	61.1	**New York, NY** (city)	61.7
New Jersey	17.5	Queens County, NY	61.0	**Bronx, NY** (borough) Bronx County	61.1
Delaware	15.2	Suffolk County, MA	58.2	**Queens, NY** (borough) Queens County	61.0
Washington	15.2	Richmond County, NY	56.9	**Jersey City, NJ** (city) Hudson County	57.6
Louisiana	14.9	San Francisco County, CA	49.1	**Boston, MA** (city) Suffolk County	57.3
Illinois	12.9	Hudson County, NJ	38.6	**Staten Island, NY** (borough) Richmond County	56.9
Maryland	10.5	Middlesex County, MA	28.0	**San Francisco, CA** (city) San Francisco County	49.1
Virginia	9.5	Atlantic County, NJ	27.1	**Union City, NJ** (city) Hudson County	44.9

Sorted by Percent in Ascending Order — U.S. = 13.0%

State	Percent	County	Percent	Place	Percent
Indiana	0.0	Baltimore County, MD	0.0	**Cape Coral, FL** (city) Lee County	0.0
Kansas	0.0	Bexar County, TX	0.0	**Charlotte, NC** (city) Mecklenburg County	0.0
Kentucky	0.0	Collier County, FL	0.0	**Davie, FL** (town) Broward County	0.0
Missouri	0.0	Denton County, TX	0.0	**Doral, FL** (city) Miami-Dade County	0.0
South Carolina	0.0	Fort Bend County, TX	0.0	**Fort Lauderdale, FL** (city) Broward County	0.0
Tennessee	0.0	Fulton County, GA	0.0	**Kendale Lakes, FL** (cdp) Miami-Dade County	0.0
North Carolina	0.3	Lee County, FL	0.0	**Linden, NJ** (city) Union County	0.0
New Mexico	1.7	Lehigh County, PA	0.0	**Phoenix, AZ** (city) Maricopa County	0.0
Alabama	2.3	Orange County, NY	0.0	**San Antonio, TX** (city) Bexar County	0.0
Nevada	2.9	San Joaquin County, CA	0.0	**Sunrise, FL** (city) Broward County	0.0

Note: (1) Ranking tables cover all states and counties, and places with an overall population of at least 125,000, OR an overall population of at least 25,000 where the Hispanic/Latino population is at least 20% of the overall population. In states where less than five places meet either of these criteria, we have included places with at least 10,000 total population with the highest percentage of Hispanic/Latino population. These places are identified with an asterisk (*); Please refer to the User's Guide for a full explanation of data.

Means of Transportation to Work: Public Transportation

(Universe: Civilian Employed Population 16 Years and Over)

South American: Uruguayan

Top 10 States, Counties, and Places[1]

Sorted by Number in Descending Order — U.S. = 3,213

State	Number	County	Number	Place	Number
New York	1,168	Queens County, NY	446	**New York, NY** (city)	970
New Jersey	991	Miami-Dade County, FL	371	**Queens, NY** (borough) Queens County	446
Florida	443	Union County, NJ	366	**Elizabeth, NJ** (city) Union County	302
Massachusetts	230	Hudson County, NJ	325		
California	61	Essex County, NJ	129		
Maryland	45	Westchester County, NY	72		
Georgia	40	Broward County, FL	57		
Pennsylvania	32	Los Angeles County, CA	47		
Virginia	26	Middlesex County, NJ	42		
Texas	14	Gwinnett County, GA	18		

Sorted by Number in Ascending Order — U.S. = 3,213

State	Number	County	Number	Place	Number
Texas	14	Harris County, TX	0	**Elizabeth, NJ** (city) Union County	302
Virginia	26	Morris County, NJ	0	**Queens, NY** (borough) Queens County	446
Pennsylvania	32	Palm Beach County, FL	0	**New York, NY** (city)	970
Georgia	40	Worcester County, MA	15		
Maryland	45	Gwinnett County, GA	18		
California	61	Middlesex County, NJ	42		
Massachusetts	230	Los Angeles County, CA	47		
Florida	443	Broward County, FL	57		
New Jersey	991	Westchester County, NY	72		
New York	1,168	Essex County, NJ	129		

Sorted by Percent in Descending Order — U.S. = 11.3%

State	Percent	County	Percent	Place	Percent
New York	36.7	Queens County, NY	67.7	**Queens, NY** (borough) Queens County	67.7
Massachusetts	19.0	Hudson County, NJ	47.1	**New York, NY** (city)	66.1
New Jersey	15.7	Union County, NJ	16.0	**Elizabeth, NJ** (city) Union County	19.0
Pennsylvania	6.5	Middlesex County, NJ	11.6		
Florida	6.1	Miami-Dade County, FL	11.1		
Maryland	5.7	Essex County, NJ	9.9		
California	3.7	Westchester County, NY	9.9		
Georgia	2.6	Los Angeles County, CA	7.3		
Virginia	2.5	Gwinnett County, GA	3.2		
Texas	1.0	Broward County, FL	3.1		

Sorted by Percent in Ascending Order — U.S. = 11.3%

State	Percent	County	Percent	Place	Percent
Texas	1.0	Harris County, TX	0.0	**Elizabeth, NJ** (city) Union County	19.0
Virginia	2.5	Morris County, NJ	0.0	**New York, NY** (city)	66.1
Georgia	2.6	Palm Beach County, FL	0.0	**Queens, NY** (borough) Queens County	67.7
California	3.7	Worcester County, MA	2.4		
Maryland	5.7	Broward County, FL	3.1		
Florida	6.1	Gwinnett County, GA	3.2		
Pennsylvania	6.5	Los Angeles County, CA	7.3		
New Jersey	15.7	Essex County, NJ	9.9		
Massachusetts	19.0	Westchester County, NY	9.9		
New York	36.7	Miami-Dade County, FL	11.1		

Note: (1) Ranking tables cover all states and counties, and places with an overall population of at least 125,000, OR an overall population of at least 25,000 where the Hispanic/Latino population is at least 20% of the overall population. In states where less than five places meet either of these criteria, we have included places with at least 10,000 total population with the highest percentage of Hispanic/Latino population. These places are identified with an asterisk (*); Please refer to the User's Guide for a full explanation of data.

Means of Transportation to Work: Public Transportation

(Universe: Civilian Employed Population 16 Years and Over)

South American: Venezuelan

Top 10 States, Counties, and Places[1]

Sorted by Number in Descending Order (U.S. = 7,299)

State	Number	County	Number	Place	Number
New York	3,661	Queens County, NY	1,339	**New York, NY** (city)	3,422
Florida	1,381	Kings County, NY	986	**Queens, NY** (borough) Queens County	1,339
New Jersey	527	Miami-Dade County, FL	934	**Brooklyn, NY** (borough) Kings County	986
California	389	New York County, NY	865	**Manhattan, NY** (borough) New York County	865
Illinois	185	Hudson County, NJ	247	**Miami, FL** (city) Miami-Dade County	304
Virginia	161	Bronx County, NY	214	**Bronx, NY** (borough) Bronx County	214
Pennsylvania	160	Broward County, FL	180	**Kendall, FL** (cdp) Miami-Dade County	87
Texas	144	Cook County, IL	144	**Miami Beach, FL** (city) Miami-Dade County	73
Maryland	120	Harris County, TX	98	**Fountainebleau, FL** (cdp) Miami-Dade County	50
Massachusetts	113	Los Angeles County, CA	89	**Orlando, FL** (city) Orange County	30

Sorted by Number in Ascending Order (U.S. = 7,299)

State	Number	County	Number	Place	Number
Arizona	0	Cobb County, GA	0	**Aventura, FL** (city) Miami-Dade County	0
Indiana	0	Dallas County, TX	0	**Coral Springs, FL** (city) Broward County	0
Louisiana	0	Fulton County, GA	0	**Country Club, FL** (cdp) Miami-Dade County	0
Missouri	0	Gwinnett County, GA	0	**Doral, FL** (city) Miami-Dade County	0
Oklahoma	0	Hillsborough County, FL	0	**Hialeah, FL** (city) Miami-Dade County	0
Tennessee	0	Lee County, FL	0	**Hollywood, FL** (city) Broward County	0
Wisconsin	0	Montgomery County, TX	0	**Kendall West, FL** (cdp) Miami-Dade County	0
North Carolina	9	Palm Beach County, FL	0	**Pembroke Pines, FL** (city) Broward County	0
Michigan	10	Seminole County, FL	0	**Sunrise, FL** (city) Broward County	0
Minnesota	10	Tarrant County, TX	0	**Tamiami, FL** (cdp) Miami-Dade County	0

Sorted by Percent in Descending Order (U.S. = 7.0%)

State	Percent	County	Percent	Place	Percent
New York	47.9	Kings County, NY	69.8	**Brooklyn, NY** (borough) Kings County	69.8
New Jersey	17.0	New York County, NY	66.8	**Manhattan, NY** (borough) New York County	66.8
Illinois	12.2	Queens County, NY	56.1	**New York, NY** (city)	58.5
Pennsylvania	10.7	Hudson County, NJ	33.3	**Queens, NY** (borough) Queens County	56.1
Maryland	8.7	Bronx County, NY	32.5	**Bronx, NY** (borough) Bronx County	32.5
Massachusetts	7.1	Cook County, IL	16.3	**Kendall, FL** (cdp) Miami-Dade County	12.0
California	6.6	Suffolk County, MA	16.3	**Miami, FL** (city) Miami-Dade County	9.8
Washington	6.3	Fairfield County, CT	13.0	**Miami Beach, FL** (city) Miami-Dade County	6.2
Connecticut	6.2	Montgomery County, MD	10.2	**Los Angeles, CA** (city) Los Angeles County	3.8
Virginia	6.2	Fairfax County, VA	10.1	**Orlando, FL** (city) Orange County	2.9

Sorted by Percent in Ascending Order (U.S. = 7.0%)

State	Percent	County	Percent	Place	Percent
Arizona	0.0	Cobb County, GA	0.0	**Aventura, FL** (city) Miami-Dade County	0.0
Indiana	0.0	Dallas County, TX	0.0	**Coral Springs, FL** (city) Broward County	0.0
Louisiana	0.0	Fulton County, GA	0.0	**Country Club, FL** (cdp) Miami-Dade County	0.0
Missouri	0.0	Gwinnett County, GA	0.0	**Doral, FL** (city) Miami-Dade County	0.0
Oklahoma	0.0	Hillsborough County, FL	0.0	**Hialeah, FL** (city) Miami-Dade County	0.0
Tennessee	0.0	Lee County, FL	0.0	**Hollywood, FL** (city) Broward County	0.0
Wisconsin	0.0	Montgomery County, TX	0.0	**Kendall West, FL** (cdp) Miami-Dade County	0.0
North Carolina	0.4	Palm Beach County, FL	0.0	**Pembroke Pines, FL** (city) Broward County	0.0
Georgia	0.6	Seminole County, FL	0.0	**Sunrise, FL** (city) Broward County	0.0
Texas	1.6	Tarrant County, TX	0.0	**Tamiami, FL** (cdp) Miami-Dade County	0.0

Note: (1) Ranking tables cover all states and counties, and places with an overall population of at least 125,000, OR an overall population of at least 25,000 where the Hispanic/Latino population is at least 20% of the overall population. In states where less than five places meet either of these criteria, we have included places with at least 10,000 total population with the highest percentage of Hispanic/Latino population. These places are identified with an asterisk (*); Please refer to the User's Guide for a full explanation of data.

Means of Transportation to Work: Public Transportation

(Universe: Civilian Employed Population 16 Years and Over)

Spaniard

Top 10 States, Counties, and Places[1]

Sorted by Number in Descending Order — U.S. = 13,801

State	Number	County	Number	Place	Number
New York	5,362	New York County, NY	1,390	**New York, NY** (city)	4,526
California	1,683	Queens County, NY	1,155	**Manhattan, NY** (borough) New York County	1,390
New Jersey	1,251	Kings County, NY	1,153	**Queens, NY** (borough) Queens County	1,155
Colorado	961	Bronx County, NY	628	**Brooklyn, NY** (borough) Kings County	1,153
Texas	634	Los Angeles County, CA	449	**Bronx, NY** (borough) Bronx County	628
Illinois	455	Cook County, IL	437	**Chicago, IL** (city) Cook County	356
District of Columbia	329	Hudson County, NJ	403	**San Francisco, CA** (city) San Francisco County	290
Virginia	304	Nassau County, NY	302	**Denver, CO** (city) Denver County	232
Washington	303	San Francisco County, CA	290	**Hempstead (town), NY** (town) Nassau County	230
Maryland	256	Essex County, NJ	287	**Staten Island, NY** (borough) Richmond County	200

Sorted by Number in Ascending Order — U.S. = 13,801

State	Number	County	Number	Place	Number
Idaho	0	Ada County, ID	0	**Anchorage, AK** (municipality)	0
Iowa	0	Brazoria County, TX	0	**Bakersfield, CA** (city) Kern County	0
Kansas	0	Brevard County, FL	0	**El Paso, TX** (city) El Paso County	0
Maine	0	Broward County, FL	0	**Fort Worth, TX** (city) Tarrant County	0
Mississippi	0	Butte County, CA	0	**Glendale, AZ** (city) Maricopa County	0
Montana	0	Cameron County, TX	0	**Jacksonville, FL** (city) Duval County	0
Nebraska	0	Cibola County, NM	0	**Las Cruces, NM** (city) Dona Ana County	0
New Hampshire	0	Clark County, WA	0	**Lubbock, TX** (city) Lubbock County	0
Oklahoma	0	Colfax County, NM	0	**Mesa, AZ** (city) Maricopa County	0
South Carolina	0	Collin County, TX	0	**Miami, FL** (city) Miami-Dade County	0

Sorted by Percent in Descending Order — U.S. = 5.5%

State	Percent	County	Percent	Place	Percent
District of Columbia	51.3	Kings County, NY	69.5	**Brooklyn, NY** (borough) Kings County	69.5
New York	31.5	New York County, NY	63.3	**Manhattan, NY** (borough) New York County	63.3
New Jersey	12.6	Bronx County, NY	50.4	**New York, NY** (city)	53.1
Massachusetts	10.3	Queens County, NY	46.5	**Bronx, NY** (borough) Bronx County	50.4
Illinois	8.4	Philadelphia County, PA	35.3	**Queens, NY** (borough) Queens County	46.5
Connecticut	8.1	Hudson County, NJ	26.2	**Philadelphia, PA** (city) Philadelphia County	35.3
Maryland	7.7	Multnomah County, OR	24.7	**Chicago, IL** (city) Cook County	28.5
Minnesota	7.5	Bergen County, NJ	22.3	**Newark, NJ** (city) Essex County	28.0
Pennsylvania	6.7	San Francisco County, CA	21.3	**San Francisco, CA** (city) San Francisco County	21.3
Hawaii	6.4	Richmond County, NY	21.2	**Staten Island, NY** (borough) Richmond County	21.2

Sorted by Percent in Ascending Order — U.S. = 5.5%

State	Percent	County	Percent	Place	Percent
Idaho	0.0	Ada County, ID	0.0	**Anchorage, AK** (municipality)	0.0
Iowa	0.0	Brazoria County, TX	0.0	**Bakersfield, CA** (city) Kern County	0.0
Kansas	0.0	Brevard County, FL	0.0	**El Paso, TX** (city) El Paso County	0.0
Maine	0.0	Broward County, FL	0.0	**Fort Worth, TX** (city) Tarrant County	0.0
Mississippi	0.0	Butte County, CA	0.0	**Glendale, AZ** (city) Maricopa County	0.0
Montana	0.0	Cameron County, TX	0.0	**Jacksonville, FL** (city) Duval County	0.0
Nebraska	0.0	Cibola County, NM	0.0	**Las Cruces, NM** (city) Dona Ana County	0.0
New Hampshire	0.0	Clark County, WA	0.0	**Lubbock, TX** (city) Lubbock County	0.0
Oklahoma	0.0	Colfax County, NM	0.0	**Mesa, AZ** (city) Maricopa County	0.0
South Carolina	0.0	Collin County, TX	0.0	**Miami, FL** (city) Miami-Dade County	0.0

Note: (1) Ranking tables cover all states and counties, and places with an overall population of at least 125,000, OR an overall population of at least 25,000 where the Hispanic/Latino population is at least 20% of the overall population. In states where less than five places meet either of these criteria, we have included places with at least 10,000 total population with the highest percentage of Hispanic/Latino population. These places are identified with an asterisk (*); Please refer to the User's Guide for a full explanation of data.

Homeownship Rate

(Universe: Occupied Housing Units)

Total Population

Top 10 States, Counties, and Places[1]

Sorted by Percent in Descending Order — U.S. = 65.1%

State	Percent	County	Percent	Place	Percent
West Virginia	73.4	Sumter County, FL	89.7	**Cooper City, FL** (city) Broward County	89.2
Minnesota	73.0	Alcona County, MI	89.6	**Streamwood, IL** (village) Cook County	88.4
Delaware	72.1	Morgan County, UT	89.1	**Oyster Bay, NY** (town) Nassau County	86.9
Iowa	72.1	Powhatan County, VA	88.5	**Richmond West, FL** (cdp) Miami-Dade County	86.5
Michigan	72.1	New Kent County, VA	88.4	**Romeoville, IL** (village) Will County	85.0
Maine	71.3	Elbert County, CO	88.1	**Sahuarita, AZ** (town) Pima County	84.4
New Hampshire	71.0	Cameron Parish, LA	87.8	**Huntington, NY** (town) Suffolk County	83.9
Vermont	70.7	Goochland County, VA	87.8	**Royal Palm Beach, FL** (village) Palm Beach County	83.8
Utah	70.4	Presque Isle County, MI	86.5	**Fortuna Foothills, AZ** (cdp) Yuma County	83.6
Idaho	69.9	Harris County, GA	85.8	**Bolingbrook, IL** (village) Will County	83.1

Sorted by Percent in Ascending Order — U.S. = 65.1%

State	Percent	County	Percent	Place	Percent
District of Columbia	42.0	Bronx County, NY	19.3	**Schofield Barracks*, HI** (cdp) Honolulu County	0.5
New York	53.3	New York County, NY	22.8	**Fort Leonard Wood*, MO** (cdp) Pulaski County	0.6
California	55.9	Kings County, NY	27.7	**Fort Campbell North*, KY** (cdp) Christian County	0.7
Hawaii	57.7	Hudson County, NJ	32.1	**Fort Hood, TX** (cdp) Bell County	0.8
Nevada	58.8	Chattahoochee County, GA	33.7	**University, FL** (cdp) Hillsborough County	13.4
Rhode Island	60.7	Suffolk County, MA	35.3	**Bronx, NY** (borough) Bronx County	19.3
Oregon	62.2	Kenedy County, TX	35.4	**Union City, NJ** (city) Hudson County	20.1
Massachusetts	62.3	San Francisco County, CA	35.8	**West New York, NJ** (town) Hudson County	21.3
Alaska	63.1	Riley County, KS	41.8	**Newark, NJ** (city) Essex County	22.1
Texas	63.7	Clarke County, GA	42.2	**Central Falls*, RI** (city) Providence County	22.4

RANKINGS & COMPARISONS

Note: (1) Ranking tables cover all states and counties, and places with an overall population of at least 125,000, OR an overall population of at least 25,000 where the Hispanic/Latino population is at least 20% of the overall population. In states where less than five places meet either of these criteria, we have included places with at least 10,000 total population with the highest percentage of Hispanic/Latino population. These places are identified with an asterisk (*); Please refer to the User's Guide for a full explanation of data.

Homeownship Rate

(Universe: Occupied Housing Units)

Hispanic or Latino (of any race)

Top 10 States, Counties, and Places[1]

Sorted by Percent in Descending Order — U.S. = 47.3%

State	Percent	County	Percent	Place	Percent
New Mexico	66.2	Chase County, KS	100.0	**Romeoville, IL** (village) Will County	86.7
Texas	57.8	Aitkin County, MN	90.0	**Cooper City, FL** (city) Broward County	86.0
Michigan	56.2	Webster County, MS	89.3	**Richmond West, FL** (cdp) Miami-Dade County	85.4
Arizona	54.4	Piscataquis County, ME	88.9	**Streamwood, IL** (village) Cook County	84.8
Florida	54.4	Wyoming County, WV	88.2	**Mission Bend, TX** (cdp) Fort Bend County	84.1
Wyoming	53.5	Cameron Parish, LA	86.0	**Atascocita, TX** (cdp) Harris County	83.1
West Virginia	53.2	Putnam County, IL	85.1	**Little Elm, TX** (city) Denton County	80.6
Idaho	53.1	Pike County, PA	84.8	**Diamond Bar, CA** (city) Los Angeles County	80.3
Kansas	53.0	Menard County, IL	84.4	**Eastvale, CA** (cdp) Riverside County	80.3
Illinois	52.6	Mora County, NM	83.4	**Sahuarita, AZ** (town) Pima County	80.0

Sorted by Percent in Ascending Order — U.S. = 47.3%

State	Percent	County	Percent	Place	Percent
New York	23.2	Chattahoochee County, GA	6.4	**Fort Hood, TX** (cdp) Bell County	0.5
Massachusetts	24.8	New York County, NY	7.3	**Fort Campbell North*, KY** (cdp) Christian County	0.8
Rhode Island	27.2	Marshall County, SD	8.7	**Schofield Barracks*, HI** (cdp) Honolulu County	1.0
District of Columbia	31.5	Bronx County, NY	11.1	**Manhattan, NY** (borough) New York County	7.3
Connecticut	33.2	Bullock County, AL	13.2	**North Atlanta, GA** (cdp) DeKalb County	7.7
North Dakota	35.4	Kings County, NY	14.1	**Bronx, NY** (borough) Bronx County	11.1
Kentucky	35.5	Nantucket County, MA	14.3	**Woonsocket*, RI** (city) Providence County	11.5
New Jersey	36.3	Carroll County, KY	14.7	**University, FL** (cdp) Hillsborough County	12.0
Hawaii	39.5	Butler County, KY	15.5	**Fitchburg*, WI** (city) Dane County	12.3
New Hampshire	39.7	Chickasaw County, IA	17.7	**Spring Valley, NY** (village) Rockland County	12.8

Note: (1) Ranking tables cover all states and counties, and places with an overall population of at least 125,000, OR an overall population of at least 25,000 where the Hispanic/Latino population is at least 20% of the overall population. In states where less than five places meet either of these criteria, we have included places with at least 10,000 total population with the highest percentage of Hispanic/Latino population. These places are identified with an asterisk (*); Please refer to the User's Guide for a full explanation of data.

Homeownship Rate

(Universe: Occupied Housing Units)

Central American, excluding Mexican

Top 10 States, Counties, and Places[1]

Sorted by Percent in Descending Order — U.S. = 39.7%

State	Percent	County	Percent	Place	Percent
West Virginia	58.5	King George County, VA	88.5	**Leander, TX** (city) Williamson County	93.8
New Mexico	55.3	Pike County, PA	87.7	**Romeoville, IL** (village) Will County	88.9
Idaho	54.0	Liberty County, TX	86.6	**Mission Bend, TX** (cdp) Fort Bend County	88.1
Arizona	53.6	Valencia County, NM	84.4	**Little Elm, TX** (city) Denton County	87.7
Arkansas	53.5	Saint John the Baptist Parish, LA	84.0	**Richmond West, FL** (cdp) Miami-Dade County	86.8
Utah	52.5	Kendall County, IL	83.9	**Schertz, TX** (city) Guadalupe County	86.0
Maryland	49.6	Hendricks County, IN	83.6	**Sahuarita, AZ** (town) Pima County	85.4
Iowa	49.2	Union County, PA	83.3	**Kyle, TX** (city) Hays County	85.1
Alaska	48.9	Yellowstone County, MT	82.6	**Cooper City, FL** (city) Broward County	85.0
Illinois	48.5	Fort Bend County, TX	82.3	**Kearns, UT** (cdp) Salt Lake County	83.4

Sorted by Percent in Ascending Order — U.S. = 39.7%

State	Percent	County	Percent	Place	Percent
District of Columbia	27.4	Ohio County, KY	6.7	**Fort Hood, TX** (cdp) Bell County	2.9
Massachusetts	28.4	Parmer County, TX	7.1	**Schofield Barracks*, HI** (cdp) Honolulu County	3.1
New York	28.8	Independence County, AR	7.4	**North Atlanta, GA** (cdp) DeKalb County	4.5
Hawaii	29.2	New York County, NY	8.2	**Spring Valley, NY** (village) Rockland County	6.1
New Jersey	29.4	Columbiana County, OH	9.1	**Fitchburg*, WI** (city) Dane County	6.5
North Dakota	29.8	Lyon County, MN	9.2	**San Rafael, CA** (city) Marin County	6.7
Kentucky	30.3	Tuscarawas County, OH	9.5	**Mayfield*, KY** (city) Graves County	8.1
Connecticut	31.9	Nantucket County, MA	10.4	**Manhattan, NY** (borough) New York County	8.2
Rhode Island	32.1	Saluda County, SC	10.5	**University, FL** (cdp) Hillsborough County	9.0
Alabama	33.3	Bronx County, NY	10.7	**West New York, NJ** (town) Hudson County	9.6

RANKINGS & COMPARISONS

Note: (1) Ranking tables cover all states and counties, and places with an overall population of at least 125,000, OR an overall population of at least 25,000 where the Hispanic/Latino population is at least 20% of the overall population. In states where less than five places meet either of these criteria, we have included places with at least 10,000 total population with the highest percentage of Hispanic/Latino population. These places are identified with an asterisk (*); Please refer to the User's Guide for a full explanation of data.

Homeownship Rate

(Universe: Occupied Housing Units)

Central American: Costa Rican

Top 10 States, Counties, and Places[1]

Sorted by Percent in Descending Order — U.S. = 46.8%

State	Percent	County	Percent	Place	Percent
Mississippi	68.2	Wayne County, MI	80.8	**Port Saint Lucie, FL** (city) Saint Lucie County	85.4
Idaho	64.3	Saint Lucie County, FL	80.7	**Richmond West, FL** (cdp) Miami-Dade County	85.2
Maine	62.5	Fort Bend County, TX	78.7	**Miami Gardens, FL** (city) Miami-Dade County	83.9
Delaware	62.1	Placer County, CA	76.5	**Oyster Bay, NY** (town) Nassau County	80.6
Michigan	61.7	Snohomish County, WA	76.4	**Brookhaven, NY** (town) Suffolk County	79.6
Louisiana	60.9	Pasco County, FL	75.3	**Lakewood, CA** (city) Los Angeles County	79.3
Minnesota	60.7	Polk County, FL	73.7	**Rialto, CA** (city) San Bernardino County	78.8
Nebraska	59.2	Clackamas County, OR	73.0	**Tamiami, FL** (cdp) Miami-Dade County	78.3
New Hampshire	59.2	Oakland County, MI	72.1	**Margate, FL** (city) Broward County	77.8
Tennessee	59.1	Orange County, NY	71.2	**Weston, FL** (city) Broward County	76.9

Sorted by Percent in Ascending Order — U.S. = 46.8%

State	Percent	County	Percent	Place	Percent
New Jersey	27.6	New York County, NY	9.5	**West New York, NJ** (town) Hudson County	9.3
Hawaii	35.5	Lancaster County, PA	17.4	**Manhattan, NY** (borough) New York County	9.5
New York	35.7	Hudson County, NJ	19.9	**Hilton Head Island*, SC** (town) Beaufort County	12.8
Rhode Island	37.3	Essex County, NJ	20.1	**Elizabeth, NJ** (city) Union County	14.0
Massachusetts	41.6	Hunterdon County, NJ	20.8	**Paterson, NJ** (city) Passaic County	15.0
Kentucky	42.6	Union County, NJ	23.4	**Bloomfield, NJ** (township) Essex County	15.1
Connecticut	42.7	Passaic County, NJ	24.1	**Plainfield, NJ** (city) Union County	17.9
South Carolina	45.7	Bronx County, NY	24.9	**Trenton, NJ** (city) Mercer County	22.3
Pennsylvania	46.4	Somerset County, NJ	24.9	**Orlando, FL** (city) Orange County	22.8
Virginia	46.4	Morris County, NJ	26.4	**Miami Beach, FL** (city) Miami-Dade County	23.1

Note: (1) Ranking tables cover all states and counties, and places with an overall population of at least 125,000, OR an overall population of at least 25,000 where the Hispanic/Latino population is at least 20% of the overall population. In states where less than five places meet either of these criteria, we have included places with at least 10,000 total population with the highest percentage of Hispanic/Latino population. These places are identified with an asterisk (*); Please refer to the User's Guide for a full explanation of data.

Homeownship Rate

(Universe: Occupied Housing Units)

Central American: Guatemalan

Top 10 States, Counties, and Places[1]

Sorted by Percent in Descending Order — U.S. = 31.9%

State	Percent	County	Percent	Place	Percent
New Mexico	56.2	Sandoval County, NM	89.2	**Round Lake Beach, IL** (village) Lake County	93.0
West Virginia	55.0	Canadian County, OK	87.5	**Streamwood, IL** (village) Cook County	93.0
Utah	50.9	Ottawa County, MI	85.7	**Little Elm, TX** (city) Denton County	91.2
Illinois	48.6	Fort Bend County, TX	85.0	**Atascocita, TX** (cdp) Harris County	90.9
Arizona	48.2	Kendall County, IL	83.0	**Richmond West, FL** (cdp) Miami-Dade County	90.6
Idaho	46.7	Henry County, GA	80.0	**Rio Rancho, NM** (city) Sandoval County	90.3
Louisiana	46.7	McHenry County, IL	78.4	**Farmers Branch, TX** (city) Dallas County	89.3
Alaska	45.5	Guadalupe County, TX	77.4	**Romeoville, IL** (village) Will County	87.5
Indiana	44.4	Johnson County, TX	76.7	**Hanover Park, IL** (village) Cook County	86.3
Nevada	43.7	Will County, IL	75.3	**Poinciana, FL** (cdp) Osceola County	85.4

Sorted by Percent in Ascending Order — U.S. = 31.9%

State	Percent	County	Percent	Place	Percent
Kentucky	19.1	Coffee County, AL	1.0	**University, FL** (cdp) Hillsborough County	2.6
New York	19.5	Kendall County, TX	4.3	**Mayfield*, KY** (city) Graves County	2.9
Mississippi	19.7	Madison County, MS	4.3	**Spring Valley, NY** (village) Rockland County	4.0
District of Columbia	22.1	Campbell County, KY	4.8	**Marietta, GA** (city) Cobb County	4.4
Tennessee	22.6	DeKalb County, GA	5.3	**San Rafael, CA** (city) Marin County	4.4
New Jersey	24.3	Monroe County, FL	5.9	**Cincinnati, OH** (city) Hamilton County	5.4
Massachusetts	24.4	Leake County, MS	6.1	**SeaTac, WA** (city) King County	5.7
South Carolina	24.6	Columbiana County, OH	6.5	**Urban Honolulu, HI** (cdp) Honolulu County	5.9
Connecticut	25.1	Independence County, AR	6.8	**West New York, NJ** (town) Hudson County	6.2
Alabama	25.2	New York County, NY	7.2	**North Atlanta, GA** (cdp) DeKalb County	6.3

Note: (1) Ranking tables cover all states and counties, and places with an overall population of at least 125,000, OR an overall population of at least 25,000 where the Hispanic/Latino population is at least 20% of the overall population. In states where less than five places meet either of these criteria, we have included places with at least 10,000 total population with the highest percentage of Hispanic/Latino population. These places are identified with an asterisk (*); Please refer to the User's Guide for a full explanation of data.

Homeownship Rate

(Universe: Occupied Housing Units)

Central American: Honduran

Top 10 States, Counties, and Places[1]

Sorted by Percent in Descending Order — U.S. = 31.9%

State	Percent	County	Percent	Place	Percent
Idaho	51.4	Hendricks County, IN	87.5	**Mission Bend, TX** (cdp) Fort Bend County	86.7
Alaska	50.0	Saint John the Baptist Parish, LA	85.3	**Little Elm, TX** (city) Denton County	83.9
New Mexico	50.0	Monroe County, PA	83.1	**Richmond West, FL** (cdp) Miami-Dade County	81.1
Arizona	46.2	Paulding County, GA	81.8	**Spring, TX** (cdp) Harris County	81.0
Utah	46.2	Fort Bend County, TX	77.6	**Poinciana, FL** (cdp) Osceola County	79.7
Nebraska	42.8	Charles County, MD	76.5	**Riverview, FL** (cdp) Hillsborough County	78.6
West Virginia	42.6	Bastrop County, TX	75.0	**Miramar, FL** (city) Broward County	78.5
Arkansas	42.2	Saint Charles Parish, LA	72.4	**Pearland, TX** (city) Brazoria County	75.0
Michigan	41.9	Fayette County, GA	71.9	**Atascocita, TX** (cdp) Harris County	74.5
Illinois	41.3	Saint Johns County, FL	69.7	**The Colony, TX** (city) Denton County	74.3

Sorted by Percent in Ascending Order — U.S. = 31.9%

State	Percent	County	Percent	Place	Percent
District of Columbia	18.0	New York County, NY	5.5	**North Atlanta, GA** (cdp) DeKalb County	1.7
New York	19.1	Franklin County, KY	7.1	**West New York, NJ** (town) Hudson County	5.4
Hawaii	20.9	Clark County, IN	7.7	**Manhattan, NY** (borough) New York County	5.5
Massachusetts	23.9	Bronx County, NY	7.8	**Biloxi*, MS** (city) Harrison County	6.5
New Hampshire	25.2	Bibb County, GA	8.3	**Birmingham, AL** (city) Jefferson County	6.7
New Jersey	27.3	Sevier County, TN	9.5	**Fort Pierce, FL** (city) Saint Lucie County	7.2
Virginia	27.5	Talbot County, MD	9.7	**Bronx, NY** (borough) Bronx County	7.8
California	28.1	DeKalb County, GA	9.8	**University, FL** (cdp) Hillsborough County	7.9
Washington	28.2	Henrico County, VA	10.7	**Hilton Head Island*, SC** (town) Beaufort County	8.3
Kentucky	28.5	Kings County, NY	13.0	**Alexandria, VA** (independent city)	8.5

Note: (1) Ranking tables cover all states and counties, and places with an overall population of at least 125,000, OR an overall population of at least 25,000 where the Hispanic/Latino population is at least 20% of the overall population. In states where less than five places meet either of these criteria, we have included places with at least 10,000 total population with the highest percentage of Hispanic/Latino population. These places are identified with an asterisk (*); Please refer to the User's Guide for a full explanation of data.

Homeownship Rate

(Universe: Occupied Housing Units)

Central American: Nicaraguan

Top 10 States, Counties, and Places[1]

Sorted by Percent in Descending Order — U.S. = 46.4%

State	Percent	County	Percent	Place	Percent
New Mexico	59.4	Lyon County, NV	87.1	**Hacienda Heights, CA** (cdp) Los Angeles County	94.1
Arizona	58.4	Union County, NC	86.7	**Chino Hills, CA** (city) San Bernardino County	90.0
Oklahoma	57.2	Saint Charles Parish, LA	83.3	**Richmond West, FL** (cdp) Miami-Dade County	88.2
West Virginia	56.8	Pasco County, FL	82.3	**La Mirada, CA** (city) Los Angeles County	82.1
Pennsylvania	55.3	Saint Tammany Parish, LA	81.3	**Royal Palm Beach, FL** (village) Palm Beach County	82.1
Maryland	54.3	Fort Bend County, TX	81.1	**Poinciana, FL** (cdp) Osceola County	81.2
Illinois	54.1	Lucas County, OH	76.5	**Menifee, CA** (city) Riverside County	80.6
Louisiana	54.1	El Dorado County, CA	75.0	**Perris, CA** (city) Riverside County	80.4
Idaho	53.8	Henry County, GA	74.2	**Pennsauken, NJ** (township) Camden County	80.2
Texas	53.3	Pinal County, AZ	72.5	**Mission Bend, TX** (cdp) Fort Bend County	79.2

Sorted by Percent in Ascending Order — U.S. = 46.4%

State	Percent	County	Percent	Place	Percent
Rhode Island	22.9	New York County, NY	8.2	**North Atlanta, GA** (cdp) DeKalb County	2.1
New York	23.1	Bronx County, NY	13.0	**Manhattan, NY** (borough) New York County	8.2
Massachusetts	31.8	Kings County, NY	16.4	**Union City, NJ** (city) Hudson County	12.9
District of Columbia	33.8	Brown County, WI	19.4	**Bronx, NY** (borough) Bronx County	13.0
Connecticut	37.0	DeKalb County, GA	20.3	**Bell Gardens, CA** (city) Los Angeles County	13.2
Hawaii	38.4	Monroe County, FL	21.0	**Newark, NJ** (city) Essex County	14.9
Kentucky	40.4	Arlington County, VA	21.7	**Providence, RI** (city) Providence County	15.0
New Jersey	41.1	Hudson County, NJ	23.3	**New York, NY** (city)	16.3
Wisconsin	42.9	Queens County, NY	23.6	**Brooklyn, NY** (borough) Kings County	16.4
South Carolina	43.1	Providence County, RI	23.8	**West New York, NJ** (town) Hudson County	16.4

RANKINGS & COMPARISONS

Note: (1) Ranking tables cover all states and counties, and places with an overall population of at least 125,000, OR an overall population of at least 25,000 where the Hispanic/Latino population is at least 20% of the overall population. In states where less than five places meet either of these criteria, we have included places with at least 10,000 total population with the highest percentage of Hispanic/Latino population. These places are identified with an asterisk (*); Please refer to the User's Guide for a full explanation of data.

Homeownship Rate

(Universe: Occupied Housing Units)

Central American: Panamanian

Top 10 States, Counties, and Places[1]

Sorted by Percent in Descending Order — U.S. = 48.8%

State	Percent	County	Percent	Place	Percent
New Mexico	62.3	Charlotte County, FL	89.3	**Richmond West, FL** (cdp) Miami-Dade County	86.5
Minnesota	61.2	Guadalupe County, TX	88.5	**Tamiami, FL** (cdp) Miami-Dade County	85.2
Utah	61.1	Charles County, MD	86.5	**Poinciana, FL** (cdp) Osceola County	84.1
Arizona	59.9	Fort Bend County, TX	84.6	**Riverview, FL** (cdp) Hillsborough County	82.7
Delaware	59.7	Hoke County, NC	82.6	**Brentwood, NY** (cdp) Suffolk County	82.2
Oklahoma	59.2	Saint Tammany Parish, LA	82.1	**Central Islip, NY** (cdp) Suffolk County	82.2
Tennessee	58.7	Newton County, GA	80.6	**Corona, CA** (city) Riverside County	80.6
South Carolina	58.6	Columbia County, GA	80.3	**Cutler Bay, FL** (town) Miami-Dade County	79.7
Mississippi	58.2	Hernando County, FL	78.3	**South Miami Heights, FL** (cdp) Miami-Dade County	79.6
West Virginia	57.4	Monroe County, PA	77.6	**McKinney, TX** (city) Collin County	78.6

Sorted by Percent in Ascending Order — U.S. = 48.8%

State	Percent	County	Percent	Place	Percent
New York	30.9	New York County, NY	14.4	**Hawthorne, CA** (city) Los Angeles County	13.0
Hawaii	35.6	Bronx County, NY	19.5	**Manhattan, NY** (borough) New York County	14.4
North Dakota	36.0	Kings County, NY	22.6	**Bayonne, NJ** (city) Hudson County	15.6
Rhode Island	37.2	Brazos County, TX	26.5	**Elizabeth, NJ** (city) Union County	17.9
District of Columbia	38.5	Hudson County, NJ	26.5	**Bronx, NY** (borough) Bronx County	19.5
Massachusetts	40.4	San Francisco County, CA	27.1	**Tallahassee, FL** (city) Leon County	19.6
Maine	41.4	Arlington County, VA	27.6	**Worcester, MA** (city) Worcester County	21.7
Kentucky	43.0	Jefferson County, NY	27.6	**Brooklyn, NY** (borough) Kings County	22.6
Nevada	46.1	Leon County, FL	29.3	**Irving, TX** (city) Dallas County	24.1
California	46.9	Essex County, MA	29.4	**Silver Spring, MD** (cdp) Montgomery County	24.2

Note: (1) Ranking tables cover all states and counties, and places with an overall population of at least 125,000, OR an overall population of at least 25,000 where the Hispanic/Latino population is at least 20% of the overall population. In states where less than five places meet either of these criteria, we have included places with at least 10,000 total population with the highest percentage of Hispanic/Latino population. These places are identified with an asterisk (*); Please refer to the User's Guide for a full explanation of data.

Homeownship Rate

(Universe: Occupied Housing Units)

Central American: Salvadoran

Top 10 States, Counties, and Places[1]

Sorted by Percent in Descending Order — U.S. = 43.9%

State	Percent	County	Percent	Place	Percent
West Virginia	63.7	Paulding County, GA	89.5	**Magna, UT** (cdp) Salt Lake County	89.7
Idaho	59.8	Liberty County, TX	88.9	**Mission Bend, TX** (cdp) Fort Bend County	89.5
Kansas	59.2	Navarro County, TX	88.1	**Little Elm, TX** (city) Denton County	87.7
Arizona	58.8	Hendricks County, IN	87.5	**Richmond West, FL** (cdp) Miami-Dade County	87.1
Arkansas	58.7	Kaufman County, TX	87.5	**The Colony, TX** (city) Denton County	86.9
Nebraska	57.8	Rockwall County, TX	85.1	**Eastvale, CA** (cdp) Riverside County	85.9
Iowa	57.7	Henry County, GA	84.7	**Spring, TX** (cdp) Harris County	85.0
Utah	55.7	Titus County, TX	84.6	**El Mirage, AZ** (city) Maricopa County	84.8
Maryland	55.1	Granville County, NC	83.9	**Buckeye, AZ** (town) Maricopa County	83.0
Indiana	54.7	Fort Bend County, TX	82.7	**Tamiami, FL** (cdp) Miami-Dade County	83.0

Sorted by Percent in Ascending Order — U.S. = 43.9%

State	Percent	County	Percent	Place	Percent
Hawaii	24.1	New York County, NY	7.1	**North Atlanta, GA** (cdp) DeKalb County	3.2
District of Columbia	27.4	Blount County, TN	8.0	**Santa Barbara, CA** (city) Santa Barbara County	6.9
New Jersey	30.4	Bronx County, NY	11.4	**Manhattan, NY** (borough) New York County	7.1
Massachusetts	30.7	Kings County, NY	11.6	**Spring Valley, NY** (village) Rockland County	9.9
Wyoming	31.5	Nantucket County, MA	11.6	**San Rafael, CA** (city) Marin County	10.6
Vermont	33.3	Harrison County, MS	17.6	**Union City, NJ** (city) Hudson County	11.3
Maine	37.2	Hudson County, NJ	18.7	**West New York, NJ** (town) Hudson County	11.3
Ohio	37.5	Charleston County, SC	18.9	**Bronx, NY** (borough) Bronx County	11.4
California	37.6	Queens County, NY	18.9	**Brooklyn, NY** (borough) Kings County	11.6
Connecticut	38.5	DeKalb County, GA	19.0	**Costa Mesa, CA** (city) Orange County	12.5

Note: (1) Ranking tables cover all states and counties, and places with an overall population of at least 125,000, OR an overall population of at least 25,000 where the Hispanic/Latino population is at least 20% of the overall population. In states where less than five places meet either of these criteria, we have included places with at least 10,000 total population with the highest percentage of Hispanic/Latino population. These places are identified with an asterisk (*); Please refer to the User's Guide for a full explanation of data.

Homeownship Rate

(Universe: Occupied Housing Units)

Cuban

Top 10 States, Counties, and Places[1]

Sorted by Percent in Descending Order — U.S. = 57.1%

State	Percent	County	Percent	Place	Percent
Delaware	66.6	Pike County, PA	90.9	**Cooper City, FL** (city) Broward County	90.2
Georgia	63.8	Walton County, FL	90.5	**Bolingbrook, IL** (village) Will County	86.8
South Carolina	63.1	Fayette County, GA	89.3	**La Porte, TX** (city) Harris County	86.7
Maryland	62.0	Calhoun County, FL	88.9	**Eastvale, CA** (cdp) Riverside County	86.2
New Hampshire	61.8	Barrow County, GA	87.9	**Richmond West, FL** (cdp) Miami-Dade County	86.0
Florida	60.6	Sandoval County, NM	87.7	**Oyster Bay, NY** (town) Nassau County	85.6
Louisiana	59.7	Franklin County, NC	87.2	**Chino Hills, CA** (city) San Bernardino County	85.5
North Carolina	58.9	Guadalupe County, TX	86.6	**Pearland, TX** (city) Brazoria County	85.4
Connecticut	58.8	Saint John the Baptist Parish, LA	86.1	**Rio Rancho, NM** (city) Sandoval County	85.1
Alabama	58.5	Forsyth County, GA	85.5	**Atascocita, TX** (cdp) Harris County	85.0

Sorted by Percent in Ascending Order — U.S. = 57.1%

State	Percent	County	Percent	Place	Percent
Nebraska	31.9	Madison County, NE	5.0	**Grand Island, NE** (city) Hall County	7.9
Hawaii	33.5	Ford County, KS	8.0	**Dodge City, KS** (city) Ford County	8.0
New York	36.2	Hall County, NE	8.2	**National City, CA** (city) San Diego County	11.4
District of Columbia	39.7	Cass County, IL	11.6	**Portland*, ME** (city) Cumberland County	13.3
North Dakota	40.5	New York County, NY	15.7	**Manhattan, NY** (borough) New York County	15.7
Wisconsin	40.5	Buchanan County, MO	16.7	**West Chicago, IL** (city) DuPage County	16.9
Rhode Island	41.2	Bronx County, NY	17.4	**Guymon*, OK** (city) Texas County	17.1
Oregon	42.4	Kings County, CA	17.9	**Bronx, NY** (borough) Bronx County	17.4
Alaska	42.7	Jefferson County, NY	20.8	**West New York, NJ** (town) Hudson County	17.8
Massachusetts	44.6	Texas County, OK	20.8	**Urban Honolulu, HI** (cdp) Honolulu County	18.3

Note: (1) Ranking tables cover all states and counties, and places with an overall population of at least 125,000, OR an overall population of at least 25,000 where the Hispanic/Latino population is at least 20% of the overall population. In states where less than five places meet either of these criteria, we have included places with at least 10,000 total population with the highest percentage of Hispanic/Latino population. These places are identified with an asterisk (*); Please refer to the User's Guide for a full explanation of data.

Homeownship Rate

(Universe: Occupied Housing Units)

Dominican Republic

Top 10 States, Counties, and Places[1]

Sorted by Percent in Descending Order — U.S. = 26.8%

State	Percent	County	Percent	Place	Percent
Florida	52.5	Hoke County, NC	93.0	**San Tan Valley, AZ** (cdp) Pinal County	88.5
South Carolina	50.4	Pike County, PA	88.2	**Cooper City, FL** (city) Broward County	84.1
Delaware	49.3	Fayette County, GA	84.6	**Richmond West, FL** (cdp) Miami-Dade County	82.8
Texas	49.2	Pinal County, AZ	81.3	**Ocoee, FL** (city) Orange County	80.5
Georgia	48.6	Brazoria County, TX	80.0	**Pennsauken, NJ** (township) Camden County	78.4
Nevada	47.7	Paulding County, GA	80.0	**Tamiami, FL** (cdp) Miami-Dade County	77.9
Michigan	47.2	Forsyth County, GA	77.8	**Deltona, FL** (city) Volusia County	76.0
Iowa	47.0	Putnam County, NY	77.7	**Oyster Bay, NY** (town) Nassau County	74.5
Maryland	47.0	Citrus County, FL	76.8	**Royal Palm Beach, FL** (village) Palm Beach County	74.0
New Mexico	46.8	Sussex County, NJ	76.0	**Bergenfield, NJ** (borough) Bergen County	73.4

Sorted by Percent in Ascending Order — U.S. = 26.8%

State	Percent	County	Percent	Place	Percent
New York	14.1	Centre County, PA	2.9	**Manhattan, NY** (borough) New York County	3.4
Massachusetts	19.7	New York County, NY	3.4	**Bronx, NY** (borough) Bronx County	7.9
Hawaii	22.0	Bronx County, NY	7.9	**New York, NY** (city)	10.1
Rhode Island	27.8	Suffolk County, MA	11.1	**Metairie, LA** (cdp) Jefferson Parish	10.6
New Hampshire	29.4	Lincoln County, NC	12.5	**West New York, NJ** (town) Hudson County	10.6
Idaho	31.3	Union County, PA	12.5	**Boston, MA** (city) Suffolk County	10.7
District of Columbia	32.1	Tompkins County, NY	12.9	**Union City, NJ** (city) Hudson County	11.8
Vermont	32.1	Jefferson County, NY	13.0	**Port Chester, NY** (village) Westchester County	12.6
Maine	32.5	Kings County, NY	13.4	**Brooklyn, NY** (borough) Kings County	13.4
New Jersey	32.9	San Francisco County, CA	14.4	**Woonsocket*, RI** (city) Providence County	13.4

Note: (1) Ranking tables cover all states and counties, and places with an overall population of at least 125,000, OR an overall population of at least 25,000 where the Hispanic/Latino population is at least 20% of the overall population. In states where less than five places meet either of these criteria, we have included places with at least 10,000 total population with the highest percentage of Hispanic/Latino population. These places are identified with an asterisk (*); Please refer to the User's Guide for a full explanation of data.

Homeownship Rate

(Universe: Occupied Housing Units)

Mexican

Top 10 States, Counties, and Places[1]

Sorted by Percent in Descending Order — U.S. = 49.8%

State	Percent	County	Percent	Place	Percent
New Mexico	64.7	Martin County, KY	100.0	**Romeoville, IL** (village) Will County	87.6
Texas	59.1	Cameron Parish, LA	87.9	**Streamwood, IL** (village) Cook County	85.4
Michigan	57.6	Putnam County, IL	86.8	**Atascocita, TX** (cdp) Harris County	84.6
Arizona	54.7	Pike County, PA	83.3	**Mission Bend, TX** (cdp) Fort Bend County	82.9
Kansas	54.5	Worth County, IA	83.3	**Burbank, IL** (city) Cook County	80.8
Illinois	54.3	Mora County, NM	83.0	**Diamond Bar, CA** (city) Los Angeles County	80.7
Idaho	53.2	Winkler County, TX	83.0	**Eastvale, CA** (cdp) Riverside County	80.5
Wyoming	52.4	Ness County, KS	82.4	**Kyle, TX** (city) Hays County	80.0
Indiana	52.2	Kendall County, IL	82.2	**Sahuarita, AZ** (town) Pima County	79.9
Iowa	51.4	Crane County, TX	81.3	**La Mirada, CA** (city) Los Angeles County	79.7

Sorted by Percent in Ascending Order — U.S. = 49.8%

State	Percent	County	Percent	Place	Percent
New York	13.9	Bronx County, NY	4.8	**Fort Hood, TX** (cdp) Bell County	0.3
New Jersey	20.8	Kings County, NY	6.9	**Schofield Barracks*, HI** (cdp) Honolulu County	0.7
District of Columbia	28.2	Marshall County, SD	7.5	**North Atlanta, GA** (cdp) DeKalb County	2.6
Connecticut	28.3	New York County, NY	7.5	**Bronx, NY** (borough) Bronx County	4.8
Rhode Island	28.4	Northumberland County, VA	8.2	**Spring Valley, NY** (village) Rockland County	6.1
Kentucky	29.8	Queens County, NY	9.5	**West New York, NJ** (town) Hudson County	6.8
Hawaii	30.7	Chattahoochee County, GA	10.3	**Brooklyn, NY** (borough) Kings County	6.9
Massachusetts	33.3	Lawrence County, MS	10.3	**University, FL** (cdp) Hillsborough County	6.9
North Dakota	34.0	McKenzie County, ND	11.1	**Union City, NJ** (city) Hudson County	7.1
South Carolina	35.6	Hudson County, NJ	11.2	**Manhattan, NY** (borough) New York County	7.5

Note: (1) Ranking tables cover all states and counties, and places with an overall population of at least 125,000, OR an overall population of at least 25,000 where the Hispanic/Latino population is at least 20% of the overall population. In states where less than five places meet either of these criteria, we have included places with at least 10,000 total population with the highest percentage of Hispanic/Latino population. These places are identified with an asterisk (*); Please refer to the User's Guide for a full explanation of data.

Homeownship Rate

(Universe: Occupied Housing Units)

Puerto Rican

Top 10 States, Counties, and Places[1]

Sorted by Percent in Descending Order — U.S. = 37.9%

State	Percent	County	Percent	Place	Percent
New Mexico	55.2	Adams County, WI	94.1	**Norco, CA** (city) Riverside County	89.5
Indiana	53.9	Wilson County, TX	91.2	**Sahuarita, AZ** (town) Pima County	87.2
Georgia	53.7	Harris County, GA	90.0	**Pueblo West, CO** (cdp) Pueblo County	85.7
Alabama	53.1	Hampton County, SC	87.5	**Diamond Bar, CA** (city) Los Angeles County	85.5
Texas	52.7	Currituck County, NC	86.5	**Richmond West, FL** (cdp) Miami-Dade County	85.5
South Carolina	52.4	Tipton County, TN	86.2	**West Whittier-Los Nietos, CA** (cdp) Los Angeles County	83.3
Maryland	52.2	Powhatan County, VA	84.6	**Cooper City, FL** (city) Broward County	82.8
Florida	52.1	Wright County, MN	84.4	**Little Elm, TX** (city) Denton County	82.6
Arizona	50.1	Geauga County, OH	84.2	**Bolingbrook, IL** (village) Will County	82.5
Tennessee	50.1	Medina County, TX	84.0	**Romeoville, IL** (village) Will County	81.1

Sorted by Percent in Ascending Order — U.S. = 37.9%

State	Percent	County	Percent	Place	Percent
Rhode Island	17.3	Chattahoochee County, GA	6.2	**Fort Hood, TX** (cdp) Bell County	0.7
Massachusetts	19.8	New York County, NY	7.0	**Schofield Barracks*, HI** (cdp) Honolulu County	1.1
New York	23.4	Hardy County, WV	9.8	**Fort Campbell North*, KY** (cdp) Christian County	2.8
Connecticut	28.3	Coos County, NH	10.3	**Central Falls*, RI** (city) Providence County	6.6
South Dakota	31.2	Bronx County, NY	13.2	**Manhattan, NY** (borough) New York County	7.0
North Dakota	31.6	Kings County, NY	13.7	**Woonsocket*, RI** (city) Providence County	8.4
New Hampshire	32.1	Beadle County, SD	13.8	**Atlantic City, NJ** (city) Atlantic County	9.7
District of Columbia	34.2	Suffolk County, MA	13.9	**Huntington Park, CA** (city) Los Angeles County	9.9
Alaska	34.9	Juniata County, PA	14.0	**Fairbanks*, AK** (city) Fairbanks North Star Borough	11.6
Wisconsin	35.0	Indiana County, PA	14.5	**Union City, NJ** (city) Hudson County	11.6

RANKINGS & COMPARISONS

Note: (1) Ranking tables cover all states and counties, and places with an overall population of at least 125,000, OR an overall population of at least 25,000 where the Hispanic/Latino population is at least 20% of the overall population. In states where less than five places meet either of these criteria, we have included places with at least 10,000 total population with the highest percentage of Hispanic/Latino population. These places are identified with an asterisk (*); Please refer to the User's Guide for a full explanation of data.

Homeownship Rate

(Universe: Occupied Housing Units)

South American

Top 10 States, Counties, and Places[1]

Sorted by Percent in Descending Order — U.S. = 48.8%

State	Percent	County	Percent	Place	Percent
New Mexico	63.0	Sumter County, FL	93.8	**Suisun City, CA** (city) Solano County	89.7
Maryland	62.8	Orange County, VA	92.3	**Streamwood, IL** (village) Cook County	89.6
Michigan	62.8	Wilson County, TN	90.5	**Little Elm, TX** (city) Denton County	88.9
Arizona	62.0	Lancaster County, SC	90.2	**Kyle, TX** (city) Hays County	87.9
Delaware	61.1	Medina County, OH	88.9	**Leander, TX** (city) Williamson County	87.5
Georgia	60.4	Newton County, GA	88.9	**Sahuarita, AZ** (town) Pima County	87.5
Indiana	59.8	Pike County, PA	88.5	**Yucaipa, CA** (city) San Bernardino County	86.9
South Carolina	59.8	Scott County, MN	87.3	**Hanover Park, IL** (village) Cook County	86.8
Tennessee	59.2	Bastrop County, TX	87.1	**Bolingbrook, IL** (village) Will County	86.6
Alaska	59.0	Calvert County, MD	87.1	**Round Lake Beach, IL** (village) Lake County	85.5

Sorted by Percent in Ascending Order — U.S. = 48.8%

State	Percent	County	Percent	Place	Percent
New York	31.0	Madison County, ID	12.5	**Spring Valley, NY** (village) Rockland County	11.1
Hawaii	36.2	New York County, NY	14.2	**Manhattan, NY** (borough) New York County	14.2
North Dakota	36.3	Bronx County, NY	16.9	**West New York, NJ** (town) Hudson County	15.9
Rhode Island	37.8	Kings County, NY	18.1	**City of Orange, NJ** (township) Essex County	16.5
District of Columbia	38.8	Montgomery County, VA	20.2	**Bronx, NY** (borough) Bronx County	16.9
New Jersey	39.2	Centre County, PA	22.1	**Twentynine Palms, CA** (city) San Bernardino County	17.1
Massachusetts	39.7	Union County, PA	22.2	**University, FL** (cdp) Hillsborough County	17.3
Montana	43.7	Bulloch County, GA	22.4	**Union City, NJ** (city) Hudson County	17.4
Wyoming	43.7	Whitman County, WA	22.4	**Brooklyn, NY** (borough) Kings County	18.1
South Dakota	46.2	Tuscaloosa County, AL	22.5	**Bell Gardens, CA** (city) Los Angeles County	18.5

Note: (1) Ranking tables cover all states and counties, and places with an overall population of at least 125,000, OR an overall population of at least 25,000 where the Hispanic/Latino population is at least 20% of the overall population. In states where less than five places meet either of these criteria, we have included places with at least 10,000 total population with the highest percentage of Hispanic/Latino population. These places are identified with an asterisk (*); Please refer to the User's Guide for a full explanation of data.

Homeownship Rate

(Universe: Occupied Housing Units)

South American: Argentinean

Top 10 States, Counties, and Places[1]

Sorted by Percent in Descending Order — U.S. = 55.0%

State	Percent	County	Percent	Place	Percent
Michigan	72.8	Will County, IL	90.3	**Cary, NC** (town) Wake County	94.9
Delaware	70.0	Galveston County, TX	87.5	**Hacienda Heights, CA** (cdp) Los Angeles County	88.1
West Virginia	68.4	Lake County, IL	86.2	**Cooper City, FL** (city) Broward County	86.0
Indiana	66.0	Charlotte County, FL	86.0	**Grand Prairie, TX** (city) Dallas County	85.7
Maryland	65.8	Forsyth County, GA	84.2	**Lake Elsinore, CA** (city) Riverside County	83.7
Ohio	65.3	Pasco County, FL	83.7	**Deltona, FL** (city) Volusia County	83.3
Kansas	64.8	Sussex County, NJ	83.1	**Oyster Bay, NY** (town) Nassau County	82.3
North Carolina	64.8	Pinal County, AZ	82.9	**Chino Hills, CA** (city) San Bernardino County	80.4
Minnesota	64.2	Burlington County, NJ	81.7	**Miramar, FL** (city) Broward County	80.1
Arizona	63.7	Monroe County, PA	81.5	**Weston, FL** (city) Broward County	79.8

Sorted by Percent in Ascending Order — U.S. = 55.0%

State	Percent	County	Percent	Place	Percent
Hawaii	36.3	New York County, NY	25.2	**West New York, NJ** (town) Hudson County	17.2
New York	42.9	Bronx County, NY	25.3	**Newark, NJ** (city) Essex County	17.8
District of Columbia	44.8	Kings County, NY	29.2	**Elizabeth, NJ** (city) Union County	20.5
Rhode Island	50.0	San Francisco County, CA	29.7	**Hilton Head Island*, SC** (town) Beaufort County	20.9
Wisconsin	51.0	Hudson County, NJ	30.4	**Union City, NJ** (city) Hudson County	22.1
California	54.0	Maui County, HI	31.1	**Perth Amboy, NJ** (city) Middlesex County	22.3
New Jersey	54.0	Suffolk County, MA	33.4	**New Haven, CT** (city/town) New Haven County	22.7
Massachusetts	54.1	Arlington County, VA	34.0	**Providence, RI** (city) Providence County	25.0
Florida	54.6	Queens County, NY	34.1	**Manhattan, NY** (borough) New York County	25.2
Montana	55.3	Honolulu County, HI	35.9	**Bronx, NY** (borough) Bronx County	25.3

Note: (1) Ranking tables cover all states and counties, and places with an overall population of at least 125,000, OR an overall population of at least 25,000 where the Hispanic/Latino population is at least 20% of the overall population. In states where less than five places meet either of these criteria, we have included places with at least 10,000 total population with the highest percentage of Hispanic/Latino population. These places are identified with an asterisk (*); Please refer to the User's Guide for a full explanation of data.

Homeownship Rate

(Universe: Occupied Housing Units)

South American: Bolivian

Top 10 States, Counties, and Places[1]

Sorted by Percent in Descending Order — U.S. = 56.4%

State	Percent	County	Percent	Place	Percent
Michigan	77.4	Will County, IL	93.8	**Miramar, FL** (city) Broward County	90.0
New Mexico	74.7	Kane County, IL	90.0	**Santa Clarita, CA** (city) Los Angeles County	89.7
Illinois	70.7	Fort Bend County, TX	88.5	**Islip, NY** (town) Suffolk County	86.3
Delaware	70.0	Anne Arundel County, MD	87.7	**Dale City, VA** (cdp) Prince William County	85.2
Iowa	69.0	Lake County, IL	82.5	**Montgomery Village, MD** (cdp) Montgomery County	79.7
Idaho	68.8	Monmouth County, NJ	82.4	**Chula Vista, CA** (city) San Diego County	76.9
West Virginia	67.4	Riverside County, CA	79.6	**Kendall West, FL** (cdp) Miami-Dade County	74.4
Maryland	67.3	Montgomery County, TX	79.4	**Sterling, VA** (cdp) Loudoun County	73.8
Kentucky	67.1	Cobb County, GA	77.6	**Springfield, VA** (cdp) Fairfax County	72.2
Kansas	66.7	Sacramento County, CA	77.4	**Kendale Lakes, FL** (cdp) Miami-Dade County	72.0

Sorted by Percent in Ascending Order — U.S. = 56.4%

State	Percent	County	Percent	Place	Percent
Arkansas	31.5	New York County, NY	18.8	**Newark, NJ** (city) Essex County	13.3
Massachusetts	41.0	Washington County, AR	23.7	**Garfield, NJ** (city) Bergen County	17.6
District of Columbia	41.2	Bronx County, NY	27.6	**Manhattan, NY** (borough) New York County	18.8
Rhode Island	42.8	Collier County, FL	29.0	**Elizabeth, NJ** (city) Union County	26.2
New York	44.4	Kings County, NY	32.6	**Bronx, NY** (borough) Bronx County	27.6
New Jersey	47.1	Hudson County, NJ	33.0	**Jersey City, NJ** (city) Hudson County	28.8
Hawaii	48.3	San Francisco County, CA	33.1	**Orlando, FL** (city) Orange County	32.4
Connecticut	50.5	Arlington County, VA	34.0	**Alexandria, VA** (independent city)	32.5
Louisiana	50.5	Suffolk County, MA	34.0	**Brooklyn, NY** (borough) Kings County	32.6
Oregon	51.7	Middlesex County, MA	35.2	**Boston, MA** (city) Suffolk County	33.0

Note: (1) Ranking tables cover all states and counties, and places with an overall population of at least 125,000, OR an overall population of at least 25,000 where the Hispanic/Latino population is at least 20% of the overall population. In states where less than five places meet either of these criteria, we have included places with at least 10,000 total population with the highest percentage of Hispanic/Latino population. These places are identified with an asterisk (*); Please refer to the User's Guide for a full explanation of data.

Homeownship Rate

(Universe: Occupied Housing Units)

South American: Chilean

Top 10 States, Counties, and Places[1]

Sorted by Percent in Descending Order — U.S. = 52.7%

State	Percent	County	Percent	Place	Percent
New Mexico	75.4	Douglas County, CO	86.4	**Richmond West, FL** (cdp) Miami-Dade County	90.0
Vermont	65.7	Ocean County, NJ	84.6	**Port Saint Lucie, FL** (city) Saint Lucie County	84.2
West Virginia	65.7	Saint Lucie County, FL	82.4	**Tamarac, FL** (city) Broward County	80.7
Tennessee	64.5	Frederick County, MD	80.7	**Tamiami, FL** (cdp) Miami-Dade County	77.0
South Carolina	64.4	Kane County, IL	80.5	**Cutler Bay, FL** (town) Miami-Dade County	76.8
Alaska	63.6	Howard County, MD	79.7	**Albuquerque, NM** (city) Bernalillo County	76.7
Maryland	63.5	Fort Bend County, TX	79.2	**Brookhaven, NY** (town) Suffolk County	76.2
Ohio	62.1	Prince William County, VA	78.4	**Miramar, FL** (city) Broward County	76.2
Michigan	62.0	Bernalillo County, NM	77.8	**Pembroke Pines, FL** (city) Broward County	76.2
Indiana	61.8	Pinal County, AZ	76.9	**Lancaster, CA** (city) Los Angeles County	75.4

Sorted by Percent in Ascending Order — U.S. = 52.7%

State	Percent	County	Percent	Place	Percent
New York	35.7	New York County, NY	15.6	**West New York, NJ** (town) Hudson County	13.5
Hawaii	38.0	Kings County, NY	17.5	**Manhattan, NY** (borough) New York County	15.6
District of Columbia	38.9	Bronx County, NY	20.6	**Brooklyn, NY** (borough) Kings County	17.5
Rhode Island	42.0	San Francisco County, CA	25.1	**Union City, NJ** (city) Hudson County	19.9
New Jersey	44.8	Hudson County, NJ	25.9	**Bronx, NY** (borough) Bronx County	20.6
Alabama	46.3	Yolo County, CA	27.7	**Jersey City, NJ** (city) Hudson County	23.1
Wisconsin	48.3	Queens County, NY	29.2	**Salt Lake City, UT** (city) Salt Lake County	23.1
Massachusetts	48.5	Providence County, RI	31.8	**New York, NY** (city)	23.6
Pennsylvania	49.8	Alachua County, FL	34.6	**New Haven, CT** (city/town) New Haven County	24.4
Montana	50.0	Erie County, NY	35.0	**San Francisco, CA** (city) San Francisco County	25.1

Note: (1) Ranking tables cover all states and counties, and places with an overall population of at least 125,000, OR an overall population of at least 25,000 where the Hispanic/Latino population is at least 20% of the overall population. In states where less than five places meet either of these criteria, we have included places with at least 10,000 total population with the highest percentage of Hispanic/Latino population. These places are identified with an asterisk (*); Please refer to the User's Guide for a full explanation of data.

Homeownship Rate

(Universe: Occupied Housing Units)

South American: Colombian

Top 10 States, Counties, and Places[1]

Sorted by Percent in Descending Order — U.S. = 50.3%

State	Percent	County	Percent	Place	Percent
Delaware	63.7	Adams County, MS	100.0	**Streamwood, IL** (village) Cook County	91.7
Maryland	62.6	Rockwall County, TX	95.6	**Altadena, CA** (cdp) Los Angeles County	90.9
Georgia	61.9	Sumter County, FL	89.5	**Bolingbrook, IL** (village) Will County	90.0
Tennessee	61.7	Lancaster County, SC	87.3	**Pennsauken, NJ** (township) Camden County	89.5
Arizona	61.6	Forsyth County, GA	87.2	**Little Elm, TX** (city) Denton County	87.5
Maine	61.5	Union County, NC	86.9	**Hanover Park, IL** (village) Cook County	86.1
South Carolina	61.2	Jackson County, GA	86.8	**Hacienda Heights, CA** (cdp) Los Angeles County	84.6
New Mexico	61.0	Barrow County, GA	86.5	**Richmond West, FL** (cdp) Miami-Dade County	84.5
North Carolina	59.8	Will County, IL	86.2	**Mission Bend, TX** (cdp) Fort Bend County	84.1
Alabama	59.3	Rockdale County, GA	84.8	**Spring, TX** (cdp) Harris County	84.0

Sorted by Percent in Ascending Order — U.S. = 50.3%

State	Percent	County	Percent	Place	Percent
North Dakota	28.4	Montgomery County, VA	8.6	**West New York, NJ** (town) Hudson County	13.4
Hawaii	31.4	Centre County, PA	12.1	**University, FL** (cdp) Hillsborough County	14.4
New York	31.9	New York County, NY	14.5	**Manhattan, NY** (borough) New York County	14.5
District of Columbia	34.6	Bronx County, NY	17.0	**Bronx, NY** (borough) Bronx County	17.0
Rhode Island	35.4	Kings County, NY	17.2	**Brooklyn, NY** (borough) Kings County	17.2
Massachusetts	35.7	Tompkins County, NY	18.2	**Union City, NJ** (city) Hudson County	17.4
South Dakota	36.0	Maui County, HI	20.0	**New London, CT** (city/town) New London County	19.0
Montana	37.9	Tippecanoe County, IN	22.8	**Boston, MA** (city) Suffolk County	19.8
New Jersey	40.1	Hudson County, NJ	23.7	**Pittsburgh, PA** (city) Allegheny County	20.6
Wyoming	43.8	Jefferson County, NY	23.8	**Central Falls*, RI** (city) Providence County	21.2

Note: (1) Ranking tables cover all states and counties, and places with an overall population of at least 125,000, OR an overall population of at least 25,000 where the Hispanic/Latino population is at least 20% of the overall population. In states where less than five places meet either of these criteria, we have included places with at least 10,000 total population with the highest percentage of Hispanic/Latino population. These places are identified with an asterisk (*); Please refer to the User's Guide for a full explanation of data.

Homeownship Rate

(Universe: Occupied Housing Units)

South American: Ecuadorian

Top 10 States, Counties, and Places[1]

Sorted by Percent in Descending Order — U.S. = 40.8%

State	Percent	County	Percent	Place	Percent
Idaho	69.6	Lake County, IN	97.2	**Royal Palm Beach, FL** (village) Palm Beach County	90.2
Arizona	66.1	Kendall County, IL	96.6	**Eastvale, CA** (cdp) Riverside County	89.4
Arkansas	65.7	Paulding County, GA	95.7	**Poinciana, FL** (cdp) Osceola County	88.9
Georgia	64.7	Pike County, PA	93.2	**Streamwood, IL** (village) Cook County	88.6
Maryland	63.5	Pinal County, AZ	89.7	**Richmond West, FL** (cdp) Miami-Dade County	88.1
South Carolina	63.5	Stafford County, VA	89.5	**Cooper City, FL** (city) Broward County	86.8
Texas	63.4	Union County, NC	88.7	**Saint Cloud, FL** (city) Osceola County	86.0
Indiana	62.5	Will County, IL	85.1	**Valley Stream, NY** (village) Nassau County	85.5
Kansas	62.4	Sussex County, NJ	84.5	**Diamond Bar, CA** (city) Los Angeles County	85.3
Missouri	62.4	Hernando County, FL	84.3	**Deltona, FL** (city) Volusia County	84.9

Sorted by Percent in Ascending Order — U.S. = 40.8%

State	Percent	County	Percent	Place	Percent
New York	26.0	New York County, NY	6.3	**Manhattan, NY** (borough) New York County	6.3
Massachusetts	36.1	Bronx County, NY	15.5	**Spring Valley, NY** (village) Rockland County	9.1
Hawaii	36.2	Kings County, NY	16.0	**City of Orange, NJ** (township) Essex County	10.6
New Jersey	36.2	Champaign County, IL	20.0	**Salt Lake City, UT** (city) Salt Lake County	12.0
District of Columbia	37.5	Bristol County, MA	20.4	**New London, CT** (city/town) New London County	14.8
Rhode Island	38.2	Rockland County, NY	23.9	**Bronx, NY** (borough) Bronx County	15.5
Connecticut	39.5	Queens County, NY	24.7	**Brooklyn, NY** (borough) Kings County	16.0
Minnesota	41.7	New London County, CT	25.0	**West New York, NJ** (town) Hudson County	18.4
New Hampshire	45.0	Plymouth County, MA	25.9	**Union City, NJ** (city) Hudson County	19.1
Oregon	45.7	Hudson County, NJ	26.5	**Hackensack, NJ** (city) Bergen County	19.2

Note: (1) Ranking tables cover all states and counties, and places with an overall population of at least 125,000, OR an overall population of at least 25,000 where the Hispanic/Latino population is at least 20% of the overall population. In states where less than five places meet either of these criteria, we have included places with at least 10,000 total population with the highest percentage of Hispanic/Latino population. These places are identified with an asterisk (*); Please refer to the User's Guide for a full explanation of data.

Homeownship Rate

(Universe: Occupied Housing Units)

South American: Paraguayan

Top 10 States, Counties, and Places[1]

Sorted by Percent in Descending Order — U.S. = 42.7%

State	Percent	County	Percent	Place	Percent
Georgia	64.8	Gwinnett County, GA	75.7	**Hempstead (town), NY** (town) Nassau County	68.6
Texas	64.2	Palm Beach County, FL	69.4	**Houston, TX** (city) Harris County	58.1
Nevada	63.6	Harris County, TX	67.9	**North Hempstead, NY** (town) Nassau County	44.8
South Carolina	60.0	Broward County, FL	64.2	**Arlington, VA** (cdp) Arlington County	43.2
Maryland	58.7	Clark County, NV	61.0	**Chicago, IL** (city) Cook County	40.5
North Carolina	57.9	Montgomery County, MD	58.6	**Miami, FL** (city) Miami-Dade County	40.0
Washington	57.8	Suffolk County, NY	58.6	**White Plains, NY** (city) Westchester County	32.4
Colorado	57.5	Fairfax County, VA	57.0	**Los Angeles, CA** (city) Los Angeles County	31.5
Florida	56.1	Prince George's County, MD	56.7	**Rye, NY** (town) Westchester County	17.6
Ohio	54.8	Maricopa County, AZ	55.9	**Queens, NY** (borough) Queens County	17.4

Sorted by Percent in Ascending Order — U.S. = 42.7%

State	Percent	County	Percent	Place	Percent
New York	23.5	New York County, NY	10.9	**Manhattan, NY** (borough) New York County	10.9
Alabama	35.0	Bronx County, NY	11.8	**Bronx, NY** (borough) Bronx County	11.8
Kansas	35.8	Kings County, NY	12.7	**Brooklyn, NY** (borough) Kings County	12.7
New Jersey	37.0	Queens County, NY	17.4	**New York, NY** (city)	16.3
Massachusetts	38.3	Middlesex County, MA	25.0	**Queens, NY** (borough) Queens County	17.4
District of Columbia	41.9	Westchester County, NY	27.2	**Rye, NY** (town) Westchester County	17.6
Missouri	42.4	Morris County, NJ	31.6	**Los Angeles, CA** (city) Los Angeles County	31.5
Minnesota	43.8	Somerset County, NJ	31.6	**White Plains, NY** (city) Westchester County	32.4
Tennessee	45.5	San Diego County, CA	40.7	**Miami, FL** (city) Miami-Dade County	40.0
Wisconsin	46.4	Los Angeles County, CA	42.3	**Chicago, IL** (city) Cook County	40.5

Note: (1) Ranking tables cover all states and counties, and places with an overall population of at least 125,000, OR an overall population of at least 25,000 where the Hispanic/Latino population is at least 20% of the overall population. In states where less than five places meet either of these criteria, we have included places with at least 10,000 total population with the highest percentage of Hispanic/Latino population. These places are identified with an asterisk (*); Please refer to the User's Guide for a full explanation of data.

Homeownship Rate

(Universe: Occupied Housing Units)

South American: Peruvian

Top 10 States, Counties, and Places[1]

Sorted by Percent in Descending Order — U.S. = 47.8%

State	Percent	County	Percent	Place	Percent
Alaska	64.3	York County, SC	92.3	**Magna, UT** (cdp) Salt Lake County	91.3
New Mexico	63.7	Union County, NC	91.5	**Poinciana, FL** (cdp) Osceola County	89.2
Arizona	61.4	Sandoval County, NM	89.3	**Carson, CA** (city) Los Angeles County	88.7
Maryland	60.6	Washington County, MN	89.3	**Chesapeake, VA** (independent city)	87.1
Vermont	60.3	Harford County, MD	86.0	**Atascocita, TX** (cdp) Harris County	86.7
Indiana	59.9	Lake County, IN	85.7	**Cooper City, FL** (city) Broward County	86.1
Michigan	59.4	Forsyth County, GA	85.1	**Wesley Chapel, FL** (cdp) Pasco County	85.1
Minnesota	58.9	Sussex County, NJ	83.7	**Diamond Bar, CA** (city) Los Angeles County	84.0
Oklahoma	58.9	Brazoria County, TX	83.6	**Mission Bend, TX** (cdp) Fort Bend County	83.7
Missouri	58.6	Carroll County, MD	81.8	**Richmond West, FL** (cdp) Miami-Dade County	83.0

Sorted by Percent in Ascending Order — U.S. = 47.8%

State	Percent	County	Percent	Place	Percent
Montana	33.9	Montgomery County, VA	9.7	**North Atlanta, GA** (cdp) DeKalb County	9.1
District of Columbia	34.4	New York County, NY	13.0	**Union City, NJ** (city) Hudson County	11.9
New York	34.5	Bronx County, NY	18.0	**Manhattan, NY** (borough) New York County	13.0
New Jersey	37.7	Kings County, NY	19.2	**City of Orange, NJ** (township) Essex County	13.6
Rhode Island	39.0	Centre County, PA	19.4	**University, FL** (cdp) Orange County	16.0
Idaho	41.9	Hudson County, NJ	22.6	**Bell Gardens, CA** (city) Los Angeles County	16.2
Hawaii	43.2	Blaine County, ID	22.7	**West New York, NJ** (town) Hudson County	16.8
Massachusetts	43.6	Monroe County, FL	24.6	**Richmond, VA** (independent city)	16.9
California	45.1	San Francisco County, CA	26.2	**University, FL** (cdp) Hillsborough County	17.2
Wisconsin	45.6	Harrison County, MS	26.8	**Tallahassee, FL** (city) Leon County	17.4

Note: (1) Ranking tables cover all states and counties, and places with an overall population of at least 125,000, OR an overall population of at least 25,000 where the Hispanic/Latino population is at least 20% of the overall population. In states where less than five places meet either of these criteria, we have included places with at least 10,000 total population with the highest percentage of Hispanic/Latino population. These places are identified with an asterisk (*); Please refer to the User's Guide for a full explanation of data.

Homeownship Rate

(Universe: Occupied Housing Units)

South American: Uruguayan

Top 10 States, Counties, and Places[1]

Sorted by Percent in Descending Order — U.S. = 44.1%

State	Percent	County	Percent	Place	Percent
Arizona	67.7	Ocean County, NJ	79.0	**Oyster Bay, NY** (town) Nassau County	85.4
Michigan	65.1	Fort Bend County, TX	76.6	**Miramar, FL** (city) Broward County	80.0
Indiana	63.2	Riverside County, CA	73.2	**Sunrise, FL** (city) Broward County	76.3
Colorado	61.9	Nassau County, NY	72.9	**Hempstead (town), NY** (town) Nassau County	75.4
Maryland	58.9	Saint Lucie County, FL	68.4	**Port Saint Lucie, FL** (city) Saint Lucie County	70.6
New Hampshire	57.6	Henry County, GA	66.7	**Tamarac, FL** (city) Broward County	70.2
Illinois	56.7	Maricopa County, AZ	66.4	**Pembroke Pines, FL** (city) Broward County	66.3
Alabama	56.3	Santa Clara County, CA	65.6	**Weston, FL** (city) Broward County	64.7
Texas	55.2	Suffolk County, NY	65.2	**The Hammocks, FL** (cdp) Miami-Dade County	64.4
Ohio	54.6	Sussex County, NJ	64.6	**Davie, FL** (town) Broward County	63.0

Sorted by Percent in Ascending Order — U.S. = 44.1%

State	Percent	County	Percent	Place	Percent
Massachusetts	31.5	Lackawanna County, PA	18.9	**West New York, NJ** (town) Hudson County	13.3
New Jersey	32.6	Hudson County, NJ	20.0	**Newark, NJ** (city) Essex County	13.6
New York	38.8	San Francisco County, CA	20.8	**Union City, NJ** (city) Hudson County	14.5
Missouri	40.7	New York County, NY	21.8	**Hilton Head Island*, SC** (town) Beaufort County	14.8
Tennessee	42.0	Kings County, NY	24.4	**Elizabeth, NJ** (city) Union County	15.1
Connecticut	44.7	Bronx County, NY	24.6	**Miami Beach, FL** (city) Miami-Dade County	16.6
Georgia	45.5	Union County, NJ	24.6	**Miami, FL** (city) Miami-Dade County	16.6
Florida	45.6	Essex County, NJ	25.8	**Kearny, NJ** (town) Hudson County	17.3
Louisiana	46.2	Worcester County, MA	29.8	**City of Orange, NJ** (township) Essex County	20.6
Pennsylvania	46.2	Fulton County, GA	30.0	**San Francisco, CA** (city) San Francisco County	20.8

Note: (1) Ranking tables cover all states and counties, and places with an overall population of at least 125,000, OR an overall population of at least 25,000 where the Hispanic/Latino population is at least 20% of the overall population. In states where less than five places meet either of these criteria, we have included places with at least 10,000 total population with the highest percentage of Hispanic/Latino population. These places are identified with an asterisk (*); Please refer to the User's Guide for a full explanation of data.

Homeownship Rate

(Universe: Occupied Housing Units)

South American: Venezuelan

Top 10 States, Counties, and Places[1]

Sorted by Percent in Descending Order — U.S. = 52.4%

State	Percent	County	Percent	Place	Percent
Alaska	67.5	Union County, NC	89.7	**Richmond West, FL** (cdp) Miami-Dade County	81.9
New Hampshire	64.5	Will County, IL	88.2	**Royal Palm Beach, FL** (village) Palm Beach County	80.8
Michigan	64.1	Warren County, OH	85.0	**Cooper City, FL** (city) Broward County	80.4
Idaho	64.0	Fort Bend County, TX	84.4	**Riverview, FL** (cdp) Hillsborough County	79.4
Nebraska	62.7	Cherokee County, GA	83.5	**Atascocita, TX** (cdp) Harris County	78.0
Maine	62.5	Forsyth County, GA	81.2	**Pearland, TX** (city) Brazoria County	77.5
Delaware	62.3	Douglas County, NE	78.4	**Deltona, FL** (city) Volusia County	75.0
Maryland	62.3	Macomb County, MI	76.7	**Ocoee, FL** (city) Orange County	75.0
New Mexico	61.3	Solano County, CA	75.9	**Saint Cloud, FL** (city) Osceola County	75.0
Minnesota	61.1	Oakland County, MI	74.4	**Winter Garden, FL** (city) Orange County	74.6

Sorted by Percent in Ascending Order — U.S. = 52.4%

State	Percent	County	Percent	Place	Percent
Hawaii	28.0	Bronx County, NY	17.1	**West New York, NJ** (town) Hudson County	12.1
New York	30.7	Kings County, NY	21.2	**Union City, NJ** (city) Hudson County	15.3
Rhode Island	38.7	New York County, NY	22.0	**Bronx, NY** (borough) Bronx County	17.1
California	41.6	Hudson County, NJ	23.4	**Tallahassee, FL** (city) Leon County	18.9
Massachusetts	42.5	Queens County, NY	23.6	**Brooklyn, NY** (borough) Kings County	21.2
District of Columbia	44.3	San Francisco County, CA	23.6	**Long Beach, CA** (city) Los Angeles County	22.0
New Jersey	45.8	Brazos County, TX	25.6	**Manhattan, NY** (borough) New York County	22.0
Connecticut	47.7	Honolulu County, HI	26.7	**New York, NY** (city)	22.4
Nevada	49.1	Suffolk County, MA	26.9	**New Rochelle, NY** (city) Westchester County	22.5
Oregon	49.5	Passaic County, NJ	29.6	**Providence, RI** (city) Providence County	22.6

RANKINGS & COMPARISONS

Note: (1) Ranking tables cover all states and counties, and places with an overall population of at least 125,000, OR an overall population of at least 25,000 where the Hispanic/Latino population is at least 20% of the overall population. In states where less than five places meet either of these criteria, we have included places with at least 10,000 total population with the highest percentage of Hispanic/Latino population. These places are identified with an asterisk (*); Please refer to the User's Guide for a full explanation of data.

Homeownship Rate

(Universe: Occupied Housing Units)

Spaniard

Top 10 States, Counties, and Places[1]

Sorted by Percent in Descending Order — U.S. = 63.7%

State	Percent	County	Percent	Place	Percent
New Mexico	76.1	Calvert County, MD	93.2	**Wesley Chapel, FL** (cdp) Pasco County	92.4
Louisiana	75.8	Humboldt County, NV	92.0	**Dale City, VA** (cdp) Prince William County	91.4
Vermont	75.7	Livingston Parish, LA	92.0	**Cooper City, FL** (city) Broward County	91.3
Delaware	74.8	Elbert County, CO	91.4	**Tamiami, FL** (cdp) Miami-Dade County	90.2
West Virginia	74.7	Forsyth County, GA	91.4	**Drexel Heights, AZ** (cdp) Pima County	90.0
Florida	71.9	Ascension Parish, LA	90.5	**Lake Magdalene, FL** (cdp) Hillsborough County	89.4
New Jersey	71.3	Delaware County, OH	89.7	**Kyle, TX** (city) Hays County	89.1
Michigan	70.0	Sussex County, NJ	89.7	**Oyster Bay, NY** (town) Nassau County	88.5
Wyoming	69.5	York County, VA	89.3	**Sunrise, FL** (city) Broward County	88.2
Connecticut	69.3	Saint Bernard Parish, LA	88.6	**Westchester, FL** (cdp) Miami-Dade County	88.1

Sorted by Percent in Ascending Order — U.S. = 63.7%

State	Percent	County	Percent	Place	Percent
District of Columbia	43.0	New York County, NY	23.4	**University, FL** (cdp) Hillsborough County	15.1
North Dakota	46.7	Bronx County, NY	27.1	**Trenton, NJ** (city) Mercer County	18.2
Rhode Island	52.4	Montgomery County, VA	27.9	**Florence-Graham, CA** (cdp) Los Angeles County	20.0
Massachusetts	52.8	Tippecanoe County, IN	30.0	**New Brunswick, NJ** (city) Middlesex County	20.8
New York	53.6	Suffolk County, MA	32.6	**San Marcos, TX** (city) Hays County	21.1
Wisconsin	54.0	Boone County, MO	32.9	**New Haven, CT** (city/town) New Haven County	22.2
Hawaii	54.1	Pulaski County, MO	33.3	**Manhattan, NY** (borough) New York County	23.4
South Dakota	55.8	Tompkins County, NY	33.8	**Bronx, NY** (borough) Bronx County	27.1
Oregon	57.0	Centre County, PA	34.5	**Union City, NJ** (city) Hudson County	28.4
Iowa	57.4	Kings County, NY	34.6	**Missoula*, MT** (city) Missoula County	28.9

Note: (1) Ranking tables cover all states and counties, and places with an overall population of at least 125,000, OR an overall population of at least 25,000 where the Hispanic/Latino population is at least 20% of the overall population. In states where less than five places meet either of these criteria, we have included places with at least 10,000 total population with the highest percentage of Hispanic/Latino population. These places are identified with an asterisk (*); Please refer to the User's Guide for a full explanation of data.

Median Home Value

Total Population

Top 10 States, Counties, and Places[1]

Sorted by Percent in Descending Order — U.S. = $188,400

State	Dollars	County	Dollars	Place	Dollars
Hawaii	537,400	Nantucket County, MA	1,000,000+	**Santa Barbara, CA** (city) Santa Barbara County	969,200
California	458,500	Marin County, CA	868,000	**Manhattan, NY** (borough) New York County	825,200
District of Columbia	443,300	New York County, NY	825,200	**San Rafael, CA** (city) Marin County	811,000
New Jersey	357,000	San Francisco County, CA	785,200	**Redwood City, CA** (city) San Mateo County	808,600
Massachusetts	352,300	San Mateo County, CA	784,800	**San Francisco, CA** (city) San Francisco County	785,200
Maryland	329,400	Teton County, WY	723,700	**Mountain View, CA** (city) Santa Clara County	779,500
New York	303,900	Santa Clara County, CA	701,000	**San Mateo, CA** (city) San Mateo County	769,000
Connecticut	296,500	Dukes County, MA	681,300	**Goleta, CA** (city) Santa Barbara County	767,100
Washington	285,400	Pitkin County, CO	670,200	**Sunnyvale, CA** (city) Santa Clara County	707,900
Rhode Island	279,300	Santa Cruz County, CA	648,700	**Coral Gables, FL** (city) Miami-Dade County	690,100

Sorted by Percent in Ascending Order — U.S. = $188,400

State	Dollars	County	Dollars	Place	Dollars
West Virginia	94,500	Shannon County, SD	18,600	**Hope*, AR** (city) Hempstead County	54,300
Mississippi	96,500	Foard County, TX	29,700	**Big Spring, TX** (city) Howard County	55,300
Arkansas	102,300	Reeves County, TX	31,400	**Port Arthur, TX** (city) Jefferson County	59,000
Oklahoma	104,300	Zavala County, TX	36,900	**Weslaco, TX** (city) Hidalgo County	64,900
North Dakota	111,300	Winkler County, TX	38,900	**Reading, PA** (city) Berks County	65,500
Kentucky	116,800	Haskell County, TX	39,200	**Buffalo, NY** (city) Erie County	65,700
Alabama	117,600	La Salle County, TX	39,600	**Pharr, TX** (city) Hidalgo County	66,200
Iowa	119,200	Culberson County, TX	39,900	**Parker*, SC** (cdp) Greenville County	68,000
South Dakota	122,200	Cochran County, TX	40,100	**Kingsville, TX** (city) Kleberg County	70,200
Kansas	122,600	Cottle County, TX	42,400	**Mayfield*, KY** (city) Graves County	71,900

RANKINGS & COMPARISONS

Note: (1) Ranking tables cover all states and counties, and places with an overall population of at least 125,000, OR an overall population of at least 25,000 where the Hispanic/Latino population is at least 20% of the overall population. In states where less than five places meet either of these criteria, we have included places with at least 10,000 total population with the highest percentage of Hispanic/Latino population. These places are identified with an asterisk (*); Please refer to the User's Guide for a full explanation of data.

Median Home Value

Hispanic or Latino (of any race)

Top 10 States, Counties, and Places[1]

Sorted by Percent in Descending Order — U.S. = $185,900

State	Dollars	County	Dollars	Place	Dollars
District of Columbia	462,200	Teton County, WY	1,000,000+	**Santa Barbara, CA** (city) Santa Barbara County	876,200
Hawaii	458,600	San Francisco County, CA	700,000	**Goleta, CA** (city) Santa Barbara County	759,100
New York	405,800	Marin County, CA	663,600	**Redwood City, CA** (city) San Mateo County	724,300
California	366,300	San Mateo County, CA	654,900	**San Mateo, CA** (city) San Mateo County	705,100
New Jersey	344,000	New York County, NY	617,100	**San Francisco, CA** (city) San Francisco County	700,000
Maryland	338,500	Maui County, HI	584,300	**Mountain View, CA** (city) Santa Clara County	687,200
Virginia	325,800	Santa Clara County, CA	577,700	**Novato, CA** (city) Marin County	661,000
Massachusetts	294,500	Kings County, NY	540,300	**San Bruno, CA** (city) San Mateo County	660,100
Connecticut	245,400	San Juan County, WA	505,700	**San Rafael, CA** (city) Marin County	643,400
New Hampshire	242,100	Santa Cruz County, CA	502,800	**Coral Gables, FL** (city) Miami-Dade County	636,700

Sorted by Percent in Ascending Order — U.S. = $185,900

State	Dollars	County	Dollars	Place	Dollars
Oklahoma	79,100	Berrien County, GA	<10,000	**Big Spring, TX** (city) Howard County	28,000
Kansas	82,400	Chattahoochee County, GA	<10,000	**Altus*, OK** (city) Jackson County	34,000
North Dakota	84,900	Georgetown County, SC	<10,000	**Hope*, AR** (city) Hempstead County	43,700
Iowa	85,700	Greene County, NC	<10,000	**Port Arthur, TX** (city) Jefferson County	44,500
Texas	89,800	Jackson County, WI	<10,000	**Greenville, TX** (city) Hunt County	44,800
Nebraska	91,200	Kit Carson County, CO	<10,000	**Mayfield*, KY** (city) Graves County	45,200
Alabama	95,000	Orleans County, VT	<10,000	**Worthington*, MN** (city) Nobles County	51,100
Arkansas	100,100	Saunders County, NE	<10,000	**Abilene, TX** (city) Taylor County	54,800
South Dakota	100,100	Teton County, ID	<10,000	**Lufkin, TX** (city) Angelina County	56,700
Indiana	105,100	Union County, FL	<10,000	**Guymon*, OK** (city) Texas County	58,300

Note: (1) Ranking tables cover all states and counties, and places with an overall population of at least 125,000, OR an overall population of at least 25,000 where the Hispanic/Latino population is at least 20% of the overall population. In states where less than five places meet either of these criteria, we have included places with at least 10,000 total population with the highest percentage of Hispanic/Latino population. These places are identified with an asterisk (*); Please refer to the User's Guide for a full explanation of data.

Median Home Value

Central American, excluding Mexican

Top 10 States, Counties, and Places[1]

Sorted by Percent in Descending Order — U.S. = $244,100

State	Dollars	County	Dollars	Place	Dollars
Hawaii	413,900	Putnam County, NY	739,600	**Mountain View, CA** (city) Santa Clara County	1,000,000+
District of Columbia	395,300	San Luis Obispo County, CA	691,400	**San Rafael, CA** (city) Marin County	790,900
California	392,600	San Francisco County, CA	673,400	**Novato, CA** (city) Marin County	788,200
New York	385,900	San Mateo County, CA	629,700	**San Mateo, CA** (city) San Mateo County	700,800
New Jersey	330,900	Napa County, CA	624,000	**San Francisco, CA** (city) San Francisco County	673,400
Maryland	330,600	Marin County, CA	622,200	**Huntington Beach, CA** (city) Orange County	632,400
Massachusetts	327,700	Santa Clara County, CA	573,000	**Costa Mesa, CA** (city) Orange County	626,300
Virginia	326,300	Santa Cruz County, CA	511,800	**Daly City, CA** (city) San Mateo County	625,500
Connecticut	297,500	Kings County, NY	499,800	**Glendale, CA** (city) Los Angeles County	622,000
Vermont	269,200	New York County, NY	496,100	**Redwood City, CA** (city) San Mateo County	615,900

Sorted by Percent in Ascending Order — U.S. = $244,100

State	Dollars	County	Dollars	Place	Dollars
Wyoming	20,500	Cass County, IN	<10,000	**Worthington*, MN** (city) Nobles County	<10,000
Kansas	89,000	Lee County, AL	<10,000	**Little Rock, AR** (city) Pulaski County	14,300
Iowa	91,700	Wayne County, NC	13,200	**Carthage*, MO** (city) Jasper County	39,000
Nebraska	93,500	Washtenaw County, MI	14,800	**Rochester, NY** (city) Monroe County	56,400
Oklahoma	94,100	DeKalb County, AL	21,100	**Chattanooga, TN** (city) Hamilton County	64,100
Missouri	97,600	Walker County, TX	22,700	**Wichita, KS** (city) Sedgwick County	66,100
Alabama	98,800	Duplin County, NC	24,200	**Albertville*, AL** (city) Marshall County	67,900
Michigan	104,500	Boulder County, CO	33,800	**Lexington*, NE** (city) Dawson County	70,300
Indiana	105,900	Franklin County, AL	39,000	**Kansas City, MO** (city) Jackson County	74,000
Texas	110,700	Nobles County, MN	45,000	**Detroit, MI** (city) Wayne County	75,800

Note: (1) Ranking tables cover all states and counties, and places with an overall population of at least 125,000, OR an overall population of at least 25,000 where the Hispanic/Latino population is at least 20% of the overall population. In states where less than five places meet either of these criteria, we have included places with at least 10,000 total population with the highest percentage of Hispanic/Latino population. These places are identified with an asterisk (*); Please refer to the User's Guide for a full explanation of data.

Median Home Value

Central American: Costa Rican

Top 10 States, Counties, and Places[1]

Sorted by Percent in Descending Order — U.S. = $267,200

State	Dollars	County	Dollars	Place	Dollars
California	468,200	Contra Costa County, CA	590,100	**Los Angeles, CA** (city) Los Angeles County	527,200
Virginia	408,900	Orange County, CA	557,000	**Brooklyn, NY** (borough) Kings County	437,800
Oregon	397,100	Suffolk County, NY	508,100	**Queens, NY** (borough) Queens County	432,900
Maryland	381,600	Union County, NJ	501,400	**New York, NY** (city)	410,300
New York	371,600	Los Angeles County, CA	469,600	**Bronx, NY** (borough) Bronx County	345,500
New Jersey	349,600	Bergen County, NJ	443,500	**Miami, FL** (city) Miami-Dade County	315,800
Connecticut	318,800	Kings County, NY	437,800	**Philadelphia, PA** (city) Philadelphia County	185,000
Washington	296,700	Queens County, NY	432,900		
Massachusetts	292,000	Passaic County, NJ	400,800		
Arizona	282,700	Fairfield County, CT	400,000		

Sorted by Percent in Ascending Order — U.S. = $267,200

State	Dollars	County	Dollars	Place	Dollars
South Carolina	137,100	Harris County, TX	131,100	**Philadelphia, PA** (city) Philadelphia County	185,000
North Carolina	149,300	Hillsborough County, FL	169,900	**Miami, FL** (city) Miami-Dade County	315,800
Texas	156,100	Philadelphia County, PA	185,000	**Bronx, NY** (borough) Bronx County	345,500
Louisiana	168,500	Broward County, FL	225,000	**New York, NY** (city)	410,300
Wisconsin	171,700	Clark County, NV	225,000	**Queens, NY** (borough) Queens County	432,900
Michigan	190,200	Mercer County, NJ	229,300	**Brooklyn, NY** (borough) Kings County	437,800
Pennsylvania	191,100	Palm Beach County, FL	246,800	**Los Angeles, CA** (city) Los Angeles County	527,200
Minnesota	196,100	Orange County, FL	248,200		
Georgia	196,900	Riverside County, CA	260,000		
Florida	209,400	Maricopa County, AZ	263,400		

Note: (1) Ranking tables cover all states and counties, and places with an overall population of at least 125,000, OR an overall population of at least 25,000 where the Hispanic/Latino population is at least 20% of the overall population. In states where less than five places meet either of these criteria, we have included places with at least 10,000 total population with the highest percentage of Hispanic/Latino population. These places are identified with an asterisk (*); Please refer to the User's Guide for a full explanation of data.

Median Home Value

Central American: Guatemalan

Top 10 States, Counties, and Places[1]

Sorted by Percent in Descending Order — U.S. = $246,100

State	Dollars	County	Dollars	Place	Dollars
District of Columbia	548,600	San Francisco County, CA	610,700	**San Rafael, CA** (city) Marin County	809,400
New York	386,300	San Mateo County, CA	603,300	**San Mateo, CA** (city) San Mateo County	713,700
California	377,000	Santa Clara County, CA	586,900	**San Francisco, CA** (city) San Francisco County	610,700
Connecticut	346,600	Rockland County, NY	581,300	**Glendale, CA** (city) Los Angeles County	603,600
Virginia	334,300	Norfolk County, MA	476,700	**Alhambra, CA** (city) Los Angeles County	594,600
Massachusetts	330,800	Ventura County, CA	455,300	**San Diego, CA** (city) San Diego County	544,600
Maryland	303,100	Arlington County, VA	450,000	**San Jose, CA** (city) Santa Clara County	544,200
New Jersey	281,700	Queens County, NY	441,100	**Downey, CA** (city) Los Angeles County	530,500
Illinois	256,400	Alameda County, CA	440,100	**Elizabeth, NJ** (city) Union County	494,200
Washington	243,800	San Diego County, CA	439,200	**Westmont, CA** (cdp) Los Angeles County	481,300

Sorted by Percent in Ascending Order — U.S. = $246,100

State	Dollars	County	Dollars	Place	Dollars
Mississippi	59,400	Hamilton County, OH	<10,000	**Richmond, VA** (independent city)	<10,000
Alabama	68,800	Lee County, AL	<10,000	**Carthage*, MO** (city) Jasper County	32,300
Missouri	70,600	DeKalb County, AL	21,100	**Chattanooga, TN** (city) Hamilton County	61,700
Kansas	85,600	Jasper County, MO	33,000	**Albertville*, AL** (city) Marshall County	68,800
Arkansas	85,900	Franklin County, AL	39,000	**Grand Island, NE** (city) Hall County	72,100
Nebraska	86,700	Gilmer County, GA	45,700	**Homestead, FL** (city) Miami-Dade County	89,000
Oklahoma	87,300	Nobles County, MN	58,100	**Oklahoma City, OK** (city) Oklahoma County	89,000
Indiana	88,000	Hamilton County, TN	61,700	**Lexington*, NE** (city) Dawson County	93,100
Iowa	98,500	Cobb County, GA	61,800	**Grand Rapids, MI** (city) Kent County	95,000
North Carolina	100,500	Marshall County, AL	63,300	**Garland, TX** (city) Dallas County	104,900

Note: (1) Ranking tables cover all states and counties, and places with an overall population of at least 125,000, OR an overall population of at least 25,000 where the Hispanic/Latino population is at least 20% of the overall population. In states where less than five places meet either of these criteria, we have included places with at least 10,000 total population with the highest percentage of Hispanic/Latino population. These places are identified with an asterisk (*); Please refer to the User's Guide for a full explanation of data.

Median Home Value

Central American: Honduran

Top 10 States, Counties, and Places[1]

Sorted by Percent in Descending Order — U.S. = $194,200

State	Dollars	County	Dollars	Place	Dollars
California	394,200	San Francisco County, CA	595,900	**Yonkers, NY** (city) Westchester County	875,000
New York	392,300	Orange County, CA	576,300	**Pasadena, CA** (city) Los Angeles County	643,400
New Jersey	331,500	Kings County, NY	528,200	**San Francisco, CA** (city) San Francisco County	595,900
District of Columbia	318,400	Santa Clara County, CA	517,700	**Miami Beach, FL** (city) Miami-Dade County	565,000
Virginia	312,400	Queens County, NY	507,800	**Brooklyn, NY** (borough) Kings County	528,200
Maryland	312,200	Ventura County, CA	474,100	**San Jose, CA** (city) Santa Clara County	517,500
Massachusetts	298,400	San Diego County, CA	467,200	**Queens, NY** (borough) Queens County	507,800
Washington	285,100	Richmond County, NY	464,400	**San Diego, CA** (city) San Diego County	492,200
Illinois	246,700	Loudoun County, VA	457,400	**Staten Island, NY** (borough) Richmond County	464,400
Utah	232,100	Los Angeles County, CA	419,400	**New York, NY** (city)	453,700

Sorted by Percent in Ascending Order — U.S. = $194,200

State	Dollars	County	Dollars	Place	Dollars
Michigan	49,300	Sampson County, NC	11,700	**Fort Worth, TX** (city) Tarrant County	71,700
Nebraska	68,400	Duplin County, NC	33,300	**Oklahoma City, OK** (city) Oklahoma County	85,500
Missouri	79,400	Galveston County, TX	67,700	**Houston, TX** (city) Harris County	89,800
Oklahoma	91,600	Jackson County, MO	68,700	**Pasadena, TX** (city) Harris County	90,000
Kentucky	93,200	Tarrant County, TX	75,300	**Austin, TX** (city) Travis County	93,200
Indiana	99,600	Elkhart County, IN	77,400	**Baltimore, MD** (independent city)	97,800
Arkansas	102,100	Oklahoma County, OK	87,300	**Memphis, TN** (city) Shelby County	109,000
Texas	103,000	Kern County, CA	89,200	**San Antonio, TX** (city) Bexar County	109,000
Ohio	106,300	Travis County, TX	96,400	**Garland, TX** (city) Dallas County	110,900
North Carolina	117,200	Clayton County, GA	99,700	**Conroe, TX** (city) Montgomery County	111,700

Note: (1) Ranking tables cover all states and counties, and places with an overall population of at least 125,000, OR an overall population of at least 25,000 where the Hispanic/Latino population is at least 20% of the overall population. In states where less than five places meet either of these criteria, we have included places with at least 10,000 total population with the highest percentage of Hispanic/Latino population. These places are identified with an asterisk (*); Please refer to the User's Guide for a full explanation of data.

Median Home Value

Central American: Nicaraguan

Top 10 States, Counties, and Places[1]

Sorted by Percent in Descending Order — U.S. = $247,100

State	Dollars	County	Dollars	Place	Dollars
District of Columbia	679,300	San Mateo County, CA	657,500	**Daly City, CA** (city) San Mateo County	660,300
New York	455,600	San Francisco County, CA	641,500	**San Francisco, CA** (city) San Francisco County	641,500
California	445,700	Sonoma County, CA	600,000	**South San Francisco, CA** (city) San Mateo County	638,600
Massachusetts	403,300	Orange County, CA	564,100	**Brooklyn, NY** (borough) Kings County	546,900
Virginia	364,800	Kings County, NY	546,900	**San Jose, CA** (city) Santa Clara County	542,900
Maryland	358,300	Santa Clara County, CA	528,200	**Hayward, CA** (city) Alameda County	498,500
Connecticut	352,400	Alameda County, CA	514,400	**Queens, NY** (borough) Queens County	479,800
Washington	351,400	Queens County, NY	479,800	**New York, NY** (city)	476,900
Oregon	292,800	Bronx County, NY	460,200	**Los Angeles, CA** (city) Los Angeles County	468,500
New Jersey	267,500	Los Angeles County, CA	436,000	**Bronx, NY** (borough) Bronx County	460,200

Sorted by Percent in Ascending Order — U.S. = $247,100

State	Dollars	County	Dollars	Place	Dollars
North Carolina	117,500	Camden County, NJ	112,500	**Houston, TX** (city) Harris County	116,200
Texas	119,800	Dallas County, TX	112,700	**Charlotte, NC** (city) Mecklenburg County	120,300
Michigan	120,000	Harris County, TX	118,200	**Austin, TX** (city) Travis County	140,300
Pennsylvania	127,300	Hillsborough County, FL	138,400	**West Little River, FL** (cdp) Miami-Dade County	163,000
Indiana	129,500	Gwinnett County, GA	159,700	**Hollywood, FL** (city) Broward County	169,900
Ohio	131,500	Bexar County, TX	161,900	**Kendale Lakes, FL** (cdp) Miami-Dade County	173,300
Missouri	156,400	Orange County, FL	166,100	**Metairie, LA** (cdp) Jefferson Parish	192,300
Georgia	162,000	Mecklenburg County, NC	167,000	**Hialeah, FL** (city) Miami-Dade County	194,000
Tennessee	163,100	Jefferson Parish, LA	186,700	**Miami Gardens, FL** (city) Miami-Dade County	199,000
Wisconsin	169,400	Palm Beach County, FL	205,700	**Kenner, LA** (city) Jefferson Parish	201,300

RANKINGS & COMPARISONS

Note: (1) Ranking tables cover all states and counties, and places with an overall population of at least 125,000, OR an overall population of at least 25,000 where the Hispanic/Latino population is at least 20% of the overall population. In states where less than five places meet either of these criteria, we have included places with at least 10,000 total population with the highest percentage of Hispanic/Latino population. These places are identified with an asterisk (*); Please refer to the User's Guide for a full explanation of data.

Median Home Value

Central American: Panamanian

Top 10 States, Counties, and Places[1]

Sorted by Percent in Descending Order — U.S. = $236,300

State	Dollars	County	Dollars	Place	Dollars
New York	438,000	Orange County, CA	584,200	**Los Angeles, CA** (city) Los Angeles County	687,500
California	405,700	Kings County, NY	551,600	**Brooklyn, NY** (borough) Kings County	551,600
Minnesota	345,300	Fairfax County, VA	537,500	**Hempstead (town), NY** (town) Nassau County	475,400
Connecticut	327,000	Hudson County, NJ	478,800	**New York, NY** (city)	470,500
New Jersey	322,200	Nassau County, NY	475,400	**Manhattan, NY** (borough) New York County	463,200
Maryland	304,500	Montgomery County, MD	475,000	**Queens, NY** (borough) Queens County	427,800
Virginia	288,900	New York County, NY	463,200	**San Diego, CA** (city) San Diego County	422,200
Washington	282,400	Los Angeles County, CA	461,000	**Bronx, NY** (borough) Bronx County	378,400
Massachusetts	279,000	Queens County, NY	427,800	**Miami, FL** (city) Miami-Dade County	334,400
Nevada	268,500	San Diego County, CA	419,000	**San Antonio, TX** (city) Bexar County	153,000

Sorted by Percent in Ascending Order — U.S. = $236,300

State	Dollars	County	Dollars	Place	Dollars
Mississippi	99,000	Cumberland County, NC	102,100	**Fayetteville, NC** (city) Cumberland County	97,500
Michigan	107,000	Bell County, TX	107,600	**Killeen, TX** (city) Bell County	112,000
Oklahoma	119,200	Dallas County, TX	123,400	**Houston, TX** (city) Harris County	137,500
Alabama	129,500	Duval County, FL	141,100	**Jacksonville, FL** (city) Duval County	141,100
Indiana	136,300	Harris County, TX	148,400	**San Antonio, TX** (city) Bexar County	153,000
Tennessee	140,000	Bexar County, TX	153,500	**Miami, FL** (city) Miami-Dade County	334,400
Wisconsin	143,800	Hillsborough County, FL	158,100	**Bronx, NY** (borough) Bronx County	378,400
North Carolina	148,300	Brevard County, FL	170,400	**San Diego, CA** (city) San Diego County	422,200
Texas	150,600	Broward County, FL	188,200	**Queens, NY** (borough) Queens County	427,800
New Mexico	154,200	Palm Beach County, FL	234,600	**Manhattan, NY** (borough) New York County	463,200

Note: (1) Ranking tables cover all states and counties, and places with an overall population of at least 125,000, OR an overall population of at least 25,000 where the Hispanic/Latino population is at least 20% of the overall population. In states where less than five places meet either of these criteria, we have included places with at least 10,000 total population with the highest percentage of Hispanic/Latino population. These places are identified with an asterisk (*); Please refer to the User's Guide for a full explanation of data.

Median Home Value

Central American: Salvadoran

Top 10 States, Counties, and Places[1]

Sorted by Percent in Descending Order — U.S. = $254,000

State	Dollars	County	Dollars	Place	Dollars
District of Columbia	391,900	San Francisco County, CA	707,800	**Whittier, CA** (city) Los Angeles County	784,400
California	383,600	New York County, NY	676,500	**San Francisco, CA** (city) San Francisco County	707,800
New York	373,100	San Mateo County, CA	622,700	**San Mateo, CA** (city) San Mateo County	698,300
New Jersey	362,500	Santa Clara County, CA	571,400	**Glendale, CA** (city) Los Angeles County	697,800
Hawaii	354,300	Arlington County, VA	503,200	**Manhattan, NY** (borough) New York County	676,500
Massachusetts	340,200	Bergen County, NJ	483,300	**Fullerton, CA** (city) Orange County	665,500
Maryland	333,300	Napa County, CA	483,300	**Daly City, CA** (city) San Mateo County	653,300
Virginia	324,300	Queens County, NY	459,800	**San Bruno, CA** (city) San Mateo County	628,000
Connecticut	253,600	Orange County, CA	457,300	**Sunnyvale, CA** (city) Santa Clara County	617,300
Rhode Island	244,900	Westchester County, NY	446,200	**Fremont, CA** (city) Alameda County	586,300

Sorted by Percent in Ascending Order — U.S. = $254,000

State	Dollars	County	Dollars	Place	Dollars
Kansas	75,500	Walker County, TX	22,700	**Wichita, KS** (city) Sedgwick County	76,900
Iowa	87,800	Montgomery County, TX	68,500	**Richmond, VA** (independent city)	77,300
Oklahoma	89,700	Sebastian County, AR	72,900	**Pasadena, TX** (city) Harris County	83,000
Nebraska	97,200	Sedgwick County, KS	77,300	**Grand Island, NE** (city) Hall County	95,200
Missouri	97,600	Galveston County, TX	80,600	**Mesquite, TX** (city) Dallas County	96,600
Michigan	98,800	Crawford County, AR	84,300	**Garland, TX** (city) Dallas County	97,600
Indiana	99,800	Jackson County, MO	87,400	**Greensboro, NC** (city) Guilford County	97,900
Idaho	106,200	Alamance County, NC	92,400	**Indianapolis, IN** (city) Marion County	98,900
Texas	108,800	Hall County, NE	95,200	**Dallas, TX** (city) Dallas County	101,100
Ohio	114,300	El Paso County, TX	98,300	**Arlington, TX** (city) Tarrant County	101,500

RANKINGS & COMPARISONS

Note: (1) Ranking tables cover all states and counties, and places with an overall population of at least 125,000, OR an overall population of at least 25,000 where the Hispanic/Latino population is at least 20% of the overall population. In states where less than five places meet either of these criteria, we have included places with at least 10,000 total population with the highest percentage of Hispanic/Latino population. These places are identified with an asterisk (*); Please refer to the User's Guide for a full explanation of data.

Median Home Value

Cuban

Top 10 States, Counties, and Places[1]

Sorted by Percent in Descending Order — U.S. = $268,500

State	Dollars	County	Dollars	Place	Dollars
District of Columbia	675,800	Sumter County, FL	914,100	**Manhattan, NY** (borough) New York County	778,700
California	512,100	Santa Clara County, CA	784,800	**San Francisco, CA** (city) San Francisco County	731,100
Hawaii	460,000	New York County, NY	778,700	**San Jose, CA** (city) Santa Clara County	712,000
New York	417,600	San Mateo County, CA	746,000	**Glendale, CA** (city) Los Angeles County	684,200
New Jersey	395,200	San Francisco County, CA	731,100	**Coral Gables, FL** (city) Miami-Dade County	642,300
Virginia	381,000	Chester County, PA	659,800	**Anaheim, CA** (city) Orange County	625,000
Massachusetts	366,700	Orange County, CA	621,400	**Downey, CA** (city) Los Angeles County	597,000
Maryland	364,500	Norfolk County, MA	597,600	**Burbank, CA** (city) Los Angeles County	575,200
Connecticut	346,100	Ventura County, CA	596,400	**Los Angeles, CA** (city) Los Angeles County	569,300
Illinois	317,500	Alameda County, CA	576,800	**North Hempstead, NY** (town) Nassau County	545,000

Sorted by Percent in Ascending Order — U.S. = $268,500

State	Dollars	County	Dollars	Place	Dollars
Kansas	113,500	Onondaga County, NY	79,400	**Rochester, NY** (city) Monroe County	34,600
Indiana	118,600	Ingham County, MI	89,800	**Syracuse, NY** (city) Onondaga County	74,000
Iowa	123,700	Philadelphia County, PA	107,600	**Philadelphia, PA** (city) Philadelphia County	107,600
Kentucky	124,400	Hendry County, FL	110,000	**Sunrise Manor, NV** (cdp) Clark County	117,200
Nebraska	126,000	Hamilton County, OH	114,400	**Milwaukee, WI** (city) Milwaukee County	118,900
Alabama	127,900	Monroe County, NY	115,000	**Louisville-Jefferson County, KY** (metropolitan govt) Jefferson County	119,700
Tennessee	142,300	Lancaster County, PA	118,800	**Houston, TX** (city) Harris County	129,300
West Virginia	143,800	Jefferson County, KY	121,700	**Kansas City, MO** (city) Jackson County	131,900
Missouri	145,400	Milwaukee County, WI	124,300	**San Antonio, TX** (city) Bexar County	132,800
Texas	147,200	Jackson County, MO	126,300	**Nashville-Davidson, TN** (metropolitan govt) Davidson County	133,200

Note: (1) Ranking tables cover all states and counties, and places with an overall population of at least 125,000, OR an overall population of at least 25,000 where the Hispanic/Latino population is at least 20% of the overall population. In states where less than five places meet either of these criteria, we have included places with at least 10,000 total population with the highest percentage of Hispanic/Latino population. These places are identified with an asterisk (*); Please refer to the User's Guide for a full explanation of data.

Median Home Value

Dominican Republic

Top 10 States, Counties, and Places[1]

Sorted by Percent in Descending Order — U.S. = $282,200

State	Dollars	County	Dollars	Place	Dollars
New York	439,000	Erie County, NY	564,500	**Weston, FL** (city) Broward County	672,800
California	435,700	Kings County, NY	549,900	**Oyster Bay, NY** (town) Nassau County	624,100
New Jersey	359,300	Queens County, NY	530,400	**Ramapo, NY** (town) Rockland County	599,200
District of Columbia	337,100	Onondaga County, NY	529,300	**Stamford, CT** (city/town) Fairfield County	592,300
Maryland	290,900	Los Angeles County, CA	505,100	**North Hempstead, NY** (town) Nassau County	563,800
Massachusetts	281,200	Westchester County, NY	483,600	**Brooklyn, NY** (borough) Kings County	549,900
Virginia	265,500	San Diego County, CA	480,900	**Queens, NY** (borough) Queens County	530,400
Washington	259,800	Bergen County, NJ	443,700	**Los Angeles, CA** (city) Los Angeles County	523,300
Arizona	250,900	Nassau County, NY	440,100	**Yonkers, NY** (city) Westchester County	497,600
Connecticut	245,400	Hudson County, NJ	415,500	**Huntington, NY** (town) Suffolk County	495,200

Sorted by Percent in Ascending Order — U.S. = $282,200

State	Dollars	County	Dollars	Place	Dollars
Michigan	98,800	Oneida County, NY	57,900	**Reading, PA** (city) Berks County	70,700
Pennsylvania	108,400	Berks County, PA	74,100	**Rochester, NY** (city) Monroe County	78,300
Ohio	114,900	Luzerne County, PA	96,000	**Syracuse, NY** (city) Onondaga County	80,700
Indiana	116,000	Kent County, MI	99,600	**Lancaster, PA** (city) Lancaster County	89,000
Alabama	127,500	Cuyahoga County, OH	100,100	**York, PA** (city) York County	92,700
Wisconsin	135,100	Philadelphia County, PA	108,200	**Cleveland, OH** (city) Cuyahoga County	92,800
Texas	139,200	Lancaster County, PA	109,800	**Grand Rapids, MI** (city) Kent County	99,900
Tennessee	144,200	York County, PA	112,500	**Hazleton, PA** (city) Luzerne County	101,200
Missouri	154,600	Lackawanna County, PA	114,300	**Camden, NJ** (city) Camden County	106,600
North Carolina	156,200	Harris County, TX	123,100	**Philadelphia, PA** (city) Philadelphia County	108,200

RANKINGS & COMPARISONS

Note: (1) Ranking tables cover all states and counties, and places with an overall population of at least 125,000, OR an overall population of at least 25,000 where the Hispanic/Latino population is at least 20% of the overall population. In states where less than five places meet either of these criteria, we have included places with at least 10,000 total population with the highest percentage of Hispanic/Latino population. These places are identified with an asterisk (*); Please refer to the User's Guide for a full explanation of data.

Median Home Value

Mexican

Top 10 States, Counties, and Places[1]

Sorted by Percent in Descending Order — U.S. = $155,200

State	Dollars	County	Dollars	Place	Dollars
District of Columbia	540,100	San Francisco County, CA	682,300	**Coral Gables, FL** (city) Miami-Dade County	1,000,000+
Hawaii	429,400	New York County, NY	667,200	**Santa Barbara, CA** (city) Santa Barbara County	868,400
New York	380,100	San Mateo County, CA	654,000	**Goleta, CA** (city) Santa Barbara County	757,000
Massachusetts	356,000	Marin County, CA	628,000	**Redwood City, CA** (city) San Mateo County	738,700
California	352,800	Kings County, NY	590,400	**North Hempstead, NY** (town) Nassau County	717,700
Maryland	328,500	Santa Clara County, CA	568,700	**San Bruno, CA** (city) San Mateo County	716,200
New Jersey	317,700	Maui County, HI	551,000	**San Francisco, CA** (city) San Francisco County	682,300
Rhode Island	266,100	Mono County, CA	537,500	**San Mateo, CA** (city) San Mateo County	673,400
Virginia	262,800	Hunterdon County, NJ	537,000	**Manhattan, NY** (borough) New York County	667,200
Connecticut	250,600	Putnam County, NY	534,500	**South San Francisco, CA** (city) San Mateo County	640,000

Sorted by Percent in Ascending Order — U.S. = $155,200

State	Dollars	County	Dollars	Place	Dollars
Alabama	70,400	Beaufort County, NC	<10,000	**Parker*, SC** (cdp) Greenville County	19,500
Oklahoma	72,200	Berrien County, GA	<10,000	**Altus*, OK** (city) Jackson County	31,900
Kansas	78,900	Fremont County, ID	<10,000	**Big Spring, TX** (city) Howard County	32,600
Iowa	80,500	Georgetown County, SC	<10,000	**Ramapo, NY** (town) Rockland County	33,000
North Carolina	83,200	Greene County, NC	<10,000	**Hope*, AR** (city) Hempstead County	43,500
Texas	86,700	Jackson County, IL	<10,000	**Greenville, TX** (city) Hunt County	43,600
Nebraska	87,400	Jackson County, WI	<10,000	**Mayfield*, KY** (city) Graves County	44,000
South Dakota	89,500	Kit Carson County, CO	<10,000	**Albertville*, AL** (city) Marshall County	46,300
Mississippi	89,600	Lenoir County, NC	<10,000	**Port Arthur, TX** (city) Jefferson County	46,800
Arkansas	91,100	Marshall County, MN	<10,000	**Reading, PA** (city) Berks County	52,100

Note: (1) Ranking tables cover all states and counties, and places with an overall population of at least 125,000, OR an overall population of at least 25,000 where the Hispanic/Latino population is at least 20% of the overall population. In states where less than five places meet either of these criteria, we have included places with at least 10,000 total population with the highest percentage of Hispanic/Latino population. These places are identified with an asterisk (*); Please refer to the User's Guide for a full explanation of data.

Median Home Value

Puerto Rican

Top 10 States, Counties, and Places[1]

Sorted by Percent in Descending Order — U.S. = $219,100

State	Dollars	County	Dollars	Place	Dollars
California	437,300	Madison County, NY	852,300	**Waianae*, HI** (cdp) Honolulu County	760,600
Hawaii	419,700	San Francisco County, CA	690,800	**San Francisco, CA** (city) San Francisco County	690,800
District of Columbia	388,900	San Mateo County, CA	690,300	**Huntington Beach, CA** (city) Orange County	677,800
New York	371,800	Marin County, CA	614,600	**Makakilo*, HI** (cdp) Honolulu County	620,700
Maryland	333,700	Monterey County, CA	605,100	**Fremont, CA** (city) Alameda County	602,300
New Jersey	302,100	New York County, NY	591,700	**Manhattan, NY** (borough) New York County	591,700
Virginia	285,100	Orange County, CA	568,900	**Coral Gables, FL** (city) Miami-Dade County	587,000
Washington	271,500	Santa Clara County, CA	558,200	**Rancho Cucamonga, CA** (city) San Bernardino County	561,400
Illinois	262,100	Kauai County, HI	543,600	**Huntington, NY** (town) Suffolk County	561,100
Oregon	260,000	Ventura County, CA	542,600	**Anaheim, CA** (city) Orange County	559,700

Sorted by Percent in Ascending Order — U.S. = $219,100

State	Dollars	County	Dollars	Place	Dollars
South Dakota	59,300	Wyoming County, NY	12,500	**Buffalo, NY** (city) Erie County	55,400
North Dakota	69,200	Yolo County, CA	19,100	**Akron, OH** (city) Summit County	57,600
Ohio	102,000	Oswego County, NY	33,800	**Rochester, NY** (city) Monroe County	61,200
Pennsylvania	110,300	Chautauqua County, NY	38,500	**Reading, PA** (city) Berks County	66,600
Michigan	114,100	Cattaraugus County, NY	42,000	**York, PA** (city) York County	67,200
Indiana	124,600	Schuylkill County, PA	57,700	**Detroit, MI** (city) Wayne County	74,300
Iowa	128,000	Ontario County, NY	62,200	**Corpus Christi, TX** (city) Nueces County	77,300
Oklahoma	129,800	Mahoning County, OH	67,500	**Philadelphia, PA** (city) Philadelphia County	81,100
Kansas	130,800	Cayuga County, NY	67,700	**Lebanon, PA** (city) Lebanon County	81,700
Alabama	131,500	Oneida County, NY	73,300	**Toledo, OH** (city) Lucas County	82,400

Note: (1) Ranking tables cover all states and counties, and places with an overall population of at least 125,000, OR an overall population of at least 25,000 where the Hispanic/Latino population is at least 20% of the overall population. In states where less than five places meet either of these criteria, we have included places with at least 10,000 total population with the highest percentage of Hispanic/Latino population. These places are identified with an asterisk (*); Please refer to the User's Guide for a full explanation of data.

Median Home Value

South American

Top 10 States, Counties, and Places[1]

Sorted by Percent in Descending Order — U.S. = $290,800

State	Dollars	County	Dollars	Place	Dollars
Hawaii	702,000	Santa Cruz County, CA	825,000	**Mountain View, CA** (city) Santa Clara County	764,100
District of Columbia	550,900	Santa Barbara County, CA	818,300	**Fullerton, CA** (city) Orange County	750,000
California	487,900	San Francisco County, CA	710,100	**San Francisco, CA** (city) San Francisco County	710,100
New York	454,700	Honolulu County, HI	706,600	**Daly City, CA** (city) San Mateo County	686,500
Virginia	381,800	Marin County, CA	698,900	**Manhattan, NY** (borough) New York County	671,500
New Jersey	367,300	San Mateo County, CA	691,400	**Redwood City, CA** (city) San Mateo County	661,800
Maryland	361,400	New York County, NY	671,500	**Irvine, CA** (city) Orange County	657,600
Massachusetts	336,000	Santa Clara County, CA	659,000	**Sunnyvale, CA** (city) Santa Clara County	636,700
Washington	327,500	Monterey County, CA	638,500	**Coral Gables, FL** (city) Miami-Dade County	616,100
Alaska	324,200	Orange County, CA	587,600	**Fremont, CA** (city) Alameda County	610,200

Sorted by Percent in Ascending Order — U.S. = $290,800

State	Dollars	County	Dollars	Place	Dollars
North Dakota	88,400	Berks County, PA	87,300	**Cleveland, OH** (city) Cuyahoga County	67,100
Oklahoma	123,600	Kent County, MI	89,300	**Reading, PA** (city) Berks County	73,500
Indiana	133,700	Bell County, TX	105,700	**Killeen, TX** (city) Bell County	108,700
Nebraska	139,200	Onondaga County, NY	114,500	**Tulsa, OK** (city) Tulsa County	109,100
Mississippi	139,300	Cleveland County, OK	115,600	**Mission Bend, TX** (cdp) Fort Bend County	113,600
South Carolina	143,500	Jackson County, MO	116,200	**Kansas City, MO** (city) Jackson County	118,300
Texas	156,600	Oklahoma County, OK	118,800	**Indianapolis, IN** (city) Marion County	122,600
Arkansas	165,900	Oneida County, NY	118,800	**North Lauderdale, FL** (city) Broward County	123,200
Iowa	167,700	Hidalgo County, TX	119,500	**Fayetteville, NC** (city) Cumberland County	130,400
Tennessee	167,900	Tulsa County, OK	119,800	**Oklahoma City, OK** (city) Oklahoma County	130,600

Note: (1) Ranking tables cover all states and counties, and places with an overall population of at least 125,000, OR an overall population of at least 25,000 where the Hispanic/Latino population is at least 20% of the overall population. In states where less than five places meet either of these criteria, we have included places with at least 10,000 total population with the highest percentage of Hispanic/Latino population. These places are identified with an asterisk (*); Please refer to the User's Guide for a full explanation of data.

Median Home Value

South American: Argentinean

Top 10 States, Counties, and Places[1]

Sorted by Percent in Descending Order — U.S. = $323,800

State	Dollars	County	Dollars	Place	Dollars
District of Columbia	575,400	Santa Clara County, CA	1,000,000	**Brooklyn, NY** (borough) Kings County	720,400
California	505,300	Kings County, NY	720,400	**Manhattan, NY** (borough) New York County	684,800
New York	496,500	Ventura County, CA	697,000	**San Francisco, CA** (city) San Francisco County	650,600
Virginia	453,400	New York County, NY	684,800	**New York, NY** (city)	607,700
Maryland	428,700	San Francisco County, CA	650,600	**Queens, NY** (borough) Queens County	583,700
Massachusetts	390,600	Alameda County, CA	599,800	**Los Angeles, CA** (city) Los Angeles County	561,000
Oregon	370,100	Queens County, NY	583,700	**San Jose, CA** (city) Santa Clara County	475,800
New Jersey	367,400	San Diego County, CA	574,700	**Bronx, NY** (borough) Bronx County	430,400
Colorado	365,000	Orange County, CA	574,600	**Hempstead (town), NY** (town) Nassau County	425,400
Connecticut	355,900	King County, WA	550,000	**San Diego, CA** (city) San Diego County	378,100

Sorted by Percent in Ascending Order — U.S. = $323,800

State	Dollars	County	Dollars	Place	Dollars
Tennessee	133,500	Tarrant County, TX	138,300	**Houston, TX** (city) Harris County	164,400
Texas	166,800	Bexar County, TX	156,700	**Miami Beach, FL** (city) Miami-Dade County	230,300
Utah	170,800	Harris County, TX	158,200	**Hialeah, FL** (city) Miami-Dade County	256,300
Ohio	175,800	Dallas County, TX	159,000	**Aventura, FL** (city) Miami-Dade County	259,400
North Carolina	191,700	Palm Beach County, FL	167,500	**Hollywood, FL** (city) Broward County	269,100
Louisiana	195,500	Travis County, TX	171,500	**Chicago, IL** (city) Cook County	271,400
Indiana	197,900	Hillsborough County, FL	176,700	**Coral Springs, FL** (city) Broward County	292,100
Minnesota	219,600	Montgomery County, TX	190,400	**Miami, FL** (city) Miami-Dade County	337,000
Michigan	221,200	Salt Lake County, UT	200,000	**Pembroke Pines, FL** (city) Broward County	351,200
South Carolina	221,400	Utah County, UT	201,300	**Doral, FL** (city) Miami-Dade County	357,200

RANKINGS & COMPARISONS

Note: (1) Ranking tables cover all states and counties, and places with an overall population of at least 125,000, OR an overall population of at least 25,000 where the Hispanic/Latino population is at least 20% of the overall population. In states where less than five places meet either of these criteria, we have included places with at least 10,000 total population with the highest percentage of Hispanic/Latino population. These places are identified with an asterisk (*); Please refer to the User's Guide for a full explanation of data.

Median Home Value

South American: Bolivian

Top 10 States, Counties, and Places[1]

Sorted by Percent in Descending Order — U.S. = $357,200

State	Dollars	County	Dollars	Place	Dollars
New York	527,500	Santa Clara County, CA	682,400	**Queens, NY** (borough) Queens County	607,300
California	482,900	Orange County, CA	616,700	**New York, NY** (city)	591,900
Virginia	418,400	Queens County, NY	607,300	**Arlington, VA** (cdp) Arlington County	579,600
Maryland	397,900	Arlington County, VA	579,600	**West Falls Church, VA** (cdp) Fairfax County	488,900
Massachusetts	382,200	Los Angeles County, CA	536,500	**Los Angeles, CA** (city) Los Angeles County	486,900
New Jersey	378,900	San Diego County, CA	451,500	**Springfield, VA** (cdp) Fairfax County	461,900
Rhode Island	278,100	Montgomery County, MD	425,200	**Annandale, VA** (cdp) Fairfax County	438,600
Illinois	273,900	Fairfax County, VA	424,400	**Providence, RI** (city) Providence County	330,800
Florida	227,600	Cook County, IL	401,100	**Dale City, VA** (cdp) Prince William County	328,400
North Carolina	206,000	Loudoun County, VA	390,300		

Sorted by Percent in Ascending Order — U.S. = $357,200

State	Dollars	County	Dollars	Place	Dollars
Texas	160,200	Harris County, TX	156,900	**Dale City, VA** (cdp) Prince William County	328,400
Pennsylvania	171,000	Palm Beach County, FL	180,900	**Providence, RI** (city) Providence County	330,800
North Carolina	206,000	Broward County, FL	200,400	**Annandale, VA** (cdp) Fairfax County	438,600
Florida	227,600	Providence County, RI	278,100	**Springfield, VA** (cdp) Fairfax County	461,900
Illinois	273,900	Prince George's County, MD	288,100	**Los Angeles, CA** (city) Los Angeles County	486,900
Rhode Island	278,100	Miami-Dade County, FL	315,900	**West Falls Church, VA** (cdp) Fairfax County	488,900
New Jersey	378,900	Prince William County, VA	374,200	**Arlington, VA** (cdp) Arlington County	579,600
Massachusetts	382,200	Loudoun County, VA	390,300	**New York, NY** (city)	591,900
Maryland	397,900	Cook County, IL	401,100	**Queens, NY** (borough) Queens County	607,300
Virginia	418,400	Fairfax County, VA	424,400		

Note: (1) Ranking tables cover all states and counties, and places with an overall population of at least 125,000, OR an overall population of at least 25,000 where the Hispanic/Latino population is at least 20% of the overall population. In states where less than five places meet either of these criteria, we have included places with at least 10,000 total population with the highest percentage of Hispanic/Latino population. These places are identified with an asterisk (*); Please refer to the User's Guide for a full explanation of data.

Median Home Value

South American: Chilean

Top 10 States, Counties, and Places[1]

Sorted by Percent in Descending Order — U.S. = $294,700

State	Dollars	County	Dollars	Place	Dollars
California	535,100	New York County, NY	1,000,000+	**Manhattan, NY** (borough) New York County	1,000,000+
New York	459,800	San Mateo County, CA	747,100	**Los Angeles, CA** (city) Los Angeles County	505,800
Virginia	399,700	Santa Clara County, CA	657,500	**New York, NY** (city)	498,900
Connecticut	392,900	Orange County, CA	644,700	**Brooklyn, NY** (borough) Kings County	470,000
Massachusetts	380,800	Westchester County, NY	588,500	**Queens, NY** (borough) Queens County	463,600
Minnesota	377,900	Alameda County, CA	562,500	**Hempstead (town), NY** (town) Nassau County	431,100
Maryland	325,800	Nassau County, NY	527,300	**Chicago, IL** (city) Cook County	268,800
New Jersey	325,200	Los Angeles County, CA	497,000	**Miami, FL** (city) Miami-Dade County	266,400
Washington	309,900	San Diego County, CA	472,100	**Kendall, FL** (cdp) Miami-Dade County	187,800
Pennsylvania	268,400	Kings County, NY	470,000		

Sorted by Percent in Ascending Order — U.S. = $294,700

State	Dollars	County	Dollars	Place	Dollars
Texas	146,200	Harris County, TX	175,300	**Kendall, FL** (cdp) Miami-Dade County	187,800
North Carolina	179,200	Salt Lake County, UT	201,300	**Miami, FL** (city) Miami-Dade County	266,400
Arizona	187,000	Broward County, FL	228,300	**Chicago, IL** (city) Cook County	268,800
Michigan	187,900	Utah County, UT	229,200	**Hempstead (town), NY** (town) Nassau County	431,100
Missouri	189,700	Maricopa County, AZ	250,500	**Queens, NY** (borough) Queens County	463,600
Wisconsin	190,700	San Bernardino County, CA	260,100	**Brooklyn, NY** (borough) Kings County	470,000
Utah	199,500	Cook County, IL	263,300	**New York, NY** (city)	498,900
Tennessee	210,800	Miami-Dade County, FL	265,100	**Los Angeles, CA** (city) Los Angeles County	505,800
Ohio	212,700	Clark County, NV	268,400	**Manhattan, NY** (borough) New York County	1,000,000+
Georgia	220,200	Palm Beach County, FL	314,500		

RANKINGS & COMPARISONS

Note: (1) Ranking tables cover all states and counties, and places with an overall population of at least 125,000, OR an overall population of at least 25,000 where the Hispanic/Latino population is at least 20% of the overall population. In states where less than five places meet either of these criteria, we have included places with at least 10,000 total population with the highest percentage of Hispanic/Latino population. These places are identified with an asterisk (*); Please refer to the User's Guide for a full explanation of data.

Median Home Value

South American: Colombian

Top 10 States, Counties, and Places[1]

Sorted by Percent in Descending Order — U.S. = $260,900

State	Dollars	County	Dollars	Place	Dollars
District of Columbia	598,000	San Francisco County, CA	814,500	**San Francisco, CA** (city) San Francisco County	814,500
California	479,900	San Mateo County, CA	695,800	**Burbank, CA** (city) Los Angeles County	632,600
New York	432,200	Norfolk County, MA	627,400	**Glendale, CA** (city) Los Angeles County	628,400
New Jersey	367,400	Orange County, CA	610,900	**Manhattan, NY** (borough) New York County	606,100
Maryland	350,100	New York County, NY	606,100	**Huntington, NY** (town) Suffolk County	581,200
Washington	341,700	Santa Clara County, CA	588,200	**Stamford, CT** (city/town) Fairfield County	554,400
Virginia	333,000	Kings County, NY	522,800	**Los Angeles, CA** (city) Los Angeles County	523,900
Massachusetts	313,600	Los Angeles County, CA	498,600	**Brooklyn, NY** (borough) Kings County	522,800
Alaska	296,700	Ventura County, CA	484,300	**North Hempstead, NY** (town) Nassau County	508,300
New Hampshire	295,700	Queens County, NY	474,100	**Englewood, NJ** (city) Bergen County	486,100

Sorted by Percent in Ascending Order — U.S. = $260,900

State	Dollars	County	Dollars	Place	Dollars
Oklahoma	115,100	Berks County, PA	85,000	**Indianapolis, IN** (city) Marion County	113,700
Indiana	122,800	Cuyahoga County, OH	108,200	**Fort Worth, TX** (city) Tarrant County	120,300
Iowa	125,700	Dallas County, TX	110,400	**North Lauderdale, FL** (city) Broward County	124,000
South Carolina	131,900	Marion County, IN	114,000	**Dallas, TX** (city) Dallas County	125,700
Nebraska	141,700	Greenville County, SC	121,900	**Houston, TX** (city) Harris County	130,500
Kansas	143,800	Hampden County, MA	130,300	**Philadelphia, PA** (city) Philadelphia County	144,500
Texas	149,600	Harris County, TX	137,200	**Phoenix, AZ** (city) Maricopa County	144,800
Louisiana	153,000	Philadelphia County, PA	144,500	**Miami Gardens, FL** (city) Miami-Dade County	145,800
Alabama	158,700	Tarrant County, TX	146,400	**Hallandale Beach, FL** (city) Broward County	157,500
Tennessee	161,400	Lancaster County, PA	149,300	**Tallahassee, FL** (city) Leon County	157,700

Note: (1) Ranking tables cover all states and counties, and places with an overall population of at least 125,000, OR an overall population of at least 25,000 where the Hispanic/Latino population is at least 20% of the overall population. In states where less than five places meet either of these criteria, we have included places with at least 10,000 total population with the highest percentage of Hispanic/Latino population. These places are identified with an asterisk (*); Please refer to the User's Guide for a full explanation of data.

Median Home Value

South American: Ecuadorian

Top 10 States, Counties, and Places[1]

Sorted by Percent in Descending Order — U.S. = $336,100

State	Dollars	County	Dollars	Place	Dollars
California	477,900	Queens County, NY	532,200	**White Plains, NY** (city) Westchester County	1,000,000+
New York	470,600	Kings County, NY	525,800	**Downey, CA** (city) Los Angeles County	621,600
Virginia	381,600	Orange County, CA	517,200	**Ossining, NY** (town) Westchester County	596,400
New Jersey	376,100	Los Angeles County, CA	500,700	**Ossining, NY** (village) Westchester County	575,800
Maryland	367,500	New York County, NY	496,400	**Stamford, CT** (city/town) Fairfield County	562,000
Nevada	349,000	Westchester County, NY	487,700	**Los Angeles, CA** (city) Los Angeles County	538,800
Washington	320,000	Santa Clara County, CA	479,000	**Queens, NY** (borough) Queens County	532,200
Massachusetts	318,500	Bergen County, NJ	463,500	**North Hempstead, NY** (town) Nassau County	529,800
Illinois	303,800	Richmond County, NY	463,100	**Brooklyn, NY** (borough) Kings County	525,800
Colorado	297,700	Nassau County, NY	460,000	**New York, NY** (city)	499,000

Sorted by Percent in Ascending Order — U.S. = $336,100

State	Dollars	County	Dollars	Place	Dollars
Oklahoma	88,700	Berks County, PA	97,300	**Philadelphia, PA** (city) Philadelphia County	116,400
Missouri	95,000	Philadelphia County, PA	116,400	**Allentown, PA** (city) Lehigh County	138,600
Michigan	114,400	Dallas County, TX	122,100	**Houston, TX** (city) Harris County	138,800
Indiana	123,000	Harris County, TX	127,400	**Charlotte, NC** (city) Mecklenburg County	159,400
Wisconsin	129,800	Lehigh County, PA	141,600	**Hialeah, FL** (city) Miami-Dade County	183,800
Texas	142,000	Tarrant County, TX	141,900	**Minneapolis, MN** (city) Hennepin County	201,100
Kansas	144,600	Delaware County, PA	147,900	**New Haven, CT** (city/town) New Haven County	203,700
South Carolina	159,200	Gwinnett County, GA	152,300	**Sunrise, FL** (city) Broward County	207,600
Iowa	161,400	Lee County, FL	159,800	**Country Club, FL** (cdp) Miami-Dade County	215,400
North Carolina	164,300	Mecklenburg County, NC	167,700	**Miramar, FL** (city) Broward County	258,200

RANKINGS & COMPARISONS

Note: (1) Ranking tables cover all states and counties, and places with an overall population of at least 125,000, OR an overall population of at least 25,000 where the Hispanic/Latino population is at least 20% of the overall population. In states where less than five places meet either of these criteria, we have included places with at least 10,000 total population with the highest percentage of Hispanic/Latino population. These places are identified with an asterisk (*); Please refer to the User's Guide for a full explanation of data.

Median Home Value

South American: Paraguayan

Top 10 States, Counties, and Places[1]

Sorted by Percent in Descending Order — U.S. = $285,300

State	Dollars	County	Dollars	Place	Dollars
New York	426,800	Queens County, NY	483,300	**New York, NY** (city)	485,600
California	419,000	Westchester County, NY	242,700	**Queens, NY** (borough) Queens County	483,300
New Jersey	351,900				
Maryland	312,800				
Florida	240,800				
Texas	144,000				

Sorted by Percent in Ascending Order — U.S. = $285,300

State	Dollars	County	Dollars	Place	Dollars
Texas	144,000	Westchester County, NY	242,700	**Queens, NY** (borough) Queens County	483,300
Florida	240,800	Queens County, NY	483,300	**New York, NY** (city)	485,600
Maryland	312,800				
New Jersey	351,900				
California	419,000				
New York	426,800				

Note: (1) Ranking tables cover all states and counties, and places with an overall population of at least 125,000, OR an overall population of at least 25,000 where the Hispanic/Latino population is at least 20% of the overall population. In states where less than five places meet either of these criteria, we have included places with at least 10,000 total population with the highest percentage of Hispanic/Latino population. These places are identified with an asterisk (*); Please refer to the User's Guide for a full explanation of data.

Median Home Value

South American: Peruvian

Top 10 States, Counties, and Places[1]

Sorted by Percent in Descending Order — U.S. = $296,500

State	Dollars	County	Dollars	Place	Dollars
Hawaii	714,500	San Francisco County, CA	787,600	**San Francisco, CA** (city) San Francisco County	787,600
District of Columbia	614,700	San Mateo County, CA	665,600	**San Jose, CA** (city) Santa Clara County	647,100
California	468,900	Santa Clara County, CA	621,200	**San Mateo, CA** (city) San Mateo County	622,600
New York	455,500	New York County, NY	619,100	**Manhattan, NY** (borough) New York County	619,100
Virginia	372,300	Ventura County, CA	593,900	**Rye, NY** (town) Westchester County	598,800
New Jersey	358,500	Orange County, CA	574,400	**Port Chester, NY** (village) Westchester County	596,700
Maryland	346,200	Kings County, NY	569,400	**Concord, CA** (city) Contra Costa County	584,000
Washington	346,200	Westchester County, NY	548,900	**Brooklyn, NY** (borough) Kings County	569,400
Connecticut	282,300	Queens County, NY	511,300	**Stamford, CT** (city/town) Fairfield County	512,100
Massachusetts	272,800	Fairfield County, CT	506,900	**Queens, NY** (borough) Queens County	511,300

Sorted by Percent in Ascending Order — U.S. = $296,500

State	Dollars	County	Dollars	Place	Dollars
Oklahoma	99,300	Travis County, TX	128,400	**Las Vegas, NV** (city) Clark County	112,500
Idaho	102,900	Dallas County, TX	134,300	**Dallas, TX** (city) Dallas County	126,300
Indiana	121,000	Philadelphia County, PA	138,700	**Garland, TX** (city) Dallas County	129,900
Ohio	146,600	Sarasota County, FL	139,400	**Philadelphia, PA** (city) Philadelphia County	138,700
Texas	154,000	Harris County, TX	143,300	**Houston, TX** (city) Harris County	142,400
Kentucky	158,300	Franklin County, OH	146,600	**Austin, TX** (city) Travis County	148,900
Louisiana	160,800	Bexar County, TX	162,900	**Hollywood, FL** (city) Broward County	151,000
Missouri	168,300	Duval County, FL	166,600	**San Antonio, TX** (city) Bexar County	158,500
North Carolina	174,600	Pinellas County, FL	169,500	**Charlotte, NC** (city) Mecklenburg County	161,700
Tennessee	174,800	Fort Bend County, TX	171,400	**Jacksonville, FL** (city) Duval County	166,600

Note: (1) Ranking tables cover all states and counties, and places with an overall population of at least 125,000, OR an overall population of at least 25,000 where the Hispanic/Latino population is at least 20% of the overall population. In states where less than five places meet either of these criteria, we have included places with at least 10,000 total population with the highest percentage of Hispanic/Latino population. These places are identified with an asterisk (*); Please refer to the User's Guide for a full explanation of data.

Median Home Value

South American: Uruguayan

Top 10 States, Counties, and Places[1]

Sorted by Percent in Descending Order — U.S. = $271,300

State	Dollars	County	Dollars	Place	Dollars
New York	469,800	Hudson County, NJ	565,800	**Queens, NY** (borough) Queens County	530,800
California	425,000	Queens County, NY	530,800	**New York, NY** (city)	465,300
Massachusetts	375,600	Los Angeles County, CA	524,100	**Elizabeth, NJ** (city) Union County	359,100
New Jersey	351,000	Westchester County, NY	479,000		
Maryland	346,900	Morris County, NJ	378,500		
Virginia	325,200	Union County, NJ	367,000		
Florida	202,400	Essex County, NJ	330,300		
Georgia	156,200	Middlesex County, NJ	280,100		
Pennsylvania	147,700	Broward County, FL	271,000		
Texas	140,200	Palm Beach County, FL	245,700		

Sorted by Percent in Ascending Order — U.S. = $271,300

State	Dollars	County	Dollars	Place	Dollars
Texas	140,200	Harris County, TX	144,400	**Elizabeth, NJ** (city) Union County	359,100
Pennsylvania	147,700	Gwinnett County, GA	161,600	**New York, NY** (city)	465,300
Georgia	156,200	Miami-Dade County, FL	213,500	**Queens, NY** (borough) Queens County	530,800
Florida	202,400	Worcester County, MA	229,300		
Virginia	325,200	Palm Beach County, FL	245,700		
Maryland	346,900	Broward County, FL	271,000		
New Jersey	351,000	Middlesex County, NJ	280,100		
Massachusetts	375,600	Essex County, NJ	330,300		
California	425,000	Union County, NJ	367,000		
New York	469,800	Morris County, NJ	378,500		

Note: (1) Ranking tables cover all states and counties, and places with an overall population of at least 125,000, OR an overall population of at least 25,000 where the Hispanic/Latino population is at least 20% of the overall population. In states where less than five places meet either of these criteria, we have included places with at least 10,000 total population with the highest percentage of Hispanic/Latino population. These places are identified with an asterisk (*); Please refer to the User's Guide for a full explanation of data.

Median Home Value

South American: Venezuelan

Top 10 States, Counties, and Places[1]

Sorted by Percent in Descending Order — U.S. = $258,400

State	Dollars	County	Dollars	Place	Dollars
California	457,500	New York County, NY	902,000	**Manhattan, NY** (borough) New York County	902,000
Massachusetts	443,200	Orange County, CA	582,100	**Miami Beach, FL** (city) Miami-Dade County	475,900
New Jersey	442,000	Fulton County, GA	469,600	**New York, NY** (city)	451,300
New York	378,300	King County, WA	450,000	**Brooklyn, NY** (borough) Kings County	450,000
Maryland	361,900	Kings County, NY	450,000	**Weston, FL** (city) Broward County	381,400
Washington	311,500	San Diego County, CA	445,100	**Doral, FL** (city) Miami-Dade County	373,600
Virginia	309,500	Middlesex County, MA	443,500	**Kendall, FL** (cdp) Miami-Dade County	369,100
Illinois	291,000	Los Angeles County, CA	412,300	**Miami, FL** (city) Miami-Dade County	368,300
Arizona	288,800	Hudson County, NJ	409,300	**Bronx, NY** (borough) Bronx County	366,700
Florida	272,800	Suffolk County, MA	383,300	**Hollywood, FL** (city) Broward County	351,400

Sorted by Percent in Ascending Order — U.S. = $258,400

State	Dollars	County	Dollars	Place	Dollars
Indiana	124,500	Pinellas County, FL	161,600	**Hialeah, FL** (city) Miami-Dade County	162,400
Oklahoma	147,800	Montgomery County, TX	168,800	**Sunrise, FL** (city) Broward County	168,800
South Carolina	168,300	Tarrant County, TX	172,600	**Davie, FL** (town) Broward County	197,300
Missouri	176,100	Dallas County, TX	174,000	**Fountainebleau, FL** (cdp) Miami-Dade County	198,600
North Carolina	180,500	Lee County, FL	175,400	**Tamiami, FL** (cdp) Miami-Dade County	215,100
Texas	188,100	Gwinnett County, GA	176,800	**Houston, TX** (city) Harris County	216,600
Michigan	192,900	Harris County, TX	180,700	**Kendall West, FL** (cdp) Miami-Dade County	220,700
Wisconsin	193,900	Travis County, TX	197,400	**Country Club, FL** (cdp) Miami-Dade County	224,400
Utah	196,000	Cobb County, GA	213,500	**Coral Springs, FL** (city) Broward County	231,500
Georgia	199,300	Hillsborough County, FL	224,000	**Orlando, FL** (city) Orange County	236,500

Note: (1) Ranking tables cover all states and counties, and places with an overall population of at least 125,000, OR an overall population of at least 25,000 where the Hispanic/Latino population is at least 20% of the overall population. In states where less than five places meet either of these criteria, we have included places with at least 10,000 total population with the highest percentage of Hispanic/Latino population. These places are identified with an asterisk (*); Please refer to the User's Guide for a full explanation of data.

Median Home Value

Spaniard

Top 10 States, Counties, and Places[1]

Sorted by Percent in Descending Order — U.S. = $241,000

State	Dollars	County	Dollars	Place	Dollars
District of Columbia	761,000	San Francisco County, CA	869,300	**San Francisco, CA** (city) San Francisco County	869,300
Hawaii	579,200	New York County, NY	868,400	**Manhattan, NY** (borough) New York County	868,400
California	452,500	Maui County, HI	724,000	**San Jose, CA** (city) Santa Clara County	668,500
New York	449,800	San Mateo County, CA	700,600	**Brooklyn, NY** (borough) Kings County	615,000
Massachusetts	386,100	Santa Clara County, CA	647,100	**Queens, NY** (borough) Queens County	604,600
New Jersey	383,300	Santa Barbara County, CA	625,000	**New York, NY** (city)	580,100
Maryland	375,900	Monterey County, CA	624,100	**Los Angeles, CA** (city) Los Angeles County	533,200
Virginia	344,100	Kings County, NY	615,000	**San Diego, CA** (city) San Diego County	506,200
Connecticut	328,300	Santa Cruz County, CA	606,100	**Oyster Bay, NY** (town) Nassau County	500,000
Washington	301,700	Queens County, NY	604,600	**Staten Island, NY** (borough) Richmond County	496,200

Sorted by Percent in Ascending Order — U.S. = $241,000

State	Dollars	County	Dollars	Place	Dollars
Oklahoma	107,100	Oklahoma County, OK	73,000	**Lubbock, TX** (city) Lubbock County	92,200
Iowa	118,300	Cibola County, NM	73,900	**Oklahoma City, OK** (city) Oklahoma County	95,000
Indiana	126,000	Lubbock County, TX	74,600	**Corpus Christi, TX** (city) Nueces County	100,400
Nebraska	128,800	Colfax County, NM	84,300	**Las Cruces, NM** (city) Dona Ana County	110,600
South Carolina	134,600	Conejos County, CO	89,500	**San Bernardino, CA** (city) San Bernardino County	115,200
Mississippi	136,300	Nueces County, TX	99,000	**Glendale, AZ** (city) Maricopa County	120,000
Texas	140,400	San Miguel County, NM	101,500	**Pueblo, CO** (city) Pueblo County	122,100
Maine	148,700	Las Animas County, CO	109,000	**Tucson, AZ** (city) Pima County	125,000
Kentucky	149,500	Doña Ana County, NM	113,000	**San Antonio, TX** (city) Bexar County	128,100
Alabama	151,500	Rio Arriba County, NM	115,000	**Fort Worth, TX** (city) Tarrant County	143,800

Note: (1) Ranking tables cover all states and counties, and places with an overall population of at least 125,000, OR an overall population of at least 25,000 where the Hispanic/Latino population is at least 20% of the overall population. In states where less than five places meet either of these criteria, we have included places with at least 10,000 total population with the highest percentage of Hispanic/Latino population. These places are identified with an asterisk (*); Please refer to the User's Guide for a full explanation of data.

Median Gross Rent

Total Population

Top 10 States, Counties, and Places[1]

Sorted by Percent in Descending Order — U.S. = $841

State	Dollars	County	Dollars	Place	Dollars
Hawaii	1,260	Nantucket County, MA	1,714	**Eastvale, CA** (cdp) Riverside County	2,000+
California	1,147	Loudoun County, VA	1,531	**Schofield Barracks*, HI** (cdp) Honolulu County	2,000+
New Jersey	1,092	Marin County, CA	1,523	**Irvine, CA** (city) Orange County	1,788
Maryland	1,091	Arlington County, VA	1,519	**Chino Hills, CA** (city) San Bernardino County	1,760
District of Columbia	1,063	Fairfax County, VA	1,492	**Weston, FL** (city) Broward County	1,736
Massachusetts	1,006	San Mateo County, CA	1,443	**Thousand Oaks, CA** (city) Ventura County	1,731
Nevada	998	Suffolk County, NY	1,427	**Laguna Hills, CA** (city) Orange County	1,727
Connecticut	982	Orange County, CA	1,423	**Richmond West, FL** (cdp) Miami-Dade County	1,711
New York	977	Montgomery County, MD	1,417	**Cooper City, FL** (city) Broward County	1,673
Alaska	972	Nassau County, NY	1,407	**Doral, FL** (city) Miami-Dade County	1,672

Sorted by Percent in Ascending Order — U.S. = $841

State	Dollars	County	Dollars	Place	Dollars
West Virginia	549	Cottle County, TX	298	**Huron*, SD** (city) Beadle County	441
North Dakota	555	Blaine County, MT	312	**San Luis, AZ** (city) Yuma County	488
South Dakota	574	Rolette County, ND	331	**Yankton*, SD** (city) Yankton County	504
Kentucky	601	Harding County, NM	333	**San Juan, TX** (city) Hidalgo County	505
Arkansas	617	Clay County, TN	334	**Butte-Silver Bow*, MT** (consolidated govt) Silver Bow County	516
Iowa	617	Menominee County, WI	336	**Eagle Pass, TX** (city) Maverick County	518
Montana	629	Dundy County, NE	340	**Beckley*, WV** (city) Raleigh County	526
Oklahoma	633	Throckmorton County, TX	342	**Spearfish*, SD** (city) Lawrence County	526
Alabama	644	Corson County, SD	346	**Williston*, ND** (city) Williams County	527
Mississippi	648	Haskell County, TX	347	**Socorro, TX** (city) El Paso County	528

Note: (1) Ranking tables cover all states and counties, and places with an overall population of at least 125,000, OR an overall population of at least 25,000 where the Hispanic/Latino population is at least 20% of the overall population. In states where less than five places meet either of these criteria, we have included places with at least 10,000 total population with the highest percentage of Hispanic/Latino population. These places are identified with an asterisk (*); Please refer to the User's Guide for a full explanation of data.

Median Gross Rent

Hispanic or Latino (of any race)

Top 10 States, Counties, and Places[1]

Sorted by Percent in Descending Order — U.S. = $877

State	Dollars	County	Dollars	Place	Dollars
Hawaii	1,294	Plaquemines Parish, LA	1,723	**Eastvale, CA** (cdp) Riverside County	2,000+
Maryland	1,199	Charles County, MD	1,663	**Schofield Barracks*, HI** (cdp) Honolulu County	2,000+
Virginia	1,152	Gladwin County, MI	1,571	**Chino Hills, CA** (city) San Bernardino County	1,804
District of Columbia	1,118	Mariposa County, CA	1,538	**Richmond West, FL** (cdp) Miami-Dade County	1,728
New Jersey	1,080	Franklin County, VT	1,475	**Diamond Bar, CA** (city) Los Angeles County	1,714
California	1,031	Anne Arundel County, MD	1,456	**Sterling, VA** (cdp) Loudoun County	1,681
New Hampshire	1,011	Fairfax County, VA	1,452	**Doral, FL** (city) Miami-Dade County	1,673
Alaska	995	Loudoun County, VA	1,446	**Elmont, NY** (cdp) Nassau County	1,657
New York	986	Putnam County, NY	1,446	**Irvine, CA** (city) Orange County	1,655
Florida	977	Hunterdon County, NJ	1,443	**Moorpark, CA** (city) Ventura County	1,655

Sorted by Percent in Ascending Order — U.S. = $877

State	Dollars	County	Dollars	Place	Dollars
North Dakota	543	Wabaunsee County, KS	194	**Willmar*, MN** (city) Kandiyohi County	457
South Dakota	567	Kent County, MD	200	**Minot*, ND** (city) Ward County	476
Arkansas	588	Haskell County, TX	226	**San Luis, AZ** (city) Yuma County	488
West Virginia	593	West Carroll Parish, LA	232	**San Juan, TX** (city) Hidalgo County	501
Kentucky	609	Johnston County, OK	240	**Butte-Silver Bow*, MT** (consolidated govt) Silver Bow County	507
Oklahoma	613	Washington County, ME	242	**Alamogordo, NM** (city) Otero County	509
Iowa	619	Concho County, TX	248	**Morgantown*, WV** (city) Monongalia County	510
Alabama	636	Jackson County, FL	272	**Eagle Pass, TX** (city) Maverick County	514
Idaho	636	Osage County, OK	276	**Altus*, OK** (city) Jackson County	517
Nebraska	642	Dickens County, TX	288	**Socorro, TX** (city) El Paso County	525

Note: (1) Ranking tables cover all states and counties, and places with an overall population of at least 125,000, OR an overall population of at least 25,000 where the Hispanic/Latino population is at least 20% of the overall population. In states where less than five places meet either of these criteria, we have included places with at least 10,000 total population with the highest percentage of Hispanic/Latino population. These places are identified with an asterisk (*); Please refer to the User's Guide for a full explanation of data.

Median Gross Rent

Central American, excluding Mexican

Top 10 States, Counties, and Places[1]

Sorted by Percent in Descending Order — U.S. = $944

State	Dollars	County	Dollars	Place	Dollars
Hawaii	1,405	Leon County, FL	1,546	**Apple Valley, CA** (town) San Bernardino County	2,000+
Connecticut	1,223	Loudoun County, VA	1,533	**Eastvale, CA** (cdp) Riverside County	2,000+
Virginia	1,206	Suffolk County, NY	1,456	**Hacienda Heights, CA** (cdp) Los Angeles County	2,000+
Alaska	1,204	Fairfax County, VA	1,423	**Chino Hills, CA** (city) San Bernardino County	1,965
Maryland	1,201	Putnam County, NY	1,413	**Oyster Bay, NY** (town) Nassau County	1,774
New Jersey	1,152	Nassau County, NY	1,412	**West Falls Church, VA** (cdp) Fairfax County	1,714
New Hampshire	1,140	Kane County, IL	1,410	**Sterling, VA** (cdp) Loudoun County	1,709
Massachusetts	1,121	Rockland County, NY	1,407	**Richmond West, FL** (cdp) Miami-Dade County	1,701
New York	1,110	Ventura County, CA	1,400	**Covina, CA** (city) Los Angeles County	1,699
Delaware	1,038	Albany County, NY	1,377	**Union City, CA** (city) Alameda County	1,693

Sorted by Percent in Ascending Order — U.S. = $944

State	Dollars	County	Dollars	Place	Dollars
Vermont	483	Smith County, TX	394	**Rubidoux, CA** (cdp) Riverside County	338
South Dakota	499	Crawford County, AR	402	**Channelview, TX** (cdp) Harris County	428
Iowa	550	Hays County, TX	443	**Lincoln, NE** (city) Lancaster County	479
Arkansas	598	DeKalb County, AL	445	**Sioux Falls, SD** (city) Minnehaha County	530
Kentucky	609	Woodbury County, IA	463	**San Jacinto, CA** (city) Riverside County	535
Idaho	610	Cleveland County, OK	474	**Colorado Springs, CO** (city) El Paso County	553
Oklahoma	618	Lancaster County, NE	479	**Tulsa, OK** (city) Tulsa County	561
West Virginia	627	Sebastian County, AR	497	**Springdale, AR** (city) Washington County	575
Nebraska	635	Douglas County, GA	513	**Grand Island, NE** (city) Hall County	584
Alabama	648	Sampson County, NC	527	**Galveston, TX** (city) Galveston County	588

Note: (1) Ranking tables cover all states and counties, and places with an overall population of at least 125,000, OR an overall population of at least 25,000 where the Hispanic/Latino population is at least 20% of the overall population. In states where less than five places meet either of these criteria, we have included places with at least 10,000 total population with the highest percentage of Hispanic/Latino population. These places are identified with an asterisk (*); Please refer to the User's Guide for a full explanation of data.

Median Gross Rent

Central American: Costa Rican

Top 10 States, Counties, and Places[1]

Sorted by Percent in Descending Order — U.S. = $1,038

State	Dollars	County	Dollars	Place	Dollars
Maryland	1,439	Contra Costa County, CA	1,701	**Queens, NY** (borough) Queens County	1,253
Virginia	1,308	Suffolk County, NY	1,675	**New York, NY** (city)	1,066
New Jersey	1,287	Somerset County, NJ	1,649	**Brooklyn, NY** (borough) Kings County	1,037
California	1,197	Morris County, NJ	1,455	**Miami, FL** (city) Miami-Dade County	995
Connecticut	1,197	Orange County, CA	1,413	**Los Angeles, CA** (city) Los Angeles County	991
Minnesota	1,125	Mercer County, NJ	1,410	**Philadelphia, PA** (city) Philadelphia County	872
Nevada	1,101	Bergen County, NJ	1,385	**Bronx, NY** (borough) Bronx County	768
New York	1,095	San Bernardino County, CA	1,350		
Washington	1,080	Fairfield County, CT	1,307		
Florida	1,031	Queens County, NY	1,253		

Sorted by Percent in Ascending Order — U.S. = $1,038

State	Dollars	County	Dollars	Place	Dollars
Oregon	539	Nassau County, NY	642	**Bronx, NY** (borough) Bronx County	768
North Carolina	639	Bronx County, NY	768	**Philadelphia, PA** (city) Philadelphia County	872
Colorado	678	Cook County, IL	777	**Los Angeles, CA** (city) Los Angeles County	991
Wisconsin	719	Orange County, FL	801	**Miami, FL** (city) Miami-Dade County	995
Tennessee	737	Harris County, TX	808	**Brooklyn, NY** (borough) Kings County	1,037
Illinois	783	Philadelphia County, PA	872	**New York, NY** (city)	1,066
Texas	811	Maricopa County, AZ	896	**Queens, NY** (borough) Queens County	1,253
Arizona	829	Hillsborough County, FL	985		
Michigan	835	Essex County, NJ	1,003		
Massachusetts	844	Broward County, FL	1,014		

Note: (1) Ranking tables cover all states and counties, and places with an overall population of at least 125,000, OR an overall population of at least 25,000 where the Hispanic/Latino population is at least 20% of the overall population. In states where less than five places meet either of these criteria, we have included places with at least 10,000 total population with the highest percentage of Hispanic/Latino population. These places are identified with an asterisk (*); Please refer to the User's Guide for a full explanation of data.

Median Gross Rent

Central American: Guatemalan

Top 10 States, Counties, and Places[1]

Sorted by Percent in Descending Order — U.S. = $941

State	Dollars	County	Dollars	Place	Dollars
Connecticut	1,398	Loudoun County, VA	1,670	**Wheaton, MD** (cdp) Montgomery County	2,000+
New York	1,215	Suffolk County, NY	1,552	**North Hempstead, NY** (town) Nassau County	1,585
New Jersey	1,199	Fairfield County, CT	1,480	**Rye, NY** (town) Westchester County	1,544
Massachusetts	1,174	Morris County, NJ	1,478	**Pasadena, CA** (city) Los Angeles County	1,511
Virginia	1,141	Putnam County, NY	1,426	**Port Chester, NY** (village) Westchester County	1,503
Maryland	1,134	Fairfax County, VA	1,422	**Islip, NY** (town) Suffolk County	1,487
Delaware	1,088	Nassau County, NY	1,412	**Stamford, CT** (city/town) Fairfield County	1,486
District of Columbia	1,037	Marin County, CA	1,408	**Brentwood, NY** (cdp) Suffolk County	1,442
Florida	1,019	Rockland County, NY	1,405	**Spring Valley, NV** (cdp) Clark County	1,414
California	991	Westchester County, NY	1,384	**Paterson, NJ** (city) Passaic County	1,405

Sorted by Percent in Ascending Order — U.S. = $941

State	Dollars	County	Dollars	Place	Dollars
South Dakota	547	DeKalb County, AL	437	**Bakersfield, CA** (city) Kern County	540
Iowa	564	Milwaukee County, WI	545	**Grand Island, NE** (city) Hall County	556
Alabama	603	Hall County, NE	556	**Sioux Falls, SD** (city) Minnehaha County	572
Kentucky	608	Minnehaha County, SD	572	**Columbus, OH** (city) Franklin County	585
Missouri	608	Franklin County, OH	585	**Carthage*, MO** (city) Jasper County	586
Oklahoma	608	Jasper County, MO	586	**Lancaster, CA** (city) Los Angeles County	631
Wisconsin	613	Floyd County, GA	600	**Oklahoma City, OK** (city) Oklahoma County	636
Nebraska	614	Hamilton County, TN	618	**Chattanooga, TN** (city) Hamilton County	639
Arkansas	617	Franklin County, AL	619	**Nashville-Davidson, TN** (metropolitan govt) Davidson County	671
Idaho	638	Gilmer County, GA	624	**Lexington*, NE** (city) Dawson County	672

RANKINGS & COMPARISONS

Note: (1) Ranking tables cover all states and counties, and places with an overall population of at least 125,000, OR an overall population of at least 25,000 where the Hispanic/Latino population is at least 20% of the overall population. In states where less than five places meet either of these criteria, we have included places with at least 10,000 total population with the highest percentage of Hispanic/Latino population. These places are identified with an asterisk (*); Please refer to the User's Guide for a full explanation of data.

Median Gross Rent

Central American: Honduran

Top 10 States, Counties, and Places[1]

Sorted by Percent in Descending Order — U.S. = $886

State	Dollars	County	Dollars	Place	Dollars
Maryland	1,255	Loudoun County, VA	1,685	**Wheaton, MD** (cdp) Montgomery County	1,804
Virginia	1,223	Montgomery County, MD	1,435	**San Jose, CA** (city) Santa Clara County	1,440
Connecticut	1,139	Fairfax County, VA	1,420	**Hempstead (village), NY** (village) Nassau County	1,386
New Jersey	1,106	Orange County, CA	1,400	**Huntington Station, NY** (cdp) Suffolk County	1,383
Massachusetts	1,077	Santa Clara County, CA	1,400	**Springfield, VA** (cdp) Fairfax County	1,368
Washington	1,054	Ventura County, CA	1,374	**Hempstead (town), NY** (town) Nassau County	1,363
New York	997	Nassau County, NY	1,354	**Huntington, NY** (town) Suffolk County	1,354
California	991	Atlantic County, NJ	1,313	**Plainfield, NJ** (city) Union County	1,280
Nevada	966	Prince William County, VA	1,302	**Miramar, FL** (city) Broward County	1,269
Florida	957	Fairfield County, CT	1,294	**Baltimore, MD** (independent city)	1,253

Sorted by Percent in Ascending Order — U.S. = $886

State	Dollars	County	Dollars	Place	Dollars
Iowa	482	Duplin County, NC	482	**Brentwood, NY** (cdp) Suffolk County	606
Utah	549	Elkhart County, IN	497	**Oklahoma City, OK** (city) Oklahoma County	609
Arkansas	577	Salt Lake County, UT	540	**Islip, NY** (town) Suffolk County	619
Oklahoma	599	Sampson County, NC	552	**Indianapolis, IN** (city) Marion County	633
Kentucky	615	Oklahoma County, OK	625	**Conroe, TX** (city) Montgomery County	634
Indiana	643	Marion County, IN	632	**Fort Worth, TX** (city) Tarrant County	636
Wisconsin	687	Tarrant County, TX	639	**Manhattan, NY** (borough) New York County	650
Arizona	694	Montgomery County, TX	645	**Pasadena, TX** (city) Harris County	655
Kansas	696	New York County, NY	650	**Aurora, CO** (city) Arapahoe County	674
Ohio	696	Arapahoe County, CO	665	**Dallas, TX** (city) Dallas County	674

Note: (1) Ranking tables cover all states and counties, and places with an overall population of at least 125,000, OR an overall population of at least 25,000 where the Hispanic/Latino population is at least 20% of the overall population. In states where less than five places meet either of these criteria, we have included places with at least 10,000 total population with the highest percentage of Hispanic/Latino population. These places are identified with an asterisk (*); Please refer to the User's Guide for a full explanation of data.

Median Gross Rent

Central American: Nicaraguan

Top 10 States, Counties, and Places[1]

Sorted by Percent in Descending Order — U.S. = $1,022

State	Dollars	County	Dollars	Place	Dollars
Virginia	1,264	Gwinnett County, GA	1,467	**Richmond, CA** (city) Contra Costa County	1,769
Maryland	1,215	Orange County, CA	1,433	**Daly City, CA** (city) San Mateo County	1,424
Connecticut	1,194	Prince William County, VA	1,411	**South San Francisco, CA** (city) San Mateo County	1,394
District of Columbia	1,130	San Mateo County, CA	1,376	**Tamiami, FL** (cdp) Miami-Dade County	1,391
New Jersey	1,124	Fairfax County, VA	1,362	**Fontana, CA** (city) San Bernardino County	1,359
California	1,123	Queens County, NY	1,359	**Queens, NY** (borough) Queens County	1,359
Nevada	1,095	Collier County, FL	1,293	**Hayward, CA** (city) Alameda County	1,358
Colorado	1,077	Clark County, NV	1,267	**Kendall, FL** (cdp) Miami-Dade County	1,352
Massachusetts	1,077	Contra Costa County, CA	1,259	**Kendale Lakes, FL** (cdp) Miami-Dade County	1,350
New York	1,077	Alameda County, CA	1,254	**Kendall West, FL** (cdp) Miami-Dade County	1,326

Sorted by Percent in Ascending Order — U.S. = $1,022

State	Dollars	County	Dollars	Place	Dollars
Ohio	527	Camden County, NJ	662	**West Little River, FL** (cdp) Miami-Dade County	520
South Carolina	584	Bexar County, TX	720	**Miramar, FL** (city) Broward County	685
Minnesota	616	Harris County, TX	777	**Kenner, LA** (city) Jefferson Parish	717
Tennessee	729	Duval County, FL	781	**Houston, TX** (city) Harris County	741
Michigan	750	Hillsborough County, FL	809	**Jacksonville, FL** (city) Duval County	781
Wisconsin	752	Cook County, IL	856	**Austin, TX** (city) Travis County	853
Texas	788	San Joaquin County, CA	863	**Chicago, IL** (city) Cook County	869
Arizona	796	Travis County, TX	865	**San Diego, CA** (city) San Diego County	888
Missouri	818	Dallas County, TX	890	**Bronx, NY** (borough) Bronx County	892
Oregon	845	Bronx County, NY	892	**Los Angeles, CA** (city) Los Angeles County	909

RANKINGS & COMPARISONS

Note: (1) Ranking tables cover all states and counties, and places with an overall population of at least 125,000, OR an overall population of at least 25,000 where the Hispanic/Latino population is at least 20% of the overall population. In states where less than five places meet either of these criteria, we have included places with at least 10,000 total population with the highest percentage of Hispanic/Latino population. These places are identified with an asterisk (*); Please refer to the User's Guide for a full explanation of data.

Median Gross Rent

Central American: Panamanian

Top 10 States, Counties, and Places[1]

Sorted by Percent in Descending Order — U.S. = $958

State	Dollars	County	Dollars	Place	Dollars
Massachusetts	1,160	Fairfax County, VA	1,707	**San Diego, CA** (city) San Diego County	1,752
California	1,146	Suffolk County, NY	1,636	**Hempstead (town), NY** (town) Nassau County	1,231
Pennsylvania	1,066	San Diego County, CA	1,612	**Queens, NY** (borough) Queens County	1,172
Virginia	1,060	Montgomery County, MD	1,425	**Miami, FL** (city) Miami-Dade County	1,043
Maryland	1,057	Broward County, FL	1,264	**Bronx, NY** (borough) Bronx County	994
Illinois	1,048	Nassau County, NY	1,231	**Los Angeles, CA** (city) Los Angeles County	961
Florida	1,019	Queens County, NY	1,172	**New York, NY** (city)	958
New Jersey	1,007	Riverside County, CA	1,163	**Brooklyn, NY** (borough) Kings County	916
New York	1,000	Prince William County, VA	1,142	**Manhattan, NY** (borough) New York County	881
Nevada	983	Palm Beach County, FL	1,132	**Killeen, TX** (city) Bell County	846

Sorted by Percent in Ascending Order — U.S. = $958

State	Dollars	County	Dollars	Place	Dollars
Alabama	622	Cumberland County, NC	619	**Fayetteville, NC** (city) Cumberland County	620
Missouri	623	Bell County, TX	693	**Jacksonville, FL** (city) Duval County	740
North Carolina	649	Duval County, FL	740	**Houston, TX** (city) Harris County	811
Kentucky	662	Pierce County, WA	749	**San Antonio, TX** (city) Bexar County	830
Colorado	676	Bexar County, TX	812	**Killeen, TX** (city) Bell County	846
South Carolina	684	Hillsborough County, FL	822	**Manhattan, NY** (borough) New York County	881
Indiana	694	Dallas County, TX	828	**Brooklyn, NY** (borough) Kings County	916
Louisiana	699	Hudson County, NJ	828	**New York, NY** (city)	958
Oklahoma	709	Harris County, TX	834	**Los Angeles, CA** (city) Los Angeles County	961
Michigan	747	New York County, NY	881	**Bronx, NY** (borough) Bronx County	994

Note: (1) Ranking tables cover all states and counties, and places with an overall population of at least 125,000, OR an overall population of at least 25,000 where the Hispanic/Latino population is at least 20% of the overall population. In states where less than five places meet either of these criteria, we have included places with at least 10,000 total population with the highest percentage of Hispanic/Latino population. These places are identified with an asterisk (*); Please refer to the User's Guide for a full explanation of data.

Median Gross Rent

Central American: Salvadoran

Top 10 States, Counties, and Places[1]

Sorted by Percent in Descending Order — U.S. = $947

State	Dollars	County	Dollars	Place	Dollars
Alaska	1,315	Frederick County, MD	1,610	**Sterling, VA** (cdp) Loudoun County	1,947
Maryland	1,234	Loudoun County, VA	1,598	**West Falls Church, VA** (cdp) Fairfax County	1,819
Hawaii	1,228	Suffolk County, NY	1,460	**Oyster Bay, NY** (town) Nassau County	1,794
Virginia	1,225	Nassau County, NY	1,444	**Islip, NY** (town) Suffolk County	1,774
New York	1,212	Ventura County, CA	1,433	**Fremont, CA** (city) Alameda County	1,761
Massachusetts	1,121	Fairfax County, VA	1,409	**Springfield, VA** (cdp) Fairfax County	1,757
New Jersey	1,113	Anne Arundel County, MD	1,397	**Glen Cove, NY** (city) Nassau County	1,721
California	987	Rockland County, NY	1,345	**Central Islip, NY** (cdp) Suffolk County	1,688
Connecticut	966	Bergen County, NJ	1,344	**North Hempstead, NY** (town) Nassau County	1,678
Florida	944	Santa Clara County, CA	1,340	**Antioch, CA** (city) Contra Costa County	1,674

Sorted by Percent in Ascending Order — U.S. = $947

State	Dollars	County	Dollars	Place	Dollars
Kentucky	523	Crawford County, AR	402	**Winston-Salem, NC** (city) Forsyth County	529
Iowa	536	Sebastian County, AR	460	**La Puente, CA** (city) Los Angeles County	548
Arkansas	580	Rutherford County, TN	548	**Springdale, AR** (city) Washington County	554
Idaho	632	Forsyth County, NC	553	**Des Moines, IA** (city) Polk County	625
Missouri	655	Hidalgo County, TX	556	**San Antonio, TX** (city) Bexar County	628
Ohio	658	Washington County, AR	565	**Pasadena, TX** (city) Harris County	639
Oklahoma	677	El Paso County, CO	594	**Jacksonville, FL** (city) Duval County	643
Nebraska	693	Benton County, AR	611	**Rogers, AR** (city) Benton County	651
New Mexico	694	Polk County, IA	625	**Arlington, TX** (city) Tarrant County	653
Texas	694	Bexar County, TX	627	**Greensboro, NC** (city) Guilford County	665

RANKINGS & COMPARISONS

Note: (1) Ranking tables cover all states and counties, and places with an overall population of at least 125,000, OR an overall population of at least 25,000 where the Hispanic/Latino population is at least 20% of the overall population. In states where less than five places meet either of these criteria, we have included places with at least 10,000 total population with the highest percentage of Hispanic/Latino population. These places are identified with an asterisk (*); Please refer to the User's Guide for a full explanation of data.

Median Gross Rent

Cuban

Top 10 States, Counties, and Places[1]

Sorted by Percent in Descending Order — U.S. = $920

State	Dollars	County	Dollars	Place	Dollars
District of Columbia	1,406	San Mateo County, CA	2,000	**San Jose, CA** (city) Santa Clara County	1,931
New Hampshire	1,335	Norfolk County, MA	1,871	**Brookhaven, NY** (town) Suffolk County	1,839
Hawaii	1,266	Ventura County, CA	1,706	**Miramar, FL** (city) Broward County	1,791
Massachusetts	1,203	Arapahoe County, CO	1,500	**Richmond West, FL** (cdp) Miami-Dade County	1,761
Maryland	1,096	San Diego County, CA	1,499	**Weston, FL** (city) Broward County	1,721
California	1,076	Nassau County, NY	1,474	**Tamarac, FL** (city) Broward County	1,644
Rhode Island	1,017	Rockland County, NY	1,408	**Oyster Bay, NY** (town) Nassau County	1,634
Connecticut	961	Orleans Parish, LA	1,385	**Royal Palm Beach, FL** (village) Palm Beach County	1,546
Virginia	955	Santa Clara County, CA	1,378	**Hempstead (town), NY** (town) Nassau County	1,511
Florida	940	Suffolk County, NY	1,377	**Doral, FL** (city) Miami-Dade County	1,508

Sorted by Percent in Ascending Order — U.S. = $920

State	Dollars	County	Dollars	Place	Dollars
West Virginia	387	Atlantic County, NJ	340	**Cutler Bay, FL** (town) Miami-Dade County	388
Kentucky	545	Forsyth County, NC	484	**Rochester, NY** (city) Monroe County	495
New Mexico	548	Bernalillo County, NM	496	**Albuquerque, NM** (city) Bernalillo County	496
Arkansas	581	Erie County, NY	529	**Louisville-Jefferson County, KY** (metropolitan govt) Jefferson County	533
Alabama	599	Jefferson County, KY	543	**West Little River, FL** (cdp) Miami-Dade County	649
Nebraska	604	Monroe County, NY	544	**University, FL** (cdp) Hillsborough County	668
Michigan	620	Kent County, MI	576	**Syracuse, NY** (city) Onondaga County	676
Oklahoma	630	Pima County, AZ	594	**Tampa, FL** (city) Hillsborough County	683
Tennessee	652	Ingham County, MI	595	**Phoenix, AZ** (city) Maricopa County	684
Utah	705	Hamilton County, OH	613	**Milwaukee, WI** (city) Milwaukee County	698

Note: (1) Ranking tables cover all states and counties, and places with an overall population of at least 125,000, OR an overall population of at least 25,000 where the Hispanic/Latino population is at least 20% of the overall population. In states where less than five places meet either of these criteria, we have included places with at least 10,000 total population with the highest percentage of Hispanic/Latino population. These places are identified with an asterisk (*); Please refer to the User's Guide for a full explanation of data.

Median Gross Rent

Dominican Republic

Top 10 States, Counties, and Places[1]

Sorted by Percent in Descending Order — U.S. = $944

State	Dollars	County	Dollars	Place	Dollars
Maryland	1,273	Burlington County, NJ	1,583	**Weston, FL** (city) Broward County	1,693
District of Columbia	1,261	Suffolk County, NY	1,350	**Doral, FL** (city) Miami-Dade County	1,607
California	1,176	Rockland County, NY	1,348	**Homestead, FL** (city) Miami-Dade County	1,598
Nevada	1,159	Los Angeles County, CA	1,324	**Buenaventura Lakes, FL** (cdp) Osceola County	1,478
New Jersey	1,070	Montgomery County, MD	1,319	**Islip, NY** (town) Suffolk County	1,454
Florida	1,018	Prince George's County, MD	1,274	**Miramar, FL** (city) Broward County	1,419
Connecticut	988	Bergen County, NJ	1,267	**Stamford, CT** (city/town) Fairfield County	1,407
Alaska	967	Richmond County, NY	1,265	**Huntington, NY** (town) Suffolk County	1,392
Virginia	962	Norfolk County, MA	1,262	**Los Angeles, CA** (city) Los Angeles County	1,383
Missouri	954	Somerset County, NJ	1,245	**Kearny, NJ** (town) Hudson County	1,349

Sorted by Percent in Ascending Order — U.S. = $944

State	Dollars	County	Dollars	Place	Dollars
Indiana	591	York County, PA	492	**Chelsea, MA** (city) Suffolk County	210
Michigan	618	Tarrant County, TX	590	**Englewood, NJ** (city) Bergen County	343
Wisconsin	680	Suffolk County, MA	597	**Valley Stream, NY** (village) Nassau County	380
Alabama	695	Kent County, MI	614	**Bethlehem, PA** (city) Northampton County	389
Tennessee	726	Volusia County, FL	653	**Elmont, NY** (cdp) Nassau County	448
Minnesota	737	Northampton County, PA	659	**York, PA** (city) York County	494
Utah	759	Berks County, PA	692	**West Little River, FL** (cdp) Miami-Dade County	544
Arizona	764	Cuyahoga County, OH	697	**Boston, MA** (city) Suffolk County	594
Texas	764	Harris County, TX	711	**Grand Rapids, MI** (city) Kent County	636
Ohio	773	Luzerne County, PA	724	**Tampa, FL** (city) Hillsborough County	640

Note: (1) Ranking tables cover all states and counties, and places with an overall population of at least 125,000, OR an overall population of at least 25,000 where the Hispanic/Latino population is at least 20% of the overall population. In states where less than five places meet either of these criteria, we have included places with at least 10,000 total population with the highest percentage of Hispanic/Latino population. These places are identified with an asterisk (*); Please refer to the User's Guide for a full explanation of data.

Median Gross Rent

Mexican

Top 10 States, Counties, and Places[1]

Sorted by Percent in Descending Order — U.S. = $842

State	Dollars	County	Dollars	Place	Dollars
Hawaii	1,509	Honolulu County, HI	1,676	**Eastvale, CA** (cdp) Riverside County	2,000+
New Jersey	1,209	Suffolk County, NY	1,657	**Schofield Barracks*, HI** (cdp) Honolulu County	2,000+
New York	1,194	Hunterdon County, NJ	1,607	**Weston, FL** (city) Broward County	1,844
District of Columbia	1,175	Ocean County, NJ	1,570	**Wheaton, MD** (cdp) Montgomery County	1,800
Maryland	1,164	Pierce County, WI	1,560	**Chino Hills, CA** (city) San Bernardino County	1,797
Massachusetts	1,139	Madison County, ID	1,542	**Diamond Bar, CA** (city) Los Angeles County	1,699
Connecticut	1,121	Anne Arundel County, MD	1,519	**Irvine, CA** (city) Orange County	1,670
California	1,021	Huron County, MI	1,517	**Islip, NY** (town) Suffolk County	1,670
Alaska	993	Nassau County, NY	1,476	**Dale City, VA** (cdp) Prince William County	1,661
Virginia	972	Fairfax County, VA	1,443	**Moorpark, CA** (city) Ventura County	1,657

Sorted by Percent in Ascending Order — U.S. = $842

State	Dollars	County	Dollars	Place	Dollars
North Dakota	526	Edgefield County, SC	200	**Willmar*, MN** (city) Kandiyohi County	458
Arkansas	587	Haskell County, TX	226	**Evanston*, WY** (city) Uinta County	481
South Dakota	593	Marquette County, WI	235	**San Luis, AZ** (city) Yuma County	488
Kentucky	595	Concho County, TX	239	**Fargo*, ND** (city) Cass County	498
Oklahoma	604	Plymouth County, IA	248	**San Juan, TX** (city) Hidalgo County	499
Alabama	622	Guadalupe County, NM	274	**Alamogordo, NM** (city) Otero County	508
Iowa	622	Osage County, OK	278	**Eagle Pass, TX** (city) Maverick County	511
New Mexico	625	Jackson County, FL	286	**Altus*, OK** (city) Jackson County	517
Idaho	630	Howard County, AR	289	**Del Rio, TX** (city) Val Verde County	526
West Virginia	633	Lewis and Clark County, MT	289	**Weslaco, TX** (city) Hidalgo County	526

Note: (1) Ranking tables cover all states and counties, and places with an overall population of at least 125,000, OR an overall population of at least 25,000 where the Hispanic/Latino population is at least 20% of the overall population. In states where less than five places meet either of these criteria, we have included places with at least 10,000 total population with the highest percentage of Hispanic/Latino population. These places are identified with an asterisk (*); Please refer to the User's Guide for a full explanation of data.

Median Gross Rent

Puerto Rican

Top 10 States, Counties, and Places[1]

Sorted by Percent in Descending Order — U.S. = $864

State	Dollars	County	Dollars	Place	Dollars
District of Columbia	1,442	Marin County, CA	1,704	**Doral, FL** (city) Miami-Dade County	1,822
Hawaii	1,231	Charles County, MD	1,661	**Murrieta, CA** (city) Riverside County	1,792
Maryland	1,176	Hoke County, NC	1,636	**Waianae*, HI** (cdp) Honolulu County	1,779
California	1,151	Anne Arundel County, MD	1,604	**Fontana, CA** (city) San Bernardino County	1,722
Alaska	1,150	Ventura County, CA	1,571	**Makakilo*, HI** (cdp) Honolulu County	1,639
Virginia	1,063	Pinal County, AZ	1,512	**Weston, FL** (city) Broward County	1,625
Nevada	1,034	Orange County, CA	1,479	**Huntington, NY** (town) Suffolk County	1,574
New Hampshire	995	Frederick County, MD	1,456	**Temecula, CA** (city) Riverside County	1,571
New Jersey	983	San Mateo County, CA	1,443	**Babylon, NY** (town) Suffolk County	1,566
Florida	973	Fairfax County, VA	1,434	**Huntington Beach, CA** (city) Orange County	1,541

Sorted by Percent in Ascending Order — U.S. = $864

State	Dollars	County	Dollars	Place	Dollars
South Dakota	501	Madera County, CA	293	**Huntsville, AL** (city) Madison County	460
Montana	513	Schuylkill County, PA	321	**West Little River, FL** (cdp) Miami-Dade County	476
North Dakota	579	Salem County, NJ	362	**Fort Wayne, IN** (city) Allen County	486
Arkansas	617	Wayne County, NC	382	**Lorain, OH** (city) Lorain County	532
Iowa	634	Schoharie County, NY	396	**Akron, OH** (city) Summit County	543
Kansas	637	Putnam County, FL	457	**Wichita, KS** (city) Sedgwick County	555
Alabama	642	Ashtabula County, OH	468	**Oklahoma City, OK** (city) Oklahoma County	565
Ohio	649	Trumbull County, OH	477	**Kansas City, MO** (city) Jackson County	572
Oklahoma	650	Elkhart County, IN	483	**Manhattan, NY** (borough) New York County	579
Idaho	670	Rensselaer County, NY	484	**Lebanon, PA** (city) Lebanon County	580

Note: (1) Ranking tables cover all states and counties, and places with an overall population of at least 125,000, OR an overall population of at least 25,000 where the Hispanic/Latino population is at least 20% of the overall population. In states where less than five places meet either of these criteria, we have included places with at least 10,000 total population with the highest percentage of Hispanic/Latino population. These places are identified with an asterisk (*); Please refer to the User's Guide for a full explanation of data.

Median Gross Rent

South American

Top 10 States, Counties, and Places[1]

Sorted by Percent in Descending Order — U.S. = $1,101

State	Dollars	County	Dollars	Place	Dollars
Hawaii	1,424	Loudoun County, VA	1,722	**Oceanside, CA** (city) San Diego County	2,000+
Virginia	1,400	Ventura County, CA	1,630	**Sterling, VA** (cdp) Loudoun County	2,000+
District of Columbia	1,306	Solano County, CA	1,596	**Thousand Oaks, CA** (city) Ventura County	2,000+
Maryland	1,261	Santa Clara County, CA	1,586	**Elmont, NY** (cdp) Nassau County	1,929
Maine	1,258	Anne Arundel County, MD	1,582	**Chino Hills, CA** (city) San Bernardino County	1,910
California	1,223	Hunterdon County, NJ	1,579	**Irvine, CA** (city) Orange County	1,766
New York	1,170	Honolulu County, HI	1,576	**Tustin, CA** (city) Orange County	1,750
Massachusetts	1,159	Clark County, WA	1,575	**Huntington Beach, CA** (city) Orange County	1,711
Connecticut	1,136	Prince William County, VA	1,563	**Santa Clarita, CA** (city) Los Angeles County	1,696
Florida	1,128	Orange County, CA	1,519	**Cooper City, FL** (city) Broward County	1,694

Sorted by Percent in Ascending Order — U.S. = $1,101

State	Dollars	County	Dollars	Place	Dollars
North Dakota	470	Weber County, UT	283	**Springfield, MA** (city) Hampden County	238
Arkansas	569	Hamilton County, TN	610	**Killeen, TX** (city) Bell County	539
Iowa	635	Champaign County, IL	622	**Cleveland, OH** (city) Cuyahoga County	641
Nebraska	642	Spartanburg County, SC	639	**East Hartford, CT** (cdp/town) Hartford County	665
Oklahoma	670	Cleveland County, OK	647	**Oklahoma City, OK** (city) Oklahoma County	672
Kentucky	674	Cameron County, TX	658	**Columbus, OH** (city) Franklin County	694
West Virginia	685	Sedgwick County, KS	665	**Pittsburgh, PA** (city) Allegheny County	701
New Mexico	703	Montgomery County, OH	666	**Salt Lake City, UT** (city) Salt Lake County	716
Ohio	707	Cache County, UT	669	**Denver, CO** (city) Denver County	717
Idaho	711	Oklahoma County, OK	671	**West Valley City, UT** (city) Salt Lake County	723

Note: (1) Ranking tables cover all states and counties, and places with an overall population of at least 125,000, OR an overall population of at least 25,000 where the Hispanic/Latino population is at least 20% of the overall population. In states where less than five places meet either of these criteria, we have included places with at least 10,000 total population with the highest percentage of Hispanic/Latino population. These places are identified with an asterisk (*); Please refer to the User's Guide for a full explanation of data.

Median Gross Rent

South American: Argentinean

Top 10 States, Counties, and Places[1]

Sorted by Percent in Descending Order — U.S. = $1,118

State	Dollars	County	Dollars	Place	Dollars
Washington	1,517	San Francisco County, CA	1,947	**Doral, FL** (city) Miami-Dade County	2,000+
District of Columbia	1,480	Contra Costa County, CA	1,836	**San Jose, CA** (city) Santa Clara County	2,000+
Virginia	1,387	Montgomery County, MD	1,827	**San Francisco, CA** (city) San Francisco County	1,947
Massachusetts	1,377	Middlesex County, MA	1,788	**Manhattan, NY** (borough) New York County	1,631
California	1,306	New York County, NY	1,631	**San Diego, CA** (city) San Diego County	1,611
New York	1,243	Travis County, TX	1,581	**Aventura, FL** (city) Miami-Dade County	1,305
Maryland	1,221	Orange County, CA	1,543	**Chicago, IL** (city) Cook County	1,261
New Jersey	1,219	Nassau County, NY	1,525	**New York, NY** (city)	1,245
Connecticut	1,180	Union County, NJ	1,512	**Queens, NY** (borough) Queens County	1,223
Florida	1,091	Fairfield County, CT	1,435	**Los Angeles, CA** (city) Los Angeles County	1,197

Sorted by Percent in Ascending Order — U.S. = $1,118

State	Dollars	County	Dollars	Place	Dollars
Louisiana	716	Utah County, UT	671	**Bronx, NY** (borough) Bronx County	829
Tennessee	719	Oakland County, MI	697	**Houston, TX** (city) Harris County	848
Pennsylvania	744	Tarrant County, TX	748	**Pembroke Pines, FL** (city) Broward County	961
Wisconsin	776	Bexar County, TX	784	**Hollywood, FL** (city) Broward County	970
Oregon	782	Montgomery County, TX	790	**Miami, FL** (city) Miami-Dade County	1,067
Michigan	803	Dallas County, TX	822	**Miami Beach, FL** (city) Miami-Dade County	1,076
Ohio	806	Bronx County, NY	829	**Hialeah, FL** (city) Miami-Dade County	1,082
Utah	813	Maricopa County, AZ	837	**Brooklyn, NY** (borough) Kings County	1,129
Arizona	828	Harris County, TX	879	**Coral Springs, FL** (city) Broward County	1,192
Missouri	835	Salt Lake County, UT	907	**Los Angeles, CA** (city) Los Angeles County	1,197

RANKINGS & COMPARISONS

Note: (1) Ranking tables cover all states and counties, and places with an overall population of at least 125,000, OR an overall population of at least 25,000 where the Hispanic/Latino population is at least 20% of the overall population. In states where less than five places meet either of these criteria, we have included places with at least 10,000 total population with the highest percentage of Hispanic/Latino population. These places are identified with an asterisk (*); Please refer to the User's Guide for a full explanation of data.

Median Gross Rent

South American: Bolivian

Top 10 States, Counties, and Places[1]

Sorted by Percent in Descending Order — U.S. = $1,240

State	Dollars	County	Dollars	Place	Dollars
Virginia	1,496	Loudoun County, VA	1,887	**Dale City, VA** (cdp) Prince William County	2,000+
New York	1,365	Orange County, CA	1,766	**Annandale, VA** (cdp) Fairfax County	1,644
California	1,310	San Diego County, CA	1,646	**Springfield, VA** (cdp) Fairfax County	1,625
New Jersey	1,234	Fairfax County, VA	1,567	**Arlington, VA** (cdp) Arlington County	1,385
Maryland	1,204	Santa Clara County, CA	1,548	**New York, NY** (city)	1,278
Florida	1,099	Arlington County, VA	1,385	**Queens, NY** (borough) Queens County	1,221
Massachusetts	996	Miami-Dade County, FL	1,280	**West Falls Church, VA** (cdp) Fairfax County	1,107
Rhode Island	930	Montgomery County, MD	1,228	**Los Angeles, CA** (city) Los Angeles County	1,063
Illinois	821	Queens County, NY	1,221	**Providence, RI** (city) Providence County	697
Texas	796	Palm Beach County, FL	1,167		

Sorted by Percent in Ascending Order — U.S. = $1,240

State	Dollars	County	Dollars	Place	Dollars
North Carolina	685	Cook County, IL	634	**Providence, RI** (city) Providence County	697
Pennsylvania	780	Prince George's County, MD	888	**Los Angeles, CA** (city) Los Angeles County	1,063
Texas	796	Providence County, RI	930	**West Falls Church, VA** (cdp) Fairfax County	1,107
Illinois	821	Harris County, TX	933	**Queens, NY** (borough) Queens County	1,221
Rhode Island	930	Los Angeles County, CA	1,117	**New York, NY** (city)	1,278
Massachusetts	996	Broward County, FL	1,147	**Arlington, VA** (cdp) Arlington County	1,385
Florida	1,099	Palm Beach County, FL	1,167	**Springfield, VA** (cdp) Fairfax County	1,625
Maryland	1,204	Queens County, NY	1,221	**Annandale, VA** (cdp) Fairfax County	1,644
New Jersey	1,234	Montgomery County, MD	1,228	**Dale City, VA** (cdp) Prince William County	2,000+
California	1,310	Miami-Dade County, FL	1,280		

Note: (1) Ranking tables cover all states and counties, and places with an overall population of at least 125,000, OR an overall population of at least 25,000 where the Hispanic/Latino population is at least 20% of the overall population. In states where less than five places meet either of these criteria, we have included places with at least 10,000 total population with the highest percentage of Hispanic/Latino population. These places are identified with an asterisk (*); Please refer to the User's Guide for a full explanation of data.

Median Gross Rent

South American: Chilean

Top 10 States, Counties, and Places[1]

Sorted by Percent in Descending Order — U.S. = $1,120

State	Dollars	County	Dollars	Place	Dollars
Maryland	1,579	Montgomery County, MD	1,916	**Kendall, FL** (cdp) Miami-Dade County	1,357
Massachusetts	1,482	Middlesex County, MA	1,756	**Brooklyn, NY** (borough) Kings County	1,315
Virginia	1,405	Orange County, CA	1,647	**Los Angeles, CA** (city) Los Angeles County	1,256
California	1,241	Santa Clara County, CA	1,491	**Hempstead (town), NY** (town) Nassau County	1,225
New York	1,167	Alameda County, CA	1,484	**New York, NY** (city)	1,183
New Jersey	1,161	Riverside County, CA	1,457	**Queens, NY** (borough) Queens County	1,180
Florida	1,144	San Mateo County, CA	1,426	**Manhattan, NY** (borough) New York County	1,140
Washington	1,121	San Diego County, CA	1,370	**Miami, FL** (city) Miami-Dade County	908
Colorado	1,096	Fairfax County, VA	1,364	**Chicago, IL** (city) Cook County	796
Georgia	1,095	Nassau County, NY	1,318		

Sorted by Percent in Ascending Order — U.S. = $1,120

State	Dollars	County	Dollars	Place	Dollars
Tennessee	292	Utah County, UT	707	**Chicago, IL** (city) Cook County	796
Minnesota	544	Salt Lake County, UT	845	**Miami, FL** (city) Miami-Dade County	908
Michigan	651	Harris County, TX	873	**Manhattan, NY** (borough) New York County	1,140
Wisconsin	668	Hudson County, NJ	988	**Queens, NY** (borough) Queens County	1,180
Ohio	714	Clark County, NV	1,031	**New York, NY** (city)	1,183
Utah	760	San Bernardino County, CA	1,081	**Hempstead (town), NY** (town) Nassau County	1,225
Pennsylvania	762	Cook County, IL	1,083	**Los Angeles, CA** (city) Los Angeles County	1,256
Missouri	813	New York County, NY	1,140	**Brooklyn, NY** (borough) Kings County	1,315
Texas	866	Maricopa County, AZ	1,146	**Kendall, FL** (cdp) Miami-Dade County	1,357
Illinois	917	Queens County, NY	1,180		

RANKINGS & COMPARISONS

Note: (1) Ranking tables cover all states and counties, and places with an overall population of at least 125,000, OR an overall population of at least 25,000 where the Hispanic/Latino population is at least 20% of the overall population. In states where less than five places meet either of these criteria, we have included places with at least 10,000 total population with the highest percentage of Hispanic/Latino population. These places are identified with an asterisk (*); Please refer to the User's Guide for a full explanation of data.

Median Gross Rent

South American: Colombian

Top 10 States, Counties, and Places[1]

Sorted by Percent in Descending Order — U.S. = $1,092

State	Dollars	County	Dollars	Place	Dollars
District of Columbia	1,430	Prince William County, VA	1,883	**Elmont, NY** (cdp) Nassau County	2,000+
Virginia	1,310	Suffolk County, NY	1,589	**Homestead, FL** (city) Miami-Dade County	1,663
Maryland	1,273	Orange County, CA	1,507	**Islip, NY** (town) Suffolk County	1,636
Alaska	1,259	Santa Clara County, CA	1,483	**Huntington, NY** (town) Suffolk County	1,628
California	1,232	Fairfax County, VA	1,477	**Stamford, CT** (city/town) Fairfield County	1,554
Massachusetts	1,210	Will County, IL	1,450	**Weston, FL** (city) Broward County	1,550
New York	1,163	Arlington County, VA	1,411	**Doral, FL** (city) Miami-Dade County	1,531
Florida	1,144	Nassau County, NY	1,411	**North Hempstead, NY** (town) Nassau County	1,508
Oregon	1,125	Prince George's County, MD	1,403	**Aventura, FL** (city) Miami-Dade County	1,486
New Jersey	1,115	Somerset County, NJ	1,370	**Miramar, FL** (city) Broward County	1,477

Sorted by Percent in Ascending Order — U.S. = $1,092

State	Dollars	County	Dollars	Place	Dollars
Arkansas	491	Pasco County, FL	463	**Brandon, FL** (cdp) Hillsborough County	647
Michigan	641	Milwaukee County, WI	556	**Central Falls*, RI** (city) Providence County	734
Nebraska	643	Franklin County, OH	567	**Fort Worth, TX** (city) Tarrant County	734
Oklahoma	664	Luzerne County, PA	672	**Dallas, TX** (city) Dallas County	740
Kentucky	667	Hall County, GA	691	**Phoenix, AZ** (city) Maricopa County	743
Ohio	734	Cuyahoga County, OH	716	**Pawtucket*, RI** (city) Providence County	789
Alabama	746	Greenville County, SC	719	**Egypt Lake-Leto, FL** (cdp) Hillsborough County	791
Delaware	748	Hampden County, MA	725	**Carrollwood, FL** (cdp) Hillsborough County	793
Wisconsin	751	Lake County, FL	743	**Indianapolis, IN** (city) Marion County	793
Indiana	752	Saint Louis County, MO	745	**North Miami Beach, FL** (city) Miami-Dade County	804

Note: (1) Ranking tables cover all states and counties, and places with an overall population of at least 125,000, OR an overall population of at least 25,000 where the Hispanic/Latino population is at least 20% of the overall population. In states where less than five places meet either of these criteria, we have included places with at least 10,000 total population with the highest percentage of Hispanic/Latino population. These places are identified with an asterisk (*); Please refer to the User's Guide for a full explanation of data.

Median Gross Rent

South American: Ecuadorian

Top 10 States, Counties, and Places[1]

Sorted by Percent in Descending Order — U.S. = $1,102

State	Dollars	County	Dollars	Place	Dollars
South Carolina	1,303	Santa Clara County, CA	1,821	**White Plains, NY** (city) Westchester County	1,609
Connecticut	1,218	Fairfax County, VA	1,674	**North Hempstead, NY** (town) Nassau County	1,551
Virginia	1,169	Ocean County, NJ	1,648	**Brookhaven, NY** (town) Suffolk County	1,532
New York	1,156	Morris County, NJ	1,463	**Norwalk, CT** (city/town) Fairfield County	1,435
California	1,154	Nassau County, NY	1,452	**Danbury, CT** (city/town) Fairfield County	1,400
New Jersey	1,127	Somerset County, NJ	1,423	**Sunrise, FL** (city) Broward County	1,399
Arizona	1,098	Suffolk County, NY	1,404	**Doral, FL** (city) Miami-Dade County	1,395
Nevada	1,088	Montgomery County, MD	1,403	**Hempstead (town), NY** (town) Nassau County	1,382
Florida	1,075	Orange County, CA	1,392	**Ossining, NY** (town) Westchester County	1,338
Kansas	1,025	Orange County, NY	1,329	**Ossining, NY** (village) Westchester County	1,338

Sorted by Percent in Ascending Order — U.S. = $1,102

State	Dollars	County	Dollars	Place	Dollars
Oklahoma	580	Dallas County, TX	695	**Charlotte, NC** (city) Mecklenburg County	739
Indiana	598	Providence County, RI	715	**Houston, TX** (city) Harris County	744
Ohio	657	Mecklenburg County, NC	742	**Hollywood, FL** (city) Broward County	773
Louisiana	659	Berks County, PA	767	**Minneapolis, MN** (city) Hennepin County	836
Wisconsin	690	Harris County, TX	789	**Central Islip, NY** (cdp) Suffolk County	853
Rhode Island	715	Osceola County, FL	796	**Manhattan, NY** (borough) New York County	859
North Carolina	755	Utah County, UT	846	**Allentown, PA** (city) Lehigh County	865
Colorado	780	Hennepin County, MN	852	**Miami, FL** (city) Miami-Dade County	886
Texas	818	New York County, NY	859	**Clifton, NJ** (city) Passaic County	931
Missouri	821	Lehigh County, PA	865	**Philadelphia, PA** (city) Philadelphia County	944

RANKINGS & COMPARISONS

Note: (1) Ranking tables cover all states and counties, and places with an overall population of at least 125,000, OR an overall population of at least 25,000 where the Hispanic/Latino population is at least 20% of the overall population. In states where less than five places meet either of these criteria, we have included places with at least 10,000 total population with the highest percentage of Hispanic/Latino population. These places are identified with an asterisk (*); Please refer to the User's Guide for a full explanation of data.

Median Gross Rent

South American: Paraguayan

Top 10 States, Counties, and Places[1]

Sorted by Percent in Descending Order — U.S. = $1,169

State	Dollars	County	Dollars	Place	Dollars
Maryland	1,461	Westchester County, NY	1,460	**Queens, NY** (borough) Queens County	1,148
New Jersey	1,361	Queens County, NY	1,148	**New York, NY** (city)	1,129
New York	1,287				
California	1,222				
Florida	986				
Texas	543				

Sorted by Percent in Ascending Order — U.S. = $1,169

State	Dollars	County	Dollars	Place	Dollars
Texas	543	Queens County, NY	1,148	**New York, NY** (city)	1,129
Florida	986	Westchester County, NY	1,460	**Queens, NY** (borough) Queens County	1,148
California	1,222				
New York	1,287				
New Jersey	1,361				
Maryland	1,461				

Note: (1) Ranking tables cover all states and counties, and places with an overall population of at least 125,000, OR an overall population of at least 25,000 where the Hispanic/Latino population is at least 20% of the overall population. In states where less than five places meet either of these criteria, we have included places with at least 10,000 total population with the highest percentage of Hispanic/Latino population. These places are identified with an asterisk (*); Please refer to the User's Guide for a full explanation of data.

Median Gross Rent

South American: Peruvian

Top 10 States, Counties, and Places[1]

Sorted by Percent in Descending Order — U.S. = $1,081

State	Dollars	County	Dollars	Place	Dollars
Virginia	1,434	Loudoun County, VA	1,696	**Doral, FL** (city) Miami-Dade County	1,814
Hawaii	1,325	Nassau County, NY	1,581	**Oyster Bay, NY** (town) Nassau County	1,762
Maryland	1,281	Fairfax County, VA	1,512	**Hempstead (town), NY** (town) Nassau County	1,750
New York	1,175	Prince William County, VA	1,442	**Santa Clarita, CA** (city) Los Angeles County	1,530
California	1,173	Middlesex County, MA	1,393	**Port Chester, NY** (village) Westchester County	1,426
District of Columbia	1,147	Orange County, CA	1,385	**Miramar, FL** (city) Broward County	1,421
Massachusetts	1,125	Santa Clara County, CA	1,366	**San Mateo, CA** (city) San Mateo County	1,409
Connecticut	1,098	Morris County, NJ	1,356	**Rye, NY** (town) Westchester County	1,399
Florida	1,092	Contra Costa County, CA	1,354	**Concord, CA** (city) Contra Costa County	1,397
New Jersey	1,092	Montgomery County, MD	1,350	**Santa Ana, CA** (city) Orange County	1,363

Sorted by Percent in Ascending Order — U.S. = $1,081

State	Dollars	County	Dollars	Place	Dollars
Missouri	625	San Joaquin County, CA	499	**Salt Lake City, UT** (city) Salt Lake County	533
South Carolina	629	Denver County, CO	578	**West Valley City, UT** (city) Salt Lake County	535
Oklahoma	636	Arapahoe County, CO	660	**Denver, CO** (city) Denver County	578
Kentucky	666	Lehigh County, PA	693	**Aurora, CO** (city) Arapahoe County	681
New Mexico	667	Salt Lake County, UT	756	**Islip, NY** (town) Suffolk County	734
Minnesota	685	Duval County, FL	766	**West New York, NJ** (town) Hudson County	740
Ohio	692	Philadelphia County, PA	769	**Jacksonville, FL** (city) Duval County	766
Indiana	693	Pinellas County, FL	830	**Philadelphia, PA** (city) Philadelphia County	769
Wisconsin	706	Dallas County, TX	838	**Dallas, TX** (city) Dallas County	804
Pennsylvania	730	Denton County, TX	854	**Tampa, FL** (city) Hillsborough County	813

RANKINGS & COMPARISONS

Note: (1) Ranking tables cover all states and counties, and places with an overall population of at least 125,000, OR an overall population of at least 25,000 where the Hispanic/Latino population is at least 20% of the overall population. In states where less than five places meet either of these criteria, we have included places with at least 10,000 total population with the highest percentage of Hispanic/Latino population. These places are identified with an asterisk (*); Please refer to the User's Guide for a full explanation of data.

Median Gross Rent

South American: Uruguayan

Top 10 States, Counties, and Places[1]

Sorted by Percent in Descending Order — U.S. = $1,033

State	Dollars	County	Dollars	Place	Dollars
Maryland	1,314	Westchester County, NY	1,314	**New York, NY** (city)	1,336
New York	1,291	Queens County, NY	1,205	**Queens, NY** (borough) Queens County	1,205
New Jersey	1,095	Morris County, NJ	1,193	**Elizabeth, NJ** (city) Union County	1,084
California	1,085	Broward County, FL	1,171		
Florida	1,044	Union County, NJ	1,128		
Virginia	1,008	Essex County, NJ	1,108		
Georgia	930	Los Angeles County, CA	1,108		
Pennsylvania	929	Hudson County, NJ	1,090		
Massachusetts	852	Palm Beach County, FL	1,085		
Texas	745	Miami-Dade County, FL	977		

Sorted by Percent in Ascending Order — U.S. = $1,033

State	Dollars	County	Dollars	Place	Dollars
Texas	745	Harris County, TX	747	**Elizabeth, NJ** (city) Union County	1,084
Massachusetts	852	Worcester County, MA	838	**Queens, NY** (borough) Queens County	1,205
Pennsylvania	929	Gwinnett County, GA	886	**New York, NY** (city)	1,336
Georgia	930	Middlesex County, NJ	902		
Virginia	1,008	Miami-Dade County, FL	977		
Florida	1,044	Palm Beach County, FL	1,085		
California	1,085	Hudson County, NJ	1,090		
New Jersey	1,095	Essex County, NJ	1,108		
New York	1,291	Los Angeles County, CA	1,108		
Maryland	1,314	Union County, NJ	1,128		

Note: (1) Ranking tables cover all states and counties, and places with an overall population of at least 125,000, OR an overall population of at least 25,000 where the Hispanic/Latino population is at least 20% of the overall population. In states where less than five places meet either of these criteria, we have included places with at least 10,000 total population with the highest percentage of Hispanic/Latino population. These places are identified with an asterisk (*); Please refer to the User's Guide for a full explanation of data.

Median Gross Rent

South American: Venezuelan

Top 10 States, Counties, and Places[1]

Sorted by Percent in Descending Order — U.S. = $1,132

State	Dollars	County	Dollars	Place	Dollars
California	1,407	Fairfax County, VA	1,786	**The Hammocks, FL** (cdp) Miami-Dade County	2,000+
Maryland	1,398	Montgomery County, MD	1,639	**Aventura, FL** (city) Miami-Dade County	1,774
Connecticut	1,301	Fort Bend County, TX	1,576	**Weston, FL** (city) Broward County	1,733
New York	1,216	Hudson County, NJ	1,403	**Doral, FL** (city) Miami-Dade County	1,707
Florida	1,212	Fairfield County, CT	1,397	**Miramar, FL** (city) Broward County	1,635
Washington	1,210	Broward County, FL	1,358	**Coral Springs, FL** (city) Broward County	1,434
New Jersey	1,204	Suffolk County, MA	1,358	**Pembroke Pines, FL** (city) Broward County	1,359
Virginia	1,190	Queens County, NY	1,309	**Los Angeles, CA** (city) Los Angeles County	1,341
Illinois	1,043	Miami-Dade County, FL	1,272	**Sunrise, FL** (city) Broward County	1,331
Texas	988	King County, WA	1,244	**Queens, NY** (borough) Queens County	1,309

Sorted by Percent in Ascending Order — U.S. = $1,132

State	Dollars	County	Dollars	Place	Dollars
Indiana	610	Salt Lake County, UT	768	**Houston, TX** (city) Harris County	945
Missouri	646	Collin County, TX	795	**Country Club, FL** (cdp) Miami-Dade County	985
Pennsylvania	764	Cobb County, GA	825	**Miami Beach, FL** (city) Miami-Dade County	1,013
Tennessee	778	Lee County, FL	885	**Kendall West, FL** (cdp) Miami-Dade County	1,046
Oklahoma	779	Middlesex County, MA	887	**Orlando, FL** (city) Orange County	1,050
Utah	799	Gwinnett County, GA	920	**Brooklyn, NY** (borough) Kings County	1,109
Wisconsin	811	Hillsborough County, FL	944	**Bronx, NY** (borough) Bronx County	1,128
Michigan	825	Harris County, TX	984	**Hialeah, FL** (city) Miami-Dade County	1,154
Ohio	838	Tarrant County, TX	992	**Davie, FL** (town) Broward County	1,164
Minnesota	842	Montgomery County, TX	1,026	**Miami, FL** (city) Miami-Dade County	1,183

RANKINGS & COMPARISONS

Note: (1) Ranking tables cover all states and counties, and places with an overall population of at least 125,000, OR an overall population of at least 25,000 where the Hispanic/Latino population is at least 20% of the overall population. In states where less than five places meet either of these criteria, we have included places with at least 10,000 total population with the highest percentage of Hispanic/Latino population. These places are identified with an asterisk (*); Please refer to the User's Guide for a full explanation of data.

Median Gross Rent

Spaniard

Top 10 States, Counties, and Places[1]

Sorted by Percent in Descending Order — U.S. = $959

State	Dollars	County	Dollars	Place	Dollars
District of Columbia	1,399	Ocean County, NJ	1,840	**Henderson, NV** (city) Clark County	1,739
Maryland	1,386	Ventura County, CA	1,821	**San Jose, CA** (city) Santa Clara County	1,626
California	1,241	Fairfax County, VA	1,698	**Manhattan, NY** (borough) New York County	1,624
Virginia	1,219	Nassau County, NY	1,676	**Hempstead (town), NY** (town) Nassau County	1,622
New York	1,206	New York County, NY	1,624	**San Francisco, CA** (city) San Francisco County	1,492
New Hampshire	1,186	Santa Clara County, CA	1,581	**San Diego, CA** (city) San Diego County	1,461
Hawaii	1,156	Orange County, CA	1,574	**Bakersfield, CA** (city) Kern County	1,289
Connecticut	1,099	Morris County, NJ	1,559	**Los Angeles, CA** (city) Los Angeles County	1,287
Massachusetts	1,081	Utah County, UT	1,504	**Fort Collins, CO** (city) Larimer County	1,255
New Jersey	1,063	San Francisco County, CA	1,492	**New York, NY** (city)	1,221

Sorted by Percent in Ascending Order — U.S. = $959

State	Dollars	County	Dollars	Place	Dollars
Wyoming	436	Cibola County, NM	412	**Santa Fe, NM** (city) Santa Fe County	454
West Virginia	439	Colfax County, NM	428	**Las Cruces, NM** (city) Dona Ana County	489
Arkansas	544	Erie County, NY	455	**Oklahoma City, OK** (city) Oklahoma County	575
Oklahoma	627	Conejos County, CO	574	**Pueblo, CO** (city) Pueblo County	635
New Mexico	630	Weber County, UT	575	**Colorado Springs, CO** (city) El Paso County	687
Idaho	642	Oklahoma County, OK	577	**Tampa, FL** (city) Hillsborough County	699
Montana	643	Las Animas County, CO	580	**Albuquerque, NM** (city) Bernalillo County	713
Maine	644	San Miguel County, NM	598	**Tucson, AZ** (city) Pima County	730
Minnesota	677	Doña Ana County, NM	601	**Fort Worth, TX** (city) Tarrant County	746
Kansas	687	Taos County, NM	608	**Portland, OR** (city) Multnomah County	749

Note: (1) Ranking tables cover all states and counties, and places with an overall population of at least 125,000, OR an overall population of at least 25,000 where the Hispanic/Latino population is at least 20% of the overall population. In states where less than five places meet either of these criteria, we have included places with at least 10,000 total population with the highest percentage of Hispanic/Latino population. These places are identified with an asterisk (*); Please refer to the User's Guide for a full explanation of data.

Median Household Income

(2010 Inflation-Adjusted Dollars)

Total Population

Top 10 States, Counties, and Places[1]

Sorted by Percent in Descending Order — U.S. = $51,914

State	Dollars	County	Dollars	Place	Dollars
Maryland	70,647	Loudoun County, VA	115,574	**Eastvale, CA** (cdp) Riverside County	105,894
New Jersey	69,811	Fairfax County, VA	105,416	**Oyster Bay, NY** (town) Nassau County	104,453
Connecticut	67,740	Los Alamos County, NM	103,643	**Chino Hills, CA** (city) San Bernardino County	103,891
Alaska	66,521	Howard County, MD	103,273	**Huntington, NY** (town) Suffolk County	102,782
Hawaii	66,420	Hunterdon County, NJ	100,980	**Moorpark, CA** (city) Ventura County	101,962
Massachusetts	64,509	Douglas County, CO	99,198	**Naperville, IL** (city) DuPage County	101,911
New Hampshire	63,277	Somerset County, NJ	97,440	**North Hempstead, NY** (town) Nassau County	100,760
Virginia	61,406	Morris County, NJ	96,747	**Thousand Oaks, CA** (city) Ventura County	98,713
California	60,883	Arlington County, VA	94,880	**Fremont, CA** (city) Alameda County	96,287
District of Columbia	58,526	Nassau County, NY	93,613	**Arlington, VA** (cdp) Arlington County	94,880

Sorted by Percent in Ascending Order — U.S. = $51,914

State	Dollars	County	Dollars	Place	Dollars
Mississippi	37,881	Brooks County, TX	19,959	**Parker*, SC** (cdp) Greenville County	22,650
West Virginia	38,380	Allendale County, SC	20,081	**University, FL** (cdp) Hillsborough County	24,235
Arkansas	39,267	Clay County, KY	20,175	**Morgantown*, WV** (city) Monongalia County	25,495
Kentucky	41,576	Holmes County, MS	21,375	**San Luis, AZ** (city) Yuma County	25,622
Alabama	42,081	Knox County, KY	21,493	**Mayfield*, KY** (city) Graves County	25,833
Oklahoma	42,979	Chicot County, AR	21,676	**San Marcos, TX** (city) Hays County	26,734
Tennessee	43,314	Zavala County, TX	21,707	**Camden, NJ** (city) Camden County	27,027
Louisiana	43,445	Leflore County, MS	22,020	**Laurel*, MS** (city) Jones County	27,056
New Mexico	43,820	Hancock County, GA	22,283	**Cleveland, OH** (city) Cuyahoga County	27,349
Montana	43,872	McCreary County, KY	22,643	**Huntington*, WV** (city) Cabell County	27,858

RANKINGS & COMPARISONS

Note: (1) Ranking tables cover all states and counties, and places with an overall population of at least 125,000, OR an overall population of at least 25,000 where the Hispanic/Latino population is at least 20% of the overall population. In states where less than five places meet either of these criteria, we have included places with at least 10,000 total population with the highest percentage of Hispanic/Latino population. These places are identified with an asterisk (*); Please refer to the User's Guide for a full explanation of data.

Median Household Income

(2010 Inflation-Adjusted Dollars)

Hispanic or Latino (of any race)

Top 10 States, Counties, and Places[1]

Sorted by Percent in Descending Order — U.S. = $41,534

State	Dollars	County	Dollars	Place	Dollars
Maryland	61,818	Union County, FL	133,698	**Eastvale, CA** (cdp) Riverside County	99,893
Virginia	57,793	Calvert County, MD	120,227	**Oyster Bay, NY** (town) Nassau County	98,982
Alaska	57,006	Harris County, GA	108,235	**Chino Hills, CA** (city) San Bernardino County	91,556
Hawaii	54,050	Marlboro County, SC	100,417	**Diamond Bar, CA** (city) Los Angeles County	88,659
District of Columbia	51,569	Marion County, WV	100,149	**Springfield, VA** (cdp) Fairfax County	85,270
New Hampshire	51,336	Delaware County, OH	98,224	**Moorpark, CA** (city) Ventura County	83,854
Vermont	50,833	Putnam County, NY	88,636	**Elmont, NY** (cdp) Nassau County	82,827
New Jersey	48,578	Hunterdon County, NJ	88,370	**Pearland, TX** (city) Brazoria County	80,152
California	47,180	Douglas County, CO	88,067	**Cooper City, FL** (city) Broward County	79,444
Illinois	47,170	Warren County, OH	86,536	**Weston, FL** (city) Broward County	79,375

Sorted by Percent in Ascending Order — U.S. = $41,534

State	Dollars	County	Dollars	Place	Dollars
Montana	32,182	Logan County, KY	2	**Holyoke, MA** (city) Hampden County	15,531
Massachusetts	32,206	McDonough County, IL	3,727	**Buffalo, NY** (city) Erie County	15,899
Arkansas	32,712	West Carroll Parish, LA	4,458	**Syracuse, NY** (city) Onondaga County	20,526
Pennsylvania	32,876	Mahaska County, IA	7,500	**Springfield, MA** (city) Hampden County	21,364
Rhode Island	33,679	Clinton County, PA	9,306	**Asheboro, NC** (city) Randolph County	21,676
Oklahoma	34,193	Warren County, PA	9,773	**York, PA** (city) York County	21,803
North Carolina	34,523	Huntingdon County, PA	10,313	**University, FL** (cdp) Hillsborough County	21,836
Tennessee	34,606	Wyoming County, NY	11,328	**Mayfield*, KY** (city) Graves County	22,006
Kentucky	34,639	Benton County, MN	11,626	**Worcester, MA** (city) Worcester County	22,213
Idaho	35,141	Scioto County, OH	12,273	**Morgantown*, WV** (city) Monongalia County	22,344

Note: (1) Ranking tables cover all states and counties, and places with an overall population of at least 125,000, OR an overall population of at least 25,000 where the Hispanic/Latino population is at least 20% of the overall population. In states where less than five places meet either of these criteria, we have included places with at least 10,000 total population with the highest percentage of Hispanic/Latino population. These places are identified with an asterisk (*); Please refer to the User's Guide for a full explanation of data.

Median Household Income

(2010 Inflation-Adjusted Dollars)

Central American, excluding Mexican

Top 10 States, Counties, and Places[1]

Sorted by Percent in Descending Order — U.S. = $43,332

State	Dollars	County	Dollars	Place	Dollars
Hawaii	61,653	Macomb County, MI	96,528	**Eastvale, CA** (cdp) Riverside County	127,750
West Virginia	61,615	Douglas County, CO	89,912	**La Mirada, CA** (city) Los Angeles County	120,272
Maryland	57,874	Rockwall County, TX	84,400	**Weston, FL** (city) Broward County	114,107
Virginia	54,930	Chester County, PA	83,750	**Murrieta, CA** (city) Riverside County	93,074
Connecticut	50,771	El Dorado County, CA	79,500	**Montclair, CA** (city) San Bernardino County	90,417
Delaware	50,315	Orange County, NY	76,719	**Lake Forest, CA** (city) Orange County	88,669
Wyoming	49,676	Charles County, MD	76,136	**San Leandro, CA** (city) Alameda County	88,160
New Jersey	49,461	Napa County, CA	75,489	**Cranston*, RI** (city) Providence County	87,762
Illinois	48,314	Washington County, MD	73,750	**Annandale, VA** (cdp) Fairfax County	86,815
Massachusetts	48,278	New London County, CT	72,969	**Hacienda Heights, CA** (cdp) Los Angeles County	84,318

Sorted by Percent in Ascending Order — U.S. = $43,332

State	Dollars	County	Dollars	Place	Dollars
Vermont	15,114	Montgomery County, TN	11,250	**Clarksville, TN** (city) Montgomery County	9,750
Idaho	26,230	DeKalb County, AL	16,888	**Reading, PA** (city) Berks County	16,953
Kentucky	31,262	Murray County, GA	20,273	**Laredo, TX** (city) Webb County	21,271
Alabama	32,722	Clarke County, GA	20,561	**Springfield, MA** (city) Hampden County	21,639
Oklahoma	32,799	Webb County, TX	21,271	**Lexington-Fayette, KY** (consolidated govt) Fayette County	21,927
Arkansas	34,589	Hampden County, MA	21,361	**Danbury, CT** (city/town) Fairfield County	22,176
Indiana	34,911	Fayette County, KY	21,927	**University, FL** (cdp) Hillsborough County	23,750
North Carolina	35,965	Shasta County, CA	22,356	**Knoxville, TN** (city) Knox County	26,615
Michigan	36,308	Hendry County, FL	23,304	**Colorado Springs, CO** (city) El Paso County	26,664
Iowa	36,326	Sampson County, NC	24,018	**Maywood, CA** (city) Los Angeles County	27,346

RANKINGS & COMPARISONS

Note: (1) Ranking tables cover all states and counties, and places with an overall population of at least 125,000, OR an overall population of at least 25,000 where the Hispanic/Latino population is at least 20% of the overall population. In states where less than five places meet either of these criteria, we have included places with at least 10,000 total population with the highest percentage of Hispanic/Latino population. These places are identified with an asterisk (*); Please refer to the User's Guide for a full explanation of data.

Median Household Income

(2010 Inflation-Adjusted Dollars)

Central American: Costa Rican

Top 10 States, Counties, and Places[1]

Sorted by Percent in Descending Order — U.S. = $50,197

State	Dollars	County	Dollars	Place	Dollars
Virginia	75,563	Contra Costa County, CA	90,455	**Queens, NY** (borough) Queens County	73,534
Maryland	73,203	Nassau County, NY	82,000	**Los Angeles, CA** (city) Los Angeles County	48,734
Colorado	64,821	Somerset County, NJ	80,053	**New York, NY** (city)	48,487
Oregon	62,868	Orange County, CA	77,794	**Bronx, NY** (borough) Bronx County	42,891
Connecticut	62,500	Queens County, NY	73,534	**Brooklyn, NY** (borough) Kings County	39,063
Massachusetts	59,653	Morris County, NJ	63,636	**Philadelphia, PA** (city) Philadelphia County	33,750
California	58,989	Fairfield County, CT	63,333	**Miami, FL** (city) Miami-Dade County	24,375
Minnesota	57,125	Bergen County, NJ	61,656		
Louisiana	56,641	San Bernardino County, CA	60,926		
Wisconsin	52,778	Broward County, FL	59,167		

Sorted by Percent in Ascending Order — U.S. = $50,197

State	Dollars	County	Dollars	Place	Dollars
Pennsylvania	28,359	Orange County, FL	29,744	**Miami, FL** (city) Miami-Dade County	24,375
North Carolina	35,568	Essex County, NJ	31,250	**Philadelphia, PA** (city) Philadelphia County	33,750
Michigan	36,211	Mercer County, NJ	33,636	**Brooklyn, NY** (borough) Kings County	39,063
Arizona	38,008	Philadelphia County, PA	33,750	**Bronx, NY** (borough) Bronx County	42,891
Florida	43,967	Passaic County, NJ	35,943	**New York, NY** (city)	48,487
Georgia	44,440	Harris County, TX	36,750	**Los Angeles, CA** (city) Los Angeles County	48,734
Tennessee	46,250	Maricopa County, AZ	38,906	**Queens, NY** (borough) Queens County	73,534
New Jersey	47,178	Kings County, NY	39,063		
Texas	48,750	Miami-Dade County, FL	39,781		
Washington	49,028	Palm Beach County, FL	42,734		

Note: (1) Ranking tables cover all states and counties, and places with an overall population of at least 125,000, OR an overall population of at least 25,000 where the Hispanic/Latino population is at least 20% of the overall population. In states where less than five places meet either of these criteria, we have included places with at least 10,000 total population with the highest percentage of Hispanic/Latino population. These places are identified with an asterisk (*); Please refer to the User's Guide for a full explanation of data.

Median Household Income

(2010 Inflation-Adjusted Dollars)

Central American: Guatemalan

Top 10 States, Counties, and Places[1]

Sorted by Percent in Descending Order — U.S. = $41,272

State	Dollars	County	Dollars	Place	Dollars
Maryland	57,952	Will County, IL	84,457	**Cranston*, RI** (city) Providence County	88,314
Wisconsin	53,750	Anne Arundel County, MD	70,056	**Moreno Valley, CA** (city) Riverside County	85,927
Delaware	50,650	Fulton County, GA	66,250	**Alhambra, CA** (city) Los Angeles County	80,429
New Hampshire	49,630	Loudoun County, VA	66,061	**Brentwood, NY** (cdp) Suffolk County	76,555
New Jersey	49,361	Rutherford County, TN	64,519	**Islip, NY** (town) Suffolk County	75,213
Illinois	47,171	Montgomery County, MD	63,778	**Wheaton, MD** (cdp) Montgomery County	74,516
Connecticut	47,048	Rockland County, NY	62,747	**Central Islip, NY** (cdp) Suffolk County	73,309
Virginia	46,597	Middlesex County, MA	61,629	**Santa Clarita, CA** (city) Los Angeles County	71,410
Massachusetts	46,583	Stanislaus County, CA	61,548	**Union City, NJ** (city) Hudson County	68,929
New Mexico	46,132	Somerset County, NJ	61,410	**West Covina, CA** (city) Los Angeles County	68,707

Sorted by Percent in Ascending Order — U.S. = $41,272

State	Dollars	County	Dollars	Place	Dollars
Kentucky	27,149	DeKalb County, AL	16,505	**Westmont, CA** (cdp) Los Angeles County	23,611
Missouri	27,712	Cherokee County, GA	17,309	**Yonkers, NY** (city) Westchester County	26,442
Kansas	30,114	Murray County, GA	20,773	**Homestead, FL** (city) Miami-Dade County	26,842
Michigan	30,299	Norfolk County, MA	23,482	**Grand Rapids, MI** (city) Kent County	27,610
Alabama	30,711	Greenville County, SC	26,343	**Carthage*, MO** (city) Jasper County	27,807
South Carolina	30,862	Hamilton County, OH	26,369	**Houston, TX** (city) Harris County	28,099
Indiana	32,147	Cobb County, GA	26,616	**Durham, NC** (city) Durham County	29,096
Georgia	32,645	Utah County, UT	27,500	**Bell, CA** (city) Los Angeles County	29,583
Oklahoma	32,897	Jasper County, MO	28,160	**Lawrence, MA** (city) Essex County	29,816
North Carolina	32,931	Marshall County, AL	28,272	**San Bernardino, CA** (city) San Bernardino County	29,861

RANKINGS & COMPARISONS

Note: (1) Ranking tables cover all states and counties, and places with an overall population of at least 125,000, OR an overall population of at least 25,000 where the Hispanic/Latino population is at least 20% of the overall population. In states where less than five places meet either of these criteria, we have included places with at least 10,000 total population with the highest percentage of Hispanic/Latino population. These places are identified with an asterisk (*); Please refer to the User's Guide for a full explanation of data.

Median Household Income

(2010 Inflation-Adjusted Dollars)

Central American: Honduran

Top 10 States, Counties, and Places[1]

Sorted by Percent in Descending Order — U.S. = $37,901

State	Dollars	County	Dollars	Place	Dollars
Maryland	56,914	Essex County, NJ	80,600	**Islip, NY** (town) Suffolk County	80,882
Virginia	51,250	Loudoun County, VA	70,596	**Brentwood, NY** (cdp) Suffolk County	80,662
Pennsylvania	48,482	Orange County, NY	70,446	**San Jose, CA** (city) Santa Clara County	65,750
Illinois	46,833	Prince William County, VA	64,829	**Wheaton, MD** (cdp) Montgomery County	64,589
Massachusetts	46,225	San Francisco County, CA	64,330	**San Francisco, CA** (city) San Francisco County	64,330
New Jersey	46,205	Philadelphia County, PA	63,112	**Philadelphia, PA** (city) Philadelphia County	63,112
Iowa	45,833	Montgomery County, MD	62,834	**Las Vegas, NV** (city) Clark County	61,566
Nevada	45,023	Santa Clara County, CA	62,321	**Newburgh, NY** (city) Orange County	60,405
Nebraska	44,293	Prince George's County, MD	60,284	**Springfield, VA** (cdp) Fairfax County	59,400
Connecticut	44,222	Fairfax County, VA	59,730	**Elizabeth, NJ** (city) Union County	54,000

Sorted by Percent in Ascending Order — U.S. = $37,901

State	Dollars	County	Dollars	Place	Dollars
Indiana	27,852	Jackson County, MO	21,935	**Manhattan, NY** (borough) New York County	22,153
Minnesota	28,173	New York County, NY	22,153	**Indianapolis, IN** (city) Marion County	26,071
Oklahoma	28,446	Oklahoma County, OK	23,179	**Miami, FL** (city) Miami-Dade County	26,325
Oregon	28,581	Salt Lake County, UT	23,269	**Houston, TX** (city) Harris County	26,586
District of Columbia	28,707	Johnston County, NC	23,611	**Fort Worth, TX** (city) Tarrant County	26,633
Tennessee	30,467	Marion County, IN	24,349	**Dallas, TX** (city) Dallas County	27,518
Utah	30,985	King County, WA	25,913	**Oklahoma City, OK** (city) Oklahoma County	29,286
Texas	31,762	Elkhart County, IN	26,825	**San Antonio, TX** (city) Bexar County	29,861
North Carolina	32,298	Lee County, FL	27,031	**Aurora, CO** (city) Arapahoe County	29,868
South Carolina	32,731	Kern County, CA	27,375	**Nashville-Davidson, TN** (metropolitan govt) Davidson County	30,273

Note: (1) Ranking tables cover all states and counties, and places with an overall population of at least 125,000, OR an overall population of at least 25,000 where the Hispanic/Latino population is at least 20% of the overall population. In states where less than five places meet either of these criteria, we have included places with at least 10,000 total population with the highest percentage of Hispanic/Latino population. These places are identified with an asterisk (*); Please refer to the User's Guide for a full explanation of data.

Median Household Income

(2010 Inflation-Adjusted Dollars)

Central American: Nicaraguan

Top 10 States, Counties, and Places[1]

Sorted by Percent in Descending Order — U.S. = $49,335

State	Dollars	County	Dollars	Place	Dollars
Michigan	71,413	Contra Costa County, CA	81,592	**Antioch, CA** (city) Contra Costa County	105,313
Connecticut	70,000	Queens County, NY	77,042	**South San Francisco, CA** (city) San Mateo County	100,263
Minnesota	67,333	King County, WA	73,413	**Richmond, CA** (city) Contra Costa County	99,412
Maryland	66,300	Montgomery County, MD	73,100	**San Jose, CA** (city) Santa Clara County	77,971
Virginia	61,956	Fairfax County, VA	68,618	**Queens, NY** (borough) Queens County	77,042
New Jersey	59,940	Orange County, CA	68,438	**Hayward, CA** (city) Alameda County	75,326
California	59,588	San Mateo County, CA	67,384	**The Hammocks, FL** (cdp) Miami-Dade County	74,657
Wisconsin	53,145	Santa Clara County, CA	66,806	**Richmond West, FL** (cdp) Miami-Dade County	72,955
Louisiana	52,868	Riverside County, CA	66,761	**Daly City, CA** (city) San Mateo County	69,250
New York	52,500	Sonoma County, CA	65,500	**Pembroke Pines, FL** (city) Broward County	68,867

Sorted by Percent in Ascending Order — U.S. = $49,335

State	Dollars	County	Dollars	Place	Dollars
South Carolina	32,472	Duval County, FL	27,061	**San Diego, CA** (city) San Diego County	19,960
Ohio	36,635	Orange County, FL	29,967	**Jacksonville, FL** (city) Duval County	27,061
District of Columbia	37,713	New York County, NY	33,417	**Oakland, CA** (city) Alameda County	28,406
Massachusetts	41,545	Bronx County, NY	35,536	**Miami, FL** (city) Miami-Dade County	29,282
Colorado	41,705	Kings County, NY	39,688	**Metairie, LA** (cdp) Jefferson Parish	31,944
Tennessee	42,333	San Diego County, CA	41,422	**Austin, TX** (city) Travis County	32,344
Florida	43,103	Miami-Dade County, FL	42,994	**Hialeah, FL** (city) Miami-Dade County	32,620
Oregon	43,514	Gwinnett County, GA	43,289	**Manhattan, NY** (borough) New York County	33,417
Pennsylvania	44,268	Palm Beach County, FL	43,309	**University Park, FL** (cdp) Miami-Dade County	33,864
Indiana	45,120	Collier County, FL	43,571	**Bronx, NY** (borough) Bronx County	35,536

Note: (1) Ranking tables cover all states and counties, and places with an overall population of at least 125,000, OR an overall population of at least 25,000 where the Hispanic/Latino population is at least 20% of the overall population. In states where less than five places meet either of these criteria, we have included places with at least 10,000 total population with the highest percentage of Hispanic/Latino population. These places are identified with an asterisk (*); Please refer to the User's Guide for a full explanation of data.

Median Household Income

(2010 Inflation-Adjusted Dollars)

Central American: Panamanian

Top 10 States, Counties, and Places[1]

Sorted by Percent in Descending Order — U.S. = $49,834

State	Dollars	County	Dollars	Place	Dollars
Minnesota	126,250	Prince William County, VA	100,106	**Hempstead (town), NY** (town) Nassau County	88,884
Connecticut	74,485	Suffolk County, NY	90,417	**Queens, NY** (borough) Queens County	69,306
Illinois	67,871	Nassau County, NY	88,884	**San Diego, CA** (city) San Diego County	66,593
Indiana	63,333	Pierce County, WA	75,093	**Fayetteville, NC** (city) Cumberland County	60,096
New Jersey	62,721	Queens County, NY	69,306	**New York, NY** (city)	46,146
Washington	62,070	Cook County, IL	68,661	**Brooklyn, NY** (borough) Kings County	44,407
Michigan	61,458	San Diego County, CA	66,743	**Houston, TX** (city) Harris County	41,435
Virginia	58,877	San Bernardino County, CA	61,597	**Jacksonville, FL** (city) Duval County	40,625
Missouri	58,750	Riverside County, CA	60,250	**Manhattan, NY** (borough) New York County	39,293
Maryland	58,415	Prince George's County, MD	59,387	**Los Angeles, CA** (city) Los Angeles County	39,174

Sorted by Percent in Ascending Order — U.S. = $49,834

State	Dollars	County	Dollars	Place	Dollars
Nevada	21,172	Clark County, NV	20,742	**Miami, FL** (city) Miami-Dade County	35,144
New Mexico	26,509	Sacramento County, CA	31,667	**San Antonio, TX** (city) Bexar County	37,763
Kentucky	29,750	Palm Beach County, FL	33,693	**Killeen, TX** (city) Bell County	39,107
Alabama	29,938	Bell County, TX	34,706	**Bronx, NY** (borough) Bronx County	39,127
Colorado	32,131	Dallas County, TX	36,771	**Los Angeles, CA** (city) Los Angeles County	39,174
Pennsylvania	41,168	Bronx County, NY	39,127	**Manhattan, NY** (borough) New York County	39,293
Massachusetts	41,458	New York County, NY	39,293	**Jacksonville, FL** (city) Duval County	40,625
Mississippi	42,292	Cumberland County, NC	39,331	**Houston, TX** (city) Harris County	41,435
Louisiana	43,603	Duval County, FL	40,625	**Brooklyn, NY** (borough) Kings County	44,407
Georgia	43,962	Hillsborough County, FL	41,712	**New York, NY** (city)	46,146

Note: (1) Ranking tables cover all states and counties, and places with an overall population of at least 125,000, OR an overall population of at least 25,000 where the Hispanic/Latino population is at least 20% of the overall population. In states where less than five places meet either of these criteria, we have included places with at least 10,000 total population with the highest percentage of Hispanic/Latino population. These places are identified with an asterisk (*); Please refer to the User's Guide for a full explanation of data.

Median Household Income

(2010 Inflation-Adjusted Dollars)

Central American: Salvadoran

Top 10 States, Counties, and Places[1]

Sorted by Percent in Descending Order — U.S. = $44,322

State	Dollars	County	Dollars	Place	Dollars
Hawaii	75,222	Orange County, NY	92,550	**Springfield, VA** (cdp) Fairfax County	87,466
Maryland	57,283	Hartford County, CT	80,020	**Annandale, VA** (cdp) Fairfax County	85,464
Connecticut	56,198	Washington County, OR	77,708	**Chino, CA** (city) San Bernardino County	79,875
Virginia	55,585	Napa County, CA	73,409	**West Falls Church, VA** (cdp) Fairfax County	78,879
New York	51,329	New Haven County, CT	71,250	**West Covina, CA** (city) Los Angeles County	73,482
Massachusetts	50,493	Fulton County, GA	69,167	**Simi Valley, CA** (city) Ventura County	72,333
New Mexico	50,236	Camden County, NJ	67,782	**Oyster Bay, NY** (town) Nassau County	72,212
Wisconsin	49,613	Somerset County, NJ	66,703	**Huntington, NY** (town) Suffolk County	70,268
New Jersey	49,035	Loudoun County, VA	66,648	**San Mateo, CA** (city) San Mateo County	70,000
Illinois	48,477	Frederick County, MD	66,406	**Modesto, CA** (city) Stanislaus County	69,423

Sorted by Percent in Ascending Order — U.S. = $44,322

State	Dollars	County	Dollars	Place	Dollars
Idaho	24,602	Forsyth County, NC	21,593	**Winston-Salem, NC** (city) Forsyth County	21,731
Kentucky	31,324	Sebastian County, AR	23,661	**Richmond, VA** (independent city)	25,566
Arkansas	31,881	Jefferson Parish, LA	25,938	**Jersey City, NJ** (city) Hudson County	26,058
Iowa	32,135	Dakota County, MN	27,360	**Mesa, AZ** (city) Maricopa County	27,031
South Carolina	32,679	Bronx County, NY	27,591	**Homestead, FL** (city) Miami-Dade County	27,035
Alabama	32,917	Franklin County, OH	27,760	**Bronx, NY** (borough) Bronx County	27,591
Louisiana	34,747	Buncombe County, NC	29,236	**Columbus, OH** (city) Franklin County	28,385
Oklahoma	35,125	Polk County, FL	30,189	**Glen Cove, NY** (city) Nassau County	29,097
Ohio	35,818	Ramsey County, MN	31,140	**Yonkers, NY** (city) Westchester County	29,861
Texas	36,764	Guilford County, NC	31,196	**Greensboro, NC** (city) Guilford County	30,272

RANKINGS & COMPARISONS

Note: (1) Ranking tables cover all states and counties, and places with an overall population of at least 125,000, OR an overall population of at least 25,000 where the Hispanic/Latino population is at least 20% of the overall population. In states where less than five places meet either of these criteria, we have included places with at least 10,000 total population with the highest percentage of Hispanic/Latino population. These places are identified with an asterisk (*); Please refer to the User's Guide for a full explanation of data.

Median Household Income

(2010 Inflation-Adjusted Dollars)

Cuban

Top 10 States, Counties, and Places[1]

Sorted by Percent in Descending Order — U.S. = $43,857

State	Dollars	County	Dollars	Place	Dollars
District of Columbia	78,417	Morris County, NJ	150,625	**North Hempstead, NY** (town) Nassau County	129,375
Hawaii	75,568	Sussex County, NJ	140,156	**Oyster Bay, NY** (town) Nassau County	116,184
New Hampshire	72,986	Fairfax County, VA	129,917	**Kearny, NJ** (town) Hudson County	111,473
Maryland	71,167	Nassau County, NY	112,994	**Weston, FL** (city) Broward County	108,421
Virginia	71,116	Ventura County, CA	109,145	**Santa Clarita, CA** (city) Los Angeles County	102,702
Connecticut	65,476	Somerset County, NJ	108,173	**Brookhaven, NY** (town) Suffolk County	97,432
Rhode Island	63,203	Monmouth County, NJ	104,844	**Hempstead (town), NY** (town) Nassau County	96,094
Georgia	57,055	Loudoun County, VA	104,073	**Islip, NY** (town) Suffolk County	87,069
California	56,167	Burlington County, NJ	103,295	**Cooper City, FL** (city) Broward County	84,821
Nebraska	55,713	San Mateo County, CA	102,583	**Alafaya, FL** (cdp) Orange County	82,218

Sorted by Percent in Ascending Order — U.S. = $43,857

State	Dollars	County	Dollars	Place	Dollars
West Virginia	14,769	Hampden County, MA	17,364	**Bell, CA** (city) Los Angeles County	18,903
Arkansas	30,078	Alachua County, FL	17,833	**Rochester, NY** (city) Monroe County	21,081
Missouri	34,252	Bronx County, NY	22,123	**Bronx, NY** (borough) Bronx County	22,123
Maine	34,453	Pima County, AZ	24,107	**Miami, FL** (city) Miami-Dade County	23,960
Utah	35,575	Davidson County, TN	26,304	**Lake Worth, FL** (city) Palm Beach County	24,911
Delaware	36,875	Jackson County, MO	26,656	**Nashville-Davidson, TN** (metropolitan govt) Davidson County	26,304
New Mexico	37,581	Lancaster County, PA	27,176	**Sunrise Manor, NV** (cdp) Clark County	26,443
Tennessee	37,587	Multnomah County, OR	27,436	**Miami Beach, FL** (city) Miami-Dade County	27,753
Kansas	37,877	Salt Lake County, UT	29,608	**Tallahassee, FL** (city) Leon County	28,784
Kentucky	38,229	Ingham County, MI	30,385	**Hallandale Beach, FL** (city) Broward County	28,864

Note: (1) Ranking tables cover all states and counties, and places with an overall population of at least 125,000, OR an overall population of at least 25,000 where the Hispanic/Latino population is at least 20% of the overall population. In states where less than five places meet either of these criteria, we have included places with at least 10,000 total population with the highest percentage of Hispanic/Latino population. These places are identified with an asterisk (*); Please refer to the User's Guide for a full explanation of data.

Median Household Income

(2010 Inflation-Adjusted Dollars)

Dominican Republic

Top 10 States, Counties, and Places[1]

Sorted by Percent in Descending Order — U.S. = $34,925

State	Dollars	County	Dollars	Place	Dollars
Nevada	71,607	Morris County, NJ	76,928	**Ramapo, NY** (town) Rockland County	125,938
Virginia	55,836	Orange County, NY	71,983	**North Hempstead, NY** (town) Nassau County	107,583
Maryland	55,000	Clark County, NV	71,161	**Oyster Bay, NY** (town) Nassau County	97,981
Illinois	53,873	Bergen County, NJ	69,880	**Plantation, FL** (city) Broward County	86,528
Missouri	53,707	Bexar County, TX	68,404	**Belleville, NJ** (township) Essex County	85,972
Alaska	50,231	Fairfax County, VA	64,531	**Elmont, NY** (cdp) Nassau County	84,521
California	48,971	Fulton County, GA	63,359	**Valley Stream, NY** (village) Nassau County	82,813
South Carolina	48,227	Somerset County, NJ	62,096	**Huntington, NY** (town) Suffolk County	80,625
Alabama	47,167	Suffolk County, NY	61,972	**Davie, FL** (town) Broward County	78,606
Indiana	46,250	Baltimore County, MD	61,635	**Richmond West, FL** (cdp) Miami-Dade County	77,917

Sorted by Percent in Ascending Order — U.S. = $34,925

State	Dollars	County	Dollars	Place	Dollars
Utah	19,516	Erie County, NY	16,083	**Syracuse, NY** (city) Onondaga County	16,961
Wisconsin	21,635	Pinellas County, FL	21,148	**Chelsea, MA** (city) Suffolk County	16,987
Tennessee	25,888	Cuyahoga County, OH	21,170	**Lynn, MA** (city) Essex County	20,206
Massachusetts	26,650	Suffolk County, MA	21,991	**Raleigh, NC** (city) Wake County	21,111
Rhode Island	26,926	Bristol County, MA	22,019	**Trenton, NJ** (city) Mercer County	21,111
Michigan	28,125	Oneida County, NY	23,542	**York, PA** (city) York County	21,597
Ohio	29,755	Onondaga County, NY	23,571	**Springfield, MA** (city) Hampden County	21,635
Pennsylvania	29,852	Berks County, PA	23,904	**Cleveland, OH** (city) Cuyahoga County	21,755
New York	31,880	York County, PA	24,514	**West Little River, FL** (cdp) Miami-Dade County	21,927
Louisiana	33,241	Philadelphia County, PA	25,668	**Boston, MA** (city) Suffolk County	21,949

Note: (1) Ranking tables cover all states and counties, and places with an overall population of at least 125,000, OR an overall population of at least 25,000 where the Hispanic/Latino population is at least 20% of the overall population. In states where less than five places meet either of these criteria, we have included places with at least 10,000 total population with the highest percentage of Hispanic/Latino population. These places are identified with an asterisk (*); Please refer to the User's Guide for a full explanation of data.

Median Household Income

(2010 Inflation-Adjusted Dollars)

Mexican

Top 10 States, Counties, and Places[1]

Sorted by Percent in Descending Order — U.S. = $40,588

State	Dollars	County	Dollars	Place	Dollars
Maryland	59,381	McPherson County, KS	100,270	**Weston, FL** (city) Broward County	144,750
Alaska	58,342	Beaver County, PA	95,199	**Miramar, FL** (city) Broward County	110,061
Vermont	54,116	Delaware County, OH	94,118	**Coral Gables, FL** (city) Miami-Dade County	104,940
Massachusetts	53,743	Waseca County, MN	90,625	**Eastvale, CA** (cdp) Riverside County	98,329
Hawaii	52,885	Norfolk County, MA	86,875	**Pembroke Pines, FL** (city) Broward County	93,717
Virginia	50,811	Jefferson County, WV	85,690	**Diamond Bar, CA** (city) Los Angeles County	91,736
District of Columbia	49,912	Chisago County, MN	85,000	**Chino Hills, CA** (city) San Bernardino County	90,193
Illinois	46,580	Saint Mary's County, MD	82,786	**Doral, FL** (city) Miami-Dade County	88,333
California	46,493	Howard County, MD	82,440	**Huntington, NY** (town) Suffolk County	87,778
Nevada	45,757	Charles County, MD	81,927	**Kendall, FL** (cdp) Miami-Dade County	81,964

Sorted by Percent in Ascending Order — U.S. = $40,588

State	Dollars	County	Dollars	Place	Dollars
North Carolina	31,065	McDonough County, IL	3,250	**Fargo*, ND** (city) Cass County	17,326
Kentucky	31,673	Coleman County, TX	12,000	**Springfield, MA** (city) Hampden County	20,781
Montana	31,872	Berrien County, GA	13,571	**Columbia, SC** (city) Richland County	21,518
Arkansas	31,878	Winona County, MN	13,693	**Waterbury, CT** (city/town) New Haven County	21,728
West Virginia	32,054	Box Butte County, NE	14,250	**Asheboro, NC** (city) Randolph County	22,064
South Carolina	32,229	Logan County, IL	14,400	**Passaic, NJ** (city) Passaic County	22,161
Tennessee	32,286	Pittsburg County, OK	15,313	**Altus*, OK** (city) Jackson County	22,222
Alabama	33,170	Dickens County, TX	15,750	**North Lauderdale, FL** (city) Broward County	23,438
Oklahoma	33,683	Antrim County, MI	15,938	**Berea*, SC** (cdp) Greenville County	23,720
Georgia	33,685	Warren County, TN	15,990	**Rapid City*, SD** (city) Pennington County	23,848

Note: (1) Ranking tables cover all states and counties, and places with an overall population of at least 125,000, OR an overall population of at least 25,000 where the Hispanic/Latino population is at least 20% of the overall population. In states where less than five places meet either of these criteria, we have included places with at least 10,000 total population with the highest percentage of Hispanic/Latino population. These places are identified with an asterisk (*); Please refer to the User's Guide for a full explanation of data.

Median Household Income

(2010 Inflation-Adjusted Dollars)

Puerto Rican

Top 10 States, Counties, and Places[1]

Sorted by Percent in Descending Order — U.S. = $38,426

State	Dollars	County	Dollars	Place	Dollars
District of Columbia	72,500	Warren County, OH	128,750	**Bergenfield, NJ** (borough) Bergen County	125,168
Maryland	70,795	Hamilton County, IN	117,679	**Coral Gables, FL** (city) Miami-Dade County	111,629
Virginia	61,449	Hunterdon County, NJ	107,045	**Elmont, NY** (cdp) Nassau County	110,893
Nebraska	61,429	Putnam County, NY	99,261	**Fremont, CA** (city) Alameda County	108,641
Nevada	57,229	Howard County, MD	96,641	**Oyster Bay, NY** (town) Nassau County	107,143
California	56,154	Loudoun County, VA	93,813	**Alexandria, VA** (independent city)	101,394
Oklahoma	54,541	Montgomery County, MD	92,521	**Rahway, NJ** (city) Union County	98,000
Wyoming	54,091	Rockland County, NY	89,659	**West Covina, CA** (city) Los Angeles County	97,813
Hawaii	50,776	Medina County, OH	89,185	**Elk Grove, CA** (city) Sacramento County	95,117
Alaska	50,431	McHenry County, IL	89,178	**Valley Stream, NY** (village) Nassau County	94,643

Sorted by Percent in Ascending Order — U.S. = $38,426

State	Dollars	County	Dollars	Place	Dollars
Massachusetts	22,816	Wyoming County, NY	10,859	**Bridgeton, NJ** (city) Cumberland County	9,519
Rhode Island	23,835	Clearfield County, PA	12,563	**Holyoke, MA** (city) Hampden County	14,664
Montana	25,917	Chautauqua County, NY	13,071	**Buffalo, NY** (city) Erie County	15,132
Pennsylvania	26,966	Cattaraugus County, NY	14,750	**Hazleton, PA** (city) Luzerne County	17,684
South Dakota	27,109	Ontario County, NY	14,808	**Worcester, MA** (city) Worcester County	18,007
Maine	29,826	Clinton County, NY	15,556	**Syracuse, NY** (city) Onondaga County	18,233
Ohio	30,691	Lackawanna County, PA	16,312	**Pawtucket***, **RI** (city) Providence County	18,318
Connecticut	31,486	Cayuga County, NY	16,466	**Boston, MA** (city) Suffolk County	18,499
Wisconsin	31,861	Brown County, WI	17,155	**University, FL** (cdp) Hillsborough County	18,750
New York	33,436	Erie County, NY	17,223	**Providence, RI** (city) Providence County	19,701

RANKINGS & COMPARISONS

Note: (1) Ranking tables cover all states and counties, and places with an overall population of at least 125,000, OR an overall population of at least 25,000 where the Hispanic/Latino population is at least 20% of the overall population. In states where less than five places meet either of these criteria, we have included places with at least 10,000 total population with the highest percentage of Hispanic/Latino population. These places are identified with an asterisk (*); Please refer to the User's Guide for a full explanation of data.

Median Household Income

(2010 Inflation-Adjusted Dollars)

South American

Top 10 States, Counties, and Places[1]

Sorted by Percent in Descending Order — U.S. = $51,747

State	Dollars	County	Dollars	Place	Dollars
New Hampshire	73,375	Rockingham County, NH	130,938	**Oyster Bay, NY** (town) Nassau County	110,417
District of Columbia	72,271	Douglas County, CO	124,432	**Placentia, CA** (city) Orange County	109,469
Maryland	66,489	Norfolk County, MA	103,075	**Thousand Oaks, CA** (city) Ventura County	99,755
Alaska	66,414	Stafford County, VA	103,026	**Elmont, NY** (cdp) Nassau County	96,208
Virginia	66,410	Cameron County, TX	100,536	**Round Rock, TX** (city) Williamson County	93,125
Hawaii	65,643	Washington County, MN	93,750	**Chino Hills, CA** (city) San Bernardino County	92,419
Arizona	60,479	Williamson County, TX	91,250	**Springfield, VA** (cdp) Fairfax County	92,396
California	58,729	Santa Cruz County, CA	89,118	**Central Islip, NY** (cdp) Suffolk County	90,729
Maine	58,333	Clark County, WA	88,750	**Huntington, NY** (town) Suffolk County	90,500
Illinois	57,836	Ada County, ID	87,629	**Fremont, CA** (city) Alameda County	86,932

Sorted by Percent in Ascending Order — U.S. = $51,747

State	Dollars	County	Dollars	Place	Dollars
Vermont	28,370	Brazos County, TX	20,036	**Tallahassee, FL** (city) Leon County	20,467
Oklahoma	33,642	Leon County, FL	21,250	**Cleveland, OH** (city) Cuyahoga County	26,563
North Dakota	38,316	Alachua County, FL	21,580	**Egypt Lake-Leto, FL** (cdp) Hillsborough County	26,782
Arkansas	38,380	Hamilton County, TN	23,264	**Saint Petersburg, FL** (city) Pinellas County	29,241
Nebraska	38,917	Cleveland County, OK	24,241	**Tulsa, OK** (city) Tulsa County	29,598
Montana	40,568	Escambia County, FL	24,327	**Margate, FL** (city) Broward County	29,772
Idaho	40,881	Oneida County, NY	26,250	**Miami Gardens, FL** (city) Miami-Dade County	30,852
Tennessee	42,404	Weber County, UT	26,287	**Inglewood, CA** (city) Los Angeles County	31,858
South Carolina	43,208	Bell County, TX	29,840	**Salt Lake City, UT** (city) Salt Lake County	32,759
Mississippi	43,260	Cache County, UT	32,455	**Reading, PA** (city) Berks County	32,847

Note: (1) Ranking tables cover all states and counties, and places with an overall population of at least 125,000, OR an overall population of at least 25,000 where the Hispanic/Latino population is at least 20% of the overall population. In states where less than five places meet either of these criteria, we have included places with at least 10,000 total population with the highest percentage of Hispanic/Latino population. These places are identified with an asterisk (*); Please refer to the User's Guide for a full explanation of data.

Median Household Income

(2010 Inflation-Adjusted Dollars)

South American: Argentinean

Top 10 States, Counties, and Places[1]

Sorted by Percent in Descending Order — U.S. = $56,918

State	Dollars	County	Dollars	Place	Dollars
Connecticut	102,386	Contra Costa County, CA	123,958	**Aventura, FL** (city) Miami-Dade County	118,438
Colorado	91,250	Fairfield County, CT	123,447	**Doral, FL** (city) Miami-Dade County	114,808
District of Columbia	84,583	Middlesex County, MA	101,434	**Manhattan, NY** (borough) New York County	100,600
Massachusetts	81,364	New York County, NY	100,600	**Hempstead (town), NY** (town) Nassau County	86,208
Maryland	78,800	Santa Clara County, CA	95,714	**San Francisco, CA** (city) San Francisco County	83,295
Indiana	78,125	Suffolk County, NY	95,174	**Pembroke Pines, FL** (city) Broward County	73,115
Missouri	75,096	Ventura County, CA	92,111	**Los Angeles, CA** (city) Los Angeles County	61,048
Virginia	74,618	Montgomery County, MD	87,105	**Houston, TX** (city) Harris County	59,286
Minnesota	69,698	Nassau County, NY	86,655	**Coral Springs, FL** (city) Broward County	59,224
Washington	66,250	San Francisco County, CA	83,295	**New York, NY** (city)	58,718

Sorted by Percent in Ascending Order — U.S. = $56,918

State	Dollars	County	Dollars	Place	Dollars
Wisconsin	32,813	Dallas County, TX	34,150	**Hialeah, FL** (city) Miami-Dade County	33,603
Utah	42,875	Riverside County, CA	34,553	**Miami Beach, FL** (city) Miami-Dade County	35,766
Florida	44,445	Utah County, UT	36,693	**Miami, FL** (city) Miami-Dade County	38,314
Tennessee	46,734	Kings County, NY	39,208	**Hollywood, FL** (city) Broward County	38,338
Nevada	48,534	Montgomery County, TX	41,402	**Brooklyn, NY** (borough) Kings County	39,208
Oregon	50,921	Lee County, FL	41,698	**Bronx, NY** (borough) Bronx County	42,500
North Carolina	51,795	Bronx County, NY	42,500	**Chicago, IL** (city) Cook County	48,208
Michigan	52,309	Orange County, FL	42,724	**San Diego, CA** (city) San Diego County	49,188
Texas	53,299	Salt Lake County, UT	43,200	**San Jose, CA** (city) Santa Clara County	51,563
South Carolina	55,287	Miami-Dade County, FL	44,317	**Queens, NY** (borough) Queens County	52,696

RANKINGS & COMPARISONS

Note: (1) Ranking tables cover all states and counties, and places with an overall population of at least 125,000, OR an overall population of at least 25,000 where the Hispanic/Latino population is at least 20% of the overall population. In states where less than five places meet either of these criteria, we have included places with at least 10,000 total population with the highest percentage of Hispanic/Latino population. These places are identified with an asterisk (*); Please refer to the User's Guide for a full explanation of data.

Median Household Income

(2010 Inflation-Adjusted Dollars)

South American: Bolivian

Top 10 States, Counties, and Places[1]

Sorted by Percent in Descending Order — U.S. = $61,501

State	Dollars	County	Dollars	Place	Dollars
Maryland	69,742	San Diego County, CA	120,682	**Springfield, VA** (cdp) Fairfax County	92,841
Virginia	67,843	Loudoun County, VA	85,750	**West Falls Church, VA** (cdp) Fairfax County	81,250
Illinois	64,297	Cook County, IL	76,750	**Annandale, VA** (cdp) Fairfax County	66,563
North Carolina	63,917	Orange County, CA	72,946	**Arlington, VA** (cdp) Arlington County	66,471
California	62,917	Fairfax County, VA	71,517	**Dale City, VA** (cdp) Prince William County	65,517
New York	58,411	Santa Clara County, CA	71,181	**Queens, NY** (borough) Queens County	55,238
New Jersey	55,923	Montgomery County, MD	70,029	**New York, NY** (city)	53,214
Texas	49,332	Arlington County, VA	66,471	**Los Angeles, CA** (city) Los Angeles County	41,735
Rhode Island	48,255	Prince George's County, MD	66,250	**Providence, RI** (city) Providence County	31,818
Pennsylvania	47,670	Prince William County, VA	64,185		

Sorted by Percent in Ascending Order — U.S. = $61,501

State	Dollars	County	Dollars	Place	Dollars
Massachusetts	39,946	Palm Beach County, FL	31,205	**Providence, RI** (city) Providence County	31,818
Florida	47,038	Harris County, TX	48,210	**Los Angeles, CA** (city) Los Angeles County	41,735
Pennsylvania	47,670	Providence County, RI	48,255	**New York, NY** (city)	53,214
Rhode Island	48,255	Los Angeles County, CA	52,892	**Queens, NY** (borough) Queens County	55,238
Texas	49,332	Broward County, FL	54,286	**Dale City, VA** (cdp) Prince William County	65,517
New Jersey	55,923	Miami-Dade County, FL	54,293	**Arlington, VA** (cdp) Arlington County	66,471
New York	58,411	Queens County, NY	55,238	**Annandale, VA** (cdp) Fairfax County	66,563
California	62,917	Prince William County, VA	64,185	**West Falls Church, VA** (cdp) Fairfax County	81,250
North Carolina	63,917	Prince George's County, MD	66,250	**Springfield, VA** (cdp) Fairfax County	92,841
Illinois	64,297	Arlington County, VA	66,471		

Note: (1) Ranking tables cover all states and counties, and places with an overall population of at least 125,000, OR an overall population of at least 25,000 where the Hispanic/Latino population is at least 20% of the overall population. In states where less than five places meet either of these criteria, we have included places with at least 10,000 total population with the highest percentage of Hispanic/Latino population. These places are identified with an asterisk (*); Please refer to the User's Guide for a full explanation of data.

Median Household Income

(2010 Inflation-Adjusted Dollars)

South American: Chilean

Top 10 States, Counties, and Places[1]

Sorted by Percent in Descending Order — U.S. = $58,579

State	Dollars	County	Dollars	Place	Dollars
Ohio	83,125	Suffolk County, NY	126,012	**Hempstead (town), NY** (town) Nassau County	70,843
Connecticut	76,903	Montgomery County, MD	82,159	**Brooklyn, NY** (borough) Kings County	65,526
Virginia	74,167	Bergen County, NJ	81,932	**Miami, FL** (city) Miami-Dade County	60,915
Oregon	71,442	Maricopa County, AZ	75,843	**Los Angeles, CA** (city) Los Angeles County	59,259
Wisconsin	71,389	Fairfax County, VA	73,542	**Queens, NY** (borough) Queens County	59,234
Illinois	70,568	Cook County, IL	73,261	**New York, NY** (city)	57,133
Maryland	69,718	Nassau County, NY	72,106	**Chicago, IL** (city) Cook County	56,985
Michigan	67,957	San Diego County, CA	70,343	**Manhattan, NY** (borough) New York County	50,739
Arizona	66,538	Kings County, NY	65,526	**Kendall, FL** (cdp) Miami-Dade County	40,100
Minnesota	66,354	San Bernardino County, CA	64,342		

Sorted by Percent in Ascending Order — U.S. = $58,579

State	Dollars	County	Dollars	Place	Dollars
Nevada	46,000	Utah County, UT	36,865	**Kendall, FL** (cdp) Miami-Dade County	40,100
Tennessee	47,132	Salt Lake County, UT	44,000	**Manhattan, NY** (borough) New York County	50,739
Pennsylvania	48,603	Clark County, NV	46,047	**Chicago, IL** (city) Cook County	56,985
Florida	51,681	Palm Beach County, FL	46,058	**New York, NY** (city)	57,133
Georgia	53,421	Harris County, TX	48,771	**Queens, NY** (borough) Queens County	59,234
Washington	54,932	Santa Clara County, CA	50,357	**Los Angeles, CA** (city) Los Angeles County	59,259
Texas	55,893	New York County, NY	50,739	**Miami, FL** (city) Miami-Dade County	60,915
Utah	56,068	Miami-Dade County, FL	52,091	**Brooklyn, NY** (borough) Kings County	65,526
Colorado	56,944	Riverside County, CA	52,093	**Hempstead (town), NY** (town) Nassau County	70,843
Missouri	57,093	Broward County, FL	53,558		

RANKINGS & COMPARISONS

Note: (1) Ranking tables cover all states and counties, and places with an overall population of at least 125,000, OR an overall population of at least 25,000 where the Hispanic/Latino population is at least 20% of the overall population. In states where less than five places meet either of these criteria, we have included places with at least 10,000 total population with the highest percentage of Hispanic/Latino population. These places are identified with an asterisk (*); Please refer to the User's Guide for a full explanation of data.

Median Household Income

(2010 Inflation-Adjusted Dollars)

South American: Colombian

Top 10 States, Counties, and Places[1]

Sorted by Percent in Descending Order — U.S. = $50,731

State	Dollars	County	Dollars	Place	Dollars
District of Columbia	84,406	Loudoun County, VA	106,484	**Elmont, NY** (cdp) Nassau County	103,068
Alaska	82,803	Burlington County, NJ	105,954	**Huntington, NY** (town) Suffolk County	98,438
Kansas	78,415	Norfolk County, MA	104,345	**Arlington, VA** (cdp) Arlington County	97,568
Virginia	73,520	Arlington County, VA	97,568	**Garfield, NJ** (city) Bergen County	85,556
New Hampshire	70,087	Dutchess County, NY	95,404	**Homestead, FL** (city) Miami-Dade County	84,635
Arizona	64,521	Fairfax County, VA	94,524	**North Hempstead, NY** (town) Nassau County	81,932
Wisconsin	64,464	Prince William County, VA	86,538	**Hempstead (town), NY** (town) Nassau County	81,338
Nebraska	63,438	Forsyth County, GA	81,842	**Oyster Bay, NY** (town) Nassau County	79,200
Maryland	60,030	Ventura County, CA	81,250	**Yonkers, NY** (city) Westchester County	78,380
Oregon	59,375	Collin County, TX	81,000	**Islip, NY** (town) Suffolk County	75,337

Sorted by Percent in Ascending Order — U.S. = $50,731

State	Dollars	County	Dollars	Place	Dollars
Oklahoma	35,579	Leon County, FL	18,156	**Tallahassee, FL** (city) Leon County	17,813
New Mexico	35,625	Alachua County, FL	22,444	**Egypt Lake-Leto, FL** (cdp) Hillsborough County	28,458
Utah	36,994	Philadelphia County, PA	32,325	**Town 'n' Country, FL** (cdp) Hillsborough County	29,428
South Carolina	38,950	Baltimore County, MD	32,368	**Passaic, NJ** (city) Passaic County	30,250
Arkansas	40,238	Marion County, IN	34,130	**Miami Beach, FL** (city) Miami-Dade County	30,288
Rhode Island	42,427	Erie County, NY	35,268	**Raleigh, NC** (city) Wake County	31,125
Tennessee	42,572	Cuyahoga County, OH	35,625	**North Lauderdale, FL** (city) Broward County	31,545
Louisiana	42,777	Volusia County, FL	35,687	**Philadelphia, PA** (city) Philadelphia County	32,325
Colorado	43,581	Salt Lake County, UT	36,167	**Hialeah, FL** (city) Miami-Dade County	33,342
Indiana	43,984	Greenville County, SC	36,480	**Hallandale Beach, FL** (city) Broward County	33,409

Note: (1) Ranking tables cover all states and counties, and places with an overall population of at least 125,000, OR an overall population of at least 25,000 where the Hispanic/Latino population is at least 20% of the overall population. In states where less than five places meet either of these criteria, we have included places with at least 10,000 total population with the highest percentage of Hispanic/Latino population. These places are identified with an asterisk (*); Please refer to the User's Guide for a full explanation of data.

Median Household Income

(2010 Inflation-Adjusted Dollars)

South American: Ecuadorian

Top 10 States, Counties, and Places[1]

Sorted by Percent in Descending Order — U.S. = $49,755

State	Dollars	County	Dollars	Place	Dollars
Iowa	82,361	Ocean County, NJ	108,438	**Oyster Bay, NY** (town) Nassau County	119,583
Maryland	66,543	Fairfax County, VA	99,107	**Brookhaven, NY** (town) Suffolk County	82,056
Washington	63,906	Santa Clara County, CA	85,313	**Central Islip, NY** (cdp) Suffolk County	71,611
Virginia	59,479	Orange County, CA	76,711	**Hempstead (town), NY** (town) Nassau County	71,339
California	57,484	Hartford County, CT	75,656	**Clifton, NJ** (city) Passaic County	70,192
South Carolina	57,188	Nassau County, NY	75,652	**Islip, NY** (town) Suffolk County	69,274
Louisiana	56,750	Burlington County, NJ	74,861	**Spring Valley, NY** (village) Rockland County	68,929
Illinois	56,284	Orange County, NY	72,500	**Port Chester, NY** (village) Westchester County	68,182
Rhode Island	54,952	Montgomery County, MD	71,978	**Rye, NY** (town) Westchester County	68,182
Kansas	52,298	Morris County, NJ	71,585	**Babylon, NY** (town) Suffolk County	67,161

Sorted by Percent in Ascending Order — U.S. = $49,755

State	Dollars	County	Dollars	Place	Dollars
Wisconsin	22,292	Clark County, NV	29,962	**Allentown, PA** (city) Lehigh County	28,661
Missouri	25,313	Seminole County, FL	31,964	**Hialeah, FL** (city) Miami-Dade County	30,227
Nevada	33,205	Lehigh County, PA	35,469	**Yonkers, NY** (city) Westchester County	30,434
Oklahoma	33,750	Philadelphia County, PA	35,701	**Houston, TX** (city) Harris County	34,762
Indiana	34,796	Berks County, PA	36,641	**Miami, FL** (city) Miami-Dade County	35,152
Oregon	35,893	Kings County, NY	37,720	**Philadelphia, PA** (city) Philadelphia County	35,701
Ohio	37,396	Bronx County, NY	38,565	**Bloomfield, NJ** (township) Essex County	36,500
Utah	39,028	Pinellas County, FL	39,000	**Charlotte, NC** (city) Mecklenburg County	37,401
Michigan	39,500	New York County, NY	39,134	**Brooklyn, NY** (borough) Kings County	37,720
Tennessee	41,591	Utah County, UT	39,398	**Paterson, NJ** (city) Passaic County	37,806

Note: (1) Ranking tables cover all states and counties, and places with an overall population of at least 125,000, OR an overall population of at least 25,000 where the Hispanic/Latino population is at least 20% of the overall population. In states where less than five places meet either of these criteria, we have included places with at least 10,000 total population with the highest percentage of Hispanic/Latino population. These places are identified with an asterisk (*); Please refer to the User's Guide for a full explanation of data.

Median Household Income

(2010 Inflation-Adjusted Dollars)

South American: Paraguayan

Top 10 States, Counties, and Places[1]

Sorted by Percent in Descending Order — U.S. = $50,930

State	Dollars	County	Dollars	Place	Dollars
Maryland	72,318	Queens County, NY	52,391	**Queens, NY** (borough) Queens County	52,391
New Jersey	55,815	Westchester County, NY	37,321	**New York, NY** (city)	50,427
Florida	53,261				
New York	49,915				
Texas	41,818				
California	29,091				

Sorted by Percent in Ascending Order — U.S. = $50,930

State	Dollars	County	Dollars	Place	Dollars
California	29,091	Westchester County, NY	37,321	**New York, NY** (city)	50,427
Texas	41,818	Queens County, NY	52,391	**Queens, NY** (borough) Queens County	52,391
New York	49,915				
Florida	53,261				
New Jersey	55,815				
Maryland	72,318				

Note: (1) Ranking tables cover all states and counties, and places with an overall population of at least 125,000, OR an overall population of at least 25,000 where the Hispanic/Latino population is at least 20% of the overall population. In states where less than five places meet either of these criteria, we have included places with at least 10,000 total population with the highest percentage of Hispanic/Latino population. These places are identified with an asterisk (*); Please refer to the User's Guide for a full explanation of data.

Median Household Income

(2010 Inflation-Adjusted Dollars)

South American: Peruvian

Top 10 States, Counties, and Places[1]

Sorted by Percent in Descending Order — U.S. = $50,179

State	Dollars	County	Dollars	Place	Dollars
Alabama	75,686	Fort Bend County, TX	135,234	**Oyster Bay, NY** (town) Nassau County	112,361
Hawaii	72,781	Denton County, TX	83,110	**San Jose, CA** (city) Santa Clara County	90,417
Missouri	71,595	Morris County, NJ	76,719	**Doral, FL** (city) Miami-Dade County	86,111
Virginia	62,451	Ventura County, CA	76,684	**San Mateo, CA** (city) San Mateo County	83,929
Maryland	62,066	Lake County, IL	76,118	**Belleville, NJ** (township) Essex County	78,333
Minnesota	59,450	Nassau County, NY	73,901	**Kearny, NJ** (town) Hudson County	74,125
Illinois	57,383	Prince William County, VA	72,199	**Hempstead (town), NY** (town) Nassau County	73,750
Washington	56,474	Loudoun County, VA	71,272	**Pembroke Pines, FL** (city) Broward County	70,994
Michigan	54,792	Riverside County, CA	70,325	**San Diego, CA** (city) San Diego County	69,750
California	53,557	Suffolk County, NY	68,393	**Weston, FL** (city) Broward County	65,147

Sorted by Percent in Ascending Order — U.S. = $50,179

State	Dollars	County	Dollars	Place	Dollars
Oklahoma	30,115	Sarasota County, FL	26,840	**Miami Beach, FL** (city) Miami-Dade County	29,667
Louisiana	35,313	Travis County, TX	28,922	**Austin, TX** (city) Travis County	30,278
Tennessee	37,737	Arapahoe County, CO	33,750	**Miami, FL** (city) Miami-Dade County	30,703
Delaware	39,225	Atlantic County, NJ	35,771	**Davie, FL** (town) Broward County	33,500
Kentucky	40,938	Suffolk County, MA	35,815	**West New York, NJ** (town) Hudson County	34,118
Indiana	41,212	Bronx County, NY	36,500	**Fountainebleau, FL** (cdp) Miami-Dade County	34,618
Kansas	42,143	Pinellas County, FL	37,061	**Perth Amboy, NJ** (city) Middlesex County	35,469
New Mexico	42,853	Osceola County, FL	37,268	**Bloomfield, NJ** (township) Essex County	35,787
South Carolina	43,917	Sacramento County, CA	40,417	**Anaheim, CA** (city) Orange County	35,859
Florida	44,237	Philadelphia County, PA	40,750	**Boston, MA** (city) Suffolk County	36,033

RANKINGS & COMPARISONS

Note: (1) Ranking tables cover all states and counties, and places with an overall population of at least 125,000, OR an overall population of at least 25,000 where the Hispanic/Latino population is at least 20% of the overall population. In states where less than five places meet either of these criteria, we have included places with at least 10,000 total population with the highest percentage of Hispanic/Latino population. These places are identified with an asterisk (*); Please refer to the User's Guide for a full explanation of data.

Median Household Income

(2010 Inflation-Adjusted Dollars)

South American: Uruguayan

Top 10 States, Counties, and Places[1]

Sorted by Percent in Descending Order — U.S. = $46,991

State	Dollars	County	Dollars	Place	Dollars
Maryland	69,676	Westchester County, NY	57,143	**New York, NY** (city)	59,333
New York	59,125	Harris County, TX	55,532	**Queens, NY** (borough) Queens County	52,303
Virginia	53,906	Morris County, NJ	54,724	**Elizabeth, NJ** (city) Union County	43,948
Texas	50,511	Los Angeles County, CA	52,955		
California	50,307	Queens County, NY	52,303		
New Jersey	49,252	Broward County, FL	51,120		
Massachusetts	44,487	Union County, NJ	49,394		
Georgia	42,094	Hudson County, NJ	45,347		
Florida	37,978	Middlesex County, NJ	44,148		
Pennsylvania	27,008	Essex County, NJ	43,810		

Sorted by Percent in Ascending Order — U.S. = $46,991

State	Dollars	County	Dollars	Place	Dollars
Pennsylvania	27,008	Miami-Dade County, FL	33,772	**Elizabeth, NJ** (city) Union County	43,948
Florida	37,978	Palm Beach County, FL	38,826	**Queens, NY** (borough) Queens County	52,303
Georgia	42,094	Gwinnett County, GA	42,708	**New York, NY** (city)	59,333
Massachusetts	44,487	Worcester County, MA	43,622		
New Jersey	49,252	Essex County, NJ	43,810		
California	50,307	Middlesex County, NJ	44,148		
Texas	50,511	Hudson County, NJ	45,347		
Virginia	53,906	Union County, NJ	49,394		
New York	59,125	Broward County, FL	51,120		
Maryland	69,676	Queens County, NY	52,303		

Note: (1) Ranking tables cover all states and counties, and places with an overall population of at least 125,000, OR an overall population of at least 25,000 where the Hispanic/Latino population is at least 20% of the overall population. In states where less than five places meet either of these criteria, we have included places with at least 10,000 total population with the highest percentage of Hispanic/Latino population. These places are identified with an asterisk (*); Please refer to the User's Guide for a full explanation of data.

Median Household Income

(2010 Inflation-Adjusted Dollars)

South American: Venezuelan

Top 10 States, Counties, and Places[1]

Sorted by Percent in Descending Order — U.S. = $52,435

State	Dollars	County	Dollars	Place	Dollars
Ohio	84,952	Fort Bend County, TX	113,085	**Hollywood, FL** (city) Broward County	89,018
Texas	78,117	Travis County, TX	91,140	**Pembroke Pines, FL** (city) Broward County	73,925
Maryland	74,417	Collin County, TX	81,429	**Weston, FL** (city) Broward County	66,042
South Carolina	67,188	Harris County, TX	78,929	**Houston, TX** (city) Harris County	62,761
Louisiana	66,926	Montgomery County, MD	76,983	**Manhattan, NY** (borough) New York County	60,754
Michigan	65,139	Tarrant County, TX	76,667	**Doral, FL** (city) Miami-Dade County	60,231
Connecticut	60,724	King County, WA	76,213	**The Hammocks, FL** (cdp) Miami-Dade County	58,068
Wisconsin	60,682	San Diego County, CA	71,424	**Miramar, FL** (city) Broward County	54,830
California	60,246	Orange County, CA	71,023	**Davie, FL** (town) Broward County	53,616
Illinois	59,167	Fairfax County, VA	66,250	**Sunrise, FL** (city) Broward County	53,264

Sorted by Percent in Ascending Order — U.S. = $52,435

State	Dollars	County	Dollars	Place	Dollars
Utah	36,440	Lee County, FL	26,320	**Los Angeles, CA** (city) Los Angeles County	31,550
Indiana	42,404	Osceola County, FL	32,631	**Tamiami, FL** (cdp) Miami-Dade County	32,179
Tennessee	42,857	Suffolk County, MA	33,095	**Aventura, FL** (city) Miami-Dade County	33,167
Minnesota	43,264	Pinellas County, FL	36,705	**Orlando, FL** (city) Orange County	35,473
Oklahoma	45,375	Salt Lake County, UT	36,902	**Country Club, FL** (cdp) Miami-Dade County	35,588
Colorado	45,605	Kings County, NY	36,920	**Miami, FL** (city) Miami-Dade County	35,725
Pennsylvania	47,119	Bronx County, NY	37,533	**Brooklyn, NY** (borough) Kings County	36,920
Florida	48,036	Orange County, FL	38,309	**Bronx, NY** (borough) Bronx County	37,533
North Carolina	49,523	Miami-Dade County, FL	48,610	**Kendall West, FL** (cdp) Miami-Dade County	38,640
Missouri	50,395	Hillsborough County, FL	49,503	**Hialeah, FL** (city) Miami-Dade County	40,240

Note: (1) Ranking tables cover all states and counties, and places with an overall population of at least 125,000, OR an overall population of at least 25,000 where the Hispanic/Latino population is at least 20% of the overall population. In states where less than five places meet either of these criteria, we have included places with at least 10,000 total population with the highest percentage of Hispanic/Latino population. These places are identified with an asterisk (*); Please refer to the User's Guide for a full explanation of data.

Median Household Income

(2010 Inflation-Adjusted Dollars)

Spaniard

Top 10 States, Counties, and Places[1]

Sorted by Percent in Descending Order — U.S. = $54,275

State	Dollars	County	Dollars	Place	Dollars
Virginia	81,370	Morris County, NJ	148,750	**Oyster Bay, NY** (town) Nassau County	146,400
Alaska	80,966	Fairfax County, VA	120,938	**Staten Island, NY** (borough) Richmond County	100,732
New Jersey	74,461	Bergen County, NJ	120,179	**Brookhaven, NY** (town) Suffolk County	82,721
Maryland	73,155	Hartford County, CT	113,641	**Hempstead (town), NY** (town) Nassau County	81,842
Connecticut	71,250	Douglas County, CO	105,820	**San Francisco, CA** (city) San Francisco County	79,833
New York	66,478	Richmond County, NY	100,732	**Kearny, NJ** (town) Hudson County	77,823
New Hampshire	65,323	Brazoria County, TX	89,464	**Glendale, AZ** (city) Maricopa County	73,542
Tennessee	64,157	Suffolk County, NY	88,352	**San Jose, CA** (city) Santa Clara County	73,095
Hawaii	62,880	Union County, NJ	88,319	**Anchorage, AK** (municipality)	70,000
Illinois	61,952	Fairfield County, CT	85,319	**Virginia Beach, VA** (independent city)	69,293

Sorted by Percent in Ascending Order — U.S. = $54,275

State	Dollars	County	Dollars	Place	Dollars
Maine	27,214	La Plata County, CO	21,359	**Las Cruces, NM** (city) Dona Ana County	22,782
Nebraska	34,450	San Miguel County, NM	22,747	**Fresno, CA** (city) Fresno County	24,983
Arkansas	35,603	Douglas County, NE	27,031	**Long Beach, CA** (city) Los Angeles County	26,419
Alabama	38,974	Conejos County, CO	27,500	**Tucson, AZ** (city) Pima County	28,594
Missouri	39,084	Colfax County, NM	28,000	**Seattle, WA** (city) King County	30,074
Oklahoma	39,494	Las Animas County, CO	28,636	**San Bernardino, CA** (city) San Bernardino County	30,507
New Mexico	41,417	Erie County, NY	29,543	**Lakewood, CO** (city) Jefferson County	30,765
South Carolina	41,661	Weber County, UT	30,568	**South Valley, NM** (cdp) Bernalillo County	33,529
Mississippi	42,500	Fresno County, CA	30,982	**Lubbock, TX** (city) Lubbock County	34,355
Oregon	43,045	Hidalgo County, TX	31,532	**Pueblo, CO** (city) Pueblo County	35,739

Note: (1) Ranking tables cover all states and counties, and places with an overall population of at least 125,000, OR an overall population of at least 25,000 where the Hispanic/Latino population is at least 20% of the overall population. In states where less than five places meet either of these criteria, we have included places with at least 10,000 total population with the highest percentage of Hispanic/Latino population. These places are identified with an asterisk (*); Please refer to the User's Guide for a full explanation of data.

Per Capita Income

(2010 Inflation-Adjusted Dollars)

Total Population

Top 10 States, Counties, and Places[1]

Sorted by Percent in Descending Order — U.S. = $27,334

State	Dollars	County	Dollars	Place	Dollars
District of Columbia	42,078	Pitkin County, CO	64,381	**Manhattan, NY** (borough) New York County	59,149
Connecticut	36,775	New York County, NY	59,149	**Arlington, VA** (cdp) Arlington County	57,724
New Jersey	34,858	Arlington County, VA	57,724	**Alexandria, VA** (independent city)	54,345
Maryland	34,849	Marin County, CA	53,940	**Coral Gables, FL** (city) Miami-Dade County	53,264
Massachusetts	33,966	Nantucket County, MA	53,410	**North Hempstead, NY** (town) Nassau County	51,663
Virginia	32,145	Los Alamos County, NM	49,474	**Scottsdale, AZ** (city) Maricopa County	51,090
New Hampshire	31,422	Fairfax County, VA	49,001	**Mountain View, CA** (city) Santa Clara County	49,403
New York	30,948	Hunterdon County, NJ	48,489	**Laguna Hills, CA** (city) Orange County	47,542
Alaska	30,726	Fairfield County, CT	48,295	**Aventura, FL** (city) Miami-Dade County	47,462
Colorado	30,151	Westchester County, NY	47,814	**Huntington, NY** (town) Suffolk County	46,862

Sorted by Percent in Ascending Order — U.S. = $27,334

State	Dollars	County	Dollars	Place	Dollars
Mississippi	19,977	Shannon County, SD	7,772	**San Luis, AZ** (city) Yuma County	7,868
West Virginia	21,232	Wheeler County, GA	10,043	**Florence, AZ** (town) Pinal County	8,577
Arkansas	21,274	Zavala County, TX	10,180	**Soledad, CA** (city) Monterey County	10,118
Kentucky	22,515	Willacy County, TX	10,800	**Delano, CA** (city) Kern County	10,739
Idaho	22,518	Hancock County, GA	10,925	**San Juan, TX** (city) Hidalgo County	10,832
New Mexico	22,966	Todd County, SD	11,010	**Florence-Graham, CA** (cdp) Los Angeles County	11,236
Alabama	22,984	Hudspeth County, TX	11,485	**Socorro, TX** (city) El Paso County	11,567
Louisiana	23,094	Holmes County, MS	11,585	**Wasco, CA** (city) Kern County	11,799
Oklahoma	23,094	Starr County, TX	11,659	**Pharr, TX** (city) Hidalgo County	11,860
Utah	23,139	Lake County, TN	11,813	**Coachella, CA** (city) Riverside County	12,019

RANKINGS & COMPARISONS

Note: (1) Ranking tables cover all states and counties, and places with an overall population of at least 125,000, OR an overall population of at least 25,000 where the Hispanic/Latino population is at least 20% of the overall population. In states where less than five places meet either of these criteria, we have included places with at least 10,000 total population with the highest percentage of Hispanic/Latino population. These places are identified with an asterisk (*); Please refer to the User's Guide for a full explanation of data.

Per Capita Income

(2010 Inflation-Adjusted Dollars)

Hispanic or Latino (of any race)

Top 10 States, Counties, and Places[1]

Sorted by Percent in Descending Order — U.S. = $15,638

State	Dollars	County	Dollars	Place	Dollars
District of Columbia	29,285	Geauga County, OH	45,113	**Coral Gables, FL** (city) Miami-Dade County	44,849
Virginia	20,949	Monongalia County, WV	37,067	**Aventura, FL** (city) Miami-Dade County	36,267
Maryland	20,490	Labette County, KS	32,745	**Oyster Bay, NY** (town) Nassau County	30,139
Vermont	20,391	Terrebonne Parish, LA	31,902	**Weston, FL** (city) Broward County	30,080
Alaska	20,010	Washakie County, WY	31,781	**Plantation, FL** (city) Broward County	29,797
New Jersey	19,221	Allegany County, NY	30,082	**Miami Lakes, FL** (town) Miami-Dade County	29,355
Florida	18,749	Los Alamos County, NM	27,682	**Miami Beach, FL** (city) Miami-Dade County	29,043
Louisiana	18,727	Calvert County, MD	27,556	**Kendall, FL** (cdp) Miami-Dade County	28,289
Hawaii	18,628	Elbert County, CO	27,351	**Doral, FL** (city) Miami-Dade County	28,229
West Virginia	18,275	Douglas County, CO	27,343	**Bergenfield, NJ** (borough) Bergen County	27,325

Sorted by Percent in Ascending Order — U.S. = $15,638

State	Dollars	County	Dollars	Place	Dollars
Arkansas	11,290	West Carroll Parish, LA	1,777	**Florence, AZ** (town) Pinal County	6,840
South Dakota	11,907	Wyoming County, NY	2,938	**Mayfield*, KY** (city) Graves County	7,209
Idaho	11,974	Johnston County, OK	3,612	**Albertville*, AL** (city) Marshall County	7,215
Oklahoma	12,191	Fulton County, IL	3,757	**Parker*, SC** (cdp) Greenville County	7,427
North Carolina	12,287	Hertford County, NC	3,808	**Big Spring, TX** (city) Howard County	7,629
Nebraska	12,519	Thurston County, NE	4,152	**Carthage*, MO** (city) Jasper County	8,056
Oregon	12,751	Mahaska County, IA	4,398	**San Luis, AZ** (city) Yuma County	8,200
Iowa	12,850	Blaine County, OK	4,830	**Marshalltown, IA** (city) Marshall County	8,203
Alabama	12,872	Calhoun County, FL	4,901	**York, PA** (city) York County	8,271
Kentucky	13,122	Coleman County, TX	5,498	**Asheboro, NC** (city) Randolph County	8,518

Note: (1) Ranking tables cover all states and counties, and places with an overall population of at least 125,000, OR an overall population of at least 25,000 where the Hispanic/Latino population is at least 20% of the overall population. In states where less than five places meet either of these criteria, we have included places with at least 10,000 total population with the highest percentage of Hispanic/Latino population. These places are identified with an asterisk (*); Please refer to the User's Guide for a full explanation of data.

Per Capita Income

(2010 Inflation-Adjusted Dollars)

Central American, excluding Mexican

Top 10 States, Counties, and Places[1]

Sorted by Percent in Descending Order — U.S. = $15,838

State	Dollars	County	Dollars	Place	Dollars
Alaska	21,586	Cumberland County, NJ	30,864	**Weston, FL** (city) Broward County	53,425
District of Columbia	19,215	El Dorado County, CA	28,527	**Miami Lakes, FL** (town) Miami-Dade County	37,150
Hawaii	18,866	Muscogee County, GA	26,606	**Coral Gables, FL** (city) Miami-Dade County	36,919
Louisiana	17,912	Chester County, PA	26,535	**Oyster Bay, NY** (town) Nassau County	29,118
Illinois	17,907	Placer County, CA	26,293	**La Mirada, CA** (city) Los Angeles County	28,925
Virginia	17,785	Douglas County, CO	25,516	**Pembroke Pines, FL** (city) Broward County	28,759
Connecticut	17,779	Williamson County, TX	24,488	**Eastvale, CA** (cdp) Riverside County	27,555
Nevada	17,466	Davis County, UT	23,816	**Fairfield, CA** (city) Solano County	27,328
New York	17,209	Kane County, IL	23,414	**Hacienda Heights, CA** (cdp) Los Angeles County	26,904
New Jersey	17,154	Richmond County, NY	23,188	**Fremont, CA** (city) Alameda County	26,763

Sorted by Percent in Ascending Order — U.S. = $15,838

State	Dollars	County	Dollars	Place	Dollars
Vermont	7,109	Gilmer County, GA	5,456	**Laredo, TX** (city) Webb County	6,446
Maine	8,976	Webb County, TX	6,436	**Albertville*, AL** (city) Marshall County	6,552
South Dakota	10,708	Hendry County, FL	6,942	**Cincinnati, OH** (city) Hamilton County	8,043
Arkansas	11,042	DeKalb County, AL	7,097	**Little Elm, TX** (city) Denton County	8,309
Kentucky	11,131	Marshall County, AL	7,918	**Grand Rapids, MI** (city) Kent County	8,450
Alabama	11,288	Etowah County, AL	7,953	**Lexington-Fayette, KY** (consolidated govt) Fayette County	8,585
Missouri	12,125	Cass County, IN	8,073	**Clarksville, TN** (city) Montgomery County	8,671
Indiana	12,236	Franklin County, AL	8,113	**Springfield, MA** (city) Hampden County	8,898
Nebraska	12,237	Sampson County, NC	8,247	**Lexington*, NE** (city) Dawson County	9,150
North Carolina	12,358	Hamilton County, OH	8,369	**Delano, CA** (city) Kern County	9,156

Note: (1) Ranking tables cover all states and counties, and places with an overall population of at least 125,000, OR an overall population of at least 25,000 where the Hispanic/Latino population is at least 20% of the overall population. In states where less than five places meet either of these criteria, we have included places with at least 10,000 total population with the highest percentage of Hispanic/Latino population. These places are identified with an asterisk (*); Please refer to the User's Guide for a full explanation of data.

Per Capita Income

(2010 Inflation-Adjusted Dollars)

Central American: Costa Rican

Top 10 States, Counties, and Places[1]

Sorted by Percent in Descending Order — U.S. = $20,657

State	Dollars	County	Dollars	Place	Dollars
Colorado	29,658	Orange County, CA	30,741	**Queens, NY** (borough) Queens County	26,058
Louisiana	26,916	Broward County, FL	26,559	**New York, NY** (city)	22,497
Illinois	26,508	Queens County, NY	26,058	**Bronx, NY** (borough) Bronx County	21,674
Oregon	25,348	Cook County, IL	25,878	**Los Angeles, CA** (city) Los Angeles County	21,143
California	24,759	Contra Costa County, CA	25,678	**Brooklyn, NY** (borough) Kings County	19,924
Texas	24,669	Harris County, TX	24,707	**Philadelphia, PA** (city) Philadelphia County	17,743
Georgia	23,569	San Diego County, CA	23,920	**Miami, FL** (city) Miami-Dade County	9,650
Virginia	23,031	Los Angeles County, CA	23,710		
Nevada	22,882	Riverside County, CA	22,587		
Massachusetts	22,112	Morris County, NJ	22,361		

Sorted by Percent in Ascending Order — U.S. = $20,657

State	Dollars	County	Dollars	Place	Dollars
Michigan	12,533	Orange County, FL	12,703	**Miami, FL** (city) Miami-Dade County	9,650
North Carolina	13,871	Passaic County, NJ	12,990	**Philadelphia, PA** (city) Philadelphia County	17,743
Tennessee	14,518	Union County, NJ	14,494	**Brooklyn, NY** (borough) Kings County	19,924
Minnesota	16,856	Mercer County, NJ	14,497	**Los Angeles, CA** (city) Los Angeles County	21,143
South Carolina	17,067	Essex County, NJ	16,200	**Bronx, NY** (borough) Bronx County	21,674
Pennsylvania	17,291	Suffolk County, NY	16,273	**New York, NY** (city)	22,497
Washington	17,451	Miami-Dade County, FL	17,101	**Queens, NY** (borough) Queens County	26,058
New Jersey	17,640	Philadelphia County, PA	17,743		
Florida	18,790	Palm Beach County, FL	19,040		
Wisconsin	19,115	Fairfield County, CT	19,060		

Note: (1) Ranking tables cover all states and counties, and places with an overall population of at least 125,000, OR an overall population of at least 25,000 where the Hispanic/Latino population is at least 20% of the overall population. In states where less than five places meet either of these criteria, we have included places with at least 10,000 total population with the highest percentage of Hispanic/Latino population. These places are identified with an asterisk (*); Please refer to the User's Guide for a full explanation of data.

Per Capita Income

(2010 Inflation-Adjusted Dollars)

Central American: Guatemalan

Top 10 States, Counties, and Places[1]

Sorted by Percent in Descending Order — U.S. = $14,281

State	Dollars	County	Dollars	Place	Dollars
District of Columbia	19,551	Stanislaus County, CA	22,272	**Hialeah, FL** (city) Miami-Dade County	26,120
Maryland	16,964	Collin County, TX	20,431	**Burbank, CA** (city) Los Angeles County	24,386
Illinois	16,726	New York County, NY	20,228	**Ontario, CA** (city) San Bernardino County	23,508
Nevada	16,359	Loudoun County, VA	20,199	**Union City, NJ** (city) Hudson County	23,474
Virginia	16,240	San Joaquin County, CA	20,106	**Brentwood, NY** (cdp) Suffolk County	23,065
Massachusetts	16,125	Suffolk County, MA	19,965	**Boston, MA** (city) Suffolk County	22,313
New York	15,915	Arlington County, VA	19,811	**Alhambra, CA** (city) Los Angeles County	21,961
New Mexico	15,884	Montgomery County, MD	19,633	**Central Islip, NY** (cdp) Suffolk County	21,856
Rhode Island	15,813	Lake County, IL	19,442	**Glendale, CA** (city) Los Angeles County	21,553
Utah	15,677	San Diego County, CA	19,264	**Islip, NY** (town) Suffolk County	21,513

Sorted by Percent in Ascending Order — U.S. = $14,281

State	Dollars	County	Dollars	Place	Dollars
Kentucky	7,896	Gilmer County, GA	5,456	**Albertville*, AL** (city) Marshall County	6,509
Idaho	8,037	Cherokee County, GA	5,967	**Cincinnati, OH** (city) Hamilton County	7,551
Missouri	8,372	Pinal County, AZ	6,082	**Grand Rapids, MI** (city) Kent County	7,830
Michigan	9,591	DeKalb County, AL	6,597	**Carthage*, MO** (city) Jasper County	8,504
South Dakota	9,714	Marshall County, AL	7,817	**West Palm Beach, FL** (city) Palm Beach County	9,317
Alabama	9,813	Franklin County, AL	8,113	**Lexington*, NE** (city) Dawson County	9,343
Indiana	9,832	Murray County, GA	8,218	**Indianapolis, IN** (city) Marion County	9,357
South Carolina	9,839	Kent County, MI	8,377	**Westmont, CA** (cdp) Los Angeles County	9,555
New Hampshire	9,903	Hamilton County, OH	8,396	**Portland, OR** (city) Multnomah County	9,872
Wisconsin	9,975	Caroline County, MD	8,669	**Sioux Falls, SD** (city) Minnehaha County	10,060

Note: (1) Ranking tables cover all states and counties, and places with an overall population of at least 125,000, OR an overall population of at least 25,000 where the Hispanic/Latino population is at least 20% of the overall population. In states where less than five places meet either of these criteria, we have included places with at least 10,000 total population with the highest percentage of Hispanic/Latino population. These places are identified with an asterisk (*); Please refer to the User's Guide for a full explanation of data.

Per Capita Income

(2010 Inflation-Adjusted Dollars)

Central American: Honduran

Top 10 States, Counties, and Places[1]

Sorted by Percent in Descending Order — U.S. = $14,264

State	Dollars	County	Dollars	Place	Dollars
District of Columbia	18,851	Orange County, NY	27,330	**Staten Island, NY** (borough) Richmond County	26,602
Nevada	18,072	Richmond County, NY	26,602	**Las Vegas, NV** (city) Clark County	24,930
New Jersey	17,537	Bergen County, NJ	21,450	**Miramar, FL** (city) Broward County	20,941
Connecticut	16,859	Clark County, NV	21,404	**Newark, NJ** (city) Essex County	19,863
Arizona	16,844	Essex County, NJ	20,760	**Brentwood, NY** (cdp) Suffolk County	19,636
Pennsylvania	16,534	Orange County, CA	20,760	**Philadelphia, PA** (city) Philadelphia County	18,915
Maryland	16,460	Osceola County, FL	20,649	**Islip, NY** (town) Suffolk County	18,421
Louisiana	16,394	Riverside County, CA	19,901	**Queens, NY** (borough) Queens County	18,188
New York	16,289	Saint Tammany Parish, LA	19,891	**San Jose, CA** (city) Santa Clara County	18,081
Massachusetts	15,995	Prince William County, VA	19,159	**Jersey City, NJ** (city) Hudson County	17,755

Sorted by Percent in Ascending Order — U.S. = $14,264

State	Dollars	County	Dollars	Place	Dollars
Indiana	10,208	Kern County, CA	7,104	**Indianapolis, IN** (city) Marion County	8,999
Arkansas	10,253	Sampson County, NC	8,331	**Durham, NC** (city) Durham County	9,241
Missouri	10,895	Elkhart County, IN	8,583	**Dallas, TX** (city) Dallas County	10,097
South Carolina	11,080	Marion County, IN	8,596	**Charlotte, NC** (city) Mecklenburg County	10,160
North Carolina	11,136	Jackson County, MO	9,015	**West Little River, FL** (cdp) Miami-Dade County	10,271
Ohio	11,553	Galveston County, TX	9,292	**Conroe, TX** (city) Montgomery County	10,481
Nebraska	11,593	Durham County, NC	9,356	**Oklahoma City, OK** (city) Oklahoma County	10,715
Kentucky	11,652	Manatee County, FL	9,702	**Garland, TX** (city) Dallas County	10,945
Alabama	11,722	Montgomery County, TX	10,076	**Miami, FL** (city) Miami-Dade County	10,977
Iowa	12,054	Lee County, FL	10,117	**Houston, TX** (city) Harris County	11,069

Note: (1) Ranking tables cover all states and counties, and places with an overall population of at least 125,000, OR an overall population of at least 25,000 where the Hispanic/Latino population is at least 20% of the overall population. In states where less than five places meet either of these criteria, we have included places with at least 10,000 total population with the highest percentage of Hispanic/Latino population. These places are identified with an asterisk (*); Please refer to the User's Guide for a full explanation of data.

Per Capita Income

(2010 Inflation-Adjusted Dollars)

Central American: Nicaraguan

Top 10 States, Counties, and Places[1]

Sorted by Percent in Descending Order — U.S. = $19,311

State	Dollars	County	Dollars	Place	Dollars
Connecticut	32,240	Fairfax County, VA	32,495	**Fontana, CA** (city) San Bernardino County	28,436
District of Columbia	31,282	Santa Clara County, CA	27,108	**Antioch, CA** (city) Contra Costa County	28,130
Virginia	23,757	Orange County, CA	26,845	**Pembroke Pines, FL** (city) Broward County	26,145
Michigan	23,538	Hudson County, NJ	26,541	**Manhattan, NY** (borough) New York County	26,114
Louisiana	23,068	Montgomery County, MD	26,135	**Hayward, CA** (city) Alameda County	26,095
Maryland	23,036	New York County, NY	26,114	**Kendall, FL** (cdp) Miami-Dade County	25,405
Illinois	22,961	Contra Costa County, CA	26,053	**San Jose, CA** (city) Santa Clara County	24,528
New York	22,202	San Mateo County, CA	25,599	**Richmond, CA** (city) Contra Costa County	24,435
Pennsylvania	22,002	Riverside County, CA	24,961	**Daly City, CA** (city) San Mateo County	24,086
New Jersey	21,926	Alameda County, CA	24,933	**South San Francisco, CA** (city) San Mateo County	23,810

Sorted by Percent in Ascending Order — U.S. = $19,311

State	Dollars	County	Dollars	Place	Dollars
Missouri	15,200	Orange County, FL	12,417	**North Miami, FL** (city) Miami-Dade County	10,384
Oregon	15,214	Hillsborough County, FL	14,494	**South Gate, CA** (city) Los Angeles County	11,636
Wisconsin	16,130	Collier County, FL	16,049	**Miami, FL** (city) Miami-Dade County	11,875
Massachusetts	16,395	Miami-Dade County, FL	16,489	**West Little River, FL** (cdp) Miami-Dade County	12,456
North Carolina	16,550	Sonoma County, CA	16,744	**Hialeah, FL** (city) Miami-Dade County	13,097
Florida	16,563	Palm Beach County, FL	16,856	**South Miami Heights, FL** (cdp) Miami-Dade County	13,317
South Carolina	17,075	Gwinnett County, GA	17,119	**Charlotte, NC** (city) Mecklenburg County	14,084
Indiana	17,360	Travis County, TX	17,515	**Sacramento, CA** (city) Sacramento County	14,245
Minnesota	17,367	Duval County, FL	17,777	**Austin, TX** (city) Travis County	14,434
Colorado	17,401	Camden County, NJ	17,785	**University Park, FL** (cdp) Miami-Dade County	14,961

Note: (1) Ranking tables cover all states and counties, and places with an overall population of at least 125,000, OR an overall population of at least 25,000 where the Hispanic/Latino population is at least 20% of the overall population. In states where less than five places meet either of these criteria, we have included places with at least 10,000 total population with the highest percentage of Hispanic/Latino population. These places are identified with an asterisk (*); Please refer to the User's Guide for a full explanation of data.

Per Capita Income

(2010 Inflation-Adjusted Dollars)

Central American: Panamanian

Top 10 States, Counties, and Places[1]

Sorted by Percent in Descending Order — U.S. = $23,572

State	Dollars	County	Dollars	Place	Dollars
Minnesota	35,867	Fairfax County, VA	39,480	**Hempstead (town), NY** (town) Nassau County	32,411
Connecticut	33,343	Cook County, IL	36,926	**Los Angeles, CA** (city) Los Angeles County	32,361
Maryland	29,615	Montgomery County, MD	36,925	**Houston, TX** (city) Harris County	30,034
Illinois	28,726	Prince William County, VA	35,947	**Queens, NY** (borough) Queens County	29,494
Virginia	28,368	Prince George's County, MD	33,632	**Manhattan, NY** (borough) New York County	27,849
New Jersey	28,305	Nassau County, NY	32,477	**San Antonio, TX** (city) Bexar County	24,203
Ohio	27,517	Los Angeles County, CA	31,967	**San Diego, CA** (city) San Diego County	23,436
California	27,151	Hudson County, NJ	31,169	**New York, NY** (city)	22,613
Louisiana	26,865	Suffolk County, NY	30,495	**Jacksonville, FL** (city) Duval County	21,699
New York	23,531	Queens County, NY	29,494	**Fayetteville, NC** (city) Cumberland County	21,511

Sorted by Percent in Ascending Order — U.S. = $23,572

State	Dollars	County	Dollars	Place	Dollars
Mississippi	10,394	Bell County, TX	15,218	**Killeen, TX** (city) Bell County	14,967
New Mexico	12,955	Sacramento County, CA	15,486	**Miami, FL** (city) Miami-Dade County	19,513
Alabama	14,058	San Bernardino County, CA	17,081	**Brooklyn, NY** (borough) Kings County	20,287
Colorado	16,344	Clark County, NV	17,163	**Bronx, NY** (borough) Bronx County	20,431
Nevada	17,676	Orange County, FL	17,580	**Fayetteville, NC** (city) Cumberland County	21,511
South Carolina	17,910	Cumberland County, NC	17,966	**Jacksonville, FL** (city) Duval County	21,699
Pennsylvania	18,568	Hillsborough County, FL	18,889	**New York, NY** (city)	22,613
Arizona	18,805	Dallas County, TX	19,376	**San Diego, CA** (city) San Diego County	23,436
Wisconsin	19,445	Pierce County, WA	19,746	**San Antonio, TX** (city) Bexar County	24,203
Oklahoma	20,137	Kings County, NY	20,287	**Manhattan, NY** (borough) New York County	27,849

Note: (1) Ranking tables cover all states and counties, and places with an overall population of at least 125,000, OR an overall population of at least 25,000 where the Hispanic/Latino population is at least 20% of the overall population. In states where less than five places meet either of these criteria, we have included places with at least 10,000 total population with the highest percentage of Hispanic/Latino population. These places are identified with an asterisk (*); Please refer to the User's Guide for a full explanation of data.

Per Capita Income

(2010 Inflation-Adjusted Dollars)

Central American: Salvadoran

Top 10 States, Counties, and Places[1]

Sorted by Percent in Descending Order — U.S. = $15,416

State	Dollars	County	Dollars	Place	Dollars
Alaska	22,515	Placer County, CA	29,077	**Fairfield, CA** (city) Solano County	33,393
Hawaii	21,168	New York County, NY	26,760	**Burbank, CA** (city) Los Angeles County	30,640
Idaho	19,735	Solano County, CA	24,314	**Manhattan, NY** (borough) New York County	26,760
Wisconsin	19,154	New Haven County, CT	23,114	**Whittier, CA** (city) Los Angeles County	26,421
Louisiana	18,739	Frederick County, MD	22,791	**Sterling, VA** (cdp) Loudoun County	25,746
Connecticut	18,654	Loudoun County, VA	22,049	**San Bruno, CA** (city) San Mateo County	25,426
New Mexico	18,385	Santa Clara County, CA	22,028	**Santa Clarita, CA** (city) Los Angeles County	24,829
District of Columbia	17,996	San Mateo County, CA	21,445	**Oyster Bay, NY** (town) Nassau County	24,292
Illinois	17,866	Williamson County, TX	21,238	**Corona, CA** (city) Riverside County	23,767
Virginia	17,364	Contra Costa County, CA	20,556	**San Mateo, CA** (city) San Mateo County	23,703

Sorted by Percent in Ascending Order — U.S. = $15,416

State	Dollars	County	Dollars	Place	Dollars
Arkansas	10,273	Polk County, FL	9,271	**Glen Cove, NY** (city) Nassau County	8,663
Kentucky	10,673	Sebastian County, AR	9,352	**Homestead, FL** (city) Miami-Dade County	9,394
Tennessee	11,945	Crawford County, AR	9,594	**Durham, NC** (city) Durham County	9,706
Indiana	11,962	Davidson County, TN	10,021	**Nashville-Davidson, TN** (metropolitan govt) Davidson County	9,972
North Carolina	12,014	Durham County, NC	10,141	**Mesquite, TX** (city) Dallas County	10,413
Georgia	12,248	Utah County, UT	10,285	**Winston-Salem, NC** (city) Forsyth County	10,620
Alabama	12,982	Benton County, AR	10,407	**San Rafael, CA** (city) Marin County	10,637
Nebraska	13,094	Walker County, TX	10,483	**Springdale, AR** (city) Washington County	10,724
Texas	13,251	Buncombe County, NC	10,535	**Hialeah, FL** (city) Miami-Dade County	10,846
Ohio	13,305	Washington County, AR	10,596	**Maywood, CA** (city) Los Angeles County	10,897

RANKINGS & COMPARISONS

Note: (1) Ranking tables cover all states and counties, and places with an overall population of at least 125,000, OR an overall population of at least 25,000 where the Hispanic/Latino population is at least 20% of the overall population. In states where less than five places meet either of these criteria, we have included places with at least 10,000 total population with the highest percentage of Hispanic/Latino population. These places are identified with an asterisk (*); Please refer to the User's Guide for a full explanation of data.

Per Capita Income

(2010 Inflation-Adjusted Dollars)

Cuban

Top 10 States, Counties, and Places[1]

Sorted by Percent in Descending Order — U.S. = $24,144

State	Dollars	County	Dollars	Place	Dollars
District of Columbia	55,976	Loudoun County, VA	86,249	**North Hempstead, NY** (town) Nassau County	52,895
Virginia	36,015	Morris County, NJ	62,646	**Coral Gables, FL** (city) Miami-Dade County	48,407
Maryland	35,791	San Mateo County, CA	60,078	**Atlanta, GA** (city) Fulton County	43,315
Connecticut	32,117	East Baton Rouge Parish, LA	51,413	**Riverside, CA** (city) Riverside County	41,527
California	31,864	Lehigh County, PA	50,237	**San Francisco, CA** (city) San Francisco County	41,126
Delaware	31,686	Fairfax County, VA	49,455	**Brookhaven, NY** (town) Suffolk County	39,937
New Hampshire	30,224	Sussex County, NJ	45,242	**Manhattan, NY** (borough) New York County	38,532
Georgia	30,047	Montgomery County, MD	44,511	**Oyster Bay, NY** (town) Nassau County	38,197
New Jersey	29,994	Montgomery County, PA	44,504	**Burbank, CA** (city) Los Angeles County	36,645
New York	29,901	Lake County, FL	43,615	**Miami Beach, FL** (city) Miami-Dade County	35,979

Sorted by Percent in Ascending Order — U.S. = $24,144

State	Dollars	County	Dollars	Place	Dollars
Rhode Island	16,288	Berks County, PA	12,471	**Lehigh Acres, FL** (cdp) Lee County	11,915
New Mexico	16,310	Sumter County, FL	12,657	**West Little River, FL** (cdp) Miami-Dade County	12,081
Iowa	16,819	Jackson County, MO	13,583	**Rochester, NY** (city) Monroe County	12,824
Oklahoma	18,686	Lancaster County, PA	13,693	**Deltona, FL** (city) Volusia County	13,507
Alabama	18,704	Ingham County, MI	13,724	**Cape Coral, FL** (city) Lee County	14,017
Kentucky	19,237	Bernalillo County, NM	13,940	**Lake Worth, FL** (city) Palm Beach County	14,078
Maine	19,449	Atlantic County, NJ	14,049	**University, FL** (cdp) Hillsborough County	15,018
Nevada	19,679	Multnomah County, OR	14,729	**Hialeah, FL** (city) Miami-Dade County	15,214
Oregon	19,969	Lee County, FL	14,791	**Homestead, FL** (city) Miami-Dade County	15,230
Wisconsin	20,006	Escambia County, FL	15,377	**Miami Gardens, FL** (city) Miami-Dade County	15,583

Note: (1) Ranking tables cover all states and counties, and places with an overall population of at least 125,000, OR an overall population of at least 25,000 where the Hispanic/Latino population is at least 20% of the overall population. In states where less than five places meet either of these criteria, we have included places with at least 10,000 total population with the highest percentage of Hispanic/Latino population. These places are identified with an asterisk (*); Please refer to the User's Guide for a full explanation of data.

Per Capita Income

(2010 Inflation-Adjusted Dollars)

Dominican Republic

Top 10 States, Counties, and Places[1]

Sorted by Percent in Descending Order — U.S. = $14,986

State	Dollars	County	Dollars	Place	Dollars
Nevada	35,248	Clark County, NV	37,097	**Deltona, FL** (city) Volusia County	28,326
California	26,198	Los Angeles County, CA	30,355	**Ramapo, NY** (town) Rockland County	27,998
Tennessee	24,527	Fairfax County, VA	26,775	**Los Angeles, CA** (city) Los Angeles County	27,303
Louisiana	23,472	Volusia County, FL	25,370	**Belleville, NJ** (township) Essex County	27,251
Texas	22,529	Bexar County, TX	24,699	**Oyster Bay, NY** (town) Nassau County	27,243
Virginia	21,967	Bergen County, NJ	24,162	**Valley Stream, NY** (village) Nassau County	26,748
Colorado	21,887	Orange County, NY	23,987	**North Hempstead, NY** (town) Nassau County	26,686
Alabama	21,784	New Castle County, DE	23,400	**Weston, FL** (city) Broward County	26,325
Delaware	21,147	Morris County, NJ	21,411	**Pembroke Pines, FL** (city) Broward County	24,807
Illinois	19,887	San Diego County, CA	21,387	**Kendale Lakes, FL** (cdp) Miami-Dade County	24,150

Sorted by Percent in Ascending Order — U.S. = $14,986

State	Dollars	County	Dollars	Place	Dollars
Utah	7,075	Oneida County, NY	6,122	**Reading, PA** (city) Berks County	8,751
Rhode Island	10,909	Ulster County, NY	8,413	**Bethlehem, PA** (city) Northampton County	8,927
Pennsylvania	11,829	Erie County, NY	8,461	**Syracuse, NY** (city) Onondaga County	9,166
Michigan	11,903	Berks County, PA	9,141	**Rochester, NY** (city) Monroe County	9,663
Massachusetts	13,170	Bristol County, MA	9,322	**Cleveland, OH** (city) Cuyahoga County	9,901
Wisconsin	14,085	Luzerne County, PA	10,076	**Chelsea, MA** (city) Suffolk County	9,993
New York	14,091	Cumberland County, NJ	10,479	**Grand Rapids, MI** (city) Kent County	10,010
North Carolina	14,977	Gwinnett County, GA	10,500	**Providence, RI** (city) Providence County	10,445
Washington	15,030	Lackawanna County, PA	10,579	**Passaic, NJ** (city) Passaic County	10,652
Georgia	15,454	Providence County, RI	10,819	**New Haven, CT** (city/town) New Haven County	11,063

RANKINGS & COMPARISONS

Note: (1) Ranking tables cover all states and counties, and places with an overall population of at least 125,000, OR an overall population of at least 25,000 where the Hispanic/Latino population is at least 20% of the overall population. In states where less than five places meet either of these criteria, we have included places with at least 10,000 total population with the highest percentage of Hispanic/Latino population. These places are identified with an asterisk (*); Please refer to the User's Guide for a full explanation of data.

Per Capita Income

(2010 Inflation-Adjusted Dollars)

Mexican

Top 10 States, Counties, and Places[1]

Sorted by Percent in Descending Order — U.S. = $13,925

State	Dollars	County	Dollars	Place	Dollars
District of Columbia	31,032	Washakie County, WY	36,069	**Weston, FL** (city) Broward County	56,248
Massachusetts	20,867	Terrebonne Parish, LA	34,541	**Coral Gables, FL** (city) Miami-Dade County	50,452
Hawaii	19,523	Arlington County, VA	29,391	**Alexandria, VA** (independent city)	45,466
Maryland	19,353	Montgomery County, MD	27,620	**Doral, FL** (city) Miami-Dade County	33,653
Virginia	18,280	Clinton County, MI	27,579	**Arlington, VA** (cdp) Arlington County	29,391
Alaska	18,130	Fairfax County, VA	27,543	**Hollywood, FL** (city) Broward County	29,296
Vermont	17,222	Howard County, MD	27,383	**Miami Beach, FL** (city) Miami-Dade County	28,105
Connecticut	17,190	Uintah County, UT	27,320	**Fort Lauderdale, FL** (city) Broward County	26,699
Wyoming	16,570	Elbert County, CO	26,569	**Kendall, FL** (cdp) Miami-Dade County	26,231
Louisiana	15,952	Loudoun County, VA	26,188	**Diamond Bar, CA** (city) Los Angeles County	26,076

Sorted by Percent in Ascending Order — U.S. = $13,925

State	Dollars	County	Dollars	Place	Dollars
North Carolina	10,021	Hertford County, NC	3,910	**North Lauderdale, FL** (city) Broward County	6,344
Arkansas	10,056	Blaine County, OK	4,263	**Carthage*, MO** (city) Jasper County	6,415
Georgia	10,753	Fulton County, IL	4,782	**Florence, AZ** (town) Pinal County	6,716
Alabama	11,113	McDonough County, IL	4,982	**Albertville*, AL** (city) Marshall County	7,005
Kentucky	11,383	Coleman County, TX	5,363	**Passaic, NJ** (city) Passaic County	7,293
Tennessee	11,392	Houston County, TX	5,422	**Parker*, SC** (cdp) Greenville County	7,398
Idaho	11,435	Decatur County, GA	5,572	**York, PA** (city) York County	7,542
South Carolina	11,522	Briscoe County, TX	5,700	**Big Spring, TX** (city) Howard County	7,718
Oklahoma	11,524	Putnam County, TN	5,745	**Ocoee, FL** (city) Orange County	7,960
South Dakota	11,696	Telfair County, GA	5,788	**Marshalltown, IA** (city) Marshall County	8,093

Note: (1) Ranking tables cover all states and counties, and places with an overall population of at least 125,000, OR an overall population of at least 25,000 where the Hispanic/Latino population is at least 20% of the overall population. In states where less than five places meet either of these criteria, we have included places with at least 10,000 total population with the highest percentage of Hispanic/Latino population. These places are identified with an asterisk (*); Please refer to the User's Guide for a full explanation of data.

Per Capita Income

(2010 Inflation-Adjusted Dollars)

Puerto Rican

Top 10 States, Counties, and Places[1]

Sorted by Percent in Descending Order — U.S. = $17,556

State	Dollars	County	Dollars	Place	Dollars
District of Columbia	40,879	Arlington County, VA	58,437	**Arlington, VA** (cdp) Arlington County	58,437
Maryland	25,984	Warren County, OH	41,184	**Huntington Beach, CA** (city) Orange County	40,793
New Mexico	24,715	Hamilton County, IN	39,341	**Alexandria, VA** (independent city)	40,030
Virginia	24,140	Loudoun County, VA	38,405	**Bergenfield, NJ** (borough) Bergen County	38,085
Arkansas	23,941	Saint Tammany Parish, LA	37,631	**Coral Gables, FL** (city) Miami-Dade County	37,886
California	23,768	Montgomery County, MD	36,803	**Stamford, CT** (city/town) Fairfield County	37,280
Nevada	22,782	San Francisco County, CA	36,766	**San Francisco, CA** (city) San Francisco County	36,766
Texas	22,499	Forsyth County, GA	35,310	**Oyster Bay, NY** (town) Nassau County	35,955
Louisiana	21,479	Fairfax County, VA	35,227	**Plantation, FL** (city) Broward County	33,314
Arizona	21,422	Marin County, CA	34,542	**Henderson, NV** (city) Clark County	32,324

Sorted by Percent in Ascending Order — U.S. = $17,556

State	Dollars	County	Dollars	Place	Dollars
Maine	10,343	Wyoming County, NY	3,276	**Bridgeton, NJ** (city) Cumberland County	6,537
Rhode Island	11,312	Cayuga County, NY	4,515	**Woonsocket*, RI** (city) Providence County	7,862
Pennsylvania	12,134	Seneca County, NY	6,020	**Hazleton, PA** (city) Luzerne County	7,981
South Dakota	12,138	Washington County, NY	6,204	**York, PA** (city) York County	7,997
North Dakota	12,426	Saint Lawrence County, NY	7,146	**Syracuse, NY** (city) Onondaga County	8,672
Massachusetts	12,608	Cattaraugus County, NY	7,167	**Buffalo, NY** (city) Erie County	8,829
Wisconsin	12,666	Franklin County, PA	7,280	**Central Falls*, RI** (city) Providence County	9,026
Montana	13,665	Northumberland County, PA	7,367	**Reading, PA** (city) Berks County	9,049
Idaho	13,740	Brown County, WI	7,681	**Holyoke, MA** (city) Hampden County	9,341
Ohio	13,745	Sumter County, FL	8,032	**Allentown, PA** (city) Lehigh County	9,513

Note: (1) Ranking tables cover all states and counties, and places with an overall population of at least 125,000, OR an overall population of at least 25,000 where the Hispanic/Latino population is at least 20% of the overall population. In states where less than five places meet either of these criteria, we have included places with at least 10,000 total population with the highest percentage of Hispanic/Latino population. These places are identified with an asterisk (*); Please refer to the User's Guide for a full explanation of data.

Per Capita Income

(2010 Inflation-Adjusted Dollars)

South American

Top 10 States, Counties, and Places[1]

Sorted by Percent in Descending Order — U.S. = $22,420

State	Dollars	County	Dollars	Place	Dollars
District of Columbia	48,046	Douglas County, CO	49,439	**Scottsdale, AZ** (city) Maricopa County	43,748
Michigan	31,427	Oakland County, MI	45,219	**Atlanta, GA** (city) Fulton County	39,726
Hawaii	28,925	Hidalgo County, TX	41,456	**Coral Gables, FL** (city) Miami-Dade County	38,753
Iowa	28,375	Douglas County, NE	40,737	**Oceanside, CA** (city) San Diego County	37,615
Wyoming	27,523	Middlesex County, CT	40,025	**San Francisco, CA** (city) San Francisco County	37,256
Alaska	27,243	Jefferson County, AL	37,728	**Thousand Oaks, CA** (city) Ventura County	36,014
Louisiana	26,871	Saint Louis County, MO	37,304	**Manhattan, NY** (borough) New York County	35,893
California	26,844	San Francisco County, CA	37,256	**Oakland, CA** (city) Alameda County	35,598
Maryland	26,527	New York County, NY	35,893	**Aventura, FL** (city) Miami-Dade County	34,533
Missouri	26,522	Washtenaw County, MI	35,749	**Lake Forest, CA** (city) Orange County	34,515

Sorted by Percent in Ascending Order — U.S. = $22,420

State	Dollars	County	Dollars	Place	Dollars
North Dakota	13,116	Weber County, UT	7,560	**Spring Valley, NY** (village) Rockland County	11,596
Idaho	13,953	Oneida County, NY	10,966	**Reading, PA** (city) Berks County	11,984
Utah	15,377	Cache County, UT	11,877	**Greenacres, FL** (city) Palm Beach County	12,512
Montana	16,302	Flagler County, FL	11,999	**Buenaventura Lakes, FL** (cdp) Osceola County	12,666
Maine	16,324	Hernando County, FL	12,570	**Miami Gardens, FL** (city) Miami-Dade County	13,160
Oklahoma	17,280	Henry County, GA	12,730	**Glendale, AZ** (city) Maricopa County	13,326
South Carolina	17,927	Cleveland County, OK	12,742	**New Brunswick, NJ** (city) Middlesex County	13,642
Rhode Island	18,079	Brazos County, TX	12,950	**Meadow Woods, FL** (cdp) Orange County	14,149
Kentucky	18,188	Berks County, PA	13,017	**Hialeah, FL** (city) Miami-Dade County	14,251
Minnesota	19,391	Hamilton County, TN	13,042	**Four Corners, FL** (cdp) Lake County	14,256

Note: (1) Ranking tables cover all states and counties, and places with an overall population of at least 125,000, OR an overall population of at least 25,000 where the Hispanic/Latino population is at least 20% of the overall population. In states where less than five places meet either of these criteria, we have included places with at least 10,000 total population with the highest percentage of Hispanic/Latino population. These places are identified with an asterisk (*); Please refer to the User's Guide for a full explanation of data.

Per Capita Income

(2010 Inflation-Adjusted Dollars)

South American: Argentinean

Top 10 States, Counties, and Places[1]

Sorted by Percent in Descending Order — U.S. = $31,616

State	Dollars	County	Dollars	Place	Dollars
District of Columbia	65,629	Oakland County, MI	71,233	**Manhattan, NY** (borough) New York County	68,661
Connecticut	49,985	New York County, NY	68,661	**San Francisco, CA** (city) San Francisco County	52,111
Michigan	46,541	Bexar County, TX	68,149	**Doral, FL** (city) Miami-Dade County	51,818
Washington	40,247	Fairfield County, CT	64,019	**Aventura, FL** (city) Miami-Dade County	46,099
Tennessee	39,627	Westchester County, NY	57,584	**Houston, TX** (city) Harris County	42,070
Pennsylvania	39,018	San Francisco County, CA	52,111	**New York, NY** (city)	39,871
Missouri	38,972	King County, WA	51,026	**San Diego, CA** (city) San Diego County	38,402
Massachusetts	38,745	Santa Clara County, CA	48,806	**Pembroke Pines, FL** (city) Broward County	32,140
New York	38,302	Orange County, CA	45,917	**Los Angeles, CA** (city) Los Angeles County	31,683
Arizona	34,897	Ventura County, CA	42,187	**Brooklyn, NY** (borough) Kings County	30,468

Sorted by Percent in Ascending Order — U.S. = $31,616

State	Dollars	County	Dollars	Place	Dollars
Utah	12,713	Utah County, UT	13,062	**Hialeah, FL** (city) Miami-Dade County	14,002
South Carolina	21,158	Salt Lake County, UT	15,660	**Hollywood, FL** (city) Broward County	21,098
Nevada	23,395	Montgomery County, TX	17,092	**Chicago, IL** (city) Cook County	22,774
Wisconsin	25,591	Orange County, FL	19,346	**Miami, FL** (city) Miami-Dade County	23,185
Florida	25,845	Travis County, TX	21,051	**Coral Springs, FL** (city) Broward County	23,851
North Carolina	27,433	Riverside County, CA	21,258	**Miami Beach, FL** (city) Miami-Dade County	24,321
Indiana	27,473	San Bernardino County, CA	22,857	**Queens, NY** (borough) Queens County	26,172
Illinois	28,486	Lee County, FL	23,126	**Bronx, NY** (borough) Bronx County	26,308
Oregon	29,313	Dallas County, TX	23,286	**San Jose, CA** (city) Santa Clara County	26,994
Louisiana	30,301	Clark County, NV	23,624	**Hempstead (town), NY** (town) Nassau County	29,318

Note: (1) Ranking tables cover all states and counties, and places with an overall population of at least 125,000, OR an overall population of at least 25,000 where the Hispanic/Latino population is at least 20% of the overall population. In states where less than five places meet either of these criteria, we have included places with at least 10,000 total population with the highest percentage of Hispanic/Latino population. These places are identified with an asterisk (*); Please refer to the User's Guide for a full explanation of data.

Per Capita Income

(2010 Inflation-Adjusted Dollars)

South American: Bolivian

Top 10 States, Counties, and Places[1]

Sorted by Percent in Descending Order — U.S. = $23,689

State	Dollars	County	Dollars	Place	Dollars
Illinois	28,751	Cook County, IL	50,166	**Springfield, VA** (cdp) Fairfax County	28,005
Texas	28,200	San Diego County, CA	39,471	**Providence, RI** (city) Providence County	24,061
California	26,318	Santa Clara County, CA	26,525	**New York, NY** (city)	23,984
New York	25,868	Montgomery County, MD	25,419	**Queens, NY** (borough) Queens County	21,012
Maryland	24,989	Orange County, CA	24,501	**Los Angeles, CA** (city) Los Angeles County	20,830
New Jersey	24,939	Los Angeles County, CA	24,150	**Arlington, VA** (cdp) Arlington County	20,421
Pennsylvania	23,676	Harris County, TX	23,487	**Annandale, VA** (cdp) Fairfax County	19,333
Florida	21,657	Miami-Dade County, FL	23,114	**Dale City, VA** (cdp) Prince William County	19,027
Virginia	21,401	Fairfax County, VA	22,310	**West Falls Church, VA** (cdp) Fairfax County	17,925
Rhode Island	21,237	Broward County, FL	22,178		

Sorted by Percent in Ascending Order — U.S. = $23,689

State	Dollars	County	Dollars	Place	Dollars
North Carolina	20,401	Palm Beach County, FL	18,252	**West Falls Church, VA** (cdp) Fairfax County	17,925
Massachusetts	20,557	Prince William County, VA	19,012	**Dale City, VA** (cdp) Prince William County	19,027
Rhode Island	21,237	Arlington County, VA	20,421	**Annandale, VA** (cdp) Fairfax County	19,333
Virginia	21,401	Queens County, NY	21,012	**Arlington, VA** (cdp) Arlington County	20,421
Florida	21,657	Providence County, RI	21,237	**Los Angeles, CA** (city) Los Angeles County	20,830
Pennsylvania	23,676	Loudoun County, VA	21,365	**Queens, NY** (borough) Queens County	21,012
New Jersey	24,939	Prince George's County, MD	21,813	**New York, NY** (city)	23,984
Maryland	24,989	Broward County, FL	22,178	**Providence, RI** (city) Providence County	24,061
New York	25,868	Fairfax County, VA	22,310	**Springfield, VA** (cdp) Fairfax County	28,005
California	26,318	Miami-Dade County, FL	23,114		

Note: (1) Ranking tables cover all states and counties, and places with an overall population of at least 125,000, OR an overall population of at least 25,000 where the Hispanic/Latino population is at least 20% of the overall population. In states where less than five places meet either of these criteria, we have included places with at least 10,000 total population with the highest percentage of Hispanic/Latino population. These places are identified with an asterisk (*); Please refer to the User's Guide for a full explanation of data.

Per Capita Income

(2010 Inflation-Adjusted Dollars)

South American: Chilean

Top 10 States, Counties, and Places[1]

Sorted by Percent in Descending Order — U.S. = $26,551

State	Dollars	County	Dollars	Place	Dollars
Connecticut	41,280	Westchester County, NY	39,240	**Chicago, IL** (city) Cook County	36,486
Ohio	29,290	New York County, NY	35,808	**Manhattan, NY** (borough) New York County	35,808
Massachusetts	29,118	Cook County, IL	31,828	**Miami, FL** (city) Miami-Dade County	32,319
New York	28,508	San Mateo County, CA	31,824	**Los Angeles, CA** (city) Los Angeles County	29,133
California	28,387	Fairfax County, VA	31,407	**New York, NY** (city)	27,395
Michigan	28,373	Suffolk County, NY	31,297	**Queens, NY** (borough) Queens County	26,199
Illinois	27,126	Santa Clara County, CA	30,648	**Hempstead (town), NY** (town) Nassau County	25,840
Virginia	27,103	Los Angeles County, CA	30,004	**Brooklyn, NY** (borough) Kings County	20,862
Minnesota	26,968	Riverside County, CA	28,738	**Kendall, FL** (cdp) Miami-Dade County	14,331
Maryland	26,458	Middlesex County, MA	27,515		

Sorted by Percent in Ascending Order — U.S. = $26,551

State	Dollars	County	Dollars	Place	Dollars
Georgia	18,956	Utah County, UT	14,904	**Kendall, FL** (cdp) Miami-Dade County	14,331
Wisconsin	19,033	San Bernardino County, CA	18,998	**Brooklyn, NY** (borough) Kings County	20,862
Colorado	19,057	Clark County, NV	20,568	**Hempstead (town), NY** (town) Nassau County	25,840
Utah	19,214	Salt Lake County, UT	20,723	**Queens, NY** (borough) Queens County	26,199
Tennessee	20,508	Kings County, NY	20,862	**New York, NY** (city)	27,395
Nevada	21,739	San Diego County, CA	21,294	**Los Angeles, CA** (city) Los Angeles County	29,133
Missouri	22,335	Palm Beach County, FL	22,488	**Miami, FL** (city) Miami-Dade County	32,319
North Carolina	22,442	Orange County, CA	22,802	**Manhattan, NY** (borough) New York County	35,808
Washington	23,032	Maricopa County, AZ	24,875	**Chicago, IL** (city) Cook County	36,486
Arizona	23,441	Miami-Dade County, FL	25,003		

RANKINGS & COMPARISONS

Note: (1) Ranking tables cover all states and counties, and places with an overall population of at least 125,000, OR an overall population of at least 25,000 where the Hispanic/Latino population is at least 20% of the overall population. In states where less than five places meet either of these criteria, we have included places with at least 10,000 total population with the highest percentage of Hispanic/Latino population. These places are identified with an asterisk (*); Please refer to the User's Guide for a full explanation of data.

Per Capita Income

(2010 Inflation-Adjusted Dollars)

South American: Colombian

Top 10 States, Counties, and Places[1]

Sorted by Percent in Descending Order — U.S. = $21,619

State	Dollars	County	Dollars	Place	Dollars
District of Columbia	46,951	New York County, NY	39,494	**Manhattan, NY** (borough) New York County	39,494
Michigan	27,832	Bucks County, PA	38,037	**Arlington, VA** (cdp) Arlington County	37,556
Virginia	27,687	Arlington County, VA	37,556	**San Jose, CA** (city) Santa Clara County	36,323
Alabama	26,829	Alameda County, CA	36,743	**San Francisco, CA** (city) San Francisco County	34,495
Missouri	26,604	Sacramento County, CA	36,506	**Coral Gables, FL** (city) Miami-Dade County	34,020
California	26,558	Fairfax County, VA	35,872	**San Diego, CA** (city) San Diego County	33,968
Alaska	26,068	Saint Louis County, MO	35,155	**Huntington, NY** (town) Suffolk County	33,048
Maryland	25,443	Oakland County, MI	34,602	**Aventura, FL** (city) Miami-Dade County	32,714
Wisconsin	25,388	San Francisco County, CA	34,495	**Linden, NJ** (city) Union County	31,097
Iowa	24,977	Santa Clara County, CA	33,769	**Englewood, NJ** (city) Bergen County	29,076

Sorted by Percent in Ascending Order — U.S. = $21,619

State	Dollars	County	Dollars	Place	Dollars
Delaware	13,879	Leon County, FL	8,261	**Tallahassee, FL** (city) Leon County	7,458
Utah	14,706	Berks County, PA	11,896	**Hialeah, FL** (city) Miami-Dade County	12,996
South Carolina	16,604	Hall County, GA	13,285	**Buenaventura Lakes, FL** (cdp) Osceola County	13,034
Nevada	16,740	Greenville County, SC	13,431	**Indianapolis, IN** (city) Marion County	13,401
Tennessee	16,853	Luzerne County, PA	13,911	**Greenacres, FL** (city) Palm Beach County	13,697
Oklahoma	16,976	Lake County, FL	14,216	**Miami Gardens, FL** (city) Miami-Dade County	14,444
Rhode Island	17,040	Hampden County, MA	14,413	**Meadow Woods, FL** (cdp) Orange County	14,764
New Mexico	17,539	Pasco County, FL	15,052	**Carrollwood, FL** (cdp) Hillsborough County	14,927
Indiana	17,866	Marion County, IN	15,275	**Passaic, NJ** (city) Passaic County	14,934
Washington	18,929	Osceola County, FL	15,349	**Town 'n' Country, FL** (cdp) Hillsborough County	15,013

Note: (1) Ranking tables cover all states and counties, and places with an overall population of at least 125,000, OR an overall population of at least 25,000 where the Hispanic/Latino population is at least 20% of the overall population. In states where less than five places meet either of these criteria, we have included places with at least 10,000 total population with the highest percentage of Hispanic/Latino population. These places are identified with an asterisk (*); Please refer to the User's Guide for a full explanation of data.

Per Capita Income

(2010 Inflation-Adjusted Dollars)

South American: Ecuadorian

Top 10 States, Counties, and Places[1]

Sorted by Percent in Descending Order — U.S. = $18,651

State	Dollars	County	Dollars	Place	Dollars
Colorado	28,716	Santa Clara County, CA	31,339	**Miami, FL** (city) Miami-Dade County	37,845
Virginia	25,717	Fairfax County, VA	30,549	**Oyster Bay, NY** (town) Nassau County	30,007
California	24,641	Orange County, CA	29,628	**Sunrise, FL** (city) Broward County	25,463
Maryland	23,065	Orange County, NY	28,514	**Los Angeles, CA** (city) Los Angeles County	25,363
Ohio	22,618	Riverside County, CA	27,675	**Doral, FL** (city) Miami-Dade County	24,566
Iowa	21,870	Monmouth County, NJ	27,559	**Houston, TX** (city) Harris County	24,071
Kansas	21,807	Gwinnett County, GA	27,336	**Paterson, NJ** (city) Passaic County	23,297
Michigan	21,475	Prince George's County, MD	27,310	**Clifton, NJ** (city) Passaic County	23,241
Arizona	20,878	Montgomery County, MD	26,960	**North Hempstead, NY** (town) Nassau County	22,901
Florida	20,673	Burlington County, NJ	25,882	**Staten Island, NY** (borough) Richmond County	22,597

Sorted by Percent in Ascending Order — U.S. = $18,651

State	Dollars	County	Dollars	Place	Dollars
Wisconsin	11,029	Delaware County, PA	11,703	**Spring Valley, NY** (village) Rockland County	10,934
Oklahoma	12,331	Pinellas County, FL	12,276	**Allentown, PA** (city) Lehigh County	11,869
Utah	13,416	Camden County, NJ	12,476	**Minneapolis, MN** (city) Hennepin County	12,119
Indiana	13,651	Hennepin County, MN	12,594	**Ossining, NY** (village) Westchester County	12,480
Minnesota	13,914	Lehigh County, PA	13,038	**Ramapo, NY** (town) Rockland County	12,584
Pennsylvania	15,479	Clark County, NV	14,099	**Norwalk, CT** (city/town) Fairfield County	12,751
South Carolina	16,291	Philadelphia County, PA	14,210	**Ossining, NY** (town) Westchester County	12,859
Nevada	16,485	Tarrant County, TX	14,311	**Orlando, FL** (city) Orange County	13,243
North Carolina	16,921	Worcester County, MA	14,796	**Hialeah, FL** (city) Miami-Dade County	13,399
New York	17,129	Westchester County, NY	14,810	**White Plains, NY** (city) Westchester County	13,852

Note: (1) Ranking tables cover all states and counties, and places with an overall population of at least 125,000, OR an overall population of at least 25,000 where the Hispanic/Latino population is at least 20% of the overall population. In states where less than five places meet either of these criteria, we have included places with at least 10,000 total population with the highest percentage of Hispanic/Latino population. These places are identified with an asterisk (*); Please refer to the User's Guide for a full explanation of data.

Per Capita Income

(2010 Inflation-Adjusted Dollars)

South American: Paraguayan

Top 10 States, Counties, and Places[1]

Sorted by Percent in Descending Order — U.S. = $23,507

State	Dollars	County	Dollars	Place	Dollars
California	51,943	Queens County, NY	21,223	**New York, NY** (city)	22,909
Texas	27,563	Westchester County, NY	14,897	**Queens, NY** (borough) Queens County	21,223
Maryland	23,514				
New Jersey	23,059				
Florida	22,271				
New York	21,045				

Sorted by Percent in Ascending Order — U.S. = $23,507

State	Dollars	County	Dollars	Place	Dollars
New York	21,045	Westchester County, NY	14,897	**Queens, NY** (borough) Queens County	21,223
Florida	22,271	Queens County, NY	21,223	**New York, NY** (city)	22,909
New Jersey	23,059				
Maryland	23,514				
Texas	27,563				
California	51,943				

Note: (1) Ranking tables cover all states and counties, and places with an overall population of at least 125,000, OR an overall population of at least 25,000 where the Hispanic/Latino population is at least 20% of the overall population. In states where less than five places meet either of these criteria, we have included places with at least 10,000 total population with the highest percentage of Hispanic/Latino population. These places are identified with an asterisk (*); Please refer to the User's Guide for a full explanation of data.

Per Capita Income

(2010 Inflation-Adjusted Dollars)

South American: Peruvian

Top 10 States, Counties, and Places[1]

Sorted by Percent in Descending Order — U.S. = $21,529

State	Dollars	County	Dollars	Place	Dollars
District of Columbia	46,300	New York County, NY	49,219	**Manhattan, NY** (borough) New York County	49,219
Michigan	32,978	Denver County, CO	34,323	**Denver, CO** (city) Denver County	34,323
Kansas	26,063	Fort Bend County, TX	33,805	**Oyster Bay, NY** (town) Nassau County	34,225
Missouri	25,585	San Diego County, CA	33,372	**Doral, FL** (city) Miami-Dade County	32,804
Maryland	25,412	San Francisco County, CA	32,177	**San Francisco, CA** (city) San Francisco County	32,177
Illinois	24,484	Fulton County, GA	31,435	**North Bergen, NJ** (township) Hudson County	31,454
Tennessee	24,214	Ventura County, CA	31,151	**San Diego, CA** (city) San Diego County	31,122
Virginia	23,740	Arlington County, VA	29,590	**Arlington, VA** (cdp) Arlington County	29,590
Louisiana	23,255	Denton County, TX	28,952	**Weston, FL** (city) Broward County	29,564
New York	23,113	Morris County, NJ	27,504	**Kendall, FL** (cdp) Miami-Dade County	29,558

Sorted by Percent in Ascending Order — U.S. = $21,529

State	Dollars	County	Dollars	Place	Dollars
Delaware	11,992	Sarasota County, FL	12,703	**Garland, TX** (city) Dallas County	13,483
Idaho	12,331	Utah County, UT	13,805	**Bloomfield, NJ** (township) Essex County	13,672
Kentucky	14,416	San Joaquin County, CA	13,964	**West New York, NJ** (town) Hudson County	13,995
Oklahoma	14,747	Atlantic County, NJ	14,612	**Kendall West, FL** (cdp) Miami-Dade County	14,301
Rhode Island	15,110	Suffolk County, MA	15,578	**West Valley City, UT** (city) Salt Lake County	14,327
Utah	15,972	Philadelphia County, PA	15,798	**Anaheim, CA** (city) Orange County	14,790
South Carolina	17,385	Solano County, CA	15,834	**Hollywood, FL** (city) Broward County	14,803
New Mexico	17,881	Osceola County, FL	15,948	**Cape Coral, FL** (city) Lee County	14,993
Indiana	18,017	Wake County, NC	16,194	**Sunrise, FL** (city) Broward County	15,180
North Carolina	18,442	Collin County, TX	16,332	**Fountainebleau, FL** (cdp) Miami-Dade County	15,183

RANKINGS & COMPARISONS

Note: (1) Ranking tables cover all states and counties, and places with an overall population of at least 125,000, OR an overall population of at least 25,000 where the Hispanic/Latino population is at least 20% of the overall population. In states where less than five places meet either of these criteria, we have included places with at least 10,000 total population with the highest percentage of Hispanic/Latino population. These places are identified with an asterisk (*); Please refer to the User's Guide for a full explanation of data.

Per Capita Income

(2010 Inflation-Adjusted Dollars)

South American: Uruguayan

Top 10 States, Counties, and Places[1]

Sorted by Percent in Descending Order — U.S. = $22,297

State	Dollars	County	Dollars	Place	Dollars
Maryland	32,692	Los Angeles County, CA	32,989	**New York, NY** (city)	29,413
California	28,701	Middlesex County, NJ	28,146	**Queens, NY** (borough) Queens County	26,517
New York	26,543	Queens County, NY	26,517	**Elizabeth, NJ** (city) Union County	13,682
Texas	22,984	Broward County, FL	25,212		
New Jersey	21,575	Hudson County, NJ	24,380		
Massachusetts	20,481	Harris County, TX	22,910		
Florida	19,246	Palm Beach County, FL	22,405		
Virginia	19,123	Union County, NJ	20,934		
Georgia	18,823	Essex County, NJ	19,451		
Pennsylvania	18,203	Gwinnett County, GA	18,730		

Sorted by Percent in Ascending Order — U.S. = $22,297

State	Dollars	County	Dollars	Place	Dollars
Pennsylvania	18,203	Worcester County, MA	14,791	**Elizabeth, NJ** (city) Union County	13,682
Georgia	18,823	Miami-Dade County, FL	16,164	**Queens, NY** (borough) Queens County	26,517
Virginia	19,123	Westchester County, NY	17,766	**New York, NY** (city)	29,413
Florida	19,246	Morris County, NJ	18,417		
Massachusetts	20,481	Gwinnett County, GA	18,730		
New Jersey	21,575	Essex County, NJ	19,451		
Texas	22,984	Union County, NJ	20,934		
New York	26,543	Palm Beach County, FL	22,405		
California	28,701	Harris County, TX	22,910		
Maryland	32,692	Hudson County, NJ	24,380		

Note: (1) Ranking tables cover all states and counties, and places with an overall population of at least 125,000, OR an overall population of at least 25,000 where the Hispanic/Latino population is at least 20% of the overall population. In states where less than five places meet either of these criteria, we have included places with at least 10,000 total population with the highest percentage of Hispanic/Latino population. These places are identified with an asterisk (*); Please refer to the User's Guide for a full explanation of data.

Per Capita Income

(2010 Inflation-Adjusted Dollars)

South American: Venezuelan

Top 10 States, Counties, and Places[1]

Sorted by Percent in Descending Order — U.S. = $24,842

State	Dollars	County	Dollars	Place	Dollars
Maryland	35,750	New York County, NY	62,922	**Manhattan, NY** (borough) New York County	62,922
New York	32,560	Middlesex County, MA	41,517	**Hollywood, FL** (city) Broward County	38,939
Wisconsin	32,441	San Diego County, CA	39,992	**New York, NY** (city)	33,107
Colorado	31,068	Dallas County, TX	37,863	**Houston, TX** (city) Harris County	31,132
Ohio	30,199	Fulton County, GA	34,918	**Aventura, FL** (city) Miami-Dade County	30,987
Texas	29,850	King County, WA	34,574	**The Hammocks, FL** (cdp) Miami-Dade County	30,743
Massachusetts	29,610	Montgomery County, MD	31,764	**Miami Beach, FL** (city) Miami-Dade County	29,829
California	28,297	Fort Bend County, TX	31,367	**Brooklyn, NY** (borough) Kings County	26,713
Washington	27,342	Tarrant County, TX	31,149	**Doral, FL** (city) Miami-Dade County	25,258
Louisiana	27,121	Travis County, TX	31,052	**Pembroke Pines, FL** (city) Broward County	24,646

Sorted by Percent in Ascending Order — U.S. = $24,842

State	Dollars	County	Dollars	Place	Dollars
Utah	14,811	Lee County, FL	11,672	**Kendall West, FL** (cdp) Miami-Dade County	14,198
Arizona	18,831	Osceola County, FL	12,596	**Hialeah, FL** (city) Miami-Dade County	16,014
Oklahoma	19,811	Salt Lake County, UT	16,205	**Tamiami, FL** (cdp) Miami-Dade County	16,469
North Carolina	20,324	Fairfield County, CT	17,442	**Fountainebleau, FL** (cdp) Miami-Dade County	16,734
Indiana	21,303	Bronx County, NY	17,695	**Coral Springs, FL** (city) Broward County	17,265
Florida	22,055	Orange County, FL	18,964	**Bronx, NY** (borough) Bronx County	17,695
South Carolina	22,518	Gwinnett County, GA	19,276	**Country Club, FL** (cdp) Miami-Dade County	19,850
Missouri	22,619	Suffolk County, MA	19,843	**Miramar, FL** (city) Broward County	20,814
Pennsylvania	23,626	Seminole County, FL	20,122	**Weston, FL** (city) Broward County	21,513
Michigan	23,858	Hillsborough County, FL	21,420	**Kendall, FL** (cdp) Miami-Dade County	21,572

Note: (1) Ranking tables cover all states and counties, and places with an overall population of at least 125,000, OR an overall population of at least 25,000 where the Hispanic/Latino population is at least 20% of the overall population. In states where less than five places meet either of these criteria, we have included places with at least 10,000 total population with the highest percentage of Hispanic/Latino population. These places are identified with an asterisk (*); Please refer to the User's Guide for a full explanation of data.

Per Capita Income

(2010 Inflation-Adjusted Dollars)

Spaniard

Top 10 States, Counties, and Places[1]

Sorted by Percent in Descending Order — U.S. = $27,912

State	Dollars	County	Dollars	Place	Dollars
District of Columbia	59,812	Morris County, NJ	63,777	**San Francisco, CA** (city) San Francisco County	54,164
Connecticut	43,980	Fairfax County, VA	60,474	**Manhattan, NY** (borough) New York County	53,800
Maryland	43,673	Montgomery County, MD	55,614	**Miami, FL** (city) Miami-Dade County	46,309
Virginia	40,112	San Francisco County, CA	54,164	**Oyster Bay, NY** (town) Nassau County	45,473
New Jersey	36,544	New York County, NY	53,800	**Philadelphia, PA** (city) Philadelphia County	40,822
Massachusetts	35,869	Fairfield County, CT	49,059	**New York, NY** (city)	39,604
New York	35,721	Ventura County, CA	48,308	**Staten Island, NY** (borough) Richmond County	37,848
Pennsylvania	32,732	Bergen County, NJ	46,233	**Dallas, TX** (city) Dallas County	36,979
Alabama	31,752	Montgomery County, PA	45,734	**Riverside, CA** (city) Riverside County	36,896
Florida	31,036	Union County, NJ	44,524	**North Las Vegas, NV** (city) Clark County	36,666

Sorted by Percent in Ascending Order — U.S. = $27,912

State	Dollars	County	Dollars	Place	Dollars
South Carolina	15,068	Utah County, UT	10,914	**San Bernardino, CA** (city) San Bernardino County	14,310
Oklahoma	16,167	Butte County, CA	11,911	**Las Cruces, NM** (city) Dona Ana County	16,774
Mississippi	17,106	Milwaukee County, WI	12,756	**Pueblo, CO** (city) Pueblo County	17,069
Wyoming	17,665	La Plata County, CO	14,764	**Rio Rancho, NM** (city) Sandoval County	17,583
Maine	18,488	Conejos County, CO	14,809	**Glendale, AZ** (city) Maricopa County	18,041
Nebraska	19,350	San Miguel County, NM	14,848	**South Valley, NM** (cdp) Bernalillo County	18,475
Missouri	19,602	Hawaii County, HI	17,041	**Lubbock, TX** (city) Lubbock County	19,350
Arkansas	20,307	Pueblo County, CO	17,199	**Paradise, NV** (cdp) Clark County	19,682
Hawaii	20,648	Cibola County, NM	17,717	**Oklahoma City, OK** (city) Oklahoma County	20,000
Wisconsin	20,887	Lubbock County, TX	17,723	**Lakewood, CO** (city) Jefferson County	20,463

Note: (1) Ranking tables cover all states and counties, and places with an overall population of at least 125,000, OR an overall population of at least 25,000 where the Hispanic/Latino population is at least 20% of the overall population. In states where less than five places meet either of these criteria, we have included places with at least 10,000 total population with the highest percentage of Hispanic/Latino population. These places are identified with an asterisk (*); Please refer to the User's Guide for a full explanation of data.

Households with $100,000+ Income

Total Population

Top 10 States, Counties, and Places[1]

Sorted by Number in Descending Order — U.S. = 23,850,374

State	Number	County	Number	Place	Number
California	3,458,070	Los Angeles County, CA	803,223	**New York, NY** (city)	696,100
New York	1,806,762	Cook County, IL	445,049	**Los Angeles, CA** (city) Los Angeles County	290,386
Texas	1,699,243	Orange County, CA	354,427	**Manhattan, NY** (borough) New York County	257,814
Florida	1,253,066	Maricopa County, AZ	308,858	**Chicago, IL** (city) Cook County	200,080
Illinois	1,094,563	Harris County, TX	304,421	**Queens, NY** (borough) Queens County	171,703
New Jersey	1,059,839	San Diego County, CA	302,695	**Brooklyn, NY** (borough) Kings County	162,415
Pennsylvania	938,986	Santa Clara County, CA	261,505	**Houston, TX** (city) Harris County	136,800
Virginia	821,409	New York County, NY	257,814	**San Diego, CA** (city) San Diego County	135,967
Massachusetts	749,692	King County, WA	248,486	**San Francisco, CA** (city) San Francisco County	122,778
Ohio	743,956	Middlesex County, MA	216,117	**San Jose, CA** (city) Santa Clara County	117,807

Sorted by Number in Ascending Order — U.S. = 23,850,374

State	Number	County	Number	Place	Number
North Dakota	40,309	Kenedy County, TX	0	**Fort Campbell North*, KY** (cdp) Christian County	13
South Dakota	41,726	Harding County, NM	17	**Parker*, SC** (cdp) Greenville County	81
Wyoming	41,945	Terrell County, TX	21	**San Luis, AZ** (city) Yuma County	92
Vermont	45,541	Briscoe County, TX	23	**Jerome*, ID** (city) Jerome County	118
Montana	52,469	Kent County, TX	31	**Fort Leonard Wood*, MO** (cdp) Pulaski County	138
Alaska	71,518	Hudspeth County, TX	33	**Hope*, AR** (city) Hempstead County	158
District of Columbia	76,064	Cottle County, TX	34	**Berea*, SC** (cdp) Greenville County	163
Delaware	77,739	Wheeler County, GA	39	**Florence, AZ** (town) Pinal County	179
Idaho	77,992	Motley County, TX	42	**Fort Hood, TX** (cdp) Bell County	192
West Virginia	78,855	Real County, TX	43	**Burley*, ID** (city) Cassia County	196

Sorted by Percent in Descending Order — U.S. = 20.9%

State	Percent	County	Percent	Place	Percent
New Jersey	33.4	Loudoun County, VA	59.1	**Eastvale, CA** (cdp) Riverside County	53.6
Maryland	33.0	Fairfax County, VA	53.2	**Chino Hills, CA** (city) San Bernardino County	52.8
Connecticut	31.6	Los Alamos County, NM	52.7	**Huntington, NY** (town) Suffolk County	52.3
Massachusetts	29.8	Howard County, MD	51.7	**Oyster Bay, NY** (town) Nassau County	52.0
District of Columbia	29.6	Hunterdon County, NJ	50.5	**Moorpark, CA** (city) Ventura County	51.4
Hawaii	28.9	Douglas County, CO	49.5	**Naperville, IL** (city) DuPage County	51.0
Alaska	28.8	Somerset County, NJ	48.7	**North Hempstead, NY** (town) Nassau County	50.5
California	27.9	Morris County, NJ	48.4	**Thousand Oaks, CA** (city) Ventura County	49.4
Virginia	27.6	Arlington County, VA	47.4	**Fremont, CA** (city) Alameda County	48.2
New Hampshire	26.5	Montgomery County, MD	46.9	**Arlington, VA** (cdp) Arlington County	47.4

Sorted by Percent in Ascending Order — U.S. = 20.9%

State	Percent	County	Percent	Place	Percent
West Virginia	10.6	Kenedy County, TX	0.0	**Fort Campbell North*, KY** (cdp) Christian County	0.5
Arkansas	11.7	Wheeler County, GA	2.3	**San Luis, AZ** (city) Yuma County	1.5
Mississippi	12.0	Shannon County, SD	2.4	**Parker*, SC** (cdp) Greenville County	2.0
Montana	13.1	Bledsoe County, TN	2.5	**Fort Hood, TX** (cdp) Bell County	2.9
South Dakota	13.2	Hudspeth County, TX	3.1	**University, FL** (cdp) Hillsborough County	3.1
Kentucky	13.3	Hancock County, GA	3.2	**Berea*, SC** (cdp) Greenville County	3.2
Idaho	13.7	Holmes County, MS	3.2	**Jerome*, ID** (city) Jerome County	3.2
Oklahoma	13.8	Long County, GA	3.2	**Reading, PA** (city) Berks County	3.8
Tennessee	14.3	Real County, TX	3.2	**York, PA** (city) York County	3.9
Alabama	14.5	Ripley County, MO	3.3	**West Little River, FL** (cdp) Miami-Dade County	4.5

Note: (1) Ranking tables cover all states and counties, and places with an overall population of at least 125,000, OR an overall population of at least 25,000 where the Hispanic/Latino population is at least 20% of the overall population. In states where less than five places meet either of these criteria, we have included places with at least 10,000 total population with the highest percentage of Hispanic/Latino population. These places are identified with an asterisk (*); Please refer to the User's Guide for a full explanation of data.

Households with $100,000+ Income

Hispanic or Latino (of any race)

Top 10 States, Counties, and Places[1]

Sorted by Number in Descending Order — U.S. = 1,605,309

State	Number	County	Number	Place	Number
California	510,555	Los Angeles County, CA	163,730	**New York, NY** (city)	81,398
Texas	229,010	Miami-Dade County, FL	78,567	**Los Angeles, CA** (city) Los Angeles County	50,371
Florida	163,881	Orange County, CA	46,316	**Queens, NY** (borough) Queens County	28,292
New York	136,343	Harris County, TX	40,385	**San Antonio, TX** (city) Bexar County	23,285
New Jersey	74,933	Cook County, IL	38,429	**Chicago, IL** (city) Cook County	22,452
Illinois	64,807	San Diego County, CA	37,696	**Houston, TX** (city) Harris County	17,779
Arizona	47,552	San Bernardino County, CA	35,466	**San Jose, CA** (city) Santa Clara County	16,570
Virginia	35,206	Riverside County, CA	32,853	**Manhattan, NY** (borough) New York County	16,194
Colorado	28,544	Maricopa County, AZ	30,673	**Bronx, NY** (borough) Bronx County	16,109
New Mexico	27,912	Bexar County, TX	30,388	**Brooklyn, NY** (borough) Kings County	15,288

Sorted by Number in Ascending Order — U.S. = 1,605,309

State	Number	County	Number	Place	Number
South Dakota	246	Adair County, OK	0	**Berea*, SC** (cdp) Greenville County	0
Maine	324	Ashe County, NC	0	**Fort Campbell North*, KY** (cdp) Christian County	0
North Dakota	341	Barbour County, AL	0	**Fort Hood, TX** (cdp) Bell County	0
Montana	413	Beaver County, UT	0	**Hope*, AR** (city) Hempstead County	0
Vermont	589	Becker County, MN	0	**Muscatine*, IA** (city) Muscatine County	0
West Virginia	675	Belmont County, OH	0	**Shelbyville*, KY** (city) Shelby County	0
Wyoming	1,637	Bent County, CO	0	**Warr Acres*, OK** (city) Oklahoma County	0
Mississippi	1,674	Benzie County, MI	0	**York, PA** (city) York County	1
New Hampshire	1,761	Bladen County, NC	0	**Portland*, ME** (city) Cumberland County	6
Alaska	1,920	Blaine County, OK	0	**Minot*, ND** (city) Ward County	7

Sorted by Percent in Descending Order — U.S. = 12.5%

State	Percent	County	Percent	Place	Percent
Maryland	23.9	Union County, FL	92.6	**Eastvale, CA** (cdp) Riverside County	49.9
Virginia	23.3	Calvert County, MD	63.4	**Oyster Bay, NY** (town) Nassau County	48.9
District of Columbia	22.9	Harris County, GA	53.3	**Chino Hills, CA** (city) San Bernardino County	45.6
Vermont	21.9	Marlboro County, SC	53.0	**Diamond Bar, CA** (city) Los Angeles County	44.5
Alaska	19.1	Marion County, WV	51.7	**Cooper City, FL** (city) Broward County	39.8
Hawaii	19.1	Newton County, TX	50.0	**Springfield, VA** (cdp) Fairfax County	39.8
New Hampshire	18.6	Miami County, KS	48.8	**Moorpark, CA** (city) Ventura County	39.2
New Jersey	17.8	Delaware County, OH	48.6	**Camarillo, CA** (city) Ventura County	37.7
California	15.5	Hunterdon County, NJ	44.7	**Coral Gables, FL** (city) Miami-Dade County	37.4
Connecticut	14.0	McPherson County, KS	44.5	**Weston, FL** (city) Broward County	37.4

Sorted by Percent in Ascending Order — U.S. = 12.5%

State	Percent	County	Percent	Place	Percent
South Dakota	4.9	Adair County, OK	0.0	**Berea*, SC** (cdp) Greenville County	0.0
Arkansas	5.4	Ashe County, NC	0.0	**Fort Campbell North*, KY** (cdp) Christian County	0.0
Montana	5.5	Barbour County, AL	0.0	**Fort Hood, TX** (cdp) Bell County	0.0
Nebraska	5.5	Beaver County, UT	0.0	**Hope*, AR** (city) Hempstead County	0.0
Oklahoma	6.0	Becker County, MN	0.0	**Muscatine*, IA** (city) Muscatine County	0.0
Idaho	6.3	Belmont County, OH	0.0	**Shelbyville*, KY** (city) Shelby County	0.0
Iowa	6.8	Bent County, CO	0.0	**Warr Acres*, OK** (city) Oklahoma County	0.0
North Carolina	6.8	Benzie County, MI	0.0	**York, PA** (city) York County	0.0
Maine	7.3	Bladen County, NC	0.0	**Portland*, ME** (city) Cumberland County	0.8
Rhode Island	7.6	Blaine County, OK	0.0	**Marshalltown, IA** (city) Marshall County	1.2

Note: (1) Ranking tables cover all states and counties, and places with an overall population of at least 125,000, OR an overall population of at least 25,000 where the Hispanic/Latino population is at least 20% of the overall population. In states where less than five places meet either of these criteria, we have included places with at least 10,000 total population with the highest percentage of Hispanic/Latino population. These places are identified with an asterisk (*); Please refer to the User's Guide for a full explanation of data.

Households with $100,000+ Income

Central American, excluding Mexican

Top 10 States, Counties, and Places[1]

Sorted by Number in Descending Order — U.S. = 126,726

State	Number	County	Number	Place	Number
California	43,083	Los Angeles County, CA	20,585	**Los Angeles, CA** (city) Los Angeles County	9,543
New York	13,503	Miami-Dade County, FL	6,690	**New York, NY** (city)	5,394
Florida	11,987	Montgomery County, MD	3,518	**Hempstead (town), NY** (town) Nassau County	2,263
Virginia	8,640	Fairfax County, VA	3,464	**Queens, NY** (borough) Queens County	2,078
Maryland	8,022	Suffolk County, NY	3,313	**Islip, NY** (town) Suffolk County	1,912
Texas	7,707	Nassau County, NY	3,137	**San Francisco, CA** (city) San Francisco County	1,855
New Jersey	6,340	Harris County, TX	2,916	**Brooklyn, NY** (borough) Kings County	1,524
Massachusetts	3,315	Prince George's County, MD	2,838	**Houston, TX** (city) Harris County	1,460
Illinois	2,690	San Bernardino County, CA	2,364	**Chicago, IL** (city) Cook County	1,035
Georgia	2,153	San Mateo County, CA	2,303	**San Jose, CA** (city) Santa Clara County	924

Sorted by Number in Ascending Order — U.S. = 126,726

State	Number	County	Number	Place	Number
South Dakota	0	Caroline County, MD	0	**Brandon, FL** (cdp) Hillsborough County	0
Vermont	0	Carroll County, AR	0	**Channelview, TX** (cdp) Harris County	0
West Virginia	0	Catawba County, NC	0	**Cincinnati, OH** (city) Hamilton County	0
Idaho	21	Clarke County, GA	0	**Clarksville, TN** (city) Montgomery County	0
Wyoming	25	Davidson County, NC	0	**Cleveland, OH** (city) Cuyahoga County	0
Maine	29	Dawson County, NE	0	**Colton, CA** (city) San Bernardino County	0
Alaska	66	DeKalb County, AL	0	**Delano, CA** (city) Kern County	0
New Hampshire	74	Floyd County, GA	0	**Deltona, FL** (city) Volusia County	0
Nebraska	88	Franklin County, AL	0	**Grand Island, NE** (city) Hall County	0
Hawaii	150	Franklin County, PA	0	**Greensboro, NC** (city) Guilford County	0

Sorted by Percent in Descending Order — U.S. = 12.0%

State	Percent	County	Percent	Place	Percent
Hawaii	21.0	Macomb County, MI	47.3	**Eastvale, CA** (cdp) Riverside County	70.8
Delaware	20.7	Douglas County, CO	47.1	**La Mirada, CA** (city) Los Angeles County	58.2
Virginia	18.9	Thurston County, WA	34.0	**Weston, FL** (city) Broward County	55.9
Maryland	18.7	Charles County, MD	33.8	**Hacienda Heights, CA** (cdp) Los Angeles County	48.7
Connecticut	15.5	Orange County, NY	33.8	**Chino, CA** (city) San Bernardino County	45.4
New York	15.1	Cumberland County, NJ	33.5	**Oyster Bay, NY** (town) Nassau County	42.5
New Jersey	14.8	Chester County, PA	32.5	**Lake Forest, CA** (city) Orange County	42.0
New Mexico	14.6	Will County, IL	32.3	**San Leandro, CA** (city) Alameda County	37.6
District of Columbia	14.5	Napa County, CA	31.8	**Chino Hills, CA** (city) San Bernardino County	36.5
Illinois	14.3	Rockwall County, TX	31.6	**Springfield, VA** (cdp) Fairfax County	36.4

Sorted by Percent in Ascending Order — U.S. = 12.0%

State	Percent	County	Percent	Place	Percent
South Dakota	0.0	Caroline County, MD	0.0	**Brandon, FL** (cdp) Hillsborough County	0.0
Vermont	0.0	Carroll County, AR	0.0	**Channelview, TX** (cdp) Harris County	0.0
West Virginia	0.0	Catawba County, NC	0.0	**Cincinnati, OH** (city) Hamilton County	0.0
Nebraska	2.0	Clarke County, GA	0.0	**Clarksville, TN** (city) Montgomery County	0.0
Idaho	2.7	Davidson County, NC	0.0	**Cleveland, OH** (city) Cuyahoga County	0.0
Arkansas	2.8	Dawson County, NE	0.0	**Colton, CA** (city) San Bernardino County	0.0
Oklahoma	4.3	DeKalb County, AL	0.0	**Delano, CA** (city) Kern County	0.0
North Carolina	5.7	Floyd County, GA	0.0	**Deltona, FL** (city) Volusia County	0.0
Kansas	6.0	Franklin County, AL	0.0	**Grand Island, NE** (city) Hall County	0.0
Utah	6.3	Franklin County, PA	0.0	**Greensboro, NC** (city) Guilford County	0.0

RANKINGS & COMPARISONS

Note: (1) Ranking tables cover all states and counties, and places with an overall population of at least 125,000, OR an overall population of at least 25,000 where the Hispanic/Latino population is at least 20% of the overall population. In states where less than five places meet either of these criteria, we have included places with at least 10,000 total population with the highest percentage of Hispanic/Latino population. These places are identified with an asterisk (*); Please refer to the User's Guide for a full explanation of data.

Households with $100,000+ Income

Central American: Costa Rican

Top 10 States, Counties, and Places[1]

Sorted by Number in Descending Order — U.S. = 6,840

State	Number	County	Number	Place	Number
California	1,794	Los Angeles County, CA	594	**New York, NY** (city)	359
Florida	809	Miami-Dade County, FL	347	**Los Angeles, CA** (city) Los Angeles County	177
New Jersey	707	Orange County, CA	234	**Queens, NY** (borough) Queens County	162
New York	550	Contra Costa County, CA	164	**Brooklyn, NY** (borough) Kings County	93
Texas	469	Queens County, NY	162	**Philadelphia, PA** (city) Philadelphia County	71
Virginia	280	Broward County, FL	148	**Miami, FL** (city) Miami-Dade County	27
Pennsylvania	210	Morris County, NJ	131	**Bronx, NY** (borough) Bronx County	13
Georgia	203	Maricopa County, AZ	114		
Maryland	197	Somerset County, NJ	103		
Illinois	189	Cook County, IL	102		

Sorted by Number in Ascending Order — U.S. = 6,840

State	Number	County	Number	Place	Number
Wisconsin	20	Orange County, FL	0	**Bronx, NY** (borough) Bronx County	13
Michigan	27	Bronx County, NY	13	**Miami, FL** (city) Miami-Dade County	27
Tennessee	27	Clark County, NV	20	**Philadelphia, PA** (city) Philadelphia County	71
Nevada	45	Passaic County, NJ	23	**Brooklyn, NY** (borough) Kings County	93
Connecticut	63	Essex County, NJ	37	**Queens, NY** (borough) Queens County	162
Minnesota	64	Hillsborough County, FL	38	**Los Angeles, CA** (city) Los Angeles County	177
Oregon	69	Suffolk County, NY	42	**New York, NY** (city)	359
Washington	73	Mercer County, NJ	45		
South Carolina	85	Palm Beach County, FL	46		
Colorado	98	Fairfield County, CT	50		

Sorted by Percent in Descending Order — U.S. = 17.7%

State	Percent	County	Percent	Place	Percent
Virginia	42.7	Contra Costa County, CA	40.0	**Queens, NY** (borough) Queens County	25.6
Maryland	34.1	Orange County, CA	36.0	**Los Angeles, CA** (city) Los Angeles County	17.0
California	25.2	Morris County, NJ	30.8	**Philadelphia, PA** (city) Philadelphia County	15.3
Illinois	25.0	Nassau County, NY	30.8	**New York, NY** (city)	14.7
Minnesota	23.4	San Bernardino County, CA	26.3	**Brooklyn, NY** (borough) Kings County	9.4
Oregon	23.4	Queens County, NY	25.6	**Miami, FL** (city) Miami-Dade County	5.6
Colorado	21.9	Riverside County, CA	24.9	**Bronx, NY** (borough) Bronx County	3.3
Texas	21.6	Maricopa County, AZ	23.8		
Washington	21.0	Somerset County, NJ	21.5		
Arizona	20.0	Cook County, IL	19.8		

Sorted by Percent in Ascending Order — U.S. = 17.7%

State	Percent	County	Percent	Place	Percent
North Carolina	8.7	Orange County, FL	0.0	**Bronx, NY** (borough) Bronx County	3.3
Connecticut	8.9	Bronx County, NY	3.3	**Miami, FL** (city) Miami-Dade County	5.6
Tennessee	9.0	Passaic County, NJ	4.0	**Brooklyn, NY** (borough) Kings County	9.4
Nevada	10.0	Essex County, NJ	5.7	**New York, NY** (city)	14.7
Florida	12.4	Clark County, NV	6.0	**Philadelphia, PA** (city) Philadelphia County	15.3
Wisconsin	13.5	Union County, NJ	6.8	**Los Angeles, CA** (city) Los Angeles County	17.0
South Carolina	13.9	Hillsborough County, FL	7.8	**Queens, NY** (borough) Queens County	25.6
Massachusetts	14.1	Palm Beach County, FL	8.2		
New Jersey	14.1	Kings County, NY	9.4		
Michigan	14.6	Fairfield County, CT	12.1		

Note: (1) Ranking tables cover all states and counties, and places with an overall population of at least 125,000, OR an overall population of at least 25,000 where the Hispanic/Latino population is at least 20% of the overall population. In states where less than five places meet either of these criteria, we have included places with at least 10,000 total population with the highest percentage of Hispanic/Latino population. These places are identified with an asterisk (*); Please refer to the User's Guide for a full explanation of data.

Households with $100,000+ Income

Central American: Guatemalan

Top 10 States, Counties, and Places[1]

Sorted by Number in Descending Order — U.S. = 26,906

State	Number	County	Number	Place	Number
California	9,676	Los Angeles County, CA	5,368	**Los Angeles, CA** (city) Los Angeles County	2,581
New York	2,299	Cook County, IL	967	**New York, NY** (city)	971
Florida	2,029	San Bernardino County, CA	716	**Chicago, IL** (city) Cook County	652
New Jersey	1,282	Miami-Dade County, FL	685	**Queens, NY** (borough) Queens County	443
Illinois	1,270	Orange County, CA	619	**Providence, RI** (city) Providence County	369
Texas	1,215	Riverside County, CA	550	**Brooklyn, NY** (borough) Kings County	301
Maryland	1,192	Providence County, RI	540	**Islip, NY** (town) Suffolk County	288
Massachusetts	1,162	Prince George's County, MD	528	**Houston, TX** (city) Harris County	278
Virginia	1,092	Suffolk County, MA	472	**San Francisco, CA** (city) San Francisco County	261
Rhode Island	552	Suffolk County, NY	462	**Stamford, CT** (city/town) Fairfield County	255

Sorted by Number in Ascending Order — U.S. = 26,906

State	Number	County	Number	Place	Number
Idaho	0	Arapahoe County, CO	0	**Cincinnati, OH** (city) Hamilton County	0
South Dakota	0	Caroline County, MD	0	**Fort Worth, TX** (city) Tarrant County	0
New Hampshire	9	Cherokee County, GA	0	**Grand Island, NE** (city) Hall County	0
Mississippi	13	Dawson County, NE	0	**Indianapolis, IN** (city) Marion County	0
Nebraska	17	DeKalb County, AL	0	**Jersey City, NJ** (city) Hudson County	0
Wisconsin	30	Floyd County, GA	0	**Lawrence, MA** (city) Essex County	0
Indiana	36	Franklin County, AL	0	**Lexington*, NE** (city) Dawson County	0
Missouri	54	Gordon County, GA	0	**Pawtucket*, RI** (city) Providence County	0
Kansas	61	Hall County, NE	0	**Reno, NV** (city) Washoe County	0
Kentucky	62	Hillsborough County, FL	0	**Salt Lake City, UT** (city) Salt Lake County	0

Sorted by Percent in Descending Order — U.S. = 10.5%

State	Percent	County	Percent	Place	Percent
Delaware	30.4	Will County, IL	44.5	**Moreno Valley, CA** (city) Riverside County	38.5
Virginia	16.1	Lee County, AL	35.1	**Central Islip, NY** (cdp) Suffolk County	38.1
New Mexico	15.8	Rutherford County, TN	32.2	**Ontario, CA** (city) San Bernardino County	31.2
District of Columbia	15.6	Denton County, TX	28.9	**Islip, NY** (town) Suffolk County	30.7
Maryland	15.0	Solano County, CA	26.9	**Brookhaven, NY** (town) Suffolk County	30.4
Tennessee	13.7	Prince William County, VA	26.5	**West Covina, CA** (city) Los Angeles County	29.6
Illinois	13.6	New Haven County, CT	25.5	**Union City, NJ** (city) Hudson County	28.1
New York	13.4	Norfolk County, MA	24.9	**West New York, NJ** (town) Hudson County	27.8
Massachusetts	12.9	Putnam County, NY	23.8	**Brentwood, NY** (cdp) Suffolk County	27.1
Connecticut	12.8	Suffolk County, MA	21.8	**Victorville, CA** (city) San Bernardino County	23.6

Sorted by Percent in Ascending Order — U.S. = 10.5%

State	Percent	County	Percent	Place	Percent
Idaho	0.0	Arapahoe County, CO	0.0	**Cincinnati, OH** (city) Hamilton County	0.0
South Dakota	0.0	Caroline County, MD	0.0	**Fort Worth, TX** (city) Tarrant County	0.0
Nebraska	0.9	Cherokee County, GA	0.0	**Grand Island, NE** (city) Hall County	0.0
Mississippi	2.6	Dawson County, NE	0.0	**Indianapolis, IN** (city) Marion County	0.0
Indiana	3.4	DeKalb County, AL	0.0	**Jersey City, NJ** (city) Hudson County	0.0
North Carolina	3.8	Floyd County, GA	0.0	**Lawrence, MA** (city) Essex County	0.0
Oklahoma	4.2	Franklin County, AL	0.0	**Lexington*, NE** (city) Dawson County	0.0
Oregon	4.2	Gordon County, GA	0.0	**Pawtucket*, RI** (city) Providence County	0.0
Georgia	4.8	Hall County, NE	0.0	**Reno, NV** (city) Washoe County	0.0
Missouri	4.8	Hillsborough County, FL	0.0	**Salt Lake City, UT** (city) Salt Lake County	0.0

Note: (1) Ranking tables cover all states and counties, and places with an overall population of at least 125,000, OR an overall population of at least 25,000 where the Hispanic/Latino population is at least 20% of the overall population. In states where less than five places meet either of these criteria, we have included places with at least 10,000 total population with the highest percentage of Hispanic/Latino population. These places are identified with an asterisk (*); Please refer to the User's Guide for a full explanation of data.

Households with $100,000+ Income

Central American: Honduran

Top 10 States, Counties, and Places[1]

Sorted by Number in Descending Order — U.S. = 14,741

State	Number	County	Number	Place	Number
California	2,237	Los Angeles County, CA	1,027	**New York, NY** (city)	1,120
New York	2,187	Miami-Dade County, FL	814	**Los Angeles, CA** (city) Los Angeles County	475
Florida	1,748	Harris County, TX	508	**Queens, NY** (borough) Queens County	363
New Jersey	1,227	Suffolk County, NY	438	**Bronx, NY** (borough) Bronx County	352
Texas	1,166	Nassau County, NY	369	**Hempstead (town), NY** (town) Nassau County	270
Louisiana	1,040	Queens County, NY	363	**Islip, NY** (town) Suffolk County	265
Virginia	957	Jefferson Parish, LA	353	**Houston, TX** (city) Harris County	244
Maryland	763	Bronx County, NY	352	**Brooklyn, NY** (borough) Kings County	238
Georgia	440	Broward County, FL	336	**Boston, MA** (city) Suffolk County	198
North Carolina	360	Fairfax County, VA	312	**Miami, FL** (city) Miami-Dade County	188

Sorted by Number in Ascending Order — U.S. = 14,741

State	Number	County	Number	Place	Number
Missouri	9	Beaufort County, SC	0	**Austin, TX** (city) Travis County	0
Utah	10	Durham County, NC	0	**Durham, NC** (city) Durham County	0
Oregon	13	Elkhart County, IN	0	**Fort Worth, TX** (city) Tarrant County	0
Nebraska	15	Hall County, GA	0	**Hialeah, FL** (city) Miami-Dade County	0
Kentucky	17	Jackson County, MO	0	**Memphis, TN** (city) Shelby County	0
Arkansas	20	Kern County, CA	0	**Miami Beach, FL** (city) Miami-Dade County	0
Alabama	29	New Haven County, CT	0	**North Miami, FL** (city) Miami-Dade County	0
Wisconsin	35	Polk County, FL	0	**Oklahoma City, OK** (city) Oklahoma County	0
Oklahoma	40	Salt Lake County, UT	0	**Chelsea, MA** (city) Suffolk County	7
Indiana	43	Sampson County, NC	0	**Garland, TX** (city) Dallas County	10

Sorted by Percent in Descending Order — U.S. = 9.2%

State	Percent	County	Percent	Place	Percent
Maryland	21.1	Essex County, NJ	39.3	**Islip, NY** (town) Suffolk County	40.4
Arizona	20.2	Riverside County, CA	31.4	**Wheaton, MD** (cdp) Montgomery County	39.7
Connecticut	16.0	Orange County, NY	30.9	**Plainfield, NJ** (city) Union County	35.5
Michigan	15.9	Suffolk County, NY	29.8	**Brentwood, NY** (cdp) Suffolk County	32.3
Virginia	15.1	Ventura County, CA	29.4	**Springfield, VA** (cdp) Fairfax County	26.7
Iowa	14.7	Saint Tammany Parish, LA	27.0	**Newburgh, NY** (city) Orange County	26.1
New Jersey	14.3	Fresno County, CA	26.3	**North Miami Beach, FL** (city) Miami-Dade County	24.4
Pennsylvania	13.7	Richmond County, NY	22.7	**Las Vegas, NV** (city) Clark County	23.2
Colorado	13.3	Alameda County, CA	22.3	**Staten Island, NY** (borough) Richmond County	22.7
Nevada	12.7	Prince George's County, MD	22.3	**Phoenix, AZ** (city) Maricopa County	21.1

Sorted by Percent in Ascending Order — U.S. = 9.2%

State	Percent	County	Percent	Place	Percent
Missouri	1.3	Beaufort County, SC	0.0	**Austin, TX** (city) Travis County	0.0
Utah	2.0	Durham County, NC	0.0	**Durham, NC** (city) Durham County	0.0
Indiana	2.4	Elkhart County, IN	0.0	**Fort Worth, TX** (city) Tarrant County	0.0
Tennessee	2.5	Hall County, GA	0.0	**Hialeah, FL** (city) Miami-Dade County	0.0
Oregon	2.7	Jackson County, MO	0.0	**Memphis, TN** (city) Shelby County	0.0
Kentucky	3.1	Kern County, CA	0.0	**Miami Beach, FL** (city) Miami-Dade County	0.0
South Carolina	3.4	New Haven County, CT	0.0	**North Miami, FL** (city) Miami-Dade County	0.0
Alabama	3.8	Polk County, FL	0.0	**Oklahoma City, OK** (city) Oklahoma County	0.0
Arkansas	4.1	Salt Lake County, UT	0.0	**Chelsea, MA** (city) Suffolk County	1.3
North Carolina	4.8	Sampson County, NC	0.0	**Nashville-Davidson, TN** (metropolitan govt) Davidson County	2.0

Note: (1) Ranking tables cover all states and counties, and places with an overall population of at least 125,000, OR an overall population of at least 25,000 where the Hispanic/Latino population is at least 20% of the overall population. In states where less than five places meet either of these criteria, we have included places with at least 10,000 total population with the highest percentage of Hispanic/Latino population. These places are identified with an asterisk (*); Please refer to the User's Guide for a full explanation of data.

Households with $100,000+ Income

Central American: Nicaraguan

Top 10 States, Counties, and Places[1]

Sorted by Number in Descending Order — U.S. = 16,352

State	Number	County	Number	Place	Number
California	6,580	Miami-Dade County, FL	3,523	**Los Angeles, CA** (city) Los Angeles County	826
Florida	4,397	Los Angeles County, CA	2,072	**New York, NY** (city)	551
New York	846	San Mateo County, CA	755	**Miami, FL** (city) Miami-Dade County	414
Texas	709	Contra Costa County, CA	730	**San Francisco, CA** (city) San Francisco County	379
Maryland	610	Alameda County, CA	529	**Daly City, CA** (city) San Mateo County	272
New Jersey	532	Montgomery County, MD	392	**The Hammocks, FL** (cdp) Miami-Dade County	271
Virginia	489	San Bernardino County, CA	379	**Tamiami, FL** (cdp) Miami-Dade County	269
Louisiana	311	San Francisco County, CA	379	**Antioch, CA** (city) Contra Costa County	243
Pennsylvania	202	Santa Clara County, CA	368	**Kendall, FL** (cdp) Miami-Dade County	232
North Carolina	193	Broward County, FL	361	**Queens, NY** (borough) Queens County	203

Sorted by Number in Ascending Order — U.S. = 16,352

State	Number	County	Number	Place	Number
Oregon	7	Orange County, FL	0	**North Miami, FL** (city) Miami-Dade County	0
South Carolina	15	Collier County, FL	22	**Sacramento, CA** (city) Sacramento County	7
Colorado	20	Gwinnett County, GA	23	**San Diego, CA** (city) San Diego County	11
Wisconsin	23	San Diego County, CA	49	**South Gate, CA** (city) Los Angeles County	17
Missouri	25	Duval County, FL	51	**Austin, TX** (city) Travis County	24
Indiana	27	Camden County, NJ	52	**Kendall West, FL** (cdp) Miami-Dade County	25
Michigan	29	San Joaquin County, CA	58	**Fontana, CA** (city) San Bernardino County	27
District of Columbia	49	Travis County, TX	59	**Charlotte, NC** (city) Mecklenburg County	28
Tennessee	53	Sacramento County, CA	68	**West Little River, FL** (cdp) Miami-Dade County	31
Ohio	59	Lee County, FL	71	**University Park, FL** (cdp) Miami-Dade County	34

Sorted by Percent in Descending Order — U.S. = 16.7%

State	Percent	County	Percent	Place	Percent
Connecticut	40.9	Contra Costa County, CA	41.1	**South San Francisco, CA** (city) San Mateo County	50.7
Maryland	32.9	Montgomery County, MD	37.5	**Antioch, CA** (city) Contra Costa County	50.4
Pennsylvania	27.0	Fairfax County, VA	36.7	**Richmond, CA** (city) Contra Costa County	48.5
Virginia	24.1	Santa Clara County, CA	33.0	**Hayward, CA** (city) Alameda County	38.1
Tennessee	23.9	Alameda County, CA	32.7	**The Hammocks, FL** (cdp) Miami-Dade County	36.2
California	23.5	Riverside County, CA	30.9	**San Jose, CA** (city) Santa Clara County	31.5
New Jersey	23.4	Stanislaus County, CA	30.9	**Kendall, FL** (cdp) Miami-Dade County	28.7
Washington	23.1	Sonoma County, CA	30.1	**Pembroke Pines, FL** (city) Broward County	27.8
Minnesota	22.2	Orange County, CA	30.0	**Richmond West, FL** (cdp) Miami-Dade County	27.2
New York	22.0	Prince William County, VA	27.8	**Queens, NY** (borough) Queens County	25.0

Sorted by Percent in Ascending Order — U.S. = 16.7%

State	Percent	County	Percent	Place	Percent
Oregon	2.2	Orange County, FL	0.0	**North Miami, FL** (city) Miami-Dade County	0.0
Wisconsin	3.5	Sacramento County, CA	7.6	**Sacramento, CA** (city) Sacramento County	1.9
Colorado	4.2	San Diego County, CA	7.6	**Hialeah, FL** (city) Miami-Dade County	3.5
South Carolina	5.9	Collier County, FL	8.0	**San Diego, CA** (city) San Diego County	4.1
Missouri	7.3	Gwinnett County, GA	8.1	**Miami, FL** (city) Miami-Dade County	4.8
Georgia	8.9	Harris County, TX	8.3	**Kendall West, FL** (cdp) Miami-Dade County	5.0
Indiana	9.6	Palm Beach County, FL	8.6	**Kendale Lakes, FL** (cdp) Miami-Dade County	5.1
Florida	11.3	Miami-Dade County, FL	11.6	**West Little River, FL** (cdp) Miami-Dade County	5.7
Michigan	12.1	Bronx County, NY	11.9	**Houston, TX** (city) Harris County	5.8
Arizona	12.5	San Joaquin County, CA	12.2	**South Gate, CA** (city) Los Angeles County	6.0

RANKINGS & COMPARISONS

Note: (1) Ranking tables cover all states and counties, and places with an overall population of at least 125,000, OR an overall population of at least 25,000 where the Hispanic/Latino population is at least 20% of the overall population. In states where less than five places meet either of these criteria, we have included places with at least 10,000 total population with the highest percentage of Hispanic/Latino population. These places are identified with an asterisk (*); Please refer to the User's Guide for a full explanation of data.

Households with $100,000+ Income

Central American: Panamanian

Top 10 States, Counties, and Places[1]

Sorted by Number in Descending Order — U.S. = 10,050

State	Number	County	Number	Place	Number
New York	1,551	Miami-Dade County, FL	612	**New York, NY** (city)	994
Florida	1,457	Los Angeles County, CA	420	**Brooklyn, NY** (borough) Kings County	411
California	1,451	Kings County, NY	411	**Queens, NY** (borough) Queens County	320
Texas	882	Queens County, NY	320	**Hempstead (town), NY** (town) Nassau County	237
Virginia	711	San Diego County, CA	272	**San Diego, CA** (city) San Diego County	153
New Jersey	612	Nassau County, NY	237	**Los Angeles, CA** (city) Los Angeles County	147
Georgia	507	Prince William County, VA	230	**Bronx, NY** (borough) Bronx County	134
Maryland	320	Broward County, FL	217	**San Antonio, TX** (city) Bexar County	102
Washington	240	Fairfax County, VA	149	**Manhattan, NY** (borough) New York County	95
Massachusetts	222	Orange County, FL	142	**Houston, TX** (city) Harris County	70

Sorted by Number in Ascending Order — U.S. = 10,050

State	Number	County	Number	Place	Number
New Mexico	6	Dallas County, TX	13	**Fayetteville, NC** (city) Cumberland County	31
Oklahoma	13	Sacramento County, CA	26	**Jacksonville, FL** (city) Duval County	36
Alabama	30	San Bernardino County, CA	28	**Killeen, TX** (city) Bell County	40
Indiana	38	Cumberland County, NC	31	**Miami, FL** (city) Miami-Dade County	43
Mississippi	51	Duval County, FL	36	**Houston, TX** (city) Harris County	70
Colorado	59	Bell County, TX	40	**Manhattan, NY** (borough) New York County	95
Nevada	61	Orange County, CA	47	**San Antonio, TX** (city) Bexar County	102
Wisconsin	64	Hudson County, NJ	48	**Bronx, NY** (borough) Bronx County	134
Kentucky	65	Brevard County, FL	51	**Los Angeles, CA** (city) Los Angeles County	147
Louisiana	75	Pierce County, WA	57	**San Diego, CA** (city) San Diego County	153

Sorted by Percent in Descending Order — U.S. = 18.4%

State	Percent	County	Percent	Place	Percent
Minnesota	60.7	Prince William County, VA	50.5	**Hempstead (town), NY** (town) Nassau County	47.5
Connecticut	39.3	Nassau County, NY	47.5	**San Diego, CA** (city) San Diego County	28.0
Missouri	32.5	Fairfax County, VA	44.1	**San Antonio, TX** (city) Bexar County	23.2
Mississippi	30.0	Suffolk County, NY	37.1	**Queens, NY** (borough) Queens County	19.8
Wisconsin	29.8	Cook County, IL	29.0	**Los Angeles, CA** (city) Los Angeles County	18.1
Virginia	29.6	Pierce County, WA	28.8	**Houston, TX** (city) Harris County	15.2
New Jersey	28.1	Riverside County, CA	27.3	**Bronx, NY** (borough) Bronx County	12.0
Kentucky	26.6	San Diego County, CA	26.9	**Miami, FL** (city) Miami-Dade County	11.3
Washington	24.2	Montgomery County, MD	24.7	**Killeen, TX** (city) Bell County	10.7
Michigan	23.9	Bexar County, TX	24.4	**New York, NY** (city)	10.3

Sorted by Percent in Ascending Order — U.S. = 18.4%

State	Percent	County	Percent	Place	Percent
New Mexico	2.8	Dallas County, TX	3.1	**Brooklyn, NY** (borough) Kings County	7.2
Oklahoma	3.9	Cumberland County, NC	5.2	**Fayetteville, NC** (city) Cumberland County	8.4
Alabama	6.1	San Bernardino County, CA	5.9	**Manhattan, NY** (borough) New York County	9.1
North Carolina	8.2	Sacramento County, CA	6.2	**Jacksonville, FL** (city) Duval County	9.7
Colorado	12.1	Kings County, NY	7.2	**New York, NY** (city)	10.3
South Carolina	12.7	Bell County, TX	8.3	**Killeen, TX** (city) Bell County	10.7
New York	13.4	New York County, NY	9.1	**Miami, FL** (city) Miami-Dade County	11.3
Arizona	14.1	Hillsborough County, FL	9.6	**Bronx, NY** (borough) Bronx County	12.0
Tennessee	14.9	Duval County, FL	9.7	**Houston, TX** (city) Harris County	15.2
Louisiana	15.2	Hudson County, NJ	11.7	**Los Angeles, CA** (city) Los Angeles County	18.1

Note: (1) Ranking tables cover all states and counties, and places with an overall population of at least 125,000, OR an overall population of at least 25,000 where the Hispanic/Latino population is at least 20% of the overall population. In states where less than five places meet either of these criteria, we have included places with at least 10,000 total population with the highest percentage of Hispanic/Latino population. These places are identified with an asterisk (*); Please refer to the User's Guide for a full explanation of data.

Households with $100,000+ Income

Central American: Salvadoran

Top 10 States, Counties, and Places[1]

Sorted by Number in Descending Order — U.S. = 48,507

State	Number	County	Number	Place	Number
California	19,829	Los Angeles County, CA	10,261	**Los Angeles, CA** (city) Los Angeles County	5,059
New York	5,679	Fairfax County, VA	2,148	**Hempstead (town), NY** (town) Nassau County	1,388
Virginia	4,916	Montgomery County, MD	2,115	**Islip, NY** (town) Suffolk County	1,248
Maryland	4,739	Suffolk County, NY	2,092	**New York, NY** (city)	1,193
Texas	3,073	Nassau County, NY	1,993	**San Francisco, CA** (city) San Francisco County	912
New Jersey	1,882	Prince George's County, MD	1,847	**Houston, TX** (city) Harris County	704
Florida	1,374	Harris County, TX	1,541	**Queens, NY** (borough) Queens County	575
Massachusetts	1,156	San Mateo County, CA	1,170	**Brentwood, NY** (cdp) Suffolk County	526
District of Columbia	760	Prince William County, VA	1,122	**San Jose, CA** (city) Santa Clara County	484
Nevada	685	Contra Costa County, CA	980	**Babylon, NY** (town) Suffolk County	374

Sorted by Number in Ascending Order — U.S. = 48,507

State	Number	County	Number	Place	Number
Idaho	0	Adams County, CO	0	**Grand Island, NE** (city) Hall County	0
Kentucky	0	Alamance County, NC	0	**Greensboro, NC** (city) Guilford County	0
Nebraska	7	Duval County, FL	0	**Hialeah, FL** (city) Miami-Dade County	0
Oklahoma	18	Forsyth County, NC	0	**Jacksonville, FL** (city) Duval County	0
Rhode Island	19	Guilford County, NC	0	**Lewisville, TX** (city) Denton County	0
Arkansas	21	Hall County, NE	0	**Maywood, CA** (city) Los Angeles County	0
Alabama	22	Henrico County, VA	0	**Portland, OR** (city) Multnomah County	0
Hawaii	22	Merced County, CA	0	**Raleigh, NC** (city) Wake County	0
Alaska	31	Polk County, FL	0	**Springdale, AR** (city) Washington County	0
Michigan	43	Rutherford County, TN	0	**Tacoma, WA** (city) Pierce County	0

Sorted by Percent in Descending Order — U.S. = 11.4%

State	Percent	County	Percent	Place	Percent
Virginia	18.2	Orange County, NY	35.7	**Springfield, VA** (cdp) Fairfax County	48.0
Maryland	17.7	Loudoun County, VA	30.8	**Oyster Bay, NY** (town) Nassau County	46.5
New York	17.5	Frederick County, MD	29.7	**Chino, CA** (city) San Bernardino County	43.1
Connecticut	16.7	Howard County, MD	29.1	**Corona, CA** (city) Riverside County	37.4
New Mexico	16.0	San Joaquin County, CA	28.6	**Modesto, CA** (city) Stanislaus County	35.8
Alaska	15.8	Washington County, OR	27.3	**Fairfield, CA** (city) Solano County	32.5
District of Columbia	15.0	Solano County, CA	26.3	**Riverside, CA** (city) Riverside County	32.5
New Jersey	13.7	Buncombe County, NC	26.2	**Santa Clarita, CA** (city) Los Angeles County	31.6
Wisconsin	13.7	Lake County, IL	26.0	**West Covina, CA** (city) Los Angeles County	31.0
Illinois	13.6	Fairfax County, VA	24.7	**Simi Valley, CA** (city) Ventura County	30.5

Sorted by Percent in Ascending Order — U.S. = 11.4%

State	Percent	County	Percent	Place	Percent
Idaho	0.0	Adams County, CO	0.0	**Grand Island, NE** (city) Hall County	0.0
Kentucky	0.0	Alamance County, NC	0.0	**Greensboro, NC** (city) Guilford County	0.0
Nebraska	0.4	Duval County, FL	0.0	**Hialeah, FL** (city) Miami-Dade County	0.0
Arkansas	0.6	Forsyth County, NC	0.0	**Jacksonville, FL** (city) Duval County	0.0
Rhode Island	1.9	Guilford County, NC	0.0	**Lewisville, TX** (city) Denton County	0.0
Oklahoma	2.6	Hall County, NE	0.0	**Maywood, CA** (city) Los Angeles County	0.0
Tennessee	3.1	Henrico County, VA	0.0	**Portland, OR** (city) Multnomah County	0.0
Alabama	3.9	Merced County, CA	0.0	**Raleigh, NC** (city) Wake County	0.0
Kansas	4.7	Polk County, FL	0.0	**Springdale, AR** (city) Washington County	0.0
Michigan	4.8	Rutherford County, TN	0.0	**Tacoma, WA** (city) Pierce County	0.0

Note: (1) Ranking tables cover all states and counties, and places with an overall population of at least 125,000, OR an overall population of at least 25,000 where the Hispanic/Latino population is at least 20% of the overall population. In states where less than five places meet either of these criteria, we have included places with at least 10,000 total population with the highest percentage of Hispanic/Latino population. These places are identified with an asterisk (*); Please refer to the User's Guide for a full explanation of data.

Households with $100,000+ Income

Cuban

Top 10 States, Counties, and Places[1]

Sorted by Number in Descending Order — U.S. = 110,896

State	Number	County	Number	Place	Number
Florida	65,553	Miami-Dade County, FL	45,283	**Miami, FL** (city) Miami-Dade County	4,647
New Jersey	8,245	Broward County, FL	7,114	**Hialeah, FL** (city) Miami-Dade County	3,495
California	8,020	Los Angeles County, CA	3,833	**New York, NY** (city)	3,412
New York	6,382	Hillsborough County, FL	2,730	**Kendall, FL** (cdp) Miami-Dade County	2,850
Texas	3,088	Palm Beach County, FL	2,425	**Tamiami, FL** (cdp) Miami-Dade County	2,311
Georgia	2,100	Bergen County, NJ	1,730	**Coral Gables, FL** (city) Miami-Dade County	2,172
Illinois	1,831	Hudson County, NJ	1,543	**Kendale Lakes, FL** (cdp) Miami-Dade County	1,858
Virginia	1,730	Orange County, FL	1,365	**Pembroke Pines, FL** (city) Broward County	1,855
Pennsylvania	1,305	New York County, NY	1,230	**Miami Lakes, FL** (town) Miami-Dade County	1,518
Maryland	1,295	Queens County, NY	1,223	**Miami Beach, FL** (city) Miami-Dade County	1,456

Sorted by Number in Ascending Order — U.S. = 110,896

State	Number	County	Number	Place	Number
Arkansas	19	Pierce County, WA	6	**Rochester, NY** (city) Monroe County	9
Maine	27	Lancaster County, PA	7	**Bell, CA** (city) Los Angeles County	10
West Virginia	30	Kern County, CA	9	**University, FL** (cdp) Hillsborough County	17
Iowa	37	Highlands County, FL	10	**Syracuse, NY** (city) Onondaga County	22
Hawaii	96	Hendry County, FL	13	**Hallandale Beach, FL** (city) Broward County	24
New Mexico	97	Jackson County, MO	24	**Lehigh Acres, FL** (cdp) Lee County	28
Nebraska	107	Onondaga County, NY	30	**Baltimore, MD** (independent city)	35
Oklahoma	112	Hampden County, MA	31	**Columbus, OH** (city) Franklin County	42
Rhode Island	115	Salt Lake County, UT	31	**Portland, OR** (city) Multnomah County	43
Mississippi	123	Arapahoe County, CO	36	**Lake Worth, FL** (city) Palm Beach County	46

Sorted by Percent in Descending Order — U.S. = 18.4%

State	Percent	County	Percent	Place	Percent
Virginia	36.7	Sussex County, NJ	67.1	**North Hempstead, NY** (town) Nassau County	58.1
District of Columbia	36.6	Morris County, NJ	66.7	**Weston, FL** (city) Broward County	57.4
Maryland	36.4	Loudoun County, VA	63.6	**Kearny, NJ** (town) Hudson County	57.1
Connecticut	35.6	Fairfax County, VA	62.6	**Oyster Bay, NY** (town) Nassau County	55.5
Delaware	33.9	Monmouth County, NJ	54.4	**Santa Clarita, CA** (city) Los Angeles County	50.9
New Hampshire	31.8	Ventura County, CA	53.0	**Islip, NY** (town) Suffolk County	48.2
Colorado	26.9	Burlington County, NJ	52.9	**Cooper City, FL** (city) Broward County	47.5
California	26.4	Lake County, IL	52.8	**Brookhaven, NY** (town) Suffolk County	46.8
New Jersey	26.0	Somerset County, NJ	52.5	**Hempstead (town), NY** (town) Nassau County	46.7
Georgia	25.7	Nassau County, NY	52.2	**Riverview, FL** (cdp) Hillsborough County	41.6

Sorted by Percent in Ascending Order — U.S. = 18.4%

State	Percent	County	Percent	Place	Percent
Arkansas	5.6	Highlands County, FL	1.4	**Lehigh Acres, FL** (cdp) Lee County	1.6
New Mexico	8.2	Lancaster County, PA	1.5	**Rochester, NY** (city) Monroe County	2.1
Maine	8.7	Hendry County, FL	2.0	**Bell, CA** (city) Los Angeles County	2.4
West Virginia	10.6	Pierce County, WA	3.6	**Hallandale Beach, FL** (city) Broward County	2.6
Iowa	10.9	Sarasota County, FL	3.9	**Cape Coral, FL** (city) Lee County	3.2
Nevada	11.1	Kern County, CA	4.0	**University, FL** (cdp) Hillsborough County	3.8
Kentucky	11.5	Lee County, FL	4.1	**West Little River, FL** (cdp) Miami-Dade County	4.2
Indiana	12.3	Onondaga County, NY	5.3	**Syracuse, NY** (city) Onondaga County	5.0
Missouri	14.0	Jackson County, MO	6.0	**Homestead, FL** (city) Miami-Dade County	5.6
Oregon	14.3	Multnomah County, OR	6.6	**West New York, NJ** (town) Hudson County	6.2

Note: (1) Ranking tables cover all states and counties, and places with an overall population of at least 125,000, OR an overall population of at least 25,000 where the Hispanic/Latino population is at least 20% of the overall population. In states where less than five places meet either of these criteria, we have included places with at least 10,000 total population with the highest percentage of Hispanic/Latino population. These places are identified with an asterisk (*); Please refer to the User's Guide for a full explanation of data.

Households with $100,000+ Income

Dominican Republic

Top 10 States, Counties, and Places[1]

Sorted by Number in Descending Order — U.S. = 37,904

State	Number	County	Number	Place	Number
New York	16,900	Queens County, NY	3,718	**New York, NY** (city)	12,136
New Jersey	6,325	Bronx County, NY	3,074	**Queens, NY** (borough) Queens County	3,718
Florida	5,770	New York County, NY	3,012	**Bronx, NY** (borough) Bronx County	3,074
Massachusetts	2,137	Kings County, NY	2,050	**Manhattan, NY** (borough) New York County	3,012
Pennsylvania	832	Miami-Dade County, FL	1,826	**Brooklyn, NY** (borough) Kings County	2,050
Connecticut	816	Bergen County, NJ	1,642	**Hempstead (town), NY** (town) Nassau County	1,134
Maryland	647	Broward County, FL	1,494	**Lawrence, MA** (city) Essex County	533
Virginia	627	Nassau County, NY	1,351	**Islip, NY** (town) Suffolk County	509
Georgia	589	Hudson County, NJ	1,346	**Yonkers, NY** (city) Westchester County	419
California	568	Suffolk County, NY	1,093	**Boston, MA** (city) Suffolk County	403

Sorted by Number in Ascending Order — U.S. = 37,904

State	Number	County	Number	Place	Number
Utah	0	Collier County, FL	0	**Chelsea, MA** (city) Suffolk County	0
South Carolina	16	Erie County, NY	0	**Cleveland, OH** (city) Cuyahoga County	0
Missouri	20	Kent County, MI	0	**Grand Rapids, MI** (city) Kent County	0
Washington	26	Oneida County, NY	0	**New Haven, CT** (city/town) New Haven County	0
Alaska	28	Lackawanna County, PA	4	**New London, CT** (city/town) New London County	0
Colorado	28	Wake County, NC	7	**North Miami Beach, FL** (city) Miami-Dade County	0
Michigan	30	Jefferson Parish, LA	8	**Pennsauken, NJ** (township) Camden County	0
Indiana	36	York County, PA	8	**Raleigh, NC** (city) Wake County	0
Alabama	46	Ulster County, NY	9	**Reading, PA** (city) Berks County	0
Delaware	52	Bristol County, MA	13	**Town 'n' Country, FL** (cdp) Hillsborough County	0

Sorted by Percent in Descending Order — U.S. = 9.5%

State	Percent	County	Percent	Place	Percent
Nevada	25.6	Fairfax County, VA	46.5	**Ramapo, NY** (town) Rockland County	51.7
Virginia	25.3	Morris County, NJ	41.9	**North Hempstead, NY** (town) Nassau County	50.2
District of Columbia	20.8	Dutchess County, NY	32.3	**Plantation, FL** (city) Broward County	45.1
Maryland	20.4	Bexar County, TX	31.9	**Elmont, NY** (cdp) Nassau County	44.5
Minnesota	20.3	Bergen County, NJ	28.0	**Weston, FL** (city) Broward County	35.4
California	18.9	Clark County, NV	27.0	**Oyster Bay, NY** (town) Nassau County	34.9
Illinois	16.5	Nassau County, NY	26.0	**Belleville, NJ** (township) Essex County	32.5
Alabama	16.2	Orange County, NY	25.3	**Davie, FL** (town) Broward County	31.9
Louisiana	15.7	Richmond County, NY	24.4	**Deltona, FL** (city) Volusia County	30.2
Arizona	15.4	Somerset County, NJ	23.1	**Huntington, NY** (town) Suffolk County	30.1

Sorted by Percent in Ascending Order — U.S. = 9.5%

State	Percent	County	Percent	Place	Percent
Utah	0.0	Collier County, FL	0.0	**Chelsea, MA** (city) Suffolk County	0.0
Rhode Island	3.1	Erie County, NY	0.0	**Cleveland, OH** (city) Cuyahoga County	0.0
Michigan	3.8	Kent County, MI	0.0	**Grand Rapids, MI** (city) Kent County	0.0
North Carolina	4.3	Oneida County, NY	0.0	**New Haven, CT** (city/town) New Haven County	0.0
Missouri	5.0	Wake County, NC	1.3	**New London, CT** (city/town) New London County	0.0
South Carolina	5.1	York County, PA	1.6	**North Miami Beach, FL** (city) Miami-Dade County	0.0
Indiana	5.4	Jefferson Parish, LA	1.8	**Pennsauken, NJ** (township) Camden County	0.0
Colorado	5.8	Berks County, PA	1.9	**Raleigh, NC** (city) Wake County	0.0
Pennsylvania	5.9	Lackawanna County, PA	1.9	**Reading, PA** (city) Berks County	0.0
Massachusetts	6.6	Bristol County, MA	2.5	**Town 'n' Country, FL** (cdp) Hillsborough County	0.0

Note: (1) Ranking tables cover all states and counties, and places with an overall population of at least 125,000, OR an overall population of at least 25,000 where the Hispanic/Latino population is at least 20% of the overall population. In states where less than five places meet either of these criteria, we have included places with at least 10,000 total population with the highest percentage of Hispanic/Latino population. These places are identified with an asterisk (*); Please refer to the User's Guide for a full explanation of data.

Households with $100,000+ Income

Mexican

Top 10 States, Counties, and Places[1]

Sorted by Number in Descending Order — U.S. = 838,495

State	Number	County	Number	Place	Number
California	385,639	Los Angeles County, CA	118,747	**Los Angeles, CA** (city) Los Angeles County	32,211
Texas	183,578	Orange County, CA	35,888	**San Antonio, TX** (city) Bexar County	19,556
Illinois	44,237	San Diego County, CA	31,160	**Chicago, IL** (city) Cook County	14,308
Arizona	38,229	Harris County, TX	29,145	**San Jose, CA** (city) Santa Clara County	13,516
Colorado	18,191	San Bernardino County, CA	28,747	**Houston, TX** (city) Harris County	12,497
Nevada	13,859	Cook County, IL	26,199	**El Paso, TX** (city) El Paso County	11,873
Washington	13,479	Riverside County, CA	25,866	**San Diego, CA** (city) San Diego County	10,978
New Mexico	12,554	Bexar County, TX	25,261	**Phoenix, AZ** (city) Maricopa County	9,852
Florida	11,664	Maricopa County, AZ	24,212	**New York, NY** (city)	8,154
New York	11,561	Santa Clara County, CA	20,542	**Santa Ana, CA** (city) Orange County	7,303

Sorted by Number in Ascending Order — U.S. = 838,495

State	Number	County	Number	Place	Number
Maine	66	Adair County, OK	0	**Allentown, PA** (city) Lehigh County	0
Vermont	137	Albany County, WY	0	**Babylon, NY** (town) Suffolk County	0
South Dakota	170	Alexander County, NC	0	**Beloit*, WI** (city) Rock County	0
Montana	217	Anderson County, TN	0	**Berea*, SC** (cdp) Greenville County	0
New Hampshire	263	Antrim County, MI	0	**Bluffton*, SC** (town) Beaufort County	0
North Dakota	265	Ashe County, NC	0	**Deltona, FL** (city) Volusia County	0
West Virginia	272	Barbour County, AL	0	**Fairbanks*, AK** (city) Fairbanks North Star Borough	0
Rhode Island	337	Beaufort County, NC	0	**Fort Campbell North*, KY** (cdp) Christian County	0
District of Columbia	696	Beaver County, UT	0	**Fort Hood, TX** (cdp) Bell County	0
Delaware	741	Becker County, MN	0	**Fort Pierce, FL** (city) Saint Lucie County	0

Sorted by Percent in Descending Order — U.S. = 10.9%

State	Percent	County	Percent	Place	Percent
District of Columbia	21.8	McPherson County, KS	53.4	**Weston, FL** (city) Broward County	67.3
Maryland	21.8	Chisago County, MN	45.6	**Coral Gables, FL** (city) Miami-Dade County	57.9
Massachusetts	20.6	Waseca County, MN	45.3	**Miramar, FL** (city) Broward County	50.4
Virginia	19.5	Richland County, OH	44.3	**Eastvale, CA** (cdp) Riverside County	48.2
Vermont	18.0	Hampshire County, MA	44.1	**Diamond Bar, CA** (city) Los Angeles County	46.0
Hawaii	17.9	Los Alamos County, NM	43.9	**Chino Hills, CA** (city) San Bernardino County	45.1
Alaska	17.4	Tolland County, CT	42.9	**Doral, FL** (city) Miami-Dade County	44.4
Connecticut	14.7	Sherburne County, MN	41.7	**Pembroke Pines, FL** (city) Broward County	39.7
California	14.6	Delaware County, OH	41.5	**Alexandria, VA** (independent city)	38.4
New Hampshire	14.5	Howard County, MD	41.4	**Haverstraw, NY** (town) Rockland County	37.0

Sorted by Percent in Ascending Order — U.S. = 10.9%

State	Percent	County	Percent	Place	Percent
Arkansas	4.2	Adair County, OK	0.0	**Allentown, PA** (city) Lehigh County	0.0
North Carolina	4.2	Albany County, WY	0.0	**Babylon, NY** (town) Suffolk County	0.0
Montana	4.4	Alexander County, NC	0.0	**Beloit*, WI** (city) Rock County	0.0
Maine	4.7	Anderson County, TN	0.0	**Berea*, SC** (cdp) Greenville County	0.0
Nebraska	4.9	Antrim County, MI	0.0	**Bluffton*, SC** (town) Beaufort County	0.0
South Dakota	5.0	Ashe County, NC	0.0	**Deltona, FL** (city) Volusia County	0.0
Idaho	5.3	Barbour County, AL	0.0	**Fairbanks*, AK** (city) Fairbanks North Star Borough	0.0
Oklahoma	5.3	Beaufort County, NC	0.0	**Fort Campbell North*, KY** (cdp) Christian County	0.0
South Carolina	5.9	Beaver County, UT	0.0	**Fort Hood, TX** (cdp) Bell County	0.0
Alabama	6.0	Becker County, MN	0.0	**Fort Pierce, FL** (city) Saint Lucie County	0.0

Note: (1) Ranking tables cover all states and counties, and places with an overall population of at least 125,000, OR an overall population of at least 25,000 where the Hispanic/Latino population is at least 20% of the overall population. In states where less than five places meet either of these criteria, we have included places with at least 10,000 total population with the highest percentage of Hispanic/Latino population. These places are identified with an asterisk (*); Please refer to the User's Guide for a full explanation of data.

Households with $100,000+ Income

Puerto Rican

Top 10 States, Counties, and Places[1]

Sorted by Number in Descending Order — U.S. = 184,689

State	Number	County	Number	Place	Number
New York	48,256	Bronx County, NY	9,074	**New York, NY** (city)	29,140
Florida	28,072	Queens County, NY	6,557	**Bronx, NY** (borough) Bronx County	9,074
New Jersey	23,461	Kings County, NY	6,341	**Queens, NY** (borough) Queens County	6,557
California	13,638	Miami-Dade County, FL	5,662	**Brooklyn, NY** (borough) Kings County	6,341
Illinois	7,971	Suffolk County, NY	5,128	**Manhattan, NY** (borough) New York County	4,059
Connecticut	7,764	Broward County, FL	4,771	**Chicago, IL** (city) Cook County	3,635
Texas	7,316	Cook County, IL	4,741	**Staten Island, NY** (borough) Richmond County	3,109
Pennsylvania	6,974	New York County, NY	4,059	**Islip, NY** (town) Suffolk County	2,085
Massachusetts	5,584	Orange County, FL	3,995	**Hempstead (town), NY** (town) Nassau County	1,808
Virginia	5,231	Westchester County, NY	3,432	**Brookhaven, NY** (town) Suffolk County	1,573

Sorted by Number in Ascending Order — U.S. = 184,689

State	Number	County	Number	Place	Number
North Dakota	0	Brown County, WI	0	**Akron, OH** (city) Summit County	0
Montana	16	Butte County, CA	0	**Columbia, SC** (city) Richland County	0
South Dakota	30	Camden County, GA	0	**Fort Hood, TX** (cdp) Bell County	0
Wyoming	46	Cattaraugus County, NY	0	**Hazleton, PA** (city) Luzerne County	0
Maine	73	Cayuga County, NY	0	**Lake Worth, FL** (city) Palm Beach County	0
Iowa	84	Centre County, PA	0	**Manchester*, NH** (city) Hillsborough County	0
Utah	98	Chemung County, NY	0	**West Little River, FL** (cdp) Miami-Dade County	0
Nebraska	105	Christian County, KY	0	**Winston-Salem, NC** (city) Forsyth County	0
West Virginia	116	Clearfield County, PA	0	**York, PA** (city) York County	1
Mississippi	124	Columbia County, FL	0	**Bridgeton, NJ** (city) Cumberland County	6

Sorted by Percent in Descending Order — U.S. = 13.1%

State	Percent	County	Percent	Place	Percent
District of Columbia	31.7	Warren County, OH	59.9	**Bergenfield, NJ** (borough) Bergen County	60.9
Maryland	29.4	Hamilton County, IN	56.1	**Fremont, CA** (city) Alameda County	57.7
Virginia	25.1	Hunterdon County, NJ	53.6	**Coral Gables, FL** (city) Miami-Dade County	57.6
California	24.0	Howard County, MD	49.1	**Elmont, NY** (cdp) Nassau County	56.9
Arkansas	21.4	Putnam County, NY	48.6	**Oyster Bay, NY** (town) Nassau County	54.1
Wyoming	20.4	Spotsylvania County, VA	46.7	**Alexandria, VA** (independent city)	53.3
Vermont	19.9	Montgomery County, MD	46.3	**Chula Vista, CA** (city) San Diego County	49.7
Colorado	18.6	Loudoun County, VA	44.8	**Rahway, NJ** (city) Union County	47.3
Texas	18.6	Medina County, OH	44.2	**Bolingbrook, IL** (village) Will County	47.2
Minnesota	18.4	Rockland County, NY	43.0	**Huntington, NY** (town) Suffolk County	46.7

Sorted by Percent in Ascending Order — U.S. = 13.1%

State	Percent	County	Percent	Place	Percent
North Dakota	0.0	Brown County, WI	0.0	**Akron, OH** (city) Summit County	0.0
Montana	3.0	Butte County, CA	0.0	**Columbia, SC** (city) Richland County	0.0
Rhode Island	5.6	Camden County, GA	0.0	**Fort Hood, TX** (cdp) Bell County	0.0
Utah	6.1	Cattaraugus County, NY	0.0	**Hazleton, PA** (city) Luzerne County	0.0
Iowa	6.3	Cayuga County, NY	0.0	**Lake Worth, FL** (city) Palm Beach County	0.0
Wisconsin	6.3	Centre County, PA	0.0	**Manchester*, NH** (city) Hillsborough County	0.0
Maine	6.4	Chemung County, NY	0.0	**West Little River, FL** (cdp) Miami-Dade County	0.0
Massachusetts	6.9	Christian County, KY	0.0	**Winston-Salem, NC** (city) Forsyth County	0.0
Pennsylvania	6.9	Clearfield County, PA	0.0	**York, PA** (city) York County	0.0
South Dakota	8.3	Columbia County, FL	0.0	**Miami Gardens, FL** (city) Miami-Dade County	0.9

Note: (1) Ranking tables cover all states and counties, and places with an overall population of at least 125,000, OR an overall population of at least 25,000 where the Hispanic/Latino population is at least 20% of the overall population. In states where less than five places meet either of these criteria, we have included places with at least 10,000 total population with the highest percentage of Hispanic/Latino population. These places are identified with an asterisk (*); Please refer to the User's Guide for a full explanation of data.

Households with $100,000+ Income

South American

Top 10 States, Counties, and Places[1]

Sorted by Number in Descending Order — U.S. = 165,425

State	Number	County	Number	Place	Number
Florida	30,556	Miami-Dade County, FL	13,533	**New York, NY** (city)	18,410
New York	30,220	Queens County, NY	10,501	**Queens, NY** (borough) Queens County	10,501
California	24,491	Los Angeles County, CA	9,532	**Manhattan, NY** (borough) New York County	3,826
New Jersey	19,153	Broward County, FL	7,382	**Los Angeles, CA** (city) Los Angeles County	3,679
Texas	9,772	Fairfax County, VA	4,153	**Hempstead (town), NY** (town) Nassau County	2,241
Virginia	8,549	Nassau County, NY	3,871	**Brooklyn, NY** (borough) Kings County	2,041
Maryland	5,270	New York County, NY	3,826	**Chicago, IL** (city) Cook County	2,041
Illinois	4,752	Hudson County, NJ	3,720	**Miami, FL** (city) Miami-Dade County	1,820
Connecticut	3,973	Harris County, TX	3,360	**Houston, TX** (city) Harris County	1,773
Massachusetts	3,315	Orange County, CA	3,152	**Doral, FL** (city) Miami-Dade County	1,429

Sorted by Number in Ascending Order — U.S. = 165,425

State	Number	County	Number	Place	Number
North Dakota	18	Flagler County, FL	0	**New London, CT** (city/town) New London County	0
Montana	29	Oneida County, NY	6	**Norfolk, VA** (independent city)	0
Maine	44	Davis County, UT	8	**Sanford, FL** (city) Seminole County	0
Vermont	50	Spartanburg County, SC	8	**Sterling, VA** (cdp) Loudoun County	0
Wyoming	86	Spokane County, WA	8	**Westchester, FL** (cdp) Miami-Dade County	0
Idaho	106	Cache County, UT	10	**Palm Springs, CA** (city) Riverside County	4
Nebraska	115	Gaston County, NC	11	**Springfield, MA** (city) Hampden County	7
West Virginia	115	Horry County, SC	11	**Reading, PA** (city) Berks County	8
Mississippi	161	Cleveland County, OK	12	**City of Orange, NJ** (township) Essex County	9
Alaska	180	Hall County, GA	15	**Stockton, CA** (city) San Joaquin County	9

Sorted by Percent in Descending Order — U.S. = 19.1%

State	Percent	County	Percent	Place	Percent
District of Columbia	34.3	Rockingham County, NH	77.3	**Placentia, CA** (city) Orange County	63.2
New Hampshire	30.4	Douglas County, CO	73.9	**Oyster Bay, NY** (town) Nassau County	52.5
Maryland	29.2	Norfolk County, MA	53.7	**Glendora, CA** (city) Los Angeles County	49.1
Virginia	28.5	Cameron County, TX	51.0	**Thousand Oaks, CA** (city) Ventura County	49.0
Wyoming	27.4	Stafford County, VA	50.9	**Elmont, NY** (cdp) Nassau County	47.1
Ohio	27.1	Washington County, MN	50.0	**Fremont, CA** (city) Alameda County	45.3
Missouri	26.5	Clark County, WA	47.4	**Round Rock, TX** (city) Williamson County	44.9
Michigan	25.8	Santa Cruz County, CA	45.1	**Modesto, CA** (city) Stanislaus County	43.7
California	25.4	Hidalgo County, TX	44.4	**Huntington, NY** (town) Suffolk County	42.9
Washington	24.1	Frederick County, MD	44.0	**Dale City, VA** (cdp) Prince William County	42.0

Sorted by Percent in Ascending Order — U.S. = 19.1%

State	Percent	County	Percent	Place	Percent
North Dakota	8.3	Flagler County, FL	0.0	**New London, CT** (city/town) New London County	0.0
Utah	10.6	Davis County, UT	1.4	**Norfolk, VA** (independent city)	0.0
Rhode Island	11.2	Gaston County, NC	2.2	**Sanford, FL** (city) Seminole County	0.0
Montana	11.6	Leon County, FL	2.2	**Sterling, VA** (cdp) Loudoun County	0.0
South Carolina	12.2	Spartanburg County, SC	3.1	**Westchester, FL** (cdp) Miami-Dade County	0.0
Oklahoma	12.3	Horry County, SC	3.3	**Reading, PA** (city) Berks County	1.0
Idaho	12.8	Cleveland County, OK	3.6	**City of Orange, NJ** (township) Essex County	1.2
Nebraska	13.5	Hall County, GA	3.8	**Miami Gardens, FL** (city) Miami-Dade County	1.8
Nevada	13.9	Oneida County, NY	3.9	**Tulsa, OK** (city) Tulsa County	1.8
North Carolina	13.9	Lancaster County, PA	4.0	**Lehigh Acres, FL** (cdp) Lee County	2.1

Note: (1) Ranking tables cover all states and counties, and places with an overall population of at least 125,000, OR an overall population of at least 25,000 where the Hispanic/Latino population is at least 20% of the overall population. In states where less than five places meet either of these criteria, we have included places with at least 10,000 total population with the highest percentage of Hispanic/Latino population. These places are identified with an asterisk (*); Please refer to the User's Guide for a full explanation of data.

Households with $100,000+ Income

South American: Argentinean

Top 10 States, Counties, and Places[1]

Sorted by Number in Descending Order — U.S. = 21,197

State	Number	County	Number	Place	Number
California	4,446	Miami-Dade County, FL	1,866	**New York, NY** (city)	1,718
Florida	3,606	Los Angeles County, CA	1,795	**Los Angeles, CA** (city) Los Angeles County	971
New York	2,892	New York County, NY	923	**Manhattan, NY** (borough) New York County	923
New Jersey	1,655	Broward County, FL	811	**Queens, NY** (borough) Queens County	394
Texas	1,236	Orange County, CA	741	**Miami, FL** (city) Miami-Dade County	368
Connecticut	685	Hudson County, NJ	451	**Houston, TX** (city) Harris County	270
Maryland	675	Fairfield County, CT	442	**Aventura, FL** (city) Miami-Dade County	269
Virginia	638	Harris County, TX	425	**San Francisco, CA** (city) San Francisco County	254
Massachusetts	616	Queens County, NY	394	**Brooklyn, NY** (borough) Kings County	217
Illinois	565	Nassau County, NY	382	**Doral, FL** (city) Miami-Dade County	217

Sorted by Number in Ascending Order — U.S. = 21,197

State	Number	County	Number	Place	Number
Tennessee	28	Utah County, UT	20	**Hialeah, FL** (city) Miami-Dade County	0
Louisiana	70	New Haven County, CT	40	**San Jose, CA** (city) Santa Clara County	46
Wisconsin	73	Tarrant County, TX	45	**Coral Springs, FL** (city) Broward County	60
Missouri	79	Salt Lake County, UT	53	**Hollywood, FL** (city) Broward County	68
Utah	86	Montgomery County, TX	57	**San Diego, CA** (city) San Diego County	70
Minnesota	121	Riverside County, CA	61	**Bronx, NY** (borough) Bronx County	90
South Carolina	126	Dallas County, TX	68	**Pembroke Pines, FL** (city) Broward County	151
North Carolina	153	Orange County, FL	72	**Hempstead (town), NY** (town) Nassau County	170
Indiana	160	Orange County, NY	84	**Miami Beach, FL** (city) Miami-Dade County	181
Ohio	161	Bronx County, NY	90	**Chicago, IL** (city) Cook County	182

Sorted by Percent in Descending Order — U.S. = 26.5%

State	Percent	County	Percent	Place	Percent
Connecticut	51.6	Fairfield County, CT	69.2	**Doral, FL** (city) Miami-Dade County	57.1
Colorado	48.5	Middlesex County, MA	54.0	**Aventura, FL** (city) Miami-Dade County	54.2
Massachusetts	45.8	Contra Costa County, CA	53.5	**Manhattan, NY** (borough) New York County	50.3
District of Columbia	44.7	New York County, NY	50.3	**San Francisco, CA** (city) San Francisco County	44.7
Oregon	40.9	Santa Clara County, CA	49.1	**Hempstead (town), NY** (town) Nassau County	42.4
Indiana	40.3	Nassau County, NY	45.0	**Pembroke Pines, FL** (city) Broward County	32.8
Washington	39.2	Montgomery County, MD	44.8	**New York, NY** (city)	29.4
Georgia	38.6	Ventura County, CA	44.8	**Los Angeles, CA** (city) Los Angeles County	28.5
Minnesota	38.2	San Francisco County, CA	44.7	**San Diego, CA** (city) San Diego County	26.8
Maryland	36.3	Oakland County, MI	41.6	**Houston, TX** (city) Harris County	26.1

Sorted by Percent in Ascending Order — U.S. = 26.5%

State	Percent	County	Percent	Place	Percent
Utah	7.0	Utah County, UT	4.0	**Hialeah, FL** (city) Miami-Dade County	0.0
Tennessee	8.9	Riverside County, CA	8.6	**Miami Beach, FL** (city) Miami-Dade County	8.4
North Carolina	13.2	Dallas County, TX	10.2	**Hollywood, FL** (city) Broward County	9.8
Nevada	16.8	San Bernardino County, CA	11.7	**Miami, FL** (city) Miami-Dade County	16.5
Wisconsin	16.9	Orange County, FL	12.0	**Coral Springs, FL** (city) Broward County	17.0
Florida	17.8	Salt Lake County, UT	13.1	**San Jose, CA** (city) Santa Clara County	17.2
Louisiana	21.1	New Haven County, CT	14.3	**Queens, NY** (borough) Queens County	17.3
Pennsylvania	22.9	Palm Beach County, FL	15.9	**Bronx, NY** (borough) Bronx County	18.4
Texas	25.3	Montgomery County, TX	16.5	**Brooklyn, NY** (borough) Kings County	20.1
Ohio	25.9	Tarrant County, TX	16.7	**Chicago, IL** (city) Cook County	25.3

RANKINGS & COMPARISONS

Note: (1) Ranking tables cover all states and counties, and places with an overall population of at least 125,000, OR an overall population of at least 25,000 where the Hispanic/Latino population is at least 20% of the overall population. In states where less than five places meet either of these criteria, we have included places with at least 10,000 total population with the highest percentage of Hispanic/Latino population. These places are identified with an asterisk (*); Please refer to the User's Guide for a full explanation of data.

Households with $100,000+ Income

South American: Bolivian

Top 10 States, Counties, and Places[1]

Sorted by Number in Descending Order — U.S. = 7,624

State	Number	County	Number	Place	Number
Virginia	2,619	Fairfax County, VA	1,347	**New York, NY** (city)	390
California	1,250	Los Angeles County, CA	535	**Arlington, VA** (cdp) Arlington County	340
Maryland	692	Montgomery County, MD	490	**Los Angeles, CA** (city) Los Angeles County	258
New York	606	Prince William County, VA	385	**Queens, NY** (borough) Queens County	194
Florida	500	Arlington County, VA	340	**Annandale, VA** (cdp) Fairfax County	153
Texas	335	Miami-Dade County, FL	215	**West Falls Church, VA** (cdp) Fairfax County	129
New Jersey	316	Loudoun County, VA	213	**Springfield, VA** (cdp) Fairfax County	109
Illinois	175	Queens County, NY	194	**Dale City, VA** (cdp) Prince William County	92
Massachusetts	149	Orange County, CA	182	**Providence, RI** (city) Providence County	40
Rhode Island	57	San Diego County, CA	174		

Sorted by Number in Ascending Order — U.S. = 7,624

State	Number	County	Number	Place	Number
Pennsylvania	18	Palm Beach County, FL	42	**Providence, RI** (city) Providence County	40
North Carolina	52	Providence County, RI	57	**Dale City, VA** (cdp) Prince William County	92
Rhode Island	57	Broward County, FL	59	**Springfield, VA** (cdp) Fairfax County	109
Massachusetts	149	Harris County, TX	94	**West Falls Church, VA** (cdp) Fairfax County	129
Illinois	175	Cook County, IL	108	**Annandale, VA** (cdp) Fairfax County	153
New Jersey	316	Santa Clara County, CA	110	**Queens, NY** (borough) Queens County	194
Texas	335	Prince George's County, MD	122	**Los Angeles, CA** (city) Los Angeles County	258
Florida	500	San Diego County, CA	174	**Arlington, VA** (cdp) Arlington County	340
New York	606	Orange County, CA	182	**New York, NY** (city)	390
Maryland	692	Queens County, NY	194		

Sorted by Percent in Descending Order — U.S. = 25.1%

State	Percent	County	Percent	Place	Percent
North Carolina	34.4	San Diego County, CA	50.9	**West Falls Church, VA** (cdp) Fairfax County	32.9
Massachusetts	33.0	Loudoun County, VA	40.4	**Springfield, VA** (cdp) Fairfax County	31.8
Maryland	32.2	Cook County, IL	40.3	**Arlington, VA** (cdp) Arlington County	31.5
Virginia	28.2	Orange County, CA	35.4	**Dale City, VA** (cdp) Prince William County	30.7
California	27.4	Montgomery County, MD	33.3	**Los Angeles, CA** (city) Los Angeles County	23.9
New Jersey	25.4	Prince William County, VA	32.4	**Annandale, VA** (cdp) Fairfax County	22.1
Illinois	25.0	Arlington County, VA	31.5	**New York, NY** (city)	20.4
New York	23.5	Prince George's County, MD	30.7	**Queens, NY** (borough) Queens County	17.3
Texas	20.3	Santa Clara County, CA	30.6	**Providence, RI** (city) Providence County	13.3
Florida	15.3	Los Angeles County, CA	30.3		

Sorted by Percent in Ascending Order — U.S. = 25.1%

State	Percent	County	Percent	Place	Percent
Pennsylvania	7.6	Broward County, FL	9.9	**Providence, RI** (city) Providence County	13.3
Rhode Island	11.2	Palm Beach County, FL	10.9	**Queens, NY** (borough) Queens County	17.3
Florida	15.3	Providence County, RI	11.2	**New York, NY** (city)	20.4
Texas	20.3	Harris County, TX	16.2	**Annandale, VA** (cdp) Fairfax County	22.1
New York	23.5	Queens County, NY	17.3	**Los Angeles, CA** (city) Los Angeles County	23.9
Illinois	25.0	Miami-Dade County, FL	21.1	**Dale City, VA** (cdp) Prince William County	30.7
New Jersey	25.4	Fairfax County, VA	26.8	**Arlington, VA** (cdp) Arlington County	31.5
California	27.4	Los Angeles County, CA	30.3	**Springfield, VA** (cdp) Fairfax County	31.8
Virginia	28.2	Santa Clara County, CA	30.6	**West Falls Church, VA** (cdp) Fairfax County	32.9
Maryland	32.2	Prince George's County, MD	30.7		

Note: (1) Ranking tables cover all states and counties, and places with an overall population of at least 125,000, OR an overall population of at least 25,000 where the Hispanic/Latino population is at least 20% of the overall population. In states where less than five places meet either of these criteria, we have included places with at least 10,000 total population with the highest percentage of Hispanic/Latino population. These places are identified with an asterisk (*); Please refer to the User's Guide for a full explanation of data.

Households with $100,000+ Income

South American: Chilean

Top 10 States, Counties, and Places[1]

Sorted by Number in Descending Order — U.S. = 9,788

State	Number	County	Number	Place	Number
California	2,270	Los Angeles County, CA	902	**New York, NY** (city)	612
New York	1,392	Miami-Dade County, FL	702	**Los Angeles, CA** (city) Los Angeles County	460
Florida	1,292	Westchester County, NY	280	**Queens, NY** (borough) Queens County	277
New Jersey	590	Queens County, NY	277	**Manhattan, NY** (borough) New York County	165
Virginia	495	Montgomery County, MD	276	**Miami, FL** (city) Miami-Dade County	121
Maryland	434	Broward County, FL	253	**Hempstead (town), NY** (town) Nassau County	115
Texas	375	Fairfax County, VA	250	**Brooklyn, NY** (borough) Kings County	114
Illinois	288	Nassau County, NY	225	**Chicago, IL** (city) Cook County	85
Massachusetts	249	Suffolk County, NY	215	**Kendall, FL** (cdp) Miami-Dade County	23
Utah	228	Hudson County, NJ	171		

Sorted by Number in Ascending Order — U.S. = 9,788

State	Number	County	Number	Place	Number
Colorado	26	Salt Lake County, UT	52	**Kendall, FL** (cdp) Miami-Dade County	23
Wisconsin	40	Utah County, UT	63	**Chicago, IL** (city) Cook County	85
Michigan	50	Clark County, NV	65	**Brooklyn, NY** (borough) Kings County	114
Nevada	72	San Mateo County, CA	73	**Hempstead (town), NY** (town) Nassau County	115
Minnesota	78	Maricopa County, AZ	74	**Miami, FL** (city) Miami-Dade County	121
Oregon	78	Riverside County, CA	74	**Manhattan, NY** (borough) New York County	165
Missouri	81	San Bernardino County, CA	79	**Queens, NY** (borough) Queens County	277
Arizona	82	San Diego County, CA	79	**Los Angeles, CA** (city) Los Angeles County	460
Tennessee	95	Alameda County, CA	82	**New York, NY** (city)	612
Georgia	128	Palm Beach County, FL	86		

Sorted by Percent in Descending Order — U.S. = 23.5%

State	Percent	County	Percent	Place	Percent
Ohio	42.0	Suffolk County, NY	66.6	**Hempstead (town), NY** (town) Nassau County	30.2
Tennessee	40.3	Bergen County, NJ	40.5	**Miami, FL** (city) Miami-Dade County	26.3
Virginia	35.9	Montgomery County, MD	40.3	**Los Angeles, CA** (city) Los Angeles County	25.6
Minnesota	35.6	Westchester County, NY	37.8	**Manhattan, NY** (borough) New York County	24.5
Connecticut	34.4	Fairfax County, VA	36.0	**Chicago, IL** (city) Cook County	21.4
Maryland	34.0	Orange County, CA	35.2	**New York, NY** (city)	19.5
Missouri	29.1	Nassau County, NY	30.4	**Brooklyn, NY** (borough) Kings County	19.4
California	28.6	Los Angeles County, CA	28.2	**Queens, NY** (borough) Queens County	18.5
Illinois	27.1	Cook County, IL	27.0	**Kendall, FL** (cdp) Miami-Dade County	10.6
Oregon	26.7	Middlesex County, MA	25.6		

Sorted by Percent in Ascending Order — U.S. = 23.5%

State	Percent	County	Percent	Place	Percent
Colorado	7.1	Clark County, NV	13.5	**Kendall, FL** (cdp) Miami-Dade County	10.6
Nevada	11.2	Utah County, UT	15.1	**Queens, NY** (borough) Queens County	18.5
Arizona	13.4	Harris County, TX	15.3	**Brooklyn, NY** (borough) Kings County	19.4
Wisconsin	14.6	Palm Beach County, FL	16.0	**New York, NY** (city)	19.5
Florida	15.4	Miami-Dade County, FL	16.9	**Chicago, IL** (city) Cook County	21.4
Georgia	16.5	Broward County, FL	17.1	**Manhattan, NY** (borough) New York County	24.5
Washington	17.2	San Diego County, CA	18.2	**Los Angeles, CA** (city) Los Angeles County	25.6
New Jersey	20.6	Queens County, NY	18.5	**Miami, FL** (city) Miami-Dade County	26.3
Texas	21.6	Salt Lake County, UT	18.6	**Hempstead (town), NY** (town) Nassau County	30.2
Massachusetts	22.3	Kings County, NY	19.4		

Note: (1) Ranking tables cover all states and counties, and places with an overall population of at least 125,000, OR an overall population of at least 25,000 where the Hispanic/Latino population is at least 20% of the overall population. In states where less than five places meet either of these criteria, we have included places with at least 10,000 total population with the highest percentage of Hispanic/Latino population. These places are identified with an asterisk (*); Please refer to the User's Guide for a full explanation of data.

Households with $100,000+ Income

South American: Colombian

Top 10 States, Counties, and Places[1]

Sorted by Number in Descending Order (U.S. = 48,775)

State	Number	County	Number	Place	Number
Florida	11,854	Miami-Dade County, FL	4,756	**New York, NY** (city)	4,935
New York	8,815	Queens County, NY	3,172	**Queens, NY** (borough) Queens County	3,172
New Jersey	6,370	Broward County, FL	3,147	**Hempstead (town), NY** (town) Nassau County	988
California	5,109	Los Angeles County, CA	1,862	**Manhattan, NY** (borough) New York County	804
Texas	3,087	Nassau County, NY	1,530	**Houston, TX** (city) Harris County	606
Virginia	1,499	Bergen County, NJ	1,386	**Miami, FL** (city) Miami-Dade County	574
Massachusetts	1,305	Harris County, TX	1,143	**Pembroke Pines, FL** (city) Broward County	563
Illinois	1,259	Suffolk County, NY	874	**Los Angeles, CA** (city) Los Angeles County	558
Connecticut	1,069	Hudson County, NJ	818	**Weston, FL** (city) Broward County	536
Georgia	1,011	New York County, NY	804	**Boston, MA** (city) Suffolk County	533

Sorted by Number in Ascending Order (U.S. = 48,775)

State	Number	County	Number	Place	Number
Delaware	16	Leon County, FL	0	**Hartford, CT** (city/town) Hartford County	0
Utah	24	Luzerne County, PA	0	**Miami Gardens, FL** (city) Miami-Dade County	0
New Mexico	29	Dane County, WI	3	**Tallahassee, FL** (city) Leon County	0
Oklahoma	29	Marion County, IN	8	**Royal Palm Beach, FL** (village) Palm Beach County	6
Arkansas	46	Hall County, GA	15	**Indianapolis, IN** (city) Marion County	8
Iowa	49	Manatee County, FL	16	**Long Beach, CA** (city) Los Angeles County	9
Nebraska	59	Cherokee County, GA	18	**Buenaventura Lakes, FL** (cdp) Osceola County	17
Kentucky	62	Lancaster County, PA	18	**Central Falls*, RI** (city) Providence County	20
Tennessee	76	Hampden County, MA	19	**Meadow Woods, FL** (cdp) Orange County	20
Alaska	108	Ulster County, NY	20	**West New York, NJ** (town) Hudson County	21

Sorted by Percent in Descending Order (U.S. = 17.4%)

State	Percent	County	Percent	Place	Percent
Kansas	35.3	Norfolk County, MA	66.2	**Elmont, NY** (cdp) Nassau County	51.3
Virginia	33.9	Burlington County, NJ	60.4	**Huntington, NY** (town) Suffolk County	46.0
Oregon	33.0	Loudoun County, VA	52.7	**Hempstead (town), NY** (town) Nassau County	42.3
District of Columbia	32.9	Fairfax County, VA	44.4	**Oyster Bay, NY** (town) Nassau County	42.2
Ohio	30.1	San Mateo County, CA	42.9	**Arlington, VA** (cdp) Arlington County	42.0
Michigan	28.9	Arlington County, VA	42.0	**North Hempstead, NY** (town) Nassau County	39.7
New Hampshire	27.5	Dutchess County, NY	41.1	**Downey, CA** (city) Los Angeles County	37.5
Arizona	27.4	Nassau County, NY	41.0	**Burbank, CA** (city) Los Angeles County	33.8
Alaska	25.7	Forsyth County, GA	40.1	**Englewood, NJ** (city) Bergen County	33.1
California	25.7	Lake County, IL	37.7	**Cooper City, FL** (city) Broward County	32.8

Sorted by Percent in Ascending Order (U.S. = 17.4%)

State	Percent	County	Percent	Place	Percent
Utah	2.9	Leon County, FL	0.0	**Hartford, CT** (city/town) Hartford County	0.0
Oklahoma	4.7	Luzerne County, PA	0.0	**Miami Gardens, FL** (city) Miami-Dade County	0.0
Delaware	6.3	Dane County, WI	2.3	**Tallahassee, FL** (city) Leon County	0.0
Rhode Island	7.0	Marion County, IN	2.5	**West New York, NJ** (town) Hudson County	2.1
Tennessee	7.0	Saint Lucie County, FL	3.5	**Indianapolis, IN** (city) Marion County	2.5
New Mexico	8.5	Cherokee County, GA	3.8	**Meadow Woods, FL** (cdp) Orange County	2.6
South Carolina	8.8	Manatee County, FL	4.2	**Royal Palm Beach, FL** (village) Palm Beach County	2.6
Florida	12.8	Polk County, FL	4.3	**Long Beach, CA** (city) Los Angeles County	2.9
Pennsylvania	13.4	Salt Lake County, UT	4.9	**Central Falls*, RI** (city) Providence County	3.0
North Carolina	13.9	Lancaster County, PA	5.1	**Fort Lauderdale, FL** (city) Broward County	3.8

Note: (1) Ranking tables cover all states and counties, and places with an overall population of at least 125,000, OR an overall population of at least 25,000 where the Hispanic/Latino population is at least 20% of the overall population. In states where less than five places meet either of these criteria, we have included places with at least 10,000 total population with the highest percentage of Hispanic/Latino population. These places are identified with an asterisk (*); Please refer to the User's Guide for a full explanation of data.

Households with $100,000+ Income

South American: Ecuadorian

Top 10 States, Counties, and Places[1]

Sorted by Number in Descending Order — U.S. = 26,975

State	Number	County	Number	Place	Number
New York	9,537	Queens County, NY	4,302	**New York, NY** (city)	6,699
New Jersey	4,756	Los Angeles County, CA	1,696	**Queens, NY** (borough) Queens County	4,302
California	3,100	Hudson County, NJ	1,204	**Bronx, NY** (borough) Bronx County	859
Florida	2,779	Miami-Dade County, FL	1,099	**Brooklyn, NY** (borough) Kings County	786
Illinois	1,298	Cook County, IL	982	**Chicago, IL** (city) Cook County	767
Connecticut	812	Suffolk County, NY	956	**Manhattan, NY** (borough) New York County	605
Texas	650	Bronx County, NY	859	**Los Angeles, CA** (city) Los Angeles County	590
Maryland	599	Kings County, NY	786	**Hempstead (town), NY** (town) Nassau County	404
Virginia	559	Nassau County, NY	745	**Islip, NY** (town) Suffolk County	348
Pennsylvania	396	Bergen County, NJ	648	**Newark, NJ** (city) Essex County	347

Sorted by Number in Ascending Order — U.S. = 26,975

State	Number	County	Number	Place	Number
Louisiana	3	Philadelphia County, PA	0	**City of Orange, NJ** (township) Essex County	0
Missouri	11	Camden County, NJ	10	**Philadelphia, PA** (city) Philadelphia County	0
Oregon	14	Utah County, UT	13	**Bridgeport, CT** (city/town) Fairfield County	9
Rhode Island	19	Delaware County, PA	15	**Country Club, FL** (cdp) Miami-Dade County	9
Oklahoma	21	Providence County, RI	19	**Orlando, FL** (city) Orange County	20
Wisconsin	22	Worcester County, MA	20	**New Haven, CT** (city/town) New Haven County	30
Indiana	28	Pinellas County, FL	21	**Allentown, PA** (city) Lehigh County	32
Iowa	28	Baltimore County, MD	25	**Hialeah, FL** (city) Miami-Dade County	36
Utah	31	Berks County, PA	27	**Downey, CA** (city) Los Angeles County	38
South Carolina	33	Clark County, NV	28	**Coral Springs, FL** (city) Broward County	41

Sorted by Percent in Descending Order — U.S. = 16.2%

State	Percent	County	Percent	Place	Percent
Washington	40.2	Ocean County, NJ	51.8	**Oyster Bay, NY** (town) Nassau County	71.6
Virginia	32.3	Fairfax County, VA	48.4	**Clifton, NJ** (city) Passaic County	42.4
Maryland	27.4	Santa Clara County, CA	45.7	**Doral, FL** (city) Miami-Dade County	39.4
California	25.7	Burlington County, NJ	44.4	**Brookhaven, NY** (town) Suffolk County	34.3
Colorado	24.8	Orange County, CA	40.0	**Islip, NY** (town) Suffolk County	30.2
Arizona	21.3	Monmouth County, NJ	38.2	**Ramapo, NY** (town) Rockland County	28.2
Tennessee	20.4	Montgomery County, MD	34.4	**Hempstead (town), NY** (town) Nassau County	26.6
Georgia	18.8	Nassau County, NY	32.9	**Central Islip, NY** (cdp) Suffolk County	25.4
Illinois	18.6	Orange County, NY	30.7	**Brentwood, NY** (cdp) Suffolk County	25.3
Texas	16.9	Will County, IL	30.5	**North Hempstead, NY** (town) Nassau County	23.7

Sorted by Percent in Ascending Order — U.S. = 16.2%

State	Percent	County	Percent	Place	Percent
Louisiana	1.5	Philadelphia County, PA	0.0	**City of Orange, NJ** (township) Essex County	0.0
Missouri	4.2	Camden County, NJ	2.9	**Philadelphia, PA** (city) Philadelphia County	0.0
Utah	4.9	Utah County, UT	4.0	**Bridgeport, CT** (city/town) Fairfield County	1.8
Indiana	6.6	Hennepin County, MN	4.1	**Country Club, FL** (cdp) Miami-Dade County	2.6
Rhode Island	7.1	Clark County, NV	5.4	**Minneapolis, MN** (city) Hennepin County	4.1
Oregon	7.5	Worcester County, MA	5.8	**Orlando, FL** (city) Orange County	4.5
Wisconsin	8.7	Delaware County, PA	6.0	**Hialeah, FL** (city) Miami-Dade County	6.0
Oklahoma	9.5	Lehigh County, PA	6.3	**New Haven, CT** (city/town) New Haven County	6.3
South Carolina	9.6	Hillsborough County, FL	6.9	**Allentown, PA** (city) Lehigh County	6.9
Minnesota	9.7	Berks County, PA	7.1	**Ossining, NY** (village) Westchester County	7.1

Note: (1) Ranking tables cover all states and counties, and places with an overall population of at least 125,000, OR an overall population of at least 25,000 where the Hispanic/Latino population is at least 20% of the overall population. In states where less than five places meet either of these criteria, we have included places with at least 10,000 total population with the highest percentage of Hispanic/Latino population. These places are identified with an asterisk (*); Please refer to the User's Guide for a full explanation of data.

Households with $100,000+ Income

South American: Paraguayan

Top 10 States, Counties, and Places[1]

Sorted by Number in Descending Order — U.S. = 1,028

State	Number	County	Number	Place	Number
New York	333	Queens County, NY	242	**New York, NY** (city)	262
Texas	105	Westchester County, NY	8	**Queens, NY** (borough) Queens County	242
New Jersey	93				
Florida	64				
Maryland	50				
California	26				

Sorted by Number in Ascending Order — U.S. = 1,028

State	Number	County	Number	Place	Number
California	26	Westchester County, NY	8	**Queens, NY** (borough) Queens County	242
Maryland	50	Queens County, NY	242	**New York, NY** (city)	262
Florida	64				
New Jersey	93				
Texas	105				
New York	333				

Sorted by Percent in Descending Order — U.S. = 18.5%

State	Percent	County	Percent	Place	Percent
Texas	26.0	Queens County, NY	30.4	**Queens, NY** (borough) Queens County	30.4
New York	18.5	Westchester County, NY	1.6	**New York, NY** (city)	24.3
New Jersey	16.7				
Maryland	14.8				
Florida	12.6				
California	8.3				

Sorted by Percent in Ascending Order — U.S. = 18.5%

State	Percent	County	Percent	Place	Percent
California	8.3	Westchester County, NY	1.6	**New York, NY** (city)	24.3
Florida	12.6	Queens County, NY	30.4	**Queens, NY** (borough) Queens County	30.4
Maryland	14.8				
New Jersey	16.7				
New York	18.5				
Texas	26.0				

Note: (1) Ranking tables cover all states and counties, and places with an overall population of at least 125,000, OR an overall population of at least 25,000 where the Hispanic/Latino population is at least 20% of the overall population. In states where less than five places meet either of these criteria, we have included places with at least 10,000 total population with the highest percentage of Hispanic/Latino population. These places are identified with an asterisk (*); Please refer to the User's Guide for a full explanation of data.

Households with $100,000+ Income

South American: Peruvian

Top 10 States, Counties, and Places[1]

Sorted by Number in Descending Order — U.S. = 28,095

State	Number	County	Number	Place	Number
California	5,648	Los Angeles County, CA	1,785	**New York, NY** (city)	2,336
New York	4,343	Miami-Dade County, FL	1,744	**Queens, NY** (borough) Queens County	1,368
New Jersey	4,008	Queens County, NY	1,368	**Manhattan, NY** (borough) New York County	604
Florida	4,001	Fairfax County, VA	1,003	**Los Angeles, CA** (city) Los Angeles County	436
Virginia	2,008	Broward County, FL	857	**Islip, NY** (town) Suffolk County	340
Maryland	1,352	Montgomery County, MD	833	**Chicago, IL** (city) Cook County	298
Texas	1,281	Hudson County, NJ	785	**Hempstead (town), NY** (town) Nassau County	296
Connecticut	828	Orange County, CA	689	**San Francisco, CA** (city) San Francisco County	273
Illinois	647	Passaic County, NJ	646	**Elizabeth, NJ** (city) Union County	271
Georgia	498	New York County, NY	604	**Kearny, NJ** (town) Hudson County	229

Sorted by Number in Ascending Order — U.S. = 28,095

State	Number	County	Number	Place	Number
Delaware	21	Sarasota County, FL	0	**Phoenix, AZ** (city) Maricopa County	0
South Carolina	22	Wake County, NC	7	**West Valley City, UT** (city) Salt Lake County	9
Idaho	27	Denver County, CO	16	**Garland, TX** (city) Dallas County	10
Kentucky	34	Baltimore County, MD	21	**West New York, NJ** (town) Hudson County	10
Rhode Island	43	Lehigh County, PA	22	**Boston, MA** (city) Suffolk County	11
Oklahoma	48	Philadelphia County, PA	22	**Hollywood, FL** (city) Broward County	12
Kansas	56	Franklin County, OH	23	**Tampa, FL** (city) Hillsborough County	12
New Mexico	56	Collier County, FL	24	**Denver, CO** (city) Denver County	16
Indiana	57	Suffolk County, MA	25	**Davie, FL** (town) Broward County	17
Louisiana	62	Utah County, UT	27	**Fort Lauderdale, FL** (city) Broward County	17

Sorted by Percent in Descending Order — U.S. = 17.7%

State	Percent	County	Percent	Place	Percent
Missouri	34.8	Fort Bend County, TX	57.3	**Oyster Bay, NY** (town) Nassau County	68.5
Minnesota	28.8	Lake County, IL	45.5	**San Jose, CA** (city) Santa Clara County	41.3
Maryland	27.7	Morris County, NJ	44.2	**Belleville, NJ** (township) Essex County	36.8
Virginia	24.2	Denton County, TX	42.7	**Manhattan, NY** (borough) New York County	35.6
District of Columbia	23.5	New York County, NY	35.6	**Islip, NY** (town) Suffolk County	32.9
Alabama	22.9	Prince William County, VA	35.3	**Brentwood, NY** (cdp) Suffolk County	32.1
California	21.4	Nassau County, NY	34.2	**Doral, FL** (city) Miami-Dade County	31.9
Michigan	21.4	Ventura County, CA	32.4	**North Bergen, NJ** (township) Hudson County	31.5
Illinois	20.9	Santa Clara County, CA	31.9	**Weston, FL** (city) Broward County	31.3
Hawaii	20.5	Orange County, NY	31.3	**Linden, NJ** (city) Union County	30.7

Sorted by Percent in Ascending Order — U.S. = 17.7%

State	Percent	County	Percent	Place	Percent
South Carolina	4.1	Sarasota County, FL	0.0	**Phoenix, AZ** (city) Maricopa County	0.0
Delaware	5.2	Wake County, NC	2.6	**Hollywood, FL** (city) Broward County	1.1
Idaho	7.7	Collier County, FL	4.6	**West New York, NJ** (town) Hudson County	2.6
Oklahoma	7.8	Suffolk County, MA	5.1	**Boston, MA** (city) Suffolk County	3.1
Kentucky	9.5	Bronx County, NY	5.3	**West Valley City, UT** (city) Salt Lake County	3.5
Utah	9.6	Lee County, FL	5.6	**Hialeah, FL** (city) Miami-Dade County	3.6
Arizona	9.9	Maricopa County, AZ	5.6	**Tampa, FL** (city) Hillsborough County	3.6
Indiana	9.9	Travis County, TX	5.8	**Garland, TX** (city) Dallas County	4.0
North Carolina	11.7	Hillsborough County, FL	6.4	**Rye, NY** (town) Westchester County	4.9
Wisconsin	12.0	Lehigh County, PA	6.5	**Fort Lauderdale, FL** (city) Broward County	5.0

Note: (1) Ranking tables cover all states and counties, and places with an overall population of at least 125,000, OR an overall population of at least 25,000 where the Hispanic/Latino population is at least 20% of the overall population. In states where less than five places meet either of these criteria, we have included places with at least 10,000 total population with the highest percentage of Hispanic/Latino population. These places are identified with an asterisk (*); Please refer to the User's Guide for a full explanation of data.

Households with $100,000+ Income

South American: Uruguayan

Top 10 States, Counties, and Places[1]

Sorted by Number in Descending Order — U.S. = 2,905

State	Number	County	Number	Place	Number
New Jersey	576	Miami-Dade County, FL	224	**New York, NY** (city)	251
New York	514	Broward County, FL	152	**Queens, NY** (borough) Queens County	126
Florida	472	Union County, NJ	149	**Elizabeth, NJ** (city) Union County	8
California	250	Queens County, NY	126		
Virginia	161	Westchester County, NY	110		
Maryland	141	Essex County, NJ	98		
Texas	125	Los Angeles County, CA	96		
Georgia	115	Middlesex County, NJ	80		
Massachusetts	64	Hudson County, NJ	76		
Pennsylvania	41	Gwinnett County, GA	52		

Sorted by Number in Ascending Order — U.S. = 2,905

State	Number	County	Number	Place	Number
Pennsylvania	41	Worcester County, MA	10	**Elizabeth, NJ** (city) Union County	8
Massachusetts	64	Palm Beach County, FL	42	**Queens, NY** (borough) Queens County	126
Georgia	115	Morris County, NJ	47	**New York, NY** (city)	251
Texas	125	Harris County, TX	49		
Maryland	141	Gwinnett County, GA	52		
Virginia	161	Hudson County, NJ	76		
California	250	Middlesex County, NJ	80		
Florida	472	Los Angeles County, CA	96		
New York	514	Essex County, NJ	98		
New Jersey	576	Westchester County, NY	110		

Sorted by Percent in Descending Order — U.S. = 15.0%

State	Percent	County	Percent	Place	Percent
Virginia	28.4	Middlesex County, NJ	29.7	**Queens, NY** (borough) Queens County	23.6
Maryland	27.4	Westchester County, NY	25.5	**New York, NY** (city)	22.7
New York	24.3	Queens County, NY	23.6	**Elizabeth, NJ** (city) Union County	0.9
California	19.5	Los Angeles County, CA	17.9		
Texas	14.3	Hudson County, NJ	16.3		
New Jersey	14.0	Gwinnett County, GA	15.3		
Georgia	12.7	Broward County, FL	12.1		
Pennsylvania	10.0	Essex County, NJ	11.4		
Florida	8.9	Harris County, TX	11.4		
Massachusetts	8.3	Morris County, NJ	11.4		

Sorted by Percent in Ascending Order — U.S. = 15.0%

State	Percent	County	Percent	Place	Percent
Massachusetts	8.3	Worcester County, MA	2.7	**Elizabeth, NJ** (city) Union County	0.9
Florida	8.9	Palm Beach County, FL	6.7	**New York, NY** (city)	22.7
Pennsylvania	10.0	Miami-Dade County, FL	9.0	**Queens, NY** (borough) Queens County	23.6
Georgia	12.7	Union County, NJ	11.2		
New Jersey	14.0	Essex County, NJ	11.4		
Texas	14.3	Harris County, TX	11.4		
California	19.5	Morris County, NJ	11.4		
New York	24.3	Broward County, FL	12.1		
Maryland	27.4	Gwinnett County, GA	15.3		
Virginia	28.4	Hudson County, NJ	16.3		

Note: (1) Ranking tables cover all states and counties, and places with an overall population of at least 125,000, OR an overall population of at least 25,000 where the Hispanic/Latino population is at least 20% of the overall population. In states where less than five places meet either of these criteria, we have included places with at least 10,000 total population with the highest percentage of Hispanic/Latino population. These places are identified with an asterisk (*); Please refer to the User's Guide for a full explanation of data.

Households with $100,000+ Income

South American: Venezuelan

Top 10 States, Counties, and Places[1]

Sorted by Number in Descending Order — U.S. = 14,836

State	Number	County	Number	Place	Number
Florida	5,533	Miami-Dade County, FL	2,695	**New York, NY** (city)	811
Texas	2,258	Broward County, FL	1,398	**Doral, FL** (city) Miami-Dade County	534
New York	1,191	Harris County, TX	768	**Manhattan, NY** (borough) New York County	456
California	1,036	New York County, NY	456	**Houston, TX** (city) Harris County	413
New Jersey	540	Fort Bend County, TX	413	**Weston, FL** (city) Broward County	401
Georgia	413	Palm Beach County, FL	315	**Miami, FL** (city) Miami-Dade County	258
Virginia	381	Orange County, FL	233	**Hollywood, FL** (city) Broward County	217
Massachusetts	317	Los Angeles County, CA	229	**Pembroke Pines, FL** (city) Broward County	206
Maryland	284	Queens County, NY	199	**Queens, NY** (borough) Queens County	199
Ohio	265	Middlesex County, MA	182	**Aventura, FL** (city) Miami-Dade County	165

Sorted by Number in Ascending Order — U.S. = 14,836

State	Number	County	Number	Place	Number
Indiana	16	Osceola County, FL	0	**Hialeah, FL** (city) Miami-Dade County	6
Utah	49	Lee County, FL	18	**Kendall West, FL** (cdp) Miami-Dade County	15
Missouri	60	Bronx County, NY	21	**Bronx, NY** (borough) Bronx County	21
Michigan	66	Suffolk County, MA	22	**Coral Springs, FL** (city) Broward County	39
Minnesota	71	Gwinnett County, GA	33	**Orlando, FL** (city) Orange County	40
Arizona	83	Fairfield County, CT	38	**Tamiami, FL** (cdp) Miami-Dade County	44
South Carolina	95	Salt Lake County, UT	49	**Fountainebleau, FL** (cdp) Miami-Dade County	55
Oklahoma	104	Hudson County, NJ	75	**Country Club, FL** (cdp) Miami-Dade County	56
Washington	108	Pinellas County, FL	76	**Miramar, FL** (city) Broward County	75
Wisconsin	110	Orange County, CA	93	**Miami Beach, FL** (city) Miami-Dade County	95

Sorted by Percent in Descending Order — U.S. = 21.6%

State	Percent	County	Percent	Place	Percent
Ohio	46.1	Fort Bend County, TX	54.0	**Hollywood, FL** (city) Broward County	48.8
Texas	37.6	Travis County, TX	44.3	**Manhattan, NY** (borough) New York County	37.0
Maryland	32.6	Collin County, TX	39.9	**Aventura, FL** (city) Miami-Dade County	29.6
New Jersey	30.2	Montgomery County, TX	39.2	**Houston, TX** (city) Harris County	29.5
Wisconsin	29.7	New York County, NY	37.0	**The Hammocks, FL** (cdp) Miami-Dade County	25.0
Connecticut	29.5	Tarrant County, TX	36.3	**Kendall, FL** (cdp) Miami-Dade County	24.7
South Carolina	29.0	San Diego County, CA	35.6	**Doral, FL** (city) Miami-Dade County	23.8
California	27.5	King County, WA	35.5	**Davie, FL** (town) Broward County	23.6
Missouri	27.0	Harris County, TX	35.0	**Sunrise, FL** (city) Broward County	23.1
Colorado	26.3	Orange County, CA	33.8	**Pembroke Pines, FL** (city) Broward County	22.4

Sorted by Percent in Ascending Order — U.S. = 21.6%

State	Percent	County	Percent	Place	Percent
Indiana	4.4	Osceola County, FL	0.0	**Hialeah, FL** (city) Miami-Dade County	1.4
Utah	8.8	Lee County, FL	2.7	**Kendall West, FL** (cdp) Miami-Dade County	3.3
North Carolina	10.0	Bronx County, NY	4.8	**Bronx, NY** (borough) Bronx County	4.8
Minnesota	15.4	Suffolk County, MA	4.9	**Fountainebleau, FL** (cdp) Miami-Dade County	5.5
Florida	16.9	Gwinnett County, GA	5.6	**Orlando, FL** (city) Orange County	6.4
Arizona	18.3	Orange County, FL	10.0	**Miami Beach, FL** (city) Miami-Dade County	9.8
Michigan	18.3	Queens County, NY	12.8	**Tamiami, FL** (cdp) Miami-Dade County	9.8
Georgia	19.6	Salt Lake County, UT	13.2	**Country Club, FL** (cdp) Miami-Dade County	11.6
Tennessee	21.3	Pinellas County, FL	13.5	**Miami, FL** (city) Miami-Dade County	12.6
Washington	21.5	Fairfield County, CT	14.0	**Queens, NY** (borough) Queens County	12.8

Note: (1) Ranking tables cover all states and counties, and places with an overall population of at least 125,000, OR an overall population of at least 25,000 where the Hispanic/Latino population is at least 20% of the overall population. In states where less than five places meet either of these criteria, we have included places with at least 10,000 total population with the highest percentage of Hispanic/Latino population. These places are identified with an asterisk (*); Please refer to the User's Guide for a full explanation of data.

Households with $100,000+ Income

Spaniard

Top 10 States, Counties, and Places[1]

Sorted by Number in Descending Order — U.S. = 48,174

State	Number	County	Number	Place	Number
California	11,920	Los Angeles County, CA	2,328	**New York, NY** (city)	2,239
Texas	4,469	Bernalillo County, NM	1,247	**Albuquerque, NM** (city) Bernalillo County	1,070
New York	4,370	Miami-Dade County, FL	1,211	**Los Angeles, CA** (city) Los Angeles County	937
Florida	4,123	San Diego County, CA	1,066	**Queens, NY** (borough) Queens County	723
New Jersey	2,818	Santa Clara County, CA	981	**San Francisco, CA** (city) San Francisco County	627
New Mexico	2,607	Orange County, CA	887	**Manhattan, NY** (borough) New York County	601
Colorado	2,036	Harris County, TX	851	**Houston, TX** (city) Harris County	430
Virginia	1,236	Maricopa County, AZ	847	**San Diego, CA** (city) San Diego County	422
Arizona	1,229	Queens County, NY	723	**San Jose, CA** (city) Santa Clara County	357
Illinois	1,116	Hillsborough County, FL	672	**Staten Island, NY** (borough) Richmond County	336

Sorted by Number in Ascending Order — U.S. = 48,174

State	Number	County	Number	Place	Number
Maine	29	Butte County, CA	0	**Lubbock, TX** (city) Lubbock County	9
Mississippi	30	Milwaukee County, WI	0	**San Bernardino, CA** (city) San Bernardino County	24
West Virginia	31	Colfax County, NM	5	**Bakersfield, CA** (city) Kern County	32
Montana	35	Utah County, UT	7	**South Valley, NM** (cdp) Bernalillo County	38
Iowa	59	La Plata County, CO	16	**Las Cruces, NM** (city) Dona Ana County	40
Kentucky	73	Lubbock County, TX	16	**Oklahoma City, OK** (city) Oklahoma County	40
Wisconsin	75	Tulare County, CA	16	**Fresno, CA** (city) Fresno County	41
Indiana	77	Conejos County, CO	17	**Fort Collins, CO** (city) Larimer County	44
New Hampshire	77	Weber County, UT	18	**Long Beach, CA** (city) Los Angeles County	51
South Carolina	79	Las Animas County, CO	23	**Corpus Christi, TX** (city) Nueces County	55

Sorted by Percent in Descending Order — U.S. = 22.1%

State	Percent	County	Percent	Place	Percent
Virginia	40.2	Morris County, NJ	72.8	**Oyster Bay, NY** (town) Nassau County	54.7
Connecticut	39.7	Fairfax County, VA	60.4	**Staten Island, NY** (borough) Richmond County	51.9
Maryland	39.7	Bergen County, NJ	59.2	**Hempstead (town), NY** (town) Nassau County	45.9
District of Columbia	38.1	Hartford County, CT	55.6	**San Francisco, CA** (city) San Francisco County	41.6
New Jersey	35.4	Douglas County, CO	52.1	**Riverside, CA** (city) Riverside County	38.4
Alaska	34.5	Richmond County, NY	51.9	**Glendale, AZ** (city) Maricopa County	37.8
New York	30.6	Brazoria County, TX	48.7	**Virginia Beach, VA** (independent city)	37.2
Hawaii	30.3	Nassau County, NY	43.4	**San Jose, CA** (city) Santa Clara County	33.9
Georgia	29.9	Fairfield County, CT	41.8	**Kearny, NJ** (town) Hudson County	33.0
Pennsylvania	28.7	San Francisco County, CA	41.6	**Brookhaven, NY** (town) Suffolk County	30.9

Sorted by Percent in Ascending Order — U.S. = 22.1%

State	Percent	County	Percent	Place	Percent
Mississippi	5.5	Butte County, CA	0.0	**Lubbock, TX** (city) Lubbock County	2.0
Montana	6.0	Milwaukee County, WI	0.0	**Pueblo, CO** (city) Pueblo County	5.0
West Virginia	6.2	Colfax County, NM	2.3	**Colorado Springs, CO** (city) El Paso County	6.7
Oklahoma	7.0	Lubbock County, TX	3.0	**Long Beach, CA** (city) Los Angeles County	6.8
South Carolina	7.7	Utah County, UT	3.3	**Fresno, CA** (city) Fresno County	6.9
Maine	8.9	Cibola County, NM	3.8	**San Bernardino, CA** (city) San Bernardino County	8.7
Indiana	9.6	Conejos County, CO	4.3	**Corpus Christi, TX** (city) Nueces County	8.9
Wisconsin	9.9	San Miguel County, NM	5.0	**South Valley, NM** (cdp) Bernalillo County	9.0
Iowa	11.8	Valencia County, NM	5.7	**Lakewood, CO** (city) Jefferson County	9.1
Colorado	12.6	La Plata County, CO	5.9	**Oklahoma City, OK** (city) Oklahoma County	9.6

Note: (1) Ranking tables cover all states and counties, and places with an overall population of at least 125,000, OR an overall population of at least 25,000 where the Hispanic/Latino population is at least 20% of the overall population. In states where less than five places meet either of these criteria, we have included places with at least 10,000 total population with the highest percentage of Hispanic/Latino population. These places are identified with an asterisk (*); Please refer to the User's Guide for a full explanation of data.

Households with Food Stamps/SNAP Benefits During Past 12 Months

Total Population

Top 10 States, Counties, and Places[1]

Sorted by Number in Descending Order U.S. = 10,583,720

State	Number	County	Number	Place	Number
Texas	890,215	Cook County, IL	209,977	**New York, NY** (city)	480,945
New York	806,295	Los Angeles County, CA	179,948	**Brooklyn, NY** (borough) Kings County	169,644
California	673,449	Kings County, NY	169,644	**Chicago, IL** (city) Cook County	152,490
Florida	605,727	Miami-Dade County, FL	138,490	**Bronx, NY** (borough) Bronx County	133,714
Ohio	498,685	Bronx County, NY	133,714	**Philadelphia, PA** (city) Philadelphia County	101,040
Michigan	484,952	Wayne County, MI	127,110	**Detroit, MI** (city) Wayne County	85,433
Pennsylvania	445,506	Harris County, TX	122,472	**Manhattan, NY** (borough) New York County	82,243
Illinois	431,798	Maricopa County, AZ	105,439	**Queens, NY** (borough) Queens County	81,582
North Carolina	372,066	Philadelphia County, PA	101,040	**Los Angeles, CA** (city) Los Angeles County	80,046
Georgia	344,023	New York County, NY	82,243	**Houston, TX** (city) Harris County	79,834

Sorted by Number in Ascending Order U.S. = 10,583,720

State	Number	County	Number	Place	Number
Wyoming	10,764	Kenedy County, TX	0	**Hanover*, NH** (town) Grafton County	0
North Dakota	19,803	Eureka County, NV	4	**Schofield Barracks*, HI** (cdp) Honolulu County	0
Alaska	21,968	Glasscock County, TX	4	**Laguna Hills, CA** (city) Orange County	53
Vermont	25,957	Greeley County, KS	8	**Fort Leonard Wood*, MO** (cdp) Pulaski County	85
South Dakota	26,885	Sterling County, TX	8	**San Dimas, CA** (city) Los Angeles County	95
District of Columbia	27,437	Terrell County, TX	10	**Florence, AZ** (town) Pinal County	105
Delaware	27,718	Irion County, TX	12	**Green River*, WY** (city) Sweetwater County	109
New Hampshire	29,881	Wallace County, KS	13	**Sahuarita, AZ** (town) Pima County	118
Hawaii	32,544	Kent County, TX	15	**Diamond Bar, CA** (city) Los Angeles County	140
Montana	32,783	Motley County, TX	15	**Badger*, AK** (cdp) Fairbanks North Star Borough	155

Sorted by Percent in Descending Order U.S. = 9.3%

State	Percent	County	Percent	Place	Percent
Louisiana	16.7	Zavala County, TX	41.7	**Pharr, TX** (city) Hidalgo County	35.8
Mississippi	14.8	Todd County, SD	40.9	**Holyoke, MA** (city) Hampden County	34.1
Kentucky	14.0	Starr County, TX	39.0	**San Luis, AZ** (city) Yuma County	33.5
Tennessee	13.8	Martin County, KY	36.6	**Eagle Pass, TX** (city) Maverick County	32.6
Maine	13.6	Dimmit County, TX	34.8	**Hartford, CT** (city/town) Hartford County	32.4
West Virginia	13.2	Willacy County, TX	34.8	**San Juan, TX** (city) Hidalgo County	32.2
Oregon	13.0	Zapata County, TX	34.2	**East Chicago, IN** (city) Lake County	31.7
Arkansas	12.6	Shannon County, SD	33.8	**Detroit, MI** (city) Wayne County	31.5
Michigan	12.6	Lake County, TN	33.7	**Reading, PA** (city) Berks County	31.5
South Carolina	11.5	Mississippi County, MO	33.7	**York, PA** (city) York County	30.9

Sorted by Percent in Ascending Order U.S. = 9.3%

State	Percent	County	Percent	Place	Percent
Wyoming	4.9	Kenedy County, TX	0.0	**Hanover*, NH** (town) Grafton County	0.0
New Jersey	5.0	Pitkin County, CO	0.5	**Schofield Barracks*, HI** (cdp) Honolulu County	0.0
California	5.4	Eureka County, NV	0.6	**Laguna Hills, CA** (city) Orange County	0.5
Colorado	5.7	Morgan County, UT	0.8	**Chino Hills, CA** (city) San Bernardino County	0.7
New Hampshire	5.8	Glasscock County, TX	0.9	**Diamond Bar, CA** (city) Los Angeles County	0.8
Minnesota	5.9	Eagle County, CO	1.1	**San Dimas, CA** (city) Los Angeles County	0.8
Nevada	5.9	Blaine County, ID	1.2	**Culver City, CA** (city) Los Angeles County	0.9
Maryland	6.0	Teton County, WY	1.2	**Hacienda Heights, CA** (cdp) Los Angeles County	1.0
Utah	6.4	Routt County, CO	1.3	**Mountain View, CA** (city) Santa Clara County	1.0
Virginia	6.9	Carson County, TX	1.4	**San Mateo, CA** (city) San Mateo County	1.0

Note: (1) Ranking tables cover all states and counties, and places with an overall population of at least 125,000, OR an overall population of at least 25,000 where the Hispanic/Latino population is at least 20% of the overall population. In states where less than five places meet either of these criteria, we have included places with at least 10,000 total population with the highest percentage of Hispanic/Latino population. These places are identified with an asterisk (*); Please refer to the User's Guide for a full explanation of data.

Households with Food Stamps/SNAP Benefits During Past 12 Months

Hispanic or Latino (of any race)

Top 10 States, Counties, and Places[1]

Sorted by Number in Descending Order — U.S. = 2,019,816

State	Number	County	Number	Place	Number
Texas	444,989	Los Angeles County, CA	108,086	**New York, NY** (city)	216,371
California	333,839	Miami-Dade County, FL	102,654	**Bronx, NY** (borough) Bronx County	89,119
New York	255,528	Bronx County, NY	89,119	**Brooklyn, NY** (borough) Kings County	48,933
Florida	192,784	Hidalgo County, TX	61,031	**Los Angeles, CA** (city) Los Angeles County	48,036
Arizona	84,788	Harris County, TX	50,131	**Manhattan, NY** (borough) New York County	43,964
Illinois	68,796	Kings County, NY	48,933	**San Antonio, TX** (city) Bexar County	42,997
Massachusetts	56,728	Bexar County, TX	47,715	**El Paso, TX** (city) El Paso County	36,161
Pennsylvania	55,522	Cook County, IL	46,278	**Chicago, IL** (city) Cook County	33,571
New Jersey	52,232	El Paso County, TX	45,287	**Houston, TX** (city) Harris County	30,923
New Mexico	45,184	New York County, NY	43,964	**Queens, NY** (borough) Queens County	30,581

Sorted by Number in Ascending Order — U.S. = 2,019,816

State	Number	County	Number	Place	Number
Vermont	350	Addison County, VT	0	**College*, AK** (cdp) Fairbanks North Star Borough	0
North Dakota	739	Athens County, OH	0	**Fort Leonard Wood*, MO** (cdp) Pulaski County	0
South Dakota	885	Augusta County, VA	0	**Salem*, NH** (town) Rockingham County	0
West Virginia	1,047	Big Horn County, WY	0	**Schofield Barracks*, HI** (cdp) Honolulu County	0
Maine	1,149	Boone County, AR	0	**Green River*, WY** (city) Sweetwater County	5
Alaska	1,200	Carlton County, MN	0	**Bozeman*, MT** (city) Gallatin County	8
Montana	1,211	Carson County, TX	0	**Laurel*, MS** (city) Jones County	8
District of Columbia	1,342	Cass County, NE	0	**Brookside*, DE** (cdp) New Castle County	13
Wyoming	1,347	Chaffee County, CO	0	**Gillette*, WY** (city) Campbell County	16
New Hampshire	1,497	Charlevoix County, MI	0	**Middle*, DE** (town) New Castle County	16

Sorted by Percent in Descending Order — U.S. = 15.7%

State	Percent	County	Percent	Place	Percent
Massachusetts	31.8	Clearfield County, PA	76.3	**Holyoke, MA** (city) Hampden County	67.0
Pennsylvania	30.1	Lawrence County, TN	64.9	**York, PA** (city) York County	53.6
Rhode Island	29.4	Johnston County, OK	62.7	**Buffalo, NY** (city) Erie County	53.1
Maine	26.0	Logan County, KY	62.5	**Woonsocket*, RI** (city) Providence County	52.6
New York	25.7	Benton County, MN	60.3	**Springfield, MA** (city) Hampden County	52.1
Connecticut	25.5	Wexford County, MI	59.9	**Lebanon, PA** (city) Lebanon County	48.4
Oregon	22.9	Wyoming County, PA	58.1	**Hartford, CT** (city/town) Hartford County	47.3
Michigan	22.7	Greene County, TN	57.5	**Reading, PA** (city) Berks County	46.3
Tennessee	21.6	Neosho County, KS	55.0	**Worcester, MA** (city) Worcester County	45.1
Ohio	21.1	Dickens County, TX	53.5	**Hazleton, PA** (city) Luzerne County	44.4

Sorted by Percent in Ascending Order — U.S. = 15.7%

State	Percent	County	Percent	Place	Percent
Virginia	6.1	Addison County, VT	0.0	**College*, AK** (cdp) Fairbanks North Star Borough	0.0
Maryland	7.2	Athens County, OH	0.0	**Fort Leonard Wood*, MO** (cdp) Pulaski County	0.0
District of Columbia	7.3	Augusta County, VA	0.0	**Salem*, NH** (town) Rockingham County	0.0
Nevada	8.5	Big Horn County, WY	0.0	**Schofield Barracks*, HI** (cdp) Honolulu County	0.0
Mississippi	9.7	Boone County, AR	0.0	**Torrance, CA** (city) Los Angeles County	1.1
Wyoming	9.9	Carlton County, MN	0.0	**Burbank, CA** (city) Los Angeles County	1.2
California	10.1	Carson County, TX	0.0	**Green River*, WY** (city) Sweetwater County	1.2
Georgia	10.9	Cass County, NE	0.0	**San Dimas, CA** (city) Los Angeles County	1.3
Alaska	11.9	Chaffee County, CO	0.0	**Chino Hills, CA** (city) San Bernardino County	1.4
Utah	11.9	Charlevoix County, MI	0.0	**La Verne, CA** (city) Los Angeles County	1.4

Note: (1) Ranking tables cover all states and counties, and places with an overall population of at least 125,000, OR an overall population of at least 25,000 where the Hispanic/Latino population is at least 20% of the overall population. In states where less than five places meet either of these criteria, we have included places with at least 10,000 total population with the highest percentage of Hispanic/Latino population. These places are identified with an asterisk (*); Please refer to the User's Guide for a full explanation of data.

Households with Food Stamps/SNAP Benefits During Past 12 Months

Central American, excluding Mexican

Top 10 States, Counties, and Places[1]

Sorted by Number in Descending Order — U.S. = 111,818

State	Number	County	Number	Place	Number
California	24,968	Los Angeles County, CA	16,227	**Los Angeles, CA** (city) Los Angeles County	10,067
Florida	17,090	Miami-Dade County, FL	11,049	**New York, NY** (city)	9,913
New York	12,864	Harris County, TX	6,016	**Miami, FL** (city) Miami-Dade County	4,124
Texas	11,777	Bronx County, NY	3,439	**Houston, TX** (city) Harris County	3,913
New Jersey	3,671	Kings County, NY	3,091	**Bronx, NY** (borough) Bronx County	3,439
Massachusetts	3,621	Cook County, IL	1,928	**Brooklyn, NY** (borough) Kings County	3,091
North Carolina	3,380	Queens County, NY	1,911	**Queens, NY** (borough) Queens County	1,911
Virginia	3,198	Suffolk County, MA	1,712	**Manhattan, NY** (borough) New York County	1,335
Maryland	3,168	Dallas County, TX	1,694	**Chicago, IL** (city) Cook County	1,288
Georgia	2,761	San Bernardino County, CA	1,631	**Hialeah, FL** (city) Miami-Dade County	1,099

Sorted by Number in Ascending Order — U.S. = 111,818

State	Number	County	Number	Place	Number
Hawaii	0	Caroline County, MD	0	**Altadena, CA** (cdp) Los Angeles County	0
West Virginia	7	Chester County, PA	0	**Annandale, VA** (cdp) Fairfax County	0
South Dakota	40	Cumberland County, NJ	0	**Belleville, NJ** (township) Essex County	0
Maine	52	Dawson County, NE	0	**Buenaventura Lakes, FL** (cdp) Osceola County	0
Vermont	54	Delaware County, PA	0	**Chesapeake, VA** (independent city)	0
Wyoming	58	Douglas County, CO	0	**Chino Hills, CA** (city) San Bernardino County	0
Idaho	106	El Dorado County, CA	0	**Concord, CA** (city) Contra Costa County	0
Alaska	120	Escambia County, FL	0	**Coral Gables, FL** (city) Miami-Dade County	0
New Hampshire	129	Frederick County, VA	0	**Covina, CA** (city) Los Angeles County	0
New Mexico	219	Garfield County, CO	0	**Cranston*, RI** (city) Providence County	0

Sorted by Percent in Descending Order — U.S. = 10.6%

State	Percent	County	Percent	Place	Percent
Vermont	58.1	Kitsap County, WA	42.9	**Springfield, MA** (city) Hampden County	50.5
Wyoming	24.3	Hillsborough County, NH	35.9	**Reading, PA** (city) Berks County	48.9
Kentucky	22.9	Hamilton County, TN	35.5	**Hartford, CT** (city/town) Hartford County	40.4
Alaska	21.8	Hays County, TX	35.4	**Westchester, FL** (cdp) Miami-Dade County	40.4
Delaware	20.9	Franklin County, AL	35.1	**Elkhart, IN** (city) Elkhart County	37.5
Tennessee	19.2	Murray County, GA	35.0	**Chattanooga, TN** (city) Hamilton County	36.3
Indiana	18.1	Elkhart County, IN	34.7	**Lubbock, TX** (city) Lubbock County	34.1
New Hampshire	17.8	Berks County, PA	34.6	**Kansas City, MO** (city) Jackson County	33.2
Rhode Island	17.6	Pitt County, NC	34.3	**Anchorage, AK** (municipality)	30.8
Maine	16.4	Henry County, GA	33.8	**Woodland, CA** (city) Yolo County	29.9

Sorted by Percent in Ascending Order — U.S. = 10.6%

State	Percent	County	Percent	Place	Percent
Hawaii	0.0	Caroline County, MD	0.0	**Altadena, CA** (cdp) Los Angeles County	0.0
West Virginia	2.3	Chester County, PA	0.0	**Annandale, VA** (cdp) Fairfax County	0.0
Nevada	5.5	Cumberland County, NJ	0.0	**Belleville, NJ** (township) Essex County	0.0
South Dakota	6.5	Dawson County, NE	0.0	**Buenaventura Lakes, FL** (cdp) Osceola County	0.0
Virginia	7.0	Delaware County, PA	0.0	**Chesapeake, VA** (independent city)	0.0
Minnesota	7.2	Douglas County, CO	0.0	**Chino Hills, CA** (city) San Bernardino County	0.0
Maryland	7.4	El Dorado County, CA	0.0	**Concord, CA** (city) Contra Costa County	0.0
California	7.9	Escambia County, FL	0.0	**Coral Gables, FL** (city) Miami-Dade County	0.0
Colorado	7.9	Frederick County, VA	0.0	**Covina, CA** (city) Los Angeles County	0.0
New Jersey	8.5	Garfield County, CO	0.0	**Cranston*, RI** (city) Providence County	0.0

Note: (1) Ranking tables cover all states and counties, and places with an overall population of at least 125,000, OR an overall population of at least 25,000 where the Hispanic/Latino population is at least 20% of the overall population. In states where less than five places meet either of these criteria, we have included places with at least 10,000 total population with the highest percentage of Hispanic/Latino population. These places are identified with an asterisk (*); Please refer to the User's Guide for a full explanation of data.

Households with Food Stamps/SNAP Benefits During Past 12 Months

Central American: Costa Rican

Top 10 States, Counties, and Places[1]

Sorted by Number in Descending Order — U.S. = 3,042

State	Number	County	Number	Place	Number
Florida	669	Miami-Dade County, FL	311	**New York, NY** (city)	422
New York	492	Broward County, FL	179	**Brooklyn, NY** (borough) Kings County	164
New Jersey	403	Kings County, NY	164	**Queens, NY** (borough) Queens County	104
California	229	Union County, NJ	118	**Bronx, NY** (borough) Bronx County	101
Massachusetts	159	Queens County, NY	104	**Miami, FL** (city) Miami-Dade County	77
Pennsylvania	150	Bronx County, NY	101	**Los Angeles, CA** (city) Los Angeles County	73
Texas	150	Essex County, NJ	86	**Philadelphia, PA** (city) Philadelphia County	49
North Carolina	148	Los Angeles County, CA	83		
Georgia	113	Palm Beach County, FL	60		
Louisiana	78	Clark County, NV	55		

Sorted by Number in Ascending Order — U.S. = 3,042

State	Number	County	Number	Place	Number
Arizona	0	Contra Costa County, CA	0	**Philadelphia, PA** (city) Philadelphia County	49
Maryland	0	Maricopa County, AZ	0	**Los Angeles, CA** (city) Los Angeles County	73
South Carolina	0	Morris County, NJ	0	**Miami, FL** (city) Miami-Dade County	77
Tennessee	0	Nassau County, NY	0	**Bronx, NY** (borough) Bronx County	101
Virginia	0	Riverside County, CA	0	**Queens, NY** (borough) Queens County	104
Wisconsin	0	San Bernardino County, CA	4	**Brooklyn, NY** (borough) Kings County	164
Colorado	13	Hillsborough County, FL	13	**New York, NY** (city)	422
Michigan	17	Orange County, FL	14		
Oregon	30	Somerset County, NJ	17		
Minnesota	31	Bergen County, NJ	19		

Sorted by Percent in Descending Order — U.S. = 7.9%

State	Percent	County	Percent	Place	Percent
Washington	15.2	Bronx County, NY	25.3	**Bronx, NY** (borough) Bronx County	25.3
Louisiana	13.8	Broward County, FL	21.0	**New York, NY** (city)	17.3
New York	13.2	Kings County, NY	16.6	**Brooklyn, NY** (borough) Kings County	16.6
Massachusetts	12.2	Clark County, NV	16.5	**Queens, NY** (borough) Queens County	16.4
Nevada	12.2	Queens County, NY	16.4	**Miami, FL** (city) Miami-Dade County	15.9
Pennsylvania	12.1	Essex County, NJ	13.2	**Philadelphia, PA** (city) Philadelphia County	10.5
Minnesota	11.4	Miami-Dade County, FL	13.1	**Los Angeles, CA** (city) Los Angeles County	7.0
Georgia	10.7	Union County, NJ	11.4		
Florida	10.2	Palm Beach County, FL	10.7		
Oregon	10.2	Philadelphia County, PA	10.5		

Sorted by Percent in Ascending Order — U.S. = 7.9%

State	Percent	County	Percent	Place	Percent
Arizona	0.0	Contra Costa County, CA	0.0	**Los Angeles, CA** (city) Los Angeles County	7.0
Maryland	0.0	Maricopa County, AZ	0.0	**Philadelphia, PA** (city) Philadelphia County	10.5
South Carolina	0.0	Morris County, NJ	0.0	**Miami, FL** (city) Miami-Dade County	15.9
Tennessee	0.0	Nassau County, NY	0.0	**Queens, NY** (borough) Queens County	16.4
Virginia	0.0	Riverside County, CA	0.0	**Brooklyn, NY** (borough) Kings County	16.6
Wisconsin	0.0	San Bernardino County, CA	1.1	**New York, NY** (city)	17.3
Colorado	2.9	Los Angeles County, CA	2.6	**Bronx, NY** (borough) Bronx County	25.3
California	3.2	Hillsborough County, FL	2.7		
Texas	6.9	Somerset County, NJ	3.6		
Illinois	7.4	Bergen County, NJ	4.4		

Note: (1) Ranking tables cover all states and counties, and places with an overall population of at least 125,000, OR an overall population of at least 25,000 where the Hispanic/Latino population is at least 20% of the overall population. In states where less than five places meet either of these criteria, we have included places with at least 10,000 total population with the highest percentage of Hispanic/Latino population. These places are identified with an asterisk (*); Please refer to the User's Guide for a full explanation of data.

Households with Food Stamps/SNAP Benefits During Past 12 Months

Central American: Guatemalan

Top 10 States, Counties, and Places[1]

Sorted by Number in Descending Order — U.S. = 27,422

State	Number	County	Number	Place	Number
California	7,487	Los Angeles County, CA	5,231	**Los Angeles, CA** (city) Los Angeles County	3,417
Florida	2,645	Cook County, IL	1,114	**New York, NY** (city)	1,271
New York	1,988	Miami-Dade County, FL	1,087	**Chicago, IL** (city) Cook County	737
Texas	1,551	Harris County, TX	981	**Houston, TX** (city) Harris County	709
Illinois	1,407	Providence County, RI	845	**Providence, RI** (city) Providence County	555
Massachusetts	1,051	Palm Beach County, FL	511	**Queens, NY** (borough) Queens County	425
North Carolina	914	San Bernardino County, CA	459	**Bronx, NY** (borough) Bronx County	418
New Jersey	856	Queens County, NY	425	**Brooklyn, NY** (borough) Kings County	387
Rhode Island	852	Bronx County, NY	418	**Miami, FL** (city) Miami-Dade County	299
Georgia	625	Kings County, NY	387	**Phoenix, AZ** (city) Maricopa County	245

Sorted by Number in Ascending Order — U.S. = 27,422

State	Number	County	Number	Place	Number
Idaho	0	Arapahoe County, CO	0	**Alhambra, CA** (city) Los Angeles County	0
New Hampshire	6	Caroline County, MD	0	**Aurora, CO** (city) Arapahoe County	0
South Dakota	29	Dawson County, NE	0	**Bell Gardens, CA** (city) Los Angeles County	0
Wisconsin	34	Denton County, TX	0	**Bonita Springs, FL** (city) Lee County	0
Kansas	45	Floyd County, GA	0	**Brentwood, NY** (cdp) Suffolk County	0
District of Columbia	63	Fort Bend County, TX	0	**Chillum, MD** (cdp) Prince George's County	0
Minnesota	72	Franklin County, OH	0	**Columbus, OH** (city) Franklin County	0
Mississippi	75	Fulton County, GA	0	**Corona, CA** (city) Riverside County	0
Ohio	99	Gilmer County, GA	0	**Cranston*, RI** (city) Providence County	0
Arkansas	114	Knox County, TN	0	**Elizabeth, NJ** (city) Union County	0

Sorted by Percent in Descending Order — U.S. = 10.7%

State	Percent	County	Percent	Place	Percent
Kentucky	28.9	Utah County, UT	45.7	**San Bernardino, CA** (city) San Bernardino County	34.8
Delaware	24.4	Polk County, FL	43.0	**Yonkers, NY** (city) Westchester County	34.0
Washington	23.8	Murray County, GA	42.8	**Winston-Salem, NC** (city) Forsyth County	33.8
Michigan	22.0	Hamilton County, TN	38.6	**Chattanooga, TN** (city) Hamilton County	33.7
North Carolina	19.4	Franklin County, AL	35.1	**Homestead, FL** (city) Miami-Dade County	29.4
Indiana	19.2	Manatee County, FL	33.3	**Pomona, CA** (city) Los Angeles County	26.8
Utah	19.1	Essex County, NJ	30.6	**Philadelphia, PA** (city) Philadelphia County	26.7
Alabama	17.3	Sussex County, DE	29.7	**Bronx, NY** (borough) Bronx County	25.6
Missouri	17.3	Forsyth County, NC	26.9	**Central Falls*, RI** (city) Providence County	25.4
Rhode Island	17.0	Philadelphia County, PA	26.7	**Hialeah, FL** (city) Miami-Dade County	25.0

Sorted by Percent in Ascending Order — U.S. = 10.7%

State	Percent	County	Percent	Place	Percent
Idaho	0.0	Arapahoe County, CO	0.0	**Alhambra, CA** (city) Los Angeles County	0.0
New Hampshire	3.7	Caroline County, MD	0.0	**Aurora, CO** (city) Arapahoe County	0.0
Kansas	4.4	Dawson County, NE	0.0	**Bell Gardens, CA** (city) Los Angeles County	0.0
Ohio	5.5	Denton County, TX	0.0	**Bonita Springs, FL** (city) Lee County	0.0
Maryland	5.6	Floyd County, GA	0.0	**Brentwood, NY** (cdp) Suffolk County	0.0
Minnesota	5.6	Fort Bend County, TX	0.0	**Chillum, MD** (cdp) Prince George's County	0.0
Nevada	6.0	Franklin County, OH	0.0	**Columbus, OH** (city) Franklin County	0.0
Georgia	7.3	Fulton County, GA	0.0	**Corona, CA** (city) Riverside County	0.0
Connecticut	7.7	Gilmer County, GA	0.0	**Cranston*, RI** (city) Providence County	0.0
New Jersey	8.0	Knox County, TN	0.0	**Elizabeth, NJ** (city) Union County	0.0

Note: (1) Ranking tables cover all states and counties, and places with an overall population of at least 125,000, OR an overall population of at least 25,000 where the Hispanic/Latino population is at least 20% of the overall population. In states where less than five places meet either of these criteria, we have included places with at least 10,000 total population with the highest percentage of Hispanic/Latino population. These places are identified with an asterisk (*); Please refer to the User's Guide for a full explanation of data.

Households with Food Stamps/SNAP Benefits During Past 12 Months

Central American: Honduran

Top 10 States, Counties, and Places[1]

Sorted by Number in Descending Order — U.S. = 23,632

State	Number	County	Number	Place	Number
New York	4,190	Miami-Dade County, FL	2,631	**New York, NY** (city)	3,675
Florida	4,160	Bronx County, NY	1,967	**Bronx, NY** (borough) Bronx County	1,967
Texas	3,182	Los Angeles County, CA	1,541	**Miami, FL** (city) Miami-Dade County	1,328
California	2,383	Harris County, TX	1,502	**Houston, TX** (city) Harris County	1,181
Louisiana	1,195	Kings County, NY	898	**Brooklyn, NY** (borough) Kings County	898
North Carolina	1,193	Jefferson Parish, LA	694	**Los Angeles, CA** (city) Los Angeles County	732
Georgia	848	Dallas County, TX	560	**Manhattan, NY** (borough) New York County	433
New Jersey	812	New York County, NY	433	**Dallas, TX** (city) Dallas County	380
Tennessee	624	Suffolk County, MA	389	**Queens, NY** (borough) Queens County	341
Massachusetts	567	Broward County, FL	380	**Charlotte, NC** (city) Mecklenburg County	331

Sorted by Number in Ascending Order — U.S. = 23,632

State	Number	County	Number	Place	Number
Michigan	31	Alameda County, CA	0	**Oakland, CA** (city) Alameda County	0
District of Columbia	40	Atlantic County, NJ	0	**North Miami Beach, FL** (city) Miami-Dade County	16
Arkansas	47	Loudoun County, VA	0	**Newburgh, NY** (city) Orange County	17
Utah	56	Prince William County, VA	12	**Plainfield, NJ** (city) Union County	17
Kansas	67	East Baton Rouge Parish, LA	13	**San Jose, CA** (city) Santa Clara County	20
Alabama	68	Arapahoe County, CO	15	**Waukegan, IL** (city) Lake County	22
Nebraska	78	Denton County, TX	15	**Fort Worth, TX** (city) Tarrant County	31
Iowa	85	Collier County, FL	19	**Raleigh, NC** (city) Wake County	36
Minnesota	87	Sampson County, NC	19	**Staten Island, NY** (borough) Richmond County	36
Colorado	93	DeKalb County, GA	21	**Newark, NJ** (city) Essex County	37

Sorted by Percent in Descending Order — U.S. = 14.7%

State	Percent	County	Percent	Place	Percent
Oregon	29.2	Philadelphia County, PA	48.9	**Philadelphia, PA** (city) Philadelphia County	48.9
Iowa	27.2	Jackson County, MO	48.8	**Phoenix, AZ** (city) Maricopa County	36.0
Missouri	26.0	King County, WA	41.0	**South Miami Heights, FL** (cdp) Miami-Dade County	34.8
Washington	25.5	New Haven County, CT	33.3	**Bronx, NY** (borough) Bronx County	32.4
Nebraska	25.4	Bronx County, NY	32.4	**Manhattan, NY** (borough) New York County	31.4
Mississippi	25.1	New York County, NY	31.4	**Long Beach, CA** (city) Los Angeles County	30.6
Arizona	24.7	Kern County, CA	30.0	**Memphis, TN** (city) Shelby County	28.8
Tennessee	23.3	Shelby County, TN	29.9	**Garland, TX** (city) Dallas County	27.9
Indiana	22.4	Johnston County, NC	29.1	**Nashville-Davidson, TN** (metropolitan govt) Davidson County	27.9
New York	21.8	Maricopa County, AZ	28.4	**Miramar, FL** (city) Broward County	26.5

Sorted by Percent in Ascending Order — U.S. = 14.7%

State	Percent	County	Percent	Place	Percent
Michigan	5.9	Alameda County, CA	0.0	**Oakland, CA** (city) Alameda County	0.0
Virginia	6.1	Atlantic County, NJ	0.0	**Plainfield, NJ** (city) Union County	3.7
Maryland	6.6	Loudoun County, VA	0.0	**San Jose, CA** (city) Santa Clara County	3.8
Colorado	6.7	Prince William County, VA	1.3	**Waukegan, IL** (city) Lake County	4.3
District of Columbia	6.9	East Baton Rouge Parish, LA	1.7	**Newburgh, NY** (city) Orange County	5.3
Nevada	8.8	DeKalb County, GA	2.9	**North Miami Beach, FL** (city) Miami-Dade County	5.4
Illinois	8.9	Prince George's County, MD	2.9	**Hempstead (town), NY** (town) Nassau County	6.1
Alabama	9.0	Collier County, FL	3.0	**Fort Worth, TX** (city) Tarrant County	6.3
New Jersey	9.5	Lake County, IL	3.2	**Raleigh, NC** (city) Wake County	6.6
Arkansas	9.6	Arapahoe County, CO	3.8	**Islip, NY** (town) Suffolk County	6.9

Note: (1) Ranking tables cover all states and counties, and places with an overall population of at least 125,000, OR an overall population of at least 25,000 where the Hispanic/Latino population is at least 20% of the overall population. In states where less than five places meet either of these criteria, we have included places with at least 10,000 total population with the highest percentage of Hispanic/Latino population. These places are identified with an asterisk (*); Please refer to the User's Guide for a full explanation of data.

Households with Food Stamps/SNAP Benefits During Past 12 Months

Central American: Nicaraguan

Top 10 States, Counties, and Places[1]

Sorted by Number in Descending Order — U.S. = 11,786

State	Number	County	Number	Place	Number
Florida	6,561	Miami-Dade County, FL	5,737	**Miami, FL** (city) Miami-Dade County	2,130
California	1,558	Los Angeles County, CA	649	**New York, NY** (city)	651
New York	737	New York County, NY	226	**Hialeah, FL** (city) Miami-Dade County	618
Texas	473	Palm Beach County, FL	220	**Los Angeles, CA** (city) Los Angeles County	435
Louisiana	289	Harris County, TX	165	**Fountainebleau, FL** (cdp) Miami-Dade County	429
New Jersey	226	Bronx County, NY	160	**Manhattan, NY** (borough) New York County	226
Virginia	201	Jefferson Parish, LA	153	**Tamiami, FL** (cdp) Miami-Dade County	223
North Carolina	200	Queens County, NY	150	**North Miami, FL** (city) Miami-Dade County	174
Maryland	166	San Francisco County, CA	148	**Bronx, NY** (borough) Bronx County	160
Pennsylvania	160	Cook County, IL	143	**Queens, NY** (borough) Queens County	150

Sorted by Number in Ascending Order — U.S. = 11,786

State	Number	County	Number	Place	Number
Connecticut	0	King County, WA	0	**Pembroke Pines, FL** (city) Broward County	0
Minnesota	0	Stanislaus County, CA	0	**Richmond, CA** (city) Contra Costa County	0
Tennessee	0	Collier County, FL	6	**South San Francisco, CA** (city) San Mateo County	0
Michigan	6	Orange County, CA	9	**Antioch, CA** (city) Contra Costa County	5
District of Columbia	13	Sonoma County, CA	12	**Fontana, CA** (city) San Bernardino County	8
Washington	20	Dallas County, TX	14	**Miramar, FL** (city) Broward County	9
Indiana	30	Gwinnett County, GA	16	**South Gate, CA** (city) Los Angeles County	12
Arizona	40	Maricopa County, AZ	16	**Hayward, CA** (city) Alameda County	18
Georgia	40	Bexar County, TX	20	**Charlotte, NC** (city) Mecklenburg County	20
Missouri	41	San Joaquin County, CA	20	**Las Vegas, NV** (city) Clark County	22

Sorted by Percent in Descending Order — U.S. = 12.0%

State	Percent	County	Percent	Place	Percent
Oregon	33.6	New York County, NY	33.4	**Sacramento, CA** (city) Sacramento County	34.4
Massachusetts	21.5	Travis County, TX	29.2	**North Miami, FL** (city) Miami-Dade County	34.1
Pennsylvania	21.4	Bronx County, NY	20.4	**Manhattan, NY** (borough) New York County	33.4
New York	19.1	Cook County, IL	20.2	**Austin, TX** (city) Travis County	29.8
South Carolina	19.0	Palm Beach County, FL	19.8	**Miami, FL** (city) Miami-Dade County	24.8
Illinois	17.3	Lee County, FL	19.4	**Fountainebleau, FL** (cdp) Miami-Dade County	21.4
Ohio	17.1	Miami-Dade County, FL	18.9	**New York, NY** (city)	21.4
Florida	16.9	Queens County, NY	18.5	**West Little River, FL** (cdp) Miami-Dade County	21.1
Wisconsin	14.9	Prince William County, VA	16.9	**Country Club, FL** (cdp) Miami-Dade County	20.6
North Carolina	13.7	Camden County, NJ	16.2	**Tamiami, FL** (cdp) Miami-Dade County	20.5

Sorted by Percent in Ascending Order — U.S. = 12.0%

State	Percent	County	Percent	Place	Percent
Connecticut	0.0	King County, WA	0.0	**Pembroke Pines, FL** (city) Broward County	0.0
Minnesota	0.0	Stanislaus County, CA	0.0	**Richmond, CA** (city) Contra Costa County	0.0
Tennessee	0.0	Orange County, CA	1.0	**South San Francisco, CA** (city) San Mateo County	0.0
Michigan	2.5	Collier County, FL	2.2	**Antioch, CA** (city) Contra Costa County	1.0
Washington	2.8	Dallas County, TX	2.2	**Miramar, FL** (city) Broward County	2.1
District of Columbia	3.5	Maricopa County, AZ	2.9	**Fontana, CA** (city) San Bernardino County	2.3
Georgia	3.8	San Mateo County, CA	3.5	**Daly City, CA** (city) San Mateo County	2.5
Nevada	4.8	Santa Clara County, CA	3.5	**South Gate, CA** (city) Los Angeles County	4.3
Arizona	4.9	Alameda County, CA	4.2	**Hayward, CA** (city) Alameda County	4.6
California	5.6	San Joaquin County, CA	4.2	**Metairie, LA** (cdp) Jefferson Parish	5.1

Note: (1) Ranking tables cover all states and counties, and places with an overall population of at least 125,000, OR an overall population of at least 25,000 where the Hispanic/Latino population is at least 20% of the overall population. In states where less than five places meet either of these criteria, we have included places with at least 10,000 total population with the highest percentage of Hispanic/Latino population. These places are identified with an asterisk (*); Please refer to the User's Guide for a full explanation of data.

Households with Food Stamps/SNAP Benefits During Past 12 Months

Central American: Panamanian

Top 10 States, Counties, and Places[1]

Sorted by Number in Descending Order — U.S. = 5,602

State	Number	County	Number	Place	Number
New York	1,901	Kings County, NY	878	**New York, NY** (city)	1,819
Florida	861	New York County, NY	387	**Brooklyn, NY** (borough) Kings County	878
Georgia	417	Bronx County, NY	329	**Manhattan, NY** (borough) New York County	387
California	272	Miami-Dade County, FL	326	**Bronx, NY** (borough) Bronx County	329
Texas	237	Queens County, NY	208	**Queens, NY** (borough) Queens County	208
Pennsylvania	176	Broward County, FL	180	**Miami, FL** (city) Miami-Dade County	101
Ohio	169	Orange County, FL	114	**Houston, TX** (city) Harris County	49
Massachusetts	144	Hillsborough County, FL	91	**Jacksonville, FL** (city) Duval County	46
Virginia	125	San Bernardino County, CA	84	**Hempstead (town), NY** (town) Nassau County	30
Maryland	118	Prince William County, VA	55	**Killeen, TX** (city) Bell County	25

Sorted by Number in Ascending Order — U.S. = 5,602

State	Number	County	Number	Place	Number
Indiana	0	Bexar County, TX	0	**San Antonio, TX** (city) Bexar County	0
Kentucky	0	Fairfax County, VA	0	**Fayetteville, NC** (city) Cumberland County	14
Mississippi	0	Pierce County, WA	3	**Los Angeles, CA** (city) Los Angeles County	15
Colorado	11	Essex County, NJ	4	**Killeen, TX** (city) Bell County	25
South Carolina	14	Orange County, CA	5	**San Diego, CA** (city) San Diego County	25
Oklahoma	17	Suffolk County, NY	14	**Hempstead (town), NY** (town) Nassau County	30
Louisiana	18	Dallas County, TX	22	**Jacksonville, FL** (city) Duval County	46
Minnesota	18	Bell County, TX	25	**Houston, TX** (city) Harris County	49
Connecticut	24	Maricopa County, AZ	25	**Miami, FL** (city) Miami-Dade County	101
New Mexico	24	San Diego County, CA	25	**Queens, NY** (borough) Queens County	208

Sorted by Percent in Descending Order — U.S. = 10.3%

State	Percent	County	Percent	Place	Percent
Wisconsin	27.9	New York County, NY	37.2	**Manhattan, NY** (borough) New York County	37.2
Ohio	24.2	Bronx County, NY	29.4	**Bronx, NY** (borough) Bronx County	29.4
Alabama	19.6	San Bernardino County, CA	17.8	**Miami, FL** (city) Miami-Dade County	26.6
Pennsylvania	18.3	Broward County, FL	16.1	**New York, NY** (city)	18.8
Georgia	16.4	Kings County, NY	15.4	**Brooklyn, NY** (borough) Kings County	15.4
New York	16.4	Orange County, FL	12.9	**Queens, NY** (borough) Queens County	12.9
Tennessee	14.0	Queens County, NY	12.9	**Jacksonville, FL** (city) Duval County	12.4
Massachusetts	12.9	Duval County, FL	12.4	**Houston, TX** (city) Harris County	10.6
Arizona	12.3	Prince William County, VA	12.1	**Killeen, TX** (city) Bell County	6.7
Washington	11.5	Miami-Dade County, FL	11.2	**Hempstead (town), NY** (town) Nassau County	6.0

Sorted by Percent in Ascending Order — U.S. = 10.3%

State	Percent	County	Percent	Place	Percent
Indiana	0.0	Bexar County, TX	0.0	**San Antonio, TX** (city) Bexar County	0.0
Kentucky	0.0	Fairfax County, VA	0.0	**Los Angeles, CA** (city) Los Angeles County	1.9
Mississippi	0.0	Essex County, NJ	0.9	**Fayetteville, NC** (city) Cumberland County	3.8
Colorado	2.3	Pierce County, WA	1.5	**San Diego, CA** (city) San Diego County	4.6
South Carolina	2.4	Orange County, CA	1.6	**Hempstead (town), NY** (town) Nassau County	6.0
Louisiana	3.7	San Diego County, CA	2.5	**Killeen, TX** (city) Bell County	6.7
California	4.3	Los Angeles County, CA	2.6	**Houston, TX** (city) Harris County	10.6
New Jersey	4.7	Suffolk County, NY	3.7	**Jacksonville, FL** (city) Duval County	12.4
Oklahoma	5.1	Bell County, TX	5.2	**Queens, NY** (borough) Queens County	12.9
North Carolina	5.2	Dallas County, TX	5.2	**Brooklyn, NY** (borough) Kings County	15.4

Note: (1) Ranking tables cover all states and counties, and places with an overall population of at least 125,000, OR an overall population of at least 25,000 where the Hispanic/Latino population is at least 20% of the overall population. In states where less than five places meet either of these criteria, we have included places with at least 10,000 total population with the highest percentage of Hispanic/Latino population. These places are identified with an asterisk (*); Please refer to the User's Guide for a full explanation of data.

Households with Food Stamps/SNAP Benefits During Past 12 Months

Central American: Salvadoran

Top 10 States, Counties, and Places[1]

Sorted by Number in Descending Order — U.S. = 38,438

State	Number	County	Number	Place	Number
California	12,476	Los Angeles County, CA	8,270	**Los Angeles, CA** (city) Los Angeles County	5,192
Texas	6,054	Harris County, TX	3,203	**New York, NY** (city)	1,955
New York	3,399	Montgomery County, MD	1,040	**Houston, TX** (city) Harris County	1,801
Maryland	2,182	Dallas County, TX	999	**Queens, NY** (borough) Queens County	659
Florida	2,045	Miami-Dade County, FL	898	**Brooklyn, NY** (borough) Kings County	643
Virginia	1,864	Prince George's County, MD	839	**Islip, NY** (town) Suffolk County	438
Massachusetts	1,416	Suffolk County, MA	773	**Irving, TX** (city) Dallas County	432
New Jersey	1,266	Fairfax County, VA	741	**Bronx, NY** (borough) Bronx County	418
North Carolina	816	San Bernardino County, CA	739	**Chelsea, MA** (city) Suffolk County	402
Georgia	718	Queens County, NY	659	**Hempstead (town), NY** (town) Nassau County	388

Sorted by Number in Ascending Order — U.S. = 38,438

State	Number	County	Number	Place	Number
Alaska	0	Brazoria County, TX	0	**Annandale, VA** (cdp) Fairfax County	0
Hawaii	0	Collin County, TX	0	**Baldwin Park, CA** (city) Los Angeles County	0
New Mexico	27	Napa County, CA	0	**Brookhaven, NY** (town) Suffolk County	0
Alabama	32	Orange County, NY	0	**Carson, CA** (city) Los Angeles County	0
Idaho	42	Placer County, CA	0	**Concord, CA** (city) Contra Costa County	0
Oklahoma	56	Washington County, AR	0	**Corona, CA** (city) Riverside County	0
Michigan	68	El Paso County, TX	2	**Gainesville, GA** (city) Hall County	0
Wisconsin	69	Henrico County, VA	5	**Glen Cove, NY** (city) Nassau County	0
Louisiana	71	Polk County, IA	6	**La Puente, CA** (city) Los Angeles County	0
Utah	78	Salt Lake County, UT	9	**Lewisville, TX** (city) Denton County	0

Sorted by Percent in Descending Order — U.S. = 9.0%

State	Percent	County	Percent	Place	Percent
Tennessee	25.0	Hartford County, CT	41.1	**Homestead, FL** (city) Miami-Dade County	41.7
Kentucky	20.1	Shelby County, TN	32.1	**Bronx, NY** (borough) Bronx County	30.2
Indiana	18.7	Bronx County, NY	30.2	**Nashville-Davidson, TN** (metropolitan govt) Davidson County	29.5
Kansas	16.6	Sedgwick County, KS	28.9	**Wichita, KS** (city) Sedgwick County	29.4
Idaho	16.5	Davidson County, TN	28.5	**Chelsea, MA** (city) Suffolk County	26.7
Massachusetts	15.3	Sebastian County, AR	26.5	**Brooklyn, NY** (borough) Kings County	26.1
South Carolina	14.9	Kings County, NY	26.1	**Austin, TX** (city) Travis County	25.6
Washington	13.6	Lee County, FL	24.9	**Santa Rosa, CA** (city) Sonoma County	23.4
Florida	13.5	Williamson County, TX	24.7	**West Falls Church, VA** (cdp) Fairfax County	23.4
Wisconsin	13.1	Pima County, AZ	23.8	**Pasadena, TX** (city) Harris County	23.1

Sorted by Percent in Ascending Order — U.S. = 9.0%

State	Percent	County	Percent	Place	Percent
Alaska	0.0	Brazoria County, TX	0.0	**Annandale, VA** (cdp) Fairfax County	0.0
Hawaii	0.0	Collin County, TX	0.0	**Baldwin Park, CA** (city) Los Angeles County	0.0
Utah	3.6	Napa County, CA	0.0	**Brookhaven, NY** (town) Suffolk County	0.0
Nevada	4.2	Orange County, NY	0.0	**Carson, CA** (city) Los Angeles County	0.0
New Mexico	5.4	Placer County, CA	0.0	**Concord, CA** (city) Contra Costa County	0.0
Alabama	5.6	Washington County, AR	0.0	**Corona, CA** (city) Riverside County	0.0
Louisiana	6.0	El Paso County, TX	0.5	**Gainesville, GA** (city) Hall County	0.0
Virginia	6.9	Salt Lake County, UT	0.9	**Glen Cove, NY** (city) Nassau County	0.0
Minnesota	7.3	Henrico County, VA	1.2	**La Puente, CA** (city) Los Angeles County	0.0
Colorado	7.6	Polk County, IA	1.5	**Lewisville, TX** (city) Denton County	0.0

Note: (1) Ranking tables cover all states and counties, and places with an overall population of at least 125,000, OR an overall population of at least 25,000 where the Hispanic/Latino population is at least 20% of the overall population. In states where less than five places meet either of these criteria, we have included places with at least 10,000 total population with the highest percentage of Hispanic/Latino population. These places are identified with an asterisk (*); Please refer to the User's Guide for a full explanation of data.

Households with Food Stamps/SNAP Benefits During Past 12 Months

Cuban

Top 10 States, Counties, and Places[1]

Sorted by Number in Descending Order — U.S. = 108,226

State	Number	County	Number	Place	Number
Florida	84,019	Miami-Dade County, FL	68,808	**Miami, FL** (city) Miami-Dade County	19,762
New York	5,525	Hillsborough County, FL	3,187	**Hialeah, FL** (city) Miami-Dade County	17,158
New Jersey	3,475	Broward County, FL	2,739	**New York, NY** (city)	4,416
Texas	1,701	Hudson County, NJ	2,124	**Miami Beach, FL** (city) Miami-Dade County	2,284
California	1,117	Palm Beach County, FL	1,890	**Fountainebleau, FL** (cdp) Miami-Dade County	2,172
Pennsylvania	1,037	New York County, NY	1,541	**Tamiami, FL** (cdp) Miami-Dade County	2,056
Nevada	1,006	Bronx County, NY	1,363	**South Miami Heights, FL** (cdp) Miami-Dade County	1,586
Illinois	993	Lee County, FL	1,296	**Manhattan, NY** (borough) New York County	1,541
Georgia	691	Clark County, NV	952	**Tampa, FL** (city) Hillsborough County	1,492
Kentucky	620	Queens County, NY	949	**Kendale Lakes, FL** (cdp) Miami-Dade County	1,486

Sorted by Number in Ascending Order — U.S. = 108,226

State	Number	County	Number	Place	Number
Hawaii	0	Baltimore County, MD	0	**Coconut Creek, FL** (city) Broward County	0
Maine	22	Bucks County, PA	0	**Glendale, CA** (city) Los Angeles County	0
New Hampshire	26	Charlotte County, FL	0	**Long Beach, CA** (city) Los Angeles County	0
Mississippi	40	Contra Costa County, CA	0	**North Hempstead, NY** (town) Nassau County	0
Delaware	58	Forsyth County, NC	0	**Oyster Bay, NY** (town) Nassau County	0
District of Columbia	59	Honolulu County, HI	0	**San Jose, CA** (city) Santa Clara County	0
Arkansas	76	Loudoun County, VA	0	**Santa Clarita, CA** (city) Los Angeles County	0
Rhode Island	79	Norfolk County, MA	0	**Burbank, CA** (city) Los Angeles County	8
Kansas	89	San Mateo County, CA	0	**Kearny, NJ** (town) Hudson County	8
Iowa	93	Santa Clara County, CA	0	**Alafaya, FL** (cdp) Orange County	9

Sorted by Percent in Descending Order — U.S. = 17.9%

State	Percent	County	Percent	Place	Percent
West Virginia	41.3	Bronx County, NY	43.3	**Bronx, NY** (borough) Bronx County	43.3
Wisconsin	32.2	Ingham County, MI	38.8	**Milwaukee, WI** (city) Milwaukee County	41.7
Iowa	27.4	Milwaukee County, WI	36.8	**West Little River, FL** (cdp) Miami-Dade County	38.7
Oklahoma	26.5	Erie County, NY	34.4	**Syracuse, NY** (city) Onondaga County	38.5
Oregon	25.2	Onondaga County, NY	31.6	**South Miami Heights, FL** (cdp) Miami-Dade County	38.4
Kentucky	23.9	Davidson County, TN	31.5	**Baltimore, MD** (independent city)	37.3
Arkansas	22.6	Essex County, MA	31.3	**Miami, FL** (city) Miami-Dade County	33.4
Florida	20.6	Hampden County, MA	30.2	**Nashville-Davidson, TN** (metropolitan govt) Davidson County	31.5
Minnesota	20.5	Lehigh County, PA	29.4	**Hialeah, FL** (city) Miami-Dade County	30.9
New York	19.5	Multnomah County, OR	28.7	**Rochester, NY** (city) Monroe County	30.9

Sorted by Percent in Ascending Order — U.S. = 17.9%

State	Percent	County	Percent	Place	Percent
Hawaii	0.0	Baltimore County, MD	0.0	**Coconut Creek, FL** (city) Broward County	0.0
California	3.7	Bucks County, PA	0.0	**Glendale, CA** (city) Los Angeles County	0.0
Virginia	5.1	Charlotte County, FL	0.0	**Long Beach, CA** (city) Los Angeles County	0.0
New Hampshire	5.8	Contra Costa County, CA	0.0	**North Hempstead, NY** (town) Nassau County	0.0
District of Columbia	6.2	Forsyth County, NC	0.0	**Oyster Bay, NY** (town) Nassau County	0.0
Maine	7.1	Honolulu County, HI	0.0	**San Jose, CA** (city) Santa Clara County	0.0
Mississippi	8.1	Loudoun County, VA	0.0	**Santa Clarita, CA** (city) Los Angeles County	0.0
Georgia	8.5	Norfolk County, MA	0.0	**Alafaya, FL** (cdp) Orange County	1.8
Colorado	8.7	San Mateo County, CA	0.0	**Spring Valley, NV** (cdp) Clark County	1.9
Maryland	8.7	Santa Clara County, CA	0.0	**Boston, MA** (city) Suffolk County	2.0

Note: (1) Ranking tables cover all states and counties, and places with an overall population of at least 125,000, OR an overall population of at least 25,000 where the Hispanic/Latino population is at least 20% of the overall population. In states where less than five places meet either of these criteria, we have included places with at least 10,000 total population with the highest percentage of Hispanic/Latino population. These places are identified with an asterisk (*); Please refer to the User's Guide for a full explanation of data.

Households with Food Stamps/SNAP Benefits During Past 12 Months

Dominican Republic

Top 10 States, Counties, and Places[1]

Sorted by Number in Descending Order — U.S. = 121,131

State	Number	County	Number	Place	Number
New York	75,289	Bronx County, NY	31,014	**New York, NY** (city)	70,528
Massachusetts	12,078	New York County, NY	21,877	**Bronx, NY** (borough) Bronx County	31,014
Florida	8,787	Kings County, NY	10,370	**Manhattan, NY** (borough) New York County	21,877
New Jersey	8,609	Queens County, NY	6,914	**Brooklyn, NY** (borough) Kings County	10,370
Pennsylvania	5,088	Essex County, MA	5,399	**Queens, NY** (borough) Queens County	6,914
Rhode Island	4,205	Providence County, RI	4,127	**Boston, MA** (city) Suffolk County	3,767
Connecticut	1,783	Suffolk County, MA	3,960	**Providence, RI** (city) Providence County	3,494
North Carolina	665	Miami-Dade County, FL	3,754	**Lawrence, MA** (city) Essex County	3,054
Georgia	639	Hudson County, NJ	2,484	**Yonkers, NY** (city) Westchester County	1,526
Maryland	500	Passaic County, NJ	2,363	**Paterson, NJ** (city) Passaic County	1,391

Sorted by Number in Ascending Order — U.S. = 121,131

State	Number	County	Number	Place	Number
Alabama	0	Fulton County, GA	0	**Englewood, NJ** (city) Bergen County	0
Nevada	5	Clark County, NV	5	**Huntington, NY** (town) Suffolk County	0
Missouri	52	Ulster County, NY	8	**Linden, NJ** (city) Union County	0
Minnesota	57	Tarrant County, TX	11	**Ramapo, NY** (town) Rockland County	0
Washington	77	Plymouth County, MA	18	**Valley Stream, NY** (village) Nassau County	6
South Carolina	80	Fairfax County, VA	21	**Plantation, FL** (city) Broward County	15
Colorado	84	Bexar County, TX	23	**Belleville, NJ** (township) Essex County	18
Alaska	87	Burlington County, NJ	26	**Kearny, NJ** (town) Hudson County	18
Indiana	89	Marion County, FL	30	**North Miami Beach, FL** (city) Miami-Dade County	18
Tennessee	93	Duval County, FL	41	**Pennsauken, NJ** (township) Camden County	21

Sorted by Percent in Descending Order — U.S. = 30.4%

State	Percent	County	Percent	Place	Percent
Utah	43.6	Hampden County, MA	57.1	**Bethlehem, PA** (city) Northampton County	66.7
Rhode Island	39.3	Oneida County, NY	54.2	**Chelsea, MA** (city) Suffolk County	54.6
Michigan	37.8	Northampton County, PA	52.2	**Rochester, NY** (city) Monroe County	52.9
New York	37.6	Berks County, PA	50.7	**Reading, PA** (city) Berks County	52.6
Massachusetts	37.1	Kent County, MI	45.6	**Worcester, MA** (city) Worcester County	49.7
Pennsylvania	36.4	Sullivan County, NY	45.6	**Cleveland, OH** (city) Cuyahoga County	48.5
Ohio	27.9	Suffolk County, MA	44.4	**Springfield, MA** (city) Hampden County	47.6
Connecticut	26.2	New York County, NY	43.7	**Grand Rapids, MI** (city) Kent County	45.6
Delaware	26.0	Bronx County, NY	43.2	**Hazleton, PA** (city) Luzerne County	44.1
Arizona	25.6	Cuyahoga County, OH	41.9	**Boston, MA** (city) Suffolk County	44.0

Sorted by Percent in Ascending Order — U.S. = 30.4%

State	Percent	County	Percent	Place	Percent
Alabama	0.0	Fulton County, GA	0.0	**Englewood, NJ** (city) Bergen County	0.0
Nevada	0.6	Clark County, NV	0.7	**Huntington, NY** (town) Suffolk County	0.0
Virginia	7.6	Tarrant County, TX	3.4	**Linden, NJ** (city) Union County	0.0
California	7.7	Fairfax County, VA	5.6	**Ramapo, NY** (town) Rockland County	0.0
Texas	8.4	Los Angeles County, CA	5.9	**Valley Stream, NY** (village) Nassau County	2.4
Missouri	13.0	Duval County, FL	6.0	**North Miami Beach, FL** (city) Miami-Dade County	4.8
Indiana	13.3	Plymouth County, MA	6.7	**Belleville, NJ** (township) Essex County	5.1
Illinois	13.5	Union County, NJ	6.8	**Pennsauken, NJ** (township) Camden County	5.2
District of Columbia	14.3	Orange County, NY	7.1	**Sunrise, FL** (city) Broward County	5.7
Georgia	15.7	Bexar County, TX	7.2	**Kearny, NJ** (town) Hudson County	5.9

Note: (1) Ranking tables cover all states and counties, and places with an overall population of at least 125,000, OR an overall population of at least 25,000 where the Hispanic/Latino population is at least 20% of the overall population. In states where less than five places meet either of these criteria, we have included places with at least 10,000 total population with the highest percentage of Hispanic/Latino population. These places are identified with an asterisk (*); Please refer to the User's Guide for a full explanation of data.

Households with Food Stamps/SNAP Benefits During Past 12 Months

Mexican

Top 10 States, Counties, and Places[1]

Sorted by Number in Descending Order — U.S. = 1,155,415

State	Number	County	Number	Place	Number
Texas	396,528	Los Angeles County, CA	87,023	**San Antonio, TX** (city) Bexar County	37,093
California	289,756	Hidalgo County, TX	58,950	**Los Angeles, CA** (city) Los Angeles County	35,911
Arizona	76,625	El Paso County, TX	43,092	**El Paso, TX** (city) El Paso County	34,465
Illinois	49,341	Bexar County, TX	41,011	**Houston, TX** (city) Harris County	24,546
Washington	31,512	Harris County, TX	39,811	**Phoenix, AZ** (city) Maricopa County	23,609
Colorado	28,693	Maricopa County, AZ	38,641	**Chicago, IL** (city) Cook County	21,144
New Mexico	27,069	Cook County, IL	31,002	**New York, NY** (city)	18,411
New York	21,792	Cameron County, TX	26,825	**Laredo, TX** (city) Webb County	15,406
Florida	21,026	Fresno County, CA	22,155	**Dallas, TX** (city) Dallas County	13,312
Oregon	20,574	San Bernardino County, CA	21,017	**Fresno, CA** (city) Fresno County	12,780

Sorted by Number in Ascending Order — U.S. = 1,155,415

State	Number	County	Number	Place	Number
Vermont	25	Albemarle County, VA	0	**Aspen Hill, MD** (cdp) Montgomery County	0
District of Columbia	206	Big Horn County, WY	0	**Babylon, NY** (town) Suffolk County	0
New Hampshire	230	Cass County, IL	0	**Bayonne, NJ** (city) Hudson County	0
Rhode Island	260	Charles County, MD	0	**Chesapeake, VA** (independent city)	0
Maine	385	Chisago County, MN	0	**Coral Gables, FL** (city) Miami-Dade County	0
North Dakota	580	Clay County, TX	0	**Dale City, VA** (cdp) Prince William County	0
South Dakota	620	Columbia County, NY	0	**Fort Hood, TX** (cdp) Bell County	0
West Virginia	624	Converse County, WY	0	**Fort Leonard Wood*, MO** (cdp) Pulaski County	0
Alaska	683	Crow Wing County, MN	0	**Garfield, NJ** (city) Bergen County	0
Wyoming	742	Delaware County, NY	0	**Kendall, FL** (cdp) Miami-Dade County	0

Sorted by Percent in Descending Order — U.S. = 15.1%

State	Percent	County	Percent	Place	Percent
Maine	27.3	Greene County, TN	74.6	**Hazleton, PA** (city) Luzerne County	50.8
Oregon	24.4	Marshall County, MN	68.7	**York, PA** (city) York County	47.0
West Virginia	24.3	Neosho County, KS	59.0	**Springfield, MA** (city) Hampden County	41.0
Michigan	23.7	Lake County, MT	57.4	**Walla Walla, WA** (city) Walla Walla County	41.0
Tennessee	23.6	Emmet County, MI	53.3	**Rapid City*, SD** (city) Pennington County	40.7
North Dakota	23.4	Polk County, MN	52.9	**Pharr, TX** (city) Hidalgo County	40.1
New York	22.8	Toombs County, GA	52.4	**Grand Rapids, MI** (city) Kent County	37.8
Washington	22.6	Blaine County, OK	52.0	**Clovis, NM** (city) Curry County	36.8
Iowa	20.5	Cass County, MN	51.5	**Carthage*, MO** (city) Jasper County	36.5
Texas	19.0	Dickens County, TX	51.5	**Weslaco, TX** (city) Hidalgo County	36.5

Sorted by Percent in Ascending Order — U.S. = 15.1%

State	Percent	County	Percent	Place	Percent
Vermont	3.3	Albemarle County, VA	0.0	**Aspen Hill, MD** (cdp) Montgomery County	0.0
District of Columbia	6.4	Big Horn County, WY	0.0	**Babylon, NY** (town) Suffolk County	0.0
Maryland	6.7	Cass County, IL	0.0	**Bayonne, NJ** (city) Hudson County	0.0
Virginia	6.9	Charles County, MD	0.0	**Chesapeake, VA** (independent city)	0.0
Wyoming	8.4	Chisago County, MN	0.0	**Coral Gables, FL** (city) Miami-Dade County	0.0
Nevada	8.9	Clay County, TX	0.0	**Dale City, VA** (cdp) Prince William County	0.0
Mississippi	9.1	Columbia County, NY	0.0	**Fort Hood, TX** (cdp) Bell County	0.0
Hawaii	9.4	Converse County, WY	0.0	**Fort Leonard Wood*, MO** (cdp) Pulaski County	0.0
Connecticut	9.6	Crow Wing County, MN	0.0	**Garfield, NJ** (city) Bergen County	0.0
California	10.9	Delaware County, NY	0.0	**Kendall, FL** (cdp) Miami-Dade County	0.0

Note: (1) Ranking tables cover all states and counties, and places with an overall population of at least 125,000, OR an overall population of at least 25,000 where the Hispanic/Latino population is at least 20% of the overall population. In states where less than five places meet either of these criteria, we have included places with at least 10,000 total population with the highest percentage of Hispanic/Latino population. These places are identified with an asterisk (*); Please refer to the User's Guide for a full explanation of data.

Households with Food Stamps/SNAP Benefits During Past 12 Months

Puerto Rican

Top 10 States, Counties, and Places[1]

Sorted by Number in Descending Order — U.S. = 344,445

State	Number	County	Number	Place	Number
New York	110,948	Bronx County, NY	42,918	**New York, NY** (city)	88,354
Pennsylvania	39,896	Kings County, NY	23,618	**Bronx, NY** (borough) Bronx County	42,918
Florida	39,253	Philadelphia County, PA	14,736	**Brooklyn, NY** (borough) Kings County	23,618
Massachusetts	36,895	Hampden County, MA	13,911	**Philadelphia, PA** (city) Philadelphia County	14,736
Connecticut	28,065	New York County, NY	13,843	**Manhattan, NY** (borough) New York County	13,843
New Jersey	21,972	Hartford County, CT	12,273	**Chicago, IL** (city) Cook County	8,896
Illinois	12,311	Cook County, IL	10,231	**Springfield, MA** (city) Hampden County	8,002
Ohio	8,108	New Haven County, CT	8,619	**Hartford, CT** (city/town) Hartford County	7,669
California	4,620	Orange County, FL	6,775	**Queens, NY** (borough) Queens County	6,047
Texas	4,591	Queens County, NY	6,047	**Boston, MA** (city) Suffolk County	4,931

Sorted by Number in Ascending Order — U.S. = 344,445

State	Number	County	Number	Place	Number
Wyoming	0	Chatham County, GA	0	**Columbia, SC** (city) Richland County	0
North Dakota	23	DeKalb County, IL	0	**Coral Gables, FL** (city) Miami-Dade County	0
Montana	46	Fayette County, GA	0	**Elmont, NY** (cdp) Nassau County	0
District of Columbia	60	Forsyth County, GA	0	**Fort Hood, TX** (cdp) Bell County	0
South Dakota	88	Guadalupe County, TX	0	**Fremont, CA** (city) Alameda County	0
West Virginia	122	Lowndes County, GA	0	**Gilbert, AZ** (town) Maricopa County	0
Alaska	154	Madera County, CA	0	**Modesto, CA** (city) Stanislaus County	0
Vermont	174	Marin County, CA	0	**Murrieta, CA** (city) Riverside County	0
Nebraska	176	Perry County, PA	0	**Oceanside, CA** (city) San Diego County	0
Mississippi	183	Pulaski County, MO	0	**Rahway, NJ** (city) Union County	0

Sorted by Percent in Descending Order — U.S. = 24.4%

State	Percent	County	Percent	Place	Percent
Massachusetts	45.7	Clearfield County, PA	96.2	**Holyoke, MA** (city) Hampden County	68.7
Maine	44.2	Wyoming County, NY	71.4	**Woonsocket*, RI** (city) Providence County	61.3
Pennsylvania	39.4	Weld County, CO	57.3	**York, PA** (city) York County	57.5
Rhode Island	39.1	Hampden County, MA	56.2	**Buffalo, NY** (city) Erie County	57.4
Connecticut	35.9	Chautauqua County, NY	55.4	**Lebanon, PA** (city) Lebanon County	56.6
Ohio	30.2	Bristol County, MA	54.2	**Worcester, MA** (city) Worcester County	54.4
New York	29.9	Lackawanna County, PA	53.9	**Springfield, MA** (city) Hampden County	53.9
Michigan	28.9	Broome County, NY	50.8	**Hartford, CT** (city/town) Hartford County	53.6
Wisconsin	28.6	Berkshire County, MA	50.6	**Rockford, IL** (city) Winnebago County	53.0
Iowa	27.8	Erie County, NY	50.1	**Hazleton, PA** (city) Luzerne County	51.8

Sorted by Percent in Ascending Order — U.S. = 24.4%

State	Percent	County	Percent	Place	Percent
Wyoming	0.0	Chatham County, GA	0.0	**Columbia, SC** (city) Richland County	0.0
District of Columbia	3.9	DeKalb County, IL	0.0	**Coral Gables, FL** (city) Miami-Dade County	0.0
California	8.1	Fayette County, GA	0.0	**Elmont, NY** (cdp) Nassau County	0.0
Virginia	8.6	Forsyth County, GA	0.0	**Fort Hood, TX** (cdp) Bell County	0.0
Montana	8.7	Guadalupe County, TX	0.0	**Fremont, CA** (city) Alameda County	0.0
Maryland	9.2	Lowndes County, GA	0.0	**Gilbert, AZ** (town) Maricopa County	0.0
Nevada	9.5	Madera County, CA	0.0	**Modesto, CA** (city) Stanislaus County	0.0
Georgia	10.8	Marin County, CA	0.0	**Murrieta, CA** (city) Riverside County	0.0
North Dakota	10.9	Perry County, PA	0.0	**Oceanside, CA** (city) San Diego County	0.0
Minnesota	11.0	Pulaski County, MO	0.0	**Rahway, NJ** (city) Union County	0.0

Note: (1) Ranking tables cover all states and counties, and places with an overall population of at least 125,000, OR an overall population of at least 25,000 where the Hispanic/Latino population is at least 20% of the overall population. In states where less than five places meet either of these criteria, we have included places with at least 10,000 total population with the highest percentage of Hispanic/Latino population. These places are identified with an asterisk (*); Please refer to the User's Guide for a full explanation of data.

Households with Food Stamps/SNAP Benefits During Past 12 Months

South American

Top 10 States, Counties, and Places[1]

Sorted by Number in Descending Order — U.S. = 70,886

State	Number	County	Number	Place	Number
New York	23,210	Queens County, NY	10,146	**New York, NY** (city)	19,948
Florida	18,420	Miami-Dade County, FL	9,333	**Queens, NY** (borough) Queens County	10,146
New Jersey	7,292	Kings County, NY	3,875	**Brooklyn, NY** (borough) Kings County	3,875
California	3,025	Broward County, FL	3,767	**Bronx, NY** (borough) Bronx County	3,442
Texas	2,288	Bronx County, NY	3,442	**Manhattan, NY** (borough) New York County	2,146
Pennsylvania	1,694	Hudson County, NJ	2,444	**Miami, FL** (city) Miami-Dade County	1,197
Illinois	1,601	New York County, NY	2,146	**Miami Beach, FL** (city) Miami-Dade County	1,128
Connecticut	1,460	Los Angeles County, CA	1,241	**Hialeah, FL** (city) Miami-Dade County	902
Massachusetts	1,283	Cook County, IL	1,193	**Chicago, IL** (city) Cook County	854
North Carolina	1,056	Passaic County, NJ	1,179	**Country Club, FL** (cdp) Miami-Dade County	687

Sorted by Number in Ascending Order — U.S. = 70,886

State	Number	County	Number	Place	Number
Mississippi	0	Allegheny County, PA	0	**Alhambra, CA** (city) Los Angeles County	0
West Virginia	0	Butler County, OH	0	**Bakersfield, CA** (city) Kern County	0
Alaska	14	Cabarrus County, NC	0	**Carrollton, TX** (city) Denton County	0
Montana	15	Cherokee County, GA	0	**Chesapeake, VA** (independent city)	0
Wyoming	25	Clark County, WA	0	**Chino Hills, CA** (city) San Bernardino County	0
Vermont	32	Denton County, TX	0	**Chino, CA** (city) San Bernardino County	0
Maine	41	Douglas County, CO	0	**Chula Vista, CA** (city) San Diego County	0
Idaho	43	Douglas County, NE	0	**Concord, CA** (city) Contra Costa County	0
Nebraska	52	Fayette County, KY	0	**Corona, CA** (city) Riverside County	0
Hawaii	54	Hamilton County, IN	0	**Covina, CA** (city) Los Angeles County	0

Sorted by Percent in Descending Order — U.S. = 8.2%

State	Percent	County	Percent	Place	Percent
North Dakota	33.3	Oneida County, NY	36.2	**Four Corners, FL** (cdp) Lake County	27.9
Rhode Island	17.1	Luzerne County, PA	33.2	**Meadow Woods, FL** (cdp) Orange County	25.8
Maine	14.7	York County, PA	25.9	**Bronx, NY** (borough) Bronx County	25.7
New York	14.1	Bronx County, NY	25.7	**Springfield, MA** (city) Hampden County	25.3
Tennessee	12.4	Middlesex County, CT	25.3	**Glendale, AZ** (city) Maricopa County	23.9
Vermont	12.1	McHenry County, IL	23.7	**Providence, RI** (city) Providence County	23.9
Delaware	12.0	Gaston County, NC	23.6	**New London, CT** (city/town) New London County	23.5
Pennsylvania	11.6	Schenectady County, NY	23.6	**Miami Gardens, FL** (city) Miami-Dade County	23.1
Oregon	10.7	Escambia County, FL	23.3	**Cleveland, OH** (city) Cuyahoga County	22.6
Ohio	9.5	Kings County, NY	21.6	**West Valley City, UT** (city) Salt Lake County	22.6

Sorted by Percent in Ascending Order — U.S. = 8.2%

State	Percent	County	Percent	Place	Percent
Mississippi	0.0	Allegheny County, PA	0.0	**Alhambra, CA** (city) Los Angeles County	0.0
West Virginia	0.0	Butler County, OH	0.0	**Bakersfield, CA** (city) Kern County	0.0
Alaska	1.6	Cabarrus County, NC	0.0	**Carrollton, TX** (city) Denton County	0.0
District of Columbia	2.6	Cherokee County, GA	0.0	**Chesapeake, VA** (independent city)	0.0
Virginia	2.8	Clark County, WA	0.0	**Chino Hills, CA** (city) San Bernardino County	0.0
California	3.1	Denton County, TX	0.0	**Chino, CA** (city) San Bernardino County	0.0
Minnesota	3.2	Douglas County, CO	0.0	**Chula Vista, CA** (city) San Diego County	0.0
Alabama	3.3	Douglas County, NE	0.0	**Concord, CA** (city) Contra Costa County	0.0
South Carolina	3.9	Fayette County, KY	0.0	**Corona, CA** (city) Riverside County	0.0
Hawaii	4.0	Hamilton County, IN	0.0	**Covina, CA** (city) Los Angeles County	0.0

Note: (1) Ranking tables cover all states and counties, and places with an overall population of at least 125,000, OR an overall population of at least 25,000 where the Hispanic/Latino population is at least 20% of the overall population. In states where less than five places meet either of these criteria, we have included places with at least 10,000 total population with the highest percentage of Hispanic/Latino population. These places are identified with an asterisk (*); Please refer to the User's Guide for a full explanation of data.

Households with Food Stamps/SNAP Benefits During Past 12 Months

South American: Argentinean

Top 10 States, Counties, and Places[1]

Sorted by Number in Descending Order — U.S. = 4,313

State	Number	County	Number	Place	Number
Florida	1,466	Miami-Dade County, FL	689	**New York, NY** (city)	710
New York	923	Broward County, FL	384	**Queens, NY** (borough) Queens County	324
California	361	Queens County, NY	324	**Miami Beach, FL** (city) Miami-Dade County	227
New Jersey	275	Los Angeles County, CA	144	**Miami, FL** (city) Miami-Dade County	183
Texas	268	Bronx County, NY	139	**Bronx, NY** (borough) Bronx County	139
Pennsylvania	174	Palm Beach County, FL	130	**Brooklyn, NY** (borough) Kings County	126
Utah	156	Kings County, NY	126	**Manhattan, NY** (borough) New York County	116
Massachusetts	105	New York County, NY	116	**Los Angeles, CA** (city) Los Angeles County	87
Oregon	80	Salt Lake County, UT	114	**Coral Springs, FL** (city) Broward County	86
Illinois	51	Harris County, TX	85	**Houston, TX** (city) Harris County	74

Sorted by Number in Ascending Order — U.S. = 4,313

State	Number	County	Number	Place	Number
District of Columbia	0	Alameda County, CA	0	**Aventura, FL** (city) Miami-Dade County	0
Indiana	0	Bexar County, TX	0	**Chicago, IL** (city) Cook County	0
Minnesota	0	Contra Costa County, CA	0	**Hialeah, FL** (city) Miami-Dade County	0
North Carolina	0	Fairfax County, VA	0	**San Diego, CA** (city) San Diego County	0
Ohio	0	Fairfield County, CT	0	**San Francisco, CA** (city) San Francisco County	0
South Carolina	0	King County, WA	0	**Doral, FL** (city) Miami-Dade County	12
Missouri	5	Lee County, FL	0	**Pembroke Pines, FL** (city) Broward County	12
Colorado	9	Middlesex County, MA	0	**Hollywood, FL** (city) Broward County	15
Georgia	11	Oakland County, MI	0	**San Jose, CA** (city) Santa Clara County	30
Virginia	12	San Francisco County, CA	0	**Hempstead (town), NY** (town) Nassau County	47

Sorted by Percent in Descending Order — U.S. = 5.4%

State	Percent	County	Percent	Place	Percent
Oregon	15.7	Bronx County, NY	28.4	**Bronx, NY** (borough) Bronx County	28.4
Utah	12.8	Salt Lake County, UT	28.1	**Coral Springs, FL** (city) Broward County	24.4
Pennsylvania	12.0	Orange County, NY	21.6	**Queens, NY** (borough) Queens County	14.2
Tennessee	11.5	Queens County, NY	14.2	**New York, NY** (city)	12.1
Louisiana	11.4	Kings County, NY	11.7	**Brooklyn, NY** (borough) Kings County	11.7
New York	10.0	Orange County, FL	11.0	**Hempstead (town), NY** (town) Nassau County	11.7
Massachusetts	7.8	Riverside County, CA	10.1	**San Jose, CA** (city) Santa Clara County	11.2
Florida	7.2	Broward County, FL	9.9	**Miami Beach, FL** (city) Miami-Dade County	10.5
Texas	5.5	Palm Beach County, FL	9.5	**Miami, FL** (city) Miami-Dade County	8.2
New Jersey	5.3	Montgomery County, TX	9.3	**Houston, TX** (city) Harris County	7.1

Sorted by Percent in Ascending Order — U.S. = 5.4%

State	Percent	County	Percent	Place	Percent
District of Columbia	0.0	Alameda County, CA	0.0	**Aventura, FL** (city) Miami-Dade County	0.0
Indiana	0.0	Bexar County, TX	0.0	**Chicago, IL** (city) Cook County	0.0
Minnesota	0.0	Contra Costa County, CA	0.0	**Hialeah, FL** (city) Miami-Dade County	0.0
North Carolina	0.0	Fairfax County, VA	0.0	**San Diego, CA** (city) San Diego County	0.0
Ohio	0.0	Fairfield County, CT	0.0	**San Francisco, CA** (city) San Francisco County	0.0
South Carolina	0.0	King County, WA	0.0	**Hollywood, FL** (city) Broward County	2.2
Virginia	0.6	Lee County, FL	0.0	**Los Angeles, CA** (city) Los Angeles County	2.6
Georgia	1.1	Middlesex County, MA	0.0	**Pembroke Pines, FL** (city) Broward County	2.6
Colorado	1.7	Oakland County, MI	0.0	**Doral, FL** (city) Miami-Dade County	3.2
Maryland	1.7	San Francisco County, CA	0.0	**Manhattan, NY** (borough) New York County	6.3

Note: (1) Ranking tables cover all states and counties, and places with an overall population of at least 125,000, OR an overall population of at least 25,000 where the Hispanic/Latino population is at least 20% of the overall population. In states where less than five places meet either of these criteria, we have included places with at least 10,000 total population with the highest percentage of Hispanic/Latino population. These places are identified with an asterisk (*); Please refer to the User's Guide for a full explanation of data.

Households with Food Stamps/SNAP Benefits During Past 12 Months

South American: Bolivian

Top 10 States, Counties, and Places[1]

Sorted by Number in Descending Order — U.S. = 1,103

State	Number	County	Number	Place	Number
New York	248	Fairfax County, VA	112	**New York, NY** (city)	132
Virginia	204	Broward County, FL	94	**Queens, NY** (borough) Queens County	82
Florida	177	Queens County, NY	82	**Providence, RI** (city) Providence County	78
California	89	Providence County, RI	78	**Arlington, VA** (cdp) Arlington County	34
Rhode Island	78	Santa Clara County, CA	47	**Annandale, VA** (cdp) Fairfax County	14
New Jersey	56	Loudoun County, VA	35	**West Falls Church, VA** (cdp) Fairfax County	10
Texas	54	Miami-Dade County, FL	35	**Dale City, VA** (cdp) Prince William County	0
Maryland	40	Arlington County, VA	34	**Los Angeles, CA** (city) Los Angeles County	0
Pennsylvania	32	Prince William County, VA	23	**Springfield, VA** (cdp) Fairfax County	0
North Carolina	18	Montgomery County, MD	22		

Sorted by Number in Ascending Order — U.S. = 1,103

State	Number	County	Number	Place	Number
Massachusetts	0	San Diego County, CA	0	**Dale City, VA** (cdp) Prince William County	0
Illinois	13	Prince George's County, MD	2	**Los Angeles, CA** (city) Los Angeles County	0
North Carolina	18	Cook County, IL	8	**Springfield, VA** (cdp) Fairfax County	0
Pennsylvania	32	Los Angeles County, CA	9	**West Falls Church, VA** (cdp) Fairfax County	10
Maryland	40	Palm Beach County, FL	9	**Annandale, VA** (cdp) Fairfax County	14
Texas	54	Orange County, CA	11	**Arlington, VA** (cdp) Arlington County	34
New Jersey	56	Harris County, TX	17	**Providence, RI** (city) Providence County	78
Rhode Island	78	Montgomery County, MD	22	**Queens, NY** (borough) Queens County	82
California	89	Prince William County, VA	23	**New York, NY** (city)	132
Florida	177	Arlington County, VA	34		

Sorted by Percent in Descending Order — U.S. = 3.6%

State	Percent	County	Percent	Place	Percent
Rhode Island	15.4	Broward County, FL	15.7	**Providence, RI** (city) Providence County	26.0
Pennsylvania	13.4	Providence County, RI	15.4	**Queens, NY** (borough) Queens County	7.3
North Carolina	11.9	Santa Clara County, CA	13.1	**New York, NY** (city)	6.9
New York	9.6	Queens County, NY	7.3	**Arlington, VA** (cdp) Arlington County	3.2
Florida	5.4	Loudoun County, VA	6.6	**West Falls Church, VA** (cdp) Fairfax County	2.6
New Jersey	4.5	Miami-Dade County, FL	3.4	**Annandale, VA** (cdp) Fairfax County	2.0
Texas	3.3	Arlington County, VA	3.2	**Dale City, VA** (cdp) Prince William County	0.0
Virginia	2.2	Cook County, IL	3.0	**Los Angeles, CA** (city) Los Angeles County	0.0
California	2.0	Harris County, TX	2.9	**Springfield, VA** (cdp) Fairfax County	0.0
Illinois	1.9	Palm Beach County, FL	2.3		

Sorted by Percent in Ascending Order — U.S. = 3.6%

State	Percent	County	Percent	Place	Percent
Massachusetts	0.0	San Diego County, CA	0.0	**Dale City, VA** (cdp) Prince William County	0.0
Illinois	1.9	Los Angeles County, CA	0.5	**Los Angeles, CA** (city) Los Angeles County	0.0
Maryland	1.9	Prince George's County, MD	0.5	**Springfield, VA** (cdp) Fairfax County	0.0
California	2.0	Montgomery County, MD	1.5	**Annandale, VA** (cdp) Fairfax County	2.0
Virginia	2.2	Prince William County, VA	1.9	**West Falls Church, VA** (cdp) Fairfax County	2.6
Texas	3.3	Orange County, CA	2.1	**Arlington, VA** (cdp) Arlington County	3.2
New Jersey	4.5	Fairfax County, VA	2.2	**New York, NY** (city)	6.9
Florida	5.4	Palm Beach County, FL	2.3	**Queens, NY** (borough) Queens County	7.3
New York	9.6	Harris County, TX	2.9	**Providence, RI** (city) Providence County	26.0
North Carolina	11.9	Cook County, IL	3.0		

Note: (1) Ranking tables cover all states and counties, and places with an overall population of at least 125,000, OR an overall population of at least 25,000 where the Hispanic/Latino population is at least 20% of the overall population. In states where less than five places meet either of these criteria, we have included places with at least 10,000 total population with the highest percentage of Hispanic/Latino population. These places are identified with an asterisk (*); Please refer to the User's Guide for a full explanation of data.

Households with Food Stamps/SNAP Benefits During Past 12 Months

South American: Chilean

Top 10 States, Counties, and Places[1]

Sorted by Number in Descending Order — U.S. = 2,164

State	Number	County	Number	Place	Number
Florida	608	Miami-Dade County, FL	443	**New York, NY** (city)	305
New York	330	Queens County, NY	169	**Queens, NY** (borough) Queens County	169
California	311	Los Angeles County, CA	139	**Brooklyn, NY** (borough) Kings County	70
New Jersey	155	Utah County, UT	87	**Los Angeles, CA** (city) Los Angeles County	68
Utah	99	Broward County, FL	79	**Manhattan, NY** (borough) New York County	46
Arizona	70	Hudson County, NJ	75	**Miami, FL** (city) Miami-Dade County	38
Illinois	53	Kings County, NY	70	**Chicago, IL** (city) Cook County	0
Oregon	52	Montgomery County, MD	47	**Hempstead (town), NY** (town) Nassau County	0
Pennsylvania	49	New York County, NY	46	**Kendall, FL** (cdp) Miami-Dade County	0
Maryland	47	Maricopa County, AZ	42		

Sorted by Number in Ascending Order — U.S. = 2,164

State	Number	County	Number	Place	Number
Colorado	0	Bergen County, NJ	0	**Chicago, IL** (city) Cook County	0
Connecticut	0	Harris County, TX	0	**Hempstead (town), NY** (town) Nassau County	0
Minnesota	0	Middlesex County, MA	0	**Kendall, FL** (cdp) Miami-Dade County	0
Wisconsin	8	San Mateo County, CA	0	**Miami, FL** (city) Miami-Dade County	38
Georgia	14	Suffolk County, NY	0	**Manhattan, NY** (borough) New York County	46
Missouri	14	Westchester County, NY	0	**Los Angeles, CA** (city) Los Angeles County	68
Nevada	14	Fairfax County, VA	10	**Brooklyn, NY** (borough) Kings County	70
North Carolina	14	Riverside County, CA	10	**Queens, NY** (borough) Queens County	169
Ohio	15	Orange County, CA	12	**New York, NY** (city)	305
Michigan	19	Salt Lake County, UT	12		

Sorted by Percent in Descending Order — U.S. = 5.2%

State	Percent	County	Percent	Place	Percent
Oregon	17.8	Utah County, UT	20.9	**Brooklyn, NY** (borough) Kings County	11.9
Arizona	11.4	Maricopa County, AZ	12.5	**Queens, NY** (borough) Queens County	11.3
Tennessee	11.4	Kings County, NY	11.9	**New York, NY** (city)	9.7
Utah	10.0	Queens County, NY	11.3	**Miami, FL** (city) Miami-Dade County	8.3
Michigan	8.8	Miami-Dade County, FL	10.6	**Manhattan, NY** (borough) New York County	6.8
Florida	7.2	Hudson County, NJ	9.8	**Los Angeles, CA** (city) Los Angeles County	3.8
Pennsylvania	7.1	Alameda County, CA	9.1	**Chicago, IL** (city) Cook County	0.0
New York	6.0	Montgomery County, MD	6.9	**Hempstead (town), NY** (town) Nassau County	0.0
Washington	5.9	New York County, NY	6.8	**Kendall, FL** (cdp) Miami-Dade County	0.0
New Jersey	5.4	San Diego County, CA	6.0		

Sorted by Percent in Ascending Order — U.S. = 5.2%

State	Percent	County	Percent	Place	Percent
Colorado	0.0	Bergen County, NJ	0.0	**Chicago, IL** (city) Cook County	0.0
Connecticut	0.0	Harris County, TX	0.0	**Hempstead (town), NY** (town) Nassau County	0.0
Minnesota	0.0	Middlesex County, MA	0.0	**Kendall, FL** (cdp) Miami-Dade County	0.0
Georgia	1.8	San Mateo County, CA	0.0	**Los Angeles, CA** (city) Los Angeles County	3.8
North Carolina	1.9	Suffolk County, NY	0.0	**Manhattan, NY** (borough) New York County	6.8
Virginia	1.9	Westchester County, NY	0.0	**Miami, FL** (city) Miami-Dade County	8.3
Nevada	2.2	Fairfax County, VA	1.4	**New York, NY** (city)	9.7
Texas	2.5	Nassau County, NY	2.6	**Queens, NY** (borough) Queens County	11.3
Massachusetts	2.8	Clark County, NV	2.9	**Brooklyn, NY** (borough) Kings County	11.9
Wisconsin	2.9	Cook County, IL	3.0		

Note: (1) Ranking tables cover all states and counties, and places with an overall population of at least 125,000, OR an overall population of at least 25,000 where the Hispanic/Latino population is at least 20% of the overall population. In states where less than five places meet either of these criteria, we have included places with at least 10,000 total population with the highest percentage of Hispanic/Latino population. These places are identified with an asterisk (*); Please refer to the User's Guide for a full explanation of data.

Households with Food Stamps/SNAP Benefits During Past 12 Months

South American: Colombian

Top 10 States, Counties, and Places[1]

Sorted by Number in Descending Order — U.S. = 24,038

State	Number	County	Number	Place	Number
Florida	8,555	Miami-Dade County, FL	4,466	**New York, NY** (city)	5,333
New York	6,155	Queens County, NY	3,600	**Queens, NY** (borough) Queens County	3,600
New Jersey	1,775	Broward County, FL	1,739	**Brooklyn, NY** (borough) Kings County	728
Texas	852	Kings County, NY	728	**Miami, FL** (city) Miami-Dade County	575
Massachusetts	680	Hudson County, NJ	582	**Manhattan, NY** (borough) New York County	512
Illinois	626	New York County, NY	512	**Bronx, NY** (borough) Bronx County	445
Connecticut	603	Bronx County, NY	445	**Hialeah, FL** (city) Miami-Dade County	433
North Carolina	569	Harris County, TX	444	**Miami Beach, FL** (city) Miami-Dade County	386
Pennsylvania	548	Cook County, IL	436	**Country Club, FL** (cdp) Miami-Dade County	365
California	535	Providence County, RI	436	**Pembroke Pines, FL** (city) Broward County	340

Sorted by Number in Ascending Order — U.S. = 24,038

State	Number	County	Number	Place	Number
Iowa	0	Baltimore County, MD	0	**Anaheim, CA** (city) Orange County	0
Kansas	0	Burlington County, NJ	0	**Austin, TX** (city) Travis County	0
Alabama	3	Cherokee County, GA	0	**Burbank, CA** (city) Los Angeles County	0
Alaska	3	Dane County, WI	0	**Coral Gables, FL** (city) Miami-Dade County	0
Oregon	10	Denton County, TX	0	**Deltona, FL** (city) Volusia County	0
Kentucky	13	Loudoun County, VA	0	**Elmont, NY** (cdp) Nassau County	0
Minnesota	22	Marion County, FL	0	**Fort Worth, TX** (city) Tarrant County	0
Nebraska	22	Marion County, IN	0	**Glendale, CA** (city) Los Angeles County	0
District of Columbia	23	Montgomery County, PA	0	**Huntington, NY** (town) Suffolk County	0
Arkansas	29	Oakland County, MI	0	**Indianapolis, IN** (city) Marion County	0

Sorted by Percent in Descending Order — U.S. = 8.6%

State	Percent	County	Percent	Place	Percent
Utah	17.5	Luzerne County, PA	32.4	**Passaic, NJ** (city) Passaic County	35.8
Rhode Island	15.9	Erie County, NY	23.7	**South Miami Heights, FL** (cdp) Miami-Dade County	29.8
New Mexico	14.9	Salt Lake County, UT	23.5	**Meadow Woods, FL** (cdp) Orange County	23.9
Tennessee	14.6	Bronx County, NY	22.6	**Hallandale Beach, FL** (city) Broward County	22.8
New York	12.5	Hampden County, MA	21.5	**Bronx, NY** (borough) Bronx County	22.6
New Hampshire	12.0	Lake County, FL	21.0	**Providence, RI** (city) Providence County	22.5
Louisiana	11.7	Kings County, NY	19.5	**North Lauderdale, FL** (city) Broward County	21.6
North Carolina	11.7	Forsyth County, GA	18.8	**Buenaventura Lakes, FL** (cdp) Osceola County	20.8
Delaware	11.5	Lancaster County, PA	18.3	**Miami Gardens, FL** (city) Miami-Dade County	20.6
Wisconsin	11.5	Providence County, RI	17.4	**Hialeah, FL** (city) Miami-Dade County	20.5

Sorted by Percent in Ascending Order — U.S. = 8.6%

State	Percent	County	Percent	Place	Percent
Iowa	0.0	Baltimore County, MD	0.0	**Anaheim, CA** (city) Orange County	0.0
Kansas	0.0	Burlington County, NJ	0.0	**Austin, TX** (city) Travis County	0.0
Alabama	0.4	Cherokee County, GA	0.0	**Burbank, CA** (city) Los Angeles County	0.0
Alaska	0.7	Dane County, WI	0.0	**Coral Gables, FL** (city) Miami-Dade County	0.0
Oregon	1.6	Denton County, TX	0.0	**Deltona, FL** (city) Volusia County	0.0
Minnesota	2.2	Loudoun County, VA	0.0	**Elmont, NY** (cdp) Nassau County	0.0
Virginia	2.4	Marion County, FL	0.0	**Fort Worth, TX** (city) Tarrant County	0.0
California	2.7	Marion County, IN	0.0	**Glendale, CA** (city) Los Angeles County	0.0
District of Columbia	2.7	Montgomery County, PA	0.0	**Huntington, NY** (town) Suffolk County	0.0
Kentucky	4.2	Oakland County, MI	0.0	**Indianapolis, IN** (city) Marion County	0.0

Note: (1) Ranking tables cover all states and counties, and places with an overall population of at least 125,000, OR an overall population of at least 25,000 where the Hispanic/Latino population is at least 20% of the overall population. In states where less than five places meet either of these criteria, we have included places with at least 10,000 total population with the highest percentage of Hispanic/Latino population. These places are identified with an asterisk (*); Please refer to the User's Guide for a full explanation of data.

Households with Food Stamps/SNAP Benefits During Past 12 Months

South American: Ecuadorian

Top 10 States, Counties, and Places[1]

Sorted by Number in Descending Order — U.S. = 20,562

State	Number	County	Number	Place	Number
New York	11,854	Queens County, NY	4,503	**New York, NY** (city)	10,423
New Jersey	2,318	Bronx County, NY	2,345	**Queens, NY** (borough) Queens County	4,503
Florida	2,184	Kings County, NY	2,345	**Bronx, NY** (borough) Bronx County	2,345
California	590	New York County, NY	1,120	**Brooklyn, NY** (borough) Kings County	2,345
Pennsylvania	519	Hudson County, NJ	1,035	**Manhattan, NY** (borough) New York County	1,120
Connecticut	463	Miami-Dade County, FL	915	**Newark, NJ** (city) Essex County	373
Illinois	407	Essex County, NJ	610	**Chicago, IL** (city) Cook County	323
Texas	358	Westchester County, NY	594	**Union City, NJ** (city) Hudson County	303
Massachusetts	279	Cook County, IL	391	**Yonkers, NY** (city) Westchester County	301
North Carolina	210	Broward County, FL	368	**Jersey City, NJ** (city) Hudson County	283

Sorted by Number in Ascending Order — U.S. = 20,562

State	Number	County	Number	Place	Number
Colorado	0	Clark County, NV	0	**Clifton, NJ** (city) Passaic County	0
Nevada	0	Hartford County, CT	0	**Coral Springs, FL** (city) Broward County	0
Washington	5	King County, WA	0	**White Plains, NY** (city) Westchester County	0
Louisiana	7	Mercer County, NJ	0	**Bloomfield, NJ** (township) Essex County	9
Iowa	9	Middlesex County, MA	0	**Babylon, NY** (town) Suffolk County	14
Indiana	10	Ocean County, NJ	0	**Oyster Bay, NY** (town) Nassau County	14
Wisconsin	10	Putnam County, NY	0	**Doral, FL** (city) Miami-Dade County	15
South Carolina	11	Santa Clara County, CA	0	**Philadelphia, PA** (city) Philadelphia County	15
Arizona	12	Tarrant County, TX	0	**New Haven, CT** (city/town) New Haven County	21
Tennessee	16	Utah County, UT	0	**Bridgeport, CT** (city/town) Fairfield County	23

Sorted by Percent in Descending Order — U.S. = 12.3%

State	Percent	County	Percent	Place	Percent
Rhode Island	38.6	Providence County, RI	40.6	**Bronx, NY** (borough) Bronx County	28.7
Missouri	31.8	Pinellas County, FL	30.8	**Plainfield, NJ** (city) Union County	28.3
Michigan	27.0	Bronx County, NY	28.7	**Spring Valley, NY** (village) Rockland County	27.1
Oregon	26.3	Orange County, NY	25.9	**Yonkers, NY** (city) Westchester County	26.3
New York	18.3	Kings County, NY	25.7	**Brooklyn, NY** (borough) Kings County	25.7
Ohio	16.8	Worcester County, MA	24.1	**Downey, CA** (city) Los Angeles County	23.7
Pennsylvania	16.1	New York County, NY	22.3	**Hialeah, FL** (city) Miami-Dade County	22.8
Massachusetts	16.0	Seminole County, FL	18.8	**Manhattan, NY** (borough) New York County	22.3
Georgia	12.5	Berks County, PA	17.8	**New York, NY** (city)	20.6
Utah	12.2	Queens County, NY	16.4	**Country Club, FL** (cdp) Miami-Dade County	19.6

Sorted by Percent in Ascending Order — U.S. = 12.3%

State	Percent	County	Percent	Place	Percent
Colorado	0.0	Clark County, NV	0.0	**Clifton, NJ** (city) Passaic County	0.0
Nevada	0.0	Hartford County, CT	0.0	**Coral Springs, FL** (city) Broward County	0.0
Washington	1.0	King County, WA	0.0	**White Plains, NY** (city) Westchester County	0.0
Arizona	1.6	Mercer County, NJ	0.0	**Bloomfield, NJ** (township) Essex County	2.2
Indiana	2.3	Middlesex County, MA	0.0	**Danbury, CT** (city/town) Fairfield County	2.6
South Carolina	3.2	Ocean County, NJ	0.0	**Minneapolis, MN** (city) Hennepin County	3.2
Iowa	3.3	Putnam County, NY	0.0	**Babylon, NY** (town) Suffolk County	3.6
Louisiana	3.5	Santa Clara County, CA	0.0	**Brookhaven, NY** (town) Suffolk County	3.6
Wisconsin	4.0	Tarrant County, TX	0.0	**Elizabeth, NJ** (city) Union County	3.9
California	4.9	Utah County, UT	0.0	**Doral, FL** (city) Miami-Dade County	4.2

Note: (1) Ranking tables cover all states and counties, and places with an overall population of at least 125,000, OR an overall population of at least 25,000 where the Hispanic/Latino population is at least 20% of the overall population. In states where less than five places meet either of these criteria, we have included places with at least 10,000 total population with the highest percentage of Hispanic/Latino population. These places are identified with an asterisk (*); Please refer to the User's Guide for a full explanation of data.

Households with Food Stamps/SNAP Benefits During Past 12 Months

South American: Paraguayan

Top 10 States, Counties, and Places[1]

Sorted by Number in Descending Order — U.S. = 307

State	Number	County	Number	Place	Number
New York	132	Queens County, NY	62	**New York, NY** (city)	118
Texas	29	Westchester County, NY	14	**Queens, NY** (borough) Queens County	62
Florida	22				
California	9				
Maryland	0				
New Jersey	0				

Sorted by Number in Ascending Order — U.S. = 307

State	Number	County	Number	Place	Number
Maryland	0	Westchester County, NY	14	**Queens, NY** (borough) Queens County	62
New Jersey	0	Queens County, NY	62	**New York, NY** (city)	118
California	9				
Florida	22				
Texas	29				
New York	132				

Sorted by Percent in Descending Order — U.S. = 5.5%

State	Percent	County	Percent	Place	Percent
New York	7.3	Queens County, NY	7.8	**New York, NY** (city)	10.9
Texas	7.2	Westchester County, NY	2.9	**Queens, NY** (borough) Queens County	7.8
Florida	4.3				
California	2.9				
Maryland	0.0				
New Jersey	0.0				

Sorted by Percent in Ascending Order — U.S. = 5.5%

State	Percent	County	Percent	Place	Percent
Maryland	0.0	Westchester County, NY	2.9	**Queens, NY** (borough) Queens County	7.8
New Jersey	0.0	Queens County, NY	7.8	**New York, NY** (city)	10.9
California	2.9				
Florida	4.3				
Texas	7.2				
New York	7.3				

Note: (1) Ranking tables cover all states and counties, and places with an overall population of at least 125,000, OR an overall population of at least 25,000 where the Hispanic/Latino population is at least 20% of the overall population. In states where less than five places meet either of these criteria, we have included places with at least 10,000 total population with the highest percentage of Hispanic/Latino population. These places are identified with an asterisk (*); Please refer to the User's Guide for a full explanation of data.

Households with Food Stamps/SNAP Benefits During Past 12 Months

South American: Peruvian

Top 10 States, Counties, and Places[1]

Sorted by Number in Descending Order — U.S. = 11,947

State	Number	County	Number	Place	Number
Florida	2,854	Miami-Dade County, FL	1,414	**New York, NY** (city)	1,997
New York	2,475	Queens County, NY	923	**Queens, NY** (borough) Queens County	923
New Jersey	2,317	Passaic County, NJ	757	**Paterson, NJ** (city) Passaic County	414
California	896	Broward County, FL	633	**Bronx, NY** (borough) Bronx County	367
Texas	396	Hudson County, NJ	581	**Brooklyn, NY** (borough) Kings County	303
Connecticut	315	Los Angeles County, CA	397	**Manhattan, NY** (borough) New York County	228
Virginia	246	Bronx County, NY	367	**Clifton, NJ** (city) Passaic County	185
Pennsylvania	245	Kings County, NY	303	**Los Angeles, CA** (city) Los Angeles County	182
Maryland	224	Essex County, NJ	265	**Staten Island, NY** (borough) Richmond County	176
Illinois	185	Palm Beach County, FL	250	**Hollywood, FL** (city) Broward County	174

Sorted by Number in Ascending Order — U.S. = 11,947

State	Number	County	Number	Place	Number
Hawaii	0	Arapahoe County, CO	0	**Aurora, CO** (city) Arapahoe County	0
Minnesota	0	Denton County, TX	0	**Belleville, NJ** (township) Essex County	0
Missouri	0	Fort Bend County, TX	0	**Cape Coral, FL** (city) Lee County	0
South Carolina	0	Lake County, IL	0	**Concord, CA** (city) Contra Costa County	0
Idaho	2	San Joaquin County, CA	0	**Davie, FL** (town) Broward County	0
Alabama	9	San Mateo County, CA	0	**Doral, FL** (city) Miami-Dade County	0
Wisconsin	21	Sarasota County, FL	0	**Fort Lauderdale, FL** (city) Broward County	0
Indiana	31	Seminole County, FL	0	**Las Vegas, NV** (city) Clark County	0
Louisiana	35	Solano County, CA	0	**Port Chester, NY** (village) Westchester County	0
Oklahoma	35	Ventura County, CA	0	**Salt Lake City, UT** (city) Salt Lake County	0

Sorted by Percent in Descending Order — U.S. = 7.5%

State	Percent	County	Percent	Place	Percent
Rhode Island	29.6	Richmond County, NY	28.1	**West New York, NJ** (town) Hudson County	29.7
Delaware	18.8	Bronx County, NY	25.6	**Staten Island, NY** (borough) Richmond County	28.1
Kentucky	15.4	Denver County, CO	25.0	**Bronx, NY** (borough) Bronx County	25.6
Tennessee	15.4	Ocean County, NJ	22.8	**Jersey City, NJ** (city) Hudson County	25.4
Kansas	13.8	Morris County, NJ	19.8	**Denver, CO** (city) Denver County	25.0
Ohio	13.2	Kings County, NY	17.7	**West Valley City, UT** (city) Salt Lake County	23.2
New Mexico	12.8	Tarrant County, TX	15.4	**Miami Beach, FL** (city) Miami-Dade County	20.8
Pennsylvania	11.6	Philadelphia County, PA	14.8	**Passaic, NJ** (city) Passaic County	20.5
New York	11.3	Franklin County, OH	14.4	**Hialeah, FL** (city) Miami-Dade County	19.4
Michigan	10.9	Passaic County, NJ	14.4	**Kendall West, FL** (cdp) Miami-Dade County	18.9

Sorted by Percent in Ascending Order — U.S. = 7.5%

State	Percent	County	Percent	Place	Percent
Hawaii	0.0	Arapahoe County, CO	0.0	**Aurora, CO** (city) Arapahoe County	0.0
Minnesota	0.0	Denton County, TX	0.0	**Belleville, NJ** (township) Essex County	0.0
Missouri	0.0	Fort Bend County, TX	0.0	**Cape Coral, FL** (city) Lee County	0.0
South Carolina	0.0	Lake County, IL	0.0	**Concord, CA** (city) Contra Costa County	0.0
Idaho	0.6	San Joaquin County, CA	0.0	**Davie, FL** (town) Broward County	0.0
Wisconsin	2.7	San Mateo County, CA	0.0	**Doral, FL** (city) Miami-Dade County	0.0
Nevada	2.9	Sarasota County, FL	0.0	**Fort Lauderdale, FL** (city) Broward County	0.0
Virginia	3.0	Seminole County, FL	0.0	**Las Vegas, NV** (city) Clark County	0.0
Alabama	3.1	Solano County, CA	0.0	**Port Chester, NY** (village) Westchester County	0.0
California	3.4	Ventura County, CA	0.0	**Salt Lake City, UT** (city) Salt Lake County	0.0

Note: (1) Ranking tables cover all states and counties, and places with an overall population of at least 125,000, OR an overall population of at least 25,000 where the Hispanic/Latino population is at least 20% of the overall population. In states where less than five places meet either of these criteria, we have included places with at least 10,000 total population with the highest percentage of Hispanic/Latino population. These places are identified with an asterisk (*); Please refer to the User's Guide for a full explanation of data.

Households with Food Stamps/SNAP Benefits During Past 12 Months

South American: Uruguayan

Top 10 States, Counties, and Places[1]

Sorted by Number in Descending Order — U.S. = 1,378

State	Number	County	Number	Place	Number
Florida	491	Miami-Dade County, FL	302	**New York, NY** (city)	92
New Jersey	224	Queens County, NY	92	**Queens, NY** (borough) Queens County	92
New York	111	Essex County, NJ	80	**Elizabeth, NJ** (city) Union County	28
Virginia	92	Palm Beach County, FL	64		
Texas	70	Hudson County, NJ	48		
Georgia	64	Harris County, TX	45		
California	37	Union County, NJ	37		
Pennsylvania	36	Broward County, FL	31		
Massachusetts	35	Los Angeles County, CA	25		
Maryland	19	Gwinnett County, GA	12		

Sorted by Number in Ascending Order — U.S. = 1,378

State	Number	County	Number	Place	Number
Maryland	19	Middlesex County, NJ	0	**Elizabeth, NJ** (city) Union County	28
Massachusetts	35	Westchester County, NY	5	**New York, NY** (city)	92
Pennsylvania	36	Morris County, NJ	8	**Queens, NY** (borough) Queens County	92
California	37	Worcester County, MA	10		
Georgia	64	Gwinnett County, GA	12		
Texas	70	Los Angeles County, CA	25		
Virginia	92	Broward County, FL	31		
New York	111	Union County, NJ	37		
New Jersey	224	Harris County, TX	45		
Florida	491	Hudson County, NJ	48		

Sorted by Percent in Descending Order — U.S. = 7.1%

State	Percent	County	Percent	Place	Percent
Virginia	16.3	Queens County, NY	17.3	**Queens, NY** (borough) Queens County	17.3
Florida	9.3	Miami-Dade County, FL	12.1	**New York, NY** (city)	8.3
Pennsylvania	8.8	Harris County, TX	10.5	**Elizabeth, NJ** (city) Union County	3.2
Texas	8.0	Hudson County, NJ	10.3		
Georgia	7.1	Palm Beach County, FL	10.2		
New Jersey	5.4	Essex County, NJ	9.3		
New York	5.3	Los Angeles County, CA	4.7		
Massachusetts	4.5	Gwinnett County, GA	3.5		
Maryland	3.7	Union County, NJ	2.8		
California	2.9	Worcester County, MA	2.7		

Sorted by Percent in Ascending Order — U.S. = 7.1%

State	Percent	County	Percent	Place	Percent
California	2.9	Middlesex County, NJ	0.0	**Elizabeth, NJ** (city) Union County	3.2
Maryland	3.7	Westchester County, NY	1.2	**New York, NY** (city)	8.3
Massachusetts	4.5	Morris County, NJ	1.9	**Queens, NY** (borough) Queens County	17.3
New York	5.3	Broward County, FL	2.5		
New Jersey	5.4	Worcester County, MA	2.7		
Georgia	7.1	Union County, NJ	2.8		
Texas	8.0	Gwinnett County, GA	3.5		
Pennsylvania	8.8	Los Angeles County, CA	4.7		
Florida	9.3	Essex County, NJ	9.3		
Virginia	16.3	Palm Beach County, FL	10.2		

Note: (1) Ranking tables cover all states and counties, and places with an overall population of at least 125,000, OR an overall population of at least 25,000 where the Hispanic/Latino population is at least 20% of the overall population. In states where less than five places meet either of these criteria, we have included places with at least 10,000 total population with the highest percentage of Hispanic/Latino population. These places are identified with an asterisk (*); Please refer to the User's Guide for a full explanation of data.

Households with Food Stamps/SNAP Benefits During Past 12 Months

South American: Venezuelan

Top 10 States, Counties, and Places[1]

Sorted by Number in Descending Order (U.S. = 4,390)

State	Number	County	Number	Place	Number
Florida	2,014	Miami-Dade County, FL	1,042	**New York, NY** (city)	719
New York	771	Broward County, FL	418	**Queens, NY** (borough) Queens County	323
Illinois	192	Queens County, NY	323	**Brooklyn, NY** (borough) Kings County	231
Texas	161	Kings County, NY	231	**Miami, FL** (city) Miami-Dade County	140
Georgia	152	Osceola County, FL	182	**Hialeah, FL** (city) Miami-Dade County	113
New Jersey	105	Cook County, IL	118	**Country Club, FL** (cdp) Miami-Dade County	90
California	89	Harris County, TX	118	**Manhattan, NY** (borough) New York County	88
Colorado	82	Orange County, FL	103	**Kendall West, FL** (cdp) Miami-Dade County	87
Pennsylvania	82	New York County, NY	88	**Kendall, FL** (cdp) Miami-Dade County	83
Tennessee	69	Bronx County, NY	77	**Bronx, NY** (borough) Bronx County	77

Sorted by Number in Ascending Order (U.S. = 4,390)

State	Number	County	Number	Place	Number
South Carolina	0	Collin County, TX	0	**Aventura, FL** (city) Miami-Dade County	0
Utah	0	Dallas County, TX	0	**Hollywood, FL** (city) Broward County	0
Oklahoma	4	Fairfield County, CT	0	**Los Angeles, CA** (city) Los Angeles County	0
Missouri	8	Fulton County, GA	0	**Miramar, FL** (city) Broward County	0
Indiana	11	Hillsborough County, FL	0	**Coral Springs, FL** (city) Broward County	8
Arizona	14	King County, WA	0	**Pembroke Pines, FL** (city) Broward County	8
Maryland	14	Los Angeles County, CA	0	**Orlando, FL** (city) Orange County	24
Connecticut	15	Middlesex County, MA	0	**The Hammocks, FL** (cdp) Miami-Dade County	27
Ohio	19	Montgomery County, MD	0	**Weston, FL** (city) Broward County	37
Wisconsin	25	Montgomery County, TX	0	**Miami Beach, FL** (city) Miami-Dade County	41

Sorted by Percent in Descending Order (U.S. = 6.4%)

State	Percent	County	Percent	Place	Percent
Illinois	17.5	Kings County, NY	29.1	**Brooklyn, NY** (borough) Kings County	29.1
Michigan	15.3	Queens County, NY	20.8	**Hialeah, FL** (city) Miami-Dade County	26.3
New York	14.8	Osceola County, FL	19.0	**Kendall, FL** (cdp) Miami-Dade County	21.1
Tennessee	12.8	Bronx County, NY	17.7	**Queens, NY** (borough) Queens County	20.8
Colorado	12.6	Cook County, IL	17.1	**Kendall West, FL** (cdp) Miami-Dade County	19.0
Louisiana	7.8	Cobb County, GA	16.7	**Country Club, FL** (cdp) Miami-Dade County	18.6
Pennsylvania	7.5	Gwinnett County, GA	9.4	**New York, NY** (city)	17.8
Georgia	7.2	Lee County, FL	7.7	**Bronx, NY** (borough) Bronx County	17.7
Wisconsin	6.8	Miami-Dade County, FL	7.1	**Davie, FL** (town) Broward County	17.3
Florida	6.2	New York County, NY	7.1	**Tamiami, FL** (cdp) Miami-Dade County	15.1

Sorted by Percent in Ascending Order (U.S. = 6.4%)

State	Percent	County	Percent	Place	Percent
South Carolina	0.0	Collin County, TX	0.0	**Aventura, FL** (city) Miami-Dade County	0.0
Utah	0.0	Dallas County, TX	0.0	**Hollywood, FL** (city) Broward County	0.0
Oklahoma	1.0	Fairfield County, CT	0.0	**Los Angeles, CA** (city) Los Angeles County	0.0
Maryland	1.6	Fulton County, GA	0.0	**Miramar, FL** (city) Broward County	0.0
Virginia	1.6	Hillsborough County, FL	0.0	**Pembroke Pines, FL** (city) Broward County	0.9
Connecticut	2.3	King County, WA	0.0	**Doral, FL** (city) Miami-Dade County	1.9
California	2.4	Los Angeles County, CA	0.0	**Weston, FL** (city) Broward County	1.9
Texas	2.7	Middlesex County, MA	0.0	**Coral Springs, FL** (city) Broward County	2.6
Indiana	3.0	Montgomery County, MD	0.0	**Houston, TX** (city) Harris County	3.6
Arizona	3.1	Montgomery County, TX	0.0	**Orlando, FL** (city) Orange County	3.9

Note: (1) Ranking tables cover all states and counties, and places with an overall population of at least 125,000, OR an overall population of at least 25,000 where the Hispanic/Latino population is at least 20% of the overall population. In states where less than five places meet either of these criteria, we have included places with at least 10,000 total population with the highest percentage of Hispanic/Latino population. These places are identified with an asterisk (*); Please refer to the User's Guide for a full explanation of data.

Households with Food Stamps/SNAP Benefits During Past 12 Months

Spaniard

Top 10 States, Counties, and Places[1]

Sorted by Number in Descending Order — U.S. = 18,301

State	Number	County	Number	Place	Number
Texas	2,601	Bernalillo County, NM	598	**Albuquerque, NM** (city) Bernalillo County	504
California	2,535	Maricopa County, AZ	406	**New York, NY** (city)	390
New Mexico	2,135	Harris County, TX	384	**San Antonio, TX** (city) Bexar County	319
Colorado	1,941	Los Angeles County, CA	371	**Pueblo, CO** (city) Pueblo County	282
Florida	1,048	Bexar County, TX	340	**Phoenix, AZ** (city) Maricopa County	219
Arizona	866	Pueblo County, CO	316	**Denver, CO** (city) Denver County	192
Washington	690	Miami-Dade County, FL	306	**Austin, TX** (city) Travis County	163
New York	670	Sacramento County, CA	291	**Santa Fe, NM** (city) Santa Fe County	160
Oregon	429	San Miguel County, NM	283	**Houston, TX** (city) Harris County	157
Michigan	414	Santa Fe County, NM	247	**Colorado Springs, CO** (city) El Paso County	152

Sorted by Number in Ascending Order — U.S. = 18,301

State	Number	County	Number	Place	Number
District of Columbia	0	Ada County, ID	0	**Brookhaven, NY** (town) Suffolk County	0
New Hampshire	0	Collin County, TX	0	**Jacksonville, FL** (city) Duval County	0
Wisconsin	7	Douglas County, CO	0	**Kearny, NJ** (town) Hudson County	0
West Virginia	26	Douglas County, NE	0	**North Las Vegas, NV** (city) Clark County	0
Kansas	27	Duval County, FL	0	**Staten Island, NY** (borough) Richmond County	0
Montana	27	Hidalgo County, TX	0	**Urban Honolulu, HI** (cdp) Honolulu County	6
Iowa	36	Hudson County, NJ	0	**Hempstead (town), NY** (town) Nassau County	10
Nebraska	39	Middlesex County, NJ	0	**Bakersfield, CA** (city) Kern County	12
Virginia	39	Morris County, NJ	0	**Virginia Beach, VA** (independent city)	13
Indiana	47	Passaic County, NJ	0	**Fort Worth, TX** (city) Tarrant County	14

Sorted by Percent in Descending Order — U.S. = 8.4%

State	Percent	County	Percent	Place	Percent
Maine	26.2	Conejos County, CO	33.4	**Pueblo, CO** (city) Pueblo County	20.5
Arkansas	25.5	Erie County, NY	31.1	**Oklahoma City, OK** (city) Oklahoma County	18.9
Kentucky	24.5	Weber County, UT	23.5	**Rio Rancho, NM** (city) Sandoval County	18.5
Oklahoma	19.8	Hawaii County, HI	23.0	**Sacramento, CA** (city) Sacramento County	18.3
Missouri	18.5	Las Animas County, CO	22.6	**Lakewood, CO** (city) Jefferson County	17.4
Alaska	17.1	Ocean County, NJ	21.1	**Las Cruces, NM** (city) Dona Ana County	17.4
Idaho	15.7	Pierce County, WA	20.6	**Riverside, CA** (city) Riverside County	17.1
Michigan	14.9	Larimer County, CO	20.1	**Phoenix, AZ** (city) Maricopa County	16.8
Washington	14.1	Kern County, CA	18.8	**Reno, NV** (city) Washoe County	16.4
South Carolina	14.0	Pueblo County, CO	18.0	**Fort Collins, CO** (city) Larimer County	16.0

Sorted by Percent in Ascending Order — U.S. = 8.4%

State	Percent	County	Percent	Place	Percent
District of Columbia	0.0	Ada County, ID	0.0	**Brookhaven, NY** (town) Suffolk County	0.0
New Hampshire	0.0	Collin County, TX	0.0	**Jacksonville, FL** (city) Duval County	0.0
Wisconsin	0.9	Douglas County, CO	0.0	**Kearny, NJ** (town) Hudson County	0.0
Virginia	1.3	Douglas County, NE	0.0	**North Las Vegas, NV** (city) Clark County	0.0
Maryland	3.0	Duval County, FL	0.0	**Staten Island, NY** (borough) Richmond County	0.0
Kansas	3.3	Hidalgo County, TX	0.0	**Urban Honolulu, HI** (cdp) Honolulu County	1.0
Massachusetts	4.2	Hudson County, NJ	0.0	**San Jose, CA** (city) Santa Clara County	1.3
Georgia	4.4	Middlesex County, NJ	0.0	**Hempstead (town), NY** (town) Nassau County	1.4
Montana	4.6	Morris County, NJ	0.0	**San Francisco, CA** (city) San Francisco County	1.4
New Jersey	4.7	Passaic County, NJ	0.0	**Aurora, CO** (city) Arapahoe County	2.1

Note: (1) Ranking tables cover all states and counties, and places with an overall population of at least 125,000, OR an overall population of at least 25,000 where the Hispanic/Latino population is at least 20% of the overall population. In states where less than five places meet either of these criteria, we have included places with at least 10,000 total population with the highest percentage of Hispanic/Latino population. These places are identified with an asterisk (*); Please refer to the User's Guide for a full explanation of data.

Poverty Rate

(Income in Past 12 Months Below Poverty Level)

Total Population

Top 10 States, Counties, and Places[1]

Sorted by Percent in Descending Order — U.S. = 13.8%

State	Percent	County	Percent	Place	Percent
Mississippi	21.2	Shannon County, SD	53.5	**Parker*, SC** (cdp) Greenville County	38.1
District of Columbia	18.5	Todd County, SD	48.8	**Morgantown*, WV** (city) Monongalia County	37.5
New Mexico	18.4	Hudspeth County, TX	46.0	**Pharr, TX** (city) Hidalgo County	37.3
Louisiana	18.1	Holmes County, MS	43.4	**San Marcos, TX** (city) Hays County	36.9
Arkansas	18.0	Willacy County, TX	43.4	**University, FL** (cdp) Hillsborough County	36.7
Kentucky	17.7	Zavala County, TX	43.0	**York, PA** (city) York County	36.6
West Virginia	17.4	Humphreys County, MS	42.9	**Camden, NJ** (city) Camden County	36.1
Alabama	17.1	Allendale County, SC	42.4	**Brownsville, TX** (city) Cameron County	35.8
Texas	16.8	East Carroll Parish, LA	40.8	**San Luis, AZ** (city) Yuma County	35.2
Tennessee	16.5	Leflore County, MS	39.7	**Hope*, AR** (city) Hempstead County	35.1

Sorted by Percent in Ascending Order — U.S. = 13.8%

State	Percent	County	Percent	Place	Percent
New Hampshire	7.8	Morgan County, UT	1.1	**Oyster Bay, NY** (town) Nassau County	3.2
Maryland	8.6	Irion County, TX	1.5	**Makakilo*, HI** (cdp) Honolulu County	3.4
New Jersey	9.1	Los Alamos County, NM	2.4	**Naperville, IL** (city) DuPage County	3.4
Connecticut	9.2	Douglas County, CO	2.9	**Moorpark, CA** (city) Ventura County	3.5
Alaska	9.5	Loudoun County, VA	3.2	**Salem*, NH** (town) Rockingham County	3.5
Hawaii	9.6	Elbert County, CO	3.5	**Eastvale, CA** (cdp) Riverside County	3.8
Wyoming	9.8	Somerset County, NJ	3.6	**Chino Hills, CA** (city) San Bernardino County	4.1
Virginia	10.3	Kendall County, IL	3.9	**Atascocita, TX** (cdp) Harris County	4.4
Massachusetts	10.5	York County, VA	3.9	**Cooper City, FL** (city) Broward County	4.4
Minnesota	10.6	Hunterdon County, NJ	4.0	**Huntington, NY** (town) Suffolk County	4.4

RANKINGS & COMPARISONS

Note: (1) Ranking tables cover all states and counties, and places with an overall population of at least 125,000, OR an overall population of at least 25,000 where the Hispanic/Latino population is at least 20% of the overall population. In states where less than five places meet either of these criteria, we have included places with at least 10,000 total population with the highest percentage of Hispanic/Latino population. These places are identified with an asterisk (*); Please refer to the User's Guide for a full explanation of data.

Poverty Rate

(Income in Past 12 Months Below Poverty Level)

Hispanic or Latino (of any race)

Top 10 States, Counties, and Places[1]

Sorted by Percent in Descending Order — U.S. = 22.4%

State	Percent	County	Percent	Place	Percent
Kentucky	31.0	Alexander County, NC	73.4	**Holyoke, MA** (city) Hampden County	51.8
Pennsylvania	31.0	Floyd County, IA	72.1	**Buffalo, NY** (city) Erie County	51.7
Tennessee	31.0	Mahaska County, IA	72.0	**Woonsocket*, RI** (city) Providence County	51.0
Arkansas	30.6	Yellow Medicine County, MN	70.9	**Albertville*, AL** (city) Marshall County	50.3
Alabama	30.5	Kent County, MD	68.0	**York, PA** (city) York County	49.4
North Carolina	29.8	McDonough County, IL	66.0	**Shelbyville*, KY** (city) Shelby County	49.0
Massachusetts	29.6	Hughes County, OK	65.5	**Carthage*, MO** (city) Jasper County	48.7
Rhode Island	28.4	Dickens County, TX	65.2	**Parker*, SC** (cdp) Greenville County	47.8
Oklahoma	28.2	McCurtain County, OK	64.9	**Worthington*, MN** (city) Nobles County	45.4
Georgia	28.1	Alleghany County, NC	62.0	**Asheboro, NC** (city) Randolph County	45.3

Sorted by Percent in Ascending Order — U.S. = 22.4%

State	Percent	County	Percent	Place	Percent
Alaska	11.6	Perry County, IL	0.7	**Fort Leonard Wood*, MO** (cdp) Pulaski County	1.4
Maryland	12.2	Harris County, GA	1.0	**San Dimas, CA** (city) Los Angeles County	2.1
Hawaii	13.7	Caroline County, VA	1.2	**Makakilo*, HI** (cdp) Honolulu County	2.3
District of Columbia	13.8	Newton County, IN	1.3	**The Colony, TX** (city) Denton County	4.0
Virginia	13.9	Los Alamos County, NM	1.5	**Leander, TX** (city) Williamson County	4.2
Wyoming	15.5	Calvert County, MD	1.6	**La Verne, CA** (city) Los Angeles County	4.3
New Hampshire	15.8	Waseca County, MN	1.7	**Suisun City, CA** (city) Solano County	4.3
New Jersey	17.6	Miami County, OH	2.0	**Marana, AZ** (town) Pima County	4.7
Illinois	18.2	Isle of Wight County, VA	2.4	**College*, AK** (cdp) Fairbanks North Star Borough	4.8
Nevada	18.2	Saint John the Baptist Parish, LA	3.1	**Miami Lakes, FL** (town) Miami-Dade County	4.9

Note: (1) Ranking tables cover all states and counties, and places with an overall population of at least 125,000, OR an overall population of at least 25,000 where the Hispanic/Latino population is at least 20% of the overall population. In states where less than five places meet either of these criteria, we have included places with at least 10,000 total population with the highest percentage of Hispanic/Latino population. These places are identified with an asterisk (*); Please refer to the User's Guide for a full explanation of data.

Poverty Rate

(Income in Past 12 Months Below Poverty Level)

Central American, excluding Mexican

Top 10 States, Counties, and Places[1]

Sorted by Percent in Descending Order — U.S. = 19.8%

State	Percent	County	Percent	Place	Percent
Vermont	43.3	Gilmer County, GA	65.4	**Albertville*, AL** (city) Marshall County	71.4
Alabama	38.2	Murray County, GA	59.7	**Cincinnati, OH** (city) Hamilton County	58.2
Kentucky	34.1	Hamilton County, OH	58.2	**Springfield, MA** (city) Hampden County	57.1
Tennessee	31.9	Marshall County, AL	58.0	**University, FL** (cdp) Hillsborough County	55.2
Arkansas	31.1	Hendry County, FL	56.4	**Rubidoux, CA** (cdp) Riverside County	55.0
Missouri	28.6	Johnston County, NC	53.8	**Clarksville, TN** (city) Montgomery County	48.4
North Carolina	28.4	Clarke County, GA	51.9	**Grand Rapids, MI** (city) Kent County	47.0
Kansas	28.3	DeKalb County, AL	51.2	**Greensboro, NC** (city) Guilford County	44.6
Georgia	28.1	Mobile County, AL	48.6	**Lexington-Fayette, KY** (consolidated govt) Fayette County	44.5
Ohio	27.8	Cherokee County, GA	48.5	**Rochester, NY** (city) Monroe County	44.4

Sorted by Percent in Ascending Order — U.S. = 19.8%

State	Percent	County	Percent	Place	Percent
Alaska	3.6	Douglas County, CO	1.0	**Rohnert Park, CA** (city) Sonoma County	1.3
District of Columbia	12.6	Saint John the Baptist Parish, LA	1.0	**Union City, CA** (city) Alameda County	1.3
Hawaii	13.3	Pinal County, AZ	1.7	**Hacienda Heights, CA** (cdp) Los Angeles County	1.6
Illinois	13.6	Harford County, MD	2.3	**Sunrise, FL** (city) Broward County	1.6
Maryland	13.7	Charles County, MD	3.2	**Culver City, CA** (city) Los Angeles County	1.9
Nevada	14.8	Shasta County, CA	3.3	**Lake Forest, CA** (city) Orange County	2.0
Wisconsin	14.9	Kane County, IL	3.4	**Lewisville, TX** (city) Denton County	2.1
Virginia	15.4	Richmond County, NY	3.5	**Fremont, CA** (city) Alameda County	2.3
Arizona	15.9	New Castle County, DE	4.1	**Monterey Park, CA** (city) Los Angeles County	2.4
New Hampshire	16.1	Spotsylvania County, VA	4.1	**Newburgh, NY** (city) Orange County	2.4

Note: (1) Ranking tables cover all states and counties, and places with an overall population of at least 125,000, OR an overall population of at least 25,000 where the Hispanic/Latino population is at least 20% of the overall population. In states where less than five places meet either of these criteria, we have included places with at least 10,000 total population with the highest percentage of Hispanic/Latino population. These places are identified with an asterisk (*); Please refer to the User's Guide for a full explanation of data.

Poverty Rate

(Income in Past 12 Months Below Poverty Level)

Central American: Costa Rican

Top 10 States, Counties, and Places[1]

Sorted by Percent in Descending Order — U.S. = 14.4%

State	Percent	County	Percent	Place	Percent
Pennsylvania	27.9	Philadelphia County, PA	43.4	**Philadelphia, PA** (city) Philadelphia County	43.4
Illinois	21.7	Mercer County, NJ	39.9	**Miami, FL** (city) Miami-Dade County	40.4
New Jersey	20.8	Orange County, FL	29.8	**Bronx, NY** (borough) Bronx County	18.2
North Carolina	20.5	Union County, NJ	28.7	**Los Angeles, CA** (city) Los Angeles County	17.3
Florida	19.1	Essex County, NJ	25.8	**Brooklyn, NY** (borough) Kings County	17.0
Michigan	19.1	Passaic County, NJ	24.9	**New York, NY** (city)	12.0
Connecticut	14.3	Miami-Dade County, FL	22.9	**Queens, NY** (borough) Queens County	3.0
Nevada	14.2	Bronx County, NY	18.2		
New York	14.1	Cook County, IL	18.0		
Oregon	14.1	Bergen County, NJ	17.2		

Sorted by Percent in Ascending Order — U.S. = 14.4%

State	Percent	County	Percent	Place	Percent
Arizona	0.7	Maricopa County, AZ	0.9	**Queens, NY** (borough) Queens County	3.0
Washington	1.8	Nassau County, NY	2.3	**New York, NY** (city)	12.0
Maryland	5.2	Queens County, NY	3.0	**Brooklyn, NY** (borough) Kings County	17.0
Tennessee	5.8	Contra Costa County, CA	3.7	**Los Angeles, CA** (city) Los Angeles County	17.3
Virginia	5.9	Palm Beach County, FL	3.9	**Bronx, NY** (borough) Bronx County	18.2
California	7.9	San Bernardino County, CA	4.1	**Miami, FL** (city) Miami-Dade County	40.4
Louisiana	10.1	Orange County, CA	7.7	**Philadelphia, PA** (city) Philadelphia County	43.4
Minnesota	10.5	San Diego County, CA	8.1		
Massachusetts	10.8	Morris County, NJ	8.6		
South Carolina	11.2	Somerset County, NJ	9.1		

Note: (1) Ranking tables cover all states and counties, and places with an overall population of at least 125,000, OR an overall population of at least 25,000 where the Hispanic/Latino population is at least 20% of the overall population. In states where less than five places meet either of these criteria, we have included places with at least 10,000 total population with the highest percentage of Hispanic/Latino population. These places are identified with an asterisk (*); Please refer to the User's Guide for a full explanation of data.

Poverty Rate

(Income in Past 12 Months Below Poverty Level)

Central American: Guatemalan

Top 10 States, Counties, and Places[1]

Sorted by Percent in Descending Order — U.S. = 23.4%

State	Percent	County	Percent	Place	Percent
Alabama	47.0	Hamilton County, OH	66.0	**Albertville*, AL** (city) Marshall County	70.7
Kentucky	43.5	Gilmer County, GA	65.4	**Cincinnati, OH** (city) Hamilton County	62.0
Mississippi	39.6	Murray County, GA	64.4	**San Bernardino, CA** (city) San Bernardino County	52.3
Georgia	38.9	Cherokee County, GA	60.0	**Grand Rapids, MI** (city) Kent County	51.4
Kansas	38.2	Marshall County, AL	59.3	**West Palm Beach, FL** (city) Palm Beach County	47.7
Missouri	35.9	DeKalb County, AL	55.8	**Marietta, GA** (city) Cobb County	44.7
Ohio	35.9	Cobb County, GA	49.0	**Homestead, FL** (city) Miami-Dade County	43.6
Oklahoma	35.1	Utah County, UT	48.0	**Chattanooga, TN** (city) Hamilton County	42.7
South Carolina	34.5	Hamilton County, TN	46.4	**Carthage*, MO** (city) Jasper County	41.2
Michigan	34.2	Kent County, MI	45.0	**Philadelphia, PA** (city) Philadelphia County	41.0

Sorted by Percent in Ascending Order — U.S. = 23.4%

State	Percent	County	Percent	Place	Percent
New Hampshire	9.8	Anne Arundel County, MD	2.2	**Cranston*, RI** (city) Providence County	1.4
Wisconsin	9.8	Osceola County, FL	2.2	**Brentwood, NY** (cdp) Suffolk County	1.6
New Mexico	11.8	Sonoma County, CA	2.7	**Islip, NY** (town) Suffolk County	3.6
Louisiana	12.7	Morris County, NJ	4.2	**Burbank, CA** (city) Los Angeles County	4.3
District of Columbia	14.1	Milwaukee County, WI	5.5	**Elizabeth, NJ** (city) Union County	5.0
Illinois	14.1	Pinal County, AZ	5.6	**Spring Valley, NV** (cdp) Clark County	5.0
Maryland	14.9	Fort Bend County, TX	5.8	**San Antonio, TX** (city) Bexar County	5.1
Nevada	15.4	Santa Fe County, NM	6.5	**Central Islip, NY** (cdp) Suffolk County	5.6
Arizona	17.0	Bexar County, TX	6.8	**Downey, CA** (city) Los Angeles County	6.2
Rhode Island	17.5	Worcester County, MA	7.5	**Norwalk, CA** (city) Los Angeles County	7.3

Note: (1) Ranking tables cover all states and counties, and places with an overall population of at least 125,000, OR an overall population of at least 25,000 where the Hispanic/Latino population is at least 20% of the overall population. In states where less than five places meet either of these criteria, we have included places with at least 10,000 total population with the highest percentage of Hispanic/Latino population. These places are identified with an asterisk (*); Please refer to the User's Guide for a full explanation of data.

Poverty Rate

(Income in Past 12 Months Below Poverty Level)

Central American: Honduran

Top 10 States, Counties, and Places[1]

Sorted by Percent in Descending Order — U.S. = 25.4%

State	Percent	County	Percent	Place	Percent
Missouri	42.6	King County, WA	55.4	**Huntington Station, NY** (cdp) Suffolk County	49.7
Washington	38.4	Jackson County, MO	53.8	**Huntington, NY** (town) Suffolk County	48.2
Kansas	35.4	Johnston County, NC	49.5	**Pasadena, CA** (city) Los Angeles County	44.7
Minnesota	34.8	Polk County, FL	42.2	**Pasadena, TX** (city) Harris County	44.7
Indiana	34.6	Kern County, CA	40.4	**Aurora, CO** (city) Arapahoe County	43.3
Tennessee	33.2	New York County, NY	40.4	**Springfield, VA** (cdp) Fairfax County	40.8
Texas	32.0	Oklahoma County, OK	40.2	**Manhattan, NY** (borough) New York County	40.4
North Carolina	30.8	Arapahoe County, CO	38.8	**Dallas, TX** (city) Dallas County	39.9
South Carolina	30.5	Davidson County, TN	38.0	**Houston, TX** (city) Harris County	38.7
Kentucky	30.3	Marion County, IN	38.0	**Nashville-Davidson, TN** (metropolitan govt) Davidson County	38.0

Sorted by Percent in Ascending Order — U.S. = 25.4%

State	Percent	County	Percent	Place	Percent
Nebraska	5.2	Orange County, NY	4.3	**Newburgh, NY** (city) Orange County	3.8
Illinois	14.3	Richmond County, NY	6.1	**Miramar, FL** (city) Broward County	5.5
Maryland	18.2	Cobb County, GA	9.0	**North Miami, FL** (city) Miami-Dade County	6.0
New Jersey	18.4	Osceola County, FL	9.3	**Staten Island, NY** (borough) Richmond County	6.1
Virginia	18.7	Atlantic County, NJ	9.4	**Hempstead (village), NY** (village) Nassau County	7.7
Pennsylvania	19.7	Denton County, TX	9.5	**Brentwood, NY** (cdp) Suffolk County	9.9
Louisiana	19.9	Lake County, IL	9.6	**Waukegan, IL** (city) Lake County	9.9
Mississippi	20.9	Alameda County, CA	9.7	**North Miami Beach, FL** (city) Miami-Dade County	11.2
Michigan	21.8	Morris County, NJ	10.7	**Queens, NY** (borough) Queens County	11.8
Nevada	21.9	Loudoun County, VA	11.0	**Islip, NY** (town) Suffolk County	12.0

Note: (1) Ranking tables cover all states and counties, and places with an overall population of at least 125,000, OR an overall population of at least 25,000 where the Hispanic/Latino population is at least 20% of the overall population. In states where less than five places meet either of these criteria, we have included places with at least 10,000 total population with the highest percentage of Hispanic/Latino population. These places are identified with an asterisk (*); Please refer to the User's Guide for a full explanation of data.

Poverty Rate

(Income in Past 12 Months Below Poverty Level)

Central American: Nicaraguan

Top 10 States, Counties, and Places[1]

Sorted by Percent in Descending Order — U.S. = 14.0%

State	Percent	County	Percent	Place	Percent
South Carolina	31.1	Gwinnett County, GA	35.9	**San Diego, CA** (city) San Diego County	37.0
Indiana	28.6	Lee County, FL	23.3	**Oakland, CA** (city) Alameda County	28.0
Georgia	25.4	Palm Beach County, FL	22.3	**Austin, TX** (city) Travis County	27.3
Massachusetts	24.4	Travis County, TX	21.6	**Sacramento, CA** (city) Sacramento County	25.9
Tennessee	24.0	San Diego County, CA	21.1	**Miami, FL** (city) Miami-Dade County	25.2
Missouri	23.4	Stanislaus County, CA	20.3	**South Gate, CA** (city) Los Angeles County	22.7
Ohio	20.8	Bronx County, NY	19.1	**Miami Gardens, FL** (city) Miami-Dade County	22.1
Minnesota	17.4	Kings County, NY	19.1	**Metairie, LA** (cdp) Jefferson Parish	20.7
Colorado	16.2	San Joaquin County, CA	18.4	**Bronx, NY** (borough) Bronx County	19.1
North Carolina	16.0	Cook County, IL	16.7	**Brooklyn, NY** (borough) Kings County	19.1

Sorted by Percent in Ascending Order — U.S. = 14.0%

State	Percent	County	Percent	Place	Percent
Connecticut	2.5	Fairfax County, VA	1.8	**Pembroke Pines, FL** (city) Broward County	1.5
Virginia	5.3	Collier County, FL	2.7	**Antioch, CA** (city) Contra Costa County	1.6
Maryland	6.2	King County, WA	2.7	**The Hammocks, FL** (cdp) Miami-Dade County	2.2
District of Columbia	7.5	Contra Costa County, CA	3.2	**Daly City, CA** (city) San Mateo County	2.3
Nevada	7.8	Bexar County, TX	4.6	**Kendall West, FL** (cdp) Miami-Dade County	2.3
Oregon	10.3	San Bernardino County, CA	5.2	**Richmond West, FL** (cdp) Miami-Dade County	2.3
Pennsylvania	11.3	San Mateo County, CA	5.2	**Fontana, CA** (city) San Bernardino County	3.0
Texas	11.5	Montgomery County, MD	6.4	**Hayward, CA** (city) Alameda County	3.0
Washington	11.6	Sonoma County, CA	7.7	**Country Club, FL** (cdp) Miami-Dade County	3.5
Arizona	11.8	San Francisco County, CA	8.2	**South San Francisco, CA** (city) San Mateo County	3.6

Note: (1) Ranking tables cover all states and counties, and places with an overall population of at least 125,000, OR an overall population of at least 25,000 where the Hispanic/Latino population is at least 20% of the overall population. In states where less than five places meet either of these criteria, we have included places with at least 10,000 total population with the highest percentage of Hispanic/Latino population. These places are identified with an asterisk (*); Please refer to the User's Guide for a full explanation of data.

Poverty Rate

(Income in Past 12 Months Below Poverty Level)

Central American: Panamanian

Top 10 States, Counties, and Places[1]

Sorted by Percent in Descending Order — U.S. = 14.0%

State	Percent	County	Percent	Place	Percent
New Mexico	34.9	Bronx County, NY	27.1	**Miami, FL** (city) Miami-Dade County	31.4
Alabama	20.6	Cook County, IL	26.7	**Bronx, NY** (borough) Bronx County	27.1
Massachusetts	20.4	Sacramento County, CA	25.7	**Killeen, TX** (city) Bell County	25.3
Tennessee	19.2	Bell County, TX	25.2	**Manhattan, NY** (borough) New York County	20.4
Illinois	17.2	Cumberland County, NC	24.8	**Fayetteville, NC** (city) Cumberland County	20.2
Ohio	17.0	Dallas County, TX	21.0	**Brooklyn, NY** (borough) Kings County	17.6
Wisconsin	16.5	New York County, NY	20.4	**New York, NY** (city)	17.5
New York	16.2	San Bernardino County, CA	20.0	**San Diego, CA** (city) San Diego County	13.6
Florida	16.0	Orange County, FL	19.8	**Queens, NY** (borough) Queens County	10.7
Indiana	15.8	Kings County, NY	17.6	**Houston, TX** (city) Harris County	10.4

Sorted by Percent in Ascending Order — U.S. = 14.0%

State	Percent	County	Percent	Place	Percent
Missouri	4.3	Pierce County, WA	0.9	**Los Angeles, CA** (city) Los Angeles County	4.7
Minnesota	4.6	Suffolk County, NY	1.6	**Hempstead (town), NY** (town) Nassau County	8.4
Virginia	7.5	Essex County, NJ	1.8	**Jacksonville, FL** (city) Duval County	8.4
Oklahoma	8.5	Harris County, TX	4.3	**San Antonio, TX** (city) Bexar County	9.6
California	8.6	Los Angeles County, CA	4.6	**Houston, TX** (city) Harris County	10.4
Louisiana	8.6	Bexar County, TX	6.8	**Queens, NY** (borough) Queens County	10.7
Washington	8.7	Riverside County, CA	6.8	**San Diego, CA** (city) San Diego County	13.6
Michigan	10.0	Broward County, FL	7.0	**New York, NY** (city)	17.5
New Jersey	10.2	Prince George's County, MD	7.1	**Brooklyn, NY** (borough) Kings County	17.6
Nevada	10.3	Montgomery County, MD	7.8	**Fayetteville, NC** (city) Cumberland County	20.2

Note: (1) Ranking tables cover all states and counties, and places with an overall population of at least 125,000, OR an overall population of at least 25,000 where the Hispanic/Latino population is at least 20% of the overall population. In states where less than five places meet either of these criteria, we have included places with at least 10,000 total population with the highest percentage of Hispanic/Latino population. These places are identified with an asterisk (*); Please refer to the User's Guide for a full explanation of data.

Poverty Rate

(Income in Past 12 Months Below Poverty Level)

Central American: Salvadoran

Top 10 States, Counties, and Places[1]

Sorted by Percent in Descending Order — U.S. = 17.8%

State	Percent	County	Percent	Place	Percent
Tennessee	33.8	Crawford County, AR	47.9	**Richmond, VA** (independent city)	49.9
Alabama	33.4	Walker County, TX	46.9	**Glen Cove, NY** (city) Nassau County	49.4
Arkansas	31.4	Forsyth County, NC	42.4	**Tacoma, WA** (city) Pierce County	48.8
Kentucky	30.1	Davidson County, TN	40.9	**Winston-Salem, NC** (city) Forsyth County	46.5
North Carolina	29.3	Pima County, AZ	38.8	**Homestead, FL** (city) Miami-Dade County	44.3
New Mexico	25.5	Marion County, IN	37.6	**Maywood, CA** (city) Los Angeles County	42.4
Indiana	24.5	Pierce County, WA	35.7	**Nashville-Davidson, TN** (metropolitan govt) Davidson County	41.0
Georgia	24.4	Durham County, NC	35.6	**Yonkers, NY** (city) Westchester County	38.5
Texas	21.8	Sebastian County, AR	35.4	**Bridgeport, CT** (city/town) Fairfield County	36.9
Florida	21.5	Fresno County, CA	35.1	**Gainesville, GA** (city) Hall County	36.4

Sorted by Percent in Ascending Order — U.S. = 17.8%

State	Percent	County	Percent	Place	Percent
Alaska	2.3	Arapahoe County, CO	4.1	**Sunnyvale, CA** (city) Santa Clara County	0.6
Illinois	9.2	Spotsylvania County, VA	5.0	**San Pablo, CA** (city) Contra Costa County	0.9
Michigan	10.5	Cuyahoga County, OH	5.5	**Fremont, CA** (city) Alameda County	1.0
Rhode Island	11.5	Napa County, CA	5.5	**Mesquite, TX** (city) Dallas County	1.1
Utah	11.5	Passaic County, NJ	5.9	**Corona, CA** (city) Riverside County	1.3
District of Columbia	11.8	Orange County, NY	6.1	**Daly City, CA** (city) San Mateo County	2.6
Louisiana	12.4	Solano County, CA	6.1	**Pittsburg, CA** (city) Contra Costa County	2.7
Hawaii	13.2	Lake County, IL	6.3	**Lewisville, TX** (city) Denton County	2.8
Maryland	13.7	Hartford County, CT	6.9	**West Covina, CA** (city) Los Angeles County	3.1
Oklahoma	14.1	Ocean County, NJ	6.9	**Sterling, VA** (cdp) Loudoun County	3.5

RANKINGS & COMPARISONS

Note: (1) Ranking tables cover all states and counties, and places with an overall population of at least 125,000, OR an overall population of at least 25,000 where the Hispanic/Latino population is at least 20% of the overall population. In states where less than five places meet either of these criteria, we have included places with at least 10,000 total population with the highest percentage of Hispanic/Latino population. These places are identified with an asterisk (*); Please refer to the User's Guide for a full explanation of data.

Poverty Rate

(Income in Past 12 Months Below Poverty Level)

Cuban

Top 10 States, Counties, and Places[1]

Sorted by Percent in Descending Order — U.S. = 15.2%

State	Percent	County	Percent	Place	Percent
Arkansas	39.7	Alachua County, FL	41.4	**Milwaukee, WI** (city) Milwaukee County	46.2
West Virginia	35.1	Milwaukee County, WI	39.9	**Lehigh Acres, FL** (cdp) Lee County	45.0
District of Columbia	31.0	Multnomah County, OR	34.2	**Baltimore, MD** (independent city)	40.5
Utah	29.5	Erie County, NY	33.1	**Lake Worth, FL** (city) Palm Beach County	36.9
Oregon	27.0	East Baton Rouge Parish, LA	30.8	**Tallahassee, FL** (city) Leon County	34.4
Wisconsin	26.6	Philadelphia County, PA	30.8	**Sunrise Manor, NV** (cdp) Clark County	33.5
New Mexico	23.8	Hampden County, MA	29.7	**Rochester, NY** (city) Monroe County	33.0
Oklahoma	23.5	Allegheny County, PA	28.9	**Philadelphia, PA** (city) Philadelphia County	30.8
Iowa	23.3	Lee County, FL	28.9	**Homestead, FL** (city) Miami-Dade County	28.1
Kentucky	22.7	Ingham County, MI	28.5	**Boston, MA** (city) Suffolk County	27.8

Sorted by Percent in Ascending Order — U.S. = 15.2%

State	Percent	County	Percent	Place	Percent
Maine	4.5	Nassau County, NY	0.9	**Santa Clarita, CA** (city) Los Angeles County	0.9
Hawaii	4.7	Montgomery County, PA	1.2	**Cooper City, FL** (city) Broward County	1.1
Virginia	7.7	Guilford County, NC	1.9	**Oakland Park, FL** (city) Broward County	1.1
Connecticut	8.3	Mercer County, NJ	2.3	**Kearny, NJ** (town) Hudson County	1.3
California	9.6	Monmouth County, NJ	2.3	**Hempstead (town), NY** (town) Nassau County	1.6
New Jersey	11.0	Henry County, GA	3.0	**Brookhaven, NY** (town) Suffolk County	2.1
New Hampshire	11.1	Sussex County, NJ	3.1	**Pembroke Pines, FL** (city) Broward County	3.2
Nebraska	11.7	Suffolk County, NY	3.4	**Downey, CA** (city) Los Angeles County	4.1
Colorado	11.9	Montgomery County, TX	3.6	**Coconut Creek, FL** (city) Broward County	4.2
Rhode Island	12.0	Fort Bend County, TX	4.1	**Weston, FL** (city) Broward County	4.7

Note: (1) Ranking tables cover all states and counties, and places with an overall population of at least 125,000, OR an overall population of at least 25,000 where the Hispanic/Latino population is at least 20% of the overall population. In states where less than five places meet either of these criteria, we have included places with at least 10,000 total population with the highest percentage of Hispanic/Latino population. These places are identified with an asterisk (*); Please refer to the User's Guide for a full explanation of data.

Poverty Rate

(Income in Past 12 Months Below Poverty Level)

Dominican Republic

Top 10 States, Counties, and Places[1]

Sorted by Percent in Descending Order — U.S. = 25.7%

State	Percent	County	Percent	Place	Percent
Wisconsin	36.0	Oneida County, NY	55.5	**Lancaster, PA** (city) Lancaster County	44.5
Rhode Island	34.5	Marion County, FL	44.4	**Chelsea, MA** (city) Suffolk County	44.2
Pennsylvania	34.1	Bristol County, MA	44.0	**Syracuse, NY** (city) Onondaga County	43.9
Utah	34.1	Luzerne County, PA	43.3	**Reading, PA** (city) Berks County	42.7
Massachusetts	32.5	Berks County, PA	41.5	**Bethlehem, PA** (city) Northampton County	42.1
Michigan	29.3	Erie County, NY	38.6	**Lynn, MA** (city) Essex County	41.9
Washington	29.3	Dallas County, TX	38.5	**Charlotte, NC** (city) Mecklenburg County	41.2
Ohio	29.2	Lancaster County, PA	38.3	**York, PA** (city) York County	40.4
North Carolina	29.1	Philadelphia County, PA	37.7	**Hazleton, PA** (city) Luzerne County	39.3
New York	28.3	Suffolk County, MA	35.9	**Philadelphia, PA** (city) Philadelphia County	37.7

Sorted by Percent in Ascending Order — U.S. = 25.7%

State	Percent	County	Percent	Place	Percent
Nevada	6.4	Saint Lucie County, FL	3.3	**Oyster Bay, NY** (town) Nassau County	0.8
Missouri	6.7	Ocean County, NJ	3.7	**Doral, FL** (city) Miami-Dade County	1.1
Alaska	8.6	Somerset County, NJ	4.9	**Port Saint Lucie, FL** (city) Saint Lucie County	1.1
South Carolina	9.7	Fairfax County, VA	6.3	**Plantation, FL** (city) Broward County	1.2
New Hampshire	10.4	Sullivan County, NY	6.4	**Belleville, NJ** (township) Essex County	1.6
Indiana	11.5	Orange County, NY	6.5	**North Hempstead, NY** (town) Nassau County	1.7
Virginia	12.9	Bexar County, TX	6.6	**Elmont, NY** (cdp) Nassau County	2.4
Texas	14.8	Clark County, NV	6.9	**Ramapo, NY** (town) Rockland County	2.7
District of Columbia	15.2	Monmouth County, NJ	8.5	**Valley Stream, NY** (village) Nassau County	4.3
Illinois	15.9	Burlington County, NJ	8.6	**Kendale Lakes, FL** (cdp) Miami-Dade County	4.6

Note: (1) Ranking tables cover all states and counties, and places with an overall population of at least 125,000, OR an overall population of at least 25,000 where the Hispanic/Latino population is at least 20% of the overall population. In states where less than five places meet either of these criteria, we have included places with at least 10,000 total population with the highest percentage of Hispanic/Latino population. These places are identified with an asterisk (*); Please refer to the User's Guide for a full explanation of data.

Poverty Rate

(Income in Past 12 Months Below Poverty Level)

Mexican

Top 10 States, Counties, and Places[1]

Sorted by Percent in Descending Order — U.S. = 24.0%

State	Percent	County	Percent	Place	Percent
North Carolina	34.9	Alexander County, NC	78.6	**North Lauderdale, FL** (city) Broward County	62.3
Kentucky	34.3	Oldham County, KY	69.2	**Carthage*, MO** (city) Jasper County	55.6
Tennessee	34.1	Yellow Medicine County, MN	67.7	**Springfield, MA** (city) Hampden County	54.5
Alabama	32.6	Putnam County, TN	66.2	**Chattanooga, TN** (city) Hamilton County	49.1
Georgia	32.5	Anderson County, TN	65.9	**Asheboro, NC** (city) Randolph County	48.4
South Carolina	32.5	McCurtain County, OK	65.4	**Worthington*, MN** (city) Nobles County	48.2
Arkansas	31.8	Dickens County, TX	65.1	**Shelbyville*, KY** (city) Shelby County	47.9
Oklahoma	29.2	Greene County, TN	63.8	**Winston-Salem, NC** (city) Forsyth County	46.8
Florida	29.0	Box Butte County, NE	62.9	**Parker*, SC** (cdp) Greenville County	46.7
Mississippi	28.9	Decatur County, GA	61.3	**Passaic, NJ** (city) Passaic County	45.6

Sorted by Percent in Ascending Order — U.S. = 24.0%

State	Percent	County	Percent	Place	Percent
Vermont	11.6	York County, VA	0.9	**Pembroke Pines, FL** (city) Broward County	1.0
Maryland	13.3	New London County, CT	1.1	**Miami Beach, FL** (city) Miami-Dade County	1.5
Hawaii	13.6	Merrimack County, NH	1.3	**San Dimas, CA** (city) Los Angeles County	2.1
Alaska	14.2	Sussex County, NJ	1.3	**Leander, TX** (city) Williamson County	3.4
New Hampshire	16.9	Miami County, OH	1.4	**Fort Leonard Wood*, MO** (cdp) Pulaski County	3.7
Wyoming	17.2	Newton County, IN	1.6	**Sahuarita, AZ** (town) Pima County	4.3
Massachusetts	18.1	Saint Tammany Parish, LA	2.5	**Rancho Cucamonga, CA** (city) San Bernardino County	4.5
Illinois	18.4	Waseca County, MN	2.5	**The Colony, TX** (city) Denton County	4.5
District of Columbia	19.4	White County, IN	2.6	**Diamond Bar, CA** (city) Los Angeles County	4.7
Virginia	19.4	Cumberland County, PA	2.7	**Kendall, FL** (cdp) Miami-Dade County	4.7

Note: (1) Ranking tables cover all states and counties, and places with an overall population of at least 125,000, OR an overall population of at least 25,000 where the Hispanic/Latino population is at least 20% of the overall population. In states where less than five places meet either of these criteria, we have included places with at least 10,000 total population with the highest percentage of Hispanic/Latino population. These places are identified with an asterisk (*); Please refer to the User's Guide for a full explanation of data.

Poverty Rate

(Income in Past 12 Months Below Poverty Level)

Puerto Rican

Top 10 States, Counties, and Places[1]

Sorted by Percent in Descending Order — U.S. = 25.1%

State	Percent	County	Percent	Place	Percent
Rhode Island	42.2	Northumberland County, PA	71.4	**Woonsocket*, RI** (city) Providence County	62.8
Massachusetts	40.0	Wyoming County, NY	70.8	**Buffalo, NY** (city) Erie County	56.3
Pennsylvania	37.6	Clearfield County, PA	67.8	**Holyoke, MA** (city) Hampden County	55.5
Maine	33.5	Cattaraugus County, NY	56.8	**Rockford, IL** (city) Winnebago County	52.7
Wisconsin	33.3	Tompkins County, NY	54.1	**Reading, PA** (city) Berks County	52.1
Iowa	31.6	Berkshire County, MA	53.1	**Bridgeton, NJ** (city) Cumberland County	51.4
Connecticut	30.5	Centre County, PA	53.1	**Pawtucket*, RI** (city) Providence County	51.1
Montana	30.1	Chautauqua County, NY	52.2	**York, PA** (city) York County	50.8
Ohio	30.1	Rensselaer County, NY	51.8	**Worcester, MA** (city) Worcester County	49.8
Michigan	29.4	Lackawanna County, PA	51.3	**Syracuse, NY** (city) Onondaga County	49.7

Sorted by Percent in Ascending Order — U.S. = 25.1%

State	Percent	County	Percent	Place	Percent
District of Columbia	9.2	Dakota County, MN	1.4	**Makakilo*, HI** (cdp) Honolulu County	0.5
Utah	10.6	Marin County, CA	1.7	**Temecula, CA** (city) Riverside County	1.2
Nevada	11.4	Charles County, MD	2.1	**Garland, TX** (city) Dallas County	1.5
Maryland	11.6	Prince William County, VA	2.2	**Fontana, CA** (city) San Bernardino County	1.6
Virginia	12.4	Lexington County, SC	2.5	**Rio Rancho, NM** (city) Sandoval County	1.6
Alaska	12.6	Butler County, OH	2.6	**Fremont, CA** (city) Alameda County	1.7
Wyoming	12.6	Sandoval County, NM	2.6	**Riverview, FL** (cdp) Hillsborough County	1.8
Arizona	14.7	Somerset County, NJ	2.6	**Coral Gables, FL** (city) Miami-Dade County	2.0
Arkansas	14.8	Montgomery County, TX	2.7	**Wesley Chapel, FL** (cdp) Pasco County	2.2
Texas	14.8	Loudoun County, VA	3.4	**Dale City, VA** (cdp) Prince William County	2.3

Note: (1) Ranking tables cover all states and counties, and places with an overall population of at least 125,000, OR an overall population of at least 25,000 where the Hispanic/Latino population is at least 20% of the overall population. In states where less than five places meet either of these criteria, we have included places with at least 10,000 total population with the highest percentage of Hispanic/Latino population. These places are identified with an asterisk (*); Please refer to the User's Guide for a full explanation of data.

Poverty Rate

(Income in Past 12 Months Below Poverty Level)

South American

Top 10 States, Counties, and Places[1]

Sorted by Percent in Descending Order — U.S. = 12.3%

State	Percent	County	Percent	Place	Percent
Idaho	22.5	Weber County, UT	49.8	**Glendale, AZ** (city) Maricopa County	43.4
West Virginia	20.4	Brazos County, TX	44.9	**Tallahassee, FL** (city) Leon County	37.7
Minnesota	18.9	Oneida County, NY	38.0	**Ossining, NY** (village) Westchester County	36.3
Tennessee	17.2	Escambia County, FL	37.0	**Ontario, CA** (city) San Bernardino County	36.0
Vermont	16.9	Leon County, FL	32.1	**Four Corners, FL** (cdp) Lake County	34.8
Pennsylvania	16.6	Yolo County, CA	31.0	**Ossining, NY** (town) Westchester County	32.6
Delaware	16.4	Montgomery County, OH	30.9	**Minneapolis, MN** (city) Hennepin County	30.4
Indiana	16.3	Champaign County, IL	30.4	**Town 'n' Country, FL** (cdp) Hillsborough County	30.0
Utah	16.3	Alachua County, FL	30.2	**New Brunswick, NJ** (city) Middlesex County	29.2
Kentucky	15.2	Gaston County, NC	27.8	**Miami Gardens, FL** (city) Miami-Dade County	28.8

Sorted by Percent in Ascending Order — U.S. = 12.3%

State	Percent	County	Percent	Place	Percent
Alaska	4.7	Pinal County, AZ	1.2	**Winston-Salem, NC** (city) Forsyth County	0.5
Mississippi	5.1	Harford County, MD	1.5	**Rahway, NJ** (city) Union County	0.6
New Hampshire	5.4	Saint Johns County, FL	1.6	**Dale City, VA** (cdp) Prince William County	0.8
Maryland	5.9	Douglas County, CO	1.8	**Royal Palm Beach, FL** (village) Palm Beach County	0.8
Virginia	8.0	Monroe County, FL	1.8	**Alhambra, CA** (city) Los Angeles County	0.9
North Dakota	8.4	Stafford County, VA	1.9	**Miami Lakes, FL** (town) Miami-Dade County	1.1
Missouri	9.0	Forsyth County, NC	2.2	**Oyster Bay, NY** (town) Nassau County	1.2
Montana	10.0	Butler County, OH	2.9	**Oceanside, CA** (city) San Diego County	1.5
Connecticut	10.3	Jackson County, MO	3.2	**Huntington, NY** (town) Suffolk County	1.6
California	10.4	Jefferson County, CO	3.2	**San Mateo, CA** (city) San Mateo County	1.6

Note: (1) Ranking tables cover all states and counties, and places with an overall population of at least 125,000, OR an overall population of at least 25,000 where the Hispanic/Latino population is at least 20% of the overall population. In states where less than five places meet either of these criteria, we have included places with at least 10,000 total population with the highest percentage of Hispanic/Latino population. These places are identified with an asterisk (*); Please refer to the User's Guide for a full explanation of data.

Poverty Rate

(Income in Past 12 Months Below Poverty Level)

South American: Argentinean

Top 10 States, Counties, and Places[1]

Sorted by Percent in Descending Order — U.S. = 10.7%

State	Percent	County	Percent	Place	Percent
Utah	23.9	Oakland County, MI	25.4	**Miami, FL** (city) Miami-Dade County	28.1
South Carolina	21.6	Essex County, NJ	25.0	**Hialeah, FL** (city) Miami-Dade County	26.3
Indiana	20.2	Palm Beach County, FL	22.0	**Brooklyn, NY** (borough) Kings County	18.5
Michigan	19.8	Utah County, UT	19.6	**Hollywood, FL** (city) Broward County	17.0
Ohio	15.7	Orange County, FL	18.8	**Bronx, NY** (borough) Bronx County	16.6
Oregon	15.4	Kings County, NY	18.5	**San Jose, CA** (city) Santa Clara County	15.7
Florida	13.5	Lee County, FL	18.5	**Coral Springs, FL** (city) Broward County	15.6
Pennsylvania	11.6	Montgomery County, TX	18.4	**Miami Beach, FL** (city) Miami-Dade County	13.4
Washington	11.4	Bronx County, NY	16.6	**Manhattan, NY** (borough) New York County	13.3
New Jersey	11.2	New York County, NY	13.3	**Chicago, IL** (city) Cook County	12.7

Sorted by Percent in Ascending Order — U.S. = 10.7%

State	Percent	County	Percent	Place	Percent
Minnesota	1.9	Suffolk County, NY	0.6	**Pembroke Pines, FL** (city) Broward County	1.1
North Carolina	1.9	Contra Costa County, CA	2.0	**Doral, FL** (city) Miami-Dade County	1.6
Missouri	3.9	Montgomery County, MD	2.3	**San Diego, CA** (city) San Diego County	3.8
Maryland	4.3	San Diego County, CA	4.0	**Aventura, FL** (city) Miami-Dade County	4.9
Colorado	5.9	Middlesex County, MA	4.4	**Houston, TX** (city) Harris County	8.5
Louisiana	5.9	Travis County, TX	4.4	**Queens, NY** (borough) Queens County	9.0
Connecticut	6.1	Nassau County, NY	4.9	**Hempstead (town), NY** (town) Nassau County	9.8
Tennessee	6.5	Fairfax County, VA	5.0	**Los Angeles, CA** (city) Los Angeles County	10.4
District of Columbia	6.9	New Haven County, CT	5.2	**New York, NY** (city)	12.3
Massachusetts	7.8	Ventura County, CA	5.4	**San Francisco, CA** (city) San Francisco County	12.6

RANKINGS & COMPARISONS

Note: (1) Ranking tables cover all states and counties, and places with an overall population of at least 125,000, OR an overall population of at least 25,000 where the Hispanic/Latino population is at least 20% of the overall population. In states where less than five places meet either of these criteria, we have included places with at least 10,000 total population with the highest percentage of Hispanic/Latino population. These places are identified with an asterisk (*); Please refer to the User's Guide for a full explanation of data.

Poverty Rate

(Income in Past 12 Months Below Poverty Level)

South American: Bolivian

Top 10 States, Counties, and Places[1]

Sorted by Percent in Descending Order — U.S. = 8.7%

State	Percent	County	Percent	Place	Percent
Illinois	16.9	Palm Beach County, FL	18.4	**Queens, NY** (borough) Queens County	16.6
Pennsylvania	14.5	Queens County, NY	16.6	**New York, NY** (city)	13.2
Texas	13.6	Harris County, TX	16.4	**Los Angeles, CA** (city) Los Angeles County	7.9
North Carolina	13.4	Miami-Dade County, FL	12.4	**Providence, RI** (city) Providence County	7.9
New Jersey	11.4	San Diego County, CA	9.9	**Arlington, VA** (cdp) Arlington County	7.7
Florida	10.5	Montgomery County, MD	9.5	**Annandale, VA** (cdp) Fairfax County	3.2
New York	9.3	Providence County, RI	8.9	**Springfield, VA** (cdp) Fairfax County	2.2
Rhode Island	8.9	Los Angeles County, CA	7.9		
Maryland	8.6	Arlington County, VA	7.7		
Virginia	7.1	Cook County, IL	7.1		

Sorted by Percent in Ascending Order — U.S. = 8.7%

State	Percent	County	Percent	Place	Percent
Massachusetts	4.7	Loudoun County, VA	1.8	**Springfield, VA** (cdp) Fairfax County	2.2
California	6.4	Santa Clara County, CA	2.1	**Annandale, VA** (cdp) Fairfax County	3.2
Virginia	7.1	Prince George's County, MD	3.0	**Arlington, VA** (cdp) Arlington County	7.7
Maryland	8.6	Orange County, CA	4.0	**Los Angeles, CA** (city) Los Angeles County	7.9
Rhode Island	8.9	Broward County, FL	4.4	**Providence, RI** (city) Providence County	7.9
New York	9.3	Fairfax County, VA	6.4	**New York, NY** (city)	13.2
Florida	10.5	Prince William County, VA	7.0	**Queens, NY** (borough) Queens County	16.6
New Jersey	11.4	Cook County, IL	7.1		
North Carolina	13.4	Arlington County, VA	7.7		
Texas	13.6	Los Angeles County, CA	7.9		

Note: (1) Ranking tables cover all states and counties, and places with an overall population of at least 125,000, OR an overall population of at least 25,000 where the Hispanic/Latino population is at least 20% of the overall population. In states where less than five places meet either of these criteria, we have included places with at least 10,000 total population with the highest percentage of Hispanic/Latino population. These places are identified with an asterisk (*); Please refer to the User's Guide for a full explanation of data.

Poverty Rate

(Income in Past 12 Months Below Poverty Level)

South American: Chilean

Top 10 States, Counties, and Places[1]

Sorted by Percent in Descending Order — U.S. = 9.0%

State	Percent	County	Percent	Place	Percent
Minnesota	29.6	Clark County, NV	19.5	**Chicago, IL** (city) Cook County	19.7
Pennsylvania	23.5	Utah County, UT	19.3	**Miami, FL** (city) Miami-Dade County	17.8
Colorado	21.7	Riverside County, CA	19.1	**Kendall, FL** (cdp) Miami-Dade County	14.8
Utah	14.8	Salt Lake County, UT	15.7	**Brooklyn, NY** (borough) Kings County	12.6
Nevada	14.3	Fairfax County, VA	14.1	**Manhattan, NY** (borough) New York County	9.4
Oregon	13.2	Hudson County, NJ	14.1	**Los Angeles, CA** (city) Los Angeles County	8.3
North Carolina	11.5	Kings County, NY	12.6	**New York, NY** (city)	7.9
Texas	10.0	Cook County, IL	12.1	**Hempstead (town), NY** (town) Nassau County	6.6
Florida	9.8	Middlesex County, MA	11.0	**Queens, NY** (borough) Queens County	5.8
Massachusetts	9.7	Montgomery County, MD	9.4		

Sorted by Percent in Ascending Order — U.S. = 9.0%

State	Percent	County	Percent	Place	Percent
Georgia	2.4	Suffolk County, NY	2.6	**Queens, NY** (borough) Queens County	5.8
Washington	2.8	Harris County, TX	3.2	**Hempstead (town), NY** (town) Nassau County	6.6
Connecticut	3.9	San Mateo County, CA	3.4	**New York, NY** (city)	7.9
Missouri	4.1	Alameda County, CA	4.2	**Los Angeles, CA** (city) Los Angeles County	8.3
Maryland	6.3	Nassau County, NY	4.7	**Manhattan, NY** (borough) New York County	9.4
New York	6.8	Westchester County, NY	4.9	**Brooklyn, NY** (borough) Kings County	12.6
Wisconsin	6.9	Queens County, NY	5.8	**Kendall, FL** (cdp) Miami-Dade County	14.8
California	7.3	Orange County, CA	6.6	**Miami, FL** (city) Miami-Dade County	17.8
Michigan	7.4	Broward County, FL	6.8	**Chicago, IL** (city) Cook County	19.7
Ohio	7.4	San Bernardino County, CA	6.8		

RANKINGS & COMPARISONS

Note: (1) Ranking tables cover all states and counties, and places with an overall population of at least 125,000, OR an overall population of at least 25,000 where the Hispanic/Latino population is at least 20% of the overall population. In states where less than five places meet either of these criteria, we have included places with at least 10,000 total population with the highest percentage of Hispanic/Latino population. These places are identified with an asterisk (*); Please refer to the User's Guide for a full explanation of data.

Poverty Rate

(Income in Past 12 Months Below Poverty Level)

South American: Colombian

Top 10 States, Counties, and Places[1]

Sorted by Percent in Descending Order — U.S. = 11.9%

State	Percent	County	Percent	Place	Percent
Arkansas	20.5	Leon County, FL	49.7	**Tallahassee, FL** (city) Leon County	57.5
Nevada	18.4	Berks County, PA	36.5	**Fort Lauderdale, FL** (city) Broward County	37.4
Pennsylvania	17.9	Alachua County, FL	28.1	**Town 'n' Country, FL** (cdp) Hillsborough County	36.2
Oklahoma	17.6	Ulster County, NY	28.0	**Phoenix, AZ** (city) Maricopa County	26.7
Tennessee	17.3	Hall County, GA	25.7	**Margate, FL** (city) Broward County	26.3
Utah	16.5	San Bernardino County, CA	25.0	**Hallandale Beach, FL** (city) Broward County	26.1
Alabama	15.9	Luzerne County, PA	23.8	**Long Beach, CA** (city) Los Angeles County	26.1
Delaware	15.2	Philadelphia County, PA	23.5	**Greenacres, FL** (city) Palm Beach County	24.3
Kansas	14.6	Brevard County, FL	21.2	**Raleigh, NC** (city) Wake County	24.2
Arizona	13.9	Cobb County, GA	20.6	**Central Falls*, RI** (city) Providence County	23.9

Sorted by Percent in Ascending Order — U.S. = 11.9%

State	Percent	County	Percent	Place	Percent
Alaska	4.1	DuPage County, IL	0.4	**Miami Lakes, FL** (town) Miami-Dade County	0.5
New Hampshire	5.2	Northampton County, PA	0.9	**Cooper City, FL** (city) Broward County	1.2
Missouri	5.3	Burlington County, NJ	1.6	**Oyster Bay, NY** (town) Nassau County	1.2
Maryland	6.7	Montgomery County, TX	1.8	**Brookhaven, NY** (town) Suffolk County	1.3
Kentucky	7.1	Oakland County, MI	1.8	**Royal Palm Beach, FL** (village) Palm Beach County	1.4
Minnesota	7.1	Bexar County, TX	2.2	**Virginia Beach, VA** (independent city)	1.6
Connecticut	8.1	Fort Bend County, TX	2.5	**Elmont, NY** (cdp) Nassau County	1.7
Iowa	8.2	Nassau County, NY	2.8	**Garfield, NJ** (city) Bergen County	2.2
Virginia	8.2	Ocean County, NJ	2.8	**Huntington, NY** (town) Suffolk County	2.5
Nebraska	8.5	Baltimore County, MD	3.0	**Downey, CA** (city) Los Angeles County	2.6

Note: (1) Ranking tables cover all states and counties, and places with an overall population of at least 125,000, OR an overall population of at least 25,000 where the Hispanic/Latino population is at least 20% of the overall population. In states where less than five places meet either of these criteria, we have included places with at least 10,000 total population with the highest percentage of Hispanic/Latino population. These places are identified with an asterisk (*); Please refer to the User's Guide for a full explanation of data.

Poverty Rate

(Income in Past 12 Months Below Poverty Level)

South American: Ecuadorian

Top 10 States, Counties, and Places[1]

Sorted by Percent in Descending Order — U.S. = 15.3%

State	Percent	County	Percent	Place	Percent
Missouri	54.8	Dallas County, TX	31.4	**Ossining, NY** (village) Westchester County	44.7
Indiana	37.1	Hennepin County, MN	31.1	**Ossining, NY** (town) Westchester County	40.9
Minnesota	28.5	Worcester County, MA	30.2	**Hialeah, FL** (city) Miami-Dade County	33.0
Rhode Island	26.4	Lehigh County, PA	29.4	**Allentown, PA** (city) Lehigh County	31.8
Utah	25.5	Providence County, RI	26.7	**Minneapolis, MN** (city) Hennepin County	31.1
Ohio	25.0	Tarrant County, TX	25.4	**City of Orange, NJ** (township) Essex County	29.0
Wisconsin	24.0	Kings County, NY	24.0	**Houston, TX** (city) Harris County	28.9
Tennessee	20.0	Camden County, NJ	23.6	**Doral, FL** (city) Miami-Dade County	28.3
Pennsylvania	19.8	Westchester County, NY	23.3	**Downey, CA** (city) Los Angeles County	28.3
Massachusetts	19.4	Philadelphia County, PA	21.1	**Brooklyn, NY** (borough) Kings County	24.0

Sorted by Percent in Ascending Order — U.S. = 15.3%

State	Percent	County	Percent	Place	Percent
Virginia	4.2	Fairfax County, VA	0.5	**Sunrise, FL** (city) Broward County	1.5
Maryland	4.5	Burlington County, NJ	0.7	**Miramar, FL** (city) Broward County	2.2
Oregon	4.5	Baltimore County, MD	0.9	**Oyster Bay, NY** (town) Nassau County	3.0
Washington	6.9	Dutchess County, NY	2.0	**Brookhaven, NY** (town) Suffolk County	3.1
Michigan	7.9	Montgomery County, MD	2.5	**Bridgeport, CT** (city/town) Fairfield County	3.5
Louisiana	8.9	Prince George's County, MD	2.9	**Hollywood, FL** (city) Broward County	3.7
Colorado	9.1	Osceola County, FL	3.3	**Brentwood, NY** (cdp) Suffolk County	4.0
Iowa	10.5	Ocean County, NJ	3.5	**Islip, NY** (town) Suffolk County	4.2
Arizona	11.3	Middlesex County, NJ	4.3	**Country Club, FL** (cdp) Miami-Dade County	4.6
Kansas	11.3	Orange County, NY	4.6	**North Bergen, NJ** (township) Hudson County	4.7

Note: (1) Ranking tables cover all states and counties, and places with an overall population of at least 125,000, OR an overall population of at least 25,000 where the Hispanic/Latino population is at least 20% of the overall population. In states where less than five places meet either of these criteria, we have included places with at least 10,000 total population with the highest percentage of Hispanic/Latino population. These places are identified with an asterisk (*); Please refer to the User's Guide for a full explanation of data.

Poverty Rate

(Income in Past 12 Months Below Poverty Level)

South American: Paraguayan

Top 10 States, Counties, and Places[1]

Sorted by Percent in Descending Order — U.S. = 12.3%

State	Percent	County	Percent	Place	Percent
New York	13.7	Queens County, NY	26.3	**Queens, NY** (borough) Queens County	26.3
California	10.3	Westchester County, NY	3.2	**New York, NY** (city)	24.1
Texas	9.0				
Florida	6.6				
New Jersey	5.7				
Maryland	4.3				

Sorted by Percent in Ascending Order — U.S. = 12.3%

State	Percent	County	Percent	Place	Percent
Maryland	4.3	Westchester County, NY	3.2	**New York, NY** (city)	24.1
New Jersey	5.7	Queens County, NY	26.3	**Queens, NY** (borough) Queens County	26.3
Florida	6.6				
Texas	9.0				
California	10.3				
New York	13.7				

Note: (1) Ranking tables cover all states and counties, and places with an overall population of at least 125,000, OR an overall population of at least 25,000 where the Hispanic/Latino population is at least 20% of the overall population. In states where less than five places meet either of these criteria, we have included places with at least 10,000 total population with the highest percentage of Hispanic/Latino population. These places are identified with an asterisk (*); Please refer to the User's Guide for a full explanation of data.

Poverty Rate

(Income in Past 12 Months Below Poverty Level)

South American: Peruvian

Top 10 States, Counties, and Places[1]

Sorted by Percent in Descending Order — U.S. = 12.1%

State	Percent	County	Percent	Place	Percent
Kentucky	30.0	Richmond County, NY	34.8	**Staten Island, NY** (borough) Richmond County	34.8
Idaho	26.4	San Joaquin County, CA	31.3	**Bronx, NY** (borough) Bronx County	28.5
Louisiana	21.7	Bronx County, NY	28.5	**West New York, NJ** (town) Hudson County	28.0
Oklahoma	19.4	Solano County, CA	28.3	**Kendall West, FL** (cdp) Miami-Dade County	27.3
Colorado	17.6	Wake County, NC	27.8	**Perth Amboy, NJ** (city) Middlesex County	27.0
Georgia	15.9	Sarasota County, FL	24.3	**Fountainebleau, FL** (cdp) Miami-Dade County	25.5
Alabama	14.8	Collin County, TX	23.9	**Miramar, FL** (city) Broward County	24.1
North Carolina	14.7	Travis County, TX	19.7	**Santa Ana, CA** (city) Orange County	23.8
South Carolina	14.5	Philadelphia County, PA	19.4	**Cape Coral, FL** (city) Lee County	23.4
Ohio	14.0	Monmouth County, NJ	18.9	**Austin, TX** (city) Travis County	23.0

Sorted by Percent in Ascending Order — U.S. = 12.1%

State	Percent	County	Percent	Place	Percent
Missouri	5.2	Denton County, TX	1.0	**Las Vegas, NV** (city) Clark County	0.4
Maryland	6.0	Somerset County, NJ	1.0	**Tampa, FL** (city) Hillsborough County	0.6
Arizona	6.7	Seminole County, FL	1.7	**Garland, TX** (city) Dallas County	1.1
Massachusetts	8.2	Riverside County, CA	1.9	**North Bergen, NJ** (township) Hudson County	1.3
Michigan	8.4	New Haven County, CT	2.0	**Long Beach, CA** (city) Los Angeles County	1.5
Virginia	8.8	Ventura County, CA	2.3	**Torrance, CA** (city) Los Angeles County	1.5
Indiana	9.4	Franklin County, OH	2.8	**Sunrise, FL** (city) Broward County	1.7
District of Columbia	10.2	Lake County, IL	2.9	**Port Chester, NY** (village) Westchester County	3.2
Nevada	10.4	Duval County, FL	4.0	**Doral, FL** (city) Miami-Dade County	3.6
Connecticut	10.5	Atlantic County, NJ	4.1	**Weston, FL** (city) Broward County	3.6

Note: (1) Ranking tables cover all states and counties, and places with an overall population of at least 125,000, OR an overall population of at least 25,000 where the Hispanic/Latino population is at least 20% of the overall population. In states where less than five places meet either of these criteria, we have included places with at least 10,000 total population with the highest percentage of Hispanic/Latino population. These places are identified with an asterisk (*); Please refer to the User's Guide for a full explanation of data.

Poverty Rate

(Income in Past 12 Months Below Poverty Level)

South American: Uruguayan

Top 10 States, Counties, and Places[1]

Sorted by Percent in Descending Order — U.S. = 13.5%

State	Percent	County	Percent	Place	Percent
Pennsylvania	19.7	Essex County, NJ	24.2	**Elizabeth, NJ** (city) Union County	24.1
New Jersey	18.3	Union County, NJ	20.1	**New York, NY** (city)	6.5
Florida	14.9	Miami-Dade County, FL	19.1	**Queens, NY** (borough) Queens County	5.6
Virginia	12.3	Hudson County, NJ	17.1		
Texas	12.2	Los Angeles County, CA	16.0		
Georgia	11.6	Westchester County, NY	14.2		
Massachusetts	11.3	Morris County, NJ	10.9		
California	8.6	Broward County, FL	9.0		
New York	7.5	Worcester County, MA	9.0		
Maryland	4.6	Gwinnett County, GA	8.4		

Sorted by Percent in Ascending Order — U.S. = 13.5%

State	Percent	County	Percent	Place	Percent
Maryland	4.6	Queens County, NY	5.6	**Queens, NY** (borough) Queens County	5.6
New York	7.5	Harris County, TX	6.0	**New York, NY** (city)	6.5
California	8.6	Middlesex County, NJ	6.6	**Elizabeth, NJ** (city) Union County	24.1
Massachusetts	11.3	Palm Beach County, FL	7.3		
Georgia	11.6	Gwinnett County, GA	8.4		
Texas	12.2	Broward County, FL	9.0		
Virginia	12.3	Worcester County, MA	9.0		
Florida	14.9	Morris County, NJ	10.9		
New Jersey	18.3	Westchester County, NY	14.2		
Pennsylvania	19.7	Los Angeles County, CA	16.0		

Note: (1) Ranking tables cover all states and counties, and places with an overall population of at least 125,000, OR an overall population of at least 25,000 where the Hispanic/Latino population is at least 20% of the overall population. In states where less than five places meet either of these criteria, we have included places with at least 10,000 total population with the highest percentage of Hispanic/Latino population. These places are identified with an asterisk (*); Please refer to the User's Guide for a full explanation of data.

Poverty Rate

(Income in Past 12 Months Below Poverty Level)

South American: Venezuelan

Top 10 States, Counties, and Places[1]

Sorted by Percent in Descending Order — U.S. = 12.6%

State	Percent	County	Percent	Place	Percent
Tennessee	31.1	Lee County, FL	26.1	**Bronx, NY** (borough) Bronx County	22.1
Minnesota	25.6	Bronx County, NY	22.1	**Hollywood, FL** (city) Broward County	21.6
Louisiana	18.5	New York County, NY	19.4	**Kendall West, FL** (cdp) Miami-Dade County	21.2
Arizona	16.7	Queens County, NY	18.8	**Miami, FL** (city) Miami-Dade County	21.0
Illinois	16.5	Suffolk County, MA	18.0	**Manhattan, NY** (borough) New York County	19.4
New York	16.0	Kings County, NY	17.9	**Davie, FL** (town) Broward County	18.8
Washington	15.1	Fairfax County, VA	16.8	**New York, NY** (city)	18.8
Florida	14.2	Osceola County, FL	16.7	**Queens, NY** (borough) Queens County	18.8
Indiana	13.6	Miami-Dade County, FL	15.6	**Brooklyn, NY** (borough) Kings County	17.9
Michigan	13.2	King County, WA	14.5	**Tamiami, FL** (cdp) Miami-Dade County	17.8

Sorted by Percent in Ascending Order — U.S. = 12.6%

State	Percent	County	Percent	Place	Percent
Missouri	0.8	Fort Bend County, TX	0.5	**Orlando, FL** (city) Orange County	4.5
Connecticut	3.6	San Diego County, CA	1.3	**Country Club, FL** (cdp) Miami-Dade County	5.1
Maryland	5.2	Collin County, TX	1.6	**Hialeah, FL** (city) Miami-Dade County	5.2
Utah	5.6	Montgomery County, MD	1.7	**Weston, FL** (city) Broward County	5.6
North Carolina	6.9	Salt Lake County, UT	3.4	**Miramar, FL** (city) Broward County	7.5
Texas	7.3	Seminole County, FL	4.8	**Houston, TX** (city) Harris County	7.8
Oklahoma	8.0	Middlesex County, MA	5.4	**Coral Springs, FL** (city) Broward County	8.0
California	8.3	Pinellas County, FL	5.6	**Kendall, FL** (cdp) Miami-Dade County	8.1
Wisconsin	9.5	Travis County, TX	5.9	**Aventura, FL** (city) Miami-Dade County	8.8
Massachusetts	9.9	Harris County, TX	6.0	**Pembroke Pines, FL** (city) Broward County	10.6

Note: (1) Ranking tables cover all states and counties, and places with an overall population of at least 125,000, OR an overall population of at least 25,000 where the Hispanic/Latino population is at least 20% of the overall population. In states where less than five places meet either of these criteria, we have included places with at least 10,000 total population with the highest percentage of Hispanic/Latino population. These places are identified with an asterisk (*); Please refer to the User's Guide for a full explanation of data.

Poverty Rate

(Income in Past 12 Months Below Poverty Level)

Spaniard

Top 10 States, Counties, and Places[1]

Sorted by Percent in Descending Order — U.S. = 12.2%

State	Percent	County	Percent	Place	Percent
Arkansas	37.5	Butte County, CA	36.3	**Fort Collins, CO** (city) Larimer County	37.1
Oklahoma	25.7	San Miguel County, NM	35.1	**Reno, NV** (city) Washoe County	34.0
Nebraska	25.1	Pasco County, FL	34.2	**Las Cruces, NM** (city) Dona Ana County	23.6
Maine	21.3	La Plata County, CO	27.6	**Long Beach, CA** (city) Los Angeles County	23.1
South Carolina	20.8	Larimer County, CO	26.8	**Westminster, CO** (city) Adams County	23.1
Iowa	19.7	Doña Ana County, NM	25.9	**Corpus Christi, TX** (city) Nueces County	20.4
Michigan	18.3	Washoe County, NV	25.0	**Tucson, AZ** (city) Pima County	20.2
Montana	16.8	Mecklenburg County, NC	24.4	**El Paso, TX** (city) El Paso County	19.9
Tennessee	16.8	Yolo County, CA	23.3	**Lakewood, CO** (city) Jefferson County	19.9
West Virginia	16.6	Hawaii County, HI	22.5	**Pueblo, CO** (city) Pueblo County	19.9

Sorted by Percent in Ascending Order — U.S. = 12.2%

State	Percent	County	Percent	Place	Percent
Virginia	4.5	Morris County, NJ	0.9	**Brookhaven, NY** (town) Suffolk County	0.5
Connecticut	5.8	Clark County, WA	1.3	**Staten Island, NY** (borough) Richmond County	2.9
Alaska	6.3	Middlesex County, NJ	2.1	**North Las Vegas, NV** (city) Clark County	4.0
New Jersey	6.8	Bergen County, NJ	2.7	**Queens, NY** (borough) Queens County	4.0
New York	7.1	Union County, NJ	2.7	**Fort Worth, TX** (city) Tarrant County	4.2
Maryland	7.9	Colfax County, NM	2.8	**Hempstead (town), NY** (town) Nassau County	4.3
Indiana	8.4	Fairfax County, VA	2.8	**Paradise, NV** (cdp) Clark County	4.6
Utah	9.0	Fairfield County, CT	2.9	**Rio Rancho, NM** (city) Sandoval County	5.4
Wyoming	9.4	Richmond County, NY	2.9	**Henderson, NV** (city) Clark County	5.5
New Hampshire	10.0	Suffolk County, NY	3.0	**Glendale, AZ** (city) Maricopa County	5.8

Note: (1) Ranking tables cover all states and counties, and places with an overall population of at least 125,000, OR an overall population of at least 25,000 where the Hispanic/Latino population is at least 20% of the overall population. In states where less than five places meet either of these criteria, we have included places with at least 10,000 total population with the highest percentage of Hispanic/Latino population. These places are identified with an asterisk (*); Please refer to the User's Guide for a full explanation of data.

Alphabetical Place Name Index

A

Abilene, TX (city) Taylor County, 903
Addison, IL (village) DuPage County, 515
Adelanto, CA (city) San Bernardino County, 92
Akron, OH (city) Summit County, 828
Alabama (state), 41
Alafaya, FL (cdp) Orange County, 372
Alamogordo, NM (city) Otero County, 731
Alaska (state), 48
Albertville, AL (city) Marshall County, 43
Albuquerque, NM (city) Bernalillo County, 731
Alexandria, VA (independent city) , 1001
Alhambra, CA (city) Los Angeles County, 93
Allentown, PA (city) Lehigh County, 857
Aloha, OR (cdp) Washington County, 847
Altadena, CA (cdp) Los Angeles County, 95
Altamonte Springs, FL (city) Seminole County, 373
Altus, OK (city) Jackson County, 839
Amarillo, TX (city) Potter County, 904
Anaheim, CA (city) Orange County, 96
Anchorage, AK (municipality) , 49
Annandale, VA (cdp) Fairfax County, 1002
Antioch, CA (city) Contra Costa County, 97
Apopka, FL (city) Orange County, 374
Apple Valley, CA (town) San Bernardino County, 99
Arizona (state), 54
Arkansas (state), 82
Arlington, TX (city) Tarrant County, 905
Arlington, VA (cdp) Arlington County, 1003
Asheboro, NC (city) Randolph County, 807
Aspen Hill, MD (cdp) Montgomery County, 589
Atascocita, TX (cdp) Harris County, 906
Atlanta, GA (city) Fulton County, 490
Atlantic City, NJ (city) Atlantic County, 686
Atwater, CA (city) Merced County, 100
Augusta-Richmond County, GA (consolidated government) Richmond County, 492
Aurora, CO (city) Arapahoe County, 325
Aurora, IL (city) Kane County, 516
Austin, TX (city) Travis County, 907
Aventura, FL (city) Miami-Dade County, 376
Avondale, AZ (city) Maricopa County, 56
Azusa, CA (city) Los Angeles County, 100

B

Babylon, NY (town) Suffolk County, 744
Badger, AK (cdp) Fairbanks North Star Borough, 51
Bakersfield, CA (city) Kern County, 101
Baldwin Park, CA (city) Los Angeles County, 103
Baltimore, MD (independent city) , 590
Banning, CA (city) Riverside County, 104
Baton Rouge, LA (city) East Baton Rouge Parish, 574
Bay Shore, NY (cdp) Suffolk County, 745
Bayonne, NJ (city) Hudson County, 687
Baytown, TX (city) Harris County, 909
Bear, DE (cdp) New Castle County, 361
Beaumont, CA (city) Riverside County, 105
Beckley, WV (city) Raleigh County, 1035
Bell Gardens, CA (city) Los Angeles County, 107
Bell, CA (city) Los Angeles County, 106
Belleville, NJ (township) Essex County, 688
Bellflower, CA (city) Los Angeles County, 108
Beloit, WI (city) Rock County, 1041
Belvidere, IL (city) Boone County, 517
Bennington, VT (town) Bennington County, 994
Berea, SC (cdp) Greenville County, 880
Bergenfield, NJ (borough) Bergen County, 690
Berwyn, IL (city) Cook County, 518
Bethlehem, PA (city) Northampton County, 858
Big Spring, TX (city) Howard County, 910
Billings, MT (city) Yellowstone County, 647
Biloxi, MS (city) Harrison County, 633
Birmingham, AL (city) Jefferson County, 44
Bloomfield, NJ (township) Essex County, 691
Bluffton, SC (town) Beaufort County, 881
Boise City, ID (city) Ada County, 508
Bolingbrook, IL (village) Will County, 519
Bonita Springs, FL (city) Lee County, 377
Boston, MA (city) Suffolk County, 602
Bozeman, MT (city) Gallatin County, 648
Brandon, FL (cdp) Hillsborough County, 378
Brattleboro, VT (town) Windham County, 994
Brea, CA (city) Orange County, 109
Brentwood, CA (city) Contra Costa County, 110
Brentwood, NY (cdp) Suffolk County, 746
Bridgeport, CT (city/town) Fairfield County, 343
Bridgeton, NJ (city) Cumberland County, 692
Brighton, CO (city) Adams County, 327
Bronx, NY (borough) Bronx County, 748
Brookhaven, NY (town) Suffolk County, 751
Brooklyn, NY (borough) Kings County, 753
Brookside, DE (cdp) New Castle County, 362
Brownsville, TX (city) Cameron County, 911
Brunswick, ME (town) Cumberland County, 582
Bryan, TX (city) Brazos County, 911
Buckeye, AZ (town) Maricopa County, 57
Buena Park, CA (city) Orange County, 111
Buenaventura Lakes, FL (cdp) Osceola County, 379
Buffalo, NY (city) Erie County, 755
Bullhead City, AZ (city) Mohave County, 58
Burbank, CA (city) Los Angeles County, 112
Burbank, IL (city) Cook County, 520
Burien, WA (city) King County, 1022
Burley, ID (city) Cassia County, 509
Burlington, VT (city) Chittenden County, 995
Butte-Silver Bow, MT (consolidated government) Silver Bow County, 648

C

Caldwell, ID (city) Canyon County, 510
Calexico, CA (city) Imperial County, 114
California (state), 89
Camarillo, CA (city) Ventura County, 114
Camden, NJ (city) Camden County, 693
Cape Coral, FL (city) Lee County, 381
Carlsbad, NM (city) Eddy County, 733
Carpentersville, IL (village) Kane County, 521
Carrollton, TX (city) Denton County, 912
Carrollwood, FL (cdp) Hillsborough County, 382
Carson City, NV (independent city) , 661
Carson, CA (city) Los Angeles County, 115
Carthage, MO (city) Jasper County, 640
Cary, NC (town) Wake County, 808
Casa Grande, AZ (city) Pinal County, 59
Casas Adobes, AZ (cdp) Pima County, 60
Casselberry, FL (city) Seminole County, 383
Cathedral City, CA (city) Riverside County, 116
Cedar Rapids, IA (city) Linn County, 551
Central Falls, RI (city) Providence County, 871
Central Islip, NY (cdp) Suffolk County, 756
Ceres, CA (city) Stanislaus County, 117
Chandler, AZ (city) Maricopa County, 60
Channelview, TX (cdp) Harris County, 913
Charlotte, NC (city) Mecklenburg County, 809
Chattanooga, TN (city) Hamilton County, 893
Chelsea, MA (city) Suffolk County, 603
Chesapeake, VA (independent city) , 1005
Cheyenne, WY (city) Laramie County, 1048
Chicago Heights, IL (city) Cook County, 524
Chicago, IL (city) Cook County, 522
Chillum, MD (cdp) Prince George's County, 591
Chino Hills, CA (city) San Bernardino County, 119
Chino, CA (city) San Bernardino County, 118
Chula Vista, CA (city) San Diego County, 120
Cicero, IL (town) Cook County, 525
Cincinnati, OH (city) Hamilton County, 829
City of Orange, NJ (township) Essex County, 694
Clarksburg, WV (city) Harrison County, 1036
Clarksville, TN (city) Montgomery County, 894
Cleburne, TX (city) Johnson County, 914
Cleveland, OH (city) Cuyahoga County, 830
Clifton, NJ (city) Passaic County, 695
Clovis, CA (city) Fresno County, 122
Clovis, NM (city) Curry County, 734
Coachella, CA (city) Riverside County, 123
Coconut Creek, FL (city) Broward County, 384
College, AK (cdp) Fairbanks North Star Borough, 51
Colorado (state), 323
Colorado Springs, CO (city) El Paso County, 328
Colton, CA (city) San Bernardino County, 123
Columbia, SC (city) Richland County, 882
Columbus, GA (city) Muscogee County, 493
Columbus, OH (city) Franklin County, 832
Commerce City, CO (city) Adams County, 329
Compton, CA (city) Los Angeles County, 124
Concord, CA (city) Contra Costa County, 125
Connecticut (state), 341
Conroe, TX (city) Montgomery County, 915
Cooper City, FL (city) Broward County, 385
Coral Gables, FL (city) Miami-Dade County, 387
Coral Springs, FL (city) Broward County, 388
Corona, CA (city) Riverside County, 127
Corpus Christi, TX (city) Nueces County, 916
Costa Mesa, CA (city) Orange County, 128
Country Club, FL (cdp) Miami-Dade County, 390
Covina, CA (city) Los Angeles County, 129
Cranston, RI (city) Providence County, 872
Culver City, CA (city) Los Angeles County, 131
Cutler Bay, FL (town) Miami-Dade County, 392

D

Dale City, VA (cdp) Prince William County, 1006
Dallas, TX (city) Dallas County, 917
Dalton, GA (city) Whitfield County, 494
Daly City, CA (city) San Mateo County, 132
Danbury, CT (city/town) Fairfield County, 345
Dania Beach, FL (city) Broward County, 393
Davie, FL (town) Broward County, 394
Dayton, OH (city) Montgomery County, 833
Deer Park, TX (city) Harris County, 919
Del Rio, TX (city) Val Verde County, 920
Delano, CA (city) Kern County, 133
Delaware (state), 360
Deltona, FL (city) Volusia County, 396
Denton, TX (city) Denton County, 921
Denver, CO (city) Denver County, 330
Derry, NH (cdp) Rockingham County, 678
Des Moines, IA (city) Polk County, 551
Desert Hot Springs, CA (city) Riverside County, 134
Detroit, MI (city) Wayne County, 617
Diamond Bar, CA (city) Los Angeles County, 135
Dickinson, ND (city) Stark County, 822
District of Columbia (state), 366
Dodge City, KS (city) Ford County, 558
Doral, FL (city) Miami-Dade County, 398
Dover, DE (city) Kent County, 363
Downey, CA (city) Los Angeles County, 136
Drexel Heights, AZ (cdp) Pima County, 62
Duncanville, TX (city) Dallas County, 922

Durham, NC (city) Durham County, 811

E

Eagle Pass, TX (city) Maverick County, 923
East Chicago, IN (city) Lake County, 542
East Hartford, CT (cdp/town) Hartford County, 347
East Los Angeles, CA (cdp) Los Angeles County, 137
East Palo Alto, CA (city) San Mateo County, 138
Eastvale, CA (cdp) Riverside County, 139
Edinburg, TX (city) Hidalgo County, 923
Egypt Lake-Leto, FL (cdp) Hillsborough County, 400
El Cajon, CA (city) San Diego County, 140
El Centro, CA (city) Imperial County, 141
El Mirage, AZ (city) Maricopa County, 63
El Monte, CA (city) Los Angeles County, 142
El Paso de Robles (Paso Robles), CA (city) San Luis Obispo County, 143
El Paso, TX (city) El Paso County, 924
Elgin, IL (city) Kane County, 526
Elizabeth, NJ (city) Union County, 697
Elk Grove, CA (city) Sacramento County, 144
Elkhart, IN (city) Elkhart County, 543
Elmont, NY (cdp) Nassau County, 758
Englewood, NJ (city) Bergen County, 699
Escondido, CA (city) San Diego County, 145
Essex, VT (town) Chittenden County, 996
Eugene, OR (city) Lane County, 848
Evanston, WY (city) Uinta County, 1049
Everett, MA (city) Middlesex County, 605

F

Fairbanks, AK (city) Fairbanks North Star Borough, 52
Fairfield, CA (city) Solano County, 146
Fallbrook, CA (cdp) San Diego County, 147
Fargo, ND (city) Cass County, 822
Farmers Branch, TX (city) Dallas County, 926
Farmington, NM (city) San Juan County, 734
Fayetteville, NC (city) Cumberland County, 813
Fitchburg, WI (city) Dane County, 1042
Fitchburg, MA (city) Worcester County, 606
Florence, AZ (town) Pinal County, 63
Florence-Graham, CA (cdp) Los Angeles County, 148
Florida (state), 369
Florin, CA (cdp) Sacramento County, 149
Fontana, CA (city) San Bernardino County, 150
Foothill Farms, CA (cdp) Sacramento County, 151
Fort Campbell North, KY (cdp) Christian County, 567
Fort Collins, CO (city) Larimer County, 332
Fort Hood, TX (cdp) Bell County, 927
Fort Lauderdale, FL (city) Broward County, 401
Fort Leonard Wood, MO (cdp) Pulaski County, 641
Fort Pierce, FL (city) Saint Lucie County, 402
Fort Wayne, IN (city) Allen County, 544
Fort Worth, TX (city) Tarrant County, 927
Fortuna Foothills, AZ (cdp) Yuma County, 64
Fountainebleau, FL (cdp) Miami-Dade County, 403
Four Corners, FL (cdp) Lake County, 405
Freeport, NY (village) Nassau County, 759
Fremont, CA (city) Alameda County, 152
Fresno, CA (city) Fresno County, 153
Fullerton, CA (city) Orange County, 155

G

Gainesville, GA (city) Hall County, 495
Gaithersburg, MD (city) Montgomery County, 592
Galveston, TX (city) Galveston County, 929
Garden City, KS (city) Finney County, 559
Garden Grove, CA (city) Orange County, 156
Gardena, CA (city) Los Angeles County, 157
Garfield, NJ (city) Bergen County, 700
Garland, TX (city) Dallas County, 930
Georgetown, TX (city) Williamson County, 932
Georgia (state), 488
Gilbert, AZ (town) Maricopa County, 65
Gillette, WY (city) Campbell County, 1049
Gilroy, CA (city) Santa Clara County, 159
Glen Cove, NY (city) Nassau County, 760
Glendale Heights, IL (village) DuPage County, 527
Glendale, AZ (city) Maricopa County, 66
Glendale, CA (city) Los Angeles County, 159
Glendora, CA (city) Los Angeles County, 161
Goleta, CA (city) Santa Barbara County, 162
Goodyear, AZ (city) Maricopa County, 67
Goshen, IN (city) Elkhart County, 545
Grand Forks, ND (city) Grand Forks County, 823
Grand Island, NE (city) Hall County, 653
Grand Prairie, TX (city) Dallas County, 933
Grand Rapids, MI (city) Kent County, 618
Great Falls, MT (city) Cascade County, 649
Greeley, CO (city) Weld County, 333
Green River, WY (city) Sweetwater County, 1050
Greenacres, FL (city) Palm Beach County, 406
Greensboro, NC (city) Guilford County, 814
Greenville, TX (city) Hunt County, 934
Guymon, OK (city) Texas County, 840

H

Hacienda Heights, CA (cdp) Los Angeles County, 163
Hackensack, NJ (city) Bergen County, 701
Hallandale Beach, FL (city) Broward County, 407
Haltom City, TX (city) Tarrant County, 935
Hammond, IN (city) Lake County, 546
Hampton, VA (independent city) , 1008
Hanford, CA (city) Kings County, 164
Hanover Park, IL (village) Cook County, 528
Hanover, NH (town) Grafton County, 679
Harlingen, TX (city) Cameron County, 935
Hartford, CT (city/town) Hartford County, 348
Haverstraw, NY (town) Rockland County, 761
Hawaii (state), 501
Hawaiian Paradise Park, HI (cdp) Hawaii County, 502
Hawthorne, CA (city) Los Angeles County, 165
Hayward, CA (city) Alameda County, 166
Hazleton, PA (city) Luzerne County, 859
Hemet, CA (city) Riverside County, 167
Hempstead, NY (town) Nassau County, 762
Hempstead, NY (village) Nassau County, 765
Henderson, NV (city) Clark County, 662
Hesperia, CA (city) San Bernardino County, 168
Hialeah, FL (city) Miami-Dade County, 409
Highland, CA (city) San Bernardino County, 169
Hillsboro, OR (city) Washington County, 849
Hilton Head Island, SC (town) Beaufort County, 883
Hobbs, NM (city) Lea County, 735
Holland, MI (charter township) Ottawa County, 620
Holland, MI (city) Ottawa County, 620
Hollister, CA (city) San Benito County, 170
Hollywood, FL (city) Broward County, 411
Holyoke, MA (city) Hampden County, 607
Homestead, FL (city) Miami-Dade County, 413
Honolulu, HI (cdp) *see* Urban Honolulu
Hope, AR (city) Hempstead County, 84
Horn Lake, MS (city) DeSoto County, 634
Houston, TX (city) Harris County, 936
Huntington Beach, CA (city) Orange County, 171
Huntington Park, CA (city) Los Angeles County, 172
Huntington Station, NY (cdp) Suffolk County, 768
Huntington, WV (city) Cabell County, 1036
Huntington, NY (town) Suffolk County, 766
Huntsville, AL (city) Madison County, 45
Huron, SD (city) Beadle County, 887
Hurst, TX (city) Tarrant County, 939

I

Idaho (state), 507
Illinois (state), 513
Imperial Beach, CA (city) San Diego County, 174
Indiana (state), 540
Indianapolis, IN (city) Marion County, 547
Indio, CA (city) Riverside County, 174
Inglewood, CA (city) Los Angeles County, 175
Iowa (state), 549
Irvine, CA (city) Orange County, 176
Irving, TX (city) Dallas County, 939
Islip, NY (town) Suffolk County, 769

J

Jackson, MS (city) Hinds County, 635
Jacksonville, FL (city) Duval County, 415
Jerome, ID (city) Jerome County, 511
Jersey City, NJ (city) Hudson County, 702
Joliet, IL (city) Will County, 528
Juneau, AK (borough) Juneau City and Borough, 53

K

Kansas (state), 556
Kansas City, KS (city) Wyandotte County, 559
Kansas City, MO (city) Jackson County, 642
Kearns, UT (cdp) Salt Lake County, 986
Kearny, NJ (town) Hudson County, 704
Kendale Lakes, FL (cdp) Miami-Dade County, 417
Kendall West, FL (cdp) Miami-Dade County, 421
Kendall, FL (cdp) Miami-Dade County, 419
Kenner, LA (city) Jefferson Parish, 575
Kennewick, WA (city) Benton County, 1023
Kentucky (state), 565
Killeen, TX (city) Bell County, 941
Kingsville, TX (city) Kleberg County, 942
Kissimmee, FL (city) Osceola County, 422
Knoxville, TN (city) Knox County, 895
Kyle, TX (city) Hays County, 943

L

La Habra, CA (city) Orange County, 178
La Mesa, CA (city) San Diego County, 179
La Mirada, CA (city) Los Angeles County, 180
La Porte, TX (city) Harris County, 944
La Presa, CA (cdp) San Diego County, 181
La Puente, CA (city) Los Angeles County, 181
La Quinta, CA (city) Riverside County, 182
La Verne, CA (city) Los Angeles County, 183
Laguna Hills, CA (city) Orange County, 184
Lake Elsinore, CA (city) Riverside County, 185
Lake Forest, CA (city) Orange County, 186
Lake Jackson, TX (city) Brazoria County, 944
Lake Magdalene, FL (cdp) Hillsborough County, 424
Lake Worth, FL (city) Palm Beach County, 425
Lakewood, CA (city) Los Angeles County, 187
Lakewood, CO (city) Jefferson County, 333
Lancaster, CA (city) Los Angeles County, 188
Lancaster, PA (city) Lancaster County, 860
Laredo, TX (city) Webb County, 945
Las Cruces, NM (city) Dona Ana County, 736
Las Vegas, NV (city) Clark County, 664

Laurel, MS (city) Jones County, 636
Lawndale, CA (city) Los Angeles County, 190
Lawrence, MA (city) Essex County, 608
Lawrenceville, GA (city) Gwinnett County, 496
Leander, TX (city) Williamson County, 946
Lebanon, PA (city) Lebanon County, 861
Lehigh Acres, FL (cdp) Lee County, 426
Lemon Grove, CA (city) San Diego County, 191
Lewiston, ME (city) Androscoggin County, 583
Lewisville, TX (city) Denton County, 947
Lexington, NE (city) Dawson County, 654
Lexington-Fayette, KY (consolidated government) Fayette County, 567
Lincoln, NE (city) Lancaster County, 655
Linden, NJ (city) Union County, 706
Little Elm, TX (city) Denton County, 948
Little Rock, AR (city) Pulaski County, 84
Livermore, CA (city) Alameda County, 192
Lodi, CA (city) San Joaquin County, 192
Lompoc, CA (city) Santa Barbara County, 193
Long Beach, CA (city) Los Angeles County, 194
Long Branch, NJ (city) Monmouth County, 707
Longmont, CO (city) Boulder County, 334
Lorain, OH (city) Lorain County, 834
Los Angeles, CA (city) Los Angeles County, 196
Los Banos, CA (city) Merced County, 199
Louisiana (state), 572
Louisville-Jefferson County, KY (metropolitan government) Jefferson County, 569
Lubbock, TX (city) Lubbock County, 949
Lufkin, TX (city) Angelina County, 950
Lynn, MA (city) Essex County, 609
Lynwood, CA (city) Los Angeles County, 199

M

Madera, CA (city) Madera County, 201
Madison, WI (city) Dane County, 1043
Magna, UT (cdp) Salt Lake County, 987
Maine (state), 581
Makakilo, HI (cdp) Honolulu County, 503
Manassas, VA (independent city) , 1009
Manchester, NH (city) Hillsborough County, 680
Manhattan, NY (borough) New York County, 771
Manteca, CA (city) San Joaquin County, 201
Marana, AZ (town) Pima County, 68
Margate, FL (city) Broward County, 428
Maricopa, AZ (city) Pinal County, 69
Marietta, GA (city) Cobb County, 497
Marshalltown, IA (city) Marshall County, 553
Martinsburg, WV (city) Berkeley County, 1037
Marumsco, VA (cdp) Prince William County, 1010
Maryland (state), 586
Massachusetts (state), 599
Mayfield, KY (city) Graves County, 570
Maywood, CA (city) Los Angeles County, 202
McAllen, TX (city) Hidalgo County, 951
McKinney, TX (city) Collin County, 952
McMinnville, OR (city) Yamhill County, 850
Meadow Woods, FL (cdp) Orange County, 429
Melrose Park, IL (village) Cook County, 529
Memphis, TN (city) Shelby County, 896
Menifee, CA (city) Riverside County, 203
Merced, CA (city) Merced County, 204
Meriden, CT (city/town) New Haven County, 349
Mesa, AZ (city) Maricopa County, 70
Mesquite, TX (city) Dallas County, 953
Metairie, LA (cdp) Jefferson Parish, 577
Miami Beach, FL (city) Miami-Dade County, 433
Miami Gardens, FL (city) Miami-Dade County, 435
Miami Lakes, FL (town) Miami-Dade County, 436
Miami, FL (city) Miami-Dade County, 430
Michigan (state), 615
Middle, DE (town) New Castle County, 364
Middletown, NY (city) Orange County, 774
Midland, TX (city) Midland County, 954
Midvale, UT (city) Salt Lake County, 988
Milwaukee, WI (city) Milwaukee County, 1044
Minneapolis, MN (city) Hennepin County, 626
Minnesota (state), 624
Minot, ND (city) Ward County, 824
Miramar, FL (city) Broward County, 437
Mission Bend, TX (cdp) Fort Bend County, 955
Mission, TX (city) Hidalgo County, 955
Mississippi (state), 632
Missoula, MT (city) Missoula County, 650
Missouri (state), 638
Mobile, AL (city) Mobile County, 46
Modesto, CA (city) Stanislaus County, 205
Monroe, NC (city) Union County, 816
Monrovia, CA (city) Los Angeles County, 206
Montana (state), 646
Montclair, CA (city) San Bernardino County, 207
Montebello, CA (city) Los Angeles County, 208
Monterey Park, CA (city) Los Angeles County, 210
Montgomery Village, MD (cdp) Montgomery County, 594
Montgomery, AL (city) Montgomery County, 46
Moorpark, CA (city) Ventura County, 211
Moreno Valley, CA (city) Riverside County, 211
Morgan Hill, CA (city) Santa Clara County, 213
Morgantown, WV (city) Monongalia County, 1037
Mount Vernon, WA (city) Skagit County, 1024
Mountain View, CA (city) Santa Clara County, 214
Mundelein, IL (village) Lake County, 530
Murrieta, CA (city) Riverside County, 215
Muscatine, IA (city) Muscatine County, 553

N

Nampa, ID (city) Canyon County, 511
Napa, CA (city) Napa County, 216
Naperville, IL (city) DuPage County, 531
Nashua, NH (city) Hillsborough County, 681
Nashville-Davidson, TN (metropolitan government) Davidson County, 898
National City, CA (city) San Diego County, 217
Nebraska (state), 651
Nevada (state), 659
New Braunfels, TX (city) Comal County, 957
New Britain, CT (city/town) Hartford County, 350
New Brunswick, NJ (city) Middlesex County, 709
New Hampshire (state), 677
New Haven, CT (city/town) New Haven County, 351
New Jersey (state), 683
New London, CT (city/town) New London County, 352
New Mexico (state), 729
New Orleans, LA (city) Orleans Parish, 578
New Rochelle, NY (city) Westchester County, 774
New York (state), 741
New York City, NY (city), 776
Newark, CA (city) Alameda County, 218
Newark, NJ (city) Essex County, 710
Newburgh, NY (city) Orange County, 779
Newport News, VA (independent city), 1011
Norco, CA (city) Riverside County, 218
Norfolk, VA (independent city), 1012
Norristown, PA (borough) Montgomery County, 862
North Atlanta, GA (cdp) DeKalb County, 498
North Bergen, NJ (township) Hudson County, 712
North Carolina (state), 805
North Chicago, IL (city) Lake County, 532
North Dakota (state), 821
North Hempstead, NY (town) Nassau County, 780
North Highlands, CA (cdp) Sacramento County, 219
North Las Vegas, NV (city) Clark County, 666
North Lauderdale, FL (city) Broward County, 439
North Miami Beach, FL (city) Miami-Dade County, 442
North Miami, FL (city) Miami-Dade County, 441
Northglenn, CO (city) Adams County, 335
Norwalk, CA (city) Los Angeles County, 220
Norwalk, CT (city/town) Fairfield County, 353
Novato, CA (city) Marin County, 221

O

Oakland Park, FL (city) Broward County, 444
Oakland, CA (city) Alameda County, 222
Oakley, CA (city) Contra Costa County, 224
Oceanside, CA (city) San Diego County, 225
Ocoee, FL (city) Orange County, 445
Odessa, TX (city) Ector County, 957
Ogden, UT (city) Weber County, 989
Ohio (state), 826
Oklahoma (state), 837
Oklahoma City, OK (city) Oklahoma County, 840
Olathe, KS (city) Johnson County, 560
Omaha, NE (city) Douglas County, 656
Ontario, CA (city) San Bernardino County, 226
Orange, CA (city) Orange County, 227
Orcutt, CA (cdp) Santa Barbara County, 229
Oregon (state), 845
Orlando, FL (city) Orange County, 446
Ossining, NY (town) Westchester County, 782
Ossining, NY (village) Westchester County, 783
Overland Park, KS (city) Johnson County, 561
Oxnard, CA (city) Ventura County, 229
Oyster Bay, NY (town) Nassau County, 784

P

Palm Desert, CA (city) Riverside County, 230
Palm Springs, CA (city) Riverside County, 231
Palmdale, CA (city) Los Angeles County, 232
Paradise, NV (cdp) Clark County, 667
Paramount, CA (city) Los Angeles County, 234
Parker, SC (cdp) Greenville County, 884
Pasadena, CA (city) Los Angeles County, 235
Pasadena, TX (city) Harris County, 958
Pascagoula, MS (city) Jackson County, 636
Pasco, WA (city) Franklin County, 1025
Passaic, NJ (city) Passaic County, 714
Paterson, NJ (city) Passaic County, 715
Pawtucket, RI (city) Providence County, 873
Pearland, TX (city) Brazoria County, 959
Pembroke Pines, FL (city) Broward County, 448
Pennsauken, NJ (township) Camden County, 717
Pennsylvania (state), 854
Peoria, AZ (city) Maricopa County, 71
Perris, CA (city) Riverside County, 236
Perth Amboy, NJ (city) Middlesex County, 718
Petaluma, CA (city) Sonoma County, 237
Pflugerville, TX (city) Travis County, 960
Pharr, TX (city) Hidalgo County, 961
Philadelphia, PA (city) Philadelphia County, 863
Phoenix, AZ (city) Maricopa County, 72
Pico Rivera, CA (city) Los Angeles County, 238
Pittsburg, CA (city) Contra Costa County, 239
Pittsburgh, PA (city) Allegheny County, 865
Placentia, CA (city) Orange County, 241
Plainfield, NJ (city) Union County, 720
Plano, TX (city) Collin County, 962
Plant City, FL (city) Hillsborough County, 450

Plantation, FL (city) Broward County, 451
Poinciana, FL (cdp) Osceola County, 452
Pomona, CA (city) Los Angeles County, 242
Port Arthur, TX (city) Jefferson County, 963
Port Chester, NY (village) Westchester County, 786
Port Saint Lucie, FL (city) Saint Lucie County, 454
Porterville, CA (city) Tulare County, 243
Portland, ME (city) Cumberland County, 583
Portland, OR (city) Multnomah County, 850
Providence, RI (city) Providence County, 875
Pueblo West, CO (cdp) Pueblo County, 337
Pueblo, CO (city) Pueblo County, 336

Q

Queens, NY (borough) Queens County, 787

R

Racine, WI (city) Racine County, 1045
Rahway, NJ (city) Union County, 721
Raleigh, NC (city) Wake County, 816
Ramapo, NY (town) Rockland County, 790
Rancho Cucamonga, CA (city) San Bernardino County, 244
Rapid City, SD (city) Pennington County, 887
Reading, PA (city) Berks County, 866
Redlands, CA (city) San Bernardino County, 245
Redwood City, CA (city) San Mateo County, 246
Reno, NV (city) Washoe County, 669
Revere, MA (city) Suffolk County, 610
Rhode Island (state), 869
Rialto, CA (city) San Bernardino County, 247
Richmond West, FL (cdp) Miami-Dade County, 455
Richmond, CA (city) Contra Costa County, 248
Richmond, VA (independent city), 1013
Rio Rancho, NM (city) Sandoval County, 737
Riverside, CA (city) Riverside County, 250
Riverview, FL (cdp) Hillsborough County, 457
Rochester, NY (city) Monroe County, 792
Rock Springs, WY (city) Sweetwater County, 1051
Rockford, IL (city) Winnebago County, 533
Rogers, AR (city) Benton County, 85
Rohnert Park, CA (city) Sonoma County, 251
Romeoville, IL (village) Will County, 534
Rosemead, CA (city) Los Angeles County, 252
Rosenberg, TX (city) Fort Bend County, 964
Roswell, NM (city) Chaves County, 738
Round Lake Beach, IL (village) Lake County, 535
Round Rock, TX (city) Williamson County, 965
Rowland Heights, CA (cdp) Los Angeles County, 253
Royal Palm Beach, FL (village) Palm Beach County, 458
Rubidoux, CA (cdp) Riverside County, 254
Rye, NY (town) Westchester County, 793

S

Sacramento, CA (city) Sacramento County, 255
Sahuarita, AZ (town) Pima County, 74
Saint Cloud, FL (city) Osceola County, 459
Saint Louis, MO (independent city), 643
Saint Paul, MN (city) Ramsey County, 628
Saint Petersburg, FL (city) Pinellas County, 460
Salem, NH (town) Rockingham County, 682
Salem, OR (city) Marion County, 852
Salinas, CA (city) Monterey County, 257
Salt Lake City, UT (city) Salt Lake County, 989
San Angelo, TX (city) Tom Green County, 966
San Antonio, TX (city) Bexar County, 967
San Bernardino, CA (city) San Bernardino County, 258
San Bruno, CA (city) San Mateo County, 259
San Buenaventura (Ventura), CA (city) Ventura County, 260
San Diego, CA (city) San Diego County, 261
San Dimas, CA (city) Los Angeles County, 263
San Francisco, CA (city) San Francisco County, 264
San Gabriel, CA (city) Los Angeles County, 266
San Jacinto, CA (city) Riverside County, 267
San Jose, CA (city) Santa Clara County, 268
San Juan Capistrano, CA (city) Orange County, 270
San Juan, TX (city) Hidalgo County, 969
San Leandro, CA (city) Alameda County, 271
San Luis, AZ (city) Yuma County, 75
San Marcos, CA (city) San Diego County, 272
San Marcos, TX (city) Hays County, 969
San Mateo, CA (city) San Mateo County, 273
San Pablo, CA (city) Contra Costa County, 274
San Rafael, CA (city) Marin County, 275
San Tan Valley, AZ (cdp) Pinal County, 76
Sanford, FL (city) Seminole County, 462
Sanford, NC (city) Lee County, 818
Santa Ana, CA (city) Orange County, 276
Santa Barbara, CA (city) Santa Barbara County, 278
Santa Clarita, CA (city) Los Angeles County, 279
Santa Fe, NM (city) Santa Fe County, 738
Santa Maria, CA (city) Santa Barbara County, 280
Santa Paula, CA (city) Ventura County, 281
Santa Rosa, CA (city) Sonoma County, 282
Savannah, GA (city) Chatham County, 499
Schertz, TX (city) Guadalupe County, 970
Schofield Barracks, HI (cdp) Honolulu County, 504
Scottsdale, AZ (city) Maricopa County, 76
Seaside, CA (city) Monterey County, 283
SeaTac, WA (city) King County, 1026
Seattle, WA (city) King County, 1026
Seguin, TX (city) Guadalupe County, 971
Shelbyville, KY (city) Shelby County, 571
Sherman, TX (city) Grayson County, 972
Shreveport, LA (city) Caddo Parish, 579
Siloam Springs, AR (city) Benton County, 86
Silver Spring, MD (cdp) Montgomery County, 595
Simi Valley, CA (city) Ventura County, 284
Sioux Falls, SD (city) Minnehaha County, 888
Socorro, TX (city) El Paso County, 972
Soledad, CA (city) Monterey County, 285
South Burlington, VT (city) Chittenden County, 996
South Carolina (state), 878
South Dakota (state), 886
South Gate, CA (city) Los Angeles County, 286
South Miami Heights, FL (cdp) Miami-Dade County, 463
South Portland, ME (city) Cumberland County, 584
South San Francisco, CA (city) San Mateo County, 287
South Sioux City, NE (city) Dakota County, 657
South Valley, NM (cdp) Bernalillo County, 739
South Whittier, CA (cdp) Los Angeles County, 288
Sparks, NV (city) Washoe County, 670
Spearfish, SD (city) Lawrence County, 889
Spokane, WA (city) Spokane County, 1028
Spring Valley, CA (cdp) San Diego County, 289
Spring Valley, NV (cdp) Clark County, 671
Spring Valley, NY (village) Rockland County, 794
Spring, TX (cdp) Harris County, 973
Springdale, AR (city) Washington County, 87
Springfield, MA (city) Hampden County, 611
Springfield, MO (city) Greene County, 644
Springfield, VA (cdp) Fairfax County, 1014
Stamford, CT (city/town) Fairfield County, 355
Stanton, CA (city) Orange County, 290
Staten Island, NY (borough) Richmond County, 796
Sterling Heights, MI (city) Macomb County, 621
Sterling, VA (cdp) Loudoun County, 1016
Stockton, CA (city) San Joaquin County, 291
Storm Lake, IA (city) Buena Vista County, 554
Streamwood, IL (village) Cook County, 535
Suisun City, CA (city) Solano County, 292
Sunnyvale, CA (city) Santa Clara County, 293
Sunrise Manor, NV (cdp) Clark County, 673
Sunrise, FL (city) Broward County, 464
Syracuse, NY (city) Onondaga County, 797

T

Tacoma, WA (city) Pierce County, 1029
Tallahassee, FL (city) Leon County, 466
Tamarac, FL (city) Broward County, 468
Tamiami, FL (cdp) Miami-Dade County, 469
Tampa, FL (city) Hillsborough County, 471
Temecula, CA (city) Riverside County, 294
Tempe, AZ (city) Maricopa County, 77
Temple, TX (city) Bell County, 974
Tennessee (state), 891
Texas (state), 900
Texas City, TX (city) Galveston County, 975
The Colony, TX (city) Denton County, 976
The Hammocks, FL (cdp) Miami-Dade County, 472
Thornton, CO (city) Adams County, 338
Thousand Oaks, CA (city) Ventura County, 295
Toledo, OH (city) Lucas County, 835
Topeka, KS (city) Shawnee County, 562
Torrance, CA (city) Los Angeles County, 297
Town 'n' Country, FL (cdp) Hillsborough County, 474
Tracy, CA (city) San Joaquin County, 298
Trenton, NJ (city) Mercer County, 722
Tucson, AZ (city) Pima County, 78
Tulare, CA (city) Tulare County, 299
Tulsa, OK (city) Tulsa County, 842
Turlock, CA (city) Stanislaus County, 300
Tustin, CA (city) Orange County, 301
Twentynine Palms, CA (city) San Bernardino County, 302
Tyler, TX (city) Smith County, 976

U

Union City, CA (city) Alameda County, 302
Union City, NJ (city) Hudson County, 724
University Park, FL (cdp) Miami-Dade County, 478
University, FL (cdp) Hillsborough County, 476
University, FL (cdp) Orange County, 477
Upland, CA (city) San Bernardino County, 303
Urban Honolulu, HI (cdp) Honolulu County, 504
Utah (state), 984

V

Vacaville, CA (city) Solano County, 305
Vallejo, CA (city) Solano County, 305
Valley Stream, NY (village) Nassau County, 799
Vancouver, WA (city) Clark County, 1030
Vermont (state), 993
Victoria, TX (city) Victoria County, 977
Victorville, CA (city) San Bernardino County, 307
Vineland, NJ (city) Cumberland County, 726
Virginia (state), 998
Virginia Beach, VA (independent city), 1017
Visalia, CA (city) Tulare County, 308
Vista, CA (city) San Diego County, 309

W

Waco, TX (city) McLennan County, 978
Waianae, HI (cdp) Honolulu County, 506
Walla Walla, WA (city) Walla Walla County, 1031

Wallkill, NY (town) Orange County, 800
Warr Acres, OK (city) Oklahoma County, 843
Warren, MI (city) Macomb County, 622
Wasco, CA (city) Kern County, 310
Washington (state), 1020
Waterbury, CT (city/town) New Haven County, 357
Waterville, ME (city) Kennebec County, 585
Watsonville, CA (city) Santa Cruz County, 310
Waukegan, IL (city) Lake County, 536
Waxahachie, TX (city) Ellis County, 979
Wenatchee, WA (city) Chelan County, 1032
Weslaco, TX (city) Hidalgo County, 980
Wesley Chapel, FL (cdp) Pasco County, 479
West Chicago, IL (city) DuPage County, 537
West Covina, CA (city) Los Angeles County, 311
West Falls Church, VA (cdp) Fairfax County, 1018
West Little River, FL (cdp) Miami-Dade County, 480
West New York, NJ (town) Hudson County, 727
West Palm Beach, FL (city) Palm Beach County, 482
West Sacramento, CA (city) Yolo County, 313
West Saint Paul, MN (city) Dakota County, 629
West Valley City, UT (city) Salt Lake County, 991
West Virginia (state), 1034
West Whittier-Los Nietos, CA (cdp) Los Angeles County, 313
Westchester, FL (cdp) Miami-Dade County, 483
Westminster, CA (city) Orange County, 314
Westminster, CO (city) Adams County, 339
Westmont, CA (cdp) Los Angeles County, 315
Weston, FL (city) Broward County, 484
Wheat Ridge, CO (city) Jefferson County, 339
Wheaton, MD (cdp) Montgomery County, 596
Wheeling, IL (village) Cook County, 538
White Plains, NY (city) Westchester County, 801
Whitney, NV (cdp) Clark County, 674
Whittier, CA (city) Los Angeles County, 316
Wichita, KS (city) Sedgwick County, 563
Wildomar, CA (city) Riverside County, 318
Williston, ND (city) Williams County, 824
Willmar, MN (city) Kandiyohi County, 630
Willowbrook, CA (cdp) Los Angeles County, 318
Wilmington, DE (city) New Castle County, 364
Winchester, NV (cdp) Clark County, 675
Windham, CT (town) Windham County, 358
Windsor, CA (town) Sonoma County, 319
Winston-Salem, NC (city) Forsyth County, 819
Winter Garden, FL (city) Orange County, 486
Wisconsin (state), 1039
Woodland, CA (city) Yolo County, 320
Woonsocket, RI (city) Providence County, 876
Worcester, MA (city) Worcester County, 613
Worthington, MN (city) Nobles County, 631
Wyoming (state), 1047

Y

Yakima, WA (city) Yakima County, 1032
Yankton, SD (city) Yankton County, 890
Yonkers, NY (city) Westchester County, 802
York, PA (city) York County, 867
Yuba City, CA (city) Sutter County, 321
Yucaipa, CA (city) San Bernardino County, 322
Yuma, AZ (city) Yuma County, 80

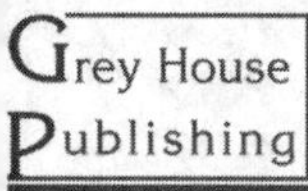

Grey House Publishing
2012 Title List

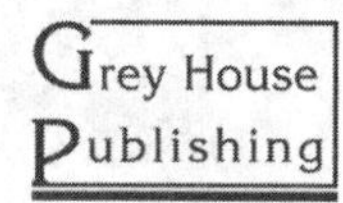

Visit **www.greyhouse.com** for Product Information, Table of Contents and Sample Pages

General Reference

America's College Museums
American Environmental Leaders: From Colonial Times to the Present
An African Biographical Dictionary
An Encyclopedia of Human Rights in the United States
Encyclopedia of African-American Writing
Encyclopedia of Gun Control & Gun Rights
Encyclopedia of Invasions & Conquests
Encyclopedia of Prisoners of War & Internment
Encyclopedia of Religion & Law in America
Encyclopedia of Rural America
Encyclopedia of the United States Cabinet, 1789-2010
Encyclopedia of War Journalism
Encyclopedia of Warrior Peoples & Fighting Groups
From Suffrage to the Senate: America's Political Women
Nations of the World
Political Corruption in America
Speakers of the House of Representatives, 1789-2009
The Environmental Debate: A Documentary History
The Evolution Wars: A Guide to the Debates
The Religious Right: A Reference Handbook
The Value of a Dollar: 1860-2009
The Value of a Dollar: Colonial Era
US Land & Natural Resource Policy
Weather America
Working Americans 1770-1869 Vol. IX: Revol. War to the Civil War
Working Americans 1880-1999 Vol. I: The Working Class
Working Americans 1880-1999 Vol. II: The Middle Class
Working Americans 1880-1999 Vol. III: The Upper Class
Working Americans 1880-1999 Vol. IV: Their Children
Working Americans 1880-2003 Vol. V: At War
Working Americans 1880-2005 Vol. VI: Women at Work
Working Americans 1880-2006 Vol. VII: Social Movements
Working Americans 1880-2007 Vol. VIII: Immigrants
Working Americans 1880-2009 Vol. X: Sports & Recreation
Working Americans 1880-2010 Vol. XI: Inventors & Entrepreneurs
Working Americans 1880-2011 Vol. XII: Our History through Music
World Cultural Leaders of the 20th & 21st Centuries

Business Information

Directory of Business Information Resources
Directory of Mail Order Catalogs
Directory of Venture Capital & Private Equity Firms
Environmental Resource Handbook
Food & Beverage Market Place
Grey House Homeland Security Directory
Grey House Performing Arts Directory
Hudson's Washington News Media Contacts Directory
New York State Directory
Sports Market Place Directory
The Rauch Guides – Industry Market Research Reports
Sweets Directory by McGraw Hill Construction

Statistics & Demographics

America's Top-Rated Cities
America's Top-Rated Small Towns & Cities
America's Top-Rated Smaller Cities
Comparative Guide to American Hospitals
Comparative Guide to American Suburbs
Profiles of... Series – State Handbooks

Health Information

Comparative Guide to American Hospitals
Complete Directory for Pediatric Disorders
Complete Directory for People with Chronic Illness
Complete Directory for People with Disabilities
Complete Mental Health Directory
Directory of Health Care Group Purchasing Organizations
Directory of Hospital Personnel
HMO/PPO Directory
Medical Device Register
Older Americans Information Directory

Education Information

Charter School Movement
Comparative Guide to American Elementary & Secondary Schools
Complete Learning Disabilities Directory
Educators Resource Directory
Special Education

Financial Ratings Series

TheStreet.com Ratings Guide to Bond & Money Market Mutual Funds
TheStreet.com Ratings Guide to Common Stocks
TheStreet.com Ratings Guide to Exchange-Traded Funds
TheStreet.com Ratings Guide to Stock Mutual Funds
TheStreet.com Ratings Ultimate Guided Tour of Stock Investing
Weiss Ratings Consumer Box Set
Weiss Ratings Guide to Banks & Thrifts
Weiss Ratings Guide to Credit Unions
Weiss Ratings Guide to Health Insurers
Weiss Ratings Guide to Life & Annuity Insurers
Weiss Ratings Guide to Property & Casualty Insurers

Bowker's Books In Print® Titles

Books In Print®
Books In Print® Supplement
American Book Publishing Record® Annual
American Book Publishing Record® Monthly
Books Out Loud™
Bowker's Complete Video Directory™
Children's Books In Print®
Complete Directory of Large Print Books & Serials™
El-Hi Textbooks & Serials In Print®
Forthcoming Books®
Law Books & Serials In Print™
Medical & Health Care Books In Print™
Publishers, Distributors & Wholesalers of the US™
Subject Guide to Books In Print®
Subject Guide to Children's Books In Print®

Canadian General Reference

Associations Canada
Canadian Almanac & Directory
Canadian Environmental Resource Guide
Canadian Parliamentary Guide
Financial Services Canada
Governments Canada
Libraries Canada
The History of Canada

Grey House Publishing
4919 Route 22, PO Box 56, Amenia NY 12501-0056 | (800) 562-2139 | www.greyhouse.com | books@greyhouse.com